DISCARD

The PF Will Accurately Grade Your Stamps

The PF is a leader in the accurate grading of U.S. and British North American stamps. Grading is a cumulative score arrived at by the careful examination of several critical components. A numeric grade is assigned based on centering, soun eal.

Application of the PF's uniform our in-house expert staff to assess your stamps fa

Scott #7 Graded 98

Scott #11 Graded 100J

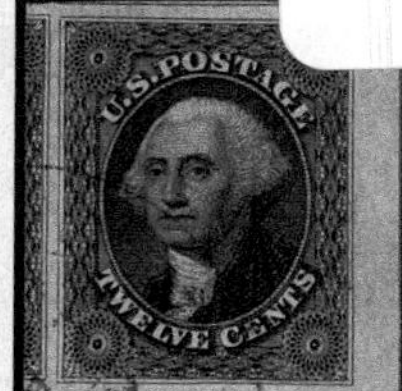
Scott #17 Graded 100J

Scott #261 Graded 98

Scott #233 Graded 98J

Scott #404 Graded 98

Scott #354 Graded 100

Scott #313 Graded 95

Scott #E8 Graded 100J

Most stamps are eligible for grading except those that have faults, been repaired, reperforated, or otherwise altered, or have natural straight edges.

Census figures for PF graded stamps can be found using the PF Search program on our website.

Our sole objective is to provide you, the collector or dealer, with the most accurately and reliably graded certificates in our hobby today.

"The Philatelic Foundation is one of the world's esteemed expertizing bodies . . . ." Linn's Editorial

COLLECT WITH CONFIDENCE—WITH A PF CERTIFICATE

The Philatelic Foundation
22 East 35th Street, 4th Floor
New York, NY 10016

Phone: 212-221-6555 **Web: www.philatelicfoundation.org**

Visit our new site

www.alanmillerstamps.com

TO VIEW OUR FREE 2019-2020 CATALOGUE OF USED UNITED STATES STAMPS AND MONTHLY ONLINE SPECIALS

All grades Listed From Seconds To Extra Fine

We have an extensive stock of the following #1-711, Airmails, Special Delivery, Postage Dues, Shanghai's, Parcel Post & Duck Stamps.

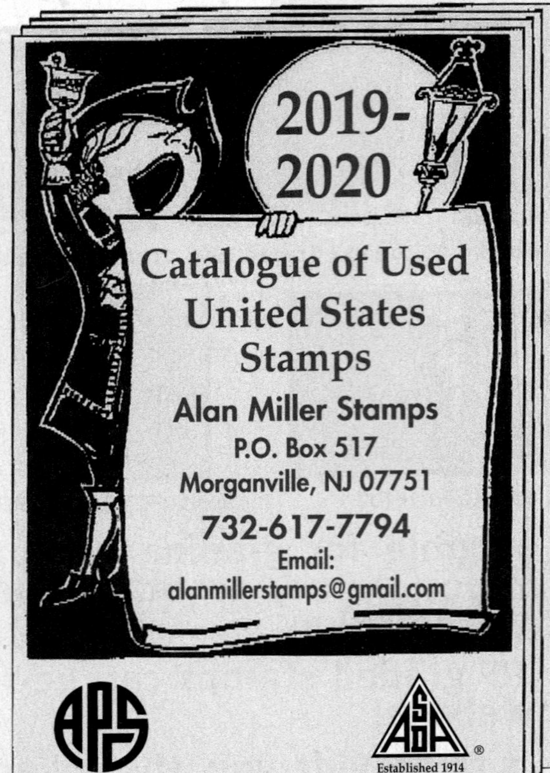

MENTION YOU SAW THIS AD IN THE SCOTT U.S. SPECIALIZED CATALOGUE OR MAIL THE COUPON TO SAVE 10% ON YOUR FIRST ORDER!!

WE ALSO BUY!

Stamps like these can be found in our FREE 28-page catalogue of used stamps.

❑ **YES!** Please Send Me Your FREE 28-Page Used Catalogue. ($1.00 Postage Appreciated).

NAME ______________________

ADDRESS ______________________

____

❑ Please contact me I have used stamps for sale.

PHONE (   ) ______________________

E-MAIL ______________________

MAIL TO:

Alan Miller Stamps

48 Years of Quality And Service

DEPT. S

P.O. Box 517 • Morganville, NJ 07751

(732) 617-7794

We Buy Used Stamps

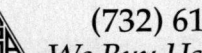

SCOTT®

2020 Specialized Catalogue of United States Stamps & Covers

NINETY-EIGHTH EDITION

CONFEDERATE STATES • CANAL ZONE • DANISH WEST INDIES
GUAM • HAWAII • UNITED NATIONS

UNITED STATES ADMINISTRATION:
Cuba • Puerto Rico • Philippines • Ryukyu Islands

EDITOR-IN-CHIEF	Jay Bigalke
EDITOR-AT-LARGE	Donna Houseman
EDITOR	Charles Snee
MANAGING EDITOR	Timothy A. Hodge
EDITOR EMERITUS	James E. Kloetzel
SENIOR EDITOR /NEW ISSUES & VALUING	Martin J. Frankevicz
ADMINISTRATIVE ASSISTANT/CATALOGUE LAYOUT	Eric Wiessinger
PRINTING AND IMAGE COORDINATOR	Stacey Mahan
SENIOR GRAPHIC DESIGNER	Cinda McAlexander
SALES DIRECTOR	David Pistello
SALES DIRECTOR	Eric Roth

Released October 2019
Includes New Stamp Listings through the August 2019 *Linn's Stamp News Monthly* Catalogue Update

Copyright© 2019 by

AMOS MEDIA
911 S. Vandemark Rd, Sidney, OH 45365-4129
Publishers of *Linn's Stamp News*,
Linn's Stamp News Monthly, Coin World and *Coin World Monthly.*

Copyright Notice

The contents of this book are owned exclusively by Amos Media Co. and all rights thereto are reserved under the Pan American and Universal Copyright Conventions.

Copyright 2019 by Amos Media Co., Sidney, OH.
Printed in U.S.A.

COPYRIGHT NOTE

Permission is hereby given for the use of material in this book and covered by copyright if:

(a) The material is used in advertising matter, circulars or price lists for the purpose of offering stamps for sale or purchase at the prices listed therein; and

(b) Such use is incidental to the business of buying and selling stamps and is limited in scope and length, i.e., it does not cover a substantial portion of the total number of stamps issued by any country or of any special category of stamps of any country; and

(c) Such material is not used as part of any catalogue, stamp album or computerized or other system based upon the Scott catalogue numbers, or in any updated valuations of stamps not offered for sale or purchase; and

(d) Such use is not competitive with the business of the copyright owner; and

(e) Such use is for editorial purposes in publications in the form of articles or commentary, except for computer software or the serialization of books in such publications, for which separate written permission is required.

Any use of the material in this book which does not satisfy all the foregoing conditions is forbidden in any form unless permission in each instance is given in writing by the copyright owner.

Trademark Notice

The terms SCOTT, SCOTT'S, SCOTT CATALOGUE NUMBERING SYSTEM, SCOTT CATALOGUE NUMBER, SCOTT NUMBER and abbreviations thereof, are trademarks of Amos Media Co., used to identify its publications and its copyrighted system for identifying and classifying postage stamps for dealers and collectors. These trademarks are to be used only with the prior consent of Amos Media Co.

No part of this work may be reproduced in any form or by any means, electronic or mechanical, including photocopying, without permission in writing from Amos Media Co., P.O. Box 4129, Sidney, Ohio 45365-4129.

Please Note

Effective as of 1978, designs of all United States stamps are copyrighted.

Scott Catalogue accepts all advertisements in good faith, but does not endorse or assume any responsibility for the contents of advertisements.

ISBN 0-89487-577-9

Library of Congress Card No. 2-3301

Scott Catalogue Mission Statement

The Scott Catalogue Team exists to serve the recreational, educational and commercial hobby needs of stamp collectors and dealers.

We strive to set the industry standard for philatelic information and products by developing and providing goods that help collectors identify, value, organize and present their collections.

Quality customer service is, and will continue to be, our highest priority. We aspire toward achieving total customer satisfaction.

SCOTT

What's new for 2020 Scott Specialized Catalogue of United States Stamps and Covers?

Many important value and editorial changes enhance the 98th edition of the Scott U.S. Specialized catalog.

Before we turn our attention to the many value changes and editorial enhancements made in the 2020 Scott *Specialized Catalogue of United States Stamps and Covers*, the Scott editors salute Scott editor emeritus James E. Kloetzel for working tirelessly on the thousands of value changes and hundreds of editorial changes. Kloetzel and the rest of the Scott editors have been busy adding and expanding listings and making significant improvements throughout the catalog.

Similar to the 2019 U.S. Specialized catalog, editorial enhancements somewhat overshadow value changes. Value changes from No. 1 through No. 771 are somewhat more than normally seen, though the overall trend is quite neutral. When the U.S. value changes in Volume 1A of the 2020 Standard catalog are brought forward, and the new 2020 U.S. Specialized value changes are added, the total is 2,680, about the same as in the 2019 U.S. Specialized catalog.

A horizontal dimension comparison of plate blocks of the Fourth Bureau series 11¢ Rutherford B. Hayes stamp printed on "special" booklet paper vs. regular orientation paper (bottom).

There are also many value changes found in the listings for 19th- and 20th-century stamps. An important stamp, the 2¢ George Washington coil stamp (Scott 321) pair in unused condition, jumps to $600,000 from $450,000 in the 2020 Vol. 1A catalog.

Overall, however, the story is steady as she goes, with very few significant increases or decreases in values.

The Columbia SCADTA consular overprint values should be studied closely, because it has been clarified that values are for stamps and covers that are actually very fine examples without the oftentimes tropicalized perforations or spotting.

Value changes made for this catalog also reflect a somewhat softening of high-value parcel post stamps (Scott Q1-Q12) and plate blocks.

It has been noted that modern stamped envelopes properly used in the time period of validity of the issued denominations (which is what Scott values reflect) are getting extremely hard to find, and values for many of these used envelopes rise in value, often significantly. These values may continue to rise in value in the future. For example, modern commemorative-themed envelopes such as the 2001 34¢ Community Colleges (Scott U648) previously had a value for a used entire at 40¢. The new value is $2.

For collectors who have been waiting to buy large die proofs of the private-die proprietary stamps, we are afraid that the ship has sailed. Values increase about 20 percent across the board for Nos. ROTC1a through RU16P1.

Christmas seals issued from 1980 to 2018 were added to the 2020 Scott U.S. Specialized catalog. Shown is a block of four of the 1991 Christmas seals featuring musical instruments (Scott WX307).

Also featured in this edition of the Scott U.S. Specialized catalog is the 24th edition of *Scott Stamp Values: U.S. Specialized by Grade*. The supplement can be easily located in this catalog by the yellow-tipped pages. Scott Stamp Values lists values for sound stamps in eight different grades. Numerical grades are assigned to the verbal grades commonly used.

Editorial enhancements

Editorial enhancements in the 2020 U.S. Specialized catalog are prolific.

Special Feature articles are included in this catalog for two important editorial enhancements.

After long research and documented proof, the Scott U.S. Specialized catalog now lists the "special" booklet paper stamps of 1928. This includes varieties from No. 563b through QE3b, 11 stamps in all. These listings will appear only in the U.S. Specialized catalog.

The second Special Feature provides details about the new "on cover" listings for the Kansas-Nebraska overprint issues of 1929 (Scott 658-679).

A significant number of new essays were added to the catalog, and approximately 100 images of essays have been updated from black-and-white to color. Collectors of essays will also be happy to know that the 1869 safety paper essays have been renumbered in a way that makes sense, including the addition of one type that was not before noted. Thank you to Scott Trepel and John Zuckerman of Robert A. Siegel Auction Galleries for the excellent research behind these changes.

Long-delayed listings of Christmas seals for the years 1980 to 2018 have been added. The Christmas seal listings sound like a routine matter, but they are everything but. I encourage you to look at this section closely. Values for early errors, covers and earliest documented uses were also are added, plus new early major varieties.

The number of new postal counterfeits discovered since the 2019 U.S. Specialized catalog was published comes as no surprise, considering their prevalence in different online marketplaces. For those collectors looking to tell the differences between these counterfeits and their genuine versions, this section in the 2020 U.S. Specialized catalog is the reference tool for you.

Jay Bigalke, Scott catalog editor-in-chief

Table of contents

We are Buying!
Waterbury and Other High-Quality Fancy Cancel Covers
What Do You Have?

The two covers above were recently purchased by us for one of our clients.
We are looking to buy more, whether a single piece or an entire collection.
Of course, immediate payment in full to any amount. Please call us to discuss a sale.

COLUMBIAN STAMP COMPANY

SCARSDALE, NEW YORK PHONE 914-649-8919 WWW.COLUMBIANSTAMP.COM

EMAIL: sonnyhagendorf@gmail.com

Acknowledgments

Our appreciation and gratitude go to the following individuals and organizations who have assisted us in preparing information included in this year's edition of the Scott *Specialized Catalogue of United States Stamps and Covers*. Some helpers prefer anonymity. Those individuals have generously shared their stamp knowledge with others through the medium of the Scott Catalogue. Those who follow provided information that is in addition to the hundreds of dealer price lists and advertisements and scores of auction catalogues and realizations which were used in producing the Catalogue Values provided herein. It is from those noted here that we have been able to obtain information on items not normally seen in published lists and advertisements. Support from these people of course goes beyond data leading to Catalogue Values, for they also are key to editorial changes.

Michael E. Aldrich (Michael E. Aldrich, Inc.)
Clifford J. Alexander (Carriers and Locals Society)
Roland Austin
Jim Bardo (Bardo Stamps)
William P. Barlow, Jr.
Harvey Bennett (Matthew Bennett International)
Bill Bergstrom (H.R. Harmer, Inc.)
John Birkinbine II
Charles R. Biro
Brian M. Bleckwenn (The Philatelic Foundation)
Roger S. Brody
Randall Brooksbank
Tom Brougham (Canal Zone Study Group)
James R. Callis, Jr. (postalstationery.com)
Gil Celli (The Gold Mine)
Ron H. Cipolla
Harry Corrigan
Tony L. Crumbley (Carolina Coin and Stamp, Inc.)
John Denune Jr.
John Denune, Sr.
Bob and Rita Dumaine (Sam Houston Duck Co.)
Mark Eastzer
Jeffrey M. Forster
Richard Friedberg
Melvin Getlan
Stan Goldfarb
Marty Graff
Fred F. Gregory
Dan Harding
Bruce Hecht (Bruce L. Hecht Co.)
Peter Hoffman
John M. Hotchner
Doug Iams
Tom Jacks (Mountainside Stamps)
Eric Jackson
Michael Jaffe (Michael Jaffe Stamps, Inc.)
Allan Katz (Ventura Stamp Co.)
Lewis Kaufman (The Philatelic Foundation)
Patricia A. Kaufmann (Confederate Stamp Alliance)
Jon Kawaguchi (Ryukyu Philatelic Specialist Society)
William V. Kriebel (Souvenir Card Collectors Society)
Ken Lawrence
James E. Lee
John R. Lewis (The William Henry Stamp Co.)
Nicholas Lombardi
Peter Martin (State Revenue Society)
Timothy M. McRee
Brian Metz
Gary Morris (Pacific Midwest Co.)
Peter Mosiondz, Jr.
Bruce M. Moyer (Moyer Stamps & Collectables)
Scott Murphy
Leonard Nadybal
Joseph M. Napp
Gerald Nylander
George Painter
Michael O. Perry
Stanley M. Piller (Stanley M. Piller & Associates)
Peter W. W. Powell
Bob Prager (Gary Posner, Inc.)
Ed Reiser (Century Stamp Co.)
Peter A. Robertson
Robert G. Rufe
Christopher Rupp
Dennis W. Schmidt
Terry R. Scott
Craig Selig
J. Randall Shoemaker (Philatelic Stamp Authentication and Grading, Inc.)
Ray Simrak
Sergio & Liane Sismondo (The Classic Collector)
Merle Spencer (The Stamp Gallery)
Alfred E. Staubus
Stephen L. Suffet
Robert E. Thompson
Alan Thomson (Plate Number Coil Collectors Club)
David R. Torre
Scott R. Trepel (Siegel Auction Galleries, Inc.)
Dan Undersander
Steven Unkrich
Philip T. Wall
Dr. Gary B. Weiss
Robert Wurdeman
Jack & Carol Yao

Expertizing Services

The following organizations will, for a fee, provide expert opinions about stamps submitted to them. Collectors should contact these organizations to find out about their fees and requirements before submitting philatelic material to them. The listing of these groups here is not intended as an endorsement by Amos Media Co.

General Expertizing Services

American Philatelic Expertizing Service (a service of the American Philatelic Society)
100 Match Factory Place
Bellefonte PA 16823-1367
Ph: (814) 933-3803
Fax: (814) 933-6128
www.stamps.org
E-mail: apsinfo@stamps.org
Areas of expertise: Worldwide

Philatelic Foundation
22 E. 35th St., 4th Floor
New York NY 10016
Ph: (212) 221-6555
Fax: (212) 221-6208
www.philatelicfoundation.org
E-mail: philatelicfoundation@verizon.net
Areas of expertise: U.S. & Worldwide

Philatelic Stamp Authentication and Grading, Inc.
PO Box 41-0880
Melbourne FL 32941-0880
Customer Service: (305) 345-9864
www.psaginc.com
E-mail: info@psaginc.com
Areas of expertise: U.S., Canal Zone, Hawaii, Philippines, Canada & Provinces

Professional Stamp Experts
PO Box 539309
Henderson NV 89053-9309
Ph: (702) 776-6522
www.gradingmatters.com
www.psestamp.com
E-mail: info@gradingmatters.com
Areas of expertise: U.S., U.S. Possessions, British Commonwealth

Expertizing Services Covering Specific Fields Or Countries

American First Day Cover Society Expertizing Committee
P.O. Box 141379
Columbus, OH 43214

Confederate Stamp Alliance Authentication Service
Gen. Frank Crown, Jr.
PO Box 278
Capshaw AL 35742-0396
Ph: (302) 422-2656
Fax: (302) 424-1990
www.csalliance.org
E-mail: csaas@knology.net
Areas of expertise: Confederate stamps and postal history

Errors, Freaks and Oddities Collectors Club Expertizing Service
138 East Lakemont Drive
Kingsland GA 31548
Ph: (912) 729-1573
Areas of expertise: U.S. errors, freaks and oddities

Hawaiian Philatelic Society Expertizing Service
PO Box 10115
Honolulu HI 96816-0115
Areas of expertise: Hawaii

Seeking, Selling or Enjoying— We are your Best Choice.

Seeking New Stamps or Covers?

Frequent Major Public Auction Sales including Specialty Sales, plus weekly Internet Sales. Also, look for our online offerings.

Selling Your Collection?

- **Consign or sell—Receive the market price *Now*!**
- **Outright purchase for *Immediate Payment***
- **Auction Consignment • Cash Advances**
- **Ask about our Guaranteed Value Program**
- **Private Treaty**

Enjoying Your Collection?

Receive our outstanding magazine—*Stamp Collector's Quarterly*
Ask us to send you a FREE copy! We'll send you a future copy when you take our short survey.
Have your article published —Share your story or passion!

Our philatelic team includes over 300 years of unparalleled professional expertise

David Coogle
Co-Chairman

Laurence Gibson
Co-Chairman

Tracy L. Carey
President & COO

Michael Rogers
President Emeritus
Kelleher & Rogers, Ltd.

Stanley J. Richmond
President Emeritus
DFK Auctions, LLC

Job opportunities at Kelleher—
Philatelists enquire, both full and part time needed

22 Shelter Rock Lane • Unit 53 • Danbury, CT 06810, USA
Toll Free: 800.212.2830 • Tel: 203.830.2500 • Fax: 203.297.6059
www.kelleherauctions.com

Addresses, Telephone Numbers & E-Mail Addresses of General & Specialized Philatelic Societies

Collectors can contact the following groups for information about the philately of the areas within the scope of these societies, or inquire about membership in these groups. Many more specialized philatelic societies exist than those listed below. Aside from the general societies, we limit this list to groups which specialize in areas covered by the Scott U.S. Specialized Catalogue. These addresses were compiled two months prior to publication, and are, to the best of our knowledge, correct and current. Groups should inform the editors of address changes whenever they occur. The editors also want to hear from other such specialized groups not listed. Unless otherwise noted, all website addresses begin with http://

American Air Mail Society
Stephen Reinhard
P.O. Box 110
Mineola NY 11501
www.americanairmailsociety.org
E-mail: sreinhard1@optonline.net

American First Day Cover Society
Douglas Kelsey
P.O. Box 16277
Tucson AZ 85732-6277
Ph: (520) 321-0880
www.afdcs.org
E-mail: afdcs@afdcs.org

American Philatelic Society
100 Match Factory Place
Bellefonte PA 16823-1367
Ph: (814) 933-3803
www.stamps.org
E-mail: apsinfo@stamps.org

American Revenue Association
Lyman Hensley
473 E. Elm St.
Sycamore IL 60178-1934
www.revenuer.org
E-mail: ilrno2@netzero.net

American Society for Philatelic Pages and Panels
Ron Walenciak
P.O. Box 1042
Washington Township NJ 07676
www.asppp.org
E-mail: rwalenciak@aol.com

American Stamp Dealers Association
P.O. Box 692
Leesport PA 19553
Ph: (800) 369-8207
www.americanstampdealer.com
E-mail: asda@americanstampdealer.com

American Topical Association
Jennifer Miller
P.O. Box 2143
Greer SC 29652-2143
www.americantopicalassn.org
E-mail: americantopical@msn.com

Auxiliary Markings Club
Jerry Johnson
6621 W. Victoria Ave.
Kennewick WA 99336
www.postal-markings.org
E-mail: membership-2016@postal-markings.org

Canal Zone Study Group
Mike Drabik
P.O. Box 281
Bolton MA 01740
www.canalzonestudygroup.com
E-mail: czsgsecretary@gmail.com

Carriers and Locals Society
John Bowman
14409 Pentridge Drive
Corpus Christi TX 78410
www.pennypost.org
E-mail: jbowman@stx.rr.com

Christmas Seal & Charity Stamp Society
John Denune
234 East Broadway
Granville OH 43023
Ph: (740) 587-0276
www.seal-society.org
E-mail: john@christmasseals.net

Confederate Stamp Alliance
Patricia A. Kaufmann
10194 N. Old State Road
Lincoln DE 19960
Ph. (302) 422-2656
www.csalliance.org
E-mail: trishkauf@comcast.net

Errors, Freaks, and Oddities Collectors Club
Scott Shaulis
P.O. Box 549
Murrysville PA 15668-0549
Ph: (724) 733-4134
www.efocc.org
E-mail: scott@shaulisstamps.com

Hawaiian Philatelic Society
Gannon Sugimura
P.O. Box 10115
Honolulu HI 96816-0115
E-mail: hiphilsoc@gmail.com

International Philippine Philatelic Society
James R. Larot, Jr.
4990 Bayleaf Court
Martinez CA 94553
Ph: (925) 260-5425
www.theipps.info
E-mail: jlarot@ccwater.com

International Society of Reply Coupon Collectors
Peter Robin
P.O. Box 353
Bala Cynwyd PA 19004
E-mail: peterrobin@verizon.net

National Duck Stamp Collectors Society
Anthony J. Monico
P.O. Box 43
Harleysville PA 19438-0043
www.ndscs.org
E-mail: ndscs@hwcn.org

National Stamp Dealers Association
Sheldon Ruckens, President
3643 Private Road 18
Pinckneyville IL 62274-3426
Ph: (800) 875-6631
www.nsdainc.org
E-mail: nsda@nsdainc,org

Plate Number Coil Collectors Club
Gene Trinks
16415 W. Desert Wren Court
Surprise AZ 85374
Ph: (623) 322-4619
www.pnc3.org
E-mail: gctrinks@cox.net

Post Mark Collectors Club
Bob Mulligan
7014 Woodland Oaks Drive
Magnolia TX 77354
Ph: (281) 259-2735
www.postmarks.org
E-mail: bob.mulligan0@gmail.com

Postal History Society
Yamil Kouri
405 Waltham St. #347
Lexington MA 02421
www.postalhistorysociety.org
E-mail: yhkouri@massmed.org

Precancel Stamp Society
Dick Kalmbach
404 Sundown Drive
Knoxville TN 37934
www.precancels.com
E-mail: promo@precancels.com

Ryukyu Philatelic Specialists Society
Laura Edmonds, Secy.
P.O. Box 240177
Charlotte NC 28224-0177
Ph: (704) 519-5157
www.ryukyustamps.org
E-mail: secretary@ryukyustamps.org

Souvenir Card Collectors Society
William V. Kriebel
1923 Manning St.
Philadelphia PA 12103-5728
E-mail: krebewv@drexel.edu

State Revenue Society
Kent Gray
P. O. Box 67842
Albuquerque NM 87193
www.staterevenue.org
E-mail: srssecretary@comcast.net

United Nations Philatelists
Blanton Clement, Jr.
P. O. Box 146
Morrisville PA 19067-0146
www.unpi.com
E-mail: bclemjr@yahoo.com

United Postal Stationery Society
Dave Kandziolka
1659 Branham Lane,
Suite F-307
San Jose CA 95118-2291
www.upss.org
E-mail: poststat@gmail.com

U.S. Cancellation Club
Roger Curran
20 University Avenue
Lewisburg PA 17837
E-mail: rcurran@dejazzd.com

U.S. Philatelic Classics Society
Rob Lund
2913 Fulton St.
Everett WA 98201-3733
www.uspcs.org
E-mail: membershipchairman@uspcs.org

U.S. Possessions Philatelic Society
Daniel F. Ring
P.O. Box 113
Woodstock IL 60098
www.uspps.net
E-mail: danielfring@hotmail.com

United States Stamp Society
Executive Secretary
Larry Ballantyne
P.O. Box 6634
Katy TX 77491-6634
www.usstamps.org
E-mail: webmaster@usstamps.org

Information on Catalogue Values, Grade and Condition

Catalogue Value

The Scott Catalogue value is a retail value; that is, an amount you could expect to pay for a stamp in the grade of Very Fine with no faults. Any exceptions to the grade valued will be noted in the text. The general introduction on the following pages and the individual section introductions further explain the type of material that is valued. The value listed for any given stamp is a reference that reflects recent actual dealer selling prices for that item.

Dealer retail price lists, public auction results, published prices in advertising and individual solicitation of retail prices from dealers, collectors and specialty organizations have been used in establishing the values found in this catalogue. Amos Media Co. values stamps, but Amos Media is not a company engaged in the business of buying and selling stamps as a dealer.

Use this catalogue as a guide for buying and selling. The actual price you pay for a stamp may be higher or lower than the catalogue value because of many different factors, including the amount of personal service a dealer offers, or increased or decreased interest in the country or topic represented by a stamp or set. An item may occasionally be offered at a lower price as a "loss leader," or as part of a special sale. You also may obtain an item inexpensively at public auction because of little interest at that time or as part of a large lot.

Stamps that are of a lesser grade than Very Fine, or those with condition problems, generally trade at lower prices than the values shown in this catalogue. Stamps of exceptional quality in both grade and condition often command higher prices than the values listed.

Values for pre-1879 unused issues are for stamps with approximately half or more of their original gum. Stamps with most or all of their original gum may be expected to sell for more, and stamps with less than half of their original gum may be expected to sell for somewhat less than the values listed. On rarer stamps, it may be expected that the original gum will be somewhat more disturbed than it will be on more common issues. Post-1879 unused issues are assumed to have full original gum. From breakpoints in most countries' listings, stamps are valued as never hinged, due to the wide availability of stamps in that condition. These notations are prominently placed in the listings and in the country information preceding the listings. Some countries also feature listings with dual values for hinged and never-hinged stamps.

Grade

A stamp's grade and condition are crucial to its value. The accompanying illustrations show examples of Very Fine stamps from different time periods, along with examples of stamps in Fine to Very Fine and Extremely Fine grades as points of reference. When a stamp seller offers a stamp in any grade from fine to superb without further qualifying statements, that stamp should not only have the centering grade as defined, but it also should be free of faults or other condition problems.

FINE stamps (illustrations not shown) have designs that are noticeably off center on two sides. Imperforate stamps may have small margins, and earlier issues may show the design touching one edge of the stamp design. For perforated stamps, perfs may barely clear the design on one side, and very early issues normally will have the perforations slightly cutting into the design. Used stamps may have heavier than usual cancellations.

FINE-VERY FINE stamps may be somewhat off center on one side, or slightly off center on two sides. Imperforate stamps will have two margins of at least normal size, and the design will not touch any edge. For perforated stamps, the perfs are well clear of the design, but are still noticeably off center. *However, early issues of a country may be printed in such a way that the design naturally is very close to the edges. In these cases, the perforations may cut into the design very slightly.* Used stamps will not have a cancellation that detracts from the design.

VERY FINE stamps may be slightly off center on one or two sides, but the design will be well clear of the edge. The stamp will present a nice, balanced appearance. Imperforate stamps will have three normal-sized margins. *However, early issues of many countries may be printed in such a way that the perforations may touch the design on one or more sides. Where this is the case, a boxed note will be found defining the centering and margins of the stamps being valued.* Used stamps will have light or otherwise neat cancellations. This is the grade used to establish Scott Catalogue values.

EXTREMELY FINE stamps are close to being perfectly centered. Imperforate stamps will have even margins that are larger than normal. Even the earliest perforated issues will have perforations clear of the design on all sides.

Amos Media Co. recognizes that there is no formally enforced grading scheme for postage stamps, and that the final price you pay or obtain for a stamp will be determined by individual agreement at the time of transaction.

Condition

Grade addresses only centering and (for used stamps) cancellation. *Condition* refers to factors other than grade that affect a stamp's desirability.

Factors that can increase the value of a stamp include exceptionally wide margins, particularly fresh color, the presence of selvage, and plate or die varieties. Unusual cancels on used stamps (particularly those of the 19th century) can greatly enhance their value as well.

Factors other than faults that decrease the value of a stamp include loss of original gum, regumming, a hinge remnant or foreign object adhering to the gum, natural inclusions, straight edges, and markings or notations applied by collectors or dealers.

Faults include missing pieces, tears, pin or other holes, surface scuffs, thin spots, creases, toning, short or pulled perforations, clipped perforations, oxidation or other forms of color changelings, soiling, stains, and such man-made changes as reperforations or the chemical removal or lightening of a cancellation.

Grading Illustrations

On the following page are illustrations of 11 different representative stamps from various time periods, 1847 to the modern era. Beginning with the 1847 10¢ Washington, examples are shown from the 1851-57 imperforates, two examples from the difficult 1857-61 perforated issues, a Black Jack representative of the 1861-67 issues, a Franklin stamp from the 1869 issue, a Bank Note stamp representative of the 1870-88 issues, an 1898 commemorative, a stamp from the 1902-03 issue, a representative 1908-22 Washington-Franklin design, and a 20th century definitive from the 1922 issue.

The editors believe these illustrations will prove useful in showing the margin size and centering that will be seen in the different time periods of U.S. stamp production.

In addition to the matters of margin size and centering, collectors are reminded that the very fine stamps valued in the Scott catalogues also will possess fresh color and intact perforations, and they will be free from defects.

Examples shown are computer-manipulated images made from single digitized master illustrations.

Stamp Illustrations Used in the Catalogue

It is important to note that the stamp images used for identification purposes in this catalogue may not be indicative of the grade of stamp being valued. Refer to the written discussion of grades on this page and to the grading illustrations on the following two pages for grading information.

	1847 ISSUE	1851-57 ISSUES	1857-61 ISSUES	1857-61 ISSUES	1861-67 ISSUES	1869 ISSUE
Fine-Very Fine →						
SCOTT CATALOGUES VALUE STAMPS IN THIS GRADE Very Fine →						
Extremely Fine →						

	1870-88 ISSUES	1898 TRANS-MISSISSIPPIS	1902-03 ISSUES	1908-20 WASHINGTON-FRANKLIN ISSUES	1922-25 ISSUES
Fine-Very Fine →					
SCOTT CATALOGUES VALUE STAMPS IN THIS GRADE Very Fine →					
Extremely Fine →					

For purposes of helping to determine the gum condition and value of an unused stamp, Scott presents the following chart which details different gum conditions and indicates how the conditions correlate with the Scott values for unused stamps. Used together, the Illustrated Grading Chart on the previous page and this Illustrated Gum Chart should allow users to better understand the grade and gum condition of stamps valued in the *Scott U.S. Specialized Catalogue*.

Gum Categories:	MINT N.H.	ORIGINAL GUM (O.G.)				NO GUM
	 **Mint Never Hinged** *Free from any disturbance*	 **Lightly Hinged** *Faint impression of a removed hinge over a small area*	 **Hinge Mark or Remnant** *Prominent hinged spot; may have part or all of the hinge remaining*	 **Large part o.g.** *Approximately half or more of the gum intact*	 **Small part o.g.** *Approximately less than half of the gum intact*	**No gum** *Only if issued with gum*
Commonly Used Symbol:	★★	★	★	★	★	(★)
PRE-1879 ISSUES	*Very fine pre-1879 stamps in these categories trade at a premium over Scott value*		Scott Value for "Unused" (Actual value will be affected by the degree of hinging and completeness of the gum.)			Scott "No Gum" Values thru No. 218
1879-1935 ISSUES	Scott "Never Hinged" Values for Nos. 182-771	Scott Value for "Unused" (Actual value will be affected by the degree of hinging of the full o.g.)				
1935 TO DATE	Scott Value for "Unused"					

Never Hinged (NH; ★★): A never-hinged stamp will have full original gum that will have no hinge mark or disturbance. The presence of an expertizer's mark does not disqualify a stamp from this designation.

Original Gum (OG; ★): Pre-1890 stamps should have approximately half or more of their original gum. On rarer stamps, it may be expected that the original gum will be somewhat more disturbed than it will be on more common issues. Stamps issued in 1890 or later should have full original gum. Original gum will show some disturbance caused by a previous hinge(s) which may be present or entirely removed. The actual value of an 1890 or later stamp will be affected by the degree of hinging of the full original gum.

Disturbed Original Gum: Gum showing noticeable effects of humidity, climate or hinging over more than half of the gum. The significance of gum disturbance in valuing a stamp in any of the Original Gum categories depends on the degree of disturbance, the rarity and normal gum condition of the issue and other variables affecting quality.

Regummed (RG; (★)): A regummed stamp is a stamp without gum that has had some type of gum privately applied at a time after it was issued. This normally is done to deceive collectors and/or dealers into thinking that the stamp has original gum and therefore has a higher value. A regummed stamp is considered the same as a stamp with none of its original gum for purposes of grading.

IMPORTANT INFORMATION REGARDING VALUES FOR NEVER-HINGED STAMPS

Collectors should be aware that the values given for never-hinged stamps from No. 182 on are for stamps in the grade of very fine. The never-hinged premium as a percentage of value will be larger for stamps in extremely fine or superb grades, and the premium will be smaller for fine-very-fine, fine or poor examples. This is particulary true of the issues of the late-19th and early 20th centuries. For example, in the grade of very fine, an unused stamp from this time period may be valued at $100 hinged and $200 never hinged. The never-hinged premium is thus 100%. But in a grade of extremely fine, this same stamp will not only sell for more hinged, but the never-hinged premium will increase, perhaps to 200%-400% or more over the higher extremely fine value. In a grade of superb, a hinged copy will sell for much more than a very fine copy, and additionally the never-hinged premium will be much larger, perhaps as large as 500%-1,000%. On the other hand, the same stamp in a grade of fine or fine-very fine not only will sell for less than a very fine stamp in hinged condition, but additionally the never-hinged premium will be smaller than the never-hinged premium on a very fine stamp, perhaps as small as 15%-30%.

Please note that the above statements and percentages are NOT a formula for arriving at the values of stamps in hinged or never-hinged condition in the grades of very good, fine, fine to very fine, extremely fine or superb. The percentages given apply only to the size of the premium for never-hinged condition that might be added to the stamp value for hinged condition. Further, the percentages given are only generalized estimates. Some stamps or grades may have percentages for never-hinged condition that are higher or lower than the ranges given. For values of the most popular U.S. stamps in the grades of very good, fine, fine to very fine, very fine to extremely fine, extremely fine, extremely fine to superb and superb, see the *Scott Stamp Values* section of this catalog.

Never-Hinged Plate Blocks

Values given for never-hinged plate blocks are for blocks in which all stamps have original gum that has never been hinged and has no disturbances, and all selvage, whether gummed or ungummed, has never been hinged.

Catalogue Values for Stamps on Covers

Definition of a Cover

Covers are philatelically defined as folded letters, folded covers or envelopes, with or without postage stamps, that have passed through the mail and bear postal or other markings of philatelic interest. Before the introduction of envelopes about 1840, people folded letters and wrote the address on the outside. Used stamped envelopes and wrappers and other items of postal stationery also are considered covers, as is a postage stamp used on a post card.

Catalogue Value

The Scott Catalogue value for a stamp on cover, as for a stamp off cover, is a retail value; that is, an amount you could expect to pay for that cover in a grade of Very Fine, as defined below. Folded letters, folded covers, envelopes, postcards, stationery entires and newspapers are valued as whole and complete, not as fronts of letter sheets or envelopes or as fragments of newspapers or circulars. Values given are for covers bearing stamps that are "tied on" by the cancellation. A stamp is said to be "tied" to a cover when the cancellation or postmark falls on both the stamp and the cover. Exceptions always will be noted. Values for bisected stamps on cover are for items on which the cancellation ties the stamp across the cut. Values for U.S. patriotic covers of the Civil War period (bearing pictorial designs of a patriotic nature) are for the most common designs.

It should be noted that conventions observed for calculating the catalogue value of a cover with several different stamps vary somewhat between types of covers. In a general way, however, the most common procedure may be summarized as follows: the stamp which has the highest "value on cover" is counted with its on-cover value, while the other stamps are added on to the total with their normal value as used stamps "off cover."

The value generally is given for the stamps as they are most commonly found on a cover. In some cases a stamp is most commonly found alone, paying a specified rate for the envelope, given its weight, destination and method of intended delivery. For instance, beginning July 1, 1863, and continuing through September 30, 1883, a one-half ounce letter sent domestically by ordinary first-class mail required three cents postage. Because such letters were very common, it follows that stamps with denominations of three cents are most often found on envelopes paying that one-half ounce domestic rate. Three-cent stamps also are found on letters together with other stamps making up different rates. A pair of three-cent stamps paid for a one-ounce domestic letter, four three-cent stamps paid for a one-ounce letter addressed to England (rate effective January 1, 1870, through June 30, 1875), and so forth. Because letters addressed abroad are less common than letters addressed domestically, the on-cover value of the three-cent stamps refers to the single usage. That is not true in all instances, because there are some stamps issued during the 19th century that are more scarce used singly than in combination with other stamps. In all these other cases, the value given is for the least scarce of the combinations. For most stamps issued during 1922-31, the value is for a specific use. For example, the value for the 1922 15-cent Statue of Liberty stamp (Scott 566) is for that stamp on a registered cover with a two-cent stamp, to pay the two-cent domestic first-class letter rate and 15-cent registry fee.

If the value of a single stamp on a cover is of particular philatelic importance, as in the case of certain stamps used to pay for reduced rates for the delivery of newspapers or other printed matter, then their different value for this use may be indicated in footnotes or as a separate listing. For example, the 3-cent George Washington stamp of 1851 (Scott 10) is specifically valued paying the 3-cent rate for a circular mailed a distance of 1,000 miles to 1,500 miles from the point of mailing. It clearly is impossible to add to a specialized catalogue of U.S. stamps the detailed information regarding the relative scarcity and value of all rates and combinations. We have limited ourselves to some of the more noteworthy and important cases.

In the majority of cases, the value of a cover assumes that the stamps on it have been used in the period contemporaneous with their issuance. Late uses are sometimes considered premium items, but in most cases late and very late uses are of no significance and detract from the value of the cover.

Condition

When evaluating a cover, care must be given to the factors that determine the overall condition of the item. It is generally more difficult to grade and evaluate a cover than a stamp. The condition of the stamps affixed to the cover must be taken into account — always in relation to the criteria for the particular issue. The Scott Catalogue does specify the grade and condition of the stamps for which a value is given, so it is important to consult this information. In addition, the condition of the cover must be taken into account. Values are for covers that are reasonably well preserved given the period of usage and the country of origin. A tiny nick or tear, or slight reduction from opening, are normal for 19th century covers. Folded letters may be expected to have tears on the reverse from opening, and often they will have file folds. Unless these factors affect the stamps or postal markings, they should not detract from the on-cover values given in the catalogue.

Just as with stamps, various factors can lower the value of a cover. Missing pieces, serious tears, holes, creases, toning, stains and alterations of postal markings are examples of factors that lower the value of a cover. The necessity of considering these factors for the cover, as well as having to consider the condition of the stamps on the cover, helps to explain why it is more difficult to determine the value of a cover than a stamp off cover.

Factors Enhancing the Value of a Cover

A further difficulty in the valuation of covers is the necessity of considering factors other than the stamps used on a cover and the condition of the stamps and the cover. As stated previously, catalogue values listed herein generally reflect the most common uses of stamps on covers that are reasonably well preserved given the period of usage. Consideration of factors that may enhance the value of covers for the most part is beyond the scope of the Scott Catalogue. However, it is critical to understand that there are many such factors. Following is a list of many of the factors that often will increase the value of a cover.

- postal markings indicating origin, transit and arrival;
- postal markings indicating rates paid, which include postage, registration, acknowledgment of receipt, express charges, insurance, postage due, forwarding and many others;
- postal markings indicating carriers such as stagecoaches, trains, ships, aircraft, etc.;
- markings applied by censors, other civilian or military authorities, and others;
- scarce or rare destinations and routings;
- interruptions in the delivery system due to accidents, wars, natural calamities, etc.;
- unusual combinations of stamps;
- printed or hand-drawn pictorial, advertising or patriotic cover designs;
- unusual quality of stamps, postal markings or cover;
- and, outside of postal history, particularly noteworthy addressee, sender or contents.

Catalogue Listing Policy

It is the intent of Amos Media Co. to list all postage stamps of the world in the *Scott Standard Postage Stamp Catalogue*. The only strict criteria for listing is that stamps be decreed legal for postage by the issuing country and that the issuing country actually have an operating postal system. Whether the primary intent of issuing a given stamp or set was for sale to postal patrons or to stamp collectors is not part of our listing criteria. Scott's role is to provide basic comprehensive postage stamp information. It is up to each stamp collector to choose which items to include in a collection.

It is Scott's objective to seek reasons why a stamp should be listed, rather than why it should not. Nevertheless, there are certain types of items that will not be listed. These include the following:

1. Unissued items that are not officially distributed or released by the issuing postal authority. If such items are officially issued at a later date by the country, they will be listed. Unissued items consist of those that have been printed and then held from sale for reasons such as change in government, errors found on stamps or something deemed objectionable about a stamp subject or design.

2. Stamps "issued" by non-existent postal entities or fantasy countries, such as Nagaland, Occusi-Ambeno, Staffa, Sedang, Torres Straits and others. Also, stamps "issued" in the names of legitimate, stamp-issuing countries that are not authorized by those countries.

3. Semi-official or unofficial items not required for postage. Examples include items issued by private agencies for their own express services. When such items are required for delivery, or are valid as prepayment of postage, they are listed.

4. Local stamps issued for local use only. Postage stamps issued by governments specifically for "domestic" use, such as Haiti Scott 219-228, or the United States non-denominated stamps, are not considered to be locals, since they are valid for postage throughout the country of origin.

5. Items not valid for postal use. For example, a few countries have issued souvenir sheets that are not valid for postage. This area also includes a number of worldwide charity labels (some denominated) that do not pay postage.

6. Egregiously exploitative issues such as stamps sold for far more than face value, stamps purposefully issued in artificially small quantities or only against advance orders, stamps awarded only to a selected audience such as a philatelic bureau's standing order customers, or stamps sold only in conjunction with other products. All of these kinds of items are usually controlled issues and/or are intended for speculation. These items normally will be included in a footnote.

7. Items distributed by the issuing government only to a limited group, such as a stamp club, philatelic exhibition or a single stamp dealer, or other private company. These items normally will be included in a footnote.

8. Stamps not available to collectors. These generally are rare items, all of which are held by public institutions such as museums. The existence of such items often will be cited in footnotes.

The fact that a stamp has been used successfully as postage, even on international mail, is not in itself sufficient proof that it was legitimately issued. Numerous examples of so-called stamps from non-existent countries are known to have been used to post letters that have successfully passed through the international mail system.

There are certain items that are subject to interpretation. When a stamp falls outside our specifications, it may be listed along with a cautionary footnote.

A number of factors are considered in our approach to analyzing how a stamp is listed. The following list of factors is presented to share with you, the catalogue user, the complexity of the listing process.

Additional printings — "Additional printings" of a previously issued stamp may range from an item that is totally different to cases where it is impossible to differentiate from the original. At least a minor number (a small-letter suffix) is assigned if there is a distinct change in stamp shade, noticeably redrawn design, or a significantly different perforation measurement. A major number (numeral or numeral and capital-letter combination) is assigned if the editors feel the "additional printing" is sufficiently different from the original that it constitutes a different issue.

Commemoratives — Where practical, commemoratives with the same theme are placed in a set. For example, the U.S. Civil War Centennial set of 1961-65 and the Constitution Bicentennial series of 1989-90 appear as sets. Countries such as Japan and Korea issue such material on a regular basis, with an announced, or at least predictable, number of stamps known in advance. Occasionally, however, stamp sets that were released over a period of years have been separated. Appropriately placed footnotes will guide you to each set's continuation.

Definitive sets — Blocks of numbers generally have been reserved for definitive sets, based on previous experience with any given country. If a few more stamps were issued in a set than originally expected, they often have been inserted into the original set with a capital-letter suffix, such as U.S. Scott 1059A. If it appears that many more stamps than the originally allotted block will be released before the set is completed, a new block of numbers will be reserved, with the original one being closed off. In some cases, such as the U.S. Transportation and Great Americans series, several blocks of numbers exist. Appropriately placed footnotes will guide you to each set's continuation.

New country — Membership in the Universal Postal Union is not a consideration for listing status or order of placement within the catalogue. The index will tell you in what volume or page number the listings begin.

"No release date" items — The amount of information available for any given stamp issue varies greatly from country to country and even from time to time. Extremely comprehensive information about new stamps is available from some countries well before the stamps are released. By contrast some countries do not provide information about stamps or release dates. Most countries, however, fall between these extremes. A country may provide denominations or subjects of stamps from upcoming issues that are not issued as planned. Sometimes, philatelic agencies, those private firms hired to represent countries, add these later-issued items to sets well after the formal release date. This time period can range from weeks to years. If these items were officially released by the country, they will be added to the appropriate spot in the set. In many cases, the specific release date of a stamp or set of stamps may never be known.

Overprints — The color of an overprint is always noted if it is other than black. Where more than one color of ink has been used on overprints of a single set, the color used is noted. Early overprint and surcharge illustrations were altered to prevent their use by forgers.

Se-tenants — Connected stamps of differing features (se-tenants) will be listed in the format most commonly collected. This includes pairs, blocks or larger multiples. Se-tenant units are not always symmetrical. An example is Australia Scott 508, which is a block of seven stamps. If the stamps are primarily collected as a unit, the major number may be assigned to the multiple, with minors going to each component stamp. In cases where continuous-design or other unit se-tenants will receive significant postal use, each stamp is given a major Scott number listing. This includes issues from the United States, Canada, Germany and Great Britain, for example.

Understanding the Listings

On the opposite page is an enlarged "typical" listing from this catalogue. Following are detailed explanations of each of the highlighted parts of the listing.

❶ **Scott number** — Stamp collectors use Scott numbers to identify specific stamps when buying, selling, or trading stamps, and for ease in organizing their collections. Each stamp issued by a country has a unique number. Therefore, U.S. Scott 219 can only refer to a single stamp. Although the Scott Catalogue usually lists stamps in chronological order by date of issue, when a country issues a set of stamps over a period of time the stamps within that set are kept together without regard to date of issue. This follows the normal collecting approach of keeping stamps in their natural sets.

When a country is known to be issuing a set of stamps over a period of time, a group of consecutive catalogue numbers is reserved for the stamps in that set, as issued. If that group of numbers proves to be too few, capital-letter suffixes are added to numbers to create enough catalogue numbers to cover all items in the set. Scott uses a suffix letter, e.g., "A," "b," etc., only once. If there is a Scott 296B in a set, there will not be a Scott 296b also.

There are times when the block of numbers is too large for the set, leaving some numbers unused. Such gaps in the sequence also occur when the editors move an item elsewhere in the catalogue or remove it from the listings entirely. Scott does not attempt to account for every possible number, but rather it does attempt to assure that each stamp is assigned its own number.

Scott numbers designating regular postage normally are only numerals. Scott numbers for other types of stamps, e.g., air post, special delivery, and so on, will have a prefix of either a capital letter or a combination of numerals and capital letters.

❷ **Illustration number** — used to identify each illustration. Where more than one stamp in a set uses the same illustration number, that number needs to be used with the description line (noted below) to be certain of the exact variety of the stamp within the set. Illustrations normally are 75, 100, or 150 percent of the original size of the stamp. An effort has been made to note all illustrations not at those percentages. Overprints are shown at 100 percent of the original, unless otherwise noted. Letters *in parentheses* which follow an illustration number refer to illustrations of overprints or surcharges.

❸ **Listing styles** — there are two principal types of catalogue listings: major and minor.

Majors may be distinguished by having as their catalogue number a numeral with or without a capital-letter suffix and with or without a prefix.

Minors have a small-letter suffix (or, only have the small letter itself shown if the listing is immediately beneath its major listing). These listings show a variety of the "normal," or major item. Examples include color variation or a different watermark used for that stamp only.

Examples of major numbers are 9X1, 16, 28A, 6LB1, C13, RW1, and TS1. Examples of minor numbers are 22b, 279Bc and C3a.

❹ **Denomination** — normally value printed on the stamp (generally known as the *face value*), which is — unless otherwise stated — the cost of the stamp at the time of issue.

❺ **Basic information on stamp or set** — introducing each stamp issue, this section normally includes the date of issue, method of printing, perforation, watermark, and sometimes additional information. New information on method of printing, watermark or perforation measurement will appear when that information changes. Dates of issue are as precise as Scott is able to confirm, either year only, month and year, or month, day and year.

In stamp sets issued over more than one date, the year or span of years will be in bold type above the first catalogue number. Individual stamps in the set will have a date-of-issue appearing in italics. Stamps without a year listed appeared during the first year of the span. Dates are not always given for minor varieties.

❻ **Color or other description** — this line provides information to solidify identification of the stamp. Historically, when stamps normally were printed in a single color, only the color appeared here. With modern printing techniques, which include multicolor presses which mix inks on the paper, earlier methods of color identification are no longer applicable. When space permits, a description of the stamp design will replace the terms "multi" or "multicolored." The color of the paper is noted in italic type when the paper used is not white.

❼ **Date of issue** — As precisely as Scott is able to confirm, either year only; month and year, or month, day and year. In some cases, the earliest documented use (edu) is given. All dates, especially where no official date of issue has been given, are subject to change as new information is obtained. Many cases are known of inadvertent sale and use of stamps prior to dates of issue announced by postal officials. These are not listed here.

❽ **Value unused and Value used** — the catalogue values are in U. S. dollars and are based on stamps that are in a grade of Very Fine unless stated otherwise. Unused values refer to items that have not seen postal or other duty for which they were intended. For pre-1890 issues, unused stamps must have at least most of their original gum; for later issues, complete gum is expected. Stamps issued without gum are noted. Unused values are for never-hinged stamps beginning at the point immediately following a prominent notice in the actual listing. Scott values for used self-adhesive stamps are for examples either on piece or off piece.

Some sections in this book have more than two columns for values. Check section introductions and watch for value column headers. See the sections "Catalogue Values" and "Understanding Valuing Notations" for an explanation of the meaning of these values.

❾ **Changes in basic set information** — bold or other type is used to show any change in the basic data between stamps within a set of stamps, e.g., perforation from one stamp to the next or a different paper or printing method or watermark.

❿ **Other varieties** — these include additional shades, plate varieties, multiples, used on cover, plate number blocks. coil line pairs, coil plate number strips of three or five, ZIP blocks, etc.

On early issues, there may be a "Cancellation" section. Values in this section refer to single stamps off cover, unless otherwise noted. Values with a "+" are added to the basic used value. See "Basic Stamp Information" for more details on stamp and cancellation varieties.

⓫ **Footnote** — Where other important details about the stamps can be found.

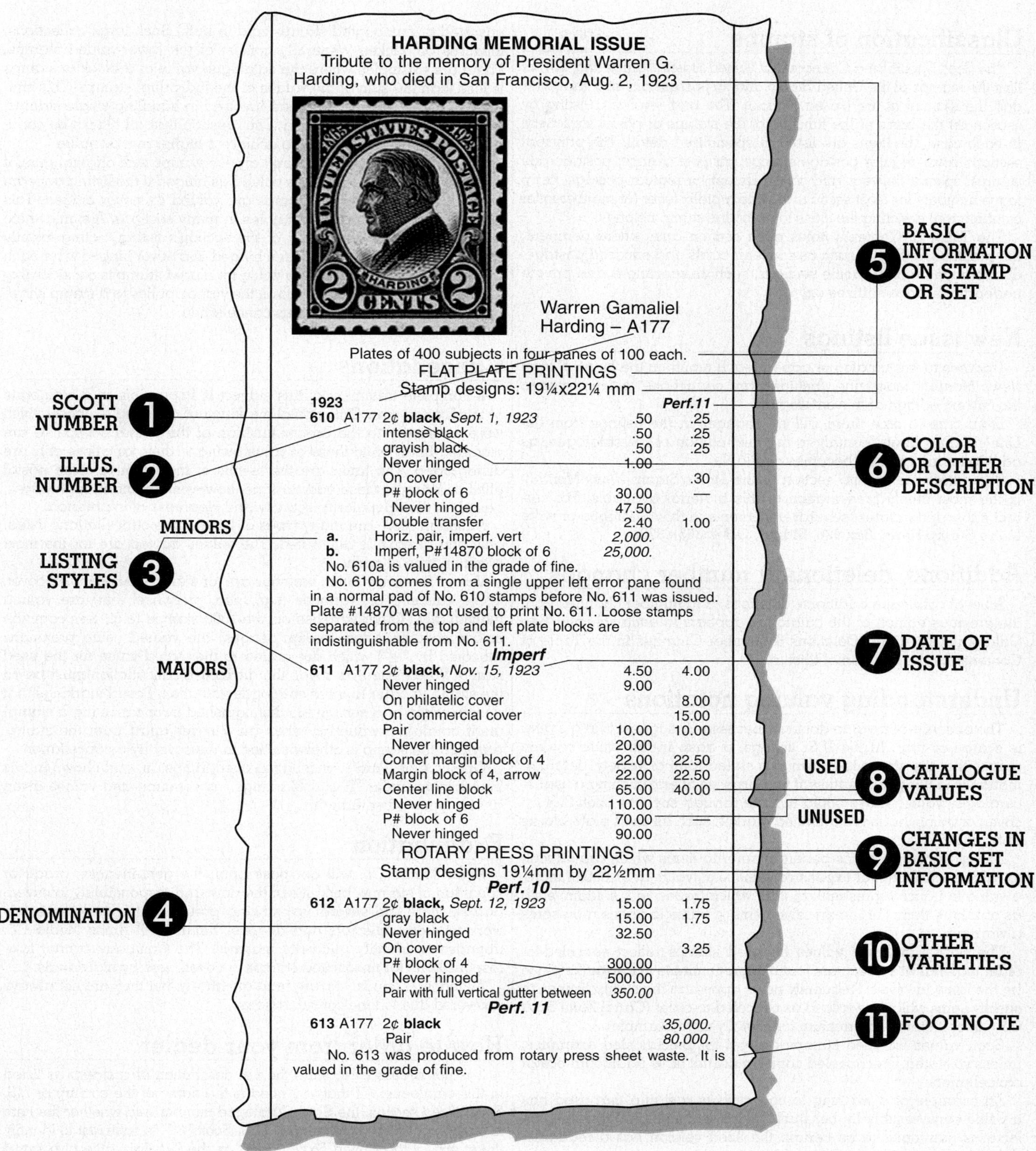
HARDING MEMORIAL ISSUE
Tribute to the memory of President Warren G. Harding, who died in San Francisco, Aug. 2, 1923
1865 UNITED STATES POSTAGE 1923
HARDING
2 CENTS 2
Warren Gamaliel Harding – A177
Plates of 400 subjects in four panes of 100 each.
FLAT PLATE PRINTINGS
Stamp designs: 19¼x22¼ mm
1923 Perf.11
610 A177 2¢ black, Sept. 1, 1923 .50 .25
intense black .50 .25
grayish black .50 .25
Never hinged 1.00
On cover .30
P# block of 6 30.00 —
Never hinged 47.50
Double transfer 2.40 1.00
a. Horiz. pair, imperf. vert 2,000.
b. Imperf, P#14870 block of 6 25,000.
No. 610a is valued in the grade of fine.
No. 610b comes from a single upper left error pane found in a normal pad of No. 610 stamps before No. 611 was issued. Plate #14870 was not used to print No. 611. Loose stamps separated from the top and left plate blocks are indistinguishable from No. 611.
Imperf
611 A177 2¢ black, Nov. 15, 1923 4.50 4.00
Never hinged 9.00
On philatelic cover 8.00
On commercial cover 15.00
Pair 10.00 10.00
Never hinged 20.00
Corner margin block of 4 22.00 22.50
Margin block of 4, arrow 22.00 22.50
Center line block 65.00 40.00
Never hinged 110.00
P# block of 6 70.00 —
Never hinged 90.00
ROTARY PRESS PRINTINGS
Stamp designs 19¼mm by 22½mm
Perf. 10
612 A177 2¢ black, Sept. 12, 1923 15.00 1.75
gray black 15.00 1.75
Never hinged 32.50
On cover 3.25
P# block of 4 300.00
Never hinged 500.00
Pair with full vertical gutter between 350.00
Perf. 11
613 A177 2¢ black 35,000.
Pair 80,000.
No. 613 was produced from rotary press sheet waste. It is valued in the grade of fine.
SCOTT NUMBER 1
ILLUS. NUMBER 2
MINORS
LISTING STYLES 3
MAJORS
DENOMINATION 4
5 BASIC INFORMATION ON STAMP OR SET
6 COLOR OR OTHER DESCRIPTION
7 DATE OF ISSUE
USED
8 CATALOGUE VALUES
UNUSED
9 CHANGES IN BASIC SET INFORMATION
10 OTHER VARIETIES
11 FOOTNOTE

Scott Numbering Practices and Special Notices

Classification of stamps

The Scott *Specialized Catalogue of United States Stamps and Covers* lists the stamps of the United States and its possessions and territories and the stamps of the United Nations. The next level is a listing by section on the basis of the function of the stamps or postal stationery. In each case, the items are listed in specialized detail. The principal sections cover regular postage stamps; air post stamps; postage due stamps, special delivery, and so on. Except for regular postage, catalogue numbers for most sections include a prefix letter (or number-letter combination) denoting the class to which the stamp belongs.

The Table of Contents notes each section and, where pertinent, the prefix used. Some, such as souvenir cards and encased postage, do not have prefixes. Some sections, such as specimens and private perforations, have suffixes only.

New issue listings

Updates to this catalogue appear each month in the *Linn's Stamp News Monthly* magazine. Included are corrections and updates to the current edition of this catalogue.

From time to time there will be changes in the listings from the *Linn's Stamp News Monthly* to the next edition of the catalogue, as additional information becomes available.

The catalogue update section of the *Linn's Stamp News Monthly* is the most timely presentation of this material available. For current subscription rates, see advertisements in this catalogue or write Linn's Stamp News, Box 926, Sidney, OH 45365-0926.

Additions, deletions & number changes

A list of catalogue additions, deletions, and number changes from the previous edition of the catalogue appears in each volume. See Catalogue Additions, Deletions & Number Changes in the Table of Contents for the location of this list.

Understanding valuing notations

The *absence of a value* does not necessarily suggest that a stamp is scarce or rare. In the U.S. listings, a dash in the value column means that the stamp is known in a stated form or variety, but information is lacking or insufficient for purposes of establishing a usable catalogue value. These could include rarities, such as Scott 3X4 on cover, or items that have a limited market, such as used plate blocks of Scott 1097.

Stamp values in *italics* generally refer to items which are difficult to value accurately. For expensive items, e.g., value at $1,000 or more, a value in italics represents an item which trades very seldom, such as a unique item. For inexpensive items, a value in italics represents a warning.

The Scott Catalogue values for used stamps reflect canceled-to-order material when such are found to predominate in the marketplace for the issue involved. Frequently notes appear in the stamp listings to specify items which are valued as canceled-to-order (Canal Zone Scott O1-O8) or if there is a premium for postally used examples.

Scott values for used stamps are not for precanceled examples, unless so stated. Precanceled copies must not have additional postal cancellations.

An example of a warning to collectors is a stamp that used has a value considerably higher than the unused version. Here, the collector is cautioned to be certain the used version has a readable, contemporaneous cancellation.

The *minimum catalogue value* of a stamp is 25 cents, to cover a dealer's costs of purchase and preparation for resale. The minimum catalogue value of a first day cover is one dollar. As noted, the sum of these values does not properly represent the "value" of a packet of unsorted or unmounted stamps sold in bulk. Such large collections, mixtures or packets generally consist of the lower-valued stamps. There are examples where the catalogue value of a block of stamps is less than the sum of the values of the individual stamps. This situation is caused by the overhead involved in handling single stamps, and should not be considered a suggestion that all blocks be separated into individual stamps to achieve a higher market value.

Values in the "unused" column are for stamps with original gum, if issued with gum. The stamp is valued as hinged if the listing appears *before* the point at which stamps are valued as never hinged. This point is marked by prominent notes in many sections. A similar note will appear at the beginning of the section's listing, noting exactly where the dividing point between hinged and never hinged is for each section of the listings. Where a value for a used stamp is considerably higher than for the unused stamp, the value applies to a stamp showing a distinct contemporaneous cancellation.

Cancellations

A complete treatment of this subject is impossible in a catalogue of this limited size. Only postal markings of meaning — those which were necessary to the proper function of the postal service — are recorded here, while those of value owing to their fanciness only are disregarded. The latter are the results of the whim of some postal official. Many of these odd designs, however, command high prices, based on their popularity, scarcity and clearness of impression.

Although there are many types of most of the cancellations listed, only one of each is illustrated. The values quoted are for the most common type of each.

Values for cancellation varieties are for stamp specimens off cover. Some cancellation varieties (e.g., pen, precancel, cut) are valued individually. Other varieties on pre-1900 stamps (e.g., less common colors, specific dates, foreign usages) are valued using premiums (denoted by "+") which are added to the stated value for the used stamp. When listed on cover, the distinctive cancellation must be on the stamp in order to merit catalogue valuation. Postal markings that denote origin or a service (as distinguished from canceling a stamp) merit catalogue valuation when on a cover apart from the stamp, provided the stamp is otherwise tied to the cover by a cancellation.

One type of "Paid" cancellation used in Boston, and shown in this introduction under "Postal Markings," is common and values given are for types other than this.

Examination

Amos Media Co. will not pass upon the genuineness, grade or condition of stamps, because of the time and responsibility involved. Rather, there are several expertizing groups which undertake this work for both collectors and dealers. Neither will Amos Media Co. appraise or identify philatelic material. The Company cannot take responsibility for unsolicited stamps or covers sent by individuals.

All letters, E-mails, etc. are read attentively, but they are not always answered due to time considerations

How to order from your dealer

It is not necessary to write the full description of a stamp as listed in this catalogue. All that you need is the name of the country or *U.S. Specialized* section, the Scott Catalogue number and whether the item is unused or used. For example, "U.S. Scott 833" is sufficient to identify the stamp of the United States listed as the 2-dollar value of a set of stamps issued between 1938-43. This stamp was issued September 29, 1938. It is yellow green and black in color, has a perforation of 11, and is printed on paper without a watermark by a flat plate press. Sections without a prefix or suffix must be mentioned by name.

Abbreviations

Amos Media Co. uses a consistent set of abbreviations throughout this catalogue and the *Standard Postage Stamp Catalogue* to conserve space while still providing necessary information. The first block shown here refers to color names only:

COLOR ABBREVIATIONS

amb....amber
anil....aniline
ap....apple
aqua....aquamarine
az....azure
bis....bister
bl....blue
bld....blood
blk....black
bril....brilliant
brn....brown
brnsh....brownish
brnz....bronze
brt....bright
brnt....burnt
car....carmine
cer....cerise
chlky....chalky
cham....chamois
chnt....chestnut
choc....chocolate
chr....chrome
cit....citron
cl....claret
cob....cobalt
cop....copper
crim....crimson
cr....cream
dk....dark
dl....dull
dp....deep
db....drab
emer....emerald
gldn....golden
grysh....grayish
grn....green
grnsh....greenish
hel....heliotrope
hn....henna
ind....indigo
int....intense
lav....lavender
lem....lemon
lil....lilac
lt....light
mag....magenta
man....manila
mar....maroon
mv....mauve
multi....multicolored
mlky....milky
myr....myrtle
ol....olive
olvn....olivine
org....orange
pck....peacock
pnksh....pinkish
Prus....Prussian
pur....purple
redsh....reddish
res....reseda
ros....rosine
ryl....royal
sal....salmon
saph....sapphire
scar....scarlet
sep....sepia
sien....sienna
sil....silver
sl....slate
stl....steel
turq....turquoise
ultra....ultramarine
ven....venetian
ver....vermilion
vio....violet
yel....yellow
yelsh....yellowish

When no color is given for an overprint or surcharge, black is the color used. Abbreviations for colors used for overprints and surcharges are: "(B)" or "(Blk)," black; "(Bl)," blue; "(R)," red; "(G)," green; etc.

Additional abbreviations used in this catalogue are shown below:

Adm....Administration
AFL....American Federation of Labor
Anniv....Anniversary
APU....Arab Postal Union
APS....American Philatelic Society
ASEAN....Association of South East Asian Nations
ASPCA....American Society for the Prevention of Cruelty to Animals
Assoc....Association

b....Born
BEP....Bureau of Engraving and Printing
Bicent....Bicentennial
Bklt....Booklet
Brit....British
btwn....Between
Bur....Bureau

c. or ca....Circa
CAR....Central African Republic
Cat....Catalogue
Cent....Centennial, century, centenary
CEPT....Conference Europeenne des Administrations des Postes et des Telecommunications
CIO....Congress of Industrial Organizations
Conf....Conference
Cong....Congress
Cpl....Corporal
CTO....Canceled to order

d....Died
Dbl....Double
DDR....German Democratic Republic (East Germany)

EC....European Community
ECU....European currency unit
EDU....Earliest documented use
EEC....European Economic Community
Engr....Engraved
Exhib....Exhibition
Expo....Exposition

FAO....Food and Agricultural Organization of the United Nations
Fed....Federation
FIP....Federation International de Philatelie

GB....Great Britain
Gen....General
GPO....General post office

Horiz....Horizontal

ICAO....International Civil Aviation Organization
ICY....International Cooperation Year
ILO....International Labor Organization
Imperf....Imperforate
Impt....Imprint
Intl....International
Invtd....Inverted
IQSY....International Quiet Sun Year
ITU....International Telecommunications Union
ITY....International Tourism Year
IWY....International Women's Year
IYC....International Year of the Child
IYD....International Year of the Disabled
IYSH....International Year of Shelter for the Homeless
IYY....International Youth Year

L....Left
Lieut....Lieutenant
Litho....Lithographed
LL....Lower left
LR....Lower right

mm....Millimeter
Ms....Manuscript

NASA....National Aeronautics and Space Administration
Natl....National
NATO....North Atlantic Treaty Organization
No....Number
NY....New York
NYC....New York City

OAU....Organization of African Unity
OPEC....Organization of Petroleum Exporting Countries
Ovpt....Overprint
Ovptd....Overprinted

P#....Plate number
Perf....Perforated, perforation
Phil....Philatelic
Photo....Photogravure
PO....Post office
Pr....Pair
P.R....Puerto Rico
PRC....People's Republic of China (Mainland China)
Prec....Precancel, precanceled
Pres....President

R....Right
Rio....Rio de Janeiro
ROC....Republic of China (Taiwan)

SEATO....South East Asia Treaty Organization
Sgt....Sergeant
Soc....Society
Souv....Souvenir
SSR....Soviet Socialist Republic
St....Saint, street
Surch....Surcharge

Typo....Typographed

UAE....United Arab Emirates
UAMPT....Union of African and Malagasy Posts and Telecommunications
UL....Upper left
UN....United Nations
UNESCO....United Nations Educational, Scientific and Cultural Organization
UNICEF....United Nations Children's Fund
Univ....University
UNPA....United Nations Postal Administration
Unwmkd....Unwatermarked
UPU....Universal Postal Union
UR....Upper right
US....United States
USPO....United States Post Office Department
USPS....United States Postal Service (also "U.S. Postage Stamp" when referring to the watermark)
USSR....Union of Soviet Socialist Republics

Vert....Vertical
VP....Vice president

WCY....World Communications Year
WFUNA....World Federation of United Nations Associations
WHO....World Health Organization
Wmk....Watermark
Wmkd....Watermarked
WMO....World Meteorological Organization
WRY....World Refugee Year
WWF....World Wildlife Fund
WWI....World War I
WWII....World War II

YAR....Yemen Arab Republic
Yemen PDR. Yemen People's Democratic Republic

Basic Stamp Information

A stamp collector's knowledge of the combined elements that make a given issue of a stamp unique determines his or her ability to identify stamps. These elements include paper, watermark, method of separation, printing, design and gum. On the following pages these important areas are described in detail.

The guide below will direct you to those philatelic terms which are not major headings in the following introductory material. The major headings are:

Plate	Paper	Gum	Postal Markings
Printing	Separation	Luminescence	General Glossary

Subheadings are shown in parentheses after the major heading for a given term.

Guide to Subjects

Arrows	See Plate (Sheet Stamps)
Bisect	See General Glossary
Blind Perforations	See General Glossary
Blocks	See Plate (Sheet Stamps)
Booklet Panes	See Plate (Sheet Stamps)
Booklets	See Plate (Sheet Stamps), General Glossary
Booklets A.E.F.	See Plate (Sheet Stamps)
Bureau Precancels	See Postal Markings
Cancellations	See Postal Markings, General Glossary
Carrier Postmarks	See Postal Markings
Coarse Perforation	See Separation (Perforations)
Coils	See Plate (Coil Stamps)
Coil Waste	See Plate (Coil Stamps)
Color Changeling	See Printing (Additional Terms
Color Registration Markings	See Plate (Sheet Stamps)
Color Trials	See Printing (Additional Terms)
Commemorative Stamps	See General Glossary
Compound Perforation	See Separation (Perforations)
Covers	See General Glossary
Cracked Plate	See Printing (Common Flaws)
Die	See Plate (Line Engraving)
Die Cutting	See Separation
Double Impression	See Printing (Additional Terms)
Double Paper	See Paper
Double Perforation	See Separation (Perforations)
Double Transfer	See Plate (Line Engraving)
Dry Printings	See note after Scott 1029
Electric Eye	See Separation (Perforations)
Embossed Printing	See Printing
End Roller Grills	See Paper (Grills)
Engraved	See Printing
Error	See General Glossary
Essay	See Printing (Additional Terms)
Fine Perforation	See Separation (Perforations)
First Day Cover	See General Glossary
Flat Plate Printing	See Printing (Additional Terms)
Fluorescent Papers	See Luminescence
Foil Application	See Printing
Foreign Entry	See Plate
Giori Press	See Printing
Gridiron Cancellation	See Postal Markings
Grills	See Paper
Gripper Cracks	See Printing (Common Flaws)
Gouge	See Printing (Additional Terms)
Guide Lines	See Plate (Sheet Stamps)
Gum Breaker Ridges	See General Glossary
Gutter	See Plate (Sheet Stamps)
Hidden Plate Number	See Plate (Coil Stamps)
Holograms	See Printing
Imperforate	See General Glossary
Imprint	See Plate (Sheet Stamps)
India Paper	See Paper
Intaglio	See Plate (Line Engraving), Printing
Inverted Center	See Printing (Additional Terms)
Joint Line	See Plate (Coil Stamps)
Laid Paper	See Paper
Line Engraved	See Printing
Line Pair	See Plate (Coil Stamps)
Lithography	See Printing
Manila Paper	See Paper
Margin	See Plate (Sheet Stamps)
Military Postmarks	See Postal Markings
Multicolored Stamps	See Printing (Additional Terms)
New York City Foreign Mail	See Postal Markings
Offset Lithography	See Printing
Original Gum	See General Glossary
Overprint	See Printing (Additional Terms), General Glossary
Pair Imperf. Between	See General Glossary
Pane	See Plate (Plate Arrangement)
Part-Perforate	See General Glossary
Paste-up	See Plate (Coil Stamps)
Paste-up Pair	See Plate (Coil Stamps)
Patent Cancellations	See Postal Markings
Pelure Paper	See Paper
Perforation Gauge	See Separation (Perforations)
Phosphor Tagged	See Luminescence
Photogravure	See Printing
Plate Flaws	See Printing (Common Flaws)
Plate Markings	See Plate (Sheet Stamps)
Plate Numbers	See Plate (Sheet Stamps)
Postmarks	See Postal Markings
Precancels	See Postal Markings
Printed on Both Sides	See Printing (Additional Terms)
Proofs	See Printing (Additional Terms)
Railroad Postmarks	See Postal Markings
Receiving Mark	See Postal Markings
Re-cut	See Plate (Line Engraving)
Re-engraved	See Plate (Line Engraving)
Re-entry	See Plate (Line Engraving)
Reissue	See Printing (Additional Terms)
Relief	See Plate (Line Engraving)
Reprint	See Printing (Additional Terms)
Retouch	See Plate (Line Engraving)
Ribbed Paper	See Paper
Rosette Crack	See Printing (Common Flaws)
Rotary Press Printing	See Printing (Additional Terms)
Rough Perforation	See Separation (Perforations)
Rouletting	See Separation
Se-Tenant	See General Glossary
Service Indicators	See Postal Markings
Sheet	See Plate (Plate Arrangement)
Shifted Transfer	See Plate (Line Engraving)
Ship Postmarks	See Postal Markings
Short Transfer	See Plate (Line Engraving)
Silk Paper	See Paper
Specimens	See General Glossary
Splice	See General Glossary
Split Grill	See Paper (Grills)
Stitch Watermark	See Paper
Supplementary Mail	See Postal Markings
Surcharge	See Printing (Additional Terms), General Glossary

PLATE

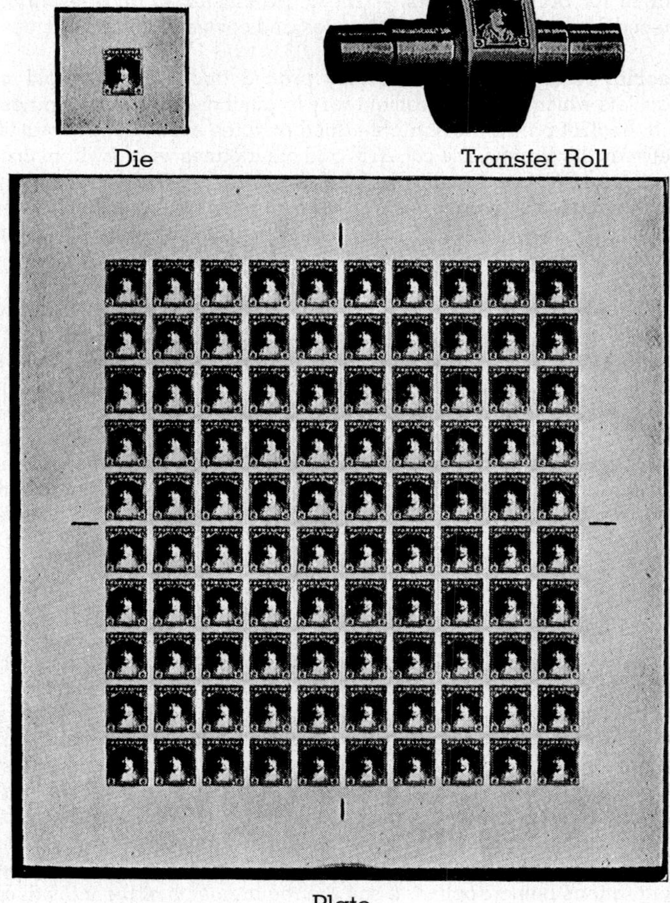

Die Transfer Roll

Plate

Line Engraving (Intaglio)

Die — Making the die is the initial operation in developing the intaglio plate. The die is a small flat piece of soft steel on which the subject (design) is recess-engraved in reverse. Dies are usually of a single-subject type, but dies exist with multiple subjects of the same design, or even different designs. After the engraving is completed, the die is hardened to withstand the stress of subsequent operations.

Transfer Roll — The next operation is making the transfer roll, which is the medium used to transfer the subject from the die to the plate. A blank roll of soft steel, mounted on a mandrel, is placed under the bearers of a transfer press. The hardened die is placed on the bed of the press and the face of the roll is brought to bear on the die. The bed is then rocked backed and forth under increasing pressure until the soft steel of the roll is forced into every line of the die. The resulting impression on the roll is known as a "relief" or "relief transfer." Several reliefs usually are rocked in on each roll. After the required reliefs are completed, the roll is hardened.

Relief — A relief is the normal reproduction of the design on the die, in reverse. A defective relief, caused by a minute piece of foreign material lodging on the die, may occur during the rocking-in process, or from other causes. Imperfections in the steel of the transfer roll may also result in a breaking away of parts of the design. If the damaged relief is continued in use, it will transfer a repeating defect to the plate. Also, reliefs sometimes are deliberately altered. "Broken relief" and "altered relief" are terms used to designate these changed conditions.

Plate — A flat piece of soft steel replaces the die on the bed of the transfer press and one of the reliefs on the transfer roll is brought to bear on this soft steel. The position of the plate is determined by guide dots, which have been lightly marked on the plate in advance. After the position of the relief is determined, pressure is brought to bear and, by following the same method used in the making of the transfer roll, a transfer is entered. This transfer reproduces, in reverse, every detail of the design of the relief. As many transfers are entered on the plate as there are to be subjects printed at one time.

After the required transfers have been entered, the guide dots, layouts and lines, scratches, etc., are burnished out. Also, any required guide lines, plate numbers, or other marginal markings are added. A proof impression is then taken and if certified (approved), the plate is machined for fitting to the press, hardened and sent to the plate vault until used.

Rotary press plates, after being certified, require additional machining. They are curved to fit the press cylinder and gripper slots are cut into the back of each plate to receive the grippers, which hold the plate securely to the press. The rotary press plate is not hardened until these additional processes are completed.

Transfer — An impression entered on the plate by the transfer roll. A relief transfer is made when entering the design of the die onto the transfer roll.

Double Transfer — The condition of a transfer on a plate that shows evidence of a duplication of all or a portion of the design. A double transfer usually is the result of the changing of the registration between the relief and the plate during the rolling of the original entry.

Occasionally it is necessary to remove the original transfer from a plate and enter the relief a second time. When the finished re-transfer shows indications of the original transfer, because of incomplete erasure, the result is known as a double transfer.

Triple Transfer — Similar to a double transfer, this situation shows evidence of a third entry or two duplications.

Foreign Entry — When original transfers are erased incompletely from a plate, they can appear with new transfers of a different design which are entered subsequently on the plate.

Re-entry — When executing a re-entry, the transfer roll is reapplied to the plate at some time after the latter has been put to press. Thus, worn-out designs may be resharpened by carefully re-entering the transfer roll. If the transfer roll is not carefully entered, the registration will not be true and a double transfer will result. With the protective qualities of chromium plating, it is no longer necessary to resharpen the plate. In fact, after a plate has been curved for the rotary press, it is impossible to make a re-entry.

Shifted Transfer (Shift) — In transferring, the metal displaced on the plate by the entry of the ridges, constituting the design on the transfer roll, is forced ahead of the roll as well as pressed out at the sides. The amount of displaced metal increases with the depth of the entry. When the depth is increased evenly, the design will be uniformly entered. Most of the displaced metal is pressed ahead of the roll. If too much pressure is exerted on any pass (rocking), the impression on the previous partial entry may be floated (pushed) ahead of the roll and cause a duplication of the final design. The duplication appears as an increased width of frame lines or a doubling of the lines.

The ridges of the displaced metal are flattened out by the hammering or rolling back of the plate along the space occupied by the subject margins.

Short Transfer — Occasionally the transfer roll is not rocked its entire length in the entering of a transfer onto a plate, with the result that the finished transfer fails to show the complete design. This is known as a short transfer.

Short transfers are known to have been made deliberately, as in the Type III of the 1-cent issue of 1851-60 (Scott 8, 21), or accidentally, as in the 10-cent 1847 (Scott 2).

Re-engraved — Either the die that has been used to make a plate or the plate itself may have its temper drawn (softened) and be re-cut. The resulting impressions for such re-engraved die or plate may differ very slightly from the original issue and are given the label "re-engraved."

Re-cut — A re-cut is the strengthening or altering of a line by use of an engraving tool on unhardened plates.

Retouch — A retouch is the strengthening or altering of a line by means of etching.

Plate Arrangement

Arrangement — The first engraved plates used to produce U.S. postage stamps in 1847 contained 200 subjects. The number of subjects to a plate varied between 100 and 300 until the issue of 1890, when the 400-subject plate was first laid down. Since that time, this size of plate has been used for a majority of the regular postal issues (those other than commemoratives). Exceptions to this practice exist, particularly among the more recent issues, and are listed under the headings of the appropriate issues in the catalogue.

Sheet — In single-color printings, the complete impression from a plate is termed a sheet. A sheet of multicolored stamps (two or more colors) may come from a single impression of a plate, i.e., many Giori-type press printings from 1957, or from as many impressions from separate plates as there are inks used for the particular stamp. Combination process printings may use both methods of multicolor production: Giori-type intaglio with offset lithography or with photogravure.

The Huck multicolor press used plates of different format (40, 72 or 80 subjects). The sheet it produced had 200 subjects for normal-sized commemoratives or 400 subjects for regular-issue stamps, similar to the regular products of other presses.

See the note on the Combination Press following the listing for Scott 1703 in this catalogue.

In casual usage, a "pane" often is referred to as a "sheet."

Pane — A pane is the part of the original sheet that is issued for sale at post offices. A pane may be the same as an entire sheet, where the plate is small, or it may be a half, quarter, or some other fraction of a sheet where the plate is large.

The illustration shown later under the subtopic "Sheet Stamps" shows the layout of a 400-subject sheet from a flat plate, which for issuance would have been divided along the intersecting guide lines into four panes of 100.

Panes are classified into normal reading position according to their location on the printed sheet: U.L., upper left; U.R., upper right; L.L., lower left; and L.R., lower right. Where only two panes appear on a sheet, they are designed "R" (right) and "L" (left) or "T" (top) and "B" (bottom), on the basis of the division of the sheet vertically or horizontally.

To fix the location of a particular stamp on any pane, except for those printed on the Combination press, the pane is held with the subjects in the normal position, and a position number is given to each stamp starting with the first stamp in the upper left corner and proceeding horizontally to the right, then staring on the second row at the left and counting across to the right, and so on to the last stamp in the lower right corner.

In describing the location of a stamp on a sheet of stamps issued prior to 1894, the practice is to give the stamp position number first, then the pane position and finally the plate number, i.e., "1R22." Beginning with the 1894 issue and on all later issues the method used is to give the plate number first, then the position of the pane, and finally the position number of the stamp, i.e., "16807LL48" to identify an example of Scott 619 or "2138L2" to refer to an example of Scott 323.

Booklet Stamps

Plates for Stamp Booklets — These are illustrated and described preceding the listing of booklet panes and covers in this catalogue.

Booklet Panes — Panes specially printed and cut to be sold in booklets which are a convenient way to purchase and store stamps. U.S. Booklet panes are straight-edged on three sides, but perforated between the stamps. Die cut, ATM and other panes will vary from this. Except for BK64 and BK65, the A.E.F. booklets, booklets were sold by the Post Office Department for a one-cent premium until 1962. Other sections of this catalogue with listings for booklet panes include Savings stamps, Telegraph stamps and Canal Zone.

A.E.F. Booklets — These were special booklets prepared principally for use by the U.S. Army Post Office in France during World War I. They were issued in 1-cent and 2-cent denominations with 30 stamps to a pane (10 x 3), bound at right or left. As soon as Gen. John J. Pershing's organization reached France, soldiers' mail was sent free by means of franked envelopes.

Stamps were required during the war for the civilian personnel, as well as for registered mail, parcel post and other types of postal service. See the individual listings for Scott 498f and 499f and booklets BK64 and BK65.

Coil Stamps

First issued in 1908-09, coil stamps originally were produced in two roll sizes, 500 and 1,000 stamps, with the individual stamps arranged endways or sideways and with or without perforations between.

Rolls of stamps for use in affixing or vending machines were first constructed by private companies and later by the Bureau of Engraving and Printing. Originally, it was customary for the Post Office Department to sell to the private vending companies and others imperforate sheets of stamps printed from the ordinary 400-subject flat plates. These sheets were then pasted together end-to-end or side-to-side by the purchaser and cut into rolls as desired, with the perforations being applied to suit the requirements of the individual machines. Such stamps with private perforations are listed in this catalogue under "Vending and Affixing Machine Perforations."

Later the Bureau produced coils by the same method, also in rolls of 500 and 1,000. These coils were arranged endways or sideways and were issued with or without perforations.

With the introduction of the Stickney rotary press, curved plates made for use on these presses were put into use at the Bureau of Engraving and Printing, and the sale of imperforate sheets was discontinued. This move marked the end of the private perforation. Rotary press coils have been printed on a number of presses over the years and have been made in roll sizes of 100, 500, 1,000, 3,000 and 10,000 stamps, etc.

Paste-up — The junction of two flat-plate printings joined by pasting the edge of one sheet onto the edge of another sheet to make coils. A two-stamp example of this joining is a "paste-up pair." See Splice.

Guide Line Pair — Attached pair of flat-plate-printed coil stamps with printed line between. This line is identical with the guide line (See listing under (Sheet Stamps) found in sheets.

Joint Line — The edges of two curved plates do not meet exactly on the press and the small space between the plates takes ink and prints a line. A pair of rotary-press-printed stamps with such a line is called a "joint line pair."

Coil stamps printed on the Multicolor Huck Press do not consistently produce such lines. Occasionally accumulated ink will print partial lines in one or more colors, and very occasionally complete lines will be printed. Stamps resulting from such situations are not listed in this catalogue. The "B" and "C" presses do not print joint lines at all.

Plate Number — for U.S. coil stamps prior to Scott 1891, Scott 1947, War Savings coils and Canal Zone:

On a rotary-press horizontal coil the top or bottom part of a plate number may show. On a vertical coil, the left or right part of a plate number may show. The number was entered on the plate to be cut off when the web was sliced into coils and is found only when the web was sliced off center. Every rotary press coil plate number was adjacent to a joint line, so both features could occur together in one strip.

For U.S. coil stamps from Scott 1891 onward (excluding Scott 1947) and Official coils:

The plate number is placed in the design area of the stamp, so it will not be trimmed off. Such items are normally collected unused with the stamp containing the plate number in the center of a strip of three or five stamps. They normally are collected used as singles. The line, if any, will be at the right of the plate-number stamp. On the Bureau's Cottrell press, the number occurs every 24th stamp, on the "B" press every 52nd stamp, on the "C," "D" and "F" presses every 48th stamp. On modern private contractor presses, the number occurs in a range from every 5th stamp to every 31st stamp, depending on the press used.

Unused plate-number strips of three and five are valued in this catalogue.

Hidden Plate Number — A plate number may be found entirely on a coil made from flat plates, but usually is hidden by a part of the next sheet which has been lapped over it.

Coil Waste — an occurrence brought about by stamps issued in perforated sheets from a printing intended for coils. These stamps came from short lengths of paper at the end of the coil run. Sometimes the salvaged sections were those which had been laid aside for mutilation because of some defect. Because the paper had been moistened during printing, it sometimes stretched slightly and provided added printing area. Sheets of 70, 100, and 170 are known. See Scott 538-541, 545-546, 578-579, and 594-595.

"T" — Letter which appears in the lower design area of Scott 2115b, which was printed on an experimental pre-phosphored paper. The stamp with the plate number is inscribed "T1."

Sheet Stamps

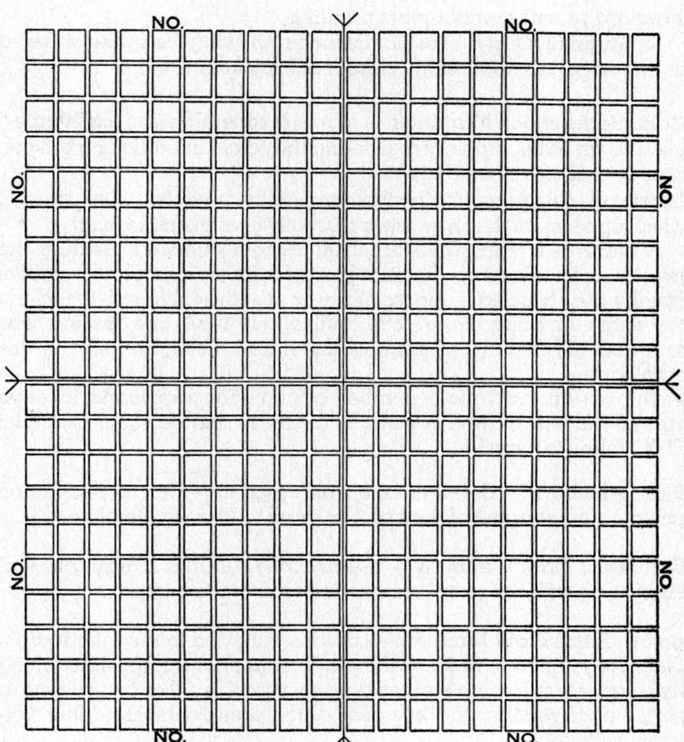

A typical 400-subject plate of 1922

Plate Markings — The illustration above shows a typical 400-subject plate of the 1922 issue, with markings as found on this type of plate. Other layouts and markings are found further in the catalogue text.

Guide Lines — Horizontal or vertical colored lines between the stamps, extending wholly or partially across the sheet. They serve as guides for the operators of perforating machines or to indicate the point of separation of the sheet into panes.

A block of stamps divided by any of the guide lines is known as a "line block" or "guide line block." The block of stamps from the exact center of the sheet, showing the crossed guide lines, is a "center line block."

Gutter — When guide lines are used to mark the division of the sheet into panes, the space between the stamps at the edge of the pane is no different than the space between any other stamps on the sheet. Some plates provide a wide space, or gutter, between the panes. These plates do not produce guide lines.

A pair of stamps with the wide space between is known as a "gutter pair," and blocks with that feature are "gutter blocks." A block of stamps from the position where four panes meet, showing the two wide spaces crossing, is a "center gutter block" or "cross gutter block."

Gutter pairs or gutter blocks must contain complete stamp images on both sides of the gutter. On pairs or blocks that had a paper foldover before proper perforating, the stamps on each side of the gutter must be complete and show perforation teeth all around, unless imperforate. Gutter pairs or blocks caused by a paper foldover may or may not contain creased stamps from the foldover; either way they qualify as the listed variety. Some gutter pairs or blocks are the result of misplaced perforations and improper cutting of the panes. These pairs or blocks may have perforations running through the stamps, either straight or at an angle. In these cases, there must be complete stamp-size images on each side of the gutter to be considered gutter pairs or blocks. These errors may have parts of two or more designs in the stamp-size images.

Arrows — Arrow-shaped markings were used in the margins of stamp sheets, in place of guide lines, on the issues of 1870 through 1894. Since 1894, guide lines with arrows at both ends have been the standard practice on flat-plate printings.

A margin block of at least four stamps, showing the arrow centered at one edge, is known as a "margin block with arrow."

Color Registration Markings — marks of different sizes and shapes, used as an aid in properly registering the colors in producing a bicolored or multicolored stamp.

Imprint — design containing the name of the producer of the stamps, which appears on the sheet margin usually near the plate number.

A block of stamps with the sheet margin attached, bearing the imprint, is known as an "imprint block." Imprints and plate numbers usually are collected in blocks of six, or of sufficient length to include the entire marking. From 1894 until about 1907, one fashion was to collect the imprints in strips of three, and these are listed in this catalogue.

The imprint and plate number combination are found in eight types I-VIII, which are illustrated at Scott 245 and Scott E3. Example: "T V" refers to Type V.

Plate Numbers — Serial numbers assigned to plates, appearing on one or more margins of the sheet or pane to identify the plate.

Flat Press Plate Numbers — usually collected in a margin block of six stamps with the plate number centered in the margin.

Rotary Press Plate Numbers — usually collected in a corner margin block large enough to show the plate number(s) and position along the margin and complete selvage on two sides. For issues with a single plate number at the corner of the pane, a block of four normally suffices.

During 1933-39, some plates had the number opposite the third stamp (up or down) from the corner of the sheet and for these the number is customarily collected in a corner block of no less than eight stamps, with most collectors preferring a block of ten stamps. Multicolored stamps may have more than one plate number in the margin and the "plate block" may then be expanded to suit the collector's desire.

The catalogue listing for plate blocks includes enough stamps to accommodate all numbers on the plate. Plate block listings for se-tenant issues include all the designs as part of the block. When a continuous design is involved, such as Scott 1629-31, the complete design will be included in the plate number block. The entire pane constitutes the plate number block for issues such as the State Birds and Flowers (Scott 1953-2002, 1953A-2002A).

Plate numbers take a further designation from the position on the sheet on which they appear, e.g. U.L. refers to upper left pane, etc.

See note following Scott 1703 for description of combination press markings.

Private Contractor Marks — On rotary plates from Scott 1789 onward: "A" denotes issues produced by private contractor American Bank Note Co., "B" by Banknote Corp of America, "D" by Dittler Brothers, "G" by Guilford Gravure, "K" by KCS Industries, "M" by 3M Corp., "P" by Ashton-Potter (USA) Ltd., "S" by Stamp Venturers, Inc. (now Sennett Security Products), "U" by U.S. Bank Note Co., "V" by Avery Dennison.

Stars — used on the flat plates to indicate a change from the previous spacing of the stamps. They also were used as a check on the assignment of the printed sheets to a perforating machine of the proper setting. Stars appear on certain rotary plates used for printing stamps for coils, appearing adjacent to the plate joint line and above stamp No. 1 on the 170-subject plates, and to the left of stamp No. 141 on the 150-subject plates.

"A" — on flat plates; used on plates having uniform vertical spacing between rows of subjects, but wider than those with the star marking.

"C.S." and "C" — plate has been chromium plated.

"E.I." — abbreviation for Electrolytic Iron. The designation is for plates made by the electrolytic process.

"F" — used to indicate the plate is ready for hardening. This appears only on flat plates and generally precedes the upper right plate number.

"O" — plate has undergone an experimental oil-hardening process during manufacture.

"Top" — marking on the top sheet margin of printings from both plates of some bicolored issues. This marking is used to check printings for "inverts." Beginning with the 6-cent bicolored airpost issue of 1938 (Scott C23), bicolored crosses also were used as an additional check.

"Coil Stamps" — appearing on the side sheet margins, designates plates used in the production of endwise coils.

"S 20," "S 30," "S 40" — marginal markings appearing on certain 150- and 170-subject rotary press plates to designate experimental variations in the depth and character of the frame line to over-come excess inking. "S 30" was adopted as the standard. Blocks showing these markings are listed as "Margin Block with S 20," etc., in this catalogue.

Initials — used in sheet margins to identify individuals in the Bureau of Engraving and Printing who participated in the production or use of the plates.

Gutter Dashes — on the first 400-subject rotary plates, 3/16-inch horizontal dashes appear in the gutter between the 10th and 11th vertical rows of stamps. This arrangement was superseded by dashes 3/16-inch at the extreme ends of the vertical and horizontal gutters, and a ¼-inch cross at the central gutter intersection. This latter arrangement continued until replaced by the scanning marks on the Electric Eye plates. See Electric Eye.

Margin — border outside the printed design or perforated area of a stamp, also known as selvage, or the similar border of a sheet of stamps. A block of stamps from the top, side or bottom of a sheet or pane to which is attached the selvage (margin) is known as a "margin block." A block of stamps from the corner of a sheet with full selvage attached to two adjoining sides is known as a "corner block."

NOTE: The descriptions and definitions above indicate that a certain number of stamps make up an arrow or plate number block. Any block of stamps, no matter how large or small, which had an arrow or plate number on its margin would be considered by that name. The usual practice is to collect flat-plate numbers in margin blocks of six and arrow blocks in margin blocks of four. Plate number blocks from rotary press printings generally are collected in blocks of 4 when the plate number appears beside the stamp at any of the four corners of the sheet. Particularly relative to bi-colored stamps, an arrow block is now separated from a plate number block. Thus, in those situations, the two individual types of blocks might form a block of eight or 10, as the situation dictates.

PRINTING

Methods Used — all four basic forms of printing have been used in producing U.S. stamps, engraved, photogravure, lithography, and typography. Holography has been used on some stamps and stamped envelopes.

Engraved (Recess or Intaglio) — process where ink is received and held in lines depressed below the surface of the plate. Initially, in printing from such plates, damp paper was forced into the depressed lines and therefore picked up ink. Consequently, ink lines on the stamp are slightly raised. This also is noted from the back of the stamp, where depressions mark where ink is placed on the front.

When the ornamental work for a stamp is engraved by a machine, the process is called "engine turned" or lathe-work engraving. An example of such lathe-work background is the 3-cent stamp of 1861

(Scott Illustration No. A25).

Engraved stamps were printed only with flat plates until 1914, when rotary press printing was introduced. "Wet" and "dry" printings are explained in the note in the text of the catalogue following Scott 1029. The various Giori presses, used to print some U.S. stamps from 1957 (see Scott 1094, 4-cent Flag issue until the early 1990s), applied two or three different colored inks simultaneously.

The Huck Multicolor press, put into service at the Bureau of Engraving and Printing in 1968, was first used to produce the 1968 Christmas stamp (Scott 1363) and the 6-cent Flag coil of 1969 (Scott 1338A). Developed by the Bureau's technical staff and the firm of graphic arts engineers whose name it bears, the Huck press printed, tagged with phosphor ink, gummed and perforated stamps in a continuous operation. Printing was accomplished in as many as nine colors. Fed by paper from a roll, the Huck Multicolor used many recess-engraved plates of smaller size than any used previously for U.S. stamp printing. Its product has certain characteristics which other U.S. stamps do not have. Post office panes of the 1969 Christmas stamp, for example, show seven or eight plate numbers in the margins. Joint lines appear after every two or four stamps. Other presses providing multiple plate numbers are the Andreotti, Champlain, Combination, Miller Offset, A Press, D Press and more.

Photogravure — the design of a stamp to be printed by photogravure usually is photographed through an extremely fine screen, lined in minute quadrille. The screen breaks up the reproduction into tiny dots, which are etched onto the plate and the depressions formed hold the ink. Somewhat similarly to engraved printing, the ink is lifted out of the recesses by the paper, which is pressed against the plate. Unlike engraved printing, however, the ink does not appear to be raised relative to the surface of the paper.

Gravure is most often used for multicolored stamps, generally using the three primary colors (red, yellow and blue) and black. By varying the dot matrix pattern and density of these colors, virtually any color can be reproduced. A typical full-color gravure stamp will be created from four printing cylinders (one for each color). The original multicolored image will have been photographically separated into its component colors.

For U.S. stamps, photogravure first appeared in 1967, with the Thomas Eakins issue (Scott 1335). The early photogravure stamps were printed by outside contractors until the Bureau obtained the multicolor Andreotti press in 1971. The earliest stamp printed on that press was the 8-cent Missouri Statehood issue of 1971 (Scott 1426).

Color control bars, dashes or dots are printed in the margin of one pane in each "Andreotti" sheet of 200, 160 or 128 stamps. These markings generally are collected in blocks of 20 or 16 (two full rows of one pane), which include the full complement of plate numbers, Mr. Zip and the Zip and Mail Early slogans.

Details on the Combination Press follow the listing for Scott 1703.

Modern gravure printing may use computer-generated dot-matrix screens, and modern plates may be of various types including metal-coated plastic. The catalogue designation of Photogravure (or "Photo") covers any of these older and more modern gravure methods of printing.

Lithography — this is the most common and least expensive process for printing stamps. In this method, the design is drawn by hand or transferred in greasy ink from an original engraving to the surface of a lithographic stone or metal plate. The stone or plate is wet with an acid fluid, which causes it to repel the printing ink except at the greasy lines of the design. A fine lithographic print closely resembles an engraving, but the lines are not raised on the face or depressed on the back. Thus there usually is a more dull appearance to the lithograph than to the engraving.

Offset Lithography (Offset Printing) — a modern development of the lithographic process. Anything that will print — type, wood-cuts, photoengravings, plates engraved or etched in intaglio, half-tone plates, linoleum blocks, lithographic stones or plates, photo-gravure plates, rubber stamps, etc. — may be used. Greasy ink is applied to the dampened plate or form and an impression made on a rubber blanket. Paper immediately is pressed against the blanket, which transfers the ink. Because of its greater flexibility, offset printing has largely displaced lithography.

Because the processes and results obtained are similar, stamps printed by either of these two methods normally are considered to be "lithographed."

The first application of lithographic printing for any U.S. items listed in this catalogue was for Post Office seals, probably using stone printing bases. See also some Confederates States general issues. Offset lithography was used for the 1914 documentary revenues (Scott R195-R216). Postage stamps followed in 1918-20 (Scott 525-536) because of war-time shortages of ink, plates and manpower relative to the regular intaglio production.

The next use of offset lithography for postage stamps was in 1964 with the Homemakers issue (Scott 1253), in combination with intaglio printing. Many similar issues followed, all of which were produced by the combination of offset lithography and intaglio. The combination process serves best for soft backgrounds and tonal effects.

Typography — an exact reverse of engraved-plate printing, this process provides for the parts of the design which are to show in color to be left at the original level of the plate and the spaces between cut away. Ink is applied to the raised lines, and the pressure of the printing forces these lines more or less into the paper. The process impresses the lines on the face of the stamp and slightly raises them on the back. Normally, a large number of electrotypes of the original are made and assembled into a plate with the requisite number of designs for printing a sheet of stamps. Stamps printed by this process show greater uniformity, and the stamps are less expensive to print than with intaglio printing.

The first U.S. postal usage of an item printed by typography, or letterpress, under national authority was the 1846 "2" surcharge on the United States City Despatch Post 3-cent carrier stamp (Scott 6LB7). The next usage was the 1865 newspaper and periodical stamp issue, which for security reasons combined the techniques of machine engraving, colorless embossing and typography. This created an unusual first.

Most U.S. stamp typography consists of overprints, such as those for the Canal Zone, the Molly Pitcher and Hawaii Sesquicentennial stamps of 1928 (Scott 646-648), the Kansas-Nebraska control markings (Scott 658-679), Bureau-printed precancels, and "specimen" markings.

Embossed (relief) Printing — method in which the design is sunk in the metal of the die and the printing is done against a platen that is forced into the depression, thus forming the design on the paper in relief. Embossing may be done without ink (blind embossing), totally with ink, or a combination thereof. The U.S. stamped envelopes are an example of this form of printing.

Typeset — made from movable type.

Typeset Stamps — printed from ordinary printer's type. Sometimes electrotype or stereotype plates are made, but because such stamps usually are printed only in small quantities for temporary use, movable type often is used for the purpose. This method of printing is apt to show broken type and lack of uniformity. See Hawaii Scott 1-4 and 12-26.

Holograms — for objects to appear as holograms on stamps, a model exactly the same size as it is to appear on the hologram must be created. Rather than using photographic film to capture the image, holography records an image on a photoresist material. In processing, chemicals eat away at certain exposed areas, leaving a pattern of constructive and destructive interference. When the photoresist is developed, the result is a pattern of uneven ridges that acts as a mold. This mold is then coated with metal, and the resulting form is used to press copies in much the same way phonograph records are produced.

A typical reflective hologram used for stamps consists of a reproduction of the uneven patterns on a plastic film that is applied to a reflective background, ususally a silver or gold foil. Light is reflected off the background through the film, making the pattern present on the film visible. Because of the uneven pattern of the film, the viewer will perceive the objects in their proper three-dimensional relationships with appropriate brightness.

The first hologram on a stamp was produced by Austria in 1988 (Scott 1441).

Foil Application — A modern technique of applying color to stamps involves the application of metallic foil to the stamp paper. A pattern of foil is applied to the stamp paper by use of a stamping die. The foil usually is flat, but it may be textured. Canada Scott 1735 has three different foil applications in pearl, bronze, and gold. The gold foil was texured using a chemical-etch copper embossing die. The printing of this stamp also involved two-colored offset lithography plus embossing.

Additional Terms

Multicolored Stamps — Until 1957 when the Giori press was introduced, bicolored stamps were printed on a flat-bed press in two runs, one for each color (example: Norse-American Issue of 1925, Scott 620-621). In the flat-press bicolors, if the sheet were fed to the press on the second run in reversed position, the part printed in the second color would be upside down, producing an "invert" such as the famed Scott C3a.

With the Giori press and subsequent presses, stamps could be printed in more than one color at the same time.

Many bicolored and multicolored stamps show varying degrees of poor color registration (alignment). Such varieties are not listed in this catalogue.

Color Changeling — a stamp which, because of exposure to the environment, has naturally undergone a change of ink colors. Orange U.S. stamps of the early 1900's are notorious for turning brown as the ink reacts with oxygen. Exposure to light can cause some inks to fade. These are not considered color-omitted errors. Exposure to other chemicals can cause ink colors to change. These stamps are merely altered stamps, and their value to collectors is greatly diminished.

Color Trials — printings in various colors, made to facilitate selection of color for the issued stamp.

Double Impression — a second impression of a stamp over the original impression.

This is not to be confused with a "double transfer," which is a plate imperfection and generally shows just bits of doubling of the design. See also "Printed on Both Sides."

Essay — a proposed design, a designer's model or an incomplete engraving. Its design differs in some way — great or small — from the issued item.

Inverted Center — bicolored or multicolored stamp with the center printed upside down relative to the remainder of the design. A stamp may be described as having an inverted center even if the center is printed first. See "Multicolored Stamps."

Flat Plate Printing — stamp printed on a flat-bed press, rather than on a rotary press. See "Plate."

Overprint — any word, inscription or image printed across the face of a stamp to alter its use or locality or otherwise to serve a special purpose. An example is U.S. Scott 646, the "Molly Pitcher" overprint, which is Scott 634 with a black overprinted inscription as a memorial to the Revolutionary War heroine. See "Surcharge."

Printed on Both Sides — Occasionally a sheet of stamps already printed will, through error, be turned over and passed through the press a second time, creating the rare "printed on both sides" variety. On one side the impression is almost always poor or incomplete. This often is confused with an "offset," which occurs when sheets of stamps are stacked while the ink is still wet.

The "printed on both sides" variety will show the design as a positive (all inscriptions reading correctly) and the offset shows a reverse impression. See "Double Impression."

Progressive Proof — a type of essay that is an incomplete engraving of the finished, accepted die.

Proofs — trial printings of a stamp made from the original die or the finished plate.

Reprints and Reissues — are impressions of stamps (usually obsolete) made from the original plates or stones. If they are valid for postage and reproduce obsolete issues (such as U.S. Scott 102-111), the stamps are *reissues*. If they are from current issues, they are designated as *second, third,* etc., *printing*. If designated for a particular purpose, they are called *special printings*.

When special printings are not valid for postage, but are made from original dies and plates by authorized persons, they are *official reprints*. *Private reprints* are made from the original plates and dies by private hands. An example of a private reprint is that of the 1871-1932 reprints made from the original die of the 1845 New Haven, Conn., postmaster's provisional. *Official reproductions* or imitations are made from new dies and plates by government authorization. Scott will list those reissues that are valid for postage if they differ significantly from the original printing.

The U.S. government made special printings of its first postage stamps in 1875. Produced were official imitations of the first two stamps (listed as Scott 3-4), reprints of the demonetized pre-1861 issues (Scott 40-47) and reissues of the 1861 stamps, the 1869 stamps and the then-current 1875 denominations. Even though the official imitations and the reprints were not valid for postage, Scott lists all of these U.S. special printings.

Most reprints or reissues differ slightly from the original stamp in some characteristic, such as gum, paper, perforation, color or watermark. Sometimes the details are followed so meticulously that only a student of that specific stamp is able to distinguish the reprint or reissue from the original.

Rotary Press Printing — stamps which have been printed on a rotary-type press from curved plates. Rotary press-printed stamps are longer or wider than stamps of the same design printed from flat plates. All rotary press printings through 1953, except coil waste (such as Scott 538), exist with horizontal "gum breaker ridges" varying from one to four per stamp. See: "Plate."

Surcharge — overprint which alters or restates the face value or denomination of the stamp to which it is applied. An example is Scott K1-K18, U.S. stamps that were surcharged for use by U.S. offices in China. Many surcharges are typeset. See: "Overprint" and "Typeset."

Common Flaws

Cracked Plate — A term to describe stamps that show evidence that the plate from which they were printed was cracked.

Plate cracks have various causes, each which may result in a different formation and intensity of the crack. Cracks similar to the above illustration are quite common in older issues and are largely due to the plate being too quickly immersed in the cooling bath when being tempered. These cracks are known as *crystallization cracks*. A jagged line running generally in one direction and most often in the gutter between stamps is due to the stress of the steel during the rolling in or transferring process.

In curved (rotary) plates, there are two types of cracks. Once is the bending or curving crack, which is quite marked and always runs in the direction in which the plate is curved.

The accompanying illustration shows the second type, the *gripper crack*. This type is caused by the cracking of the plate over the slots cut in the underside of the plate, which receive the "grippers" that fasten the plate to the press. These occur only on curved plates and are to be found in the row of stamps adjoining the plate joint. These appear on the printed impression as light, irregularly colored lines, usually parallel to the plate joint line.

Rosette Crack — cluster of fine cracks radiating from a central point in irregular lines. These usually are caused by the plate receiving a blow.

Scratched Plate — caused by foreign matter scratching the plate, these usually are too minor to mention. See: "Gouge."

Gouge — exceptionally heavy and usually short scratches, these may be caused by a tool falling onto the plate.

Surface Stains — irregular surface marks resembling the outline of a point on a map. Experts differ on the cause. These are too minor to list.

PAPER

Paper falls broadly into two types: wove and laid. The difference in the appearance is caused by the wire cloth upon which the pulp is first formed.

Paper also is distinguished as thick or thin, hard or soft, and by its color (such as bluish, yellowish, greenish, etc.).

Wove — where the wire cloth is of even and closely woven nature, producing a sheet of uniform texture throughout. This type shows no light or dark figures when held to the light.

Laid — where the wire cloth is formed of closely spaced parallel wires crossed at much wider intervals by cross wires. The resultant paper shows alternate light and dark lines. The distances between the widely spaced lines and the thickness of these lines may vary, but on any one piece of paper they will be the same.

Pelure — type of paper which is very thin and semi-transparent. It may be either wove or laid.

Bluish — The 1909 so-called "bluish" paper was made with 35 percent rag stock instead of all wood pulp. The bluish (actually grayish-blue) color goes through the paper, showing clearly on back and face. See the note with Scott 331.

Manila — a coarse paper formerly made of Manila hemp fiber. Since about 1890, so-called "manila" paper has been manufactured entirely from wood fiber. It is used for cheaper grades of envelopes and newspaper wrappers and normally is a natural light brown. Sometimes color is added, such as in the U.S. "amber manila" envelopes. It may be either wove or laid.

Silk — refers to two kinds of paper found by stamp collectors.

One type has one or more threads of silk embedded in the substance of the paper, extending across the stamp. In the catalogues, this type of paper usually is designated as "with silk threads."

The other type, used to print many U.S. revenue stamps, has short silk fibers strewn over it and impressed into it during manufacture. This is simply called "silk paper."

Ribbed — paper which shows fine parallel ridges on one or both sides of a stamp.

India — a soft, silky appearing wove paper, usually used for proof impressions.

Double Paper — as patented by Charles F. Steel, this style of paper consists of two layers, a thin surface paper and a thicker backing paper. Double paper was supposed to be an absolute safeguard against cleaning cancellations off stamps to permit reuse, for any attempt to remove the cancellation would result in the destruction of the upper layer. The Continental Bank Note Co. experimented with this paper in the course of printing Scott 156-165. See "Rotary Press Double Paper."

China Clay Paper — See note preceding Scott 331.

Fluorescent or Bright Paper — See "Luminescence."

Rotary Press Double Paper — Rotary press printings occasionally are found on a double sheet of paper. The web (roll) of paper used on the press must be continuous. Therefore, any break in the web during the process of manufacture must be lapped and pasted. The overlapping portion, when printed upon, is known as a "double paper" variety. In some cases, the lapped ends are joined with colored or transparent adhesive tape.

Such results of splicing normally are removed from the final printed material, although some slip through quality control efforts.

In one instance known, two splices have been made, thus leaving three thicknesses of paper. All rotary press stamps may exist on double paper.

Watermarks — Closely allied to the study of paper, watermarks normally are formed in the process of paper manufacture. Watermarks used on U.S. items consist of the letters "USPS" (found on postage stamps). "USPOD" (found on postal cards), the Seal of the United States (found on official seals), "USIR" (found on revenue items), and various monograms of letters, numbers, and so on, found on stamped envelopes.

The letters may be single- or double-lined and are formed from dies made of wire or cut from metal and soldered to the frame on which the pulp is caught or to a roll under which it is passed. The action of these dies is similar to the wires causing the prominent lines of laid paper, with the designs making thin places in the paper which show by more easily transmitting light.

The best method of detecting watermarks is to lay the stamp face down on a dark tray and immerse the stamp in a commercial brand of watermark fluid, which brings up the watermark in dark lines against a lighter background. **When collectors discuss watermarks, they refer to their appearance as viewed from the back of the stamp.**

Note: This method of detecting watermarks may damage certain stamps printed with inks that run when immersed (such as U.S. Scott 1260 and 1832). It is advisable to first test a damaged stamp of the same type, if possible.

Wmk. 191
PERIOD OF USE
Postage: 1895-1910 Revenue: none

In the 1895-1903 U.S. issues, the paper was fed through the press so that the watermark letters read horizontally on 400 subject sheets and vertically on 200 subject sheets.

The "USPS" in watermark 191 is known in two different orientations: a "backward-stepping" version in which each row of letters begins one letter to the left of the row above (shown above), and a second variety, called a "forward-stepping" variety, in which each row of letters begins one letter to the right of the row above. For more detail, see the notes and diagrams before No. 264 in the postage section of this catalogue.

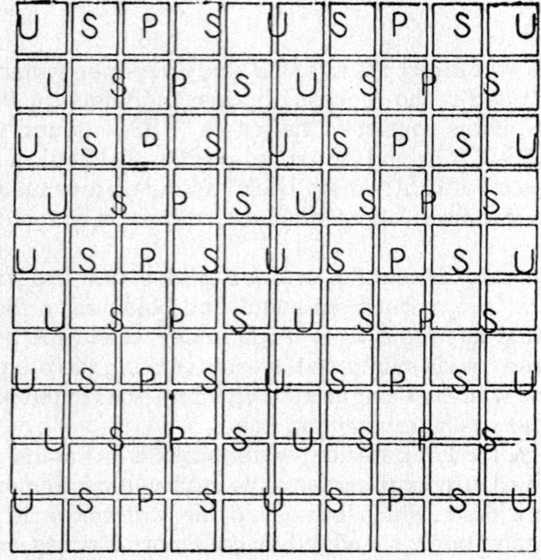

Wmk. 190
PERIOD OF USE
Postage: 1910-1916 Revenue: 1914

USIR

Wmk. 191R
PERIOD OF USE
Postage (unintentionally): 1895 (Scott 271a, 272a), 1951 (832b) Revenue: 1878-1958

Paper watermarked "USPOD" was used for postal cards from 1873 to 1875. For watermarks used on stamped envelopes, see Stamped Envelopes & Wrappers section in this catalogue.

Watermarks may be found normal, reversed, inverted, inverted reversed and sideways, as seen from the back of the stamp. See illustrated diagrams before No. 264.

Stitch Watermark — a type of watermark consisting of a row of short parallel lines. This is caused by the stitches which join the ends of the band on which the paper pulp is first formed. Stitch watermarks have been found on a great many issues, and may exist on all.

Grills

The grill consists of small square pyramids in parallel rows, impressed or embossed on the stamp. The object of the process is to break the fibers of the paper so that the ink from the cancellation would soak into the paper and make washing for reuse impossible. Grill impressions, when viewed from the face of the stamp, may be either "points up" or "points down." This process was used on U.S. Scott 79-101, 112-122 and 134-144, as well as some examples of 156-165 and 178-179.

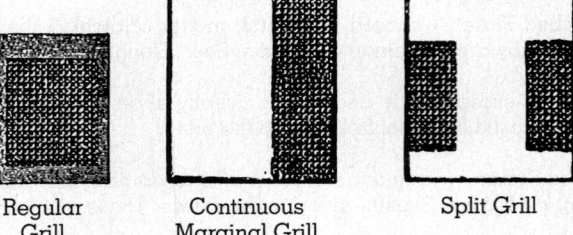

Regular Grill

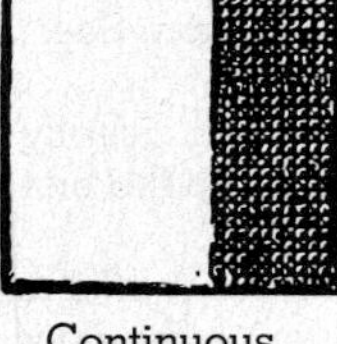

Continuous Marginal Grill

Split Grill

Continuous Marginal Grill — includes continuous rows of grill points impressed by the untrimmed parts of the ends of the grill rollers, noted as "end roller grill" on the 1870 and 1873 issues, and those grills which came from a continuous band lengthwise of the roller.

Split Grill — situation on a stamp showing parts of two or more grills, caused by a sheet being fed under the grill roller off center.

Double (or Triple) Grill — stamp showing two or more separate grill impressions. This is not to be confused with a split grill, which shows two or four partial impressions from a single grill impression.

Rotary Grills — grilled appearance occasionally found on rotary press printings that was produced unintentionally by a knurled roller during the perforating process.

Similarly, grill-like impressions can be left on stamps dispensed from vending machines.

SEPARATION

"Separation" is the general term used to describe methods used to separate stamps. The standard forms currently in use in the United States are perforating and die-cutting. These methods are done during the stamp production process, after printing. Sometimes these methods are done on-press or sometimes as a separate step. The earliest issues, such as the 1847 5¢ Franklin (Scott 1), did not have any means provided for separation. It was expected the stamps would be cut apart with scissors or folded and torn. These are examples of imperforate stamps. Many stamps were first issued in imperforate formats and were later issued with perforations. Therefore, care must be observed in buying single imperforate stamps, to be certain they were issued imperforate and are not perforated examples that have been altered by having the perforations trimmed away. Stamps issued imperforate usually are valued as singles. However, imperforate varieties of normally perforated stamps should be collected in pairs or larger multiples as indisputable evidence of their imperforate character.

Perforations

The chief style of separation of U.S. stamps has been perforating. This is produced by cutting away the paper between the stamps in a line of holes (usually round) and leaving little bridges of paper between the stamps. These little bridges are the "teeth" of the perforation and, of course, project from the stamp when it is torn from the pane.

Because the gauge of the perforation often is the distinguishing difference among stamps, it is necessary to measure and describe perforations by a gauge number. The standard for this measurement is the number of such teeth within two centimeters. Thus, we say that a stamp is perforated 12 or 10½ to note that there are either 12 or 10½ teeth counted within two centimeters.

Some later U.S. stamps are "stroke" perforated rather than "line" perforated. While it is difficult to tell the difference on a single stamp, with a block of four or more stamps the difference is more easily seen where the horizontal and vertical perforations cross. On the stroke-perforated items, the crossing point is clean and no holes are out of line. On the line-perforated stamps, the crossing point only rarely is perfect and generally there is a roughness.

Perforation Gauge — tool for measuring perforation, as described above.

Fine Perforation — perforation with small holes and teeth close together.

Coarse Perforation — perforation with large holes and teeth far apart, frequently irregularly spaced.

Rough Perforation — holes not clean cut, but jagged.

Compound Perforation — normally where perforations at the top and bottom differ from the perforations at the sides of the stamp. In describing compound perforations, the gauge of the top is given first, then the sides.

Some stamps are found where one side will differ from the other three, and in this case the reading will be the top first, then the right side, then the bottom, then the left side.

Double Perforation — often found on early U.S. revenue stamps and occasionally on postage issues, double perforations are applied in error. They do not generally command a premium over catalogue values of properly perforated stamps and are not to be confused with a variety found on occasional rotary press printings, where stamps adjacent to the center gutters will show the entire width of the gutter and a line of perforations on the far end of the gutter. These are caused by the sheet having been cut off center and are called "gutter snipes." They command a small premium.

Many double perforations were privately made to increase the value of the stamp, and are to be considered damaged stamps.

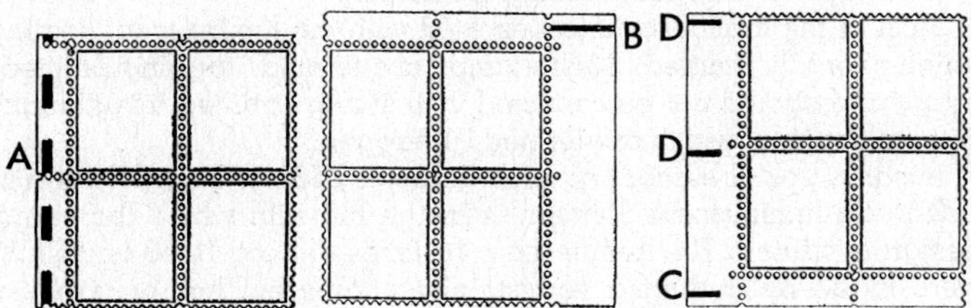

Electric Eye — an electronically controlled mechanical device acting as a guide in the operation of the perforating machine. Positive identification of stamps perforated by the electric eye process may be made by means of the distinctive marks in the gutters and margins of the full sheets on the printed web of paper. The original marks consisted of a series of heavy dashes dividing the vertical sheet gutter between the left and right panes (illustration A), together with a single line (margin line, illustration B), in the right sheet margin at the end of the horizontal sheet gutter between the upper and lower panes.

They first were used in 1933 on 400-subject plates for Scott 634, which was distributed to post offices in 1935 (used were plates 21149-50 and 21367-68). On these plates the plate numbers were placed opposite the ends of the third row of stamps from the top or bottom of the full sheet.

In later experiments, the margin line was broken into closely spaced thin vertical lines. Then it was again returned to its original form, but somewhat narrower.

In 1939, the Bureau of Engraving and Printing installed a new perforating machine which required a different layout to operate the centering mechanism. The vertical dashes remained the same, but the margin line was removed from the right sheet margin and a corresponding line ("gutter bar," illustration C) was placed in the left sheet margin at the end of the horizontal sheet gutter. Additional horizontal lines ("frame bars," illustration D) were added in the left sheet margin opposite the top frame line of the adjacent stamp design of all horizontal rows except the upper horizontal row of each left pane, where the frame bar is omitted. The plate numbers were moved back to their normal positions adjoining the corner stamps. Plates for the two types of machines could not be interchanged.

Later in 1939, a "convertible" plate was employed, consisting of a combination of the two previous layouts, the current one with the addition of a margin line (B) in its former position in the right sheet margin, thus making the perforation possible on either machine.

Originally laid out as 400-subject plates, electric-eye plates were later used for 200-subject horizontal or vertical format (commemorative, special delivery and airpost issues), 280-subject (Famous Americans and those with similar formats) and 180- and 360-subject plates (booklet panes of definitives, airpost, postal savings and war savings issues).

In laying out the plates for the 400-subject and 200-subject horizontal format issues, the marks retained the same relative position to the stamp designs. This was changed, however, in entering the design for the stamps of the 200-subject vertical format and 280-subject issues because the stamp designs were turned 90 degrees. That is, the designs were entered on the plates with the longer dimension horizontal. Although the electric eye marks were entered on the plates in the usual positions, on the printed sheet they appear as though shifted 90 degrees when the stamps are held in the customary upright position.

Thus a "horizontal" mark on a 400-subject or 200-subject horizontal format sheet would become a "vertical" mark on a 200-subject vertical format or 280-subject sheet. This situation has caused confusion among collectors and dealers in determining a definite description of the various marks. The designation of the position of the plate numbers also has not been uniform for the "turned" designs.

To solve this confusion, the United States Stamp Society (formerly the Bureau Issues Association) adopted a standard terminology for all the marks appearing on the electric eye sheets. Dashes (A), Margin Line (B), Gutter Bar (C) and Frame Bars (D), whereby each type of mark may be identified readily without referring to its plate-number position. The plate-number designation of the panes will continue to be established by holding the pane of stamps with the designs in an upright position; the corner of the pane on which the plate number appears will determine whether the pane is upper left, upper right, lower left, or lower right.

Die Cutting

The other major form of U.S. stamp separation is die-cutting. This is a method where a die in the pattern of separation is created that later cuts the stamp paper in a stroke motion. This process is used for self-adhesive postage stamps. Die-cutting can appear in straight lines, such as U.S. Scott 2522; shapes, such as U.S. Scott 1552; or imitating the appearance of perforations, such as U.S. Scott 2920. On stamps where the die cutting is unintentionally omitted, the terms "die cutting omitted" or "imperforate" may be used interchangeably.

Rouletting

A third type of separation is seen on a few revenue stamps. In rouletting, the stamp paper is cut partly or wholly through in a series of short consecutive cuts, with no paper removed. The number of cuts made in a two-centimeter space determines the gauge of the rouletting, just as the number of perforations in two centimeters determines the gauge of the perforation.

GUM

The Illustrated Gum Chart in the first part of this introduction shows and defines various types of gum condition. Because gum condition has an important impact on the value of unused stamps, we recommend studying this chart and the accompanying text carefully.

The gum on the back of a stamp may be shiny, dull, smooth, rough, dark, white, colored or tinted. Most stamp gumming adhesives use gum arabic or dextrine as a base. Certain polymers such as polyvinyl alcohol (PVA) have been used extensively since World War II.

The Scott *Standard Postage Stamp Catalogue* does not list items by types of gum. The Scott *Specialized Catalogue of United States Stamps and Covers* does differentiate among some types of gum for certain issues.

Because collectors generally prefer unused stamps with original gum, many unused stamps with no gum have been regummed to make them more desirable (and costly) to collectors who want stamps with full original gum. Some used stamps with faint cancels have had these cancels chemically removed and have been regummed. Skillful regumming can be difficult to detect, particularly on imperforate stamps. Certification of such stamps by competent authorities is suggested.

Reprints of stamps may have gum differing from the original issues. In addition, some countries have used different gum formulas for different seasons. These adhesives have different properties that may become more apparent over time.

Many stamps have been issued without gum, and this catalogue will note this fact. See United States Scott PR33-PR56.

LUMINESCENCE

Kinds of Luminescence — Fluorescence and phosphorescence, two different luminescent qualities, are found in U.S. postage stamps and postal stationery. While all luminescent stamps glow when exposed to short-wave ultraviolet (UV) light, only those with phosphorescent properties display brief afterglow when the UV light source is extinguished.

Fluorescent or "Hi-Bright" Papers — The Bureau of Engraving and Printing, at one point accepting paper for the printing of stamps without regard to fluorescent properties, unknowingly used a mix of paper with infinitely varying amounts of fluorescent optical brighteners added during the papermaking process. In March 1964, to preserve uniformity of product and as a safeguard for an emerging but still incomplete plan for nationwide use of luminescent stamps, BEP purchasing specifications were amended to limit the use of fluorescent paper brighteners. The amended specification permitted paper with some brightener content, but excluded brilliantly glowing papers known in the printing trade as "hi-bright."

Stamps printed on such papers emit a distinctive, intense whitish-violet glow when viewed with either long or short-wave UV. In following years, stamps were produced on papers with lower levels of fluorescence permitted by amended specifications.

Tagged Stamps — The Post Office Department (now the U.S. Postal Service) field-tested automated mail-handling equipment to face, cancel and sort mail at rates up to 30,000 pieces an hour, by sensing UV-light-activated afterglow from phosphorescent substances. For the first tests at Dayton, Ohio, started after August 1, 1963, the 8-cent carmine airpost stamp (Scott C64a) was overprinted (tagged) with a so-called "nearly-invisible" calcium silicate compound which phosphoresces orange-red when exposed to short-wave UV. A facer-canceler, with modifications that included a rapidly cycling on-off UV light, activated the phosphor-tagged airpost stamps and extracted envelopes bearing them from the regular flow of mail.

While the airpost extraction test was still in progress, the entire printing of the City Mail Delivery commemorative (Scott 1238) was ordered tagged with a yellow-green glowing zinc orthosilicate compound intended for use with the automated recognition circuits to be tested with surface-transported letter mail.

After the first-day ceremonies October 26, 1963, at Washington, D.C., it was learned the stamps had been tagged to publicize the innovative test by coupling tagging with stamps memorializing "100 years of postal progress" and to provide the first national distribution of tagged stamps for collectors. Between October 28 and November 2, to broaden the scope of the test in the Dayton area, the 4-cent and 5-cent denominations of the regular issue then in use were issued with the same yellow-green glowing compound applied in an experimental tagging format (Scott 1036e, 1213b, 1213c, and 1229a).

By June 1964, testing had proven sufficiently effective for the Post Office Department to order all 8-cent airpost adhesive stamps phosphor-tagged for general distribution. By January 1966, all airpost stamps, regardless of denomination, were ordered tagged. Meanwhile, from 1963 through 1965, limited quantities of the Christmas issues were tagged for use in the continuing test in the Dayton area on the use of tagging to automatically position (face) and cancel mail. (Scott 1240a, 1254a-1257a, and 1276a).

On May 19, 1966, the use of phosphor-tagged stamps was expanded to the Cincinnati Postal Region, which then included offices in Ohio, Kentucky and Indiana. During the last half of 1966, primarily to meet postal needs of that region, phosphor-tagged issues were authorized to include additional denominations of regular issues, some postal stationery, and about 12 percent of each commemorative issue, starting with the National Park Service 5-cent issue (Scott 1314a) and continuing through the Mary Cassatt 5-cent commemorative (Scott 1322a). After January 1, 1967, most regular values through the 16-cent, all commemoratives, and additional items of postal stationery were ordered tagged.

Adhesive stamps precanceled by the Bureau of Engraving and Printing (Bureau precancels), however, were not tagged, with the exception of Scott 1394, 1596, 1608, and 1610. Because there was no need to cancel mail with these stamps and since precancel permit holders post such mail already faced, postal officials by-passed facer-canceler operations and avoided the cost of tagging.

Overall phosphorescent overprints, when newly issued, are practically invisible in ordinary light. After aging three to five years, the tagging can discolor and become more easily visible. When viewed with UV light, there is little change in the hue of either orange-red or yellow-green emitted light. Even though observable discoloration exists, the presence or absence of tagging is best determined by examination with UV light.

Bar, or block, tagging, instead of the usual overall phosphorescent overprint, was used for some stamps beginning with the Andreotti-printed Mail Order Business commemorative (Scott 1468). These are much easier to identify than the overall overprint, often without need for a UV light.

Band tagging, a bar extending across two or more stamps, was first used with Scott 1489-1498.

Beginning in the 1990s, many stamps are printed on prephosphored paper. Unlike overall tagging, in which the tagging substance is applied to the entire stamp after it is printed, prephosphored paper has the tagging substance added to the surface of the paper during the paper-making process, before printing occurs.

In the late 1990s, some stamps appeared with the tagging formed in the shape of the stamp design elements.

Most of the luminescent issues exist with the luminescent coating unintentionally omitted. Such stamps are termed "tagging omitted" errors and should not be confused with stamps printed intentionally without tagging, which are termed "untagged."

In some postal stationery, such as Scott U551, UC40, UX48a and UX55, the luminescent element is in the ink with which the stamp design is printed. The luminescent varieties of Scott U550 and UC37 were made by adding a vertical phosphorescent bar or panel to the left of the stamp imprint. On Scott UC42, this "glow-bar" passes through the tri-globe design.

The Scott *Specialized Catalogue of United States Stamps and Covers* lists different tagging types when more than one type is known on a stamp. Currently, these types can be large or small block tagging, overall tagging and prephosphored paper. Prephosphored paper is further broken down into two types, each listed separately. In the first case, the tagging compound is applied to uncoated paper, seeping into its fibers and creating a highly mottled, or blotchy, appearance under short-wave UV light. This type is designated in the catalogue listings as "prephosphored uncoated paper with embedded tagging showing a mottled appearance." Some specialists shorten this to "embedded phosphor paper (EP)." In the second case, the tagging compound is mixed with the substance used to coat the surface when making coated paper. The taggant lies on top of the paper and can be removed if the coating is scraped off. This surface phosphor can have a number of different appearances, including solid (or smooth), grainy solid, uneven or randomly wavy. These variations should not be confused with the heavy and irregular mottled appearance of embedded tagging. This second type of prephosphored paper is designated in the catalogue listings as "prephosphored coated paper with surface tagging showing a solid [or grainy solid, or uneven, etc.] appearance." Some specialists shorten this to "surface phosphor paper (SP)." In instances where different prephosphored coated papers are used in the printing or printings of a single stamp, giving rise to surface phosphor paper with different appearances as noted above, such differences are mentioned in footnotes.

NOTE: Users of UV light should avoid prolonged exposure, which can burn the eyes. Sunglasses (particularly those that feature a "UV block") or prescription eyeglasses, tinted or plain, screen the rays and provide protection.

POSTAL MARKINGS

Postal markings are those marks placed by postal employees of this and other countries on the stamp or cover or both. These marks may indicate the mailing place of a letter, date, rate, route, accounting between post offices, and so on.

In addition to the basic town designations, there are many varieties of supplemental markings. Among these are rate marks, route marks, obliterators, special dating markings usually found on advertised or dead-letter covers, transportation markings (rail, steam, ship, airpost, etc.), and service markings (advertised, forwarded, missent, second delivery, mail route, too late, charged, paid box, due, returned for postage, soldier's letter, held for postage, short paid, unpaid, not paid, paid, free, dead letter office, etc.).

These markings originated, for material mailed in what is now the United States, in the Colonial period when manuscript postal markings were first introduced under the Ordinance of December 10, 1672, of New York, which established an inland postal system between the colonies. A "Post Payd" is found on the first letter ever sent under the system, on January 22, 1673. Manuscript postal markings continued in use right through the pre-stamp period and even can be found on some letters today.

The earliest handstamp associated with American service is a "NEW/YORK" blank handstamp found on letters conveyed via the Bristol Packet line in 1710-12 between New York and England. Following the demise of this operation, the first regular handstamp postal markings were introduced at New York in 1756, when a post office packet service was established between Falmouth, England, and New York. The marking merely was "NEW YORK" on two lines of type. The marking (see illustration), with each word of the city name on a separate line, is represented in presentations such as this as "NEW/YORK." Similar markings were later introduced at other towns, such as ANNA/POLIS, by 1766; CHARLES/TOWN, by 1770; PHILA/DELPHIA, by 1766; HART/FORD, by 1766; while other offices received a single-line marking: BOSTON, by 1769; ALBANY, by 1773; PENSACOLA, by 1772; SAVANNA, by 1765; BALTIMORE, by 1772; and WMSBURG, by 1770.

Some of these early letters also bear a circular datestamp containing the month in abbreviated form, i.e., "IV" for June and "IY" for July, and the date in a 14-17mm circle (see illustration). Known from at least nine towns, these are called "Franklin marks" after Benjamin Franklin, then deputy postmaster general for the English crown. The marks also are known as "American Bishopmarks," to distinguish them from the Bishopmark used in England, which has a center line.

First U.S. Handstamp

Franklin Mark

During 1774-75, an American provisional postal system was established in opposition to that of the English crown. Both manuscript and handstamp markings have been attributed to it. This system was taken over by Congress on July 26, 1775, and the same markings were continued in use. The earliest reported Congressional marks are a manuscript "Camb Au 8" and a blue-green straightline "NEW*YORK*AU*24." Postal markings are known throughout Revolution, including English occupation markings. Most are manuscript.

In the post-war Confederation period, handstamped circular markings were introduced at Charleston, South Carolina, in 1778-1780, and later at New London, Connecticut. Straightlines and manuscripts continued to dominate until the use of oval markings became widespread about 1800, with circles becoming the predominant markings shortly thereafter.

Handstamp rate markings are known as early as the 1789 pennyweight markings of Albany. Such types of markings became more common in the 1830's and almost the standard by the "5"and- "10"-cent rate period which began on July 1, 1845. This period also is when envelopes began to replace folded letter sheets. Before that date, envelopes were charged with an extra rate of postage. These "5," "10," and succeeding "3," "6," "5," and "10" rates of 1851-56 were common on domestic mail until prepayment became compulsory April 1, 1855, on all but drop or local letters domestically. The markings were common on foreign mail through about 1875.

Only 1.3 percent of all letters posted between 1847 and 1852 bore stamps. This proportion increased to 25 percent in 1852, 32 percent in 1853, 34 percent in 1854, 40 percent in 1855, and 64 percent in 1856. Stampless covers are commonplace, although there are some that are highly prized on the basis of their markings. Most are more common than stamped covers of the same period.

While the government began issuing handstamps as early as 1799 and obliterators in 1847, many postmasters were required, or at least permitted, to purchase their own canceling devices or to use pen strokes. Pen cancellations continued to be common in the smaller offices into the 1880's. Because of collector prejudice against pen-canceled stamps, many have ended up being "cleaned" (having the pen cancel removed). These are sold either as unused or with a different, faked cancellation to cover the evidence of cleaning. Ultraviolet light (long-wave) usually will reveal traces of the original pen markings.

From around 1850 until 1900, many postmasters used obliterators cut from wood or cork. Many bear fanciful designs, such as bees, bears, chickens, locks, eagles, Masonic symbols, flags, numerals and so on. Some of the designs symbolized the town of origin. These are not listed in this catalogue, for they owe their origin to the whim of some individual rather than a requirement of the postal regulations. Many command high prices and are eagerly sought by collectors. This has led to extensive forgery of such markings so that collectors are advised to check them carefully.

Rapid machine cancellations were introduced at Boston in 1880-90 and later spread across the country. Each of the various canceling machine types had identifiable characteristics, and collectors form collections based on type. One sub-specialty is that of flag cancellations. While handstamp flag designs are known earlier, the first machine flag cancellation was that of Boston in November-December 1894.

Specialists have noted that different canceling inks are used at different times, depending partly on the type of canceling device used. Rubber handstamps, prohibited in 1893 although used for parcel post and precanceling after that date, require a different type of ink from the boxwood or type-metal cancelers of the classic period, while a still different ink is used for the steel devices of the machine cancels.

Registry of letters was first authorized in this country in the Dutch colony of New Netherlands on overseas mail. Records of valuable letters were kept by postmasters throughout the stampless period while an "R" marking was introduced at Philadelphia in 1845 for registered mail. Cincinnati also had such a registry system. The first appearance of the word "registered" is on mail in November 1847, in manuscript, and in handstamp in May 1850. The official registration for U.S. mail, however, did not begin until July 1, 1855.

In recent years, the handstamped and machine types of cancellations have been standardized by the U.S. Postal Service and supplied to the various post offices.

Postmarks — markings to indicate the office of origin or manner of postal conveyance. In general terms, the postmark refers to the post office of origin, but sometimes there also are receiving postmarks of the post office of destination or of transit. Other post office markings include: advertised, forwarded, mail route, missent, paid, not paid, second delivery, too late, etc. Postmarks often serve to cancel postage stamps with or without additional obliterating cancels.

Cancellations — postal markings that make further use of stamps impossible. As used in the listings in this catalogue, cancellations include both postmarks used as cancellations and obliterations intended primarily to cancel (or "kill") the stamp.

Carrier Postmarks — usually show the words "Carrier" "City Delivery," or "U.S.P.O. Dispatch." They were applied to letters to indicate the delivery of mail by U.S. Government carriers. These markings should not be confused with those of local posts or other private mail services that used postmarks of their own. Free delivery of city mail by carriers was begun on July 1, 1863.

Free — handstamp generally used on free, franked mail. The marking occasionally is seen on early adhesives of the United States, used as a canceling device.

Railroad Postmarks — usually handstamps, the markings were used to postmark unpouched mail received by route agents of the Post Office Department traveling on trains on railway mail route. The route name in an agent's postmark often was similar to the name of the railroad or included the terminals of the route. The earliest known use of the word "Railroad" as a postmark is 1838. Route agents gradually became R.P.O. clerks, and some continued to use their handstamps after the route-agent service ceased June 30, 1882. The railroad postmarks of the 1850 period and later usually carried the name of the railroad.

A sub-group of railroad postmarks is made up of those applied in the early days by railroad station agents, using the railroad's ticket dating handstamp as a postmark. Sometimes the station agent was also the postmaster.

In 1864, the Post Office Department equipped cars for the general distribution of mails between Chicago and Clinton, Iowa.

Modern railroad marks, such as "R.P.O.," indicate transportation by railroad, and include Railway Post Office, Terminal Railway Post Office, Transfer Office, Closed Mail Service, Air Mail Field, and Highway Post Office.

Effective November 1, 1949, the Railway Mail Service was merged with others of like nature under the consolidated title Postal Transportation Service (PTS). The service was discontinued June 30, 1977.

The modern "railway marks" are quite common and are not the types referred to under cancellations as listed in this catalogue.

Way Markings — Way letters are those received by a mail carrier on his way between post offices and delivered at the first post office he reached. The postmaster ascertained where the carrier received them and charged, in his postbills, the postage from those places to destination. He wrote "Way" against those charges in his bills and also wrote or stamped "Way" on each letter. If the letter was exempt from postage, it should have been marked "Free."

The term "mail carrier" above refers to any carrier under contract to carry U.S. mail: a stage line, a horseback rider, or a steamboat or railroad that did not have a route agent on board. Only unpouched mail (not previously placed in a post office) was eligible for a Way fee of one cent. The postmaster paid this fee to the carrier, if demanded, for the carrier's extra work of bringing the letter individually to the post office. For a limited time at certain post offices, the Way fee was added to the regular postage. This explains the use of a numeral with the "Way" marking.

Packet Markings — Packet markings listed in this catalogue are those applied on a boat traveling on inland or coastal waterways. This group does not include mail to foreign countries that contains the words "British Packet," "American Packet," etc, or their abbreviations. These are U.S. foreign-mail exchange-office markings.

Listed packet markings are in two groups: 1) waterways route-agent markings that denote service exactly the same as that of the railroad route-agent markings, except that the route agent traveled on a boat instead of a train; 2) name-of-boat markings placed on the cover to advertise the boat or, as some believe, to expedite payment of Way and Steam fees at the post office where such letters entered the U.S. mails.

Occasionally waterways route-agent markings included the name of a boat, "S.B.," "STEAMBOAT," or merely a route number. Such supplemental designations do not alter the character of the markings as those of a route-agent.

19th Century U.S. Express Mail Postmarks — In pre-stamp days these represented either an extra-fast mail service or mail under the care of an express-mail messenger who also carried out-of-mail express packages. The service was permitted as a practical means of competing with package express companies that also carried mail in competition with the U.S. Mail. Several of these early postmarks were later used by U.S. Mail route agents on the New York-Boston and New York-Albany runs, or by U.S. steamboat letter carriers on the coastal run between Boston and St. John, New Brunswick.

Steamboat or **Steam Markings** — Except for the circular markings "Maysville Ky. Steam" and "Terre Haute Stb." and the rectangular "Troy & New York Steam Boat," these markings contain only the word "STEAMBOAT" or "STEAM," with or without a rating numeral. They represent the same service as that of Way markings, except that the carrier was an inland or coastal steamer that had no contract to carry U.S. mails. Such boats, however, were required by law to carry to the nearest post office any mail given them at landings. The boat owner was paid a two-cent fee for each letter so delivered, except on Lake Erie where the fee was one-cent. At some post offices, the Steamboat fee was added to regular postage. In 1861, the two-cent fee was again added to the postage, and in 1863 double postage was charged.

Ship Postmarks — postal markings indicating arrival on a private ship (one not under contract to carry mail). This marking was applied to letters delivered by such ships to the post office at their port of entry as required by law, for which they received a fee and the letters were taxed with a specified fee for the service in place of the ordinary open postage.

The use of U.S. postage stamps on ship letters is unusual, except for letters from Hawaii, because the U.S. inland postage on ship letters from a foreign point did not need to be prepaid. "U.S. SHIP" is a special marking applied to mail posted on naval vessels, especially during the Civil War period.

Steamship Postmarks — akin to Ship postmarks, but they appear to have been used mostly on mail from Caribbean or Pacific ports to New Orleans or Atlantic ports carried on steamships having a U.S. mail contract. An associated numeral usually designates the through rate from where the letter was received by the ship to its inland destination.

Receiving Mark — postal marking placed on the back of envelopes by the receiving post office to indicate the name of the office and date of arrival. It also is known as a "backstamp." Generally discontinued about 1913, the marking was employed for a time on airmail service until it was found the practice slowed the service. Receiving markings now are used on regisered and special-delivery mail.

Miscellaneous Route Markings — wordings associated with the previously described markings include "Bay Route," "River Mail," "Steamer," "Mail Route," etc. Classification of the marking ordinarily is evident from the use, or it can be identified from publications on postal markings.

U.S. Foreign-Mail Exchange-Office Markings — These served to meet the accounting requirements of the various mail treaties before the Universal Postal Union was established. The markings usually designate the exchange office or the carrier (British Packet, Bremen Packet, American Packet, etc.). Sometimes these markings are a restatement of the through rate, or a numeral designating the amount credited or debited to the foreign country as a means of allocating the respective parts of the total postage, according to conditions of route, method of transit, weight, etc.

Gridiron Cancellation — most common type of cancellation on early U.S. stamps. The marking consists of a circle enclosing parallel lines. There are many varieties of grid cancellations.

Paid Markings — generally consist of the word "PAID," sometimes within a frame, indicating regular postage prepaid by the sender of a letter. They are found as separate handstamps, within town or city postmarks, and as a part of obliterating cancels. In each case, the "paid" marking may be used with or without an accompanying or combined rate numeral indication.

Precancels — stamps having the cancellation applied before the article is presented for mailing. The purpose is to reduce handling and speed up the mails. A permit is required for use by the public, except for special cases, such as the experiments using Scott 1384a, 1414a-1418a, or 1552 for Christmas mail. Normally the precanceling is done with devices not used for ordinary postal service. Most precancellations consist of the city and state names between two lines or bars.

Precancels are divided into two groups: locals and Bureaus. Locals were printed, usually from 100-subject plates, or handstamped, usually by means of a 10- or 25-subject device having a rubber, metal or vinyl surface, at the town using the stamps. Most locals were made with devices furnished by the Post Office Department and the Postal Service, but a number were made with devices created in the city using them. Early locals include the printed "PAID" or "paid" on Scott 7 and 9, "CUMBERLAND, ME." on Scott 24-26 and the Glen Allen, Virginia stars. The U.S. Postal Service discontinued the practice of local precanceling as of July 5, 2007.

Many styles of precancellation are known. More than 600,000 different precancels exist from more than 20,000 post offices in the United States.

The Bureaus, or Bureau Prints, were precancels furnished to the post offices by the Post Office Department in Washington. For 75 years these were printed by the Bureau of Engraving and Printing, hence the name "Bureaus."

In late 1991, the American Bank Note Co. and J.W. Fergusson and Sons for Stamp Venturers also began producing precanceled stamps under contract with the Postal Service. Other companies have followed. Because the stamps go to the local post office from the same source, the Postal Service, and the method of production is essentially the same as used by the BEP, the term "Bureau precancel" has been retained in this catalogue. The cancellations consist of the name of the city and state where the stamps are to be used, lines or the class of mail. They originated in 1916, when postal officials were seeking ways to reduce costs as well as increase the legibility of the overprint. The BEP was low bidder in three cities, which resulted in the "experimentals." These 16 denominations, including two postage dues, were issued for Augusta, Maine (one value); Springfield, Massachusetts (14 values); and New Orleans (six values) in quanities ranging from 4,000,000 down to 10,000. Electrotype plates mounted on a flat-bed press were used to print the precancellations.

Regular production of Bureau precancels began on May 2, 1923, with Scott 581 precanceled "New York, N.Y." All regular Bureaus until 1954 were produced by the Stickney rotary press, whereby the stamps, immediately after printing, pass under the precanceling plates. Then the roll is gummed, perforated and cut into sheets or coils. Since 1954, a variety of printing methods have been used.

Precancels are listed in this catalogue only if the precanceled stamp is different from the nonprecanceled version (untagged stamps such as Scott 1582a); or, if the stamp only exists precanceled (Scott 2265). Classic locals and experimental Bureaus also are included as cancellations. See Service Indicator.

Service Indicator — inscription included in the design of the stamp to indicate the category of postal service to be rendered. The first regular postage stamp to include a service indicator was the 1976 7.9-cent Drum coil stamp of the Americana series (Scott 1615), which was for bulk rate mailings. This stamp was issued with Bureau precancels for proper usage from 107 cities. Examples without the Bureau precancellation were for philatelic purposes.

A second category of service indicator came about when the USPS began to include the service inscription between the lines of the Bureau precancellation. Examples of this group are "Bulk Rate" and "Nonprofit Organization."

Finally, with the 16.7-cent Transportation coil (Scott 2261), issued July 7, 1988, the USPS went back to including the service indicator in the design, with the indicator serving as the cancellation. With the precancellation now part of the design, the USPS stopped offering tagged versions of the stamps for collectors. The only so-called precancels currently in use are the service class/rate inscribed coils, and mailers' postmarks. This change was announced in *Postal Bulletin* 22210, dated July 5, 2007.

In all cases, the "service indicator" stamp does not normally receive an additional cancellation when used for the indicated service. For examples see Postal Markings - Bureau Precancels.

Tied On — when the cancellation (or postmark) extends from the stamp to the envelope.

Postal Markings - Cancellation Examples

Numerals
Values are for rating marks such as those illustrated. Later types of numerals in grids targets, etc., are common.

The common Boston Paid cancellation
(Values are for types other than this)

PAID ALL
PAID

Steamship

STEAMBOAT

SHIP STEAM

FREE

Steamboat
(Route agent marking)

ST. LOUIS, CAIRO AND NEW ORLEANS
RAILROAD LINE STEAMER
CHAMPION
LEAVES NEW ORLEANS FOR
CAIRO AND ST LOUIS.
MAR 25

Packet Boat
(Name-of-boat marking)

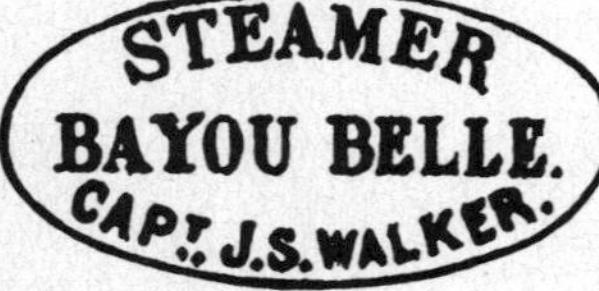

Packet Boat
(Name-of-boat marking)

Packet Boat
(Name-of-boat marking)

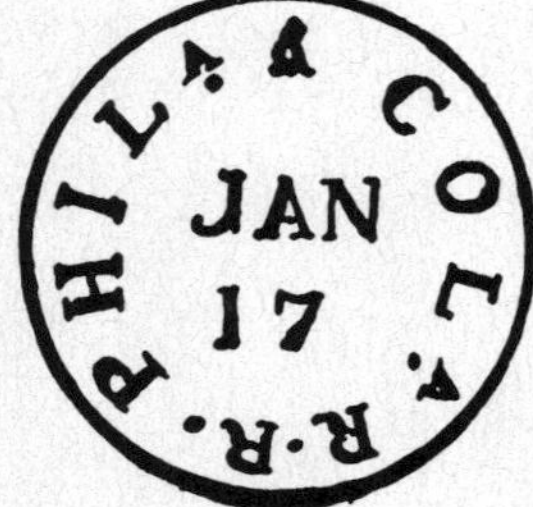

Railroad
(Route agent marking)

U.S. Express Mail
(Route agent marking)

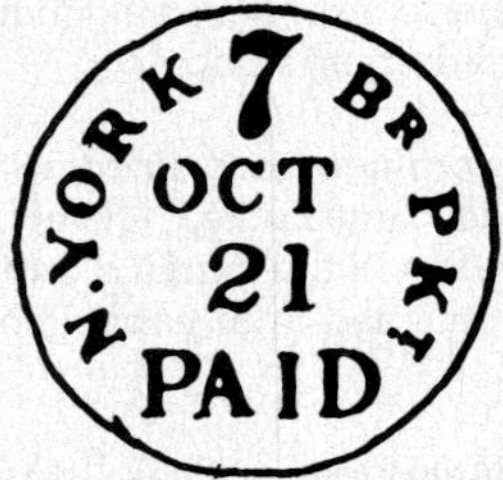

(In red on letter to Germany via Prussian Closed Mail, via British Packet. Credits 7 cents to Prussia.)

Express Company

Carrier

BANKS' DIVISION
OCT
4

Army Field Post

Canadian

Town

Fort

Year dated

Vera Cruz, Mexico 1914

U.S. Postmark used in China

Exposition Station
Used while exposition is open. Many styles.

U.S. Postmark
used in Japan

Exposition advertising
Used before exposition opens. Many styles.

New York City Foreign Mail — A group of design cancellations used between 1871 and 1877 in New York City on outgoing foreign mail only. This group of handstamps totals about 200 different fancy stars, geometric designs, wheels conventionalized flowers, etc., the majority within a circle 26-29 mm in diameter.

Patent Defacing Cancellations — When adhesive stamps came into general use, the Post Office Department made constant efforts to find a type of cancellation which would make the reuse of the stamp impossible. Many patents were granted to inventors, and some of the cancellations (killers) came into more or less general use. Some of them appear in combination with the town postmarks.

About 125 different types are known on the stamps issued up to about 1887. Their principal use and greatest variety occur on Scott 65, 147, 158, 183 and 184.

Patent cancellations generally fall into three groups:

1) Small pins or punches which pierce the paper or depress it sufficiently to break the fiber.

2) Sharp blades or other devices for cutting the paper.

3) Rotation of a portion of the canceler so that part of the paper is scraped away.

1. Dot punches through paper

2. Blades cut the paper

2. Small circle cuts the paper

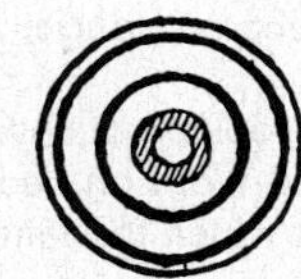

3. Scraped in the shaded circle

Supplementary Mail — markings which designate the special post office service of dispatching mail after the regular mail closed. Two kinds of supplementary mail were available:

1. Foreign mail. For New York, the postmaster general established in 1853 a fee of double the regular rate. This paid to get the mail aboard ship after the regular mail closing and before sailing time. The service continued until 1939. Postmark Types A, D, E, F, and G were used.

2. Domestic mail. For Chicago, at no extra fee, supplementary mail entitled a letter to catch the last eastbound train. Postmark Types B and C were used. No foreign destination was implied.

Similar service with "Supplementary" in the postmark apparently was available in Philadelphia and possibly elsewhere.

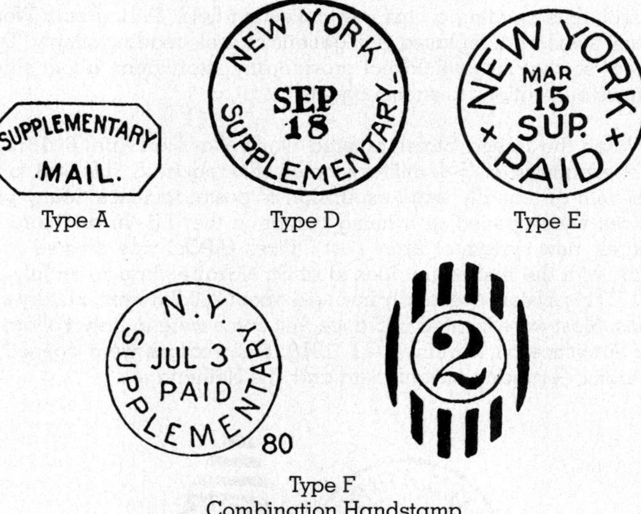

Type A Type D Type E

Type F
Combination Handstamp
(Also comes with numeral "1")
(Stamps with numeral cancel alone do not qualify for Supplementary Mail cancel premiums.)

Type G (also with other numerals)

Type B Type C

Military Postmarks – Although mail from soldiers and sailors exists for all of the wars back to the American Revolution, such early letters were ordinarily sent through nearby civilian post offices. In fact, the first postal stations specifically for the handling of military mail were opened during the Spanish-American War in 1898. They were initially set up at training camps in the U.S. However, as the actual conflict took place in the Spanish colonies in the Caribbean and the Pacific, 77 special post offices were opened to handle military mail in Cuba, Puerto Rico, Guam and the Philippines. Most of these offices were issued cancels inscribed "Military Postal Station No. __" with the name of the town and territory in which they were located.

For many years, the warships of the U.S. Navy did not have post offices, so sailors' mail was simply deposited at the next convenient port. However, in 1908 the creation of on-board postal facilities was authorized, resulting in new postmarks showing the name of each vessel, thus creating a vast new collecting field. During both World Wars, these were replaced with generic cancels reading simply "U.S. Navy" so that they would not provide any information about ships' names or locations to enemy agents.

When the United States entered World War I on April 6, 1917, a vast expansion of U.S. military forces was required. This had to be met with an equally large expansion of postal facilities. Many post offices were opened at training camps in the U.S. In addition, an entirely new system of Army Post Offices (APOs) was created overseas, with the first being opened at St. Nazaire, France, on July 10, 1917. This system eventually involved about 200 different military stations. Most were located in France, but some were in Italy. Following the Armistice on November 11, 1918, other offices were opened in Belgium, Germany, Luxembourg and The Netherlands.

At first, members of the AEF were allowed to send mail from the APOs to the U.S., its territories and possessions at domestic postage rates, which were 1¢ for postcards and 2¢ for letters. However, from October 4, 1917, the troops were granted free postage for such items, although they were still required to pay at domestic rates for special services such as registration, special delivery and parcel post.

Civilians serving with the army, war correspondents and workers with welfare organizations, including the American Red Cross, YMCA, Knights of Columbus and Salvation Army, were permitted to use the APOs but had to pay domestic postage, including the war tax of 1¢ per piece that was in effect from November 2, 1917, until June 30, 1919.

Some American units participated in the Allied intervention in Russia in 1918-1920, including Siberia and North Russia. A U.S. postal agency was opened in Vladivostok, Siberia, to handle mail from the AEF-Siberia, but the troops in North Russia used the British postal facilities (with their so-called "Polar Bear" markings).

Elsewhere, American forces were involved in military interventions in China, the Caribbean and Latin America (Cuba, Dominican Republic, Haiti, Mexico and Nicaragua). In each case, U.S. military postal facilities were opened to serve the troops, thus creating new postal markings that are collected by specialists.

During World War II, the first new U.S. military post offices were opened in connection with the bases acquired from Great Britain in exchange for a fleet of old destroyers. The first of these offices was opened on January 15, 1941, using a postmark inscribed "American Forces in Newfoundland." When other offices opened, the inscription was changed to "American Base Forces" and an APO number added. After the U.S. entered the war on December 7, 1941, there was a vast expansion of the system, and the postmarks were changed to "U.S. Army Postal Service" with an APO number.

During the course of the war and its aftermath, more than 1,000 APOs were created, serving Army and Air Force personnel around the world. Some of these were open for very short periods, and their postmarks are scarce. As in World War I, the troops were granted free franking for surface cards and letters from April 1, 1942, to December 31, 1947, but postage was required for special services, including airmail, at normal domestic rates.

More recently, of course, there is military mail from the conflicts in Korea, Vietnam, Kuwait, Afghanistan and Iraq, not to mention smaller events in places like Grenada, Panama and Kosovo. It should be noted that the APO numbering system was switched over to five digits in 1965, to bring it in line with the civilian zip code designations.

In looking at covers, collectors will find that most military mail from World War I on bears evidence of military and/or civilian censorship, after which the letters were permitted to be forwarded.

Readers desiring more information on military postal markings, censorship and the handling of military mail, or a list of available publications on these and related subjects, are invited to visit www.MilitaryPHS.org, the website of the Military Postal History Society.

Postal Markings - Bureau Precancels

AUGUSTA
MAINE

NEW
ORLEANS
LA.

SPRINGFIELD
MASS.

Experimentals

PERU
IND.

LANSING
MICH.

SAINT LOUIS
MO.

New Orleans
La.

San Francisco
Calif.

PORTLAND
ME.

LAKEWOOD
N. J.

KANSAS
CITY
MO.

POUGHKEEPSIE
N. Y.

LONG ISLAND
CITY, N. Y.

CORPUS
CHRISTI
TEXAS

ATLANTA
GEORGIA

ATLANTA
GA.

PEORIA
IL

CINCINNATI
OH

Postal Markings - Service Indicators

Blk. Rt.
CAR-RT
SORT

Bulk Rate

Nonprofit
Org.

Nonprofit
Org.

PRESORTED
FIRST-CLASS

ZIP+4

Postal Markings - Local Precancels

QUINCY
ILLINOIS

FITCHBURG
MASS.

LOS ANGELES
CALIF.

Fergus Falls
Minn.

COVINGTON
KY.

REDWOOD CITY
CALIF.

BELMONT
CALIF.

ELGIN
ILLINOIS

Electroplates

Ashland
Wis.

PALMYRA
N. Y.

Northhampton
MASS.

DES PLAINES
ILL.

RICHMOND
VA.

BROOKFIELD
ILLINOIS

PAONIA
COLO.

GOSHEN
IND

TOWER CITY
N. DAK.

NEW BRUNSWICK
N. J.

ORLANDO,
FLA.

RICHTON PARK
ILL.

MULINO,
OREG.

PINE HILL
N.Y.

FARRELL,
PA

SACRAMENTO
CA

Handstamps

GENERAL GLOSSARY

Scott Publishing Co. uses the following terms in its catalogues, as appropriate. Definitions follow each term.

Imperforate — stamps without perforations, rouletting, or other form of separation. Some self-adhesive stamps are die cut with straight lines. They look imperforate, but they are not.

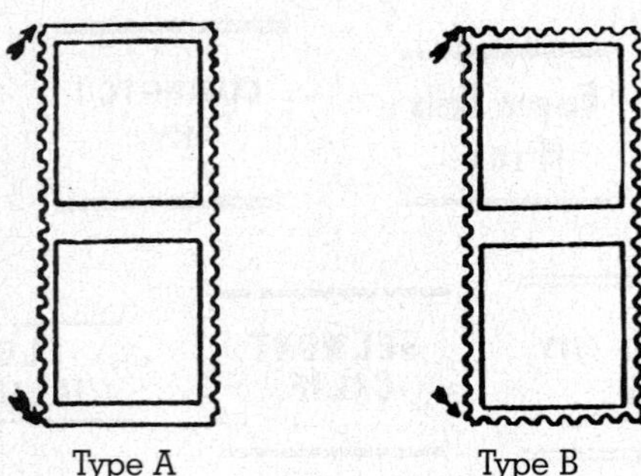

Type A Type B

Part-Perforate — Stamps with perforations on the two opposite sides, the other two sides remaining imperforate. See Coil Stamps.

Vertical Pair, Imperforate Horizontally — (Type A illustrated) indicating that a pair of stamps is fully perforated vertically, but has no horizontal perforations.

Horizontal Pair, Imperforate Vertically — (Type A) indicating that a pair of stamps is fully perforated horizontally but has no vertical perforations.

Vertical Pair, Imperforate Between — (Type B illustrated) indicating that the vertical pair is fully perforated at the top, sides and bottom, but has no perforations between the stamps.

Horizontal Pair, Imperforate Between — (Type B) indicating that the horizontal pair is fully perforated at the top, sides and bottom, but has no perforations between the stamps.

Note: Of the above two types (A and B), Type A is the more common.

Blind Perforations — the slight impressions left by the perforating pins if they fail to puncture the paper. While multiples of stamps showing blind perforations may command a slight premium over normally perforated stamps, they are not imperforate errors. Fakers have removed gum from stamps to make blind perforations less evident.

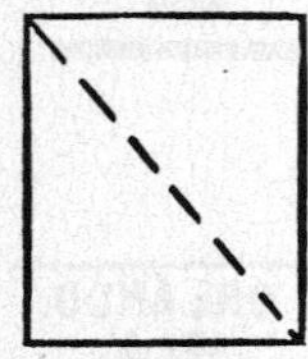

Diagonal

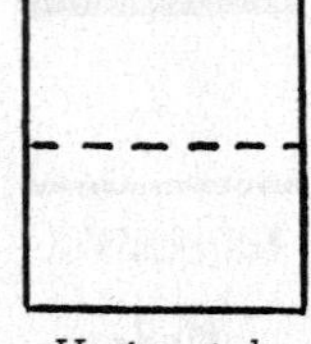

Horizontal

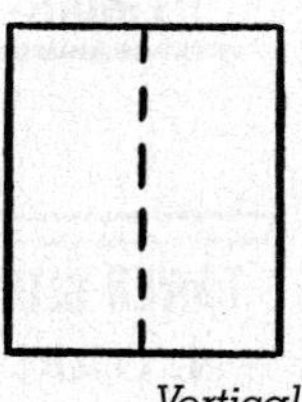

Vertical

Bisect — Stamps cut in half so that each part prepaid postage. These items were used in emergencies where no stamps of the lower denomination were available. These may be diagonal, horizontal or vertical,as shown. Listings are for bisects on full covers with the bisected stamp tied to the cover on the cut side. Those on piece or part of a cover sell for considerably less. "Half-stamps" that receive a surcharge or overprint are not considered bisects.

This catalogue does not list unofficial bisects after the 1880's.

Block of Four, Imperforate Within — Examples exist of blocks of four stamps that are perforated on all four outside edges, but lack both horizontal and vertical perforations within the block. Scott 2096c, the Smokey the Bear commemorative, is an accidental example of this phenomenon. Scott RS173j and RS174j are examples of a situation where internal perforations were omitted intentionally to create 4-cent "stamps" from four 1-cent stamps.

Rouletting — short consecutive cuts in the paper to facilitate separation of the stamps, made with a toothed wheel or disc.

Booklets — Many countries have issued stamps in booklets for the convenience of users. This idea is becoming increasingly popular today in many countries. Booklets have been issued in all sizes and forms, often with advertising on the covers, on the panes of stamps or on the interleaving.

The panes may be printed from special plates or made from regular sheets. All panes from booklets issued by the United States and many from those of other countries are imperforate on three sides, but perforated between the stamps. Any stamplike unit in the pane, either printed or blank, which is not a postage stamp, is considered a *label* in the catalogue listings. The part of the pane through which stitches or staples bind the booklet together, or which affixes the pane to the booklet cover, is considered to be a *binding stub* or *tab*.

Scott lists and values booklets in this volume. Except for panes from Canal Zone, handmade booklet panes are not listed when they are fashioned from existing sheet stamps and, therefore, are not distinguishable from the sheet-stamp foreign counterparts.

Panes usually do not have a "used" value because there is little market activity in used panes, even though many exist used.

Cancellations — the marks or obliterations put on a stamp by the authorities to show that it has done service and is no longer valid for use. If made with a pen, it is a "pen cancellation." When the location of the post office appears in the cancellation, it is a "town cancellation." When calling attention to a cause or celebration, it is a "slogan cancellation." Many other types and styles of cancellations exist, such as duplex, numerals, targets, etc.

Coil Stamps — stamps issued in rolls for use in dispensers, affixing and vending machines. Those of the United States and its territories are perforated horizontally or vertically only, with the outer edges imperforate. Coil stamps of some countries, such as Great Britain, are perforated on all four sides.

Commemorative Stamps — Special issues that commemorate some anniversary or event or person. Usually such stamps are available for a limited period concurrently with the regular issue of stamps. Examples of commemorative issues are Scott 230-245, 620-621, 946, 1266, C68, and U218-U221.

Covers — envelopes, with or without adhesive postage stamps, which have passed through the mail and bear postal or other markings of philatelic interest. Before the introduction of envelopes in about 1840, people folded letters and wrote the address on the outside. Many people covered their letters with an extra sheet of paper on the outside for the address, producing the term "cover." Used air letter sheets and stamped envelopes also are considered covers. Stamps on paper used to cover parcels are said to be "on wrapper." ("Wrapper" also is the term used for postal stationery items that were open at both sides and wrapped around newspapers or pamphlets.) Often stamps with high face values are rare on cover, but more common on wrapper. Some stamps and postal stationery items are difficult to find used in the manner for which they were intended, but quite common when used to make philatelic items such as flight or first day covers. High face-value stamps also may be more common on package address tags. See Postal Cards.

Earliest Documented Use (EDU) — For stamps that do not have a designated first day of issue, the earliest documented use is the date when a stamp was first used in the U.S. mails. These dates are listed in the U.S. Specialized catalogue, and new dates must be documented with recognized certificates from leading expertizing committees.

Error — stamps having some unintentional major deviation from the normal. Errors include, but are not limited to, mistakes in color, paper, or watermark; inverted centers or frames on multicolor printing; missing color;inverted or double surcharges or overprints; imperforates and part-perforates; unintentionally omitted tagging; and double impressions. A factually wrong or misspelled inscription, if it appears on all examples of a stamp, even if corrected later, is not classified as a philatelic error.

Color-Omitted Errors — This term refers to stamps where a missing color is caused by the complete failure of the printing plate to deliver ink to the stamp paper or any other paper. Generally, this is caused by the printing plate not being engaged on the press or by the ink station running dry of ink during printing.

Color-Missing Errors — This term refers to stamps where a color or colors were printed somewhere but do not appear on the finished stamp. There are four different classes of color-missing errors, and this catalogue indicates with a two-letter code appended to each such listing what caused the color to be missing. This same terminology is used in the listings of many modern perforation/die cutting missing errors.

FO = A *foldover* of the stamp sheet during printing may block ink from appearing on a stamp. Instead, the color will appear on the back of the foldover (where it might fall on the back of the selvage or perhaps on the back of another stamp). FO also will be used in the case of foldunders, where the paper may fold underneath the other stamp paper and the color will print on the platen.

EP = A piece of *extraneous paper* falling across the plate or stamp paper will receive the printed ink. When the extraneous paper is removed, an unprinted area of stamp paper remains and shows partially or totally missing colors.

CM = A misregistration of the printing plates during printing will result in a *color misregistration*, and such a misregistration may result in a color not appearing on the finished stamp.

PS = A *perforation shift* after printing may remove a color from the finished stamp. Normally, this will occur on a row of stamps at the edge of the stamp pane.

First Day Cover — A philatelic term to designate the use of a certain stamp (on cover) or postal stationery item on the first day of issue at a place officially designated for such issue or so postmarked. Current U.S. stamps may have such a postal marking applied considerably after the actual issue date.

Gum Breaker Ridges — Colorless marks across the backs of some rotary press stamps, impressed during manufacture to prevent curling. Many varieties of "gum breaks" exist.

Measurements — When measurements are given in the Scott catalogues for stamp size, grill size or any other reason, the first measurement given is always for the top and bottom dimension, while the second measurement will be for the sides (just as perforation gauges are measured). Thus, a stamp size of 15mm x 21mm will indicate a vertically oriented stamp 15mm wide at top and bottom, and 21mm tall at the sides. The same principle holds for measuring or counting items such as U.S. grills. A grill count of 22x18 points (B grill) indicates that there are 22 grill points across by 18 grill points down.

Original Gum — A stamp is described as "O.G." if it has the original gum as applied when printed. Some are issued without gum, such as Scott 730, 731, 735, 752, etc; government reproductions, such as Scott 3 and 4; and official reprints.

Overprinted and Surcharged Stamps — Overprinting is a wording or design placed on stamps to alter the place of use (e.g., "Canal Zone" on U.S. stamps), to adapt them for a special purpose ("I.R." on 1-cent and 2-cent U.S. stamps of the 1897-1903 regular issue for use as revenue stamps. Scott R153-R155A), or for a special occasion (U.S. Scott 647-648).

Surcharge is an overprint that changes or restates the face value of the item.

Surcharges and overprints may be handstamped, typeset or, occasionally, lithographed or engraved. A few handwritten overprints and surcharges are known. The world's first surcharge was a handstamped "2" on the United States City Despatch Post stamps of 1846.

Postal Cards — cards that have postage printed on them. Ones without printed stamps are referred to as "postcards."

Proofs and Essays — *Proofs* are impressions taken from an approved die, plate or stone in which the design and color are the same as the stamp issued to the public. *Trial color proofs* are impressions taken from approved dies, plates or stones in varying colors. An *essay* is the impression of a design that differs in some way from the stamp as issued.

Provisionals — stamps issued on short notice and intended for temporary use pending the arrival of regular (definitive) issues. They usually are issued to meet such contingencies as changes in government or currency, shortage of necessary denominations, or military occupation.

In the 1840's, postmasters in certain American cities issued stamps that were valid only at specific post offices. Postmasters of the Confederate States also issued stamps with limited validity. These are known as "postmaster's provisionals." See U.S. Scott 9X1-9X3 and Confederate States Scott 51X1.

Se-Tenant — joined, referring to an unsevered pair, strip or block of stamps differing in design, denomination or overprint. See U.S. Scott 2158a. Unless the se-tenant item has a continuous design (see U.S. Scott 1451a, 1694a), the stamps do not have to be in the same order as shown in the catalogue (see U.S. Scott 2158a).

Tete Beche — A pair of stamps in which one is upside down in relation to the other. Some of these are the result of intentional sheet arrangements, i.e. Morocco Scott B10-B11. Others occurred when one or more electrotypes accidentally were placed upside down on the plate. See Hawaii Scott 21a and 22a. Separation of the stamps, of course, destroys the tete beche variety.

Specimens — One of the regulations of the Universal Postal Union requires member nations to send samples of all stamps they put into service to the International Bureau in Switzerland. Member nations of the UPU receive these specimens as samples of what stamps are valid for postage. Many are overprinted, handstamped or initial-perforated "Specimen," "Canceled" or "Muestra."Stamps distributed to government officials or for publicity purposes, and stamps submitted by private security printers for official approval also may receive such defacements.

These markings prevent postal use, and all such items generally are known as "specimens." There is a section in this catalogue devoted to this type of material. U.S. officials with "specimen" overprints and printings are listed in the Special Printings section.

Splice — The junction of two rotary-press printings by butting the ends of the web (roll) of paper together and pasting a strip of perforated translucent paper on the back of the junction. The two-stamp specimen to show this situation is a "spliced pair."

Splices occur when a web breaks and is repaired or when one web is finished and another begins.

Territorial and Statehood Dates

	Territorial Date	Statehood Date	
Alabama	Sept. 25, 1817	Dec. 14, 1819	Territory by enabling act of March 3, 1817, effective Sept. 25, 1817. Created out of part of existing Mississippi Territory.
Alaska	Oct. 18, 1867	Jan. 3, 1959	A district from Oct. 18, 1867, until it became an organized territory Aug. 24, 1912.
Arizona	Feb. 24, 1863	Feb. 14, 1912	This region was sometimes called Arizona before 1863 though still in the Territory of New Mexico.
Arkansas	July 5, 1819*	June 15, 1836	The territory was larger than the state. After statehood, the left-over area to the west had post offices that continued for some years to use an Arkansas abbreviation in the postmarks although really they were in the "Indian Country."
California		Sept. 9, 1850	Ceded by Mexico by the Treaty of Guadalupe-Hidalgo, concluded Feb. 2, 1848, and proclaimed July 4, 1848. From then until statehood, California had first a military government until Dec. 20, 1849, and then a local civil government. It never had a territorial form of government.
Colorado	Feb. 28, 1861	Aug. 1, 1876	
Connecticut		Jan. 9, 1788	The fifth of the original 13 colonies.
Delaware		Dec. 7, 1787	The first of the original 13 colonies.
Dakota	March 2, 1861	Nov. 2, 1889	Became two states: North and South Dakota.
Deseret	March 5, 1849		Brigham Young created the unofficial territory of Deseret. In spite of the fact that Utah Territory was created Sept. 9, 1850, Deseret continued to exist unofficially, in what is now Utah, at least as late as 1862.
Frankland or Franklin			This unofficial state was formed in Aug. 1784, in the northeast corner of what is now Tennessee, and the government existed until 1788. In reality it was part of North Carolina.
Florida	March 30, 1822	March 3, 1845	
Georgia		Jan. 2, 1788	The fourth of the original 13 colonies.
Hawaii	Aug. 12, 1898	Aug. 21, 1959	The territorial date given is that of the formal transfer to the United States, with Sanford B. Dole as first Governor.
Idaho	March 3, 1863	July 3, 1890	
Illinois	March 2, 1809*	Dec. 3, 1818	
Indiana	July 5, 1800*	Dec. 11, 1816	There was a residue of Indiana Territory which continued to exist under that name from Dec. 11, 1816 until Dec. 3, 1818, when it was attached to Michigan Territory.
Indian Territory		Nov. 16, 1907	In the region first called the "Indian Country," established June 30, 1834. It never had a territorial form of government. Finally, with Oklahoma Territory, it became the State of Oklahoma on Nov. 16, 1907.
Iowa	July 4, 1838	Dec. 28, 1846	
Jefferson	Oct. 24, 1859		An unofficial territory from Oct. 24, 1859, to Feb. 28, 1861. In reality it included parts of Kansas, Nebraska, Utah and New Mexico Territories, about 30% being in each of the first three and 10% in New Mexico. The settled portion was mostly in Kansas Territory until Jan. 29, 1861, when the State of Kansas was formed from the eastern part of Kansas Territory. From this date the heart of "Jefferson" was in unorganized territory until Feb. 28, 1861, when it became the Territory of Colorado.
Kansas	May 30, 1854	Jan. 29, 1861	
Kentucky		June 1, 1792	Never a territory, it was part of Virginia until statehood.
District of Louisiana	Oct. 1, 1804		An enormous region, it encompassed all of the Louisiana Purchase except the Territory of Orleans. Created by Act of March 26, 1804, effective Oct. 1, 1804, and attached for administrative purposes to the Territory of Indiana.
Territory of Louisiana	July 4, 1805		By Act of March 3, 1805, effective July 4, 1805, the District of Louisiana became the Territory of Louisiana.
Louisiana		April 30, 1812	With certain boundary changes, had been the Territory of Orleans.
District of Maine		March 16, 1820	Before statehood, what is now the State of Maine was called the District of Maine and belonged to Massachusetts.
Maryland		April 28, 1788	The seventh of the original 13 colonies.
Massachusetts		Feb. 6, 1788	The sixth of the original 13 colonies.
Michigan	July 1, 1805	Jan. 26, 1837	
Minnesota	March 3, 1849	May 11, 1858	
Mississippi	May 7, 1798	Dec. 10, 1817	Territory by Act of April 7, 1798, effective May 7, 1798.
Missouri	Dec. 7, 1812	Aug. 10, 1821	The state was much smaller than the territory. The area to the west and northwest of the state, which had been in the territory, was commonly known as the "Missouri Country" until May 30, 1854, and certain of the post offices in this area show a Missouri abbreviation in the postmark.
Montana	May 26, 1864	Nov. 8, 1889	
Nebraska	May 30, 1854	March 1, 1867	
Nevada	March 2, 1861	Oct. 31, 1864	
New Hampshire		June 21, 1788	The ninth of the original 13 colonies.
New Jersey		Dec. 18, 1787	The third of the original 13 colonies.
New Mexico	Dec. 13, 1850	Jan. 6, 1912	
New York		July 26, 1788	The 11th of the original 13 colonies.
North Carolina		Nov. 21, 1789	The 12th of the original 13 colonies.
North Dakota		Nov. 2, 1889	Had been part of the Territory of Dakota.
Northwest Territory	July 13, 1787		Ceased to exist March 1, 1803, when Ohio became a state. The date given is in dispute, Nov. 29, 1802 often being accepted.
Ohio		March 1, 1803	Had been part of Northwest Territory until statehood.
Oklahoma	May 2, 1890	Nov. 16, 1907	The state was formed from Oklahoma Territory and Indian Territory.
Oregon	Aug. 14, 1848	Feb. 14, 1859	
Orleans	Oct. 1, 1804		A territory by Act of March 26, 1804, effective Oct. 1, 1804. With certain boundary changes, it became the State of Louisiana, April 30, 1812.
Pennsylvania		Dec. 12, 1787	The second of the original 13 colonies.
Rhode Island		May 29, 1790	The 13th of the original 13 colonies.
South Carolina		May 23, 1788	The eighth of the original 13 colonies.
South Dakota		Nov. 2, 1889	Had been part of Dakota Territory.
Southwest Territory			Became the State of Tennessee, with minor boundary changes, June 1, 1796.
Tennessee		June 1, 1796	Had been Southwest Territory before statehood.
Texas		Dec. 29, 1845	Had been an independent Republic before statehood.
Utah	Sept. 9, 1850	Jan. 4, 1896	
Vermont		March 4, 1791	Until statehood, had been a region claimed by both New York and New Hampshire.
Virginia		June 25, 1788	The 10th of the original 13 colonies.
Washington	March 2, 1853	Nov. 11, 1889	
West Virginia		June 20, 1863	Had been part of Virginia until statehood.
Wisconsin	July 4, 1836	May 29, 1848	The state was smaller than the territory, and the left-over area continued to be called the Territory of Wisconsin until March 3, 1849.
Wyoming	July 29, 1868	July 10, 1890	

* The dates followed by an asterisk are one day later than those generally accepted. The reason is that the Act states, with Arkansas for example, "from and after July 4." While it was undoubtedly the intention of Congress to create Arkansas as a Territory on July 4, the U.S. Supreme Court decided that "from and after July 4," for instance, meant "July 5."

Territorial and statehood data compiled by Dr. Carroll Chase and Richard McP. Cabeen.

Domestic Letter Rates

Effective Date	Prepaid	
1845, July 1		
Reduction from 6¢ to 25¢ range on single-sheet letters		
Under 300 miles, per ½ oz	5¢	5¢
Over 300 miles, per ½ oz	10¢	10¢
Drop letters	2¢	
1847-1848		
East, to or from Havana (Cuba) per ½ oz	12½¢	12½¢
East, to or from Chagres (Panama) per ½ oz	20¢	20¢
East, to or from Panama, across Isthmus, per ½ oz	30¢	30¢
To or from Astoria (Ore.) or Pacific Coast, per ½ oz	40¢	40¢
Along Pacific Coast, per ½ oz	12½¢	12½¢
1847, July 1		
Unsealed circulars		
1 oz. or less	3¢	
1851, July 1		
Elimination of rates of 1847-1848 listed above		
Up to 3,000 miles, per ½ oz.	3¢	5¢
Over 3,000 miles, per ½ oz	6¢	10¢
Drop letters	1¢	
Unsealed circular		
1 oz. or less up to 500 miles	1¢	
Over 500 miles to 1,500 miles	2¢	
Over 1,500 miles to 2,500 miles	3¢	
Over 2,500 miles to 3,500 miles	4¢	
Over 3,500 miles	5¢	
1852, September 30		
Unsealed circulars		
3 oz. or less anywhere in U.S.	1¢	
Each additional ounce	1¢	
(Double charge if collect)		
1855, April 1		
Prepayment made compulsory		
Not over 3,000 miles, per ½ oz.	3¢	
Over 3,000 miles, per ½ oz.	10¢	
Drop letters	1¢	
1863, July 1		
Distance differential eliminated		
All parts of United States, per ½ oz.	3¢	

Effective Date	Prepaid
1883, October 1	
Letter rate reduced one-third	
All parts of United States, per ½ oz.	2¢
1885, July 1	
Weight increased to 1 oz.	
All parts of United States, per 1 oz.	2¢
1896, October 1	
Rural Free Delivery started	
1917, November 2	
War emergency	
All parts of United States, per 1 oz.	3¢
1919, July 1	
Restoration of pre-war rate	
All parts of United States, per 1 oz.	2¢
1932, July 6	
Rise due to depression	
All parts of United States, per 1 oz.	3¢
1958, August 1	
All parts of United States, per 1 oz.	4¢
1963, January 7	
All parts of United States, per 1 oz.	5¢
1968, January 7	
All parts of United States, per 1 oz.	6¢
1971, May 16	
All parts of United States, per 1 oz.	8¢
1974, March 2	
All parts of United States, per 1 oz.	10¢
1975, December 31	
All parts of United States, 1st oz.	13¢
1978, May 29	
All parts of United States, 1st oz.	15¢
1981, March 22	
All parts of United States, 1st oz.	18¢
1981, November 1	
All parts of United States, 1st oz.	20¢
1985, February 17	
All parts of United States, 1st oz.	22¢

Effective Date	Prepaid
1988, April 3	
All parts of United States, 1st oz.	25¢
1991, February 3	
All parts of United States, 1st oz.	29¢
1995, January 1	
All parts of United States, 1st oz.	32¢
1999, January 10	
All parts of United States, 1st oz.	33¢
2001, January 7	
All parts of United States, 1st oz.	34¢
2002, June 30	
All parts of United States, 1st oz.	37¢
2006, January 8	
All parts of United States, 1st oz.	39¢
2007, May 14	
All parts of United States, 1st oz.	41¢
2008, May 12	
All parts of United States, 1st oz.	42¢
2009, May 11	
All parts of United States, 1st oz.	44¢
2012, January 22	
All parts of United States, 1st oz.	45¢
2013, January 27	
All parts of United States, 1st oz.	46¢
2014, January 26	
All parts of United States, 1st oz.	49¢
2016, April 10	
All parts of United States, 1st oz.	47¢
2017, January 22	
All parts of United States, 1st oz.	49¢
2018, January 21	
All parts of United States, 1st oz.	50¢
2019, January 27	
All parts of United States, 1st oz.	55¢

Domestic Air Mail Rates

Effective Date	Prepaid
1911-1916 – The Pioneer Period	
Special official Post Office Flights at Fairs, aviation meets, etc., per 1 oz.	2¢
Postal cards and postcards	1¢
(Regulations prohibited an additional charge for air service on Post Office authorized flights.)	
1918, May 15 - July 13, 1918	
Service between Washington, DC, New York and Philadelphia (including 10¢ special delivery fee), per 1 oz.	24¢
1918, July 15-Dec. 14, 1918	
Service between Washington, DC, New York and Philadelphia (including 10¢ special delivery fee), per 1 oz.	16¢
Additional ounces	6¢
1918, Dec. 15-July 17, 1919	
Service between selected cities (other cities added later, special delivery no longer included), per 1 oz.	6¢
1919, July 18-June 29, 1924	
No specific airmail rate: mail carried by airplane on space available basis but airmail service not guaranteed, per 1 oz.	2¢
Postal cards and postcards, per 1 oz.	1¢
1924, June 30-Jan. 31, 1927	
Airmail service per zone (New York-Chicago; Chicago-Cheyenne, Wyo.; Cheyenne-San Francisco), per 1 oz. (each zone or portion thereof)	8¢
1925, July 1-Jan. 31, 1927	
Special overnight service New York-Chicago (with three intermediate stops), per 1 oz.	10¢
1926, Feb. 15-Jan. 31, 1927	
Contract routes not exceeding 1,000 miles (first flight Feb. 15) per 1 oz. (each route or portion thereof)	10¢
Contract routes between 1,000 and 1,500 miles (Seattle-Los Angeles, first flight Sept. 15) per 1 oz.	15¢
Mail traveling less than entire Seattle-Los Angeles route per 1 oz.	10¢
Contract routes exceeding 1,500 miles (none established during this rate period) per 1 oz.	20¢
Additional service on govt. route, per 1 oz. (each route or portion thereof)	5¢
1927, Feb. 1-July 31, 1928	
All contract routes or govt. zones, or combinations thereof, per ½ oz.	10¢

Effective Date	Prepaid
1928, Aug. 1-July 5, 1932	
All routes, 1st oz.	5¢
Each additional ounce or fraction thereof	10¢
1932, July 6-June 30, 1934	
All routes, 1st oz.	8¢
Each additional ounce or fraction thereof	13¢
1934, July 1-Mar. 25, 1944	
All routes, per oz.	6¢
1944, Mar. 26-Sept. 30, 1946	
All routes, per oz.	8¢
1946, Oct. 1-Dec. 31, 1948	
All routes, per oz.	5¢
1949, Jan. 1-July 31, 1958	
All routes, per oz.	6¢
Postal cards and postcards, per oz.	4¢
1958, Aug. 1-Jan. 6, 1963	
All routes, per oz.	7¢
Postal cards and postcards, per oz.	5¢
1963, Jan. 7-Jan. 6, 1968	
All routes, per oz.	8¢
Postal cards and postcards, per oz.	6¢
1968, Jan. 7-May 15, 1971	
All routes, per oz.	10¢
Postal cards and postcards, per oz.	8¢
1971, May 16-Mar. 1, 1974	
All routes, per oz.	11¢
Postal cards and postcards, per oz.	9¢
1974, Mar. 2-Oct. 10, 1975	
All routes, per oz.	13¢
Postal cards and postcards, per oz.	11¢

As of Oct. 11, 1975, separate domestic airmail service was abolished, although at least one more airmail rate was published; effective Dec. 28, 1975, 17¢ per 1st oz., 15¢ each additional oz., 14¢ for postal cards and postcards. It lasted until May 1, 1977.

Many thanks to the American Air Mail Society for sharing information on airmail rates. For further study, we highly recommend the society's book, ***Via Airmail, An Aerophilatelic Survey of Events, Routes, and Rates;*** Simine Short, editor; James R. Adams, author (available from the American Airmail Society, P.O. Box 110, Mineola, NY 11501. Price: $20, plus $2.50 postage to U.S. addresses; $3.50 to addresses outside the U.S.).

IDENTIFIER OF DEFINITIVE ISSUES

This section covers only listed postage stamps. See the Proofs section for imperforate items in the stamp colors mentioned which are not listed here and the Trial Color Proofs section for items in other colors.

ISSUES OF 1847-75

Benjamin Franklin
A1

Reproduction
A3

5¢ On the originals the left side of the white shirt frill touches the oval on a level with the top of the "F" of "Five." On the reproductions it touches the oval about on a level with the top of the figure "5."

George
Washington
A2

Reproduction
A4

Top image original, bottom image reproduction

10¢ On the originals line of coat (A) points to "T" of TEN and (B) it points between "T" and "S" of CENTS.

On the reproductions line of coat (A) points to right tip of "X" and line of coat (B) points to center of "S."

On the reproductions, the gap between the bottom legs of the left "X" is noticeably wider than the gap on the right "X." On the originals, the gaps are of equal width.

On the reproductions the eyes have a sleepy look, the line of the mouth is straighter, and in the curl of the hair near the left cheek is a strong black dot, while the originals have only a faint one.

Imperforate and Unwatermarked

Design Number		*Scott Number*
A1	5¢ red brown	**1**
A1	5¢ blue (reproduction)	**948a**
A3	5¢ red brown (reproduction, Special Printing)	**3**
A2	10¢ black	**2**
A2	10¢ brown orange (reproduction)	**948b**
A4	10¢ black (reproduction, Special Printing)	**4**

ISSUE OF 1851-75

Franklin — A5

A5

Type I Has a curved line outside the labels with "U.S. Postage" and "One Cent." The scrolls below the lower label are turned under, forming little balls. The scrolls and outer line at top are complete.

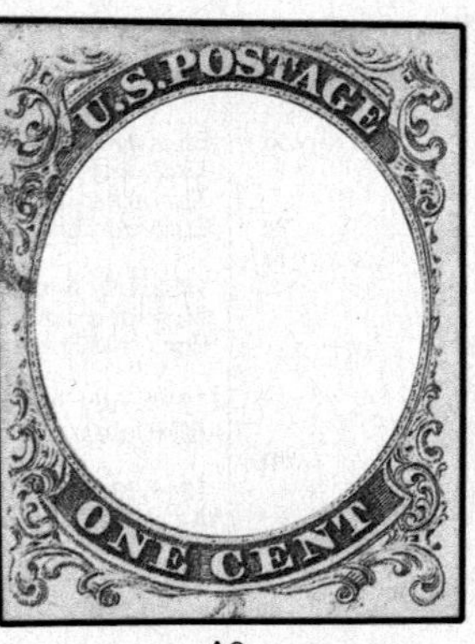

A6

Type Ia Same as I at bottom but top ornaments and outer line at top are partly cut away.

Type Ib Same as I but balls below the bottom label are not so clear. The plume-like scrolls at bottom are not complete.

Type Ic Same as type Ia, but bottom right plume and ball ornament is incomplete. The bottom left plume is complete or almost complete.

A7

Type II The little balls of the bottom scrolls and the bottoms of the lower plume ornaments are missing. The side ornaments are complete.

A8

Type III The top and bottom curved lines outside the labels are broken in the middle. The side ornaments are complete.

Type IIIa Similar to III with the outer line broken at top or bottom but not both. Type IIIa from Plate IV generally shows signs of plate erasure between the horizontal rows. Those from Plate IE show only a slight break in the line at top or bottom.

Type IV Similar to II, but with the curved lines outside the labels recut at top or bottom or both — A9

Type V Similar to type III of 1851-56 but with side ornaments partly cut away — A20

The seven types listed account for most of the varieties of recutting.

A5	1¢ blue, type I, imperf.	**5**
A5	1¢ blue, type Ib, imperf.	**5A**
A5	1¢ blue, type I, perf. 15½	**18**
A5	1¢ bright blue, perf. 12 (Special Printing)	**40**
A5	(47¢) tan & blue, serpentine die cut 10¾, self-adhesive	**5079b**
A6	1¢ blue, type Ia, imperf.	**6**
A6	1¢ blue, type Ic, imperf.	**6b**
A6	1¢ blue, type Ia, perf. 15½	**19**
A6	1¢ blue, type Ic, perf. 15½	**19b**
A7	1¢ blue, type II, imperf.	**7**
A7	1¢ blue, type II, perf. 15½	**20**
A8	1¢ blue, type III, imperf.	**8**
A8	1¢ blue, type IIIa, imperf.	**8A**
A8	1¢ blue, type III, perf. 15½	**21**
A8	1¢ blue, type IIIa, perf. 15½	**22**
A9	1¢ blue, type IV, imperf.	**9**
A9	1¢ blue, type IV, perf. 15½	**23**
A20	1¢ blue, type V, perf. 15½	**24**

A20 1¢ blue, type V, perf. 15½, laid paper........**24b**

Washington, Type I — A10

Type I

Type I. There is an outer frame line on all four sides. The outer frame lines at the sides are always recut, but the inner lines at the sides are not.

Type II

Type II. As type I, but with the inner lines at the sides also recut.

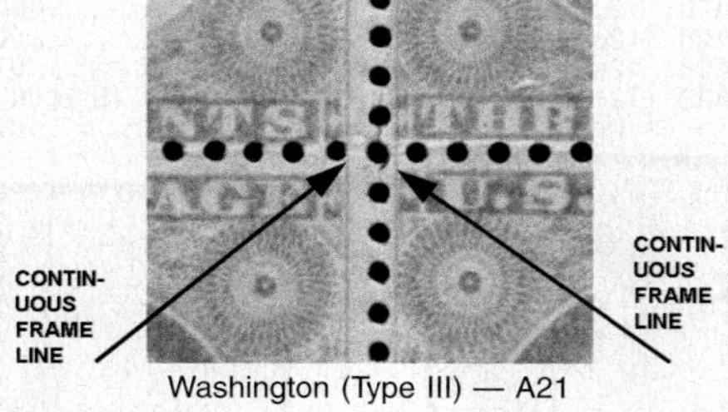

Washington (Type III) — A21

Type III. There are no outer frame lines at top and bottom. The side frame lines were recut so as to be continuous from the top to the bottom of the plate.

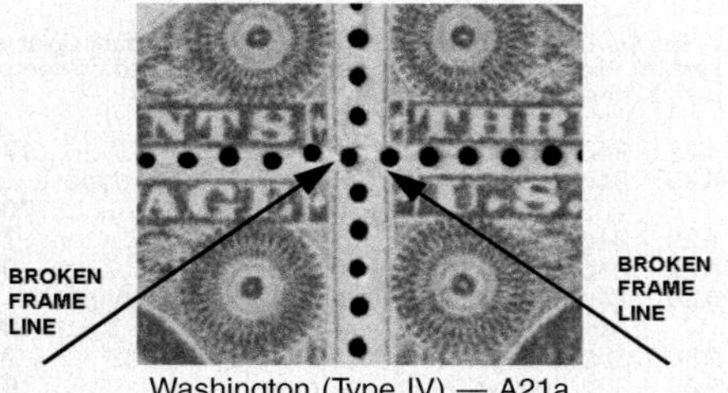

Washington (Type IV) — A21a

Type IV — As type III, but the side frame lines extend only to the top and bottom of the stamp design. All Type IV stamps are from plates 10 and 11 (each of which exists in three states), and these plates produced only Type IV. The side frame lines were recut individually for each stamp, thus being broken between the stamps vertically.

Beware of type III stamps with frame lines that stop at the top of the design (from top row of plate) or bottom of the design (from bottom row of plate). These are often mistakenly offered as No. 26A.

Jefferson, Type I There are projections on all four sides. — A11

Type II, The projections at top and bottom are partly cut away. Several minor types could be made according to the extent of cutting of the projections. — A22

Nos. 40-47 are reprints produced by the Continental Bank Note Co. The stamps are on white paper without gum, perf. 12. They were not good for postal use. They also exist imperforate.

A10 3¢ orange brown, type I, imperf....................**10**
A10 3¢ orange brown, type II, imperf................ **10A**
A10 3¢ dull red, type I, imperf.............................**11**
A10 3¢ dull red, type II, imperf......................... **11A**
A10 3¢ rose, type I, perf. 15½..............................**25**
A10 3¢ rose, type II, perf. 15½......................... **25A**
A10 3¢ scarlet, perf. 12 (Special Printing)..........**41**
A21 3¢ dull red, type III, perf. 15½.....................**26**
A21a 3¢ dull red, type IV, perf. 15½.................**26A**
A11 5¢ red brown, type I, imperf..........................**12**
A11 5¢ brick red, type I, perf. 15½ **27**
A11 5¢ red brown, type I, perf. 15½ **28**
A11 5¢ Indian red, type I, perf. 15½ **28A**
A11 5¢ brown, type I, perf. 15½............................**29**
A22 5¢ orange brown, type II, perf. 15½ **30**
A22 5¢ brown, type II, perf. 15½....................... **30A**
A22 5¢ orange brown, type II, perf. 12 (Special Printing)..**42**

Washington,Type I — A12

Washington — A16

A12 Type I The shells at the lower corners are practically complete. The outer line below the label is very nearly complete. The outer lines are broken above the middle of the top label and the "X" in each upper corner.

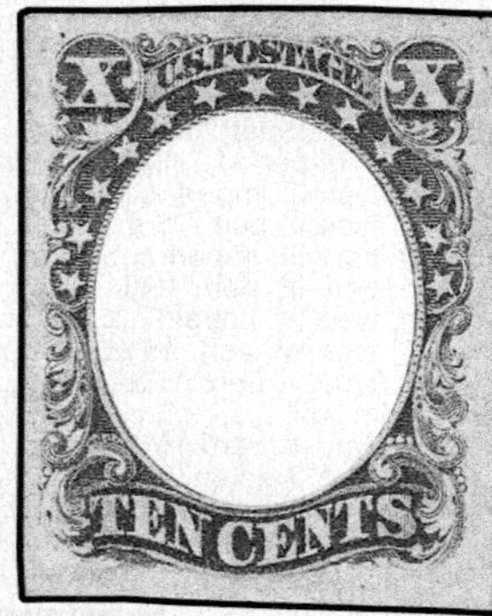

A13 Type II The design is complete at the top. The outer line at the bottom is broken in the middle. The shells are partly cut away.

A14 Type III The outer lines are broken above the top label and the "X" numerals. The outer line at the bottom and the shells are partly cut away as in Type II.

A15 Type IV The outer lines have been recut at top or bottom or both.

Example I Example II

A23 Type V The side ornaments are slightly cut away. Usually only one pearl remains at each end of the lower label but some stamps show two or three pearls at the right side. At the bottom, the outer line is complete and the shells nearly so. The outer lines at top are complete except over the right "X."

A12 10¢ green, type I, imperf. **13**
A12 10¢ green, type I, perf. 15½ **31**
A12 10¢ blue green, perf. 12 (Special Printing) **43**
A13 10¢ green, type II, imperf. **14**
A13 10¢ green, type II, perf. 15½ **32**
A14 10¢ green, type III, imperf. **15**
A14 10¢ green, type III, perf. 15½ **33**
A15 10¢ green, type IV, imperf. **16**
A15 10¢ green, type IV, perf. 15½ **34**
A23 10¢ green, type V, perf. 15½ **35**
A16 12¢ black, imperf. **17**
A16 12¢ black, plate 1, perf. 15½ **36**
A16 12¢ black, plate 3 .... **36B**
A16 12¢ greenish black, perf. 12 .... **44**
A16 (47¢) tan & black, serpentine die cut 10¾, self-adhesive **5079a**

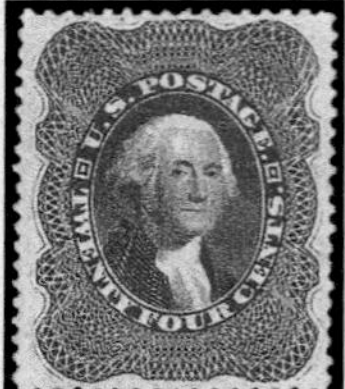

Washington — A17

Franklin — A18

Washington — A19

A17 24¢ gray lilac, perf. 15½ **37**
A17 24¢ blackish violet, perf. 12 (Special Printing) **45**
A17 (47¢) tan & black, serpentine die cut 10¾, self-adhesive **5079c**
A18 30¢ orange, perf. 15½ **38**
A18 30¢ yellow orange, perf. 12 (Special Printing) **46**
A19 90¢ blue, perf. 15½ **39**
A19 90¢ deep blue, perf. 12 (Special Printing) **47**
A19 (47¢) tan & blue, serpentine die cut 10¾, self-adhesive **5079d**

ISSUES OF 1861-75

Franklin — A24

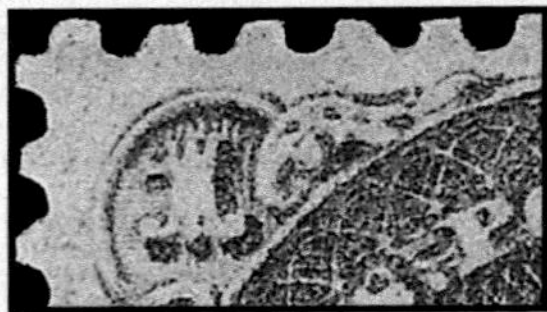

A24 See the essay section for type A24 in indigo on perf. 12 thin, semi-transparent paper without the dash under the tip of the ornament at the right of the numeral in the upper left corner.

A24 1¢ blue, perf. 12 .... **63**
A24 1¢ blue, same, laid paper **63c**
A24 1¢ blue, "Z" grill **85A**
A24 1¢ blue, "E" grill **86**
A24 1¢ blue, "F" grill **92**
A24 1¢ blue, no grill, hard white paper (Special Printing) **102**
A24 (47¢) tan & blue, serpentine die cut 10¾, self-adhesive **5079f**

Washington — A25

A25 See the essay section for type A25 in brown rose on perf. 12 thin, semi-transparent paper with smaller ornaments in the corners which do not end in a small ball.

A25 3¢ pink, no grill, perf. 12 .... **64**
A25 3¢ lake, same (Special Printing) **66**
A25 3¢ scarlet, same (Special Printing) **74**
A25 3¢ rose, same **65**
A25 3¢ rose, same, laid paper **65b**
A25 3¢ rose, grilled all over **79**
A25 3¢ rose, "B" grill **82**
A25 3¢ rose, "C" grill **83**
A25 3¢ rose, "D" grill **85**
A25 3¢ rose, "Z" grill **85C**
A25 3¢ rose, "E" grill **88**
A25 3¢ red, "F" grill **94**
A25 3¢ brown red, no grill, hard white paper (Special Printing) **104**

Jefferson — A26

A26 See the essay section for type A26 in brown on perf. 12 thin, semi-transparent paper without the leaflet in the foliated ornament at each corner.

A26 5¢ buff, no grill **67**
A26 5¢ red brown, no grill **75**
A26 5¢ brown, no grill **76**
A26 5¢ brown, laid paper **76b**
A26 5¢ brown, grilled all over **80**
A26 5¢ brown, "F" grill **95**
A26 5¢ brown, no grill, hard white paper **105**

A27a

Washington — A27

A27 A heavy curved line has been cut below the stars and an outer line added to the ornaments above them.

A27a 10¢ dark green, thin paper, no grill **62B**
A27 10¢ green, no grill **68**
A27 10¢ green, "Z" grill **85D**
A27 10¢ green, "E" grill **89**
A27 10¢ yellow green, "F" grill **96**
A27 10¢ green, no grill, hard white paper (Special Printing) **106**

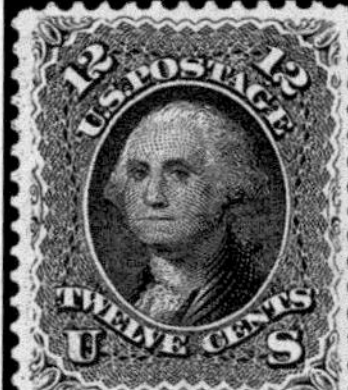

Washington — A28

A28 See the essay section for type A28 in black on perf. 12 thin, semi-transparent paper without corner ornaments.

A28 12¢ black, no grill **69**
A28 12¢ black, "Z" grill **85E**
A28 12¢ black, "E" grill **90**
A28 12¢ black, "F" grill **97**
A28 12¢ black, no grill, hard white paper, (Special Printing) **107**

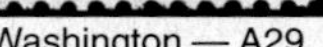

Washington — A29

Franklin — A30

See the Trial Color proof section for type A29 in dark violet on perf. 12 thin paper without grill and type A30 in red orange on perf. 12 thin paper without grill.

A29 24¢ red lilac, no grill **70**
A29 24¢ violet, no grill, thin, transparent paper **70c**
A29 24¢ lilac, no grill **78**
A29 24¢ gray lilac, "F" grill **99**
A29 24¢ deep violet, no grill, hard white paper, (Special Printing) **109**
A30 30¢ orange, no grill **71**
A30 30¢ orange, grilled all over **81**

A30 30¢ orange, "F" grill **100**
A30 30¢ brownish orange, no grill, hard white paper, (Special Printing) **110**

Washington — A31

A31 See the essay section for type A31 in dull blue on perf. 12 thin semi-transparent paper without dashes between the parallel lines which form the angle above the ribbon with "U.S. Postage," and without the point of color at the apex of the lower line.

A31 90¢ blue, no grill **72**
A31 90¢ blue, "F" grill **101**
A31 90¢ blue, no grill, hard white paper, (Special Printing) **111**

ISSUES OF 1861-75

Jackson — A32

Lincoln — A33

Perf. 12, Unwmkd.

A32 2¢ black, no grill **73**
A32 2¢ black, laid paper **73g**
A32 2¢ black, "D" grill **84**
A32 2¢ black, "Z" grill **85B**
A32 2¢ black, "E" grill **87**
A32 2¢ black, "F" grill **93**
A32 2¢ black, no grill, hard white paper, (Special Printing) **103**
A33 15¢ black, no grill **77**
A33 15¢ black, "Z" grill **85F**
A33 15¢ black, "E" grill **91**
A33 15¢ black, "F" grill **98**
A33 15¢ black, no grill, hard white paper, (Special Printing) **108**
A33 (47¢) tan & black, serpentine die cut 10¾, self-adhesive **5079e**

ISSUES OF 1869-80

Franklin — A34

A34 1¢ buff, "G" grill **112**
A34 1¢ buff, no grill **112b**
A34 1¢ buff, no grill, hard white paper (Special Printing) **123**
A34 1¢ buff, no grill, soft porous paper (Special Printing) **133**
A34 1¢ brown orange, same without gum (Special Printing) **133a**

Pony Express — A35

Baldwin 4-4-0 Locomotive, c. 1857 — A36

A35 2¢ brown, "G" grill **113**
A35 2¢ brown, no grill **113b**
A35 2¢ brown, no grill, hard white paper (Special Printing) **124**
A36 3¢ ultramarine, "G" grill **114**
A36 3¢ ultramarine, no grill **114a**
A36 3¢ blue, no grill, hard white paper (Special Printing) **125**

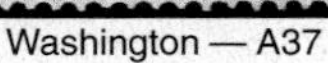
Washington — A37

Shield and Eagle — A38

S.S. Adriatic — A39

A37 6¢ ultramarine, "G" grill **115**
A37 6¢ blue, no grill, hard white paper (Special Printing) **126**
A38 10¢ yellow, "G" grill **116**
A38 10¢ yellow, no grill, hard white paper (Special Printing) **127**
A39 12¢ green, "G" grill **117**
A39 12¢ green, no grill, hard white paper (Special Printing) **128**

Landing of Columbus — A40

A40 Type I Picture unframed

A40a Type II Picture framed

Type III same as Type I but without the fringe of brown shading lines around central vignette.

A40 15¢ brown & blue, type I, "G" grill **118**
A40 15¢ brown & blue, type I, no grill **118a**
A40 15¢ brown & blue, type III, no grill, hard white paper (Special Printing) **129**
A40a 15¢ brown & blue, type II, "G" grill **119**

The Declaration of Independence — A41

Shield, Eagle and Flags — A42

Lincoln — A43

A41 24¢ green & violet, "G" grill **120**
A41 24¢ green & violet, no grill **120a**
A41 24¢ green & violet, no grill, hard white paper (Special Printing) **130**
A42 30¢ ultramarine & carmine, "G" grill **121**
A42 30¢ ultramarine & carmine, no grill **121a**
A42 30¢ ultramarine & carmine, no grill, hard white paper (Special Printing) **131**
A43 90¢ carmine & black, "G" grill **122**
A43 90¢ carmine & black, no grill **122a**
A43 90¢ carmine & black, no grill, hard white paper (Special Printing) **132**
A43 90¢ carmine & black, 28x28mm, imperf., litho. & engraved **2433a**
A43 90¢ blue & brown, 28x28mm, imperf., litho. & engraved **2433b**
A43 90¢ green & blue, 28x28mm, imperf., litho. & engraved **2433c**
A43 90¢ scarlet & blue, 28x28mm, imperf., litho. & engraved **2433d**

ISSUES OF 1870-88

The secret mark shown in the detail of A45a is seldom found on the actual stamps. Stamps Nos. 146 and 157 are best identified by color which is red brown for No. 146 and brown for No. 157.

Note I: Special printings of 1880-83 — All denominations of this series were printed on special order from the Post Office Department during the period the stamps were current. The paper being the same as used on current issue, the special printings are extremely difficult to identify. The 2¢ brown, 7¢ scarlet vermilion, 12¢ blackish purple and 24¢ dark violet are easily distinguished by the soft porous paper as these denominations were never previously printed on soft paper. The other denominations can be distinguished by shades only, those of the special printings being slightly deeper and richer than the regular issue. The special printings except No. 211B were issued without gum. The only certain way to identify them is by comparison with stamps previously established as special printings.

Franklin — A44

A44

A44a With secret mark. In the pearl at the left of the numeral "1" there is a small dash.

A44b Re-engraved. The vertical lines in the upper part of the stamp have been so deepened that the background often appears to be solid. Lines of shading have been added to the upper arabesques.

A44 1¢ ultramarine, "H" grill **134**
A44 1¢ ultramarine, no grill **145**
A44a 1¢ ultramarine, white wove paper no grill **156**
A44a 1¢ ultramarine, with grill **156e**
A44a 1¢ ultramarine, hard white paper, without gum (Special Printing) **167**
A44a 1¢ dark ultra, soft porous paper **182**
A44a 1¢ dark ultra, soft porous paper, without gum (Special Printing, see note I) **192**
A44b 1¢ gray blue **206**

Jackson — A45

A45

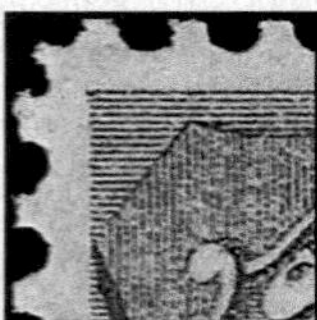
A45a Under the scroll at the left of "U.S." there is a small diagonal line.

A45 2¢ red brown, "H" grill **135**
A45 2¢ red brown, "I" grill **135A**
A45 2¢ red brown, no grill **146**
A45a 2¢ brown, white wove paper no grill **157**
A45a 2¢ brown, with grill **157c**
A45a 2¢ dark brown, hard white paper, without gum (Special Printing) **168**
A45a 2¢ black brown, soft porous paper, without gum (Special Printing) **193**
A45a 2¢ vermilion, yellowish paper **178**
A45a 2¢ vermilion, same, with grill **178c**
A45a 2¢ vermilion, soft porous paper **183**
A45a 2¢ carmine vermilion, hard white paper, without gum (Special Printing) **180**
A45a 2¢ scarlet vermilion, soft porous paper, without gum (Special Printing, see note I) **203**

Washington — A46

A46

A46a With secret mark. The under part of the tail of the left ribbon is heavily shaded.

A46b Re-engraved. The shading at the sides of the central oval appears only about one half the previous width. A short horizontal dash has been cut about 1mm. below the "TS" of "CENTS."

A46 3¢ green, "H" grill **136**
A46 3¢ green, "I" grill **136A**
A46 3¢ green, no grill **147**
A46a 3¢ green, white wove paper, no grill **158**
A46a 3¢ green, same, with grill **158e**
A46a 3¢ blue green, hard white paper, without gum (Special Printing) **169**
A46a 3¢ green, soft porous paper **184**
A46a 3¢ blue green, soft porous paper, without gum (Special Printing see note I) **194**
A46b 3¢ blue green, re-engraved **207**
A46b 3¢ vermilion re-engraved **214**

Lincoln — A47

A47

A47a With secret mark. The first four vertical lines of the shading in the lower part of the left ribbon have been strengthened.

A47b Re-engraved. On the original stamps four vertical lines can be counted from the edge of the panel to the outside of the stamp. On the re-engraved stamps there are three lines in the same place.

A47 6¢ carmine, "H" grill **137**
A47 6¢ carmine, "I" grill **137A**
A47 6¢ carmine, no grill **148**
A47a 6¢ dull pink, no grill, white wove paper **159**
A47a 6¢ dull pink, with grill **159b**
A47a 6¢ dull rose, hard white paper, without gum (Special Printing) **170**
A47a 6¢ pink, soft porous paper **186**
A47a 6¢ dull rose, soft porous paper, without gum (Special Printing see note I) **195**
A47b 6¢ rose, re-engraved **208**

Edwin McMasters Stanton — A48

Thomas Jefferson — A49

A48

A48a With secret mark. Two small semi-circles are drawn around the ends of the lines which outline the ball in the lower right hand corner.

A49

A49a With secret mark. A small semi-circle in the scroll at the right end of the upper label.

A49b Re-engraved. On the original stamps there are five vertical lines between the left side of the oval and the edge of the shield. There are only four lines on the re-engraved stamps. In the lower part of the re-engraved stamps the horizontal lines of the background have been strengthened.

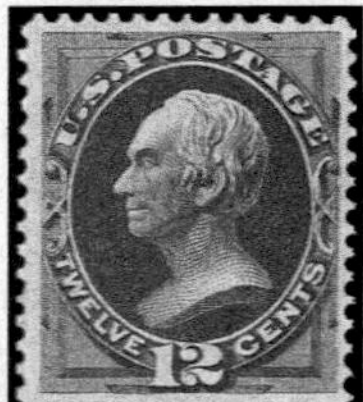
Henry Clay — A50

A50

A50a With secret mark. The balls of the figure "2" are crescent shaped.

A48 7¢ vermilion, "H" grill **138**
A48 7¢ vermilion, "I" grill **138A**
A48 7¢ vermilion, no grill **149**
A48a 7¢ orange verm., white wove paper no grill **160**
A48a 7¢ orange verm., same, with grill **160a**
A48a 7¢ reddish verm., hard white paper, without gum (Special Printing) **171**
A48a 7¢ scarlet verm., soft porous paper, without gum (Special Printing) **196**
A49 10¢ brown, "H" grill **139**
A49 10¢ brown, "I" grill **139A**
A49 10¢ brown, no grill **150**
A49 10¢ brown, soft porous paper **187**
A49a 10¢ brown, white wove paper no grill **161**
A49a 10¢ brown, with grill **161c**
A49a 10¢ pale brown, hard white paper, without gum (Special Printing) **172**
A49a 10¢ brown, soft porous paper **188**
A49a 10¢ deep brown, soft porous paper, without gum (Special Printing, see note I) **197**
A49b 10¢ brown, re-engraved **209**
A50 12¢ dull violet, "H" grill **140**
A50 12¢ dull violet, "I" grill **140A**
A50 12¢ dull violet, no grill **151**
A50a 12¢ blackish violet, white wove paper, no grill **162**
A50a 12¢ blackish violet, with grill **162a**
A50a 12¢ dark violet, hard white paper, without gum (Special Printing) **173**

A50a 12¢ blackish purple, soft porous paper, without gum (Special Printing) **198**

Webster — A51

A51

A51a With secret mark. In the lower part of the triangle in the upper left corner two lines have been made heavier forming a "V." This mark can be found on some of the Continental and American (1879) printings, but not all stamps show it.

A51 15¢ orange, "H" grill **141**
A51 15¢ orange, "I" grill **141A**
A51 15¢ bright orange, no grill **152**
A51a 15¢ yellow orange, white wove paper, no grill **163**
A51a 15¢ yellow orange, with grill **163a**
A51a 15¢ bright orange, hard white paper, without gum (Special Printing) **174**
A51a 15¢ red orange, soft porous paper **189**
A51a 15¢ orange, soft porous paper, without gum (Special Printing, see note I) **199**

General Winfield Scott — A52

Hamilton — A53

Perry — A54

Secret marks were added to the dies of the 24¢, 30¢ and 90¢ but new plates were not made from them. The various printings of these stamps can be distinguished only by the shades and paper.

A52 24¢ purple, with grill **142**
A52 24¢ purple, no grill **153**
A52 24¢ purple, vertically ribbed white wove paper, no grill **164**
A52 24¢ dull purple, hard white paper, without gum (Special Printing) **175**
A52 24¢ dark violet, soft porous paper, without gum (Special Printing) **200**
A53 30¢ black, "H" grill **143**
A53 30¢ black, "I" grill **143A**
A53 30¢ black, no grill **154**
A53 30¢ full black, soft porous paper **190**
A53 30¢ gray black, white wove paper, no grill **165**
A53 30¢ greenish black, with grill **165c**
A53 30¢ greenish black, hard white paper, without gum (Special Printing) **176**
A53 30¢ greenish black, soft porous paper, without gum (Special Printing, see note I) **201**
A53 30¢ orange brown **217**
A54 90¢ carmine, "H" grill **144**
A54 90¢ carmine, "I" grill **144A**
A54 90¢ carmine, no grill **155**
A54 90¢ carmine, soft porous paper **191**
A54 90¢ rose carmine, white wove paper **166**
A54 90¢ violet carmine, hard white paper, without gum (Special Printing) **177**
A54 90¢ dull carmine, soft porous paper, without gum (Special Printing, see note I) **202**
A54 90¢ purple **218**

ISSUES OF 1875-88

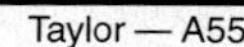

Taylor — A55

Garfield — A56

Perf. 12, Unwmkd.

A55 5¢ blue, yellowish wove paper, no grill **179**
A55 5¢ blue, with grill **179c**
A55 5¢ bright blue, hard, white wove paper, without gum (Special Printing) **181**
A55 5¢ blue, soft porous paper **185**
A55 5¢ deep blue, soft porous paper, without gum (Special Printing, see note I) **204**
A56 5¢ yellow brown **205**
A56 5¢ gray brown, soft porous paper, without gum (Special Printing, see note I) **205C**
A56 5¢ indigo **216**

Washington — A57

Jackson — A58

A57 2¢ red brown **210**
A57 2¢ pale red brown, soft porous paper (Special Printing, see note I) **211B**
A57 2¢ green **213**
A58 4¢ blue green **211**
A58 4¢ deep blue green, soft porous paper, without gum (Special Printing, see note I) **211D**
A58 4¢ carmine **215**

Franklin — A59

A59 1¢ ultramarine **212**

ISSUES OF 1890-93

Franklin — A60

Washington — A61

Jackson — A62

Lincoln — A63

Grant — A64

Garfield — A65

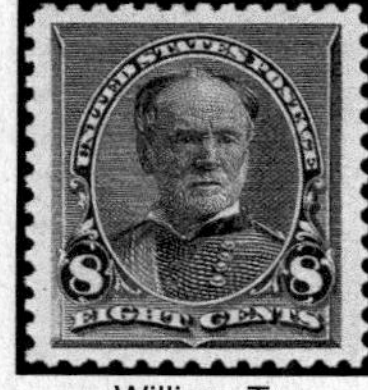

William T. Sherman — A66

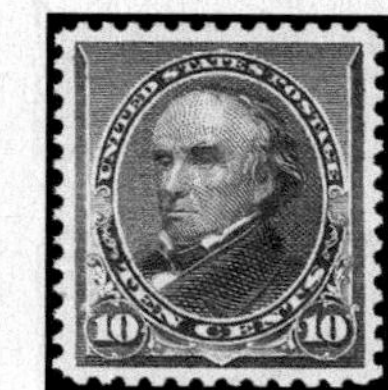

Daniel Webster — A67

Henry Clay — A68

Jefferson — A69

Perry — A70

A60 1¢ dull blue **219**
A61 2¢ lake **219D**
A61 2¢ carmine **220**
A62 3¢ purple **221**
A63 4¢ dark brown **222**
A64 5¢ chocolate **223**
A65 6¢ brown red **224**
A66 8¢ lilac **225**
A67 10¢ green **226**
A68 15¢ indigo **227**
A69 30¢ black **228**
A70 90¢ orange **229**

ISSUES OF 1894-1903

This series, the first to be printed by the Bureau of Engraving and Printing, closely resembles the 1890 series but is identified by the triangles which have been added to the upper corners of the designs.

The Catalogue divides this group into three separate series, the first of which was issued in 1894 and is unwatermarked. In 1895 the paper used was watermarked with the double line letters USPS (United States Postage Stamp). The stamps show one complete letter of the watermark or parts of two or more letters.

This watermark appears on all United States stamps issued from 1895 until 1910.

In 1898 the colors of some of the denominations were changed, which created the third series noted in the Catalogue.

Other than the watermark, or lack of it, there are three styles of the corner triangles used on the 2 cent stamps and two variations of designs are noted on the 10 cent and $1 denomination. In the following list all of these variations are illustrated and described immediately preceding the denominations on which they appear.

USPS

Wmkd. (191) Horizontally

USPS

or Vertically

(Actual size of letter)

Franklin — A87

Washington — A88

Jackson — A89

Lincoln — A90

Grant — A91

Garfield — A92

Sherman — A93

Webster — A94

Clay — A95

Jefferson — A96

Perry — A97

James Madison — A98

John Marshall — A99

A87	1¢ ultramarine, unwmkd.	**246**
A87	1¢ blue, unwmkd.	**247**
A87	1¢ blue, wmkd.	**264**
A87	1¢ deep green, wmkd.	**279**
A87	1¢ on 1¢ yellow green, "CUBA"	**Cuba 221**
A87	1¢ deep green, "GUAM"	**Guam 1**
A87	1¢ yellow green, "PHILIPPINES"	**Phil. 213**
A87	1¢ yellow green, "PORTO RICO"	**P.R. 210**
A87	1¢ yellow green, "PUERTO RICO"	**P.R. 215**

Triangle A (Type I) The horizontal lines of the ground work run across the triangle and are of the same thickness within it as without.

Triangle B (Type II) The horiztonal lines cross the triangle but are thinner within it than without. Other minor differences exist, but the change to Triangle B is a sufficient determinant.

Triangle C (Types III & IV) Type III: The horizontal lines do not cross the double lines of the triangle. The lines within the triangle are thin, as in Triangle B.

The rest of the design is the same as Type II, except that most of the designs had the dot in the "S" of "CENTS" removed. Stamps with this dot are listed; some specialists refer to them as "Type IIIa" varieties.

Type IV: Same triangle C as type III, but other design differences including (1) recutting and lengthening of hairline, (2) shaded toga button, (3) strengthening of lines on sleeve, (4) additional dots on ear, (5) "T" of "TWO" straight at right, (6) background lines extend into white oval opposite "U" of "UNITED." Many other differences exist.

A88	2¢ pink, type I, unwmkd.	**248**
A88	2¢ carmine lake, type I, unwmkd.	**249**
A88	2¢ carmine, type I, unwmkd.	**250**
A88	2¢ carmine, type I, wmkd.	**265**
A88	2¢ carmine, type II, unwmkd.	**251**
A88	2¢ carmine, type II, wmkd.	**266**
A88	2¢ carmine, type III, unwmkd.	**252**
A88	2¢ carmine, type III, wmkd.	**267**
A88	2¢ red, type IV, wmkd.	**279B**
A88	2¢ booklet pane of 6, wmkd., single stamps with 1 or 2 straight edges	**279Bj**
A88	2c on 2¢ reddish carmine, type III "CUBA"	**Cuba 222**
A88	2c on 2¢ reddish carmine, type IV, "CUBA"	**Cuba 222A**
A88	2½c on 2¢ reddish carmine, type III, "CUBA"	**Cuba 223**
A88	2½c on 2¢ reddish carmine, type IV, "CUBA"	**Cuba 223A**
A88	2¢ red, type IV, "GUAM"	**Guam 2**
A88	2¢ red, type IV, "PHILIPPINES"	**Phil. 214**
A88	Same, booklet pane of 6	**Phil. 214b**
A88	2¢ reddish carmine, type IV, "PORTO RICO"	**P.R. 211**
A88	Same, "PUERTO RICO"	**P.R. 216**
A89	3¢ purple, unwmkd.	**253**
A89	3¢ purple, wmkd.	**268**
A89	3¢ on 3¢ purple, "CUBA"	**Cuba 224**
A89	3¢ purple, "GUAM"	**Guam 3**
A89	3¢ purple "PHILIPPINES"	**Phil. 215**
A90	4¢ dark brown, unwmkd.	**254**
A90	4¢ dark brown, wmkd.	**269**
A90	4¢ rose brown, wmkd.	**280**
A90	4¢ lilac brown, "GUAM"	**Guam 4**
A90	4¢ orange brown, "PHILIPPINES"	**Phil. 220**
A91	5¢ chocolate, unwmkd.	**255**
A91	5¢ chocolate, wmkd.	**270**
A91	5¢ dark blue, wmkd.	**281**
A91	5¢ on 5¢ blue, "CUBA"	**Cuba 225**
A91	5¢ blue, "GUAM"	**Guam 5**
A91	5¢ blue, "PHILIPPINES"	**Phil. 216**
A91	5¢ blue, "PORTO RICO"	**P.R. 212**
A92	6¢ dull brown, unwmkd.	**256**
A92	6¢ dull brown, wmkd. USPS	**271**
A92	6¢ dull brown, wmkd. USIR	**271a**
A92	6¢ lake, wmkd.	**282**
A92	6¢ lake, "GUAM"	**Guam 6**
A92	6¢ lake, "PHILIPPINES"	**Phil. 221**
A93	8¢ violet brown, unwmkd.	**257**
A93	8¢ violet brown, wmkd. USPS	**272**
A93	8¢ violet brown, wmkd. USIR	**272a**
A93	8¢ violet brown, "GUAM"	**Guam 7**
A93	8¢ violet brown, "PHILIPPINES"	**Phil. 222**
A93	8¢ violet brown, "PORTO RICO"	**P.R. 213**

Type I The tips of the foliate ornaments do not impinge on the white curved line below "ten cents."

Type II The tips of the ornaments break the curved line below the "e" of "ten" and the "t" of "cents."

A94	10¢ dark green, unwmkd.	**258**
A94	10¢ dark green, wmkd.	**273**
A94	10¢ brown, type I, wmkd.	**282C**
A94	10¢ orange brown, type II, wmkd.	**283**
A94	10¢ on 10¢ brown, type I, "CUBA"	**Cuba 226**
A94	Same, type II, "CUBA"	**Cuba 226A**
A94	10¢ brown, type I, "GUAM"	**Guam 8**
A94	10¢ brown, type II, "GUAM"	**Guam 9**
A94	10¢ brown, type I, "PHILIPPINES"	**Phil. 217**
A94	10¢ orange brown, type II, "PHILIPPINES"	**Phil. 217A**
A94	10¢ brown, type I, "PORTO RICO"	**P.R. 214**
A95	15¢ dark blue, unwmkd.	**259**
A95	15¢ dark blue, wmkd.	**274**
A95	15¢ olive green, wmkd.	**284**
A95	15¢ olive green, "GUAM"	**Guam 10**
A95	15¢ olive green, "PHILIPPINES"	**Phil. 218**
A96	50¢ orange, unwmkd.	**260**
A96	50¢ orange, wmkd.	**275**
A96	50¢ orange, "GUAM"	**Guam 11**
A96	50¢ orange, unwmkd., "PHILIPPINES"	**Phil. 212**
A96	50¢ orange, wmkd., "PHILIPPINES"	**Phil. 219**

A97 Type I The circles enclosing "$1" are broken where they meet the curved line below "One Dollar."

A97 Type II The circles are complete.

A97	$1 black, type I, unwmkd.	**261**
A97	$1 black, type I, wmkd.	**276**
A97	$1 black, type II, unwmkd.	**261A**
A97	$1 black, type II, wmkd.	**276A**
A97	$1 black, type I, "GUAM"	**Guam 12**
A97	$1 black, type II, "GUAM"	**Guam 13**
A97	$1 black, type I, "PHILIPPINES"	**Phil. 223**
A97	$1 black, type II, "PHILIPPINES"	**Phil. 223A**
A98	$2 bright blue, unwmkd.	**262**
A98	$2 blue, perf. 11, tagged	**2875a**
A98	$2 bright blue, wmkd.	**277**
A98	$2 dark blue, "PHILIPPINES"	**Phil. 224**
A99	$5 dark green, unwmkd.	**263**
A99	$5 dark green, wmkd.	**278**
A99	$5 dark green, "PHILIPPINES"	**Phil. 225**

ISSUES OF 1902-17

Franklin — A115

Washington — A116

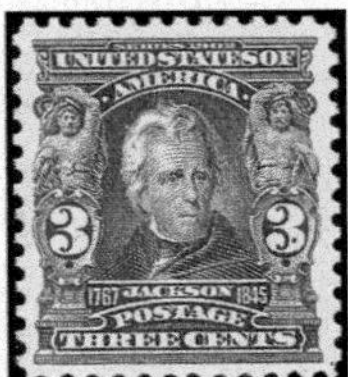

Jackson — A117

Grant — A118

Lincoln — A119

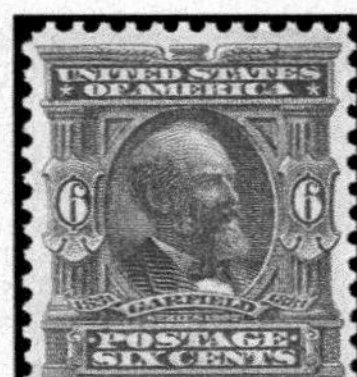

Garfield — A120

Martha Washington — A121

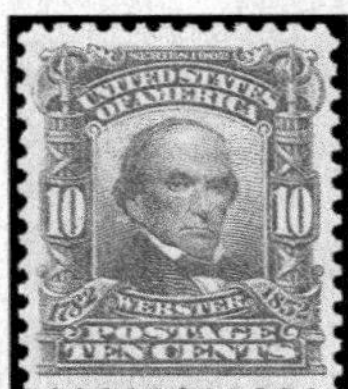

Daniel Webster — A122

Benjamin Harrison — A123

Henry Clay — A124

Jefferson — A125

David G. Farragut — A126

Madison — A127

Marshall — A128

Unless otherwise noted all stamps are Perf. 12 and Wmkd. (191)

Single stamps from booklet panes show 1 or 2 straight edges.

A115	1¢ blue green	**300**
A115	1¢ booklet pane of 6	**300b**
A115	1¢ blue green, imperf.	**314**
A115	1¢ blue green, perf. 12 horiz., pair	**316**
A115	1¢ blue green, perf. 12 vert., pair	**318**
A115	1¢ blue green, "CANAL ZONE PANAMA"	**C.Z. 4**
A115	1¢ blue green, "PHILIPPINES"	**Phil. 226**
A116	2¢ carmine	**301**
A116	2¢ booklet pane of 6	**301c**
A116	2¢ carmine, "PHILIPPINES"	**Phil. 227**
A117	3¢ bright violet	**302**
A117	3¢ bright violet, "PHILIPPINES"	**Phil. 228**
A118	4¢ brown	**303**
A118	4¢ brown, imperf.	**314A**
A118	4¢ brown, "PHILIPPINES"	**Phil. 229**
A119	5¢ blue	**304**
A119	5¢ blue, imperf.	**315**
A119	5¢ blue, perf. 12 horiz. pair	**317**
A119	5¢ blue, "CANAL ZONE PANAMA"	**C.Z. 6**
A119	5¢ blue, "PHILIPPINES"	**Phil. 230**
A120	6¢ claret	**305**
A120	6¢ brownish lake, "PHILIPPINES"	**Phil. 231**
A121	8¢ violet black	**306**
A121	8¢ violet black, "CANAL ZONE PANAMA"	**C.Z. 7**
A121	8¢ violet black, "PHILIPPINES"	**Phil. 232**
A122	10¢ pale red brown	**307**
A122	10¢ pale red brown, "CANAL ZONE PANAMA"	**C.Z. 8**
A122	10¢ pale red brown, "PHILIPPINES"	**Phil. 233**
A123	13¢ purple black	**308**
A123	13¢ purple black, "PHILIPPINES"	**Phil. 234**
A124	15¢ olive green	**309**
A124	15¢ olive green, "PHILIPPINES"	**Phil. 235**
A125	50¢ orange	**310**
A125	50¢ orange, "PHILIPPINES"	**Phil. 236**
A126	$1 black	**311**
A126	$1 black, "PHILIPPINES"	**Phil. 237**
A127	$2 dark blue	**312**
A127	$2 dark blue, unwmkd., perf. 10	**479**
A127	$2 dark blue, "PHILIPPINES"	**Phil. 238**
A128	$5 dark green	**313**
A128	$5 light green, unwmkd., perf. 10	**480**
A128	$5 dark green, "PHILIPPINES"	**Phil. 239**

ISSUES OF 1903

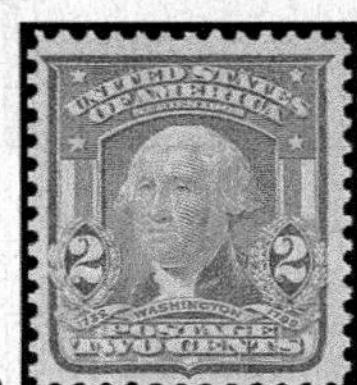

Washington — A129

Type I

Type II

The two large arrows in the illustrations highlight the two major differences of the type II stamps: closing of the thin left border line next to the laurel leaf, and strengthening of the inner frame line at the lower left corner. The small arrows point out three minor differences that are not always easily discernible: strengthening of shading lines under the ribbon just above the "T" of "TWO," a shorter shading line to the left of the "P" in "POSTAGE," and shortening of a shading line in the left side ribbon.

Specialists recognize over a hundred shades of this stamp in various hues of vermilion, red, carmine and lake. The Scott Catalogue lists only the most striking differences.

The Government coil stamp, No. 322 should not be confused with the scarlet vermilion coil of the International Vending Machine Co., which is perforated 12½ to 13.

A129	2¢ carmine, type I, wmkd.	**319**
A129	2¢ lake, type II	**319f**
A129	2¢ carmine, type I, booklet pane of 6	**319g**
A129	Same, type II	**319h**
A129	2¢ carmine, type I, imperf.	**320**
A129	2¢ lake, type II, imperf.	**320a**
A129	2¢ carmine, perf. 12 horiz. pair	**321**

A129 2¢ carmine, perf. 12 vert. pair **322**
A129 2¢ carmine, "CANAL ZONE PANAMA"... **C.Z. 5**
A129 2¢ carmine, "PHILIPPINES"............... **Phil. 240**
A129 2¢ carmine, same, booklet pane of 6.............. .... **Phil. 240a**

ISSUES OF 1908-09

This series introduces for the first time the single line watermark USPS. Only a small portion of several letters is often all that can be seen on a single stamp.

Franklin — A138

Washington — A139

Wmk. 190

A138 1¢ green, perf. 12, double line wmk. **331**
A138 1¢ green, perf. 12, single line wmk. **374**
A138 1¢ green, perf. 12, bluish paper.................. **357**
A138 1¢ green, imperf., double line wmk............. **343**
A138 1¢ green, imperf., single line wmk............. **383**
A138 1¢ green, perf. 12 horiz., double line wmk. **348**
A138 1¢ green, perf. 12 horiz., single line wmk. **385**
A138 1¢ green, perf. 12 vert., double line wmk......... .... **352**
A138 1¢ green, perf. 12 vert., single line wmk. ... **387**
A138 1¢ green, perf. 8½ horiz., single line wmk. **390**
A138 1¢ green, perf. 8½ vert., single line wmk. **392**
A139 2¢ carmine, perf. 12, double line wmk. **332**
A139 2¢ carmine, perf. 12, single line wmk......... **375**
A139 2¢ carmine, perf. 12, bluish paper............. **358**
A139 2¢ carmine, perf. 11, double line wmk. **519**
A139 2¢ carmine, imperf., double line wmk.......... **344**
A139 2¢ carmine, imperf., single line wmk. **384**
A139 2¢ carmine, perf. 12 horiz., double line wmk. **349**
A139 2¢ carmine, perf. 12 horiz., single line wmk..... .... **386**
A139 2¢ carmine, perf. 12 vert., double line wmk. **353**
A139 2¢ carmine, perf. 12 vert., single line wmk. **388**
A139 2¢ carmine, perf. 8½ horiz. single line wmk..... .... **391**
A139 2¢ carmine, perf. 8½ vert., single line wmk. **393**

Single stamps from booklet panes show 1 or 2 straight edges.

A138 1¢ green, perf. 12, double line wmk., booklet pane of 6 .... **331a**
A138 1¢ green, perf.12, single line wmk., booklet pane of 6 .... **374a**
A139 2¢ carmine, perf. 12, double line wmk., booklet pane of 6.................................... **332a**
A139 2¢ carmine, perf. 12, single line wmk., booklet pane of 6 .... **375a**

ISSUES OF 1908-21
FLAT BED AND ROTARY PRESS STAMPS

The Rotary Press Stamps are printed from plates that are curved to fit around a cylinder. This curvature produces stamps that are slightly larger, either horizontally or vertically, than those printed from flat plates. Designs of stamps from flat plates measure about 18½-19mm. wide by 22mm. high. When the impressions are placed sidewise on the curved plates the designs are 19½-20mm. wide; when they are placed vertically the designs are 22½ to 22¾mm. high. A line of color (not a guide line) shows where the curved plates meet or join on the press.

Rotary Press Coil Stamps were printed from plates of 170 subjects for stamps coiled sidewise, and from plates of 150 subjects for stamps coiled endwise.

Washington — A140

1¢ A138 Portrait of Franklin, value in words.
2¢ A139 Portrait of Washington, value in words.
A140 Portrait of Washington, value in numerals.

A140 1¢ green, perf. 12, single line wmk. **405**
A140 1¢ green, same, booklet pane of 6........... **405b**
A140 1¢ green, perf. 11, flat plate, unwmkd........ **498**
A140 1¢ green, same, booklet pane of 6........... **498e**
A140 1¢ green, same, booklet pane of 30.......... **498f**
A140 1¢ green, perf. 11, rotary press measuring 19mmx22½mm, unwmkd........................... **544**
A140 1¢ green, same, measuring 19½ to 20mmx22mm **545**
A140 1¢ gray green, perf. 11, offset, unwmkd..... **525**
A140 1¢ gray green, perf. 12½............................ **536**
A140 1¢ green, perf. 11x10................................ **538**
A140 1¢ green, perf. 10x11................................ **542**
A140 1¢ green, perf. 10, single line wmk. **424**
A140 1¢ green, same, perf. 12x10................... **423A**
A140 1¢ green, same, perf. 10x12................... **423D**
A140 1¢ green, perf.10, single line wmk., booklet pane of 6 .... **424d**
A140 1¢ green, perf. 10, flat plate, unwmkd........ **462**
A140 1¢ green, same, booklet pane of 6........... **462a**
A140 1¢ green, perf. 10, rotary press, unwmkd. **543**
A140 1¢ green, imperf., single line wmk............. **408**
A140 1¢ green, imperf., unwmkd. **481**
A140 1¢ green, imperf., offset........................... **531**
A140 1¢ green, perf. 10 horiz., flat plate, single line wmk.. **441**
A140 1¢ green, same, rotary press..................... **448**
A140 1¢ green, perf. 10 horiz., rotary press, unwmkd... **486**
A140 1¢ green, perf. 10 vert., flat plate, single line wmk.. **443**
A140 1¢ green, same, rotary press..................... **452**
A140 1¢ green, perf. 10 vert., rotary press, unwmkd. **490**
A140 1¢ green, perf. 8½ horiz. single line wmk. **410**
A140 1¢ green, perf. 8½ vert., same **412**

TYPES OF TWO CENTS

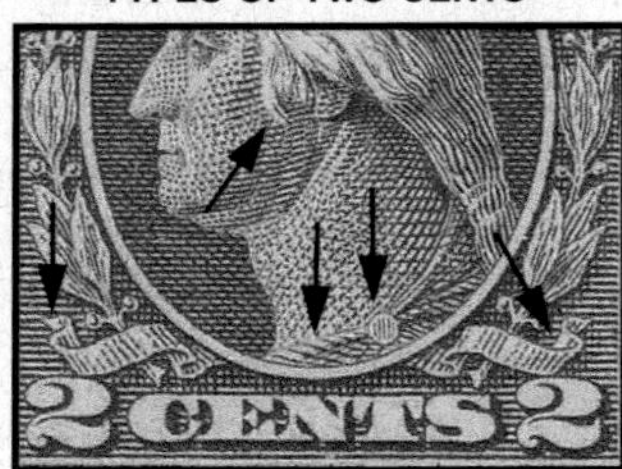

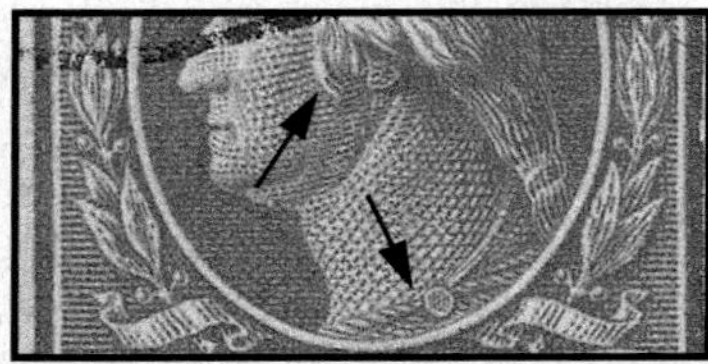

Type Ia — The design characteristics are similar to type I except that all of the lines of the design are stronger.

The toga button, toga rope and rope shading lines are heavy. The latter characteristics are those of type II, which, however, occur only on impressions from rotary plates.

Used only on flat plates 10208 and 10209.

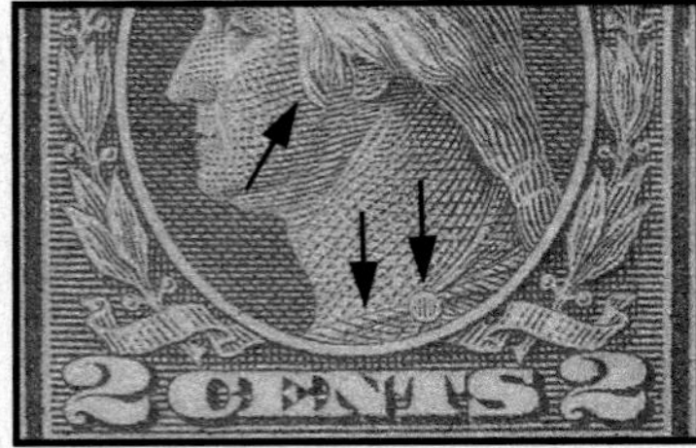

Type II — Shading lines in ribbons as on type I.

The toga button, rope and rope shading lines are heavy.

The shading lines of the face at the lock of hair end in a strong, vertical curved line.

Used on rotary press printings only.

Type III — Two lines of shading in the curves of the ribbons.

Other characteristics similar to type II.

Used on rotary press printings only.

Type IV — Top line of the toga rope is broken.

The shading lines in the toga button are so arranged that the curving of the first and last form "ID."

The line of color in the left "2" is very thin and usually broken. Used on offset printings only.

Type V — Top line of the toga is complete.

There are five vertical shading lines in the toga button.

The line of color in the left "2" is very thin and usually broken.

The shading dots on the nose are as shown on the diagram.

Used on offset printings only.

Type Va — Characteristics are the same as type V except in the shading dots of the nose. The third row of dots from the bottom has four dots instead of six. The overall height is ⅓mm shorter than type V.

Used on offset printings only.

Type VI — General characteristics the same as type V except that the line of color in the left "2" is very heavy. Used on offset printings only.

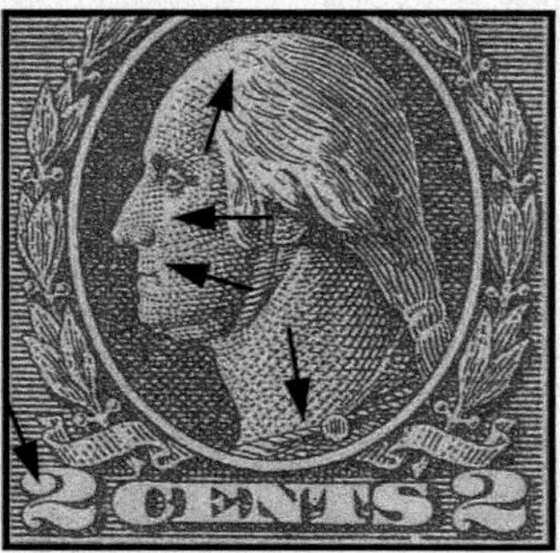

Type VII — The line of color in the left "2" is invariably continuous, clearly defined and heavier than in type V or Va but not as heavy as type VI.
An additional vertical row of dots has been added to the upper lip.
Numerous additional dots have been added to the hair on top of the head.
Used on offset printings only.

A140 2¢ carmine, perf. 12, type I, single line wmk. **406**
A140 2¢ carmine, same, booklet pane of 6 .... **406a**
A140 2¢ pale car. red, perf. 11, single line wmk., type I **461**
A140 2¢ rose, perf. 11, flat plate, unwmkd., type I **499**
A140 2¢ rose, same, booklet pane of 6 .... **499e**
A140 2¢ rose, same, booklet pane of 30 .... **499f**
A140 2¢ deep rose, perf. 11, unwmkd., type Ia ... **500**
A140 2¢ carmine rose, perf. 11, rotary press, unwmkd., type III **546**
A140 2¢ carmine, perf. 11, offset, unwmkd., type IV **526**
A140 2¢ carmine, same, type V **527**
A140 2¢ carmine, same, type Va **528**
A140 2¢ carmine, same, type VI **528A**
A140 2¢ carmine, same, type VII **528B**
A140 2¢ carmine rose, perf. 11x10, type II **539**
A140 2¢ carmine rose, same, type III **540**
A140 2¢ rose red, perf. 10x12, single line wmk., type I **423B**
A140 2¢ rose red, perf. 12x10, single line wmk., type I **423E**
A140 2¢ rose red, perf. 10, single line wmk., type I **425**
A140 2¢ rose red, same, perf. 10, booklet pane of 6 .... **425e**
A140 2¢ carmine, perf. 10, unwmkd., type I **463**
A140 2¢ carmine, same, booklet pane of 6 .... **463a**
A140 2¢ carmine, imperf., flat plate, single line wmk., type I **409**
A140 2¢ carmine, imperf., rotary press, single line wmk., type I **459**
A140 2¢ carmine, imperf., flat plate, unwmkd., type I **482**
A140 2¢ deep rose, same, type Ia **482A**
A140 2¢ carmine rose, imperf., offset, unwmkd., type IV **532**
A140 2¢ carmine rose, same, type V **533**
A140 2¢ carmine, same, type Va **534**
A140 2¢ carmine, same, type VI **534A**
A140 2¢ carmine, same, type VII **534B**
A140 2¢ carmine, perf. 10 horiz., flat plate, single line wmk., type I **442**
A140 2¢ red, same, rotary press **449**
A140 2¢ carmine, same, type III **450**
A140 2¢ carmine, perf. 10 horiz., rotary press unwmkd., type II **487**
A140 2¢ carmine, same, type III **488**
A140 2¢ carmine, perf. 10 vert., flat plate, single line wmk., type I **444**
A140 2¢ carmine rose, same, rotary press **453**
A140 2¢ red, same, type II **454**
A140 2¢ carmine, same, type III **455**
A140 2¢ carmine, perf. 10 vert., rotary press, unwmkd., type II **491**
A140 2¢ carmine, same, type III **492**
A140 2¢ carmine, perf. 8½ horiz., type I **411**
A140 2¢ carmine, perf. 8½ vert., type I **413**

TYPES OF THREE CENTS

Type I — The top line of the toga rope is weak and the rope shading lines are thin. The 5th line from the left is missing. The line between the lips is thin.

Type II — The top line of the toga rope is strong and the rope shading lines are heavy and complete.
The line between the lips is heavy.
Used on both flat plate and rotary press printings.

Type III — The top line of the toga rope is strong but the 5th shading line is missing as in type I.
Center shading line of the toga button consists of two dashes with a central dot.
The "P" and "O" of "POSTAGE" are separated by a line of color.
The frame line at the bottom of the vignette is complete.
Used on offset printings only.

Type IV — The shading lines of the toga rope are complete.
The second and fourth shading lines in the toga button are broken in the middle and the third line is continuous with a dot in the center.
The "P" and "O" of "POSTAGE" are joined.
The frame line at the bottom of the vignette is broken.
Used on offset printings only.

A140 3¢ deep violet, perf. 12, double line wmk., type I **333**
A140 3¢ deep violet, perf. 12, single line wmk., type I **376**
A140 3¢ deep violet, perf. 12, bluish paper, type I **359**
A140 3¢ light violet, perf. 11, unwmkd., type I **501**
A140 3¢ light violet, same, booklet pane of 6 .... **501b**
A140 3¢ dark violet, perf. 11, unwmkd., type II **502**
A140 3¢ dark violet, same, booklet pane of 6 .... **502b**
A140 3¢ violet, perf. 11, offset, type III **529**
A140 3¢ purple, same, type IV **530**
A140 3¢ violet, perf. 11x10, type II **541**
A140 3¢ deep violet, perf. 10, single line wmk., type I **426**
A140 3¢ violet, perf. 10, unwmkd., type I **464**
A140 3¢ deep violet, imperf., double line wmk., type I **345**
A140 3¢ violet, imperf., unwmkd., type I **483**
A140 3¢ violet, same, type II **484**
A140 3¢ violet, imperf., offset, type IV **535**
A140 3¢ deep violet, perf. 12 vert., single line wmk., type I **389**
A140 3¢ violet, perf. 10 vert., flat plate, single line wmk., type I **445**
A140 3¢ violet, perf. 10 vert., rotary press, single line wmk., type I **456**
A140 3¢ violet, perf. 10 vert., rotary press, unwmkd., type I **493**
A140 3¢ violet, same, type II **494**
A140 3¢ violet, perf. 10 horiz., type I **489**
A140 3¢ deep violet, perf. 8½ vert., type I **394**
A140 4¢ orange brown, perf. 12, double line wmk. **334**
A140 4¢ orange brown, perf. 12, bluish paper **360**
A140 4¢ brown, perf. 12, single line wmk. **377**
A140 4¢ brown, perf. 11, unwmkd. **503**
A140 4¢ brown, perf. 10, single line wmk. **427**
A140 4¢ orange brown, perf. 10, unwmkd. **465**
A140 4¢ orange brown, imperf. **346**
A140 4¢ orange brown, perf. 12 horiz. **350**
A140 4¢ orange brown, perf. 12 vert. **354**
A140 4¢ brown, perf. 10 vert., flat plate, single line wmk. **446**
A140 4¢ brown, same, rotary press **457**
A140 4¢ orange brown, perf. 10 vert., rotary press, unwmkd. **495**
A140 4¢ brown, perf. 8½ vert., single line wmk. **395**
A140 5¢ blue, perf. 12, double line wmk. **335**
A140 5¢ blue, perf. 12 bluish paper **361**
A140 5¢ blue, perf. 12, single line wmk. **378**
A140 5¢ blue, perf. 11, unwmkd. **504**
A140 5¢ rose (error), same **505**
A140 5¢ carmine (error), perf. 10, unwmkd. **467**
A140 5¢ blue, perf. 10, single line wmk. **428**
A140 5¢ blue, perf. 12x10 .... **423C**
A140 5¢ blue, perf. 10, unwmkd. **466**
A140 5¢ blue, imperf. **347**
A140 5¢ carmine (error), imperf. **485**
A140 5¢ blue, perf. 12 horiz. **351**
A140 5¢ blue, perf. 12 vert. **355**
A140 5¢ blue, perf. 10 vert., flat plate, single line wmk. **447**
A140 5¢ blue, same, rotary press **458**
A140 5¢ blue, perf. 10 vert., rotary press, unwmkd. **496**
A140 5¢ blue, perf. 8½ vert. **396**
A140 6¢ red orange, perf. 12, double line wmk. **336**
A140 6¢ red orange, perf. 12, bluish paper **362**
A140 6¢ red orange, perf. 12, single line wmk. ... **379**
A140 6¢ red orange, perf. 11, unwmkd. **506**
A140 6¢ red orange, perf. 10, single line wmk. ... **429**
A140 6¢ red orange, perf. 10, unwmkd. **468**
A140 7¢ black, perf. 12, single line wmk. **407**
A140 7¢ black, perf. 11, unwmkd. **507**
A140 7¢ black, perf. 10, single line wmk. **430**
A140 7¢ black, perf. 10, unwmkd. **469**
A140 8¢ olive green, perf. 12, double line wmk. **337**
A140 8¢ olive green, perf. 12, bluish paper **363**
A140 8¢ olive green, perf. 12, single line wmk. ... **380**
A140 10¢ yellow, perf. 12, double line wmk. **338**
A140 10¢ yellow, perf. 12, bluish paper **364**
A140 10¢ yellow, perf. 12, single line wmk. **381**
A140 10¢ yellow, perf. 12 vert. **356**
A140 13¢ blue green, perf. 12, double line wmk. **339**
A140 13¢ blue green, perf. 12, bluish paper **365**
A140 15¢ pale ultra, perf. 12, double line wmk. **340**
A140 15¢ pale ultra, perf. 12, bluish paper **366**
A140 15¢ pale ultra, perf. 12, single line wmk. ... **382**
A140 50¢ violet **341**
A140 $1 violet brown **342**

ISSUES OF 1912-19

A148

Franklin — A149

Designs of 8¢ to $1 denominations differ only in figures of value.

A148 8¢ pale olive green, perf. 12, single line wmk. **414**
A148 8¢ olive bister, perf. 11, unwmkd. **508**
A148 8¢ pale olive grn., perf. 10, single line wmk. **431**
A148 8¢ olive green, perf. 10, unwmkd. **470**
A148 9¢ salmon red, perf. 12, single line wmk. **415**
A148 9¢ salmon red, perf. 11, unwmkd. **509**
A148 9¢ salmon red, perf. 10, single line wmk. **432**
A148 9¢ salmon red, perf. 10, unwmkd. **471**
A148 10¢ orange yellow, perf. 12, single line wmk. **416**
A148 10¢ orange yellow, perf. 11, unwmkd. **510**
A148 10¢ orange yellow, perf. 10, single line wmk. **433**
A148 10¢ orange yellow, perf. 10, unwmkd. **472**
A148 10¢ orange yellow, perf. 10 vert., same **497**
A148 11¢ light green, perf. 11, unwmkd. **511**
A148 11¢ dark green, perf. 10, single line wmk. **434**
A148 11¢ dark green, perf. 10, unwmkd. **473**
A148 12¢ claret brown, perf. 12, single line wmk. **417**
A148 12¢ claret brown, perf. 11, unwmkd. **512**
A148 12¢ claret brown, perf. 10, single line wmk. **435**
A148 12¢ claret brown, perf. 10, unwmkd. **474**
A148 13¢ apple green, perf. 11, unwmkd. **513**
A148 15¢ gray, perf. 12, single line wmk. **418**
A148 15¢ gray, perf. 11, unwmkd. **514**
A148 15¢ gray, perf. 10, single line wmk. **437**
A148 15¢ gray, perf. 10, unwmkd. **475**
A148 20¢ ultramarine, perf. 12, single line wmk. **419**
A148 20¢ light ultra., perf. 11, unwmkd. **515**
A148 20¢ ultramarine, perf. 10, single line wmk. **438**
A148 20¢ light ultra, perf. 10, unwmkd. **476**
A148 30¢ orange red, perf. 12, single line wmk. **420**
A148 30¢ orange red, perf. 11, unwmkd. **516**
A148 30¢ orange red, perf. 10, single line wmk. **439**
A148 30¢ orange red, perf. 10, unwmkd. **476A**
A148 50¢ violet, perf. 12, single line wmk. **421**
A148 50¢ violet, perf. 12, double line wmk. **422**
A148 50¢ red violet, perf. 11, unwmkd. **517**
A148 50¢ violet, perf. 10, single line wmk. **440**
A148 50¢ light violet, perf. 10, unwmkd. **477**
A148 $1 violet brown, perf. 12, double line wmk. **423**
A148 $1 violet brown, perf. 11, unwmkd. **518**
A148 $1 violet black, perf. 10, double line wmk. **460**
A148 $1 violet black, perf. 10, unwmkd. **478**

ISSUES OF 1918-20
Perf. 11 Unwmkd.

A149 $2 orange red & black **523**
A149 $2 carmine & black **547**
A149 $5 deep green & black **524**

ISSUES OF 1922-32

Nathan Hale — A154

Franklin — A155

Warren G. Harding — A156

Washington — A157

Lincoln — A158

Martha Washington — A159

Theodore Roosevelt — A160

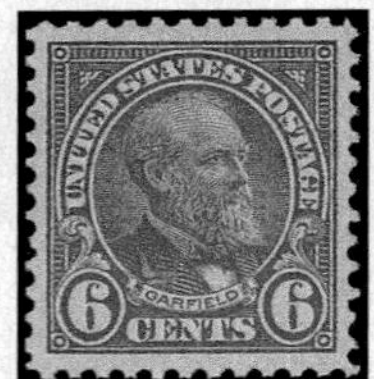

Garfield — A161

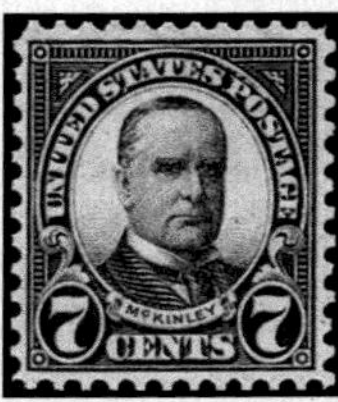

McKinley — A162

Grant — A163

Jefferson — A164

Monroe — A165

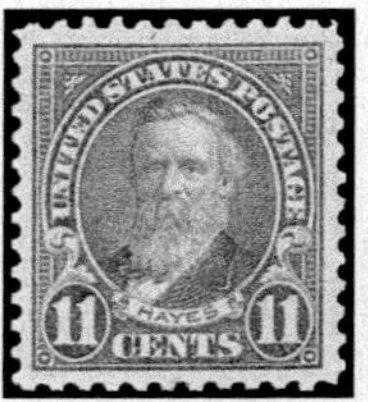

Hayes — A166

Cleveland — A167

American Indian — A168

Statue of Liberty — A169

Golden Gate — A170

Niagara Falls — A171

Buffalo — A172

Arlington Amphitheater and Tomb of the Unknown Soldier — A173

Lincoln Memorial — A174

United States Capitol — A175

"America" — A176

Canal Zone Overprints:
Type A has flat-topped "A's" in "CANAL."
Type B has sharp-pointed "A's" in "CANAL."

Unwmkd.

A154 ½¢ olive brown, perf. 11 .... **551**
A154 ½¢ olive brown, perf. 11x10½ **653**
A154 ½¢ olive brown, "CANAL ZONE" .... **C.Z. 70**
A155 1¢ deep green, perf. 11, flat plate **552**
A155 1¢ deep green, booklet pane of 6 .... **552a**
A155 1¢ green, perf. 11, rotary press 19¾x22¼mm **594**
A155 1¢ green, same, 191/4x22½mm (used) **596**
A155 1¢ green, perf. 11x10, rotary press **578**
A155 1¢ green, perf. 10 .... **581**
A155 1¢ green, perf. 11x10½ **632**
A155 1¢ green, same, booklet pane of 6 .... **632a**
A155 1¢ green, ovpt. Kans. **658**
A155 1¢ green, ovpt. Nebr. **669**
A155 1¢ green, imperf. **575**
A155 1¢ green, perf. 10 vert. **597**
A155 1¢ yellow green, perf. 10 horiz. **604**
A155 1¢ deep green, "CANAL ZONE" type A, perf. 11 .... **C.Z. 71**
A155 1¢ deep green, same, booklet pane of 6 .... **C.Z. 71e**
A155 1¢ green, "CANAL ZONE" type B, perf. 11x10½ .... **C.Z. 100**
A156 1½¢ yellow brown, perf. 11 .... **553**
A156 1½¢ yellow brown, perf. 11x10½ **633**
A156 1½¢ brown, ovpt. Kans **659**
A156 1½¢ brown, ovpt. Nebr **670**
A156 1½¢ brown, perf. 10 .... **582**
A156 1½¢ brown, perf. 10 vert. **598**
A156 1½¢ yellow brown, perf. 10 horiz. **605**
A156 1½¢ yellow brown, imperf., flat plate **576**
A156 1½¢ yellow brown, imperf., rotary press, 19¼x22½mm **631**
A156 1½¢ yellow brown "CANAL ZONE" .... **C.Z. 72**

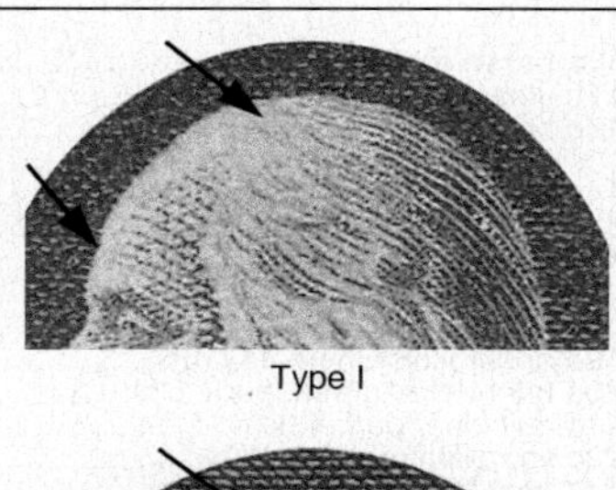

Type I

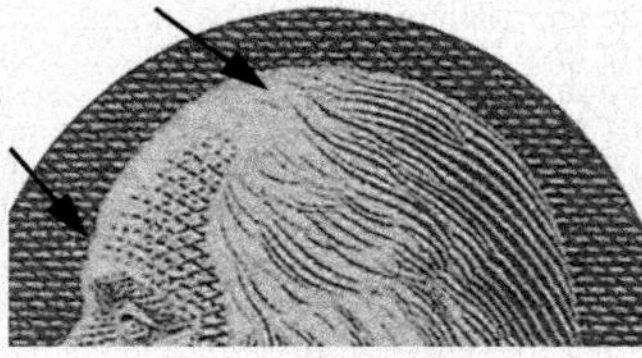

Type II

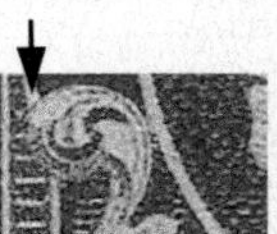

Type I

Type II

TYPE I. No line outlining forehead. No heavy hair lines at top center of head. Outline of left acanthus scroll generally faint at top and toward base at left side.

TYPE II. Thin line outlining forehead. Three heavy hair lines at top center of head; two being outstanding in the white area. Outline of left acanthus scroll very strong and clearly defined at top (under left edge of lettered panel) and at lower curve (above and to left of numeral oval). This type appears only on Nos. 599A and 634A.

A157 2¢ carmine, perf. 11, flat plate.................... **554**
A157 2¢ carmine, same, booklet pane of 6....... **554c**
A157 2¢ carmine, perf. 11, rotary press, 19¾x22¼mm.. **595**
A157 2¢ carmine, perf. 11x10............................ **579**
A157 2¢ carmine, perf. 11x10½, type I............... **634**
A157 2¢ carmine, perf. 11x10½, type II........... **634A**
A157 2¢ carmine lake, same, type I **634b**
A157 2¢ carmine lake, same, booklet pane of 6 .... **634d**
A157 2¢ carmine, overprt. Molly Pitcher............. **646**
A157 2¢ carmine, overprt. Hawaii 1778-1928...... **647**
A157 2¢ carmine, overprt. Kans........................ **660**
A157 2¢ carmine, overprt. Nebr......................... **671**
A157 2¢ carmine, perf. 10.................................. **583**
A157 2¢ carmine, same, booklet pane of 6....... **583a**
A157 2¢ carmine, imperf.................................... **577**
A157 2¢ carmine, perf. 10 vert., type I **599**
A157 2¢ carmine, same, type II **599A**
A157 2¢ carmine, perf. 10 horiz......................... **606**
A157 2¢ carmine, "CANAL ZONE" type A, perf. 11 .... **C.Z. 73**
A157 2¢ carmine, same, booklet pane of 6.............. .... **C.Z. 73a**
A157 2¢ carmine, "CANAL ZONE" type B, perf. 11 .... **C.Z. 84**
A157 2¢ carmine, same, booklet pane of 6.............. .... **C.Z. 84d**
A157 2¢ carmine, "CANAL ZONE" type B, perf. 10 .... **C.Z. 97**
A157 2¢ carmine, same, booklet pane of 6.............. .... **C.Z. 97b**
A157 2¢ carmine, "CANAL ZONE" type B, perf. 11x10½.. **C.Z. 101**
A157 2¢ carmine, same, booklet pane of 6.............. .... **C.Z. 101a**
A158 3¢ violet, perf. 11 .... **555**
A158 3¢ violet, perf. 11x10½.............................. **635**
A158 3¢ violet, overprt. Kans............................. **661**
A158 3¢ violet, overprt. Nebr............................. **672**
A158 3¢ violet, perf. 10....................................... **584**
A158 3¢violet, perf. 10 vert. **600**
A158 3¢ violet, "CANAL ZONE" perf. 11........ **C.Z. 85**
A158 3¢ violet, "CANAL ZONE" perf. 10........ **C.Z. 98**
A158 3¢ violet, "CANAL ZONE" perf. 11x10½.......... .... **C.Z. 102**
A159 4¢ yellow brown, perf. 11 .... **556**
A159 4¢ yellow brown, perf. 11x10½.................... **636**
A159 4¢ yellow brown, ovrpt. Kans...................... **662**
A159 4¢ yellow brown, ovrpt. Nebr. **673**
A159 4¢ yellow brown, perf. 10........................... **585**
A159 4¢ yellow brown, perf. 10 vert.................... **601**
A160 5¢ dark blue, perf. 11................................. **557**
A160 5¢ dark blue, perf. 11x10½......................... **637**
A160 5¢ dark blue, ovpt. Hawaii 1778-1928........ **648**
A160 5¢ deep blue, ovpt. Kans........................... **663**
A160 5¢ deep blue, ovpt. Nebr........................... **674**
A160 5¢ blue, perf. 10.. **586**
A160 5¢ dark blue, perf. 10 vert. **602**
A160 5¢ dark blue, "CANAL ZONE" type A, perf. 11 .... **C.Z. 74**
A160 5¢ dark blue, same, type B................... **C.Z. 86**
A160 5¢ dark blue, same, perf. 11x10½...... **C.Z. 103**
A161 6¢ red orange, perf. 11 .... **558**
A161 6¢ red orange, perf. 11x10½ **638**
A161 6¢ red orange, ovrpt. Kans......................... **664**
A161 6¢ red orange, ovrpt. Nebr.......................... **675**
A161 6¢ red orange, perf. 10 .... **587**
A161 6¢ deep orange, perf. 10 vert. **723**
A162 7¢ black, perf. 11... **559**
A162 7¢ black, perf. 11x10½................................ **639**
A162 7¢ black, ovrpt. Kans.................................. **665**
A162 7¢ black, ovrpt. Nebr................................... **676**
A162 7¢ black, perf. 10... **588**
A163 8¢ olive green, perf. 11 .... **560**
A163 8¢ olive green, perf. 11x10½ **640**
A163 8¢ olive green, ovrpt. Kans. **666**
A163 8¢ olive green, ovrpt. Nebr. **677**
A163 8¢ olive green, perf. 10 .... **589**
A164 9¢ rose, perf. 11... **561**
A164 9¢ orange red, perf. 11x10½ **641**
A164 9¢ light rose, ovrpt. Kans............................ **667**
A164 9¢ light rose, ovrpt. Nebr. **678**
A164 9¢ rose, perf. 10... **590**
A165 10¢ orange, perf. 11...................................... **562**
A165 10¢ orange, perf. 11x10½.............................. **642**
A165 10¢ orange yellow, ovrpt. Kans..................... **668**
A165 10¢ orange yellow, ovrpt. Nebr..................... **679**
A165 10¢ orange, perf. 10...................................... **591**
A165 10¢ orange, perf. 10 vert.............................. **603**
A165 10¢ orange, "CANAL ZONE" type A, perf. 11 .... **C.Z. 75**
A165 10¢ orange, same, type B.................... **C.Z. 87**
A165 10¢ orange, same, perf. 10................... **C.Z. 99**
A165 10¢ orange, same, perf. 11x10½........ **C.Z. 104**
A166 11¢ light blue, perf. 11 .... **563**
A166 11¢ light blue, perf. 11x10½ **692**
A167 12¢ brown violet, perf. 11 .... **564**
A167 12¢ brown violet, perf. 11x10½.................... **693**
A167 12¢ brown violet, "CANAL ZONE" type A .... **C.Z. 76**
A167 12¢ brown violet, same, type B .... **C.Z. 88**
A168 14¢ blue, perf. 11 .... **565**
A168 14¢ dark blue, perf. 11x10½......................... **695**
A168 14¢ dark blue, "CANAL ZONE" type A, perf. 11 .... **C.Z. 77**
A168 14¢ dark blue, same, type B................. **C.Z. 89**
A168 14¢ dark blue, same, perf. 11x10½.... **C.Z. 116**
A169 15¢ gray, perf. 11 .... **566**
A169 15¢ gray, perf. 11x10½ **696**
A169 15¢ gray, "CANAL ZONE" type A......... **C.Z. 78**
A169 15¢ gray, "CANAL ZONE" type B......... **C.Z. 90**
A170 20¢ carmine rose, perf. 11........................... **567**
A170 20¢ carmine rose, perf. 10½x11.................... **698**
A170 20¢ carmine rose, "CANAL ZONE" ...... **C.Z. 92**
A171 25¢ yellow green, perf. 11............................ **568**
A171 25¢ blue green, perf. 10½x11...................... **699**
A172 30¢ olive brown, perf. 11............................. **569**
A172 30¢ brown, perf. 10½x11.............................. **700**
A172 30¢ olive brown, "CANAL ZONE" type A.......... .... **C.Z. 79**
A172 30¢ olive brown, "CANAL ZONE" type B.......... .... **C.Z. 93**
A173 50¢ lilac, perf. 11... **570**
A173 50¢ lilac, perf. 10½x11................................... **701**
A173 50¢ lilac, "CANAL ZONE" type A.......... **C.Z. 80**
A173 50¢ lilac, "CANAL ZONE" type B.......... **C.Z. 94**
A174 $1 violet brown, perf. 11 .... **571**
A174 $1 violet brown, perf. 10¾x10½.............. **4075a**
A174 $1 violet brown, "CANAL ZONE" type A.......... .... **C.Z. 81**
A174 $1 violet brown, "CANAL ZONE" type B.......... .... **C.Z. 95**
A175 $2 deep blue, perf. 11................................. **572**
A175 $2 deep blue, perf. 10¾x10½................. **4075b**
A176 $5 carmine & blue, perf. 11.......................... **573**
A176 $5 carmine & blue, perf. 10¾x10½ **4075c**

REGULAR ISSUES OF 1925-26, 1930 and 1932

Harrison — A186

Wilson — A187

A186 13¢ green, perf. 11.. **622**
A186 13¢ yellow green, perf. 11x10½.................... **694**
A187 17¢ black, perf. 11.. **623**
A187 17¢ black, perf. 10½x11................................ **697**
A187 17¢ black, "CANAL ZONE" .... **C.Z. 91**

Harding — A203

Taft — A204

A203 1½¢ brown, perf. 11x10½............................ **684**
A203 1½¢ brown, perf. 10 vert............................... **686**
A204 4¢ brown, perf. 11x10½................................ **685**
A204 4¢ brown, perf. 10 vert.................................. **687**

Washington — A226

A226 3¢ deep violet, perf. 11x10½ **720**
A226 3¢ deep violet, same, booklet pane of 6 **720b**
A226 3¢ deep violet, perf. 10 vert........................ **721**
A226 3¢ deep violet, perf. 10 horiz. **722**
A226 3¢ deep violet, "CANAL ZONE"......... **C.Z. 115**

PRESIDENTIAL ISSUE OF 1938

Benjamin Franklin — A275

George Washington — A276

Martha Washington — A277

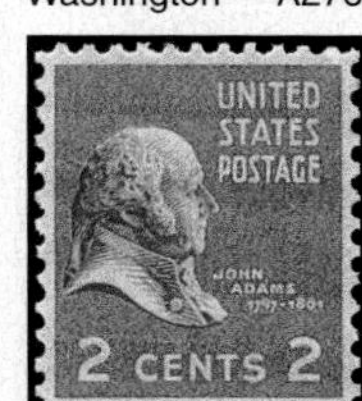

John Adams — A278

Thomas Jefferson — A279

James Madison — A280

The White House — A281

James Monroe — A282

John Quincy Adams — A283

Martin Van Buren — A285

John Tyler — A287

Zachary Taylor — A289

Franklin Pierce — A291

Abraham Lincoln — A293

Ulysses S. Grant — A295

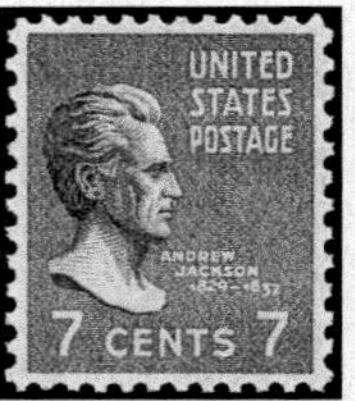

Andrew Jackson — A284

William H. Harrison — A286

James K. Polk — A288

Millard Fillmore — A290

James Buchanan — A292

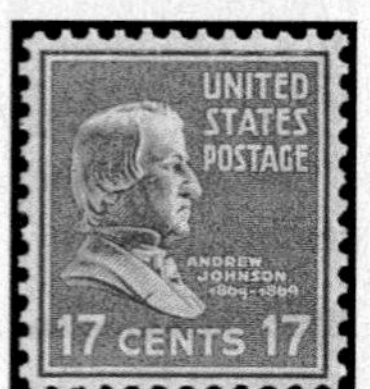

Andrew Johnson — A294

Rutherford B. Hayes — A296

James A. Garfield — A297

Grover Cleveland — A299

William McKinley — A301

William Howard Taft — A303

Warren G. Harding — A305

Chester A. Arthur — A298

Benjamin Harrison — A300

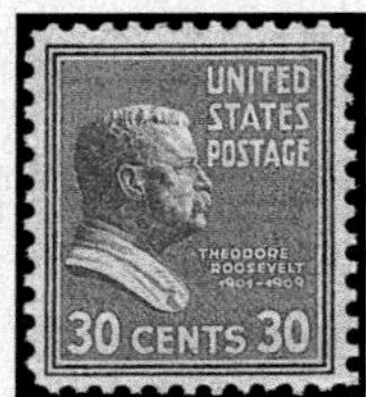

Theodore Roosevelt — A302

Woodrow Wilson — A304

Calvin Coolidge — A306

Rotary Press Printing
Unwmkd.

A275 ½¢ deep orange, perf. 11x10½ **803**
A275 ½¢ red orange, "CANAL ZONE" .... **C.Z. 118**
A276 1¢ green, perf. 11x10½ **804**
A276 1¢ green, booklet pane of 6 .... **804b**
A276 1¢ green, perf. 10 vert. **839**
A276 1¢ green, perf. 10 horiz. **848**
A277 1½¢ bister brown, perf. 11x10½ **805**
A277 1½¢ bister brown, perf. 10 vert. **840**
A277 1½¢ bister brown, perf. 10 horiz. **849**
A277 1½¢ bister brown, "CANAL ZONE" .... **C.Z. 119**
A278 2¢ rose carmine, perf. 11x10½ **806**
A278 2¢ booklet pane of 6 .... **806b**
A278 2¢ rose carmine, perf. 10 vert. **841**
A278 2¢ rose carmine, perf. 10 horiz. **850**
A279 3¢ deep violet, perf. 11x10½ **807**
A279 3¢ deep violet, booklet pane of 6 .... **807a**
A279 3¢ deep violet, perf. 10 vert. **842**
A279 3¢ deep violet, perf. 10 horiz. **851**
A280 4¢ red violet, perf. 11x10½ **808**
A280 4¢ red violet, perf. 10 vert. **843**
A281 4½¢ dark gray, perf. 11x10½ **809**
A281 4½¢ dark gray, perf. 10 vert. **844**
A282 5¢ bright blue, perf. 11x10½ **810**
A282 5¢ bright blue, perf. 10 vert. **845**
A283 6¢ red orange, perf. 11x10½ **811**
A283 6¢ red orange, perf. 10 vert. **846**
A284 7¢ sepia, perf. 11x10½ **812**
A285 8¢ olive green, perf. 11x10½ **813**
A286 9¢ rose pink, perf. 11x10½ **814**
A287 10¢ brown red, perf. 11x10½ **815**
A287 10¢ brown red, perf. 10 vert. **847**
A288 11¢ ultramarine, perf. 11x10½ **816**
A289 12¢ bright violet, perf. 11x10½ **817**
A290 13¢ blue green, perf. 11x10½ **818**
A291 14¢ blue, perf. 11x10½ **819**
A292 15¢ blue gray, perf. 11x10½ **820**
A293 16¢ black, perf. 11x10½ **821**
A294 17¢ rose red, perf. 11x10½ **822**
A295 18¢ brn. carmine, perf. 11x10½ **823**
A296 19¢ bright violet, perf. 11x10½ **824**
A297 20¢ bright blue green, perf. 11x10½ **825**
A298 21¢ dull blue, perf. 11x10½ **826**
A299 22¢ vermilion, perf. 11x10½ **827**
A300 24¢ gray black, perf. 11x10½ **828**
A301 25¢ dp. red lilac, perf. 11x10½ **829**
A302 30¢ deep ultra, perf. 11x10½ **830**
A303 50¢ lt. red violet, perf. 11x10½ **831**

Flat Plate Printing
Perf. 11

A304 $1 pur. & blk., unwmkd. **832**
A304 $1 pur. & blk., wmkd. USIR **832b**
A304 $1 red vio. & blk., thick white paper, smooth colorless gum **832c**
A305 $2 yellow green & black **833**
A306 $5 carmine & black **834**

LIBERTY ISSUE 1954-80

Benjamin Franklin — A477

George Washington — A478

Palace of the Governors, Santa Fe — A478a

Mount Vernon — A479

Thomas Jefferson — A480

Bunker Hill Monument and Massachusetts Flag 1776 — A481

Statue of Liberty — A482

Abraham Lincoln — A483

The Hermitage — A484

James Monroe — A485

Theodore Roosevelt — A486

Woodrow Wilson — A487

Statue of Liberty (Rotary and flat plate printing) — A488

Design slightly altered; see position of torch (Giorgi press printing) — A489

The Alamo — A490

Independence Hall — A491

Statue of Liberty — A491a

Benjamin Harrison — A492

John Jay — A493

Monticello — A494

Paul Revere — A495

Robert E. Lee — A496

John Marshall — A497

Susan B. Anthony — A498

Patrick Henry — A499

Alexander Hamilton — A500

Unwmkd.

A477 ½¢ red orange, perf. 11x10½ **1030**
A478 1¢ dark green, perf. 11x10½ **1031**
A478 1¢ dark green, perf. 10 vert. **1054**
A478a 1¼¢ turquoise, perf. 10½x11 .... **1031A**
A478a 1¼¢ turquoise, perf. 10 horiz. **1054A**
A479 1½¢ brown carmine, perf. 10½x11 .... **1032**
A480 2¢ carmine rose, perf. 11x10 .... **1033**
A480 2¢ carmine rose, perf. 10 vert. **1055**
A481 2½¢ gray blue, perf. 11x10½ **1034**
A481 2½¢ gray blue, perf. 10 vert. **1056**
A482 3¢ deep violet, perf. 11x10½ **1035**
A482 3¢ deep violet, perf. 10 vert. **1057**
A482 3¢ deep violet, imperf., size: 24x28mm **1075a**
A483 4¢ red violet, perf. 11x10½ **1036**
A483 4¢ red violet, perf. 10 vert. **1058**
A484 4½¢ blue green, perf. 10½x11 .... **1037**
A484 4½¢ blue green, perf. 10 horiz. **1059**
A485 5¢ deep blue, perf. 11x10½ **1038**
A486 6¢ carmine, perf. 11x10½ **1039**
A487 7¢ rose carmine, same **1040**
A488 8¢ dark violet blue & carmine, flat plate printing, perf. 11, mapprox. 22.7mm high **1041**
A488 8¢ dark violet blue & carmine, rotary press printing, perf. 11, appprox. 22.9mm high **1041B**
A488 8¢ dark violet blue & carmine, imperf., size: 24x28mm **1075b**
A489 8¢ dark violet blue & carmine, perf. 11 ... **1042**
A490 9¢ rose lilac, perf. 10½x11 .... **1043**
A491 10¢ rose lake, same **1044**
A491a 11¢ carmine & dark violet blue, perf. 11 .... **1044A**
A492 12¢ red, perf. 11x10½ **1045**
A493 15¢ rose lake, perf. 11x10½ **1046**
A494 20¢ ultramarine, perf. 10½x11 .... **1047**
A495 25¢ green, perf. 11x10½ **1048**
A495 25¢ green, perf. 10 vert. **1059A**
A496 30¢ black, perf. 11x10½ **1049**
A497 40¢ brown red, perf. 11x10½ **1050**
A498 50¢ bright purple, perf. 11x10½ **1051**
A499 $1 purple, perf. 11x10½ **1052**
A500 $5 black, perf. 11 .... **1053**

FLAG ISSUE 1963

Flag over White House — A645

A645 5¢ blue & red, perf. 11 .... **1208**

ISSUE OF 1962-66

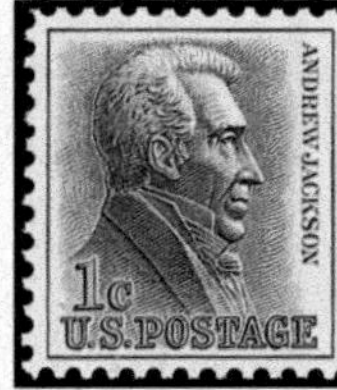
Andrew Jackson — A646

George Washington — A650

John J. Pershing — A651

A646 1¢ green, perf. 11x10½ **1209**
A646 1¢ green, perf. 10 vert. **1225**
A650 5¢ dk. bl. gray, perf. 11x10½ **1213**
A650 5¢ dk. bl. gray, perf. 10 vert. **1229**
A651 8¢ brown, perf. 11x10½ **1214**

PROMINENT AMERICANS ISSUE 1965-81

Thomas Jefferson — A710

Albert Gallatin — A711

Frank Lloyd Wright and Guggenheim Museum, New York — A712

Francis Parkman — A713

Abraham Lincoln — A714

George Washington — A715

Re-engraved — A715a

Franklin D. Roosevelt — A716

Franklin D. Roosevelt (vertical coil) — A727a

Benjamin Franklin and his signature — A816

Albert Einstein — A717

Andrew Jackson — A718

Henry Ford and 1909 Model I — A718a

John F. Kennedy — A719

Fiorello H. LaGuardia and New York skyline — A817a

Oliver Wendell Holmes — A720

Oliver Wendell Holmes — A720a

Ernest (Ernie) Taylor Pyle — A818

Dr. Elizabeth Blackwell — A818a

George C. Marshall — A721

Amadeo P. Giannini — A818b

Frederick Douglass — A722

John Dewey — A723

Thomas Paine — A724

Lucy Stone — A725

Eugene O'Neill — A726

John Bassett Moore — A727

Types of 15¢:

I — Necktie barely touches coat at bottom; crosshatching of tie strong and complete. Flag of "5" is true horizontal. Crosshatching of "15" is colorless when visible.

II — Necktie does not touch coat at bottom; LL to UR crosshatching lines strong, UL to LR lines very faint. Flag of "5" slants down slightly at right. Crosshatching of "15" is colored and visible when magnified.

A third type, used only for No. 1288B, is smaller in overall size, and "15¢" is ¾mm closer to head.

Unwmkd.

Rotary Press Printing

A710 1¢ green, perf. 11x10½ **1278**
A710 1¢ green, perf. 10, vert., tagged **1299**
A711 1¼¢ light green, perf. 11x10½ **1279**
A712 2¢ dk. bl. gray, perf. 11x10½ **1280**
A713 3¢ violet, perf. 10½x11 .... **1281**
A713 3¢ violet, perf. 10 horiz. **1297**
A714 4¢ black, perf. 11x10½ **1282**
A714 4¢ black, perf. 10, vert. **1303**
A715 5¢ blue, perf. 11x10½ **1283**
A715 5¢ blue, perf. 10 vert. **1304**
A715a 5¢ blue, perf. 11x10½ **1283B**
A715a 5¢ blue, perf. 10 vert. **1304C**
A716 6¢ gray brown, perf. 10½x11 .... **1284**
A716 6¢ gray brown, perf. 10 horiz., tagged **1298**
A727a 6¢ gray brown, perf. 10 vert., tagged **1305**
A816 7¢ bright blue, perf. 10½x11 .... **1393D**
A717 8¢ violet, perf. 11x10½ **1285**
A718 10¢ lilac, perf. 11x10½ **1286**
A718a 12¢ black, perf. 10½x11 .... **1286A**
A719 13¢ brown, perf. 11x10½ **1287**
A817a 14¢ gray brown, perf. 11x10½ **1397**
A720 15¢ magenta, perf. 11x10½ **1288**
A720a 15¢ magenta, perf. 10 (booklet panes only) **1288B**
A720 15¢ magenta, perf. 10 vert. **1305E**
A818 16¢ brown **1398**
A818a 18¢ violet, perf. 11x10½ **1399**
A721 20¢ deep olive, perf. 11x10½ **1289**
A818b 21¢ green, perf. 11x10½ **1400**
A722 25¢ rose lake, perf. 11x10½ **1290**
A723 30¢ red lilac, perf. 10½x11 .... **1291**
A724 40¢ blue black, perf. 11x10½ **1292**
A725 50¢ rose magenta, perf. 11x10½ **1293**
A726 $1 dull purple, perf 11x10½ **1294**
A726 $1 dull purple, perf. 10 vert, tagged..... **1305C**
A727 $5 gray black, perf 11x10½ **1295**

Dwight D. Eisenhower — A815

A815a

A815 6¢ dark blue gray, perf. 11x10½ **1393**
A815 6¢ dk. bl. gray, perf. 10, vert. **1401**
A815 8¢ deep claret, perf. 11x10½ (booklet panes only) **1395**
A815 8¢ deep claret, perf. 10 vert **1402**
A815a 8¢ blk., red & bl. gray, perf. 11 .... **1394**

FLAG ISSUE 1968-71

Flag and White House — A760

A760 6¢ dark blue, red & green, perf. 11, size: 19x22mm **1338**
A760 6¢ dark blue, red & green, perf. 11x10½, size: 18¼x21mm **1338D**
A760 6¢ dark blue, red & green, perf. 10 vert., size: 18¼x21mm **1338A**
A760 8¢ multicolored, perf. 11x10½ **1338F**
A760 8¢ multicolored, perf. 10 vert. **1338G**

REGULAR ISSUE 1971-74

U.S. Postal Service Emblem — A817

50-Star and 13-Star Flags — A923

Jefferson Memorial and quotation from Declaration of Independence A924

Mail Transport and "Zip Code" A925

Liberty Bell — A926

A817 8¢ multicolored, perf. 11x10½ **1396**
A923 10¢ red & blue, perf 11x10½ **1509**
A923 10¢ red & blue, perf. 10 vert. **1519**
A924 10¢ blue, perf. 11x10½ **1510**
A924 10¢ blue, perf. 10 vert. **1520**
A925 10¢ multicolored, perf. 11x10½ **1511**
A926 6.3¢ brick red, perf. 10 vert. **1518**

AMERICANA ISSUE 1975-81

Inkwell and Quill — A984

Speaker's Stand — A985

Early Ballot Box — A987

Books, Bookmark, Eyeglasses — A988

Dome of Capitol — A994

Contemplation of Justice — A995

Early American Printing Press — A996

Torch Statue of Liberty — A997

Liberty Bell — A998

Eagle and Shield — A999

Ft. McHenry Flag — A1001

Head Statue of Liberty — A1002

Old North Church — A1003

Ft. Nisqually — A1004

Sandy Hook Lighthouse A1005

Morris Township School No. 2, Devil's Lake A1006

Iron "Betty" Lamp Plymouth Colony, 17th-18th Centuries — A1007

Rush Lamp and Candle Holder — A1008

Kerosene Table Lamp — A1009

Railroad Conductors Lantern, c. 1850 — A1010

COIL STAMPS

Six-string guitar — A1011

Weaver violins — A1199

Saxhorns — A1012

Drum — A1013

Steinway Grand Piano, 1857 — A1014

A984 1¢ dark blue, greenish, perf. 11x10½...... **1581**
A984 1¢ dark blue, greenish, perf. 10 vert. **1811**
A985 2¢ red brown, greenish, perf. 11x10½ **1582**
A987 3¢ olive, greenish, perf 11x10½ **1584**
A988 4¢ rose magenta, cream, perf. 11x10½ **1585**
A994 9¢ slate green, perf. 11x10½ (booklet panes only).. **1590**
A994 9¢ slate green, perf. 10x9¾ (booklet panes only).. **1590A**
A994 9¢ slate green, gray, perf. 11x10½.......... **1591**
A994 9¢ slate green, gray, perf. 10 vert. **1616**
A995 10¢ violet, gray, perf. 10 vert.................. **1617**
A995 10¢ violet, gray, perf. 11x10½ **1592**
A996 11¢ orange, gray, perf. 11x10½ **1593**
A997 12¢ red brown, beige, perf. 11x10½ **1594**
A997 12¢ red brown, beige, perf. 10 vert **1816**
A998 13¢ brown, perf. 11x10½......................... **1595**
A998 13¢ brown, perf. 10 vert. **1618**
A999 13¢ multicolored....................................... **1596**
A1001 15¢ gray, dark blue & red, perf. 11 .... **1597**
A1001 15¢ gray, dark blue & red, perf. 11x10½ (booklet panes only)............................. **1598**
A1001 15¢ gray, dark blue & red, perf. 10 vert. **1618C**
A1002 16¢ blue, perf. 11x10½............................. **1599**
A1002 16¢ blue, perf. 10 vert. **1619**
A1003 24¢ red, blue, perf. 11x10½ **1603**
A1004 28¢ brown, blue, perf. 11x10½.................. **1604**
A1005 29¢ blue, blue, perf. 11x10½.................... **1605**
A1006 30¢ green, perf. 11x10½ **1606**
A1007 50¢ black & orange, perf. 11 .... **1608**
A1008 $1 brown, orange & yellow, tan, perf. 11 .... **1610**
A1009 $2 dark green & red, tan, perf. 11........... **1611**
A1010 $5 red brown, yellow & orange, tan, perf. 11 .... **1612**
A1011 3.1¢ brown, yellow, perf. 10 vert. **1613**
A1199 3.5¢ purple, yellow, perf. 10 vert. **1813**
A1012 7.7¢ brown, bright yellow, perf. 10 vert. **1614**
A1013 7.9¢ carmine, yellow, perf. 10 vert. **1615**
A1014 8.4¢ dark blue, yellow, perf. 10 vert..... **1615C**

FLAG ISSUE 1975-77

13-star Flag over Independence Hall — A1015

Flag over Capitol — A1016

A1015 13¢ dark blue & red, perf. 11x10¾ **1622**
A1015 13¢ dark blue & red, perf. 11¼ **1622C**
A1015 13¢ dark blue & red, perf. 10 vert. **1625**
A1016 13¢ blue & red, perf. 11x10½ (booklet panes only)... **1623**
A1016 13¢ blue & red, perf. 10x9¾ (booklet panes only).. **1623B**

REGULAR ISSUE 1978

Indian Head, Penny, 1877 A1123

Dolley Madison A1209

Red Masterpiece and Medallion Roses — A1126

A1123 13¢ brown & blue, green, bister, perf. 11........ .... **1734**
A1126 15¢ multicolored, perf 10 (booklet panes only)... **1737**
A1209 15¢ red brown & sepia, perf. 11.............. **1822**

REGULAR ISSUE 1978-85

"A" Eagle — A1124

"B" Eagle — A1207

"C" Eagle A1332

"C" Eagle (Booklet) A1333

"D" Eagle
A1496

"D" Eagle
(Booklet)
A1497

A1124 (15¢) orange, perf. 11 .... **1735**
A1124 (15¢) orange, perf. 11x10½ (booklet panes only) **1736**
A1124 (15¢) orange, perf. 10 vert. **1743**
A1207 (18¢) violet, perf. 11x10½ **1818**
A1207 (18¢) violet, perf. 10 (booklet panes only) **1819**
A1207 (18¢) violet, perf. 10 vert. **1820**
A1332 (20¢) brown, perf. 11x10½ **1946**
A1332 (20¢) brown, perf. 10 vert. **1947**
A1333 (20¢) brown, perf. 11x10½ (booklet panes only) **1948**
A1496 (22¢) green, perf. 11 .... **2111**
A1496 (22¢) green, perf. 10 vert. **2112**
A1497 (22¢) green, perf. 11 (booklet panes only) **2113**

GREAT AMERICANS ISSUE 1980-99

A1231

A1551

A1232

A1552

A1233

A1553

A1234

A1554

A1235

A1555

A1556

A1236

A1237

A1238

A1239

A1240

A1557

A1241

A1242

A1243

A1558

A1559

A1244

A1560

A1245

A1246

A1247

A1248

A1249

A1561

A1562

A1250

A1563

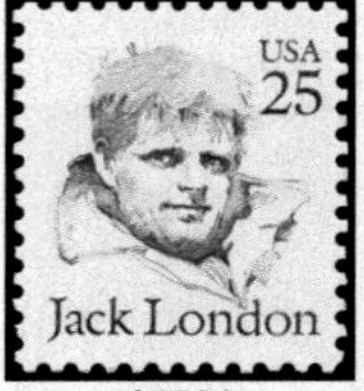

A1564

A1565

A1566

A1567

A1251

A2248

A2249

A2250

A2251

A1252

A1568

A1253

A1254

A1255

A1569

A1570

A2253

A1256

A1571

A2255

A2256

A1572

A1573

A1574

A2257

A2258

A1575

A1576

A1577

A1578

A1231 1¢ black, perf. 11 ... **1844**
A1551 1¢ brownish vermilion, perf. 11 ... **2168**
A1232 2¢ brown black, perf. 11x10½ ... **1845**
A1552 2¢ bright blue, perf. 11 ... **2169**
A1233 3¢ olive green, perf. 11x10½ ... **1846**
A1553 3¢ bright blue, perf. 11 ... **2170**
A1234 4¢ violet, perf. 11x10½ ... **1847**
A1554 4¢ blue violet, perf. 11 ... **2171**
A1235 5¢ henna brown, perf. 11x10½ ... **1848**
A1555 5¢ dark olive green, perf. 11 ... **2172**
A1556 5¢ carmine, perf. 11 ... **2173**
A1236 6¢ orange vermilion, perf. 11 ... **1849**
A1237 7¢ bright carmine, perf. 11 ... **1850**
A1238 8¢ olive black, perf. 11 ... **1851**
A1239 9¢ dark green, perf. 11 ... **1852**
A1240 10¢ Prussian blue, perf. 11 ... **1853**
A1557 10¢ lake, perf. 11 ... **2175**
A1241 11¢ dark blue, perf. 11 ... **1854**
A1242 13¢ light maroon, perf. 11x10½ ... **1855**
A1243 14¢ slate green, perf. 11 ... **1856**
A1558 14¢ crimson, perf. 11 ... **2176**
A1559 15¢ claret, perf. 11 ... **2177**
A1244 17¢ green, perf. 11x10½ ... **1857**
A1560 17¢ dull blue green, perf. 11 ... **2178**
A1245 18¢ dark blue, perf. 11x10½ ... **1858**
A1246 19¢ brown, perf. 11x10½ ... **1859**
A1247 20¢ claret, perf. 11x10½ ... **1860**
A1248 20¢ green, perf. 11x10½ ... **1861**
A1249 20¢ black, perf. 11 ... **1862**
A1561 20¢ red brown, perf. 11 ... **2179**
A1562 21¢ blue violet, perf. 11 ... **2180**
A1250 22¢ dark chalky blue, perf. 11 ... **1863**
A1563 23¢ purple, perf. 11 ... **2181**
A1564 25¢ blue, perf. 11 ... **2182**
A1564 25¢ blue, perf. 10 ... **2197**
A1565 28¢ myrtle green, perf. 11 ... **2183**
A1566 29¢ blue, perf. 11 ... **2184**
A1567 29¢ indigo, perf. 11½x11 ... **2185**
A1251 30¢ olive gray, perf. 11 ... **1864**
A2248 32¢ brown, perf.11.1 ... **2933**
A2249 32¢ green, perf. 11.2 ... **2934**
A2250 32¢ lake, perf. 11.2 ... **2935**
A2251 32¢ blue, perf. 11.2x11.1 ... **2936**
A1252 35¢ gray, perf. 11x10½ ... **1865**
A1568 35¢ black, perf. 11 ... **2186**
A1253 37¢ blue, perf. 11x10½ ... **1866**
A1254 39¢ rose lilac, perf. 11 ... **1867**
A1255 40¢ dark green, perf. 11 ... **1868**
A1569 40¢ dark blue, perf. 11 ... **2187**
A1570 45¢ bright blue, perf. 11 ... **2188**
A2253 46¢ carmine, perf. 11.1 ... **2938**
A1256 50¢ brown, perf. 11 ... **1869**
A1571 52¢ purple, perf. 11 ... **2189**
A2255 55¢ green, perf. 11 ... **2940**
A2256 55¢ black, serpentine die cut 11½, self-adhesive ... **2941**
A1572 56¢ scarlet, perf. 11 ... **2190**
A1573 65¢ dark blue, perf. 11 ... **2191**
A1574 75¢ deep magenta, perf. 11 ... **2192**
A2257 77¢ blue, perf.11.8x11.6 ... **2942**
A2258 78¢ purple, perf. 11.2 ... **2943**
A1575 $1 dark Prussian green, perf. 11 ... **2193**
A1576 $1 dark blue, perf. 11 ... **2194**
A1577 $2 bright violet, perf. 11 ... **2195**

A1578 $5 copper red, perf. 11 ... **2196**

WILDLIFE ISSUES 1981-82

Bighorn — A1267

Puma — A1268

Harbor Seal — A1269

Bison — A1270

Brown bear — A1271

Polar bear — A1272

Elk (wapiti) — A1273

Moose — A1274

White-tailed deer A1275

Pronghorn A1276

Rocky Mountain Bighorn — A1334

FROM BOOKLET PANES

A1267 18¢ dark brown, perf. 11 ... **1880**
A1268 18¢ dark brown, perf. 11 ... **1881**
A1269 18¢ dark brown, perf. 11 ... **1882**
A1270 18¢ dark brown, perf. 11 ... **1883**
A1271 18¢ dark brown, perf. 11 ... **1884**
A1272 18¢ dark brown, perf. 11 ... **1885**
A1273 18¢ dark brown, perf. 11 ... **1886**
A1274 18¢ dark brown, perf. 11 ... **1887**
A1275 18¢ dark brown, perf. 11 ... **1888**
A1276 18¢ dark brown, perf. 11 ... **1889**
A1334 20¢ dark blue, perf. 11 ... **1949**

FLAG ISSUES 1981-85

A1277

A1278

Field of 1777 flag — A1279

A1280

A1281

A1498

Of the People, By the People, For the People
A1499

A1277 18¢ multicolored, perf. 11 1890
A1278 18¢ multicolored, perf. 10 vert. 1891
A1279 6¢ perf. 11 (booklet panes only)..................... 1892
A1280 18¢ perf. 11 (booklet panes only)..................... 1893
A1281 20¢ black, dark blue & red, perf. 11 1894
A1281 20¢ black, dark blue & red, perf. 10 vert. 1895
A1281 20¢ black, dark blue & red, perf. 11x10½ (booklet panes only) 1896
A1498 22¢ blue, red & black, perf. 11 2114
A1498 22¢ blue, red & black, perf. 10 vert. 2115
A1499 22¢ blue, red & black, perf. 10 horiz. (booklet panes only) 2116

TRANSPORTATION ISSUE 1981-95

A1283

A1604a

A1284

A1604b

A1284a

A1622

A1506

A1285

A1810

A1286

A1811

A1812

A1624

A1288

A1510

A1625

A1507

A1623

A1811a

A1287

A1508

A1509

A1289

A1511

A1626

A1290

A1816

A1291

A1514

A1516

A1629

A1630

A1512

A1627

A1513

A1292

A1515

A1628

A1517

A1631

A1293

A1518

A1632

A1294

A1295

A1633

A1822

A1634

A1635

A1823

A1636

A1519

A1825

A1827

A1283 1¢ violet **1897**
A1604a 1¢ violet **2225**
A1284 2¢ black **1897A**
A1604b 2¢ black **2226**
A1284a 3¢ dark green **1898**
A1622 3¢ claret **2252**
A1506 3.4¢ dark bluish green **2123**
A1285 4¢ reddish brown, inscription 19 ½mm long **1898A**
A1285 4¢ reddish brown, inscription 17mm long **2228**
A1810 4¢ claret **2451**
A1507 4.9¢ brown black **2124**
A1286 5¢ gray green **1899**
A1623 5¢ black **2253**

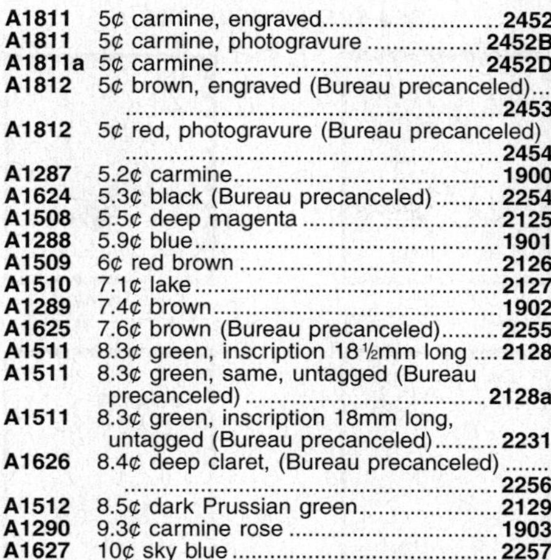

A1811 5¢ carmine, engraved **2452**
A1811 5¢ carmine, photogravure **2452B**
A1811a 5¢ carmine **2452D**
A1812 5¢ brown, engraved (Bureau precanceled) **2453**
A1812 5¢ red, photogravure (Bureau precanceled) **2454**
A1287 5.2¢ carmine **1900**
A1624 5.3¢ black (Bureau precanceled) **2254**
A1508 5.5¢ deep magenta **2125**
A1288 5.9¢ blue **1901**
A1509 6¢ red brown **2126**
A1510 7.1¢ lake **2127**
A1289 7.4¢ brown **1902**
A1625 7.6¢ brown (Bureau precanceled) **2255**
A1511 8.3¢ green, inscription 18 ½mm long **2128**
A1511 8.3¢ green, same, untagged (Bureau precanceled) **2128a**
A1511 8.3¢ green, inscription 18mm long, untagged (Bureau precanceled) **2231**
A1626 8.4¢ deep claret, (Bureau precanceled) **2256**
A1512 8.5¢ dark Prussian green **2129**
A1290 9.3¢ carmine rose **1903**
A1627 10¢ sky blue **2257**
A1816 10¢ green, engraved (Bureau precanceled) **2457**
A1816 10¢ green, photogravure (Bureau precanceled **2458**
A1513 10.1¢ slate blue **2130**
A1291 10.9¢ purple **1904**
A1292 11¢ red **1905**
A1514 11¢ dark green **2131**
A1515 12¢ dark blue **2132**
A1516 12.5¢ olive green **2133**
A1628 13¢ black, (Bureau precanceled) **2258**
A1629 13.2¢ slate green, (Bureau precanceled) **2259**
A1517 14¢ sky blue **2134**
A1630 15¢ violet **2260**
A1631 16.7¢ rose, (Bureau precanceled) **2261**
A1293 17¢ ultramarine **1906**
A1518 17¢ sky blue **2135**
A1632 17.5¢ dark violet **2262**
A1294 18¢ dark brown **1907**
A1295 20¢ vermilion **1908**
A1633 20¢ blue violet **2263**
A1822 20¢ green **2463**
A1634 20.5¢ rose, (Bureau precanceled) **2264**
A1635 21¢ olive green, (Bureau precanceled) **2265**
A1823 23¢ dark blue **2464**
A1636 24.1¢ deep ultramarine, (Bureau precanceled) **2266**
A1519 25¢ orange brown **2136**
A1825 32¢ blue **2466**
A1811 50¢ red, imperf. **4905c**
A1827 $1 dark blue & scarlet **2468**

REGULAR ISSUE 1983-99

A1894

A1897

A1898

A2532

A1758

Eagle and Moon A1296

A1895

Eagle and Half Moon — A1505

A1898a

A2533

A1896

A1894 $2.90 multicolored, perf. 11 .... **2540**
A1897 $2.90 multicolored, perf. 11x10½.......... **2543**
A1898 $3 multicolored, perf. 11 .... **2544**
A2532 $3.20 multicolored, serpentine die cut 11.5 .... **3261**
A1758 $8.75 multicolored, perf. 11 .... **2394**
A1296 $9.35 multicolored, perf. 10 vert. (booklet panes only) **1909**
A1296 $9.35 multicolored, booklet pane of 3 .... **1909a**
A1895 $9.95 multicolored, perf. 11 .... **2541**
A1505 $10.75 multicolored, perf. 10 vert. (booklet panes only) **2122**
A1898a $10.75 multicolored, perf. 11 .... **2544A**
A2533 $11.75 multicolored, serpentine die cut 11.5 .... **3262**
A1896 $14 multicolored, perf. 11 .... **2542**

REGULAR ISSUE 1982-85

George Washington Washington Monument — A1532

Consumer Education — A1390

Sealed Envelopes — A1533

A1532 18¢ multicolored, perf. 10 vert. **2149**
A1532 18¢ multicolored, same, untagged (Bureau precanceled) **2149a**
A1390 20¢ sky blue, perf. 10 vert. **2005**
A1533 21.1¢ multicolored, perf. 10 vert. **2150**
A1533 21.1¢ multicolored, same, untagged (Bureau precanceled) **2150a**

SEA SHELLS ISSUE 1985

Frilled Dogwinkle — A1500

Reticulated Helmet — A1501

New England Neptune — A1502

Calico Scallop — A1503

Lightning Whelk — A1504

A1500 22¢ black and brown, perf. 10 on 2 or 3 sides (booklet panes only).................... **2117**
A1501 22¢ black and multicolored, perf. 10 on 2 or 3 sides (booklet panes only) **2118**
A1502 22¢ black and brown, perf. 10 on 2 or 3 sides (booklet panes only).................... **2119**
A1503 22¢ black and violet, perf. 10 on 2 or 3 sides (booklet panes only) **2120**
A1504 22¢ black and multicolored, perf. 10 on 2 or 3 sides (booklet panes only) **2121**

REGULAR ISSUE 1987-88

A1646

A1647

A1648

A1649

A1646 22¢ multicolored, perf. 11........................ **2276**
A1647 (25¢) multicolored, perf. 11..................... **2277**
A1647 (25¢) multicolored, perf. 10 on 2 or 3 sides (booklet panes only) **2282**
A1647 (25¢) multicolored, perf. 10 vert. **2279**
A1648 25¢ multicolored, perf. 11........................ **2278**
A1648 25¢ multicolored, perf. 10...................... **2285A**
A1649 25¢ multicolored, perf. 10 vert. **2280**

FLORA & FAUNA ISSUE 1988-2001

A1840

A1841

A2335

A1842

A2336

A1843

A1847

A2350

A1649a

A1649b

A1649c

A1649d

A1848

A1849

A1852

A1853

A1854

A1875

A1879

A1844

A1850

A1851

A2351

A2550

A2551

A2552

A2553

A2634

A2635

A2636

A2637

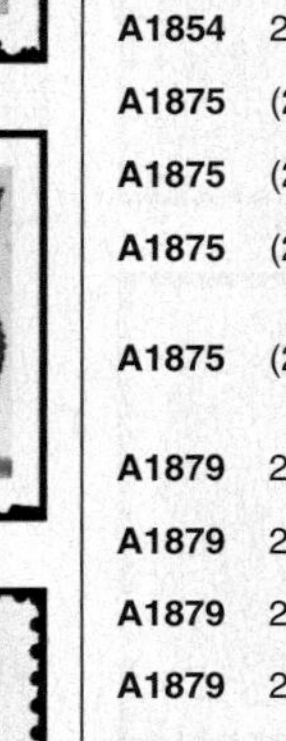
A2694

A2695

A1845

A2339

A1846

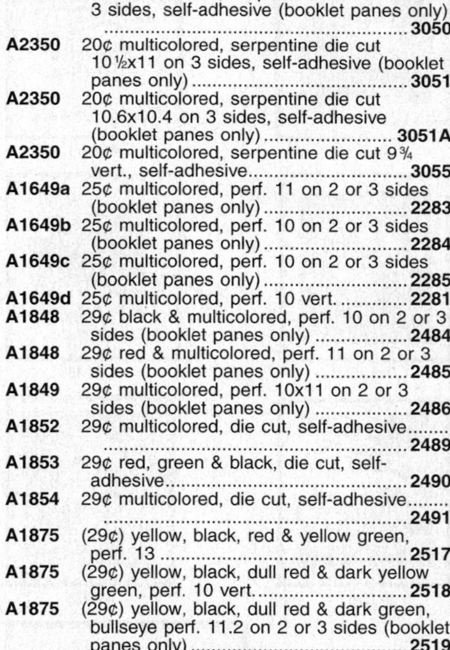

A1840 1¢ multicolored, perf. 11 .... **2476**
A1841 1¢ multicolored, perf. 11.2 .... **2477**
A1841 1¢ multicolored, serpentine die cut 10½, self-adhesive **3031**
A1841 1¢ multicolored, blue inscriptions, serpentine die cut 11¼, self-adhesive **3031A**
A1841 1¢ multicolored, perf. 9¾ vert. **3044**
A2335 2¢ multicolored, perf. 11 .... **3032**
A2335 2¢ multicolored, perf. 9¾ vert. **3045**
A1842 3¢ multicolored, perf. 11 .... **2478**
A2336 3¢ multicolored, perf. 11 .... **3033**
A1843 19¢ multicolored, perf. 11 .... **2479**
A1847 20¢ multicolored, perf. 10.9x9.8 on 2 or 3 sides (booklet panes only) **2483**
A1847 20¢ multicolored, serpentine die cut 10.4x10.8 on 2 or 3 sides, self-adhesive (booklet panes only) **3048**
A1847 20¢ multicolored, serpentine die cut 11½ vert., self-adhesive **3053**
A2350 20¢ multicolored, serpentine die cut 11.2 on 3 sides, self-adhesive (booklet panes only) **3050**
A2350 20¢ multicolored, serpentine die cut 10½x11 on 3 sides, self-adhesive (booklet panes only) **3051**
A2350 20¢ multicolored, serpentine die cut 10.6x10.4 on 3 sides, self-adhesive (booklet panes only) **3051A**
A2350 20¢ multicolored, serpentine die cut 9¾ vert., self-adhesive **3055**
A1649a 25¢ multicolored, perf. 11 on 2 or 3 sides (booklet panes only) **2283**
A1649b 25¢ multicolored, perf. 10 on 2 or 3 sides (booklet panes only) **2284**
A1649c 25¢ multicolored, perf. 10 on 2 or 3 sides (booklet panes only) **2285**
A1649d 25¢ multicolored, perf. 10 vert. **2281**
A1848 29¢ black & multicolored, perf. 10 on 2 or 3 sides (booklet panes only) **2484**
A1848 29¢ red & multicolored, perf. 11 on 2 or 3 sides (booklet panes only) **2485**
A1849 29¢ multicolored, perf. 10x11 on 2 or 3 sides (booklet panes only) **2486**
A1852 29¢ multicolored, die cut, self-adhesive **2489**
A1853 29¢ red, green & black, die cut, self-adhesive **2490**
A1854 29¢ multicolored, die cut, self-adhesive **2491**
A1875 (29¢) yellow, black, red & yellow green, perf. 13 .... **2517**
A1875 (29¢) yellow, black, dull red & dark yellow green, perf. 10 vert. **2518**
A1875 (29¢) yellow, black, dull red & dark green, bullseye perf. 11.2 on 2 or 3 sides (booklet panes only) **2519**
A1875 (29¢) pale yellow, black, red & bright green, perf. 11 on 2 or 3 sides (booklet panes only) **2520**
A1879 29¢ dull yellow, black, red & yellow green, perf. 11 .... **2524**
A1879 29¢ dull yellow, black, red & yellow green, perf. 13x12¾ **2524A**
A1879 29¢ pale yellow, black, red & yellow green, roulette 10 vert. **2525**
A1879 29¢ pale yellow, black, red & yellow green, perf. 10 vert. **2526**
A1879 29¢ pale yellow, black, red & bright green, perf. 11 on 2 or 3 sides (booklet panes only) **2527**
A1844 30¢ multicolored, perf. 11 .... **2480**
A1850 32¢ multicolored, perf. 11x10 on 2 or 3 sides (booklet panes only) **2487**
A1850 32¢ multicolored, serpentine die cut 8.8 on 2, 3 or 4 sides, self-adhesive (booklet panes only) **2493**
A1850 32¢ multicolored, serpentine die cut 8.8 vert., self-adhesive **2495**

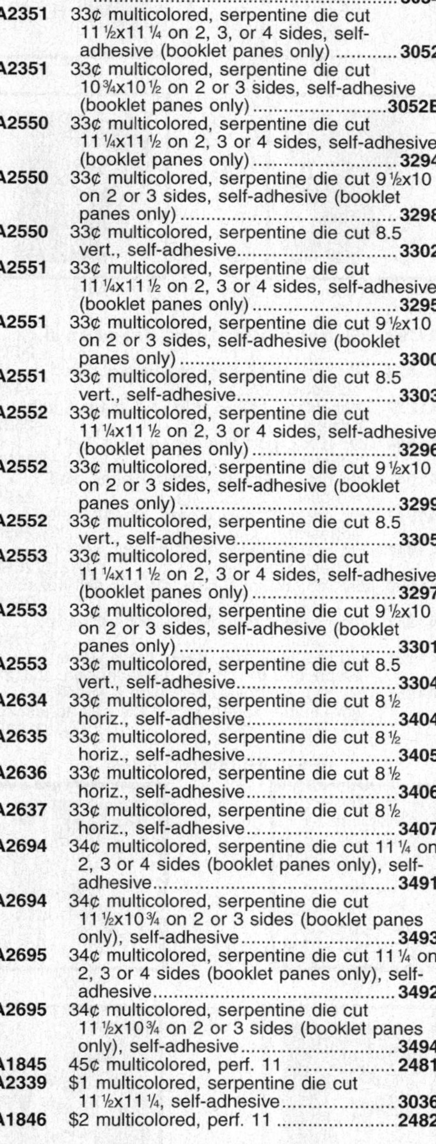

A1851 32¢ multicolored, perf. 11x10 on 2 or 3 sides (booklet panes only) **2488**
A1851 32¢ multicolored, serpentine die cut 8.8 on 2, 3 or 4 sides, self-adhesive (booklet panes only) **2494**
A1851 32¢ multicolored, serpentine die cut 8.8 vert., self-adhesive **2495A**
A1853 32¢ pink, green & black, serpentine die cut 11.3x11.7 on 2, 3 or 4 sides, self-adhesive (booklet panes only) **2492**
A1853 32¢ yellow, orange, green & black, serpentine die cut 11.3x11.7 on 2, 3 or 4 sides, self-adhesive (booklet panes only) **3049**
A1853 32¢ yellow, magenta, black & green, serpentine die cut 9¾ vert., self-adhesive **3054**
A2351 33¢ multicolored, serpentine die cut 11½x11¼ on 2, 3, or 4 sides, self-adhesive (booklet panes only) **3052**
A2351 33¢ multicolored, serpentine die cut 10¾x10½ on 2 or 3 sides, self-adhesive (booklet panes only) **3052E**
A2550 33¢ multicolored, serpentine die cut 11¼x11½ on 2, 3 or 4 sides, self-adhesive (booklet panes only) **3294**
A2550 33¢ multicolored, serpentine die cut 9½x10 on 2 or 3 sides, self-adhesive (booklet panes only) **3298**
A2550 33¢ multicolored, serpentine die cut 8.5 vert., self-adhesive **3302**
A2551 33¢ multicolored, serpentine die cut 11¼x11½ on 2, 3 or 4 sides, self-adhesive (booklet panes only) **3295**
A2551 33¢ multicolored, serpentine die cut 9½x10 on 2 or 3 sides, self-adhesive (booklet panes only) **3300**
A2551 33¢ multicolored, serpentine die cut 8.5 vert., self-adhesive **3303**
A2552 33¢ multicolored, serpentine die cut 11¼x11½ on 2, 3 or 4 sides, self-adhesive (booklet panes only) **3296**
A2552 33¢ multicolored, serpentine die cut 9½x10 on 2 or 3 sides, self-adhesive (booklet panes only) **3299**
A2552 33¢ multicolored, serpentine die cut 8.5 vert., self-adhesive **3305**
A2553 33¢ multicolored, serpentine die cut 11¼x11½ on 2, 3 or 4 sides, self-adhesive (booklet panes only) **3297**
A2553 33¢ multicolored, serpentine die cut 9½x10 on 2 or 3 sides, self-adhesive (booklet panes only) **3301**
A2553 33¢ multicolored, serpentine die cut 8.5 vert., self-adhesive **3304**
A2634 33¢ multicolored, serpentine die cut 8½ horiz., self-adhesive **3404**
A2635 33¢ multicolored, serpentine die cut 8½ horiz., self-adhesive **3405**
A2636 33¢ multicolored, serpentine die cut 8½ horiz., self-adhesive **3406**
A2637 33¢ multicolored, serpentine die cut 8½ horiz., self-adhesive **3407**
A2694 34¢ multicolored, serpentine die cut 11¼ on 2, 3 or 4 sides (booklet panes only), self-adhesive **3491**
A2694 34¢ multicolored, serpentine die cut 11½x10¾ on 2 or 3 sides (booklet panes only), self-adhesive **3493**
A2695 34¢ multicolored, serpentine die cut 11¼ on 2, 3 or 4 sides (booklet panes only), self-adhesive **3492**
A2695 34¢ multicolored, serpentine die cut 11½x10¾ on 2 or 3 sides (booklet panes only), self-adhesive **3494**
A1845 45¢ multicolored, perf. 11 .... **2481**
A2339 $1 multicolored, serpentine die cut 11½x11¼, self-adhesive **3036**
A1846 $2 multicolored, perf. 11 .... **2482**

REGULAR ISSUE 1989-98

A1793

A1834

A1877

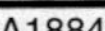
A1884

A1947

A1950

A1951

A1793 25¢ multicolored, die cut, self-adhesive **2431**
A1834 25¢ dark red & dark blue, die cut, self-adhesive **2475**
A1877 (29¢) black, blue & dark red, die cut, self-adhesive **2522**
A1884 29¢ black, gold & green, die cut, self-adhesive **2531A**
A1947 29¢ brown & multicolored, die cut, self-adhesive **2595**
A1947 29¢ green & multicolored, die cut, self-adhesive **2596**
A1947 29¢ red & multicolored, die cut, self-adhesive **2597**
A1950 29¢ red, cream & blue, die cut, self-adhesive **2598**
A1951 29¢ multicolored, die cut, self-adhesive **2599**
A1951 32¢ red, light blue, dark blue & yellow, serpentine die cut 11, self-adhesive **3122**
A1951 32¢ red, light blue, dark blue & yellow, serpentine die cut 11.5x11.8, self-adhesive **3122E**

REGULAR ISSUE 1990-94

A1876

A1802

A1881

A1882

A1878

A1880

A1883

A1876 (4¢) bister & carmine, perf. 11 .... **2521**
A1802 15¢ multicolored, perf. 11 (booklet panes only) **2443**
A1881 19¢ multicolored, perf. 10 vert., two rope loops on piling **2529**
A1881 19¢ multicolored, perf. 10 vert., one rope loop on piling **2529C**
A1882 19¢ multicolored, perf. 10 (booklet panes only) **2530**
A1878 29¢ multicolored, engraved, perf. 10 vert. **2523**
A1878 29¢ multicolored, photogravure, perf. 10 vert. **2523A**
A1880 29¢ multicolored, perf. 11 (booklet panes only) **2528**
A1883 29¢ multicolored, perf. 11 .... **2531**

REGULAR ISSUE 1991-98

A1956

A1957

A2534

A1959

A1960

A1946

A1961

A1939

A1942

A1944

A1956 (10¢) multicolored, perf. 10 vert. (Bureau precanceled) **2602**
A1957 (10¢) orange yellow & multicolored, perf. 10 vert. (Bureau precanceled) **2603**
A1957 (10¢) gold & multicolored, perf. 10 vert. (Bureau precanceled) **2604**
A1957 (10¢) gold & multicolored, serpentine die cut 11.5 vert, self-adhesive **2907**
A2534 (10¢) multicolored, perf. 9.9 vert. (Bureau precanceled) **3270**
A2534 (10¢) multicolored, serpentine die cut 9.9 vert., self-adhesive (Bureau precanceled) **3271**
A1959 (23¢) multicolored, perf. 10 vert. (Bureau precanceled) **2605**
A1960 23¢ multicolored, perf. 10 vert., "First-Class" 9½mm long (Bureau precanceled) **2606**
A1960 23¢ multicolored, perf. 10 vert., "First-Class" 9mm long (Bureau precanceled) **2607**
A1960 23¢ violet blue, red & black, perf. 10 vert., "First Class" 8½mm long (Bureau precanceled) **2608**
A1946 29¢ black & multicolored, perf. 10 (booklet panes only) **2593**
A1946 29¢ black & multicolored, perf. 11x10 (booklet panes only) **2593B**
A1946 29¢ red & multicolored, perf. 11x10 (booklet panes only) **2594**
A1961 29¢ blue & red, perf. 10 vert. **2609**
A1939 32¢ red brown, perf. 11.2 .... **2587**
A1942 $1 blue, perf. 11½ **2590**
A1944 $5 slate green, perf. 11½ **2592**

G RATE ISSUE 1994-95

A2206

A2210

A2207

A2209

A2208

A2206 (3¢) tan, bright blue & red, perf. 11x10.8 .... **2877**
A2206 (3¢) tan, dark blue & red, perf. 10.8x10.9 .... **2878**
A2210 (5¢) green & multicolored, perf. 9.8 vert. (Bureau precanceled) **2893**
A2207 (20¢) black "G," yellow & multicolored, perf. 11.2x11.1 .... **2879**
A2207 (20¢) red "G," yellow & multicolored, perf. 11x10.9 .... **2880**

A2209 (25¢) black "G," blue & multicolored, perf. 9.8 vert.(Bureau precanceled) **2888**
A2208 (32¢) black "G" & multicolored, perf. 11.2x11.1 .... **2881**
A2208 (32¢) black "G" & multicolored, perf. 10x9.9 (booklet panes only) **2883**
A2208 (32¢) black "G" & multicolored, die cut, self-adhesive, small number of blue shading dots in white stripes below blue field ... **2886**
A2208 (32¢) black "G" & multicolored, die cut, self-adhesive, thin translucent paper, more blue shading dots in white stripes below blue field **2887**
A2208 (32¢) black "G" & multicolored, perf. 9.8 vert. **2889**
A2208 (32¢) red "G" & multicolored, perf. 11x10.9, distance from bottom of "G" to top of flag is 13¾mm **2882**
A2208 (32¢) red "G" & multicolored, perf. 11x10.9 on 2 or 3 sides (booklet panes only), distance from bottom of "G" to top of flag is 13½mm **2885**
A2208 (32¢) red "G" & multicolored, perf. 9.8 vert. **2891**
A2208 (32¢) red "G" & multicolored, rouletted. 9.8 vert. **2892**
A2208 (32¢) blue "G" & multicolored, perf. 10.9 (booklet panes only) **2884**
A2208 (32¢) blue "G" & multicolored, perf. 9.8 vert. **2890**

REGULAR ISSUE 1995-2008

A2217

A2218

A2489

A2853

A2220

A2509

A2223

A2724

A2225

A2225a

A2490

A2212

A2230

A2217 (5¢) yellow, red & blue, perf. 9.8 vert. (Bureau precanceled) **2902**
A2217 (5¢) yellow, red & blue, serpentine die cut 11.5 vert, self-adhesive (Bureau precanceled) **2902B**
A2218 (5¢) purple & multicolored, perf. 9.9 vert. (Bureau precanceled) **2903**
A2218 (5¢) purple & multicolored, serpentine die cut 11.2 vert., self-adhesive (Bureau precanceled) **2904A**
A2218 (5¢) purple & multicolored, serpentine die cut 9.8 vert., self-adhesive (Bureau precanceled) **2904B**
A2218 (5¢) blue & multicolored, perf. 9.9 vert. (Bureau precanceled) **2904**
A2489 (5¢) multicolored, perf. 10 vert. (Bureau precanceled) **3207**
A2489 (5¢) multicolored, serpentine die cut 9.7 vert., self-adhesive (Bureau precanceled).... .... **3207A**
A2853 (5¢) multicolored, serpentine die cut 8½ vert., "2002" date, self-adhesive (Bureau precanceled) **3693**
A2853 (5¢) multicolored, perf. 9¾ vert., "2003" date in blue, unclear dots in surf (Bureau precanceled) **3775**
A2853 (5¢) multicolored, black "2003" year date, serpentine die cut 9½x10 (coil stamp), self-adhesive (Bureau precanceled) **3785**
A2853 (5¢) multicolored, perf. 9¾ vert., "2004" date in black, rows of dots in surf (Bureau precanceled) **3864**
A2853 (5¢) multicolored, serpentine die cut 10 vert., "2003" date in black, self-adhesive (Bureau precanceled) **3874**
A2853 (5¢) multicolored, serpentine die cut 11½ vert., "2004" date in black, self-adhesive (Bureau precanceled) **3875**
A2853 (5¢) multicolored, perf. 9¾ vert., "2008" date in black, with microprinted "USPS" (Bureau precanceled) **4348**
A2220 (10¢) black, red brown & brown, perf. 9.8 vert. (Bureau precanceled) **2905**
A2220 (10¢) black, red brown & brown, serpentine die cut 11.5 vert., self-adhesive (Bureau precanceled) **2906**
A2509 (10¢) multicolored, serpentine die cut 9.8 vert., self-adhesive (Bureau precanceled).... .... **3228**
A2509 (10¢) multicolored, perf 9.9 vert. (Bureau precanceled) **3229**
A2223 (15¢) dark orange, yellow & multicolored (dark, bold colors, heavy shading lines, heavily shaded chrome), blue "2005" year date, perf. 9.8 vert. **2908**
A2223 (15¢) buff & multicolored (more subdued colors, finer details, shinier chrome), black "2005" year date, perf. 9.8 vert. **2909**
A2223 (15¢) buff & multicolored, serpentine die cut 11.5 vert., self-adhesive **2910**
A2724 (15¢) multicolored, serpentine die cut 11½ vert., self-adhesive (Bureau precanceled **3522**
A2225 (25¢) dark red, dark yellow green & multicolored (dark, saturated colors, dark blue lines in music selection board), perf. 9.8 vert. **2911**
A2225 (25¢) dark red, yellow green & multicolored, serpentine die cut 9.8 vert, self-adhesive **2912B**
A2225 (25¢) bright orange red, bright yellow green & multicolored (bright colors, less shading and light blue lines in music selection board), perf. 9.8 vert. **2912**
A2225 (25¢) bright orange red, bright yellow green & multicolored, serpentine die cut 11.5 vert., self-adhesive **2912A**

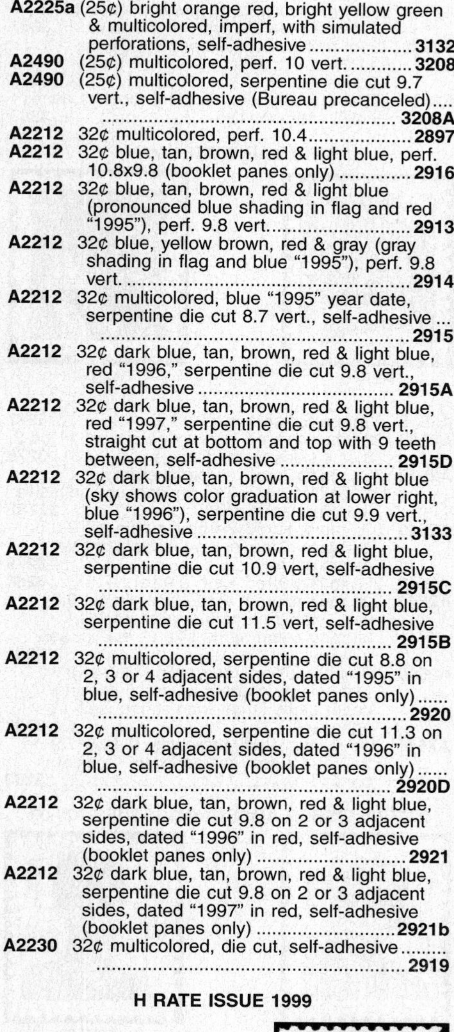

A2225a (25¢) bright orange red, bright yellow green & multicolored, imperf, with simulated perforations, self-adhesive **3132**
A2490 (25¢) multicolored, perf. 10 vert. **3208**
A2490 (25¢) multicolored, serpentine die cut 9.7 vert., self-adhesive (Bureau precanceled).... .... **3208A**
A2212 32¢ multicolored, perf. 10.4 .... **2897**
A2212 32¢ blue, tan, brown, red & light blue, perf. 10.8x9.8 (booklet panes only) **2916**
A2212 32¢ blue, tan, brown, red & light blue (pronounced blue shading in flag and red "1995"), perf. 9.8 vert. **2913**
A2212 32¢ blue, yellow brown, red & gray (gray shading in flag and blue "1995"), perf. 9.8 vert. **2914**
A2212 32¢ multicolored, blue "1995" year date, serpentine die cut 8.7 vert., self-adhesive **2915**
A2212 32¢ dark blue, tan, brown, red & light blue, red "1996," serpentine die cut 9.8 vert., self-adhesive **2915A**
A2212 32¢ dark blue, tan, brown, red & light blue, red "1997," serpentine die cut 9.8 vert., straight cut at bottom and top with 9 teeth between, self-adhesive **2915D**
A2212 32¢ dark blue, tan, brown, red & light blue (sky shows color graduation at lower right, blue "1996"), serpentine die cut 9.9 vert., self-adhesive **3133**
A2212 32¢ dark blue, tan, brown, red & light blue, serpentine die cut 10.9 vert, self-adhesive **2915C**
A2212 32¢ dark blue, tan, brown, red & light blue, serpentine die cut 11.5 vert, self-adhesive **2915B**
A2212 32¢ multicolored, serpentine die cut 8.8 on 2, 3 or 4 adjacent sides, dated "1995" in blue, self-adhesive (booklet panes only)...... .... **2920**
A2212 32¢ multicolored, serpentine die cut 11.3 on 2, 3 or 4 adjacent sides, dated "1996" in blue, self-adhesive (booklet panes only)...... .... **2920D**
A2212 32¢ dark blue, tan, brown, red & light blue, serpentine die cut 9.8 on 2 or 3 adjacent sides, dated "1996" in red, self-adhesive (booklet panes only) **2921**
A2212 32¢ dark blue, tan, brown, red & light blue, serpentine die cut 9.8 on 2 or 3 adjacent sides, dated "1997" in red, self-adhesive (booklet panes only) **2921b**
A2230 32¢ multicolored, die cut, self-adhesive......... .... **2919**

H RATE ISSUE 1999

A2529

A2530

A2531

A2529 (1¢) multicolored, white USA, black "1998," perf. 11.2 .... **3257**
A2529 (1¢) multicolored, pale blue USA, blue "1998," perf. 11.2 .... **3258**
A2530 22¢ multicolored, serpentine die cut 10.8, self-adhesive **3259**
A2530 22¢ multicolored, serpentine die cut 9.9 vert, self-adhesive **3263**
A2530 22¢ multicolored, perf. 9¾ vert. **3353**
A2531 (33¢) multicolored, perf. 11.2 .... **3260**
A2531 (33¢) multicolored, perf. 9.8 vert. **3264**
A2531 (33¢) multicolored, serpentine die cut 9.9 vert., stamp corners at right angles, backing paper same size as stamp, self-adhesive **3265**
A2531 (33¢) multicolored, serpentine die cut 9.9 vert., stamp corners rounded, backing paper larger than stamp, self-adhesive....... .... **3266**

A2531 (33¢) multicolored, serpentine die cut 9.9, (booklet panes only), self-adhesive **3267**
A2531 (33¢) multicolored, serpentine die cut 11.2x11.1 (booklet panes only), self-adhesive **3268**
A2531 (33¢) multicolored, die cut 8 (booklet panes only), self-adhesive **3269**

REGULAR ISSUE 1999

A2540  A2541

A2540 33¢ multicolored, perf. 11.2 ...... **3277**
A2540 33¢ multicolored, serpentine die cut 11 on 2, 3 or 4 sides, self-adhesive **3278**
A2540 33¢ multicolored, serpentine die cut 11½x11¾ on 2, 3 or 4 sides, self-adhesive (booklet panes only) **3278F**
A2540 33¢ multicolored, serpentine die cut 9.8 on 2, 3 or 4 sides, self-adhesive (booklet panes only) **3279**
A2540 33¢ multicolored, perf. 9.9 vert. **3280**
A2540 33¢ multicolored, serpentine die cut 9.8 vert., stamp corners at right angles, backing paper same size as stamp, self-adhesive **3281**
A2540 33¢ multicolored, serpentine die cut 9.8 vert., stamp corners rounded, backing paper same larger than stamp, self-adhesive **3282**
A2541 33¢ multicolored, serpentine die cut 7.9 on 2, 3 or 4 sides, self-adhesive (booklet panes only) **3283**

DISTINGUISHED AMERICANS ISSUE 2000-09

A2650  A2652  A2656  A2657  A2657a  A2658  A2660  A2661  A2661a  A2661b  A2662  A2663  A2664

A2650 10¢ red & black, perf 11 ...... **3420**
A2652 23¢ red & black, litho. & engr., serpentine die cut 11¼x10¾, self-adhesive **3422**
A2652 23¢ red & black, litho., serpentine die cut 11¼x10¾ on 3 sides, self-adhesive (booklet panes only) **3436**
A2656 33¢ red & black, perf 11 ...... **3426**
A2657 58¢ red & black, serpentine die cut 11, self-adhesive **3427**
A2657a 59¢ multicolored, serpentine die cut 11¼x10¾, self-adhesive **3427A**
A2658 63¢ red & black, serpentine die cut 11¼x11, self-adhesive **3428**
A2660 75¢ red & black, serpentine die cut 11¼x10¾, self-adhesive **3430**
A2661 76¢ red & black, serpentine die cut 11, self-adhesive **3431**
A2661 76¢ red & black, serpentine die cut 11½x11, self-adhesive **3432**
A2661a 76¢ multicolored, serpentine die cut 11¼x10¾, self-adhesive **3432A**
A2661b 78¢ multicolored, serpentine die cut 11¼x10¾, self-adhesive **3432B**
A2662 83¢ red & black, "2002" year date, serpentine die cut 11x11¾, self-adhesive **3433**
A2663 83¢ red & black, "2003" year date, serpentine die cut 11¼, self-adhesive **3434**
A2664 87¢ red & black, serpentine die cut 11¼x11, self-adhesive **3435**

AMERICAN CULTURE ISSUE 2000-03

A2677  A2722  A2875

A2677 (10¢) multicolored, serpentine die cut 11½ vert., self adhesive (Bureau precanceled) **3447**
A2677 (10¢) multicolored, perf. 10 vert. (Bureau precanceled) **3769**
A2722 (10¢) multicolored, "2001" year date, serpentine die cut 8½ vert., self-adhesive (Bureau precanceled) **3520**
A2722 (10¢) multicolored, "2003" year date, serpentine die cut 11 vert., self-adhesive (Bureau precanceled) **3770**
A2875 $1 multicolored, serpentine die cut 11¼x11 vert., self-adhesive **3766**

REGULAR ISSUE 2000-03

A2686  A2687  A2678  A2679  A2680  A2681  A2682  A2683  A2684  A2685  A2688  A2689  A2690  A2691

A2692

A2693

A2696

A2686 20¢ dark carmine, serpentine die cut 11¼x11 on 3 sides (booklet panes only), self-adhesive **3482**
A2686 20¢ dark carmine, serpentine die cut 10½x11 on 3 sides (booklet panes only), self-adhesive **3483**
A2687 21¢ multicolored, perf. 11¼.......... **3467**
A2687 21¢ multicolored, serpentine die cut 11¼ on 3 sides, self-adhesive (booklet panes only) **3484**
A2687 21¢ multicolored, serpentine die cut 10½x11¼ on 3 sides, self-adhesive (booklet panes only.......... **3484A**
A2687 21¢ multicolored, serpentine die cut 11, self-adhesive **3468**
A2687 21¢ multicolored, serpentine die cut 8½ vert., self-adhesive **3475**
A2686 23¢ green, perf. 11¼.......... **3616**
A2686 23¢ green, serpentine die cut 11¼x11¾, self-adhesive **3468A**
A2686 23¢ green, "2001" year date, serpentine die cut 8½ vert., self-adhesive (Banknote Corp. Printing).......... **3475A**
A2686 23¢ gray green, "2002" year date, serpentine die cut 8½ vert., self-adhesive (Avery Printing).......... **3617**
A2686 23¢ green, serpentine die cut 11¼x11 on 3 sides, self-adhesive (booklet panes only) **3618**
A2686 23¢ green, serpentine die cut 10½x11¼ on 3 sides, self-adhesive (booklet panes only) **3619**
A2686 23¢ gray green, serpentine die cut 11, self-adhesive (Avery Printing).......... **3819**
A2678 (34¢) multicolored, perf. 111/4 .... **3448**
A2678 (34¢) multicolored, serpentine die cut 11¼, self-adhesive **3449**
A2678 (34¢) multicolored, serpentine die cut 8 on 2, 3 or 4 sides (booklet panes only), self-adhesive **3450**
A2679 (34¢) multicolored, serpentine die cut 11 on 2, 3 or 4 sides (booklet panes only), self-adhesive **3451**
A2680 (34¢) multicolored, perf. 9¾ vert. **3452**
A2680 (34¢) multicolored, serpentine die cut 10 vert., self-adhesive **3453**
A2681 (34¢) purple & multicolored, serpentine die cut 10½x10¾ on 2 or 3 sides (booklet panes only), self-adhesive **3454**
A2681 (34¢) purple & multicolored, serpentine die cut 11½x11¾ on 2 or 3 sides (booklet panes only), self-adhesive **3458**
A2681 (34¢) purple & multicolored, serpentine die cut 8½ vert., self-adhesive.......... **3465**
A2682 (34¢) tan & multicolored, serpentine die cut 10½x10¾ on 2 or 3 sides (booklet panes only), self-adhesive **3455**
A2682 (34¢) tan & multicolored, serpentine die cut 11½x11¾ on 2 or 3 sides (booklet panes only), self-adhesive **3459**
A2682 (34¢) tan & multicolored, serpentine die cut 8½ vert., self-adhesive.......... **3464**
A2683 (34¢) green & multicolored, serpentine die cut 10½x10¾ on 2 or 3 sides (booklet panes only), self-adhesive **3456**
A2683 (34¢) green & multicolored, serpentine die cut 11½x11¾ on 2 or 3 sides (booklet panes only), self-adhesive **3460**
A2683 (34¢) green & multicolored, serpentine die cut 8½ vert., self-adhesive.......... **3462**
A2684 (34¢) red & multicolored, serpentine die cut 10½x10¾ on 2 or 3 sides (booklet panes only), self-adhesive **3457**
A2684 (34¢) red & multicolored, serpentine die cut 11½x11¾ on 2 or 3 sides (booklet panes only), self-adhesive **3461**

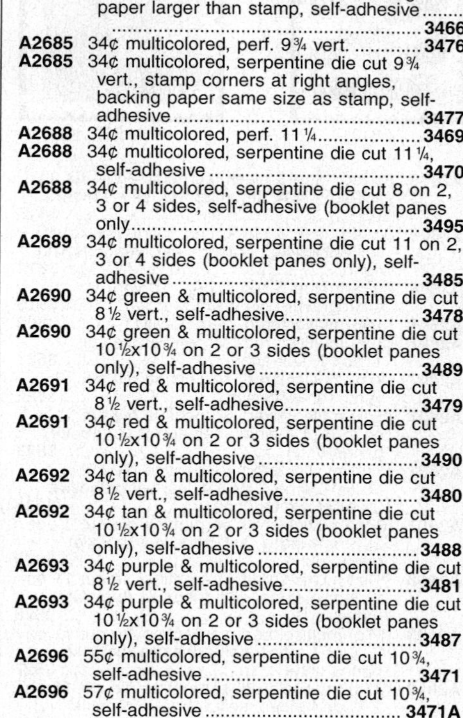

A2684 (34¢) red & multicolored, serpentine die cut 8½ vert., self-adhesive.......... **3463**
A2685 34¢ multicolored, serpentine die cut 9¾ vert., stamp corners rounded, backing paper larger than stamp, self-adhesive **3466**
A2685 34¢ multicolored, perf. 9¾ vert. **3476**
A2685 34¢ multicolored, serpentine die cut 9¾ vert., stamp corners at right angles, backing paper same size as stamp, self-adhesive **3477**
A2688 34¢ multicolored, perf. 11¼.......... **3469**
A2688 34¢ multicolored, serpentine die cut 11¼, self-adhesive **3470**
A2688 34¢ multicolored, serpentine die cut 8 on 2, 3 or 4 sides, self-adhesive (booklet panes only).......... **3495**
A2689 34¢ multicolored, serpentine die cut 11 on 2, 3 or 4 sides (booklet panes only), self-adhesive **3485**
A2690 34¢ green & multicolored, serpentine die cut 8½ vert., self-adhesive.......... **3478**
A2690 34¢ green & multicolored, serpentine die cut 10½x10¾ on 2 or 3 sides (booklet panes only), self-adhesive **3489**
A2691 34¢ red & multicolored, serpentine die cut 8½ vert., self-adhesive.......... **3479**
A2691 34¢ red & multicolored, serpentine die cut 10½x10¾ on 2 or 3 sides (booklet panes only), self-adhesive **3490**
A2692 34¢ tan & multicolored, serpentine die cut 8½ vert., self-adhesive.......... **3480**
A2692 34¢ tan & multicolored, serpentine die cut 10½x10¾ on 2 or 3 sides (booklet panes only), self-adhesive **3488**
A2693 34¢ purple & multicolored, serpentine die cut 8½ vert., self-adhesive.......... **3481**
A2693 34¢ purple & multicolored, serpentine die cut 10½x10¾ on 2 or 3 sides (booklet panes only), self-adhesive **3487**
A2696 55¢ multicolored, serpentine die cut 10¾, self-adhesive **3471**
A2696 57¢ multicolored, serpentine die cut 10¾, self-adhesive **3471A**

WASHINGTON VIEWS ISSUE 2001-03

A2697

A2818

A2698

A2819

A2697 $3.50 multicolored, serpentine die cut 11¼x11½, self-adhesive **3472**
A2818 $3.85 multicolored, serpentine die cut 11¼, self-adhesive, dated "2002" **3647**
A2818 $3.85 multicolored, serpentine die cut 11x10¾, self-adhesive, dated "2003" **3647A**
A2698 $12.25 multicolored, serpentine die cut 11¼x11½, self-adhesive **3473**
A2819 $13.65 multicolored, serpentine die cut 11¼, self-adhesive **3648**

UNITED WE STAND ISSUE 2001-02

A2744

A2744 34¢ multicolored, serpentine die cut 11¼ on 2, 3 or 4 sides, self-adhesive (booklet panes only) **3549**
A2744 34¢ multicolored, serpentine die cut 10½x10¾ on 2 or 3 sides, self-adhesive (booklet panes only) **3549B**
A2744 34¢ multicolored, serpentine die cut 9¾ vert., stamp corners at right angles, backing paper same size as stamp, self-adhesive **3550**
A2744 34¢ multicolored, serpentine die cut 9¾ vert., stamp corners rounded, backing paper larger than stamp, self-adhesive **3550A**

AMERICAN DESIGN ISSUE 2002-14

A2866

A2858

A2868

A2859

A2805

A2860

A2866 1¢ multicolored, "2007" year date, serpentine die cut 11¼x11, self-adhesive **3749**

A2866 1¢ multicolored, "2008" year date, serpentine die cut 11, self-adhesive **3749A**
A2866 1¢ multicolored, perf. 9¾ vert., photo., without microprinting, dated "2003" **3758**
A2866 1¢ multicolored, perf. 9¾ vert., litho., with microprinting, dated "2008" **3758A**
A2858 2¢ multicolored, serpentine die cut 11, without microprinting,self-adhesive, dated "2004" **3750**
A2858 2¢ multicolored, without microprinting, serpentine die cut 11¼x11½, self-adhesive, dated "2006" **3751**
A2858 2¢ multicolored, with microprinting at right, serpentine die cut 11¼x11, self-adhesive, dated "2006" **3752**
A2858 2¢ multicolored, with microprinting at left, serpentine die cut 11¼x10¾, self-adhesive, date "2007" **3753**
A2858 2¢ multicolored, perf. 9¾ vert. **3758B**
A2868 3¢ multicolored, serpentine die cut 11¼x11, self-adhesive **3754**
A2868 3¢ multicolored, perf. 9¾ vert. **3759**
A2859 4¢ multicolored, serpentine die cut 10¾x10¼, self-adhesive **3755**
A2859 4¢ multicolored, perf. 9¾ vert., "2007" date (Sennett printing) **3761**
A2859 4¢ multicolored, perf. 9¾ vert., "2013" date (Ashton-Potter printing) **3761A**
A2805 5¢ multicolored, "2004" year date, serpentine die cut 11¼x11¾, photo., without microprinting, self-adhesive **3756**
A2805 5¢ multicolored, "2007" year date, serpentine die cut 11¼x10¾, photo., with microprinting, self-adhesive **3756A**
A2805 5¢ multicolored, perf. 9¾ vert. **3612**
A2860 10¢ multicolored, serpentine die cut 11¼x11, self-adhesive **3757**
A2860 10¢ multicolored, "2006" year date, perf. 9¾ vert., photo., without microprinting **3762**
A2860 10¢ multicolored, "2008" year date, perf. 9¾ vert., litho., with microprinting **3763**

REGULAR ISSUE 2002-05

A2806

A2807

A2808

A2809

A2810

A2811

A2813

A2814

A2815

A2816

A2812

A2817

A2806 3¢ red, blue & black, serpentine die cut 11, self-adhesive, lithographed, year at lower left **3613**
A2806 3¢ red, blue & black, serpentine die cut 10, self-adhesive, photogravure, year at lower right **3614**
A2806 3¢ red, blue & black, perf. 10 vert., photogravure, year at lower left **3615**
A2807 (37¢) multicolored, perf. 11¼x11 .... **3620**
A2807 (37¢) multicolored, serpentine die cut 11¼x11, self-adhesive **3621**
A2807 (37¢) multicolored, serpentine die cut 10 vert., self-adhesive **3622**
A2807 (37¢) multicolored, serpentine die cut 11¼ on 2, 3 or 4 sides, self-adhesive (booklet panes only) **3623**
A2807 (37¢) multicolored, serpentine die cut 10½x10¾ on 2 or 3 sides, self-adhesive (booklet panes only) **3624**
A2807 (37¢) multicolored, serpentine die cut 8 on 2, 3 or 4 sides, self-adhesive (booklet panes only) **3625**
A2808 (37¢) multicolored, serpentine die cut 11 on 2, 3 or 4 sides, self-adhesive (booklet panes only) **3626**
A2809 (37¢) multicolored, serpentine die cut 11 on 2, 3 or 4 sides, self-adhesive (booklet panes only) **3627**
A2810 (37¢) multicolored, serpentine die cut 11 on 2, 3 or 4 sides, self-adhesive (booklet panes only) **3628**
A2811 (37¢) multicolored, serpentine die cut 11 on 2, 3 or 4 sides, self-adhesive (booklet panes only) **3629**
A2812 37¢ multicolored, perf. 11¼ **3629F**
A2812 37¢ multicolored, serpentine die cut 11¼x11, self-adhesive **3630**
A2812 37¢ multicolored, perf. 9¾ vert. **3631**
A2812 37¢ multicolored, serpentine die cut 9¾ vert., self-adhesive **3632**
A2812 37¢ multicolored, serpentine die cut 10¼ vert., self-adhesive, lacking points of stars at upper left **3632A**
A2812 37¢ multicolored, serpentine die cut 11¾ vert., self-adhesive **3632C**
A2812 37¢ multicolored, serpentine die cut 8½ vert., rounded corners, self-adhesive ... **3633**
A2812 37¢ multicolored, serpentine die cut 8½ vert., right angle corners, self-adhesive **3633A**
A2812 37¢ multicolored, serpentine die cut 9½ vert., with microprinted "USA" in top red stripe, self-adhesive **3633B**
A2812 37¢ multicolored, serpentine die cut 11 on 3 sides, self-adhesive (booklet panes only) **3634**
A2812 37¢ multicolored, serpentine die cut 11¼ on 2 or 3 sides, self-adhesive (booklet panes only) **3635**
A2812 37¢ multicolored, serpentine die cut 10½x10¾ on 2 or 3 sides, self-adhesive (booklet panes only) **3636**
A2812 37¢ multicolored, serpentine die cut 11¼x11 on 2 or 3 sides, self-adhesive (booklet panes only) **3636D**
A2812 37¢ multicolored, serpentine die cut 8 on 2, 3 or 4 sides, self-adhesive (booklet panes only) **3637**
A2813 37¢ multicolored, serpentine die cut 8½ horiz., self-adhesive **3638**
A2813 37¢ multicolored, serpentine die cut 11 on 2, 3 or 4 sides, self-adhesive (booklet panes only) **3643**
A2814 37¢ multicolored, serpentine die cut 8½ horiz., self-adhesive **3639**
A2814 37¢ multicolored, serpentine die cut 11 on 2, 3 or 4 sides, self-adhesive (booklet panes only) **3642**
A2815 37¢ multicolored, serpentine die cut 8½ horiz., self-adhesive **3640**
A2815 37¢ multicolored, serpentine die cut 11 on 2, 3 or 4 sides, self-adhesive (booklet panes only) **3645**
A2816 37¢ multicolored, serpentine die cut 8½ horiz., self-adhesive **3641**
A2816 37¢ multicolored, serpentine die cut 11 on 2, 3 or 4 sides, self-adhesive (booklet panes only) **3644**

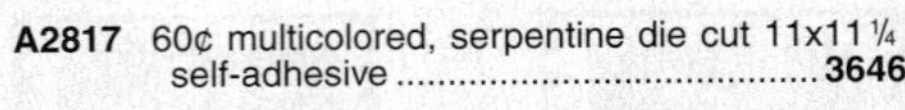

A2817 60¢ multicolored, serpentine die cut 11x11¼ self-adhesive **3646**

PURPLE HEART ISSUE 2003-15

A2891

A3458

A3587

A2891 37¢ multicolored, serpentine die cut 11¼x10¾, self-adhesive **3784**
A2891 37¢ multicolored, serpentine die cut 10¾x10¼, self-adhesive **3784A**
A2891 39¢ multicolored, serpentine die cut 11¼x11, self-adhesive **4032**
A2891 41¢ multicolored, serpentine die cut 11¼x10¾, self-adhesive **4164**
A2891 42¢ multicolored, perf. 11¼ **4263**
A2891 42¢ multicolored, serpentine die cut 11¼x10¾, self-adhesive **4264**
A2891 44¢ multicolored, serpentine die cut 11¼x10¾, self-adhesive **4390**
A3458 (44¢) multicolored, serpentine die cut 11¼x10¾, self-adhesive **4529**
A3587 (45¢) multicolored, serpentine die cut 11, photo., without microprinted "USPS," self-adhesive, dated "2012" **4704**
A3587 (49¢) multicolored, serpentine die cut 11, photo., without microprinted "USPS," self-adhesive, dated "2014" **4704b**
A3587 (49¢) multicolored, serpentine die cut 11, litho., with microprinted "USPS," self-adhesive, dated "2014" **5035**

EAGLE ISSUE 2003-04

A2898

A2899

A2898 (25¢) gray & gold, serpentine die 11¾ vert. **3792**
A2898 (25¢) gray & gold, perf. 9¾ vert. **3844**
A2898 (25¢) dull blue & gold, serpentine die 11¾ vert. **3794**
A2898 (25¢) dull blue & gold, perf. 9¾ vert. **3852**
A2898 (25¢) green & gold, serpentine die 11¾ vert. **3796**
A2898 (25¢) green & gold, perf. 9¾ vert. **3850**
A2898 (25¢) Prussian blue & gold, serpentine die 11¾ vert. **3798**
A2898 (25¢) Prussian blue & gold, perf. 9¾ vert. **3848**
A2898 (25¢) red & gold, serpentine die cut 11¾ vert. **3800**
A2898 (25¢) red & gold, perf. 9¾ vert. **3846**
A2899 (25¢) gold & red, serpentine die cut 11¾ vert. **3793**
A2899 (25¢) gold & red, perf. 9¾ vert. **3853**
A2899 (25¢) gold & Prussian blue, serpentine die cut 11¾ vert. **3795**
A2899 (25¢) gold & Prussian blue, perf. 9¾ vert. **3851**
A2899 (25¢) gold & gray, serpentine die cut 11¾ vert. **3797**
A2899 (25¢) gold & gray, perf. 9¾ vert. **3849**
A2899 (25¢) gold & dull blue, serpentine die cut 11¾ vert. **3799**
A2899 (25¢) gold & dull blue, perf. 9¾ vert. **3847**
A2899 (25¢) gold & green, serpentine die cut 11¾ vert. **3801**
A2899 (25¢) gold & green, perf. 9¾ vert. **3845**

WILDLIFE ISSUE 2003-15

A3564

A3151

A3837

A3152

A3340

A3718

A2925

A3230

A3341

A3564 1¢ multicolored, serpentine die cut 10 vert., self-adhesive **4672**
A3564 1¢ multicolored, perf. 9¾ vert. **4802**
A3151 17¢ multicolored, without microprinting, serpentine die cut 11, self-adhesive **4138**
A3151 17¢ multicolored, without microprinting, serpentine die cut 11 vert., self-adhesive **4140**
A3837 (22¢) multicolored, serpentine die cut 10¾, self-adhesive **4989**
A3837 (22¢) multicolored, serpentine die cut 11 vert., self-adhesive **4990**
A3152 26¢ multicolored, with microprinting, perf. 11¼x11 .... **4137**
A3152 26¢ multicolored, with microprinting, serpentine die cut 11¼x11 .... **4139**
A3152 26¢ multicolored, with microprinting, serpentine die cut 11 vert. **4141**
A3152 26¢ multicolored, without microprinting, serpentine die cut 11¼x11 on 3 sides (booklet panes only) **4142**
A3340 28¢ multicolored, serpentine die cut 11¼x11 self-adhesive **4387**
A3340 28¢ multicolored, serpentine die cut 8½ vert., self-adhesive **4389**
A3718 34¢ multicolored, serpentine die cut 11¼x10¾, self-adhesive **4857**
A3718 34¢ multicolored, serpentine die cut 9½ vert., self-adhesive **4858**
A2925 37¢ multicolored, serpentine die cut 8½ vert., self-adhesive **3829**
A2925 37¢ multicolored, serpentine die cut 9½ vert., self-adhesive **3829A**
A2925 37¢ multicolored, without microprinting, serpentine die cut 11½x11 on 2, 3 or 4 sides, self-adhesive (booklet panes only) **3830**
A2925 37¢ multicolored, with microprinting, serpentine die cut 11½x11 on 2, 3 or 4 sides, self-adhesive (booklet panes only) **3830D**
A3230 62¢ multicolored, serpentine die cut 11¼x11, self-adhesive **4267**
A3341 64¢ multicolored, serpentine die cut 11, self-adhesive **4388**

FLAG AND STATUE OF LIBERTY ISSUE 2005-06

A3038

A3040

A3038 (39¢) multicolored, with microprinting, perf. 11¼ **3965**
A3038 (39¢) multicolored, with microprinting, serpentine die cut 11¼x10¾, self-adhesive **3966**
A3038 (39¢) multicolored, without microprinting, perf. 9¾ vert. **3967**
A3038 (39¢) multicolored, without microprinting, serpentine die cut 8½ vert., self-adhesive **3968**
A3038 (39¢) multicolored, without microprinting, serpentine die cut 10¼ vert., self-adhesive **3969**
A3038 (39¢) multicolored, with microprinting, serpentine die cut 9½ vert., self-adhesive **3970**
A3038 (39¢) multicolored, without microprinting, bright blue sky above date, serpentine die cut 11¼x10¾ on 2 or 3 sides, self-adhesive (Avery Dennison printing, booklet panes only) **3972**
A3038 (39¢) multicolored, without microprinting, bright blue sky above date, serpentine die cut 10½x10¾ on 2 or 3 sides, self-adhesive (Sennett printing, booklet panes only) **3973**
A3038 (39¢) multicolored, photogravure, without microprinting, dark blue sky above date, serpentine die cut 11¼x10¾ on 2 or 3 sides, self-adhesive (Sennett printing, booklet panes only) **3974**
A3038 (39¢) multicolored, without microprinting, serpentine die cut 8 on 2, 3 or 4 sides, self-adhesive (booklet panes only) **3975**
A3040 39¢ multicolored, with microprinting, serpentine die cut 11¼x10¾, self-adhesive **3978**
A3040 39¢ multicolored, without microprinting, perf. 9¾ vert. **3979**
A3040 39¢ multicolored, without microprinting, serpentine die cut 11 vert., self-adhesive **3980**
A3040 39¢ multicolored, with microprinting, serpentine die cut 9½ vert., self-adhesive **3981**
A3040 39¢ multicolored, without microprinting, serpentine die cut 10¼ vert., self-adhesive **3982**
A3040 39¢ multicolored, without microprinting, serpentine die cut 8½ vert., self-adhesive **3983**
A3040 39¢ multicolored, without microprinting, serpentine die cut 11¼x10¾ on 2 or 3 sides, self-adhesive (booklet panes only) **3985**

REGULAR ISSUE 2006

A3053

A3054

A3055

A3056

A3057

A3058

A3053 24¢ multicolored, perf. 11¼ **4000**
A3053 24¢ multicolored, serpentine die cut 11, self-adhesive **4001**
A3053 24¢ multicolored, serpentine die cut 8½ horiz., self-adhesive **4002**
A3054 39¢ multicolored, serpentine die cut 10¼ horiz., self-adhesive **4003**
A3054 39¢ multicolored, serpentine die cut 10¾x10½ on 2 or 3 sides, self-adhesive (booklet panes only) **4012**
A3054 39¢ multicolored, serpentine die cut 10¾x11¼ on 2 or 3 sides, self-adhesive (booklet panes only) **4013**
A3055 39¢ multicolored, serpentine die cut 10¼ horiz., self-adhesive **4004**
A3055 39¢ multicolored, serpentine die cut 10¾x10½ on 2 or 3 sides, self-adhesive (booklet panes only) **4011**
A3055 39¢ multicolored, serpentine die cut 10¾x11¼ on 2 or 3 sides, self-adhesive (booklet panes only) **4017**
A3056 39¢ multicolored, serpentine die cut 10¼ horiz., self-adhesive **4005**
A3056 39¢ multicolored, serpentine die cut 10¾x10½ on 2 or 3 sides, self-adhesive (booklet panes only) **4010**
A3056 39¢ multicolored, serpentine die cut 10¾x11¼ on 2 or 3 sides, self-adhesive (booklet panes only) **4016**
A3057 39¢ multicolored, serpentine die cut 10¼ horiz., self-adhesive **4006**
A3057 39¢ multicolored, serpentine die cut 10¾x10½ on 2 or 3 sides, self-adhesive (booklet panes only) **4009**
A3057 39¢ multicolored, serpentine die cut 10¾x11¼ on 2 or 3 sides, self-adhesive (booklet panes only) **4015**
A3058 39¢ multicolored, serpentine die cut 10¼ horiz., self-adhesive **4007**
A3058 39¢ multicolored, serpentine die cut 10¾x10½ on 2 or 3 sides, self-adhesive (booklet panes only) **4008**
A3058 39¢ multicolored, serpentine die cut 10¾x11¼ on 2 or 3 sides, self-adhesive (booklet panes only) **4014**

X-PLANES ISSUE 2006

A3059

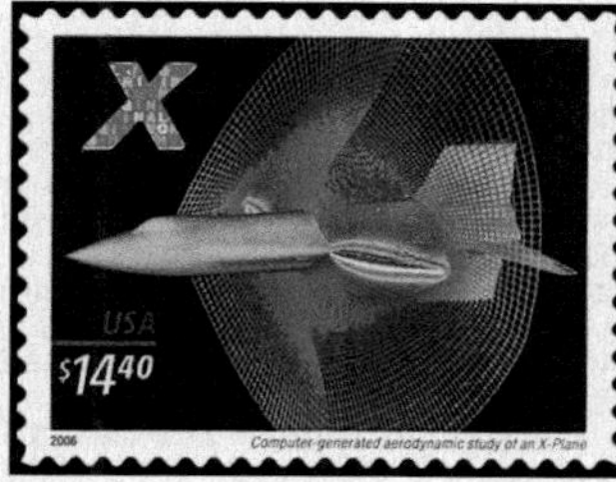

A3060

A3059 $4.05 multicolored, serpentine die cut 10¾x10½, self-adhesive **4018**
A3060 $14.40 multicolored, serpentine die cut 10¾x10½, self-adhesive **4019**

LIBERTY BELL (FOREVER) ISSUE 2007-10

A3148

Large Microprinting (#4125, 4128)

Small Microprinting (#4126)

Medium Microprinting (#4127)

A3148 (41¢) multicolored, large microprinting, bell 16mm wide, serpentine die cut 11¼x10¾ on 2 or 3 sides, self-adhesive (booklet panes only) **4125**
A3148 (41¢) multicolored, large microprinting, bell 16mm wide, serpentine die cut 8 on 2, 3 or 4 sides, self-adhesive (booklet panes only) **4128**
A3148 (41¢) multicolored, small microprinting, bell 16mm wide, serpentine die cut 11¼x10¾ on 2 or 3 sides, self-adhesive (booklet panes only) **4126**
A3148 (41¢) multicolored, medium microprinting, bell 15mm wide, serpentine die cut 11¼x10¾ on 2 or 3 sides, self-adhesive (booklet panes only) **4127**
A3148 (44¢) multicolored, medium microprinting, bell 16mm wide, serpentine die cut 11¼x10¾ on 2, 3 or 4 sides, dated "2009", self-adhesive (booklet panes only) **4437**

FLAG ISSUE 2007

A3149 A3184

A3149 (41¢) multicolored, perf. 11¼ **4129**
A3149 (41¢) multicolored, serpentine die cut 11¼x10¾, self-adhesive **4130**
A3149 (41¢) multicolored, perf. 9¾ vert. **4131**
A3149 (41¢) multicolored, serpentine die cut 9½ vert., with perpendicular corners, self-adhesive **4132**
A3149 (41¢) multicolored, serpentine die cut 11 vert., with perpendicular corners, self-adhesive **4133**
A3149 (41¢) multicolored, serpentine die cut 8½ vert., with perpendicular corners, self-adhesive **4134**
A3149 (41¢) multicolored, serpentine die cut 11 vert., with rounded corners, self-adhesive **4135**
A3184 41¢ multicolored, serpentine die cut 9½ vert., with "USPS" microprinted on right side of flagpole, self-adhesive **4186**
A3184 41¢ multicolored, serpentine die cut 11 vert., with "USPS" microprinted on left side of flagpole, self-adhesive, with perpendicular corners **4187**
A3184 41¢ multicolored, serpentine die cut 8½ vert., without "USPS" microprinted on flagpole, self-adhesive, with perpendicular corners **4188**
A3184 41¢ multicolored, serpentine die cut 11 vert., without "USPS" microprinted on flagpole, self-adhesive, with rounded corners..... **4189**
A3184 41¢ multicolored, serpentine die cut 11¼x10¾ on 3 sides, with "USPS" microprinted on right side of flagpole, self-adhesive (booklet panes only).............. **4190**
A3184 41¢ multicolored, serpentine die cut 11¼x10¾ on 2 or 3 sides, with "USPS" microprinted on leftt side of flagpole, self-adhesive (booklet panes only).............. **4191**

PRESIDENTIAL AIRCRAFT ISSUE 2007

A3154

A3155

A3154 $4.60 multicolored, serpentine die cut 10¾, self-adhesive **4144**
A3155 $16.25 multicolored, serpentine die cut 10¾, self-adhesive **4145**

PATRIOTIC BANNER ISSUE 2007-09

Patriotic Banner — A3167

A3167 (10¢) multicolored, serpentine die cut 11 vert., photo., self-adhesive.................. **4157**
A3167 (10¢) multicolored, serpentine die cut 11¾ vert., litho., self-adhesive.................... **4158**
A3167 (10¢) multicolored, perf. 9¾ vert. **4385**

FLOWERS ISSUE 2007

Iris — A3174

Dahlia — A3175

Magnolia — A3176

Red Gerbera Daisy — A3177

Coneflower — A3178

Tulip — A3179

Water Lily — A3180

Poppy — A3181

Chrysanthemum A3182

Orange Gerbera Daisy A3183

A3174 41¢ multicolored, serpentine die cut 9½ vert., self-adhesive **4166**
A3174 41¢ multicolored, serpentine die cut 11¼x11½ on 2 or 3 sides, self-adhesive (booklet pane only) **4178**
A3175 41¢ multicolored, serpentine die cut 9½ vert., self-adhesive **4167**
A3174 41¢ multicolored, serpentine die cut 11¼x11½ on 2 or 3 sides, self-adhesive (booklet pane only) **4179**
A3176 41¢ multicolored, serpentine die cut 9½ vert., self-adhesive **4168**
A3176 41¢ multicolored, serpentine die cut 11¼x11½ on 2 or 3 sides, self-adhesive (booklet pane only) **4180**
A3177 41¢ multicolored, serpentine die cut 9½ vert., self-adhesive **4169**
A3177 41¢ multicolored, serpentine die cut 11¼x11½ on 2 or 3 sides, self-adhesive (booklet pane only) **4181**
A3178 41¢ multicolored, serpentine die cut 9½ vert., self-adhesive **4170**
A3178 41¢ multicolored, serpentine die cut 11¼x11½ on 2 or 3 sides, self-adhesive (booklet pane only) **4184**
A3179 41¢ multicolored, serpentine die cut 9½ vert., self-adhesive **4171**
A3179 41¢ multicolored, serpentine die cut 11¼x11½ on 2 or 3 sides, self-adhesive (booklet pane only) **4185**
A3180 41¢ multicolored, serpentine die cut 9½ vert., self-adhesive **4172**
A3180 41¢ multicolored, serpentine die cut 11¼x11½ on 2 or 3 sides, self-adhesive (booklet pane only) **4182**
A3181 41¢ multicolored, serpentine die cut 9½ vert., self-adhesive **4173**
A3181 41¢ multicolored, serpentine die cut 11¼x11½ on 2 or 3 sides, self-adhesive (booklet pane only) **4183**
A3182 41¢ multicolored, serpentine die cut 9½ vert., self-adhesive **4174**
A3182 41¢ multicolored, serpentine die cut 11¼x11½ on 2 or 3 sides, self-adhesive (booklet pane only) **4176**
A3183 41¢ multicolored, serpentine die cut 9½ vert., self-adhesive **4175**
A3183 41¢ multicolored, serpentine die cut 11¼x11½ on 2 or 3 sides, self-adhesive (booklet pane only) **4177**

FLAG ISSUE 2008

Flag at Dusk — A3214

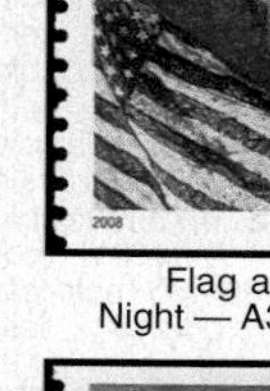

Flag at Night — A3215

Flag at Dawn — A3216

Flag at Midday — A3217

A3214 42¢ multicolored, perf. 10 vert., without microprinting.......... **4228**
A3214 42¢ multicolored, serpentine die cut 9½ vert., with microprinting, self-adhesive, with perpendicular corners.......... **4232**
A3214 42¢ multicolored, perf. 11 vert., without microprinting, self-adhesive, with perpendicular corners.......... **4236**
A3214 42¢ multicolored, serpentine die cut 8½ vert., without microprinting, self-adhesive, with perpendicular corners.......... **4240**
A3214 42¢ multicolored, serpentine die cut 11 vert., without microprinting, self-adhesive, with rounded corners.......... **4244**
A3215 42¢ multicolored, perf. 10 vert., without microprinting.......... **4229**
A3215 42¢ multicolored, serpentine die cut 9½ vert., with microprinting, self-adhesive, with perpendicular corners.......... **4233**
A3215 42¢ multicolored, perf. 11 vert., without microprinting, self-adhesive, with perpendicular corners.......... **4237**
A3215 42¢ multicolored, serpentine die cut 8½ vert., without microprinting, self-adhesive, with perpendicular corners.......... **4241**
A3215 42¢ multicolored, serpentine die cut 11 vert., without microprinting, self-adhesive, with rounded corners.......... **4245**
A3216 42¢ multicolored, perf. 10 vert., without microprinting.......... **4230**
A3216 42¢ multicolored, serpentine die cut 9½ vert., with microprinting, self-adhesive, with perpendicular corners.......... **4234**
A3216 42¢ multicolored, perf. 11 vert., without microprinting, self-adhesive, with perpendicular corners.......... **4238**
A3216 42¢ multicolored, serpentine die cut 8½ vert., without microprinting, self-adhesive, with perpendicular corners.......... **4242**
A3216 42¢ multicolored, serpentine die cut 11 vert., without microprinting, self-adhesive, with rounded corners.......... **4246**
A3217 42¢ multicolored, perf. 10 vert., without microprinting.......... **4231**
A3217 42¢ multicolored, serpentine die cut 9½ vert., with microprinting, self-adhesive, with perpendicular corners.......... **4235**
A3217 42¢ multicolored, perf. 11 vert., without microprinting, self-adhesive, with perpendicular corners.......... **4239**
A3217 42¢ multicolored, serpentine die cut 8½ vert., without microprinting, self-adhesive, with perpendicular corners.......... **4243**
A3217 42¢ multicolored, serpentine die cut 11 vert., without microprinting, self-adhesive, with rounded corners.......... **4247**

TROPICAL FRUIT ISSUE 2008

Pomegranate A3223

Star Fruit A3224

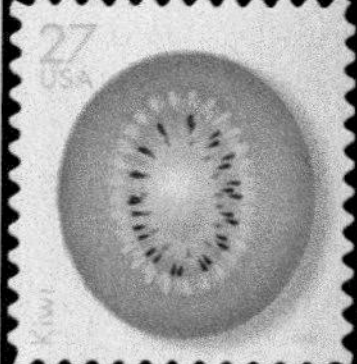

Kiwi — A3225

Papaya — A3226

Guava — A3227

A3223 27¢ multicolored, serpentine die cut 11¼x10¾, self-adhesive.......... **4253**
A3223 42¢ multicolored, serpentine die cut 8½ vert., self-adhesive.......... **4260**
A3224 27¢ multicolored, serpentine die cut 11¼x10¾, self-adhesive.......... **4254**
A3224 42¢ multicolored, serpentine die cut 8½ vert., self-adhesive.......... **4261**
A3225 27¢ multicolored, serpentine die cut 11¼x10¾, self-adhesive.......... **4255**
A3225 42¢ multicolored, serpentine die cut 8½ vert., self-adhesive.......... **4262**
A3226 27¢ multicolored, serpentine die cut 11¼x10¾, self-adhesive.......... **4256**
A3226 42¢ multicolored, serpentine die cut 8½ vert., self-adhesive.......... **4258**
A3227 27¢ multicolored, serpentine die cut 11¼x10¾, self-adhesive.......... **4257**
A3227 42¢ multicolored, serpentine die cut 8½ vert., self-adhesive.......... **4259**

AMERICAN LANDMARKS ISSUE 2008-19

Mount Rushmore A3231

Mackinac Bridge, Michigan A3381

Redwood Forest A3332

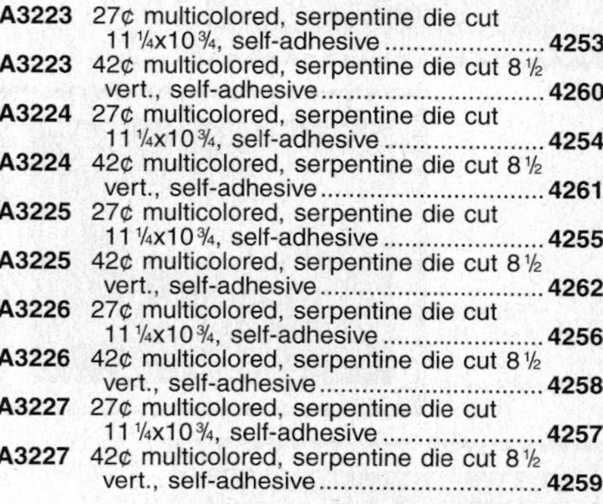

New River Gorge Bridge, West Virginia A3450

Sunshine Skyway Bridge, Florida A3541

Arlington Green Bridge, Vermont A3612

Verrazano-Narrows Bridge, New York — A3726

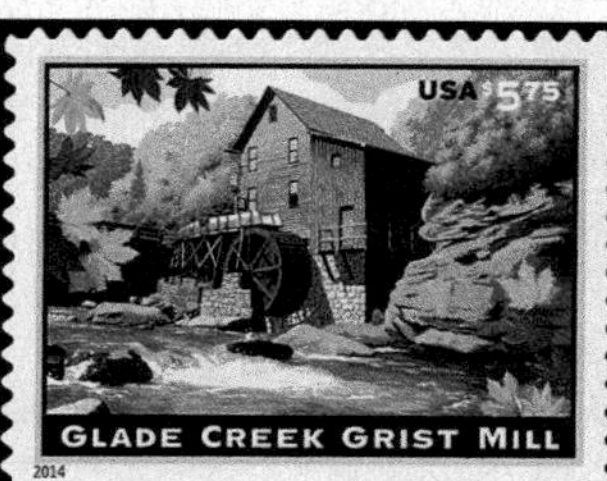

Glade Creek Grist Mill, West Virginia A3780

La Cueva del Indio, Puerto Rico — A3875

Lili'uokalani Gardens, Hilo, Hawaii A3986

Byodo-In Temple, Kaneohe, Hawaii A4096

Joshua Tree — A4191

Hoover Dam — A3232

Old Faithful A3333

Bixby Creek Bridge, California A3382

Carmel Mission, Carmel, CA — A3542

Grand Central Terminal, New York City — A3613

USS Arizona Memorial, Hawaii A3727

Columbia River Gorge A3876

Gateway Arch, St. Louis, Missouri A3987

Sleeping Bear Dunes, Michigan A4097

Bethesda Fountain, Central Park, New York City — A4192

A3231 $4.80 multicolored, serpentine die cut 10¾x10½, self-adhesive 4268
A3381 $4.90 multicolored, serpentine die cut 10¾x10½, self-adhesive 4438
A3332 $4.95 multicolored, serpentine die cut 10¾x10½, self-adhesive 4378
A3450 $4.95 multicolored, serpentine die cut 10¾x10½, self-adhesive 4511
A3541 $5.15 multicolored, serpentine die cut 10¾x10½, self-adhesive 4649
A3612 $5.60 multicolored, serpentine die cut 10¾x10½, self-adhesive 4738
A3726 $5.60 multicolored, serpentine die cut 10¾x10½, self-adhesive 4872
A3780 $5.75 multicolored, serpentine die cut 10¾x10½, self-adhesive 4927
A3875 $6.45 multicolored, serpentine die cut 10¾x10½, self-adhesive 5040
A3986 $6.65 multicolored, serpentine die cut 10¾x10½, self-adhesive 5156
A4096 $6.70 multicolored, serpentine die cut 10¾x10½, self-adhesive 5257
A4191 $7.35 multicolored, serpentine die cut 10¾x10½, self-adhesive 5347
A3232 $16.50 multicolored, serpentine die cut 10¾x10½, self-adhesive 4269
A3333 $17.50 multicolored, serpentine die cut 10¾x10½, self-adhesive 4379
A3382 $18.30 multicolored, serpentine die cut 10¾x10½, self-adhesive 4439
A3542 $18.95 multicolored, serpentine die cut 10¾x10½, self-adhesive 4650
A3613 $19.95 multicolored, serpentine die cut 10¾x10½, self-adhesive 4739
A3727 $19.99 multicolored, serpentine die cut 10¾x10½, self-adhesive 4873
A3876 $22.95 multicolored, serpentine die cut 10¾x10½, self-adhesive 5041
A3987 $23.75 multicolored, serpentine die cut 10¾x10½, self-adhesive 5157
A4097 $24.70 multicolored, serpentine die cut 10¾x10½, self-adhesive 5258
A4192 $25.50 multicolored, serpentine die cut 10¾x10½, self-adhesive 5348

SUNFLOWER ISSUE 2008

Sunflower — A3309

A3309 42¢ multicolored, serpentine die cut 11¼x10¾ on 2 or 3 sides, self-adhesive (booklet panes only) 4259

FLAG ISSUE 2009

Flag — A3342

A3342 44¢ multicolored, perf 9¾ vert. 4391
A3342 44¢ multicolored, serpentine die cut 11 vert., with pointed corners, litho., self-adhesive 4392
A3342 44¢ multicolored, serpentine die cut 9½ vert., with pointed corners, litho., self-adhesive 4393
A3342 44¢ multicolored, serpentine die cut 8½ vert., with pointed corners, litho., self-adhesive 4394
A3342 44¢ multicolored, serpentine die cut 11 vert., with rounded corners, photo., self-adhesive 4395
A3342 44¢ multicolored, serpentine die cut 11¼x10¾ on 3 sides, photo., self-adhesive (booklet panes only) 4396

STATUE OF LIBERTY AND FLAG ISSUE 2010-11

Replica of Statue of Liberty, Las Vegas — A3429

Flag — A3430

A3429 (44¢) multicolored, serpentine die cut 9½ vert., "4evR" microprinting, litho., self-adhesive 4486
A3429 (44¢) multicolored, serpentine die cut 11 vert., "4evr" microprinting, litho., self-adhesive 4488
A3429 (44¢) multicolored, serpentine die cut 8½ vert., "4EVR" microprinting, photo., self-adhesive 4490
A3429 (44¢) multicolored, serpentine die cut 11¼x11 on 2, 3 or 4 sides, "4evr" microprinting, litho., thin paper, self-adhesive (booklet panes only)............. 4518
A3429 (44¢) multicolored, serpentine die cut 11¼x11 on 2 or 3 sides, "4evR" microprinting, litho., self-adhesive (booklet panes only) 4559
A3429 (44¢) multicolored, serpentine die cut 11¼x11 on 2, 3 or 4 sides, "4evr" microprinting, litho., self-adhesive (booklet panes only) 4561

A3429 (44¢) multicolored, serpentine die cut 11¼x11½ on 2 or 3 sides, "4EVR" microprinting, photo., self-adhesive (booklet panes only) **4563**
A3430 (44¢) multicolored, serpentine die cut 9½ vert., "4evR" microprinting, litho., self-adhesive **4487**
A3430 (44¢) multicolored, serpentine die cut 11 vert., "4evr" microprinting, litho., self-adhesive **4489**
A3430 (44¢) multicolored, serpentine die cut 8½ vert., "4EVR" microprinting, photo., self-adhesive **4491**
A3430 (44¢) multicolored, serpentine die cut 11¼x11 on 2, 3 or 4 sides, "4evr" microprinting, litho., thin paper, self-adhesive (booklet panes only) **4519**
A3430 (44¢) multicolored, serpentine die cut 11¼x11 on 2 or 3 sides, "4evR" microprinting, litho., self-adhesive (booklet panes only) **4560**
A3430 (44¢) multicolored, serpentine die cut 11¼x11 on 2 or 3 sides, "4evr" microprinting, litho., self-adhesive (booklet panes only) **4562**
A3430 (44¢) multicolored, serpentine die cut 11¼x11½ on 2 or 3 sides, "4EVR" microprinting, photo., self-adhesive (booklet panes only) **4564**

REGULAR ISSUE 2011

Art Deco Bird — A3434

George Washington — A3443

Oregano — A3444

Flax — A3445

Foxglove — A3446

Lavender — A3447

Sage — A3448

Quill and Inkwell — A3435

A3434 (5¢) multicolored, serpentine die cut 10 vert., self-adhesive **4495**
A3443 20¢ multicolored, serpentine die cut 11¼x10¾, self-adhesive **4504**
A3443 20¢ multicolored, serpentine die cut 9½ vert., self-adhesive **4512**
A3444 29¢ multicolored, serpentine die cut 11, self-adhesive **4505**
A3444 29¢ multicolored, serpentine die cut 8½ vert., self-adhesive **4516**
A3445 29¢ multicolored, serpentine die cut 11, self-adhesive **4506**
A3445 29¢ multicolored, serpentine die cut 8½ vert., self-adhesive **4517**
A3446 29¢ multicolored, serpentine die cut 11, self-adhesive **4507**
A3446 29¢ multicolored, serpentine die cut 8½ vert., self-adhesive **4513**
A3447 29¢ multicolored, serpentine die cut 11, self-adhesive **4508**
A3447 29¢ multicolored, serpentine die cut 8½ vert., self-adhesive **4514**
A3448 29¢ multicolored, serpentine die cut 11, self-adhesive **4509**
A3448 29¢ multicolored, serpentine die cut 8½ vert., self-adhesive **4515**
A3435 44¢ multicolored, serpentine die cut 11¾ vert., self-adhesive **4496**

DISTINGUISHED AMERICANS ISSUE 2011-17

José Ferrer (1912-92), Actor — A3558

C. Alfred "Chief" Anderson (1907-96), Aviator — A3733

Robert Panara (1920-2014), Educator of the Deaf — A4020

Oveta Culp Hobby — A3449

A3558 (45¢) multicolored, serpentine die cut 10¾x11, self-adhesive **4666**
A3733 70¢ multicolored, serpentine die cut 10¾x11, self-adhesive **4879**
A4020 (70¢) multicolored, serpentine die cut 10¾, self-adhesive **5191**
A3449 84¢ multicolored, serpentine die cut 11, self-adhesive **4510**

EAGLES ISSUE 2012-15

A3504

A3504 (25¢) green behind "USA," serpentine die cut 11 vert., photo., self-adhesive, dated "2012" **4585**
A3504 (25¢) green behind "USA," serpentine die cut 10¼ vert., litho., self-adhesive, dated "2015" **5013**
A3504 (25¢) blue green behind "USA", serpentine die cut 11 vert., photo., self-adhesive, dated "2012" **4586**
A3504 (25¢) blue green behind "USA", serpentine die cut 10¼ vert., litho., self-adhesive, dated "2015" **5014**
A3504 (25¢) blue behind "USA", serpentine die cut 11 vert., photo., self-adhesive, dated "2012" **4587**
A3504 (25¢) blue behind "USA", serpentine die cut 10¼ vert., litho., self-adhesive, dated "2015" **5015**
A3504 (25¢) red violet behind "USA", serpentine die cut 11 vert., photo., self-adhesive, dated "2012" **4588**
A3504 (25¢) red violet behind "USA", serpentine die cut 10¼ vert., litho., self-adhesive, dated "2015" **5016**
A3504 (25¢) brown orange behind "USA", serpentine die cut 11 vert., photo., self-adhesive, dated "2012" **4589**
A3504 (25¢) brown orange behind "USA", serpentine die cut 10¼ vert., litho., self-adhesive, dated "2015" **5017**

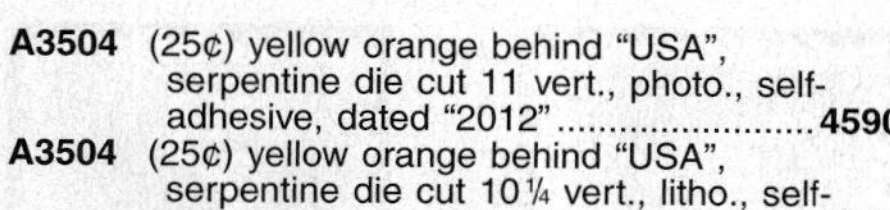

A3504 (25¢) yellow orange behind "USA", serpentine die cut 11 vert., photo., self-adhesive, dated "2012" **4590**
A3504 (25¢) yellow orange behind "USA", serpentine die cut 10¼ vert., litho., self-adhesive, dated "2015" **5018**

ALOHA SHIRTS ISSUE 2012

Surfers and Palm Trees — A3506

Surfers — A3507

Bird of Paradise Flowers — A3508

Shells — A3509

Fossil Fish, Shells and Starfish — A3510

A3506 32¢ multicolored, serpentine die cut 11, photo., self-adhesive **4592**
A3506 32¢ multicolored, serpentine die cut 11 vert., litho., self-adhesive **4598**
A3506 32¢ multicolored, serpentine die cut 11¼x10¾ on 3 sides, litho., self-adhesive (booklet panes only) **4682**
A3507 32¢ multicolored, serpentine die cut 11, photo., self-adhesive **4593**
A3507 32¢ multicolored, serpentine die cut 11vert., litho., self-adhesive **4599**
A3507 32¢ multicolored, serpentine die cut 11¼x10¾ on 3 sides, litho., self-adhesive (booklet panes only) **4685**
A3508 32¢ multicolored, serpentine die cut 11, photo., self-adhesive **4594**
A3508 32¢ multicolored, serpentine die cut 11vert., litho., self-adhesive **4600**
A3508 32¢ multicolored, serpentine die cut 11¼x10¾ on 3 sides, litho., self-adhesive (booklet panes only) **4683**
A3509 32¢ multicolored, serpentine die cut 11, photo., self-adhesive **4595**
A3509 32¢ multicolored, serpentine die cut 11 vert., litho., self-adhesive **4601**
A3509 32¢ multicolored, serpentine die cut 11¼x10¾ on 3 sides, litho., self-adhesive (booklet panes only) **4686**
A3510 32¢ multicolored, serpentine die cut 11, photo., self-adhesive **4596**
A3510 32¢ multicolored, serpentine die cut 11 vert., litho., self-adhesive **4597**
A3510 32¢ multicolored, serpentine die cut 11¼x10¾ on 3 sides, litho., self-adhesive (booklet panes only) **4684**

DOGS AT WORK ISSUE 2012

Seeing Eye Dog — A3512

Therapy Dog — A3513

Military Dog — A3514

Rescue Dog — A3515

A3512 65¢ multicolored, serpentine die cut 10¾, self-adhesive **4604**
A3513 65¢ multicolored, serpentine die cut 10¾, self-adhesive **4605**
A3514 65¢ multicolored, serpentine die cut 10¾, self-adhesive **4606**
A3515 65¢ multicolored, serpentine die cut 10¾, self-adhesive **4607**

BIRDS OF PREY ISSUE 2012

Northern Goshawk — A3516

Peregrine Falcon — A3517

Golden Eagle — A3518

Osprey — A3519

Northern Harrier — A3520

A3516 85¢ multicolored, serpentine die cut 10¾, self-adhesive **4608**
A3517 85¢ multicolored, serpentine die cut 10¾, self-adhesive **4609**
A3518 85¢ multicolored, serpentine die cut 10¾, self-adhesive **4610**
A3519 85¢ multicolored, serpentine die cut 10¾, self-adhesive **4611**
A3520 85¢ multicolored, serpentine die cut 10¾, self-adhesive **4612**

WEATHER VANES ISSUE 2012

Rooster With Perch — A3521

Cow — A3522

Eagle — A3523

Rooster Without Perch — A3524

Centaur — A3525

A3521 45¢ multicolored, serpentine die cut 11¾ vert., self-adhesive **4613**
A3522 45¢ multicolored, serpentine die cut 11¾ vert., self-adhesive **4614**
A3523 45¢ multicolored, serpentine die cut 11¾ vert., self-adhesive **4615**
A3524 45¢ multicolored, serpentine die cut 11¾ vert., self-adhesive **4616**
A3525 45¢ multicolored, serpentine die cut 11¾ vert., self-adhesive **4617**

FLAG ISSUE 2012

Flag and "Equality" — A3537

Flag and "Justice" — A3538

Flag and "Freedom" — A3539

Flag and "Liberty" — A3540

A3537 (45¢) multicolored, serpentine die cut 8½ vert., photo., self-adhesive.................. **4629**
A3537 (45¢) multicolored, serpentine die cut 9½ vert., litho., self-adhesive **4633**
A3537 (45¢) multicolored, serpentine die cut 11 vert., litho., self-adhesive **4637**
A3537 (45¢) multicolored, serpentine die cut 11¼x10¾ on 2 or 3 sides, litho., colored dots in stars, 18½mm from lower left to lower right corner of flag, self-adhesive (booklet panes only) **4643**
A3537 (45¢) multicolored, serpentine die cut 11¼x10¾ on 2 or 3 sides, litho., dark dots only in stars, 19mm from lower left to lower right corner of flag, self-adhesive (booklet panes only) **4647**
A3537 (45¢) multicolored, serpentine die cut 11¼x10¾ on 2 or 3 sides, photo., colored dots in stars, 19¼mm from lower left to lower right corner of flag, self-adhesive (booklet panes only) **4675**
A3537 (45¢) multicolored, serpentine die cut 11¼x10¾ on 2, 3 or 4 sides, litho., colored dots in stars, 18½mm from lower left to lower right corner of flag, self-adhesive (booklet panes only) **4708**
A3538 (45¢) multicolored, serpentine die cut 8½ vert., photo., self-adhesive.................. **4630**
A3538 (45¢) multicolored, serpentine die cut 9½ vert., litho., self-adhesive **4634**
A3538 (45¢) multicolored, serpentine die cut 11 vert., litho., self-adhesive **4638**
A3538 (45¢) multicolored, serpentine die cut 11¼x10¾ on 2 or 3 sides, litho., colored dots in stars, 18½mm from lower left to lower right corner of flag, self-adhesive (booklet panes only) **4644**
A3538 (45¢) multicolored, serpentine die cut 11¼x10¾ on 2 or 3 sides, litho., dark dots only in stars, 19mm from lower left to lower right corner of flag, self-adhesive (booklet panes only) **4648**
A3538 (45¢) multicolored, serpentine die cut 11¼x10¾ on 2 or 3 sides, photo., colored dots in stars, 19¼mm from lower left to lower right corner of flag, self-adhesive (booklet panes only) **4676**
A3538 (45¢) multicolored, serpentine die cut 11¼x10¾ on 2, 3 or 4 sides, litho., colored dots in stars, 18½mm from lower left to lower right corner of flag, self-adhesive (booklet panes only) **4709**
A3539 (45¢) multicolored, serpentine die cut 8½ vert., photo., self-adhesive.................. **4631**
A3539 (45¢) multicolored, serpentine die cut 9½ vert., litho., self-adhesive **4635**
A3539 (45¢) multicolored, serpentine die cut 11 vert., litho., self-adhesive **4639**
A3539 (45¢) multicolored, serpentine die cut 11¼x10¾ on 2 or 3 sides, litho., colored dots in stars, 18½mm from lower left to lower right corner of flag, self-adhesive (booklet panes only) **4641**
A3539 (45¢) multicolored, serpentine die cut 11¼x10¾ on 2 or 3 sides, litho., dark dots only in stars, 19mm from lower left to lower right corner of flag, self-adhesive (booklet panes only) **4645**
A3539 (45¢) multicolored, serpentine die cut 11¼x10¾ on 2 or 3 sides, photo., colored dots in stars, 19¼mm from lower left to lower right corner of flag, self-adhesive (booklet panes only) **4673**
A3539 (45¢) multicolored, serpentine die cut 11¼x10¾ on 2, 3 or 4 sides, litho., colored dots in stars, 18½mm from lower left to lower right corner of flag, self-adhesive (booklet panes only) **4706**
A3540 (45¢) multicolored, serpentine die cut 8½ vert., photo., self-adhesive.................. **4632**
A3540 (45¢) multicolored, serpentine die cut 9½ vert., litho., self-adhesive **4636**
A3540 (45¢) multicolored, serpentine die cut 11 vert., litho., self-adhesive **4640**
A3540 (45¢) multicolored, serpentine die cut 11¼x10¾ on 2 or 3 sides, litho., colored dots in stars, 18½mm from lower left to lower right corner of flag, self-adhesive (booklet panes only) **4642**
A3540 (45¢) multicolored, serpentine die cut 11¼x10¾ on 2 or 3 sides, litho., dark dots only in stars, 19mm from lower left to lower right corner of flag, self-adhesive (booklet panes only) **4646**
A3540 (45¢) multicolored, serpentine die cut 11¼x10¾ on 2 or 3 sides, photo., colored dots in stars, 19¼mm from lower left to lower right corner of flag, self-adhesive (booklet panes only) **4674**
A3540 (45¢) multicolored, serpentine die cut 11¼x10¾ on 2, 3 or 4 sides, litho., colored dots in stars, 18½mm from lower left to lower right corner of flag, self-adhesive (booklet panes only) **4707**

WAVES OF COLOR ISSUE 2012

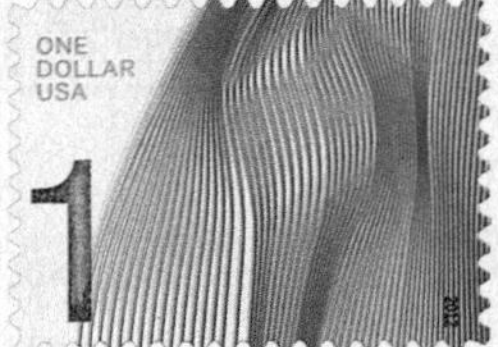

A3596

A3597

A3598

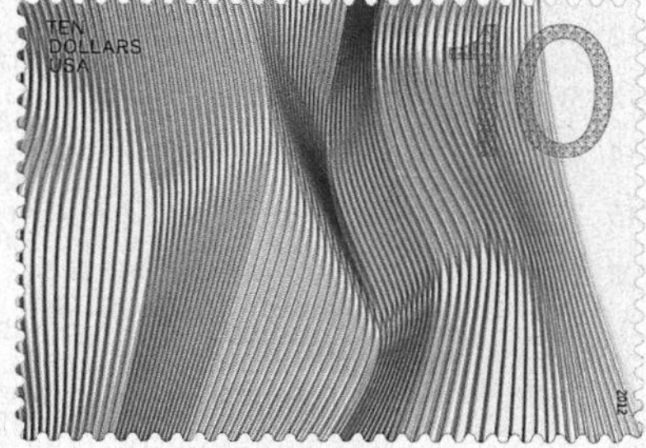

A3599

A3596 $1 multicolored, serpentine die cut 11, self-adhesive **4717**
A3597 $2 multicolored, serpentine die cut 11, self-adhesive **4718**
A3598 $5 multicolored, serpentine die cut 10¾, self-adhesive **4719**
A3599 $10 multicolored, serpentine die cut 11, self-adhesive **4720**

KALEIDOSCOPE FLOWERS ISSUE 2013

A3601

A3602

A3603

A3604

A3601 46¢ multicolored, yellow orange large outer leaves, serpentine die cut 11 vert., self-adhesive **4722**
A3602 46¢ multicolored, yellow green large outer leaves, serpentine die cut 11 vert., self-adhesive **4723**
A3603 46¢ multicolored, red violet large outer leaves, serpentine die cut 11 vert., self-adhesive **4724**
A3604 46¢ multicolored, red large outer leaves, serpentine die cut 11 vert., self-adhesive **4725**

APPLES ISSUE 2013

Northern Spy Apple — A3606

Golden Delicious Apple — A3607

Granny Smith Apple — A3608

Baldwin Apple — A3609

A3606 33¢ multicolored, serpentine die cut 11¼x10¾, self-adhesive **4727**
A3606 33¢ multicolored, serpentine die cut 11 vert., self-adhesive **4732**
A3607 33¢ multicolored, serpentine die cut 11¼x10¾, self-adhesive **4728**
A3607 33¢ multicolored, serpentine die cut 11 vert., self-adhesive **4733**
A3608 33¢ multicolored, serpentine die cut 11¼x10¾, self-adhesive **4729**
A3608 33¢ multicolored, serpentine die cut 11 vert., self-adhesive **4734**
A3609 33¢ multicolored, serpentine die cut 11¼x10¾, self-adhesive **4730**
A3609 33¢ multicolored, serpentine die cut 11 vert., self-adhesive **4731**

REGULAR ISSUE 2013

Patriotic Star — A3623

Tufted Puffins — A3611

A3623 46¢ multicolored, serpentine die cut 10¾ vert., self-adhesive **4749**
A3611 86¢ multicolored, dated "2013" in orange, serpentine die cut 11¼x10¾, self-adhesive **4737**
A3611 86¢ multicolored, dated "2013" in black, serpentine die cut 11¼x10¾, self-adhesive **4737A**

CIRCULAR STAMPS ISSUE 2013-17

Earth — A3614

Wreath — A3677

Map of Sea Surface Temperatures A3746

Silver Bells Wreath — A3789

Echeveria A4027

Moon — A3890

A3614 ($1.10) multicolored, serpentine die cut, self-adhesive **4740**
A3677 ($1.10) multicolored, serpentine die cut, self-adhesive **4814**
A3746 ($1.15) multicolored, serpentine die cut, self-adhesive **4893**
A3789 ($1.15) multicolored, serpentine die cut, self-adhesive **4936**
A4027 ($1.15) multicolored, serpentine die cut, self-adhesive **5198**
A3890 ($1.20) multicolored, serpentine die cut, self-adhesive **5058**

FLAG FOR ALL SEASONS ISSUE 2013

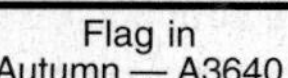
Flag in Autumn — A3640

Flag in Winter — A3641

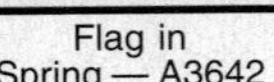
Flag in Spring — A3642

Flag in Summer — A3643

A3640 (46¢) multicolored, serpentine die cut 8½ vert., photo., self-adhesive.................... **4766**
A3640 (46¢) multicolored, serpentine die cut 9½ vert., litho., self-adhesive...................... **4770**
A3640 (46¢) multicolored, serpentine die cut 11 vert., litho., self-adhesive...................... **4777**
A3640 (46¢) multicolored, serpentine die cut 11¼x10¾ on 2 or 3 sides, litho., with "USPS" microprinted at lower left corner of flag, self-adhesive (booklet panes only)... **4780**
A3640 (46¢) multicolored, serpentine die cut 11¼x10¾ on 2 or 3 sides, litho., with "USPS" microprinted near top of pole, self-adhesive (booklet panes only).............. **4784**
A3640 (46¢) multicolored, serpentine die cut 11¼x11½ on 2 or 3 sides, photo., self-adhesive (booklet panes only).............. **4798**
A3641 (46¢) multicolored, serpentine die cut 8½ vert., photo., self-adhesive.................... **4767**
A3641 (46¢) multicolored, serpentine die cut 9½ vert., litho., self-adhesive...................... **4771**
A3641 (46¢) multicolored, serpentine die cut 11 vert., litho., self-adhesive...................... **4774**
A3641 (46¢) multicolored, serpentine die cut 11¼x10¾ on 2 or 3 sides, litho., with "USPS" microprinted at lower left corner of flag, self-adhesive (booklet panes only)... **4781**
A3641 (46¢) multicolored, serpentine die cut 11¼x10¾ on 2 or 3 sides, litho., with "USPS" microprinted near top of pole, self-adhesive (booklet panes only).............. **4785**
A3641 (46¢) multicolored, serpentine die cut 11¼x11½ on 2 or 3 sides, photo., self-adhesive (booklet panes only).............. **4799**
A3642 (46¢) multicolored, serpentine die cut 8½ vert., photo., self-adhesive.................... **4768**
A3642 (46¢) multicolored, serpentine die cut 9½ vert., litho., self-adhesive...................... **4772**
A3642 (46¢) multicolored, serpentine die cut 11 vert., litho., self-adhesive...................... **4775**
A3642 (46¢) multicolored, serpentine die cut 11¼x10¾ on 2 or 3 sides, litho., with "USPS" microprinted at lower left corner of flag, self-adhesive (booklet panes only)... **4778**
A3642 (46¢) multicolored, serpentine die cut 11¼x10¾ on 2 or 3 sides, litho., with "USPS" microprinted near top of pole, self-adhesive (booklet panes only).............. **4782**
A3642 (46¢) multicolored, serpentine die cut 11¼x11½ on 2 or 3 sides, photo., self-adhesive (booklet panes only).............. **4796**
A3643 (46¢) multicolored, serpentine die cut 8½ vert., photo., self-adhesive.................... **4769**
A3643 (46¢) multicolored, serpentine die cut 9½ vert., litho., self-adhesive...................... **4773**
A3643 (46¢) multicolored, serpentine die cut 11 vert., litho., self-adhesive...................... **4776**
A3643 (46¢) multicolored, serpentine die cut 11¼x10¾ on 2 or 3 sides, litho., with "USPS" microprinted at lower left corner of flag, self-adhesive (booklet panes only)... **4779**
A3643 (46¢) multicolored, serpentine die cut 11¼x10¾ on 2 or 3 sides, litho., with "USPS" microprinted at lower left corner near rope, self-adhesive (booklet panes only)... **4783**
A3643 (46¢) multicolored, serpentine die cut 11¼x11½ on 2 or 3 sides, photo., self-adhesive (booklet panes only).............. **4797**

SNOWFLAKES ISSUE 2013

A3672

A3673

A3674

A3675

A3676

A3672 10¢ light blue & multicolored, serpentine die cut 11 vert., self-adhesive.................... **4808**
A3673 10¢ pale blue & multicolored, serpentine die cut 11 vert., self-adhesive.................... **4809**
A3674 10¢ light blue & multicolored, serpentine die cut 11 vert., self-adhesive.................... **4810**
A3675 10¢ pale blue & multicolored, serpentine die cut 11 vert., self-adhesive.................... **4811**
A3676 10¢ lilac & multicolored, serpentine die cut 11 vert., self-adhesive.......................... **4812**

FERNS ISSUE 2014-15

Fortune's Holly Fern — A3711

Soft Shield Fern — A3712

Autumn Fern — A3713

Goldie's Wood Fern — A3714

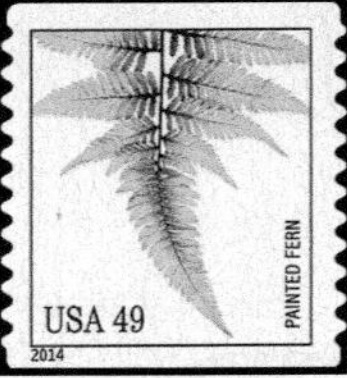

Painted Fern — A3715

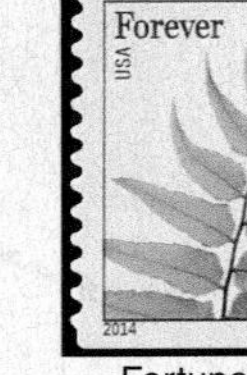

Fortune's Holly Fern — A3728

Soft Shield Fern — A3729

Autumn Fern — A3730

Goldie's Wood Fern — A3731

Painted Fern — A3732

A3711 49¢ multicolored, serpentine die cut 11 vert., self-adhesive.. **4848**
A3712 49¢ multicolored, serpentine die cut 11 vert., self-adhesive.. **4849**
A3713 49¢ multicolored, serpentine die cut 11 vert., self-adhesive.. **4850**
A3714 49¢ multicolored, serpentine die cut 11 vert., self-adhesive.. **4851**
A3715 49¢ multicolored, serpentine die cut 11 vert., self-adhesive.. **4852**
A3728 (49¢) multicolored, serpentine die cut 11 vert., photo., without microprinting, self-adhesive.. **4874**
A3728 (49¢) multicolored, serpentine die cut 11 vert., litho., with microprinting, self-adhesive... **4977**
A3729 (49¢) multicolored, serpentine die cut 11 vert., photo., without microprinting, self-adhesive.. **4875**
A3729 (49¢) multicolored, serpentine die cut 11 vert., litho., with microprinting, self-adhesive... **4973**
A3730 (49¢) multicolored, serpentine die cut 11 vert., photo., without microprinting, self-adhesive.. **4876**
A3730 (49¢) multicolored, serpentine die cut 11 vert., litho., with microprinting, self-adhesive... **4974**
A3731 (49¢) multicolored, serpentine die cut 11 vert., photo., without microprinting, self-adhesive.. **4877**
A3731 (49¢) multicolored, serpentine die cut 11 vert., litho., with microprinting, self-adhesive... **4975**
A3732 (49¢) multicolored, serpentine die cut 11 vert., photo., without microprinting, self-adhesive.. **4878**
A3732 (49¢) multicolored, serpentine die cut 11 vert., litho., with microprinting, self-adhesive... **4976**

FORT MCHENRY FLAG AND FIREWORKS ISSUE 2014

A3716

A3716 (49¢) multicolored, serpentine die cut 8½ vert., self-adhesive.............................. **4853**
A3716 (49¢) multicolored, serpentine die cut 9½ vert., self-adhesive.............................. **4854**
A3716 (49¢) multicolored, litho., serpentine die cut 11¼x10¾ on 2 or 3 sides, microprinting on lowest white stripe, self-adhesive (booklet panes only).. **4855**
A3716 (49¢) multicolored, serpentine die cut 11 vert., self-adhesive.............................. **4868**
A3716 (49¢) multicolored, photo., serpentine die cut 11¼x11½ on 2 or 3 sides, without microprinting, self-adhesive (booklet panes only).. **4869**
A3716 (49¢) multicolored, litho., serpentine die cut 11¼x10¾ on 2 or 3 sides, microprinting in fireworks above flagpole, self-adhesive (booklet panes only).......................... **4870**
A3716 (49¢) multicolored, litho., serpentine die cut 11¼x11 on 2, 3 or 4 sides, microprinting in fireworks above flagpole, self-adhesive (booklet panes only).......................... **4871**

ABRAHAM LINCOLN ISSUE 2014

A3720

A3720 21¢ multicolored, serpentine die cut 11 vert., self-adhesive **4860**
A3720 21¢ multicolored, serpentine die cut 8½ vert., self-adhesive **4861**

FLAG ISSUE 2014

Flag With 5 Full and 3 Partial Stars — A3747

Flag With 3 Full Stars — A3748

Flag With 4 Full and 2 Partial Stars — A3749

Flag With 2 Full and 2 Partial Stars — A3750

A3747 (49¢) blue & red, serpentine die cut 11 vert., self-adhesive **4894**
A3748 (49¢) blue & red, serpentine die cut 11 vert., self-adhesive **4895**
A3749 (49¢) blue & red, serpentine die cut 11 vert., self-adhesive **4896**
A3750 (49¢) blue & red, serpentine die cut 11 vert., self-adhesive **4897**

HOT ROD ISSUE 2014

Rear of 1932 Ford "Deuce" Roadster — A3761

Front of 1932 Ford "Deuce" Roadster — A3762

A3761 (49¢) multicolored, serpentine die cut 11¾x11¼ on 2 or 3 sides, self-adhesive (booklet panes only) **4909**
A3762 (49¢) multicolored, serpentine die cut 11¾x11¼ on 2 or 3 sides, self-adhesive (booklet panes only) **4910**

PATRIOTIC WAVES ISSUE 2015

A3806

A3807

A3806 $1 multicolored, serpentine die cut 11, self-adhesive **4953**
A3807 $2 multicolored, serpentine die cut 11, self-adhesive **4954**

FLOWERS ISSUE 2015

Rose and Heart — A3812

Tulip and Heart — A3813

Tulip and Heart — A3845

A3812 (49¢) red & black, serpentine die cut 11, self-adhesive **4959**
A3813 70¢ black & red, serpentine die cut 11, self-adhesive **4960**
A3845 (71¢) black & red, serpentine die cut 11, self-adhesive **5002**

FLAGS ISSUE 2015

Stripes at Left, Stars at Right — A3814

Stars and White Stripe — A3815

Stars at Left, Stripes at Right — A3816

A3814 (10¢) multicolored, serpentine die cut 11 vert., self-adhesive **4961**
A3815 (10¢) multicolored, serpentine die cut 11 vert., self-adhesive **4962**
A3816 (10¢) multicolored, serpentine die cut 11 vert., self-adhesive **4963**

COASTAL BIRDS ISSUE 2015

Red Knot — A3838

King Eider — A3839

Spoonbill — A3840

Frigatebird — A3841

A3838 (35¢) multicolored, serpentine die cut 11¼x11, self-adhesive **4991**
A3838 (35¢) multicolored, serpentine die cut 9½ vert., self-adhesive **4997**
A3839 (35¢) multicolored, serpentine die cut 11¼x11, self-adhesive **4992**
A3839 (35¢) multicolored, serpentine die cut 9½ vert., self-adhesive **4998**
A3840 (35¢) multicolored, serpentine die cut 11¼x11, self-adhesive **4993**
A3840 (35¢) multicolored, serpentine die cut 9½ vert., self-adhesive **4995**
A3841 (35¢) multicolored, serpentine die cut 11¼x11, self-adhesive **4994**
A3841 (35¢) multicolored, serpentine die cut 9½ vert., self-adhesive **4996**

FRUIT ISSUE 2016-18

Albemarle Pippin Apples — A3872

Meyer Lemons — A4095

Strawberries A4030

Pinot Noir Grapes A3873

Red Pears — A3874

A3872 1¢ multicolored, serpentine die cut 10 vert., self-adhesive **5037**
A4095 2¢ multicolored, serpentine die cut 10¾ vert., self-adhesive **5256**
A4030 3¢ multicolored, serpentine die cut 10 vert., self-adhesive **5201**
A3873 5¢ multicolored, serpentine die cut 10 vert., self-adhesive **5038**
A3873 5¢ multicolored, serpentine die cut 11¼x11, self-adhesive **5177**
A3874 10¢ multicolored, serpentine die cut 10¾ vert., self-adhesive **5039**
A3873 10¢ multicolored, serpentine die cut 11¼x11, self-adhesive **5178**

FLAG ISSUE 2016

Flag — A3887

A3887 (49¢) multicolored, serpentine die cut 11 vert., microprinted "USPS" to right of pole under flag, self-adhesive....................... **5052**
A3887 (49¢) multicolored, serpentine die cut 9½ vert., microprinted "USPS" on second white flag stripe, self-adhesive....................... **5053**
A3887 (49¢) multicolored, serpentine die cut 11¼x10¾ on 2 or 3 sides, microprinted "USPS" to right of pole under flag, self-adhesive (booklet panes only).............. **5054**
A3887 (49¢) multicolored, serpentine die cut 11¼x10¾ on 2 or 3 sides, microprinted "USPS" to second white flag stripe, self-adhesive (booklet panes only).............. **5055**

USA AND STARS ISSUE 2016-17

"USA" and Star — A3893

"USA" and Star With Blue Frame — A3994

A3893 (5¢) multicolored, serpentine die cut 10 vert., self-adhesive (Bureau precanceled)..... **5061**
A3994 (5¢) multicolored, serpentine die cut 10 vert., self-adhesive (Bureau precanceled)..... **5172**

STAR QUILTS ISSUE 2016

A3929

A3930

A3929 (25¢) multicolored, serpentine die cut 11 vert., self-adhesive (Bureau precanceled)... **5098**
A3930 (25¢) multicolored, serpentine die cut 11 vert., self-adhesive (Bureau precanceled)... **5099**

PATRIOTIC SPIRAL ISSUE 2016

Stars — A3961

A3961 (47¢) multicolored, serpentine die cut 10 vert., self-adhesive................................ **5130**
A3961 (47¢) multicolored, serpentine die cut 11 on 2 or 3 sides, self-adhesive (booklet panes only)... **5131**

FLAG ISSUE 2017

Flag — A3988

A3988 (49¢) multicolored, serpentine die cut 11 vert., microprinted "USPS" on right end of fourth red stripe, self-adhesive (Banknote printing).. **5158**
A3988 (49¢) multicolored, serpentine die cut 9½ vert., microprinted "USPS" on right end of second white flag stripe, self-adhesive (Ashton-Potter printing)........................ **5159**
A3988 (49¢) multicolored, serpentine die cut 11¼x10¾ on 2 or 3 sides, microprinted "USPS" on right end of fourth red stripe, self-adhesive (Banknote printing, booklet panes only).. **5160**
A3988 (49¢) multicolored, serpentine die cut 11¼x10¾ on 2 or 3 sides, microprinted "USPS" on right end of second white flag stripe, self-adhesive (Ashton-Potter printing, booklet panes only)............................... **5161**
A3988 (49¢) multicolored, serpentine die cut 11¼x10¾ on 2, 3 or 4 sides, microprinted "USPS" on left end of second white flag stripe near blue field, thin paper, self-adhesive (Ashton-Potter printing, booklet panes only).. **5162**

SHELLS ISSUE 2017

Queen Conch — A3989

Pacific Calico Scallop — A3990

Alphabet Cone — A3991

Zebra Nerite — A3992

A3989 (34¢) multicolored, serpentine die cut 11¼x10¾, self-adhesive....................... **5163**
A3989 (34¢) multicolored, serpentine die cut 9¾ vert., self-adhesive............................... **5169**
A3990 (34¢) multicolored, serpentine die cut 11¼x10¾, self-adhesive....................... **5164**
A3990 (34¢) multicolored, serpentine die cut 9¾ vert., self-adhesive............................... **5170**
A3991 (34¢) multicolored, serpentine die cut 11¼x10¾, self-adhesive....................... **5165**
A3991 (34¢) multicolored, serpentine die cut 9¾ vert., self-adhesive............................... **5167**
A3992 (34¢) multicolored, serpentine die cut 11¼x10¾, self-adhesive....................... **5166**
A3992 (34¢) multicolored, serpentine die cut 9¾ vert., self-adhesive............................... **5168**

UNCLE SAM'S HAT ISSUE 2017-19

People Wearing Uncle Sam Hats — A4006

A4006 (15¢) multicolored, serpentine die cut 11 vert., self-adhesive............................... **5341**
A4006 (21¢) multicolored, serpentine die cut 11¼x11, self-adhesive......................... **5174**

FLAG ISSUE 2018

Flag — A4099

A4099 (50¢) multicolored, serpentine die cut 9½ vert., self-adhesive, microprinted "USPS" at left of flag fold on fourth white stripe.... **5260**
A4099 (50¢) multicolored, serpentine die cut 11 vert., self-adhesive, microprinted "USPS" at right of flag fold on fifth white stripe..... **5261**
A4099 (50¢) multicolored, serpentine die cut 11¼x10¾ on 2 or 3 sides, self-adhesive, microprinted "USPS" at left of flag fold on fourth red stripe (booklet panes only) **5262**
A4099 (50¢) multicolored, serpentine die cut 11¼x10¾ on 2 or 3 sides, self-adhesive, microprinted "USPS" at right of flag fold on fifth white stripe (booklet panes only) **5263**

PEACE ROSE ISSUE 2018

Peace Rose — A4116

A4116 (50¢) multicolored, serpentine die cut 11¼x10¾ on 2 or 3 sides, self-adhesive (booklet panes only)............................ **5280**

STATUE OF FREEDOM ISSUE 2018

Head of Statue of Freedom on U.S. Capitol Dome A4130

A4130 $1 emerald, gold & black, serpentine die cut 10¾x10½, self-adhesive....................... **5295**
A4130 $2 indigo, gold & black, serpentine die cut 10¾x10½, self-adhesive....................... **5296**
A4130 $5 brick red, gold & black, serpentine die cut 10¾x10½, self-adhesive....................... **5297**

FLAG ISSUE 2019

Flag — A4189

A4189 (55¢) multicolored, serpentine die cut 9½ horiz., self-adhesive, microprinted "USPS" at lower flag grommet.......................... **5342**
A4189 (55¢) multicolored, serpentine die cut 11 horiz., self-adhesive, microprinted "USPS" to right of sixth red flag stripe.............. **5343**
A4189 (55¢) multicolored, serpentine die cut 10¾x11¼ on 2 or 3 sides, self-adhesive, microprinted "USPS" at upper left corner of flag (booklet panes only)...................... **5344**
A4189 (55¢) multicolored, serpentine die cut 10¾x11¼ on 2 or 3 sides, self-adhesive, microprinted "USPS" to right of sixth red flag stripe (booklet panes only)........... **5345**

STAR RIBBON ISSUE 2019

Star Ribbon — A4205

A4205 (55¢) multicolored, serpentine die cut 11¼x10¾, self-adhesive **5361**
A4205 (55¢) multicolored, serpentine die cut 10¾ vert., self-adhesive **5362**

CORAL REEFS ISSUE 2019

Elkhorn Coral and French Angelfish — A4206

Brain Coral and Spotted Moray Eel — A4207

Pillar Coral, Coney Grouper and Neon Gobies — A4208

Staghorn Coral and Blue-striped Grunts — A4209

A4206 (35¢) multicolored, serpentine die cut 11¼x10¾, self-adhesive **5363**
A4206 (35¢) multicolored, serpentine die cut 9½ vert., self-adhesive **5369**
A4207 (35¢) multicolored, serpentine die cut 11¼x10¾, self-adhesive **5364**
A4207 (35¢) multicolored, serpentine die cut 9½ vert., self-adhesive **5370**
A4208 (35¢) multicolored, serpentine die cut 11¼x10¾, self-adhesive **5365**
A4208 (35¢) multicolored, serpentine die cut 9½ vert., self-adhesive **5367**
A4209 (35¢) multicolored, serpentine die cut 11¼x10¾, self-adhesive **5366**
A4209 (35¢) multicolored, serpentine die cut 9½ vert., self-adhesive **5368**

SUBJECT INDEX OF REGULAR, COMMEMORATIVE & AIR POST ISSUES

Additions, Deletions & Number Changes

Postage

Number in 2019 Catalogue	Number in 2020 Catalogue
new	490a
new	492a
new	495a
new	563b
new	564b
new	566a
new	567b
new	568a
new	569a
new	1416d
new	1472a
new	2091a
new	2107b
new	2182h
2281b	2281i
new	2419d
new	2433f
new	2523Ae
new	2884c
new	2884d
new	3187q
new	3258a
new	3505e
new	3622b
new	4782c
new	4783c
new	4784c
new	4785j
new	4817a-4820a
4820a	4820b
4820b	4820c
new	4820d
new	4820e
4820c	4820f
4820d	4820g
new	4823e
4823e	4823f
4823f	4823g
new	5036c
new	5172a
new	5306b
new	5310b
new	5315b

Air Post Stamps

Number in 2019 Catalogue	Number in 2020 Catalogue
new	C11b

Special Delivery Stamps

Number in 2019 Catalogue	Number in 2020 Catalogue
new	E13a

Postage Due Stamps

Number in 2019 Catalogue	Number in 2020 Catalogue
J78	J78a
J78a	J78b
J78b	J78
J79	J79a
J79a	J79
J80	J80a
J80a	J80b
J80b	J80
J81	J81a
J81a	J81b
J81b	J81
J82	J82a
J82a	J82b
J82b	J82
J83	J83a
J83a	J83b
J83b	J83
J84	J84a
J84a	J84b
J84b	J84
J85	J85a
J85a	J85
J86	J86a
J86a	J86

Special Handling stamps

Number in 2019 Catalogue	Number in 2020 Catalogue
new	QE1b
new	QE2b
new	QE3b

Booklets

Number in 2019 Catalogue	Number in 2020 Catalogue
new	BK143a
4820b	4820c
new	4820e
4820d	4820g

Computer Vended Postage

Number in 2019 Catalogue	Number in 2020 Catalogue
new	CVP101a
CVP102	CVP91b
CVP103	CVP94a
CVP104	CVP89Ad
CVP105	CVP95a
CVP106	CVP96a
CVP107	CVP97a
new	CVPT17A

Carriers' Stamps

Number in 2019 Catalogue	Number in 2020 Catalogue
new	6LB4a

Stamped Envelopes and Wrappers

Number in 2019 Catalogue	Number in 2020 Catalogue
new	W384a
new	U596g
new	U682a
new	U682b
new	UO75a

Postal Cards

Number in 2019 Catalogue	Number in 2020 Catalogue
new	UX120l

Revenue Stamps

Number in 2019 Catalogue	Number in 2020 Catalogue
new	R2d
R106b	deleted
new	R157a
new	R278b
new	R287
new	R287A
new	R301a
new	R303a
new	R304a
new	RG55a
RO16b	RO16d

Hunting Permit Stamps

Number in 2019 Catalogue	Number in 2020 Catalogue
RW1a	deleted
RW1b	deleted

Essays

Number in 2019 Catalogue	Number in 2020 Catalogue
115-E3a	115-ESP1
115-E3b	116-ESP1
115-E3c	121-ESP1
115-E4a	115-ESP2
115-E4b	116-ESP2
115-E4c	121-ESP2
115-E5a	115-ESP3
115-E5b	116-ESP3
115-E5c	121-ESP3
115-E6a	115-ESP4
115-E6b	116-ESP4
115-E6c	121-ESP4
115-E7a	115-ESP5
115-E7b	116-ESP5
115-E7c	121-ESP5
115-E8a	115-ESP6
115-E8b	116-ESP6
115-E8c	121-ESP6
115-E9a	115-ESP7
115-E9b	116-ESP7
115-E9c	121-ESP7
115-E10a	115-ESP8
115-E10b	116-ESP8
129-E3	118-ESP9
129-E4	118-ESP10
129-E5	118-ESP11
129-E6	118-ESP12
115-E11a	115-ESP13
115-E11b	116-ESP13
115-E11c	121-ESP13
115-E12a	115-ESP14
115-E12b	116-ESP14
115-E12c	121-ESP14
115-E13a	115-ESP15

Essays

Number in 2019 Catalogue	Number in 2020 Catalogue
115-E13b	121-ESP15
115-E14a	115-ESP16
115-E14b	116-ESP16
115-E15a	115-ESP17
115-E15b	121-ESP17
115-E16a	115-ESP18
115-E16b	116-ESP18
115-E16c	121-ESP18
116-E6a	116-ESP19
116-E6b	121-ESP19
116-E7a	116-ESP20
116-E7b	deleted
116-E8	116-ESP21
115-E17a	115-ESP22
115-E17b	116-ESP22
115-E18	115-ESP23
115-E19b	116-ESP24
115-E19a	115-ESP25
new	116-ESP25
115-E19c	deleted
115-E20	115-ESP26
146-E8	211-E2
new	1105-E1
new	1105-E2
new	1105-E3
new	1105-E4
new	1128-E1
new	1128-E2
new	1139-E1
new	1139-E2
new	1139-E3
new	1139-E4
new	1139-E5
new	1139-E6
new	1139-E7
new	1139-E8
new	1139-E9
new	1141-E1
new	1141-E2
new	1141-E3
new	1141-E4
new	1141-E5
new	1141-E6
new	1141-E7
new	1141-E8
new	1141-E9
new	1141-E10
new	1141-E11
new	1141-E12
new	1147-E1
new	1147-E2
new	1147-E3
new	1147-E4
new	1147-E5
new	2646a-E1
new	2646a-E2
new	2646a-E3
new	2646a-E4
new	2646a-E5
new	2646a-E6

Trial Color, Die, Plate Proofs

Number in 2019 Catalogue	Number in 2020 Catalogue
178P1	deleted
179P1	deleted
new	1178P1b
new	RK40P1a
new	PS7TC1

Postal Counterfeits

Number in 2019 Catalogue	Number in 2020 Catalogue
250(CF1)	250(CF2)
250(CF2)	250(CF1)
267(CF1)	252(CF1)
3281(CF1)a	deleted
new	3281(CF2)
new	3622(CF2)
new	3982(CF2)
new	3982(CF3)
new	3982(CF4)
new	4125(CF2)

Postal Counterfeits

Number in 2019 Catalogue	Number in 2020 Catalogue
new	4125(CF3)
new	4235(CF2)
new	4390(CF1)
new	4393(CF9)
new	4393(CF10)
new	4394(CF2)
new	4629(CF1)
new	4631(CF1)
new	4632(CF1)
new	4770(CF1)
new	4771(CF1)
new	4772(CF1)
new	4773(CF1)
new	4854(CF1)
new	4854(CF2)
new	4854(CF3)
new	4854(CF4)
new	4868(CF2)
new	4868(CF3)
new	4868(CF4)
new	4991(CF1)
new	4992(CF1)
new	4993(CF1)
new	4994(CF1)
new	5052(CF1)
new	5053(CF2)
new	5053(CF3)
new	5053(CF4)
new	5053(CF5)
new	5131(CF2)
new	5155(CF2)
new	5158(CF2)
new	5158(CF3)
new	5158(CF4)
new	5159(CF1)
new	5161(CF1)
new	5255(CF1)
new	5260(CF1)
new	5260(CF2)
new	5260(CF3)
new	5260(CF4)
new	5262(CF1)
new	5262(CF2)
new	5262(CF3)

Nonpostal and Revenue Counterfeits

Number in 2019 Catalogue	Number in 2020 Catalogue
new	RC3ca(CF1)
new	R86c(CF1)

Test Stamps

Number in 2019 Catalogue	Number in 2020 Catalogue
new	TD27B
new	TD54C
TD71	deleted
new	TD87H

Test Booklets

Number in 2019 Catalogue	Number in 2020 Catalogue
new	TDB4C
new	TDB11e
new	TDB16e
new	TDB16f
TDB27a	deleted
TDB31a	deleted
TDB32a	deleted
new	TDB32A
TDB33a	deleted
new	TDB35A
new	TDB35Ab
new	TDB35C
new	TDB35Cd
TDB36a	deleted
TDB36B	TDB36A
TDB36Bc	TDB36Ab
new	TDB61a
new	TDB61b
new	TDB84B
new	TDB84Bc
new	TDB84D
new	TDB84De
new	TDB84F
new	TDB84Fg

Additions, Deletions & Number Changes

Test Booklets

Number in 2019 Catalogue	Number in 2020 Catalogue
new	TDB93Ab
new	TDB99B
new	TDB99Bc
new	TDB99D
new	TDB88De

Christmas Seals

Number in 2019 Catalogue	Number in 2020 Catalogue
new	WX1a
new	WX1b
new	WX1c
new	WX2a
WX3h	WX3H
new	WX9A
new	WX9B
WX12a	WX12A
new	WX14
new	WX268-WX270
new	WX271-WX273
new	WX274-WX276
new	WX274a
new	WX277-WX279
new	WX277a
new	WX280-WX282
new	WX280a
new	WX283-WX288
new	WX283a
new	WX289-WX290
new	WX289a-WX290a
new	WX292-WX295
new	WX292a
new	WX296-WX298
new	WX298a
new	WX299-WX302
new	WX299a
new	WX303-WX306
new	WX303a
new	WX307-WX311
new	WX307a
new	WX312-WX315
new	WX312a
new	WX316-WX318
new	WX316a
new	WX319-WX321
new	WX319a
new	WX322-WX326
new	WX326a
new	WX327-WX330
new	WX327a
new	WX331-WX334
new	WX331a
new	WX335-WX338
new	WX336a
new	WX339-WX341
new	WX340a
new	WX342-WX344
new	WX343a
new	WX345-WX348
new	WX348a
new	WX349-WX354
new	WX351a
new	WX355-WX357
new	WX355a
new	WX358-WX360
new	WX359a
new	WX361
new	WX361a-WX361b
new	WX362
new	WX362a-WX362b
new	WX363
new	WX363a-WX363b
new	WX364-WX364a
new	WX365-WX365a
new	WX366-WX366a
new	WX367-WX367a
new	WX368-WX368a
new	WX369-WX369a
new	WX370
new	WX371-WX372
new	WX373-WX374
new	WX375-WX376
new	WX377-WX378

Confederate 3¢ 1861 Postmasters' Provisionals

Number in 2019 Catalogue	Number in 2020 Catalogue
new	8AXU1

Confederate Postmasters' Provisionals

Number in 2019 Catalogue	Number in 2020 Catalogue
new	150XU1
new	151XU1
new	152XU1

Canal Zone

Number in 2019 Catalogue	Number in 2020 Catalogue
new	55g
new	55h
new	61e
new	87b
new	115a

Hawaii

Number in 2019 Catalogue	Number in 2020 Catalogue
new	15d
new	62f

Ryukyu Islands

Number in 2019 Catalogue	Number in 2020 Catalogue
new	2X1a
new	2X4b
new	2X8a
new	2X9a
new	2X21a
new	3X1a
new	3X2d
new	3X4a
new	3X5a
new	3X6a
new	3X7a
new	3X8a
new	3X8b
new	3X11a
new	3X12a
new	3X12b
new	3X13a
new	3X15a
new	3X16a
new	3X17b
new	3X17c
new	3X18a
new	3X20a
new	3X21a
new	3X21b
new	3X21c
new	3X22b
new	3X22c
new	3X28b
new	3X31a
new	4X2b
new	4X2c
new	4X3a
new	4X4a
new	5X6a
new	5X7a
new	5X7b
new	5X8a
new	5X10a
new	5X10b
new	UZE22b
new	3XR1a
new	3XR2b
new	3XR2c
new	3XR2d
new	3XR3a
new	3XR3b
new	3XR4b
new	3XR4c
new	3XR5a
new	3XR5b
new	3XR6a
new	3XR7b

POSTMASTERS' PROVISIONALS

The Act of Congress of March 3, 1845, effective July 1, 1845, established rates of postage as follows:

"For every single letter in manuscript or paper of any kind by or upon which information shall be asked or communicated in writing or by marks designs, conveyed in the mail, for any distance under 300 miles, five cents; and for any distance over 300 miles, ten cents; and for a double letter there shall be charged double these rates; and for a treble letter, treble these rates; and for a quadruple letter, quadruple these rates; and every letter or parcel not exceeding half an ounce in weight shall be deemed a single letter, and every additional weight of half an ounce, shall be charged with an additional single postage. All drop letters, or letters placed in any post office, not for transmission through the mail but for delivery only, shall be charged with postage at the rate of two cents each."

Circulars were charged 2 cents, magazines and pamphlets 2½ cents; newspapers according to size.

Between the time of the Act of 1845, effecting uniform postage rates, and the Act of Congress of March 3, 1847, authorizing the postmaster-general to issue stamps, postmasters in various cities issued provisional stamps.

Before adhesive stamps were introduced, prepaid mail was marked "Paid" either with pen and ink or handstamps of various designs. Unpaid mail occasionally was marked "Due." Most often, however, unpaid mail did not have a "Due" marking, only the amount of postage to be collected from the recipient, e.g. "5," "10," "18¾," etc. Thus, if a letter was not marked "Paid," it was assumed to be unpaid. These "stampless covers" are found in numerous types and usually carry the town postmark.

New York Postmaster Robert H. Morris issued the first postmaster provisional in July 1845. Other postmasters soon followed. The provisionals served until superseded by the federal government's 5c and 10c stamps issued July 1, 1847.

Postmasters recognized the provisionals as indicating postage prepaid. On several provisionals, the signature of initials of the postmaster vouched for their legitimate use.

On July 12, 1845, Postmaster Morris sent examples of his new stamp to the postmasters of Boston, Philadelphia, Albany and Washington, asking that they be treated as unpaid until they reached the New York office. Starting in that year, the New York stamps were distributed to other offices. Postmaster General Cave Johnson reportedly authorized this practice with the understanding that these stamps were to be sold for letters directed to or passing through New York. This was an experiment to test the practicality of the use of adhesive postage stamps.

ALEXANDRIA, VA.

Daniel Bryan, Postmaster

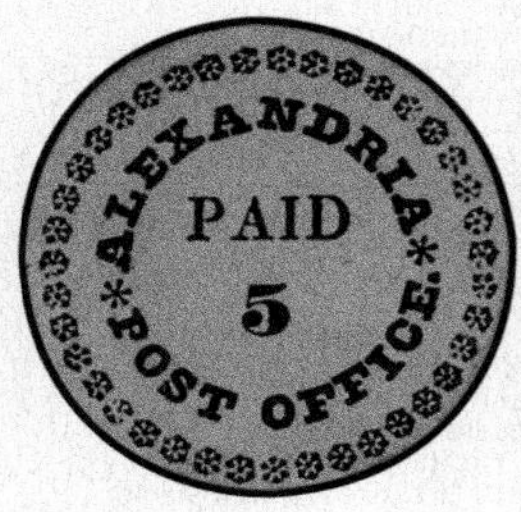

A1

All known examples are cut to shape.
Type I — 40 asterisks in circle.
Type II — 39 asterisks in circle.

1846 **Typeset** ***Imperf.***

1X1 A1 5c **black,** *buff,* type I *325,000.*
a. 5c black, *buff,* type II *625,000.*
On cover (I or II) *500,000.*
1X2 A1 5c **black,** *blue,* type I, on cover *1,180,000.*

Cancellations

Red circular town
Black "PAID"
Black ms. accounting number ("No. 45," "No. 70")

The approximately 6 examples of Nos. 1X1 and 1X1a known on cover or cover front are generally not tied by postmark and some are uncanceled. The value for "on cover" is for a stamp obviously belonging on a cover which bears the proper circular dated town, boxed "5" and straight line "PAID" markings.

No. 1X2 is unique. Value represents realization in a 2019 auction sale. It is canceled with a black straight line "PAID" marking which is repeated on the cover. The cover also bears a black circular "Alexandria Nov. 25" postmark.

ANNAPOLIS, MD.

Martin F. Revell, Postmaster
ENVELOPE

E1

1846 **Printed in upper right corner of envelope**

2XU1 E1 5c **carmine red,** *white* *500,000.*

No. 2XU1 exists in two sizes of envelope.

Envelopes and letter sheets are known showing the circular design and figure "2" handstamped in blue or red. They were used locally. Value, blue $17,500, red $30,000.

Letter sheets are known showing the circular design and figure "5" handstamped in blue or red. Value, blue $10,000, red $12,500.

Similar circular design in blue without numeral or "PAID" is known to have been used as a postmark.

BALTIMORE, MD.

James Madison Buchanan, Postmaster

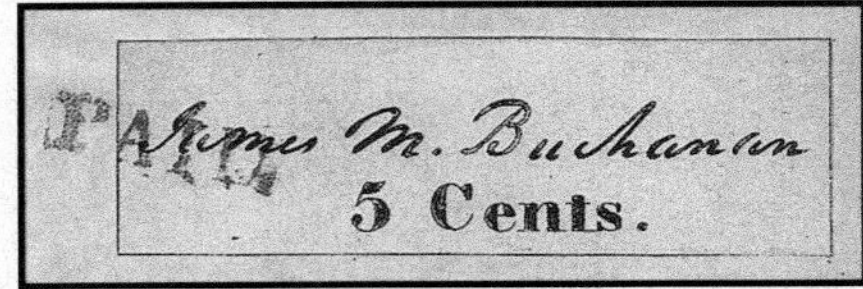

Signature of Postmaster — A1

Printed from a plate of 12 (2x6) containing nine 5c stamps (Pos. 1-6, 8, 10, 12) and three 10c (Pos. 7, 9, 11).

1845 **Engr.** ***Imperf.***

3X1 A1 5c **black** *6,000.*
On cover *15,000.*
Vertical pair on cover *125,000.*
3X2 A1 10c **black,** on cover *80,000.*
3X3 A1 5c **black,** *bluish* *65,000.* *6,000.*
On cover *13,500.*
3X4 A1 10c **black,** *bluish* *50,000.*
On cover —

Earliest documented uses: Jan. 15, 1846 (No. 3X1); Aug. 3, 1845 (No. 3X3).

Nos. 3X3-3X4 preceded Nos. 3X1-3X2 in use.

No. 3X3 unused is unique. Value is based on 1997 auction sale.

Cancellations

Blue circular town
Blue straight line "PAID"
Blue "5" in oval
Blue "10" in oval
Black pen

Off cover values are for stamps canceled by either pen or handstamp. Stamps on covers tied by handstamps command premiums.

Envelopes

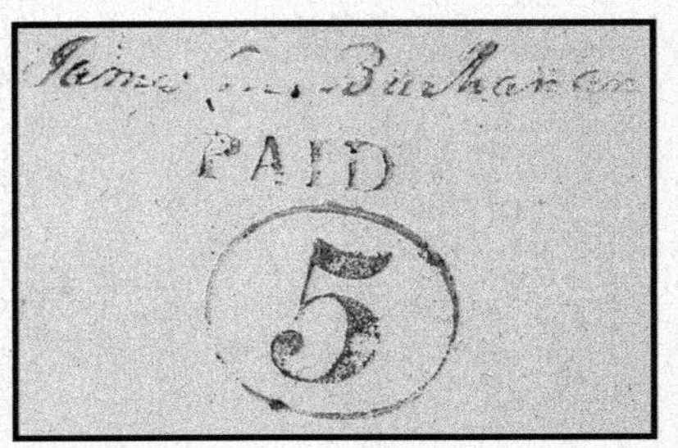

E1

Three Separate Handstamps

The "PAID" and "5" in oval were handstamped in blue or red, always both in the same color on the same entire. "James M. Buchanan" was handstamped in black, blue or red. Blue town and rate with black signature was issued first and sells for more.

The paper is manila, buff, white, salmon or grayish. Manila is by far the most frequently found 5c envelope. All 10c envelopes are rare, with manila or buff the more frequent. Of the 10c on salmon, only one example is known.

The general attractiveness of the envelope and the clarity of the handstamps primarily determine the value.

The color listed is that of the "PAID" and "5" in oval.

1845 **Various Papers** **Handstamped**

3XU1 E1 5c **blue** *6,500.*
3XU2 E1 5c **red** *10,000.*
3XU3 E1 10c **blue** *20,000.*
3XU4 E1 10c **red** *20,000.*

Earliest documented uses: Sept. 7, 1845 (No. 3UX1); Apr. 27, 1846 (No. 3XU2); Nov. 16, 1845 (No. 3XU3); June 12, 1846 (No. 3XU4).

Cancellations

Blue circular town
Blue "5" in oval

The second "5" in oval on the unlisted "5 + 5" envelopes is believed not to be part of the basic prepaid marking, but envelopes bearing this marking merit a premium over the values for Nos. 3XU1-3XU2.

BOSCAWEN, NH.

Worcester Webster, Postmaster

A1

1846 (?) **Typeset** ***Imperf.***

4X1 A1 5c **dull blue,** *yellowish,* on cover *300,000.*

One example known, uncanceled on cover with ms. postal markings.

BRATTLEBORO, VT.

Frederick N. Palmer, Postmaster

Initials of Postmaster (FNP) — A1

Printed from plate of 10 (5x2) separately engraved subjects with imprint "Eng'd by Thos. Chubbuck, Bratto." below the middle stamp of the lower row (Pos. 8).

1846 ***Imperf.***

Thick Softwove Paper Colored Through

5X1 A1 5c **black,** *buff* *7,500.*
On cover *25,000.*
Two singles on cover —

Earliest documented use: Aug. 28, 1846.

Cancellations

Red straight line "PAID"
Red pen
Blue "5" (unique)
Red grid (unique)

The red pen-marks are small and lightly applied. They were used to invalidate a single sample sheet. One example of each plate position is known so canceled.

LOCKPORT, N.Y.

Hezekiah W. Scovell, Postmaster

A1

"Lockport, N.Y." oval and "PAID" separately handstamped in red, "5" in black ms.

1846 ***Imperf.***

6X1 A1 5c **red,** *buff,* on cover — *300,000.*

Cancellation

Black ms. "X"

One example of No. 6X1 is known. Small fragments of two other stamps adhering to one cover also exist.

MILLBURY, MASS.

Asa H. Waters, Postmaster

George Washington — A1

Printed from a woodcut, singly, on a hand press.

1846 ***Imperf.***

7X1 A1 5c **black,** *bluish* — *50,000.*
On cover — *350,000.*

Earliest documented use: Aug. 21, 1846.

Cancellations

Red straight line "PAID"
Red circular "MILBURY, MS.," date in center

NEW HAVEN, CONN.

Edward A. Mitchell, Postmaster
ENVELOPES

E1

Impressed from a brass handstamp at upper right of envelope.

Signed in blue, black or magenta ms., as indicated in parentheses.

1845

8XU1 E1 5c **red** (M) — *100,000.*
Cut square — *50,000.*
Cut to shape — *15,000.*
8XU2 E1 5c **red,** *light bluish* (Bk) — *125,000.*
8XU3 E1 5c **dull blue,** *buff* (Bl) — *75,000.*
Cut to shape (Bk) — *55,000.*
8XU4 E1 5c **dull blue** (Bl) — *60,000.*

Values of Nos. 8XU1-8XU4 are a guide to value. They are based on auction realizations and other sales, and take condition into consideration. All New Haven envelopes are of equal rarity (each is unique), with the exception of No. 8XU2, of which two exist. An entire of No. 8XU2 is the finest example known, and this is reflected in the value shown. The other envelopes are valued according to condition, and cut squares also are valued according to condition as much as rarity.

REPRINTS

Twenty reprints in dull blue on white paper, signed by E. A. Mitchell in lilac rose ink, were made in 1871 for W. P. Brown and others, value $1,750. Thirty reprints in carmine on hard white paper, signed in dark blue, red or black (rare), were made in 1874 for Cyrus B. Peets, Chief Clerk for Mitchell, value $1,200. Unsigned reprints in dull red on soft yellowish white paper were made for N. F. Seebeck and others about 1872, value $400.

Edward A. Mitchell, grandson of the Postmaster, in 1923 delivered reprints in lilac on soft white wove paper, dated "1923" in place of the signature, value $400.

In 1932, the New Haven Philatelic Society bought the original handstamp and gave it to the New Haven Colony Historical Society. To make the purchase possible (at the $1000 price) it was decided to print 260 stamps from the original handstamp. Of these, 130 were in red and 130 in dull blue, all on hard, white wove paper, value approximately $250 each.

According to Carroll Alton Means' booklet on the New Haven Provisional Envelope, after this last reprinting the brass handstamp was so treated that further reprints cannot be made. The reprints were sold originally at $5 each. A facsimile signature of the postmaster, "E. A. Mitchell," (blue on the red reprints, black on the blue) was applied with a rubber handstamp. These 260 reprints are all numbered to correspond with the number of the booklet issued then.

NEW YORK, N.Y.

Robert H. Morris, Postmaster

George Washington — A1

Printed by Rawdon, Wright & Hatch from a plate of 40 (5x8). The die for Washington's head on the contemporary bank notes was used for the vignette. It had a small flaw—a line extending from the corner of the mouth down the chin—which is quite visible on the paper money. This was corrected for the stamp.

The stamps were usually initialed "ACM" (Alonzo Castle Monson) in magenta ink as a control before being sold or passed through the mails. There are four or five styles of these initials. The most common is "ACM" without periods. The scarcest is "A.C.M.", believed written by Marcena Monson. The rare initials "RHM" (Robert H. Morris, the postmaster) and "MMJr" (Marcena Monson) are listed separately.

The stamps were printed on a variety of wove papers varying in thickness from pelure to thick, and in color from gray to bluish and blue. A thick brown gum was used first, succeeded by a thin whitish transparent gum. Some stamps appear to have a slight ribbing or mesh effect. A few also show letters of a double-line papermaker's watermark, a scarce variety. All used true blue copies carry "ACM" without periods; of the three unused copies, two lack initials.

Nos. 9X1-9X3 and varieties unused are valued without gum. Examples with original gum are extremely scarce and will command higher prices.

Earliest documented use: July 15, 1845 (No. 9X1e).

1845-46 Engr. Bluish Wove Paper ***Imperf.***

9X1 A1 5c **black,** signed ACM, connected, *1846* — 1,500. — 475.
On cover — 600.
On cover to France or England — *2,250.*
On cover to other European countries — *5,500.*
Pair — 5,750. — 1,450.
Pair on cover — 2,000.
Pair on cover to England — *4,500.*
Pair on cover to Canada — *5,500.*
Vertical pair, 9X1 and 9X1e — *85,000.*
Strip of 3 — *5,000.*
Strip of 3 on cover — *9,000.*
Strip of 4 — *12,500.*
Strip of 4 on cover — *100,000.*
Block of 4 — *50,000.*
Double transfer at bottom (Pos. 2) — 1,700. — 550.
Double transfer at top (Pos. 7) — 1,700. — 550.
Bottom frame line double (Pos. 31) — 1,700. — 550.
Top frame line double (Pos. 36) — 1,700. — 550.

The unused pair of Nos. 9X1 and 9X1e is unique.

The only blocks currently known are a used block of 4 off cover (faulty), a repaired block of 6 on cover, and a block of 9 on cover.

Cancellations

Blue pen — 475.
Black pen — +25.
Magenta pen — +100.
Red square grid (New York) — +100.
Black circular date stamp — —
Red round grid (Boston) — +350.
Blue numeral (Philadelphia) — +750.
Red "U.S" in octagon frame (carrier) — +1,200.
Red "PAID" — +100.
Red N.Y. circular date stamp — +150.
Large red N.Y. circular date stamp containing "5" — +125.
Small red "5" — —
Large red "5" — +1,000.

a. Signed ACM, AC connected — 1,750. — 550.
On cover — 700.
On cover to France or England — *2,250.*
On cover to other European countries — *6,000.*
Pair — 5,750. — 1,750.
Pair, on cover — *2,250.*
Strip of 4, on cover — *100,000.*
Pair, Nos. 9X1, 9X1a — — — 4,750.
Pair, Nos. 9X1 and 9X1a, on cover — *15,000.*
Double transfer at bottom (Pos. 2) — 1,800. — 675.
Double transfer at top (Pos. 7) — 1,800. — 675.
Bottom frame line double (Pos. 31) — 1,800. — 675.
Top frame line double (Pos. 36) — 1,800. — 675.

Cancellations

Blue pen — 550.
Black pen — +25.
Magenta pen — +100.
Red N.Y. circular date stamp — +125.
Large red N.Y. circular date stamp with "5" — +150.
Red square grid — +100.
Red "PAID" — +50.

b. Signed A.C.M. — *4,500.* — *675.*
On cover — *825.*
On cover to France or England — *2,750.*
On cover to other European countries — *6,000.*
Pair — *2,400.*
Pair on cover — *3,250.*
Double transfer at bottom (Pos. 2) — — — *925.*
Double transfer at top (Pos. 7) — — — *925.*
Bottom frame line double (Pos. 31) — *925.*
Top frame line double (Pos. 36) — *925.*

Cancellations

Blue pen — *675.*
Black pen — +25.
Red square grid — +100.
Red N.Y. circular date stamp — +100.
Large red N.Y. circular date stamp containing "5" — +150.
Red "PAID" — +75.

c. Signed MMJr — *10,000.*
On cover — —
Pair on cover front — *26,500.*

The No. 9X1c pair on cover front is unique. Value reflects auction sale price in 1992.

d. Signed RHM — *13,000.* — *3,500.*
Pair — *12,000.*
On cover — *5,500.*
On cover from New Hamburgh, N.Y. — *12,500.*

Cancellations

Blue pen — *3,500.*
Black pen — +150.
Red square grid — +250.
Red N.Y. circular date stamp — +400.
Red "PAID" — +300.

Earliest documented use: July 17, 1845.

e. Without signature — *3,750.* — 900.
On cover — 1,350.
On cover to France or England — *2,500.*
On cover to other European countries — *6,000.*
On cover, July 15, 1845 — *27,500.*
Pair — *2,600.*
Pair on cover — *2,900.*
Double transfer at bottom (Pos. 2) — *4,000.* — *1,000.*
Double transfer at top (Pos. 7) — *4,000.* — *1,000.*
Bottom frame line double (Pos. 31) — *4,000.* — *1,000.*
Top frame line double (Pos. 36) — *4,000.* — *1,000.*
Ribbed paper — — — —

Cancellations

Blue pen — 900.
Black pen — +25.
Magenta pen — +100.
Red square grid — +100.
Red N.Y. circular date stamp — +100.
Large red N.Y. circular date stamp containing "5" — +150.
Red "PAID" — +100.

Known used from Albany, Boston, Jersey City, N.J., New Hamburgh, N.Y., Philadelphia, Sing Sing, N.Y., Washington, D.C., and Hamilton, Canada, as well as by route agents on the Baltimore R.R. Covers originating in New Hamburgh are known only with No. 9X1d (one also bearing the U.S. City Despatch Post carrier); one also known used to Holland.

1847 Engr. Blue Wove Paper ***Imperf.***

9X2 A1 5c **black,** signed ACM connected — *6,500.* — 3,750.
On cover — *5,750.*
Pair — *13,000.*
Pair on cover — —
Double transfer at bottom (Pos. 2) — 4,250.

Double transfer at top (Pos. 7) 4,250.
Bottom frame line double (Pos. 31) 4,250.
Top frame line double (Pos. 36) 4,250.
a. Signed RHM —
b. Signed ACM, AC connected *8,000.*
d. Without signature *25,000.* *7,500.*

Earliest documented use: Mar. 4, 1847.

Cancellations

Red square grid 3,750.
Red "PAID" +100.
Red N.Y. circular date stamp +650.

All used true blue examples carry "ACM" without periods; of the three unused examples, two lack initials.
On the only example known of No. 9X2a the "R" is illegible and does not match those of the other "RHM" signatures.
No. 9X2b is unique.

1847 Engr. Gray Wove Paper *Imperf.*

9X3 A1 5c **black,** signed ACM connected 5,250. 2,250.
On cover *5,250.*
On cover to Europe *8,500.*
Pair *7,750.*
Pair on cover *8,750.*
Double transfer at bottom (Pos. 2) 2,600.
Double transfer at top (Pos. 7) 2,600.
Bottom frame line double (Pos. 31) 2,600.
Top frame line double (Pos. 36) 2,600.
a. Signed RHM *8,500.*
b. Without signature *13,000.*

Earliest documented use: Feb. 8, 1847.

Cancellations

Red square grid 2,250.
Red N.Y. circular date stamp 2,250.
Red "PAID" +100.

All known used examples of No. 9X3a have red square grid or red "PAID" in arc cancel.

The first plate was of nine subjects (3x3). Each subject differs slightly from the others, with Position 8 showing the white stock shaded by crossed diagonal lines. At some point prints were struck from this plate in black on deep blue and white bond paper, as well as in blue, green, scarlet and brown on white bond paper. These are listed in the Proof and Trial Color Proof sections. Stamps from this plate were not issued, and it is possible that it is an essay, as the design differs slightly from the issued stamps from the sheet of 40. No examples from the plate of nine are known used.

ENVELOPES

Postmaster Morris, according to newspaper reports of July 2 and 7, 1845, issued envelopes. The design was not stated and no example has been seen. It is possible that these items were envelopes to which stamps had been affixed.

PROVIDENCE, R.I.

Welcome B. Sayles, Postmaster

A1 & A2

Engraved on copper plate containing 12 stamps (3x4). Upper right corner stamp (Pos. 3) "TEN"; all others "FIVE." The stamps were engraved directly on the plate, each differing from the other. The "TEN" and Pos. 4, 5, 6, 9, 11 and 12 have no period after "CENTS."

Yellowish White Handmade Paper

Earliest documented use: Aug. 25, 1846 (No. 10X1).

1846, Aug. 24 *Imperf.*

10X1 A1 5c **gray black** 350. *2,250.*
No gum 200.
On cover, tied by postmark *21,500.*
On cover, tied by pen cancel *11,000.*
On cover, pen canceled *7,000.*
Two on cover —
Pair 725.
Block of four 1,450.
10X2 A2 10c **gray black** 1,150. *16,500.*
No gum 700.
On cover, pen canceled *45,000.*
a. Se-tenant with 5c *2,000.*
Complete sheet *5,500.*
No gum *3,500.*

Cancellations

Black pen check mark
Red circular town
Red straight line "PAID" (2 types)
Red "5"

All canceled examples of Nos. 10X1-10X2, whether or not bearing an additional handstamped cancellation, are obliterated with a black pen check mark. There is only one known certified used example off cover of No. 10X2, and it has a minor fault. Value represents a 1997 sale. All genuine covers must bear the red straight line "PAID," the red circular town postmark, and the red numeral "5" or "10" rating mark.

Reprints were made in 1898. In general, each stamp bears one of the following letters on the back: B. O. G. E. R. T. D. U. R. B. I. N. However, some reprint sheets received no such printing on the reverse. All reprints are without gum. Value for 5c, $65; for 10c, $160; for sheet, $1,000. Reprints without the printing on the reverse sell for more.

ST. LOUIS, MO.

John M. Wimer, Postmaster

A1

A2

Missouri Coat of Arms — A3

Printed from a copper plate of 6 (2x3) subjects separately engraved by J. M. Kershaw.

The plate in its first state, referred to as Plate 1, comprised: three 5c stamps in the left vertical row and three 10c in the right vertical row. The stamps vary slightly in size, measuring from 17¾ to 18¼ by 22 to 22½mm.

Later a 20c denomination was believed necessary. So two of the 5c stamps, types I (pos. 1) and II (pos. 3) were changed to 20c by placing the plate face down on a hard surface and hammering on the back of the parts to be altered until the face was driven flush at those points. The new numerals were then engraved. Both 20c stamps show broken frame lines and the paw of the rights bear on type II is missing. The 20c type II (pos. 3) also shows retouching in the dashes under "SAINT" and "LOUIS." The characteristics of types I and II of the 5c also serve to distinguish the two types of the 20c. This altered, second state of the plate is referred to as Plate 2. It is the only state to contain the 20c.

The demand for the 20c apparently proved inadequate, and the plate was altered again. The "20" was erased and the "5" engraved in its place, resulting in noticeable differences from the 5c stamps from Plate 1. In type I (pos. 1) reengraved, the "5" is twice as far from the top frame line as in the original state, and the four dashes under "SAINT" and "LOUIS" have disappeared except for about half of the upper dash under each word. In type II (pos. 3) reengraved, the ornament in the flag of the "5" is a diamond instead of a triangle; the diamond in the bow is much longer than in the first state, and the ball of the "5," originally blank, contains a large dot. At right of the shading of the "5" is a short curved line which is evidently a remnant of the "0" of "20." Type III (pos. 5) of the 5c was slightly retouched. This second alteration of the plate is referred to as Plate 3.

Type characteristics common to Plates 1, 2 and 3:

5 Cent. Type I (pos. 1). Haunches of both bears almost touch frame lines.

Type II (pos. 3). Bear at right almost touches frame line, but left bear is about ¼mm from it.

Type III (pos. 5). Haunches of both bears about ½mm from frame lines. Small spur on "S" of "POST."

10 Cent. Type I (pos. 2). Three dashes below "POST OFFICE."

Type II (pos. 4). Three pairs of dashes.

Type III (pos. 6). Pairs of dashes (with rows of dots between) at left and right. Dash in center with row of dots above it.

20 Cent. Type I. See 5c Type I.

Type II. See 5c Type II.

Nos. 11X1-11X8 unused are valued without gum.

Values for used off-cover examples of Nos. 11X1-11X8 are for pen-canceled examples. Handstamp-canceled stamps sell for much more. Values for stamps on cover are for examples with pen cancels. Covers with the stamps tied by handstamp sell at considerable premiums depending upon the condition of the stamps and the general attractiveness of the cover. In general, covers with multiple frankings (unless separately valued) are valued at the "on cover" value of the highest-valued stamp, plus the "off cover" value of the other stamps.

Earliest documented use of St. Louis "Bears": Nov. 13, 1845 (No. 11X2).

Wove Paper Colored Through

1845, Nov.-1846 *Imperf.*

11X1 A1 5c **black,** *greenish* *50,000.* *8,000.*
On cover *17,500.*
Pair — *18,000.*
Two on cover *25,000.*
Strip of 3 *35,000.*
Strip of 3 plus single on cover *45,000.*
11X2 A2 10c **black,** *greenish* *50,000.* *8,000.*
On cover *14,000.*
Pair *18,000.*
Pair on cover *22,500.*
Strip of 3 *32,500.*
Strip of 3 on cover *70,000.*
Five on cover *225,000.*
On cover, #11X2, 11X6 *125,000.*
11X3 A3 20c **black,** *greenish* *160,000.*
On cover —
On cover, #11X5, two #11X3 *325,000.*

Printed from Plate 1 (3 varieties each of the 5c and 10c) and Plate 2 (1 variety of the 5c, 3 of the 10c, 2 of the 20c).

1846

11X4 A1 5c **black,** (III), *gray lilac* — *55,000.*
On cover —
11X5 A2 10c **black,** *gray lilac* *50,000.* *12,500.*
On cover *16,000.*
Pair *29,000.*
Pair, 10c (III), 5c (III) *90,000.*
Strip of 3 *52,500.*
Strip of 3 on cover *160,000.*
Pair 10c (II), 10c (III) se-tenant with 5c (III) *70,000.*
Strip of 3 10c (I, II, III) se-tenant with 5c (III) *300,000.*

Earliest documented use: Feb. 27, 1846.

11X6 A3 20c **black,** *gray lilac* *100,000.* *60,000.*
On cover *70,000.*
Pair *130,000.*
Pair on cover *145,000.*
On cover, #11X6 and #11X5 *75,000.*
On cover, #11X6 and 2 #11X4, tied by handstamp cancel (unique) *125,000.*
Pair, #11X6 and #11X5 *155,000.*
Pair, #11X6 and #11X5, on cover *210,000.*
Strip of 3, 2#11X6 and #11X4 *175,000.*

Printed from Plate 2 (1 variety of the 5c, 3 of the 10c, 2 of the 20c).

No. 11X6 unused is unique. It is in the grade of fine and is valued thus.

The used pair of No. 11X6 is unique. The left margin cuts into the frameline, and it is valued thus.

1847 Pelure Paper

11X7 A1 5c **black,** *bluish* — *11,000.*
On cover *16,000.*
Pair *40,000.*
Two on cover *37,500.*
11X8 A2 10c **black,** *bluish* *17,500.* *15,000.*
On cover *20,000.*
a. Impression of 5c on back *77,500.*

Printed from Plate 3 (3 varieties each of the 5c, 10c).
Earliest documented use: Nov. 25, 1846 (#11X8).
No. 11X8 unused is unique. No. 11X8a is unique.

Cancellations, Nos. 11X1-11X8

Black pen
Ms. initials of postmaster (#11X2, type I)
Red circular town
Red straight line "PAID"
Red grid (#11X7)

Values of Nos. 11X7-11X8, on and off cover, reflect the usual poor condition of these stamps, which were printed on fragile pelure paper. Attractive examples with minor defects sell for considerably more.

POSTAGE

GENERAL ISSUES

Please Note:
Stamps are valued in the grade of very fine unless otherwise indicated.
Values for early and valuable stamps are for examples with certificates of authenticity from acknowledged expert committees, or examples sold with the buyer having the right of certification. This applies to examples with original gum as well as examples without gum. Beware of stamps offered "as is," as the gum on some unused stamps offered with "original gum" may be fraudulent, and stamps offered as unused without gum may in some cases be altered or faintly canceled used stamps.

Color Cancellations

Additional values for color cancellations listed in the "cancellations" section after stamps from No. 1 through No. 218 are for full or nearly full unfaded strikes on very fine stamps. Premiums for such strikes on extremely fine or superb stamps often are much larger, and premiums for strikes on stamps in grades lower than very fine are smaller.

Issues from 1847 through 1894 are unwatermarked.

Benjamin Franklin — A1

Double transfer of top frame line — (A) position 80R1

Double transfer of top and bottom frame lines — (B) position 90R1

Double transfer of bottom frame line and lower part of left frame line — (C)

Double transfer of top, bottom and left frame lines, also numerals — (D)

Double transfer of "U," "POST OFFICE" and left numeral — (E)

Double transfer of top frame line, upper part of side frame lines, "U," and "POST OFFICE" — (F)

This issue was authorized by an Act of Congress, approved March 3, 1847, to take effect July 1, 1847, from which date the use of Postmasters' Stamps or any which were not authorized by the Postmaster General became illegal.

This issue was declared invalid as of July 1, 1851.

Produced by Rawdon, Wright, Hatch & Edson.
Plates of 200 subjects in two panes of 100 each.

1847, July 1 **Engr.** ***Imperf.***

Thin Bluish Wove Paper

No.		Description	Unused	Used
1	A1	5c **red brown**	6,000.	350.
		pale brown	6,000.	350.
		brown	6,500.	350.
		No gum	2,100.	
		On cover		425.
		On cover to England or France		2,500.
		On cover to other European countries		3,000.
		Pair	15,000.	800.
		Pair on cover		1,000.
		Strip of 3	*25,000.*	1,750.
		Strip of 4		5,000.
		Block of 4	*50,000.*	*27,500.*
		Block of 4 on cover		*240,000.*
		Dot in "S" in upper right corner	7,000.	400.
		Cracked plate (69R1)		*3,000.*
		Recut left frame line	—	*1,150.*
a.		5c **dark brown**	7,000.	400.
		No gum	2,400.	
		On cover		900.
		Pair	*21,000.*	2,000.
		Block of 4	*55,000.*	
		grayish brown	9,000.	950.
		No gum	3,500.	
		Pair		2,200.
		blackish brown	10,000.	*1,500.*
		No gum	3,750.	
		Pair	*25,000.*	*3,250.*
b.		5c **orange brown**	10,000.	725.
		No gum	3,500.	
		On cover		825.
		Pair		2,000.
		Block of 4 on cover		—
c.		5c **red orange**	*25,000.*	*9,000.*
		No gum	*9,500.*	
		On cover		*10,500.*
		Pair		*30,000.*
d.		5c **brown orange**	—	1,000.
		No gum	*4,500.*	
		On cover		1,150.
		Pair on cover		—
(A)		Double transfer of top frame line (80R1)		550.
(B)		Double transfer of top and bottom frame lines (90R1)	*50,000.*	550.
		No gum	*5,000.*	
(C)		Double transfer shows best on bottom frame line and lower part of left frame line, also shows on top and right frame lines and in "5"s and "Five Cents"		*10,500.*
(D)		Double transfer on all frame lines (most noticeable at top right and lower left corners), also numerals		*11,000.*
(E)		Double transfer of "U," "POST OFFICE" and left numeral		*1,750.*
		On cover		*3,500.*
(F)		Double transfer of top frame line, upper part of side frame lines, "U," and "POST OFFICE"		*14,000.*

The "B double transfer" with original gum is in a pair and is valued thus. A second example with original gum is known, a single with faults.

Some students believe that the "E double transfer" actually shows plate scratches instead.

Earliest documented use: July 7, 1847.

Cancellations

Cancellation	Value
Red	350.
Red town	+150.
Orange red	+50.
Orange red town	+220.
Blue	+40.
Blue town	+125.
Black	+75.
Black town	+350.
Magenta	+275.
Orange	+750.
Ultramarine	+900.
Violet	+1,000.
Violet town	—
Green	+1,250.
"Paid"	+50.
"Paid" in grid (demonetized usage)	+300.
"Free"	+400.
Railroad	+200.
U. S. Express Mail (on the cover)	+100.
U. S. Express Mail (on stamp)	—
U. S. Express Mail in black (on stamp) (demonetized usage)	+12,500.
"Way"	+250.
"Way" with numeral	+500.
"Steamboat"	+350.
"Steam"	+200.
"Steamship"	+300.
Philadelphia RR	+250.
On cover	+500.
Hotel (on the cover)	*+2,000.*
Numeral	+100.
Canada	+3,000.
Wheeling, Va., grid	+6,000.
Pen Cancel	190.

George Washington — A2

Double transfer in "X" at lower right — (A)

Double transfer in "Post Office" — (B)

Double transfer in "X" at lower left and lower right, plus bottom frame line — (C)

Double transfer of left and bottom frame line — (D)

Double transfer of several letters at top, also top frame line recut — (E)

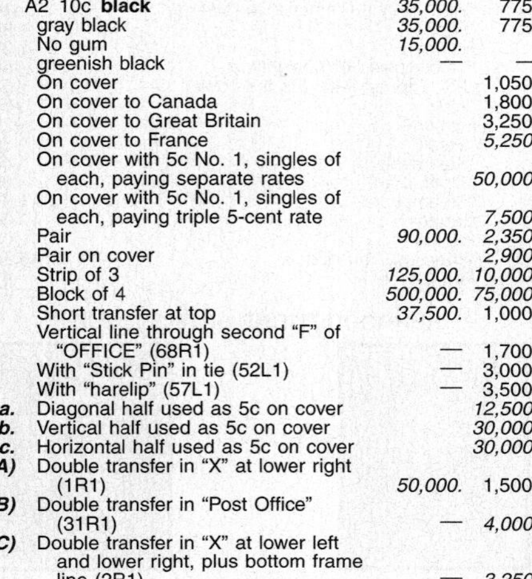

2	A2 10c **black**	*35,000.*	775.
	gray black	*35,000.*	775.
	No gum	*15,000.*	
	greenish black	—	—
	On cover		1,050.
	On cover to Canada		1,800.
	On cover to Great Britain		3,250.
	On cover to France		*5,250.*
	On cover with 5c No. 1, singles of each, paying separate rates		*50,000.*
	On cover with 5c No. 1, singles of each, paying triple 5-cent rate		*7,500.*
	Pair	*90,000.*	*2,350.*
	Pair on cover		*2,900.*
	Strip of 3	*125,000.*	*10,000.*
	Block of 4	*500,000.*	*75,000.*
	Short transfer at top	*37,500.*	1,000.
	Vertical line through second "F" of "OFFICE" (68R1)	—	1,700.
	With "Stick Pin" in tie (52L1)	—	3,000.
	With "harelip" (57L1)	—	3,500.
a.	Diagonal half used as 5c on cover		*12,500.*
b.	Vertical half used as 5c on cover		*30,000.*
c.	Horizontal half used as 5c on cover		*30,000.*
(A)	Double transfer in "X" at lower right (1R1)	*50,000.*	1,500.
(B)	Double transfer in "Post Office" (31R1)	—	*4,000.*
(C)	Double transfer in "X" at lower left and lower right, plus bottom frame line (2R1)	—	*3,250.*

How do you get the best price for your collection?

PUZZLED?

We offer you two options:

1. We will buy the collection outright. We spent over half a million dollars last year on collections from collectors all across the country. Plus, we will buy your entire collection – not just the best parts.
2. We are among the top sellers on Ebay and can sell your collections through our Ebay Consignment Program. We have been selling on Ebay since 1996 and have amassed over 75,000 positive comments from those we have sold stamps to over the years. We get top prices for quality material and fair prices for stamps that are not of top quality. With a collector base of over 100,000 collectors worldwide, your stamps receive absolute maximum exposure. We will break down your collection to lots with a value as low as $25. And with our low commissions, you get to put more in your pocket. Contact us for details.

IF YOU HAVE A COLLECTION THAT YOU ARE CONSIDERING SELLING...

it would be worth your time to contact us today. We handle stamps from any country in the world. A quick note to either our email address or by phone to our office detailing the contents of your collection can get the ball rolling. We will let you know if the collection is more suited for consignment or direct purchase.

CONTACT US TODAY!

2310 SE Delaware Ave, Ste G, #278
Ankeny, IA 50021
515-963-8099
email: info@southweststamps.com

(D)	Double transfer of left and bottom frame line (41R1)	—	2,150.
(E)	Double Transfer of several letters at top, also top frame line recut		2,150.

Earliest documented use: July 2, 1847.

Two examples of the unused block are recorded, only one of which is available to collectors.

The value for the used block of 4 represents a block with manuscript cancel. One block is recorded with a handstamp cancellation and it is worth significantly more.

Cancellations

Red	775.
Orange red	+100.
Blue	+50.
Orange	+500.
Black	+250.
Magenta	+650.
Violet	+950.
Green	+3,500.
Ultramarine	+1,500.
"Paid"	+100.
"Paid" in grid (demonetized usage)	+400.
"Free"	+900.
Railroad	+1,000.
Philadelphia RR straightline	+500.
U.S. Express Mail (on the cover)	+500.
"Way"	+550.
Numeral	+250.
"Steam"	+350.
"Steamship"	+400.
"Steamboat"	+650.
"Steamer 10"	+1,000.
Canada	+3,000.
Panama	—
Wheeling, Va., grid	+5,500.
Pen Cancel	475.

REPRODUCTIONS of 1847 ISSUE

A3

A4

Actually, official imitations made from new plates of 50 subjects made by the Bureau of Engraving and Printing by order of the Post Office Department. These were not valid for postal use.

Reproductions. The letters R. W. H. & E. at the bottom of each stamp are less distinct on the reproductions than on the originals.

5c. On the originals the left side of the white shirt frill touches the oval on a level with the top of the "F" of "Five." On the reproductions it touches the oval about on a level with the top of the figure "5." On the originals, the bottom of the right leg of the "N" in "CENTS" is blunt. On the reproductions, the "N" comes to a point at the bottom.

10c. On the originals line of coat at left points to "T" of TEN and at right it points between "T" and "S" of "CENTS."

On the reproductions line of coat at left points to right tip of "X" and line of coat at right points to center of "S."

The bottom of the right leg of the "N" of "CENTS" shows the same difference as on the 5c originals and reproductions.

On the reproductions, the gap between the bottom legs of the left "X" is noticeably wider than the gap on the right "X." On the originals, the gaps are of equal width.

On the reproductions the eyes have a sleepy look, the line of the mouth is straighter, and in the curl of the hair near the left cheek is a strong black dot, while the originals have only a faint one.

(See Nos. 948a and 948b for 1947 reproductions — 5c blue and 10c brown orange in larger size.)

1875	**Bluish paper, without gum**	***Imperf.***
3	A3 5c **red brown** *(4779)*	900.
	brown	900.
	dark brown	900.
	Pair	2,000.
	Block of 4	*8,000.*
4	A4 10c **black** *(3883)*	1,100.
	gray black	1,100.
	Pair	2,450.
	Block of 4	*10,000.*

Numbers in parentheses are quantities sold.

Except as noted here and in footnotes for selected issues, values for 1851-57 issues are for examples that clearly show all of the illustrated type characteristics. Stamps that have weakly defined or missing type characteristics sell for less.

In Nos. 5-17, the 1¢, 3¢ and 12¢ have very small margins between the stamps. The 5¢ and 10¢ have moderate size margins. The values of these stamps take the margin size into consideration.

Values for Nos. 5A, 6b and 19b are for the less distinct positions. Best examples sell for more.

Values for No. 16 are for outer line recut at top. Other recuts sell for more.

Produced by Toppan, Carpenter, Casilear & Co.

Stamps of the 1851-57 series were printed from plates consisting of 200 subjects and the sheets were divided into two panes of 100 each. Stamps printed from different positions on the plate often have characteristics which make them more valuable than the basic listing. It is, therefore, necessary to be able to clearly identify each position on the plates used to print these stamps. In order that each stamp in the sheet and within each pane could be identified easily in regard to its relative position it was devised that the stamps in each pane be numbered from one to one hundred, starting with the top horizontal row and numbering consecutively from left to right. Thus the first stamp at the upper left corner would be 1 and the last stamp at the bottom right corner, would be 100. The left and right panes are indicated by the letters "L" or "R." The number of the plate is given last. As an example, the best-known of the scarce type III, one cent 1851 being the 99th stamp in the right pane of Plate No. 2 is listed as (99R2), *i.e.* 99th stamp, right pane, Plate No. 2.

One plate of the one cent and several plates of the three cents were reentered after they had been in use. The original state of the plate is called "Early" and the reentered state is termed "Late." If the plate was reentered twice, the inbetween state is called "Intermediate." Identification of "Early," "Intermediate" or "Late" state is explained by the addition of the letters "E," "i" or "L" after the plate numbers. The sixth stamp of the right pane of Plate No. 1 from the "Early" state would be 6R1E. The same plate position from the "Late" state would be 6R1L. Many varieties occur on the same position in each of the states of the plate. The state of the plate is mentioned only if that variety does not show on the other states.

One plate of the three cent stamp never had a plate number and is referred to by specialists as "Plate O."

The position of the stamp in the sheet is placed within parentheses, for example: (99R2).

The different values of this issue were intended primarily for the payment of specific rates, though any value might be used in making up a rate. The one cent stamp was to pay the postage on newspapers, drop letters and circulars, and the one cent carrier fee in some cities from 1856. The three cent stamp represented the rate on ordinary letters and two of them made up the rate for distances over 3000 miles prior to April 1, 1855. The five cent stamp was originally for the registration fee but the fee was usually paid in cash. Occasionally two of them were used to pay the rate over 3000 miles, after it was changed in April, 1855. Singles paid the "Shore to ship" rate to certain foreign countries and, from 1857, triples paid the fifteen-cent rate to France. Ten cents was the rate to California and points distant more than 3000 miles. The twelve cent stamp was for quadruple the ordinary rate. Twenty-four cents represented the single letter rate to Great Britain. Thirty cents was the rate to Germany. The ninety cent stamp was apparently intended to facilitate the payment of large amounts of postage.

Act of Congress, March 3, 1851. "From and after June 30, 1851, there shall be charged the following rates: Every single letter not exceeding 3000 miles, prepaid postage, 3 cents; not prepaid, 5 cents; for any greater distance, double these rates. Every single letter or paper conveyed wholly or in part by sea, and to or from a foreign country over 2500 miles, 20 cents; under 2500 miles, 10 cents. Drop or local letters, 1 cent each. Letters uncalled for and advertised, to be charged 1 cent in addition to the regular postage."

Act of Congress, March 3, 1855. "For every single letter, in manuscript or paper of any kind, in writing, marks or signs, conveyed in the mail between places in the United States not exceeding 3000 miles, 3 cents; and for any greater distance, 10 cents. Drop or local letters, 1 cent."

The Act of March 3, 1855, made the prepayment of postage on domestic letters compulsory April 1, 1855, and prepayment of postage on domestic letters compulsory by stamps effective January 1, 1856.

The Act authorized the Postmaster to establish a system for the registration of valuable letters, and to require prepayment of postage on such letters as well as registration fee of five cents. Stamps to prepay the registry fee were not required until June 1, 1867.

Franklin — A5

Type I

Type Ib

ONE CENT. Issued July 1, 1851.

Type I. Has complete curved lines outside the labels with "U. S. Postage" and "One Cent." The scrolls below the lower label are turned under, forming little balls. The ornaments at top are substantially complete.

Type Ib. As type I, but balls below bottom label are not as clear. Plume-like scrolls at bottom are incomplete.

1851-57			***Imperf.***
5	A5 1c **blue,** type I (7R1E)	*135,000.*	*55,000.*
	dark blue		—
	On cover		*110,000.*
	Pair, types I, Ib		*110,000.*
	On cover, pair, one stamp type I		—

It takes a team of philately's most qualified professionals to create the finest auction catalog ever produced.

Put us to work for you.

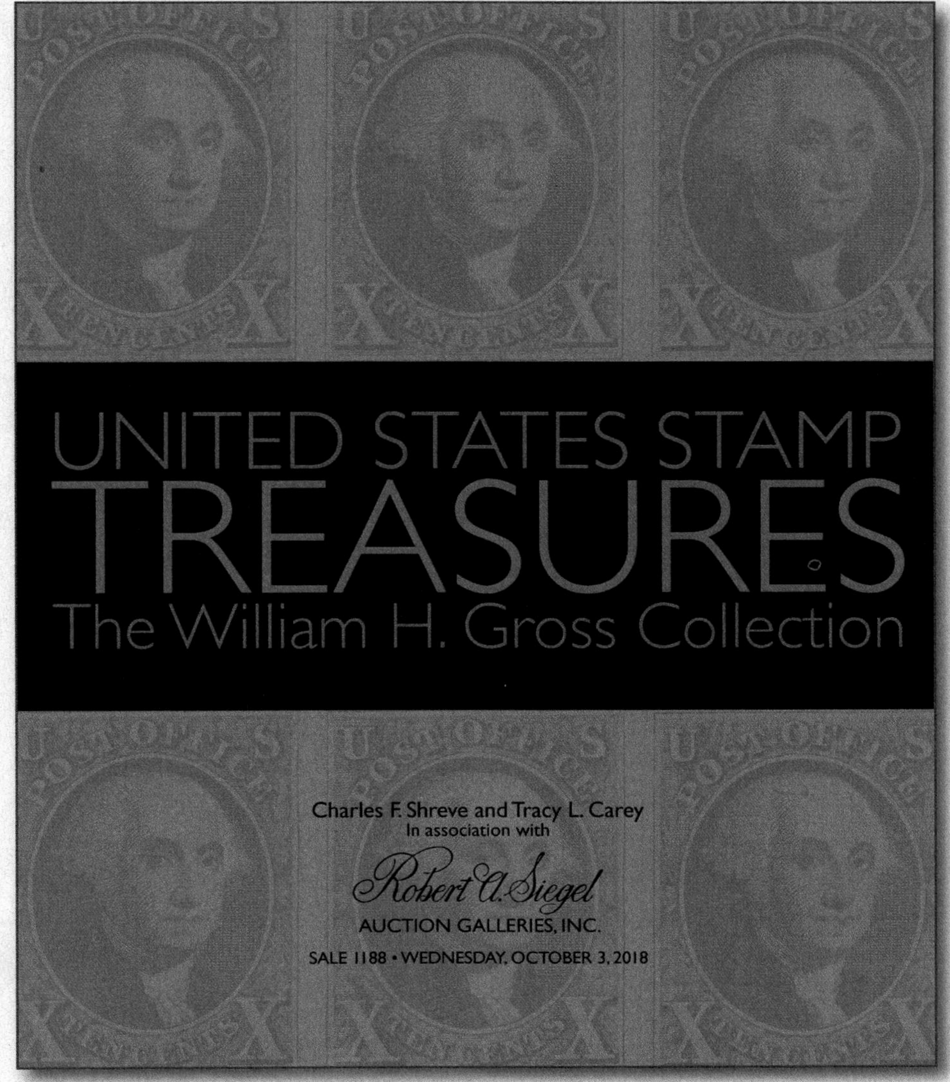

To discuss the sale of your U.S. stamps or postal history, call Scott Trepel at 212-753-6421.
If you have a worldwide collection, call Charles Shreve at 214-754-5991.

Robert A. Siegel
AUCTION GALLERIES, INC.
siegelauctions.com

6 WEST 48TH STREET, NEW YORK, N.Y. 10036 212-753-6421 STAMPS@SIEGELAUCTIONS.COM

Strip of 3, one stamp type I	*125,000.*	
On cover, strip of 3, one stamp type I		*200,000.*

Only one example of No. 5 in the dark blue shade is recorded.

Earliest documented use: July 5, 1851.

Cancellations

Blue	+1,000.
Blue town	—
Red grid	+3,000.
Red town	—
Red "Paid"	—

Values for No. 5 are for examples with margins touching or cutting slightly into the design, or for examples with four margins and minor faults. Very few sound examples with the design untouched exist, and these sell for much more than the values shown.

Value for No. 5 unused is for a stamp with no gum. Only one example unused with original gum is recorded. It is in a multiple and is creased.

5A	A5 1c **blue,** type Ib, *July 1, 1851* (Less distinct examples 3-5, 9R1E)	*32,500.*	*7,000.*
	No gum	*12,000.*	
	Pair	*70,000.*	*16,000.*
	On cover		*8,500.*
	blue, type Ib (Best examples 6, 8R1E)	*45,000.*	*11,000.*
	No gum	*18,000.*	
	On cover		*15,500.*
	Pair, type Ib, II		*12,000.*
	Block of 4, pair type Ib, pair type IIIa (8-9, 18-19R1E)		—

Earliest documented use: July 1, 1851 (FDC).

Cancellations

Blue town	+300.
Red town	+550.
Red Carrier	+550.
Red "Paid"	+550.
Pen (3, 4, 5 or 9R1E)	*3,500.*
Pen (6 or 8R1E)	*5,500.*

Values for No. 5A are for sound examples with margins just clear to just touching the design on one or two sides. Examples with margins well clear of the design all around are scarce and will sell for more than the values shown.

A6

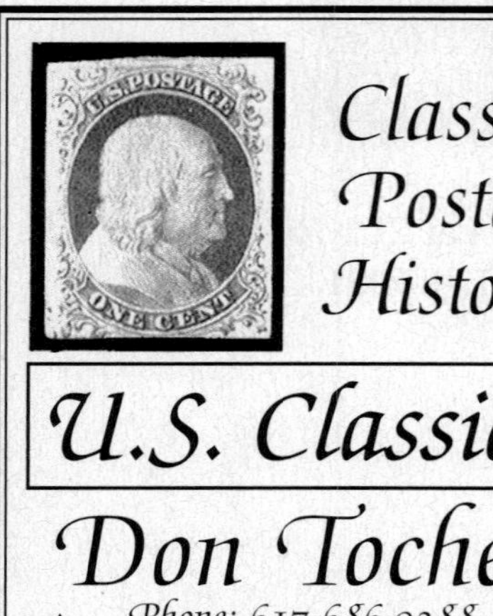

Type Ic

Type Ia. Same as type I at bottom, but top ornaments and outer line at top are partly cut away. Type Ia comes only from the bottom row of both panes of Plate 4. All type Ia stamps have the flaw below "U" of "U.S.," but this flaw also appears on some stamps of types Ic, III and IIIa of Plate 4.

Type Ic. Same as type Ia, but bottom right plume and ball ornament incomplete. Bottom left plume is complete or nearly complete. Best examples are from bottom row, "F" relief, positions 91 and 96R4. Less distinct examples are "E" reliefs from 5th and 9th rows, positions 47L, 49L, 83L, 49R, 81R, 82R, and 89R, Plate 4, and early impressions of 41R4.

6	A6 1c **blue,** type Ia, *1857*	*45,000.*	*9,500.*
	No gum	*20,000.*	
	On cover		*14,000.*
	Pair	—	*23,000.*
	Strip of 3 on cover		*67,500.*
	Pair, types Ia, Ic		*22,500.*
	Horizontal strip of 3, (95-97R4) types Ia, Ic, Ia		*37,500.*
	Vertical pair, types Ia, III	*75,000.*	*14,500.*
	Vertical pair, types Ia, IIIa	*55,000.*	*13,500.*
	Block of 4, types Ia, IIIa	*120,000.*	
	"Curl on shoulder" (97L4)	*47,500.*	*11,000.*
	"Curl in C" (97R4)	*47,500.*	*11,000.*

The horizontal strip of 3 represents positions 95-97R4, position 96R4 being type 1c.

Earliest documented use: Apr. 19, 1857.

Cancellations

Blue	+300.
Black Carrier	+350.
Red Carrier	+700.
Pen Cancel	*4,750.*

6b	A6 1c **blue,** type Ic ("E" relief, less distinct examples)	*7,000.*	*3,000.*
	No gum	*3,000.*	
	On cover		*4,000.*
	Horizontal pair (81-82R4)		—
	Pair, types Ic, III		—
	Pair, types Ic, IIIa		—
	blue, type Ic ("F" relief, best examples, 91, 96R4)	*27,500.*	*9,000.*
	No gum	*12,500.*	
	On cover		*10,000.*
	Vertical pair (81-91R4)		—

Earliest documented use: May 20, 1857 (dated cancel on off-cover stamp); June 6, 1857 (on cover).

Cancellations

Blue ("E" relief)	—
Red ("E" relief)	—
Blue town ("F" relief)	—
Red ("F" relief)	—
Black carrier ("F" relief)	—
Pen ("E" relief)	*1,500.*
Pen ("F" relief)	*4,500.*

A7

Type II — Same as Type I at top, but the little balls of the bottom scrolls and the bottoms of the lower plume ornaments are missing. The side ornaments are substantially complete.

7	A7 1c **blue,** type II, (Plates 1E, 2); *July 1, 1851* (Plate 1E)	1,000.	130.
	No gum	375.	
	On cover		155.
	Pair	2,300.	275.
	Strip of 3	8,500.	425.
	Block of 4 (Plate 1E)	—	—
	Block of 4 (Plate 2)	*9,500.*	1,100.
	P# block of 8, Impt. (Plate 2)	*47,500.*	
	Design complete at top (10R1E only)	—	*2,000.*
	Pair, types II, IIIa (Plate 1E)	7,500.	1,450.
	Double transfer (Plate 1E or 2)	1,100.	155.
	Double transfer (65R1E)		*500.*
	Double transfer (89R2)	1,150.	190.
	Double transfer, one inverted (71L1E)	1,500.	375.
	Triple transfer, one inverted (91L1E)	1,500.	400.
	Major cracked plate (2L, 13L, 23L, Plate 2)	1,300.	450.
	Intermediate cracked plate (12L2)	900.	340.
	Minor cracked plate (33L2)	900.	230.
	Plate 1L (4R1L only, double transfer), *June 1852*	2,000.	350.
	Pair, types II (4R1L), IV	*3,800.*	*650.*
	Plate 3, *May, 1856*	*2,000.*	350.
	On cover		550.
	Pair	—	750.
	Strip of 3		—
	Block of 4	—	—
	Double transfer		450.
	Major plate crack (22L, 24L, 31L, 33L, 34L, 8R, Plate 3)		800.
	Plate 4, *April, 1857*	*3,250.*	*900.*
	On cover		*1,250.*
	Pair	—	*2,100.*
	Pair (vert.), types II, III	—	—
	Pair (vert.), types II, IIIa	—	—
	Vertical strip of 3 (9L, 19L, 29L; Plate 4), types II, III, III, on cover		—
	Block of 4, type II and types III, IIIa	—	
	"Curl in hair" (3R, 4R4)	—	*1,100.*
	Double transfer (10R4)	—	—
	Perf. 12½, unofficial	*22,500.*	*8,000.*
	On cover		*35,000.*
	On cover with strip of 3 No. 11		*25,000.*

Please note: Regardless of the strength or weakness of the design at bottom, all stamps originating from the top row of plate 4 are classified as type II.

See note concerning unofficial perfs following listings for No. 11.

Earliest documented uses: July 1, 1851 (Plate 1E) (FDC); Dec. 5, 1855 (Plate 2); May 6, 1856 (Plate 3).

Cancellations

Blue	+7.50
Red	+20.00
Magenta	+80.00
Ultramarine	+175.00
Green	+400.00
Orange	+500.
1855 year date	+10.00
1856 year date	+5.00
1857 year date	+2.50
1858 year date	—
"Paid"	+5.00
"Way"	+35.00
Red "Too Late"	+200.00
Numeral	+25.00
Railroad	+50.00
"Steam"	+60.00
"Steamboat"	+80.00
Red Carrier	+45.00
Black Carrier	+25.00
U. S. Express Mail	+25.00
Territorial	+200.00
Printed precancel "PAID"	+2,500.
Printed precancel "paid"	+2,500.
Pen Cancel	55.00

A8

Theater A1139

Folk Dance A1140

Modern Dance A1141

Designed by John Hill.

PHOTOGRAVURE (Andreotti)
Plates of 192 subjects in four panes of 48 (6x8).

1978, Apr. 26	**Tagged**	***Perf. 11***	
1749 A1138 13c **multicolored**		.25	.25
1750 A1139 13c **multicolored**		.25	.25
1751 A1140 13c **multicolored**		.25	.25
1752 A1141 13c **multicolored**		.25	.25
a. Block of 4, #1749-1752		1.00	1.00
P# block of 12, 6#		3.25	—
P# block of 16, 6#, Mr. Zip and copyright		4.50	—
Margin block of 4, Mr. Zip, copyright		1.05	—

AMERICAN BICENTENNIAL ISSUE

French Alliance, signed in Paris, Feb. 6, 1778 and ratified by Continental Congress, May 4, 1778.

King Louis XVI and Benjamin Franklin, by Charles Gabriel Sauvage — A1142

Designed by Bradbury Thompson after 1785 porcelain sculpture in Du Pont Winterthur Museum, Delaware.

GIORI PRESS PRINTING
Plates of 160 subjects in four panes of 40.

1978, May 4	**Tagged**	***Perf. 11***	
1753 A1142 13c **blue, black & red**		.25	.25
P# block of 4		1.10	—
Margin block of 4, Mr. Zip		1.00	—
a. Red missing (PS)		—	

EARLY CANCER DETECTION ISSUE

George Papanicolaou, M.D. (1883-1962), cytologist and developer of Pap Test, early cancer detection in women.

Dr. Papanicolaou and Microscope — A1143

Designed by Paul Calle.

ENGRAVED
Plates of 200 subjects in four panes of 50.

1978, May 18	**Tagged**	***Perf. 10½x11***	
1754 A1143 13c **brown**		.25	.25
P# block of 4		1.10	—
Margin block of 4, Mr. Zip		1.00	—

PERFORMING ARTS SERIES

Jimmie Rodgers (1897-1933), the "Singing Brakeman, Father of Country Music" (No. 1755); George M. Cohan (1878-1942), actor and playwright (No. 1756).

Jimmie Rodgers with Guitar and Brakeman's Cap, Locomotive — A1144

George M. Cohan, "Yankee Doodle Dandy" and Stars — A1145

Designed by Jim Sharpe.

PHOTOGRAVURE (Andreotti)
Plates of 200 subjects in four panes of 50.

1978	**Tagged**	***Perf. 11***	
1755 A1144 13c **multicolored,** *May 24*		.25	.25
P# block of 12, 6#		4.00	—
Margin block of 4, Mr. Zip		1.25	—
1756 A1145 15c **multicolored,** *July 3*		.30	.25
P# block of 12, 6#		4.00	—
Margin block of 4, Mr. Zip		1.25	—

CAPEX ISSUE

CAPEX '78, Canadian International Philatelic Exhibition, Toronto, Ont., June 9-18.

Wildlife from Canadian-United States Border — A1146

Illustration reduced.

Designed by Stanley Galli.

LITHOGRAPHED, ENGRAVED (Giori)
Plates of 24 subjects in four panes of 6 each.

1978, June 10	**Tagged**	***Perf. 11***	
1757 A1146 Block of 8, **multicolored**		2.00	2.00
a. 13c Cardinal		.25	.25
b. 13c Mallard		.25	.25
c. 13c Canada goose		.25	.25
d. 13c Blue jay		.25	.25
e. 13c Moose		.25	.25
f. 13c Chipmunk		.25	.25
g. 13c Red fox		.25	.25
h. 13c Raccoon		.25	.25
P# block of 8		2.25	—
Margin block of 8, Mr. Zip and copyright		2.10	—
Pane of 6 No. 1757, P#, Mr. Zip and copyright		13.00	—
i. As No. 1757, yellow, green, red, brown, blue, black (litho) omitted		*6,000.*	
j. Strip of 4 (a-d), imperf. vert.		*5,000.*	
k. Strip of 4 (e-h), imperf. vert.		*2,000.*	
l. As No. 1757, "d" and "h" with black (engr.) omitted		—	
m. As No. 1757, "b" with blue missing (PS)		—	
n. As No. 1757, tagging omitted		—	
o. Strip of 4 (e-h), all colors except black missing on "e," "f" and "g," all colors except black and brown missing on "h" (PS)		*1,250.*	
p. As No. 1757, yellow, red, brown omitted, pane of 48		—	

No. 1757k is worth more when contained in the block of 8. Value is for strip only.

PHOTOGRAPHY ISSUE

Photography's contribution to communications and understanding.

Camera, Lens, Color Filters, Adapter Ring, Studio Light Bulb and Album — A1147

Designed by Ben Somoroff.

PHOTOGRAVURE (Andreotti)
Plates of 160 subjects in four panes of 40.

1978, June 26	**Tagged**	***Perf. 11***	
1758 A1147 15c **multicolored**		.30	.25
P# block of 12, 6#		4.00	—
Margin block of 4, Mr. Zip and copyright		1.25	—
P# block of 16, 6#, Mr. Zip and copyright		5.00	—

VIKING MISSIONS TO MARS ISSUE

Second anniv. of landing of Viking 1 on Mars.

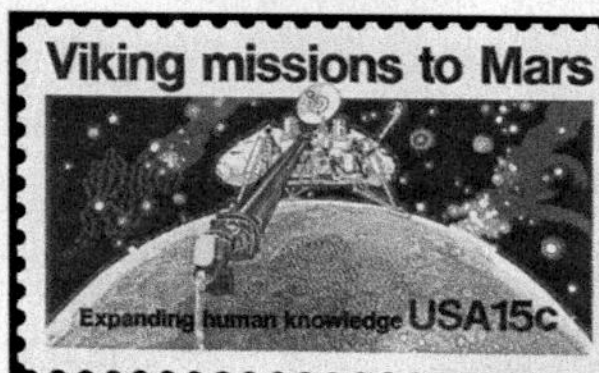

Viking 1 Lander Scooping up Soil on Mars — A1148

Designed by Robert McCall.

LITHOGRAPHED, ENGRAVED (Giori)
Plates of 200 subjects in four panes of 50.

1978, July 20	**Tagged**	***Perf. 11***	
1759 A1148 15c **multicolored**		.30	.25
P# block of 4		1.35	—
Margin block of 4, Mr. Zip		1.25	—
a. Tagging omitted		*75.00*	

WILDLIFE CONSERVATION

Nos. 1760-1761 alternate in one horizontal row. Nos. 1762-1763 in the next.

Great Gray Owl — A1149

Saw-whet Owl — A1150

Barred Owl — A1151

Great Horned Owl — A1152

Designed by Frank J. Waslick.

LITHOGRAPHED, ENGRAVED (Giori)

Plates of 200 subjects in four panes of 50.

1978, Aug. 26 **Tagged** ***Perf. 11***

1760	A1149	15c	**multicolored**	.30	.25
1761	A1150	15c	**multicolored**	.30	.25
1762	A1151	15c	**multicolored**	.30	.25
1763	A1152	15c	**multicolored**	.30	.25
a.			Block of 4, #1760-1763	1.25	1.25
			P# block of 4	1.40	—
			Margin block of 4, Mr. Zip	1.25	—
b.			As "a," tagging omitted		—
c.			As "a," yellow and orange (litho.) omitted	—	

Two panes of No. 1763c have been reported. On one pane, the black (engr.) is shifted to the left.

AMERICAN TREES ISSUE

Nos. 1764-1765 alternate in 1st row, Nos. 1766-1767 in 2nd.

Giant Sequoia A1153

White Pine — A1154

White Oak — A1155

Gray Birch — A1156

Designed by Walter D. Richards.

PHOTOGRAVURE (Andreotti)

Plates of 160 subjects in four panes of 40.

1978, Oct. 9 **Tagged** ***Perf. 11***

1764	A1153	15c	**multicolored**	.30	.25
1765	A1154	15c	**multicolored**	.30	.25
1766	A1155	15c	**multicolored**	.30	.25
1767	A1156	15c	**multicolored**	.30	.25
a.			Block of 4, #1764-1767	1.25	1.25
			P# block of 12, 6#	4.00	—
			P# block of 16, 6#, Mr. Zip and copyright	5.25	—
			Margin block of 4, Mr. Zip, copyright	1.30	—
b.			As "a," imperf. horiz.	*17,500.*	

No. 1767b is unique.

CHRISTMAS ISSUE

Madonna and Child with Cherubim, by Andrea della Robbia — A1157

Child on Hobby Horse and Christmas Trees — A1158

Designed by Bradbury Thompson (No. 1768) after terra cotta sculpture in National Gallery, Washington, D.C. by Dolli Tingle (No. 1769).

PHOTOGRAVURE (Andreotti)

Plates of 400 subjects in four panes of 100.

1978, Oct. 18 ***Perf. 11***

1768	A1157	15c	**blue & multicolored**	.30	.25
			P# block of 12, 6#	4.00	—
			Margin block of 4, "Use Correct Zip Code"	1.25	—
			Pair with full horiz. gutter between	—	
a.			Imperf., pair	*70.00*	

Value for No. 1768a is for an uncreased pair.

1769	A1158	15c	**red & multicolored**	.30	.25
			P# block of 12, 6#	4.00	—
			Margin block of 4, "Use Correct Zip Code"	1.25	—
			Pair with full horiz. gutter btwn.	—	
a.			Imperf., pair	*75.00*	
b.			Vert. pair, imperf. horiz.	*1,000.*	

ROBERT F. KENNEDY ISSUE

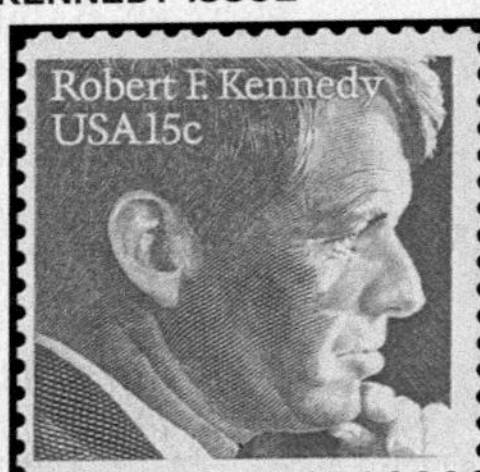

Robert F. Kennedy — A1159

Designed by Bradbury Thompson after photograph by Stanley Tretick.

ENGRAVED

Plates of 192 subjects in four panes of 48 (8x6).

1979, Jan. 12 **Tagged** ***Perf. 11***

1770	A1159	15c	**blue**	.35	.25
			P# block of 4	1.50	—
			Margin block of 4, Mr. Zip	1.40	—
a.			Tagging omitted	*50.00*	

BLACK HERITAGE SERIES

Dr. Martin Luther King, Jr. (1929-1968), Civil Rights leader.

Martin Luther King, Jr. and Civil Rights Marchers — A1160

Designed by Jerry Pinkney.

PHOTOGRAVURE (Andreotti)

Plates of 200 subjects in four panes of 50.

1979, Jan. 13 **Tagged** ***Perf. 11***

1771	A1160	15c	**multicolored**	.40	.25
			P# block of 12, 6#	5.75	—
			Margin block of 4, Mr. Zip	1.75	—
a.			Imperf., pair	*800.00*	
b.			Tagging omitted		—

INTERNATIONAL YEAR OF THE CHILD ISSUE

Children of Different Races A1161

Designed by Paul Calle.

ENGRAVED

Plates of 200 subjects in four panes of 50.

1979, Feb. 15 **Tagged** ***Perf. 11***

1772	A1161	15c	**orange red**	.30	.25
			P# block of 4	1.40	—
			Margin block of 4, Mr. Zip	1.25	—

LITERARY ARTS SERIES

John Steinbeck (1902-1968), Novelist — A1162

Designed by Bradbury Thompson after photograph by Philippe Halsman.

ENGRAVED

Plates of 200 subjects in four panes of 50.

1979, Feb. 27 **Tagged** ***Perf. 10½x11***

1773	A1162	15c	**dark blue**	.30	.25
			P# block of 4	1.40	—
			Margin block of 4, Mr. Zip	1.25	—

ALBERT EINSTEIN ISSUE

Albert Einstein (1879-1955), Theoretical Physicist — A1163

Designed by Bradbury Thompson after photograph by Hermann Landshoff.

ENGRAVED

Plates of 200 subjects in four panes of 50.

1979, Mar. 4	**Tagged**	***Perf. 10½x11***	
1774 A1163 15c **chocolate**		.30	.25
P# block of 4		1.60	—
Margin block of 4, Mr. Zip		1.45	—
Pair, horiz. gutter btwn.		—	

AMERICAN FOLK ART SERIES

Pennsylvania Toleware, c. 1800.

Coffeepot — A1164

Tea Caddy — A1165

Sugar Bowl — A1166

Coffeepot — A1167

Designed by Bradbury Thompson.

PHOTOGRAVURE (Andreotti)

Plates of 160 subjects in four panes of 40.

1979, Apr. 19	**Tagged**	***Perf. 11***	
1775 A1164 15c **multicolored**		.30	.25
1776 A1165 15c **multicolored**		.30	.25
1777 A1166 15c **multicolored**		.30	.25
1778 A1167 15c **multicolored**		.30	.25
a. Block of 4, #1775-1778		1.25	1.25
P# block of 10, 5#		3.25	—
P# block of 16, 5#; Mr. Zip and copyright		5.25	—
Margin block of 6, Mr. Zip and copyright		2.00	—
b. As "a," imperf. horiz.		*2,000.*	

AMERICAN ARCHITECTURE SERIES

Nos. 1779-1780 alternate in 1st row, Nos. 1781-1782 in 2nd.

Virginia Rotunda, by Thomas Jefferson — A1168

Baltimore Cathedral, by Benjamin Latrobe — A1169

Boston State House, by Charles Bulfinch — A1170

Philadelphia Exchange, by William Strickland — A1171

Designed by Walter D. Richards.

ENGRAVED (Giori)

Plates of 192 subjects in four panes of 48 (6x8).

1979, June 4	**Tagged**	***Perf. 11***	
1779 A1168 15c **black & brick red**		.30	.25
1780 A1169 15c **black & brick red**		.30	.25
1781 A1170 15c **black & brick red**		.30	.25
1782 A1171 15c **black & brick red**		.30	.25
a. Block of 4, #1779-1782		1.25	1.25
P# block of 4		1.45	—
Margin block of 4, Mr. Zip		1.30	—
b. As "a," tagging omitted		—	

ENDANGERED FLORA ISSUE

Nos. 1783-1784 alternate in one horizontal row. Nos. 1785-1786 in the next.

Persistent Trillium — A1172

Hawaiian Wild Broadbean — A1173

Contra Costa Wallflower — A1174

Antioch Dunes Evening Primrose — A1175

Designed by Frank J. Waslick.

PHOTOGRAVURE (Andreotti)

Plates of 200 subjects in four panes of 50.

1979, June 7	**Tagged**	***Perf. 11***	
1783 A1172 15c **multicolored**		.30	.25
1784 A1173 15c **multicolored**		.30	.25
1785 A1174 15c **multicolored**		.30	.25
1786 A1175 15c **multicolored**		.30	.25
a. Block of 4, #1783-1786		1.25	1.25
P# block of 12, 6#		4.00	—
P# block of 20, 6#, Mr. Zip and copyright		6.50	—
Margin block of 4, Mr. Zip		1.30	—
As "a," full vert. gutter btwn.		*800.00*	
b. As "a," imperf.		*200.00*	

SEEING EYE DOGS ISSUE

1st guide dog program in the US, 50th anniv.

German Shepherd Leading Man — A1176

Designed by Joseph Csatari.

PHOTOGRAVURE (Combination Press)

Plates of 230 (10x23) subjects in panes of 50 (10x5).

1979, June 15	**Tagged**	***Perf. 11***	
1787 A1176 15c **multicolored**		.30	.25
P# block of 20, 5-8#, 1-2 copyright		6.50	—
a. Imperf., pair		*325.00*	
b. Tagging omitted		15.00	

See Combination Press note after No. 1703.

SPECIAL OLYMPICS ISSUE

Special Olympics for special children, Brockport, N.Y., Aug. 8-13.

Child Holding Winner's Medal — A1177

Designed by Jeff Cornell.

PHOTOGRAVURE (Andreotti)

Plates of 200 subjects in four panes of 50.

1979, Aug. 9	**Tagged**	***Perf. 11***	
1788 A1177 15c **multicolored**		.30	.25
P# block of 10, 5#		3.25	—
Zip block of 4		1.25	—

JOHN PAUL JONES ISSUE

John Paul Jones (1747-1792), Naval Commander, American Revolution.

John Paul Jones, by Charles Willson Peale — A1178

Designed after painting in Independence National Historical Park, Philadelphia.
Printed by American Bank Note Co. and J. W. Fergusson and Sons.

Designed by Bradbury Thompson.

PHOTOGRAVURE (Champlain)

Plates of 200 subjects in four panes of 50.

1979, Sept. 23	**Tagged**	***Perf. 11x12***	
1789	A1178 15c **multicolored**	.30	.25
	P# block of 10, 5#+A	3.25	—
	Zip block of 4	1.25	—
c.	Vert. pair, imperf. horiz.	*125.00*	

Imperforates on gummed stamp paper, including gutter pairs and blocks, are proofs from the ABNCo. archives. See No. 1789P in Proofs section.

	Perf. 11		
1789A	A1178 15c **multicolored**	.55	.25
	P# block of 10, 5#+A	5.75	—
	Zip block of 4	3.25	—
d.	Vertical pair, imperf. horiz.	*115.00*	

	Perf. 12		
1789B	A1178 15c **multicolored**	*3,000.*	*3,500.*
	On cover		*14,000.*
	P# block of 10, 5#+A	*37,500.*	
	Zip block of 4	*15,000.*	—

OLYMPIC GAMES ISSUE

22nd Summer Olympic Games, Moscow, July 19-Aug. 3, 1980. Nos. 1791-1792 alternate in one horizontal row, Nos. 1793-1794 in next.

Javelin — A1179

Running A1180

Swimming A1181

Equestrian A1183

Designed by Robert M. Cunningham.

PHOTOGRAVURE

Plates of 200 subjects in four panes of 50.

1979, Sept. 5	**Tagged**	***Perf. 11***	
1790	A1179 10c **multicolored**	.25	.25
	P# block of 12, 6#	3.25	—
	Zip block of 4	1.00	—

1979, Sept. 28			
1791	A1180 15c **multicolored**	.30	.25
1792	A1181 15c **multicolored**	.30	.25
1793	A1182 15c **multicolored**	.30	.25
1794	A1183 15c **multicolored**	.30	.25
a.	Block of 4, #1791-1794	1.25	1.25
	P# block of 12, 6#	4.00	—
	Zip block of 4	1.30	—
	P# block of 20, 6#, zip, copyright	6.50	—
b.	As "a," imperf.	*900.00*	

OLYMPIC GAMES ISSUE

13th Winter Olympic Games, Lake Placid, N.Y., Feb. 12-24. Nos. 1795-1796 alternate in one horizontal row, Nos. 1797-1798 in next.

Speed Skating A1184

Downhill Skiing A1185

Ski Jump — A1186

Ice Hockey A1187

Designed by Robert M. Cunningham

PHOTOGRAVURE

Plates of 200 subject in four panes of 50.

1980, Feb. 1	**Tagged**	***Perf. 11¼x10½***	
1795	A1184 15c **multicolored**	.35	.25
1796	A1185 15c **multicolored**	.35	.25
1797	A1186 15c **multicolored**	.35	.25
1798	A1187 15c **multicolored**	.35	.25
b.	Block of 4, #1795-1798	1.50	1.40
	P# block of 12, 6#	4.50	—
	Zip block of 4	1.55	—
	P# block of 20, 6#, zip and copyright	7.50	—

	Perf. 11		
1795A	A1184 15c **multicolored**	1.00	.60
1796A	A1185 15c **multicolored**	1.00	.60
1797A	A1186 15c **multicolored**	1.00	.60
1798A	A1187 15c **multicolored**	1.00	.60
c.	Block of 4, #1795A-1798A	4.00	3.50
	P# block of 12, 6#	14.00	—
	Zip block of 4	4.25	—
	P# block of 20, 6#, zip and copyright	26.00	—

CHRISTMAS ISSUE

Virgin and Child by Gerard David — A1188

Santa Claus, Christmas Tree Ornament — A1189

Designed by Bradbury Thompson (No. 1799) and by Eskil Ohlsson (No. 1800).

No. 1799 is designed after a painting in National Gallery of Art, Washington, D.C.

PHOTOGRAVURE (Andreotti)

Plates of 400 subjects in four panes of 100.

1979, Oct. 18	**Tagged**	***Perf. 11***	
1799	A1188 15c **multicolored**	.30	.25
	P# block of 12, 6#	4.00	—
	Zip block of 4	1.25	—
	P# block of 20, 6#, zip, copyright	6.50	—
a.	Imperf., pair	70.00	
b.	Vert. pair, imperf. horiz.	*450.00*	
c.	Vert. pair, imperf. between	*950.00*	
d.	Tagging omitted		—

	Perf. 11x10½		
1800	A1189 15c **multicolored**	.30	.25
	P# block of 12, 6#	4.00	—
	Zip block of 4	1.25	—
	P# block of 20, 6#, zip, copyright	6.50	—
a.	Green & yellow omitted	*400.00*	
b.	Green, yellow & tan omitted	*400.00*	
c.	Vert. se-tenant pair, #1800a & 1800b	*850.00*	

Nos. 1800a and 1800b always have the remaining colors misaligned.
Nos. 1800a, 1800b and 1800c are valued in the grade of fine.

VALUES FOR HINGED STAMPS AFTER NO. 771

This catalogue does not value unused stamps after No. 771 in hinged condition. Hinged unused stamps from No. 772 to the present are worth considerably less than the values given for unused stamps, which are for never-hinged examples.

PERFORMING ARTS SERIES

Will Rogers (1879-1935), Actor and Humorist — A1190

Designed by Jim Sharpe.

PHOTOGRAVURE (Andreotti)

Plates of 200 subjects in four panes of 50.

1979, Nov. 4	**Tagged**	***Perf. 11***	
1801	A1190 15c **multicolored**	.30	.25
	P# block of 12, 6#	4.00	—
	Zip block of 4	1.25	—
	P# block of 20, 6#, zip, copyright	6.50	—
a.	Imperf., pair	*135.00*	

VIETNAM VETERANS ISSUE

A tribute to veterans of the Vietnam War.

Ribbon for Vietnam

Designed by Stevan Dohanos.

PHOTOGRAVURE (Andreotti)
Plates of 200 subjects in four panes of 50.

1979, Nov. 11 **Tagged** ***Perf. 11***

1802 A1191 15c **multicolored**	.30	.25
P# block of 10, 5#	3.25	—
Zip block of 4	1.25	—

PERFORMING ARTS SERIES

W.C. Fields (1880-1946), actor and comedian.

W.C. Fields — A1192

Designed by Jim Sharpe.

PHOTOGRAVURE
Plates of 200 subjects in four panes of 50.

1980, Jan. 29 **Tagged** ***Perf. 11***

1803 A1192 15c **multicolored**	.30	.25
P# block of 12, 6#	4.00	—
Zip block of 4	1.25	—
P# block of 20, 6#, zip, copyright	6.50	—
a. Imperf., pair	—	

BLACK HERITAGE SERIES

Benjamin Banneker (1731-1806), astronomer and mathematician.

Benjamin Banneker — A1193

Designed by Jerry Pinkney.

Printed by American Bank Note Co. and J. W. Fergusson and Sons.

PHOTOGRAVURE
Plates of 200 subjects in four panes of 50.

1980, Feb. 15 **Tagged** ***Perf. 11***

1804 A1193 15c **multicolored**	.30	.25
P# block of 12, 6#+A	4.00	—
Zip block of 4	1.25	—
Plate block of 20, 6#+A, zip, copyright	6.50	—
a. Horiz. pair, imperf. vert.	*275.00*	

Imperfs, including gutter pairs and blocks, exist from printer's waste. These have been fraudulently perforated to simulate No. 1804a. Genuine examples of No. 1804a do not have colors misregistered.

NATIONAL LETTER WRITING WEEK ISSUE

National Letter Writing Week, Feb. 24-Mar. 1. Nos. 1805-1810 are printed vertically se-tenant.

Letters Preserve Memories — A1194

P.S. Write Soon — A1195

Letters Lift Spirits — A1196

Letters Shape Opinions — A1197

Designed by Randall McDougall.

Plates of 240 subjects in four panes of 60 (10x6) each.

PHOTOGRAVURE

1980, Feb. 25 **Tagged** ***Perf. 11***

1805 A1194 15c **multicolored**	.30	.25
1806 A1195 15c **purple & multi**	.30	.25
1807 A1196 15c **multicolored**	.30	.25
1808 A1195 15c **green & multi**	.30	.25
1809 A1197 15c **multicolored**	.30	.25
1810 A1195 15c **red & multi**	.30	.25
a. Vertical strip of 6, #1805-1810	1.85	*2.00*
P# block of 36, 6#	13.00	—
Zip block of 12	3.75	—
Nos. 1805-1810 (6)	1.80	1.50

AMERICANA TYPE

Weaver Violins — A1199

Designer: 3.5c, George Mercer.

COIL STAMPS

1980-81 **Engr.** ***Perf. 10 Vertically***

1811 A984 1c **dark blue,** *greenish,* shiny gum, *Mar. 6, 1980*	.25	.25
Pair	.50	.50
Joint line pair	.60	—
Dull gum	.35	
Joint line pair	1.75	
a. Imperf., pair	*60.00*	
Joint line pair	*150.00*	
b. Tagging omitted	—	
1813 A1199 3.5c **purple,** *yellow, June 23, 1980*	.25	.25
Pair	.50	.50
Joint line pair	1.00	—
a. Untagged (Bureau precanceled, lines only)	.25	.25
Pair	.50	.50
Joint line pair	1.95	—
b. Imperf., pair	*125.00*	
Joint line pair	*375.00*	
1816 A997 12c **red brown,** *beige, Apr. 8, 1981*	.25	.25
Pair	.50	.50
Joint line pair	2.00	—
a. Untagged (Bureau precanceled), **red brown,** *beige*	1.25	1.25
Pair	2.60	2.60
Joint line pair	40.00	—
b. Imperf., pair	135.00	
Joint line pair	275.00	
c. As "a," **brownish red,** *reddish beige*	1.25	1.25
Pair	2.60	2.60
Joint line pair	*37.50*	—
Nos. 1811-1816 (3)	.75	.75

Bureau Precancels: No. 1816a, lines only (valued), lines and PRESORTED/FIRST CLASS (values: unused $75, pair $150, joint line pair $2,250); No. 1816c, lines and PRESORTED/FIRST CLASS.

Eagle — A1207

PHOTOGRAVURE
Plates of 400 subjects in four panes of 100.

1981, Mar. 15 **Tagged** ***Perf. 11x10½***

1818 A1207 (18c) **violet**	.35	.25
P# block of 4	1.60	—
Zip block of 4	1.50	—
Pair with full vert. gutter between	—	
Cross gutter block of 10	*3,000.*	

The cross gutter block, caused by a foldover and misperforated horizontally, is unique.

BOOKLET STAMP
ENGRAVED
Perf. 10 on 2 or 3 Sides

1819 A1207 (18c) **violet**	.40	.25
a. Booklet pane of 8	3.50	2.25

COIL STAMP
Perf. 10 Vert.

1820 A1207 (18c) **violet**	.40	.25
Pair	.80	.50
Joint line pair	1.60	—
a. Imperf., pair	*75.00*	
Joint line pair	*120.00*	

FRANCES PERKINS ISSUE

Frances Perkins (1882-1965), Secretary of Labor, 1933-1945 (first woman cabinet member).

Frances Perkins — A1208

Designed by F.R. Petrie.

ENGRAVED
Plates of 200 subjects in four panes of 50.

1980, Apr. 10 **Tagged** ***Perf. 10½x11***

1821 A1208 15c **Prussian blue**	.30	.25
P# block of 4	1.30	—
Zip block of 4	1.25	—

DOLLEY MADISON ISSUE

Dolley Madison (1768-1849), First Lady, 1809-1817.

Dolley Madison — A1209

Designed by Esther Porter.

ENGRAVED
Plates of 600 subjects in four panes of 150.

1980, May 20 **Tagged** ***Perf. 11***

1822 A1209 15c **red brown & sepia**	.30	.25
P# block of 4	1.40	—
Zip block of 4	1.25	—
a. Red brown missing (PS)	*575.00*	

EMILY BISSELL ISSUE

Emily Bissell (1861-1948), social worker; introduced Christmas seals in United States.

Emily Bissell — A1210

Designed by Stevan Dohanos.

ENGRAVED

Plates of 200 subjects in four panes of 50.

1980, May 31 **Tagged** ***Perf. 11***

1823 A1210 15c **black & red** .30 .25
P# block of 4 1.60 —
Zip block of 4 1.45 —
a. Vert. pair, imperf. horiz. *250.00*
b. All colors missing (EP) —
c. Red missing (FO) —
d. Red omitted —

On No. 1823d, traces of black are present.

HELEN KELLER ISSUE

Helen Keller (1880-1968), blind and deaf writer and lecturer taught by Anne Sullivan (1867-1936).

Helen Keller and Anne Sullivan — A1211

Designed by Paul Calle.

LITHOGRAPHED AND ENGRAVED

Plates of 200 subjects in four panes of 50.

1980, June 27 **Tagged** ***Perf. 11***

1824 A1211 15c **multicolored** .30 .25
P# block of 4 1.30 —
Zip block of 4 1.25 —

VETERANS ADMINISTRATION, 50th ANNIV.

Veterans Administration Emblem — A1212

Designed by Malcolm Grear.

Printed by American Bank Note Co. and J. W. Fergusson and Sons.

PHOTOGRAVURE

Plates of 200 subjects in four panes of 50.

1980, July 21 **Tagged** ***Perf. 11***

1825 A1212 15c **carmine & violet blue** .30 .25
P# block of 4, 2#+A 1.30 —
Zip block of 4 1.25 —
a. Horiz. pair, imperf. vert. *375.00*

BERNARDO DE GALVEZ ISSUE

Gen. Bernardo de Galvez (1746-1786), helped

Gen. Bernardo de Galvez — A1213

Designed by Roy H. Andersen.

LITHOGRAPHED & ENGRAVED

Plates of 200 subjects in four panes of 50.

1980, July 23 **Tagged** ***Perf. 11***

1826 A1213 15c **multicolored** .30 .25
P# block of 4 1.30 —
Zip block of 4 1.25 —
a. Red, brown & blue (engr.) omitted *550.00*
b. Light yellow, red, blue & brown (litho.) omitted *550.00*

CORAL REEFS ISSUE

Nos. 1827-1828 alternate in one horizontal row, Nos. 1829-1830 in the next.

Brain Coral, Beaugregory Fish — A1214

Elkhorn Coral, Porkfish — A1215

Chalice Coral, Moorish Idol — A1216

Finger Coral, Sabertooth Blenny — A1217

Coral Reefs U
Finger Coral: Hawaii

Normal

Coral Reefs U
Finger Coral. Hawaii

Cylinder Flaw

Designed by Chuck Ripper.

PHOTOGRAVURE

Plates of 200 subjects in four panes of 50.

1980, Aug. 26 **Tagged** ***Perf. 11***

1827 A1214 15c **multi** .30 .25
1828 A1215 15c **multi** .30 .25
1829 A1216 15c **multi** .30 .25
1830 A1217 15c **multi** .30 .25
Cylinder flaw (period between "Finger

a. Block of 4, #1827-1830 1.25 1.10
P# block of 12, 6# 5.00 —
Zip block of 4 1.30 —
b. As "a," imperf. *350.00*
c. As "a," vert. imperf. between *1,750.*
d. As "a," imperf. vert. *2,750.*

ORGANIZED LABOR ISSUE

American Bald Eagle — A1218

Designed by Peter Cocci.

PHOTOGRAVURE

Plates of 200 subjects in four panes of 50.

1980, Sept. 1 **Tagged** ***Perf. 11***

1831 A1218 15c **multi** .30 .25
P# block of 12, 6# 3.50 —
Zip block of 4 1.25 —
a. Imperf., pair *275.00*

LITERARY ARTS SERIES

Edith Wharton (1862-1937), novelist.

Edith Wharton — A1219

Designed by Bradbury Thompson after 1905 photograph.

ENGRAVED

Plates of 200 subjects in four panes of 50.

1980, Sept. 5 **Tagged** ***Perf. 10½x11***

1832 A1219 15c **purple** .30 .25
P# block of 4 1.30 —
Zip block of 4 1.25 —

EDUCATION ISSUE

"Homage to the Square: Glow" by Josef Albers — A1220

Designed by Bradbury Thompson

Printed by American Bank Note Co. and J. W. Fergusson and Sons.

PHOTOGRAVURE

Plates of 200 subjects in four panes of 50.

1980, Sept. 12 **Tagged** ***Perf. 11***

1833 A1220 15c **multi** .30 .25
P# block of 6, 3#+A 1.90 —
Zip block of 4 1.25 —
a. Horiz. pair, imperf. vert. *150.00*

AMERICAN FOLK ART SERIES

Pacific Northwest Indian Masks

Heiltsuk, Bella Bella Tribe — A1221

Chilkat Tlingit Tribe — A1222

Tlingit Tribe — A1223

Bella Coola Tribe — A1224

Designed by Bradury Thompson after photographs.

PHOTOGRAVURE

Plates of 160 subjects in four panes of 40.

1980, Sept. 25	**Tagged**	***Perf. 11***	
1834 A1221 15c **multi**		.35	.25
1835 A1222 15c **multi**		.35	.25
1836 A1223 15c **multi**		.35	.25
1837 A1224 15c **multi**		.35	.25
a. Block of 4, #1834-1837		1.50	1.25
P# block of 10, 5#		5.00	—
Zip, copyright block of 6		2.25	—

AMERICAN ARCHITECTURE SERIES

Smithsonian A1225

Trinity Church A1226

Penn Academy A1227

Lyndhurst A1228

Designed by Walter D. Richards.

ENGRAVED (Giori)

Plates of 160 subjects in four panes of 40.

1980, Oct. 9	**Tagged**	***Perf. 11***	
1838 A1225 15c **black & red**		.30	.25
a. Red missing (PS)			—
1839 A1226 15c **black & red**		.30	.25
1840 A1227 15c **black & red**		.30	.25
1841 A1228 15c **black & red**		.30	.25
a. Block of 4, #1838-1841		1.25	1.25
P# block of 4		1.50	—
Zip block of 4		1.30	—
b. As "a," red missing on Nos. 1838, 1839 (PS)		*400.00*	
c. As "a," tagging omitted		—	

CHRISTMAS ISSUE

Madonna and Child — A1229

Wreath and Toys — A1230

Designed by Esther Porter (No. 1842) after Epiphany Window, Washington Cathedral, and by Bob Timberlake (No. 1843).

PHOTOGRAVURE

Plate of 200 subjects in four panes of 50.

1980, Oct. 31	**Tagged**	***Perf. 11***	
1842 A1229 15c **multi**		.30	.25
P# block of 12, 6#		4.00	—
Zip block of 4		1.25	—
Pair with full vert. gutter btwn.		—	
a. Imperf., pair		40.00	

PHOTOGRAVURE (Combination Press)

Plates of 230 subjects (10x23) in panes of 50 (10x5).

1843 A1230 15c **multi**	.30	.25
P# block of 20, 5-8 #, 1-2 copyright	6.50	—
a. Imperf., pair	40.00	
b. Buff omitted	22.50	
c. Vert. pair, imperf. horiz.		—
d. Horiz. pair, imperf. between	*3,250.*	
e. Tagging omitted	125.00	—

No. 1843b is difficult to identify and should have a competent certificate.

See Combination Press note after No. 1703.

GREAT AMERICANS ISSUE

A1231

A1232

A1233

A1234

A1235

A1236

A1237

A1238

A1239

A1240

A1241

A1242

A1243

A1244

A1245

A1246

A1247

A1248

A1249

A1250

A1251

A1252

A1253

A1254

A1255

A1256

Designers: 1c, Bernie Fuchs. 2c, Burt Silverman, 3c, 17c, 40c, Ward Brackett. 4c, 7c, 10c, 18c, 30c, Richard Sparks. 5c, Paul Calle. 6c, No. 1861, Dennis Lyall. 8c, Arthur Lidov. 9c, 11c, Robert Alexander Anderson. 13c, Brad Holland. 14c, Bradbury Thompson. 19c, 39c, Roy H. Andersen. No. 1860, Jim Sharpe. No. 1862, 22c, 50c, 37c, Christopher Calle. 35c, Nathan Jones.

ENGRAVED

Perf. 11x10½, 11 (1c, 6c-11c, 14c, No. 1862, 22c, 30c, 39c, 40c, 50c)

1980-85 **Tagged**

1844 A1231 1c **black,** perf. 11.2, small block tagging, *Sept. 23, 1983* .25 .25
P# block of 6 .75 —
P# block of 20, 1-2 #, 1-2 copyright 3.50 —
a. Imperf., pair *250.00*
b. Vert. pair, imperf. btwn. and with natural straight edge at bottom *1,000.*
c. Perf. 10.9, small block tagging .25 .25
P# block of 6 1.50 —
P# block of 20, 1-2 #, 1-2 copyright 3.50 —
d. Perf. 10.9, large block tagging, *1985* .25 .25
P# block of 6 1.50 —
P# block of 20, 1-2 #, 1-2 copyright 3.50 —
e. Vert. pair, imperf. horiz. *1,000.*

1845 A1232 2c **brn blk,** overall tagging, *Nov. 18, 1982* .25 .25
P# block of 4 .60 —
Zip block of 4 .50 —
Pair with full horiz. gutter between —
a. Tagging omitted 125.00

The pair with gutter between of No. 1845 is also misperfed, with horiz. perfs running through the stamps.

1846 A1233 3c **olive green,** overall tagging, *July 13, 1983* .25 .25
deep olive green .25 .25
P# block of 4 1.00 —
Zip block of 4 .80 —
a. Tagging omitted 9.00

1847 A1234 4c **violet,** overall tagging, *June 3, 1983* .25 .25
P# block of 4 1.00 —
Zip block of 4 1.00 —
a. Tagging omitted 9.00

1848 A1235 5c **henna brown,** overall tagging, *June 25, 1983* .30 .25
P# block of 4 1.50 —
Zip block of 4 1.25 —

1849 A1236 6c **orange vermilion,** large block tagging, *Sept. 19, 1985* .25 .25
P# block of 6 1.50 —
P# block of 20, 1-2 #, 1-2 zip, 1-2 copyright 5.00 —
a. Vert. pair, imperf. between and with natural straight edge at bottom *1,000.*

1850 A1237 7c **bright carmine,** small block tagging, *Jan. 25, 1985* .25 .25
P# block of 6 1.50 —
P# block of 20, 1-2 #, 1-2 zip, 1-2 copyright 4.00 —

1851 A1238 8c **olive black,** overall tagging, *July 25, 1985* .25 .25
P# block of 4 1.00 —
Zip block of 4 1.00 —
a. Tagging omitted *150.00*

1852 A1239 9c **dark green,** small block tagging, *June 7, 1985* .25 .25
P# block of 6 1.50 —
P# block of 20, 1-2 #. 1-2 zip, 1-2 copyright 5.00 —

1853 A1240 10c **Prussian blue,** small block tagging, *May 31, 1984* .25 .25
P# block of 6 2.00 —
P# block of 20, 1-2 #, 1-2 copyright, 1-2 zip 9.00 —
a. Large block tagging .30 .25
P# block of 6 2.25 —
P# block of 20, 1-2 #, 1-2 copyright, 1-2 zip 9.00 —
b. Vert. pair, imperf. between *550.00*
c. Horiz. pair, imperf. between *1,250.*
d. Vert. pair, imperf horiz. —

Almost all examples of No. 1853b also have a natural straight edge at bottom. At least one pair has perfs at bottom and partial perfs at top.

Completely imperforate tagged or untagged stamps are from printer's waste. Known unused and used.

1854 A1241 11c **dark blue,** overall tagging, *Feb. 12, 1985* .40 .25
P# block of 4 2.00 —
Zip block of 4 1.60 —
a. Tagging omitted 30.00

1855 A1242 13c **light maroon,** overall tagging, *Jan. 15, 1982* .40 .25
P# block of 4 2.25 —
Zip block of 4 1.60 —
a. Tagging omitted 22.50

1856 A1243 14c **slate green,** small block tagging, *Mar. 21, 1985* .30 .25
P# block of 6 2.25 —
P# block of 20, 1-2 #, 1-2 zip, 1-2 copyright 10.00 —
a. Large block tagging .30 .25
P# block of 6 2.25 —
P# block of 20, 1-2 #, 1-2 zip, 1-2 copyright 9.00 —
b. Vert. pair, imperf. horiz. *90.00*
c. Horiz. pair, imperf. between 8.00 —
d. Vert. pair, imperf. between *1,250.*
e. All color omitted —

No. 1856e comes from a partially printed pane and should be collected as a vertical strip of 10, one stamp normal, one stamp transitional and 8 stamps with color omitted.

1857 A1244 17c **green,** overall tagging, *May 28, 1981* .35 .25
P# block of 4 2.00 —
Zip block of 4 1.40 —
a. Tagging omitted 17.50

1858 A1245 18c **dark blue,** overall tagging, *May 7, 1981* .35 .25
P# block of 4 3.00 —
Zip block of 4 1.40 —
Pair with full horiz. gutter between —
a. Tagging omitted 15.00

1859 A1246 19c **brown,** overall tagging, *Dec. 27, 1980* .45 .25
P# block of 4 2.75 —
Zip block of 4 1.90 —

1860 A1247 20c **claret,** overall tagging, *Jan. 12, 1982* .40 .25
P# block of 4 3.25 —
Zip block of 4 1.65 —
a. Tagging omitted 12.50

1861 A1248 20c **green,** overall tagging, *June 10, 1983* .50 .25
P# block of 4 4.00 —
Zip block of 4 2.00 —
a. Tagging omitted *225.00*

1862 A1249 20c **black,** perf 10.9, small block tagging, dull gum, *Jan. 26, 1984* .40 .25
P# block of 6 4.50 —
P# block of 20, 1-2 #, 1-2 copyright, 1-2 zip 11.00 —
a. Perf. 11.2, large block tagging, dull gum .75 .25
Corner P# block of 4 4.50 —
Zip block of 4 3.00 —
b. Perf. 11.2, overall tagging, dull gum, *1990* .40 —
Corner P# block of 4 3.75 —
Zip block of 4 1.60 —
c. Tagging omitted, perf. 11.2 10.00
d. Prephosphored uncoated paper with embedded tagging showing a mottled appearance, shiny gum, perf. 11.2, *1993* .40 .25
Corner P# block of 4 2.50
Zip block of 4 1.60

1863 A1250 22c **dark chalky blue,** small block tagging, *Apr. 23, 1985* .75 .25
P# block of 6 9.00 —
P# block of 20, 1-2 #, 1-2 zip, 1-2 copyright 16.00 —
a. Large block tagging 1.00 .25
P# block of 6 12.50 —
P# block of 20, 1-2 #, 1-2 zip, 1-2 copyright 22.50 —
b. Perf. 11.2, large block tagging, *1987* .75 .25
Corner P# block of 4 8.00 —
Zip block of 4 3.25 —
c. Tagging omitted 17.50
d. Vert. pair, imperf. horiz. *1,300.*
f. Horiz. pair, imperf. between *1,300.*
g. Vert. pair, imperf. between —

1864 A1251 30c **olive gray,** small block tagging, *Sept. 2, 1984* .60 .25
P# block of 6 3.75 —
P# block of 20, 1-2 #, 1-2 copyright, 1-2 zip 17.50 —
a. Perf. 11.2, large block tagging .70 .25
Corner P# block of 4 4.50 —
Zip block of 4 3.00 —
b. Perf. 11.2, overall tagging 3.75 .25
Corner P# block of 4 30.00 —
Zip block of 4 16.00 —
c. Tagging omitted *225.00*

1865 A1252 35c **gray,** overall tagging, *June 3, 1981* .75 .25
P# block of 4 4.25 —
Zip block of 4 3.25 —
a. Tagging omitted 85.00

1866 A1253 37c **blue,** overall tagging, *Jan. 26, 1982* .80 .25
P# block of 4 3.75 —
Zip block of 4 3.25 —
a. Tagging omitted 30.00

1867 A1254 39c **rose lilac,** perf 10.9, small block tagging, *Mar. 20, 1985* 1.00 .25
P# block of 6 6.50 —
P# block of 20, 1-2 #, 1-2 zip, 1-2 copyright 21.00 —
a. Vert. pair, imperf. horiz. *350.00*
b. Vert. pair, imperf. between *1,500.*
c. Large block tagging, perf 10.9 .90 .25
P# block of 6 5.75 —
P# block of 20, 1-2 #, 1-2 zip, 1-2 copyright 20.00 —
d. Perf. 11.2, large block tagging .90 .25
Corner P# block of 4 8.00 —
Zip block of 4 3.75 —

1868 A1255 40c **dark green,** perf 10.9, small block tagging, *Feb. 24, 1984* 1.00 .25
P# block of 6 6.50 —
P# block of 20, 1-2 #, 1-2 copyright, 1-2 zip 21.00 —
a. Perf. 11.2, large block tagging .90 .25
Corner P# block of 4 5.50 —
Zip block of 4 3.75 —

1869 A1256 50c **brown,** perf 10.9, overall tagging, shiny gum, *Feb. 22, 1985* 1.00 .25
P# block of 4 7.50 —
Zip block of 4 4.25 —
a. Perf. 11.2, medium block tagging, dull gum 1.00 .25
P# block of 4 6.25 —
Zip block of 4 4.25 —
b. Tagging omitted, perf. 10.9, shiny gum 22.50
c. Tagging omitted, perf. 11.2, dull gum 12.50
d. Perf. 11.2, overall tagging, dull gum 3.50 .25
P# block of 4 35.00 —
Zip block of 4 15.00 —
e. Perf. 11.2, prephosphored uncoated paper with embedded tagging showing a mottled appearance, shiny gum, *1992* 1.00 .25
P# block of 4 5.00 —
Zip block of 4 4.25 —
f. Perf. 11.2, large block tagging, dull gum —
P# block of 4 —
Nos. 1844-1869 (26) 12.00 6.50

The medium block tagging, No. 1869a, measures 19x21.5mm. The large block tagging, No. 1869f, measures 20x24mm.

EVERETT DIRKSEN (1896-1969)

Senate minority leader, 1960-1969.

A1261

Designed by Ron Adair.

ENGRAVED

Plates of 200 subjects in four panes of 50.

1981, Jan. 4	**Tagged**	***Perf. 11***	
1874 A1261 15c **gray**		.30	.25
P# block of 4		1.40	—
Zip block of 4		1.25	—
a. All color omitted		*500.00*	

No. 1874a comes from a partially printed pane and may be collected as a vertical strip of 3 or 5 (1 or 3 stamps normal, one stamp transitional and one stamp with color omitted) or as a pair with one partially printed stamp.

BLACK HERITAGE SERIES

Whitney Moore Young, Jr. (1921-1971), civil rights leader.

A1262

Designed by Jerry Pinkney.

PHOTOGRAVURE

Plates of 200 subjects in four panes of 50.

1981, Jan. 30	**Tagged**	***Perf. 11***	
1875 A1262 15c **multi**		.35	.25
P# block of 4, 6#		1.60	—
Zip block of 4		1.50	—

FLOWER ISSUE

A1263

A1264

A1265

A1266

Illustration reduced.

Designed by Lowell Nesbitt.

PHOTOGRAVURE

Plates of 192 subjects in four panes of 48 (8x6).

1981, Apr. 23	**Tagged**	***Perf. 11***	
1876 A1263 18c **multicolored**		.35	.25
1877 A1264 18c **multicolored**		.35	.25
1878 A1265 18c **multicolored**		.35	.25
1879 A1266 18c **multicolored**		.35	.25
a. Block of 4, #1876-1879		1.40	1.25
P# block of 4, 6#		1.75	—
Zip block of 4		1.45	—

AMERICAN WILDLIFE

A1267

A1268

A1269

A1270

A1271

A1272

A1273

A1274

A1275

A1276

Designs from photographs by Jim Brandenburg.

No. 1880, Bighorn. No. 1881, Puma. No. 1882, Harbor seal. No. 1883, American Buffalo. No. 1884, Brown bear. No. 1885, Polar bear. No. 1886, Elk (wapiti). No. 1887, Moose. No. 1888, White-tailed deer. No. 1889, Pronghorn.

ENGRAVED

Perf. 11 on 2 or 3 Sides

1981, May 14	**Tagged**	**Dark brown**	
1880 A1267 18c multicolored		.50	.25
a. Tagging omitted			—
1881 A1268 18c multicolored		.50	.25
1882 A1269 18c multicolored		.50	.25
1883 A1270 18c multicolored		.50	.25
1884 A1271 18c multicolored		.50	.25
1885 A1272 18c multicolored		.50	.25
1886 A1273 18c multicolored		.50	.25
a. Tagging omitted			—
1887 A1274 18c multicolored		.50	.25
a. Tagging omitted			—
1888 A1275 18c multicolored		.50	.25
1889 A1276 18c multicolored		.50	.25
a. Booklet pane of 10, #1880-1889		5.00	5.00
b. Tagging omitted			—
Nos. 1880-1889 (10)		5.00	2.50

Nos. 1880-1889 issued in booklet only. All stamps have one or two straight edges.

Imperfs are from printer's waste.

FLAG AND ANTHEM ISSUE

A1277

A1278

A1279

A1280

Designed by Peter Cocci.

ENGRAVED

Plates of 460 subjects (20x23) in panes of 100 (10x10).

1981, Apr. 24	**Tagged**	***Perf. 11***	
1890 A1277 18c **multicolored**		.35	.25
P# block of 6		2.25	—
P# block of 20, 1-2 #		10.00	—
a. Imperf., pair		75.00	
b. Vert. pair, imperf. horiz.		*550.00*	
c. Vert. pair, imperf. between		*550.00*	
d. Tagging omitted		125.00	
e. As "a," tagging omitted		—	

See Combination Press note after No. 1703.

Coil Stamp

Perf. 10 Vert.

1891 A1278 18c **multicolored**	.35	.25
Pair	.70	.25
P# strip of 3, #1	45.00	
P# strip of 3, #2	11.50	
P# strip of 3, #3	80.00	
P# strip of 3, #4	3.00	
P# strip of 3, #5	3.00	
P# strip of 3, #6	*525.00*	
P# strip of 3, #7	7.50	
P# strip of 5, #1	100.00	
P# strip of 5, #2	27.50	
P# strip of 5, #3	550.00	
P# strip of 5, #4	3.50	
P# strip of 5, #5	3.50	
P# strip of 5, #6	*1,900.*	
P# strip of 5, #7	8.00	
P# single, #1	—	2.50
P# single, #2	—	.80
P# single, #3	—	9.00
P# single, #4	—	.80
P# single, #5	—	1.00
P# single, #6	—	*500.00*
P# single, #7	—	9.00
a. Imperf., pair	17.50	—
b. Pair, imperf. between	*1,750.*	
c. Tagging omitted		—

Beware of pairs offered as No. 1891b that have faint blind perfs.

Vertical pairs and blocks exist from printer's waste.

Booklet Stamps

Perf. 11x10½ on 3 Sides

1892 A1279 6c **dark blue & red**	.50	.25
a. Tagging omitted	35.00	

Perf. 11x10½ on 2 or 3 Sides

1893 A1280 18c **multicolored**	.30	.25
a. Booklet pane of 8 (2 #1892, 6 #1893)	3.00	2.50
b. As "a," vert. imperf. between	60.00	

c. Se-tenant pair, #1892 & #1893 .90 1.00
d. As "a," tagging omitted *675.00*
e. As No. 1893, tagging omitted 100.00

Bureau Precanceled Coils

Starting with No. 1895b, Bureau precanceled coil stamps are valued unused as well as used. The coils issued with dull gum may be difficult to distinguish.

When used normally these stamps do not receive any postal markings so that used stamps with an additional postal cancellation of any kind are worth considerably less than the values shown here.

FLAG OVER SUPREME COURT ISSUE

A1281

Designed by Dean Ellis

ENGRAVED

Plates of 460 subjects (20x23) in panes of 100 (10x10)

1981, Dec. 17 **Tagged** ***Perf. 11***

1894 A1281 20c **black, dark blue & red,** dull gum .40 .25
P# block of 6 2.75 —
P# block of 20, 1-2 # 9.00 —
a. As "e," vert. pair, imperf. 30.00
b. Vert. pair, imperf. horiz. *350.00*
c. Dark blue omitted *60.00*
d. Black omitted *225.00*
e. Perf. 11.2, shiny gum .35 .25
P# block of 6 2.50 —
P# block of 20, 1-2 # 8.50 —
f. Tagging omitted —

Counterfeits exist of No. 1894. See the Postal Counterfeits section of this catalog.

Coil Stamp

Perf. 10 Vert.

1895 A1281 20c **black, dark blue & red,** wide block tagging .40 .25
Pair .80 .50
P# strip of 3, #1 1.75
P# strip of 3, #2 3.00
P# strip of 3, #3 3.00
P# strip of 3, #5 3.00
P# strip of 3, #11 3.00
P# strip of 3, #13, 14 3.00
P# strip of 5, #1 25.00
P# strip of 5, #2 3.75
P# strip of 5, #3 3.25
P# strip of 5, #5 3.25
P# strip of 5, #11 3.75
P# strip of 5, #13, 14 3.25
P# single, #1 — .75
P# single, #2-3 — .50
P# single, #5 — .50
P# single, #11 — 3.00
P# single, #13, 14 — .50
a. Narrow block tagging .40 .25
Pair .80 .50
P# strip of 3, #4 110.00
P# strip of 3, #6 35.00
P# strip of 3, #8 2.75
P# strip of 3, #9-10 2.75
P# strip of 3, #12 3.00
P# strip of 5, #4 *250.00*
P# strip of 5, #6 85.00
P# strip of 5, #8 8.00
P# strip of 5, #9 3.50
P# strip of 5, #10 4.25
P# strip of 5, #12 4.00
P# single, #4 — .80
P# single, #6 — 2.25
P# single, #8 — .40
P# single, #9 — .40
P# single, #10 — .60
P# single, #12 — .40
b. Untagged (Bureau precanceled, lines only) .50 .50
P# strip of 3, #14 27.50
P# strip of 5, #14 32.50
P# single, #14 30.00
c. Tagging omitted (not Bureau precanceled) *25.00* —
P# strip of 3, #4 —
P# strip of 3, #3, 5, 8, 10, 11, 14 —
P# strip of 5, #5, 10, 11, 14 —
P# single, #5, 8-11, 14 — —
d. Imperf., pair, narrow block tagging 8.00 —
e. Pair, imperf. between *600.00*
f. Black omitted *45.00*
g. Dark blue omitted *1,000.*
h. Black field of stars instead of blue —
i. As "d," tagging omitted —
j. Imperf., pair, wide block tagging 20.00 —

The wide block tagging on No. 1895 and narrow block tagging on No. 1895a differentiate stamps printed on two different presses. The wide blocks are approximately 20-21mm high by 18mm wide with a 4mm untagged gutter between tagging blocks.

The narrow blocks are approximately 21-22mm high and approximately 16-16½mm wide with a 5½-6½ untagged gutter between tagging blocks.

BOOKLET STAMP

Perf. 11x10½ on 2 or 3 Sides

1896 A1281 20c **black, dark blue & red,** small block tagging .40 .25
a. Booklet pane of 6 3.00 2.25
Scored perforations 3.00 2.25
b. Booklet pane of 10, *June 1, 1982* 5.25 3.25
Scored perforations 7.50 5.00
c. As "b," tagging omitted — —
d. Large block tagging ('83) .40 .25
e. As "d," booklet pane of 10 5.25 3.25
Scored perforations 5.25 3.25
f. As "a," tagging omitted —
g. As No. 1896, tagging omitted —

Booklets containing two panes of ten of No. 1896e were issued Nov. 17, 1983.

The small block tagging is 16x18mm (Nos. 1896-1896b). The large block tagging is 18x21mm (Nos. 1896d-1896e).

TRANSPORTATION ISSUE

A1283

A1284

Designer: 1c, 2c, David Stone.

COIL STAMPS

ENGRAVED

1981-84 **Tagged** ***Perf. 10 Vert.***

1897 A1283 1c **violet,** *Aug. 19, 1983* .25 .25
Pair .25 .25
P# strip of 3, line, #1, 2 .40
P# strip of 3, line, #3, 4 .50
P# strip of 3, line, #5, 6 .40
P# strip of 5, line, #1, 2 .50
P# strip of 5, line, #3, 4 .50
P# strip of 5, line, #5, 6 .50
P# single, #1, 2 — .25
P# single, #3, 4 — .55
P# single, #5, 6 — .30
b. Imperf., pair *325.00*
Joint line pair, P# —
e. Tagging omitted *150.00*

See No. 2225.

1897A A1284 2c **black,** *May 20, 1982* .25 .25
Pair .25 .25
P# strip of 3, line, #2-4, 6, 8, 10 .45
P# strip of 5, line, #2-4, 6, 8, 10 .50
P# single, #2-4, 6, 8, 10 — .40
c. Imperf., pair 45.00
Joint line pair, P# —
d. Tagging omitted 40.00

See No. 2226.

A1284a

A1285

Designers: 3c, Walter Brooks. 4c, Jim Schleyer.

1898 A1284a 3c **dark green,** *Mar. 25, 1983* .25 .25
Pair .25 .25
P# strip of 3, line, #1-4 .55
P# strip of 5, line, #1-4 .75
P# single, #1-4 — .50
1898A A1285 4c **reddish brown,** *Aug. 19, 1982* .25 .25
Pair .25 .25
P# strip of 3, line, #1-4 .75
P# strip of 3, line, #5-6 1.25
P# strip of 5, line, #1-4 .90
P# strip of 5, line, #5-6 1.75
P# single, #1-4 — .75
P# single, #5-6 — 1.50
b. Untagged (Bureau precanceled, Nonprofit Org.) .25 .25
P# strip of 3, line, #3-6 2.50
P# strip of 5, line, #3-6 3.00
P# single, #3, 4 — 2.90
P# single, #5, 6 — 2.90
c. As "b," imperf., pair *375.00*
d. As No. 1898A, imperf. pair *400.00* —
e. Tagging omitted (not Bureau precanceled) *50.00* *35.00*

See No. 2228.

A1286

A1287

Designers: 5c, 5.2c, Walter Brooks.

1899 A1286 5c **gray green,** *Oct. 10, 1983* .25 .25
Pair .25 .25
P# strip of 3, line, #1-4 .80
P# strip of 5, line, #1-4 .90
P# single, #1-4 — .65
a. Imperf., pair *1,750.*
b. Tagging omitted 25.00 —
1900 A1287 5.2c **carmine,** *Mar. 21, 1983* .25 .25
Pair .35 .35
P# strip of 3, line, #1-2 2.00
P# strip of 3, line, #3 150.00
P# strip of 3, line, #5 90.00
P# strip of 5, line, #1-2 3.00
P# strip of 5, line, #3 190.00
P# strip of 5, line, #5 125.00
P# single, #1-2 — 2.50
P# single, #3 — *110.00*
P# single, #5 — *100.00*
a. Untagged (Bureau precanceled, lines only) .25 .25
P# strip of 3, line, #1-3 3.75
P# strip of 3, line, #4 4.75
P# strip of 3, line, #5 4.00
P# strip of 3, line, #6 4.50
P# strip of 5, line, #1-3 4.50
P# strip of 5, line, #4, 6 7.50
P# strip of 5, line, #5 4.50
P# single, #1, 2 — 2.25
P# single, #3 — 1.50
P# single, #4 — 7.00
P# single, #5 — 1.75
P# single, #6 — 7.50
b. Tagging omitted *150.00*

A1288

A1289

Designers: 5.9c, David Stone. 7.4c, Jim Schleyer.

1901 A1288 5.9c **blue,** *Feb. 17, 1982* .25 .25
Pair .50 .50
P# strip of 3, line, #3-4 2.75
P# strip of 5, line, #3-4 3.75
P# single, #3-4 — 3.50
a. Untagged (Bureau precanceled, lines only) .25 .25
P# strip of 3, line, #3-4 10.00
P# strip of 3, line, #5-6 50.00
P# strip of 5, line, #3-4 17.50
P# strip of 5, line, #5-6 75.00
P# single, #3-4 — 5.00
P# single, #5-6 — 50.00
b. As "a," imperf., pair *140.00*
1902 A1289 7.4c **brown,** *Apr. 7, 1984* .25 .25
Pair .50 .50
P# strip of 3, #2 3.25
P# strip of 5, #2 3.50
P# single, #2 — 4.00
a. Untagged (Bureau precanceled, Blk. Rt. CAR-RT SORT) .25 .25
P# strip of 3, #2 3.00
P# strip of 5, #2 3.25
P# single, #2 — 3.50

A1290

A1291

Designers: 9.3c, Jim Schleyer. 10.9c, David Stone.

1903 A1290 9.3c **carmine rose,** *Dec. 15* .30 .25
Pair .60 .50
P# strip of 3, line, #1-2 3.00
P# strip of 3, line, #3-4 5.00
P# strip of 3, line, #5-6 125.00
P# strip of 5, line, #1-2 3.75
P# strip of 5, line, #3-4 11.00
P# strip of 5, line, #5-6 260.00
P# single, #1-2 — 2.00
P# single, #3-4 — 7.50
P# single, #5-6 — 150.00
a. Untagged (Bureau precanceled, lines only) .25 .25
P# strip of 3, line, #1 3.25
P# strip of 3, line, #2 3.25
P# strip of 3, line, #3 5.25
P# strip of 3, line, #4 3.50
P# strip of 3, line, #5-6 1.25
P# strip of 3, line, #8 150.00
P# strip of 5, line, #1 5.00
P# strip of 5, line, #2 5.00
P# strip of 5, line, #3 10.00
P# strip of 5, line, #4 5.50
P# strip of 5, line, #5-6 1.75
P# strip of 5, line, #8 200.00
P# single, #1-2 — 3.25
P# single, #3 — 5.25
P# single, #4 — 3.50
P# single, #5-6 — 1.25
P# single, #8 — 150.00
b. As "a," imperf., pair 90.00

1904 A1291 10.9c **purple,** *Mar. 26, 1982* .30 .25
Pair .60 .50
P# strip of 3, line, #1-2 4.00
P# strip of 5, line, #1-2 9.00
P# single, #1-2 — 6.00
a. Untagged (Bureau precanceled, lines only) .30 .25
P# strip of 3, line, #1-2 10.00
P# strip of 3, line, #3-4 50.00
P# strip of 5, line, #1-2 15.00
P# strip of 5, line, #3-4 200.00
P# single, #1-2 — 7.00
P# single, #3-4 — 50.00
b. As "a," imperf., pair 125.00
Joint line pair, P# —

A1292

A1293

Designers: 11c, Jim Schleyer. 17c Chuck Jaquays.

1905 A1292 11c **red,** *Feb. 3, 1984* .30 .25
Pair .60 .50
P# strip of 3, #1 1.90
P# strip of 5, #1 2.25
P# single, #1 — 2.25
a. Untagged *Sept. 1991* .25 .25
Pair .50 .50
P# strip of 3, #1 1.50
P# strip of 3, #2 1.70
P# strip of 5, #1 2.25
P# strip of 5, #2 2.25
P# single, #1 — 2.25
P# single, #2 — 2.00

Untagged stamps from plate 1 come only Bureau precanceled with lines. Untagged stamps from plate 2 come only without precancel lines.

1906 A1293 17c **ultramarine,** *June 25* .35 .25
Pair .70 .50
P# strip of 3, line, #1-5 1.50
P# strip of 3, line, #6 6.00
P# strip of 3, line, #7 2.25
P# strip of 5, line, #1-5 2.00
P# strip of 5, line, #6 7.00
P# strip of 5, line, #7 2.75
P# single, #1-5 — 1.50
P# single, #6 — 7.50
P# single, #7 — 3.00
a. Untagged (Bureau precanceled, Presorted First Class) .35 .35
P# strip of 3, line, #1, 2 4.00
P# strip of 3, line, #3-5 2.50
P# strip of 3, line, #6, 7 6.00
P# strip of 5, line, #1, 2 6.00
P# strip of 5, line, #3-5 5.00
P# strip of 5, line, #6-7 7.00
P# single, #1, 2 — 6.00
P# single, #3-5 — 3.00
P# single, #6, 7 — 7.50
b. Imperf., pair 130.00
c. As "a," imperf., pair *400.00*
d. As No. 1906, tagging omitted —

Three different precancel styles exist with differences in the font used: Type A has thin lines and the "T" in "PRESORTED" is tall with a short cross bar (most common); Type B has thicker lines and the "T" is shorter with a longer cross bar (least common); Type C has thicker lines still and the "T" has a shorter stem with a cross bar longer than on Types A or B. Lengths of the precancel increase with the types and the wider spacing of the letters, though the imprecise manufacture of the precancel mats led to significant variations in length. Combination pairs exist of Types A and B.

A1294

A1295

Designers: 18c, David Stone. 20c, Jim Schleyer.

1907 A1294 18c **dark brown,** *May 18* .35 .25
Pair .70 .50
P# strip of 3, line, #1 15.00
P# strip of 3, line, #2 2.00
P# strip of 3, line, #3, 4 17.50
P# strip of 3, line, #5, 6 2.50
P# strip of 3, line, #7 6.00
P# strip of 3, line, #8 2.50
P# strip of 3, line, #9-12 4.75
P# strip of 3, line, #13, 14 2.50
P# strip of 3, line, #15, 16 6.00
P# strip of 3, line, #17, 18 2.50
P# strip of 5, line, #1 45.00
P# strip of 5, line, #2 3.00
P# strip of 5, line, #3-4 45.00
P# strip of 5, line, #5, 6 3.00
P# strip of 5, line, #7 7.00
P# strip of 5, line, #8 3.00
P# strip of 5, line, #9-12 6.00
P# strip of 5, line, #13, 14 3.00
P# strip of 5, line, #15, 16 7.50
P# strip of 5, line, #17, 18 3.00
P# single, #1 — 8.00
P# single, #2 — .75
P# single, #3, 4 — 8.00
P# single, #5, 6 — .75
P# single, #7 — 7.00
P# single, #8 — .75
P# single, #9-14 — 3.25
P# single, #15, 16 — 10.00
P# single, #17, 18 — 2.75
a. Imperf., pair 95.00
b. Tagging omitted —

1908 A1295 20c **vermilion,** *Dec. 10* .35 .25
Pair .70 .50
P# strip of 3, line, #1 12.50
P# strip of 3, line, #2 90.00
P# strip of 3, line, #3, 4 2.50
P# strip of 3, line, #5 2.25
P# strip of 3, line, #6 9.00
P# strip of 3, line, #7, 8 20.00
P# strip of 3, line, #9, 10 2.25
P# strip of 3, line, #11 9.00
P# strip of 3, line, #12 4.00
P# strip of 3, line, #13 2.50
P# strip of 3, line, #14 4.00
P# strip of 3, line, #15, 16 2.75
P# strip of 5, line, #1 55.00
P# strip of 5, line, #2 400.00
P# strip of 5, line, #3, 4 3.00
P# strip of 5, line, #5 2.75
P# strip of 5, line, #6 20.00
P# strip of 5, line, #7-8 140.00
P# strip of 5, line, #9-10 2.75
P# strip of 5, line, #11 50.00
P# strip of 5, line, #12 5.00
P# strip of 5, line, #13 3.25
P# strip of 5, line, #14 5.00
P# strip of 5, line, #15-16 3.25
P# single, #1 — .65
P# single, #2 — 7.50
P# single, #3, 4 — .65
P# single, #5 — .75
P# single, #6 — 1.25
P# single, #7, 8 — 1.10
P# single, #9, 10 — .75
P# single, #11 — 1.00
P# single, #12 — 5.00
P# single, #13 — .65
P# single, #14 — 5.00
P# single, #15, 16 — 2.00
a. Imperf., pair 75.00
b. Tagging omitted *100.00* —
Nos. 1897-1908 (14) 3.95 3.50

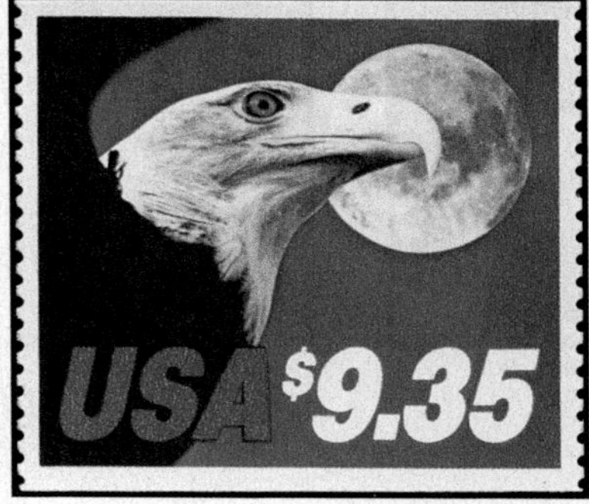

Eagle and Moon
A1296

Booklet Stamp
PHOTOGRAVURE
Perf. 10 Vert. on 1 or 2 Sides

1983, Aug. 12 **Untagged**
1909 A1296 $9.35 **multicolored** 19.00 15.00
a. Booklet pane of 3 57.50 —

AMERICAN RED CROSS CENTENNIAL

A1297

Designed by Joseph Csatari.

PHOTOGRAVURE
Plates of 200 subjects in four panes of 50.

1981, May 1 **Tagged** ***Perf. 10½x11***
1910 A1297 18c **multicolored** .35 .25
P# block of 4, 6# 1.75 —
Zip block of 4 1.40 —

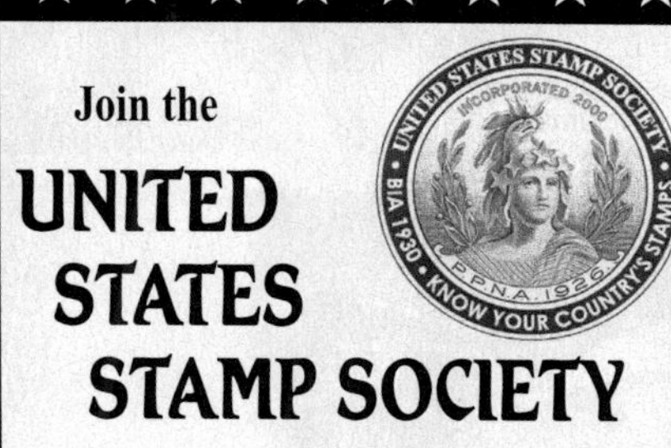

Since 1930, **THE** society for U.S. collectors and publishers of the ***Durland Standard Plate Number Catalog*** and other U.S. philatelic references. The Durland is the reference for plate number collectors with illustrations of marginal marking types and data on sheets, coils and booklet panes. Other publications include ***"The Prexies," "The Transports" and "United States Saving Stamps."***

Sample copy of the society's journal, the ***United States Specialist*** is available for $2. Membership information and a complete list of publications from:

USSS, PO Box 3508
Joliet, IL 60434-3508
www.usstamps.org

SAVINGS & LOAN SESQUICENTENNIAL

A1298

Designed by Don Hedin.

PHOTOGRAVURE

Plates of 200 subjects in four panes of 50.

1981, May 8	**Tagged**	***Perf. 11***	
1911 A1298 18c **multicolored**		.35	.25
P# block of 4, 6#		1.75	—
Zip block of 4		1.40	—

SPACE ACHIEVEMENT ISSUE

Moon Walk — A1299

Skylab — A1302

Space Shuttle Columbia A1300

Space Shuttle Columbia A1301

Pioneer 11 — A1303

Telescope — A1306

Space Shuttle Columbia A1304

Space Shuttle Columbia A1305

Designed by Robert McCall.

PHOTOGRAVURE

Plates of 192 subjects in four panes of 48 each.

1981, May 21	**Tagged**	***Perf. 11***	
1912 A1299 18c **multicolored**		.35	.25
1913 A1300 18c **multicolored**		.35	.25
1914 A1301 18c **multicolored**		.35	.25
1915 A1302 18c **multicolored**		.35	.25
1916 A1303 18c **multicolored**		.35	.25
1917 A1304 18c **multicolored**		.35	.25
1918 A1305 18c **multicolored**		.35	.25
1919 A1306 18c **multicolored**		.35	.25
a. Block of 8, #1912-1919		2.80	3.00
P# block of 8, 6#		3.00	—
Zip, copyright block of 8		2.90	—
b. As "a," imperf.		*5,500.*	
c. As "a," imperf. vert.		*2,000.*	
d. As "a," tagging omitted		*1,000.*	
e. As "a," top 4 stamps part perf, bottom 4 stamps imperf		—	

No. 1919c is unique and has blind horiz. perfs.

PROFESSIONAL MANAGEMENT EDUCATION CENTENARY

Joseph Wharton (Founder of Wharton School of Business) A1307

Designed by Rudolph de Harak.

PHOTOGRAVURE

Plates of 200 subject in four panes of 50.

1981, June 18	**Tagged**	***Perf. 11***	
1920 A1307 18c **blue & black**		.35	.25
P# block of 4, 2#		1.50	—
Zip block of 4		1.40	—

PRESERVATION OF WILDLIFE HABITATS

Great Blue Heron — A1308

Badger — A1309

Grizzly Bear — A1310

Ruffed Grouse — A1311

Designed by Chuck Ripper.

PHOTOGRAVURE

Plates of 200 subjects in four panes of 50.

1981, June 26	**Tagged**	***Perf. 11***	
1921 A1308 18c **multicolored**		.35	.25
1922 A1309 18c **multicolored**		.35	.25
1923 A1310 18c **multicolored**		.35	.25
1924 A1311 18c **multicolored**		.35	.25
a. Block of 4, #1921-1924		1.50	1.25
P# block of 4, 5#		2.50	—
Zip block of 4		1.50	—

INTERNATIONAL YEAR OF THE DISABLED

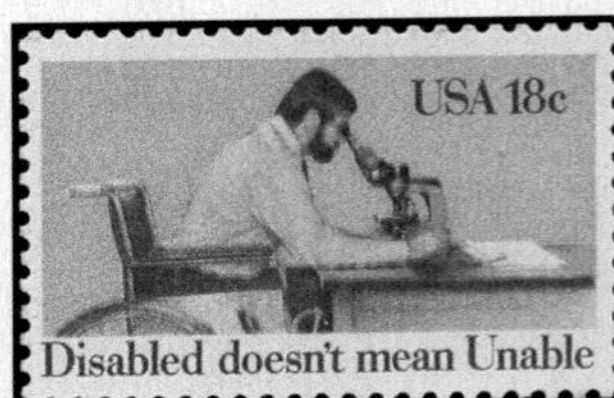

Man Using Microscope A1312

Designed by Martha Perske.

PHOTOGRAVURE

Plates of 200 subjects in four panes of 50.

1981, June 29	**Tagged**	***Perf. 11***	
1925 A1312 18c **multicolored**		.35	.25
P# block of 4, 6#		1.50	—
Zip block of 4		1.40	—
a. Vert. pair, imperf. horiz.		*1,500.*	

EDNA ST. VINCENT MILLAY ISSUE

A1313

Designed by Glenora Case Richards.

LITHOGRAPHED AND ENGRAVED

Plates of 200 subjects in four panes of 50.

1981, July 10	**Tagged**	***Perf. 11***	
1926 A1313 18c **multicolored**		.35	.25
P# block of 4, 7#		1.50	—
Zip block of 4		1.40	—
a. Black (engr., inscriptions) omitted		*200.00*	—

ALCOHOLISM

A1314

Designed by John Boyd.

ENGRAVED

Plates of 230 (10x23) subjects in panes of 50 (5x10)

1981, Aug. 19 **Tagged** ***Perf. 11***

1927 A1314 18c **blue & black,** large block tagging .45 .25
P# block of 6 9.00 —
P# block of 20, 1-2 #, 1-2 copyright, 1-2 Zip 15.00 —
a. Imperf., pair *325.00*
b. Vert. pair, imperf. horiz. *2,000.*
c. Small block tagging *2.50*

See Combination Press note after No. 1703.

AMERICAN ARCHITECTURE SERIES

New York University Library by Stanford White A1315

Biltmore House By Richard Morris Hunt — A1316

Palace of the Arts by Bernard Maybeck A1317

National Farmer's Bank by Louis Sullivan A1318

Designed by Walter D. Richards.

ENGRAVED

Plates of 160 subjects in four panes of 40.

1981, Aug. 28 **Tagged** ***Perf. 11***

1928 A1315 18c **black & red** .40 .25
a. Tagging omitted —
1929 A1316 18c **black & red** .40 .25
a. Red missing (PS) —
1930 A1317 18c **black & red** .40 .25
a. Tagging omitted —
b. Red missing (PS) —
1931 A1318 18c **black & red** .40 .25
a. Block of 4, #1928-1931 1.65 1.65
P# block of 4 2.10 —
Zip block of 4 1.80 —
b. As "a," tagging omitted —

SPORTS PERSONALITIES

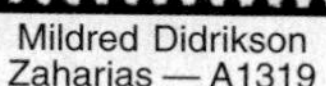

Mildred Didrikson Zaharias — A1319

Robert Tyre Jones — A1320

Designed by Richard Gangel.

ENGRAVED

Plates of 200 subjects in four panes of 50.

1981, Sept. 22 **Tagged** ***Perf. 10½x11***

1932 A1319 18c **purple** .40 .25
P# block of 4 3.00 —
Zip block of 4 1.75 —
1933 A1320 18c **green** .60 .25
P# block of 4 3.25 —
Zip block of 4 2.50 —

FREDERIC REMINGTON

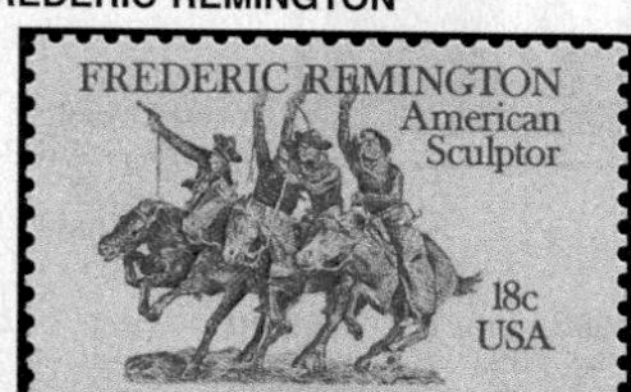

Coming Through the Rye — A1321

Designed by Paul Calle.

LITHOGRAPHED AND ENGRAVED

Plates of 200 in four panes of 50.

1981, Oct. 9 **Tagged** ***Perf. 11***

1934 A1321 18c **gray, olive green & brown** .35 .25
P# block of 4, 3# 1.75 —
Zip block of 4 1.50 —
a. Vert. pair, imperf. between *160.00*
b. Brown omitted *190.00*

JAMES HOBAN

Irish-American Architect of the White House A1322

Designed by Ron Mercer and Walter D. Richards.

PHOTOGRAVURE

Plates of 200 in four panes of 50.

1981, Oct. 13 **Tagged** ***Perf. 11***

1935 A1322 18c **multicolored** .35 .25
P# block of 4, 6# 1.60 —
Zip block of 4 1.50 —
1936 A1322 20c **multicolored** .35 .25
P# block of 4, 6# 2.00 —
Zip block of 4 1.50 —

See Ireland No. 504.

AMERICAN BICENTENNIAL

Battle of Yorktown A1323

Battle of the Virginia Capes A1324

Designed by Cal Sacks.

LITHOGRAPHED AND ENGRAVED

Plates of 200 in four panes of 50.

1981, Oct. 16 **Tagged** ***Perf. 11***

1937 A1323 18c **multicolored** .35 .25
1938 A1324 18c **multicolored** .35 .25
a. Pair, #1937-1938 .90 .75
P# block of 4, 7# 2.00 —
Zip block of 4 1.65 —
b. As "a," black (engr., inscriptions) omitted *275.00*
c. As "a," tagging omitted *120.00*
d. As "a," black (litho.) omitted —

CHRISTMAS

Madonna and Child, Botticelli — A1325

Felt Bear on Sleigh A1326

Designed by Bradbury Thompson (No. 1939) and by Naiad Einsel (No. 1940).

PHOTOGRAVURE

Plates of 400 in four panes of 100 (No. 1939)
Plates of 200 in four panes of 50 (No. 1940)

1981, Oct. 28 **Tagged** ***Perf. 11***

1939 A1325 (20c) **multicolored** .40 .25
P# block of 4, 6# 1.75 —
Zip block of 4 1.65 —
a. Imperf., pair *90.00*
b. Vert. pair, imperf. horiz. *750.00*
c. Tagging omitted *17.50*
1940 A1326 (20c) **multicolored** .40 .25
P# block of 4, 5# 1.75 —
Zip block of 4 1.65 —
a. Imperf., pair *175.00*
b. Vert. pair, imperf. horiz. *2,000.*

JOHN HANSON

First President of the Continental Congress — A1327

Designed by Ron Adair.

PHOTOGRAVURE

Plates of 200 in panes of 50

1981, Nov. 5 **Tagged** ***Perf. 11***

1941 A1327 20c **multicolored** .40 .25
P# block of 4, 5# 1.75 —
Zip block of 4 1.65 —

DESERT PLANTS

Barrel Cactus — A1328

Agave — A1329

Beavertail Cactus — A1330

Saguaro — A1331

Designed by Frank J. Waslick.

LITHOGRAPHED AND ENGRAVED
Plates of 160 in four panes of 40

1981 Dec. 11 Tagged *Perf. 11*

1942	A1328 20c **multicolored**	.35	.25
1943	A1329 20c **multicolored**	.35	.25
1944	A1330 20c **multicolored**	.35	.25
1945	A1331 20c **multicolored**	.35	.25
a.	Block of 4, #1942-1945	1.50	1.25
	P# block of 4, 7#	1.90	—
	Zip block of 4	1.55	—
b.	As "a," deep brown (litho.) omitted	*3,000.*	
c.	No. 1945 imperf., vert. pair	*3,000.*	
d.	As "a," dark green & dark blue (engr.) missing (EP)	—	
e.	As "a," dark green (engr.) missing on left stamp (EP)	—	
f.	As "a," tagging omitted		—

Designed by Bradbury Thompson.

PHOTOGRAVURE
Plates of 400 in panes of 100.

1981, Oct. 11 Tagged *Perf. 11x10½*

1946	A1332 (20c) **brown**	.40	.25
	P# block of 4	2.00	—
	Zip block of 4	1.65	—
a.	Tagging omitted	10.00	
b.	All color omitted	*425.00*	

No. 1946b comes from a partially printed pane with most stamps normal. It must be collected as a vertical pair or strip with normal or partially printed stamps attached.

Counterfeits exist of No. 1946. See the Postal Counterfeits section of this catalog.

ENGRAVED
COIL STAMP
Perf. 10 Vert.

1947	A1332 (20c) **brown**	.60	.25
	Pair	1.20	.25
	Joint line pair	1.50	—
a.	Imperf. pair	*700.00*	
	Joint line pair	—	

BOOKLET STAMPS
Perf. 11 on 2 or 3 Sides

1948	A1333 (20c) **brown**	.40	.25
a.	Booklet pane of 10	4.50	3.25
b.	Tagging omitted	—	

Rocky Mountain Bighorn — A1334

BOOKLET STAMP
ENGRAVED

1982, Jan. 8 Tagged ***Perf. 11 on 2 or 3 Sides***

1949	A1334 20c **dark blue**	.50	.25
a.	Booklet pane of 10	5.00	2.50
b.	As "a," imperf. vert.	*90.00*	
c.	Type II	1.40	.25
d.	Type II, booklet pane of 10	14.00	—
e.	As #1949, tagging omitted	5.00	—
f.	As "e," booklet pane of 10	*55.00*	—

No. 1949 is 18¾mm wide and has overall tagging. No. 1949c is 18½mm wide and has block tagging.

See No. 1880.

FRANKLIN DELANO ROOSEVELT

A1335

Designed by Clarence Holbert.

ENGRAVED
Plates of 192 in four panes of 48

1982, Jan. 30 Tagged *Perf. 11*

1950	A1335 20c **blue**	.40	.25
	P# block of 4	1.75	—
	Zip block of 4	1.65	—

LOVE ISSUE

A1336

Designed by Mary Faulconer.

PHOTOGRAVURE
Plates of 200 in four panes of 50.

1982, Feb. 1 Tagged *Perf. 11¼*

1951	A1336 20c **multicolored**	.50	.25
	P# block of 4, 5#	2.25	—
	Zip block of 4	2.10	—
d.	Yellow omitted	*600.00*	
e.	Purple omitted	—	
f.	Tagging omitted	75.00	—

No. 1951c is valued in the grade of fine.

Perf. 11¼x10½

1951A	A1336 20c **multicolored**	.90	.25
	P# block of 4, 5#	3.75	—
	Zip block of 4	3.75	—

GEORGE WASHINGTON

A1337

Designed by Mark English.

PHOTOGRAVURE
Plates of 200 in four panes of 50.

1982, Feb. 22 Tagged *Perf. 11*

1952	A1337 20c **multicolored**	.40	.25
	P# block of 4, 6#	1.75	—
	Zip block of 4	1.65	—

STATE BIRDS AND FLOWERS ISSUE

Illustration reduced.

Designed by Arthur and Alan Singer.

PHOTOGRAVURE (Andreotti)
Plates of 200 subjects in four panes of 50.

1982, Apr. 14 Tagged *Perf. 10½x11¼*

1953	A1338 20c Alabama	.55	.30
1954	A1339 20c Alaska	.55	.30
1955	A1340 20c Arizona	.55	.30
1956	A1341 20c Arkansas	.55	.30
1957	A1342 20c California	.55	.30
1958	A1343 20c Colorado	.55	.30
1959	A1344 20c Connecticut	.55	.30
1960	A1345 20c Delaware	.55	.30
1961	A1346 20c Florida	.55	.30
1962	A1347 20c Georgia	.55	.30
1963	A1348 20c Hawaii	.55	.30
1964	A1349 20c Idaho	.55	.30
1965	A1350 20c Illinois	.55	.30
1966	A1351 20c Indiana	.55	.30
1967	A1352 20c Iowa	.55	.30
1968	A1353 20c Kansas	.55	.30
1969	A1354 20c Kentucky	.55	.30
1970	A1355 20c Louisiana	.55	.30
1971	A1356 20c Maine	.55	.30
1972	A1357 20c Maryland	.55	.30
1973	A1358 20c Massachusetts	.55	.30
1974	A1359 20c Michigan	.55	.30
1975	A1360 20c Minnesota	.55	.30
1976	A1361 20c Mississippi	.55	.30
1977	A1362 20c Missouri	.55	.30
1978	A1363 20c Montana	.55	.30
1979	A1364 20c Nebraska	.55	.30
1980	A1365 20c Nevada	.55	.30
1981	A1366 20c New Hampshire	.55	.30
b.	Black missing (EP)	*4,000.*	
1982	A1367 20c New Jersey	.55	.30
1983	A1368 20c New Mexico	.55	.30
1984	A1369 20c New York	.55	.30
1985	A1370 20c North Carolina	.55	.30
1986	A1371 20c North Dakota	.55	.30
1987	A1372 20c Ohio	.55	.30
1988	A1373 20c Oklahoma	.55	.30
1989	A1374 20c Oregon	.55	.30
1990	A1375 20c Pennsylvania	.55	.30
1991	A1376 20c Rhode Island	.55	.30
b.	Black missing (EP)	*4,000.*	
1992	A1377 20c South Carolina	.55	.30
1993	A1378 20c South Dakota	.55	.30
1994	A1379 20c Tennessee	.55	.30
1995	A1380 20c Texas	.55	.30
1996	A1381 20c Utah	.55	.30
1997	A1382 20c Vermont	.55	.30
1998	A1383 20c Virginia	.55	.30
1999	A1384 20c Washington	.55	.30
2000	A1385 20c West Virginia	.55	.30
2001	A1386 20c Wisconsin	.55	.30
b.	Black missing (EP)	*4,000.*	
2002	A1387 20c Wyoming	.55	.30
b.	A1338-A1387 Pane of 50, Nos. 1953-2002	27.50	20.00
d.	Pane of 50, imperf.	*21,000.*	

Perf. 11¼x11

1953A	A1338 20c Alabama	.60	.30
1954A	A1339 20c Alaska	.60	.30
1955A	A1340 20c Arizona	.60	.30
1956A	A1341 20c Arkansas	.60	.30
1957A	A1342 20c California	.60	.30
1958A	A1343 20c Colorado	.60	.30

1961A	A1346	20c	Florida	.60	.30
1962A	A1347	20c	Georgia	.60	.30
1963A	A1348	20c	Hawaii	.60	.30
1964A	A1349	20c	Idaho	.60	.30
1965A	A1350	20c	Illinois	.60	.30
1966A	A1351	20c	Indiana	.60	.30
1967A	A1352	20c	Iowa	.60	.30
1968A	A1353	20c	Kansas	.60	.30
1969A	A1354	20c	Kentucky	.60	.30
1970A	A1355	20c	Louisiana	.60	.30
1971A	A1356	20c	Maine	.60	.30
1972A	A1357	20c	Maryland	.60	.30
1973A	A1358	20c	Massachusetts	.60	.30
1974A	A1359	20c	Michigan	.60	.30
1975A	A1360	20c	Minnesota	.60	.30
1976A	A1361	20c	Mississippi	.60	.30
1977A	A1362	20c	Missouri	.60	.30
1978A	A1363	20c	Montana	.60	.30
1979A	A1364	20c	Nebraska	.60	.30
1980A	A1365	20c	Nevada	.60	.30
1981A	A1366	20c	New Hampshire	.60	.30
1982A	A1367	20c	New Jersey	.60	.30
1983A	A1368	20c	New Mexico	.60	.30
1984A	A1369	20c	New York	.60	.30
1985A	A1370	20c	North Carolina	.60	.30
1986A	A1371	20c	North Dakota	.60	.30
1987A	A1372	20c	Ohio	.60	.30
1988A	A1373	20c	Oklahoma	.60	.30
1989A	A1374	20c	Oregon	.60	.30
1990A	A1375	20c	Pennsylvania	.60	.30
1991A	A1376	20c	Rhode Island	.60	.30
1992A	A1377	20c	South Carolina	.60	.30
1993A	A1378	20c	South Dakota	.60	.30
1994A	A1379	20c	Tennessee	.60	.30
1995A	A1380	20c	Texas	.60	.30
1996A	A1381	20c	Utah	.60	.30
1997A	A1382	20c	Vermont	.60	.30
1998A	A1383	20c	Virginia	.60	.30
1999A	A1384	20c	Washington	.60	.30
2000A	A1385	20c	West Virginia	.60	.30
2001A	A1386	20c	Wisconsin	.60	.30
2002A	A1387	20c	Wyoming	.60	.30
c.			A1338-A1387 Pane of 50, Nos. 1953A-2002A	30.00	22.50

Nos. 1953-2002 are line perforated. The perforations do not meet perfectly at the corners of each stamp and extend into the narrow selvage margins of an intact pane. Nos. 1953A-2002A are comb perforated. The perforations meet perfectly at the corners of each stamp and do not extend into the narrow selvage margins of an intact pane (shown).

The dull, dry gum on this State Birds and Flowers issue is essentially invisible, making the stamps appear to have no gum. This is normal for the issue.

US-NETHERLANDS

200th Anniv. of Diplomatic Recognition by The Netherlands
A1388

Designed by Heleen Tigler Wybrandi-Raue.

PHOTOGRAVURE

Plates of 230 (10x23) subjects in panes of 50 (5x10).

1982, Apr. 20 — Tagged — *Perf. 11*

2003	A1388 20c **multicolored**	.40	.25
	P# block of 6	3.50	—
	P# block of 20, 1-2 #, 1-2 copyright, 1-2 zip	10.00	—
a.	Imperf., pair	*250.00*	

See Combination Press note after No. 1703.
See Netherlands Nos. 640-641.

LIBRARY OF CONGRESS

A1389

Designed by Bradbury Thompson.

ENGRAVED

Plates of 200 subjects in four panes of 50.

1982, Apr. 21 — Tagged — *Perf. 11*

2004	A1389 20c **red & black**	.40	.25
	P# block of 4	1.75	—
	Zip block of 4	1.65	—
a.	All color missing	—	

No. 2004a must be collected as a right margin horiz. strip of 3, 4 or 5 with one No. 2004a, one transitional stamp and one or more normal stamps.

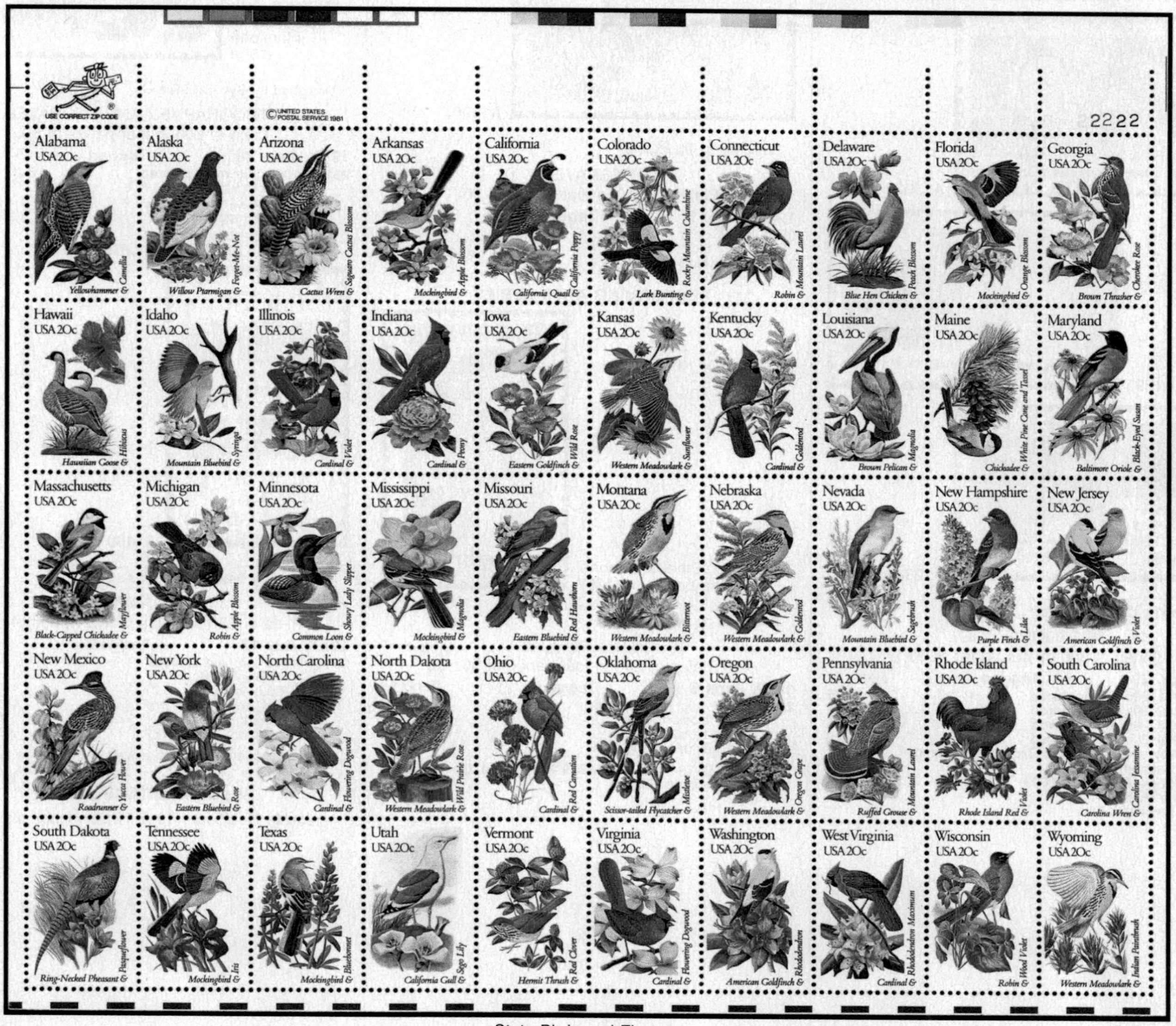

State Birds and Flowers
A1338-A1387

CONSUMER EDUCATION

A1390

Designed by John Boyd.

ENGRAVED
Coil Stamp

1982, Apr. 27	Tagged	Perf. 10 Vert.	
2005 A1390 20c **sky blue**		.55	.25
Pair		1.10	.50
P# strip of 3, line, #1-4		9.00	
P# strip of 5, line, #1-2		40.00	
P# strip of 5, line, #3-4		40.00	
P# single, #1-4		—	1.50
a. Imperf., pair		70.00	
b. Tagging omitted		*15.00*	

KNOXVILLE WORLD'S FAIR

A1391

A1392

A1393

A1394

Designed by Charles Harper.

PHOTOGRAVURE
Plates of 200 in four panes of 50.

1982, Apr. 29	Tagged	Perf. 11	
2006 A1391 20c **multicolored**		.45	.25
2007 A1392 20c **multicolored**		.45	.25
2008 A1393 20c **multicolored**		.45	.25
2009 A1394 20c **multicolored**		.45	.25
Any single on cover, Expo. station hand-stamp cancel			10.00
a. Block of 4, #2006-2009		1.80	1.50
P# block of 4, 6#		2.40	—
Zip block of 4		1.90	—

HORATIO ALGER

A1395

Designed by Robert Hallock.

ENGRAVED
Plates of 200 in four panes of 50.

1982, Apr. 30	Tagged	Perf. 11	
2010 A1395 20c **red & black,** *tan*		.40	.25
P# block of 4		1.75	—
Zip block of 4		1.65	—
a. Red and black omitted		—	
b. Tagging omitted			—

The Philatelic Foundation has issued a certificate for a pane of 50 with red and black colors omitted. Recognition of this error is by the paper and by a tiny residue of red ink from the tagging roller. The engraved plates did not strike the paper.

AGING TOGETHER

A1396

Designed by Paul Calle.

ENGRAVED
Plates of 200 in four panes of 50.

1982, May 21	Tagged	Perf. 11	
2011 A1396 20c **brown**		.40	.25
P# block of 4		1.75	—
Zip block of 4		1.65	—

PERFORMING ARTS SERIES

John, Ethel and Lionel Barrymore — A1397

Designed by Jim Sharpe.

PHOTOGRAVURE
Plates of 200 in four panes of 50.

1982, June 8	Tagged	Perf. 11	
2012 A1397 20c **multicolored**		.40	.25
P# block of 4, 6#		1.75	—
Zip block of 4		1.65	—
a. Black missing (EP)		—	

John (1882-1942), Ethel (1879-1959), and Lionel (1878-1954) Barrymore, actors.

DR. MARY WALKER

Dr. Mary Walker — A1398

Designed by Glenora Richards.

PHOTOGRAVURE
Plate of 200 in four panes of 50.

1982, June 10	Tagged	Perf. 11	
2013 A1398 20c **multicolored**		.40	.25
P# block of 4, 6#		1.75	—
Zip block of 4		1.65	—

Dr. Mary Walker (1832-1919), 1865 recipient of Medal of Honor.

INTERNATIONAL PEACE GARDEN

Dunseith, ND-Boissevain, Manitoba A1399

Designed by Gyo Fujikawa.

LITHOGRAPHED AND ENGRAVED
Plate of 200 in four panes of 50.

1982, June 30	Tagged	Perf. 11	
2014 A1399 20c **multicolored**		.45	.25
P# block of 4, 5#		2.00	—
Zip block of 4		1.90	—
a. Black (engr.) omitted		*200.00*	

AMERICA'S LIBRARIES

A1400

Designed by Bradbury Thompson.

ENGRAVED
Plate of 200 subjects in four panes of 50.

1982, July 13	Tagged	Perf. 11	
2015 A1400 20c **red & black**		.40	.25
P# block of 4		1.75	—
Zip block of 4		1.65	—
a. Vert. pair, imperf. horiz.		*200.00*	
b. Tagging omitted		*12.50*	
c. All colors missing (EP)		*175.00*	

On No. 2015c, an albino impression of the design is present.

BLACK HERITAGE SERIES

Jackie Robinson (1919-72), baseball player.

A1401

Designed by Jerry Pinkney.

PHOTOGRAVURE

Plate of 200 subjects in four panes of 50.

1982, Aug. 2 **Tagged** ***Perf. 10½x11***

2016	A1401 20c **multicolored**	1.00	.25
	P# block of 4, 5#	5.00	—
	Zip block of 4	4.25	—

TOURO SYNAGOGUE

Oldest Existing Synagogue Building in the U.S. — A1402

Designed by Donald Moss and Bradbury Thompson.

PHOTOGRAVURE AND ENGRAVED

Plates of 230 (10x23) subjects in panes of 50 (5x10).

1982, Aug. 22 **Tagged** ***Perf. 11***

2017	A1402 20c **multicolored**	.40	.25
	P# block of 20, 6-12 #, 1-2 copyright, 1-2 zip	11.50	—
a.	Imperf., pair	*1,400.*	

See Combination Press note after No. 1703.

WOLF TRAP FARM PARK

A1403

Designed by Richard Schlecht.

PHOTOGRAVURE

Plates of 200 in four panes of 50.

1982, Sept. 1 **Tagged** ***Perf. 11***

2018	A1403 20c **multicolored**	.40	.25
	P# block of 4, 5#	1.75	—
	Zip block of 4	1.65	—

AMERICAN ARCHITECTURE SERIES

A1404

A1405

A1406

A1407

Designed by Walter D. Richards.

ENGRAVED

Plates of 160 subjects in four panes of 40.

1982, Sept. 30 **Tagged** ***Perf. 11***

2019	A1404 20c **black & brown**	.45	.25
a.	Tagging omitted		—
b.	Red missing (PS)	—	
2020	A1405 20c **black & brown**	.45	.25
a.	Red missing (PS)	—	
2021	A1406 20c **black & brown**	.45	.25
2022	A1407 20c **black & brown**	.45	.25
a.	Block of 4, #2019-2022	2.00	1.75
	P# block of 4	2.50	—
	Zip block of 4	2.10	—

FRANCIS OF ASSISI

A1408

Designed by Ned Seidler.

Printed by American Bank Note Co. and J.W. Fergusson and Sons.

PHOTOGRAVURE

Plates of 200 subjects in four panes of 50.

1982, Oct. 7 **Tagged** ***Perf. 11***

2023	A1408 20c **multicolored**	.40	.25
	P# block of 4, 6#+A	1.75	—
	Zip block of 4	1.65	—

PONCE DE LEON

A1409

Designed by Richard Schlecht.

PHOTOGRAVURE (Combination press)

Plates of 230 subjects (10x23) in panes of 50 (5x10).

1982, Oct. 12 **Tagged** ***Perf. 11***

2024	A1409 20c **multicolored**	.40	.25
	P# block of 6, 5#	3.00	—
	P# block of 20, 5 or 10 #, 1-2 zip, 1-2 copyright	10.50	—
a.	Imperf., pair	*250.00*	
b.	Vert. pair, imperf. between and at top	*500.00*	
c.	Tagging omitted		—

See Combination Press note after No. 1703.

CHRISTMAS ISSUES

A1410

A1411

A1412

A1413

A1414

A1415

PHOTOGRAVURE

Plates of 200 subjects in four panes of 50

Designed by Chuck Ripper.

1982, Nov. 3 **Tagged**

2025	A1410 13c **multicolored**	.25	.25
	P# block of 4	1.40	—
	Zip block of 4	1.10	—
a.	Imperf., pair	*300.00*	

PHOTOGRAVURE (Combination Press)

Plates of 230 subjects (10x23) in panes of 50 (5x10).

Designed by Bradbury Thompson.

1982, Oct. 28 **Tagged**

2026	A1411 20c **multicolored**	.40	.25
	P# block of 6	3.00	—
	P# block of 20, 5 or 10 #, 1-2 copyright, 1-2 zip	11.00	—
a.	Imperf. pair	90.00	
b.	Horiz. pair, imperf. vert.	*900.00*	
c.	Vert. pair, imperf. horiz.	—	

See Combination Press note after No. 1703.

PHOTOGRAVURE
Plates of 200 in four panes of 50.

Designed by Dolli Tingle.

2027 A1412 20c **multicolored**		.60	.25
2028 A1413 20c **multicolored**		.60	.25
2029 A1414 20c **multicolored**		.60	.25
2030 A1415 20c **multicolored**		.60	.25
a.	Block of 4, #2027-2030	2.40	1.50
	P# block of 4, 4#	2.50	—
	Zip block of 4	2.40	—
b.	As "a," imperf.	*1,250.*	
c.	As "a," imperf. horiz.	*700.00*	
	Nos. 2025-2030 (6)	3.05	1.50

SCIENCE & INDUSTRY

A1416

Designed by Saul Bass.

LITHOGRAPHED AND ENGRAVED
Plates of 200 in four panes of 50.

1983, Jan. 19 **Tagged** ***Perf. 11***

2031 A1416 20c **multicolored**		.40	.25
	P# block of 4, 4#	1.75	—
	Zip block of 4	1.65	—
a.	Black (engr.) omitted	*750.00*	
b.	Tagging omitted		—

BALLOONS

Intrepid — A1417

Explorer II — A1420

A1418

A1419

Designed by Davis Meltzer.

PHOTOGRAVURE
Plates of 160 in four panes of 40.

1983, Mar. 31 **Tagged** ***Perf. 11***

2035 A1420 20c **multicolored**		.50	.25
a.	Block of 4, #2032-2035	2.00	1.50
	P# block of 4, 5#	2.25	—
	Zip block of 4	2.10	—
b.	As "a," imperf.	*2,750.*	
c.	As "a," right stamp perf., otherwise imperf.	*2,750.*	

US-SWEDEN

Benjamin Franklin
A1421

Designed by Czeslaw Slania, court engraver of Sweden.

ENGRAVED
Plates of 200 in four panes of 50.

1983, Mar. 24 **Tagged** ***Perf. 11***

2036 A1421 20c **blue, blk & red brn**		.40	.25
	P# block of 4	1.75	—
	Zip block of 4	1.65	—

See Sweden No. 1453.

CCC, 50th ANNIV.

A1422

Designed by David K. Stone.

PHOTOGRAVURE
Plates of 200 in four panes of 50.

1983, Apr. 5 **Tagged** ***Perf. 11***

2037 A1422 20c **multicolored**		.40	.25
	P# block of 4, 6#	1.75	—
	Zip block of 4	1.65	—
a.	Imperf., pair	*2,250.*	
b.	Vert. pair, imperf. horiz.	—	

JOSEPH PRIESTLEY

Joseph Priestley (1733-1804), Discoverer of Oxygen — A1423

Designed by Dennis Lyall.

Printed by American Bank Note Company and J.W. Fergusson and Sons.

PHOTOGRAVURE
Plates of 200 in four panes of 50.

1983, Apr. 13 **Tagged** ***Perf. 11***

2038 A1423 20c **multicolored**		.40	.25
	P# block of 4, 6#+A	1.75	—
	Zip block of 4	1.65	—

VOLUNTEERISM

A1424

Designed by Paul Calle.

ENGRAVED (Combination Press)
Plates of 230 subjects (10x23) in panes of 50 (5x10).

1983, Apr. 20 **Tagged** ***Perf. 11***

2039 A1424 20c **red & black**		.40	.25
	P# block of 6	3.00	—
	P# block of 20, 1-2 #, 1-2 copyright, 1-2 zip	10.00	—
a.	Imperf., pair	*225.00*	

See Combination Press note after No. 1703.

US-GERMANY

A1425

Designed by Richard Schlecht.

ENGRAVED
Plates of 200 in four panes of 50.

1983, Apr. 29 **Tagged** ***Perf. 11***

2040 A1425 20c **brown**		.40	.25
	P# block of 4	1.75	—
	Zip block of 4	1.65	—
a.	Tagging omitted	—	—

See Germany No. 1397.

BROOKLYN BRIDGE

A1426

Normal

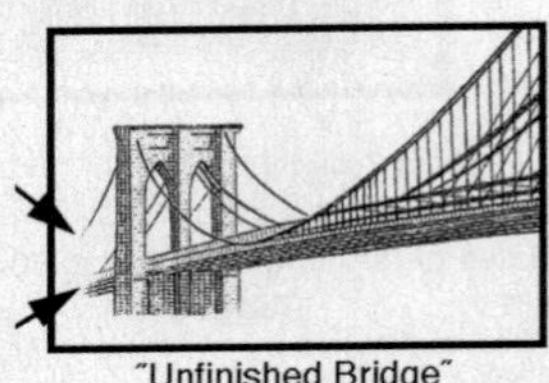
"Unfinished Bridge"
Short Transfer

Designed by Howard Koslow.

ENGRAVED
Plates of 200 in four panes of 50.

1983, May 17 **Tagged** ***Perf. 11***

2041 A1426 20c **blue**		.40	.25
	P# block of 4	1.75	—
	Zip block of 4	1.65	—
	Short transfer (unfinished bridge) (UL 2)	9.00	.75
	P# block of 4	15.00	—
a.	Tagging omitted	*125.00*	
b.	All color missing (EP)	*90.00*	

On No. 2041b, an albino impression of part of the design is evident.

TVA

Norris

Designed by Howard Koslow.

PHOTOGRAVURE AND ENGRAVED (Combination Press)
Plates of 230 in panes of 50

1983, May 18	**Tagged**	***Perf. 11***	
2042 A1427 20c **multicolored**		.40	.25
P# block of 20, 5-10 #, 1-2 copyright, 1-2 zip		10.00	—

Runners, Electrocardiograph Tracing — A1428

Designed by Donald Moss.

PHOTOGRAVURE (Combination Press)
Plates of 230 in panes of 50.

1983, May 14	**Tagged**	***Perf. 11***	
2043 A1428 20c **multicolored**		.40	.25
P# block of 6, 4#		3.00	—
P# block of 20, 4-8 #, 1-2 copyright, 1-2 zip		10.00	—

BLACK HERITAGE SERIES

Scott Joplin (1868-1917), Ragtime composer.

A1429

Designed by Jerry Pinkney.

PHOTOGRAVURE
Plates of 200 in four panes of 50.

1983, June 9	**Tagged**	***Perf. 11***	
2044 A1429 20c **multicolored**		.50	.25
P# block of 4, 6#		2.40	—
Zip block of 4		2.10	—
a. Imperf., pair		*300.00*	
b. Tagging omitted		*300.00*	—

MEDAL OF HONOR

A1430

Designed by Dennis J. Hom.

LITHOGRAPHED AND ENGRAVED
Plates of 160 in four panes of 40.

1983, June 7	**Tagged**	***Perf. 11***	
2045 A1430 20c **multicolored**		.55	.25
P# block of 4, 5#		2.50	—
Zip block of 4		2.25	—
a. Red omitted		*150.00*	

GEORGE HERMAN RUTH (1895-1948)

A1431

Designed by Richard Gangel.

ENGRAVED
Plates of 200 in four panes of 50.

1983, July 6	**Tagged**	***Perf. 10½x11***	
2046 A1431 20c **blue**		1.00	.25
P# block of 4		5.00	—
Zip block of 4		4.25	—

LITERARY ARTS SERIES

Nathaniel Hawthorne (1804-1864), novelist.

A1432

Designed by Bradbury Thompson after 1851 painting by Cephus Giovanni Thompson.

PHOTOGRAVURE
Plates of 200 in four panes of 50.

1983, July 8	**Tagged**	***Perf. 11***	
2047 A1432 20c **multicolored**		.40	.25
P# block of 4, 4#		1.90	—
Zip block of 4		1.70	—

1984 SUMMER OLYMPICS

Los Angeles, July 28-August 12

Discus A1433

High Jump — A1434

Archery A1435

Boxing A1436

Designed by Bob Peak.

PHOTOGRAVURE
Plates of 200 in four panes of 50.

1983, July 28	**Tagged**	***Perf. 11***	
2048 A1433 13c **multicolored**		.35	.25
2049 A1434 13c **multicolored**		.35	.25
2050 A1435 13c **multicolored**		.35	.25
2051 A1436 13c **multicolored**		.35	.25
a. Block of 4, #2048-2051		1.50	1.25
P# block of 4, 4#		1.75	—
Zip block of 4		1.65	—

SIGNING OF TREATY OF PARIS

John Adams, B. Franklin, John Jay, David Hartley A1437

Designed by David Blossom after an unfinished painting by Benjamin West in Winterthur Museum.

PHOTOGRAVURE
Plates of 160 in four panes of 40.

1983, Sept. 2	**Tagged**	***Perf. 11***	
2052 A1437 20c **multicolored**		.40	.25
P# block of 4, 4#		1.75	—
Zip block of 4		1.65	—
a. Tagging omitted			—

CIVIL SERVICE

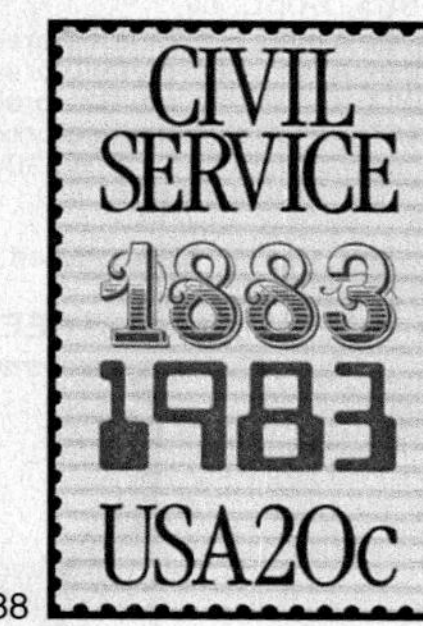

A1438

Designed by MDB Communications, Inc.

PHOTOGRAVURE AND ENGRAVED
Plates of 230 in four panes of 50.

1983, Sept. 9	**Tagged**	***Perf. 11***	
2053 A1438 20c **buff, blue & red**		.40	.25
P# block of 20, 1-2P#, 1-2 Zip, 1-2 Copyright		10.00	—
a. Tagging omitted		—	—

METROPOLITAN OPERA

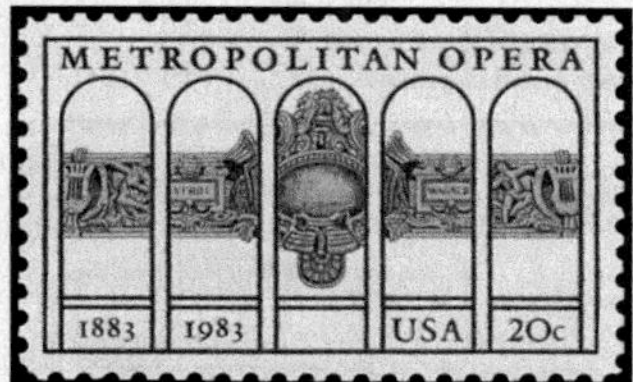

Original State Arch and Current 5-arch Entrance A1439

Designed by Ken Davies.

LITHOGRAPHED AND ENGRAVED
Plates of 200 in four panes of 50.

1983, Sept. 14	**Tagged**	***Perf. 11***	
2054 A1439 20c **yellow & maroon**		.40	.25
P# block of 4, 2#		1.75	—
Zip block of 4		1.65	—
a. Tagging omitted		*12.50*	

AMERICAN INVENTORS

Charles Steinmetz and Curve on Graph A1440

Edwin Armstrong and Frequency Modulator A1441

Nikola Tesla and Induction Motor A1442

Philo T. Farnsworth and First Television Camera A1443

Designed by Dennis Lyall.

LITHOGRAPHED AND ENGRAVED
Plates of 200 in four panes of 50.

1983, Sept. 21	**Tagged**	***Perf. 11***	
2055 A1440 20c **multicolored**		.50	.25
2056 A1441 20c **multicolored**		.50	.25
2057 A1442 20c **multicolored**		.50	.25
2058 A1443 20c **multicolored**		.50	.25
a. Block of 4, #2055-2058		2.00	1.50
P# block of 4, 2#		2.75	—
Zip block of 4		2.10	—
b. As "a," black omitted		*275.00*	

STREETCARS

A1444

A1445

A1446

A1447

Designed by Richard Leech.

PHOTOGRAVURE AND ENGRAVED
Plates of 200 in four panes of 50.

1983, Oct. 8	**Tagged**	***Perf. 11***	
2059 A1444 20c **multicolored**		.50	.25
2060 A1445 20c **multicolored**		.50	.25
a. Horiz. pair, black (engr.) missing on Nos. 2059, 2060 (EP)		—	
2061 A1446 20c **multicolored**		.50	.25
a. Vert. pair, black (engr.) missing on Nos. 2059, 2061 (EP)		—	
2062 A1447 20c **multicolored**		.50	.25
a. Block of 4, #2059-2062		2.00	1.50
P# block of 4, 5#		2.75	—
Zip block of 4		2.10	—
b. As "a," black (engr.) omitted		*250.00*	
c. As "a," black (engr.) omitted on #2059, 2061		—	

CHRISTMAS

Niccolini-Cowper Madonna, by Raphael — A1448

Santa Claus — A1449

Designed by Bradbury Thompson (No. 2063), and John Berkey (No. 2064).

PHOTOGRAVURE
Plates of 200 in four panes of 50 (No. 2063),
Plates of 230 in panes of 50 (Combination Press, No. 2064)

1983, Oct. 28	**Tagged**	***Perf. 11***	
2063 A1448 20c **multicolored**		.40	.25
P# block of 4, 5#		1.75	—
Zip block of 4		1.65	—
2064 A1449 20c **multicolored**		.40	.25
P# block of 6, 5#		3.00	—
P# block of 20, 5-10 P#, 1-2 copyright, 1-2 zip		11.50	—
a. Imperf., pair		*100.00*	
b. Tagging omitted		—	

See Combination Press note after No. 1703.

MARTIN LUTHER

Martin Luther (1483-1546), German Religious Leader, Founder of Lutheran Church — A1450

Designed by Bradbury Thompson.

Printed by American Bank Note Company.

PHOTOGRAVURE
Plates of 200 in four panes of 50.

1983, Nov. 11	**Tagged**	***Perf. 11***	
2065 A1450 20c **multicolored**		.40	.25
P# block of 4, 5#+A		1.75	—
Zip block of 4		1.65	—

ALASKA STATEHOOD, 25th ANNIV.

Caribou and Alaska Pipeline — A1451

Designed by Bill Bond.

Printed by American Bank Note Company and J.W. Ferguson and Sons.

PHOTOGRAVURE
Plates of 200 in four panes of 50.

1984, Jan. 3	**Tagged**	***Perf. 11***	
2066 A1451 20c **multicolored**		.40	.25
P# block of 4, 5#+A		1.75	—
Zip block of 4		1.65	—
a. Vert. pair, imperf. horiz.			—

14th WINTER OLYMPIC GAMES

Sarajevo, Yugoslavia, Feb. 8-19

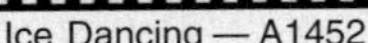

Ice Dancing — A1452

Downhill Skiing — A1453

Cross-country Skiing — A1454

Hockey — A1455

Designed by Bob Peak.

PHOTOGRAVURE
Plates of 200 in four panes of 50.

1984, Jan. 6	**Tagged**	***Perf. 10½x11***	
2067 A1452 20c **multicolored**		.55	.25
2068 A1453 20c **multicolored**		.55	.25
2069 A1454 20c **multicolored**		.55	.25
2070 A1455 20c **multicolored**		.55	.25
a. Block of 4, #2067-2070		2.20	1.75
P# block of 4, 4#		3.00	—
Zip block of 4		2.25	—

FEDERAL DEPOSIT INSURANCE CORPORATION, 50TH ANNIV.

Pillar, Dollar Sign — A1456

Designed by Michael David Brown.

PHOTOGRAVURE
Plates of 200 in four panes of 50
(1 pane each #2071, 2074, 2075 and 2081)

1984, Jan. 12 Tagged *Perf. 11*

2071 A1456 20c **multicolored** .40 .25
P# block of 4, 6#, UL only 2.00 —
Zip block of 4 1.65 —

LOVE

A1457

Designed by Bradbury Thompson.

PHOTOGRAVURE AND ENGRAVED (Combination Press)
Plates of 230 in four panes of 50.

1984, Jan. 31 Tagged *Perf. 11x10½*

2072 A1457 20c **multicolored** .40 .25
P# block of 20, 6-12#, 1-2 copyright, 1-2 zip 10.00 —
a. Horiz. pair, imperf. vert. *125.00*
b. Tagging omitted *10.00*

See Combination Press note after No. 1703.

BLACK HERITAGE SERIES

Carter G. Woodson (1875-1950), Historian.

A1458

Designed by Jerry Pinkney.

Printed by American Bank Note Company.

PHOTOGRAVURE
Plates of 200 in four panes of 50.

1984, Feb. 1 Tagged *Perf. 11*

2073 A1458 20c **multicolored** .40 .25
P# block of 4, 6#+A 2.00 —
Zip block of 4 1.65 —
a. Horiz. pair, imperf. vert. *800.00*

SOIL & WATER CONSERVATION

A1459

Designed by Michael David Brown.

See No. 2071 for printing information.

1984, Feb. 6 Tagged *Perf. 11*

2074 A1459 20c **multicolored** .40 .25
P# block of 4, 6#, UR only 1.75 —
Zip block of 4 1.65 —

50TH ANNIV. OF CREDIT UNION ACT

Dollar Sign, Coin — A1460

Designed by Michael David Brown.

See No. 2071 for printing information.

1984, Feb. 10 Tagged *Perf. 11*

2075 A1460 20c **multicolored** .40 .25
P# block of 4, 6#, LR only 1.75 —
Zip block of 4 1.65 —

ORCHIDS

Wild Pink — A1461

Yellow Lady's-slipper A1462

Spreading Pogonia — A1463

Pacific Calypso — A1464

Designed by Manabu Saito.

PHOTOGRAVURE
Plates of 192 in four panes of 48.

1984, Mar. 5 Tagged *Perf. 11*

2076 A1461 20c **multicolored** .50 .25
2077 A1462 20c **multicolored** .50 .25
2078 A1463 20c **multicolored** .50 .25
2079 A1464 20c **multicolored** .50 .25
a. Block of 4, #2076-2079 2.00 1.50
P# block of 4, 5# 2.50 —
Zip block of 4 2.10 —

HAWAII STATEHOOD, 25th ANNIV.

Eastern Polynesian Canoe, Golden Plover, Mauna Loa Volcano A1465

Designed by Herb Kane.

Printed by American Bank Note Company.

PHOTOGRAVURE
Plates of 200 in four panes of 50.

1984, Mar. 12 Tagged *Perf. 11*

2080 A1465 20c **multicolored** .40 .25
P# block of 4, 5#+A 2.00 —
Zip block of 4 1.65 —

50TH ANNIV., NATIONAL ARCHIVES

Abraham Lincoln, George Washington — A1466

Designed by Michael David Brown.

See No. 2071 for printing information.

1984, Apr. 16 Tagged *Perf. 11*

2081 A1466 20c **multicolored** .40 .25
P# block of 4, 6#, LL only 2.00 —
Zip block of 4 1.65 —

LOS ANGELES SUMMER OLYMPICS

July 28-August 12

Diving — A1467 Long Jump — A1468

Wrestling — A1469 Kayak — A1470

Designed by Bob Peak.

PHOTOGRAVURE

Plates of 200 in four panes of 50.

1984, May 4 **Tagged** ***Perf. 11***

2082 A1467 20c **multicolored** .55 .25
2083 A1468 20c **multicolored** .55 .25
2084 A1469 20c **multicolored** .55 .25
2085 A1470 20c **multicolored** .55 .25
a. Block of 4, #2082-2085 2.40 1.90
P# block of 4, 4# 3.00 —
Zip block of 4 2.50 —
b. As "a," imperf between vertically *9,500.*

LOUISIANA WORLD EXPOSITION

New Orleans, May 12-Nov. 11

Bayou Wildlife A1471

Designed by Chuck Ripper.

PHOTOGRAVURE

Plates of 160 in four panes of 40.

1984, May 11 **Tagged** ***Perf. 11***

2086 A1471 20c **multicolored** .50 .25
On cover, Expo. station pictorial hand-stamp cancel 2.50
P# block of 4, 5# 2.60 —
Zip block of 4 2.10 —

HEALTH RESEARCH

Lab Equipment A1472

Designed by Tyler Smith.

Printed by American Bank Note Company.

PHOTOGRAVURE

Plates of 200 in four panes of 50.

1984, May 17 **Tagged** ***Perf. 11***

2087 A1472 20c **multicolored** .40 .25
P# block of 4, 5#+A 2.00 —
Zip block of 4 1.65 —

PERFORMING ARTS

Douglas Fairbanks (1883-1939), Actor — A1473

Designed by Jim Sharpe.

PHOTOGRAVURE AND ENGRAVED (Combination Press)

Plates of 230 in panes of 50.

1984, May 23 **Tagged** ***Perf. 11***

2088 A1473 20c **multicolored** .40 .25
P# block of 20, 5-10#, 1-2 copyright, 1-2 zip 12.50 —
a. Tagging omitted *20.00*
b. Horiz. pair, imperf between —

See Combination Press note after No. 1703.

JIM THORPE

Jim Thorpe (1888-1953), Athlete — A1474

Designed by Richard Gangel.

ENGRAVED

Plates of 200 in four panes of 50.

1984, May 24 **Tagged** ***Perf. 11***

2089 A1474 20c **dark brown** .60 .25
P# block of 4 3.50 —
Zip block of 4 1.90 —
a. All color omitted —

On No. 2089a, an albino impression of the design is evident.

PERFORMING ARTS

John McCormack (1884-1945), Operatic Tenor — A1475

Designed by Jim Sharpe (US) and Ron Mercer (Ireland).

PHOTOGRAVURE

Plates of 200 in four panes of 50.

1984, June 6 **Tagged** ***Perf. 11***

2090 A1475 20c **multicolored** .40 .25
P# block of 4, 5# 2.00 —
Zip block of 4 1.65 —

See Ireland No. 594.

ST. LAWRENCE SEAWAY, 25th ANNIV.

Aerial View of Seaway, Freighters A1476

Designed by Ernst Barenscher (Canada).

Printed by American Bank Note Company.

PHOTOGRAVURE

Plates of 200 in four panes of 50.

1984, June 26 **Tagged** ***Perf. 11***

2091 A1476 20c **multicolored** .40 .25
P# block of 4, 4#+A 1.75 —
Zip block of 4 1.65 —
a. Tagging omitted —

WATERFOWL PRESERVATION ACT, 50th ANNIV.

"Mallards Dropping In" by Jay N. Darling A1477

Design adapted from Darling's work (No. RW1) by Donald M. McDowell.

ENGRAVED

Plates of 200 in four panes of 50.

1984, July 2 **Tagged** ***Perf. 11***

2092 A1477 20c **blue** .50 .25
P# block of 4 2.50 —
Zip block of 4 2.25 —
a. Horiz. pair, imperf. vert. *275.00*

ROANOKE VOYAGES

The Elizabeth — A1478

Designed by Charles Lundgren.

Printed by American Bank Note Company.

PHOTOGRAVURE

Plates of 200 in four panes of 50.

1984, July 13 **Tagged** ***Perf. 11***

2093 A1478 20c **multicolored** .40 .25
P# block of 4, 5#+A 1.75 —
Zip block of 4 1.65 —
Pair with full horiz. gutter btwn. —

LITERARY ARTS SERIES

Herman Melville (1819-1891), Author — A1479

Designed by Bradbury Thompson.

ENGRAVED

Plates of 200 in four panes of 50.

1984, Aug. 1 **Tagged** ***Perf. 11***

2094 A1479 20c **sage green** .40 .25
P# block of 4 1.75 —
Zip block of 4 1.65 —
a. Tagging omitted 75.00 —

HORACE MOSES (1862-1947)

Horace Moses, Junior Achievement Founder — A1480

Designed by Dennis Lyall.

ENGRAVED (Combination Press)
Plates of 200 in panes of 50.

1984, Aug. 6	**Tagged**	***Perf. 11***	
2095 A1480 20c **orange & dark brown**		.40	.25
P# block of 6		3.00	—
P# block of 20, 1-2#, 1-2 copyright, 1-2 zip		10.00	—

See Combination Press note after No. 1703.

SMOKEY BEAR

Smokey Bear — A1481

Designed by Rudolph Wendelin.

LITHOGRAPHED AND ENGRAVED
Plates of 200 in panes of 50.

1984, Aug. 13	**Tagged**	***Perf. 11***	
2096 A1481 20c **multicolored**		.40	.25
P# block of 4, 5#		2.25	—
Zip block of 4		1.65	—
a. Horiz. pair, imperf. btwn.		*175.00*	
b. Vert. pair, imperf. btwn.		*150.00*	
c. Block of 4, imperf. btwn. vert. and horiz.		*2,500.*	
d. Horiz. pair, imperf. vert.		*450.00*	
e. Tagging omitted		*275.00*	—

ROBERTO CLEMENTE (1934-1972)

Clemente Wearing Pittsburgh Pirates Cap, Puerto Rican Flag — A1482

Designed by Juan Lopez-Bonilla.

PHOTOGRAVURE
Plates of 200 in panes of 50.

1984, Aug. 17	**Tagged**	***Perf. 11***	
2097 A1482 20c **multicolored**		1.00	.25
P# block of 4, 6#		5.00	—
Zip block of 4		4.25	—
a. Horiz. pair, imperf. vert.		*1,250.*	

DOGS

Beagle and Boston Terrier A1483

Chesapeake Bay Retriever and Cocker Spaniel A1484

Alaskan Malamute and Collie A1485

Black and Tan Coonhound and American Foxhound A1486

Designed by Roy Andersen.

PHOTOGRAVURE
Plates of 160 in panes of 40.

1984, Sept. 7	**Tagged**	***Perf. 11***	
2098 A1483 20c **multicolored**		.50	.25
2099 A1484 20c **multicolored**		.50	.25
2100 A1485 20c **multicolored**		.50	.25
2101 A1486 20c **multicolored**		.50	.25
a. Block of 4, #2098-2101		2.00	1.90
P# block of 4, 4#		3.00	—
Zip block of 4		2.10	—
b. As "a," imperf horiz.		*5,500.*	

CRIME PREVENTION

McGruff, the Crime Dog — A1487

Designed by Randall McDougall.

Printed by American Bank Note Company.

PHOTOGRAVURE
Plates of 200 in panes of 50.

1984, Sept. 26	**Tagged**	***Perf. 11***	
2102 A1487 20c **multicolored**		.40	.25
P# block of 4, 4#+A		2.00	—
Zip block of 4		1.65	—

HISPANIC AMERICANS

A1488

Designed by Robert McCall.

PHOTOGRAVURE
Plates of 160 in four panes of 40.

1984, Oct. 31	**Tagged**	***Perf. 11***	
2103 A1488 20c **multicolored**		.40	.25
P# block of 4, 6#		2.00	—
Zip block of 4		1.65	—
a. Vert. pair, imperf. horiz.		*1,250.*	

FAMILY UNITY

Stick Figures — A1489

Designed by Molly LaRue.

PHOTOGRAVURE AND ENGRAVED (Combination Press)
Plates of 230 in panes of 50.

1984, Oct. 1	**Tagged**	***Perf. 11***	
2104 A1489 20c **multicolored**		.40	.25
P# block of 20, 3-6#, 1-2 copyright, 1-2 zip		10.00	—
a. Horiz. pair, imperf. vert.		*325.00*	
b. Tagging omitted		*12.50*	
c. Vert. pair, imperf. btwn. and at bottom			—
d. Horiz. pair, imperf. between			—

See Combination Press note after No. 1703.
Used untagged imperfs exist from printer's waste.

ELEANOR ROOSEVELT (1884-1962)

A1490

Designed by Bradbury Thompson.

ENGRAVED
Plates of 192 in panes of 48.

1984, Oct. 11	**Tagged**	***Perf. 11***	
2105 A1490 20c **deep blue**		.40	.25
P# block of 4		2.00	—
Zip block of 4		1.65	—

NATION OF READERS

Abraham Lincoln Reading to Son, Tad — A1491

Design adapted from Anthony Berger daguerrotype by Bradbury Thompson.

ENGRAVED
Plates of 200 in panes of 50.

1984, Oct. 16	**Tagged**	***Perf. 11***	
2106 A1491 20c **brown & maroon**		.40	.25
P# block of 4		2.00	—
Zip block of 4		1.65	—

CHRISTMAS

Madonna and Child by Fra Filippo Lippi — A1492

Santa Claus — A1493

Designed by Bradbury Thompson (No. 2107) and Danny La Boccetta (No. 2108).

PHOTOGRAVURE
Plates of 200 in panes of 50.

1984, Oct. 30 **Tagged** ***Perf. 11***

2107 A1492 20c **multicolored** .40 .25
P# block of 4, 5# 2.00 —
Zip block of 4 1.65 —
a. Imperf., pair *1,400.*
b. Tagging omitted —

2108 A1493 20c **multicolored** .40 .25
P# block of 4, 5# 2.00 —
Zip block of 4 1.65 —
a. Horiz. pair, imperf. vert. *750.00*

No. 2108a is valued in the grade of fine.

VIETNAM VETERANS MEMORIAL

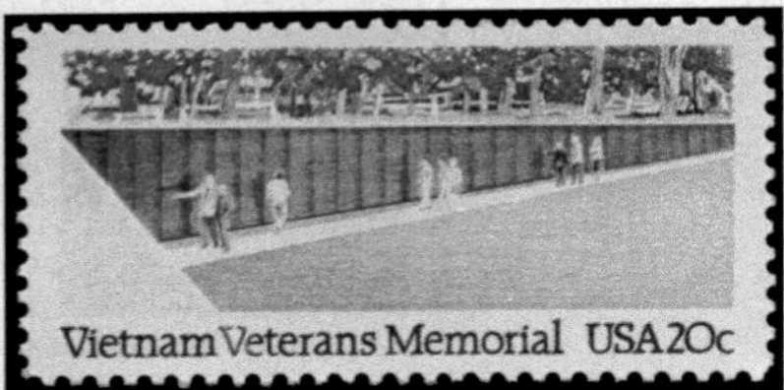

Memorial and Visitors — A1494

Designed by Paul Calle.

ENGRAVED
Plates of 160 in panes of 40.

1984, Nov. 10 **Tagged** ***Perf. 11***

2109 A1494 20c **multicolored** .50 .25
P# block of 4 3.00 —
Zip block of 4 2.10 —
a. Tagging omitted *65.00*

PERFORMING ARTS

Jerome Kern (1885-1945), Composer — A1495

Designed by Jim Sharpe.

Printed by the American Bank Note Company.

PHOTOGRAVURE
Plates of 200 in four panes of 50.

1985, Jan. 23 **Tagged** ***Perf. 11***

2110 A1495 22c **multicolored** .45 .25
P# block of 4, 5#+A 2.00 —
Zip block of 4 1.65 —
a. Tagging omitted *12.50*

A1496

A1497

Designed by Bradbury Thompson.

PHOTOGRAVURE
Plates of 460 (20x23) in panes of 100.

1985, Feb. 1 **Tagged** ***Perf. 11***

2111 A1496 (22c) **green** .60 .25
P# block of 6 4.50 —
P# block of 20, 1-2 #, 1-2 Zip, 1-2 Copyright 17.50 —
a. Vert. pair, imperf. 35.00
b. Vert. pair, imperf. horiz. *750.00*
c. Tagging omitted —

Counterfeits exist of No. 2111. See the Postal Counterfeits section of this catalog.

COIL STAMP

Perf. 10 Vert.

2112 A1496 (22c) **green** .60 .25
Pair 1.20 .25
P# strip of 3, #1, 2 3.00
P# strip of 5, #1, 2 4.00
P# single, #1, 2 — .50
a. Imperf., pair *45.00*
b. As "a," tagging omitted *100.00*
c. As No. 2112, tagging omitted *250.00* —

BOOKLET STAMP

ENGRAVED

Perf. 11 on 2 or 3 Sides

2113 A1497 (22c) **green** .70 .25
a. Booklet pane of 10 7.00 3.00
b. As "a," Horiz. imperf. btwn. *1,850.*

Two examples of No. 2113b are reported, both in unexploded booklet No. BK143a.

A1498

Flag Over Capitol Dome A1499

Designed by Frank Waslick.

ENGRAVED
Plates of 400 subjects in panes of 100.

1985, Mar. 29 **Tagged** ***Perf. 11***

2114 A1498 22c **blue, red & black** .45 .25
P# block of 4 2.10 —
Zip block of 4 1.85 —
Pair with full horizontal gutter *125.00*
a. All color missing (EP) —
b. Tagging omitted — *25.00*

No. 2114a should be collected se-tenant with a normal or a partially printed stamp.

COIL STAMP

Perf. 10 Vert.

2115 A1498 22c **blue, red & black,** wide block tagging, 19mmx21.5mm (B press) .45 .25
Pair .90 .50
P# strip of 3, #2, 4, 6, 10 2.50
P# strip of 3, #13 5.50
P# strip of 3, #14 17.50
P# strip of 3, #15, 16, 21 2.25
P# strip of 5, #2, 4, 6, 10 3.00
P# strip of 5, #13 6.50
P# strip of 5, #14 25.00
P# strip of 5, #15, 16, 21 2.75
P# single, #2 — .50
P# single, #4 — .50
P# single, #6 — 5.50
P# single, #10 — .65
P# single, #13 — 8.00
P# single, #14 — 22.00
P# single, #21 — 2.25
a. Narrow block tagging, 17.5mmx21.5mm (C press) .40 .25
P# strip of 3, #1 3.75
P# strip of 3, #3 8.00
P# strip of 3, #5 2.00
P# strip of 3, #7 3.50
P# strip of 3, #8, 11-12, 17-20, 22 2.25
P# strip of 5, #1 6.00
P# strip of 5, #3 30.00
P# strip of 5, #5 3.00
P# strip of 5, #7 6.00
P# strip of 5, #8, 11-12, 17-20, 22 3.00
P# single, #1, 3, 5 — .70
P# single, #7-8 — .70
P# single, #11 — .70
P# single, #12 — .70
P# single, #17-18 — 2.00
P# single, #19 — .75
P# single, #20 — 1.75
P# single, #22 — .75
b. Wide and tall block tagging, 19.5mmx23mm (D press) .40 .25
P# strip of 3, #8 —
P# strip of 3, #18 *37.50*
P# strip of 3, #20 *55.00*
P# strip of 3, #22 *55.00*
P# strip of 5, #2 (B press) *225.00*
P# strip of 5, #8 *125.00*
P# strip of 5, #18 *55.00*
P# strip of 5, #20 *75.00*
P# strip of 5, #22 *150.00*
P# single, #2 (B press) — *115.00*
P# single, #8 — *40.00*
P# single, #18 — *40.00*
P# single, #20 — *40.00*
P# single, #22 — *37.50*
c. Inscribed "T" at bottom, *May 23, 1987* .55 .40
P# strip of 3, #1 2.00
P# strip of 5, #1 3.00
P# single, #1 — 2.50
d. Black field of stars instead of blue — —
e. Tagging omitted 10.00
f. Imperf., pair, wide block tagging 10.00
g. Imperf., pair, narrow block tagging 10.00

No. 2115 is known with capitol in bluish black color, apparently from contaminated ink. Specialists often refer to this as "Erie blue."

No. 2115 plate number 2 exists with block tagging similar to that found on No. 2115b. Plate number 2 was used only on the B press and could not be used on either the C or D presses. The similar tagging is an anomaly, and specialists consider it to have been caused by excessive anvil roller pressure on the B press tagging mat, resulting in a tagging ink squeeze.

BOOKLET STAMP

Perf. 10 Horiz.

2116 A1499 22c **blue, red & black** .50 .25
a. Booklet pane of 5 2.50 1.25
Scored perforations 2.50 —

BOOKLET STAMPS

Frilled Dogwinkle — A1500

Reticulated Helmet — A1501

New England Neptune — A1502

Calico Scallop — A1503

Lightning Whelk — A1504

Designed by Pete Cocci.

ENGRAVED

1985, Apr. 4 **Tagged** ***Perf. 10 on 2 or 3 Sides***

2117 A1500 22c **black & brown** .45 .25
a. Tagging omitted —

2118 A1501 22c **black & multi** .45 .25

2120 A1503 22c **black & violet** .45 .25
2121 A1504 22c **black & multi** .45 .25
a. Booklet pane of 10, 2 ea #2117-2121 4.50 3.00
b. As "a," violet omitted on both Nos. 2120 *400.00*
c. As "a," vert. imperf. between *350.00*
d. As "a," imperf. —
e. Strip of 5, Nos. 2117-2121 2.00 —

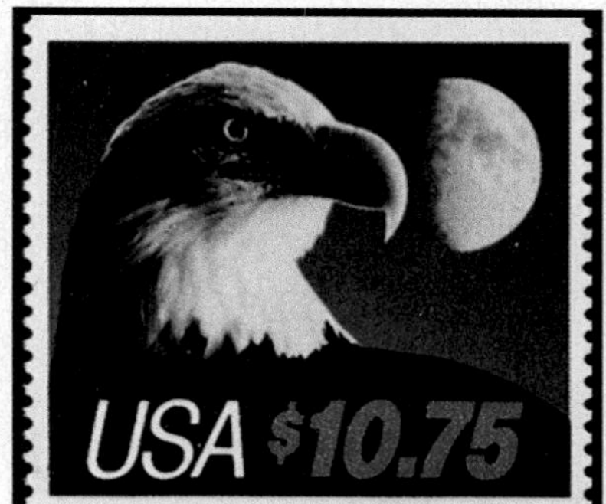

Eagle and Half Moon — A1505

Designed by Young & Rubicam.

TYPE I: washed out, dull appearance most evident in the black of the body of the eagle, and the red in the background between the eagle's shoulder and the moon. "$10.75" appears splotchy or grainy (P# 11111).

TYPE II: brighter, more intense colors most evident in the black on the eagle's body, and red in the background. "$10.75" appears smoother, brighter, and less grainy (P# 22222).

PHOTOGRAVURE

Perf. 10 Vert. on 1 or 2 Sides

1985, Apr. 29 **Untagged**
2122 A1505 $10.75 **multicolored,** type I 20.00 7.50
a. Booklet pane of 3 60.00 —
b. Type II, *June 19, 1989* 20.00 10.00
c. As "b," booklet pane of 3 60.00 —

Coil Plate No. Strips of 3
Beginning with No. 2123, coil plate No. strips of 3 usually sell at the level of strips of 5 minus the face value of two stamps.

TRANSPORTATION ISSUE

A1506

Buckboard 1880s USA 4.9

A1507

A1508

Tricycle 1880s 6 USA

A1509

A1510

Ambulance 1860s 8.3 USA

A1511

A1512

A1513

A1514

A1515

A1516

A1517

A1518

Bread Wagon 1880s 25 USA

A1519

Designers: 3.4c, 17c, Lou Nolan. 4.9c, 8.5c, 14c, 25c, William H. Bond. 5.5c, David K. Stone. 6c, 8.3c, 10.1c, 12.5c. James Schleyer. 7.1c, 11c, 12c, Ken Dallison.

COIL STAMPS

ENGRAVED

1985-89 **Tagged** ***Perf. 10 Vert.***
2123 A1506 3.4c **dark bluish green,** *June 8* .25 .25
Pair .50 .50
P# strip of 5, line, #1-2 .90
P# single, #1-2 — .75
a. Untagged (Bureau precancel, Non-profit Org. CAR-RT SORT) .25 .25
P# strip of 5, line, #1-2 2.75
P# single, #1-2 — 2.75
2124 A1507 4.9c **brown black,** *June 21* .25 .25
Pair .50 .50
P# strip of 5, line, #3-4 .90
P# single, #3-4 — .65
a. Untagged (Bureau precancel, Non-profit Org.) .25 .25
P# strip of 5, line, #1-6 1.25
P# single, #1-6 — 1.10
b. Tagging omitted —
2125 A1508 5.5c **deep magenta,** *Nov. 1, 1986* .25 .25
Pair .50 .50
P# strip of 5, #1 1.35
P# single, #1 — 1.10
a. Untagged (Bureau precancel, Non-profit Org. CAR-RT SORT) .25 .25
P# strip of 5, #1 1.30
P# strip of 5, #2 1.50
P# single, #1 — 1.10
P# single, #2 — 1.75
b. Tagging omitted —

On No. 2125a, both vignette and the precancel inscription were printed from a single printing sleeve.

2126 A1509 6c **red brown,** *May 6* .35 .25
Pair .70 .50
P# strip of 5, #1 1.50
P# single, #1 — 1.00
a. Untagged (Bureau precancel, Non-profit Org.) .25 .25
P# strip of 5, #1 1.50
P# strip of 5, #2 3.00
P# single, #1 — 1.00
P# single, #2 — 2.50
b. As "a," imperf., pair *175.00*
c. Tagging omitted —
2127 A1510 7.1c **lake,** *Feb. 6, 1987* .25 .25
Pair .50 .50
P# strip of 5, #1 1.50
P# single, #1 — 1.40
a. Untagged (Bureau precancel "Non-profit Org." in black), *Feb. 6, 1987* .25 .25
P# strip of 5, #1 1.75
P# single, #1 — 1.50
b. Untagged (Bureau precancel "Non-profit 5-Digit Zip + 4" in black), *May 26, 1989* .25 .25
P# strip of 5, #1 1.40
P# single, #1 — 1.25
c. As "a," black (precancel) omitted —

On Nos. 2127a and 2127b, both the vignette and the precancel inscription were printed from a single printing sleeve.

On No. 2127c, an albino impression of the precancel is present.

2128 A1511 8.3c **green,** *June 21* .25 .25
Pair .50 .50
P# strip of 5, line, #1-2 1.40
P# single, #1-2 — 1.00
a. Untagged (Bureau precancel, Blk. Rt. CAR-RT SORT) .25 .25
P# strip of 5, line, #1-2 1.25
P# strip of 5, line, #3-4 2.00
P# single, #1-2 — 1.10
P# single, #3-4 — 3.50

On No. 2231 "Ambulance 1860s" is 18mm long; on No. 2128, 18⅓mm long.

2129 A1512 8.5c **dark Prussian green,** *Jan. 24, 1987* .25 .25
Pair .50 .50
P# strip of 5, #1 1.90
P# single, #1 — 1.50
a. Untagged (Bureau precancel, Non-profit Org.) .25 .25
P# strip of 5, #1 2.00
P# strip of 5, #2 5.75
P# single, #1 — 1.75
P# single, #2 — 5.75
2130 A1513 10.1c **slate blue,** *Apr. 18* .55 .25
Pair 1.10 .50
P# strip of 5, #1 2.50
P# single, #1 — 1.60
a. Untagged (Bureau precancel "Bulk Rate Carrier Route Sort" in red), *June 27, 1988* .25 .25
P# strip of 5, #2-3 2.00
P# single, #2-3 — 1.50
Untagged (Bureau precancel "Bulk Rate" and lines in black) .25 .25
P# strip of 5, #1-2 2.00
P# single, #1-2 — 1.60
b. As "a," red precancel, imperf, pair 15.00
As "a," black precancel, imperf, pair 70.00
2131 A1514 11c **dark green,** *June 11* .25 .25
Pair .50 .50
P# strip of 5, line, #1-4 1.40
P# single, #1-4 — 1.00
a. Tagging omitted *250.00*
2132 A1515 12c **dark blue,** type I, *Apr. 2* .35 .25
Pair .70 .50
P# strip of 5, line, #1-2 2.25
P# single, #1-2 — 1.25
a. Untagged, type I (Bureau precancel, PRESORTED FIRST-CLASS), *Apr. 2* .25 .25
P# strip of 5, line, #1-2 1.90
P# single, #1-2 — 1.50
b. Untagged, type II, (Bureau precancel, PRESORTED FIRST-CLASS) *1987* .40 .30
P# strip of 5, no line, #1 12.50
P# single, #1 — 12.50
c. Tagging omitted, type I, (not Bureau precanceled), *1987* 15.00

Type II has "Stanley Steamer 1909" ⅕mm shorter (17⅘mm) than No. 2132 (18mm).

2133 A1516 12.5c **olive green,** *Apr. 18* .35 .25
Pair .70 .50
P# strip of 5, #1 2.50
P# strip of 5, #2 3.00
P# single, #1 — 2.00
P# single, #2 — 2.75
a. Untagged (Bureau precancel, Bulk Rate) .25 .25
P# strip of 5, #1 2.00
P# strip of 5, #2 2.50
P# single, #1 — 1.40
P# single, #2 — 2.60
b. As "a," imperf., pair 40.00

All No. 2133 from plate 1 and some No. 2133a from plate 1 were printed with luminescent ink that is orange under long wave UV light.

2134 A1517 14c **sky blue,** type I, *Mar. 23* .30 .25
Pair .60 .50
P# strip of 5, line, #1-4 2.00
P# single, #1-4 — 1.50
a. Imperf., pair 75.00
b. Type II, *Sept. 30, 1986* .30 .25
P# strip of 5, no line, #2 2.60
P# single, #2 — 2.40
c. Tagging omitted, type I 35.00 —

Type II design is ¼mm narrower (17¼mm) than the original stamp (17½mm) and has block tagging. No. 2134 has overall tagging.

2135 A1518 17c **bright blue,** *Aug. 20, 1986* .75 .25
Pair 1.50 .50
P# strip of 5, #2 5.50
P# single, #2 — 1.50
a. Imperf., pair *300.00*
2136 A1519 25c **orange brown,** *Nov. 22, 1986* .50 .25
Pair 1.00 .50
P# strip of 5, #1-5 3.00
P# single, #1 — 1.00
P# single, #2-4 — .55
P# single, #5 — 2.25
a. Imperf., pair 10.00
b. Pair, imperf. between *525.00*
c. Tagging omitted *50.00*
d. As "a," tagging omitted —
Nos. 2123-2136 (14) 4.90 3.50

Precancellations on Nos. 2125a, 2127a do not have lines. Precancellation on No. 2129a is in red. See No. 2231.

BLACK HERITAGE SERIES

Mary McLeod Bethune (1875-1955), Educator — A1520

Designed by Jerry Pinkney from a photograph.

Printed by American Bank Note Company.

PHOTOGRAVURE

Plates of 200 in four panes of 50.

1985, Mar. 5	**Tagged**	***Perf. 11***	
2137 A1520 22c **multicolored**		.60	.25
	P# block of 4, 6#+A	3.25	—
	Zip block of 4	2.50	—
a.	Tagging omitted	—	—

AMERICAN FOLK ART SERIES

Duck Decoys

Broadbill A1521

Mallard A1522

Canvasback A1523

Redhead A1524

Designed by Stevan Dohanos.

Printed by American Bank Note Company.

PHOTOGRAVURE

Plates of 200 in four panes of 50.

1985, Mar. 22	**Tagged**	***Perf. 11***	
2138 A1521 22c **multicolored**		.90	.25
2139 A1522 22c **multicolored**		.90	.25
2140 A1523 22c **multicolored**		.90	.25
2141 A1524 22c **multicolored**		.90	.25
a.	Block of 4, #2138-2141	3.60	2.75
	P# block of 4, 5#+A	4.00	—
	Zip block of 4	3.75	—
b.	As "a," tagging omitted	—	

WINTER SPECIAL OLYMPICS

Ice Skater, Emblem, Skier — A1525

Designed by Jeff Carnell.

PHOTOGRAVURE

Plates of 160 in four panes of 40.

1985, Mar. 25	**Tagged**	***Perf. 11***	
2142 A1525 22c **multicolored**		.50	.25
	P# block of 4, 6#	2.75	—
	Zip block of 4	2.10	—
a.	Vert. pair, imperf. horiz.	*300.00*	

LOVE

A1526

Designed by Corita Kent.

PHOTOGRAVURE

Plates of 200 in four panes of 50.

1985, Apr. 17	**Tagged**	***Perf. 11***	
2143 A1526 22c **multicolored**		.45	.25
	P# block of 4, 6#	2.00	—
	Zip block of 4	1.90	—
a.	Imperf., pair	*800.00*	

RURAL ELECTRIFICATION ADMINISTRATION

REA Power Lines, Farmland A1527

Designed by Howard Koslow.

PHOTOGRAVURE & ENGRAVED (Combination Press)

Plates of 230 in panes of 50.

1985, May 11	**Tagged**	***Perf. 11***	
2144 A1527 22c **multicolored**		.50	.25
	P# block of 20, 5-10 #, 1-2 Zip, 1-2 Copyright	16.00	—
a.	Vert. pair, imperf between	—	

See Combination Press note after No. 1703.

AMERIPEX '86

US No. 134 — A1528

Designed by Richard Sheaff.

LITHOGRAPHED & ENGRAVED

Plates of 192 in four panes of 48

1985, May 25	**Tagged**	***Perf. 11***	
2145 A1528 22c **multicolored**		.45	.25
	P# block of 4, 3#	2.10	—
	Zip block of 4	1.90	—
a.	Red, black & blue (engr.) omitted	*110.00*	
b.	Red & black omitted	*1,250.*	
c.	Red omitted	*1,750.*	
d.	Black missing (PS)	—	

ABIGAIL ADAMS (1744-1818)

A1529

Designed by Bart Forbes.

PHOTOGRAVURE

Plates of 200 in four panes of 50.

1985, June 14	**Tagged**	***Perf. 11***	
2146 A1529 22c **multicolored**		.45	.25
	P# block of 4, 4#	2.10	—
	Zip block of 4	1.90	—
a.	Imperf., pair	*200.00*	

FREDERIC AUGUSTE BARTHOLDI (1834-1904)

Architect and Sculptor, Statue of Liberty A1530

Designed by Howard Paine from paintings by Jose Frappa and James Dean.

LITHOGRAPHED & ENGRAVED

Plates of 200 in four panes of 50.

1985, July 18	**Tagged**	***Perf. 11***	
2147 A1530 22c **multicolored**		.45	.25
	P# block of 4, 5#	2.10	—
	Zip block of 4	1.90	—

Examples of No. 2147 exist with most, but not all, of the engraved black omitted.

George Washington, Washington Monument — A1532

Sealed Envelopes — A1533

Designed by Thomas Szumowski (#2149) based on a portrait by Gilbert Stuart, and Richard Sheaff (#2150).

COIL STAMPS

PHOTOGRAVURE

1985		***Perf. 10 Vertically***	
2149 A1532	18c **multicolored,** low gloss gum, *Nov. 6*	.40	.25
	Pair	.80	.50
	P# strip of 5, #1112	2.75	
	P# strip of 5, #3333	3.00	
	P# single, #1112	—	2.00
	P# single, #3333	—	3.00
a.	Untagged (Bureau precanceled), low gloss gum	.35	.35
	P# strip of 5, #11121	4.00	
	P# strip of 5, #33333	2.75	
	P# single, #11121	—	4.00
	P# single, #33333	—	1.50
	Dull gum	.35	
	P# strip of 5, #33333	4.00	
	P# strip of 5, #43444	5.00	
	P# single, #43444	—	5.00
b.	Imperf., pair	*750.00*	

c. As "a," imperf., pair 575.00
d. Tagging omitted (not Bureau precanceled) 75.00 —
e. As "a," tagged (error), dull gum 2.00 1.75
Pair 4.00 3.75
P# strip of 5, #33333 45.00
P# single, #33333 — 10.00
Low gloss gum 2.00
P# strip of 5, #33333 150.00
P# single, #33333 — 35.00

2150 A1533 21.1c **multicolored,** *Oct. 22* .40 .25
Pair .80 .50
P# strip of 5, #111111 3.00
P# strip of 5, #111121 3.25
P# single, #111111 — 2.25
P# single, #111121 — 3.50
a. Untagged (Bureau Precancel) .40 .40
Pair .80 .80
P# strip of 5, #111111 3.25
P# strip of 5, #111121 3.50
P# single, #111111 — 2.50
P# single, #111121 — 2.75
b. As "a," tagged (error) .50 .50
Pair 1.00 1.00
P# strip of 5, #111111 3.25
P# strip of 5, #111121 4.25
P# single, #111111 — 3.00
P# single, #111121 — 3.50

Precancellations on Nos. 2149a ("PRESORTED FIRST-CLASS"), 2150a and 2150b ("ZIP+4") do not have lines.

No. 2150b shows obvious tagging. All No. 2150a P#111121 and some P#111111 show a very faint block tagging due to contamination of a lacquer coating that was applied to the face of the stamps to keep the ink from smearing.

KOREAN WAR VETERANS

American Troops in Korea
A1535

Designed by Richard Sheaff from a photograph by David D. Duncan.

ENGRAVED
Plates of 200 in four panes of 50.

1985, July 26 **Tagged** ***Perf. 11***
2152 A1535 22c **gray green & rose red** .45 .25
P# block of 4 2.50 —
Zip block of 4 1.90 —

SOCIAL SECURITY ACT, 50th ANNIV.

Men, Women, Children, Corinthian Columns
A1536

Designed by Robert Brangwynne.

Printed by American Bank Note Company.

PHOTOGRAVURE
Plates of 200 in four panes of 50.

1985, Aug. 14 **Tagged** ***Perf. 11***
2153 A1536 22c **deep & light blue** .45 .25
P# block of 4, 2#+A 2.10 —
Zip block of 4 1.90 —

WORLD WAR I VETERANS

The Battle of Marne, France
A1537

Designed by Richard Sheaff from Harvey Dunn's charcoal drawing.

ENGRAVED
Plates of 200 in four panes of 50.

1985, Aug. 26 **Tagged** ***Perf. 11***
2154 A1537 22c **gray green & rose red** .45 .25
P# block of 4 2.50 —
Zip block of 4 1.90 —
a. Red missing (PS) 200.00
b. Tagging omitted — —

HORSES

Quarter Horse
A1538

Morgan
A1539

Saddlebred
A1540

Appaloosa
A1541

Designed by Roy Andersen.

PHOTOGRAVURE
Plates of 160 in four panes of 40.

1985, Sept. 25 **Tagged** ***Perf. 11***
2155 A1538 22c **multicolored** 1.10 .25
2156 A1539 22c **multicolored** 1.10 .25
2157 A1540 22c **multicolored** 1.10 .25
2158 A1541 22c **multicolored** 1.10 .25
a. Block of 4, #2155-2158 4.40 4.00
P# block of 4, 5# 6.00 —
Zip block of 4 4.75 —

PUBLIC EDUCATION IN AMERICA

Quill Pen, Apple, Spectacles, Penmanship Quiz — A1542

Designed by Uldis Purins.

Printed by American Bank Note Company

PHOTOGRAVURE
Plates of 200 in four panes of 50.

1985, Oct. 1 **Tagged** ***Perf. 11***
2159 A1542 22c **multicolored** .45 .25
P# block of 4, 5#+A 2.75 —
Zip block of 4 1.85 —
a. Tagging omitted —

INTERNATIONAL YOUTH YEAR

YMCA Youth Camping, Cent.
A1543

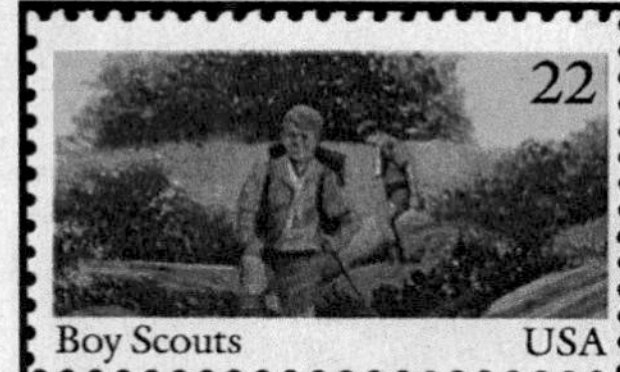

Boy Scouts, 75th Anniv.
A1544

Big Brothers / Big Sisters Federation, 40th Anniv.
A1545

Camp Fire Inc., 75th Anniv.
A1546

Designed by Dennis Luzak.

Printed by American Bank Note Company.

PHOTOGRAVURE
Plates of 200 in four panes of 50.

1985, Oct. 7 **Tagged** ***Perf. 11***
2160 A1543 22c **multicolored** .70 .25
2161 A1544 22c **multicolored** .70 .25
2162 A1545 22c **multicolored** .70 .25
2163 A1546 22c **multicolored** .70 .25
a. Block of 4, #2160-2163 3.00 2.25
P# block of 4, 5#+A 4.00 —
Zip block of 4 3.25 —

HELP END HUNGER

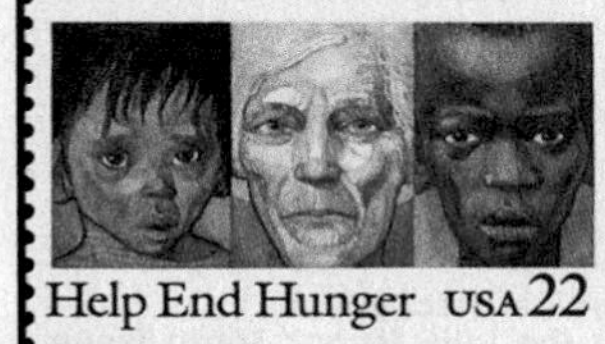

Youths and Elderly Suffering from Malnutrition
A1547

Designed by Jerry Pinkney.

Printed by the American Bank Note Company.

PHOTOGRAVURE
Plates of 200 in four panes of 50.

1985, Oct. 15 **Tagged** ***Perf. 11***
2164 A1547 22c **multicolored** .45 .25
P# block of 4, 5#+A 2.25 —
Zip block of 4 1.90 —
a. Tagging omitted —

CHRISTMAS

Genoa Madonna, Enameled Terra-Cotta by Luca Della Robbia (1400-1482) — A1548

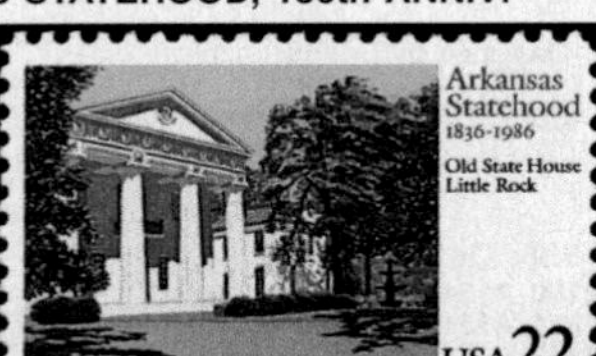

Poinsettia Plants A1549

Designed by Bradbury Thompson (No. 2165) and James Dean (No. 2166).

PHOTOGRAVURE
Plates of 200 in panes of 50.

1985, Oct. 30 Tagged *Perf. 11*

2165 A1548 22c **multicolored**	.45	.25
P# block of 4, 4#	2.00	—
Zip block of 4	1.90	—
a. Imperf., pair	*55.00*	
b. Tagging omitted		—
2166 A1549 22c **multicolored**	.45	.25
P# block of 4, 5#	2.00	—
Zip block of 4	1.90	—
Vert. pair with full horiz. gutter between	—	
a. Imperf., pair	*50.00*	

ARKANSAS STATEHOOD, 150th ANNIV.

Old State House, Little Rock — A1550

Designed by Roger Carlisle.

Printed by the American Bank Note Company

PHOTOGRAVURE
Plates of 200 in four panes of 50.

1986, Jan. 3 Tagged *Perf. 11*

2167 A1550 22c **multicolored**	.65	.25
P# block of 4, 6#+A	3.25	—
Zip block of 4	2.75	—
a. Vert. pair, imperf. horiz.	*500.00*	
b. Tagging omitted		—

Marginal Inscriptions
Beginning with the Luis Munoz Marin issue a number of stamps include a descriptive inscription in the selvage.

GREAT AMERICANS ISSUE

A1551

A1552

Designed by Ron Adair.

Printed by the Bureau of Engraving & Printing.

ENGRAVED
Panes of 100 (#2168-2193, 2195), Panes of 20 (#2194, 2196)

Perf. 11, 11½x11 (#2185), 11.2x11.1 (#2179)

1986-94 Tagged

2168 A1551 1c **brownish vermilion,** large block tagging, *June 30*	.25	.25
P# block of 4	.50	—
Zip block of 4	.50	—
a. Tagging omitted	*15.00*	
b. 1c **red brown**	.30	.30
2169 A1552 2c **bright blue,** large block tagging, *Feb. 28, 1987*	.25	.25
P# block of 4	.50	—
Zip block of 4	.50	—
a. Untagged	.40	.25
P# block of 4	1.75	—
Zip block of 4	1.60	—
b. Tagging omitted	—	—

The tagging omitted error No. 2169b appeared before No. 2169a was issued. Plate blocks from plate 1 are the error if untagged. No. 2169a is from plate 3. Other blocks and singles can be distinguished if se-tenant with tagged stamps. No. 2169a and 2169b also can be distinguished using a long wave ultraviolet light. The paper of No. 2169b will appear brownish, while the paper of No. 2169a appears almost white.

A1553

A1554

Designed by Christopher Calle.

Printed by the Bureau of Engraving & Printing.

2170 A1553 3c **bright blue,** large block tagging, dull gum, *Sept. 15*	.25	.25
P# block of 4	.50	—
Zip block of 4	.50	—
a. Untagged, dull gum, *1994*	.30	.25
P# block of 4	1.00	—
Zip block of 4	1.00	—
Shiny gum, *1994*	.35	.25
P# block of 4	1.50	—
Zip block of 4	1.40	—
b. Tagging omitted	*75.00*	—

No. 2170a with dull gum can be distinguished from No. 2170a with shiny gum, because the paper on the latter is significantly whiter in color.

The tagging omitted error No. 2170b appeared before No. 2170a was issued. Plate blocks from plates 2 and 3 are the error if untagged. No. 2170a is from plate 4. Other blocks and singles are indistiguishable, unless se-tenant with tagged stamps.

2171 A1554 4c **blue violet,** large block tagging, *July 14*	.25	.25
P# block of 4	.60	—
Zip block of 4	.50	—
a. 4c **grayish violet,** untagged	.25	.25
P# block of 4	1.00	—
Zip block of 4	1.00	—
b. 4c **deep grayish blue,** untagged, *1993*	.35	.25
P# block of 4	1.50	—
Zip block of 4	1.40	—
c. As No. 2171, tagging omitted		—
d. All color missing (EP)	—	

No. 2171c was found on a USPS souvenir page with first day cancel. No. 2171a and 2171b were not available on the first day of issue.

No. 2171d has an albino impression, and it also may be collected with a fully or partially printed stamp.

A1555

A1556

Designers: No. 2172, Christopher Calle. No. 2173, Juan Maldonado.

Printed by the Bureau of Engraving & Printing.

2172 A1555 5c **dark olive green,** large block tagging, *Feb. 27*	.25	.25
P# block of 4	1.00	—
Zip block of 4	1.00	—
a. As No. 2172, tagging omitted	*150.00*	—
b. 5c **light olive green,** large block tagging	.35	.25
P# block of 4	1.50	—
Zip block of 4	1.40	—
2173 A1556 5c **carmine,** overall tagging, *Feb. 18, 1990*	.25	.25
P# block of 4	1.25	—
P# zip block of 4	1.00	—
Zip block of 4	1.00	—
a. Untagged, *1991*	.25	.25
P# block of 4	1.00	—
P# zip block of 4	1.00	—
Zip block of 4	1.00	—
b. Tagging omitted	—	—

The tagging omitted error No. 2173b appeared before No. 2173a was issued. Plate blocks from plate 1 are the error if untagged. No. 2173a is from plate 2. Other blocks and singles are indistinguishable, unless se-tenant with tagged stamps.

A1557

A1558

Designers: 10c, Robert Anderson. 14c, Ward Brackett.

Printed by the Bureau of Engraving & Printing.

2175 A1557 10c **lake,** large block tagging, dull gum, *Aug. 15, 1987*	.25	.25
P# block of 4	1.10	—
Zip block of 4	1.00	—
a. Overall tagging, dull gum, *1990*	1.35	.25
P# block of 4	11.00	—
Zip block of 4	5.50	—
b. Tagging omitted	*25.00*	
c. Prephosphored coated paper with surface tagging showing a solid appearance, dull gum, *1991*	1.50	.25
P# block of 4	7.50	—
Zip block of 4	6.25	—
d. Prephosphored uncoated paper with embedded tagging showing a mottled appearance, shiny gum, *1993*	1.50	.25
P# block of 4	7.50	—
Zip block of 4	6.25	—
e. 10c **carmine,** prephosphored uncoated paper with embedded tagging showing a mottled appearance, shiny gum, *1994*	.80	.25
P# block of 4	6.00	—
Zip block of 4	3.00	—
f. As "c," all color omitted	*125.00*	

No. 2175f may be collected se-tenant with a partially printed stamp or longer vertical strip. Stamps not se-tenant with a partially printed stamp are identified by a light setoff on the gum side.

2176 A1558 14c **crimson,** large block tagging, *Feb. 12, 1987*	.30	.25
P# block of 4	1.50	—
Zip block of 4	1.20	—
a. Tagging omitted	—	

A1559

A1560

Designers: 15c, Jack Rosenthal. 17c, Christopher Calle.

Printed by the Bureau of Engraving & Printing.

2177 A1559 15c **claret,** large block tagging, *June 6, 1988*	1.00	.25
P# block of 4	12.00	—
Zip block of 4	4.25	—
a. Overall tagging, *1990*	.30	—
P# block of 4	3.25	—
Zip block of 4	1.20	—
b. Prephosphored coated paper with surface tagging showing a solid appearance	.60	—
P# block of 4	3.75	—
Zip block of 4	2.40	—
c. Tagging omitted	*15.00*	—
d. All color omitted	*200.00*	

No. 2177d resulted from partially printed panes. It must be collected se-tenant with a partially printed stamp or in a longer horizontal strip showing error stamps plus partially/completely printed stamps.

2178 A1560 17c **dull blue green,** large block tagging, *June 18*	.35	.25
P# block of 4	2.00	—
Zip block of 4	1.40	—
Pair with full horizontal gutter be-		

A1561

A1562

Designers: 20c, Robert Anderson. 21c, Susan Sanford.

Printed by: 20c, Banknote Corporation of America. 21c, Bureau of Engraving & Printing.

2179 A1561 20c **red brown,** prephosphored coated paper with surface tagging showing a grainy solid appearance, *Oct. 24, 1994* .40 .25
P# block of 4, 1#+B 2.00 —
a. 20c **orange brown,** prephosphored coated paper with surface tagging showing a grainy solid appearance .75 .25
P# block of 4, 1#+B 4.00 —
b. 20c **bright red brown,** prephosphored coated paper with surface tagging showing a grainy solid appearance 1.25 .25
P# block of 4, 1#+B 8.50 —

2180 A1562 21c **blue violet,** large block tagging, *Oct. 21, 1988* .45 .25
P# block of 4 2.50 —
Zip block of 4 1.65 —
a. Tagging omitted —

No. 2180 is known with worn tagging mats on which horizontal untagged areas have taggant giving the appearance of vertical band tagging.

A1563

A1564

Designers: 23c, Dennis Lyall. 25c, Richard Sparks.

Printed by the Bureau of Engraving & Printing.

2181 A1563 23c **purple,** large block tagging, dull gum, *Nov. 4, 1988* .45 .25
P# block of 4 2.50 —
Zip block of 4 1.90 —
a. Overall tagging, dull gum .75 —
P# block of 4 6.50 —
Zip block of 4 3.25 —
b. Prephosphored coated paper with surface tagging showing a solid appearance, dull gum 1.00 —
P# block of 4 6.50 —
Zip block of 4 4.25 —
c. Prephosphored uncoated paper with embedded tagging showing a mottled appearance, shiny gum 1.50 .25
P# block of 4 8.50 —
Zip block of 4 6.25 —
d. Tagging omitted *7.50*

2182 A1564 25c **blue,** large block tagging, *Jan. 11* .50 .25
P# block of 4 2.75 —
Zip block of 4 2.00 —
a. Booklet pane of 10, perf. 11 ¼, *May 3, 1988* 5.00 3.75
b. As #2182, tagging omitted — —
c. As "a," tagging omitted —
d. Horiz. pair, imperf between *750.00*
e. As "a," all color omitted on right stamps *1,250.*
f. As No. 2182 (sheet stamp), vert. pair, bottom stamp all color omitted —
g. As "a," tagging omitted on two stamps —
h. As "a," all color omitted on left stamps *1,250.*

No. 2182f may be collected se-tenant with a partially printed stamp or longer vertical strip.

Counterfeits exist of No. 2182. See the Postal Counterfeits section of this catalog.

See Nos. 2197, 2197a.

A1565

A1566

Designers: 28c, Robert Anderson. 29c, Christopher Calle.

Printed by: No. 2183, Bureau of Engraving & Printing. No. 2184, Canadian Bank Note Co. for Stamp Venturers.

2183 A1565 28c **myrtle green,** large block tagging, *Sept. 14, 1989* .65 .35
P# block of 4 3.75 —
Zip block of 4 2.60 —

2184 A1566 29c **blue,** prephosphored uncoated paper with embedded tagging showing a mottled appearance, *Mar. 9, 1992* .70 .25
P# block of 4, ##+S 4.00 —
Zip block of 4 3.00 —

A1567

A1568

Designed by Christopher Calle.

Printed by: No. 2185, Stamp Venturers. 2186, Canadian Bank Note Co. for Stamp Venturers.

2185 A1567 29c **indigo,** prephosphored coated paper with surface tagging showing a solid appearance, *Apr. 13, 1993* .65 .25
P# block of 4, 1#+S 3.50 —
Zip block of 4 2.70 —

2186 A1568 35c **black,** prephosphored uncoated paper with embedded tagging showing a mottled appearance, *Apr. 3, 1991* .75 .25
P# block of 4, ##+S 4.00 —
Zip block of 4 3.00 —

A1569

A1570

Designers: 40c, Christopher Calle. 45c, Bradbury Thompson.

Printed by: 40c, 45c, Bureau of Engraving & Printing.

2187 A1569 40c **dark blue,** overall tagging, dull gum, *Sept. 6, 1990* .85 .25
P# block of 4 5.00 —
Zip block of 4 3.50 —
a. Prephosphored coated paper with surface tagging, dull gum 1.25 .35
P# block of 4 6.50 —
Zip block of 4 5.25 —
Low gloss gum, *1998* 1.25 .35
P# block of 4 6.50 —
Zip block of 4 5.25 —
c. Prephosphored uncoated paper with embedded tagging showing a mottled appearance, shiny gum, *1994* 1.00 .25
P# block of 4 10.00 —
Zip block of 4 4.25 —
d. Tagging omitted *75.00*

No. 2187a exists on two types of surface-tagged paper that exhibit either a solid appearance (dull gum) or a grainy solid appearance (low gloss gum).

2188 A1570 45c **bright blue,** large block tagging, *June 17, 1988* 1.00 .25
P# block of 4 5.00 —
Zip block of 4 4.00 —
a. 45c **blue,** overall tagging, *1990* 2.75 .25
P# block of 4 27.50 —
Zip block of 4 12.00 —
b. Tagging omitted *17.50*

The blue on No. 2188a is noticeably lighter than on No. 2188. Color variety specialists, as well as tagging specialists, will want to consider it as a second variety of this stamp.

Almost all examples of No. 2188a are in the grade of fine or fine-very fine. Values are for stamps in the grade of fine-very fine.

A1571

A1572

Designers: 52c, John Berkey. 56c, Robert Anderson.

Printed by the Bureau of Engraving & Printing.

2189 A1571 52c **purple,** prephosphored coated paper with surface tagging showing a solid appearance, dull gum, *June 3, 1991* 1.10 .25
P# block of 4 7.00 —
Zip block of 4 4.50 —
a. Prephosphored uncoated paper with embedded tagging showing a mottled appearance, shiny gum, *1993* 1.25 —
P# block of 4 10.00 —
Zip block of 4 5.50 —

Selvage inscriptions from the original printing of No. 2189 from plate 1 show the incorrect dates for Humphrey's vice-presidential term ("1964 to 1968"). Corrected plate 1 and plate 2 printings (No. 2189a) show the dates correctly as 1965 to 1969. Values for the two varieties of inscription blocks of 6 are approximately the same: $10 each.

2190 A1572 56c **scarlet,** large block tagging, *Sept. 3* 1.20 .25
P# block of 4 5.25 —
Zip block of 4 4.80 —
a. Tagging omitted —

No. 2190 known with a "tagging spill" making stamp appear overall tagged.

A1573

A1574

Designed by Christopher Calle.

Printed by the Bureau of Engraving & Printing.

2191 A1573 65c **dark blue,** large block tagging, *Nov. 5, 1988* 1.30 .25
P# block of 4 6.50 —
Zip block of 4 5.20 —
a. Tagging omitted *22.50*

2192 A1574 75c **deep magenta,** prephosphored coated paper with surface tagging showing a solid appearance, dull gum, *Feb. 16, 1992* 1.75 .25
P# block of 4 8.00 —
Zip block of 4 7.25 —
a. Prephosphored uncoated paper with embedded tagging showing a mottled appearance, shiny gum 1.90 —
P# block of 4 10.00 —
Zip block of 4 7.75 —

A1575

A1576

"Lipstick on Shirt Front" double gouge plate flaw

Designers: No. 2193, Tom Broad. No. 2194, Bradbury Thompson.

Printed by the Bureau of Engraving & Printing.

2193 A1575 $1 **dark Prussian green,** large block tagging, *Sept. 23* 3.00 .50
- P# block of 4 13.00 —
- Zip block of 4 12.00 —
- *a.* All color omitted —
- *b.* Tagging omitted *75.00*

No. 2193a must be collected se-tenant vertically with partially printed stamps.

2194 A1576 $1 **intense deep blue,** large block tagging, dull gum, *June 7, 1989* 2.25 .50
- P# block of 4 10.00 —
- Pane of 20 48.00
- Double gouge plate flaw ("Lipstick on Shirt Front"), (pos. 6 on one plate #1 pane) *375.00*
- P# block of 4, UL, plate flaw at LL *425.00*
- Pane of 20, plate flaw at pos. 6 *575.00*
- *b.* $1 **deep blue,** overall tagging, dull gum, *1990* 2.50 .50
- P# block of 4 13.00 —
- Pane of 20 52.50
- *c.* Tagging omitted *17.50*
- *d.* $1 **dark blue,** prephosphored coated paper with surface tagging showing a solid appearance, dull gum, *1992* 2.50 .50
- P# block of 4 13.00 —
- Pane of 20 52.50
- *e.* $1 **blue,** prephosphored uncoated paper with embedded tagging showing a mottled appearance, shiny gum, *1993* 2.75 .60
- P# block of 4 14.00 —
- Pane of 20 58.00
- *f.* $1 **blue,** prephosphored coated paper with surface tagging showing a grainy solid appearance, low gloss gum, *1998* 2.75 .50
- P# block of 4 14.00 —
- Pane of 20 58.00

No. 2194 issued in pane of 20 (see No. 2196.)

The intense deep blue of No. 2194 is much deeper than the deep blue and dark blue of the other $1 varieties.

The "Lipstick on Shirt Front" flaw was discovered during production and the position was repaired. Very few have been found.

A1577

A1578

Designers: $2, Tom Broad. $5, Arthur Lidov.

Printed by the Bureau of Engraving & Printing.

2195 A1577 $2 **bright violet,** large block tagging, *Mar. 19* 4.50 .50
- P# block of 4 20.00 —
- Zip block of 4 17.00 —
- *a.* Tagging omitted *300.00 100.00*

No. 2195 is known with worn tagging mats on which horizontal untagged areas have taggant giving the appearance of vertical band tagging.

2196 A1578 $5 **copper red,** large block tagging, *Aug. 25, 1987* 9.00 1.00
- P# block of 4 42.50 —
- Pane of 20 185.00
- *a.* Tagging omitted *225.00* —
- *b.* Prephosphored coated paper with surface tagging showing a solid appearance, *1992* 11.00 —
- P# block of 4 45.00 —
- Pane of 20 220.00
- *Nos. 2168-2196 (28)* 33.90 8.60

Booklet Stamp

Perf. 10 on 2 or 3 Sides

2197 A1564 25c **blue,** large block tagging, *May 3, 1988* .55 .25
- *a.* Booklet pane of 6 3.30 2.50
- *b.* Tagging omitted 20.00
- *c.* As "b," booklet pane of 6 150.00

UNITED STATES - SWEDEN STAMP COLLECTING

Handstamped Cover, Philatelic Memorabilia A1581

Boy Examining Stamp Collection A1582

No. 836 Under Magnifying Glass, Sweden Nos. 268, 271 — A1583

1986 Presidents Miniature Sheet on First Day Cover — A1584

Designed by Richard Sheaff and Eva Jern (No. 2200).

BOOKLET STAMPS
LITHOGRAPHED & ENGRAVED

Perf. 10 Vert. on 1 or 2 Sides

1986, Jan. 23 **Tagged**

- **2198** A1581 22c **multicolored** .45 .25
- **2199** A1582 22c **multicolored** .45 .25
- **2200** A1583 22c **multicolored** .45 .25
- **2201** A1584 22c **multicolored** .45 .25
- *a.* Bklt. pane of 4, #2198-2201 2.00 1.75
- *b.* As "a," black omitted on Nos. 2198, 2201 50.00 —
- *c.* As "a," blue (litho.) omitted on Nos. 2198-2200 *1,500.*
- *d.* As "a," buff (litho.) omitted —
- *e.* As "a," tagging omitted —

See Sweden Nos. 1585-1588.

LOVE ISSUE

A1585

Designed by Saul Mandel.

Plates of 200 in four panes of 50.
PHOTOGRAVURE

1986, Jan. 30 **Tagged** ***Perf. 11***

2202 A1585 22c **multicolored** .55 .25
- P# block of 4, 5# 2.50 —
- Zip block of 4 2.25 —
- Pair with full vert. gutter btwn. —
- *a.* Tagging omitted *325.00*

BLACK HERITAGE SERIES

Sojourner Truth (c. 1797-1883), Human Rights Activist — A1586

Designed by Jerry Pinkney.

Printed by American Bank Note Co.

Plates of 200 in four panes of 50
PHOTOGRAVURE

1986, Feb. 4 **Tagged** ***Perf. 11***

2203 A1586 22c **multicolored** .55 .25
- P# block of 4, 6#+A 2.75 —
- Zip block of 4 2.25 —
- *a.* Tagging omitted —

REPUBLIC OF TEXAS, 150th ANNIV.

Texas State Flag and Silver Spur — A1587

Designed by Don Adair.

Printed by the American Bank Note Co.

Plates of 200 in four panes of 50.
PHOTOGRAVURE

1986, Mar. 2 **Tagged** ***Perf. 11***

2204 A1587 22c **dark blue, dark red & grayish black** .50 .25
- P# block of 4, 3#+A 2.50 —
- Zip block of 4 2.25 —
- *a.* Horiz. pair, imperf. vert. *600.00*
- *b.* Dark red omitted *1,750.*
- *c.* Dark blue omitted *5,000.*

FISH

Muskellunge — A1588

Atlantic Cod A1589

Largemouth Bass — A1590

Bluefin Tuna A1591

Catfish A1592

Designed by Chuck Ripper.

BOOKLET STAMPS
PHOTOGRAVURE

Perf. 10 Horiz. on 1 or 2 Sides

1986, Mar. 21		**Tagged**	
2205	A1588 22c **multicolored**	1.00	.25
2206	A1589 22c **multicolored**	1.00	.25
2207	A1590 22c **multicolored**	1.00	.25
2208	A1591 22c **multicolored**	1.00	.25
2209	A1592 22c **multicolored**	1.00	.25
a.	Bklt. pane of 5, #2205-2209	5.00	2.75

The magenta used to print this issue is extremely fugitive. Dangerous fakes purported to be magenta omitted exist. No genuine examples are known. Panes apparently lacking red must be certified, and examples presently with certificates should be recertified.

PUBLIC HOSPITALS

A1593

Designed by Uldis Purins.

Printed by the American Bank Note Co.

PHOTOGRAVURE
Plates of 200 in four panes of 50.

1986, Apr. 11	**Tagged**	***Perf. 11***	
2210	A1593 22c **multicolored**	.45	.25
	P# block of 4, 5#+A	2.00	—
	Zip block of 4	1.90	—
a.	Vert. pair, imperf. horiz.	*250.00*	
b.	Horiz. pair, imperf. vert.	*800.00*	

PERFORMING ARTS

Edward Kennedy "Duke" Ellington (1899-1974), Jazz Composer — A1594

Designed by Jim Sharpe.
Printed by the American Bank Note Co.

PHOTOGRAVURE
Plates of 200 in four panes of 50.

1986, Apr. 29	**Tagged**	***Perf. 11***	
2211	A1594 22c **multicolored**	.45	.25
	P# block of 4, 6#+A	2.50	—
	Zip block of 4	1.90	—
a.	Vert. pair, imperf. horiz.	*500.00*	

AMERIPEX '86 ISSUE

Miniature Sheets

A1599a

Presidents of
the United States: II
AMERIPEX 86
International
Stamp Show
Chicago, Illinois
May 22-June 1, 1986

A1599b

A1599c

Presidents — A1599d

Illustrations reduced.

No. 2216: a, George Washington. b, John Adams. c, Thomas Jefferson. d, James Madison. e, James Monroe. f, John Quincy Adams. g, Andrew Jackson. h, Martin Van Buren. i, William H. Harrison.

No. 2217: a, John Tyler. b, James Knox Polk. c, Zachary Taylor. d, Millard Fillmore. e, Franklin Pierce. f, James Buchanan. g, Abraham Lincoln. h, Andrew Johnson. i, Ulysses S. Grant.

No. 2218: a, Rutherford B. Hayes. b, James A. Garfield. c, Chester A. Arthur. d, Grover Cleveland. e, Benjamin Harrison. f, William McKinley. g, Theodore Roosevelt. h, William H. Taft. i, Woodrow Wilson.

No. 2219: a, Warren G. Harding. b, Calvin Coolidge. c, Herbert Hoover. d, Franklin Delano Roosevelt. e, White House. f, Harry S. Truman. g, Dwight D. Eisenhower. h, John F. Kennedy. i, Lyndon B. Johnson.

Designed by Jerry Dadds.

LITHOGRAPHED & ENGRAVED

1986, May 22		**Tagged**		*Perf. 11*
2216	A1599a	Pane of 9	6.50	4.00
a.-i.		22c, any single	.65	.40
j.		Blue (engr.) omitted	*1,800.*	
k.		Black inscription omitted	*1,000.*	
l.		Imperf.	*10,500.*	
m.		As "k," double impression of red	—	
n.		Blue omitted on b-c, e-f, i	—	
o.		Tagging omitted on a, d, g	*225.00*	
p.		Tagging omitted	—	
2217	A1599b	Pane of 9	6.50	4.00
a-i.		22c, any single	.65	.40
j.		Black inscription omitted	*1,500.*	
k.		Tagging omitted	*225.00*	
2218	A1599c	Pane of 9	6.50	4.00
a.-i.		22c, any single	.65	.40
j.		Brown (engr.) omitted	—	
k.		Black inscription omitted	*1,500.*	
l.		Tagging omitted	*400.00*	
2219	A1599d	Pane of 9	6.50	4.00
a.-i.		22c, any single	.65	.40
j.		Blackish blue (engr.) inscription omitted on a-b, d-e, g-h	*2,250.*	
k.		Tagging omitted on c, f, i	*2,750.*	
l.		Blackish blue (engr.) omitted on all stamps	—	
m.		Tagging omitted on a-b, d-e, g-h	—	
n.		Tagging omitted on a, b, and i	—	
o.		Tagging omitted on b-c, e-f, h-i	—	
		Nos. 2216-2219 (4)	26.00	16.00

Issued in conjunction with AMERIPEX '86 Intl. Philatelic Exhibition, Chicago, IL May 22-June 1. Pane size: 120x207mm (pane size varied).

ARCTIC EXPLORERS

Elisha Kent Kane — A1600

Adolphus W. Greely A1601

Vilhjalmur Stefansson A1602

Robert E. Peary, Matthew Henson A1603

Designed by Dennis Lyall.
Printed by the American Bank Note Company

PHOTOGRAVURE

Plates of 200 in four panes of 50.

1986, May 28		**Tagged**		*Perf. 11*
2220	A1600	22c **multicolored**	.65	.25
2221	A1601	22c **multicolored**	.65	.25
2222	A1602	22c **multicolored**	.65	.25
2223	A1603	22c **multicolored**	.65	.25
a.		Block of 4, #2220-2223	2.75	2.25
		P# block of 4, 5#+A	4.50	—
		Zip block of 4	3.00	—
b.		As "a," black omitted	*4,500.*	
c.		As "a," Nos. 2220, 2221 black omitted	*1,000.*	
d.		As "a," Nos. 2222, 2223 black omitted	*1,000.*	

STATUE OF LIBERTY, 100th ANNIVERSARY

A1604

Designed by Howard Paine.

ENGRAVED

Plates of 200 in four panes of 50.

1986, July 4		**Tagged**		*Perf. 11*
2224	A1604	22c **scarlet & dark blue**	.45	.25
		P# block of 4	2.25	—
		Zip block of 4	1.65	—
a.		Scarlet omitted	—	

On No. 2224a, virtually all of the dark blue also is omitted, so the error stamp should be collected as part of a transition strip. See France No. 2014.

Coil Plate No. Strips of 3
Beginning with No. 2123, coil plate no. strips of 3 usually sell at the level of strips of 5 minus

TRANSPORTATION ISSUE

Types of 1982-85 and

A1604a

A1604b

Designers: 1c, 2c, David Stone.

COIL STAMPS
ENGRAVED

1986-90		**Tagged**		*Perf. 10 Vert.*
2225	A1604a	1c **violet,** large block tagging, dull gum, *Nov. 26*	.25	.25
		Pair	.30	.50
		P# strip of 5, #1, 2	.55	
		P# single, #1, 2	—	.40
a.		Prephosphored uncoated paper with embedded tagging showing a mottled appearance (error), shiny gum	3.00	.25
		Pair	6.00	.50
		P# strip of 5, #3	35.00	
		P# single, #3	—	35.00
b.		Untagged, dull gum	.25	.25
		Pair	.35	.50
		P# strip of 5, #2-3	.60	
		P# single, #2-3	—	.45
		Shiny gum	.25	
		P# strip of 5, #3	.70	
		Low gloss gum	.25	
		P# strip of 5, #3	2.50	
c.		Imperf., pair	*1,750.*	
d.		As No. 2225, tagging omitted (error), P# single, #1		—
2226	A1604b	2c **black,** dull gum, *Mar. 6, 1987*	.25	.25
		Pair	.25	.50
		P# strip of 5, #1	.40	
		P# single, #1	—	.35
a.		Untagged, dull gum	.25	.25
		Pair	.50	.50
		P# strip of 5, #2	1.00	
		P# single, #2	—	.45
		Shiny gum	.25	
		P# strip of 5, #2	2.00	

REDUCED SIZE

2228	A1285	4c **reddish brown,** large block tagging, *Aug.*	.25	.25
		Pair	.50	.50
		P# strip of 5, #1	1.10	
		P# single, #1	—	.85
a.		Overall tagging, *1990*	.70	.25
		Pair	1.40	.50
		P# strip of 5, #1	6.00	
		P# single, #1	—	5.75
b.		Imperf., pair	175.00	

Earliest known usage of No. 2228: Aug. 15, 1986.

On No. 2228 "Stagecoach 1890s" is 17¾mm long; on No. 1898A, 19½mm long.

Untagged

2231	A1511	8.3c **green** (Bureau precancel, Blk. Rt./CAR-RT/SORT), *Aug. 29*	.65	.25
		Pair	1.30	.50
		P# strip of 5, #1	3.75	
		P# strip of 5, #2	4.50	
		P# single, #1	—	3.00
		P# single, #2	—	4.50
		Nos. 2225-2231 (4)	1.40	1.00

On No. 2231 "Ambulance 1860s" is 18mm long; on No. 2128, 18⅓mm long.

Joint lines do not appear on Nos. 2225-2231.

AMERICAN FOLK ART SERIES

Navajo Art

A1605

A1606

A1607

A1608

Designed by Derry Noyes.

LITHOGRAPHED & ENGRAVED
Plates of 200 in four panes of 50.

1986, Sept. 4	**Tagged**	***Perf. 11***	
2235 A1605 22c **multicolored**		.80	.25
a. Black (engr.) omitted		65.00	
2236 A1606 22c **multicolored**		.80	.25
a. Black (engr.) omitted		65.00	
2237 A1607 22c **multicolored**		.80	.25
a. Black (engr.) omitted		65.00	
2238 A1608 22c **multicolored**		.80	.25
a. Black (engr.) omitted		65.00	
b. Block of 4, #2235-2238		3.25	2.25
P# block of 4, 5#		4.25	—
Zip block of 4		3.50	—
c. As "b," black (engr.) omitted		*275.00*	

LITERARY ARTS SERIES

T.S. Eliot (1888-1965), Poet — A1609

Designed by Bradbury Thompson.

ENGRAVED
Plates of 200 in four panes of 50.

1986, Sept. 26	**Tagged**	***Perf. 11***	
2239 A1609 22c **copper red**		.45	.25
P# block of 4		2.25	—
Zip block of 4		2.00	—
a. Tagging omitted			—

AMERICAN FOLK ART SERIES
Woodcarved Figurines

A1610

A1611

A1612 A1613

Designed by Bradbury Thompson.
Printed by the American Bank Note Company

PHOTOGRAVURE
Plates of 200 in four panes of 50.

1986, Oct. 1	**Tagged**	***Perf. 11***	
2240 A1610 22c **multicolored**		.50	.25
2241 A1611 22c **multicolored**		.50	.25
2242 A1612 22c **multicolored**		.50	.25
2243 A1613 22c **multicolored**		.50	.25
a. Block of 4, #2240-2243		2.00	1.50
P# block of 4, 5#+A		3.75	—
Zip block of 4		2.25	—
b. As "a," imperf. vert.		*750.00*	

CHRISTMAS

Madonna, National Gallery, by Perugino (c. 1450-1513) A1614

Village Scene A1615

Designed by Bradbury Thompson (#2244) & Dolli Tingle (#2245).

PHOTOGRAVURE
Panes of 100

1986, Oct. 24	**Tagged**	***Perf. 11***	
2244 A1614 22c **multicolored**		.45	.25
P# block of 4, 5#		2.10	—
Zip block of 4		1.90	—
a. Imperf., pair		*400.00*	
2245 A1615 22c **multicolored**		.45	.25
P# block of 4, 6#		2.10	—
Zip block of 4		1.90	—

MICHIGAN STATEHOOD, 150th ANNIV.

White Pine — A1616

Designed by Robert Wilbert.

PHOTOGRAVURE
Plates of 200 in four panes of 50.

1987, Jan. 26	**Tagged**	***Perf. 11***	
2246 A1616 22c **multicolored**		.50	.25
P# block of 4, 5#		2.25	—
Zip block of 4		2.10	—
Pair with full vert. gutter between		—	

PAN AMERICAN GAMES
Indianapolis, Aug. 7-25

Runner in Full Stride A1617

Designed by Lon Busch.

PHOTOGRAVURE
Plates of 200 in four panes of 50.

1987, Jan. 29	**Tagged**	***Perf. 11***	
2247 A1617 22c **multicolored**		.45	.25
P# block of 4, 5#		2.10	—
Zip block of 4		1.90	—
a. Silver omitted		*550.00*	

No. 2247a is valued in the grade of fine.

LOVE ISSUE

A1618

Designed by John Alcorn.

PHOTOGRAVURE
Panes of 100

1987, Jan. 30	**Tagged**	***Perf. 11½x11***	
2248 A1618 22c **multicolored**		.45	.25
P# block of 4, 5#		2.10	—
Zip block of 4		1.90	—
Pair with full horiz. gutter between		*125.00*	

BLACK HERITAGE SERIES

Jean Baptiste Pointe du Sable (c. 1750-1818), Pioneer Trader, Founder of Chicago — A1619

Designed by Thomas Blackshear.

PHOTOGRAVURE
Plates of 200 in four panes of 50.

1987, Feb. 20	**Tagged**	***Perf. 11***	
2249 A1619 22c **multicolored**		.40	.25
P# block of 4, 5#		2.25	—
Zip block of 4		2.00	—
a. Tagging omitted		*20.00*	

PERFORMING ARTS SERIES

Enrico Caruso (1873-1921), Opera Tenor — A1620

Designed by Jim Sharpe.
Printed by American Bank Note Co.

PHOTOGRAVURE

Plates of 200 in four panes of 50.

1987, Feb. 27 **Tagged** ***Perf. 11***

2250 A1620 22c **multicolored** .45 .25
P# block of 4, 4#+A 2.00 —
Zip block of 4 1.90 —
a. Black omitted *3,500.*
b. Tagging omitted —

GIRL SCOUTS, 75TH ANNIVERSARY

Fourteen Achievement Badges — A1621

Designed by Richard Sheaff.

LITHOGRAPHED & ENGRAVED

Plates of 200 in four panes of 50.

1987, Mar. 12 **Tagged** ***Perf. 11***

2251 A1621 22c **multicolored** .45 .25
P# block of 4, 6# 2.25 —
Zip block of 4 1.90 —
a. All litho. colors omitted *1,600.*
b. Red & black (engr.) omitted *1,500.*

All known examples of No. 2251a have been expertized and certificate must accompany purchase. The unique pane of No. 2251b has been expertized and a certificate exists for the pane of 50.

Coil Plate No. Strips of 3

Beginning with No. 2123, coil plate no. strips of 3 usually sell at the level of strips of 5 minus the face value of two stamps.

TRANSPORTATION ISSUE

A1622

A1623

A1624

A1625

A1626

A1627

A1628

A1629

A1630

A1631

A1632

A1633

A1634

A1635

A1636

Designers: 3c, 7.6c, 13.2c, 15c, Richard Schlecht. 5c, 5.3c, 16.7c, Lou Nolan. 8.4c, 20.5c, 24.1c, Christopher Calle. 10c, William H. Bond. 13c, Joe Brockert. 17.5c, Tom Broad. 20c, Dan Romano. 21c, David Stone.

COIL STAMPS

ENGRAVED

1987-95 ***Perf. 10 Vert.***

Tagged, Untagged (5.3c, 7.6c, 8.4c, 13c, 13.2c, 16.7c, 20.5c, 21c, 24.1c)

2252 A1622 3c **claret,** dull gum, *Feb. 29, 1988* .25 .25
Pair .35 .35
P# strip of 5, #1 .85
P# single, #1 — .60
a. Untagged, dull gum .25 .25
P# strip of 5, #2-3 1.35
P# single, #2 — 1.10
P# single, #3 — .90
Shiny gum, *1995* .25
P# strip of 5, #3 1.00
P# strip of 5, #5 7.00
P# strip of 5, #6 1.00
P# single, #3 1.00
P# single, #5 — 6.00
P# single, #6 — 1.10
Low gloss gum .40
P# strip of 5, #5 7.50
P# single, #5 6.00
b. As "a," imperf pair, shiny gum *1,350.*

The plate #5 on No. 2252a with low gloss gum is smaller than the #5 on No. 2252a with shiny gum. The smaller plate #5 represents a different printing sleeve (plate).

2253 A1623 5c **black,** *Sept. 25* .25 .25
Pair .50 .50
P# strip of 5, #1 .90
P# single, #1 — .65

2254 A1624 5.3c **black** (Bureau precancel "Nonprofit Carrier Route Sort" in red), *Sept. 16, 1988* .25 .25
Pair .50 .50
P# strip of 5, #1 1.40
P# single, #1 — .90

2255 A1625 7.6c **brown** (Bureau precancel "Nonprofit" in red), *Aug. 30, 1988* .25 .25
Pair .50 .50
P# strip of 5, #1-2 1.75
P# strip of 5, #3 3.25
P# single, #1-2 — 1.50
P# single, #3 — 4.00

2256 A1626 8.4c **deep claret** (Bureau precancel "Nonprofit" in red), *Aug. 12, 1988* .25 .25
Pair .50 .50
P# strip of 5, #1-2 1.75
P# strip of 5, #3 5.25
P# single, #1-2 — 1.00
P# single, #3 — 5.00
a. Imperf., pair *350.00*

2257 A1627 10c **blue,** large block tagging, dull gum, *Apr. 11* .40 .25
Pair .80 .50
P# strip of 5, #1 1.75
P# single, #1 — 1.00
a. Overall tagging, dull gum, *1993* 1.50 .25
Pair 3.00 .50
P# strip of 5, #1 9.00
P# single, #1 — 8.00
Shiny gum, *1994* .25 .25
Pair .50 .50
P# strip of 5, #4 3.25
P# single, #4 — 2.50
b. Prephosphored uncoated paper with embedded tagging showing a mottled appearance, shiny gum .25 .25
Pair .50 .50
P# strip of 5, #1, 2 3.00
P# strip of 5, #3, 4 3.75
P# single, #1, 2 — 2.90
P# single, #3, 4 — 2.90
c. Prephosphored coated paper with surface tagging showing a solid appearance, low gloss gum .25 .25
Pair .50 .50
P# strip of 5, #5 4.50
P# single, #5 — 4.00
d. Tagging omitted, shiny gum *15.00*
e. Imperf, pair, large block tagging *1,000.*

2258 A1628 13c **black** (Bureau precancel "Presorted First-Class" in red), *Oct. 29, 1988* .65 .25
Pair 1.30 .50
P# strip of 5, #1 3.50
P# single, #1 — 2.25

2259 A1629 13.2c **slate green** (Bureau precancel "Bulk Rate" in red), *July 19, 1988* .25 .25
Pair .50 .50
P# strip of 5, #1-2 2.50
P# single, #1-2 — 1.60
a. Imperf., pair 75.00

2260 A1630 15c **violet,** large block tagging, *July 12, 1988* .30 .25
Pair .60 .50
P# strip of 5, #1 2.00
P# strip of 5, #2 2.25
P# single, #1 — 1.00
P# single, #2 — 1.75
a. Overall tagging, *1990* .40 .30
Pair .80 .60
P# strip of 5, #2 3.00
P# single, #2 — 2.25
b. Tagging omitted *4.25*
c. As "a," imperf. pair *500.00*

2261 A1631 16.7c **rose** (Bureau precancel "Bulk Rate " in black), *July 7, 1988* .30 .30
Pair .60 .60
P# strip of 5, #1 2.25
P# strip of 5, #2 2.50
P# single, #1 — 1.60
P# single, #2 — 2.50
a. Imperf., pair *125.00*

All known examples of No. 2261a are miscut top to bottom.

2262 A1632 17.5c **dark violet,** *Sept. 25* .75 .25
Pair 1.50 .50
P# strip of 5, #1 3.50
P# single, #1 — 3.25
a. Untagged (Bureau Precancel "ZIP + 4 Presort" in red) .65 .30
Pair 1.30 .60
P# strip of 5, #1 4.00
P# single, #1 — 2.75
b. Imperf., pair *1,250.*

2263 A1633 20c **blue violet,** large block tagging, *Oct. 28, 1988* .35 .25
Pair .70 .50
P# strip of 5, #1-2 3.00
P# single, #1-2 — 1.75
a. Imperf., pair 50.00
b. Overall tagging, *1990* 1.00 .25
Pair 2.00 .50
P# strip of 5, #2 7.50
P# single, #2 — 5.75

2264 A1634 20.5c **rose** (Bureau precancel "ZIP + 4 Presort" in black), *Sept. 28, 1988* .75 .40
Pair 1.50 .80
P# strip of 5, #1 4.25
P# single, #1 — 3.00

2265 A1635 21c **olive green** (Bureau precancel "Presorted First-Class" in red), *Aug. 16, 1988* .50 .40
Pair 1.00 .80
P# strip of 5, #1-2 3.00
P# single, #1-2 — 2.50
a. Imperf., pair 35.00

2266 A1636 24.1c **deep ultra** (Bureau precancel ZIP + 4 in red), *Oct. 26, 1988* .80 .45
Pair 1.60 .90
P# strip of 5, #1 3.75
P# single, #1 — 2.25
Nos. 2252-2266 (15) 6.30 4.30

5.3c, 7.6c, 8.4c, 13.2c, 16.7c, 20.5c, 21c and 24.1c only available precanceled.

See Nos. 1897-1908, 2123-2136, 2225-2231, 2451-2468.

SPECIAL OCCASIONS

A1637

A1638

A1639

A1640

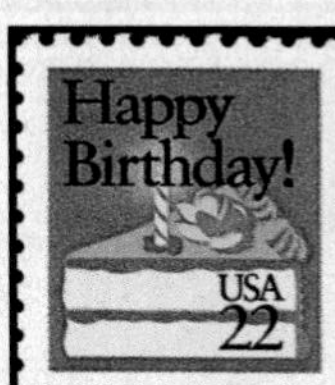

A1641

A1642

A1643

A1644

Designed by Oren Sherman.

BOOKLET STAMPS
PHOTOGRAVURE

1987, Apr. 20 Tagged ***Perf. 10 on 1, 2 or 3 Sides***

2267	A1637	22c **multicolored**	.75	.25
2268	A1638	22c **multicolored**	.90	.25
2269	A1639	22c **multicolored**	.90	.25
2270	A1640	22c **multicolored**	.90	.25
2271	A1641	22c **multicolored**	.90	.25
2272	A1642	22c **multicolored**	.75	.25
2273	A1643	22c **multicolored**	1.50	.25
2274	A1644	22c **multicolored**	.90	.25
a.		Bklt. pane of 10 (#2268-2271, 2273-2274, 2 each #2267, 2272)	9.00	5.00
		Nos. 2267-2274 (8)	7.50	2.00

UNITED WAY, 100th ANNIV.

Six Profiles
A1645

Designed by Jerry Pinkney.

LITHOGRAPHED & ENGRAVED
Plates of 200 in four panes of 50.

1987, Apr. 28 Tagged ***Perf. 11***

2275	A1645	22c **multicolored**	.45	.25
		P# block of 4, 6#	2.00	—
		Zip block of 4	1.90	—

A1646

A1647

A1648

A1649

Pheasant — A1649a

Grosbeak — A1649b

Owl — A1649c

Honeybee — A1649d

Designs: Nos. 2276, 2278, 2280, Peter Cocci. Nos. 2277, 2279, 2282, Robert McCall. Nos. 2281, 2283-2285, Chuck Ripper.

PHOTOGRAVURE (Nos. 2276-2279)
Panes of 100

1987-88 Tagged ***Perf. 11***

2276	A1646	22c **multicolored,** *May 9*	.45	.25
		P# block of 4, 4#	2.00	—
		Zip block of 4	1.90	—
a.		Booklet pane of 20, *Nov. 30*	9.00	—
b.		As "a," vert. pair, imperf. btwn.	*1,450.*	
c.		As "a," miscut and inserted upside down into booklet cover, imperf between stamps and right selvage	—	
d.		Yellow omitted	—	

All documented examples of No. 2276d show significant misregistration of the red ink.

2277	A1647	(25c) **multi,** *Mar. 22, 1988*	.50	.25
		P# block of 4, 4#	2.25	—
		Zip block of 4	2.10	—
a.		Tagging omitted	—	
2278	A1648	25c **multi,** *May 6, 1988*	.50	.25
		P# block of 4, 4#	2.25	—
		Zip block of 4	2.10	—
		Pair with full vert. gutter between	*125.00*	
a.		Tagging omitted	—	
		Nos. 2276-2278 (3)	1.45	.75

COIL STAMPS

Perf. 10 Vert.

2279	A1647	(25c) **multi,** *Mar. 22, 1988*	.50	.25
		Pair	1.00	.50
		P# strip of 5, #1111	3.00	
		P# strip of 5, #1211	3.25	
		P# strip of 5, #1222	3.00	
		P# strip of 5, #2222	3.25	
		P# single, #1111	—	.50
		P# single, #1211	—	1.10
		P# single, #1222	—	.90
		P# single, #2222	—	3.25
a.		Imperf., pair	60.00	—
b.		Tagging omitted		—

Engr.

2280	A1649	25c **multi,** large block tagging, *May 20, 1988*	.50	.25
		Pair	1.00	.50
		P# strip of 5, #1	3.50	
		P# strip of 5, #2-5	3.00	
		P# strip of 5, #7	3.50	
		P# strip of 5, #8	3.00	
		P# strip of 5, #9	6.00	
		P# single, #1	—	2.50
		P# single, #2-5	—	.75
		P# single, #7	—	1.75
		P# single, #8	—	.65
		P# single, #9	—	2.00
a.		Prephosphored uncoated paper with embedded tagging showing a mottled appearance *Feb. 14, 1989*	.45	.25
		P# strip of 5, #1	17.50	
		P# strip of 5, #2, 3	3.00	
		P# strip of 5, #5	5.25	
		P# strip of 5, #6	5.75	
		P# strip of 5, #7-11, 13-14	3.00	
		P# strip of 5, #15	4.25	
		P# single, #1	—	15.00
		P# single, #2	—	.60
		P# single, #3	—	.60
		P# single, #5	—	1.10
		P# single, #6	—	5.00
		P# single, #7-11, 13-14	—	.60
		P# single, #15	—	2.00
b.		Imperf., pair, large block tagging	25.00	
c.		Imperf., pair, prephosphored uncoated paper with embedded tagging showing a mottled appearance	10.00	
d.		Tagging omitted	*5.00*	
e.		Black trees	*90.00*	—
		P# strip of 5, #4, 5, 9	*700.00*	
f.		Pair, imperf. between	*375.00*	

Litho. & Engr.

2281	A1649d	25c **multi,** small block tagging *Sept. 2, 1988*	.50	.25
		Pair	1.00	.50
		P# strip of 5, #1	3.50	
		P# single, #1	—	.50
a.		As No. 2281, imperf. pair	45.00	
c.		Black (litho. - "25 USA") omitted	*500.00*	
d.		Pair, imperf. between	*600.00*	
e.		Yellow (litho.) omitted	*700.00*	
f.		Large block tagging	.45	.25
		Pair	.90	
		P# strip of 5, #1	3.50	
		P# strip of 5, #2	3.25	
		P# single, #1	—	.60
		P# single, #2	—	.50
g.		As "f," imperf, pair	45.00	
h.		As "f," tagging omitted	85.00	—
i.		As "f," black (engr. - details on bee) omitted	45.00	—
		Nos. 2279-2281 (3)	1.50	.75

No. 2281 from plate #1 is known with three types of "1" on the plate-numbered stamps. The original tall "1" was later shortened manually by removing the top of the "1," including the serif, so it would not penetrate the design. A short "1" with top serif also exists. Value of P# strip of 5 with tall "1," $17.50.

Beware of stamps with traces of the litho. black that are offered as No. 2281c.

Vertical pairs or blocks of No. 2281 and imperfs. with the engr. black missing are from printer's waste.

BOOKLET STAMPS

Printed by American Bank Note Co. (#2283)

PHOTOGRAVURE

Perf. 10 on 2 or 3 Sides

2282	A1647	(25c) **multi,** *Mar. 22, 1988*	.50	.25
a.		Booklet pane of 10	6.50	3.50
		Scored perforations	6.50	—

Perf. 11 on 2 or 3 Sides

2283	A1649a	25c **multi,** *Apr. 29, 1988*	.50	.25
a.		Booklet pane of 10	6.00	3.50
b.		25c multicolored, red removed from sky	4.50	.25
c.		As "b," bklt. pane of 10	45.00	—
d.		Vert. pair, imperf. btwn.	*275.00*	

Imperf. panes exist from printers waste, and a large number exist. No. 2283d resulted from a foldover. Non-foldover pairs and multiples are printer's waste.

Perf. 10 on 2 or 3 Sides

2284	A1649b	25c **multi,** *May 28, 1988*	.50	.25
2285	A1649c	25c **multi,** *May 28, 1988*	.50	.25
b.		Bklt. pane of 10, 5 each #2284-2285	5.00	3.50
d.		Pair, Nos. 2284-2285	1.10	.50
e.		As "d," tagging omitted	14.00	
f.		As "b," tagging omitted	*110.00*	

2285A	A1648	25c	**multi,** *July 5, 1988*	.50	.25
c.			Booklet pane of 6	3.00	2.00
			Nos. 2282-2285A (5)	2.50	1.25

NORTH AMERICAN WILDLIFE

Illustration reduced.

Designed by Chuck Ripper.

PHOTOGRAVURE

Plates of 200 in four panes of 50.

1987, June 13 **Tagged** ***Perf. 11***

2286	A1650	22c	Barn swallow	1.00	.50
2287	A1651	22c	Monarch butterfly	1.00	.50
2288	A1652	22c	Bighorn sheep	1.00	.50
2289	A1653	22c	Broad-tailed hummingbird	1.00	.50
2290	A1654	22c	Cottontail	1.00	.50
2291	A1655	22c	Osprey	1.00	.50
2292	A1656	22c	Mountain lion	1.00	.50
2293	A1657	22c	Luna moth	1.00	.50
2294	A1658	22c	Mule deer	1.00	.50
2295	A1659	22c	Gray squirrel	1.00	.50
2296	A1660	22c	Armadillo	1.00	.50
2297	A1661	22c	Eastern chipmunk	1.00	.50
2298	A1662	22c	Moose	1.00	.50
2299	A1663	22c	Black bear	1.00	.50
2300	A1664	22c	Tiger swallowtail	1.00	.50
2301	A1665	22c	Bobwhite	1.00	.50
2302	A1666	22c	Ringtail	1.00	.50
2303	A1667	22c	Red-winged blackbird	1.00	.50
2304	A1668	22c	American lobster	1.00	.50
2305	A1669	22c	Black-tailed jack rabbit	1.00	.50
2306	A1670	22c	Scarlet tanager	1.00	.50
2307	A1671	22c	Woodchuck	1.00	.50
2308	A1672	22c	Roseate spoonbill	1.00	.50
2309	A1673	22c	Bald eagle	1.00	.50
2310	A1674	22c	Alaskan brown bear	1.00	.50
2311	A1675	22c	Iiwi	1.00	.50
2312	A1676	22c	Badger	1.00	.50
2313	A1677	22c	Pronghorn	1.00	.50
2314	A1678	22c	River otter	1.00	.50
2315	A1679	22c	Ladybug	1.00	.50
2316	A1680	22c	Beaver	1.00	.50
2317	A1681	22c	White-tailed deer	1.00	.50
2318	A1682	22c	Blue jay	1.00	.50
2319	A1683	22c	Pika	1.00	.50
2320	A1684	22c	Bison	1.00	.50
2321	A1685	22c	Snowy egret	1.00	.50
2322	A1686	22c	Gray wolf	1.00	.50
2323	A1687	22c	Mountain goat	1.00	.50
2324	A1688	22c	Deer mouse	1.00	.50
2325	A1689	22c	Black-tailed prairie dog	1.00	.50
2326	A1690	22c	Box turtle	1.00	.50
2327	A1691	22c	Wolverine	1.00	.50
2328	A1692	22c	American elk	1.00	.50
2329	A1693	22c	California sea lion	1.00	.50
2330	A1694	22c	Mockingbird	1.00	.50
2331	A1695	22c	Raccoon	1.00	.50
2332	A1696	22c	Bobcat	1.00	.50
2333	A1697	22c	Black-footed ferret	1.00	.50
2334	A1698	22c	Canada goose	1.00	.50
2335	A1699	22c	Red fox	1.00	.50
a.			Pane of 50, #2286-2335	50.00	35.00
c.			Pane of 50, tagging omitted	—	
2286b-2335b			Any single, red omitted	*2,000.*	

NORTH AMERICAN WILDLIFE ISSUE — A1650-A1699

RATIFICATION OF THE CONSTITUTION BICENTENNIAL

A1700

A1701

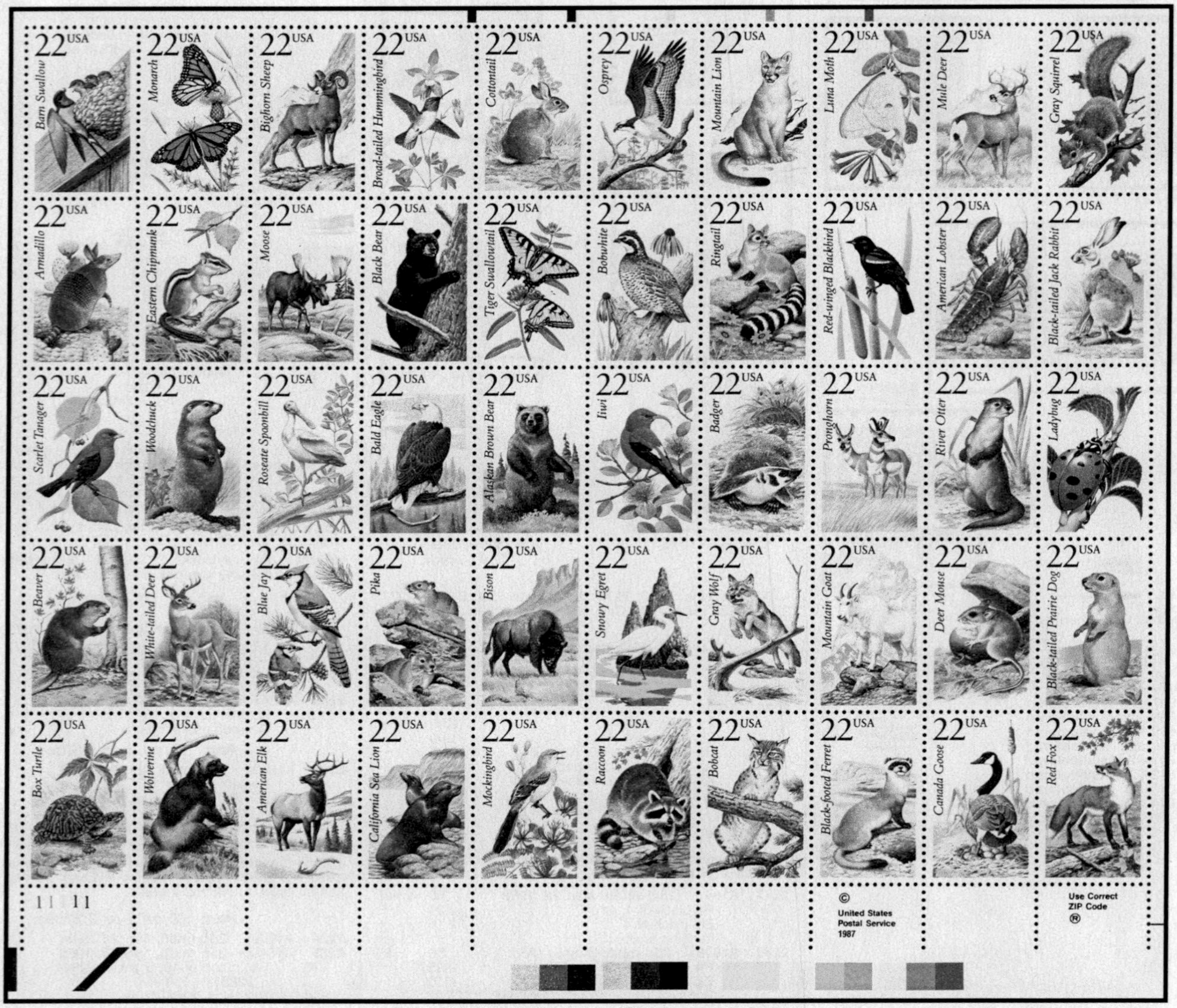

A1702

A1703

A1704

A1705

A1706

A1707

A1708

A1709

A1710

A1711

A1712

Designers: Nos. 2336-2337, 2341 Richard Sheaff. No. 2338, Jim Lamb. No. 2339, Greg Harlin. No. 2340, Christopher Calle. No. 2342, Stephen Hustvedt. Nos. 2343, 2347, Bob Timberlake. No. 2344, Thomas Szumowski. No. 2345, Pierre Mion. No. 2346, Bradbury Thompson. No. 2348, Robert Brangwynne.

Printed by the Bureau of Engraving & Printing, J.W. Fergusson and Sons (Nos. 2337, 2338), American Bank Note Co. (Nos. 2339, 2343-2344, 2347).

LITHOGRAPHED & ENGRAVED, PHOTOGRAVURE (#2337-2339, 2343-2344, 2347), ENGRAVED (#2341).

Plates of 200 in four panes of 50.

1987-90 Tagged *Perf. 11*

2336	A1700 22c **multi,** *July 4*	.55	.25
	P# block of 4, 5#	2.50	—
	Zip block of 4	2.40	—
2337	A1701 22c **multi,** *Aug. 26*	.55	.25
	P# block of 4, 5#+A	2.50	—
	Zip block of 4	2.40	—
2338	A1702 22c **multi,** *Sept. 11*	.55	.25
	P# block of 4, 5#+A	2.50	—
	Zip block of 4	2.40	—
a.	Black (engr.) omitted	*2,750.*	
2339	A1703 22c **multi,** *Jan. 6, 1988*	.55	.25
	P# block of 4, 5#+A	2.50	—
	Zip block of 4	2.40	—
2340	A1704 22c **multi,** *Jan. 9, 1988*	.55	.25
	P# block of 4, 5#	2.50	—
	Zip block of 4	2.40	—
2341	A1705 22c **dark blue & dark red,** *Feb. 6, 1988*	.55	.25
	P# block of 4, 1#	2.50	—
	Zip block of 4	2.40	—
2342	A1706 22c **multi,** *Feb. 15, 1988*	.55	.25
	P# block of 4, 6#	2.50	—
	Zip block of 4	2.40	—
2343	A1707 25c **multi,** *May 23, 1988*	.55	.25
	P# block of 4, 5#+A	2.50	—
	Zip block of 4	2.40	—
a.	Strip of 3, vert. imperf btwn.	*12,500.*	
b.	Red missing (PS)	—	
2344	A1708 25c **multi,** *June 21, 1988*	.55	.25
	P# block of 4, 4#+A	2.50	—
	Zip block of 4	2.40	—
a.	Red missing (PS)	—	
2345	A1709 25c **multi,** *June 25, 1988*	.55	.25
	P# block of 4, 5#	2.50	—
	Zip block of 4	2.40	—
2346	A1710 25c **multi,** *July 26, 1988*	.55	.25
	P# block of 4, 5#	2.50	—
	Zip block of 4	2.40	—
2347	A1711 25c **multi,** *Aug. 22, 1989*	.55	.25
	P# block of 4, 5#+A	2.50	—
	Zip block of 4	2.40	—
2348	A1712 25c **multi,** *May 29, 1990*	.55	.25
	P# block of 4, 7#	2.50	—
	Zip block of 4	2.40	—
	Nos. 2336-2348 (13)	7.15	3.25

No. 2343b resulted either from a shifting of all colors or from a shift of both the perforations and the cutting of the pane.

US-MOROCCO DIPLOMATIC RELATIONS, 200th ANNIV.

Arabesque, Dar Batha Palace Door, Fez — A1713

Designed by Howard Paine.

LITHOGRAPHED & ENGRAVED

Plates of 200 in four panes of 50.

1987, July 17 Tagged *Perf. 11*

2349	A1713 22c **scarlet & black**	.50	.25
	P# block of 4, 2#	2.10	—
	Zip block of 4	2.00	—
a.	Black (engr.) omitted	*180.00*	

See Morocco No. 642.

LITERARY ARTS SERIES

William Faulkner (1897-1962), Novelist — A1714

Designed by Bradbury Thompson.

ENGRAVED

Plates of 200 in four panes of 50

1987, Aug. 3 Tagged *Perf. 11*

2350	A1714 22c **bright green**	.50	.25
	P# block of 4	2.50	—
	Zip block of 4	2.25	—

Used untagged imperfs exist from printer's waste.

AMERICAN FOLK ART SERIES
Lacemaking

A1715

A1716

A1717

A1718

Designed by Libby Thiel.

LITHOGRAPHED & ENGRAVED
Plates of 160 in four panes of 40.

1987, Aug. 14	**Tagged**	***Perf. 11***	
2351 A1715 22c **ultra & white**		.45	.25
2352 A1716 22c **ultra & white**		.45	.25
2353 A1717 22c **ultra & white**		.45	.25
2354 A1718 22c **ultra & white**		.45	.25
a. Block of 4, #2351-2354		1.90	1.90
P# block of 4, 4#		3.25	—
Zip block of 4		2.00	—
b. As "a," white omitted		*350.00*	
c. Any single stamp, white omitted		*90.00*	

DRAFTING OF THE CONSTITUTION BICENTENNIAL
Excerpts from the Preamble

The Bicentennial of the Constitution of the United States of America 1787-1987 USA 22

A1719

We the people of the United States, in order to form a more perfect Union... Preamble, U.S. Constitution USA 22

A1720

Establish justice, insure domestic tranquility, provide for the common defense, promote the general welfare... Preamble, U.S. Constitution USA 22

A1721

And secure the blessings of liberty to ourselves and our posterity... Preamble, U.S. Constitution USA 22

A1722

Do ordain and establish this Constitution for the United States of America. Preamble, U.S. Constitution USA 22

A1723

Designed by Bradbury Thompson.

BOOKLET STAMPS
PHOTOGRAVURE
Perf. 10 Horiz. on 1 or 2 Sides

1987, Aug. 28	**Tagged**	
2355 A1719 22c **multicolored**	.75	.25
a. Grayish green (background) omitted	*400.00*	
2356 A1720 22c **multicolored**	.75	.25
a. Grayish green (background) omitted	*400.00*	
2357 A1721 22c **multicolored**	.75	.25
a. Grayish green (background) omitted	*400.00*	
2358 A1722 22c **multicolored**	.75	.25
a. Grayish green (background) omitted	*400.00*	
2359 A1723 22c **multicolored**	.75	.25
a. Bklt. pane of 5, #2355-2359	3.75	2.25
b. Grayish green (background) omitted	*400.00*	

SIGNING OF THE CONSTITUTION

A1724

Designed by Howard Koslow.

LITHOGRAPHED & ENGRAVED
Plates of 200 in four panes of 50.

1987, Sept. 17	**Tagged**	***Perf. 11***	
2360 A1724 22c **multicolored**		.55	.25
P# block of 4, 6#		2.75	—
Zip block of 4		2.25	—

CERTIFIED PUBLIC ACCOUNTING

A1725

Designed by Lou Nolan.

LITHOGRAPHED & ENGRAVED
Plates of 200 in four panes of 50.

1987, Sept. 21	**Tagged**	***Perf. 11***	
2361 A1725 22c **multicolored**		.70	.25
P# block of 4, 5#		3.50	—
Zip block of 4		3.00	—
a. Black (engr.) omitted		*425.00*	

LOCOMOTIVES

Stourbridge Lion, 1829
A1726

Best Friend of Charleston, 1830
A1727

John Bull, 1831
A1728

Brother Jonathan, 1832
A1729

Gowan & Marx, 1839
A1730

Designed by Richard Leech.

BOOKLET STAMPS
LITHOGRAPHED & ENGRAVED
Perf. 10 Horiz. on 1 or 2 Sides

1987, Oct. 1	**Tagged**	
2362 A1726 22c **multicolored**	.50	.25
a. Red (litho.) omitted		—
2363 A1727 22c **multicolored**	.50	.25
a. Red (litho.) omitted		—
2364 A1728 22c **multicolored**	.50	.25
a. Red (litho.) omitted		—
2365 A1729 22c **multicolored**	.50	.25
a. Red omitted	*1,000.*	*250.00*
2366 A1730 22c **multicolored**	.50	.25
a. Bklt. pane of 5, #2362-2366	2.50	2.00
b. As No. 2366, black (engr.) omitted (single)	—	
c. As No. 2366, blue omitted (single)		—

CHRISTMAS

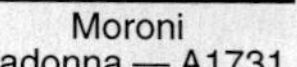
Moroni Madonna — A1731

Christmas Ornaments — A1732

Designed by Bradbury Thompson (No. 2367) and Jim Dean (No. 2368).

PHOTOGRAVURE
Plates of 800 in eight panes of 100.

1987, Oct. 23	**Tagged**	***Perf. 11***	
2367 A1731 22c **multicolored**		.45	.25
P# block of 4, 6#		2.25	—
Zip block of 4		1.90	—
2368 A1732 22c **multicolored**		.45	.25
P# block of 4, 6#		2.10	—
Zip block of 4		1.90	—
Pair with full vert. gutter between		—	

1988 WINTER OLYMPICS, CALGARY

Skiing — A1733

Designed by Bart Forbes.

Printed by the American Bank Note Company

PHOTOGRAVURE
Plates of 200 in four panes of 50.

1988, Jan. 10	**Tagged**	***Perf. 11***	
2369 A1733 22c **multicolored**		.50	.25
P# block of 4, 4#+A		3.00	—
Zip block of 4		2.10	—

AUSTRALIA BICENTENNIAL

Caricature of an Australian Koala and an American Bald Eagle — A1734

Designed by Roland Harvey.

PHOTOGRAVURE

Plates of 160 in four panes of 40.

1988, Jan. 26 **Tagged** *Perf. 11*

2370	A1734 22c **multicolored**	.45	.25
	P# block of 4, 5#	2.10	—
	Zip block of 4	1.90	—

See Australia No. 1052.

BLACK HERITAGE SERIES

James Weldon Johnson (1871-1938), Author and Lyricist — A1735

Designed by Thomas Blackshear.

Printed by the American Bank Note Co.

PHOTOGRAVURE

Plates of 200 in four panes of 50.

1988, Feb. 2 **Tagged** *Perf. 11*

2371	A1735 22c **multicolored**	.50	.25
	P# block of 4, 5#+A	2.60	—
	Zip block of 4	2.10	—
a.	Tagging omitted		—

CATS

Siamese and Exotic Shorthair A1736

Abyssinian and Himalayan A1737

Maine Coon and Burmese A1738

American Shorthair and Persian A1739

Designed by John Dawson.

Printed by the American Bank Note Co.

PHOTOGRAVURE

Plates of 160 in four panes of 40.

1988, Feb. 5 **Tagged** *Perf. 11*

2372	A1736 22c **multicolored**	.70	.25
2373	A1737 22c **multicolored**	.70	.25
2374	A1738 22c **multicolored**	.70	.25
2375	A1739 22c **multicolored**	.70	.25
a.	Block of 4, #2372-2375	2.80	1.90
	P# block of 4, 5#+A	4.00	—
	Zip block of 4	3.00	—

AMERICAN SPORTS

Knute Rockne (1888-1931), Notre Dame football coach.

A1740

Designed by Peter Cocci and Thomas Hipschen.

LITHOGRAPHED & ENGRAVED

Plates of 200 in four panes of 50.

1988, Mar. 9 **Tagged** *Perf. 11*

2376	A1740 22c **multicolored**	.50	.25
	P# block of 4, 7#	2.60	—
	Zip block of 4	2.10	—

AMERICAN SPORTS

Francis Ouimet (1893-1967), 1st amateur golfer to win the US Open championship.

A1741

Designed by M. Gregory Rudd.
Printed by the American Bank Note Co.

PHOTOGRAVURE

Plates of 200 in four panes of 50.

1988, June 13 **Tagged** *Perf. 11*

2377	A1741 25c **multicolored**	.60	.25
	P# block of 4, 5#+A	3.00	—
	Zip block of 4	2.50	—

LOVE ISSUE (Roses)

A1742

A1743

Designed by Richard Sheaff.

PHOTOGRAVURE

Plates of 400 in four panes of 100 (25c).

Plates of 200 in four panes of 50 (45c).

1988 **Tagged** *Perf. 11*

2378	A1742 25c **multicolored**, *July 4*	.50	.25
	P# block of 4, 5#	2.25	—
	Zip block of 4	2.10	—
	Pair with full horiz. gutter between	—	
a.	Imperf., pair	*1,500.*	
2379	A1743 45c **multicolored**, *Aug, 8*	.85	.25
	P# block of 4, 4#	3.75	—
	Zip block of 4	3.50	—
a.	Tagging omitted	—	

1988 SUMMER OLYMPICS, SEOUL

Gymnastic Rings — A1744

Designed by Bart Forbes.

PHOTOGRAVURE

Plates of 200 in four panes of 50

1988, Aug. 19 **Tagged** *Perf. 11*

2380	A1744 25c **multicolored**	.50	.25
	P# block of 4, 5#	2.25	—
	Zip block of 4	2.10	—

CLASSIC AUTOMOBILES

1928 Locomobile A1745

1929 Pierce-Arrow — A1746

1931 Cord A1747

1932 Packard A1748

1935 Duesenberg — A1749

Designed by Ken Dallison.

LITHOGRAPHED & ENGRAVED

BOOKLET STAMPS

Perf. 10 Horiz. on 1 or 2 Sides

1988, Aug. 25 **Tagged**

2381	A1745 25c **multicolored**	.65	.25
2382	A1746 25c **multicolored**	.65	.25
2383	A1747 25c **multicolored**	.65	.25

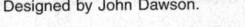

2384	A1748 25c **multicolored**	.65	.25
2385	A1749 25c **multicolored**	.65	.25
a.	Bklt. pane of 5, #2381-2385	3.25	2.50

ANTARCTIC EXPLORERS

Nathaniel Palmer (1799-1877) A1750

Lt. Charles Wilkes (1798-1877) A1751

Richard E. Byrd (1888-1957) A1752

Lincoln Ellsworth (1880-1951) A1753

Designed by Dennis Lyall.

Printed by the American Bank Note Co.

PHOTOGRAVURE
Plates of 160 in four panes of 40.

1988, Sept. 14 **Tagged** ***Perf. 11***

2386	A1750 25c **multicolored**	.65	.25
2387	A1751 25c **multicolored**	.65	.25
2388	A1752 25c **multicolored**	.65	.25
2389	A1753 25c **multicolored**	.65	.25
a.	Block of 4, #2386-2389	2.75	2.00
	P# block of 4, 6#+A	4.50	—
	Zip block of 4	3.00	—
b.	As "a," black omitted	*750.00*	
c.	As "a," imperf. horiz.	*1,500.*	

AMERICAN FOLK ART SERIES
Carousel Animals

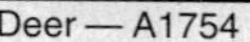

Deer — A1754

Horse — A1755

Camel — A1756

Goat — A1757

Designed by Paul Calle.

LITHOGRAPHED & ENGRAVED
Plates of 200 in four panes of 50.

1988, Oct. 1 **Tagged** ***Perf. 11***

2390	A1754 25c **multicolored**	.75	.25
2391	A1755 25c **multicolored**	.75	.25
2392	A1756 25c **multicolored**	.75	.25
2393	A1757 25c **multicolored**	.75	.25
a.	Block of 4, #2390-2393	3.00	2.00
	P# block of 4, 7#	4.00	—
	Zip block of 4	3.25	—
b.	As "a," red omitted	*800.00*	

EXPRESS MAIL RATE

Eagle and Moon — A1758

Designed by Ned Seidler.

LITHOGRAPHED & ENGRAVED
Panes of 20

1988, Oct. 4 **Tagged** ***Perf. 11***

2394	A1758 $8.75 **multicolored**	16.00	8.00
	P# block of 4, 7#	70.00	—

SPECIAL OCCASIONS

Happy Birthday A1759

Best Wishes A1760

Thinking of You A1761

Love You A1762

Designed by Harry Zelenko

Printed by the American Bank Note Co.

BOOKLET STAMPS
PHOTOGRAVURE

1988, Oct. 22 **Tagged** ***Perf. 11 on 2 or 3 Sides***

2395	A1759 25c **multicolored**	.50	.25
2396	A1760 25c **multicolored**	.50	.25
a.	Bklt. pane of 6, 3 #2395 + 3 #2396 with gutter between	3.50	3.25
2397	A1761 25c **multicolored**	.50	.25
2398	A1762 25c **multicolored**	.50	.25
a.	Bklt. pane of 6, 3 #2397 + 3 #2398 with gutter between	3.50	3.25
b.	As "a," imperf. horiz.	*2,250.*	
c.	As "a," imperf.	—	
	Nos. 2395-2398 (4)	2.00	1.00

CHRISTMAS

Madonna and Child, by Botticelli — A1763

One-horse Open Sleigh and Village Scene — A1764

"Missing Curlicue on Sleigh Runner" Cylinder Flaw

"Partially Missing Curlicue on Sleigh Runner" Cylinder Flaw

Designed by Bradbury Thompson (No. 2399) and Joan Landis (No. 2400).

LITHOGRAPHED & ENGRAVED (No. 2399),
PHOTOGRAVURE (No. 2400)
Plates of 300 in 6 Panes of 50

1988, Oct. 20 **Tagged** ***Perf. 11½***

2399	A1763 25c **multicolored**	.50	.25
	P# block of 4, 5+1#	2.25	—
	Zip, copyright block of 4	2.10	—
	Pair with full vert. gutter btwn.	—	
a.	Gold omitted	25.00	

The pair with vert. gutter of No. 2399 also is misperfed through the stamps and the gutter.

2400	A1764 25c **multicolored**	.50	.25
	P# block of 4, 5#	2.25	—
	Zip, copyright block of 4	2.10	—
	Pair with full vert. gutter btwn.	*225.00*	
	Cylinder flaw (missing curlicue on sleigh runner, 11111UR19)	15.00	—
	Cylinder flaw (partially missing curlicue on sleigh runner, 11111TopCenter46)	10.00	—

MONTANA STATEHOOD, 100th ANNIV.

C.M. Russell and Friends, by Charles M. Russell (1865-1926) A1765

Designed by Bradbury Thompson.

LITHOGRAPHED & ENGRAVED
Plates of 200 in four panes of 50.

1989, Jan. 15 **Tagged** ***Perf. 11***

2401 A1765 25c **multicolored**	.55	.25
P# block of 4, 5#	2.75	—
Zip block of 4	2.25	—
a. Tagging omitted	—	—

Imperfs without gum exist from printer's waste.

BLACK HERITAGE SERIES

A. Philip Randolph (1889-1979), Labor and Civil Rights Leader — A1766

Designed by Thomas Blackshear.

PHOTOGRAVURE
Plates of 200 in four panes of 50.

1989, Feb. 3 **Tagged** ***Perf. 11***

2402 A1766 25c **multicolored**	.50	.25
P# block of 4, 5#	2.50	—
Zip block of 4	2.10	—

NORTH DAKOTA STATEHOOD, 100th ANNIV.

Grain Elevator A1767

Designed by Wendell Minor.

Printed by the American Bank Note Co.

PHOTOGRAVURE
Plates of 200 in four panes of 50.

1989, Feb. 21 **Tagged** ***Perf. 11***

2403 A1767 25c **multicolored**	.50	.25
P# block of 4, 4#+A	3.00	—
Zip block of 4	2.10	—

WASHINGTON STATEHOOD, 100th ANNIV.

Mt. Rainier — A1768

Designed by Howard Rogers.

Printed by the American Bank Note Co.

PHOTOGRAVURE
Plates of 200 in four panes of 50.

1989, Feb. 22 **Tagged** ***Perf. 11***

2404 A1768 25c **multicolored**	.50	.25
P# block of 4, 4#+A	2.50	—
Zip block of 4	2.10	—

STEAMBOATS

Experiment, 1788-90 — A1769

Phoenix, 1809 A1770

New Orleans, 1812 A1771

Washington, 1816 — A1772

Walk in the Water, 1818 A1773

Designed by Richard Schlecht.

LITHOGRAPHED & ENGRAVED
BOOKLET STAMPS
Perf. 10 Horiz. on 1 or 2 Sides

1989, Mar. 3 **Tagged**

2405 A1769 25c **multicolored**	.60	.25
2406 A1770 25c **multicolored**	.60	.25
2407 A1771 25c **multicolored**	.60	.25
2408 A1772 25c **multicolored**	.60	.25
2409 A1773 25c **multicolored**	.60	.25
a. Booklet pane of 5, #2405-2409	3.00	1.75
b. As "a," tagging omitted	—	—

WORLD STAMP EXPO '89

Nov. 17-Dec. 3. Washington, D.C.

No. 122 — A1774

Designed by Richard Sheaff.

LITHOGRAPHED & ENGRAVED
Plates of 200 in four panes of 50.

1989, Mar. 16 **Tagged** ***Perf. 11***

2410 A1774 25c **grayish brn, blk & car rose**	.50	.25
P# block of 4, 4#	2.25	—
Zip block of 4	2.10	—

PERFORMING ARTS

Arturo Toscanini (1867-1957), Conductor — A1775

Designed by Jim Sharpe

Printed by the American Bank Note Co.

PHOTOGRAVURE
Plates of 200 in four panes of 50.

1989, Mar. 25 **Tagged** ***Perf. 11***

2411 A1775 25c **multicolored**	.50	.25
P# block of 4, 5#+A	2.25	—
Zip block of 4	2.10	—

CONSTITUTION BICENTENNIAL SERIES

House of Representatives A1776

Senate A1777

Executive Branch — A1778

Supreme Court — A1779

Designed by Howard Koslow

LITHOGRAPHED & ENGRAVED
Plates of 200 in four panes of 50.

1989-90 **Tagged** ***Perf. 11***

2412 A1776 25c **multi,** *Apr. 4, 1989*	.50	.25
P# block of 4, 4#	2.25	—
Zip block of 4	2.10	—
2413 A1777 25c **multi,** *Apr. 6, 1989*	.50	.25
P# block of 4, 4#	3.25	—
Zip block of 4	2.10	—
2414 A1778 25c **multi,** *Apr. 16, 1989*	.50	.25
P# block of 4, 4#	2.25	—
Zip block of 4	2.10	—
2415 A1779 25c **multi,** *Feb. 2, 1990*	.50	.25
P# block of 4, 4#	2.25	—
Zip block of 4	2.10	—
Nos. 2412-2415 (4)	2.00	1.00

SOUTH DAKOTA STATEHOOD, 100th ANNIV.

Pasque Flowers, Pioneer Woman and Sod House on Grasslands A1780

Designed by Marian Henjum.

Printed by the American Bank Note Co.

PHOTOGRAVURE

Plates of 200 in four panes of 50.

1989, May 3	Tagged	*Perf. 11*	
2416 A1780 25c **multicolored**		.60	.25
P# block of 4, 4#+A		3.00	—
Zip block of 4		2.50	—

Imperfs exist from printer's waste.

AMERICAN SPORTS

Lou Gehrig (1903-1941), New York Yankee Baseball Player — A1781

Designed by Bart Forbes.

Printed by the American Bank Note Co.

PHOTOGRAVURE

Plates of 200 in four panes of 50.

1989, June 10	Tagged	*Perf. 11*	
2417 A1781 25c **multicolored**		.60	.25
P# block of 4, 6#+A		3.00	—
Zip block of 4		2.50	—

LITERARY ARTS SERIES

Ernest Hemingway (1899-1961), 1954 Nobel Prize Winner for Literature — A1782

Designed by M. Gregory Rudd.

Printed by the American Bank Note Co.

PHOTOGRAVURE

Plates of 200 in four panes of 50.

1989, July 17	Tagged	*Perf. 11*	
2418 A1782 25c **multicolored**		.50	.25
P# block of 4, 5#+A		2.25	—
Zip block of 4		2.10	—
a. Vert. pair, imperf horiz.		*800.00*	

Imperforates on gummed stamp paper, including gutter pairs and blocks, are proofs from the ABNCo. archives. See No. 2418P in Proofs section.

MOON LANDING, 20TH ANNIVERSARY

Raising of the Flag on the Lunar Surface, July 20, 1969 — A1783

Designed by Christopher Calle.

LITHOGRAPHED & ENGRAVED

Panes of 20

1989, July 20	Tagged	*Perf. 11x11½*	
2419 A1783 $2.40 **multicolored**		4.75	2.00
P# block of 4, 6#		20.00	—
Pane of 20		100.00	—
a. Black (engr.) omitted		*1,350.*	
b. Imperf., pair		*375.00*	
c. Black (litho.) omitted		*1,500.*	
d. Tagging omitted			—

No. 2419 exists with a gray background instead of the normal dark blue. Some of these may have been caused by a chemical wiping of the blue plate. However, the same or extremely similar stamps can be produced by exposing normal stamps to sunlight or fluorescent light for varying time periods.

LETTER CARRIERS

A1784

Designed by Jack Davis.

Printed by the American Bank Note Co.

PHOTOGRAVURE

Plates of 160 in four panes of 40.

1989, Aug. 30	Tagged	*Perf. 11*	
2420 A1784 25c **multicolored**		.50	.25
P# block of 4, 5#+A		2.25	—
Zip block of 4		2.10	—

CONSTITUTION BICENTENNIAL

Bill of Rights — A1785

Designed by Lou Nolan.

LITHOGRAPHED & ENGRAVED

Plates of 200 in four panes of 50.

1989, Sept. 25	Tagged	*Perf. 11*	
2421 A1785 25c **multicolored**		.50	.25
P# block of 4		3.25	—
Zip block of 4		2.10	—
a. Black (engr.) omitted		*225.00*	

PREHISTORIC ANIMALS

Tyrannosaurus Rex — A1786

Pteranodon A1787

Stegosaurus A1788

Brontosaurus A1789

Designed by John Gurche.

LITHOGRAPHED & ENGRAVED

Plates of 160 in four panes of 40.

1989, Oct. 1	Tagged	*Perf. 11*	
2422 A1786 25c **multicolored**		.70	.25
a. Black (engr.) omitted		80.00	—
2423 A1787 25c **multicolored**		.70	.25
a. Black (engr.) omitted		80.00	
2424 A1788 25c **multicolored**		.70	.25
a. Black (engr.) omitted		80.00	
2425 A1789 25c **multicolored**		.70	.25
a. Black (engr.) omitted		80.00	
b. Block of 4, #2422-2425		2.80	2.00
P# block of 4, 6#		3.50	—
Zip block of 4		3.00	—
c. As "b," black (engr.) omitted		*325.00*	

No. 2425c is valued in the grade of fine. Very fine blocks exist and sell for approximately $600.

PRE-COLUMBIAN AMERICA ISSUE

Southwest Carved Figure, A.D. 1150-1350 — A1790

Designed by Lon Busch.

Printed by the American Bank Note Company.

PHOTOGRAVURE

Plates of 200 in four panes of 50.

1989, Oct. 12	Tagged	*Perf. 11*	
2426 A1790 25c **multicolored**		.60	.25
P# block of 4, 6#+A		3.00	—
Zip block of 4		2.50	—
a. Tagging omitted		—	—

See No. C121.

CHRISTMAS

Madonna and Child, by Carracci — A1791

Sleigh Full of Presents — A1792

Designed by Bradbury Thompson (#2427 & 2429) and Steven Dohanos (#2428).

Printed by the Bureau of Engraving and Printing (#2427 & 2429) and American Bank Note Company (#2428).

LITHOGRAPHED & ENGRAVED,
PHOTOGRAVURE (#2428-2429)
Sheets of 300 in six panes of 50.

1989, Oct. 19 **Tagged** ***Perf. 11¼***

2427	A1791 25c **multicolored**	.50	.25
	P# block of 4, 5#	2.25	—
	Zip, copyright block of 4	2.10	—
	Pair with full horiz. gutter between	—	
a.	Booklet pane of 10	5.00	3.50
b.	Red (litho.) omitted	*400.00*	
c.	As "a," imperf.	—	

Perf. 11½

2428	A1792 25c **multicolored**	.50	.25
	P# block of 4, 5#+A	2.25	—
	Zip, copyright block of 4	2.10	—
a.	Vert. pair, imperf. horiz.	*500.00*	

BOOKLET STAMP

Perf. 11½ on 2 or 3 Sides

2429	A1792 25c **multicolored**	.50	.25
a.	Booklet pane of 10	5.00	3.50
b.	Vert. pair, imperf. btwn. (from miscut bklt pane)	*500.00*	
c.	As "a," horiz. imperf. between	*2,250.*	
d.	As "a," red omitted	*3,250.*	
e.	Imperf., pair	*750.00*	

Marked differences exist between Nos. 2428 and 2429: No. 2429 was printed in four colors, No. 2428 in five colors. The runners on the sleigh in No. 2429 are twice as thick as those on No. 2428. On No. 2429 the package at the upper left in the sleigh has a red bow, whereas the same package in No. 2428 has a red and black bow; and the ribbon on the upper right package in No. 2429 is green, whereas the same ribbon in No. 2428 is black.

Eagle and Shield — A1793

Designed by Jay Haiden.

Printed by the American Bank Note Company.

PHOTOGRAVURE
BOOKLET STAMP

1989, Nov. 10 **Tagged** **Self-Adhesive** ***Die Cut***

2431	A1793 25c **multicolored** ⓢ	.50	.25
a.	Booklet pane of 18	10.00	
b.	Vert. pair, die cutting omitted between	*325.00*	
c.	Die cutting omitted, pair	*200.00*	

Panes sold for $5.

Also available in strips of 18 with stamps spaced for use in affixing machines to service first day covers. Sold for $5.

No. 2431c will include part of the margins around the stamps.

Sold only in 15 test cities (Atlanta, Chicago, Cleveland, Columbus, OH, Dallas, Denver, Houston, Indianapolis, Kansas City, MO, Los Angeles, Miami, Milwaukee, Minneapolis, Phoenix, St. Louis) and through the philatelic agency.

ⓢ: Adhesive residue sometimes remains on the back of examples of No. 2431 after soaking. See note after No. 1549.

WORLD STAMP EXPO '89
Washington, DC, Nov. 17-Dec. 3

WORLD STAMP EXPO'89 SM
The classic 1869 U.S. Abraham Lincoln stamp is reborn in these four larger versions commemorating World Stamp Expo'89, held in Washington, D.C. during the 20th Universal Postal Congress of the UPU. These stamps show the issued colors and three of the trial proof color combinations.

A1794

Illustration reduced.

Designed by Richard Sheaff.

LITHOGRAPHED & ENGRAVED

1989, Nov. 17 **Tagged** ***Imperf.***

2433	A1794 Pane of 4	16.00	14.00
a.	90c like No. 122	4.00	3.00
b.	90c like 132TC4j	4.00	3.00
c.	90c like 132TC4i	4.00	3.00
d.	90c like 132TC4d	4.00	3.00
e.	As No. 2433, tagging omitted	—	
f.	Double impression of all 4 frames	—	

20th UPU CONGRESS
Traditional Mail Delivery

Stagecoach, c. 1850 — A1795

Paddlewheel Steamer — A1796

Biplane — A1797

Depot-hack Type Automobile — A1798

Designed by Mark Hess.

LITHOGRAPHED & ENGRAVED
Plates of 160 in four panes of 40.

1989, Nov. 19 **Tagged** ***Perf. 11***

2434	A1795 25c **multicolored**	.50	.25
2435	A1796 25c **multicolored**	.50	.25
2436	A1797 25c **multicolored**	.50	.25
2437	A1798 25c **multicolored**	.50	.25
a.	Block of 4, #2434-2437	2.00	1.75
	P# block of 4, 5#	3.75	—
	Zip block of 4	2.25	—
b.	As "a," dark blue (engr.) omitted	*300.00*	
c.	As No. 2437a, tagging omitted	—	

No. 2437b is valued in the grade of fine. Very fine blocks exist and sell for approximately $450.

Souvenir Sheet
LITHOGRAPHED & ENGRAVED

1989, Nov. 28 **Tagged** ***Imperf.***

2438	0 0 Sheet of 4	5.00	3.75
a.	A1795 25c **multicolored**	1.25	.80
b.	A1796 25c **multicolored**	1.25	.80
c.	A1797 25c **multicolored**	1.25	.80
d.	A1798 25c **multicolored**	1.25	.80
e.	Dark blue & gray (engr.) omitted	*4,000.*	

20th Universal Postal Union Congress.

VALUES FOR HINGED STAMPS AFTER NO. 771
This catalogue does not value unused stamps after No. 771 in hinged condition. Hinged unused stamps from No. 772 to the present are worth considerably less than the values given for unused stamps, which are for never-hinged examples.

IDAHO STATEHOOD, 100th ANNIV.

Mountain Bluebird, Sawtooth Mountains — A1799

Designed by John Dawson.

Printed by the American Bank Note Company.

PHOTOGRAVURE
Plates of 200 in four panes of 50.

1990, Jan. 6 **Tagged** ***Perf. 11***

2439	A1799 25c **multicolored**	.55	.25
	P# block of 4, 5#+A	3.50	—
	Zip block of 4	2.25	—

LOVE

A1800

Designed by Jayne Hertko.

Printed by the U.S. Banknote Company (#2440) and the Bureau of Engraving and Printing (#2441).

PHOTOGRAVURE
Plates of 200 in four panes of 50.

1990, Jan. 18 **Tagged** ***Perf. 12½x13***

2440	A1800 25c **multicolored**	.50	.25
	P# block of 4, 4#	2.25	—
	Zip, copyright block of 4	2.10	—
a.	Imperf., pair	*550.00*	

BOOKLET STAMP

Perf. 11½ on 2 or 3 Sides

2441	A1800 25c **multicolored**	.50	.25
a.	Booklet pane of 10	5.00	3.50
b.	Bright pink omitted	*80.00*	
c.	As "a," bright pink omitted	*950.00*	
d.	As "a," tagging omitted	—	

No. 2441b may be obtained from booklet panes containing both normal and color-omitted stamps.

BLACK HERITAGE SERIES

Ida B. Wells (1862-1931), Journalist — A1801

Designed by Thomas Blackshear.

Printed by American Bank Note Company.

PHOTOGRAVURE
Plates of 200 in four panes of 50.

1990, Feb. 1 **Tagged** ***Perf. 11***

2442	A1801 25c **multicolored**	.75	.25
	P# block of 4, 5#+A	3.75	—
	Zip block of 4	3.25	—

Beach Umbrella — A1802

Designed by Pierre Mion.

BOOKLET STAMP
PHOTOGRAVURE

1990, Feb. 3	**Tagged**	***Perf. 11 on 2 or 3 Sides***	
2443 A1802 15c **multicolored**		.30	.25
a. Booklet pane of 10		3.00	2.50
b. Blue omitted		*100.00*	
c. As "a," blue omitted		*900.00*	

WYOMING STATEHOOD, 100th ANNIV.

High Mountain Meadows, by Conrad Schwiering A1803

Designed by Jack Rosenthal.

LITHOGRAPHED & ENGRAVED
Plates of 200 in four panes of 50.

1990, Feb. 23	**Tagged**	***Perf. 11***	
2444 A1803 25c **multicolored**		.80	.25
P# block of 4, 5#		4.00	—
Zip block of 4		3.25	—
a. Black (engr.) omitted		*900.00*	—

CLASSIC FILMS

Judy Garland and Toto (The Wizard of Oz) — A1804

Clark Gable & Vivien Leigh (Gone With the Wind) — A1805

Gary Cooper (Beau Geste) — A1806

John Wayne (Stagecoach) A1807

Designed by Thomas Blackshear.

Printed by the American Bank Note Company.

PHOTOGRAVURE
Plates of 160 in four panes of 40.

1990, Mar. 23	**Tagged**	***Perf. 11***	
2445 A1804 25c **multicolored**		1.25	.25
2446 A1805 25c **multicolored**		1.25	.25
2447 A1806 25c **multicolored**		1.25	.25
2448 A1807 25c **multicolored**		1.25	.25
a. Block of 4, #2445-2448		5.00	3.50
P# block of 4, 5#+A		5.50	—
Zip block of 4		5.25	—

LITERARY ARTS SERIES

Marianne Moore (1887-1972), Poet — A1808

Designed by M. Gregory Rudd.

Printed by the American Bank Note Company.

PHOTOGRAVURE
Plates of 200 in four panes of 50.

1990, Apr. 18	**Tagged**	***Perf. 11***	
2449 A1808 25c **multicolored**		.55	.25
P# block of 4, 3#+A		2.50	—
Zip block of 4		2.40	—
a. All colors missing (EP)		—	

No. 2449a must be collected se-tenant with a partially printed stamp or in longer horizontal strips with a partially printed stamp and normal stamps.

Coil Plate No. Strips of 3
Beginning with No. 2123, coil plate no. strips of 3 usually sell at the level of strips of 5 minus the face value of two stamps.

TRANSPORTATION ISSUE

A1810

A1811

A1811a

A1812

A1816

A1822

A1823

A1825

A1827

Designers: 4c, 32c, Richard Schlecht. Nos. 2452, 2452B, 2452D, Susan Sanford. No. 2453, Paul Calle. 10c, David K. Stone. 20c, 23c, Robert Brangwynne. $1, Chuck Hodgson.

Printed by: Guilford Gravure for American Bank Note Co. (No. 2452B), J.W. Fergusson & Sons for Stamp Venturers (No. 2454), Stamp Venturers (No, 2452D), others by BEP.

COIL STAMPS
ENGRAVED, PHOTOGRAVURE (#2452B, 2452D, 2454, 2458)

1990-95 ***Perf. 9.8 Vert.***
Tagged, Untagged (Nos. 2452B, 2452D, 2453, 2454, 2457-2458)

2451 A1810 4c **claret,** *Jan. 25, 1991*	.25	.25
Pair	.50	.50
P# strip of 5, #1	.90	
P# single, #1	—	.65
a. Imperf., pair	*450.00*	
b. Untagged	.25	.25
Pair	.50	.50
P# strip of 5, #1	.90	
P# single, #1	—	.65
2452 A1811 5c **carmine,** dull gum, *Aug. 31*	.25	.25
Pair	.50	.50
P# strip of 5, #1	.90	
P# single, #1	—	.65
a. Untagged, dull gum	.25	.25
Pair	.50	.50
P# strip of 5, #1	2.50	
P# single, #1	—	2.25
Low gloss gum	.25	
Pair	.50	
P# strip of 5, #2	2.00	
P# single, #2	—	1.60
c. Imperf., pair	*350.00*	

No. 2452c is valued in the grade of fine.

2452B A1811 5c **carmine,** *Dec. 8, 1992*	.25	.25
Pair	.50	.50
P# strip of 5, #A1-A2	1.25	
P# single, #A1-A2	—	.90
f. Printed with luminescent ink	.40	.25
Pair	.80	.50
P# strip of 5, #A3	3.00	
P# single, #A3	—	2.00
2452D A1811a 5c **carmine,** low gloss gum, *Mar. 20, 1995*	.25	.25
Pair	.50	.50
P# strip of 5, #S1-S2	1.25	
P# single, #S1-S2	—	1.00
e. Imperf., pair	*115.00*	
g. Printed with luminescent ink, shiny gum	.25	.25
Pair	.50	.50
P# strip of 5, #S2	2.00	
P# single, #S2	—	1.60
Low gloss gum	.25	
P# strip of 5, #S3	2.00	
P# single, #S3	—	1.75
h. As "g," low gloss gum, imperf. pair	—	
2453 A1812 5c **brown** (Bureau precancel, Additional Nonprofit Postage Paid, in gray), *May 25, 1991*	.40	.25
Pair	.80	.50
P# strip of 5, #1-3	1.50	
P# single, #1-3	—	1.00
a. Imperf., pair	*225.00*	
b. Gray omitted		—

No.	Design	Description	Unused	Used
2454	A1812	5c **red** (Bureau precancel, Additional Nonprofit Postage Paid, in gray), shiny gum, *Oct. 22, 1991*	.45	.25
		Pair	.90	.50
		P# strip of 5, #S11	1.25	
		P# single, #S11	—	1.00
		Low gloss gum	.65	
		Pair	1.30	
		P# strip of 5, #S11	4.00	
2457	A1816	10c **green** (Bureau precancel, Additional Presort Postage Paid, in gray), *May 25, 1991*	.45	.25
		Pair	.90	.50
		P# strip of 5, #1	2.25	
		P# single, #1	—	1.40
a.		Imperf., pair	*110.00*	
b.		All color omitted	—	

No. 2457b must be accompanied by a 2012 certificate of authentication confirming that stamps are from the discovery coil roll that also contained normal and partially printed stamps.

No.	Design	Description	Unused	Used
2458	A1816	10c **green** (Bureau precancel, Additional Presort Postage Paid, in black), *May 25, 1994*	.55	.25
		Pair	1.10	.50
		P# strip of 5, #11, 22	3.50	
		P# single, #11, 22	—	1.75
2463	A1822	20c **green,** *June 9, 1995*	.40	.25
		Pair	.80	.50
		P# strip of 5, #1-2	3.00	
		P# single, #1-2	—	2.00
a.		Imperf., pair	*75.00*	
2464	A1823	23c **dark blue,** prephosphored coated paper with surface tagging showing a solid appearance, dull gum, *Apr. 12, 1991*	.45	.25
		Pair	.90	.50
		P# strip of 5, #2-3	3.25	
		P# single, #2-3	—	1.75
a.		Prephosphored uncoated paper with embedded tagging showing a mottled appearance, dull gum, *1993*	1.20	.25
		Pair	2.40	.50
		P# strip of 5, #3	9.00	
		Shiny gum, *1993*	.45	
		Pair	.90	
		P# strip of 5, #3	3.75	
		P# strip of 5, #4	9.00	
		P# strip of 5, #5	4.00	
		P# single, #3		2.00
		P# single, #4		8.00
		P# single, #5	—	4.00
b.		Imperf., pair, prephosphored coated paper	*100.00*	
c.		Imperf., pair, prephosphored uncoated paper	*110.00*	
2466	A1825	32c **blue,** prephosphored uncoated paper with embedded tagging showing a mottled appearance, shiny gum, *June 2, 1995*	.80	.25
		Pair	1.60	.50
		P# strip of 5, #2	4.50	
		P# strip of 5, #3	5.00	
		P# strip of 5, #4	4.75	
		P# strip of 5, #5	6.50	
		P# single, #2, 3	—	2.25
		P# single, #4	—	2.50
		P# single, #5	—	3.50
		Low gloss gum	1.10	
		Pair	2.20	
		P# strip of 5, #3	10.00	
		P# strip of 5, #4	12.00	
		P# strip of 5, #5	10.00	
		P# single, #3	—	
		P# single, #4	—	
		P# single, #5	—	
a.		Imperf., pair, shiny gum	*375.00*	
		Low gloss gum	*475.00*	
b.		32c **bright blue,** prephosphored uncoated paper with embedded tagging showing a mottled appearance, low gloss gum	3.00	2.25
		Pair	6.00	5.50
		P# strip of 5, #5	90.00	
		P# single, #5	—	90.00

Some specialists refer to No. 2466b as "Bronx blue," and it is considered to be an error of color.

No.	Design	Description	Unused	Used
2468	A1827	$1 **blue & scarlet,** overall tagging, dull gum, *Apr. 20*	2.25	.50
		Pair	4.50	1.00
		P# strip of 5, #1	12.50	
		P# single, #1	—	5.00
a.		Imperf., pair	*1,750.*	*1,150.*
b.		Prephosphored uncoated paper with embedded tagging showing a mottled appearance, shiny gum, *1993*	2.50	.50
		Pair	5.00	1.00
		P# strip of 5, #3	13.00	
		P# single, #3	—	5.00
c.		Prephosphored coated paper with surface tagging showing a grainy solid appearance, low gloss gum, *1998*	3.00	.50
		Pair	6.00	1.00
		P# strip of 5, #3	16.00	
		P# single, #3	—	10.00
		Nos. 2451-2468 (12)	6.75	3.25

Some mint pairs of No. 2468 appear to be imperf. but have faint blind perforations on the gum. Beware of examples with the gum removed.

LIGHTHOUSES

Admiralty Head, WA — A1829

Cape Hatteras, NC — A1830

West Quoddy Head, ME — A1831

American Shoals, FL — A1832

Sandy Hook, NJ — A1833

Designed by Howard Koslow.

BOOKLET STAMPS
LITHOGRAPHED & ENGRAVED

Perf. 10 Vert. on 1 or 2 Sides

1990, Apr. 26			**Tagged**	
2470	A1829	25c **multicolored**	1.50	.25
2471	A1830	25c **multicolored**	1.50	.25
2472	A1831	25c **multicolored**	1.50	.25
2473	A1832	25c **multicolored**	1.50	.25
2474	A1833	25c **multicolored**	1.50	.25
a.		Bklt. pane of 5, #2470-2474	7.50	2.00
b.		As "a," white ("USA 25") omitted	85.00	—

Perforations on Lighthouse booklet panes separate very easily. Careful handling is required.

FLAG Ⓢ

25 USA

A1834

Designed by Harry Zelenko.

Printed by Avery International Corp.

PHOTOGRAVURE

1990, May 18 Untagged Self-adhesive *Die Cut*
Printed on Plastic

2475	A1834	25c **dark red & dark blue**	.55	.25
a.		Pane of 12	6.60	

Sold only in panes of 12; peelable plastic backing inscribed in light ultramarine. Available for a test period of six months at 22 First National Bank automatic teller machines in Seattle.

Ⓢ: Adhesive residue sometimes remains on the back of examples of No. 2475 after soaking. See note after No. 1549.

FLORA AND FAUNA

American Kestrel — A1840

USA 1¢
American Kestrel

American Kestrel — A1841

Eastern Bluebird — A1842

19 USA

Fawn — A1843

Cardinal — A1844

Pumpkinseed Sunfish — A1845

Bobcat A1846

Designers: 1c, 3c, 45c, Michael Matherly. 19c, Peter Cocci. 30c, Robert Giusti. $2, Chuck Ripper.

Printed by: No. 2476 and No. 2478, American Bank Note Co. No. 2477, No. 2479 and No. 2482, Bureau of Engraving & Printing. No. 2480, Stamp Venturers. No. 2481, Stamp Venturers (engraved) and The Press, Inc. (lithographed).

LITHOGRAPHED

Panes of 100

1990-95 Untagged (1c, 3c) *Perf. 11, 11.2 (#2477)*

No.	Design	Description	Unused	Used
2476	A1840	1c **multicolored,** *June 22, 1991*	.25	.25
		P# block of 4, 4#+A	.50	—
		Zip block of 4	.50	—
a.		Quadruple impression of black inscriptions and denomination	*850.00*	
b.		Quintuple impression of black inscriptions and denomination	*1,500.*	
c.		Triple impression of black inscriptions and denomination	—	

Other colors on Nos. 2476a, 2476b and 2476c are misregistered and the stamps are poorly centered.

No.	Design	Description	Unused	Used
2477	A1841	1c **multicolored,** shiny gum, *May 10, 1995*	.25	.25
		P# block of 4, 4#	.50	—
		Low gloss gum	.25	
		P# block of 4, 4#	.50	
a.		Tagged (error), shiny gum	—	
2478	A1842	3c **multicolored,** *June 22, 1991*	.25	.25
		P# block of 4, 4#+A	.50	—
		Zip block of 4	.50	—
a.		Vert. pair, imperf horiz.	—	
b.		Double impression of all colors except yellow	*200.00*	
c.		Double impression of blue, triple impression of black	—	

Other colors on No. 2478c are misregistered and all kown examples have fine centering.

Imperforates on gummed stamp paper, plus imperforate and perforated gutter pairs and blocks (including imperforate and perforated gutter pairs and blocks of No. 2476 se-tenant with No. 2478), are proofs from the ABNCo. archives. See Nos. 2476P and 2478P in Proofs section.

See Nos. 3031, 3031A, 3044. Compare design A1842 with design A2336.

PHOTOGRAVURE
Plates of 400 in four panes of 100.

Tagged *Perf. 11*

2479 A1843 19c **multicolored,** *Mar. 11, 1991* .35 .25
P# block of 4, 5# 1.75 —
Zip block of 4 1.50 —
a. Tagging omitted *10.00*
b. Red omitted *425.00*
c. Imperf, pair *900.00*

On No. 2479b other colors are shifted.

2480 A1844 30c **multicolored,** *June 22, 1991* .60 .25
P# block of 4, 4#+S 2.75 —
Zip block of 4 2.50 —

LITHOGRAPHED & ENGRAVED
Panes of 100
Perf. 11

2481 A1845 45c **multicolored,** *Dec. 2, 1992* .90 .25
P# block of 4, 5#+S 4.25 —
Zip block of 4 3.75 —
a. Black (engr.) omitted *300.00* —

Panes of 20

2482 A1846 $2 **multicolored,** *June 1, 1990* 3.50 1.25
P# block of 4, 5# 14.00 —
Pane of 20 70.00
a. Black (engr.) omitted *200.00*
b. Tagging omitted 22.50
Nos. 2476-2482 (7) 6.10 2.75

Blue Jay — A1847

Wood Duck — A1848

African Violets — A1849

Peach — A1850

Pear — A1851

Red Squirrel — A1852

Rose — A1853

Pine Cone — A1854

Designed by Robert Giusti (#2483-2485), Ned Seidler (#2486-2488, 2493-2495A), Michael R. Matherly (#2489), Gyo Fujikawa (#2490), Paul Breeden (#2491), Gyo Fujikawa (#2492).

Printed by Stamp Venturers (#2483, 2492), Bureau of Engraving and Printing (#2484, 2487-2488), J.W. Fergusson & Sons for KCS Industries, Inc. (#2485), KCS Industries (#2486), Dittler Brothers, Inc. (#2489), Stamp Venturers (#2490), Banknote Corporation of America (#2491), Avery-Dennison (#2493-2495, 2495A).

PHOTOGRAVURE
BOOKLET STAMPS

1991-95 ***Perf. 10.9x9.8 on 2 or 3 Sides***
Tagged

2483 A1847 20c **multicolored,** *June 15, 1995* .50 .25
a. Booklet pane of 10 5.25 2.50
b. As "a," imperf —

Perf. 10 on 2 or 3 sides

2484 A1848 29c **black & multi,** overall tagging, *Apr. 12, 1991* .60 .25
a. Booklet pane of 10 6.00 3.75
b. Vert. pair, imperf. horiz. *175.00*
c. As "b," bklt. pane of 10 *875.00*
d. Prephosphored coated paper with surface tagging showing a solid appearance .60 .25
e. As "d," booklet pane of 10 6.00 3.75
f. Vert. pair, imperf between and with natural straight edge at top or bottom *175.00*
g. As "f," bklt. pane of 10 *875.00*

Perf. 11 on 2 or 3 Sides

2485 A1848 29c **red & multi,** *Apr. 12, 1991* .60 .25
a. Booklet pane of 10 6.00 4.00
b. Vert. pair, imperf. between *2,500.*
c. Imperf, pair *4,500.*

Perf. 10x11 on 2 or 3 Sides

2486 A1849 29c **multicolored,** *Oct. 8, 1993* .60 .25
a. Booklet pane of 10 6.00 4.00

Perf. 11x10 on 2 or 3 Sides

2487 A1850 32c **multicolored,** *July 8, 1995* .65 .25
2488 A1851 32c **multicolored,** *July 8, 1995* .65 .25
a. Booklet pane, 5 each #2487-2488 6.50 4.25
b. Pair, #2487-2488 1.30 .30

PHOTOGRAVURE, ENGRAVED (#2491)

1993-95 **Tagged** ***Die Cut***
Self-Adhesive
Booklet Stamps

2489 A1852 29c **multicolored,** *June 25* .60 .25
a. Booklet pane of 18 11.00
b. As "a," die cutting omitted —
2490 A1853 29c **red, green & black,** *Aug. 19* .60 .25
a. Booklet pane of 18 11.00

Nos. 2489-2490 also available in strips with stamps spaced for use in affixing machines to service first day covers. No plate numbers. Stamps removed from strips are virtually indistinguishable from booklet stamps. The stamps from strips have minutely rounded corners, whereas the corners of the booklet stamps are squared.

2491 A1854 29c **multicolored,** *Nov. 5* .60 .25
a. Booklet pane of 18 11.00
b. Horiz. pair, die cutting omitted between *175.00 125.00*
c. Coil with plate # B1 — 6.00
P# strip of 5, #B1 7.50

Stamps without plate number from coil strips are indistinguishable from booklet stamps once they are removed from the backing paper.

Serpentine Die Cut 11.3x11.7 on 2, 3 or 4 Sides

2492 A1853 32c **pink, green & black,** *June 2, 1995* .65 .25
a. Booklet pane of 20 + label 13.00
b. Booklet pane of 15 + label 9.75
c. Horiz. pair, die cutting omitted between —
d. As "a," 2 stamps and parts of 7 others printed on backing liner —
e. Booklet pane of 14 20.00
f. Booklet pane of 16 20.00
g. Coil with plate # S111 — 5.50
P# strip of 5, #S111 7.00
h. Vert. pair, die cutting omitted between (from No. 2492b) *400.00*
i. As "a," 6 pairs plus stamp and label die cutting omitted vert. btwn. (due to miscutting) *800.00*
j. As "f," with 2 vert. pairs at bottom die cutting omitted horiz., in full bklt. #BK178D —
k. As "a," horiz. die cutting omitted —

Nos. 2492, 2492a and 2492b exist on two types of surface-tagged paper that exhibit either a solid or a grainy solid appearance. Values are the same. Nos. 2492e, 2492f and 2492g have tagging with a solid appearance, while Nos. 2492c, 2492d and 2492h have tagging with a grainy solid appearance.

Stamps on plate # strips are separated on backing larger than the stamps. Stamps without plate # from coil strips are indistinquishable from interior position booklet stamps once they are removed from the backing paper.

For booklet panes containing No. 2492f with one stamp removed, see Nos. BK178B, BK178D-BK178E in Booklets section.

Serpentine Die Cut 8.8 on 2, 3 or 4 Sides

2493 A1850 32c **multicolored,** *July 8, 1995* .65 .25
2494 A1851 32c **multicolored,** *July 8, 1995* .65 .25
a. Booklet pane of 20, 10 each #2493-2494 + label 13.00
b. Pair, #2493-2494 1.30
c. As "b," die cutting omitted —

COIL STAMPS
Serpentine Die Cut 8.8 Vert.

2495 A1850 32c **multicolored,** *July 8, 1995* 2.00 .25
2495A A1851 32c **multicolored,** *July 8, 1995* 2.00 .25
b. Pair, #2495-2495A 4.00
P# strip of 5, 3 #2495A, 2 #2495, P#V11111 13.00
P# single, #V11111 — 6.75

See Nos. 3048-3049, 3053-3054.

Values for used self-adhesive stamps are for examples either on piece or off piece.

OLYMPIANS

Jesse Owens, 1936 — A1855

Ray Ewry, 1900-08 A1856

Hazel Wightman, 1924 — A1857

Eddie Eagan, 1920, 1932 — A1858

Helene Madison, 1932 — A1859

Designed by Bart Forbes.

Printed by the American Bank Note Company.

PHOTOGRAVURE
Panes of 35.

1990, July 6 **Tagged** ***Perf. 11***

2496 A1855 25c **multicolored** .60 .25
2497 A1856 25c **multicolored** .60 .25
2498 A1857 25c **multicolored** .60 .25
2499 A1858 25c **multicolored** .60 .25

2500 A1859 25c **multicolored** .60 .25
a. Strip of 5, #2496-2500 3.25 2.50
P# block of 10, 4#+A 8.00 —
Zip, inscription block of 10 6.50 —
b. As "a," blue omitted —

Imperforates on gummed stamp paper, including gutter pairs, strips and blocks, are proofs from the ABNCo. archives. See No. 2500aP in Proofs section.

INDIAN HEADDRESSES

Assiniboin A1860

Cheyenne A1861

Comanche A1862

Flathead A1863

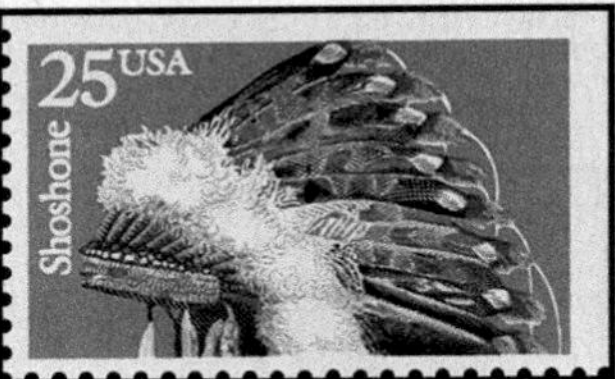

Shoshone A1864

Designed by Lunda Hoyle Gill.

LITHOGRAPHED & ENGRAVED
BOOKLET STAMPS

1990, Aug. 17 Tagged *Perf. 11 on 2 or 3 Sides*
2501 A1860 25c **multicolored** .80 .25
2502 A1861 25c **multicolored** .80 .25
2503 A1862 25c **multicolored** .80 .25
a. Black (engr.) omitted —
2504 A1863 25c **multicolored** .80 .25
a. Black (engr.) omitted —
2505 A1864 25c **multicolored** .80 .25
a. Bklt. pane of 10, 2 each #2501-2505 8.00 6.00
b. As "a," black (engr.) omitted *2,500.*
c. Strip of 5, #2501-2505 4.00 2.50
d. As "a," horiz. imperf. between *2,250.*

At least one of the examples of No. 2505d that have been reported is actually split at the booklet fold and is a block of 4 and a block of 6.

MICRONESIA & MARSHALL ISLANDS

Canoe and Flag of the Federated States of Micronesia A1865

Stick Chart, Canoe and Flag of the Republic of the Marshall Islands A1866

LITHOGRAPHED & ENGRAVED
Sheets of 200 in four panes of 50.

1990, Sept. 28 Tagged *Perf. 11*
2506 A1865 25c **multicolored** .50 .25
2507 A1866 25c **multicolored** .50 .25
a. Pair, #2506-2507 1.00 .75
P# block of 4, 6# 2.75 —
Zip block of 4 2.10 —
b. As "a," black (engr.) omitted *1,400.*

See Micronesia Nos. 124-126, Marshall Islands No. 381.

SEA CREATURES

Killer Whales A1867

Northern Sea Lions — A1868

Sea Otter — A1869

Common Dolphin A1870

Designed by Peter Cocci (Nos. 2508, 2511), Vladimir Beilin, USSR (Nos. 2509-2510).

LITHOGRAPHED & ENGRAVED
Sheets of 160 in four panes of 40.

1990, Oct. 3 Tagged *Perf. 11*
2508 A1867 25c **multicolored** .55 .25
2509 A1868 25c **multicolored** .55 .25
2510 A1869 25c **multicolored** .55 .25
2511 A1870 25c **multicolored** .55 .25
a. Block of 4, #2508-2511 2.25 1.90
P# block of 4, 5# 2.75 —
Zip block of 4 2.30 —
b. As "a," black (engr.) omitted *250.00*
c. As "a," tagging omitted —

See Russia Nos. 5933-5936.

PRE-COLUMBIAN AMERICA ISSUE

Grand Canyon A1871

Designed by Mark Hess.

Printed by the American Bank Note Company.

PHOTOGRAVURE
Plates of 200 in four panes of 50.
(3 panes of #2512, 1 pane of #C127)

1990, Oct. 12 Tagged *Perf. 11*
2512 A1871 25c **multicolored** .55 .25
P# block of 4, 4#+A, UR, LL, LR 2.75 —
Zip block of 4 2.25 —

See No. C127.

DWIGHT D. EISENHOWER, BIRTH CENTENARY

A1872

Designed by Ken Hodges.

Printed by the American Bank Note Company.

PHOTOGRAVURE
Plates of 160 in four panes of 40.

1990, Oct. 13 Tagged *Perf. 11*
2513 A1872 25c **multicolored** .80 .25
P# block of 4, 5#+A 4.00 —
P# block of 8, 5#+A and inscriptions 8.00 —
Zip block of 4 3.75 —

Imperforates on gummed stamp paper are proofs from the ABNCo. archives. See No. 2513P in Proofs section.

CHRISTMAS

Madonna & Child, by Antonello — A1873

Christmas Tree — A1874

Designed by Bradbury Thompson (#2514) and Libby Thiel (#2515-2516).

Printed by the Bureau of Engraving and Printing or the American Bank Note Company (#2515).

LITHOGRAPHED & ENGRAVED
Sheets of 300 in six panes of 50 (#2414-2415).

1990, Oct. 18 Tagged *Perf. 11¼x11½*
2514 A1873 25c **multicolored**, large block tagging .50 .25
P# block of 4, 5# 2.25 —
Zip, copyright block of 4 2.10 —
a. Large block tagging over prephosphored coated paper with surface tagging showing a solid appearance .50 .25
b. As "a," bklt. pane of 10 5.00 3.25

PHOTOGRAVURE
Perf. 11

2515 A1874 25c **multicolored** .50 .25
P# block of 4, 4#+A 2.25 —
Zip block of 4 2.10 —
Pair with full horiz. gutter btwn. —
a. Vert. pair, imperf. horiz. *500.00*
b. All colors missing (EP) —

No. 2515b must be collected se-tenant with normal and/or partially printed stamp(s).

BOOKLET STAMP

Perf. 11½x11 on 2 or 3 Sides

2516 A1874 25c **multicolored** .60 .25
a. Booklet pane of 10 6.00 3.25

Marked differences exist between Nos. 2515 and 2516. The background red on No. 2515 is even while that on No. 2516 is splotchy. The bands across the tree and "Greetings" are blue green on No. 2515 and yellow green on No. 2516.

A1875

A1876

Designed by Wallace Marosek (Nos. 2517-2520), Richard Sheaff (No. 2521).

Printed by U.S. Bank Note Company (No. 2517), Bureau of Engraving and Printing (No. 2518-2519), KCS Industries (No. 2520), American Bank Note Company (No. 2521).

PHOTOGRAVURE
Sheets of 100

1991, Jan. 22 Tagged *Perf. 13*

2517 A1875 (29c) **yel, blk, red & yel grn** .60 .25
P# block of 4, 4#+U 2.75 —
Zip block of 4 2.50 —
a. Imperf., pair *1,000.*
b. Horiz. pair, imperf. vert. *1,000.*

See note after No. 2518.

Gutter pairs and blocks, and cross gutter blocks, all perforated, are proofs from the ABNCo. archives. See No. 2517P in Proofs section.

No. 2517a is usually collected as a vertical pair, though No. 2517 can be distinguished from the other "F" stamp issues.

COIL STAMP

Perf. 10 Vert.

2518 A1875 (29c) **yel, blk, dull red & dk yel grn** .60 .25
Pair 1.20 .25
P# strip of 5, #1111 2.75
P# strip of 5, #1211 6.50
P# strip of 5, #1222 3.25
P# strip of 5, #2211 3.50
P# strip of 5, #2222 3.25
P# single, #1111 — .50
P# single, #1211 — 11.50
P# single, #1222 — .50
P# single, #2211 — 3.00
P# single, #2222 — .50
a. Imperf., pair 25.00

"For U.S. addresses only" is 17½mm long on No. 2517, 16½mm long on No. 2518. Design of No. 2517 measures 21½x17½mm, No. 2518, 21x18mm.

BOOKLET STAMPS

Perf. 11 on 2 or 3 Sides

2519 A1875 (29c) **yel, blk, dull red & dk grn** .60 .25
a. Booklet pane of 10 6.50 4.50

2520 A1875 (29c) **pale yel, blk, red & brt grn** 1.50 .25
a. Booklet pane of 10 15.00 4.50
b. As "a," imperf. horiz. —
c. Horiz. pair, imperf btwn., in error booklet pane of 12 stamps *450.00*
d. Imperf. vert., pair —

No. 2519 has bullseye perforations that measure approximately 11.2. No. 2520 has less pronounced black lines in the leaf, which is a much brighter green than on No. 2519.

No. 2520c is from a paper foldover before perforating.

LITHOGRAPHED
Panes of 100

1991, Jan. 22 Untagged *Perf. 11*

2521 A1876 (4c) **bister & carmine** .25 .25
P# block of 4, 2# .60 —
Zip block of 4 .50 —
a. Vert. pair, imperf. horiz. 70.00
b. Imperf., pair 60.00

FLAG 

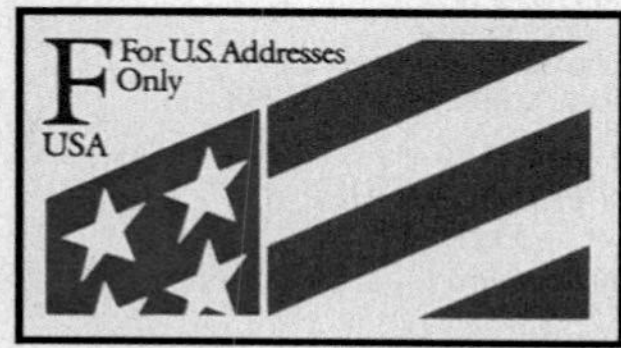

A1877

Designed by Harry Zelenko. Printed by Avery International Corp.

PHOTOGRAVURE

1991, Jan. 22 Untagged Self-Adhesive *Die Cut*
Printed on Plastic

2522 A1877 (29c) **blk, blue & dk red** .60 .25
a. Pane of 12 7.25

Sold only in panes of 12; peelable plastic backing inscribed in light ultramarine. Available during a test period at First National Bank automatic teller machines in Seattle.

Ⓢ: Adhesive residue sometimes remains on the back of examples of No. 2522 after soaking. See note after No. 1549.

Flag Over Mt. Rushmore — A1878

Designed by Clarence Holbert.

COIL STAMPS
ENGRAVED

1991, Mar. 29 Tagged *Perf. 10 Vert.*

2523 A1878 29c **blue, red & claret,** prephosphored uncoated paper with embedded tagging showing a mottled appearance .75 .25
Pair 1.50 .25
P# strip of 5, #1-7 4.00
P# strip of 5, #8 4.75
P# strip of 5, #9 5.25
P# single, #1 — .40
P# single, #2-4 — .50
P# single, #5 — 2.25
P# single, #6, 7 — .45
P# single, #8 — 2.50
P# single, #9 — 2.00
b. Imperf., pair 20.00
c. **blue, red & brown,** prephosphored uncoated paper with embedded tagging showing a mottled appearance 3.00 —
Pair 6.00
P# strip of 5, #1 *4,000.*
P# strip of 5, #7 *135.00*
P# single, #1 — *1,450.*
P# single, 7 — *120.00*
d. Prephosphored coated paper with surface tagging showing a solid appearance 5.00 —
Pair 10.00 —
P# strip of 5, #2 *1,500.*
P# strip of 5, #6 *225.00*
P# single, #2 — *200.00*
P# single, #6 — *150.00*

Specialists often call No. 2523c the "Toledo brown" variety, and No. 2523d "Lenz paper." It was from No. 2523d that it was discovered that "solid tagging" on prephosphored paper resulted from the application of taggant to coated paper.

COIL STAMP
PHOTOGRAVURE

Printed by American Bank Note Co.

1991, July 4 *Perf. 10 Vert.*

2523A A1878 29c **bl, red, lt brn, med brn & dk brn** .75 .25
Pair 1.50 .25
P# strip of 5, #A11111, A22211 4.25
P# single, #A11111, A22211 — 2.25
e. Medium brown omitted —

On No. 2523A, USA and 29 are not outlined in white and are farther from the bottom of the design.

A1879

Designed by Wallace Marosek.

Printed by U.S. Bank Note Co. (#2524), J.W. Fergusson & Sons for Stamp Venturers (#2525, 2526), J.W. Fergusson & Sons, Inc. for KCS Industries, Inc. (#2527).

PHOTOGRAVURE
Panes of 100

1991-92 Tagged *Perf. 11*

2524 A1879 29c **dull yel, blk, red & yel grn,** *Apr. 5, 1991* .60 .25
P# block of 4, 4#+U 2.75 —
Zip block of 4 2.50 —

See note after No. 2527.

Perf. 13x12¾

2524A A1879 29c **dull yel, blk, red & yel grn,** *Apr. 5, 1991* 1.00 .25
P# block of 4, 4#+U 40.00 —
Zip block of 4 6.50 —

COIL STAMPS

Rouletted 10 Vert.

2525 A1879 29c **pale yel, blk, red & yel grn,** *Aug. 16, 1991* .60 .25
Pair 1.20 .30
P# strip of 5, #S1111, S2222 4.00
P# single, #S1111, S2222 — .75

Perf. 10 Vert.

2526 A1879 29c **pale yel, blk, red & yel grn,** *Mar. 3, 1992* .80 .25
Pair 1.60 .30
P# strip of 5, #S2222 4.25
P# single, #S2222 — 2.25

BOOKLET STAMP

Perf. 11 on 2 or 3 Sides

2527 A1879 29c **pale yel, blk, red & bright grn,** *Apr. 5* .60 .25
a. Booklet pane of 10 6.00 3.50
b. Horiz. pair, imperf. between —
c. Horiz. pair, imperf. vert. *150.00*
d. As "a," imperf. horiz. *750.00*
e. As "a," imperf. vert. *500.00*

Flower on Nos. 2524-2524A has grainy appearance, inscriptions look rougher.

No. 2527b resulted from a foldover.

Flag, Olympic Rings — A1880

Designed by John Boyd.

Printed by KCS Industries, Inc.

BOOKLET STAMP
PHOTOGRAVURE

1991, Apr. 21 Tagged *Perf. 11 on 2 or 3 Sides*

2528 A1880 29c **multicolored** .60 .25
a. Booklet pane of 10 6.00 3.50
b. As "a," imperf. horiz. *2,750.*
c. Vert. pair, imperf. between, perfed at top and bottom *225.00*
d. Vert. strip of 3, top or bottom pair imperf. between —
e. Vert. pair, imperf. horiz. *650.00*
f. As "d," two pairs in #2528a with foldover —

No. 2528c comes from misperfed booklet panes. No. 2528d resulted from paper foldovers after normal perforating and before cutting into panes. Two No. 2528d are known. No. 2528e is valued in the grade of fine.

Fishing Boat — A1881

Designed by Pierre Mion.

Printed by: Multi-Color Corp. for American Bank Note Co (type I); Guilford Gravure (type II); J. W. Fergusson & Sons for Stamp Venturers (No. 2529C).

COIL STAMPS
PHOTOGRAVURE

1991, Aug. 8 Tagged *Perf. 9.8 Vert.*

2529 A1881 19c **multicolored,** type I .40 .25
Pair .80 .50
P# strip of 5, #A1111, A1212, A2424 3.00
P# strip of 5, #A1112 4.00
P# single, #A1111, A1212, A2424 — 2.25
P# single, #A1112 — 4.00
a. Type II, *1993* .40 .25
Pair .80 .50
P# strip of 5, #A5555, A5556, A6667, A7667, A7679, A7766, A7779 3.00
P# single, same # — 2.25
b. As "a," untagged, *1993* 1.00 .40
Pair 2.00 .80
P# strip of 5, #A5555 5.75
P# single, #A5555 — 4.25

Design on Type II stamps is created by a finer dot pattern. Vertical sides of "1" are smooth on Type II and jagged on Type I stamps.

Imperforates are from printer's waste. Also, No. 2529a, Plate #A7767 is known only from printer's waste.

Nos. 2529 and 2529a have two loops of rope tying boat to piling.

1994, June 25 **Tagged** ***Perf. 9.8 Vert.***

2529C A1881 19c **multicolored**	.50	.25
Pair	1.00	.50
P# strip of 5, #S111	4.00	
P# single, #S111	—	2.75

No. 2529C has one loop of rope tying boat to piling.

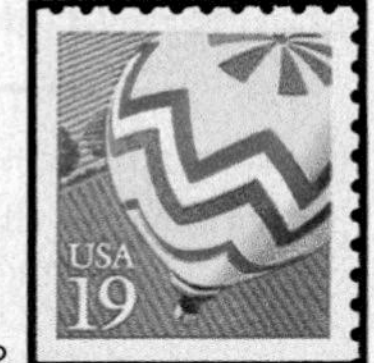

Balloon — A1882

BOOKLET STAMP

1991, May 17 **Tagged** ***Perf. 10 on 2 or 3 Sides***

2530 A1882 19c **multicolored**	.40	.25
a. Booklet pane of 10	4.00	2.75

Flags on Parade — A1883

Designed by Frank J. Waslick and Peter Cocci.

PHOTOGRAVURE
Panes of 100

1991, May 30 **Tagged** ***Perf. 11***

2531 A1883 29c **multicolored**, overall tagging	.60	.25
P# block of 4, 4#	2.75	—
Zip block of 4	2.50	—
b. Prephosphored coated paper with surface tagging showing a solid appearance	.75	.25
P# block of 4, 4#	6.50	—
Zip block of 4	3.25	—

Counterfeits exist of No. 2531. See the Postal Counterfeits section of this catalog.

Liberty Torch — A1884

Designed by Harry Zelenko.

Printed by Avery Dennison Co.

PHOTOGRAVURE

1991, June 25 **Tagged** ***Die Cut***

Self-Adhesive

2531A A1884 29c **black, gold & green**, prephosphored coated paper with surface tagging showing a solid appearance ⑤	.60	.25
b. Booklet pane of 18	11.00	
c. Die cutting omitted, pair	*1,000.*	
d. Overall tagging, *1992*	.60	.25
e. As "d," booklet pane of 18	11.00	

Sold only in panes of 18; peelable paper backing inscribed in light blue. Available for consumer testing at First National Bank automatic teller machines in Seattle, WA.

⑤: Adhesive residue sometimes remains on the back of examples of No. 2531A after soaking. See note after No. 1549.

SWITZERLAND

Switzerland, 700th Anniv. A1887

Designed by Hans Hartman, Switzerland.

Printed by the American Bank Note Company.

PHOTOGRAVURE
Plates of 160 in four panes of 40

1991, Feb. 22 **Tagged** ***Perf. 11***

2532 A1887 50c **multicolored**	1.00	.25
P# block of 4, 5#+A	5.00	—
Zip block of 4	4.25	—
a. Vert. pair, imperf. horiz.	*1,400.*	

See Switzerland No. 888.
Imperfs exist from printer's waste.

VERMONT STATEHOOD, 200th ANNIV.

A1888

Designed by Sabra Field.

Printed by the American Bank Note Company.

PHOTOGRAVURE
Plates of 200 in four panes of 50

1991, Mar. 1 **Tagged** ***Perf. 11***

2533 A1888 29c **multicolored**	.80	.25
P# block of 4, 4#+A	4.00	—
Zip block of 4	3.50	—

SAVINGS BONDS, 50TH ANNIVERSARY

A1889

Designed by Primo Angeli.

PHOTOGRAVURE
Plates of 200 in four panes of 50

1991, Apr. 30 **Tagged** ***Perf. 11***

2534 A1889 29c **multicolored**	.60	.25
P# block of 4, 6#	2.75	—
Zip block of 4	2.50	—
a. Tagging omitted	—	

LOVE

A1890

A1891

Designed by Harry Zelenko (#2535-2536) and Nancy L. Krause (#2537).

Printed by U.S. Banknote Co. (#2535), the Bureau of Engraving and Printing (#2536) and American Bank Note Co. (#2537).

PHOTOGRAVURE
Panes of 50

1991, May 9 **Tagged** ***Perf. 12½x13***

2535 A1890 29c **multicolored**	.60	.25
P# block of 4, 5#+U	2.75	—
Zip, copyright block of 4	2.50	—
b. Imperf., pair	*1,650.*	

Perf. 11

2535A A1890 29c **multicolored**	1.00	.25
P# block of 4, 5#+U	5.00	—
Zip, copyright block of 4	4.00	—

BOOKLET STAMP

Perf. 11.1x11.3 on 2 or 3 Sides

2536 A1890 29c **multicolored**	.60	.25
a. Booklet pane of 10	6.00	3.50

"29" is closer to edge of design on No. 2536 than on No. 2535.

Sheets of 200 in panes of 50

Perf. 11

2537 A1891 52c **multicolored**	.90	.25
P# block of 4, 3#+A	4.50	—
Zip block of 4	4.00	—

LITERARY ARTS SERIES

William Saroyan (1908-81), Author A1892

Designed by Ren Wicks.

Printed by J.W. Fergusson for American Bank Note Co.

PHOTOGRAVURE
Sheets of 200 in four panes of 50

1991, May 22 **Tagged** ***Perf. 11***

2538 A1892 29c **multicolored**	.60	.25
P# block of 4, 5#+A	2.75	—
Zip block of 4	2.50	—
a. All colors missing (EP)		—
b. All colors except black missing (EP)	11,000.	

No. 2538a must be collected se-tenant with a partially printed stamp. On No. 2538b, only part of the black is present; it is unique.

See Russia No. 6002.

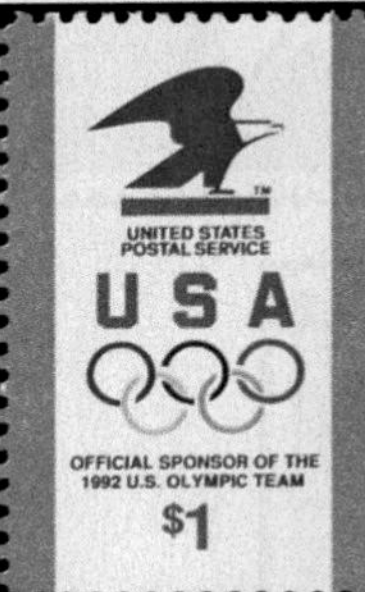

Eagle, Olympic Rings — A1893

Eagle — A1894

Eagle and Olympic Rings — A1895

Eagle in Flight — A1896

Futuristic Space Shuttle A1897

Space Shuttle Challenger A1898

Space Shuttle Endeavour — A1898a

Designed by: Terrence McCaffrey (Nos. 2539-2541), Timothy Knapp (No. 2542), Ken Hodges (No. 2543), Phil Jordan (Nos. 2544-2544A).

Printed by: J.W. Fergusson & Sons for Stamp Venturers (No. 2539); American Bank Note Co (Nos. 2540-2541); Jeffries Banknote Co. for the American Bank Note Co (No. 2542).

Nos. 2540, 2543-2544 for priority mail rate. Nos. 2541, 2544A for domestic express mail rate. No. 2542 for international express mail rate.
Nos. 2544-2544A printed by Ashton-Potter (USA) Ltd.

Sheet of 180 in nine panes of 20 (No. 2539)
Sheet of 120 in six panes of 20 (Nos. 2540-2542, 2544-2544A)
Pane of 40 (No. 2543)

PHOTOGRAVURE

Copyright information appears in the center of the top and bottom selvage.

1991, Sept. 29 Tagged *Perf. 11*
2539 A1893 $1 **gold & multi** 2.00 .50
P# block of 4, 6#+S 10.00 —
Pane of 20 50.00
a. Black omitted —

LITHOGRAPHED & ENGRAVED

1991, July 7 Tagged *Perf. 11*
2540 A1894 $2.90 **multicolored** 6.00 1.50
P# block of 4, 5#+A 24.00 —
Pane of 20 120.00
a. Vert. pair, imperf horiz. *900.00*
b. Black (engr.) omitted *750.00*

Imperforates on gummed stamp paper, including gutter pairs and blocks, are proofs from the ABNCo. archives. From the same source also come imperforate progressive proofs. See No. 2540P in Proofs section.

1991, June 16 Untagged *Perf. 11*
2541 A1895 $9.95 **multicolored** 20.00 6.00
P# block of 4, 5#+A 80.00 —
Pane of 20 400.00
a. Imperf., pair —

No. 2541 exists imperf plus black (engr.) omitted from printer's waste.

1991, Aug. 31 Untagged *Perf. 11*
2542 A1896 $14 **multicolored** 25.00 15.00
P# block of 4, 5#+A 100.00 —
Pane of 20 500.00
a. Red (engr. inscriptions) omitted *750.00*

No. 2542 exists imperf plus red omitted from printer's waste.

PHOTOGRAVURE

1993, June 3 Tagged *Perf. 11x10¾*
2543 A1897 $2.90 **multicolored** 6.00 1.75
P# block of 4, 6# 27.50 —
Zip block of 4 25.00 —
a. Tagging omitted —

Faked examples of No. 2543, unused and used, exist with red omitted due to bleaching.

1995, June 22 Tagged *Perf. 11.2*
2544 A1898 $3 **multicolored,** dated "1995" 5.75 1.75
P# block of 4, 5#+P 23.50 —
Pane of 20 120.00 —
b. Dated "1996" 5.75 1.75
P# block of 4, 5#+P 23.50 —
Pane of 20 120.00 —
c. As "b," horiz. pair, imperf between *1,000.*
d. As "b," imperf pair *800.00*

1995, Aug. 4 Tagged *Perf. 11*
2544A A1898a $10.75 **multicolored** 20.00 9.00
P# block of 4, 5#+P 82.50 —
Pane of 20 425.00 —

No. 2544A was printed on paper embedded with red fibers.

FISHING FLIES

Royal Wulff — A1899

Jock Scott — A1900

Apte Tarpon Fly — A1901

Lefty's Deceiver A1902

Muddler Minnow A1903

Designed by Chuck Ripper.

Printed by American Bank Note Co.

PHOTOGRAVURE
BOOKLET STAMPS

Perf. 11 Horiz. on 1 or 2 Sides

1991, May 31 Tagged
2545 A1899 29c **multicolored** 1.10 .25
a. Black omitted —
b. Horiz. pair, imperf. btwn., in #2549a with foldover *2,400.*
2546 A1900 29c **multicolored** 1.10 .25
a. Black omitted —
2547 A1901 29c **multicolored** 1.10 .25
a. Black omitted —
2548 A1902 29c **multicolored** 1.10 .25
2549 A1903 29c **multicolored** 1.10 .25
a. Bklt. pane of 5, #2545-2549 5.50 3.00

Horiz. pairs, imperf vert., exist from printer's waste.
No. 2545b is unique and resulted from a foldover after perfing but before cutting. Both stamps are creased.

PERFORMING ARTS

Cole Porter (1891-1964), Composer — A1904

Designed by Jim Sharpe.

Printed by American Bank Note Co.

PHOTOGRAVURE
Panes of 50

1991, June 8 Tagged *Perf. 11*
2550 A1904 29c **multicolored** .60 .25
P# block of 4, 5#+A 2.75 —
Zip block of 4 2.50 —
a. Vert. pair, imperf. horiz. *400.00*

OPERATIONS DESERT SHIELD & DESERT STORM

S. W. Asia Service Medal — A1905

Designed by Jack Williams.

Printed by J.W. Fergusson Co. for Stamp Venturers (No. 2551), Multi-Color Corp. for the American Bank Note Co. (No. 2552).

PHOTOGRAVURE
Panes of 50

1991, July 2 Tagged *Perf. 11*
2551 A1905 29c **multicolored** .60 .25
P# block of 4, 7#+S 2.75 —
Zip block of 4 2.50 —
a. Vert. pair, imperf. horiz. *600.00*

No. 2551 is 21mm wide.

BOOKLET STAMP

Perf. 11 Vert. on 1 or 2 Sides

2552 A1905 29c **multicolored** .60 .25
a. Booklet pane of 5 3.00 2.25

No. 2552 is 20½mm wide. Inscriptions are shorter than on No. 2551.

No. 2552 Vert. pairs, imperf horiz., are from printer's waste.

1992 SUMMER OLYMPICS, BARCELONA

Pole Vault — A1907

Discus A1908

Women's Sprints A1909

Javelin A1910

Women's Hurdles A1911

Designed by Joni Carter.

Printed by the American Bank Note Co.

PHOTOGRAVURE

Panes of 40

1991, July 12	**Tagged**	***Perf. 11***	
2553 A1907 29c **multicolored**		.60	.25
2554 A1908 29c **multicolored**		.60	.25
2555 A1909 29c **multicolored**		.60	.25
2556 A1910 29c **multicolored**		.60	.25
2557 A1911 29c **multicolored**		.60	.25
a. Strip of 5, #2553-2557		3.00	2.25
P# block of 10, 5#+A		8.00	—
Zip block of 10		6.00	—

NUMISMATICS

1858 Flying Eagle Cent, 1907 Standing Liberty Double Eagle, Series 1875 $1 Note, Series 1902 $10 National Currency Note — A1912

Designed by V. Jack Ruther.

LITHOGRAPHED & ENGRAVED

Sheets of 200 in four panes of 50

1991, Aug. 13	**Tagged**	***Perf. 11***	
2558 A1912 29c **multicolored**		.60	.25
P# block of 4, 7#		2.75	—
Zip block of 4		2.50	—

WORLD WAR II

A1913

Illustration reduced.

Designed by William H. Bond.

Designs and events of 1941: a, Military vehicles (Burma Road, 717-mile lifeline to China). b, Recruits (America's first peacetime draft). c, Shipments for allies (U.S. supports allies with Lend-Lease Act). d, Franklin D. Roosevelt, Winston Churchill (Atlantic Charter sets war aims of allies). e, Tank (America becomes the "arsenal of democracy.") f, Sinking of Destoyer Reuben James, Oct. 31. g, Gas mask, helmet (Civil defense mobilizes Americans at home). h, Liberty Ship, sea gull (First Liberty ship delivered December 30). i, Sinking ships (Japanese bomb Pearl Harbor, December 7). j, Congress in session (U.S. declares war on Japan, December 8). Central label is the size of 15 stamps and shows world map, extent of axis control.

LITHOGRAPHED & ENGRAVED

Plates of eight subjects in four panes of 2 each

1991, Sept. 3	**Tagged**	***Perf. 11***	
2559 A1913 Block of 10		7.50	5.00
Pane of 20		15.00	—
a.-j. 29c any single		.75	.45
k. Black (engr.) omitted		*6,500.*	
l. As "c," tagging omitted		—	

No. 2559 has selvage at left and right and either top or bottom.

BASKETBALL, 100TH ANNIVERSARY

Basketball, Hoop, Players' Arms — A1914

Designed by Lon Busch.

PHOTOGRAVURE

Sheets of 200 in four panes of 50

1991, Aug. 28	**Tagged**	***Perf. 11***	
2560 A1914 29c **multicolored**		.60	.25
P# block of 4, 4#		3.50	—
Zip block of 4		2.50	—

DISTRICT OF COLUMBIA BICENTENNIAL

Capitol Building from Pennsylvania Avenue, Circa 1903 — A1915

Designed by Pierre Mion.

LITHOGRAPHED & ENGRAVED

Plates of 200 in four panes of 50

1991, Sept. 7	**Tagged**	***Perf. 11***	
2561 A1915 29c **multicolored**		.60	.25
P# block of 4, 5#		2.75	—
Zip block of 4		2.50	—
a. Black (engr.) omitted		*85.00*	

COMEDIANS

Stan Laurel (1890-1965) and Oliver Hardy (1892-1957) A1916

Edgar Bergen (1903-1978) and Charlie McCarthy A1917

Jack Benny (1894-1974) A1918

Fanny Brice (1891-1951) A1919

Bud Abbott (1895-1974) and Lou Costello (1908-1959) A1920

Designed by Al Hirschfeld.

LITHOGRAPHED & ENGRAVED
BOOKLET STAMPS

1991, Aug. 29	**Tagged**	***Perf. 11 on 2 or 3 Sides***	
2562 A1916 29c **multicolored**		1.00	.25
2563 A1917 29c **multicolored**		1.00	.25
2564 A1918 29c **multicolored**		1.00	.25
2565 A1919 29c **multicolored**		1.00	.25
2566 A1920 29c **multicolored**		1.00	.25
a. Strip of 5, #2562-2566		5.00	2.25
b. Bklt. pane of 10, 2 each #2562-2566		10.00	5.00
c. As "b," scar & brt violet (engr.) omitted		*350.00*	

BLACK HERITAGE SERIES

Jan E. Matzeliger (1852-1889), Inventor — A1921

Designed by Higgins Bond.
Printed by J.W. Fergusson & Sons for the American Bank Note Co.

PHOTOGRAVURE
Plates of 200 in four panes of 50

1991, Sept. 15	**Tagged**	***Perf. 11***	
2567	A1921 29c **multicolored**	.60	.25
	P# block of 4, 6#+A	3.00	—
	Zip block of 4	2.50	—
a.	Horiz. pair, imperf. vert.	*600.00*	
b.	Vert. pair, imperf. horiz.	*550.00*	
c.	Imperf., pair	*275.00*	

SPACE EXPLORATION

Mercury, Mariner 10 A1922

Venus, Mariner 2 A1923

Earth, Landsat A1924

Moon, Lunar Orbiter A1925

Mars, Viking Orbiter A1926

Jupiter,

Saturn, Voyager 2 A1928

Uranus, Voyager 2 A1929

Neptune, Voyager 2 A1930

Pluto — A1931

Designed by Ron Miller.

PHOTOGRAVURE
BOOKLET STAMPS

1991, Oct. 1	**Tagged**	***Perf. 11 on 2 or 3 Sides***	
2568	A1922 29c **multicolored**	.90	.25
2569	A1923 29c **multicolored**	.90	.25
2570	A1924 29c **multicolored**	.90	.25
2571	A1925 29c **multicolored**	.90	.25
2572	A1926 29c **multicolored**	.90	.25
2573	A1927 29c **multicolored**	.90	.25
2574	A1928 29c **multicolored**	.90	.25
2575	A1929 29c **multicolored**	.90	.25
2576	A1930 29c **multicolored**	.90	.25
2577	A1931 29c **multicolored**	.90	.25
a.	Bklt. pane of 10, #2568-2577	9.00	4.50

CHRISTMAS

Madonna and Child by Antoniazzo Romano — A1933

Santa Claus in Chimney — A1934

Santa Checking List — A1935

Santa with Present — A1936

Santa at Fireplace — A1937

Santa and Sleigh — A1938

Designed by Bradbury Thompson (#2578) and John Berkey (#2579-2585).
Printed by the Bureau of Engraving and Printing (#2578); J.W. Fergusson & Sons (#2579) and Multi-Color Corp. (#2580-2585) for the American Bank Note Co.

LITHOGRAPHED & ENGRAVED
Sheets of 300 in six panes of 50

1991, Oct. 17	**Tagged**	***Perf. 11¼***	
2578	A1933 (29c) **multicolored**	.60	.25
	P# block of 4, 5#	2.75	—
	Zip, copyright block of 4	2.50	—
a.	Booklet pane of 10	6.00	3.25
b.	Red & black (engr.) omitted	*2,250.*	

PHOTOGRAVURE
Perf. 11

2579	A1934 (29c) **multicolored**	.60	.25
	P# block of 4, 3#+A	2.50	—
	Zip block of 4	2.25	—
a.	Horiz. pair, imperf. vert.	175.00	
b.	Vert. pair, imperf. horiz.	*350.00*	

BOOKLET STAMPS
Size: 25x18½mm
Perf. 11 on 2 or 3 Sides

2580	A1934 (29c) **multicolored**, type I	2.00	.25
2581	A1934 (29c) **multicolored**, type II	2.00	.25
a.	Pair #2580-2581	4.00	.55
b.	Bklt. pane, 2 each, #2580-2581	8.00	1.25
2582	A1935 (29c) **multicolored**	.60	.25
a.	Bklt. pane of 4	2.40	1.25
2583	A1936 (29c) **multicolored**	.60	.25
a.	Bklt. pane of 4	2.40	1.25
2584	A1937 (29c) **multicolored**	.60	.25
a.	Bklt. pane of 4	2.40	1.25
2585	A1938 (29c) **multicolored**	.60	.25
a.	Bklt. pane of 4	2.40	1.25
	Nos. 2578-2585 (8)	7.60	2.00

The far left brick from the top row of the chimney is missing from Type II, No. 2581.
Imperfs of Nos. 2581, 2583-2585 are printer's waste.

Pres. James K. Polk (1795-1849) A1939

"The Surrender of General Burgoyne at Saratoga," by John Trumbull A1942

Presidents George Washington and Andrew Jackson — A1944

Printed by Banknote Corporation of America (No. 2587), Stamp Venturers (Nos. 2590, 2592).

ENGRAVED

Sheets of 400 in four panes of 100 (No. 2587)
Sheets of 120 in six panes of 20 (Nos. 2590, 2592)

1994-95 **Tagged** ***Perf. 11.2***

2587 A1939 32c **red brown,** *Nov. 2, 1995* .65 .25
P# block of 4, 1#+B 3.25 —

Perf. 11.5

2590 A1942 $1 **blue,** *May 5, 1994* 1.90 .50
P# block of 4, 1#+S 7.60 —
Pane of 20 38.00 —
2592 A1944 $5 **slate green,** *Aug. 19, 1994* 8.00 2.50
P# block of 4, 1#+S 40.00 —
Pane of 20 160.00 —

Some plate blocks contain either inscription or plate position diagram.

Flag — A1946

Eagle and Shield — A1947

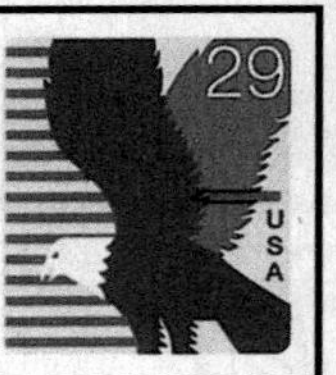

Eagle — A1950

Statue of Liberty — A1951

Designed by Lou Nolan (#2593-2594), Jay Haiden (#2595-2597), Richard Sheaff (#2598), Tom Engeman (#2599).
Printed by Bureau of Engraving & Printing (#2593), Stamp Venturers for KCS Industries (#2594), Banknote Corporation of America (#2595), Dittler Brothers, Inc. (#2596, 2599), Stamp Venturers (#2597), National Label Co. for 3M (#2598).

BOOKLET STAMPS
PHOTOGRAVURE

1992, Sept. 8 **Tagged** ***Perf. 10 on 2 or 3 Sides***

2593 A1946 29c **black & multi** .60 .25
a. Booklet pane of 10 6.00 4.25
d. Imperf, pair *500.00*

Perf. 11x10 on 2 or 3 Sides

2593B A1946 29c **black & multi,** shiny gum 2.50 .50
Low gloss gum 3.50
c. Bklt. pane of 10, shiny gum 30.00 7.50
Low gloss gum 40.00

1993, Apr. 8 (?) ***Perf. 11x10 on 2 or 3 Sides***

2594 A1946 29c **red & multi** .65 .25
a. Booklet pane of 10 6.50 4.25

Denomination is red on #2594 and black on #2593 and 2593B.

LITHOGRAPHED & ENGRAVED (#2595), PHOTOGRAVURE

1992, Sept. 25 **Tagged** ***Die Cut***
Self-Adhesive

2595 A1947 29c **brown & multicolored** .75 .25
a. Bklt. pane of 17 + label 12.75
b. Die cutting omitted, pair *90.00*
c. Brown omitted *250.00*
d. As "a," die cutting omitted *725.00*
2596 A1947 29c **green & multicolored** .75 .25
a. Bklt. pane of 17 + label 12.75
2597 A1947 29c **red & multicolored** .75 .25
a. Bklt. pane of 17 + label 12.75

Plate No. and inscription reads down on No. 2595a and up on Nos. 2596a-2597a. Design is sharper and more finely detailed on Nos. 2595, 2597.
Nos. 2595a-2597a sold for $5 each.
Nos. 2595-2597 also available in strips with stamps spaced for use in affixing machines to service first day covers.

PHOTOGRAVURE

1994 **Tagged** ***Die Cut***
Self-Adhesive

2598 A1950 29c **red, cream & blue,** *Feb. 4* .60 .25
a. Booklet pane of 18 11.00
b. Coil with P#111 — 5.00
P# strip of 5, #111 7.00
c. Die cutting omitted, pair *1,000.*

2599 A1951 29c **multicolored,** *June 24* .60 .25
a. Booklet pane of 18 11.00
b. Coil with P#D1111 — 5.00
P# strip of 5, #D1111 8.00

Except for No. 2599b with plate number, coil stamps of this issue are indistinguishable from booklet stamps once they are removed from the backing paper. For No. 2598b, however, the stamps from the coil strips have minutely rounded corners, whereas the corners of the booklet stamps are squared.
See Nos. 3122-3122E.

Scott values for used self-adhesive stamps are for examples either on piece or off piece.

Eagle and Shield — A1956

Eagle and Shield — A1957

Flag — A1959

Flag — A1960

Flag Over White House — A1961

Designed by Chris Calle (#2602-2604), Terrence McCaffrey (#2605), Lon Busch (#2606-2608), V. Jack Ruther (29c).
Printed by Guildford Gravure, Inc. for the American Bank Note Co. (#2602, 2606), Bureau of Engraving and Printing (#2603, 2607), Stamp Venturers (#2604, 2608), American Bank Note Co. (#2605).

PHOTOGRAVURE
COIL STAMPS

1991-93 **Untagged** ***Perf. 10 Vert.***

2602 A1956 (10c) **multi** (Bureau precancel, Bulk Rate, in blue), *Dec. 13* .30 .25
Pair .60 .50
P# strip of 5, #A11111, A11112, A21112, A21113, A22112, A22113, A33333, A43325, A43326, A43334, A43335, A53335, A54444, A54445, A77777, A88888 1.90
P# strip of 5, #A12213 5.00
P# strip of 5, #A34424, A34426, A43324, A88889 2.75
P# strip of 5, #A32333 *160.00*
P# strip of 5, #A33334 10.00
P# strip of 5, #A33335, A43426, A89999, A99998, A99999, A1010101010, A1011101011, A1011101012, A1110101010, A1110111010, A1111101010, A1111111010, A1411101010, A1411101011, A1412111110, A1412111111 2.25
P# strip of 5, #A1011101010 3.25
P# strip of 5, #A1211101010 3.00
P# strip of 5, #A1110101011 4.00
P# single, #A11111, A11112, A21112, A21113, A22112, A22113, A43324, A43325, A43326, A43334, A43335, A43426, A53335, A54444, A54445, A77777, A88888, A89999, A99998, A99999 — 1.75
P# single, #A12213 — 5.00
P# single, #A32333 — 175.00
P# single, #A33333, A33335, A34424, A34426 — 2.50
P# single, #A33334 — 45.00
P# single, #A53335, A88889, A1010101010, A1011101011, A1011101012, A1110101010, A1110111010, A1111101010, A1111111010, A1411101010, A1411101011, A1412111110, A1412111111 — 2.50
P# single, #A1011101010 — 3.00
P# single, #A1211101010 — 4.00
P# single, #A1110101011 — 7.00
a. Imperf., pair *3,500.*
2603 A1957 (10c) **org yel & multi,** shiny gum (Bureau precancel, Bulk Rate, in red), *May 29, 1993* .30 .25
Pair .60 .50
P# strip of 5, #11111, 22221, 22222 2.25
P# single, same — 1.75
Low gloss gum .25
Pair .50
P# strip of 5, #22222, 33333, 44444 3.00
P# strip of 5, #11111 15.00
P# single, #33333, 44444 — 2.00
a. Imperf., pair 20.00
b. Tagged (error), shiny gum 2.00 1.50
Pair 4.00 3.50
P# strip of 5, #11111, 22221 9.00
P# strip of 5, #22222 *400.00*
P# single, #11111, 22221 — 10.00
P# single, #22222 — *350.00*

All examples of Nos. 2603, 2603a and 2603b were printed with luminescent ink.
See No. 2907.

2604 A1957 (10c) **gold & multi,** low gloss gum (Bureau precancel, Bulk Rate, in red), *May 29, 1993* .25 .25
Pair .50 .50
P# strip of 5, #S11111 2.00
P# strip of 5, #S22222 1.75
P# single, #S11111 — 1.50
Shiny gum .50
Pair 1.00
P# strip of 5, #S22222 4.00
P# single, same — 1.50
2605 A1959 23c **multi** (Bureau precancel in blue), *Sept. 27* .45 .40
Pair .90 .80
P# strip of 5, #A111, A212, A222 3.00
P# strip of 5, #A112, A122, A333 3.25
P# single, #A111, A112, A122, A212, A222, A333 — 2.25
a. Imperf, pair —

Vertical pairs uncut between on gummed stamp paper are proofs from the ABNCo. archives. See No. 2605P in Proofs section.

2606 A1960 23c **multi** (Bureau precanceled), *July 21, 1992* .45 .40
Pair .90 .80
P# strip of 5, #A1111, A2222, A2232, A2233, A3333, A4364, A4443, A4444, A4453 3.50
P# single, same # — 2.50

"First-Class" is 9½mm long and "23" is 6mm long on No. 2606.

2607 A1960 23c **multi,** shiny gum (Bureau precanceled), *Oct. 9, 1992* .45 .40
Pair .90 .80
P# strip of 5, #1111 4.00
P# single, #1111 — 1.75
Low gloss gum .45
Pair .90
P# strip of 5, #1111 4.00
a. Tagged (error), shiny gum 5.00 4.50
Pair 10.00 9.00
P# strip of 5, #1111 125.00
P# single, #1111 — 95.00
c. Imperf., pair 65.00

"First-Class" is 9mm long and "23" is 6½mm long on No. 2607.

2608 A1960 23c **vio bl, red & blk** (Bureau precanceled), *May 14, 1993* .80 .40
Pair 1.60 .80
P# strip of 5, #S111 4.25
P# single, #S111 — 2.25

"First-Class" is 8½mm long and "23" is 6½mm long on No. 2608.

ENGRAVED
Tagged

2609 A1961 29c **blue & red,** *Apr. 23, 1992* .60 .25
Pair 1.20 .50
P# strip of 5, #1-8 4.00
P# strip of 5, #9-16 4.50
P# strip of 5, #18 5.50
P# single, #1-4 — .50
P# single, #5 — 2.00
P# single, #6-8 — .50
P# single, #9 — 2.25
P# single, #10-16 — .80
P# single, #18 — 4.50
a. Imperf., pair 15.00 *25.00*
b. Pair, imperf. between 75.00
c. 29c **Indigo blue & red** *22.50* —
Pair *45.00* —
Nos. 2602-2609 (8) 3.60 2.60

Beware of pairs with blind perfs sometimes offered as No. 2609b.
See Nos. 2907, 3270-3271.

WINTER OLYMPICS

Hockey
A1963

Figure Skating
A1964

Speed Skating
A1965

Skiing
A1966

Bobsledding
A1967

Designed by Lon Busch. Printed by J.W. Fergusson & Sons for Stamp Venturers.

PHOTOGRAVURE
Panes of 35

1992, Jan. 11	**Tagged**	***Perf. 11***	
2611 A1963 29c **multicolored**		.60	.25
2612 A1964 29c **multicolored**		.60	.25
2613 A1965 29c **multicolored**		.60	.25
2614 A1966 29c **multicolored**		.60	.25
2615 A1967 29c **multicolored**		.60	.25
a. Strip of 5, #2611-2615		3.00	2.50
P# block of 10, 4#+S		7.00	—
Zip, copyright block of 15		9.00	—

Inscriptions on six marginal tabs.

WORLD COLUMBIAN STAMP EXPO

Features detail from No. 129 — A1968

Designed by Richard Sheaff.

LITHOGRAPHED & ENGRAVED
Plates of 200 in four panes of 50

1992, Jan. 24	**Tagged**	***Perf. 11***	
2616 A1968 29c **multicolored**		.60	.25
P# block of 4, 4#		3.00	—
Zip block of 4		2.50	—
a. Tagging omitted		10.00	

BLACK HERITAGE SERIES

W.E.B. Du Bois (1868-1963), Civil Rights Leader — A1969

Designed by Higgins Bond.

LITHOGRAPHED & ENGRAVED
Plates of 200 in four panes of 50

1992, Jan. 31	**Tagged**	***Perf. 11***	
2617 A1969 29c **multicolored**		.60	.25
P# block of 4, 7#		2.75	—
Zip block of 4		2.50	—

LOVE

Heart in Envelope — A1970

Designed by Uldis Purins. Printed by the U.S. Bank Note Co.

PHOTOGRAVURE
Panes of 50

1992, Feb. 6	**Tagged**	***Perf. 11***	
2618 A1970 29c **multicolored**		.60	.25
P# block of 4, U+5#		2.75	—
Zip, copyright block of 4		2.50	—
a. Horiz. pair, imperf. vert.		*300.00*	
b. As "a," green omitted on right stamp		*1,250.*	

OLYMPIC BASEBALL

Baseball Players
A1971

Designed by Anthony DeLuz.

PHOTOGRAVURE
Plates of 200 in four panes of 50

1992, Apr. 3	**Tagged**	***Perf. 11***	
2619 A1971 29c **multicolored**		.60	.25
P# block of 4, 5#		2.75	—
Zip block of 4		2.50	—

VOYAGES OF COLUMBUS

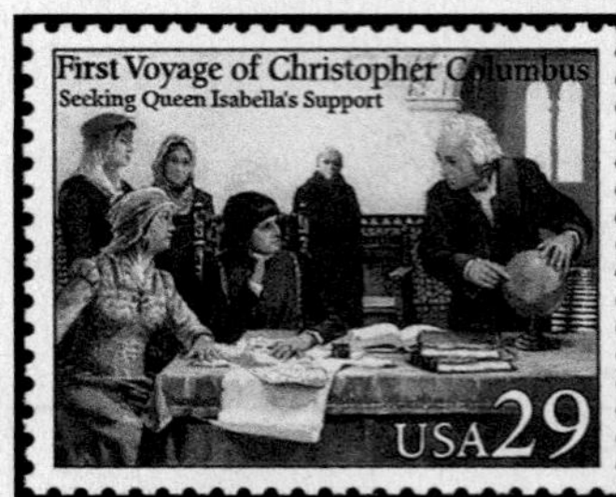

Seeking Queen Isabella's Support
A1972

Crossing the Atlantic
A1973

Approaching Land
A1974

Coming Ashore
A1975

Designed by Richard Schlecht.

LITHOGRAPHED & ENGRAVED
Plates of 160 in four panes of 40

1992, Apr. 24	**Tagged**	***Perf. 11***	
2620 A1972 29c **multicolored**		.65	.25
2621 A1973 29c **multicolored**		.65	.25
2622 A1974 29c **multicolored**		.65	.25
2623 A1975 29c **multicolored**		.65	.25
a. Block of 4, #2620-2623		2.60	2.00
P# block of 4, 5#		2.75	—
Zip block of 4		2.60	—

See Italy Nos. 1877-1880.

Souvenir Sheets

A1976

A1977

A1978

A1979

A1980

Christopher Columbus
The United States Postal Service celebrates the 500th anniversary of the voyages of Christopher Columbus. This set is based on the first U.S. stamps in commemorative format, engraved a century ago.

A1981

Illustrations reduced.

Designed by Richard Sheaff.

Printed by the American Bank Note Co. Margins on Nos. 2624-2628 are lithographed. Nos. 2624a-2628c, 2629 are similar in design to Nos. 230-245 but are dated 1492-1992.

LITHOGRAPHED & ENGRAVED

1992, May 22 *Perf. 10½*

Tagged (15c-$5), Untagged

2624	A1976	Pane of 3	2.25	1.50
a.	A71 1c **deep blue**		.25	.25
b.	A74 4c **ultramarine**		.25	.25
c.	A82 $1 **salmon**		1.75	1.00
d.	As No. 2624, tagging omitted on "c"		*1,000.*	
2625	A1977	Pane of 3	7.50	5.00
a.	A72 2c **brown violet**		.25	.25
b.	A73 3c **green**		.25	.25
c.	A85 $4 **crimson lake**		7.00	4.00
2626	A1978	Pane of 3	1.75	1.25
a.	A75 5c **chocolate**		.25	.25
b.	A80 30c **orange brown**		.60	.30
c.	A81 50c **slate blue**		.90	.50
d.	As No. 2626, tagging omitted on "c"		—	—
2627	A1979	Pane of 3	6.00	3.75
a.	A76 6c **purple**		.25	.25
b.	A77 8c **magenta**		.25	.25
c.	A84 $3 **yellow green**		5.50	3.00
2628	A1980	Pane of 3	4.25	3.00
a.	A78 10c **black brown**		.25	.25
b.	A79 15c **dark green**		.30	.25
c.	A83 $2 **brown red**		3.50	2.00
d.	As No. 2628, tagging omitted on "b"		*500.00*	
2629	A1981 $5 Pane of 1		8.75	6.00
a.	A86 $5 **black**, single stamp		8.50	5.00
	Nos. 2624-2629 (6)		30.50	20.50

See Italy Nos. 1883-1888, Portugal Nos. 1918-1923 and Spain Nos. 2677-2682.

Imperforate souvenir sheets on gummed stamp paper, singly or in pairs and blocks, are proofs from the ABNCo. archives. Additionally, one imperforate essay, with the background of No. 2622 combined with the stamps of No. 2620, is recorded. See Nos. 2624P-2629P in Proofs section.

NEW YORK STOCK EXCHANGE BICENTENNIAL

A1982

Designed by Richard Sheaff.

Printed by the Jeffries Bank Note Co. for the American Bank Note Co.

LITHOGRAPHED & ENGRAVED

Panes of 40

1992, May 17 **Tagged** *Perf. 11*

2630	A1982 29c **green, red & black**		.60	.25
	P# block of 4, 3#+A		2.75	—
	Zip, Olympic block of 4		2.50	—
a.	Black missing (EP)		*4,000.*	
b.	Black missing (CM)		*4,000.*	
c.	Center (black engr.) inverted		*17,000.*	
d.	Se-tenant pair, #2630b and #2630c		*22,500.*	

No. 2630a resulted from extraneous paper that blocked the black from appearing on the stamp paper. It is from a unique pane that contained four color-missing errors plus a fifth stamp missing half the black center.

No. 2630a must be collected se-tenant with a normal stamp or with a stamp with half of black engraving missing, or se-tenant with a normal stamp and an additional 2630a.

No. 2630b may be collected alone or se-tenant with No. 2630c.

Two panes, each containing 28 No. 2630c and 12 No. 2630b, have been documented.

SPACE ACCOMPLISHMENTS

Cosmonaut, US Space Shuttle — A1983

Astronaut, Russian Space Station, Russian Space Shuttle — A1984

Sputnik, Vostok, Apollo Command & Lunar Modules — A1985

Soyuz, Mercury & Gemini Spacecraft — A1986

"Toaster Cord" Plate Flaw

Designed by Vladimir Beilin (Russia) and Robert T. McCall.

PHOTOGRAVURE

Plates of 200 in four panes of 50

1992, May 29 **Tagged** *Perf. 11*

2631	A1983 29c **multicolored**		.60	.25
2632	A1984 29c **multicolored**		.60	.25
2633	A1985 29c **multicolored**		.60	.25
	Black line below space capsule, "Toaster Cord" plate flaw (plate 1111 LL 49 and LR 49)		4.50	2.50
2634	A1986 29c **multicolored**		.60	.25
a.	Block of 4, #2631-2634		2.40	2.00
	P# block of 4, 4#		3.25	—
	Zip block of 4		2.50	—
b.	As "a," yellow omitted		*4,750.*	

The yellow color in Nos. 2631-2634 is easily removed by exposure to sunlight. Expertization of No. 2634b is essential.

See Russia Nos. 6080-6083.

ALASKA HIGHWAY, 50th ANNIVERSARY

A1987

Designed by Byron Birdsall.

LITHOGRAPHED & ENGRAVED
Plates of 200 in four panes of 50

1992, May 30	**Tagged**	***Perf. 11***	
2635 A1987 29c **multicolored**		.60	.25
P# block of 4, 6#		2.75	—
Zip block of 4		2.50	—
a. Black (engr.) omitted		*575.00*	—

Almost half the recorded No. 2635a errors are poorly centered. These sell for approximately $400.

KENTUCKY STATEHOOD BICENTENNIAL

A1988

Designed by Joseph Petro.

Printed by J.W. Fergusson & Sons for Stamp Venturers.

PHOTOGRAVURE
Plates of 200 in four panes of 50

1992, June 1	**Tagged**	***Perf. 11***	
2636 A1988 29c **multicolored**		.60	.25
P# block of 4, 5#+S		2.75	—
Zip block of 4		2.50	—
a. Dark blue missing (EP)		—	
b. Dark blue and red missing (EP)		—	
c. All colors missing (EP)		—	

Nos. 2636a-2636c must be collected se-tenant with normal stamps.

SUMMER OLYMPICS

Soccer
A1989

Gymnastics
A1990

Volleyball
A1991

Boxing
A1992

Swimming
A1993

Designed by Richard Waldrep.

Printed by J.W. Fergusson & Sons for Stamp Venturers.

PHOTOGRAVURE
Panes of 35

1992, June 11	**Tagged**	***Perf. 11***	
2637 A1989 29c **multicolored**		.60	.25
2638 A1990 29c **multicolored**		.60	.25
2639 A1991 29c **multicolored**		.60	.25
2640 A1992 29c **multicolored**		.60	.25
2641 A1993 29c **multicolored**		.60	.25
a. Strip of 5, #2637-2641		3.00	2.50
P# block of 10, 5#+S		6.50	—
Zip, copyright block of 15		9.00	—

Inscriptions on six marginal tabs.

HUMMINGBIRDS

Ruby-throated
A1994

Broad-billed
A1995

Costa's — A1996

Rufous — A1997

Calliope — A1998

Designed by Chuck Ripper.

Printed by Multi-Color Corp. for the American Bank Note Co.

PHOTOGRAVURE
BOOKLET STAMPS
Perf. 11 Vert. on 1 or 2 Sides

1992, June 15	**Tagged**	
2642 A1994 29c **multicolored**	.60	.25
2643 A1995 29c **multicolored**	.60	.25
2644 A1996 29c **multicolored**	.60	.25
2645 A1997 29c **multicolored**	.60	.25
2646 A1998 29c **multicolored**	.60	.25
a. Bklt. pane of 5, #2642-2646	3.00	2.50

Imperforate singles, booklet panes and pane multiples or varieties on gummed stamp paper are proofs from the ABNCo. archives. From the same source also come imperforate progressive proofs. See No. 2646aP in Proofs section.

WILDFLOWERS

Illustration reduced.

Designed by Karen Mallary.

Printed by Ashton-Potter America, Inc.

LITHOGRAPHED
Plates of 300 in six panes of 50 and
Plates of 200 in four panes of 50

1992, July 24	**Tagged**	***Perf. 11***	
2647 A1999 29c Indian paintbrush		.60	.60
2648 A2000 29c Fragrant water lily		.60	.60
2649 A2001 29c Meadow beauty		.60	.60
2650 A2002 29c Jack-in-the-pulpit		.60	.60
2651 A2003 29c California poppy		.60	.60
2652 A2004 29c Large-flowered trillium		.60	.60
2653 A2005 29c Tickseed		.60	.60
2654 A2006 29c Shooting star		.60	.60
2655 A2007 29c Stream violet		.60	.60
2656 A2008 29c Bluets		.60	.60
2657 A2009 29c Herb Robert		.60	.60
2658 A2010 29c Marsh marigold		.60	.60
2659 A2011 29c Sweet white violet		.60	.60
2660 A2012 29c Claret cup cactus		.60	.60
2661 A2013 29c White mountain avens		.60	.60
2662 A2014 29c Sessile bellwort		.60	.60
2663 A2015 29c Blue flag		.60	.60
2664 A2016 29c Harlequin lupine		.60	.60
2665 A2017 29c Twinflower		.60	.60
2666 A2018 29c Common sunflower		.60	.60
2667 A2019 29c Sego lily		.60	.60
2668 A2020 29c Virginia bluebells		.60	.60
2669 A2021 29c Ohi'a lehua		.60	.60
2670 A2022 29c Rosebud orchid		.60	.60
2671 A2023 29c Showy evening primrose		.60	.60
2672 A2024 29c Fringed gentian		.60	.60
2673 A2025 29c Yellow lady's slipper		.60	.60
2674 A2026 29c Passionflower		.60	.60
2675 A2027 29c Bunchberry		.60	.60
2676 A2028 29c Pasqueflower		.60	.60
2677 A2029 29c Round-lobed hepatica		.60	.60
2678 A2030 29c Wild columbine		.60	.60
2679 A2031 29c Fireweed		.60	.60
2680 A2032 29c Indian pond lily		.60	.60
2681 A2033 29c Turk's cap lily		.60	.60
2682 A2034 29c Dutchman's breeches		.60	.60
2683 A2035 29c Trumpet honeysuckle		.60	.60
2684 A2036 29c Jacob's ladder		.60	.60
2685 A2037 29c Plains prickly pear		.60	.60
2686 A2038 29c Moss campion		.60	.60
2687 A2039 29c Bearberry		.60	.60
2688 A2040 29c Mexican hat		.60	.60
2689 A2041 29c Harebell		.60	.60
2690 A2042 29c Desert five spot		.60	.60
2691 A2043 29c Smooth Solomon's seal		.60	.60
2692 A2044 29c Red maids		.60	.60
2693 A2045 29c Yellow skunk cabbage		.60	.60
2694 A2046 29c Rue anemone		.60	.60
2695 A2047 29c Standing cypress		.60	.60
2696 A2048 29c Wild flax		.60	.60
a. A1999-A2048 Pane of 50, #2647-2696		30.00	—

Sheet margin selvage contains a diagram of the plate layout with each pane's position shaded in gray.

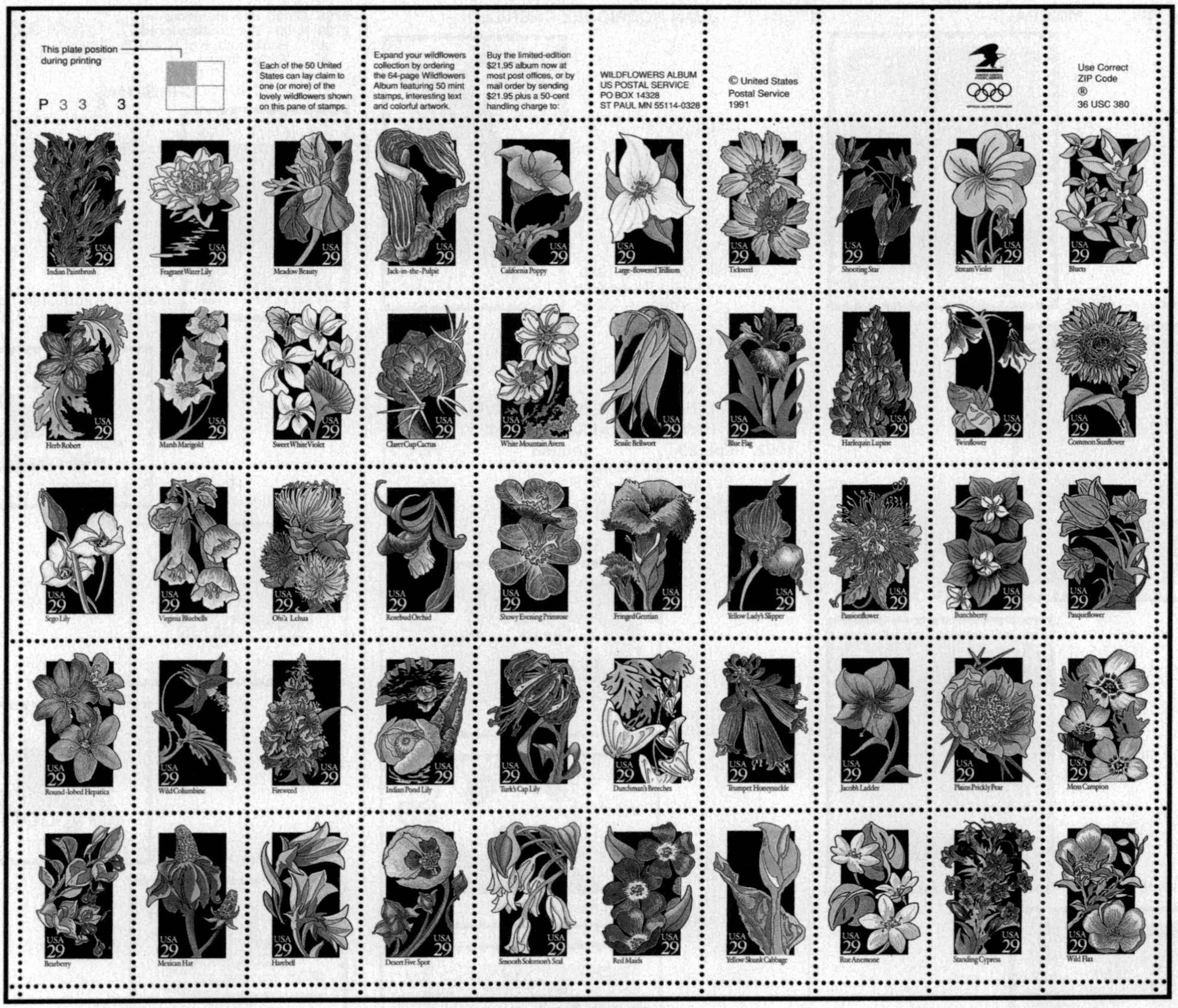

WILDFLOWERS
A1999-A2048

WORLD WAR II

A2049

Illustration reduced.

Designed by William H. Bond.

No. 2697 — Events of 1942: a, B-25's take off to raid Tokyo, Apr. 18. b, Ration coupons (Food and other commodities rationed). c, Divebomber and deck crewman (US wins Battle of the Coral Sea, May). d, Prisoners of war (Corregidor falls to Japanese, May 6). e, Dutch Harbor buildings on fire (Japan invades Aleutian Islands, June). f, Headphones, coded message (Allies decipher secret enemy codes). g, Yorktown lost, U.S. wins at Midway. h, Woman with drill (Millions of women join war effort). i, Marines land on Guadalcanal, Aug. 7. j, Tank in desert (Allies land in North Africa, Nov.).

Central label is the size of 15 stamps and shows world map, extent of axis control.

LITHOGRAPHED & ENGRAVED

Plates of 80 in four panes of 20 each

1992, Aug. 17		**Tagged**	***Perf. 11***	
2697	A2049	Block of 10	7.50	5.00
		Pane of 20	15.00	—
a.-j.		29c any single	.75	.30
k.		Red (litho.) omitted	*4,000.*	

No. 2697 has selvage at left and right and either top or bottom.

LITERARY ARTS SERIES

Dorothy Parker (1893-1967), Writer — A2050

Designed by Greg Rudd.

Printed by J.W. Fergusson & Sons for Stamp Venturers.

PHOTOGRAVURE

Plates of 200 in four panes of 50

1992, Aug. 22		**Tagged**	***Perf. 11***	
2698	A2050	29c **multicolored**	.60	.25
		P# block of 4, 5# + S	2.75	—
		Zip block of 4	2.50	—

THEODORE VON KARMAN

Theodore Von Karman (1881-1963), Rocket Scientist — A2051

Designed by Chris Calle.

Printed by J.W. Fergusson & Sons for Stamp Venturers.

PHOTOGRAVURE

Plates of 200 in four panes of 50

1992, Aug. 31		**Tagged**	***Perf. 11***	
2699	A2051	29c **multicolored**	.60	.25
		P# block of 4, 4# + S	2.75	—
		Zip block of 4	2.50	—

MINERALS

Azurite — A2052

Copper — A2053

Variscite — A2054

Wulfenite — A2055

Designed by Len Buckley.

LITHOGRAPHED & ENGRAVED
Sheets of 160 in four panes of 40.

1992, Sept. 17 **Tagged** ***Perf. 11***

2700 A2052 29c **multicolored** .60 .25
2701 A2053 29c **multicolored** .60 .25
2702 A2054 29c **multicolored** .60 .25
2703 A2055 29c **multicolored** .60 .25
a. Block or strip of 4, #2700-2703 2.40 2.00
P# block of 4, 6# 3.50 —
Zip block of 4 2.50 —
b. As "a," silver (litho.) omitted *6,000.*
d. As "a," silver omitted on two stamps —
e. As "a," tagging omitted —

JUAN RODRIGUEZ CABRILLO

Cabrillo (d. 1543), Ship, Map of San Diego Bay Area — A2056

Designed by Ren Wicks.

Printed by The Press and J.W. Fergusson & Sons for Stamp Venturers.

LITHOGRAPHED & ENGRAVED
Plates of 200 in four panes of 50

1992, Sept. 28 **Tagged** ***Perf. 11***

2704 A2056 29c **multicolored** .60 .25
P# block of 4, 7# + 2 "S"s 3.50 —
Zip, Olympic block of 4 2.50 —
a. Black (engr.) omitted *1,750.*

WILD ANIMALS

Giraffe A2057

Giant Panda — A2058

Flamingo A2059

King Penguins A2060

White Bengal Tiger — A2061

Designed by Robert Giusti.

Printed by J.W. Fergusson & Sons for Stamp Venturers.

PHOTOGRAVURE
BOOKLET STAMPS
Perf. 11 Horiz. on 1 or 2 Sides

1992, Oct. 1 **Tagged**

2705 A2057 29c **multicolored** .65 .25
2706 A2058 29c **multicolored** .65 .25
2707 A2059 29c **multicolored** .65 .25
2708 A2060 29c **multicolored** .65 .25
2709 A2061 29c **multicolored** .65 .25
a. Booklet pane of 5, #2705-2709 3.25 2.25
b. As "a," imperf. *2,000.*

CHRISTMAS

Madonna and Child, by Giovanni Bellini — A2062

Horse and Rider — A2063

Fire Pumper — A2064

Train Engine — A2065

Riverboat — A2066

Designed by Bradbury Thompson (#2710) and Lou Nolan (#2711-2719).

Printed by the Bureau of Engraving and Printing, Ashton-Potter America, Inc. (#2711-2714), the Multi-Color Corporation for American Bank Note Company (#2715-2718), and Avery Dennison (#2719).

LITHOGRAPHED & ENGRAVED
Sheets of 300 in six panes of 50 (#2710, 2714a)

1992 **Tagged** ***Perf. 11¼***

2710 A2062 29c **multicolored,** *Oct. 22* .60 .25
P# block of 4, 5# 2.75 —
Zip, copyright block of 4 2.50 —
a. Booklet pane of 10 6.00 3.50

LITHOGRAPHED
Perf. 11¼x11

2711 A2063 29c **multicolored,** *Oct. 22* .75 .25
2712 A2064 29c **multicolored,** *Oct. 22* .75 .25
2713 A2065 29c **multicolored,** *Oct. 22* .75 .25
2714 A2066 29c **multicolored,** *Oct. 22* .75 .25
a. Block of 4, #2711-2714 3.00 1.10
P# block of 4, 5# + P 3.75 —
Zip, copyright block of 6 4.50 —

Booklet Stamps
PHOTOGRAVURE
Perf. 11 on 2 or 3 Sides

2715 A2063 29c **multicolored,** *Oct. 22* .90 .25
2716 A2064 29c **multicolored,** *Oct. 22* .90 .25
2717 A2065 29c **multicolored,** *Oct. 22* .90 .25
2718 A2066 29c **multicolored,** *Oct. 22* .90 .25
a. Booklet pane of 4, #2715-2718 3.60 1.25

Imperforates and part-perforates on gummed stamp paper are proofs from the ABNCo. archives. From the same source come imperforates with Toys only and imperforates without denominations. See No. 2718aP in Proofs section.

Self-Adhesive

Die Cut

2719	A2065 29c **multicolored,** *Oct. 28*	.65	.25
a.	Booklet pane of 18	12.00	

"Greetings" is 27mm long on Nos. 2711-2714, 25mm long on Nos. 2715-2718 and 21½mm long on No. 2719. Nos. 2715-2719 differ in color from Nos. 2711-2714.

CHINESE NEW YEAR

Year of the Rooster
A2067

Designed by Clarence Lee.

Printed by the American Bank Note Co.

LITHOGRAPHED & ENGRAVED

Panes of 20

1992, Dec. 30 **Tagged** ***Perf. 11***

2720	A2067 29c **multicolored,** prephosphored uncoated paper with embedded tagging showing a mottled appearance, plus block tagging under the engraved portion of the design	.60	.25
	P# block of 4, 5#+A	2.50	—
	Pane of 20	11.50	—
a.	Prephosphored uncoated paper with embedded tagging showing a mottled appearance, plus block tagging on top of printed design	1.50	—
	P# block of 4, 5#+A	—	
b.	Prephosphored uncoated paper with embedded tagging showing a mottled appearance	*125.00*	—

See No. 3895j.

AMERICAN MUSIC SERIES

Elvis Presley
A2068

Oklahoma!
A2069

Hank Williams
A2070

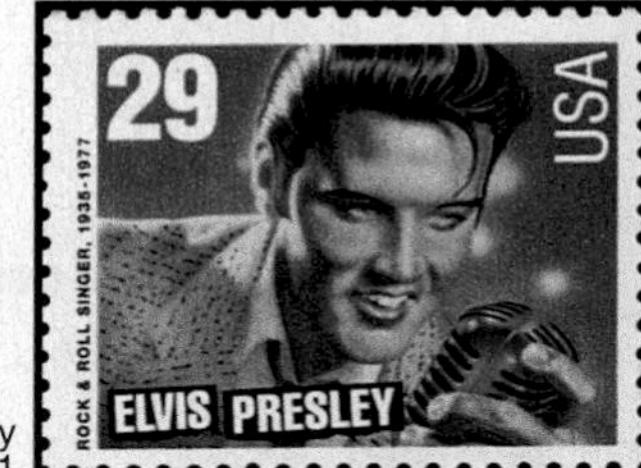

Elvis Presley
A2071

Bill Haley — A2072

Clyde McPhatter
A2073

Ritchie Valens
A2074

Otis Redding
A2075

Buddy Holly — A2076

Dinah Washington
A2077

Designed by Mark Stutzman (#2721, 2724-2725, 2727, 2729, 2731-2732, 2734, 2736), Wilson McLean (#2722), Richard Waldrep (#2723), John Berkey (#2726, 2728, 2730, 2733, 2735, 2737).

Printed by the Bureau of Engraving and Printing (#2721), Stamp Venturers (#2722-2730), Multi-color Corp. for American Bank Note Co. (#2731-2737).

PHOTOGRAVURE

Panes of 40, Panes of 35 (#2724-2730)

1993 **Tagged** ***Perf. 11***

2721	A2068 29c **multicolored,** *Jan. 8*	.60	.25
	P# block of 4, 5#	2.75	—
	Zip, copyright block of 4	2.50	—
a.	Imperf, pair	—	

Perf. 10

2722	A2069 29c **multicolored,** *Mar. 30*	.60	.25
	P# block of 4, 4#+S	3.25	—
	Zip block of 4	2.50	—
2723	A2070 29c **multicolored,** *June 9*	.75	.25
	P# block of 4, 6#+S	4.25	—
	Zip block of 4	3.25	—

Perf. 11.2x11.5

2723A	A2070 29c **multicolored,** *June 9*	12.00	10.00
	P# block of 4, 6#+S	95.00	—
	Zip block of 4	65.00	—

1993, June 16 ***Perf. 10***

2724	A2071 29c **multicolored**	.70	.25
2725	A2072 29c **multicolored**	.70	.25
2726	A2073 29c **multicolored**	.70	.25
2727	A2074 29c **multicolored**	.70	.25
2728	A2075 29c **multicolored**	.70	.25
2729	A2076 29c **multicolored**	.70	.25
2730	A2077 29c **multicolored**	.70	.25
a.	Vert. strip of 7, #2724-2730	5.50	3.00
	Horiz. P# block of 10, 2 sets of 6P#+S, + top label	10.00	—
	Vert. P# block of 8, 6#+S	7.75	—
	Pane of 35	29.00	—

No. 2730a with Nos. 2724-2730 in numerical sequence cannot be obtained from the pane of 35.

Booklet Stamps

Perf. 11 Horiz. on 1 or 2 Sides

2731	A2071 29c **multicolored**	.65	.25
2732	A2072 29c **multicolored**	.65	.25
2733	A2073 29c **multicolored**	.65	.25
2734	A2074 29c **multicolored**	.65	.25
2735	A2075 29c **multicolored**	.65	.25
2736	A2076 29c **multicolored**	.65	.25
2737	A2077 29c **multicolored**	.65	.25
a.	Booklet pane, 2 #2731, 1 each #2732-2737	5.25	2.25
b.	Booklet pane, #2731, 2735-2737 + tab	2.60	1.50

Nos. 2731-2737 have smaller design sizes, brighter colors and shorter inscriptions than Nos. 2724-2730, as well as framelines around the designs and other subtle design differences.

No. 2737b without tab is indistinguishable from broken No. 2737a.

Imperforates of both No. 2737a and 2737b on gummed stamp paper are proofs from the ABNCo. archives. Perforated booklet pane multiples and varieties also exist from the same source. See Nos. 2737aP-2737bP in Proofs section.

See Nos. 2769, 2771, 2775 and designs A2112-A2117.

SPACE FANTASY

A2086

A2087

A2088

A2089

A2090

Designed by Stephen Hickman.

PHOTOGRAVURE
BOOKLET STAMPS

1993, Jan. 25 **Tagged** ***Perf. 11 Vert.***

2741	A2086 29c **multicolored**	.60	.25
2742	A2087 29c **multicolored**	.60	.25
2743	A2088 29c **multicolored**	.60	.25
2744	A2089 29c **multicolored**	.60	.25
2745	A2090 29c **multicolored**	.60	.25
a.	Booklet pane of 5, #2741-2745	3.00	2.25

BLACK HERITAGE SERIES

Percy Lavon Julian (1899-1975), Chemist — A2091

Designed by Higgins Bond.

LITHOGRAPHED & ENGRAVED
Panes of 50

1993, Jan. 29 **Tagged** ***Perf. 11***

2746	A2091 29c **multicolored**	.60	.25
	P# block of 4, 7#	2.75	—
	Zip block of 4	2.50	—

OREGON TRAIL

A2092

Designed by Jack Rosenthal.

LITHOGRAPHED & ENGRAVED
Panes of 50

1993, Feb. 12 **Tagged** ***Perf. 11***

2747	A2092 29c **multicolored**	.60	.25
	P# block of 4, 6#	3.00	—
	Zip block of 4	2.50	—
a.	Tagging omitted	25.00	
b.	Blue omitted	*650.00*	

WORLD UNIVERSITY GAMES

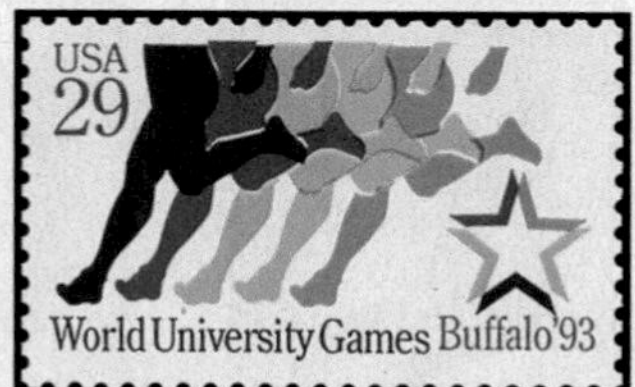

A2093

Designed by David Buck.

PHOTOGRAVURE
Panes of 50

1993, Feb. 25 **Tagged** ***Perf. 11***

2748	A2093 29c **multicolored**	.60	.25
	P# block of 4, 5#	2.75	—
	Zip block of 4	2.50	—

GRACE KELLY (1929-1982)

Actress, Princess of Monaco — A2094

Designed by Czeslaw Slania.

Printed by Stamp Venturers.

ENGRAVED
Panes of 50

1993, Mar. 24 **Tagged** ***Perf. 11***

2749	A2094 29c **blue**	.60	.25
	P# block of 4, 1# +S	2.75	—
	Zip block of 4	2.50	—

See Monaco No. 1851.

CIRCUS

Clown — A2095

Ringmaster — A2096

Trapeze Artist — A2097

Elephant — A2098

Designed by Steve McCracken.

Printed by Ashton Potter America.

LITHOGRAPHED
Panes of 40

1993, Apr. 6 **Tagged** ***Perf. 11***

2750	A2095 29c **multicolored**	.60	.25
2751	A2096 29c **multicolored**	.60	.25
2752	A2097 29c **multicolored**	.60	.25
2753	A2098 29c **multicolored**	.60	.25
a.	Block of 4, #2750-2753	2.40	1.75
	P# block of 6, 5#+P	7.50	—
	Zip block of 6	3.75	—

Plate and zip blocks of 6 and copyright blocks of 9 contain one #2753a with continuous design (complete spotlight).

CHEROKEE STRIP LAND RUN, CENTENNIAL

A2099

Designed by Harold T. Holden.

Printed by American Bank Note. Co.

LITHOGRAPHED & ENGRAVED
Panes of 20

1993, Apr. 17 **Tagged** ***Perf. 11***

2754	A2099 29c **multicolored**	.60	.25
	P# block of 4, 5#+A	2.50	—
	Pane of 20	12.50	—

Imperforates on gummed stamp paper, including gutter pairs and blocks, are proofs from the ABNCo. archives. From the same source also come perforated gutter pairs and blocks, plus imperforates missing the red text and black denomination and "USA." An approved die proof also is recorded. See No. 2754P in Proofs section.

DEAN ACHESON (1893-1971)

Secretary of State — A2100

Designed by Christopher Calle.

Printed by Stamp Venturers.

ENGRAVED
Sheets of 300 in six panes of 50

1993, Apr. 21 ***Perf. 11***

2755	A2100 29c **greenish gray**	.60	.25
	P# block of 4, 1#+S	2.75	—
	Zip block of 4	2.50	—

SPORTING HORSES

Steeplechase
A2101

Thoroughbred Racing
A2102

Harness Racing
A2103

Polo — A2104

Designed by Michael Dudash.

Printed by Stamp Venturers.

LITHOGRAPHED & ENGRAVED
Panes of 40

1993, May 1 **Tagged** ***Perf. 11x11½***

2756 A2101 29c **multicolored** .60 .25
2757 A2102 29c **multicolored** .60 .25
2758 A2103 29c **multicolored** .60 .25
2759 A2104 29c **multicolored** .60 .25
a. Block of 4, #2756-2759 2.40 2.00
P# block of 4, 5#+S 2.75 —
Zip block of 4 2.50 —
b. As "a," black (engr.) omitted *500.00*

GARDEN FLOWERS

Hyacinth — A2105

Tulip — A2107

Iris — A2108

Lilac — A2109

Daffodil — A2106

Designed by Ned Seidler.

LITHOGRAPHED & ENGRAVED
BOOKLET STAMPS

1993, May 15 **Tagged** ***Perf. 11 Vert.***

2760 A2105 29c **multicolored** .60 .25
2761 A2106 29c **multicolored** .60 .25
2762 A2107 29c **multicolored** .60 .25
2763 A2108 29c **multicolored** .60 .25
2764 A2109 29c **multicolored** .60 .25
a. Booklet pane of 5, #2760-2764 3.00 2.25
b. As "a," black (engr.) omitted *135.00*
c. As "a," imperf. *700.00*
d. As "a," tagging omitted *650.00*

WORLD WAR II

A2110

Illustration reduced.

Designed by William H. Bond.

Designs and events of 1943: a, Destroyers (Allied forces battle German U-boats). b, Military medics treat the wounded. c, Amphibious landing craft on beach (Sicily attacked by Allied forces, July). d, B-24s hit Ploesti refineries, August. e, V-mail delivers letters from home. f, PT boat (Italy invaded by Allies, Sept.). g, Nos. WS7, WS8, savings bonds, (Bonds and stamps help war effort). h, "Willie and Joe" keep spirits high. i, Banner in window (Gold Stars mark World War II losses). j, Marines assault Tarawa, Nov.

Central label is the size of 15 stamps and shows world map with extent of Axis control and Allied operations.

LITHOGRAPHED & ENGRAVED
Plates of 80 in four panes of 20 each

1993, May 31 **Tagged** ***Perf. 11***

2765 A2110 Block of 10 7.50 5.00
Pane of 20 15.00 —
a.-j. 29c any single .75 .40
k. As No. 2765, tagging omitted on a.-e. —
l. As No. 2765, tagging omitted on f.-j. — —

No. 2765 has selvage at left and right and either top or bottom.

JOE LOUIS (1914-1981)

A2111

Designed by Thomas Blackshear.

LITHOGRAPHED & ENGRAVED
Plates of 200 in four panes of 50

1993, June 22 **Tagged** ***Perf. 11***

2766 A2111 29c **multicolored** .60 .25
P# block of 4, 5# 2.75 —
Zip block of 4 2.50 —

AMERICAN MUSIC SERIES

Oklahoma! Type and

Show Boat — A2112

Porgy & Bess — A2113

My Fair Lady — A2114

Designed by Wilson McLean.

Printed by Multi-Color Corp.

BOOKLET STAMPS
PHOTOGRAVURE

Perf. 11 Horiz. on 1 or 2 Sides

1993, July 14 **Tagged**

2767 A2112 29c **multicolored** .60 .25
2768 A2113 29c **multicolored** .60 .25
2769 A2069 29c **multicolored** .60 .25
2770 A2114 29c **multicolored** .60 .25
a. Booklet pane of 4, #2767-2770 2.75 2.25

No. 2769 has smaller design size, brighter colors and shorter inscription than No. 2722, as well as a frameline around the design and other subtle design differences.

Imperforate booklet panes, singly or in multiples, on gummed stamp paper are proofs from the ABNCo. archives. From the same source come imperforate progressive proofs, plus imperforate proofs/essays showing slightly altered designs. See No. 2770aP in Proofs section.

AMERICAN MUSIC SERIES

Hank Williams Type and

Patsy Cline — A2115

The Carter Family A2116

Bob Wills — A2117

Designed by Richard Waldrep.

Printed by Stamp Venturers (#2771-2774) and American Bank Note Co. (#2775-2778).

PHOTOGRAVURE

Panes of 20

1993, Sept. 25		**Tagged**	***Perf. 10***	
2771	A2070 29c **multicolored**		.75	.25
2772	A2115 29c **multicolored**		.75	.25
2773	A2116 29c **multicolored**		.75	.25
2774	A2117 29c **multicolored**		.75	.25
a.	Block or horiz. strip of 4, #2771-2774		3.00	1.75
	Horiz. P# block of 8, 2 sets of 6#+S + top label		6.50	—
	P# block of 4, 6#+S		3.25	—
	Pane of 20		16.00	—

Booklet Stamps

Perf. 11 Horiz. on one or two sides

With Black Frameline

2775	A2070 29c **multicolored**	.60	.25
2776	A2116 29c **multicolored**	.60	.25
2777	A2115 29c **multicolored**	.60	.25
2778	A2117 29c **multicolored**	.60	.25
a.	Booklet pane of 4, #2775-2778	2.50	2.00

Inscription at left measures 27½mm on No. 2723, 27mm on No. 2771 and 22mm on No. 2775. No. 2723 shows only two tuning keys on guitar, while No. 2771 shows those two and parts of two others.

Imperforate booklet panes on gummed stamp paper, singly or in multiples, are proofs from the ABNCo. archives. From the same source come panes perfed horiz. but uncut vertically, plus imperforate progressive proofs and other die proof varieties. See No. 2778aP in Proofs section.

NATIONAL POSTAL MUSEUM

Independence Hall, Benjamin Franklin, Printing Press, Colonial Post Rider — A2118

Pony Express Rider, Civil War Soldier, Concord Stagecoach A2119

JN-4H Biplane, Charles Lindbergh, Railway Mail Car, 1931 Model A Ford Mail Truck — A2120

California Gold Rush Miner's Letter, Nos. 39, 295, C3a, C13, Barcode and Circular Date Stamp A2121

Designed by Richard Schlecht.

Printed by American Bank Note Co.

LITHOGRAPHED AND ENGRAVED

1993, July 30		**Tagged**	***Perf. 11***	
2779	A2118 29c **multicolored**		.60	.25
2780	A2119 29c **multicolored**		.60	.25
2781	A2120 29c **multicolored**		.60	.25
2782	A2121 29c **multicolored**		.60	.25
a.	Block or strip of 4, #2779-2782		2.40	2.00
	P# block of 4, 7#+A		2.50	—
	Pane of 20		12.50	—
b.	As "a," engr. maroon (USA/29) and black ("My dear...") omitted		*2,500.*	
c.	As "a," imperf		*2,500.*	

AMERICAN SIGN LANGUAGE

A2122

A2123

Designed by Chris Calle.

Printed by Stamp Venturers.

PHOTOGRAVURE

1993, Sept. 20		**Tagged**	***Perf. 11½***	
2783	A2122 29c **multicolored**		.60	.25
2784	A2123 29c **multicolored**		.60	.25
a.	Pair, #2783-2784		1.20	.75
	P# block of 4, 4#+S		2.50	—
	Pane of 20		12.50	—

CLASSIC BOOKS

A2124

A2125

A2126

A2127

Designed by Jim Lamb.

Printed by American Bank Note Co.

Designs: No. 2785, Rebecca of Sunnybrook Farm, by Kate Douglas Wiggin. No. 2786, Little House on the Prairie, by Laura Ingalls Wilder. No. 2787, The Adventures of Huckleberry Finn, by Mark Twain. No. 2788, Little Women, by Louisa May Alcott.

LITHOGRAPHED & ENGRAVED

Panes of 40

1993, Oct. 23		**Tagged**	***Perf. 11***	
2785	A2124 29c **multicolored**		.60	.25
2786	A2125 29c **multicolored**		.60	.25
2787	A2126 29c **multicolored**		.60	.25
2788	A2127 29c **multicolored**		.60	.25
a.	Block or horiz. strip of 4, #2785-2788		2.40	2.00
	P# block of 4, 5#+A		5.00	—
	Zip block of 4		2.50	—

Imperforates on gummed stamp paper, including gutter pairs and blocks, are proofs from the ABNCo. archives. See No. 2788aP in Proofs section.

CHRISTMAS

Madonna and Child in a Landscape, by Giovanni Battista Cima — A2128

Jack-in-the-Box A2129

Red-Nosed Reindeer A2130

Snowman — A2131

Toy Soldier Blowing Horn — A2132

Designed by Bradbury Thompson (#2789-2790), Peter Good (#2791-2803).

Printed by Bureau of Engraving and Printing (#2789, 2791-2798), KCS Industries (#2790), Avery Dennison (#2799-2803).

LITHOGRAPHED & ENGRAVED
Panes of 50 (#2789, 2791-2794)

1993, Oct. 21 **Tagged** ***Perf. 11***

2789 A2128 29c **multicolored** .60 .25
P# block of 4, 4# 2.75 —
Zip, copyright block of 4 2.50 —

Booklet Stamp

Size: 18x25mm

Perf. 11½x11 on 2 or 3 Sides

2790 A2128 29c **multicolored** .60 .25
a. Booklet pane of 4 2.40 1.75
b. Imperf., pair —
c. As "a," imperf —

Nos. 2789-2790 have numerous design differences.

1993 ***Perf. 11½***

PHOTOGRAVURE

2791 A2129 29c **multicolored,** *Oct. 21* .60 .25
2792 A2130 29c **multicolored,** *Oct. 21* .60 .25
2793 A2131 29c **multicolored,** *Oct. 21* .60 .25
2794 A2132 29c **multicolored,** *Oct. 21* .60 .25
a. Block or strip of 4, #2791-2794 2.40 2.00
P# block of 4, 6# 4.00 —
Zip, copyright block of 4 2.50 —

Booklet Stamps

Size: 18x21mm

Perf. 11x10 on 2 or 3 Sides

2795 A2132 29c **multicolored,** *Oct. 21* .85 .25
2796 A2131 29c **multicolored,** *Oct. 21* .85 .25
2797 A2130 29c **multicolored,** *Oct. 21* .85 .25
2798 A2129 29c **multicolored,** *Oct. 21* .85 .25
a. Booklet pane, 3 each #2795-2796, 2 each #2797-2798 8.50 4.00
b. Booklet pane, 3 each #2797-2798, 2 each #2795-2796 8.50 4.00
c. Block of 4, #2795-2798 3.40 1.75

Self-Adhesive

Size: 19½x26½mm

Die Cut

2799 A2131 29c **multicolored,** *Oct. 28* .75 .25
a. Coil with plate # V1111111 — 6.00
b. Horiz. coil strip of 4, #2799-2802 3.00
P# strip of 5, 1 each #2799-2801, 2 #2802, P#V1111111 9.00
P# strip of 8, 2 each #2799-2802, P#V1111111 12.00
2800 A2132 29c **multicolored,** *Oct. 28* .75 .25
2801 A2129 29c **multicolored,** *Oct. 28* .75 .25
2802 A2130 29c **multicolored,** *Oct. 28* .75 .25
a. Booklet pane, 3 each #2799-2802 9.00
b. Block of 4, #2799-2802 3.00

Except for No. 2799a with plate number, coil stamps are indistinguishable from booklet stamps once they are removed from the backing paper.

Size: 17x20mm

2803 A2131 29c **multicolored,** *Oct. 28* ® .60 .25
a. Booklet pane of 18 11.00

Snowman on Nos. 2793, 2799 has three buttons and seven snowflakes beneath nose (placement differs on both stamps). No. 2796 has two buttons and five snowflakes beneath nose. No. 2803 has two orange buttons and four snowflakes beneath nose.

Adhesive residue may remain on some examples of No. 2803 after soaking. See note after No. 1549.

MARIANA ISLANDS

A2133

Designed by Herb Kane.

LITHOGRAPHED AND ENGRAVED

1993, Nov. 4 **Tagged** ***Perf. 11***

2804 A2133 29c **multicolored** .60 .25
P# block of 4, 6# 3.25 —
Pane of 20 15.50 —

COLUMBUS' LANDING IN PUERTO RICO, 500th ANNIVERSARY

A2134

Designed by Richard Schlecht.

Printed by Stamp Venturers.

PHOTOGRAVURE
Panes of 50

1993, Nov. 19 **Tagged** ***Perf. 11.2***

2805 A2134 29c **multicolored** .60 .25
P# block of 4, 5#+S 2.75 —
Zip block of 4 2.50 —

AIDS AWARENESS

A2135

Designed by Tom Mann.
Printed by Stamp Venturers.

PHOTOGRAVURE
Panes of 50

1993, Dec. 1 **Tagged** ***Perf. 11.2***

2806 A2135 29c **black & red** .60 .25
P# block of 4, 3#+S 2.75 —
Zip, copyright block of 6 2.50 —
a. Perf. 11 vert. on 1 or 2 sides, from bklt. pane .70 .25
b. As "a," booklet pane of 5 3.50 2.00

WINTER OLYMPICS

Slalom — A2136

Luge — A2137

Ice Dancing — A2138

Cross-Country Skiing — A2139

Ice Hockey — A2140

Designed by Lon Busch.
Printed by Ashton-Potter.

LITHOGRAPHED
Sheets of 120 in six panes of 20

1994, Jan. 6 **Tagged** ***Perf. 11.2***

2807 A2136 29c **multicolored** .60 .25
2808 A2137 29c **multicolored** .60 .25
2809 A2138 29c **multicolored** .60 .25
2810 A2139 29c **multicolored** .60 .25
2811 A2140 29c **multicolored** .60 .25
a. Strip of 5, #2807-2811 3.00 2.50
Horiz. P# block of 10, 2 sets of 4#+P and inscriptions 6.50 —
Horiz. P# block of 10, 2 sets of 4#+P 6.00 —
Pane of 20 12.50 —

EDWARD R. MURROW, JOURNALIST (1908-65)

A2141

Designed by Chris Calle.

ENGRAVED
Panes of 50

1994, Jan. 21 **Tagged** ***Perf. 11.2***

2812 A2141 29c **brown** .60 .25
P# block of 4, 1# 3.50 —

LOVE

A2142

A2143

A2144

Designed by Peter Good (#2813), Lon Busch (#2814-2815).

Printed by Banknote Corp. of America (#2813), American Banknote Co. (#2814) and Bureau of Engraving and Printing (#2814C, 2815).

Booklet Stamps
LITHOGRAPHED & ENGRAVED

1994 **Tagged** ***Die Cut***
Self-adhesive

2813	A2142 29c **multicolored,** *Jan. 27*	.60	.25
a.	Booklet pane of 18	11.00	
b.	Coil with plate # B1	—	5.00
	P# strip of 5, #B1	7.00	

Except for No. 2813b with plate number, coil stamps are indistinguishable from booklet stamps once they are removed from the backing paper.

PHOTOGRAVURE
Perf. 10.9x11.1 on 2 or 3 sides

2814	A2143 29c **multicolored,** *Feb. 14*	.60	.25
a.	Booklet pane of 10	6.00	3.50
b.	Imperf, pair	—	
d.	As "a," imperf.	—	

Horiz. pairs, imperf between, are printer's waste.

LITHOGRAPHED & ENGRAVED
Sheets of 300 in six panes of 50
Tagged
Perf. 11.1

2814C	A2143 29c **multicolored,** *June 11*	.70	.25
	P# block of 4, 5#	3.00	—

Size of No. 2814C is 20x28mm. No. 2814 is 18x24½mm.

PHOTOGRAVURE & ENGRAVED
Sheet of 300 in six panes of 50
Perf. 11.2

2815	A2144 52c **multicolored,** *Feb. 14*	1.00	.25
	P# block of 4, 5#	5.00	—
	P# block of 10, 2 sets of 5#, plate diagram, copyright and pane price inscriptions	11.00	—

BLACK HERITAGE SERIES

Dr. Allison Davis (1902-83), Social Anthropologist, Educator — A2145

Designed by Chris Calle.

Printed by Stamp Venturers.

ENGRAVED

1994, Feb. 1 **Tagged** ***Perf. 11.2***

2816	A2145 29c **red brown & brown**	.60	.25
	P# block of 4, 1#+S	2.50	—
	Pane of 20	12.50	—

CHINESE NEW YEAR

Year of the Dog — A2146

Designed by Clarence Lee.

Printed by J.W. Fergusson & Sons for Stamp Venturers.

PHOTOGRAVURE
Sheets of 180 in nine panes of 20

1994, Feb. 5 **Tagged** ***Perf. 11.2***

2817	A2146 29c **multicolored**	.80	.25
	P# block of 4, 4#+S	3.50	—
	Pane of 20	17.50	—

See No. 3895k.

BUFFALO SOLDIERS

A2147

Designed by Mort Kuntsler.

Printed by Stamp Venturers.

LITHOGRAPHED & ENGRAVED
Plates of 180 in nine panes of 20

1994, Apr. 22 **Tagged** ***Perf. 11.5x11.2***

2818	A2147 29c **multicolored**	.60	.25
	P# block of 4, 5#+S	2.50	—
	Pane of 20	12.50	—
a.	Double impression (second impression light) of red brown (engr. inscriptions)	—	

SILENT SCREEN STARS

Rudolph Valentino (1895-1926) — A2148

Clara Bow (1905-65) — A2149

Charlie Chaplin (1889-1977) — A2150

Lon Chaney (1883-1930) — A2151

John Gilbert (1895-1936) — A2152

Zasu Pitts (1898-1963) — A2153

Harold Lloyd (1894-1971) — A2154

Keystone Cops — A2155

Theda Bara (1885-1955) — A2156

Buster Keaton (1895-1966) — A2157

Designed by Al Hirschfeld.

LITHOGRAPHED & ENGRAVED
Plates of 160 in four panes of 40

1994, Apr. 27 **Tagged** ***Perf. 11.2***

2819	A2148 29c **red, black & bright violet**	1.10	.30
2820	A2149 29c **red, black & bright violet**	1.10	.30
2821	A2150 29c **red, black & bright violet**	1.10	.30
2822	A2151 29c **red, black & bright violet**	1.10	.30
2823	A2152 29c **red, black & bright violet**	1.10	.30
2824	A2153 29c **red, black & bright violet**	1.10	.30
2825	A2154 29c **red, black & bright violet**	1.10	.30
2826	A2155 29c **red, black & bright violet**	1.10	.30
2827	A2156 29c **red, black & bright violet**	1.10	.30
2828	A2157 29c **red, black & bright violet**	1.10	.30
a.	Block of 10, #2819-2828	11.00	5.00
	P# block of 10, 4#, plate diagram and copyright inscription	12.00	—
	Half pane of 20	23.00	—
b.	As "a," black (litho.) omitted	—	
c.	As "a," blk, red & brt vio (litho.) omitted	—	

GARDEN FLOWERS

Gladiola — A2160

Marigold — A2161

Rose — A2162

Designed by Ned Seidler.

LITHOGRAPHED & ENGRAVED

1994, Apr. 28 Tagged *Perf. 10.9 Vert.*

Booklet Stamps

2829	A2158 29c **multicolored**	.60	.25
2830	A2159 29c **multicolored**	.60	.25
2831	A2160 29c **multicolored**	.60	.25
2832	A2161 29c **multicolored**	.60	.25
2833	A2162 29c **multicolored**	.60	.25
a.	Booklet pane of 5, #2829-2833	3.00	2.25
b.	As "a," imperf	*400.00*	
c.	As "a," black (engr.) omitted	*125.00*	
d.	As "a," tagging omitted	—	

1994 WORLD CUP SOCCER CHAMPIONSHIPS

A2163

A2163a

A2164

A2165

Illustration reduced.

Designed by Michael Dudash.

Printed by J.W. Fergusson & Sons for Stamp Venturers. Design: 40c, Soccer player, diff.

PHOTOGRAVURE

Plates of 180 in nine panes of 20

1994, May 26 Tagged *Perf. 11.1*

2834	A2163 29c **multicolored**	.60	.25
	P# block of 4, 4#+S	2.50	—
	Pane of 20	12.50	—
2835	A2163a 40c **multicolored**	.80	.25
	P# block of 4, 4#+S	3.20	—
	Pane of 20	16.00	—
2836	A2164 50c **multicolored**	1.00	.25
	P# block of 4, 4#+S	4.00	—
	Pane of 20	20.00	—
	Nos. 2834-2836 (3)	2.40	.75

Souvenir Sheet

2837	A2165 Sheet of 3, #a.-c.	4.50	3.00

Nos. 2834-2836 are printed on phosphor-coated paper while Nos. 2837a (29c), 2837b (40c), 2837c (50c) are block tagged. No. 2837c has a portion of the yellow map in the LR corner.

Printer's waste exists for No. 2835, including imperf. pairs, imperf. pairs with gutter between, imperf. with all colors except black omitted, and imperf. with black omitted.

WORLD WAR II

A2166

Illustration reduced.

Designed by William H. Bond.

Designs and events of 1944: a, Allied forces retake New Guinea. b, P-51s escort B-17s on bombing raids. c, Troops running from landing craft (Allies in Normandy, D-Day, June 6). d, Airborne units spearhead attacks. e, Officer at periscope (Submarines shorten war in Pacific). f, Parade (Allies free Rome, June 4; Paris, Aug. 25). g, Soldier firing flamethrower (US troops clear Saipan bunkers). h, Red Ball Express speeds vital supplies. i, Battleship firing main battery (Battle for Leyte Gulf, Oct. 23-26). j, Soldiers in snow (Bastogne and Battle of the Bulge, Dec.).

Central label is size of 15 stamps and shows world map with extent of Axis control and Allied operations.

LITHOGRAPHED & ENGRAVED

Plates of eight subjects in four panes of 2 each

1994, June 6 Tagged *Perf. 10.9*

2838	A2166 Block of 10	17.00	10.00
	Pane of 20	34.00	—
a.-j.	29c any single	1.70	.50

No. 2838 has selvage at left and right and either top or bottom.

NORMAN ROCKWELL

A2167

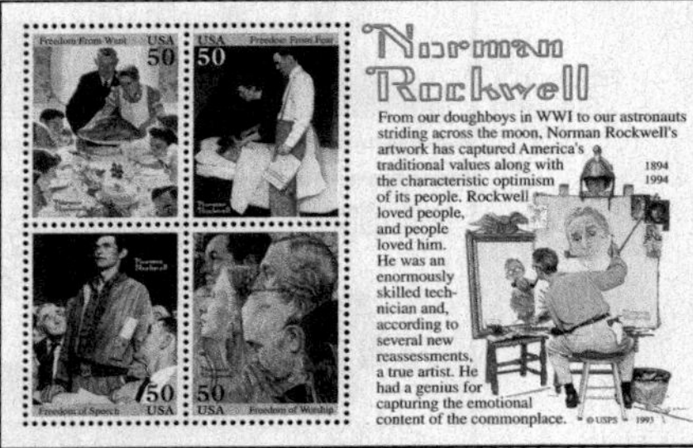

A2168

Illustration reduced.

Designed by Richard Sheaff based on Rockwell's works.

LITHOGRAPHED & ENGRAVED

Sheets of 200 in four panes of 50

1994, July 1 Tagged *Perf. 10.9x11.1*

2839	A2167 29c **multicolored**	.60	.25
	P# block of 4, 5#	2.75	—

Souvenir Sheet

LITHOGRAPHED

2840	A2168 Sheet of 4	4.50	2.75
a.	50c Freedom From Want	1.10	.65
b.	50c Freedom From Fear	1.10	.65
c.	50c Freedom of Speech	1.10	.65
d.	50c Freedom of Worship	1.10	.65

Panes of No. 2839 contain two plate blocks, one containing a plate position diagram.

Moon Landing, 25th Anniv.

A2169

A2170

Designed by Paul and Chris Calle.

Printed by Stamp Venturers (#2841) and Banknote Corp. of America (#2842).

Miniature Sheet
LITHOGRAPHED

1994, July 20 **Tagged** ***Perf. 11.2x11.1***

2841	A2169	29c Sheet of 12	10.50	—
a.		Single stamp	.85	.60

LITHOGRAPHED & ENGRAVED
Sheets of 120 in six panes of 20

Perf. 10.7x11.1

2842	A2170	$9.95 **multicolored**	20.00	16.00
		P# block of 4, 5#+B	82.50	—

LOCOMOTIVES

Hudson's General A2171

McQueen's Jupiter — A2172

Eddy's No. 242 — A2173

Ely's No. 10 — A2174

Buchanan's No. 999 — A2175

Designed by Richard Leech.

Printed by J.W. Ferguson & Sons for Stamp Venturers.

PHOTOGRAVURE

1994, July 28 **Tagged** ***Perf. 11 Horiz.***

Booklet Stamps

2843	A2171 29c **multicolored**		.75	.25
2844	A2172 29c **multicolored**		.75	.25
2845	A2173 29c **multicolored**		.75	.25
2846	A2174 29c **multicolored**		.75	.25
2847	A2175 29c **multicolored**		.75	.25
a.	Booklet pane of 5, #2843-2847		3.75	2.00
b.	As "a," imperf.		*2,500.*	

GEORGE MEANY, LABOR LEADER (1894-1980)

A2176

Designed by Chris Calle.

ENGRAVED
Sheets of 200 in four panes of 50

1994, Aug. 16 **Tagged** ***Perf. 11.1x11***

2848	A2176 29c **blue**		.60	.25
	P# block of 4, 1#		2.50	—

Panes of No. 2848 contain two plate blocks, one containing a plate position diagram.

AMERICAN MUSIC SERIES
Popular Singers

Al Jolson (1886-1950) A2177

Bing Crosby (1904-77) A2178

Ethel Waters (1896-1977) A2179

Nat "King" Cole (1919-65) A2180

Ethel Merman (1908-84) A2181

Jazz Singers

Bessie Smith (1894-1937) A2182

Muddy Waters (1915-83) A2183

Billie Holiday (1915-59) A2184

Robert Johnson (1911-38) A2185

Jimmy Rushing (1902-72) A2186

"Ma" Rainey (1886-1939) A2187

Mildred Bailey (1907-51) A2188

Howlin' Wolf (1910-76) A2189

Designed by Chris Payne (#2849-2853), Howard Koslow (#2854, 2856, 2858, 2860), Julian Allen (#2855, 2857, 2859, 2861).

Printed by J.W. Fergusson & Sons for Stamp Venturers (#2849-2853), Manhardt-Alexander for Ashton-Potter (USA) Ltd. (#2854-2861).

PHOTOGRAVURE
Plates of 180 in nine panes of 20, Plates of 210 in six panes of 35 (#2854-2861)

1994, Sept. 1 **Tagged** ***Perf. 10.1x10.2***

2849 A2177 29c **multicolored** .85 .25
2850 A2178 29c **multicolored** .85 .25
2851 A2179 29c **multicolored** .85 .25
2852 A2180 29c **multicolored** .85 .25
2853 A2181 29c **multicolored** .85 .25
a. Vert. strip of 5, #2849-2853 4.25 2.00
Vert. P# block of 6, 6#+S 8.50 —
Horiz. P# block of 12, 2 sets of 6#+S, + top label 16.50 —
Pane of 20 23.50 —
b. Pane of 20, imperf *10,000.*

Some plate blocks of 6 will contain plate position diagram and copyright inscription, others will contain pane price inscription.

1994, Sept. 17 ***Perf. 11x10.8***

LITHOGRAPHED

2854 A2182 29c **multicolored** 1.50 .25
2855 A2183 29c **multicolored** 1.50 .25
2856 A2184 29c **multicolored** 1.50 .25
2857 A2185 29c **multicolored** 1.50 .25
2858 A2186 29c **multicolored** 1.50 .25
2859 A2187 29c **multicolored** 1.50 .25
2860 A2188 29c **multicolored** 1.50 .25
2861 A2189 29c **multicolored** 1.50 .25
a. Block of 10, #2854-2861 +2 additional stamps 15.00 4.50
Vert. P# block of 10, 5#+P 16.00 —
P# block of 10, 2 sets of 5#+P, + top label 17.00 —
Pane of 35 55.00 —

Vertical plate blocks contain either pane price inscription or copyright inscription.

LITERARY ARTS SERIES

James Thurber (1894-1961) — A2190

Designed by Richard Sheaff based on drawing by James Thurber.

LITHOGRAPHED & ENGRAVED
Plates of 200 in four panes of 50

1994, Sept. 10 **Tagged** ***Perf. 11***

2862 A2190 29c **multicolored** .60 .25
P# block of 4, 2# 2.75 —

Panes of No. 2862 contain two plate blocks, one containing a plate position diagram.

WONDERS OF THE SEA

Diver, Motorboat A2191

Diver, Ship — A2192

Diver, Ship's Wheel — A2193

Diver, Coral — A2194

Designed by Charles Lynn Bragg.

Printed by Barton Press for Banknote Corporation of America.

LITHOGRAPHED
Plates of 216 in nine panes of 24

1994, Oct. 3 **Tagged** ***Perf. 11x10.9***

2863 A2191 29c **multicolored** .75 .25
2864 A2192 29c **multicolored** .75 .25
2865 A2193 29c **multicolored** .75 .25
2866 A2194 29c **multicolored** .75 .25
a. Block of 4, #2863-2866 3.00 1.50
P# block of 4, 4#+B 3.25 —
Pane of 24 19.00 —
b. As "a," imperf *450.00*

CRANES

Black-Necked A2195

Whooping — A2196

Designed by Clarence Lee based on illustrations by Zhan Gengxi.

Printed by Barton Press for Banknote Corporation of America.

LITHOGRAPHED & ENGRAVED
Sheets of 120 in six panes of 20

1994, Oct. 9 **Tagged** ***Perf. 10.8x11***

2867 A2195 29c **multicolored** .70 .25
2868 A2196 29c **multicolored** .70 .25
a. Pair, #2867-2868 1.40 .75
P# block of 4, 5#+B 3.00 —
Pane of 20 14.50
b. As "a," black & magenta (engr.) omitted *1,250.*
c. As "a," double impression of engr. black (Birds' names and "USA") & magenta ("29") *3,000.*
d. As "a," double impression of engr. black ("USA") & magenta ("29") *3,000.*

See People's Republic of China Nos. 2528-2529.

Uncut Press Sheets

Typical Vertical Pair with Horizontal Gutter

Typical Horizontal Pair with Vertical Gutter

Cross Gutter Block of 8

Illustrations reduced.

Beginning with No. 2869, the U.S. Postal Service made available for sale uncut press sheets of selected commemorative and definitive issues. These sheets are noted in footnotes following each issue. These sheets generally contain cross-gutter blocks and pairs with gutters between (typical examples shown above) and sometimes other collectible pair or block formats. The cross-gutter blocks and the pairs with gutters between are valued in the footnotes. Other possible formats not noted sell for a premium, but they are not listed or valued herein.

See note before No. 4694 for uncut press sheets without die cutting (imperforates).

LEGENDS OF THE WEST

A2197

Illustration reduced.

g. Bill Pickett (1870-1932) (Revised)

Designed by Mark Hess.

Printed by J.W. Fergusson & Sons for Stamp Venturers.

Designs: a, Home on the Range. b, Buffalo Bill Cody (1846-1917). c, Jim Bridger (1804-81). d, Annie Oakley (1860-1926). e, Native American Culture. f, Chief Joseph (c. 1840-1904). h, Bat Masterson (1853-1921). i, John C. Fremont (1813-90). j, Wyatt Earp (1848-1929). k, Nellie Cashman (c. 1849-1925). l, Charles Goodnight (1826-1929). m, Geronimo (1823-1909). n, Kit Carson (1809-68). o, Wild Bill Hickok (1837-76). p, Western Wildlife. q, Jim Beckwourth (c. 1798-1866). r, Bill Tilghman (1854-1924). s, Sacagawea (c. 1787-1812). t, Overland Mail.

PHOTOGRAVURE

Sheets of 120 in six panes of 20

1994, Oct. 18		**Tagged**	***Perf. 10.1x10***	
2869	A2197	Pane of 20	15.00	10.00
a.-t.		29c any single	.75	.50
u.		As No. 2869, a.-e. imperf. f.-j. part perf.	—	

Uncut press sheets of No. 2869 were made available for sale. Values: cross-gutter block of 20, $27.50; pairs with gutters between, $2.50 each.

See note after No. 2868.

LEGENDS OF THE WEST (Recalled)

g. Bill Pickett (Recalled)

Nos. 2870b-2870d, 2870f-2870o, 2870q-2870s have a frameline around the vignette that is half the width of the frameline on similar stamps in No. 2869. Other design differences may exist.

PHOTOGRAVURE

Sheets of 120 in six panes of 20

1994	**Tagged**	***Perf. 10.1x10***	
2870 A2197 29c Pane of 20		125.00	—

150,000 panes of No. 2870 were made available through a drawing. Panes were delivered in an envelope. Value is for pane without envelope. Panes with envelopes sell for somewhat more.

CHRISTMAS

Madonna and Child, by Elisabetta Sirani — A2200

Stocking — A2201

Santa Claus — A2202

Cardinal in Snow — A2203

Designed by Bradbury Thompson (#2871), Lou Nolan (#2872), Harry Zelenko (#2873), Peter Good (#2874).

Printed by Bureau of Engraving and Printing (#2871), Ashton-Potter USA, Ltd. (#2872), Avery Dennison (#2873-2874).

LITHOGRAPHED & ENGRAVED

Sheets of 300 in six panes of 50

1994, Oct. 20		**Tagged**	***Perf. 11¼***	
2871	A2200	29c **multicolored,** shiny gum	.60	.25
		P# block of 4, 5#	2.75	—
		Low gloss gum	.60	
		P# block of 4, 5#	2.75	

BOOKLET STAMP

Perf. 9¾x11

2871A	A2200	29c **multicolored**	.60	.25
b.		Booklet pane of 10	6.25	3.50
c.		Imperf, pair	*350.00*	

LITHOGRAPHED

Sheets of 400 in eight panes of 50

Perf. 11¼

2872	A2201	29c **multicolored**	.60	.25
		P# block of 4, 5#+P	2.50	—
a.		Booklet pane of 20	12.50	6.00
b.		Imperf., pair	—	
c.		Vert. pair, imperf. horiz.	—	
d.		Quadruple impression of black, triple impression of blue, double impression of red and yellow, green normal	*900.00*	
e.		Vert. pair, imperf. between	*125.00*	
f.		As "a," imperf.	—	

Panes of Nos. 2871-2872 contain four plate blocks, one containing pane position diagram.

PHOTOGRAVURE

BOOKLET STAMPS

Self-Adhesive

Die Cut

2873	A2202	29c **multicolored**	.70	.25
a.		Booklet pane of 12	8.50	
b.		Coil with plate #V1111	—	5.75
		P# strip of 5, #V1111	7.25	

Except for No. 2873b with plate number, coil stamps are indistinguishable from booklet stamps once they are removed from the backing paper.

2874	A2203	29c **multicolored** ⓢ	.60	.25
a.		Booklet pane of 18	11.00	

ⓢ: Adhesive residue may adhere to the back of some examples of No. 2874 after soaking. See note after No. 1549.

BUREAU OF ENGRAVING & PRINTING

Souvenir Sheet

A2204

Double Impression of Brown Lettering Panel

Major Double Transfer

Minor Double Transfer

Illustration A2204 reduced.

Designed by Peter Cocci, using original die for Type A98.

LITHOGRAPHED & ENGRAVED

1994, Nov. 3		**Tagged**	***Perf. 11***	
2875	A2204	$2 Pane of 4	16.00	13.50
a.		Single stamp	4.00	2.00
		Pane of 4 with major double transfer on right stamp	*65.00*	—
		Major double transfer, single stamp	—	—
		Pane of 4 with minor double transfer on right stamp	*22.50*	—
		Minor double transfer, single stamp	—	—
b.		Pane of 4 with double impression of the brown lettering panel	*1,200.*	—
c.		As "b," tagging omitted	*1,100.*	

The double impression is clear, but may be seen best in the scrolls at lower right. The major double transfer is most evident in the extra line at the bottom of the design. The minor double transfer is in the same area, but it is much less distinct.

CHINESE NEW YEAR

Year of the Boar — A2205

Designed by Clarence Lee.

Printed by Stamp Venturers.

PHOTOGRAVURE
Panes of 20

1994, Dec. 30 Tagged *Perf. 11.2x11.1*
2876 A2205 29c **multicolored** .70 .25
P# block of 4, 5#+S 3.00 —
Pane of 20 15.00 —

See No. 3895l.

A2206

A2207

A2208

A2208a

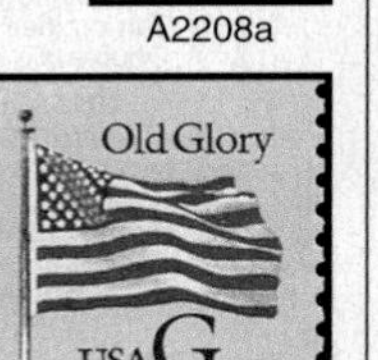

A2209

Designed by Richard D. Sheaff (#2877-2878), Lou Nolan (#2879-2892).

Printed by American Bank Note Co. (#2877, 2884, 2890), Bureau of Engraving and Printing (#2879, 2881, 2883, 2889), Stamp Venturers (#2878, 2880, 2882, 2888, 2891-2892), KCS Industries (#2885), Avery-Dennison (#2886-2887).

Coil Plate No. Strips of 3
Beginning with No. 2123, coil plate no. strips of 3 usually sell at the level of strips of 5 minus the face value of two stamps.

LITHOGRAPHED
Sheets of 100

1994, Dec. 13 Untagged *Perf. 11x10.8*
2877 A2206 (3c) **tan, bright blue & red** .25 .25
P# block of 4, 3#+A .50 —
Zip block of 4 .30 —
a. Imperf., pair *115.00*
b. Double impression of red *175.00*

No. 2877 imperf and with blue omitted is known from printer's waste.

Perf. 10.8x10.9
Untagged
2878 A2206 (3c) **tan, dark blue & red** .25 .25
P# block of 4, 3#+S .50 —
Zip block of 4 .50 —

Inscriptions on #2877 are in a thin typeface. Those on #2878 are in heavy, bold type.

PHOTOGRAVURE
Tagged
Perf. 11.2x11.1
2879 A2207 (20c) **black "G," yellow & multi** .40 .25
P# block of 4, 5# 7.50 —
Zip block of 4 1.75 —
a. Imperf., pair —

Perf. 11x10.9
2880 A2207 (20c) **red "G," yellow & multi** .75 .25
P# block of 4, 5#+S 15.00 —
Zip block of 4 3.25 —

Perf. 11.2x11.1
2881 A2208 (32c) **black "G" & multi** 1.25 .25
P# block of 4, 4# 60.00 —
Zip block of 4 5.50 —

a. Booklet pane of 10 12.50 5.00

Perf. 11x10.9
2882 A2208a (32c) **red "G" & multi** .60 .25
P# block of 4, 4#+S 4.00 —
Zip block of 4 2.75 —

Distance on #2882 from bottom of red G to top of flag immediately above is 13¾mm. Illustration A2208a shows #2885 superimposed over #2882.

BOOKLET STAMPS
Perf. 10x9.9 on 2 or 3 Sides
2883 A2208 (32c) **black "G" & multi** .65 .25
a. Booklet pane of 10 6.50 3.75

Perf. 10.9 on 2 or 3 Sides
2884 A2208 (32c) **blue "G" & multi** .65 .25
a. Booklet pane of 10 6.50 3.75
b. As "a," imperf *4,500.*
c. Horiz. pair, imperf. btwn. due to miscut —
d. Horiz. pair, imperf. vert. —

Perf. 11x10.9 on 2 or 3 Sides
2885 A2208a (32c) **red "G" & multi** .90 .25
a. Booklet pane of 10 9.00 4.50
b. Horiz. pair, imperf vert. *750.00*
c. Horiz. pair, imperf. btwn., in #2885a with foldover —

Distance on #2885 from bottom of red G to top of flag immediately above is 13½mm. See note below #2882.

No. 2885c resulted from a paper foldover after perforating and before cutting into panes.

A2208b

A2208c

Self-Adhesive *Die Cut*
2886 A2208b (32c) **gray, blue, light blue, red & black** .70 .25
a. Booklet pane of 18 12.50
b. Coil with plate # V11111 — 9.50
P# strip of 5, same # 10.00

No. 2886 is printed on surface-tagged paper which is opaque, thicker and brighter than that of No. 2887 and has only a small number of blue shading dots in the white stripes immediately below the flag's blue field.

Except for No. 2886b with plate number, coil stamps are indistinguishable from booklet stamps once they are removed from the backing paper.

2887 A2208c (32c) **black, blue & red** ® .70 .25
a. Booklet pane of 18 12.50

No. 2887 has noticeable blue shading in the white stripes immediately below the blue field and has overall tagging. The paper is translucent, thinner and duller than No. 2886.

®: Adhesive residue may remain on some examples of No. 2887 after soaking. See note after No. 1549.

COIL STAMPS
Perf. 9.8 Vert.
2888 A2209 (25c) **black "G," blue & multi** .90 .50
Pair 1.80 1.00
P# strip of 5, #S11111 4.00
P# single, #S11111 2.50
2889 A2208 (32c) **black "G" & multi** 1.50 .25
Pair 3.00 .30
P# strip of 5, #1111, 2222 8.00
P# single, #1111, 2222 — 4.00
a. Imperf., pair *250.00*
2890 A2208 (32c) **blue "G" & multi** .65 .25
Pair 1.25 .50
P# strip of 5, #A1111, A1112, A1113, A1211, A1212, A1311, A1313, A1324, A2211, A2212, A2213, A2214, A3113, A3314, A3323, A3324, A3433, A3435, A3436, A4427, A5327, A5417, A5427 4.00
P# strip of 5, #A1222, A1314, A4426, A5437 4.25
P# strip of 5, #A1417, A2223 6.50
P# strip of 5, #A1433 6.00
P# strip of 5, #A2313 6.50
P# strip of 5, #A3114, A3315, A3423 6.50
P# strip of 5, #A3426 5.25
P# strip of 5, #A4435 *175.00*
P# single, #A1111, A1313, A2214, A3113, A3314, A3324, A4427, A5427 — 1.00
P# single, #A1212, A3323 — 3.00
P# single, #A2212, A3435 — 3.50
P# single, #A1112, A1311, A1324, A2213, A5327 — 2.50
P# single, #A1113, A5437 — 3.75
P# single, #A3315, A3423, A3426 4.75
P# single, #A1222, A2211, A3114 — 4.25
P# single, #A1211, A1314, A4426 — 4.00
P# single, #A1417, A1433 — 6.75
P# single, #A2223, A2313 — 6.00
P# single, #A3433, A3436 — 2.00
P# single, #A4435 — *190.00*
P# single, #A5417 3.00

2891 A2208 (32c) **red "G" & multi** .85 .25
Pair 1.70 .30
P# strip of 5, #S1111 4.25
P# single, #S1111 — 1.00

Rouletted 9.8 Vert.
2892 A2208 (32c) **red "G" & multi** .75 .25
Pair 1.50 .50
P# strip of 5, #S1111, S2222 4.75
P# single, #S1111, S2222 — 1.00

A2210

Flag Over Porch — A2212

Designed by Lou Nolan (#2893), Dave LaFleur (#2897).

Printed by American Bank Note Co. (#2893), Stamp Venturers (#2897).

PHOTOGRAVURE
COIL STAMP

1995 Untagged *Perf. 9.8 Vert.*
2893 A2210 (5c) **green & multi** .50 .25
Pair 1.00 .50
P# strip of 5, #A11111 3.00
P# strip of 5, #A21111 2.50
P# single, #A11111 3.00
P# single, #A21111 2.00

No. 2893 was only available through the Philatelic Fullfillment Center (and, for a short time, at the L'Enfant Plaza Philatelic Center in Washington, DC) after its announcement 1/12/95. Covers submitted for first day cancels received a 12/13/94 cancel, even though the stamps were not available on that date.

Sheets of 400 in four panes of 100

1995, May 19 Tagged *Perf. 10.4*
2897 A2212 32c **multicolored,** .75 .25
P# block of 4, 5#+S 4.25 —
a. Imperf., vert. pair 55.00

See Nos. 2913-2916, 2920-2921, 3133. For booklet see No. BK243.

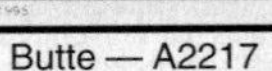
Butte — A2217

Mountain — A2218

Auto — A2220

Auto Tail Fin — A2223

Juke Box — A2225

Flag Over Field — A2230

Designed by Tom Engeman (#2902-2904B), Robert Brangwynne (#2905-2906), Chris Calle (#2907), Bill Nelson (#2908-2912B), Dave LaFleur (#2913-2916, 2921), Sabra Field (#2919).

Printed by J.W. Fergusson & Sons for Stamp Venturers (#2902, 2905, 2909, 2912, 2914), Bureau of Engraving and Printing (#2903, 2904B, 2908, 2911, 2912B, 2913, 2915A, 2915C-2915D, 2916, 2921), Stamp Venturers (#2902B, 2904,

2906-2907, 2910, 2912A, 2915B), Avery Dennison (#2904A, 2915, 2919, 2920).

Coil Plate No. Strips of 3
Beginning with No. 2123, coil plate No. strips of 3 usually sell at the level of strips of 5 minus the face value of two stamps.

COIL STAMPS

PHOTOGRAVURE

1995-97 ***Perf. 9.8 Vert.***

Untagged (Nos. 2902-2912B)

Self-Adhesive (#2902B, 2904A-2904B, 2906-2907, 2910, 2912A, 2912B, 2915-2915D, 2919-2921)

2902 A2217 (5c) **yellow, red & blue,** *Mar. 10* .25 .25
Pair .50 .50
P# strip of 5, #S111, S222, S333 1.10
P# single, #S111, S222, S333 — .90
a. Imperf., pair 350.00

Serpentine Die Cut 11.5 Vert.

2902B A2217 (5c) **yellow, red & blue,** *June 15, 1996* .35 .25
Pair .70
P# strip of 5, #S111 1.75
P# single, #S111 — .80

Perf. 9.8 Vert.

2903 A2218 (5c) **purple & multi,** *Mar. 16, 1996* .25 .25
Pair .50 .50
P# strip of 5, #11111 1.10
P# single, #11111 — .90
a. Tagged (error) 4.00 3.50
P# strip of 5, #11111 40.00
P# single, #11111 — 40.00

Letters of inscription "USA NONPROFIT ORG." outlined in purple on No. 2903. No. 2903 has purple "1996" at left bottom.

2904 A2218 (5c) **blue & multi,** *Mar. 16, 1996* .25 .25
Pair .50 .50
P# strip of 5, #S111 1.10
P# single, #S111 — 1.00
c. Imperf., pair 225.00

Letters of inscription have no outline on No. 2904. No. 2904 has blue "1996" at bottom left.

Serpentine Die Cut 11.2 Vert.

2904A A2218 (5c) **purple & multi,** *June 15, 1996* .40 .25
Pair .80
P# strip of 5, #V222222, V333323, V333342 4.00
P# strip of 5, #V333333 2.50
P# strip of 5, #V333343 3.00
P# single, #V222222, V333323, V333333, V333342 — 2.50
P# single, #V333343 4.50

Serpentine Die Cut 9.8 Vert.

2904B A2218 (5c) **purple & multi,** *Jan. 24, 1997* .25 .25
Pair .50
P# strip of 5, #1111 1.40
P# single, #1111 — 1.00

Letters of inscription outlined in purple on No. 2904B, not outlined on No. 2904A. No. 2904A has large purple "1996" at bottom left. No. 2904B has small purple "1997" at bottom left.

No. 2904B shows 10 "peaks" at left and 10 at right, or 9 "peaks" at left and 10 at right. The 9 "peaks" variety is extremely scarce. Values: mint $30, used $15; P# strip of 5, $2,500, used P# single $400.

Perf. 9.8 Vert.

2905 A2220 (10c) **black, red brown & brown,** small "1995" date, *Mar. 10* .25 .25
Pair .50 .50
P# strip of 5, #S111 2.00
P# single, #S111 — 1.25
a. Medium "1995" date .35 .25
Pair .70 .50
P# strip of 5, #S222 2.00
P# single, #S222 1.40
b. Large "1995" date, *1996* .60 .25
Pair 1.20 .50
P# strip of 5, #S333 3.00
P# single, #S333 — 1.50
c. As "b," brown omitted, P#S33 single *400.00*

Date on 2905 is approximately 1.9mm long, on No. 2905a 2mm long, and on No. 2905b 2.1mm long.

Serpentine Die Cut 11.5 Vert.

2906 A2220 (10c) **black, brown & red brown,** *June 15, 1996* .50 .25
Pair 1.00
P# strip of 5, #S111 2.40
P# single, #S111 — 2.00

2907 A1957 (10c) **gold & multi,** *May 21, 1996* .75 .25
Pair 1.50
P# strip of 5, #S11111 3.75
P# single, #S11111 — 2.50

Perf. 9.8 Vert.

2908 A2223 (15c) **dark orange yellow & multi,** *Mar. 17* .30 .30
Pair .60 .60
P# strip of 5, #11111 2.00
P# single, #11111 — 1.60

No. 2908 has "1995" in blue and has dark, bold colors, heavy shading lines and heavily shaded chrome.

2909 A2223 (15c) **buff & multi,** *Mar. 17* .30 .30
Pair .60 .60
P# strip of 5, #S11111 2.00
P# single, #S11111 — 1.50

No. 2909 has "1995" in black and has shinier chrome, more subdued colors and finer details than No. 2908.

Serpentine Die Cut 11.5 Vert.

2910 A2223 (15c) **buff & multi,** *June 15, 1996* .30 .30
Pair .60
P# strip of 5, #S11111 2.00
P# single, #S11111 — 1.50

Perf. 9.8 Vert.

2911 A2225 (25c) **dark red, dark yellow green & multi,** *Mar. 17* .50 .50
Pair 1.00 1.00
P# strip of 5, #111111, 212222, 222222, 332222 3.50
P# single, #111111, 212222, 222222 — 2.25
P# single, #332222 — 2.75
a. Imperf, pair *400.00*

No. 2911 has dark, saturated colors and dark blue lines in the music selection board.

See No. 3132.

2912 A2225 (25c) **bright orange red, bright yellow green & multi,** *Mar. 17* .75 .50
Pair 1.50 1.00
P# strip of 5, #S11111, S22222 3.75
P# single, same # — 2.00

No. 2912 has bright colors, less shading and light blue lines in the music selection board.

Serpentine Die Cut 11.5 Vert.

2912A A2225 (25c) **bright orange red, bright yellow green & multi,** *June 15, 1996* .50 .50
Pair 1.00
P# strip of 5, #S11111, S22222 3.75
P# single, same # — 1.75

Serpentine Die Cut 9.8 Vert.

2912B A2225 (25c) **dark red, dark yellow green & multi,** *Jan. 24, 1997* .75 .50
Pair 1.50
P# strip of 5, #111111 3.50
P# strip of 5, #222222 4.00
P# single, #111111 — 1.50
P# single, #222222 — 3.50
c. Tagged (prephosphored coated paper, solid appearance) —
P# single, #222222 —

Tagged (Nos. 2913-2921)

Perf. 9.8 Vert.

2913 A2212 32c **blue, tan, brown, red & light blue,** shiny gum, *May 19* .65 .25
Pair 1.30 .30
P# strip of 5, #11111, 22221 5.00
P# strip of 5, #22222 5.25
P# single, #11111, 22222 — 1.50
P# single, #22221 — 1.75
Low gloss gum .65
Pair 1.30
P# strip of 5, #11111 4.75
P# strip of 5, #22222 6.00
P# strip of 5, #33333, 34333, 44444, 45444, 66646, 77767, 78767, 91161, 99969 4.50
P# strip of 5, #22322 6.75
P# strip of 5, #66666 9.00
P# single, #22322 — 5.75
P# single, #33333, 44444, 45444, 66646, 77767 — 1.50
P# single, #34333 — 5.00
P# single, #66666 — 5.00
P# single, #78767, 91161, 99969 — 2.25
a. Imperf., pair 30.00

No. 2913 has pronounced light blue shading in the flag and red "1995" at left bottom. See No. 3133.

2914 A2212 32c **blue, yellow brown, red & gray,** *May 19* .80 .25
Pair 1.60 .30
P# strip of 5, #S11111 4.50
P# single, #S11111 — 2.25

No. 2914 has pale gray shading in the flag and blue "1995" at left bottom.

Serpentine Die Cut 8.7 Vert.

2915 A2212 32c **multicolored,** *Apr. 18* 1.25 .30
Pair 2.50
P# strip of 5, #V11111 9.00
P# single, #V11111 — 7.50

No. 2915 has blue "1995" at bottom left.

Serpentine Die Cut 9.8 Vert.

2915A A2212 32c **dk blue, tan, brown, red & light blue,** *May 21, 1996* .65 .25
Pair 1.30
P# strip of 5, #11111, 22222, 23222, 33333, 44444, 45444, 55555, 66666, 88888, 99999, 11111A, 13231A, 13311A, 22222A, 33333A, 44444A, 55555A, 66666A, 77777A, 88888A 4.25
P# strip of 5, #78777 —
P# strip of 5, #78777A 30.00
P# strip of 5, #87888 20.00
P# strip of 5, #87898 10.00
P# strip of 5, #88898 *75.00*
P# strip of 5, #89878 *1,500.*
P# strip of 5, #89888 14.00
P# strip of 5, #89898, 97898 10.00
P# strip of 5, #89899 *350.00*
P# strip of 5, #99899 100.00
P# strip of 5, #13211A 60.00
P# single, #11111, 22222, 23222, 33333, 44444, 45444, 55555, 66666, 88888, 99999, 11111A, 13231A,13311A, 22222A, 33333A, 44444A, 55555A, 66666A, 77777A, 88888A — 1.00
P# single, #78777 — 300.00
P# single, #78777A 16.00
P# single, #87888 — *12.00*
P# single, #87898, 97898 — 4.00
P# single, #89878 50.00
P# single, #88898 — *75.00*
P# single, #89888 — 9.00
P# single, #89898 — 2.75
P# single, #89899 — 175.00
P# single, #99899 — 25.00
P# single, #13211A — *60.00*
h. Die cutting omitted, pair 32.50 —
i. Tan omitted
j. Double die cutting 30.00

No. 2915A has red "1996" at left bottom.

Die cutting on No. 2915A shows either 10 serpentine "peaks" on each side, 11 "peaks" on the left side and 10 "peaks" on the right side, or 10 "peaks" on the left side and 11 "peaks" on the right side. The last configuration is considered by specialists to be an error, and it is rare.

Sky on No. 3133 shows color gradation at LR not on No. 2915A.

On No. 2915Ai all other colors except brown are severely shifted.

On No. 2915Aj, the second die cutting is a different gauge than the normal 9.8.

Plate number 99999 strips of No. 2915A are known with the brown plate number shifted one stamp to the right of the stamp with the other plate numbers. Such strips are scarce. Value of mint never hinged P# strip of 5 or 6, $1,500. Used examples are rare.

Serpentine Die Cut 11.5 Vert.

2915B A2212 32c **dk blue, tan, brown, red & light blue,** *June 15, 1996* 1.00 *.90*
Pair 2.00
P# strip of 5, #S11111 5.00
P# single, #S11111 — 2.75

Serpentine Die Cut 10.9 Vert.

2915C A2212 32c **dk blue, tan, brown, red & light blue,** *May 21, 1996* 3.50 .40
Pair 7.00
P# strip of 5, #55555, 66666 25.00
P# single, #55555, 66666 — 3.50
P# single, #88888 *3,000.*

Plate number 55555 strips of No. 2915C are known with the tan plate number shifted one stamp to the left of the stamp with the other plate numbers. Extremely scarce. Value of P# strip approximately $5,000.

Serpentine Die Cut 9.8 Vert.

2915D A2212 32c **dark blue, tan, brown, red & light blue,** *Jan. 24, 1997* 2.00 *.90*
Pair 4.00
P# strip of 5, #11111 9.00
P# single, #11111 — 6.00

No. 2915D shows 9 "peaks" at left and 10 at right or 10 "peaks" at left and 10 at right.

Stamps on multiples of No. 2915A touch, and are on a peelable backing the same size as the stamps, while those of No. 2915D are separated on the peelable backing, which is larger than the stamps.

No. 2915D has red "1997" at left bottom; No. 2915A has red "1996" at left bottom.

Sky on No. 3133 shows color gradation at LR not on No. 2915D, and it has blue "1996" at left bottom.

BOOKLET STAMPS

Perf. 10.8x9.8 on 2 or 3 Adjacent Sides

2916 A2212 32c **blue, tan, brown, red & light blue,** *May 19* .65 .25
a. Booklet pane of 10 6.50 3.25
b. As "a," imperf. —

Die Cut

2919 A2230 32c **multicolored,** *Mar. 17* ⓢ .65 .25
a. Booklet pane of 18 12.00
b. Vert. pair, die cutting omitted btwn. —

ⓢ: Adhesive may adhere to some examples of No. 2919 after soaking. See note after No. 1549.

Serpentine Die Cut 8.7 on 2, 3 or 4 Adjacent Sides

2920	A2212	32c **multicolored,** dated blue "1995," *Apr. 18*	.65	.25
a.		Booklet pane of 20+label	13.00	
b.		Small date	6.00	.35
c.		As "b," booklet pane of 20+label	110.00	
f.		As No. 2920, pane of 15+label	9.75	
g.		As "a," partial pane of 10, 3 stamps and parts of 7 stamps printed on backing liner	—	
h.		As No. 2920, booklet pane of 15	*47.50*	
i.		As No. 2920, die cutting omitted, pair	—	
j.		Dark blue omitted (from No. 2920a)	*2,100.*	
k.		Vert. pair, die cutting missing btwn., three examples in No. 2920a with shift in die cutting (PS)	—	

Date on No. 2920 is nearly twice as large as date on No. 2920b. No. 2920f comes in various configurations.

No. 2920h is a pane of 16 with one stamp removed. The missing stamp is the lower right stamp in the pane or (more rarely) the upper left stamp. No. 2920h cannot be made from No. 2920f, a pane of 15 + label. The label is located in the sixth or seventh row of the pane and is die cut. If the label is removed, an impression of the die cutting appears on the backing paper.

Serpentine Die Cut 11.3 on 3 sides

2920D	A2212	32c **multicolored,** dated blue "1996," *Jan. 20, 1996*	.80	.25
e.		Booklet pane of 10	8.00	

Serpentine Die Cut 9.8 on 2 or 3 Adjacent Sides

2921	A2212	32c **dk bl, tan, brn, red & lt bl,** dated red 1996, *May 21, 1996*	.90	.25
a.		Booklet pane of 10, dated red "1996"	9.00	
b.		As No. 2921, dated red "1997," *Jan. 24, 1997*	1.20	.25
c.		As "a," dated red "1997"	12.00	
d.		Booklet pane of 5 + label, dated red "1997," *Jan. 24, 1997*	8.00	
e.		As "a," die cutting omitted	*200.00*	

Scott values for used self-adhesive stamps are for examples either on piece or off piece.

GREAT AMERICANS ISSUE

A2248

A2249

A2250

A2251

A2253

A2255

A2256

A2257

A2258

Designed by Dennis Lyall (#2933-2934), Richard Sheaff (#2935), Howard Paine (#2936, 2941-2942), Roy Andersen (#2938), Chris Calle (#2940, 2943).

Printed by Banknote Corporation of America (#2933-2935, 2940-2943), Ashton-Potter (USA) Ltd. (#2936), Bureau of Engraving & Printing (#2938).

ENGRAVED

Sheets of 400 in four panes of 100

Sheets of 160 in eight panes of 20 (#2935)

Sheets of 120 in six panes of 20 (#2936, 2941-2942)

1995-99 **Tagged**

Self-Adhesive (#2941-2942)

Perf. 11.2, Serpentine Die Cut 11.7x11.5 (#2941-2942)

2933	A2248	32c **brown,** prephosphored coated paper with surface tagging showing a solid appearance, *Sept. 13, 1995*	.75	.25
		P# block of 4, 1#+B	3.50	—
2934	A2249	32c **green,** prephosphored coated paper with surface tagging showing a solid appearance, *Apr. 26, 1996*	.75	.25
		P# block of 4, 1#+B	3.50	—

No. 2934 exists on two types of surface-tagged paper that exhibit either a solid or grainy solid appearance.

2935	A2250	32c **lake,** prephosphored coated paper with surface tagging showing a grainy solid appearance, *Apr. 3, 1998*	.65	.35
		P# block of 4, 1#+B	3.00	—
		Pane of 20	14.75	
2936	A2251	32c **gray blue,** prephosphored coated paper with surface tagging showing a solid appearance, *July 16, 1998*	.65	.35
		P# block of 4, 1#+P	3.00	—
		Pane of 20	14.75	—
a.		32c **light blue**	2.00	.50
		P# block of 4, 1#+P	9.00	—
		Pane of 20	40.00	—
2938	A2253	46c **carmine,** prephosphored uncoated paper with embedded tagging showing a mottled appearance, *Oct. 20, 1995*	.90	.30
		P# block of 4, 1#	4.50	—

Counterfeits exist of No. 2938. See the Postal Counterfeits section of this catalog.

2940	A2255	55c **green,** prephosphored coated paper with surface tagging showing a grainy solid appearance, *July 11, 1995*	1.15	.25
		P# block of 4, 1#+B	6.00	—
a.		Imperf, pair	—	
2941	A2256	55c **black,** prephosphored coated paper with surface tagging showing a solid appearance, *July 17, 1999*	1.10	.25
		P# block of 4, 1#+B	4.40	
		Pane of 20	22.00	
2942	A2257	77c **blue,** prephosphored coated paper with surface tagging showing a solid appearance, *Nov. 9, 1998*	1.50	.40
		P# block of 4, 1#+B	6.00	
		Pane of 20	30.00	
2943	A2258	78c **bright violet,** prephosphored coated paper with surface tagging showing a solid appearance, *Aug. 18, 1995*	1.60	.25
		P# block of 4, 1#+B	7.50	—
a.		78c **dull violet,** prephosphored coated paper with surface tagging showing a grainy solid appearance	1.60	.25
		P# block of 4, 1#+B	7.50	—
b.		78c **pale violet,** prephosphored coated paper with surface tagging showing a grainy solid appearance	3.00	.30
		P# block of 4, 1#+B	16.00	—
		Nos. 2933-2943 (9)	9.05	2.65

The pale violet ink on No. 2943b luminesces bright pink under long-wave ultraviolet light.

LOVE

Cherub from Sistine Madonna, by Raphael
A2263 A2264

Designed by Terry McCaffrey.

Printed by the Bureau of Engraving and Printing (#2948) and Banknote Corp. of America (#2949).

LITHOGRAPHED & ENGRAVED

Sheets of 300 in six panes of 50

1995, Feb. 1 **Tagged** ***Perf. 11.2***

2948	A2263	(32c) **multicolored**	.65	.25
		P# block of 4, 5#	3.00	—

Self-Adhesive

Die Cut

2949	A2264	(32c) **multicolored**	.65	.25
a.		Booklet pane of 20 + label	13.00	
b.		Red (engr.) omitted	*100.00*	
c.		As "a," red (engr.) omitted	*2,000.*	
d.		Red (engr.) missing (CM)	—	

No. 2949d must be collected se-tenant with a normal stamp.

See Nos. 2957-2960, 3030.

FLORIDA STATEHOOD

Florida Statehood, 150th Anniv.
A2265

Designed by Laura Smith.
Printed by Ashton-Potter (USA) Ltd.

LITHOGRAPHED

Sheets of 160 in eight panes of 20

1995, Mar. 3 **Tagged** ***Perf. 11.1***

2950	A2265	32c **multicolored**	.65	.25
		P# block of 4, 5#+P	3.00	—
		Pane of 20	15.00	—

EARTH DAY

Earth Clean-Up
A2266

Solar Energy
A2267

Tree Planting A2268

Beach Clean-Up A2269

Designed by Christy Millard (#2951), Jennifer Michalove (#2952), Brian Hailes (#2953) and Melody Kiper (#2954).
Printed by Ashton-Potter (USA) Ltd.

LITHOGRAPHED
Sheets of 96 in six panes of 16

1995, Apr. 20 **Tagged** ***Perf. 11.1x11***

2951 A2266 32c **multicolored**	.65	.25
2952 A2267 32c **multicolored**	.65	.25
2953 A2268 32c **multicolored**	.65	.25
2954 A2269 32c **multicolored**	.65	.25
a. Block of 4, #2951-2954	2.60	1.75
P# block of 4, 5#+P	2.60	—
Horiz. P# block of 8, 2 sets of 5#+P, + top or bottom label	5.25	—
Pane of 16	10.50	—

RICHARD M. NIXON
37th President (1913-94)

A2270

Designed by Daniel Schwartz.
Printed by Barton Press and Bank Note Corp. of America.

LITHOGRAPHED & ENGRAVED
Sheets of 200 in four panes of 50

1995, Apr. 26 **Tagged** ***Perf. 11.2***

2955 A2270 32c **multicolored**	.65	.25
P# block of 4, 5#+B	3.00	—
a. Red (engr.) missing (CM)	*800.00*	

No. 2955 is known with red (engr. "Richard Nixon") inverted, and with red engr. omitted but only half the Nixon portrait present, both from printer's waste. No. 2955a shows a complete Nixon portrait.

BLACK HERITAGE SERIES
Bessie Coleman (d. 1926), Aviator

A2271

ENGRAVED
Sheets of 200 in four panes of 50

1995, Apr. 27 **Tagged** ***Perf. 11.2***

2956 A2271 32c **red & black**	.85	.25
P# block of 4, 1#	3.75	—

LOVE

A2272

A2273

Cherubs from Sistine Madonna, by Raphael — A2274

Designed by Terry McCaffrey.
Printed by Bureau of Engraving and Printing (#2957-2959), Bank Note Corp. of America (#2960).

LITHOGRAPHED & ENGRAVED
Sheets of 300 in six panes of 50

1995, May 12 **Tagged** ***Perf. 11.2***

2957 A2272 32c **multicolored**	.65	.25
P# block of 4, 5#	3.00	—
Copyright block of 6	4.25	—

Compare with No. 3030. For booklet see No. BK244.

2958 A2273 55c **multicolored**	1.10	.25
P# block of 4, 5#	5.50	—

BOOKLET STAMPS
Perf. 9.8x10.8

2959 A2272 32c **multicolored**	.65	.25
a. Booklet pane of 10	6.50	3.25
b. Imperf, pair	*100.00*	
c. As "a," imperf.	*500.00*	

Self-Adhesive
Die Cut

2960 A2274 55c **multicolored**	1.10	.25
a. Booklet pane of 20 + label	22.50	

RECREATIONAL SPORTS

Volleyball A2275

Softball A2276

Bowling A2277

Tennis A2278

Golf — A2279

Designed by Don Weller.
Printed by Bank Note Corp. of America.

LITHOGRAPHED
Sheets of 120 in six panes of 20

1995, May 20 **Tagged** ***Perf. 11.2***

2961 A2275 32c **multicolored**	.65	.25
2962 A2276 32c **multicolored**	.65	.25
2963 A2277 32c **multicolored**	.65	.25
2964 A2278 32c **multicolored**	.65	.25
2965 A2279 32c **multicolored**	.65	.25
a. Vert. strip of 5, #2961-2965	3.25	2.00
P# block of 10, 2 sets of 4#+B	6.50	—
P# block of 8, 2 sets of 4#+B	5.50	—
Pane of 20	13.00	—
b. As "a," imperf	*1,750.*	
c. As "a," yellow omitted	*1,600.*	
d. As "a," yellow, blue & magenta omitted	*1,600.*	

PRISONERS OF WAR & MISSING IN ACTION

A2280

Designed by Carl Herrman.
Printed by Ashton-Potter (USA) Ltd.

LITHOGRAPHED
Sheets of 160 in eight panes of 20

1995, May 29 **Tagged** ***Perf. 11.2***

2966 A2280 32c **multicolored**	.65	.25
P# block of 4, 5#+P	2.50	—
Pane of 20	12.50	—

The five plate numbers do not include a sixth plate number for the plate that applied a transparent laquer "color."

LEGENDS OF HOLLYWOOD

Marilyn Monroe (1926-62) — A2281

Designed by Michael Deas.
Printed by Stamp Venturers.

PHOTOGRAVURE
Sheets of 120 in six panes of 20

1995, June 1 **Tagged** ***Perf. 11.1***

2967 A2281 32c **multicolored**	.80	.25
P# block of 4, 6#+S	5.00	—
Pane of 20	24.00	
a. Imperf., pair	*225.00*	
Pane of 20, imperf.	*3,250.*	

Perforations in corner of each stamp are star-shaped.
Uncut press sheets of No. 2967 were made available for sale.

TEXAS STATEHOOD

A2282

Designed by Laura Smith.
Printed by Sterling Sommer for Ashton-Potter (USA) Ltd.

LITHOGRAPHED
Sheets of 120 in six panes of 20

1995, June 16 **Tagged** ***Perf. 11.2***

2968	A2282 32c **multicolored**	.70	.25
	P# block of 4, 6#+P	2.80	—
	Pane of 20	14.00	—

GREAT LAKES LIGHTHOUSES

Split Rock, Lake Superior — A2283

St. Joseph, Lake Michigan — A2284

Spectacle Reef, Lake Huron — A2285

Marblehead, Lake Erie — A2286

Thirty Mile Point, Lake Ontario — A2287

Designed by Howard Koslow.
Printed by Stamp Venturers.

PHOTOGRAVURE
BOOKLET STAMPS

1995, June 17 **Tagged** ***Perf. 11.2 Vert.***

2969	A2283 32c **multicolored**	.90	.30
2970	A2284 32c **multicolored**	.90	.30
2971	A2285 32c **multicolored**	.90	.30
2972	A2286 32c **multicolored**	.90	.30
2973	A2287 32c **multicolored**	.90	.30
a.	Booklet pane of 5, #2969-2973	4.50	2.50
b.	As "a," two vert. pairs imperf. horiz. of #2972 and 2973, in pane of 7+ stamps in cplt. bklt. #BK230 (due to foldover)	—	

U.N., 50th ANNIV.

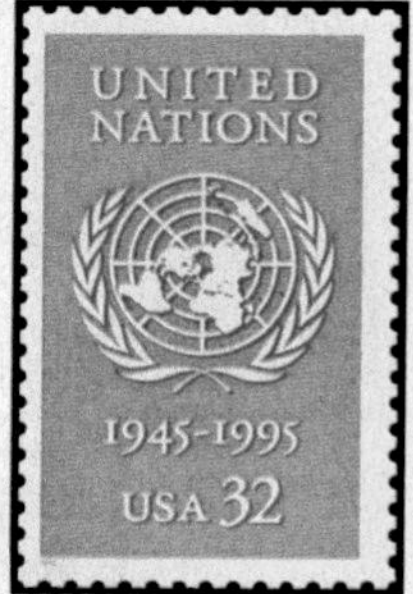

A2288

Designed by Howard Paine.
Printed by Banknote Corp. of America.

ENGRAVED
Sheets of 180 in nine panes of 20

1995, June 26 **Tagged** ***Perf. 11.2***

2974	A2288 32c **blue**	.65	.25
	P# block of 4, 1#+B	2.60	—
	Pane of 20	13.00	—

CIVIL WAR

A2289

Illustration reduced.

Designed by Mark Hess.

Printed by Stamp Venturers.

Designs: a, Monitor and Virginia. b, Robert E. Lee. c, Clara Barton. d, Ulysses S. Grant. e, Battle of Shiloh. f, Jefferson Davis. g, David Farragut. h, Frederick Douglass. i, Raphael Semmes. j, Abraham Lincoln. k, Harriet Tubman. l, Stand Watie. m, Joseph E. Johnston. n, Winfield Hancock. o, Mary Chesnut. p, Battle of Chancellorsville. q, William T. Sherman. r, Phoebe Pember. s, "Stonewall" Jackson. t, Battle of Gettysburg.

PHOTOGRAVURE
Sheets of 120 in six panes of 20

1995, June 29 **Tagged** ***Perf. 10.1***

2975	A2289 Pane of 20	32.50	17.50
a.-t.	32c any single	1.50	.60
u.	As No. 2975, a.-e. imperf, f.-j. part perf, others perf	*800.00*	
v.	As No. 2975, k.-t. imperf, f.-j. part perf, others perf	*1,250.*	
w.	As No. 2975, imperf	*800.00*	
x.	Block of 9 (f.-h., k.-m., p.-r.) k.-l. & p.-q. imperf. vert.	*800.00*	
y.	As No. 2975, a.-b. perf, c., f.-h. part perf, others imperf	*800.00*	
z.	As No. 2975, o. and t. imperf, j., n. & s. part perf, others perf	—	
aa.	As No. 2975, c.-e. imperf, b., g.-j. part perf, others perf	*500.00*	

Uncut press sheets of No. 2975 were made available for sale. Values: cross-gutter block of 20, $45; pairs with gutters between, $5.50 each. See note after No. 2868.

AMERICAN FOLK ART SERIES
Carousel Horses

A2290

A2291

A2292

A2293

Designed by Paul Calle.
Printed at Sterling Sommer for Ashton-Potter (USA) Ltd.

LITHOGRAPHED
Sheets of 160 in eight panes of 20

1995, July 21 **Tagged** ***Perf. 11***

2976	A2290 32c **multicolored**	.65	.25
2977	A2291 32c **multicolored**	.65	.25
2978	A2292 32c **multicolored**	.65	.25
2979	A2293 32c **multicolored**	.65	.25
a.	Block or strip of 4, #2976-2979	2.60	2.00
	P# block of 4, 5#+P	2.60	—
	Pane of 20	13.00	—

WOMAN SUFFRAGE

A2294

Designed by April Greiman.
Printed by Ashton-Potter (USA) Ltd.

LITHOGRAPHED & ENGRAVED
Sheets of 160 in four panes of 40

1995, Aug. 26 **Tagged** ***Perf. 11.1x11***

2980	A2294 32c **multicolored**	.65	.25
	P# block of 4, 5#+P	3.00	—
a.	Black (engr.) omitted	*275.00*	
b.	Imperf., pair	*750.00*	
c.	Vert. pair, imperf between and at bottom	*500.00*	

No. 2980a is valued in the grade of fine. Very fine examples exist and sell for much more.

WORLD WAR II

A2295

Illustration reduced.

Designed by Bill Bond.

Designs and events of 1945: a, Marines raise flag on Iwo Jima. b, Fierce fighting frees Manila by March 3, 1945. c, Soldiers advancing (Okinawa, the last big battle). d, Destroyed bridge (US and Soviets link up at Elbe River). e, Allies liberate Holocaust survivors. f, Germany surrenders at Reims. g, Refugees (By 1945, World War II has uprooted millions). h, Truman announces Japan's surrender. i, Sailor kissing nurse (News of victory hits home). j, Hometowns honor their returning veterans.
Central label is size of 15 stamps and shows world map with extent of Axis control and Allied operations.

LITHOGRAPHED & ENGRAVED
Plates of eight subjects in four panes of 2 each

1995, Sept. 2	**Tagged**	***Perf. 11.1***	
2981 A2295	Block of 10	15.00	7.50
	Pane of 20	30.00	—
a.-j.	32c any single	1.50	.50

No. 2981 has selvage at left and right and either top or bottom.

AMERICAN MUSIC SERIES

Louis Armstrong (1901-71) A2296

Coleman Hawkins (1904-69) A2297

James P. Johnson (1894-1955) A2298

Jelly Roll Morton (1890-1941) A2299

Charlie Parker (1920-55) A2300

Eubie Blake (1883-1983) A2301

Charles Mingus (1922-79) A2302

Thelonious Monk (1917-82) A2303

John Coltrane (1926-67) A2304

Erroll Garner (1921-77) A2305

Designed by Dean Mitchell (#2982-2984, 2987, 2989, 2991-2992) and Thomas Blackshear (others).

Printed by Ashton-Potter (USA) Ltd. (#2982), Sterling Sommer for Ashton-Potter (USA) Ltd. (#2983-2992).

LITHOGRAPHED
Plates of 120 in six panes of 20

1995	**Tagged**	***Perf. 11.1x11***	
2982 A2296	32c **white denomination,** *Sept. 1*	.90	.25
	P# block of 4, 4#+P	3.60	—
	Pane of 20	18.00	—
a.	Imperf, pair	—	
2983 A2297	32c **multicolored,** *Sept. 16*	2.25	.30
2984 A2296	32c **black denomination,** *Sept. 16*	2.25	.30
2985 A2298	32c **multicolored,** *Sept. 16*	2.25	.30
2986 A2299	32c **multicolored,** *Sept. 16*	2.25	.30
2987 A2300	32c **multicolored,** *Sept. 16*	2.25	.30
2988 A2301	32c **multicolored,** *Sept. 16*	2.25	.30
2989 A2302	32c **multicolored,** *Sept. 16*	2.25	.30
2990 A2303	32c **multicolored,** *Sept. 16*	2.25	.30
2991 A2304	32c **multicolored,** *Sept. 16*	2.25	.30
2992 A2305	32c **multicolored,** *Sept. 16*	2.25	.30
a.	Vert. block of 10, #2983-2992	23.00	7.50
	P# block of 10	23.00	—
	Pane of 20	46.00	—
b.	Pane of 20, dark blue (inscriptions) omitted	—	
c.	Imperf pair of Nos. 2991-2992	*5,000.*	

GARDEN FLOWERS

Aster A2306

Chrysanthemum A2307

Dahlia — A2308

Hydrangea — A2309

Rudbeckia — A2310

Designed by Ned Seidler.

LITHOGRAPHED & ENGRAVED
BOOKLET STAMPS

1995, Sept. 19	**Tagged**	***Perf. 10.9 Vert.***	
2993 A2306	32c **multicolored**	.65	.25
2994 A2307	32c **multicolored**	.65	.25
2995 A2308	32c **multicolored**	.65	.25
2996 A2309	32c **multicolored**	.65	.25
2997 A2310	32c **multicolored**	.65	.25
a.	Booklet pane of 5, #2993-2997	3.25	2.25
b.	As "a," imperf	*2,250.*	

EDDIE RICKENBACKER (1890-1973), AVIATOR

A2311

Designed by Davis Meltzer.

PHOTOGRAVURE
Panes of 50

1995, Sept. 25	**Tagged**	***Perf. 11¼***	
2998 A2311	60c **multicolored,** small "1995" year date	1.40	.50
	P# block of 4, 5#	8.00	—
a.	Large "1995" date, *Oct., 1999*	2.00	.50
	P# block of 4, 5#	17.50	

REPUBLIC OF PALAU

A2312

Designed by Herb Kane.
Printed by Sterling Sommer for Ashton-Potter (USA) Ltd.

LITHOGRAPHED
Sheets of 200 in four panes of 50

1995, Sept. 29	**Tagged**		***Perf. 11.1***	
2999	A2312 32c **multicolored**		.65	.25
	P# block of 4, 5#+P		3.00	—

See Palau Nos. 377-378.

COMIC STRIPS

A2313

Illustration reduced.

Designed by Carl Herrman.

Printed by Stamp Venturers.

Designs: a, The Yellow Kid. b, Katzenjammer Kids. c, Little Nemo in Slumberland. d, Bringing Up Father. e, Krazy Kat. f, Rube Goldberg's Inventions. g, Toonerville Folks. h, Gasoline Alley. i, Barney Google. j, Little Orphan Annie. k, Popeye. l, Blondie. m, Dick Tracy. n, Alley Oop. o, Nancy. p, Flash Gordon. q, Li'l Abner. r, Terry and the Pirates. s, Prince Valiant. t, Brenda Starr, Reporter.

PHOTOGRAVURE
Sheets of 120 in six panes of 20

1995, Oct. 1	**Tagged**	***Perf. 10.1***	
3000	A2313 Pane of 20	13.00	10.00
a.-t.	32c any single	.65	.50
u.	As No. 3000, a.-h. imperf., i.-l. part perf	*3,250.*	
v.	As No. 3000, m.-t. imperf., i.-l. part perf	*3,250.*	
w.	As No. 3000, a.-l. imperf.,m.-t. imperf vert.	*3,250.*	
x.	As No. 3000, imperf	*4,250.*	

Inscriptions on back of each stamp describe the comic strip.
Uncut press sheets of No. 3000 were made available for sale. Values: cross-gutter block of 20, $35; pairs with gutters between, $3.75 each. See note after No. 2868.

U.S. NAVAL ACADEMY, 150th ANNIVERSARY

A2314

Designed by Dean Ellis. Printed by Sterling-Sommer for Aston-Potter (USA) Ltd.

LITHOGRAPHED
Sheets of 160 in eight panes of 20

1995, Oct. 10	**Tagged**	***Perf. 10.9***	
3001	A2314 32c **multicolored**	.65	.25
	P# block of 4, 5#+P	3.25	—
	Pane of 20	16.00	—

LITERARY ARTS SERIES

Tennessee Williams (1911-83)
A2315

Designed by Michael Deas. Printed by Sterling-Sommer for Ashton-Potter (USA) Ltd.

LITHOGRAPHED
Sheets of 160 in eight panes of 20

1995, Oct. 13	**Tagged**	***Perf. 11.1***	
3002	A2315 32c **multicolored**	.65	.25
	P# block of 4, 5#+P	3.25	—
	Pane of 20	16.00	—

CHRISTMAS

Madonna and Child, by Giotto di Bondone — A2316

Santa Claus Entering Chimney — A2317

Child Holding Jumping Jack — A2318

Child Holding Tree — A2319

Santa Claus Working on Sled — A2320

Midnight Angel — A2321

Children Sledding — A2322

Designed by Richard Sheaff (#3003), John Grossman & Laura Alders (#3004-3018).

Printed by Bureau of Engraving and Printing (#3003), Sterling-Sommer for Ashton-Potter (USA) Ltd. (#3004-3007), Avery Dennison (#3008-3011, 3013-3017), Banknote Corporation of America (#3012, 3018).

LITHOGRAPHED & ENGRAVED
Sheets of 300 in six panes of 50

1995	**Tagged**	***Perf. 11.2***	
3003	A2316 32c **multicolored**, *Oct. 19*	.65	.25
	P# block of 4, 5#	3.00	—
c.	Black (engr., denomination) omitted	*200.00*	—
d.	Tagging omitted	75.00	—

BOOKLET STAMP
Perf. 9.8x10.9

3003A	A2316 32c **multicolored**, *Oct. 19*	.65	.25
b.	Booklet pane of 10	6.50	4.00

LITHOGRAPHED
Sheets of 200 in four panes of 50
Perf. 11.25

3004	A2317 32c **multicolored**, *Sept. 30*	.70	.25
3005	A2318 32c **multicolored**, *Sept. 30*	.70	.25
3006	A2319 32c **multicolored**, *Sept. 30*	.70	.25
3007	A2320 32c **multicolored**, *Sept. 30*	.70	.25
a.	Block or strip of 4, #3004-3007	2.80	1.25
	P# block of 4, 4#+P	4.00	—
b.	Booklet pane of 10, 3 each #3004-3005, 2 each #3006-3007	8.00	4.00
c.	Booklet pane of 10, 2 each #3004-3005, 3 each #3006-3007	8.00	4.00
d.	As "a," imperf	*325.00*	
e.	As "b," miscut and inserted upside down into booklet cover, with full bottom selvage		—

PHOTOGRAVURE
Self-Adhesive Stamps
Serpentine Die Cut 11.25 on 2, 3 or 4 sides

3008	A2320 32c **multicolored**, *Sept. 30*	.95	.25
3009	A2318 32c **multicolored**, *Sept. 30*	.95	.25
3010	A2317 32c **multicolored**, *Sept. 30*	.95	.25
3011	A2319 32c **multicolored**, *Sept. 30*	.95	.25
a.	Booklet pane of 20, 5 each #3008-3011 + label	19.00	
b.	Strip of 4, #3008-3011	3.80	

LITHOGRAPHED
Serpentine Die Cut 11.3x11.6 on 2, 3 or 4 sides

3012	A2321 32c **multicolored**, *Oct. 19*	.65	.25
a.	Booklet pane of 20 + label	13.00	
b.	Vert. pair, die cutting omitted between	—	
c.	Booklet pane of 15 + label, *1996*	12.00	
d.	Booklet pane of 15	*30.00*	

No. 3012a comes either with no die cutting in the label (1995 printing) or with the die cutting from the 1996 printing.
No. 3012d is a pane of 16 with one stamp removed. The missing stamp can be from either row 1, 2, 3, 7 or 8 of the pane. No. 3012d cannot be made from No. 3012c, a pane of 15 + label. The label is die cut. If the label is removed, an impression of the die cutting appears on the backing paper.

PHOTOGRAVURE
Die Cut

3013	A2322 32c **multicolored**, *Oct. 19* ⓢ	.65	.25
a.	Booklet pane of 18	12.00	
b.	As "a," tagging omitted	—	

ⓢ: Adhesive residue may adhere to the back of some examples of No. 3013 after soaking. See note after No. 1549.

Self-Adhesive Coil Stamps
Serpentine Die Cut 11.2 Vert.

3014	A2320 32c **multicolored**, *Sept. 30*	3.00	.30
3015	A2318 32c **multicolored**, *Sept. 30*	3.00	.30
3016	A2317 32c **multicolored**, *Sept. 30*	3.00	.30
3017	A2319 32c **multicolored**, *Sept. 30*	3.00	.30
a.	Strip of 4, #3014-3017	12.00	
	P# strip of 5, 1 each #3014-3017 + 1 stamp, P#V1111	25.00	
	P# strip of 8, 2 each #3014-3017, P#V1111	35.00	
	P# single (#3017), #V1111	—	12.50

LITHOGRAPHED
Serpentine Die Cut 11.6 Vert.

3018	A2321 32c **multicolored**, *Oct. 19*	1.10	.30
	Pair	2.20	.60
	P# strip of 5, #B1111	8.00	
	P# single, #B1111	—	6.00

Nos. 3014-3018 were only available through the Philatelic Fullfillment Center in Kansas City.
Nos. 3005-3006 have "USA" printed in green. It is red on the self-adhesive stamps.

ANTIQUE AUTOMOBILES

1893 Duryea
A2323

1894 Haynes
A2324

1898 Columbia
A2325

1899 Winton
A2326

1901 White
A2327

Designed by Ken Dallison.
Printed by Stamp Venturers.

PHOTOGRAVURE
Sheets of 200 in eight panes of 25

1995, Nov. 3 **Tagged** ***Perf. 10.1x11.1***

3019 A2323 32c **multicolored** .90 .25
3020 A2324 32c **multicolored** .90 .25
3021 A2325 32c **multicolored** .90 .25
3022 A2326 32c **multicolored** .90 .25
3023 A2327 32c **multicolored** .90 .25
a. Vert. or horiz. strip of 5, #3019-3023 4.50 2.00
Vert. or Horiz. P# block of 10, 2 sets of 4#+S 10.00 —
Pane of 25 24.00 —

Vert. and horiz. strips are all in different order.

UTAH STATEHOOD CENTENARY

Delicate Arch, Arches Natl. Park — A2328

Designed by McRay Magleby.
Printed by Sterling Sommer for Ashton-Potter (USA) Ltd.

LITHOGRAPHED
Sheets of 200 in four panes of 50

1996, Jan. 4 **Tagged** ***Perf. 11.1***

3024 A2328 32c **multicolored** .75 .25
P# block of 4, 5#+P 4.00 —

For booklet see No. BK245.

GARDEN FLOWERS

Crocus — A2329

Winter Aconite — A2330

Pansy — A2331

Snowdrop — A2332

Anemone — A2333

Designed by Ned Seidler.

LITHOGRAPHED & ENGRAVED
BOOKLET STAMPS

1996, Jan. 19 **Tagged** ***Perf. 10.9 Vert.***

3025 A2329 32c **multicolored** .65 .25
3026 A2330 32c **multicolored** .65 .25
3027 A2331 32c **multicolored** .65 .25
3028 A2332 32c **multicolored** .65 .25
3029 A2333 32c **multicolored** .65 .25
a. Booklet pane of 5, #3025-3029 3.25 2.50
b. As "a," imperf. —

LOVE

Cherub from Sistine Madonna, by Raphael — A2334

Designed by Terry McCaffrey.
Printed by Banknote Corporation of America.

LITHOGRAPHED & ENGRAVED
BOOKLET STAMP

Serpentine Die Cut 11.3x11.7

1996, Jan. 20 **Tagged**

Self-Adhesive

3030 A2334 32c **multicolored** .65 .25
a. Booklet pane of 20 + label 13.00
b. Booklet pane of 15 + label 9.75
e. Double impression of red (engr. "Love") *450.00*
f. Die cutting omitted, pair *225.00*
g. As "a," stamps 1-5 double impression of red (engr. "LOVE") *1,000.*
h. As "a," red (engr. "LOVE") omitted *1,200.*
i. As "a," die cutting omitted —
j As "e," two examples in booklet pane of 20 (No. 3030a) *1,000.*

No. 3030d must be collected se-tenant with a stamp bearing the red engraving.

FLORA AND FAUNA SERIES

Kestrel, Blue Jay and Rose Types of 1993-95 and

Red-headed Woodpecker
A2335

Eastern Bluebird
A2336

Red Fox — A2339

Ring-necked Pheasant — A2350

Coral Pink Rose — A2351

Designed by Michael Matherly (#3031-3033, 3044-3045); Terry McCaffrey (#3050-3051, 3055); Derry Noyes (#3036, 3052, 3052E).

Printed by Banknote Corporation of America (#3031A, 3036); Bureau of Engraving & Printing (#3031-3033, 3044-3045); Stamp Venturers (#3048-3049, 3053); Avery Dennison (#3050-3051A). American Packaging Corp. for Sennett Security Products (#3052); Sennett Security Products (#3052E).

LITHOGRAPHED
Sheets of 300 in six panes of 50 (#3031).
Sheets of 400 in eight panes of 50 (#3031A).
Sheets of 400 in four panes of 100 (#3032-3033).
Sheets of 120 in six panes of 20 (#3036).
Sheets of 200 in ten panes of 20 (#3036a)

1996-2002 **Untagged** ***Serpentine Die Cut 10½***

Self-Adhesive (#3031, 3031A)

3031 A1841 1c **multicolored,** *Nov. 19, 1999* .25 .25
P# block of 4, 4# or 4# + A, B or C .50
c. Die cutting omitted, pair —

Serpentine Die Cut 11¼

3031A A1841 1c **multicolored,** *Nov. 2000* .25 .25
P# block of 4, 6# + B .50
b. Die cutting omitted, pane of 50 *325.00*

No. 3031A has blue inscription and year.

Perf. 11

3032 A2335 2c **multicolored,** *Feb. 2* .25 .25
P# block of 4, 5# .50 —
3033 A2336 3c **multicolored,** *Apr. 3* .25 .25
P# block of 4, 5# .50 —

Some plate blocks contain plate position diagram.

Tagged

Serpentine Die Cut 11½x11¼

Self-Adhesive

3036 A2339 $1 **multicolored,** *Aug. 14, 1998* 4.50 .50
P# block of 4, 4#+B 18.00
Pane of 20 90.00
a. Serpentine die cut 11¾x11, *2002* 4.75 .50
P# block of 4, 4#+B 19.00
Pane of 20 95.00

The tagging of No. 3036 has a bright yellow-green appearance under shortwave ultraviolet light while that of No. 3036a appears light blue green. Nos. 3036 and 3036a are dated 1998 at left bottom.

A hidden 3-D image (a small fox) can be seen on Nos. 3036

Beginning with Nos. 3036 and 3036a, hidden 3-D images can be seen on some stamps when they are viewed with a special "Stamp Decoder" lens sold by the USPS. Stamps with 3-D images are 3036-3036a, 3167, 3168-3172, 3178, 3206, 3230-3234, 3238-3242, 3261-3262, 3321-3324, 3472-3473, 3647-3648, 3651, 3771, 3787-3791, 3808-3811, 3838 and 3862.

COIL STAMPS

Untagged

Perf. 9¾ Vert.

3044	A1841 1c **multicolored,** small date, *Jan. 20*	.25	.25
	Pair	.25	.25
	P# strip of 5, #1111 in black, yellow, blue, magenta order	.65	
	P# single, same	—	.60
	P# strip of 5, #1111 in black, blue, yellow, magenta order	3.00	
	P# single, same	—	3.00
a.	Large date	.25	.25
	Pair	.25	.25
	P# strip of 5, #1111, 2222, 3333, 4444 in yellow, magenta, blue, black order	.70	
	P# single, same	—	.70

Date on No. 3044 is 1mm long, on No. 3044a 1.5mm long.

Untagged

3045	A2335 2c **multicolored,** *June 22, 1999*	.25	.25
	Pair	.25	.25
	P# strip of 5, #11111	.70	—
	P# strip of 5, #22222	1.25	
	P# single, #11111	—	.65
	P# single, #22222	—	.85

BOOKLET STAMPS

PHOTOGRAVURE

Serpentine Die Cut 10.4x10.8 on 3 Sides

Tagged

Self-Adhesive

3048	A1847 20c **multicolored,** *Aug. 2, 1996*	.40	.25
a.	Booklet pane of 10	4.00	
b.	Booklet pane of 4	70.00	
c.	Booklet pane of 6	100.00	

No. 3048 and 3048a exist on two types of surface-tagged paper that exhibit either a solid appearance (P# S1111) or a grainy solid appearance (P# S1111 and S2222).

Nos. 3048b-3048c are from the vending machine booklet No. BK237 that has a glue strip at the top edge of the top pane, the peelable strip removed and the rouletting line 2mm lower than on No. 3048a on some booklets, when the panes are compared with bottoms aligned. Vending booklets with plate #S2222 always have gauge 8½ rouletting on booklet covers. Convertible booklets (No. 3048a) with plate #S2222 always have gauge 12½ rouletting on booklet covers. Vending booklets with plate #S1111 can have either 8½ or 12½ gauge rouletting on booklet cover, and it may be impossible to tell a vending booklet with 12½ gauge rouletting and plate #S1111 from a convertible booklet with peelable strip removed.

Serpentine Die Cut 11.3x11.7 on 2, 3 or 4 Sides

3049	A1853 32c **yellow, orange, green & black,** *Oct. 24, 1996*	.65	.25
a.	Booklet pane of 20 + label	13.00	
b.	Booklet pane of 4, *Dec. 1996*	2.60	
c.	Booklet pane of 5 + label, *Dec. 1996*	3.50	
	P# single, #S1111	.85	*1.00*
d.	Booklet pane of 6, *Dec. 1996*	4.00	
	Booklet pane of 6 containing P# single	6.00	
	P# single, #S1111	2.50	*1.00*

The plate # single in No. 3049c is on the lower left stamp. In No. 3049d it is the lower right stamp on the bottom pane of the booklet.

Serpentine Die Cut 11.2 on 3 Sides

3050	A2350 20c **multicolored,** *July 31, 1998*	.65	.25
a.	Booklet pane of 10, all stamps upright	6.50	
b.	Serpentine die cut 11	3.25	.25
c.	As "b," booklet pane of 10, all stamps upright	35.00	

Serpentine Die Cut 10½x11 on 3 Sides

3051	A2350 20c **multicolored,** *July 1999*	.75	.25

Serpentine Die Cut 10.6x10.4 on 3 Sides

3051A	A2350 20c **multicolored**	7.00	.50
b.	Booklet pane of 5, 4 #3051, 1 #3051A turned sideways at top	10.00	
c.	Booklet pane of 5, 4 #3051, 1 #3051A turned sideways at bottom	10.00	

No. 3051 represents the eight upright stamps on the booklet panes Nos. 3051Ab and 3051Ac. The two stamps turned sideways on those panes are No. 3051A.

Specialists should note that 3051 can be either die cut 10.4 at top and 10.6 at bottom or 10.6 at top and 10.4 at bottom. These two varieties exist in equal numbers.

Serpentine Die Cut 11½x11¼ on 2, 3 or 4 Sides

3052	A2351 33c **multicolored,** *Aug. 13, 1999*	.90	.25
a.	Booklet pane of 4	3.60	
b.	Booklet pane of 5 + label	4.50	
c.	Booklet pane of 6	5.50	
d.	Booklet pane of 20 + label	17.50	
j.	Die cutting omitted, pair	—	
k.	As "d," die cutting omitted	*5,500.*	

Serpentine Die Cut 10¾x10½ on 2 or 3 sides

3052E	A2351 33c **multi,** *Apr. 7, 2000* ®	.75	.25
f.	Booklet pane of 20	15.00	
g.	Black ("33 USA," etc.) omitted	350.00	
h.	As "f," all 12 stamps on one side with black omitted	—	
i.	Horiz. pair, die cutting missing between (PS)	—	
j.	As "f," vert. die cutting missing between (PS)	—	

No. 3052Ef is a double-sided booklet pane with 12 stamps on one side and 8 stamps plus label on the other side.

See note after No. 1549.

COIL STAMPS

Serpentine Die Cut 11½ Vert.

3053	A1847 20c **multicolored,** *Aug. 2, 1996*	.50	.25
	Pair	1.00	
	P# strip of 5, #S1111	3.75	
	P# single, #S1111	—	1.00
a.	Die cutting omitted, pair	*2,100.*	

Yellow Rose, Ring-necked Pheasant Types of 1996-98

Printed by Bureau of Engraving and Printing (#3054-3055).

COIL STAMPS

LITHOGRAPHED

Serpentine Die Cut 9¾ Vert.

Tagged

Self-Adhesive

3054	A1853 32c **yellow, magenta, black & green,** *Aug. 1, 1997*	.65	.25
	Pair	1.30	
	P# strip of 5, #1111, 1112, 1122, 2222, 2223, 2333, 3344, 4455, 5455, 5555, 5556, 5566, 5666, 6666, 7777	4.50	
	P# strip of 5, #2233, 3444	6.00	
	P# strip of 5, #6677, 6777, 8888	7.50	
	P# single, #1111, 1112, 1122, 4455, 5555, 5556, 5566, 5666, 6666, 7777	—	1.50
	P# single, #2222, 2333	—	2.50
	P# single, #2223, 8888	—	2.75
	P# single, #2233, 3444	—	4.50
	P# single, #3344, 5455, 6677	—	3.50
	P# single, #6777	—	5.50
a.	Die cutting omitted, pair	*85.00*	
b.	Black, yellow & green omitted	—	
c.	Black, yellow & green omitted, die cutting omitted, pair	—	
d.	Black omitted	*250.00*	
e.	Black omitted, die cutting omitted, pair	—	
f.	All colors omitted, die cutting omitted	—	
g.	Pair, die cutting omitted, containing one stamp each of "c" and "e"	—	

Nos. 3054b and 3054d also are miscut and with shifted die cuttings.

No. 3054f must be collected se-tenant with a partially printed stamp(s).

3055	A2350 20c **multicolored,** *July, 31, 1998*	.40	.25
	Pair	.80	
	P# strip of 5, P#1111, 2222	3.00	
	P# single, same	—	1.25
a.	Die cutting omitted, pair	*125.00*	

No. 3055a exists miscut. It is more common in this form and is valued thus.

BLACK HERITAGE SERIES

Ernest E. Just (1883-1941), Marine Biologist — A2358

Designed by Richard Sheaff.
Printed by Banknote Corporation of America.

LITHOGRAPHED

Sheets of 160 in eight panes of 20

1996, Feb. 1 **Tagged** ***Perf. 11.1***

3058	A2358 32c **gray & black**	.65	.25
	P# block of 4, 4#+B	2.60	—
	Pane of 20	13.00	—

SMITHSONIAN INSTITUTION, 150TH ANNIVERSARY

A2359

Designed by Tom Engeman.
Printed by Ashton-Potter (USA) Ltd.

LITHOGRAPHED

Sheets of 160 in eight panes of 20

1996, Feb. 7 **Tagged** ***Perf. 11.1***

3059	A2359 32c **multicolored**	.65	.25
	P# block of 4, 4#+P	2.60	—
	Pane of 20	13.00	—

CHINESE NEW YEAR

Year of the Rat — A2360

Designed by Clarence Lee.
Printed by Stamp Venturers.

PHOTOGRAVURE

Sheets of 180 in nine panes of 20

1996, Feb. 8 **Tagged** ***Perf. 11.1***

3060	A2360 32c **multicolored**	.90	.25
	P# block of 4, 4#+S	4.25	—
	Pane of 20	19.00	—
a.	Imperf., pair	*550.00*	

See No. 3895a.

PIONEERS OF COMMUNICATION

Eadweard Muybridge (1830-1904), Photographer A2361

Ottmar Mergenthaler (1854-99), Inventor of Linotype A2362

Frederic E. Ives (1856-1937), Developer of Halftone Process A2363

William Dickson (1860-1935), Co-developer of Kinetoscope
A2364

Designed by Fred Otnes.
Printed by Ashton-Potter USA.

LITHOGRAPHED

Sheets of 120 in six panes of 20

1996, Feb. 22	**Tagged**	***Perf. 11.1x11***	
3061 A2361 32c **multicolored**		.65	.25
3062 A2362 32c **multicolored**		.65	.25
3063 A2363 32c **multicolored**		.65	.25
3064 A2364 32c **multicolored**		.65	.25
a. Block or strip of 4, #3061-3064		2.60	2.00
P# block of 4, 5#+P		2.60	—
Pane of 20		13.00	—

FULBRIGHT SCHOLARSHIPS, 50th ANNIVERSARY

A2365

Designed by Richard D. Sheaff.

LITHOGRAPHED & ENGRAVED

Sheets of 200 in four panes of 50

1996, Feb. 28	**Tagged**	***Perf. 11.1***	
3065 A2365 32c **multicolored**		.75	.25
P# block of 4, 5#		4.25	—

For booklet see No. BK246.

JACQUELINE COCHRAN (1910-80), PILOT

A2366

Designed by Davis Meltzer.

LITHOGRAPHED & ENGRAVED

Sheets of 300 in six panes of 50

1996, Mar. 9	**Tagged**	***Perf. 11.1***	
3066 A2366 50c **multicolored**		1.00	.40
P# block of 4, 5#		5.00	—
a. Black (engr.) omitted		45.00	

MARATHON

A2367

Designed by Michael Bartalos.

LITHOGRAPHED

Sheets of 160 in eight panes of 20

1996, Apr. 11	**Tagged**	***Perf. 11.1***	
3067 A2367 32c **multicolored**		.65	.25
P# block of 4, 4#+B		2.60	—
Pane of 20		13.00	—

1996 SUMMER OLYMPIC GAMES

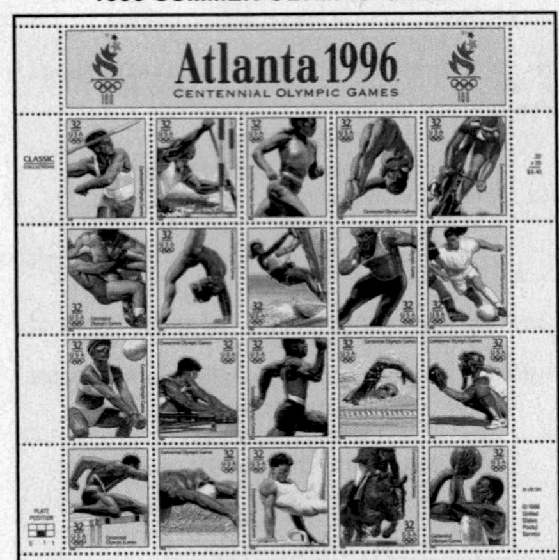

A2368

Illustration reduced.

Designed by Richard Waldrep. Printed by Stamp Venturers.

Designs: a, Decathlon (javelin). b, Men's canoeing. c, Women's running. d, Women's diving. e, Men's cycling. f, Freestyle wrestling. g, Women's gymnastics. h, Women's sailboarding. i, Men's shot put. j, Women's soccer. k, Beach volleyball. l, Men's rowing. m, Men's sprints. n, Women's swimming. o, Women's softball. p, Men's hurdles. q, Men's swimming. r, Men's gymnastics (pommel horse). s, Equestrian. t, Men's basketball.

PHOTOGRAVURE

Sheets of 120 in six panes of 20

1996, May 2	**Tagged**	***Perf. 10.1***	
3068 A2368 Pane of 20		14.00	10.00
a.-t. 32c any single		.70	.50
u. As No. 3068, imperf		*700.00*	
v. As No. 3068, back inscriptions omitted on a., f., k. & p., incorrect back inscriptions on others		—	
w. As No. 3068, e. imperf, d., i.-j. part perf, all others perf		*750.00*	

Inscription on back of each stamp describes the sport shown.

Uncut press sheets of No. 3068 were made available for sale. Values: cross-gutter block of 20, $45; pairs with gutters between, $4 each. See note after No. 2868.

GEORGIA O'KEEFFE (1887-1986)

A2369

Designed by Margaret Bauer. Printed by Stamp Venturers.

PHOTOGRAVURE

Sheets of 90 in six panes of 15

1996, May 23	**Tagged**	***Perf. 11.6x11.4***	
3069 A2369 32c **multicolored**		.85	.25
P# block of 4, 5#+S		5.00	—
Pane of 15		15.00	9.00
a. Imperf., pair		*110.00*	
Pane of 15, imperf.		*675.00*	—

For booklet see No. BK247.

TENNESSEE STATEHOOD BICENTENNIAL

A2370

Designed by Phil Jordan. Printed by Stamp Venturers.

PHOTOGRAVURE

Sheets of 200 in four panes of 50.

1996, May 31	**Tagged**	***Perf. 11.1***	
3070 A2370 32c **multicolored**		.65	.25
P# block of 4, 5#+S		3.00	—

For booklet see No. BK248.

Booklet Stamp

Self-Adhesive

Serpentine Die Cut 9.9x10.8

3071 A2370 32c **multicolored**		.65	.30
a. Booklet pane of 20, #S11111		13.00	
b. Horiz. pair, die cutting omitted btwn.		*300.00*	—
c. Die cutting omitted, pair		—	
d. Horiz. pair, die cutting omitted vert.		—	—

AMERICAN INDIAN DANCES

Fancy — A2371

Butterfly — A2372

Traditional — A2373

Raven — A2374

Hoop — A2375

Designed by Keith Birdsong. Printed by Ashton-Potter (USA) Ltd.

LITHOGRAPHED

Sheets of 120 in six panes of 20.

1996, June 7	**Tagged**	***Perf. 11.1***	
3072 A2371 32c **multicolored**		1.20	.25

3075 A2374 32c **multicolored** 1.20 .25
3076 A2375 32c **multicolored** 1.20 .25
a. Strip of 5, #3072-3076 6.00 2.50
P# block of 10, 4#+P 12.50 —
Pane of 20 25.00 —

For booklet see No. BK249.

PREHISTORIC ANIMALS

Eohippus
A2376

Woolly
Mammoth
A2377

Mastodon
A2378

Saber-tooth
Cat — A2379

Designed by Davis Meltzer. Printed by Ashton-Potter (USA) Ltd.

LITHOGRAPHED

Sheets of 120 in six panes of 20

1996, June 8 **Tagged** ***Perf. 11.1x11***
3077 A2376 32c **multicolored** .65 .25
3078 A2377 32c **multicolored** .65 .25
3079 A2378 32c **multicolored** .65 .25
3080 A2379 32c **multicolored** .65 .25
a. Block or strip of 4, #3077-3080 2.60 2.00
P# block of 4, 4#+P 2.60 —
Pane of 20 13.00 —

BREAST CANCER AWARENESS

A2380

Designed by Tom Mann. Printed by Ashton-Potter (USA) Ltd.

LITHOGRAPHED

Sheets of 120 in six panes of 20

1996, June 15 **Tagged** ***Perf. 11.1***
3081 A2380 32c **multicolored** .65 .25
P# block of 4, 5#+P 2.60 —
Pane of 20 13.00 —

LEGENDS OF HOLLYWOOD

James Dean, (1931-55) — A2381

Designed by Michael Deas.

Printed by Stamp Venturers.

PHOTOGRAVURE

Sheets of 120 in six panes of 20.

1996, June 24 **Tagged** ***Perf. 11.1***
3082 A2381 32c **multicolored** .65 .25
P# block of 4, 7#+S 4.25 —
Pane of 20 20.00 10.00
a. Imperf., pair *100.00*
Pane of 20, imperf. *1,250.* —
b. As "a," red (USA 32c) missing (CM) and tan (JAMES DEAN) omitted —
c. As "a," tan (JAMES DEAN) omitted —
d. As "a," top stamp red missing (CM) and tan (JAMES DEAN) omitted, bottom stamp tan omitted —
e. As No. 3082 pane of 20, right two columns perf, left three columns imperf *1,750.*

Perforations in corner of each stamp are star-shaped. No. 3082 was also available on the first day of issue in at least 127 Warner Bros. Studio stores.

Uncut press sheets of No. 3082 were made available for sale. Values: cross-gutter block of 8, $35; pairs with gutters between, $4.25 each. See note after No. 2868.

For booklet see No. BK250.

Nos. 3082b-3082d come from the same error pane. The top row is No. 3082b; rows 2-4 are No. 3082c. No. 3082d is a vertical pair with one stamp from No. 3082b at top and one stamp from No. 3082c at bottom.

FOLK HEROES

A2382

A2383

A2384

A2385

Designed by David LaFleur.

Printed by Ashton-Potter (USA) Ltd.

LITHOGRAPHED

Sheets of 120 in six panes of 20

1996, July 11 **Tagged** ***Perf. 11.1x11***
3083 A2382 32c **multicolored** .65 .25
3084 A2383 32c **multicolored** .65 .25
3085 A2384 32c **multicolored** .65 .25
3086 A2385 32c **multicolored** .65 .25
a. Block or strip of 4, #3083-3086 2.60 2.00
P# block of 4, 4#+P 2.60 —
Pane of 20 13.00 —

For booklet see No. BK251.

CENTENNIAL OLYMPIC GAMES

Myron's Discobolus — A2386

Designed by Carl Herrman.

Printed by Ashton-Potter (USA) Ltd.

ENGRAVED

Sheets of 80 in four panes of 20

1996, July 19 **Tagged** ***Perf. 11.1***
3087 A2386 32c **brown** .75 .25
P# block of 4, 1#+P 4.25 —
Pane of 20 20.00 10.00

Sheet margin of the pane of 20 is lithographed.

For booklet see No. BK252.

IOWA STATEHOOD, 150TH ANNIVERSARY

Young Corn, by Grant Wood — A2387

Designed by Carl Herrman.

Printed by Ashton-Potter (USA) Ltd. (#3088), Banknote Corporation of America (#3089)

LITHOGRAPHED

Sheets of 200 in four panes of 50

1996, Aug. 1 **Tagged** ***Perf. 11.1***
3088 A2387 32c **multicolored** .80 .25
P# block of 4, 4#+P 3.75 —

For booklet see No. BK253.

BOOKLET STAMP

Self-Adhesive

Serpentine Die Cut 11.6x11.4

3089 A2387 32c **multicolored** .65 .30
a. Booklet pane of 20 13.00

RURAL FREE DELIVERY, CENT.

A2388

Designed by Richard Sheaff.

LITHOGRAPHED & ENGRAVED
Sheets of 120 in six panes of 20

1996, Aug. 7 **Tagged** ***Perf. 11.2x11***

3090 A2388 32c **multicolored**		.80	.25
	P# block of 4, 5#	3.50	—
	Pane of 20	17.50	—

For booklet see No. BK254.

RIVERBOATS

Robt. E. Lee — A2389

Sylvan Dell — A2390

Far West — A2391

Rebecca Everingham A2392

Bailey Gatzert A2393

Designed by Dean Ellis.

Printed by Avery Dennison.

PHOTOGRAVURE
Sheets of 200 in 10 panes of 20
Serpentine Die Cut 11x11.1

1996, Aug. 22 **Tagged**

Self-Adhesive

3091 A2389 32c **multicolored**		.65	.40
3092 A2390 32c **multicolored**		.65	.40
3093 A2391 32c **multicolored**		.65	.40
3094 A2392 32c **multicolored**		.65	.40
3095 A2393 32c **multicolored**		.65	.40
a.	Vert. strip of 5, #3091-3095	3.25	
	P# block of 10, 5#+V	6.50	
	Pane of 20	13.00	
b.	Strip of 5, #3091-3095, with special die cutting, die cut 11¼	*45.00*	*45.00*
	P# block of 10, 5#+V	*90.00*	
	Pane of 20	*180.00*	

The serpentine die cutting runs through the peelable backing to which Nos. 3091-3095 are affixed. No. 3095a exists with stamps in different sequences.

On the long side of each stamp in No. 3095b, the die cutting is missing 3 "perforations" between the stamps, one near each end and one in the middle. This allows a complete strip to be removed from the backing paper for use on a first day cover. No. 3095b was also used to make Souvenir Page No. 1215.

For booklet see No. BK255.

AMERICAN MUSIC SERIES
Big Band Leaders

Count Basie — A2394

Tommy & Jimmy Dorsey A2395

Glenn Miller — A2396

Benny Goodman A2397

Songwriters

Harold Arlen — A2398

Johnny Mercer A2399

Hoagy Carmichael A2401

Designed by Bill Nelson (#3096-3099), Gregg Rudd (#3100-3103).

Printed by Ashton-Potter (USA) Ltd.

LITHOGRAPHED
Sheets of 120 in six panes of 20

1996, Sept. 11 **Tagged** ***Perf. 11.1x11***

3096 A2394 32c **multicolored**		.75	.25
3097 A2395 32c **multicolored**		.75	.25
3098 A2396 32c **multicolored**		.75	.25
3099 A2397 32c **multicolored**		.75	.25
a.	Block or strip of 4, #3096-3099	3.00	2.00
	P# block of 4, 6#+P	4.00	—
	P# block of 8, 2 sets of P# + top label	7.00	—
	Pane of 20	19.00	—
3100 A2398 32c **multicolored**		.75	.25
3101 A2399 32c **multicolored**		.75	.25
3102 A2400 32c **multicolored**		.75	.25
3103 A2401 32c **multicolored**		.75	.25
a.	Block or strip of 4, #3100-3103	3.00	2.00
	P# block of 4, 6#+P	3.50	—
	P# block of 8, 2 sets of P# + top label	5.75	—
	Pane of 20	16.00	—

LITERARY ARTS SERIES

F. Scott Fitzgerald (1896-1940) A2402

Designed by Michael Deas.

PHOTOGRAVURE
Sheets of 200 in four panes of 50

1996, Sept. 27 **Tagged** ***Perf. 11.1***

3104 A2402 23c **multicolored**		.55	.25
	P# block of 4, 4#	4.00	—
	Pair with full horiz. gutter between		—

ENDANGERED SPECIES

A2403

Illustration reduced.

Designed by James Balog. Printed by Ashton-Potter (USA) Ltd.

Designs: a, Black-footed ferret. b, Thick-billed parrot. c, Hawaiian monk seal. d, American crocodile. e, Ocelot. f, Schaus swallowtail butterfly. g, Wyoming toad. h, Brown pelican. i, California condor. j, Gila trout. k, San Francisco garter snake. l, Woodland caribou. m, Florida panther. n, Piping plover. o, Florida manatee.

LITHOGRAPHED
Sheets of 90 in six panes of 15

1996, Oct. 2	**Tagged**	***Perf. 11.1x11***	
3105 A2403	Pane of 15	12.00	8.00
a.-o.	32c any single	.80	.50

See Mexico No. 1995. For booklet see No. BK256.

COMPUTER TECHNOLOGY

A2404

Designed by Nancy Skolos & Tom Wedell.

Printed by Ashton-Potter (USA) Ltd.

LITHOGRAPHED & ENGRAVED
Sheets of 160 in four panes of 40

1996, Oct. 8	**Tagged**	***Perf. 10.9x11.1***	
3106 A2404 32c **multicolored**		.65	.25
P# block of 4, 6#+P		3.00	—

CHRISTMAS

Madonna and Child from Adoration of the Shepherds, by Paolo de Matteis — A2405

Family at Fireplace — A2406

Decorating Tree — A2407

Dreaming of Santa Claus — A2408

Holiday Shopping — A2409

Skaters — A2410

Designed by Richard D. Sheaff (#3107, 3112), Julia Talcott (#3108-3111, 3113-3117).

Printed by Bureau of Engraving and Printing (#3107, 3112), Ashton-Potter (USA) Ltd. (#3108-3111), Banknote Corporation of America (#3113-3116), Avery-Dennison (#3117).

LITHOGRAPHED & ENGRAVED
Sheets of 300 in six panes of 50

1996	**Tagged**	***Perf. 11.1x11.2***	
3107 A2405 32c **multicolored,** *Nov. 1*		.65	.25
	P# block of 4, 5#	3.00	—
a.	Black (engr.) omitted at bottom	*600.00*	

On No. 3107a, an albino impression of the lettering at bottom is present, but there is no trace of black ink.
For booklet see No. BK257.

LITHOGRAPHED
Perf. 11.3

3108 A2406 32c **multicolored,** *Oct. 8*		.65	.25
3109 A2407 32c **multicolored,** *Oct. 8*		.65	.25
3110 A2408 32c **multicolored,** *Oct. 8*		.65	.25
3111 A2409 32c **multicolored,** *Oct. 8*		.65	.25
a.	Block or strip of 4, #3108-3111	2.60	1.75
	P# block of 4, 4#+P	3.00	—
b.	Strip of 4, #3110-3111, 3108-3109, with #3109 imperf., #3108 imperf. at right	*1,000.*	
c.	Strip of 4, #3108-3111, with #3111 imperf, #3110 imperf at right	*1,000.*	

BOOKLET STAMPS
Self-Adhesive
LITHOGRAPHED & ENGRAVED
Serpentine Die Cut 10 on 2, 3 or 4 Sides

3112 A2405 32c **multicolored,** *Nov. 1*		.75	.25
a.	Booklet pane of 20 + label	15.00	
b.	Die cutting omitted, pair	40.00	
c.	As "a," die cutting omitted	*400.00*	
d.	As "a," top seven stamps with black (engr.) missing (PS)	—	

No. 3112d is missing the black lettering at bottom due to a small upward shift of the horizontal perforations. This lettering is the only engraved black on the stamp.

LITHOGRAPHED
Serpentine Die Cut 11.8x11.5 on 2, 3 or 4 Sides

3113 A2406 32c **multicolored,** *Oct. 8*		.65	.25
3114 A2407 32c **multicolored,** *Oct. 8*		.65	.25
3115 A2408 32c **multicolored,** *Oct. 8*		.65	.25
3116 A2409 32c **multicolored,** *Oct. 8*		.65	.25
a.	Booklet pane of 20, 5 ea #3113-3116	13.00	
b.	Strip of 4, #3113-3116	2.60	
c.	As "a," die cutting omitted	*1,250.*	
d.	As "b," die cutting omitted	*500.00*	
e.	Block of 6, die cutting omitted	*700.00*	

PHOTOGRAVURE
Die Cut

3117 A2410 32c **multicolored,** *Oct. 8*		.65	.25
a.	Booklet pane of 18	12.00	

HANUKKAH

A2411

Designed by Hannah Smotrich.

Printed by Avery Dennison.

PHOTOGRAVURE
Sheets of 200 in 10 panes of 20

1996, Oct. 22	**Tagged**	***Serpentine Die Cut 11.1***	
	Self-Adhesive		
3118 A2411 32c **multicolored**		.65	.25
	P# block of 4, 5#+V	2.60	
	Pane of 20	13.00	

Backing on No. 3118 is die cut with continuous vertical wavy lines. The 1997 reprint is die cut with two short vertical lines on each side of a semi-circle on the backing of each stamp.
See Nos. 3352, 3547, 3672, Israel No. 1289. For booklet see No. BK258.

CYCLING
Souvenir Sheet

A2412

Illustration reduced.

Designed by McRay Magleby.

Printed by Stamp Venturers.

PHOTOGRAVURE

1996, Nov. 1	**Tagged**	***Perf. 11x11.1***	
3119 A2412	Sheet of 2	2.75	2.00
a.	50c orange & multi	1.30	1.00
b.	50c blue green & multi	1.30	1.00

No. 3119 exists overprinted in gold and in silver for the Tour of China '96. This overprint is a private production. Value, set of 2 sheets $12.50.

CHINESE NEW YEAR

Year of the Ox — A2413

Designed by Clarence Lee.

Printed by Stamp Venturers.

PHOTOGRAVURE
Sheets of 180 in 9 panes of 20

1997, Jan. 5	**Tagged**	***Perf. 11.2***	
3120 A2413 32c **multicolored**		.80	.25
	P# block of 4, 4#+S	3.20	—
	Pane of 20	16.00	—

See No. 3895b.

BLACK HERITAGE SERIES

Brig. Gen. Benjamin O. Davis, Sr. (1880-1970) — A2414

Designed by Richard Sheaff.

Printed by Banknote Corp. of America.

LITHOGRAPHED
Sheets of 120 in six panes of 20

1997, Jan. 28	**Tagged**	***Serpentine Die Cut 11.4***	
	Self-Adhesive		
3121 A2414 32c **multicolored**		.70	.25
	P# block of 4, 4#+B	2.75	
	Pane of 20	14.00	

Statue of Liberty Type of 1994

Printed by Avery-Dennison.

PHOTOGRAVURE
Serpentine Die Cut 11 on 2, 3 or 4 Sides

1997, Feb. 1		**Tagged**	
	Self-Adhesive		
3122 A1951 32c **red, light blue, dark blue & yellow**		.70	.25
a.	Booklet pane of 20 + label	14.00	
b.	Booklet pane of 4	2.80	
c.	Booklet pane of 5 + label	3.75	
	P# single, #V1111	.95	1.00
d.	Booklet pane of 6	4.25	
	Booklet pane of 6 containing P# single	6.00	
	P# single, #V1111	2.50	1.00
h.	As "a," die cutting omitted	—	

The plate # single in No. 3122c is the lower left stamp and should be collected unused with the reorder label to its right to differentiate it from the plate # single in No. 3122d which is the lower left stamp in the bottom pane of the booklet and should be collected with a normal stamp adjoining it at right. In used condition, these plate # singles are indistinguishable.

Serpentine Die Cut 11.5x11.8 on 2, 3 or 4 Sides

1997 **Tagged**

Self-Adhesive

3122E A1951 32c **red, light blue, dark blue & yellow** 1.50 .25
- ***f.*** Booklet pane of 20 + label 40.00
- ***g.*** Booklet pane of 6 9.00
- Booklet pane of 6 containing P# single 13.50
- P# single, #V1111 5.50 2.00

The plate # single in No. 3122Eg is the lower left stamp in the bottom pane of the booklet.

LOVE

Swans

A2415 A2416

Designed by Marvin Mattelson.

Printed by Banknote Corp. of America.

LITHOGRAPHED

Serpentine Die Cut 11.8x11.6 on 2, 3 or 4 Sides

1997, Feb. 4 **Tagged**

Self-Adhesive

3123 A2415 32c **multicolored** .65 .25
- ***a.*** Booklet pane of 20 + label 13.00
- ***b.*** Die cutting omitted, pair *100.00*
- ***c.*** As "a," die cutting omitted *1,000.*
- ***d.*** As "a," black omitted —

Serpentine Die Cut 11.6x11.8 on 2, 3 or 4 Sides

3124 A2416 55c **multicolored** 1.10 .25
- ***a.*** Booklet pane of 20 + label 22.00

HELPING CHILDREN LEARN

A2417

Designed by Chris Van Allsburg.

Printed by Avery-Dennison.

PHOTOGRAVURE

Sheets of 160 in eight panes of 20

Serpentine Die Cut 11.6x11.7

1997, Feb. 18 **Tagged**

Self-Adhesive

3125 A2417 32c **multicolored** .65 .25
- P# block of 4, 4#+V 2.60
- Pane of 20 13.00

The die cut perforations of #3125 are fragile and separate easily.

MERIAN BOTANICAL PRINTS

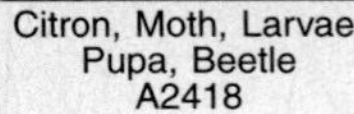

Citron, Moth, Larvae, Pupa, Beetle A2418

Flowering Pineapple, Cockroaches A2419

No. 3128 (r), No. 3129 (l), No. 3128a below

Designed by Phil Jordan based on works by Maria Sibylla Merian (1647-1717).

Printed by Stamp Venturers.

PHOTOGRAVURE

Serpentine Die Cut 10.9x10.2 on 2, 3 or 4 Sides

1997, Mar. 3 **Tagged**

Self-Adhesive

3126 A2418 32c **multicolored** .65 .25

3127 A2419 32c **multicolored** .65 .25
- ***a.*** Booklet pane, 10 ea #3126-3127 + label 13.00
- ***b.*** Pair, #3126-3127 1.30
- ***c.*** Vert. pair, die cutting omitted between *350.00*

Size: 18.5x24mm

Serpentine Die Cut 11.2x10.8 on 2 or 3 Sides

3128 A2418 32c **multicolored** 1.00 .25
- ***a.*** See footnote 2.50 .25
- ***b.*** Booklet pane, 2 ea #3128-3129, 1 #3128a 6.50

3129 A2419 32c **multicolored** 1.00 .25
- ***a.*** See footnote 4.50 .35
- ***b.*** Booklet pane, 2 ea #3128-3129, 1 #3129a 8.50
- ***c.*** Pair, #3128-3129 2.00

Nos. 3128a-3129a are placed sideways on the pane and are serpentine die cut 11.2 on top and bottom, 10.8 on left side. One of the two No. 3128a per pane has a straight edge at left. The right side is 11.2 broken by a sloping die cut where the stamp meets the vertical die cutting of the two stamps above it. See illustration above.

PACIFIC 97

Sailing Ship — A2420

Stagecoach — A2421

Designed by Richard Sheaff.

Printed by Banknote Corporation of America.

ENGRAVED

Sheets of 96 in six panes of 16

1997, Mar. 13 **Tagged** *Perf. 11.2*

3130 A2420 32c **blue** .65 .30

3131 A2421 32c **red** .65 .30
- ***a.*** Pair, #3130-3131 1.30 .75
- P# block of 4, 1#+B 2.60 —
- Pane of 16 10.50 7.50

Uncut press sheets of Nos. 3130-3131 were made available for sale. Values: cross-gutter block of 16 (8 #3131a), $30; pairs with gutters between, $7.50 each. See note after No. 2868.

Flag Over Porch Type of 1995 and

Juke Box — A2225a

Designed by Bill Nelson (#3132), Dave LaFleur (#3133).

Printed by Stamp Venturers.

PHOTOGRAVURE

COIL STAMPS

1997, Mar. 14 **Untagged** ***Imperf.***

Self-Adhesive

3132 A2225a (25c) **bright orange red, bright yellow green & multi** 1.50 .50
- Pair 3.00
- P# strip of 5, #M11111 7.50
- P#, single, #M11111 5.00

Tagged

Serpentine Die Cut 9.9 Vert.

3133 A2212 32c **dark blue, tan, brown, red & light blue** 1.75 .25
- Pair 3.50
- P# strip of 5, #M11111 9.00
- P#, single, #M11111 4.00

Nos. 3132-3133 were issued without backing paper. No. 3132 has simulated perforations ending in black bars at the top and bottom edges of the stamp. Sky on No. 3133 shows color gradation at LR not on Nos. 2915A or 2915D, and it has blue "1996" at left bottom.

LITERARY ARTS SERIES

Thornton Wilder (1897-1975) A2422

Designed by Phil Jordan.

Printed by Ashton-Potter (USA) Ltd.

LITHOGRAPHED

Sheets of 180 in nine panes of 20

1997, Apr. 17 **Tagged** *Perf. 11.1*

3134 A2422 32c **multicolored** .65 .25
- P# block of 4, 4#+P 2.60 —
- Pane of 20 13.00 —

RAOUL WALLENBERG (1912-47)

Wallenberg and Jewish Refugees A2423

Designed by Howard Paine.

Printed by Sterling Sommer for Ashton-Potter (USA) Ltd.

LITHOGRAPHED

Sheets of 180 in nine panes of 20

1997, Apr. 24 **Tagged** *Perf. 11.1*

3135 A2423 32c **multicolored** .65 .25
- P# block of 4, 4#+P 2.60 —
- Pane of 20 13.00 —

DINOSAURS

A2424

Illustration reduced.

Designed by James Gurney.
Printed by Sterling Sommer for Ashton-Potter (USA) Ltd.

Designs: a, Ceratosaurus. b, Camptosaurus. c, Camarasaurus. d, Brachiosaurus. e, Goniopholis. f, Stegosaurus. g, Allosaurus. h, Opisthias. i, Edmontonia. j, Einiosaurus. k, Daspletosaurus. l, Palaeosaniwa. m, Corythosaurus. n, Ornithomimus. o, Parasaurolophus.

LITHOGRAPHED

1997, May 1 **Tagged** ***Perf. 11x11.1***

3136	A2424 Sheet of 15	10.00	8.00
a.-o.	32c any single	.65	.50
p.	As No. 3136, bottom 7 stamps imperf.	*2,500.*	
q.	As No. 3136, top 8 stamps imperf	*2,500.*	
r.	As No. 3136, all colors and tagging missing (EP)		—

No. 3136r resulted from double sheeting in the sheet-fed press. It is properly gummed and perforated.

BUGS BUNNY

A2425

Designed by Warner Bros.

Printed by Avery Dennison.

PHOTOGRAVURE

1997, May 22 **Tagged** ***Serpentine Die Cut 11***
Self-Adhesive

3137	Pane of 10 #3137a	6.75	
a.	A2425 32c single	.65	.25
b.	Pane of 9 #3137a	6.00	
c.	Pane of 1 #3137a	.65	

Die cutting on No. 3137 does not extend through the backing paper.

Nos. 3137b-3137c and 3138b-3138c are separated by a vertical line of microperforations that are absent on the uncut sheet of 60.

Uncut press sheets of No. 3137 were made available for sale. Values: top sheet of 60, $250; bottom sheet of 60 with P#, $450; cross-gutter block of 7, $200; pairs with gutters between, $30 each. See note after No. 2868.

3138	Pane of 10, #3138c, 9 #3138a	130.00
a.	A2425 32c single	2.75
b.	Pane of 9 #3138a	20.00
c.	Pane of 1, no die cutting	100.00

Die cutting on No. 3138b extends through the backing paper.

An untagged promotional piece similar to No. 3137c exists on the same backing paper as the pane, with the same design image, but without Bugs' signature and the single stamp. Replacing the stamp is an enlarged "32 / USA" in the same style as used on the stamp. This promotional piece was not valid for postage.

PACIFIC 97

Franklin — A2426

Washington — A2427

Designed by Richard Sheaff. Selvage on Nos. 3139-3140 is lithographed.

LITHOGRAPHED & ENGRAVED

1997 **Tagged** ***Perf. 10.5x10.4***

3139	Pane of 12, *May 29*	12.00	9.00
a.	A2426 50c single	1.00	.50
3140	Pane of 12, *May 30*	14.50	11.00
a.	A2427 60c single	1.20	.60

Nos. 3139-3140 were sold through June 8.

MARSHALL PLAN, 50TH ANNIV.

Gen. George C. Marshall, Map of Europe A2428

Designed by Richard Sheaff.

Printed by Stevens Security Press for Ashton-Potter (USA) Ltd.

LITHOGRAPHED & ENGRAVED
Sheets of 120 in six panes of 20

1997, June 4 **Tagged** ***Perf. 11.1***

3141	A2428 32c **multicolored**	.65	.25
	P# block of 4, 5#+P	2.60	—
	Pane of 20	13.00	—

CLASSIC AMERICAN AIRCRAFT

A2429

Illustration reduced.

Designed by Phil Jordan.

Printed by Stamp Venturers.

Designs: a, Mustang. b, Model B. c, Cub. d, Vega. e, Alpha. f, B-10. g, Corsair. h, Stratojet. i, GeeBee. j, Staggerwing. k, Flying Fortress. l, Stearman. m, Constellation. n, Lightning. o, Peashooter. p, Tri-Motor. q, DC-3. r, 314 Clipper. s, Jenny. t, Wildcat.

PHOTOGRAVURE
Sheets of 120 in six panes of 20

1997, July 19 **Tagged** ***Perf. 10.1***

3142	A2429 Pane of 20	13.00	10.00
a.-t.	32c any single	.65	.50

Inscriptions on back of each stamp describe the airplane.

Uncut press sheets of No. 3142 were made available for sale. Values: cross-gutter block of 20, $27.50; pairs with gutters between, $2.75 each. See note after No. 2868.

FOOTBALL COACHES

Bear Bryant A2430

Pop Warner A2431

Vince Lombardi A2432

George Halas A2433

Designed by Carl Herrman.

Printed by Sterling Sommer for Ashton-Potter (USA) Ltd.

LITHOGRAPHED
Sheets of 120 in six panes of 20

1997 **Tagged** ***Perf. 11.2***

3143	A2430 32c **multicolored,** *July 25*	.65	.25
3144	A2431 32c **multicolored,** *July 25*	.65	.25
3145	A2432 32c **multicolored,** *July 25*	.65	.25
3146	A2433 32c **multicolored,** *July 25*	.65	.25
a.	Block or strip of 4, #3143-3146	2.60	1.50
	P# block of 4, 5#+P	2.60	1.75
	P# block of 8, 2 sets of P# + top label	5.25	—
	Pane of 20	13.00	

With Red Bar Above Coach's Name

Perf. 11

3147	A2432 32c **multicolored,** *Aug. 5*	.65	.45
	P# block of 4, 4#+P	3.00	—
	Pane of 20	14.50	—
3148	A2430 32c **multicolored,** *Aug. 7*	.65	.45
	P# block of 4, 4#+P	3.00	—
	Pane of 20	14.50	—
3149	A2431 32c **multicolored,** *Aug. 8*	.65	.45
	P# block of 4, 4#+P	3.25	—
	Pane of 20	15.50	—
3150	A2433 32c **multicolored,** *Aug. 16*	.65	.45
	P# block of 4, 4#+P	3.25	—
	Pane of 20	15.50	—

AMERICAN DOLLS

A2434

Illustration reduced.

Designed by Derry Noyes.

Printed by Sterling Sommer for Ashton-Potter (USA) Ltd.

Designs: a, "Alabama Baby," and doll by Martha Chase. b, "Columbian Doll." c, Johnny Gruelle's "Raggedy Ann." d, Doll by Martha Chase. e, "American Child." f, "Baby Coos." g, Plains Indian. h, Doll by Izannah Walker. i, "Babyland Rag." j, "Scootles." k, Doll by Ludwig Greiner. l, "Betsy McCall." m, Percy Crosby's "Skippy." n, "Maggie Mix-up." o, Dolls by Albert Schoenhut.

LITHOGRAPHED

Sheets of 90 in six panes of 15

1997, July 28	**Tagged**	***Perf. 10.9x11.1***	
3151 A2434	Pane of 15	13.50	—
a.-o.	32c any single	.90	.60

For booklet see No. BK266.

LEGENDS OF HOLLYWOOD

Humphrey Bogart (1899-1957).

A2435

Designed by Carl Herrman.

Printed by Stamp Venturers.

PHOTOGRAVURE

Sheets of 120 in six panes of 20

1997, July 31	**Tagged**	***Perf. 11.1***	
3152 A2435 32c **multicolored**		.85	.25
P# block of 4, 5#+S		3.50	—
Pane of 20		17.50	—

Perforations in corner of each stamp are star-shaped.

Uncut press sheets of No. 3152 were made available for sale. Values: cross-gutter block of 8, $19; pairs with gutters between, $3 each. See note after No. 2868.

For booklet see No. BK267.

"THE STARS AND STRIPES FOREVER!"

A2436

Designed by Richard Sheaff.

Sheets of 300 in six panes of 50

PHOTOGRAVURE

1997, Aug. 21	**Tagged**	***Perf. 11.1***	
3153 A2436 32c **multicolored**		.65	.25
P# block of 4, 4#		3.00	—

For booklet see No. BK268.

AMERICAN MUSIC SERIES

Opera Singers

Lily Pons — A2437

Richard Tucker A2438

Lawrence Tibbett A2439

Rosa Ponselle A2440

Classical Composers & Conductors

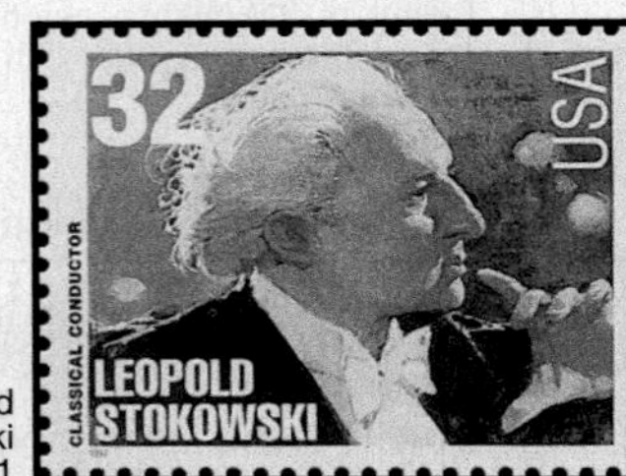

Leopold Stokowski A2441

Arthur Fiedler A2442

George Szell — A2443

Eugene Ormandy A2444

Samuel Barber A2445

Ferde Grofé A2446

Charles Ives — A2447

Louis Moreau Gottschalk A2448

Designed by Howard Paine.

Printed by Ashton-Potter (USA) Ltd.

LITHOGRAPHED

Sheets of 120 in six panes of 20

1997	**Tagged**	***Perf. 11***	
3154 A2437 32c **multicolored,** *Sept. 10*		.75	.25
3155 A2438 32c **multicolored,** *Sept. 10*		.75	.25
3156 A2439 32c **multicolored,** *Sept. 10*		.75	.25
3157 A2440 32c **multicolored,** *Sept. 10*		.75	.25
a. Block or strip of 4, #3154-3157		3.00	2.00
P# block of 4, 5#+P		3.00	—
P# block of 8, 2 sets of P# + top label		6.00	—
Pane of 20		15.00	—
3158 A2441 32c **multicolored,** *Sept. 12*		1.50	.25
3159 A2442 32c **multicolored,** *Sept. 12*		1.50	.25
3160 A2443 32c **multicolored,** *Sept. 12*		1.50	.25
3161 A2444 32c **multicolored,** *Sept. 12*		1.50	.25
3162 A2445 32c **multicolored,** *Sept. 12*		1.50	.25
3163 A2446 32c **multicolored,** *Sept. 12*		1.50	.25
3164 A2447 32c **multicolored,** *Sept. 12*		1.50	.25
3165 A2448 32c **multicolored,** *Sept. 12*		1.50	.25
a. Block of 8, #3158-3165		12.00	4.00
P# block of 8, 2 sets of 5P#+P + top label		14.00	—
Pane of 20		32.50	

PADRE FÉLIX VARELA (1788-1853)

A2449

Designed by Carl Herrman.

Printed by Sterling Sommer for Ashton-Potter (USA) Ltd.

LITHOGRAPHED

Sheets of 120 in six panes of 20

1997, Sept. 15 **Tagged** ***Perf. 11.2***

3166 A2449 32c **purple**	.65	.25
P# block of 4, 1#+P	2.60	—
Pane of 20	13.00	—

DEPARTMENT OF THE AIR FORCE, 50TH ANNIV.

Thunderbirds Aerial Demonstration Squadron A2450

Designed by Phil Jordan.

Printed by Sterling Sommer for Ashton-Potter (USA) Ltd.

LITHOGRAPHED

Sheets of 180 in nine panes of 20

1997, Sept. 18 **Tagged** ***Perf. 11.2x11.1***

3167 A2450 32c **multicolored**	.65	.25
P# block of 4, 4#+P	2.60	—
Pane of 20	13.00	—

A hidden 3-D image (USAF repeated) can be seen on the stamp when it is viewed with a special "Stamp Decoder" lens sold by the USPS.

CLASSIC MOVIE MONSTERS

Lon Chaney as The Phantom of the Opera — A2451

Bela Lugosi as Dracula — A2452

Boris Karloff as Frankenstein's Monster — A2453

Boris Karloff as The Mummy — A2454

Lon Chaney, Jr. as The Wolf Man — A2455

Designed by Derry Noyes.

Printed by Stamp Venturers.

PHOTOGRAVURE

Sheets of 180 in nine panes of 20

1997, Sept. 30 **Tagged** ***Perf. 10.2***

3168 A2451 32c **multicolored**	.75	.25
3169 A2452 32c **multicolored**	.75	.25
3170 A2453 32c **multicolored**	.75	.25
3171 A2454 32c **multicolored**	.75	.25
3172 A2455 32c **multicolored**	.75	.25
a. Strip of 5, #3168-3172	3.75	2.25
P# block of 10, 5#+S	7.50	—
Pane of 20	15.00	—

Plate blocks may contain top label.

For booklet see No. BK269.

Hidden 3-D images can be seen on these stamps when they are viewed with a special "Stamp Decoder" lens sold by the USPS. No. 3168, two masquerade masks; No. 3169, three flying bats; No. 3170, three electricity bolts; No. 3171, two Egyptian deities; No. 3172, two howling wolves.

Uncut press sheets of Nos. 3168-3172 were made available for sale. Values: cross-gutter block of 8, $20; pairs with gutters between, $2.75 each. See note after No. 2868.

FIRST SUPERSONIC FLIGHT, 50TH ANNIV.

A2456

Designed by Phil Jordan.

Printed by Banknote Corporation of America.

LITHOGRAPHED

Sheets of 180 in nine panes of 20

1997, Oct. 14 **Tagged** ***Serpentine Die Cut 11.4***

Self-Adhesive

3173 A2456 32c **multicolored**	.65	.25
P# block of 4, 4#+B	2.60	
Pane of 20	13.00	

WOMEN IN MILITARY SERVICE

A2457

Designed by Derry Noyes.

Printed by Banknote Corporation of America.

LITHOGRAPHED

Sheets of 120 in six panes of 20

1997, Oct. 18 **Tagged** ***Perf. 11.1***

3174 A2457 32c **multicolored**	.65	.25
P# block of 4, 6#+B	2.60	—
Pane of 20	13.00	

KWANZAA

A2458

Designed by Synthia Saint James. Printed by Avery Dennison.

PHOTOGRAVURE

Sheets of 250 in five panes of 50

1997, Oct. 22 **Tagged** ***Serpentine Die Cut 11***

Self-Adhesive

3175 A2458 32c **multicolored**	.65	.25
P# block of 4, 4#+V	3.00	

See Nos. 3368, 3548, 3673.

Uncut press sheets of No. 3175 were made available for sale. Values: horiz. pairs with vert. gutters between, $11 each. See note after No. 2868.

CHRISTMAS

Madonna and Child, by Sano di Pietro — A2459

Holly — A2460

Designed by Richard D. Sheaff (#3176), Howard Paine (#3177).

Printed by Bureau of Engraving and Printing (#3176), Banknote Corporation of America (#3177).

LITHOGRAPHED

Serpentine Die Cut 9.9 on 2, 3 or 4 Sides

1997 **Tagged**

Booklet Stamps

Self-Adhesive

3176 A2459 32c **multicolored,** *Oct. 27*	.65	.25
a. Booklet pane of 20 + label	13.00	

Serpentine Die Cut 11.2x11.6 on 2, 3 or 4 Sides

3177 A2460 32c **multicolored,** *Oct. 30*	.65	.25
a. Booklet pane of 20 + label	13.00	
b. Booklet pane of 4	2.60	
c. Booklet pane of 5 + label	3.25	
d. Booklet pane of 6	3.90	

MARS PATHFINDER

Souvenir Sheet

Mars Rover Sojourner — A2461

Illustration reduced.

Designed by Terry McCaffrey. Printed by Stamp Venturers.

PHOTOGRAVURE

1997, Dec. 10 **Tagged** ***Perf. 11x11.1***

3178 A2461 $3 **multicolored**	6.00	4.00
a. $3, single stamp	5.50	3.00
b. Single souvenir sheet from sheet of 18	7.50	—

The perforations at the bottom of the stamp contain the letters "USA." Vertical rouletting extends from the vertical perforations of the stamp to the bottom of the souvenir sheet.

Uncut press sheets of Nos. 3178 were made available for sale. Values: pane of 18 with perforations on one or two sides, $145; vert. pair with horiz. gutter between, $17.50. See note after No. 2868.

A hidden 3-D image (USPS and MARS PATHFINDER JULY 4, 1997 repeated) can be seen when viewed with a special "Stamp Decoder" lens sold by the USPS.

CHINESE NEW YEAR

Year of the Tiger — A2462

Designed by Clarence Lee. Printed by Stamp Venturers.

PHOTOGRAVURE

Sheets of 180 in nine panes of 20

1998, Jan. 5 **Tagged** ***Perf. 11.2***

3179 A2462 32c **multicolored**	.80	.25
P# block of 4, 4#+S	3.75	—
Pane of 20	18.00	

See No. 3895c.

ALPINE SKIING

A2463

Designed by Michael Schwab.

Printed by Banknote Corporation of America.

LITHOGRAPHED

Sheets of 180 in nine panes of 20

1998, Jan. 22 **Tagged** ***Perf. 11.2***

3180 A2463 32c **multicolored**	.75	.25
P# block of 4, 6#+B	4.00	—
Pane of 20	19.00	

BLACK HERITAGE SERIES

Madam C.J. Walker (1867-1919), Entrepreneur.

A2464

Designed by Richard Sheaff. Printed by Banknote Corp. of America.

LITHOGRAPHED

Sheets of 180 in nine panes of 20

Serpentine Die Cut 11.6x11.3

1998, Jan. 28 **Tagged**

Self-Adhesive

3181 A2464 32c **sepia & black**	.70	.25
P# block of 4, 3#+B	3.00	
Pane of 20	15.00	

CELEBRATE THE CENTURY

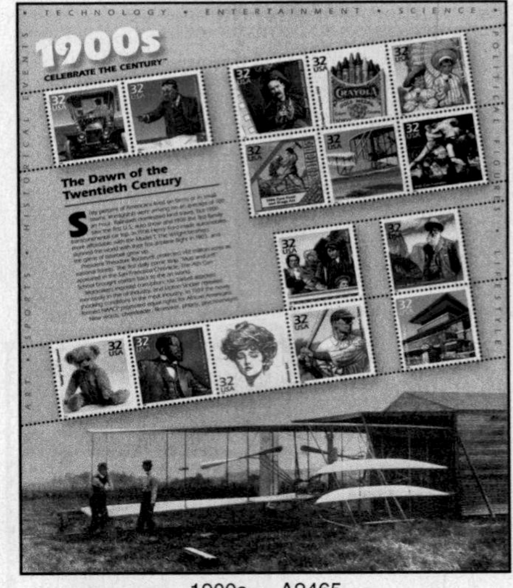

1900s — A2465

No. 3182: a, Model T Ford. b, Theodore Roosevelt. c, Motion picture "The Great Train Robbery," 1903. d, Crayola Crayons introduced, 1903. e, St. Louis World's Fair, 1904. f, Design used on Hunt's Remedy stamp (#RS56), Pure Food & Drug Act, 1906. g, Wright Brothers first flight, Kitty Hawk, 1903. h, Boxing match shown in painting "Stag at Sharkey's," by George Bellows of the Ash Can School. i, Immigrants arrive. j, John Muir, preservationist. k, "Teddy" Bear created. l, W.E.B. Du Bois, social activist. m, Gibson Girl. n, First baseball World Series, 1903. o, Robie House, Chicago, designed by Frank Lloyd Wright.

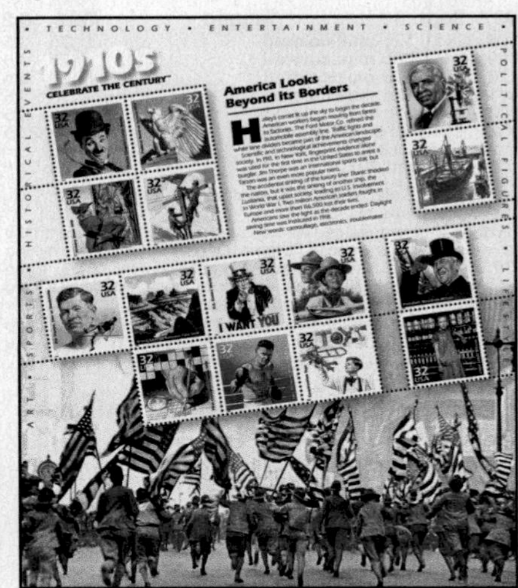

1910s — A2466

No. 3183: a, Charlie Chaplin as the Little Tramp. b, Federal Reserve System created, 1913. c, George Washington Carver. d, Avant-garde art introduced at Armory Show, 1913. e, First transcontinental telephone line, 1914. f, Panama Canal opens, 1914. g, Jim Thorpe wins decathlon at Stockholm Olympics, 1912. h, Grand Canyon National Park, 1919. i, U.S. enters World War I. j, Boy Scouts started in 1910, Girl Scouts formed in 1912. k, Woodrow Wilson. l, First crossword puzzle published, 1913. m, Jack Dempsey wins heavyweight title, 1919. n, Construction toys. o, Child labor reform.

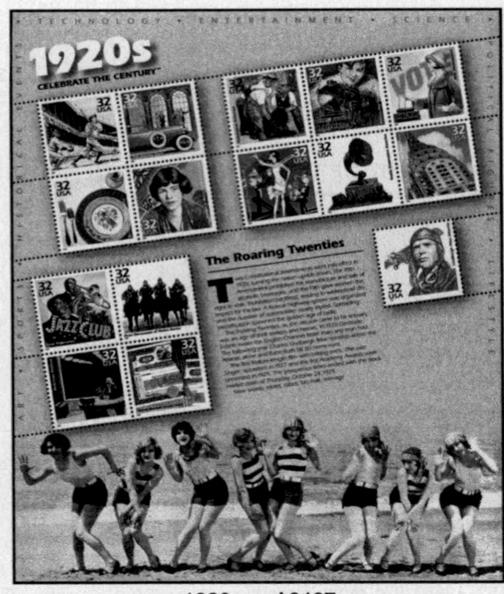

1920s — A2467

No. 3184: a, Babe Ruth. b, The Gatsby style. c, Prohibition enforced. d, Electric toy trains. e, 19th Amendment (woman voting). f, Emily Post's Etiquette. g, Margaret Mead, anthropologist. h, Flappers do the Charleston. i, Radio entertains America. j, Art Deco style (Chrysler Building). k, Jazz flourishes. l, Four Horsemen of Notre Dame. m, Lindbergh flies the Atlantic. n, American realism (Automat, by Edward Hopper). o, Stock Market crash, 1929.

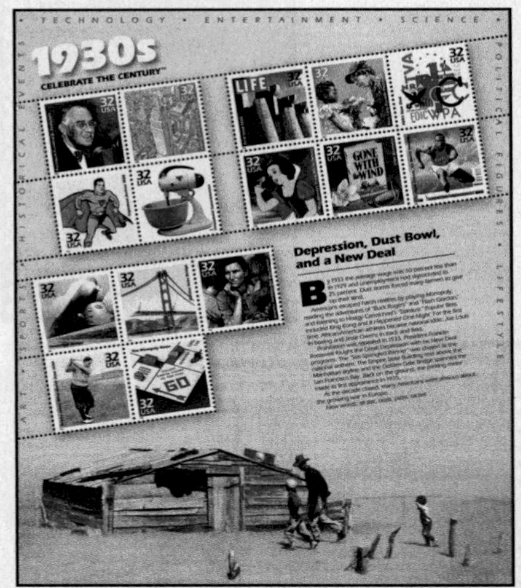

1930s — A2468

No. 3185: a, Franklin D. Roosevelt. b, The Empire State Building. c, 1st Issue of Life Magazine, 1936. d, Eleanor Roosevelt. e, FDR's New Deal. f, Superman arrives, 1938. g, Household conveniences. h, "Snow White and the Seven Dwarfs," 1937. i, "Gone with the Wind," 1936. j, Jesse Owens. k, Streamline design. l, Golden Gate Bridge. m, America survives the Depression. n, Bobby Jones wins golf Grand Slam, 1938. o, The Monopoly Game.

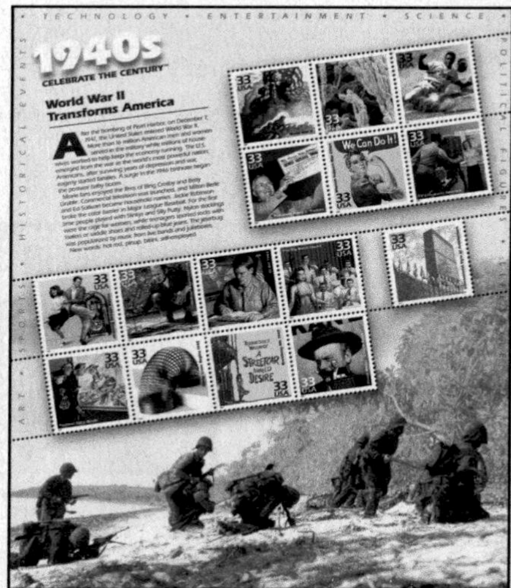

1940s — A2469

No. 3186: a, World War II. b, Antibiotics save lives. c, Jackie Robinson. d, Harry S Truman. e, Women support war effort. f, TV entertains America. g, Jitterbug sweeps nation. h, Jackson Pollock, Abstract Expressionism. i, GI Bill, 1944. j, Big Band Sound. k, Intl. style of architecture (UN Headquarters). l, Postwar baby boom. m, Slinky, 1945. n, "A Streecar Named Desire," 1947. o, Orson Welles' "Citizen Kane."

1950s — A2470

No. 3187: a, Polio vaccine developed. b, Teen fashions. c, The "Shot Heard 'Round the World." d, US launches satellites. e, Korean War. f, Desegregating public schools. g, Tail fins, chrome. h, Dr. Seuss' "The Cat in the Hat." i, Drive-in movies. j, World Series rivals. k, Rocky Marciano, undefeated boxer. l, "I Love Lucy." m, Rock 'n Roll. n, Stock car racing. o, Movies go 3-D.

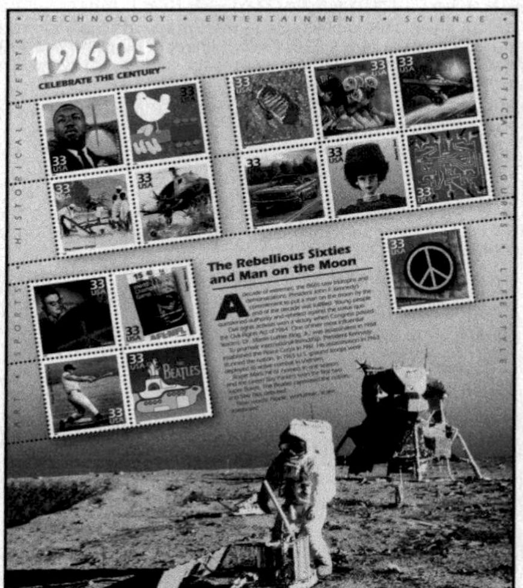

1960s — A2471

No. 3188: a, Martin Luther King, Jr., "I Have a Dream." b, Woodstock. c, Man walks on the moon. d, Green Bay Packers. e, Star Trek. f, The Peace Corps. g, Viet Nam War. h, Ford Mustang. i, Barbie Doll. j, Integrated circuit. k, Lasers. l, Super Bowl I. m, Peace symbol. n, Roger Maris, 61 in '61. o, The Beatles "Yellow Submarine."

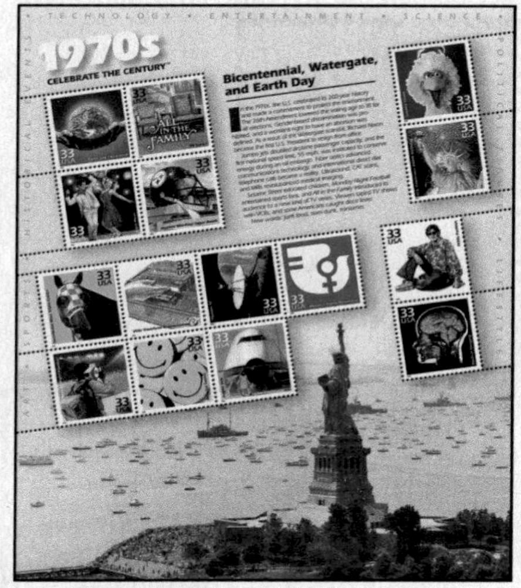

1970s — A2472

No. 3189: a, Earth Day celebrated. b, "All in the Family" television series. c, "Sesame Street" television series character, Big Bird. d, Disco music. e, Pittsburgh Steelers win four Super Bowls. f, US Celebrates 200th birthday. g, Secretariat wins Triple Crown. h, VCRs transform entertainment. i, Pioneer 10. j, Women's rights movement. k, 1970s fashions. l, "Monday Night Football." m, Smiley face buttons. n, Jumbo jets. o, Medical imaging.

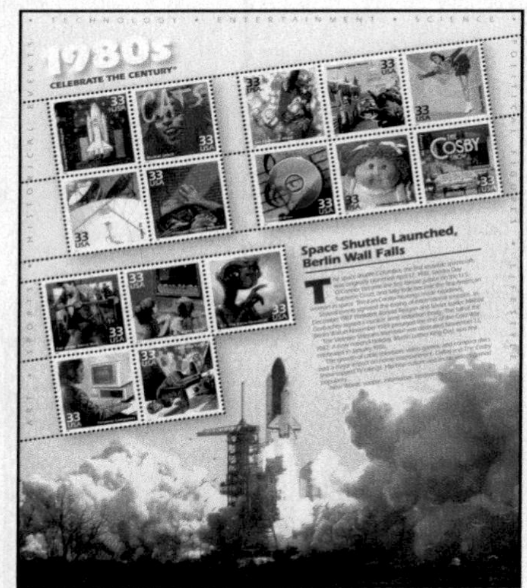

1980s — A2473

No. 3190: a, Space shuttle program. b, "Cats" Broadway show. c, San Francisco 49ers. d, Hostages in Iran come home. e, Figure skating. f, Cable TV. g, Vietnam Veterans Memorial. h, Compact discs. i, Cabbage Patch Kids. j, "The Cosby Show" television series. k, Fall of the Berlin Wall. l, Video games. m, "E. T. The Extra-Terrestrial" movie. n, Personal computers. o, Hip-hop culture.

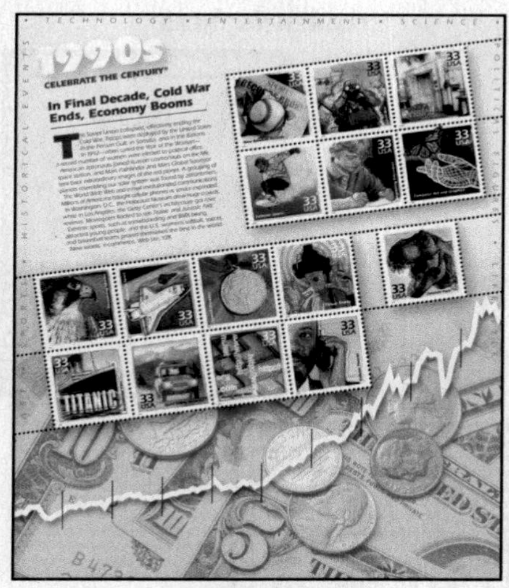

1990s — A2474

No. 3191: a, New baseball records. b, Gulf War. c, "Seinfeld" television series. d, Extreme sports. e, Improving education. f, Computer art and graphics. g, Recovering species. h, Return to space. i, Special Olympics. j, Virtual reality. k, Movie "Jurassic Park." l, Movie "Titanic." m, Sport utility vehicles. n, World Wide Web. o, Cellular phones.

Designed by Richard Waldrep (#3182), Dennis Lyall (#3183), Carl Herrman (#3184, 3188, 3190), Howard Paine (#3185-3187, 3189, 3191).

All illustrations reduced.

Printed by Ashton-Potter (USA) Ltd.

LITHOGRAPHED, ENGRAVED (#3182m, 3183f, 3184m, 3185b, 3186k, 3187a, 3188c, 3189h)

1998-2000		**Tagged**	***Perf. 11½***	
3182	A2465	Pane of 15, *Feb. 3, 1998*	10.00	8.50
a.-o.		32c any single	.75	.65
p.		Engr. red (No. 3182m, Gibson girl) omitted, in pane of 15	*3,000.*	
3183	A2466	Pane of 15, *Feb. 3, 1998*	10.00	8.50
a.-o.		32c any single	.75	.65
p.		Nos. 3183g, 3183 l-3183o imperf, in pane of 15	*7,000.*	
3184	A2467	Pane of 15, *May 28, 1998*	12.50	8.50
a.-o.		32c any single	.80	.65
3185	A2468	Pane of 15, *Sept. 10, 1998*	12.50	8.50
a.-o.		32c any single	.80	.65
3186	A2469	Pane of 15, *Feb. 18, 1999*	13.00	8.50
a.-o.		33c any single	.85	.65
p.		Tagging omitted on b-j and m-o	—	
q.		Tagging omitted on a-f, j-k, n-o	—	
3187	A2470	Pane of 15, *May 26, 1999*	13.00	8.50
a.-o.		33c any single	.85	.65
p.		Tagging omitted	—	
q.		Nos. "a" and "k" tagged, all others tagging omitted	—	
3188	A2471	Pane of 15, *Sept. 17, 1999*	13.00	8.50
a.-o.		33c any single	.85	.65
3189	A2472	Pane of 15, *Nov. 18, 1999*	13.00	8.50
a.-o.		33c any single	.85	.65
3190	A2473	Pane of 15, *Jan. 12, 2000*	13.00	8.50
a.-o.		33c any single	.85	.65
3191	A2474	Pane of 15, *May 2, 2000*	13.00	8.50
a.-o.		33c any single	.85	.65
		Nos. 3182-3191 (10)	123.00	85.00

Uncut press sheets of Nos. 3182-3191 were made available for sale. See note after No. 2868.

"REMEMBER THE MAINE"

A2475

Designed by Richard Sheaff.

LITHOGRAPHED & ENGRAVED

Sheets of 120 in six panes of 20

1998, Feb. 15	**Tagged**	***Perf. 11.2x11***	
3192 A2475 32c **red & black**		.70	.25
P# block of 4, 2#		3.00	—
Pane of 20		15.00	

FLOWERING TREES

Southern Magnolia — A2476

Blue Paloverde — A2477

Yellow Poplar — A2478

Prairie Crab Apple — A2479

Pacific Dogwood — A2480

Designed by Howard Paine.

Printed by Banknote Corporation of America.

LITHOGRAPHED
Sheets of 120 in six panes of 20

1998, Mar. 19 **Tagged** ***Die Cut Perf 11.3***
Self-Adhesive

3193	A2476 32c **multicolored**	1.50	.40
3197	A2480 32c **multicolored**	1.50	.40
a.	Strip of 5, #3193-3197	7.50	
	P# block of 10, 2 sets of B+6#	15.00	
	Pane of 20	30.00	
b.	As "a," die cutting omitted	—	

ALEXANDER CALDER (1898-1976), SCULPTOR

Black Cascade, 13 Verticals, 1959 — A2481

Untitled, 1965 — A2482

Rearing Stallion, 1928 — A2483

Portrait of a Young Man, c. 1945 — A2484

Un Effet du Japonais, 1945 — A2485

Designed by Derry Noyes. Printed by Stamp Venturers.

PHOTOGRAVURE
Sheets of 120 in six panes of 20

1998, Mar. 25 **Tagged** ***Perf. 10.2***

3201	A2484 32c **multicolored**	.65	.25
3202	A2485 32c **multicolored**	.65	.25
a.	Strip of 5, #3198-3202	3.25	2.25
	P# block of 10, 2 sets of S+6#	7.00	—
	Pane of 20	14.00	—

Uncut press sheets of Nos. 3198-3202 were made available for sale. Values: cross-gutter block of 20, $37.50; pairs with gutters between, $4 each. See note after No. 2868.

CINCO DE MAYO

A2486

Designed by Carl Herrman.

Printed by Stamp Venturers.

PHOTOGRAVURE
Sheets of 180 in nine panes of 20
Serpentine Die Cut 11.7x10.9

1998, Apr. 16 **Tagged**
Self-Adhesive

3203	A2486 32c **multicolored**	.65	.25
	P# block of 4, 5#+S	2.60	
	Pane of 20	13.00	

See Mexico No. 2066. For 33c version, see No. 3309.

Uncut press sheets of No. 3203 were made available for sale. Values: cross-gutter block of 4, $15; pairs with gutters between, $2.50 each. See note after No. 2868.

SYLVESTER & TWEETY

A2487

Designed by Brenda Guttman.

Printed by Avery Dennison.

PHOTOGRAVURE

1998, Apr. 27 **Tagged** ***Serpentine Die Cut 11.1***
Self-Adhesive

3204	Pane of 10 #3204a	6.75	
a.	A2487 32c single	.65	.25
b.	Pane of 9 #3204a	6.00	
c.	Pane of 1 #3204a	.65	

Die cutting on No. 3204b does not extend through the backing paper. Pane with plate number comes from bottom uncut sheet of 60.

Uncut press sheets of No. 3204 were made available for sale. Values: top sheet of 60, $70; bottom sheet of 60 with P#, $110; cross-gutter block of 7, $45; pairs with gutters between, $10 each. See note after No. 2868.

3205	Pane of 10, #3205c, 9 #3205a	11.00	
a.	A2487 32c single	.90	
b.	Pane of 9 #3205a	*7.00*	
c.	Pane of 1, no die cutting	*3.00*	

Die cutting on #3205a extends through the backing paper.

Nos. 3204b-3204c and 3205b-3205c are separated by a vertical line of microperforations, which is absent on the uncut sheets of 60.

WISCONSIN STATEHOOD

A2488

Designed by Phil Jordan.

Printed by Sennett Security Products.

PHOTOGRAVURE
Sheets of 120 in six panes of 20
Serpentine Die Cut 10.8x10.9

1998, May 29 **Tagged**

Self-Adhesive

3206	A2488 32c **multicolored**	.65	.30
	P# block of 4, 4#+S	3.00	
	Pane of 20	15.00	

A hidden 3-D image (a badger) can be seen on this stamp when it is viewed with a special "Stamp Decoder" lens sold by the USPS.

Wetlands — A2489

Diner — A2490

Designer by Phil Jordan (#3207-3207A), Carl Herrman (#3208, 308A).

Printed by Sennett Security Products (#3207, 3208), Bureau of Engraving and Printing (#3207A, 3208A).

PHOTOGRAVURE
COIL STAMPS

1998 **Untagged** ***Perf. 10 Vert.***

3207	A2489 (5c) **multicolored,** *June 5*		.25	.25
	Pair		.25	.25
	P# strip of 5, #S1111		1.25	
	P#, single, #S1111		—	.75

Serpentine Die Cut 9.8 Vert.

Self-adhesive

Untagged

3207A	A2489 (5c) **multicolored,** small date, *Dec.14*	.25	.25
	Pair	.50	
	P# strip of 5, #1111, 2222, 3333	1.40	
	P# single, same #	—	.80
b.	Large date	.30	.25
	Pair	.60	
	P# strip of 5, #4444, 5555, 6666	1.50	
	P# single, same #	—	.80

Date on No. 3207A is approximately 1.4mm long, on No. 3207Ab approx. 1.6mm long.

Perf. 10 Vert.

Untagged

3208	A2490 (25c) **multicolored,** *June 5*	.50	.50
	Pair	1.00	1.00
	P# strip of 5, #S11111	3.50	
	P#, single, #S11111	—	2.00

Serpentine Die Cut 9.8 Vert.

Self-Adhesive

Untagged

3208A	A2490 (25c) **multicolored,** *Sept. 30*	.50	.50
	Pair	1.00	
	P# strip of 5, #11111, 22211, 22222, 33333, 44444, 55555	3.50	
	P# single, same #	—	2.00

1898 TRANS-MISSISSIPPI STAMPS, CENT.

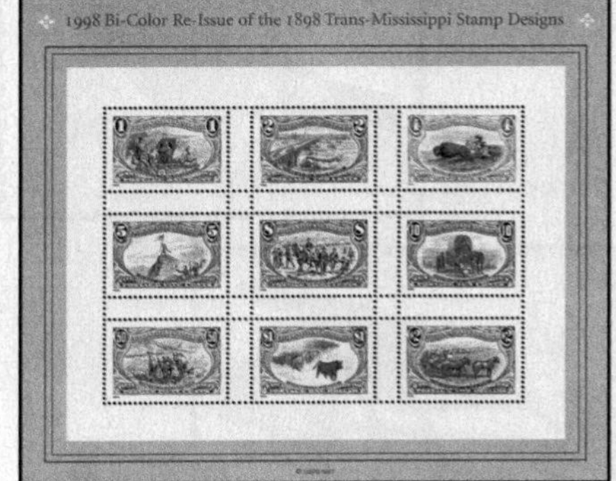

A2491

Illustration reduced.

Designed by Raymond Ostrander Smith (1898), Richard Sheaff (1998).
Printed by Banknote Corporation of America.

LITHOGRAPHED & ENGRAVED
Sheets of 54 in six panes of 9

1998, June 18 **Tagged** ***Perf. 12x12.4***

3209	A2491 Pane of 9	9.50	7.00
a.	A100 1c green & black	.25	.25
b.	A108 2c red brown & black	.25	.25
c.	A102 4c orange & black	.25	.25
d.	A103 5c blue & black	.25	.25
e.	A104 8c dark lilac & black	.25	.25
f.	A105 10c purple & black	.25	.25
g.	A106 50c green & black	1.25	.60
h.	A107 $1 red & black	2.50	1.25
i.	A101 $2 red brown & black	4.25	2.50

Vignettes on Nos. 3209b and 3209i are reversed in comparison to the original issue.

3210	A107 $1 Pane of 9 #3209h	22.50	—

Uncut press sheets of Nos. 3209-3210 were made available for sale. The press sheets have 3 panes of No. 3209 at left and 3 panes of No. 3210 at right. Values: cross-gutter block of 12, $60; pairs with gutters between, $10 each. See note after No. 2868.

BERLIN AIRLIFT, 50th ANNIV.

A2492

Designed by Bill Bond.
Printed by Banknote Corporation of America.

PHOTOGRAVURE
Sheets of 120 in six panes of 20

1998, June 26 **Tagged** ***Perf. 11.2***

3211	A2492 32c **multicolored**	.65	.25
	P# block of 4, 4#+B	2.60	—
	Pane of 20	13.00	—

AMERICAN MUSIC SERIES
Folk Singers

Huddie "Leadbelly" Ledbetter (1888-1949)
A2493

Woody Guthrie (1912-67)
A2494

Sonny Terry (1911-86)
A2495

Josh White (1908-69)
A2496

Designed by Howard Paine.
Printed by American Packaging Corp. for Sennett Security Products.

PHOTOGRAVURE
Sheets of 180 in nine panes of 20

1998, June 26 **Tagged** ***Perf. 10.1x10.2***

3212	A2493 32c **multicolored**	.90	.25
3213	A2494 32c **multicolored**	.90	.25
3214	A2495 32c **multicolored**	.90	.25
3215	A2496 32c **multicolored**	.90	.25
a.	Block or strip of 4, #3212-3215	3.60	2.00
	P# block of 4, 5#+S	4.25	—
	P# block of 8, 2 sets of P# + top label	8.50	—
	Pane of 20	21.00	—

AMERICAN MUSIC SERIES
Gospel Singers

Mahalia Jackson (1911-72)
A2497

Roberta Martin (1917-69)
A2498

Clara Ward (1924-73)
A2499

Sister Rosetta Tharpe (1921-73)
A2500

Designed by Howard Paine.
Printed by American Packaging Corp. for Sennett Security Products.

PHOTOGRAVURE
Sheets of 120 in six panes of 20

1998, July 15 **Tagged** ***Perf. 10.1x10.3***

3216 A2497 32c **multicolored** 1.00 .25
3217 A2498 32c **multicolored** 1.00 .25
3218 A2499 32c **multicolored** 1.00 .25
3219 A2500 32c **multicolored** 1.00 .25
a. Block or strip of 4, #3216-3219 4.00 2.00
P# block of 4, 6#+S 5.00 —
P# block of 8, 2 sets of P# + top label 10.00 —
Pane of 20 24.00 —

SPANISH SETTLEMENT OF THE SOUTHWEST

La Mision de San Miguel de San Gabriel, Espanola, NM — A2501

Designed by Richard Sheaff.
Printed by Banknote Corporation of America.

LITHOGRAPHED
Sheets of 180 in nine panes of 20

1998, July 11 **Tagged** ***Perf. 11.2***

3220 A2501 32c **multicolored** .65 .25
P# block of 4, 4#+B 2.60 —
Pane of 20 13.00 —

LITERARY ARTS SERIES

Stephen Vincent Benét (1898-43)
A2502

Designed by Carl Herrman.
Printed by Ashton-Potter (USA) Ltd.

LITHOGRAPHED
Sheets of 180 in nine panes of 20

1998, July 22 **Tagged** ***Perf. 11.2***

3221 A2502 32c **multicolored** .65 .25
P# block of 4, 4#+P 2.60 —
Pane of 20 13.00 —

TROPICAL BIRDS

Antillean Euphonia
A2503

Green-throated Carib — A2504

Crested Honeycreeper
A2505

Cardinal Honeyeater
A2506

Designed by Phil Jordan.
Printed by Banknote Corporation of America.

LITHOGRAPHED
Sheets of 180 in nine panes of 20

1998, July 29 **Tagged** ***Perf. 11.2***

3222 A2503 32c **multicolored** .65 .25
3223 A2504 32c **multicolored** .65 .25
3224 A2505 32c **multicolored** .65 .25
3225 A2506 32c **multicolored** .65 .25
a. Block or strip of 4, #3222-3225 2.60 2.00
P# block of 4, 4#+B 2.60 —
Pane of 20 13.00 —

For booklet see No. BK272.

LEGENDS OF HOLLYWOOD

Alfred Hitchcock (1899-1980) — A2507

Designed by Richard Sheaff.
Printed at American Packaging Corp. for Sennett Security Products.

PHOTOGRAVURE
Sheets of 120 in six panes of 20

1998, Aug. 3 **Tagged** ***Perf. 11.1***

3226 A2507 32c **multicolored** .75 .25
P# block of 4, 4#+S 4.50 —
Pane of 20 20.00 12.50

Perforations in corner of each stamp are star-shaped. Hitchcock's profile in the UL corner of each stamp is laser cut.

Uncut press sheets of No. 3226 were made available for sale. Values: cross-gutter block of 8, $20; pairs with gutters between, $3.50 each. See note after No. 2868.

ORGAN & TISSUE DONATION

A2508

Designed by Richard Sheaff. Printed by Avery Dennison.

PHOTOGRAVURE
Sheets of 160 in eight panes of 20

1998, Aug. 5 **Tagged** ***Serpentine Die Cut 11.7***
Self-Adhesive

3227 A2508 32c **multicolored** .65 .25
P# block of 4 5#+V 2.60
Pane of 20 13.00

MODERN BICYCLE

A2509

Designed by Richard Sheaff. Printed by Bureau of Engraving and Printing (#3228), Sennett Security Printers (#3229).

PHOTOGRAVURE
COIL STAMP
Serpentine Die Cut 9.8 Vert.

1998, Aug. 14 **Untagged**
Self-Adhesive (#3228)

3228 A2509 (10c) **multicolored,** small "1998" year date .25 .25
Pair .50
P# strip of 5, P#111, 221, 222, 333, 344, 444, 555 2.10
P# single, same # 1.90
a. Large date .35 .25
Pair .70
P# strip of 5, #666, 777, 888, 999 2.25
P# single, #666, 777, 888, 999 — 2.25

Date on No. 3228a is approximately 1½mm; on No. 3228 approximately 1mm.

Untagged
Perf. 9.9 Vert.

3229 A2509 (10c) **multicolored** .25 .25
Pair .50 .50
P# strip of 5, P#S111 1.75
P# single, same # — 1.40

Date on No. 3229 is approximately 2mm wide.

BRIGHT EYES

Dog — A2510

Fish — A2511

Cat — A2512

Parakeet
A2513

Hamster
A2514

Designed by Carl Herrman. Printed at Guilford Gravure for Banknote Corp. of America.

PHOTOGRAVURE

Sheets of 180 in nine panes of 20

1998, Aug. 20 Tagged *Serpentine Die Cut 9.9*

Self-Adhesive

3230 A2510 32c **multicolored**	.75	.40
3231 A2511 32c **multicolored**	.75	.40
3232 A2512 32c **multicolored**	.75	.40
3233 A2513 32c **multicolored**	.75	.40
3234 A2514 32c **multicolored**	.75	.40
a. Strip of 5, #3230-3234	3.75	
P# block of 8, 2 sets of 6#+B	7.50	
Pane of 20	15.00	

Hidden 3-D images can be seen on each stamp when viewed with a special "Stamp Decoder" lens sold by the USPS. No. 3230, bone and doghouse; No. 3231, eight bubbles; No. 3232, paw print and mouse; No. 3233, birdcage; No. 3234, exercise wheel.

Plate blocks may contain top label.

KLONDIKE GOLD RUSH, CENTENNIAL

A2515

Designed by Howard Paine. Printed at Sterling Sommer for Ashton Potter (USA) Ltd.

LITHOGRAPHED

Sheets of 180 in nine panes of 20

1998, Aug. 21 Tagged *Perf. 11.1*

3235 A2515 32c **multicolored**	.65	.25
P# block of 4, 5#+P	2.60	—
Pane of 20	13.00	—

AMERICAN ART

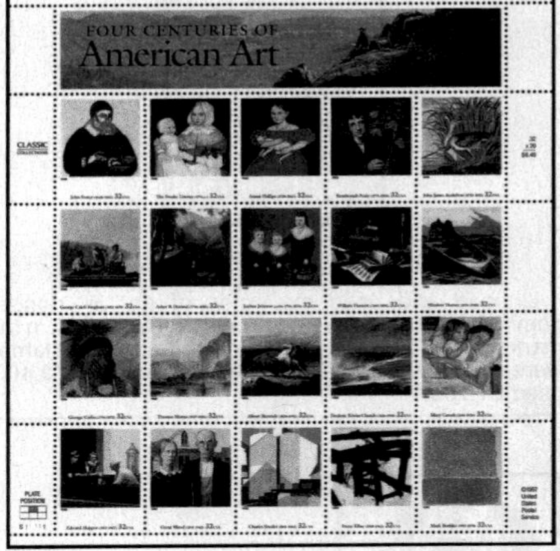

A2516

Illustration reduced.

Designed by Howard Paine. Printed by Sennett Security Products.

Paintings: a, "Portrait of Richard Mather," by John Foster. b, "Mrs. Elizabeth Freake and Baby Mary," by The Freake Limner. c, "Girl in Red Dress with Cat and Dog," by Ammi Phillips. d, "Rubens Peale with a Geranium," by Rembrandt Peale. e, "Long-billed Curlew, Numenius Longrostris," by John James Audubon. f, "Boatmen on the Missouri," by George Caleb Bingham. g, "Kindred Sprits," by Asher B. Durand. h, "The Westwood Children," by Joshua Johnson. i, "Music and Literature," by William Harnett. j, "The Fog Warning," by Winslow Homer. k, "The White Cloud, Head Chief of the Iowas," by George Catlin. l, "Cliffs of Green River," by Thomas Moran. m, "The Last of the Buffalo," by Alfred Bierstadt. n, "Niagara," by Frederic Edwin Church. o, "Breakfast in Bed," by Mary Cassatt. p, "Nighthawks," by Edward Hopper. q, "American Gothic," by Grant Wood. r, "Two Against the White," by Charles Sheeler. s, "Mahoning," by Franz Kline. t, "No. 12," by Mark Rothko.

PHOTOGRAVURE

Sheets of 120 stamps in six panes of 20

1998, Aug. 27 Tagged *Perf. 10.2*

3236 A2516 Pane of 20	18.00	10.00
a.-t. 32c any single	.90	.60

Inscriptions on the back of each stamp describe the painting and the artist.

Uncut press sheets of No. 3236 were made available for sale. Values: cross-gutter block of 20, $40; pairs with gutters between, $4 each. See note after No. 2868.

AMERICAN BALLET

A2517

Designed by Derry Noyes. Printed by Sterling Sommer for Ashton-Potter (USA) Ltd.

LITHOGRAPHED

Sheets of 120 in six panes of 20

1998, Sept. 16 Tagged *Perf. 10.9x11.1*

3237 A2517 32c **multicolored**	.65	.25
P# block of 4, 4#+P	3.00	—
Pane of 20	14.50	—

For booklet see No. BK273.

Uncut press sheets of No. 3237 were made available for sale. Values: cross-gutter block of 4, $17.50; pairs with gutters between, $3.25 each. See note after No. 2868.

SPACE DISCOVERY

A2518

A2519

A2520

A2521

A2522

Designed by Phil Jordan. Printed at American Packaging Corp. for Sennett Security Products.

PHOTOGRAVURE

Sheets of 180 in nine panes of 20

1998, Oct. 1 Tagged *Perf. 11.1*

3238 A2518 32c **multicolored**	.65	.25
3239 A2519 32c **multicolored**	.65	.25
3240 A2520 32c **multicolored**	.65	.25
3241 A2521 32c **multicolored**	.65	.25
3242 A2522 32c **multicolored**	.65	.25
a. Strip of 5, #3238-3242	3.25	2.25
P# block of 10, 2 sets of 5#+S	6.50	—
Pane of 20	13.00	

Hidden 3-D images can be seen on each stamp when viewed with a special "Stamp Decoder" lens sold by the USPS. No. 3238, large spacecraft, small spacecraft and figure; No. 3239, small spacecraft; No. 3240, small spacecraft; No. 3241, small spacecraft; No. 3242, large spacecraft and small spacecraft.

Plate blocks may contain top label.

Uncut press sheets of Nos. 3238-3242 were made available for sale. Values: cross-gutter block of 10, $22.50; pairs with gutters between, $2.50 each. See note after No. 2868.

For booklet see No. BK274.

GIVING AND SHARING

A2523

Designed by Bob Dinetz.

Printed by Avery Dennison.

PHOTOGRAVURE

Sheets of 200 in 10 panes of 20

1998, Oct. 7 Tagged *Serpentine Die Cut 11.1*

Self-Adhesive

3243 A2523 32c **multicolored**	.65	.25
P# block of 4, 4#+V	2.60	—
Pane of 20	13.00	—

CHRISTMAS

Madonna and Child, Florence, 15th Cent. — A2524

Evergreen Wreath — A2525

Victorian Wreath — A2526

Chili Pepper Wreath — A2527

Tropical Wreath — A2528

Designed by Richard D. Sheaff (#3244), Lilian Dinihanian (A2525), George de Bruin (A2526), Chris Crinklaw (A2527), Micheale Thunin (A2528).

Printed by Bureau of Engraving and Printing (#3244), Banknote Corporation of America (#3245-3252).

LITHOGRAPHED

Sheets of 160 in 8 panes of 20 (#3249-3252)

Serpentine Die Cut 10.1x9.9 on 2, 3 or 4 Sides

1998, Oct. 15 Tagged

Self-Adhesive

Booklet Stamps

3244 A2524 32c **multicolored**	.65	.25
a. Booklet pane of 20 + label	13.00	
b. Die cutting omitted, pair	—	

Size: 22x25mm

Serpentine Die Cut 11.3x11.7 on 2 or 3 Sides

3245 A2525 32c **multicolored**		3.25	.25
3246 A2526 32c **multicolored**		3.25	.25
3247 A2527 32c **multicolored**		3.25	.25
3248 A2528 32c **multicolored**		3.75	.25
a.	Booklet pane of 4, #3245-3248	13.00	
b.	Booklet pane of 5, #3245-3246, 3248, 2 #3247 + label	16.25	
c.	Booklet pane of 6, #3247-3248, 2 each #3245-3246	19.50	
d.	As "a," die cutting omitted	—	
e.	As "b," die cutting omitted	—	
f.	As "c," die cutting omitted	—	
g.	Block of 4, #3245-3248	13.00	

Size: 23x30mm

Serpentine Die Cut 11.4x11.5 on 2, 3, or 4 Sides

3249 A2525 32c **multicolored**		1.35	.25
a.	Serp. die cut 11.7x11.6 on 2, 3, or 4 sides	1.75	.25
3250 A2526 32c **multicolored**		1.35	.25
a.	Serp. die cut 11.7x11.6 on 3 or 4 sides	1.75	.25
3251 A2527 32c **multicolored**		1.35	.25
a.	Serp. die cut 11.7x11.6 on 3 or 4 sides	1.75	.25
3252 A2528 32c **multicolored + label**		1.35	.25
a.	Serp. die cut 11.7x11.6 on 2, 3, or 4 sides	1.75	.25
b.	Block or strip of 4, #3249-3252	5.40	
	P# block of 4, 6#+B	6.00	
	Pane of 20	27.00	
c.	Booklet pane of 20, 5 each #3249-3252 + label	30.00	
d.	Block or strip of 4, #3249a-3252a	7.00	
e.	Booklet pane of 20, 5 each #3249a-3252a + label	35.00	
f.	Block or strip of 4, #3249-3252, red ("Greetings 32 USA" and "1998") omitted on #3249, 3252	*625.00*	
g.	Block or strip of 4, #3249-3252, red ("Greetings 32 USA" and "1998") omitted on #3249, 3252; green (same) omitted on #3250, 3251	—	
h.	As "b," die cutting omitted	—	
i.	As "c," die cutting omitted	*4,500.*	

Dedicated printing plates were used to print the red and green denominations, salutations and dates. Red and green appearing in the wreaths come from other plates and, therefore, are not part of the color omissions.

Specialists will want to note that the "1998" date on the flat pane of 20 is about .1mm wider than the date on the corresponding booklet pane (No. 3252c). The measurements are approximately 1.3mm versus 1.2mm, respectively. Therefore, unused and used singles can be distinguished.

Weather Vane — A2529

Uncle Sam — A2530

Uncle Sam's Hat — A2531

Space Shuttle Landing A2532

Piggyback Space Shuttle A2533

Designed by Terry McCaffrey (#3257-3258, 3260, 3264-3269), Richard Sheaff (#3259, 3263), Phil Jordan (#3261-3262).

Printed by Ashton Potter (USA) Ltd. (#3257), American Packaging Corp. for Sennett Security Products (#3259), Stamp Venturers (#3260), Banknote Corporation of America (#3258, 3261-3262), Bureau of Engraving and Printing (#3263-3267), Avery Dennison (#3268-3269).

LITHOGRAPHED

Sheets of 400 in eight panes of 50 (#3257, 3260), Sheets of 300 in six panes of 50 (#3258), Sheets of 160 in eight panes of 20 (#3259), Sheets of 120 in six panes of 20 (#3261-3262)

1998 Untagged *Perf. 11.2*

3257 A2529 (1c) **multicolored** *Nov. 9*		.25	.25
	P# block of 4, 5# + P	.25	—
a.	Black omitted	125.00	
b.	Horiz. pair, imperf. vert. and at top	—	
3258 A2529 (1c) **multicolored,** *Nov. 9*		.25	.25
	P# block of 4, 5# + B	.25	—
a.	Black missing (PS)	—	

No. 3257 is 18mm high, has thin letters, white USA, and black 1998. No. 3258 is 17mm high, has thick letters, pale blue USA and blue 1998.

PHOTOGRAVURE

Tagged

Serpentine Die Cut 10.8

Self-Adhesive (#3259, 3261-3263, 3265-3269)

3259 A2530 22c **multicolored,** *Nov. 9*		.45	.25
a.	Die cut 10.8x10.5	2.50	.25
b.	Vert. pair, No. 3259 + 3259a	3.50	
	P# block of 4, 4# + S, all No. 3259	2.50	
	P# block of 4, top stamps No. 3259, bottom stamps No. 3259a	—	
	P# block of 4, top stamps No. 3259a, bottom stamps No. 3259	7.50	
	Pane of 20, all No. 3259	9.00	
	Pane of 20, row 1 No. 3259a, rows 2-4 No. 3259	—	
	Pane of 20, row 2 No. 3259a, rows 1, 3-4 No. 3259	35.00	
	Pane of 20, row 3 No. 3259a, rows 1-2, 4 No. 3259	22.50	
	Pane of 20, row 4 No. 3259a, rows 1-3 No. 3259	30.00	

See No. 3353.

Perf. 11.2

3260 A2531 (33c) **multicolored,** shiny gum, *Nov. 9*		.65	.25
	P# block of 4 4#+S	2.75	—
	Low-gloss gum	.65	.25
	P# block of 4 4#+S	2.75	—

LITHOGRAPHED

Serpentine Die Cut 11.5

3261 A2532 $3.20 **multicolored,** *Nov. 9*		6.00	1.50
	P# block of 4, 4#+B	24.00	
	Pane of 20	120.00	
3262 A2533 $11.75 **multicolored,** *Nov. 19*		22.50	10.00
	P# block of 4, 4#+B	90.00	
	Pane of 20	450.00	

Hidden 3-D images (ENTERPRISE/COLUMBIA /CHALLENGER/ATLANTIS/ENDEAVOR/DISCOVERY) can be seen on Nos. 3261 and 3262 when viewed with a special "Stamp Decoder" lens sold by the USPS.

COIL STAMPS

PHOTOGRAVURE

Serpentine Die Cut 9.9 Vert.

3263 A2530 22c **multicolored,** *Nov. 9*		.45	.25
	Pair	.90	
	P# strip of 5, #1111	4.25	
	P# single, same #		1.75
a.	Die cutting omitted, pair	*750.00*	

See No. 3353.

Perf. 9.8 Vert.

3264 A2531 (33c) **multicolored,** *Nov. 9*		.65	.25
	Pair	1.30	.50
	P# strip of 5, #1111, 3333, 3343, 3444	5.75	
	P# strip of 5, #3344	9.50	
	P# single, #1111, 3333, 3343, 3444		3.75
	P# single, #3344		4.50
a.	Imperf, pair	*325.00*	

On No. 3264, the black plate #1 of plate #1111 used in printing rolls of 100 places the plate digit "1" farther from the black printing in the vignette than does the black plate #1 of plate #1111 used in printing rolls of 3,000. These are referred to as "Low black 1" and "Hi black 1" and are used by plate number

Serpentine Die Cut 9.9 Vert.

3265 A2531 (33c) **multicolored,** *Nov. 9*		.80	.25
	Pair	1.60	
	P# strip of 5, #1111, 2222, 3333	6.00	
	P# strip of 5, #1131	8.50	
	P# single, #1111, 2222, 3333		1.50
	P# single, #1131		3.00
a.	Die cutting omitted, pair	65.00	—
b.	Red omitted	*300.00*	
c.	Black omitted	*1,400.*	
d.	Black omitted, die cutting omitted, pair	*675.00*	
e.	Red omitted, die cutting omitted, pair	*500.00*	
f.	Blue omitted	—	

Unused examples of No. 3265 are on backing paper the same size as the stamps. Corners of the stamp are 90 degree angles.

On No. 3265b, the blue and gray colors are shifted down and to the right.

On No. 3265f, the red is misregistered to right by 10½ stamps and gray by 3mm.

Serpentine Die Cut 9.9 Vert.

3266 A2531 (33c) **multicolored,** *Nov. 9*		2.25	.25
	Pair	4.50	
	P# strip of 5, #1111	14.00	
	P# single, same #		4.00

Unused examples of No. 3266 are on backing paper larger than the stamps, and the stamps are spaced approximately 2mm. apart. Corners of stamps are rounded.

BOOKLET STAMPS

Serpentine Die Cut 9.9 on 2 or 3 Sides

3267 A2531 (33c) **multicolored,** *Nov. 9*		.75	.25
a.	Booklet pane of 10	7.50	

Serpentine Die Cut 11¼ on 3 Sides (#3268, 3268a) or 11 on 2, 3 or 4 sides (#3268b, 3268c)

3268 A2531 (33c) **multicolored,** *Nov. 9*		.75	.25
a.	Booklet pane of 10	7.50	
b.	Serpentine die cut 11	.75	.25
c.	As "b," booklet pane of 20 + label	15.00	

Die Cut 8 on 2, 3 or 4 Sides

3269 A2531 (33c) **multicolored,** *Nov. 9* ⓢ		.65	.25
a.	Booklet pane of 18	12.00	

ⓢ: Adhesive residue may remain on the backs of some examples of No. 3269 after soaking. See note after No. 1549.

Unused and used examples of an "H" nondenominated stamp inscribed "Postcard Rate" exist in the marketplace. There is no evidence that these stamps were ever officially issued. Values: unused $2,400; used $1,750.

A2534

Designed by Chris Calle.

PHOTOGRAVURE

COIL STAMPS

1998, Dec. 14 Untagged *Perf. 9.8 Vert.*

3270 A2534 (10c) **multicolored,** small date		.25	.25
	Pair	.50	—
	P# strip of 5, #11111	2.25	
	P# single, #11111		1.75
a.	Large date	.45	.25
	Pair	.90	—
	P# strip of 5, #22222	7.00	—
	P# single, same #	—	5.00

Self-Adhesive

Serpentine Die Cut 9.9 Vert.

3271 A2534 (10c) **multicolored,** small date		.25	.25
	Pair	.50	
	P# strip of 5, #11111, 22222	2.00	
	P# single, #11111, 22222		1.75
a.	Large date	1.00	.25
	Pair	2.00	
	P# strip of 5, #33333	5.25	

Pair 2.50
P# strip of 5, #11111 8.00
P# single, #11111 — 8.50

No. 3271 is known with eagle in red brown rather than the normal golden brown, apparently from contaminated ink. Values slightly higher than normal No. 3271.

Dates on Nos. 3270a and 3271a are approximately 1¾mm; on Nos. 3270-3271 approximately 1¼mm.

Compare to Nos. 2602-2604, 2907.

Scott values for used self-adhesive stamps are for examples either on piece or off piece.

CHINESE NEW YEAR

Year of the Rabbit A2535

Designed by Clarence Lee.

Printed at American Packaging Corp. for Sennett Security Printers.

PHOTOGRAVURE
Sheets of 180 in nine panes of 20

1999, Jan. 5 Tagged *Perf. 11.2*

3272	A2535 33c **multicolored**	.80	.25
	P# block of 4, 4#+S	3.25	—
	Pane of 20	17.00	—

See No. 3895d.

BLACK HERITAGE SERIES

Malcolm X (1925-65), Civil Rights Activist — A2536

Designed by Richard Sheaff. Printed by Banknote Corp. of America.

LITHOGRAPHED
Sheets of 180 in nine panes of 20

1999, Jan. 20 Tagged *Serpentine Die Cut 11.4*
Self-Adhesive

3273	A2536 33c **multicolored**	.85	.25
	P# block of 4, 3#+B	3.75	
	Pane of 20	18.50	

VICTORIAN LOVE

A2537

A2538

Designed by John Grossman, Holly Sudduth.

Printed by Avery Dennison.

PHOTOGRAVURE

1999, Jan. 28 Tagged *Die Cut*
Booklet Stamp
Self-Adhesive

3274	A2537 33c **multicolored**	.65	.25
a.	Booklet pane of 20	13.00	
b.	Die cutting omitted, pair	*100.00*	
c.	As "a," die cutting omitted	*1,000.*	

Sheets of 160 in eight panes of 20

3275	A2538 55c **multicolored**	1.10	.25
	P# block of 4, 7#+B	4.40	
	Pane of 20	22.00	

HOSPICE CARE

A2539

Designed by Phil Jordan.

Printed by Banknote Corp. of America.

LITHOGRAPHED
Sheets of 120 in six panes of 20

1999, Feb. 9 Tagged *Serpentine Die Cut 11.4*

3276	A2539 33c **multicolored**	.65	.25
	P# block of 4, 4#+B	2.80	
	Pane of 20	13.50	
a.	Horiz. pair, vert. die cutting omitted	—	

Flag and City — A2540

Designed by Richard Sheaff. Printed by Bureau of Engraving and Printing (#3277, 3279-3282), Avery Dennison (#3278, 3278F, 3283).

PHOTOGRAVURE
Sheets of 400 in four panes of 100 (#3277),
Sheets of 200 in 10 panes of 20 (#3278)

1999, Feb. 25 Tagged *Perf. 11.2*
Self-Adhesive (#3278, 3278F, 3279, 3281-3282)

3277	A2540 33c **multicolored**	.70	.25
	P# block of 4, 4#	60.00	—

No. 3277 has red date.

Serpentine Die Cut 11 on 2, 3 or 4 Sides

3278	A2540 33c **multicolored**	.65	.25
	P# block of 4, 4#+V	5.00	
	Pane of 20	22.50	
a.	Booklet pane of 4	2.60	
b.	Booklet pane of 5 + label	3.25	
	P# single, #V1111, V1112, V1121, V1122, V1212, V2212	.80	1.00
c.	Booklet pane of 6	3.90	
d.	Booklet pane of 10	13.00	
e.	Booklet pane of 20 + label	17.00	
h.	As "e," die cutting omitted	—	
i.	Serpentine die cut 11¼	.90	.25
j.	As "i," booklet pane of 10	9.00	

No. 3278 has black date.
The plate # single in No. 3278b is the lower left stamp.

BOOKLET STAMPS
Serpentine Die Cut 11½x11¾ on 2, 3 or 4 Sides

3278F	A2540 33c **multicolored**	1.40	.25
g.	Booklet pane of 20 + label	28.00	

No. 3278F has black date.

Serpentine Die Cut 9.8 on 2 or 3 Sides

3279	A2540 33c **multicolored**	.85	.25
a.	Booklet pane of 10	8.50	

No. 3279 has red date.

COIL STAMPS
Perf. 9.9 Vert.

3280	A2540 33c **multicolored,** small "1999" year date	.65	.25
	Pair	1.30	.50
	P# strip of 5, #1111, 2222	4.25	
	P# single, same #		2.00
a.	Large date	2.00	.25
	Pair	4.00	.50
	P# strip of 5, #3333	11.00	
	P# single, same #	—	6.50
b.	As No. 3280, imperf pair	*200.00*	*150.00*

Serpentine Die Cut 9.8 Vert.

Two types of No. 3281: Type I, Long vertical feature at left and right of tallest building consists of 3 separate lines; Type II, Same features consist of solid color.

3281	A2540 33c **multicolored,** type I, large "1999" year date	.65	.25
	Pair	1.30	
	P# strip of 5, #6666, 7777, 8888, 9999, 1111A, 2222A, 3333A, 4444A, 5555A, 6666A, 7777A, 8888A, 1111B, 2222B	4.75	
	P# single, same #	—	.85
	P# single, 1111B, 2222B	—	1.50
a.	As No. 3281, die cutting omitted, pair	30.00	
b.	Light blue and yellow omitted	*275.00*	
c.	Small date, type II	.65	.25
	Pair	1.30	
	P# strip of 5, #1111, 2222, 3333, 3433, 4443, 4444, 5555	4.75	
	P# single, same #	—	.85
d.	Small date, type I	5.00	.30
	Pair	10.00	
	P# strip of 5, #9999A	40.00	
	P# single, same #		3.50
e.	As "c," die cutting omitted, pair	—	

Corners are square on No. 3281. Unused examples are on backing paper the same size as the stamps, and the stamps are adjoining.

Date on Nos. 3280a and 3281 is approximately 1¾mm; on Nos. 3280, 3281c and 3281d approximately 1¼mm.

Counterfeits exist of No. 3281. See the Postal Counterfeits section of this catalog.

3282	A2540 33c **multicolored**	.65	.25
	Pair	1.30	
	P# strip of 5, #1111, 2222	4.25	
	P# single, same #		3.25

Corners are rounded on #3282. Unused examples are on backing paper larger than the stamps, and the stamps are spaced approximately 2mm. apart.

Flag and Chalkboard — A2541

PHOTOGRAVURE
Serpentine Die Cut 7.9 on 2, 3 or 4 Sides

1999, Mar. 13 Tagged
Self-Adhesive
BOOKLET STAMP

3283	A2541 33c **multicolored**	.65	.25
a.	Booklet pane of 18	12.00	
b.	Die cutting omitted, pair	—	

IRISH IMMIGRATION

A2542

Designed by Howard Paine. Printed by Ashton-Potter (USA) Ltd.

LITHOGRAPHED
Sheets of 180 in nine panes of 20

1999, Feb. 26 Tagged *Perf. 11.2*

3286	A2542 33c **multicolored**	.65	.25
	P# block of 4, 4#+P	2.60	—
	Pane of 20	13.00	—

See Ireland No. 1168.

PERFORMING ARTS SERIES

Alfred Lunt (1892-1977), Lynn Fontanne (1887-1983), Actors

A2543

Designed by Carl Herrman. Printed by Sterling Sommer for Ashton-Potter (USA) Ltd.

LITHOGRAPHED
Sheets of 180 in nine panes of 20

1999, Mar. 2 **Tagged** ***Perf. 11.2***

3287	A2543 33c **multicolored**	.65	.25
	P# block of 4, 4#+P	2.60	—
	Pane of 20	13.00	—

ARCTIC ANIMALS

Arctic Hare — A2544

Arctic Fox — A2545

Snowy Owl — A2546

Polar Bear — A2547

Gray Wolf — A2548

Designed by Derry Noyes. Printed by Banknote Corp. of America.

LITHOGRAPHED
Sheets of 90 in six panes of 15

1999, Mar. 12 **Tagged** ***Perf. 11***

3288	A2544 33c **multicolored**	.85	.25
3289	A2545 33c **multicolored**	.85	.25
3290	A2546 33c **multicolored**	.85	.25
3291	A2547 33c **multicolored**	.85	.25
3292	A2548 33c **multicolored**	.85	.25
a.	Strip of 5, #3288-3292	4.25	—
	Pane of 15, 6#+B	13.00	—

While the normal definition of a plate block dictates a block of 10, this would require collectors to discard the decorative label and top row of stamps from the pane of 15. To avoid destroying the more collectible entire, we list the entire pane as the plate block.

SONORAN DESERT Ⓢ

A2549

Illustration reduced.

Designed by Ethel Kessler. Printed by Banknote Corporation of America.

Designs: a, Cactus wren, brittlebush, teddy bear cholla. b, Desert tortoise. c, White-winged dove, prickly pear. d, Gambel quail. e, Saguaro cactus. f, Desert mule deer. g, Desert cottontail, hedgehog cactus. h, Gila monster. i, Western diamondback rattlesnake, cactus mouse. j, Gila woodpecker.

LITHOGRAPHED
Sheets of 60 in six panes of 10
Serpentine Die Cut Perf 11.2

1999, Apr. 6 **Tagged**

Self-Adhesive

3293	A2549 Pane of 10	8.00	
a.-j.	33c any single	.80	.50

Uncut press sheets of No. 3293 were made available for sale. See note after No. 2868.
See note after No. 1549.

BERRIES

Blueberries
A2550

Raspberries
A2551

Strawberries
A2552

Blackberries
A2553

Designed by Howard Paine. Printed by Guilford Gravure for Banknote Corporation of America.

PHOTOGRAVURE
Serpentine Die Cut 11¼x11½ on 2, 3 or 4 Sides (Nos. 3294-3297), or 2 or 3 sides (Nos. 3294a-3297a)

1999, Apr. 10 **Tagged**

Self-Adhesive

3294	A2550 33c **multicolored**	.85	.25
a.	Dated "2000," *Mar. 15, 2000*	1.25	.25
3295	A2551 33c **multicolored**	.85	.25
a.	Dated "2000," *Mar. 15, 2000*	1.25	.25
3297	A2553 33c **multicolored**	.85	.25
a.	Dated "2000," *Mar. 15, 2000*	1.25	.25
b.	Booklet pane of 20, 5 each #3294-3297 + label	17.50	
c.	Block or strip of 4, #3294-3297	3.50	
d.	Booklet pane of 20, 5 #3297e + label	25.00	
e.	Block of 4, #3294a-3297a	5.00	

No. 3297d is a double-sided booklet pane, with 12 stamps on one side and eight stamps plus label on the other side.

Serpentine Die Cut 9½x10 on 2 or 3 Sides

3298	A2550 33c **multicolored**	1.00	.25
3299	A2552 33c **multicolored**	1.00	.25
3300	A2551 33c **multicolored**	1.00	.25
3301	A2553 33c **multicolored**	1.00	.25
a.	Booklet pane of 4, #3298-3301	4.00	
b.	Booklet pane of 5, #3298, 3299, 3301, 2 #3300 + label	5.00	
c.	Booklet pane of 6, #3300, 3301, 2 #3298, 3299	6.00	
d.	Block of 4, #3298-3301	4.00	

COIL STAMPS
Serpentine Die Cut 8.5 Vert.

3302	A2550 33c **multicolored**	2.25	.25
3303	A2551 33c **multicolored**	2.25	.25
3304	A2553 33c **multicolored**	2.25	.25
3305	A2552 33c **multicolored**	2.25	.25
a.	Strip of 4, #3302-3305	9.00	
	P# strip of 5, 2 #3302, 1 ea #3303-3305, P#B1111, B1112, B2211, B2221, B2222	12.50	
	P# strip of 9, 2 ea #3302-3303, 3305, 3 #3304, same P#	22.50	
	P# single (#3304), same P#	—	1.10

See Nos. 3404-3407.

DAFFY DUCK

A2554

Designed by Ed Wieczyk.
Printed by Avery Dennison.

PHOTOGRAVURE

1999, Apr. 16 **Tagged** ***Serpentine Die Cut 11.1***

Self-Adhesive

3306	Pane of 10 #3306a	6.75	
a.	A2554 33c single	.65	.25
b.	Pane of 9 #3306a	6.00	
c.	Pane of 1 #3306a	.65	

Nos. 3306b-3306c and 3307b-3307c are separated by a vertical line of microperforations, which is absent on the uncut sheet of 60.

Die cutting on No. 3306b does not extend through the backing paper.

Uncut press sheets of No. 3306 were made available for sale. Values: top sheet of 60, $40; bottom sheet of 60 with P#, $47.50; cross-gutter block of 7, $15; pairs with gutters between, $3 each. See note after No. 2868.

3307	Pane of 10, #3307c, 9 #3307a	13.00	
a.	A2554 33c single	1.10	
b.	Pane of 9 #3307a	10.00	
c.	Pane of 1, no die cutting	2.75	
d.	As "a," vert. pair, die cutting omitted btwn. pos. 6 and 9 (unique)	*4,250.*	

Die cutting on #3307b extends through the backing paper.

LITERARY ARTS SERIES

Ayn Rand (1905-82) — A2555

Designed by Phil Jordan

LITHOGRAPHED
Sheets of 180 in nine panes of 20

1999, Apr. 22	Tagged	*Perf. 11.2*	
3308 A2555 33c **multicolored**		.65	.25
P# block of 4, 4#+P		2.60	—
Pane of 20		13.00	—

Cinco De Mayo Type of 1998

Designed by Carl Herrman.

Printed by Banknote Corporation of America.

LITHOGRAPHED
Sheets of 160 in eight panes of 20
Serpentine Die Cut 11.6x11.3

1999, Apr. 27 **Tagged**

Self-Adhesive

3309 A2486 33c **multicolored**	.70	.25
P# block of 4, 6#+B	3.00	
Pane of 20	15.00	

TROPICAL FLOWERS

Bird of Paradise A2556

Royal Poinciana A2557

Gloriosa Lily — A2558

Chinese Hibiscus A2559

Designed by Carl Herrman.

Printed by Sennett Security Products.

PHOTOGRAVURE
BOOKLET STAMPS
Serpentine Die Cut 10.9 on 2 or 1 Sides

1999, May 1 **Tagged**

Self-Adhesive

3310 A2556 33c **multicolored**	.65	.30
3311 A2557 33c **multicolored**	.65	.30
3312 A2558 33c **multicolored**	.65	.30
3313 A2559 33c **multicolored**	.65	.30
a. Block of 4, #3310-3313	2.60	
b. Booklet pane, 5 each #3313a	13.00	

No. 3313b is a double-sided booklet pane with 12 stamps on one side and 8 stamps plus label on the other side.

JOHN (1699-1777) & WILLIAM (1739-1823) BARTRAM, BOTANISTS

A2560

Designed by Phil Jordan. Printed by Banknote Corporation of America.

Design: 33c, Franklinia alatamaha, by William Bartram.

LITHOGRAPHED
Sheets of 180 in nine panes of 20

1999, May 18 **Tagged** ***Serpentine Die Cut 11½***

Self-Adhesive

3314 A2560 33c **multicolored**	.65	.25
P# block of 4, 4#+B	2.60	
Pane of 20	13.00	

PROSTATE CANCER AWARENESS

A2561

Designed by Michael Cronan. Printed by Avery Dennison.

PHOTOGRAVURE
Sheets of 200 in 10 panes of 20

1999, May 28 **Tagged** ***Serpentine Die Cut 11***

Self-Adhesive

3315 A2561 33c **multicolored**	.65	.25
P# block of 4, 5#+V	2.60	
Pane of 20	13.00	

CALIFORNIA GOLD RUSH, 150TH ANNIV.

A2562

Designed by Howard Paine. Printed by Ashton-Potter (USA) Ltd.

LITHOGRAPHED
Sheets of 180 in nine panes of 20

1999, June 18	Tagged	*Perf. 11¼*	
3316 A2562 33c **multicolored**		.65	.25
P# block of 4, 5#+P		2.60	—
Pane of 20		13.00	—

AQUARIUM FISH Ⓢ

A2563

A2564

A2565

Reef Fish — A2566

Designed by Richard Sheaff. Printed by Banknote Corporation of America.

Designs: No. 3317, Yellow fish, red fish, cleaner shrimp. No. 3318, Fish, thermometer. No. 3319, Red fish, blue & yellow fish. No. 3320, Fish, heater/aerator.

LITHOGRAPHED
Sheets of 120 in six panes of 20

1999, June 24 **Tagged** ***Serpentine Die Cut 11½***

Self-Adhesive

3317 A2563 33c **multicolored,** block tagging	.65	.30
a. Overall tagging	15.00	*12.50*
3318 A2564 33c **multicolored,** block tagging	.65	.30
a. Overall tagging	15.00	*12.50*
3319 A2565 33c **multicolored,** block tagging	.65	.30
a. Overall tagging	15.00	*12.50*
3320 A2566 33c **multicolored,** block tagging	.65	.30
a. Overall tagging	15.00	*12.50*
b. Strip of 4, #3317-3320	2.60	
P# block of 8, 2 sets of 4#+B	5.20	
Pane of 20	13.00	
c. Strip of 4, #3317a-3320a	50.00	
P# block of 8, 2 sets of 4#+B	110.00	
Pane of 20	275.00	

Plate blocks will have either top label or list of fish shown on bottom selvage.

Uncut press sheets of Nos. 3317-3320 were made available for sale. Values: cross-gutter block of 8, $60; pairs with gutters between, $8.25 each. Press sheets were printed with large block tagging. See note after No. 2868.

See note after No. 1549.

EXTREME SPORTS

Skateboarding — A2567

BMX Biking — A2568

Snowboarding — A2569

Inline Skating — A2570

Designed by Carl Herrman. Printed by Avery Dennison.

PHOTOGRAVURE

Sheets of 160 in eight panes of 20

1999, June 25 Tagged *Serpentine Die Cut 11*

Self-Adhesive

3321 A2567 33c **multicolored**	.75	.30
3322 A2568 33c **multicolored**	.75	.30
3323 A2569 33c **multicolored**	.75	.30
3324 A2570 33c **multicolored**	.75	.30
a. Block or strip of 4, #3321-3324	3.00	
P# block of 4, 4#+V	3.00	
Pane of 20	15.00	

Uncut press sheets of Nos. 3321-3324 were made available for sale. Values: top sheet of 80, $62.50; bottom sheet of 80 with P#, $67.50; cross-gutter block of 8, $12.50; pairs with gutters between, $3 each. See note after No. 2868.

Hidden 3-D images can be seen on each of these stamps when viewed with a special "Stamp Decoder" lens sold by the USPS. No. 3321, GNARLY; No. 3322, RAD; No. 3323, SWEET; No. 3324, PHAT.

AMERICAN GLASS

Free-Blown Glass — A2571

Mold-Blown Glass — A2572

Pressed Glass — A2573

Art Glass — A2574

Designed by Richard Sheaff. Printed by Sterling Sommer for Ashton-Potter (USA) Ltd.

LITHOGRAPHED

Sheets of 90 in six panes of 15

1999, June 29 Tagged *Perf. 11*

3325 A2571 33c **multicolored**	1.90	.25
3326 A2572 33c **multicolored**	1.90	.25
3327 A2573 33c **multicolored**	1.90	.25
3328 A2574 33c **multicolored**	1.90	.25
a. Strip or block of 4, #3325-3328	7.75	3.00
Pane of 15, 4 each #3325, 3327-3328, 3 #3326	28.50	12.50

LEGENDS OF HOLLYWOOD

James Cagney (1899-1986) — A2575

Designed by Howard Paine.

Printed by Sennett Security Products.

PHOTOGRAVURE

Sheets of 120 in six panes of 20

1999, July 22 Tagged *Perf. 11*

3329 A2575 33c **multicolored**	.80	.25
P# block of 4, 5#+S	4.75	—
Pane of 20	22.00	—

Perforations in corner of each stamp are star-shaped.

Uncut press sheets of No. 3329 were made available for sale. Values: cross-gutter block of 8, $17.50; pairs with gutters between, $3.50. See note after No. 2868.

GEN. WILLIAM "BILLY" L. MITCHELL (1879-1936), AVIATION PIONEER

A2576

Designed by Phil Jordan.

Printed by Guilford Gravure for Banknote Corporation of America.

PHOTOGRAVURE

Sheets of 180 in nine panes of 20

1999, July 30 Tagged *Serpentine Die Cut 9¾x10*

Self-Adhesive

3330 A2576 55c **multicolored**	1.10	.30
P# block of 4, 5#+B	4.40	
Pane of 20	22.00	

HONORING THOSE WHO SERVED

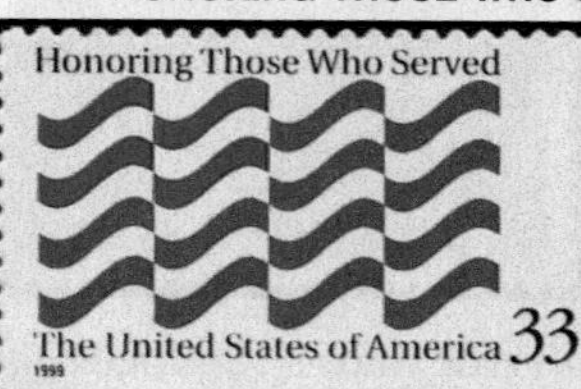

A2577

Designed by Richard Sheaff and Uldis Purins.

Printed by Avery Dennison.

PHOTOGRAVURE

Sheets of 200 in 10 panes of 20

1999, Aug. 16 Tagged *Serpentine Die Cut 11*

Self-Adhesive

3331 A2577 33c **black, blue & red**	.65	.25
P# block of 4, 3#+V	2.60	
Pane of 20	13.00	

UNIVERSAL POSTAL UNION

A2578

Designed by Gerald Gallo.

Printed by Sterling Sommer for Ashton-Potter (USA) Ltd.

LITHOGRAPHED

Sheets of 180 in nine panes of 20

1999, Aug. 25 Tagged *Perf. 11*

3332 A2578 45c **multicolored**	1.00	.45
P# block of 4, 3#+P	4.50	—
Pane of 20	22.00	—

FAMOUS TRAINS

Daylight A2579

Congressional A2580

20th Century Limited A2581

Hiawatha A2582

Super Chief — A2583

Designed by Howard Paine.

Printed by Ashton-Potter (USA) Ltd.

LITHOGRAPHED

Sheets of 120 in six panes of 20

1999, Aug. 26 Tagged *Perf. 11*

3333 A2579 33c **multicolored**	.75	.25
3334 A2580 33c **multicolored**	.75	.25
3335 A2581 33c **multicolored**	.75	.25
3336 A2582 33c **multicolored**	.75	.25
3337 A2583 33c **multicolored**	.75	.25
a. Strip of 5, #3333-3337	3.75	—
Pane of 20, 4 #3337a	15.00	—
P# block of 8, 2 sets of 4#+P	6.00	—

Stamps in No. 3337a are arranged in four different orders. Plate block may contain top label.

Uncut press sheets of Nos. 3333-3337 were made available for sale. Values: cross-gutter block of 8, $25; pairs with gutters between, $3.50 each. See note after No. 2868.

FREDERICK LAW OLMSTED (1822-1903), LANDSCAPE ARCHITECT

A2584

Designed by Ethel Kessler.
Printed by Ashton-Potter (USA) Ltd.

LITHOGRAPHED
Sheets of 120 in six panes of 20

1999, Sept. 12	**Tagged**	***Perf. 11***	
3338 A2584 33c **multicolored**		.65	.25
P# block of 4, 4#+P		2.60	—
Pane of 20		13.00	—

AMERICAN MUSIC SERIES
Hollywood Composers

Max Steiner (1888-1971) A2585

Dimitri Tiomkin (1894-1975) A2586

Bernard Herrmann (1911-75) A2587

Franz Waxman (1906-67) A2588

Alfred Newman (1907-70) A2589

Erich Wolfgang Korngold (1897-1957) A2590

Designed by Howard Paine.
Printed by Sterling Sommer for Ashton-Potter (USA) Ltd.

LITHOGRAPHED
Sheets of 120 in six panes of 20

1999, Sept. 16	**Tagged**	***Perf. 11***	
3339 A2585 33c **multicolored**		1.40	.25
3340 A2586 33c **multicolored**		1.40	.25
3341 A2587 33c **multicolored**		1.40	.25
3342 A2588 33c **multicolored**		1.40	.25
3343 A2589 33c **multicolored**		1.40	.25
3344 A2590 33c **multicolored**		1.40	.25
a. Block of 6, #3339-3344		8.50	4.50
P# block of 6, 5#+P		8.50	—
P# block of 8, 2 sets of 5#+P + top label		11.50	—
Pane of 20		28.50	—

AMERICAN MUSIC SERIES
Broadway Songwriters

Ira (1896-1983) & George (1898-1937) Gershwin A2591

Alan Jay Lerner (1918-86) & Frederick Loewe (1901-88) A2592

Lorenz Hart (1895-1943) A2593

Richard Rodgers (1902-79) & Oscar Hammerstein II (1895-1960) A2594

Meredith Willson (1902-84) A2595

Frank Loesser (1910-69) A2596

Designed by Howard Paine.
Printed by Sterling Sommer for Ashton-Potter (USA) Ltd.

LITHOGRAPHED
Sheets of 120 in six panes of 20

1999, Sept. 21	**Tagged**	***Perf. 11***	
3345 A2591 33c **multicolored**		1.25	.25
3346 A2592 33c **multicolored**		1.25	.25
3347 A2593 33c **multicolored**		1.25	.25
3348 A2594 33c **multicolored**		1.25	.25
3349 A2595 33c **multicolored**		1.25	.25
3350 A2596 33c **multicolored**		1.25	.25
a. Block of 6, #3345-3350		7.50	4.50
P# block of 6, 5#+P		7.50	—
P# block of 8, 2 sets of 5#+P + top label		10.00	—
Pane of 20		25.00	—

INSECTS & SPIDERS

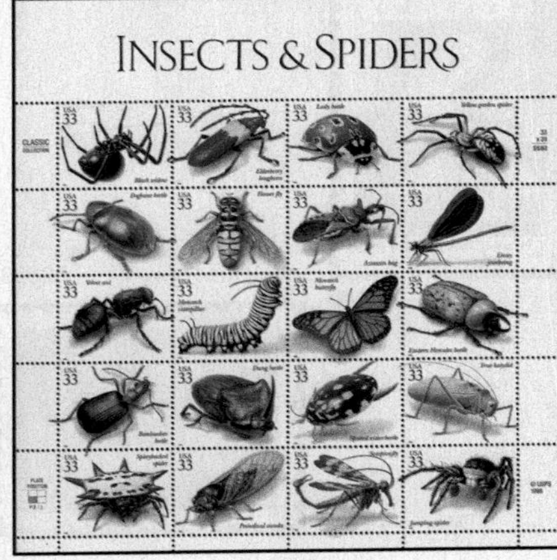

A2597

Illustration reduced.

Designed by Carl Herrman.
Printed by Ashton-Potter (USA) Ltd.

Designs: a, Black widow. b, Elderberry longhorn. c, Lady beetle. d, Yellow garden spider. e, Dogbane beetle. f, Flower fly. g, Assassin bug. h, Ebony jewelwing. i, Velvet ant. j, Monarch caterpillar. k, Monarch butterfly. l, Eastern Hercules beetle. m, Bombardier beetle. n, Dung beetle. o, Spotted water beetle. p, True katydid. q, Spinybacked spider. r, Periodical cicada. s, Scorpionfly. t, Jumping spider.

LITHOGRAPHED
Sheets of 80 in four panes of 20

1999, Oct. 1	**Tagged**	***Perf. 11***	
3351 A2597 Pane of 20		14.00	10.00
a.-t. 33c any single		.70	.50

Uncut press sheets of No. 3351 were made available for sale. Values: cross-gutter block of 20, $30; pairs with gutters between, $2.50 each. See note after No. 2868.

Hanukkah Type of 1996

Designed by Hannah Smotrich.
Printed by Avery Dennison.

PHOTOGRAVURE
Sheets of 200 in 10 panes of 20

1999, Oct. 8 **Tagged** ***Serpentine Die Cut 11***
Self-Adhesive

3352 A2411 33c **multicolored** .65 .25
P# block of 4, 5#+V 2.60
Pane of 20 13.00

Uncle Sam Type of 1998

Designed by Richard Sheaff.
Printed by Bureau of Engraving and Printing.

COIL STAMP
PHOTOGRAVURE

1999, Oct. 8 **Tagged** ***Perf. 9¾ Vert.***

3353 A2530 22c **multicolored** .45 .25
Pair .90 .50
P# strip of 5, #1111 3.25 —
P# single, same # — 2.25

NATO, 50TH ANNIV.

A2598

Designed by Michael Cronan.
Printed by Ashton-Potter (USA) Ltd.

LITHOGRAPHED
Sheets of 180 in nine panes of 20

1999, Oct. 13 **Tagged** ***Perf. 11¼***

3354 A2598 33c **multicolored** .65 .25
P# block of 4, 4#+P 2.60 —
Pane of 20 13.00 —

CHRISTMAS

Madonna and Child, by Bartolomeo Vivarini — A2599

Deer — A2600

Designed by Richard Sheaff (#3355), Tom Nikosey (#3356-3367).
Printed by Banknote Corp. of America.

LITHOGRAPHED
Serpentine Die Cut 11¼ on 2 or 3 sides

1999, Oct. 20 **Tagged**
Booklet Stamp
Self-Adhesive

3355 A2599 33c **multicolored** .90 .25
a. Booklet pane of 20 18.00

Sheets of 120 in six panes of 20
Serpentine Die Cut 11¼

3356 A2600 33c **gold & red** 2.25 .25
3357 A2600 33c **gold & blue** 2.25 .25
3358 A2600 33c **gold & purple** 2.25 .25
3359 A2600 33c **gold & green** 2.25 .25
a. Block or strip of 4, #3356-3359 9.00
P# block of 4, 6#+B 9.00
Pane of 20 45.00

Booklet Stamps
Serpentine Die Cut 11¼ on 2, 3 or 4 sides

3360 A2600 33c **gold & red** 1.10 .25
3361 A2600 33c **gold & blue** 1.10 .25
3362 A2600 33c **gold & purple** 1.10 .25
3363 A2600 33c **gold & green** 1.10 .25
a. Booklet pane of 20, 5 each #3360-3363 22.50
b. Block or strip of 4, #3360-3363 4.40
c. As "b," die cutting omitted *100.00*
d. As "a," die cutting omitted *500.00*

Size: 21x19mm
Serpentine Die Cut 11½x11¼ on 2 or 3 sides

3364 A2600 33c **gold & red** 1.35 .25
3365 A2600 33c **gold & blue** 1.35 .25
3366 A2600 33c **gold & purple** 1.35 .25
3367 A2600 33c **gold & green** 1.35 .25
a. Booklet pane of 4, #3364-3367 5.50
b. Booklet pane of 5, #3364, 3366, 3367, 2 #3365 + label 7.00
c. Booklet pane of 6, #3365, 3367, 2 each #3364 & 3366 8.00
d. Block of 4, #3364-3367 5.50

The frame on Nos. 3356-3359 is narrow and the space between it and the hoof is a hairline. The frame on Nos. 3360-3363 is much thicker, and the space between it and the hoof is wider.

Kwanzaa Type of 1997

Designed by Synthia Saint James
Printed by Avery Dennison.

PHOTOGRAVURE
Sheets of 240 in 12 panes of 20

1999, Oct. 29 **Tagged** ***Serpentine Die Cut 11***
Self-Adhesive

3368 A2458 33c **multicolored** .65 .25
P# block of 4, 4#+V 2.60
Pane of 20 13.00

YEAR 2000

Baby New Year — A2601

Designed by Carl Herrman.
Printed by Banknote Corporation of America.

LITHOGRAPHED
Sheets of 120 in six panes of 20

1999, Dec. 27 **Tagged** ***Serpentine Die Cut 11¼***
Self-Adhesive

3369 A2601 33c **multicolored** .65 .25
P# block of 4, 5#+B 3.00
Pane of 20 14.50

CHINESE NEW YEAR

Year of the Dragon A2602

Designed by Clarence Lee.
Printed by Sterling Sommer.

LITHOGRAPHED
Sheets of 180 in nine panes of 20

2000, Jan. 6 **Tagged** ***Perf. 11¼***

3370 A2602 33c **multicolored** .80 .25
P# block of 4, 4#+P 3.25 —
Pane of 20 15.50 —

See No. 3895e.

BLACK HERITAGE SERIES

Patricia Roberts Harris (1924-85), First Black Woman Cabinet Secretary — A2603

Designed by Richard Sheaff.
Printed by Ashton-Potter (USA) Ltd.

LITHOGRAPHED
Sheets of 180 in nine panes of 20
Serpentine Die Cut 11½x11¼

2000, Jan. 27 **Tagged**
Self-Adhesive

3371 A2603 33c **indigo** .65 .25
P# block of 4, 4#+P 2.75
Pane of 20 13.50

SUBMARINES

S Class — A2604

Los Angeles Class A2605

Ohio Class — A2606

USS Holland A2607

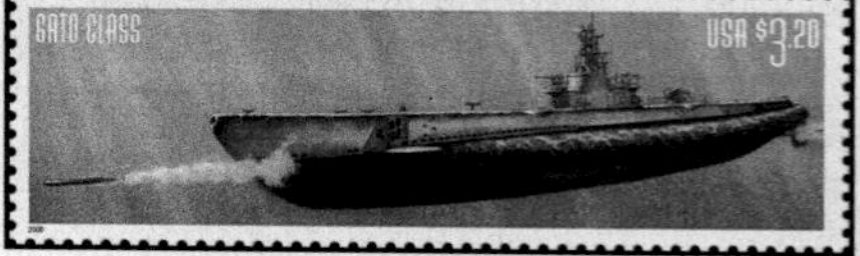

Gato Class — A2608

Illustration of No. 3377 reduced.

Designed by Carl Herrman.
Printed by Banknote Corporation of America.

LITHOGRAPHED
Sheets of 180 in nine panes of 20

2000, Mar. 27 **Tagged** ***Perf. 11***

3372 A2605 33c **multicolored,** with microprinted "USPS" at base of sail .75 .25
P# block of 4, 4#+B 3.00 —
Pane of 20 15.00 —

BOOKLET STAMPS

3373 A2604 22c **multicolored** .75 .75
3374 A2605 33c **multicolored,** no microprinting 1.00 1.00
3375 A2606 55c **multicolored** 1.50 1.25
3376 A2607 60c **multicolored** 1.75 1.50
3377 A2608 $3.20 **multicolored** 10.00 5.00
a. Booklet pane of 5, #3373-3377 15.00 —

No. 3377a was issued with two types of text in the selvage.

PACIFIC COAST RAIN FOREST

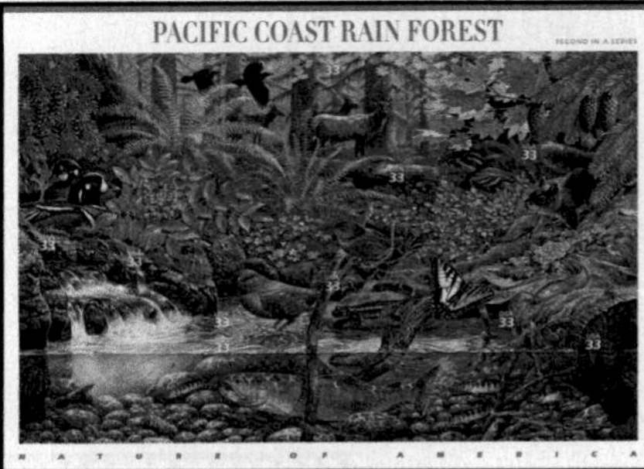

A2609

Illustration reduced.

Designed by Ethel Kessler.
Printed by Banknote Corporation of America.

Designs: a, Harlequin duck. b, Dwarf oregongrape, snail-eating ground beetle. c, American dipper, horiz. d, Cutthroat trout, horiz. e, Roosevelt elk. f, Winter wren. g, Pacific giant salamander, Rough-skinned newt. h, Western tiger swallowtail, horiz. i, Douglas squirrel, foliose lichen. j, Foliose lichen, banana slug.

LITHOGRAPHED
Sheets of 60 in six panes of 10

Serpentine Die Cut 11¼x11½, 11½ (horiz. stamps)
2000, Mar. 29 Tagged

Self-Adhesive

3378	A2609 Pane of 10	10.00	
a.-j.	33c any single	1.00	.50

Uncut press sheets of No. 3378 were made available for sale. See note after No. 2868.

LOUISE NEVELSON (1899-1988), SCULPTOR

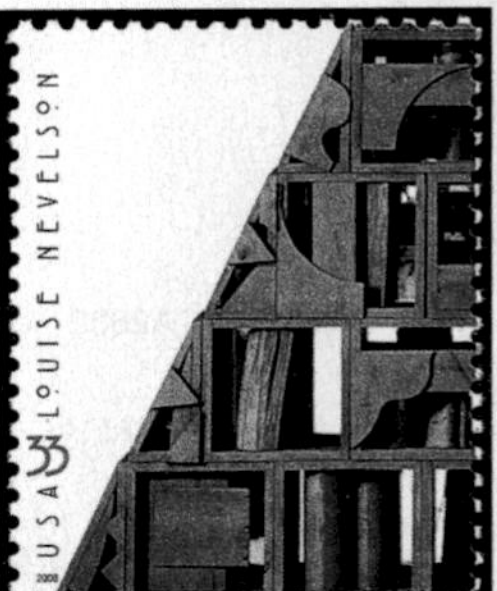

Silent Music I — A2610

Royal Tide I — A2611

Black Chord — A2612

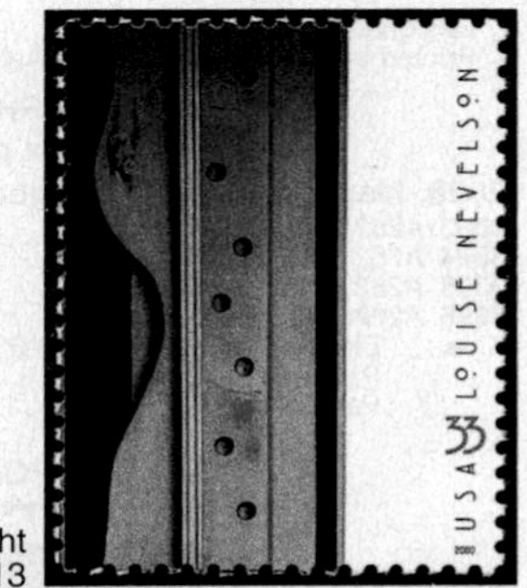

Nightsphere-Light A2613

Dawn's Wedding Chapel I — A2614

Designed by Ethel Kessler.
Printed by Ashton-Potter (USA) Ltd.

LITHOGRAPHED
Sheets of 80 in four panes of 20.

2000, Apr. 6 Tagged *Perf. 11x11¼*

3379	A2610 33c **multicolored**	.65	.25
3380	A2611 33c **multicolored**	.65	.25
3381	A2612 33c **multicolored**	.65	.25
3382	A2613 33c **multicolored**	.65	.25
3383	A2614 33c **multicolored**	.65	.25
a.	Strip of 5, #3379-3383	3.25	—
	P# block of 10, 4#+P	6.50	—
	Pane of 20	13.00	—

HUBBLE SPACE TELESCOPE IMAGES

Eagle Nebula — A2615

Ring Nebula — A2616

Lagoon Nebula — A2617

Egg Nebula — A2618

Galaxy NGC 1316 — A2619

Designed by Phil Jordan. Printed at American Packaging Corp. for Sennett Security Products.

PHOTOGRAVURE
Sheets of 120 in six panes of 20.

2000, Apr. 10 Tagged *Perf. 11*

3384	A2615 33c **multicolored**	.65	.25
3385	A2616 33c **multicolored**	.65	.25
3386	A2617 33c **multicolored**	.65	.25
3387	A2618 33c **multicolored**	.65	.25
3388	A2619 33c **multicolored**	.65	.25
a.	Strip of 5, #3384-3388	3.25	2.00
	P# block of 10, 6#+S	6.50	—
	Pane of 20	13.00	—
b.	As "a," imperf	*900.00*	
	As "b," pane of 20	*4,500.*	

AMERICAN SAMOA

Samoan Double Canoe A2620

Designed by Howard Paine.
Printed by Ashton-Potter (USA) Ltd.

LITHOGRAPHED
Sheets of 120 in six panes of 20

2000, Apr. 17 Tagged *Perf. 11*

3389	A2620 33c **multicolored**	.85	.25
	P# block of 4, 4#+P	4.25	—
	Pane of 20	21.00	—

LIBRARY OF CONGRESS

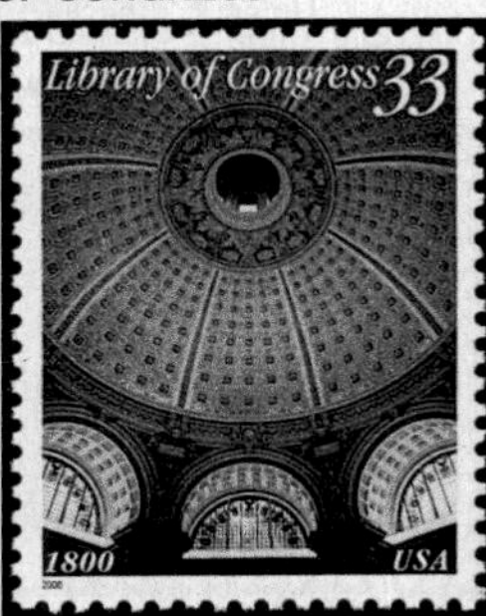

Interior Dome and Arched Windows in Main Reading Room, Thomas Jefferson Building — A2621

Designed by Ethel Kessler.
Printed by Ashton-Potter (USA) Ltd.

LITHOGRAPHED
Sheets of 120 in six panes of 20

2000, Apr. 24 Tagged *Perf. 11*

3390	A2621 33c **multicolored**	.65	.25
	P# block of 4, 5#+P	2.60	—
	Pane of 20	13.00	—

ROAD RUNNER & WILE E. COYOTE

A2622

Designed by Ed Wleczyk, Warner Bros.
Printed by Banknote Corp. of America, Inc.

LITHOGRAPHED

2000, Apr. 26 Tagged *Serpentine Die Cut 11*
Self-Adhesive

3391	Pane of 10 #3391a	10.00	
a.	A2622 33c single	.85	.25
b.	Pane of 9 #3391a	8.00	
c.	Pane of 1 #3391a	1.50	
d.	All die cutting omitted, pane of 10	2,250.	

Die cutting on #3391b does not extend through the backing paper.

Uncut press sheets of No. 3391 were made available for sale. Values: top sheet of 60 with P# on reverse, $60; bottom sheet of 60 with P#, $62.50; cross-gutter block of 7, $17.50; pairs with gutters between, $3.50 each. See note after No. 2868.

3392	Pane of 10, #3392c, 9 #3392a	30.00	
a.	A2622 33c single	2.75	
b.	Pane of 9 #3392a	25.00	
c.	Pane of 1, no die cutting	5.00	

Die cutting on #3392a extends through the backing paper. Used examples of No. 3392a are identical to those of No. 3391a.

Nos. 3391b-3391c and 3392b-3392c are separated by a vertical line of microperforations.

DISTINGUISHED SOLDIERS

Maj. Gen. John L. Hines (1868-1968) A2623

Gen. Omar N. Bradley (1893-1981) A2624

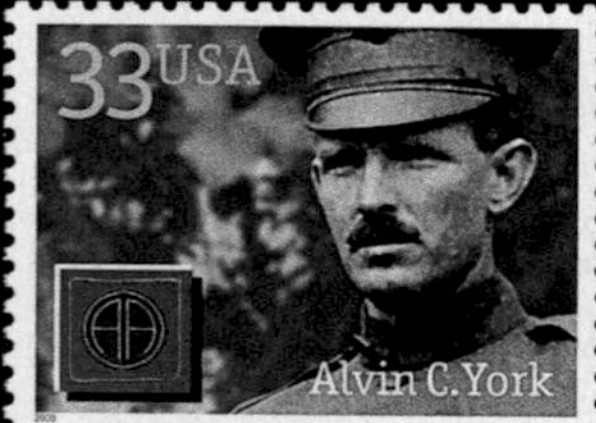

Sgt. Alvin C. York (1887-1964) A2625

Second Lt. Audie L. Murphy (1924-71)

Designed by Phil Jordan.
Printed by Sterling Sommer for Ashton-Potter (USA) Ltd.

LITHOGRAPHED
Sheets of 120 in six panes of 20

2000, May 3 Tagged *Perf. 11*

3393 A2623 33c **multicolored**		.70	.25
3394 A2624 33c **multicolored**		.70	.25
3395 A2625 33c **multicolored**		.70	.25
3396 A2626 33c **multicolored**		.70	.25
a.	Block or strip of 4, #3393-3396	2.80	1.50
	P# block of 4, 4#+P	2.80	—
	Pane of 20	14.00	—

SUMMER SPORTS

Runners A2627

Designed by Richard Sheaff.
Printed by Ashton-Potter (USA) Ltd.

LITHOGRAPHED
Sheets of 120 in six panes of 20

2000, May 5 Tagged *Perf. 11*

3397 A2627 33c **multicolored**		.65	.25
	P# block of 4, 4#+P	2.60	—
	Pane of 20	13.00	—

ADOPTION Ⓢ

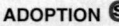

Stick Figures — A2628

Designed by Greg Berger.
Printed by Banknote Corporation of America.

LITHOGRAPHED
Sheets of 120 in six panes of 20

2000, May 10 Tagged *Serpentine Die Cut 11½*
Self-Adhesive

3398 A2628 33c **multicolored**		.65	.25
	P# block of 4, 5#+B	2.60	
	Pane of 20	13.00	
a.	Die cutting omitted, pair	*2,500.*	

See note after No. 1549.

YOUTH TEAM SPORTS

Basketball — A2629

Football — A2630

Soccer — A2631

Baseball — A2632

Designed by Derry Noyes.
Printed by Sterling Sommer for Ashton-Potter (USA) Ltd.

LITHOGRAPHED
Sheets of 120 in six panes of 20

2000, May 27 Tagged *Perf. 11*

3399 A2629 33c **multicolored**		.70	.25
3400 A2630 33c **multicolored**		.70	.25
3401 A2631 33c **multicolored**		.70	.25
3402 A2632 33c **multicolored**		.70	.25
a.	Block or strip of 4, #3399-3402	2.80	1.75
	P# block of 4, 4#+P	2.80	—
	Pane of 20	14.00	—

THE STARS AND STRIPES

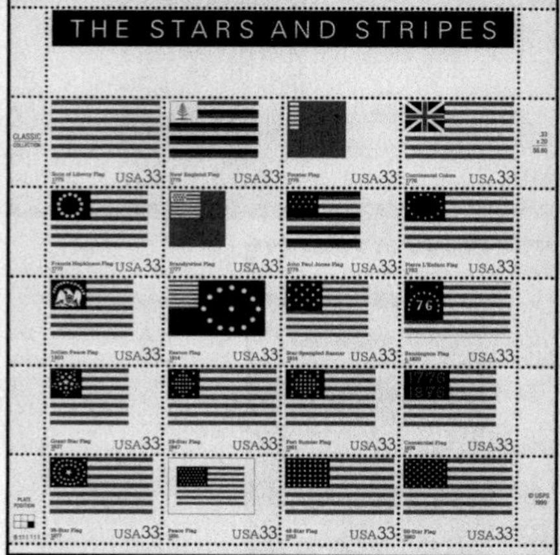

A2633

Illustration reduced.

Designed by Richard Sheaff.
Printed by Banknote Corp. of America.

Designs: a, Sons of Liberty Flag, 1775. b, New England Flag, 1775. c, Forster Flag, 1775. d, Continental Colors, 1776. e,

Indian Peace Flag, 1803. j, Easton Flag, 1814. k, Star-Spangled Banner, 1814. l, Bennington Flag, c. 1820. m, Great Star Flag, 1837. n, 29-Star Flag, 1847. o, Fort Sumter Flag, 1861. p, Centennial Flag, 1876. q, 38-Star Flag, 1877. r, Peace Flag, 1891. s, 48-Star Flag, 1912. t, 50-Star Flag, 1960.

LITHOGRAPHED

2000, June 14 Tagged *Perf. 10½x11*

3403	A2633	Pane of 20	15.00	11.00
a.-t.		33c any single	.75	.50

Inscriptions on the back of each stamp describe the flag.

Uncut press sheets of No. 3403 were made available for sale. Values: cross-gutter block of 20, $30; pairs with gutters between, $3.25 each. See note after No. 2868.

BERRIES

Blueberries — A2634

Strawberries — A2635

Blackberries — A2636

Raspberries — A2637

Designed by Howard Paine. Printed by Guilford Gravure.

See designs A2550-A2553.

PHOTOGRAVURE
COIL STAMPS

Serpentine Die Cut 8½ Horiz.

2000, June 16 Tagged

Self-Adhesive

3404	A2634 33c **multicolored**		3.50	.25
3405	A2635 33c **multicolored**		3.50	.25
3406	A2636 33c **multicolored**		3.50	.25
3407	A2637 33c **multicolored**		3.50	.25
a.	Strip of 4, #3404-3407		15.00	
	P# strip of 5, 2 #3404, 1 each #3405-3407, #G1111		30.00	
	P# strip of 9, 2 each #3404-3405, 3407, 3 #3406, #G1111		45.00	
	P# single (#3406), #G1111		—	1.25

Nos. 3404-3407 are linerless coils issued without backing paper. The adhesive is strong and can remove the ink from stamps in the roll.

LEGENDS OF BASEBALL

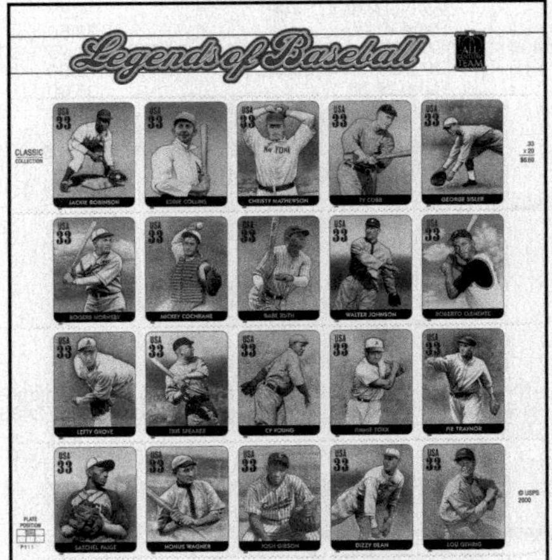

A2638

Illustration reduced.

Designed by Phil Jordan. Printed by Ashton-Potter (USA) Ltd.

Designs: a, Jackie Robinson. b, Eddie Collins. c, Christy Mathewson. d, Ty Cobb. e, George Sisler. f, Rogers Hornsby. g, Mickey Cochrane. h, Babe Ruth. i, Walter Johnson. j, Roberto Clemente. k, Lefty Grove. l, Tris Speaker. m, Cy Young. n, Jimmie Foxx. o, Pie Traynor. p, Satchel Paige. q, Honus Wagner. r, Josh Gibson. s, Dizzy Dean. t, Lou Gehrig.

LITHOGRAPHED

Sheets of 120 in six panes of 20

2000, July 6 Tagged *Serpentine Die Cut 11¼*

Self-Adhesive

3408	A2638	Pane of 20	15.00	
a.-t.		33c any single	.75	.50

Uncut press sheets of No. 3408 were made available for sale. Values: cross-gutter block of 20, $32.50; pairs with gutters between, $3 each. See note after No. 2868.

SPACE

Souvenir Sheets

Probing the Vastness of Space — A2639

Exploring the Solar System — A2640

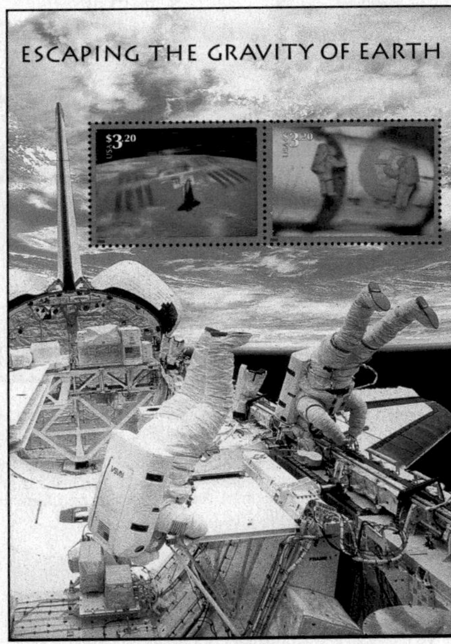

Escaping the Gravity of Earth — A2641

Space Achievement and Exploration — A2642

Landing on the Moon — A2643

Illustrations reduced.

Designed by Richard Sheaff. Printed by American Packaging Corporation for Sennett Security Products.

Designs: No. 3409: a, Hubble Space Telescope. b, Radio interferometer very large array, New Mexico. c, Optical and infrared telescopes, Keck Observatory, Hawaii. d, Optical telescopes, Cerro Tololo Observatory, Chile. e, Optical telescope, Mount Wilson Observatory, California. f, Radio telescope, Arecibo Observatory, Puerto Rico.

No. 3410: a, Sun and corona. b, Cross-section of sun. c, Sun and earth. d, Sun and solar flare. e, Sun and clouds.

No. 3411: a, Space Shuttle and Space Station. b, Astronauts working in space.

PHOTOGRAVURE

2000 Tagged *Perf. 10½x11*

3409	A2639	Sheet of 6, *July 10*	15.00	7.00
a.-f.		60c any single	2.25	1.00

Perf. 10¾

3410	A2640	Sheet of 5 + label, *July 11*	17.50	10.00
a.-e.		$1 any single	3.00	1.75
f.		As No. 3410, imperf	*2,000.*	
g.		As No. 3410, with hologram from No. 3411b applied	*1,500.*	

Untagged

Photogravure with Hologram Affixed

Perf. 10½, 10¾ (#3412)

3411	A2641	Sheet of 2, *July 9*	22.50	10.00
a.-b.		$3.20 any single	10.00	4.00
c.		Hologram omitted on right stamp	—	
3412	A2642	**multicolored,** *July 7*	40.00	17.50
a.		$11.75 single	35.00	15.00
b.		Hologram omitted	—	
c.		Hologram omitted on No. 3412 in uncut sheet of 5 panes	—	
3413	A2643	**multicolored,** *July 8*	40.00	17.50
a.		$11.75 single	35.00	15.00
b.		Double hologram	*3,000.*	
c.		Double hologram on No. 3413 in uncut sheet of 5 panes	—	
d.		Hologram omitted on No. 3413 in uncut sheet of 5 panes	—	
		Nos. 3409-3413 (5)	135.00	62.00

The holograms on Nos. 3411-3413 scratch easily. Values are for examples with minimal scratches. Examples without scratches are worth more.

Warning: Soaking in water may affect holographic images.

Uncut press sheets containing Nos. 3409-3413 were made available for sale. Value, sheet of five panes, $140. See note after No. 2868.

STAMPIN' THE FUTURE CHILDREN'S STAMP DESIGN CONTEST WINNERS

By Zachary Canter
A2644

By Sarah Lipsey
A2645

By Morgan Hill — A2646

By Ashley Young
A2647

Designed by Richard Sheaff. Printed by Ashton-Potter (USA) Ltd.

LITHOGRAPHED

Sheets of 120 in six panes of 20

2000, July 13 Tagged *Serpentine Die Cut 11¼*

Self-Adhesive

3414	A2644	33c **multicolored**	.65	.30
3415	A2645	33c **multicolored**	.65	.30
3416	A2646	33c **multicolored**	.65	.30
3417	A2647	33c **multicolored**	.65	.30
a.		Horiz. strip of 4, #3414-3417	2.60	
		P# block of 8, 2 sets of 5#+P	5.25	
		Pane of 20	13.00	

Plate block may contain top label.

DISTINGUISHED AMERICANS

Gen. Joseph W. Stilwell (1883-1946)
A2650

Wilma Rudolph (1940-94), Athlete
A2652

Sen. Claude Pepper (1900-89)
A2656

Sen. Margaret Chase Smith (1897-1995)
A2657

James A. Michener (1907-97), Author — A2657a

Dr. Jonas Salk (1914-95), Polio Vaccine Pioneer — A2658

Harriet Beecher Stowe (1811-96), Author
A2660

Sen. Hattie Caraway (1878-1950)
A2661

Edward Trudeau (1848-1915), Phthisiologist — A2661a

Mary Lasker (1900-94), Philanthropist — A2661b

Edna Ferber (1887-1968), Writer — A2662

Edna Ferber (With Curving Shoulder) — A2663

Dr. Albert Sabin (1906-93), Polio Vaccine Pioneer — A2664

Designed by: 10c, 23c, 33c, 58c, 59c, 63c, 75c, Nos. 3431-3432, 83c, 87c Richard Sheaff; No. 3432A, Howard E. Paine, 78c, Ethel Kessler.

Printed by Banknote Corporation of America (#3420-3433). Ashton-Potter (USA) Ltd. (#3422, 3427, 3428, 3432A, 3234B 3434). Banknote Corporation of America for Sennett Security Products, (#3427A, 3430).

LITHOGRAPHED & ENGRAVED, LITHOGRAPHED (#3427A, 3432A, 3432B, 3436)

Sheets of 120 in six panes of 20

Sheets of 300 in 15 panes of 20 (#3427A)

Perf. 11 (#3420, 3426), Serpentine Die Cut 11¼x10¾ (#3422, 3430, 3432B), 11¼x11 (#3427A, 3428, 3432A, 3435), 11 (#3427, 3431), 11½x11 (#3432), 11x11¾ (#3433), 11¼ (#3434)

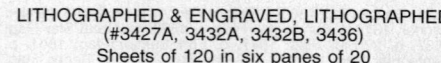

2000-09 Tagged

Self-Adhesive (All Except #3420, 3426)

3420	A2650	10c **red & black,** *Aug. 24*	.25	.25
		P# block of 4, 3#+B	.80	—
		Pane of 20	4.00	—
a.		Imperf, pair	*200.00*	
3422	A2652	23c **red & black,** *July 14, 2004*	.45	.25
		P# block of 4, 2#+P	1.80	
		Pane of 20	9.00	
a.		Imperf, pair	—	
3426	A2656	33c **red & black,** *Sept. 7*	.65	.25
		P# block of 4, 3#+B	2.60	—
		Pane of 20	13.00	—
3427	A2657	58c **red & black,** *June 13, 2007*	1.25	.25
		P# block of 4, 3#+P	5.50	
		Pane of 20	27.00	
b.		Black (engr.) omitted	*400.00*	
3427A	A2657a	59c **multicolored,** *May 12, 2008*	1.30	.25
		P# block of 4, 5#+S	6.50	
		Pane of 20	32.00	
c.		Blue, magenta and yellow omitted	*1,500.*	
d.		Blue and yellow omitted	—	

On No. 3427Ad, traces of magenta are present.

3428	A2658	63c **red & black** *Mar. 8, 2006*	1.25	.25
		P# block of 4, 3#+P	5.50	
		Pane of 20	27.00	
a.		Black (litho.) omitted	*275.00*	
3430	A2660	75c **red & black,** *June 13, 2007*	1.50	.25
		P# block of 4, 3#+S	6.00	
		Pane of 20	30.00	
3431	A2661	76c **red & black,** *Feb. 21, 2001*	1.50	.25
		P# block of 4, 3#+B	6.00	
		Pane of 20	30.00	
3432	A2661	76c **red & black**	4.00	*2.00*
		P# block of 4, 3#+B	16.00	
		Pane of 20	80.00	
3432A	A2661a	76c **multicolored,** *May 12, 2008* ⓢ	2.00	.25
		P# block of 4, 4#+P	8.50	
		Pane of 20	42.50	

See note after No. 1549.

3432B	A2661b	78c **multicolored,** *May 15, 2009*	1.60	.25
		P# block of 4, 4#+P	8.00	
		Pane of 20	38.50	
3433	A2662	83c **red & black,** *July 29, 2002*	1.70	.30
		P# block of 4, 3#+B1	7.00	
		Pane of 20	35.00	

The previously listed "Big Mouth" flaw on No. 3433 has been discovered to be not a constant plate flaw but rather the result of extraneous matter on the plate affecting a reported 15 panes before the matter fell off, or was removed from, the plate.

3434	A2663	83c **red & black,** *Aug. 2003*	1.60	.30
		P# block of 4, 3#+P	6.50	
		Pane of 20	32.50	
3435	A2664	87c **red & black,** *Mar. 8, 2006*	1.75	.30
		P# block of 4, 2#+S	7.00	
		Pane of 20	35.00	

BOOKLET STAMP

Serpentine Die Cut 11¼x10¾ on 3 Sides

Self-Adhesive

3436	A2652	23c **red & black,** *July 14, 2004*	.45	.25
a.		Booklet pane of 4	1.80	
b.		Booklet pane of 6	2.70	
c.		As "a" & "b" in cplt booklet of 10 (No. BK279A), die cutting omitted and peel strip intact, P#P44	—	
d.		Booklet pane of 10	4.50	
e.		As "d," die cutting omitted	—	—

The backing on No. 3436b has a different product number (672900) than that found on the lower portion of No. 3436d (673000).

CALIFORNIA STATEHOOD, 150TH ANNIV.

Big Sur and Iceplant — A2668

Designed by Carl Herrman.
Printed by Avery Dennison.

PHOTOGRAVURE
Sheets of 200 in 10 panes of 20

2000, Sept. 8 **Tagged** ***Serpentine Die Cut 11***
Self-Adhesive

3438 A2668 33c **multicolored**	.75	.25
P# block of 4, 5#+V	3.00	
Pane of 20	15.00	

DEEP SEA CREATURES

Fanfin Anglerfish A2669

Sea Cucumber A2670

Fangtooth A2671

Amphipod A2672

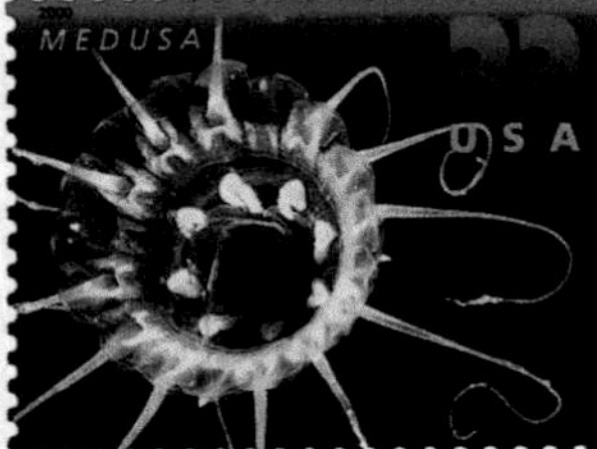

Medusa A2673

Designed by Ethel Kessler.
Printed by American Packaging Corp. for Sennett Security Products.

PHOTOGRAVURE
Sheets of 135 in nine panes of 15

2000, Oct. 2 **Tagged** ***Perf. 10x10¼***

3439 A2669 33c **multicolored**	.75	.25
3440 A2670 33c **multicolored**	.75	.25
3441 A2671 33c **multicolored**	.75	.25
3442 A2672 33c **multicolored**	.75	.25
3443 A2673 33c **multicolored**	.75	.25
a. Vert. strip of 5, #3439-3443	3.75	2.00
Pane of 15, 4#+S	11.25	—

See note under No. 3292 regarding lack of plate block listing.
Uncut press sheets of Nos. 3439-3443 were made available for sale. Values: cross-gutter block of 10, $20; pairs with gutters between, $3 each. See note after No. 2868.

LITERARY ARTS SERIES

Thomas Wolfe (1900-38), Novelist A2674

Designed by Phil Jordan.
Printed by Ashton-Potter (USA) Ltd.

LITHOGRAPHED
Sheets of 120 in six panes of 20

2000, Oct. 3 **Tagged** ***Perf. 11***

3444 A2674 33c **multicolored**	.65	.25
P# block of 4, 5#+P	2.60	—
Pane of 20	13.00	—

WHITE HOUSE, 200TH ANNIV.

A2675

Designed by Derry Noyes.
Printed by Ashton-Potter (USA) Ltd.

LITHOGRAPHED
Sheets of 180 in nine panes of 20

2000, Oct. 18 **Tagged** ***Serpentine Die Cut 11¼***
Self-Adhesive

3445 A2675 33c **multicolored**	1.00	.25
P# block of 4, 4#+P	4.00	
Pane of 20	20.00	

LEGENDS OF HOLLYWOOD

Edward G. Robinson (1893-1973), Actor — A2676

Designed by Howard Paine.
Printed by American Packaging Corporation for Sennett Security Products.

PHOTOGRAVURE
Sheets of 120 in six panes of 20

2000, Oct. 24 **Tagged** ***Perf. 11***

3446 A2676 33c **multicolored**	1.60	.25
P# block of 4, 7#+S	7.50	—
Pane of 20	37.50	12.50

Perforations in corner of each stamp are star-shaped.
Uncut press sheets of No. 3446 were made available for sale. Values: cross-gutter block of 8, $32.50; pairs with gutters between, $5 each. See note after No. 2868.

New York Public Library Lion — A2677

Designed by Carl Herrman.
Printed by American Packaging Corporation for Sennett Security Products.

PHOTOGRAVURE
COIL STAMP
Serpentine Die Cut 11½ Vert.

2000, Nov. 9 **Untagged**
Self-Adhesive

3447 A2677 (10c) **multicolored,** "2000" year date	.25	.25
Pair	.40	
P# strip of 5, #S11111, S22222, S33333, S44444, S66666, S77777	2.25	
P# single, #S11111, S22222, S33333, S44444	—	1.50
P# single, #S66666	—	1.75
P# single, #S77777	—	1.90
a. "2003" year date	.25	.25
Pair	.40	
P# strip of 5, #S55555	2.75	
P# single, #S55555	—	2.00
b. As No. 3447, prephosphored coated paper with surface tagging showing a solid appearance (error)		—
P# single, #S66666		—

No. 3447 also is known with extremely faint phosphor splotches. No. 3447b has full-strength tagging. Values with faint tagging: unused and used singles, $2; P# strip of 5, #S33333 and S44444 $10 each, #S77777 $25; P# single used, #S33333 and S44444 $20 each, #77777 $20.
See No. 3769.

Flag Over Farm — A2678

Designed by Richard Sheaff.
Printed by Sterling Sommer for Ashton-Potter (USA) Ltd. (#3448), Ashton-Potter (USA) Ltd. (#3449), Avery Dennison (#3450).

LITHOGRAPHED (#3448-3449), PHOTOGRAVURE (#3450)
Sheets of 120 in six panes of 20

2000, Dec. 15 **Tagged** ***Perf. 11¼***

3448 A2678 (34c) **multicolored**	1.00	.25
P# block of 4, 4# + P	10.00	—
Pane of 20	45.00	—

Self-Adhesive
Serpentine Die Cut 11¼

3449 A2678 (34c) **multicolored**	1.00	.25
P# block of 4, 4# + P	6.50	
Pane of 20	30.00	

Booklet Stamp
Self-Adhesive
Serpentine Die Cut 8 on 2, 3 or 4 Sides

3450 A2678 (34c) **multicolored**	.85	.25
a. Booklet pane of 18	16.00	
b. Die cutting omitted, pair	—	

A2679

Statue of Liberty — A2680

Designed by Derry Noyes.
Printed by Avery Dennison (#3451), Bureau of Engraving and Printing (#3452-3453).

PHOTOGRAVURE
Serpentine Die Cut 11 on 2, 3 or 4 Sides

2000, Dec. 15 **Tagged**
Self-Adhesive (#3451, 3453)
Booklet Stamp

3451 A2679 (34c) **multicolored**	1.10	.25
a. Booklet pane of 20	22.00	
b. Booklet pane of 4	4.40	
Booklet pane of 4 containing P# single	4.50	
P# single, #V1111, V2222	1.50	.70
c. Booklet pane of 6	6.60	
d. As "a," die cutting omitted	—	

The plate # single in No. 3451b is the lower right stamp of the right pane of 4 of the booklet.

Coil Stamps
Perf. 9¾ Vert.

3452 A2680 (34c) **multicolored**	1.10	.25
Pair	1.40	.30
P# strip of 5, #1111	5.00	—

P# single, same # — 2.25

Serpentine Die Cut 10 Vert.

3453 A2680 (34c) **multicolored**, small date .70 .25
Pair 1.40
P# strip of 5, #1111 6.50
P# single, same # — 1.50
a. Die cutting omitted, pair *300.00*
b. Large date .75 .25
Pair 1.50
P# strip of 5, #1111 7.25
P# single, same # — 1.50

The date on No. 3453 is 1.4mm long, on No. 3453b 1.55mm long and darker in color.

A2681

A2682

A2683

Flowers — A2684

Designed by Derry Noyes.
Printed by American Packaging Corporation for Sennett Security Products (#3454-3461), Guilford Gravure for Banknote Corporation of America, Inc. (#3462-3465).

PHOTOGRAVURE

Serpentine Die Cut 10½x10¾ on 2 or 3 Sides

2000, Dec. 15 **Tagged**

Booklet Stamps

Self-Adhesive

3454 A2681 (34c) **purple & multi** 1.10 .25
3455 A2682 (34c) **tan & multi** 1.10 .25
3456 A2683 (34c) **green & multi** 1.10 .25
3457 A2684 (34c) **red & multi** 1.10 .25
a. Block of 4, #3454-3457 4.40
b. Booklet pane of 4, #3454-3457 4.40
c. Booklet pane of 6, #3456, 3457, 2 each #3454-3455 7.00
d. Booklet pane of 6, #3454, 3455, 2 each #3456-3457 7.00
e. Booklet pane of 20, 5 each #3454-3457 + label 22.50

No. 3457e is a double-sided booklet pane, with 12 stamps on one side and eight stamps plus label on the other side.

Serpentine Die Cut 11½x11¾ on 2 or 3 Sides

3458 A2681 (34c) **purple & multi** 5.00 .25
3459 A2682 (34c) **tan & multi** 5.00 .25
3460 A2683 (34c) **green & multi** 5.00 .25
3461 A2684 (34c) **red & multi** 5.00 .25
a. Block of 4, #3458-3461 20.00
b. Booklet pane of 20, 2 each #3461a, 3 each #3457a 55.00
c. Booklet pane of 20, 2 each #3457a, 3 each #3461a 90.00

Nos. 3461b and 3461c are double-sided booklet panes, with 12 stamps on one side and eight stamps plus label on the other side.

Coil Stamps

Serpentine Die Cut 8½ Vert.

3462 A2683 (34c) **green & multi** 4.50 .25
3463 A2684 (34c) **red & multi** 4.50 .25
3464 A2682 (34c) **tan & multi** 4.50 .25
3465 A2681 (34c) **purple & multi** 4.50 .25
a. Strip of 4, #3462-3465 20.00
P# strip of 5, 2 #3462, 1 each #3463-3465, P#B1111 27.50
P# strip of 9, 2 each #3462-3463, 3465, 3 #3464, same P# 45.00
P# single (#3464) — 1.25

Lettering on No. 3462 has black outline not found on No. 3456. Zeroes of "2000" are rounder on Nos. 3454-3457 than on Nos. 3462-3465.

Statue of Liberty
A2685

George Washington
A2686

American
Buffalo — A2687

Flag Over
Farm — A2688

Statue of
Liberty — A2689

A2690

A2691

A2692

Flowers — A2693

Apple — A2694

Orange — A2695

Eagle — A2696

Capitol
Dome — A2697

Washington
Monument — A2698

Designed by Carl Herrman (#3467, 3468, 3471, 3471A, 3475, 3484, 3484A), Richard Sheaff (#3468A, 3469, 3470, 3475A, 3482-3483, 3495), Derry Noyes (#3466, 3472-3473, 3476, 3477-3481, 3485, 3487-3490), Ned Seidler (#3491-3494).

Printed by Sterling Sommer for Ashton-Potter (USA) Ltd. (#3467), Avery Dennison (#3468, 3475, 3485, 3495) Ashton-Potter (USA) Ltd. (#3469-3470, 3482-3484A), American Packaging Corporation for Sennett Security Printers (#3471, 3471A, 3487-3490), Bureau of Engraving and Printing (#3466, 3476-3477), Guilford Gravure, Inc. for Banknote Corporation of America (#3475A, 3478-3481), Banknote Corporation of America (#3468A, 3472-3473, 3491-3494).

PHOTOGRAVURE

Serpentine Die Cut 9¾ Vert.

2001, Jan. 7 **Tagged**

Coil Stamp

Self-Adhesive

3466 A2685 34c **multicolored** .70 .25
Pair 1.40
P# strip of 5, #1111, 2222 5.00
P# single, same # — 2.50

Sheets of 400 in four panes of 100 (#3467), Sheets of 200 in 10 panes of 20 (#3468), Sheets of 200 in two panes of 100 (#3469), Sheets of 120 in six panes of 20 (#3468A, 3470-3473), Sheets of 160 in eight panes of 20 (#3471A)

Self-Adhesive (#3468-3468A, 3470-3473)

2001 **Photo.** **Tagged** ***Perf. 11¼x11***

3467 A2687 21c **multicolored**, *Sept. 20* .50 .25
P# block of 4, 6#+P 27.50 —

Serpentine Die Cut 11

3468 A2687 21c **multicolored**, *Feb. 22* .50 .25
P# block of 4, 4#+V 4.00
Pane of 20 18.00

Litho.

Serpentine Die Cut 11¼x11¾

3468A A2686 23c **green**, *Sept. 20* .50 .25
P# block of 4, 3#+B 3.00
Pane of 20 14.00

Photo.

Perf. 11¼

3469 A2688 34c **multicolored**, *Feb. 7* .75 .25
P# block of 4, 4#+P 25.00 —

Serpentine Die Cut 11¼

3470 A2688 34c **multicolored**, *Mar. 6* 1.00 .25
P# block of 4, 4#+P 7.50
Pane of 20 34.00

Serpentine Die Cut 10¾

3471 A2696 55c **multicolored**, *Feb. 22* 1.10 .25
P# block of 4, 5#+S 4.40
Pane of 20 22.00
3471A A2696 57c **multicolored**, *Sept. 20* 1.10 .25
P# block of 4, 5#+S 4.40
Pane of 20 22.00

Serpentine Die Cut 11¼x11½

Litho.

3472 A2697 $3.50 **multicolored**, *Jan. 29* 7.00 2.00
P# block of 4, 4#+B 28.00
Pane of 20 140.00
a. Die cutting omitted, pair *500.00*
3473 A2698 $12.25 **multicolored**, *Jan. 29* 22.50 10.00
P# block of 4, 4#+B 90.00
Pane of 20 450.00

Hidden images can be seen on Nos. 3472 and 3473 when viewed with a special "Stamp Decoder" lens sold by the USPS. No. 3472, PRIORITY MAIL; No. 3473, EXPRESS MAIL.

COIL STAMPS

Self-Adhesive (#3475-3475A, 3477-3481)

Photo.

Serpentine Die Cut 8½ Vert.

3475 A2687 21c **multicolored**, *Feb. 22* .50 .25
Pair 1.00 .50
P# strip of 5, #V1111, V2222 2.50 —
P# single, same # — 1.00
3475A A2686 23c **green**, *Sept. 20* .75 .25
Pair 1.50
P# strip of 5, #B11 3.25
P# single, same # — .85

Compare No. 3475A ("2001" date at lower left) with No. 3617 ("2002" date at lower left).

Perf. 9¾ Vert.

3476 A2685 34c **multicolored,** prephosphored coated paper, *Feb. 7* .90 .25
Pair 1.80 .50
P# strip of 5, #1111 5.50 —
P# single, #1111 — 2.75

No. 3476 exists on two types of surface-tagged paper that exhibit either a solid or a grainy solid appearance.

Serpentine Die Cut 9¾ Vert.

3477 A2685 34c **multicolored,** *Feb. 7* .80 .25
Pair 1.60 .50
P# strip of 5, #1111, 2222, 3333, 4444, 5555, 6666 5.00 —
P# single, same # — 1.00
P# strip of 5, #7777 12.00 —
P# single, #7777 — 7.00
a. Die cutting omitted, pair *65.00*

No. 3477 has right angle corners and backing paper as high as the stamp. No. 3466 has rounded corners and is on backing paper larger than the stamp.

Serpentine Die Cut 8½ Vert.

3478 A2690 34c **green & multi,** *Feb. 7* 1.50 .25
3479 A2691 34c **red & multi,** *Feb. 7* 1.50 .25
3480 A2692 34c **tan & multi,** *Feb. 7* 1.50 .25
3481 A2693 34c **purple & multi,** *Feb. 7* 1.50 .25
a. Strip of 4, #3478-3481 6.00
P# strip of 5, 2 #3478, 1 each #3479-3481, P#B1111, B2111, B2122, B2211, B2222 10.00
P# strip of 9, 3 #3480, 2 each #3478-3479, 3481, P# B1111, B2111, B2122, B2211, B2222 15.00 —
P# single, (#3480), same # — 2.00

BOOKLET STAMPS

Litho.

Self-Adhesive

Serpentine Die Cut 11¼x11 on 3 Sides

3482 A2686 20c **dark carmine,** *Feb. 22* .55 .25
a. Booklet pane of 10 5.50
b. Booklet pane of 4 2.20
c. Booklet pane of 6 3.30

Serpentine Die Cut 10½x11 on 3 Sides

3483 A2686 20c **dark carmine,** *Feb. 22* 5.50 1.25
a. Booklet pane of 4, 2 #3482 at L, 2 #3483 at R 12.50
b. Booklet pane of 6, 3 #3482 at L, 3 #3483 at R 20.00
c. Booklet pane of 10, 5 #3482 at L, 5 #3483 at R 30.00
d. Booklet pane of 4, 2 #3483 at L, 2 #3482 at R 12.50
e. Booklet pane of 6, 3 #3483 at L, 3 #3482 at R 20.00
f. Booklet pane of 10, 5 #3483 at L, 5 #3482 at R 30.00
g. Pair, #3482 at L, #3483 at R 6.00
h. Pair, #3483 at L, #3482 at R 6.00

Serpentine Die Cut 11¼ on 3 Sides

3484 A2687 21c **multicolored,** *Sept. 20* .60 .25
b. Booklet pane of 4 2.40
c. Booklet pane of 6 3.60
d. Booklet pane of 10 6.00

Serpentine Die Cut 10½x11¼

3484A A2687 21c **multicolored,** *Sept. 20* 5.50 1.50
e. Booklet pane of 4, 2 #3484 at L, 2 #3484A at R 12.50
f. Booklet pane of 6, 3 #3484 at L, 3 #3484A at R 20.00
g. Booklet pane of 10, 5 #3484 at L, 5 #3484A at R 30.00
h. Booklet pane of 4, 2 #3484A at L, 2 #3484 at R 12.50
i. Booklet pane of 6, 3 #3484A at L, 3 #3484 at R 20.00
j. Booklet pane of 10, 5 #3484A at L, 5 #3484 at R 30.00
k. Pair, #3484 at L, #3484A at R 6.00
l. Pair, #3484A at L, #3484 at R 6.00

Photo.

Serpentine Die Cut 11 on 2, 3 or 4 Sides

3485 A2689 34c **multicolored,** *Feb. 7* .70 .25
a. Booklet pane of 10 7.00
b. Booklet pane of 20 14.00
c. Booklet pane of 4 3.00
Booklet pane of 4 containing P# single 4.00
P# single, #V1111, V1122, V2212, V2222 1.50 1.50
P# single, #V1112, V1121 — —
d. Booklet pane of 6 4.50
e. Die cutting omitted, pair (from No. 3485b) —
f. As "e," booklet pane of 20 —

The plate # single in No. 3485c is the lower right stamp of the right pane of 4 of the booklet.

Serpentine Die Cut 10½x10¾ on 2 or 3 Sides

3487 A2693 34c **purple & multi,** *Feb. 7* .85 .25
3488 A2692 34c **tan & multi,** *Feb. 7* .85 .25
3489 A2690 34c **green & multi,** *Feb. 7* .85 .25
3490 A2691 34c **red & multi,** *Feb. 7* .85 .25
a. Block of 4, #3487-3490 3.50
b. Booklet pane of 4, #3487-3490 3.50
c. Booklet pane of 6, #3489-3490, 2 each #3487-3488 5.00
d. Booklet pane of 6, #3487-3488, 2 each #3489-3490 5.00
e. Booklet pane of 20, 5 each #3490a + label 20.00

No. 3490e is a double-sided booklet pane, with 12 stamps on one side and eight stamps plus label on the other side.

Litho.

Serpentine Die Cut 11¼ on 2, 3 or 4 Sides

3491 A2694 34c **multicolored,** *Mar. 6* .70 .25
3492 A2695 34c **multicolored,** *Mar. 6* .70 .25
a. Pair, #3491-3492 1.40
b. Booklet pane, 10 each #3491-3492 14.00
c. As "a," black ("34 USA") omitted —
d. As "a," die cutting omitted *1,100.*
e. As "b," die cutting omitted *5,500.*
f. As "b," right four stamps yellow omitted *3,500.*

Serpentine Die Cut 11½x10¾ on 2 or 3 Sides

3493 A2694 34c **multicolored,** *May* 1.05 .25
3494 A2695 34c **multicolored,** *May* 1.05 .25
a. Pair, #3493-3494 2.10
b. Booklet pane, 2 each #3493-3494 4.20
Booklet pane, 2 each #3493-3494, containing P# single 5.50
P# single, #B1111 2.25 2.00
c. Booklet pane, 3 each #3493-3494, #3493 at UL 6.30
d. Booklet pane, 3 each #3493-3494, #3494 at UL 6.30

Serpentine Die Cut 8 on 2, 3, or 4 Sides

3495 A2688 34c **multicolored,** *Dec. 17* 1.10 .25
a. Booklet pane of 18 18.00

See Nos. 3616-3619, 3819.

LOVE

Rose, Apr. 20, 1763 Love Letter by John Adams — A2699

Rose, Apr. 20, 1763 Love Letter by John Adams — A2700

Rose, Aug. 11, 1763 Love Letter by Abigail Smith (Abigail Adams in 1764) — A2701

Designed by Lisa Catalone. Printed by Banknote Corporation of America, Inc.

LITHOGRAPHED

Sheets of 180 in nine panes of 20 (#3499)

Serpentine Die Cut 11¼ on 2, 3 or 4 Sides

2001 **Tagged**

Self-Adhesive

Booklet Stamps (Nos. 3496-3498)

3496 A2699 (34c) **multicolored,** *Jan. 19* 1.10 .25
a. Booklet pane of 20 22.00
b. Vert. pair, die cutting omitted between —

Serpentine Die Cut 11¼ on 2, 3 or 4 Sides

3497 A2700 34c **multicolored,** *Feb. 14* .90 .25
a. Booklet pane of 20 18.00
b. Vertical pair, die cutting omitted between —

Size: 18x21mm

Serpentine Die Cut 11½x10¾ on 2 or 3 Sides

3498 A2700 34c **multicolored,** *Feb. 14* .85 .25
a. Booklet pane of 4 3.50
Booklet pane of 4 containing P# single 5.50
P# single, #B1111 2.00 2.00
b. Booklet pane of 6 5.10

Plate number single on No. 3498 is on the lower left stamp of the bottom pane of 4 of the booklet.

Serpentine Die Cut 11¼

3499 A2701 55c **multicolored,** *Feb. 14* 1.10 .25
P# block of 4, 4#+B 4.50
Pane of 20 22.50

See No. 3551.

CHINESE NEW YEAR

Year of the Snake — A2702

Designed by Clarence Lee. Printed by Sterling Sommer for Ashton-Potter (USA) Ltd.

LITHOGRAPHED

Sheets of 180 in nine panes of 20

2001, Jan. 20 **Tagged** ***Perf. 11¼***

3500 A2702 34c **multicolored** .75 .25
P# block of 4, 5#+P 3.00 —
Pane of 20 15.00 —

See No. 3895f.

BLACK HERITAGE SERIES

Roy Wilkins (1901-81), Civil Rights Leader — A2703

Designed by Richard Sheaff. Printed by Ashton-Potter (USA) Ltd.

LITHOGRAPHED

Sheets of 180 in nine panes of 20

Serpentine Die Cut 11½x11¼

2001, Jan. 24 **Tagged**

Self-Adhesive

3501 A2703 34c **blue** .70 .25
P# block of 4, 2#+P 2.80
Pane of 20 14.00

AMERICAN ILLUSTRATORS

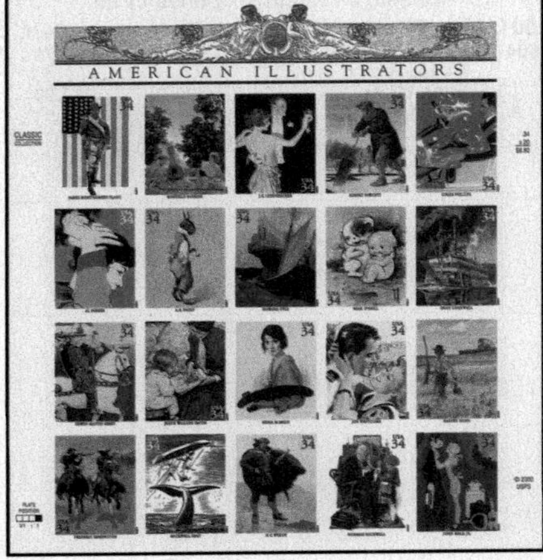

A2704

Illustration reduced.

Designed by Carl Herrman.
Printed by Avery Dennison.

No. 3502: a, Marine Corps poster "First in the Fight, Always Faithful," by James Montgomery Flagg. b, "Interlude (The Lute Players)," by Maxfield Parrish. c, Advertisement for Arrow Collars and Shirts, by J. C. Leyendecker. d, Advertisement for Carrier Corp. Refrigeration, by Robert Fawcett. e, Advertisement for Luxite Hosiery, by Coles Phillips. f, Illustration for correspondence school lesson, by Al Parker. g, "Br'er Rabbit," by A. B. Frost. h, "An Attack on a Galleon," by Howard Pyle. i, Kewpie and Kewpie Doodle Dog, by Rose O'Neill. j, Illustration for cover of True Magazine, by Dean Cornwell. k, "Galahad's Departure," by Edwin Austin Abbey. l, "The First Lesson," by Jessie Willcox Smith. m, Illustration for cover of McCall's Magazine, by Neysa McMein. n, "Back Home For Keeps," by Jon Whitcomb. o, "Something for Supper," by Harvey Dunn. p, "A Dash for the Timber," by Frederic Remington. q, Illustration for

"Moby Dick," by Rockwell Kent. r, "Captain Bill Bones," by N. C. Wyeth. s, Illustration for cover of The Saturday Evening Post, by Norman Rockwell. t, "The Girl He Left Behind," by John Held, Jr.

PHOTOGRAVURE
Sheets of 80 in four panes of 20

2001, Feb. 1 Tagged *Serpentine Die Cut 11¼*
Self-Adhesive

3502 A2704 Pane of 20 19.00
a.-t. 34c any single .90 .60

Uncut press sheets of No. 3502 were made available for sale. Values: block of 20 diff. stamps with vert. gutter btwn. any 2 columns, $40; pairs with vert. gutters btwn., $4 each. See note after No. 2868.

DIABETES AWARENESS

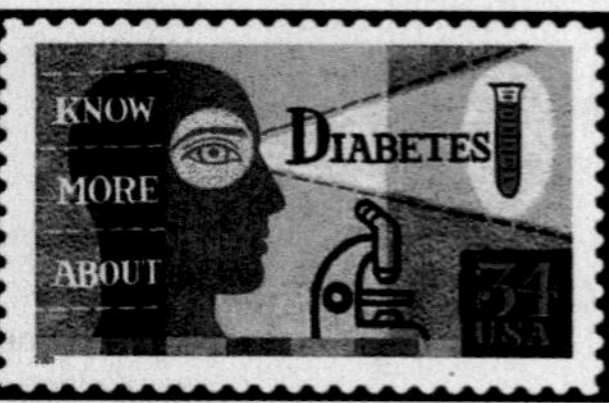

A2705

Designed by Richard Sheaff. Printed by Ashton-Potter (USA) Ltd.

LITHOGRAPHED
Sheets of 180 in nine panes of 20
Serpentine Die Cut 11¼x11½

2001, Mar. 16 Tagged
Self-Adhesive

3503 A2705 34c **multicolored** .65 .25
P# block of 4, 4#+P 2.60
Pane of 20 13.00

NOBEL PRIZE CENTENARY

Alfred Nobel and Obverse of Medals A2706

Designed by Olof Baldursdottir of Sweden. Printed by De La Rue Security Printing.

LITHOGRAPHED & ENGRAVED
Sheets of 120 in six panes of 20

2001, Mar. 22 Tagged *Perf. 11*

3504 A2706 34c **multicolored** .70 .25
P# block of 4, 3#+S 2.80 —
Pane of 20 14.00 —
a. Imperf, pair —

See Sweden No. 2415.

PAN-AMERICAN EXPOSITION INVERT STAMPS, CENT.

A2707

Illustration reduced.

No. 3505: Reproductions (dated 2001) of: a, #294a. b, #295a. c, #296a. d, Commemorative "cinderella" stamp depicting a buffalo.

Designed by Richard Sheaff. Printed by Banknote Corporation of America.

LITHOGRAPHED (#3505d), ENGRAVED (others)
Sheets of 28 in four panes of 7

2001, Mar. 29 *Perf. 12 (#3505d), 12½x12 (others)*
Tagged (#3505d), Untagged (others)

3505 A2707 Pane of 7, #3505a-3505c, 4 #3505d 10.00 7.00
a. A109 1c **green & black** .75 .25
b. A110 2c **carmine & black** .75 .25
c. A111 4c **deep red brown & black** .75 .25
d. 80c **red & blue** 1.90 .35
e. As #3505, all colors except black (vignettes) missing on a.-c. (CM) *15,000.*

On No. 3505e, the green, carmine and deep red brown frames appear 4mm above Nos. 3505a-3505c on the pane.

Uncut press sheets of No. 3505 were made available for sale. Value: pane with vert. gutter, 80c stamps at left, Nos. 3505a-3505c at right, $22.50. See note after No. 2868.

GREAT PLAINS PRAIRIE Ⓢ

A2708

Illustration reduced.

Designed by Ethel Kessler. Printed by Ashton-Potter (USA) Ltd.

No. 3506 — Wildlife and flowers: a, Pronghorns, Canada geese. b, Burrowing owls, American buffalos. c, American buffalo, Black-tailed prairie dogs, wild alfalfa, horiz. d, Black-tailed prairie dog, American buffalos,. e, Painted lady butterfly, American buffalo, prairie coneflowers, prairie wild roses, horiz. f, Western meadowlark, camel cricket, prairie coneflowers, prairie wild roses. g, Badger, harvester ants. h, Eastern short-horned lizard, plains pocket gopher. i, Plains spadefoot, dung beetle, prairie wild roses, horiz. j, Two-striped grasshopper, Ord's kangaroo rat.

LITHOGRAPHED
Sheets of 60 in six panes of 10

2001, Apr. 19 Tagged *Serpentine Die Cut 10*
Self-Adhesive

3506 A2708 Pane of 10 10.00
a.-j. 34c Any single 1.00 .50

Uncut press sheets of No. 3506 were made available for sale. See note after No. 2868.

See note after No. 1549.

PEANUTS COMIC STRIP

Snoopy A2709

Designed by Paige Braddock. Printed by Ashton-Potter (USA) Ltd.

LITHOGRAPHED
Sheets of 180 in nine panes of 20
Serpentine Die Cut 11¼x11½

2001, May 17 Tagged
Self-Adhesive

3507 A2709 34c **multicolored** .80 .25
P# block of 4, 5#+P 3.50
Pane of 20 17.50

HONORING VETERANS

A2710

Designed by Carl Herrman. Printed by Ashton-Potter (USA) Ltd.

LITHOGRAPHED
Sheets of 180 in nine panes of 20
Serpentine Die Cut 11¼x11½

2001, May 23 Tagged
Self-Adhesive

3508 A2710 34c **multicolored** .80 .25
P# block of 4, 4#+P 3.25
Pane of 20 16.50 11.00

FRIDA KAHLO (1907-54), PAINTER

Self-portrait — A2711

Designed by Richard Sheaff. Printed by Sterling Sommer for Ashton-Potter (USA) Ltd..

LITHOGRAPHED
Sheets of 80 in four panes of 20

2001, June 21 Tagged *Perf. 11¼*

3509 A2711 34c **multicolored** .70 .25
P# block of 4, 4#+P 3.25 —
Pane of 20 16.00 —

LEGENDARY PLAYING FIELDS

Ebbets Field — A2712

Tiger Stadium A2713

Crosley Field — A2714

Yankee Stadium A2715

Polo Grounds A2716

Forbes Field — A2717

Fenway Park — A2718

Comiskey Park — A2719

Shibe Park — A2720

Wrigley Field — A2721

Designed by Phil Jordan. Printed by Avery Dennison.

PHOTOGRAVURE
Sheets of 160 in eight panes of 20
Serpentine Die Cut 11¼x11½

2001, June 27	**Tagged**	**Self-Adhesive**	
3510 A2712 34c	**multicolored**	.90	.60
3511 A2713 34c	**multicolored**	.90	.60
3512 A2714 34c	**multicolored**	.90	.60
3513 A2715 34c	**multicolored**	.90	.60
3514 A2716 34c	**multicolored**	.90	.60
3515 A2717 34c	**multicolored**	.90	.60
3516 A2718 34c	**multicolored**	.90	.60
3517 A2719 34c	**multicolored**	.90	.60
3518 A2720 34c	**multicolored**	.90	.60
3519 A2721 34c	**multicolored**	.90	.60
a.	Block of 10, #3510-3519	9.00	
	P# block of 10, 4#+V	9.00	
	Pane of 20	18.00	

Uncut press sheets of Nos. 3510-3519 were made available for sale. Values: cross-gutter block of 12, $27.50; pairs with gutters between, $3 each. See note after No. 2868.

ATLAS STATUE, NEW YORK CITY

A2722

Designed by Kevin Newman. Printed by Banknote Corporation of America.

PHOTOGRAVURE
COIL STAMP
Serpentine Die Cut 8½ Vert.

2001, June 29		**Untagged**	
	Self-Adhesive		
3520 A2722 (10c)	**multicolored**, dated "2001"	.25	.25
	Pair	.40	
	P# strip of 5, #B1111	2.25	
	P# single, same #	—	1.40

No. 3520 is dated 2001. See No. 3770.

No. 3520 is known with extremely faint tagging, most likely from contamination in the paper-making process.

LEONARD BERNSTEIN (1918-90), CONDUCTOR

A2723

Designed by Howard Paine. Printed by Sterling Sommer for Ashton-Potter (USA) Ltd.

LITHOGRAPHED
Sheets of 180 in nine panes of 20

2001, July 10	**Tagged**	***Perf. 11¼***	
3521 A2723 34c	**multicolored**	.70	.25
	P# block of 4, 4#+P	2.80	—
	Pane of 20	14.00	—

WOODY WAGON

A2724

Designed by Kevin Newman. Printed by American Packaging Corporation for Sennett Security Products.

PHOTOGRAVURE
COIL STAMP
Serpentine Die Cut 11½ Vert.

2001, Aug. 3		**Untagged**	
	Self-Adhesive		
3522 A2724 (15c)	**multicolored**	.30	.25
	Pair	.60	
	P# strip of 5, #S11111	2.75	
	P# single, same #	—	2.00

LEGENDS OF HOLLYWOOD

Lucille Ball (1911-89) — A2725

Designed by Derry Noyes. Printed by Banknote Corporation of America.

LITHOGRAPHED
Sheets of 180 in nine panes of 20

2001, Aug. 6	**Tagged**	***Serpentine Die Cut 11***	
	Self-Adhesive		
3523 A2725 34c	**multicolored**	1.00	.25
	P# block of 4, 4#+B	5.00	
	Pane of 20	24.00	13.00
a.	Die cutting omitted, pair	*700.00*	
	As "a," pane of 20	—	

Uncut press sheets of No. 3523 were made available for sale. Values: cross-gutter block of 8, $30; pairs with gutters between, $3.25 each. See note after No. 2868.

AMERICAN TREASURES SERIES
Amish Quilts

Diamond in the Square, c. 1920 — A2726

Lone Star, c. 1920 — A2727

Sunshine and Shadow, c. 1910 — A2728

Double Ninepatch Variation — A2729

Designed by Derry Noyes. Printed by Ashton-Potter (USA) Ltd.

LITHOGRAPHED

Sheets of 120 in six panes of 20

Serpentine Die Cut 11¼x11½

2001, Aug. 9 **Tagged**

Self-Adhesive

3524 A2726 34c **multicolored**	.70	.30
3525 A2727 34c **multicolored**	.70	.30
3526 A2728 34c **multicolored**	.70	.30
3527 A2729 34c **multicolored**	.70	.30
a. Block or strip of 4, #3524-3527	2.80	
P# block of 4, 5#+P	2.80	
Pane of 20	14.00	

CARNIVOROUS PLANTS

Venus Flytrap — A2730

Yellow Trumpet — A2731

Cobra Lily — A2732

English Sundew — A2733

Designed by Steve Buchanan.
Printed by Avery Dennison.

PHOTOGRAVURE

Sheets of 160 in eight panes of 20

2001, Aug. 23 **Tagged** ***Serpentine Die Cut 11½***

Self-Adhesive

3528 A2730 34c **multicolored**	.70	.25
3529 A2731 34c **multicolored**	.70	.25
3530 A2732 34c **multicolored**	.70	.25
3531 A2733 34c **multicolored**	.70	.25
a. Block or strip of 4, #3528-3531	2.80	
P# block of 4, 4#+V	2.80	
Pane of 20	14.00	

EID

"Eid Mubarak" — A2734

Designed by Mohamed Zakariya.
Printed by Avery Dennison.

PHOTOGRAVURE

Sheets of 240 in 12 panes of 20

2001, Sept. 1 **Tagged** ***Serpentine Die Cut 11¼***

Self-Adhesive

3532 A2734 34c **multicolored**	.70	.25
P# block of 4, 3#+V	2.80	
Pane of 20	14.00	

See Nos. 3674, 4117, 4202, 4351, 4416.

ENRICO FERMI (1901-54), PHYSICIST

A2735

Designed by Richard Sheaff. Printed by Sterling Sommer for Ashton-Potter (USA) Ltd.

LITHOGRAPHED

Sheets of 180 in nine panes of 20

2001, Sept. 29 **Tagged** ***Perf. 11***

3533 A2735 34c **multicolored**	.70	.25
P# block of 4, 4#+P	2.80	—
Pane of 20	14.00	—

THAT'S ALL FOLKS!

Porky Pig at Mailbox — A2736

Designed by Ed Wleczyk, Warner Bros. Printed by Avery Dennison.

PHOTOGRAVURE

2001, Oct. 1 **Tagged** ***Serpentine Die Cut 11***

Self-Adhesive

3534 Pane of 10 #3534a	7.00	
a. A2736 34c single	.70	.25
b. Pane of 9 #3534a	6.25	
c. Pane of 1 #3534a	.70	

Die cutting on No. 3534b does not extend through the backing paper.

Uncut press sheets of No. 3534 were made available for sale. Values: sheet of 60 with no P#s, $50; sheet of 60 with P# on front and reverse, $55; cross-gutter block of 7, $17.50; pairs with gutters between, $4 each. See note after No. 2868.

3535 Pane of 10, #3535c, 9 #3535a	50.00	
a. A2736 34c single	2.75	
b. Pane of 9 #3535a	25.00	
c. Pane of 1, no die cutting	25.00	

Die cutting on No. 3535a extends through backing paper.

Nos. 3534b-3534c and 3535b-3535c are separated by a vertical line of microperforations.

CHRISTMAS

Virgin and Child, by Lorenzo Costa — A2737

A2738 A2739

A2740 A2741

19th Century Chromolithographs of Santa Claus

Designed by Richard Sheaff.
Printed by Guilford Gravure, Inc., for Banknote Corporation of America (#3536), American Packaging Corporation for Sennett Security Products (#3537-3540), Avery Dennison (#3541-3544).

PHOTOGRAVURE

Sheets of 160 in eight panes of 20 (#3537-3540)

Serpentine Die Cut 11½ on 2, 3 or 4 Sides

2001, Oct. 10 **Tagged**

Self-Adhesive

Booklet Stamps (#3536, 3537a-3540a, 3537b, 3538b, 3539b, 3540e, 3541-3544)

3536 A2737 34c **multicolored**	.75	.25
a. Booklet pane of 20	15.00	

Serpentine Die Cut 10¾x11

Black Inscriptions

3537 A2738 34c **multicolored,** large date	.70	.25
a. Small date (from booklet pane) ⓢ	.90	.25
b. Large date (from booklet pane)	2.00	.25
3538 A2739 34c **multicolored,** large date	.70	.25
a. Small date (from booklet pane) ⓢ	.90	.25
b. Large date (from booklet pane)	2.00	.25
3539 A2740 34c **multicolored,** large date	.70	.25
a. Small date (from booklet pane) ⓢ	.90	.25
b. Large date (from booklet pane)	2.00	.25
3540 A2741 34c **multicolored,** large date	.70	.25
a. Small date (from booklet pane) ⓢ	.90	.25
b. Block or strip of 4, #3537-3540	2.80	
P# block of 4, 4#+S	3.50	
Pane of 20	17.00	
c. Block of 4, small date, #3537a-3540a	3.60	
d. Booklet pane of 20, 5 #3540c + label	18.00	
e. Large date (from booklet pane)	2.00	.25
f. Block of 4, large date, #3537b-3539b, 3540e	8.00	
g. Booklet pane of 20, 5 #3540f + label	40.00	

Nos. 3540d and 3540g are double-sided booklet panes, with 12 stamps on one side and eight stamps plus label on the other side.

Numerals "3" and "4" are distinctly separate on Nos. 3537-3540, and touching or separated by a slight hairline on the booklet pane stamps.

Designs of booklet stamps Nos. 3537a-3539a and 3537b-3539b are slightly taller than Nos. 3537-3539. Nos. 3540a and 3540e measure the same as No. 3540.

See note after No. 1549

Serpentine Die Cut 11 on 2 or 3 Sides

Size: 21x18½mm

Green and Red Inscriptions

3541 A2738 34c **multicolored**	.90	.25
3542 A2739 34c **multicolored**	.90	.25
3543 A2740 34c **multicolored**	.90	.25

3544 A2741 34c **multicolored**	.90	.25
a. Block of 4, #3541-3544	3.60	
b. Booklet pane of 4, #3541-3544	3.60	
c. Booklet pane of 6, #3543-3544, 2 #3541-3542	5.40	
d. Booklet pane of 6, #3541-3542, 2 #3543-3544	5.40	
Nos. 3536-3544 (9)	7.15	2.25

JAMES MADISON (1751-1836)

Madison and His Home, Montpelier A2742

Designed by John Thompson.

Printed by Banknote Corporation of America.

LITHOGRAPHED & ENGRAVED
Sheets of 120 in six panes of 20

2001, Oct. 18 Tagged *Perf. 11x11¼*

3545 A2742 34c **green & black**	.70	.25
P# block of 4, 2#+B	2.80	—
Pane of 20	14.00	—

Uncut press sheets of No. 3545 were made available for sale. Values: cross-gutter block of 4, $10; pairs with gutters between, $3.50 each. See note after No. 2868.

THANKSGIVING

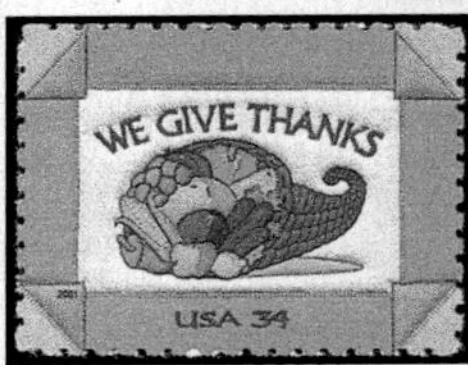

Cornucopia — A2743

Designed by Richard Sheaff.

Printed by Ashton-Potter (USA) Ltd.

LITHOGRAPHED
Sheets of 180 in nine panes of 20

2001, Oct. 19 Tagged *Serpentine Die Cut 11¼*
Self-Adhesive

3546 A2743 34c **multicolored**	.70	.25
P# block of 4, 4#+P	2.80	
Pane of 20	14.00	

Hanukkah Type of 1996

Designed by Hannah Smotrich.

Printed by Avery Dennison.

PHOTOGRAVURE
Sheets of 200 in 10 panes of 20

2001, Oct. 21 Tagged *Serpentine Die Cut 11*
Self-Adhesive

3547 A2411 34c **multicolored**	.70	.25
P# block of 4, 5#+V	2.80	
Pane of 20	14.00	

Kwanzaa Type of 1997

Designed by Synthia Saint James.

Printed by Avery Dennison.

PHOTOGRAVURE
Sheets of 240 in 12 panes of 20

2001, Oct. 21 Tagged *Serpentine Die Cut 11*
Self-Adhesive

3548 A2458 34c **multicolored**	.70	.25
P# block of 4, 4#+V	2.80	
Pane of 20	14.00	

UNITED WE STAND

A2744

Designed by Terry McCaffrey.

Printed by Banknote Corporation of America (#3549), Bureau of Engraving and Printing (#3550).

LITHOGRAPHED
BOOKLET STAMPS
Serpentine Die Cut 11¼ on 2, 3, or 4 Sides

2001, Oct. 24 Tagged
Self-Adhesive

3549 A2744 34c **multicolored**	.75	.25
a. Booklet pane of 20	15.00	

PHOTOGRAVURE
Serpentine Die Cut 10½x10¾ on 2 or 3 Sides

2002, Jan. Tagged
Self-Adhesive

3549B A2744 34c **multicolored**	.85	.25
c. Booklet pane of 4	3.40	
d. Booklet pane of 6	5.10	
e. Booklet pane of 20	18.00	

No. 3549Be is a double-sided booklet pane, with 12 stamps on one side and eight stamps plus label on the other side. "First day covers" of No. 3549B are dated Oct. 24, 2001.

COIL STAMPS

Serpentine Die Cut 9¾ Vert.

2001, Oct. 24 Tagged
Self-Adhesive

3550 A2744 34c **multicolored,** perpendicular corners	1.25	.25
Pair	2.50	
P# strip of 5, #1111, 2222	5.50	
P# strip of 5, #3333	8.50	
P# single, #1111, 2222	—	1.00
P# single, #3333	—	3.00
3550A A2744 34c **multicolored**	1.75	.25
Pair	3.50	
P# strip of 5, #1111	9.50	
P# single, same #	—	3.00

No. 3550 has right angle corners and backing paper as high as the stamp. No. 3550A has rounded corners, the backing paper larger than the stamp, and the stamps are spaced approximately 2mm apart.

Love Letters Type of 2001

Designed by Lisa Catalone.
Printed by Banknote Corporation of America.

LITHOGRAPHED
Sheets of 160 in eight panes of 20

2001, Nov. 19 Tagged *Serpentine Die Cut 11¼*
Self-Adhesive

3551 A2701 57c **multicolored**	1.10	.25
P# block of 4, 4# + B	5.00	
Pane of 20	24.00	

WINTER OLYMPICS

Ski Jumping A2745

Snowboarding A2746

Ice Hockey A2747

Figure Skating A2748

Designed by Jager Di Paola Kemp. Printed by American Packaging Corporation for Sennett Security Products.

PHOTOGRAVURE
Sheets of 180 in nine panes of 20
Serpentine Die Cut 11½x10¾

2002, Jan. 8 Tagged
Self-Adhesive

3552 A2745 34c **multicolored**	.70	.35
3553 A2746 34c **multicolored**	.70	.35
3554 A2747 34c **multicolored**	.70	.35
3555 A2748 34c **multicolored**	.70	.35
a. Block or strip of 4, #3552-3555	2.80	
P# block of 4, 6#+S (UL and UR only)	4.50	
Pane of 20	19.00	
b. Die cutting inverted, pane of 20	—	
c. Die cutting omitted, block of 4	*825.00*	
As "c," pane of 20	—	

Uncut press sheets of Nos. 3552-3555 were made available for sale. Values: cross-gutter block of 8, $25; pairs with gutters between, $3 each. See note after No. 2868.

MENTORING A CHILD

Child and Adult — A2749

Designed by Lance Hidy. Printed by American Packaging Corporation for Sennett Security Products.

PHOTOGRAVURE
Sheets of 120 in six panes of 20
Serpentine Die Cut 11x10¾

2002, Jan. 10 Tagged
Self-Adhesive

3556 A2749 34c **multicolored**	.70	.25
P# block of 4, 5#+S	2.80	
Pane of 20	14.00	

BLACK HERITAGE SERIES

Langston Hughes (1902-67), Writer — A2750

Designed by Richard Sheaff. Printed by Banknote Corporation of America.

LITHOGRAPHED
Sheets of 120 in six panes of 20
Serpentine Die Cut 10¼x10½

2002, Feb. 1 Tagged
Self-Adhesive

3557 A2750 34c **multicolored**	.70	.25
P# block of 4, 5#+B	3.00	
Pane of 20	15.00	
a. Die cutting omitted, pair	*850.00*	
As "a," pane of 20	—	

Beware of pairs/panes with extremely faint die cutting offered as imperf errors.

HAPPY BIRTHDAY

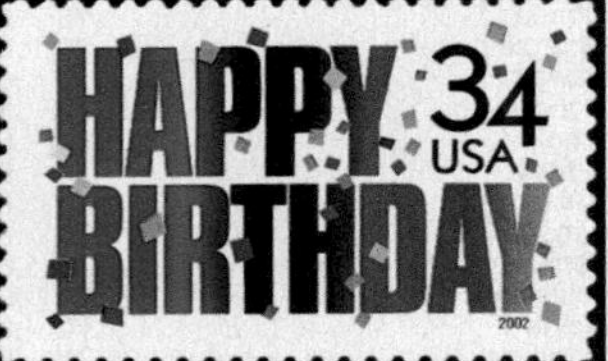

A2751

Designed by Harry Zelenko. Printed by Avery Dennison.

PHOTOGRAVURE
Sheets of 200 in 10 panes of 20

2002, Feb. 8 Tagged *Serpentine Die Cut 11*
Self-Adhesive

3558 A2751 34c **multicolored** .75 .25
P# block of 4, 4#+V 3.00
Pane of 20 15.00

See Nos. 3695, 4079.

CHINESE NEW YEAR

Year of the Horse A2752

Designed by Clarence Lee. Printed by Banknote Corporation of America.

LITHOGRAPHED
Sheets of 120 in six panes of 20
Serpentine Die Cut 10½x10¼

2002, Feb. 11 Tagged
Self-Adhesive

3559 A2752 34c **multicolored** .75 .25
P# block of 4, 5#+B 3.00
Pane of 20 15.00
a. Horiz. pair, vert. die cutting omitted *5,000.*

See No. 3895g.

U.S. MILITARY ACADEMY, BICENT.

Military Academy Coat of Arms — A2753

Designed by Derry Noyes. Printed by American Packaging Corp. for Sennett Security Products.

PHOTOGRAVURE
Sheets of 180 in nine panes of 20
Serpentine Die Cut 10½x11

2002, Mar. 16 Tagged
Self-Adhesive

3560 A2753 34c **multicolored** .75 .25
P# block of 4, 6#+S 3.00
Pane of 20 15.00

GREETINGS FROM AMERICA

Illustration reduced.

Designed by Richard Sheaff. Printed by American Packaging Corp. for Sennett Security Products.

PHOTOGRAVURE
Sheets of 100 in two panes of 50

2002, Apr. 4 Tagged *Serpentine Die Cut 10¾*
Self-Adhesive

3561 A2754 34c Alabama .70 .60
3562 A2755 34c Alaska .70 .60
3563 A2756 34c Arizona .70 .60
3564 A2757 34c Arkansas .70 .60
3565 A2758 34c California .70 .60
3566 A2759 34c Colorado .70 .60
3567 A2760 34c Connecticut .70 .60
3568 A2761 34c Delaware .70 .60
3569 A2762 34c Florida .70 .60
3570 A2763 34c Georgia .70 .60
3571 A2764 34c Hawaii .70 .60
3572 A2765 34c Idaho .70 .60
3573 A2766 34c Illinois .70 .60
3574 A2767 34c Indiana .70 .60
3575 A2768 34c Iowa .70 .60
3576 A2769 34c Kansas .70 .60
3577 A2770 34c Kentucky .70 .60
3578 A2771 34c Louisiana .70 .60
3579 A2772 34c Maine .70 .60
3580 A2773 34c Maryland .70 .60
3581 A2774 34c Massachusetts .70 .60
3582 A2775 34c Michigan .70 .60
3583 A2776 34c Minnesota .70 .60
3584 A2777 34c Mississippi .70 .60
3585 A2778 34c Missouri .70 .60
3586 A2779 34c Montana .70 .60
3587 A2780 34c Nebraska .70 .60
3588 A2781 34c Nevada .70 .60
3589 A2782 34c New Hampshire .70 .60
3590 A2783 34c New Jersey .70 .60
3591 A2784 34c New Mexico .70 .60
3592 A2785 34c New York .70 .60
3593 A2786 34c North Carolina .70 .60
3594 A2787 34c North Dakota .70 .60
3595 A2788 34c Ohio .70 .60
3596 A2789 34c Oklahoma .70 .60
3597 A2790 34c Oregon .70 .60
3598 A2791 34c Pennsylvania .70 .60
3599 A2792 34c Rhode Island .70 .60
3600 A2793 34c South Carolina .70 .60
3601 A2794 34c South Dakota .70 .60
3602 A2795 34c Tennessee .70 .60
3603 A2796 34c Texas .70 .60
3604 A2797 34c Utah .70 .60
3605 A2798 34c Vermont .70 .60
3606 A2799 34c Virginia .70 .60
3607 A2800 34c Washington .70 .60
3608 A2801 34c West Virginia .70 .60
3609 A2802 34c Wisconsin .70 .60
3610 A2803 34c Wyoming .70 .60
a. Pane of 50, #3561-3610 35.00

See Nos. 3696-3745.

Uncut press sheets of Nos. 3561-3610 were made available for sale. Values: block of 50 diff. stamps with vert. gutter btwn. any 2 columns, $40; pairs with vert. gutters between, $3 each. See note after No. 2868.

LONGLEAF PINE FOREST

A2804

Illustration reduced.

Designed by Ethel Kessler. Printed by American Packaging Corp. for Sennett Security Products.

No. 3611 — Wildlife and flowers: a, Bachman's sparrow. b, Northern bobwhite, yellow pitcher plants. c, Fox squirrel, red-bellied woodpecker. d, Brown-headed nuthatch. e, Broadhead skink, yellow pitcher plants, pipeworts. f, Eastern towhee, yellow pitcher plants, Savannah meadow beauties, toothache grass. g, Gray fox, gopher tortoise, horiz. h, Blind click beetle, sweetbay, pine woods treefrog. i, Rosebud orchid, pipeworts, southern toad, yellow pitcher plants. j, Grass-pink orchid, yellow-sided skimmer, pipeworts, yellow pitcher plants, horiz.

PHOTOGRAVURE
Sheets of 90 in nine panes of 10
Serpentine Die Cut 10½x10¾, 10¾x10½

2002, Apr. 26 Tagged
Self-Adhesive

3611 A2804 Pane of 10 19.00
a.-j. 34c Any single 1.90 .50
k. As No. 3611, die cutting omitted *2,500.*

Uncut press sheets of No. 3611 were made available for sale. See note after No. 2868.

AMERICAN DESIGN SERIES

Toleware Coffeepot — A2805

Designed by Derry Noyes.
Printed by American Packaging Corp. for Sennett Security Products.

PHOTOGRAVURE
COIL STAMP

2002, May 31 Untagged *Perf. 9¾ Vert.*

3612 A2805 5c **multicolored** .25 .25
Pair .50 .50
P# strip of 5, #S1111111 1.10 —
P# single, #S1111111 — .70
a. Imperf, pair —

No. 3612a is valued with disturbed gum. It is also known without gum and is valued only slightly less thus.
See Nos. 3756-3756A.

Star — A2806

Designed by Phil Jordan. Printed by Banknote Corporation of America.

LITHOGRAPHED, PHOTOGRAVURE (No. 3614, 3615)
Sheets of 400 in eight panes of 50

2002, June 7 Untagged *Serpentine Die Cut 11*
Self-Adhesive (#3613-3614)
Year at Lower Left

3613 A2806 3c **red, blue & black** .25 .25
P# block of 4, 3#+B .25
a. Die cutting omitted, pair —

Serpentine Die Cut 10
Year at Lower Right
Untagged

3614 A2806 3c **red, blue & black** .25 .25
P# block of 4, 3#+B .25

Coil Stamp
Perf. 9¾ Vert.
Year at Lower Left
Untagged

3615 A2806 3c **red, blue & black** .25 .25
Pair .25 .25
P# strip of 5, #S111 .90 —
P# single, same # — .70
a. Prephosphored coated paper with surface tagging showing a solid appearance (error) .40 .25
Pair .80 .50
P# strip of 5, #S111 8.00 —
P# single, same # — 8.00

Washington Type of 2001

Designed by Richard Sheaff. Printed by Ashton-Potter (USA) Ltd. (#3616, 3618, 3619), Avery Dennison (#3617).

LITHOGRAPHED, PHOTOGRAVURE (#3617)
Sheets of 400 in four panes of 100 (#3616)

2002, June 7 Tagged *Perf. 11¼*

3616 A2686 23c **green** .50 .25
P# block of 4, 1#+P 25.00

Self-Adhesive
Coil Stamp
Serpentine Die Cut 8½ Vert.

3617 A2686 23c **gray green** .45 .25
Pair .90
P# strip of 5, #V11, V13, V21, V22, V24, V35, V36, V45, V46 3.25
P# single, same # — 1.00
a. Die cutting omitted, pair —

Compare No. 3617 ("2002" date at lower left) with No. 3475A ("2001" date at lower left).

Booklet Stamps
Serpentine Die Cut 11¼x11 on 3 Sides

3618 A2686 23c **green** .50 .25
a. Booklet pane of 4 2.00
b. Booklet pane of 6 3.00
c. Booklet pane of 10 5.00

Serpentine Die Cut 10½x11 on 3 Sides

3619 A2686 23c **green** 4.50 1.75
a. Booklet pane of 4, 2 #3619 at L, 2 #3618 at R 10.00
b. Booklet pane of 6, 3 #3619 at L, 3 #3618 at R 15.00
c. Booklet pane of 4, 2 #3618 at L, 2 #3619 at R 10.00
d. Booklet pane of 6, 3 #3618 at L, 3 #3619 at R 15.00
e. Booklet pane of 10, 5 #3619 at L, 5#3618 at R 27.50
f. Booklet pane of 10, 5 #3618 at L, 5 #3619 at R 27.50
g. Pair, #3619 at L, #3618 at R 5.00
h. Pair, #3618 at L, #3619 at R 5.00
i. Nos. 3619c and 3619d, in bklt. of 10 (#BK289A), imperf. vert. btwn. on both panes —

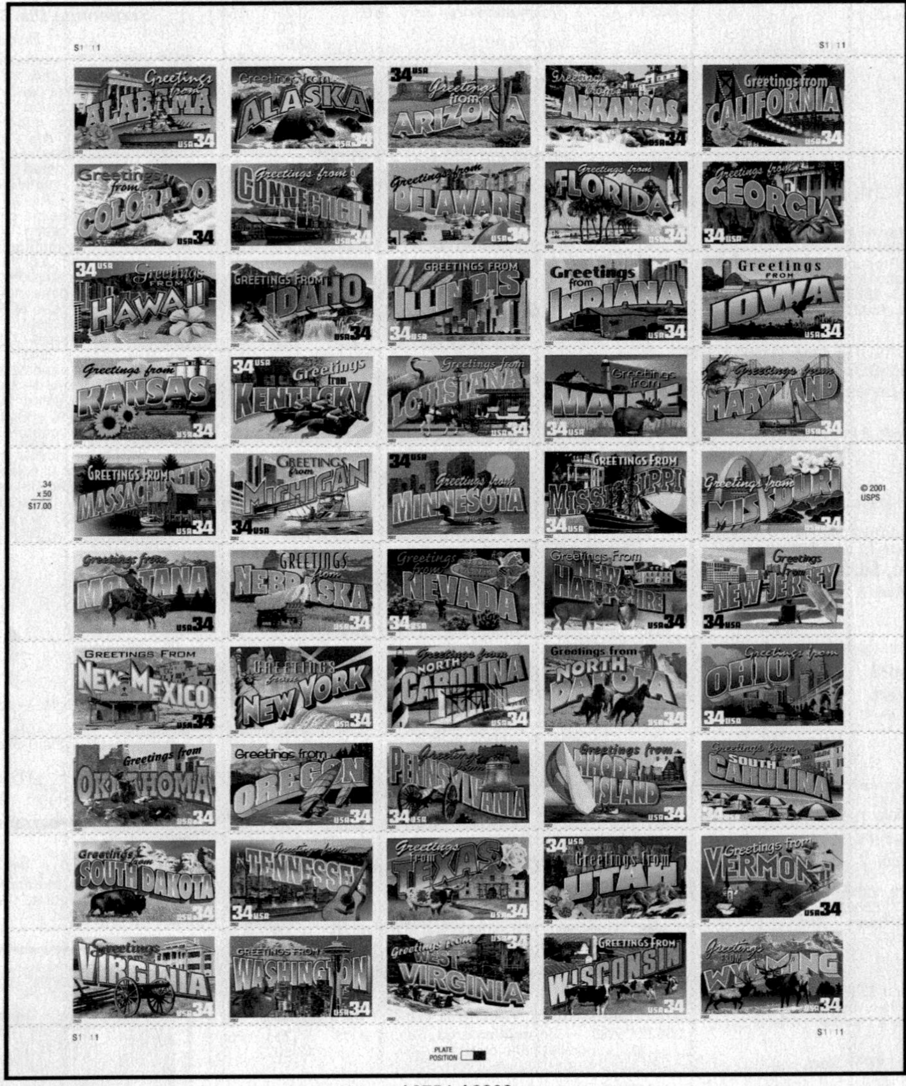

A2754-A2803

Flag — A2807

Designed by Terrence W. McCaffrey. Printed by Sterling Sommer for Ashton-Potter (USA) Ltd. (#3620), Ashton-Potter (USA) Ltd. (#3621), Bureau of Engraving and Printing (#3622), Banknote Corporation of America (#3623), American Packaging Corporation for Sennett Security Products (#3624), Avery Dennison (#3625).

LITHOGRAPHED, PHOTOGRAVURE (#3622, 3624, 3625)

Sheets of 400 in four panes of 100 (#3620), Sheets of 120 in six panes of 20 (#3621)

2002, June 7 Tagged *Perf. 11¼x11*

3620 A2807 (37c) **multicolored** 1.10 .25
P# block of 4, 4#+P 25.00 —

Self-Adhesive

Serpentine Die Cut 11¼x11

3621 A2807 (37c) **multicolored** 1.10 .25
P# block of 4, 4#+P 8.00
Pane of 20 36.00

Coil Stamp

Serpentine Die Cut 10 Vert.

3622 A2807 (37c) **multicolored** 1.10 .25
Pair 1.50
P# strip of 5, #1111, 2222 7.00
P# single, same # — 1.00
a. Die cutting omitted, pair —
b. Yellow omitted —

Counterfeits exist of No. 3622. See the Postal Counterfeits section of this catalog.

Booklet Stamps

Serpentine Die Cut 11¼ on 2, 3 or 4 Sides

3623 A2807 (37c) **multicolored** 1.10 .25
a. Booklet pane of 20 22.00

No. 3623 has "USPS" microprinted in the top red stripe of the flag.

Serpentine Die Cut 10½x10¾ on 2 or 3 Sides

3624 A2807 (37c) **multicolored** 1.10 .25
a. Booklet pane of 4 4.40
b. Booklet pane of 6 6.60
c. Booklet pane of 20 22.00

No. 3624 does not have a microprinted "USPS."

Serpentine Die Cut 8 on 2, 3 or 4 Sides

3625 A2807 (37c) **multicolored** 1.10 .25
a. Booklet pane of 18 19.00

Toy Mail Wagon — A2808

Toy Locomotive — A2809

Toy Taxicab — A2810

Toy Fire Pumper — A2811

Designed by Derry Noyes. Printed by Avery Dennison

PHOTOGRAVURE

Serpentine Die Cut 11 on 2, 3 or 4 Sides

2002, June 7 Tagged

Booklet Stamps

Self-Adhesive

3626 A2808 (37c) **multicolored** 1.10 .25
3627 A2809 (37c) **multicolored** 1.10 .25
3628 A2810 (37c) **multicolored** 1.10 .25
3629 A2811 (37c) **multicolored** 1.10 .25
a. Block or strip of 4, #3626-3629 4.40
b. Booklet pane of 4, #3626-3629 4.40
c. Booklet pane of 6, #3627, 3629, 2 each #3626, 3628 6.60
d. Booklet pane of 6, #3626, 3628, 2 each #3627, 3629 6.60
e. Booklet pane of 20, 5 each #3626-3629 22.00

Flag — A2812

Designed by Terrence W. McCaffrey. Printed by Ashton-Potter (USA) Ltd. (#3629F, 3630, 3633B), American Packaging Corporation for Sennett Security Products (#3631, 3632A, 3632C, 3636), Bureau of Engraving and Printing (#3632), Banknote Corporation of America (#3633, 3635), Guilford Gravure for Banknote Corporation of America (#3633A), Avery Dennison (#3634, 3634b, 3636D, 3637).

LITHOGRAPHED, PHOTOGRAVURE (#3631-3633, 3634, 3636, 3636D)

Sheets of 400 in four panes of 100

2002-05 Tagged *Perf. 11¼*

3629F A2812 37c **multicolored,** *Nov. 24, 2003* .90 .25
P# block of 4, 4#+P 25.00 —
g. Imperf, pair *100.00*

No. 3629F has microprinted "USA" in top red stripe of flag.

Sheets of 120 in six panes of 20

Serpentine Die Cut 11¼x11

Self-Adhesive (#3630, 3632-3637)

3630 A2812 37c **multicolored,** *June 7* .90 .25
P# block of 4, 4#+P 5.00
Pane of 20 23.50

No. 3630 has microprinted "USA" in top red stripe of flag.

COIL STAMPS

Perf. 9¾ Vert.

3631 A2812 37c **multicolored,** *June 7* .75 .25
Pair 1.50 —
P# strip of 5, #S1111 5.25 —
P# single, same # — 2.00

No. 3631 is known printed with non-reactive yellow ink and also with luminescent yellow ink that makes the red flag stripes glow orange under long wave ultraviolet light.

Serpentine Die Cut 9¾ Vert.

3632 A2812 37c **multicolored,** *June 7* .75 .25
Pair 1.50
P# strip of 5, #1111, 2222, 3333, 4444, 5555, 6666, 7777, 8888, 9999, 1111A, 2222A, 3333A, 4444A, 5555A, 6666A 5.00
P# single, same # — 1.00
b. Die cutting omitted, pair 55.00 55.00

On plate #s 1111 through 9999 and 5555A-6666A, the color laydown order of plate numbers is yellow, magenta, cyan, black. Plate #s 1111A through 4444A have a laydown order of cyan, magenta, yellow, black.

Serpentine Die Cut 10¼ Vert.

3632A A2812 37c **multicolored,** prephosphored coated paper, *Aug. 7, 2003* .75 .25
Pair 1.50
P# strip of 5, #S1111, S2222, S3333, S4444 5.25
P# single, #S1111, S2222, S3333, S4444 — 1.00
f. Die cutting omitted, pair *250.00*
g. Vert. pair, horiz. die-cut slits omitted *750.00*

No. 3632A lacks points of stars at margin at left top, and was printed in "logs" of adjacent coil rolls that are connected at the top or bottom, wherein each roll could be separated from an adjacent roll as needed.

No. 3632 has "2002" date at left bottom. No. 3632A has "2003" date at left bottom.

No. 3632A exists on two types of surface-tagged paper that exhibit either a solid or an uneven appearance. Value of plate #S4444 strip of 5 with solid tagging, $90; used plate #S4444 single with solid tagging, $60.

On No. 3632A, P# S3333 was printed with yellow ink that makes the red flag stripes glow orange under long wave ultraviolet light as well as with non-reactive yellow ink. P# S4444 was printed with and without luminescent yellow ink. Values the same.

Serpentine Die Cut 11¾ Vert.

3632C A2812 37c **multicolored,** prephosphored coated paper, *2004* 1.50 .25
Pair 3.00
P# strip of 5, #S1111 8.50
P# single, #S1111 — 2.50
d. Tagging omitted —

No. 3632C is the only 37c Flag coil stamp with a "2004" date at left bottom.

No. 3632C exists on two types of surface-tagged paper that exhibit either a solid or an uneven appearance. Values are the same.

Serpentine Die Cut 8½ Vert.

3633 A2812 37c **multicolored,** *June 7* .75 .25
Pair 1.50
P# strip of 5, #B1111 5.00
P# single, same # — 1.75

3633A A2812 37c **multicolored** *April, 2003* 2.25 .25
Pair 4.50
P# strip of 5 #B1111 12.50
P# single, same # — 1.50

No. 3633A has right angle corners and backing paper as high as the stamp, and is dated "2003." No. 3633 is dated "2002," has rounded corners, the backing paper larger than the stamp, and the stamps are spaced approximately 2mm apart.

Serpentine Die Cut 9½ Vert.

3633B A2812 37c **multicolored** *June 7, 2005* 9.00 .25
Pair 18.00
P# strip of 5, #P1111 50.00
P# single, #P1111 — 3.00

No. 3633B has microprinted "USA" in top red stripe of flag, and has "2005" date at bottom left.

Booklet Stamps

Serpentine Die Cut 11.1 on 3 Sides (#3634)

3634 A2812 37c **multicolored,** large "2002" year date, *June 7* .75 .25
a. Booklet pane of 10 7.50
b. Small "2003," die cut 11, *Oct. 23, 2003* .75 .25
c. Booklet pane, 4 #3634b 3.00
d. Booklet pane, 6 #3634b 4.50
e. As #3634, die cut 11.3 1.00 .25
f. As "e," booklet pane of 10 10.00

Serpentine Die Cut 11.3 on 2, 3 or 4 Sides

3635 A2812 37c **multicolored,** *June 7* .75 .25
a. Booklet pane of 20 15.00
b. Black omitted *3,000.*

No. 3635 has "USPS" microprinted in the top red flag stripe and has a small "2002" year date. Counterfeits exist of No. 3635. See the Postal Counterfeits section of this catalog.

Serpentine Die Cut 10½x10¾ on 2 or 3 Sides

3636 A2812 37c **multicolored,** *June 7* .75 .25
a. Booklet pane of 4 3.00
b. Booklet pane of 6 4.50
c. Booklet pane of 20 15.00
f. As "c," 11 stamps and part of 12th stamp on reverse printed on backing liner, the 8 stamps on front side die cutting omitted —

No. 3636c is a double-sided booklet pane, with 12 stamps on one side and eight stamps plus label on the other side.

Nos. 3636a and 3636b were issued on three types of prephosphored coated paper, with solid, grainy solid and uneven tagging characteristics. No. 3636c was issued on two types of prephosphored coated paper, with solid and uneven tagging.

Serpentine Die Cut 11¼x11 on 2 or 3 Sides

3636D A2812 37c **multicolored,** *July, 2004* 1.25 .25
e. Booklet pane of 20 25.00

No. 3636D lacks points of stars at margin at UL. No. 3636D is the only 37c Flag booklet stamp with a "2004" date at left bottom. No. 3636De is a double-sided booklet pane with 12 stamps on one side and eight stamps plus label on the other side.

Serpentine Die Cut 8 on 2, 3 or 4 Sides

3637 A2812 37c **multicolored,** *Feb. 4, 2003* .75 .25
a. Booklet pane of 18 13.50

Toy Locomotive — A2813

Toy Mail Wagon — A2814

Toy Fire Pumper — A2815

Toy Taxicab — A2816

Designed by Derry Noyes. Printed by Banknote Corporation of America, Avery Dennison (#3642-3645).

PHOTOGRAVURE

2002-03 Tagged *Serpentine Die Cut 8½ Horiz.*

Self-Adhesive

Coil Stamps

3638 A2813 37c **multicolored,** *July 26* 1.50 .25
3639 A2814 37c **multicolored,** *July 26* 1.50 .25
3640 A2815 37c **multicolored,** *July 26* 1.50 .25
3641 A2816 37c **multicolored,** *July 26* 1.50 .25
a. Strip of 4, #3638-3641 6.00
P# strip of 5, 2 #3638, 1 each #3639-3641, #B11111, B12222 8.25
P# strip of 9, 2 each #3638-3639, 3641, 3 #3640, #B11111, B12222 14.00
P# single (#3640), #B11111, B12222 — 1.25

Serpentine Die Cut 11 on 2, 3 or 4 Sides

Booklet Stamps

3642 A2814 37c **multicolored,** "2002" year date, *July 26* .75 .25
a. Serpentine die cut 11x11¼ on 2 or 3 sides, dated "2003," *Sept. 3, 2003* .75 .25
3643 A2813 37c **multicolored,** "2002" year date, *July 26* .75 .25
a. Serpentine die cut 11x11¼ on 2 or 3 sides, dated "2003," *Sept. 3, 2003* .75 .25
3644 A2816 37c **multicolored,** "2002" year date, *July 26* .75 .25
a. Serpentine die cut 11x11¼ on 2 or 3 sides, dated "2003," *Sept. 3, 2003* .75 .25
3645 A2815 37c **multicolored,** "2002" year date, *July 26* .75 .25
a. Block or strip of 4, #3642-3645 3.00
b. Booklet pane of 4, #3642-3645 3.00
c. Booklet pane of 6, #3643, 3645, 2 each #3642, 3644 4.50
d. Booklet pane of 6, #3642, 3644, 2 each #3643, 3645 4.50
e. Booklet pane of 20, 5 each #3642-3645 15.00
f. Serpentine die cut 11x11¼ on 2 or 3 sides, dated "2003," *Sept. 3, 2003* .75 .25
g. Block of 4, #3642a, 3643a, 3644a, 3645f 3.00
h. Booklet pane of 20, 5 #3645g 15.00

No. 3645h is a double-sided booklet with 12 stamps on one side and 8 stamps plus label (booklet cover) on the other side. Nos. 3642a, 3643a, 3644a and 3645f have slightly narrower designs than Nos. 3642-3645.

Coverlet Eagle — A2817

Designed by Richard Sheaff. Printed by Ashton-Potter (USA) Ltd.

LITHOGRAPHED

Sheets of 120 in six panes of 20

Serpentine Die Cut 11x11¼

2002, July 12 Tagged

Self-Adhesive

3646 A2817 60c **multicolored** 1.25 .25
P# block of 4, 4#+P 5.00
Pane of 20 25.00

Jefferson Memorial A2818

Capitol Dome — A2819

Designed by Derry Noyes. Printed by Banknote Corporation of America (#3647-3648), American Packaging Corporation for Sennett Security Printers (#3647A).

LITHOGRAPHED

Sheets of 180 in nine panes of 20

Serpentine Die Cut 11¼ (#3647, 3648), 11x10¾ (#3647A)

2002-03 Tagged

Self-Adhesive

3647 A2818 $3.85 **multicolored,** *July 30* 7.50 2.00
P# block of 4, 4#+B 30.00
Pane of 20 150.00
3647A A2818 $3.85 **multicolored,** *Nov. 2003* 9.00 2.00
P# block of 4, 5#+S 40.00
Pane of 20 195.00

3648 A2819 $13.65 **multicolored,** *July 30* 27.50 10.00
P# block of 4, 4#+B 110.00
Pane of 20 550.00

No. 3647 is dated 2002, and No. 3647A is dated 2003.
Hidden images can be seen on Nos. 3647-3648 when viewed with a special "Stamp Decoder" lens sold by the USPS. Nos. 3647-3647A, Jefferson's signature; No. 3648, a U.S. flag.

MASTERS OF AMERICAN PHOTOGRAPHY

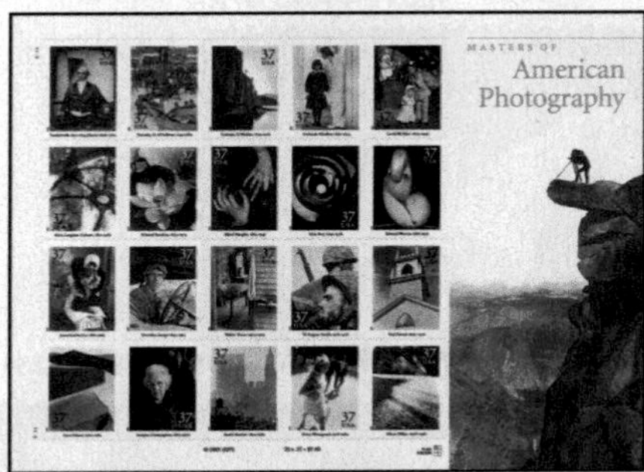

A2820

Illustration reduced.

Designed by Derry Noyes. Printed by American Packaging Corporation for Sennett Security Products.

No. 3649: a, Portrait of Daniel Webster, by Albert Sands Southworth and Josiah Johnson Hawes. b, Gen. Ulysses S. Grant and Officers, by Timothy H. O'Sullivan. c, "Cape Horn, Columbia River," by Carleton E. Watkins. d, "Blessed Art Thou Among Women," by Gertrude Käsebier. e, "Looking for Lost Luggage, Ellis Island," by Lewis W. Hine. f, "The Octopus," by Alvin Langdon Coburn. g, "Lotus, Mount Kisco, New York," by Edward Steichen. h, "Hands and Thimble," by Alfred Stieglitz. i, "Rayograph," by Man Ray. j, "Two Shells," by Edward Weston. k, "My Corsage," by James VanDerZee. l, "Ditched, Stalled, and Stranded, San Joaquin Valley, California," by Dorothea Lange. m, "Washroom and Dining Area of Floyd Burroughs' Home, Hale County, Alabama," by Walker Evans. n, "Frontline Soldier with Canteen, Saipan," by W. Eugene Smith. o, "Steeple," by Paul Strand. p, "Sand Dunes, Sunrise," by Ansel Adams. q, "Age and Its Symbols," by Imogen Cunningham. r, New York cityscape, by André Kertész. s, Photograph of pedestrians, by Garry Winogrand. t, "Bristol, Vermont," by Minor White.

PHOTOGRAVURE
Sheets of 120 in six panes of 20
Serpentine Die Cut 10½x10¾
2002, June 13 **Tagged**
Self-Adhesive

3649 A2820 Pane of 20 22.50
a.-t. 37c Any single 1.00 .50
u. As No. 3649, die cutting omitted —

Uncut press sheets of No. 3649 were made available for sale. Values: cross-gutter block of 20, $47.50; pairs with gutters between, $4 each. See note after No. 2868.

AMERICAN TREASURES SERIES

Scarlet and Louisiana Tanagers, by John James Audubon — A2821

Designed by Derry Noyes. Printed by American Pacakaging Corporation for Sennett Security Products.

PHOTOGRAVURE
Sheets of 120 in six panes of 20
2002, June 27 **Tagged** ***Serpentine Die Cut 10¾***
Self-Adhesive

3650 A2821 37c **multicolored** 1.00 .25
P# block of 4, 7#+S 6.00
Pane of 20 27.50

HARRY HOUDINI (1874-1926), MAGICIAN

A2822

Designed by Richard Sheaff. Printed by Ashton-Potter (USA) Ltd.

LITHOGRAPHED
Sheets of 180 in nine panes of 20
2002, July 3 **Tagged** ***Serpentine Die Cut 11¼***
Self-Adhesive

3651 A2822 37c **multicolored** .75 .25
P# block of 4, 4#+P 3.00 —
Pane of 20 15.00 —

A hidden 3-D image (Houdini in chains) can be seen on this stamp when it is viewed with a special "Stamp Decoder" lens sold by the USPS.

ANDY WARHOL (1928-87), ARTIST

Self-Portrait — A2823

Designed by Richard Sheaff.
Printed by American Packaging Corporation for Sennett Security Products.

PHOTOGRAVURE
Sheets of 80 in four panes of 20
Serpentine Die Cut 10½x10¾
2002, Aug. 9 **Tagged**
Self-Adhesive

3652 A2823 37c **multicolored** .75 .25
P# block of 4, 6#+S 4.00
Pane of 20 19.00

TEDDY BEARS, CENTENNIAL

Bruin Bear, c. 1907 — A2824

"Stick" Bear, 1920s — A2825

Gund Bear, c. 1948 — A2826

Ideal Bear, c. 1905 — A2827

Designed by Margaret Bauer.
Printed by American Packaging Corporation for Sennett Security Products.

PHOTOGRAVURE
Sheets of 120 in six panes of 20
2002, Aug. 15 **Tagged** ***Serpentine Die Cut 10½***
Self-Adhesive

3653 A2824 37c **multicolored** 1.00 .30
3654 A2825 37c **multicolored** 1.00 .30
3655 A2826 37c **multicolored** 1.00 .30
3656 A2827 37c **multicolored** 1.00 .30
a. Block or vert. strip of 4, #3653-3656 4.00
P# block of 4, 7#+S 5.00
P# block of 10, 2 sets of P# + top label 15.00
Pane of 20 27.50

Uncut press sheets of Nos. 3653-3656 were made available for sale. Values: cross-gutter block of 8, $30; pairs with gutters between, $3.50 each. See note after No. 2868.

LOVE

A2828

A2829

Designed by Michael Osborne.
Printed by Banknote Corporation of America (#3657), Avery Dennison.

LITHOGRAPHED (#3657), PHOTOGRAVURE
Sheets of 200 in 10 panes of 20 (#3658)
Serpentine Die Cut 11 on 2, 3 or 4 Sides
2002, Aug. 16 **Tagged**
Booklet Stamp (#3657)
Self-Adhesive

3657 A2828 37c **multicolored** .75 .25
a. Booklet pane of 20 15.00
b. As "a," silver ("Love 37 USA") missing on top five stamps (CM) *750.00*
c. Strip of 5, silver ("Love 37 USA") omitted on one stamp *1,000.*

Serpentine Die Cut 11

3658 A2829 60c **multicolored** 1.25 .25
P# block of 4, 5#+V 5.00
Pane of 20 25.00

Beware of examples of No. 3658 with gold ink fraudulently removed.

LITERARY ARTS

Ogden Nash (1902-71), Poet — A2830

Designed by Carl T. Herrman.
Printed by Avery Dennison.

PHOTOGRAVURE
Sheets of 200 in 10 panes of 20

2002, Aug. 19 Tagged *Serpentine Die Cut 11*
Self-Adhesive

3659 A2830 37c **multicolored** .75 .25
P# block of 4, 8#+V 3.00
Pane of 20 15.00

DUKE KAHANAMOKU (1890-1968), "FATHER OF SURFING" AND OLYMPIC SWIMMER

Kahanamoku and Surfers at Waikiki Beach — A2831

Designed by Carl T. Herrman.
Printed by Avery Dennison.

PHOTOGRAVURE
Sheets of 200 in 10 panes of 20
Serpentine Die Cut 11½x11¾

2002, Aug. 24 Tagged
Self-Adhesive

3660 A2831 37c **multicolored** .75 .25
P# block of 4, 4#+V 3.00
Pane of 20 15.00

AMERICAN BATS

Red Bat — A2832

Leaf-nosed Bat — A2833

Pallid Bat — A2834

Spotted Bat — A2835

Designed by Phil Jordan.
Printed by American Packaging Corporation for Sennett Security Products.

PHOTOGRAVURE
Sheets of 120 in six panes of 20

2002, Sept. 13 Tagged *Serpentine Die Cut 10¾*
Self-Adhesive

3661 A2832 37c **multicolored** .75 .30

3664 A2835 37c **multicolored** .75 .30
a. Block or strip of 4, #3661-3664 3.00
P# block of 4, 7#+S 3.25
P# block of 8, 2 sets of P# + top label 6.50
Pane of 20 16.00

WOMEN IN JOURNALISM

Nellie Bly (1864-1922) A2836

Ida M. Tarbell (1857-1944) A2837

Ethel L. Payne (1911-91) A2838

Marguerite Higgins (1920-66) A2839

Designed by Fred Otnes.
Printed by American Packaging Corporation for Sennett Security Products.

PHOTOGRAVURE
Sheets of 120 in six panes of 20
Serpentine Die Cut 11x10½

2002, Sept. 14 Tagged
Self-Adhesive

3665 A2836 37c **multicolored** 1.25 .35
3666 A2837 37c **multicolored** 1.25 .35
3667 A2838 37c **multicolored** 1.25 .35
3668 A2839 37c **multicolored** 1.25 .35
a. Block or horiz. strip of 4, #3665-3668 5.00
P# block of 4, 5#+S 5.25
P# block of 8, 2 sets of P# + top label 10.50
Pane of 20 25.00

IRVING BERLIN (1888-1989), COMPOSER

Berlin and Score of "God Bless America" — A2840

PHOTOGRAVURE
Sheets of 200 in 10 panes of 20

2002, Sept. 15 Tagged *Serpentine Die Cut 11*
Self-Adhesive

3669 A2840 37c **multicolored** .75 .25
P# block of 4, 4#+V 3.00
Pane of 20 15.00

NEUTER AND SPAY

Kitten — A2841

Puppy A2842

Designed by Derry Noyes. Printed by American Packaging Corporation for Sennett Security Products.

PHOTOGRAVURE
Sheets of 120 in six panes of 20
Serpentine Die Cut 10¾x10½

2002, Sept. 20 Tagged
Self-Adhesive

3670 A2841 37c **multicolored** 1.00 .25
3671 A2842 37c **multicolored** 1.00 .25
a. Horiz. or vert. pair, #3670-3671 2.00
P# block of 4, 5#+S 4.00
P# block of 8, 2 sets of P# + top label 8.00
Pane of 20 20.00

Hanukkah Type of 1996

Designed by Hannah Smotrich.
Printed by Avery Dennison.

PHOTOGRAVURE
Sheets of 200 in 10 panes of 20

2002, Oct. 10 Tagged *Serpentine Die Cut 11*
Self-Adhesive

3672 A2411 37c **multicolored** .75 .25
P# block of 4, 5#+V 3.00
Pane of 20 15.00

Kwanzaa Type of 1997

Designed by Synthia Saint James.
Printed by Avery Dennison.

PHOTOGRAVURE
Sheets of 200 in 10 panes of 20

2002, Oct. 10 Tagged *Serpentine Die Cut 11*
Self-Adhesive

3673 A2458 37c **multicolored** .75 .25
P# block of 4, 4#+V 3.00
Pane of 20 15.00

Eid Type of 2001

Designed by Mohamed Zakariya.
Printed by Avery Dennison.

PHOTOGRAVURE
Sheets of 240 in 12 panes of 20

2002, Oct. 10 Tagged *Serpentine Die Cut 11*
Self-Adhesive

3674 A2734 37c **multicolored** .75 .25
P# block of 4, 3#+V 3.00
Pane of 20 15.00

CHRISTMAS

Madonna and Child, by Jan Gossaert — A2843

Designed by Richard Sheaff.
Printed by Banknote Corporation of America.

LITHOGRAPHED

Serpentine Die Cut 11x11¼ on 2, 3 or 4 Sides

2002, Oct. 10 **Tagged**

Self-Adhesive

Booklet Stamp

Design size: 19x27mm

3675	A2843 37c **multicolored**		.75	.25
a.	Booklet pane of 20		15.00	

Compare to No. 3820, which measures 19½x28mm

CHRISTMAS

Snowman with Red and Green Plaid Scarf — A2844

Snowman with Blue Plaid Scarf — A2845

Snowman with Pipe — A2846

Snowman with Top Hat — A2847

Snowman with Blue Plaid Scarf — A2848

Snowman with Pipe — A2849

Snowman with Top Hat — A2850

Snowman with Red and Green Plaid Scarf — A2851

Designed by Derry Noyes.

Printed by Avery Dennison (#3676-3679, 3688-3691), Guilford Gravure (#3680-3683), and American Packaging Corp. for Sennett Security Products (#3684-3687).

PHOTOGRAVURE

Sheets of 200 in 10 panes of 20

2002, Oct. 28 **Tagged** ***Serpentine Die Cut 11***

Self-Adhesive

3676	A2844 37c **multicolored**	.90	.25
3677	A2845 37c **multicolored**	.90	.25
3678	A2846 37c **multicolored**	.90	.25
3679	A2847 37c **multicolored**	.90	.25
a.	Block or vert. strip of 4, #3676-3679	3.75	
	P# block of 4, 4#+V	4.25	
	Pane of 20	21.00	

COIL STAMPS

Serpentine Die Cut 8½ Vert.

3680	A2848 37c **multicolored**	3.25	.25
3681	A2849 37c **multicolored**	3.25	.25
3682	A2850 37c **multicolored**	3.25	.25
3683	A2851 37c **multicolored**	3.25	.25
a.	Strip of 4, #3680-3683	13.00	
	P# strip of 5, 2 #3680, 1 each #3681-3683, #G1111, G1112	17.50	
	P# strip of 9, 2 each #3680, 3681, 3683, 3 #3682, same #	30.00	
	P# single (#3682), same #	—	2.00

BOOKLET STAMPS

Serpentine Die Cut 10¾x11 on 2 or 3 Sides

3684	A2844 37c **multicolored**	1.25	.25
3685	A2845 37c **multicolored**	1.25	.25
3686	A2846 37c **multicolored**	1.25	.25
3687	A2847 37c **multicolored**	1.25	.25
a.	Block of 4, #3684-3687	5.00	
b.	Booklet pane of 20, 5 #3687a + label	25.00	

No. 3687b is a double-sided booklet pane with 12 stamps on one side and eight stamps plus label on the other side.

Colors of Nos. 3684-3687 are deeper and designs are slightly smaller than those found on Nos. 3676-3679.

Serpentine Die Cut 11 on 2 or 3 Sides

3688	A2851 37c **multicolored**	1.15	.25
3689	A2848 37c **multicolored**	1.15	.25
3690	A2849 37c **multicolored**	1.15	.25
3691	A2850 37c **multicolored**	1.15	.25
a.	Block of 4, #3688-3691	4.60	
b.	Booklet pane of 4, #3688-3691	4.60	
c.	Booklet pane of 6, #3690-3691, 2 each #3688-3689	7.00	
d.	Booklet pane of 6, #3688-3689, 2 each #3690-3691	7.00	
	Nos. 3676-3691 (16)	26.20	4.00

LEGENDS OF HOLLYWOOD

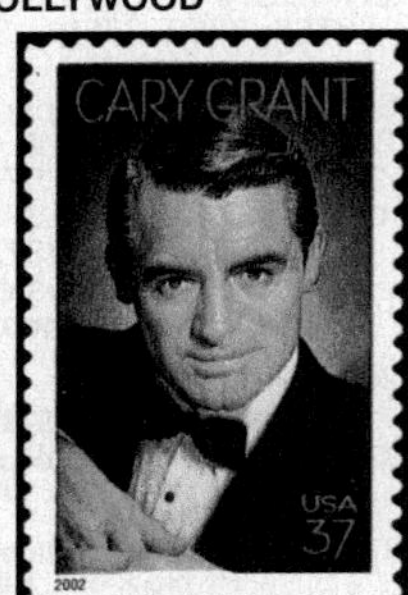

Cary Grant (1904-86), Actor — A2852

Designed by Carl Herrman.

Printed by American Packaging Corporation for Sennett Security Products.

PHOTOGRAVURE

Sheets of 120 in six panes of 20

2002, Oct. 15 **Tagged** ***Serpentine Die Cut 10¾***

Self-Adhesive

3692	A2852 37c **multicolored**	1.25	.25
	P# block of 4, 6#+S	5.00	
	Pane of 20	25.00	

Uncut press sheets of No. 3692 were made available for sale. Values: cross-gutter block of 8, $27.50; pairs with gutters between, $4 each. See note after No. 2868.

Sea Coast — A2853

Designed by Tom Engeman.

Printed by Banknote Corporation Of America.

PHOTOGRAVURE

COIL STAMP

Serpentine Die Cut 8½ Vert.

2002, Oct. 21 **Tagged**

Self-Adhesive

3693	A2853 (5c) **multicolored**, dated "2002"	.25	.25
	Pair	.50	
	P# strip of 5, #B111	1.30	
	P# single, #B111	—	.90

See Nos. 3775, 3785, 3864, 3874, 3875, 4348.

HAWAIIAN MISSIONARY STAMPS

A2854

Illustration reduced.

Designed by Richard Sheaff.

Printed by Banknote Corporation of America.

No. 3694: a, 2c stamp of 1851 (Hawaii Scott 1). b, 5c stamp of 1851 (Hawaii Scott 2) c, 13c stamp of 1851 (Hawaii Scott 3). d, 13c stamp of 1852 (Hawaii Scott 4).

LITHOGRAPHED

Sheets of 24 in six panes of 4

2002, Oct. 24 **Tagged** ***Perf. 11***

3694	A2854 Pane of 4	5.00	2.50
a.-d.	37c Any single	1.25	.50

Uncut press sheets of No. 3694 were made available for sale. See note after No. 2868.

Happy Birthday Type of 2002

Designed by Harry Zelenko.

Printed by Avery Dennison.

PHOTOGRAVURE

Sheets of 200 in 10 panes of 20

2002, Oct. 25 **Tagged** ***Serpentine Die Cut 11***

Self-Adhesive

3695	A2751 37c **multicolored**	.75	.25
	P# block of 4, 4#+V	3.00	
	Pane of 20	15.00	

Greetings From America Type of 2002

Designed by Richard Sheaff. Printed by American Packaging Corp. for Sennett Security Products.

PHOTOGRAVURE

Sheets of 100 in two panes of 50

2002, Oct. 25 **Tagged** ***Serpentine Die Cut 10¾***

Self-Adhesive

3696	A2754 37c Alabama	.75	.60
3697	A2755 37c Alaska	.75	.60
3698	A2756 37c Arizona	.75	.60
3699	A2757 37c Arkansas	.75	.60
3700	A2758 37c California	.75	.60
3701	A2759 37c Colorado	.75	.60
3702	A2760 37c Connecticut	.75	.60
3703	A2761 37c Delaware	.75	.60
3704	A2762 37c Florida	.75	.60
3705	A2763 37c Georgia	.75	.60
3706	A2764 37c Hawaii	.75	.60
3707	A2765 37c Idaho	.75	.60
3708	A2766 37c Illinois	.75	.60
3709	A2767 37c Indiana	.75	.60
3710	A2768 37c Iowa	.75	.60
3711	A2769 37c Kansas	.75	.60
3712	A2770 37c Kentucky	.75	.60
3713	A2771 37c Louisiana	.75	.60
3714	A2772 37c Maine	.75	.60
3715	A2773 37c Maryland	.75	.60
3716	A2774 37c Massachusetts	.75	.60
3717	A2775 37c Michigan	.75	.60
3718	A2776 37c Minnesota	.75	.60
3719	A2777 37c Mississippi	.75	.60
3720	A2778 37c Missouri	.75	.60
3721	A2779 37c Montana	.75	.60
3722	A2780 37c Nebraska	.75	.60

3723	A2781	37c Nevada	.75	.60
3724	A2782	37c New Hampshire	.75	.60
3725	A2783	37c New Jersey	.75	.60
3726	A2784	37c New Mexico	.75	.60
3727	A2785	37c New York	.75	.60
3728	A2786	37c North Carolina	.75	.60
3729	A2787	37c North Dakota	.75	.60
3730	A2788	37c Ohio	.75	.60
3731	A2789	37c Oklahoma	.75	.60
3732	A2790	37c Oregon	.75	.60
3733	A2791	37c Pennsylvania	.75	.60
3734	A2792	37c Rhode Island	.75	.60
3735	A2793	37c South Carolina	.75	.60
3736	A2794	37c South Dakota	.75	.60
3737	A2795	37c Tennessee	.75	.60
3738	A2796	37c Texas	.75	.60
3739	A2797	37c Utah	.75	.60
3740	A2798	37c Vermont	.75	.60
3741	A2799	37c Virginia	.75	.60
3742	A2800	37c Washington	.75	.60
3743	A2801	37c West Virginia	.75	.60
3744	A2802	37c Wisconsin	.75	.60
3745	A2803	37c Wyoming	.75	.60
a.		Pane of 50, #3696-3745	37.50	

BLACK HERITAGE SERIES

Thurgood Marshall (1908-93), Supreme Court Justice — A2855

Designed by Richard Sheaff. Printed by Ashton-Potter (USA) Ltd.

LITHOGRAPHED

Sheets of 180 in nine panes of 20

2003, Jan. 7 Tagged *Serpentine Die Cut 11½*

Self-Adhesive

3746	A2855	37c **black & gray**	.75	.25
		P# block of 4, 3#+P	3.00	
		Pane of 20	15.00	

CHINESE NEW YEAR

Year of the Ram — A2856

Designed by Clarence Lee. Printed by Banknote Corporation of America.

LITHOGRAPHED

Sheets of 120 in six panes of 20

2003, Jan. 15 Tagged *Serpentine Die Cut 11½*

Self-Adhesive

3747	A2856	37c **multicolored**	.75	.25
		P# block of 4, 4#+B	3.00	
		Pane of 20	15.00	
a.		Tagging omitted	—	

See No. 3895h.

LITERARY ARTS

Zora Neale Hurston (1891-1960), Writer A2857

Designed by Howard E. Paine. Printed by American Packaging Corporation for Sennett Security Products.

PHOTOGRAVURE

Sheets of 120 in six panes of 20

2003, Jan. 24 Tagged *Serpentine Die Cut 10¾*

Self-Adhesive

3748	A2857	37c **multicolored**	.90	.25
		P# block of 4, 5#+S	3.60	
		Pane of 20	18.00	

AMERICAN DESIGN SERIES

Toleware Coffeepot Type of 2002 and

Navajo Necklace — A2858

Chippendale Chair — A2859

American Clock — A2860

Tiffany Lamp — A2866

Silver Coffeepot — A2868

Designed by Derry Noyes. Printed by Ashton-Potter (USA) Ltd. (#3749, 3752, 3755, 3757), American Packaging Corp. for Sennett Security Products (#3751, 3756, 3758, 3759, 3761, 3762), Banknote Corporation of America for Sennett Security Products (#3749A, 3753, 3754, 3756A, 3758A, 3758B, 3763), Avery Dennison (#3750), Guildford Gravure for Ashton-Potter (USA) Ltd. (#3761A).

LITHOGRAPHED, PHOTOGRAVURE (#3750, 3751, 3756, 3758, 3758A, 3758B, 3759, 3761, 3761A, 3762)

Sheets of 300 in 15 panes of 20 (#3749A), Sheets of 280 in 14 panes of 20, Sheets of 240 in 12 panes of 20 (#3751, 3752, 3757), Sheets of 200 in 10 panes of 20 (#3749, 3753, 3754, 3756A), Sheets of 120 in six panes of 20 (#3755), Sheets of 160 in eight panes of 20 (#3756).

Self-Adhesive (#3749-3757)

2003-14 *Serpentine Die Cut 11¼x11*

Untagged (#3749-3756A, 3758-3762, 3763a)

3749	A2866	1c **multicolored**, *Mar. 16, 2007*	.25	.25
		P# block of 4, 6#+P	.50	
		Pane of 20	3.00	
3749A	A2866	1c **multicolored**, *Mar. 7, 2008*	.25	.25
		P# block of 4, 5#+S	.50	
		Pane of 20	3.00	

No. 3749A has "USPS" microprinted on a white field high on the lamp stand, just below the shade and is dated "2008." No. 3749 has "USPS" microprinted lower on the lamp stand and not on a white field and is dated "2007."

Serpentine Die Cut 11

3750	A2858	2c **multicolored**, *Aug. 20, 2004*	.25	.25
		P# block of 4, 5#+V	.50	
		Pane of 20	3.00	

A reprinting of No. 3750 shows the borders in a much brighter deep turquoise blue shade.

Serpentine Die Cut 11¼x11½

3751	A2858	2c **multicolored**, *Dec. 8, 2005*	1.00	.25
		P# block of 4, 6#+S	5.00	
		Pane of 20	21.50	

Serpentine Die Cut 11¼x11

With "USPS" Microprinting

3752	A2858	2c **multicolored**, *Dec. 8, 2005*	.25	.25
		P# block of 4, 5#+P	.50	
		Pane of 20	3.00	

Serpentine Die Cut 11¼x10¾

3753	A2858	2c **multicolored**, *May 12, 2007*	.25	.25
		P# block of 4, 6#+S	.50	
		Pane of 20	3.00	

Serpentine Die Cut 11¼x11

3754	A2868	3c **multicolored**, *Mar. 16, 2007*	.25	.25
		P# block of 4, 4#+S	.50	
		Pane of 20	3.00	

Microprinted "USPS" on No. 3752 is found on top silver appendage next to and below the middle turquoise stone on the right side of the necklace. Microprinting on No. 3753 is found on the top silver appendage next to and below the lower turquoise stone on the left side of the necklace. Nos. 3751 and 3752 are dated "2006." No. 3753 is dated "2007."

Serpentine Die Cut 10¾x10¼

3755	A2859	4c **multicolored**, *Mar. 5, 2004*	.25	.25
		P# block of 4, 4#+P	.50	
		Pane of 20	3.00	

Serpentine Die Cut 11¼x11¾

3756	A2805	5c **multicolored**, *June 25, 2004*	.25	.25
		P# block of 4, 7#+S	.50	
		Pane of 20	2.50	

Serpentine Die Cut 11¼x10¾

3756A	A2805	5c **multicolored**, *Aug. 2008*	.25	.25
		P# block of 4, 7#+S	.50	
		Pane of 20	3.00	
b.		Die cutting omitted, pair	400.00	

No. 3756A has microprinting on the lower part of the coffeepot handle and is dated "2007." No. 3756 has no microprinting and is dated "2004." Existence of No. 3756A was reported in Aug. 2008.

No. 3756A is known printed with non-reactive cream-colored background ink and also with luminescent cream-colored ink that glows orange under both shortwave and longwave ultraviolet light.

Serpentine Die Cut 11¼x11

Tagged

3757	A2860	10c **multicolored**, prephosphored coated paper with surface tagging showing a solid appearance, plus block tagging on top of the printed design *Jan. 24*	.25	.25
		P# block of 4, 4#+P	1.00	
		Pane of 20	5.00	
a.		Die cutting omitted, pair		—
b.		10c **multicolored**, overall tagging, *2013*	.25	.25
		P# block of 4, 4#+P	1.00	
		Pane of 20	5.00	

No. 3757b was printed from plates P6666 and P7777.

COIL STAMPS

Perf. 9¾ Vert.

3758	A2866	1c **multicolored**, *Mar. 1*	.25	.25
		Pair	.25	.25
		P# strip of 5, #S11111	.60	—
		P# single, #S11111	—	.35
3758A	A2866	1c **multicolored**, *June 7, 2008*	.25	.25
		Pair	.25	.25
		P# strip of 5, #S11111	.80	—
		P# single, #S11111	—	.45

No. 3758A has microprinted "USPS" on lamp stand just below the lampshade and is dated "2008." No. 3758 lacks microprinting and is dated "2003."

3758B	A2858	2c **multicolored**, *Feb. 12, 2011*	.25	.25
		Pair	.35	.40
		P# strip of 5, #S111111	1.00	—
		P# single, #S111111	—	.50
3759	A2868	3c **multicolored**, *Sept. 16, 2005*	.25	.25
		Pair	.40	.40
		P# strip of 5, #S1111	.80	—
		P# single, #S1111	—	.55
		P# strip of 5, #S2222	2.00	—
		P# single, #S2222	—	1.90
3761	A2859	4c **multicolored**, dated "2007" at LL, *July 19, 2007*	.25	.25
		Pair	.40	.40
		P# strip of 5, #S1111	1.00	—
		P# single, #S1111	—	.90
3761A	A2859	4c **multicolored**, dated "2013" at UL, *Jan. 2, 2014*	.25	.25
		Pair	.40	.40
		P# strip of 5, #P1111	1.35	—
		P# single, #P1111	—	1.25

On plate number singles, the plate number is at the lower right on No. 3761 and centered at bottom on No. 3761A.

3762	A2860	10c **multicolored**, *Aug. 4, 2006*	.25	.25
		Pair	.50	.50
		P# strip of 5, #S1111	1.90	—
		P# single, #S1111	—	1.30
3763	A2860	10c **multicolored** *July 15, 2008*	.25	.25
		Pair	.50	.50
		P# strip of 5, #S1111	2.50	—
		P# single, #S1111	—	2.00
a.		Untagged, *2013*	.25	.25
		Pair	.50	.50
		P# strip of 5, #S2222	3.00	—
		P# single, #S2222	—	3.00

Nos. 3763 and 3763a are dated "2008," have a microprinted "USPS" as the middle "I" in "VIII," and have network of beige dots on clock face. No. 3762 is dated "2006," lacks microprinting, and has network of gray dots on clock face.

This is an ongoing set. Numbers may change.

See No. 3612.

AMERICAN CULTURE SERIES

Wisdom, Rockefeller Center, New York City — A2875

Designed by Carl Herrman. Printed by Ashton-Potter (USA) Ltd.

LITHOGRAPHED
Sheets of 120 in six panes of 20
Serpentine Die Cut 11¼x11

2003, Feb. 28 **Tagged**

Self-Adhesive

3766 A2875 $1 **multicolored** 2.00 .40
P# block of 4, 5# + P 8.00
Pane of 20 40.00
a. Dated "2008" ⓢ 2.00 .40
P# block of 4, 5# + P 8.00
Pane of 20 40.00

See note after No. 1549.

New York Public Library Lion Type of 2000

Designed by Carl Herrman. Printed by American Packaging Corporation for Sennett Security Products.

PHOTOGRAVURE
COIL STAMP

2003, Feb. 4 **Untagged** ***Perf. 9¾ Vert.***

3769 A2677 (10c) **multicolored** .25 .25
Pair .50 .50
P# strip of 5, #S11111 2.25 —
P# single, #S11111 — 1.60

Atlas Statue Type of 2001

Designed by Kevin Newman. Printed by Avery Dennison.

PHOTOGRAVURE

2003, Oct. **Untagged** ***Serpentine Die Cut 11 Vert.***

Coil Stamp

Self-Adhesive

3770 A2722 (10c) **multicolored** .25 .25
Pair .50
P# strip of 5, #V11111, V11222, V12222, V21111, V21211, V22111, V22112, V22211, V23113, V32332, V33333, V33332 2.25
P# strip of 5, #V12111 *60.00*
P# strip of 5, #V22222 10.00
P# single, #V11111, V11222, V21111, V21211, V22111, V22112, V22211, V23113, V32332, V33332 — 2.00
P# single, # V12111 *75.00*
P# single, # V12222 *1.00*
P# single, # V13222 *250.00*
P# single, # V22222 8.50
P# single, # V21113 *1,600.*
P# single, # V33333 1.00
a. Tagged, error —
P# single, # V21211 —

No. 3770 is dated 2003.

SPECIAL OLYMPICS

Athlete with Medal — A2879

Designed by Lance Hidy. Printed by Avery Dennison.

PHOTOGRAVURE
Sheets of 200 in 10 panes of 20

2003, Feb. 13 **Tagged** ***Serpentine Die Cut 11***

Self-Adhesive

3771 A2879 80c **multicolored** 1.60 .35
P# block of 4, 6# + V 6.40
Pane of 20 32.00

A hidden 3-D image (Special Olympics logo) can be seen on this stamp when it is viewed with a special "Stamp Decoder" lens sold by the USPS.

AMERICAN FILMMAKING: BEHIND THE SCENES

A2880

Illustration reduced.

Designed by Imaginary Forces. Printed by American Packaging Corporation for Sennett Security Products.

No. 3772: a, Screenwriting (segment of script from *Gone With the Wind*). b, Directing (John Cassavetes). c, Costume design (Edith Head). d, Music (Max Steiner working on score). e, Makeup (Jack Pierce working on Boris Karloff's makeup for *Frankenstein*). f, Art direction (Perry Ferguson working on sketch for *Citizen Kane*). g, Cinematography (Paul Hill, assistant cameraman for *Nagana*). h, Film editing (J. Watson Webb editing *The Razor's Edge*). i, Special effects (Mark Siegel working on model for *E.T. The Extra-Terrestrial*). j, Sound (Gary Summers works on control panel).

PHOTOGRAVURE
Sheets of 60 in six panes of 10
Serpentine Die Cut 11 Horiz.

2003, Feb. 25 **Tagged**

Self-Adhesive

3772 A2880 Pane of 10 12.00
a.-j. 37c Any single 1.20 .50

Uncut press sheets of No. 3772 were made available for sale. Values: block of 10 with vert. gutter btwn., $15. See note after No. 2868.

OHIO STATEHOOD BICENTENNIAL

Aerial View of Farm Near Marietta — A2881

Designed by Phil Jordan. Printed by Banknote Corporation of America.

LITHOGRAPHED
Sheets of 120 in six panes of 20
Serpentine Die Cut 11¾x11½

2003, Mar. 1 **Tagged**

Self-Adhesive

3773 A2881 37c **multicolored** .75 .25
P# block of 4, 4# + B 3.00
Pane of 20 15.00

PELICAN ISLAND NATIONAL WILDLIFE REFUGE, CENT.

Brown Pelican — A2882

Designed by Carl T. Herrman. Printed by Banknote Corporation of America.

LITHOGRAPHED
Sheets of 120 in six panes of 20
Serpentine Die Cut 12x11½

2003, Mar. 14 **Tagged**

Self-Adhesive

3774 A2882 37c **multicolored** .75 .25
P# block of 4, 4#+B 3.00
Pane of 20 15.00

Sea Coast Type of 2002

Designed by Tom Engeman. Printed by Banknote Corporation of America.

PHOTOGRAVURE
COIL STAMP

2003, Mar. 19 **Untagged** ***Perf. 9¾ Vert.***

3775 A2853 (5c) **multicolored** .25 .25
Pair .50 —
P# strip of 5, #B111 1.30
P# single, #B111 .90

See No. 3864. No. 3775 has "2003" year date in blue, dots that run together in surf area, and a distinct small orange cloud. No. 3864 has "2004" year date in black, rows of distinctly separated dots in surf area, and the small orange cloud is indistinct.

OLD GLORY

Uncle Sam on Bicycle with Liberty Flag, 20th Cent. — A2883

1888 Presidential Campaign Badge — A2884

1893 Silk Bookmark — A2885

Modern Hand Fan — A2886

Carving of Woman with Flag and Sword, 19th Cent. — A2887

Designed by Richard Sheaff. Printed by Ashton-Potter (USA) Ltd.

LITHOGRAPHED
BOOKLET STAMPS

2003, Apr. 3 Tagged *Serpentine Die Cut 10x9¾*
Self-Adhesive

3776	A2883 37c **multicolored**	.75	.50
3777	A2884 37c **multicolored**	.75	.50
3778	A2885 37c **multicolored**	.75	.50
3779	A2886 37c **multicolored**	.75	.50
3780	A2887 37c **multicolored**	.75	.50
a.	Horiz. strip of 5, #3776-3780	3.75	
b.	Booklet pane, 2 #3780a	7.50	

Nos. 3776-3780 were issued in booklets containing two No. 3780b, each with a different backing.

CESAR E. CHAVEZ (1927-93), LABOR ORGANIZER

A2888

Designed by Carl Herrman. Printed by Banknote Corporation of America.

LITHOGRAPHED
Sheets of 120 in six panes of 20
Serpentine Die Cut 11¾x11½

2003, Apr. 23 Tagged
Self-Adhesive

3781	A2888 37c **multicolored**	.75	.25
	P# block of 4, 4# + B	3.00	
	Pane of 20	15.00	

LOUISIANA PURCHASE, BICENTENNIAL

English Translation of Treaty, Map of U.S., Treaty Signers — A2889

Designed by Richard Sheaff. Printed by American Packaging Corporation for Sennett Security Products

PHOTOGRAVURE
Sheets of 120 in six panes of 20

2003, Apr. 30 Tagged *Serpentine Die Cut 10¾*
Self-Adhesive

3782	A2889 37c **multicolored**	.95	.40
	P# block of 4, 6# + S	4.00	
	Pane of 20	20.00	

FIRST FLIGHT OF WRIGHT BROTHERS, CENT.

Orville Wright Piloting 1903 Wright Flyer — A2890

Designed by McRay Magleby. Printed by Avery Dennison.

PHOTOGRAVURE

2003, May 22 Tagged *Serpentine Die Cut 11*
Self-Adhesive

3783	Pane of 10	9.00	
a.	A2890 37c single	.90	.40
b.	Pane of 9 #3783a	8.00	
c.	Pane of 1 #3783a	.90	

PURPLE HEART

A2891

Designed by Carl Herrman. Printed by Banknote Corporation of America (#3784), Ashton-Potter (USA) Ltd. (#3784A).

LITHOGRAPHED
Sheets of 200 in 10 panes of 20 (#3784), Sheets of 120 in six panes of 20 (#3784A)

2003 Tagged *Serpentine Die Cut 11¼x10¾*
Self-Adhesive

3784	A2891 37c **multicolored,** *May 30*	.75	.25
	P# block of 4, 4#+B	3.00	
	Pane of 20	15.00	
b.	Printed on back of backing paper	—	
d.	Die cutting omitted, pair	—	

Serpentine Die Cut 10¾x10¼

3784A	A2891 37c **multicolored,** *Aug. 1*	.75	.25
	P# block of 4, 4#+P	3.00	
	Pane of 20	15.00	
e.	Die cutting omitted, pair	150.00	
	Pane of 20	*1,600.*	

See Nos. 4032, 4164, 4263-4264, 4390.

Sea Coast Type of 2002

Designed by Tom Engeman. Printed by J.W. Ferguson & Sons for Ashton-Potter (USA) Ltd.

COIL STAMP
PHOTOGRAVURE

2003, June Untagged *Serpentine Die Cut 9½x10*
Self-Adhesive

3785	A2853 (5c) **multicolored**	.25	.25
	Pair	.50	
	P# strip of 5, #P1111	1.40	
	P# single, same #	—	1.00
a.	Serp. die cut 9¼x10	.25	.25
	Pair	.50	
	P# strip of 5, #P2222	1.50	
	P# single, same #	—	1.00
b.	As "a," tagged (error)	3.25	2.50
	P# strip of 5, #P2222	62.50	
	P# single, same #	—	50.00

On No. 3785, the stamps are spaced on backing paper that is taller than the stamps.

One printing of No. 3785 has more of a scarlet shade in the sky than do other examples of Nos. 3785 and 3785a. Nos. 3785 and 3785a have black "2003" year date.

LEGENDS OF HOLLYWOOD

Audrey Hepburn (1929-93), Actress — A2892

Designed by Michael J. Deas. Printed by American Packaging Corporation for Sennett Security Products.

PHOTOGRAVURE
Sheets of 120 in six panes of 20

2003, June 11 Tagged *Serpentine Die Cut 10¾*
Self-Adhesive

3786	A2892 37c **multicolored**	1.25	1.00
	P# block of 4, 6#+S	6.00	
	Pane of 20	29.00	

Uncut press sheets of No. 3786 were made available for sale. Values: cross-gutter block of 8, $27.50; pairs with gutters between, $4.25 each. See note after No. 2868.

SOUTHEASTERN LIGHTHOUSES

Old Cape Henry, Virginia — A2893

Cape Lookout, North Carolina — A2894

Morris Island, South Carolina — A2895

Tybee Island, Georgia — A2896

Hillsboro Inlet, Florida — A2897

Designed by Howard E. Paine. Printed by American Packaging Corporation for Sennett Security Products.

PHOTOGRAVURE
Sheets of 120 in six panes of 20

2003, June 13 Tagged *Serpentine Die Cut 10¾*
Self-Adhesive

3787	A2893 37c **multicolored**	1.10	.30
3788	A2894 37c **multicolored**	1.10	.30
a.	Bottom of "USA" even with top of upper half-diamond of lighthouse (pos. 2)	4.00	2.50
3789	A2895 37c **multicolored**	1.10	.30
3790	A2896 37c **multicolored**	1.10	.30
3791	A2897 37c **multicolored**	1.10	.30
a.	Strip of 5, #3787-3791	5.50	
b.	Strip of 5, #3787, 3788a, 3789-3791	9.50	
	P# block of 10, 2 sets of 6#+S	17.50	
	Pane of 20	37.00	

Hidden 3-D images can be seen on Nos. 3787-3791 when viewed with a special "Stamp Decoder" lens sold by the USPS. No. 3787, 1792; No. 3788 and 3788a, 1859; No. 3789, 1876; No. 3790, 1867; No. 3791, 1907.

Eagle in Gold on Colored Background
A2898

Colored Eagle on Gold Background
A2899

Designed by Tom Engeman. Printed by American Packaging Corporation for Sennett Security Products.

PHOTOGRAVURE
COIL STAMPS
Dated "2003"

Serpentine Die Cut 11¾ Vert.

2003, June 26 **Untagged**

Self-Adhesive

3792 A2898 (25c) **gray & gold** .50 .25
a. Tagged —
3793 A2899 (25c) **gold & red** .50 .25
a. Tagged —
3794 A2898 (25c) **dull blue & gold** .50 .25
a. Tagged —
3795 A2899 (25c) **gold & Prussian blue** .50 .25
a. Tagged —
3796 A2898 (25c) **green & gold** .50 .25
a. Tagged —
3797 A2899 (25c) **gold & gray** .50 .25
a. Tagged —
3798 A2898 (25c) **Prussian blue & gold** .50 .25
a. Tagged —
3799 A2899 (25c) **gold & dull blue** .50 .25
a. Tagged —
3800 A2898 (25c) **red & gold** .50 .25
a. Tagged —
3801 A2899 (25c) **gold & green** .50 .25
a. Tagged —
b. Strip of 10, #3792-3801 5.00
P# strip of 11, 2 #3801, 1 each #3792-3800, #S1111111, S2222222, S3333333 8.00
P# strip of 21, 3 #3796, 2 each #3792-3795, 3797-3801, same # 16.00
P# single (#3796), #S1111111, S2222222 — 1.50
P# single (#3796), #S3333333 — 1.00
c. Strip of 10, #3792a-3801a —
P# strip of 11, 2 #3801a, 1 each #3792a-3800a, #S3333333 —
P# strip of 21, 3 #3796a, 2 each #3792a-3795a, 3797a-3801a, same # —
P# single (#3796a), same # — —

Dated "2005"

Serpentine Die Cut 11½ Vert.

2005, Aug. 5 **Untagged**

3792d A2898 (25c) **gray & gold** .50 .25
3793d A2899 (25c) **gold & red** .50 .25
3794d A2898 (25c) **dull blue & gold** .50 .25
3795d A2899 (25c) **gold & Prussian blue** .50 .25
3796d A2898 (25c) **green & gold** .50 .25
3797d A2899 (25c) **gold & gray** .50 .25
3798d A2898 (25c) **Prussian blue & gold** .50 .25
3799d A2899 (25c) **gold & dull blue** .50 .25
3800d A2898 (25c) **red & gold** .50 .25
3801d A2899 (25c) **gold & green** .50 .25
e. Strip of 10, #3792d-3801d 5.00
P# strip of 11, 2 #3801d, 1 each #3792d-3800d, P#S1111111 9.00
P# strip of 21, 3 #3796d, 2 each #3792d-3795d, 3797d-3800d, 3801d, P#S1111111 20.00
P# single (#3796d), #S1111111 3.25

See Nos. 3844-3853.

ARCTIC TUNDRA

A2900

Illustration reduced.

Designed by Ethel Kessler. Printed by Banknote Corporation of America.

No. 3802 — Wildlife and vegetation: a, Gyrfalcon. b, Gray wolf, vert. c, Common raven, vert. d, Musk oxen and caribou, vert. e, Grizzly bears, caribou. f, Caribou, willow ptarmigans. g, Arctic ground squirrel, vert. h, Willow ptarmigan, bearberry. i, Arctic grayling. j, Singing vole, thin-legged wolf spider, lingonberry, Labrador tea.

LITHOGRAPHED
Sheets of 80 in eight panes of 10

Serpentine Die Cut 10¾x10½, 10½x10¾

2003, July 2 **Tagged**

Self-Adhesive

3802 A2900 Pane of 10 8.50
a.-j. 37c Any single .85 .50

Uncut press sheets of No. 3802 were made available for sale. See note after No. 2868.

KOREAN WAR VETERANS MEMORIAL

Memorial in Snow — A2901

Designed by Richard Sheaff. Printed by Banknote Corporation of America.

LITHOGRAPHED
Sheets of 120 in six panes of 20

Serpentine Die Cut 11½x11¾

2003, July 27 **Tagged**

Self-Adhesive

3803 A2901 37c **multicolored** .75 .25
P# block of 4, 4#+B 3.00
Pane of 20 15.00

MARY CASSATT PAINTINGS

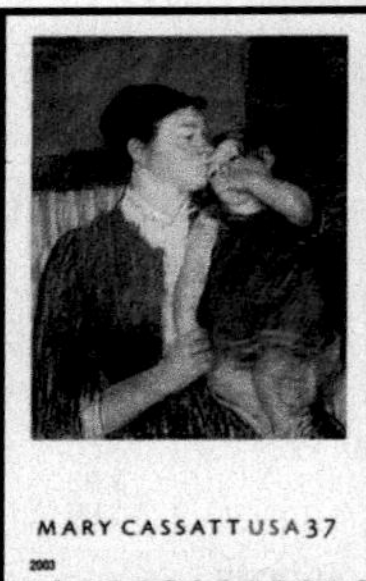

Young Mother, 1888 — A2902

Children Playing on the Beach, 1884 — A2903

On a Balcony, 1878-79 — A2904

Child in a Straw Hat, c. 1886 — A2905

Designed by Derry Noyes. Printed by American Packaging Corporation for Sennett Security Products.

PHOTOGRAVURE

Serpentine Die Cut 10¾ on 2 or 3 Sides

2003, Aug. 7 **Tagged**

Self-Adhesive
Booklet Stamps

3804 A2902 37c **multicolored** .75 .30
3805 A2903 37c **multicolored** .75 .30
3806 A2904 37c **multicolored** .75 .30
3807 A2905 37c **multicolored** .75 .30
a. Block of 4, #3804-3807 3.00
b. Booklet pane of 20, 5 #3807a 15.00

No. 3807b is a double-sided booklet with 12 stamps on one side and 8 stamps plus label (booklet cover) on the other side.

EARLY FOOTBALL HEROES

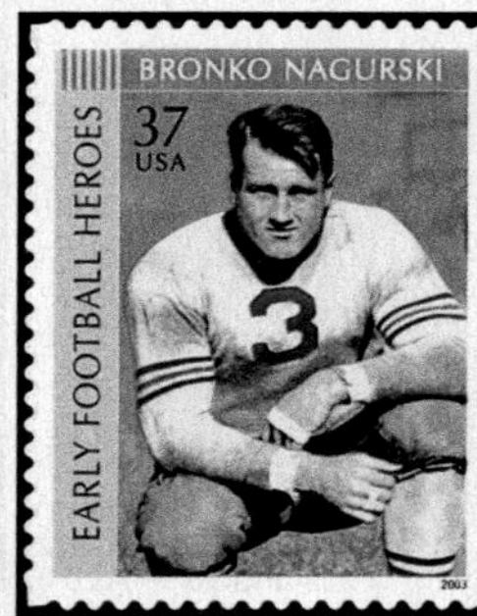

Bronko Nagurski (1908-90) — A2906

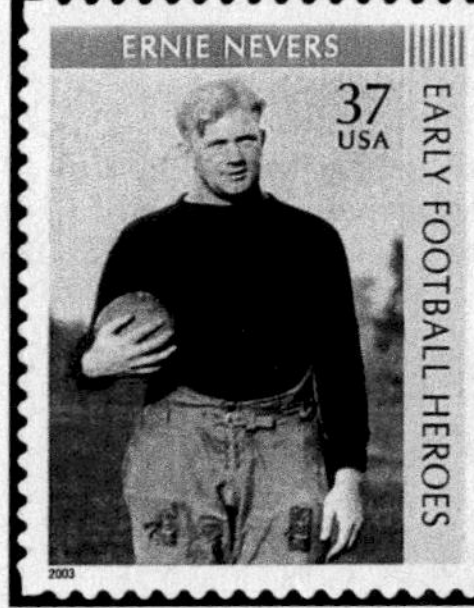

Ernie Nevers (1903-76) — A2907

Walter Camp (1859-1925) — A2908

Red Grange (1903-91) — A2909

Designed by Richard Sheaff. Printed by Avery Dennison.

PHOTOGRAVURE
Sheets of 200 in 10 panes of 20

Serpentine Die Cut 11½x11¾

2003, Aug. 8 **Tagged**

Self-Adhesive

3808 A2906 37c **multicolored** .75 .35
3809 A2907 37c **multicolored** .75 .35
3810 A2908 37c **multicolored** .75 .35
3811 A2909 37c **multicolored** .75 .35
a. Block or strip of 4, #3808-3811 3.00
P# block of 4, 7#+V 3.00
Pane of 20 15.00

Hidden 3-D images (a stylized football player) can be seen on Nos. 3808-3811 when viewed with a special "Stamp Decoder" lens sold by the USPS.

ROY ACUFF

Acuff (1903-92), Country Music Artist, and Fiddle — A2910

Designed by Richard Sheaff.
Printed by Avery Dennison.

PHOTOGRAVURE
Sheets of 200 in 10 panes of 20

2003, Sept. 13 Tagged *Serpentine Die Cut 11*
Self-Adhesive

3812 A2910 37c **multicolored**		.75	.25
P# block of 4, 4#+V		3.00	
Pane of 20		15.00	

DISTRICT OF COLUMBIA

Map, National Mall, Row Houses and Cherry Blossoms — A2911

Designed by Greg Berger.
Printed by American Packaging Corporation for Sennett Security Products.

PHOTOGRAVURE
Sheets of 128 in eight panes of 16

2003, Sept. 23 Tagged *Serpentine Die Cut 11*
Self-Adhesive

3813 A2911 37c **multicolored**		.80	.25
P# block of 4, 8#+S		3.75	
Pane of 16		18.00	

REPTILES AND AMPHIBIANS

Scarlet Kingsnake A2912

Blue-Spotted Salamander A2913

Reticulate Collared Lizard A2914

Ornate Chorus Frog — A2915

Ornate Box Turtle A2916

Designed by Steve Buchanan. Printed by Avery Dennison.

PHOTOGRAVURE
Sheets of 200 in 10 panes of 20

2003, Oct. 7 Tagged *Serpentine Die Cut 11*
Self-Adhesive

3814 A2912 37c **multicolored**		.80	.40
3815 A2913 37c **multicolored**		.80	.40
3816 A2914 37c **multicolored**		.80	.40
3817 A2915 37c **multicolored**		.80	.40
3818 A2916 37c **multicolored**		.80	.40
a.	Vert. strip of 5, #3814-3818	4.00	
	P# block of 10, 4#+V	8.00	
	Pane of 20	16.00	

Washington Type of 2002

Designed by Richard Sheaff.

Printed by Avery Dennison.

PHOTOGRAVURE
Sheets of 200 in 10 panes of 20

2003, Oct. Tagged *Serpentine Die Cut 11*
Self-Adhesive

3819 A2686 23c **gray green**		2.00	.25
P# block of 4, 2#+V		10.00	
Pane of 20		50.00	

Christmas Type of 2002

Designed by Richard Sheaff.

Printed by Ashton-Potter (USA) Ltd.

LITHOGRAPHED
Serpentine Die Cut 11¼ on 2 or 3 Sides

2003, Oct. 23 Tagged
Self-Adhesive
Booklet Stamp
Size: 19½x28mm

3820 A2843 37c **multicolored**		.75	.25
a.	Booklet pane of 20	15.00	
b.	Die cutting omitted, pair	—	

No. 3820a is a double-sided booklet with 12 stamps on one side and 8 stamps plus label (booklet cover) on the other side. Compare to No. 3675, which measures 19x27mm.

CHRISTMAS

Reindeer with Pan Pipes — A2917

Santa Claus with Drum — A2918

Santa Claus with Trumpet — A2919

Reindeer with Horn — A2920

Reindeer with Pan Pipes — A2921

Santa Claus with Drum — A2922

Santa Claus with Trumpet — A2923

Reindeer with Horn — A2924

Designed by Ethel Kessler.

Printed by American Packaging Corp. for Sennett Security Products.

PHOTOGRAVURE
Sheets of 160 in eight panes of 20
Serpentine Die Cut 11¾x11

2003, Oct. 23 Tagged
Self-Adhesive

3821 A2917 37c **multicolored**		1.00	.25
3822 A2918 37c **multicolored**		1.00	.25
3823 A2919 37c **multicolored**		1.00	.25
3824 A2920 37c **multicolored**		1.00	.25
a.	Block or strip of 4, #3821-3824	4.00	
	P# block of 4, 4#+S	4.00	
	Pane of 20	20.00	
b.	Booklet pane of 20, 5 each #3821-3824	20.00	

No. 3824b is a double-sided booklet with 12 stamps on one side and 8 stamps plus label (booklet cover) on the other side.

BOOKLET STAMPS
Serpentine Die Cut 10½x10¾ on 2 or 3 Sides

3825 A2921 37c **multicolored**		1.00	.25
3826 A2922 37c **multicolored**		1.00	.25
3827 A2923 37c **multicolored**		1.00	.25
3828 A2924 37c **multicolored**		1.00	.25
a.	Block of 4, #3825-3828	4.00	
b.	Booklet pane of 4, #3825-3828	4.00	
c.	Booklet pane of 6, #3827-3828, 2 each #3825-3826	6.00	
d.	Booklet pane of 6, #3825-3826, 2 each #3827-3828	6.00	

Snowy Egret — A2925

Designed by Carl T. Herrman.

Printed by Avery Dennison (#3829), Ashton-Potter (USA) Ltd. (#3829A, 3830, 3830D).

COIL STAMPS
PHOTOGRAVURE

2003-04 Tagged *Serpentine Die Cut 8½ Vert.*
Self-Adhesive

3829 A2925 37c **multicolored,** *Oct. 24, 2003* .75 .25
Pair 1.50
P# strip of 5, #V1111, V2111, V3212, V3222 4.50
P# strip of 5, #V3221 250.00
P# single, #V1111, V2111, V3212, V3222 — 1.25
P# single, #V2121 *475.00*
P# single, #V3211 *400.00*
P# single, #V3221 — *115.00*
b. Black omitted — —

LITHOGRAPHED
Serpentine Die Cut 9½ Vert.

3829A A2925 37c **multicolored,** *Mar. 2004* .85 .25
Pair 1.70
P# strip of 5, #P11111, P22222, P33333, P44444, P55555 6.00
P# single, same # — 1.75

Serpentine Die Cut 11½x11 on 2, 3 or 4 Sides
Booklet Stamps
PHOTOGRAVURE

3830 A2925 37c **multicolored,** *Jan. 30, 2004* .75 .25
a. Booklet pane of 20 15.00
b. As "a," die cutting omitted —

With "USPS" Microprinted on Bird's Breast
Litho.

3830D A2925 37c **multicolored,** *2004* *5.00* .25
e. Booklet pane of 20 *100.00*
f. Die cutting omitted, pair *150.00*
g. As "e," die cutting omitted *1,200.*

PACIFIC CORAL REEF

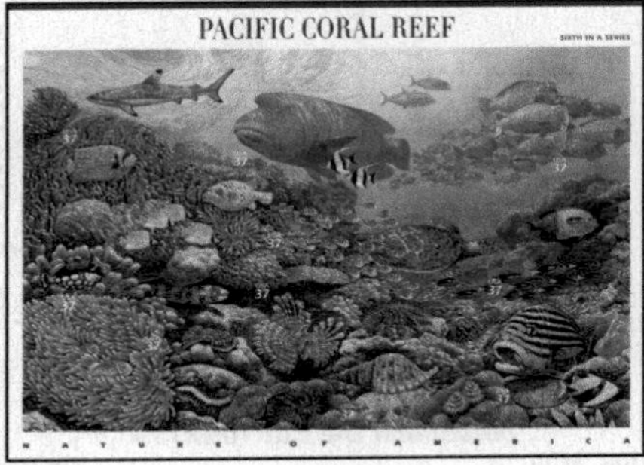

A2926

Illustration reduced.

Designed by Ethel Kessler. Printed by Avery Dennison.

No. 3831 — Marine life: a, Emperor angelfish, blue coral, mound coral, vert. b, Humphead wrasse, Moorish idol. c, Bumphead parrotfish, vert. d, Black-spotted puffer, threadfin butterflyfish, staghorn coral. e, Hawksbill turtle, palette surgeonfish. f, Pink anemonefish, magnificent sea anemone, vert. g, Snowflake moray eel, Spanish dancer. h, Lionfish, vert. i, Triton's trumpet. j, Oriental sweetlips, bluestreak cleaner wrasse, mushroom coral, vert.

PHOTOGRAVURE
Sheets of 80 in eight panes of 10

2004, Jan. 2 Tagged *Serpentine Die Cut 10¾*
Self-Adhesive

3831 A2926 Pane of 10 9.00
a.-j. 37c Any single .90 .40

Uncut press sheets of No. 3831 were made available for sale. See note after No. 2868.

CHINESE NEW YEAR

Year of the Monkey
A2927

Designed by Clarence Lee. Printed by American Packaging Corporation for Sennett Security Products.

PHOTOGRAVURE
Sheets of 120 in six panes of 20

2004, Jan. 13 Tagged *Serpentine Die Cut 10¾*
Self-Adhesive

3832 A2927 37c **multicolored** .75 .25
P# block of 4, 4# + S 3.00
Pane of 20 15.00
a. Yellow omitted —

See No. 3895i.

LOVE

Candy Hearts — A2928

Designed by Michael Osborne. Printed by Avery Dennison.

PHOTOGRAVURE
BOOKLET STAMP

Serpentine Die Cut 10¾ on 2, 3 or 4 Sides
2004, Jan. 14 Tagged
Self-Adhesive

3833 A2928 37c **multicolored** .75 .25
a. Booklet pane of 20 15.00

BLACK HERITAGE SERIES

Paul Robeson (1898-1976), Actor, Singer, Athlete and Activist — A2929

Designed by Richard Sheaff. Printed by American Packaging Corporation for Sennett Security Products.

PHOTOGRAVURE
Sheets of 120 in six panes of 20

2004, Jan. 20 Tagged *Serpentine Die Cut 10¾*
Self-Adhesive

3834 A2929 37c **multicolored** .85 .25
P# block of 4, 4# + S 3.40
Pane of 20 17.00

THEODOR SEUSS GEISEL (DR. SEUSS)

Dr. Seuss (1904-91), Children's Book Writer, and Book Characters
A2930

Designed by Carl T. Herrman. Printed by American Packaging Corporation for Sennett Security Products.

PHOTOGRAVURE
Sheets of 180 in nine panes of 20
Serpentine Die Cut 10¾x10½

2004, Mar. 2 Tagged
Self-Adhesive

3835 A2930 37c **multicolored** .85 .25
P# block of 4, 6#+S 3.50
Pane of 20 17.50
a. Die cutting omitted, pair *1,400.*

FLOWERS

White Lilacs and Pink Roses — A2931

Five Varieties of Pink Roses — A2932

Designed by Richard Sheaff. Printed by Ashton-Potter (USA) Ltd. (#3836), American Packaging Corporation for Sennett Security Products.

LITHOGRAPHED (#3836), PHOTOGRAVURE
BOOKLET STAMP (#3836)
Sheets of 160 in eight panes of 20 (#3837)

Serpentine Die Cut 10¾ on 2, 3 or 4 Sides
2004, Mar. 4 Tagged
Self-Adhesive

3836 A2931 37c **multicolored** .75 .25
a. Booklet pane of 20 15.00

Serpentine Die Cut 11½x11

3837 A2932 60c **multicolored** 2.00 .25
P# block of 4, 5#+S 10.00
Pane of 20 45.00

UNITED STATES AIR FORCE ACADEMY, 50TH ANNIV.

Cadet Chapel
A2933

Designed by Phil Jordan. Printed by American Packaging Corporation for Sennett Security Products.

PHOTOGRAVURE
Sheets of 120 in six panes of 20

2004, Apr. 1 Tagged *Serpentine Die Cut 10¾*
Self-Adhesive

3838 A2933 37c **multicolored** .75 .25
P# block of 4, 6# + S 3.00
Pane of 20 15.00

A hidden 3-D image (a stylized falcon) can be seen on this stamp when it is viewed with a special "Stamp Decoder" lens sold by the USPS.

HENRY MANCINI

Henry Mancini (1924-94), Composer, and Pink Panther
A2934

Designed by Carl Herrman. Printed by American Packaging Corporation for Sennett Security Products.

PHOTOGRAVURE
Sheets of 120 in six panes of 20

2004, Apr. 13 Tagged *Serpentine Die Cut 10¾*
Self-Adhesive

3839 A2934 37c **multicolored** .75 .25
P# block of 4, 6#+S 3.00
Pane of 20 15.00

AMERICAN CHOREOGRAPHERS

Martha Graham (1893-1991)
A2935

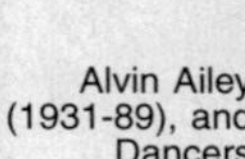

Alvin Ailey (1931-89), and Dancers A2936

Agnes de Mille (1909-93), and Dancers A2937

George Balanchine (1904-83), and Dancers A2938

Designed by Ethel Kessler. Printed by Ashton-Potter (USA) Ltd.

LITHOGRAPHED
Sheets of 120 in six panes of 20

2004, May 4 Tagged *Serpentine Die Cut 10¾*

Self-Adhesive

3840	A2935 37c **multicolored**	.75	.35
3841	A2936 37c **multicolored**	.75	.35
3842	A2937 37c **multicolored**	.75	.35
3843	A2938 37c **multicolored**	.75	.35
a.	Horiz. strip of 4, #3840-3843	3.00	
	P# block of 8, 2 sets of P#, 6#+P	6.00	
	Pane of 20	15.00	
b.	Strip of 4, die cutting omitted	*300.00*	
	Pane of 20	*1,750.*	
c.	Pane of 20 misprinted and miscut to show 5 #3843 and half of 5 #3842 at left, lower center plate position diagram at center, and 10 blank stamps at right.	—	
d.	As "a," block tagging omitted	55.00	

Normal tagging on Nos. 3840-3843 is prephosphored paper with additional block tagging on top of the printed designs.

Eagle Types of 2003

Designed by Tom Engeman. Printed by American Packaging Corporation for Sennett Security Products.

PHOTOGRAVURE
COIL STAMPS

2004, May 12 Untagged *Perf. 9¾ Vert.*

3844	A2898 (25c) **gray & gold**	.95	.25
3845	A2899 (25c) **gold & green**	.95	.25
3846	A2898 (25c) **red & gold**	.95	.25
3847	A2899 (25c) **gold & dull blue**	.95	.25
3848	A2898 (25c) **Prussian blue & gold**	.95	.25
3849	A2899 (25c) **gold & gray**	.95	.50
3850	A2898 (25c) **green & gold**	.95	.25
3851	A2899 (25c) **gold & Prussian blue**	.95	.25
3852	A2898 (25c) **dull blue & gold**	.95	.25
3853	A2899 (25c) **gold & red**	.95	.25
a.	Strip of 10, #3844-3853	9.50	—
	P# strip of 11, 2 #3844, 1 each #3845-3853, #S1111111	15.00	—
	P# strip of 21, 3 #3849, 2 each #3844-3848, 3850-3853, #S1111111	30.00	—
	P# single (#3849), same #	—	.50

LEWIS & CLARK EXPEDITION, BICENTENNIAL

Meriwether Lewis (1774-1809) and William Clark (1770-1838) On Hill — A2939

Lewis — A2940

Clark — A2941

Designed by Michael J. Deas. Printed by Banknote Corporation of America for Sennett Security Products (#3854), Ashton-Potter (USA) Ltd.

LITHOGRAPHED & ENGRAVED
Sheets of 180 in nine panes of 20

2004, May 14 Tagged *Serpentine Die Cut 10¾*

Self-Adhesive

3854	A2939 37c **green & multicolored**	1.10	.25
	P# block of 4, 6#+S	4.50	
	Pane of 20	22.50	

Uncut press sheets of No. 3854 were made available for sale. Values: cross-gutter block of 4, $18; pairs with gutters between, $3 each. See note after No. 2868.

Booklet Stamps

Serpentine Die Cut 10½x10¾

3855	A2940 37c **blue & multicolored** ⓢ	.90	.45
3856	A2941 37c **red & multicolored** ⓢ	.90	.45
a.	Horiz. or vert. pair, #3855-3856	1.80	
b.	Booklet pane, 5 each #3855-3856	9.00	

Nos. 3855-3856 were issued in booklets containing two No. 3856b, each with a different backing. The booklets sold for $8.95.

ⓢ: Portrait ink can flake off during water soak. See note after No. 1549.

ISAMU NOGUCHI (1904-88), SCULPTOR

Akari 25N — A2942

Margaret La Farge Osborn — A2943

Black Sun — A2944

Mother and Child — A2945

Figure (Detail) — A2946

Designed by Derry Noyes. Printed by Ashton-Potter (USA) Ltd.

LITHOGRAPHED
Sheets of 120 in six panes of 20
Serpentine Die Cut 10½x10¾

2004, May 18 Tagged

Self-Adhesive

3857	A2942 37c **black**	.90	.40
3858	A2943 37c **black**	.90	.40
3859	A2944 37c **black**	.90	.40
3860	A2945 37c **black**	.90	.40
3861	A2946 37c **black**	.90	.40
a.	Horiz. strip of 5, #3857-3861	4.50	
	P# block of 6 (3 across x 2 down), 2#+P	6.00	
	P# block of 8, 2 sets of 2#+P + left label	8.00	
	Pane of 20	20.00	

Uncut press sheets of Nos. 3857-3861 were made available for sale. Values: cross-gutter block of 8, $25; pairs with gutters between, $3 each. See note after No. 2868.

NATIONAL WORLD WAR II MEMORIAL

A2947

Designed by Howard E. Paine. Printed by Ashton-Potter (USA) Ltd.

LITHOGRAPHED
Sheets of 180 in nine panes of 20

2004, May 29 Tagged *Serpentine Die Cut 10¾*
Self-Adhesive

3862 A2947 37c **multicolored** .75 .25
P# block of 4, 4#+P 3.00
Pane of 20 15.00

A hidden 3-D image (a U.S. flag) can be seen on this stamp when it is viewed with a special "Stamp Decoder" lens sold by the USPS.

Scott values for used self-adhesive stamps are for examples either on piece or off piece.

OLYMPIC GAMES, ATHENS, GREECE Ⓢ

Stylized Runner A2948

Designed by Richard Sheaff. Printed by Ashton-Potter (USA) Ltd.

LITHOGRAPHED
Sheets of 120 in six panes of 20

2004, June 9 Tagged *Serpentine Die Cut 10¾*
Self-Adhesive

3863 A2948 37c **multicolored** .75 .25
P# block of 4, 4#+P 3.00
Pane of 20 15.00

Ⓢ: Ink cracks and flakes off during water soak. See note after No. 1549.

Sea Coast Type of 2002

Designed by Tom Engeman. Printed by American Packaging Corp. for Sennett Security Products.

PHOTOGRAVURE
COIL STAMP

2004, June 11 Untagged *Perf. 9¾ Vert.*

3864 A2853 (5c) **multicolored** .25 .25
Pair .50 —
P# strip of 5, #S1111 1.40 —
P# single, same # — 1.00

No. 3864 has "2004" year date in black, rows of distinctly separated dots in surf area, and the small orange cloud is indistinct. No. 3775 has "2003" year date in blue, dots that run together in surf area, and a distinct small orange cloud.

No. 3864 known with red ink that glows orange under long wave ultraviolet light. Values the same.

THE ART OF DISNEY: FRIENDSHIP

Goofy, Mickey Mouse, Donald Duck — A2949

Bambi, Thumper — A2950

Mufasa, Simba — A2951

Jiminy Cricket, Pinocchio — A2952

Designed by David Pacheco. Printed by American Packaging Corporation for Banknote Corporation of America/Sennett Security Products.

LITHOGRAPHED
Sheets of 180 in nine panes of 20
Serpentine Die Cut 10½x10¾

2004, June 23 Tagged
Self-Adhesive

3865 A2949 37c **multicolored** 1.00 .30
3866 A2950 37c **multicolored** 1.00 .30
3867 A2951 37c **multicolored** 1.00 .30
3868 A2952 37c **multicolored** 1.00 .30
a. Block or vert. strip of 4, #3865-3868 4.00
P# block of 4, 4#+S 4.00
Pane of 20 20.00

U.S.S. CONSTELLATION

A2953

Designed by Howard E. Paine. Printed by Ashton-Potter (USA) Ltd.

ENGRAVED
Sheets of 180 in nine panes of 20

2004, June 30 Tagged *Serpentine Die Cut 10½*
Self-Adhesive

3869 A2953 37c **brown** .75 .25
P# block of 4, 1#+P 3.00
Pane of 20 15.00

R. BUCKMINSTER FULLER (1895-1983), ENGINEER

Time Magazine Cover Depicting Fuller, by Boris Artzybasheff — A2954

Designed by Carl T. Herrman. Printed by Ashton-Potter (USA) Ltd.

LITHOGRAPHED
Sheets of 120 in six panes of 20
Serpentine Die Cut 10½x10¾

2004, July 12 Tagged
Self-Adhesive

3870 A2954 37c **multicolored** .75 .25
P# block of 4, 5#+P 3.00
Pane of 20 15.00

LITERARY ARTS

James Baldwin (1924-87), Writer A2955

Designed by Phil Jordan. Printed by Ashton-Potter (USA) Ltd.

LITHOGRAPHED
Sheets of 180 in nine panes of 20

2004, July 23 Tagged *Serpentine Die Cut 10¾*
Self-Adhesive

3871 A2955 37c **multicolored** .75 .25
P# block of 4, 5#+P 3.00
Pane of 20 15.00
a. Die cutting omitted, pair *750.00*

AMERICAN TREASURES SERIES

Giant Magnolias on a Blue Velvet Cloth, by Martin Johnson Heade A2956

Designed by Derry Noyes. Printed by American Packaging Corporation for Sennett Security Products.

PHOTOGRAVURE
BOOKLET STAMP
Serpentine Die Cut 10¾ on 2 or 3 Sides

2004, Aug. 12 Tagged
Self-Adhesive

3872 A2956 37c **multicolored** .70 .25
a. Booklet pane of 20 15.00
b. Die cutting omitted, pair, in #3872a with foldover —

No. 3872a is a double-sided booklet pane with 12 stamps on one side and eight stamps plus label on the other side.

ART OF THE AMERICAN INDIAN

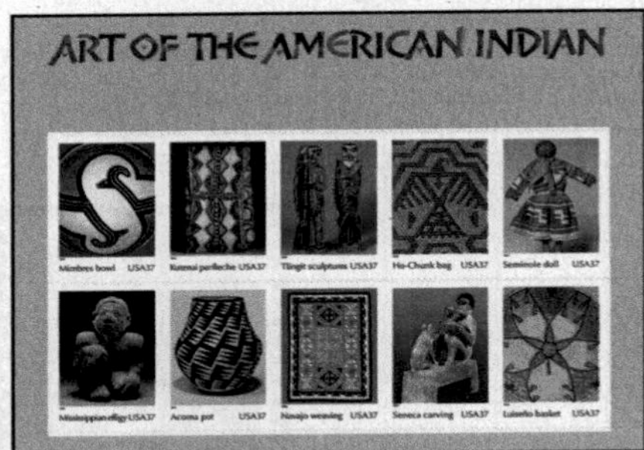

A2957

Illustration reduced.

Designed by Richard Sheaff. Printed by Avery Dennison.

No. 3873: a, Mimbres bowl. b, Kutenai parfleche. c, Tlingit sculptures. d, Ho-Chunk bag. e, Seminole doll. f, Mississippian effigy. g, Acoma pot. h, Navajo weaving. i, Seneca carving. j, Luiseño basket.

PHOTOGRAVURE
Serpentine Die Cut 10¾x11

2004, Aug. 21 Tagged
Self-Adhesive

3873 A2957 Pane of 10 25.00
a.-j. 37c Any single 2.50 .40

Sea Coast Type of 2002

Designed by Tom Engeman.

Printed by Ashton-Potter (USA), Ltd. (#3874); American Packaging Corporation for Sennett Security Products (#3875).

PHOTOGRAVURE
COIL STAMPS

2004-05 Untagged *Serpentine Die Cut 10 Vert.*
Self-Adhesive

3874 A2853 (5c) **multicolored,** large "2003" year date .25 .25
Pair .50
P# strip of 5, #P2222 1.50
P# single, #P2222 — 1.10
a. Small "2003" year date, *2005* ⓢ .25 .25
Pair .50
P# strip of 5, #P3333, P4444, P5555, P6666, P7777, P8888, P9999 1.50
P# single, #P3333, P4444, P5555, P6666 — 1.10
P# single, #P7777, P8888, P9999 — .75

On Nos. 3874 and 3874a, the stamps are spaced on backing paper that is taller than the stamps.

On No. 3874 the color laydown order of plate numbers is cyan, magenta, yellow, black. On No. 3874a, the order is BCMY.

ⓢ: Later printings of No. 3874a do not respond to a water soak. See note after No. 1549.

Serpentine Die Cut 11½ Vert.
Untagged

3875 A2853 (5c) **multicolored,** "2004" year date .25 .25
Pair .50
P# strip of 5, #S1111 1.40
P# single, #S1111 — 1.10

On Nos. 3874, 3874a and 3875, the stamps are spaced on backing paper that is taller than the stamps.

No. 3875 exists with very faint traces of tagging.

LEGENDS OF HOLLYWOOD

John Wayne (1907-79), Actor — A2958

Designed by Derry Noyes.

Printed by American Packaging Corporation for Sennett Security Products.

PHOTOGRAVURE
Sheets of 120 in six panes of 20

2004, Sept. 9 Tagged *Serpentine Die Cut 10¾*
Self-Adhesive

3876 A2958 37c **multicolored** .85 .25
P# block of 4, 6#+S 3.50
Pane of 20 18.00

Uncut press sheets of No. 3876 were made available for sale. Values: cross-gutter block of 8, $27.50; pairs with gutters between, $3.50 each. See note after No. 2868.

SICKLE CELL DISEASE AWARENESS

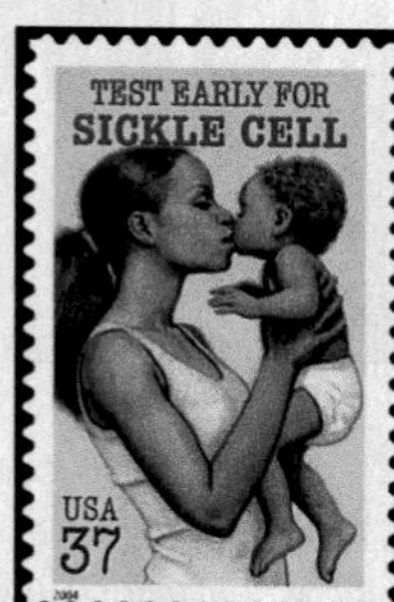

Mother and Child — A2959

Designed by Howard Paine.

Printed by Avery Dennison.

PHOTOGRAVURE
Sheets of 200 in ten panes of 20

2004, Sept. 29 Tagged *Serpentine Die Cut 11*
Self-Adhesive

3877 A2959 37c **multicolored** .75 .25

CLOUDSCAPES

A2960

Illustration reduced.

Designed by Howard E. Paine. Printed by Avery Dennison.

No. 3878 — Clouds: a, Cirrus radiatus. b, Cirrostratus fibratus. c, Cirrocumulus undulatus. d, Cumulonimbus mammatus. e, Cumulonimbus incus. f, Altocumulus stratiformis. g, Altostratus translucidus. h, Altocumulus undulatus. i, Altocumulus castellanus. j, Altocumulus lenticularis. k, Stratocumulus undulatus. l, Stratus opacus. m, Cumulus humilis. n, Cumulus congestus. o, Cumulonimbus with tornado.

PHOTOGRAVURE

2004, Oct. 4 Tagged *Serpentine Die Cut 11*
Self-Adhesive

3878 A2960 Pane of 15 15.00
a.-o. 37c Any single 1.00 .50

CHRISTMAS

Madonna and Child, by Lorenzo Monaco — A2961

Designed by Richard Sheaff.
Printed by Ashton-Potter (USA), Ltd.

LITHOGRAPHED
BOOKLET STAMP

Serpentine Die Cut 10¾x11 on 2 or 3 Sides
2004, Oct. 14 Tagged
Self-Adhesive

3879 A2961 37c **multicolored** .75 .25
a. Booklet pane of 20 15.00
b. As "a," die cutting omitted —

No. 3879a is a double-sided booklet pane with 12 stamps on one side and eight stamps plus label that serves as a booklet cover on the other side.

HANUKKAH

Dreidel — A2962

Designed by Ethel Kessler.
Printed by Banknote Corporation of America for Sennett Security Products.

LITHOGRAPHED
Sheets of 300 in fifteen panes of 20

2004, Oct. 15 Tagged *Serpentine Die Cut 10¾*
Self-Adhesive

3880 A2962 37c **multicolored** .75 .25
P# block of 4, 4#+S 3.00
Pane of 20 15.00
a. Die cuts applied to wrong sides of stamp (hyphen-hole die cuts and wavy line

KWANZAA

People in Robes — A2963

Designed by Derry Noyes.
Printed by Ashton-Potter (USA), Ltd.

LITHOGRAPHED
Sheets of 160 in eight panes of 20

2004, Oct. 16 Tagged *Serpentine Die Cut 10¾*
Self-Adhesive

3881 A2963 37c **multicolored** .75 .25
P# block of 4, 6#+P 3.00
Pane of 20 15.00

See Nos. 4119, 4220, 4373.

LITERARY ARTS

Moss Hart (1904-61), Playwright A2964

Designed by Ethel Kessler.
Printed by Avery Dennison.

PHOTOGRAVURE
Sheets of 200 in ten panes of 20

2004, Oct. 25 Tagged *Serpentine Die Cut 11*
Self-Adhesive

3882 A2964 37c **multicolored** .75 .25
P# block of 4, 5#+V 3.00
Pane of 20 15.00

CHRISTMAS

Purple Santa Ornament — A2965

Green Santa Ornament — A2966

Blue Santa Ornament — A2967

Red Santa Ornament — A2968

Purple Santa Ornament — A2969

Green Santa Ornament — A2970

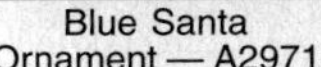

Blue Santa Ornament — A2971

Red Santa Ornament — A2972

Designed by Derry Noyes. Printed by American Packaging Corporation for Sennett Security Printers. (#3883-3890), Avery Dennison (#3891-3894).

PHOTOGRAVURE

Sheets of 160 in eight panes of 20

Serpentine Die Cut 11½x11

2004, Nov. 16 **Tagged**

Self-Adhesive

3883 A2965 37c **purple & multicolored** 1.00 .25
3884 A2966 37c **green & multicolored** 1.00 .25
3885 A2967 37c **blue & multicolored** 1.00 .25
3886 A2968 37c **red & multicolored** 1.00 .25
a. Block or strip of 4, #3883-3886 4.00
P# block of 4, 4#+S 4.00
Pane of 20 20.00
b. Booklet pane of 20, 5 #3886a blocks 20.00

Booklet Stamps

Serpentine Die Cut 10¼x10¾ on 2 or 3 Sides

3887 A2969 37c **purple & multicolored** .90 .25
3888 A2970 37c **green & multicolored** .90 .25
3889 A2971 37c **blue & multicolored** .90 .25
3890 A2972 37c **red & multicolored** .90 .25
a. Block of 4, #3887-3890 3.60
b. Booklet pane of 4, #3887-3890 3.60
c. Booklet pane of 6, #3889-3890, 2 each #3887-3888 5.50
d. Booklet pane of 6, #3887-3888, 2 each #3889-3890 5.50

Serpentine Die Cut 8 on 2, 3 or 4 Sides

3891 A2970 37c **green & multicolored** 2.00 .25
3892 A2969 37c **purple & multicolored** 2.00 .25
3893 A2972 37c **red & multicolored** 2.00 .25
3894 A2971 37c **blue & multicolored** 2.00 .25
a. Block of 4, #3891-3894 8.00
b. Booklet pane of 18, 6 each #3891, 3893, 3 each # 3892, 3894 36.00
Nos. 3883-3894 (12) 15.60 3.00

No. 3886b is a double-sided booklet with 12 stamps on one side and 8 stamps plus label that serves as a booklet cover on the other side.

The design of No. 3894b shows ornaments in a wooden box. The pattern of the wooden box dividers creates three types of each design. Rows 1 and 4 are Type 1, with a top horizontal strip of frame extending from edge to edge while the bottom strip of frame stops at the design's width. Rows 2 and 5 are Type 2, with both top and bottom strips of frame stopping at the design's width. Rows 3 and 6 are Type 3, with the top strip of frame stopping at design's width while the bottom strip of frame extends from edge to edge. Each variety is equally common.

Chinese New Year Types of 1992-2004

Designed by Clarence Lee. Printed by American Packaging Corporation for Sennett Security Products.

PHOTOGRAVURE

2005, Jan. 6 **Tagged** ***Serpentine Die Cut 10¾***

Self-Adhesive

3895 Double sided pane of 24, 2 each #a-l 18.00
a. A2360 37c Rat .75 .40
b. A2413 37c Ox .75 .40
c. A2462 37c Tiger .75 .40
d. A2535 37c Rabbit .75 .40
e. A2602 37c Dragon .75 .40
f. A2702 37c Snake .75 .40
g. A2752 37c Horse .75 .40
h. A2856 37c Ram .75 .40
i. A2927 37c Monkey .75 .40
j. A2067 37c Rooster .75 .40
k. A2146 37c Dog .75 .40
l. A2205 37c Boar .75 .40
m. As No. 3895, die cutting missing on "a," "b," and "c" on reverse side (PS) *1,100.*

No. 3895h has "2005" year date and is photogravure while No. 3747 has "2003" year date and is lithographed.

Stamps are on the right side of the front and on the left side of the reverse.

BLACK HERITAGE SERIES

Marian Anderson (1897-1993), Singer — A2973

Designed by Richard Sheaff. Printed by American Packaging Corporation for Sennett Security Products.

PHOTOGRAVURE

Sheets of 120 in six panes of 20

2005, Jan. 27 **Tagged** ***Serpentine Die Cut 10¾***

Self-Adhesive

3896 A2973 37c **multicolored** .85 .25
P# block of 4, 4# + S 3.40
Pane of 20 17.00

RONALD REAGAN

Ronald Reagan (1911-2004), 40th President — A2974

Designed by Howard E. Paine. Printed by American Packaging Corporation for Sennett Security Products.

PHOTOGRAVURE

Sheets of 120 in six panes of 20

2005, Feb. 9 **Tagged** ***Serpentine Die Cut 10¾***

Self-Adhesive

3897 A2974 37c **multicolored** .75 .25
P# block of 4, 4#+S 3.00
Pane of 20 15.00

The bottom center stamp (pos. 18) shows a small portion of the pane position diagram in the bottom margin, due to the too-high placement of the diagram in the selvage. There are three varieties of the portion appearing on the stamp, depending on the pane position on the press sheet.

Uncut press sheets of No. 3897 were made available for sale. Values: cross-gutter block of 4, $9.50; pairs with gutters between, $3 each. See note after No. 2868.

See No. 4078.

LOVE

Hand and Flower Bouquet — A2975

Designed by Derry Noyes. Printed by Avery Dennison.

PHOTOGRAVURE

BOOKLET STAMP

Serpentine Die Cut 10¾x11 on 2, 3 or 4 Sides

2005, Feb. 18 **Tagged**

Self-Adhesive

3898 A2975 37c **multicolored** .75 .25
a. Booklet pane of 20 15.00

NORTHEAST DECIDUOUS FOREST

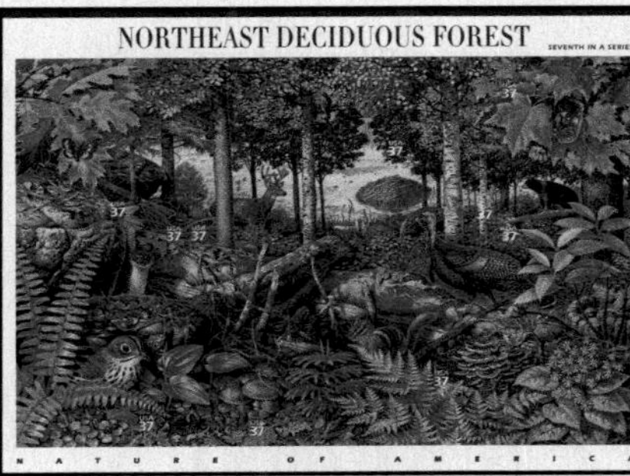

A2976

Illustration reduced.

Designed by Ethel Kessler. Printed by Avery Dennison.

No. 3899 — Wildlife: a, Eastern buckmoth, vert. b, Red-shouldered hawk. c, Eastern red bat. d, White-tailed deer. e, Black bear. f, Long-tailed weasel, vert. g, Wild turkey, vert. h, Ovenbird, vert. i, Red eft. j, Eastern chipmunk.

PHOTOGRAVURE

Sheets of 80 in eight panes of 10

2005, Mar. 3 **Tagged** ***Serpentine Die Cut 10¾***

Self-Adhesive

3899 A2976 Pane of 10 8.50
a.-j. 37c Any single .85 .40

Uncut press sheets of No. 3899 were made available for sale. See note after No. 2868.

SPRING FLOWERS

Hyacinth — A2977

Daffodil — A2978

Tulip — A2979

Iris — A2980

Designed by Derry Noyes. Printed by Ashton-Potter (USA) Ltd.

LITHOGRAPHED

BOOKLET STAMPS

Serpentine Die Cut 10¾ on 2 or 3 Sides

2005, Mar. 15 **Tagged**

Self-Adhesive

3900 A2977 37c **multicolored** .85 .30
3901 A2978 37c **multicolored** .85 .30
3902 A2979 37c **multicolored** .85 .30
3903 A2980 37c **multicolored** .85 .30
a. Block of 4, #3900-3903 3.40
b. Booklet pane of 20, 5 each #3900-3903 17.00
c. As "b," die cutting omitted on side with 8 stamps —

No. 3903b is a double-sided booklet with 12 stamps on one side and 8 stamps plus label (booklet cover) on the other side.

LITERARY ARTS

Robert Penn Warren (1905-89), Writer A2981

Designed by Carl Herrman. Printed by American Packaging Corporation for Sennett Security Products.

PHOTOGRAVURE
Sheets of 120 in six panes of 20

2005, Apr. 22 Tagged *Serpentine Die Cut 10¾*
Self-Adhesive

3904 A2981 37c **multicolored** .75 .25
P# block of 4, 5#+S 3.00
Pane of 20 15.00

EDGAR Y. "YIP" HARBURG

Harburg (1896-1981), Lyricist A2982

Designed by Ethel Kessler. Printed by Banknote Corporation of America for Sennett Security Products.

LITHOGRAPHED
Sheets of 120 in six panes of 20

2005, Apr. 28 Tagged *Serpentine Die Cut 10¾*
Self-Adhesive

3905 A2982 37c **multicolored** .75 .25
P# block of 4, 4#+S 3.00
Pane of 20 15.00

AMERICAN SCIENTISTS

Barbara McClintock (1902-92), Geneticist A2983

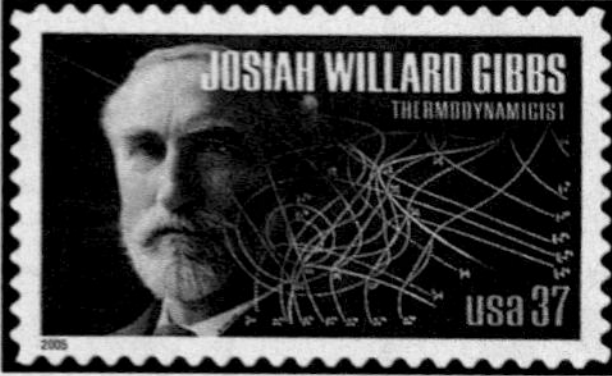

Josiah Willard Gibbs (1839-1903), Thermodynamicist — A2984

John von Neumann (1903-57), Mathematician A2985

Richard Feynman (1918-88), Physicist A2986

Designed by Carl Herrman. Printed by Banknote Corporation of America for Sennett Security Products.

LITHOGRAPHED
Sheets of 180 in nine panes of 20

2005, May 4 Tagged *Serpentine Die Cut 10¾*
Self-Adhesive

3906 A2983 37c **multicolored** 1.00 .35
3907 A2984 37c **multicolored** 1.00 .35
3908 A2985 37c **multicolored** 1.00 .35
a. Vert. pair, die cutting omitted, #3906 & 3908 —
3909 A2986 37c **multicolored** 1.00 .35
a. Block or horiz. strip of 4, #3906-3909 4.00
P# block of 8, 2 sets of P# + top label, 5#+S 8.00
P# block of 4, 5#+S 4.00
Pane of 20 20.00
b. All colors omitted, tagging omitted, pane of 20 —
c. As "a," printing on back of stamps omitted —
d. Vert. pair, die cutting omitted, #3907 & 3909 —

On No. 3909b, the printing on the back of the pane and all die cutting is normal.

MODERN AMERICAN ARCHITECTURE

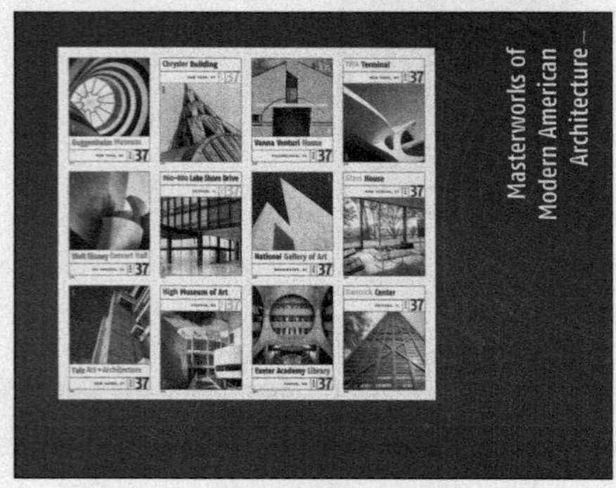

A2987

Illustration reduced.

Designed by Margaret Bauer. Printed by Ashton-Potter (USA) Ltd.

No. 3910 — Buildings: a, Guggenheim Museum, New York. b, Chrysler Building, New York. c, Vanna Venturi House, Philadelphia. d, TWA Terminal, New York. e, Walt Disney Concert Hall, Los Angeles. f, 860-880 Lake Shore Drive, Chicago. g, National Gallery of Art, Washington, DC. h, Glass House, New Canaan, CT. i, Yale Art and Architecture Building, New Haven, CT. j, High Museum of Art, Atlanta. k, Exeter Academy Library, Exeter, NH. l, Hancock Center, Chicago.

LITHOGRAPHED
Serpentine Die Cut 10¾x11

2005, May 19 Tagged
Self-Adhesive

3910 A2987 Pane of 12 11.00
a.-l. 37c Any single .90 .50
m. As No. 3910, orange yellow omitted *400.00* —

No. 3910m exists on a first day cover.

LEGENDS OF HOLLYWOOD

Henry Fonda (1905-82), Actor — A2988

Designed by Derry Noyes. Printed by Ashton-Potter (USA) Ltd.

LITHOGRAPHED
Sheets of 180 in nine panes of 20
Serpentine Die Cut 11x10¾

2005, May 20 Tagged
Self-Adhesive

3911 A2988 37c **multicolored** .90 .25
P# block of 4, 5#+P 4.50
Pane of 20 22.00

Uncut press sheets of No. 3911 were made available for sale. Values: cross-gutter block of 8, $22.50; pairs with gutters between, $3.50 each. See note after No. 2868.

THE ART OF DISNEY: CELEBRATION

Pluto, Mickey Mouse — A2989

Mad Hatter, Alice — A2990

Flounder, Ariel — A2991

Snow White, Dopey — A2992

Designed by David Pacheco. Printed by Banknote Corporation of America for Sennett Security Products.

LITHOGRAPHED
Sheets of 180 in nine panes of 20
Serpentine Die Cut 10½x10¾

2005, June 30 Tagged
Self-Adhesive

3912 A2989 37c **multicolored** .85 .30
3913 A2990 37c **multicolored** .85 .30
3914 A2991 37c **multicolored** .85 .30
3915 A2992 37c **multicolored** .85 .30
a. Block or vert. strip of 4, #3912-3915 3.40
P# block of 4, 6#+S 3.40
P# block of 10, 2 sets of P# + top label 8.25
Pane of 20 17.00
b. Die cutting omitted, pane of 20 *5,500.* *1,400.*
c. Printed on backing paper, pane of 20 —

On the unique used pane of No. 3915b, the outer selvage was removed by cutting.

ADVANCES IN AVIATION

Boeing 247 — A2993

Consolidated PBY Catalina A2994

Grumman F6F Hellcat A2995

Republic P-47 Thunderbolt A2996

Engineering and Research Corporation Ercoupe 415 — A2997

Lockheed P-80 Shooting Star — A2998

Consolidated B-24 Liberator A2999

Boeing B-29 Superfortress A3000

Beechcraft 35 Bonanza A3001

Northrop YB-49 Flying Wing — A3002

Designed by Phil Jordan. Printed by Ashton-Potter (USA) Ltd.

LITHOGRAPHED
Sheets of 180 in nine panes of 20
Serpentine Die Cut 10¾x10½

2005, July 29 **Tagged**

Self-Adhesive

3916	A2993	37c	**multicolored**	.80	.40
3917	A2994	37c	**multicolored**	.80	.40
3918	A2995	37c	**multicolored**	.80	.40
3919	A2996	37c	**multicolored**	.80	.40
3920	A2997	37c	**multicolored**	.80	.40
3921	A2998	37c	**multicolored**	.80	.40
3922	A2999	37c	**multicolored**	.80	.40
3923	A3000	37c	**multicolored**	.80	.40
3924	A3001	37c	**multicolored**	.80	.40
3925	A3002	37c	**multicolored**	.80	.40
a.	Block of 10, #3916-3925			8.00	
	P# block of 10, 7#+P			8.00	
	Pane of 20			16.00	
b.	As "a," tagging omitted			—	

No. 3925b currently is in a pane of 20 format. Only one pane is recorded.

RIO GRANDE BLANKETS

A3003

A3004

A3005

A3006

Designed by Derry Noyes. Printed by Ashton-Potter (USA) Ltd.

LITHOGRAPHED
BOOKLET STAMPS
Serpentine Die Cut 10¾ on 2 or 3 Sides

2005, July 30 **Tagged**

Self-Adhesive

3926	A3003	37c	**multicolored**	.75	.30
3927	A3004	37c	**multicolored**	.75	.30
3928	A3005	37c	**multicolored**	.75	.30
3929	A3006	37c	**multicolored**	.75	.30
a.	Block of 4, #3926-3929			3.00	
b.	Booklet pane, 5 each #3926-3929			15.00	

No. 3929b is a double-sided booklet with 12 stamps on one side and 8 stamps plus label (booklet cover) on the other side.

PRESIDENTIAL LIBRARIES ACT, 50th ANNIV.

Presidential Seal — A3007

Designed by Howard E. Paine. Printed by Banknote Corporation of America for Sennett Security Products.

LITHOGRAPHED
Sheets of 180 in nine panes of 20

2005, Aug. 4 **Tagged** ***Serpentine Die Cut 10¾***

Self-Adhesive

3930	A3007	37c	**multicolored**	.80	.25
	P# block of 4, 3#+S			3.25	
	Pane of 20			16.50	

Uncut press sheets of No. 3930 were made available for sale. Values: cross-gutter block of 4, $9.50; pairs with gutters between, $3.50 each. See note after No. 2868.

SPORTY CARS OF THE 1950S

1953 Studebaker Starliner A3008

1954 Kaiser Darrin A3009

1953 Chevrolet Corvette A3010

1952 Nash Healey A3011

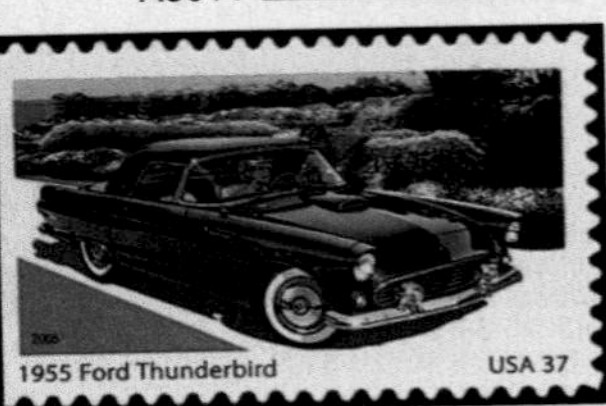

1955 Ford Thunderbird A3012

Designed by Art M. Fitzpatrick. Printed by Ashton-Potter (USA) Ltd.

LITHOGRAPHED
BOOKLET STAMPS

Serpentine Die Cut 10¾ on 2 or 3 Sides

2005, Aug. 20 **Tagged**

Self-Adhesive

3931	A3008 37c **multicolored**	1.60	.40
3932	A3009 37c **multicolored**	1.60	.40
3933	A3010 37c **multicolored**	1.60	.40
3934	A3011 37c **multicolored**	1.60	.40
3935	A3012 37c **multicolored**	1.60	.40
a.	Vert. strip of 5, #3931-3935	8.00	
b.	Booklet pane, 4 each #3931-3935	32.00	

Stamps in No. 3935a are not adjacent, as rows of selvage are between stamps one and two, and between stamps three and four.

No. 3935b is a double-sided booklet pane with 12 stamps on one side (2 each #3931, 3933, 3935, and 3 each #3932, 3934) and eight stamps (1 each #3932, 3934, and 2 each #3931, 3933, 3935) plus label on the other side.

ARTHUR ASHE

Arthur Ashe (1943-93), Tennis Player — A3013

Designed by Carl T. Herrman. Printed by Ashton-Potter (USA) Ltd.

LITHOGRAPHED
Sheets of 240 in twelve panes of 20

2005, Aug. 27 **Tagged** ***Serpentine Die Cut 10¾***

Self-Adhesive

3936	A3013 37c **multicolored**	.75	.25
	P# block of 4, 5#+P	3.00	
	Pane of 20	15.00	

TO FORM A MORE PERFECT UNION

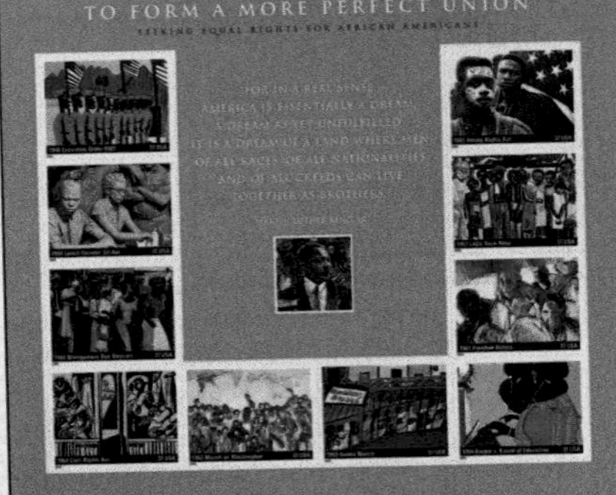

A3014

Illustration reduced.

Designed by Ethel Kessler. Printed by Ashton-Potter (USA) Ltd.

No. 3937 — Inscriptions and artwork: a, 1948 Executive Order 9981 (Training for War, by William H. Johnson). b, 1965 Voting Rights Act (Youths on the Selma March, 1965, photograph by Bruce Davidson). c, 1960 Lunch Counter Sit-ins (National Civil Rights Museum exhibits, by StudioEIS). d, 1957 Little Rock Nine (America Cares, by George Hunt). e, 1955 Montgomery Bus Boycott (Walking, by Charles Alston). f, 1961 Freedom Riders (Freedom Riders, by May Stevens). g, 1964 Civil Rights Act (Dixie Café, by Jacob Lawrence). h, 1963 March on Washington (March on Washington, by Alma Thomas). i, 1965 Selma March (Selma March, by Bernice Sims). j, 1954 Brown v. Board of Education (The Lamp, by Romare Bearden).

LITHOGRAPHED

Serpentine Die Cut 10¾x10½

2005, Aug. 30 **Tagged**

Self-Adhesive

3937	A3014 Pane of 10	11.00	
a.-j.	37c Any single	1.10	.40

CHILD HEALTH

Child and Doctor — A3015

Designed by Craig Frazier.

Printed by Avery Dennison.

PHOTOGRAVURE
Sheets of 200 in ten panes of 20

Serpentine Die Cut 10½x11

2005, Sept. 7 **Tagged**

Self-Adhesive

3938	A3015 37c **multicolored**	.75	.25
	P# block of 4, 4#+V	3.00	
	Pane of 20	15.00	

LET'S DANCE

Merengue — A3016

Salsa — A3017

Cha Cha Cha — A3018

Mambo — A3019

Designed by Ethel Kessler.

Printed by American Packaging Corporation for Sennett Security Products.

PHOTOGRAVURE
Sheets of 120 in six panes of 20

2005, Sept. 17 **Tagged** ***Serpentine Die Cut 10¾***

Self-Adhesive

3939	A3016 37c **multicolored**	1.00	.35
3940	A3017 37c **multicolored**	1.00	.35
3941	A3018 37c **multicolored**	1.00	.35
3942	A3019 37c **multicolored**	1.00	.35
a.	Vert. strip of 4, #3939-3942	4.00	
	P# block of 8, 8#+S	8.00	
	Pane of 20	20.00	

Stamps in the vertical strip are not adjacent as rows of selvage are between the stamps. The backing paper of stamps from the 2nd and 4th columns have Spanish inscriptions, while the other columns have English inscriptions.

GRETA GARBO

Garbo (1905-90), Actress — A3020

Designed by Carl T. Herrman.

Printed by Banknote Corporation of America for Sennett Security Products.

ENGRAVED
Sheets of 120 in six panes of 20
2005, Sept. 23 Tagged *Serpentine Die Cut 10¾*
Self-Adhesive

3943 A3020 37c **black**		.75	.25
P# block of 4, 1#+S		3.00	
Pane of 20		15.00	

See Sweden No. 2517.

JIM HENSON AND THE MUPPETS

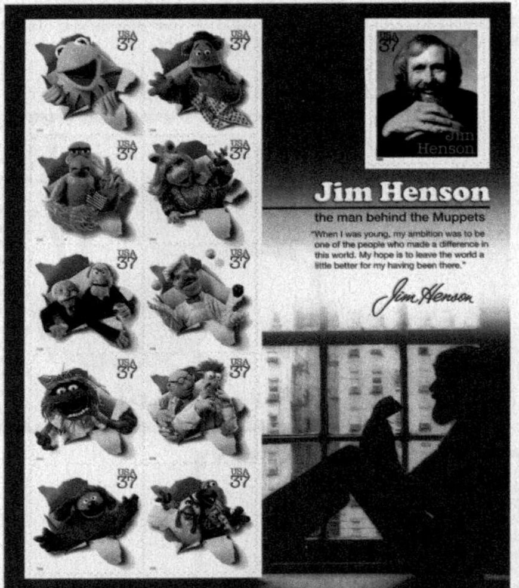

A3021

Illustration reduced.

Designed by Edward Eyth.

Printed by Avery Dennison.

No. 3944: a, Kermit the Frog. b, Fozzie Bear. c, Sam the Eagle and flag. d, Miss Piggy. e, Statler and Waldorf. f, The Swedish Chef and fruit. g, Animal. h, Dr. Bunsen Honeydew and Beaker. i, Rowlf the Dog. j, The Great Gonzo and Camilla the Chicken. k, Jim Henson.

Nos. 3944a-3944j are 30x30mm; No. 3944k, 28x37mm.

PHOTOGRAVURE
Serpentine Die Cut 10½, 10½x10¾ (#3944k)
2005, Sept. 28 Tagged
Self-Adhesive

3944 A3021	Pane of 11	9.00	
a.-k.	37c Any single	.80	.50

CONSTELLATIONS Ⓢ

Leo — A3022

Orion — A3023

Lyra — A3024

Pegasus — A3025

Designed by McRay Magleby.

Printed by Ashton-Potter (USA) Ltd.

LITHOGRAPHED
Sheets of 240 in twelve panes of 20
2005, Oct. 3 Tagged *Serpentine Die Cut 10¾*
Self-Adhesive

3945 A3022 37c **multicolored**		.85	.35
3946 A3023 37c **multicolored**		.85	.35
3947 A3024 37c **multicolored**		.85	.35
3948 A3025 37c **multicolored**		.85	.35
a.	Block or vert. strip of 4, #3945-3948	3.40	
	P# block of 4, 6#+P	3.40	
	P# block of 10, 2 sets of P# + top label	8.25	
	Pane of 20	17.00	
b.	As "a," die cutting omitted	750.00	

Ⓢ: Ink on Nos. 3945-3948 cracks and flakes off during water soak. See note after No. 1549.

CHRISTMAS COOKIES

Santa Claus — A3026

Snowmen — A3027

Angel — A3028

Elves — A3029

Santa Claus — A3030

Snowmen — A3031

Angel — A3032

Elves — A3033

Designed by Derry Noyes.

Printed by Banknote Corporation of America for Sennett Security Products (#3949-3952), American Packaging Corporation for Sennett Security Products (#3953-3960).

LITHOGRAPHED, PHOTOGRAVURE (#3953-3960)
Serpentine Die Cut 10¾x11
2005, Oct. 20 Tagged
Self-Adhesive
Design Size: 19x26mm

3949 A3026 37c **multicolored**		.85	.25
3950 A3027 37c **multicolored**		.85	.25
3951 A3028 37c **multicolored**		.85	.25
3952 A3029 37c **multicolored**		.85	.25
a.	Block or vert. strip of 4, #3949-3952	3.50	
	P# block of 4, 4#+S	3.50	
	Pane of 20	17.50	

Booklet Stamps
Serpentine Die Cut 10¾x11 on 2 or 3 Sides
Design Size: 19½x27mm

3953 A3026 37c **multicolored**		1.00	.25
3954 A3027 37c **multicolored**		1.00	.25
3955 A3028 37c **multicolored**		1.00	.25
3956 A3029 37c **multicolored**		1.00	.25
a.	Block of 4, #3953-3956	4.00	
b.	Booklet pane of 20, 5 #3956a	20.00	

Serpentine Die Cut 10½x10¾

3957 A3030 37c **multicolored**		1.10	.25
3958 A3031 37c **multicolored**		1.10	.25
3959 A3032 37c **multicolored**		1.10	.25
3960 A3033 37c **multicolored**		1.10	.25
a.	Block of 4, #3957-3960	4.50	
b.	Booklet pane of 4, #3957-3960	4.50	
c.	Booklet pane of 6, #3959-3960, 2 each #3957-3958	7.00	
d.	Booklet pane of 6, #3957-3958, 2 each #3959-3960	7.00	

No. 3956b is a double-sided booklet pane with 12 stamps on one side and eight stamps plus label that serves as a booklet cover on the other side. Nos. 3949-3952 have a small "2005" year date, while Nos. 3953-3956 have a large year date. Other design differences caused by different cropping of the images can be found, with Nos. 3953-3956 showing slightly more design features on one or more sides.

DISTINGUISHED MARINES

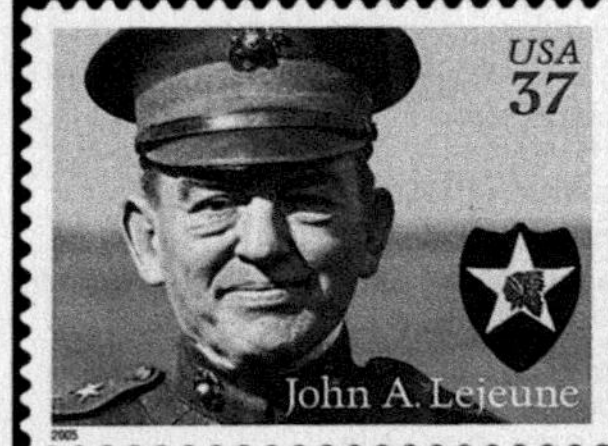

Lt. Gen. John A. Lejeune (1867-1942), 2nd Infantry Division Insignia A3034

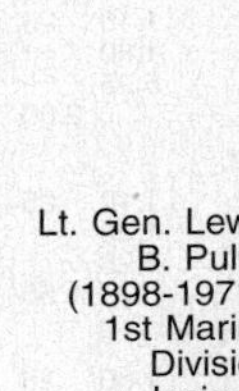
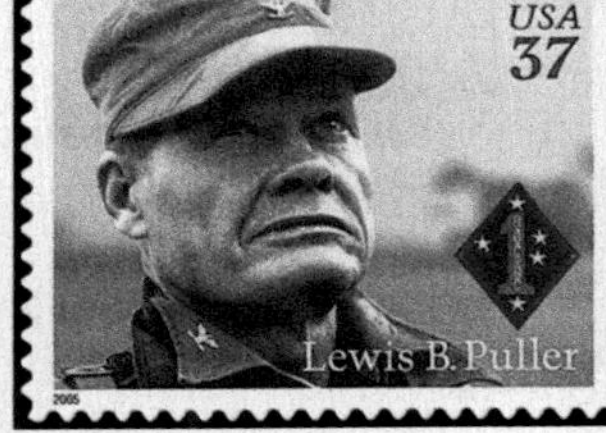

Lt. Gen. Lewis B. Puller (1898-1971), 1st Marine Division Insignia A3035

Sgt. John Basilone (1916-45), 5th Marine Division Insignia A3036

Sgt. Major Daniel J. Daly (1873-1937), 73rd Machine Gun Company, 6th Marine Regiment Insignia A3037

Designed by Phil Jordan. Printed by Ashton-Potter (USA) Ltd.

LITHOGRAPHED
Sheets of 180 in nine panes of 20
Serpentine Die Cut 11x10½
2005, Nov. 10 Tagged
Self-Adhesive

3961 A3034 37c **multicolored**		1.00	.35
3962 A3035 37c **multicolored**		1.00	.35
3963 A3036 37c **multicolored**		1.00	.35
3964 A3037 37c **multicolored**		1.00	.35
a.	Block or horiz. strip of 4, #3961-3964	4.00	
	P# block of 4, 6#+P	4.50	
	P# block of 8, 2 sets of P# + top panel	9.00	
	Pane of 20	23.00	

Flag and Statue of Liberty — A3038

Designed by Carl and Ann Purcell. Printed by Sterling Sommer, Inc. for Ashton-Potter (USA) Ltd. (#3965), Ashton-Potter (USA) Ltd. (#3966, 3970), American Packaging Corporation for Sennett Security Printers (#3967, 3969, 3973), Avery Dennison (#3968, 3972, 3975), Banknote Corporation of America for Sennett Security Products (#3974).

LITHOGRAPHED (#3965, 3966, 3970, 3974), PHOTOGRAVURE

Sheets of 400 in four panes of 100 (#3965), Sheets of 120 in six panes of 20 (#3966)

2005, Dec. 8 **Tagged** ***Perf. 11¼***

3965 A3038 (39c) **multicolored** 1.10 .25
P# block of 4, 4#+P 12.50 —

Self-Adhesive (#3966, 3968-3975)

Serpentine Die Cut 11¼x10¾

3966 A3038 (39c) **multicolored** 1.10 .25
P# block of 4, 4#+P 4.00
Pane of 20 18.50
a. Booklet pane of 20 22.00
b. As "a," die cutting omitted —

COIL STAMPS

Perf. 9¾ Vert.

3967 A3038 (39c) **multicolored** 1.10 .25
Pair 1.60 —
P# strip of 5, #S1111 5.25 —
P# single, #S1111 2.00

Serpentine Die Cut 8½ Vert.

3968 A3038 (39c) **multicolored** 1.10 .25
Pair 1.60
P# strip of 5, #V1111 5.25
P# single, #V1111 1.50

Serpentine Die Cut 10¼ Vert.

3969 A3038 (39c) **multicolored** 1.50 .25
Pair 3.00
P# strip of 5, #S1111 8.00
P# single, #S1111 1.50

Serpentine Die Cut 9½ Vert.

3970 A3038 (39c) **multicolored** 3.50 .25
Pair 7.00
P# strip of 5, #P1111, P2222 20.00
P# single, #P1111, P2222 2.00

BOOKLET STAMPS

Serpentine Die Cut 11¼x10¾ on 2 or 3 Sides

3972 A3038 (39c) **multicolored** 1.10 .25
a. Booklet pane of 20 22.00

Serpentine Die Cut 10½x10¾ on 2 or 3 Sides

3973 A3038 (39c) **multicolored** 1.10 .25
a. Booklet pane of 20 22.00

On both Nos. 3972 and 3973, the sky immediately above the date is bright blue and extends from the left side to beyond the "6" in the date, the left arm of the star at the upper left barely touches the frame line and is without the "USPS" microprinting. They are distinguishable by the die cutting. Nos. 3872a and 3973a are double-sided booklet panes with 12 stamps on one side and eight stamps plus label that serves as a booklet cover on the other side.

No. 3973 was not available until January 2006.

Serpentine Die Cut 11¼x10¾ on 2 or 3 Sides

3974 A3038 (39c) **multicolored** 1.10 .25
a. Booklet pane of 4 4.40
b. Booklet pane of 6 6.60

Serpentine Die Cut 8 on 2, 3 or 4 Sides

3975 A3038 (39c) **multicolored** 1.10 .25
a. Booklet pane of 18 20.00
Nos. 3965-3975 (10) 13.80 2.50

Nos. 3965-3975 are dated "2006."

On No. 3966, the sky immediately above the date is bright blue and extends from the left side to beyond the "6" in the date, the left arm of the star at upper left is clear of the top frame, and "USPS" is microprinted on the top red flag stripe.

On No. 3974, the sky immediately above the date is dark blue and extends from the left side to the second "0" in the date, the left arm of the star at upper left touches the top frame, and lacks the microprinting found on No. 3966.

Nos. 3965 and 3970 also have "USPS" microprinted on the top red flag stripe.

Nos. 3966a and 3972a are double-sided booklet panes with 12 stamps on one side and eight stamps plus label that serves as a booklet cover on the other side. On No. 3966a, the stamps on one side are upside-down with relation to the stamps on the other side. On No. 3972a the stamps are all aligned the same on both sides.

LOVE

Birds — A3039

Designed by Craig Frazier. Printed by Avery Dennison.

PHOTOGRAVURE

Serpentine Die Cut 11 on 2, 3, or 4 Sides

2006, Jan. 3 **Tagged**

BOOKLET STAMP
Self-Adhesive

3976 A3039 (39c) **multicolored** 1.10 .25
a. Booklet pane of 20 22.00

Flag and Statue of Liberty — A3040

Designed by Carl and Ann Purcell. Printed by American Packaging Corporation for Sennett Security Products (#3979, 3982), Ashton-Potter (USA) Ltd. (#3978, 3981). Avery Dennison (#3980, 3985).

LITHOGRAPHED (#3978, 3981), PHOTOGRAVURE (#3979-3980, 3982-3983, 3985)

Sheets of 120 in six panes of 20

2006 **Tagged** ***Serpentine Die Cut 11¼x10¾***

Self-Adhesive (#3978, 3980-3985)

3978 A3040 39c **multicolored,** *Apr. 8* .85 .25
P# block of 4, 4#+P 5.00
Pane of 20 24.00
a. Booklet pane of 10 8.50
b. Booklet pane of 20 17.00
c. As "b," die cutting omitted on side with 8 stamps —

No. 3978 has "USPS" microprinted on top red flag stripe.

No. 3978b is a double-sided booklet with 12 stamps on one side and 8 stamps plus label (booklet cover) on the other side.

COIL STAMPS

Perf. 9¾ Vert.

3979 A3040 39c **multicolored,** *Mar. 8* 1.00 .25
Pair 2.00 —
P# strip of 5, #S1111 5.25 —
P# single, #S1111 — 2.50

Serpentine Die Cut 11 Vert.

3980 A3040 39c **multicolored,** overall tagging, *Jan. 9* ⓢ .80 .25
Pair 1.60
P# strip of 5, #V1111 5.25
P# single, #V1111 2.50
a. Prephosphored coated paper with surface tagging showing a solid appearance — —
Pair —
P# strip of 5, #V1111 —

No. 3980 has rounded corners and lacks microprinting. Unused examples are on backing paper taller than the stamp, and the stamps are spaced approximately 3mm apart.

See note after No. 1549.

Serpentine Die Cut 9½ Vert.

3981 A3040 39c **multicolored,** *Apr. 8* 1.40 .25
Pair 2.80
P# strip of 5, #P1111 8.00
P# single, #P1111 1.75
a. Die cutting omitted, pair *150.00*

No. 3981 has "USPS" microprinted on top red flag stripe.

Counterfeits exist of No. 3981. See the Postal Counterfeits section of this catalog.

Serpentine Die Cut 10¼ Vert.

3982 A3040 39c **multicolored,** *Apr. 8* 1.25 .25
Pair 2.50
P# strip of 5, #S1111 6.50
P# single, #S1111 1.75
a. Vert. pair, unslit between *500.00*

Counterfeits exist of No. 3982. See the Postal Counterfeits section of this catalog.

Serpentine Die Cut 8½ Vert.

3983 A3040 39c **multicolored,** *Apr. 8* .80 .25
Pair 1.60
P# strip of 5, #V1111 5.25
P# single, #V1111 — 1.50

BOOKLET STAMP

Serpentine Die Cut 11¼x10¾ on 2 or 3 Sides

3985 A3040 39c **multicolored,** *Apr. 8* .80 .25
a. Booklet pane of 20 16.00
b. Serpentine die cut 11.1 on 2 or 3 sides, *Nov. 8* .80 .25
c. Booklet pane of 4 #3985b 3.20
d. Booklet pane of 6 #3985b 4.80

Nos. 3983 and 3985 lack the microprinting found on Nos. 3978 and 3981. No. 3982 was not made available until June, despite the official first day of issue. No. 3983 was not made available until July and No. 3985 was not made available until August, despite the official first day of issue. No. 3985a is a double-sided booklet with 12 stamps on one side and 8 stamps plus label (booklet cover) on the other side.

CHILDREN'S BOOK ANIMALS

The Very Hungry Caterpillar, from *The Very Hungry Caterpillar,* by Eric Carle — A3041

Wilbur, from *Charlotte's Web,* by E. B. White — A3042

Fox in Socks, from *Fox in Socks,* by Dr. Seuss — A3043

Maisy, from *Maisy's ABC,* by Lucy Cousins — A3044

Wild Thing, from *Where the Wild Things Are,* by Maurice Sendak — A3045

Curious George, from *Curious George,* by Margaret and H. A. Rey — A3046

Olivia, from *Olivia,* by Ian Falconer — A3047

Frederick, from *Frederick,* by Leo Lionni — A3048

Designed by Derry Noyes. Printed by American Packaging Corporation for Sennett Security Products.

PHOTOGRAVURE

Sheets of 96 in six panes of 16

2006, Jan. 10 Tagged *Serpentine Die Cut 10¾*

Self-Adhesive

3987 A3041 39c **multicolored** .80 .40
3988 A3042 39c **multicolored** .80 .40
3989 A3043 39c **multicolored** .80 .40
3990 A3044 39c **multicolored** .80 .40
3991 A3045 39c **multicolored** .80 .40
3992 A3046 39c **multicolored** .80 .40
3993 A3047 39c **multicolored** .80 .40
3994 A3048 39c **multicolored** .80 .40
a. Block of 8, #3987-3994 6.50
P# block of 8, 9# + S 6.50
Pane of 16 13.00

Uncut press sheets of Nos. 3987-3994 were made available for sale. Values: cross-gutter block of 8, $17; pairs with gutters between, $2.25 each. See note after No. 2868.

See Great Britain Nos. 2340-2341.

2006 WINTER OLYMPICS, TURIN, ITALY

Skier — A3049

Designed by Derry Noyes. Printed by Banknote Corporation of America for Sennett Security Products.

LITHOGRAPHED

Sheets of 240 in twelve panes of 20

2006, Jan. 11 Tagged *Serpentine Die Cut 10¾*

Self-Adhesive

3995 A3049 39c **multicolored** .80 .25
P# block of 4, 4# + S 3.20
Pane of 20 16.00

BLACK HERITAGE SERIES

Hattie McDaniel (1895-1952), Actress — A3050

Designed by Ethel Kessler. Printed by Banknote Corporation of America for Sennett Security Products.

LITHOGRAPHED

Sheets of 240 in twelve panes of 20

2006, Jan. 25 Tagged *Serpentine Die Cut 10¾*

Self-Adhesive

3996 A3050 39c **multicolored** .80 .25
P# block of 4, 4# + S 3.20
Pane of 20 16.00

Chinese New Year Types of 1992-2004

Designed by Clarence Lee. Printed by Banknote Corporation of America for Sennett Security Products.

LITHOGRAPHED

2006, Jan. 29 Tagged *Serpentine Die Cut 10¾*

Self-Adhesive

3997 Pane of 12 12.00
a. A2360 39c Rat 1.00 .50
b. A2413 39c Ox 1.00 .50
c. A2462 39c Tiger 1.00 .50
d. A2535 39c Rabbit 1.00 .50
e. A2602 39c Dragon 1.00 .50
f. A2702 39c Snake 1.00 .50
g. A2752 39c Horse 1.00 .50
h. A2856 39c Ram 1.00 .50
i. A2927 39c Monkey 1.00 .50
j. A2067 39c Rooster 1.00 .50
k. A2146 39c Dog 1.00 .50
l. A2205 39c Boar 1.00 .50

WEDDING DOVES

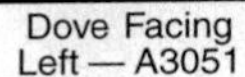

Dove Facing Left — A3051

Dove Facing Right — A3052

Designed by Michael Osborne. Printed by Ashton-Potter (USA) Ltd.

LITHOGRAPHED

BOOKLET STAMPS

Serpentine Die Cut 10¾x11 on 2, 3 or 4 Sides

2006, Mar. 1 Tagged

Self-Adhesive

3998 A3051 39c **pale lilac** .80 .25
a. Booklet pane of 20 16.00
b. As "a," die cutting omitted —

Serpentine Die Cut 10¾x11

3999 A3052 63c **pale yellow green** 1.40 .50
a. Booklet pane, 20 each #3998-3999 45.00
b. Horiz. pair, #3998-3999 with vertical gutter between 2.25 1.50

Common Buckeye Butterfly — A3053

Designed by Carl T. Herrman. Printed by Sterling Sommer, Inc. for Ashton-Potter (USA) Ltd. (#4000), Avery Dennison (#4001-4002).

LITHOGRAPHED (#4000), PHOTOGRAVURE (#4001-4002)

Sheets of 400 in four panes of 100 (#4000), Sheets of 280 in fourteen panes of 20 (#4001)

2006, Mar. 8 Tagged *Perf. 11¼*

4000 A3053 24c **multicolored** .50 .25
P# block of 4, 4#+P 12.50 —

Self-Adhesive

Serpentine Die Cut 11

4001 A3053 24c **multicolored** .55 .25
P# block of 4, 4#+V 3.00
Pane of 20 14.50
a. Serpentine die cut 10¾x11¼ on 3 sides (from booklet panes) .50 .25
b. Booklet pane of 10 #4001a 5.00
c. Booklet pane of 4 #4001a 2.00
d. Booklet pane of 6 #4001a 3.00

Some panes of No. 4001 contain bottom-row stamps that are 1mm taller than the other stamps on the pane. This most likely was caused by a shift up by one row of the die cutting blade cylinder on a low percentage of sheets in the press run.

No. 4001b is a convertible booklet that was sold flat. It has a self-adhesive panel that covers the rouletting on the inside of the booklet cover. Nos. 4001c and 4001d are component panes of a vending machine booklet, which was sold pre-folded and sealed, and which does not have the self-adhesive panel covering the rouletting on the inside of the booklet cover.

COIL STAMP

Serpentine Die Cut 8½ Horiz.

4002 A3053 24c **multicolored** .50 .25
Pair 1.00
P# strip of 5, #V1111 3.50
P# single, #V1111 — 1.75

CROPS OF THE AMERICAS

Chili Peppers — A3054

Beans — A3055

Sunflower and Seeds — A3056

Squashes — A3057

Corn — A3058

Designed by Phil Jordan. Printed by American Packaging Corporation for Sennett Security Products (#4003-4012), Banknote Corporation of America for Sennett Security Products (#4013-4017).

PHOTOGRAVURE (#4003-4012), LITHOGRAPHED (#4013-4017)

Serpentine Die Cut 10¼ Horiz.

2006, Mar. 16 Tagged

Self-Adhesive

Coil Stamps

4003 A3054 39c **multicolored** 2.40 .35
4004 A3055 39c **multicolored** 2.40 .35
4005 A3056 39c **multicolored** 2.40 .35
4006 A3057 39c **multicolored** 2.40 .35
4007 A3058 39c **multicolored** 2.40 .35
a. Strip of 5, #4003-4007 12.00
P# strip of 5, #4003-4007, #S1111 15.00 —
P# strip of 11, 3 #4005, 2 each #4003-4004, 4006-4007 27.50
P# single (#4005), #S1111 — 2.00

Booklet Stamps

Serpentine Die Cut 10¾x10½ on 2 or 3 Sides

4008 A3058 39c **multicolored** 1.25 .35
4009 A3057 39c **multicolored** 1.25 .35
4010 A3056 39c **multicolored** 1.25 .35
4011 A3055 39c **multicolored** 1.25 .35
4012 A3054 39c **multicolored** 1.25 .35
a. Horiz. strip of 5, #4008-4012 6.25

b. Booklet pane, 4 each #4008-4012 25.00

Serpentine Die Cut 10¾x11¼ on 2 or 3 Sides

4013 A3054 39c **multicolored** 1.10 .35
4014 A3058 39c **multicolored** 1.10 .35
4015 A3057 39c **multicolored** 1.10 .35
4016 A3056 39c **multicolored** 1.10 .35
a. Booklet pane of 4, #4013-4016 4.50
4017 A3055 39c **multicolored** 1.10 .35
a. Horiz. strip of 5, #4013-4017 5.50
b. Booklet pane of 4, #4013-4015, 4017 4.50
c. Booklet pane of 6, #4013-4016, 2 #4017 6.75
d. Booklet pane of 6, #4013-4015, 4017, 2 #4016 6.75

Stamps in Nos. 4012a and 4017a are not adjacent, as one or two rows of selvage is between stamps (or a blank space where selvage was removed by the manufacturer).

No. 4012b is a double-sided booklet with 12 stamps on one side and 8 stamps plus label (booklet cover) on the other side.

"USA" is at right of "39" on No. 4004, at left of "39" on Nos. 4011, 4017. Top of "USA" is aligned with top of "39" on No. 4013, with bottom of "39" on Nos. 4003, 4012.

The peelable selvage strips were removed by the manufacturer from 1 million of the 11 million vending booklets produced (containing Nos. 4017b, 4017c and 4017d).

X-PLANES

A3059

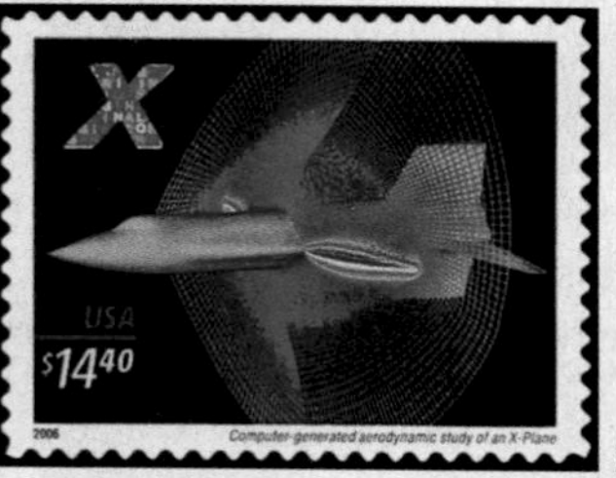

A3060

Designed by Phil Jordan. Printed by Banknote Corporation of America for Sennett Security Products.

LITHOGRAPHED WITH HOLOGRAM AFFIXED

Sheets of 120 in six panes of 20

Serpentine Die Cut 10¾x10½

2006, Mar. 17 Tagged Self-Adhesive

4018 A3059 $4.05 **multicolored** 8.00 5.00
P# block of 4, 4#+S 40.00
Pane of 20 160.00
a. Silver foil ("X") omitted —
4019 A3060 $14.40 **multicolored** 27.50 15.00
P# block of 4, 4#+S 110.00
Pane of 20 550.00

Beware of Nos. 4018 and 4019 with "X" hologram chemically removed. Certification is strongly recommended.

SUGAR RAY ROBINSON (1921-89), BOXER

A3061

Designed by Carl T. Herrman. Printed by Avery Dennison.

PHOTOGRAVURE

Sheets of 200 in ten panes of 20

2006, Apr. 7 Tagged *Serpentine Die Cut 11*
Self-Adhesive

4020 A3061 39c **red & blue** .80 .25

BENJAMIN FRANKLIN (1706-90)

Statesman A3062

Scientist A3063

Printer A3064

Postmaster A3065

Designed by Richard Sheaff. Printed by Avery Dennison.

PHOTOGRAVURE

Sheets of 200 in ten panes of 20

Serpentine Die Cut 11

2006, Apr. 7 Tagged Self-Adhesive

4021 A3062 39c **multicolored** 1.25 .35
4022 A3063 39c **multicolored** 1.25 .35
4023 A3064 39c **multicolored** 1.25 .35
4024 A3065 39c **multicolored** 1.25 .35
a. Block or horiz. strip of 4 5.00
P# block of 4, 4#+V 6.00
Pane of 20 29.00

THE ART OF DISNEY: ROMANCE

Mickey and Minnie Mouse — A3066

Beauty and the Beast — A3068

Lady and Tramp — A3069

Designed by David Pacheco. Printed by Ashton-Potter (USA) Ltd.

LITHOGRAPHED

Sheets of 180 in nine panes of 20

Serpentine Die Cut 10½x10¾

2006, Apr. 21 Tagged

Self-Adhesive

4025 A3066 39c **multicolored** .80 .30
4026 A3067 39c **multicolored** .80 .30
4027 A3068 39c **multicolored** .80 .30
4028 A3069 39c **multicolored** .80 .30
a. Block or vert. strip of 4, #4025-4028 3.20
P# block of 4, 6#+P 3.50
Pane of 20 17.50

LOVE

Birds — A3070

Designed by Craig Frazier. Printed by Avery Dennison.

PHOTOGRAVURE

Serpentine Die Cut 11 on 2, 3 or 4 Sides

2006, May 1 Tagged

Self-Adhesive
Booklet Stamp

4029 A3070 39c **multicolored** .95 .25
a. Booklet pane of 20 19.00

LITERARY ARTS

Katherine Anne Porter (1890-1980), Author A3071

Designed by Derry Noyes. Printed by Banknote Corporation of America for Sennett Security Products.

LITHOGRAPHED

Sheets of 240 in twelve panes of 20

2006, May 15 Tagged *Serpentine Die Cut 10¾*
Self-Adhesive

AMBER ALERT

Mother and Child — A3072

Designed by Derry Noyes. Printed by Avery Dennison.

PHOTOGRAVURE
Sheets of 160 in eight panes of 20

2006, May 25 Tagged *Serpentine Die Cut 10¾*
Self-Adhesive

4031	A3072 39c **multicolored**		.80	.25
	P# block of 4, 6#+V		3.20	
	Pane of 20		16.00	

Purple Heart Type of 2003

Designed by Carl T. Herrman. Printed by Ashton-Potter (USA) Ltd.

LITHOGRAPHED
Sheets of 120 in six panes of 20
Serpentine Die Cut 11¼x11

2006, May 26 Tagged
Self-Adhesive

4032	A2891 39c **multicolored**	.80	.25
	P# block of 4, 4#+P	3.20	
	Pane of 20	16.00	

WONDERS OF AMERICA

Illustration reduced.

Designed by Richard Sheaff. Printed by Avery Dennison.

Designs: No. 4033, American alligator, largest reptile. No. 4034, Moloka'i, highest sea cliffs. No. 4035, Saguaro, tallest cactus. No. 4036, Bering Glacier, largest glacier. No. 4037, Great Sand Dunes, tallest dunes. No. 4038, Chesapeake Bay, largest estuary. No. 4039, Cliff Palace, largest cliff dwelling. No. 4040, Crater Lake, deepest lake. No. 4041, American bison, largest land mammal. No. 4042, Off the Florida Keys, longest reef. No. 4043, Pacific Crest Trail, longest hiking trail. No. 4044, Gateway Arch, tallest man-made monument. No. 4045, Appalachians, oldest mountains. No. 4046, American lotus, largest flower. No. 4047, Lake Superior, largest lake. No. 4048, Pronghorn, fastest land animal. No. 4049, Bristlecone pines, oldest trees. No. 4050, Yosemite Falls, tallest waterfall. No. 4051, Great Basin, largest desert. No. 4052, Verrazano-Narrows Bridge, longest span. No. 4053, Mount Washington, windiest place. No. 4054, Grand Canyon, largest canyon. No. 4055, American bullfrog, largest frog. No. 4056, Oroville Dam, tallest dam. No. 4057, Peregrine falcon, fastest bird. No. 4058, Mississippi River Delta, largest delta. No. 4059, Steamboat, tallest geyser. No. 4060, Rainbow Bridge, largest natural bridge. No. 4061, White sturgeon, largest freshwater fish. No. 4062, Rocky Mountains, longest mountain chain. No. 4063, Coast redwoods, tallest trees. No. 4064, American beaver, largest rodent. No. 4065, Mississippi-Missouri, longest river system. No. 4066, Mount Wai'ale'ale, rainiest spot. No. 4067, Kilauea, most active volcano. No. 4068, Mammoth Cave, longest cave. No. 4069, Blue whale, loudest animal. No. 4070, Death Valley, hottest spot. No. 4071, Cornish-Windsor Bridge, longest covered bridge. No. 4072, Quaking aspen, largest plant.

PHOTOGRAVURE
Sheets of 80 in two panes of 40

2006, May 27 Tagged *Serpentine Die Cut 10¾*
Self-Adhesive

4033	A3073 39c **multicolored**	.80	.60
4034	A3074 39c **multicolored**	.80	.60
4035	A3075 39c **multicolored**	.80	.60
4036	A3076 39c **multicolored**	.80	.60
4037	A3077 39c **multicolored**	.80	.60
4038	A3078 39c **multicolored**	.80	.60
4039	A3079 39c **multicolored**	.80	.60
4040	A3080 39c **multicolored**	.80	.60
4041	A3081 39c **multicolored**	.80	.60
4042	A3082 39c **multicolored**	.80	.60
4043	A3083 39c **multicolored**	.80	.60
4044	A3084 39c **multicolored**	.80	.60
4045	A3085 39c **multicolored**	.80	.60
4046	A3086 39c **multicolored**	.80	.60
4047	A3087 39c **multicolored**	.80	.60
4048	A3088 39c **multicolored**	.80	.60
4049	A3089 39c **multicolored**	.80	.60
4050	A3090 39c **multicolored**	.80	.60
4051	A3091 39c **multicolored**	.80	.60
4052	A3092 39c **multicolored**	.80	.60
4053	A3093 39c **multicolored**	.80	.60
4054	A3094 39c **multicolored**	.80	.60
4055	A3095 39c **multicolored**	.80	.60
4056	A3096 39c **multicolored**	.80	.60
4057	A3097 39c **multicolored**	.80	.60
4058	A3098 39c **multicolored**	.80	.60
4059	A3099 39c **multicolored**	.80	.60
4060	A3100 39c **multicolored**	.80	.60
4061	A3101 39c **multicolored**	.80	.60
4062	A3102 39c **multicolored**	.80	.60
4063	A3103 39c **multicolored**	.80	.60
4064	A3104 39c **multicolored**	.80	.60
4065	A3105 39c **multicolored**	.80	.60
4066	A3106 39c **multicolored**	.80	.60
4067	A3107 39c **multicolored**	.80	.60
4068	A3108 39c **multicolored**	.80	.60
4069	A3109 39c **multicolored**	.80	.60
4070	A3110 39c **multicolored**	.80	.60
4071	A3111 39c **multicolored**	.80	.60
4072	A3112 39c **multicolored**	.80	.60
a.	Pane of 40, #4033-4072	32.00	

Uncut press sheets of Nos. 4033-4072 were made available for sale. Values: block of 40 diff. stamps with horiz. gutter btwn. any two rows, $37.50; pairs with horiz. gutter btwn., $2.25 each. See note after No. 2868.

EXPLORATION OF EAST COAST BY SAMUEL DE CHAMPLAIN, 400TH ANNIV.

Ship and Map — A3113

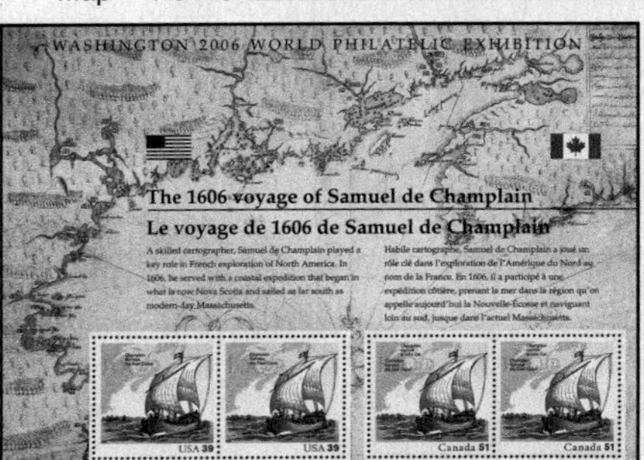

A3114

Illustration reduced.

Designed by Rejean Myette and Francois Martin, Canada (#4073), Terrence W. McCaffrey and Francois Martin (#4074). Printed by Ashton-Potter (USA) Ltd. Illustration A3114 is reduced.

LITHOGRAPHED & ENGRAVED
Sheets of 120 in six panes of 20 (#4073), Sheets of 24 in six panes of 4 (#4074)

2006, May 28 Tagged *Serpentine Die Cut 10¾*
Self-Adhesive (#4073)

4073	A3113 39c **multicolored**	.85	.25
	P# block of 4, 6#+P	3.75	
	Pane of 20	18.50	

Souvenir Sheet
Perf. 11

4074	A3114 Pane of 4, 2 each #4074a, Canada #2156a	8.50	8.50
a.	A3113 39c **multicolored**	2.00	.25

Washington 2006 World Philatelic Exhibition (#4074). Canada No. 2156, which was sold only by Canada Post, has a bar code in the lower left margin of the pane. No. 4074, which was sold only by the United States Postal Service for $1.75, lacks this bar code.

Uncut press sheets of No. 4074 were made available for sale. Values: cross-gutter block of 4 Canadian and 4 American stamps, $22.50; horiz. pair of Canadian and American stamps with vert. gutter btwn., $4. See note after No. 2868.

WASHINGTON 2006 WORLD PHILATELIC EXHIBITION

Souvenir Sheet

A3115

Illustration reduced.

Designed by Richard Sheaff. Printed by Banknote Corporation of America for Sennett Security Products.

LITHOGRAPHED (MARGIN) & ENGRAVED
Sheets of 18 in six panes of 3

2006, May 29 Tagged *Perf. 10¾x10½*

4075	A3115 Pane of 3	16.00	6.00
a.	A174 $1 **violet brown**	2.00	.50
b.	A175 $2 **deep blue**	4.00	1.00
c.	A176 $5 **carmine & blue**	10.00	2.50

Uncut press sheets of No. 4075 were made available for sale. Values: cross-gutter block of 4 panes, $67.50; pairs of panes with gutters between, $35 each. See note after No. 2868.

DISTINGUISHED AMERICAN DIPLOMATS

Souvenir Sheet

A3116

Illustration reduced.

Designed by Howard E. Paine. Printed by Avery Dennison.

No. 4076: a, Robert D. Murphy (1894-1978). b, Frances E. Willis (1899-1983). c, Hiram Bingham IV (1903-88). d, Philip C. Habib (1920-92). e, Charles E. Bohlen (1904-74). f, Clifton R. Wharton, Sr. (1899-1990).

Sheets of 90 in fifteen panes of 6

PHOTOGRAVURE

2006, May 29 Tagged *Serpentine Die Cut 10¾*
Self-Adhesive

4076	A3116 Pane of 6	6.00	
a.-f.	39c any single	1.00	.40

Uncut press sheets of No. 4076 were made available for sale. Values: cross-gutter block of 6, $9; pairs with gutters between, $3 each. See note after No. 2868.

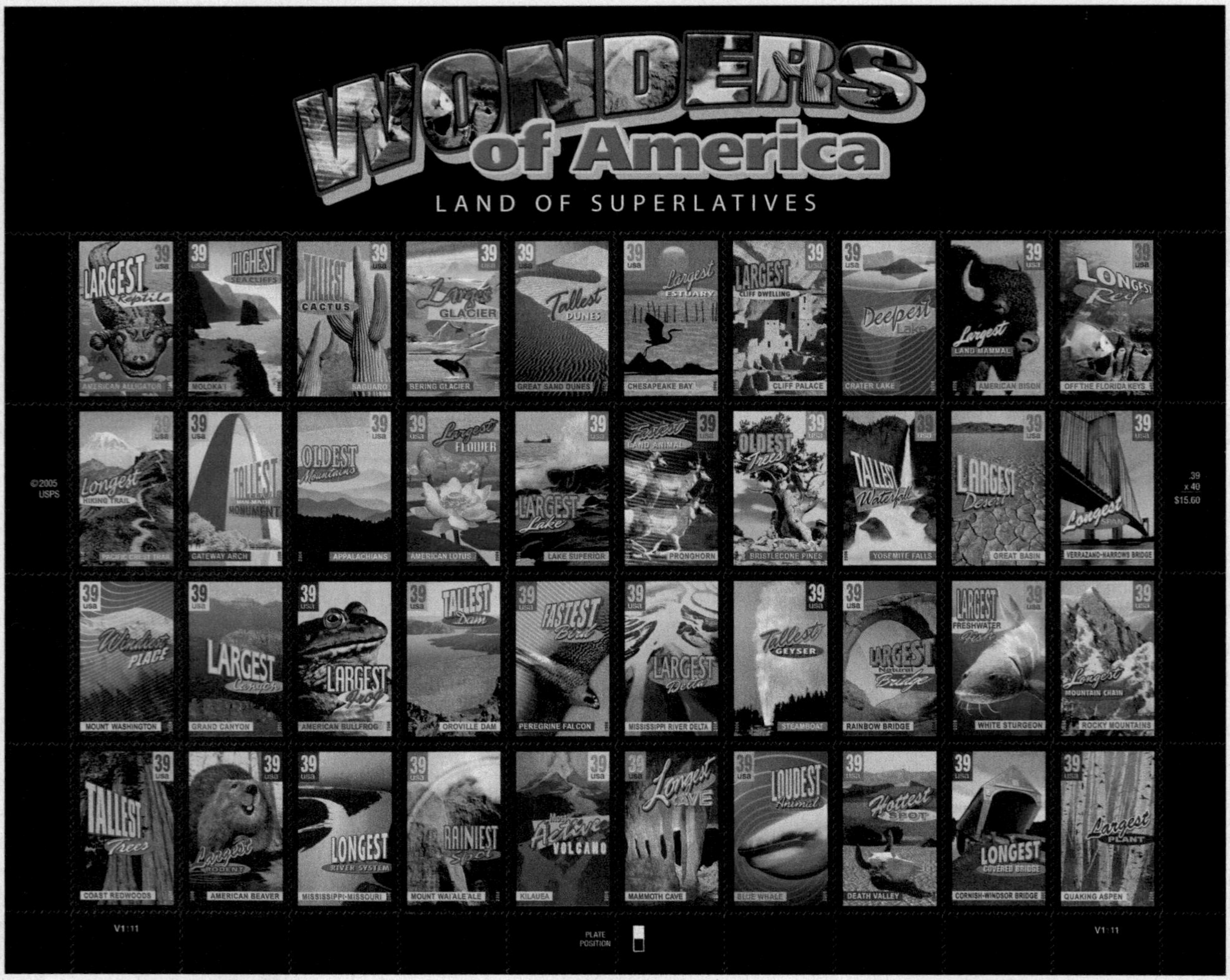

A3073-A3112

LEGENDS OF HOLLYWOOD

Judy Garland (1922-69), Actress — A3117

Designed by Ethel Kessler. Printed by Banknote Corporation of America for Sennett Security Products.

LITHOGRAPHED

Sheets of 120 in six panes of 20

2006, June 10 Tagged *Serpentine Die Cut 10¾*

Self-Adhesive

4077	A3117 39c **multicolored**	1.00	.25
	P# block of 4, 4#+S	5.50	
	Pane of 20	24.00	
a.	Pair, die cutting omitted	—	

Uncut press sheets of No. 4077 were made available for sale. Values: cross-gutter block of 8, $25; pairs with gutters between, $3.75 each. See note after No. 2868.

Ronald Reagan Type of 2005

Designed by Howard E. Paine. Printed by American Packaging Corporation for Sennett Security Products.

PHOTOGRAVURE

Sheets of 120 in six panes of 20

2006, June 14 Tagged *Serpentine Die Cut 10¾*

Self-Adhesive

4078	A2974 39c **multicolored**	.90	.25
	P# block of 4, 4#+S	3.60	
	Pane of 20	18.00	

Happy Birthday Type of 2002

Designed by Harry Zelenko. Printed by Avery Dennison.

PHOTOGRAVURE

Sheets of 200 in ten panes of 20

2006, June 23 Tagged *Serpentine Die Cut 11*

Self-Adhesive

4079	A2751 39c **multicolored**	.80	.25
	P# block of 4, 4#+V	3.20	
	Pane of 20	16.00	

BASEBALL SLUGGERS

Roy Campanella (1921-93) — A3118

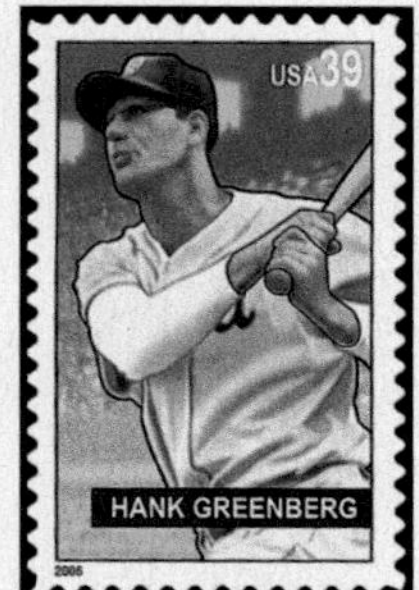

Hank Greenberg (1911-86) — A3119

Mel Ott (1909-58) — A3120

Mickey Mantle (1931-95) — A3121

Designed by Phil Jordan. Printed by Avery Dennison.

PHOTOGRAVURE

Sheets of 120 in six panes of 20

2006, July 15 Tagged *Serpentine Die Cut 10¾*

Self-Adhesive

4080	A3118 39c **multicolored**	.80	.30
4081	A3119 39c **multicolored**	.80	.30
4082	A3120 39c **multicolored**	.80	.30
4083	A3121 39c **multicolored**	.80	.30
a.	Block or vert. strip of 4, #4080-4083	3.20	
	P# block of 4, 6#+V	3.20	
	P# block of 10, 2 sets of P# + top label	8.00	
	Pane of 20	16.00	

Uncut press sheets of Nos. 4080-4083 were made available for sale. Values: cross-gutter block of 8, $20; pairs with gutters between, $3.75 each. See note after No. 2868.

DC COMICS SUPERHEROES

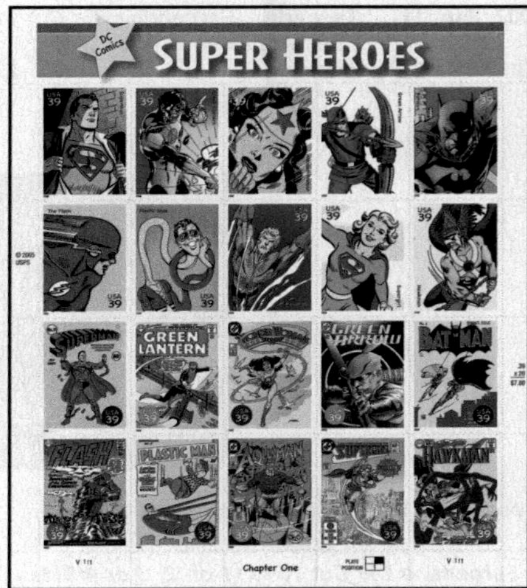

A3122

Illustration reduced.

Designed by Carl T. Herrman. Printed by Avery Dennison.

No. 4084: a, Superman. b, Green Lantern. c, Wonder Woman. d, Green Arrow. e, Batman. f, The Flash. g, Plastic Man. h, Aquaman. i, Supergirl. j, Hawkman. k, Cover of *Superman #11*. l, Cover of *Green Lantern #4*. m, Cover of *Wonder Woman #22 (Second Series)*. n, Cover of *Green Arrow #15*. o, Cover of *Batman #1*. p, Cover of *The Flash #111*. q, Cover of *Plastic Man #4*. r, Cover of *Aquaman #5 (of 5)*. s, Cover of *The Daring New Adventures of Supergirl #1*. t, Cover of *The Brave and the Bold Presents Hawkman #36*.

PHOTOGRAVURE

Sheets of 80 in four panes of 20

Serpentine Die Cut 10½x10¾

2006, July 20 **Tagged**

Self-Adhesive

4084	A3122	Pane of 20	16.00	
a.-t.		39c Any single	.80	.50
u.		As No. 4084, all inscriptions omitted on reverse	*2,000.*	

Uncut press sheets of No. 4084 were made available for sale. Values: cross-gutter block of 20, $25; pairs with gutters between, $3.50 each. See note after No. 2868.

MOTORCYCLES

1940 Indian Four — A3123

1918 Cleveland A3124

Generic "Chopper," c. 1970 — A3125

1965 Harley-Davidson Electra-Glide — A3126

Designed by Richard Sheaff. Printed by Avery Dennison.

PHOTOGRAVURE

Sheets of 160 in eight panes of 20

Serpentine Die Cut 10¾x10½

2006, Aug. 7 **Tagged**

Self-Adhesive

4085	A3123	39c	**multicolored**	1.00	.35
4086	A3124	39c	**multicolored**	1.00	.35
4087	A3125	39c	**multicolored**	1.00	.35
4088	A3126	39c	**multicolored**	1.00	.35
a.			Block or horiz. strip of 4, #4085-4088	4.00	
			P# block of 4, 5#+V	4.00	
			P# block of 8, 2 sets of P# + top label	8.00	
			Pane of 20	20.00	

AMERICAN TREASURES SERIES
Quilts of Gee's Bend, Alabama

Housetop Variation, by Mary Lee Bendolph — A3127

Pig in a Pen Medallion, by Minnie Sue Coleman — A3128

Nine Patch, by Ruth P. Mosely — A3129

Housetop Four Block Half Log Cabin Variation, by Lottie Mooney — A3130

Roman Stripes Variation, by Loretta Pettway — A3131

Chinese Coins Variation, by Arlonzia Pettway — A3132

Blocks and Strips, by Annie Mae Young — A3133

Medallion, by Loretta Pettway — A3134

Bars and String-pieced Columns, by Jessie T. Pettway — A3135

Medallion With Checkerboard Center, by Patty Ann Williams — A3136

Designed by Derry Noyes. Printed by American Packaging Corporation for Sennett Security Products.

PHOTOGRAVURE

BOOKLET STAMPS

Serpentine Die Cut 10¾ on 2 or 3 Sides

2006, Aug. 24 **Tagged**

Self-Adhesive

4089	A3127	39c	**multicolored**	1.10	.40
4090	A3128	39c	**multicolored**	1.10	.40
4091	A3129	39c	**multicolored**	1.10	.40
4092	A3130	39c	**multicolored**	1.10	.40
4093	A3131	39c	**multicolored**	1.10	.40
4094	A3132	39c	**multicolored**	1.10	.40
4095	A3133	39c	**multicolored**	1.10	.40
4096	A3134	39c	**multicolored**	1.10	.40
4097	A3135	39c	**multicolored**	1.10	.40
4098	A3136	39c	**multicolored**	1.10	.40
a.			Block of 10, #4089-4098	11.00	
b.			Booklet pane of 20, 2 each #4089-4098	22.50	

No. 4098b is a double-sided booklet pane with 12 stamps on one side (1 each #4090-4093, 4095-4098, and 2 each #4089, 4094) and eight stamps (1 each #4090-4093, 4095-4098) plus label (booklet cover) on the other side.

SOUTHERN FLORIDA WETLAND

A3137

Illustration reduced.

Designed by Ethel Kessler. Printed by Avery Dennison.

No. 4099 — Wildlife: a, Snail kite. b, Wood storks. c, Florida panther. d, Bald eagle, horiz. e, American crocodile, horiz. f, Roseate spoonbills, horiz. g, Everglades mink. h, Cape Sable seaside sparrow, horiz. i, American alligator, horiz. j, White ibis.

PHOTOGRAVURE
Sheets of 80 in eight panes of 10
2006, Oct. 4 Tagged *Serpentine Die Cut 10¾*
Self-Adhesive

4099 A3137 Pane of 10 9.00
a.-j. 39c any single .90 .40

Uncut press sheets of No. 4099 were made available for sale. Value: See note after No. 2868.

CHRISTMAS

Madonna and Child with Bird, by Ignacio Chacón — A3138

Snowflake — A3139

Snowflake — A3140

Snowflake — A3141

Snowflake — A3142

Designed by Michael Osborne (#4100), Richard Sheaff. Printed by Ashton-Potter (USA) Ltd. (#4100), Banknote Corporation of America for Sennett Security Products (#4101-4112), Avery Dennison (#4113-4116).

LITHOGRAPHED, PHOTOGRAVURE (#4113-4116)
Sheets of 240 in twelve panes of 20 (#4101-4104)
Serpentine Die Cut 10¾x11 on 2 or 3 Sides
2006 Tagged
Self-Adhesive
Booklet Stamps (#4100, 4105-4116)

4100 A3138 39c **multicolored,** *Oct. 17* ⓢ .80 .25
a. Booklet pane of 20 16.00

ⓢ: The ink of No. 4100 cracks and flakes off during a water soak. See note after No. 1549.

Base of Denomination Higher Than Year Date
Serpentine Die Cut 11¼x11

4101 A3139 39c **multicolored,** *Oct. 5* .90 .25
4102 A3140 39c **multicolored,** *Oct. 5* .90 .25
4103 A3141 39c **multicolored,** *Oct. 5* .90 .25
4104 A3142 39c **multicolored,** *Oct. 5* .90 .25
a. Block or vert. strip of 4, #4101-4104 3.60
P# block of 4, 4#+S 3.60
Pane of 20 18.00

Base of Denominations Even With Year Date
Serpentine Die Cut 11¼x11½ on 2 or 3 Sides

4105 A3139 39c **multicolored,** *Oct. 5* .90 .25
a. Red missing (PS) —
4106 A3140 39c **multicolored,** *Oct. 5* .90 .25
a. Red missing (PS) —
4107 A3141 39c **multicolored,** *Oct. 5* .90 .25
4108 A3142 39c **multicolored,** *Oct. 5* .90 .25
a. Block of 4, #4105-4108 3.60
b. Booklet pane of 20, 5 #4108a 18.00
c. As "a," red ("USA") and green ("39") omitted —

Serpentine Die Cut 11¼x10¾ on 2 or 3 Sides

4109 A3139 39c **multicolored,** *Oct. 5* 1.00 .25
4110 A3140 39c **multicolored,** *Oct. 5* 1.00 .25
4111 A3141 39c **multicolored,** *Oct. 5* 1.00 .25
4112 A3142 39c **multicolored,** *Oct. 5* 1.00 .25
a. Block of 4, #4109-4112 4.00
b. Booklet pane of 4, #4109-4112 4.00
c. Booklet pane of 6, #4111-4112, 2 each #4109-4110 6.00
d. Booklet pane of 6, #4109-4110, 2 each #4111-4112 6.00

Serpentine Die Cut 8 on 2, 3 or 4 Sides

4113 A3139 39c **multicolored,** *Oct. 5* 1.50 .35
a. Red and green missing (PS) —
4114 A3141 39c **multicolored,** *Oct. 5* 1.50 .35
4115 A3140 39c **multicolored,** *Oct. 5* 1.50 .35
4116 A3142 39c **multicolored,** *Oct. 5* 1.50 .35
a. Block or strip of 4, #4113-4116 6.00
b. Booklet pane of 18, 4 each #4114, 4116, 5 each #4113, 4115 27.00
Nos. 4100-4116 (17) 18.00 4.65

No. 4108b is a double-sided booklet pane with 12 stamps on one side and eight stamps plus label that serves as a booklet cover on the other side. Snowflakes on Nos. 4101-4104 are slightly smaller than those on Nos. 4105-4116.

Eid Type of 2001

Designed by Mohamed Zakariya. Printed by Avery Dennison.

PHOTOGRAVURE
Sheets of 240 in twelve panes of 20
2006, Oct. 6 Tagged *Serpentine Die Cut 11*
Self-Adhesive

4117 A2734 39c **multicolored** .80 .25
P# block of 4, 3#+V 3.50
Pane of 20 17.50

Hanukkah Type of 2004

Designed by Ethel Kessler. Printed by Banknote Corporation of America for Sennett Security Products.

LITHOGRAPHED
Sheets of 240 in twelve panes of 20
2006, Oct. 6 Tagged *Serpentine Die Cut 10¾x11*
Self-Adhesive

4118 A2962 39c **multicolored** .80 .25
P# block of 4, 4#+S 3.20
Pane of 20 16.00
a. Die cutting omitted, pane of 20 —

Kwanzaa Type of 2004

Designed by Derry Noyes. Printed by Ashton-Potter (USA) Ltd.

LITHOGRAPHED
Sheets of 160 in eight panes of 20
2006, Oct. 6 Tagged *Serpentine Die Cut 11x10¾*
Self-Adhesive

4119 A2963 39c **multicolored** .80 .25
P# block of 4, 6#+P 3.50
Pane of 20 17.50

BLACK HERITAGE SERIES

Ella Fitzgerald (1917-96), Singer — A3143

Designed by Ethel Kessler. Printed by Ashton-Potter (USA) Ltd.

LITHOGRAPHED
Sheets of 120 in six panes of 20
2007, Jan. 10 Tagged *Serpentine Die Cut 11*
Self-Adhesive

4120 A3143 39c **multicolored** ⓢ .80 .25
P# block of 4, 6# + P 3.20
Pane of 20 16.00

ⓢ: Ink on No. 4120 cracks and flakes off during water soak. See note after No. 1549.

OKLAHOMA STATEHOOD, 100TH ANNIV.

Cimarron River — A3144

Designed by Phil Jordan. Printed by Ashton-Potter (USA) Ltd.

LITHOGRAPHED
Sheets of 120 in six panes of 20
2007, Jan. 11 Tagged *Serpentine Die Cut 11*
Self-Adhesive

4121 A3144 39c **multicolored** .80 .25
P# block of 4, 5# + P 3.20
Pane of 20 16.00

LOVE

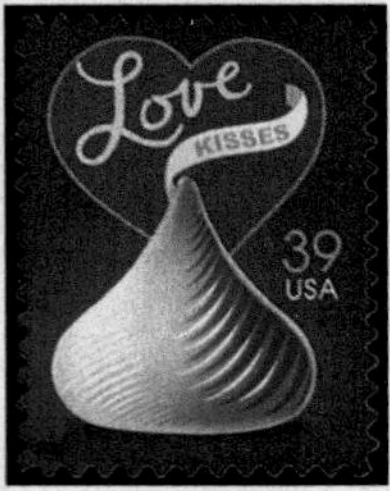

Hershey's Kiss — A3145

Designed by Derry Noyes. Printed by Avery Dennison.

PHOTOGRAVURE
Serpentine Die Cut 10¾x11 on 2, 3 or 4 Sides
2007, Jan. 13 Tagged
BOOKLET STAMP
Self-Adhesive

4122 A3145 39c **multicolored** .80 .25
a. Booklet pane of 20 16.00

INTERNATIONAL POLAR YEAR ⓢ
Souvenir Sheet

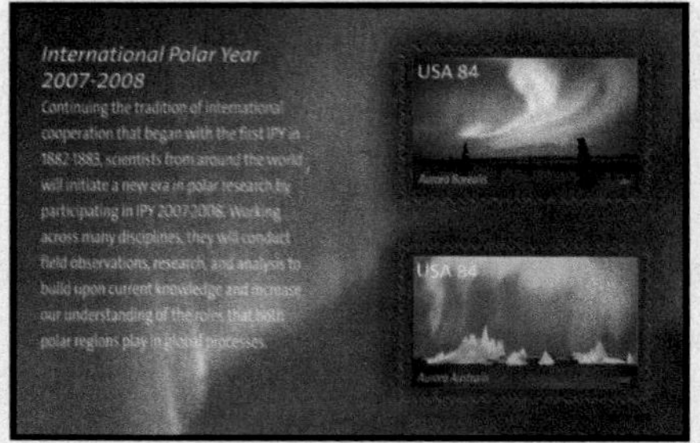

A3146

Illustration reduced.

Designed by Phil Jordan. Printed by Ashton-Potter (USA) Ltd.

No. 4123: a, Aurora borealis. b, Aurora australis.

LITHOGRAPHED
Sheets of 30 in fifteen panes of 2
2007, Feb. 21 Tagged *Serpentine Die Cut 10¾*
Self-Adhesive

4123 A3146 Pane of 2 4.00
a.-b. 84c Either single 2.00 .50

ⓢ: Ink on Nos. 4123a and 4123b cracks and flakes off during water soak. See note after No. 1549.

Uncut press sheets of No. 4123 were made available for sale. Values: cross-gutter block of 4 stamps, $15; vert pair of stamps with horiz. gutter between, $4.50. See note after No. 2868.

LITERARY ARTS

Henry Wadsworth Longfellow (1807-82), Poet — A3147

Designed by Howard E. Paine. Printed by Ashton-Potter (USA) Ltd.

LITHOGRAPHED
Sheets of 120 in six panes of 20
2007, Mar. 15 Tagged *Serpentine Die Cut 10¾*
Self-Adhesive

4124 A3147 39c **multicolored** .80 .25
P# block of 4, 5#+P 3.20
Pane of 20 16.00

Beginning with No. 4125, the United States Postal Service began issuing "Forever" stamps that satisfy the domestic 1-ounce first-class letter rate and the 1-ounce international letter rate regardless of future rate increases. The denomination in parentheses in the catalogue listing represents the face value at the time of issue. The face value increases to the new letter rate whenever rates change.

"FOREVER" STAMP

Liberty Bell — A3148

Large Microprinting (#4125, 4128)

Small Microprinting (#4126)

Medium Microprinting (#4127)

Designed by Carl T. Herrman. Printed by Avery Dennison (#4125, 4128), Ashton-Potter (USA) Ltd. (#4126), Banknote Corporation of America for Sennett Security Products (#4127)

PHOTOGRAVURE, LITHOGRAPHED (#4126, 4127)

Serpentine Die Cut 11¼x10¾ on 2 or 3 Sides

2007-09 **Tagged**

Booklet Stamps

Self-Adhesive

Large Microprinting, Bell 16mm Wide

4125 A3148 (41c) **multicolored**, dated "2007," *Apr. 12* 1.10 .25
a. Booklet pane of 20 22.00
b. (42c) Dated "2008," *Aug. 22, 2008* ⓢ 1.10 .25
c. Booklet pane of 20 #4125b 22.00
d. As "c," copper ("FOREVER") omitted *1,000.*
e. As "c," copper ("FOREVER") omitted on side with 12 stamps, copper splatters on side with 8 stamps —
f. (44c) Dated "2009," *Aug. 7, 2009* ⓢ 1.10 .25
g. Booklet pane of 20 #4125f 22.00
h. As No. 4125, copper ("FOREVER") omitted —
On cover —
i. As No. 4125, die cutting missing, horiz. pair (PS) —
j. As "b," copper ("FOREVER") omitted —

Counterfeits exist of No. 4125. See the Postal Counterfeits section of this catalog.

Small Microprinting, Bell 16mm Wide

4126 A3148 (41c) **multicolored**, dated "2007," *April 12* 1.10 .25
a. Booklet pane of 20 22.00
b. (42c) Dated "2008," *Aug. 22, 2008* ⓢ 1.10 .25
c. Booklet pane of 20 #4126b 22.00
d. (44c) Dated "2009" in copper, *Aug. 7, 2009* ⓢ 1.10 .25
e. Booklet pane of 20 #4126d 22.00
f. As "b," copper ("FOREVER") omitted *1,400.*
g. As "c," die cutting omitted —

Medium Microprinting, Bell 15mm Wide

4127 A3148 (41c) **multicolored**, dated "2007," prephosphored coated paper, *April 12* 1.10 .25
a. Booklet pane of 20 22.00
b. Booklet pane of 4 4.40
c. Booklet pane of 6 6.60
d. (42c) Dated "2008," *May 12, 2008* 1.10 .25
e. As "d," booklet pane of 20 22.00
f. (42c) Dated "2008," date in smaller type, *Oct. 25, 2008* 1.10 .25
g. As "f," booklet pane of 4 4.40
h. As "f," booklet pane of 6 6.60
i. (44c) Dated "2009" in copper, *May 15, 2009* 1.10 .25
j. As "i," booklet pane of 20 22.00
k. As "i," die cutting omitted, pair —
l. As No. 4127, copper ("FOREVER") and "USA FIRST-CLASS" missing (PS) —
m. As "e," die cutting omitted *500.00*

Large Microprinting, Bell 16mm Wide

Serpentine Die Cut 8 on 2, 3 or 4 Sides

4128 A3148 (41c) **multicolored**, dated "2007", *April 12* ⓢ 1.10 .25
a. Booklet pane of 18 20.00
b. (42c) Dated "2009" in black, *Feb. 24, 2009* ⓢ 1.10 .25
c. As "b," booklet pane of 18 20.00
Nos. 4125-4128 (4) 4.40 1.00

Nos. 4125-4128 were sold for 41c on the day of issue and will be valid for the one ounce first class postage rate after any new rates go into effect. As of May 12, 2008, any "Forever" stamp (Nos. 4125-4128 and 4127d) in stock was sold for 42c. As of May 15, 2009, all "Forever" stamps in stock were sold for 44c, etc.

Nos. 4125a, 4125c, 4126a, 4126c, 4127a, 4127e and 4127j are double-sided booklet panes, with 12 stamps on one side and eight stamps plus a label that serves as a booklet cover on the other side.

No. 4127a and its varieties exist on two types of surface-tagged paper that exhibit either an uneven or solid appearance, as follows: tagging on No. 4127a appears uneven on both sides (most common), solid on both sides (value, $80), uneven on eight-stamp side and solid on 12-stamp side (extremely scarce), solid on eight stamp side and uneven on 12-stamp side (extremely scarce); tagging on No. 4127e appears solid on both sides, or solid on eight-stamp side and uneven on 12-stamp side (value, $25); tagging on No. 4127j appears solid.

Nos. 4127b and 4127c exist with rouletting on backing paper of either gauge 9½ or 13.

See No. 4437.

ⓢ: Examples of No. 4128 with a shiny surface do not respond to a water soak. See note after No. 1549.

Flag — A3149

Designed by Richard Sheaff. Printed by Ashton-Potter (USA) Ltd. (#4129, 4130, 4132), Banknote Corporation of America for Sennett Security Products (#4131, 4133), Avery Dennison (#4134, 4135).

LITHOGRAPHED, PHOTOGRAVURE (#4134, 4135)
Sheets of 400 in four panes of 100 (#4129), Sheets of 120 in six panes of 20 (#4130)

2007, Apr. 12 **Tagged** ***Perf. 11¼***

4129 A3149 (41c) **multicolored** .90 .40
P# block of 4, 4#+P 18.00 —

Self-Adhesive (#4130, 4132-4135)

Serpentine Die Cut 11¼x10¾

4130 A3149 (41c) **multicolored** 1.10 .25
P# block of 4, 4#+P 3.75
Pane of 20 18.00

COIL STAMPS

Perf. 9¾ Vert.

4131 A3149 (41c) **multicolored** 1.10 .40
Pair 1.80 .80
P# strip of 5, #S1111 6.50 —
P# single, #S1111 — 2.75

With Perpendicular Corners

Serpentine Die Cut 9½ Vert.

4132 A3149 (41c) **multicolored** 1.20 .25
Pair 2.40
P# strip of 5, #P1111 7.00
P# single, #P1111 — 1.75

Serpentine Die Cut 11 Vert.

4133 A3149 (41c) **multicolored** 1.20 .25
Pair 2.40
P# strip of 5, #S1111 7.00
P# single, #S1111 — 1.50
a. Die cutting omitted, pair *1,250.*

Counterfeits exist of No. 4133. See the Postal Counterfeits section of this catalog.

Serpentine Die Cut 8½ Vert.

4134 A3149 (41c) **multicolored**, overall tagging 1.10 .25
Pair 1.80
P# strip of 5, #V1111 5.75
P# single, #V1111 — 1.75
a. Prephosphored coated paper with surface tagging — —

With Rounded Corners

Serpentine Die Cut 11 Vert.

4135 A3149 (41c) **multicolored** 1.25 .75
Pair 2.50
P# strip of 5, #V1111 9.00
P# single, #V1111 — 2.25
Nos. 4129-4135 (7) 7.85 2.55

Nos. 4132-4134 are on backing paper as high as the stamp. No. 4135 is on backing paper that is larger than the stamp.

SETTLEMENT OF JAMESTOWN, 400TH ANNIV.

Ships Susan Constant, Godspeed and Discovery — A3150

Illustration reduced.

Designed by Richard Sheaff. Printed by Banknote Corporation of America for Sennett Security Products.

LITHOGRAPHED
Double-sided panes of 20 (19 on one side, 1 on other side)

Serpentine Die Cut 10½x10½x10¾

2007, May 11 **Tagged**

Self-Adhesive

4136 A3150 41c **multicolored** 1.10 .25
Pane of 20 22.00

WILDLIFE

Bighorn Sheep — A3151

Florida Panther — A3152

Designed by Carl T. Herrman. Printed by Ashton-Potter (USA) Ltd. (#4137, 4139), Avery Dennison (#4138, 4142), Banknote Corporation of America for Sennett Security Products (#4140, 4141).

LITHOGRAPHED, PHOTOGRAVURE (#4138, 4142)
Sheets of 400 in four panes of 100 (#4137), Sheets of 280 in fourteen panes of 20 (#4138), Sheets of 120 in six panes of 20 (#4139)

2007 **Tagged** ***Perf. 11¼x11***

4137 A3152 26c **multicolored**, *May 12* .60 .25
P# block of 4, 4#+P 15.00 —

Self-Adhesive

Serpentine Die Cut 11

4138 A3151 17c **multicolored**, overall tagging, *May 14* .35 .25
P# block of 4, 4#+V 1.75
Pane of 20 9.00
a. Prephosphored paper .35 .25

Serpentine Die Cut 11¼x11

4139 A3152 26c **multicolored**, *May 12* .55 .25
P# block of 4, 4#+P 2.25
Pane of 20 11.00

Coil Stamps

Serpentine Die Cut 11 Vert.

4140 A3151 17c **multicolored**, *May 21* .35 .25
Pair .70
P# strip of 5, #S11111111 3.50
P# single, #S11111111 — 2.25
4141 A3152 26c **multicolored**, prephosphored coated paper, *May 12* .75 .25
Pair 1.50
P# strip of 5, #S1111 4.50
P# single, #S1111 — 2.25
a. Die cutting omitted, pair *500.00*

No. 4140 and No. 4141 exist on two types of surface-tagged paper that exhibit either a solid or uneven appearance. Stamps with solid tagging are scarcer for No. 4141. Values: P# strip of 5, #S1111, $120; used P# single, $120.

Booklet Stamp

Serpentine Die Cut 11¼x11 on 3 Sides

4142 A3152 26c **multicolored**, *May 12* .55 .25
a. Booklet pane of 10 5.50

Nos. 4137 and 4139 have microprinted "USPS" to the left and above the lower left whisker. No. 4140 has microprinted "USPS" on right horn. No. 4141 has microprinted "USPS" along the right edge of the stamp just above the panther. Nos. 4138 and 4142 lack microprinting.

PREMIERE OF MOVIE "STAR WARS," 30TH ANNIVERSARY

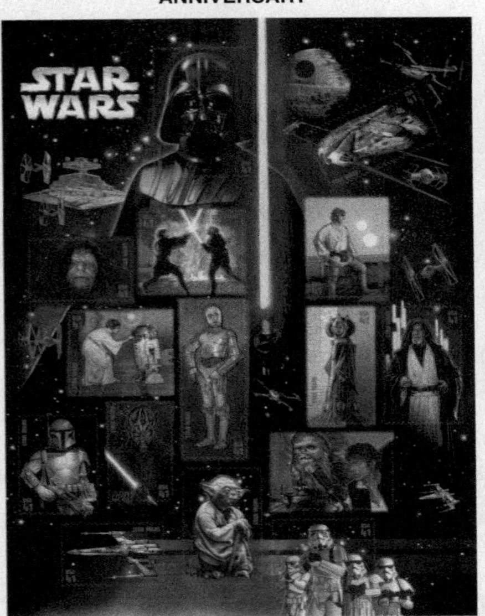

A3153

Illustration reduced.

Designed by Terrence McCaffrey and William J. Gicker, Jr.. Printed by Banknote Corporation of America for Sennett Security Products.

No. 4143: a, Darth Vader (40x53mm). b, Millennium Falcon (47x25mm). c, Emperor Palpatine (41x26mm). d, Anakin Skywalker and Obi-Wan Kenobi (41x33mm). e, Luke Skywalker (31x41mm). f, Princess Leia and R2-D2 (41x33mm). g, C-3PO (21x65mm). h, Queen Padmé Amidala (26x48mm). i, Obi-Wan Kenobi (31x48mm). j, Boba Fett (32x40mm). k, Darth Maul (26x41mm). l, Chewbacca and Han Solo (48x31mm). m, X-wing Starfighter (41x26mm). n, Yoda (31x48mm). o, Stormtroopers (41x31mm).

LITHOGRAPHED

Sheets of 45 in three panes of 15

2007, May 25 Tagged *Serpentine Die Cut 11*

Self-Adhesive

4143 A3153 Pane of 15 15.00
a.-o. 41c Any single 1.00 .50

Uncut press sheets of No. 4143 were made available for sale. Values: block of 15 with vert. gutter (6 stamps at left, 9 stamps at right), $18. See note after No. 2868.

PRESIDENTIAL AIRCRAFT

Air Force One — A3154

Marine One — A3155

Designed by Phil Jordan. Printed by Ashton-Potter (USA) Ltd. (#4144), Banknote Corporation of America for Sennett Security Products (#4145).

LITHOGRAPHED & ENGRAVED (#4144), LITHOGRAPHED (#4145)

Sheets of 120 in six panes of 20

2007, June 13 Tagged *Serpentine Die Cut 10¾*

Self-Adhesive

4144 A3154 $4.60 **multicolored** 9.25 5.00
P# block of 4, 6#+P 37.50
Pane of 20 190.00
a. Black (engr.) omitted *225.00*

4145 A3155 $16.25 **multicolored** 30.00 16.00
P# block of 4, 5#+S 120.00
Pane of 20 600.00

PACIFIC LIGHTHOUSES

Diamond Head Lighthouse, Hawaii — A3156

Five Finger Lighthouse, Alaska — A3157

Grays Harbor Lighthouse, Washington — A3158

Umpqua River Lighthouse, Oregon — A3159

St. George Reef Lighthouse, California — A3160

Designed by Howard E. Paine. Printed by Avery Dennison.

PHOTOGRAVURE

Sheets of 160 in eight panes of 20

2007, June 21 Tagged *Serpentine Die Cut 11*

Self-Adhesive

4146 A3156 41c **multicolored** 1.20 .40
4147 A3157 41c **multicolored** 1.20 .40
4148 A3158 41c **multicolored** 1.20 .40
4149 A3159 41c **multicolored** 1.20 .40
4150 A3160 41c **multicolored** 1.20 .40
a. Horiz. strip of 5, #4146-4150 6.00
P# block of 10, 5#+V 12.00
Pane of 20 24.00

WEDDING HEARTS

Heart With Lilac Background — A3161

Heart With Pink Background — A3162

Designed by Carl T. Herrman. Printed by Ashton-Potter (USA) Ltd. (#4151), Avery Dennison (#4152).

LITHOGRAPHED (#4151), PHOTOGRAVURE (#4152)

BOOKLET STAMP (#4151)

Sheets of 240 in twelve panes of 20 (#4152)

Serpentine Die Cut 10¾ on 2, 3 or 4 Sides

2007, June 27 Tagged

Self-Adhesive

4151 A3161 41c **multicolored** 1.00 .25
a. Booklet pane of 20 20.00

Serpentine Die Cut 10¾x11

4152 A3162 58c **multicolored** 1.25 .25
P# block of 4, 4#+V 5.00
Pane of 20 25.00

POLLINATION

Purple Nightshade, Morrison's Bumblebee A3163

Hummingbird Trumpet, Calliope Hummingbird A3164

Saguaro, Lesser Long-nosed Bat — A3165

Prairie Ironweed, Southern Dogface Butterfly A3166

Designed by Steve Buchanan. Printed by Ashton-Potter (USA) Ltd.

No. 4153: Type I, Tip of bird wing is directly under center of "U" in "USA," straight edge at left. Type II, Tip of bird wing is directly under the right line of the "U" in "USA," straight edge at right.

No. 4154: Type I, Tip of bird wing is even with the top of denomination, straight edge at right. Type II, Tip of bird wing is well above denomination, straight edge at left.

No. 4155: Type I, Top of "USA" is even with the lower portion of the nearest unopened green saguaro flower bud, straight edge at left. Type II, Top of "USA" is even with the point where the flower and unopened green saguaro bud meet, straight edge at right.

No. 4156: Type I, Bottom of denomination is even with top point of the white triangle found between the bottom of the purple flower and the green leaf below it, straight edge at right. Type II, Bottom of denomination is even with the lower point of the white triangle found between the bottom of the purple flower and the green leaf below it, straight edge at left.

LITHOGRAPHED

Serpentine Die Cut 11 on 2, 3 or 4 Sides

2007, June 29 Tagged

Self-Adhesive

Booklet Stamps

4153 A3163 41c **multicolored,** Type I .85 .30
a. Type II .85 .30
4154 A3164 41c **multicolored,** Type I .85 .30
a. Type II .85 .30
4155 A3165 41c **multicolored,** Type I .85 .30
a. Type II .85 .30
4156 A3166 41c **multicolored,** Type I .85 .30
a. Type II .85 .30
b. Block of 4, #4153-4156 3.40
c. Block of 4, #4153a-4156a 3.40
d. Booklet pane of 20, 3 each #4153-4156, 2 each #4153a-4156a 17.00

No. 4156d is a double-sided booklet with 12 stamps (2 each #4153-4156, 1 each #4153a-4156a) on one side and 8 stamps plus label (booklet cover) on the other side.

Patriotic Banner — A3167

Designed by Michael Osborne. Printed by Avery-Dennison (#4157), Banknote Corporation of America for Sennett Security Products (#4158).

PHOTOGRAVURE (#4157), LITHOGRAPHED (#4158)

Serpentine Die Cut 11 Vert.

2007, July 4 **Untagged**

Coil Stamps

Self-Adhesive

4157 A3167 (10c) **red, gold & blue** ⓢ .25 .25
Pair .40
P# strip of 5, #V111, V222 2.25
P# strip of 5, V333 2.75
P# single, #V111, V222 — 1.40
P# single, #V333 2.75

Later printings of No. 4157 do not respond to a water soak. See note after No. 1549.

Serpentine Die Cut 11¾ Vert.

4158 A3167 (10c) **red, gold & blue** .25 .25
Pair .40
P# strip of 5, #S111 2.75
P# single, #S111 — 1.25

A later printing of No. 4158 shows the red and blue in somewhat darker shades.
See No. 4385.

MARVEL COMICS SUPERHEROES

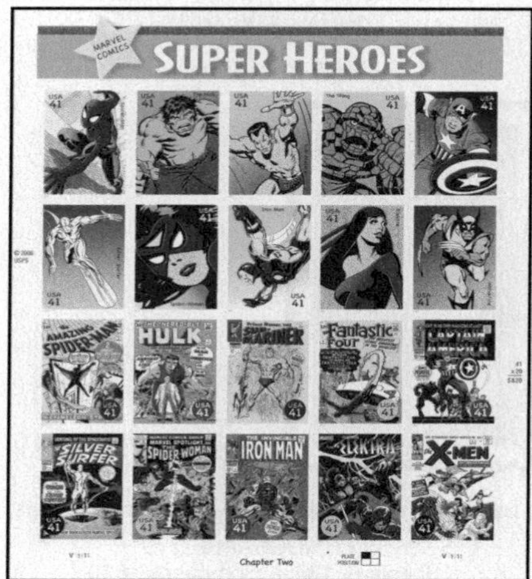

A3168

Illustration reduced.
Designed by Carl T. Herrman. Printed by Avery Dennison.
No. 4159: a, Spider-man. b, The Hulk. c, Sub-Mariner. d, The Thing. e, Captain America. f, Silver Surfer. g, Spider-Woman. h, Iron Man. i, Elektra. j, Wolverine. k, Cover of *The Amazing Spider-Man #1*. l, Cover of *The Incredible Hulk #1*. m, Cover of *Sub-Mariner #1*. n, Cover of *The Fantastic Four #3*. o, Cover of *Captain America #100*. p, Cover of *The Silver Surfer #1*. q, Cover of *Marvel Spotlight on The Spider-Woman #32*. r, Cover of *Iron Man #1*. s, Cover of *Daredevil #176 Featuring Elektra*. t, Cover of *The X-Men #1*.

PHOTOGRAVURE

Sheets of 80 in four panes of 20

Serpentine Die Cut 10½x10¾

2007, July 26 **Tagged**

Self-Adhesive

4159 A3168 Pane of 20 20.00
a.-t. 41c Any single 1.00 .50

Uncut press sheets of No. 4159 were made available for sale. Values: cross-gutter block of 20, $30; pairs with gutters between, $3.25 each. See note after No. 2868.

VINTAGE MAHOGANY SPEEDBOATS ⓢ

1915 Hutchinson — A3169

1954 Chris-Craft — A3170

1939 Hacker-Craft A3171

1931 Gar Wood — A3172

Designed by Carl T. Herrman. Printed by Ashton-Potter (USA) Ltd.

LITHOGRAPHED

Sheets of 72 in six panes of 12

2007, Aug. 4 **Tagged** ***Serpentine Die Cut 10½***

Self-Adhesive

4160 A3169 41c **multicolored** .85 .35
4161 A3170 41c **multicolored** .85 .35
4162 A3171 41c **multicolored** .85 .35
4163 A3172 41c **multicolored** .85 .35
a. Horiz. strip of 4, #4160-4163 3.40
P# block of 8, 4#+P 7.25
Pane of 12 10.50

See note after No. 1549.

Purple Heart Type of 2003

Designed by Carl T. Herrman. Printed by Ashton-Potter (USA) Ltd.

LITHOGRAPHED

Sheets of 120 in six panes of 20

Serpentine Die Cut 11¼x10¾

2007, Aug. 7 **Tagged**

Self-Adhesive

4164 A2891 41c **multicolored** ⓢ .85 .25
P# block of 4, 4#+P 3.40
Pane of 20 17.00

See note after No. 1549.

AMERICAN TREASURES SERIES

Magnolia and Irises, Stained Glass by Louis Comfort Tiffany — A3173

Designed by Derry Noyes. Printed by Ashton-Potter (USA) Ltd.

LITHOGRAPHED

BOOKLET STAMP

Serpentine Die Cut 10¾ on 2 or 3 Sides

2007, Aug. 9 **Tagged**

Self-Adhesive

4165 A3173 41c **multicolored** .85 .25
a. Booklet pane of 20 17.00

No. 4165a is a double-sided booklet pane with 12 stamps on one side and eight stamps plus label (booklet cover) on the other side.

FLOWERS

Iris — A3174

Dahlia — A3175

Magnolia — A3176

Red Gerbera Daisy — A3177

Coneflower — A3178

Tulip — A3179

Water Lily — A3180

Poppy — A3181

Chrysanthemum A3182

Orange Gerbera Daisy A3183

Designed by Carl T. Herrman. Printed by Ashton-Potter (USA) Ltd. (#4166-4175), Avery Dennison (#4176-4185)

LITHOGRAPHED, PHOTOGRAVURE (#4176-4185)

Serpentine Die Cut 9½ Vert.

2007, Aug. 10 **Tagged**

COIL STAMPS Ⓢ

Self-Adhesive

4166 A3174 41c **multicolored** 2.00 .35
4167 A3175 41c **multicolored** 2.00 .35
4168 A3176 41c **multicolored** 2.00 .35
4169 A3177 41c **multicolored** 2.00 .35
4170 A3178 41c **multicolored** 2.00 .35
4171 A3179 41c **multicolored** 2.00 .35
4172 A3180 41c **multicolored** 2.00 .35
4173 A3181 41c **multicolored** 2.00 .35
4174 A3182 41c **multicolored** 2.00 .35
4175 A3183 41c **multicolored** 2.00 .35
a. Strip of 10, #4166-4175 20.00
P# strip of 11, 2 # 4175, 1 each #4166-4174, #P1111, P2222 25.00 —
P# single (#4170), same # — 2.00

Some later printings of Nos. 4166-4175 do not respond to a water soak. See note after No. 1549.

BOOKLET STAMPS

Serpentine Die Cut 11¼x11½ on 2 or 3 Sides

4176 A3182 41c **multicolored** 1.25 .35
4177 A3183 41c **multicolored** 1.25 .35
4178 A3174 41c **multicolored** 1.25 .35
4179 A3175 41c **multicolored** 1.25 .35
4180 A3176 41c **multicolored** 1.25 .35
4181 A3177 41c **multicolored** 1.25 .35
4182 A3180 41c **multicolored** 1.25 .35
4183 A3181 41c **multicolored** 1.25 .35
4184 A3178 41c **multicolored** 1.25 .35
4185 A3179 41c **multicolored** 1.25 .35
a. Booklet pane of 20, 2 each #4176-4185 25.00
b. As "a," die cutting missing on Nos. 4178 & 4183 on side with 8 stamps (PS) *1,000.*

No. 4185a is a double-sided booklet pane with 12 stamps on one side (2 each #4176-4177, 1 each #4178-4185) and eight stamps (#4178-4185) plus label (booklet cover) on the other side.

Flag — A3184

Designed by Richard Sheaff. Printed by Avery Dennison (#4188, 4189), Ashton-Potter (USA) Ltd. (#4186, 4190), Banknote Corporation of America for Sennett Security Products (#4187, 4191).

LITHOGRAPHED, PHOTOGRAVURE (#4188, 4189)

Serpentine Die Cut 9½ Vert.

2007, Aug. 15 **Tagged**

COIL STAMPS

Self-Adhesive

With "USPS" Microprinted on Right Side of Flagpole

With Perpendicular Corners

4186 A3184 41c **multicolored** 1.20 .25
Pair 2.40
P# strip of 5, #P11111 7.25
P# single, #P11111 — 2.00

With "USPS" Microprinted on Left Side of Flagpole

Serpentine Die Cut 11 Vert.

4187 A3184 41c **multicolored,** prephosphored coated paper 1.20 .25
Pair 2.40
P# strip of 5, #S11111 7.50
P# single, #S11111 — 2.00

No. 4187 exists on two types of surface-tagged paper that exhibit either a solid or an uneven appearance.

No. 4186 was not sold to the public until October 2007 and No. 4187 was not sold to the public until November 2007.

Counterfeits exist of No. 4187. See the Postal Counterfeits section of this catalog.

Without "USPS" Microprinting on Flagpole

Serpentine Die Cut 8½ Vert.

4188 A3184 41c **multicolored,** overall tagging .85 .25
Pair 1.70
P# strip of 5, #V11111 6.00
P# single, same # — 2.00
a. Prephosphored coated paper with surface tagging showing a solid appearance 1.00 .25
Pair 2.00
P# strip of 5, #V22222 6.50
P# single, #V22222 — 2.00
c. As "a," light blue ("41 USA") omitted, on cover —

Serpentine Die Cut 11 Vert.

With Rounded Corners

4189 A3184 41c **multicolored** .85 .25
Pair 1.60
P# strip of 5, #V11111 6.00
P# single, #V11111 — 2.00

No. 4188 is on backing paper as high as the stamp. No. 4189 is on backing paper that is larger than the stamp.

BOOKLET STAMPS

Serpentine Die Cut 11¼x10¾ on 3 Sides

With "USPS" Microprinted on Right Side of Flagpole

4190 A3184 41c **multicolored** .85 .25
a. Booklet pane of 10 8.50

With "USPS" Microprinted on Left Side of Flagpole

Serpentine Die Cut 11¼x10¾ on 2 or 3 Sides

4191 A3184 41c **multicolored** .85 .25
a. Booklet pane of 20 17.00

The microprinting on Nos. 4190 and 4191 is under the ball of the flagpole. The flagpole is light gray on No. 4190 and dark gray on No. 4191. No. 4191a is a double-sided booklet with 12 stamps on one side of the peelable backing and 8 stamps plus label (booklet cover) on the other side.

THE ART OF DISNEY: MAGIC

Mickey Mouse — A3185

Peter Pan and Tinker Bell — A3186

Dumbo and Timothy Mouse — A3187

Aladdin and Genie — A3188

Designed by David Pacheco. Printed by Avery Dennison.

PHOTOGRAVURE

Sheets of 160 in eight panes of 20

Serpentine Die Cut 10½x10¾

2007, Aug. 16 **Tagged**

Self-Adhesive

4192 A3185 41c **multicolored** .85 .30
4193 A3186 41c **multicolored** .85 .30
4194 A3187 41c **multicolored** .85 .30
4195 A3188 41c **multicolored** .85 .30
a. Block or strip of 4, #4192-4195 3.40
P# block of 4, 6#+V 3.40
P# block of 10, 2 sets of P# + top label 8.50
Pane of 20 17.00

CELEBRATE

A3189

Designed by Ethel Kessler. Printed by Banknote Corporation of America for Sennett Security Products.

LITHOGRAPHED

Sheets of 160 in eight panes of 20

2007, Aug. 17 **Tagged** ***Serpentine Die Cut 10¾***

Self-Adhesive

4196 A3189 41c **multicolored** .85 .25
P# block of 4, 4#+S 3.40
Pane of 20 17.00

See Nos. 4335, 4407.

LEGENDS OF HOLLYWOOD

James Stewart (1908-97), Actor — A3190

Designed by Phil Jordan. Printed by Ashton-Potter (USA) Ltd.

LITHOGRAPHED

Sheets of 180 in nine panes of 20

2007, Aug. 17 **Tagged** ***Serpentine Die Cut 10¾***

Self-Adhesive

4197 A3190 41c **multicolored** Ⓢ 1.00 .25
P# block of 4, 4#+P 5.00
Pane of 20 20.00

Ⓢ: Ink on No. 4197 cracks and flakes off during water soak. See note after No. 1549.

Uncut press sheets of No. 4197 were made available for sale. Values: cross-gutter block of 8, $24; pairs with gutters between, $3.25 each. See note after No. 2868.

ALPINE TUNDRA

A3191

Illustration reduced.

Designed by Ethel Kessler. Printed by Banknote Corporation of America for Sennett Security Products.

No. 4198 — Wildlife: a, Elk. b, Golden eagle, horiz. c, Yellow-bellied marmot. d, American pika. e, Bighorn sheep. f, Magdalena alpine butterfly. g, White-tailed ptarmigan. h, Rocky Mountain parnassian butterfly. i, Melissa arctic butterfly, horiz. j, Brown-capped rosy-finch, horiz.

PHOTOGRAVURE
Sheets of 80 in eight panes of 10

2007, Aug. 28 Tagged *Serpentine Die Cut 10¾*
Self-Adhesive

4198 A3191 Pane of 10 8.50
a.-j. 41c any single .85 .40

Uncut press sheets of Nos. 4198 were made available for sale. See note after No. 2868.

GERALD R. FORD Ⓢ

Gerald R. Ford (1913-2006), 38th President — A3192

Designed by Ethel Kessler. Printed by Ashton-Potter (USA) Ltd.

LITHOGRAPHED
Sheets of 120 in six panes of 20

2007, Aug. 31 Tagged *Serpentine Die Cut 11*
Self-Adhesive

4199 A3192 41c **multicolored** .85 .25
P# block of 4, 5#+P 3.40
Pane of 20 17.00

Uncut press sheets of No. 4199 were made available for sale. Values: cross-gutter block of 4, $9; pairs with gutters between, $3 each. See note after No. 2868.
See note after No. 1549.

JURY DUTY Ⓢ

Twelve Jurors — A3193

Designed by Carl T. Herrman. Printed by Ashton-Potter (USA) Ltd.

LITHOGRAPHED
Sheets of 120 in six panes of 20

2007, Sept. 12 Tagged *Serpentine Die Cut 10½*
Self-Adhesive

4200 A3193 41c **multicolored** .85 .25
P# block of 4, 5#+P 3.40
Pane of 20 17.00

See note after No. 1549.

MENDEZ v. WESTMINSTER, 60th ANNIV. Ⓢ

A3194

Designed by Ethel Kessler. Printed by Ashton-Potter (USA) Ltd.

LITHOGRAPHED
Sheets of 120 in six panes of 20

2007, Sept. 14 Tagged *Serpentine Die Cut 11*
Self-Adhesive

4201 A3194 41c **multicolored** .85 .25
P# block of 4, 4#+P 3.40
Pane of 20 17.00

See note after No. 1549.

Eid Type of 2001

Designed by Mohamed Zakariya. Printed by Avery Dennison.

PHOTOGRAVURE
Sheets of 240 in twelve panes of 20

2007, Sept. 28 Tagged *Serpentine Die Cut 11*
Self-Adhesive

4202 A2734 41c **multicolored** .90 .25
P# block of 4, 3#+V 4.50
Pane of 20 22.00

AURORAS Ⓢ

Aurora Borealis A3195

Aurora Australis A3196

Designed by Phil Jordan. Printed by Ashton-Potter (USA) Ltd.

LITHOGRAPHED
Sheets of 120 in six panes of 20

2007, Oct. 1 Tagged *Serpentine Die Cut 10¾*
Self-Adhesive

4203 A3195 41c **multicolored** 1.25 .30
4204 A3196 41c **multicolored** 1.25 .30
a. Horiz. or vert. pair, #4203-4204 2.50
P# block of 4, 5#+P 6.00
Pane of 20 29.00

See note after No. 1549.

YODA

A3197

Designed by Greg Breeding. Printed by Banknote Corporation of America for Sennett Security Products.

LITHOGRAPHED
Sheets of 120 in six panes of 20
Serpentine Die Cut 10½x10¾

2007, Oct. 25 Tagged
Self-Adhesive

4205 A3197 41c **multicolored** 1.00 .25
P# block of 4, 5#+S 4.00
Pane of 20 20.00

Uncut part press sheets of No. 4205 of 3 panes each (1x3) were made available for sale. Value: vertical pair with horizontal gutter, $3. See note after No. 2868.

CHRISTMAS

Madonna of the Carnation, by Bernardino Luini — A3198

Knit Reindeer — A3199

Knit Christmas Tree — A3200

Knit Snowman — A3201

Knit Bear — A3202

Knit Reindeer — A3203

Knit Christmas Tree — A3204

Knit Snowman — A3205

Knit Bear — A3206

Designed by Richard Sheaff (#4206), Carl T. Herrman.
Printed by Ashton-Potter (USA) Ltd. (#4206), Banknote Corporation of America for Sennett Security Products (#4207-4214), Avery Dennison (#4215-4218).

LITHOGRAPHED, PHOTOGRAVURE (#4215-4218)
Sheets of 160 in eight panes of 20 (#4207-4210)
Serpentine Die Cut 10¾x11 on 2 or 3 Sides

2007, Oct. 25 Tagged
Self-Adhesive

Booklet Stamps (#4206, 4210b, 4211-4218)

4206 A3198 41c **multicolored** Ⓢ .85 .25
a. Booklet pane of 20 17.00

No. 4206a is a double-sided booklet pane with 12 stamps on one side and eight stamps plus label that serves as a booklet cover on the other side.

Ink on No. 4206 cracks and flakes off during a water soak. See note after No. 1549.

Serpentine Die Cut 10¾ on 2, 3 or 4 Sides

4207 A3199 41c **multicolored,** overall tagging .85 .25
a. Prephosphored coated paper with surface tagging showing an uneven appearance .85 .25

4208 A3200 41c **multicolored**, overall tagging .85 .25
a. Prephosphored coated paper with surface tagging showing an uneven appearance .85 .25
4209 A3201 41c **multicolored**, overall tagging .85 .25
a. Prephosphored coated paper with surface tagging showing an uneven appearance .85 .25
4210 A3202 41c **multicolored**, overall tagging .85 .25
a. Prephosphored coated paper with surface tagging showing an uneven appearance .85 .25
b. Block or vert. strip of 4, #4207-4210 3.40
P# block of 4, 4#+S 3.40
Pane of 20 17.00
c. Block of 4, #4207a-4210a 3.40
d. Booklet pane of 20, 5 each #4207a-4210a 17.00

No. 4210d is a double-sided booklet pane with 12 stamps on one side and eight stamps plus label that serves as a booklet cover on the other side.

Tagging on stamps from panes of 20 has a solid appearance; tagging on stamps from booklets has an uneven appearance.

Serpentine Die Cut 11¼x11 on 2 or 3 Sides

4211 A3203 41c **multicolored** 1.25 .25
4212 A3204 41c **multicolored** 1.25 .25
4213 A3205 41c **multicolored** 1.25 .25
4214 A3206 41c **multicolored** 1.25 .25
a. Block of 4, #4211-4214 5.00
b. Booklet pane of 4, #4211-4214 5.00
c. Booklet pane of 6, #4213-4214, 2 each #4211-4212 7.50
d. Booklet pane of 6, #4211-4212, 2 each #4213-4214 7.50

Serpentine Die Cut 8 on 2, 3 or 4 Sides

4215 A3203 41c **multicolored** Ⓢ 1.30 .25
4216 A3204 41c **multicolored** Ⓢ 1.30 .25
4217 A3205 41c **multicolored** Ⓢ 1.30 .25
4218 A3206 41c **multicolored** Ⓢ 1.30 .25
a. Block or strip of 4, #4215-4218 5.20
b. Booklet pane of 18, 4 each #4215, 4218, 5 each #4216, 4217 23.50
Nos. 4206-4218 (13) 14.45 3.25

See note after No. 1549.

Hanukkah Type of 2004

Designed by Ethel Kessler. Printed by Banknote Corporation of America for Sennett Security Products.

LITHOGRAPHED

Sheets of 160 in eight panes of 20

Serpentine Die Cut 10¾x11

2007, Oct. 26 Tagged

Self-Adhesive

4219 A2962 41c **multicolored** .85 .25
P# block of 4, 4#+S 3.40
Pane of 20 17.00

Kwanzaa Type of 2004

Designed by Derry Noyes. Printed by Ashton-Potter (USA) Ltd.

LITHOGRAPHED

Sheets of 160 in eight panes of 20

Serpentine Die Cut 11x10¾

2007, Oct. 26 Tagged

Self-Adhesive

4220 A2963 41c **multicolored** Ⓢ .85 .25
P# block of 4, 6#+P 3.40
Pane of 20 17.00

See note after No. 1549.

CHINESE NEW YEAR

Year of the Rat — A3207

Designed by Ethel Kessler. Printed by Avery Dennison

PHOTOGRAVURE

Sheets of 108 in nine panes of 12

Serpentine Die Cut 10¾

2008, Jan. 9 Tagged Self-Adhesive

4221 A3207 41c **multicolored** .85 .25
Pane of 12 10.50

Uncut press sheets of No. 4221 were made available for sale. Values: cross-gutter block of 4, $9; pairs with gutters between, $2.25 each. See note after No. 2868.

BLACK HERITAGE SERIES

Charles W. Chesnutt (1858-1932), Writer — A3208

Designed by Howard E. Paine. Printed by Avery Dennison.

PHOTOGRAVURE

Sheets of 200 in ten panes of 20

Serpentine Die Cut 11

2008, Jan. 31 Tagged Self-Adhesive

4222 A3208 41c **multicolored** .85 .25
P# block of 4, 4# + V 3.40
Pane of 20 17.00

LITERARY ARTS SERIES

Marjorie Kinnan Rawlings (1896-1953), Writer A3209

Designed by Carl T. Herrman. Printed by Avery Dennison.

PHOTOGRAVURE

Sheets of 200 in ten panes of 20

2008, Feb. 21 Tagged *Serpentine Die Cut 11*

Self-Adhesive

4223 A3209 41c **multicolored** .85 .25
P# block of 4, 4# + V 3.40
Pane of 20 17.00

AMERICAN SCIENTISTS

Gerty Cori (1896-1957), Biochemist A3210

Linus Pauling (1901-94), Structural Chemist A3211

Edwin Hubble (1889-1953), Astronomer A3212

John Bardeen (1908-91), Theoretical Physicist A3213

Designed by Victor Stabin. Printed by Avery Dennison.

PHOTOGRAVURE

Sheets of 160 in eight panes of 20

2008, Mar. 6 Tagged *Serpentine Die Cut 11*

Self-Adhesive

4224 A3210 41c **multicolored** 1.00 .35
4225 A3211 41c **multicolored** 1.00 .35
4226 A3212 41c **multicolored** 1.00 .35
4227 A3213 41c **multicolored** 1.00 .35
a. Horiz. strip of 4, #4224-4227 4.00
P# block of 8, 2 sets of 4# + V 8.00
Pane of 20 20.00

Plate block may contain top label.

Flag at Dusk — A3214

Flag at Night — A3215

Flag at Dawn — A3216

Flag at Midday — A3217

Designed by Phil Jordan. Printed by American Packaging Corporation for Sennett Security Products (#4228-4231), Ashton-Potter (USA) Ltd. (#4232-4235), Banknote Corporation of America for Sennett Security Products (#4236-4239), Avery Dennison (#4240-4247).

PHOTOGRAVURE (#4228-4231, 4240-4247), LITHOGRAPHED (#4232-4239)

2008, Apr. 18 Tagged *Perf. 9¾ Vert.*

COIL STAMPS

4228 A3214 42c **multicolored** 2.50 .40
4229 A3215 42c **multicolored** 2.50 .40
4230 A3216 42c **multicolored** 2.50 .40
4231 A3217 42c **multicolored** 2.50 .40
a. Horiz. strip of 4, #4228-4231 10.00 1.60
P# strip of 5, 2 #4228, 1 each #4229-4231, #S1111111 15.00 —
P# strip of 9, 3 #4230, 2 each #4228-4229, 4230, P#S1111111 27.50 —
P# single, #S1111111 (#4230) — 2.00

Counterfeits exist of Nos. 4228-4231. See the Postal Counterfeits section of this catalog.

Self-Adhesive

With Perpendicular Corners

Serpentine Die Cut 9½ Vert.

4232 A3214 42c **multicolored** Ⓢ 2.25 .25
4233 A3215 42c **multicolored** Ⓢ 2.25 .25
4234 A3216 42c **multicolored** Ⓢ 2.25 .25
4235 A3217 42c **multicolored** Ⓢ 2.25 .25
a. Horiz. strip of 4, #4232-4235 9.00
P# strip of 5, 2 #4232, 1 each #4233-4235, #P1111 13.00
P# strip of 9, 3 #4234, 2 each #4232-4233, 4235, P#P1111 21.50
P# single, #P1111 (#4234) — 2.00

Counterfeits exist of Nos. 4232-4235. See the Postal Counterfeits section of this catalog.

Serpentine Die Cut 11 Vert.

4236 A3214 42c **multicolored** 2.50 .25
4237 A3215 42c **multicolored** 2.50 .25
4238 A3216 42c **multicolored** 2.50 .25
4239 A3217 42c **multicolored** 2.50 .25
a. Horiz. strip of 4, #4236-4239 10.00
P# strip of 5, 2 #4236, 1 each #4237-4239, #S1111 16.00
P# strip of 9, 3 #4238, 2 each #4236-4237, 4239, P#S1111 25.00
P# single, #S1111 (#4238) — 2.00

Serpentine Die Cut 8½ Vert.

4240 A3214 42c **multicolored** 2.00 .25
4241 A3215 42c **multicolored** 2.00 .25
4242 A3216 42c **multicolored** 2.00 .25
4243 A3217 42c **multicolored** 2.00 .25
a. Horiz. strip of 4, #4240-4243 8.00
P# strip of 5, 2 #4240, 1 each #4241-4243, #V1111, V2222 12.50
P# strip of 9, 3 #4242, 2 each #4240-4241, 4244, P#V1111, V2222 20.00
P# single, same # (#4242) — 2.00

Serpentine Die Cut 11 Vert.

With Rounded Corners

4244	A3214 42c **multicolored**	1.25	.30
4245	A3215 42c **multicolored**	1.25	.30
4246	A3216 42c **multicolored**	1.25	.30
4247	A3217 42c **multicolored**	1.25	.30
a.	Horiz. strip of 4, #4244-4247	6.00	
	P# strip of 5, 2 #4244, 1 each #4245-4247, #V1111, V2222	11.00	
	P# strip of 9, 3 #4246, 2 each #4244-4245, 4247, P#V1111, V2222	17.00	
	P# single, same # (#4246)	—	2.00
	Nos. 4228-4247 (20)	42.00	5.80

Nos. 4232-4243 are on backing paper as high as the stamp. See note after No. 1549.

Nos. 4244-4247 are on backing paper that is larger than the stamp. Nos. 4232-4235 have "USPS" microprinted on the right side of a white flag stripe. Nos. 4236-4239 have "USPS" micorprinted on red flag stripes. On Nos. 4244-4247, the paper, vignette size and "2008" year date are slightly larger than those features on Nos. 4236-4239.

AMERICAN JOURNALISTS ⓢ

Martha Gellhorn (1908-98) A3218

John Hersey (1914-93) A3219

George Polk (1913-48) A3220

Ruben Salazar (1928-70) A3221

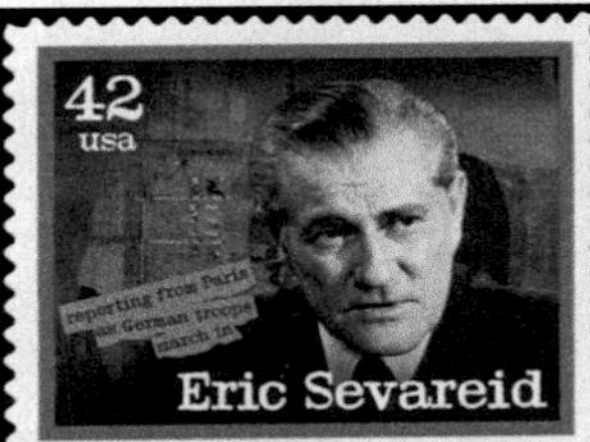

Eric Sevareid (1912-92) A3222

Designed by Howard E. Paine. Printed by Ashton-Potter (USA) Ltd.

LITHOGRAPHED

Sheets of 180 in nine panes of 20

Serpentine Die Cut 10¾x10½

2008, Apr. 22 **Tagged**

Self-Adhesive

4248	A3218 42c **multicolored**	1.40	.40
4249	A3219 42c **multicolored**	1.40	.40
4250	A3220 42c **multicolored**	1.40	.40
4251	A3221 42c **multicolored**	1.40	.40
4252	A3222 42c **multicolored**	1.40	.40
a.	Vert. strip of 5, #4248-4252	7.00	
	P# block of 10, 2 sets of 4# + P	14.00	
	P# block of 8, 2 sets of 4# +P	12.50	
	Pane of 20	28.00	

See note after No. 1549.

TROPICAL FRUIT

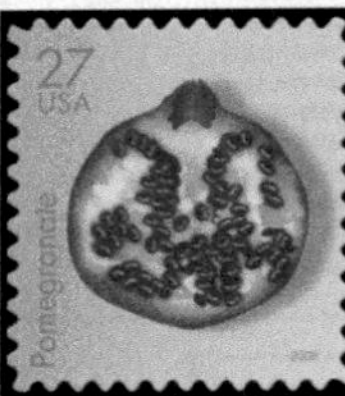

Pomegranate A3223

Star Fruit A3224

Kiwi — A3225

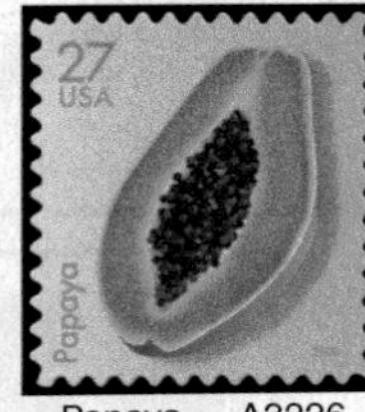

Papaya — A3226

Guava — A3227

Designed by Ethel Kessler. Printed by Ashton-Potter (USA) Ltd. (#4253-4257), Avery Dennison (#4258-4262)

LITHOGRAPHED (#4253-4257), PHOTOGRAVURE (#4258-4262)

Serpentine Die Cut 11¼x10¾

2008, Apr. 25 **Tagged**

Self-Adhesive

4253	A3223 27c **multicolored** ⓢ	.90	.25
4254	A3224 27c **multicolored** ⓢ	.90	.25
4255	A3225 27c **multicolored** ⓢ	.90	.25
4256	A3226 27c **multicolored** ⓢ	.90	.25
4257	A3227 27c **multicolored** ⓢ	.90	.25
a.	Horiz. strip of 5, #4253-4257	4.50	
	P# block of 10, 2 sets of 4# + P	9.00	
	Pane of 20	18.00	

See note after No. 1549.

COIL STAMPS

Serpentine Die Cut 8½ Vert.

4258	A3226 27c **multicolored**	1.80	.25
4259	A3227 27c **multicolored**	1.80	.25
4260	A3223 27c **multicolored**	1.80	.25
4261	A3224 27c **multicolored**	1.80	.25
4262	A3225 27c **multicolored**	1.80	.25
a.	Strip of 5, #4258-4262	9.00	
	P# strip of 5, #V1111111	11.00	
	P# strip of 11, 3 #4260, 2 each #4258-4259, 4261, 4262, #V1111111	22.50	
	P# single, #V1111111 (#4260)	—	3.00
b.	As No. 4262, light green ("27 USA," "Kiwi" and year date) omitted	—	
	Nos. 4253-4262 (10)	13.50	2.50

Purple Heart Type of 2003

Designed by Carl T. Herrman. Printed by Ashton-Potter (USA) Ltd.

LITHOGRAPHED

Sheets of 400 in four panes of 100 (#4263), Sheets of 120 in six panes of 20 (#4264)

2008, Apr. 30 **Tagged** ***Perf. 11¼***

4263	A2891 42c **multicolored**	.90	.25
	P# block of 4, 4#+P	35.00	—

Self-Adhesive

Serpentine Die Cut 11¼x10¾

4264	A2891 42c **multicolored** ⓢ	.85	.25
	P# block of 4, 4#+P	3.40	
	Pane of 20	17.00	

See note after No. 1549.

FRANK SINATRA

Frank Sinatra (1915-98), Singer and Actor — A3228

Designed by Richard Sheaff. Printed by Ashton-Potter (USA) Ltd.

LITHOGRAPHED

Sheets of 120 in six panes of 20

2008, May 13 **Tagged** ***Serpentine Die Cut 10¾***

Self-Adhesive

4265	A3228 42c **multicolored** ⓢ	.85	.25
	P# block of 4, 4#+P	3.40	
	Pane of 20	17.00	

See note after No. 1549.

Uncut press sheets of No. 4265 were made available for sale. Values: cross-gutter block of 4, $9; pairs with gutters between, $2.25 each. See note after No. 2868.

MINNESOTA STATEHOOD, 150th ANNIV. ⓢ

Bridge Over Mississippi River Near Winona — A3229

Designed by Ethel Kessler. Printed by Ashton-Potter (USA) Ltd.

LITHOGRAPHED

Sheets of 120 in six panes of 20

2008, May 17 **Tagged** ***Serpentine Die Cut 10¾***

Self-Adhesive

4266	A3229 42c **multicolored**	.85	.25
	P# block of 4, 4#+P	3.40	
	Pane of 20	17.00	

See note after No. 1549.

WILDLIFE

Dragonfly — A3230

Designed by Carl T. Herrman. Printed by Banknote Corporation of America for Sennett Security Products.

LITHOGRAPHED

Sheets of 400 in twenty panes of 20

Serpentine Die Cut 11¼x11

2008, May 19 **Tagged**

Self-Adhesive

4267	A3230 62c **multicolored**	2.50	.25
	P# block of 4, 4#+S	10.00	
	Pane of 20	50.00	

AMERICAN LANDMARKS

Mount Rushmore A3231

Hoover Dam — A3232

Designed by Carl T. Herrman. Printed by Ashton-Potter (USA) Ltd. (#4268), Banknote Corporation of America for Sennett Security Products (#4269).

LITHOGRAPHED

Sheets of 180 in nine panes of 20 (#4268), Sheets of 120 in six panes of 20 (#4269)

2008 **Tagged** ***Serpentine Die Cut 10¾x10½***

Self-Adhesive

4268 A3231 $4.80 **multicolored,** *June 6* Ⓢ 12.00 5.00
P# block of 4, 4#+P 48.00
Pane of 20 240.00
4269 A3232 $16.50 **multicolored,** *June 20* 35.00 17.00
P# block of 4, 5#+S 140.00
Pane of 20 700.00

See note after No. 1549.

LOVE

Man Carrying Heart — A3233

Designed by Ethel Kessler. Printed by Avery Dennison.

PHOTOGRAVURE

Serpentine Die Cut 10¾ on 2, 3, or 4 Sides

2008, June 10 **Tagged**

Booklet Stamp

Self-Adhesive

4270 A3233 42c **multicolored** Ⓢ .95 .25
a. Booklet pane of 20 19.00

See note after No. 1549.

WEDDING HEARTS Ⓢ

Heart With Light Green Background — A3234

Heart With Buff Background — A3235

Designed by Carl T. Herrman. Printed by Ashton-Potter (USA) Ltd. (#4271), Avery Dennison (#4272).

LITHOGRAPHED (#4271), PHOTOGRAVURE (#4272)

BOOKLET STAMP (#4271)

Sheets of 240 in twelve panes of 20 (#4272)

Serpentine Die Cut 10¾ on 2, 3 or 4 Sides

2008, June 10 **Tagged**

Self-Adhesive

4271 A3234 42c **multicolored** .90 .25
a. Booklet pane of 20 18.00

Serpentine Die Cut 10¾

4272 A3235 59c **multicolored** 1.25 .25
P# block of 4, 3#+V 5.00
Pane of 20 25.00

See note after No. 1549.

FLAGS OF OUR NATION

American Flag and Clouds A3236

Alabama Flag and Shrimp Boat A3237

Alaska Flag and Humpback Whale — A3238

American Samoa Flag and Island Peaks and Trees A3239

Arizona Flag and Saguaro Cacti A3240

Arkansas Flag and Wood Duck A3241

California Flag and Coast A3242

Colorado Flag and Mountain A3243

Connecticut Flag, Sailboats and Buoy — A3244

Delaware Flag and Beach A3245

Designed by Howard E. Paine. Printed by American Packaging Corp. for Sennett Security Products.

PHOTOGRAVURE

Serpentine Die Cut 11 Vert.

2008, June 14 **Tagged**

Self-Adhesive

Coil Stamps

4273 A3236 42c **multicolored** 1.00 .30
4274 A3237 42c **multicolored** 1.00 .30
4275 A3238 42c **multicolored** 1.00 .30
4276 A3239 42c **multicolored** 1.00 .30
4277 A3240 42c **multicolored** 1.00 .30
a. Strip of 5, #4273-4277 5.00
4278 A3241 42c **multicolored** 1.00 .30
4279 A3242 42c **multicolored** 1.00 .30
4280 A3243 42c **multicolored** 1.00 .30
4281 A3244 42c **multicolored** 1.00 .30
4282 A3245 42c **multicolored** 1.00 .30
a. Strip of 5, #4278-4282 5.00
b. P # set of 10, #4277a + 4282a 10.00
P# strip of 11, #4273-4277, 4279-4282, 2 #4278, S#111111111 13.00
P# strip of 21, 3 #4273, 2 each #4274-4282, S#111111111 30.00

No. 4273 always has a plate number. No. 4282b may be collected as one continuous strip, but the item will not fit in any standard album.

District of Columbia Flag and Cherry Tree A3246

Florida Flag and Anhinga A3247

Georgia Flag, Fence and Lamppost A3248

Guam Flag, Fish and Tropicbird A3249

Hawaii Flag and Ohia Lehua Flowers A3250

Idaho Flag and Rainbow Trout A3251

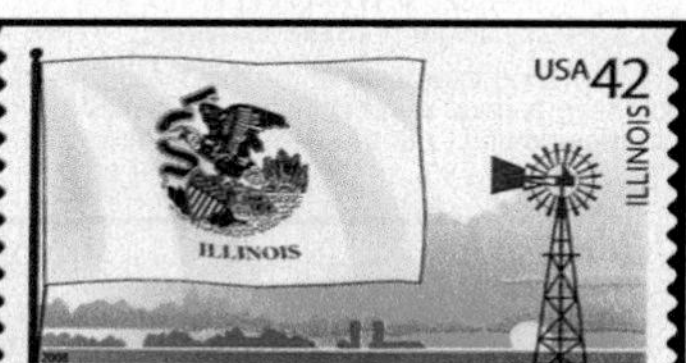

Illinois Flag and Windmill A3252

Indiana Flag and Tractor A3253

Iowa Flag, Farm Field and Cornstalks — A3254

Kansas Flag and Farm Buildings A3255

Designed by Howard E. Paine. Printed by American Packaging Corp. for Sennett Security Products.

PHOTOGRAVURE

Serpentine Die Cut 11 Vert.

2008, Sept. 2 **Tagged**

Self-Adhesive

Coil Stamps

4283 A3246 42c **multicolored** 1.00 .30
4284 A3247 42c **multicolored** 1.00 .30
4285 A3248 42c **multicolored** 1.00 .30
4286 A3249 42c **multicolored** 1.00 .30
4287 A3250 42c **multicolored** 1.00 .30
a. Strip of 5, #4283-4287 5.00
4288 A3251 42c **multicolored** 1.00 .30
4289 A3252 42c **multicolored** 1.00 .30
4290 A3253 42c **multicolored** 1.00 .30
4291 A3254 42c **multicolored** 1.00 .30
4292 A3255 42c **multicolored** 1.00 .30
a. Strip of 5, #4288-4292 5.00
b. P # set of 10, #4287a + 4192a 10.00
P# strip of 11, #4283-4287, 4289-4292, 2 #4288, S#111111111 13.00
P# strip of 21, 3 #4283, 2 each #4284-4292, S#111111111 30.00

No. 4283 always has a plate number. No. 4292b may be collected as one continuous strip, but the item will not fit in any standard album.

Kentucky Flag, Fence and Horses A3256

Louisiana Flag and Brown Pelicans A3257

Maine Flag and Moose A3258

Maryland Flag and Red-winged Blackbird — A3259

Massachusetts Flag, Sea Birds and Sailboats — A3260

Michigan Flag and Great Lakes Ships A3261

Minnesota Flag, Swans and Grain Elevator A3262

Mississippi Flag and Black Bears A3263

Missouri Flag and Paddle Wheeler A3264

American Flag and Wheat A3265

Designed by Howard E. Paine. Printed by American Packaging Corp. for Sennett Security Products.

PHOTOGRAVURE

2009, Aug. 6 **Tagged** ***Serpentine Die Cut 11 Vert.***

Self-Adhesive

Coil Stamps

4293 A3256 44c **multicolored** 1.00 .30
4294 A3257 44c **multicolored** 1.00 .30
4295 A3258 44c **multicolored** 1.00 .30
4296 A3259 44c **multicolored** 1.00 .30
4297 A3260 44c **multicolored** 1.00 .30
a. Strip of 5, #4293-4297 5.00
4298 A3261 44c **multicolored** 1.00 .30
4299 A3262 44c **multicolored** 1.00 .30
4300 A3263 44c **multicolored** 1.00 .30
4301 A3264 44c **multicolored** 1.00 .30
4302 A3265 44c **multicolored** 1.00 .30
a. Strip of 5, #4298-4302 5.00
b. P # set of 10, #4297a + 4302a 10.00
P# strip of 11, #4293-4297, 4299-4302, 2 #4298, P#S111111111 13.00
P# strip of 21, 3 #4293, 2 each #4294-4302, S#111111111 30.00

No. 4293 always has a plate number. No. 4302b may be collected as one continuous strip, but the item will not fit in any standard album.

American Flag and Mountains A3266

Montana Flag and Mountain Lion A3267

Nebraska Flag and Central-pivot Irrigation System — A3268

Nevada Flag, Mountains and Ocotillos A3269

New Hampshire Flag and Loon
A3270

New Jersey Flag and Sand Castle
A3271

New Mexico Flag, Mountains and Hot Air Balloons
A3272

New York Flag, Fireboats and City Skyline
A3273

North Carolina Flag, Great Blue Heron and Cape Hatteras Lighthouse — A3274

North Dakota Flag and Elk
A3275

Designed by Howard E. Paine. Printed by American Packaging Corp. for Sennett Security Products.

PHOTOGRAVURE

2010, Apr. 16 ***Serpentine Die Cut 11 Vert.***

Self-Adhesive

Coil Stamps

4303	A3266 44c **multicolored**	1.00	.30
4304	A3267 44c **multicolored**	1.00	.30
4305	A3268 44c **multicolored**	1.00	.30
4306	A3269 44c **multicolored**	1.00	.30
4307	A3270 44c **multicolored**	1.00	.30
a.	Strip of 5, #4303-4307	5.00	
4308	A3271 44c **multicolored**	1.00	.30
4309	A3272 44c **multicolored**	1.00	.30
4310	A3273 44c **multicolored**	1.00	.30
4311	A3274 44c **multicolored**	1.00	.30
4312	A3275 44c **multicolored**	1.00	.30
a.	Strip of 5, #4308-4312	5.00	
b.	P # set of 10, #4307a + 4312a	10.00	
	P# strip of 11, #4303-4307, 4309-4312, 2 #4308, P#S111111111	13.00	
	P# strip of 21, 3 #4303, 2 each #4304-4312, S#111111111	30.00	

No. 4303 always has a plate number. No. 4312b may be collected as one continuous strip, but the item will not fit in any standard album.

Northern Marianas Flag, Beach and Palm Trees
A3276

Ohio Flag, Butterfly, Milkweed Flowers and River
A3277

Oklahoma Flag and Oil Pumps
A3278

Oregon Flag, Mount Hood and Camas Lilies
A3279

Pennsylvania Flag and White-tailed Deer — A3280

Puerto Rico Flag and Puerto Rican Tody Bird
A3281

Rhode Island Flag and Sailboat
A3282

South Carolina Flag, Marsh and Gazebo
A3283

South Dakota Flag and Bison
A3284

Tennessee Flag and Scarlet Tanagers
A3285

Designed by Howard E. Paine. Printed by American Packaging Corp. for Sennett Security Products.

PHOTOGRAVURE

Serpentine Die Cut 11 Vert.

2011, Aug. 11 **Tagged**

Self-Adhesive

Coil Stamps

4313	A3276 (44c) **multicolored**	1.25	.30
4314	A3277 (44c) **multicolored**	1.25	.30
4315	A3278 (44c) **multicolored**	1.25	.30
4316	A3279 (44c) **multicolored**	1.25	.30
4317	A3280 (44c) **multicolored**	1.25	.30
a.	Strip of 5, #4313-4317	6.25	
4318	A3281 (44c) **multicolored**	1.25	.30
4319	A3282 (44c) **multicolored**	1.25	.30
4320	A3283 (44c) **multicolored**	1.25	.30
4321	A3284 (44c) **multicolored**	1.25	.30
4322	A3285 (44c) **multicolored**	1.25	.30
a.	Strip of 5, #4318-4322	6.25	
b.	P# set of 10, #4317a + 4322a	12.50	
	P# strip of 11, #4313-4317, 4319-4322, 2 #4318, P#S111111111	15.00	
	P# strip of 21, 3 #4313, 2 each #4314-4322, #S111111111	32.50	—
	P# single (#4313), same #	—	2.00

Alternating examples of the five examples of No. 4313 in the roll have a plate number. No. 4322b may be collected as one continuous strip, but the item will not fit in any standard album.

Texas Flag, Cotton Plant and Field
A3286

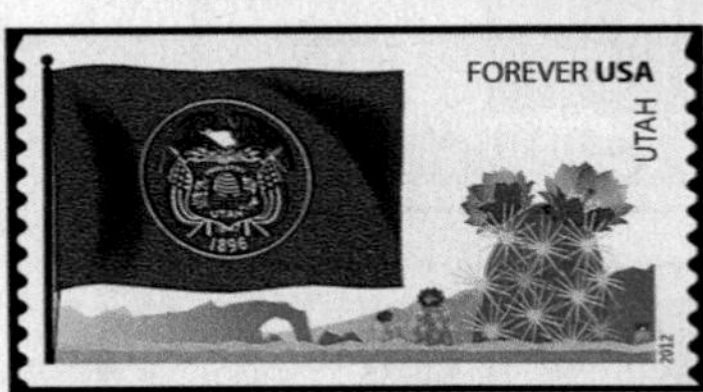

Utah Flag, Cactus and Rock Arch
A3287

Vermont Flag and Owls
A3288

Virgin Islands Flag, Sailfish and Boat
A3289

Virginia Flag and Replicas of Ships that Carried Settlers to Jamestown — A3290

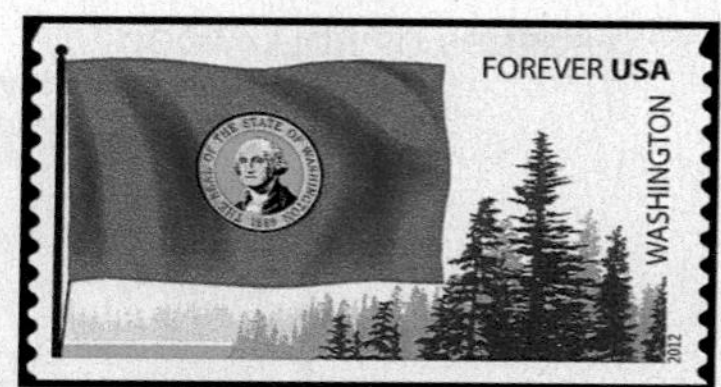

Washington Flag and Evergreen Forest — A3291

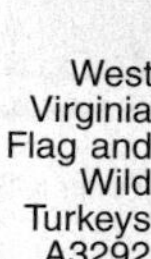

West Virginia Flag and Wild Turkeys A3292

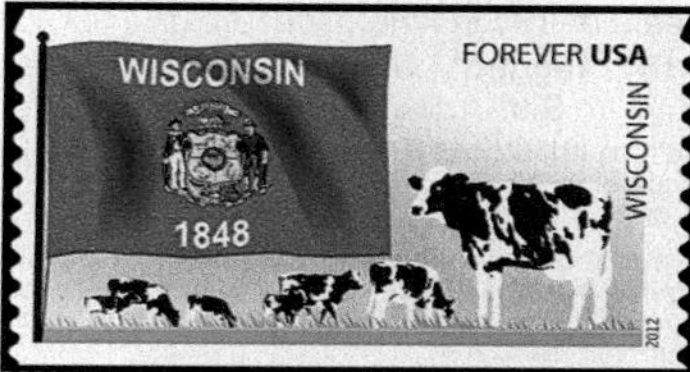

Wisconsin Flag and Dairy Cows A3293

Wyoming Flag and Bighorn Sheep A3294

American Flag and Fruited Plain A3295

Designed by Howard E. Paine. Printed by American Packaging Corp. for Sennett Security Products.

PHOTOGRAVURE

Serpentine Die Cut 11 Vert.

2012, Aug. 16 **Tagged**

Self-Adhesive

Coil Stamps

4323	A3286 (45c) **multicolored**	1.50	.30
4324	A3287 (45c) **multicolored**	1.50	.30
4325	A3288 (45c) **multicolored**	1.50	.30
4326	A3289 (45c) **multicolored**	1.50	.30
4327	A3290 (45c) **multicolored**	1.50	.30
a.	Strip of 5, #4323-4327	7.50	
4328	A3291 (45c) **multicolored**	1.50	.30
4329	A3292 (45c) **multicolored**	1.50	.30
4330	A3293 (45c) **multicolored**	1.50	.30
4331	A3294 (45c) **multicolored**	1.50	.30
4332	A3295 (45c) **multicolored**	1.50	.30
a.	Strip of 5, #4328-4332	7.50	
b.	P# set of 10, #4327a + 4332a	15.00	
	P# strip of 11, #4323-4327, 4329-4332, 2 #4328, P#S11111111	17.50	
	P# strip of 21, 3 #4323, 2 each #4324-4332, #S11111111	37.50	—
	P# single (#4323), same #	—	2.00

Alternating examples of the five examples of No. 4323 in the roll have a plate number. No. 4332b may be collected as one continuous strip, but the item will not fit in any standard album.

CHARLES (1907-78) AND RAY (1912-88) EAMES, DESIGNERS Ⓢ

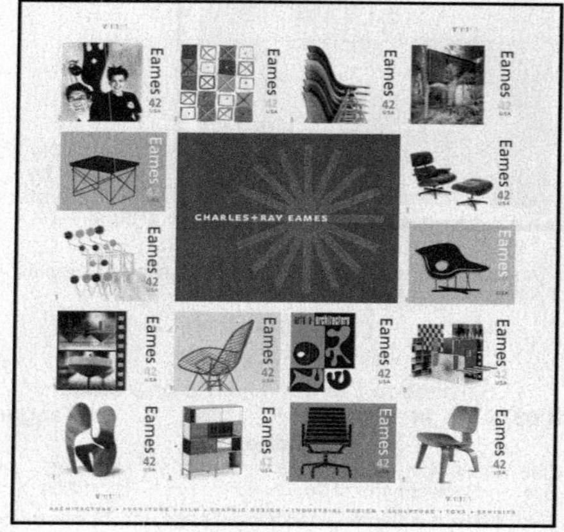

A3296

Illustration reduced.

Designed by Derry Noyes. Printed by Avery Dennison.

No. 4333: a, Christmas card depicting Charles and Ray Eames. b, "Crosspatch" fabric design. c, Stacking chairs. d, Case Study House #8, Pacific Palisades, CA. e, Wire-base table. f, Lounge chair and ottoman. g, Hang-it-all. h, La Chaise. i, Scene from film, "Tops." j, Wire mesh chair. k, Cover of May 1943 edition of *California Arts & Architecture* Magazine. l, House of Cards. m, Molded plywood sculpture. n, Eames Storage Unit. o, Aluminum group chair. p, Molded plywood chair.

PHOTOGRAVURE

Sheets of 160 in ten panes of 16

Serpentine Die Cut 10¾x10½

2008, June 17 **Tagged**

Self-Adhesive

4333	A3296 Pane of 16 + label	18.00	
a.-p.	42c Any single	1.10	.50

See note after No. 1549.

SUMMER OLYMPIC GAMES, BEIJING, CHINA

Gymnast A3297

Designed by Clarence Lee. Printed by Banknote Corporation of America for Sennett Security Products.

LITHOGRAPHED

Sheets of 180 in nine panes of 20

2008, June 19 **Tagged** ***Serpentine Die Cut 10¾***

Self-Adhesive

4334	A3297 42c **multicolored**	.85	.25
	P# block of 4, 6#+S	3.40	
	Pane of 20	17.00	

Celebrate Type of 2007

Designed by Ethel Kessler. Printed by Banknote Corporation of America for Sennett Security Products.

LITHOGRAPHED

Sheets of 240 in twelve panes of 20

2008, July 10 **Tagged** ***Serpentine Die Cut 10¾***

Self-Adhesive

4335	A3189 42c **multicolored**	.85	.25
	P# block of 4, 4# + S	3.40	
	Pane of 20	17.00	

VINTAGE BLACK CINEMA Ⓢ

Poster for "Black and Tan" — A3298

Poster for "The Sport of the Gods" — A3299

Poster for "Prinsesse Tam-Tam" — A3300

Poster for "Caldonia" — A3301

Poster for "Hallelujah" — A3302

Designed by Carl T. Herrman. Printed by Ashton-Potter (USA) Ltd.

LITHOGRAPHED

Sheets of 120 in six panes of 20

2008, July 16 **Tagged** ***Serpentine Die Cut 10¾***

Self-Adhesive

4336	A3298 42c **multicolored**	.95	.45
4337	A3299 42c **multicolored**	.95	.45
4338	A3300 42c **multicolored**	.95	.45
4339	A3301 42c **multicolored**	.95	.45
4340	A3302 42c **multicolored**	.95	.45
a.	Horiz. strip of 5, #4336-4340	4.75	
	P# block of 10, 2 sets of 4# + P	9.50	
	Pane of 20	19.00	

Plate block may contain top label.

Uncut press sheets of Nos. 4336-4340 were made available for sale. Values: cross-gutter block of 8, $19; pairs with gutters between, $2.75 each. See note after No. 2868.

See note after No. 1549.

"TAKE ME OUT TO THE BALLGAME," CENT.

Baseball Players and First Six Notes of Song — A3303

Designed by Richard Sheaff. Printed by Avery Dennison.

PHOTOGRAVURE
Sheets of 200 in ten panes of 20

2008, July 16 Tagged *Serpentine Die Cut 11*
Self-Adhesive

4341 A3303 42c **multicolored** .85 .25
P# block of 4, 4# + V 3.40
Pane of 20 17.00

THE ART OF DISNEY: IMAGINATION Ⓢ

Pongo and Pup — A3304

Steamboat Willie — A3305

Princess Aurora, Flora, Fauna and Merryweather A3306

Mowgli and Baloo — A3307

Designed by David Pacheco. Printed by Avery Dennison.

PHOTOGRAVURE
Sheets of 160 in eight panes of 20
Serpentine Die Cut 10½x10¾

2008, Aug. 7 Tagged
Self-Adhesive

4342 A3304 42c **multicolored** .85 .30
4343 A3305 42c **multicolored** .85 .30
4344 A3306 42c **multicolored** .85 .30
4345 A3307 42c **multicolored** .85 .30
a. Block or strip of 4, #4342-4345 3.40
P# block of 4, 6#+V 3.40
P# block of 10, 2 sets of P# + top label 8.50
Pane of 20 17.00

See note after No. 1549.

AMERICAN TREASURES SERIES

Valley of the Yosemite, by Albert Bierstadt A3308

Designed by Derry Noyes. Printed by Banknote Corporation of America for Sennett Security Products.

LITHOGRAPHED
BOOKLET STAMP
Serpentine Die Cut 11 on 2 or 3 Sides

2008, Aug. 14 Tagged
Self-Adhesive

4346 A3308 42c **multicolored** .85 .25
a. Booklet pane of 20 17.00

No. 4346a is a double-sided booklet pane with 12 stamps on one side and eight stamps plus label (booklet cover) on the other side.

Sunflower — A3309

Designed by Derry Noyes. Printed by Ashton-Potter (USA) Ltd.

LITHOGRAPHED
BOOKLET STAMP
Serpentine Die Cut 11¼x10¾ on 2 or 3 Sides

2008, Aug. 15 Tagged
Self-Adhesive

4347 A3309 42c **multicolored** Ⓢ .85 .25
a. Booklet pane of 20 17.00

No. 4347a is a double-sided booklet pane with 12 stamps on one side and eight stamps plus label (booklet cover) on the other side.

See note after No. 1549.

Sea Coast Type of 2002

Designed by Tom Engeman. Printed by Banknote Corporation of America for Sennett Security Products.

LITHOGRAPHED
COIL STAMP

2008, Sept. 5 Untagged *Perf. 9¾ Vert.*

4348 A2853 (5c) **multicolored** .25 .25
Pair .50 —
P# strip of 5, #S11111 1.50
P# single, #S11111 1.10

No. 4348 has "2008" year date in black, and microprinted "USPS" at the end of the purple rock to the right of the crashing wave.

LATIN JAZZ Ⓢ

Musicians A3310

Designed by Richard Sheaff. Printed by Avery Dennison.

PHOTOGRAVURE
Sheets of 200 in ten panes of 20
Serpentine Die Cut 11x10¾

2008, Sept. 8 Tagged
Self-Adhesive

4349 A3310 42c **multicolored** .85 .25
P# block of 4, 4#+V 3.75
Pane of 20 19.00

See note after No. 1549.

LEGENDS OF HOLLYWOOD

Bette Davis (1908-89), Actress — A3311

Designed by Richard Sheaff. Printed by Ashton-Potter (USA) Ltd.

LITHOGRAPHED
Sheets of 180 in nine panes of 20

2008, Sept. 18 Tagged *Serpentine Die Cut 10¾*
Self-Adhesive

4350 A3311 42c **multicolored** Ⓢ 1.00 .25
P# block of 4, 4#+P 4.00
Pane of 20 20.00

Uncut press sheets of No. 4350 were made available for sale. Values: cross-gutter block of 8, $20; pairs with gutters between, $3 each. See note after No. 2868.

See note after No. 1549.

Eid Type of 2001

Designed by Mohamed Zakariya. Printed by Avery Dennison.

PHOTOGRAVURE
Sheets of 240 in twelve panes of 20

2008, Sept. 23 Tagged *Serpentine Die Cut 11*
Self-Adhesive

4351 A2734 42c **multicolored** .85 .25
P# block of 4, 3#+V 3.40
Pane of 20 17.00

GREAT LAKES DUNES

A3312

Illustration reduced.

Designed by Ethel Kessler. Printed by Avery Dennison.

No. 4352 — Wildlife: a, Vesper sparrow. b, Red fox, vert. c, Piping plover. d, Eastern hognose snake. e, Common mergansers. f, Spotted sandpiper, vert. g, Tiger beetle, vert. h, White-footed mouse, vert. i, Piping plover nestlings. j, Red admiral butterfly, vert.

PHOTOGRAVURE
Sheets of 80 in eight panes of 10

2008, Oct. 2 Tagged *Serpentine Die Cut 10¾*
Self-Adhesive

4352 A3312 Pane of 10 10.00
a.-j. 42c Any single 1.00 .40

Uncut press sheets of No. 4352 were made available for sale. See note after No. 2868.

AUTOMOBILES OF THE 1950s

1959 Cadillac Eldorado A3313

1957 Studebaker Golden Hawk A3314

1957 Pontiac Safari A3315

1957 Lincoln Premiere A3316

1957 Chrysler 300C A3317

Designed by Carl T. Herrman. Printed by Banknote Corporation of America for Sennett Security Products.

LITHOGRAPHED

Sheets of 180 in nine panes of 20

2008, Oct. 3 **Tagged** ***Serpentine Die Cut 10¾***

Self-Adhesive

4353 A3313 42c **multicolored**	.85	.45
4354 A3314 42c **multicolored**	.85	.45
4355 A3315 42c **multicolored**	.85	.45
4356 A3316 42c **multicolored**	.85	.45
4357 A3317 42c **multicolored**	.85	.45
a. Vert. strip of 5, #4353-4357	4.25	
Vert. P# block of 10, 2 sets of 4# + S	8.50	
Horiz. P# block of 8, 2 sets of 4# + S	7.00	
Pane of 20	17.00	

ALZHEIMER'S DISEASE AWARENESS ⓢ

A3318

Designed by Ethel Kessler. Printed by Avery Dennison.

PHOTOGRAVURE

Sheets of 240 in twelve panes of 20

2008, Oct. 17 **Tagged** ***Serpentine Die Cut 10¾***

Self-Adhesive

4358 A3318 42c **multicolored**	.85	.25
P# block of 4, 6#+V	3.50	
Pane of 20	17.50	

See note after No. 1549.

CHRISTMAS

Virgin and Child with the Young John the Baptist, by Sandro Botticelli — A3319

Drummer Nutcracker — A3320

Santa Claus Nutcracker — A3321

King Nutcracker — A3322

Soldier Nutcracker — A3323

Drummer Nutcracker — A3324

Santa Claus Nutcracker — A3325

King Nutcracker — A3326

Soldier Nutcracker — A3327

Designed by Richard Sheaff (#4359), Derry Noyes.
Printed by Ashton-Potter (USA) Ltd. (#4359), Banknote Corporation of America for Sennett Security Products (#4360-4367), Avery Dennison (#4368-4371).

LITHOGRAPHED, PHOTOGRAVURE (#4368-4371)

Serpentine Die Cut 10¾x11 on 2 or 3 Sides

2008, Oct. 23 **Tagged**

Self-Adhesive

Booklet Stamps

4359 A3319 42c **multicolored** ⓢ	.85	.25
a. Booklet pane of 20	17.00	
b. Die cutting omitted, pair	—	
4360 A3320 42c **multicolored**	1.00	.25
4361 A3321 42c **multicolored**	1.00	.25
4362 A3322 42c **multicolored**	1.00	.25
4363 A3323 42c **multicolored**	1.00	.25
a. Block of 4, #4360-4363	4.00	
b. Booklet pane of 20, 5 each #4360-4363	20.00	

No. 4359a is a double-sided booklet pane with 12 stamps on one side and eight stamps plus label that serves as a booklet cover on the other side. No. 4363b is a double-sided booklet pane with 12 stamps on one side (3 each of Nos. 4360-4363) and eight stamps (2 each of Nos. 4360-4363) plus label that serves as a booklet cover on the other side.

See note after No. 1549.

Serpentine Die Cut 11¼x11 on 2 or 3 Sides

4364 A3324 42c **multicolored**	1.25	.25
4365 A3325 42c **multicolored**	1.25	.25
4366 A3326 42c **multicolored**	1.25	.25
4367 A3327 42c **multicolored**	1.25	.25
a. Block of 4, #4364-4367	5.00	
b. Booklet pane of 4, #4364-4367	5.00	
c. Booklet pane of 6, #4366-4367, 2 each #4364-4365	7.50	
d. Booklet pane of 6, #4364-4365, 2 each #4366-4367	7.50	

Serpentine Die Cut 8 on 2, 3 or 4 Sides

4368 A3324 42c **multicolored** ⓢ	1.25	.25
4369 A3325 42c **multicolored** ⓢ	1.25	.25
4370 A3326 42c **multicolored** ⓢ	1.25	.25
4371 A3327 42c **multicolored** ⓢ	1.25	.25
a. Block or strip of 4, #4368-4371	5.00	
b. Booklet pane of 18, 5 each #4368-4369, 4 each #4370-4371	22.50	
Nos. 4359-4371 (13)	14.85	3.25

See note after No. 1549.

Hanukkah Type of 2004

Designed by Ethel Kessler. Printed by Banknote Corporation of America for Sennett Security Products.

LITHOGRAPHED

Sheets of 240 in twelve panes of 20

Serpentine Die Cut 10¾x11

2008, Oct. 24 **Tagged**

Self-Adhesive

4372 A2962 42c **multicolored**	.85	.25
P# block of 4, 4#+S	3.40	
Pane of 20	17.00	

Kwanzaa Type of 2004

Designed by Derry Noyes. Printed by Ashton-Potter (USA) Ltd.

LITHOGRAPHED

Sheets of 160 in eight panes of 20

Serpentine Die Cut 11x10¾

2008, Oct. 24 **Tagged**

Self-Adhesive

4373 A2963 42c **multicolored** ⓢ	.85	.25
P# block of 4, 6#+P	3.40	
Pane of 20	17.00	

See note after No. 1549.

ALASKA STATEHOOD, 50TH ANNIV.

Dogsledder Near Rainy Pass — A3328

Designed by Phil Jordan. Printed by Banknote Corporation of America for Sennett Security Products.

LITHOGRAPHED

Sheets of 180 in nine panes of 20

2009, Jan. 3 **Tagged** ***Serpentine Die Cut 10¾***

Self-Adhesive

4374 A3328 42c **multicolored**	.85	.25
P# block of 4, 4#+S	3.40	
Pane of 20	17.00	

CHINESE NEW YEAR

Year of the Ox — A3329

Designed by Ethel Kessler. Printed by Banknote Corporation of America for Sennett Security Products.

LITHOGRAPHED

Sheets of 108 in nine panes of 12

2009, Jan. 8 Tagged *Serpentine Die Cut 10¾*

Self-Adhesive

4375 A3329 42c **multicolored**	.85	.25
Pane of 12	10.50	

Uncut press sheets of No. 4375 were made available for sale. Values: cross-gutter block of 4, $9; pairs with gutters between, $2.25 each. See note after No. 2868.

OREGON STATEHOOD, 150TH ANNIV.

Pacific Coast of Oregon A3330

Designed by Derry Noyes. Printed by Banknote Corporation of America for Sennett Security Products.

LITHOGRAPHED

Sheets of 180 in nine panes of 20

2009, Jan. 14 Tagged *Serpentine Die Cut 10¾*

Self-Adhesive

4376 A3330 42c **multicolored**	.85	.25
P# block of 4, 5# + S	3.40	
Pane of 20	17.00	

EDGAR ALLAN POE Ⓢ

Edgar Allan Poe (1809-49), Writer — A3331

Designed by Carl T. Herrman. Printed by Avery Dennison.

PHOTOGRAVURE

Sheets of 160 in eight panes of 20

2009, Jan. 16 Tagged *Serpentine Die Cut 10¾*

Self-Adhesive

4377 A3331 42c **multicolored**	.90	.25
P# block of 4, 5# + V	5.00	
Pane of 20	23.50	

See note after No. 1549.

AMERICAN LANDMARKS

Redwood Forest A3332

Old Faithful A3333

Designed by Carl T. Herrman. Printed by Ashton-Potter (USA) Ltd.

LITHOGRAPHED

Sheets of 180 in nine panes of 20

Serpentine Die Cut 10¾x10½

2009, Jan. 16 Tagged

Self-Adhesive

4378 A3332 $4.95 **multicolored** Ⓢ	11.00	5.00
P# block of 4, 4# + P	45.00	
Pane of 20	220.00	
4379 A3333 $17.50 **multicolored** Ⓢ	40.00	20.00
P# block of 4, 4# + P	160.00	
Pane of 20	800.00	

See note after No. 1549.

ABRAHAM LINCOLN (1809-65), 16TH PRESIDENT Ⓢ

Lincoln as Rail-splitter A3334

Lincoln as Lawyer A3335

Lincoln as Politician A3336

Lincoln as President A3337

Designed by Richard Sheaff. Printed by Ashton-Potter (USA) Ltd.

LITHOGRAPHED

Sheets of 120 in six panes of 20

2009, Feb. 9 Tagged *Serpentine Die Cut 10¾*

Self-Adhesive

4380 A3334 42c **multicolored**	1.50	.35
4381 A3335 42c **multicolored**	1.50	.35
4382 A3336 42c **multicolored**	1.50	.35
4383 A3337 42c **multicolored**	1.50	.35
a. Horiz. strip of 4, #4380-4383	6.00	
P# block of 8, 2 sets of 4# + P	12.00	
Pane of 20	28.00	

Uncut press sheets of Nos. 4380-4383 were made available for sale. Values: cross-gutter block of 8, $27.50; pairs with gutters between, $4 each. See note after No. 2868.
See note after No. 1549.

CIVIL RIGHTS PIONEERS Ⓢ

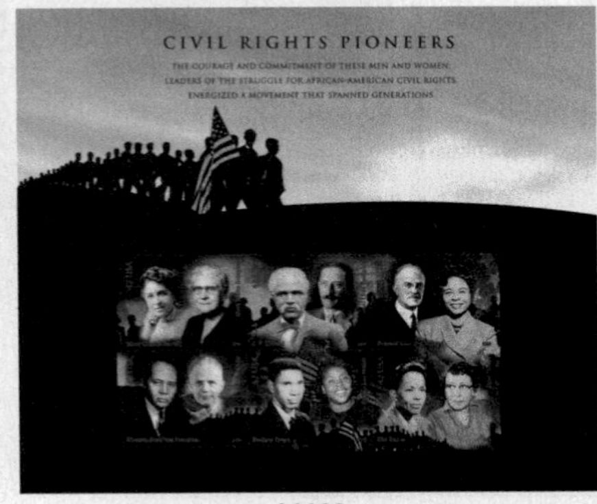

A3338

Illustration reduced.

Designed by Greg Berger. Printed by Avery Dennison.

No. 4384: a, Mary Church Terrell (1863-1954), writer, Mary White Ovington (1865-1951), journalist. b, J. R. Clifford (1848-1933), attorney, Joel Elias Spingarn (1875-1939), educator. c, Oswald Garrison Villard (1872-1949), co-founder of National Association for the Advancement of Colored People (NAACP), Daisy Gatson Bates (1914-99), mentor of black Little Rock Central High School students. d, Charles Hamilton Houston (1895-1950), lawyer, Walter White (1893-1955), chief secretary of NAACP. e, Medgar Evers (1925-63), assassinated Mississippi NAACP field secretary, Fannie Lou Hamer (1917-77), voting rights activist. f, Ella Baker (1903-86), activist, Ruby Hurley (1909-80), NAACP Southeast Regional Director.

PHOTOGRAVURE

Sheets of 48 in eight panes of 6

2009, Feb. 21 Tagged *Serpentine Die Cut 10¾*

Self-Adhesive

4384 A3338 Pane of 6	9.00	
a.-f. 42c Any single	1.50	.40

See note after No. 1549.

Patriotic Banner Type of 2007

Designed by Michael Osborne. Printed by Banknote Corporation of America for Sennett Security Products.

LITHOGRAPHED

COIL STAMP

2009, Feb. 24 Untagged *Perf. 9¾ Vert.*

4385 A3167 (10c) **multicolored**	.25	.25
Pair	.40	—
P# strip of 5, #S111	2.50	—
P# single, #S111	—	2.10

LITERARY ARTS

Richard Wright (1908-60), Author A3339

Designed by Carl T. Herrman. Printed by Ashton-Potter (USA) Ltd.

LITHOGRAPHED

Sheets of 120 in six panes of 20

2009, Apr. 9 Tagged *Serpentine Die Cut 10¾*

Self-Adhesive

4386 A3339 61c **multicolored** Ⓢ	1.25	.25
P# block of 4, 6# + P	5.00	
Pane of 20	25.00	

See note after No. 1549.

WILDLIFE

Polar Bear — A3340

Dolphin — A3341

Designed by Carl T. Herrman. Printed by Banknote Corporation of America for Sennett Security Products (#4387), Avery Dennison (#4388, 4389)

LITHOGRAPHED (#4387), PHOTOGRAVURE

Sheets of 300 in 15 panes of 20 or sheets of 200 in 10 panes of 20 (#4387)

Sheets of 280 in 14 panes of 20 (#4388)

2009 Tagged ***Serpentine Die Cut 11¼x11***

Self-Adhesive

4387 A3340 28c **multicolored,** *Apr. 16* .75 .25
P# block of 4, 4# + S 3.00
Pane of 20 15.00
a. Die cutting omitted, pane of 20 *7,250.*

Serpentine Die Cut 11

4388 A3341 64c **multicolored,** *June 12* Ⓢ 1.40 .25
P# block of 4, 5#+V 5.60
Pane of 20 28.00

COIL STAMP

Serpentine Die Cut 8½ Vert.

4389 A3340 28c **multicolored,** *Apr. 16* Ⓢ .60 .25
P# strip of 5, #V11111 4.25
P# single, #V11111 — 2.00

See note after No. 1549.

Purple Heart Type of 2003

Designed by Carl T. Herrman. Printed by Ashton-Potter (USA) Ltd.

LITHOGRAPHED

Sheets of 120 in six panes of 20

Serpentine Die Cut 11¼x10¾

2009, Apr. 28 Tagged

Self-Adhesive

4390 A2891 44c **multicolored** Ⓢ .90 .25
P# block of 4, 4#+P 3.60
Pane of 20 18.00

Counterfeits exist of No. 4390. See the Postal Counterfeits section of this catalog.

See note after No. 1549.

Flag — A3342

Designed by Terrence W. McCaffrey. Printed by Banknote Corporation of America for Sennett Security Products (#4391, 4392), Ashton-Potter (USA) Ltd. (#4393), Avery Dennison (#4394, 4395, 4396).

LITHOGRAPHED, PHOTOGRAVURE (#4394, 4395, 4396)

2009 Tagged ***Perf. 9¾ Vert.***

COIL STAMPS

4391 A3342 44c **multicolored,** *May 1* 1.00 1.00
Pair 2.00
P# strip of 5, #S111 6.25
P# single, #S111 — 3.50

Self-Adhesive

Serpentine Die Cut 11 Vert.

With Pointed Corners

4392 A3342 44c **multicolored,** *May 8* 2.00 .25
Pair 4.00
P# strip of 5, #S111 12.50
P# single, #S111 — 2.50
a. Die cutting omitted, pair —

Counterfeits exist of No. 4392. See the Postal Counterfeits section of this catalog.

Serpentine Die Cut 9½ Vert.

4393 A3342 44c **multicolored,** *May 8* Ⓢ 1.50 .25
Pair 3.00
P# strip of 5, #P1111 8.00
P# single, #P1111 — 2.50

Counterfeits exist of No. 4393. See the Postal Counterfeits section of this catalog.

Serpentine Die Cut 8½ Vert.

4394 A3342 44c **multicolored,** *May 8* Ⓢ 1.50 .25
Pair 3.00
P# strip of 5, #V1111 8.00
P# single, #V1111 — 2.50

Counterfeits exist of No. 4394. See the Postal Counterfeits section of this catalog.

Serpentine Die Cut 11 Vert.

With Rounded Corners

4395 A3342 44c **multicolored,** *May 1* Ⓢ 1.25 .25
Pair 2.50
P# strip of 5, #V1111 6.75
P# single, #V1111 — 2.00

BOOKLET STAMP

Serpentine Die Cut 11¼x10¾ on 3 Sides

4396 A3342 44c **multicolored,** *June 5* Ⓢ .90 .25
a. Booklet pane of 10 9.00

Nos. 4392-4394 are on backing paper as high as the stamp. No. 4395 is on backing paper that is taller than the stamp. No. 4393 has microprinted "USPS" on white stripe below the blue field.

See note after No. 1549.

WEDDINGS

Wedding Rings — A3343

Wedding Cake — A3344

Designed by Ethel Kessler. Printed by Banknote Corporation of America for Sennett Security Products (#4397), Avery Dennison (#4398)

LITHOGRAPHED, PHOTOGRAVURE (#4398)

Sheets of 160 in eight panes of 20, Sheets of 240 in twelve panes of 20 (#4398)

2009, May 1 Tagged ***Serpentine Die Cut 10¾***

Self-Adhesive

4397 A3343 44c **multicolored** .90 .25
P# block of 4, 5#+S 3.60
Pane of 20 18.00
4398 A3344 61c **multicolored** Ⓢ 1.25 .25
P# block of 4, 6#+V 5.00
Pane of 20 25.00

See Nos. 4521, 4602, 4735, 4867.

See note after No. 1549.

THE SIMPSONS TELEVISION SHOW, 20TH ANNIV.

Homer Simpson — A3345

Marge Simpson — A3346

Bart Simpson — A3347

Lisa Simpson — A3348

Maggie Simpson — A3349

Designed by Matt Groening. Printed by Banknote Corporation of America for Sennett Security Products.

LITHOGRAPHED

BOOKLET STAMPS

Serpentine Die Cut 10¾ on 2, 3 or 4 Sides

2009, May 7 Tagged

Self-Adhesive

4399 A3345 44c **multicolored** 1.15 .40
4400 A3346 44c **multicolored** 1.15 .40
4401 A3347 44c **multicolored** 1.15 .40
4402 A3348 44c **multicolored** 1.15 .40
4403 A3349 44c **multicolored** 1.15 .40
a. Horiz. strip of 5, #4399-4403 5.75
b. Booklet pane of 20, 4 each #4399-4403 23.00

LOVE

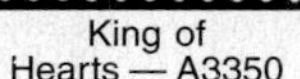
King of Hearts — A3350

Queen of Hearts — A3351

Designed by Jeanne Greco. Printed by Avery Dennison.

PHOTOGRAVURE

BOOKLET STAMPS

Serpentine Die Cut 10¾ on 2, 3 or 4 Sides

2009, May 8 Tagged

Self-Adhesive

4404 A3350 44c **multicolored** Ⓢ 1.15 .25
4405 A3351 44c **multicolored** Ⓢ 1.15 .25
a. Horiz. or vert. pair, #4404-4405 2.30
b. Booklet pane of 20, 10 each #4404-4405 23.00

See note after No. 1549.

BOB HOPE Ⓢ

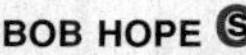

Bob Hope (1903-2003), Actor, Comedian — A3352

Designed by Derry Noyes. Printed by Ashton-Potter (USA) Ltd.

LITHOGRAPHED

Sheets of 180 in nine panes of 20

2009, May 29 Tagged ***Serpentine Die Cut 10¾***

Self-Adhesive

4406 A3352 44c **multicolored** 1.00 .25
P# block of 4, 4#+P 4.00
Pane of 20 20.00

Uncut press sheets of No. 4406 were made available for sale. Values: cross-gutter block of 8, $20; pairs with gutters between, $2.50 each. See note after No. 2868.

See note after No. 1549.

Celebrate Type of 2007

Designed by Ethel Kessler. Printed by Banknote Corporation of America for Sennett Security Products.

LITHOGRAPHED

Sheets of 240 in twelve panes of 20

2009, June 10 Tagged ***Serpentine Die Cut 10¾***

Self-Adhesive

4407 A3189 44c **multicolored** .90 .25
P# block of 4, 4#+S 3.60
Pane of 20 18.00
a. Die cutting omitted, pair —

BLACK HERITAGE

Anna Julia Cooper (c. 1858-1964), Educator — A3353

Designed by Ethel Kessler. Printed by Ashton-Potter (USA) Ltd.

LITHOGRAPHED
Sheets of 120 in six panes of 20

2009, June 11 Tagged *Serpentine Die Cut 10¾*
Self-Adhesive

4408	A3353 44c **multicolored** ⓢ	.90	.25
	P# block of 4, 5#+P	3.60	
	Pane of 20	18.00	

See note after No. 1549.

GULF COAST LIGHTHOUSES ⓢ

Matagorda Island Lighthouse, Texas — A3354

Sabine Pass Lighthouse, Louisiana — A3355

Biloxi Lighthouse, Mississippi — A3356

Sand Island Lighthouse, Alabama — A3357

Fort Jefferson Lighthouse, Florida — A3358

Designed by Howard E. Paine. Printed by Ashton-Potter (USA) Ltd.

LITHOGRAPHED
Sheets of 120 in six panes of 20
Serpentine Die Cut 11x10¾

2009, July 23 Tagged
Self-Adhesive

4409	A3354 44c **multicolored**	.90	.40
4410	A3355 44c **multicolored**	.90	.40
4411	A3356 44c **multicolored**	.90	.40
4412	A3357 44c **multicolored**	.90	.40
4413	A3358 44c **multicolored**	.90	.40
a.	Horiz. strip of 5, #4409-4413	4.50	
	P# block of 10, 2 sets of 4#+P	10.00	
	Pane of 20	19.00	

Plate block may contain top label.
See note after No. 1549.

EARLY TV MEMORIES ⓢ

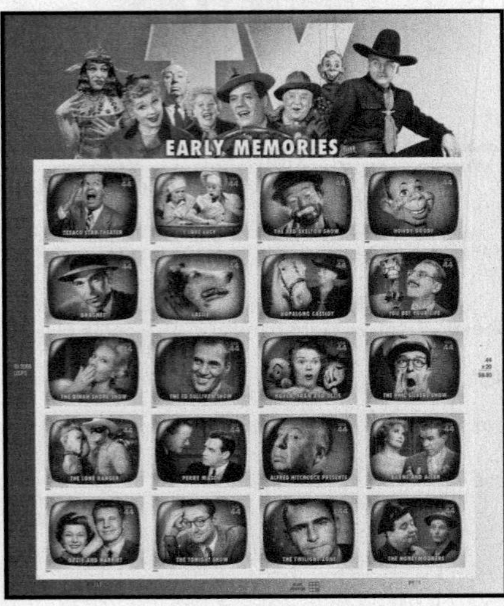

A3359

Illustration reduced.

Designed by Carl T. Herrman. Printed by Ashton-Potter (USA) Ltd.

No. 4414: a, Milton Berle in "Texaco Star Theater." b, Lucille Ball and Vivian Vance in "I Love Lucy." c, Red Skelton in "The Red Skelton Show." d, Marionette Howdy Doody in "Howdy Doody." e, Jack Webb in "Dragnet." f, Lassie in "Lassie." g, William Boyd and horse, Topper, in "Hopalong Cassidy." h, Groucho Marx in "You Bet Your Life." i, Dinah Shore in "The Dinah Shore Show." j, Ed Sullivan in "The Ed Sullivan Show." k, Fran Allison and puppets, Kukla and Ollie in "Kukla, Fran and Ollie." l, Phil Silvers in "The Phil Silvers Show." m, Clayton Moore and horse, Silver, in "The Lone Ranger." n, Raymond Burr and William Talman in "Perry Mason." o, Alfred Hitchcock in "Alfred Hitchcock Presents." p, George Burns and Gracie Allen in "Burns and Allen." q, Ozzie and Harriet Nelson in "Ozzie and Harriet." r, Steve Allen in "The Tonight Show." s, Rod Serling in "The Twilight Zone." t, Jackie Gleason and Art Carney in "The Honeymooners."

LITGHOGRAPHED
Sheets of 180 in nine panes of 20
Serpentine Die Cut 10¾x10½

2009, Aug. 11 Tagged
Self-Adhesive

4414	A3359 Pane of 20	20.00	
a.-t.	44c Any single	1.00	.50

Uncut press sheets of No. 4414 were made available for sale. Values: cross-gutter block of 20, $30; pairs with gutters between, $3.75 each. See note after No. 2868.
See note after No. 1549.

HAWAII STATEHOOD, 50TH ANNIV. ⓢ

Surfer and Outrigger Canoe A3360

Designed by Phil Jordan. Printed by Avery Dennison.

PHOTOGRAVURE
Sheets of 200 in ten panes of 20

2009, Aug. 21 Tagged *Serpentine Die Cut 11*
Self-Adhesive

4415	A3360 44c **multicolored**	1.25	.25
	P# block of 4, 4#+V	7.00	
	Pane of 20	28.00	

See note after No. 1549.

Eid Type of 2001

Designed by Mohamed Zakariya. Printed by Avery Dennison.

PHOTOGRAVURE
Sheets of 240 in twelve panes of 20

2009, Sept. 3 Tagged *Serpentine Die Cut 11*
Self-Adhesive

4416	A2734 44c **multicolored** ⓢ	.90	.25
	P# block of 4, 3#+V	3.60	
	Pane of 20	18.00	

See note after No. 1549.

THANKSGIVING DAY PARADE ⓢ

Crowd, Street Sign, Bear Balloon A3361

Drum Major, Musicians A3362

Musicians, Balloon, Horse A3363

Cowboy, Turkey Balloon, Crowd, Television Cameraman A3364

Designed by Howard E. Paine. Printed by Avery Dennison.

PHOTOGRAVURE
Sheets of 200 in ten panes of 20
Serpentine Die Cut 11x10¾

2009, Sept. 9 Tagged
Self-Adhesive

4417	A3361 44c **multicolored**	.90	.35
4418	A3362 44c **multicolored**	.90	.35
4419	A3363 44c **multicolored**	.90	.35
4420	A3364 44c **multicolored**	.90	.35
a.	Horiz. strip of 4, #4417-4420	3.60	
	P# block of 8, 2 sets of 6#+V	8.75	
	Pane of 20	19.00	

See note after No. 1549.

LEGENDS OF HOLLYWOOD

Gary Cooper (1901-61), Actor — A3365

Designed by Phil Jordan. Printed by Avery Dennison.

PHOTOGRAVURE

Sheets of 160 in eight panes of 20

2009, Sept. 10 Tagged *Serpentine Die Cut 11*

Self-Adhesive

4421 A3365 44c **multicolored** Ⓢ 1.00 .25
P# block of 4, 4#+V 4.00
Pane of 20 20.00

Uncut press sheets of No. 4421 were made available for sale. Values: cross-gutter block of 8, $20; pairs with gutters between, $3 each. See note after No. 2868.

See note after No. 1549.

SUPREME COURT JUSTICES Ⓢ

Souvenir Sheet

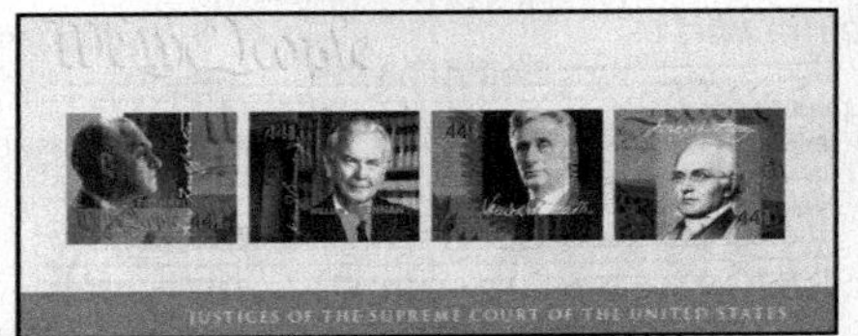

A3366

Illustration reduced.

Designed by Howard E. Paine. Printed by Avery Dennison.

No. 4422: a, Felix Frankfurter (1882-1965). b, William J. Brennan, Jr. (1906-97). c, Louis D. Brandeis (1856-1941). d, Joseph Story (1779-1845).

LITHOGRAPHED

Serpentine Die Cut 11x10½

2009, Sept. 22 Tagged

Self-Adhesive

4422 A3366 Pane of 4 4.00
a.-d. 44c Any single 1.00 .30

See note after No. 1549.

KELP FOREST Ⓢ

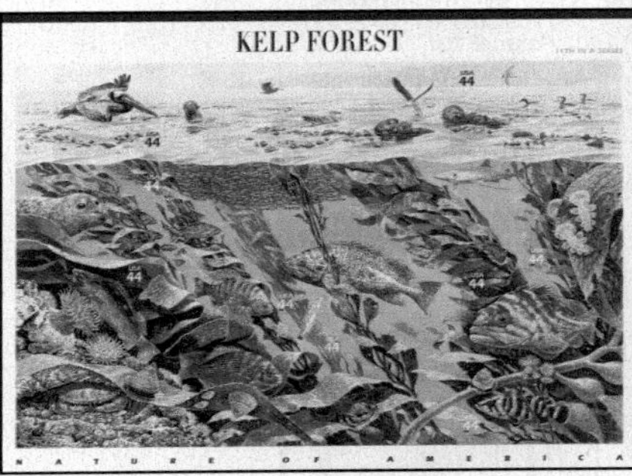

A3367

Illustration reduced.

Designed by Ethel Kessler. Printed by Avery Dennison.

Wildlife: a, Brown pelican. b, Western gull, southern sea otters, red sea urchin. c, Harbor seal. d, Lion's mane nudibranch, vert. e, Yellowtail rockfish, white-spotted rose anemone. f, Vermilion rockfish. g, Copper rockfish. h, Pacific rock crab, jeweled top snail. i, Northern kelp crab, vert. j, Treefish, Monterey turban snail, brooding sea anemones.

PHOTOGRAVURE

Sheets of 80 in eight panes of 10

2009, Oct. 1 Tagged *Serpentine Die Cut 10¾*

Self-Adhesive

4423 A3367 Pane of 10 11.00
a.-j. 44c Any single 1.10 .40

Uncut press sheets of No. 4423 were made available for sale. See note after No. 2868.

See note after No. 1549.

CHRISTMAS

Madonna and Sleeping Child, by Sassoferrato (Giovanni Battista Salvi) — A3368

Reindeer — A3369

Snowman — A3370

Gingerbread Man — A3371

Toy Soldier — A3372

Reindeer — A3373

Snowman — A3374

Gingerbread Man — A3375

Toy Soldier — A3376

Designed by Carl T. Herrman (#4424), Richard Sheaff.

Printed by Ashton-Potter (USA) Ltd. (#4424), Banknote Corporation of America for Sennett Security Products (#4425-4428), Avery Dennison (#4429-4432).

LITHOGRAPHED, PHOTOGRAVURE (#4429-4432)

Serpentine Die Cut 10¾x11 on 2 or 3 Sides

2009 Tagged

Self-Adhesive

Booklet Stamps

4424 A3368 44c **multicolored,** *Oct. 20* Ⓢ .90 .25
a. Booklet pane of 20 18.00
4425 A3369 44c **multicolored,** *Oct. 8* 1.10 .25
4426 A3370 44c **multicolored,** *Oct. 8* 1.10 .25
4427 A3371 44c **multicolored,** *Oct. 8* 1.10 .25
4428 A3372 44c **multicolored,** *Oct. 8* 1.10 .25
a. Block of 4, #4425-4428 4.40
b. Booklet pane of 20, 5 each #4425-4428 22.00
c. As "b," die cutting omitted on side with 12 stamps —
d. As "b," die cutting omitted on side with 8 stamps —
e. As "a," die cutting omitted *375.00*

Serpentine Die Cut 8 on 2, 3 or 4 Sides

4429 A3373 44c **multicolored,** *Oct. 8* Ⓢ 1.10 .25
4430 A3374 44c **multicolored,** *Oct. 8* Ⓢ 1.10 .25
4431 A3375 44c **multicolored,** *Oct. 8* Ⓢ 1.10 .25
4432 A3376 44c **multicolored,** *Oct. 8* Ⓢ 1.10 .25
a. Block or strip of 4, #4429-4432 4.40
b. Booklet pane of 18, 5 each #4429, 4431, 4 each #4430, 4432 20.00
Nos. 4424-4432 (9) 9.70 2.25

No. 4424a is a double-sided booklet pane with 12 stamps on one side and eight stamps plus label that serves as a booklet cover on the other side. No. 4428b is a double-sided booklet pane with 12 stamps on one side (3 each of Nos. 4425-4428) and eight stamps (2 each of Nos. 4425-4428) plus label that serves as a booklet cover on the other side.

See note after No. 1549.

HANUKKAH

Menorah — A3377

Designed by Carl T. Herrman. Printed by Banknote Corporation of America for Sennett Security Products.

LITHOGRAPHED

Sheets of 200 in ten panes of 20

2009, Oct. 9 Tagged *Serpentine Die Cut 10¾x11*

Self-Adhesive

4433 A3377 44c **multicolored** .90 .25
P# block of 4, 6#+S 3.60
Pane of 20 18.00

KWANZAA

Family — A3378

Designed by Carl T. Herrman. Printed by Ashton-Potter (USA) Ltd.

LITHOGRAPHED

Sheets of 160 in eight panes of 20

2009, Oct. 9 Tagged *Serpentine Die Cut 10¾x11*

Self-Adhesive

4434 A3378 44c **multicolored** Ⓢ .90 .25
P# block of 4, 4#+P 3.60
Pane of 20 18.00

See note after No. 1549.

CHINESE NEW YEAR

Year of the Tiger A3379

Designed by Ethel Kessler. Printed by Avery Dennison.

PHOTOGRAVURE
Sheets of 108 in nine panes of 12

2010, Jan. 14 Tagged *Serpentine Die Cut 11*
Self-Adhesive

4435 A3379 44c **multicolored** ⓢ	1.10	.25
Pane of 12	13.50	

Uncut press sheets of No. 4435 were made available for sale. Values: cross-gutter block of 4, $10; pairs with gutters between, $2.50 each. See note after No. 2868.
See note after No. 1549.

2010 WINTER OLYMPICS, VANCOUVER ⓢ

Snowboarder — A3380

Designed by Howard E. Paine. Printed by Avery Dennison.

PHOTOGRAVURE
Sheets of 160 in eight panes of 20

2010, Jan. 22 Tagged *Serpentine Die Cut 11*
Self-Adhesive

4436 A3380 44c **multicolored**	.90	.25
P# block of 4, 6# + V	4.00	
Pane of 20	20.00	

See note after No. 1549.

"Forever" Liberty Bell Type of 2007

Printed by Ashton-Potter (USA) Ltd.

Serpentine Die Cut 11¼x10¾ on 2, 3 or 4 Sides
2010, Feb. 3 Litho.
Booklet Stamp
Self-Adhesive
Medium Microprinting, Bell 16mm Wide
Dated "2009" in Copper

4437 A3148 (44c) **multicolored** ⓢ	1.10	.25
a. Booklet pane of 18	20.00	

On No. 4437, the "2009" date is smaller than that on No. 4127i, which has a 15mm wide bell. The bell on No. 4437 is also 17mm tall while No. 4127i is 16mm tall. The microprinted "Forever" is on a dotted background on No. 4437 and on a white background on No. 4127i.
See also No. 4128c.
See note after No. 1549.

AMERICAN LANDMARKS

Mackinac Bridge, Michigan A3381

Bixby Creek Bridge, California A3382

Designed by Carl T. Herrman. Printed by Avery Dennison.

PHOTOGRAVURE
Sheets of 200 in ten panes of 20
Serpentine Die Cut 10¾x10½
2010, Feb. 3 Tagged
Self-Adhesive

4438 A3381 $4.90 **multicolored** ⓢ	11.00	5.00
P# block of 4, 4# +V	45.00	
Pane of 20	220.00	
4439 A3382 $18.30 **multicolored** ⓢ	45.00	18.00
P# block of 4, 4# +V	180.00	
Pane of 20	900.00	

See note after No. 1549.

DISTINGUISHED SAILORS ⓢ

Admiral William S. Sims (1858-1936), Emblem of USS W.S. Sims — A3383

Admiral Arleigh A. Burke (1901-96), Emblem of USS Arleigh Burke A3384

Lieutenant Commander John McCloy (1876-1945), Emblem of USS McCloy A3385

Petty Officer 3rd Class Doris Miller (1919-43), Emblem of USS Miller A3386

Designed by Phil Jordan. Printed by Avery Dennison.

PHOTOGRAVURE
Sheets of 200 in ten panes of 20
Serpentine Die Cut 10¾x10½
2010, Feb. 4 Tagged
Self-Adhesive

4440 A3383 44c **multicolored**	.90	.40
4441 A3384 44c **multicolored**	.90	.40
4442 A3385 44c **multicolored**	.90	.40
4443 A3386 44c **multicolored**	.90	.40
a. Block or horiz. strip of 4, #4440-4443	3.60	
P# block of 4, 6# + V	4.00	
P# block of 8, 2 sets of 6# + V + top label	7.20	
Pane of 20	19.50	

See note after No. 1549.

ABSTRACT EXPRESSIONISTS ⓢ

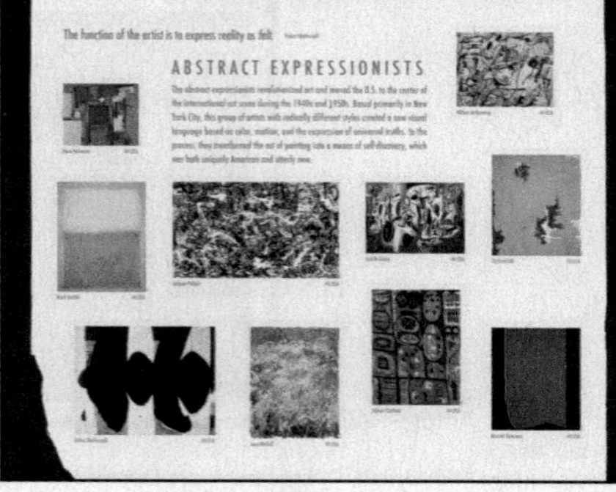

A3387

Illustration reduced.
Designed by Ethel Kessler. Printed by Ashton-Potter (USA) Ltd.
No. 4444: a, The Golden Wall, by Hans Hofmann (30x30mm). b, Asheville, by Willem de Kooning (38x38mm). c, Orange and Yellow, by Mark Rothko (35x49mm). d, Convergence, by Jackson Pollock (63x43mm). e, The Liver Is the Cock's Comb, by Arshile Gorky (39x32mm). f, 1948-C, by Clyfford Still (35x49mm). g, Elegy to the Spanish Republic No. 34, by Robert Motherwell (54x49mm). h, La Grande Vallée 0, by Joan Mitchell (35x49mm). i, Romanesque Façade, by Adolph Gottlieb (35x49mm). j, Achilles, by Barnett Newman (35x49mm).

LITHOGRAPHED
Serpentine Die Cut 10¾x11, 10¾ (#4444a, 4444b, 4444e), 11x10¾ (#4444d)
2010, Mar. 11 Tagged
Self-Adhesive

4444 A3387 Pane of 10	11.00	
a.-j. 44c Any single	1.10	.40

See note after No. 1549.

BILL MAULDIN (1921-2003), CARTOONIST ⓢ

Mauldin and His Characters, Willie and Joe A3388

Designed by Terrence W. McCaffrey. Printed by Ashton-Potter (USA) Ltd.

LITHOGRAPHED
Sheets of 120 in six panes of 20
2010, Mar. 31 Tagged *Serpentine Die Cut 10¾*
Self-Adhesive

4445 A3388 44c **multicolored**	.90	.25
P# block of 4, 4# + P	3.60	
Pane of 20	18.00	

See note after No. 1549.

COWBOYS OF THE SILVER SCREEN ⓢ

Roy Rogers (1911-98) — A3389

Tom Mix (1880-1940) — A3390

William S. Hart (1864-1946) — A3391

Gene Autry (1907-98) — A3392

Designed by Carl T. Herrman. Printed by Ashton-Potter (USA) Ltd.

LITHOGRAPHED

Sheets of 180 in nine panes of 20

Serpentine Die Cut 10½x10¾

2010, Apr. 17 **Tagged**

Self-Adhesive

4446 A3389 44c **multicolored**	1.25	.35
4447 A3390 44c **multicolored**	1.25	.35
4448 A3391 44c **multicolored**	1.25	.35
4449 A3392 44c **multicolored**	1.25	.35
a. Block or strip of 4, #4446-4449	5.00	
P# block of 4, 4# + P	5.00	
Pane of 20	25.00	

Uncut press sheets of Nos. 4446-4449 were made available for sale. Values: cross-gutter block of 8, $25; pairs with gutters between, $3.75 each. See note after No. 2868.

See note after No. 1549.

LOVE

Pansies in a Basket — A3393

Designed by Derry Noyes. Printed by Avery Dennison.

PHOTOGRAVURE

Sheets of 240 in twelve panes of 20

2010, Apr. 22 **Tagged** ***Serpentine Die Cut 10¾***

Self-Adhesive

4450 A3393 44c **multicolored** ⓢ	.90	.25
P# block of 4, 5# + V	3.60	
Pane of 20	18.00	

See note after No. 1549.

ANIMAL RESCUE

Wire-haired Jack Russell Terrier — A3394

Maltese — A3395

Calico — A3396

Yellow Labrador Retriever — A3397

Golden Retriever — A3398

Gray, White and Tan Cat — A3399

Black, White and Tan Cat — A3400

Australian Shepherd — A3401

Boston Terrier — A3402

Orange Tabby — A3403

Designed by Derry Noyes. Printed by Banknote Corporation of America for Sennett Security Products.

LITHOGRAPHED

Sheets of 160 in eight panes of 20

2010, Apr. 30 **Tagged** ***Serpentine Die Cut 10¾***

Self-Adhesive

4451 A3394 44c **multicolored**	1.25	.40
4452 A3395 44c **multicolored**	1.25	.40
4453 A3396 44c **multicolored**	1.25	.40
4454 A3397 44c **multicolored**	1.25	.40
4455 A3398 44c **multicolored**	1.25	.40
4456 A3399 44c **multicolored**	1.25	.40
4457 A3400 44c **multicolored**	1.25	.40
4458 A3401 44c **multicolored**	1.25	.40
4459 A3402 44c **multicolored**	1.25	.40
4460 A3403 44c **multicolored**	1.25	.40
a. Block of 10, #4451-4460	12.50	
P# block of 10, 8# + S	12.50	
Pane of 20	25.00	

Uncut press sheets of Nos. 4451-4460 were made available for sale. Values: cross-gutter block of 10, $20; pairs with gutters between, $3.25 each. See note after No. 2868.

LEGENDS OF HOLLYWOOD

Katharine Hepburn (1907-2003), Actress — A3404

Designed by Derry Noyes. Printed by Avery Dennison.

PHOTOGRAVURE

Sheets of 80 in four panes of 20

2010, May 12 **Tagged** ***Serpentine Die Cut 10¾***

Self-Adhesive

4461 A3404 44c **black** ⓢ	1.00	.25
P# block of 4, 2#+V	4.25	
Pane of 20	21.00	

Uncut press sheets of No. 4461 were made available for sale. Values: cross-gutter block of 8, $20; pairs with gutters between, $2.50 each. See note after No. 2868.

See note after No. 1549.

MONARCH BUTTERFLY ⓢ

A3405

Designed by Derry Noyes. Printed by Avery Dennison.

PHOTOGRAVURE

Sheets of 200 in ten panes of 20

2010, May 17 **Tagged** ***Serpentine Die Cut 10½***

Self-Adhesive

4462 A3405 64c **multicolored**	1.50	.25
P# block of 4, 6#+V	6.00	
Pane of 20	30.00	

See note after No. 1549.

KATE SMITH Ⓢ

Kate Smith (1907-86), Singer — A3406

Designed by Ethel Kessler. Printed by Avery Dennison.

PHOTOGRAVURE
Sheets of 160 in eight panes of 20

2010, May 27 Tagged *Serpentine Die Cut 11*
Self-Adhesive

4463 A3406 44c **multicolored**	.90	.25
P# block of 4, 4#+V	3.60	
Pane of 20	18.00	

See note after No. 1549.

BLACK HERITAGE

Oscar Micheaux (1884-1951), Film Director — A3407

Designed by Derry Noyes. Printed by Avery Dennison.

PHOTOGRAVURE
Sheets of 200 in ten panes of 20

2010, June 22 Tagged *Serpentine Die Cut 11*
Self-Adhesive

4464 A3407 44c **multicolored** Ⓢ	.90	.25
P# block of 4, 4#+V	3.60	
Pane of 20	18.00	

See note after No. 1549.

NEGRO LEAGUES BASEBALL Ⓢ

Play at the Plate — A3408

Andrew "Rube" Foster (1879-1930), Founder of Negro National League A3409

Designed by Howard E. Paine. Printed by Avery Dennison.

PHOTOGRAVURE
Sheets of 200 in ten panes of 20

2010, July 15 Tagged *Serpentine Die Cut 11*
Self-Adhesive

4465 A3408 44c **multicolored**	.90	.30
4466 A3409 44c **multicolored**	.90	.30
a. Horiz. pair, #4465-4466	1.80	
P# block of 4, 5#+V	3.60	
Pane of 20	18.00	

SUNDAY FUNNIES

Beetle Bailey — A3410

Calvin and Hobbes — A3411

Archie — A3412

Garfield — A3413

Dennis the Menace — A3414

Designed by Ethel Kessler. Printed by Banknote Corporation of America for Sennett Security Products.

LITHOGRAPHED
Sheets of 180 in nine panes of 20
Serpentine Die Cut 10½x10¾

2010, July 16 Tagged
Self-Adhesive

4467 A3410 44c **multicolored**	1.00	.30
4468 A3411 44c **multicolored**	1.00	.30
4471 A3414 44c **multicolored**	1.00	.30
a. Horiz. strip of 5, #4467-4471	5.00	
P# block of 10, 2 sets of 9#+S	10.00	
Pane of 20	20.00	

Uncut press sheets of Nos. 4467-4471 were made available for sale. Panes that are vertically adjacent are tete-beche in relation to each other. Values: cross-gutter block of 10 with or without top panel, $19; pairs with gutters between, $2.50 each. See note after No. 2868.

BOY SCOUTS OF AMERICA, CENTENNIAL Ⓢ

Boy Scouts — A3415

Designed by Derry Noyes. Printed by Avery Dennison.

PHOTOGRAVURE
Sheets of 160 in eight panes of 20

2010, July 27 Tagged *Serpentine Die Cut 11*
Self-Adhesive

4472 A3415 44c **multicolored**	.90	.25
P# block of 4, 6#+V	3.60	
Pane of 20	18.00	

See note after No. 1549.

AMERICAN TREASURES SERIES

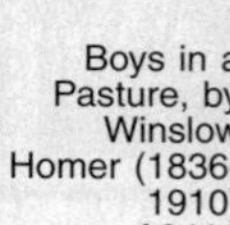

Boys in a Pasture, by Winslow Homer (1836-1910) A3416

Designed by Derry Noyes. Printed by Banknote Corporation of America for Sennett Security Products.

PHOTOGRAVURE
Sheets of 180 in nine panes of 20

2010, Aug. 12 Tagged *Serpentine Die Cut 10¾*
Self-Adhesive

4473 A3416 44c **multicolored**	1.00	.25
P# block of 4, 5#+S	4.00	
Pane of 20	20.00	

HAWAIIAN RAIN FOREST

A3417

Designed by Ethel Kessler. Printed by Banknote Corporation of America for Sennett Security Products.

No. 4474: a, Hawaii 'amakihi, Hawaii 'elepaio, ohi'a lehua. b, 'Akepa, 'ope'ape'a, vert. c, 'I'iwi, haha. d, 'Oma'o, kanawao, 'ohelo kau la'au, vert. e, 'Oha, vert. f, Pulelehua butterfly, kolea lau nui, 'ilihia. g, Koele Mountain damselfly, 'akala, vert. h, 'Apapane, Hawaiian mint, vert. i, Jewel orchid, vert. j, Happyface spider, 'ala'ala wai nui, vert.

LITHOGRAPHED
Sheets of 80 in eight panes of 10

2010, Sept. 1 Tagged *Serpentine Die Cut 10¾*
Self-Adhesive

4474 A3417 Pane of 10 10.00
a.-j. 44c Any single 1.00 .40

Uncut press sheets of No. 4474 were made available for sale. See note after No. 2868.

MOTHER TERESA Ⓢ

Mother Teresa (1910-97), Humanitarian, 1979 Nobel Peace Laureate — A3418

Designed by Derry Noyes. Printed by Avery Dennison.

PHOTOGRAVURE
Sheets of 200 in ten panes of 20

2010, Sept. 5 Tagged *Serpentine Die Cut 11*
Self-Adhesive

4475 A3418 44c **multicolored** .90 .25
P# block of 4, 4#+V 3.60
Pane of 20 18.00

See note after No. 1549.

LITERARY ARTS

Julia de Burgos (1914-53), Poet — A3419

Designed by Howard E. Paine. Printed by Avery Dennison.

PHOTOGRAVURE
Sheets of 200 in ten panes of 20

2010, Sept. 14 Tagged *Serpentine Die Cut 11*
Self-Adhesive

4476 A3419 44c **multicolored** Ⓢ .90 .25
P# block of 4, 4#+V 3.60
Pane of 20 18.00

See note after No. 1549.

CHRISTMAS

Angel with Lute, Detail of Fresco by Melozzo da Forli — A3420

Ponderosa Pine — A3421

Eastern Red Cedar — A3422

Balsam Fir — A3423

Blue Spruce — A3424

Ponderosa Pine — A3425

Eastern Red Cedar — A3426

Balsam Fir — A3427

Blue Spruce — A3428

Designed by Terrence W. McCaffrey (#4477), Howard E. Paine
Printed by Avery Dennison (#4477), Banknote Corporation of America for Sennett Security Products (#4478-4481), Ashton-Potter (USA) Ltd. (#4482-4485).

PHOTOGRAVURE (#4477), LITHOGRAPHED
Sheets of 240 in twelve panes of 20 (#4477)

2010, Oct. 21 Tagged *Serpentine Die Cut 10¾*
Self-Adhesive

4477 A3420 44c **multicolored** Ⓢ 1.00 .25
P# block of 4, 5#+V 4.00
Pane of 20 20.00

Booklet Stamps
Serpentine Die Cut 11 on 2 or 3 Sides

4478 A3421 (44c) **multicolored** 1.10 .25
4479 A3422 (44c) **multicolored** 1.10 .25
4480 A3423 (44c) **multicolored** 1.10 .25
4481 A3424 (44c) **multicolored** 1.10 .25
a. Block of 4, #4478-4481 4.40
b. Booklet pane of 20, 5 each #4478-4481 22.00
c. As "a," die cutting omitted — *500.00*
d. As "b," die cutting omitted on side with 12 stamps *700.00*
e. As "b," die cutting omitted on side with 8 stamps *700.00*
f. As "b," die cutting omitted on side with 12 stamps, die cutting omitted on bottom 4 stamps on side with 8 stamps —

Serpentine Die Cut 11¼x10¾ on 2, 3 or 4 Sides

4482 A3425 (44c) **multicolored** Ⓢ 1.10 .25
4483 A3426 (44c) **multicolored** Ⓢ 1.10 .25
4484 A3427 (44c) **multicolored** Ⓢ 1.10 .25
4485 A3428 (44c) **multicolored** Ⓢ 1.10 .25
a. Block or strip of 4, #4482-4485 4.40
b. Booklet pane of 18, 5 each #4482, 4484, 4 each #4483, 4485 20.00
Nos. 4477-4485 (9) 9.80 2.25

No. 4481b is a double-sided booklet pane with 12 stamps on one side (3 each of Nos. 4478-4481) and eight stamps (2 each of Nos. 4478-4481) plus label that serves as a booklet cover on the other side.
See note after No. 1549.

Replica of Statue of Liberty, Las Vegas — A3429

Flag — A3430

Designed by Terrence W. McCaffrey. Printed by Ashton-Potter (USA) Ltd. (#4486-4487), Banknote Corporation of America for Sennett Security Products (#4488-4489), Avery Dennison (#4490-4491).

LITHOGRAPHED (#4486-4489), PHOTOGRAVURE
Serpentine Die Cut 9½ Vert.

2010, Dec. 1 Tagged
COIL STAMPS
Self-Adhesive

4486 A3429 (44c) **multicolored** Ⓢ 1.50 .25
4487 A3430 (44c) **multicolored** Ⓢ 1.50 .25
a. Pair, #4486-4487 3.00
P# strip of 5, 3 #4487, 2 #4486 8.50
P# single (#4487), #P111111 — 2.00

Serpentine Die Cut 11 Vert.

4488 A3429 (44c) **multicolored** 1.50 .25
a. Vert. pair, horiz. unslit btwn. —
4489 A3430 (44c) **multicolored** 1.50 .25
a. Pair, #4488-4489 3.00
P# strip of 5, 3 #4489, 2 #4488 8.50
P# single (#4489), #S111111 — 2.00
b. Block of 4 (one pair each from two different coil rolls), horiz. unslit btwn. —

Serpentine Die Cut 8½ Vert.

4490 A3429 (44c) **multicolored** Ⓢ 1.50 .25
4491 A3430 (44c) **multicolored** Ⓢ 1.50 .25
a. Pair, #4490-4491 3.00
P# strip of 5, 3 #4491, 2 #4490 8.50
P# single (#4491), #V111111 — 2.00
Nos. 4486-4491 (6) 9.00 1.50

Microprinting reads "4evR" on Nos. 4486-4487, "4evr" on Nos. 4488-4489, and "4EVR" on Nos. 4490-4491. The microprinting is found above the Statue of Liberty's hair, and at the bottom of the lowest red stripe of the flag.
Counterfeits exist of Nos. 4490-4491. See the Postal Counterfeits section of this catalog.
See Nos. 4518-4519, 4559-4564.
See note after No. 1549.

CHINESE NEW YEAR

Year of the Rabbit A3431

Designed by Ethel Kessler. Printed by Avery Dennison.

PHOTOGRAVURE
Sheets of 108 in nine panes of 12

2011, Jan. 22 Tagged *Serpentine Die Cut 11*
Self-Adhesive

4492 A3431 (44c) **multicolored** Ⓢ 1.10 .25
Pane of 12 13.25

Uncut press sheets of No. 4492 were made available for sale. Values: cross-gutter block of 4, $9; pairs with gutters between, $2.50 each. See note after No. 2868.
See note after No. 1549.

KANSAS STATEHOOD, 150TH ANNIV. Ⓢ

Windmill and Wind Turbines A3432

Designed by Howard E. Paine. Printed by Ashton-Potter (USA) Ltd.

LITHOGRAPHED
Sheets of 180 in nine panes of 20

2011, Jan. 27 Tagged *Serpentine Die Cut 11*
Self-Adhesive

4493 A3432 (44c) **multicolored**		1.10	.25
	P# block of 4, 5# + P	4.40	
	Pane of 20	22.00	

See note after No. 1549.

PRES. RONALD REAGAN (1911-2004)

Pres. Ronald Reagan — A3433

Designed by Ethel Kessler. Printed by Avery Dennison.

PHOTOGRAVURE
Sheets of 200 in ten panes of 20

2011, Feb. 10 Tagged *Serpentine Die Cut 10½*
Self-Adhesive

4494 A3433 (44c) **multicolored**		1.10	.25
	P# block of 4, 6#+V	4.40	
	Pane of 20	22.00	

Uncut press sheets of No. 4494 were made available for sale. Values: cross-gutter block of 4, $8; pairs with gutters between, $2.50 each. See note after No. 2868.

See note after No. 1549.

Art Deco Bird — A3434

Designed by Carl T. Herrman. Printed by Ashton-Potter (USA) Ltd.

LITHOGRAPHED
Serpentine Die Cut 10 Vert.

2011, Feb. 11 Untagged
COIL STAMP
Self-Adhesive

4495 A3434 (5c) **multicolored** ⓢ		.25	.25
	Pair	.50	
	P# strip of 5, #P1111	1.25	
	P# strip of 5, #P2222	1.60	
	P# strip of 5, #P3333	2.50	
	P# single, #P1111	—	1.75
	P# single, #P2222, P3333	—	2.00

See note after No. 1549.

Quill and Inkwell — A3435

Designed by Craig Frazier. Printed by Banknote Corporation of America for Sennett Security Products.

LITHOGRAPHED
Serpentine Die Cut 11¾ Vert.

2011, Feb. 14 Tagged
COIL STAMP
Self-Adhesive

4496 A3435 44c **multicolored**		.95	.25
	Pair	1.90	
	P# strip of 5, #S11111	6.25	
	P# single, #S11111	—	2.00

LATIN MUSIC LEGENDS

Tito Puente (1923-2000) — A3436

Carmen Miranda (1909-55) — A3437

Selena (1971-95) — A3438

Carlos Gardel (1890-35) — A3439

Celia Cruz (1925-2003) — A3440

Designed by Ethel Kessler. Printed by Avery Dennison.

PHOTOGRAVURE
Sheets of 240 in twelve panes of 20

2011, Mar. 16 Tagged *Serpentine Die Cut 10¾*
Self-Adhesive

4497 A3436 (44c) **multicolored**		1.10	.40
4498 A3437 (44c) **multicolored**		1.10	.40
4499 A3438 (44c) **multicolored**		1.10	.40
4500 A3439 (44c) **multicolored**		1.10	.40
4501 A3440 (44c) **multicolored**		1.10	.40
a.	Horiz. strip of 5, #4497-4501	5.50	
	P# block of 10, 2 sets of 4#+V	11.00	
	Pane of 20	22.00	

See note after No. 1549.

CELEBRATE

A3441

Designed by Phil Jordan. Printed by American Packaging Corporation for Sennett Security Products.

PHOTOGRAVURE
Sheets of 160 in eight panes of 20
Serpentine Die Cut 11x11½

2011, Mar. 25 Tagged
Self-Adhesive

4502 A3441 (44c) **multicolored**		1.10	.25
	P# block of 4, 6#+S	4.40	
	Pane of 20	22.00	

Compare with type A3855.

JAZZ

Musicians — A3442

Designed by Howard E. Paine. Printed by Avery Dennison.

PHOTOGRAVURE
Sheets of 200 in ten panes of 20

2011, Mar. 26 Tagged *Serpentine Die Cut 10¾*
Self-Adhesive

4503 A3442 (44c) **multicolored**		1.10	.25
	P# block of 4, 4#+V	4.40	
	Pane of 20	22.00	

See note after No. 1549.

Statue of Liberty and Flag Types of 2010 and

George Washington — A3443

Oregano — A3444

Flax — A3445

Foxglove — A3446

Lavender — A3447

Sage — A3448

Oveta Culp Hobby (1905-95), First Health, Education and Welfare Department Secretary — A3449

New River Gorge Bridge, West Virginia — A3450

Designed by Derry Noyes (#4504, 4512), Phil Jordan (#4505-4510, 4513-4517), Carl T. Herrman (#4511). Printed by Ashton-

Potter (USA) Ltd. (#4504, 4511, 4512), Avery Dennison (4505-4510, 4513-4517), Banknote Corporation of America for Sennett Security Products (#4518-4519).

LITHOGRAPHED (#4504, 4511, 4512, 4518-4519), PHOTOGRAVURE (#4505-4510, 4513-4517)

Sheets of 200 in ten panes of 20 (#4504), Sheets of 420 in twenty-one panes of 20 (#4505-4509), Sheets of 240 in twelve panes of 20 (#4510), Sheets of 120 in six panes of 20 (#4511)

2011 Tagged *Serpentine Die Cut 11¼x10¾*

Self-Adhesive

4504 A3443 20c **multicolored,** *Apr. 11* Ⓢ .40 .25
P# block of 4, 5#+P 1.60
Pane of 20 8.00

Serpentine Die Cut 11

4505 A3444 29c **multicolored,** *Apr. 7* Ⓢ 1.00 .25
4506 A3445 29c **multicolored,** *Apr. 7* Ⓢ 1.00 .25
4507 A3446 29c **multicolored,** *Apr. 7* Ⓢ 1.00 .25
4508 A3447 29c **multicolored,** *Apr. 7* Ⓢ 1.00 .25
4509 A3448 29c **multicolored,** *Apr. 7* Ⓢ 1.00 .25
a. Horiz. strip of 5, #4505-4509 5.00
P# block of 10, 2 sets of 5#+V 10.00
Pane of 20 20.00
4510 A3449 84c **multicolored,** *Apr. 15* Ⓢ 1.75 .35
P# block of 4, 5#+V 7.00
Pane of 20 35.00

Serpentine Die Cut 10¾x10½

4511 A3450 $4.95 **multicolored,** *Apr. 11* Ⓢ 10.00 5.00
P# block of 4, 4#+P 40.00
Pane of 20 200.00
Nos. 4504-4511 (7) 15.40 6.50

Coil Stamps

Serpentine Die Cut 9½ Vert.

4512 A3443 20c **multicolored,** *Apr. 11* Ⓢ .40 .25
Pair .80
P# strip of 5, #P11111, P22222 3.50
P# single, #P11111, P22222 — 2.50
a. Imperf., on cover —

No. 4512a is recorded only on a single cover bearing a strip of 9 and three strips of 10. The editors would welcome reports of unused examples.

Serpentine Die Cut 8½ Vert.

4513 A3446 29c **multicolored,** *Apr. 7* Ⓢ 1.20 .25
4514 A3447 29c **multicolored,** *Apr. 7* Ⓢ 1.20 .25
4515 A3448 29c **multicolored,** *Apr. 7* Ⓢ 1.20 .25
4516 A3444 29c **multicolored,** *Apr. 7* Ⓢ 1.20 .25
4517 A3445 29c **multicolored,** *Apr. 7* Ⓢ 1.20 .25
a. Horiz. strip of 5, #4513-4517 6.00
P# strip of 5, #4513-4517, #V11111 8.00
P# strip of 11, 3 #4515, 2 each #4513-4514, 4516-4517, #V11111 16.00
P# single (#4515), #V11111 — 2.00
Nos. 4512-4517 (6) 6.40 1.50

See note after No. 1549.

Booklet Stamps

Thin Paper

Serpentine Die Cut 11¼x10¾ on 2, 3, or 4 Sides

4518 A3429 (44c) **multicolored,** *Apr. 8* 1.10 .25
4519 A3430 (44c) **multicolored,** *Apr. 8* 1.10 .25
a. Pair, #4518-4519 2.20
b. Booklet pane of 18, 9 each #4518-4519 20.00

Wedding Cake Type of 2009 With "USA" in Serifed Type and

Wedding Roses — A3450a

Designed by Ethel Kessler. Printed by Banknote Corporation of America for Sennett Security Products (#4520). Printed by Avery Dennison (#4521).

LITHOGRAPHED (#4520), PHOTOGRAVURE (#4521)

Sheets of 200 in Ten Panes of 20 (#4520), Sheets of 120 in twelve panes of 20 (#4521)

2011 Tagged *Serpentine Die Cut 11*

Self-Adhesive

4520 A3450a (44c) **multicolored,** *Apr. 21* 1.50 .25
P# block of 4, 5#+S 6.00
Pane of 20 30.00
a. Die cutting omitted, pair —
4521 A3344 64c **multicolored,** *Apr. 11* Ⓢ 1.35 .25
P# block of 4, 5#+V 5.40
Pane of 20 27.00

See note after No. 1549.

CIVIL WAR SESQUICENTENNIAL

Battle of Fort Sumter — A3451

First Battle of Bull Run — A3452

Designed by Phil Jordan. Printed by Ashton-Potter (USA) Ltd.

LITHOGRAPHED

Double-sided sheets of 72 in six panes of 12 (60 on one side, 12 on other side)

2011, Apr. 12 Tagged *Serpentine Die Cut 11*

Self-Adhesive

4522 A3451 (44c) **multicolored** Ⓢ 1.10 .30
4523 A3452 (44c) **multicolored** Ⓢ 1.10 .30
a. Pair, #4522-4523 2.20
Pane of 12 12.00

Uncut press sheets of Nos. 4522-4523 were made available for sale. See note after No. 2868.

See note after No. 1549.

GO GREEN Ⓢ

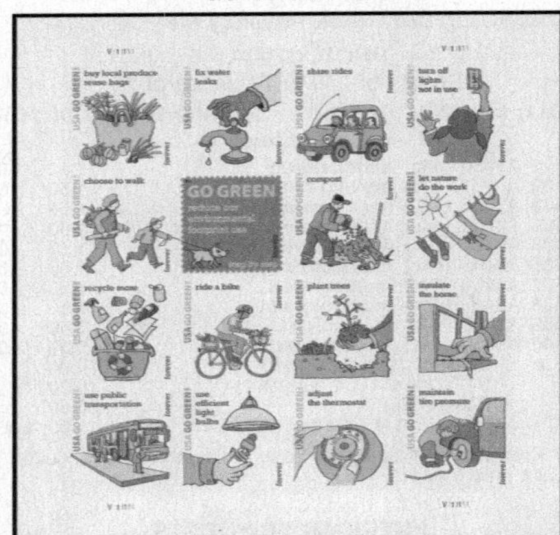

A3453

Illustration reduced.

Designed by Derry Noyes. Printed by Avery Dennison.

No. 4524 — Messages: a, Buy local produce, reuse bags. b, Fix water leaks. c, Share rides. d, Turn off lights not in use. e, Choose to walk. f, Go Green, reduce our environmental footprint step by step. g, Compost. h, Let nature do the work. i, Recycle more. j, Ride a bike. k, Plant trees. l, Insulate the home. m, Use public transportation. n, Use efficient light bulbs. o, Adjust the thermostat. p, Maintain tire pressure.

PHOTOGRAVURE

Sheets of 144 in nine panes of 16

2011, Apr. 14 Tagged *Serpentine Die Cut 10¾*

Self-Adhesive

4524 A3453 Pane of 16 17.50
a.-p. (44c) Any single 1.10 .50

Uncut press sheets of No. 4524 were made available for sale. Values: cross-gutter block of 16, $22.50; pairs with gutters between, $3.25 each. See note after No. 2868.

See note after No. 1549.

HELEN HAYES Ⓢ

Helen Hayes (1900-93), Actress — A3454

Designed by Howard E. Paine. Printed by Avery Dennison.

PHOTOGRAVURE

Sheets of 200 in ten panes of 20

2011, Apr. 25 Tagged *Serpentine Die Cut 11*

Self-Adhesive

4525 A3454 (44c) **multicolored** 1.10 .25
P# block of 4, 5#+V 4.40
Pane of 20 22.00

Uncut press sheets of No. 4525 were made available for sale. Values: cross-gutter block of 8, $20; pairs with gutters between, $2.50 each. See note after No. 2868.

See note after No. 1549.

LEGENDS OF HOLLYWOOD

Gregory Peck (1916-2003), Actor — A3455

Designed by Phil Jordan. Printed by Avery Dennison.

PHOTOGRAVURE

Sheets of 80 in four panes of 20

2011, Apr. 28 Tagged *Serpentine Die Cut 10¾*

Self-Adhesive

4526 A3455 (44c) **black** Ⓢ 1.25 .25
P# block of 4, 4#+V 4.00
Pane of 20 20.00

Uncut press sheets of No. 4526 were made available for sale. Values: cross-gutter block of 8, $20; pairs with gutters between, $2.50 each. See note after No. 2868.

See note after No. 1549.

SPACE FIRSTS

Alan B. Shepard, Jr. (1923-98), First American in Space A3456

Messenger, First Spacecraft to Orbit Mercury A3457

Designed by Phil Jordan. Printed by Banknote Corporation of America for Sennett Security Products.

LITHOGRAPHED

Sheets of 240 in twelve panes of 20

2011, May 4 Tagged *Serpentine Die Cut 11*

Self-Adhesive

4527	A3456 (44c) **multicolored**	1.10	.30
4528	A3457 (44c) **multicolored**	1.10	.30
a.	Horiz. pair, #4527-4528	2.20	
	P# block of 4, 6#+S	4.40	
	Pane of 20	22.00	

Uncut press sheets of Nos. 4527-4528 were made available for sale. Values: cross-gutter block of 4, $9; pairs with gutters between, $2.50 each. See note after No. 2868.

Purple Heart and Ribbon — A3458

Designed by Jennifer Arnold. Printed by Banknote Corporation of America for Sennett Security Products.

LITHOGRAPHED

Sheets of 80 in four panes of 20

Serpentine Die Cut 11¼x10¾

2011, May 5 Tagged

Self-Adhesive

4529	A3458 (44c) **multicolored**	1.10	.25
	P# block of 4, 8#+S	4.40	
	Pane of 20	22.00	

INDIANAPOLIS 500, CENT.

Ray Harroun Driving Marmon Wasp A3459

Designed by Phil Jordan. Printed by Banknote Corporation of America for Sennett Security Products.

LITHOGRAPHED

Sheets of 240 in 12 panes of 20

2011, May 20 Tagged *Serpentine Die Cut 10¾*

Self-Adhesive

4530	A3459 (44c) **multicolored**	1.10	.25
	P# block of 4, 6#+S	4.40	
	Pane of 20	22.00	

GARDEN OF LOVE Ⓢ

Pink Flower — A3460

Red Flower — A3461

Blue Flowers — A3462

Butterfly — A3463

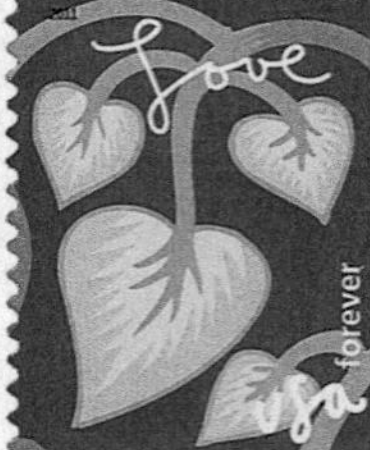

Green Vine Leaves — A3464

Blue Flower — A3465

Doves — A3466

Orange Red Flowers — A3467

Strawberry — A3468

Yellow Orange Flowers — A3469

Designed by Derry Noyes. Printed by Avery Dennison.

PHOTOGRAVURE

Sheets of 240 in 12 panes of 20

2011, May 23 Tagged *Serpentine Die Cut 10¾*

Self-Adhesive

4531	A3460 (44c) **multicolored**	1.50	.40
4532	A3461 (44c) **multicolored**	1.50	.40
4533	A3462 (44c) **multicolored**	1.50	.40
4534	A3463 (44c) **multicolored**	1.50	.40
4535	A3464 (44c) **multicolored**	1.50	.40
4536	A3465 (44c) **multicolored**	1.50	.40
4537	A3466 (44c) **multicolored**	1.50	.40
4538	A3467 (44c) **multicolored**	1.50	.40
4539	A3468 (44c) **multicolored**	1.50	.40
4540	A3469 (44c) **multicolored**	1.50	.40
a.	Block of 10, #4531-4540	15.00	
	P# block of 10, 2 sets of 4#+V	16.00	
	Pane of 20	32.50	
	Nos. 4531-4540 (10)	15.00	4.00

The two blocks of 10 on the pane are separated by a gutter. See note after No. 1549.

AMERICAN SCIENTISTS

Melvin Calvin (1911-97), Chemist A3470

Asa Gray (1810-88), Botanist A3471

Maria Goeppert Mayer (1906-72), Physicist A3472

Severo Ochoa (1905-93), Biochemist A3473

Designed by Greg Berger. Printed by Banknote Corporation of America for Sennett Security Products.

LITHOGRAPHED

Sheets of 240 in twelve panes of 20

2011, June 16 Tagged *Serpentine Die Cut 11*

Self-Adhesive

4541	A3470 (44c) **multicolored**	1.10	.50
4542	A3471 (44c) **multicolored**	1.10	.50
4543	A3472 (44c) **multicolored**	1.10	.50
4544	A3473 (44c) **multicolored**	1.10	.50
a.	Horiz. strip of 4, #4541-4544	4.40	
	P# block of 8, 2 sets of 8#+S	8.80	
	Pane of 20	22.00	
b.	Horiz. strip of 4, die cutting missing on backing paper (from misaligned die-cutting mat)	*375.00*	

LITERARY ARTS

Mark Twain (Samuel L. Clemens) (1835-1910), Writer A3474

Designed by Phil Jordan. Printed by Avery Dennison.

PHOTOGRAVURE

Sheets of 160 in eight panes of 20

2011, June 25 Tagged *Serpentine Die Cut 11*

Self-Adhesive

4545	A3474 (44c) **multicolored** Ⓢ	1.10	.25
	P# block of 4, 4#+V	4.40	
	Pane of 20	22.00	

See note after No. 1549.

PIONEERS OF AMERICAN INDUSTRIAL DESIGN Ⓢ

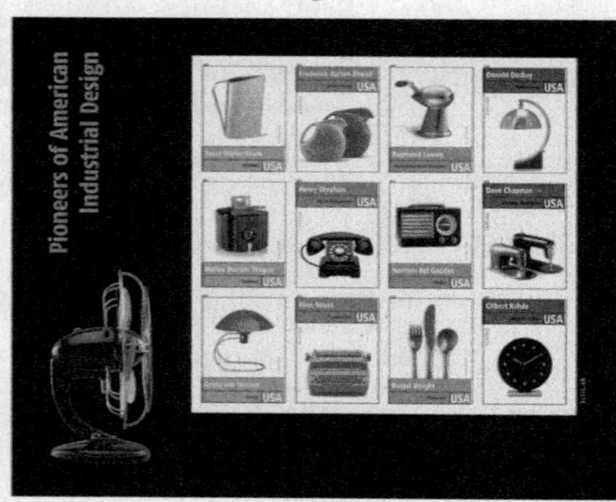

A3475

Designed by Derry Noyes. Printed by Avery Dennison.

No. 4546: a, "Normandie" pitcher, designed by Peter Müller-Munk (1904-67). b, Fiesta dinnerware, designed by Frederick Hurten Rhead (1880-1942). c, Streamlined pencil sharpener, designed by Raymond Loewy (1893-1986). d, Table lamp, designed by Donald Deskey (1894-1989). e, Kodak "Baby Brownie" camera, designed by Walter Dorwin Teague (1883-1960). f, Model 302 Bell telephone, designed by Henry Dreyfuss (1904-72). g, Emerson "Patriot" radio, designed by Norman Bel Geddes (1893-1958). h, Streamlined sewing machines, designed by Dave Chapman (1909-78). i, "Any-where" lamp, designed by Greta von Nessen (1900-74). j, IBM

"Selectric" typewriter, designed by Eliot Noyes (1910-77). k, "Highlight/Pinch" flatware, designed by Russel Wright (1904-76). l, Herman Miller electric clock, designed by Gilbert Rohde (1894-1944).

PHOTOGRAVURE

2011, June 29 Tagged *Serpentine Die Cut 10¾*
Self-Adhesive

4546 A3475 Pane of 12 13.25
a.-l. (44c) Any single 1.10 .50

See note after No. 1549.

OWNEY, THE POSTAL DOG Ⓢ

Owney, His Medals and Tags — A3476

Designed by Bill Bond. Printed by Avery Dennison.

PHOTOGRAVURE
Sheets of 200 in 10 panes of 20

2011, July 27 Tagged *Serpentine Die Cut 11*
Self-Adhesive

4547 A3476 (44c) **multicolored** 1.50 .25
P# block of 4, 5#+V 6.00
Pane of 20 30.00

Uncut press sheets of No. 4547 were made available for sale. Values: cross-gutter block of 4, $10; pairs with gutters between, $2.50 each. See note after No. 2868.

See note after No. 1549.

U.S. MERCHANT MARINE Ⓢ

Clipper Ship — A3477

Auxiliary Steamship A3478

Liberty Ship — A3479

Container Ship — A3480

Designed by Carl T. Herrman. Printed by Avery Dennison.

PHOTOGRAVURE
Sheets of 240 in 12 panes of 20

2011, July 28 Tagged *Serpentine Die Cut 11*
Self-Adhesive

4548 A3477 (44c) **multicolored** 1.10 .35
4549 A3478 (44c) **multicolored** 1.10 .35
4550 A3479 (44c) **multicolored** 1.10 .35
4551 A3480 (44c) **multicolored** 1.10 .35
a. Block or horiz. strip of 4, #4548-4551 4.40
P# block of 4, 6#+V 4.50
Pane of 20 24.00

See note after No. 1549.

EID

"Eid Mubarak" — A3481

Designed by Mohamed Zakariya.
Printed by Avery Dennison.

PHOTOGRAVURE
Sheets of 240 in 12 panes of 20

2011, Aug. 12 Tagged *Serpentine Die Cut 11¼*
Self-Adhesive

4552 A3481 (44c) **maroon, gray & gold** Ⓢ 1.10 .25
P# block of 4, 3#+V 4.40
Pane of 20 22.00

See note after No. 1549.

CHARACTERS FROM DISNEY-PIXAR FILMS

Send a Hello Ⓢ

Lightning McQueen and Mater from *Cars* — A3482

Remy the Rat and Linguini from *Ratatouille* — A3483

Buzz Lightyear and Aliens from *Toy Story* — A3484

Carl Fredricksen and Dug the Dog from *Up* — A3485

WALL-E from *WALL-E* — A3486

Designed by Terrence W. McCaffrey and William J. Gicker. Printed by Avery Dennison.

PHOTOGRAVURE
Sheets of 80 in four panes of 20

2011, Aug. 19 Tagged *Serpentine Die Cut 10½*
Self-Adhesive

4553 A3482 (44c) **multicolored** 1.10 .40
4554 A3483 (44c) **multicolored** 1.10 .40
4555 A3484 (44c) **multicolored** 1.10 .40
4556 A3485 (44c) **multicolored** 1.10 .40
4557 A3486 (44c) **multicolored** 1.10 .40
a. Horiz. strip of 5, #4553-4557 5.50
P# block of 10, 4#+V 11.00
Pane of 20 22.00

Adjacent horizontal or vertical stamps have selvage between the stamps. Plate block may contain top label.

Uncut press sheets of Nos. 4553-4557 were made available for sale. Values: cross gutter block of 10 (four stamps from one side of the sheet and six stamps from the other side), $22.50; pairs with gutters between, $2.50. See note after No. 2868.

See note after No. 1549.

AMERICAN TREASURES SERIES

The Long Leg, by Edward Hopper (1882-1967) A3487

Designed by Derry Noyes. Printed by Avery Dennison.

PHOTOGRAVURE
Sheets of 200 in 10 panes of 20

2011, Aug. 24 Tagged *Serpentine Die Cut 11*
Self-Adhesive

4558 A3487 (44c) **multicolored** Ⓢ 1.10 .25
P# block of 4, 5#+V 5.00
Pane of 20 24.00

See note after No. 1549.

Statue of Liberty and Flag Types of 2010

Designed by Terrence W. McCaffrey. Printed by Ashton-Potter (USA) Ltd. (#4559-4560), Banknote Corporation of America for Sennett Security Products (#4561-4562), Avery Dennison (#4563-4564).

LITHOGRAPHED (#4559-4562), PHOTOGRAVURE
Serpentine Die Cut 11¼x11 on 2 or 3 Sides

2011, Sept. 14 Tagged

BOOKLET STAMPS
Self-Adhesive

4559 A3429 (44c) **multicolored** Ⓢ 1.25 .25
4560 A3430 (44c) **multicolored** Ⓢ 1.25 .25
a. Pair, #4559-4560 2.50
b. Booklet pane of 20, 10 each #4559-4560 25.00
4561 A3429 (44c) **multicolored** 1.10 .25
4562 A3430 (44c) **multicolored** 1.10 .25
a. Pair, #4561-4562 2.20
b. Booklet pane of 20, 10 each #4561-4562 22.00

Serpentine Die Cut 11¼x11½ on 2 or 3 Sides

4563 A3429 (44c) **multicolored** Ⓢ 1.10 .25
4564 A3430 (44c) **multicolored** Ⓢ 1.10 .25
a. Pair, #4563-4564 2.20
b. Booklet pane of 20, 10 each #4563-4564 22.00
Nos. 4559-4564 (6) 6.90 1.50

Microprinting reads "4evR" on Nos. 4559-4560, "4evr" on Nos. 4561-4562, and "4EVR" on Nos. 4563-4564. The microprinting is found above the Statue of Liberty's hair, and at the bottom of the lowest red stripe of the flag. Nos. 4560b, 4562b and 4564b are double-sided booklet panes with 12 stamps one one side (6 each of types A3429-A3430) and 8 stamps (4 each of types A3429-A3430) on the other side. The paper used on Nos. 4561-4562 is thicker than that used on Nos. 4518-4519.

See note after No. 1549.

BLACK HERITAGE

Barbara Jordan (1936-96), Congresswoman — A3488

Designed by Richard Sheaff. Printed by Ashton-Potter (USA) Ltd.

LITHOGRAPHED

Sheets of 180 in nine panes of 20

2011, Sept. 16 Tagged ***Serpentine Die Cut 10¾***

Self-Adhesive

4565 A3488 (44c) **multicolored** Ⓢ 1.10 .25
P# block of 4, 5#+P 4.40
Pane of 20 22.00

See note after No. 1549.

ART OF ROMARE BEARDEN (1911-88) Ⓢ

Conjunction — A3489

Odysseus: Poseidon, The Sea God - Enemy of Odysseus — A3490

Prevalence of Ritual: Conjur Woman — A3491

Falling Star — A3492

Designed by Margaret Bauer. Printed by Avery Dennison.

PHOTOGRAVURE

Sheets of 128 in six panes of 16

2011, Sept. 28 Tagged ***Serpentine Die Cut 10¾***

Self-Adhesive

4566 A3489 (44c) **multicolored** 1.10 .40

4569 A3492 (44c) **multicolored** 1.10 .40
a. Horiz. strip of 4, #4566-4569 4.40
P# block of 6 (#4567, 4569, 2 each #4566, 4568), 5#+V 6.60
Pane of 16 17.50

See note after No. 1549.

CHRISTMAS

Madonna of the Candelabra, by Raphael — A3493

A3494  A3495

A3496  A3497

A3498  A3499

Ornaments

A3500 A3501

Designed by Richard Sheaff (#4570), William J. Gicker. Printed by Banknote Corporation of America for Sennett Security Products (#4570, 4575-4582), Ashton-Potter (USA) Ltd. (#4571-4574).

LITHOGRAPHED

Serpentine Die Cut 10¾x 11 on 2 or 3 Sides

2011, Oct. 13 Tagged

Booklet Stamps
Self-Adhesive

4570 A3493 (44c) **multicolored** 1.10 .25
a. Booklet pane of 20 22.00

With "USPS" Microprinted on Collar of Ornament

4571 A3494 (44c) **multicolored** Ⓢ 1.10 .25
4572 A3495 (44c) **multicolored** Ⓢ 1.10 .25
4573 A3496 (44c) **multicolored** Ⓢ 1.10 .25
4574 A3497 (44c) **multicolored** Ⓢ 1.10 .25
a. Block of 4, #4571-4574 4.40
b. Booklet pane of 20, 5 each #4571-4574 22.00

See note after No. 1549.

Microprinted "USPS" in Places Other Than Collar of Ornament

4575 A3494 (44c) **multicolored** 1.10 .25
Cylinder flaw ("USPS" microprinting doubled) — —
4576 A3495 (44c) **multicolored** 1.10 .25
Cylinder flaw ("USPS" microprinting doubled) — —
4577 A3496 (44c) **multicolored** 1.10 .25
Cylinder flaw ("USPS" microprinting doubled) — —
4578 A3497 (44c) **multicolored** 1.10 .25
Cylinder flaw ("USPS" microprinting doubled) — —
a. Block of 4, #4575-4578 4.40
b. Booklet pane of 20, 5 each #4575-4578 22.00

Serpentine Die Cut 11¼x11 on 2, 3 or 4 Sides

4579 A3498 (44c) **multicolored** 1.10 .25
4580 A3499 (44c) **multicolored** 1.10 .25
4581 A3500 (44c) **multicolored** 1.10 .25
4582 A3501 (44c) **multicolored** 1.10 .25
a. Block or strip of 4, #4579-4582 4.40
b. Booklet pane of 18, 5 each #4579, 4582, 4 each #4580-4581 20.00
Nos. 4570-4582 (13) 14.30 3.25

The microprinted "USPS" is to the left of the third stripe on Nos. 4575 and 4579, on the left side of the bottom ribbon of the ribbon cluster above the ornament collar on Nos. 4576 and 4578, below the bottom stripe near the bottom tip on No. 4577, on the vertical ribbon on No. 4580, on a curved ribbon above the collar on No. 4581, and on the left side of the ornament, below the collar, on No. 4582.

No. 4570a is a double-sided booklet with 12 stamps on one side and eight stamps plus a label that serves as a booklet cover on the other side. Nos. 4574b and 4578b are double sided booklets with 12 stamps (3 each of types A3494-A3497) on one side and eight stamps (2 each of types A3494-A3497) plus a label that serves as a booklet cover on the other side.

The cylinder flaw on Nos. 4575-4578 always appears on the four stamps to the left on the 12-stamp side of the booklet.

HANUKKAH

A3502

Designed by Suzanne Kleinwaks. Printed by Banknote Corporation of America for Sennett Security Products.

LITHOGRAPHED

Sheets of 200 in 10 panes of 20

Serpentine Die Cut 11x10¾

2011, Oct. 14 Tagged

Self-Adhesive

4583 A3502 (44c) **multicolored** 1.10 .25
P# block of 4, 5#+S 4.40
Pane of 20 22.00

KWANZAA

Family — A3503

Designed by Derry Noyes. Printed by Ashton-Potter (USA) Ltd.

LITHOGRAPHED

Sheets of 160 in eight panes of 20

Serpentine Die Cut 10¾x11

2011, Oct. 14 Tagged

Self-Adhesive

4584 A3503 (44c) **multicolored** Ⓢ 1.10 .25
P# block of 4, 4#+P 4.40
Pane of 20 22.00

See note after No. 1549.

Eagle — A3504

Designed by Ethel Kessler. Printed by Avery Dennison.

PHOTOGRAVURE

Serpentine Die Cut 11 Vert.

2012, Jan. 3 **Untagged**

Coil Stamps

Self-Adhesive

Color Behind "USA"

4585	A3504 (25c) **green** Ⓢ	.50	.25
4586	A3504 (25c) **blue green** Ⓢ	.50	.25
4587	A3504 (25c) **blue** Ⓢ	.50	.25
4588	A3504 (25c) **red violet** Ⓢ	.50	.25
4589	A3504 (25c) **brown orange** Ⓢ	.50	.25
4590	A3504 (25c) **yellow orange** Ⓢ	.50	.25
a.	Strip of 6, #4585-4590	3.00	
	P# strip of 7, 2 #4585, 1 each #4586-4590, #V11111, V11112	5.00	
	P# strip of 13, 3 #4588, 2 each #4585-4587, 4589-4590, #V11111, V11112	9.00	
	P# single (#4588), #V11111, V11112	—	2.50

See note after No. 1549.

NEW MEXICO STATEHOOD CENTENNIAL Ⓢ

Sanctuary II, Painting by Doug West — A3505

Designed by Richard Sheaff. Printed by Avery Dennison.

PHOTOGRAVURE

Sheets of 160 in eight panes of 20

2012, Jan. 6 **Tagged** ***Serpentine Die Cut 11***

Self-Adhesive

4591	A3505 (44c) **multicolored**	1.10	.25
	P# block of 4, 4#+V	4.40	
	Pane of 20	22.00	

See note after No. 1549.

ALOHA SHIRTS

Surfers and Palm Trees — A3506

Surfers — A3507

Bird of Paradise Flowers — A3508

Kilauea Volcano — A3509

Fossil Fish, Shells and Starfish — A3510

Designed by Carl T. Herrman. Printed by Avery Dennison (#4592-4596), Banknote Corporation of America for Sennett Security Products (#4597-4601).

PHOTOGRAVURE, LITHOGRAPHED (#4597-4601)

Sheets of 420 in 21 panes of 20

2012, Jan. 19 **Tagged** ***Serpentine Die Cut 11***

Self-Adhesive

4592	A3506 32c **multicolored** Ⓢ	2.00	.30
4593	A3507 32c **multicolored** Ⓢ	2.00	.30
4594	A3508 32c **multicolored** Ⓢ	2.00	.30
4595	A3509 32c **multicolored** Ⓢ	2.00	.30
4596	A3510 32c **multicolored** Ⓢ	2.00	.30
a.	Horiz. strip of 5, #4592-4596	10.00	
	P# block of 10, 7#+V	20.00	
	Pane of 20	40.00	

Coil Stamps

Serpentine Die Cut 11 Vert.

4597	A3510 32c **multicolored**	2.00	.30
4598	A3506 32c **multicolored**	2.00	.30
4599	A3507 32c **multicolored**	2.00	.30
4600	A3508 32c **multicolored**	2.00	.30
4601	A3509 32c **multicolored**	2.00	.30
a.	Strip of 5, #4597-4601	10.00	
	P# strip of 5, #4597-4601, #S1111111	12.00	
	P# strip of 11, 3 #4599, 2 each #4597-4598, 4600-4601, #S1111111	24.00	
	P# single (#4599), same #	—	3.00
b.	As "a," die cutting omitted	—	
	Nos. 4592-4601 (10)	20.00	3.00

On Nos. 4592-4596, the top of the shirt collars are all higher than the cross line of the "A" in "USA," and on Nos. 4597-4601, they are even with or slightly below the cross line.

See Nos. 4682-4686.
See note after No. 1549.

Wedding Cake Type of 2009

Designed by Ethel Kessler. Printed by Banknote Corporation of America for Sennett Security Products.

LITHOGRAPHED

Sheets of 160 in eight panes of 20

2012, Jan. 20 **Tagged** ***Serpentine Die Cut 10¾***

Self-Adhesive

4602	A3344 65c **multicolored**	1.35	.25
	P# block of 4, 6#+S	5.40	
	Pane of 20	27.00	

BALTIMORE CHECKERSPOT BUTTERFLY Ⓢ

A3511

Designed by Derry Noyes. Printed by Avery Dennison.

PHOTOGRAVURE

Sheets of 200 in 10 panes of 20

2012, Jan. 20 **Tagged** ***Serpentine Die Cut 10¾***

Self-Adhesive

4603	A3511 65c **multicolored**	1.50	.25
	P# block of 4, 4#+V	7.00	
	Pane of 20	34.00	

See note after No. 1549.

DOGS AT WORK Ⓢ

Seeing Eye Dog — A3512

Therapy Dog — A3513

Military Dog — A3514

Rescue Dog — A3515

Designed by Howard E. Paine. Printed by Avery Dennison.

PHOTOGRAVURE

Sheets of 240 in 12 panes of 20

2012, Jan. 20 **Tagged** ***Serpentine Die Cut 10¾***

Self-Adhesive

4604	A3512 65c **multicolored**	1.30	.30
4605	A3513 65c **multicolored**	1.30	.30
4606	A3514 65c **multicolored**	1.30	.30
4607	A3515 65c **multicolored**	1.30	.30
a.	Block or vert. strip of 4, #4604-4607	5.20	
	P# block of 4, 4#+V	5.20	
	Pane of 20	26.00	

See note after No. 1549.

BIRDS OF PREY Ⓢ

Northern Goshawk — A3516

Peregrine Falcon — A3517

Golden Eagle — A3518

Osprey — A3519

Northern Harrier — A3520

Designed by Howard E. Paine. Printed by Ashton-Potter (USA) Ltd.

LITHOGRAPHED

Sheets of 120 in six panes of 20

Serpentine Die Cut 11¼x10¾

2012, Jan. 20 **Tagged**

Self-Adhesive

4608	A3516 85c **multicolored**	1.75	.35
4609	A3517 85c **multicolored**	1.75	.35
4610	A3518 85c **multicolored**	1.75	.35
4611	A3519 85c **multicolored**	1.75	.35
4612	A3520 85c **multicolored**	1.75	.35
a.	Horiz. strip of 5, #4608-4612	8.75	
	P# block of 10, 4#+P	17.50	
	Pane of 20	35.00	

See note after No. 1549.

WEATHER VANES

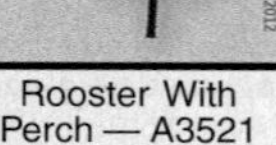

Rooster With Perch — A3521

Cow — A3522

Eagle — A3523

Rooster Without Perch — A3524

Centaur — A3525

Designed by Derry Noyes. Printed by Banknote Corporation of America for Sennett Security Products.

LITHOGRAPHED

Serpentine Die Cut 11¾ Vert.

2012, Jan. 20 **Tagged**

Coil Stamps
Self-Adhesive

4613 A3521 45c **multicolored**		1.50	.30
4614 A3522 45c **multicolored**		1.50	.30
4615 A3523 45c **multicolored**		1.50	.30
4616 A3524 45c **multicolored**		1.50	.30
4617 A3525 45c **multicolored**		1.50	.30
a.	Strip of 5, #4613-4617	7.50	
	P# strip of 5, #4613-4617, #S1111111	8.50	
	P# strip of 11, 3 #4615, 2 each #4613-4614, 4616-4617, #S1111111	17.50	
	P# single (#4615), same #	—	2.75

BONSAI Ⓢ

Sierra Juniper — A3526

Black Pine — A3527

Banyan — A3528

Trident Maple — A3529

Azalea — A3530

Designed by Ethel Kessler. Printed by Ashton-Potter (USA) Ltd.

LITHOGRAPHED

Serpentine Die Cut 11x10¾ on 2 or 3 Sides

2012, Jan. 23 **Tagged**

Booklet Stamps
Self-Adhesive

4618 A3526 (45c) **multicolored**		2.00	.40
4619 A3527 (45c) **multicolored**		2.00	.40
4620 A3528 (45c) **multicolored**		2.00	.40
4621 A3529 (45c) **multicolored**		2.00	.40
4622 A3530 (45c) **multicolored**		2.00	.40
a.	Vert. strip of 5, #4618-4622	10.00	
b.	Booklet pane of 20, 4 each #4618-4622	40.00	

Stamps in No. 4622a are not adjacent, as rows of selvage are between stamps two and three, and between stamps four and five.

No. 4622b is a double-sided booklet with 12 stamps on one side (3 each #4618, 4621, 2 each #4619, 4620, 4622) and eight stamps (#4618, 4621, 2 each #4619, 4620, 4622) plus label that serves as a booklet cover on the other side.

See note after No. 1549.

CHINESE NEW YEAR

Year of the Dragon A3531

Designed by Ethel Kessler. Printed by Avery Dennison.

PHOTOGRAVURE

Sheets of 108 in nine panes of 12

Serpentine Die Cut 11x10¾

2012, Jan. 23 **Tagged**

Self-Adhesive

4623 A3531 (45c) **multicolored** Ⓢ		1.15	.25
	Pane of 12	14.00	

Uncut press sheets of No. 4623 were made available for sale. Values: cross-gutter block of 4, $10; pairs with gutters between, $2.50 each. See note after No. 2868.

See note after No. 1549.

BLACK HERITAGE

John H. Johnson (1918-2005), Magazine Publisher — A3532

Designed by Howard E. Paine. Printed by Ashton-Potter (USA) Ltd.

LITHOGRAPHED

Sheets of 120 in six panes of 20

2012, Jan. 31 **Tagged** ***Serpentine Die Cut 10¾***

Self-Adhesive

4624 A3532 (45c) **multicolored** Ⓢ		1.10	.25
	P# block of 4, 5#+P	4.40	
	Pane of 20	22.00	

Uncut press sheets of No. 4624 were made available for sale. Values: cross-gutter block of 4, $10; pairs with gutters between, $2.50 each. See note after No. 2868.

See note after No. 1549.

HEART HEALTH Ⓢ

Tree, Man, Sun and Apple — A3533

Designed by Derry Noyes. Printed by Avery Dennison.

PHOTOGRAVURE

Sheets of 200 in 10 panes of 20

2012, Feb. 9 **Tagged** ***Serpentine Die Cut 11***

Self-Adhesive

4625 A3533 (45c) **multicolored**		1.10	.25
	P# block of 4, 6#+V	4.40	
	Pane of 20	22.00	

See note after No. 1549.

LOVE

Ribbons — A3534

Designed by Louise Fili. Printed by Banknote Corporation of America for Sennett Security Products.

LITHOGRAPHED

Sheets of 200 in 10 panes of 20

2012, Feb. 14 **Tagged** ***Serpentine Die Cut 10¾***

Self-Adhesive

4626 A3534 (45c) **red**		1.10	.25
	P# block of 4, 2#+S	4.40	
	Pane of 20	22.00	
a.	Die cutting omitted, pair	—	

Postal Service officials declared on Feb. 2 that No. 4626 could be sold in post offices as of that date to make the stamp available to customers before St. Valentine's Day, but the first day ceremony for the stamp was held Feb. 14 in Colorado Springs, CO. Official first day covers have that date and city.

ARIZONA STATEHOOD CENTENNIAL Ⓢ

Cathedral Rock — A3535

Designed by Richard Sheaff. Printed by Avery Dennison.

PHOTOGRAVURE

Sheets of 200 in 10 panes of 20

2012, Feb. 14 **Tagged** ***Serpentine Die Cut 11***

Self-Adhesive

4627 A3535 (45c) **multicolored**		1.10	.25
	P# block of 4, 5#+V	4.40	
	Pane of 20	22.00	

See note after No. 1549.

DANNY THOMAS

Thomas (1912-91), Comedian, and St. Jude's Children's Research Hospital, Memphis A3536

Designed by Greg Breeding. Printed by Banknote Corporation of America for Sennett Security Products.

LITHOGRAPHED

Sheets of 180 in nine panes of 20

Serpentine Die Cut 10¾x10½

2012, Feb. 16 **Tagged**

Self-Adhesive

4628 A3536 (45c) **multicolored** 1.10 .25
P# block of 4, 5#+S 4.40
Pane of 20 22.00

Flag and "Equality" — A3537

Flag and "Justice" — A3538

Flag and "Freedom" — A3539

Flag and "Liberty" — A3540

Designed by Howard E. Paine. Printed by Avery Dennison (#4629-4632), Ashton-Potter (USA) Ltd. (#4633-4636, 4641-4644), Banknote Corporation of America for Sennett Security Products (#4637-4640, 4645-4648).

PHOTOGRAVURE (#4629-4632), LITHOGRAPHED (#4633-4648)

Serpentine Die Cut 8½ Vert.

2012, Feb. 22 **Tagged**

Coil Stamps
Self-Adhesive

4629 A3537 (45c) **multicolored** Ⓢ 1.50 .25
4630 A3538 (45c) **multicolored** Ⓢ 1.50 .25
4631 A3539 (45c) **multicolored** Ⓢ 1.50 .25
4632 A3540 (45c) **multicolored** Ⓢ 1.50 .25
a. Strip of 4, #4629-4632 6.00
P# strip of 5, 2 #4629, 1 each #4630-4632, #V1111 8.50
P# strip of 9, 3# 4631, 2 each #4629-4630, 4632, #V1111 16.00
P# single, #V1111 (#4631) — 2.75

Counterfeits exist of Nos. 4629-4632. See the Postal Counterfeits section of this catalog.

Serpentine Die Cut 9½ Vert.

4633 A3537 (45c) **multi**, overall tagging Ⓢ 1.10 .25
a. Prephosphored coated paper with surface tagging showing a solid appearance Ⓢ 1.10 .25
4634 A3538 (45c) **multi**, overall tagging Ⓢ 1.10 .25
a. Prephosphored coated paper with surface tagging showing a solid appearance Ⓢ 1.10 .25
4635 A3539 (45c) **multi**, overall tagging Ⓢ 1.10 .25
a. Prephosphored coated paper with surface tagging showing a solid appearance Ⓢ 1.10 .25
4636 A3540 (45c) **multi**, overall tagging Ⓢ 1.10 .25
a. Prephosphored coated paper with surface tagging showing a solid appearance Ⓢ 1.10 .25
b. Strip of 4, #4633-4636 4.40
P# strip of 5, 2 #4633, 1 each #4634-4636, #P1111 6.25
P# strip of 9, 3 #4635, 2 each #4633-4634, 4636, #P1111 11.50
P# single, #P1111 (#4635) — 2.75
c. Strip of 4, #4633a-4636a 4.40
P# strip of 5, 2 #4633a, 1 each #4634a-4636a, #P2222 7.00
P# strip of 9, 3 #4635a, 2 each #4633a-4634a, 4636a, #P2222 12.50
P# single, #P2222 (#4635a) — 3.00

Nos. 4633-4636 were printed on nonphosphored paper with tagging applied after the stamps were printed.

Serpentine Die Cut 11 Vert.

4637 A3537 (45c) **multicolored** 1.50 .25
4638 A3538 (45c) **multicolored** 1.50 .25
4639 A3539 (45c) **multicolored** 1.50 .25
4640 A3540 (45c) **multicolored** 1.50 .25
a. Strip of 4, #4637-4640 6.00
P# strip of 5, 2 #4637, 1 each #4638-4640, #S11111, S22222 7.00
P# strip of 9, 3# 4639, 2 each #4637-4638, 4640, #S11111, S22222 13.00
P# single, #S11111, S22222 (#4639) — 2.75
b. As "a," die cutting omitted *350.00*
Nos. 4629-4640 (12) 16.40 3.00

Counterfeits exist of Nos. 4637-4640. See the Postal Counterfeits section of this catalog.

Booklet Stamps
Colored Dots in Stars
18½mm From Lower Left to Lower Right Corners of Flag

Serpentine Die Cut 11¼x10¾ on 2 or 3 Sides

4641 A3539 (45c) **multi**, overall tagging Ⓢ 1.25 .25
a. Prephosphored coated paper with surface tagging showing a solid appearance Ⓢ 1.25 .25
4642 A3540 (45c) **multi**, overall tagging Ⓢ 1.25 .25
a. Prephosphored coated paper with surface tagging showing a solid appearance Ⓢ 1.25 .25
4643 A3537 (45c) **multi**, overall tagging Ⓢ 1.25 .25
a. Prephosphored coated paper with surface tagging showing a solid appearance Ⓢ 1.25 .25
4644 A3538 (45c) **multi**, overall tagging Ⓢ 1.25 .25
a. Prephosphored coated paper with surface tagging showing a solid appearance Ⓢ 1.25 .25
b. Block of 4, #4641-4644 5.00
c. Booklet pane of 20, 5 each #4641-4644 25.00
d. Block of 4, #4641a-4644a 5.00
e. Booklet pane of 20, 5 each #4641a-4644a 25.00

Dark Dots Only in Stars
19mm from Lower Left to Lower Right Corners of Flag

4645 A3539 (45c) **multicolored** 1.50 .25
4646 A3540 (45c) **multicolored** 1.50 .25
4647 A3537 (45c) **multicolored** 1.50 .25
4648 A3538 (45c) **multicolored** 1.50 .25
a. Block of 4, #4645-4648 6.00
b. Booklet pane of 20, 5 each #4645-4648 30.00
Nos. 4641-4648 (8) 11.00 2.00

On Nos. 4641-4644, the blue canton of the flag is made up of blue and red inks. The paper is tagged over each block of 4, with no tagging on the paper between the blocks. The tagging is a dull yellow green under ultraviolet light. The tagging on Nos. 4641a-4644a is a bright yellow green under ultraviolet ligtht. The words are slightly longer than those on Nos. 4645-4648.

On Nos. 4645-4648, the blue canton is made up of blue and dull blue inks. The paper is prephosphored with the tagging appearing bright yellow green under ultraviolet light. The words are slightly shorter than those on Nos. 4641-4644.

No. 4644c is a double-sided booklet with 12 stamps on one side (3 each #4641-4644) and eight stamps (2 each #4641-4644) plus label that serves as a booklet cover on the other side.

No. 4644e is a double-sided booklet with 12 stamps on one side (3 each #4641a-4644a) and eight stamps (2 each #4641a-4644a) plus label that serves as a booklet cover on the other side.

No. 4648b is a double-sided booklet with 12 stamps on one side (3 each #4645-4648) and eight stamps (2 each #4645-4648) plus label that serves as a booklet cover on the other side.

See Nos. 4673-4676.
See note after No. 1549.

AMERICAN LANDMARKS ISSUE

Sunshine Skyway Bridge, Florida A3541

Carmel Mission, Carmel, CA — A3542

Designed by Carl T. Hermann (#4649), Phil Jordan (#4650). Printed by Banknote Corporation of America for Sennett Security Products (#4649), Ashton-Potter (USA) Ltd. (#4650).

LITHOGRAPHED

Sheets of 180 in nine panes of 20 (#4649), Sheets of 60 in six panes of 10 (#4650)

Serpentine Die Cut 10¾x10½

2012, Feb. 28 **Tagged**

Self-Adhesive

4649 A3541 $5.15 **multicolored** 11.00 5.75
P# block of 4, 5#+S 45.00
Pane of 20 220.00
4650 A3542 $18.95 **multicolored** Ⓢ 42.50 19.00
P# block of 4, 5#+S 170.00
Pane of 10 425.00

See note after No. 1549.

CHERRY BLOSSOM CENTENNIAL Ⓢ

Cherry Blossoms and Washington Monument A3543

Cherry Blossoms and Jefferson Memorial A3544

Designed by Phil Jordan. Printed by Ashton-Potter (USA) Ltd.

LITHOGRAPHED

Sheets of 120 in six panes of 20

2012, Mar. 24 **Tagged** ***Serpentine Die Cut 10¾***

Self-Adhesive

4651 A3543 (45c) **multicolored** 1.10 .25
4652 A3544 (45c) **multicolored** 1.10 .25
a. Horiz. pair, #4651-4652 2.20
P# block of 4, 5#+P 4.40
P# block of 8, 2 sets of 5#+P, + top label 8.80
Pane of 20 22.00

See Japan No. 3413.
See note after No. 1549.

AMERICAN TREASURES SERIES

Flowers, by William H. Johnson (1901-70) — A3545

Designed by Derry Noyes. Printed by Avery Dennison.

PHOTOGRAVURE
Sheets of 200 in 10 panes of 20

2012, Apr. 11 Tagged *Serpentine Die Cut 10¾*
Self-Adhesive

4653 A3545 (45c) **multicolored** ⓢ		1.15	.35
	P# block of 4, 6#+V	4.60	
	P# block of 10, 2 sets of 6#+V, + top label	11.50	
	Pane of 20	23.00	

See note after No. 1549.

TWENTIETH CENTURY POETS ⓢ

Joseph Brodsky (1940-96) — A3546

Gwendolyn Brooks (1917-2000) — A3547

William Carlos Williams (1883-1963) — A3548

Robert Hayden (1913-80) — A3549

Sylvia Plath (1932-63) — A3550

Elizabeth Bishop (1911-79) — A3551

Wallace Stevens (1879-1955) — A3552

Denise Levertov (1923-97) — A3553

E. E. Cummings (1894-1962) — A3554

Theodore Roethke (1908-63) — A3555

Designed by Derry Noyes. Printed by Ashton-Potter (USA) Ltd.

LITHOGRAPHED
Sheets of 160 in eight panes of 20
Serpentine Die Cut 10¾x11

2012, Apr. 21 Tagged
Self-Adhesive

4654 A3546 (45c) **multicolored**		2.00	.50
4655 A3547 (45c) **multicolored**		2.00	.50
4656 A3548 (45c) **multicolored**		2.00	.50
4657 A3549 (45c) **multicolored**		2.00	.50
4658 A3550 (45c) **multicolored**		2.00	.50
4659 A3551 (45c) **multicolored**		2.00	.50
4660 A3552 (45c) **multicolored**		2.00	.50
4661 A3553 (45c) **multicolored**		2.00	.50
4662 A3554 (45c) **multicolored**		2.00	.50
4663 A3555 (45c) **multicolored**		2.00	.50
a.	Block of 10, #4654-4663	20.00	
	P# block of 10, 6#+P	20.00	
	Pane of 20	40.00	
	Nos. 4654-4663 (10)	20.00	5.00

See note after No. 1549.

CIVIL WAR SESQUICENTENNIAL

Battle of New Orleans — A3556

Battle of Antietam — A3557

Designed by Phil Jordan. Printed by Ashton-Potter (USA) Ltd.

LITHOGRAPHED
Double-sided sheets of 72 in six panes of 12 (60 on one side, 12 on other side)

2012, Apr. 24 Tagged *Serpentine Die Cut 11*
Self-Adhesive

4664 A3556 (45c) **multicolored** ⓢ		1.10	.30
4665 A3557 (45c) **multicolored** ⓢ		1.10	.30
a.	Pair, #4664-4665	2.20	
	Pane of 12	13.25	

Uncut press sheets of Nos. 4664-4665 were made available for sale. See note after No. 2868.
See note after No. 1549.

DISTINGUISHED AMERICANS

José Ferrer (1912-92), Actor — A3558

Designed by Antonio Alcala. Printed by Ashton-Potter (USA) Ltd.

LITHOGRAPHED
Sheets of 160 in eight panes of 20
Serpentine Die Cut 10¾x11

2012, Apr. 26 Tagged
Self-Adhesive

4666 A3558 (45c) **multicolored** ⓢ		1.10	.25
	P# block of 4, 7#+P	4.40	
	Pane of 20	22.00	

See note after No. 1549.

LOUISIANA STATEHOOD BICENTENNIAL ⓢ

Sunset Over Flat Lake — A3559

Designed by Phil Jordan. Printed by Avery Dennison.

PHOTOGRAVURE
Sheets of 160 in eight panes of 20

2012, Apr. 30 Tagged *Serpentine Die Cut 11*
Self-Adhesive

4667 A3559 (45c) **multicolored**		1.10	.25
	P# block of 4, 5#+V	4.40	
	Pane of 20	22.00	

See note after No. 1549.

GREAT FILM DIRECTORS ⓢ

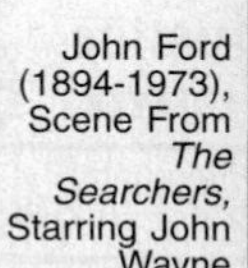

John Ford (1894-1973), Scene From *The Searchers,* Starring John Wayne A3560

Frank Capra (1897-1991), Scene From *It Happened One Night,* Starring Clark Gable and Claudette Colbert A3561

Billy Wilder (1906-2002), Scene From *Some Like It Hot,* Starring Marilyn Monroe A3562

John Huston (1906-87), Scene From *The Maltese Falcon,* Starring Humphrey Bogart A3563

Designed by Derry Noyes. Printed by Avery Dennison.

PHOTOGRAVURE
Sheets of 200 in 10 panes of 20

2012, May 23 Tagged *Serpentine Die Cut 10¾*
Self-Adhesive

4668 A3560 (45c) **multicolored**		1.10	.40
4669 A3561 (45c) **multicolored**		1.10	.40
4670 A3562 (45c) **multicolored**		1.10	.40
4671 A3563 (45c) **multicolored**		1.10	.40
a.	Block or horiz. strip of 4, #4668-4671	4.40	
	P# block of 4, 5#+V	4.40	
	P# block of 8, 2 sets of 5#+V, + top label	4.40	
	Pane of 20	22.00	

See note after No. 1549.

WILDLIFE

Bobcat — A3564

Designed by Carl T. Herrman. Printed by Ashton-Potter (USA) Ltd.

LITHOGRAPHED

Serpentine Die Cut 10 Vert.

2012, June 1 **Untagged**

Coil Stamp

Self-Adhesive

4672 A3564 1c **multicolored** Ⓢ .25 .25
Pair .25
P# strip of 5, #P1111, P2222 .80
P# single, #P1111, P2222 — .55
a. Dated "2015," *Feb. 21, 2015* .25 .25
Pair .25
P# strip of 5, #P1111 .75
P# single, #P1111 — .60

Microprinting is on bobcat's ear on No. 4672 and on the bobcat's leg on No. 4672a. See No. 4802. See note after No. 1549.

Flags Type of 2012

Designed by Howard E. Paine. Printed by Avery Dennison.

PHOTOGRAVURE

Serpentine Die Cut 11¼x10¾ on 3 Sides

2012, June 1 **Tagged**

Booklet Stamps

Self-Adhesive

Colored Dots in Stars

19¼mm From Lower Left to Lower Right Corners of Flag

4673 A3539 (45c) **multicolored** Ⓢ 1.10 .25
4674 A3540 (45c) **multicolored** Ⓢ 1.10 .25
4675 A3537 (45c) **multicolored** Ⓢ 1.10 .25
4676 A3538 (45c) **multicolored** Ⓢ 1.10 .25
a. Block of 4, #4673-4676 4.40
b. Booklet pane of 10, 3 each #4673-4674, 2 each #4675-4676 11.00

Nos. 4673 and No. 4675 have straight edge on left side only. Nos. 4674 and 4676 have straight edge on right side only. Nos. 4641-4648 each have a straight edge at top or bottom. The letters in the "USPS" microprinting on Nos. 4673-4676, found at the right side of the bottom white flag stripe, are printed in a distinct curve, with the tops of the middle letters, "SP," being below the tops of the outside letters, "U" and "S," and the letters can be difficult to distinguish against the shading on the stripe. The letters in the microprinting on Nos. 4641-4648, found in the same place on the stamp, are printed in a straight line, and are printed boldly, making them easily distinguishable from the shading. The lettering on Nos. 4673-4767 has a fuzzier, less distinct appearance under magnification than the lettering on Nos. 4641-4648, which is most evident in the year "2012."

See note after No. 1549.

CHARACTERS FROM DISNEY-PIXAR FILMS

Mail a Smile Ⓢ

Flik and Dot From *A Bug's Life* — A3565

Bob Parr and Dashiell Parr From *The Incredibles* — A3566

Nemo and Squirt From *Finding Nemo* — A3567

Jessie, Woody and Bullseye From *Toy Story 2* — A3568

Boo, Mike Wazowski and James P. "Sulley" Sullivan From *Monsters, Inc.* — A3569

Designed by William J. Gicker. Printed by Avery Dennison.

PHOTOGRAVURE

Sheets of 80 in four panes of 20

2012, June 1 **Tagged** ***Serpentine Die Cut 10½***

Self-Adhesive

4677 A3565 (45c) **multicolored** 1.20 .40
4678 A3566 (45c) **multicolored** 1.20 .40
4679 A3567 (45c) **multicolored** 1.20 .40
4680 A3568 (45c) **multicolored** 1.20 .40
4681 A3569 (45c) **multicolored** 1.20 .40
a. Horiz. strip of 5, #4677-4681 6.00
P# block of 10, 4#+V 12.00
Pane of 20 24.00

Adjacent horizontal or vertical stamps have selvage between the stamps. Plate block may contain top label.

Uncut press sheets of Nos. 4677-4681 were made available for sale. Values: cross-gutter block of 10 (four stamps from one side of the sheet and six stamps from the other side), $25; pairs with gutters between, $2.50 each. See note after No. 2868.

See note after No. 1549.

Aloha Shirts Type of 2012

Designed by Carl T. Herrman. Printed by Ashton-Potter (USA) Ltd.

LITHOGRAPHED

Tagged

Serpentine Die Cut 11¼x10¾ on 3 Sides

2012, June 2

Booklet Stamps

Self-Adhesive

4682 A3506 32c **multicolored** Ⓢ 4.50 .30
4683 A3508 32c **multicolored** Ⓢ 4.50 .30
4684 A3510 32c **multicolored** Ⓢ 4.50 .30
4685 A3507 32c **multicolored** Ⓢ 4.50 .30
4686 A3509 32c **multicolored** Ⓢ 4.50 .30
a. Vert. strip of 5, #4682-4686 22.50
b. Booklet pane of 10, 2 each #4682-4686 45.00

Stamps in No. 4686a are not adjacent, as a row of selvage is between stamps two and three.

See note after No. 1549.

BICYCLING Ⓢ

Child on Bicycle with Training Wheels A3570

Commuter on Bicycle with Panniers A3571

Road Racer A3572

BMX Rider A3573

Designed by Phil Jordan. Printed by Ashton-Potter (USA) Ltd.

LITHOGRAPHED

Sheets of 120 in six panes of 20

2012, June 7 **Tagged** ***Serpentine Die Cut 10¾***

Self-Adhesive

4687 A3570 (45c) **multicolored** 1.10 .35
4688 A3571 (45c) **multicolored** 1.10 .35
4689 A3572 (45c) **multicolored** 1.10 .35
4690 A3573 (45c) **multicolored** 1.10 .35
a. Horiz. strip of 4, #4687-4690 4.40
P# block of 8, 5#+P 8.00
Pane of 20 20.00

Uncut press sheets of Nos. 4687-4690 were made available for sale. Values: cross-gutter block of 8, $12.50; pairs with gutters between, $2.50 each. See note after No. 2868.

See note after No. 1549.

GIRL SCOUTS OF AMERICA, CENT.

Girl Scouts — A3574

Designed by Derry Noyes. Printed by Banknote Corporation of America for Sennett Security Products.

LITHOGRAPHED

Sheets of 180 in nine panes of 20

2012, June 9 **Tagged** ***Serpentine Die Cut 10¾***

Self-Adhesive

4691 A3574 (45c) **multicolored** 1.10 .25
P# block of 4, 6#+S 4.40
Pane of 20 22.00
a. Die cutting omitted, pair —

Uncut press sheets of No. 4691 were made available for sale. Values: cross-gutter block of 4, $10; pairs with gutters between, $2.50 each. See note after No. 2868.

MUSICIANS (S)

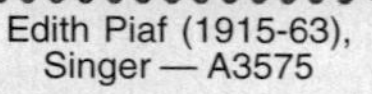

Edith Piaf (1915-63), Singer — A3575

Miles Davis (1926-91), Jazz Trumpet Player — A3576

Designed by Greg Breeding. Printed by Avery Dennison.

PHOTOGRAVURE

Sheets of 80 in four panes of 20

Serpentine Die Cut 10¾x11

2012, June 12 **Tagged**

Self-Adhesive

4692	A3575 (45c) **multicolored**	1.20	.30
4693	A3576 (45c) **multicolored**	1.20	.30
a.	Pair, #4692-4693	2.40	
	P# block of 5, 6#+V	6.00	
	P# block of 10, 6#+V, + top label	12.00	
	Pane of 20	24.00	

See France Nos. 4256-4257.

Uncut press sheets of Nos. 4692-4693 were made available for sale. Values: cross-gutter block of 10 (five stamps from each side of the sheet), $15; pairs with gutters between, $2.50 each. See note after No. 2868.

See note after No. 1549.

Imperforate Uncut Press Sheets

Beginning with Nos. 4694-4697, the U.S. Postal Service made available for sale imperforate uncut press sheets of selected commemorative and definitive issues. These sheets are noted in footnotes following each issue, and imperforate singles, small panes and booklets are listed and valued in the main listings. Imperforate pairs are valued at twice the value of imperforate singles. Like the perforated and die cut uncut press sheets, the imperforate uncut press sheets generally contain cross-gutter blocks and pairs with gutters between. Other collectible pair or block formats might also appear on selected sheets. The cross-gutter blocks, plus blocks and pairs with gutters between, are valued in the footnotes. The other possible formats not noted sell for a premium, but they are not listed or valued herein.

See note before No. 2869 for descriptions and illustrations of typical press-sheet multiples.

MAJOR LEAGUE BASEBALL ALL-STARS (S)

Ted Williams (1918-2002) A3577

Larry Doby (1923-2003) A3578

Willie Stargell (1940-2001) A3579

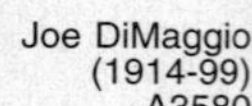

Joe DiMaggio (1914-99) A3580

Designed by Phil Jordan. Printed by Avery Dennison.

PHOTOGRAVURE

Sheets of 120 in six panes of 20

Serpentine Die Cut 10¾x11

2012, July 20 **Tagged**

Self-Adhesive

4694	A3577 (45c) **multicolored**	1.10	.30
	P# block of 4, 5#+V	4.40	
	P# block of 8, 2 sets of 5#+V, + top panel	8.80	
	Pane of 20	22.00	
a.	Imperforate	2.50	—
	Pane of 20	50.00	
4695	A3578 (45c) **multicolored**	1.10	.30
	P# block of 4, 5#+V	4.40	
	P# block of 8, 2 sets of 5#+V, + top panel	8.80	
	Pane of 20	22.00	
a.	Imperforate	2.50	—
	Pane of 20	50.00	
4696	A3579 (45c) **multicolored**	1.10	.30
	P# block of 4, 5#+V	4.40	
	P# block of 8, 2 sets of 5#+V, + top panel	8.80	
	Pane of 20	22.00	
a.	Imperforate	2.50	—
	Pane of 20	50.00	
4697	A3580 (45c) **multicolored**	1.10	.30
	P# block of 4, 5#+V	4.40	
	P# block of 8, 2 sets of 5#+V, + top panel	8.80	
	Pane of 20	22.00	
a.	Imperforate	2.50	—
	Pane of 20	50.00	
b.	Horiz. strip or block of 4, #4694-4697	4.40	
	P# block of 4, 5#+V	4.40	
	P# block of 8, 2 sets of 5#+V, + top panel	8.80	
	Pane of 20, 5 each #4694-4697	22.00	
c.	Imperf. horiz. strip or block of 4, #4694a-4697a	14.00	—
	Pane of 20, 5 each #4694a-4697a	70.00	

Panes containing 20 of the same stamp were issued on July 21 in Boston, MA (for No. 4694), Cleveland, OH (for No. 4695), Pittsburgh, PA (for No. 4696) and New York, NY (for No. 4697). Imperforate uncut press sheets of these single stamps were also made available for sale on that day. Imperforate uncut press sheets containing the four different stamps were also made available for sale. These press sheets sold out prior to the day of issue. Values: cross-gutter block of 8 (from sheet containing all four stamps), $40; cross-gutter blocks of 4 (from sheets containing identical stamps), $15 each; pairs with gutters between, $6 each. See note after No. 4693.

See note after No. 1549.

INNOVATIVE CHOREOGRAPHERS

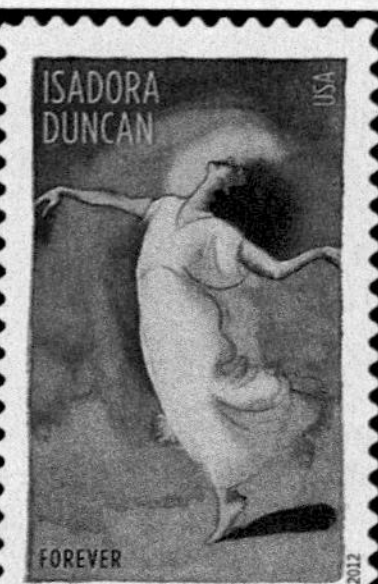

Isadora Duncan (1877-1927) — A3581

José Limón (1908-72) — A3582

Katherine Dunham (1909-2006) — A3583

Bob Fosse (1927-87) — A3584

Designed by Ethel Kessler. Printed by Banknote Corporation of America for Sennett Security Products.

LITHOGRAPHED

Sheets of 180 in nine panes of 20

Serpentine Die Cut 10¾x11

2012, July 28 **Tagged**

Self-Adhesive

4698	A3581 (45c) **multicolored**	1.10	.35
4699	A3582 (45c) **multicolored**	1.10	.35
4700	A3583 (45c) **multicolored**	1.10	.35
4701	A3584 (45c) **multicolored**	1.10	.35
a.	Vert. strip of 4, #4698-4701	4.40	
	P# block of 8, 2 sets of P#, 6#+S	8.80	
	Pane of 20	22.00	

Uncut press sheets of Nos. 4698-4701 were made available for sale. Values: cross-gutter block of 16, $24; pairs with gutters between, $2.50 each. Panes that are vertically adjacent are tete-beche in relation to each other. See note after No. 2868.

EDGAR RICE BURROUGHS

Edgar Rice Burroughs (1875-1950), Writer, and Tarzan — A3585

Designed by Phil Jordan. Printed by Banknote Corporation of America for Sennett Security Products.

LITHOGRAPHED

Sheets of 180 in nine panes of 20

2012, Aug. 17 **Tagged** ***Serpentine Die Cut 10¾***

Self-Adhesive

4702	A3585 (45c) **multicolored**	1.10	.25
	P# block of 4, 6#+S	4.40	
	Pane of 20	22.00	

WAR OF 1812 BICENTENNIAL (S)

Painting of U.S.S. Constitution, by Michele Felice Corné A3586

Designed by Greg Breeding. Printed by Avery Dennison.

PHOTOGRAVURE

Sheets of 100 in five panes of 20

Serpentine Die Cut 10¾x10½

2012, Aug. 18 **Tagged**

Self-Adhesive

4703	A3586 (45c) **multicolored**	1.75	.25
	Pane of 20	30.00	
a.	Imperforate	2.75	—
	Pane of 20	55.00	

Die-cut and imperforate uncut press sheets of No. 4703 were made available for sale. Values: pairs with gutters between, $4.25 each. See note after No. 2868.

See note after No. 1549.

Purple Heart and Ribbon — A3587

Designed by Jennifer Arnold. Printed by Avery Dennison or CCL Label, Inc.

PHOTOGRAVURE

Sheets of 420 in 21 panes of 20

2012, Sept. 4 Tagged *Serpentine Die Cut 11*

Self-Adhesive

4704 A3587 (45c) **multicolored** Ⓢ 1.10 .25
P# block of 4, 6#+V or C 4.40
Pane of 20 22.00
a. Imperforate 2.50 —
Pane of 20 45.00
b. Dated "2014," *Oct. 11, 2014* Ⓢ 1.10 .25
P# block of 4, 6#+C 4.40
Pane of 20 22.00

Compare with Type A3458. See No. 5035.

Imperforate partial uncut press sheets of three vertical panes of No. 4704 were made available for sale. Values: vert. pair with horiz. gutter, $4.50. See note after No. 4693.

No. 4704b sold for 49c on day of issue.

See note after No. 1549.

LITERARY ARTS

O. Henry (William S. Porter) (1862-1910), New York City Buildings and Elevated Trains A3588

Designed by Ethel Kessler. Printed by Avery Dennison.

PHOTOGRAVURE

Sheets of 160 in eight panes of 20

2012, Sept. 11 Tagged *Serpentine Die Cut 11*

Self-Adhesive

4705 A3588 (45c) **multicolored** Ⓢ 1.10 .25
P# block of 4, 5#+V 4.40
Pane of 20 22.00

Uncut press sheets of No. 4705 were made available for sale. Values: cross-gutter block of 4, $10; pairs with gutters between, $2.50 each. See note after No. 2868.

See note after No. 1549.

Flags Type of 2012

Designed by Howard E. Paine. Printed by Ashton-Potter (USA) Ltd.

LITHOGRAPHED

Serpentine Die Cut 11¼x10¾ on 2, 3 or 4 Sides

2012, Sept. 22 Tagged

Booklet Stamps
Self-Adhesive
Colored Dots in Stars
18½mm From Lower Left to Lower Right Corners of Flag
Thin Paper

4706 A3539 (45c) **multicolored** Ⓢ 1.10 .25
4707 A3540 (45c) **multicolored** Ⓢ 1.10 .25
4708 A3537 (45c) **multicolored** Ⓢ 1.10 .25
4709 A3538 (45c) **multicolored** Ⓢ 1.10 .25
a. Block or strip of 4, #4706-4709 4.40
b. Booklet pane of 18, 5 each #4706-4707, 4 each #4708-4709 20.00
Nos. 4706-4709 (4) 4.40 1.00

The overall-tagged paper used for Nos. 4706-4709 is glossier than that used on Nos. 4641-4644. The blue canton of the flag on Nos. 4706-4709 is made up of blue and red inks, similar to Nos. 4641-4644.

See note after No. 1549.

EARTHSCAPES

EARTHSCAPES

A3589

Designed by Howard E. Paine. Printed by Banknote Corporation of America for Sennett Security Products.

No. 4710: a, Glacier and icebergs. b, Volcanic crater. c, Geothermal spring. d, Butte in early morning fog. e, Inland marsh. f, Salt evaporation ponds. g, Log rafts on way to sawmill. h, Center-pivot irrigation. i, Cherry orchard. j, Cranberry harvest. k, Residential subdivision. l, Barge fleeting. m, Railroad roundhouse. n, Skyscraper apartments. o, Highway interchange.

LITHOGRAPHED

Sheets of 135 in nine panes of 15

2012, Oct. 1 Tagged *Serpentine Die Cut 10¾*

Self-Adhesive

4710 A3589 Pane of 15 25.00
a.-o. (45c) Any single 1.65 .50
p. Imperforate pane of 15 75.00

Imperforate uncut press sheets of No. 4710 were made available for sale. Values: pairs with gutters between, $8.50 each. Panes that are vertically adjacent are tete-beche in relation to each other. See note after No. 4693.

CHRISTMAS

Holy Family and Donkey — A3590

Reindeer in Flight, Moon — A3591

Santa Claus and Sleigh — A3592

Reindeer Over Roof — A3593

Snow-covered Buildings — A3594

Designed by Greg Breeding (#4711), Howard E. Paine. Printed by Banknote Corporation of America for Sennett Security Products (#4711), Ashton-Potter (USA) Ltd. (#4712-4715).

LITHOGRAPHED

Serpentine Die Cut 11 on 2 or 3 Sides

2012 Tagged

Booklet Stamps
Self-Adhesive

4711 A3590 (45c) **multicolored,** "2012" year date, *Oct. 10* 1.10 .25
a. Booklet pane of 20 22.00
b. Imperforate 1.75 —
c. Imperforate booklet pane of 20 35.00

Serpentine Die Cut 11x10¾ on 2 or 3 sides

4712 A3591 (45c) **multicolored,** *Oct. 13* Ⓢ 1.10 .25
4713 A3592 (45c) **multicolored,** *Oct. 13* Ⓢ 1.10 .25
4714 A3593 (45c) **multicolored,** *Oct. 13* Ⓢ 1.10 .25
4715 A3594 (45c) **multicolored,** *Oct. 13* Ⓢ 1.10 .25
a. Block of 4, #4712-4715 4.40
b. Booklet pane of 20, 5 each #4712-4715 22.00
c. Imperforate block of 4 8.00 —
d. Imperforate booklet pane of 20 40.00
Nos. 4711-4715 (5) 4.50 1.25

No. 4711a is a double-sided booklet with 12 stamps on one side and eight stamps plus a label that serves as a booklet cover on the other side. No. 4715b is a double-sided booklet with 12 stamps on one side (3 each of Nos. 4712-4715) and eight stamps (2 each of Nos. 4712-4715) plus a label that serves as a booklet cover on the other side.

Imperforate uncut press sheets of 10 booklet panes of Nos. 4711 and 4712-4715 were made available for sale, along with cut-down sheets containing three imperforate panes. Values: cross-gutter blocks of 4 of Nos. 4711 or 4712-4715 with marginal markings, $10 each; block of Nos. 4712-4715 with vert. gutter between, $10; pairs of Nos. 4711 or 4712-4715 with gutters between, $4.25 each. See note after No. 4693.

See note after No. 1549.

See No. 4813.

LADY BIRD JOHNSON Ⓢ

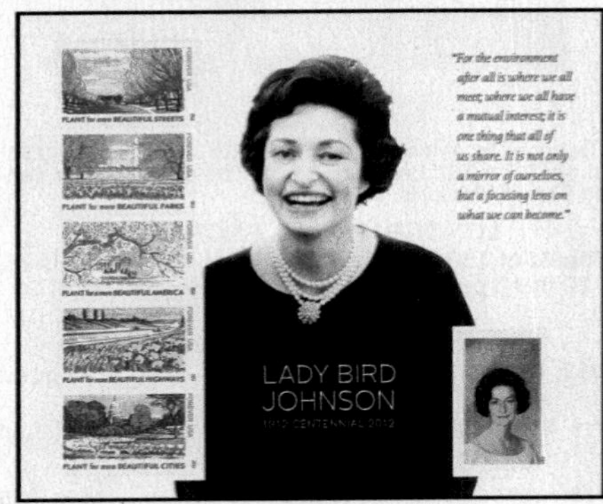

A3595

Designed by Antonio Alcalá. Printed by Ashton-Potter (USA) Ltd.

No. 4716: a, Blooming crab apples lining avenue (Plant for more Beautiful Streets). b, Washington Monument, Potomac River and daffodils (Plant for more Beautiful Parks). c, Jefferson Memorial, Tidal Basin and cherry blossoms (Plant for a more Beautiful America). d, Poppies and lupines along highway (Plant for more Beautiful Highways). e, Capitol, azaleas and tulips (Plant for more Beautiful Cities). f, Lady Bird Johnson (1912-2007), First Lady, vert.

LITHOGRAPHED

Sheets of 96 in 16 panes of six

2012, Nov. 30 Tagged *Serpentine Die Cut 10¾*

Self-Adhesive

4716 A3595 Pane of 6 6.60
a.-f. (45c) Any single 1.10 .40
g. Imperforate pane of 6 25.00

Imperforate uncut press sheets of No. 4716 were made available for sale. Values: vert. pairs with horiz. gutters, $6.50 each. See note after No. 4693.

See note after No. 1549.

WAVES OF COLOR

A3596

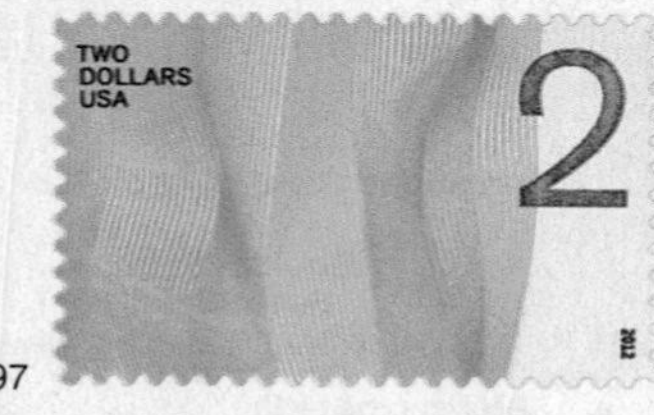

A3597

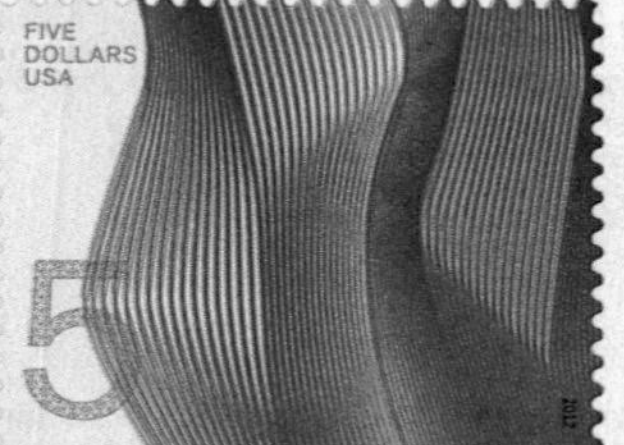

A3598

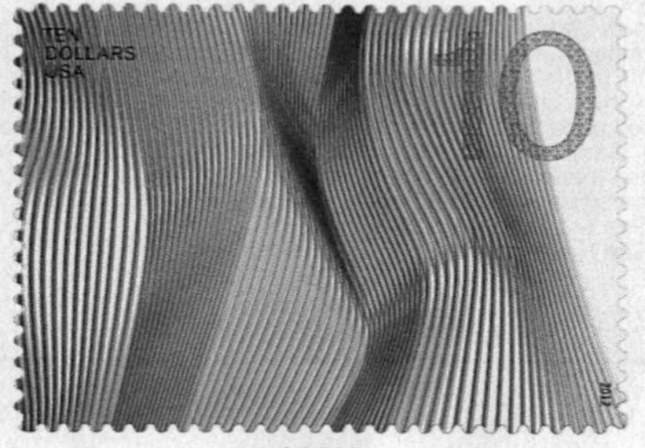

A3599

Designed by Antonio Alcalá. Printed by Ashton-Potter (USA) Ltd. (#4717-4718), Banknote Corporation of America for Sennett Security Products (#4719-4720).

LITHOGRAPHED & ENGRAVED

Sheets of 150 in 15 panes of 10 (#4717), Sheets of 120 in 12 panes of 10 (#4718, 4719), Sheets of 90 in nine panes of 10 (#4720)

Serpentine Die Cut 11, 10¾ (#4719)

2012, Dec. 1 **Tagged**

Self-Adhesive

4717 A3596 $1 **multicolored** Ⓢ 3.25 .50
P# block of 4, 7#+P 12.00
Pane of 10 30.00
4718 A3597 $2 **multicolored** Ⓢ 4.50 1.25
P# block of 4, 7#+P 18.00
Pane of 10 45.00
4719 A3598 $5 **multicolored** 8.75 2.50
P# block of 4, 8#+S 35.00
Pane of 10 87.50
4720 A3599 $10 **multicolored** 17.50 9.00
P# block of 4, 8#+S 70.00
Pane of 10 175.00
Nos. 4717-4720 (4) 34.00 13.25

Adjacent horizontal or vertical stamps have selvage between the stamps. Plate blocks have sheet margins on the top or bottom and both sides.

See note after No. 1549.

EMANCIPATION PROCLAMATION, 150th ANNIV.

Ⓢ

A3600

Designed by Gail Anderson. Printed by Avery Dennison.

PHOTOGRAVURE

Sheets of 200 in 10 panes of 20

2013, Jan. 1 **Tagged** ***Serpentine Die Cut 11***

Self-Adhesive

4721 A3600 (45c) **multicolored** 1.10 .25
P# block of 4, 4#+V 4.40
P# block of 8, 2 sets of 4#+V + side panel 8.80
Pane of 20 22.00
a. Imperforate 2.00 —
Pane of 20 40.00

Die cut and imperforate uncut press sheets of No. 4721 were made available for sale. Values: cross-gutter block of 4, $12.50; pairs with gutters between, $4.50 each. See note after No. 4693.

See note after No. 1549.

KALEIDOSCOPE FLOWERS

A3601

A3602

A3603

A3604

Designed by Antonio Alcalá. Printed by Banknote Corporation of America for Sennett Security Products.

LITHOGRAPHED

Serpentine Die Cut 11 Vert.

2013, Jan. 14 **Tagged**

Coil Stamps
Self-Adhesive
Color of Large Outer Leaves

4722 A3601 46c **yellow orange** 1.25 .25
4723 A3602 46c **yellow green** 1.25 .25
4724 A3603 46c **red violet** 1.25 .25
4725 A3604 46c **red** 1.25 .25
a. Strip of 4, #4722-4725 5.00
P# strip of 5, 2 #4722, 1 each #4723-4725, #S11111 7.00
P# strip of 9, 3# 4724, 2 each #4722-4723, 4725, #S11111 12.50
P# single, #S1111 (#4724) — 2.75
Nos. 4722-4725 (4) 5.00 1.00

CHINESE NEW YEAR

Year of the Snake A3605

Designed by Ethel Kessler. Printed by Avery Dennison.

PHOTOGRAVURE

Sheets of 108 in nine panes of 12

2013, Jan. 16 **Tagged** ***Serpentine Die Cut 11***

Self-Adhesive

4726 A3605 (45c) **multicolored** Ⓢ 1.10 .25
Pane of 12 13.25
a. Imperforate 2.00 —
Pane of 12 24.00

Die cut and imperforate uncut press sheets of No. 4726 were made available for sale. Values: cross-gutter block of 4, $12.50; pairs with gutters between, $4.75 each. See note after No. 4693.

See note after No. 1549.

APPLES

Northern Spy Apple — A3606

Golden Delicious Apple — A3607

Granny Smith Apple — A3608

Baldwin Apple — A3609

Designed by Derry Noyes. Printed by Banknote Corporation of America for Sennett Security Products.

LITHOGRAPHED

Sheets of 200 in 10 panes of 20

Serpentine Die Cut 11¼x10¾

2013, Jan. 17 **Tagged**

Self-Adhesive

4727 A3606 33c **multicolored** 1.00 .25
4728 A3607 33c **multicolored** 1.00 .25
4729 A3608 33c **multicolored** 1.00 .25
4730 A3609 33c **multicolored** 1.00 .25
a. Block or strip of 4, #4727-4730 4.00
P# block of 4, 5#+S 4.00
Pane of 20 20.00
b. Imperforate block or strip of 4 6.50 —
Pane of 20 32.50

Die cut and imperforate uncut press sheets of Nos. 4727-4730 were made available for sale. Values: cross gutter-block of 8, $15; pairs with gutters between, $3 each. See note after No. 4693.

Coil Stamps

Serpentine Die Cut 11 Vert.

4731 A3609 33c **multicolored** 1.25 .25
4732 A3606 33c **multicolored** 1.25 .25
4733 A3607 33c **multicolored** 1.25 .25
4734 A3608 33c **multicolored** 1.25 .25
a. Strip of 4, #4731-4734 5.00
P# strip of 5, 2 #4731, 1 each #4732-4734, #S11111 8.00
P# strip of 9, 3 #4733, 2 each #4731-4732, 4734, #S11111 13.50
P# single #S1111 (#4733) — 2.75
Nos. 4727-4734 (8) 9.00 2.00

Wedding Cake Type of 2009

Designed by Ethel Kessler. Printed by Banknote Corporation of America for Sennett Security Products.

LITHOGRAPHED

Sheets of 200 in 10 panes of 20

2013, Jan. 18 **Tagged** ***Serpentine Die Cut 10¾***

Self-Adhesive

4735 A3344 66c **multicolored** 1.40 .25
P# block of 4, 6#+S 5.60
Pane of 20 28.00
a. Imperforate 3.50 —
Pane of 20 70.00

Die cut and imperforate uncut press sheets of No. 4735 were made available for sale. Values: cross-gutter block of 4, $17.50; pairs with gutters between, $8.50 each. See note after No. 4693.

SPICEBUSH SWALLOWTAIL BUTTERFLY (S)

A3610

Designed by Derry Noyes. Printed by Avery Dennison.

PHOTOGRAVURE

Sheets of 200 in 10 panes of 20

2013, Jan. 23 Tagged ***Serpentine Die Cut 10¾***

Self-Adhesive

4736	A3610 66c **multicolored**	1.40	.25
	P# block of 4, 7#+V	5.60	
	Pane of 20	28.00	
a.	Imperforate	3.00	—
	Pane of 20	60.00	

Die cut and imperforate uncut press sheets of No. 4736 were made available for sale. Values: cross-gutter block of 4, $15; pairs with gutters between, $5.50 each. See note after No. 4693.

See note after No. 1549.

TUFTED PUFFINS (S)

A3611

Designed by Derry Noyes. Printed by Ashton-Potter (USA) Ltd.

LITHOGRAPHED

Sheets of 120 in six panes of 20

Serpentine Die Cut 11¼x10¾

2013, Jan. 23 Tagged

"2013" in Orange Red
Solid Color in "Tufted Puffins" and "86"
Self-Adhesive

4737	A3611 86c **multicolored**	1.80	.35
	P# block of 4, 5#+P	7.25	
	Pane of 20	36.00	
b.	Imperforate	4.00	—
	Pane of 20	80.00	

Die cut and imperforate uncut press sheets of No. 4737 were made available for sale. Values: cross-gutter block of 4, $22.50; pairs with gutters between, $9 each. See note after No. 4693.

"2013" in Black
With Dots in "Tufted Puffins" and "86"

4737A	A3611 86c **multicolored** (S)	2.50	.35
	P# block of 4, 4#+P	8.00	
	Pane of 20	40.00	

See note after No. 1549.

AMERICAN LANDMARKS ISSUE

Arlington Green Bridge, Vermont A3612

Grand Central Terminal, New York City — A3613

Designed by Derry Noyes (#4738), Phil Jordan (#4739). Printed by Avery Dennison.

PHOTOGRAVURE

Sheets of 80 in eight panes of 10 (#4738), Sheets of 100 in ten panes of 10 (#4739)

2013 Tagged ***Serpentine Die Cut 10¾x10½***

Self-Adhesive

4738	A3612 $5.60 **multicolored**, *Jan. 25* (S)	11.00	6.25
	P# block of 4, 4#+V	44.00	
	Pane of 10	110.00	
4739	A3613 $19.95 **multicolored**, *Feb. 1*	40.00	21.00
	P# block of 4, 4#+V	160.00	
	Pane of 10	400.00	

See note after No. 1549.

Earth — A3614

Designed by Greg Breeding. Printed by Avery Dennison.

PHOTOGRAVURE

Sheets of 80 in four panes of 20

2013, Jan. 28 Tagged ***Serpentine Die Cut***

Self-Adhesive

4740	A3614 ($1.10) **multicolored** (S)	2.25	.50
	P# block of 4, 6#+V	9.00	
	P# block of 8, 2 sets of 6#+V, + top label	18.00	
	Pane of 20	45.00	
a.	Imperforate	5.00	—
	Pane of 20	100.00	

Unused values are for stamps with surrounding selvage. Adjacent stamps are separated by rouletting.

Die cut and imperforate uncut press sheets of No. 4740 were made available for sale. Values: cross-gutter block of 4, $16.50; pairs with gutters between, $7 each. See note after No. 4693.

See note after No. 1549.

LOVE

Envelope With Wax Seal — A3615

Designed by Louise Fili. Printed by Avery Dennison.

PHOTOGRAVURE

Sheets of 120 in six panes of 20

2013, Jan. 30 Tagged ***Serpentine Die Cut 10¾***

Self-Adhesive

4741	A3615 (46c) **multicolored** (S)	1.10	.25
	P# block of 4, 5#+V	4.40	
	Pane of 20	22.00	
a.	Imperforate	2.00	—
	Pane of 20	40.00	

Die cut and imperforate uncut press sheets of No. 4741 were made available for sale. Values: cross-gutter block of 4, $11; pairs with gutters between, $4.50 each. See note after No. 4693.

See note after No. 1549.

ROSA PARKS (S)

Parks (1913-2005), Civil Rights Pioneer — A3616

Designed by Derry Noyes. Printed by Avery Dennison.

PHOTOGRAVURE

Sheets of 200 in 10 panes of 20

2013, Feb. 4 Tagged ***Serpentine Die Cut 10¾***

Self-Adhesive

4742	A3616 (46c) **multicolored**	1.10	.25
	P# block of 4, 5#+V	4.40	
	P# block of 8, 2 sets of 5#+V + side panel	8.80	
	Pane of 20	22.00	
a.	Imperforate	2.00	—
	Pane of 20	40.00	

Die cut and imperforate uncut press sheets of No. 4742 were made available for sale. Values: cross-gutter block of 4, $12; pairs with gutters between, $5 each. See note after No. 4693.

See note after No. 1549.

MUSCLE CARS (S)

1969 Dodge Charger Daytona A3617

1966 Pontiac GTO — A3618

1967 Ford Mustang Shelby GT 500 — A3619

1970 Chevrolet Chevelle SS — A3620

1970 Plymouth Hemi Barracuda A3621

Designed by Carl T. Herrman. Printed by Avery Dennison.

PHOTOGRAVURE
Sheets of 200 in 10 panes of 20

2013, Feb. 22 Tagged *Serpentine Die Cut 10¾*
Self-Adhesive

4743 A3617 (46c) **multicolored** 1.10 .30
4744 A3618 (46c) **multicolored** 1.10 .30
4745 A3619 (46c) **multicolored** 1.10 .30
4746 A3620 (46c) **multicolored** 1.10 .30
4747 A3621 (46c) **multicolored** 1.10 .30
a. Vert. strip of 5, #4743-4747 5.50
Vert. P# block of 10, 5# + V 11.00
Horiz. P# block of 8, 2 sets of 5# + V 8.80
Pane of 20 22.00
b. Imperforate vert. strip of 5 10.00 —
Pane of 20 40.00
Nos. 4743-4747 (5) 5.50 1.50

Die cut and imperforate uncut press sheets of Nos. 4743-4747 were made available for sale. Values: cross-gutter block of 10, $27.50; pairs with gutters between, $4.75 each. See note after No. 4693.

See note after No. 1549.

MODERN ART IN AMERICA Ⓢ

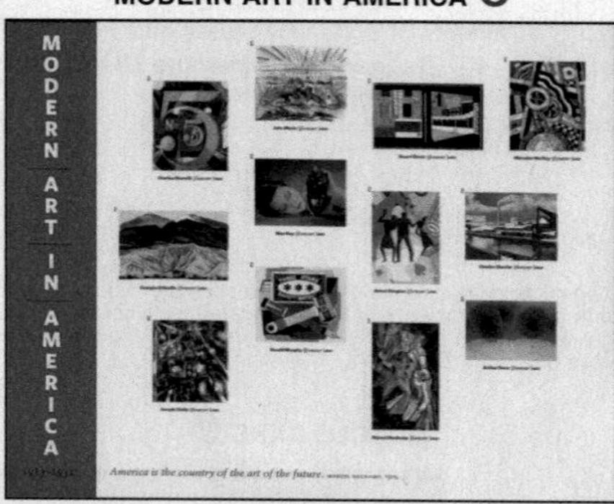

A3622

Designed by Margaret Bauer. Printed by Avery Dennison.

No. 4748: a, I Saw the Figure 5 in Gold, by Charles Demuth (37x51mm). b, Sunset, Maine Coast, by John Marin (43x43mm). c, House and Street, by Stuart Davis (51x41mm). d, Painting, Number 5, by Marsden Hartley (37x51mm). e, Black Mesa Landscape, New Mexico/Out Back of Marie's II, by Georgia O'Keeffe (51x41mm). f, Noire et Blanche, by Man Ray (43x41mm). g, The Prodigal Son, by Aaron Douglas (34x51mm). h, American Landscape, by Charles Sheeler (43x41mm). i, Brooklyn Bridge, by Joseph Stella (38x47mm). j, Razor, by Gerald Murphy (43x43mm). k, Nude Descending a Staircase, No. 2, by Marcel Duchamp (34x58mm). l, Fog Horns, by Arthur Dove (43x37mm).

PHOTOGRAVURE
Sheets of 48 in four panes of 12

2013, Mar. 7 Tagged *Serpentine Die Cut 10½*
Self-Adhesive

4748 A3622 Pane of 12 13.25
a.-l. (46c) Any single 1.10 .50
m. Imperforate pane of 12 70.00

Armory Show, cent.

Die cut and imperforate uncut press sheets of No. 4748 were made available for sale. See note after No. 4693.

See note after No. 1549.

Patriotic Star — A3623

Designed by Greg Breeding. Printed by Banknote Corporation of America for Sennett Security Products.

LITHOGRAPHED
Serpentine Die Cut 10¾ Vert.

2013, Mar. 19 Tagged
Coil Stamp
Self-Adhesive

4749 A3623 46c **multicolored** 1.10 .25
Pair 2.20
P# strip of 5, #S111 6.50
P# single, #S111 — 2.75

LA FLORIDA Ⓢ

A3624 A3625

A3626 A3627

Designed by Ethel Kessler. Printed by Avery Dennison.

PHOTOGRAVURE
Sheets of 160 in 10 panes of 16

2013, Apr. 3 Tagged *Serpentine Die Cut 10½*
Self-Adhesive

4750 A3624 (46c) **multicolored** 1.10 .25
4751 A3625 (46c) **multicolored** 1.10 .25
4752 A3626 (46c) **multicolored** 1.10 .25
4753 A3627 (46c) **multicolored** 1.10 .25
a. Block of 4, #4750-4753 4.40
P# block of 4, 9#+V 4.40
Pane of 16 17.50
b. Imperforate block of 4 10.00 —
Pane of 16 40.00
Nos. 4750-4753 (4) 4.40 1.00

Naming of Florida, 500th anniv.

Die cut and imperforate uncut press sheets of Nos. 4750-4753 were made available for sale. Values: cross-gutter block of 4, $15; pairs with gutters between, $5.50 each. See note after No. 4693.

See note after No. 1549.

VINTAGE SEED PACKETS Ⓢ

Phlox — A3628

Calendula — A3629

Digitalis — A3630

Linum — A3631

Alyssum — A3632

Zinnias — A3633

Pinks — A3634

Cosmos — A3635

Aster — A3636

Primrose — A3637

Designed by Antonio Alcalá. Printed by Avery Dennison.

PHOTOGRAVURE
Serpentine Die Cut 10¾ on 2 or 3 Sides

2013, Apr. 5 Tagged
Booklet Stamps
Self-Adhesive

4754 A3628 (46c) **multicolored** 2.50 .25
4755 A3629 (46c) **multicolored** 2.50 .25
4756 A3630 (46c) **multicolored** 2.50 .25
4757 A3631 (46c) **multicolored** 2.50 .25
4758 A3632 (46c) **multicolored** 2.50 .25
4759 A3633 (46c) **multicolored** 2.50 .25
4760 A3634 (46c) **multicolored** 2.50 .25
4761 A3635 (46c) **multicolored** 2.50 .25
4762 A3636 (46c) **multicolored** 2.50 .25
4763 A3637 (46c) **multicolored** 2.50 .25
a. Block of 10, #4754-4763 25.00
b. Booklet pane of 20, 2 each #4754-4763 50.00
Nos. 4754-4763 (10) 25.00 2.50

No. 4763b is a double-sided booklet pane with 12 stamps on one side (2 each #4754, 4759, 1 each #4755-4758, 4760-4763), and eight stamps (1 each #4755-4758, 4760-4763) plus label (booklet cover) on the other side.

See note after No. 1549.

WEDDING FLOWERS

Flowers — A3638

Flowers and "Yes I Do" — A3639

Designed by Michael Osborne. Printed by Banknote Corporation of America for Sennett Security Products (#4764), Ashton-Potter (USA) Ltd. (#4765).

LITHOGRAPHED

Sheets of 160 in eight panes of 20 (#4764), Sheets of 180 in nine panes of 20 (#4765)

2013, Apr. 11 Tagged *Serpentine Die Cut 10¾*
Self-Adhesive

4764 A3638 (46c) **multicolored** 1.10 .25
P# block of 4, 9#+S 4.40
Pane of 20 22.00
a. Dated "2014" 1.10 .25
P# block of 4, 9#+S 4.40
Pane of 20 22.00
b. Imperforate 2.50 —
Pane of 20 50.00
4765 A3639 66c **multicolored** ⓢ 1.40 .30
P# block of 4, 4#+P 5.60
Pane of 20 28.00
a. Imperforate 3.00 —
Pane of 20 60.00

Die cut and imperforate uncut press sheets of Nos. 4764 and 4765 were made available for sale. Values: No. 4764 cross-gutter block of 4, $12; No. 4765 cross-gutter block of 4, $14; No. 4764 pairs with gutters between, $5.50 each; No. 4765 pairs with gutters between, $6.50 each. See note after No. 4693.

See note after No. 1549.

No. 4764a was issued 5/2/14, and sold for 49c on day of issue.

See No. 4881.

Flag in Autumn — A3640

Flag in Winter — A3641

Flag in Spring — A3642

Flag in Summer — A3643

Designed by Phil Jordan. Printed by Avery Dennison (#4766-4769), Ashton-Potter (USA) Ltd. (#4770-4773, 4778-4781), Banknote Corporation of America for Sennett Security Products (#4774-4777, 4782-4785).

PHOTOGRAVURE (#4766-4769), LITHOGRAPHED (#4770-4785)

2013 Tagged *Serpentine Die Cut 8½ Vert.*
Coil Stamps
Self-Adhesive

4766 A3640 (46c) **multicolored,** *May 3* ⓢ 2.25 .25
4767 A3641 (46c) **multicolored,** *May 3* ⓢ 2.25 .25
4768 A3642 (46c) **multicolored,** *May 3* ⓢ 2.25 .25
4769 A3643 (46c) **multicolored,** *May 3* ⓢ 2.25 .25
a. Strip of 4, #4766-4769 9.00
P# strip of 5, 2 #4766, 1 each #4767-4769, #V1111 15.00
P# strip of 9, 3# 4768, 2 each #4766-4767, 4769, #V1111 20.00
P# single, #V1111 (#4768) — 2.75

Serpentine Die Cut 9½ Vert.

4770 A3640 (46c) **multicolored,** *May 3* ⓢ 2.25 .25
4771 A3641 (46c) **multicolored,** *May 3* ⓢ 2.25 .25
4772 A3642 (46c) **multicolored,** *May 3* ⓢ 2.25 .25
4773 A3643 (46c) **multicolored,** *May 3* ⓢ 2.25 .25
a. Strip of 4, #4770-4773 9.00
P# strip of 5, 2 #4770, 1 each #4771-4773, #P1111 15.00
P# strip of 9, 3 #4772, 2 each #4770-4771, 4773, #P1111 20.00
P# single, #P1111 (#4772) — 2.75

Counterfeits exist of Nos. 4770-4773. See the Postal Counterfeits section of this catalog.

Serpentine Die Cut 11 Vert.

4774 A3641 (46c) **multicolored,** *May 3* 3.00 .25
4775 A3642 (46c) **multicolored,** *May 3* 3.00 .25
4776 A3643 (46c) **multicolored,** *May 3* 3.00 .25
4777 A3640 (46c) **multicolored,** *May 3* 3.00 .25
a. Strip of 4, #4774-4777 12.00
b. Block of 28 (4x7), #4774-4777, with no horiz. slits —
P# strip of 5, 2 #4774, 1 each #4775-4777, #S1111 17.50
P# strip of 9, 3 #4776, 2 each #4774-4775, 4777, #S1111 25.00
P# single, #S1111 (#4776) — 2.75
P# strip of 5, #S1111, seven strips (5x7) with no horiz. slits —
P# strip of 9, #S1111, block of seven strips (9x7) with no horiz. slits —
Nos. 4766-4777 (12) 30.00 3.00

Nos. 4774-4777 were produced as "sticks" or "logs" of ten coil rolls of 100 with partial horizontal slits that allowed individual rolls to be snapped off for retail sale. Customers could buy an entire "log" if desired. No. 4777b has no horizontal slits and therefore is an error that can be collected as pairs or larger units of strips "imperf." horizontally.

Booklet Stamps
With Microprinted "USPS" at Lower Left Corner of Flag

Serpentine Die Cut 11¼x10¾ on 2 or 3 Sides

4778 A3642 (46c) **multicolored,** *May 17* ⓢ 1.25 .25
4779 A3643 (46c) **multicolored,** *May 17* ⓢ 1.25 .25
4780 A3640 (46c) **multicolored,** *May 17* ⓢ 1.25 .25
4781 A3641 (46c) **multicolored,** *May 17* ⓢ 1.25 .25
a. Block of 4, #4778-4781 6.00
b. Booklet pane of 20, 5 each #4778-4781 30.00

With Microprinted "USPS" Near Top of Pole or at Lower Left Corner Near Rope (#4783, 4783b)
Pre-phosphored Paper

4782 A3642 (46c) **multicolored,** *May 17* 1.10 .25
a. Overall tagging, *Aug. 16* 1.10 .25
b. As #4782, dated "2014," overall tagging, *Mar. 17, 2014* 1.10 .25
c. Tagging omitted —
4783 A3643 (46c) **multicolored,** *May 17* 1.10 .25
a. Overall tagging, *Aug. 16* 1.10 .25
b. As #4783, dated "2014," overall tagging, *Mar. 17, 2014* 1.10 .25
c. Tagging omitted —
4784 A3640 (46c) **multicolored,** *May 17* 1.10 .25
a. Overall tagging, *Aug. 16* 1.10 .25
b. As #4784, dated "2014," overall tagging, *Mar. 17, 2014* 1.10 .25
c. Tagging omitted —
4785 A3641 (46c) **multicolored,** *May 17* 1.10 .25
a. Overall tagging, *Aug. 16* 1.10 .25
b. As #4785, dated "2014," overall tagging, *Mar. 17, 2014* 1.10 .25
c. Block of 4, #4782-4785 4.40
d. Booklet pane of 20, 5 each #4782-4785 22.00
e. Block of 4, #4782a, 4783a, 4784a, 4785a 4.00
f. Booklet pane of 10, 3 each #4782a, 4783a, 2 each #4784a, 4785a 11.00
g. Block of 4, #4782b, 4783b, 4784b, 4785b 4.40
h. Booklet pane of 20, 5 each #4782b, 4783b, 4784b, 4785b 22.00
i. As "h," die cutting omitted on side with 8 stamps and 3 pairs on side with 12 stamps —
j. Tagging omitted —
Nos. 4778-4785 (8) 9.40 2.00

No. 4781b is a double-sided booklet with 12 stamps on one side (3 each #4778-4781) and eight stamps (2 each #4778-4781) plus label that serves as a booklet cover on the other side.

No. 4785d is a double-sided booklet with 12 stamps on one side (3 each #4782-4785) and eight stamps (2 each #4782-4785) plus label that serves as a booklet cover on the other side.

A microprinted "USPS" is found on tree trunk to the left of the "F" in "Forever" on No. 4766, on tree trunk near lower left corner of flag on No. 4767, on white flag stripe at lower right on No. 4768, and on the top of the flagpole below the ball on No. 4769. Nos. 4770-4773 are microprinted "USPS" in the same places as on Nos. 4778-4781. Nos. 4774-4777 are microprinted "USPS" in the same places as on Nos. 4782-4785.

See Nos. 4796-4799.

All examples of No. 4782a will have straight edge on the left side only, left side and top, or left side and bottom. All examples of No. 4783a will have straight edge on the right side only, right side and top, or right side and bottom. No. 4784a has the straight edge on the left side of the stamp. No. 4785a has the straight edge on the right side of the stamp. One-sided straight-edged examples of Nos. 4784 and 4785 will have the straight edge on the bottom of the stamps. One-sided straight-edged examples of Nos. 4782 and 4783 will have the straight edge on the top of the stamps.

See note after No. 1549.

Nos. 4782b, 4783b, 4784b and 4785b each sold for 49c on day of issue.

MUSIC ICONS

Lydia Mendoza (1916-2007), Tejano Music Recording Artist — A3644

Designed by Patrick Donohue and Neal Ashby. Printed by Avery Dennison.

PHOTOGRAVURE

Sheets of 128 in eight panes of 16

2013, May 15 Tagged *Serpentine Die Cut 10¾*
Self-Adhesive

4786 A3644 (46c) **multicolored** ⓢ 1.10 .25
Pane of 16 17.50
a. Imperforate 1.75 —
Pane of 16 28.00

Adjacent horizontal or vertical stamps have selvage between the stamps.

Die cut and imperforate uncut press sheets of No. 4786 were made available for sale. Values: cross-gutter block of 4, $11; pairs with gutters between, $4.50 each. See note after No. 4693.

See note after No. 1549.

CIVIL WAR SESQUICENTENNIAL

Battle of Vicksburg — A3645

Battle of Gettysburg — A3646

Designed by Phil Jordan. Printed by Ashton-Potter (USA) Ltd.

LITHOGRAPHED

Double-sided sheets of 72 in six panes of 12 (60 on one side, 12 on other side)

2013, May 23 Tagged *Serpentine Die Cut 11*
Self-Adhesive

4787 A3645 (46c) **multicolored** ⓢ 1.10 .30
4788 A3646 (46c) **multicolored** ⓢ 1.10 .30
a. Pair, #4787-4788 2.20
Pane of 12 13.25
b. Imperforate pair, #4787-4788 5.50 —
Imperforate pair with wide spacing 6.00 —
Pane of 12 28.00

Die cut and imperforate uncut press sheets of Nos. 4787-4788 were made available for sale. See note after No. 4693.

See note after No. 1549.

MUSIC ICONS

Johnny Cash (1932-2003), Country Music Recording Artist — A3647

Designed by Greg Breeding. Printed by Avery Dennison.

PHOTOGRAVURE

Sheets of 128 in eight panes of 16

2013, June 5 Tagged *Serpentine Die Cut 10¾*
Self-Adhesive

4789 A3647 (46c) **multicolored** ⓢ 1.10 .25
Pane of 16 17.50
a. Imperforate 1.75 —
Pane of 16 28.00

Die cut and imperforate uncut press sheets of No. 4789 were made available for sale. Values: cross-gutter block of 4, $9; pairs with gutters between, $4.25 each. See note after No. 4693.

See note after No. 1549.

WEST VIRGINIA STATEHOOD, 150th ANNIV. Ⓢ

Hills in Monongahela National Forest — A3648

Designed by Greg Breeding. Printed by Avery Dennison.

PHOTOGRAVURE

Sheets of 200 in 10 panes of 20

2013, June 20 Tagged *Serpentine Die Cut 11*

Self-Adhesive

4790 A3648 (46c) **multicolored** 1.10 .25
P# block of 4, 4#+V 4.40
Pane of 20 22.00
a. Imperforate 1.75 —
Pane of 20 35.00

Die cut and imperforate uncut press sheets of No. 4790 were made available for sale. Values: cross-gutter block of 4, $9; pairs with gutters between, $4.25 each. See note after No. 4693.

See note after No. 1549.

NEW ENGLAND COASTAL LIGHTHOUSES

Portland Head Lighthouse, Maine — A3649

Portsmouth Harbor Lighthouse, New Hampshire — A3650

Boston Harbor Lighthouse, Massachusetts A3651

Point Judith Lighthouse, Rhode Island A3652

New London Harbor Lighthouse, Connecticut — A3653

Designed by Howard E. Paine. Printed by Banknote Corpora-

LITHOGRAPHED

Sheets of 120 in six panes of 20

Serpentine Die Cut 11x10¾

2013, July 13 Tagged

Self-Adhesive

4791 A3649 (46c) **multicolored** 1.10 .40
a. "FOREVER" and "USA" 1mm higher than normal (pos. 1) 2.00 1.00
b. Horiz. strip of 5, #4791a, 4792-4795 6.00
4792 A3650 (46c) **multicolored** 1.10 .40
4793 A3651 (46c) **multicolored** 1.10 .40
4794 A3652 (46c) **multicolored** 1.10 .40
4795 A3653 (46c) **multicolored** 1.10 .40
a. Horiz. strip of 5, #4791-4795 5.50
P# block of 10, 2 sets of 4#+S 11.00
Pane of 20 22.00
b. Imperforate horiz. strip of 5 11.00 —
c. Imperforate horiz. strip of 5, pos. 1 as No. 4791a 13.00 —
Pane of 20 44.00
Nos. 4791-4795 (5) 5.50 2.00

Die cut and imperforate uncut press sheets of Nos. 4791-4795 were made available for sale. Values: cross gutter block of 10 (four stamps from one side of the sheet and six stamps from the other side), $22.50 each; vert. pair with horiz. gutter, $4 each; horiz. pair with vert. gutter, $4.25 each; horiz. strip of 5 without die cuts, $9. See note after No. 2868.

Flag Types of 2013

Designed by Phil Jordan. Printed by Avery Dennison.

PHOTOGRAVURE

Serpentine Die Cut 11¼x11½ on 2 or 3 Sides

2013, Aug. 8 Tagged

Booklet Stamps

Self-Adhesive

4796 A3642 (46c) **multicolored** Ⓢ 1.25 .25
4797 A3643 (46c) **multicolored** Ⓢ 1.25 .25
4798 A3640 (46c) **multicolored** Ⓢ 1.25 .25
4799 A3641 (46c) **multicolored** Ⓢ 1.25 .25
a. Block of 4, #4796-4799 5.00
b. Booklet pane of 20, 5 each #4796-4799 25.00
Nos. 4796-4799 (4) 5.00 1.00

No. 4799b is a double-sided booklet with 12 stamps on one side (3 each #4796-4799) and eight stamps (2 each #4796-4799) plus label that serves as a booklet cover on the other side. Nos. 4796-4799 are microprinted "USPS" in the same places as Nos. 4766-4769.

See note after No. 1549.

EID

"Eid Mubarak" — A3654

Designed by Mohamed Zakariya. Printed by Ashton-Potter (USA) Ltd.

LITHOGRAPHED

Sheets of 160 in eight panes of 20

2013, Aug. 8 Tagged *Serpentine Die Cut 11*

Self-Adhesive

4800 A3654 (46c) **dark green, gray & gold** Ⓢ 1.10 .25
P# block of 4, 3#+P 4.40
Pane of 20 22.00
a. Imperforate 2.00 —
Pane of 20 40.00

Imperforate uncut press sheets of No. 4800 were made available for sale. Values: cross-gutter block of 4, $10; pairs with gutters between, $4.50 each. See note after No. 4693.

See note after No. 1549.

BUILDING A NATION Ⓢ

Airplane Mechanic, Photograph by Lewis

Derrick Man on Empire State Building, Photograph by Lewis Hine — A3656

Millinery Apprentice, Photograph by Lewis Hine — A3657

Man on Hoisting Ball on Empire State Building, Photograph by Lewis Hine — A3658

Linotype Operator, Photograph by Lewis Hine — A3659

Welder on Empire State Building, Photograph by Lewis Hine — A3660

Coal Miner, by Anonymous Photographer A3661

Riveters on Empire State Building, Photograph by Lewis Hine — A3662

Powerhouse Mechanic, Photograph by Lewis Hine — A3663

Railroad Track Walker, Photograph by Lewis Hine — A3664

Textile Worker, Photograph by Lewis Hine — A3665

Man Guiding Beam on Empire State Building, Photograph by Lewis Hine — A3666

Designed by Derry Noyes. Printed by Avery Dennison.

PHOTOGRAVURE
Sheets of 60 in five panes of 12
Serpentine Die Cut 10½x10¾

2013, Aug. 8 **Tagged**

Self-Adhesive

4801	Pane of 12	12.00	
a.	A3655 (46c) **black & gray**	1.10	.50
b.	A3656 (46c) **black & gray**	1.10	.50
c.	A3657 (46c) **black & gray**	1.10	.50
d.	A3658 (46c) **black & gray**	1.10	.50
e.	A3659 (46c) **black & gray**	1.10	.50
f.	A3660 (46c) **black & gray**	1.10	.50
g.	A3661 (46c) **black & gray**	1.10	.50
h.	A3662 (46c) **black & gray**	1.10	.50
i.	A3663 (46c) **black & gray**	1.10	.50
j.	A3664 (46c) **black & gray**	1.10	.50
k.	A3665 (46c) **black & gray**	1.10	.50
l.	A3666 (46c) **black & gray**	1.10	.50
m.	Imperforate pane of 12	70.00	

No. 4801 was printed with five different sheet margins depicting coal miner from No. 4801g, man on hoisting ball on Empire State Building, man measuring bearings in large gearwheel, man on cable at Empire State Building, and woman welder. Value is for sheet with any margin. Value, set of 5 panes, $60.00.

Die cut and imperforate uncut press sheets of No. 4801 were made available for sale. Value, set of 5 individual imperforate panes of 12, $350. See note after No. 4693.

See note after No. 1549.

Bobcat Type of 2012

Designed by Carl T. Herrman. Printed by Banknote Corporation of America for Sennett Security Products.

LITHOGRAPHED

2013, Aug. 9 **Untagged** ***Perf. 9¾ Vert.***

Coil Stamp

4802	A3564 1c **multicolored**	.25	.25
	Pair	.25	.25
	P# strip of 5, #S111111	.60	
	P# single, #S111111	—	.50

BLACK HERITAGE

Althea Gibson (1927-2003), Tennis Player — A3667

Designed by Derry Noyes. Printed by Avery Dennison.

PHOTOGRAVURE
Sheets of 200 in 10 panes of 20

2013, Aug. 23 **Tagged** ***Serpentine Die Cut 11***

Self-Adhesive

4803	A3667 (46c) **multicolored** Ⓢ	1.10	.25
	P# block of 4, 4#+V	4.00	
	Pane of 20	20.00	
a.	Imperforate	1.75	—
	Pane of 20	35.00	

Die cut and imperforate uncut press sheets of No. 4803 were made available for sale. Values: cross-gutter block of 4, $9; pairs with gutters between, $4.25 each. See note after No. 4693.

See note after No. 1549.

MARCH ON WASHINGTON, 50th ANNIV.

Marchers and Washington Monument — A3668

Designed by Antonio Alcalá. Printed by Avery Dennison.

PHOTOGRAVURE
Sheets of 200 in 10 panes of 20

2013, Aug. 23 **Tagged** ***Serpentine Die Cut 10¾***

Self-Adhesive

4804	A3668 (46c) **multicolored** Ⓢ	1.10	.25
	P# block of 4, 5#+V	4.00	
	P# block of 2, 2 sets of 5#+V, + side panel	8.00	
	Pane of 20	20.00	
a.	Imperforate	1.75	—
	Pane of 20	35.00	

Die cut and imperforate uncut press sheets of No. 4804 were made available for sale. Values: cross-gutter block of 4, $9; pairs with gutters between, $4.25 each. See note after No. 4693.

See note after No. 1549.

WAR OF 1812 BICENTENNIAL

Painting of Battle of Lake Erie, by William Henry Powell A3669

Designed by Greg Breeding. Printed by Ashton-Potter (USA) Ltd.

LITHOGRAPHED
Sheets of 120 in six panes of 20

2013, Sept. 10 **Tagged** ***Serpentine Die Cut 10¾***

Self-Adhesive

4805	A3669 (46c) **multicolored** Ⓢ	1.10	.25
	Pane of 20	22.00	
a.	Imperforate	1.75	—
	Pane of 20	35.00	

Die-cut and imperforate uncut press sheets of No. 4805 were made available for sale. Values: cross-gutter block of 4, $9; pairs with gutters between, $4.25 each. See note after No. 4693.

See note after No. 1549.

INVERTED JENNY Ⓢ

Miniature Sheet

A3670

Designed by Antonio Alcalá. Printed by Banknote Corporation of America for Sennett Security Products.

LITHOGRAPHED & ENGRAVED

Sheets of 36 in six panes of 6

Serpentine Die Cut 10½x11¼

2013, Sept. 22 **Untagged**

Self-Adhesive

4806 A3670	Pane of 6	24.00	
a.	$2 Single stamp	4.00	1.25
b.	Imperforate pane of 6	72.50	—
c.	As "b," single stamp	12.00	—
d.	Pane of 6, airplane right-side up	*70,000.*	
e.	As "d," single stamp	*13,500.*	

No. 4806, along with a piece of white cardboard backing, was placed in a sealed envelope. The envelope, along with a piece of gray cardboard backing, was inside a sealed plastic outerwrap. One hundred panes were produced that contain the airplane right-side up. These panes were included in the same envelope and outerwrap and were distributed somewhat randomly. No returns or refunds were offered for any opened packages. Values for No. 4806 are for panes removed from the envelope.

A book containing an unused and a first-day canceled example of No. 4806, along with items that are termed "proofs" and "die wipes" sold for $200.

Die-cut and imperforate uncut press sheets of No. 4806 were made available for sale. Values: cross-gutter block of 4 with die cuts, $27.50; cross-gutter block of 4 without die cuts, $60; pairs with gutters between, die cut, $11 each; pairs with gutters between, without die cuts, $25 each. See note after No. 4693.

MUSIC ICONS

Ray Charles (1930-2004), Recording Artist — A3671

Designed by Ethel Kessler. Printed by Banknote Corporation of America for Sennett Security Products.

LITHOGRAPHED

Sheets of 144 in nine panes of 16

2013, Sept. 23 **Tagged** ***Serpentine Die Cut 10½***

Self-Adhesive

4807 A3671 (46c)	**multicolored**	1.10	.25
	Pane of 16	17.50	
a.	Imperforate	1.75	—
	Pane of 16	35.00	

Adjacent horizontal or vertical stamps have selvage between the stamps.

Die cut and imperforate uncut press sheets of No. 4807 were made available for sale. Values: cross gutter block of 4, $9; pairs with gutters between, $4.25 each. See note after No. 4693.

SNOWFLAKES Ⓢ

A3672

A3673

A3674

A3675

A3676

PHOTOGRAVURE

2013, Oct. 1 **Tagged** ***Serpentine Die Cut 11 Vert.***

Coil Stamps

Self-Adhesive

4808 A3672 (10c)	**light blue & multicolored**	.25	.25
4809 A3673 (10c)	**pale blue & multicolored**	.25	.25
4810 A3674 (10c)	**light blue & multicolored**	.25	.25
4811 A3675 (10c)	**pale blue & multicolored**	.25	.25
4812 A3676 (10c)	**lilac & multicolored**	.25	.25
a.	Strip of 5, #4808-4812	1.25	
	P# strip of 5, #4808-4812, #C11111111	2.50	
	P# strip of 11, 3 #4810, 2 each #4808-4809, 4811-4812, #C11111111	4.00	
	P# single (#4810), same #	—	2.00
	Nos. 4808-4812 (5)	1.25	1.25

See note after No. 1549.

Holy Family and Donkey Type of 2012 Dated "2013" and

Wreath — A3677

Virgin and Child, by Jan Gossaert — A3678

Poinsettia — A3679

Gingerbread House With Red Door — A3680

Gingerbread House With Blue Door — A3681

Gingerbread House With Green Door — A3682

Gingerbread House With Orange Door — A3683

Poinsettia — A3684

Designed by Greg Breeding (#4813), William J. Gicker (#4814), Richard Sheaff (#4815), Ethel Kessler (#4816, 4821), Derry Noyes (#4817-4820). Printed by Banknote Corporation of

LITHOGRAPHED, PHOTOGRAVURE (#4821)

Sheets of 200 in 10 panes of 20 (#4813), Sheets of 60 in six panes of 10 (#4814)

2013 **Tagged** ***Serpentine Die Cut 11***

Self-Adhesive

4813 A3590 (46c)	**multicolored,** "2013" year date, *Oct. 11*	1.10	.25
	P# block of 4, 5#+S	4.40	
	Pane of 20	22.00	
a.	Imperforate	1.75	—
	Pane of 20	35.00	

Serpentine Die Cut

4814 A3677 ($1.10)	**multicolored,** *Oct. 24* Ⓢ	2.25	.50
	P# block of 4, 6#+P	9.00	
	Pane of 10	22.50	
a.	Imperforate	4.00	—
	Pane of 10	40.00	

Booklet Stamps

Serpentine Die Cut 11 on 2 or 3 Sides

4815 A3678 (46c)	**multicolored,** *Oct. 11*	1.10	.25
a.	Booklet pane of 20	22.00	
b.	Imperforate	1.75	—
c.	Imperforate booklet pane of 20	35.00	
4816 A3679 (46c)	**multicolored,** *Oct. 10*	1.10	.25
a.	Booklet pane of 20	22.00	
b.	Dated "2014"	1.10	.25
c.	As #4816a, dated "2014"	22.00	
d.	Imperforate, dated "2013"	1.75	—
e.	Imperforate booklet pane of 20	35.00	
4817 A3680 (46c)	**multicolored,** overall tagging on prephosphored paper, *Nov. 6*	1.10	.25
a.	Strong overall tagging only	1.10	.25
4818 A3681 (46c)	**multicolored,** overall tagging on prephosphored paper, *Nov. 6*	1.10	.25
a.	Strong overall tagging only	1.10	.25
4819 A3682 (46c)	**multicolored,** overall tagging on prephosphored paper, *Nov. 6*	1.10	.25
a.	Strong overall tagging only	1.10	.25
4820 A3683 (46c)	**multicolored,** overall tagging on prephosphored paper, *Nov. 6*	1.10	.25
a.	Strong overall tagging only	1.10	.25
b.	Block of 4, #4817-4820	4.40	
c.	Booklet pane of 20, 5 each #4817-4820	22.00	
d.	Block of 4, #4817a-4820a	4.40	
e.	Booklet pane of 20, 5 each #4817a-4820a	22.00	
f.	Imperforate block of 4	8.00	—
g.	Imperforate booklet pane of 20	40.00	

Serpentine Die Cut 8 on 2, 3 or 4 Sides

4821 A3684 (46c)	**multicolored,** *Oct. 10* Ⓢ	1.10	.25
a.	Booklet pane of 18	18.00	
	Nos. 4815-4821 (7)	7.70	1.75

Die cut and imperforate uncut press sheets of No. 4813 were made available for sale. Values: cross gutter block of 4, $9; pairs with gutters between, $4 each.

Die cut and imperforate uncut press sheets of No. 4814 were made available for sale. Values: cross gutter block of 4, $20; pairs with gutters between, $8.50 each.

Die cut and imperforate uncut press sheets of No. 4815 were made available for sale. Values for varieties from die cut press sheets: cross gutter block of 4 with booklet cover, imperf. within, $10; cross gutter block of 4, imperf. within, $10; vert. pair, imperf. between, $4; horiz. pair, imperf. between, $6. Values for varieties from imperforate press sheets: cross gutter block of 4 with booklet cover, $10; horiz. pair with booklet cover and gutter between, $6.

Die cut and imperforate uncut press sheets of No. 4816 were made available for sale. Values for varieties from die cut press sheets: cross gutter block of 4 with booklet cover, imperf. within, $10; cross gutter block of 4, imperf. within, $10; vert. pair, imperf. between, $4; horiz. pair, imperf. between, $6. Values for varieties from imperforate press sheets: cross gutter block of 4 with booklet cover, $10; horiz pair with booklet cover and gutter between, $6.

Die cut and imperforate uncut press sheets of No. 4817-4820 were made available for sale. Values for varieties from die cut press sheets: cross gutter block of 4 with booklet cover, imperf. within, $10: cross gutter block of 4, imperf. within, $10; vert. pair, imperf. between, $4; horiz. pair, imperf. between, $6. Values for varieties from imperforate press sheets: cross gutter block of 4 with booklet cover, $10; vert. pair with gutter between, $4; horiz. pair with booklet cover and gutter between, $6. See note after No. 4693.

See note after No. 1549.

Issued: No. 4816b, 8/21/14. No. 4816b sold for 49c on day of issue. Nos. 4815a, 4815c, 4816a, 4816c, 4816e, 4820c, 4820e, and 4820g are complete double-sided booklets. Eight stamps plus and the label that serves as a booklet cover are on one side of the peelable backing and 12 stamps are on the other side of the backing.

MEDALS OF HONOR

Navy Medal of Honor — A3685

Army Medal of Honor — A3686

Designed by Antonio Alcalá. Printed by Banknote Coporation of America for Sennett Security Products.

LITHOGRAPHED

Sheets of 60 in three panes of 20 (Panes are folded into a folio with 18 stamps on back side of folded pane and 2 stamps on the front side)

2013, Nov. 11 Tagged *Serpentine Die Cut 11*

Self-Adhesive

4822	A3685 (46c) **multicolored**	1.10	.30
a.	Dated "2014," *July 26, 2014*	1.10	.30
b.	Dated "2015," *May 25, 2015*	1.10	.30
4823	A3686 (46c) **multicolored**	1.10	.30
a.	Dated "2014," *July 26, 2014*	1.10	.30
b.	Dated "2015," *May 25, 2015*	1.10	.30
c.	Pair, #4822-4823	2.20	
	P# block of 4, 6#+S	4.40	
	Folio of 20	22.00	
d.	Pair, #4822a-4823a	2.20	
	Dated "2014," P# block of 4, 6#+S	4.40	
	Dated "2014," folio of 20	22.00	
e.	Pair, 4822b-4823b	2.20	
f.	Imperf. pair, #4822-4823	4.50	—
	Imperf. pair with wide margins	7.00	—
	Folio of 20	47.50	
g.	Imperf. pair, #4822a-4823a	4.50	—
	Imperf. pair with wide margins	7.00	—
	Folio of 20	47.50	

Die cut and imperforate uncut press sheets of Nos. 4822-4823 and 4822a-4823a were made available for sale. Values: vert. pairs with gutters between, $4.50 each. See note after No. 4693.

Nos. 4822a, 4822b, 4823a and 4823b sold for 49c on day of issue. Folios containing Nos. 4822a and 4823a have different images of Medal of Honor recipients, product numbers (on folio margins) and text on the paper backing than that found on the folios with Nos. 4822 and 4823. Nos. 4822b and 4823b were in a folio with No. 4988.

HANUKKAH

Menorah — A3687

Designed by Ethel Kessler. Printed by Ashton-Potter (USA) Ltd.

LITHOGRAPHED

Sheets of 160 in eight panes of 20

2013, Nov. 19 Tagged *Serpentine Die Cut 11*

Self-Adhesive

4824	A3687 (46c) **multicolored** Ⓢ	1.10	.25
	P# block of 4, 5#+P	4.40	
	Pane of 20	22.00	
a.	Imperforate	1.75	—
	Pane of 20	35.00	

Postal Service officials declared on Nov. 8 that No. 4824 could be sold in post offices on Nov. 9, but the first day ceremony was held on Nov. 19 in New York, NY. Official first day covers have that date and city.

Imperforate uncut press sheets of No. 4824 were made available for sale. Values: cross gutter block of 4, $9; pairs with gutters between, $4.25 each. See note after No. 4693.

See note after No. 1549.

SCENES FROM HARRY POTTER MOVIES Ⓢ

Harry Potter — A3688

Harry Potter and Ron Weasley A3689

Harry Potter, Ron Weasley, Hermione Granger A3690

Hermione Granger — A3691

Harry Potter and Fawkes the Phoenix A3692

Hedwig the Owl — A3693

Dobby the House Elf — A3694

Harry Potter and Buckbeak the Hippogriff A3695

Headmaster Albus Dumbledore — A3696

Professor Severus Snape A3697

Rubeus Hagrid A3698

Professor Minerva McGonagall — A3699

Harry Potter, Ron Weasley, Hermione Granger A3700

Luna Lovegood — A3701

Fred and George Weasley — A3702

Ginny Weasley A3703

Draco Malfoy — A3704

Harry Potter A3705

Lord Voldemort A3706

Bellatrix Lestrange — A3707

Designed by Greg Breeding. Printed by Ashton-Potter (USA) Ltd.

LITHOGRAPHED

2013, Nov. 19 Tagged *Serpentine Die Cut 11*

Booklet Stamps

Self-Adhesive

4825	A3688 (46c) **multicolored**	1.10	.30
4826	A3689 (46c) **multicolored**	1.10	.30
4827	A3690 (46c) **multicolored**	1.10	.30
4828	A3691 (46c) **multicolored**	1.10	.30
a.	Booklet pane of 4, #4825-4828, + central label	4.40	
b.	Imperf. booklet pane of 4	12.50	—
4829	A3692 (46c) **multicolored**	1.10	.30
4830	A3693 (46c) **multicolored**	1.10	.30
4831	A3694 (46c) **multicolored**	1.10	.30
4832	A3695 (46c) **multicolored**	1.10	.30
a.	Booklet pane of 4, #4829-4832, + central label	4.40	
b.	Imperf. booklet pane of 4	12.50	—
4833	A3696 (46c) **multicolored**	1.10	.30
4834	A3697 (46c) **multicolored**	1.10	.30
4835	A3698 (46c) **multicolored**	1.10	.30
4836	A3699 (46c) **multicolored**	1.10	.30
a.	Booklet pane of 4, #4833-4836, + central label	4.40	
b.	Imperf. booklet pane of 4	12.50	—
4837	A3700 (46c) **multicolored**	1.10	.30
4838	A3701 (46c) **multicolored**	1.10	.30
4839	A3702 (46c) **multicolored**	1.10	.30
4840	A3703 (46c) **multicolored**	1.10	.30
a.	Booklet pane of 4, #4837-4840, + central label	4.40	
b.	Imperf. booklet pane of 4	12.50	—
4841	A3704 (46c) **multicolored**	1.10	.30
4842	A3705 (46c) **multicolored**	1.10	.30
4843	A3706 (46c) **multicolored**	1.10	.30
4844	A3707 (46c) **multicolored**	1.10	.30
a.	Booklet pane of 4, #4841-4844, + central label	4.40	
b.	Imperf. booklet pane of 4	12.50	—
	Nos. 4825-4844 (20)	22.00	6.00

Die cut and imperforate uncut press sheets of Nos. 4825-4844 were made available for sale. Values: imperforate singles, $3.50 each. See note after No. 4693.

See note after No. 1549.

KWANZAA

People, Candles and Book — A3708

Designed by Antonio Alcalá. Printed by Ashton-Potter (USA) Ltd.

LITHOGRAPHED

Sheets of 160 in 8 panes of 20

2013, Nov. 26 Tagged *Serpentine Die Cut 11*

Self-Adhesive

4845	A3708 (46c) **multicolored** Ⓢ	1.00	.25
	P# block of 4, 6#+P	4.40	
	Pane of 20	22.00	
a.	Imperforate	1.75	—
	Pane of 20	35.00	

Imperforate uncut press sheets of No. 4845 were made available for sale. Values: cross gutter block of 4, $9; pairs with gutters between, $4.25 each. See note after No. 4693.

See note after No. 1549.

CHINESE NEW YEAR

Year of the Horse A3709

Designed by Ethel Kessler. Printed by CCL Label, Inc.

PHOTOGRAVURE

Sheets of 108 in nine panes of 12

2014, Jan. 15 Tagged *Serpentine Die Cut 11*

Self-Adhesive

4846	A3709 (46c) **multicolored** Ⓢ	1.00	.25
	Pane of 12	13.25	
a.	Imperforate	2.00	—
	Pane of 12	24.00	

Die cut and imperforate uncut press sheets of No. 4846 were made available for sale. Values: cross gutter block of 4, $9; pairs with gutters between, $4.25 each. See note after No. 4693.

See note after No. 1549.

LOVE

Heart — A3710

Designed by Antonio Alcalá. Printed by CCL Label, Inc.

PHOTOGRAVURE

Sheets of 120 in six panes of 20

2014, Jan. 21 Tagged *Serpentine Die Cut 10¾*

Self-Adhesive

4847	A3710 (46c) **multicolored** Ⓢ	1.00	.25
	P# block of 4, 3#+C	4.40	
	Pane of 20	22.00	
a.	Imperforate	2.00	—
	Pane of 20	40.00	

Die cut and imperforate uncut press sheets of No. 4847 were made available for sale. Values: cross gutter block of 4, $10; pairs with gutters between, $4.25 each. See note after No. 4693.

See note after No. 1549.

FERNS Ⓢ

Fortune's Holly Fern — A3711

Soft Shield Fern — A3712

Autumn Fern — A3713

Goldie's Wood Fern — A3714

Painted Fern — A3715

Designed by Phil Jordan. Printed by CCL Label, Inc.

PHOTOGRAVURE

Serpentine Die Cut 11 Vert.

2014, Jan. 27 Tagged

Coil Stamps

Self-Adhesive

4848	A3711 49c **multicolored**	1.50	.25
4849	A3712 49c **multicolored**	1.50	.25
4850	A3713 49c **multicolored**	1.50	.25
4851	A3714 49c **multicolored**	1.50	.25
4852	A3715 49c **multicolored**	1.50	.25
a.	Strip of 5, #4848-4852	7.50	
	P# strip of 5, #4848-4852, #C1111	10.50	
	P# strip of 11, 3# 4850, 2 each #4848-4849, 4851-4852, #C1111	18.00	
	P# single, #C1111 (#4850)	—	3.00
	Nos. 4848-4852 (5)	7.50	1.25

Fort McHenry Flag and Fireworks — A3716

Designed by Phil Jordan. Printed by CCL Label, Inc. (#4853), Ashton-Potter (USA) Ltd. (#4854-4855).

PHOTOGRAVURE (#4853), LITHOGRAPHED (#4854-4855)

Serpentine Die Cut 8½ Vert.

2014, Jan. 28 Tagged

Coil Stamps

Self-Adhesive

4853	A3716 (49c) **multicolored** Ⓢ	1.10	.25
	Pair	2.20	
	P# strip of 5, #C11111	7.50	

P# single, #C11111 — 3.50

Serpentine Die Cut 9½ Vert.

4854 A3716 (49c) **multicolored** Ⓢ 1.10 .25
Pair 2.20
P# strip of 5, #P1111, P2222 7.50
P# single, #P1111, P2222 — 3.50
a. Die cutting omitted, pair 200.00

Booklet Stamp

Serpentine Die Cut 11¼x10¾ on 2 or 3 Sides

4855 A3716 (49c) **multicolored** Ⓢ 1.10 .25
a. Booklet pane of 20 22.00

No. 4855a is a double-sided booklet with 12 stamps on one side and eight stamps plus a label that serves as the booklet cover on the other side.

Nos. 4854 and 4855 each have a microprinted "USPS" on the right side of the lowest white stripe of the flag.

Counterfeits exist of No. 4854. See the Postal Counterfeits section of this catalog.

See note after No. 1549.

See Nos. 4868-4871.

BLACK HERITAGE

Shirley Chisholm (1924-2005), Congresswoman — A3717

Designed by Ethel Kessler. Printed by CCL Label, Inc.

PHOTOGRAVURE

Sheets of 200 in 10 panes of 20

2014, Jan. 31 Tagged *Serpentine Die Cut 11*

Self-Adhesive

4856 A3717 (49c) **multicolored** Ⓢ 1.10 .25
P# block of 4, 4#+C 4.40
Pane of 20 22.00
a. Imperforate 2.00 —
Pane of 20 40.00

Die cut and imperforate uncut press sheets of No. 4856 were made available for sale. Values: cross gutter block of 4, $10; pairs with gutters between, $4.25 each. See note after No. 4693.

See note after No. 1549.

WILDLIFE ISSUE

Hummingbird — A3718

Designed by Carl T. Herrman. Printed by Ashton-Potter (USA) Ltd.

LITHOGRAPHED

Sheets of 200 in 10 panes of 20

Serpentine Die Cut 11¼x10¾

2014, Feb. 7 Tagged

Self-Adhesive

4857 A3718 34c **multicolored** Ⓢ .70 .25
P# block of 4, 5#+P 2.80
Pane of 20 14.00

Coil Stamp

Serpentine Die Cut 9½ Vert.

4858 A3718 34c **multicolored,** prephosphored coated paper with surface tagging showing a solid appearance Ⓢ .70 .25
Pair 1.40
P# strip of 5, #P11111 5.25
P# single #P11111 — 2.75
a. Overall tagging .70 .25
Pair 1.40
P# strip of 5, #P22222 5.25
P# single #P22222 — 2.75
b. As "a," die cutting omitted, pair —

See note after No. 1549.

GREAT SPANGLED FRITILLARY BUTTERFLY Ⓢ

A3719

Designed by Derry Noyes. Printed by CCL Label, Inc.

PHOTOGRAVURE

Sheets of 200 in 10 panes of 20

2014, Feb. 10 Tagged *Serpentine Die Cut 10¾*

Self-Adhesive

4859 A3719 70c **multicolored** 1.40 .25
P# block of 4, 7#+C 5.60
Pane of 20 28.00
a. Imperforate 3.25 —
Pane of 20 65.00

Die cut and imperforate uncut press sheets of No. 4859 were made available for sale. Values: cross gutter block of 4, $18; pairs with gutters between, $7.50 each. See note after No. 4693.

See note after No. 1549.

Statue of Abraham Lincoln in Lincoln Memorial — A3720

Designed by Derry Noyes. Printed by CCL Label, Inc.

PHOTOGRAVURE

Sheets of 60 in three panes of 20

2014, Feb. 12 Tagged *Serpentine Die Cut 11*

Self-Adhesive

4860 A3720 21c **multicolored** Ⓢ .45 .25
P# block of 4, 3#+C 1.80
Pane of 20 9.00
a. Imperforate 1.25 —
Pane of 20 25.00

Die cut and imperforate uncut press sheets of No. 4860 were made available for sale. Value: vert. pair with gutter between, $2.75. See note after No. 4693.

See note after No. 1549.

Coil Stamp

Serpentine Die Cut 8½ Vert.

4861 A3720 21c **multicolored** Ⓢ .45 .25
Pair .90
P# strip of 5, #C111 3.75
P# single #C111 — 2.25

See note after No. 1549.

WINTER FLOWERS

Amaryllis — A3721

Cyclamen — A3722

Paperwhite — A3723

Christmas Cactus — A3724

Designed by Ethel Kessler. Printed by Banknote Corporation of America for Sennett Security Products.

LITHOGRAPHED

Serpentine Die Cut 11 on 2 or 3 Sides

2014, Feb. 14 Tagged

Booklet Stamps

Self-Adhesive

4862 A3721 (49c) **multicolored** 1.10 .30
4863 A3722 (49c) **multicolored** 1.10 .30
4864 A3723 (49c) **multicolored** 1.10 .30
4865 A3724 (49c) **multicolored** 1.10 .30
a. Block of 4, #4862-4865 4.40
b. Booklet pane of 20, 5 each #4862-4865 22.00
c. Imperforate block of 4 7.00 —
d. Imperforate booklet pane of 20 35.00
Nos. 4862-4865 (4) 4.40 1.20

Nos. 4865b and 4865d are double-sided booklet panes with 12 stamps on one side (3 each Nos. 4862-4865), and eight stamps (2 each Nos. 4862-4865) plus label (booklet cover) on the other side.

Die cut and imperforate uncut press sheets of No. 4862-4865 were made available for sale. Values for varieties from die cut press sheets: cross gutter block of 4 with booklet cover, imperf. within, $10; cross gutter block of 4, imperf. within, $10; vert. pair, imperf. between, $4; horiz. pair, imperf. between, $6. Values for varieties from imperforate press sheets: cross gutter block of 4 with booklet cover, $10; vert. pair with gutter between, $4; horiz. pair with booklet cover and gutter between, $6. See note after No. 4693.

LITERARY ARTS

Ralph Ellison (1913-94), Buildings in Harlem A3725

Designed by Ethel Kessler. Printed by CCL Label, Inc.

PHOTOGRAVURE

Sheets of 200 in 10 panes of 20

2014, Feb. 18 Tagged *Serpentine Die Cut 11*

Self-Adhesive

4866 A3725 91c **multicolored** Ⓢ 1.90 .45
P# block of 4, 5#+C 7.60
Pane of 20 38.00
a. Imperforate 4.00 —
Pane of 20 80.00

Die cut and imperforate uncut press sheets of No. 4866 were made available for sale. Values: cross-gutter block of 4, $22.50; pairs with gutters between, $10 each. See note after No. 4693.

See note after No. 1549.

Wedding Cake Type of 2009

Designed by Ethel Kessler. Printed by Banknote Corporation of America for Sennett Security Products.

LITHOGRAPHED

Sheets of 200 in 10 panes of 20

2014, Feb. 22 Tagged *Serpentine Die Cut 10¾*

Self-Adhesive

4867 A3344 70c **multicolored** 1.40 .25
P# block of 4, 6#+S 5.60
Pane of 20 28.00

Fort McHenry Flag and Fireworks Type of 2014

Designed by Phil Jordan. Printed by Banknote Corporation of America for Sennett Security Products (#4868, 4870-4871), CCL Label, Inc. (#4869).

LITHOGRAPHED (#4868, 4870-4871), PHOTOGRAVURE (#4869)

Coil Stamp

Self-Adhesive

With "USPS" Microprinted in Fireworks Above Flagpole

2014, Mar. 3 Tagged *Serpentine Die Cut 11 Vert.*

4868 A3716 (49c) **multicolored** 1.10 .25
Pair
P# strip of 5, #S11111 7.00
P# single, #S11111 — 3.00
a. Vert. strip of 3 (one single each from three different coil rolls), horiz. unslit between 60.00
b. Pair, die cutting omitted —

Counterfeits exist of No. 4868. See the Postal Counterfeits section of this catalog.

Booklet Stamps

Without Microprinted "USPS"

Serpentine Die Cut 11¼x11½ on 2 or 3 Sides

4869 A3716 (49c) **multicolored** Ⓢ 1.10 .25
a. Booklet pane of 20 22.00

With "USPS" Microprinted in Fireworks Above Flagpole

Serpentine Die Cut 11¼x10¾ on 2 or 3 Sides

4870	A3716 (49c) **multicolored**	1.10	.25
a.	Booklet pane of 20	22.00	

The actual design images on Nos. 4855, 4869 and 4870 differ slightly in size. This is easiest seen by measuring the height of the flagpole: No. 4855 is 13mm, No. 4869 is 14mm, and No. 4870 is 12mm.

Thin Paper

Serpentine Die Cut 11¼x11 on 2, 3 or 4 Sides

4871	A3716 (49c) **multicolored**	1.10	.25
a.	Booklet pane of 18	20.00	

Nos. 4869a and 4870a are double-sided booklet panes with 12 stamps on one side and eight stamps plus a label that serves as the booklet cover on the other side.

See note after No. 1549.

AMERICAN LANDMARKS ISSUE

Verrazano-Narrows Bridge, New York — A3726

USS Arizona Memorial, Hawaii A3727

Designed by Phil Jordan. Printed by Ashton-Potter (USA) Ltd. (#4872), Banknote Corporation of America for Sennett Security Products (#4873).

LITHOGRAPHED

Sheets of 120 in 12 panes of 10 (#4872), Sheets of 30 in three panes of 10 (#4873)

2014 Tagged *Serpentine Die Cut 10¾x10½*

Self-Adhesive

4872	A3726 $5.60 **multicolored**, *Mar. 4*	11.00	6.25
	P# block of 4, 4#+P	44.00	
	Pane of 10	110.00	
4873	A3727 $19.99 **multicolored**, *Mar. 13*	40.00	21.00
	P# block of 4, 4#+S	160.00	
	Pane of 10	400.00	
a.	Imperforate	55.00	—
	Pane of 10	500.00	

Die cut and imperforate press sheets of No. 4873 were made available for sale. Value: horiz. pair with gutter between, $125. See note after No. 4693.

See note after No. 1549.

FERNS

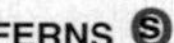

Fortune's Holly Fern — A3728

Soft Shield Fern — A3729

Autumn Fern — A3730

Goldie's Wood Fern — A3731

Painted Fern — A3732

Designed by Phil Jordan. Printed by CCL Label, Inc.

PHOTOGRAVURE

2014, Mar. 6 Tagged *Serpentine Die Cut 11 Vert.*

Coil Stamps

Self-Adhesive

4874	A3728 (49c) **multicolored**	2.00	.25
4875	A3729 (49c) **multicolored**	2.00	.25
4876	A3730 (49c) **multicolored**	2.00	.25
4877	A3731 (49c) **multicolored**	2.00	.25
4878	A3732 (49c) **multicolored**	2.00	.25
a.	Strip of 5, #4874-4878	10.00	
	P# strip of 5, #4874-4878, #C1111	15.00	
	P# strip of 11, 3# 4876, 2 each #4874-4875, 4877-4878, #C1111	25.00	
	P# single, #C1111 (#4876)	—	3.00
	Nos. 4874-4878 (5)	10.00	1.25

See note after No. 1549.

DISTINGUISHED AMERICANS

C. Alfred "Chief" Anderson (1907-96), Aviator — A3733

Designed by Phil Jordan. Printed by Ashton-Potter (USA) Ltd.

LITHOGRAPHED

Sheets of 160 in eight panes of 20

Serpentine Die Cut 10¾x11

2014, Mar. 13 Tagged

Self-Adhesive

4879	A3733 70c **multicolored**	1.40	.30
	P# block of 4, 5#+P	5.60	
	Pane of 20	28.00	
a.	Imperforate	3.00	—
	Pane of 20	60.00	

Die cut and imperforate press sheets of No. 4879 were made available for sale. Values: cross gutter block of 4, $12; pairs with gutters between, $5 each. See note after No. 4693.

See note after No. 1549.

MUSIC ICONS

Jimi Hendrix (1942-70), Rock Guitarist — A3734

Designed by Greg Breeding. Printed by Banknote Corporation of America for Sennett Security Products.

PHOTOGRAVURE

Sheets of 144 in nine panes of 16

2014, Mar. 13 Tagged *Serpentine Die Cut 10½*

Self-Adhesive

4880	A3734 (49c) **multicolored**	1.10	.25
	Pane of 16	17.50	
a.	Imperforate	1.75	—
	Pane of 16	28.00	

Adjacent horizontal or vertical stamps have selvage between the stamps. Any stamp on the pane is rotated 90 degrees with respect to any adjacent stamp, so that any block of four has stamps oriented in each of the four directions.

Die cut and imperforate uncut press sheets of No. 4880 were made available for sale. Values: cross gutter block of 4, $9; pairs with gutters between, $4.25 each. See note after No. 4693.

See note after No. 1549.

Flowers and "Yes I Do" Type of 2013

Designed by Michael Osborne. Printed by Ashton-Potter (USA) Ltd.

LITHOGRAPHED

Sheets of 180 in nine panes of 20

2014, Mar. 21 Tagged *Serpentine Die Cut 10¾*

Self-Adhesive

4881	A3639 70c **multicolored**	1.40	.30
	P# block of 4, 4#+P	5.60	
	Pane of 20	28.00	

See note after No. 1549.

SONGBIRDS

Western Meadowlark — A3735

Mountain Bluebird — A3736

Western Tanager — A3737

Painted Bunting — A3738

Baltimore Oriole — A3739

Evening Grosbeak — A3740

Scarlet Tanager — A3741

Rose-breasted Grosbeak — A3742

American Goldfinch — A3743

White-throated Sparrow — A3744

Designed by Derry Noyes. Printed by Ashton-Potter (USA) Ltd.

LITHOGRAPHED

Serpentine Die Cut 10¾ on 2 or 3 Sides

2014, Apr. 5 **Tagged**

Booklet Stamps
Self-Adhesive

4882	A3735 (49c) **multicolored**	1.10	.40
4883	A3736 (49c) **multicolored**	1.10	.40
4884	A3737 (49c) **multicolored**	1.10	.40
4885	A3738 (49c) **multicolored**	1.10	.40
4886	A3739 (49c) **multicolored**	1.10	.40
4887	A3740 (49c) **multicolored**	1.10	.40
4888	A3741 (49c) **multicolored**	1.10	.40
4889	A3742 (49c) **multicolored**	1.10	.40
4890	A3743 (49c) **multicolored**	1.10	.40
4891	A3744 (49c) **multicolored**	1.10	.40
a.	Block of 10, #4882-4891	11.00	
b.	Booklet pane of 20, 2 each #4882-4891	22.00	
c.	Imperforate block of 10	20.00	—
d.	Imperforate booklet pane of 20	40.00	
	Nos. 4882-4891 (10)	11.00	4.00

Nos. 4891b and 4891d are double-sided booklet panes with 12 stamps on one side (Nos. 4883-4886, 4888-4891, 2 each Nos. 4882, 4887) and eight stamps (Nos. 4883-4886, 4888-4891) plus label (booklet cover) on the other side.

Die cut and imperforate uncut press sheets of Nos. 4882-4891 were made available for sale. Values for varieties from die cut press sheets: cross gutter block of 4 with booklet cover, imperf. within, $10; cross gutter block of 4, imperf. within, $10; vert. pair, imperf. between, $4; horiz. pair, imperf. between, $6. Values for varieties from imperforate press sheets: cross gutter block of 4 with booklet cover, $10; vert. pair with gutter between, $4; horiz. pair with booklet cover and gutter between, $6. See note after No. 4693.

See note after No. 1549.

LEGENDS OF HOLLYWOOD

Charlton Heston (1923-2008), Actor — A3745

Designed by Greg Breeding. Printed by Ashton-Potter (USA) Ltd.

LITHOGRAPHED

Sheets of 180 in nine panes of 20

2014, Apr. 11 **Tagged** ***Serpentine Die Cut 11***

Self-Adhesive

4892	A3745 (49c) **multicolored** Ⓢ	1.10	.25
	P# block of 4, 4#+P	4.40	
	Pane of 20	22.00	
a.	Imperforate	1.75	—
	Pane of 20	35.00	

Die cut and imperforate uncut press sheets of No. 4892 were made available for sale. Values: cross gutter block of 4, $9; pairs with gutters between, $4 each. See note after No. 4693.

See note after No. 1549.

Map of Sea Surface Temperatures A3746

Designed by William J. Gicker. Printed by Ashton-Potter (USA) Ltd.

LITHOGRAPHED

Sheets of 50 in five panes of 10

2014, Apr. 22 **Tagged** ***Serpentine Die Cut***

Self-Adhesive

4893	A3746 ($1.15) **multicolored** Ⓢ	2.40	.50
	P# block of 4, 6#+P	10.00	
	Pane of 10	24.00	
a.	Imperforate	3.50	—
	Pane of 10	35.00	

Unused values are for stamps with surrounding selvage. Adjacent stamps are separated by rouletting.

Die cut and imperforate uncut press sheets of No. 4893 were made available for sale. Value: vert. pair with gutter between, $8. See note after No. 4693.

See note after No. 1549.

FLAGS Ⓢ

Flag With 5 Full and 3 Partial Stars — A3747

Flag With 3 Full Stars — A3748

Flag With 4 Full and 2 Partial Stars — A3749

Flag With 2 Full and 2 Partial Stars — A3750

Designed by Ethel Kessler. Printed by CCL Label, Inc.

PHOTOGRAVURE

Serpentine Die Cut 11 Vert.

2014, Apr. 25 **Tagged**

Coil Stamps
Self-Adhesive

4894	A3747 (49c) **blue & red**	1.10	.25
4895	A3748 (49c) **blue & red**	1.10	.25
4896	A3749 (49c) **blue & red**	1.10	.25
4897	A3750 (49c) **blue & red**	1.10	.25
a.	Strip of 4, #4894-4897	4.40	
	P# strip of 5, #4895-4897, 2 #4894, #C11, C12	7.00	
	P# strip of 9, 3# 4896, 2 each #4894-4895, 4897, #C11, C12	12.00	
	P# single, #C11, C12 (#4896)	—	3.00
	Nos. 4894-4897 (4)	4.40	1.00

See note after No. 1549.

CIRCUS POSTERS

Barnum and Bailey Circus Poster With Clown — A3751

Sells-Floto Circus Poster — A3752

Ringling Bros. Barnum and Bailey Circus Poster With Dainty Miss Leitzel — A3753

Al G. Barnes Wild Animal Circus Poster — A3754

Ringling Bros. Shows Poster With Hillary Long — A3755

Barnum and Bailey Circus Poster With Tiger — A3756

Ringling Bros. Barnum and Bailey Circus Poster With Elephant — A3757

Carl Hagenbeck-Wallace Circus Poster — A3758

A3758a

Designed by Jennifer Arnold, Joe Brockert (#4905c). Printed by Banknote Coporation of America for Sennett Security Products.

LITHOGRAPHED, ENGRAVED (50c), SHEET MARGIN (#4905b) LITHOGRAPHED WITH FOIL APPLICATION

Sheets of 96 in six panes of 16

2014, May 5 ***Serpentine Die Cut 11***

Tagged, Untagged (No. 4905c)

Self-Adhesive

No.	Design	Description	Unused	Used
4898	A3751	(49c) **multicolored**	1.10	.45
4899	A3752	(49c) **multicolored**	1.10	.45
4900	A3753	(49c) **multicolored**	1.10	.45
4901	A3754	(49c) **multicolored**	1.10	.45
4902	A3755	(49c) **multicolored**	1.10	.45
4903	A3756	(49c) **multicolored**	1.10	.45
4904	A3757	(49c) **multicolored**	1.10	.45
4905	A3758	(49c) **multicolored**	1.10	.45
a.		Block of 8, #4898-4905	8.80	
		Pane of 16	17.50	
b.		Imperforate block of 8	16.00	—
		Pane of 16	32.00	
c.		A3758a Imperforate souvenir sheet of 3, #4905e, 2 #4905d, *Dec. 10*	9.00	—
d.		A1811 50c **red**, imperforate	2.25	—
e.		$1 **multicolored** (57x48mm stamp similar to #4898), imperforate	4.50	—
f.		As "c," gold omitted in sheet margin	—	
		Nos. 4898-4905 (8)	8.80	3.60

Die cut and imperforate uncut press sheets of Nos. 4898-4905 were made available for sale. Values: cross gutter block of 8, $22.50; block of 8 with horiz. gutter between, $17.50; pairs with gutters between, $4.25 each; No. 4905c in cross gutter block of 4, $40; pair of No. 4905c with horiz. gutter between, $17.50; pair of No. 4905c with wide horiz. gutter between, $20. See note after No. 4693.

No. 4905c was printed only in press sheets containing 12 souvenir sheets. No. 4905c has die cutting around the souvenir sheet margin, but values for unused examples are for souvenir sheets having the white press sheet margin surrounding the die cutting. Examples of No. 4905c with serpentine die cutting around the three stamps were sold only with the USPS 2014 Stamp Yearbook, which sold for $64.95. The souvenir sheets sold with the yearbook are punched out from the press sheets and lack the white press sheet margin.

HARVEY MILK

Harvey Milk (1930-78), Homosexual Rights Advocate and Politician — A3759

Designed by Antonio Alcalá. Printed by Banknote Corporation of America for Sennett Security Products.

LITHOGRAPHED

Sheets of 240 in 12 panes of 20

2014, May 22 **Tagged** ***Serpentine Die Cut 10¾***

Self-Adhesive

No.	Design	Description	Unused	Used
4906	A3759	(49c) **multicolored**	1.10	.25
		P# block of 4, 4#+S	4.40	
		Pane of 20	22.00	
a.		Imperforate	1.75	—
		Pane of 20	35.00	

Die cut and imperforate uncut press sheets of No. 4906 were made available for sale. Values: cross gutter block of 4, $9; pairs with gutters between, $4.25 each. See note after No. 4693.

NEVADA STATEHOOD, 150th ANNIV.

Fire Canyon A3760

Designed by Antonio Alcalá. Printed by Banknote Corporation of America for Sennett Security Products.

LITHOGRAPHED

Sheets of 240 in 12 panes of 20

2014, May 29 **Tagged** ***Serpentine Die Cut 10¾***

Self-Adhesive

No.	Design	Description	Unused	Used
4907	A3760	(49c) **multicolored**	1.10	.25
		P# block of 4, 6#+S	4.40	
		Pane of 20	22.00	
a.		Imperforate	1.75	—
		Pane of 20	35.00	

Die cut and imperforate uncut press sheets of No. 4907 were made available for sale. Values: cross gutter block of 4, $9; pairs with gutters between, $4.25 each. See note after No. 4693.

HOT RODS Ⓢ

Rear of 1932 Ford "Deuce" Roadster — A3761

Front of 1932 Ford "Deuce" Roadster — A3762

Designed by Derry Noyes. Printed by CCL Label, Inc.

PHOTOGRAVURE

Serpentine Die Cut 11¾x11¼ on 2 or 3 Sides

2014, June 6 **Tagged**

Booklet Stamps

Self-Adhesive

No.	Design	Description	Unused	Used
4908	A3761	(49c) **multicolored**	1.10	.25
4909	A3762	(49c) **multicolored**	1.10	.25
a.		Pair, #4908-4909	2.20	
b.		Booklet pane of 20, 10 each #4908-4909	22.00	
c.		Imperforate pair	4.00	—
d.		Imperforate booklet pane of 20	40.00	

Nos. 4909b and 4909d are double-sided booklet panes with 12 stamps on one side (6 each Nos. 4908-4909) and eight stamps (4 each Nos. 4908-4909) plus label (booklet cover) on the other side.

Die cut and imperforate uncut press sheets of Nos. 4908-4909 were made available for sale. Values for varieties from die cut press sheets: horiz. pair, imperf. between, $4.50. Values for varieties from imperforate press sheets: horiz. pair with booklet cover, $6. See note after No. 4693.

See note after No. 1549.

CIVIL WAR SESQUICENTENNIAL

Battle of Petersburg — A3763

Battle of Mobile Bay — A3764

Designed by Phil Jordan. Printed by Banknote Corporation of America for Sennett Security Products.

LITHOGRAPHED

Double-sided sheets of 72 in six panes of 12 (60 on one side, 12 on other side)

2014, July 30 **Tagged** ***Serpentine Die Cut 11***

Self-Adhesive

No.	Design	Description	Unused	Used
4910	A3763	(49c) **multicolored**	1.10	.35
4911	A3764	(49c) **multicolored**	1.10	.35
a.		Pair, #4910-4911	2.20	
		Pane of 12	13.25	
b.		Imperforate pair	5.00	—
		Imperf. pair with wide spacing	7.00	
		Pane of 12	32.00	

Die cut and imperforate uncut press sheets of Nos. 4910-4911 were made available for sale. Values: vert. pairs with gutters between, $4.50 each. See note after No. 4693.

FARMERS MARKETS Ⓢ

Breads — A3765

Fruits and Vegetables — A3766

Flowers — A3767

Plants — A3768

Designed by Greg Breeding. Printed by Ashton-Potter (USA) Ltd.

LITHOGRAPHED

Sheets of 100 in five panes of 20

2014, Aug. 7 Tagged ***Serpentine Die Cut 10¾***

Self-Adhesive

4912	A3765 (49c) **multicolored**	1.10	.30
4913	A3766 (49c) **multicolored**	1.10	.30
4914	A3767 (49c) **multicolored**	1.10	.30
4915	A3768 (49c) **multicolored**	1.10	.30
a.	Horiz. strip of 4, #4912-4915	4.40	
	P# block of 8, 4#+P	8.80	
	Pane of 20	22.00	
b.	Imperf. horiz. strip of 4	9.00	—
	Pane of 20	45.00	
	Nos. 4912-4915 (4)	4.40	1.20

Die cut and imperforate uncut press sheets of Nos. 4912-4915 were made available for sale. Value: horiz. strip of 4 with vert. gutter between, $11. See note after No. 4693.

See note after No. 1549.

MUSIC ICONS

Janis Joplin (1943-70), Rock Singer — A3769

Designed by Antonio Alcalá. Printed by Ashton-Potter (USA) Ltd.

LITHOGRAPHED

Sheets of 144 in nine panes of 16

2014, Aug. 8 Tagged ***Serpentine Die Cut 10½***

Self-Adhesive

4916	A3769 (49c) **multicolored** Ⓢ	1.10	.25
	Pane of 16	17.50	
a.	Imperforate	1.75	—
	Pane of 16	28.00	

Die cut and imperforate uncut press sheets of No. 4916 were made available for sale. Values: cross gutter block of 4, $9; pairs with gutters between, $4.25 each. See note after No. 4693.

See note after No. 1549.

HUDSON RIVER SCHOOL PAINTINGS Ⓢ

Grand Canyon, by Thomas Moran (1837-1926) A3770

Summer Afternoon, by Asher B. Durand (1796-1886) A3771

Sunset, by Frederic Edwin Church (1826-1900) A3772

Distant View of Niagara Falls, by Thomas Cole (1801-48) A3773

Designed by Derry Noyes. Printed by CCL Label, Inc.

PHOTOGRAVURE

Serpentine Die Cut 10¾ on 2 or 3 Sides

2014, Aug. 21 Tagged

Booklet Stamps

Self-Adhesive

4917	A3770 (49c) **multicolored**	1.10	.30
4918	A3771 (49c) **multicolored**	1.10	.30
4919	A3772 (49c) **multicolored**	1.10	.30
4920	A3773 (49c) **multicolored**	1.10	.30
a.	Block of 4, #4917-4920	4.40	
b.	Booklet pane of 20, 5 each #4917-4920	22.00	
c.	Imperforate block of 4	8.00	—
d.	Imperforate booklet pane of 20	40.00	
	Nos. 4917-4920 (4)	4.40	1.20

Nos. 4920b and 4920d are double-sided booklet panes with 12 stamps on one side (3 each Nos. 4917-4920), and eight stamps (2 each Nos. 4917-4920) plus label (booklet cover) on the other side.

Die cut and imperforate uncut press sheets of Nos. 4917-4920 were made available for sale. Values for varieties from die cut press sheets: block of 4, vert. imperf. between, $10. Values for varieties from imperforate press sheets: block of 4 with vert. gutter, $10. See note after No. 4693.

See note after No. 1549.

WAR OF 1812 BICENTENNIAL

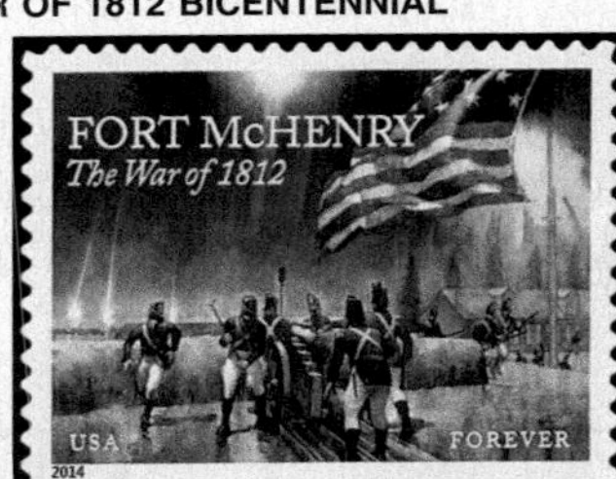

Bombardment of Fort McHenry A3774

Designed by Greg Breeding. Printed by CCL Label, Inc.

PHOTOGRAVURE

Sheets of 100 in five panes of 20

Serpentine Die Cut 10¾x10½

2014, Sept. 13 Tagged

Self-Adhesive

4921	A3774 (49c) **multicolored** Ⓢ	1.10	.25
	Pane of 20	22.00	
a.	Imperforate	1.75	—
	Pane of 20	35.00	

Die-cut and imperforate uncut press sheets of No. 4921 were made available for sale. Value, pair with gutter between, $4. See note after No. 4693.

See note after No. 1549.

CELEBRITY CHEFS Ⓢ

Edna Lewis (1916-2006) — A3775

Felipe Rojas-Lombardi (1946-91) — A3776

Joyce Chen (1917-94) — A3777

James Beard (1903-85) — A3778

Julia Child (1912-2004) — A3779

Designed by Greg Breeding. Printed by Ashton-Potter (USA) Ltd.

LITHOGRAPHED

Sheets of 180 in nine panes of 20

Serpentine Die Cut 11x10¾

2014, Sept. 26 Tagged

Self-Adhesive

4922	A3775 (49c) **multicolored**	1.20	.45
4923	A3776 (49c) **multicolored**	1.20	.45
4924	A3777 (49c) **multicolored**	1.20	.45
4925	A3778 (49c) **multicolored**	1.20	.45
4926	A3779 (49c) **multicolored**	1.20	.45
a.	Horiz. strip of 5, #4922-4926	6.00	
	P# block of 10, 2 sets of 5#+P	12.00	
	Pane of 20	24.00	
b.	Imperf. horiz. strip of 5	8.00	—
	Pane of 20	32.50	
	Nos. 4922-4926 (5)	6.00	2.25

The gray shading of the inner curve of the dinner plate shown in the margin of the pane continues into the white frames surrounding some of the stamps in the pane's outer rows and columns.

Die cut and imperforate uncut press sheets of Nos. 4922-4926 were made available for sale. Values: cross gutter block of 10, $22.50; pairs with gutters between, $4.25 each. See note after No. 4693.

See note after No. 1549.

AMERICAN LANDMARKS ISSUE

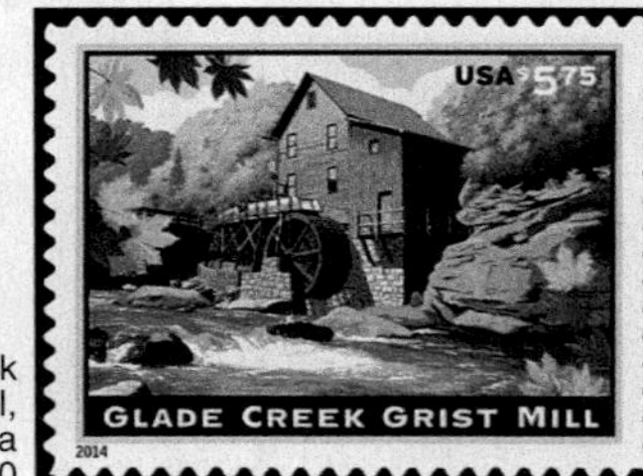

Glade Creek Grist Mill, West Virginia
A3780

Designed by Derry Noyes. Printed by Ashton-Potter (USA) Ltd.

LITHOGRAPHED
Sheets of 60 in six panes of 10

Serpentine Die Cut 10¾x10½

2014, Sept. 29 **Tagged**

Self-Adhesive

4927	A3780 $5.75 **multicolored** Ⓢ	11.50	6.50
	P# block of 4, 4#+P	46.00	
	Pane of 10	115.00	
a.	Imperforate	15.00	—
	Pane of 10	150.00	

Die cut and imperforate press sheets of No. 4927 were made available for sale. Values: s cross gutter block of 4, $80; pairs with gutter between, $30 each. See note after No. 2868.

See note after No. 1549.

BATMAN

Bat Signal — A3781

Bat Signal — A3782

Bat Signal — A3783

Bat Signal — A3784

Batman — A3785

Batman and Bat Signal — A3786

Batman and Rope — A3787

Batman — A3788

Designed by Greg Breeding. Printed by Baknote Corporation of America for Sennett Security Products.

LITHOGRAPHED
Sheets of 180 in nine panes of 20

2014, Oct. 9 **Tagged** ***Serpentine Die Cut***

Self-Adhesive

4928	A3781 (49c) **multicolored**	1.75	.40
4929	A3782 (49c) **multicolored**	1.75	.40
4930	A3783 (49c) **multicolored**	1.75	.40
4931	A3784 (49c) **multicolored**	1.75	.40

Serpentine Die Cut 11x10¾

4932	A3785 (49c) **multicolored**	1.10	.40
4933	A3786 (49c) **multicolored**	1.10	.40
4934	A3787 (49c) **multicolored**	1.10	.40
4935	A3788 (49c) **multicolored**	1.10	.40
a.	Vert. block of 8, #4928-4935	11.50	
	Pane of 20, #4928-4931, 4 each #4932-4935	23.00	
b.	Imperf. vert. block of 8	20.00	—
	Pane of 20	40.00	
	Nos. 4928-4935 (8)	11.40	3.20

Die cut and imperforate press sheets of Nos. 4928-4935 were made available for sale. See note after No. 4693.

Silver Bells Wreath — A3789

Designed by Michael Owens and William J. Gicker. Printed by Banknote Corporation of America for Sennett Security Products.

LITHOGRAPHED
Sheets of 60 in six panes of 10

2014, Oct. 23 **Tagged** ***Serpentine Die Cut***

Self-Adhesive

4936	A3789 ($1.15) **multicolored**	2.50	.50
	P# block of 4, 5#+S	10.00	
	Pane of 10	25.00	
a.	Imperforate	4.00	—
	Pane of 10	40.00	

Unused values are for stamps with surrounding selvage. Adjacent stamps are separated by rouletting.

Die cut and imperforate uncut press sheets of No. 4936 were made available for sale. Values: cross gutter block of 4, $21; pairs with gutters between, $9.50 each. See note after No. 4693.

WINTER FUN Ⓢ

Skaters — A3790

Child Making Snowman — A3791

Cardinal — A3792

Child Making Snow Angel — A3793

Skaters — A3794

Child Making Snowman — A3795

Cardinal — A3796

Child Making Snow Angel — A3797

Designed by Ethel Kessler. Printed by CCL Label, Inc. (Nos. 4937-4940), Ashton-Potter (USA) Ltd. (Nos. 4941-4944).

PHOTOGRAVURE (Nos. 4937-4940),
LITHOGRAPHED (Nos. 4941-4944)

Serpentine Die Cut 10¾x11 on 2 or 3 Sides

2014, Oct. 23 **Tagged**

Booklet Stamps
Self-Adhesive

4937	A3790 (49c) **multicolored**	1.10	.30
4938	A3791 (49c) **multicolored**	1.10	.30
4939	A3792 (49c) **multicolored**	1.10	.30
4940	A3793 (49c) **multicolored**	1.10	.30
a.	Block of 4, #4937-4940	4.40	
b.	Booklet pane of 20, 5 each #4937-4940	22.00	
c.	Imperforate block of 4	7.00	—
d.	Imperf. booklet pane of 20	35.00	

Serpentine Die Cut 11¼x11 on 2, 3 or 4 Sides

Thin Paper

4941	A3794 (49c) **multicolored**	1.50	.30
4942	A3795 (49c) **multicolored**	1.50	.30
4943	A3796 (49c) **multicolored**	1.50	.30
4944	A3797 (49c) **multicolored**	1.50	.30
a.	Block or strip of 4, #4941-4944	6.00	
b.	Booklet pane of 18, 5 each #4941-4942, 4 each #4943-4944	27.00	
	Nos. 4937-4944 (8)	10.40	2.40

Nos. 4940b and 4940d are double-sided booklet panes with 12 stamps on one side (3 each Nos. 4937-4940) and eight stamps (2 each Nos. 4937-4940) plus label (booklet cover) on the other side.

Die cut and imperforate uncut press sheets of Nos. 4937-4940 were made available for sale. Values for varieties from die cut press sheets: block of 4, horiz. imperf. between, $9. Values for varieties from imperforate sheets: block of 4 with horiz. gutter, $9. See note after No. 4693.

See note after No. 1549.

CHRISTMAS

Magi — A3798

Rudolph, the Red-Nosed Reindeer — A3799

Hermey and Rudolph — A3800

Santa Claus — A3801

Bumble — A3802

Designed by Greg Breeding.
Printed by Banknote Corporation of America for Sennett Security Products (#4945), CCL Label, Inc. (#4946-4949).

LITHOGRAPHED (#4945), PHOTOGRAVURE

Serpentine Die Cut 10¾x11 on 2 or 3 Sides

2014 **Tagged**

Booklet Stamps
Self-Adhesive

4945	A3798 (49c) **multicolored,** *Nov. 19*	1.10	.25
a.	Booklet pane of 20	22.00	
b.	Imperforate	1.75	—
c.	Imperf. booklet pane of 20	35.00	

Serpentine Die Cut 11x10¾ on 2 or 3 sides

4946	A3799 (49c) **multicolored,** *Nov. 6* Ⓢ	1.20	.30
4947	A3800 (49c) **multicolored,** *Nov. 6* Ⓢ	1.20	.30
4948	A3801 (49c) **multicolored,** *Nov. 6* Ⓢ	1.20	.30
4949	A3802 (49c) **multicolored,** *Nov. 6* Ⓢ	1.20	.30
a.	Block of 4, #4946-4949	4.80	
b.	Booklet pane of 20, 5 each #4946-4949	24.00	
c.	Imperf. block of 4	7.50	—
d.	Imperf. booklet pane of 20	37.50	
	Nos. 4945-4949 (5)	5.90	1.45

Premiere of *Rudolph, the Red-Nosed Reindeer* animated television show, 50th anniv.

Nos. 4945a and 4945c are double-sided booklet panes with 12 stamps on one side and eight stamps plus a label that serves as a booklet cover on the other side. Nos. 4949b and 4949d are double-sided booklet panes with 12 stamps on one side (3 each of Nos. 4946-4949) and eight stamps (2 each of Nos. 4946-4949) plus a label that serves as a booklet cover on the other side.

Die cut and imperforate uncut press sheets of eight booklet panes of Nos. 4945 were made available for sale. Values for varieties from die cut press sheets: cross gutter block of 4 with booklet cover, imperf. within, $10; cross gutter block of 4, imperf. within, $10; vert. pair, imperf. between, $4; horiz. pair, imperf. between, $6. Values for varieties from imperforate press sheets: cross gutter block of 4 with booklet cover, $10; horiz. pair with booklet cover and gutter between, $6.

Die cut and imperforate uncut press sheets of Nos. 4946-4949 were made available for sale. Values for varieties from die cut press sheets: block of 4, vert. imperf. between, $8.50. Values for varieties from imperforate press sheets: block of 4, vert. gutter between, $8.50.

See note after No. 4693.
See note after No. 1549.

WILT CHAMBERLAIN (1936-99), BASKETBALL PLAYER

Chamberlain in Philadelphia Warriors Uniform — A3803

Chamberlain in Los Angeles Lakers Uniform — A3804

Designed by Antonio Alcalá. Printed by Banknote Corporation of America for Sennett Security Products.

LITHOGRAPHED

Sheets of 144 in eight panes of 18

2014, Dec. 5 Tagged *Serpentine Die Cut 11x10¾*

Self-Adhesive

4950	A3803 (49c) **multicolored**	1.10	.25
4951	A3804 (49c) **multicolored**	1.10	.25
a.	Pair, #4950-4951	2.20	
	P# block of 4, 4#+S	4.40	
	Pane of 18	22.00	
b.	Imperforate pair	3.50	—
	Pane of 18	35.00	

Die cut and imperforate uncut press sheets of Nos. 4950-4951 were made available for sale. Values: cross gutter block of 6, $9; pairs with gutters between, $4.25 each.

See note after No. 4693.

WAR OF 1812 BICENTENNIAL

Battle of New Orleans A3805

Designed by Greg Breeding. Printed by CCL Label, Inc.

PHOTOGRAVURE

Sheets of 100 in five panes of 20

Serpentine Die Cut 10¾x10½

2015, Jan. 8 **Tagged**

Self-Adhesive

4952	A3805 (49c) **multicolored** Ⓢ	1.10	.25
	Pane of 20	20.00	
a.	Imperforate	1.75	—
	Pane of 20	35.00	

Die cut and imperforate uncut press sheets of No. 4952 were made available for sale. Value: vert. pair with gutter between, $4.25. See note after No. 4693.

See note after No. 1549.

PATRIOTIC WAVES Ⓢ

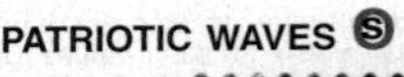

A3806

A3807

Designed by Michael Dyer. Printed by Ashton-Potter (USA) Ltd.

LITHOGRAPHED

Sheets of 140 in 14 panes of 10 (#4953), Sheets of 100 in 10 panes of 10 (#4954)

2015 Tagged *Serpentine Die Cut 11*

Self-Adhesive

4953	A3806 $1 **multicolored,** *Jan. 12*	2.00	.50
	P# block of 4, 3#+P	8.00	
	Pane of 10	20.00	
a.	Imperforate	3.00	—
	Pane of 10	30.00	
4954	A3807 $2 **multicolored,** *Jan. 30*	4.00	1.00
	P# block of 4, 3#+P	16.00	
	Pane of 10	40.00	
a.	Imperforate	5.00	—
	Pane of 10	50.00	

Die-cut and imperforate uncut press sheets of No. 4953 were made available for sale. Values: cross gutter block of 4, $16.50; pairs with gutters between, $6.75 each.

Die-cut and imperforate uncut press sheets of No. 4954 were made available for sale. Values: cross gutter block of 4, $27.50; pairs with gutters between, $12.50 each. See note after No. 4693.

See note after No. 1549.

LOVE Ⓢ

A3808

A3809

Designed by Antonio Alcalá and Jessica Hische. Printed by CCL Label, Inc.

LITHOGRAPHED

Sheets of 120 in six panes of 20

2015, Jan. 22 Tagged *Serpentine Die Cut 11*

Self-Adhesive

4955	A3808 (49c) **red**	1.10	.25
4956	A3809 (49c) **red & gray**	1.10	.25
a.	Pair, #4955-4956	2.20	
	P# block of 4, 2#+C	4.40	
	Pane of 20	22.00	
b.	Imperforate pair	3.50	—
	Pane of 20	35.00	

Die cut and imperforate uncut press sheets of Nos. 4955-4956 were made available for sale. Values: cross gutter block of 4, $9; pairs with gutters between, $4.25 each.

Counterfeits exist of Nos. 4955-4956. See the Postal Counterfeits section of this catalog.

See note after No. 4693. See note after No. 1549.

CHINESE NEW YEAR

Year of the Ram — A3810

Designed by Ethel Kessler. Printed by Banknote Corporation of America for Sennett Security Products.

LITHOGRAPHED

Sheets of 144 in 12 panes of 12

2015, Feb. 7 Tagged *Serpentine Die Cut 11*

Self-Adhesive

4957	A3810 (49c) **multicolored**	1.10	.25
	Pane of 12	13.25	
a.	Imperforate	1.75	—
	Pane of 12	18.00	

Die cut and imperforate uncut press sheets of No. 4957 were made available for sale. Values: cross gutter block of 4, $9; pairs with gutters between, $3.75 each. See note after No. 4693.

BLACK HERITAGE

Robert Robinson Taylor (1868-1942), Architect — A3811

Designed by Derry Noyes. Printed by Ashton-Potter (USA) Ltd.

LITHOGRAPHED

Sheets of 120 in six panes of 20

2015, Feb. 12 Tagged *Serpentine Die Cut 11*

Self-Adhesive

4958	A3811 (49c) **multicolored** Ⓢ	1.10	.25
	P# block of 4, 4#+P	4.40	
	Pane of 20	22.00	

a. Imperforate 2.25 —
Pane of 20 45.00

Die cut and imperforate uncut press sheets of No. 4958 were made available for sale. Values: cross gutter block of 4, $9; pairs with gutters between, $4.25 each. See note after No. 4693.

See note after No. 1549.

FLOWERS

Rose and Heart — A3812

Tulip and Heart — A3813

Designed by Jeanne Greco. Printed by Banknote Corporation of America for Sennett Security Products.

ENGRAVED

Sheets of 240 in 12 panes of 20

Serpentine Die Cut 10¾x 11

2015, Feb. 14 **Tagged**

Self-Adhesive

4959 A3812 (49c) **red & black** 1.10 .25
P# block of 4, 2#+S 4.40
Pane of 20 22.00
a. Imperforate 1.75 —
Pane of 20 35.00
b. Tagging omitted —
4960 A3813 70c **black & red** 1.50 .30
P# block of 4, 2#+S 6.00
Pane of 20 30.00
a. Imperforate 2.50 —
Pane of 20 50.00

Die cut and imperforate uncut press sheets of No. 4959 were made available for sale. Values: cross gutter block of 4, $9; pairs with gutters between, $4.25 each.

Counterfeits exist of No. 4959. See the Postal Counterfeits section of this catalog.

Die cut and imperforate uncut press sheets of No. 4960 were made available for sale. Values: cross gutter block of 4, $13.50; pairs with gutters between, $5.75 each.

See note after No. 4693.

FLAGS

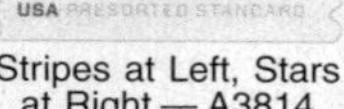

Stripes at Left, Stars at Right — A3814

Stars and White Stripe — A3815

Stars at Left, Stripes at Right — A3816

Designed by Greg Breeding. Printed by Banknote Corporation of America for Sennett Security Products.

LITHOGRAPHED

Serpentine Die Cut 11 Vert.

2015, Feb. 27 **Tagged**

Coil Stamps
Self-Adhesive

4961 A3814 (10c) **multicolored** .25 .25
4962 A3815 (10c) **multicolored** .25 .25
4963 A3816 (10c) **multicolored** .25 .25
a. Strip of 3, #4961-4963 .75
P# strip of 5, #4962, 2 each #4961, 4963, #S111, B111 3.00
P# strip of 7, 3# 4962, 2 each #4961, 4963, #S111, B111 4.50
P# single, #S111, B111 (#4962) — 2.25
Nos. 4961-4963 (3) .75 .75

WATER LILIES

Pale Pink Water Lily — A3817

Red Water Lily — A3818

Purple Water Lily — A3819

White Water Lily — A3820

Designed by Phil Jordan. Printed by Banknote Corporation of America for Sennett Security Products.

LITHOGRAPHED

Serpentine Die Cut 11x11¼ on 2 or 3 Sides

2015, Mar. 20 **Tagged**

Booklet Stamps
Self-Adhesive

4964 A3817 (49c) **multicolored** 1.10 .25
4965 A3818 (49c) **multicolored** 1.10 .25
4966 A3819 (49c) **multicolored** 1.10 .25
4967 A3820 (49c) **multicolored** 1.10 .25
a. Block of 4, #4964-4967 4.40
b. Booklet pane of 20, 5 each #4964-4967 22.00
c. Imperf. block of 4 7.00 —
d. Imperf. booklet pane of 20 35.00
Nos. 4964-4967 (4) 4.40 1.00

No. 4967b is known with the block of 4 at left on the 12-stamp side having no gum. Such booklets are rare and fragile.

Nos. 4967b and 4967d are double-sided booklet panes with 12 stamps on one side (3 each Nos. 4964-4967) and eight stamps (2 each Nos. 4964-4967) plus label (booklet cover) on the other side.

Die cut and imperforate uncut press sheets of Nos. 4964-4967 were made available for sale. Values for varieties from die cut press sheets: cross gutter block of 4 with booklet cover, imperf. within, $10; cross gutter block of 4, imperf. within, $10; block of 4, vert. imperf. between, $8.50; block of 4 with booklet cover, horiz. imperf. between, $10. Values for varieties from imperforate press sheets: cross gutter block of 4 with booklet cover, $10; block of 4 with booklet cover between, $10; block of 4 with vert. gutter between, $8.50. See note after No. 4693.

ART BY MARTIN RAMIREZ (1895-1963)

Untitled (Horse and Rider With Trees), 1954 — A3821

Untitled (Man Riding Donkey), c. 1960-63 — A3822

Untitled (Deer), c. 1960-63 — A3824

Untitled (Tunnel with Cars and Buses), 1954 — A3825

Designed by Antonio Alcalá. Printed by Banknote Corporation of America for Sennett Security Products.

LITHOGRAPHED

Sheets of 240 in 12 panes of 20

2015, Mar. 26 **Tagged** ***Serpentine Die Cut 10¾***

Self-Adhesive

4968 A3821 (49c) **multicolored** 1.10 .40
4969 A3822 (49c) **multicolored** 1.10 .40
4970 A3823 (49c) **multicolored** 1.10 .40
4971 A3824 (49c) **multicolored** 1.10 .40
4972 A3825 (49c) **multicolored** 1.10 .40
a. Vert. strip of 5, #4968-4972 5.50
P# block of 10, 5#+S 11.00
Pane of 20 22.00
b. Imperf. vert. strip of 5 7.50 —
Pane of 20 30.00

Die cut and imperforate uncut press sheets of Nos. 4968-4972 were made available for sale. Values: cross gutter block of 10, $22.50; pairs with gutters between, $3.75 each.

See note after No. 4693.

Ferns Types of 2014

Designed by Phil Jordan. Printed by Banknote Corporation of America for Sennett Security Products.

LITHOGRAPHED

Serpentine Die Cut 11 Vert.

2015, Mar. 27 **Tagged**

Coil Stamps
Self-Adhesive
With Microprinted "USPS"
Dated "2014"

4973 A3729 (49c) **multicolored** 1.10 .25
a. Dated "2015" 1.10 .25
4974 A3730 (49c) **multicolored** 1.10 .25
a. Dated "2015" 1.10 .25
4975 A3731 (49c) **multicolored** 1.10 .25
a. Dated "2015" 1.10 .25
4976 A3732 (49c) **multicolored** 1.10 .25
a. Dated "2015" 1.10 .25
4977 A3728 (49c) **multicolored** 1.10 .25
a. Dated "2015" 1.10 .25
b. Strip of 5, #4973-4977 5.50
P# strip of 5, #4973-4977, #S1111 7.00
P# strip of 11, 3# 4975, 2 each #4973-4974, 4976-4977, #S1111 13.00
P# single, #S1111 (#4975) — 3.00
c. Strip of 5, #4973a-4977a 5.50
P# strip of 5, #4973a-4977a, #S1111 7.00
P# strip of 11, 3# 4975a, 2 each #4973a-4974a, 4976a-4977a, #S1111 13.00
P# single, #S1111 (#4975a) — 3.00
Nos. 4973-4977 (5) 5.50 1.25

Nos. 4973a-4977a are from coil rolls containing 3,000 stamps. Nos. 4973-4977 are from coil rolls containing 10,000 stamps. Microprinted "USPS" is near the end of the upper left fern branch on No. 4973 and near the base of the fern's stem on Nos. 4974-4977. Nos. 4973a-4977a have same microprinting locations as Nos. 4973-4977. Nos. 4874-4878 lack microprinted "USPS."

FROM ME TO YOU Ⓢ

A3826

Designed by Michael Osborne. Printed by Ashton-Potter (USA) Ltd.

LITHOGRAPHED
Sheets of 120 in six panes of 20

2015, Apr. 1 Tagged *Serpentine Die Cut 11*
Self-Adhesive

4978	A3826 (49c) **multicolored**	1.25	.25
	P# block of 10, 5#+P + top panel	12.50	
	Pane of 20 + 20 stickers	25.00	
a.	Imperforate	2.00	—
	Pane of 20 + 20 stickers	40.00	

Die cut and imperforate uncut press sheets of No. 4978 were made available for sale. Values: cross gutter block of 4, $11; pairs with gutters between, $4.25 each. See note after No. 4693.

See note after No. 1549.

MAYA ANGELOU (1928-2014), WRITER

Angelou and Quotation
A3827

Designed by Ethel Kessler. Printed by Banknote Corporation of America for Sennett Security Products.

LITHOGRAPHED
Sheets of 96 in eight panes of 12

2015, Apr. 7 Tagged *Serpentine Die Cut 11*
Self-Adhesive

4979	A3827 (49c) **multicolored**	1.10	.25
	P# block of 4, 6#+S	4.40	
	Pane of 12	13.25	
a.	Imperforate	1.75	—
	Pane of 12	21.00	

The quotation on the stamp is not Angelou's but is similar to a quote by Joan Walsh Anglund.

Die cut and imperforate uncut press sheets of No. 4979 were made available for sale. Values: cross gutter block of 4, $9; pairs with gutters between, $4.25 each. See note after No. 4693.

CIVIL WAR SESQUICENTENNIAL

Battle of Five Forks — A3828

Surrender at Appomattox Court House — A3829

Designed by Phil Jordan. Printed by Banknote Corporation of America for Sennett Security Products.

LITHOGRAPHED
Double-sided sheets of 72 in six panes of 12 (60 on one side, 12 on other side)

2015, Apr. 9 Tagged *Serpentine Die Cut 11*
Self-Adhesive

4980	A3828 (49c) **multicolored**	1.10	.30
4981	A3829 (49c) **multicolored**	1.10	.30
a.	Pair, #4980-4981	2.20	
	Pane of 12	13.25	
b.	Imperforate pair	*27.50*	—
	Imperforate pair with wide spacing	*37.50*	—
	Pane of 12	*175.00*	

Die cut and imperforate uncut press sheets of Nos. 4980-4981 were made available for sale. See note after No. 4693.

GIFTS OF FRIENDSHIP Ⓢ

Lincoln Memorial and Cherry Blossoms
A3830

U.S. Capitol and Dogwood Blossoms
A3831

Japanese Diet, Tokyo, and Cherry Blossoms
A3832

Clock Tower, Tokyo, and Dogwood Blossoms
A3833

Designed by William J. Gicker. Printed by Ashton-Potter (USA) Ltd.

LITHOGRAPHED
Sheets of 72 in six panes of 12

2015, Apr. 10 Tagged *Serpentine Die Cut 11*
Self-Adhesive

4982	A3830 (49c) **multicolored**	1.10	.30
4983	A3831 (49c) **multicolored**	1.10	.30
a.	Horiz. pair, #4982-4983	2.20	
b.	Imperforate pair	4.50	—
4984	A3832 (49c) **multicolored**	2.50	.30
4985	A3833 (49c) **multicolored**	2.50	.30
a.	Horiz. pair, #4984-4985	5.00	
	Pane of 12 (#4984-4985, 5 each #4982-4983)	16.00	
b.	Imperforate pair	12.50	—
	Imperforate pane of 12	35.00	
	Nos. 4982-4985 (4)	7.20	1.20

Die cut and imperforate uncut press sheets of Nos. 4982-4985 were made available for sale. See note after No. 4693.

See note after No. 1549.

See Japan No. 3814

SPECIAL OLYMPICS WORLD GAMES

Emblem — A3834

Designed by Greg Breeding. Printed by Banknote Corporation of America for Sennett Security Products.

LITHOGRAPHED
Sheets of 80 in four panes of 20

2015, May 9 Tagged *Serpentine Die Cut 10¾*
Self-Adhesive

4986	A3834 (49c) **multicolored**	1.10	.25
	P# block of 4, 6#+S	4.40	
	Pane of 20	22.00	
a.	Imperforate	1.75	—
	Pane of 20	35.00	

Die cut and imperforate uncut press sheets of No. 4986 were made available for sale. Values: horiz. pair with vert. gutter between, $3.75. See note after No. 4693.

HELP FIND MISSING CHILDREN

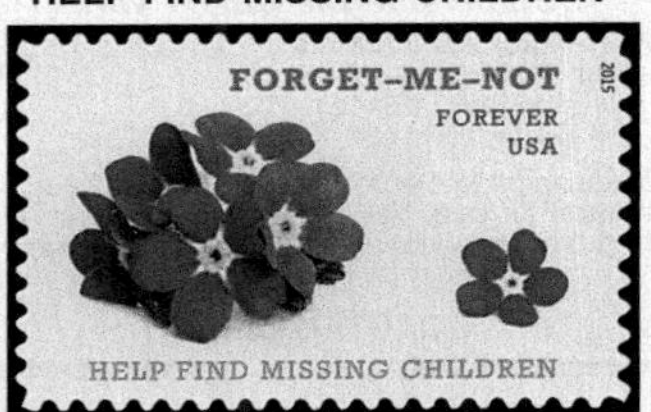

Forget-me-nots — A3835

Designed by Ethel Kessler. Printed by Ashton-Potter (USA) Ltd.

LITHOGRAPHED
Sheets of 120 in six panes of 20

2015, May 18 Tagged *Serpentine Die Cut 10¾*
Self-Adhesive

4987	A3835 (49c) **multicolored** Ⓢ	1.10	.25
	P# block of 4, 5#+P	4.40	
	Pane of 20	22.00	
a.	Imperforate	1.75	—
	Pane of 20	35.00	

Die cut and imperforate uncut press sheets of No. 4987 were made available for sale. Values: cross gutter block of 4, $9, pairs with gutters between, $4 each. See note after No. 4693.

See note after No. 1549.

MEDAL OF HONOR

Air Force Medal of Honor — A3836

Designed by Antonio Alcalá. Printed by Banknote Corporation of America for Sennett Security Products.

LITHOGRAPHED
Sheets of 72 in three panes of 24 (Panes are folded into a folio with 12 stamps on each side of the folded pane)

2015, May 25 Tagged *Serpentine Die Cut 11*
Self-Adhesive

4988	A3836 (49c) **multicolored**	1.10	.25
a.	Horiz. strip of 3, #4822b, 4823b, 4988	3.30	
	P# block of 6, 6#+S	6.60	

Folio of 24 26.50
b. Imperforate strip of 3 6.00 —
Folio of 24 48.00

Die cut and imperforate uncut press sheets of Nos. 4988, 4822b and 4823b were made available for sale. Values: vert. pairs with horiz. gutters between, $4.50 each. See note after No. 4693.

WILDLIFE ISSUE

Emperor Penguins — A3837

Designed by Carl T. Herrman. Printed by Banknote Corporation of America for Sennett Security Products.

LITHOGRAPHED
Sheets of 200 in ten panes of 20
Serpentine Die Cut 11¼x11

2015, June 1 **Tagged**

Self-Adhesive

4989 A3837 (22c) **multicolored** .45 .25
P# block of 4, 4#+S 1.90
Pane of 20 9.00
a. Imperforate 1.00 —
Pane of 20 20.00

Coil Stamp
Serpentine Die Cut 11 Vert.

4990 A3837 (22c) **multicolored** .45 .25
Pair .90
P# strip of 5, #S1111 3.50
P# single, #S1111 — 2.00

Die cut and imperforate uncut press sheets of No. 4989 were made available for sale. Values: cross gutter block of 4, $4.50; pairs with gutters between, $2 each. See note after No. 4693.

COASTAL BIRDS

Red Knot — A3838

King Eider — A3839

Spoonbill — A3840

Frigatebird — A3841

Designed by Greg Breeding. Printed by Banknote Corporation of America for Sennett Security Products (#4991-4994), Ashton-Potter (USA) Ltd. (#4995-4998).

LITHOGRAPHED
Sheets of 200 in ten panes of 20
Serpentine Die Cut 11¼x11

2015, June 1 **Tagged**

Self-Adhesive

4991 A3838 (35c) **multicolored** .70 .25
4992 A3839 (35c) **multicolored** .70 .25
4993 A3840 (35c) **multicolored** .70 .25
4994 A3841 (35c) **multicolored** .70 .25
a. Block or vert. strip of 4, #4991-4994 2.80
P# block of 4, 4#+S 2.80
Pane of 20 14.00
b. Imperforate block or vert. strip of 4 4.50 —
Pane of 20 22.50

Counterfeits exist of Nos. 4991-4994. See the Postal Counterfeits section of this catalog.

Coil Stamps
Serpentine Die Cut 9½ Vert.

4995 A3840 (35c) **multicolored** Ⓢ .70 .25
4996 A3841 (35c) **multicolored** Ⓢ .70 .25
4997 A3838 (35c) **multicolored** Ⓢ .70 .25
4998 A3839 (35c) **multicolored** Ⓢ .70 .25
a. Horiz. strip of 4, #4995-4998 2.80
P# strip of 5, #4996-4998, 2 #4995, #P1111 5.50
P# strip of 9, 2 each #4995-4996, 4998, 3 #4997, #P1111 9.25
P# single, #P1111 (#4997) — 2.75

Die cut and imperforate uncut press sheets of No. 4991-4994 were made available for sale. Values: cross gutter block of 8, $15; pairs with gutters between, $3.25 each. See note after No. 4693.

See note after No. 1549.

EASTERN TIGER SWALLOWTAIL BUTTERFLY

A3842

Designed by Derry Noyes. Printed by Ashton-Potter (USA) Ltd.

LITHOGRAPHED
Sheets of 120 in six panes of 20

2015, June 1 **Tagged** ***Serpentine Die Cut 10½***

Self-Adhesive

4999 A3842 (71c) **multicolored** Ⓢ 1.50 .25
P# block of 4, 5#+P 6.00
Pane of 20 30.00
a. Imperforate 2.50 —
Pane of 20 50.00

Die cut and imperforate uncut press sheets of No. 4999 were made available for sale. Values: cross gutter block of 4, $18, pairs with gutters between, $7.50 each. See note after No. 4693.

See note after No. 1549.

Wedding Cake — A3843

Designed by Ethel Kessler. Printed by Banknote Corporation of America for Sennett Security Products.

LITHOGRAPHED
Sheets of 160 in eight panes of 20

2015, June 1 **Tagged** ***Serpentine Die Cut 10¾***

Self-Adhesive

5000 A3843 (71c) **multicolored** 1.50 .25
P# block of 4, 6#+S 6.00
Pane of 20 30.00

Flowers and "Yes, I Do" — A3844

Designed by Michael Osborne. Printed by Ashton-Potter (USA), Ltd.

LITHOGRAPHED
Sheets of 120 in six panes of 20

2015, June 1 **Tagged** ***Serpentine Die Cut 10¾***

Self-Adhesive

5001 A3844 (71c) **multicolored** Ⓢ 1.50 .25
P# block of 4, 5#+P 6.00
Pane of 20 30.00

See note after No. 1549.

Tulip and Heart — A3845

Designed by Jeanne Greco. Printed by Banknote Corporation of America for Sennett Security Products.

ENGRAVED
Sheets of 240 in 12 panes of 20

2015, June 1 **Tagged** ***Serpentine Die Cut 11***

Self-Adhesive

5002 A3845 (71c) **black & red** 1.50 .25
P# block of 4, 2#+S 6.00
Pane of 20 30.00

LITERARY ARTS

Flannery O'Connor (1925-64), Novelist A3846

Designed by Phil Jordan. Printed by Ashton-Potter (USA) Ltd.

LITHOGRAPHED
Sheets of 120 in six panes of 20

2015, June 5 **Tagged** ***Serpentine Die Cut 10¾***

Self-Adhesive

5003 A3846 (93c) **multicolored** Ⓢ 1.90 .30
P# block of 4, 6#+P 7.60
Pane of 20 38.00
a. Imperforate 2.50 —
Pane of 20 50.00

Die cut and imperforate uncut press sheets of No. 5003 were made available for sale. Values: cross gutter block of 4, $18; pairs with gutters between, $7.50 each. See note after No. 4693.

See note after No. 1549.

SUMMER HARVEST Ⓢ

Watermelon — A3847

Sweet Corn — A3848

Cantaloupes — A3849

Tomatoes — A3850

Designed by Antonio Alcalá. Printed by Ashton-Potter (USA) Ltd.

LITHOGRAPHED
Serpentine Die Cut 11¼x10¾ on 2 or 3 Sides

2015, July 11 **Tagged**

Booklet Stamps
Self-Adhesive

5004 A3847 (49c) **multicolored** 1.10 .30
5005 A3848 (49c) **multicolored** 1.10 .30
5006 A3849 (49c) **multicolored** 1.10 .30
5007 A3850 (49c) **multicolored** 1.10 .30
a. Block of 4, #5004-5007 4.40
b. Booklet pane of 20, 5 each #5004-5007 22.00
c. As "a," imperforate 7.00 —
d. As "b," imperforate 35.00
Nos. 5004-5007 (4) 4.40 1.20

Nos. 5007b and 5007d are double-sided booklet panes with 12 stamps on one side (3 each Nos. 5004-5007), and eight stamps (2 each Nos. 5004-5007) plus label (booklet cover) on the other side.

Die cut and imperforate uncut press sheets of Nos. 5004-5007 were made available for sale. Values for varieties from die cut press sheets: cross gutter block of 4 with booklet cover, imperf. within, $10; cross gutter block of 4, imperf. within, $10; block of 4, horiz. imperf. between, $8; block of 4, vert. imperf. between, $8. Values for varieties from imperforate press sheets: cross gutter block of 4 with booklet cover, $10; block of 4 with horiz. gutter between, $8.50; block of 4 with vert. gutter between, $8.50. See note after No. 4693.

See note after No. 1549.

COAST GUARD

MH-65 Dolphin Helicopter and Cutter *Eagle* A3851

Designed by Phil Jordan. Printed by Banknote Corporation of America for Sennett Security Products.

LITHOGRAPHED

Sheets of 120 in six panes of 20

2015, Aug. 4 Tagged *Serpentine Die Cut 10¾*
Self-Adhesive

5008 A3851 (49c) **multicolored** 1.10 .25
P# block of 4, 4#+S 4.40
Pane of 20 22.00
a. Imperforate 1.75 —
Pane of 20 35.00

Die cut and imperforate uncut press sheets of No. 5008 were made available for sale. Values: cross gutter block of 4, $9; pairs with gutters between, $4 each. See note after No. 4693.

MUSIC ICONS

Elvis Presley (1935-77), Singer — A3852

Designed by Antonio Alcalá and Leslie Badani. Printed by Ashton-Potter (USA) Ltd.

LITHOGRAPHED

Sheets of 144 in nine panes of 16

2015, Aug. 12 Tagged *Serpentine Die Cut 10½*
Self-Adhesive

5009 A3852 (49c) **multicolored** ⓢ 1.10 .25
Pane of 16 17.50
a. Imperforate 1.75 —
Pane of 16 28.00

Die cut and imperforate uncut press sheets of No. 5009 were made available for sale. Values: cross gutter block of 4, $9; pairs with gutters between, $4 each. See note after No. 4693.

See note after No. 1549.

2016 WORLD STAMP SHOW, NEW YORK CITY ⓢ

Star — A3853

Designed by Michael Dyer. Printed by Ashton-Potter (USA), Ltd.

LITHOGRAPHED

Sheets of 120 in six panes of 20

2015, Aug. 20 Tagged *Serpentine Die Cut 11*
Self-Adhesive

5010 A3853 (49c) **red** 1.10 .25
5011 A3853 (49c) **blue** 1.10 .25
a. Pair, #5010-5011 2.20
P# block of 4, 2#+P 4.40
Pane of 20 22.00
b. As "a," imperforate 4.00 —
Pane of 20 40.00

Die cut and imperforate uncut press sheets of Nos. 5010-5011 were made available for sale. Values: cross gutter block of 4, $12; pairs with gutters between, $4 each.

See note after No. 4693. See note after No. 1549.

LEGENDS OF HOLLYWOOD

Ingrid Bergman (1915-82), Actress — A3854

Designed by Ethel Kessler. Printed by Banknote Corporation of America for Sennett Security Products.

LITHOGRAPHED

Sheets of 180 in nine panes of 20

2015, Aug. 20 Tagged *Serpentine Die Cut 11*
Self-Adhesive

5012 A3854 (49c) **multicolored** 1.10 .25
P# block of 4, 4#+S 4.40
Pane of 20 22.00
a. Imperforate 1.75 —
Pane of 20 35.00

Die cut and imperforate uncut press sheets of No. 5012 were made available for sale. Values: cross gutter block of 4, $9; pairs with gutters between, $4 each. See note after No. 4693.

See Sweden Nos. 2756-2758.

Eagle Type of 2012

Designed by Ethel Kessler. Printed by Ashton-Potter (USA) Ltd.

LITHOGRAPHED

Serpentine Die Cut 10¼ Vert.

2015, Sept. 2 Untagged
Coil Stamps
Self-Adhesive
Color Behind "USA"

5013 A3504 (25c) **green** ⓢ .50 .25
5014 A3504 (25c) **blue green** ⓢ .50 .25
5015 A3504 (25c) **blue** ⓢ .50 .25
5016 A3504 (25c) **red violet** ⓢ .50 .25
5017 A3504 (25c) **orange** ⓢ .50 .25
5018 A3504 (25c) **yellow orange** ⓢ .50 .25
a. Strip of 6, #5013-5018 3.00
P# strip of 7, 2 #5013, 1 each #5014-5018, #P1111 5.00
P# strip of 13, 3 #5016, 2 each #5013-5015, 5017-5018, #P1111 9.00
P# single (#5016), #P1111 — 2.50
Nos. 5013-5018 (6) 3.00 1.50

Nos. 5013-5018 were printed using two offset plates on the same cylinder. One plate was 15 stamps high and the other 12 stamps high for a total circumference of 27. This was done to keep the plate numbers on the same design. However, it caused a three-stamp immediate repeat once every revolution. The end of the 15-high plate had the same color stamps as the first three on the 12-high plate.

See note after No. 1549.

CELEBRATE

A3855

Designed by Phil Jordan. Printed by Banknote Corporation of America for Sennett Security Products.

LITHOGRAPHED

Sheets of 160 in eight panes of 20

2015, Sept. 9 Tagged *Serpentine Die Cut 10¾*
Self-Adhesive

5019 A3855 (49c) **multicolored** 1.10 .25
P# block of 4, 4#+S or 4#+B 4.40
Pane of 20 22.00

Compare with type A3441.

PAUL NEWMAN (1925-2008), ACTOR AND PHILANTHROPIST

A3856

Designed by Derry Noyes. Printed by Banknote Corporation of America for Sennett Security Products.

LITHOGRAPHED

Sheets of 120 in six panes of 20

2015, Sept. 18 Tagged *Serpentine Die Cut 10¾*
Self-Adhesive

5020 A3856 (49c) **multicolored** 1.10 .25
P# block of 4, 4#+S 4.40
Pane of 20 22.00
a. Imperforate 1.75 —
Pane of 20 35.00

Die cut and imperforate uncut press sheets of No. 5020 were made available for sale. Values: horiz. pair with vert. gutter between, $3.75. See note after No. 4693.

CHRISTMAS

Charlie Brown Carrying Christmas Tree — A3857

Charlie Brown, Pigpen and Dirty Snowman — A3858

Snoopy, Lucy, Violet, Sally and Schroeder Skating — A3859

Characters, Dog House and Christmas Tree — A3860

Linus and Christmas Tree — A3861

Charlie Brown Looking in Mailbox — A3862

Charlie Brown and Linus Behind Brick Wall — A3863

Charlie Brown, Linus and Christmas Tree — A3864

Charlie Brown Screaming, Snoopy Decorating Dog House — A3865

Charlie Brown Hanging Ornament on Christmas Tree — A3866

Designed by Antonio Alcalá. Printed by Banknote Corporation of America for Sennett Security Products.

LITHOGRAPHED

Serpentine Die Cut 10¾ on 2 or 3 Sides

2015, Oct. 1 **Tagged**

Booklet Stamps
Self-Adhesive

5021 A3857 (49c) **multicolored**	1.20	.40
5022 A3858 (49c) **multicolored**	1.20	.40
5023 A3859 (49c) **multicolored**	1.20	.40
5024 A3860 (49c) **multicolored**	1.20	.40
5025 A3861 (49c) **multicolored**	1.20	.40
5026 A3862 (49c) **multicolored**	1.20	.40
5027 A3863 (49c) **multicolored**	1.20	.40
5028 A3864 (49c) **multicolored**	1.20	.40
5029 A3865 (49c) **multicolored**	1.20	.40
5030 A3866 (49c) **multicolored**	1.20	.40
a. Block of 10, #5021-5030	12.00	
b. Booklet pane of 20, 2 each #5021-5030	24.00	
c. As "a," imperforate	17.50	—
d. As "b," imperforate	35.00	
Nos. 5021-5030 (10)	12.00	4.00

Premiere of *A Charlie Brown Christmas* animated television show, 50th anniv.

Nos. 5030b and 5030d are double-sided booklet panes with 12 stamps on one side (Nos. 5023-5030, 2 each Nos. 5021-5022) and eight stamps (Nos. 5023-5030) plus label (booklet cover) on the other side.

Die cut and imperforate uncut press sheets of Nos. 5021-5030 were made available for sale. Values for varieties from die cut press sheets: cross gutter block of 4 with booklet cover, imperf. within, $10; cross gutter block of 4, imperf. within, $10; horiz. pair, imperf. between, $4; vert. pair, imperf. between, $4. Values for varieties from imperforate press sheets: cross gutter block of 4 with booklet cover, $10; pair with horiz. gutter between, $4; pair with vert. gutter between, $4. See note after No. 4693.

GEOMETRIC SNOWFLAKES

A3867

A3868

A3869

A3870

Designed by Antonio Alcalá. Printed by Banknote Corporation of America for Sennett Security Products.

LITHOGRAPHED

Serpentine Die Cut 11¼x10¾ on 2 or 3 Sides

2015, Oct. 23 **Tagged**

Booklet Stamps
Self-Adhesive
Snowflake Colors

5031 A3867 (49c) **purple & lilac**	1.10	.30
5032 A3868 (49c) **dark blue & blue**	1.10	.30
5033 A3869 (49c) **dark green & green**	1.10	.30
5034 A3870 (49c) **crimson & pink**	1.10	.30
a. Block of 4, #5031-5034	4.40	
b. Booklet pane of 20, 5 each #5031-5034	22.00	
c. As "a," imperforate	7.00	—
d. As "b," imperforate	35.00	
Nos. 5031-5034 (4)	4.40	1.20

Nos. 5034b and 5034d are double-sided booklet panes with 12 stamps on one side (3 each Nos. 5031-5034), and eight stamps (2 each Nos. 5031-5034) plus label (booklet cover) on the other side.

Die cut and imperforate uncut press sheets of Nos. 5031-5034 were made available for sale. Values for varieties from die cut press sheets: cross gutter block of 4 with booket cover, imperf. within, $10; cross gutter block of 4, imperf. within, $10; block of 4 vert. imperf. between, $8.50; block of 4, horiz. imperf. between, $8.50. Values for varieties from imperforate press sheets: cross gutter block of 4 with booklet cover, $10; block of 4 with horiz. gutter between, $8.50; block of 4 with vert. gutter between, $8.50. See note after No. 4693.

Purple Heart and Ribbon Type of 2012

Designed by Jennifer Arnold. Printed by Banknote Corporation of America for Sennett Security Products.

LITHOGRAPHED

Sheets of 200 in 10 panes of 20

2015, Oct. **Tagged** ***Serpentine Die Cut 11***

Self-Adhesive
With "USPS" Microprinted At Left of Ribbon

5035 A3587 (49c) **multicolored**	1.10	.25
P# block of 4, 6#+S or 6#+B	4.40	
Pane of 20	22.00	

LOVE

Quilled Paper Heart — A3871

Designed by Antonio Alcalá. Printed by Banknote Corporation of America for Sennett Security Products.

LITHOGRAPHED

Sheets of 200 in ten panes of 20

2016, Jan. 12 **Tagged** ***Serpentine Die Cut 10¾***

Self-Adhesive

5036 A3871 (49c) **multicolored,** overall tagged	1.10	.25
P# block of 4, 5#+S or 5#+B	4.40	
Pane of 20	22.00	
a. Imperforate	1.75	—
Pane of 20	35.00	
b. Die cutting omitted, P#B11111 block of 4	*100.00*	
c. Prephosphored paper	1.10	.25
P# block of 4, 5#+S or 5#+B	4.40	
Pane of 20	22.00	

Die cut and imperforate uncut press sheets of No. 5036 were made available for sale. Values: cross gutter block of 4, $9; pairs with gutters between, $4 each. See note after No. 4693.

No. 5036b was printed from P#B11111 only and may also be collected in plate blocks of 6, half panes of 10 and full panes of 20. Pairs or other multiples without P#B11111 selvage attached cannot be distinguished from No. 5036a, which was printed only from P#S11111.

FRUIT

Albemarle Pippin Apples — A3872

Pinot Noir Grapes — A3873

Red Pears — A3874

Designed by Derry Noyes. Printed by Ashton-Potter (USA), Ltd. (Nos. 5037-5038), Banknote Corporation of America for Sennett Security Products (No. 5039).

LITHOGRAPHED

2016 **Untagged** ***Serpentine Die Cut 10 Vert.***

Coil Stamps
Self-Adhesive

5037 A3872 1c **multicolored,** *Aug. 12*	.25	.25
Pair	.25	
P# strip of 5, #P111111	.60	
P# single, #P111111	—	.50
5038 A3873 5c **multicolored,** *Feb. 19* ⓢ	.25	.25
Pair	.25	
P# strip of 5, #P111111	1.00	
P# single, #P111111	—	1.00
Serpentine Die Cut 10¾ Vert.		
5039 A3874 10c **multicolored,** *Jan. 17*	.25	.25
Pair	.40	
P# strip of 5, #S111111, #B111111	3.00	
P# single, #S111111, #B111111	—	2.50

See note after No. 1549.

See Nos. 5177-5178 for sheet versions of Nos. 5038-5039.

AMERICAN LANDMARKS ISSUE

La Cueva del Indio, Puerto Rico — A3875

Columbia River Gorge A3876

Designed by Greg Breeding (#5040), Phil Jordan (#5041). Printed by Ashton-Potter (USA) Ltd. (#5040), Banknote Corporation of America (#5041).

LITHOGRAPHED

Sheets of 60 in six panes of 10 (#5040), Sheets of 150 in 15 panes of 10 (#5041)

Serpentine Die Cut 10¾x10½

2016, Jan. 17 **Tagged**

Self-Adhesive

5040	A3875 $6.45 **multicolored** ⓖ		13.00	7.50
	P# block of 4, 4#+P		52.00	
	Pane of 10		130.00	
a.	Imperforate		17.50	—
	Pane of 10		175.00	
5041	A3876 $22.95 **multicolored**		45.00	24.00
	P# block of 4, 4#+B		180.00	
	Pane of 10		450.00	
a.	Imperforate		*150.00*	—
	Pane of 10		*1,500.*	

Die cut and imperforate press sheets of No. 5040 were made available for sale. Value: cross gutter block of 4, $90; pairs with gutter between, $42.50.

Die cut and imperforate partial press sheets (containing 30 stamps) of No. 5041 were made available for sale. Value: vert. pair with horiz. gutter between, $290. See note after No. 4693.

See note after No. 1549.

BOTANICAL ART Ⓢ

Corn Lilies — A3877

Tulips — A3878

Tulips — A3879

Dahlias — A3880

Stocks — A3881

Roses — A3882

Japanese Irises — A3883

Tulips — A3884

Petunias — A3885

Jonquils — A3886

Designed by Ethel Kessler. Printed by Ashton-Potter (USA) Ltd.

LITHOGRAPHED

Serpentine Die Cut 10¾ on 2 or 3 Sides

2016, Jan. 29 **Tagged**

Booklet Stamps
Self-Adhesive

5042	A3877 (49c) **multicolored**	1.20	.40
5043	A3878 (49c) **multicolored**	1.20	.40
5044	A3879 (49c) **multicolored**	1.20	.40
5045	A3880 (49c) **multicolored**	1.20	.40
5046	A3881 (49c) **multicolored**	1.20	.40
5047	A3882 (49c) **multicolored**	1.20	.40
5048	A3883 (49c) **multicolored**	1.20	.40
5049	A3884 (49c) **multicolored**	1.20	.40
5050	A3885 (49c) **multicolored**	1.20	.40
5051	A3886 (49c) **multicolored**	1.20	.40
a.	Block of 10, #5042-5051	12.00	
b.	Booklet pane of 10, #5042-5051	12.00	
c.	Booklet pane of 20, 2 each #5042-5051	24.00	
d.	Imperforate block of 10	90.00	—
e.	Imperforate booklet pane of 20	150.00	
f.	As "c," horiz. die cutting missing between all stamps front and reverse	—	
	Nos. 5042-5051 (10)	12.00	4.00

Nos. 5051c and 5051e are double-sided booklet panes with 12 stamps on one side (Nos. 5042-5049, 2 each Nos. 5050-5051) and eight stamps (Nos. 5042-5049) plus label (booklet cover) on the other side.

No. 5051f resulted from a misregistration of the die cutting/pane cutting and the printed web. The horizontal rows are reversed from their normal positions, and horizontal die cutting appears at the top and bottom of the pane.

Die cut and imperforate uncut press sheets of Nos. 5042-5051 were made available for sale. Values for varieties from die cut press sheets: cross gutter block of 4 with booklet cover, imperf. within, $10; cross gutter block of 4, imperf. within, $10; vert. pair, imperf. between, $4; horiz. pair, imperf. between, $6. Values for varieties from imperforate press sheets: cross gutter block of 4 with booklet cover, $60; cross gutter block of 10, $250; pair with vert. gutter between, $20; horiz. pair with booklet cover and gutter between, $25. See note after No. 4693.

See note after No. 1549.

Flag — A3887

Designed by Greg Breeding. Printed by Banknote Corporation of America for Sennett Security Products. (#5052, 5054), Ashton-Potter (USA) Ltd. (#5053, 5055).

LITHOGRAPHED

Serpentine Die Cut 11 Vert.

2016, Jan. 29 **Tagged**

Coil Stamps
Self-Adhesive
Microprinted "USPS" To Right of Pole Under Flag

5052	A3887 (49c) **multicolored**	1.10	.25
	Pair	2.20	
	P# strip of 5, #S11111, #B11111	7.50	
	P# single, #S11111, #B11111	—	2.50
a.	Die cutting omitted, pair	—	
b.	As "a," grayish blue (inscription and date) omitted	—	

Counterfeits exist of No. 5052. See the Postal Counterfeits section of this catalog.

Serpentine Die Cut 9½ Vert.

Microprinted "USPS" on Second White Flag Stripe

5053	A3887 (49c) **multicolored** ⓖ	1.10	.25
	Pair	2.20	
	P# strip of 5, #P11111	7.50	
	P# single, #P11111	—	2.50

Counterfeits exist of No. 5053. See the Postal Counterfeits section of this catalog.

Booklet Stamps
Microprinted "USPS" To Right of Pole Under Flag

Serpentine Die Cut 11¼x10¾ on 2 or 3 Sides

5054	A3887 (49c) **multicolored**	1.10	.25
a.	Booklet pane of 10	11.00	
b.	Booklet pane of 20	22.00	
c.	As "b," horiz. die cutting omitted on side with 12 stamps	—	

Microprinted "USPS" on Second White Flag Stripe

5055	A3887 (49c) **multicolored** ⓖ	1.10	.25
a.	Booklet pane of 20	22.00	

Nos. 5054b and 5055a are double-sided booklets with 12 stamps on one side and eight stamps plus a label that serves as the booklet cover on the other side.

See note after No. 1549.

BLACK HERITAGE

Richard Allen (1760-1831), Founder of African Methodist Episcopal Church — A3888

Designed by Greg Breeding. Printed by Ashton-Potter (USA) Ltd.

LITHOGRAPHED

Sheets of 120 in six panes of 20

2016, Feb. 2 **Tagged** *Serpentine Die Cut 10¾*

Self-Adhesive

5056	A3888 (49c) **multicolored** ⓖ	1.10	.25
	P# block of 4, 5#+P	4.40	
	Pane of 20	22.00	
a.	Imperforate	2.75	—
	Pane of 20	55.00	

Die cut and imperforate uncut press sheets of No. 5056 were made available for sale. Values: cross gutter block of 4, $18; pairs with gutters between, $7.25 each. See note after No. 4693.

See note after No. 1549.

CHINESE NEW YEAR

Year of the Monkey A3889

Designed by Ethel Kessler. Printed by Banknote Corporation of America for Sennett Security Products.

LITHOGRAPHED

Sheets of 144 in 12 panes of 12

2016, Feb. 5 **Tagged** *Serpentine Die Cut 10¾*

Self-Adhesive

5057	A3889 (49c) **multicolored**	1.10	.25
	Pane of 12	13.25	
a.	Imperforate	1.50	—
	Pane of 12	18.00	

Die cut and imperforate uncut partial press sheets (containing 72 stamps) of No. 5057 were made available for sale. Values: cross gutter block of 4, $9; pairs with gutters between, $3.75 each. See note after No. 4693.

Moon — A3890

Designed by Greg Breeding. Printed by Banknote Corporation of America.

LITHOGRAPHED

Sheets of 100 in ten panes of 10

2016, Feb. 22 **Tagged** *Serpentine Die Cut*

Self-Adhesive

5058	A3890 ($1.20) **multicolored**	2.40	.50
	P# block of 4, 6#+B	9.60	
	Pane of 10	24.00	

Unused values are for stamps with surrounding selvage. Adjacent stamps are separated by rouletting.

Die cut uncut press sheets of No. 5058 were made available for sale. Values: cross gutter block of 4, $20; pairs with gutters between, $8.75 each. See note after No. 4693.

MUSIC ICONS

Sarah Vaughan (1924-90), Singer — A3891

Designed by Ethel Kessler. Printed by Ashton-Potter (USA) Ltd.

LITHOGRAPHED

Sheets of 144 in nine panes of 16

2016, Mar. 29 Tagged *Serpentine Die Cut 10½*

Self-Adhesive

5059 A3891 (49c) **multicolored** Ⓢ	1.10	.25
Pane of 16	17.50	

Die cut uncut press sheets of No. 5059 were made available for sale. Values: cross gutter block of 4, $9; pairs with gutters between, $3.75 each. See note after No. 4693.

See note after No. 1549.

LEGENDS OF HOLLYWOOD

Shirley Temple (1928-2014), Actress and Diplomat — A3892

Designed by Ethel Kessler. Printed by Ashton-Potter (USA) Ltd.

LITHOGRAPHED

Sheets of 180 in nine panes of 20

2016, Apr. 18 Tagged *Serpentine Die Cut 10¾*

Self-Adhesive

5060 A3892 (47c) **multicolored** Ⓢ	1.10	.25
P# block of 4, 5#+P	4.40	
Pane of 20	22.00	

Die cut uncut press sheets of No. 5060 were made available for sale. Values: cross gutter block of 8, $9; pairs with gutters between, $4.25 each. See note after No. 4693.

See note after No. 1549.

"USA" and Star — A3893

Designed by Antonio Alcalá and Leslie Badani. Printed by Ashton-Potter (USA) Ltd.

LITHOGRAPHED

Serpentine Die Cut 10 Vert.

2016, Apr. 28 Untagged

COIL STAMP

Self-Adhesive

5061 A3893 (5c) **multicolored** Ⓢ	.25	.25
Pair	.50	
P# strip of 5, #P111	1.60	
P# single, #P1111	—	1.25

See note after No. 1549.

2016 WORLD STAMP SHOW, NEW YORK CITY

Star — A3894

Designed by Michael Dyer. Printed by Banknote Corporation of America.

ENGRAVED

Sheets of 96 in four folios of 24

2016, May 28 Tagged *Serpentine Die Cut 10¾*

Self-Adhesive

5062 A3894 (47c) **blue**	1.10	.25
5063 A3894 (47c) **red**	1.10	.25
a. Pair, #5062-5063	2.20	
Folio of 24, 12 each #5062-5063	26.50	

Die cut uncut press sheets of Nos. 5062-5063 were made available for sale. Values: cross gutter block of 4, $9; pairs with gutters between, $4.25 each.

See note after No. 4693.

REPEAL OF THE STAMP ACT, 250TH ANNIV.

Man Posting Notice of Repeal on Tree — A3895

Designed by Antonio Alcalá. Printed by Banknote Corporation of America.

LITHOGRAPHED

Sheets of 120 in 12 panes of 10

2016, May 29 Tagged *Serpentine Die Cut 10¾*

Self-Adhesive

5064 A3895 (47c) **multicolored**	1.10	.25
Pane of 10	11.00	

Die cut uncut press sheets of No. 5064 were made available for sale. Values: cross gutter block of 4, $9; pairs with gutters between, $4.25 each.

See note after No. 4693.

SERVICE CROSS MEDALS

Distinguished Service Cross — A3896

Navy Cross — A3897

Air Force Cross — A3898

Coast Guard Cross — A3899

Designed by Greg Breeding. Printed by Banknote Corporation of America.

LITHOGRAPHED

Sheets of 144 in 12 panes of 12

2016, May 30 Tagged *Serpentine Die Cut 10¾*

Self-Adhesive

5065 A3896 (47c) **multicolored**	1.10	.30
5066 A3897 (47c) **multicolored**	1.10	.30
5067 A3898 (47c) **multicolored**	1.10	.30
5068 A3899 (47c) **multicolored**	1.10	.30
a. Block or horiz. strip of 4, #5065-5068	4.40	
Pane of 12	13.25	
Nos. 5065-5068 (4)	4.40	1.20

Die cut uncut press sheets of Nos. 5065-5068 were made available for sale. Values: cross gutter block of 4, $9; pairs with gutters between, $4.25 each.

See note after No. 4693.

VIEWS OF OUR PLANETS Ⓢ

Mercury — A3900

Venus — A3901

Earth — A3902

Mars — A3903

Jupiter — A3904

Saturn — A3905

Uranus — A3906

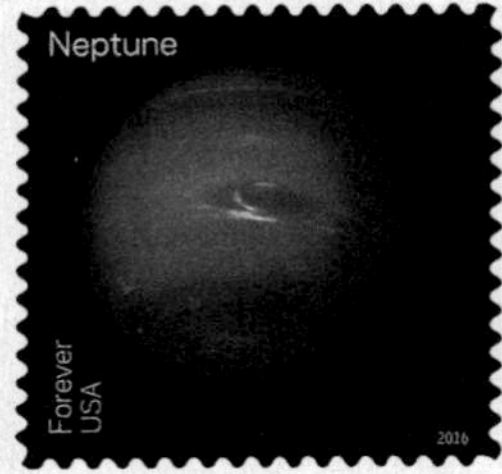

Neptune — A3907

Designed by Antonio Alcalá. Printed by Ashton-Potter (USA) Ltd.

LITHOGRAPHED
Sheets of 128 in eight panes of 16

2016, May 31 Tagged *Serpentine Die Cut 10½*
Self-Adhesive

5069	A3900 (47c) **multicolored**		1.50	.40
5070	A3901 (47c) **multicolored**		1.50	.40
5071	A3902 (47c) **multicolored**		1.50	.40
5072	A3903 (47c) **multicolored**		1.50	.40
5073	A3904 (47c) **multicolored**		1.50	.40
5074	A3905 (47c) **multicolored**		1.50	.40
5075	A3906 (47c) **multicolored**		1.50	.40
5076	A3907 (47c) **multicolored**		1.50	.40
a.	Block of 8, #5069-5076		12.00	
	P# block of 8, 5#+P		12.00	
	Pane of 16		24.00	
	Nos. 5069-5076 (8)		12.00	3.20

Die cut uncut press sheets of Nos. 5069-5076 were made available for sale. Values: cross gutter block of 8, $18; pairs with gutters between, $4.25 each. See note after No. 4693.

See note after No. 1549.

PLUTO EXPLORED

Pluto — A3908

New Horizons Probe — A3909

Designed by Antonio Alcalá. Printed by Ashton-Potter (USA) Ltd.

LITHOGRAPHED
Sheets of 56 in 14 panes of 4

2016, May 31 Tagged *Serpentine Die Cut 10½*
Self-Adhesive

5077	A3908 (47c) **multicolored**	1.10	.25
5078	A3909 (47c) **multicolored**	1.10	.25
a.	Pair, #5077-5078	2.20	
	Pane of 4, 2 each #5077-5078	4.40	

Die cut uncut press sheets of Nos. 5077-5078 were made available for sale. Values: cross gutter block of 4, $9; pairs with gutters between, $4.25 each. See note after No. 4693.

See note after No. 1549.

CLASSICS FOREVER

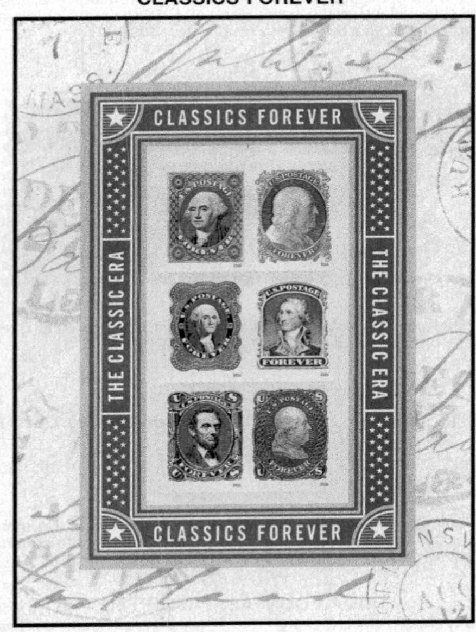

A3910

Designed by Antonio Alcalá. Printed by Banknote Corporation of America.

No. 5079: a, George Washington (redrawn type A16). b, Benjamin Franklin (redrawn type A5). c, Washington (redrawn type A17). d, Washington (redrawn type A19). e, Abraham Lincoln (redrawn type A33). f, Franklin (redrawn type A24).

LITHOGRAPHED & ENGRAVED
Sheets of 60 in 10 panes of six

2016, June 1 Tagged *Serpentine Die Cut 10¾*
Self-Adhesive

5079	A3910 Pane of 6	6.60	
a.	(47c) tan & black	1.10	.40
b.	(47c) tan & blue	1.10	.40
c.	(47c) tan & black	1.10	.40
d.	(47c) tan & blue	1.10	.40
e.	(47c) tan & black	1.10	.40
f.	(47c) tan & blue	1.10	.40

Die cut uncut press sheets of No. 5079 were made available for sale. Values: cross gutter block of 6, $12; pairs with gutters between, $4.25 each. See note after No. 4693.

NATIONAL PARK SERVICE, CENT.

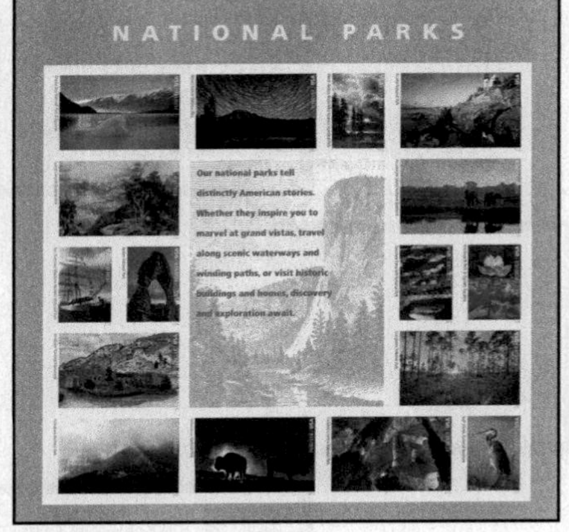

A3911

Designed by Ethel Kessler. Printed by Banknote Corporation of America.

No. 5080: a, Iceberg in Glacier Bay National Park and Preserve, Alaska (48x31mm). b, Mount Rainier National Park (48x31mm). c, *Scenery in the Grand Tetons,* painting by Albert Bierstadt, at Marsh-Billings-Rockefeller National Historic Park, Vermont (24x31mm). d, Bass Harbor Head Lighthouse, Acadia National Park, Maine (48x31mm). e, *The Grand Canyon of Arizona,* painting by Thomas Moran, at Grand Canyon National Park, Arizona (48x31mm). f, Horses at Assateague Island National Seashore, Virginia and Maryland (48x31mm). g, Ship *Balclutha,* at San Francisco Maritime National Historic Park, California (24x31mm). h, Stone arch at Arches National Park, Utah (24x31mm). i, Aerial view of Theodore Roosevelt National Park, North Dakota (24x31mm). j, Water lily at Kenilworth Park and Aquatic Gardens, Washington, D.C. (24x31mm). k, *Administration Building at Frijoles Canyon,* drawing by Helmuth Naumer, Sr., at Bandelier National Monument, New Mexico (48x31mm). l, Everglades National Park, Florida (48x31mm). m, Rainbow at Haleakala National Park, Hawaii (48x31mm). n, Bison at Yellowstone National Park, Idaho, Montana and Wyoming (48x31mm). o, Carlsbad Caverns National Park, New Mexico (48x31mm). p, Heron at Gulf Islands National Seashore, Florida and Mississippi (24x31mm).

LITHOGRAPHED
Sheets of 144 in nine panes of 16
Serpentine Die Cut 10½x10¾

2016, June 2 Tagged
Self-Adhesive

5080	A3911 Pane of 16 + label	17.50	
a.-p.	(47c) Any single	1.10	.50

Die cut uncut press sheets of No. 5080 were made available for sale. Values: pairs with gutters between, $4.25 each. See note after No. 4693.

COLORFUL CELEBRATIONS

Bird and Flowers — A3912

Birds and Flowers — A3913

Flowers — A3914

Flowers — A3915

Flowers — A3916

Flowers — A3917

Birds and Flower — A3918

Bird and Flower — A3919

Flowers — A3920

Birds and Flower — A3921

Designed by Sally Anderson-Bruce. Printed by Banknote Corporation of America.

LITHOGRAPHED

Serpentine Die Cut 11 on 2 or 3 Sides

2016, June 3 **Tagged**

Booklet Stamps
Self-Adhesive

5081 A3912 (47c) **light blue** 1.10 .40
5082 A3913 (47c) **orange** 1.10 .40
5083 A3914 (47c) **violet** 1.10 .40
5084 A3915 (47c) **rose pink** 1.10 .40
5085 A3916 (47c) **light blue** 1.10 .40
5086 A3917 (47c) **orange** 1.10 .40
5087 A3918 (47c) **violet** 1.10 .40
5088 A3919 (47c) **rose pink** 1.10 .40
5089 A3920 (47c) **rose pink** 1.10 .40
5090 A3921 (47c) **violet** 1.10 .40
a. Block of 10, #5081-5090 11.00
b. Booklet pane of 20, 2 each #5081-5090 22.00
Nos. 5081-5090 (10) 11.00 4.00

No. 5090b is a double-sided booklet pane with 12 stamps on

Die cut uncut press sheets of Nos. 5081-5090 were made available for sale. Values of varieties: cross gutter block of 4 with booklet cover, imperf. within, $10; cross gutter block of 4, imperf. within, $10; horiz. pair, imperf. between, $4. See note after No. 4693.

INDIANA STATEHOOD, 200th ANNIV. Ⓢ

Corn Field Near Milford A3922

Designed by Derry Noyes. Printed by Ashton-Potter (USA) Ltd.

LITHOGRAPHED
Sheets of 120 in six panes of 20

2016, June 7 **Tagged** ***Serpentine Die Cut 10¾***
Self-Adhesive

5091 A3922 (47c) **multicolored** 1.10 .25
P# block of 4, 4#+P 4.40
Pane of 20 22.00

Die cut uncut press sheets of No. 5091 were made available for sale. Values: cross gutter block of 4, $9; pairs with gutters between, $4.25 each. See note after No. 4693.

EID

"Eidukum Mubarak" — A3923

Designed by Mohamed Zakariya. Printed by Banknote Corporation of America.

LITHOGRAPHED
Sheets of 160 in eight panes of 20

2016, June 10 **Tagged** ***Serpentine Die Cut 11***
Self-Adhesive

5092 A3923 (47c) **multicolored** 1.10 .25
P# block of 4, 3#+B 4.40
Pane of 20 22.00

Die cut uncut press sheets of No. 5092 were made available for sale. Values: cross gutter block of 4, $9; pairs with gutters between, $4.25 each. See note after No. 4693.

SODA FOUNTAIN FAVORITES

Ice Cream Cone — A3924

Egg Cream — A3925

Banana Split A3926

Root Beer Float — A3927

Hot Fudge Sundae — A3928

Designed by Ethel Kessler. Printed by Banknote Corporation of America.

LITHOGRAPHED

2016, June 30 **Tagged** ***Serpentine Die Cut 10¾***
Booklet Stamps
Self-Adhesive

5093 A3924 (47c) **multicolored** 1.10 .40
5094 A3925 (47c) **multicolored** 1.10 .40
5095 A3926 (47c) **multicolored** (long sloping die cut at bottom) 1.10 .40
a. Long sloping die cut at top 1.10 .40
5096 A3927 (47c) **multicolored** 1.10 .40
5097 A3928 (47c) **multicolored** 1.10 .40
a. Horiz. strip of 5, #5093-5097 5.50
b. Horiz. strip of 5, #5093-5094, 5095a, 5096-5097 5.50
c. Booklet pane of 20, 4 each #5093-5094, 5096-5097, 2 each #5095, 5095a 22.00
Nos. 5093-5097 (5) 5.50 2.00

Die cut uncut press sheets of Nos. 5093-5095 were made available for sale. Values: cross gutter block of 10 with booklet cover, $27.50; pairs with gutters between, $3.75 each. See note after No. 4693.

STAR QUILTS

A3929 A3930

Designed by Derry Noyes. Printed by Banknote Corporation of America.

LITHOGRAPHED

2016, July 6 **Tagged** ***Serpentine Die Cut 11 Vert.***
Coil Stamps
Self-Adhesive

5098 A3929 (25c) **multicolored** .50 .25
5099 A3930 (25c) **multicolored** .50 .25
a. Pair, #5098-5099 1.00
P# strip of 5, 3 #5098, 2 #5099, #B11111 3.50
P# single, #B11111 (#5098) — 2.50

JAIME ESCALANTE

Jaime Escalante (1930-2010), High School Calculus Teacher — A3931

Designed by Greg Breeding. Printed by Banknote Corporation of America.

LITHOGRAPHED
Sheets of 180 in nine panes of 20

2016, July 13 **Tagged** ***Serpentine Die Cut 10¾***
Self-Adhesive

5100 A3931 (47c) **multicolored** 1.10 .25
P# block of 4, 6#+B 4.40
Pane of 20 22.00

Adjacent horizontal or vertical stamps have selvage between the stamps.

PICKUP TRUCKS

1938 International Harvester D-2 — A3932

1953 Chevrolet — A3933

1948 Ford F-1 — A3934

1965 Ford F-100 — A3935

Designed by Antonio Alcalá. Printed by Banknote Corporation of America.

LITHOGRAPHED

Serpentine Die Cut 11 on 2 or 3 Sides

2016, July 15 **Tagged**

Booklet Stamps
Self-Adhesive

5101	A3932 (47c) **multicolored**	1.10	.30
5102	A3933 (47c) **multicolored**	1.10	.30
5103	A3934 (47c) **multicolored**	1.10	.30
5104	A3935 (47c) **multicolored**	1.10	.30
a.	Block of 4, #5101-5104	4.40	
b.	Booklet pane of 20, 5 each #5101-5104	22.00	
	Nos. 5101-5104 (4)	4.40	1.20

No. 5104b is a double-sided booklet pane with 12 stamps on one side (3 each Nos. 5101-5104) and eight stamps (2 each Nos. 5101-5104) plus label (booklet cover) on the other side.

Die cut uncut press sheets of Nos. 5101-5104 were made available for sale. Values of varieties: cross gutter block of 4 with booklet cover, $10; cross gutter block of 4, imperf. within, $10; block of 4, vert. imperf. between, $8. See note after No. 4693.

LITERARY ARTS

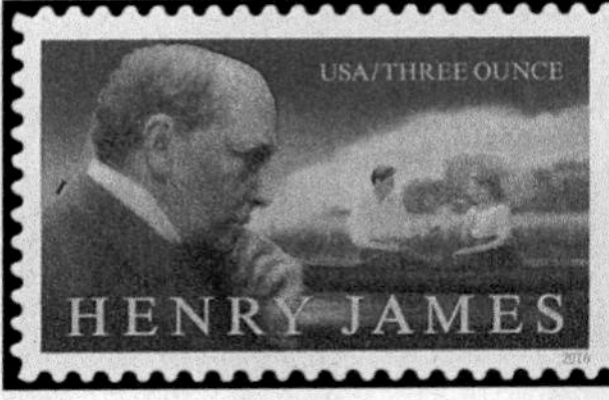

Henry James (1843-1916), Novelist A3936

Designed by Kate Simmons. Printed by Banknote Corporation of America.

LITHOGRAPHED

Sheets of 120 in six panes of 20

2016, July 31 **Tagged** ***Serpentine Die Cut 11***

Self-Adhesive

5105	A3936 (89c) **multicolored**	1.90	.30
	P# block of 4, 5#+B	7.60	
	Pane of 20	38.00	

Die cut uncut press sheets of No. 5105 were made available for sale. Values: cross gutter block of 4, $18; pairs with gutters between, $7.50 each. See note after No. 4693.

PETS

Puppy — A3937

Betta Fish — A3938

Iguana — A3939

Hamster — A3940

Goldfish — A3941

Kitten — A3942

Rabbit — A3943

Tortoise — A3944

Guinea Pig — A3945

Parrot — A3946

Corn Snake — A3947

Mouse — A3948

Hermit Crab — A3949

Chinchilla — A3950

Gerbil — A3951

Gecko — A3952

Cat — A3953

Horse — A3954

Parakeets — A3955

Dog — A3956

Designed by Derry Noyes. Printed by Ashton-Potter (USA), Ltd.

LITHOGRAPHED

Serpentine Die Cut 11 on 2 or 3 Sides

2016, Aug. 2 **Tagged**

Booklet Stamps
Self-Adhesive

5106	A3937	(47c)	**multicolored**	1.10	.50
5107	A3938	(47c)	**multicolored**	1.10	.50
5108	A3939	(47c)	**multicolored**	1.10	.50
5109	A3940	(47c)	**multicolored**	1.10	.50
5110	A3941	(47c)	**multicolored**	1.10	.50
5111	A3942	(47c)	**multicolored**	1.10	.50
5112	A3943	(47c)	**multicolored**	1.10	.50
5113	A3944	(47c)	**multicolored**	1.10	.50
5114	A3945	(47c)	**multicolored**	1.10	.50
5115	A3946	(47c)	**multicolored**	1.10	.50
5116	A3947	(47c)	**multicolored**	1.10	.50
5117	A3948	(47c)	**multicolored**	1.10	.50
5118	A3949	(47c)	**multicolored**	1.10	.50
5119	A3950	(47c)	**multicolored**	1.10	.50
5120	A3951	(47c)	**multicolored**	1.10	.50
5121	A3952	(47c)	**multicolored**	1.10	.50
5122	A3953	(47c)	**multicolored**	1.10	.50
5123	A3954	(47c)	**multicolored**	1.10	.50
5124	A3955	(47c)	**multicolored**	1.10	.50
5125	A3956	(47c)	**multicolored**	1.10	.50
a.	Booklet pane of 20, #5106-5125			22.00	
	Nos. 5106-5125 (20)			22.00	10.00

No. 5125a is a double-sided booklet pane with 12 stamps on one side (Nos. 5106-5117) and eight stamps (Nos. 5118-5125) plus label (booklet cover) on the other side.

Die cut uncut press sheets of Nos. 5106-5125 were made available for sale. Values of varieties: cross gutter block of 4 with booklet cover, imperf. within, $10; cross gutter block of 4, imperf. within, $10; horiz. pair, imperf. between, $4. See note after No. 4693.

SONGBIRDS IN SNOW

Golden-crowned Kinglets — A3957

Cedar Waxwing — A3958

Northern Cardinal — A3959

Red-breasted Nuthatches — A3960

Designed by Derry Noyes. Printed by Ashton-Potter (USA), Ltd.

LITHOGRAPHED

Serpentine Die Cut 10¾ on 2 or 3 Sides

2016, Aug. 4 **Tagged**

Booklet Stamps
Self-Adhesive

5126	A3957	(47c)	**multicolored**	1.10	.30
5127	A3958	(47c)	**multicolored**	1.10	.30
5128	A3959	(47c)	**multicolored**	1.10	.30
5129	A3960	(47c)	**multicolored**	1.10	.30
a.	Block of 4, #5126-5129			4.40	
b.	Booklet pane of 20, 5 each #5126-5129			22.00	
	Nos. 5126-5129 (4)			4.40	1.20

No. 5129b is a double-sided booklet pane with 12 stamps on one side (3 each Nos. 5126-5129) and eight stamps (2 each Nos. 5126-5129) plus label (booklet cover) on the other side.

Die cut uncut press sheets of Nos. 5126-5129 were made available for sale. Values of varieties: cross gutter block of 4 with booklet cover, imperf. within, $10; block of 4, vert. imperf. between, $8. See note after No. 4693.

PATRIOTIC SPIRAL

Stars — A3961

Designed by Polygraph. Printed by Ashton-Potter (USA), Ltd.

LITHOGRAPHED

Serpentine Die Cut 10 Vert.

2016, Aug. 19 **Tagged**

Coil Stamp
Self-Adhesive

5130	A3961	(47c)	**multicolored**	1.10	.25
	Pair			2.00	
	P# strip of 5, #P1111			7.50	
	P# single, #P1111			—	2.50

Booklet Stamp

Serpentine Die Cut 11 on 2 or 3 Sides

5131	A3961	(47c)	**multicolored**	1.10	.25
a.	Booklet pane of 10			11.00	

Counterfeits exist of No. 5131. See the Postal Counterfeits section of this catalog.

STAR TREK TELEVISION SHOW, 50TH ANNIV

Starship Enterprise and Starfleet Insignia — A3962

Crewman in Transporter — A3963

Starship Enterprise and Planet — A3964

Starship Enterprise, Planet, Vulcan Hand Salute — A3965

Designed by The Heads of State. Printed by Ashton-Potter (USA), Ltd.

LITHOGRAPHED

Sheets of 120 in six panes of 20

2016, Sept. 2 **Tagged** ***Serpentine Die Cut 11***

Self-Adhesive

5132	A3962	(47c)	**multicolored**	1.10	.30
5133	A3963	(47c)	**multicolored**	1.10	.30
5134	A3964	(47c)	**multicolored**	1.10	.30
5135	A3965	(47c)	**multicolored**	1.10	.30
a.	Block or vert. strip of 4, #5132-5135			4.40	
	P# block of 4, 8#+P			8.80	
	Pane of 20			22.00	
	Nos. 5132-5135 (4)			4.40	1.20

Die cut uncut press sheets of No. 5132-5135 were made available for sale. Values: cross gutter block of 8, $18; pairs with gutters between, $4.25 each. See note after No. 4693.

EASTERN TAILED-BLUE BUTTERFLY

A3966

Designed by Derry Noyes. Printed by Ashton-Potter (USA) Ltd.

LITHOGRAPHED

Sheets of 120 in six panes of 20

2016, Sept. 24 **Tagged** ***Serpentine Die Cut 10½***

Self-Adhesive

5136	A3966	(68c)	**multicolored**	1.40	.25
	P# block of 4, 4#+P			5.60	
	Pane of 20			28.00	

Die cut uncut press sheets of No. 5136 were made available for sale. Values: cross gutter block of 4, $18, pairs with gutters between, $7.50 each. See note after No. 4693.

JACK-O'-LANTERNS

Four Teeth — A3967

Five Teeth — A3968

Three Teeth — A3969

Nine Teeth — A3970

LITHOGRAPHED

Serpentine Die Cut 11x10¾ on 2 or 3 Sides

2016, Sept. 29 **Tagged**

Booklet Stamps
Self-Adhesive

5137	A3967 (47c) **multicolored**	1.10	.30
5138	A3968 (47c) **multicolored**	1.10	.30
5139	A3969 (47c) **multicolored**	1.10	.30
5140	A3970 (47c) **multicolored**	1.10	.30
a.	Block of 4, #5137-5140	4.40	
b.	Booklet pane of 20, 5 each #5137-5140	22.00	
	Nos. 5137-5140 (4)	4.40	1.20

No. 5140b is a double-sided booklet pane with 12 stamps on one side (3 each Nos. 5137-5140) and eight stamps (2 each Nos. 5137-5140) plus label (booklet cover) on the other side.

Die cut uncut press sheets of Nos. 5137-5140 were made available for sale. Values of varieties: cross gutter block of 4 with booklet cover, imperf. within, $10; cross gutter block of 4, imperf. within, $10; block of 4, vert. imperf.between, $8.50; block of 4, horiz. imperf. between, $7.50. See note after No. 4693.

KWANZAA

Woman, Fruits and Vegetables — A3971

Designed by Greg Breeding. Printed by Banknote Corporation of America.

LITHOGRAPHED

Sheets of 160 in eight panes of 20

2016, Oct. 1 **Tagged** ***Serpentine Die Cut 11***

Self-Adhesive

5141	A3971 (47c) **multicolored**	1.10	.25
	P# block of 4, 4#+B	4.40	
	Pane of 20	22.00	

Die cut uncut press sheets of No. 5141 were made available for sale. Values: cross gutter block of 4, $9; pairs with gutters between, $4.25 each. See note after No. 4693.

DIWALI

Diya — A3972

Designed by Greg Breeding. Printed by Ashton-Potter (USA) Ltd.

LITHOGRAPHED

Sheets of 160 in eight panes of 20

2016, Oct. 5 **Tagged** ***Serpentine Die Cut 11***

Self-Adhesive

5142	A3972 (47c) **multicolored**	1.10	.25
	P# block of 4, 4#+P	4.40	
	Pane of 20	22.00	

Die cut uncut press sheets of No. 5142 were made available for sale. Values: cross gutter block of 4, $9; pairs with gutters between, $4.25 each. See note after No. 4693.

Counterfeits exist of No. 5142. See the Postal Counterfeits section of this catalog.

CHRISTMAS

Madonna and Child, by a Follower of Fra Filippo Lippi and Peselino — A3973

Nativity — A3974

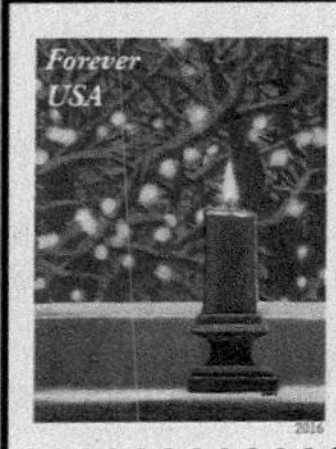

Candle in Window — A3975

Wreath in Window — A3976

Star in Window — A3977

Christmas Tree in Window — A3978

Designed by William J. Gicker (No. 5143), Greg Breeding (No. 5144), Ethel Kessler (Nos. 5145-5148). Printed by Ashton-Potter (USA) Ltd. (Nos. 5143-5144), Banknote Corporation of America (Nos. 5145-5148).

LITHOGRAPHED

Serpentine Die Cut 10¾x11 on 2 or 3 Sides

2016 **Tagged**

Booklet Stamps
Self-Adhesive

5143	A3973 (47c) **multicolored,** *Oct. 18*	1.10	.25
a.	Booklet pane of 20	22.00	
5144	A3974 (47c) **multicolored,** *Nov. 3*	1.10	.25
a.	Booklet pane of 20	22.00	
5145	A3975 (47c) **multicolored,** *Oct. 6*	1.10	.25
5146	A3976 (47c) **multicolored,** *Oct. 6*	1.10	.25
5147	A3977 (47c) **multicolored,** *Oct. 6*	1.10	.25
5148	A3978 (47c) **multicolored,** *Oct. 6*	1.10	.25
a.	Block of 4, #5145-5148	4.40	
b.	Booklet pane of 20, 5 each #5145-5148	22.00	
	Nos. 5143-5148 (6)	6.60	1.50

Nos. 5143a and 5144a are double-sided booklet panes with 12 stamps on one side and eight stamps plus label (booklet cover) on the other side. No. 5148b is a double-sided booklet pane with 12 stamps on one side (3 each Nos. 5145-5148) and eight stamps (2 each Nos. 5145-5148) plus label (booklet cover) on the other side.

Die cut uncut press sheets of Nos. 5143, 5144, and 5145-5148 were made available for sale. Values of varieties: cross gutter block of 4 with booklet cover, imperf. within, $10; cross gutter block of 4, imperf. within, $10; blocks of 4 (Nos. 5145-5148), imperf. vert. or horiz. between, $7.50 each; vert. pair, imperf. between, $4; horiz. pair, imperf. between, $6. See note after No. 4693.

WONDER WOMAN, 75TH ANNIVERSARY

Modern Age Wonder Woman — A3979

Bronze Age Wonder Woman — A3980

Silver Age Wonder Woman — A3981

Golden Age Wonder Woman — A3982

Designed by Greg Breeding. Printed by Banknote Corporation of America.

LITHOGRAPHED

Sheets of 180 in nine panes of 20

2016, Oct. 7 **Tagged** ***Serpentine Die Cut 11***

Self-Adhesive

5149	A3979 (47c) **multicolored**	1.10	.30
5150	A3980 (47c) **multicolored**	1.10	.30
5151	A3981 (47c) **multicolored**	1.10	.30
5152	A3982 (47c) **multicolored**	1.10	.30
a.	Vert. strip of 4, #5149-5152	4.40	
	P# block of 8, 4#+B	8.80	
	Pane of 20	22.00	
	Nos. 5149-5152 (4)	4.40	1.20

Die cut uncut press sheets of Nos. 5149-5152 were made available for sale. Values: cross gutter block of 8, $18; pairs with gutters between, $3.75 each. See note after No. 4693.

HANUKKAH

Menorah — A3983

Designed by Ethel Kessler. Printed by Banknote Corporation of America.

LITHOGRAPHED

Sheets of 160 in eight panes of 20

2016, Nov. 1 **Tagged** ***Serpentine Die Cut 11***

Self-Adhesive

5153	A3983 (47c) **multicolored**	1.10	.25
	P# block of 4, 5#+B	4.40	
	Pane of 20	22.00	

Die cut uncut press sheets of No. 5153 were made available for sale. Values: cross gutter block of 4, $9; pairs with gutters between, $4.25 each. See note after No. 4693.

CHINESE NEW YEAR

Year of the Rooster A3984

Designed by Ethel Kessler. Printed by Banknote Corporation of America.

LITHOGRAPHED

Sheets of 144 in 12 panes of 12

2017, Jan. 5 **Tagged** ***Serpentine Die Cut 10¾***

Self-Adhesive

5154	A3984 (47c) **multicolored**	1.10	.25
	Pane of 12	13.25	

Die cut partial press sheets (containing 72 stamps) of No. 5154 were made available for sale. Values: cross gutter block of 4, $9; pairs with gutters between, $4.25 each. See note after No. 4693.

LOVE

Airplane and Skywriting — A3985

Designed by Louise Fili. Printed by Banknote Corporation of America.

LITHOGRAPHED
Sheets of 160 in eight panes of 20

2017, Jan. 7 Tagged *Serpentine Die Cut 11x10¾*
Self-Adhesive

5155 A3985 (47c) **light blue** 1.10 .25
P# block of 4, 1#+B 4.40
Pane of 20 22.00

Die cut uncut press sheets of No. 5155 were made available for sale. Values: cross gutter block of 4, $9; pairs with gutters between, $4.25 each. See note after No. 4693.

Counterfeits exist of No. 5155. See the Postal Counterfeits section of this catalog.

AMERICAN LANDMARKS ISSUE

Lili'uokalani Gardens, Hilo, Hawaii A3986

Gateway Arch, St. Louis, Missouri A3987

Designed by Greg Breeding. Printed by Ashton-Potter (USA) Ltd.

LITHOGRAPHED
Sheets of 40 in 10 panes of 4 (#5156), Sheets of 20 in 5 panes of 4 (#5157)
Serpentine Die Cut 10¾x10½

2017, Jan. 22 Tagged
Self-Adhesive

5156 A3986 $6.65 **multicolored** ⓢ 13.50 7.75
Pane of 4 54.00
5157 A3987 $23.75 **multicolored** ⓢ 47.50 25.00
Pane of 4 190.00

Flag — A3988

Designed by Greg Breeding. Printed by Banknote Corporation of America (#5158, 5160), Ashton-Potter (USA) Ltd. (#5159, 5161, 5162).

LITHOGRAPHED
Serpentine Die Cut 11 Vert.

2017, Jan. 27 Tagged
Coil Stamps
Self-Adhesive
Microprinted "USPS" On Right End of Fourth Red Stripe

5158 A3988 (49c) **multicolored** ⓢ 1.10 .25
Pair 2.20
P# strip of 5, #B1111 7.50
P# single, #B1111 — 2.50
a. Die cutting omitted, pair —

Counterfeits exist of No. 5158. See the Postal Counterfeits section of this catalog.

Serpentine Die Cut 9½ Vert.
Microprinted "USPS" on Right End of Second White Flag Stripe

5159 A3988 (49c) **multicolored** ⓢ 1.10 .25
Pair 2.20
P# strip of 5, #P1111 7.50
P# single, #P1111 — 2.50

Counterfeits exist of No. 5159. See the Postal Counterfeits section of this catalog.

Booklet Stamps
Microprinted "USPS" on Right End of Fourth Red Stripe
Serpentine Die Cut 11¼x10¾ on 2 or 3 Sides

5160 A3988 (49c) **multicolored** ⓢ 1.10 .25
a. Booklet pane of 10 11.00
b. Booklet pane of 20 22.00

Microprinted "USPS" on Right End of Second White Flag Stripe

5161 A3988 (49c) **multicolored** ⓢ 1.10 .25
a. Booklet pane of 20 22.00

Counterfeits exist of No. 5161. See the Postal Counterfeits section of this catalog.

Microprinted "USPS" on Left End of Second White Flag Stripe Near Blue Field
Thin Paper
Serpentine Die Cut 11¼x10¾ on 2, 3 or 4 Sides

5162 A3988 (49c) **multicolored** ⓢ 2.75 .25
a. Booklet pane of 18 50.00
Nos. 5160-5162 (3) 4.95 .75

Nos. 5160b and 5161a are double-sided booklets with 12 stamps on one side and eight stamps plus a label that serves as the booklet cover on the other side.

SHELLS

Queen Conch — A3989

Pacific Calico Scallop — A3990

Alphabet Cone — A3991

Zebra Nerite — A3992

Designed by Greg Breeding. Printed by Ashton-Potter (USA) Ltd.

LITHOGRAPHED
Sheets of 200 in ten panes of 20
Serpentine Die Cut 11¼x10¾

2017, Jan. 28 Tagged
Self-Adhesive

5163 A3989 (34c) **multicolored** ⓢ .70 .25
5164 A3990 (34c) **multicolored** ⓢ .70 .25
5165 A3991 (34c) **multicolored** ⓢ .70 .25
5166 A3992 (34c) **multicolored** ⓢ .70 .25
a. Horiz. or vert. strip of 4, #5163-5166 2.80
P# block of 8, 6#+P 5.60
Pane of 20 14.00
Nos. 5163-5166 (4) 2.80 1.00

Coil Stamps
Serpentine Die Cut 9¾ Vert.

5167 A3991 (34c) **multicolored** ⓢ .70 .25
5168 A3992 (34c) **multicolored** ⓢ .70 .25
5169 A3989 (34c) **multicolored** ⓢ .70 .25
5170 A3990 (34c) **multicolored** ⓢ .70 .25
a. Horiz. strip of 4, #5167-5170 2.80
P# strip of 5, #5168-5170, 2 #5167, #P111111 5.50
P# strip of 9, 2 each #5167-5168, 5170, 3 #5169, #P111111 9.25
P# single, #P111111 (#5169) — 2.75
Nos. 5167-5170 (4) 2.80 1.00

BLACK HERITAGE

Dorothy Height (1912-2010), President of National Council of Negro Women — A3993

Designed by Derry Noyes. Printed by Ashton-Potter (USA) Ltd.

LITHOGRAPHED
Sheets of 120 in six panes of 20

2017, Feb. 1 Tagged *Serpentine Die Cut 11*
Self-Adhesive

5171 A3993 (49c) **multicolored** ⓢ 1.10 .25
P# block of 4, 4#+P 4.40
Pane of 20 22.00

Die cut uncut press sheets of No. 5171 were made available for sale. Values: cross gutter block of 4, $9; pairs with gutters between, $3.75 each. See note after No. 4693.

"USA" and Star With Blue Frame — A3994

Designed by Antonio Alcalá and Leslie Badani. Printed by Ashton-Potter (USA) Ltd.

LITHOGRAPHED
Serpentine Die Cut 10 Vert.

2017, Feb. 10 Untagged
COIL STAMP
Self-Adhesive

5172 A3994 (5c) **multicolored** ⓢ .25 .25
Pair .50
P# strip of 5, #P111 .85
P# single, #P111 — .50
a. Red omitted —

See note after No. 1549.
The discovery example of No. 5172a is on piece, uncanceled.

OSCAR DE LA RENTA ⓢ

Oscar de la Renta (1932-2014), Fashion Designer A3995

A3996

A3997

A3998

A3999

A4000

A4001

A4002

A4003

A4004

A4005

Designed by Derry Noyes. Printed by Ashton-Potter (USA) Ltd.

LITHOGRAPHED

Sheets of 99 in nine panes of 11

Serpentine Die Cut 11x10¾ (No. 5173a), 10¾x11

2017, Feb. 16 **Tagged**

Self-Adhesive

5173	Pane of 11	12.00	
a.	A3995 (49c) **multicolored**	1.10	.50
b.	A3996 (49c) **multicolored**	1.10	.50
c.	A3997 (49c) **multicolored**	1.10	.50
d.	A3998 (49c) **multicolored**	1.10	.50
e.	A3999 (49c) **multicolored**	1.10	.50
f.	A4000 (49c) **multicolored**	1.10	.50
g.	A4001 (49c) **multicolored**	1.10	.50
h.	A4002 (49c) **multicolored**	1.10	.50
i.	A4003 (49c) **multicolored**	1.10	.50
j.	A4004 (49c) **multicolored**	1.10	.50
k.	A4005 (49c) **multicolored**	1.10	.50

Die cut uncut press sheets of No. 5173 were made available for sale. See note after No. 4693.

See note after No. 1549.

People Wearing Uncle Sam Hats — A4006

Designed by Antonio Alcalá. Printed by Banknote Corporation of America.

LITHOGRAPHED

Sheets of 200 in 10 panes of 20

Serpentine Die Cut 11¼x11

2017, Feb. 18 **Tagged**

Self-Adhesive

5174	A4006 (21c) **multicolored** ⓢ	.45	.25
	P# block of 4, 7#+B	1.80	
	Pane of 20	9.00	

See note under No. 1549.

PRES. JOHN F. KENNEDY (1917-63) ⓢ

Pres. John F. Kennedy — A4007

Designed by Derry Noyes. Printed by Banknote Corporation of America.

LITHOGRAPHED

Sheets of 96 in eight panes of 12

2017, Feb. 20 **Tagged** ***Serpentine Die Cut 10¾***

Self-Adhesive

5175	A4007 (49c) **brown**	1.10	.25
	P# block of 4, 2#+B	4.40	
	Pane of 12	13.25	

Die cut uncut press sheets of No. 5175 were made available for sale. Values: cross gutter block of 4, $9; pairs with gutters between, $3.75 each. See note after No. 4693.

See note after No. 1549.

Fruits Type of 2016

Designed by Derry Noyes. Printed by Ashton-Potter (USA) Ltd. (No. 5177); Banknote Corporation of America (No. 5178).

Designs: 5c, Pinot Noir Grapes. 10c, Red Pears.

LITHOGRAPHED

Sheets of 200 in 10 panes of 20

2017 ***Serpentine Die Cut 11¼x11***

Untagged (#5177), Tagged (#5178)

Self-Adhesive

5177	A3873 5c **multicolored,** *Feb. 24* ⓢ	.25	.25
	P# block of 4, 6#+P	.40	
	Pane of 20	2.00	
5178	A3874 10c **multicolored,** *Mar. 23* ⓢ	.25	.25
	P# block of 4, 6#+B	.80	
	Pane of 20	4.00	

See note after No. 1549.

NEBRASKA STATEHOOD, 150th ANNIV. ⓢ

Sandhill Cranes Flying Over Platte River A4008

Designed by Derry Noyes. Printed by Ashton-Potter (USA) Ltd.

LITHOGRAPHED
Sheets of 120 in six panes of 20

2017, Mar. 1 Tagged *Serpentine Die Cut 10¾*
Self-Adhesive

5179 A4008 (49c) **multicolored**		1.10	.25
	P# block of 4, 4#+P	4.40	
	Pane of 20	22.00	

Die cut uncut press sheets of No. 5179 were made available for sale. Values: cross gutter block of 4, $9; pairs with gutters between, $3.75 each. See note after No. 4693.
See note after No. 1549.

WORKS PROGRESS ADMINISTRATION (WORK PROJECTS ADMINISRATION) POSTERS Ⓢ

See America Welcome to Montana Poster — A4009

Work Pays America Poster — A4010

Field Day Poster — A4011

Discover Puerto Rico Poster — A4012

City of New York Municipal Airports Poster — A4013

Foreign Trade Zone Poster — A4014

Visit the Zoo Poster — A4015

Work with Care Poster — A4016

The National Parks Preserve Wild Life Poster — A4017

Hiking Poster — A4018

Designed by Antonio Alcalá. Printed by Ashton-Potter (USA) Ltd.

LITHOGRAPHED
Serpentine Die Cut 11 on 2 or 3 Sides

2017, Mar. 7 Tagged
Booklet Stamps
Self-Adhesive

5180 A4009 (49c) **multicolored**		1.10	.40
5181 A4010 (49c) **multicolored**		1.10	.40
5182 A4011 (49c) **multicolored**		1.10	.40
5183 A4012 (49c) **multicolored**		1.10	.40
5184 A4013 (49c) **multicolored**		1.10	.40
5185 A4014 (49c) **multicolored**		1.10	.40
5186 A4015 (49c) **multicolored**		1.10	.40
5187 A4016 (49c) **multicolored**		1.10	.40
5188 A4017 (49c) **multicolored**		1.10	.40
5189 A4018 (49c) **multicolored**		1.10	.40
a.	Block of 10, #5180-5189	11.00	
b.	Booklet pane of 20, 2 each #5180-5189	22.00	
	Nos. 5180-5189 (10)	11.00	4.00

No. 5189b is a double-sided booklet pane with 12 stamps on one side (Nos. 5181-5184, 5186-5189, 2 each Nos. 5180, 5185) and eight stamps (Nos. 5181-5184, 5186-5189) plus label (booklet cover) on the other side.

Die cut uncut press sheets of Nos. 5180-5189 were made available for sale. Values of varieties: cross gutter block of 4 with booklet cover, imperf. within, $10; cross gutter block of 4, imperf. within, $10; vert. pair, imperf. between, $4; horiz. pair imperf. between, $6. See note after No. 4693.
See note after No. 1549.

MISSISSIPPI STATEHOOD, 200th ANNIV. Ⓢ

Guitarist A4019

Designed by Greg Breeding. Printed by Ashton-Potter (USA) Ltd.

LITHOGRAPHED
Sheets of 120 in six panes of 20

2017, Mar. 31 Tagged *Serpentine Die Cut 10¾*
Self-Adhesive

5190 A4019 (49c) **multicolored**		1.10	.25
	P# block of 4, 4#+P	4.40	
	Pane of 20	22.00	

Die cut uncut press sheets of No. 5190 were made available for sale. Values: cross gutter block of 4, $9; pairs with gutters between, $3.75 each. See note after No. 4693.
See note after No. 1549.

DISTINGUISHED AMERICANS

Robert Panara (1920-2014), Educator of the Deaf — A4020

Designed by Ethel Kessler. Printed by Banknote Corporation of America.

LITHOGRAPHED
Sheets of 120 in six panes of 20

2017, Apr. 11 Tagged *Serpentine Die Cut 10¾*
Self-Adhesive

5191 A4020 (70c) **multicolored** Ⓢ		1.40	.25
	P# block of 4, 4#+B	5.60	
	Pane of 20	28.00	

Adjacent horizontal or vertical stamps have selvage between the stamps. See note after No. 1549.

DELICIOSO (LATIN AMERICAN DISHES) Ⓢ

Tamales — A4021

Flan — A4022

Sancocho — A4023

Empanadas — A4024

Chile Relleno — A4025

Ceviche — A4026

Designed by Antonio Alcalá. Printed by Banknote Corporation of America.

LITHOGRAPHED
Serpentine Die Cut 11 on 2 or 3 Sides

2017, Apr. 20 Tagged
Booklet Stamps
Self-Adhesive

5192 A4021 (49c) **multicolored**		1.10	.40
5193 A4022 (49c) **multicolored**		1.10	.40
5194 A4023 (49c) **multicolored**		1.10	.40
5195 A4024 (49c) **multicolored**		1.10	.40
5196 A4025 (49c) **multicolored**		1.10	.40
5197 A4026 (49c) **multicolored**		1.10	.40
a.	Block of 6, #5192-5197	6.60	
b.	Booklet pane of 20, 4 each #5192-5193, 3 each #5194-5197	22.00	
	Nos. 5192-5197 (6)	6.60	2.40

No. 5197b is a double-sided booklet pane with 12 stamps on one side (2 each Nos. 5192-5197) and eight stamps (Nos. 5194-5197, 2 each Nos. 5192-5193) plus label (booklet cover) on the other side.

Die cut uncut press sheets of Nos. 5192-5197 were made available for sale. Values of varieties: cross gutter block of 4

with booklet cover, imperf. within, $10; cross gutter block of 4, imperf. within, $10; vert. pair, imperf. between, $6; horiz. pair, imperf. between, $4. See note after No. 4693.
See note after No. 1549.

Echeveria
A4027

Designed by Greg Breeding. Printed by Ashton-Potter (USA) Ltd.

LITHOGRAPHED
Sheets of 90 in nine panes of 10

2017, Apr. 28 **Tagged** ***Serpentine Die Cut***
Self-Adhesive

5198 A4027 ($1.15) **multicolored** ⓢ	2.40	.50
P# block of 4, 5#+P	9.60	
Pane of 10	24.00	

Unused values are for stamps with surrounding selvage. Adjacent stamps are separated by rouletting.

CELEBRATION FLOWERS ⓢ

Boutonniere — A4028 Corsage — A4029

Designed by Ethel Kessler. Printed by Banknote Corporation of America.

LITHOGRAPHED
Sheets of 200 in 10 panes of 20

2017, May 2 **Tagged** ***Serpentine Die Cut 10¾***
Self-Adhesive

5199 A4028 (49c) **multicolored** ⓢ	1.10	.25
P# block of 4, 5#+B	4.40	
Pane of 20	22.00	
5200 A4029 (70c) **multicolored** ⓢ	1.40	.25
P# block of 4, 5#+B	5.60	
Pane of 20	28.00	

See note after No. 1549.

FRUIT

Strawberries — A4030

Designed by Derry Noyes. Printed by Ashton-Potter (USA), Ltd.

LITHOGRAPHED
Serpentine Die Cut 10 Vert.

2017, May 5 **Untagged**
Coil Stamps
Self-Adhesive

5201 A4030 3c **multicolored** ⓢ	.25	.25
Pair	.25	
P# strip of 5, #P1111	1.25	
P# single, #P1111	—	.55

See note after No. 1549.

HENRY DAVID THOREAU ⓢ

Henry David Thoreau (1817-62), Writer, and Sumac Leaves
A4031

Designed by Greg Breeding. Printed by Banknote Corporation of America.

LITHOGRAPHED
Sheets of 180 in nine panes of 20

2017, May 23 **Tagged** ***Serpentine Die Cut 10¾***
Self-Adhesive

5202 A4031 (49c) **multicolored**	1.10	.25
P# block of 4, 4#+B	4.40	
Pane of 20	22.00	

Die cut uncut press sheets of No. 5202 were made available for sale. Values: cross gutter block of 4, $9; pairs with gutters between, $3.75 each. See note after No. 4693.
See note after No. 1549.

SPORTS BALLS ⓢ

Football — A4032

Volleyball — A4033

Soccer Ball — A4034

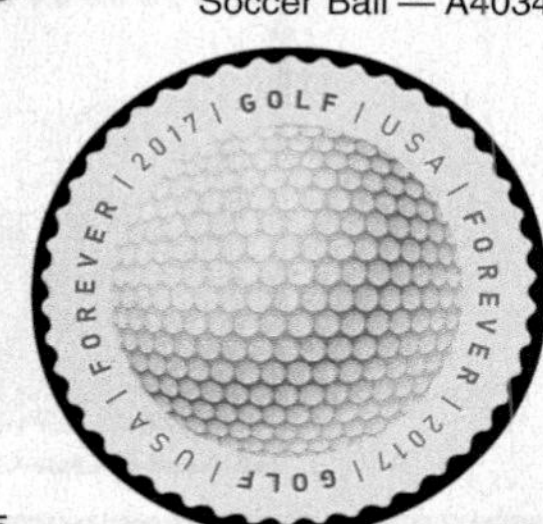

Golf Ball — A4035

Baseball — A4036

Basketball — A4037

Tennis Ball — A4038

Kickball — A4039

Designed by Greg Breeding. Printed by Ashton-Potter (USA) Ltd.

LITHOGRAPHED & TYPOGRAPHED
Sheets of 128 in eight panes of 16

2017, June 14 **Tagged** ***Serpentine Die Cut***
Self-Adhesive

5203 A4032 (49c) **multicolored**	1.10	.40
5204 A4033 (49c) **multicolored**	1.10	.40
5205 A4034 (49c) **multicolored**	1.10	.40
5206 A4035 (49c) **multicolored**	1.10	.40
5207 A4036 (49c) **multicolored**	1.10	.40
5208 A4037 (49c) **multicolored**	1.10	.40
5209 A4038 (49c) **multicolored**	1.10	.40
5210 A4039 (49c) **multicolored**	1.10	.40
a. Block of 8, #5203-5210	8.80	
P# block of 8, 5#+P	8.80	
Pane of 16	17.50	
Nos. 5203-5210 (8)	8.80	3.20

The typographed printing imitates the texture of the ball.
Die cut uncut press sheets of Nos. 5203-5210 were made available for sale. Values: cross gutter block of 8, $18; pairs with gutters between, $3.75 each. See note after No. 4693.
See note after No. 1549.

AUGUST 21, 2017, TOTAL SOLAR ECLIPSE ⓢ

Total Solar Eclipse — A4040

Designed by Antonio Alcalá. Printed by Banknote Corporation of America.

LITHOGRAPHED

Sheets of 128 in eight panes of 16

2017, June 20 Tagged *Serpentine Die Cut 10½*

Self-Adhesive

5211	A4040 (49c) **multicolored**	1.10	.25
	P# block of 4, 5#+B	4.40	
	Pane of 16	17.50	

The moon, directly in front of the sun, is covered with a circle of thermochromic ink, which when warmed, allows the moon and the corona of the sun around the moon to be seen.

Die cut uncut press sheets of No. 5202 were made available for sale. Values: cross gutter block of 4, $9; pairs with gutters between, $3.75 each. See note after No. 4693.

See note after No. 1549.

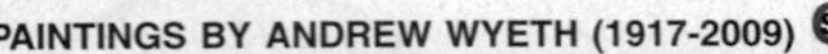

PAINTINGS BY ANDREW WYETH (1917-2009) Ⓢ

Wind from the Sea, 1947 A4041

Big Room, 1988 A4042

Christina's World, 1948 A4043

Alvaro and Christina, 1968 A4044

Frostbitten, 1962 A4045

Sailor's Valentine, 1985 A4046

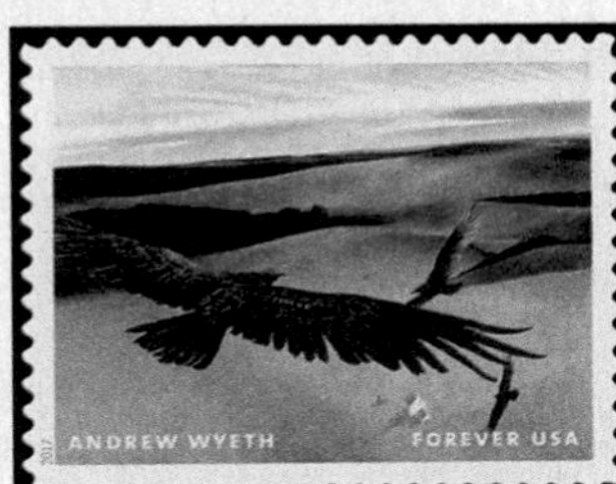

Soaring, 1942-50 A4047

North Light, 1984 A4048

Spring Fed, 1967 A4049

The Carry, 2003 A4050

Young Bull, 1960 A4051

My Studio,

Designed by Derry Noyes. Printed by Ashton-Potter (USA) Ltd.

LITHOGRAPHED

Sheets of 108 in nine panes of 12

Serpentine Die Cut 10¾x10½

2017, July 12 Tagged

Self-Adhesive

5212	Pane of 12	13.00	
a.	A4041 (49c) **multicolored**	1.10	.50
b.	A4042 (49c) **multicolored**	1.10	.50
c.	A4043 (49c) **multicolored**	1.10	.50
d.	A4044 (49c) **multicolored**	1.10	.50
e.	A4045 (49c) **multicolored**	1.10	.50
f.	A4046 (49c) **multicolored**	1.10	.50
g.	A4047 (49c) **multicolored**	1.10	.50
h.	A4048 (49c) **multicolored**	1.10	.50
i.	A4049 (49c) **multicolored**	1.10	.50
j.	A4050 (49c) **multicolored**	1.10	.50
k.	A4051 (49c) **multicolored**	1.10	.50
l.	A4052 (49c) **multicolored**	1.10	.50

Die cut uncut press sheets of No. 5212 were made available for sale. Values: cross gutter block of 12, $18; pairs with gutters between, $4.25 each. See note after No. 4693.

See note after No. 1549.

DISNEY VILLAINS Ⓢ

The Queen from *Snow White and the Seven Dwarfs* — A4053

Honest John from *Pinocchio* — A4054

Lady Tremaine from *Cinderella* — A4055

Queen of Hearts from *Alice in Wonderland* — A4056

Captain Hook from *Peter Pan* — A4057

Maleficent from *Sleeping Beauty* — A4058

Cruella De Vil from *One Hundred and One Dalmatians* — A4059

Ursula from *The Little Mermaid* — A4060

Gaston from *Beauty and the Beast* — A4061

Scar from *The Lion King* — A4062

Designed by Derry Noyes. Printed by Ashton-Potter (USA) Ltd.

LITHOGRAPHED
Sheets of 120 in six panes of 20
Serpentine Die Cut 10½x10¾

2017, July 15 **Tagged**

Self-Adhesive

5213	A4053 (49c) **multicolored**		1.10	.40
5214	A4054 (49c) **multicolored**		1.10	.40
5215	A4055 (49c) **multicolored**		1.10	.40
5216	A4056 (49c) **multicolored**		1.10	.40
5217	A4057 (49c) **multicolored**		1.10	.40
5218	A4058 (49c) **multicolored**		1.10	.40
5219	A4059 (49c) **multicolored**		1.10	.40
5220	A4060 (49c) **multicolored**		1.10	.40
5221	A4061 (49c) **multicolored**		1.10	.40
5222	A4062 (49c) **multicolored**		1.10	.40
a.	Block of 10, #5213-5222		11.00	
	P# block of 10, 2 sets of 5#+P		11.00	
	Pane of 20		22.00	
	Nos. 5213-5222 (10)		11.00	4.00

Die cut uncut press sheets of Nos. 5213-5222 were made available for sale. Values: cross gutter block of 10, $18; pairs with gutters between, $4.25 each. See note after No. 4693.

See note after No. 1549.

SHARKS 

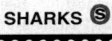

Mako Shark A4063

Whale Shark A4064

Thresher Shark A4065

Hammerhead Shark A4066

Great White Shark A4067

Designed by Derry Noyes. Printed by Banknote Corporation of America.

LITHOGRAPHED
Sheets of 180 in nine panes of 20

2017, July 26 **Tagged** ***Serpentine Die Cut 10¾***

Self-Adhesive

5223	A4063 (49c) **multicolored**		1.10	.40
5224	A4064 (49c) **multicolored**		1.10	.40
5225	A4065 (49c) **multicolored**		1.10	.40
5226	A4066 (49c) **multicolored**		1.10	.40
5227	A4067 (49c) **multicolored**		1.10	.40
a.	Vert. strip of 5, #5223-5227		5.50	
	P# block of 10, 4#+B		11.00	
	Pane of 20		22.00	
	Nos. 5223-5227 (5)		5.50	2.00

Die cut uncut press sheets of Nos. 5223-5227 were made available for sale. Values: cross gutter block of 10, $18; pairs with gutters between, $4.25 each. See note after No. 4693.

See note after No. 1549.

PROTECT POLLINATORS Ⓢ

Monarch Butterfly on Purple Coneflower A4068

Western Honeybee on Golden Ragwort A4069

Monarch Butterfly on Red Zinnia A4070

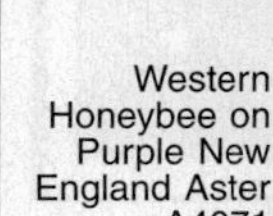

Western Honeybee on Purple New England Aster A4071

Monarch Butterfly on Goldenrod A4072

Designed by Derry Noyes. Printed by Ashton-Potter (USA) Ltd.

LITHOGRAPHED

Sheets of 180 in nine panes of 20

2017, Aug. 3 Tagged ***Serpentine Die Cut 10¾***

Self-Adhesive

5228 A4068 (49c) **multicolored** 1.10 .40
5229 A4069 (49c) **multicolored** 1.10 .40
5230 A4070 (49c) **multicolored** 1.10 .40
5231 A4071 (49c) **multicolored** 1.10 .40
5232 A4072 (49c) **multicolored** 1.10 .40
a. Vert. strip of 5, #5228-5232 5.50
P# block of 10, 4#+P 11.00
Pane of 20 22.00
Nos. 5228-5232 (5) 5.50 2.00

Die cut uncut press sheets of Nos. 5228-5232 were made available for sale. Values: cross gutter block of 10, $18; pairs with gutters between, $4.25 each. See note after No. 4693.

See note after No. 1549.

FLOWERS FROM THE GARDEN Ⓢ

Red Camellias and Yellow Forsythia in Yellow Pitcher — A4073

White Peonies and Pink Tree Peonies in Clear Vase — A4074

Blue Hydrangeas in Blue Pot — A4075

Assorted Flowers in White Vase — A4076

Red Camellias and Yellow Forsythia in Yellow Pitcher — A4077

Assorted Flowers in White Vase — A4078

White Peonies and Pink Tree Peonies in Clear Vase — A4079

Blue Hydrangeas in Blue Pot — A4080

Designed by Derry Noyes. Printed by Banknote Corporation of America.

LITHOGRAPHED

Serpentine Die Cut 10¾ Vert.

2017, Aug. 16 Tagged

Coil Stamps

Self-Adhesive

5233 A4073 (49c) **multicolored** 1.10 .30
5234 A4074 (49c) **multicolored** 1.10 .30
5235 A4075 (49c) **multicolored** 1.10 .30
5236 A4076 (49c) **multicolored** 1.10 .30
a. Strip of 4, #5233-5236 4.40
P# strip of 5, #5234-5236, 2 #5233, #B1111 7.00
P# strip of 9, 3# 5235, 2 each #5233-5234, 5236, #B1111 12.00
P# single, #B1111 (#5235) — 3.00
Nos. 5233-5236 (4) 4.40 1.20

Booklet Stamps

Serpentine Die Cut 11 on 2 or 3 Sides

5237 A4077 (49c) **multicolored** 1.10 .30
5238 A4078 (49c) **multicolored** 1.10 .30
5239 A4079 (49c) **multicolored** 1.10 .30
5240 A4080 (49c) **multicolored** 1.10 .30
a. Block of 4, #5237-5240 4.40
b. Booklet pane of 20, 5 each #5237-5240 22.00
Nos. 5237-5240 (4) 4.40 1.20

No. 5240b is a double-sided booklet pane with 12 stamps on one side (3 each Nos. 5237-5240) and eight stamps (2 each Nos. 5237-5240) plus label (booklet cover) on the other side.

Die cut uncut press sheets of Nos. 5237-5240 were made available for sale. Values of varieties: cross gutter block of 4 with booklet cover, imperf. within, $10; cross gutter block of 4, imperf. within, $10; block of 4, horiz. imperf. between, $7.50; block of 4, vert. imperf. between, $8.50. See note after No. 4693.

See note after No. 1549.

FATHER THEODORE ("TED") HESBURGH

Hesburgh (1917-2015), President of University of Notre Dame — A4081

Designed by Ethel Kessler. Printed by Ashton-Potter (USA) Ltd.

LITHOGRAPHED

Sheets of 120 in six panes of 20

2017, Sept. 1 Tagged ***Serpentine Die Cut 11***

Self-Adhesive

5241 A4081 (49c) **multicolored** Ⓢ 1.10 .25
P# block of 4, 5#+P 4.40
Pane of 20 22.00

Coil Stamp

Serpentine Die Cut 9½ Horiz.

5242 A4081 (49c) **multicolored** Ⓢ 1.10 .25
P# strip of 5, #P11111 7.00
P# single, #P11111 — 3.00

Die cut uncut press sheets of No. 5241 were made available for sale. Values: cross gutter block of 4, $9; pairs with gutters between, $3.75 each. See note after No. 4693. See note after No. 1549.

"THE SNOWY DAY," BY EZRA JACK KEATS Ⓢ

Peter Making Snowball — A4082

Peter Sliding Down Mountain of Snow — A4083

Peter Making Snow Angel — A4084

Peter Leaving Footprints in Snow — A4085

Designed by Antonio Alcalá. Printed by Ashton-Potter (USA), Ltd.

LITHOGRAPHED

Serpentine Die Cut 10¾ on 2 or 3 Sides

2017, Oct. 4 Tagged

Booklet Stamps

Self-Adhesive

5243 A4082 (49c) **multicolored** 1.10 .30
5244 A4083 (49c) **multicolored** 1.10 .30
5245 A4084 (49c) **multicolored** 1.10 .30
5246 A4085 (49c) **multicolored** 1.10 .30
a. Block of 4, #5243-5246 4.40
b. Booklet pane of 20, 5 each #5243-5246 22.00
Nos. 5243-5246 (4) 4.40 1.20

No. 5246b is a double-sided booklet pane with 12 stamps on one side (3 each Nos. 5243-5246), and eight stamps (2 each Nos. 5243-5246) plus label (booklet cover) on the other side.

Die cut uncut press sheets of Nos. 5243-5246 were made available for sale. Values of varieties: cross gutter block of 4 with booklet cover, imperf. within, $10; cross gutter block of 4, imperf. within, $10; block of 4, horiz. imperf. between, $8.50; horiz. pair, imperf. between, $4. See note after No. 4693.

CHRISTMAS CAROLS Ⓢ

Christmas Lights, Cookies, and Line From "Deck the Halls" — A4086

Star of Bethlehem, Lamb, and Line From "Silent Night" — A4087

Snowflakes, Horse, and Line From "Jingle Bells" — A4088

Child, Santa Claus, and Line From "Jolly Old St. Nicholas" — A4089

Designed by Howard E. Paine. Printed by Banknote Corporation of America.

LITHOGRAPHED

Serpentine Die Cut 10¾ on 2 or 3 Sides

2017, Oct. 5 Tagged

Booklet Stamps

Self-Adhesive

5247 A4086 (49c) **multicolored** 1.10 .30
5248 A4087 (49c) **multicolored** 1.10 .30
5249 A4088 (49c) **multicolored** 1.10 .30
5250 A4089 (49c) **multicolored** 1.10 .30
a. Block of 4, #5247-5250 4.40
b. Booklet pane of 20, 5 each #5247-5250 22.00
Nos. 5247-5250 (4) 4.40 1.20

No. 5250b is a double-sided booklet pane with 12 stamps on one side (3 each Nos. 5247-5250), and eight stamps (2 each Nos. 5247-5250) plus label (booklet cover) on the other side.

Die cut uncut press sheets of Nos. 5247-5250 were made available for sale. Values of varieties: cross gutter block of 4 with booklet cover, imperf. within, $10; cross gutter block of 4, imperf. within, $10; block of 4, horiz. imperf. between, $8.50; block of 4, vert. imperf. between, $7.50. See note after No. 4693.

NATIONAL MUSEUM OF AFRICAN AMERICAN HISTORY AND CULTURE Ⓢ

Museum Building, Washington, D.C. — A4090

Designed by Antonio Alcalá. Printed by Banknote Corporation of America.

LITHOGRAPHED
Sheets of 180 in nine panes of 20
Serpentine Die Cut 10¾x10½

2017, Oct. 13 **Tagged**

Self-Adhesive

5251 A4090 (49c) **multicolored** 1.10 .25
P# block of 4, 4#+B 4.40
Pane of 20 22.00

Die cut uncut press sheets of No. 5251 were made available for sale. Values: cross gutter block of 4, $9; pairs with gutters between, $3.75 each. See note after No. 4693.
See note after No. 1549.

HISTORY OF ICE HOCKEY Ⓢ

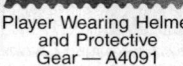

Player Wearing Helmet and Protective Gear — A4091

Player Wearing Hat and Scarf — A4092

Designed by Subplot Design, Inc. Printed by Ashton-Potter (USA), Ltd.

LITHOGRAPHED
Sheets of 120 in six panes of 20

2017, Oct. 20 **Tagged** ***Serpentine Die Cut 11***

Self-Adhesive

5252 A4091 (49c) **multicolored** 1.10 .25
a. As No. 5252, matte-finish stamp 1.10 .25
5253 A4092 (49c) **multicolored** 1.10 .25
a. As No. 5253, matte-finish stamp 1.10 .25
b. Vert. pair, #5252-5253 2.20
c. Souvenir sheet of 2, #5252a-5253a 2.20
P# block of 4, 4#+P 4.40
Pane of 20 22.00

On Nos. 5253b and 5253c, stamps are printed tete-beche. Stamps from No. 5253b have a glossier finish than those on No. 5253c. The matte finish on Nos. 5252a and 5253a is due to block tagging. Adjacent horizontal stamps have selvage between them.

Die cut uncut press sheets of No. 5252-5253 were made available for sale. Values: cross gutter block of 4, $9; pairs with gutters between, $3.75 each. See note after No. 4693.
See note after No. 1549.
See Canada Nos. 3039-3041.

CHINESE NEW YEAR Ⓢ

Year of the Dog — A4093

Designed by Ethel Kessler. Printed by Banknote Corporation of America.

LITHOGRAPHED
Sheets of 144 in 12 panes of 12

2018, Jan. 11 **Tagged** ***Serpentine Die Cut 10¾***

Self-Adhesive

5254 A4093 (49c) **multicolored** 1.10 .25
Pane of 12 13.25

Die cut partial press sheets (containing 72 stamps) of No. 5254 were made available for sale. Values: cross gutter block of 4, $9; pairs with gutters between, $4.25 each. See note after No. 4693. See note after No. 1549.

LOVE Ⓢ

Flowers — A4094

Designed by Greg Breeding. Printed by Banknote Corporation of America.

LITHOGRAPHED
Sheets of 160 in eight panes of 20
Serpentine Die Cut 11x10¾

2018, Jan. 18 **Tagged**

Self-Adhesive

5255 A4094 (49c) **multicolored** 1.10 .25
P# block of 4, 5#+B 4.40
Pane of 20 22.00

Die cut uncut press sheets of No. 5255 were made available for sale. Values: cross gutter block of 4, $9; pairs with gutters between, $4.25 each. See note after No. 4693. See note after No. 1549.

Counterfeits exist of No. 5255. See the Postal Counterfeits section of this catalog.

FRUIT Ⓢ

Meyer Lemons — A4095

Designed by Derry Noyes. Printed by Banknote Corporation of America.

LITHOGRAPHED
Serpentine Die Cut 10¾ Vert.

2018, Jan. 19 **Untagged**

Coil Stamp
Self-Adhesive

5256 A4095 2c **multicolored** .25 .25
Pair .25
P# strip of 5, #B11111 1.25
P# single, #B11111 — .50

See note after No. 1549.

AMERICAN LANDMARKS ISSUE

Byodo-In Temple, Kaneohe, Hawaii A4096

Sleeping Bear Dunes, Michigan A4097

Designed by Greg Breeding. Printed by Ashton-Potter (USA) Ltd.

LITHOGRAPHED
Sheets of 48 in 12 panes of 4 (#5257), Sheets of 24 in six panes of 4 (#5258)
Serpentine Die Cut 10¾x10½

2018, Jan. 21 **Tagged**

Self-Adhesive

5257 A4096 $6.70 **multicolored** Ⓢ 13.50 7.75
Pane of 4 54.00
5258 A4097 $24.70 **multicolored** Ⓢ 50.00 25.00
Pane of 4 200.00

See note after No. 1549.

BLACK HERITAGE

Lena Horne (1917-2010), Singer — A4098

Designed by Ethel Kessler. Printed by Banknote Corporation of America.

LITHOGRAPHED
Sheets of 240 in 12 panes of 20

2018, Jan. 30 **Tagged** ***Serpentine Die Cut 10¾***

Self-Adhesive

5259 A4098 (50c) **multicolored** Ⓢ 1.10 .25
P# block of 4, 5#+B 4.40
Pane of 20 22.00

Die cut partial press sheets (containing 120 stamps) of No. 5259 were made available for sale. Values: cross gutter block of 4, $9; pairs with gutters between, $3.75 each. See note after No. 4693. See note after No. 1549.

Flag — A4099

Designed by Kit Hinrichs. Printed by Ashton-Potter (USA) Ltd. (#5260, 5262), Banknote Corporation of America. (#5261, 5263).

LITHOGRAPHED
Serpentine Die Cut 9½ Vert.

2018, Feb. 9 **Tagged**

Coil Stamps
Self-Adhesive
Microprinted "USPS" at Left of Flag Fold on Fourth White Stripe

5260 A4099 (50c) **multicolored** Ⓢ 1.10 .25
Pair 2.20
P# strip of 5, #P111 7.50
P# single, #P111 — 2.50

Counterfeits exist of No. 5260. See the Postal Counterfeits section of this catalog.

Serpentine Die Cut 11 Vert.

Microprinted "USPS" at Right of Flag Fold on Fifth White Stripe

5261 A4099 (50c) **multicolored** Ⓢ 1.10 .25
Pair 2.20
P# strip of 5, #B111 7.50
P# single, #B111 — 2.50

Booklet Stamps Microprinted "USPS" at Left of Flag Fold on Fourth Red Stripe

Serpentine Die Cut 11¼x10¾ on 2 or 3 Sides

5262 A4099 (50c) **multicolored** Ⓢ 1.10 .25
a. Booklet pane of 20 22.00

Counterfeits exist of No. 5262. See the Postal Counterfeits section of this catalog.

Microprinted "USPS" at Right of Flag Fold on Fifth White Stripe

5263 A4099 (50c) **multicolored** Ⓢ 1.10 .25
a. Booklet pane of 20 22.00

Nos. 5262a and 5263a are double-sided booklets with 12 stamps on one side and eight stamps plus a label that serves as the booklet cover on the other side.

See note after No. 1549.

BIOLUMINESCENT LIFE Ⓢ

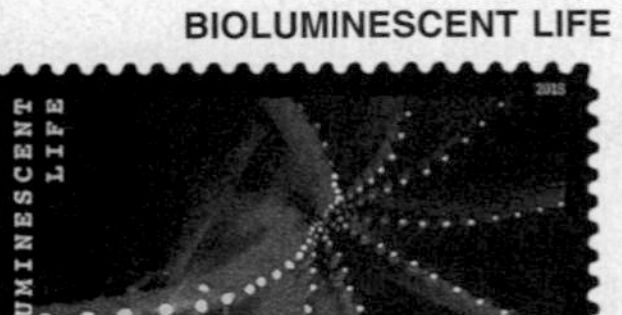

Octopus A4100

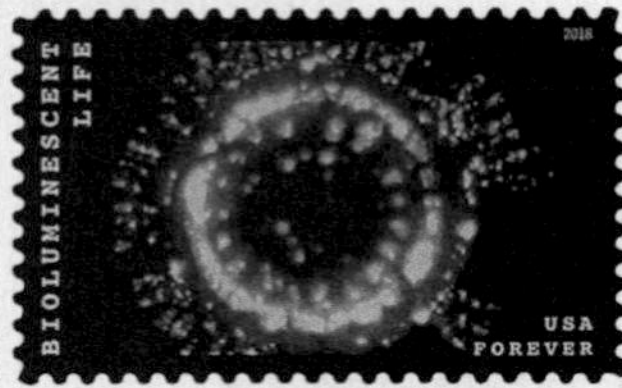

Jellyfish A4101

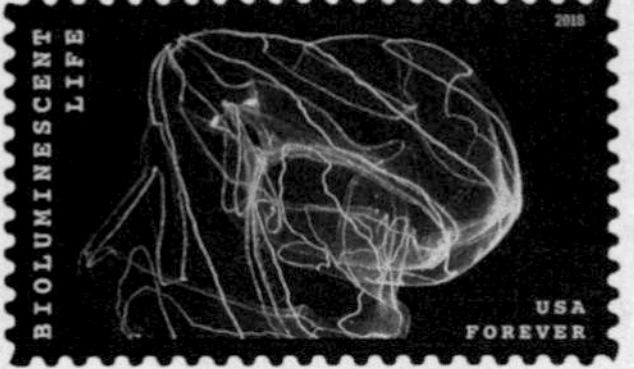

Comb Jelly — A4102

Mushrooms A4103

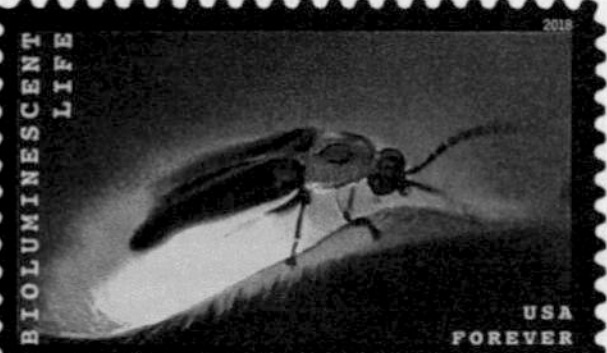

Firefly A4104

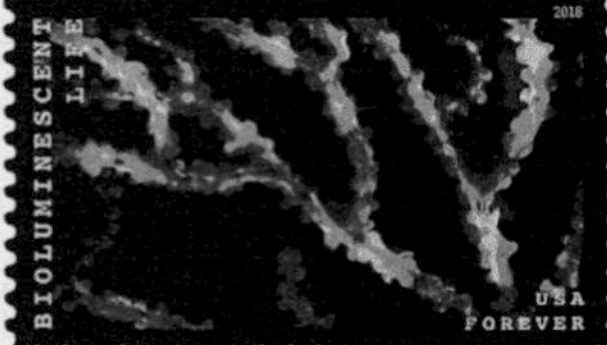

Bamboo Coral — A4105

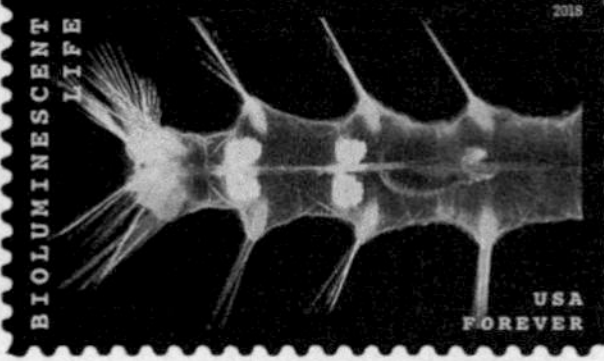

Marine Worm A4106

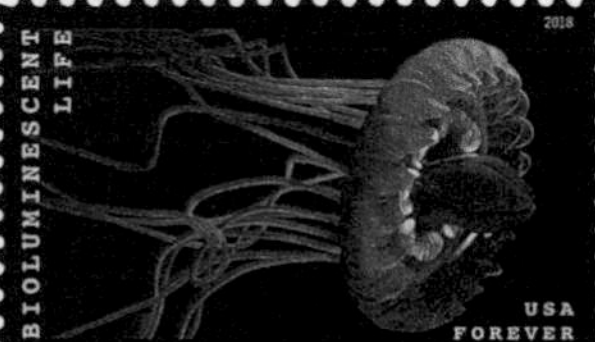

Crown Jellyfish A4107

Marine Worm A4108

Sea Pen — A4109

Designed by Derry Noyes. Printed by Banknote Corporation of America.

LITHOGRAPHED

Sheets of 180 in nine panes of 20

2018, Feb. 22 Tagged *Serpentine Die Cut 11*

Self-Adhesive

5264	A4100 (50c) **multicolored**		1.10	.40
5265	A4101 (50c) **multicolored**		1.10	.40
5266	A4102 (50c) **multicolored**		1.10	.40
5267	A4103 (50c) **multicolored**		1.10	.40
5268	A4104 (50c) **multicolored**		1.10	.40
5269	A4105 (50c) **multicolored**		1.10	.40
5270	A4106 (50c) **multicolored**		1.10	.40
5271	A4107 (50c) **multicolored**		1.10	.40
5272	A4108 (50c) **multicolored**		1.10	.40
5273	A4109 (50c) **multicolored**		1.10	.40
a.	Block of 10, #5264-5273		11.00	
	Pane of 20		22.00	
	Nos. 5264-5273 (10)		11.00	4.00

Die cut uncut press sheets of Nos. 5264-5273 were made available for sale. Values: cross gutter block of 10, $18; pairs with gutters between, $4.25 each. See note after No. 4693.

See note after No. 1549.

ILLINOIS STATEHOOD, 200TH ANNIV.

Map of Illinois and Sun Rays — A4110

Designed by Michael Konetzka. Printed by Banknote Corporation of America.

LITHOGRAPHED

Sheets of 240 in 12 panes of 20

2018, Mar. 5 Tagged *Serpentine Die Cut 11*

Self-Adhesive

5274	A4110 (50c) **multicolored** Ⓢ	1.10	.25
	P# block of 4, 7#+B	4.40	
	Pane of 20	22.00	

Die cut partial press sheets (containing 120 stamps) of No. 5274 were made available for sale. Values: cross gutter block of 4, $9; pairs with gutters between, $3.75 each. See note after No. 4693. See note after No. 1549.

MISTER ROGERS

Fred Rogers (1928-2003), Host of Children's

Designed by Derry Noyes. Printed by Banknote Corporation of America.

LITHOGRAPHED

Sheets of 240 in 12 panes of 20

2018, Mar. 23 Tagged *Serpentine Die Cut 11*

Self-Adhesive

5275	A4111 (50c) **multicolored** Ⓢ	1.10	.25
	P# block of 4, 6#+B	4.40	
	Pane of 20	22.00	

Die cut partial press sheets (containing 120 stamps) of No. 5275 were made available for sale. Values: cross gutter block of 4, $9; pairs with gutters between, $3.75 each. See note after No. 4693. See note after No. 1549.

SCIENCE, TECHNOLOGY, ENGINEERING AND MATHEMATICS (STEM) EDUCATION

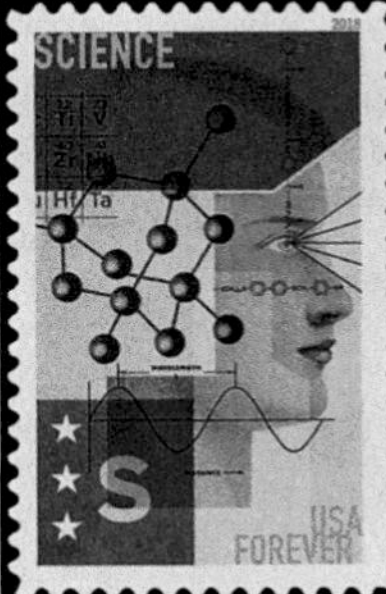

Head and Symbols of Science Education — A4112

Head and Symbols of Technology Education — A4113

Head and Symbols of Engineering Education — A4114

Head and Symbols of Mathematics Education — A4115

Designed by David Plunkert. Printed by Ashton-Potter (USA) Ltd.

LITHOGRAPHED

Sheets of 240 in 12 panes of 20

2018, Apr. 6 Tagged *Serpentine Die Cut 11*

Self-Adhesive

5276	A4112 (50c) **multicolored** Ⓢ	1.10	.30
5277	A4113 (50c) **multicolored** Ⓢ	1.10	.30
5278	A4114 (50c) **multicolored** Ⓢ	1.10	.30
5279	A4115 (50c) **multicolored** Ⓢ	1.10	.30
a.	Vert. strip of 4, #5276-5279	4.40	
	P# block of 8, 4#+P	8.80	
	Pane of 20	22.00	
	Nos. 5276-5279 (4)	4.40	1.20

Die cut partial press sheets (containing 120 stamps) of Nos. 5276-5279 were made available for sale. Values: cross gutter block of 8, $18; pairs with gutters between, $3.75 each. See note after No. 4693. See note after No. 1549.

Peace Rose — A4116

Designed by Ethel Kessler. Printed by Ashton-Potter (USA) Ltd.

LITHOGRAPHED

Serpentine Die Cut 11¼x10¾ on 2 or 3 Sides

2018, Apr. 21 **Tagged**

Booklet Stamp
Self-Adhesive

5280 A4116 (50c) **multicolored** Ⓢ 1.10 .25
a. Booklet pane of 20 22.00

No. 5280a is a double-sided booklet with 12 stamps on one side and eight stamps plus a label that serves as the booklet cover on the other side.
See note after No. 1549.

AIR MAIL, CENT.

Curtiss JN-4H "Jenny" Biplane A4117

Designed by Dan Gretta. Printed by Ashton-Potter (USA) Ltd.

ENGRAVED

Sheets of 120 in six panes of 20

2018 **Tagged** ***Serpentine Die Cut 10¾***

Self-Adhesive

5281 A4117 (50c) **blue,** *May 1* Ⓢ 1.10 .25
P# block of 4, 1#+P 4.40
Pane of 20 22.00
5282 A4117 (50c) **carmine lake,** *Aug. 11* Ⓢ 1.10 .25
P# block of 4, 1#+P 4.40
Pane of 20 22.00

Die cut press sheets of Nos. 5281 and 5282 were each made available for sale. Values: cross gutter block of 4, $9; pairs with gutters between, $3.75 each. See note after No. 4693. See note after No. 1549.

SALLY RIDE

Sally Ride (1951-2012), First American Woman in Space, and Space Shuttle Launch — A4118

Designed by Ethel Kessler. Printed by Ashton-Potter (USA), Ltd.

LITHOGRAPHED

Sheets of 180 in nine panes of 20

Serpentine Die Cut 10½x10¾

2018, May 23 **Tagged**

Self-Adhesive

5283 A4118 (50c) **multicolored** Ⓢ 1.10 .25
P# block of 4, 5#+P 4.00
Pane of 20 20.00

Die cut press sheets of No. 5283 were made available for sale. Values: cross gutter block of 4, $9; pairs with gutters between, $3.75 each. See note after No. 4693. See note after No. 1549.

FLAG ACT OF 1818, BICENT.

20-Star Flag — A4119

Designed by Kit Hinrichs. Printed by Ashton-Potter (USA) Ltd.

LITHOGRAPHED

Sheets of 120 in six panes of 20

2018, June 9 **Tagged** ***Serpentine Die Cut 10¾***

Self-Adhesive

5284 A4119 (50c) **multicolored** Ⓢ 1.10 .25
P# block of 4, 4#+P 4.40
Pane of 20 22.00

FROZEN TREATS Ⓢ

A4120

A4121

A4122

A4123

A4124

A4125

A4126

A4127

A4128

A4129

Designed by Leslie Baldani. Printed by Ashton-Potter (USA) Ltd.

LITHOGRAPHED

Serpentine Die Cut 11¼x10¾ on 2 or 3 Sides

2018, June 20 **Tagged**

Booklet Stamps
Self-Adhesive

5285 A4120 (50c) **multicolored** 1.10 .40
5286 A4121 (50c) **multicolored** 1.10 .40
5287 A4122 (50c) **multicolored** 1.10 .40
5288 A4123 (50c) **multicolored** 1.10 .40
5289 A4124 (50c) **multicolored** 1.10 .40
5290 A4125 (50c) **multicolored** 1.10 .40
5291 A4126 (50c) **multicolored** 1.10 .40
5292 A4127 (50c) **multicolored** 1.10 .40
5293 A4128 (50c) **multicolored** 1.10 .40
5294 A4129 (50c) **multicolored** 1.10 .40
a. Block of 10, #5285-5294 11.00
b. Booklet pane of 20, 2 each #5285-5294 22.00
Nos. 5285-5294 (10) 11.00 4.00

Nos. 5294b has a scratch-and-sniff coating with a fruity aroma, and is a double-sided booklet with 12 stamps on one side (Nos. 5286-5289, 5291-5294, 2 each Nos 5285, 5290), and eight stamps (Nos. 5286-5289, 5291-5294) plus a label that serves as the booklet cover on the other side.
Die cut uncut press sheets of Nos. 5285-5294 were made available for sale. Values: cross gutter block of 10 with booklet cover, $17; block of 10 with horiz. gutter between, $17. See note after No. 4693.
See note after No. 1549.

STATUE OF FREEDOM Ⓢ

Head of Statue of Freedom on U.S. Capitol Dome — A4130

Designed by Greg Breeding. Printed by Banknote Corporation of America.

LITHOGRAPHED & ENGRAVED

Sheets of 60 in six panes of 10 (#5295-5296),
Sheets of 40 in 10 panes of 4 (#5297)

Serpentine Die Cut 10¾x10½

2018, June 27 **Tagged**

Self-Adhesive

5295 A4130 $1 **emer, reddsh pink & black** 2.00 .50
P# block of 4, 3#+B 8.00
Pane of 10 20.00
5296 A4130 $2 **indigo, reddsh pink & black** 4.00 1.00
P# block of 4, 3#+B 16.00
Pane of 10 40.00
5297 A4130 $5 **brick red, reddsh pink & black** 10.00 2.50
Pane of 4 40.00
Nos. 5295-5297 (3) 16.00 4.00

Optically-variable ink was used for the numerals in the denominations.

O BEAUTIFUL Ⓢ

Death Valley National Park, California and Nevada — A4131

Three Fingers Mountain, Washington — A4132

Double Rainbow Over Field, Kansas — A4133

Great Smoky Mountains National Park, North Carolina and Tennessee — A4134

Field of Wheat, Wisconsin — A4135

Plowed Wheat Fields, Palouse Hills, Washington — A4136

Grasslands Wildlife Management Area, Merced County, California — A4137

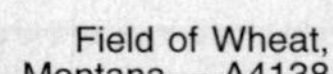

Field of Wheat, Montana — A4138

Yosemite National Park, California — A4139

Crater Lake National Park, Oregon — A4140

Monument Valley Navajo Tribal Park

Maroon Bells, Colorado — A4142

Sunrise Near Orinda, California — A4143

Pigeon Point, Near Pescadero, California — A4144

Edna Valley, San Luis Obispo County, California — A4145

Livermore, California — A4146

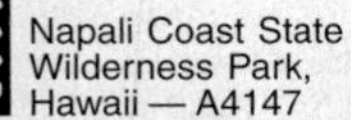

Napali Coast State Wilderness Park, Hawaii — A4147

Canaveral National Seashore, Florida — A4149

Bailey Island, Maine — A4150

Designed by Ethel Kessler. Printed by Ashton-Potter (USA), Ltd.

LITHOGRAPHED

Sheets of 120 in six panes of 20

2018, July 4 Tagged *Serpentine Die Cut 10½*

Self-Adhesive

5298	Pane of 20	22.00	
a.	A4131 (50c) **multicolored**	1.10	.50
b.	A4132 (50c) **multicolored**	1.10	.50
c.	A4133 (50c) **multicolored**	1.10	.50
d.	A4134 (50c) **multicolored**	1.10	.50
e.	A4135 (50c) **multicolored**	1.10	.50
f.	A4136 (50c) **multicolored**	1.10	.50
g.	A4137 (50c) **multicolored**	1.10	.50
h.	A4138 (50c) **multicolored**	1.10	.50
i.	A4139 (50c) **multicolored**	1.10	.50
j.	A4140 (50c) **multicolored**	1.10	.50
k.	A4141 (50c) **multicolored**	1.10	.50
l.	A4142 (50c) **multicolored**	1.10	.50
m.	A4143 (50c) **multicolored**	1.10	.50
n.	A4144 (50c) **multicolored**	1.10	.50
o.	A4145 (50c) **multicolored**	1.10	.50
p.	A4146 (50c) **multicolored**	1.10	.50
q.	A4147 (50c) **multicolored**	1.10	.50
r.	A4148 (50c) **multicolored**	1.10	.50
s.	A4149 (50c) **multicolored**	1.10	.50
t.	A4150 (50c) **multicolored**	1.10	.50

Die cut uncut press sheets of Nos. 5298 were made available for sale. Values: cross gutter block of 20, $30; pairs with gutters between, $4.25 each.

See note after No. 4693. See note after No. 1549.

SCOOBY-DOO

Cartoon Character Scooby-Doo Watering Plant A4151

Designed by Greg Breeding. Printed by Ashton-Potter (USA), Ltd.

LITHOGRAPHED

Sheets of 72 in six panes of 12

Serpentine Die Cut 10¾x10½

2018, July 14 Tagged

Self-Adhesive

5299	A4151 (50c) **multicolored** ⓢ	1.10	.25
	P# block of 4, 5#+P	4.40	
	Pane of 12	13.25	

Die cut press sheets of No. 5299 were made available for sale. Values: cross gutter block of 4, $9; pairs with gutters between, $3.75 each. See note after No. 4693. See note after No. 1549.

WORLD WAR I, CENT.

Member of American Expedtionary Force Holding Flag — A4152

Designed by Greg Breeding. Printed by Ashton-Potter (USA), Ltd.

LITHOGRAPHED

Sheets of 120 in six panes of 20

2018, July 27 Tagged *Serpentine Die Cut 10¾*

Self-Adhesive

5300 A4152 (50c) **multicolored** ⓢ 1.10 .25
P# block of 4, 7#+P 4.40
Pane of 20 22.00

Die cut press sheets of No. 5300 were made available for sale. Values: cross gutter block of 4, $9; pairs with gutters between, $3.75 each. See note after No. 4693. See note after No. 1549.

THE ART OF MAGIC ⓢ

Rabbit in Hat — A4153

Fortune Teller and Crystal Ball — A4154

Levitating Woman and Hoop — A4155

Empty Bird Cage — A4156

Bird Emerging From Flower — A4157

Designed by Greg Breeding. Printed by Banknote Corporation of America.

LITHOGRAPHED (Nos. 5301-5305), TYPOGRAPHED WITH LENTICULAR LENS AFFIXED (No. 5306)

Sheets of 120 in six panes of 20 (Nos. 5301-5305)

Serpentine Die Cut 10½x10¾

2018, Aug. 7 Tagged

Self-Adhesive

5301 A4153 (50c) **multicolored** 1.10 .40
5302 A4154 (50c) **multicolored** 1.10 .40
5303 A4155 (50c) **multicolored** 1.10 .40
5304 A4156 (50c) **multicolored** 1.10 .40
5305 A4157 (50c) **multicolored** 1.10 .40
a. Horiz. strip of 5, #5301-5305 5.50
P# block of 10, 9#+B 11.00
Pane of 20 22.00
Nos. 5301-5305 (5) 5.50 2.00

Souvenir Sheet

5306 Sheet of 3 #5306a 3.30
a. A4153 (50c) Single stamp 1.10 .30
b. As No. 5306, die cutting omitted *1,000.*

The printing method used on No. 5306a makes the rabbit in the vignette appear and disappear when the stamp is tilted. Die cut press sheets of No. 5301-5305 were made available for sale. Values: cross gutter block of 4, $9; pairs with gutters between, $3.75 each. See note after No. 4693. See note after No. 1549.

DRAGONS ⓢ

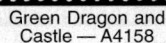

Green Dragon and Castle — A4158

Purple Dragon and Castle — A4159

Black Dragon and Ship — A4160

Orange Dragon and Pagoda — A4161

Designed by Greg Breeding. Printed by Banknote Corporation of America.

LITHOGRAPHED WITH FOIL APPLICATION

Sheets of 64 in four panes of 16

2018, Aug. 9 Tagged *Serpentine Die Cut 10¾*

Self-Adhesive

5307 A4158 (50c) **multicolored** 1.10 .30
5308 A4159 (50c) **multicolored** 1.10 .30
5309 A4160 (50c) **multicolored** 1.10 .30
5310 A4161 (50c) **multicolored** 1.10 .30
a. Strip or block of 4, #5307-5310 4.40
b. Horiz. strip of 4, #5307-5310, with die cutting missing (PS) —
P# block of 4, 4#+B 4.40
Pane of 16 17.50
Nos. 5307-5310 (4) 4.40 1.20

Die cut press sheets of Nos. 5307-5310 were made available for sale. Values: cross gutter block of 4, $9; pairs with gutters between, $3.75 each. See note after No. 4693. See note after No. 1549.

Poinsettia A4162

Designed by Greg Breeding. Printed by Banknote Corporation of America.

LITHOGRAPHED

Sheets of 60 in six panes of 10

2018, Aug. 26 Tagged *Serpentine Die Cut*

Self-Adhesive

5311 A4162 ($1.15) **multicolored** ⓢ 2.40 .50
P# block of 4, 5#+B 9.60
Pane of 10 24.00

Unused values are for stamps with surrounding selvage. Adjacent stamps are separated by rouletting.

MUSIC ICONS

John Lennon (1940-80), Rock Musician — A4163

Designed by Neal Ashby. Printed by Banknote Corporation of America.

LITHOGRAPHED

Sheets of 96 in six panes of 16

2018, Sept. 7 Tagged *Serpentine Die Cut 10¾*

Self-Adhesive

Color of Shoulders

5312 A4163 (50c) **red** ⓢ 1.10 .30
5313 A4163 (50c) **red lilac** ⓢ 1.10 .30
5314 A4163 (50c) **dark violet** ⓢ 1.10 .30

5315 A4163 (50c) **blue** Ⓢ 1.10 .30
a. Vert. strip of 4, #5312-5315 4.40
Pane of 16 17.50
b. As "a," die cutting omitted —
Nos. 5312-5315 (4) 4.40 1.20

Adjacent horizontal or vertical stamps have selvage between the stamps.

Die cut press sheets of Nos. 5312-5315 were made available for sale. Values: cross gutter block of 8, $18; pairs with gutters between, $3.75 each. See note after No. 4693. See note after No. 1549.

FIRST RESPONDERS

Firefighter, Paramedic, and Law Enforcement Officer
A4164

Designed by Antonio Alcalá. Printed by Ashton-Potter (USA), Ltd.

LITHOGRAPHED

Sheets of 120 in six panes of 20

2018, Sept. 13 Tagged *Serpentine Die Cut 11*

Self-Adhesive

5316 A4164 (50c) **multicolored** Ⓢ 1.10 .25
P# block of 4, 4#+P 4.40
Pane of 20 22.00

Die cut press sheets of No. 5316 were made available for sale. Values: cross gutter block of 4, $9; pairs with gutters between, $3.75 each. See note after No. 4693. See note after No. 1549.

BIRDS IN WINTER Ⓢ

Black-capped Chickadee — A4165

Northern Cardinal — A4166

Red-bellied Woodpecker — A4167

Blue Jay — A4168

Designed by Antonio Alcalá. Printed by Banknote Corporation of America.

LITHOGRAPHED

Serpentine Die Cut 10¾ on 2 or 3 Sides

2018, Sept. 22 Tagged

Booklet Stamps

Self-Adhesive

5317 A4165 (50c) **multicolored** 1.10 .30
5318 A4166 (50c) **multicolored** 1.10 .30
5319 A4167 (50c) **multicolored** 1.10 .30
5320 A4168 (50c) **multicolored** 1.10 .30
a. Block of 4, #5317-5320 4.40
b. Booklet pane of 20, 5 each #5317-5320 22.00
Nos. 5317-5320 (4) 4.40 1.20

No. 5320b is a double-sided booklet pane with 12 stamps on one side (3 each Nos. 5317-5320), and eight stamps (2 each Nos. 5317-5320) plus label (booklet cover) on the other side.

Die cut uncut press sheets of Nos. 5317-5320 were made available for sale. Values of varieties: cross gutter block of 4 with booklet cover, imperf. within, $10; cross gutter block of 4, imperf. within, $10; block of 4, horiz. imperf. between, $8.50; horiz. pair, imperf. between, $4. See note after No. 4693. See note after No. 1549.

HOT WHEELS TOY CARS, 50TH ANNIV. Ⓢ

Purple Passion
A4169

Rocket-Bye-Baby — A4170

Rigor Motor
A4171

Rodger Dodger
A4172

Mach Speeder
A4173

Twin Mill
A4174

Bone Shaker
A4175

HW40
A4176

Deora II
A4177

Sharkruiser
A4178

Designed by Greg Breeding. Printed by Banknote Corporation of America.

LITHOGRAPHED

Sheets of 160 in eight panes of 20

2018, Sept. 29 Tagged *Serpentine Die Cut 10¾*

Self-Adhesive

5321 A4169 (50c) **multicolored** 1.10 .40
5322 A4170 (50c) **multicolored** 1.10 .40
5323 A4171 (50c) **multicolored** 1.10 .40
5324 A4172 (50c) **multicolored** 1.10 .40
5325 A4173 (50c) **multicolored** 1.10 .40
5326 A4174 (50c) **multicolored** 1.10 .40
5327 A4175 (50c) **multicolored** 1.10 .40
5328 A4176 (50c) **multicolored** 1.10 .40
5329 A4177 (50c) **multicolored** 1.10 .40
5330 A4178 (50c) **multicolored** 1.10 .40
Pane of 20, 2 each #5321-5330, 2 sets of 5#+P 22.00
Nos. 5321-5330 (10) 11.00 4.00

Die cut press sheets of No. 5321-5330 were made available for sale. Values: pairs with gutters between, $3.75 each. See note after No. 4693. See note after No. 1549.

CHRISTMAS Ⓢ

Madonna and Child, by Bachiacca — A4179

Head of Santa Claus, by Haddon Sundblom — A4180

Santa Claus and Wreath, by Sundblom — A4181

Santa Claus and Book, by Sundblom — A4182

Santa Claus and Card, by Sundblom — A4183

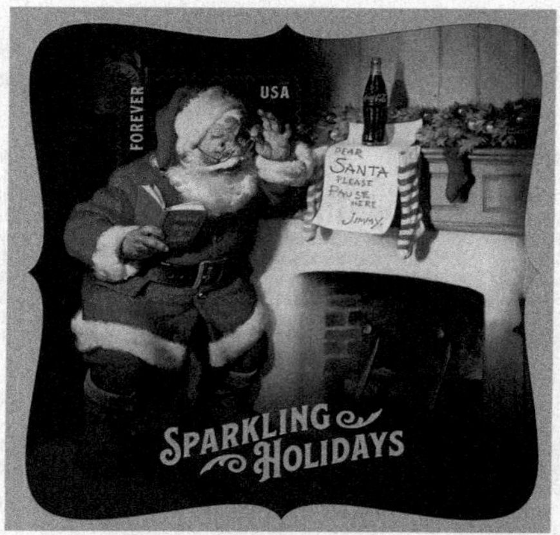

Santa Claus and Book, by Sundblom — A4184

Designed by Greg Breeding. Printed by Banknote Corporation of America (No. 5331), Ashton-Potter (USA) Ltd. (Nos. 5332-5336).

LITHOGRAPHED

Serpentine Die Cut 10¾x11 on 2 or 3 Sides

2018 **Tagged**

Booklet Stamps
Self-Adhesive

5331 A4179 (50c) **multicolored,** *Oct. 3* 1.10 .25
a. Booklet pane of 20 22.00
5332 A4180 (50c) **multicolored,** *Oct. 11* 1.10 .30
5333 A4181 (50c) **multicolored,** *Oct. 11* 1.10 .30
5334 A4182 (50c) **multicolored,** *Oct. 11* 1.10 .30
5335 A4183 (50c) **multicolored,** *Oct. 11* 1.10 .30
a. Block of 4, #5332-5335 4.40
b. Booklet pane of 20, 5 each #5332-5335 22.00
Nos. 5331-5335 (5) 5.50 1.45

Souvenir Sheet

Serpentine Die Cut 10¾

5336 A4184 (50c) **multicolored,** *Oct. 11* 1.10 .25

No. 5331a is a double-sided booklet panes with 12 stamps on one side and eight stamps plus label (booklet cover) on the other side. No. 5335b is a double-sided booklet pane with 12 stamps on one side (3 each Nos. 5332-5335) and eight stamps (2 each Nos. 5332-5335) plus label (booklet cover) on the other side.

Die cut uncut press sheets of Nos. 5331 and 5332-5335 were made available for sale. Values of varieties: cross gutter block of 4 with booklet cover, imperf. within, $10; cross gutter block of 4, imperf. within, $10; blocks of 4 (Nos. 5332-5335), imperf. vert. or horiz. between, $7.50 each; vert. pair, imperf. between, $4; horiz. pair, imperf. between, $6. See note after No. 4693. See note after No. 1549.

KWANZAA Ⓢ

Family and Kinara — A4185

Designed by Derry Noyes. Printed by Banknote Corporation of America.

LITHOGRAPHED

Sheets of 120 in six panes of 20

2018, Oct. 10 **Tagged** ***Serpentine Die Cut 10¾***

Self-Adhesive

5337 A4185 (50c) **multicolored** 1.10 .25
P# block of 4, 4#+B 4.00
Pane of 20 20.00

Die cut uncut press sheets of No. 5337 were made available for sale. Values: cross gutter block of 4, $9; pairs with gutters between, $4.25 each. See note after No. 4693. See note after No. 1549.

HANUKKAH Ⓢ

Menorah — A4186

Designed by Ethel Kessler. Printed by Banknote Corporation of America.

LITHOGRAPHED

Sheets of 120 in six panes of 20

2018, Oct. 16 **Tagged** ***Serpentine Die Cut 10¾***

Self-Adhesive

5338 A4186 (50c) **multicolored** 1.10 .25
P# block of 4, 5#+B 4.00
Pane of 20 20.00

Die cut uncut press sheets of No. 5338 were made available for sale. Values: cross gutter block of 4, $9; pairs with gutters between, $4.25 each. See note after No. 4693. See note after No. 1549.

See Israel No. 2200.

LOVE Ⓢ

Hearts — A4187

Designed by Antonio Alcalá. Printed by Banknote Corporation of America.

LITHOGRAPHED

Sheets of 160 in eight panes of 20

Serpentine Die Cut 10¾x11

2019, Jan. 10 **Tagged**

Self-Adhesive

5339 A4187 (50c) **multicolored** 1.10 .25
P# block of 4, 5#+B 4.40
Pane of 20 22.00

Die cut uncut press sheets of No. 5339 were made available for sale. Values: cross gutter block of 4, $9; pairs with gutters between, $4.25 each. See note after No. 4693. See note after No. 1549.

CHINESE NEW YEAR Ⓢ

Year of the Boar — A4188

Designed by Ethel Kessler. Printed by Banknote Corporation of America.

LITHOGRAPHED

Sheets of 144 in 12 panes of 12

2019, Jan. 17 **Tagged** ***Serpentine Die Cut 10¾***

Self-Adhesive

5340 A4188 (50c) **multicolored** 1.10 .25
Pane of 12 12.00

Die cut partial press sheets (containing 72 stamps) of No. 5340 were made available for sale. Values: cross gutter block of 4, $9; pairs with gutters between, $4.25 each. See note after No. 4693. See note after No. 1549.

People Wearing Uncle Sam Hats Type of 2017

Designed by Antonio Alcalá. Printed by Banknote Corporation of America.

LITHOGRAPHED

Serpentine Die Cut 11 Vert.

2019, Jan. 27 **Tagged**

Coil Stamp
Self-Adhesive

5341 A4006 (15c) **multicolored** Ⓢ .30 .25
Pair .60
P# strip of 5, #B1111111 2.25
P# single, #B1111111 — .60

See note after No. 1549.

Flag — A4189

Designed by Antonio Alcalá. Printed by Ashton-Potter (USA) Ltd. (#5342, 5344), Banknote Corporation of America. (#5343, 5345).

LITHOGRAPHED

Serpentine Die Cut 9½ Horiz.

2019, Jan. 27 **Tagged**

Coil Stamps
Self-Adhesive
Microprinted "USPS" at Lower Flag Grommet

5342 A4189 (55c) **multicolored** Ⓢ 1.10 .25
Pair 2.20
P# strip of 5, #P1111 7.75
P# single, #P111 — 2.75

Serpentine Die Cut 11 Horiz.

Microprinted "USPS" to Right of Sixth Red Flag Stripe

5343 A4189 (55c) **multicolored** Ⓢ 1.10 .25
Pair 2.20
P# strip of 5, #B1111 7.75
P# single, #B1111 — 2.75

Booklet Stamps

Microprinted "USPS" at Upper Left Corner of Flag

Serpentine Die Cut 10¾x11¼ on 2 or 3 Sides

5344 A4189 (55c) **multicolored** Ⓢ 1.10 .25
a. Booklet pane of 20 22.00

Microprinted "USPS" to Right of Sixth Red Flag Stripe

5345 A4189 (55c) **multicolored** Ⓢ 1.10 .25
a. Booklet pane of 20 22.00

Nos. 5344a and 5345a are double-sided booklets with 12 stamps on one side and eight stamps plus a label that serves as the booklet cover on the other side.

See note after No. 1549.

CALIFORNIA DOGFACE BUTTERFLY Ⓢ

A4190

Designed by Derry Noyes. Printed by Banknote Corporation of America.

LITHOGRAPHED

Sheets of 120 in six panes of 20

2019, Jan. 27 **Tagged** ***Serpentine Die Cut 10½***

Self-Adhesive

5346 A4190 (70c) **multicolored** 1.40 .25
P# block of 4, 6#+B 5.60
Pane of 20 28.00

See note after No. 1549.

AMERICAN LANDMARKS ISSUE

Joshua Tree — A4191

Bethesda Fountain, Central Park, New York City — A4192

Designed by Greg Breeding. Printed by Ashton-Potter (USA) Ltd.

LITHOGRAPHED

Sheets of 48 in 12 panes of 4 (#5347), Sheets of 24 in six panes of 4 (#5348)

Serpentine Die Cut 10¾x10½

2019, Jan. 27 **Tagged**

Self-Adhesive

5347 A4191 $7.35 **multicolored** ⓢ 15.00 7.50
Pane of 4 60.00
5348 A4192 $25.50 **multicolored** ⓢ 50.00 25.00
Pane of 4 200.00

See note after No. 1549.

BLACK HERITAGE

Gregory Hines (1946-2003), Tap Dancer — A4193

Designed by Derry Noyes. Printed by Ashton-Potter (USA) Ltd.

LITHOGRAPHED

Sheets of 240 in 12 panes of 20

2019, Jan. 28 **Tagged** ***Serpentine Die Cut 10¾***

Self-Adhesive

5349 A4193 (55c) **multicolored** ⓢ 1.10 .25
P# block of 4, 4#+P 4.40
Pane of 20 22.00

Die cut partial press sheets (containing 120 stamps) of No. 5349 were made available for sale. Values: cross gutter block of 4, $9; pairs with gutters between, $4 each. See note after No. 4693. See note after No. 1549.

CACTUS FLOWERS ⓢ

Opuntia Engelmannii — A4194

Rebutia Minuscula — A4195

Echinocereus Dasyacanthus — A4196

Echinocereus Poselgeri — A4197

Echinocereus Coccineus — A4198

Pelecyphora Aselliformis — A4199

Parodia Microsperma — A4200

Echinocactus Horizonthalonius A4201

Thelocactus Heterochromus A4202

Parodia Scopa — A4203

Designed by Ethel Kessler. Printed by Banknote Corporation of America.

LITHOGRAPHED

Serpentine Die Cut 11 on 2 or 3 Sides

2019, Feb. 15 **Tagged**

Booklet Stamps
Self-Adhesive

5350 A4194 (55c) **multicolored** 1.10 .40
5351 A4195 (55c) **multicolored** 1.10 .40
5352 A4196 (55c) **multicolored** 1.10 .40
5353 A4197 (55c) **multicolored** 1.10 .40
5354 A4198 (55c) **multicolored** 1.10 .40
5355 A4199 (55c) **multicolored** 1.10 .40
5356 A4200 (55c) **multicolored** 1.10 .40
5357 A4201 (55c) **multicolored** 1.10 .40
5358 A4202 (55c) **multicolored** 1.10 .40
5359 A4203 (55c) **multicolored** 1.10 .40
a. Block of 10, #5350-5359 11.00
b. Booklet pane of 20, 2 each #5350-5359 22.00
Nos. 5350-5359 (10) 11.00 4.00

No. 5359b is a double-sided booklet pane with 12 stamps on one side (Nos. 5352-5359, 2 each Nos. 5350-5351), and eight stamps (Nos. 5352-5359) plus label (booklet cover) on the other side.

Die cut uncut press sheets of Nos. 5350-5359 were made available for sale. Values of varieties: cross gutter block of 4 with booklet cover, imperf. within, $11; cross gutter block of 4, imperf. within, $11; block of 4, horiz. imperf. between, $9; block of 4, vert. imperf. between, $8. See note after No. 4693. See note after No. 1549.

ALABAMA STATEHOOD, BICENT. ⓢ

Pulpit Rock, Cheaha State Park — A4204

Designed by Greg Breeding. Printed by Banknote Corporation of America.

LITHOGRAPHED

Sheets of 240 in 12 panes of 20

Serpentine Die Cut 11x10¾

2019, Feb. 23 **Tagged**

Self-Adhesive

5360 A4204 (55c) **multicolored** 1.10 .25
P# block of 4, 5#+B 4.40
Pane of 20 22.00

Die cut partial press sheets of No. 5360 (containing 120 stamps) were made available for sale. Values: cross gutter block of 4, $9; pairs with gutters between, $4 each. See note after No. 4693. See note after No. 1549.

Star Ribbon — A4205

Designed by Aaron Draplin. Printed by Banknote Corporation of America.

LITHOGRAPHED

Sheets of 200 in 10 panes of 20

Serpentine Die Cut 11¼x10¾

2019, Mar. 22 **Tagged**

Self-Adhesive

5361 A4205 (55c) **multicolored** ⓢ 1.10 .25
P# block of 4, 3#+B 4.40
Pane of 20 22.00

Coil Stamp

Serpentine Die Cut 10¾ Vert.

5362 A4205 (55c) **multicolored** ⓢ 1.10 .25
Pair 2.20
P# strip of 5, #B111 8.00
P# single, #B111 — 2.50

See note after No. 1549.

CORAL REEFS Ⓢ

Elkhorn Coral and French Angelfish — A4206

Brain Coral and Spotted Moray Eel — A4207

Pillar Coral, Coney Grouper and Neon Gobies — A4208

Staghorn Coral and Blue-striped Grunts — A4209

Designed by Tyler Lang. Printed by Ashton-Potter (USA) Ltd.

LITHOGRAPHED
Sheets of 200 in 10 panes of 20
Serpentine Die Cut 11¼x10¾

2019, Mar. 29 **Tagged**

Self-Adhesive

5363 A4206 (35c) **multicolored** .70 .25
5364 A4207 (35c) **multicolored** .70 .25
5365 A4208 (35c) **multicolored** .70 .25
5366 A4209 (35c) **multicolored** .70 .25
a. Horiz. or vert. strip of 4, #5363-5366 2.80
P# block of 8, 1 or 2 sets of 6#+P 5.60
Pane of 20 14.00
Nos. 5363-5366 (4) 2.80 1.00

Coil Stamps
Serpentine Die Cut 9½ Vert.

5367 A4208 (35c) **multicolored** .70 .25
5368 A4209 (35c) **multicolored** .70 .25
5369 A4206 (35c) **multicolored** .70 .25
5370 A4207 (35c) **multicolored** .70 .25
a. Horiz. strip of 4, #5367-5370 2.80
P# strip of 5, #5368-5370, 2 #5367, #P111111 5.50
P# strip of 9, 2 each #5367-5368, 5370, 3 #5369, #P111111 10.00
P# single, #P111111 (#5369) — 3.00
Nos. 5367-5370 (4) 2.80 1.00

MUSIC ICONS

Marvin Gaye (1939-84), Singer — A4210

Designed by Derry Noyes. Printed by Banknote Corporation of America.

LITHOGRAPHED
Sheets of 144 in nine panes of 16

2019, Apr. 2 **Tagged** ***Serpentine Die Cut 10½***

Self-Adhesive

5371 A4210 (55c) **multicolored** Ⓢ 1.10 .25
Pane of 16 18.00

Die cut uncut press sheets of No. 5371 were made available for sale. Values: cross gutter block of 4, $9; pairs with gutters between, $4 each. See note after No. 4693.
See note after No. 1549.

POST OFFICE MURALS Ⓢ

Piggott, Arkansas Mural *Air Mail,* by Daniel Rhodes — A4211

Florence, Colorado Mural, *Antelope,* by Olive Rush — A4212

Rockville, Maryland Mural, *Sugarloaf Mountain,* by Judson Smith — A4213

Anadarko, Oklahoma Mural, *Kiowas Moving Camp,* by Stephen Mopope, James Auchiah, and Spencer Asah — A4214

Deming, New Mexico Mural, *Mountains and Yucca,* by Kenneth Miller Adams — A4215

Designed by Antonio Alcalá. Printed by Ashton-Potter (USA) Ltd.

LITHOGRAPHED
Sheets of 50 in five panes of 10
Serpentine Die Cut 11½x11

2019, Apr. 10 **Tagged**

Self-Adhesive

5372 A4211 (55c) **multicolored** 1.10 .40
5373 A4212 (55c) **multicolored** 1.10 .40
5374 A4213 (55c) **multicolored** 1.10 .40
5375 A4214 (55c) **multicolored** 1.10 .40
5376 A4215 (55c) **multicolored** 1.10 .40
a. Vert. strip of 5, #5372-5376 5.50
Pane of 10 11.00
Nos. 5372-5376 (5) 5.50 2.00

Die cut uncut press sheets of Nos. 5372-5376 were made available for sale. Values: cross gutter block of 10, $16; pairs with gutters between, $4 each. See note after No. 4693.
See note after No. 1549.

MAUREEN CONNOLLY BRINKER

Maureen "Little Mo" Connolly Brinker (1934-69), Tennis Player — A4216

Designed by Derry Noyes. Printed by Banknote Corporation of America.

LITHOGRAPHED
Sheets of 120 in six panes of 20

2019, Apr. 23 **Tagged** ***Serpentine Die Cut 10¾***

Self-Adhesive

5377 A4216 (55c) **multicolored** Ⓢ 1.10 .25
P# block of 4, 4#+B 4.40
Pane of 20 22.00

Die cut press sheets of No. 5377 were made available for sale. Values: cross gutter block of 4, $9; pairs with gutters between, $4 each. See note after No. 4693. See note after No. 1549.

TRANSCONTINENTAL RAILROAD, 150th ANNIV. Ⓢ

Jupiter Locomotive — A4217

Golden Spike — A4218

No. 119 Locomotive — A4219

Designed by Greg Breeding. Printed by Banknote Corporation of America.

LITHOGRAPHED WITH FOIL APPLICATION
Sheets of 72 in four panes of 18
Serpentine Die Cut 10¾x10½

2019, May 10 **Tagged**

Self-Adhesive

5378 A4217 (55c) **multicolored** 1.10 .30
5379 A4218 (55c) **multicolored** 1.10 .30
5380 A4219 (55c) **multicolored** 1.10 .30
a. Horiz. strip of 3, #5378-5380 3.30
P# block of 6, 4# + B 6.60
Pane of 18 20.00
Nos. 5378-5380 (3) 3.30 .90

Die cut uncut press sheets of Nos. 5378-5380 were made available for sale. Values: cross gutter block of 6, $10; pairs with gutters between, $4.25 each. See note after No. 4693.

A boxed set containing a pane of Nos. 5378-5380, imperforate panes of single-color progressive proofs in gold, cyan, magenta, yellow, and black, an imperforate proof pane with all colors except gold, a protective sleeve, a commemorative book, and a certificate of authenticity were sold together for $79.95.

See note after No. 1549.

WILD AND SCENIC RIVERS Ⓢ

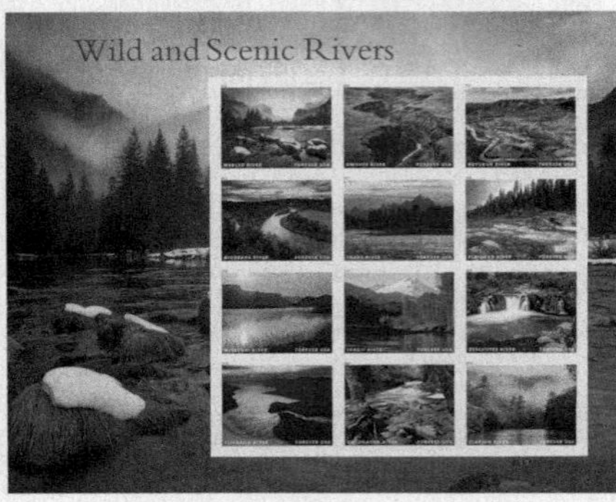

A4220

Designed by Derry Noyes. Printed by Banknote Corporation of America.

No. 5381: a, Merced River. b, Owyhee River. c, Koyukuk River. d, Niobrara River. e, Snake River. f, Flathead River. g, Missouri River. h, Skagit River. i, Deschutes River. j, Tlikakila River. k, Ontonagon River. l, Clarion River.

LITHOGRAPHED
Sheets of 108 in nine panes of 12
Serpentine Die Cut 10¾x10½

2019, May 21 **Tagged**

Self-Adhesive

5381 A4220 Pane of 12 13.50
a.-l. (55c) Any single 1.10 .50

Die cut uncut press sheets of No. 5381 were made available for sale. Values: pairs with gutters between, $4 each. See note after No. 4693. See note after No. 1549.

ART OF ELLSWORTH KELLY (1923-2015) Ⓢ

Yellow White, 1961 — A4221

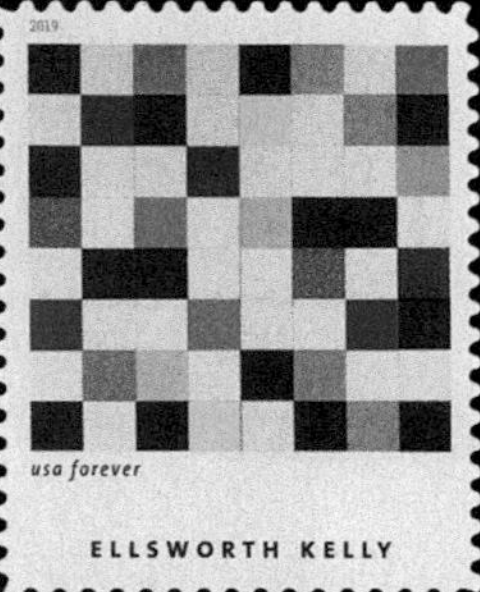

Colors for a Large Wall, 1951 — A4222

Blue Red Rocker, 1963 — A4223

Spectrum I, 1953 — A4224

South Ferry, 1956 — A4225

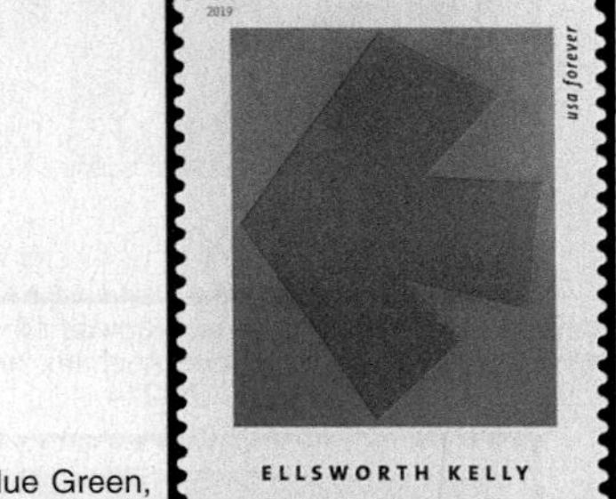

Blue Green, 1962 — A4226

Orange Red Relief (for Delphine Seyrig), 1990 — A4227

Meschers, 1951 — A4228

Red Blue, 1964 — A4229

Gaza, 1956 — A4230

Designed by Derry Noyes. Printed by Banknote Corporation of America.

LITHOGRAPHED
Sheets of 120 in six panes of 20
Serpentine Die Cut 10½x10¾

2019, May 31 **Tagged**

Self-Adhesive

5382 A4221 (55c) **multicolored** 1.10 .40
5383 A4222 (55c) **multicolored** 1.10 .40
5384 A4223 (55c) **multicolored** 1.10 .40
5385 A4224 (55c) **multicolored** 1.10 .40
5386 A4225 (55c) **multicolored** 1.10 .40
5387 A4226 (55c) **multicolored** 1.10 .40
5388 A4227 (55c) **multicolored** 1.10 .40
5389 A4228 (55c) **multicolored** 1.10 .40
5390 A4229 (55c) **multicolored** 1.10 .40
5391 A4230 (55c) **multicolored** 1.10 .40
a. Block of 10, #5382-5391 11.00
P# block of 10, 5# + B 11.00
Pane of 20 20.00
Nos. 5382-5391 (10) 11.00 4.00

Die cut uncut press sheets of Nos. 5382-5391 were made available for sale. Values: cross gutter block of 10, $18; pairs with gutters between, $4.25 each. See note after No. 4693.

See note after No. 1549.

COMMISSIONING OF U.S.S. MISSOURI, 75th ANNIV.

U.S.S. Missouri — A4231

Designed by Greg Breeding. Printed by Banknote Corporation of America.

LITHOGRAPHED
Sheets of 180 in nine panes of 20

2019, June 11 Tagged *Serpentine Die Cut 10¾*
Self-Adhesive

5392 A4231 (55c) **multicolored** ⓢ 1.10 .25
P# block of 4, 5#+B 4.40
Pane of 20 22.00

Die cut press sheets of No. 5392 were made available for sale. Values: cross gutter block of 4, $9; pairs with gutters between, $4 each. See note after No. 4693. See note after No. 1549.

GEORGE HERBERT WALKER BUSH

George Herbert Walker Bush (1924-2018), 41st President — A4232

Designed by Phil Jordan. Printed by Banknote Corporation of America.

LITHOGRAPHED
Sheets of 120 in six panes of 20

2019, June 12 Tagged *Serpentine Die Cut 10¾*
Self-Adhesive

5393 A4232 (55c) **multicolored** ⓢ 1.10 .25
P# block of 4, 5#+B 4.40
Pane of 20 22.00

Die cut press sheets of No. 5393 were made available for sale. Values: cross gutter block of 4, $9; pairs with gutters between, $4 each. See note after No. 4693. See note after No. 1549.

SESAME STREET CHILDREN'S TELEVISION SHOW, 50th ANNIV. ⓢ

Muppet Characters — A4233

Designed by Derry Noyes. Printed by Ashton-Potter (USA) Ltd.

No. 5394: a, Big Bird. b, Ernie. c, Bert. d, Cookie Monster. e, Rosita. f, The Count. g, Oscar the Grouch. h, Abby Cadabby. i, Herry Monster. j, Julia. k, Guy Smiley. l, Snuffleupagus. m, Elmo. n, Telly. o, Grover. p, Zoe.

LITHOGRAPHED
Sheets of 160 in 10 panes of 16

2019, June 22 Tagged *Serpentine Die Cut 10¾*
Self-Adhesive

5394 A4233 Pane of 16 18.00
a.-p. (55c) Any single 1.10 .50

Die cut uncut press sheets of No. 5394 were made available for sale. Values: pairs with gutters between, $4 each. See note after No. 4693. See note after No. 1549.

FROGS ⓢ

Pacific Tree Frog — A4234

Northern Leopard Frog — A4235

American Green Tree Frog — A4236

Squirrel Tree Frog — A4237

Designed by William J. Gicker. Printed by Banknote Corporation of America.

LITHOGRAPHED
Serpentine Die Cut 11x10¾ on 2 or 3 Sides

2019, July 9 Tagged

Booklet Stamps
Self-Adhesive

5395 A4234 (55c) **multicolored** 1.10 .30
5396 A4235 (55c) **multicolored** 1.10 .30
5397 A4236 (55c) **multicolored** 1.10 .30
5398 A4237 (55c) **multicolored** 1.10 .30
a. Block of 4, #5395-5398 4.40
b. Booklet pane of 20, 5 each #5395-5398 22.00
Nos. 5395-5398 (4) 4.40 1.20

No. 5398b is a double-sided booklet pane with 12 stamps on one side (3 each Nos. 5395-5398), and eight stamps (2 each Nos. 5395-5398) plus label (booklet cover) on the other side. See note after No. 1549.

2019 END-OF-YEAR ISSUES

The USPS has announced that the following items will be released in late 2019. Dates, denominations and cities are tentative.

Woodstock Music Festival, 50th Anniv., Pane of 20 (55c) forever stamps, *Aug. 8,* New York, NY.

Tyrannosaurus Rex, Four (55c) forever stamps in a pane of 16, *Aug. 29,* Washington, DC.

Walt Whitman, Pane of 20 (95c) three-ounce rate forever stamps, *Sept. 12,* Huntington Station, NY.

Winter Berries, Four (55c) forever stamps: Winter berry, juniper berry, beauty berry, soapberry; double-sided convertible booklet pane of 20, *Sept. 17,* Tulsa, OK.

Spooky Silhouettes, Four (55c) forever stamps: Cat and raven, two ghosts, spider and web, three bats, *Oct.*

Purple Heart Medal, Pane of 20 (55c) forever stamps, *Oct.,* Noblesville, IN.

Flag, (55c) stamped envelope.

Post Traumatic Stress Disorder, Semi-postal stamp.

Listings as of 10AM, September 4, 2019.

2018 U.S. Pre-Mounted Supplement

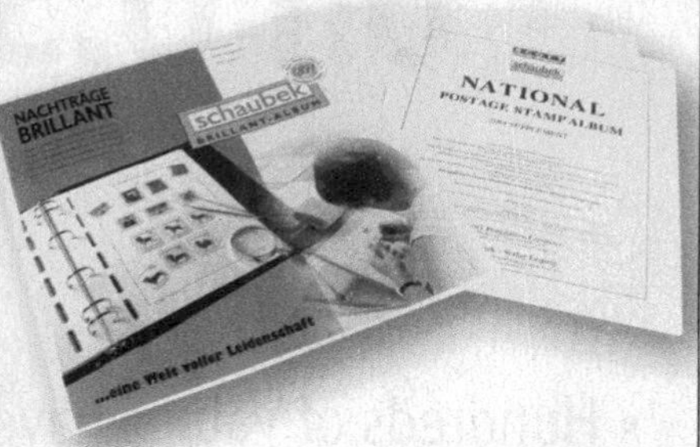

Make life easier with fully mounted United States 2018 album pages. These brilliant pages are equipped with stamp mounts for each stamp so it takes the work out of collecting. As a bonus the supplements contain Scott numbers for easy referencing and valuing. For complete list of available album pages visit AmosAdvantage.com.

Item#	Description	Retail	AA
HUSA2018	2018 U.S. Supp.	$78.99	**$67.99**

Senator Binder & Slipcase

Don't forget to pick up your binder and slipcase when you order the 2018 Schaubek/Scott supplement!

Item#	Description	Retail	AA
HRB001	Blue Binder	$39.99	**$34.99**
HRS001	Blue Slipcase	$19.99	**$16.99**

Call
800-572-6885
Outside U.S. & Canada call:
(937) 498-0800
Visit
www.AmosAdvantage.com

Ordering Information: *AA prices apply to paid subscribers of Amos Media titles, or for orders placed online. Prices, terms and product availability subject to change. Shipping & Handling: U.S.: Orders total $0-$10.00 charged $3.99 shipping. U.S. Order total $10.01-$79.99 charged $7.99 shipping. U.S. Order total $80.00 or more charged 10% of order total for shipping. Taxes will apply in CA, OH, & IL. Canada: 20% of order total. Minimum charge $19.99 Maximum charge $200.00. Foreign orders are shipped via FedEx Intl. or USPS and billed actual freight.

Introducing the New
Scott Catalogue of Errors on U.S. Postage Stamps
17th Edition

- Hundreds of Values have been Updated
- Dozens of New Full Color Illustrations
- 50+ New Listings!
- Identified by Scott Numbers
- Includes Known Quantities
- Thoroughly Reviewed and Updated

Item#	Retail	AA
ERSTPE17	$49.99	$39.99

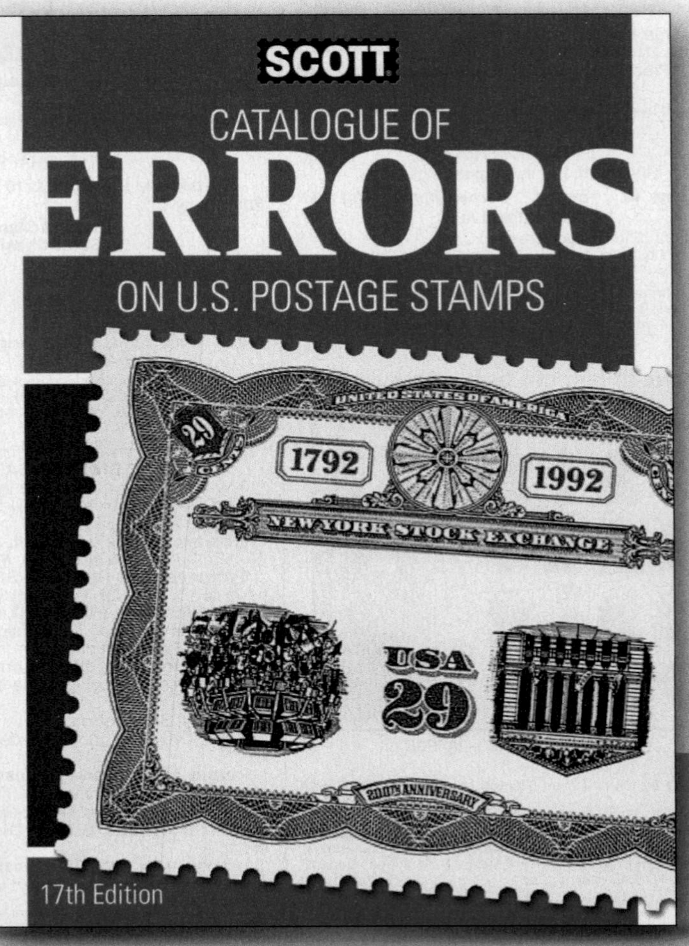

Available Now!
Order your Copy Today!

Visit www.AmosAdvantage.com

Call 800-572-6885

Outside U.S. & Canada call: (937) 498-0800

Ordering Information: *AA prices apply to paid subscribers of Amos Media titles, or for orders placed online. Prices, terms and product availability subject to change. Shipping & Handling: U.S.: Orders total $0-$10.00 charged $3.99 shipping. U.S. Order total $10.01-$79.99 charged $7.99 shipping. U.S. Order total $80.00 or more charged 10% of order total for shipping. Taxes will apply in CA, OH, & IL. Canada: 20% of order total. Minimum charge $19.99 Maximum charge $200.00. Foreign orders are shipped via FedEx Intl. or USPS and billed actual freight.

2020 SCOTT® STAMP VALUES

U.S. SPECIALIZED BY GRADE

Extended Values in Eight Different Grades for Selected United States Stamps

This is the twenty-fourth edition of *Scott Stamp Values: U. S. Specialized by Grade.* Editions before 2011 had been issued as stand-alone pamphlets, and this twenty-fourth edition is the tenth included in the *Scott Specialized Catalogue of United States Stamps and Covers.* We believe that including this information in the U.S. Specialized catalog enhances the value of the publication for collectors and dealers. All the Scott United States valuing information is now housed in one comprehensive book. *Scott Stamp Values* lists values for sound stamps in eight different grades and, in addition, numerical grades are assigned to the verbal grades commonly used. Thus, all stamps are now valued in the grades of Superb-98, Extremely Fine-Superb-95, Extremely Fine-90, Very Fine-Extremely Fine-85, Very Fine-80, Fine-Very Fine-75, Fine-70 and Very Good-50.

The stamps listed are generally those with higher catalog values and greater susceptibility to value differentials based on grade changes. They consist of Scott 1 through 715 (including coil pairs, coil guide line and joint line pairs, and booklet panes), 720b, 832-834a, 1053, C1-C31, E1-E14, F1, J1-J86, K1-K18, O1-O126 (including the special printings), PR1-PR125, Q1-Q12, JQ1-JQ5, QE1-QE4a and RW1-RW84A.

This publication is designed to fill the needs of collectors who want to know what they might expect to pay for stamps in grades other than Scott's benchmark grade of Very Fine. You will note that the values for Very Fine in *Scott Stamp Values* are the same as they are in the corresponding sections of the U.S. Specialized catalog. *Scott Stamp Values* should aid those who want to buy higher-grade stamps and need to know what kinds of premiums over the benchmark Very Fine value they might be required to pay. It also will aid budget-conscious collectors who want to know what discounts they might expect to receive when buying stamps in grades lower than Very Fine. And for those interested in selling stamps, this important valuing information should help form more realistic expectations.

All the stamps valued herein are sound stamps. Stamps with faults will sell for less, no matter what grade they would fall into if sound. Different collectors rate faults in different ways. A small margin tear is very significant to some, less so to others. If a stamp has somewhat short perforations but has extremely fine or superb centering, some collectors will shy away from paying a high price, while others seem quite content to overlook the perforations and will pay a very high price. Similarly, some collectors tend to accept a beautiful stamp with a small thin at only a slight discount (especially if it's a very scarce item), while others would shy away at the same price, holding out for a faultless gem.

The description of stamp grades on the following page notes that stamps valued in *Scott Stamp Values* are assumed to have margins of a normal size for the issue. For Superb or Extremely Fine stamps, the margins may be slightly larger than normal. But the values shown are NOT for large-margined, "jumbo" examples of Very Fine or higher-grade stamps. A Very Fine "jumbo" stamp will sell for more than the value shown here for a Very Fine stamp, and "jumbo" stamps in higher grades will sell for more than the respective non-"jumbo" stamps of the same grades. In grades lower than Very Fine, the fact that a stamp has "jumbo" margins has little influence on the stamp's value.

For stamps in unused, original-gum (OG) condition, the illustrated gum chart will be helpful in assessing value based on the condition of the gum and the degree of hinging. This chart was developed in conjunction with Robert A. Siegel Auction Galleries and has become the standard concise reference on this subject in the stamp marketplace as well as in the Scott catalog.

Used stamps present the challenge of assessing cancellations as well as centering, perforations and freshness. It may be assumed that as a stamp's grade ascends from Very Good through Superb, its cancellation will become neater, cleaner and less defacing of the design. A fresh, superbly centered stamp with a heavy blob of a cancel directly on the vignette cannot be considered a Superb used stamp. The value of such a stamp will be determined in the marketplace based on the preferences of individual collectors. Similarly, while a stamp with perforations cutting into the design may in all cases be considered to fall into the Very Good grade, a stamp with this centering but with a very neat and non-defacing cancel will sell for more than the same stamp with a heavier cancel.

Just as "jumbo" margins enhance the values of higher-grade stamps, so do scarcer color cancels and fancy cancels enhance the values of used stamps. The values in *Scott Stamp Values* represent used stamps with normal cancels. Stamps with scarcer color cancels and fancy cancels may be expected to sell for more, often much more.

We believe that a generally common and appropriate system for grading the highest-grade stamps is being consistently adhered to by all the main participants who are in the businesses of publishing valuing guides and/or actually grading stamps. Those participants are Amos Media Co., Professional Stamp Experts in California, The Philatelic Foundation in New York, and Philatelic Stamp Authentication and Grading, Inc. in Florida. While many collectors and dealers desire a certificate from one of these organizations attesting to the authenticity and grade of a stamp, the values in *Scott Stamp Values* are not tied to any expertizing body. Many expert collectors and dealers are capable of exercising their own judgment on matters of grading, and as long as their grading is consistent with the standards set forth within these pages, the values shown will serve as an accurate guide to value.

Warning: Collectors should be cautious of United States stamps graded by other than a recognized expertizing service that are offered with the grade descriptions and/or prices that are tied to the grades and values listed in *Scott Stamp Values: U.S. Specialized by Grade.* It is strongly recommended that such stamps be subject to examination by a recognized third-party expertizing service.

See the next two pages for definitions of grade, an illustrated gum chart and illustrations of representative stamps in each of the eight grades that are valued herein for each stamp. Please study both definitions and illustrations carefully. The values in this publication match the grades described and illustrated. Descriptions used by some buyers and sellers of stamps may not match the grades described and illustrated in this *Scott Stamp Values* publication. We believe strongly that the Scott standards and definitions match most accurately the traditional marketplace uses. Therefore, in order to accurately judge a stamp's value, it is essential that users match values and grades accurately in accordance with the strict standards of *Scott Stamp Values.*

Scott Stamp Values will be included in each year's edition of the Scott U.S. Specialized catalog. Just as values for Very Fine stamps are updated each year, the extended values in *Scott Stamp Values* also will be updated in each edition.

A Description of Stamp Grades for Sound United States Stamps (excluding the 1857-61 Issue and the 1875 Reprints thereof)*

SUPERB-98: The stamp is essentially perfectly centered within margins of a normal size or margins somewhat larger than normal. Stamps that are essentially perfectly centered within very large "jumbo" margins may be expected to sell for even more than the listed values for the superb grade. Color, impression and freshness will be excellent. Essentially, this will be a perfect stamp.

EXTREMELY FINE-SUPERB-95: Extremely well centered within margins that are at least of normal size or perhaps slightly larger than normal. Close examination by unaided normal eyesight will reveal that the stamp is not perfectly centered. Extremely well-centered stamps with very large "jumbo" margins may be expected to sell for even more than the listed values for the extremely fine-superb grade. Color, impression and freshness will be very nice. All in all, an extremely choice example of the stamp.

EXTREMELY FINE-90: A very well-centered stamp within margins that are normal or slightly larger than normal. A discerning collector will be able to tell rather easily that the stamp is a little bit off in one or two directions. As with the preceding grades, good color, impression and freshness should be evident. And, again, stamps with "jumbo" margins will sell for more than the values shown. This will be a premium example of the stamp.

VERY FINE-EXTREMELY FINE-85: A well-centered stamp with margins of a normal size. In all respects an excellent example of the issue.

VERY FINE-80: The stamp is just slightly off-center on one or two sides. All frame lines will be well clear of the perforations (except for the 1857-61 first perforated issue (Scott 18-39) and most of the 1875 Reprints of the 1857-61 issue (Scott 41-46)). With exceptions as noted in the catalogs, Very Fine is the benchmark grade valued in the Scott Standard Volume 1 and the *Scott Specialized Catalogue of United States Stamps and Covers.* A Very Fine stamp is, in all cases, a very desirable example of the issue.

FINE-VERY FINE-75: The stamp is noticeably off-center, with the perforations close to the design on one or two sides, resulting in margins that are narrow but with some white space between the perforations and the design. In this and lower grades, the color, impression and freshness may be somewhat below the levels of the higher grades.

FINE-70: The stamp is quite off-center, with the perforations on one or two sides very close to the design but not quite touching it. There is white space between the perforations and the design that is minimal but evident to the unaided eye.

VERY GOOD-50: The perforations just slightly cut into the design on one or two sides. This grade also is commonly referred to as AVERAGE.

*See the Illustrated Gum Chart below and also the introduction to the *Scott Specialized Catalogue of United States Stamps and Covers* for additional information concerning gum.

Illustrated Gum Chart

For purposes of helping to determine the gum condition and value of an unused stamp, Scott Publishing Co. presents the following chart which details different gum conditions and indicates how the conditions correlate with the Scott values for unused stamps. Used together, the Illustrated Grading Chart on the next page and this Illustrated Gum Chart should allow catalog users to better understand the grade and gum condition of stamps valued in the Scott catalogs.

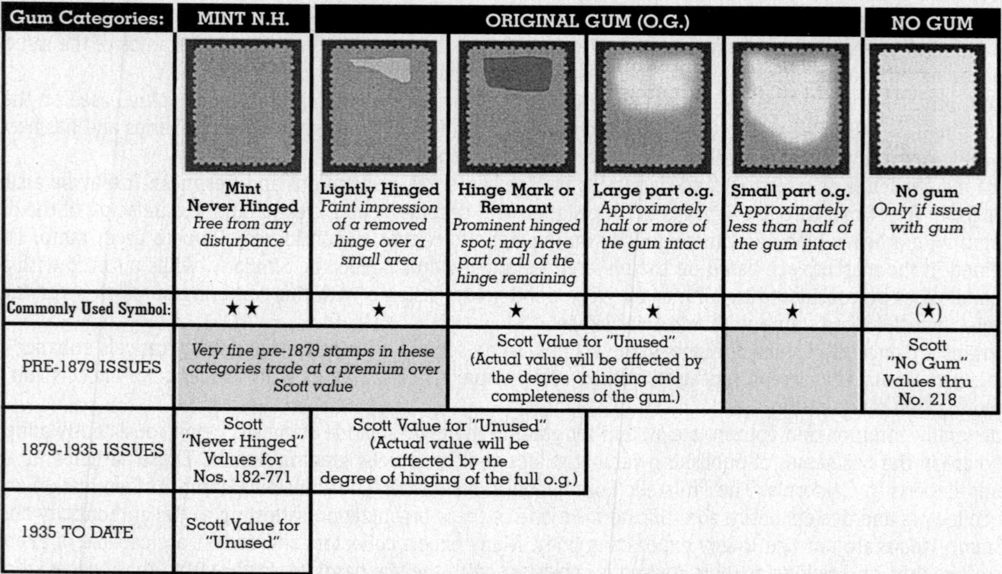

Gum Categories:	MINT N.H.	ORIGINAL GUM (O.G.)				NO GUM
	Mint Never Hinged *Free from any disturbance*	**Lightly Hinged** *Faint impression of a removed hinge over a small area*	**Hinge Mark or Remnant** *Prominent hinged spot; may have part or all of the hinge remaining*	**Large part o.g.** *Approximately half or more of the gum intact*	**Small part o.g.** *Approximately less than half of the gum intact*	**No gum** *Only if issued with gum*
Commonly Used Symbol:	★★	★	★	★	★	(★)
PRE-1879 ISSUES	*Very fine pre-1879 stamps in these categories trade at a premium over Scott value*		Scott Value for "Unused" (Actual value will be affected by the degree of hinging and completeness of the gum.)			Scott "No Gum" Values thru No. 218
1879-1935 ISSUES	Scott "Never Hinged" Values for Nos. 182-771	Scott Value for "Unused" (Actual value will be affected by the degree of hinging of the full o.g.)				
1935 TO DATE	Scott Value for "Unused"					

Never Hinged (NH; ★★): A never-hinged stamp will have full original gum that will have no hinge mark or disturbance. The presence of an expertizer's mark does not disqualify a stamp from this designation.

Original Gum (OG; ★): Pre-1879 stamps should have approximately half or more of their original gum. On rarer stamps, it may be expected that the original gum will be somewhat more disturbed that it will be on more common issues. From 1879, stamps should have full original gum. Original gum will show some disturbance caused by a previous hinge(s) which may be present or entirely removed. The actual value of an 1879 or later stamp will be affected by the degree of hinging of the full original gum.

Disturbed Original Gum: Gum showing noticeable effects of humidity, climate or hinging over more than half of the gum. The significance of gum disturbance in valuing a stamp in any of the Original Gum categories depends on the degree of disturbance, the rarity and normal gum condition of the issue and other variables affecting quality.

Regummed (RG; (★)): A regummed stamp is a stamp without gum that has had some type of gum privately applied at a time after it was issued. This normally is done to deceive collectors and/or dealers into thinking that the stamp has original gum and therefore has a higher value. A regummed stamp is considered the same as a stamp with none of its original gum for purposes of grading.

Illustrated Grading Chart

Superb-98

Extremely Fine-Superb-95

Extremely Fine-90

Very Fine-Extremely Fine-85

Very Fine-80

Fine-Very Fine-75

Fine-70

Very Good-50

Superb-98

Extremely Fine-Superb-95

Extremely Fine-90

Very Fine-Extremely Fine-85

Very Fine-80

Fine-Very Fine-75

Fine-70

Very Good-50

1847 REGULAR ISSUES

SCT#	DENOM	COLOR	CONDITION	VG 50	F 70	F-VF 75	VF 80	VF-XF 85	XF 90	XF-SUP 95	SUP 98
1	5¢	red	Used	100	160	250	350	450	625	1,250	3,850
		brown	Unused NG	475	825	1,400	2,100	2,400	3,500	5,000	—
			Unused OG	1,500	2,650	4,250	6,000	7,500	11,500	17,500	—
1a	5¢	dark	Used	95	165	275	400	500	1,100	2,000	4,500
		brown	Unused NG	550	950	1,600	2,400	2,750	3,400	4,600	7,000
			Unused OG	1,450	2,700	4,400	7,000	9,000	14,500	22,500	35,000
1b	5¢	orange	Used	175	300	475	725	850	1,050	2,250	4,250
		brown	Unused NG	875	1,700	2,500	3,500	4,000	4,750	6,250	—
			Unused OG	2,400	4,000	6,900	10,000	12,000	16,000	29,000	—
1c	5¢	red	Used	2,850	4,250	6,400	9,000	11,000	15,000	25,000	—
		orange	Unused NG	2,750	4,500	7,000	9,500	—	—	—	—
			Unused OG	5,750	10,000	15,500	25,000	—	—	—	—
1d	5¢	brown	Used	225	425	750	1,000	1,300	2,150	4,750	
		orange	Unused NG	—	—	—	4,500	—			
			Unused OG	—	—	—	—	—			
2	10¢	black	Used	200	400	550	775	1,200	1,500	3,500	6,000
			Unused NG	3,000	6,000	10,000	15,000	17,000	21,000	30,000	—
			Unused OG	7,000	13,000	22,500	35,000	45,000	75,000	—	—

1875 REPRODUCTIONS OF 1847 ISSUE

SCT#	DENOM	COLOR	CONDITION	VG 50	F 70	F-VF 75	VF 80	VF-XF 85	XF 90	XF-SUP 95	SUP 98
3	5¢	red brown	Unused NGAI	275	400	650	900	1,000	1,250	1,850	3,000
4	10¢	black	Unused NGAI	325	550	800	1,100	1,250	1,650	2,500	4,250

1851-57 REGULAR ISSUE (IMPERFORATE)

SCT#	DENOM	COLOR	CONDITION	VG 50	F 70	F-VF 75	VF 80	VF-XF 85	XF 90	XF-SUP 95	SUP 98
5	1¢	blue	Used	47,500	55,000	95,000	145,000	240,000	380,000		
		type I	Unused OG	—	135,000	—	—				
5A	1¢	blue	Used	4,250	7,000	8,750	10,000	13,250	17,500	26,500	45,000
		type Ib	Unused NG	6,500	12,000	14,000	16,500	20,000	32,500	—	—
			Unused OG	14,000	32,500	38,500	45,000	55,000	77,500		—
6	1¢	blue	Used	2,850	5,500	7,250	9,500	15,000	25,000	42,500	85,000
		type Ia	Unused NG	7,000	12,000	14,000	20,000	26,000	35,000	—	—
			Unused OG	14,000	22,500	32,500	45,000	72,500	115,000	—	—
6b	1¢	blue	Used	900	1,400	2,000	3,000	4,000	6,250	15,000	—
		type Ic	Unused NG	1,000	1,500	2,100	3,000	3,500	4,000	6,000	—
		E relief	Unused OG	2,250	3,500	5,000	7,000	9,000	14,000	—	—
		type Ic	Used	2,500	4,500	5,750	9,000	11,750	20,000	31,500	—
		F relief pos.	Unused NG	3,250	6,000	8,500	12,500	15,500	22,500	—	—
		91 & 96R4	Unused OG	5,750	15,000	22,500	27,500	40,000	—	—	—
7	1¢	blue	Used	27.50	47.50	77.50	125	200	325	750	2,000
		type II	Unused NG	85	150	250	375	450	550	850	1,400
			Unused OG	250	475	750	1,000	1,325	2,200	4,500	9,250
8	1¢	blue	Used	375	800	1,200	1,600	2,750	4,500	7,750	17,500
		type III	Unused NG	1,650	3,000	5,000	7,500	9,000	15,000	—	—
			Unused OG	4,700	9,500	13,750	25,000	37,500	62,500	—	—
(8) (99R2)	1¢	blue type III	Used	1,025	2,200	3,700	5,750	9,500	12,500	19,500	—
			Unused NG	2,700	4,600	7,100	10,000	15,000	22,500	—	—
			Unused OG	6,250	14,500	25,000	35,000	50,000	—	—	—
8A	1¢	blue	Used	200	375	500	800	1,150	2,100	4,250	9,000
		type IIIa	Unused NG	500	775	1,475	2,250	2,750	3,500	5,000	—
			Unused OG	1,200	1,800	3,600	6,000	8,000	17,500	—	—
9	1¢	blue	Used	22.50	35	65	90	140	210	550	1,400
		type IV	Unused NG	55	100	160	240	270	350	600	900
			Unused OG	140	[illegible]	[illegible]	[illegible]	[illegible]	[illegible]	[illegible]	[illegible]

SCT#	DENOM	COLOR	CONDITION	VG 50	F 70	F-VF 75	VF 80	VF-XF 85	XF 90	XF-SUP 95	SUP 98
10	3¢	orange	Used	38.50	85	125	185	300	700	2,250	3,500
		brown	Unused NG	215	575	950	1,500	1,700	2,000	2,700	4,000
		type I	Unused OG	625	1,325	2,350	4,000	5,000	7,500	13,750	—
10A	3¢	orange	Used	18.50	62.50	95	145	225	350	1,125	2,650
		brown	Unused NG	200	475	775	1,250	1,450	1,700	2,250	—
		type II	Unused OG	500	1,125	2,000	3,250	4,200	6,000	11,500	—
11	3¢	dull	Used	3.50	5	10	15	45	85	250	500
		red	Unused NG	22.50	45	70	100	125	175	300	450
		type I	Unused OG	45	90	135	250	350	500	900	1,450
11A	3¢	dull	Used	3.50	5	10	15	42.50	82.50	225	525
		red	Unused NG	20	37.50	60	85	100	130	225	375
		type II	Unused OG	47.50	110	145	250	375	525	1,000	2,250
12	5¢	red	Used	160	300	500	700	825	1,300	2,000	4,250
		brown	Unused NG	1,850	4,000	7,000	11,000	12,500	15,000	19,000	—
		type I	Unused OG	5,000	10,000	19,000	30,000	40,000	55,000	—	—
13	10¢	green	Used	180	400	550	800	1,100	1,450	2,500	6,000
		type I	Unused NG	1,575	3,700	5,400	8,500	9,750	12,500	—	—
			Unused OG	3,250	8,000	12,000	19,000	27,500	45,000	—	—
14	10¢	green	Used	32.50	60	105	140	175	305	550	1,175
		type II	Unused NG	400	725	1,175	1,800	2,000	2,300	3,000	—
			Unused OG	1,000	2,200	3,200	5,000	6,000	8,750	16,500	32,500
15	10¢	green	Used	32.50	60	105	140	175	305	550	1,175
		type III	Unused NG	400	725	1,175	1,800	2,000	2,300	3,000	4,250
			Unused OG	1,000	2,200	3,200	5,000	6,000	8,750	16,500	32,500
16	10¢	green	Used	450	800	1,125	1,600	2,100	2,750	6,500	13,000
		type IV	Unused NG	3,000	7,000	10,000	15,000	18,500	22,500	—	—
			Unused OG	7,500	22,500	30,000	37,500	47,500	75,000	—	—
17	12¢	gray	Used	45	105	145	250	315	500	1,100	2,250
		black	Unused NG	550	950	1,500	2,100	2,400	2,900	4,000	—
			Unused OG	1,650	2,750	4,000	6,250	9,000	12,000	21,500	37,500

1857-61 REGULAR ISSUE (PERFORATED)

SCT#	DENOM	COLOR	CONDITION	VG 50	F 70	F-VF 75	VF 80	VF-XF 85	XF 90	XF-SUP 95	SUP 98
18	1¢	blue	Used	70	150	305	450	700	1,000	6,250	—
		type I	Unused NG	140	320	490	800	1,000	1,200	1,900	2,500
			Unused OG	375	850	1,325	2,100	2,800	4,250	8,750	14,500
19	1¢	blue	Used	5,000	9,000	10,500	13,000	21,000	30,000	80,000	240,000
		type Ia	Unused NG	11,500	20,000	25,000	30,000	37,500	45,000	—	—
			Unused OG	20,000	42,500	47,500	55,000	65,000	80,000	—	—
19b	1¢	blue	Used	1,250	2,500	3,250	4,000	5,250	8,000	27,500	—
		type Ic	Unused NG	850	1,750	2,150	3,000	3,500	5,500	—	—
		E relief	Unused OG	2,000	4,250	5,500	7,000	9,000	14,000	—	—
		type Ic	Used	4,500	7,250	9,500	11,000	12,500	20,000	—	—
		F relief pos.	Unused NG	4,000	9,000	10,250	11,500	13,000	21,000	—	—
		91 & 96R4	Unused OG	8,500	20,000	22,500	25,000	30,000	52,500	—	—
20	1¢	blue	Used	47	93.50	165	260	400	800	2,500	—
		type II	Unused NG	70	140	260	375	475	750	1,250	—
			Unused OG	150	325	525	850	1,250	2,500	4,000	7,100
21	1¢	blue	Used	350	725	1,100	1,600	2,250	4,250	9,000	—
		type III	Unused NG	1,300	2,500	3,700	6,000	7,000	8,750	—	—
			Unused OG	4,000	7,250	10,500	17,500	24,000	37,500	—	—
(21) (99R2)	1¢	blue type II	Used	2,200	4,000	5,600	8,000	—	—		
22	1¢	blue	Used	85	170	315	475	800	1,700	4,500	—
		type IIIa	Unused NG	150	325	525	825	1,025	1,300	2,250	—
			Unused OG	425	875	1,525	2,200	3,250	5,500	12,000	—
23	1¢	blue	Used	375	700	1,000	1,200	1,500	3,000	7,500	—
		type IV	Unused NG	1,750	4,250	5,000	6,250	7,000	8,000	—	—
			Unused OG	4,750	10,000	12,500	16,500	19,000	24,000	—	—
24	1¢	blue	Used	8.50	14	25	37.50	120	275	800	2,500
		type V	Unused NG	16.50	27.50	40	60	72.50	87.50	130	190
			Unused OG	25	60	95	140	200	375	675	1,100
25	3¢	rose	Used	75	180	200	240	575	1,250	2,400	5,000
		type I	Unused NG	400	950	1,100	1,250	1,500	2,000	—	—
			Unused OG	1,350	2,750	3,250	4,000	5,000	8,000	—	—
25A	3¢	rose	Used	385	850	950	1,100	2,250	5,500	—	—
		type II	Unused NG	1,750	4,000	5,000	6,000	7,250	9,000	—	—
			Unused OG	4,250	9,000	10,250	11,500	13,000	21,000	—	—
26	3¢	dull	Used	1.75	3.25	5	10	35	120	400	800
		red	Unused NG	5	9.75	16.50	27.50	32.50	50	80	115

SCT#	DENOM	COLOR	CONDITION	VG 50	F 70	F-VF 75	VF 80	VF-XF 85	XF 90	XF-SUP 95	SUP 98
26A	3¢	dull	Used	32	60	97.50	150	260	460	1,400	5,500
		red	Unused NG	50	115	180	260	320	400	600	—
		type IV	Unused OG	85	190	360	600	800	1,200	2,600	—
27	5¢	brick	Used	275	575	925	1,450	2,500	4,750	13,500	—
		red	Unused NG	4,650	7,750	13,000	20,000	25,000	—	—	
		type I	Unused OG	22,500	35,000	60,000	80,000	120,000	—		
28	5¢	red	Used	290	500	700	1,100	1,800	3,000	9,500	25,000
		brown	Unused NG	3,450	6,100	9,500	15,000	17,250	21,500	—	
		type I	Unused OG	12,000	21,000	36,000	60,000	75,000	90,000	—	
28b	5¢	bright red	Used	575	875	1,675	2,250	3,150	4,750	9,500	—
		red brown	Unused NG	5,550	9,250	12,250	20,000	22,500	—	—	
		type I	Unused OG	15,000	25,000	42,500	70,000	90,000	—	—	
28A	5¢	Indian	Used	900	1,650	2,350	3,500	4,500	6,750	19,000	
		red	Unused NG	13,250	18,000	28,000	40,000	—			
		type I	Unused OG	100,000	160,000						
29	5¢	brown	Used	75	150	260	350	600	1,000	4,250	10,750
		type I	Unused NG	350	750	1,175	1,750	2,250	3,000	—	—
			Unused OG	1,100	2,000	3,250	5,500	8,250	12,500	—	—
30	5¢	orange	Used	225	500	825	1,300	1,850	3,250	9,750	—
		brown	Unused NG	92.50	210	340	500	600	750	1,175	1,650
		type II	Unused OG	275	575	800	1,200	2,000	3,150	8,250	—
30A	5¢	brown	Used	67.50	125	175	280	450	825	2,600	8,500
		type II	Unused NG	210	375	550	825	975	1,200	2,000	—
			Unused OG	500	875	1,475	2,200	2,800	5,000	12,000	—
31	10¢	green	Used	230	460	725	1,100	1,650	4,250	11,500	—
		type I	Unused NG	1,725	3,750	7,250	11,500	14,500	18,500	26,000	—
			Unused OG	7,000	12,000	22,000	35,000	57,500	90,000	—	—
32	10¢	green	Used	47.50	84.50	130	190	275	700	3,000	9,750
		type II	Unused NG	475	800	1,175	2,000	2,450	3,100	4,400	—
			Unused OG	1,350	2,100	3,350	5,750	7,750	13,000	21,500	—
33	10¢	green	Used	45	80	125	180	280	600	2,250	15,000
		type III	Unused NG	475	800	1,175	2,000	2,450	3,100	4,400	—
			Unused OG	1,350	2,100	3,350	5,750	7,750	13,000	22,500	—
34	10¢	green	Used	465	850	1,350	2,100	3,000	4,900	9,750	—
		type IV	Unused NG	4,000	8,500	11,000	20,000	25,000	33,500	—	—
			Unused OG	11,000	16,000	27,500	50,000	72,500	110,000	—	
35	10¢	green	Used	10	25	40	55	85	160	475	1,450
		type V	Unused NG	22.50	37.50	62.50	95	115	140	210	—
			Unused OG	52.50	75	135	210	325	600	1,250	1,850
36	12¢	black	Used	65	125	185	300	460	800	2,400	8,500
		plate 1	Unused NG	100	180	270	500	625	875	1,525	—
			Unused OG	340	725	1,150	1,700	3,000	5,650	9,000	—
36B	12¢	black	Used	55	87.50	150	250	350	725	2,250	6,000
		plate 3	Unused NG	75	150	210	325	410	525	1,000	—
			Unused OG	125	250	475	700	1,000	1,700	3,500	6,500
37	24¢	gray	Used	70	140	250	375	525	1,025	3,650	7,500
		lilac	Unused NG	90	180	300	500	600	750	1,250	2,000
			Unused OG	300	575	1,025	1,450	1,900	3,250	6,500	—
37a	24¢	gray	Used	70	140	250	375	525	1,025	3,650	7,500
			Unused NG	90	180	300	500	600	750	1,250	2,000
			Unused OG	290	550	1,025	1,450	2,000	3,150	6,500	—
38	30¢	orange	Used	85	150	285	425	750	1,100	4,000	10,000
			Unused NG	105	210	440	700	800	1,000	1,800	2,500
			Unused OG	380	825	1,225	1,900	2,850	4,650	11,000	—
39	90¢	blue	Used	2,350	5,000	7,750	11,000	17,500	25,000	50,000	—
			Unused NG	260	490	875	1,300	1,600	2,000	3,250	4,500
			Unused OG	700	1,300	2,100	3,000	4,000	6,500	13,000	—

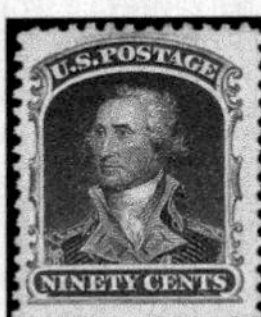

1875 REPRINTS OF THE 1857-61 ISSUE

SCT#	DENOM	COLOR	CONDITION	VG 50	F 70	F-VF 75	VF 80	VF-XF 85	XF 90	XF-SUP 95	SUP 98
40	1¢	bright blue	Unused NGAI	130	225	370	575	675	825	1,575	5,000
41	3¢	scarlet	Unused NGAI	1,050	2,750	3,450	4,800	5,750	8,750	12,500	—
42	5¢	orange brown	Unused NGAI	675	1,150	1,825	2,500	3,750	5,750	12,000	—
43	10¢	blue green	Unused NGAI	950	2,500	2,700	3,850	5,000	9,000	13,000	—
44	12¢	greenish black	Unused NGAI	1,050	2,750	3,250	4,150	5,500	9,500	—	—
45	24¢	blackish violet	Unused NGAI	1,175	3,000	3,600	4,600	5,750	9,750	—	—
46	30¢	yellow orange	Unused NGAI	1,175	3,000	3,600	4,600	5,500	9,000	—	—
47	90¢	deep blue	Unused NGAI	900	1,575	2,450	3,500	5,000	7,750	13,500	—

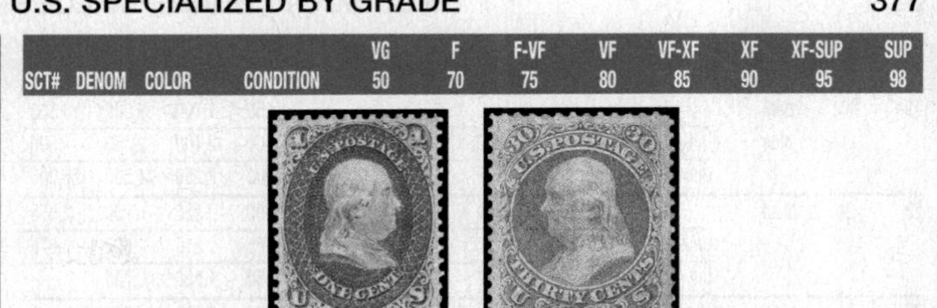

1861-66 REGULAR ISSUES

SCT#	DENOM	COLOR	CONDITION	VG 50	F 70	F-VF 75	VF 80	VF-XF 85	XF 90	XF-SUP 95	SUP 98
62B	10¢	dark	Used	475	850	1,250	1,600	2,350	4,250	9,000	—
		green	Unused NG	850	1,500	2,250	3,600	4,750	6,500	8,750	—
			Unused OG	2,650	4,750	6,500	8,500	13,000	22,000	47,500	—
63	1¢	blue	Used	9	17.50	30	45	100	150	575	2,100
			Unused NG	25	42.50	65	100	120	145	240	380
			Unused OG	50	97.50	170	275	365	650	1,500	2,500
63a	1¢	ultramarine	Used	500	850	1,200	1,900	2,650	4,000	—	—
			Unused NG	250	390	625	1,000	1,200	1,500	2,750	—
			Unused OG	575	975	1,600	2,500	3,250	4,750	8,500	—
63b	1¢	dark	Used	220	380	550	875	1,200	1,900	3,800	—
		blue	Unused NG	77.50	135	200	300	375	500	900	—
			Unused OG	180	330	525	800	1,025	1,400	3,150	—
64	3¢	pink	Used	170	300	440	600	1,100	2,750	5,500	—
			Unused NG	1,275	2,250	3,200	5,000	5,500	6,500	—	—
			Unused OG	3,250	5,500	8,500	14,000	17,000	23,500	—	—
64a	3¢	pigeon	Used	1,500	2,150	3,000	4,500	6,000	8,250	21,000	—
		blood	Unused NG	3,500	6,250	9,250	15,000	18,000	22,500	—	
		pink	Unused OG	12,500	20,000	32,500	50,000	70,000	90,000	—	
64b	3¢	rose	Used	42.50	80	110	150	275	425	1,350	4,000
		pink	Unused NG	70	110	160	250	300	360	600	950
			Unused OG	135	240	375	600	800	1,200	2,500	4,800
65	3¢	rose	Used	0.50	1.10	2	3	22.50	75	200	500
			Unused NG	12.50	20	32.50	50	60	80	125	—
			Unused OG	25	47.50	72.50	125	175	290	575	1,150
67	5¢	buff	Used	190	375	550	750	1,350	2,750	6,000	—
			Unused NG	2,500	4,750	7,000	10,500	12,500	16,000	—	
			Unused OG	7,250	13,500	18,000	27,500	42,500	—		
67a	5¢	brown	Used	275	575	800	1,100	1,900	3,000	7,250	—
		yellow	Unused NG	2,900	5,500	8,000	11,500	13,500	17,000	—	
			Unused OG	7,500	14,000	20,000	30,000	—	—		
67b	5¢	olive	Used	1,200	2,000	3,250	4,750	7,250	14,750	—	
		yellow									
68	10¢	green	Used	11.50	22.50	37.50	55	130	275	800	2,500
			Unused NG	80	150	225	375	525	750	1,150	—
			Unused OG	190	360	625	950	1,525	2,400	5,250	11,000
68a	10¢	dark	Used	17	32.50	45	85	130	250	1,000	2,500
		green	Unused NG	120	220	335	500	600	750	1,250	1,950
			Unused OG	265	480	825	1,350	2,050	3,150	6,500	13,500
69	12¢	black	Used	20	42.50	62.50	95	190	310	750	2,850
			Unused NG	150	300	475	675	800	1,000	1,600	2,750
			Unused OG	400	650	1,050	1,700	2,450	4,000	9,000	—
70	24¢	red	Used	77.50	115	180	300	500	800	3,000	—
		lilac	Unused NG	260	475	775	1,150	1,450	1,900	3,250	—
			Unused OG	700	1,300	2,000	3,000	4,250	8,000	16,000	—
70a	24¢	brown	Used	80	125	190	325	525	850	2,650	6,750
		lilac	Unused NG	300	575	850	1,250	1,500	2,000	3,250	—
			Unused OG	750	1,450	2,100	3,250	4,500	7,000	14,000	—
70b	24¢	steel	Used	235	380	550	850	1,350	2,400	7,250	—
		blue	Unused NG	1,450	2,650	4,100	6,250	7,250	8,750	—	—
			Unused OG	4,250	7,000	10,500	16,500	21,500	32,500	—	
70c	24¢	violet	Used	525	975	1,475	2,250	3,250	5,250	11,500	—
			Unused NG	3,150	6,750	10,500	13,500	15,500	20,000	—	—
			Unused OG	7,750	15,000	22,500	35,000	42,500	55,000	100,000	
70d	24¢	pale	Used	750	1,400	2,600	3,250	4,500	6,750	18,000	—
		gray	Unused NG	1,300	2,250	4,000	6,000	7,000	8,500	13,000	—
		violet	Unused OG	5,000	7,750	14,500	25,000	35,000	55,000	—	
71	30¢	orange	Used	55	90	130	210	320	575	2,250	5,500
			Unused NG	240	425	650	950	1,150	1,600	2,850	—
			Unused OG	550	950	1,550	2,600	4,000	7,500	—	—
72	90¢	blue	Used	150	265	400	575	875	1,150	4,000	11,500
			Unused NG	325	500	775	1,200	1,350	1,700	2,750	4,000
			Unused OG	700	1,100	1,850	3,000	4,250	6,750	13,500	22,500
72a	90¢	pale	Used	175	300	425	650	925	1,300	4,250	11,500
		blue	Unused NG	325	500	775	1,200	1,350	1,675	2,500	3,650
			Unused OG	700	1,100	1,850	3,000	4,150	6,450	12,500	21,000

SCT#	DENOM	COLOR	CONDITION	VG 50	F 70	F-VF 75	VF 80	VF-XF 85	XF 90	XF-SUP 95	SUP 98
72b	90¢	dark	Used	250	450	625	950	1,250	1,700	6,000	14,000
		blue	Unused NG	375	650	975	1,500	1,700	2,100	2,750	4,500
			Unused OG	800	1,325	2,100	3,750	5,000	7,250	14,500	26,000
73	2¢	black	Used	12.50	20	40	55	100	225	750	2,500
			Unused NG	30	50	85	140	165	210	500	875
			Unused OG	75	140	230	325	550	1,150	2,750	—
75	5¢	red	Used	125	210	300	425	675	1,200	4,250	—
		brown	Unused NG	525	925	1,400	2,100	2,400	2,850	4,300	—
			Unused OG	1,250	2,300	3,850	5,750	7,500	11,000	—	—
76	5¢	brown	Used	30	50	75	120	195	375	1,400	3,000
			Unused NG	150	260	375	550	750	950	1,400	2,000
			Unused OG	340	575	875	1,400	2,150	3,500	6,000	—
76a	5¢	black	Used	90	150	230	400	625	1,150	3,000	8,500
		brown	Unused NG	180	375	525	850	1,000	1,250	2,000	—
			Unused OG	475	825	1,300	2,250	3,250	4,750	10,000	—
77	15¢	black	Used	47.50	82.50	120	175	285	550	2,250	5,250
			Unused NG	450	800	1,150	1,900	2,250	2,750	3,750	6,000
			Unused OG	1,100	1,750	3,000	5,000	6,750	10,500	20,000	—
78	24¢	lilac	Used	97	170	255	400	600	1,000	3,750	7,250
			Unused NG	210	400	625	950	1,150	1,500	2,450	—
			Unused OG	550	1,000	1,750	2,750	4,000	6,250	12,000	—
78a	24¢	grayish	Used	115	185	255	425	650	1,100	3,850	7,750
		lilac	Unused NG	200	350	575	950	1,150	1,525	2,450	—
			Unused OG	525	950	1,800	2,750	4,000	7,250	—	—
78b	24¢	gray	Used	120	200	275	450	675	1,200	4,000	8,000
			Unused NG	200	360	575	950	1,150	1,475	2,400	—
			Unused OG	525	925	1,700	2,750	4,000	6,250	12,500	—
78c	24¢	blackish	Used	4,750	8,750	12,250	17,500	27,500	45,000	62,500	
		violet	Unused NG		—	30,000					
			Unused OG	35,000	72,500	95,000					

1867-68 GRILLED ISSUES

SCT#	DENOM	COLOR	CONDITION	VG 50	F 70	F-VF 75	VF 80	VF-XF 85	XF 90	XF-SUP 95	SUP 98
79	3¢	rose	Used	800	1,000	1,300	4,600	9,000	16,000	—	
			Unused NG	1,100	1,750	2,750	5,000	—	—	—	
			Unused OG	3,250	5,500	8,500	17,000	—	—	—	
80	5¢	brown	Used	400,000							
80a	5¢	dark brown	Used	400,000							
81	30¢	orange	Used	225,000							
82	3¢	rose	Used	—	900,000						
83	3¢	rose	Used	230	440	625	1,100	1,500	2,750	8,500	—
			Unused NG	500	825	1,300	2,000	2,500	3,250	5,250	—
			Unused OG	1,050	2,100	3,550	5,500	7,500	13,000	27,500	50,000
84	2¢	black	Used	2,500	4,750	5,750	8,000	10,750	18,000	37,500	67,500
			Unused NG	3,000	6,500	8,000	10,000	—	—	—	
			Unused OG	9,000	16,000	23,000	32,500	—	—	—	
85	3¢	rose	Used	325	500	775	1,100	1,525	2,600	8,000	22,500
			Unused NG	625	1,125	1,575	2,400	3,250	5,000	7,250	—
			Unused OG	1,850	3,500	5,250	8,000	12,500	20,000	—	—
85A	1¢	blue	Used						3,000,000		
85B	2¢	black	Used	340	525	725	1,100	1,800	3,000	9,750	22,500
			Unused NG	1,700	3,000	4,600	6,750	7,500	8,750	12,500	—
			Unused OG	4,250	8,500	12,000	17,500	21,000	27,500	55,000	—
85C	3¢	rose	Used	1,150	1,725	2,200	3,250	5,500	8,000	21,000	32,500
			Unused NG	2,850	4,750	6,500	9,000	15,000	—		
			Unused OG	5,000	10,000	16,000	25,000	40,000	65,000		
85D	10¢	green	Used	350,000	475,000	600,000	750,000	1,200,000			
85E	12¢	black	Used	600	950	1,450	2,400	3,350	5,500	19,000	42,500
			Unused NG	2,400	4,250	6,250	8,500	11,500	15,000	—	
			Unused OG	5,250	10,000	17,000	25,000	35,000	47,500	—	
85F	15¢	black	Used	1,600,000		two known			2,000,000		
86	1¢	blue	Used	100	180	285	425	775	1,450	4,750	13,500
			Unused NG	285	550	725	1,100	1,400	1,850	—	—

SCT#	DENOM	COLOR	CONDITION	VG 50	F 70	F-VF 75	VF 80	VF-XF 85	XF 90	XF-SUP 95	SUP 98
86a	1¢	dull	Used	92.50	170	275	400	750	1,300	4,250	12,500
		blue	Unused NG	285	550	725	1,100	1,400	1,900	3,000	—
			Unused OG	750	1,200	2,100	3,000	4,750	7,750	16,500	—
87	2¢	black	Used	42.50	77.50	120	190	310	600	1,900	4,250
			Unused NG	160	275	435	650	775	975	1,600	2,400
			Unused OG	400	825	1,075	1,700	3,000	4,500	—	—
88	3¢	rose	Used	7	12	18	30	55	175	750	—
			Unused NG	82.50	160	220	350	450	625	950	—
			Unused OG	190	360	625	950	1,525	2,500	4,750	9,000
88a	3¢	lake	Used	19	30	45	75	135	265	1,350	—
		red	Unused NG	115	210	300	475	575	725	1,100	1,625
			Unused OG	250	450	800	1,250	1,750	2,750	5,500	10,500
89	10¢	green	Used	75	110	185	325	500	850	2,250	7,000
			Unused NG	475	800	1,275	2,000	2,500	3,100	5,250	7,250
			Unused OG	1,100	2,000	3,200	5,000	7,500	12,500	24,000	—
90	12¢	black	Used	95	125	210	375	575	1,050	3,250	9,500
			Unused NG	450	750	1,200	1,900	2,250	2,750	—	—
			Unused OG	1,050	2,000	3,500	4,750	6,250	11,500	—	—
91	15¢	black	Used	150	265	410	600	825	1,450	5,750	—
			Unused NG	1,100	1,900	3,000	4,500	5,250	6,500	—	—
			Unused OG	2,750	4,750	7,500	12,500	17,500	25,000	—	—
92	1¢	blue	Used	120	180	285	425	700	1,200	4,250	13,000
			Mint NG	250	425	625	925	1,250	2,000	3,250	4,000
			Unused OG	625	1,125	1,725	2,800	4,250	7,500	16,500	—
92a	1¢	pale	Used	95	140	250	375	575	1,000	3,250	11,000
		blue	Unused NG	170	300	475	700	925	1,250	2,150	3,250
			Unused OG	525	950	1,450	2,300	3,750	6,000	11,000	—
93	2¢	black	Used	15	22.50	35	55	100	250	2,600	6,000
			Unused NG	40	70	110	155	220	300	750	1,250
			Unused OG	100	205	340	450	800	1,500	4,500	8,000
94	3¢	red	Used	2.10	3.50	5.50	10	35	90	500	900
			Mint NG	40	70	100	150	185	260	500	—
			Unused OG	85	130	240	350	575	950	2,500	—
94a	3¢	rose	Used	2.10	3.50	5.50	10	35	75	300	800
			Unused NG	42.50	72.50	105	155	200	270	525	875
			Unused OG	85	130	240	350	575	950	2,500	4,500
95	5¢	brown	Used	230	450	625	850	1,325	2,150	9,500	—
			Unused NG	300	485	750	1,200	1,500	2,100	3,000	—
			Unused OG	750	1,300	2,100	3,250	5,000	8,000	17,500	—
95a	5¢	black	Used	600	925	1,450	2,300	3,450	5,500	15,000	—
		brown	Unused NG	450	775	1,175	1,750	2,000	2,650	3,500	—
			Unused OG	975	1,700	2,750	4,500	6,250	10,000	—	—
96	10¢	yellow	Used	69.50	115	160	240	385	725	2,500	—
		green	Mint NG	210	360	525	825	1,050	1,500	2,150	3,250
			Unused OG	550	900	1,550	2,500	3,750	6,000	12,500	—
97	12¢	black	Used	72.50	115	165	250	375	675	2,250	8,500
			Unused NG	250	475	650	1,000	1,250	1,700	3,000	4,250
			Unused OG	600	1,025	1,725	2,800	4,250	6,750	13,000	23,000
98	15¢	black	Used	77.50	140	200	275	525	825	2,750	9,500
			Unused NG	375	675	1,025	1,600	1,875	2,500	4,500	7,000
			Unused OG	900	1,750	2,850	4,250	7,250	11,500	22,500	42,500
99	24¢	gray	Used	450	575	950	1,500	2,000	3,150	10,000	—
		lilac	Unused NG	800	1,450	2,100	3,250	3,750	4,750	7,500	—
			Unused OG	1,750	3,000	5,750	8,500	12,500	18,500	32,500	—
100	30¢	orange	Used	265	450	650	950	1,275	2,000	9,750	—
			Unused NG	850	1,325	2,050	3,300	4,000	5,000	—	—
			Unused OG	1,900	3,500	6,000	9,000	13,250	20,000	—	
101	90¢	blue	Used	575	900	1,500	2,250	3,750	5,000	14,000	22,500
			Unused NG	1,400	2,400	3,500	5,500	6,500	8,000	12,000	—
			Unused OG	3,000	5,500	8,750	14,500	22,500	37,500	60,000	—

1875 RE-ISSUES OF THE 1861-66 ISSUES

SCT#	DENOM	COLOR	CONDITION	VG 50	F 70	F-VF 75	VF 80	VF-XF 85	XF 90	XF-SUP 95	SUP 98
102	1¢	blue	Used	500	850	1,150	1,600	1,850	2,750	5,000	10,000
			Unused NG	68	125	210	300	365	525	875	1,150
			Unused OG	180	375	575	750	975	1,450	2,650	5,650
103	2¢	black	Used	4,500	6,250	8,250	11,000	22,000	27,500	—	—
			Unused NG	350	650	975	1,600	2,150	3,000	4,250	6,250

SCT#	DENOM	COLOR	CONDITION	VG 50	F 70	F-VF 75	VF 80	VF-XF 85	XF 90	XF-SUP 95	SUP 98
104	3¢	brown	Used	5,500	8,250	11,750	14,000	20,000	35,000	—	—
		red	Unused NG	440	775	1,125	1,700	2,150	3,000	5,500	—
			Unused OG	950	1,875	2,650	3,750	5,150	8,500	15,000	—
105	5¢	brown	Used	1,725	2,800	4,500	6,500	8,000	11,000	19,000	52,500
			Unused NG	300	500	750	1,150	1,600	2,100	3,250	—
			Unused OG	650	1,250	1,800	2,500	4,000	5,750	11,000	—
106	10¢	green	Used	45,000	67,500	92,500	125,000	135,000	150,000	—	—
			Unused NG	325	575	875	1,400	1,750	2,750	4,500	—
			Unused OG	650	1,200	1,900	2,900	3,750	6,350	10,000	19,000
107	12¢	black	Used	4,000	8,250	10,000	13,000	17,500	27,500	52,500	—
			Unused NG	400	700	1,025	1,600	2,100	3,500	6,000	—
			Unused OG	950	1,575	2,450	3,500	5,150	8,750	12,500	18,500
108	15¢	black	Used	10,000	16,250	23,000	32,500	—	—	—	
			Unused NG	500	900	1,325	2,100	2,650	3,500	5,000	—
			Unused OG	1,250	2,250	3,300	4,500	6,250	10,000	17,000	—
109	24¢	deep	Used	5,750	9,000	12,500	18,000	28,500	42,500	—	—
		violet	Unused NG	700	1,200	1,775	2,750	3,500	4,500	6,500	10,500
			Unused OG	1,500	3,000	4,500	6,000	8,500	12,500	21,000	—
110	30¢	brownish	Used	6,000	10,000	14,500	18,000	—	—	—	—
		orange	Unused NG	700	1,100	1,800	2,800	3,400	4,250	6,000	10,000
			Unused OG	1,400	2,800	3,700	5,750	8,000	11,000	20,000	—
111	90¢	blue	Used		160,000	190,000	225,000		275,000		
			Unused NG	850	1,600	2,250	3,500	4,250	5,500	7,500	—
			Unused OG	1,750	3,500	5,250	7,000	11,500	15,500	—	—

1869 PICTORIAL ISSUE

SCT#	DENOM	COLOR	CONDITION	VG 50	F 70	F-VF 75	VF 80	VF-XF 85	XF 90	XF-SUP 95	SUP 98
112	1¢	buff	Used	40	62.50	100	130	195	325	1,300	3,250
			Unused NG	52.50	92.50	130	210	260	325	500	725
			Unused OG	145	260	425	575	875	1,750	3,750	5,500
113	2¢	brown	Used	17.50	32.50	60	80	135	275	950	2,150
			Unused NG	47.50	85	135	190	230	300	450	700
			Unused OG	110	190	310	500	750	1,500	3,750	—
114	3¢	ultramarine	Used	3.50	7	11	16	35	85	400	1,000
			Unused NG	17	37.50	65	90	120	145	225	325
			Unused OG	40	80	140	225	325	550	1,150	2,000
115	6¢	ultramarine	Used	50	80	120	200	290	525	2,500	5,250
			Unused NG	250	400	650	1,000	1,225	1,550	2,350	3,350
			Unused OG	500	900	1,625	2,500	3,500	6,000	13,500	22,500
116	10¢	yellow	Used	20	35	67.50	110	175	325	850	2,750
			Unused NG	180	300	460	725	850	1,100	1,700	2,250
			Unused OG	400	700	1,200	1,850	2,800	4,500	11,500	19,500
117	12¢	green	Used	22.50	37.50	80	130	200	375	825	2,150
			Unused NG	180	300	460	725	850	1,075	1,650	—
			Unused OG	500	900	1,200	1,850	3,000	4,650	10,250	19,000
118	15¢	brown	Used	200	350	500	800	950	1,450	3,500	11,000
		& blue	Unused NG	775	1,400	2,200	3,250	3,700	4,400	6,250	—
		type I	Unused OG	1,900	3,600	5,750	9,000	13,000	20,000	35,000	—
119	15¢	brown	Used	55	75	120	190	275	500	1,900	4,500
		& blue	Unused NG	225	400	600	975	1,125	1,350	2,300	3,250
		type II	Unused OG	575	1,150	1,900	2,750	4,250	7,000	13,500	—
119b	15¢	invert	Used	12,000	22,500	45,000					
			Unused NG	—	700,000						
			Unused OG		1,000,000						
120	24¢	green	Used	130	230	375	600	850	1,500	4,500	15,000
		& violet	Unused NG	600	1,075	1,675	2,600	3,000	3,850	6,500	—
			Unused OG	1,600	2,600	4,750	7,500	12,500	18,500	36,000	—
120b	24¢	invert	Used	20,000	37,500	55,000	100,000				
			Unused NG	350,000	750,000						
121	30¢	ultramarine	Used	95	150	260	375	600	1,100	3,500	—
		& carmine	Unused NG	360	575	875	1,450	1,800	2,350	4,500	—
			Unused OG	900	1,425	2,650	4,000	6,250	16,500	32,000	—
121b	30¢	invert	Used	42,500	65,000	80,000	90,000	120,000	150,000		
			Unused NG	115,000	180,000	240,000	300,000				
			Unused OG		—	—	750,000				
122	90¢	carmine	Used	500	850	1,300	1,800	2,750	4,250	9,000	21,000
		& black	Unused NG	850	1,500	2,600	3,750	4,500	6,000	10,500	—
			Unused OG	1,900	3,250	7,000	11,000	17,500	27,500	77,500	—

1875-81 RE-ISSUES OF THE 1869 ISSUE

SCT#	DENOM	COLOR	CONDITION	VG 50	F 70	F-VF 75	VF 80	VF-XF 85	XF 90	XF-SUP 95	SUP 98
123	1¢	buff	Used	110	170	265	425	650	1,075	3,000	5,250
			Unused NG	57.50	100	160	220	300	450	700	—
			Unused OG	100	200	335	525	750	1,150	2,250	—
124	2¢	brown	Used	190	375	550	750	1,050	1,750	4,000	—
			Unused NG	57.50	105	170	250	350	475	775	—
			Unused OG	110	210	360	600	950	1,400	3,500	—
125	3¢	blue	Used	16,000	20,000	27,500	40,000	55,000	80,000	—	—
			Unused NG	650	1,150	1,650	2,500	3,000	4,000	6,500	—
			Unused OG	1,125	2,000	3,500	5,000	7,750	13,500	—	—
126	6¢	blue	Used	925	1,525	2,100	3,000	4,250	650	15,000	32,500
			Unused NG	195	385	525	800	1,050	1,325	2,100	—
			Unused OG	350	600	1,100	1,800	2,500	3,750	7,000	—
127	10¢	yellow	Used	625	1,000	1,350	1,800	3,250	5,250	9,500	—
			Unused NG	150	300	460	700	925	1,250	2,000	—
			Unused OG	315	575	1,000	1,600	2,250	3,000	6,000	10,000
128	12¢	green	Used	1,000	1,650	2,200	3,000	4,250	6,250	14,000	—
			Unused NG	220	415	600	900	1,350	2,100	4,000	—
			Unused OG	425	900	1,250	2,000	2,800	4,750	9,000	19,000
129	15¢	brown	Used	325	600	750	1,000	1,275	2,250	5,250	—
		blue	Unused NG	170	300	450	625	850	1,050	1,850	—
		type III	Unused OG	290	550	875	1,300	1,850	3,000	5,250	—
130	24¢	green	Used	500	800	1,150	1,600	2,100	3,000	7,000	—
		& violet	Unused NG	210	475	575	900	1,200	1,700	2,600	4,250
			Unused OG	400	725	1,200	2,000	2,650	4,250	7,750	15,500
131	30¢	ultramarine	Used	825	1,275	1,900	2,750	3,500	4,500	11,500	19,500
		& carmine	Unused NG	235	430	650	1,000	1,250	1,650	2,850	4,500
			Unused OG	475	800	1,300	2,250	3,000	5,000	7,750	15,000
132	90¢	carmine	Used	2,000	3,200	4,250	6,000	7,500	11,500	22,500	—
		& black	Unused NG	375	700	975	1,500	2,150	3,000	4,500	7,250
			Unused OG	80	1,500	2,600	3,750	5,000	7,500	17,500	27,500
133	1¢	buff	Used	185	285	415	550	825	1,350	2,250	—
			Unused NG	35	65	95	140	185	280	420	—
			Unused OG	67.50	130	205	325	475	750	1,350	—
133a	1¢	brown	Used	140	200	350	500	675	850	1,050	—
		orange	Unused NGAI	82.50	150	215	325	525	825	1,250	2,350

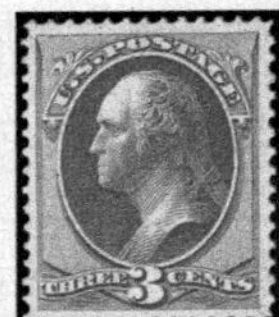

1870-71 NATIONAL BANK NOTE ISSUE (WITH "H" GRILL)

SCT#	DENOM	COLOR	CONDITION	VG 50	F 70	F-VF 75	VF 80	VF-XF 85	XF 90	XF-SUP 95	SUP 98
134	1¢	ultramarine	Used	57.50	90	125	200	250	400	1,500	4,500
			Unused NG	175	310	460	700	850	1,100	1,750	2,750
			Unused OG	400	700	1,150	2,000	3,250	5,250	10,000	—
135	2¢	red	Used	19	32.50	52.50	75	105	180	420	1,400
		brown	Unused NG	80	160	230	360	450	575	825	—
			Unused OG	200	375	625	1,000	1,500	2,250	4,500	—
136	3¢	green	Used	6	11.50	20	32.50	45	110	425	1,250
			Unused NG	45	85	120	190	275	350	475	775
			Unused OG	115	220	375	575	950	1,500	2,750	5,750
137	6¢	carmine	Used	120	210	280	400	600	950	2,750	8,250
			Unused NG	450	825	1,225	1,750	2,150	2,650	3,650	—
			Unused OG	1,025	2,000	3,150	5,000	7,150	10,500	19,000	—
138	7¢	vermilion	Used	150	250	360	500	650	950	3,000	10,500
			Unused NG	375	725	1,025	1,550	1,875	2,350	3,150	—
			Unused OG	850	1,600	2,650	4,250	6,150	9,250	12,500	—
139	10¢	brown	Used	200	330	550	800	1,000	1,325	4,750	12,000
			Unused NG	700	1,200	1,800	2,700	3,200	3,750	5,500	—
			Unused OG	1,500	2,750	4,500	7,500	10,000	14,000	27,500	—
140	12¢	dull	Used	1,175	1,850	2,650	3,500	5,000	7,500	—	—
		violet	Unused NG	4,000	8,250	12,500	17,500	21,500	26,000	—	—
			Unused OG	6,750	13,500	21,000	32,500	40,000	50,000	—	—

SCT#	DENOM	COLOR	CONDITION	VG 50	F 70	F-VF 75	VF 80	VF-XF 85	XF 90	XF-SUP 95	SUP 98
141	15¢	orange	Used	400	700	1,050	1,500	1,825	2,600	6,500	14,000
			Unused NG	625	1,125	1,700	2,500	3,150	4,000	5,500	—
			Unused OG	1,500	2,800	5,000	7,500	10,500	16,500	28,000	—
142	24¢	purple	Used	2,150	3,850	5,250	6,500	9,000	13,000	—	—
143	30¢	black	Used	1,025	1,875	2,700	3,750	5,000	8,500	18,500	—
			Unused NG	1,900	3,650	5,250	7,500	9,250	12,000	—	—
			Unused OG	4,500	8,500	13,250	20,000	26,500	37,500	—	—
144	90¢	carmine	Used	575	1,025	1,525	2,250	3,250	5,000	12,500	—
			Unused NG	2,100	3,900	6,500	10,000	12,000	16,000	—	—
			Unused OG	5,300	8,750	16,250	25,000	37,500	62,500	—	—

1870-71 NATIONAL BANK NOTE ISSUE (WITH "I" GRILL)

SCT#	DENOM	COLOR	CONDITION	VG 50	F 70	F-VF 75	VF 80	VF-XF 85	XF 90	XF-SUP 95	SUP 98
134A	1¢	ultramarine	Used	87.50	170	250	375	500	1,000		
			Unused NG	230	355	525	800	975	1,600		
			Unused OG	725	975	1,575	2,750	4,450	8,250		
135A	2¢	red	Used	85	140	210	325	450	650	1,100	—
		brown	Unused NG				1,000	1,150			
			Unused OG	400	850	1,350	2,000	3,000	4,750		
136A	3¢	green	Used	25	42.50	67.50	100	135	230	1,150	
			Unused NG				—	—	400		
			Unused OG	145	300	460	800	1,200	1,800		
137A	6¢	carmine	Used	225	375	625	950	1,325	2,900		
			Unused NG				—				
			Unused OG	1,250	2,500	4,000	7,000	9,500	15,000	—	
138A	7¢	vermilion	Used	225	400	575	850	1,500	2,750	—	
			Unused NG	650	1,000	1,500	2,200	3,200	4,500	6,500	9,000
			Unused OG	1,050	2,250	3,850	6,500	9,000	15,000		
139A	10¢	brown	Used	1,975	3,200	5,650	8,500	12,500	21,500		
			UnusedOG			—	17,500	—			
140A	12¢	dull violet	Unused OG	—	7,750	—	30,000				
141A	15¢	orange	Used	2,000	3,300	4,750	7,500	8,500	—	12,500	
			Unused OG		7,500	—	16,500				
143A	30¢	black	Unused OG			75,000					
144A	90¢	carmine	Used	4,500	8,000	—	15,000				
			Unused OG				—				

1870-71 NATIONAL BANK NOTE ISSUE (WITHOUT GRILL)

SCT#	DENOM	COLOR	CONDITION	VG 50	F 70	F-VF 75	VF 80	VF-XF 85	XF 90	XF-SUP 95	SUP 98
145	1¢	ultramarine	Used	4.50	7.50	11.50	20	30	70	350	700
			Unused NG	52.50	95	160	240	310	400	650	900
			Unused OG	125	240	435	650	950	1,850	4,500	—
146	2¢	red	Used	4.25	7	10.50	17.50	27.50	70	325	950
		brown	Unused NG	32.50	50	87.50	135	165	200	300	—
			Unused OG	65	100	200	325	500	850	1,800	—
147	3¢	green	Used	0.45	0.90	1.25	1.80	8	37.50	250	550
			Unused NG	20	32.50	50	80	100	150	200	—
			Unused OG	40	70	130	200	335	525	—	—
148	6¢	carmine	Used	4.50	8.50	14.50	22.50	45	85	375	950
			Unused NG	65	120	190	290	375	500	800	—
			Unused OG	160	300	550	900	1,450	2,250	4,500	8,500
149	7¢	vermilion	Used	25	40	67.50	90	115	190	625	1,650
			Unused NG	72.50	120	190	290	375	525	850	—
			Unused OG	160	315	550	900	1,800	2,900	4,750	—
150	10¢	brown	Used	8	12.50	20	35	50	100	325	975
			Unused NG	190	400	550	800	950	1,200	1,500	2,250
			Unused OG	375	800	1,250	2,000	2,750	4,250	—	—
151	12¢	dul	Used	50	77.50	130	200	275	450	1,200	3,350
		viiolet	Unused NG	240	450	725	1,050	1,250	1,650	2,250	—
			Unused OG	550	1,050	1,900	2,850	3,900	6,500	—	—
152	15¢	bright	Used	52.50	82.50	135	210	285	500	1,250	3,500
		orange	Unused NG	300	525	850	1,300	1,450	1,600	2,200	—
			Unused OG	650	1,225	2,150	3,500	4,750	6,750	13,500	—
153	24¢	purple	Used	60	85	135	210	300	425	1,250	3,100
			Unused NG	145	280	400	600	775	950	1,450	2,250
			Unused OG	325	575	1,025	1,700	2,850	4,750	9,250	—
154	30¢	black	Used	70	110	170	275	400	650	2,000	5,250
			Unused NG	650	1,175	1,725	2,600	3,000	4,000	5,000	—
			Unused OG	1,400	2,600	4,350	7,000	8,750	14,000	37,500	—
155	90¢	carmine	Used	82.50	140	215	325	450	700	2,250	6,250
			Unused NG	380	750	1,200	1,800	2,150	2,600	3,100	—
			Unused OG	900	1,825	3,200	5,000	7,000	11,000	19,000	—

1873 CONTINENTAL BANK NOTE ISSUE

SCT#	DENOM	COLOR	CONDITION	VG 50	F 70	F-VF 75	VF 80	VF-XF 85	XF 90	XF-SUP 95	SUP 98
156	1¢	ultramarine	Used	1.20	2	3.25	5.75	12	45	250	575
			Unused NG	20	37.50	62.50	90	110	145	—	—
			Unused OG	40	70	120	200	300	600	1,200	—
157	2¢	brown	Used	6	9	14.50	22.50	32.50	90	300	950
			Unused NG	27.50	55	85	125	150	205	—	—
			Unused OG	60	130	210	325	500	950	1,750	—
158	3¢	green	Used	0.25	0.25	0.40	1	8	32.50	110	400
			Unused NG	8.75	18	27.50	40	52.50	77.50	100	—
			Unused OG	20	40	70	110	170	275	500	1,250
159	6¢	dull pink	Used	4.50	7.75	12.50	18	27.50	75	225	800
			Unused NG	27.50	52.50	85	120	150	210	300	—
			Unused OG	70	130	230	375	600	925	1,700	3,250
160	7¢	orange	Used	21.50	35	57.50	85	120	180	525	1,750
		vermilion	Unused NG	87.50	160	230	350	415	600	850	—
			Unused OG	200	370	625	1,000	1,500	2,500	5,250	8,750
161	10¢	brown	Used	6	9	15	25	35	85	275	850
			Unused NG	62.50	115	170	250	300	500	725	—
			Unused OG	140	300	465	800	1,100	1,650	4,250	8,250
162	12¢	black	Used	27.50	65	92.50	135	185	290	775	1,900
		violet	Unused NG	180	315	525	725	875	1,250	1,750	—
			Unused OG	475	875	1,425	2,200	3,500	5,500	10,500	—
163	15¢	yellow	Used	35	57.50	95	150	225	375	1,100	—
		orange	Unused NG	165	285	460	650	825	1,200	1,900	3,150
			Unused OG	380	675	1,225	1,900	2,850	5,000	9,750	—
164	24¢	purple	Used	357,500		—					
165	30¢	gray	Used	30	57.50	85.50	135	180	290	800	2,450
		black	Unused NG	300	575	850	1,200	1,350	1,900	3,150	—
			Unused OG	775	1,450	2,300	3,750	5,500	8,750	17,500	—
166	90¢	rose	Used	70	125	175	275	400	575	1,750	—
		carmine	Unused NG	175	325	500	700	850	1,025	1,500	—
			Unused OG	450	875	1,400	2,100	3,000	4,500	7,750	17,500

1875 SPECIAL PRINTINGS OF THE 1873 ISSUE

SCT#	DENOM	COLOR	CONDITION	VG 50	F 70	F-VF 75	VF 80	VF-XF 85	XF 90	XF-SUP 95	SUP 98
167	1¢	ultramarine	Unused NGAI	5,500	8,500	11,250	14,000	23,500	45,000		
168	2¢	dark brown	Unused NGAI	2,200	3,900	4,650	6,000	15,000	—		
169	3¢	blue green	Unused NGAI	8,250	12,750	17,250	21,500	—	—		
170	6¢	dull rose	Unused NGAI	6,750	11,250	13,750	18,000	27,500	50,000		
171	7¢	reddish vermilion	Unused NGAI	2,000	2,850	3,400	4,000	8,500	15,000	27,500	
172	10¢	pale brown	Unused NGAI	7,500	11,750	14,500	17,000	25,000	40,000		
173	12¢	dark violet	Unused NGAI	2,200	3,750	4,400	5,500	9,500	17,000	25,000	
174	15¢	bright orange	Unused NGAI	6,850	10,750	13,250	15,500	27,500	45,000		
175	24¢	dull	Used	22,500							
		purple	Unused NGAI	1,450	2,450	2,700	3,400	7,000	14,000	22,500	
176	30¢	greenish black	Unused NGAI	5,250	9,000	10,000	12,000	20,000			
177	90¢	violet carmine	Unused NGAI	8,000	13,500	15,500	18,000	29,000	50,000		

1875 CONTINENTAL BANK NOTE & SPECIAL PRINTINGS

SCT#	DENOM	COLOR	CONDITION	VG 50	F 70	F-VF 75	VF 80	VF-XF 85	XF 90	XF-SUP 95	SUP 98
178	2¢	vermilion	Used	3.50	6	9	15	22.50	55	275	850
			Unused NG	25	47.50	72.50	100	125	145	225	325
			Unused OG	60	115	210	325	420	600	1,300	2,500
179	5¢	blue	Used	6.50	10	15	25	37.50	95	350	1,000
			Unused NG	52.50	85	145	225	270	330	470	700
			Unused OG	150	240	450	700	900	1,350	2,500	5,750

1875 Special Printings of the 1875 Issue

SCT#	DENOM	COLOR	CONDITION	VG 50	F 70	F-VF 75	VF 80	VF-XF 85	XF 90	XF-SUP 95	SUP 98
180	2¢	carmine vermilion	Unused NGAI	22,500	36,000	55,000	70,000	82,500	120,000		
181	5¢	bright blue	Unused NGAI	150,000	210,000	310,000	450,000	—	765,000		

1879 AMERICAN BANK NOTE ISSUE

SCT#	DENOM	COLOR	CONDITION	VG 50	F 70	F-VF 75	VF 80	VF-XF 85	XF 90	XF-SUP 95	SUP 98
182	1¢	dark ultramarine	Used	1.10	2.30	3.40	6	12.50	67.50	210	625
			Unused NG	20	35	52.50	80	100	135	230	—
			Unused OG	47.50	80	125	200	325	525	1,100	2,100
			Mint NH	67.50	120	270	675	1,200	2,200	6,500	—
183	2¢	vermilion	Used	1.20	2.40	3.50	5	11	50	170	525
			Unused NG	9	17	25	40	47.50	60	92.50	—
			Unused OG	19	45	67.50	100	140	225	625	1,025
			Mint NH	32.50	62.50	160	370	550	850	2,500	—
184	3¢	green	Used	0.25	0.30	0.70	1	15	55	125	475
			Unused NG	8.25	14.50	22	35	45	57.50	85	—
			Unused OG	17.50	35	57.50	90	125	180	360	750
			Mint NH	25	62.50	150	325	525	800	2,250	7,500
185	5¢	blue	Used	4.25	6.75	10	16	32.50	92.50	300	950
			Unused NG	40	72.50	105	155	180	220	300	450
			Unused OG	100	210	335	500	675	900	1,450	3,500
			Mint NH	150	295	750	1,600	2,250	4,000	11,500	—
186	6¢	pink	Used	5.75	9	15	22.50	50	100	375	1,150
			Unused NG	70	130	190	275	310	360	500	800
			Unused OG	190	375	625	900	1,200	1,800	3,150	6,250
			Mint NH	310	625	1,425	3,100	4,500	7,750	18,500	—
187	10¢	brown (no mark)	Used	9.50	16	25	40	65	170	550	2,500
			Unused NG	250	450	675	1,000	1,200	1,500	1,900	—
			Unused OG	625	1,200	2,000	3,000	4,000	6,000	10,000	—
			Mint NH	950	2,100	5,750	10,000	13,500	20,000	45,000	—
188	10¢	brown (mark)	Used	7	12	18.50	30	50	130	375	1,200
			Unused NG	150	300	415	650	825	975	1,350	—
			Unused OG	350	725	1,150	1,800	2,300	3,850	6,500	12,500
			Mint NH	600	1,275	2,850	6,000	8,500	14,000	33,500	—
189	15¢	red orange	Used	6.50	12	18.50	27.50	45	160	375	1,050
			Unused NG	16.50	35	47.50	70	82.50	97.50	135	220
			Unused OG	42.50	80	120	180	250	375	750	1,500
			Mint NH	62.50	140	350	600	900	1,750	4,250	8,500
190	30¢	full black	Used	20	32.50	52.50	90	130	250	700	1,900
			Unused NG	75	150	210	300	350	425	525	825
			Unused OG	200	350	600	850	1,125	1,600	3,250	6,000
			Mint NH	280	550	1,250	2,800	4,500	7,250	17,500	—
191	90¢	carmine	Used	87.50	150	220	350	475	800	2,750	—
			Unused NG	160	300	475	650	725	950	1,350	2,000
			Unused OG	400	750	1,500	2,000	2,750	4,000	7,000	14,500
			Mint NH	700	1,650	4,500	7,000	10,500	15,000	35,000	—

1880 SPECIAL PRINTINGS OF THE 1879 ISSUE

SCT#	DENOM	COLOR	CONDITION	VG 50	F 70	F-VF 75	VF 80	VF-XF 85	XF 90	XF-SUP 95	SUP 98
192	1¢	dark ultramarine	Unused NGAI	25,000	57,500	65,000	77,500	105,000	120,000	—	—
193	2¢	black brown	Unused NGAI	6,250	9,500	12,500	16,000	26,500	37,500		
194	3¢	blue green	Unused NGAI	65,000	120,000	150,000	185,000	210,000	290,000		
195	6¢	dull rose	Unused NGAI	26,500	42,500	57,500	67,500	82,500	105,000		
196	7¢	scarlet vermilion	Unused NGAI	3,150	4,500	5,650	6,750	11,500	18,000	—	
197	10¢	deep brown	Unused NGAI	14,500	22,000	27,000	34,500	55,000	72,500		
198	12¢	blackish purple	Unused NGAI	4,300	6,050	7,500	9,500	13,500	17,000	27,500	
199	15¢	orange	Unused NGAI	9,000	16,000	22,500	29,000	42,500	57,500	90,000	
200	24¢	dark violet	Unused NGAI	3,150	4,950	6,750	9,000	13,000	19,000		
201	30¢	greenish black	Unused NGAI	7,750	10,500	15,000	20,000	30,000	42,500	57,500	
202	90¢	dull carmine	Unused NGAI	8,250	14,500	21,000	29,000	40,000	57,500		
203	2¢	scarlet vermilion	Unused NGAI	38,500	60,000	77,500	100,000	145,000	180,000		
204	5¢	deep blue	Unused NGAI	92,500	135,000	185,000	240,000	300,000	350,000	425,000	500,000

1881-1885 AMERICAN BANK NOTE ISSUES & SPECIAL PRINTINGS

SCT#	DENOM	COLOR	CONDITION	VG 50	F 70	F-VF 75	VF 80	VF-XF 85	XF 90	XF-SUP 95	SUP 98
205	5¢	yellow brown	Used	3	5.50	9	15	30	130	300	825
			Unused NG	20	37.50	62.50	90	110	130	185	290
			Unused OG	57.50	115	175	240	400	600	1,150	2,000
			Mint NH	135	250	485	775	1,200	1,950	5,500	10,500
205C	5¢	gray brown	Unused NGAI	21,000	30,000	38,500	50,000	60,000	75,000	100,000	
206	1¢	gray blue	Used	0.25	0.35	0.60	1	10	37.50	115	350
			Unused NG	6	11	17	25	32.50	42.50	60	—
			Unused OG	16	30	47.50	70	95	140	375	650
			Mint NH	37.50	90	140	225	350	550	2,250	—
207	3¢	blue green	Used	0.25	0.30	0.55	0.80	10	32.50	105	750
			Unused NG	6	12.50	18	27.50	37.50	60	87.50	—
			Unused OG	20	35	52.50	80	105	170	325	675
			Mint NH	42.50	92.50	150	250	575	975	3,750	7,250
208	6¢	rose	Used	22.50	45	70	100	135	240	1,000	1,900
			Unused NG	52.50	100	160	240	265	310	425	625
			Unused OG	190	325	525	800	1,075	1,400	2,400	7,000
			Mint NH	370	925	1,575	2,500	3,400	5,250	9,250	—
208a	6¢	deep brown red	Used	45	80	120	170	235	400	1,250	2,950
			Unused NG	37.50	67.50	100	150	175	210	310	450
			Unused OG	120	230	340	550	700	1,025	1,825	4,200
			Mint NH	300	650	1,075	1,750	2,650	4,100	7,750	—
209	10¢	brown	Used	1.50	2.75	4.25	6	12.50	45	200	500
			Unused NG	15	32.50	50	65	72.50	82.50	115	—
			Unused OG	35	70	100	160	225	300	675	1,300
			Mint NH	75	160	280	475	650	1,050	3,250	12,500
209b	10¢	black brown	Used	80	140	245	375	480	800	2,250	5,000
			Unused NG	220	375	550	950	1,100	1,350	—	
			Unused OG	600	1,100	1,750	3,000	4,000	5,250	7,500	
			Mint NH	1,100	2,250	4,000	6,000	8,000	11,000		
210	2¢	red brown	Used	0.30	0.40	0.55	0.75	10	45	110	350
			Unused NG	3.75	7.50	11	17	22.50	35	55	—
			Unused OG	11.50	21	29	45	62.50	87.50	180	425
			Mint NH	26	50	90	135	230	500	1,100	3,450
211	4¢	blue green	Used	6.25	11	17	25	37.50	120	300	850
			Unused NG	20	30	50	80	100	125	200	—
			Unused OG	57.50	100	150	225	340	650	1,125	2,500
			Mint NH	150	300	500	800	1,100	2,150	5,250	11,500
211B	2¢	pale red brown	Unused NG	37.50	57.50	87.50	130	145	160	200	260
			Unused OG	85	180	250	375	475	650	1,100	2,000
			Mint NH	170	330	575	900	1,300	2,250	5,250	—
211D	4¢	deep blue green	Unused NGAI	17,750	27,000	35,500	47,500	62,500	85,000		

1887-88 AMERICAN BANK NOTE ISSUES

SCT#	DENOM	COLOR	CONDITION	VG 50	F 70	F-VF 75	VF 80	VF-XF 85	XF 90	XF-SUP 95	SUP 98
212	1¢	ultramarine	Used	0.60	1.05	1.70	2.50	12.50	32.50	140	425
			Unused NG	8.25	14.50	22.50	35	42.50	52.50	75	110
			Unused OG	22.50	40	60	90	145	275	—	—
			Mint NH	50	110	180	290	450	725	2,250	6,500
213	2¢	green	Used	0.25	0.25	0.45	0.60	10	45	125	375
			Unused NG	3.75	6.50	10	15	20	35	55	—
			Unused OG	9	18	25	40	55	80	170	350
			Mint NH	20	47.50	77.50	120	185	375	950	3,750
214	3¢	vermilion	Used	11.50	20	35	50	75	160	400	1,200
			Unused NG	5.75	10	15	25	35	52.50	75	—
			Unused OG	12.50	25	40	60	80	115	210	500
			Mint NH	35	67.50	115	180	275	450	1,400	4,750
215	4¢	carmine	Used	5.50	11	17	25	40	90	300	1,000
			Unused NG	14	25	40	60	70	82.50	130	—
			Unused OG	50	90	135	180	260	400	700	1,350
			Mint NH	95	190	335	525	800	1,500	4,000	10,000
216	5¢	indigo	Used	4.25	8	12	17.50	25	80	225	700
			Unused NG	16	35	50	75	90	120	165	—
			Unused OG	50	100	135	200	325	450	900	1,900
			Mint NH	110	225	400	625	1,100	2,250	6,250	10,000
217	30¢	orange brown	Used	22.50	40	62.50	90	120	175	750	1,600
			Unused NG	18	35	52.50	80	92.50	110	185	280
			Unused OG	60	115	175	250	375	550	1,100	2,350
			Mint NH	160	300	575	900	1,250	2,150	6,250	17,500
218	90¢	purple	Used	57.50	100	160	225	325	475	1,500	—
			Unused NG	60	120	160	250	290	350	425	725
			Unused OG	200	375	550	800	1,050	1,550	2,500	6,750
			Mint NH	440	900	1,600	2,500	3,750	6,500	26,500	—

1890-93 AMERICAN BANK NOTE ISSUE

SCT#	DENOM	COLOR	CONDITION	VG 50	F 70	F-VF 75	VF 80	VF-XF 85	XF 90	XF-SUP 95	SUP 98
219	1¢	dull blue	Used	0.25	0.35	0.50	0.75	8	30	100	300
			Unused OG	4	8.50	12.50	20	27.50	45	100	180
			Mint NH	10	22.50	40	65	120	210	875	3,500
219D	2¢	lake	Used	1.60	2.50	3.80	5.50	12.50	50	225	650
			Unused OG	40	72.50	110	160	210	350	750	1,350
			Mint NH	90	190	325	500	850	1,500	4,500	19,000
220	2¢	carmine	Used	0.25	0.30	0.50	0.70	8	30	105	275
			Unused OG	4	8.50	12.50	20	30	45	130	275
			Mint NH	8	17.50	37.50	60	100	250	750	2,400
220a	2¢	cap left 2	Used	2.75	5.75	9.75	12.50	25	67.50	210	650
			Unused OG	30	65	100	150	200	350	550	1,050
			Mint NH	60	150	260	425	600	1,075	2,500	—
220c	2¢	cap both 2s	Used	8	15	25	35	60	170	475	1,200
			Unused OG	135	250	460	650	800	1,100	1,800	—
			Mint NH	270	575	1,000	1,800	2,750	5,000	11,000	—
221	3¢	purple	Used	1.75	4	6	9	15	55	190	575
			Unused OG	12.50	22.50	37.50	55	75	120	275	525
			Mint NH	32.50	67.50	105	175	275	550	1,800	7,000
222	4¢	dark brown	Used	1	1.90	3.25	4.75	12.50	47.50	185	500
			Unused OG	17.50	35	50	80	110	160	375	—
			Mint NH	40	87.50	150	240	400	700	2,400	7,500
223	5¢	chocolate	Used	1	1.90	3.25	4.75	12.50	47.50	175	525
			Unused OG	13	26	40	60	85	140	280	500
			Mint NH	32.50	70	110	185	300	550	1,825	5,750
224	6¢	brown red	Used	5.75	10	18	25	40	120	275	775
			Unused OG	11	21	33.50	50	75	120	275	525
			Mint NH	25.50	60	97.50	160	250	475	1,800	5,000
225	8¢	lilac	Used	4	7.25	11.50	17	35	100	325	650
			Unused OG	9.50	19	30	45	65	115	225	425
			Mint NH	20	42.50	85	135	250	425	1,450	4,250
226	10¢	green	Used	1.10	2.20	3.60	5	12.50	40	175	525
			Unused OG	35	70	105	160	225	300	550	1,200
			Mint NH	77.50	165	295	475	800	1,400	4,250	11,250
227	15¢	indigo	Used	6	11	17.50	25	45	115	325	800
			Unused OG	45	82.50	125	180	250	450	800	1,650
			Mint NH	92.50	200	365	550	950	2,000	5,500	—
228	30¢	black	Used	6.50	12.50	20	30	52.50	175	425	1,100
			Unused OG	70	130	180	280	400	600	1,050	1,950
			Mint NH	150	330	575	850	1,150	2,750	7,250	17,500
229	90¢	orange	Used	30	60	87.50	130	190	300	850	1,750
			Unused OG	105	200	310	450	650	1,000	1,650	2,750
			Mint NH	240	490	875	1,350	2,250	3,850	10,000	19,000

1893 COLUMBIAN EXPOSITION ISSUE

SCT#	DENOM	COLOR	CONDITION	VG 50	F 70	F-VF 75	VF 80	VF-XF 85	XF 90	XF-SUP 95	SUP 98
230	1¢	deep blue	Used	0.25	0.25	0.30	0.40	5	30	130	400
			Unused OG	3	6	9.25	14	20	30	60	145
			Mint NH	5.25	12	22.50	32.50	50	85	325	1,125
231	2¢	brown violet	Used	0.25	0.25	0.25	0.30	4	32.50	120	375
			Unused OG	2.75	5.50	8.25	12.50	17.50	27.50	50	125
			Mint NH	5	11.50	22.50	31	50	125	375	1,300
231 var	2¢	broken hat	Used	0.80	1.60	2.40	3.50	17.50	110	400	1,000
			Unused OG	12.50	25	37.50	55	70	120	225	500
			Mint NH	30	57.50	115	160	220	350	850	3,000
232	3¢	green	Used	3.75	7.25	10.25	15	30	77.50	260	650
			Unused OG	8	14	25	35	42.50	60	120	300
			Mint NH	20	32.50	65	97.50	125	190	575	2,000
233	4¢	ultramarine	Used	1.75	3.50	5.50	8	15	50	200	525
			Unused OG	10	20	35	50	70	100	235	425
			Mint NH	27.50	52.50	92.50	140	190	325	925	2,250
233a	4¢	blue (error)	Used	5,500	7,500	11,500	16,500	—	—		
			Unused OG	6,000	9,250	13,250	17,500	23,000	30,000		
			Mint NH	9,000	13,000	22,500	32,500	—	—		
234	5¢	chocolate	Used	2	3.75	5.75	8.50	17.50	52.50	225	775
			Unused OG	10	20	35	50	65	90	225	550
			Mint NH	27.50	52.50	92.50	140	225	450	825	2,500
235	6¢	purple	Used	6	10	16	22.50	40	95	280	725
			Unused OG	10	20	35	50	62.50	87.50	240	575
			Mint NH	27.50	52.50	92.50	140	210	375	900	4,150
235a	6¢	red violet	Used	6	10	16	22.50	40	95	280	725
			Unused OG	10	20	35	50	62.50	87.50	290	725
			Mint NH	27.50	52.50	92.50	140	210	375	900	4,150
236	8¢	magenta	Used	2.25	4.50	7.25	10	22.50	60	240	600
			Unused OG	9	18	32.50	47.50	60	80	175	425
			Mint NH	27.50	52.50	92.50	140	200	325	1,500	5,000
237	10¢	black brown	Used	1.80	3.75	5.50	8	22.50	90	240	650
			Unused OG	22.50	40	60	90	120	170	375	750
			Mint NH	45	82.50	160	250	335	525	2,000	5,000
238	15¢	dark green	Used	15	32.50	52.50	72.50	110	250	775	1,850
			Unused OG	50	90	140	200	260	375	700	1,500
			Mint NH	130	240	385	600	850	1,850	6,000	11,500
239	30¢	orange brown	Used	22.50	42.50	62.50	90	140	250	775	2,000
			Unused OG	55	105	150	225	280	400	550	1,500
			Mint NH	130	270	450	675	850	1,125	2,600	6,500
240	50¢	slate blue	Used	47.50	82.50	125	175	240	400	1,150	2,650
			Unused NG	40	75	125	190	225	400	950	—
			Unused OG	100	190	290	425	525	700	1,500	3,250
			Mint NH	225	475	850	1,250	1,850	3,500	8,750	38,500
241	$1	salmon	Used	125	250	365	525	675	900	2,400	—
			Unused NG	125	240	340	500	600	725	1,000	1,450
			Unused OG	250	450	675	1,000	1,200	1,500	3,450	7,500
			Mint NH	650	1,350	2,250	3,400	5,250	12,000	34,000	—
242	$2	brown red	Used	125	250	365	525	675	1,050	3,250	9,000
			Unused NG	125	240	340	500	600	750	1,150	1,850
			Unused OG	260	445	700	1,050	1,250	1,700	4,000	8,250
			Mint NH	725	1,400	2,350	3,500	6,000	1,400	47,500	85,000
243	$3	yellow green	Used	190	300	525	750	1,000	1,600	4,750	10,000
			Unused NG	180	270	475	675	800	1,000	1,500	2,050
			Unused OG	360	625	925	1,350	1,550	2,250	4,500	8,000
			Mint NH	900	1,700	2,700	4,250	7,250	12,000	65,000	—

SCT#	DENOM	COLOR	CONDITION	VG 50	F 70	F-VF 75	VF 80	VF-XF 85	XF 90	XF-SUP 95	SUP 98
243a	$3	olive	Used	190	300	525	750	1,000	1,600	4,750	10,000
		green	Unused NG	180	270	475	675	800	1,000	1,500	2,050
			Unused OG	360	625	925	1,350	1,550	2,250	4,500	8,000
			Mint NH	900	1,700	2,700	4,250	7,250	12,000	65,000	—
244	$4	crimson	Used	215	430	675	950	1,450	2,000	6,000	11,000
		lake	Unused NG	250	450	725	1,000	1,175	1,375	1,850	2,600
			Unused OG	575	875	1,325	2,000	2,500	3,500	6,500	13,250
			Mint NH	1,250	2,500	4,500	7,000	11,500	16,500	55,000	—
244a	$4	rose	Used	215	430	675	950	1,450	2,000	6,000	11,000
		carmine	Unused NG	250	450	725	1,000	1,150	1,375	1,850	2,600
			Unused OG	575	875	1,325	2,000	2,500	3,500	6,500	13,250
			Mint NH	1,250	2,500	4,500	7,000	11,500	16,500	55,000	—
245	$5	black	Used	300	525	850	1,150	1,550	2,600	6,250	12,500
			Unused NG	350	575	775	1,150	1,350	1,600	2,000	2,950
			Unused OG	625	925	1,550	2,300	3,000	3,750	6,250	14,500
			Mint NH	1,750	3,600	6,250	9,500	17,500	30,000	85,000	—

1894 FIRST BUREAU OF ENGRAVING AND PRINTING ISSUE (UNWATERMARKED)

SCT#	DENOM	COLOR	CONDITION	VG 50	F 70	F-VF 75	VF 80	VF-XF 85	XF 90	XF-SUP 95	SUP 98
246	1¢	ultramarine	Used	1.50	3	4.50	7	15	57.50	240	1,025
			Unused OG	7.50	13.50	20	30	45	62.50	125	250
			Mint NH	16	27.50	60	90	145	240	850	2,900
247	1¢	blue	Used	1	1.60	2.75	4	12.50	55	220	850
			Unused OG	12.50	25	42.50	60	80	110	260	525
			Mint NH	32.50	62.50	110	175	310	500	2,100	—
248	2¢	pink	Used	2.10	3.60	6	9	22.50	70	300	1,000
		type I	Unused OG	7	12	20	30	42.50	65	115	260
			Mint NH	17.50	30	55	90	150	300	1,400	4,250
249	2¢	carmine	Used	1.60	2.90	4.50	7	17.50	65	250	950
		lake	Unused OG	35	67.50	105	150	200	275	650	1,100
		type I	Mint NH	90	200	300	450	675	1,225	4,250	15,000
250	2¢	carmine	Used	0.85	1.20	2.10	3	12.50	65	200	725
		type	Unused OG	6.75	11.50	19.50	29	42.50	67.50	125	240
			Mint NH	16.50	28.50	52.50	85	140	310	1,250	3,000
250a	2¢	rose	Used	1.50	2.75	4.25	6	16	70	210	750
		type I	Unused OG	8.25	14.50	24	36	52.50	82.50	150	260
			Mint NH	22.50	37.50	67.50	105	165	335	1,250	3,250
250b	2¢	scarlet	Used	0.85	1.20	2.10	3	12.50	65	200	725
		type I	Unused OG	6.25	10.50	17.50	26	40	61.50	120	235
			Mint NH	15.50	27.50	50	80	135	290	1,050	2,900
251	2¢	carmine	Used	3	5.50	9.25	14	35	95	380	—
		type II	Unused OG	100	185	265	400	500	650	1,350	2,200
			Mint NH	260	550	800	1,200	1,800	3,250	9,500	—
251a	2¢	scarlet	Used	2.75	5.50	9	13	32.50	95	360	1,300
		type II	Unused OG	95	170	245	375	475	625	1,300	2,150
			Mint NH	225	430	750	1,125	1,775	3,100	9,750	—
252	2¢	carmine	Used	2.75	5.50	9	13	32.50	90	375	1,250
		type III	Unused OG	35	60	90	135	155	225	485	925
			Mint NH	85	160	260	400	600	1,200	5,250	10,500
252a	2¢	scarlet	Used	3.25	6.25	10.75	15	37.50	100	450	1,400
		type III	Unused OG	30	55	85	120	150	220	475	900
			Mint NH	80	130	240	360	550	950	3,750	10,000
253	3¢	purple	Used	2.60	4.75	8.25	12	30	95	340	1,200
			Unused OG	30	55	85	120	150	220	475	—
			Mint NH	80	130	240	360	550	950	4,250	1,700
254	4¢	dark	Used	2.60	5	7.50	11	25	70	300	1,250
		brown	Unused OG	45	87.50	125	200	240	300	500	—
			Mint NH	120	225	375	600	850	1,275	4,250	11,500
255	5¢	chocolate	Used	2.25	4	6	9	22.50	90	260	1,100
			Unused OG	30	55	85	120	150	220	475	900
			Mint NH	80	130	240	360	550	1,000	2,750	9,000
256	6¢	dull	Used	6.50	12	18.50	27.50	60	160	525	1,400
		brown	Unused OG	37.50	70	110	160	200	260	575	1,150
			Mint NH	75	150	300	475	650	1,150	3,750	15,000

SCT#	DENOM	COLOR	CONDITION	VG 50	F 70	F-VF 75	VF 80	VF-XF 85	XF 90	XF-SUP 95	SUP 98
257	8¢	violet	Used	4.50	9	13.25	20	40	110	425	1,400
		brown	Unused OG	37.50	67.50	110	160	200	260	500	1,050
			Mint NH	75	150	300	475	700	1,100	3,500	12,500
258	10¢	dark	Used	4.50	9	13.25	20	40	125	425	1,400
		green	Unused OG	70	130	190	275	360	480	1,050	2,000
			Mint NH	140	300	550	850	1,275	2,350	6,600	20,000
259	15¢	dark	Used	15	30	45	65	130	300	850	2,900
		blue	Unused OG	70	130	190	275	360	480	1,050	2,050
			Mint NH	140	300	550	850	1,275	2,750	7,250	20,000
260	50¢	orange	Used	35	67.50	105	140	235	400	1,450	4,250
			Unused OG	115	220	320	475	575	750	1,650	3,250
			Mint NH	260	550	925	1,425	2,100	3,500	11,000	28,500
261	$1	black	Used	85	160	240	350	550	1,000	3,250	7,750
		type I	Unused NG	100	185	270	400	475	600	800	—
			Unused OG	250	425	675	1,000	1,250	1,750	3,500	6,250
			Mint NH	550	1,100	1,900	3,150	4,750	7,500	21,500	37,500
261A	$1	black	Used	200	375	550	800	1,200	1,900	6,250	15,500
		type II	Unused NG	220	365	575	850	950	1,125	1,500	—
			Unused OG	550	950	1,475	2,100	3,000	4,250	6,750	10,500
			Mint NH	1,250	2,150	4,000	6,500	8,500	14,000	31,000	—
262	$2	bright	Used	300	575	900	1,200	1,900	3,000	9,000	—
		blue	Unused NG	300	500	700	1,100	1,250	1,475	2,000	2,750
			Unused OG	675	1,275	1,900	2,750	3,600	4,750	8,000	17,500
			Mint NH	1,700	3,600	5,900	8,750	12,500	20,000	—	—
263	$5	dark	Used	700	1,200	1,800	2,600	3,600	6,000	17,500	40,000
		green	Unused NG	525	925	1,400	2,100	2,400	2,850	4,000	7,500
			Unused OG	1,000	1,875	2,800	4,000	5,250	7,250	12,500	20,000
			Mint NH	2,600	4,900	8,750	14,000	26,500	—	—	—

1895 BUREAU ISSUE (DOUBLE LINE WATERMARK)

SCT#	DENOM	COLOR	CONDITION	VG 50	F 70	F-VF 75	VF 80	VF-XF 85	XF 90	XF-SUP 95	SUP 98
264	1¢	blue	Used	0.25	0.30	0.40	0.60	8	30	95	475
			Unused OG	1.40	3	4.25	6	8.25	13.50	30	75
			Mint NH	3	5	11	17.50	30	60	325	850
265	2¢	carmine	Used	0.80	1	2.10	3.50	13.50	50	200	875
		type I	Unused OG	8.25	15	22.50	35	55	80	125	230
			Mint NH	20	35	70	105	175	310	925	3,000
266	2¢	carmine	Used	1.40	2	3.50	5.50	17.50	65	240	950
		type II	Unused OG	9.25	17	26	40	57.50	85	170	300
			Mint NH	22.50	42.50	77.50	120	210	400	1,100	4,000
267	2¢	carmine	Used	0.25	0.25	0.35	0.50	8	35	135	400
		type III	Unused OG	1.40	2.50	3.75	5.50	8.75	14	32.50	72.50
			Mint NH	3.50	5.75	10	16	27.50	60	275	925
267a	2¢	pink	Used	1.20	2.20	3.50	5	22.50	90	350	—
			Unused OG	4.80	9.50	14	20	35	60	120	260
			Mint NH	12	22.50	37.50	60	150	300	1,150	2,250
267b	2¢	vermilion	Used	6	7.50	11.25	15	40	135	400	—
		type III	Unused OG	11	21	32.50	50	85	170	800	—
267c	2¢	rose carmine	Used	—	—	—	—	—	—	—	—
		type III	Unused OG	—	—	—	—	—	—	—	—
268	3¢	purple	Used	0.55	1	1.55	2.25	14	55	175	725
			Unused OG	9	17.50	25	37.50	50	67.50	110	250
			Mint NH	22.50	40	67.50	115	175	275	1,500	8,000
269	4¢	dark	Used	0.85	2.15	2.80	3.50	20	65	210	925
		brown	Unused OG	10.75	19	28	42.50	55	75	140	280
			Mint NH	25	45	75	125	190	375	1,500	6,500
270	5¢	chocolate	Used	0.90	2	2.45	3.50	16	60	200	850
			Unused OG	8.50	17	24	35	45	60	125	260
			Mint NH	20.50	37	62	105	165	300	850	3,000
271	6¢	dull	Used	2.15	4	6	8.50	25	75	350	1,100
		brown	Unused OG	25	50	70	110	145	200	425	900
			Mint NH	50	105	200	325	450	800	4,000	13,500
272	8¢	violet	Used	0.70	1	1.75	2.75	15	45	150	450
		brown	Unused OG	17.50	32.50	47	70	85	115	210	500
			Mint NH	37.50	70	130	210	325	700	1,600	6,500
273	10¢	dark	Used	0.55	0.80	1.45	2.25	11	45	180	675
		green	Unused OG	25	42.50	67.50	95	130	175	375	750
			Mint NH	50	100	190	280	440	725	3,250	13,500
274	15¢	dark	Used	4.40	8	12	17.50	55	105	425	1,450
		blue	Unused OG	50	87.50	140	200	260	360	950	1,600
			Mint NH	105	210	380	625	925	1,350	5,250	16,500

SCT#	DENOM	COLOR	CONDITION	VG 50	F 70	F-VF 75	VF 80	VF-XF 85	XF 90	XF-SUP 95	SUP 98
275	50¢	orange	Used	10	16	26	40	85	225	725	1,950
			Unused OG	60	115	155	240	325	425	1,100	1,950
			Mint NH	135	280	480	775	1,200	2,600	9,000	22,500
275a	50¢	red	Used	11.75	20	33	47.50	95	240	750	2,100
		orange	Unused OG	77.50	140	210	325	400	550	1,200	2,100
			Mint NH	165	350	600	975	1,400	2,500	7,750	22,500
276	$1	black	Used	22.50	42.50	65	95	150	325	950	2,500
		type I	Unused NG	60	110	165	250	300	400	525	—
			Unused OG	150	275	400	600	750	1,100	2,500	5,250
			Mint NH	325	650	1,100	1,800	2,750	4,250	14,000	—
276A	$1	black	Used	50	85	135	200	300	450	1,250	4,000
		type II	Unused NG	100	200	350	500	575	675	975	—
			Unused OG	290	525	825	1,250	1,500	2,400	5,500	—
			Mint NH	700	1,400	2,400	3,750	5,750	9,500	25,000	—
277	$2	bright	Used	105	190	280	400	525	725	2,500	7,500
		blue	Unused NG	95	175	250	375	435	525	725	—
			Unused OG	225	375	600	900	1,100	1,500	2,650	5,250
			Mint NH	525	1,100	1,825	2,900	4,500	7,250	22,000	—
277a	$2	dark	Used	105	190	280	400	525	725	2,500	7,500
		blue	Unused NG	95	175	250	375	435	525	725	—
			Unused OG	225	375	600	900	1,050	1,400	2,650	5,250
			Mint NH	525	1,100	1,825	2,900	4,500	7,250	22,000	—
278	$5	dark	Used	150	280	420	600	775	1,000	3,750	10,000
		green	Unused NG	200	350	550	800	900	1,025	1,225	—
			Unused OG	500	950	1,325	2,000	2,400	3,000	4,750	9,000
			Mint NH	1,200	2,500	4,150	6,250	8,750	15,000	38,500	70,000

1897-1903 REGULAR ISSUE

SCT#	DENOM	COLOR	CONDITION	VG 50	F 70	F-VF 75	VF 80	VF-XF 85	XF 90	XF-SUP 95	SUP 98
279	1¢	deep	Used	0.25	0.25	0.40	0.50	10	25	90	325
		green	Unused OG	2.25	4	6	9	12	18	47.50	125
			Mint NH	5	9.75	16	25	42.50	85	400	1,200
279B	2¢	red	Used	0.25	0.25	0.30	0.40	8	25	95	500
		type IV	Mint NH	5	9.75	16	25	45	110	350	1,250
279Bc	2¢	rose	Used	50	72.50	150	220	330	550	1,450	3,650
		carmine	Unused OG	70	120	195	275	375	500	1,300	—
		type IV	Mint NH	180	340	575	850	1,250	2,250	7,500	15,000
279Bd	2¢	orange	Used	0.75	0.90	1.65	2	15	50	150	450
		red	Unused OG	2.75	5.25	8	11.50	17.50	27.50	65	150
		type IV	Mint NH	6	12	20	32.50	60	110	400	1,500
279Bf	2¢	carmine	Used	0.80	1	1.60	2	22.50	90	250	550
		type IV	Unused OG	2.50	4	6.75	10	14	25	60	125
			Mint NH	5.50	11	17	27.50	47.50	90	400	1,250
279Bg	2¢	pink	Used	1.50	2.55	4.30	7.50	32.50	115	310	700
		type IV	Unused OG	14	25	40	55	82.50	130	275	—
			Mint NH	30	65	105	165	300	600	2,200	—
279Bh	2¢	vermilion	Used	1.10	1.35	2.45	3	30	165	650	2,000
		type IV	Unused OG	3	5.75	8.75	12.50	17.50	27.50	65	150
			Mint NH	6.50	13.50	22.50	35	60	100	375	—
279Bi	2¢	brown	Used	37.50	50	70	100	230	575	1,300	—
		orange	Unused OG	—	175	285	400	600	—	—	—
		type IV	Mint NH	—	400	625	950	1,450	—	—	—
279Bj	2¢	red type IV	Used	1,000	1,800	2,300	3,000	3,500	—		
Booklet Pane of 6			Unused OG	220	320	400	500	575	675	900	—
Horiz. wmk.			Mint NH	350	600	800	1,000	1,175	1,500	2,500	—
279Bk	2¢	red type IV	Used	—	—	—	—	—	—	—	—
Booklet Pane of 6			Unused OG	220	320	400	500	575	675	900	—
Vert. wmk.			Mint NH	550	900	1,200	1,500	1,775	2,250	3,750	—
280	4¢	rose	Used	0.55	1.25	1.90	3.25	12.50	65	325	900
		brown	Unused OG	7.50	13.50	21	30	42.50	57.50	125	—
			Mint NH	13.50	27.50	47.50	80	125	225	1,250	3,000
280a	4¢	lilac	Used	0.55	1.25	1.90	3.25	12.50	65	325	700
		brown	Unused OG	7.50	13.50	21	30	42.50	57.50	125	—
			Mint NH	13.50	27.50	47.50	80	125	225	1,250	3,650
280b	4¢	orange	Used	0.50	0.95	1.75	3	10	55	260	675
		brown	Unused OG	7.50	13.50	21	30	42.50	57.50	125	—
			Mint NH	13.50	27.50	47.50	80	125	225	1,250	4,500
281	5¢	dark	Used	0.55	0.85	1.40	2.25	14	42.50	160	725
		blue	Unused OG	8.25	14	21	32.50	45	57.50	125	240
			Mint NH	18	37.50	62.50	100	150	300	1,500	5,250

SCT#	DENOM	COLOR	CONDITION	VG 50	F 70	F-VF 75	VF 80	VF-XF 85	XF 90	XF-SUP 95	SUP 98
282	6¢	lake	Used	1.65	3	4.50	6.50	20	75	500	—
			Unused OG	11.25	21	32	45	55	75	160	325
			Mint NH	26.50	48	87.50	140	220	475	1,375	3,750
282a	6¢	purple	Used	5.25	9	13.50	20	40	100	—	—
		lake	Unused OG	18	32.50	52.50	75	97.50	135	295	625
			Mint NH	37.50	72.50	140	225	375	700	1,850	6,250
282C	10¢	brown	Used	1.65	2.50	4	6.50	12.50	70	300	1,100
		type I	Unused OG	45	77.50	115	175	230	350	525	1,200
			Mint NH	110	200	350	525	825	1,425	4,750	15,500
283	10¢	orange	Used	1.50	3.25	4.25	6	11	65	250	850
Horiz. wmk.		brown	Unused OG	37.50	65	105	150	190	260	550	975
		type II	Mint NH	76.50	155	260	450	725	1,250	3,850	13,500
283a	10¢	orange	Used	3.75	7	9.50	15	40	115	575	1,500
Vert. wmk.		brown	Unused OG	55	100	160	250	350	500	1,000	1,850
		type II	Mint NH	140	275	500	775	1,100	2,000	7,000	16,500
284	15¢	olive	Used	3.25	6	9	13	37.50	115	450	1,500
		green	Unused OG	37.50	65	100	150	200	275	600	1,200
			Mint NH	87.50	170	310	475	750	1,500	4,750	15,000

1898 TRANS-MISSISSIPPI EXPOSITION ISSUE

SCT#	DENOM	COLOR	CONDITION	VG 50	F 70	F-VF 75	VF 80	VF-XF 85	XF 90	XF-SUP 95	SUP 98
285	1¢	dark	Used	2.15	3.50	5	7	30	65	275	850
		yellow	Unused OG	7	12	18.50	27.50	37.50	60	110	230
		green	Mint NH	16.50	32.50	55	82.50	140	240	750	2,000
286	2¢	copper	Used	0.65	1	2	2.75	15	55	225	725
		red	Unused OG	6.50	11	17	25	32.50	55	105	220
			Mint NH	13.50	30	47.50	72.50	120	250	775	2,500
287	4¢	orange	Used	6.25	11.75	17.50	25	47.50	120	525	1,500
			Unused OG	25	45	77.50	110	150	220	425	850
			Mint NH	50	105	220	330	475	725	2,000	11,000
288	5¢	dull	Used	6	11	17	25	45	120	450	1,100
		blue	Unused OG	22.50	42.50	70	100	135	210	415	850
			Mint NH	47.50	95	190	300	450	725	1,800	10,250
289	8¢	violet	Used	13.50	21	35	47.50	75	180	700	1,800
		brown	Unused OG	32.50	57.50	90	140	180	300	750	1,350
			Mint NH	75	145	265	430	650	1,325	5,000	19,500
290	10¢	gray	Used	8.50	15	24	35	50	165	650	1,800
		violet	Unused OG	30	62.50	92.50	140	180	275	465	1,025
			Mint NH	77.50	140	260	425	625	925	3,000	11,500
291	50¢	sage	Used	45	75	125	175	260	475	1,100	3,400
		green	Unused OG	150	280	450	600	725	1,000	1,625	4,000
			Mint NH	350	675	1,250	1,800	2,750	5,000	12,500	57,500
292	$1	black	Used	180	315	575	700	875	1,400	3,750	12,000
			Unused NG	215	400	575	850	925	1,025	1,175	1,325
			Unused OG	375	650	1,000	1,500	1,700	2,250	3,750	8,250
			Mint NH	800	1,450	2,450	3,750	5,750	8,750	20,000	75,000
293	$2	orange	Used	265	500	750	1,050	1,450	2,750	8,500	—
		brown	Unused NG	230	400	600	950	1,075	1,300	1,750	—
			Unused OG	475	825	1,275	1,900	2,250	2,900	5,500	17,000
			Mint NH	1,100	2,000	3,800	5,750	8,000	15,500	57,500	—
285-293		9 stamps	Used	527.05	953.25	1,550.50	2,067	2,847.50	5,330	16,175	23,175
Set			Unused OG	1,123.50	1,985.50	3,090.50	4,542.50	5,390	7,270	13,145	33,775
			Mint NH	2,530	4,672.50	8,537.50	12,940	18,960	33,440	103,325	189,250

1901 PAN-AMERICAN EXPOSITION ISSUE

SCT#	DENOM	COLOR	CONDITION	VG 50	F 70	F-VF 75	VF 80	VF-XF 85	XF 90	XF-SUP 95	SUP 98
294	1¢	green	Used	0.75	1.20	2.10	3	17.50	70	250	875
		& black	Unused OG	3.25	6.25	10	16	20.50	27.50	52.50	110
			Mint NH	6.50	14	25	40	57.50	110	325	1,300
294a	1¢	invert	Used	10,500	16,500	21,000	25,000	33,500	42,500		
			Unused OG	5,250	7,000	10,500	12,500	22,500	40,000		
			Mint NH	—	—	—	22,500		—		
295	2¢	carmine	Used	0.25	0.45	0.75	1	8	45	125	625
		& black	Unused OG	3.25	6	9.75	15	20	30	50	90
			Mint NH	7	14	23.50	37.50	55	105	350	1,000

SCT#	DENOM	COLOR	CONDITION	VG 50	F 70	F-VF 75	VF 80	VF-XF 85	XF 90	XF-SUP 95	SUP 98
295a	2¢	invert	Used	22,500	30,000	37,500	55,000	75,000	—		
			Unused OG	20,000	35,000	47,500	55,000	90,000	120,000	—	220,000
296	4¢	deep	Used	5	8.50	13.50	18	25	110	325	1,000
		red brown	Unused OG	16	30	50	70	80	100	170	325
		& black	Mint NH	30	67.50	110	170	220	400	1,000	4,750
296a	4¢	invert	Unused OG	30,000	55,000	72,500	85,000	175,000	600,000	—	—
297	5¢	ultramarine	Used	4.50	7.50	12	17	35	110	380	1,700
		& black	Unused OG	17.50	32.50	50	75	90	120	190	375
			Mint NH	30	75	120	180	230	375	1,100	3,750
298	8¢	brown	Used	12.50	22.50	37.50	50	77.50	125	500	1,750
		violet	Unused OG	20	45	62.50	90	105	140	225	400
		& black	Mint NH	42.50	97.50	150	230	300	475	1,150	3,750
299	10¢	yellow	Used	7.25	12	21	30	57.50	140	600	—
		brown	Unused OG	47.50	52.50	80	115	135	175	275	475
		& black	Mint NH	52.50	115	195	300	425	775	2,250	7,250
294-299		6 stamps	Used	30.25	52.15	86.85	119	220.50	600	2,180	5,950
Set			Unused OG	107.50	172.25	262.25	381	450.50	592.50	962.50	1,775
			Mint NH	168.50	383	623.50	957.50	1,287.50	2,240	6,175	21,800

1902-03 REGULAR ISSUE

SCT#	DENOM	COLOR	CONDITION	VG 50	F 70	F-VF 75	VF 80	VF-XF 85	XF 90	XF-SUP 95	SUP 98
300	1¢	blue	Used	0.25	0.25	0.25	0.25	8	25	100	300
		green	Unused OG	3	5.50	8.50	12	17.50	25	50	110
			Mint NH	6.50	13	20	30	45	80	240	775
300b	1¢	blue	Used			9,000	11,500				
Booklet		green	Unused OG	225	325	500	600	675	750	1,100	
Pane of 6			Mint NH	375	575	950	1,150	1,350	1,600	3,000	
301	2¢	carmine	Used	0.25	0.25	0.40	0.50	10	30	140	475
			Unused OG	3.75	6.50	10	15	19	26	47.50	105
			Mint NH	7.50	15	25	37.50	60	100	400	1,850
301c	2¢	carmine	Used	—	—	—	6,000				
Booklet			Unused OG	190	260	400	500	575	700	1,050	
Pane of 6			Mint NH	300	420	775	950	1,150	1,400	2,750	
302	3¢	bright	Used	1	1.90	2.80	3.75	14	65	210	650
		violet	Unused OG	13	22.50	37.50	55	67.50	82.50	150	325
			Mint NH	30	57.50	95	140	200	375	850	2,600
303	4¢	brown	Used	0.55	0.90	1.65	2.25	11.25	22.50	150	550
			Unused OG	12.50	25	40	55	67.50	90	150	325
			Mint NH	25	52.50	87.50	140	200	400	1,250	3,250
304	5¢	blue	Used	0.50	0.90	1.40	2	11	60	225	650
			Unused OG	14	27.50	42.50	60	75	100	150	350
			Mint NH	27.50	55	95	150	210	350	950	3,250
305	6¢	claret	Used	1.40	2.20	3.85	5.50	14.50	40	145	800
			Unused OG	14.75	27	40	60	75	95	175	350
			Mint NH	27.50	57.50	97.50	150	250	475	1,200	4,000
306	8¢	violet	Used	0.85	1.65	2.80	3.25	11.50	32.50	150	475
		black	Unused OG	10	20	32.50	45	55	67.50	125	260
			Mint NH	20	42.50	72.50	110	160	265	875	3,500
307	10¢	pale	Used	0.75	1.45	2	3	22.50	55	210	550
		red	Unused OG	13.50	27.50	40	60	75	100	180	400
		brown	Mint NH	25	57.50	100	150	230	350	1,250	4,500
308	13¢	purple	Used	2.50	4.50	7	10	17.50	67.50	210	675
		black	Unused OG	9	17.50	27	40	55	70	100	225
			Mint NH	17.50	37.50	62.50	100	160	275	850	2,400
309	15¢	olive	Used	2.60	4.50	8	12.50	22.50	55	210	800
		green	Unused OG	40	80	120	185	225	280	525	1,100
			Mint NH	100	200	325	475	725	1,250	3,700	11,000
310	50¢	orange	Used	8	15	22.50	35	47.50	110	325	—
			Unused OG	100	180	275	400	460	575	1,025	2,000
			Mint NH	250	500	800	1,150	1,650	2,250	8,500	27,000
311	$1	black	Used	22.50	40	62.50	90	115	215	550	1,050
			Unused NG	62.50	100	170	240	275	400	—	—
			Unused OG	145	290	410	600	650	800	1,275	2,250
			Mint NH	325	650	1,100	1,800	2,250	3,250	9,000	34,000
312	$2	dark	Used	47.50	85	135	190	285	450	1,200	3,250
		blue	Unused NG	82.50	155	225	325	370	465	700	—
			Unused OG	190	375	500	800	900	1,200	1,900	4,450
			Mint NH	450	950	1,600	2,500	3,500	5,750	16,500	—

SCT#	DENOM	COLOR	CONDITION	VG 50	F 70	F-VF 75	VF 80	VF-XF 85	XF 90	XF-SUP 95	SUP 98
313	$5	dark	Used	180	340	500	675	850	1,100	3,500	7,750
		green	Unused NG	190	345	550	750	825	900	1,000	—
			Unused OG	500	900	1,300	2,000	2,350	2,750	4,500	7,000
			Mint NH	1,100	2,200	3,650	6,250	8,250	14,000	—	—
300-313		14 stamps	Used	268.65	498.50	750.15	1,033	1,440.25	2,327.50	7,325	17,975
Set			Unused OG	1,068.50	2,004	2,883	4,387	5,091.50	6,261	10,352.50	19,250
			Mint NH	2,411.50	4,888	8,130	13,182.50	17,890	29,170	45,565	98,125
314	1¢	blue	Used	4.25	8	12.50	17.50	22.50	32.50	70	195
		green	Unused OG	3.25	6.50	9.50	14	16	19	25	40
			Mint NH	5.50	11	18.50	30	35	42.50	77.50	180
314A	4¢	brown	Used	21,500	33,500	45,000	50,000	57,500	75,000		
Sgl.			Unused OG	30,500	47,500	67,500	100,000	—	—		
			Mint NH				230,000	245,000			
314A	4¢	brown	Unused OG	—	122,500	177,500	250,000		500,000		
Pair											
314A	4¢	brown	Unused OG			375,000			460,000		
LP											
315	5¢	blue	Used	375	575	900	1,250	1,500	2,150	3,250	—
			Unused OG	55	130	210	300	340	400	475	650
			Mint NH	115	210	405	575	625	675	750	950
316	1¢	blue	Unused OG	—	—	160,000					
Sgl.		green									
316	1¢	blue	Unused OG	150,000	225,000	375,000					
Pair		green									
316	1¢	blue	Unused OG		325,000	500,000					
LP		green									
317	5¢	blue	Used	—	—	—	—	—	—		
Sgl.			Unused OG	2,250	—	—	6,000	11,500	26,500	—	
			Mint NH	—	—	—	12,000	—	—		
317	5¢	blue	Unused OG	6,000	9,500	12,500	15,000	18,000	25,000		
Pair			Mint NH	—	—	—	45,000	—	—		
317	5¢	blue	Unused OG			55,000	70,000				
LP			Mint NH			160,000					
318	1¢	blue	Unused OG	—	4,250	4,950	6,150	—	—		
Sgl.			Mint NH		9,500						
318	1¢	blue	Unused OG	4,200	6,250	8,000	11,000	12,000	14,000		
Pair		green									
318	1¢	blue	Unused OG			27,500	35,000				
LP		green									
319	2¢	carmine	Used	0.25	0.25	0.25	0.25	8	40	100	325
		type I	Unused OG	1.25	2.75	4.25	6	9	12.50	25	50
			Mint NH	2.70	5.75	9.50	15	27.50	45	250	950
319b	2¢	carmine	Used	0.25	0.25	0.30	0.40	9	25	125	325
		rose	Unused OG	3.15	6.75	10	15	17.50	22.50	40	100
		type I	Mint NH	7.50	17.50	30	45	70	100	800	1,750
319c	2¢	scarlet	Used	0.25	0.25	0.25	0.30	8	27.50	90	300
		type I	Unused OG	2.10	4.50	6.75	10	12.50	16	40	95
			Mint NH	4.25	9.50	16	25	50	125	900	—
319g	2¢	carmine	Used	165	250	340	450	525	675	—	
Booklet		type I	Unused OG	50	75	95	125	145	180	350	
Pane of 6			Mint NH	75	125	175	240	300	400	850	
319n	2¢	carmine	Used	275	400	525	700	850	1,100	—	
Booklet		rose	Unused OG	110	160	210	275	350	475	950	
Pane of 6		type I	Mint NH	160	220	335	500	725	1,000	2,750	
319p	2¢	scarlet	Used	225	325	455	625	750	1,000	—	
Booklet		type I	Unused OG	77.50	105	140	185	240	325	850	
Pane of 6			Mint NH	120	160	270	350	500	750	2,250	
319F	2¢	lake	Used	0.25	0.25	0.25	0.30	8	22.50	90	300
		type II	Unused OG	2.10	4.50	6.75	10	12.50	16	40	95
			Mint NH	4.25	9.50	16	25	45	70	425	1,750
319Fi	2¢	carmine	Used	12.50	22.50	35	50	70	110	275	—
		type II	Unused OG	13	27.50	45	65	78	97.50	165	—
			Mint NH	30	60	100	150	225	350	900	2,400
319Fj	2¢	carmine	Used	0.45	0.80	1.20	1.75	20	100	225	—
		rose	Unused OG	20	45	67.50	100	125	160	240	425
		type II	Mint NH	45	90	145	225	340	600	1,200	3,000
319Fk	2¢	scarlet	Used	0.75	0.90	1.50	2	7	15	50	150
		type II	Unused OG	15	30	47.50	70	85	115	210	350
			Mint NH	32.50	65	105	160	240	440	1,200	—
319Fh	2¢	carmine type II	Unused OG	360	550	675	900	1,100	1,250	2,000	
Booklet Pane of 6			Mint NH	500	825	1,150	1,500	1,750	2,400	4,500	
319Fq	2¢	lake	Used	320	450	625	800	950	1,150	—	
Booklet		type II	Unused OG	120	185	235	300	375	500	1,250	
Pane of 6			Mint NH	215	350	440	575	800	1,250	2,500	
320	2¢	carmine	Used	4.60	9	14	19	22.50	30	65	175
		type I	Unused OG	3.25	6.50	10	15	16.50	19	22.50	32.50
			Mint NH	6	12.50	21	32.50	37.50	45	67.50	140

SCT#	DENOM	COLOR	CONDITION	VG 50	F 70	F-VF 75	VF 80	VF-XF 85	XF 90	XF-SUP 95	SUP 98
320b	2¢	scarlet	Used	3.50	7	10	15	22.50	37.50	90	240
		type I	Unused OG	4.25	8	11.75	17.50	19	22.50	27.50	42.50
			Mint NH	7	14	22.50	37.50	42.50	50	90	165
320c	2¢	carmine	Used	11	18.50	27.50	42.50	52.50	67.50	120	310
		rose	Unused OG	15	32	47	75	80	90	105	140
		type I	Mint NH	25	58	100	150	165	180	200	325
320A	2¢	lake	Used	12	22	32.50	50	60	75	120	300
		type II	Unused OG	10	20	32.50	45	50	57.50	70	95
			Mint NH	18	37.50	65	100	115	135	180	325
320Ad	2¢	carmine	Used	—	—	—	—	—	—	—	—
		type II	Unused OG	27.50	55	97.50	135	175	—	—	—
			Mint NH	85	105	135	200	235	—	—	—
321	2¢	carmine	Unused OG		475,000	600,000	—				
Pair		type I									
322	2¢	carmine	Unused OG	2,650	4,250	5,500	7,000	8,250	10,000	12,500	16,000
Sgl.		type II	Mint NH	—	—	—	15,000	—	—		
322	2¢	carmine	Unused OG	7,750	11,750	14,500	17,500	20,000	25,000		
Pair		type II									
322	2¢	carmine	Unused OG				35,000				
LP		type II									

1904 LOUISIANA PURCHASE EXPOSITION ISSUE

SCT#	DENOM	COLOR	CONDITION	VG 50	F 70	F-VF 75	VF 80	VF-XF 85	XF 90	XF-SUP 95	SUP 98
323	1¢	green	Used	1.20	2.20	3.50	4.75	20	40	200	575
			Unused OG	5.50	10	15.50	22.50	30	40	85	180
			Mint NH	10.50	21	40	60	90	140	525	2,050
324	2¢	carmine	Used	0.50	1	1.40	2	12	32.50	140	475
			Unused OG	5.50	10	15.50	22.50	30	40	87.50	175
			Mint NH	10.50	21	40	60	90	140	500	1,950
325	3¢	violet	Used	7	11.50	19.50	27.50	50	115	280	900
			Unused OG	15	30	47.50	65	80	110	190	400
			Mint NH	30	65	105	170	225	450	1,250	3,650
326	5¢	dark	Used	6	10.25	15.50	22.50	42.50	90	250	700
		blue	Unused OG	16	32.50	50	70	85	120	210	475
			Mint NH	30	60	115	180	300	525	1,400	4,850
327	10¢	red	Used	7	11	20	27.50	47.50	97.50	325	950
		brown	Unused OG	30	60	82.50	125	160	240	350	700
			Mint NH	57.50	110	185	300	425	700	2,100	6,750
323-327		5 stamps	Used	21.70	35.95	59.90	84.25	172	375	1,195	3,600
Set			Unused OG	72	142.50	211	305	385	550	922.50	1,930
			Mint NH	138.50	277	485	770	1,130	1,955	5,775	19,250

1907 JAMESTOWN EXPOSITION ISSUE

SCT#	DENOM	COLOR	CONDITION	VG 50	F 70	F-VF 75	VF 80	VF-XF 85	XF 90	XF-SUP 95	SUP 98
328	1¢	green	Used	1.15	2.15	3.40	4.50	16	50	275	800
			Unused OG	5.75	11	16.50	27.50	45	75	180	350
			Mint NH	12	22.50	42.50	70	130	235	700	1,950
329	2¢	carmine	Used	1	1.85	2.90	4	15	50	240	650
			Unused OG	6	12	20	30	47.50	80	165	300
			Mint NH	13.25	24	48	80	140	375	3,250	12,000
330	5¢	blue	Used	7.50	13	20	30	55	125	400	1,150
			Unused OG	27.50	65	90	140	170	225	400	800
			Mint NH	52.50	110	175	350	475	1,000	3,000	11,500
328-330		3 stamps	Used	9.65	17	26.30	38.50	86	225	915	2,600
Set			Unused OG	39.25	88	126.50	197.50	262.50	380	745	1,450
			Mint NH	77.75	156.50	265.50	500	745	1,610	6,950	25,450

1908-09 WASHINGTON-FRANKLIN ISSUE (DOUBLE LINE WATERMARK)

SCT#	DENOM	COLOR	CONDITION	VG 50	F 70	F-VF 75	VF 80	VF-XF 85	XF 90	XF-SUP 95	SUP 98
331	1¢	green	Used	0.25	0.25	0.30	0.40	8	17.50	55	170
			Unused OG	1.50	2.80	4.65	6.25	8.25	11.50	22.50	65
			Mint NH	3.40	6.50	10.25	16	30	60	170	600
331a	1¢	green	Used	300	425	550	700	800	1,000	1,300	—
Booklet			Unused OG	70.50	89	115	150	190	250	525	—
Pane of 6			Mint NH	120	155	220	300	420	600	1,150	—
332	2¢	carmine	Used	0.25	0.25	0.25	0.35	8	20	60	180
			Unused OG	1.40	2.75	3.75	5.75	7.50	11	22.50	52.50
			Mint NH	2.80	5.50	9.25	14	25	37.50	160	500
332a	2¢	carmine	Used	210	290	390	500	600	800	1,050	—
Booklet			Unused OG	50	75	100	135	160	200	475	—
Pane of 6			Mint NH	75.50	120	170	240	340	490	1,250	—
333	3¢	deep	Used	0.75	1.40	2.10	3	12.50	32.50	125	425
		violet	Unused OG	6.25	13	18.50	27.50	35	45	80	225
			Mint NH	12.50	27.50	42.50	70	105	160	525	1,725
334	4¢	orange	Used	0.35	0.70	1.05	1.50	10	30	110	340
		brown	Unused OG	8	17	23.50	35	42.50	52.50	100	240
			Mint NH	15	32.50	55	87.50	130	200	700	2,400
335	5¢	blue	Used	0.55	1.05	1.55	2.25	9	27.50	110	325
			Unused OG	10	20	30	45	55	80	140	270
			Mint NH	20	42.50	70	110	175	260	925	2,500
336	6¢	red	Used	1.50	3	4.40	6	13.50	45	140	475
		orange	Unused OG	13.75	27.50	40	60	75	100	175	375
			Mint NH	25	52.50	90	140	200	350	1,000	3,600
337	8¢	olive	Used	0.70	1.25	2	2.75	9.25	32.50	120	375
		green	Unused OG	10	20.50	31.50	45	55	70	110	280
			Mint NH	20	42.50	70	110	175	260	925	2,900
338	10¢	yellow	Used	0.45	0.90	1.35	1.80	8	27.50	120	360
			Unused OG	15	32.50	45	67.50	80	95	160	380
			Mint NH	25	62.50	100	160	225	350	1,200	4,000
339	13¢	blue	Used	4.50	8	12	17.50	27.50	70	210	650
		green	Unused OG	8.50	15	25	37.50	45	60	110	250
			Mint NH	16	32.50	60	90	135	240	725	2,000
340	15¢	pale	Used	1.50	2.75	4.35	6	13.50	42.50	130	450
		ultramarine	Unused OG	15	27.50	42	65	75	95	170	370
			Mint NH	25	55	95	150	210	360	1,150	3,850
341	50¢	violet	Used	5	9.25	14	20	30	70	230	750
			Unused OG	67.50	130	180	275	350	450	725	1,550
			Mint NH	130	270	420	650	900	1,500	5,000	13,500
342	$1	violet	Used	22.50	40	62.50	90	120	210	700	2,150
		brown	Unused OG	110	210	300	450	550	725	1,275	2,500
			Mint NH	220	450	675	1,050	1,500	2,500	8,000	19,500
343	1¢	green	Used	1.20	2.40	3.50	5	6.50	10	32.50	75
			Unused OG	1	2	3	4.50	5.50	6.75	8	15
			Mint NH	1.60	3.60	5.75	9	11.50	17.50	30	60
344	2¢	carmine	Used	0.65	1.25	1.80	2.75	4.25	6.50	32.50	75
			Unused OG	1	2	3	4.50	5.50	6.75	8	15
			Mint NH	1.60	3.60	5.75	9	11.50	17.50	30	60
345	3¢	deep	Used	5	9	14.25	20	23.50	27.50	55	125
		violet	Unused OG	2.25	4	6	9	11	14	20	30
		type I	Mint NH	3.75	8	12	19	22.50	27.50	45	95
346	4¢	orange	Used	5.25	8.75	13.25	20	24	30	60	145
		brown	Unused OG	2.75	5.50	8.50	12.50	14	16	20	37.50
			Mint NH	4.50	8.75	15.50	25	30	37.50	65	140
347	5¢	blue	Used	8.25	13.75	21	32.50	37.50	50	95	210
			Unused OG	5.50	10.75	16.50	25	27.50	32.50	50	65
			Mint NH	8.25	17.50	30	50	55	62.50	115	230
348	1¢	green	Used	11	22.50	35	55	80	175	275	600
Sgl.			Unused OG	7	15	25	40	45	55	90	175
			Mint NH	12.25	26.50	50	80	100	125	225	500
348	1¢	green	Used	50	82.50	115	160	190	400	625	—
Pair			Unused OG	20	45	67.50	100	110	130	225	425
			Mint NH	30	80	150	225	260	325	500	1,200
348	1¢	green	Used	300	450	575	800	1,000	1,300	2,750	—
LP			Unused OG	105	165	220	300	350	435	650	975
			Mint NH	175	300	450	650	750	1,200	2,700	4,000
349	2¢	carmine	Used	32.50	62.50	87.50	150	225	375	575	—
Sgl.			Unused OG	20	45	65	100	120	150	250	500
			Mint NH	37.50	77.50	135	225	320	450	1,000	—
349	2¢	carmine	Used	115	190	250	400	650	1,150	1,750	—
Pair			Unused OG	60	115	165	260	305	390	625	1,075
			Mint NH	115	215	360	600	775	1,150	2,500	4,250
349	2¢	carmine	Used	550	700	975	1,300	1,750	2,750	—	—
LP			Unused OG	210	310	400	550	650	800	1,100	1,750
			Mint NH	375	650	925	1,350	1,825	2,250	4,650	10,000
350	4¢	orange	Used	77.50	105	160	240	375	775	1,500	—
Sgl.		brown	Unused OG	28	63	84	140	170	210	350	600
			Mint NH	55	120	185	325	475	750	2,000	3,250
350	4¢	orange	Used	300	400	550	750	1,150	1,950	—	—
Pair		brown	Unused OG	80	160	225	375	450	575	875	1,525
			Mint NH	150	335	550	900	1,250	2,000	6,000	8,500

SCT#	DENOM	COLOR	CONDITION	VG 50	F 70	F-VF 75	VF 80	VF-XF 85	XF 90	XF-SUP 95	SUP 98
350	4¢	orange	Used	1,600	2,200	2,900	4,000	5,000	6,500	12,000	—
LP		brown	Unused OG	425	625	850	1,175	1,375	1,650	3,250	5,000
			Mint NH	800	1,275	1,700	2,600	3,750	4,750	9,500	15,500
351	5¢	blue	Used	90	140	190	300	450	725	1,500	—
Sgl.			Unused OG	27.50	60	85	140	170	210	350	625
			Mint NH	50	120	190	325	450	675	1,500	2,950
351	5¢	blue	Used	250	385	575	825	1,200	1,850	3,850	—
Pair			Unused OG	85	175	250	400	450	525	875	1,400
			Mint NH	130	300	525	850	1,125	1,650	3,250	8,250
351	5¢	blue	Used	1,050	1,600	2,000	3,000	4,000	5,750	12,750	—
LP			Unused OG	400	575	775	1,075	1,250	1,500	1,900	2,700
			Mint NH	650	1,100	1,525	2,350	3,000	4,250	8,000	11,500
352	1¢	green	Used	60	110	150	225	325	550	1,150	—
Sgl.			Unused OG	21	42	60	100	115	175	300	550
			Mint NH	37.50	80	120	230	315	440	900	2,100
352	1¢	green	Used	180	300	425	650	950	1,500	3,750	—
Pair			Unused OG	55	110	160	250	320	450	750	1,175
			Mint NH	85	185	310	550	825	1,200	3,000	6,000
352	1¢	green	Used	550	875	1,150	1,650	2,250	3,250	6,500	—
LP			Unused OG	200	450	575	825	950	1,100	1,600	—
			Mint NH	425	875	1,200	1,800	2,750	3,850	8,000	—
353	2¢	carmine	Used	55	110	145	220	350	625	1,250	—
Sgl.			Unused OG	17.50	37.50	52.50	90	115	140	215	425
			Mint NH	30	70	100	200	275	400	1,250	—
353	2¢	carmine	Used	175	275	375	575	850	1,400	2,750	—
Pair			Unused OG	45	95	135	225	280	350	525	950
			Mint NH	80	170	275	500	800	1,100	3,250	—
353	2¢	carmine	Used	925	1,300	1,675	2,500	3,250	4,500	—	—
LP			Unused OG	300	400	475	750	900	1,250	2,000	2,750
			Mint NH	475	850	1,100	1,750	2,750	5,000	8,500	—
354	4¢	orange	Used	72.50	120	180	275	450	750	1,750	3,000
Sgl.		brown	Unused OG	40	87.50	120	200	250	325	450	1,100
			Mint NH	65	150	225	425	625	900	1,850	4,400
354	4¢	orange	Used	300	410	525	825	1,350	2,250	5,500	—
Pair		brown	Unused OG	90	200	300	475	550	775	1,100	1,900
			Mint NH	160	350	575	1,050	1,400	2,100	4,500	—
354	4¢	orange	Used	850	1,100	1,500	2,000	2,750	4,250	7,250	12,500
LP		brown	Unused OG	525	750	950	1,400	1,700	2,250	3,000	4,500
			Mint NH	900	1,375	1,850	3,000	4,250	6,000	12,500	—
355	5¢	blue	Used	70	110	175	300	450	725	1,550	3,850
Sgl.			Unused OG	42.50	85	125	210	250	300	450	850
			Mint NH	65	150	260	450	650	1,000	2,150	5,000
355	5¢	blue	Used	310	465	625	875	1,250	2,000	3,750	—
Pair			Unused OG	105	220	310	525	600	1,000	1,500	—
			Mint NH	180	375	575	1,100	1,500	3,250	7,750	—
355	5¢	blue	Used	1,250	2,000	2,800	4,000	5,250	7,000	—	—
LP			Unused OG	550	800	1,025	1,500	1,750	2,250	2,750	—
			Mint NH	975	1,500	2,000	3,250	4,500	7,250	12,000	—
356	10¢	yellow	Used	2,000	2,850	4,000	6,000	7,250	9,000	—	—
Sgl.			Unused OG	1,025	1,750	2,200	3,250	3,600	4,000	6,250	—
			Mint NH	2,000	3,000	5,250	8,000	9,250	11,750	—	
356	10¢	yellow	Used	4,250	6,500	9,000	15,000	18,500	22,500		
Pair			Unused OG	2,150	3,600	4,500	7,000	8,000	9,500	13,000	—
			Mint NH	—	—	—	17,500	—	25,000	30,000	
356	10¢	yellow	Used				29,000		one known		
LP			Unused OG	5,500	9,000	12,000	16,000	—	—		
			Mint NH			27,500	45,000				

1909 BLUISH PAPERS

SCT#	DENOM	COLOR	CONDITION	VG 50	F 70	F-VF 75	VF 80	VF-XF 85	XF 90	XF-SUP 95	SUP 98
357	1¢	green	Used	40	72.50	105	160	205	275	650	1,500
			Unused OG	20	40	62.50	90	105	130	225	425
			Mint NH	37	74	110	190	290	420	1,150	3,600
358	2¢	carmine	Used	37.50	67.50	97.50	150	190	260	600	1,500
			Unused OG	18	38	55	80	97.50	120	180	400
			Mint NH	30	62.50	100	170	260	450	1,650	4,250
359	3¢	deep	Used	3,500	5,500	7,250	12,500	14,250	17,250	—	—
		violet	Unused OG	450	900	1,225	1,800	2,150	2,500	3,500	6,500
		type I	Mint NH	750	1,600	2,500	4,000	6,000	8,500	18,500	—
360	4¢	orange	Unused OG	9,000	15,000	20,000	27,500	42,500	80,000	—	
		brown	Mint NH	—	40,000	60,000	80,000	110,000	—	—	
361	5¢	blue	Used	—	—	—	20,000	—	—		
			Unused OG	1,600	3,000	4,250	5,750	6,900	8,750	13,000	24,000
			Mint NH	4,500	7,500	10,000	14,500	20,000	32,500	55,000	—
362	6¢	red	Used	4,250	6,500	9,500	12,500	16,000	22,500	—	—
		orange	Unused OG	310	625	850	1,250	1,500	1,900	2,750	4,750
			Mint NH	675	1,300	2,150	3,000	4,500	7,000	14,500	37,500
363	8¢	olive	Unused OG	8,500	16,500	23,000	30,000	35,000	42,500	—	—
		green	Mint NH	—	—	—	85,000	—	—		
364	10¢	yellow	Used	2,750	5,000	7,000	10,000	12,000	15,000	22,500	—
			Unused OG	350	800	1,125	1,600	1,850	2,250	3,250	6,250
			Mint NH	650	1,500	2,750	4,000	6,000	8,750	19,000	—
365	13¢	blue	Used	1,200	1,950	2,850	4,000	4,500	5,500	10,000	—
		green	Unused OG	675	1,300	2,000	2,600	3,100	3,750	5,250	9,250
			Mint NH	1,050	2,300	4,000	6,000	9,000	13,500	30,000	—
366	15¢	pale	Used	3,750	6,750	9,750	12,500	14,000	16,500	—	—
		ultramarine	Unused OG	275	650	850	1,250	1,450	1,950	2,850	5,000
			Mint NH	500	1,200	1,900	3,000	4,500	7,000	14,500	—

1909 COMMEMORATIVES

SCT#	DENOM	COLOR	CONDITION	VG 50	F 70	F-VF 75	VF 80	VF-XF 85	XF 90	XF-SUP 95	SUP 98
367	2¢	carmine	Used	0.35	0.70	1.30	1.75	8.75	22.50	105	280
			Unused OG	1.05	1.80	2.70	4.50	6.50	12.50	35	65
			Mint NH	1.45	3.60	6.25	9.50	16	32.50	115	350
368	2¢	carmine	Used	4.25	8.50	12.75	19	22.50	32.50	75	170
		imperforate	Unused OG	2.25	4	7.50	12.50	15	22.50	40	52.50
			Mint NH	4	8.75	14.50	24	29	37.50	65	125
369	2¢	carmine	Used	60	115	160	225	300	475	950	2,750
		bluish	Unused OG	27.50	70	100	150	170	200	275	450
		paper	Mint NH	47.50	125	200	300	400	525	1,050	3,500
370	2¢	carmine	Used	0.40	0.80	1.30	2	9	27.50	80	310
			Unused OG	1.60	3.60	4.50	6.75	8	12	25	50
			Mint NH	3.25	6.50	9.50	15	30	55	115	325
371	2¢	carmine	Used	5	8.75	11.75	21	25	35	70	155
		imperforate	Unused OG	2.40	4.50	8.25	14	16	19	27.50	40
			Mint NH	4.75	10.50	18.50	30	35	45	75	125
372	2¢	carmine	Used	1	2	3.25	4.75	12.50	47.50	130	425
			Unused OG	1.65	4	6	10	14	20	35	60
			Mint NH	3	8	12	21	45	85	210	600
373	2¢	carmine	Used	7	12.50	18	27.50	32.50	45	85	180
		imperforate	Unused OG	3.80	8	12	20	22	24.50	32.50	45
			Mint NH	6	14	26	40	42.50	47.50	75	145

1910-11 WASHINGTON-FRANKLIN ISSUE (SINGLE LINE WATERMARK)

SCT#	DENOM	COLOR	CONDITION	VG 50	F 70	F-VF 75	VF 80	VF-XF 85	XF 90	XF-SUP 95	SUP 98
374	1¢	green	Used	0.25	0.25	0.25	0.25	10	20	50	150
			Unused OG	1.30	2.75	4.15	6	8	11	22.50	65
			Mint NH	2.90	6.50	9.25	14	25	47.50	140	500
374a	1¢	green	Used	150	240	315	400	500	650	1,150	—
Booklet			Unused OG	90	135	175	225	260	340	575	—
Pane of 6			Mint NH	130	190	270	375	450	650	1,250	—
375	2¢	carmine	Used	0.25	0.25	0.25	0.25	10	22.50	52.50	125
			Unused OG	1.30	2.75	4.60	6	8	11	22.50	60
			Mint NH	3	6.50	9.25	14	25	47.50	140	500
375a	2¢	carmine	Used	120	180	235	300	375	500	800	—
Booklet			Unused OG	50	75	97	125	155	200	375	—
Pane of 6			Mint NH	75	110	150	200	250	345	700	—
375b	2¢	lake	Unused OG	180	400	600	800	1,100	1,500	2,450	—
			Mint NH	325	725	1,200	1,750	2,450	3,500	—	—
376	3¢	deep	Used	0.45	0.90	1.40	2	12.50	35	100	375
		violet	Unused OG	4.25	8	12.50	18	22.50	27.50	57.50	125
		type I	Mint NH	7.50	16	26	40	62.50	100	275	1,100

SCT#	DENOM	COLOR	CONDITION	VG 50	F 70	F-VF 75	VF 80	VF-XF 85	XF 90	XF-SUP 95	SUP 98
377	4¢	brown	Used	0.25	0.45	0.65	1	11	27.50	90	300
			Unused OG	6	12.50	20	27.50	35	45	90	190
			Mint NH	11	24	42.50	65	90	160	400	1,150
378	5¢	blue	Used	0.30	0.40	0.60	0.75	4	22.50	85	290
			Unused OG	5.50	12.50	19	27.50	35	45	87.50	175
			Mint NH	11	24	42.50	65	95	160	475	1,450
379	6¢	red	Used	0.30	0.55	0.80	1.25	12.50	35	90	300
		orange	Unused OG	7.50	17.50	23.50	37.50	45	57.50	95	210
			Mint NH	15	32.50	50	85	115	170	480	1,600
380	8¢	olive	Used	4.50	8	11	15	25	70	225	575
		green	Unused OG	20	42.50	60	90	110	160	310	525
			Mint NH	37.50	80	130	200	290	425	1,100	4,500
381	10¢	yellow	Used	1.50	3.20	4.40	6	15	60	150	450
			Unused OG	20	40	60	85	100	125	225	450
			Mint NH	40	85	140	200	300	4,250	1,225	3,750
382	15¢	pale	Used	5.25	9	13.25	20	30	75	260	750
		ultramarine	Unused OG	50	100	150	225	260	375	525	1,000
			Mint NH	85	190	310	500	725	1,050	2,650	6,750
383	1¢	green	Used	0.60	1.10	1.85	2.75	6	21.50	42.50	100
			Unused OG	0.55	1.10	1.65	2.50	5.75	18	26.50	35
			Mint NH	0.90	2.10	3.15	5	10	18.50	27.50	47.50
384	2¢	carmine	Used	0.60	1	1.80	2.75	5.50	18.50	37.50	90
			Unused OG	0.85	1.50	2.60	4	8	20	30	—
			Mint NH	1.35	3.45	5.25	8	11.50	18.50	28.50	55
385	1¢	green	Used	11	18.50	28	50	82.50	140	350	925
Sgl.			Unused OG	10	20	30	45	55	70	105	175
			Mint NH	18	35	60	100	140	325	850	1,350
385	1¢	green	Used	70	125	175	250	325	500	950	—
Pair			Unused OG	22.50	50	70	110	130	160	225	375
			Mint NH	37.50	95	150	240	325	750	1,900	3,000
385	1¢	green	Used	340	450	650	850	1,000	1,500	2,900	—
LP			Unused OG	175	225	350	450	550	700	1,000	1,750
			Mint NH	325	425	750	1,000	1,300	1,800	4,000	8,500
386	2¢	carmine	Used	22.50	45	62.50	90	250	750	1,500	—
Sgl.			Unused OG	25	57.50	85	120	150	200	325	650
			Mint NH	47.50	100	165	260	375	675	1,550	4,250
386	2¢	carmine	Used	90	190	280	375	490	750	1,400	—
Pair			Unused OG	52.50	130	180	275	320	425	700	1,400
			Mint NH	100	230	390	600	900	1,750	4,000	9,000
386	2¢	carmine	Used	1,000	1,500	2,100	2,500	3,500	5,000	10,000	—
LP			Unused OG	485	850	1,150	1,600	1,850	2,250	5,250	—
			Mint NH	800	1,500	2,400	3,500	4,500	5,500	11,500	—
387	1¢	green	Used	27.50	55	77.50	140	210	360	725	1,500
Sgl.			Unused OG	40	90	130	190	240	310	575	950
			Mint NH	67.50	170	265	400	675	1,125	2,500	6,000
387	1¢	green	Used	140	240	310	425	950	2,250	3,500	—
Pair			Unused OG	100	230	325	475	600	800	1,250	2,150
			Mint NH	180	445	675	1,050	1,800	3,600	8,250	12,000
387	1¢	green	Used	825	1,350	2,000	2,500	3,250	4,500	7,500	—
LP			Unused OG	420	675	950	1,250	1,575	2,250	3,350	—
			Mint NH	625	1,250	1,675	2,500	3,750	6,250	13,500	—
388	2¢	carmine	Used	575	1,100	1,600	2,250	3,500	5,250	8,500	—
Sgl.			Unused OG	260	600	875	1,400	1,600	2,000	3,000	6,000
			Mint NH	425	1,150	2,000	3,250	5,000	7,750	14,000	19,000
388	2¢	carmine	Used	2,500	3,250	5,250	7,500	10,250	14,000	18,500	—
Pair			Unused OG	800	1,750	2,500	3,500	4,250	5,500	7,000	—
			Mint NH	1,250	3,250	4,750	7,500	12,000	17,500	—	—
388	2¢	carmine	Used			50,000					
LP			Unused OG	3,250	5,250	6,800	9,000	11,000	13,500	—	—
			Mint NH	—	—	14,500	24,000	—	—		
389	3¢	deep	Used	5,500	10,000	12,000	14,500	22,000	32,500	—	—
Sgl.		violet	Unused OG	—	110,000	—	—				
		type I	Mint NH		240,000						
389	3¢	deep violet	Used	—	42,500						
Pair		type I	Unused OG	170,000	240,000	340,000					
390	1¢	green	Used	3	5.50	9	14	22.50	35	85	220
Sgl.			Unused OG	1	2.15	3	4.50	9	20	37.50	55
			Mint NH	1.80	4.25	6.25	10	25	55	140	225
390	1¢	green	Used	12.50	22.50	32.50	45	65	115	225	400
Pair			Unused OG	2.25	5	7	10.50	20	45	85	125
			Mint NH	4	10	14.50	22	55	130	350	700
390	1¢	green	Used	30	65	85	125	200	350	1,200	—
LP			Unused OG	8.50	17.50	25	35	45	65	150	325
			Mint NH	12.50	30	50	72.50	90	175	400	1,000
391	2¢	carmine	Used	8	16	32.50	50	85	150	310	600
Sgl.			Unused OG	9	20	27.50	42.50	50	65	95	160
			Mint NH	14	37.50	55	90	135	225	525	1,000
391	2¢	carmine	Used	45	82.50	115	170	475	1,200	—	—
Pair			Unused OG	22.50	50	75	110	130	170	210	350
			Mint NH	40	100	155	240	350	500	950	2,100
391	2¢	carmine	Used	450	850	1,100	1,500	2,000	3,250	5,250	—
LP			Unused OG	75	140	180	260	300	375	500	800
			Mint NH	125	250	375	575	700	950	2,000	4,250
392	1¢	green	Used	9	16	30	50	72.50	125	300	525
Sgl.			Unused OG	5.50	12	16.50	27.50	35	42.50	60	110
			Mint NH	11	25	42.50	65	90	140	350	800
392	1¢	green	Used	40	70	100	145	225	425	700	1,200
Pair			Unused OG	13.50	30	45	67.50	80	110	150	250
			Mint NH	23.50	55	90	145	200	300	750	1,750
392	1¢	green	Used	150	280	375	500	675	1,000	1,900	3,000
LP			Unused OG	52.50	95	135	190	225	260	355	600
			Mint NH	85	180	265	400	475	700	1,500	3,000
393	2¢	carmine	Used	11	15	37.50	55	85	130	260	425
Sgl.			Unused OG	9.50	20	30	45	55	70	115	190
			Mint NH	19	42.50	67.50	105	140	215	450	1,000
393	2¢	carmine	Used	37.50	65	95	140	190	310	575	—
Pair			Unused OG	22.50	55	77.50	120	145	175	250	400
			Mint NH	40	105	155	260	325	475	1,000	2,200
393	2¢	carmine	Used	125	240	325	450	550	900	2,250	—
LP			Unused OG	75	150	210	300	350	425	575	975
			Mint NH	130	280	425	650	850	1,200	2,250	4,750
394	3¢	deep	Used	17.50	35	45	65	95	160	350	625
Sgl.		violet	Unused OG	13	30	42.50	60	75	100	150	250
		type I	Mint NH	21	57.50	85	135	190	275	600	1,100
394	3¢	deep	Used	50	100	140	200	275	425	850	—
Pair		violet	Unused OG	30	70	100	145	175	225	325	550
		type I	Mint NH	52.50	140	210	325	450	625	1,500	3,000
394	3¢	deep	Used	180	350	450	650	900	1,400	2,750	—
LP		violet	Unused OG	115	200	300	425	500	600	825	1,300
		type I	Mint NH	210	410	625	925	1,150	1,500	3,500	6,750
395	4¢	brown	Used	15	30	42.50	65	95	175	400	925
Sgl.			Unused OG	12.50	25	42.50	60	72.50	90	135	280
			Mint NH	20	52.50	87.50	135	185	250	600	1,250
395	4¢	brown	Used	57.50	95	140	190	275	430	850	2,150
Pair			Unused OG	30	65	100	140	170	220	320	600
			Mint NH	50	135	210	325	430	575	1,250	2,650
395	4¢	brown	Used	150	325	475	650	875	1,250	2,650	—
LP			Unused OG	100	225	320	475	550	650	875	1,500
			Mint NH	200	475	725	1,100	1,350	1,900	3,250	6,750
396	5¢	blue	Used	14	28	45	65	115	240	450	850
Sgl.			Unused OG	12.50	27.50	40	60	75	95	140	250
			Mint NH	21	60	87.50	135	175	250	525	1,000
396	5¢	blue	Used	45	90	135	190	275	550	1,100	2,250
Pair			Unused OG	32.50	72.50	105	160	175	225	350	550
			Mint NH	60	150	235	375	475	600	1,200	2,250
396	5¢	blue	Used	210	400	575	825	1,150	1,700	3,500	—
LP			Unused OG	120	225	310	425	500	600	825	1,300
			Mint NH	200	450	650	975	1,350	2,250	3,750	6,500

1913-15 PANAMA-PACIFIC EXPOSITION ISSUE

SCT#	DENOM	COLOR	CONDITION	VG 50	F 70	F-VF 75	VF 80	VF-XF 85	XF 90	XF-SUP 95	SUP 98
397	1¢	green	Used	0.45	0.90	1.30	2	10	40	100	280
			Unused OG	3.25	6.75	9.75	15	20	27.50	45	95
			Mint NH	7	12.50	20	35	55	90	180	550
398	2¢	carmine	Used	0.25	0.35	0.55	1	8	25	87.50	250
			Unused OG	3.75	7	11	16	20	27.50	45	95
			Mint NH	6.25	12.50	20	35	50	90	180	525
398a	2¢	carmine	Unused OG	425	850	1,100	1,500	2,000	2,750	3,250	4,500
		lake	Mint NH	625	1,250	1,825	2,500	3,250	4,500	6,000	
398b	2¢	lake	Used				3,000				
			Unused OG	—	2,650	4,000	5,250	6,400	7,250	12,000	16,500
			Mint NH		—	7,250	8,500	—			
399	5¢	blue	Used	2.50	5	7.50	10	22.50	60	180	600
			Unused OG	16	30	45	65	80	100	150	310
			Mint NH	30	57.50	95	150	210	300	675	1,650
400	10¢	orange	Used	5	10	14	20	35	90	225	775
		yellow	Unused OG	25	55	75	110	130	160	240	500
			Mint NH	42.50	105	165	250	350	490	850	2,600

SCT#	DENOM	COLOR	CONDITION	VG 50	F 70	F-VF 75	VF 80	VF-XF 85	XF 90	XF-SUP 95	SUP 98
400A	10¢	orange	Used	4.75	10	15	22.50	45	80	240	625
			Unused OG	32.50	72.50	110	175	220	300	450	775
			Mint NH	85	165	265	390	525	750	1,350	4,000
401	1¢	green	Used	1.75	3.50	4.75	7	15	45	190	475
			Unused OG	5.75	11.25	17	25	35	60	100	250
			Mint NH	10.25	21	40	60	80	125	350	1,000
402	2¢	carmine	Used	0.85	1.40	2	3	11	37.50	140	400
			Unused OG	15	32.50	45	65	77.50	100	140	300
			Mint NH	25	60	105	160	225	325	850	2,100
403	5¢	blue	Used	3.70	7	11	17.50	30	75	210	650
			Unused OG	35	77.50	105	150	170	200	320	600
			Mint NH	57.50	140	235	375	475	750	1,350	3,500
404	10¢	orange	Used	17.50	32.50	50	70	95	180	450	950
			Unused OG	150	330	450	650	725	825	1,250	2,100
			Mint NH	265	650	1,025	1,600	1,825	2,100	4,000	8,250
397-404 Set		9 stamps	Used	36.75	70.65	106.10	153	271.50	632.50	1,823	5,005
			Unused OG	286.25	622.50	867.75	1,271	1,477.50	1,800	2,740	5,025
			Mint NH	528.50	1,223.50	1,970	3,055	3,795	5,020	9,785	24,175

1912-14 WASHINGTON-FRANKLIN ISSUE

SCT#	DENOM	COLOR	CONDITION	VG 50	F 70	F-VF 75	VF 80	VF-XF 85	XF 90	XF-SUP 95	SUP 98
405	1¢	green	Used	0.25	0.25	0.25	0.25	4	30	65	150
			Unused OG	1.50	3	4.50	6.50	12	20	32.50	70
			Mint NH	3	6.25	9.50	15	25	42.50	130	400
405b Booklet Pane of 6	1¢	green	Used	22.50	40	55	75	90	110	300	—
			Unused OG	17.50	35	50	65	77.50	92.50	225	—
			Mint NH	30	60	85	110	140	180	500	—
406	2¢	carmine type I	Used	0.20	0.20	0.20	0.25	3.50	25	60	140
			Unused OG	1.50	3	4.50	6.50	9	12.50	25	70
			Mint NH	3	6.25	9.50	15	25	40	135	425
406a Booklet Pane of 6	2¢	dark carmine	Used	27.50	55	70	90	110	130	350	—
			Unused OG	17.50	35	50	65	77.50	92.50	225	—
			Mint NH	30	60	85	110	140	180	500	—
406c	2¢	lake type I	Used	—	—	—	6,000	7,250	—	—	
			Unused OG	600	1,100	1,500	2,000	2,400	3,000	—	—
			Mint NH	975	1,875	2,700	3,750	5,750	8,000	—	—
407	7¢	black type I	Used	4	6.50	9	14	24	65	200	600
			Unused OG	17.50	32.50	47.50	70	85	115	200	475
			Mint NH	30	57.50	95	150	210	325	1,000	3,400
408	1¢	green	Used	0.30	0.45	0.70	1	2.50	5	10	35
			Unused OG	0.25	0.40	0.60	1	6	15	19	25
			Mint NH	0.35	0.75	1.10	2	10	22.50	27.50	42.50
409	2¢	carmine type I	Used	0.35	0.55	0.85	1.20	6	10	17.50	37.50
			Unused OG	0.25	0.50	0.75	1.20	5	10	17.50	22.50
			Mint NH	0.40	0.85	1.25	2.40	3	5	12	35
410 Sgl.	1¢	green	Used	2.80	5.75	9	12.50	25	65	250	450
			Unused OG	1.50	2.75	4.25	6	10	15	25	50
			Mint NH	2.50	5	8.50	13	22.50	40	80	250
410 Pair	1¢	green	Used	10.25	21.50	30	42.50	95	165	450	900
			Unused OG	3.50	7	10	15	22.50	35	57.50	110
			Mint NH	5.25	14	21	32.50	50	85	180	575
410 LP	1¢	green	Used	23.50	50	72	100	200	475	1,450	—
			Unused OG	7.50	16	22.50	30	37.50	50	90	175
			Mint NH	12.50	32.50	45	65	90	140	325	550
411 Sgl.	2¢	carmine type I	Used	3.50	7.50	10.50	17.50	27.50	65	160	375
			Unused OG	2.40	4.75	7	10	14	22.50	40	70
			Mint NH	4.25	10	14.50	22.50	30	45	100	230
411 Pair	2¢	carmine type I	Used	17	37.50	54.50	75	135	275	625	—
			Unused OG	5.50	12	16.50	25	32.50	50	90	160
			Mint NH	9	22.50	37.50	55	75	135	275	900
411 LP	2¢	carmine type I	Used	59.50	110	150	190	300	460	1,300	—
			Unused OG	12.50	27.50	40	55	65	85	150	250
			Mint NH	22.50	60	85	125	160	240	425	900
412 Sgl.	1¢	green	Used	8	13.50	26.50	40	80	135	260	525
			Unused OG	5.75	12	17	25	30	37.50	60	100
			Mint NH	9	22.50	35	55	70	100	200	475
412 Pair	1¢	green	Used	21.50	42.50	87.50	130	200	325	650	1,250
			Unused OG	13.50	27.50	40	60	75	95	150	225
			Mint NH	22.50	60	87.50	130	170	240	475	1,100
412 LP	1¢	green	Used	57.50	120	170	250	375	600	1,050	2,000
			Unused OG	30	65	85	120	140	170	250	425
			Mint NH	55	120	180	260	325	425	850	1,700

SCT#	DENOM	COLOR	CONDITION	VG 50	F 70	F-VF 75	VF 80	VF-XF 85	XF 90	XF-SUP 95	SUP 98
413 Sgl.	2¢	carmine	Used	10	16.50	32.50	50	85	140	260	500
			Unused OG	13.50	30	45	60	72.50	90	145	240
			Mint NH	20	60	85	130	165	230	500	800
413 Pair	2¢	carmine	Used	21	35	67.50	100	185	400	1,000	—
			Unused OG	29	62.50	92.50	125	155	190	315	500
			Mint NH	43.50	125	175	260	400	500	1,200	3,000
413 LP	2¢	carmine	Used	72.50	160	260	325	500	900	—	—
			Unused OG	72.50	145	200	275	340	500	625	—
			Mint NH	100	275	390	575	750	1,400	2,650	4,750
414	8¢	pale olive green	Used	0.50	1	1.40	2	12.50	35	130	425
			Unused OG	8.50	19	27.50	37.50	45	55	110	250
			Mint NH	17.50	35	57.50	90	120	170	550	1,800
415	9¢	salmon red	Used	3.50	6.50	9.50	14	25	57.50	200	750
			Unused OG	11	21	35	47.50	57.50	75	130	250
			Mint NH	20	42.50	70	110	145	210	600	2,750
416	10¢	orange yellow	Used	0.25	0.30	0.55	0.80	8	35	95	310
			Unused OG	8.50	19	27.50	37.50	47.50	60	110	225
			Mint NH	17.50	35	57.50	90	125	200	600	1,675
416a	10¢	brown yellow	Unused OG	430	700	850	1,250	1,450	1,750	2,250	4,500
			Mint NH	700	1,250	1,825	2,750	3,600	5,500	—	—
417	12¢	claret brown	Used	1.25	2.40	3.60	5	11.50	40	150	500
			Unused OG	8.50	19	27.50	37.50	47.50	65	140	260
			Mint NH	17.50	35	57.50	90	125	200	625	1,850
418	15¢	gray	Used	1	2	3	4	15	40	130	500
			Unused OG	18	36.50	52.50	77.50	90	110	210	435
			Mint NH	32.50	67.50	110	175	220	325	750	2,150
419	20¢	ultramarine	Used	4.25	7.25	11.50	17.50	30	70	230	750
			Unused OG	45	82.50	115	175	205	250	450	800
			Mint NH	62.50	145	250	375	500	700	1,450	4,500
420	30¢	orange red	Used	4.25	7.25	11.50	17.50	30	110	300	850
			Unused OG	25	50	70	105	130	160	260	500
			Mint NH	40	87.50	145	230	325	425	1,250	3,000
421	50¢	violet	Used	5.50	10	18.50	27.50	45	110	325	925
			Unused OG	75	150	225	325	360	425	850	1,350
			Mint NH	115	300	490	725	925	1,450	4,000	10,000
422	50¢	violet	Used	4.50	9	15	25	40	105	300	900
			Unused OG	45	92.50	130	200	225	275	550	1,250
			Mint NH	67.50	200	300	450	625	950	2,750	9,000
423	$1	violet brown	Used	25	37.50	55	80	115	225	475	1,500
			Unused OG	105	200	310	450	500	575	950	1,800
			Mint NH	165	430	625	950	1,350	2,400	6,000	17,750

1914 COMPOUND PERFORATION ISSUES

SCT#	DENOM	COLOR	CONDITION	VG 50	F 70	F-VF 75	VF 80	VF-XF 85	XF 90	XF-SUP 95	SUP 98
423A	1¢	green	Used	2,700	4,350	5,500	7,500	9,000	11,500		
			Unused OG	6,250	9,500	14,000	19,000	—			
			Mint NH				—				
423B	2¢	rose red type I	Used	6,000	9,000	12,500	19,000	22,000	25,500		
			Unused OG				175,000		only one known		
423C	5¢	blue	Used	7,250	10,750	16,000	20,000	22,000	25,000		
423D	1¢	green	Used		7,000	9,000	14,000				
423E	2¢	rose red type I	Used			—			only one known		

1913-15 WASHINGTON-FRANKLIN ISSUE (SINGLE LINE WATERMARK)

SCT#	DENOM	COLOR	CONDITION	VG 50	F 70	F-VF 75	VF 80	VF-XF 85	XF 90	XF-SUP 95	SUP 98
424	1¢	green	Used	0.25	0.25	0.25	0.25	8	20	75	200
			Unused OG	0.55	1.10	1.55	2.25	3.40	7.50	20	40
			Mint NH	0.90	1.80	2.95	4.75	10.50	16.50	80	270
424d Booklet Pane of 6	1¢	green	Used	2	4.25	5.75	7.50	10	15	40	—
			Unused OG	1.25	2.50	3.80	5.25	6.50	8.50	20	—
			Mint NH	1.75	4	5.75	8.75	12.50	20	50	—
425	2¢	rose red type I	Used	0.25	0.25	0.25	0.25	8	20	75	200
			Unused OG	0.50	1	1.35	2.10	3.25	7.25	19	40
			Mint NH	0.75	1.75	2.70	4.25	9.50	15.50	77.50	260
425e Booklet Pane of 6	2¢	rose red type I	Used	7.50	14	19	25	35	50	130	—
			Unused OG	4.25	8.50	12.50	17.50	22.50	30	70	—
			Mint NH	7.50	13.50	20	30	47.50	70	145	—

SCT#	DENOM	COLOR	CONDITION	VG 50	F 70	F-VF 75	VF 80	VF-XF 85	XF 90	XF-SUP 95	SUP 98
426	3¢	deep	Used	0.30	0.60	0.90	1.25	8.25	20	100	325
		violet	Unused OG	3.50	6.50	9.25	14	17.50	25	50	130
		type I	Mint NH	6.50	13	21	32.50	50	75	325	950
427	4¢	brown	Used	0.25	0.35	0.60	0.90	8	17.50	100	300
			Unused OG	8	15	22.50	32.50	40	55	95	245
			Mint NH	13.25	30	52.50	75	110	175	575	1,600
428	5¢	blue	Used	0.25	0.35	0.60	0.90	8	17.50	100	300
			Unused OG	8	15	22.50	32.50	42.50	55	125	300
			Mint NH	13.25	30	52.50	75	115	170	550	1,950
429	6¢	red	Used	0.50	0.90	1.30	2	11.50	25	120	350
		orange	Unused OG	10.75	22.50	32.50	45	57.50	75	120	300
			Mint NH	18.50	42.50	70	105	160	210	775	2,150
430	7¢	black	Used	1.25	2.50	3.60	4.75	12	37.50	160	450
			Unused OG	18	37.50	55	80	95	125	210	500
			Mint NH	32.50	72.50	115	180	260	425	1,300	4,500
431	8¢	pale	Used	0.75	1.40	2	3	12.50	35	130	425
		olive	Unused OG	7.25	14.50	20	30	40	55	100	225
		green	Mint NH	12.25	27.50	45	72.50	110	210	675	1,850
432	9¢	salmon	Used	2.10	4	5.75	8	15.50	50	175	550
		red	Unused OG	9	20	27.50	40	50	65	115	290
			Mint NH	17.50	37.50	62.50	95	145	235	800	2,250
433	10¢	orange	Used	0.30	0.40	0.65	1	10	30	100	300
		yellow	Unused OG	9	20	27.50	40	52.50	72.50	115	290
			Mint NH	16.50	37.50	60	95	140	250	750	2,400
434	11¢	dark	Used	2	3.75	5.75	8	15	50	165	575
		green	Unused OG	5	10	13	20	27.50	37.50	75	180
			Mint NH	7.50	20	32	50	75	115	450	1,450
435	12¢	claret	Used	1.40	2.65	3.75	5.50	11	37.50	140	475
		brown	Unused OG	5.50	11	15	22.50	30	40	75	180
			Mint NH	9.25	25	35	60	90	150	525	1,400
435a	12¢	copper	Used	1.65	3.25	4.65	6.50	13	42.50	150	500
		red	Unused OG	7	13.75	19	27.50	35	45	85	200
			Mint NH	12.50	27.50	40	67.50	100	175	625	2,000
437	15¢	gray	Used	2	3.75	5.75	8	17.50	47.50	150	450
			Unused OG	26	52.50	77.50	110	130	170	290	700
			Mint NH	45	100	155	250	350	550	1,500	4,250
438	20¢	ultramarine	Used	1.75	3.50	5.25	7	15	45	145	450
			Unused OG	42.50	92.50	135	185	220	290	500	1,125
			Mint NH	72.50	175	280	425	575	950	2,650	6,000
439	30¢	orange	Used	5	9	13.50	20	32.50	70	225	725
		red	Unused OG	47.50	100	140	210	250	310	625	1,100
			Mint NH	77.50	200	310	475	675	950	3,250	9,000
440	50¢	violet	Used	5	9	13.50	20	32.50	70	250	900
			Unused OG	110	210	300	425	500	625	950	2,200
			Mint NH	180	400	625	1,000	1,300	1,800	4,500	10,500
441 Sgl.	1¢	green	Used	0.40	0.60	0.95	1.50	8.50	25	45	125
			Unused OG	0.25	0.45	0.70	1	7.50	22.50	40	65
			Mint NH	0.35	0.70	1.25	2	9	30	65	125
441 Pair	1¢	green	Used	1.75	3.70	5.25	7	22.50	100	225	375
			Unused OG	0.65	1.30	1.80	2.75	16	50	85	140
			Mint NH	0.90	2	3.50	5.75	20	65	140	275
441 LP	1¢	green	Used	10	22	29	40	60	125	400	700
			Unused OG	2	4	6	8	15	55	90	190
			Mint NH	4	7.75	12.50	17.50	30	70	375	650
442 Sgl.	2¢	carmine	Used	11	21	30	45	75	150	300	500
		type I	Unused OG	2.50	5	7	10	15	25	50	80
			Mint NH	4.25	8.50	14	22.50	32.50	55	115	225
442 Pair	2¢	carmine	Used	25	50	85	130	210	375	875	—
		type I	Unused OG	6	12	17	25	35	57.50	110	175
			Mint NH	10	20	35	55	75	125	250	475
442 LP	2¢	carmine	Used	82.50	140	215	300	500	900	1,750	—
		type I	Unused OG	15	30	42.50	60	80	125	200	325
			Mint NH	25	60	85	130	180	350	700	1,500
443 Sgl.	1¢	green	Used	10.50	20	30	45	80	150	275	525
			Unused OG	7.25	15	21	30	40	60	90	140
			Mint NH	11	25	42.50	65	85	130	250	450
443 Pair	1¢	green	Used	30	57.50	90	135	225	375	850	1,150
			Unused OG	17.50	35	50	75	95	140	200	310
			Mint NH	25	65	100	160	210	300	550	1,000
443 LP	1¢	green	Used	70	140	200	250	450	850	1,500	—
			Unused OG	37.50	80	110	155	180	250	425	625
			Mint NH	60	150	210	325	425	575	1,100	1,900
444 Sgl.	2¢	carmine	Used	8	13.50	25	40	70	140	275	475
		type I	Unused OG	12.50	25	35	50	62.50	80	140	240
			Mint NH	20	50	77.50	120	160	210	475	875
444 Pair	2¢	carmine	Used	27.50	55	85	125	200	375	725	1,000
		type I	Unused OG	27.50	57.50	80	120	150	225	325	625
			Mint NH	42.50	105	165	250	340	500	1,050	2,150
444 LP	2¢	carmine	Used	52.50	100	135	210	400	1,000	2,000	—
		type I	Unused OG	75	150	220	300	375	500	825	1,250
			Mint NH	125	280	425	650	850	1,500	2,750	4,500
444a Sgl.	2¢	lake	Used	600	1,100	1,500	2,000				
445 Sgl.	3¢	violet	Used	55	115	165	250	350	525	775	1,150
			Unused OG	45	100	150	210	260	375	525	1,000
			Mint NH	77.50	200	325	500	650	900	1,750	3,000
445 Pair	3¢	violet	Used	195	380	525	750	1,000	1,250	1,750	2,500
			Unused OG	120	250	345	500	625	775	1,100	1,750
			Mint NH	190	455	700	1,100	1,375	1,925	3,600	—
445 LP	3¢	violet	Used	700	1,500	2,000	2,750	3,750	4,750	9,500	—
			Unused OG	300	600	825	1,200	1,400	1,650	2,250	3,750
			Mint NH	500	1,100	1,650	2,600	3,250	4,250	8,000	13,000
446 Sgl.	4¢	brown	Used	27.50	65	90	150	200	300	650	1,200
			Unused OG	27.50	65	90	130	160	200	280	500
			Mint NH	32.50	110	185	280	350	500	1,050	2,250
446 Pair	4¢	brown	Used	70	165	250	425	550	800	1,500	—
			Unused OG	60	150	200	300	350	425	600	1,050
			Mint NH	85	260	425	650	825	1,100	2,250	4,750
446 LP	4¢	brown	Used	300	650	900	1,250	1,550	2,000	4,000	—
			Unused OG	165	350	490	700	825	950	1,300	2,100
			Mint NH	210	675	1,000	1,550	1,900	2,600	4,500	8,000
447 Sgl.	5¢	blue	Used	20	50	75	110	160	250	575	—
			Unused OG	9	22.50	35	45	55	70	110	225
			Mint NH	13.50	40	62.50	100	125	175	350	750
447 Pair	5¢	blue	Used	80	160	250	375	525	900	1,750	—
			Unused OG	19	50	75	105	130	175	275	500
			Mint NH	30	95	140	220	300	400	800	1,650
447 LP	5¢	blue	Used	250	500	700	950	1,225	1,600	3,500	—
			Unused OG	65	120	165	240	275	315	440	700
			Mint NH	80	250	365	525	675	850	1,650	3,000
448 Sgl.	1¢	green	Used	3.50	5.75	11	17.50	47.50	100	210	425
			Unused OG	1.80	3.65	5	7.50	9.50	14	25	45
			Mint NH	2.50	6	10	16	30	50	140	400
448 Pair	1¢	green	Used	10	20	32.50	50	130	250	525	1,100
			Unused OG	4.10	8.75	11.75	17.50	22.50	35	60	110
			Mint NH	7	17.50	27.50	40	70	115	325	900
448 LP	1¢	green	Used	42.50	87.50	165	250	375	700	1,100	—
			Unused OG	15	30	45	60	80	110	160	275
			Mint NH	22.50	57.50	85	125	250	500	1,200	—
449 Sgl.	2¢	red	Used	150	300	425	600	750	1,000	1,800	3,750
		type I	Unused OG	800	1,350	1,825	2,500	2,900	3,500	5,500	8,500
			Mint NH	1,550	2,750	3,750	5,500	6,500	8,250	13,000	—
449 Pair	2¢	red	Used	2,300	4,200	6,100	8,000	9,250	11,500	—	—
		type I	Unused OG	2,100	3,400	4,500	6,000	6,750	8,250	—	—
			Mint NH	4,000	7,000	10,000	12,500	14,500	18,500	—	—
449 LP	2¢	red	Used	8,500	15,000	19,000	25,000	32,500	—	—	—
		type I	Unused OG	5,000	7,250	10,000	13,500	15,000	17,750	—	—
			Mint NH	7,000	13,500	19,500	28,000	32,500	40,000	55,000	—
450 Sgl.	2¢	carmine	Used	3.75	7.50	15	25	57.50	100	210	375
		type III	Unused OG	3.10	6	8.50	12.50	16	22	35	55
			Mint NH	5	10.50	16.50	27.50	45	125	400	1,100
450 Pair	2¢	carmine	Used	7	17.50	39	70	150	300	625	925
		type III	Unused OG	7.50	15	21	30	40	52.50	80	125
			Mint NH	11	22.50	42.50	65	105	275	950	3,000
450 LP	2¢	carmine	Used	82.50	165	215	300	450	750	1,350	—
		type III	Unused OG	55	115	160	240	360	550	1,050	—
			Mint NH	90	190	380	550	1,650	2,500	—	—
452 Sgl.	1¢	green	Used	3	5.25	11.50	17.50	45	90	240	500
			Unused OG	2.50	4.75	6.75	10	12	15	22.50	40
			Mint NH	4	8	13.50	21	27.50	42.50	95	220
452 Pair	1¢	green	Used	10	18.50	37.50	55	125	250	525	—
			Unused OG	6.25	12.50	17	25	30	37.50	55	95
			Mint NH	10	22	35	55	65	95	225	450
452 LP	1¢	green	Used	40	80	135	200	375	625	975	—
			Unused OG	18	37.50	55	75	90	110	150	225
			Mint NH	32.50	72.50	100	160	200	275	475	850
453 Sgl.	2¢	carmine	Used	12.50	22.50	30	45	90	190	400	700
		rose	Unused OG	30	70	92.50	140	170	205	325	500
		type I	Mint NH	50	130	195	300	390	600	1,100	2,250
453 Pair	2¢	carmine	Used	27.50	50	90	140	225	425	900	1,600
		rose	Unused OG	67.50	150	205	300	375	450	700	1,050
		type I	Mint NH	110	270	410	625	825	1,700	2,600	4,750
453 LP	2¢	carmine	Used	125	250	400	600	850	1,250	2,500	—
		rose	Unused OG	180	350	500	675	825	1,025	1,400	2,100
		type I	Mint NH	280	625	975	1,450	2,000	2,800	5,500	—

SCT#	DENOM	COLOR	CONDITION	VG 50	F 70	F-VF 75	VF 80	VF-XF 85	XF 90	XF-SUP 95	SUP 98
454	2¢	red	Used	5.75	11.25	16	22.50	45	100	425	750
Sgl.		type II	Unused OG	16	35	47.50	70	80	92.50	130	225
			Mint NH	25	57.50	95	160	190	240	485	1,000
454	2¢	red	Used	15	27.50	45	70	120	225	525	—
Pair		type II	Unused OG	37.50	82.50	110	165	190	205	290	500
			Mint NH	57.50	140	230	360	425	550	1,100	2,100
454	2¢	red	Used	130	300	400	600	800	1,150	2,250	—
LP		type II	Unused OG	100	210	275	400	460	550	700	1,050
			Mint NH	150	425	575	850	1,050	1,500	2,500	—
455	2¢	carmine	Used	0.90	1.60	2.50	3.50	15	30	90	240
Sgl.		type III	Unused OG	2	4	5.50	8	12.50	25	40	60
			Mint NH	3.25	7	11.50	18	22.50	30	70	200
455	2¢	carmine	Used	7	13.50	19	27.50	75	250	500	—
Pair		type III	Unused OG	5	10	13	20	26.50	55	90	135
			Mint NH	7	17.50	26	42.50	50	70	150	450
455	2¢	carmine	Used	45	80	120	175	275	650	1,000	—
LP		type III	Unused OG	12	24	35	47.50	650	95	150	—
			Mint NH	19	47.50	72.50	105	150	230	500	1,650
456	3¢	violet	Used	40	80	120	170	240	360	900	1,400
Sgl.		type I	Unused OG	57.50	115	150	225	250	300	475	775
			Mint NH	87.50	200	325	500	600	750	1,600	3,150
456	3¢	violet	Used	130	325	440	650	775	1,100	2,650	3,200
Pair		type I	Unused OG	140	275	360	550	625	675	1,000	1,650
			Mint NH	200	475	725	1,150	1,400	1,800	3,500	6,500
456	3¢	violet	Used	875	1,500	2,000	3,000	3,250	4,000	8,500	—
LP		type I	Unused OG	325	650	875	1,250	1,350	1,500	2,000	3,250
			Mint NH	450	1,200	1,650	2,600	3,100	4,000	8,000	—
457	4¢	brown	Used	7.25	15	20	30	50	90	225	350
Sgl.			Unused OG	6.25	12	17.50	25	30	37.50	60	90
			Mint NH	10	21	35	55	70	95	175	390
457	4¢	brown	Used	27.50	47.50	70	95	155	250	575	1,050
Pair			Unused OG	15	30	42.50	60	70	85	125	190
			Mint NH	25	60	92.50	140	170	225	475	1,350
457	4¢	brown	Used	66	130	180	275	400	750	1,100	2,000
LP			Unused OG	40	85.50	105	160	185	215	330	480
			Mint NH	60	160	210	325	425	550	1,050	2,400
458	5¢	blue	Used	7	14	20	30	55	95	240	375
Sgl.			Unused OG	6.50	13.50	18.50	27.50	35	42.50	65	110
			Mint NH	9	22.50	37.50	60	77.50	115	225	475
458	5¢	blue	Used	22.50	45	65	95	170	300	600	1,250
Pair			Unused OG	16	32.50	45	67.50	85	100	150	240
			Mint NH	22.50	62.50	95	150	185	300	500	1,050
458	5¢	blue	Used	60	120	165	250	350	650	1,750	—
LP			Unused OG	40	80	110	160	185	220	275	475
			Mint NH	70	165	225	350	445	575	1,125	2,000
459	2¢	carmine	Used	425	750	900	1,300	1,450	1,600	2,250	—
Sgl.		type I	Unused OG	60	100	130	200	220	260	290	—
			Mint NH	85	165	195	300	325	360	400	500
459	2¢	carmine	Used	900	1,750	2,250	3,500	3,500	4,000	5,500	—
Pair		type I	Unused OG	130	210	275	425	460	550	600	—
			Mint NH	180	345	425	650	675	725	850	1,100
459	2¢	carmine type I	Unused OG	175	270	365	500	525	550	575	625
LP		with crease	Mint NH	240	400	600	875	925	975	1,025	1,200
		carmine	Used	—	—	—	50,000				
		type I	Unused OG	250	385	600	850	900	950	1,050	1,150
		without crease	Mint NH	300	550	1,025	1,500	1,575	1,700	1,900	3,350
460	$1	violet	Used	30	70	90	140	185	280	800	1,900
		black	Unused OG	165	325	425	650	725	825	1,250	2,200
			Mint NH	275	650	925	1,450	1,750	2,250	5,250	12,500
461	2¢	pale I	Used	140	200	290	375	500	1,100	—	—
		carmine red	Unused OG	40	75	100	150	180	215	350	925
		type 1	Mint NH	60	140	200	325	450	650	1,600	5,750

1916-22 WASHINGTON-FRANKLIN ISSUE (UNWATERMARKED)

SCT#	DENOM	COLOR	CONDITION	VG 50	F 70	F-VF 75	VF 80	VF-XF 85	XF 90	XF-SUP 95	SUP 98
462	1¢	green	Used	0.25	0.25	0.25	0.35	8	22.50	85	325
			Unused OG	1.75	3.50	4.75	7	9	12.50	32.50	85
			Mint NH	3	6.50	10	16	27.50	45	200	850
462a	1¢	green	Used	4.70	7.50	10	12.50	16.50	22.50	60	—
Booklet			Unused OG	3	5	7	9.50	12	15	30	—
Pane of 6			Mint NH	4.25	8.50	11.75	16	20	27.50	60	—
463	2¢	carmine	Used	0.25	0.25	0.30	0.40	9	22.50	75	300
		type I	Unused OG	1.10	2.20	3	4.50	11	17.50	35	72.50
			Mint NH	1.60	4	6.25	10	20	35	160	600
463a	2¢	carmine	Used	40	57.50	80	110	130	160	325	—
Booklet		type I	Unused OG	30	57.50	80	110	125	150	240	—
Pane of 6			Mint NH	40	85	120	180	210	250	450	—
464	3¢	violet	Used	5.50	8.25	12	17.50	30	72.50	225	675
		type I	Unused OG	16	32.50	50	65	80	100	180	425
			Mint NH	27.50	65	110	165	210	310	1,000	3,300
465	4¢	orange	Used	0.70	1.15	1.60	2.25	8	27.50	125	375
		brown	Unused OG	11	22.50	30	45	57.50	80	150	325
			Mint NH	18.50	42.50	65	105	160	225	675	2,000
466	5¢	blue	Used	0.65	1.15	1.60	2.25	8	30	125	375
			Unused OG	16	32.50	45	65	80	100	145	410
			Mint NH	27.50	60	100	150	235	375	1,250	4,500
467	5¢	carmine	Used	1,000	1,400	2,000	3,000	3,500	4,250	8,500	—
			Unused OG	90	190	290	425	475	575	825	—
			Mint NH	140	290	525	800	1,025	1,400	4,250	10,500
467	5¢	carmine	Used	—	2,200	2,800	3,500	3,900	4,750	—	—
Block			Unused OG	—	325	600	900	1,000	1,125	1,600	—
of 9			Mint NH	—	825	1,150	1,550	1,850	2,350	5,350	—
467	5¢	carmine	Used	—	2,800	3,700	5,000	5,700	7,150	—	—
Block			Unused OG	—	975	1,300	1,750	1,900	2,250	3,500	—
of 12			Mint NH	—	1,500	2,000	2,900	3,250	4,250	12,000	—
468	6¢	red	Used	2.20	4	5.50	8	16	55	200	600
		orange	Unused OG	17.50	40	57.50	80	100	135	240	525
			Mint NH	25	72.50	115	180	270	425	1,150	3,400
469	7¢	black	Used	3.25	6	9	13	22.50	65	225	675
			Unused OG	22.50	55	75	110	135	170	350	750
			Mint NH	40	97.50	155	250	350	500	1,450	3,650
470	8¢	olive	Used	1.75	3.50	5	7	15	47.50	160	550
		green	Unused OG	11	25	35	50	67.50	85	160	360
			Mint NH	20	45	72.50	115	160	250	850	2,150
471	9¢	salmon	Used	4.25	8.75	12.25	17.50	32.50	90	300	925
		red	Unused OG	12.50	27.50	37.50	55	70	95	160	380
			Mint NH	22.50	52.50	80	125	165	250	800	2,200
472	10¢	orange	Used	0.80	1.50	2.10	3	15	40	145	450
		yellow	Unused OG	22.50	50	67.50	100	120	155	240	575
			Mint NH	37.50	92.50	145	230	300	425	1,250	4,750
473	11¢	dark	Used	4.50	9.50	13.50	19	32.50	77.50	225	725
		green	Unused OG	9.50	21.50	30	42.50	50	70	125	260
			Mint NH	14	32.50	60	90	130	210	675	1,900
474	12¢	claret	Used	2	4	5.75	8	15	47.50	160	525
		brown	Unused OG	11	24	33.50	47.50	65	87.50	160	350
			Mint NH	18	45	70	110	190	325	1,100	3,250
475	15¢	gray	Used	3.50	8	10.50	15	27.50	65	200	650
			Unused OG	37.50	85	115	170	210	260	450	850
			Mint NH	62.50	155	240	375	525	800	2,250	6,250
476	20¢	ultramarine	Used	4.50	8.75	12.25	17.50	30	65	190	625
			Unused OG	47.50	100	135	200	230	300	550	1,100
			Mint NH	82.50	195	300	475	600	1,050	2,900	7,000
476A	30¢	orange	Unused OG	1,250	2,000	3,250	5,750				
		red	Mint NH	2,150	4,250	6,400	8,500				
477	50¢	light violet	Used	22.50	40	55	80	125	210	550	1,650
			Unused OG	190	425	600	850	975	1,125	1,500	3,000
			Mint NH	370	900	1,300	2,000	2,400	3,150	6,600	17,500
478	$1	violet black	Used	7	14	20	27.50	42.50	105	240	875
			Unused OG	140	300	415	600	675	775	1,075	2,150
			Mint NH	270	575	900	1,400	1,750	2,150	5,250	15,000
479	$2	dark blue	Used	9.50	21	28	40	57.50	95	325	750
			Unused OG	50	105	150	210	240	275	350	550
			Mint NH	77.50	180	310	475	600	800	1,400	2,750
480	$5	light green	Used	8.25	17.50	25	35	55	110	275	1,000
			Unused OG	35	85	115	170	190	215	265	475
			Mint NH	62.50	160	250	375	450	600	1,200	2,500
481	1¢	green	Used	0.30	0.45	0.75	0.95	1.75	5	9	35
			Unused OG	0.35	0.55	0.85	1.25	2.65	6.50	14.50	19.50
			Mint NH	0.30	0.75	1.25	1.90	6	12.50	22.50	32.50
482	2¢	carmine	Used	0.25	0.60	0.95	1.30	2.25	5.50	11	42.50
		type I	Unused OG	0.35	0.75	1.05	1.50	7.50	11.50	14.50	20
			Mint NH	0.50	1.05	1.70	2.60	7	13.50	24	35
482A	2¢	deep rose	Used	35,000	47,500	55,000	65,000	90,000	125,000	—	—
		type Ia									
482A	2¢	deep rose	Used	140,000							
Pair		type Ia									

SCT#	DENOM	COLOR	CONDITION	VG 50	F 70	F-VF 75	VF 80	VF-XF 85	XF 90	XF-SUP 95	SUP 98
483	3¢	violet	Used	2.50	5	7.25	10	12.50	19	40	100
		type I	Unused OG	2.75	5.75	8	12	14.50	18	27.50	37.50
			Mint NH	4	9	16	24	26	30	47.50	60
484	3¢	violet	Used	2.40	4	6	8	10	18	42.50	100
		type II	Unused OG	2.50	5	7.25	10	12.50	16	25	35
			Mint NH	3.35	7.75	12.75	20	23	27.50	45	57.50
485	5¢	carmine	Unused OG	2,700	4,800	6,450	9,000	9,500	10,000	—	—
			Mint NH	—	5,250	8,750	13,000	13,750	15,000	17,500	22,500
485	5¢	carmine	Unused OG	—	10,000	12,750	16,500	17,500	18,750	20,500	22,500
Block of 9			Mint NH	—	12,500	16,000	22,000	23,000	24,500	26,500	31,500
485	5¢	carmine	Unused OG	—	15,000	21,000	25,000	26,500	28,000	31,500	35,500
Block of 12			Mint NH	—	20,000	26,500	32,500	34,500	36,500	40,000	45,000
486	1¢	green	Used	0.40	0.45	0.65	0.85	9	15	40	125
Sgl.			Unused OG	0.25	0.45	0.55	0.85	2	5	20	40
			Mint NH	0.35	0.75	1.15	1.75	3.50	10	37.50	80
486	1¢	green	Used	0.75	1.40	1.85	2.50	27.50	45	125	350
Pair			Unused OG	0.50	1	1.45	2	4.50	12.50	42.50	85
			Mint NH	0.85	1.80	2.90	4.25	8	22.50	85	175
486	1¢	green	Used	3.75	7.50	10	15	32.50	85	200	350
LP			Unused OG	1.35	2.30	3.30	4.50	6.25	9	20	40
			Mint NH	2	4.50	6.50	9.50	17.50	45	130	300
487	2¢	carmine	Used	3	5.50	9.50	14	25	47.50	160	—
Sgl.		type II	Unused OG	3.25	6.25	8.25	12.50	15	22.50	35	70
			Mint NH	4.75	11	18	27.50	35	50	125	375
487	2¢	carmine	Used	8.50	17.50	25	37.50	70	130	375	—
Pair		type II	Unused OG	7	15	20	30	35	50	77.50	150
			Mint NH	11	26	42.50	65	85	120	300	900
487	2¢	carmine	Used	32.50	50	95	140	260	650	1,150	—
LP		type II	Unused OG	30	55	85	120	140	180	230	525
			Mint NH	50	125	175	275	385	525	1,500	2,100
488	2¢	carmine	Used	1.25	2.40	3.40	5	12.50	32.50	95	240
Sgl.		type III	Unused OG	0.70	1.50	2	3	6	12.50	30	65
			Mint NH	1.10	2.60	4.25	6.50	15	32.50	67.50	160
488	2¢	carmine	Used	4.25	8.50	11.50	17.50	35	95	240	600
Pair		type III	Unused OG	1.90	4	5.25	8	15	27.50	65	140
			Mint NH	3	7	11.50	17.50	35	70	175	550
488	2¢	carmine	Used	32.50	62.50	87.50	110	225	450	750	—
LP		type III	Unused OG	11	20	27.50	40	62.50	90	125	275
			Mint NH	15	30	60	90	150	240	550	950
489	3¢	violet	Used	0.55	1.10	1.50	2.25	5	19	65	150
Sgl.		type I	Unused OG	1.05	2.20	3	4.50	8	14	20	35
			Mint NH	1.80	4	6.50	10	15	25	60	150
489	3¢	violet	Used	2.10	4.50	6	9	17.50	60	225	575
Pair		type I	Unused OG	2.40	5.25	7	10.50	17.50	32.50	45	75
			Mint NH	4	9	14	22.50	35	60	145	350
489	3¢	violet	Used	11.50	19	30	40	70	300	850	—
LP		type I	Unused OG	8	17	22	32.50	45	60	90	175
			Mint NH	14.50	32.50	45	70	120	250	800	1,250
490	1¢	green	Used	0.25	0.30	0.50	0.60	2.40	15	60	120
Sgl.			Unused OG	0.25	0.25	0.35	0.50	3	12.50	25	40
			Mint NH	0.25	0.45	0.70	1.05	12.50	25	45	130
490	1¢	green	Used	0.55	1.35	1.50	2.25	6.75	35	130	260
Pair			Unused OG	0.30	0.65	0.80	1.25	6.50	27.50	55	85
			Mint NH	0.45	1.05	1.75	2.60	27.50	30	100	300
490	1¢	green	Used	2.75	4	8.25	12.50	50	140	325	—
LP			Unused OG	0.95	1.60	2.40	3.25	8	16	35	70
			Mint NH	1.60	3.25	5	7	12.50	30	150	350
491	2¢	carmine	Used	350	475	650	800	875	1,000	1,400	2,350
Sgl.		type II	Unused OG	750	1,250	1,925	2,500	3,000	3,500	4,250	6,000
			Mint NH	1,300	2,650	3,800	5,250	8,500	22,500	—	—
491	2¢	carmine	Used	1,250	2,000	2,750	3,750	4,500	6,000	9,500	—
Pair		type II	Unused OG	2,000	2,900	4,600	5,750	6,700	8,000	10,000	14,750
			Mint NH	3,850	7,200	9,500	12,500	18,500	45,000	—	—
491	2¢	carmine	Used	6,500	10,500	16,000	20,000	29,500	—	—	—
LP		type II	Unused OG	3,700	6,500	9,250	13,000	14,500	17,000	22,000	—
			Mint NH	7,250	13,000	19,000	26,000	35,000	—	—	—
492	2¢	carmine	Used	0.30	0.50	0.70	1	5	22.50	75	145
Sgl.		type III	Unused OG	2.25	4.50	6	9	11	14	25	47.50
			Mint NH	3.50	7.75	12	19	26	37.50	100	375
492	2¢	carmine	Used	1	2.25	3.50	5	20	70	175	300
Pair		type III	Unused OG	5.25	10.50	14.50	21.50	25	35	60	110
			Mint NH	8	18	30	45	55	85	225	800
492	2¢	carmine	Used	11.50	17.50	25	35	70	165	350	—
LP		type III	Unused OG	16	30	37.50	55	65	80	110	210
			Mint NH	25	57.50	75	115	140	350	575	—
493	3¢	violet	Used	1	2.25	3.20	4.50	12.50	42.50	120	325
Sgl.		type I	Unused OG	3.25	7	9.25	14	17	21	32.50	60
			Mint NH	5.50	12.50	19	30	40	55	140	300

SCT#	DENOM	COLOR	CONDITION	VG 50	F 70	F-VF 75	VF 80	VF-XF 85	XF 90	XF-SUP 95	SUP 98
493	3¢	violet	Used	3.30	6.25	8	12.50	32.50	115	275	700
Pair		type I	Unused OG	9	17.50	24	35	40	47.50	72.50	130
			Mint NH	12.50	32.50	45	75	100	120	310	625
493	3¢	violet	Used	22.50	32.50	62.50	90	160	400	925	—
LP		type I	Unused OG	37.50	55	80	110	125	140	200	350
			Mint NH	50	105	140	230	290	400	800	1,650
494	3¢	violet	Used	0.55	1.25	1.90	2.50	10	35	110	450
Sgl.		type II	Unused OG	2.30	5	6.50	10	12	16	27.50	55
			Mint NH	3.75	9	13.50	21.50	29	40	105	210
494	3¢	violet	Used	2.25	4.50	6.25	9	22.50	75	230	950
Pair		type II	Unused OG	5	12	16	24	32.50	42.50	70	135
			Mint NH	9	22.50	35	50	67.50	90	250	750
494	3¢	violet	Used	5.50	11	15	22.50	45	175	—	—
LP		type II	Unused OG	20	40	50	75	90	120	180	325
			Mint NH	32.50	75	105	160	225	290	950	1,600
495	4¢	orange	Used	1.75	3.50	4.90	7	25	80	160	450
Sgl.		brown	Unused OG	2.40	5	6.50	10	12	15	25	50
			Mint NH	3.75	9	13.50	21.50	29	42.50	100	375
495	4¢	orange	Used	5.25	10	15	20	60	200	425	975
Pair		brown	Unused OG	5.50	12	16	24	30	37.50	60	110
			Mint NH	9	22.50	32.50	50	70	100	225	850
495	4¢	orange	Used	11.25	22.50	32.50	45	75	180	375	750
LP		brown	Unused OG	20	37.50	55	75	90	110	170	325
			Mint NH	32.50	75	105	160	225	325	675	1,300
496	5¢	blue	Used	0.65	1.25	1.70	2.50	12.50	35	190	475
Sgl.			Unused OG	0.80	1.60	2.20	3.25	7	14	26	50
			Mint NH	1.20	3	4.50	7	11	20	45	140
496	5¢	blue	Used	2.20	3.90	5.50	10	40	85	260	500
Pair			Unused OG	1.90	4	5.25	8	17.50	32.50	60	110
			Mint NH	3	6	11	17.50	27.50	50	120	325
496	5¢	blue	Used	5.50	11	15	22.50	37.50	115	350	525
LP			Unused OG	8.50	17.50	21.50	30	37.50	47.50	60	115
			Mint NH	12.50	30	40	65	90	135	275	600
497	10¢	orange	Used	3.75	8.25	11.50	17.50	35	95	225	525
Sgl.		yellow	Unused OG	4.25	8.25	12	17.50	20	27.50	40	65
			Mint NH	6	13	23.50	35	42.50	60	115	300
497	10¢	orange	Used	14	27.50	40	57.50	100	250	525	1,250
Pair		yellow	Unused OG	9	20	27.50	40	45	62.50	90	150
			Mint NH	14.25	35	57.50	85	105	150	275	650
497	10¢	orange	Used	50	80	150	200	290	475	725	1,550
LP		yellow	Unused OG	32.50	5	92.50	120	130	145	160	260
			Mint NH	50	120	185	260	300	375	625	950

1917-19 WASHINGTON-FRANKLIN ISSUE (PERF. 11)

SCT#	DENOM	COLOR	CONDITION	VG 50	F 70	F-VF 75	VF 80	VF-XF 85	XF 90	XF-SUP 95	SUP 98
498	1¢	green	Used	0.25	0.25	0.25	0.25	8	17.50	70	180
			Unused OG	0.25	0.25	0.25	0.35	1.75	8	17.50	30
			Mint NH	0.25	0.35	0.50	0.75	4	15	70	200
498e	1¢	green	Used	0.60	1.10	1.50	2	2.50	3.50	12.50	—
Booklet			Unused OG	0.80	1.40	1.90	2.50	4	6.50	11	—
Pane of 6			Mint NH	1.10	2.10	3	4.25	6.50	10.75	30	—
498f	1¢	green	Used				12,500				
Booklet			Unused OG	300	650	825	1,050	1,175	1,450	2,000	—
Pane of 30			Mint NH	400	850	1,225	1,700	2,000	2,500	3,750	—
499	2¢	rose	Used	0.25	0.25	0.25	0.25	8	17.50	70	190
		type I	Unused OG	0.25	0.25	0.25	0.35	1.75	8	17.50	30
			Mint NH	0.25	0.35	0.50	0.75	4	15	85	300
499e	2¢	rose	Used	0.80	1.50	1.90	2.50	3.75	6	17.50	—
Booklet		type I	Unused OG	0.95	2.20	3	4	5.75	8	17.50	—
Pane of 6			Mint NH	1.25	3.10	4.50	6.75	10	15	40	—
499f	2¢	rose type I	Unused OG	7,250	12,750	16,750	20,000	—	—	—	
Booklet Pane of 30			Mint NH	13,000	21,500	24,000	29,000	—	—	—	
499h	2¢	lake	Used	320	480	600	800	—	—	—	—
		type I	Unused OG	130	275	375	500	625	825	1,600	—
			Mint NH	200	460	650	1,000	1,300	1,900	—	—
500	2¢	deep	Used	85	140	180	240	275	400	1,100	2,650
		rose	Unused OG	62.50	125	170	250	275	340	525	1,000
		type Ia	Mint NH	100	250	365	550	700	1,050	2,350	5,250
501	3¢	light	Used	0.25	0.25	0.30	0.40	9	20	75	225
		violet	Unused OG	2.25	4.50	6	9	11.50	16	32.50	70
		type I	Mint NH	3.50	8.50	12.50	20	35	55	145	475

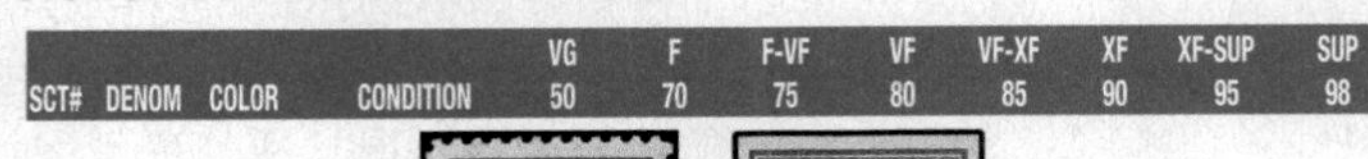

SCT#	DENOM	COLOR	CONDITION	VG 50	F 70	F-VF 75	VF 80	VF-XF 85	XF 90	XF-SUP 95	SUP 98
501b	3¢	light	Used	30	50	62.50	80	95	125	175	—
Booklet		violet	Unused OG	25	40	55	75	85	110	220	—
Pane of 6		type I	Mint NH	35	67.50	95	125	160	210	425	—
502	3¢	dark	Used	0.20	0.35	0.50	0.75	9	22.50	95	300
		violet	Unused OG	3	6	8	12	15	20	42.50	90
		type II	Mint NH	4.50	12	18.50	27.50	42.50	70	275	1,050
502b	3¢	dark	Used	25	45	57.50	75	85	100	190	—
Booklet		violet	Unused OG	18	35	45	60	72.50	85	160	—
Pane of 6		type II	Mint NH	27.50	52.50	72.50	100	120	150	300	—
503	4¢	brown	Used	0.25	0.25	0.30	0.40	8	20	80	270
			Unused OG	2.10	4.25	6	8.50	10.25	13.50	27.50	65
			Mint NH	3.50	8.50	12.50	19	30	47.50	190	450
504	5¢	blue	Used	0.25	0.25	0.25	0.35	8	20	80	250
			Unused OG	1.75	3.75	4.90	7.50	9.50	12.50	25	55
			Mint NH	3	7.50	11	17	27.50	50	180	525
505	5¢	rose	Used	225	350	475	600	900	1,250	2,250	5,750
			Unused OG	100	170	235	325	360	400	550	900
			Mint NH	135	300	440	625	775	1,000	1,750	3,750
505	5¢	rose	Used	475	650	875	1,100	1,300	1,650	—	—
Block			Unused OG	250	350	490	650	700	825	1,550	—
of 9			Mint NH	305	625	750	1,000	1,100	1,250	2,750	—
505	5¢	rose	Used	1,200	1,900	2,400	3,000	3,500	4,000	—	—
Block			Unused OG	450	750	925	1,200	1,350	1,500	2,100	—
of 12			Mint NH	575	1,075	1,400	1,850	2,000	2,250	3,250	—
506	6¢	red	Used	0.25	0.25	0.30	0.40	8	20	80	270
		orange	Unused OG	2.75	5.50	7.25	11	13	17.50	30	70
			Mint NH	4.75	11	16.50	25	35	50	165	600
507	7¢	black	Used	0.30	0.60	0.90	1.25	11	25	90	325
			Unused OG	5.25	12.25	16.50	24	30	40	85	160
			Mint NH	10	21	37.50	55	80	125	350	1,250
508	8¢	olive	Used	0.25	0.30	0.45	0.65	9	22.50	90	300
		bister	Unused OG	2.75	5.50	7.25	11	13	17.50	30	80
			Mint NH	4.75	11	16.50	25	35	50	175	600
509	9¢	salmon	Used	0.35	0.80	1.15	1.60	10	25	90	325
		red	Unused OG	2.75	5.50	7.25	11	14	20	40	85
			Mint NH	4.75	11	16.50	25	37.50	57.50	175	550
510	10¢	orange	Used	0.25	0.25	0.25	0.25	8	17.50	75	260
		yellow	Unused OG	3.75	7.50	10	15	18	22.50	42.50	95
			Mint NH	6	13.50	21.50	34	52.50	110	375	825
510a	10¢	brown	Unused OG	375	800	1,075	1,400	1,600	1,900	—	—
		yellow	Mint NH	725	1,450	2,150	3,250	4,000	5,250	—	—
511	11¢	light	Used	0.60	1.15	1.60	2.25	8	27.50	90	325
		green	Unused OG	1.75	3.75	5.25	7.50	9	11	25	55
			Mint NH	3.50	7.50	11.25	17	30	45	135	425
512	12¢	claret	Used	0.25	0.25	0.30	0.40	9	20	80	260
		brown	Unused OG	1.75	3.75	5.25	7.50	9	11	25	55
			Mint NH	3	7.50	11.25	17	27.50	45	150	450
512a	12¢	brown	Used	0.25	0.25	0.40	0.50	9	22.50	85	270
		carmine	Unused OG	2.10	4.25	6	8.50	11	15	30	100
			Mint NH	3.50	8.50	12.50	19	30	50	135	475
513	13¢	apple	Used	1.50	2.75	4	5.50	12.50	40	130	500
		green	Unused OG	2.10	4.50	6.75	9.50	11.50	15	35	70
			Mint NH	3.75	9.50	13.25	21	32.50	65	200	575
514	15¢	gray	Used	0.40	0.70	0.95	1.40	9.50	30	110	375
			Unused OG	8	16.50	22.50	32.50	40	55	100	215
			Mint NH	13	30	50	75	105	150	500	1,000
515	20¢	light	Used	0.25	0.25	0.30	0.45	9	22.50	100	280
		ultramarine	Unused OG	9	20	27.50	40	50	65	130	245
			Mint NH	14.50	35	55	85	120	190	500	1,250
516	30¢	orange	Used	0.45	0.75	1.10	1.50	9	25	95	325
		red	Unused OG	6.50	13.75	19	27.50	35	47.50	100	220
			Mint NH	11.50	25	45	65	95	125	450	1,000
517	50¢	red	Used	0.25	0.35	0.50	0.75	9	22.50	100	325
		violet	Unused OG	11	22.50	30	45	52.50	65	120	270
			Mint NH	18	47.50	70	110	135	165	475	1,000
518	$1	violet	Used	0.45	0.75	1.15	1.50	10	25	110	340
		brown	Unused OG	8.25	19	25	37.50	45	55	110	190
			Mint NH	15	35	60	95	110	140	500	1,500
518b	$1	deep	Used	600	1,075	1,250	1,800	2,250	3,000	5,750	—
		brown	Unused OG	900	1,650	1,900	2,900	3,500	4,250	7,000	—
			Mint NH	1,250	3,000	4,000	6,500	7,500	8,750	16,500	—
519	2¢	carmine	Used	675	1,100	1,400	1,800	2,200	2,750	4,750	—
			Unused OG	110	215	285	425	475	600	850	1,550
			Mint NH	190	425	600	900	1,300	1,850	3,500	8,000
523	$2	orange	Used	75	120	170	240	300	425	850	1,750
		red	Unused OG	115	250	335	500	575	650	775	1,250
		& black	Mint NH	200	460	725	1,100	1,300	1,650	3,000	7,250
524	$5	deep	Used	8	16	20	30	42.50	67.50	170	350
		green	Unused OG	40	80	110	160	185	230	320	525
		& black	Mint NH	60	145	210	340	400	500	950	2,450

1918-20 OFFSET ISSUES

SCT#	DENOM	COLOR	CONDITION	VG 50	F 70	F-VF 75	VF 80	VF-XF 85	XF 90	XF-SUP 95	SUP 98
525	1¢	gray	Used	0.25	0.45	0.65	0.90	9	22.50	100	325
		green	Unused OG	0.60	1.20	1.70	2.50	8	15	30	45
			Mint NH	1.10	2.45	3.95	6	10	19	85	375
525a	1¢	dark	Used	0.40	0.85	1.25	1.75	10	25	100	325
		green	Unused OG	2.25	5	6.75	10	12.50	20	37.50	52.50
			Mint NH	4.25	8.25	15	25	35	50	140	575
526	2¢	carmine	Used	1.10	2	2.75	4	11	35	125	400
			Unused OG	5.50	12.50	16	25	30	37.50	62.50	125
			Mint NH	9.25	22.50	35	57.50	95	160	525	1,500
527	2¢	carmine	Used	0.30	0.60	0.85	1.25	9	25	90	300
		type V	Unused OG	4.05	9	12.50	18	22.50	28	45	90
			Mint NH	6.75	18	26	40	62.50	110	350	1,100
528	2¢	carmine	Used	0.25	0.25	0.25	0.40	8	17.50	75	250
		type	Unused OG	1.90	4	5.50	8	12.50	25	32.50	45
		Va	Mint NH	3.50	8.75	12.75	20	30	50	190	550
528A	2¢	carmine	Used	0.50	1	1.40	2	10	30	95	300
		type VI	Unused OG	10.75	23.50	31.50	47.50	55	62.50	95	200
			Mint NH	18.50	42.50	72.50	115	160	240	825	2,250
528B	2¢	carmine	Used	0.25	0.35	0.50	0.75	9	22.50	95	300
		type VII	Unused OG	4.45	9.75	13.25	20	25	30	50	100
			Mint NH	8.25	18	32.50	50	72.50	125	400	1,250
529	3¢	violet	Used	0.25	0.25	0.30	0.50	9	17.50	75	250
		type III	Unused OG	0.80	1.70	2.35	3.50	7	17.50	30	45
			Mint NH	1.45	3	5	7.75	12.50	40	175	525
530	3¢	purple	Used	0.25	0.25	0.25	0.30	8	16	70	240
			Unused OG	0.45	1	1.20	2	5	15	25	40
			Mint NH	0.80	1.60	3	4.50	7.50	16	80	330
531	1¢	green	Used	2.50	4	7.50	12	15	20	50	125
			Unused OG	2.25	4	7.25	12	14.50	18	21	30
			Mint NH	3.50	6.50	11.75	21	22.50	25	40	85
532	2¢	carmine	Used	9.75	15.50	25.50	42.50	47.50	55	105	230
		rose	Unused OG	6.75	14.50	22.50	37.50	41.50	46	55	85
		type IV	Mint NH	8.75	22.50	42.50	70	75	85	130	260
533	2¢	carmine	Used	42.50	60	92.50	150	165	190	260	600
		type V	Unused OG	17.50	45	75	110	120	135	145	160
			Mint NH	22.50	65	100	175	190	210	260	450
534	2¢	carmine	Used	2.60	5.50	8.25	15	20	30	55	110
		type Va	Unused OG	3	6.50	9.75	15	17.50	22.50	30	45
			Mint NH	3.30	9.50	14.50	26	30	37.50	65	135
534A	2¢	carmine	Used	9.50	16	24	40	45	55	100	210
		type VI	Unused OG	8.50	17	23	40	42.50	47.50	57.50	85
			Mint NH	11.50	26	47.50	75	85	95	140	280
534B	2¢	carmine	Used	575	750	1,075	1,500	1,600	1,750	1,900	2,500
		type VII	Unused OG	625	900	1,350	2,000	2,100	2,250	2,450	2,800
			Mint NH	1,100	1,600	2,500	3,750	4,000	4,250	4,600	5,500
535	3¢	violet	Used	1.50	3	4.25	6	9.50	15	40	90
		type IV	Unused OG	2	4	6.50	10	12.50	16	25	37.50
			Mint NH	2.95	6.75	10.75	18	20	22.50	35	72.50
536	1¢	gray	Used	11.50	16.50	22.50	35	50	82.50	180	—
		green	Unused OG	4.25	8.75	12.50	20	24	30	45	90
			Mint NH	7.25	16	26	45	67.50	120	375	1,175

1919-21 ISSUES

SCT#	DENOM	COLOR	CONDITION	VG 50	F 70	F-VF 75	VF 80	VF-XF 85	XF 90	XF-SUP 95	SUP 98
537	3¢	violet	Used	0.75	1.60	2.10	3.25	11	30	100	240
			Unused OG	2.40	5	7	10	12	15	20	40
			Mint NH	3.75	8	13.25	20	27.50	35	105	280
537a	3¢	deep	Used	725	1,750	2,200	3,000	3,300	3,650	—	—
		red	Unused OG	525	1,250	1,450	2,250	2,650	3,000	—	—
		violet	Mint NH	950	2,300	3,100	4,250	4,500	5,000	—	—
537b	3¢	light	Used	12.50	25	37.50	50	75	140	280	—
		reddish	Unused OG	32.50	75	90	150	180	225	310	440
		violet	Mint NH	52.50	145	180	300	400	525	1,275	—

SCT#	DENOM	COLOR	CONDITION	VG 50	F 70	F-VF 75	VF 80	VF-XF 85	XF 90	XF-SUP 95	SUP 98
537c	3¢	red	Used	15	30	42.50	60	85	150	290	550
		violet	Unused OG	45	100	130	200	225	275	375	525
			Mint NH	67.50	185	250	400	500	625	1,350	—
538	1¢	green	Used	2.25	4.50	6	9	17.50	50	185	500
			Unused OG	2.25	5	6.25	10	12	16	25	50
			Mint NH	4.15	9.25	14.75	23	32.50	60	190	675
539	2¢	carmine	Used	10,000	17,500	22,500	30,000	—			
		rose	Unused OG	1,800	2,700	3,500	5,650	6,650	8,250	—	—
		type II	Mint NH	2,750	4,250	7,000	11,000	14,500	18,500	—	—
540	2¢	carmine	Used	2.50	4.75	6.75	9.50	20	55	200	550
		rose	Unused OG	2.75	6	7.75	12	14	17.50	30	55
		type III	Mint NH	4.50	11	18.50	27.50	37.50	70	260	925
541	3¢	violet	Used	9.25	18.50	25	37.50	60	150	400	1,250
		type II	Unused OG	9	20	27.50	40	47.50	60	92.50	180
			Mint NH	16	37.50	65	100	145	220	750	2,350
542	1¢	green	Used	0.35	0.70	1	1.50	10	25	90	275
			Unused OG	2.90	6.75	8.50	12.50	16	22.50	32.50	62.50
			Mint NH	5.25	11	20	30	47.50	72.50	260	850
543	1¢	green	Used	0.25	0.25	0.25	0.40	8	19	72.50	200
			Unused OG	0.25	0.35	0.45	0.70	1.25	3	7.50	15
			Mint NH	0.40	0.60	1.20	1.75	10	25	75	250
544	1¢	green	Used	2,750	3,500	4,750	6,500	7,750	11,000	18,000	—
			Unused OG	—	22,500	31,000	40,000	—	—	—	—
			Mint NH	—	35,000	60,000	87,500	100,000	—	—	—
545	1¢	green	Used	57.50	100	140	200	260	380	950	2,250
			Unused OG	40	85	115	170	215	260	425	750
			Mint NH	80	160	280	450	575	875	2,250	8,500
546	2¢	carmine	Used	55	95	125	190	230	350	900	2,150
		rose	Unused OG	22.50	45	70	105	125	155	250	450
		type III	Mint NH	40	82.50	150	230	310	525	1,500	5,250
547	$2	carmine	Used	8.75	17.50	24	35	50	85	190	375
		& black	Unused OG	25	55	75	110	125	150	300	475
			Mint NH	42.50	90	160	240	310	400	725	2,350
547a	$2	lake	Used	8.75	17.50	24	35	50	85	190	375
		& black	Unused OG	42.50	95	135	190	225	270	375	650
			Mint NH	70	140	270	400	500	650	1,750	3,750
548	1¢	green	Used	0.50	1	1.35	2	14	32.50	95	325
			Unused OG	0.85	1.80	2.50	3.75	8	15	27.50	47.50
			Mint NH	1.50	3.25	5.75	9.25	14	30	140	425
549	2¢	carmine	Used	0.40	0.80	1.10	1.60	13.50	27.50	95	375
		rose	Unused OG	1.15	2.50	3.35	5	9	17.50	30	55
			Mint NH	2.10	4.15	7.50	12	25	50	175	625
550	5¢	deep	Used	3.50	6.75	9	12.50	27.50	60	200	625
		blue	Unused OG	6	15	20	30	35	45	90	150
			Mint NH	8.75	25	42.50	65	95	170	425	1,500

1922-25 REGULAR ISSUE

SCT#	DENOM	COLOR	CONDITION	VG 50	F 70	F-VF 75	VF 80	VF-XF 85	XF 90	XF-SUP 95	SUP 98
551	½¢	olive	Used	0.25	0.25	0.25	0.25	8	20	95	200
		brown	Unused OG	0.25	0.25	0.25	0.25	2	8	15	25
			Mint NH	0.25	0.25	0.30	0.50	2	10	40	140
552	1¢	deep	Used	0.25	0.25	0.25	0.25	8	20	70	200
		green	Unused OG	0.25	0.60	0.90	1.25	1.65	3.50	10	25
			Mint NH	0.35	1.10	1.85	2.75	6.50	14	55	230
552a	1¢	deep	Used	1.25	2.30	3	4	5	6	15	—
Booklet		green	Unused OG	2.40	4.40	5.75	7.50	9.50	12.50	22.50	—
Pane of 6			Mint NH	3.30	6.50	9	12.50	16	22.50	675	—
553	1½¢	yellow	Used	0.25	0.25	0.25	0.25	8	17.50	70	200
		brown	Unused OG	0.50	1	1.40	2	2.65	7	17.50	45
			Mint NH	0.70	1.80	2.90	4.10	8	15	62.50	230
554	2¢	carmine	Used	0.25	0.25	0.25	0.25	8	20	70	200
			Unused OG	0.25	0.50	0.75	1.10	1.75	3	12.50	25
			Mint NH	0.40	1	1.65	2.50	6	15	55	225
554c	2¢	carmine	Used	0.90	1.75	2.25	3	3.60	4.50	12	—
Booklet			Unused OG	2.20	4.15	5.50	7	9.25	12.50	25	—
Pane of 6			Mint NH	3.25	7	9.25	12	16	24	70	—
555	3¢	violet	Used	0.30	0.60	0.85	1.20	9	22.50	87.50	290
			Unused OG	3	6	8.75	13	16.50	21	35	80
			Mint NH	4.50	11	18.50	27.50	40	65	235	650
556	4¢	yellow	Used	0.25	0.25	0.35	0.50	9	17.50	67.50	215
		brown	Unused OG	4	8	11	16	20	25	45	105
			Mint NH	6	14	22.50	35	55	77.50	275	900
557	5¢	dark	Used	0.25	0.25	0.25	0.30	8	20	70	225
		blue	Unused OG	4	8	11	16	20	26.50	45	100
			Mint NH	6	14	22.50	35	55	85	225	900
558	6¢	red	Used	0.25	0.50	0.70	1	10	22.50	85	275
		orange	Unused OG	7.50	13	20	30	35	42.50	65	150
			Mint NH	9.50	22.50	42.50	65	85	125	300	1,250
559	7¢	black	Used	0.25	0.35	0.50	0.75	11	20	80	240
			Unused OG	1.75	3.75	5.25	7.25	9	11	20	45
			Mint NH	2.75	6.25	10.25	15.50	25	40	85	310
560	8¢	olive	Used	0.25	0.50	0.70	1	9	22.50	85	275
		green	Unused OG	8.50	19	25	37.50	45	57.50	75	200
			Mint NH	13.50	30	50	80	100	150	360	1,250
561	9¢	rose	Used	0.30	0.65	0.90	1.25	11	24	90	300
			Unused OG	2.50	5.50	7.25	11	13.50	16	27.50	55
			Mint NH	4.75	9.50	16	25	35	60	150	475
562	10¢	orange	Used	0.25	0.25	0.25	0.35	9	19	70	210
			Unused OG	3.50	6.75	9.50	13.50	16	20	37.50	90
			Mint NH	5.25	12	20	30	42.50	75	190	775
563	11¢	light	Used	0.25	0.25	0.40	0.60	10	17.50	70	225
		blue	Unused OG	0.25	0.65	0.85	1.25	1.95	4.15	10	17.50
			Mint NH	0.50	1	1.80	2.75	5.50	20	65	240
563a	11¢	light	Used	0.25	0.25	0.40	0.60	10	17.50	70	225
		bluish	Unused OG	0.25	0.65	0.85	1.25	1.95	4.15	10	17.50
		green	Mint NH	0.50	1	1.80	2.75	5.50	16	55	220
564	12¢	brown	Used	0.25	0.25	0.25	0.35	9	17.50	67.50	200
		violet	Unused OG	1.15	2.35	3.40	4.75	6.50	10	17.50	32.50
			Mint NH	1.60	4.40	6.75	10.50	16	27.50	80	275
565	14¢	blue	Used	0.25	0.45	0.65	0.90	10	20	85	275
			Unused OG	1.05	2.15	2.90	4.25	6	9	14	32.50
			Mint NH	1.40	3.85	6	9.50	15	27.50	75	240
566	15¢	gray	Used	0.25	0.25	0.25	0.30	9	17.50	65	210
			Unused OG	4	8	10.50	16	20	25	45	95
			Mint NH	6	14	22.50	35	47.50	72.50	180	675
567	20¢	carmine	Used	0.25	0.25	0.25	0.30	9	17.50	70	220
		rose	Unused OG	4	8	10.50	16	19	24	47.50	97.50
			Mint NH	6	14	22.50	35	47.50	80	190	825
568	25¢	yellow	Used	0.25	0.35	0.50	0.75	10	20	90	250
		green	Unused OG	3.25	6.75	9	13.50	16.50	21.50	45	90
			Mint NH	5	12.50	18.50	30	40	75	190	725
569	30¢	olive	Used	0.25	0.25	0.35	0.60	9	18	75	230
		brown	Unused OG	5.50	11.25	15	22.50	27.50	35	50	135
			Mint NH	8.50	20	35	50	70	120	260	800
570	50¢	lilac	Used	0.25	0.25	0.30	0.40	9	20	65	260
			Unused OG	7	16.50	22.50	32.50	37.50	47.50	75	160
			Mint NH	11	27.50	47.50	70	85	115	300	825
571	$1	violet	Used	0.25	0.30	0.50	0.80	11.50	35	110	325
		brown	Unused OG	7.50	17.50	23.50	35	40	50	80	150
			Mint NH	10.75	27.50	47.50	75	85	115	210	775
572	$2	deep	Used	2.25	4.50	6.50	9	15	37.50	115	375
		blue	Unused OG	12.50	27.50	37.50	55	65	80	120	250
			Mint NH	17.50	50	70	120	140	180	300	675
573	$5	carmine	Used	3.75	7.50	10.50	15	20	42.50	150	450
		& blue	Unused OG	20	45	67.50	90	100	125	150	275
			Mint NH	30	67.50	110	180	200	245	390	950
573a	$5	carmine	Used	7.50	15	21	30	40	60	175	525
		lake &	Unused OG	42.50	82.50	120	175	200	230	275	370
		dark blue	Mint NH	70	165	250	350	400	475	750	1,450
551-573		23 stamps	Used	11.35	18.95	25.95	36.35	229.50	508.50	1,903	5,850
Set			Unused OG	102.20	218	304.20	439.60	523	672.15	1,059	2,280
			Mint NH	152.20	365.65	597	940.60	1,211.50	1,809	4,272.50	14,340
575	1¢	green	Used	0.90	2	3.25	5	7	9	27.50	75
			Unused OG	0.85	1.90	3.35	5	5.50	6	7	11
			Mint NH	1.30	3.15	6.75	11	12.50	16	25	57.50
576	1½¢	yellow	Used	0.30	0.70	1	1.50	2.50	5	12.50	50
		brown	Unused OG	0.25	0.60	0.85	1.25	1.60	2	3.75	6.50
			Mint NH	0.40	1	1.80	2.70	4	6	12.50	32.50
577	2¢	carmine	Used	0.25	0.60	0.85	1.25	2.25	4	11.50	45
			Unused OG	0.25	0.55	0.85	1.30	1.70	2.25	4.25	7
			Mint NH	0.40	1.10	1.80	2.90	4.25	6.50	14	25

1923 COIL WASTE ISSUES (PERF. 11X10)

SCT#	DENOM	COLOR	CONDITION	VG 50	F 70	F-VF 75	VF 80	VF-XF 85	XF 90	XF-SUP 95	SUP 98
578	1¢	green	Used	55	85	120	160	200	275	800	—
			Unused OG	17.50	37.50	52.50	75	87.50	105	175	340
			Mint NH	25	57.50	100	150	200	290	825	2,750
579	2¢	carmine	Used	40	75	100	140	185	260	775	2,000
			Unused OG	16	35	47.50	70	85	100	165	315
			Mint NH	21	52.50	92.50	140	200	260	750	2,500

1923-25 REGULAR ISSUE (PERF. 10)

SCT#	DENOM	COLOR	CONDITION	VG 50	F 70	F-VF 75	VF 80	VF-XF 85	XF 90	XF-SUP 95	SUP 98
581	1¢	green	Used	0.25	0.40	0.55	0.75	9	20	85	260
			Unused OG	2.25	5	6.75	10	13	20	40	95
			Mint NH	3.25	8.50	13.50	21	32.50	47.50	210	750
582	1½¢	brown	Used	0.25	0.30	0.50	0.65	9	19	80	250
			Unused OG	1.20	3	4.10	6	8.75	12	25	52.50
			Mint NH	2	5.25	8.50	13	21.50	32.50	150	525
583	2¢	carmine	Used	0.25	0.25	0.25	0.30	8	17.50	50	200
			Unused OG	0.65	1.45	2	3	4.65	7	14	30
			Mint NH	1	2.50	4	6.25	10	20	85	360
583a	2¢	carmine	Used	47.50	95	120	150	185	240	350	—
Booklet			Unused OG	35	60	85	110	135	150	300	—
Pane of 6			Mint NH	45	105	145	200	240	300	675	—
584	3¢	violet	Used	0.65	1.50	2.20	3	12.50	30	115	380
			Unused OG	6.50	13.50	18.50	27.50	40	55	95	175
			Mint NH	11	22.50	38.50	60	87.50	135	450	1,075
585	4¢	yellow	Used	0.25	0.30	0.45	0.65	10	20	75	260
		brown	Unused OG	4.25	8.75	12.50	17.50	22.50	35	62.50	145
			Mint NH	7	15	23.50	37.50	55	77.50	250	825
586	5¢	blue	Used	0.25	0.25	0.25	0.40	10	20	65	200
			Unused OG	4.25	8.75	12.50	17.50	22.50	35	62.50	145
			Mint NH	7	15	23.50	37.50	55	90	350	1,000
587	6¢	red	Used	0.25	0.25	0.40	0.60	10	20	70	240
		orange	Unused OG	2.20	4.50	6.50	9.25	12.50	20	35	90
			Mint NH	3.50	7.50	12.50	20	35	55	250	800
588	7¢	black	Used	1.55	3.20	4.50	6.25	15	50	160	475
			Unused OG	3	6.25	8.25	12.50	17.50	25	45	100
			Mint NH	4.50	10	16.50	26	42.50	65	275	950
589	8¢	olive	Used	1	2.30	3.30	4.50	12.50	35	135	420
		green	Unused OG	6.75	13.50	17.50	27.50	37.50	50	90	180
			Mint NH	10	24	36	57.50	82.50	120	350	1,250
590	9¢	rose	Used	0.60	1.20	1.80	2.50	12.50	30	110	350
			Unused OG	1.40	3	4.25	6	9	12.50	30	75
			Mint NH	2.20	5	8	12.50	21	32.50	150	625
591	10¢	orange	Used	0.25	0.25	0.30	0.50	9	18	65	230
			Unused OG	9	20	27.50	40	55	75	130	250
			Mint NH	13	32.50	50	85	110	150	325	1,200
581-591		11 stamps	Used	5.55	10.20	14.50	20.10	117.50	279.50	1,010	3,265
Set			Unused OG	41.45	87.70	120.35	176.75	242.90	346.50	629	1,338
			Mint NH	64.45	147.75	234.50	376.25	552.50	825	2,845	9,360

1923 COIL AND SHEET WASTE ISSUES (PERF. 11)

SCT#	DENOM	COLOR	CONDITION	VG 50	F 70	F-VF 75	VF 80	VF-XF 85	XF 90	XF-SUP 95	SUP 98
594	1¢	green	Used	7,000	10,500	15,000	22,500	42,500	82,500		
			Unused NG	20,000	35,000	—	—				
			Unused OG	—	65,000						
595	2¢	carmine	Used	105	200	300	375	450	575	1,500	3,750
			Unused OG	65	120	170	240	260	290	450	825
			Mint NH	90	190	300	450	625	875	2,000	7,000

SCT#	DENOM	COLOR	CONDITION	VG 50	F 70	F-VF 75	VF 80	VF-XF 85	XF 90	XF-SUP 95	SUP 98
596	1¢	green	Used, Machine cancel	175,000	250,000	300,000			five known		
			Used, Precancel	125,000	200,000	250,000			ten known		

1923-29 REGULAR ISSUE COILS

SCT#	DENOM	COLOR	CONDITION	VG 50	F 70	F-VF 75	VF 80	VF-XF 85	XF 90	XF-SUP 95	SUP 98
597	1¢	green	Used	0.25	0.25	0.25	0.25	0.45	2	20	120
Sgl.			Unused OG	0.25	0.25	0.30	0.35	0.40	2.60	5.75	11.75
			Mint NH	0.25	0.25	0.40	0.60	3	27.50	75	190
597	1¢	green	Used	0.25	0.25	0.25	0.25	1	5	35	170
Pair			Unused OG	0.25	0.25	0.35	0.65	1.40	4.75	11	22.50
			Mint NH	0.30	0.60	0.95	1.40	7	60	175	375
597	1¢	green	Used	0.25	0.30	0.50	0.75	3	12.50	47.50	210
LP			Unused OG	0.45	1.25	1.60	2	4	10	20	45
			Mint NH	0.75	2.05	2.90	4	12.50	50	200	425
598	1½¢	brown	Used	0.25	0.25	0.25	0.25	0.45	2	17.50	80
Sgl.			Unused OG	0.25	0.40	0.65	0.90	1.50	3	7.50	15
			Mint NH	0.35	0.75	1.25	1.80	10	20	55	160
598	1½¢	brown	Used	0.25	0.25	0.25	0.25	1	4.75	40	175
Pair			Unused OG	0.30	0.85	1.30	1.90	3.10	6.25	16	32.50
			Mint NH	0.65	1.65	2.50	3.80	21	45	125	325
598	1½¢	brown	Used	0.25	0.45	0.60	0.75	3	10	42.50	200
LP			Unused OG	0.95	2.10	3.20	4.50	7.50	11	16	25
			Mint NH	1.70	4.15	6.25	9	20	35	160	450
599	2¢	carmine	Used	0.25	0.25	0.25	0.25	4	17.50	45	130
Sgl.		type I	Unused OG	0.25	0.25	0.25	0.35	1.25	4.50	9	15
			Mint NH	0.25	0.30	0.45	0.70	3	25	45	125
599	2¢	carmine	Used	0.25	0.25	0.25	0.25	9	40	100	300
Pair		type I	Unused OG	0.25	0.35	0.55	0.75	2.60	9.50	20	35
			Mint NH	0.25	0.65	0.90	1.50	6.50	55	110	300
599	2¢	carmine	Used	0.50	0.50	0.70	1	12.50	55	200	400
LP		type I	Unused OG	0.45	1.20	1.60	2.25	10	20	60	100
			Mint NH	0.65	2.15	3.10	4.50	22.50	55	175	325
599b	2¢	carmine lake	Mint NH	—	150	195	300	340	500	—	—
Sgl.		type I									
599b	2¢	carmine lake	Mint NH	—	270	430	650	725	1,100	2,000	—
Pair		type I									
599b	2¢	carmine lake	Used		300	500	700	1,050	1,550		
LP		type I	Mint NH	—	475	625	950	1,025	1,100	2,250	—
599A	2¢	carmine	Used	4	7.25	11	16	45	100	250	325
Sgl.		type II	Unused OG	27.50	50	72.50	100	115	135	185	325
			Mint NH	45	100	140	200	240	340	550	1,350
599A	2¢	carmine	Used	12.50	25	45	60	95	225	525	900
Pair		type II	Unused OG	60	110	150	210	240	285	400	750
			Mint NH	100	215	300	425	500	725	1,400	2,850
599A	2¢	carmine	Used	105	160	275	400	460	550	1,150	—
LP		type II	Unused OG	165	290	400	550	650	775	1,050	—
			Mint NH	265	550	800	1,150	1,450	2,400	3,750	—
599	2¢	carmine	Used	260	370	725	1,000	1,200	—	—	—
599A		type I & II	Unused OG	200	370	500	700	775	900	1,300	—
LP			Mint NH	325	650	950	1,350	1,700	2,500	4,100	—
600	3¢	violet	Used	0.25	0.25	0.25	0.25	0.45	3	37.50	200
Sgl.			Unused OG	1.50	3	4.20	6.25	6.75	7.75	11	25
			Mint NH	2.40	5	8.25	12.50	16	20	55	160
600	3¢	violet	Used	0.25	0.25	0.30	0.45	1.95	14.25	110	575
Pair			Unused OG	3	6.50	8.50	13	15	17.50	25	55
			Mint NH	4.95	10.50	17.50	26	35	42.50	125	350
600	3¢	violet	Used	1	2	2.75	4	20	65	220	500
LP			Unused OG	9	16	22	30	33.50	37.50	42.50	77.50
			Mint NH	13.25	27.50	42.50	60	72.50	87.50	175	425
601	4¢	yellow	Used	0.25	0.25	0.30	0.35	0.75	5	65	225
Sgl.		brown	Unused OG	0.85	1.80	2.50	3.75	4.50	5.50	9	20
			Mint NH	1.40	3	5	7.50	11	20	55	135
601	4¢	yellow	Used	0.20	0.50	0.60	0.95	2.50	17.50	140	500
Pair		brown	Unused OG	2	4	5.75	8.25	9.75	12.50	20	45
			Mint NH	3	6.25	11	16.50	22.50	45	120	290
601	4¢	yellow	Used	2.50	5	7	10	29	115	315	1,550
LP		brown	Unused OG	7.25	14	20	27.50	32.50	40	52.50	120
			Mint NH	13	27.50	40	55	80	150	400	625
602	5¢	dark	Used	0.25	0.25	0.25	0.25	0.75	4	95	250
Sgl.		blue	Unused OG	0.40	0.80	1.15	1.75	3	6.50	10	20
			Mint NH	0.60	1.40	2.35	3.50	7.50	19	45	135

SCT#	DENOM	COLOR	CONDITION	VG 50	F 70	F-VF 75	VF 80	VF-XF 85	XF 90	XF-SUP 95	SUP 98
602	5¢	dark	Used	0.25	0.25	0.25	0.35	2	9	200	525
Pair		blue	Unused OG	0.90	1.85	2.50	3.75	6.50	14	22.50	45
			Mint NH	1.30	3	5	7.50	15	40	95	290
602	5¢	dark	Used	0.60	1.70	2.30	3	12	60	250	1,200
LP		blue	Unused OG	2.75	5.75	8.50	11	15	22.50	35	75
			Mint NH	4.80	10.75	15.50	22.50	37.50	115	300	925
603	10¢	orange	Used	0.25	0.25	0.25	0.25	0.50	5	40	200
Sgl.			Unused OG	0.85	1.70	2.30	3.50	4.25	5.25	7.50	15
			Mint NH	1.30	2.70	4.50	7	13.50	27.50	120	260
603	10¢	orange	Used	0.25	0.25	0.25	0.25	2	11.50	90	425
Pair			Unused OG	2	4	5.25	8	9.50	12	17.50	32.50
			Mint NH	2.75	6.25	10.50	16	30	60	250	575
603	10¢	orange	Used	0.90	2.25	3.25	4.50	12.50	80	300	1,250
LP			Unused OG	6.75	12.50	18	25	30	37.50	60	110
			Mint NH	10	22	35	50	65	95	300	900
604	1¢	green	Used	0.25	0.25	0.25	0.25	2	17.50	60	160
Sgl.			Unused OG	0.25	0.25	0.25	0.40	1.25	4.50	8	17.50
			Mint NH	0.25	0.35	0.45	0.80	4	15	40	125
604	1¢	green	Used	0.25	0.25	0.25	0.25	4.25	37.50	125	350
Pair			Unused OG	0.25	0.30	0.55	0.85	2.60	9.50	17.50	40
			Mint NH	0.25	0.65	0.95	1.70	8.50	32.50	100	275
604	1¢	green	Used	0.40	0.55	0.80	1.25	4	25	105	525
LP			Unused OG	0.85	1.65	2.40	3.50	8.50	20	32.50	45
			Mint NH	1.40	2.90	4.70	7	25	65	150	500
605	1½¢	brown	Used	0.25	0.25	0.25	0.25	2	17.50	55	190
Sgl.			Unused OG	0.25	0.25	0.25	0.40	1.40	2.50	5	12
			Mint NH	0.25	0.40	0.60	0.80	2.25	15	55	130
605	1½¢	brown	Used	0.25	0.25	0.25	0.35	4.50	40	130	425
Pair			Unused OG	0.25	0.45	0.55	0.85	3	5.50	11	25
			Mint NH	0.25	0.80	1.25	1.70	4.75	32.50	150	280
605	1½¢	brown	Used	1.35	1.60	2.65	4	12	30	90	525
LP			Unused OG	0.90	1.85	2.65	3.50	6	10	20	40
			Mint NH	1.60	3.45	5	7	25	65	125	450
606	2¢	carmine	Used	0.25	0.25	0.25	0.25	1.25	15	110	220
Sgl.			Unused OG	0.25	0.25	0.25	0.40	0.90	3	6	12
			Mint NH	0.25	0.40	0.60	0.80	7.50	25	45	110
606	2¢	carmine	Used	0.25	0.25	0.30	0.45	3	35	200	450
Pair			Unused OG	0.25	0.45	0.55	0.85	2	6.50	12.50	25
			Mint NH	0.25	0.80	1.25	1.70	16	55	95	230
606	2¢	carmine	Used	0.90	1.75	2.45	3.50	10	85	300	600
			Unused OG	0.65	1.30	1.75	2.50	5	12.50	35	80
			Mint NH	1	2.30	3.50	5	15	55	150	350
606a	2¢	carmine	Unused OG	—	32.50	50	75	90	120	—	—
Sgl.		lake	Mint NH	—	60	100	150	175	200	225	275
606a	2¢	carmine	Unused OG		75	115	170	230	325	—	—
Pair		lake	Mint NH	—	135	225	350	450	500	550	600
606a	2¢	carmine	Mint NH	—	360	525	775	875	1,025	1,250	—
LP		lake									

1923-29 ISSUES

SCT#	DENOM	COLOR	CONDITION	VG 50	F 70	F-VF 75	VF 80	VF-XF 85	XF 90	XF-SUP 95	SUP 98
610	2¢	black	Used	0.25	0.25	0.25	0.25	3	12.50	50	190
			Unused OG	0.25	0.25	0.30	0.50	1.25	3.50	20	40
			Mint NH	0.25	0.35	0.70	1	2.25	15	47.50	180
611	2¢	black	Used	0.65	1.75	2.75	4	6	10	27.50	90
			Unused OG	0.90	2	3	4.50	5	7.50	12.50	20
			Mint NH	1.40	3.75	6	9	13.25	19	35	52.50
612	2¢	black	Used	0.40	0.90	1.30	1.75	10	27.50	95	325
			Unused OG	3.25	7.50	10	15	19	24	35	75
			Mint NH	6	13.50	20	32.50	42.50	60	150	475
613	2¢	black	Used	22,500	35,000	55,000	77,500	90,000	120,000	—	—
614	1¢	dark	Used	0.65	1.40	2.10	3	11	30	105	325
		green	Unused OG	0.50	1.20	1.45	2.30	3.85	11.50	32.50	62.50
			Mint NH	0.70	1.90	2.85	4.25	9	22.50	72.50	310
615	2¢	carmine	Used	0.45	1	1.50	2.25	12	30	100	325
		rose	Unused OG	0.80	1.90	2.65	3.75	5.50	10	27.50	55
			Mint NH	1.15	2.80	4.60	7	12.50	27.50	90	375
616	5¢	dark	Used	3	6	9	13	20	42.50	140	450
		blue	Unused OG	3	7	9.50	15	17.50	20	40	105
			Mint NH	4.75	12	19	27.50	37.50	65	190	650
617	1¢	green	Used	0.55	1.10	1.75	2.50	12	27.50	95	280
			Unused OG	0.45	0.90	1.35	2	3	9	17.50	47.50
			Mint NH	0.65	1.50	2.45	3.75	7.50	13.50	35	135
618	2¢	carmine	Used	0.90	1.90	2.90	4	12.50	37.50	115	340
		rose	Unused OG	0.70	1.75	2.45	3.50	4.25	9	17.50	42.50
			Mint NH	1.10	2.50	4.25	6.50	9	17	42.50	145
619	5¢	dark	Used	4	6.50	9.50	13	20	42.50	145	450
		blue	Unused OG	2.80	7	9.75	14	17.50	22.50	37.50	65
			Mint NH	4.40	11.25	16.50	26	30	45	115	290
620	2¢	carmine	Used	0.65	1.30	1.90	2.75	9.50	27.50	95	300
		& black	Unused OG	0.60	1.50	2.10	3	5.50	12	20	40
			Mint NH	1	2.50	4.15	6	10.50	20	47.50	150
621	5¢	dark	Used	2.60	4.50	6.75	9	14	30	95	295
		blue	Unused OG	2	4.50	6.50	9	11	13.50	22.50	47.50
		& black	Mint NH	3.50	8	12	19	25	35	60	230
622	13¢	green	Used	0.25	0.25	0.35	0.75	9	22.50	85	275
			Unused OG	2	4.50	6	9	11	14	25	55
			Mint NH	3.50	7.50	12	19	25	32.50	90	240
623	17¢	black	Used	0.25	0.25	0.25	0.30	8	15	60	200
			Unused OG	2	4.50	6	9	11	12.50	22.50	47.50
			Mint NH	3.50	7.50	12	19	25	35	80	210
627	2¢	carmine	Used	0.25	0.25	0.25	0.50	8	17.50	65	200
		rose	Unused OG	0.45	1.10	1.60	2.25	3.25	6	12.50	30
			Mint NH	0.70	1.65	2.80	4	7.50	15	40	150
628	5¢	gray	Used	0.75	1.50	2.25	3.25	8.50	27.50	95	330
		lilac	Unused OG	1	2.50	3.60	5	6	7.50	12.50	30
			Mint NH	1.50	3.80	5.75	8.50	11	22.50	60	190
629	2¢	carmine	Used	0.40	0.80	1.25	1.70	10	20	90	250
		rose	Unused OG	0.30	0.80	1.10	1.60	3	6	10	22.50
			Mint NH	0.45	1.30	1.90	2.75	6.50	17.50	50	175
630	2¢	carmine	Used	180	260	350	450	475	525	700	—
		rose	Unused OG	100	160	220	275	310	360	475	—
		S/S	Mint NH	150	250	370	500	550	600	700	—
631	1½¢	yellow	Used	0.45	0.85	1.25	1.70	3.25	8	17.50	55
		brown	Unused OG	0.40	1	1.45	2	2.20	2.45	4	7.50
		imperforate	Mint NH	0.50	1.30	1.95	3	5	10	20	40
632	1¢	green	Used	0.25	0.25	0.25	0.25	7	15	65	210
			Unused OG	0.25	0.25	0.25	0.25	1.25	7.50	12.50	30
			Mint NH	0.25	0.25	0.25	0.35	3.50	20	75	175
632a	1¢	green	Used	1.20	2.25	3	4	5	6.50	17.50	—
Booklet			Unused OG	1.10	2	3.50	5	6.25	8	14	—
Pane of 6			Mint NH	1.50	2.80	5	8	10	13.50	35	—
633	1½¢	yellow	Used	0.25	0.25	0.25	0.25	7	15	65	200
		brown	Unused OG	0.25	0.80	1.20	1.70	4	11	22.50	40
			Mint NH	0.40	1.15	1.70	2.60	6	22.50	62.50	200
634	2¢	carmine	Used	0.25	0.25	0.25	0.25	7	15	65	200
		type I	Unused OG	0.25	0.25	0.25	0.25	1.25	7.50	12.50	30
			Mint NH	0.25	0.25	0.25	0.30	3	20	70	175
634b	2¢	carmine	Used	—	—	—	500	—	—		
		lake	Unused OG	—	—	125	180	235	300	550	
		type I	Mint NH	—	—	300	425	525	700	950	
634e	2¢	carmine	Used			—	1,000	—	—		
		lake	UnusedOG			—	400	—			
		type I	Mint NH			—	750	—			
634d	2¢	carmine	Used	0.50	0.85	1.15	1.50	1.90	2.50	9	—
Booklet		type I	Unused OG	0.40	0.75	1.05	1.50	2	2.75	7	—
Pane of 6			Mint NH	0.50	1.10	1.70	2.50	3.25	5	12.50	—
634e	2¢	carmine	Unused OG			—	400	—	—		
Booklet		lake	Mint NH			—	750	—	—		
Pane of 6		type I									
634A	2¢	carmine	Used	4.25	7	10	13.50	18.50	30	110	375
		type II	Unused OG	85	150	210	300	340	375	475	875
			Mint NH	140	270	425	600	675	800	2,000	4,400
635	3¢	violet	Used	0.25	0.25	0.25	0.25	7	15	65	200
			Unused OG	0.25	0.25	0.45	0.75	2.20	6.25	15	37.50
			Mint NH	0.35	0.40	0.80	1.20	5.25	24	70	200
635a	3¢	bright	Used	0.25	0.25	0.25	0.25	5	12.50	55	175
		violet	Unused OG	0.25	0.25	0.30	0.35	1.75	5	12.50	35
			Mint NH	0.25	0.30	0.30	0.45	2.75	16	47.50	175
636	4¢	yellow	Used	0.25	0.25	0.25	0.25	7	15	60	200
		brown	Unused OG	0.40	0.95	1.30	1.90	3	7	15	35
			Mint NH	0.50	1.30	2	3	7.50	20	65	210
637	5¢	dark	Used	0.25	0.25	0.25	0.25	7	15	60	200
		blue	Unused OG	0.40	0.95	1.30	1.90	3	7	15	35
			Mint NH	0.50	1.30	2	3	7.50	20	85	220

SCT#	DENOM	COLOR	CONDITION	VG 50	F 70	F-VF 75	VF 80	VF-XF 85	XF 90	XF-SUP 95	SUP 98
638	6¢	red	Used	0.25	0.25	0.25	0.25	7	15	60	200
		orange	Unused OG	0.40	1	1.35	2	3	7	15	35
			Mint NH	0.55	1.40	2.15	3.20	8.25	22.50	95	225
639	7¢	black	Used	0.25	0.25	0.25	0.25	7	15	60	200
			Unused OG	0.40	1	1.35	2	3	7	15	35
			Mint NH	0.55	1.40	2.15	3.20	8.25	22.50	80	225
640	8¢	olive	Used	0.25	0.25	0.25	0.25	7	15	60	200
		green	Unused OG	0.40	1	1.35	2	3	7	15	35
			Mint NH	0.55	1.40	2.15	3.20	8.25	22.50	90	250
641	9¢	rose	Used	0.25	0.25	0.25	0.25	7	15	60	200
			Unused OG	0.40	0.95	1.30	1.90	3	7	15	35
			Mint NH	0.50	1.30	2	3	7.50	22.50	80	225
642	10¢	orange	Used	0.25	0.25	0.25	0.25	7	15	60	200
			Unused OG	0.65	1.55	2.20	3.25	4	8	1.50	37.50
			Mint NH	0.95	2.60	3.75	5.50	15	32.50	100	290
643	2¢	carmine	Used	0.25	0.40	0.55	0.80	10	22.50	80	290
		rose	Unused OG	0.25	0.60	0.90	1.20	2.50	6	12.50	30
			Mint NH	0.35	0.85	1.40	2	5	12	32.50	135
644	2¢	carmine	Used	0.45	1	1.50	2.10	11	25	100	325
		rose	Unused OG	0.60	1.45	2.10	3	4.50	7.50	12.50	35
			Mint NH	0.95	2.15	3.50	5.25	8	16.50	47.50	155
645	2¢	carmine	Used	0.25	0.25	0.25	0.50	8	17.50	65	230
		rose	Unused OG	0.25	0.55	0.75	1.15	2.50	5	11	27.50
			Mint NH	0.30	0.80	1.25	1.80	6.75	16.50	45	160
645a	2¢	lake	Unused OG	—	—	—	—	—	—	—	—
			Mint NH	—	—	—	—	—	—	—	—
646	2¢	carmine	Used	0.25	0.45	0.70	1	10	22.50	90	325
			Unused OG	0.25	0.50	0.70	1	2	3.90	9	22.50
			Mint NH	0.25	0.75	1.10	1.60	4.25	13	45	160
646b	2¢	carmine	Unused OG			—	2,500	—			
		lake									
647	2¢	carmine	Used	0.90	1.80	2.75	4	11	30	115	325
			Unused OG	0.80	2	2.85	4	4.65	5.75	11	30
			Mint NH	1.40	3.50	4.90	7.25	10	25	80	275
648	5¢	dark	Used	3.70	6	8.75	12.50	17.50	35	140	525
		blue	Unused OG	2.20	4.50	7.75	11	12.50	14	22	52.50
			Mint NH	4	10	15	21.50	30	40	110	350
649	2¢	carmine	Used	0.25	0.40	0.60	0.80	12	24	95	325
		rose	Unused OG	0.25	0.55	0.75	1.10	2	4	9	22.50
			Mint NH	0.30	0.75	1.20	1.75	5	10	35	140
650	5¢	blue	Used	0.70	1.60	2.40	3.25	11	25	105	375
			Unused OG	0.90	2.25	3.10	4.50	5.25	6.50	11	30
			Mint NH	1.40	3.25	4.75	7	11	17.50	40	160
651	2¢	carmine	Used	0.25	0.25	0.25	0.50	8	17.50	67.50	250
		& black	Unused OG	0.25	0.35	0.50	0.70	1.40	3.75	10	25
			Mint NH	0.25	0.50	0.75	1.15	3.75	15	55	175
653	½¢	olive	Used	0.25	0.25	0.25	0.25	6	15	60	200
		brown	Unused OG	0.25	0.25	0.25	0.25	1.25	3.75	10	20
			Mint NH	0.30	0.30	0.30	0.35	3.50	10	30	120
654	2¢	carmine	Used	0.25	0.30	0.45	0.65	9	20	85	275
		rose	Unused OG	0.25	0.30	0.45	0.65	1.50	9	35	35
			Mint NH	0.25	0.55	0.80	1.20	4.50	12.50	40	160
655	2¢	carmine	Used	0.25	0.25	0.25	0.25	8	15	60	200
		rose	Unused OG	0.25	0.35	0.45	0.65	1.75	4	10	22.50
			Mint NH	0.25	0.35	0.65	1.10	4.50	11	45	190
656 Sgl.	2¢	carmine	Used	0.45	0.85	1.25	1.75	8	40	110	275
		rose	Unused OG	2	5	7	10	11	13	20	47.50
			Mint NH	3.50	9	14.25	20	26	35	70	160
656 Pair	2¢	carmine	Used	1	2	3	4	17.50	45	130	425
		rose	Unused OG	5.50	11	16	22.50	27	32.50	45	100
			Mint NH	10	20	31	45	60	75	150	340
656 LP	2¢	carmine	Used	8	15	21	27.50	40	125	350	750
		rose	Unused OG	13.50	27.50	40	55	62.50	72.50	100	200
			Mint NH	22.50	50	80	110	130	175	350	900
657	2¢	carmine	Used	0.25	0.30	0.40	0.55	7.50	18.50	50	150
		rose	Unused OG	0.25	0.30	0.35	0.55	1.40	3.25	9.50	22.50
			Mint NH	0.25	0.45	0.65	0.95	3.25	10	35	135
657a	2¢	lake	Used		—	—	250	—	—		
			Unused OG	110	200	275	375	425	500	600	1,000
			Mint NH	150	275	425	625	725	850	1,600	3,250

1929 KANSAS OVERPRINTS

SCT#	DENOM	COLOR	CONDITION	VG 50	F 70	F-VF 75	VF 80	VF-XF 85	XF 90	XF-SUP 95	SUP 98
658	1¢	green	Used	0.45	1	1.45	2	10	27.50	110	350
			Unused OG	0.50	1.25	1.75	2.50	4	6.25	11	25
			Mint NH	0.90	2.20	3.50	5	9.50	27.50	90	320
659	1½¢	brown	Used	0.70	1.40	2.10	2.90	12.50	32.50	120	400
			Unused OG	0.65	1.50	2.10	3.25	5.25	7.50	11	30
			Mint NH	1.15	2.90	4.40	6.50	9.25	25	82.50	325
660	2¢	carmine	Used	0.25	0.55	0.75	1	10	25	125	325
			Unused OG	0.80	1.95	2.85	4	5.50	7.50	10	30
			Mint NH	1.35	3.20	4.80	7.50	11	32.50	85	360
661	3¢	violet	Used	4.25	7.50	11	15	25	50	160	525
			Unused OG	3.75	8.75	11.75	17.50	20	25	37.50	90
			Mint NH	6.50	14	22.50	35	45	65	200	675
662	4¢	yellow	Used	2.25	4.50	6.50	9	17.50	42.50	150	475
		brown	Unused OG	3.75	8.75	11.50	17.50	20	22.50	42.50	100
			Mint NH	6.50	14	22.50	35	47.50	70	225	625
663	5¢	deep	Used	2.40	4.75	7	9.75	20	45	150	325
		blue	Unused OG	2.50	6.25	8.75	12.50	15	18	27.50	65
			Mint NH	4	9.50	15	25	35	47.50	200	750
664	6¢	red	Used	4.50	9	13	18	25	50	160	550
		orange	Unused OG	5	12.50	17	25	27.50	32.50	65	160
			Mint NH	8.25	19	32.50	50	67.50	95	325	1,000
665	7¢	black	Used	7	13	19	27.50	37.50	60	175	675
			Unused OG	4.25	12.50	15	25	27.50	32.50	55	140
			Mint NH	8.25	17.50	30	50	67.50	90	325	1,000
666	8¢	olive	Used	18.50	40	50	65	92.50	145	475	—
		green	Unused OG	15	37.50	50	72.50	80	87.50	145	280
			Mint NH	25	60	90	145	170	200	400	1,400
667	9¢	light	Used	2.50	5	7.75	11.50	20	45	140	500
		rose	Unused OG	3	7	9.50	14	15	16.50	30	72.50
			Mint NH	4.75	11	17	27.50	40	55	160	650
668	10¢	orange	Used	3	6	8.25	12.50	22.50	45	150	525
		yellow	Unused OG	3.75	10.50	15	22.50	25	30	47.50	120
			Mint NH	6.25	18	27	45	62.50	115	300	1,050
658-668 Set	11 stamps		Used	45.80	92.70	126.80	174.15	292.50	567.50	1,915	4,650
			Unused OG	42.95	108.45	145.20	216.25	244.75	285.75	482	1,113
			Mint NH	72.90	171.30	269.20	431.50	564.75	822.50	2,392.50	8,155

1929 NEBRASKA OVERPRINTS

SCT#	DENOM	COLOR	CONDITION	VG 50	F 70	F-VF 75	VF 80	VF-XF 85	XF 90	XF-SUP 95	SUP 98
669	1¢	green	Used	0.50	1.10	1.60	2.25	12.50	30	110	400
			Unused OG	0.85	1.55	2.35	3.25	4.50	5.75	10	30
			Mint NH	1.30	2.60	4.15	6.50	10	27.50	90	300
670	1½¢	brown	Used	0.50	1.25	1.75	2.50	12.50	30	105	210
			Unused OG	0.60	1.50	2.05	3	4	6	12	25
			Mint NH	1.05	2.35	3.90	6	10	25	77.50	325
671	2¢	carmine	Used	0.25	0.60	0.90	1.30	12	25	100	350
			Unused OG	0.60	1.50	2.05	3	4	6	12	25
			Mint NH	1.05	2.35	3.90	6	10	25	75	300
672	3¢	violet	Used	3	5.75	8.25	12	22.50	50	155	525
			Unused OG	2.20	5.50	7.25	11	13.75	16.50	32	77.50
			Mint NH	4.35	9.25	13.75	22	32	47.50	170	600
673	4¢	yellow	Used	3.75	7.50	11	15	24	50	160	550
		brown	Unused OG	3.50	8.75	11.50	17.50	22.50	27.50	45	95
			Mint NH	5.50	13.50	21	35	47.50	65	225	700
674	5¢	deep	Used	3.75	7.50	11	15	25	50	160	500
		blue	Unused OG	2.80	7.50	9.50	15	19	30	40	90
			Mint NH	4.75	11.50	19	30	45	62.50	220	750
675	6¢	red	Used	6	12	17	24	32.50	62.50	175	625
		orange	Unused OG	7	18.50	25	35	40	50	82.50	180
			Mint NH	11.50	27.50	45	70	90	115	375	900
676	7¢	black	Used	4.50	9	13	18	27.50	50	160	575
			Unused OG	4.50	10.50	15	22.50	27.50	32	50	120
			Mint NH	8	17.50	28.50	45	62.50	85	300	950

SCT#	DENOM	COLOR	CONDITION	VG 50	F 70	F-VF 75	VF 80	VF-XF 85	XF 90	XF-SUP 95	SUP 98
677	8¢	olive	Used	6.50	12.50	17.50	25	35	57.50	170	650
		green	Unused OG	6	15	21	30	35	45	60	160
			Mint NH	9	23.50	36.50	60	80	125	325	1,400
678	9¢	light	Used	7	14	20	27.50	37.50	62.50	180	700
		rose	Unused OG	7	16.50	25	35	40	47.50	80	200
			Mint NH	11.50	27.50	45	70	87.50	115	330	1,100
679	10¢	orange	Used	5.50	11	16	22.50	32.50	55	160	600
		yellow	Unused OG	18	45	57.50	90	100	115	135	300
			Mint NH	30	72.50	115	180	220	280	350	950
669-679		11 stamps	Used	41.25	82.20	118	165.05	273.50	522.50	1,635	5,685
Set			Unused OG	53.05	131.80	178.20	265.25	310.25	381.25	558.50	1,303
			Mint NH	88	210.05	335.70	530.50	694.50	972.50	2,538	8,275

1929-56 ISSUES

SCT#	DENOM	COLOR	CONDITION	VG 50	F 70	F-VF 75	VF 80	VF-XF 85	XF 90	XF-SUP 95	SUP 98
680	2¢	carmine	Used	0.25	0.30	0.40	0.65	8.50	19	85	290
		rose	Unused OG	0.25	0.30	0.40	0.65	1.40	4	10	22.50
			Mint NH	0.25	0.45	0.70	1	3	10	37.50	130
681	2¢	carmine	Used	0.25	0.30	0.35	0.55	8.50	20	70	275
		rose	Unused OG	0.25	0.30	0.35	0.55	1.25	3	9	22.50
			Mint NH	0.25	0.45	0.60	0.90	2.85	8.50	40	135
681a	2¢	lake	Used			—	—	—			
			Unused OG			—	425	—			
			Mint NH			—	650	—			
682	2¢	carmine	Used	0.25	0.25	0.35	0.50	8	17.50	70	250
		rose	Unused OG	0.25	0.30	0.45	0.65	1.60	3.70	9.25	22.50
			Mint NH	0.25	0.40	0.60	0.95	3.25	10	30	145
683	2¢	carmine	Used	0.25	0.50	0.70	1	9.50	21.50	95	325
		rose	Unused OG	0.25	0.50	0.70	1	2.10	3.75	9	24.50
			Mint NH	0.25	0.70	1	1.50	4	12	35	165
684	1½¢	brown	Used	0.25	0.25	0.25	0.25	7	15	60	210
			Unused OG	0.25	0.25	0.30	0.50	1.40	4.25	10	30
			Mint NH	0.25	0.30	0.50	0.70	3.75	17.50	40	170
685	4¢	brown	Used	0.25	0.25	0.25	0.25	7	15	60	210
			Unused OG	0.25	0.30	0.55	0.80	1.50	4	11	25
			Mint NH	0.25	0.45	0.75	1.25	5	15	52.50	190
686	1½¢	brown	Used	0.25	0.25	0.25	0.25	2.50	5	25	85
Sgl.			Unused OG	0.35	0.80	1.20	1.75	2.50	4	10	20
			Mint NH	0.45	1.15	1.65	2.60	7.50	35	65	150
686	1½¢	brown	Used	0.25	0.20	0.25	0.30	6	15	60	200
Pair			Unused OG	0.80	1.80	2.55	3.75	5.25	8.50	22.50	45
			Mint NH	1.10	2.60	4	5.75	16	60	135	350
686	1½¢	brown	Used	0.25	0.20	0.30	0.75	7.50	45	150	325
LP			Unused OG	1.70	3.75	5.25	7.50	9	12.50	20	45
			Mint NH	2.20	5.25	7.75	11.50	25	60	150	350
687	4¢	brown	Used	0.20	0.20	0.25	0.45	2	10	190	400
Sgl.			Unused OG	60	1.45	2.10	3	4.50	7	12.50	25
			Mint NH	0.90	2.10	3.10	4.50	9	18.50	42.50	120
687	4¢	brown	Used	0.20	0.50	0.70	1	4.50	24	325	—
Pair			Unused OG	1.40	3	4.50	6.25	10	15	26	55
			Mint NH	1.80	4.25	6.25	9.50	20	40	90	250
687	4¢	brown	Used	0.50	1.25	1.75	2.50	7.50	32.50	135	425
LP			Unused OG	3	5.50	7.50	11	14	20	35	75
			Mint NH	4.75	10	14	22	40	65	175	350
688	2¢	carmine	Used	0.25	0.40	0.60	0.85	8	22.50	90	300
		rose	Unused OG	0.25	0.45	0.55	0.85	1.30	6.25	10.50	23.50
			Mint NH	0.25	0.55	0.85	1.30	3	11	37.50	140
689	2¢	carmine	Used	0.25	0.25	0.25	0.50	8	17.50	70	250
		rose	Unused OG	0.25	0.25	0.30	0.50	1.25	4.50	9	20
			Mint NH	0.25	0.25	0.40	0.75	2.25	7.50	22.50	100
690	2¢	carmine	Used	0.25	0.25	0.25	0.25	6	13	62.50	200
		rose	Unused OG	0.25	0.25	0.25	0.30	0.75	3	9	17.50
			Mint NH	0.25	0.25	0.25	0.40	2.50	7	22.50	105
692	11¢	light	Used	0.25	0.25	0.25	0.25	7	13	62.50	200
		blue	Unused OG	0.55	1.25	1.75	2.50	3	3.75	9.50	25
			Mint NH	0.70	1.50	2.50	3.75	9	30	80	250
693	12¢	brown	Used	0.25	0.25	0.25	0.25	5	12.50	60	190
		violet	Unused OG	1	2.50	3.50	5	6.50	8.50	10	32.50
			Mint NH	1.50	3.50	5.50	8	12.50	30	75	300
694	13¢	yellow	Used	0.25	0.25	0.25	0.25	5	13	62.50	200
		green	Unused OG	0.45	1.15	1.65	2.25	2.75	3.50	9	22.50
			Mint NH	0.65	1.45	2.20	3.50	8	22.50	75	300
695	14¢	dark	Used	0.25	0.25	0.35	0.60	8	21	75	230
		blue	Unused OG	0.80	2	2.75	4	5	6.50	9	22.50
			Mint NH	1.15	2.50	4	6.25	12.50	35	110	325

SCT#	DENOM	COLOR	CONDITION	VG 50	F 70	F-VF 75	VF 80	VF-XF 85	XF 90	XF-SUP 95	SUP 98
696	15¢	gray	Used	0.25	0.25	0.25	0.25	5	13	62.50	200
			Unused OG	1.55	3.75	5.25	7.75	8.50	9.50	12.50	35
			Mint NH	2	4.75	7.50	12	17.50	30	85	300
697	17¢	black	Used	0.25	0.25	0.25	0.25	5	13	62.50	200
			Unused OG	0.95	2.35	3.35	4.75	6	7.50	12	30
			Mint NH	1.25	2.80	4.75	7.25	12.50	30	90	325
698	20¢	carmine	Used	0.25	0.25	0.25	0.25	5	13	62.50	200
		rose	Unused OG	1.50	3.75	5.50	7.75	8.50	9.50	12.50	35
			Mint NH	2.10	4.95	7.75	12.50	17.50	30	85	300
699	25¢	blue	Used	0.25	0.25	0.25	0.25	5	13	62.50	200
		green	Unused OG	1.60	4	5.75	8	8.75	10	14	37.50
			Mint NH	2.25	5.25	8.25	13	18	35	110	375
700	30¢	brown	Used	0.25	0.25	0.25	0.25	5	13	62.50	200
			Unused OG	2.50	6.25	8.25	12.50	14	17.50	35	75
			Mint NH	3.50	8.50	13	21	32.50	50	115	360
701	50¢	lilac	Used	0.25	0.25	0.25	0.25	5	13	62.50	200
			Unused OG	6	15	21	30	32.50	35	37.50	90
			Mint NH	8.50	20	32.50	50	57.50	75	165	525
702	2¢	black	Used	0.25	0.25	0.25	0.25	5	14	60	190
		& red	Unused OG	0.25	0.25	0.25	0.25	0.75	3	11	20
			Mint NH	0.25	0.25	0.25	0.35	2	10	30	125
703	2¢	carmine	Used	0.25	0.25	0.25	0.25	5	13	65	200
		rose	Unused OG	0.25	0.25	0.25	0.35	0.60	0.75	6.50	16
		& black	Mint NH	0.25	0.25	0.30	0.50	2.50	9	32.50	190
703a	2¢	lake	Used	0.25	0.40	0.55	0.75	7	17.50	70	220
		& black	Unused OG	0.90	2.25	3.20	4.50	7.50	12.50	20	50
			Mint NH	1.20	2.50	4.10	6.25	10	20	65	240
703b	2¢	dark lake	Unused OG	90	200	295	400	450	525	700	1,150
		& black	Mint NH	165	340	525	750	900	1,100	1,500	2,400
704	½¢	olive	Used	0.25	0.25	0.25	0.25	1	3	17.50	60
		brown	Unused OG	0.25	0.25	0.25	0.25	0.50	1.90	8.75	20
			Mint NH	0.25	0.25	0.25	0.35	4	12.50	35	150
705	1¢	green	Used	0.25	0.25	0.25	0.25	1	3	17.50	60
			Unused OG	0.25	0.25	0.25	0.25	0.50	1.90	8.75	20
			Mint NH	0.25	0.25	0.25	0.35	4	12.50	35	140
706	1½¢	brown	Used	0.25	0.25	0.25	0.25	1	3	17.50	60
			Unused OG	0.25	0.25	0.35	0.45	0.90	2.50	10	25
			Mint NH	0.25	0.35	0.45	0.60	5	14	35	130
707	2¢	carmine	Used	0.25	0.25	0.25	0.25	1	3	17.50	60
		rose	Unused OG	0.25	0.25	0.25	0.30	0.60	2.25	9.50	24
			Mint NH	0.25	0.25	0.35	0.45	4.50	12.50	35	135
708	3¢	deep	Used	0.25	0.25	0.25	0.25	1	3	17.50	60
		violet	Unused OG	0.25	0.30	0.40	0.55	1.25	3	11	27.50
			Mint NH	0.25	0.40	0.55	0.80	4.50	12.50	35	150
709	4¢	light	Used	0.25	0.25	0.25	0.25	1	3	17.50	60
		brown	Unused OG	0.25	0.35	0.45	0.60	1.15	3.75	10	25
			Mint NH	0.35	0.45	0.65	0.85	6.75	15	40	150
710	5¢	blue	Used	0.25	0.25	0.25	0.25	1	3	17.50	60
			Unused OG	0.30	0.60	0.95	1.40	2.50	4.75	15	37.50
			Mint NH	0.40	1	1.50	2.25	5	15	40	150
711	6¢	red	Used	0.25	0.25	0.25	0.25	1	3	17.50	60
		orange	Unused OG	0.55	1.40	1.90	2.75	4.75	9.50	22.50	47.50
			Mint NH	0.85	2	3.10	4.50	9	16	40	150
712	7¢	black	Used	0.25	0.25	0.25	0.25	1	3	17.50	60
			Unused OG	0.25	0.30	0.40	0.60	1.25	3.25	11	30
			Mint NH	0.30	0.45	0.60	0.85	5	15	37.50	140
713	8¢	olive	Used	0.25	0.25	0.35	0.50	1.50	5	20	65
		bister	Unused OG	0.55	1.20	1.75	2.50	4.50	9	20	37.50
			Mint NH	0.85	1.75	2.50	4	7.50	16	37.50	140
714	9¢	pale	Used	0.25	0.25	0.25	0.25	1	3	16	55
		red	Unused OG	0.40	1	1.35	2	4.75	8	15	32.50
			Mint NH	0.70	1.40	2.25	3.25	6.50	15	35	165
715	10¢	orange	Used	0.25	0.25	0.25	0.25	1	3	17.50	60
		yellow	Unused OG	1.80	4.50	6.25	9	12	16	25	60
			Mint NH	2.70	6.25	10	15	16	17.50	32.50	125
720b	3¢	deep	Used	3.40	5	8.25	12.50	14	17.50	35	—
Booklet		violet	Unused OG	12.50	18.50	25.50	35	38.50	45	80	—
Pane of 6			Mint NH	17.50	35	45	60	67.50	85	160	—
832	$1	purple	Used	0.25	0.25	0.25	0.25	0.90	1.50	6	25
		& black	Mint NH	1.50	2.70	4.60	7	12.50	25	40	180
832b	$1	watermarked	Used	15	30	45	65	75	90	125	250
			Mint NH	45	90	135	200	220	245	275	350
832c	$1	watermarked	Used	0.25	0.25	0.25	0.25	0.80	1.40	5.75	22.50
			Mint NH	1.40	2.60	4.50	6	12	22.50	37.50	175
833	$2	yellow green	Used	0.70	1.60	2.50	3.75	5	8	17.50	50
		& black	Mint NH	3.75	6.75	10.75	16	18.50	26	75	240
834	$5	carmine	Used	0.75	1.40	2.10	3	4	6.50	16	50
		& black	Mint NH	16	32.50	55	75	85	115	170	400
803-834 Set		32 stamps	Mint NH	30	52.50	87.50	140	275	500	975	3,450
834a	$5	red	Used				7,000				
		brown	Unused OG	500	825	1,400	1,850	2,000	2,200	2,500	2,800
		& black	Mint NH	700	1,375	2,000	3,000	3,150	3,400	3,650	—
1053	$5	black	Used	1.35	3	5	6.75	7.50	12.50	19	55
			Mint NH	11.50	20	37.50	47.50	55	65	85	190

1918-23 FIRST AND SECOND AIRMAIL ISSUES

SCT#	DENOM	COLOR	CONDITION	VG 50	F 70	F-VF 75	VF 80	VF-XF 85	XF 90	XF-SUP 95	SUP 98
C1	6¢	orange	Used	8.50	15	18.50	28	37.50	80	220	475
			Unused OG	14	30	42.50	55	67.50	85	125	200
			Mint NH	20	42.50	70	110	130	180	375	1,900
C2	16¢	green	Used	8.50	15	20	30	42.50	95	220	500
			Unused OG	15	32.50	45	60	72.50	90	140	260
			Mint NH	22.50	50	75	120	140	200	425	1,375
C3	24¢	carmine	Used	8.50	15	21	30	45	85	240	500
		rose	Unused OG	17	35	50	65	77.50	95	140	290
		& blue	Mint NH	25	52.50	82.50	130	160	210	425	1,200
C3a	24¢	invert	Unused OG	250,000	350,000	400,000	450,000	675,000	—	1,350,000	
			Mint NH		—	675,000	850,000				
C4	8¢	dark	Used	3.50	6.25	8.25	12.50	22.50	50	125	325
		green	Unused OG	3.75	8.25	11.50	17.50	20	25	40	67.50
			Mint NH	7	14	24	35	47.50	70	145	450
C5	16¢	dark	Used	6.50	13	18.50	27.50	37.50	80	220	475
		blue	Unused OG	15	32.50	45	60	70	85	130	225
			Mint NH	22.50	50	75	120	145	200	375	1,400
C6	24¢	carmine	Used	6.50	13	18.50	27.50	42.50	85	210	475
			Unused OG	17.50	35	50	65	75	92.50	140	250
			Mint NH	25	55	82.50	130	150	175	350	1,125
C1-C6		6 stamps	Used	42	77.25	104.75	155.50	227.50	475	1,235	2,750
Set			Unused OG	82.25	173.25	244	322.50	382.50	472.50	715	1,293
			Mint NH	122	264	409	645	772.50	1,035	2,095	7,450

1926-30 AIRMAILS

SCT#	DENOM	COLOR	CONDITION	VG 50	F 70	F-VF 75	VF 80	VF-XF 85	XF 90	XF-SUP 95	SUP 98
C7	10¢	dark	Used	0.25	0.25	0.25	0.35	2	17.50	60	200
		blue	Unused OG	0.45	1.15	1.65	2.25	4	10	35	55
			Mint NH	0.60	1.60	2.65	4	8	25	75	250
C8	15¢	olive	Used	0.70	1.25	1.80	2.50	7.50	27.50	105	325
		brown	Unused OG	0.50	1.15	1.70	2.50	3.50	9	30	50
			Mint NH	0.85	1.90	3.25	4.75	10	25	80	240
C9	20¢	yellow	Used	0.55	1	1.45	2	6	27.50	105	325
		green	Unused OG	1.30	3.25	4.75	6.50	8	15	30	60
			Mint NH	2.30	5	8	12.50	18.50	32.50	80	230
C10	10¢	dark	Used	0.70	1.25	1.85	2.50	6	25	110	325
		blue	Unused OG	1.40	3.50	4.75	7	8.50	15	22.50	40
			Mint NH	2.75	5.25	7.50	12.50	20	35	120	360
C10a	10¢	dark	Used	22.50	39	50	65	80	110	225	—
Booklet		blue	Unused OG	20	40	52.50	70	80	92.50	150	—
Pane of 3			Mint NH	25	47.50	72.50	115	145	180	310	—
C11	5¢	carmine	Used	0.25	0.40	0.55	0.75	5	30	80	260
		& blue	Unused OG	1.10	2.45	3.85	5.50	7.75	11	22	38.50
			Mint NH	1.80	3.50	6.25	10	17.50	35	100	375
C12	5¢	violet	Used	0.20	0.25	0.40	0.50	2.50	25	80	250
			Unused OG	1.90	4.75	6.50	9.50	11	13	20	40
			Mint NH	2.75	7	11	17.50	25	40	105	375

1930 GRAF ZEPPELIN ISSUE

SCT#	DENOM	COLOR	CONDITION	VG 50	F 70	F-VF 75	VF 80	VF-XF 85	XF 90	XF-SUP 95	SUP 98
C13	65¢	green	Used	80	95	120	150	200	250	385	850
			Unused OG	70	95	130	175	205	235	250	450
			Mint NH	77.50	110	155	240	300	425	600	1,550
C14	$1.30	brown	Used	170	225	280	350	445	550	775	1,950
			Unused OG	135	185	260	360	385	425	475	625
			Mint NH	150	265	400	550	625	700	1,200	2,850
C15	$2.60	blue	Used	275	330	400	550	675	850	1,175	2,700
			Unused OG	225	275	390	525	575	675	750	900
			Mint NH	285	425	650	825	1,000	1,200	1,650	4,000
C13-C15		3 stamps	Used	525	650	800	1,050	1,320	1,650	2,335	5,500
Set			Unused OG	430	555	780	1,060	1,165	1,335	1,475	1,975
			Mint NH	512.50	800	1,205	1,615	1,925	2,325	3,450	8,400

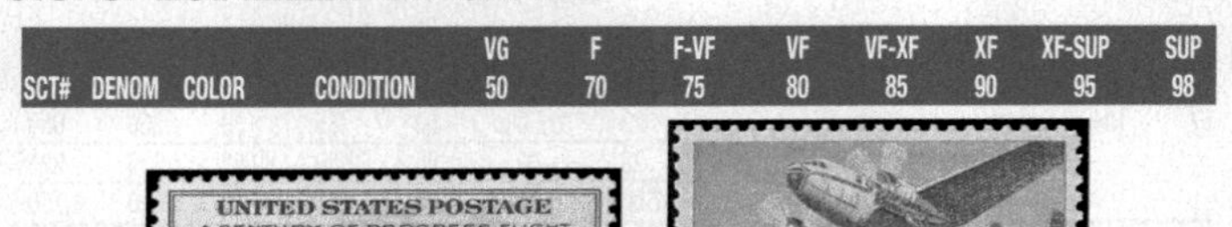

1931-44 AIRMAILS

SCT#	DENOM	COLOR	CONDITION	VG 50	F 70	F-VF 75	VF 80	VF-XF 85	XF 90	XF-SUP 95	SUP 98
C16	5¢	violet	Used	0.25	0.35	0.45	0.60	3	25	85	275
			Unused OG	0.95	2.40	3.35	4.75	6.25	10	22.50	50
			Mint NH	1.55	3.90	5.75	8.50	17	82.50	200	675
C17	8¢	olive	Used	0.25	0.25	0.25	0.40	2	20	75	260
		bister	Unused OG	0.60	1.05	1.50	2.25	3.25	9	22.50	65
			Mint NH	0.75	1.50	2.35	3.75	16.50	70	250	850
C18	50¢	green	Used	16.50	21.50	31	47.50	60	80	180	325
			Unused OG	16	22.50	34	45	52	61	76.50	110
			Mint NH	20	30	45	75	85	115	170	500
C19	6¢	dull	Used	0.25	0.25	0.25	0.25	1.50	20	75	270
		orange	Mint NH	0.70	1.50	2.20	3.50	15	85	20	1,250
C20	25¢	blue	Used	0.30	0.50	0.70	1	3	7	20	55
			Mint NH	0.30	0.60	0.85	1.40	5	12.50	50	180
C21	20¢	green	Used	0.50	0.90	1.20	1.75	5.50	10	27.50	80
			Mint NH	2	4.25	6.75	10	15	20	57.50	350
C22	50¢	carmine	Used	1.40	2.60	3.70	5	10	16.50	40	125
			Mint NH	2	4.25	6.75	10	15	20	57.50	220
C23	6¢	dark blue	Used	0.25	0.25	0.25	0.25	2	5	27.50	80
		& carmine	Mint NH	0.25	0.25	0.35	0.70	3.50	12.50	65	230
C24	30¢	blue	Used	0.35	0.70	1	1.50	6	14	35	115
			Mint NH	2	4.25	7	11	16	27.50	75	300
C25	6¢	carmine	Used	0.25	0.25	0.25	0.25	2	5	30	90
			Mint NH	0.25	0.25	0.25	0.25	2	12.50	40	175
C25a	6¢	carmine	Used	0.45	0.90	1.15	1.50	2	3	7.50	15
Booklet Pane of 3			Mint NH	0.90	1.85	2.65	3.50	4.75	7	12	25
C26	8¢	olive	Used	0.25	0.25	0.25	0.25	2	5	27.50	90
		green	Mint NH	0.25	0.25	0.25	0.25	1.50	12.50	40	150
C27	10¢	violet	Used	0.25	0.25	0.25	0.25	2	5	27.50	90
			Mint NH	0.25	0.50	0.70	1.10	3.50	10	40	150
C28	15¢	brown	Used	0.25	0.25	0.25	0.35	2.50	5.50	30	95
		carmine	Mint NH	0.40	0.95	1.40	2.10	6	12	37.50	160
C29	20¢	bright	Used	0.25	0.25	0.25	0.30	2.25	5.25	27.50	90
		green	Mint NH	0.40	0.95	1.40	2.10	6	12	37.50	160
C30	30¢	blue	Used	0.25	0.25	0.25	0.35	2.50	5.50	30	95
			Mint NH	0.40	0.95	1.40	2.10	6	11	35	130
C31	50¢	orange	Used	0.75	1.75	2.40	3.25	6.50	12.50	45	125
			Mint NH	2	4.25	7.25	11	15	25	47.50	175

1885-1925 SPECIAL DELIVERY ISSUES

SCT#	DENOM	COLOR	CONDITION	VG 50	F 70	F-VF 75	VF 80	VF-XF 85	XF 90	XF-SUP 95	SUP 98
E1	10¢	blue	Used	17	40	50	80	120	190	325	825
			Unused OG	110	225	335	550	625	750	1,300	2,500
			Mint NH	180	450	825	1,250	2,000	3,250	7,500	29,000
E2	10¢	blue	Used	11	18	30	45	70	120	300	650
			Unused OG	95	220	300	500	600	750	1,350	2,600
			Mint NH	200	450	675	1,150	1,900	3,250	7,750	32,500
E3	10¢	orange	Used	12.50	25	32.50	50	80	135	250	900
			Unused OG	62.50	135	185	300	340	400	600	1,275
			Mint NH	100	250	425	650	875	1,250	3,850	—
E4	10¢	blue	Used	27.50	45	62.50	110	140	220	425	1,000
			Unused OG	200	400	575	850	975	1,300	2,150	4,250
			Mint NH	335	750	1,300	2,000	3,100	5,250	13,000	32,500
E5	10¢	blue	Used	2.50	4.50	7	12.50	27.50	42.50	125	325
			Unused OG	45	82.50	135	210	240	300	475	1,000
			Mint NH	85	175	285	475	625	1,000	2,750	7,250
E5a	10¢	blue	Used	12.50	25	32.50	50	67.50	95	250	600
		Dots	Unused OG	85	165	260	400	425	450	675	1,250
		in frame	Mint NH	150	285	500	800	950	1,300	3,500	8,500
E6	10¢	ultramarine	Used	2.75	5	7.25	10	25	50	145	375
			Unused OG	50	90	140	225	260	325	525	1,200
			Mint NH	90	180	320	500	775	1,400	3,750	7,500
E6a	10¢	blue	Used	3.50	6.25	9	12.50	30	60	175	450
			Unused OG	65	120	200	300	350	425	750	1,500
			Mint NH	120	255	475	750	900	1,500	4,000	8,500

SCT#	DENOM	COLOR	CONDITION	VG 50	F 70	F-VF 75	VF 80	VF-XF 85	XF 90	XF-SUP 95	SUP 98
E7	10¢	green	Used	14	22	32.50	50	85	130	260	650
			Unused OG	15	25	40	65	72.50	82.50	120	225
			Mint NH	21	47.50	75	140	165	235	500	1,150
E8	10¢	ultramarine	Used	2.75	5	7	10	17.50	30	100	300
			Unused OG	22.50	45	60	110	115	125	180	360
			Mint NH	40	90	150	240	300	475	1,050	2,100
E8b	10¢	violet blue	Used	4	7	10	14	27.50	50	140	350
			Unused OG	35	70	95	160	180	220	350	600
			Mint NH	57.50	125	220	350	425	600	1,300	2,750
E9	10¢	ultramarine	Used	3	5	8	12	25	45	130	450
			Unused OG	35	80	110	190	210	240	375	700
			Mint NH	60	150	280	425	500	700	1,100	2,750
E9a	10¢	blue	Used	3	6	10	15	30	55	150	375
			Unused OG	47.50	95	145	260	285	310	475	800
			Mint NH	77.50	185	315	575	650	850	1,250	3,250
E10	10¢	pale ultramarine	Used	12.50	22.50	35	50	85	150	280	650
			Unused OG	60	125	175	320	350	400	575	1,000
			Mint NH	100	275	400	700	800	1,000	1,500	3,250
E10a	10¢	blue	Used	12.50	25	32.50	50	92.50	150	280	650
			Unused OG	75	150	225	375	425	500	800	1,400
			Mint NH	130	300	475	800	950	1,250	2,250	4,750
E11	10¢	ultramarine	Used	0.25	0.25	0.40	0.75	5	20	75	225
			Unused OG	6.25	10	13	20	22.50	30	47.50	80
			Mint NH	9	17.50	27.50	45	90	150	260	750
E11b	10¢	gray violet	Used	0.80	1	1.60	3	9	25	150	1,000
			Unused OG	11.50	22.50	30	35	52.50	75	125	190
			Mint NH	30	45	62.50	75	150	275	600	1,100
E11c	10¢	blue	Used	1.50	2.50	3.50	5	12.50	30	110	350
			Unused OG	20	35	60	100	110	135	175	300
			Mint NH	32.50	70	110	210	265	360	850	1,800
E12	10¢	gray violet	Used	0.65	1.20	1.75	3	10	20	75	325
			Unused OG	10	16	25	45	50	57.50	95	175
			Mint NH	15	32.50	55	95	115	180	450	975
E12a	10¢	deep ultramarine	Used	0.95	1.60	2.25	3.50	11.50	32.50	115	350
			Unused OG	13.50	22.50	35	55	60	67.50	115	210
			Mint NH	22.50	42.50	65	130	150	220	500	1,000
E13	15¢	deep orange	Used	0.90	1.50	2.25	3.75	12	32.50	135	375
			Unused OG	8	16	22.50	40	45	50	85	125
			Mint NH	12.50	27.50	45	75	90	115	170	375
E14	20¢	black	Used	0.30	0.50	0.70	1	4	20	70	250
			Unused OG	0.50	1	1.25	2	3.50	7.50	20	35
			Mint NH	0.60	1.30	2.25	4	6.50	15	45	150

1911 REGISTRATION STAMP

SCT#	DENOM	COLOR	CONDITION	VG 50	F 70	F-VF 75	VF 80	VF-XF 85	XF 90	XF-SUP 95	SUP 98
F1	10¢	ultramarine	Used	2.80	4.75	7.50	14	25	40	125	375
			Unused OG	15	30	47.50	75	82.50	95	140	260
			Mint NH	22.50	50	87.50	160	210	275	450	775

1879-1956 POSTAGE DUES

SCT#	DENOM	COLOR	CONDITION	VG 50	F 70	F-VF 75	VF 80	VF-XF 85	XF 90	XF-SUP 95	SUP 98
J1	1¢	brown	Used	4.50	6.75	9.75	14	16.50	22.50	65	190
			Unused OG	18	40	57.50	90	110	135	250	425
			Mint NH	35	90	150	260	325	525	975	2,200
J2	2¢	brown	Used	6	9	15	25	27.50	40	100	275
			Unused OG	90	175	250	425	475	575	950	1,500
			Mint NH	125	325	600	1,050	1,250	1,750	3,000	—
J3	3¢	brown	Used	1.75	2.90	4.25	6	9	17.50	40	125
			Unused OG	22.50	47.50	72.50	100	130	165	260	475
			Mint NH	37.50	95	165	280	350	575	1,050	—
J4	5¢	brown	Used	17	32.50	45	70	77.50	125	275	700
			Unused OG	150	300	450	800	900	1,150	1,600	—
			Mint NH	250	650	1,025	1,950	2,150	2,750	4,900	—
J5	10¢	brown	Used	17	32.50	45	70	77.50	125	300	700
			Unused OG	180	375	550	900	1,000	1,200	1,800	—

SCT#	DENOM	COLOR	CONDITION	VG 50	F 70	F-VF 75	VF 80	VF-XF 85	XF 90	XF-SUP 95	SUP 98
J6	30¢	brown	Used	17.50	30	40	65	82.50	125	275	675
			Unused OG	65	140	200	350	390	450	725	1,250
			Mint NH	100	260	475	800	1,000	1,800	—	—
J7	50¢	brown	Used	24	42	60	90	125	225	450	1,100
			Unused OG	125	250	370	600	675	875	1,400	—
			Mint NH	210	525	900	1,600	1,850	2,500	4,250	—
J8	1¢	deep brown	Unused OG	6,850	10,750	12,500	16,000	22,000	27,500	—	—
J9	2¢	deep brown	Unused OG	5,000	9,750	11,750	15,000	21,000	27,000	—	—
J10	3¢	deep brown	Unused OG	8,500	12,000	16,500	20,000	27,000	37,500	—	—
J11	5¢	deep brown	Unused OG	4,750	8,750	10,500	13,000	17,250	24,000	—	—
J12	10¢	deep brown	Unused OG	2,100	3,750	5,000	6,500	8,750	11,500	—	—
J13	30¢	deep brown	Unused OG	2,300	4,250	5,500	7,000	9,250	12,500	—	—
J14	50¢	deep brown	Unused OG	2,300	4,250	5,500	7,000	9,250	12,500	—	—
J15	1¢	red brown	Used	1.65	3.20	4.50	7	12	20	650	125
			Unused OG	15	27.50	42.50	70	80	110	160	280
			Mint NH	27.50	70	90	190	260	360	650	1,375
J16	2¢	red brown	Used	1.45	2.70	4	6	10	25	55	160
			Unused OG	17.50	40	52.50	80	100	135	225	400
			Mint NH	35	80	140	225	325	450	850	1,800
J17	3¢	red brown	Used	92.50	150	220	350	450	625	1,200	2,250
			Unused OG	225	425	625	1,050	1,150	1,450	2,100	—
			Mint NH	360	900	1,375	2,500	2,750	3,750	—	—
J18	5¢	red brown	Used	12	22.50	30	50	62.50	85	190	525
			Unused OG	110	220	330	550	625	750	1,200	—
			Mint NH	180	450	750	1,300	1,600	2,150	3,250	—
J19	10¢	red brown	Used	10	16.50	22.50	35	47.50	70	160	425
			Unused OG	110	220	330	550	625	750	1,200	2,200
			Mint NH	180	450	750	1,300	1,600	2,150	3,250	5,250
J20	30¢	red brown	Used	20	32	45	70	81.50	115	290	750
			Unused OG	42.50	80	125	190	220	260	475	750
			Mint NH	60	150	215	475	625	875	4,750	3,000
J21	50¢	red brown	Used	65	110	160	250	325	500	875	1,700
			Unused OG	360	725	1,050	1,800	1,950	2,150	2,850	—
			Mint NH	525	1,225	2,000	3,750	4,250	5,000	7,500	—
J22	1¢	bright claret	Used	0.55	0.85	1.25	2	4	10	25	80
			Unused OG	6	12.50	17.50	30	37.50	47.50	85	145
			Mint NH	11	27.50	45	85	110	170	350	750
J23	2¢	bright claret	Used	0.55	0.85	1.25	2	3.75	11	30	85
			Unused OG	7	14	21	32.50	40	50	85	160
			Mint NH	11	30	50	90	120	200	425	825
J24	3¢	bright claret	Used	4.50	7.75	10.50	16	17.50	25	70	200
			Unused OG	13.50	27.50	45	67.50	95	120	190	280
			Mint NH	22.50	57.50	100	180	250	360	650	2,400
J25	5¢	bright claret	Used	4.50	7.75	10.50	16	17.50	24	65	190
			Unused OG	22.50	47.50	65	100	120	160	275	475
			Mint NH	35	90	160	290	375	550	1,000	2,700
J26	10¢	bright claret	Used	8.50	14.50	20	30	37.50	50	120	325
			Unused OG	27.50	70	110	165	195	250	425	725
			Mint NH	55	150	260	500	575	750	1,300	3,000
J27	30¢	bright claret	Used	60	105	150	225	280	400	975	2,150
			Unused OG	120	240	350	575	675	850	1,300	2,750
			Mint NH	210	525	850	1,700	1,900	2,500	4,500	—
J28	50¢	bright claret	Used	60	105	150	225	300	450	975	2,400
			Unused OG	125	250	360	600	700	875	1,300	2,850
			Mint NH	200	525	900	1,750	1,850	2,000	3,500	—
J29	1¢	vermilion	Used	185	330	475	725	900	1,275	2,000	4,500
			Unused OG	525	900	1,350	2,250	2,600	3,350	5,000	—
			Mint NH	900	2,000	3,250	5,750	7,250	11,500	—	—
J30	2¢	vermilion	Used	85	160	235	350	450	625	1,300	2,900
			Unused OG	140	300	500	775	900	1,250	2,750	—
			Mint NH	275	600	900	1,900	2,200	2,650	4,250	—
J31	1¢	deep claret	Used	3	5.75	8.25	12	14.50	20	50	150
			Unused OG	13.50	27.50	45	72.50	82.50	105	170	300
			Mint NH	25	65	130	260	300	390	750	1,800
J32	2¢	deep claret	Used	2.50	4.65	6.75	10	15	27.50	50	150
			Unused OG	12.50	25	40	62.50	72.50	100	160	275
			Mint NH	22.50	60	120	240	300	375	800	1,650
J33	3¢	deep claret	Used	12.50	25	32.50	50	57.50	80	200	500
			Unused OG	37.50	82.50	115	200	220	260	400	700
			Mint NH	67.50	150	260	575	650	800	1,450	3,000
J34	5¢	deep claret	Used	13.75	27.50	37.50	55	65	90	225	550
			Unused OG	60	120	170	300	350	450	725	1,150
			Mint NH	95	250	425	850	1,000	1,500	2,250	—
J35	10¢	deep claret	Used	10	19	26	40	50	70	175	475
			Unused OG	65	130	200	350	400	525	775	1,300
			Mint NH	115	275	500	1,000	1,200	1,650	2,400	5,000
J36	30¢	deep claret	Used	65	115	170	250	300	425	825	1,850
			Unused OG	92.50	190	325	550	625	750	1,000	1,500

SCT#	DENOM	COLOR	CONDITION	VG 50	F 70	F-VF 75	VF 80	VF-XF 85	XF 90	XF-SUP 95	SUP 98
J36a	30¢	carmine	Used	70	130	180	275	310	450	875	1,900
			Unused OG	105	205	340	675	725	775	1,000	2,350
			Mint NH	170	410	775	1,600	1,725	2,000	3,000	—
J36b	30¢	pale	Used	50	97.50	130	200	240	325	600	1,350
		rose	Unused OG	85	170	270	450	500	550	800	1,400
			Mint NH	130	310	550	1,100	1,225	1,375	2,200	4,400
J37	50¢	deep	Used	200	375	525	800	975	1,400	2,500	5,000
		claret	Unused OG	400	750	1,075	1,800	2,100	2,500	3,650	—
			Mint NH	650	1,400	2,500	4,250	4,500	5,750	13,000	—
J37a	50¢	pale	Used	185	350	500	725	875	1,300	2,350	5,000
		rose	Unused OG	350	650	900	1,600	1,800	2,250	3,250	—
			Mint NH	700	1,600	2,500	3,750	4,250	5,500	12,000	—
J38	1¢	deep	Used	0.25	0.40	0.60	1	2	4	15	55
		claret	Unused OG	3.25	5.50	8	13.50	16	20	30	55
			Mint NH	7	15	27.50	40	60	90	275	600
J39	2¢	deep	Used	0.30	0.35	0.55	1	1.75	3	12.50	55
		claret	Unused OG	3.25	5.50	8	13.50	16	20	30	55
			Mint NH	7	15	27.50	40	60	90	275	600
J40	3¢	deep	Used	1.25	2.25	3.50	5	7	10.50	27.50	125
		claret	Unused OG	18	37.50	60	100	115	135	190	340
			Mint NH	27.50	60	120	225	290	425	825	1,600
J41	5¢	deep	Used	1.25	2.25	3.50	5	7	10.50	27.50	125
		claret	Unused OG	22.50	45	70	110	130	175	250	425
			Mint NH	37.50	92.50	175	280	360	500	875	1,750
J42	10¢	deep	Used	1.90	3.50	5	7.50	10.50	17.50	45	140
		claret	Unused OG	22.50	45	70	110	130	175	250	425
			Mint NH	37.50	92.50	175	280	360	500	950	1,750
J43	30¢	deep	Used	19	35	50	75	100	140	300	700
		claret	Unused OG	115	225	360	600	700	850	1,250	2,600
			Mint NH	190	440	825	1,500	1,750	2,250	3,500	—
J44	50¢	deep	Used	15	30	42.50	60	75	95	225	600
		claret	Unused OG	75	150	250	375	450	550	850	1,400
			Mint NH	115	27.50	500	925	1,150	1,650	2,500	—
J45	1¢	deep	Used	1.25	2.25	3.25	5	9	16	37.50	100
		claret	Unused OG	9	18	27.50	40	50	65	100	175
			Mint NH	15	40	75	115	160	240	400	850
J45a	1¢	rose	Used	1.25	2.25	3.25	5	9	16	37.50	100
		carmine	Unused OG	8	16	24	35	45	65	95	160
			Mint NH	13	35	67.50	105	140	225	375	750
J46	2¢	deep	Used	0.55	0.85	1.25	2	4	8	17.50	60
		claret	Unused OG	9	18	27.50	40	50	65	100	175
			Mint NH	15	40	75	115	160	240	400	850
J46a	2¢	rose	Used	0.55	0.85	1.25	2	4	8	17.50	60
		carmine	Unused OG	8	16	24	35	45	5	95	160
			Mint NH	13	35	67.50	105	140	225	375	750
J47	3¢	deep	Used	15	29	39	60	80	140	275	650
		claret	Unused OG	130	250	400	625	725	900	1,250	2,000
			Mint NH	200	500	925	1,600	1,850	2,650	5,000	—
J48	5¢	deep	Used	3	5.75	8.75	12	15	24	50	150
		claret	Unused OG	22.50	45	77.50	120	140	170	250	400
			Mint NH	37.50	92.50	185	275	350	475	750	1,400
J48a	5¢	rose	Used	3	5.75	8.75	12	15	24	50	150
		carmine	Unused OG	22.50	45	77.50	120	140	170	250	400
			Mint NH	37.50	92.50	185	275	350	475	750	1,400
J49	10¢	deep	Used	5	9.25	13	20	22.50	30	75	225
		claret	Unused OG	27.50	50	85	125	145	180	260	425
			Mint NH	37.50	92.50	185	280	360	475	750	1,400
J49a	10¢	rose	Used	5	9.25	13	20	22.50	30	72.50	225
		carmine	Unused OG	27.50	50	85	125	145	180	260	425
			Mint NH	37.50	92.50	185	280	360	475	750	1,400
J50	50¢	deep	Used	52.50	95	135	200	230	350	750	1,400
		claret	Unused OG	230	425	675	1,100	1,250	1,450	2,250	—
			Mint NH	375	875	1,600	2,900	3,250	4,250	7,500	—
J50a	10¢	rose	Used	47.50	87.50	130	190	225	350	775	1,375
		carmine	Unused OG	240	450	700	1,150	1,300	1,500	2,400	—
			Mint NH	390	900	1,650	3,000	3,350	4,500	7,750	—
J52	1¢	carmine	Used	3.75	7.25	10	15	17.50	25	70	200
		lake	Unused OG	15	35	55	80	95	125	175	300
			Mint NH	25	67.50	125	220	275	350	575	1,000
J52a	1¢	dull	Used	3.70	7.25	10	15	17.50	25	70	200
		rose	Unused OG	15	35	55	85	97.50	125	175	300
			Mint NH	27.50	72.50	130	230	290	375	600	1,100
J53	2¢	carmine	Used	0.40	0.50	0.60	1	2	4	17.50	65
		lake	Unused OG	11.50	25	40	62.50	72.50	90	125	210
			Mint NH	17	42.50	80	170	200	260	500	900
J53a	2¢	dull	Used	0.50	0.70	1.20	2	4	8	21	75
		rose	Unused OG	12	30	45	67.50	80	100	140	225
			Mint NH	20	47.50	85	180	210	275	500	950
J53b	2¢	vermilion	Used	0.65	0.80	1.20	2	3.75	6	21	75
			Unused OG	12	30	45	67.50	80	100	140	225
			Mint NH	20	47.50	85	180	210	275	500	950

SCT#	DENOM	COLOR	CONDITION	VG 50	F 70	F-VF 75	VF 80	VF-XF 85	XF 90	XF-SUP 95	SUP 98
J54	3¢	carmine	Used	20	35	50	75	90	125	275	700
		lake	Unused OG	225	400	650	1,050	1,200	1,600	2,300	—
			Mint NH	375	900	1,700	3,000	3,600	4,250	6,750	—
J54a	3¢	dull	Used	17	35	47.50	75	90	125	275	700
		rose	Unused OG	220	385	625	1,000	1,150	1,525	2,200	—
			Mint NH	360	850	1,600	2,900	3,400	4,000	6,500	—
J55	5¢	carmine	Used	1.45	2.75	4	6	9	17.50	45	140
		lake	Unused OG	11	22.50	35	50	60	75	135	200
			Mint NH	17.50	50	87.50	140	180	270	475	1,000
J55a	5¢	dull	Used	0.95	1.85	2.50	4	7	12.50	30	110
		rose	Unused OG	10	20	30	45	55	70	125	190
			Mint NH	16	45	82.50	130	175	260	450	925
J56	10¢	carmine	Used	0.95	1.85	2.50	4	7	12.50	30	110
		lake	Unused OG	12.50	30	50	75	85	100	170	275
			Mint NH	20	55	110	200	250	325	500	1,100
J56a	10¢	dull	Used	1.25	2.25	3.50	5	8	12.50	35	125
		rose	Unused OG	13.50	32.50	55	80	92.50	110	185	300
			Mint NH	22.50	60	115	210	260	350	550	1,150
J57	30¢	carmine	Used	13.50	26	37.50	55	60	85	220	525
		lake	Unused OG	45	90	150	225	260	325	550	850
			Mint NH	70	175	330	525	675	950	1,375	2,750
J58	50¢	carmine	Used	425	850	1,200	1,700	2,400	3,250	—	—
		lake	Unused OG	4,350	7,750	11,500	16,000	—	—	—	—
			Mint NH	6,250	—	21,000	—	—	—	—	—
J59	1¢	rose	Used	175	300	475	750	900	1,200	2,600	—
			Unused OG	900	1,600	2,500	4,000	4,750	6,500	11,500	—
			Mint NH	1,400	3,250	5,250	9,000	12,000	17,500	30,000	—
J60	2¢	rose	Used	20	35	50	75	87.50	110	220	375
			Unused OG	42.50	92.50	145	250	340	425	650	1,050
			Mint NH	72.50	170	300	625	825	1,000	1,500	3,250
J61	1¢	carmine	Used	0.25	0.25	0.25	0.25	1.50	3.50	12.50	50
		rose	Unused OG	0.70	1.30	1.75	2.75	3.75	5	9	25
			Mint NH	1.80	3.75	5.50	9	16	35	90	300
J61a	1¢	rose	Used	0.25	0.25	0.25	0.25	1.50	3.50	12.50	50
		red	Unused OG	0.70	1.30	1.75	2.75	3.75	5	9	25
			Mint NH	1.80	3.75	5.50	9	16	35	90	300
J61b	1¢	deep	Used	0.25	0.25	0.25	0.25	1.50	3.50	12.50	50
		claret	Unused OG	0.70	1.30	1.75	2.75	3.75	5	9	25
			Mint NH	1.80	3.75	5.50	9	16	35	90	300
J62	2¢	carmine	Used	0.25	0.25	0.25	0.25	1.50	3.50	12.50	50
		rose	Unused OG	0.70	1.30	1.75	2.75	3.75	5	9	25
			Mint NH	1.80	3.75	5.50	9	16	35	90	300
J62a	2¢	rose	Used	0.25	0.25	0.25	0.25	1.50	3.50	12.50	50
		red	Unused OG	0.70	1.30	1.75	2.75	3.75	5	9	25
			Mint NH	1.80	3.75	5.50	9	16	35	90	300
J62b	2¢	deep	Used	0.25	0.25	0.25	0.25	1.50	3.50	12.50	50
		claret	Unused OG	0.70	1.30	1.75	2.75	3.75	5	9	25
			Mint NH	1.80	3.75	5.50	9	16	35	90	300
J63	3¢	carmine	Used	0.25	0.40	0.55	0.80	1.60	3.75	13.50	60
		rose	Unused OG	2.75	5.50	8	13.50	16	19	27.50	45
			Mint NH	5.50	11	20	35	47.50	85	225	550
J63a	3¢	rose	Used	0.25	0.40	0.55	0.80	1.60	3.75	13.50	60
		red	Unused OG	2.75	5.50	8	13.50	16	19	27.50	45
			Mint NH	5.50	11	20	35	47.50	85	200	550
J63b	3¢	deep	Used	0.25	0.40	0.55	0.80	1.60	3.75	13.50	60
		claret	Unused OG	2.75	5.50	8	13.50	16	19	27.50	45
			Mint NH	5.50	11	20	35	47.50	85	200	550
J64	5¢	carmine	Used	0.25	0.40	0.55	0.80	1.60	3.75	13.50	60
		rose	Unused OG	2.75	5	7.50	11	14	17.50	25	40
			Mint NH	5	10	19	32.50	45	80	190	525
J64a	5¢	rose	Used	0.25	0.40	0.55	0.80	1.60	3.75	13.50	60
		red	Unused OG	2.75	5	7.50	11	14	17.50	25	40
			Mint NH	5	10	19	32.50	45	80	190	525
J64b	5¢	deep	Used	0.25	0.40	0.55	0.80	1.60	3.75	13.50	60
		claret	Unused OG	2.75	5	7.50	11	14	17.50	25	40
			Mint NH	5	10	19	32.50	45	80	190	525
J65	10¢	carmine	Used	0.25	0.50	0.75	1	1.75	4.25	17.50	70
		rose	Unused OG	5.50	10	15	22.50	27.50	32.50	42.50	85
			Mint NH	10.50	19	37.50	65	82.50	115	325	675
J65a	10¢	rose	Used	0.25	0.50	0.75	1	1.75	4.25	17.50	70
		red	Unused OG	5.50	10	15	22.50	27.50	32.50	42.50	85
			Mint NH	10.50	19	37.50	65	82.50	115	325	675
J65b	10¢	deep	Used	0.25	0.50	0.75	1	1.75	4.25	17.50	70
		claret	Unused OG	5.50	10	15	22.50	27.50	32.50	42.50	85
			Mint NH	10.50	19	37.50	65	82.50	115	325	675
J66	30¢	carmine	Used	0.50	0.80	1.20	2	4	9.50	27.50	100
		rose	Unused OG	15	35	50	80	92.50	120	175	300
			Mint NH	25	60	120	220	260	350	575	1,200
J66a	30¢	deep	Used	0.50	0.80	1.20	2	4	9.50	27.50	100
		claret	Unused OG	15	35	50	80	92.50	120	175	300
			Mint NH	25	60	120	220	260	350	575	1,200

SCT#	DENOM	COLOR	CONDITION	VG 50	F 70	F-VF 75	VF 80	VF-XF 85	XF 90	XF-SUP 95	SUP 98
J67	50¢	carmine	Used	0.25	0.50	0.75	1	1.75	4.25	18	70
		rose	Unused OG	27.50	47.50	75	140	155	175	275	450
			Mint NH	40	97.50	175	325	400	500	800	1,650
J67a	50¢	rose	Used	0.25	0.50	0.75	1	1.75	4.25	18	70
		red	Unused OG	27.50	47.50	75	140	155	175	275	450
			Mint NH	40	97.50	175	325	400	500	800	1,650
J67b	50¢	deep	Used	0.25	0.50	0.75	1	1.75	4.25	18	70
		claret	Unused OG	27.50	47.50	75	140	155	175	275	450
			Mint NH	40	97.50	175	325	400	500	800	1,650
J68	½¢	dull	Used	0.25	0.25	0.25	0.25	1.50	3.50	14	50
		red	Unused OG	0.25	0.45	0.65	1	1.40	2.10	5.50	12.50
			Mint NH	0.40	0.70	1.10	1.75	3.50	7	22.50	92.50
J69	½¢	carmine	Used	0.45	0.90	1.20	1.90	3	9.50	30	110
			Unused OG	1	2	2.75	4.25	5	6	9.75	22.50
			Mint NH	2	4	6.25	9.50	15	24	100	250
J70	1¢	carmine	Used	0.30	0.30	0.30	0.35	1.10	3.75	13	50
			Unused OG	0.65	1.30	1.85	2.75	3.50	4.50	8	15
			Mint NH	1.25	2.75	4.50	6.25	11.50	18	90	210
J71	2¢	carmine	Used	0.25	0.25	0.25	0.35	1.10	3.75	13	50
			Unused OG	0.95	1.70	2.50	3.75	4.50	5.75	9	17.50
			Mint NH	1.75	3.75	5.50	8.50	13.50	22.50	105	250
J72	3¢	carmine	Used	0.65	1.30	1.75	2.75	5	12.50	35	125
			Unused OG	4.75	8.50	11.50	20	24	30	42.50	67.50
			Mint NH	7.50	16.50	26	47.50	62.50	95	210	425
J73	5¢	carmine	Used	1.25	2.35	3.25	5	9	19	72.50	200
			Unused OG	3.75	7.50	10.50	18	20	24	37.50	55
			Mint NH	7.50	14.50	24	42.50	55	85	190	380
J74	10¢	carmine	Used	0.55	0.85	1.25	2	4	11	32.50	115
			Unused OG	8.50	15	23.50	42.50	47.50	55	85	130
			Mint NH	16	37.50	70	95	115	150	300	625
J75	30¢	carmine	Used	1	1.75	2.50	4	10	37.50	120	250
			Unused OG	16.50	50	82.50	125	140	175	250	375
			Mint NH	37.50	85	150	275	325	400	625	1,250
J76	50¢	carmine	Used	0.50	0.90	1.25	2	4	11	32.50	115
			Unused OG	32.50	65	110	175	200	260	350	525
			Mint NH	55	120	220	375	425	550	925	1,750
J77	$1	carmine	Used	0.25	0.25	0.25	0.35	1.50	3.50	15	50
			Unused OG	6.50	11.50	18.50	32.50	37.50	42.50	55	85
			Mint NH	11.50	20	37.50	65	80	110	240	500
J77a	$1	scarlet	Used	0.25	0.25	0.25	0.35	1.50	3.50	15	50
			Unused OG	5	9.50	16.50	27.50	32.50	37.50	45	72.50
			Mint NH	9.50	17.50	30	55	70	100	220	475
J78	$5	dull	Used	0.25	0.25	0.25	0.35	1.50	3.50	15	50
		carmine	Unused OG	6.50	14	22.50	37.50	42.50	55	80	115
			Mint NH	9.50	26	47.50	85	100	140	290	625
J78a	$5	scarlet	Used	0.25	0.25	0.25	0.35	1.10	3.50	15	50
			Unused OG	5.50	12	18.50	32.50	37.50	45	62.50	90
			Mint NH	10	22.50	40	70	85	125	240	550
J79	½¢	dull	Used	0.25	0.25	0.25	0.25	0.80	2	8.50	40
		carmine	Unused OG	0.25	0.40	0.60	0.90	1.40	2	4.50	10
			Mint NH	0.25	0.55	0.80	1.30	3	10	22.50	40
J79a	½¢	scarlet	Used	0.25	0.25	0.25	0.25	0.80	2	8.50	40
			Unused OG	0.25	0.40	0.60	0.90	1.40	2	4.50	10
			Mint NH	0.25	0.55	0.80	1.30	3	10	22.50	40
J80	1¢	dull	Used	0.25	0.25	0.25	0.25	0.80	2	8.50	40
		carmine	Unused OG	0.25	0.25	0.25	0.25	0.45	0.90	2.75	7.75
			Mint NH	0.25	0.25	0.25	0.30	1.50	5	12.50	50
J80a	1¢	scarlet	Used	0.25	0.25	0.25	0.25	0.80	2	8.50	40
			Unused OG	0.25	0.25	0.25	0.25	0.45	0.90	2.75	7.75
			Mint NH	0.25	0.25	0.25	0.30	1.50	5	12.50	50
J81	2¢	dull	Used	0.25	0.25	0.25	0.25	0.80	2	8.50	40
		carmine	Unused OG	0.25	0.25	0.25	0.25	0.45	0.90	2.75	7.75
			Mint NH	0.25	0.25	0.25	0.30	1.50	5	12.50	50
J81a	2¢	scarlet	Used	0.25	0.25	0.25	0.25	0.80	2	8.50	40
			Unused OG	0.25	0.25	0.25	0.25	0.45	0.90	2.75	7.75
			Mint NH	0.25	0.25	0.25	0.30	1.50	5	12.50	50
J82	3¢	dull	Used	0.25	0.25	0.25	0.25	0.80	2	8.50	40
		carmine	Unused OG	0.25	0.25	0.25	0.25	0.55	1.10	3	8.50
			Mint NH	0.25	0.25	0.25	0.40	2	6	15	50
J82a	3¢	scarlet	Used	0.25	0.25	0.25	0.25	0.80	2	8.50	40
			Unused OG	0.25	0.25	0.25	0.25	0.55	1.10	3	8.50
			Mint NH	0.25	0.25	0.30	0.45	2	6	15	50
J83	5¢	dull	Used	0.25	0.25	0.25	0.25	0.80	2	8.50	40
		carmine	Unused OG	0.25	0.25	0.25	0.40	0.80	1.60	4.50	9.50
			Mint NH	0.25	0.25	0.35	0.60	3	8	20	40
J83a	5¢	scarlet	Used	0.25	0.25	0.25	0.25	0.80	2	8.50	40
			Unused OG	0.25	0.25	0.25	0.40	0.80	1.60	4.50	9.50
			Mint NH	0.25	0.25	0.35	0.60	3	8	20	40
J84	10¢	dull	Used	0.25	0.25	0.25	0.25	0.80	2	8.50	40
		carmine	Unused OG	0.25	0.50	0.70	1.10	1.40	2	5.25	11
			Mint NH	0.35	0.75	1.05	1.80	5	10	25	47.50
J84a	10¢	scarlet	Used	0.25	0.25	0.25	0.25	0.80	2	8.50	40
			Unused OG	0.30	0.55	0.80	1.25	1.60	2.40	5.25	11
			Mint NH	0.35	0.80	1.10	1.90	5.25	10	27.50	47.50
J85	30¢	dull	Used	0.25	0.25	0.25	0.25	0.90	2.50	9.50	45
		carmine	Unused OG	1.85	3.50	4.60	7.50	9.75	16	30	70
			Mint NH	2	4.25	7.25	11.50	16	30	75	160
J85a	30¢	scarlet	Used	0.25	0.25	0.25	0.25	0.90	2.50	9.50	45
			Unused OG	1.85	3.50	4.60	7.50	9.75	16	30	70
			Mint NH	2	4.25	7.25	11.50	16	30	75	160
J86	50¢	dull	Used	0.25	0.25	0.25	0.25	0.90	2.50	9.50	45
		carmine	Unused OG	2.25	4.25	5.75	9	11.50	20	37.50	85
			Mint NH	2.50	5.75	8.50	15	20	32.50	75	160
J86a	50¢	scarlet	Used	0.25	0.25	0.25	0.25	0.90	2.50	9.50	45
			Unused OG	2.20	4.25	6	9	11.50	20	37.50	85
			Mint NH	2.50	5.75	8.50	15	20	32.50	75	160
J87	50¢	scarlet	Used	0.25	0.25	0.25	0.25	0.90	2.50	9.50	45
			Unused OG	7	14	20	30	32.50	37.50	55	115
			Mint NH	9	19.50	32.50	52.50	62.50	90	150	325

1919-22 U.S. POSTAL AGENCY IN CHINA

SCT#	DENOM	COLOR	CONDITION	VG 50	F 70	F-VF 75	VF 80	VF-XF 85	XF 90	XF-SUP 95	SUP 98
K1	2¢/1¢	green	Used	17.50	32.50	50	70	100	160	425	1,100
			Unused OG	4.50	11.25	15	22.50	27.50	37.50	70	125
			Mint NH	12.50	30	45	67.50	87.50	140	450	1,050
K2	4¢/2¢	rose	Used	17.50	32.50	50	70	100	160	425	1,050
		type I	Unused OG	4.50	11.25	15	22.50	27.50	37.50	70	125
			Mint NH	12.50	30	45	67.50	87.50	140	450	1,050
K3	6¢/3¢	violet	Used	35	70	97.50	140	210	325	900	2,250
		type II	Unused OG	11.50	22.50	40	55	67.50	75	150	275
			Mint NH	21	52.50	88.50	140	190	320	1,050	2,250
K4	8¢/4¢	brown	Used	35	70	97.50	140	210	325	975	2,100
			Unused OG	11.50	22.50	40	55	67.50	75	150	275
			Mint NH	21	52.50	88.50	140	190	320	1,050	2,250
K5	10¢/5¢	blue	Used	35	70	97.50	140	210	400	950	2,250
			Unused OG	12.50	25	42.50	60	70	80	155	280
			Mint NH	23.50	57.50	95	160	210	325	1,100	2,500
K6	12¢/6¢	red	Used	50	100	145	210	290	500	1,200	2,750
		orange	Unused OG	17.50	37.50	52.50	80	90	110	210	375
			Mint NH	32.50	77.50	145	210	250	375	1,350	3,000
K7	14¢/7¢	black	Used	55	110	150	210	310	450	1,250	2,750
			Unused OG	20	40	55	82.50	92.50	120	220	390
			Mint NH	35	80	150	215	260	400	1,400	3,100
K8	16¢/8¢	olive	Used	37.50	77.50	110	160	225	360	1,000	2,750
		bister	Unused OG	15	30	45	65	77.50	100	175	300
			Mint NH	25	65	105	170	240	400	1,200	2,650
K8a	16¢/8¢	olive	Used	37.50	72.50	100	140	210	350	975	2,650
		green	Unused OG	11.50	22.50	40	55	67.50	75	150	275
			Mint NH	22.50	65	95	150	200	320	1,075	2,500
K9	18¢/9¢	salmon	Used	45	87.50	135	175	260	425	1,050	3,250
		red	Unused OG	13.50	27.50	42.50	60	67.50	100	180	—
			Mint NH	22.50	65	95	150	200	300	1,075	2,500
K10	20¢/10¢	orange	Used	37.50	70	100	140	215	325	850	2,100
		yellow	Unused OG	12.75	27.50	40	55	67.50	90	160	300
			Mint NH	21	57.50	87.50	140	225	375	1,450	2,600
K11	24¢/12¢	brown	Used	37.50	75	105	160	240	360	1,250	2,600
		carmine	Unused OG	15	37.50	52.50	75	87.50	110	210	375
			Mint NH	30	75	120	190	260	475	1,250	3,000
K11a	24¢/12¢	claret	Used	65	125	150	240	325	500	1,400	3,250
		brown	Unused OG	22.50	50	75	110	130	170	290	500
			Mint NH	40	95	180	275	350	500	1,500	3,250
K12	30¢/15¢	gray	Used	62.50	110	150	230	320	525	1,400	3,150
			Unused OG	20	40	57.50	82.50	95	120	225	400
			Mint NH	32.50	80	135	200	290	425	1,300	3,500
K13	40¢/20¢	deep	Used	77.50	150	210	325	450	700	1,900	4,250
		ultramarine	Unused OG	25	60	82.50	120	145	175	350	575
			Mint NH	50	120	200	300	450	750	1,850	3,750
K14	60¢/30¢	orange	Used	70	130	185	275	400	750	1,650	3,750
		red	Unused OG	22.50	50	75	110	130	165	340	550
			Mint NH	45	100	170	260	400	700	1,800	3,650

SCT#	DENOM	COLOR	CONDITION	VG 50	F 70	F-VF 75	VF 80	VF-XF 85	XF 90	XF-SUP 95	SUP 98
K15	$1/50¢	light violet	Used	240	485	675	1,000	1,350	2,250	5,750	—
			Unused OG	110	240	385	550	650	800	1,400	2,350
			Mint NH	200	450	825	1,200	1,600	2,500	6,000	12,500
K16	$2/$1	violet brown	Used	200	425	575	750	1,150	1,800	4,750	10,500
			Unused OG	85	190	285	425	500	600	1,000	1,750
			Mint NH	170	340	600	925	1,250	2,250	5,000	10,000
K17	2¢/1¢	green	Used	57.50	105	160	225	340	500	1,250	3,250
			Unused OG	20	45	67.50	100	125	155	275	480
			Mint NH	35	90	150	225	300	425	1,450	3,000
K18	4¢/2¢	carmine	Used	47.50	97.50	145	200	350	500	1,250	2,900
			Unused OG	20	40	60	90	110	145	250	425
			Mint NH	32.50	77.50	135	210	310	425	1,350	2,750

OFFICIAL STAMPS

1873 Agriculture Department

SCT#	DENOM	COLOR	CONDITION	VG 50	F 70	F-VF 75	VF 80	VF-XF 85	XF 90	XF-SUP 95	SUP 98
O1	1¢	yellow	Used	55	110	145	200	250	375	850	—
			Unused NG	50	90	115	170	190	215	265	—
			Unused OG	90	155	205	300	430	625	1,350	—
			Mint NH	110	190	350	650	925	1,400	3,250	—
O2	2¢	yellow	Used	30	52.50	67.50	100	130	175	500	—
			Unused NG	32.50	60	72.50	110	120	140	225	—
			Unused OG	75	130	170	275	400	550	1,100	—
			Mint NH	100	175	315	575	800	1,200	2,700	—
O3	3¢	yellow	Used	4.75	9	12	17.50	22.50	37.50	125	—
			Unused NG	25	47.50	60	85	95	110	185	—
			Unused OG	52.50	100	155	225	320	435	875	—
			Mint NH	82.50	145	265	475	675	1,000	2,200	—
O4	6¢	yellow	Used	20	35	42.50	60	85	125	375	—
			Unused NG	32.50	57.50	77.50	110	120	140	225	435
			Unused OG	62.50	125	185	275	400	525	1,175	—
			Mint NH	100	180	315	575	800	1,200	2,650	—
O5	10¢	yellow	Used	60	110	140	200	260	350	700	—
			Unused NG	65	110	155	220	250	275	425	—
			Unused OG	150	250	370	525	700	1,050	2,000	—
			Mint NH	275	400	650	1,150	1,650	2,500	5,250	—
O6	12¢	yellow	Used	80	135	180	260	350	475	1,100	—
			Unused NG	80	110	175	250	260	275	375	—
			Unused OG	135	245	300	450	625	900	1,700	—
			Mint NH	250	385	525	950	1,350	2,050	4,500	—
O7	15¢	yellow	Used	70	120	160	230	320	450	1,000	1,800
			Unused NG	55	85	160	225	250	300	425	700
			Unused OG	115	225	285	425	600	825	1,625	—
			Mint NH	225	350	525	950	1,350	2,000	4,500	—
O8	24¢	yellow	Used	80	130	170	250	310	425	950	—
			Unused NG	55	85	160	225	255	300	425	—
			Unused OG	115	225	285	425	600	900	1,750	—
			Mint NH	225	350	550	950	1,350	2,100	4,500	—
O9	30¢	yellow	Used	82.50	145	190	280	375	500	1,100	—
			Unused NG	75	110	175	275	300	350	550	—
			Unused OG	175	300	400	550	850	1,200	2,250	—
			Mint NH	300	450	675	1,200	1,700	2,650	5,500	—

1873 Executive

SCT#	DENOM	COLOR	CONDITION	VG 50	F 70	F-VF 75	VF 80	VF-XF 85	XF 90	XF-SUP 95	SUP 98
O10	1¢	carmine	Used	175	280	390	550	800	1,150	2,600	—
			Unused NG	125	175	300	450	475	550	750	—
			Unused OG	240	425	625	900	1,175	1,600	2,950	—
			Mint NH	425	750	1,250	2,250	3,000	4,750	10,500	—
O11	2¢	carmine	Used	82.50	135	185	260	370	550	1,250	—
			Unused NG	67.50	105	180	250	280	340	525	—
			Unused OG	130	210	390	575	725	1,150	2,200	3,400
			Mint NH	275	400	700	1,250	1,750	2,650	5,900	—
O12	3¢	carmine	Used	70	115	160	225	310	455	1,025	—
			Unused NG	80	125	190	270	300	375	625	—
			Unused OG	200	350	475	700	950	1,350	2,750	—
			Mint NH	350	550	900	1,600	2,200	3,450	7,500	—
O12a	3¢	violet rose	Used	85	140	200	275	360	500	1,100	—
			Unused NG	105	175	260	375	425	475	575	—
			Unused OG	300	450	700	1,000	1,250	1,650	2,900	—
			Mint NH	440	700	1,275	2,250	3,150	—	—	—
O13	6¢	carmine	Used	170	300	435	600	875	1,300	2,850	—
			Unused NG	90	150	275	325	350	425	650	—
			Unused OG	225	400	600	900	1,150	1,750	3,000	—
			Mint NH			—	—	—			—
O14	10¢	carmine	Used	325	500	725	1,000	1,375	1,825	4,000	—
			Unused NG	150	275	450	600	650	775	1,200	—
			Unused OG	325	575	825	1,200	1,550	2,250	4,000	—
			Mint NH			—	—	—			—

1873 Interior

SCT#	DENOM	COLOR	CONDITION	VG 50	F 70	F-VF 75	VF 80	VF-XF 85	XF 90	XF-SUP 95	SUP 98
O15	1¢	vermilion	Used	3	5	7	10	14	25	75	175
			Unused NG	9	15	20	30	35	45	70	—
			Unused OG	20	40	55	75	110	170	300	—
			Mint NH	35	70	110	170	245	390	800	—
O16	2¢	vermilion	Used	3.75	6	8.75	12	17	28	80	—
			Unused NG	8.75	15	20	30	35	42.50	65	—
			Unused OG	20	40	50	70	105	165	300	—
			Mint NH	35	70	100	160	225	390	800	—
O17	3¢	vermilion	Used	1.75	3	4.25	6	8.50	17.50	50	—
			Unused NG	10.50	17.50	25	35	40	50	75	—
			Unused OG	25	45	60	80	140	200	375	—
			Mint NH	40	75	110	175	275	425	850	—
O18	6¢	vermilion	Used	3	5	7.25	10	13.50	25	70	—
			Unused NG	8	14	20	27.50	34	42.50	65	—
			Unused OG	20	40	50	70	105	165	300	—
			Mint NH	40	75	110	160	225	390	800	—
O19	10¢	vermilion	Used	6	10	15	20	28	50	125	—
			Unused NG	8	14	20	27.50	34	42.50	65	—
			Unused OG	20	40	50	70	105	170	300	—
			Mint NH	40	75	90	160	225	375	800	—
O20	12¢	vermilion	Used	3.75	6	8.75	12	17	35	90	—
			Unused NG	11	18	26	35	42.50	55	85	—
			Unused OG	25	50	65	90	130	225	400	—
			Mint NH	45	80	110	200	275	425	950	—
O21	15¢	vermilion	Used	7.75	12.50	18	25	35	60	145	—
			Unused NG	25	40	57.50	80	92.50	110	165	—
			Unused OG	55	110	135	200	280	425	825	—
			Mint NH	95	175	250	450	625	975	2,200	—
O22	24¢	vermilion	Used	6.75	11	14	20	28	50	125	—
			Unused NG	20	35	45	60	77.50	100	150	—
			Unused OG	50	100	125	180	260	400	750	—
			Mint NH	90	170	225	400	550	950	1,950	—
O23	30¢	vermilion	Used	6.25	10	14	20	28	50	125	—
			Unused NG	32.50	60	80	110	125	150	230	—
			Unused OG	75	150	200	290	400	600	1,225	—
			Mint NH	125	225	375	625	850	1,350	3,050	—
O24	90¢	vermilion	Used	15	25	37.50	50	72.50	125	275	—
			Unused NG	35	60	85	120	135	190	275	—
			Unused OG	90	160	225	325	450	625	1,250	—
			Mint NH	140	240	400	700	925	1,550	3,400	—

1873 Justice

SCT#	DENOM	COLOR	CONDITION	VG 50	F 70	F-VF 75	VF 80	VF-XF 85	XF 90	XF-SUP 95	SUP 98
O25	1¢	purple	Used	30	50	72	100	140	250	500	—
			Unused NG	30	50	72.50	100	115	135	220	—
			Unused OG	70	130	175	250	350	500	900	—
			Mint NH	125	200	325	550	775	1,200	2,650	—

SCT#	DENOM	COLOR	CONDITION	VG 50	F 70	F-VF 75	VF 80	VF-XF 85	XF 90	XF-SUP 95	SUP 98
O26	2¢	purple	Used	32.50	55	80	110	150	225	500	—
			Unused NG	35	65	90	120	135	175	300	—
			Unused OG	90	160	225	310	450	625	1,225	—
			Mint NH	140	240	400	700	975	1,450	3,300	—
O27	3¢	purple	Used	10.50	17.50	25	35	50	75	180	—
			Unused NG	30	60	90	110	125	150	230	—
			Unused OG	95	165	230	320	450	675	1,300	—
			Mint NH	150	250	425	725	950	1,575	3,450	—
O28	6¢	purple	Used	13.50	22.50	32.50	45	60	95	250	—
			Unused NG	35	65	90	110	125	150	230	—
			Unused OG	90	160	225	310	440	650	1,150	—
			Mint NH	140	240	400	700	975	1,450	3,300	—
O29	10¢	purple	Used	30	50	70	100	140	210	475	—
			Unused NG	35	65	90	120	135	160	250	—
			Unused OG	90	160	225	310	460	650	1,250	—
			Mint NH	140	240	400	700	975	1,450	3,300	—
O30	12¢	purple	Used	22.50	37.50	52.50	75	105	155	400	—
			Unused NG	27.50	47.50	70	95	110	125	200	—
			Unused OG	67.50	120	175	260	350	525	1,050	—
			Mint NH	110	200	325	575	825	1,250	2,750	—
O31	15¢	purple	Used	60	110	140	200	280	425	1,000	—
			Unused NG	62.50	100	155	220	240	300	470	—
			Unused OG	145	265	340	500	700	1,050	2,000	—
			Mint NH	260	500	675	1,100	1,575	2,400	5,250	—
O32	24¢	purple	Used	135	215	300	425	600	900	2,250	—
			Unused NG	145	225	375	550	575	700	1,100	—
			Unused OG	325	600	900	1,250	1,650	2,250	4,250	—
			Mint NH			—	—	—			—
O33	30¢	purple	Used	100	175	250	350	500	750	1,800	—
			Unused NG	140	250	400	550	575	700	1,100	—
			Unused OG	350	525	900	1,300	1,800	2,500	4,450	—
			Mint NH			—	—	—			—
O34	90¢	purple	Used	240	450	600	900	1,350	2,000	4,500	—
			Unused NG	175	300	575	800	850	1,050	1,500	—
			Unused OG	425	725	1,200	1,900	2,300	3,250	5,500	—
			Mint NH			—	—	—			—

1873 Navy

SCT#	DENOM	COLOR	CONDITION	VG 50	F 70	F-VF 75	VF 80	VF-XF 85	XF 90	XF-SUP 95	SUP 98
O35	1¢	ultramarine	Used	14	25	37.50	50	70	105	250	—
			Unused NG	16	30	47.50	65	72.50	85	125	—
			Unused OG	42.50	75	110	160	225	325	600	—
			Mint NH	75	125	200	350	475	850	1,800	—
O35a	1¢	dull	Used	14	25	35	50	70	105	250	—
		blue	Unused NG	17.50	32.50	50	70	77.50	92.50	135	—
			Unused OG	47.50	82.50	120	175	225	350	—	—
			Mint NH	82.50	140	220	385	525	925	—	—
O36	2¢	ultramarine	Used	7.50	12.50	17.50	25	35	55	140	—
			Unused NG	16	30	47.50	65	72.50	85	125	—
			Unused OG	42.50	75	110	160	225	325	600	—
			Mint NH	75	125	200	350	475	850	1,800	—
O36a	2¢	dull	Used	7.25	12.50	18	25	35	55	140	—
		blue	Unused NG	17.50	32.50	50	70	77.50	92.50	135	—
			Unused OG	47.50	82.50	120	175	240	350	650	—
			Mint NH	82.50	140	220	385	525	925	2,000	—
O37	3¢	ultramarine	Used	4.50	7.50	10.50	15	22.50	35	90	—
			Unused NG	18	33.50	45	60	75	90	130	—
			Unused OG	45	85	110	170	250	350	675	—
			Mint NH	80	140	210	375	525	900	1,900	—
O37a	3¢	dull	Used	4.50	7.50	10.50	15	22.50	35	90	—
		blue	Unused NG	19	35	47.50	62.50	75	95	145	—
			Unused OG	47.50	82.50	120	175	250	360	700	—
			Mint NH	82.50	140	220	385	525	925	2,000	—
O38	6¢	ultramarine	Used	7.50	12.50	18	25	35	60	125	—
			Unused NG	17.50	27.50	40	55	67.50	85	130	—
			Unused OG	40	70	105	150	215	325	650	—
			Mint NH	75	120	185	325	450	775	1,700	—
O38a	6¢	dull	Used	7.50	12.50	18	25	35	60	140	—
		blue	Unused NG	21.50	35	50	67.50	82.50	105	160	—
			Unused OG	50	92.50	115	175	260	400	700	—
			Mint NH	90	160	235	385	525	900	1,950	—

SCT#	DENOM	COLOR	CONDITION	VG 50	F 70	F-VF 75	VF 80	VF-XF 85	XF 90	XF-SUP 95	SUP 98
O39	7¢	ultramarine	Used	70	120	165	230	340	500	1,200	—
			Unused NG	82.50	130	200	275	310	375	600	—
			Unused OG	190	325	485	700	950	1,350	2,600	—
			Mint NH			—	—	—			—
O39a	7¢	dull	Used	70	120	165	230	340	500	1,200	—
		blue	Unused NG	82.50	130	200	275	310	375	600	—
			Unused OG	210	350	525	750	1,025	1,450	2,750	—
			Mint NH			—	—	—			—
O40	10¢	ultramarine	Used	13.50	24	32.50	45	62.50	100	240	—
			Unused NG	22.50	37.50	55	75	85	100	160	—
			Unused OG	55	110	150	210	260	425	825	—
			Mint NH	95	200	300	475	675	1,100	2,250	—
O40a	10¢	dull	Used	13.50	24	32.50	45	62.50	100	240	—
		blue	Unused NG	25	40	57.50	80	90	105	170	—
			Unused OG	60	120	160	225	300	450	875	—
			Mint NH	100	210	315	500	700	1,150	2,350	—
O41	12¢	ultramarine	Used	13.50	24	32.50	45	62.50	100	240	—
			Unused NG	27.50	50	72.50	100	115	140	215	—
			Unused OG	60	120	160	240	325	525	950	—
			Mint NH	100	210	290	525	725	1,200	2,500	—
O42	15¢	ultramarine	Used	22.50	37.50	53	75	105	160	375	—
			Unused NG	47.50	77.50	115	160	180	215	350	—
			Unused OG	115	200	285	425	575	875	1,650	3,500
			Mint NH			—	—	—			—
O43	24¢	ultramarine	Used	25	42.50	60	85	120	180	425	—
			Unused NG	47.50	75	110	160	180	215	350	—
			Unused OG	120	225	280	425	575	875	1,650	3,500
			Mint NH			—	—	—			—
O43a	24¢	dull	Used	22.50	40	55	80	110	170	400	—
		blue	Unused NG	47.50	75	110	160	180	215	350	—
			Unused OG	120	225	280	425	575	875	1,650	—
			Mint NH			—	—	—			—
O44	30¢	ultramarine	Used	15	25	37.50	50	70	110	250	—
			Unused NG	40	67.50	100	140	155	190	290	—
			Unused OG	92.50	170	235	350	475	750	1,350	2,950
			Mint NH			—	—	—			—
O45	90¢	ultramarine	Used	115	190	265	375	525	725	1,700	—
			Unused NG	110	185	300	450	475	625	850	—
			Unused OG	275	500	725	1,050	1,400	2,100	3,550	—
			Mint NH			—	—	—			—

1873 Post Office

SCT#	DENOM	COLOR	CONDITION	VG 50	F 70	F-VF 75	VF 80	VF-XF 85	XF 90	XF-SUP 95	SUP 98
O47	1¢	black	Used	3.50	6.50	8.75	12	17	27.50	50	95
			Unused NG	3	6	8.50	12	13.50	17.50	25	40
			Unused OG	7	12	17.50	25	37.50	55	—	—
			Mint NH	12	20	35	60	85	160	500	—
O48	2¢	black	Used	3	5.50	7	10	14	20	40	85
			Unused NG	4	6.50	9.50	13	15	18.50	26.50	42.50
			Unused OG	8	14	20	30	47.50	70	120	260
			Mint NH	14	25	42.50	75	110	170	390	—
O49	3¢	black	Used	0.65	1	1.25	2	3.50	10	17.50	32.50
			Unused NG	0.90	1.50	2.10	3	4	6.50	15	30
			Unused OG	2.50	4.25	7	10	15	22.50	42.50	75
			Mint NH	4.25	7.50	14	25	36	55	160	—
O50	6¢	black	Used	2.40	4	5.75	8	11	17.50	35	70
			Unused NG	3.60	6	8.75	12	14.50	18	25	40
			Unused OG	8	14	20	30	45	70	120	260
			Mint NH	14	25	42.50	75	110	170	400	—
O51	10¢	black	Used	15	27.50	37.50	55	80	115	180	350
			Unused NG	13	25	42.50	60	67.50	85	125	225
			Unused OG	35	70	100	140	200	275	525	—
			Mint NH	55	120	200	325	460	700	1,550	—
O52	12¢	black	Used	3.60	6	8.75	12	17	24	45	95
			Unused NG	12	20	28	40	50	65	85	150
			Unused OG	30	57.50	80	120	170	260	450	925
			Mint NH	47.50	90	150	275	390	625	1,375	—
O53	15¢	black	Used	6	10	14	20	30	43.50	85	175
			Unused NG	15	25	35	50	62.50	70	110	180
			Unused OG	35	70	100	140	200	280	525	1,050
			Mint NH	55	125	200	325	460	700	1,550	—
O54	24¢	black	Used	7.75	12.50	17.50	25	35	47.50	80	160
			Unused NG	25	42.50	60	85	100	120	175	300
			Unused OG	57.50	105	165	225	310	450	850	1,500
			Mint NH	85	160	300	500	675	1,000	2,250	—

SCT#	DENOM	COLOR	CONDITION	VG 50	F 70	F-VF 75	VF 80	VF-XF 85	XF 90	XF-SUP 95	SUP 98
O55	30¢	black	Used	7.75	12.50	17.50	25	35	47.50	80	160
			Unused NG	20	35	50	70	82.50	100	155	250
			Unused OG	50	95	145	200	275	425	850	1,800
			Mint NH	77.50	145	275	450	650	1,000	2,150	—
O56	90¢	black	Used	7.50	12.50	17.50	25	35	47.50	80	160
			Unused NG	24	40	55	80	95	115	170	300
			Unused OG	60	115	145	220	300	440	875	1,900
			Mint NH	95	170	290	500	700	1,100	2,450	—

1873 State

SCT#	DENOM	COLOR	CONDITION	VG 50	F 70	F-VF 75	VF 80	VF-XF 85	XF 90	XF-SUP 95	SUP 98
O57	1¢	dark	Used	22.50	37.50	52.50	75	120	165	250	475
		green	Unused NG	25	42.50	75	110	120	145	225	375
			Unused OG	65	105	175	260	330	525	900	1,900
			Mint NH	100	175	320	575	800	1,250	2,900	—
O58	2¢	dark	Used	30	50	70	100	140	200	325	600
		green	Unused NG	35	60	85	120	130	165	250	475
			Unused OG	75	125	200	310	420	625	1,250	2,500
			Mint NH	—	—	—	—	—	—	—	—
O59	3¢	dark	Used	7.50	12.50	17.50	25	35	47.50	80	160
		green	Unused NG	22.50	37.50	60	85	100	120	170	300
		bright	Unused OG	55	87.50	145	220	300	475	875	1,750
		green	Mint NH	85	150	275	500	675	1,000	2,400	—
O60	6¢	bright	Used	9	15	21	30	42.50	62.50	100	200
		green	Unused NG	30	50	77.50	110	130	155	220	375
			Unused OG	62.50	100	165	250	350	550	950	1,850
			Mint NH	92.50	165	315	550	750	1,100	2,500	—
O61	7¢	dark	Used	19	32.50	45	65	95	175	300	500
		green	Unused NG	28	47.50	67.50	95	110	140	200	375
			Unused OG	72.50	115	200	290	400	600	1,150	2,250
			Mint NH	110	200	350	650	900	1,350	3,100	—
O62	10¢	dark	Used	16	27.50	40	55	75	105	175	360
		green	Unused NG	27.50	45	75	110	125	160	250	470
			Unused OG	62.50	105	165	250	325	500	950	1,750
			Mint NH	100	175	300	575	775	1,200	2,750	—
O63	12¢	dark	Used	42.50	62.50	90	125	180	260	400	750
		green	Unused NG	35	55	90	140	150	190	260	475
			Unused OG	77.50	125	200	310	400	625	1,200	—
			Mint NH	120	210	375	700	950	1,400	3,200	—
O64	15¢	dark	Used	27.50	45	62.50	90	130	185	275	450
		green	Unused NG	45	75	105	150	165	210	315	575
			Unused OG	87.50	135	230	350	465	675	1,325	2,650
			Mint NH	135	235	430	775	1,075	1,650	3,650	—
O65	24¢	dark	Used	70	115	165	230	340	485	725	1,250
		green	Unused NG	50	90	200	275	325	400	650	975
			Unused OG	130	210	350	525	650	975	1,800	3,000
			Mint NH			—	—	—			
O66	30¢	dark	Used	55	90	125	180	260	375	575	1,000
		green	Unused NG	50	80	160	240	275	325	400	650
			Unused OG	125	200	340	500	600	800	1,600	2,750
			Mint NH			—	—	—			
O67	90¢	dark	Used	97.50	165	225	325	475	675	1,050	1,750
		green	Unused NG	100	175	350	525	575	700	1,125	—
			Unused OG	235	370	650	1,050	1,250	1,700	2,900	—
			Mint NH			—	—	—			
O68	$2	green	Used	950	1,500	2,100	3,000	3,500	4,500	—	—
		& black	Unused NG	200	350	575	850	975	1,275	—	—
			Unused OG	450	825	1,200	1,750	2,450	3,850	—	—
			Mint NH	625	1,125	2,100	3,750	5,400	8,000	—	—
O69	$5	green	Used	4,000	6,500	9,000	13,000	17,000	22,500	—	—
		& black	Unused NG	900	1,500	2,600	3,500	4,000	5,000	—	—
			Unused OG	1,850	3,600	5,000	7,500	10,250	16,500	—	—
			Mint NH			—	—	—			
O70	$10	green	Used	2,000	3,750	5,000	7,500	9,000	12,500	—	—
		& black	Unused NG	750	1,350	1,850	2,500	3,000	3,750	—	—
			Unused OG	1,150	2,000	3,000	4,500	6,500	10,000	—	—
			Mint NH	1,850	3,250	6,000	10,500	15,000	24,000	—	—
O71	$20	green	Used	1,650	2,750	4,000	5,500	7,000	10,000	—	—
		& black	Unused NG	675	1,200	1,600	2,250	2,750	3,250	—	—
			Unused OG	1,250	2,350	3,500	5,000	6,500	11,000	—	—
			Mint NH	2,000	3,500	6,500	11,500	16,500	26,000	—	—

1873 Treasury

SCT#	DENOM	COLOR	CONDITION	VG 50	F 70	F-VF 75	VF 80	VF-XF 85	XF 90	XF-SUP 95	SUP 98
O72	1¢	brown	Used	3	5	7.25	10	15	22.50	45	95
			Unused NG	13.50	24	32.50	45	55	70	105	160
			Unused OG	32.50	60	75	120	190	275	525	950
			Mint NH	55	100	140	250	360	575	1,250	—
O73	2¢	brown	Used	2.40	4	5.75	8	12	17.50	40	85
			Unused NG	14	25	30	45	57.50	75	115	190
			Unused OG	40	70	80	125	215	300	575	1,050
			Mint NH	65	125	155	275	440	650	1,450	—
O74	3¢	brown	Used	0.60	1	1.40	2	4	12.50	27.50	55
			Unused NG	12	19	27.50	40	52.50	65	95	160
			Unused OG	27.50	55	70	110	160	250	475	950
			Mint NH	45	100	130	230	340	625	1,350	—
O75	6¢	brown	Used	1.20	2	2.80	4	8	17.50	30	70
			Unused NG	13.50	22.50	32.50	45	55	70	100	160
			Unused OG	35	65	80	120	180	275	500	1,000
			Mint NH	55	110	140	250	425	650	1,400	—
O76	7¢	brown	Used	10.50	17.50	24	35	50	75	130	275
			Unused NG	27.50	47.50	67.50	95	110	130	200	325
			Unused OG	62.50	105	165	250	360	500	1,000	2,050
			Mint NH	125	190	300	550	825	1,200	2,450	—
O77	10¢	brown	Used	3.75	6	8.75	12	17.50	27.50	50	110
			Unused NG	27.50	42.50	65	90	105	125	190	300
			Unused OG	60	95	155	240	350	500	950	1,900
			Mint NH	110	225	300	525	800	1,175	2,450	—
O78	12¢	brown	Used	3.25	5	7.25	10	15	22.50	47.50	90
			Unused NG	35	62.50	87.50	125	145	175	280	425
			Unused OG	92.50	170	235	350	500	675	1,275	2,450
			Mint NH	160	260	460	750	1,075	1,625	3,500	—
O79	15¢	brown	Used	3.75	6	8.75	12	18.50	25	45	100
			Unused NG	27.50	50	70	100	115	140	225	325
			Unused OG	75	140	200	300	400	600	1,100	2,100
			Mint NH	135	220	400	650	925	1,400	3,100	—
O80	24¢	brown	Used	27.50	50	70	100	140	210	325	575
			Unused NG	85	145	210	290	310	400	700	1,075
			Unused OG	200	365	525	725	950	1,400	2,700	—
			Mint NH			—	—	—			
O81	30¢	brown	Used	3.75	6	8.75	12	17.50	25	47.50	110
			Unused NG	42.50	70	100	140	155	190	300	450
			Unused OG	100	190	285	400	550	825	1,600	—
			Mint NH			—	—	—			
O82	90¢	brown	Used	4.50	7.50	11	15	22.50	35	70	210
			Unused NG	47.50	80	115	160	175	215	345	525
			Unused OG	120	225	340	475	650	975	1,900	—
			Mint NH			—	—	—			

1873 War

SCT#	DENOM	COLOR	CONDITION	VG 50	F 70	F-VF 75	VF 80	VF-XF 85	XF 90	XF-SUP 95	SUP 98
O83	1¢	rose	Used	4.50	7.50	10.50	15	22.50	35	60	130
			Unused NG	27.50	45	65	90	105	130	190	325
			Unused OG	70	125	160	240	350	500	950	1,600
			Mint NH	125	225	320	525	725	1,100	2,550	—
O84	2¢	rose	Used	4.50	7.50	10.50	15	21	32.50	60	120
			Unused NG	32.50	55	80	110	130	160	225	375
			Unused OG	75	135	175	260	375	550	1,025	1,725
			Mint NH	145	260	365	600	825	1,250	2,900	—
O85	3¢	rose	Used	1.50	2.50	3.50	5	7	15	27.50	55
			Unused NG	37.50	60	87.50	120	140	175	250	425
			Unused OG	80	145	185	275	400	600	1,150	2,000
			Mint NH	145	260	365	600	825	1,250	2,900	
O86	6¢	rose	Used	2.75	5	7	10	15	21.50	45	95
			Unused NG	82.50	140	200	275	305	385	600	875
			Unused OG	185	340	460	675	950	1,400	2,750	4,500
			Mint NH	300	600	800	1,450	2,000	3,100	7,000	—

SCT#	DENOM	COLOR	CONDITION	VG 50	F 70	F-VF 75	VF 80	VF-XF 85	XF 90	XF-SUP 95	SUP 98
O87	7¢	rose	Used	25	47.50	65	90	130	190	300	550
			Unused NG	22.50	40	65	90	100	120	170	310
			Unused OG	50	82.50	120	175	250	350	650	1,200
			Mint NH	72.50	135	210	375	525	775	1,825	—
O88	10¢	rose	Used	7.50	12.50	18	25	35	50	100	190
			Unused NG	13.50	22.50	30	45	57.50	75	110	210
			Unused OG	35	70	95	140	190	300	550	1,000
			Mint NH	55	125	185	300	425	700	1,650	—
O89	12¢	rose	Used	3.50	6	8.75	12	17.50	26	45	150
			Unused NG	30	55	80	110	125	145	200	375
			Unused OG	70	135	180	275	375	525	1,100	1,850
			Mint NH	120	220	350	600	825	1,250	3,000	—
O90	15¢	rose	Used	4.50	7.50	10.50	15	22.50	32.50	60	120
			Unused NG	9	15	22.50	30	37.50	50	75	135
			Unused OG	20	40	55	85	120	180	350	625
			Mint NH	35	75	110	190	260	450	1,050	—
O91	24¢	rose	Used	3.50	6	8.75	12	17.50	27.50	50	100
			Unused NG	9	15	22.50	30	37.50	50	75	135
			Unused OG	20	40	55	85	120	190	350	650
			Mint NH	35	75	110	190	260	450	1,050	—
O92	30¢	rose	Used	3.50	6	8.75	12	17.50	27.50	50	100
			Unused NG	13.50	22.50	32.50	45	57.50	75	110	175
			Unused OG	32.50	60	85	130	180	275	500	900
			Mint NH	55	110	160	275	400	675	1,500	—
O93	90¢	rose	Used	17.50	30	42.50	60	80	110	180	325
			Unused NG	22.50	40	57.50	80	92.50	115	175	260
			Unused OG	57.50	110	150	225	310	475	850	1,600
			Mint NH	100	200	300	500	700	1,200	2,750	—

1879 American Bank Note Issues (Soft Paper)

SCT#	DENOM	COLOR	CONDITION	VG 50	F 70	F-VF 75	VF 80	VF-XF 85	XF 90	XF-SUP 95	SUP 98
O94	1¢	yellow	Unused NGAI	1,950	3,500	4,350	5,500	6,000	7,250	13,500	18,500
O95	3¢	yellow	Used	34	62.50	91	125	170	250	400	750
			Unused NG	50	90	150	240	260	325	475	800
			Unused OG	135	250	365	550	725	1,150	2,000	3,500
			Mint NH	250	400	700	1,250	1,775	2,750	5,650	—
O96	1¢	vermilion	Used	115	205	275	400	675	1,150	—	2350--
			Unused NG	30	55	115	160	170	220	300	525
			Unused OG	65	120	200	300	375	575	1,050	—
			Mint NH	110	200	350	550	775	1,200	2,700	—
O97	2¢	vermilion	Used	0.85	1.50	2.10	3	7	15	25	55
			Unused NG	0.85	1.50	2.10	3	5	10	17.50	27.50
			Unused OG	2.50	4	6.75	10	15	22.50	42.50	80
			Mint NH	3	5.25	9.75	17.50	27.50	45	100	—
O98	3¢	vermilion	Used	0.80	1.50	2.10	3	7	15	25	55
			Unused NG	0.85	1.50	2.10	3	5	10	17.50	27.50
			Unused OG	2.50	4	6.75	10	15	22.50	42.50	80
			Mint NH	3.75	6.75	12.50	22.50	32.50	52.50	115	—
O99	6¢	vermilion	Used	3.50	6	8.50	12.50	18.50	27.50	47.50	100
			Unused NG	0.85	1.50	2.25	3	5	10	17.50	27.50
			Unused OG	2.50	4	6.75	10	15	35	60	120
			Mint NH	3	5.25	9.25	17.50	27.50	50	100	—
O100	10¢	vermilion	Used	22	40	55	75	110	155	230	400
			Unused NG	17.50	32.50	45	60	67.50	85	130	225
			Unused OG	27.50	47.50	75	110	165	240	450	875
			Mint NH	42.50	75	140	250	360	550	1,300	—
O101	12¢	vermilion	Used	35	62.50	87.50	115	165	250	375	650
			Unused NG	40	55	90	130	140	175	250	475
			Unused OG	57.50	95	155	230	300	400	825	1,600
			Mint NH	90	160	290	525	700	1,100	2,600	—
O102	15¢	vermilion	Used	150	270	365	500	625	775	—	—
			Unused NG	60	100	140	200	225	300	475	825
			Unused OG	97.50	195	270	400	550	825	1,500	2,500
			Mint NH	155	270	500	900	1,275	1,900	4,250	—
O103	24¢	vermilion	Used	—	—	—	6,250	—	—	—	—
			Unused NG	675	1,100	1,575	2,100	2,250	3,000	—	—
			Unused OG	1,300	2,250	3,400	4,500	5,750	8,250	—	—
			Mint NH	1,750	3,000	5,500	10,000	14,000	21,000	—	—
O106	3¢	bluish	Used	37.50	62.50	87.50	125	175	225	375	700
		purple	Unused NG	30	55	80	110	120	145	200	375

SCT#	DENOM	COLOR	CONDITION	VG 50	F 70	F-VF 75	VF 80	VF-XF 85	XF 90	XF-SUP 95	SUP 98
O107	6¢	bluish	Used	87.50	150	225	300	425	575	850	1,500
		purple	Unused NG	62.50	105	150	210	230	300	450	750
			Unused OG	120	190	315	475	625	825	1,600	3,200
			Mint NH	180	315	575	1,050	1,500	2,400	5,250	—
O108	3¢	black	Used	2.75	4.50	7	10	15	25	40	100
			Unused NG	3	5	7.25	10	12.50	16	22.50	37.50
			Unused OG	7.50	12	20	30	42.50	67.50	120	230
			Mint NH	12	21	40	70	100	155	325	—
O109	3¢	brown	Used	2.75	4.50	7	10	15	25	45	100
			Unused NG	10.50	17.50	25	35	40	47.50	65	110
			Unused OG	20	32.50	52.50	80	115	175	300	600
			Mint NH	30	52.50	97.50	175	250	400	850	—
O110	6¢	brown	Used	15	25	36.50	50	70	100	150	275
			Unused NG	20	32.50	45	65	75	90	140	240
			Unused OG	50	82.50	130	200	275	425	800	1,450
			Mint NH	77.50	135	250	450	650	975	2,200	—
O111	10¢	brown	Used	22.50	40	55	80	115	160	275	475
			Unused NG	37.50	60	87.50	120	145	175	260	360
			Unused OG	70	110	185	275	370	575	1,000	2,000
			Mint NH	110	200	360	650	875	1,300	3,000	—
O112	30¢	brown	Used	130	215	300	425	550	850	1,500	2,500
			Unused NG	250	440	625	875	975	1,200	1,750	2,750
			Unused OG	625	1,200	1,650	2,400	3,250	4,750	8,500	15,500
			Mint NH			—	—	—			
O113	90¢	brown	Used	200	375	475	750	900	1,250	1,850	3,000
			Unused NG	975	1,625	2,400	3,250	3,600	4,000	—	—
			Unused OG	2,500	4,750	7,000	10,000	12,250	15,000	—	—
			Mint NH			—	—	—			
O114	1¢	rose	Used	1.20	2	2.90	4	7.50	15	25	45
		red	Unused NG	0.90	1.40	1.85	2.75	5	11	17.50	27.50
			Unused OG	1.75	3	5	7.50	12.50	22.50	40	75
			Mint NH	2.60	4.50	8.25	15	26	47.50	115	—
O115	2¢	rose	Used	1.10	2	2.75	4	7.50	15	25	45
		red	Unused NG	1.50	2.50	3.45	5	9.50	18	27.50	50
			Unused OG	3.75	6	10.25	15	22.50	32.50	57.50	110
			Mint NH	5.25	9	17.50	30	47.50	87.50	175	—
O116	3¢	rose	Used	0.60	1	1.40	2	4	9	17.50	35
		red	Unused NG	1.50	2.50	3.50	5	9.50	18	27.50	50
			Unused OG	3.75	6	10.25	15	22.50	32.50	57.50	110
			Mint NH	5.25	9	17.50	30	47.50	87.50	175	—
O117	6¢	rose	Used	0.90	1.50	2.10	3	5.50	12	20	37.50
		red	Unused NG	1.35	2.25	3.10	4.50	8.50	16	25	45
			Unused OG	3.15	5	8.50	12.50	19	27.50	50	100
			Mint NH	4.40	7.50	13.75	25	40	75	160	—
O118	10¢	rose	Used	15	25	37.50	50	70	100	170	325
		red	Unused NG	8.25	13.75	19	27.50	35	42.50	57.50	105
			Unused OG	19	30	50	75	105	160	290	525
			Mint NH	25	45	82.50	150	220	375	700	—
O119	12¢	rose	Used	4	7	9.75	14	20	27.50	45	110
		red	Unused NG	7.50	12.50	19	25	32.50	45	62.50	90
			Unused OG	17.50	28	45	70	100	150	290	450
			Mint NH	25	42.50	77.50	140	195	350	700	—
O120	30¢	rose	Used	30	50	70	100	130	180	325	600
		red	Unused NG	27	45	65	90	100	120	190	300
			Unused OG	60	95	150	225	330	475	900	1,800
			Mint NH	80	150	280	500	700	1,150	3,150	—

1875 Special Printings (Overprinted "SPECIMEN")

SCT#	DENOM	COLOR	CONDITION	VG 50	F 70	F-VF 75	VF 80	VF-XF 85	XF 90	XF-SUP 95	SUP 98
O1S	1¢	yellow	Unused NGAI	7.50	12.50	22.50	32.50	45	70	130	235
O2S	2¢	yellow	Unused NGAI	13	22.50	37.50	55	82.50	120	200	325
O3S	3¢	yellow	Unused NGAI	92.50	180	265	400	550	800	1,400	—
O4S	6¢	yellow	Unused NGAI	92.50	180	265	400	550	800	1,400	—
O5S	10¢	yellow	Unused NGAI	92.50	180	265	400	550	800	1,400	—
O6S	12¢	yellow	Unused NGAI	92.50	180	265	400	550	800	1,400	—
O7S	15¢	yellow	Unused NGAI	92.50	180	265	400	550	800	1,400	—
O8S	24¢	yellow	Unused NGAI	92.50	180	265	400	550	800	1,400	—
O9S	30¢	yellow	Unused NGAI	92.50	180	265	400	550	800	1,400	—
O10S	1¢	carmine	Unused NGAI	7.50	12.50	22.50	32.50	45	70	130	235
O11S	2¢	carmine	Unused NGAI	13	22.50	38.50	55	80	120	200	330

SCT#	DENOM	COLOR	CONDITION	VG 50	F 70	F-VF 75	VF 80	VF-XF 85	XF 90	XF-SUP 95	SUP 98
014S	10¢	carmine	Unused NGAI	16	27.50	47.50	67.50	95	150	240	400
015S	1¢	vermilion	Unused NGAI	14	25	42.50	60	87.50	130	220	350
016S	2¢	vermilion	Unused NGAI	35	62.50	95	140	200	300	450	850
017S	3¢	vermilion	Unused NGAI	600	1,175	1,750	2,500	3,200	5,000	7,500	—
018S	6¢	vermilion	Unused NGAI	600	1,175	1,750	2,500	3,200	5,000	7,500	—
019S	10¢	vermilion	Unused NGAI	600	1,175	1,750	2,500	3,200	5,000	7,500	—
020S	12¢	vermilion	Unused NGAI	600	1,175	1,750	2,500	3,200	5,000	7,500	—
021S	15¢	vermilion	Unused NGAI	600	1,175	1,750	2,500	3,200	5,000	7,500	—
022S	24¢	vermilion	Unused NGAI	600	1,175	1,750	2,500	3,200	5,000	7,500	—
023S	30¢	vermilion	Unused NGAI	600	1,175	1,750	2,500	3,200	5,000	7,500	—
024S	90¢	vermilion	Unused NGAI	600	1,175	1,750	2,500	3,200	5,000	7,500	—
025S	1¢	purple	Unused NGAI	7.50	12.50	22.50	32.50	45	70	130	235
026S	2¢	purple	Unused NGAI	13	22.50	38.50	55	80	120	200	325
027S	3¢	purple	Unused NGAI	290	550	875	1,250	1,800	2,650	4,150	—
028S	6¢	purple	Unused NGAI	290	550	875	1,250	1,800	2,650	4,150	—
029S	10¢	purple	Unused NGAI	290	550	875	1,250	1,800	2,650	4,150	—
030S	12¢	purple	Unused NGAI	290	550	875	1,250	1,800	2,650	4,150	—
031S	15¢	purple	Unused NGAI	290	550	875	1,250	1,800	2,650	4,150	—
032S	24¢	purple	Unused NGAI	290	550	875	1,250	1,800	2,650	4,150	—
033S	30¢	purple	Unused NGAI	290	550	875	1,250	1,800	2,650	4,150	—
034S	90¢	purple	Unused NGAI	290	550	875	1,250	1,800	2,650	4,150	—
035S	1¢	ultramarine	Unused NGAI	8	15	25	35	50	77.50	140	250
036S	2¢	ultramarine	Unused NGAI	17.50	31.50	53	75	105	160	275	500
037S	3¢	ultramarine	Unused NGAI	400	775	1,200	1,750	2,250	3,500	5,500	—
038S	6¢	ultramarine	Unused NGAI	400	775	1,200	1,750	2,250	3,500	5,500	—
039S	7¢	ultramarine	Unused NGAI	120	255	400	550	800	1,150	2,150	—
040S	10¢	ultramarine	Unused NGAI	400	775	1,200	1,750	2,250	3,500	5,500	—
041S	12¢	ultramarine	Unused NGAI	400	775	1,200	1,750	2,250	3,500	5,500	—
042S	15¢	ultramarine	Unused NGAI	400	775	1,200	1,750	2,250	3,500	5,500	—
043S	24¢	ultramarine	Unused NGAI	400	775	1,200	1,750	2,250	3,500	5,500	—
044S	30¢	ultramarine	Unused NGAI	400	775	1,200	1,750	2,250	3,500	5,500	—
045S	90¢	ultramarine	Unused NGAI	400	775	1,200	1,750	2,250	3,500	5,500	—
047S	1¢	black	Unused NGAI	10	20	32.50	45	62.50	95	180	325
048S	2¢	black	Unused NGAI	77.50	150	220	325	450	700	1,100	1,750
049S	3¢	black	Unused NGAI	375	725	1,050	1,600	2,050	3,250	5,000	—
050S	6¢	black	Unused NGAI	375	725	1,050	1,600	2,050	3,250	5,000	—
051S	10¢	black	Unused NGAI	225	450	725	1,000	1,325	2,200	3,400	—
052S	12¢	black	Unused NGAI	375	725	1,050	1,600	2,050	3,250	5,000	—
053S	15¢	black	Unused NGAI	375	725	1,050	1,600	2,050	3,250	5,000	—
054S	24¢	black	Unused NGAI	375	725	1,050	1,600	2,050	3,250	5,000	—
055S	30¢	black	Unused NGAI	375	725	1,050	1,600	2,050	3,250	5,000	—
056S	90¢	black	Unused NGAI	375	725	1,050	1,600	2,050	3,250	5,000	—
057S	1¢	bluish green	Unused NGAI	7.50	12.50	22.50	32.50	45	70	130	235
058S	2¢	bluish green	Unused NGAI	21	40	65	90	135	190	340	550
059S	3¢	bluish green	Unused NGAI	32.50	65	100	140	205	300	475	850
060S	6¢	bluish green	Unused NGAI	82.50	160	240	350	500	750	1,150	2,100
061S	7¢	bluish green	Unused NGAI	32	64	100	140	205	300	475	850
062S	10¢	bluish green	Unused NGAI	125	260	375	550	725	1,150	1,750	—
063S	12¢	bluish green	Unused NGAI	130	255	375	550	725	1,150	1,750	—
064S	15¢	bluish green	Unused NGAI	140	280	425	600	800	1,250	1,900	—
065S	24¢	bluish green	Unused NGAI	140	280	425	600	800	1,250	1,900	—
066S	30¢	bluish green	Unused NGAI	140	280	425	600	800	1,250	1,900	—
067S	90¢	bluish green	Unused NGAI	140	280	425	600	800	1,250	1,900	—
068S	$2	green & black	Unused NGAI	5,250	9,250	13,500	19,000	22,500	29,500	—	—
069S	$5	green & black	Unused NGAI	14,500	27,000	36,000	50,000	—	—	—	—
070S	$10	green & black	Unused NGAI	27,500	55,000	77,500	110,000	—	—	—	—
071S	$20	green & black	Unused NGAI	40,000	80,000	112,500	160,000	—	—	—	—
072S	1¢	dark brown	Unused NGAI	18.50	37.50	57.50	80	125	175	275	500
073S	2¢	dark brown	Unused NGAI	105	205	300	450	600	950	1,450	2,650
074S	3¢	dark brown	Unused NGAI	375	725	1,050	1,600	2,050	3,250	5,000	—
075S	6¢	dark brown	Unused NGAI	375	725	1,050	1,600	2,050	3,250	5,000	—
076S	7¢	dark brown	Unused NGAI	225	445	650	950	1,250	1,900	3,000	—
077S	10¢	dark brown	Unused NGAI	375	725	1,050	1,600	2,050	3,250	5,000	—
078S	12¢	dark brown	Unused NGAI	375	725	1,050	1,600	2,050	3,250	5,000	—
079S	15¢	dark brown	Unused NGAI	375	725	1,050	1,600	2,050	3,250	5,000	—
080S	24¢	dark brown	Unused NGAI	375	725	1,050	1,600	2,050	3,250	5,000	—
081S	30¢	dark brown	Unused NGAI	375	725	1,050	1,600	2,050	3,250	5,000	—
082S	90¢	dark brown	Unused NGAI	390	750	1,075	1,650	2,150	3,350	5,250	—
083S	1¢	deep rose	Unused NGAI	8	15	25	35	50	75	130	225
084S	2¢	deep rose	Unused NGAI	27.50	57.50	90	125	165	260	425	750
085S	3¢	deep rose	Unused NGAI	325	675	950	1,400	1,875	2,850	4,000	—
086S	6¢	deep rose	Unused NGAI	325	675	950	1,400	1,875	2,850	4,000	—
087S	7¢	deep rose	Unused NGAI	100	200	290	425	625	900	1,400	—
088S	10¢	deep rose	Unused NGAI	325	625	950	1,400	1,800	2,800	4,500	—
089S	12¢	deep rose	Unused NGAI	325	675	950	1,400	1,800	2,800	4,500	—
090S	15¢	deep rose	Unused NGAI	325	675	950	1,400	1,800	2,800	4,500	—
091S	24¢	deep rose	Unused NGAI	325	675	950	1,400	1,800	2,800	4,500	—
092S	30¢	deep rose	Unused NGAI	325	675	950	1,400	1,800	2,800	4,500	—
093S	90¢	deep rose	Unused NGAI	325	675	950	1,400	1,800	2,800	4,500	—
010xS	1¢	violet rose	Unused NGAI	22.50	42.50	65	95	140	200	350	575
035xS	1¢	gray blue	Unused NGAI	23.50	45	70	100	140	220	360	600
057xS	1¢	yellow green	Unused NGAI	42.50	82.50	125	180	240	390	675	1,150

1910-11 POSTAL SAVINGS MAIL STAMPS

SCT#	DENOM	COLOR	CONDITION	VG 50	F 70	F-VF 75	VF 80	VF-XF 85	XF 90	XF-SUP 95	SUP 98
O121	2¢	black	Used	0.65	1	1.40	2	5.50	12	20	40
			Unused OG	4	9	12	17.50	22.50	37.50	62.50	100
			Mint NH	7.50	15	25	40	55	75	180	375
O122	50¢	dark green	Used	18	32.50	45	60	90	130	200	350
			Unused OG	40	87.50	115	175	220	355	600	975
			Mint NH	85	170	260	425	600	875	1,850	3,400
O123	$1	ultramarine	Used	4.50	8	11	15	22.50	32.50	60	120
			Unused OG	50	100	125	200	275	400	675	1,050
			Mint NH	90	180	270	450	650	950	2,250	3,750
O124	1¢	dark violet	Used	0.60	1	1.40	2	5.50	12	20	40
			Unused OG	2.35	5	6.75	10	13.50	17.50	30	50
			Mint NH	4.40	8.50	13.50	22.50	32.50	50	110	250
O125	2¢	black	Used	2	3.75	5	7	12.50	20	40	85
			Unused OG	15	32.50	45	65	82.50	130	215	350
			Mint NH	25	52.50	85	150	210	310	650	1,325
O126	10¢	carmine	Used	0.55	1	1.60	2	5.50	12	20	40
			Unused OG	4.25	10	13.50	20	27.50	42.50	75	125
			Mint NH	9	20	32.50	50	65	105	220	475

NEWSPAPER AND PERIODICAL STAMPS

1865 Issues

SCT#	DENOM	COLOR	CONDITION	VG 50	F 70	F-VF 75	VF 80	VF-XF 85	XF 90	XF-SUP 95	SUP 98
PR1	5¢	dark	Used	600	1,200	1,600	2,000	2,300	2,750	—	
		blue	Unused NGAI	180	380	550	750	1,100	1,650	2,250	—
PR1a	5¢	light	Used	—	—	—	4,250	—	—		
		blue	Unused NGAI	325	675	950	1,350	1,900	2,850	3,500	—
PR2	10¢	blue	Used	650	1,300	1,750	2,000	2,350	2,800	—	
		green	Unused NGAI	75	150	215	300	425	575	900	—
PR2a	10¢	green	Used	445	1,000	1,225	2,000	2,350	2,800	—	
			Unused NGAI	75	150	215	300	400	575	900	—
PR3	25¢	orange	Used	1,000	1,650	2,100	2,500	2,850	3,400	—	
		red	Unused NGAI	105	210	265	400	525	700	1,150	—
PR3a	25¢	carmine	Used	1,000	1,650	2,100	2,500	2,850	3,400	—	
		red	Unused NGAI	125	245	315	475	600	800	1,300	—
PR4	5¢	light	Used	1,150	2,500	3,250	5,000	5,750	6,750	—	
		blue	Unused NGAI	170	350	500	750	900	1,175	1,800	—
PR4a	5¢	dark blue	Unused NGAI	170	350	500	750	900	1,175	1,800	—

1875 Reprints of the 1865 Issues

SCT#	DENOM	COLOR	CONDITION	VG 50	F 70	F-VF 75	VF 80	VF-XF 85	XF 90	XF-SUP 95	SUP 98
PR5	5¢	dull blue	Unused NGAI	90	150	175	225	350	500	800	—
PR6	10¢	dark bluish green	Unused NGAI	110	175	200	250	375	550	850	—
PR7	25¢	dark carmine	Unused NGAI	75	150	215	300	400	575	900	—
PR8	5¢	dark blue	Unused NGAI	165	325	450	650	1,100	2,250	3,500	—

1875 Issue

SCT#	DENOM	COLOR	CONDITION	VG 50	F 70	F-VF 75	VF 80	VF-XF 85	XF 90	XF-SUP 95	SUP 98
PR9	2¢	black	Used	12.50	30	40	62.50	85	125	—	—
			Unused NG	37.50	65	87.50	120	140	175	—	—
			Unused OG	75	150	215	300	400	575	—	—
PR10	3¢	black	Used	13.25	32.50	45	70	92.50	130	—	—
			Unused NG	37.50	65	92.50	120	140	175	—	—
			Unused OG	75	150	215	300	400	575	—	—
PR11	4¢	black	Used	12.50	30	40	62.50	85	125	—	—
			Unused NG	37.50	65	92.50	120	140	175	—	—
			Unused OG	75	150	215	300	400	575	—	—
PR12	6¢	black	Used	13.25	32.50	45	70	92.50	140	—	—
			Unused NG	37.50	65	92.50	120	140	175	—	—
			Unused OG	75	150	215	300	400	575	—	—
PR13	8¢	black	Used	22.50	47.50	65	100	135	185	—	—
			Unused NG	37.50	72.50	92.50	135	150	200	—	—
			Unused OG	90	180	260	350	450	600	—	—
PR14	9¢	black	Used	35	72.50	125	185	250	345	—	—
			Unused NG	65	120	165	225	260	350	—	—
			Unused OG	150	300	400	600	750	1,000	—	—
PR15	10¢	black	Used	18.50	45	60	97.50	140	205	—	—
			Unused NG	42.50	67.50	97.50	135	150	185	—	—
			Unused OG	97.50	195	255	375	450	625	—	—
PR16	12¢	rose	Used	27.50	65	100	150	200	290	—	—
			Unused NG	90	160	225	325	375	475	—	—
			Unused OG	250	400	550	800	1,050	1,400	2,100	—
PR17	24¢	rose	Used	30	67.50	125	150	200	300	625	—
			Unused NG	85	125	225	350	400	475	—	—
			Unused OG	275	450	600	850	1,100	1,450	—	—
PR18	36¢	rose	Used	57.50	115	150	180	240	375	—	—
			Unused NG	85	160	225	350	400	475	—	—
			Unused OG	260	425	575	850	1,100	1,450	—	—
PR19	48¢	rose	Used	120	280	400	600	725	900	—	—
			Unused NG	150	225	300	450	525	675	—	—
			Unused OG	375	625	850	1,250	1,600	2,250	—	—
PR20	60¢	rose	Used	32.50	70	115	175	225	350	—	—
			Unused NG	150	225	300	450	500	650	—	—
			Unused OG	375	625	850	1,250	1,600	2,250	—	—
PR21	72¢	rose	Used	110	240	375	550	700	925	—	—
			Unused NG	175	275	365	550	675	825	—	—
			Unused OG	450	750	1,000	1,500	1,950	2,500	—	—
PR22	84¢	rose	Used	110	240	375	550	700	925	—	—
			Unused NG	200	325	450	650	750	1,050	—	—
			Unused OG	575	925	1,300	1,850	2,300	3,250	—	—
PR23	96¢	rose	Used	70	165	250	360	525	700	—	—
			Unused NG	215	330	550	775	925	1,100	—	—
			Unused OG	550	1,000	1,400	2,000	2,600	3,250	—	—
PR24	$1.92	dark	Used	67.50	165	250	375	480	625	—	—
		brown	Unused NG	200	325	480	700	800	975	—	—
			Unused OG	575	875	1,225	1,750	2,250	3,000	—	—
PR25	$3	vermilion	Used	165	330	450	625	775	1,000	—	—
			Unused NG	315	490	675	975	1,150	1,400	—	—
			Unused OG	800	1,175	1,675	2,500	3,100	4,000	—	—
PR26	$6	ultramarine	Used	240	550	750	1,125	1,400	1,900	—	—
			Unused NG	475	800	1,075	1,600	1,875	2,400	—	—
			Unused OG	1,225	2,000	2,650	4,000	5,000	6,750	—	—
PR27	$9	yellow	Used	900	2,000	2,750	4,000	5,000	6,500	—	—
		orange	Unused NG	525	875	1,225	1,750	2,150	2,850	—	—
			Unused OG	1,350	2,250	3,100	4,500	5,500	8,000	—	—
PR28	$12	blue	Used	500	1,100	1,450	2,150	2,650	3,350	—	—
		green	Unused NG	475	950	1,275	1,850	2,100	2,500	—	—
			Unused OG	1,275	2,250	3,250	4,750	5,500	7,500	—	—
PR29	$24	dark	Used	575	1,200	1,675	2,500	3,200	4,150	—	—
		gray	Unused NG	465	950	1,275	1,850	2,100	2,500	—	—
		violet	Unused OG	1,300	2,250	3,250	4,750	5,500	7,500	—	—
PR30	$36	brown	Used	650	1,400	1,925	2,750	3,450	4,350	—	—
		rose	Unused NG	500	1,050	1,400	2,000	2,250	2,800	—	—
			Unused OG	1,400	2,350	3,350	5,000	6,750	9,000	—	—
PR31	$48	red	Used	750	1,600	2,200	3,250	3,850	4,700	—	—
		brown	Unused NG	650	1,350	1,800	2,600	3,150	3,750	—	—
			Unused OG	2,000	3,750	5,000	7,000	9,000	11,500	—	—
PR32	$60	violet	Used	850	1,750	2,300	3,350	4,000	5,000	—	—
			Unused NG	600	1,250	1,650	2,400	2,900	3,500	—	—
			Unused OG	1,850	3,500	4,650	6,500	8,250	10,750	—	—

1875 Special Printings of the 1875 Issue

SCT#	DENOM	COLOR	CONDITION	VG 50	F 70	F-VF 75	VF 80	VF-XF 85	XF 90	XF-SUP 95	SUP 98
PR33	2¢	gray black	Unused NGAI	170	325	480	700	900	1,300	—	—
PR33a	2¢	gray black	Unused NGAI	135	290	435	525	800	1,175	—	—
PR34	3¢	gray black	Unused NGAI	170	325	480	700	900	1,300	—	—
PR34a	3¢	gray black	Unused NGAI	120	265	395	525	800	1,175	—	—
PR35	4¢	gray black	Unused NGAI	165	320	470	700	950	1,350	—	—
PR36	6¢	gray black	Unused NGAI	210	390	575	900	1,300	1,800	—	—
PR37	8¢	gray black	Unused NGAI	230	435	675	975	1,400	2,000	—	—

SCT#	DENOM	COLOR	CONDITION	VG 50	F 70	F-VF 75	VF 80	VF-XF 85	XF 90	XF-SUP 95	SUP 98
PR38	9¢	gray black	Unused NGAI	240	475	700	1,050	1,475	2,100	—	—
PR39	10¢	gray black	Unused NGAI	325	625	950	1,400	1,900	2,750	3,500	—
PR40	12¢	pale rose	Unused NGAI	360	700	1,025	1,500	2,100	2,900	4,000	—
PR41	24¢	pale rose	Unused NGAI	500	950	1,425	2,100	3,000	4,250	—	—
PR42	36¢	pale rose	Unused NGAI	650	1,250	1,900	2,800	3,750	5,500	—	—
PR43	48¢	pale rose	Unused NGAI	875	1,650	2,500	3,750	4,900	7,250	—	—
PR44	60¢	pale rose	Unused NGAI	1,100	2,100	3,150	4,750	6,000	9,000	—	—
PR45	72¢	pale rose	Unused NGAI	1,025	2,050	3,000	4,500	6,250	8,750	—	
PR46	84¢	pale rose	Unused NGAI	1,200	2,400	3,600	5,250	—	—	—	
PR47	96¢	pale rose	Unused NGAI	2,000	3,850	5,650	8,500	11,500	15,000	—	
PR48	$1.92	dark brown	Unused NGAI	4,650	10,000	15,000	20,000	23,000	29,000	—	
PR49	$3	vermilion	Unused NGAI	—	26,500	34,500	45,000	—	—		
PR50	$6	ultramarine	Unused NGAI	37,500	80,000	90,000	110,000	—			
PR51	$9	yellow orange	Unused NGAI				350,000				
PR52	$12	blue green	Unused NGAI	—	175,000	—	—	—			
PR53	$24	dark gray violet	Unused NGAI	—	500,000						
PR54	$36	brown rose	Unused NGAI		400,000				one example known		
PR55	$48	red brown	Unused NGAI	—	—	—	—				
PR56	$60	violet	Unused NGAI	—	—	—	—				

1879 American Bank Note Issue (Soft Paper)

SCT#	DENOM	COLOR	CONDITION	VG 50	F 70	F-VF 75	VF 80	VF-XF 85	XF 90	XF-SUP 95	SUP 98
PR57	2¢	black	Used	4.50	11	15	25	32.50	45	110	—
			Unused NG	7	12	16	30	32.50	37.50	45	—
			Unused OG	16	27.50	40	75	85	110	160	—
PR58	3¢	black	Used	6.50	15	20	32.50	40	50	100	—
			Unused NG	8	15	20	35	37.50	42.50	60	—
			Unused OG	20	30	45	85	100	125	225	—
PR59	4¢	black	Used	6.50	15	20	32.50	40	50	100	—
			Unused NG	8	15	20	35	37.50	42.50	60	—
			Unused OG	20	30	45	85	100	125	225	—
PR60	6¢	black	Used	10	23.50	35	50	62.50	80	140	—
			Unused NG	12.50	27.50	37.50	50	55	70	100	—
			Unused OG	30	60	85	125	160	210	425	—
PR61	8¢	black	Used	10	23.50	35	50	62.50	80	140	—
			Unused NG	15	30	42.50	55	62.50	80	115	—
			Unused OG	32.50	65	90	135	160	225	475	—
PR62	10¢	black	Used	10	23.50	35	50	62.50	80	140	—
			Unused NG	15	30	42.50	55	62.50	80	115	—
			Unused OG	32.50	65	90	135	160	225	475	—
PR63	12¢	red	Used	42.50	87.50	125	190	240	300	600	—
			Unused NG	52.50	115	145	210	235	275	445	—
			Unused OG	120	225	325	500	650	875	1,650	—
PR64	24¢	red	Used	42.50	87.50	125	190	240	300	600	—
			Unused NG	52.50	115	145	210	235	275	445	—
			Unused OG	120	225	325	500	650	875	1,650	—
PR65	36¢	red	Used	110	220	325	475	575	725	1,350	—
			Unused NG	120	250	330	475	525	675	1,100	—
			Unused OG	240	450	700	1,000	1,500	2,100	3,500	—
PR66	48¢	red	Used	95	190	300	425	525	675	—	—
			Unused NG	105	225	310	450	500	650	—	—
			Unused OG	240	450	700	1,000	1,400	2,100	—	—
PR67	60¢	red	Used	75	160	275	390	485	750	—	—
			Unused NG	140	285	380	550	600	800	—	—
			Unused OG	300	550	850	1,250	1,750	2,500	—	—
PR68	72¢	red	Used	140	280	425	625	750	1,000	—	—
			Unused NG	170	365	485	700	750	950	—	—
			Unused OG	360	700	1,000	1,500	2,000	2,750	—	—
PR69	84¢	red	Used	90	200	350	525	625	875	—	—
			Unused NG	140	300	400	575	625	800	—	—
			Unused OG	300	575	825	1,250	1,750	2,500	—	—

SCT#	DENOM	COLOR	CONDITION	VG 50	F 70	F-VF 75	VF 80	VF-XF 85	XF 90	XF-SUP 95	SUP 98
PR70	96¢	red	Used	82.50	170	275	425	525	800	—	—
			Unused NG	130	275	360	525	575	750	—	—
			Unused OG	275	550	800	1,200	1,675	2,400	—	—
PR71	$2	pale brown	Used	50	100	175	260	325	475	—	—
			Unused NG	55	120	150	225	250	325	—	—
			Unused OG	130	255	365	550	750	1,150	—	—
PR72	$3	red vermilion	Used	62.50	125	200	290	375	550	—	—
			Unused NG	60	125	170	250	275	375	—	—
			Unused OG	150	280	425	625	825	1,250	—	—
PR73	$6	blue	Used	160	300	425	650	850	1,200	—	—
			Unused NG	90	200	265	400	450	600	—	—
			Unused OG	250	470	700	1,050	1,450	2,000	3,200	—
PR74	$9	orange	Used	110	225	335	475	575	925	—	—
			Unused NG	80	165	220	325	350	425	2,400	—
			Unused OG	180	365	550	800	1,000	1,650	—	—
PR75	$12	yellow green	Used	125	250	365	500	650	900	—	—
			Unused NG	82.50	165	220	325	375	500	—	—
			Unused OG	205	385	575	850	1,150	1,750	—	—
PR76	$24	dark violet	Used	150	300	425	600	800	1,150	—	—
			Unused NG	70	150	200	300	325	450	—	—
			Unused OG	185	360	525	800	925	1,500	2,250	—
PR77	$36	indian red	Used	175	350	525	700	925	1,250	—	—
			Unused NG	80	175	240	350	375	450	—	—
			Unused OG	190	350	550	850	1,050	1,650	—	—
PR78	$48	yellow brown	Used	225	450	650	950	1,250	1,850	—	—
			Unused NG	80	175	240	350	375	450	700	—
			Unused OG	210	390	600	900	1,150	1,700	2,400	—
PR79	$60	purple	Used	200	400	575	825	1,100	1,650	—	—
			Unused NG	80	175	240	350	475	700	1,100	—
			Unused OG	200	375	575	850	1,100	1,500	2,350	—

1883 Special Printing of the 1879 Issue

SCT#	DENOM	COLOR	CONDITION	VG 50	F 70	F-VF 75	VF 80	VF-XF 85	XF 90	XF-SUP 95	SUP 98
PR80	2¢	intense black	Unused NGAI Note Issue	425	875	1,175	1,750	2,150	2,850	—	—

1885 American Bank Note Issue

SCT#	DENOM	COLOR	CONDITION	VG 50	F 70	F-VF 75	VF 80	VF-XF 85	XF 90	XF-SUP 95	SUP 98
PR81	1¢	black	Used	3.90	8.25	12.50	21	34	52.50	135	—
			Unused NG	9.75	21.50	27.50	42.50	57.50	80	135	—
			Unused OG	20	40	62.50	95	130	200	425	—
PR82	12¢	carmine	Used	9	19	30	45	70	110	225	—
			Unused NG	20	42.50	57.50	85	97.50	130	215	—
			Unused OG	42.50	95	135	200	275	375	675	—
PR83	24¢	carmine	Used	9	19	32.50	45	75	150	300	—
			Unused NG	22.50	47.50	65	95	110	145	225	—
			Unused OG	47.50	105	150	225	310	425	750	—
PR84	36¢	carmine	Used	20	40	57.50	85	115	190	375	—
			Unused NG	35	72.50	100	145	175	225	400	—
			Unused OG	82.50	160	230	350	475	650	1,150	—
PR85	48¢	carmine	Used	23.50	47.50	75	110	145	225	500	—
			Unused NG	45	90	125	180	210	280	500	—
			Unused OG	100	185	275	425	625	900	1,800	—
PR86	60¢	carmine	Used	35	70	100	150	210	300	625	—
			Unused NG	57.50	120	160	240	280	360	650	—
			Unused OG	125	250	365	550	850	1,200	2,000	—
PR87	72¢	carmine	Used	37.50	80	115	170	250	360	775	—
			Unused NG	57.50	120	160	240	280	360	650	—
			Unused OG	125	250	365	550	850	1,200	2,000	—
PR88	84¢	carmine	Used	72.50	145	250	375	525	850	1,600	—
			Unused NG	82.50	180	230	350	410	550	900	—
			Unused OG	210	400	575	900	1,225	1,600	3,000	—
PR89	96¢	carmine	Used	55	110	190	290	350	500	1,000	—
			Unused NG	70	150	200	300	350	450	775	—
			Unused OG	175	350	500	750	1,000	1,400	2,500	—

1894 First Bureau Issue (Unwatermarked)

SCT#	DENOM	COLOR	CONDITION	VG 50	F 70	F-VF 75	VF 80	VF-XF 85	XF 90	XF-SUP 95	SUP 98
PR90	1¢	intense black	Used	—	5,000	—	—	—	—	—	—
			Unused NG	37.50	80	110	160	185	250	410	—
			Unused OG	95	185	280	400	575	775	1,375	—
			Mint NH	215	400	575	900	1,300	1,800	3,400	—
PR91	2¢	intense black	Unused NG	40	82.50	125	190	215	270	400	—
			Unused OG	105	210	310	450	600	875	1,450	—
			Mint NH	250	470	700	1,075	1,575	2,200	4,000	—

SCT#	DENOM	COLOR	CONDITION	VG 50	F 70	F-VF 75	VF 80	VF-XF 85	XF 90	XF-SUP 95	SUP 98
PR92	4¢	intense	Used	—	—	—	13,500	—	—	—	—
		black	Unused NG	50	105	140	210	235	275	475	—
			Unused OG	125	240	360	550	725	1,000	1,800	—
			Mint NH	290	575	825	1,275	1,875	2,650	4,800	—
PR93	6¢	intense	Unused NG	450	950	1,250	1,900	2,250	2,800	—	—
		black	Unused OG	1,100	2,000	3,000	4,500	6,500	9,000	—	15,000
			Mint NH	—	—	—	11,500	—	—	—	—
PR94	10¢	intense	Unused NG	120	265	355	525	575	750	1,300	—
		black	Unused OG	325	600	850	1,300	1,725	2,450	4,400	—
PR95	12¢	pink	Used	—	4,500	—	—	—	—	—	—
			Unused NG	260	550	750	1,100	1,325	1,750	—	—
			Unused OG	650	1,175	1,775	2,600	3,500	5,000	9,250	12,500
PR96	24¢	pink	Used	—	8,000	—	—	—	—	—	—
			Unused NG	440	925	1,225	1,850	2,000	2,500	—	—
			Unused OG	950	1,700	2,500	3,750	5,500	8,000	13,500	—
PR97	36¢	pink	Unused NG	—	—	—	—	—	—	—	—
			Unused OG	32,500	50,000	—	—				
PR98	60¢	pink	Used	—	16,000	—	—	—	—	—	—
			Unused NG	—	—	—	—	—	—	—	—
			Unused OG	30,000	40,000	—	—				
PR99	96¢	pink	Unused NG	—	—	—	—	—	—	—	—
			Unused OG	22,500	35,000	50,000	—	—			
PR100	$3	scarlet	Unused NG	—	—	—	—	—	—	—	—
			Unused OG	22,500	35,000	50,000	—	—			
PR101	$6	pale	Unused NG	—	—	25,000	—	—	—	—	—
		blue	Unused OG	22,500	35,000	50,000	—	—			

1895 Second Bureau Issue (Unwatermarked)

SCT#	DENOM	COLOR	CONDITION	VG 50	F 70	F-VF 75	VF 80	VF-XF 85	XF 90	XF-SUP 95	SUP 98
PR102	1¢	black	Used	35	67.50	125	180	260	425	750	—
			Unused NG	22.50	45	60	90	100	120	170	—
			Unused OG	52.50	105	150	230	300	425	750	—
			Mint NH	92.50	200	325	500	800	1,200	2,450	—
PR103	2¢	black	Used	35	67.50	125	180	260	425	750	—
			Unused NG	22.50	45	60	90	100	120	170	—
			Unused OG	52.50	105	150	230	300	425	750	—
			Mint NH	62.50	200	325	500	800	1,200	2,450	—
PR104	5¢	black	Used	110	215	300	425	600	875	1,600	—
			Unused NG	30	55	82.50	125	140	160	225	—
			Unused OG	70	145	200	300	425	575	1,000	—
			Mint NH	125	250	400	650	1,000	1,550	3,250	—
PR105	10¢	black	Used	165	335	400	600	750	1,050	1,925	—
			Unused NG	60	115	160	240	270	310	450	—
			Unused OG	145	265	405	600	850	1,125	2,000	—
			Mint NH	250	500	875	1,300	2,000	3,200	5,000	—
PR106	25¢	carmine	Used	175	350	500	700	975	1,300	2,500	—
			Unused NG	75	150	200	300	340	400	575	—
			Unused OG	175	350	500	750	1,050	1,450	2,600	—
			Mint NH	265	650	1,075	1,650	2,500	3,850	6,250	—
PR107	50¢	carmine	Used	325	550	800	1,075	1,400	2,100	3,750	—
			Unused NG	220	440	600	875	975	1,100	1,375	—
			Unused OG	700	1,300	1,800	2,750	3,250	4,000	6,000	—
			Mint NH	1,350	2,600	4,250	6,250	8,500	12,000	16,500	—
PR108	$2	scarlet	Used	450	800	1,100	1,550	2,100	2,900	4,250	—
			Unused NG	215	430	575	850	925	1,075	1,850	—
			Unused OG	525	1,050	1,475	2,250	3,000	4,500	7,000	—
			Mint NH	925	2,000	3,250	5,000	7,000	11,000	17,500	—
PR109	$5	ultramarine	Used	875	1,750	2,250	3,000	3,750	5,000	8,000	—
			Unused NG	200	400	525	800	875	1,000	1,500	—
			Unused OG	525	975	1,450	2,100	2,900	4,000	6,250	—
			Mint NH	850	1,800	2,850	4,500	7,000	11,000	—	—
PR110	$10	green	Used	1,000	2,000	2,750	3,750	4,750	5,250	10,500	—
			Unused NG	225	450	600	900	975	1,150	1,750	—
			Unused OG	575	1,100	1,675	2,500	3,250	4,750	7,000	—
			Mint NH	1,100	2,200	3,400	5,250	7,750	13,000	—	—
PR111	$20	slate	Used	1,200	2,500	4,000	4,500	5,500	7,000	10,000	—
			Unused NG	300	600	800	1,200	1,350	1,600	2,400	—
			Unused OG	725	1,400	2,050	3,250	4,250	5,750	10,000	—
			Mint NH	1,500	2,750	4,250	6,750	9,750	16,000	—	—
PR112	$50	dull	Used	425	950	1,100	1,500	2,150	3,250	—	—
		rose	Unused NG	265	525	700	1,050	1,200	1,425	2,000	—
			Unused OG	650	1,250	1,825	2,750	3,500	5,000	9,000	—
			Mint NH	1,400	2,600	4,150	6,250	9,500	15,000	—	—
PR113	$100	purple	Used	4,000	7,000	11,000	15,000	—	—	—	—
			Unused NG	350	700	925	1,400	1,525	1,700	2,500	—
			Unused OG	800	1,600	2,300	3,500	4,750	6,500	11,500	—
			Mint NH	1,600	3,100	4,500	7,250	11,500	—	—	—

1895-97 Bureau Issue (Double Line Watermark)

SCT#	DENOM	COLOR	CONDITION	VG 50	F 70	F-VF 75	VF 80	VF-XF 85	XF 90	XF-SUP 95	SUP 98
PR114	1¢	black	Used	6	12	17	25	35	55	110	200
			Unused NG	0.70	1.40	1.75	2.75	4	7.50	12.50	20
			Unused OG	1.75	3.75	5.50	8	10	14	22.50	35
			Mint NH	3.60	8	12.50	20	30	42.50	75	140
PR115	2¢	black	Used	6	12	17	25	35	55	110	200
			Unused NG	0.70	1.40	1.75	2.75	4	7.50	12.50	20
			Unused OG	1.75	3.75	5.50	8	10	14	22.50	35
			Mint NH	3.60	8	12.50	20	30	42.50	75	140
PR116	5¢	black	Used	12	22.50	29	40	55	80	140	225
			Unused NG	1	2.10	2.75	4.25	5.50	9	17.50	27.50
			Unused OG	3	5.75	8.75	13	16	20	32.50	60
			Mint NH	5.25	11	18	27.50	42.50	60	100	150
PR117	10¢	black	Used	6	12	17	25	35	55	110	200
			Unused NG	1	2.10	2.75	4.25	5.50	9	17.50	27.50
			Unused OG	3	5.75	8.75	13	16	20	32.50	60
			Mint NH	5.25	11	18	27.50	37.50	50	80	150
PR118	25¢	carmine	Used	13	25	42.50	65	95	130	225	375
			Unused NG	1.70	3.50	4.60	7	8.50	12	18.50	30
			Unused OG	5	9.25	13.75	20	26	37.50	60	100
			Mint NH	8.25	18	27	45	65	90	170	275
PR119	50¢	carmine	Used	22.50	40	50	75	110	150	250	425
			Unused NG	2.10	4.25	5.75	8.50	10	12.50	20	32.50
			Unused OG	5.50	11.25	16.50	25	30	40	65	120
			Mint NH	9	22	35	55	70	105	175	350
PR120	$2	scarlet	Used	32.50	60	82.50	110	160	220	375	625
			Unused NG	2.50	5	6.50	10	12	16	25	40
			Unused OG	6.75	13.25	20	30	37.50	50	87.50	160
			Mint NH	12.75	30	50	75	100	180	310	525
PR121	$5	dark	Used	55	92.50	110	175	240	310	550	925
		blue	Unused NG	3.35	6.75	9	13.50	16	20	30	42.50
			Unused OG	9	18.50	27.50	40	47.50	65	110	190
			Mint NH	17.50	37.50	62.50	100	130	190	325	650
PR121a	$5	light	Used	130	250	350	500	725	1,000	1,725	2,800
		blue	Unused NG	17.50	35	45	67.50	75	87.50	125	200
			Unused OG	45	900	130	200	250	325	475	775
			Mint NH	85	200	310	500	700	975	1,600	2,750
PR122	$10	green	Used	45	87.50	120	175	240	330	575	975
			Unused NG	3.50	7	9.50	14	16.50	22.50	32.50	45
			Unused OG	9.75	20	27.50	42.50	52.50	70	110	190
			Mint NH	18	40	65	105	135	180	325	625
PR123	$20	slate	Used	55	100	140	200	290	400	675	1,100
			Unused NG	3.75	7.50	10	15	17.50	23.50	35	47.50
			Unused OG	10.50	19	27.50	45	55	75	125	210
			Mint NH	20	42.50	67.50	110	145	210	375	700
PR124	$50	dull	Used	87.50	150	200	300	415	550	975	1,650
		rose	Unused NG	6.75	14	18	27.50	30	35	47.50	70
			Unused OG	17	35	50	75	100	140	250	400
			Mint NH	30	70	105	170	275	400	775	1,300
PR125	$100	purple	Used	80	150	195	275	375	775	1,650	3,000
			Unused NG	5.50	11.25	15	22.50	24	29	42.50	65
			Unused OG	15	30	50	65	85	125	180	350
			Mint NH	25	62.50	105	150	210	300	550	1,100

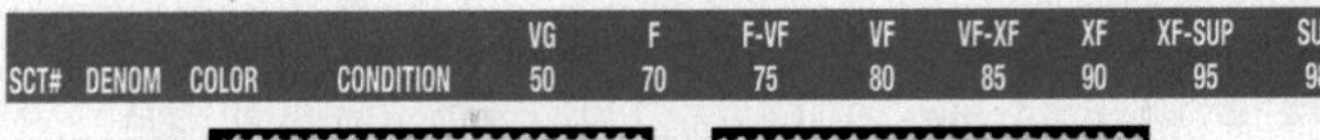

1912-13 PARCEL POST ISSUES

SCT#	DENOM	COLOR	CONDITION	VG 50	F 70	F-VF 75	VF 80	VF-XF 85	XF 90	XF-SUP 95	SUP 98
Q1	1¢	carmine	Used	0.30	0.70	1.15	1.60	9.50	32.50	125	350
		rose	Unused OG	0.95	1.90	3	4.25	6	12	32.50	47.50
			Mint NH	2	4.50	7.50	12	25	45	200	575
Q2	2¢	carmine	Used	0.25	0.55	0.90	1.25	5.25	22.50	105	325
		rose	Unused OG	1.10	2.15	3.55	5	7.50	12.50	30	57.50
			Mint NH	2.10	4.75	8	12.50	25	47.50	325	775
Q2a	2¢	lake	Unused OG	1,000	1,500	1,750	2,200				
Q2b	2¢	carmine lake	Unused OG	90	150	225	350	—	—		
Q3	3¢	carmine	Used	1.40	2.75	4.25	6	10.50	32.50	130	425
		rose	Unused OG	2.25	4.25	6.25	9	12	17.50	47.50	85
			Mint NH	4.85	7.50	15	24	45	85	325	900
Q4	4¢	carmine	Used	0.75	1.50	2.15	3	7	27.50	120	400
		rose	Unused OG	6.50	12.50	18.50	27.50	40	70	150	350
			Mint NH	9	20	42.50	77.50	100	175	700	1,800
Q5	5¢	carmine	Used	0.60	1.10	1.55	2.25	4.50	27.50	120	375
		rose	Unused OG	5.25	9.75	15	22.50	30	50	115	190
			Mint NH	9.25	21	37	62.50	105	175	525	1,500
Q6	10¢	carmine	Used	0.75	1.50	2.15	3	6	25	125	375
		rose	Unused OG	8	15	28	40	47.50	72.50	165	360
			Mint NH	14.50	30	57.50	90	125	200	575	2,200
Q7	15¢	carmine	Used	4	6.25	10	13.50	22.50	75	190	600
		rose	Unused OG	11	25	40	60	67.50	82.50	175	325
			Mint NH	25	50	110	170	215	325	725	3,150
Q8	20¢	carmine	Used	6.75	12.50	18.50	25	42.50	105	250	650
		rose	Unused OG	25	50	77.50	110	125	160	350	575
			Mint NH	35	82.50	150	260	375	600	1,250	4,000
Q9	25¢	carmine	Used	1.90	3.75	5.75	8	15	42.50	150	425
		rose	Unused OG	11	21.50	35	52.50	62.50	82.50	190	350
			Mint NH	20	42.50	85	145	215	325	850	2,250
Q10	50¢	carmine	Used	12	22.50	32.50	45	67.50	165	375	1,150
		rose	Unused OG	42.50	90	125	200	240	325	525	1,050
			Mint NH	70	135	250	500	725	1,250	2,250	6,750
Q11	75¢	carmine	Used	8.75	15	24	35	57.50	150	325	1,000
		rose	Unused OG	15	30	52.50	80	95	125	220	425
			Mint NH	25	55	90	180	280	425	950	2,750
Q12	$1	carmine	Used	9	17.50	27.50	40	57.50	140	350	975
		rose	Unused OG	57.50	125	170	250	310	400	600	1,250
			Mint NH	90	220	355	600	775	1,250	2,500	7,500
Q1-Q12	12 stamps		Used	46.45	85.60	130.40	183.60	305.25	845	2,365	7,050
Set			Unused OG	186.05	387.05	574.30	860.75	1,043	1,409.50	2,600	5,065
			Mint NH	306.70	672.75	1,207.50	2,133.50	3,010	4,902.50	11,175	34,150

1912 PARCEL POST POSTAGE DUE ISSUES

SCT#	DENOM	COLOR	CONDITION	VG 50	F 70	F-VF 75	VF 80	VF-XF 85	XF 90	XF-SUP 95	SUP 98
JQ1	1¢	dark	Used	0.85	1.80	2.80	4	9	27.50	125	375
		green	Unused OG	1.65	3.75	5.75	8	11.50	16	27.50	47.50
			Mint NH	4	7.50	12.50	22.50	37.50	70	225	475
JQ2	2¢	dark	Used	3.80	8	12	16	27.50	67.50	210	625
		green	Unused OG	13	25	42.50	60	75	97.50	190	300
			Mint NH	25	52.50	100	160	260	400	775	1,450
JQ3	5¢	dark	Used	1	2.10	3.25	4.50	9.50	30	120	375
		green	Unused OG	2.10	4.20	5.75	9	13.50	20	37.50	62.50
			Mint NH	4.25	9	12.75	24	45	90	300	650
JQ4	10¢	dark	Used	10.50	20	30	40	65	150	375	1,000
		green	Unused OG	20	50	70	110	150	225	400	650
			Mint NH	45	100	175	290	420	700	1,325	2,650
JQ5	25¢	dark	Used	1	2	3.15	4.50	11.50	35	175	475
		green	Unused OG	18.50	32.50	52.50	70	87.50	120	200	375
			Mint NH	30	60	115	185	290	450	875	1,700

1925-29 SPECIAL HANDLING ISSUES

SCT#	DENOM	COLOR	CONDITION	VG 50	F 70	F-VF 75	VF 80	VF-XF 85	XF 90	XF-SUP 95	SUP 98
QE1	10¢	yellow	Used	0.25	0.45	0.65	1	3	10	35	125
		green	Unused OG	0.45	1	1.40	2	4	12.50	20	40
		wet printing	Mint NH	0.85	1.70	2.75	4.25	8	15	40	180
QE1a	10¢	yellow	Used			125	150	—			
		green	Unused OG	1.15	2.40	3.35	5	8	15	27.50	47.50
		dry printing	Mint NH	2	4.75	7.25	11	16	27.50	75	200
QE2	15¢	yellow	Used	0.25	0.40	0.60	0.90	3	10	35	125
		green	Unused OG	0.40	0.95	1.50	2.25	4.50	13.50	22.50	42.50
		wet printing	Mint NH	0.90	1.90	3.10	4.75	9	16.50	42.50	190
QE2a	15¢	yellow	Used			125	150	—			
		green	Unused OG	1.20	2.25	3.25	5	7.50	11	18	30
		dry printing	Mint NH	2.75	4.25	6.50	10	15	25	70	210
QE3	20¢	yellow	Used	0.40	0.70	1	1.50	3.75	12.50	45	135
		green	Unused OG	0.85	1.90	2.50	3.75	5	9	17.50	32.50
		wet printing	Mint NH	1.50	3	5.25	7.75	10.50	15	45	175
QE3a	20¢	yellow	Used			125	150	—			
		green	Unused OG	1.25	3.50	5.25	7.50	9	13.50	27.50	50
		dry printing	Mint NH	2.40	6	9.50	15	20	32.50	85	200
QE4	25¢	deep	Used	1	1.80	2.50	3.75	11	20	75	175
		green	Unused OG	3.50	9.50	14	20	22.50	27.50	37.50	60
			Mint NH	6.25	15	25	37.50	45	60	170	360
QE4a	25¢	yellow	Used	5.25	10	15	22.50	37.50	60	140	425
		green	Unused OG	3.25	7.50	11	16.50	19	25	35	55
			Mint NH	5	14	21	32.50	40	55	150	325

HUNTING PERMIT (DUCK) STAMPS

SCT#	DENOM	COLOR	CONDITION	VG 50	F 70	F-VF 75	VF 80	VF-XF 85	XF 90	XF-SUP 95	SUP 98
RW1	$1	blue	Used	50	95	135	175	185	210	260	425
			Unused NG	67.50	105	150	175	190	220	245	425
			Unused OG	82.50	150	210	300	325	360	425	—
			Mint NH	130	270	575	750	850	1,125	2,100	4,750
RW2	$1	rose	Used	57.50	97.50	125	160	175	190	210	360
		lake	Unused NG	72.50	100	145	175	185	200	225	340
			Unused OG	115	190	270	375	390	420	460	600
			Mint NH	180	300	550	750	875	1,100	1,650	4,150
RW3	$1	brown	Used	25	47.50	80	100	110	135	150	175
		black	Unused NG	17.50	35	70	90	95	105	125	160
			Unused OG	42.50	82.50	120	150	160	180	210	300
			Mint NH	70	165	230	325	375	500	900	1,550
RW4	$1	light	Used	15	27.50	47.50	65	75	82.50	95	165
		green	Unused NG	22.50	40	62.50	85	97.50	115	130	190
			Unused OG	37.50	70	110	140	155	175	250	365
			Mint NH	62.50	125	200	300	425	575	875	2,300
RW5	$1	light	Used	20	37.50	60	75	87.50	105	120	170
		violet	Unused NG	22.50	40	62.50	85	97.50	115	130	190
			Unused OG	45	100	125	200	215	245	285	425
			Mint NH	72.50	145	260	425	550	925	1,475	4,650
RW6	$1	chocolate	Used	14	28	37.50	50	57.50	67.50	90	150
			Unused NG	18	32.50	47.50	60	67.50	80	105	170
			Unused OG	25	55	77.50	115	125	145	190	250
			Mint NH	45	100	180	250	280	325	800	1,500
RW7	$1	sepia	Used	14	28	37.50	50	57.50	67.50	90	150
			Unused NG	18	32.50	47.50	60	67.50	80	105	170
			Unused OG	25	55	77.50	115	125	145	190	250
			Mint NH	45	100	180	250	280	325	700	2,250
RW8	$1	brown	Used	14	28	37.50	50	57.50	67.50	90	150
		carmine	Unused NG	15	22.50	35	45	50	60	72.50	140
			Unused OG	22.50	45	65	95	105	120	135	200
			Mint NH	40	90	160	225	270	350	625	1,250

SCT#	DENOM	COLOR	CONDITION	VG 50	F 70	F-VF 75	VF 80	VF-XF 85	XF 90	XF-SUP 95	SUP 98
RW9	$1	violet	Used	12.50	25	35	45	52.50	62.50	75	140
		brown	Unused NG	15	25	35	45	50	60	75	130
			Unused OG	22.50	45	65	95	105	120	160	200
			Mint NH	40	90	160	225	280	375	850	2,000
RW10	$1	deep	Used	10	17.50	24	35	40	50	62.50	100
		rose	Unused NG	14	20	28.50	35	40	52.50	65	87.50
			Unused OG	21	27.50	42.50	55	61.50	72.50	92.50	150
			Mint NH	30	42.50	72.50	120	140	180	310	700
RW11	$1	red	Used	8	14	22	35	40	47.50	57.50	90
		orange	Unused NG	14	20	27.50	35	42.50	52.50	65	87.50
			Unused OG	15	22.50	35	45	55	67.50	160	200
			Mint NH	27.50	47.50	72.50	125	160	240	600	2,150
RW12	$1	black	Used	9	12.50	20	25	30	37.50	50	70
			Unused NG	14	17.50	25	35	40	50	65	92.50
			Unused OG	11.50	20	35	45	52.50	75	100	135
			Mint NH	18.50	32.50	67.50	100	130	180	475	850
RW13	$1	red	Used	4.75	6.25	8.75	12.50	14.25	16.50	23.50	52.50
		brown	Unused NG	5.75	10	13.25	15	17	21	27.50	50
			Mint NH	11	20	35	50	65	110	210	750
RW14	$1	black	Used	5.75	7.50	10.50	15	17	20	27.50	62.50
			Unused NG	7	12	16	18	20	25	35	65
			Mint NH	12	20	35	55	70	130	190	450
RW15	$1	bright	Used	3.75	6	8.50	12	13.50	16	25	60
		blue	Unused NG	5.75	10	12.50	15	17	21	30	62.50
			Mint NH	15	27.50	45	70	90	135	200	475
RW16	$2	bright	Used	5	7.50	11	15	17	20	30	62.50
		green	Unused NG	7	11.50	16	20	24	30	35	50
			Mint NH	13	27.50	42.50	70	85	135	220	525
RW17	$2	violet	Used	5	7.50	11	15	17	20	30	62.50
			Unused NG	7	11.50	16	20	24	30	35	50
			Mint NH	19	40	67.50	90	105	130	210	425
RW18	$2	gray	Used	5	7.50	11	15	17	20	30	62.50
		black	Unused NG	7	11.50	16	20	24	30	37.50	52.50
			Mint NH	19	40	67.50	90	105	140	220	450
RW19	$2	deep	Used	5	7.50	11	15	17	20	30	62.50
		ultra	Unused NG	7	11.50	16	20	24	30	37.50	52.50
			Mint NH	19	40	67.50	90	105	140	240	575
RW20	$2	rose	Used	5	7.50	11	15	17	20	30	62.50
		brown	Unused NG	7	11.50	16	20	24	30	37.50	52.50
			Mint NH	19	40	67.50	90	115	145	260	700
RW21	$2	black	Used	5	7.50	11	15	17	20	30	62.50
			Unused NG	7.50	11	16	20	26	30	35	57.50
			Mint NH	18	37.50	65	85	100	130	180	380
RW22	$2	dark	Used	4	7.25	9.75	12.50	15	20	27.50	45
		blue	Unused NG	7.50	11	16	20	26	30	35	57.50
			Mint NH	18	37.50	65	85	100	130	170	330
RW23	$2	black	Used	4	7.25	9.75	12.50	15	20	27.50	45
			Unused NG	7.50	11	16	20	26	30	35	55
			Mint NH	18	37.50	65	85	100	125	160	300
RW24	$2	emerald	Used	4	7.25	9.75	12.50	15	20	27.50	45
			Unused NG	7.50	11	16	20	26	30	35	55
			Mint NH	18	37.50	65	85	100	120	155	300
RW25	$2	black	Used	4	7.25	9.75	12.50	15	20	27.50	45
			Unused NG	7.50	11	16	20	26	30	35	55
			Mint NH	18	37.50	65	85	100	125	175	375
RW26	$3	multicolor	Used	4.25	7.25	9.75	12.50	16	21	32.50	60
			Unused NG	12.50	22.50	30	45	50	60	75	90
			Mint NH	32.50	60	95	130	145	170	230	400
RW27	$3	multicolor	Used	4	7.25	9.75	12.50	16	21	32.50	60
			Unused NG	12	21.50	25	30	32.50	35	37.50	50
			Mint NH	25	40	75	95	110	125	160	325
RW28	$3	multicolor	Used	4	7.25	9.75	12.50	16	21	32.50	60
			Unused NG		15	21.50	30	32.50	35	37.50	60
			Mint NH		47.50	70	95	110	140	190	350
RW29	$3	multicolor	Used	4	7.25	9.75	12.50	16	21	32.50	60
			Unused NG		17.50	25	35	37.50	42.50	50	75
			Mint NH		55	77.50	110	125	150	225	375
RW30	$3	multicolor	Used	4	7.25	9.75	12.50	16	21	32.50	60
			Unused NG		17.50	25	35	37.50	42.50	50	75
			Mint NH		42.50	65	100	110	135	185	340
RW31	$3	multicolor	Used	4	7.25	9.75	12.50	16	21	32.50	60
			Unused NG		17.50	25	35	37.50	42.50	50	75
			Mint NH		42.50	65	100	115	140	190	350
RW32	$3	multicolor	Used	4	7.25	9.75	12.50	16	21	32.50	60
			Unused NG		20	28.50	40	44	50	57.50	85
			Mint NH		42.50	65	100	110	140	185	350
RW33	$3	multicolor	Used	4	7.25	9.75	12.50	16	21	32.50	60
			Unused NG		20	27.50	40	44	50	57.50	85
			Mint NH		42.50	65	100	110	140	185	350
RW34	$3	multicolor	Used	4	7.25	9.75	12.50	16	21	32.50	60
			Unused NG		20	27.50	40	43	48.50	57.50	80
			Mint NH		42.50	65	100	115	155	210	405

SCT#	DENOM	COLOR	CONDITION	VG 50	F 70	F-VF 75	VF 80	VF-XF 85	XF 90	XF-SUP 95	SUP 98
RW35	$3	multicolor	Used	4	7.25	9.75	12.50	16	21	32.50	60
			Unused NG		9.50	14	20	22	25	29	45
			Mint NH		30	45	65	80	110	225	525
RW36	$3	multicolor	Used	2.50	4	6	8	10	14	22.50	30
			Unused NG		9.50	14	20	22	25	29	45
			Mint NH		30	45	65	80	110	225	525
RW37	$3	multicolor	Used	2.50	4	6	8	10	14	22.50	30
			Unused NG		9.50	14	20	22	25	29	45
			Mint NH		30	45	65	80	110	190	325
RW38	$3	multicolor	Used	2.50	4	6	8	9	10	12	26
			Unused NG		6	11.25	15	16	17.50	19	22.50
			Mint NH		19	32.50	42.50	50	70	100	195
RW39	$5	multicolor	Used	2.15	3.20	5.25	6	7.75	10.50	12.50	21.50
			Unused NG		4	6	8	9.50	11.50	13.50	25
			Mint NH		13.50	24	30	47.50	80	120	210
RW40	$5	multicolor	Used	2	3	4.75	6	8	10	12.50	22.50
			Unused NG		3.50	5.25	7	8.25	10	12	22
			Mint NH		9	13.50	18	25	45	55	115
RW41	$5	multicolor	Used		2.50	4	5	7	9	11.50	18
			Unused NG		4	5	6	8	10	12.50	20
			Mint NH		9	13.50	18	27.50	45	70	140
RW42	$5	multicolor	Used		2.50	4	5	7	9	11.50	18
			Unused NG		4.60	5.75	7	9	11.50	15	24
			Mint NH		7.50	10	15	22.50	42.50	75	170
RW43	$5	green & black	Used		2.50	4	5	7	9	11.50	18
			Unused NG		4.60	5.75	7	9	11.50	15	24
			Mint NH		5	6.75	10	15	25	60	140
RW44	$5	multicolor	Used		2.50	4	5	7	9	11.50	18
			Unused NG		4.60	5.75	7	9	11.50	15	24
			Mint NH		5	6.75	10	15	25	60	140
RW45	$5	multicolor	Used		2.50	4	5	7	9	11.50	18
			Unused NG		2.80	4.50	7	8	9.50	11.50	19.50
			Mint NH		5	6.75	10	17.50	40	55	120
RW46	$7.50	multicolor	Used		3	5	6	8	10	12.50	22.50
			Unused NG		4	6	8	9.50	11.50	13.50	25
			Mint NH		6.25	8.25	12.50	17.50	40	60	155
RW47	$7.50	multicolor	Used		3	4.75	6	8	10	12.50	22.50
			Unused NG		4	6	8	9.50	11.50	13.50	25
			Mint NH		6.25	8.25	12.50	19	40	60	140
RW48	$7.50	multicolor	Used		3	4.75	6	8	10	12.50	22.50
			Unused NG		4	6	8	9.50	11.50	13.50	25
			Mint NH		6.25	8.25	12.50	19	40	60	140
RW49	$7.50	multicolor	Used		3.75	5.50	7	8	10	12.50	22.50
			Unused NG		4	6	9	10	12	15	25
			Mint NH		7.50	10	15	22.50	42.50	65	160
RW50	$7.50	multicolor	Used		3.75	5.50	7	8	10	12.50	22.50
			Unused NG		3.25	4.65	7	7.75	9.25	11.50	20
			Mint NH		7.50	10	15	22.50	37.50	65	160
RW51	$7.50	multicolor	Used		3.75	5.50	7	8	10	12.50	22.50
			Unused NG		3.25	4.65	7	7.75	9.25	12.50	20
			Mint NH		6.25	8.25	12.50	17.50	27.50	50	140
RW52	$7.50	multicolor	Used		4	6	8	9	11	14	25
			Unused NG		3.25	4.65	7	8	10	12.50	20
			Mint NH		7.50	10	15	22.50	37.50	65	155
RW53	$7.50	multicolor	Used		4	6	8	9	11	14	25
			Unused NG		4	6	9	10	12	15	25
			Mint NH		7.50	10	15	22.50	37.50	65	160
RW54	$10	multicolor	Used		4	6	8	9	11	14	25
			Unused NG		4	5.75	8	9.50	11.50	15	22.50
			Mint NH		8.75	12	17.50	27.50	40	70	145
RW55	$10	multicolor	Used		4	6	8	9	11	14	25
			Unused NG		4	5.75	8	9.50	11.50	18	22.50
			Mint NH		8.75	12	17.50	27.50	40	65	150
RW56	$12.50	multicolor	Used			5.50	8	9.25	10.25	13.50	24
			Unused NG			6.50	9	11	14	18.50	25
			Mint NH			16	21.50	30	42.50	62.50	150
RW57	$12.50	multicolor	Used			5.50	8	9.50	10.25	13.50	24
			Unused NG			6.50	9	11	14	18.50	25
			Mint NH			15	20	27.50	40	57.50	110
RW58	$15	multicolor	Used			5.50	8	9.50	10.25	13.50	24
			Unused NG			12	15	17.50	20	27.50	52.50
			Mint NH			22.50	30	37.50	60	87.50	175
RW59	$15	multicolor	Used			7.50	10	12	14	17	27.50
			Unused NG			11.50	15	16.50	19	22.50	50
			Mint NH			22.50	30	37.50	55	160	260
RW60	$15	multicolor	Used			6.25	9	11	13	16	25
			Unused NG			11.50	15	16.50	19	23.50	42
			Mint NH			20	27.50	32	37.50	55	115
RW61	$15	multicolor	Used			7.50	10	12	14	17	27.50
			Unused NG			11.50	15	16.50	19	23.50	40
			Mint NH			[illegible]	[illegible]	[illegible]	[illegible]	[illegible]	[illegible]

SCT#	DENOM	COLOR	CONDITION	VG 50	F 70	F-VF 75	VF 80	VF-XF 85	XF 90	XF-SUP 95	SUP 98
RW62	$15	multicolor	Used			9	12	14	17	22.50	35
			Unused NG			12	15	17.50	20	25	45
			Mint NH			22.50	32.50	37.50	50	67.50	140
RW63	$15	multicolor	Used			9	12	14	17	22.50	35
			Unused NG			11	12.50	15	19	22.50	40
			Mint NH			22.50	32.50	37.50	50	75	145
RW64	$15	multicolor	Used			9	12	14	17	22.50	35
			Unused NG			11	15	17	18	20	40
			Mint NH			20	27.50	32.50	40	65	135
RW65	$15	multicolor	Used			16	22.50	25	30	45	65
			Unused NG			16	22.50	25	30	37.50	52.50
			Mint NH			35	42.50	50	65	105	160
RW65A	$15	multicolor	Used			14	17.50	18.50	21	24	32.50
			Unused NG				15	16	17.50	22.50	32.50
			Mint NH				35	37.50	40	50	95
RW66	$15	multicolor	Used			15	20	23.50	30	37.50	55
			Unused NG			19	22.50	25	30	37.50	50
			Mint NH			32.50	40	45	55	75	135
RW66A	$15	multicolor	Used			10	12	13	14.50	18	25
			Unused NG				15	16	17.50	22.50	32.50
			Mint NH				25	29	35	47.50	90
RW67	$15	multicolor	Used			12	15	18	20	22.50	45
			Unused NG			15	17.50	19	22	25	50
			Mint NH			25	32.50	37.50	47.50	75	135
RW67A	$15	multicolor	Used			12	14	15.50	17	19	27.50
			Unused NG				17.50	19	20	22.50	32.50
			Mint NH				25	29	35	47.50	90
RW68	$15	multicolor	Used			13.50	18	20	22.50	25	37.50
			Unused NG			15	17.50	19	22	25	50
			Mint NH			22.50	30	33.50	42.50	65	120
RW68A	$15	multicolor	Used			12	14	15	17	21	27.50
			Unused NG				15	16	17.50	22.50	32.50
			Mint NH				25	29	35	47.50	90
RW69	$15	multicolor	Used			12	16	18	20	22.50	35
			Unused NG			15	17.50	19	22	25	50
			Mint NH			22.50	30	33.50	42.50	65	125
RW69A	$15	multicolor	Used			10	12	13.50	15	18	24
			Unused NG				15	16	17.50	22.50	32.50
			Mint NH				25	29	35	47.50	90
RW70	$15	multicolor	Used			13	16	18	20	22.50	25
			Unused NG			14	17.50	19	22	25	45
			Mint NH			24	30	37.50	47.50	70	140
RW70A	$15	multicolor	Used			10	12	13.50	15	18	24
			Unused NG				15	16	17.50	22.50	32.50
			Mint NH				25	29	35	47.50	90
RW71	$15	multicolor	Used			12.75	16	18	21.50	25	35
			Unused NG			13.75	17	18.50	21	25	45
			Mint NH			24	30	40	50	75	125
RW71A	$15	multicolor	Used			10	12	13.50	15	18	24
			Unused NG				15	16	18	22.50	32.50
			Mint NH				25	27.50	32.50	45	90
RW72	$15	multicolor	Used			13	16	17.50	21	24	32.50
		type I	Unused NG			13	16	17	19	24	42.50
			Mint NH			20	25	32.50	42.50	65	115
RW72b black signature	$15	multicolor	Mint NH			1,450	1,750	1,950	2,250	2,650	3,400
RW72b blue signature	$15	multicolor	Mint NH		—	2,100	2,500	2,750	3,250	3,750	4,250
RW72b gold signature	$15	multicolor	Mint NH		—	2,500	3,000	3,250	3,800	4,500	5,500
RW72c	$15	multicolor	Used			13	16	17.50	21	24	32.50
		type II	Unused NG			13	16	17	19	24	42.50
			Mint NH			18	22.50	30	40	65	95
RW72A	$15	multicolor	Used			9	11	12	13	15	21.50
			Unused NG				15	16	18	22.50	32.50
			Mint NH				22.50	25	30	45	90
RW73	$15	multicolor	Used			9	11	12	14	16	22.50
			Unused NG			12.50	15	16	17.50	22.50	40
			Mint NH			18	22.50	31.50	42.50	65	100
RW73b 1 signature	$15	multicolor	Mint NH			95	120	135	165	205	250
RW73b 2 signatures	$15	multicolor	Mint NH			110	150	170	190	240	350
RW73A	$15	multicolor	Used			9	11	12	13	15	21.50
			Unused NG				15	16	18	22.50	32.50
			Mint NH				22.50	24	27.50	42.50	90
RW74	$15	multicolor	Used			9	11	12	14	16	21.50
			Unused NG			13.50	16	17	18	22.50	40
			Mint NH			22	27.50	36	47.50	75	105
RW74b	$15	multicolor	Mint NH			90	125	135	155	215	400
RW74A	$15	multicolor	Used			9	11	12	13	15	21.50
			Unused NG				15	16	18	22.50	30
			Mint NH				22.50	24	27.50	42.50	90
RW75	$15	multicolor	Used			9	11	12	14	16	19
			Unused NG			13.50	16	17	18	22.50	40
			Mint NH			22	27.50	36	47.50	75	105
RW75b	$15	multicolor	Mint NH			50	70	77.50	90	140	260
RW75A	$15	multicolor	Used			9	11	12	13	15	21.50
			Unused NG				25	28	32.50	45	67.50
			Mint NH				22.50	24	27.50	42.50	90
RW76	$15	multicolor	Used			9	11	12	14	16	21.50
			Unused NG				16	17	18	22.50	40
			Mint NH				27.50	36	47.50	75	105
RW76b	$15	multicolor	Mint NH			42.50	60	72.50	95	150	250
RW76A	$15	multicolor	Used			9	11	12	13	15	21.50
			Unused NG				20	21.50	24	30	40
			Mint NH				22.50	24	27.50	42.50	90
RW77	$15	multicolor	Used			9	11	12	14	16	21.50
			Unused NG				16	17	18	22.50	40
			Mint NH				27.50	36	47.50	75	105
RW77b	$15	multicolor	Mint NH			35	50	60	75	125	220
RW77A	$15	multicolor	Used			9	11	12	14	16	21.50
			Unused NG				20	21.50	24	30	45
			Mint NH				25	27	30	47.50	100
RW78	$15	multicolor	Used			9	11	12	14	16	21.50
			Unused NG				16	17	18	22.50	40
			Mint NH				27.50	36	47.50	75	105
RW78b	$15	multicolor	Mint NH			42.50	60	70	85	125	225
RW78A	$15	multicolor	Used			9	11	12	14	16	21.50
			Unused NG				20	21.50	24	30	45
			Mint NH				25	27	30	47.50	100
RW79	$15	multicolor	Used			9	11	12	14	16	21.50
			Unused NG				16	17	18	22.50	40
			Mint NH				27.50	36	47.50	75	105
RW79b	$15	multicolor	Mint NH			42.50	60	70	85	125	225
RW79A	$15	multicolor	Used			9	11	12	14	16	21.50
			Unused NG				20	21.50	24	30	45
			Mint NH				25	27	30	47.50	100
RW80	$15	multicolor	Used			9	11	12	14	16	21.50
			Unused NG				16	17	18	22.50	40
			Mint NH				27.50	36	47.50	75	105
RW80b	$15	multicolor	Mint NH			42.50	60	70	90	120	210
RW80A	$15	multicolor	Used			9	11	12	14	16	21.50
			Unused NG				20	21.50	24	30	45
			Mint NH				25	27	30	47.50	100
RW81	$15	multicolor	Used			9	11	12	14	16	21.50
			Unused NG				16	17	18	22.50	40
			Mint NH				27.50	36	47.50	75	105
RW81A	$15	multicolor	Used			10	12.50	14	16	18	25
			Unused NG				20	22	24	30	47.50
			Mint NH				25	27	30	45	100
RW82	$25	multicolor	Used			10	12	13	14	17.50	22.50
			Unused NG				25	27.50	29	32.50	45
			Mint NH				37.50	42.50	50	77.50	130
RW82A	$25	multicolor	Used			10	12	13	14	17.50	22.50
			Unused NG				32.50	35	37.50	40	45
			Mint NH				37.50	40	42.50	52.50	110
RW83	$25	multicolor	Used			12.50	15	16.50	18.50	22.50	28.50
			Unused NG				35	38.50	42.50	47.50	62.50
			Mint NH				55	62.50	72.50	115	175
RW83A	$25	multicolor	Used			10	12.50	13.50	15	18	24
			Unused NG				32.50	35	37.50	40	45
			Mint NH				37.50	40	42.50	52.50	110
RW84	$25	multicolor	Used			10	12.50	13.50	15	18	24
			Unused NG				25	27.50	29	32.50	45
			Mint NH				37.50	42.50	50	77.50	130
RW84A	$25	multicolor	Used			10	12.50	13.50	15	18	24
			Unused NG				32.50	35	37.50	40	45
			Mint NH				37.50	40	42.50	52.50	110
RW85	$25	multicolor	Used			10	12.50	13.50	15	18	24
			Unused NG				25	27.50	29	32.50	45
			Mint NH				37.50	42.50	50	77.50	130
RW85A	$25	multicolor	Mint NH			10	12.50	13.50	15	18	24
RW86	$25	multicolor	Used			10	12.50	13.50	15	18	24
			Unused NG				25	27.50	29	32.50	45
			Mint NH				37.50	42.50	50	77.50	130
RW86A	$25	multicolor	Mint NH			10	12.50	13.50	15	18	24

SEMI-POSTAL STAMPS

The genesis of the U.S. semi-postal stamp program was a July 1997 bill passed by both houses of Congress that directed the USPS to issue a stamp to benefit breast-cancer research. On August 13, the President signed it into law. The surcharge was to be up to 25% of the current first-class rate.

BREAST CANCER RESEARCH

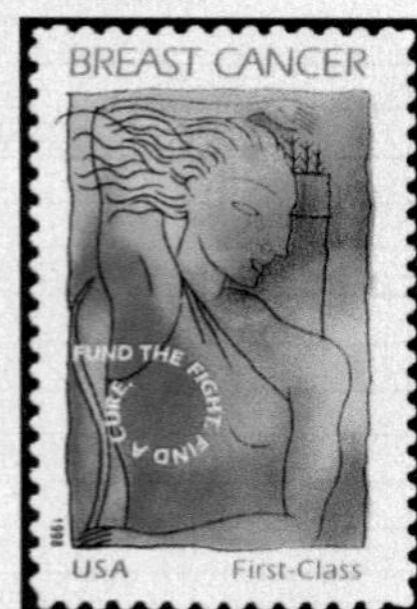

SP1

Designed by Ethel Kessler. Printed by Avery Dennison.

PHOTOGRAVURE

Sheets of 160 in eight panes of 20

1998, July 29 Tagged *Serpentine Die Cut 11*

Self-Adhesive

B1	SP1 (32c+8c) **multicolored**	1.10	.25
	P# block of 4, 6#+V	4.40	
	Pane of 20	22.00	

The 8c surtax was for cancer research. After the Jan. 10, 1999, first class postage rate changes, No. B1 became a 33c stamp with a 7c surtax; after Jan. 7, 2001, it became a 34c stamp with a 6c surtax. Effective Mar. 23, 2002, the stamp was sold for 45c, but the face value remained at 34c until June 30, 2002, at which time the face value rose to 37c. On Jan. 8, 2006, the face value rose to 39c, and on May 14, 2007, the face value rose to 41c and the stamp sold for 55c.

Sales of No. B1 were suspended Jan. 1, 2004, but resumed Feb. 2, 2004, after Congress extended the sales period through Dec. 31, 2005. Subsequently, the sales period was again extended, with the postage value matching changes in the first-class postage rates.

HEROES OF 2001

Firemen Atop World Trade Center Rubble — SP2

Designed by Derry Noyes. Printed by Ashton-Potter (USA) Ltd..

LITHOGRAPHED

Sheets of 120 in six panes of 20

2002, June 7 Tagged *Serpentine Die Cut 11¼*

Self-Adhesive

B2	SP2 (34c+11c) **multicolored**	1.10	.35
	P# block of 4, 4#+P	4.40	
	Pane of 20	22.00	

The 11c surtax was for assistance to families of emergency relief personnel killed or permanently disabled in the line of duty in connection with the terrorist attacks of Sept. 11, 2001. No. B2 became a 37c stamp with an 8c surtax June 30, 2002.

STOP FAMILY VIOLENCE

SP3

Designed by Carl T. Herrman.

Printed by Avery Dennison.

PHOTOGRAVURE

Sheets of 200 in 10 panes of 20

2003, Oct. 8 Tagged *Serpentine Die Cut 11*

Self-Adhesive

B3	SP3 (37c+8c) **multicolored**	1.10	.45
	P# block of 4, 4#+V	4.40	
	Pane of 20	22.00	

The 8¢ surtax was for the U.S. Department of Health and Humans Services to support programs aimed at reducing domestic violence. On Jan. 8, 2006, the face value rose to 39¢. Sales were suspended Dec. 31, 2006.

SAVE VANISHING SPECIES Ⓢ

Amur Tiger Cub — SP4

Designed by Derry Noyes.

Printed by Avery Dennison.

PHOTOGRAVURE

Sheets of 160 in eight panes of 20

2011, Sept. 20 Tagged *Serpentine Die Cut 10¾*

Self-Adhesive

B4	SP4 (44c+11c) **multicolored**	1.10	.50
	P# block of 4, 7#+V	4.40	
	Pane of 20	22.00	

The 11c surtax was for the Multinational Species Conservation Funds of the U.S. Fish and Wildlife Service. The stamp was sold for 55c when the first class franking value was at 45c and 46c, with the surtax being decreased in each instance. Sales of No. B4 were suspended on Jan. 1, 2014, but resumed in Oct. 2014, selling for 60c (49c franking value and 11c surtax) after Congress extended the sales period through Dec. 31, 2018.

See note after No. 1549.

Breast Cancer Awareness Type of 1998

Designed by Ethel Kessler. Printed by Banknote Corporation of America for Sennett Security Products.

LITHOGRAPHED

Sheets of 240 in 12 panes of 20

Design Size: 20x35mm

Serpentine Die Cut 11x10¾

2014, Sept. 30 Tagged

Dated 2014

Self-Adhesive

B5	SP1 (49c+11c) **multicolored**	1.40	.50
	P# block of 4, 6#+S or 6#+B	4.40	
	Pane of 20	22.00	
a.	Imperforate	2.25	—
	Pane of 20	45.00	

Die cut and imperforate uncut press sheets of No. B5 were made available for sale. Values: cross gutter block of 4, $12.50; pairs with gutters between, $5.50 each. See note after No. 4693.

ALZHEIMER'S DISEASE AWARENESS Ⓢ

SP5

Designed by Ethel Kessler. Printed by Banknote Corporation of America.

LITHOGRAPHED

Sheets of 120 in six panes of 20

Serpentine Die Cut 10½x10¾

2017, Nov. 30 Tagged

Self-Adhesive

B6	SP5 (49c+11c) **multicolored**	1.40	.60
	P# block of 4, 6#+B	4.40	
	Pane of 20	22.00	

The 11c surtax was for the National Institutes of Health.

See note after No. 1549.

AIR POST STAMPS

Air mail in the U. S. postal system developed in three stages: pioneer period (with many unofficial or semi-official flights before 1918), government flights and contract air mail (C.A.M.). Contract air mail began on February 15, 1926.

All C.A.M. contracts were canceled on February 19, 1934, and air mail was carried by Army planes for six months. After that the contract plan was resumed. Separate domestic airmail service was abolished Oct. 11, 1975.

See Domestic Air Mail Rates chart in introduction.

Curtiss Jenny — AP1

No. C3 first used on airplane mail service between Washington, Philadelphia and New York, on May 15, 1918, but was valid for ordinary postage. The rate of postage was 24 cents per ounce, which included immediate individual delivery.

Rate of postage was reduced to 16 cents for the first ounce and 6 cents for each additional ounce, which included 10 cents for immediate individual delivery, on July 15, 1918, by Postmaster General's order of June 26, 1918. No. C2 was first used for air mail in the tri-city service on July 15. Covers may be dated earlier than July 15, but they were held until the July 15 flight.

Rate of postage was reduced on December 15, 1918, by Postmaster General's order of November 30, 1918, to 6 cents per ounce. No. C1 was first used for air mail (same three-way service) on Dec. 16.

FLAT PLATE PRINTINGS

Plates of 100 subjects.

1918	**Unwmk.** **Engr.**		***Perf. 11***
C1	AP1 6c **orange,** *Dec. 10*	55.	28.
	pale orange	55.	28.
	Never hinged	110.	
	On cover		50.
	First flight cover, *Dec. 16*		2,000.
	Margin block of 4, arrow top or left	250.	140.
	Center line block	275.	150.
	P# block of 6, arrow	700.	—
	Never hinged	1,000.	
	Double transfer (#9155-14)	85.	45.
C2	AP1 16c **green,** *July 11*	60.	30.
	dark green	60.	30.
	Never hinged	120.	
	On cover		55.
	First flight cover, *July 15*		800.
	Margin block of 4, arrow top or left	250.	175.
	Center line block	275.	190.
	P# block of 6, arrow	900.	—
	Never hinged	1,350.	
C3	AP1 24c **carmine rose & blue,** *May 14*	65.	30.
	dark carmine rose & blue	65.	30.
	Never hinged	130.	
	On cover		75.
	First flight cover, *May 15*		750.
	Margin block of 4, arrow top or left	275.	150.
	Margin block of 4, arrow bottom	300.	160.
	Margin block of 4, arrow right	325.	200.
	Center line block	350.	175.
	P# block of 4, red P# only	*750.*	—
	P# block of 12, two P#, arrow & two "TOP"	1,250.	—
	Never hinged	2,000.	
	P# block of 12, two P#, arrow & blue "TOP" only	*12,500.*	
	Never hinged	*16,500.*	
a.	Center inverted	*450,000.*	
	Never hinged	*850,000.*	
	Block of 4	*2,000,000.*	
	Block of 4 with horiz. guide line	*2,100,000.*	
	Corner margin block of 4 with siderographer's initials	*2,400,000.*	
	Center line block	*2,100,000.*	
	P# block of 4, blue P#	*5,000,000.*	
	Nos. C1-C3 (3)	180.00	88.00
	Nos. C1-C3, never hinged	360.00	

Plate Blocks

Scott values for plate blocks printed from flat plates are for very fine side and bottom positions. Top position plate blocks with full wide selvage sell for more.

Airplane Radiator and Wooden Propeller — AP2

Air Service Emblem — AP3

DeHavilland Biplane — AP4

Nos. C4-C6 were issued primarily for use in the new night-flying air mail service between New York and San Francisco, but valid for all purposes. Three zones were established; New York-Chicago, Chicago-Cheyenne, Cheyenne-San Francisco, and the rate of postage was 8 cents an ounce for each zone. Service was inaugurated on July 1, 1924.

These stamps were placed on sale at the Philatelic Agency at Washington on the dates indicated in the listings but were not issued to postmasters at that time.

Plates of 400 subjects in four panes of 100 each.

1923	**Unwmk.**		***Perf. 11***
C4	AP2 8c **dark green,** *Aug. 15*	17.50	12.50
	deep green	17.50	12.50
	Never hinged	35.00	
	On cover		22.50
	P# block of 6	240.00	—
	Never hinged	330.00	
	Double transfer	35.00	20.00
C5	AP3 16c **dark blue,** *Aug. 17*	60.00	27.50
	Never hinged	120.00	
	On cover		47.50
	P# block of 6	1,300.	—
	Never hinged	2,000.	
	Double transfer	110.00	42.50
C6	AP4 24c **carmine,** *Aug. 21*	65.00	27.50
	Never hinged	130.00	
	On cover		42.50
	P# block of 6	1,700.	—
	Never hinged	2,500.	
	Double transfer (Pl. 14841)	150.00	40.00
	Nos. C4-C6 (3)	142.50	67.50
	Nos. C4-C6, never hinged	285.00	

Map of United States and Two Mail Planes — AP5

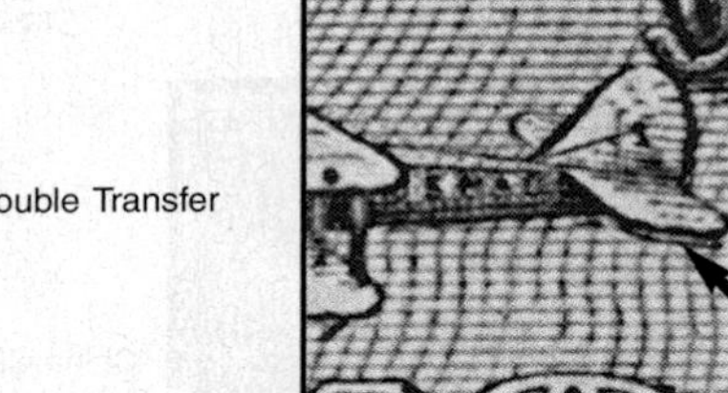
Double Transfer

The Act of Congress of February 2, 1925, created a rate of 10 cents per ounce for distances to 1000 miles, 15 cents per ounce for 1500 miles and 20 cents for more than 1500 miles on contract air mail routes.

Plates of 200 subjects in four panes of 50 each.

1926-27	**Unwmk.**		***Perf. 11***
C7	AP5 10c **dark blue,** *Feb. 13, 1926*	2.25	.35
	light blue	2.25	.35
	Never hinged	4.00	
	P# block of 6	32.50	—
	Never hinged	45.00	
	Double transfer (18246 UL 11)	12.50	1.25
C8	AP5 15c **olive brown,** *Sept. 18, 1926*	2.50	2.50
	light brown	2.50	2.50
	Never hinged	4.75	
	P# block of 6	32.50	—
	Never hinged	45.00	
C9	AP5 20c **yellow green,** *Jan. 25, 1927*	6.50	2.00
	green	6.50	2.00
	Never hinged	12.50	
	P# block of 6	70.00	—
	Never hinged	95.00	
	Nos. C7-C9 (3)	11.25	4.85
	Nos. C7-C9, never hinged	21.25	

Lindbergh's Plane "Spirit of St. Louis" and Flight Route — AP6

Double Impression

A tribute to Col. Charles A. Lindbergh, who made the first non-stop (and solo) flight from New York to Paris, May 20-21, 1927.

Plates of 200 subjects in four panes of 50 each.

1927, June 18	**Unwmk.**		***Perf. 11***
C10	AP6 10c **dark blue**	7.00	2.50
	Never hinged	12.50	
	P# block of 6	90.00	—
	Never hinged	130.00	
	Double transfer	11.00	3.25
a.	Booklet pane of 3, *May 26, 1928*	70.00	*65.00*
	Never hinged	115.00	
b.	Double impression		*16,500.*

No. C10b is unique.

Beacon on Rocky Mountains AP7

Issued to meet the new rate, effective August 1, of 5 cents per ounce.

Plates of 100 subjects in two panes of 50

1928, July 25	**Unwmk.**		***Perf. 11***
C11	AP7 5c **carmine and blue**	5.50	.85
	Never hinged	10.00	
	On cover, first day of 5c airmail rate, Aug. 1		3.00
	Margin block of 4, arrow, (line) right or left	25.00	4.50
	P# block of 6, two P# & red "TOP"	42.50	—
	Never hinged	57.50	
	P# block of 6, two P# & blue "TOP"	42.50	—
	Never hinged	57.50	
	P# block of 6, two P# & double "TOP"	110.00	—
	Never hinged	160.00	
	P# block of 6, two P# only (no "TOP")	200.00	—
	Never hinged	300.00	
	Recut frame line at left	8.00	1.50
	Double transfer	—	—
a.	Vert. pair, imperf. between	*7,000.*	
b.	Printed on "special" booklet paper, *1928* (see note before #551)	9.00	2.00
	Never hinged	17.50	
	On cover		6.00
	Block of 4	40.00	
	P# block of 6, 2 P#	100.00	
	Never hinged	150.00	

No. C11a is unique. It is torn and valued thus.

Winged Globe — AP8

Plates of 200 subjects in four panes of 50 each.

1930, Feb. 10 Unwmk. *Perf. 11*

Stamp design: 46½x19mm

C12 AP8 5c **violet** 9.50 .50
Never hinged 17.50
P# block of 6 130.00 —
Never hinged 180.00
Double transfer (Pl. 20189) 19.00 1.25
a. Horiz. pair, imperf. between *4,500.*

See Nos. C16-C17, C19.

GRAF ZEPPELIN ISSUE

Zeppelin Over Atlantic Ocean — AP9

Zeppelin Between Continents — AP10

Zeppelin Passing Globe — AP11

Issued for use on mail carried on the first Europe-Pan-America round trip flight of the Graf Zeppelin in May, 1930. They were withdrawn from sale June 30, 1930.

Plates of 200 subjects in four panes of 50 each.

1930, Apr. 19 Unwmk. *Perf. 11*

C13 AP9 65c **green** 175. 150.
Never hinged 240.
On cover or card 160.
Block of 4 750. 750.
P# block of 6 1,500. —
Never hinged 2,200.
C14 AP10 $1.30 **brown** 360. 350.
Never hinged 550.
On cover 375.
Block of 4 1,600. 1,500.
P# block of 6 3,600. —
Never hinged 5,000.
C15 AP11 $2.60 **blue** 525. 550.
Never hinged 825.
On cover 575.
Block of 4 2,400. 2,400.
P# block of 6 5,250. —
Never hinged 8,000.
Nos. C13-C15 (3) 1,060. 1,050.
Nos. C13-C15, never hinged 1,640.

ROTARY PRESS PRINTING

Plates of 200 subjects in four panes of 50 each.

1931-32 Unwmk. *Perf. 10½x11*

Stamp design: 47½x19mm

C16 AP8 5c **violet,** *Aug. 19, 1931* 4.75 .60
Never hinged 8.50
Block of 4 21.00 2.00
P# block of 4 75.00 —
Never hinged 95.00

Issued to conform with new air mail rate of 8 cents per ounce which became effective July 6, 1932.

C17 AP8 8c **olive bister,** *Sept. 26, 1932* 2.25 .40
Never hinged 3.75
Block of 4 10.00 2.00
P# block of 4 27.50 —

CENTURY OF PROGRESS ISSUE

"Graf Zeppelin," Federal Building at Chicago Exposition and Hangar at Friedrichshafen — AP12

Issued in connection with the flight of the airship "Graf Zeppelin" in October, 1933, to Miami, Akron and Chicago and from the last city to Europe.

FLAT PLATE PRINTING

Plates of 200 subjects in four panes of 50 each.

1933, Oct. 2 Unwmk. *Perf. 11*

C18 AP12 50c **green** 45.00 47.50
Never hinged 75.00
On cover 80.00
Block of 4 200.00 *275.00*
P# block of 6 475.00 —
Never hinged 675.00

Catalogue values for unused stamps in this section, from this point to the end, are for Never Hinged items.

Type of 1930 Issue

ROTARY PRESS PRINTING

Issued to conform with new air mail rate of 6 cents per ounce which became effective July 1, 1934.

Plates of 200 subjects in four panes of 50 each.

1934, June 30 Unwmk. *Perf. 10½x11*

C19 AP8 6c **dull orange** 3.50 .25
On cover, first day of 6c airmail rate, July 1 10.00
Block of 4 14.00 1.10
P# block of 4 20.00 —
Horiz. pair with full vert. gutter btwn. *425.00*
Vert. pair with full horiz. gutter btwn. *700.00*

TRANSPACIFIC ISSUES

"China Clipper" over Pacific — AP13

Issued to pay postage on mail transported by the Transpacific air mail service, inaugurated Nov. 22, 1935.

FLAT PLATE PRINTING

Plates of 200 subjects in four panes of 50 each.

1935, Nov. 22 Unwmk. *Perf. 11*

C20 AP13 25c **blue** 1.40 1.00
P# block of 6 20.00 —

"China Clipper" over Pacific — AP14

Issued primarily for use on the Transpacific service to China, but valid for all air mail purposes.

FLAT PLATE PRINTING

Plates of 200 subjects in four panes of 50 each.

1937, Feb. 15 Unwmk. *Perf. 11*

C21 AP14 20c **green** 10.00 1.75
dark green 10.00 1.75
Block of 4 40.00 8.50
P# block of 6 85.00 —
C22 AP14 50c **carmine** 10.00 5.00
Block of 4 40.00 21.00
P# block of 6 85.00 —

Wide full selvage top margin plate blocks of No. C22 are extremely scarce and sell for $3,000 or more in the grades of very fine and higher.

Eagle Holding Shield, Olive Branch and Arrows — AP15

FLAT PLATE PRINTING

Frame plates of 100 subjects in two panes of 50 each separated by a 1½-inch wide vertical gutter with central guide line, and vignette plates of 50 subjects. Some plates were made of iron, then chromed; several of these carry an additional imprint, "E.I." (Electrolytic Iron).

1938, May 14 Unwmk. *Perf. 11*

C23 AP15 6c **dark blue & carmine** .70 .25
Margin block of 4, bottom or side arrow 3.00 2.25
P# block of 4, 2 P# 7.00 —
Center line block 4.50 3.50
Top P# block of 10, with two P#, arrow, two "TOP" and two registration markers 15.00
a. Vert. pair, imperf. horiz. *300.00 300.00*
On cover 1,750.
Center line block *1,000.*
P# block of 4, 2 P# *1,750.*
b. Horiz. pair, imperf. vert. *12,500.*
P# block of 4, 2 P# *37,500.*
c. 6c **ultramarine & carmine** 200.00 *2,000.*
On cover *2,250.*
Center line block *1,200.*
P# block of 4, 2 P# *1,500.*

Top plate number blocks of No. C23 are found both with and without top arrow.

The plate block of No. C23b is unique and never hinged; value is based on 1994 auction sale.

TRANSATLANTIC ISSUE

Winged Globe — AP16

Inauguration of Transatlantic air mail service.

FLAT PLATE PRINTING

Plates of 200 subjects in four panes of 50 each.

1939, May 16 Unwmk. *Perf. 11*

C24 AP16 30c **dull blue** 11.00 1.50
P# block of 6 110.00 —

Twin-Motored Transport Plane — AP17

ROTARY PRESS PRINTING

E. E. Plates of 200 subjects in four panes of 50 each.

1941-44 Unwmk. *Perf. 11x10½*

C25 AP17 6c **carmine,** *June 25, 1941* .25 .25
P# block of 4 .60 —
Pair with full vert. gutter btwn. *225.00*
Pair with full horiz. gutter btwn. —
a. Booklet pane of 3, *Mar. 18, 1943* 3.50 1.50
b. Horiz. pair, imperf. between *2,250.*

Singles from No. C25a are imperf. at sides or at sides and bottom.

Value of No. C25b is for pair without blue crayon P. O. rejection mark on front. Very fine pairs with crayon mark sell for about $1,500.

C26 AP17 8c **olive green,** *Mar. 21, 1944* .25 .25
P# block of 4 1.10 —
Pair with full horiz. gutter btwn. *325.00*
a. All color omitted —

No. C26a has an albino impression and exists as a pair of stamps within a double-paper spliced strip of six stamps.

C27 AP17 10c **violet,** *Aug. 15, 1941* 1.10 .25
P# block of 4 5.00 —
C28 AP17 15c **brown carmine,** *Aug. 19, 1941* 2.10 .35
P# block of 4 9.00 —
C29 AP17 20c **bright green,** *Aug. 27, 1941* 2.10 .30

C31 AP17 50c **orange,** *Oct. 29, 1941* 11.00 3.25
P# block of 4 47.50 —
Nos. C25-C31 (7) 18.90 5.00

DC-4 Skymaster AP18

ROTARY PRESS PRINTING
E. E. Plates of 200 subjects in four panes of 50 each.

1946, Sept. 25 Unwmk. *Perf. 11x10½*
C32 AP18 5c **carmine** .25 .25
P# block of 4 .45 —

DC-4 Skymaster — AP19

ROTARY PRESS PRINTING
E. E. Plates of 400 subjects in four panes of 100 each.

1947, Mar. 26 Unwmk. *Perf. 10½x11*
C33 AP19 5c **carmine** .25 .25
P# block of 4 .60 —

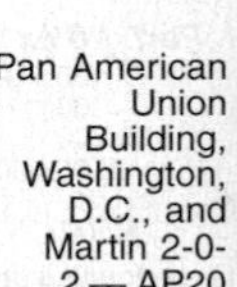

Pan American Union Building, Washington, D.C., and Martin 2-0-2 — AP20

Statue of Liberty, New York Skyline and Lockheed Constellation AP21

San Francisco-Oakland Bay Bridge and Boeing B377 Stratocruiser — AP22

Designed by Victor S. McCloskey, Jr., Leon Helguera and William K. Schrage.

ROTARY PRESS PRINTING
E. E. Plates of 200 subjects in four panes of 50 each.

1947 Unwmk. *Perf. 11x10½*
C34 AP20 10c **black,** *Aug. 30* .25 .25
P# block of 4 1.10 —
a. Dry printing .40 .25
P# block of 4 (#25613, 25614) 1.75 —
C35 AP21 15c **bright blue green,** *Aug. 20* .35 .25
blue green .35 .25
P# block of 4 1.50 —
Pair with full horiz. gutter btwn. *650.00*
a. Horiz. pair, imperf. between *1,500.*
b. Dry printing .55 .25
P# block of 4 (#25492 and up) 2.50 —
C36 AP22 25c **blue,** *July 30* .90 .25
P# block of 4 4.00 —
a. Dry printing 1.20 .25
P# block of 4 (#25615 and up) 5.25 —
Nos. C34-C36 (3) 1.50 .75

See note on wet and dry printings following No. 1029.
No. C35a is valued in the grade of fine.

Type of 1947
ROTARY PRESS COIL STAMP

1948, Jan. 15 Unwmk. *Perf. 10 Horizontally*
C37 AP19 5c **carmine** 1.00 .80
Pair 2.10 1.75
Joint line pair 10.00 3.00

NEW YORK CITY ISSUE

Map of Five Boroughs, Circular Band and Planes — AP23

50th anniv. of the consolidation of the five boroughs of New York City.

ROTARY PRESS PRINTING
E. E. Plates of 400 subjects in four panes of 100 each.

1948, July 31 Unwmk. *Perf. 11x10½*
C38 AP23 5c **bright carmine** .25 .25
P# block of 4 3.50 —

Type of 1947
ROTARY PRESS PRINTING
E. E. Plates of 400 subjects in four panes of 100 each.

1949 Unwmk. *Perf. 10½x11*
C39 AP19 6c **carmine,** *Jan. 18* .25 .25
P# block of 4 .50 —
Pair with full horiz. gutter btwn. *600.00*
a. Booklet pane of 6, *Nov. 18* 12.00 5.00
b. Dry printing .50 .25
P# block of 4 (#25340 and up) 2.25 —
c. As "a," dry printing 25.00 —

See note on wet and dry printings following No. 1029.

ALEXANDRIA BICENTENNIAL ISSUE

Home of John Carlyle, Alexandria Seal and Gadsby's Tavern AP24

200th anniv. of the founding of Alexandria, Va.

ROTARY PRESS PRINTING
E. E. Plates of 200 subjects in four panes of 50 each.

1949, May 11 Unwmk. *Perf. 11x10½*
C40 AP24 6c **carmine** .25 .25
P# block of 4 .55 —

Type of 1947
ROTARY PRESS COIL STAMP

1949, Aug. 25 Unwmk. *Perf. 10 Horizontally*
C41 AP19 6c **carmine** 3.00 .25
Pair 6.25 .25
Joint line pair 14.00 1.35

UNIVERSAL POSTAL UNION ISSUE

Post Office Department Building AP25

Globe and Doves Carrying Messages AP26

Boeing Stratocruiser and Globe — AP27

Universal Postal Union, 75th Anniv.

ROTARY PRESS PRINTING
E. E. Plates of 200 subjects in four panes of 50 each.

1949 Unwmk. *Perf. 11x10½*
C42 AP25 10c **violet,** *Nov. 18* .25 .25
P# block of 4 1.40 —
C43 AP26 15c **ultramarine,** *Oct. 7* .30 .25
P# block of 4 1.25 —
C44 AP27 25c **rose carmine,** *Nov. 30* .60 .40
P# block of 4 4.00 —
Nos. C42-C44 (3) 1.15 .90

WRIGHT BROTHERS ISSUE

Wilbur and Orville Wright and their Plane, 1903 — AP28

46th anniv. of the 1st successful flight in a motor-powered airplane, Dec. 17, 1903, at Kill Devil Hill near Kitty Hawk, NC, by Wilbur (1867-1912) and Orville Wright (1871-1948) of Dayton, OH. The plane flew 852 feet in 59 seconds.

ROTARY PRESS PRINTING
E. E. Plates of 200 subjects in four panes of 50 each.

1949, Dec. 17 Unwmk. *Perf. 11x10½*
C45 AP28 6c **magenta** .25 .25
P# block of 4 .70 —

Diamond Head, Honolulu, Hawaii AP29

ROTARY PRESS PRINTING
E. E. Plates of 200 subjects in four panes of 50 each.

1952, Mar. 26 Unwmk. *Perf. 11x10½*
C46 AP29 80c **bright red violet** 4.50 1.25
P# block of 4 19.00 —

POWERED FLIGHT, 50th ANNIV.

First Plane and Modern Plane — AP30

ROTARY PRESS PRINTING
E. E. Plates of 200 subjects in four panes of 50 each.

1953, May 29 Unwmk. *Perf. 11x10½*
C47 AP30 6c **carmine** .25 .25
P# block of 4 .55 —

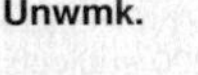

Eagle in Flight — AP31

Issued primarily for use on domestic post cards.

ROTARY PRESS PRINTING

E. E. Plates of 400 subjects in four panes of 100 each.

1954, Sept. 3 **Unwmk.** ***Perf. 11x10½***

C48 AP31 4c **bright blue** .25 .25
P# block of 4 1.10 —

AIR FORCE, 50th ANNIV.

B-52 Stratofortress and F-104 Starfighters AP32

Designed by Alexander Nagy, Jr.

ROTARY PRESS PRINTING

E. E. Plates of 200 subjects in four panes of 50 each.

1957, Aug. 1 **Unwmk.** ***Perf. 11x10½***

C49 AP32 6c **blue** .25 .25
P# block of 4 .70 —

Type of 1954

Issued primarily for use on domestic post cards.

1958, July 31 **Unwmk.** ***Perf. 11x10½***

C50 AP31 5c **red** .25 .25
P# block of 4 1.00 —

Silhouette of Jet Airliner — AP33

Designed by William H. Buckley and Sam Marsh.

ROTARY PRESS PRINTING

E. E. Plates of 400 subjects in four panes of 100 each.

1958, July 31 **Unwmk.** ***Perf. 10½x11***

C51 AP33 7c **blue** .25 .25
P# block of 4 .60 —
a. Booklet pane of 6 6.50 5.00
b. Vert. pair, imperf. between (from booklet pane) *4,000.*

No. C51b resulted from a paper foldover after perforating and before cutting into panes. Two or three pairs are believed to exist.

ROTARY PRESS COIL STAMP

Perf. 10 Horizontally

C52 AP33 7c **blue** 2.00 .25
Pair 4.25 .40
Joint line pair 15.00 1.25
Small holes 7.50 —
Pair 15.00
Joint line pair 240.00 75.00

ALASKA STATEHOOD ISSUE

Big Dipper, North Star and Map of Alaska — AP34

Designed by Richard C. Lockwood.

ROTARY PRESS PRINTING

E. E. Plates of 200 subjects in four panes of 50 each.

1959, Jan. 3 **Unwmk.** ***Perf. 11x10½***

C53 AP34 7c **dark blue** .25 .25
P# block of 4 .80 —

BALLOON JUPITER ISSUE

Balloon and Crowd — AP35

Designed by Austin Briggs.

Centenary of the carrying of mail by the balloon Jupiter from Lafayette to Crawfordsville, Ind.

GIORI PRESS PRINTING

Plates of 200 subjects in four panes of 50 each.

1959, Aug. 17 **Unwmk.** ***Perf. 11***

C54 AP35 7c **dark blue & red** .30 .25
P# block of 4 1.60 —

HAWAII STATEHOOD ISSUE

Alii Warrior, Map of Hawaii and Star of Statehood AP36

Designed by Joseph Feher.

ROTARY PRESS PRINTING

E. E. Plates of 200 subjects in four panes of 50 each.

1959, Aug. 21 **Unwmk.** ***Perf. 11x10½***

C55 AP36 7c **rose red** .25 .25
P# block of 4 .85 —

PAN AMERICAN GAMES ISSUE

Runner Holding Torch — AP37

Designed by Suren Ermoyan.

3rd Pan American Games, Chicago, Aug. 27-Sept. 7, 1959.

GIORI PRESS PRINTING

Plates of 200 subjects in four panes of 50 each.

1959, Aug. 27 **Unwmk.** ***Perf. 11***

C56 AP37 10c **red, white & blue** .25 .25
P# block of 4 1.25 —

Liberty Bell — AP38

Statue of Liberty AP39

Abraham Lincoln AP40

GIORI PRESS PRINTING

Plates of 200 subjects in four panes of 50 each.

1959-66 **Unwmk.** ***Perf. 11***

C57 AP38 10c **black & green,** *June 10, 1960* 1.00 .70
P# block of 4 4.50 —
C58 AP39 15c **black & orange,** *Nov. 20, 1959* .35 .25
P# block of 4 1.50 —
C59 AP40 25c **black & maroon,** *Apr. 22, 1960* .50 .25
P# block of 4 2.00 —
a. Tagged, *Dec. 29, 1966* .60 .30
P# block of 4 2.50 —
Nos. C57-C59 (3) 1.85 1.20

See Luminescence data in Information for Collectors section.

Type of 1958

ROTARY PRESS PRINTING

E. E. Plates of 400 subjects in four panes of 100 each.

1960, Aug. 12 **Unwmk.** ***Perf. 10½x11***

C60 AP33 7c **carmine** .25 .25
P# block of 4 .60 —
Pair with full horiz. gutter btwn. 300.00
a. Booklet pane of 6, *Aug. 19* 7.00 6.00
b. Vert. pair, imperf between (from booklet pane) *5,500.*

No. C60b resulted from a paper foldover after perforating and before cutting into panes. Two pairs are known.

Type of 1958

ROTARY PRESS COIL STAMP

1960, Oct. 22 **Unwmk.** ***Perf. 10 Horizontally***

C61 AP33 7c **carmine** 4.00 .25
Pair 8.25 .55
Joint line pair 27.50 3.75

Type of 1959-60 and

Statue of Liberty AP41

GIORI PRESS PRINTING

Plates of 200 subjects in four panes of 50 each.

1961-67 **Unwmk.** ***Perf. 11***

C62 AP38 13c **black & red,** *June 28, 1961* .40 .25
P# block of 4 1.65 —
a. Tagged, *Feb. 15, 1967* .75 .50
P# block of 4 7.50 —
C63 AP41 15c **black & orange,** *Jan. 13, 1961* .30 .25
P# block of 4 1.25 —
a. Tagged, *Jan. 11, 1967* .35 .25
P# block of 4 1.50 —
b. As "a," horiz. pair, imperf. vert. *15,000.*
c. As "a," horiz. pair, imperf between and at left *2,750.*
d. All color omitted *100.00*

On No. C63d, there is a clear albino plate impression.

Designed by Henry K. Bencsath.

ROTARY PRESS PRINTING

E.E. Plates of 400 subjects in four panes of 100 each.

1962, Dec. 5 **Unwmk.** ***Perf. 10½x11***

C64 AP42 8c **carmine**		.25	.25
	P# block of 4	.65	—
a.	Tagged, *Aug. 1, 1963*	.25	.25
	P# block of 4	.65	—
	As "a," pair with full horiz. gutter between	—	
b.	Booklet pane of 5 + label	6.00	3.00
c.	As "b," tagged, *1964*	1.75	.75

Nos. C64a and C64c were made by overprinting Nos. C64 and C64b with phosphorescent ink. No. C64a was first issued at Dayton, Ohio, for experiments in high speed mail sorting. The tagging is visible in shortwave ultraviolet light.

COIL STAMP; ROTARY PRESS

Perf. 10 Horizontally

C65 AP42 8c **carmine**		.40	.25
	Pair	.80	.50
	Joint line pair	4.00	.55
a.	Tagged, *Sept. 1964*	.35	.25
	Pair	.70	.50
	Joint line pair	1.75	.60

Earliest documented use of C65a: Jan. 14, 1965.

MONTGOMERY BLAIR ISSUE

Montgomery Blair — AP43

Designed by Robert J. Jones

Montgomery Blair (1813-83), Postmaster General (1861-64), who called the 1st Intl. Postal Conf., Paris, 1863, forerunner of the UPU.

GIORI PRESS PRINTING

Plates of 200 subjects in four panes of 50 each.

1963, May 3 **Unwmk.** ***Perf. 11***

C66 AP43 15c **dull red, dark brown & blue**		.55	.50
	P# block of 4	2.25	—

Bald Eagle — AP44

Designed by V. S. McCloskey, Jr.

Issued primarily for use on domestic post cards.

ROTARY PRESS PRINTING

E.E. Plates of 400 subjects in four panes of 100 each.

1963, July 12 **Unwmk.** ***Perf. 11x10½***

C67 AP44 6c **red**		.25	.25
	P# block of 4	1.40	—
a.	Tagged, *Feb. 15, 1967*	4.00	3.00
	P# block of 4	100.00	—

AMELIA EARHART ISSUE

Amelia Earhart and Lockheed Electra — AP45

Designed by Robert J. Jones.

Amelia Earhart (1898-1937), 1st woman to fly across the Atlantic.

GIORI PRESS PRINTING

Plates of 200 subjects in four panes of 50 each.

1963, July 24 **Unwmk.** ***Perf. 11***

C68 AP45 8c **carmine & maroon**		.25	.25
	P# block of 4	1.00	—

ROBERT H. GODDARD ISSUE

Robert H. Goddard, Atlas Rocket and Launching Tower, Cape Kennedy AP46

Designed by Robert J. Jones.

Dr. Robert H. Goddard (1882-1945), physicist and pioneer rocket researcher.

GIORI PRESS PRINTING

Plates of 200 subjects in four panes of 50 each.

1964, Oct. 5 **Tagged** ***Perf. 11***

C69 AP46 8c **blue, red & bister**		.35	.25
	P# block of 4	1.60	—
	Margin block of 4, Mr. Zip and "Use Zip Code"	1.65	—
a.	Tagging omitted		—

Luminescence

Air Post stamps issued after mid-1964 are tagged.

ALASKA PURCHASE ISSUE

Tlingit Totem, Southern Alaska — AP47

Designed by Willard R. Cox

Centenary of the Alaska Purchase. The totem pole shown is in the Alaska State Museum, Juneau.

GIORI PRESS PRINTING

Plates of 200 subjects in four panes of 50 each.

1967, Mar. 30 **Unwmk.** ***Perf. 11***

C70 AP47 8c **brown**		.25	.25
	P# block of 4	1.20	—
	Margin block of 4, Mr. Zip and "Use Zip Code"	1.05	—
a.	Tagging omitted		—

"Columbia Jays" by John James Audubon — AP48

GIORI PRESS PRINTING

Designed by Robert J. Jones.

Plates of 200 subjects in four panes of 50 each.

1967, Apr. 26 ***Perf. 11***

C71 AP48 20c **multicolored**		.75	.25
	P# block of 4	3.25	—
	Margin block of 4, Mr. Zip and "Use Zip Code"	3.10	—
a.	Tagging omitted	*12.50*	

See note over No. 1241.

Fifty-Star Runway — AP49

ROTARY PRESS PRINTING

Designed by Jaan Born.

E. E. Plates of 400 subjects in four panes of 100 each.

1968, Jan. 5 **Unwmk.** ***Perf. 11x10½***

C72 AP49 10c **carmine**		.25	.25
	P# block of 4	.90	—
	Margin block of 4, "Use Zip Codes"	5.00	—
	Vert. pair with full horiz. gutter between	—	
b.	Booklet pane of 8	2.25	2.00
c.	Booklet pane of 5 + label, *Jan. 6*	3.50	1.25
d.	Vert. pair, imperf. btwn., in #C72b with foldover	*5,250.*	
e.	Tagging omitted	*12.50*	—
f.	As "b," tagging omitted	—	—
g.	As "c," tagging omitted	—	

Red is the normal color of the tagging. Examples of No. C72b exist that have a mixture of the two tagging compounds.

No. C72d resulted from a paper foldover after perforating and before cutting into panes. Two pairs are recorded from different panes.

ROTARY PRESS COIL STAMP

Perf. 10 Vertically

C73 AP49 10c **carmine**		.30	.25
	Pair	.65	.50
	Joint line pair	1.75	.55
a.	Imperf., pair	*450.00*	
	Joint line pair	*750.00*	

$1 Airlift

This stamp, listed as No. 1341, was issued Apr. 4, 1968, to pay for airlift of parcels to and from U.S. ports to servicemen overseas and in Alaska, Hawaii and Puerto Rico.

It was "also valid for paying regular rates for other types of mail," the Post Office Department announced to the public in a philatelic release dated Mar. 10, 1968. The stamp is inscribed "U.S. Postage" and is untagged.

On Apr. 26, 1969, the P.O.D. stated in its Postal Manual (for postal employees) that this stamp "may be used toward paying the postage or fees for special services on *airmail* articles." On Jan. 1, 1970, the Department told postal employees through its Postal Bulletin that this $1 stamp "can only be used to pay the airlift fee or toward payment of postage or fees on *airmail* articles."

Some collectors prefer to consider No. 1341 an airmail stamp.

50th ANNIVERSARY OF AIR MAIL ISSUE

Curtiss Jenny — AP50

Designed by Hordur Karlsson.

50th anniv. of regularly scheduled air mail service.

LITHOGRAPHED, ENGRAVED (GIORI)

Plates of 200 subjects in four panes of 50 each.

1968, May 15 ***Perf. 11***

C74 AP50 10c **blue, black & red**		.25	.25
	P# block of 4	1.30	—
	Margin block of 4, Mr. Zip and "Use Zip Code"	1.05	—
b.	Tagging omitted	*8.00*	

"USA" and Jet — AP51

Designed by John Larrecq.

LITHOGRAPHED, ENGRAVED (GIORI)

Plates of 200 subjects in four panes of 50 each.

1968, Nov. 22 ***Perf. 11***

C75 AP51 20c **red, blue & black** .35 .25
- P# block of 4 1.75 —
- Margin block of 4, Mr. Zip and "Use Zip Code" 1.50 —
- *a.* Tagging omitted *10.00*

See No. C81.

MOON LANDING ISSUE

First Man on the Moon AP52

Designed by Paul Calle.

Man's first landing on the moon July 20, 1969, by U.S. astronauts Neil A. Armstrong and Col. Edwin E. Aldrin, Jr., with Lieut. Col. Michael Collins piloting Apollo 11.

LITHOGRAPHED, ENGRAVED (GIORI)

Plates of 128 subjects in four panes of 32 each.

1969, Sept. 9 ***Perf. 11***

C76 AP52 10c **yellow, black, lt. blue, ultra., rose red & carmine** .25 .25
- P# block of 4 1.10 —
- Margin block of 4, Mr. Zip and "Use Zip Code" 1.05 —
- *a.* Rose red (litho.) omitted *500.00* —
- *b.* Tagging omitted *550.00* —

On No. C76a, the lithographed rose red is missing from the entire vignette-the dots on top of the yellow areas as well as the flag shoulder patch.

Silhouette of Delta Wing Plane — AP53

Silhouette of Jet Airliner — AP54

Winged Airmail Envelope — AP55

Statue of Liberty AP56

Designed by George Vander Sluis (9c, 11c), Nelson Gruppo (13c) and Robert J. Jones (17c).

ROTARY PRESS PRINTING

E. E. Plates of 400 subjects in four panes of 100 each.

1971-73 ***Perf. 10½x11***

C77 AP53 9c **red,** *May 15, 1971* .25 .25
- P# block of 4 .90 —
- Margin block of 4, "Use Zip Codes" .85 —
- *a.* Tagging omitted —

No. C77 issued primarily for use on domestic post cards.

Perf. 11x10½

C78 AP54 11c **carmine,** *May 7, 1971* .25 .25
- P# block of 4 .90 —
- Margin block of 4, "Use Zip Codes" .85 —
- Pair with full vert. gutter btwn. —
- *a.* Booklet pane of 4 + 2 labels 1.25 1.00
- *b.* Untagged (Bureau precanceled) .85 .85
- P# block of 4 27.50 —
- Margin block of 4, "Use Zip Codes" 13.75 —
- *c.* Tagging omitted (not Bureau precanceled) 7.50
- *d.* As "a," tagging omitted —

C79 AP55 13c **carmine,** *Nov. 16, 1973* .25 .25
- P# block of 4 1.10 —
- Margin block of 4, "Use Zip Codes" 1.05 —
- *a.* Booklet pane of 5 + label, *Dec. 27, 1973* 1.50 1.00
- *b.* Untagged (Bureau precanceled) .85 .85
- P# block of 4 20.00 —
- Margin block of 4, "Use Zip Codes" 9.50 —
- *c.* Green instead of red tagging (single from booklet pane) —
- *d.* Tagging omitted (not precanceled) 7.50 —

No. C78b Bureau precanceled "WASHINGTON D.C." (or "DC" - more valuable thus), No. C79b "WASHINGTON DC" only; both for use of Congressmen, but available to any permit holder.

Red is the normal color of the tagging. Examples also exist that have a mixture of the two tagging compounds.

GIORI PRESS PRINTING

Panes of 200 subjects in four panes of 50 each.

Perf. 11

C80 AP56 17c **bluish black, red, & dark green,** *July 13, 1971* .35 .25
- P# block of 4 1.60 —
- Margin block of 4, Mr. Zip and "Use Zip Code" 1.50 —
- *a.* Tagging omitted 12.50 —

"USA" & Jet Type of 1968

LITHOGRAPHED, ENGRAVED (GIORI)

Plates of 200 subjects in four panes of 50 each.

Perf. 11

C81 AP51 21c **red, blue & black,** *May 21, 1971* .40 .25
- P# block of 4 2.00 —
- Margin block of 4, Mr. Zip and "Use Zip Code" 1.75 —
- *a.* Tagging omitted *10.00*
- *b.* Black (engr.) missing (FO) *2,750.*

The two recorded examples of No. C81b are in a single full pane. Catalogue value is for both errors.

COIL STAMPS

ROTARY PRESS PRINTING

1971-73 ***Perf. 10 Vertically***

C82 AP54 11c **carmine,** *May 7, 1971* .25 .25
- Pair .50 .50
- Joint line pair .85 .60
- *a.* Imperf., pair *200.00*
- Joint line pair *375.00*
- *b.* Tagging omitted 10.00

C83 AP55 13c **carmine,** *Dec. 27, 1973* .30 .25
- Pair .60 .50
- Joint line pair 1.10 —
- *a.* Imperf., pair 65.00
- Joint line pair 150.00
- *b.* Tagging omitted —

NATIONAL PARKS CENTENNIAL ISSUE

City of Refuge, Hawaii

Kii Statue and Temple — AP57

Designed by Paul Rabut.

Centenary of national parks. This 11c honors the City of Refuge National Historical Park, established in 1961 at Honaunau, island of Hawaii.

LITHOGRAPHED, ENGRAVED (GIORI)

Plates of 200 subjects in four panes of 50 each.

1972, May 3 ***Perf. 11***

C84 AP57 11c **orange & multicolored** .25 .25
- P# block of 4 .90 —
- Margin block of 4, Mr. Zip and "Use Zip Code" .85 —
- *a.* Blue & green (litho.) omitted *500.00 900.00*
- *b.* Tagging omitted — —

OLYMPIC GAMES ISSUE

Skiing and Olympic Rings — AP58

Designed by Lance Wyman.

11th Winter Olympic Games, Sapporo, Japan, Feb. 3-13, and 20th Summer Olympic Games, Munich, Germany, Aug. 26-Sept. 11.

PHOTOGRAVURE (Andreotti)

Plates of 200 subjects in four panes of 50 each.

1972, Aug. 17 ***Perf. 11x10½***

C85 AP58 11c **black, blue, red, emerald & yellow** .25 .25
- P# block of 10, 5 P# 2.40 —
- Margin block of 4, "Use Zip Code" .85 —

ELECTRONICS PROGRESS ISSUE

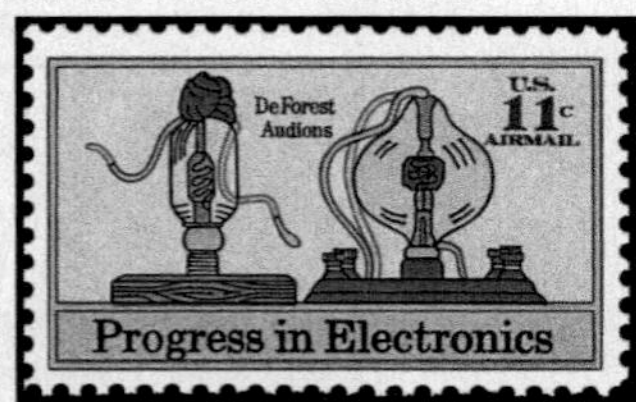

De Forest Audions AP59

Designed by Walter and Naiad Einsel.

LITHOGRAPHED, ENGRAVED (GIORI)

Plates of 200 subjects in four panes of 50 each.

1973, July 10 ***Perf. 11***

C86 AP59 11c **vermilion, lilac, pale lilac, olive, brown, deep carmine & black** .30 .25
- P# block of 4 1.25 —
- Margin block of 4, Mr. Zip and "Use Zip Code" 1.20 —
- *a.* Vermilion & olive (litho.) omitted *700.00*
- *b.* Tagging omitted *60.00*
- *c.* Olive omitted *1,000.*

Statue of Liberty AP60

Mt. Rushmore National Memorial AP61

Designed by Robert (Gene) Shehorn.

GIORI PRESS PRINTING

Panes of 200 subjects in four panes of 50 each.

1974 ***Perf. 11***

C87 AP60 18c **carmine, black & ultramarine,** *Jan. 11* .35 .30
- P# block of 4, 2# 1.50 —
- Margin block of 4, Mr. Zip and "Use Zip Code" 1.45 —
- *a.* Tagging omitted *22.50*

C88 AP61 26c **ultramarine, black & carmine,** *Jan. 2* .60 .25
- P# block of 4 2.30 —
- Margin block of 4, Mr. Zip and "Use Zip Code" 2.20 —
- Horiz. pair with full vert. gutter btwn. *1,600.*
- *a.* Tagging omitted *22.50*
- *b.* Yellow-green instead of orange-red tagging — —

Plane and Globes AP62

Plane, Globes and Flags — AP63

Designed by David G. Foote.

GIORI PRESS PRINTING
Panes of 200 subjects in four panes of 50 each.

1976, Jan. 2 *Perf. 11*

C89 AP62 25c **red, blue & black** .50 .25
P# block of 4 2.25 —
Margin block of 4, Mr. Zip and "Use Zip Code" 2.10 —
a. Tagging omitted *40.00* —
C90 AP63 31c **red, blue & black** .60 .25
P# block of 4 2.60 —
Margin block of 4, Mr. Zip and "Use Zip Code" 2.50 —
a. Tagging omitted *10.00*
b. All colors omitted —

On No. C90b, there is a colorless embossed image and a tagging ghost plane visible under UV light.

WRIGHT BROTHERS ISSUE

Orville and Wilbur Wright, and Flyer A — AP64

Wright Brothers, Flyer A and Shed — AP65

Designed by Ken Dallison.

75th anniv. of 1st powered flight, Kill Devil Hill, NC, Dec. 17, 1903.

LITHOGRAPHED, ENGRAVED (GIORI)
Plates of 400 subjects in four panes of 100 each.

1978, Sept. 23 *Perf. 11*

C91 AP64 31c **ultramarine & multicolored** .65 .30
C92 AP65 31c **ultramarine & multicolored** .65 .30
a. Vert. pair, #C91-C92 1.30 1.20
P# block of 4 2.75 —
Margin block of 4, "Use Correct Zip Code" 2.75 —
b. As "a," ultra. & black (engr.) omitted *475.00*
c. As "a," black (engr.) omitted *1,750.*
d. As "a," black, yellow, magenta, blue & brown (litho.) omitted *1,750.*

OCTAVE CHANUTE ISSUE

Chanute and Biplane Hang-glider — AP66

Biplane Hang-glider and Chanute — AP67

Designed by Ken Dallison.

Octave Chanute (1832-1910), civil engineer and aviation pioneer.

LITHOGRAPHED, ENGRAVED (GIORI)
Plates of 400 subjects in four panes of 100 each.

1979, Mar. 29 **Tagged** *Perf. 11*

C93 AP66 21c **blue & multicolored** .70 .35
C94 AP67 21c **blue & multicolored** .70 .35
a. Vert. pair, #C93-C94 1.40 1.20
P# block of 4 3.00 —
Margin block of 4, Mr. Zip 2.85 —
b. As "a," ultra & black (engr.) omitted *4,000.*

WILEY POST ISSUE

Wiley Post and "Winnie Mae" — AP68

NR-105-W, Post in Pressurized Suit, Portrait — AP69

Designed by Ken Dallison.

Wiley Post (1899-1935), first man to fly around the world alone and high-altitude flying pioneer.

LITHOGRAPHED, ENGRAVED (GIORI)
Plates of 400 subjects in four panes of 100 each.

1979, Nov. 20 **Tagged** *Perf. 11*

C95 AP68 25c **blue & multicolored** .90 .45
C96 AP69 25c **blue & multicolored** .90 .45
a. Vert. pair, #C95-C96 1.80 1.50
P# block of 4 4.75 —
Margin block of 4, Mr. Zip 3.75 —

OLYMPIC GAMES ISSUE

High Jump — AP70

Designed by Robert M. Cunningham.

22nd Olympic Games, Moscow, July 19-Aug. 3, 1980.

PHOTOGRAVURE
Plates of 200 subjects in four panes of 50 each.

1979, Nov. 1 **Tagged** *Perf. 11*

C97 AP70 31c **multicolored** .70 .30
P# block of 12, 6# 9.50 —
Zip block of 4 3.00 —

PHILIP MAZZEI (1730-1816)

Italian-born Political Writer — AP71

Designed by Sante Graziani

PHOTOGRAVURE
Plates of 200 subjects in four panes of 50 each.

1980, Oct. 13 **Tagged** *Perf. 11*

C98 AP71 40c **multicolored** .80 .25
P# block of 12, 6# 10.00 —
Zip block of 4 3.50 —
b. Imperf., pair *2,250.*
d. Tagging omitted *11.00*

1982 **Tagged** *Perf. 10½x11¼*

C98A AP71 40c **multicolored** 5.00 1.50
P# block of 12, 6# 80.00 —
c. Horiz. pair, imperf. vert. *3,250.*

BLANCHE STUART SCOTT (1886-1970)

First Woman Pilot — AP72

Designed by Paul Calle.

PHOTOGRAVURE
Plates of 200 subjects in four panes of 50.

1980, Dec. 30 **Tagged** *Perf. 11*

C99 AP72 28c **multicolored** .60 .25
P# block of 12, 6# 8.50 —
Zip block of 4 2.50 —
a. Imperf., pair *2,000.*

GLENN CURTISS (1878-1930)

Aviation Pioneer and Aircraft Designer AP73

Designed by Ken Dallison.

PHOTOGRAVURE
Plates of 200 subjects in four panes of 50.

1980, Dec. 30 **Tagged** *Perf. 11*

C100 AP73 35c **multicolored** .65 .25
P# block of 12, 6# 9.00 —
Zip block of 4 2.75 —
a. Light blue (background) omitted *2,000.*

SUMMER OLYMPICS 1984

Women's Gymnastics — AP74

Hurdles — AP75

Women's Basketball — AP76

Soccer — AP77

Designed by Robert Peak.

23rd Olympic Games, Los Angeles, July 28-Aug. 12, 1984.

PHOTOGRAVURE
Plates of 200 subjects in four panes of 50.

1983, June 17 **Tagged** *Perf. 11*

C101 AP74 28c **multicolored** 1.00 .30
C102 AP75 28c **multicolored** 1.00 .30
C103 AP76 28c **multicolored** 1.00 .30
C104 AP77 28c **multicolored** 1.00 .30
a. Block of 4, #C101-C104 4.25 2.50
P# block of 4, 4# 5.25 —
Zip block of 4 4.25 —
b. As "a," imperf. vert. *5,000.*

Shot Put — AP78

Men's Gymnastics AP79

Women's Swimming AP80

Weight Lifting — AP81

1983, Apr. 8	**Tagged**	***Perf. 11.2 Bullseye***	
C105	AP78 40c **multicolored**	.90	.40
a.	Perf. 11 line	1.00	.45
C106	AP79 40c **multicolored**	.90	.40
a.	Perf. 11 line	1.00	.45
C107	AP80 40c **multicolored**	.90	.40
a.	Perf. 11 line	1.00	.45
C108	AP81 40c **multicolored**	.90	.40
a.	Perf. 11 line	1.00	.45
b.	Block of 4, #C105-C108	4.25	3.00
	P# block of 4, 4#	5.00	—
	Zip block of 4	4.50	—
c.	Block of 4, #C105a-C108a	5.00	4.00
	P# block of 4, 4#	7.50	—
d.	Block of 4, imperf.	*650.00*	

Women's Fencing AP82

Cycling AP83

Women's Volleyball AP84

Pole Vaulting AP85

1983, Nov. 4	**Tagged**	***Perf. 11***	
C109	AP82 35c **multicolored**	.90	.55
C110	AP83 35c **multicolored**	.90	.55
C111	AP84 35c **multicolored**	.90	.55
C112	AP85 35c **multicolored**	.90	.55
a.	Block of 4, #C109-C112	4.00	3.25
	P# block of 4, 4#	6.00	—
	Zip block of 4	4.25	—

AVIATION PIONEERS

Alfred V. Verville (1890-1970), Inventor, Verville-Sperry R-3 Army Racer — AP86

Lawrence Sperry (1892-1923), Aircraft Designer, and Father Elmer (1860-1930), Designer and Pilot, 1st Seaplane AP87

Designed by Ken Dallison (No. C113) and Howard Koslow (No. C114)

PHOTOGRAVURE

Plates of 200 in four panes of 50 (2 panes each, No. C113 and No. C114)

Plates of 200 in four panes of 50 (No. C114)

1985, Feb. 13	**Tagged**	***Perf. 11***	
C113	AP86 33c **multicolored**	.65	.25
	P# block of 4, 5#, UL, LR	3.25	—
	Zip block of 4	2.90	—
a.	Imperf., pair	*600.00*	
C114	AP87 39c **multicolored**	.80	.25
	P# block of 4, 5#, UR, LL	3.75	—
	P# block of 4, 4#	3.75	—
	Zip block of 4	3.50	—
a.	Imperf., pair	*1,250.*	

Philatelic Foundation certificates issued prior to August 1994 for No. C114 with magenta missing have been rescinded. At this time no genuine magenta missing examples are known. The magenta color is very fugitive, fading rapidly when exposed to sunlight.

TRANSPACIFIC AIRMAIL
50th Anniversary

Martin M-130 China Clipper AP88

Designed by Chuck Hodgson.

PHOTOGRAVURE

Plates of 200 in four panes of 50

1985, Feb. 15	**Tagged**	***Perf. 11***	
C115	AP88 44c **multicolored**	.85	.25
	P# block of 4, 4#	4.00	—
	Zip block of 4	3.50	—
a.	Imperf., pair	*600.00*	

FR. JUNIPERO SERRA (1713-1784)
California Missionary

Outline Map of Southern California, Portrait, San Gabriel Mission AP89

Designed by Richard Schlecht from a Spanish stamp.

PHOTOGRAVURE

Plates of 200 in four panes of 50

1985, Aug. 22	**Tagged**	***Perf. 11***	
C116	AP89 44c **multicolored**	1.00	.35
	P# block of 4	7.00	—
	Zip block of 4	4.25	—
a.	Imperf., pair	*900.00*	

SETTLING OF NEW SWEDEN, 350th ANNIV.

Settler, Two Indians, Map of New Sweden, Swedish Ships "Kalmar Nyckel" and "Fogel Grip" — AP90

Designed by Goran Osterland based on an 18th century illustration from a Swedish book about the Colonies.

LITHOGRAPHED AND ENGRAVED

Plates of 200 in four panes of 50

1988, Mar. 29	**Tagged**	***Perf. 11***	
C117	AP90 44c **multicolored**	1.00	.25
	P# block of 4, 5#	6.50	—
	Zip block of 4	5.00	—

See Sweden No. 1672 and Finland No. 768.

SAMUEL P. LANGLEY (1834-1906)

Langley and Unmanned Aerodrome No. 5 — AP91

Designed by Ken Dallison.

LITHOGRAPHED AND ENGRAVED

Plates of 200 in four panes of 50

1988, May 14	**Tagged**	***Perf. 11***	
C118	AP91 45c **multicolored,** large block tagging	1.00	.25
	P# block of 4, 7#	5.00	—
	Zip block of 4	4.25	—
a.	Overall tagging	3.50	.50
	P# block of 4, 7#	45.00	—
	Zip block of 4	15.00	—

IGOR SIKORSKY (1889-1972)

Sikorsky and 1939 VS300 Helicopter AP92

Designed by Ren Wicks.

PHOTOGRAVURE AND ENGRAVED

Plates of 200 in four panes of 50

1988, June 23	**Tagged**	***Perf. 11***	
C119	AP92 36c **multicolored**	.70	.25
	P# block of 4, 6#	3.25	—
	Zip block of 4	3.10	—
a.	Red, dk blue & black (engraved) omitted	*1,250.*	

Beware of examples with traces of engraved red offered as "red omitted" varieties.

FRENCH REVOLUTION BICENTENNIAL

Liberty, Equality and Fraternity — AP93

Designed by Richard Sheaff.

LITHOGRAPHED AND ENGRAVED
Plates of 120 in four panes of 30.

1989, July 14 **Tagged** ***Perf. 11½x11***

C120 AP93 45c **multicolored**	.95	.25
P# block of 4, 4#	4.75	—
Zip block of 4	4.00	—

See France Nos. 2143-2145a.

PRE-COLUMBIAN AMERICA ISSUE

Southeast Carved Figure, 700-1430 A.D. — AP94

Designed by Lon Busch.

PHOTOGRAVURE
Plates of 200 in four panes of 50

1989, Oct. 12 ***Perf. 11***

C121 AP94 45c **multicolored**	.90	.25
P# block of 4, 4#	5.25	—
Zip block of 4	3.75	—

20th UPU CONGRESS
Futuristic Mail Delivery

Spacecraft — AP95

Air-suspended Hover Car — AP96

Moon Rover — AP97

Space Shuttle — AP98

Designed by Ken Hodges.

LITHOGRAPHED & ENGRAVED
Plates of 160 in four panes of 40.

1989, Nov. 27 **Tagged** ***Perf. 11***

C122 AP95 45c **multicolored**	1.00	.50
C123 AP96 45c **multicolored**	1.00	.50
C124 AP97 45c **multicolored**	1.00	.50
C125 AP98 45c **multicolored**	1.00	.50
a. Block of 4, #C122-C125	4.00	3.00
P# block of 4, 5#	5.00	—
Zip block of 4	4.25	—
b. As "a," light blue (engr.) omitted	*500.00*	

Souvenir Sheet
LITHOGRAPHED & ENGRAVED

1989, Nov. 24 **Tagged** ***Imperf.***

C126 Sheet of 4	5.00	4.00
a. AP95 45c multicolored	1.25	.50
b. AP96 45c multicolored	1.25	.50
c. AP97 45c multicolored	1.25	.50
d. AP98 45c multicolored	1.25	.50
e. As No. C126, tagging omitted	*650.00*	

PRE-COLUMBIAN AMERICA ISSUE

Tropical Coast — AP99

Designed by Mark Hess.
Printed by the American Bank Note Company.

PHOTOGRAVURE
Plates of 200 in four panes of 50
(3 panes of #2512, 1 pane of #C127)

1990, Oct. 12 **Tagged** ***Perf. 11***

C127 AP99 45c **multicolored**	.90	.25
P# block of 4, 4#, UL only	7.00	—
Zip block of 4	3.75	—
a. Vert. pair, imperf. btwn. and at top	—	

No. C127a is the upper left pair in a pane of 50 with a paper foldover before perforating. The pair has diagonal perforations from rows other than the top and between perforations.

HARRIET QUIMBY, 1ST AMERICAN WOMAN PILOT

Quimby (1884-1912), Bleriot Airplane AP100

Designed by Howard Koslow. Printed by Stamp Venturers.

PHOTOGRAVURE
Panes of 200 in four panes of 50

1991, Apr. 27 **Tagged** ***Perf. 11***

C128 AP100 50c **multicolored**, overall tagging	1.00	.25
P# block of 4, #S1111	5.25	—
Zip block of 4	4.25	—
a. Vert. pair, imperf. horiz.	*850.00*	
b. Perf. 11.2 bullseye, prephosphored uncoated paper (mottled tagging), *1993*	1.25	.25
P# block of 4, #S2222	6.50	—
Zip block of 6	5.00	—

WILLIAM T. PIPER, AIRCRAFT MANUFACTURER

Piper and Piper Cub — AP101

Designed by Ren Wicks.
Printed by J. W. Fergusson and Sons for American Bank Note Co.

PHOTOGRAVURE
Panes of 200 in four panes of 50

1991, May 17 **Tagged** ***Perf. 11***

C129 AP101 40c **multicolored**	.80	.25
P# block of 4, 4#+A	3.75	—
Zip block of 4	3.50	—

Blue sky is plainly visible all the way across stamp above Piper's head.

See No. C132.

ANTARCTIC TREATY, 30TH ANNIVERSARY

AP102

Designed by Howard Koslow. Printed by Stamp Venturers.

PHOTOGRAVURE
Sheets of 200 in four panes of 50

1991, June 21 **Tagged** ***Perf. 11***

C130 AP102 50c **multicolored**	1.00	.35
P# block of 4, 4#+S	5.00	—
Zip block of 4	4.25	—

PRE-COLUMBIAN AMERICA ISSUE

Bering Land Bridge AP103

Designed by Richard Schlect.

PHOTOGRAVURE
Sheets of 200 in four panes of 50

1991, Oct. 12 **Tagged** ***Perf. 11***

C131 AP103 50c **multicolored**	1.00	.35
P# block of 4, 6#	5.25	—
Zip block of 4	4.75	—

Piper Type of 1991

Printed by Stamp Venturers.

PHOTOGRAVURE
Sheets of 200 in four panes of 50

1993 **Tagged** ***Perf. 11.2 Bullseye***

C132 AP101 40c **multicolored**	3.50	.65
P# block of 4, 4#+S	40.00	—
Zip block of 4	16.00	—

Piper's hair touches top edge of design. No selvage inscriptions.

"All LC (Letters and Cards) mail receives First-Class Mail service in the United States, is dispatched by the fastest transportation available, and travels by airmail or priority service in the destination country. All LC mail should be marked 'AIRMAIL' or 'PAR AVION.'" (U.S. Postal Service, Pub. 51).

No. C133 listed below was issued to meet the LC rate to Canada and Mexico and is inscribed with the silhouette of a jet plane next to the denomination indicating the need for airmail service. This is unlike No. 2998, which met the LC rate to other countries, but contained no indication that it was intended for that use.

Future issues that meet a specific international airmail rate and contain the airplane silhouette will be treated by Scott as Air Post stamps. Stamps similar to No. 2998 will be listed in the Postage section.

SCENIC AMERICAN LANDSCAPES

Niagara Falls — AP104

Designed by Ethel Kessler. Printed by Avery Dennison.

PHOTOGRAVURE
Sheets of 200 in 10 panes of 20

1999, May 12 Tagged ***Serpentine Die Cut 11***
Self-Adhesive

C133 AP104 48c **multicolored**	.95	.25
P# block of 4, 5#+V	4.00	
Pane of 20	20.00	

Rio Grande AP105

Designed by Ethel Kessler. Printed by Avery Dennison.

PHOTOGRAVURE
Sheets of 200 in 10 panes of 20

1999, July 30 Tagged ***Serpentine Die Cut 11***
Self-Adhesive

C134 AP105 40c **multicolored**	.80	.60
P# block of 4, 5#+V	3.20	
Pane of 20	16.00	

Grand Canyon AP106

Designed by Ethel Kessler.
Printed by Banknote Corp. of America.

LITHOGRAPHED
Sheets of 180 in nine panes of 20
Serpentine Die Cut 11¼x11½

2000, Jan. 20 Tagged
Self-Adhesive

C135 AP106 60c **multicolored**	1.25	.25
P# block of 4, 4#+B	5.00	
Pane of 20	25.00	
a. Die cutting omitted, pair	*1,250.*	
b. Vert. pair, die cutting omitted horiz.	—	
c. Horiz. pair, die cutting omitted between	—	
d. Horiz. pair, die cutting omitted vert.	—	

Nine-Mile Prairie, Nebraska AP107

Designed by Ethel Kessler. Printed by Ashton-Potter (USA) Ltd.

LITHOGRAPHED
Sheets of 180 in nine panes of 20
Serpentine Die Cut 11¼x11½

2001, Mar. 6 Tagged
Self-Adhesive

C136 AP107 70c **multicolored**	1.40	.30
P# block of 4, 5#+P	5.60	
Pane of 20	28.00	

Mt. McKinley AP108

Designed by Ethel Kessler. Printed by Avery Dennison.

PHOTOGRAVURE
Sheets of 200 in ten panes of 20.

2001, Apr. 17 Tagged ***Serpentine Die Cut 11***
Self-Adhesive

C137 AP108 80c **multicolored**	1.60	.35
P# block of 4, 5 #+V	6.40	
Pane of 20	32.00	

Acadia National Park — AP109

Designed by Ethel Kessler. Printed by Banknote Corporation of America, Banknote Corporation of America for Sennett Security Printers (No. C138b).

LITHOGRAPHED
Sheets of 180 in nine panes of 20 (#C138), Sheets of 120 in six panes of 20 (#C138a)
Serpentine Die Cut 11.25x11.5 (No. C138), 11.5x11.9 (No. C138a)

2001-05 Tagged
Self-Adhesive

C138 AP109 60c **multicolored**, prephosphored coated paper (solid tagging), *May 30, 2001*	1.25	.25
P# block of 4, 4# + B	5.00	
Pane of 20	25.00	
a. Overall tagging, dated "2001," *March 2003*	1.25	.25
P# block of 4, 4# + B	5.00	
Pane of 20	25.00	
b. As "a," with "2005" year date, *Jan. 2005*	1.25	.25
P# block of 4, 4#+S	6.00	
Pane of 20	29.00	
c. As "b," printed on back of backing paper	—	

Bryce Canyon National Park — AP110

Great Smoky Mountains National Park — AP111

Designed by Ethel Kessler. Printed by Banknote Corporation of America for Sennett Security Products (#C139), Ashton-Potter (USA) Ltd. (#C140), Avery Dennison (#C141).

LITHOGRAPHED, PHOTOGRAVURE (#C141)
Sheets of 180 in nine panes of 20 and sheets of 160 in eight panes of 20 (#C139), Sheets of 120 in six panes of 20 (#C140), Sheets of 200 in ten panes of 20 (#C141)

2006, Feb. 24 Tagged ***Serpentine Die Cut 10¾***
Self-Adhesive

C139 AP110 63c **multicolored**	1.25	.25
P# block of 4, 5#+S	5.00	
Pane of 20	25.00	
a. Die cutting omitted, pair	*450.00*	
C140 AP111 75c **multicolored**	1.50	.35
P# block of 4, 5#+P	6.00	
Pane of 20	30.00	
a. Die cutting omitted, pair	*500.00*	

Two printings of No. C139 with different plate # order. Sheet of 180 has gray plate # first (and has glossier finish). Sheet of 160 has gray plate # last.

Yosemite National Park — AP112

Serpentine Die Cut 11

C141 AP112 84c **multicolored**	1.75	.35
P# block of 4, 5#+V	7.00	
Pane of 20	35.00	
Nos. C139-C141 (3)	4.50	.95

Okefenokee Swamp, Georgia and Florida AP113

Hagatña Bay, Guam AP114

Designed by Ethel Kessler. Printed by Ashton-Potter (USA) Ltd. (#C142), Avery Dennison (#C143).

LITHOGRAPHED (#C142), PHOTOGRAVURE (#C143)
Sheets of 120 in six panes of 20 (#C142), Sheets of 200 in ten panes of 20 (#C143)

2007, June 1 Tagged ***Serpentine Die Cut 10¾***
Self-Adhesive

C142 AP113 69c **multicolored**	1.40	.30
P# block of 4, 5#+P	5.60	
Pane of 20	28.00	

Serpentine Die Cut 11

C143 AP114 90c **multicolored**	1.80	.40
P# block of 4, 5#+V	7.75	
Pane of 20	38.00	

13-Mile Woods, New Hampshire AP115

Trunk Bay, St. John, Virgin Islands AP116

Designed by Ethel Kessler. Printed by Banknote Corporation of America for Sennett Security Products (#C144), Avery Dennison (#C145).

LITHOGRAPHED (#C144), PHOTOGRAVURE (#C145)

Sheets of 180 in nine panes of 20 (#C144), Sheets of 200 in ten panes of 20 (#C145)

2008, May 16 Tagged *Serpentine Die Cut 10¾*

Self-Adhesive

C144 AP115 72c **multicolored** 1.50 .30
P# block of 4, 5#+S 6.50
Pane of 20 32.00

Serpentine Die Cut 11

C145 AP116 94c **multicolored** ⓢ 1.90 .45
P# block of 4, 5#+V 8.00
Pane of 20 40.00

See note after No. 1549.

Zion National Park, Utah — AP117

Grand Teton National Park, Wyoming AP118

Designed by Ethel Kessler. Printed by Ashton-Potter (USA) Ltd. (#C146), Avery Dennison (#C147).

LITHOGRAPHED, PHOTOGRAVURE (#C147)

Sheets of 120 in six panes of 20 (#C146), Sheets of 200 in ten panes of 20 (#C147)

2009, June 28 Tagged *Serpentine Die Cut 10¾*

Self-Adhesive

C146 AP117 79c **multicolored** ⓢ 1.75 .35
P# block of 4, 5#+P 7.00
Pane of 20 35.00

Serpentine Die Cut 11

C147 AP118 98c **multicolored** ⓢ 2.00 .45
P# block of 4, 5#+V 8.00
Pane of 20 40.00

See note after No. 1549.

Voyageurs National Park, Minnesota AP119

Designed by Ethel Kessler. Printed by Ashton-Potter (USA) Ltd.

LITHOGRAPHED

Sheets of 180 in nine panes of 20

2011, Apr. 11 Tagged *Serpentine Die Cut 10¾*

Self-Adhesive

C148 AP119 80c **multicolored** ⓢ 1.60 .25
P# block of 4, 5#+P 6.40
Pane of 20 32.00

See note after No. 1549.

Glacier National Park, Montana AP120

Amish Horse and Buggy on Road, Lancaster County, Pennsylvania AP121

Designed by Ethel Kessler. Printed by Ashton-Potter (USA) Ltd. (#C149), Banknote Corporation of America for Sennett Security Products (#C150).

LITHOGRAPHED

Sheets of 120 in six panes of 20 (#C149), Sheets of 240 in 12 panes of 20 (#C150)

2012 Tagged *Serpentine Die Cut 10¾*

Self-Adhesive

C149 AP120 85c **multi,** *Jan. 19* ⓢ 1.75 .35
P# block of 4, 5#+P 7.00
Pane of 20 35.00

C150 AP121 $1.05 **multicolored,** *Jan. 20* 2.10 .45
P# block of 4, 5#+S 8.40
Pane of 20 42.50
a. Die cutting omitted on front, pair *700.00*
b. Silver (airplane silhouette) missing (PS) —

See note after No. 1549.

AIR POST SPECIAL DELIVERY STAMPS

Great Seal of United States APSD1

No. CE1 was issued for the prepayment of the air postage and the special delivery fee in one stamp. First day sale was at the American Air Mail Society Convention.

FLAT PLATE PRINTING

Plates of 200 subjects in four panes of 50 each.

1934, Aug. 30 Unwmk. *Perf. 11*

CE1 APSD1 16c **dark blue** .70 .80
blue .70 .80
Never hinged .90
P# block of 6 14.00 —
Never hinged 22.50
First day cover, Chicago *(40,171)* 25.00
First day cover, Washington, D.C., *Aug. 31* 15.00

For imperforate variety see No. 771.

Great Seal of United States APSD2

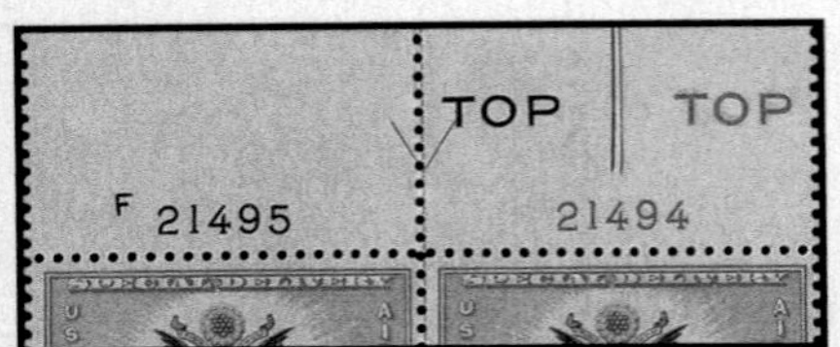

Type 1 - Thin red line with a thin blue line

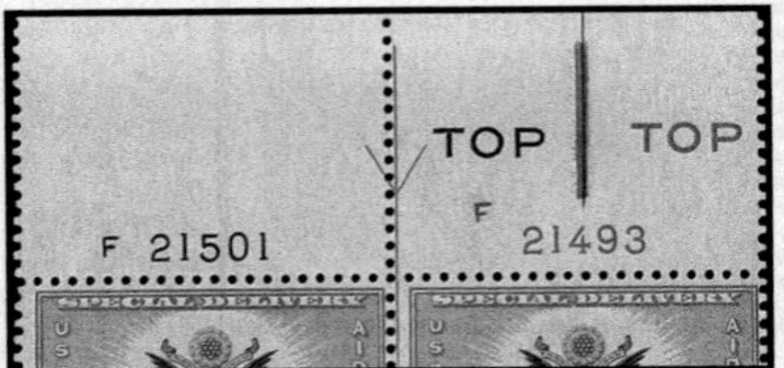

Type 2 - Thick red line with a thin blue line

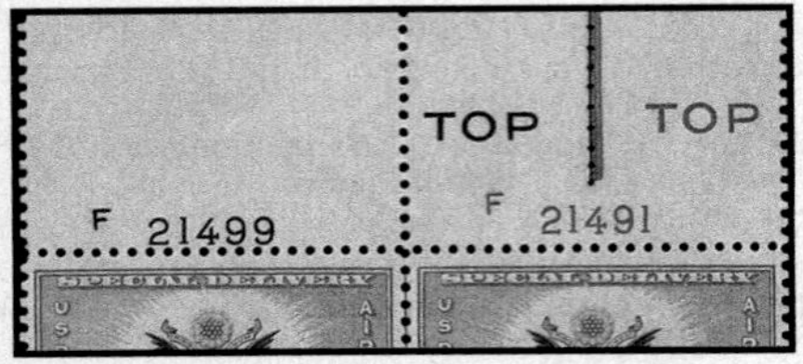

Type 3 - Thick red line with a dotted blue line

Type 4 - Thick red line with a thick blue line

Frame plates of 100 subjects in two panes of 50 each separated by a 1½ inch wide vertical gutter with central guide line, and vignette plates of 50 subjects.

The "seal" design for No. CE2 was from a new engraving, slightly smaller than that used for No. CE1.

Issued in panes of 50 each.

1936, Feb. 10

CE2 APSD2 16c **red & blue** .45 .35
Never hinged .65
Center line block 2.50 3.00
Never hinged 3.60
First day cover, Washington, D.C. *(72,981)* 20.00

Type 1 Marginal Markings, *Feb. 10, 1936*

P# block of 4, 2#, two "TOP," thin red and thin blue registration markers 10.00 —
Never hinged 12.50
Bottom margin block of 4, thin red and thin blue registration markers below right stamp 2.00 2.00
Left or right margin horizontal line block of 4 with thin red and thin blue registration markers, no red arrow 2.00 2.00

Type 2 Marginal Markings, *Aug. 1940*

P# block of 4, 2#, two "TOP," thick red and thin blue registration markers 80.00 —
Never hinged 100.00
Bottom margin block of 4, thick red and thin blue registration markers below right stamp 10.00 10.00
Left or right margin horizontal line block of 4 with thick red and thin blue registration markers, no red arrow 10.00 10.00

Type 3 Marginal Markings, *June 1941*

P# block of 4, 2#, two "TOP," thick red and thin blue dotted registration markers 100.00 —
Never hinged 130.00
P# block of 10, 2#, two "TOP," thick red and thin blue dotted registration markers, thick red vertical inversion marker over stamps 1 & 5 110.00 —
Never hinged 140.00
Bottom margin arrow block of 4, thick red and thin blue dotted registration markers over center line 15.00 15.00
Left or right margin horizontal line block of 4 with thick red and thin blue dotted registration markers, no red arrow 15.00 15.00

Type 4 Marginal Markings, *May 1942*

P# block of 4, 2#, two "TOP," thick red and thick blue registration markers 15.00 —
Never hinged 18.00
P# block of 10, 2#, two "TOP," thick red and thick blue registration markers, thick red vertical inversion and thick blue horizontal inversion markers over stamps 1 & 5 25.00 —
Never hinged 30.00
Bottom margin arrow block of 4, thick red and thick blue registration markers over center line 3.00 3.00
Left or right margin horizontal line block of 4, thick red and thick blue registration markers, no red arrow 3.00 3.00
a. Horiz. pair, imperf. vert. *4,250.*
Never hinged *5,250.*
P# block of 6, 2#, two "TOP," thick red and thick blue registration markers, thick red vertical and thick blue horizontal inversion markers over stamp 1 *60,000.*

The No. CE2a plate block is unique. Value represents sale in 2008.

Warning: Special care should be exercised when buying or selling type 3 printings. Some printers, when wiping a blue plate prior to printing, accidentally removed a portion of the blue ink from the blue registration marker. This exposed some of the blue dots that were used for type 3 printings, making a type 4 plate block appear to be a type 3 printing.

Three types of experimental versions of the type 1 plate block registration markers are known, often given the letters A, B, and C. Type 1A has 3 thin red lines and one thin blue line. type 1B has 2 thin red lines and one thin blue line, and type 1C has one long thin red line, one short thin red line and one thin blue line. These experimental markings are seldom seen and are worth much more than the values shown for type 1 plate blocks.

Quantities issued: #CE1, 9,215,750; #CE2, 72,517,850.

AIR POST SEMI-OFFICIAL STAMPS

Buffalo Balloon

This stamp was privately issued by John F. B. Lillard, a Nashville reporter. It was used on covers carried on a balloon ascension of June 18, 1877, which began at Nashville and landed at Gallatin, Tenn., and possibly on other flights. The balloon was owned and piloted by Samuel Archer King. The stamp was reported to have been engraved by (Mrs.?) J. H. Snively and printed in tete beche pairs from a single die. Lillard wrote that 300 were printed and 23 used.

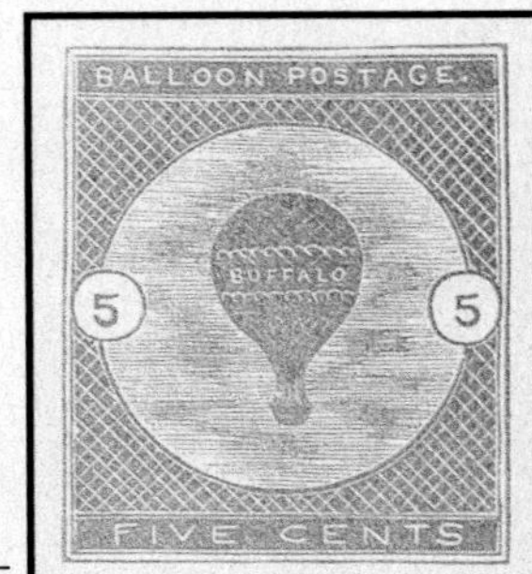

Buffalo Balloon — APSO1

1877, June 18 **Typo.** ***Imperf.***

CL1 APSO1 5c **deep blue** 7,500.
Never hinged 10,000.
On cover with 3c #158 150,000.
On cover with 1c #156 & 2c #178 100,000.
a. Tête bêche pair, vertical 22,500.
Never hinged 27,500.

A black proof exists of No. CL1, value *$17,500.*

Rodgers Aerial Post

This stamp was privately issued by Calbraith Perry Rodgers' wife who acted as unofficial postmaster during her husband's cross-country airplane flight in 1911. Rodgers was competing for the $50,000 prize offered by William Randolph Hearst to whomever completed the trip within a 30-day period. Rodgers' flight was sponsored by the Armour meat-packing company, makers of the soft drink, Vin Fiz.

The stamp probably was first available in Texas about October 19. Recorded dated examples exist from Oct. 19 to Nov. 8.

Each of the thirteen known examples is trimmed close to the design on one or more sides.

APSO2

1911, Oct. ***Imperf.***

CL2 APSO2 25c **black** *55,000.*
On postcard with 1c #374 *75,000.*
Tied on cover with 1c #374 *115,000.*

No. CL2 is the first stamp in the world to picture an airplane.

Four examples are recorded off cover and without cancel (unused column). Only one of these has original gum. The unused value is for a stamp without gum. The example tied on cover is unique. Seven examples are recorded used on postcards.

COLOMBIA (SCADTA) CONSULAR OVERPRINTS

In July 1920, SCADTA was given authority by the Colombian government to operate exclusive airmail service in Colombia and to print its own postage stamps, while retaining all profits. Transportation in Colombia at this time was slow and difficult. This SCADTA airmail service enabled commerce to flourish.

Overprinted stamps were available at Colombian consulates, trade missions and agencies that were maintained by the SCADTA Company. These stamps paid the airmail service within Colombia once the mail arrived at a Colombian port.

Due to currency fluctuations between countries, two-letter overprints were applied by hand, and later by machine, denoting country of origin. The letters for the United States were "E.U." (Estados Unidos). For the SCADTA stamps used from countries other than the United States, see the Colombia listings in the *Scott Classic Specialized Catalogue of Stamps and Covers.*

The SCADTA system was extensively used throughout the world. In the United States, all mail that was sent singularly and not under separate cover was to have United States postage affixed for delivery to a Colombian port city post office and/or for delivery locally in Colombia. It was then processed and delivered to a ship destined for Colombia under normal international delivery agreements. Other mail was taken directly to ships by SCADTA agents, and on those no U.S. Stamps were required.

On Dec. 31, 1931, the Colombian government took over all airmail service in Colombia.

Values for unused stamps are for examples with no gum faults. Stamps with "tropicalized" gum sell at a substantial discount.

UNITED STATES DISPATCH FOR EXPEDITED AIR-MAIL SERVICE WITHIN COLOMBIA

Colombia (SCADTA) Consular Overprints Sociedad Colombo-Alemana de Transportes Aereos (S.C.A.D.T.A.)

Establishing an office in New York, the SCADTA Company sold the following two issues, each bearing the agent's signature, "G Mejia" (Gonzalo Mejia), in red ink, to designate use from the United States.

Colombia Nos. C14, C16 with ms "G Mejia" in red

Quantity printed of each value in parentheses.

1920, November

CLEU1	AP3 30c blk, *rose* (5,000)	100.00	350.00
	Never hinged	150.00	
	On cover		3,000.
CLEU2	AP3 50c green (1,000)	100.00	500.00
	Never hinged	150.00	
	On cover		7,000.
a.	Black signature		—

Two examples of No. CLEU2 on cover are known. Nos. CLEU1 and CLEU2 exist together on a unique cover.

E.U. or EU - STAMPS FOR USE IN THE UNITED STATES

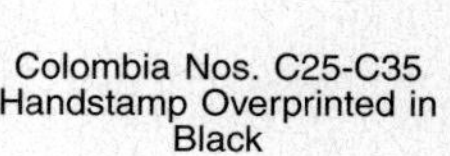

Colombia Nos. C25-C35 Handstamp Overprinted in Black

Letters 6½mm high

1921-23

CLEU3	AP4 5c org yel	20.00	15.00
	Never hinged	25.00	
	On cover		100.00
CLEU4	AP4 10c sl grn	20.00	15.00
	Never hinged	25.00	
	On cover		100.00
CLEU5	AP4 15c org brn	20.00	15.00
	Never hinged	25.00	
	On cover		150.00
CLEU6	AP4 20c red brown	20.00	15.00
	Never hinged	25.00	
	On cover		100.00
CLEU7	AP4 30c green	15.00	10.00
	Never hinged	20.00	
	On cover		150.00
CLEU8	AP4 50c blue	20.00	15.00
	Never hinged	25.00	
	On cover		200.00
CLEU9	AP4 60c vermilion	30.00	25.00
	Never hinged	37.50	
	On cover		300.00
CLEU10	AP5 1p gray black	35.00	30.00
	Never hinged	45.00	
	On cover		200.00
CLEU11	AP5 2p rose	75.00	70.00
	Never hinged	125.00	
	On cover		300.00
CLEU12	AP5 3p violet	100.00	100.00
	Never hinged	150.00	
	On cover		500.00
CLEU13	AP5 5p ol grn	425.00	400.00
	Never hinged	550.00	
	On cover		800.00
	Nos. CLEU3-CLEU13 (11)	780.00	710.00
	Nos. CLEU3-CLEU13, never hinged	1,052.50	

Same Overprint in Violet on Colombia Nos. C25-C35

1921-23

CLEU14	AP4 5c org yel	15.00	17.50
	Never hinged	20.00	
	On cover		125.00
CLEU15	AP4 10c sl grn	12.50	17.50
	Never hinged	17.50	
	On cover		125.00
CLEU16	AP4 15c org brn	12.50	17.50
	Never hinged	17.50	
	On cover		200.00
CLEU17	AP4 20c red brown	12.50	17.50
	Never hinged	17.50	
	On cover		80.00
CLEU18	AP4 30c green	9.00	12.00
	Never hinged	12.50	
	On cover		125.00
a.	Double overprint	*750.00*	
b.	Double overprint, vert.	—	
CLEU19	AP4 50c blue	12.50	17.50
	Never hinged	17.50	
	On cover		150.00
CLEU20	AP4 60c vermilion	30.00	25.00
	Never hinged	40.00	
	On cover		200.00
CLEU21	AP5 1p gray black	27.50	37.50
	Never hinged	40.00	
	On cover		200.00
CLEU22	AP5 2p rose	62.50	72.50
	Never hinged	90.00	
	On cover		250.00
CLEU23	AP5 3p violet	112.50	125.00
	Never hinged	165.00	
	On cover		500.00
CLEU24	AP5 5p ol grn	375.00	400.00
	Never hinged	500.00	
	On cover		800.00
	Nos. CLEU14-CLEU24 (11)	681.50	759.50
	Nos. CLEU14-CLEU24, never hinged	937.50	

Same overprint in black on Colombia Nos. C38//51, CF1

No. CLEU29

No. CLEU32

1923

CLEU25	AP6 5c org yel	20.00	12.50
	Never hinged	30.00	
	On cover		100.00
CLEU26	AP6 10c green	20.00	12.50
	Never hinged	30.00	
	On cover		100.00
CLEU27	AP6 15c carmine	25.00	15.00
	Never hinged	30.00	
	On cover		100.00
CLEU28	AP6 20c gray	20.00	15.00
	Never hinged	30.00	
	On cover		100.00
CLEU29	AP6 30c blue	7.50	5.00
	Never hinged	10.00	
	On cover		75.00
CLEU30	AP6 50c green	20.00	10.00
	Never hinged	30.00	
	On cover		225.00
CLEU31	AP6 60c brown	20.00	10.00
	Never hinged	30.00	
	On cover		250.00
CLEU32	AP7 1p black	30.00	20.00
	Never hinged	40.00	
	On cover		250.00
CLEU33	AP7 2p red org	35.00	27.50
	Never hinged	45.00	
	On cover		300.00
CLEU34	AP7 3p violet	75.00	50.00
	Never hinged	100.00	
	On cover		400.00
CLEU35	AP7 5p ol grn	125.00	87.50
	Never hinged	175.00	
	On cover		600.00
CFLEU1	AP6 20c gray	75.00	37.50
	Never hinged	150.00	
	On cover		500.00
	Nos. CLEU25-CLEU35, CFLEU1 (12)	472.50	302.50
	Nos. CLEU25-CLEU35, CFLEU1, never hinged	432.50	

Same Overprint in Black on Colombia No. C51

1923

CLEU36 AP6 30c on 20c gray (C) *1,500. 600.00*
On cover *750.00*
a. "60" instead of "30" at left, on cover —

No. CLEU36a is unique.

Same Overprint in Violet on Colombia Nos. C38//C50, CF1

1923

CLEU37 AP6 5c org yel 12.50 12.50
Never hinged 17.50
On cover 75.00
CLEU38 AP6 10c green 12.50 12.50
Never hinged 17.50
On cover 75.00
CLEU39 AP6 15c carmine 12.50 12.50
Never hinged 17.50
On cover 75.00
CLEU40 AP6 20c gray 12.50 12.50
Never hinged 17.50
On cover 75.00
CLEU41 AP6 30c blue 5.00 5.00
Never hinged 7.50
On cover 75.00
CLEU42 AP6 50c green 10.00 10.00
Never hinged 15.00
On cover 150.00
CLEU43 AP6 60c brown 10.00 10.00
Never hinged 15.00
On cover 175.00
CLEU44 AP7 1p black 20.00 20.00
Never hinged 30.00
On cover 175.00
CLEU45 AP7 2p red org 25.00 25.00
Never hinged 35.00
On cover 200.00
CLEU46 AP7 3p violet 50.00 50.00
Never hinged 75.00
On cover 350.00
CLEU47 AP7 5p ol grn 125.00 87.50
Never hinged 175.00
On cover 500.00
CFLEU2 AP6 20c gray 50.00 50.00
Never hinged 75.00
On cover 300.00
Nos. CLEU37-CLEU47, CFLEU2 (12) 345.00 307.50
Nos. CLEU37-CLEU47, CFLEU2, never hinged 500.00

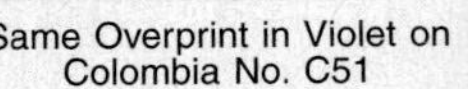

Same Overprint in Violet on Colombia No. C51

1923

CLEU48 AP6 30c on 20c gray (C) 45.00 22.50
Never hinged 90.00
On cover 200.00

Same Overprint in Red on Colombia No. C41

1923

CLEU49 AP6 20c gray 60.00 *60.00*
Never hinged 90.00
On cover 200.00

Colombia Nos. C38//C50, CF1 Lithograph Overprinted in Black, by the Reichsdruckerei, Berlin, Germany

No. CLEU50

No. CLEU58

Quantity printed of each value in parentheses.

Letters 10mm high

1923, June 4

CLEU50 AP6 5c org yel (7500) 4.50 4.50
Never hinged 7.50
On cover 75.00
CLEU51 AP6 10c green (15,000) 2.00 2.00
Never hinged 3.00
On cover 75.00
CLEU52 AP6 15c carmine (11,600) 3.00 3.00
Never hinged 4.00
On cover 75.00
CLEU53 AP6 20c gray (45,000) 6.00 6.00
Never hinged 9.00
On cover 75.00
CLEU54 AP6 30c blue (170,000) 2.00 2.00
Never hinged 3.00
On cover 50.00
CLEU55 AP6 50c green (5,000) 5.00 5.00
Never hinged 7.50
On cover
CLEU56 AP6 60c brown (55,000) 2.75 2.75
Never hinged 4.00
On cover 125.00
CLEU57 AP7 1p black (8,400) 6.75 6.00
Never hinged 8.00
On cover 150.00
a. Double impression of basic stamp *1,250.*
CLEU58 AP7 2p red org (3,800) 17.50 17.50
Never hinged 25.00
On cover 200.00
CLEU59 AP7 3p violet (3,200) 37.50 40.00
Never hinged 50.00
On cover 300.00
CLEU60 AP7 5p ol grn (3,400) 55.00 55.00
Never hinged 75.00
On cover 500.00

CFLEU3 AP6 20c gray (2,000) 25.00 12.50
Never hinged 50.00
On cover 180.00
Nos. CLEU50-CLEU60, CFLEU3 (12) 167.00 156.25
Nos. CLEU50-CLEU60, CFLEU3, never hinged 221.00

Colombia Nos. C40, C42 Lithograph Overprinted in Black

Letters 10mm high

1928, Sept. 25

CLEU61 AP6 15c carmine (1,500) 15.00 15.00
Never hinged 30.00
On cover 100.00
a. Inverted overprint *400.00 300.00*
CLEU62 AP6 30c blue (49,000) 5.00 5.00
Never hinged 10.00
On cover 35.00
a. Inverted overprint *450.00 450.00*
b. Double overprint *500.00 500.00*

Nos. CLEU61 and CLEU62 were lithograph overprinted in New York in a slightly different font by Fleming & Benedict for the New York agency. There were two printings of the 30c value, the first generally centered toward the top of the stamp, the second toward the bottom.

Nos. CLC68-CLC79, CLCF2 were sold abroad in the equivalent of U.S. gold dollars, thus eliminating the need to identify the various sales offices because of changes in rates of exchange. They were valid on mail sent to Colombia from outside its borders, and they were used from the United States in the same manner as the consular overprinted issues, which were still available and valid for use. Values for stamps on cover are for covers with United States postage as well as the Colombia gold dollar issues.

AP10

AP11

1929, June 1 **Wmk. 127** ***Perf. 14***

CLC68 AP10 5c yellow org 6.25 *7.25*
Never hinged 9.50
On cover 40.00
CLC69 AP10 10c red brown 1.25 *3.00*
Never hinged 1.80
On cover 35.00
CLC70 AP10 15c deep green 1.25 *3.00*
Never hinged 1.80
On cover 35.00
CLC71 AP10 20c carmine 1.25 *3.75*
Never hinged 1.80
On cover 35.00
CLC72 AP10 25c violet blue 1.25 .85
Never hinged 1.80
On cover 20.00
CLC73 AP10 30c gray blue 1.25 .95
Never hinged 1.80
On cover 20.00
CLC74 AP10 50c dk olive grn 1.25 *1.90*
Never hinged 1.80
On cover 35.00
CLC75 AP10 60c brown 2.50 *3.00*
Never hinged 3.60
On cover 35.00
CLC76 AP11 1p blue 5.50 *7.25*
Never hinged 7.50
On cover 60.00
CLC77 AP11 2p red orange 8.50 *10.00*
Never hinged 12.50
On cover 75.00
CLC78 AP11 3p violet 100.00 100.00
Never hinged 135.00
On cover 250.00
CLC79 AP11 5p olive green 125.00 *140.00*
Never hinged 165.00
On cover 350.00
CLCF2 AP8 20c carmine 8.00 7.00
Never hinged 12.00
On cover 100.00
Nos. CLC68-CLC79, CLCF2 (13) 263.25 *287.95*

Nos. CLC68-CLC79, CLCF2 unused are valued with fresh original gum. Stamps often are found with tropicalized gum or with no gum, and such examples sell for less.

On December 1, 1931, all airmail services were taken over from SCADTA by the government of Colombia.

R.F. OVERPRINTS

Authorized as a control mark by the United States Fleet Post Office during 1944-45 for the accommodation of and exclusive use by French naval personnel on airmail correspondence to the United States and Canada. All "R.F." (Republique Francaise) mail had to be posted on board French ships or at one of their western Mediterranean or northwest African naval bases and had to bear the return address, rank and/or serial number of a French officer or seaman. It also had to be reviewed by a censor.

All "R.F." overprints were handstamped by the French naval authorities after the stamps were affixed for mailing. The stamps had to be canceled by a special French naval cancellation. The status of unused stamps seems questionable; they are alleged to have been handstamped at a later date.

Several types of "R.F." overprints other than those illustrated are known, but their validity is doubtful.

United States No. C25 Handstamped in Black

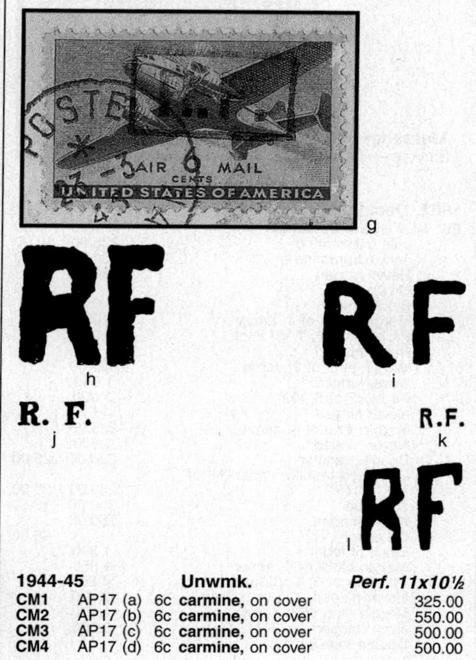

1944-45 **Unwmk.** ***Perf. 11x10½***

CM1	AP17 (a)	6c **carmine,** on cover	325.00
CM2	AP17 (b)	6c **carmine,** on cover	550.00
CM3	AP17 (c)	6c **carmine,** on cover	500.00
CM4	AP17 (d)	6c **carmine,** on cover	500.00
CM5	AP17 (e)	6c **carmine,** on cover	600.00
CM6	AP17 (f)	6c **carmine,** on cover	500.00
CM7	AP17 (g)	6c **carmine,** on cover	600.00
CM8	AP17 (h)	6c **carmine,** on cover	600.00
CM9	AP17 (i)	6c **carmine,** on cover	750.00
CM10	AP17 (j)	6c **carmine,** on cover	—
CM11	AP17 (k)	6c **carmine,** on cover	—
CM12	AP17 (l)	6c **carmine,** on cover	—

Counterfeits of several types exist.

No. 907 is known with type "c" overprint; Nos. 804 and 928 with type "f"; No. C19 with type "e"; No. C25a (single) with type "c","d," "f," and "l"; No. C26 with type "a," "d" or "f."; and No. C28 with type "c." Type "i" exists in several very minor variations.

STAMPED ENVELOPES

Nos. UC3, UC4 or UC6 Handstamped in Black

1944-45

UCM1	UC2 (a)	6c **orange,** entire	300.00
UCM2	UC2 (b)	6c **orange,** entire	500.00
a.		6c **orange,** entire, type "a" and type "b" overprints	*600.00*
UCM3	UC2 (d)	6c **orange,** entire	375.00
UCM3A	UC2 (e)	6c **orange,** entire	*1,450.*
UCM4	UC2 (f)	6c **orange,** entire	650.00
a.		6c **orange,** entire, type "a" and type "f" overprints	*750.00*
UCM5	UC2 (h)	6c **orange,** entire	—
UCM6	UC2 (i)	6c **orange,** entire	—
UCM7	UC2 (j)	6c **orange,** entire	*2,500.*
UCM8	UC2 (k)	6c **orange,** entire	—

Values for Nos. UCM1-UCM8 reflect the scarcity of the actual overprint types. Use of No. UC6 envelopes was by far the most common. Overprints on Nos. UC3 or UC4 merit a premium.

Specialist collectors question the existence of No. UCM6. The editors will be deleting this number if authenticated evidence of its existence is not provided.

SPECIAL DELIVERY STAMPS

Special Delivery service was instituted by the Act of Congress of March 3, 1885, and put into operation on October 1, 1885. The Act limited the service to free delivery offices and such others as served places with a population of 4,000 or more, and its privileges were thus operative in but 555 post offices. The Act of August 4, 1886, made the stamps and service available at all post offices and upon any article of mailable matter, beginning Oct. 1, 1886. To consume the supply of stamps of the first issue, Scott No. E2 was withheld until September 6, 1888.

A Special Delivery stamp, when affixed to any stamped letter or article of mailable matter, secured later delivery during daytime and evening at most post offices, so that the item did not have to wait until the next day for delivery.

Messenger Running SD1

ENGRAVED

Printed by the American Bank Note Co.

Plates of 100 subjects in two panes of 50 each

Flat Plate Printing

1885 **Unwmk.** ***Perf. 12***

E1 SD1 10c **blue**	550.00	80.00
deep blue	550.00	80.00
Never hinged	1,250.	
On cover		225.00
First day of service cover (Oct. 1)		*27,500.*
Block of four	2,500.	
P# block of 8, Impt. 495 or 496	*25,000.*	
Margin strip of 4, same	6,250.	
Double transfer at top	825.00	200.00

Earliest documented use: Sept. 29, 1885, on a cover delivered Oct. 1. There is also a Sept. 30 cover recorded, received for delivery at 7:00 a.m. Oct. 1.

Messenger Running SD2

1888, Sept. 6

E2 SD2 10c **blue**	500.00	45.00
deep blue	500.00	45.00
Never hinged	1,150.	
On cover		135.00
Block of four	2,100.	
P# block of 8, Impt. 73 or 552	*17,500.*	
Never hinged	*25,000.*	
Margin strip of 4, same	5,250.	

Earliest documented use: Oct. 7, 1888.

See note above No. E3.

COLUMBIAN EXPOSITION ISSUE

Though not issued expressly for the Exposition, No. E3 is considered to be part of that issue. It was released in orange because No. E2 was easily confused with the 1c Columbian, No. 230.

From Jan. 24, 1893, until Jan. 5, 1894, the special delivery stamp was printed in orange; the issue in that color continued until May 19, 1894, when the stock on hand was exhausted. The stamp in blue was not issued from Jan. 24, 1893 to May 19, 1894. However, on Jan. 5, 1894, printing of the stamp in blue was resumed. Presumably it was reissued from May 19, 1894 until the appearance of No. E4 on Oct. 10, 1894. The emissions of the blue stamp of this design before Jan. 24, 1893 and after Jan. 5, 1894 are indistinguishable.

1893, Jan. 24

E3 SD2 10c **orange**	300.00	50.00
deep orange	300.00	50.00
Never hinged	650.00	
On cover		200.00
On cover, Columbian Expo. station machine canc.		1,250.
On cover, Columbian Expo. station duplex handstamp cancel		1,500.
Block of four	1,250.	
P# block of 8, Impt. 73 or 552	*13,000.*	
Never hinged	*16,500.*	
Margin strip of 4, same	4,250.	

Earliest documented use: Feb. 11, 1893.

Messenger Running SD3

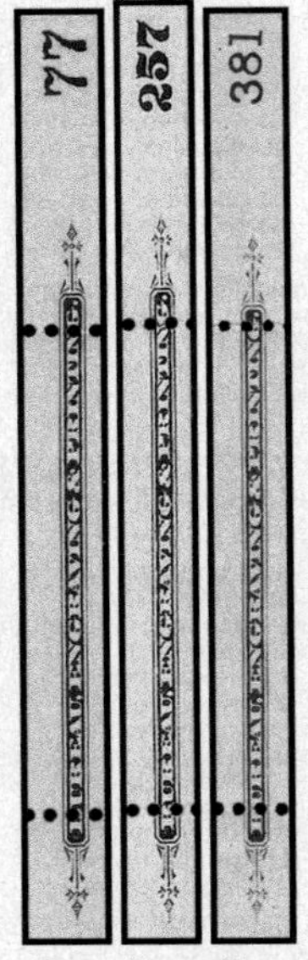

Type III Type VI Type VII

Printed by the Bureau of Engraving and Printing.

1894, Oct. 10

Line under "TEN CENTS"

E4	SD3 10c **blue**	850.00	110.00
	dark blue	850.00	110.00
	bright blue	1,050.	130.00
	Never hinged	2,000.	
	On cover		300.00
	Block of four	3,750.	
	Margin block of 4, arrow	4,000.	
	P#77 block of 6, T III Impt.	*21,000.*	
	Never hinged	*27,500.*	
	Margin strip of 3, same	5,250.	
	Never hinged	8,000.	
	Double transfer	—	—

Earliest documented use: Oct. 25, 1894.

Imperfs of No. E4 on stamp paper, currently listed as No. E4aP, may not be proofs, but it is also unlikely that they were regularly issued. They most likely are from printer's waste.

No. E5a

1895, Aug. 16 **Wmk. 191**

E5	SD3 10c **blue**	210.00	12.50
	dark blue	210.00	12.50
	deep blue	210.00	12.50
	Never hinged	475.00	
	On cover		25.00
	Block of four	900.00	
	Margin block of 4, arrow	925.00	
	P# block of 6, T III, VI or VII Impt.	*5,000.*	
	Never hinged	*7,000.*	
	Margin strip of 3, same	900.00	
	Never hinged	1,600.	
	Double transfer	—	80.00
	Line of color through "POSTAL DELIVERY," from bottom row of Plates 1257-1260	350.00	80.00
	Never hinged	700.00	
a.	Dots in curved frame above messenger (Pl. 882)	400.00	50.00
	Never hinged	800.00	
	P# block of 6, Impt.	*10,000.*	
b.	Printed on both sides		—

Earliest documented use: Oct. 3, 1895.

The existence of No. E5b has been questioned by specialists. The editors would like to see authenticated evidence of its existence.

See Die and Plate Proofs for imperf. on stamp paper.

Messenger on Bicycle — SD4

1902, Dec. 9

E6	SD4 10c **ultramarine**	225.00	10.00
	pale ultramarine	225.00	10.00
	dark ultramarine	250.00	10.00
	Never hinged	500.00	
	On cover		22.50
	Block of four	1,000.	
	Margin block of 4, arrow	1,050.	
	P# block of 6, T VII Impt.	*3,250.*	
	Never hinged	*4,750.*	
	Margin strip of 3, same	850.00	
	Never hinged	1,850.	
	P# block of 6, "09"	*3,000.*	
	Never hinged	*4,500.*	
	Margin strip of 3, same	825.00	
	Never hinged	1,800.	
	Double transfer	*250.00*	25.00
	Damaged transfer under "N" of "CENTS"	250.00	25.00
a.	10c **blue**	300.00	12.50
	Never hinged	750.00	
	On cover		65.00
	Block of four	1,300.	
	Margin block of 4, arrow	1,350.	
	P# block of 6, T VII Impt.	*4,250.*	
	Never hinged	*6,000.*	
	Margin strip of 3, same	1,100.	
	Never hinged	3,000.	
	Double transfer	—	—

Earliest documented use: Jan. 15, 1903.

No. E6 was re-issued in 1909 from new plates 5240, 5243-5245. After a few months use the Bureau added "09" to these plate numbers. The stamp can be identified only by plate number. The plate numbers without the "09" are scarcer and worth more.

Helmet of Mercury — SD5

Designed by Whitney Warren.

Plates of 280 subjects in four panes of 70 each

1908, Dec. 12

E7	SD5 10c **green**	65.00	50.00
	dark green	65.00	50.00
	yellowish green	65.00	50.00
	Never hinged	140.00	
	On cover		400.00
	Block of four	300.00	
	Margin strip of 3, P# and T V Impt.	300.00	
	Never hinged	500.00	
	P# block of 6, T V Impt.	*1,075.*	—
	Never hinged	*1,500.*	
	Double transfer	160.00	100.00

Earliest documented use: Dec. 14, 1908.

Plates of 200 subjects in four panes of 50 each

1911, Jan. **Wmk. 190** ***Perf. 12***

E8	SD4 10c **ultramarine**	110.00	10.00
	pale ultramarine	110.00	10.00
	dark ultramarine	110.00	10.00
	Never hinged	240.00	
	On cover		30.00
	Block of four	460.00	
	P# block of 6, T VII Impt.	*1,850.*	
	Never hinged	*2,750.*	
	P# block of 6	*1,700.*	
	Never hinged	*2,500.*	
	Top frame line missing (Pl. 5514)	150.00	22.50
	Never hinged	325.00	
b.	10c **violet blue**	160.00	14.00
	Never hinged	350.00	
	On cover		25.00
	Block of four	675.00	
	P# block of 6, T VII Impt.	*2,100.*	
	Never hinged	*3,250.*	
	P# block of 6	*1,900.*	
	Never hinged	*2,750.*	

Earliest documented use: Jan. 14, 1911.

1914, Sept. ***Perf. 10***

E9	SD4 10c **ultramarine**	190.00	12.00
	pale ultramarine	190.00	12.00
	Never hinged	425.00	
	On cover		65.00
	Block of four	800.00	
	P# block of 6, T VII Impt.	*4,000.*	—
	Never hinged	*6,000.*	
	P# block of 6	*3,000.*	—
	Never hinged	*4,500.*	
	P# block of 8, T VII Impt. (side)	—	
a.	10c **blue**	260.00	15.00
	Never hinged	575.00	
	On cover		65.00
	Block of four	1,150.	
	P# block of 6, T VII Impt.	*5,000.*	—
	Never hinged	*7,500.*	
	P# block of 6	*4,000.*	—
	Never hinged	*6,000.*	
	P# block of 8, T VII Impt. (side)	*6,500.*	

Earliest documented use: Oct. 26, 1914.

1916, Oct. 19 **Unwmk.** ***Perf. 10***

E10	SD4 10c **pale ultramarine**	320.00	50.00
	ultramarine	350.00	55.00
	Never hinged	700.00	
	On cover		200.00
	Block of four	1,400.	
	P# block of 6, T VII Impt. 5520	*5,500.*	—
	Never hinged	*7,750.*	
	P# block of 6	*5,000.*	—
	Never hinged	*7,250.*	
a.	10c **blue**	375.00	50.00
	Never hinged	800.00	
	On cover		110.00
	Block of four	1,650.	
	P# block of 6, T VII Impt. 5520	*5,750.*	—
	P# block of 6	*5,000.*	—

Earliest documented use: Nov. 4, 1916.

1917, May 2 **Unwmk.** ***Perf. 11***

E11	SD4 10c **ultramarine**	20.00	.75
	pale ultramarine	20.00	.75
	dark ultramarine	25.00	2.00
	Never hinged	45.00	
	On cover		4.00
	Block of four	85.00	
	P# block of 6, T VII Impt.	725.00	—
	Never hinged	1,100.	
	P# block of 6	225.00	—
	Never hinged	340.00	
	P# block of 8, T VII Impt. (side)	—	
b.	10c **gray violet**	35.00	3.00
	Never hinged	75.00	
	On cover		4.00
	Block of four	150.00	
	P# block of 6, T VII Impt.	850.00	—
	Never hinged	1,300.	
	P# block of 6	325.00	—
	Never hinged	475.00	
	P# block of 8, T VII Impt. (side)	*2,500.*	
c.	10c **blue**	100.00	5.00
	Never hinged	210.00	
	On cover		30.00
	Block of four	425.00	
	P# block of 6, T VII Impt.	2,100.	
	P# block of 6	725.00	
	P# block of 8, T VII Impt. (side)	*2,850.*	
d.	Perf. 10 at left	—	

Earliest documented use: June 12, 1917.

The aniline ink used on some printings of No. E11 permeated the paper causing a pink tinge to appear on the back. Such stamps are called "pink backs." They are scarce and valued at approximately five times the value of the normal stamp.

Motorcycle Delivery SD6

1922, July 12 **Unwmk.** ***Perf. 11***

E12	SD6 10c **gray violet**	45.00	3.00
	Never hinged	95.00	
	On cover		3.50
	First day cover		500.00
	P# block of 6	525.00	—
	Never hinged	800.00	
	Double transfer	—	—
a.	10c **deep ultramarine**	55.00	3.50
	Never hinged	130.00	
	On cover		5.00
	P# block of 6	650.00	—
	Never hinged	1,000.	
	Double transfer	—	—

Post Office Truck — SD7

FLAT PLATE PRINTING

1925 **Unwmk.** ***Perf. 11***

Issued to facilitate special delivery service for parcel post.

E13	SD6 15c **deep orange,** *Apr. 11, 1925*	40.00	3.75
	Never hinged	75.00	
	On cover		55.00
	First day cover		400.00
	P# block of 6	450.00	—
	Never hinged	700.00	
	Double transfer	47.50	4.00
a.	Printed on "special" booklet paper, *1928* (see note before #551)	85.00	10.00
	Never hinged	160.00	
	On cover		100.00
	Block of 4	350.00	
	P# block of 6	—	
	Never hinged	—	
E14	SD7 20c **black,** *Apr. 25, 1925*	2.00	1.00
	Never hinged	4.00	
	On cover		25.00
	First day cover		175.00
	P# block of 6	50.00	
	Never hinged	70.00	

Motorcycle Type of 1922

ROTARY PRESS PRINTING

1927-31 **Unwmk.** ***Perf. 11x10½***

E15	SD6 10c **gray violet,** *Nov. 29, 1927*	1.00	.25
	violet	1.00	.25
	Never hinged	1.75	
	On cover		.50
	First day cover		130.00
	First day cover, electric eye plate, *Sept. 8, 1941*		50.00
	P# block of 4	5.50	—
	Never hinged	9.00	
	Gashed plate 19280 LR 35	70.00	*75.00*
a.	10c **red lilac**	.80	.25
	Never hinged	1.40	
b.	10c **gray lilac**	.90	.25
	Never hinged	1.60	
c.	Horiz. pair, imperf. btwn., red lilac shade	*350.00*	
	Never hinged	*575.00*	

E16	SD6 15c **orange,** *Aug. 1931*	.60	.25
	Never hinged	.90	
	On cover		1.50
	First day cover, Washington, D.C., *Aug. 13, 1931*		125.00
	P# block of 4	2.50	—
	Never hinged	4.00	

The Washington, D.C. Aug. 13, 1931 first day cover reflects the first day of sale at the philatelic agency. The actual earliest documented use of No. E16 is Aug. 6, 1931, at Easton, PA; value, $2,000.

Catalogue values for unused stamps in this section, from this point to the end, are for Never Hinged items.

ROTARY PRESS PRINTING

E. E. Plates of 200 subjects in four panes of 50 each.

1944-51 **Unwmk.** ***Perf. 11x10½***

E17	SD6 13c **blue,** *Oct. 30, 1944*	.60	.25
	First day cover		15.00
	P# block of 4	2.75	—
E18	SD6 17c **orange yellow,** *Oct. 30, 1944*	3.50	2.50
	On commercial cover		65.00
	First day cover		20.00
	First day cover, Nos. E17 & E18		45.00
	P# block of 4	20.00	—
E19	SD7 20c **black,** *Nov. 30, 1951*	1.20	.25
	First day cover		5.00
	P# block of 4	5.00	—

Special Delivery Letter, Hand to Hand — SD8

ROTARY PRESS PRINTING

E.E. Plates of 200 subjects in four panes of 50 each

1954, Oct. 13 **Unwmk.** ***Perf. 11x10½***

E20	SD8 20c **deep blue**	.40	.25
	light blue	—	—
	First day cover, Boston *(194,043)*		3.00
	P# block of 4	2.00	—

1957, Sept. 3

E21	SD8 30c **lake**	.50	.25
	First day cover, Indianapolis, Ind. *(111,451)*		2.25
	P# block of 4	2.25	—

Arrows — SD9

Designed by Norman Ives.

GIORI PRESS PRINTING

Plates of 200 subjects in four panes of 50 each

1969, Nov. 21 **Unwmk.** ***Perf. 11***

E22	SD9 45c **carmine & violet blue**	1.20	.25
	First day cover, New York, N.Y.		4.00
	P# block of 4	5.00	—
	Margin block of 4, Mr. Zip and "Use Zip Code"	4.90	—

1971, May 10 ***Perf. 11***

E23	SD9 60c **violet blue & carmine**	1.25	.25
	First day cover, Phoenix, Ariz. *(129,562)*		3.50
	P# block of 4	5.50	—
	Margin block of 4, Mr. Zip and "Use Zip Code"	5.25	

From 1885 to the present, special delivery stamps have not been and are not valid for the payment of postage of any description, nor for registry fees.

U.S. REGISTRY EXCHANGE LABELS (1883-1911)

Registry exchange labels resulted from the implementation of an 1882 Universal Postal Union resolution requiring that international registered mail matter bear a label or impression of a stamp with a capital letter "R" in Roman text. The United States Post Office Department opted for gummed labels which, for the most part, were produced through the joint efforts of the Government Printing Office (printing) and the Bureau of Engraving and Printing (gumming, perforating and distributing). The use of these labels by those post offices authorized to handle inbound and outbound foreign registered mail became effective Jan. 1, 1883, and stayed in effect, virtually unchanged, until Jan. 24, 1911. Such postal facilities were designated "exchange offices," and the labels have thus come to be known as "registry exchange labels" or simply "exchange labels."

During the time period these labels were in use, there were thirty-seven exchange offices that were authorized to use them. Labels are recorded from just twenty-eight of these offices.

Values shown are for complete registered covers with the most common franking. Although condition is always a factor in the determination of any philatelic item, it is somewhat less so with regard to many of the registry exchange label covers due to the small number available from many of the offices.

Numbers in parentheses following the office headings and catalog numbers represent the numbers of currently documented examples of the particular types of registry exchange labels.

Example of Cover Bearing Registry Exchange Label With the Narrow Roman Letter "R". — No. FX-NY1a(i)(i)

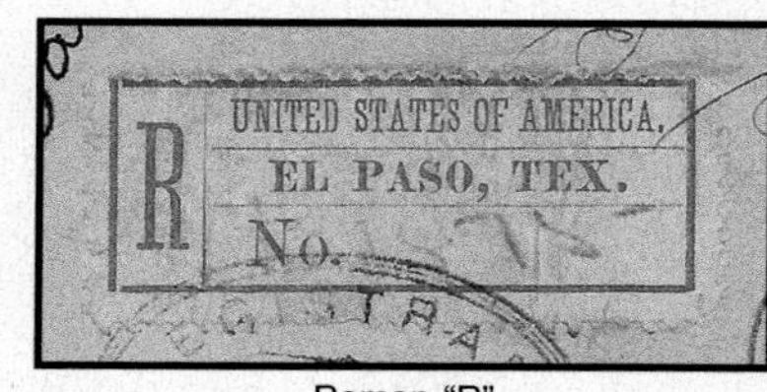

Roman "R"

Gothic "R"

Baltimore, MD (11)

FX-BA2	Handstamped name (9)	*1,500.*
FX-BA3	Manuscript name (2)	*3,000.*

Boston, MA (101)

FX-BO1	Printed name (100)	*150.*
FX-BO2	Handstamped name (1)	*500.*

Brownsville, TX (1)

FX-BR2	Handstamped name	*10,000.*

Cristobal, CZ (82)

FX-CZ1	Printed name (69)	400.
FX-CZ2	Handstamped name (12)	500.
FX-CZ4	Blank, no name (1)	—

Douglas, AZ (3)

FX-DO2	Handstamped name	*3,000.*

Eagle Pass, TX (7)

FX-EG2	Handstamped name (5)	*2,000.*
FX-EG3	Manuscript name (2)	*3,000.*

El Paso, TX (53)

FX-EP1	Printed name	
a.	Gothic letter "R" (14)	*500.*
b.	Narrow Roman letter "R" (29)	*450.*
FX-EP2	Handstamped name	
a.	All capital letters (5)	*600.*
b.	Upper & lower case letters (1)	*700.*

	Used as official seals, on cover, unique	*750.*
FX-EP4	Blank, no name (1)	*700.*

Labels on two covers are torn and missing the letter "R." Sub-type unreported for one label.

Havana, Cuba (13)

FX-HA1	Printed name	*2,000.*

Honolulu, HI (10)

FX-HO1	Printed name (8)	*2,000.*
FX-HO2	Handstamped name (2)	*3,000.*

Jacksonville, FL (8)

FX-JA2	Handstamped name (5)	*2,500.*
FX-JA3	Manuscript name (1)	*3,000.*
FX-JA4	Blank, no name (2)	*2,000.*

Key West, FL (3)

FX-KW3	Manuscript name	*1,500.*

Laredo, TX (28)

FX-LA1	Printed name	1,000.

Miami, FL (1)

FX-MA2	Handstamped name (1)	*5,000.*

Mobile, AL (80)

FX-MO1	Printed name (61)	*400.*
FX-MO2	Handstamped name	
	a. Cursive letters (3)	*1,000.*
	b. Block letters (2)	*1,000.*
FX-MO3	Manuscript name (6)	*850.*

Sub-type unreported for eight labels.

Naco, AZ (4)

FX-NA2	Handstamped name	
	a. Cursive letters (2)	*3,500.*
	b. Block letters (2)	*3,500.*

New Orleans, LA (45)

FX-NO1	Printed name (29)	600.
FX-NO4	Blank, no name (14)	525.

Sub-type unreported for two labels.

New York, NY

FX-NY1	Printed name		
	a(i)(i). "Exchange" label with narrow Roman letter "R" 2.5 mm in width, "United States of America." 25.5 mm in length	50.	
	a(i)(ii). "Exchange" label with narrow Roman letter "R" 3 mm in width, "United States of America." 26.5 mm in length	50.	
	a(ii). "Exchange" label with Gothic letter "R", "United States of America." 22 mm in length	150.	
	a(iii). "Exchange" label with Gothic letter "R", "United States of America." 28 mm in length	100.	
	Used as official seals, on cover	200.	
	Sheet of 50		*100.*
	a(iv). "Exchange" label with narrow Gothic letter "R", "United States of America." 26 mm in length	100.	
	b(i). "City" in small letters followed by a period, Gothic letter "R," "United States of America." 28 mm in length	50.	
	b(ii). "City" in large letters followed by a period, Gothic letter "R," "United States of America." 27 mm in length	50.	
	b(iii). "City" in sans-serif letters, no period, narrow Roman letter "R"	250.	
	c. Printed name without "City" or "Exchange"	*500.*	
	d. Printed name and "3rd - 4th CLASS"	*1,000.*	
	Used as official seals, on cover	200.	
FX-NY4	Blank, no name	250.	

Nogales, AZ (18)

FX-NOG1	Printed name (13)	*1,000.*
FX-NOG2	Handstamped name (5)	*1,300.*

Philadelphia, PA (19)

FX-PH1	Printed name	
	a. Name in sans-serif letters (2)	*1,000.*
	b. Name in serif letters (17)	*400.*

St. Louis, MO (17)

FX-STL1	Printed name (14)	*700.*
FX-STL2	Handstamped name (3)	*1,200.*

San Antonio, TX (7)

FX-SA1	Printed name	*2,000.*

San Diego, CA (2)

FX-SD3	Manuscript name (1)	*4,500.*
FX-SD4	Blank, no name (1)	*4,500.*

San Francisco, CA (235)

FX-SF1	Printed name	
	a. Name in sans-serif letters (206)	100.
	b. Name in serif letters (29)	400.

San Juan, PR (11)

FX-SJ1	Printed name	*2,000.*

Seattle, WA (34)

FX-SE1	Printed name	
	a. Gothic letter "R" (20)	*500.*
	b. Narrow Roman letter "R" (11)	*800.*

Sub-type unreported for three labels.

Shanghai, China (52)

FX-SH1	Printed name	
	a. Gothic red letter "R" (19)	*2,000.*
	b. Narrow red Roman letter "R" (14)	*2,000.*
	c. Gothic black letter "R" (10)	*4,000.*
	d. Narrow black Roman letter "R" (9)	*4,000.*

Nos. FX-SH1c and FX-SH1d were produced locally in China while awaiting arrival of red labels.

Tacoma, WA (15)

FX-TA1	Printed name	*750.*

Tampa, FL (2)

FX-TP2	Handstamped name	*2,000.*

A cover with a registry label bearing a manuscript "Tampa" (Florida) has been discovered. It is held in the collection of a historical society and is not available to collectors.

REGISTRATION STAMP

The Registry System for U.S. mail went into effect July 1, 1855, the fee being 5 cents. On June 30, 1863, the fee was increased to 20 cents. On January 1, 1869, the fee was reduced to 15 cents and on January 1, 1874, to 8 cents. On July 1, 1875, the fee was increased to 10 cents. On January 1, 1893 the fee was again reduced to 8 cents and again it was increased to 10 cents on November 1, 1909.

Early registered covers with various stamps, rates and postal markings are of particular interest to collectors.

Registry stamps (10c ultramarine) were issued on December 1, 1911, to prepay registry fees (not postage), but ordinary stamps were valid for registry fees then as now. These special stamps were abolished May 28, 1913, by order of the Postmaster General, who permitted their use until supplies on hand were exhausted.

Eagle — RS1

ENGRAVED

1911, Dec. 1	**Wmk. 190**	***Perf. 12***
F1 RS1 10c **ultramarine**	75.00	14.00
pale ultramarine	75.00	15.00
Never hinged	160.00	
On cover		85.00
Block of 4	375.00	*100.00*
P# block of 6, Impt. & "A"	*1,800.*	—
Never hinged	*2,750.*	
First day cover		*20,000.*

CERTIFIED MAIL STAMP

Certified Mail service was started on June 6, 1955, for use on first class mail for which no indemnity value is claimed, but for which proof of mailing and proof of delivery are available at less cost than registered mail. The mailer receives one receipt and the addressee signs another when the postman delivers the letter. The second receipt is kept on file at the post office for six months. The Certified Mail charge, originally 15 cents, is in addition to regular postage, whether surface mail, air mail, or special delivery.

Catalogue value for the unused stamp in this section is for a Never Hinged item.

Letter Carrier — CM1

ROTARY PRESS PRINTING

E. E. Plates of 200 subjects in four panes of 50

1955, June 6	**Unwmk.**	***Perf. 10½x11***	
FA1 CM1 15c **red**		.75	.75
P# block of 4		5.50	—
First day cover			10.00

POSTAGE DUE STAMPS

Postage due stamps were authorized by an act of Congress, approved March 3, 1879, and effective July 1, 1879. By law, postage due stamps were to be affixed by clerks to any piece of mailable matter to denote the amount collected from the addressee because of insufficient prepayment of postage.

Although the Post Office Department required postage to be prepaid beginning in 1855, there were many instances when full postage was not required, and postage due payment had to be collected in cash from the addressees. These instances included insufficiently prepaid letters, advertised letters, and unpaid ship letters and steamboat letters.

The reason for the appearance of postage due stamps may be summed up in one word: accountability. The 1880 *Report of the Postmaster General* noted that the former system of collecting postage due had one great weakness: "In securing the full returns of (the postage due collected in cash) the department was entirely dependent on the fidelity of the postmasters." Postage due stamps, affixed to underpaid mail as receipts for the underpayment collected, solved that problem by requiring postmasters to account for cash receipts that would balance any postage due stamps no longer in stock, in the same way that they had to account for regular postage stamp sales.

The last postage due stamps were printed in early November, 1985. With the advent of postage meters, the scrapping of the last Cottrell press in November 1985 (the last press capable of printing the current postage due stamps as designed), and finally new regulations requiring full prepayment of postage in all cases, postage due stamps became anachronistic, and their use ceased.

D1

Printed by the American Bank Note Co.

Plates of 200 subjects in two panes of 100 each.

1879 **Unwmk.**	**Engr.**	***Perf. 12***	
J1 D1 1c **brown**		90.00	14.00
pale brown		90.00	14.00
deep brown		90.00	14.00
Never hinged		260.00	
Block of 4		400.00	75.00
P# block of 10, Impt.		*1,700.*	

Earliest documented use: July 5, 1879.

J2 D1 2c **brown**	425.00	25.00
pale brown	425.00	25.00
Never hinged	1,050.	
Block of 4	1,800.	—

Earliest documented use: July 27, 1879.

J3 D1 3c **brown**	100.00	6.00
pale brown	100.00	6.00
deep brown	100.00	6.00
yellowish brown	*110.00*	7.00
Never hinged	280.00	
Block of 4	440.00	32.50
P# block of 10, Impt.	*1,750.*	

Earliest documented use: June 18, 1879.

J4 D1 5c **brown**	800.00	70.00
pale brown	800.00	70.00
deep brown	800.00	70.00
Never hinged	1,950.	
Block of 4	3,400.	—

Earliest documented use: July 7, 1879.

J5 D1 10c **brown,** *Sept. 19*	900.00	70.00
pale brown	900.00	70.00
deep brown	900.00	70.00
Never hinged	*2,500.*	
Block of 4	4,000.	—
a. Imperf., pair	*2,500.*	

Earliest documented use: Oct. 7, 1879.

J6 D1 30c **brown,** *Sept. 19*	350.00	65.00
pale brown	350.00	65.00
Never hinged	800.00	
Block of 4	1,500.	—
P# block of 10, Impt.	*4,500.*	
J7 D1 50c **brown,** *Sept. 19*	600.00	90.00
pale brown	600.00	90.00
Never hinged	1,600.	
Block of 4	2,750.	—
P# block of 10, Impt.	*12,000.*	
Nos. J1-J7 (7)	3,265.	340.00

SPECIAL PRINTING

1879 **Unwmk.**	***Perf. 12***	

Soft porous paper

Printed by the American Bank Note Co.

J8 D1 1c deep brown *(9,420)*	*16,000.*	
Never hinged	—	
No gum	*6,500.*	
J9 D1 2c deep brown *(1,361)*	*15,000.*	
No gum	*6,000.*	
J10 D1 3c deep brown *(436)*	*20,000.*	
No gum	*8,000.*	
J11 D1 5c deep brown *(249)*	*13,000.*	
No gum	*5,250.*	
J12 D1 10c deep brown *(174)*	*6,500.*	
No gum	*2,750.*	
J13 D1 30c deep brown *(179)*	*7,000.*	
No gum	*3,000.*	
J14 D1 50c deep brown *(179)*	*7,000.*	
No gum	*3,000.*	

Identifying characteristics for the final 8,920 examples of No. J8 delivered to the Post Office are unknown, and it is likely that these were regular issue stamps (No. J1) that were then sold as special printings.

1884 **Unwmk.**	***Perf. 12***	
J15 D1 1c **red brown**	70.00	7.00
pale red brown	70.00	7.00
deep red brown	70.00	7.00
Never hinged	190.00	
Block of 4	325.00	45.00
P# block of 10, Impt.	*1,400.*	
J16 D1 2c **red brown**	80.00	6.00
pale red brown	80.00	6.00
deep red brown	80.00	6.00
Never hinged	225.00	
Block of 4	360.00	37.50
P# block of 10, Impt.	*1,550.*	
J17 D1 3c **red brown**	1,050.	350.00
deep red brown	1,050.	350.00
Never hinged	2,500.	
Block of 4	4,750.	—
J18 D1 5c **red brown**	550.00	50.00
pale red brown	550.00	50.00
deep red brown	550.00	50.00
Never hinged	1,300.	
Block of 4	2,500.	—
J19 D1 10c **red brown**	550.00	35.00
deep red brown	550.00	35.00
Never hinged	1,300.	
Block of 4	2,500.	—
P# block of 10, Impt.	*17,000.*	
J20 D1 30c **red brown**	190.00	70.00
deep red brown	190.00	70.00
Never hinged	475.00	
Block of 4	900.00	450.00
P# block of 10, Impt.	*3,250.*	
Never hinged	*6,500.*	
J21 D1 50c **red brown**	1,800.	250.00
Never hinged	3,750.	
Block of 4	7,750.	—

1891 **Unwmk.**	***Perf. 12***	
J22 D1 1c **bright claret**	30.00	2.00
light claret	30.00	2.00
dark claret	30.00	2.00
Never hinged	85.00	
Block of 4	140.00	11.00
P# block of 10, Impt.	*650.00*	
Never hinged	*2,000.*	
J23 D1 2c **bright claret**	32.50	2.00
light claret	32.50	2.00
dark claret	32.50	2.00
Never hinged	90.00	

Block of 4 150.00 11.00
P# block of 10, Impt. *675.00*
J24 D1 3c **bright claret** 67.50 16.00
dark claret 67.50 16.00
Never hinged 180.00
Block of 4 325.00 80.00
P# block of 10, Impt. *1,050.*
Never hinged —
J25 D1 5c **bright claret** 100.00 16.00
light claret 100.00 16.00
dark claret 100.00 16.00
Never hinged 290.00
Block of 4 450.00 80.00
P# block of 10, Impt. *1,450.*
J26 D1 10c **bright claret** 165.00 30.00
light claret 165.00 30.00
Never hinged 500.00
Block of 4 725.00 190.00
P# block of 10, Impt. *2,450.*
J27 D1 30c **bright claret** 575.00 225.00
Never hinged 1,700.
Block of 4 2,450. —
P# block of 10, Impt. *8,250.*
Never hinged 11,000.
J28 D1 50c **bright claret** 600.00 225.00
dark claret 600.00 225.00
Never hinged 1,750.
Block of 4 2,600. —
P# block of 10, Impt. *10,000.*
Nos. J22-J28 (7) 1,570. 516.00

See Die and Plate Proofs for imperfs. on stamp paper.

The color on Nos. J29-J44 will run when immersed in water. Extreme caution is advised.

D2

Printed by the Bureau of Engraving and Printing.

1894 **Unwmk.** ***Perf. 12***

J29 D2 1c **vermilion,** *Aug. 14, 1894* 2,250. 725.
pale vermilion 2,250. 725.
Never hinged *5,750.*
Block of 4 *10,000.* *3,250.*
P# strip of 3, Impt. 8,750.
P# block of 6, Impt. *13,000.*

Only one plate block of No. J29 exists in private hands. It has VG-F centering and small faults, and it is valued thus.

Earliest documented use: Nov. 15, 1894.

J30 D2 2c **vermilion,** *July 20, 1894* 775. 350.
deep vermilion 775. 350.
Never hinged 1,900.
Block of 4 3,500.
P# strip of 3, Impt. 3,250.
P# block of 6, Impt. *6,750.*
Never hinged *19,000.*

Earliest documented use: July 31, 1894.

1894-95

J31 D2 1c **deep claret** 72.50 12.00
claret 72.50 12.00
lake 72.50 12.00
Never hinged 260.00
Block of 4 325.00 65.00
P# strip of 3, Impt. 300.00
P# block of 6, Impt. 650.00
Never hinged 1,850.
b. Vertical pair, imperf. horiz. —

Earliest documented use: Oct. 6, 1894.

See Die and Plate Proofs for imperf. on stamp paper.

J32 D2 2c **deep claret** 62.50 10.00
claret 62.50 10.00
lake 62.50 10.00
Never hinged 240.00
Block of 4 290.00 65.00
P# strip of 3, Impt. 275.00
P# block of 6, Impt. 600.00
Never hinged 1,700.

Earliest documented use: Oct. 30, 1894.

J33 D2 3c **deep claret,** *Apr. 27, 1895* 200.00 50.00
lake 200.00 50.00
Never hinged 575.00
Block of 4 875.00 —
P# strip of 3, Impt. 850.00
P# block of 6, Impt. 2,650.
Never hinged *4,750.*
J34 D2 5c **deep claret,** *Apr. 27, 1895* 300.00 55.00
claret 300.00 55.00
Never hinged 850.00
Block of 4 1,300. —
P# strip of 3, Impt. 1,250.
P# block of 6, Impt. 3,250.
Never hinged *7,750.*
J35 D2 10c **deep claret,** *Sept. 24, 1894* 350.00 40.00
Never hinged 1,000.
Block of 4 1,550. —
P# strip of 3, Impt. 1,500.
P# block of 6, Impt. 4,000.
Never hinged *7,500.*
J36 D2 30c **deep claret,** *Apr. 27, 1895* 550.00 250.00
claret 550.00 250.00
Never hinged 1,250.
Block of 4 2,500. —
P# strip of 3, Impt. 2,250.
P# block of 6, Impt. 4,500.
Never hinged 8,750.
a. 30c **carmine** 675.00 275.00
Never hinged 1,600.
Block of 4 3,250. —
P# strip of 3, Impt. 3,250.
P# block of 6, Impt. 5,500.
Never hinged *11,000.*
b. 30c **pale rose** 450.00 200.00
Never hinged 1,100.
Block of 4 2,000. —
P# strip of 3, Impt. 1,850.
P# block of 6, Impt. 4,000.
Never hinged *8,500.*
J37 D2 50c **deep claret,** *Apr. 27, 1895* 1,800. 800.00
Never hinged 4,250.
Block of 4 8,000. —
P# strip of 3, Impt. 7,500.
P# block of 6, Impt. *14,000.*
a. 50c **pale rose** 1,600. 725.00
Never hinged 3,750.
Block of 4 7,000. —
P# strip of 3, Impt. 6,500.
P# block of 6, Impt. *12,000.*

Shades are numerous in the 1894 and later issues.

Wmk. 191 Horizontally or Vertically

1895-97 ***Perf. 12***

J38 D2 1c **deep claret,** *Aug. 29, 1895* 13.50 1.00
claret 13.50 1.00
carmine 13.50 1.00
lake 13.50 1.00
Never hinged 40.00
Block of 4 57.50 8.50
P# strip of 3, Impt. 60.00
Never hinged 175.00
P# block of 6, Impt. 270.00
Never hinged 450.00
J39 D2 2c **deep claret,** *Sept. 14, 1895* 13.50 1.00
claret 13.50 1.00
carmine 13.50 1.00
lake 13.50 1.00
Never hinged 40.00
Block of 4 57.50 8.50
P# strip of 3, Impt. 60.00
Never hinged 175.00
P# block of 6, Impt. 270.00
Never hinged 450.00
Double transfer —

In October, 1895, the Postmaster at Jefferson, Iowa, surcharged a few 2 cent stamps with the words "Due I cent" in black on each side, subsequently dividing the stamps vertically and using each half as a 1 cent stamp. Twenty of these were used. Value, tied across cut, on cover, $6,000.

J40 D2 3c **deep claret,** *Oct. 30, 1895* 100.00 5.00
claret 100.00 5.00
rose red 100.00 5.00
carmine 100.00 5.00
Never hinged 225.00
Block of 4 425.00 27.50
P# strip of 3, Impt. 425.00
Never hinged 1,000.
P# block of 6, Impt. 950.00
Never hinged 1,750.
J41 D2 5c **deep claret,** *Oct. 15, 1895* 110.00 5.00
claret 110.00 5.00
carmine rose 110.00 5.00
Never hinged 280.00
Block of 4 475.00 27.50
P# strip of 3, Impt. 450.00
Never hinged 1,050.
P# block of 6, Impt. 1,000.
Never hinged 2,000.
J42 D2 10c **deep claret,** *Sept. 14, 1895* 110.00 7.50
claret 110.00 7.50
carmine 110.00 7.50
lake 110.00 7.50
Never hinged 280.00
Block of 4 475.00 47.50
P# strip of 3, Impt. 450.00
Never hinged 1,050.
P# block of 6, Impt. 1,000.
Never hinged 2,000.
J43 D2 30c **deep claret,** *Aug. 21, 1897* 600.00 75.00
claret 600.00 75.00
Never hinged 1,500.
Block of 4 2,750. 450.00
P# strip of 3, Impt. 2,500.
P# block of 6, Impt. *6,000.*
J44 D2 50c **deep claret,** *Mar. 17, 1896* 375.00 60.00
claret 375.00 60.00
Never hinged 925.00
Block of 4 1,700. 275.00
P# strip of 3, Impt. 1,750.
P# block of 6, Impt. *4,500.* —
Nos. J38-J44 (7) 1,322. 154.50

Plates of 400 subjects in four panes of 100.

1910-12 **Wmk. 190** ***Perf. 12***

J45 D2 1c **deep claret,** *Dec., 1910* 40.00 5.00
Never hinged 115.00
Block of 4 (2 or 3mm spacing) 220.00 20.00
P# block of 6, Impt. & star 575.00
Never hinged 950.00
a. 1c **rose carmine** 35.00 5.00
Never hinged 105.00
Block of 4 (2 or 3mm spacing) 180.00 20.00
P# block of 6, Impt. & star 500.00
Never hinged 850.00
J46 D2 2c **deep claret,** *Nov. 25, 1910* 40.00 2.00
lake 40.00 2.00
Never hinged 115.00
Block of 4 (2 or 3mm spacing) 220.00 7.50
P# block of 6, Impt. & star 550.00 —
Never hinged 925.00
P# block of 6 600.00
Never hinged 1,000.
a. 2c **rose carmine** 35.00 2.00
Never hinged 105.00
Block of 4 (2 or 3mm spacing) 180.00 7.50
P# block of 6, Impt. & star 500.00 —
Never hinged 850.00
P# block of 6 550.00
Never hinged 900.00
Double transfer — —
J47 D2 3c **deep claret,** *Aug. 31, 1910* 625.00 60.00
lake 625.00 60.00
Never hinged 1,600.
Block of 4 (2 or 3mm spacing) 2,750. 325.00
P# block of 6, Impt. & star 6,000.
Never hinged *11,500.*
J48 D2 5c **deep claret,** *Aug. 31, 1910* 120.00 12.00
Never hinged 275.00
a. 5c **rose carmine** 120.00 12.00
Never hinged 275.00
Block of 4 (2 or 3mm spacing) 500.00 60.00
P# block of 6, Impt. & star 1,100.
Never hinged *2,000.*
J49 D2 10c **deep claret,** *Aug. 31, 1910* 125.00 20.00
Never hinged 280.00
Block of 4 (2 or 3mm spacing) 550.00 120.00
P# block of 6, Impt. & star 1,400.
a. 10c **rose carmine** 125.00 20.00
Never hinged 280.00
J50 D2 50c **deep claret,** *Sept. 23, 1912* 1,100. 200.00
Never hinged 2,900.
Block of 4 (2 or 3mm spacing) 4,750. *1,150.*
P# block of 6, Impt. & star *9,500.*
a. 50c **rose carmine** 1,150. 190.00
Never hinged *3,000.*

1914 ***Perf. 10***

J52 D2 1c **carmine lake** 80.00 15.00
deep carmine lake 80.00 15.00
Never hinged 220.00
Block of 4 (2 or 3mm spacing) 360.00 80.00
P# block of 6, Impt. & star 700.00 —
Never hinged 1,700.
a. 1c **dull rose** 85.00 15.00
Never hinged 230.00
Block of 4 (2 or 3mm spacing) 375.00 85.00
P# block of 6, Impt. & star 750.00 —
Never hinged 1,750.
J53 D2 2c **carmine lake** 62.50 1.00
Never hinged 170.00
Block of 4 275.00 8.00
P# block of 6 600.00 —
Never hinged 1,200.
a. 2c **dull rose** 67.50 2.00
Never hinged 180.00
Block of 4 15.00
b. 2c **vermilion** 67.50 2.00
Never hinged 180.00
Block of 4 300.00 14.00
P# block of 6 625.00 —
Never hinged 1,300.
J54 D2 3c **carmine lake** 1,050. 75.00
Never hinged 3,000.
Block of 4 (2 or 3mm spacing) 4,750. —
P# block of 6, Impt. & star *9,000.* —
a. 3c **dull rose** 1,000. 75.00
Never hinged 2,900.
Block of 4 (2 or 3mm spacing) 4,500. —
P# block of 6, Impt. & star *8,750.* —
J55 D2 5c **carmine lake** 50.00 6.00
Never hinged 140.00
Block of 4 (2 or 3mm spacing) 220.00 30.00
P# block of 6, Impt. & star 425.00 —
Never hinged 1,100.
a. 5c **dull rose** 45.00 4.00
carmine rose 45.00 4.00
Never hinged 130.00
deep claret — —
Block of 4 (2 or 3mm spacing) 200.00 20.00
P# block of 6, Impt. & star 400.00 —
Never hinged 1,050.
J56 D2 10c **carmine lake** 75.00 4.00
Never hinged 200.00
Block of 4 (2 or 3mm spacing) 340.00 22.50
P# block of 6, Impt. & star 800.00 —
a. 10c **dull rose** 80.00 5.00
carmine rose 80.00 5.00
Never hinged 210.00
Block of 4 (2 or 3mm spacing) 360.00 25.00
P# block of 6, Impt. & star 900.00 —
Never hinged 1,650.
J57 D2 30c **carmine lake** 225.00 55.00
Never hinged 525.00
Block of 4 (2 or 3mm spacing) 1,000. 325.00
P# block of 6, Impt. & star 2,750. —
J58 D2 50c **carmine lake** *11,500.* 1,700.
Never hinged *21,000.*
Precanceled 750.00
Block of 4 (2 or 3mm spacing) *50,000.* *7,500.*
P# block of 6, Impt. & star *90,000.*

No. J58 unused is valued in the grade of fine to very fine.

Only one plate block of No. J58 exists in private hands. It has full top selvage with perforations cutting into the design at top, and is valued thus.

No. J58, precanceled, was used at Buffalo (normal, inverted) and Chicago (normal, inverted, double, double inverted).

1916 Unwmk. *Perf. 10*

Item	Unused	Used
J59 D2 1c **rose**	4,000.	750.00
Never hinged	9,000.	
Block of 4 (2 or 3mm spacing)	19,000.	*3,750.*
P# block of 6, Impt. & star	*30,000.*	
Experimental bureau precancel, New Orleans		*400.00*
J60 D2 2c **rose**	250.00	75.00
Never hinged	625.00	
Block of 4	1,100.	375.00
P# block of 6	2,000.	—
Experimental bureau precancel, New Orleans		50.00

1917 Unwmk. *Perf. 11*

Item	Unused	Used
J61 D2 1c **carmine rose**	2.75	.25
Never hinged	9.00	
dull rose	5.00	.25
Never hinged	15.00	
a. 1c **rose red**	2.75	.25
Never hinged	9.00	
b. 1c **deep claret**	2.75	.25
claret brown	2.75	.25
Never hinged	9.00	
Block of 4 (2 or 3mm spacing)	12.00	2.00
Never hinged	42.50	
P# block of 6, Impt. & star	150.00	—
Never hinged	350.00	
P# block of 6	45.00	—
Never hinged	100.00	
c. Vert. pair, imperf. horiz.	—	
J62 D2 2c **carmine rose**	2.75	.25
Never hinged	9.00	
a. 2c **rose red**	2.75	.25
Never hinged	9.00	
b. 2c **deep claret**	2.75	.25
claret brown	2.75	1.10
Never hinged	9.00	
Block of 4	12.00	2.00
Never hinged	42.50	
P# block of 6	55.00	—
Never hinged	125.00	
Double transfer	—	—
J63 D2 3c **carmine rose**	13.50	.80
Never hinged	35.00	
a. 3c **rose red**	13.50	.80
Never hinged	35.00	
b. 3c **deep claret**	13.50	.80
claret brown	13.50	.80
Never hinged	35.00	
Block of 4 (2 or 3mm spacing)	60.00	5.00
Never hinged	155.00	
P# block of 6, Impt. & star	150.00	—
Never hinged	300.00	
P# block of 6	125.00	—
Never hinged	275.00	
J64 D2 5c **carmine**	11.00	.80
carmine rose	11.00	.80
Never hinged	32.50	
a. 5c **rose red**	11.00	.80
Never hinged	32.50	
b. 5c **deep claret**	11.00	.80
claret brown	11.00	.80
Never hinged	32.50	
Block of 4 (2 or 3mm spacing)	47.50	6.00
Never hinged	140.00	
P# block of 6, Impt. & star	125.00	—
Never hinged	275.00	
P# block of 6	105.00	—
Never hinged	250.00	
J65 D2 10c **carmine rose**	22.50	1.00
Never hinged	65.00	
a. 10c **rose red**	22.50	1.00
Never hinged	65.00	
b. 10c **deep claret**	22.50	1.00
claret brown	22.50	1.00
Never hinged	65.00	
Block of 4 (2 or 3mm spacing)	100.00	7.50
Never hinged	300.00	
P# block of 6, Impt. & star	220.00	—
Never hinged	475.00	
P# block of 6	240.00	—
Never hinged	525.00	
Double transfer		—
J66 D2 30c **carmine rose**	80.00	2.00
Never hinged	220.00	
a. 30c **deep claret**	80.00	2.00
claret brown	80.00	2.00
Never hinged	220.00	
Block of 4 (2 or 3mm spacing)	350.00	14.00
Never hinged	950.00	
P# block of 6, Impt. & star	700.00	—
Never hinged	*1,500.*	
P# block of 6	750.00	—
Never hinged	*1,650.*	
b. As "a," perf 10 at top, precanceled		*21,000.*

No. J66b is valued with small faults and fine centering, as the two recorded examples are in this condition and grade. One is precanceled St. Louis, Mo., and the other is precanceled Minneapolis, Minn.

Item	Unused	Used
J67 D2 50c **carmine rose**	140.00	1.00
Never hinged	325.00	
a. 50c **rose red**	140.00	1.00
Never hinged	325.00	
b. 50c **deep claret**	140.00	1.00
claret brown	140.00	1.00
Never hinged	325.00	
Block of 4 (2 or 3mm spacing)	600.00	7.50
Never hinged	1,400.	
P# block of 6, Impt. & star	1,100.	—
Never hinged	2,400.	
P# block of 6	1,200.	—

1925, Apr. 13

Item	Unused	Used
J68 D2 ½c **dull red**	1.00	.25
Never hinged	1.75	
Block of 4	4.00	1.50
Never hinged	7.00	
P# block of 6	12.50	—
Never hinged	17.50	

D3

D4

1930 Unwmk. *Perf. 11*

Design measures 19x22mm

Item	Unused	Used
J69 D3 ½c **carmine**	4.25	1.90
Never hinged	9.50	
P# block of 6	50.00	—
Never hinged	80.00	
J70 D3 1c **carmine**	2.75	.35
Never hinged	6.25	
P# block of 6	55.00	—
Never hinged	100.00	
J71 D3 2c **carmine**	3.75	.35
Never hinged	8.50	
P# block of 6	50.00	—
Never hinged	95.00	
J72 D3 3c **carmine**	20.00	2.75
Never hinged	47.50	
P# block of 6	300.00	—
Never hinged	500.00	
J73 D3 5c **carmine**	18.00	5.00
Never hinged	42.50	
P# block of 6	300.00	—
Never hinged	500.00	
J74 D3 10c **carmine**	42.50	2.00
Never hinged	95.00	
P# block of 6	550.00	—
Never hinged	1,000.	
J75 D3 30c **carmine**	125.00	4.00
Never hinged	275.00	
P# block of 6	1,150.	—
Never hinged	*2,250.*	
J76 D3 50c **carmine**	175.00	2.00
Never hinged	375.00	
P# block of 6	1,750.	—
Never hinged	*3,250.*	

Design measures 22x19mm

Item	Unused	Used
J77 D4 $1 **carmine**	32.50	.35
Never hinged	65.00	
P# block of 6	250.00	—
Never hinged	475.00	
a. $1 **scarlet**	27.50	.35
Never hinged	55.00	
P# block of 6	275.00	—
Never hinged	500.00	
J78 D4 $5 **dull carmine,** wet printing	37.50	.35
Never hinged	85.00	
P# block of 6	300.00	—
Never hinged	600.00	
a. **scarlet,** wet printing	32.50	.35
Never hinged	70.00	
P# block of 6	300.00	—
Never hinged	600.00	
b. $5 **scarlet,** dry printing	32.50	.35
Never hinged	70.00	
P# block of 6	260.00	—
Never hinged	525.00	

See note on Wet and Dry Printings following No. 1029.

Type of 1930-31 Issue

Rotary Press Printing

Ordinary and Electric Eye Plates

Design measures 19x22½mm

1931 Unwmk. *Perf. 11x10½*

Item	Unused	Used
J79 D3 ½c **dull carmine**	.90	.25
Never hinged	1.30	
P# block of 4	20.00	—
Never hinged	30.00	
a. ½c **scarlet**	.90	.25
Never hinged	1.30	
J80 D3 1c **dull carmine,** wet printing	.25	.25
Never hinged	.30	
P# block of 4	1.50	—
Never hinged	2.25	
a. 1c **scarlet,** wet printing	.25	.25
Never hinged	.30	
P# block of 4	1.75	—
Never hinged	2.60	
Pair with full vertical gutter between	—	
b. 1c **scarlet,** dry printing	.25	.25
Never hinged	.30	
P# block of 4 (#25635, 25636)	1.50	—
Never hinged	2.25	
J81 D3 2c **dull carmine,** wet printing	.25	.25
Never hinged	.30	
P# block of 4	1.50	—
Never hinged	2.25	
a. 2c **scarlet,** wet printing	.25	.25
Never hinged	.30	
P# block of 4	2.00	—
Never hinged	3.00	
b. 2c **scarlet,** dry printing	.25	.25
Never hinged	.30	
P# block of 4 (#25637, 25638)	1.50	—
Never hinged	2.25	
J82 D3 3c **dull carmine,** wet printing	.25	.25
Never hinged	.40	
P# block of 4	2.25	—
Never hinged	3.40	
a. 3c **scarlet,** wet printing	.30	.25
Never hinged	.45	
P# block of 4	2.50	—
Never hinged	3.75	
b. 3c **scarlet,** dry printing	.25	.25
Never hinged	.40	
P# block of 4 (#25641, 25642)	2.25	—
Never hinged	3.40	
J83 D3 5c **dull carmine,** wet printing	.40	.25
Never hinged	.60	
P# block of 4	3.00	—
Never hinged	4.50	
a. 5c **scarlet,** wet printing	.50	.25
Never hinged	.75	
P# block of 4	3.50	—
Never hinged	5.25	
b. 5c **scarlet,** dry printing	.40	.25
Never hinged	.60	
P# block of 4 (#25643, 25644)	3.00	—
Never hinged	4.50	
J84 D3 10c **dull carmine,** wet printing	1.10	.25
Never hinged	1.80	
P# block of 4	6.50	—
Never hinged	9.75	
a. 10c **scarlet,** wet printing	1.25	.25
Never hinged	1.90	
P# block of 4	7.00	—
Never hinged	10.50	
b. 10c **scarlet,** dry printing	1.10	.25
Never hinged	1.80	
P# block of 4 (#25645, 25646)	6.50	—
Never hinged	9.75	
J85 D3 30c **dull carmine**	7.50	.25
Never hinged	11.50	
P# block of 4	35.00	—
Never hinged	60.00	
a. 30c **scarlet**	7.50	.25
Never hinged	11.50	
J86 D3 50c **dull carmine**	9.00	.25
Never hinged	15.00	
P# block of 4	52.50	—
Never hinged	85.00	
a. 50c **scarlet**	9.00	.25
Never hinged	15.00	

Alan E. Cohen
Dealer in
High Grade Stamps

Visit our website today.
www.alanecohen.com
P. O. Box 929
New York, NY 10025
212-280-7865
e-mail: alanecohen@mindspring.com

Design measures 22½x19mm

1956 *Perf. 10½x11*

J87 D4 $1 **scarlet** 30.00 .25
Never hinged 52.50
P# block of 4 190.00 —
Never hinged 290.00
Nos. J79-J87 (1) 30.00 .25

Catalogue values for unused stamps in this section, from this point to the end, are for Never Hinged items.

D5

Denominations added in black by rubber plates in an operation similar to precanceling.

Rotary Press Printing

1959, June 19 **Unwmk.** *Perf. 11x10½*

Denomination in Black

J88 D5 ½c **carmine rose** 1.50 1.10
P# block of 4 120.00 —
J89 D5 1c **carmine rose**, shiny gum .25 .25
P# block of 4 .50 —
Dull gum .25
P# block of 4 6.50
a. Denomination omitted 150.00
P# block of 4 — —
b. Pair, one without "1 CENT" 350.00
J90 D5 2c **carmine rose**, shiny gum .25 .25
P# block of 4 .55 —
Wide spacing, pair *120.00*
Dull gum .40
P# block of 4 12.50
J91 D5 3c **carmine rose**, shiny gum .25 .25
P# block of 4 .60 —
Dull gum .50
P# block of 4 17.50
a. Pair, one without "3 CENTS" *550.00*
J92 D5 4c **carmine rose** .25 .25
P# block of 4 1.10 —
Wide spacing, pair *190.00*
J93 D5 5c **carmine rose**, shiny gum .25 .25
P# block of 4 1.10 —
Dull gum .45
P# block of 4 8.00
a. Pair, one without "5 CENTS" *1,100.*
J94 D5 6c **carmine rose**, shiny gum .25 .25
P# block of 4 1.10 —
Pair with full vertical gutter between —
Dull gum *70.00*
P# block of 4 *1,250.*
a. Pair, one without "6 CENTS" *700.00*
J95 D5 7c **carmine rose**, shiny gum .25 .25
P# block of 4 1.10 —
Wide spacing, pair *120.00*
Dull gum *550.00*
P# block of 4 *3,500.*
J96 D5 8c **carmine rose** .25 .25
P# block of 4 1.10 —
Wide spacing, pair *120.00*
a. Pair, one without "8 CENTS" *750.00*
J97 D5 10c **carmine rose**, shiny gum .25 .25
P# block of 4 1.10 —
Wide spacing, pair —
Dull gum .35
P# block of 4 8.00
J98 D5 30c **carmine rose**, shiny gum .70 .25
P# block of 4 3.25 —
Dull gum 1.00
P# block of 4 16.00
J99 D5 50c **carmine rose**, shiny gum 1.10 .25
P# block of 4 5.00 —
Dull gum 1.75
P# block of 4 22.50

Straight Numeral Outlined in Black

J100 D5 $1 **carmine rose, shiny gum** 2.00 .25
P# block of 4 8.50 —
Dull gum 2.50
P# block of 4 22.50
J101 D5 $5 **carmine rose**, shiny gum 9.00 .25
P# block of 4 37.50 —
Dull gum 11.00
P# block of 4 55.00 —
Nos. J88-J101 (14) 16.55 4.35

All single stamps with denomination omitted are catalogued as No. J89a.

Rotary Press Printing

1978-85 **Denomination in Black** *Perf. 11x10½*

J102 D5 11c **carmine rose,** *Jan. 3, 1978* .25 .25
P# block of 4 1.75 —
J103 D5 13c **carmine rose,** *Jan. 3, 1978* .25 .25
P# block of 4 1.75 —
J104 D5 17c **carmine rose,** *June 10, 1985* .40 .35
P# block of 4 22.50 —

U.S. POSTAL AGENCY IN CHINA

Postage stamps of the 1917-19 U.S. series (then current) were issued to the U.S. Postal Agency, Shanghai, China, surcharged at double the original value of the stamps.

These stamps were intended for sale at Shanghai at their surcharged value in local currency, valid for prepayment on mail despatched from the U.S. Postal Agency at Shanghai to addresses in the U.S.

Stamps were first issued May 24, 1919, and were placed on sale at Shanghai on July 1, 1919. These stamps were not issued to postmasters in the U.S. The Shanghai post office, according to the U.S.P.O. Bulletin, was closed in December 1922. The stamps were on sale at the Philatelic Agency in Washington, D.C. for a short time after that.

Italicized numbers in parentheses indicate quantities shipped to the postal agency in Shanghai and to the Washington Philatelic Agency. In the case of Nos. K17-K18, the numbers are the quantity locally overprinted. All Nos. K16a, K17 and K18 are believed to have been sold. The final disposition of remainders of the others is not known. Neither the records of the Shanghai Postal Agency nor the records of the Washington Philatelic Agency have been located at this time. Authority for quantities shipped is the research of Joseph M. Napp, who in turn benefitted by the research of Meyer Tuchinsky.

The cancellations of the China office included "U.S. Postal Agency Shanghai China", "U.S. Pos. Service Shanghai China" duplexes, and the Shanghai parcel post roller cancel. Used stamps are valued bearing legible cancels showing Chinese origin.

United States Stamps #498-499, 502-504, 506-510, 512, 514-518 Surcharged in Black or Red (Nos. K7, K16)

1919 **Unwmk.** *Perf. 11*

K1 A140 2c on 1c **green** *(355,000)* 22.50 *70.00*
Never hinged 67.50
Block of 4 100.00 *375.00*
P# block of 6 300.00 —
Never hinged 600.00
Double transfer 40.00
Never hinged 105.00

Earliest documented use: July 2, 1919.

K2 A140 4c on 2c **rose**, type I *(355,000)* 22.50 *70.00*
Never hinged 67.50
Block of 4 100.00 *375.00*
P# block of 6 300.00 —
Never hinged 600.00

Earliest documented use: July 2, 1919.

K3 A140 6c on 3c **violet**, type II, *(113,000)* 55.00 *140.00*
Never hinged 140.00
Block of 4 240.00 *675.00*
P# block of 6 675.00 —
Never hinged 1,150.
K4 A140 8c on 4c **brown** *(113,000)* 55.00 *140.00*
Never hinged 140.00
Block of 4 240.00 *675.00*
P# block of 6 675.00 —
Never hinged 1,150.
K5 A140 10c on 5c **blue** *(113,000)* 60.00 *140.00*
Never hinged 160.00
Block of 4 260.00 *675.00*
P# block of 6 600.00
Never hinged 1,100.
K6 A140 12c on 6c **red orange** *(113,000)* 80.00 *210.00*
Never hinged 210.00
Block of 4 360.00 *1,100.*
P# block of 6 800.00
Never hinged *1,500.*
K7 A140 14c on 7c **black** *(113,000)* 82.50 *210.00*
Never hinged 215.00
Block of 4 380.00 *1,100.*
P# block of 6 1,050.
Never hinged *1,650.*
K8 A148 16c on 8c **olive bister** *(13,000)* 65.00 *160.00*
Never hinged 170.00
Block of 4 280.00 *850.00*
P# block of 6 625.00
Never hinged 1,150.
a. 16c on 8c **olive green** *(100,000)* 55.00 *140.00*
Never hinged 150.00
Block of 4 240.00 *750.00*
P# block of 6 575.00
Never hinged 1,000.
K9 A148 18c on 9c **salmon red** *(113,000)* 60.00 *175.00*
Never hinged 150.00
Block of 4 260.00 *850.00*
P# block of 6 700.00
Never hinged 1,200.
K10 A148 20c on 10c **orange yellow** *(113,000)* 55.00 *140.00*
Never hinged 140.00
Block of 4 240.00 *675.00*
P# block of 6 725.00
Never hinged 1,300.
K11 A148 24c on 12c **brown carmine** *(50,000)* 75.00 *160.00*
Never hinged 190.00
Block of 4 325.00 *750.00*
P# block of 6 1,000.
Never hinged 1,750.
a. 24c on 12c **claret brown** *(8,000)* 110.00 *240.00*
Never hinged 275.00
Block of 4 475.00 *1,150.*
P# block of 6 1,200.
Never hinged *2,100.*
K12 A148 30c on 15c **gray** *(58,000)* 82.50 *230.00*
Never hinged 200.00
Block of 4 360.00 —
P# block of 6 1,150.
Never hinged *2,000.*
K13 A148 40c on 20c **deep ultramarine** *(58,000)* 120.00 *325.00*
Never hinged 300.00
Block of 4 525.00 *1,800.*
P# block of 6 1,300.
Never hinged *2,250.*
K14 A148 60c on 30c **orange red** *(58,000)* 110.00 *275.00*
Never hinged 260.00
Block of 4 475.00 *1,500.*
P# block of 6 1,050.
Never hinged *1,800.*
K15 A148 $1 on 50c **light violet** *(14,000)* 550.00 *1,000.*
Never hinged 1,200.
Block of 4 2,400. *6,250.*
P# block of 6 *17,500.*
K16 A148 $2 on $1 **violet brown** *(13,800)* 425.00 *750.00*
Never hinged 925.00
Block of 4 1,900. *4,900.*
Margin block of 4, arrow, right or left 2,000.
P# block of 6 *7,000.*
Never hinged *11,000.*
a. Double surcharge *(200)* *10,500.* *12,500.*
Never hinged *17,500.*
Block of 4 *45,000.*
Nos. K1-K16 (16) 1,920. *4,195.*

Fake surcharges exist, but most are rather crudely made.

United States Stamps Nos. 498 and 528B Locally Surcharged

1922, July 3

K17 A140 2c on 1c **green** (*10,000*)	100.00	*225.00*
Never hinged	225.00	
Block of 4	425.00	*1,050.*
P# block of 6	850.00	
Never hinged	1,750.	
K18 A140 4c on 2c **carmine,** type VII (*10,000*)	90.00	*200.00*
Never hinged	210.00	
Block of 4	400.00	*900.00*
P# block of 6	800.00	
Never hinged	1,400.	
a. "SHANGHAI" omitted	*7,500.*	
b. "CHINA" only	*15,000.*	

OFFICIAL STAMPS

The original official stamps were authorized by Act of Congress, approved March 3, 1873, abolishing the franking privilege. Stamps for each executive government department were issued July 1, 1873.

Penalty franks were first authorized in 1877, and their expanded use after 1879 reduced the need for official stamps, the use of which was finally abolished on July 5, 1884.

DESIGNS. Stamps for departments other than the Post Office picture the same busts used in the regular postage issue: 1c Franklin, 2c Jackson, 3c Washington, 6c Lincoln, 7c Stanton, 10c Jefferson, 12c Clay, 15c Webster, 24c Scott, 30c Hamilton, and 90c Perry. William H. Seward appears on the $2, $5, $10 and $20.

Designs of the various denominations are not identical, but resemble those illustrated.

PLATES. Plates of 200 subjects in two panes of 100 were used for Post Office Department 1c, 3c, 6c; Treasury Department 1c, 2c, 3c, and War Department 2c, 3c. Plates of 10 subjects were used for State Department $2, $5, $10 and $20. Plates of 100 subjects were used for all other Official stamps up to No. O120.

CANCELLATIONS. Odd or Town cancellations on Departmental stamps are relatively much scarcer than those appearing on the general issues of the same period. Town cancellations, especially on the 1873 issue, are scarce. The "Kicking Mule" cancellation is found used on stamps of the War Department and has also been seen on some stamps of the other Departments. Black is usual.

AGRICULTURE

Printed by the Continental Bank Note Co.

O1

Thin Hard Paper

1873 Engr. Unwmk. *Perf. 12*

O1 O1 1c **yellow**	300.00	*200.00*
Never hinged	650.00	
No gum	170.00	
On wrapper		*2,500.*
Block of 4	1,250.	
Ribbed paper	340.00	225.00
Cancellations		
Magenta		+7.50
Violet		+7.50
Blue		+5.00
Red		+50.00
Town		+7.50
Fort		+150.00
O2 O1 2c **yellow**	275.00	100.00
Never hinged	575.00	
No gum	110.00	
On cover		*4,000.*
Block of 4	1,050.	
P# block of 12	—	
Ribbed paper	240.00	110.00
Cancellations		
Blue		+3.00
Violet		+3.00
Red		+15.00
Magenta		+5.00
Town		+5.00
O3 O1 3c **yellow**	225.00	17.50
Never hinged	475.00	
No gum	85.00	
On cover		*900.00*
Block of 4	1,000.	—
P# block of 12, Impt., never hinged	*3,900.*	
Ribbed paper	240.00	22.50
Double transfer	—	—
Short transfer at upper left (pos. 10, 18, 28)	—	—

The never hinged, bottom left plate block of No. O3 is the only plate block of this number recorded.

Cancellations		
Blue		+.50
Purple		+1.00
Magenta		+1.00
Violet		+1.00
Red		+17.50
Indigo		+10.00
Green		+200.00
Brown		+20.00
Town		+4.00
"Paid"		+27.50
Numeral		+35.00
Railroad		+75.00
Express Company		+900.00
O4 O1 6c **yellow**	275.00	60.00
Never hinged	575.00	
No gum	110.00	
On cover		*7,500.*
Block of 4	1,250.	
Cancellations		
Blue		+3.00
Magenta		+4.00
Violet		+5.00
Red		+50.00
Town		+7.00
"Paid"		+27.50
Numeral		+35.00
Express Company		—
Revenue		—
O5 O1 10c **yellow**	525.00	200.00
Never hinged	1,150.	
No gum	220.00	
On cover (parcel label)		*6,000.*
Block of 4	2,500.	
Cancellations		
Violet		+5.00
Blue		+5.00
Red		+50.00
Town		+25.00
O6 O1 12c **yellow**	450.00	260.00
Never hinged	950.00	
No gum	250.00	
On cover		*12,000.*
Block of 4	1,950.	
Cancellations		
Violet		+10.00
Blue		+10.00
Red		+50.00
Town		+30.00
O7 O1 15c **yellow**	425.00	230.00
Never hinged	950.00	
No gum	225.00	
Block of 4	1,850.	
Recut top left frame line (pos. 100)	—	—
Cancellations		
Purple		+10.00
Blue		+10.00
O8 O1 24c **yellow**	425.00	250.00
Never hinged	950.00	
No gum	225.00	
On parcel label		—
Block of 4	1,850.	
Cancellation		
Violet		+10.00
O9 O1 30c **yellow**	550.00	280.00
Never hinged	1,200.	
No gum	275.00	
Block of 4	2,500.	
Cancellations		
Blue		+10.00
Red		+65.00

EXECUTIVE

Franklin — O2

1873

O10 O2 1c **carmine**	900.00	550.00
deep carmine	900.00	550.00
Never hinged	2,250.	
No gum	450.00	
On cover with No. O11		*3,250.*
On cover, single franking		*3,100.*
Block of 6	*4,250.*	

The only known block is with original gum and is off-center with perfs just cutting into design. It is valued thus.

Cancellations		
Violet		+10.00
Blue favor		+10.00
Red		+50.00
Town		+30.00
NYC number		—
O11 O2 2c **carmine**	575.00	260.00
deep carmine	575.00	260.00
Never hinged	1,250.	
No gum	250.00	
On cover, single franking		*3,750.*
Block of 4	*3,250.*	
Foreign entry of 6c Agriculture (pos. 40)	*2,500.*	*1,000.*
Cancellations		
Violet		+10.00
Blue favor		+10.00
Red		+50.00
O12 O2 3c **carmine**	700.00	225.00
Never hinged	1,600.	
No gum	270.00	
On cover		*1,200.*
On cover from Long Branch, N.J.		*4,500.*
Block of 4	*3,250.*	
a. 3c **violet rose**	1,000.	275.00
Never hinged	2,250.	
No gum	375.00	
On cover		—
Cancellations		
Blue favor		+10.00
Violet		+10.00
Indigo		+20.00
Red		+50.00
Town		+35.00
O13 O2 6c **carmine**	900.00	600.00
Never hinged	—	
No gum	325.00	
On cover		*5,000.*
On cover from Long Branch, N.J.		*5,750.*
Block of 4	*4,000.*	
Double transfer (pos. 6)	*2,600.*	*1,000.*
Cancellations		
Violet		+15.00
Blue favor		+15.00
Town		+50.00
New York Foreign Mail		—
O14 O2 10c **carmine**	1,200.	1,000.
Never hinged	—	
No gum	600.00	
On cover		—
Block of 4	*5,500.*	
Cancellations		
Violet		+15.00
Blue favor		+15.00
Negative "2" numeral (New York)		—

INTERIOR

O3

1873

	Unused	Used
O15 O3 1c **vermilion**	75.00	10.00
dull vermilion	75.00	10.00
bright vermilion	75.00	10.00
Never hinged	170.00	
No gum	30.00	
On cover		160.00
Block of 4	325.00	*325.00*
P# block of 10, Impt.	*1,000.*	
Never hinged	*1,850.*	
Ribbed paper	85.00	20.00
Short transfer at bottom right (pos. 91)	—	—

Cancellations

Violet	+1.00
Blue	+1.00
Red	+12.50
Ultramarine	+8.00
Town	+3.00

	Unused	Used
O16 O3 2c **vermilion**	70.00	12.00
dull vermilion	70.00	12.00
bright vermilion	70.00	12.00
Never hinged	160.00	
No gum	30.00	
On cover		65.00
Block of 4	300.00	*300.00*
P# block of 10, Impt.	*950.00*	
P# block of 12, Impt.	*1,050.*	

Cancellations

Purple	+.75
Violet	+75
Blue	+.75
Red	+6.00
Town	+7.50
Numeral	+20.00
"Paid"	+20.00

	Unused	Used
O17 O3 3c **vermilion**	80.00	6.00
dull vermilion	80.00	6.00
bright vermilion	80.00	6.00
Never hinged	175.00	
No gum	35.00	
On cover		40.00
First day cover, Nos. O17, O18, *July 1, 1873*		*10,000.*
Block of 4	350.00	*350.00*
P# block of 10, Impt.	*975.00*	
Ribbed paper	100.00	10.00

Cancellations

Violet	+1.00
Blue	+1.00
Indigo	+3.00
Magenta	+5.00
Red	+15.00
Green	+65.00
Town	+7.50
Numeral	+20.00
Express Company	+75.00
"Paid"	+20.00
Fort	—

	Unused	Used
O18 O3 6c **vermilion**	70.00	10.00
dull vermilion	70.00	10.00
bright vermilion	70.00	10.00
scarlet vermilion	70.00	10.00
Never hinged	160.00	
No gum	27.50	
On cover		95.00
Block of 4	350.00	—
P# block of 10, Impt.	*950.00*	

Cancellations

Violet	+1.00
Blue	+1.00
Red	+15.00
Town	+7.50
Express Company	—
Railroad	—
Fort	—

See No. O17 for first day cover listing.

	Unused	Used
O19 O3 10c **vermilion**	70.00	20.00
dull vermilion	70.00	20.00
bright vermilion	70.00	20.00
Never hinged	160.00	
No gum	27.50	
On cover		*600.00*
Block of 4	350.00	—
P# block of 12, Impt.	*1,000.*	

Cancellations

Violet	+1.00
Blue	+1.00
Indigo	+10.00
Red	+25.00
Town	+10.00
Fort	—
New York Foreign Mail	+300.00

	Unused	Used
O20 O3 12c **vermilion**	90.00	12.00
bright vermilion	90.00	12.00
Never hinged	200.00	
No gum	35.00	
On cover		*575.00*
Block of 4	400.00	500.00
P# block of 10, Impt.	*1,150.*	
Short transfer at right (pos. 6)	—	—

Cancellations

Violet	+1.00
Magenta	+1.00
Blue	+1.00
Red	+15.00
Brown	+20.00
Town	+7.50
Fort	—

	Unused	Used
O21 O3 15c **vermilion**	200.00	25.00
bright vermilion	200.00	25.00
Never hinged	450.00	
No gum	80.00	
On cover		*650.00*
Block of 4	900.00	—
P# block of 12, Impt.	—	
Double transfer of left side (pos. 37, 47, 57, and 67)	275.00	37.50

Cancellations

Blue	+1.50
Violet	+1.50
Town	+5.00

	Unused	Used
O22 O3 24c **vermilion**	180.00	20.00
dull vermilion	180.00	20.00
bright vermilion	180.00	20.00
Never hinged	400.00	
No gum	60.00	
On cover		*2,500.*
Block of 4	775.00	*2,000.*
P# block of 12, Impt.	*2,500.*	
a. Double impression		—

Cancellations

Violet	+1.50
Blue	+1.50
Red	+15.00
Town	+5.00

	Unused	Used
O23 O3 30c **vermilion**	290.00	20.00
bright vermilion	290.00	20.00
Never hinged	625.00	
No gum	110.00	
On parcel label		*6,000.*
Block of 4	1,250.	—
P# block of 12, Impt.	*4,250.*	

Cancellations

Violet	+2.00
Blue	+2.00
Red	+50.00
Town	+7.50

	Unused	Used
O24 O3 90c **vermilion**	325.00	50.00
bright vermilion	325.00	50.00
Never hinged	700.00	
No gum	120.00	
On cover		
Block of 4	1,650.	—
P# block of 12, Impt.	*5,000.*	
Double transfer	390.00	
Major double transfer (Pos. 17)	*600.00*	*250.00*
Short transfer at right (Pos. 56)		—
Silk paper	—	

Cancellations

Violet	+4.00
Blue	+4.00
Magenta	+10.00
Red	+50.00
Brown	+60.00
Town	+17.50

JUSTICE

O4

1873

	Unused	Used
O25 O4 1c **purple**	250.00	100.00
dark purple	250.00	100.00
Never hinged	550.00	
No gum	100.00	
On cover		*1,750.*
On cover with No. O26		*4,000.*
Block of 4	1,100.	
Double transfer	—	—

Cancellations

Violet	+3.00
Blue	+3.00
Indigo	+5.00
Magenta	+5.00
Red	+20.00
Town	+7.50

	Unused	Used
O26 O4 2c **purple**	310.00	110.00
light purple	310.00	110.00
Never hinged	700.00	
No gum	120.00	
On cover		*1,500.*
Block of 4	1,400.	
Short transfer at right side (pos. 3)	—	—

Cancellations

Violet	+4.00
Blue	+4.00
Ultramarine	+10.00
Indigo	+5.00
Magenta	+5.00
Red	+20.00
Town	+20.00

	Unused	Used
O27 O4 3c **purple**	320.00	35.00
dark purple	320.00	35.00
bluish purple	320.00	35.00
Never hinged	725.00	
No gum	110.00	
On cover		*575.00*
Block of 4	1,450.	
Double transfer	—	

Cancellations

Violet	+2.00
Magenta	+2.00
Blue	+2.00
Ultramarine	+10.00
Indigo	+5.00
Red	+12.00
Green	+100.00
Town	+15.00

	Unused	Used
O28 O4 6c **purple**	310.00	45.00
light purple	310.00	45.00
bluish purple	310.00	45.00
Never hinged	700.00	
No gum	110.00	
On cover		*1,200.*
Block of 4	1,400.	

Cancellations

Violet	+2.00
Blue	+2.00
Indigo	+5.00
Magenta	+5.00
Red	+15.00
Town	+17.50

	Unused	Used
O29 O4 10c **purple**	310.00	100.00
bluish purple	310.00	100.00
Never hinged	700.00	
No gum	120.00	
On cover		*4,000.*
Block of 4	1,400.	
P# block of 10, Impt.	*6,500.*	
Double transfer		—

Cancellations

Violet	+4.00
Blue	+4.00
Magenta	+5.00
Town	+17.50

	Unused	Used
O30 O4 12c **purple**	260.00	75.00
dark purple	260.00	75.00
Never hinged	575.00	
No gum	95.00	
On cover		*1,750.*
Block of 4	1,200.	

Cancellations

Purple	+2.00
Violet	+2.00
Blue	+2.00
Magenta	+5.00
Red	+35.00
Town	+17.50

	Unused	Used
O31 O4 15c **purple**	500.00	200.00
Never hinged	1,100.	
No gum	220.00	
On cover		*1,250.*
Block of 4	*3,100.*	
Double transfer		—

Cancellations

Violet	+5.00
Blue	+5.00
Indigo	+5.00
Magenta	+10.00
Red	+35.00
Town	+10.00

The block of 4 of No. O31 is unique. It is in the grade of fine and is valued thus.

	Unused	Used
O32 O4 24c **purple**	1,250.	425.00
Never hinged	—	
No gum	550.00	
On cover		*8,000.*
Short transfer (pos. 98)	—	—

Cancellations

Violet	+10.00
Blue	+10.00
Magenta	+10.00
Red	+35.00
Town	+40.00

	Unused	Used
O33 O4 30c **purple**	1,300.	350.00
Never hinged	—	
No gum	550.00	
On cover with Nos. O27 & O28		*17,500.*
Block of 4	*7,500.*	
Double transfer at top	1,400.	375.00

Cancellations

Purple	+10.00
Violet	+10.00
Blue	+10.00
Magenta	+10.00
Red	+50.00
Town	+40.00

The block of 4 of No. O33 is unique. It is in the grade of fine and is valued thus.

	Unused	Used
O34 O4 90c **purple**	1,900.	900.00
dark purple	1,900.	900.00
Never hinged	—	
No gum	800.00	
On cover with No. O33		*26,000.*
Pair	—	
Double plate scratch	—	
Triple transfer at top	—	—

Cancellations

Purple	+25.00
Violet	+25.00
Blue	+25.00
Magenta	+25.00

No. O34 on cover is unique. The cover bears three No. O34 and four No. O33.

NAVY

O5

1873

	Unused	Used
O35 O5 1c **ultramarine**	160.00	50.00
dark ultramarine	160.00	50.00
Never hinged	350.00	
No gum	65.00	
On cover		*750.00*
On cover with No. O36		*2,000.*
Block of 4	750.00	
P# block of 12, Impt.	*2,250.*	
a. 1c **dull blue**	175.00	50.00
Never hinged	375.00	
No gum	70.00	
Cancellations		
Violet		+2.00
Blue		+2.00
Indigo		+5.00
Red		+20.00
Town		+7.50
Steamship		+100.00
New York Foreign Mail		—
O36 O5 2c **ultramarine**	160.00	25.00
dark ultramarine	160.00	25.00
Never hinged	350.00	
No gum	65.00	
On cover		*500.00*
Block of 4	750.00	
P# block of 12, Impt.	*2,250.*	
Double transfer		—
a. 2c **dull blue**	175.00	25.00
gray blue	175.00	25.00
Never hinged	385.00	
No gum	70.00	
Block of 4	825.00	

The 2c deep green and the 2c black, both perforated and imperforate, are trial color proofs.

	Unused	Used
Cancellations		
Violet		+1.50
Blue		+1.50
Indigo		+5.00
Red		+15.00
Green		+75.00
Town		+10.00
Steamship		+100.00
New York Foreign Mail		—
O37 O5 3c **ultramarine**	170.00	15.00
pale ultramarine	170.00	15.00
dark ultramarine	170.00	15.00
Never hinged	375.00	
No gum	60.00	
On cover		*250.00*
Block of 4	775.00	*1,000.*
P# block of 12, Impt.	*2,500.*	
Double transfer	—	—
a. 3c **dull blue**	175.00	15.00
Never hinged	385.00	
No gum	62.50	
Cancellations		
Violet		+1.50
Blue		+1.50
Indigo		+5.00
Ultramarine		+10.00
Magenta		+5.00
Red		+15.00
Town		+5.00
Blue town		+15.00
Steamship		+75.00
O38 O5 6c **ultramarine**	150.00	25.00
bright ultramarine	150.00	25.00
Never hinged	325.00	
No gum	55.00	
On cover		*750.00*
Block of 4	700.00	—
P# block of 12, Impt.	*2,400.*	
Vertical line through "N" of "Navy"	175.00	35.00
Double transfer	—	—
a. 6c **dull blue**	175.00	25.00
Never hinged	385.00	
No gum	67.50	
Cancellations		
Violet		+1.50
Purple		+1.50
Blue		+1.50
Magenta		+10.00
Red		+17.50
Green		+100.00
Town		+5.00
Steamship		+100.00
New York Foreign Mail		—
O39 O5 7c **ultramarine**	700.00	230.00
dark ultramarine	700.00	230.00
Never hinged	—	
No gum	275.00	
On cover		*3,000.*
Block of 4	*3,000.*	
Double transfer	—	—
a. 7c **dull blue**	750.00	230.00
Never hinged	—	
No gum	275.00	
Cancellations		
Blue		+10.00
Violet		+10.00
Magenta		+10.00
Red		+45.00
Town		+25.00
O40 O5 10c **ultramarine**	210.00	45.00
dark ultramarine	210.00	45.00
Never hinged	475.00	
No gum	75.00	
On cover		*6,500.*
Block of 4	1,000.	
P# block of 12, Impt.	*2,900.*	
Plate scratch (pos. 3)	*325.00*	—
Ribbed paper	225.00	60.00
a. 10c **dull blue**	225.00	45.00
Never hinged	500.00	
No gum	80.00	
Cancellations		
Violet		+2.00
Blue		+2.00
Brown		+20.00
Red		+25.00
Town		+10.00
Steamship		+100.00
New York Foreign Mail		—
O41 O5 12c **ultramarine**	240.00	45.00
pale ultramarine	240.00	45.00
dark ultramarine	240.00	45.00
Never hinged	525.00	
No gum	100.00	
On cover		—
Block of 4	1,100.	
P# strip of 6, Impt.	—	
Short transfer at lower right (pos. 10)	—	
Double transfer of left side (pos. 50)	400.00	250.00
Cancellations		
Violet		+2.50
Magenta		+2.50
Blue		+2.50
Red		+25.00
Town		+10.00
Supplementary Mail		+80.00
Steamship		+200.00
New York Foreign Mail		+325.00
O42 O5 15c **ultramarine**	425.00	75.00
dark ultramarine	425.00	75.00
Never hinged	—	
No gum	160.00	
On cover		*21,000.*
Block of 4	1,800.	
P# strip of 6, Impt.	—	
Short transfer at upper left (pos. 26)	—	
Cancellations		
Violet		+2.50
Blue		+2.50
Red		+35.00
Yellow		—
Town		+20.00
O43 O5 24c **ultramarine**	425.00	85.00
dark ultramarine	425.00	85.00
Never hinged	—	
No gum	160.00	
On cover		*30,000.*
Block of 4	2,000.	
Recut at upper right (pos. 33, 92)	—	—
a. 24c **dull blue**	425.00	80.00
Never hinged	—	
No gum	160.00	
Cancellations		
Violet		+5.00
Magenta		+5.00
Red		+50.00
Blue		+5.00
Green		+150.00
Town		+40.00
Steamship		+125.00
New York Foreign Mail		—
O44 O5 30c **ultramarine**	350.00	50.00
dark ultramarine	350.00	50.00
Never hinged	—	
No gum	140.00	
On cover		*25,000.*
Block of 4	1,600.	*3,000.*
Double transfer	375.00	55.00
Cancellations		
Blue		+4.00
Red		+30.00
Violet		+4.00
Town		+20.00
Supplementary Mail		+125.00
Steamship		+150.00
New York Foreign Mail		+400.00
O45 O5 90c **ultramarine**	1,050.	375.00
Never hinged	—	
No gum	450.00	
Block of 4	*6,250.*	
Short transfer at upper left (pos. 1, 5)	—	—
a. Double impression		*20,000.*
Cancellations		
Purple		+15.00
Violet		+15.00
Red		+75.00
Town		+40.00

POST OFFICE

Stamps of the Post Office Department are often on paper with a gray surface. This is essentially a wiping problem, caused by an over-milled carbon black pigment that released acid and etched the plates. There is no premium for stamps on paper with a gray surface.

O6

1873

	Unused	Used
O47 O6 1c **black**	25.00	12.00
gray black	25.00	12.00
Never hinged	60.00	
No gum	12.00	
On cover		75.00
Block of 4	110.00	—
P# block of 12, Impt.	400.00	
Never hinged	550.00	
Cancellations		
Purple		+1.00
Violet		+1.00
Magenta		+1.00
Blue		+1.00
Red		+12.50
Town		+3.50
O48 O6 2c **black**	30.00	10.00
gray black	30.00	10.00
Never hinged	75.00	
No gum	13.00	
On cover		175.00
Block of 4	140.00	—
P# block of 12, Impt.	475.00	
a. Double impression	*1,000.*	600.00
Cancellations		
Purple		+1.00
Violet		+1.00
Blue		+1.00
Indigo		+5.00
Magenta		+1.00
Red		+12.50
Town		+3.50
Blue town		+7.50
New York Foreign Mail		—
O49 O6 3c **black**	10.00	2.00
gray black	10.00	2.00
Never hinged	25.00	
No gum	3.00	
On cover		25.00
Block of 4	45.00	—
P# block of 12, Impt.	*200.00*	
Never hinged	*350.00*	
Cracked plate	—	—
Double transfer at bottom	—	—
Double paper	—	—
Vertical ribbed paper	—	—
a. Printed on both sides		*7,500.*
Cancellations		
Purple		+.75
Violet		+.75
Blue		+.75
Indigo		+5.00
Ultramarine		+1.50
Magenta		+.75
Red		+10.00
Brown		+20.00
Green		+60.00
Numeral		+20.00
Town		+1.50
Railroad		+25.00
"Paid"		+12.00
O50 O6 6c **black**	30.00	8.00
gray black	30.00	8.00
Never hinged	75.00	
No gum	12.00	
On cover		85.00
Block of 4	150.00	—
P# block of 14, Impt.	550.00	
Vertical ribbed paper	—	12.50
Double transfer of top frame (pos. 96L, 99L)	—	—
a. Diagonal half used as 3c on cover		*5,000.*
b. Double impression		*3,000.*
Cancellations		
Purple		+.75
Violet		+.75
Magenta		+.75
Blue		+.75
Indigo		+5.00
Red		+12.00
Brown		+20.00
Numeral		+20.00
Town		+2.50
"Paid"		+15.00
O51 O6 10c **black**	140.00	55.00
gray black	140.00	55.00
Never hinged	325.00	
No gum	60.00	
On cover		*400.00*
Block of 4	700.00	—
P# block of 12, Impt.	*1,950.*	
Cancellations		
Violet		+3.50
Red		+15.00
Magenta		+3.50
Blue		+3.50
Town		+10.00
O52 O6 12c **black**	120.00	12.00
gray black	120.00	12.00
Never hinged	275.00	
No gum	40.00	
On cover		*1,000.*

Block of 4 575.00 *1,250.*
P# block of 12, Impt. *1,850.*
Plate scratch above small "12" — —

Cancellations

Purple +1.00
Magenta +1.00
Blue +1.00
Indigo +5.00
Red +12.50
Town +4.00

O53 O6 15c **black** 140.00 20.00
gray black 140.00 20.00
Never hinged 325.00
No gum 50.00
On cover *5,000.*
Block of 4 675.00 —
P# block of 10, Impt. *2,250.*
Double transfer — —

Cancellations

Violet +1.50
Magenta +1.50
Red +20.00
Blue +1.50
Town +7.50
New York Foreign Mail —

O54 O6 24c **black** 225.00 25.00
gray black 225.00 25.00
Never hinged 500.00
No gum 85.00
Block of 4 900.00 —
P# block of 12, Impt. —
Double paper —

Cancellations

Violet +1.50
Blue +1.50
Red +20.00
Town +7.50
New York Foreign Mail —

O55 O6 30c **black** 200.00 25.00
gray black 200.00 25.00
Never hinged 450.00
No gum 70.00
On cover *17,500.*
Block of 4 900.00 750.00
P# block of 12, Impt. *2,900.*

Cancellations

Purple +1.50
Blue +1.50
Red +20.00
Magenta +1.50
Town +12.50

O56 O6 90c **black** 220.00 25.00
gray black 220.00 25.00
Never hinged 500.00
No gum 80.00
Block of 4 950.00 *1,250.*
P# block of 12, Impt. *3,000.*
Double transfer — —
Double paper — —
Silk paper —

Cancellations

Purple +1.50
Magenta +1.50
Blue +1.50
Town +6.50

STATE

Franklin — O7

William H. Seward — O8

1873

O57 O7 1c **dark green** 260.00 75.00
a. dark yellow green 260.00 75.00
Never hinged 575.00
No gum 110.00
On cover —
Block of 4 1,250.
Plate scratch at left (pos. 51) —

Cancellations

Violet +2.00
Blue favor +2.00
Red +17.50
Town +7.50

O58 O7 2c **dark green** 310.00 100.00
a. yellow green 310.00 100.00
Never hinged —
No gum 120.00
On cover *1,000.*
Double transfer at bottom (pos. 98) 600.00 —

Cancellations

Violet +5.00
Blue favor +5.00
Indigo +5.00
Red +50.00
Town +25.00

O59 O7 3c **dark green** 220.00 25.00
a. yellow green 220.00 25.00
Never hinged 500.00
No gum 85.00
On cover *600.00*
First day cover, *July 1, 1873* —
Block of 4 1,100. —
Double paper — —
Short transfer at right (pos. 85) —

Cancellations

Violet +1.50
Blue favor +1.50
Indigo +1.50
Red +10.00
Town +6.50

O60 O7 6c **dark green** 250.00 30.00
a. yellow green 250.00 30.00
Never hinged 550.00
No gum 110.00
On cover *800.00*
Block of 4 1,100. —
P# block of 12, Impt. —
Double transfer — —
Foreign entry of 6c Executive (pos. 41, 91) — *500.00*
Double transfer plus foreign entry of 6c Executive (pos. 61) —
Plate scratch in margin (pos. 26, right; 27, left) *325.00* *275.00*

Cancellations

Violet +2.00
Blue favor +10.00
Indigo +2.00
Red +20.00
Town +17.50

O61 O7 7c **dark green** 290.00 65.00
a. yellow green 290.00 65.00
Never hinged 650.00
No gum 95.00
On cover *1,000.*
Block of 4 1,500.
Ribbed paper 310.00 70.00

Cancellations

Violet +2.00
Blue favor +2.00
Indigo +2.00
Red +25.00
Town +10.00

O62 O7 10c **dark green** 250.00 55.00
a. yellow green 250.00 —
Never hinged 575.00
No gum 110.00
On cover *2,000.*
Block of 4 1,150.
P# block of 12, Impt. —
Short transfer (pos. 34) 275.00 67.50

Cancellations

Violet +2.50
Blue favor +2.50
Indigo +2.50
Red +35.00
Town +25.00
New York Foreign Mail +325.00

O63 O7 12c **dark green** 310.00 125.00
a. yellow green —
Never hinged 700.00
No gum 140.00
On cover *1,500.*
Block of 4 1,650.

Cancellations

Violet +5.00
Blue favor +5.00
Red +30.00
Town +15.00

O64 O7 15c **dark green** 350.00 90.00
a. yellow green 350.00 90.00
Never hinged 775.00
No gum 150.00
On cover *5,750.*
Block of 4 1,750.
Short transfer at upper right 450.00
Plate scratch at lower left (pos. 91) *450.00*
Plate scratch in margin (pos. 95, right; 96, left) —
Damaged plate at left (pos. 63) —

Cancellations

Violet +2.50
Blue favor +2.50
Red +30.00
Town +30.00

O65 O7 24c **dark green** 525.00 230.00
a. yellow green 525.00 230.00
Never hinged —
No gum 275.00
On cover *17,500.*
Block of 4 *3,100.*
Short transfer at bottom left (pos. 10) *600.00*
Plate gashes in forehead (pos. 76) *750.00* 725.00
Plate scratch (pos. 66) *800.00* —

Cancellations

Violet +15.00
Blue favor +15.00
Indigo +15.00
Red +85.00
Town +55.00

O66 O7 30c **dark green** 500.00 180.00
a. yellow green 500.00 180.00
Never hinged —
No gum 240.00
On cover *12,500.*
Block of 4 *4,500.*

Cancellations

Violet +5.00
Blue favor +5.00
Indigo +5.00

Red +50.00
Town +50.00
New York Foreign Mail —

O67 O7 90c **dark green** 1,050. 325.00
a. yellow green —
Never hinged —
No gum 525.00
On parcel wrapper front or with Nos. O60 & O66 *50,000.*

Cancellations

Violet +15.00
Blue favor +15.00
Red +85.00
Red New York Foreign Mail —
Town +90.00

O68 O8 $2 **green & black** 1,750. 3,000.
a. yellow green & black 1,750. 3,000.
Never hinged *3,750.*
No gum 850.00
On parcel label *175,000.*
Block of 4 *19,000.*
Ribbed paper —

The No. O68 on parcel label is unique.

Cancellations

Violet +25.00
Blue favor +25.00
Red +175.00
Town +125.00
Red New York Foreign Mail +3,000.
Pen Cancel *350.00*

O69 O8 $5 **green & black** 7,500. *13,000.*
a. yellow green & black 7,500. *13,000.*
Never hinged —
No gum 3,500.
Irregular block of 6 *60,000.*

Cancellations

Blue favor +250.00
Red favor +250.00
Pen Cancel *2,000.*

O70 O8 $10 **green & black** 4,500. *7,500.*
a. yellow green & black 4,500. *7,500.*
Never hinged 10,500.
No gum 2,500.
Block of 4 *24,000.*
P# sheet of 10, Impt. *62,500.*
Ribbed paper —

Cancellations

Blue favor +200.00
Pen Cancel *1,250.*

O71 O8 $20 **green & black** 5,000. 5,500.
a. yellow green & black 5,000. 5,500.
Never hinged 11,500.
No gum 2,250.
Block of 4 *27,000.*
Block of 4, presentation pen cancel *10,000.*
P# sheet of 10, Impt. *70,000.*

No. O71 used is valued with a blue or red handstamp favor cancel.

Cancellations

Blue favor 5,500.
Red favor 5,500.
Pen presentation 1,750.
Cork and manuscript +15,000.

The design of Nos. O68 to O71 measures 25½x39½mm.

TREASURY

O9

1873

O72 O9 1c **brown** 120.00 10.00
dark brown 120.00 10.00
yellow brown 120.00 10.00
Never hinged 250.00
No gum 45.00
On cover 100.00
Block of 4 525.00 *325.00*
P# block of 10, Impt. *2,100.*
Never hinged *4,000.*
Double transfer 135.00 12.50

Cancellations

Purple +1.00
Violet +1.00
Magenta +1.00
Blue +1.00
Red +10.00
Brown +20.00
Green +200.00
Town +2.00
Blue town +4.00
New York Foreign Mail —

O73 O9 2c **brown** 125.00 8.00
dark brown 125.00 8.00
yellow brown 125.00 8.00
Never hinged 275.00
No gum 45.00
On cover 75.00
Block of 4 550.00 *325.00*
P# block of 14, Impt. *2,000.*
Double transfer — 12.50

	Unused	Used
Plate scratch (pos. 3R)		—
Cancellations		
Purple		+1.00
Violet		+1.00
Magenta		+1.00
Blue		+1.00
Indigo		+3.00
Red		+10.00
Town		+2.00
Blue town		+4.00
New York Foreign Mail		+275.00
O74 O9 3c **brown**	110.00	2.00
dark brown	110.00	2.00
yellow brown	110.00	2.00
Never hinged	230.00	
No gum	40.00	
On cover		100.00
First day cover, *July 1, 1873*		*11,000.*
Block of 4	475.00	*250.00*
P# block of 14, Impt.	*1,850.*	
Double paper	—	
Shaded circle outside of right frame line	—	—
Short transfer at bottom (pos. 36 R 29)	—	—
a. Double impression	*5,000.*	
Cancellations		
Purple		+.50
Violet		+.50
Blue		+.50
Indigo		+3.00
Ultramarine		+2.00
Magenta		+.50
Red		+3.50
Brown		+20.00
Green		+200.00
Town		+1.00
Railroad		+20.00
"Paid"		+10.00
O75 O9 6c **brown**	120.00	4.00
dark brown	120.00	4.00
yellow brown	120.00	4.00
Never hinged	250.00	
No gum	45.00	
On cover		75.00
On cover with 6c War #O86		*12,000.*
Block of 4	525.00	*500.00*
P# block of 12, Impt.	*1,900.*	
Never hinged	*3,500.*	
Dirty plate	120.00	6.00
Double transfer		—
Cancellations		
Purple		+.50
Violet		+.50
Magenta		+.50
Blue		+.50
Indigo		+3.00
Ultramarine		+1.50
Red		+5.00
Green		+200.00
"Paid"		+20.00
Town		+1.50
New York Foreign Mail		—
O76 O9 7c **brown**	250.00	35.00
dark brown	250.00	35.00
yellow brown	250.00	35.00
Never hinged	550.00	
No gum	95.00	
On cover		750.00
Block of 4	1,100.	*1,000.*
P# block of 12, Impt.	—	
Cancellations		
Purple		+2.00
Violet		+2.00
Blue		+2.00
Indigo		+3.00
Red		+30.00
Green		+200.00
Town		+7.50
Blue town		+12.50
New York Foreign Mail		—
O77 O9 10c **brown**	240.00	12.00
dark brown	240.00	12.00
yellow brown	240.00	12.00
Never hinged	525.00	
No gum	90.00	
On cover		*450.00*
Block of 4	1,075.	*325.00*
P# block of 12, Impt.	—	
Double paper	—	—
Double transfer		—
Cancellations		
Purple		+1.00
Violet		+1.00
Blue		+1.00
Indigo		+3.00
Ultramarine		+4.00
Magenta		+1.00
Red		+12.00
Brown		+20.00
Green		+200.00
Town		+4.00
Blue town		+8.50
O78 O9 12c **brown**	350.00	10.00
dark brown	350.00	10.00
yellow brown	350.00	10.00
Never hinged	750.00	
No gum	125.00	
On cover		600.00
Block of 4	1,500.	*325.00*
Cancellations		
Purple		+.50
Blue		+.50
Ultramarine		+10.00
Red		+10.00
Green		+200.00
Town		+2.50
Railroad		+20.00
O79 O9 15c **brown**	300.00	12.00
yellow brown	300.00	12.00
Never hinged	650.00	
No gum	100.00	
On cover		*850.00*
Block of 4	1,400.	*325.00*
P# block of 12, Impt.	*4,250.*	
Never hinged	*6,000.*	
Cancellations		
Blue		+1.00
Purple		+1.00
Red		+10.00
Green		+200.00
Town		+2.50
Blue town		+7.50
Numeral		+15.00
Steamship		+100.00
O80 O9 24c **brown**	725.00	100.00
dark brown	725.00	100.00
yellow brown	725.00	100.00
Never hinged	—	
No gum	290.00	
Block of 4	3,250.	
Block of 14		
Double transfer at top	775.00	—
Short transfer at top (pos. 61)		—
Cancellations		
Violet		+10.00
Blue		+5.00
Ultramarine		+10.00
Magenta		+5.00
Red		+30.00
Brown		+20.00
Town		+15.00
Blue town		+25.00
New York Foreign Mail		—
O81 O9 30c **brown**	400.00	12.00
dark brown	400.00	12.00
yellow brown	400.00	12.00
Never hinged	—	
No gum	140.00	
On cover		*5,000.*
Block of 4	1,750.	*500.00*
Short transfer at left top (pos. 95)	450.00	25.00
Short transfer at right top (pos. 45)	450.00	25.00
Block of 4, one pos. 45	—	
Short transfer across entire top (pos. 41)	450.00	25.00
Cancellations		
Purple		+1.00
Blue		+1.00
Magenta		+1.00
Red		+12.00
Green		+200.00
Town		+3.50
Blue town		+7.50
O82 O9 90c **brown**	475.00	15.00
dark brown	475.00	15.00
yellow brown	475.00	15.00
Never hinged	—	
No gum	160.00	
Block of 4	2,400.	*375.00*
P# strip of 6, Impt.	—	
Double paper	—	—
Cancellations		
Purple		+1.00
Magenta		+1.00
Blue		+1.00
Red		+30.00
Brown		+7.50
Green		+200.00
Town		+3.50
Blue town		+7.50

WAR

O10

1873

	Unused	Used
O83 O10 1c **rose**	240.00	15.00
rose red	240.00	15.00
Never hinged	525.00	
No gum	90.00	
On cover		140.00
Block of 4	1,050.	
Block of 10		—
P# block of 12, Impt.	*3,250.*	
Cancellations		
Purple		+1.00
Blue		+1.00
Magenta		+5.00
Red		+15.00
Town		+3.50
Fort		+100.00
Numeral		+12.50
"Paid"		—
O84 O10 2c **rose**	260.00	15.00
rose red	260.00	15.00
Never hinged	600.00	
No gum	110.00	
On cover		70.00
Block of 4	1,100.	—
P# block of 14, Impt.	*3,750.*	
Ribbed paper	275.00	17.50
Cancellations		
Purple		+1.50
Magenta		+1.50
Blue		+1.50
Red		+15.00
Town		+4.00
Fort		+100.00
O85 O10 3c **rose**	275.00	5.00
rose red	275.00	5.00
Never hinged	600.00	
No gum	120.00	
On cover		40.00
Block of 4	1,150.	*550.00*
P# block of 14, Impt.	*3,750.*	
Cancellations		
Purple		+1.00
Blue		+1.00
Ultramarine		+10.00
Magenta		+1.00
Red		+20.00
Green		+35.00
Town		+1.50
Fort		+250.00
"Paid"		+12.00
O86 O10 6c **rose**	675.00	10.00
pale rose	675.00	10.00
Never hinged	1,450.	
No gum	275.00	
On cover		60.00
On cover with 6c Treasury #O75		*12,000.*
Block of 4	*3,000.*	—
P# block of 12, Impt.	—	
Cancellations		
Purple		+1.50
Blue		+1.50
Indigo		+3.00
Magenta		+3.00
Red		+15.00
Town		+3.50
Blue town		+6.50
Fort		+100.00

Examples of Nos. O114-O117 which bear Continental Bank Note Co. imprints are often mistaken for/offered as Nos. O83-O86. If there are doubts, expert opinions should be requested.

	Unused	Used
O87 O10 7c **rose**	175.00	90.00
pale rose	175.00	90.00
rose red	175.00	90.00
Never hinged	375.00	
No gum	90.00	
On cover		*2,000.*
Block of 4	725.00	*725.00*
P# block of 10, Impt.	*2,250.*	
Cancellations		
Purple		+2.50
Blue		+3.50
Magenta		+10.00
Red		+25.00
Town		+7.50
Fort		+300.00
O88 O10 10c **rose**	140.00	25.00
rose red	140.00	25.00
Never hinged	300.00	
No gum	45.00	
On cover		*2,000.*
Block of 4	600.00	*900.00*
P# block of 10, Impt.	*2,000.*	

All examples of No. O88 show a crack at lower left. It was on the original die.

	Unused	Used
Cancellations		
Purple		+1.00
Blue		+1.00
Town		+3.50
Fort		+100.00
O89 O10 12c **rose**	275.00	12.00
Never hinged	600.00	
No gum	110.00	
On cover		450.00
Block of 4	1,250.	*550.00*
P# block of 12, Impt.	*3,850.*	
Never hinged	*7,750.*	
Ribbed paper	300.00	20.00
Cancellations		
Purple		+1.00
Magenta		+1.00
Blue		+1.00
Indigo		+5.00
Red		+10.00
Town		+3.00
Fort		+100.00
O90 O10 15c **rose**	85.00	15.00
pale rose	85.00	15.00
rose red	85.00	15.00
Never hinged	190.00	
No gum	30.00	
On cover		3,250.
Block of 4	375.00	—
P# block of 12, Impt.	*1,100.*	
Ribbed paper	92.50	20.00
Short transfer at upper right (pos. 74)		—
Cancellations		
Purple		+1.00
Blue		+1.00
Ultramarine		+10.00
Magenta		+3.00
Red		+10.00
Town		+2.50
Fort		+200.00
Express Company		+1,000.
O91 O10 24c **rose**	85.00	12.00
pale rose	85.00	12.00
rose red	85.00	12.00
Never hinged	190.00	

No gum 30.00
On cover *20,000.*
Block of 4 375.00 *2,250.*
P# block of 10, Impt. *1,300.*
Cancellations
Purple +1.00
Blue +1.00
Magenta +5.00
Town +2.50
Fort +100.00
O92 O10 30c **rose** 130.00 12.00
rose red 130.00 12.00
Never hinged 275.00
No gum 45.00
On cover *20,000.*
Block of 4 575.00 *350.00*
P# block of 12, Impt. *1,850.*
Ribbed paper 140.00 15.00
Cancellations
Purple +1.00
Magenta +1.00
Blue +1.00
Red +20.00
Town +2.50
Fort +100.00
O93 O10 90c **rose** 225.00 60.00
rose red 225.00 60.00
Never hinged 500.00
No gum 80.00
On parcel label *3,500.*
Block of 4 975.00 *2,000.*
P# block of 12, Impt. *3,750.*
Cancellations
Purple +2.00
Magenta +2.00
Blue +2.00
Red +20.00
Numeral +40.00
Town +7.50
Fort +125.00

The used block of 4 of No. O93 is unique. It has fine centering and is valued thus.

AGRICULTURE

Printed by the American Bank Note Co.

The Continental Bank Note Co. was consolidated with the American Bank Note Co. on February 4, 1879. The American Bank Note Company used many plates of the Continental Bank Note Company to print the ordinary postage, Departmental and Newspaper stamps. Therefore, stamps bearing the Continental Company's imprint were not always its product.

1879 Soft Porous Paper

O94 O1 1c **yellow** (issued without gum) 5,500.
Block of 4 *27,500.*
O95 O1 3c **yellow** 550.00 150.00
Never hinged 1,250.
No gum 240.00
Block of 4 2,750. *1,400.*
P# block of 12, Impt. *7,250.*
Cancellations
Purple +5.00
Blue +5.00
Town +30.00

Two examples of the O95 plate block of 6 with imprint exist, both contained in a unique pane of 100.

INTERIOR

O96 O3 1c **vermilion** 300.00 *400.00*
pale vermilion 300.00 *400.00*
Never hinged 550.00
No gum 160.00
Block of 4 1,450. —
P# block of 12, Impt. *4,500.*
Short transfer at lower right (pos. 91) 600.00
Cancellations
Purple +5.00
Blue +5.00
Town +15.00
O97 O3 2c **vermilion** 10.00 3.00
pale vermilion 10.00 3.00
scarlet vermilion 10.00 3.00
Never hinged 17.50
No gum 3.00
On cover 150.00
Block of 4 47.50 *250.00*
P# block of 12, Impt. *225.00*
Cancellations
Purple +.50
Violet +.50
Blue +.50
Red +5.00
Town +1.50
Blue town +3.00
Railroad +40.00
Fort +100.00
O98 O3 3c **vermilion** 10.00 3.00
pale vermilion 10.00 3.00
Never hinged 22.50
No gum 3.00
On cover 30.00
Block of 4 47.50 —
P# block of 10, Impt. *225.00*
Cancellations
Purple +.50
Violet +.50
Blue +.50
Red +5.00
Town +1.50
Blue town +3.00
Railroad +40.00
Numeral +5.00
O99 O3 6c **vermilion** 10.00 *12.50*
pale vermilion 10.00 *12.50*
scarlet vermilion 10.00 *12.50*
Never hinged 17.50
No gum 3.00
On cover 200.00
Block of 4 47.50 —
P# block of 12, Impt. *250.00*
Cancellations
Purple +.50
Blue +.50
Red +5.00
Town +1.50
Fort +100.00
O100 O3 10c **vermilion** 110.00 75.00
pale vermilion 110.00 75.00
Never hinged 250.00
No gum 60.00
On cover *1,200.*
Block of 4 500.00
P# block of 12, Impt. *1,650.*
Cancellations
Purple +5.00
Blue +5.00
Town +10.00
O101 O3 12c **vermilion** 230.00 115.00
pale vermilion 230.00 115.00
Never hinged 525.00
No gum 130.00
On cover —
Block of 4 1,075. *575.00*
Block of 6 *1,500.*
P# block of 12, Impt. *2,900.*
Short transfer at lower right (pos. 6) — —
Cancellation
Violet +5.00
O102 O3 15c **pale vermilion** 400.00 500.00
Never hinged 900.00
No gum 200.00
Block of 4 1,750.
P# block of 12, Impt. —
On cover *6,500.*
Double transfer 450.00 —
Cancellations
Purple +5.00
Blue +5.00
O103 O3 24c **pale vermilion** 4,500. *6,250.*
Never hinged 10,000.
No gum 2,100.
Block of 4 *22,500.*
P# strip of 6, Impt. —
Cancellation
Blue —

JUSTICE

O106 O4 3c **bluish purple** 225.00 125.00
deep bluish purple 190.00 125.00
Never hinged 525.00
No gum 110.00
On cover 1,250.
Block of 4 800.00
Cancellations
Violet +5.00
Blue +5.00
Indigo +5.00
Ultramarine +10.00
O107 O4 6c **bluish purple** 475.00 300.00
Never hinged 1,050.
No gum 210.00
On cover *1,000.*
Block of 4 2,250.
Cancellations
Blue +10.00
Indigo +5.00
Town +20.00

No. O107 on cover is unique, but the stamp is damaged. It is valued thus.

POST OFFICE

O108 O6 3c **black** 30.00 10.00
gray black 30.00 10.00
Never hinged 70.00
No gum 10.00
On cover —
Block of 4 130.00 —
P# block of 14, Impt. *475.00*
Cancellations
Purple +1.00
Violet +1.00
Blue +1.00
Indigo +10.00
Magenta +1.00
Red +20.00
Green +40.00
Town +2.00
"Paid" +12.00

TREASURY

O109 O9 3c **brown** 80.00 10.00
yellow brown 80.00 10.00
Never hinged 175.00
No gum 35.00
On cover 110.00
Block of 4 400.00 *900.00*
P# block of 14, Impt. *1,450.*
Cancellations
Purple +1.50
Blue +1.50
Indigo +3.00
Town +2.00
Numeral +7.50
O110 O9 6c **brown** 200.00 50.00
yellow brown 200.00 50.00
dark brown 200.00 50.00
Never hinged 450.00
No gum 65.00
On cover 300.00
Block of 4 950.00 —
P# block of 12, Impt. *2,900.*
Cancellations
Purple +6.00
Magenta +6.00
Blue +6.00
O111 O9 10c **brown** 275.00 80.00
yellow brown 275.00 80.00
dark brown 275.00 80.00
Never hinged 650.00
No gum 120.00
On cover *750.00*
Block of 4 1,250. —
P# block of 12, Impt. *4,500.*
Cancellations
Purple +2.50
Blue +2.50
Magenta +5.00
Town +7.50
O112 O9 30c **brown** 2,400. 425.00
Never hinged —
No gum 875.00
Block of 4 *12,000.*
Short transfer at right top 2,600.
Cancellations
Blue +25.00
Indigo +25.00
Town +50.00
O113 O9 90c **brown** 10,000. 750.00
dark brown 10,000. 750.00
Never hinged —
No gum 3,250.
Block of 4 *45,000.*
Cancellations
Purple +25.00
Blue +25.00
Town +75.00

WAR

O114 O10 1c **rose red** 7.50 4.00
rose 7.50 4.00
dull rose red 7.50 4.00
brown rose 7.50 4.00
Never hinged 15.00
No gum 2.75
On cover 55.00
Block of 4 32.50 —
P# block of 12, Impt. *150.00*
Never hinged *220.00*
Cancellations
Purple +.50
Blue +.50
Town +1.00
Fort +100.00
O115 O10 2c **rose red** 15.00 4.00
dark rose red 15.00 4.00
Never hinged 30.00
No gum 5.00
On cover 40.00
Block of 4 65.00 —
P# block of 12, Impt. *200.00*
Never hinged *325.00*
Cancellations
Purple +.50
Blue +.50
Magenta +.50
Green +35.00
Town +2.00
Fort +100.00
O116 O10 3c **rose red** 15.00 2.00
dull rose red 15.00 2.00
Never hinged 30.00
No gum 5.00
On cover 35.00
Block of 4 65.00 —
P# block of 14, Impt. *200.00*
Never hinged *325.00*
Double transfer 20.00 6.00
Plate flaw at upper left (32 R 11) — —
a. Imperf., pair *5,000.*
b. Double impression *7,500.*
Cancellations
Purple +.50
Violet +.50
Blue +.50
Ultramarine +5.00
Magenta +1.00
Red +5.00
Town +1.00
Fort +100.00
O117 O10 6c **rose red** 12.50 3.00
dull rose red 12.50 3.00
dull vermilion — —
Never hinged 25.00
No gum 4.50
On cover 50.00
Block of 4 52.50 —
P# block of 12, Impt. *190.00*
Cancellations
Purple +.50
Blue +.50
Magenta +1.00
Brown +20.00
Town +1.00
Fort +100.00
Numeral +7.50
O118 O10 10c **rose red** 75.00 50.00
dull rose red 75.00 50.00
Never hinged 150.00
No gum 27.50
On cover *1,800.*
Block of 4 325.00
P# block of 10, Impt. *950.00*

Cancellations

Violet +3.00
Town +5.00
Fort +100.00

O119 O10 12c **rose red** 70.00 14.00
dull rose red 70.00 14.00
brown rose 70.00 14.00
Never hinged 140.00
No gum 25.00
On cover —
Block of 4 300.00 —
P# block of 10, Impt. *775.00*

Cancellations

Purple +1.00
Violet +1.00
Red +10.00
Green —
Town +2.50
Fort +150.00

O120 O10 30c **rose red** 225.00 100.00
dull rose red 225.00 100.00
Never hinged 500.00
No gum 90.00
Block of 4 975.00 —
P# block of 10, Impt. *3,500.*

Cancellations

Violet +5.00
Town +10.00
Fort +125.00

SPECIAL PRINTINGS

Special printings of Official stamps were made in 1875 at the time the other Reprints, Re-issues and Special Printings were printed. They are ungummed. Though overprinted "SPECIMEN," these stamps are Special Printings, and they are not considered to be in the same category as the stamps listed in the Specimen section of this catalogue.

Although perforated, these stamps were sometimes (but not always) cut apart with scissors. As a result the perforations may be mutilated and the design damaged. Values are for very fine stamps with intact perforations.

Number sold indicated in parentheses.

All values exist imperforate.

The "SEPCIMEN" error appears once on some panes of 100. The error was discovered and corrected part way through the printing. Blocks of 4 or larger with the "SEPCIMEN" error are rare and worth much more than the value of the individual stamps.

Printing flaws which resemble broken type (but are not) are commonly found on the SPECIMEN overprint on these and other overprinted stamps. The variety listed as a "small dotted i" is actually an "i"; it is not one of the printing flaws noted in the preceding sentence. All "small dotted 'i'" varieties are on ribbed paper from the second special printings. They occur in positions 7 and 26.

Printed by the Continental Bank Note Co.
Similar to Type D, without period, 11mm long

AGRICULTURE

Overprinted in Block Letters

Thin, hard white paper
Carmine Overprint

1875 *Perf. 12*

O1S D 1c **yellow** (10,234) 32.50
Block of 4 *350.00*
P# block of 12, Impt. *2,600.*
a. "Sepcimen" error *2,500.*
b. Horiz. ribbed paper (10,000) 37.50
Block of 4 *425.00*
P# strip of 6, Impt. *1,100.*
c. As "b," small dotted "i" in "Specimen" 500.00
Block of 4, one stamp small dotted "i" 750.00

O2S D 2c **yellow** (4,192) 55.00
Block of 4 *625.00*
P# block of 8, Impt. —
a. "Sepcimen" error *3,000.*
Block of 4, one stamp "Sepcimen" error *7,250.*

O3S D 3c **yellow** (389) 400.00
a. "Sepcimen" error *19,000.*

O4S D 6c **yellow** (373) 400.00
a. "Sepcimen" error *22,500.*

O5S D 10c **yellow** (390) 400.00
P# strip of 5, Impt. —
a. "Sepcimen" error *19,000.*

O6S D 12c **yellow** (379) 400.00
a. "Sepcimen" error *15,000.*

O7S D 15c **yellow** (370) 400.00
a. "Sepcimen" error *12,500.*

O8S D 24c **yellow** (352) 400.00
a. "Sepcimen" error *12,500.*

O9S D 30c **yellow** (354) 400.00
a. "Sepcimen" error *13,500.*

EXECUTIVE

Blue Overprint

O10S D 1c **carmine** (10,000) 32.50
Block of 4 *350.00*
P# block of 14, Impt. *20,000.*
a. Horiz. ribbed paper (10,000) 40.00
Block of 4 *375.00*
P# strip of 7, Impt. *3,250.*
b. As "a," small dotted "i" in "Specimen" 500.00

O11S D 2c **carmine** (7,430) 55.00
Block of 4 550.00
Foreign entry of 6c Agriculture (pos. 40) *2,250.*

O12S D 3c **carmine** (3,735) 67.50
Block of 4 —

O13S D 6c **carmine** (3,485) 67.50
Block of 4 —

O14S D 10c **carmine** (3,461) 67.50
Block of 4 —

INTERIOR

Blue Overprint

O15S D 1c **vermilion** (7,194) 60.00
Block of 4 *650.00*
P# block of 12, impt. *3,750.*

O16S D 2c **vermilion** (1,263) 140.00
Block of 4 1,600.
P# Block of 12, Impt. *7,500.*
a. "Sepcimen" error —

The existence of a genuine example of No. O16Sa has been questioned by specialists. The editors would like to see authenticated evidence of the existence of the single reported example.

O17S D 3c **vermilion** (88) *2,500.*
O18S D 6c **vermilion** (83) *2,500.*
O19S D 10c **vermilion** (82) *2,500.*
O20S D 12c **vermilion** (75) *2,500.*
O21S D 15c **vermilion** (78) *2,500.*
Double transfer at left *3,000.*
O22S D 24c **vermilion** (77) *2,500.*
O23S D 30c **vermilion** (75) *2,500.*
O24S D 90c **vermilion** (77) *2,500.*

JUSTICE

Blue Overprint

O25S D 1c **purple** (10,000) 32.50
Block of 4 *350.00*
P# block of 12, Impt. *3,250.*
a. "Sepcimen" error *1,900.*
b. Horiz. ribbed paper (9,729) 35.00
Block of 4 *550.00*
P# block of 12, Impt. *4,000.*
c. As "b," small dotted "i" in "Specimen" 500.00
P# block of 21, two stamps small dotted "i" *6,000.*

O26S D 2c **purple** (3,395) 55.00
Block of 4 650.00
P# block of 12, Impt. *5,500.*
a. "Sepcimen" error *3,500.*
Block of 4, one stamp "Sepcimen" error *9,750.*

O27S D 3c **purple** (178) 1,250.
Plate scratches —
a. "Sepcimen" error *11,000.*

O28S D 6c **purple** (163) 1,250.
O29S D 10c **purple** (163) 1,250.
O30S D 12c **purple** (154) 1,250.
a. "Sepcimen" error *19,000.*
O31S D 15c **purple** (157) 1,250.
a. "Sepcimen" error *25,000.*
O32S D 24c **purple** (150) 1,250.
a. "Sepcimen" error *20,000.*
O33S D 30c **purple** (150) 1,250.
a. "Sepcimen" error *15,000.*
O34S D 90c **purple** (152) 1,250.

NAVY

Carmine Overprint

O35S D 1c **ultramarine** (10,000) 35.00
Block of 4 *375.00*
a. "Sepcimen" error *2,750.*
Block of 4, one stamp "Sepcimen" error *6,250.*
b. Double "Specimen" overprint *1,900.*

O36S D 2c **ultramarine** (1,748) 75.00
Block of 4 *750.00*
P# strip of 6, Impt. *1,600.*
a. "Sepcimen" error *4,500.*
Block of 4, one stamp "Sepcimen" error *10,500.*

O37S D 3c **ultramarine** (126) 1,750.
O38S D 6c **ultramarine** (116) 1,750.
Vertical line through "N" of "Navy" *2,100.*

O39S D 7c **ultramarine** (501) 550.00
Block of 4 *5,000.*
a. "Sepcimen" error *10,000.*
Block of 4, one stamp "Sepcimen" error *30,000.*

O40S D 10c **ultramarine** (112) 1,750.
a. "Sepcimen" error *17,500.*

O41S D 12c **ultramarine** (107) 1,750.
Double transfer at left side, pos. 50 —
a. "Sepcimen" error *21,000.*

O42S D 15c **ultramarine** (107) 1,750.
a. "Sepcimen" error *16,000.*

O43S D 24c **ultramarine** (106) 1,750.
a. "Sepcimen" error *15,000.*

O44S D 30c **ultramarine** (104) 1,750.
Double transfer —
a. "Sepcimen" error *17,500.*

O45S D 90c **ultramarine** (102) 1,750.

POST OFFICE

Carmine Overprint

O47S D 1c **black** (6,015) 45.00
Block of 4 *475.00*
P# block of 12, Impt. *4,500.*
P# block of 14, Impt. *4,750.*
a. "Sepcimen" error *3,250.*
Block of 4, one stamp "SEPCIMEN" error *7,000.*
b. Inverted overprint *2,500.*

O48S D 2c **black** (590) 325.00
Block of 4 *3,250.*
a. "Sepcimen" error *15,000.*
Block of 4, one stamp "Sepcimen" error *30,000.*

O49S D 3c **black** (91) 1,600.
a. "Sepcimen" error *37,500.*
O50S D 6c **black** (87) 1,600.
O51S D 10c **black** (177) 1,000.
a. "Sepcimen" error *15,000.*
O52S D 12c **black** (93) 1,600.
O53S D 15c **black** (82) 1,600.
a. "Sepcimen" error *26,000.*
O54S D 24c **black** (84) 1,600.
a. "Sepcimen" error *22,000.*
O55S D 30c **black** (81) 1,600.
O56S D 90c **black** (82) 1,600.
a. "Sepcimen" error *25,000.*

STATE

Carmine Overprint

O57S D 1c **bluish green** (10,000) 32.50
Block of 4 *250.00*
a. "Sepcimen" error *1,900.*
Block of 4, one stamp "Sepcimen" error *4,500.*
b. Horiz. ribbed paper (10,000) 35.00
Block of 4 *425.00*
c. As "b," small dotted "i" in "Specimen" 650.00
d. Double "Specimen" overprint *3,850.*
Block of 4 —

O58S D 2c **bluish green** (5,145) 90.00
Block of 4 *850.00*
Double transfer at bottom (pos. 98) *750.00*
a. "Sepcimen" error *2,500.*
Block of 4, one stamp "Sepcimen" error *16,500.*

O59S D 3c **bluish green** (793) 140.00
Block of 4 —
a. "Sepcimen" error *7,000.*
Block of 4, one stamp "Sepcimen" error *11,000.*

O60S D 6c **bluish green** (467) 350.00
Foreign entry of 6c Executive *600.00*
a. "Sepcimen" error *12,500.*

O61S D 7c **bluish green** (791) 175.00
Block of 4 *1,500.*
a. "Sepcimen" error *9,000.*
Block of 4, one stamp "Sepcimen" error *21,500.*

O62S D 10c **bluish green** (346) 550.00
Short transfer, pos. 34 *2,200.*
a. "Sepcimen" error *27,500.*

O63S D 12c **bluish green** (280) 550.00
a. "Sepcimen" error *19,000.*
O64S D 15c **bluish green** (257) 600.00
O65S D 24c **bluish green** (253) 600.00
a. "Sepcimen" error *25,000.*
O66S D 30c **bluish green** (249) 600.00
a. "Sepcimen" error *27,500.*
O67S D 90c **bluish green** (245) 600.00
a. "Sepcimen" error *27,500.*
O68S D $2 **green & black** (32) *19,000.*
O69S D $5 **green & black** (12) *50,000.*
O70S D $10 **green & black** (8) *110,000.*
O71S D $20 **green & black** (7) *160,000.*

TREASURY

Blue Overprint

O72S D 1c **dark brown** (2,185) 80.00
Block of 4 *975.00*
Double transfer —

O73S D 2c **dark brown** (309) 450.00
Block of 4 *3,250.*
P# block of 14, Impt. *17,500.*

The only two recorded plate blocks of No. O73S are contained in a unique left pane of 100 stamps.

O74S D 3c **dark brown** (84) 1,600.
O75S D 6c **dark brown** (85) 1,600.
O76S D 7c **dark brown** (198) 950.00
Block of 4 9,000.
P# block of 12, Impt. 30,000.

The only recorded plate block of No. O76S is contained in a half sheet of 50 stamps.

O77S D 10c **dark brown** (82) 1,600.
O78S D 12c **dark brown** (75) 1,600.
O79S D 15c **dark brown** (75) 1,600.
O80S D 24c **dark brown** (99) 1,600.
O81S D 30c **dark brown** (74) 1,600.
Short transfer at left top (pos. 95) (1) —
Short transfer at right top (pos. 45) (1) —

O82S D 90c **dark brown** (72) 1,650.

WAR

Blue Overprint

O83S D 1c **deep rose** (9,610) 35.00
Block of 4 *375.00*
P# strip of 6, Impt. *1,300.*
a. "Sepcimen" error *3,000.*
Block of 4, one stamp "Sepcimen" error *7,500.*

O84S D 2c **deep rose** (1,618) 125.00
Block of 4 *1,400.*
P# block of 12 *9,000.*
a. "Sepcimen" error *3,500.*
Block of 4, one stamp "Sepcimen" error *9,750.*

O85S D 3c **deep rose** (118) 1,400.
a. "Sepcimen" error *30,000.*

O86S D 6c **deep rose** (111) 1,400.
a. "Sepcimen" error *32,000.*

O87S D 7c **deep rose** (539) 425.00
Block of 4 *2,750.*
a. "Sepcimen" error *17,500.*

O88S D 10c **deep rose** (119) 1,400.
a. "Sepcimen" error *27,500.*

O89S D 12c **deep rose** (105) 1,400.
a. "Sepcimen" error *32,000.*

O90S D 15c **deep rose** (105) 1,400.
a. "Sepcimen" error *30,000.*

O91S D 24c **deep rose** (106) 1,400.
a. "Sepcimen" error *30,000.*

O92S D 30c **deep rose** (104) 1,400.
a. "Sepcimen" error *30,000.*

O93S D 90c **deep rose** (106) 1,400.
a. "Sepcimen" error *30,000.*

EXECUTIVE

Printed by the American Bank Note Co. Soft Porous Paper

1881 **Blue Overprint**

O10xS D 1c **violet rose** (4,652) 95.00
Block of 4 *1,100.*
P# block of 14, Impt. *32,500.*

NAVY

Carmine Overprint

O35xS D 1c **gray blue** (4,182) 100.00
deep blue 100.00
Block of 4 *1,150.*
P# block of 12, Impt. *8,000.*
a. Double overprint 1,200.

STATE

O57xS D 1c **yellow green** (1,672) 180.00
Block of 4 *2,500.*
P# strip of 6, Impt. *3,000.*

OFFICIAL POSTAL SAVINGS MAIL

The Act of Congress, approved June 25, 1910, establishing postal savings depositories, provided:

"Sec. 2. That the Postmaster General is hereby directed to prepare and issue special stamps of the necessary denominations for use, in lieu of penalty or franked envelopes, in the transmittal of free mail resulting from the administration of this act."

The use of postal savings official stamps was discontinued by the Act of Congress, approved September 23, 1914. Postmasters were notified of the discontinuance in mid-October 1914. The unused stamps in the hands of postmasters were returned and destroyed.

O11

Printed by the Bureau of Engraving & Printing

1910-11 **Engr.** **Wmk. 191**

O121 O11 2c **black**, *Dec. 22, 1910* 17.50 2.00
Never hinged 40.00
On cover 12.50
Block of 4 (2mm spacing) 80.00 11.00
Block of 4 (3mm spacing) 77.50 10.00
P# block of 6, Impt. & Star 350.00
Double transfer 22.50 4.00

O122 O11 50c **dark green**, *Feb. 1, 1911* 175.00 60.00
Never hinged 425.00
On cover 225.00
Block of 4 (2mm spacing) 675.00 300.00
Block of 4 (3mm spacing) 650.00 300.00
Margin block of 4, arrow 675.00
P# block of 6, Impt. & Star 2,400.
Never hinged *3,500.*

O123 O11 $1 **ultramarine**, *Feb. 1, 1911* 200.00 15.00
Never hinged 450.00
On cover 110.00
Block of 4 (2mm spacing) 850.00 75.00
Block of 4 (3mm spacing) 825.00 75.00
Margin block of 4, arrow 850.00
P# block of 6, Impt. & Star 2,400. —

Wmk. 190

O124 O11 1c **dark violet**, *Mar. 27, 1911* 10.00 2.00
Never hinged 22.50
On cover 15.00
Block of 4 (2mm spacing) 45.00 9.00
Block of 4 (3mm spacing) 42.50 8.50
P# block of 6, Impt. & Star 190.00 —
Never hinged 350.00

O125 O11 2c **black** 65.00 7.00
Never hinged 150.00
On cover 25.00
Block of 4 (2mm spacing) 240.00 32.50
Block of 4 (3mm spacing) 225.00 32.50
P# block of 6, Impt. & Star 700.00
Double transfer 60.00 8.00

O126 O11 10c **carmine**, *Feb. 1, 1911* 20.00 2.00
Never hinged 50.00
On cover 20.00
Block of 4 (2mm spacing) 87.50 30.00
Block of 4 (3mm spacing) 82.50 10.00
P# block of 6, Impt. & Star 370.00
Double transfer 25.00 3.50

Catalogue values for unused stamps in this section, from this point to the end, are for Never Hinged items.

Catalogue values for used stamps are for regularly used examples, not for examples removed from first day covers.

From No. O127 onward, all official stamps are tagged unless noted.

OFFICIAL MAIL

O12

Designed by Bradbury Thompson

Engraved

1983, Jan. 12-1985 **Unwmk.** ***Perf. 11***

O127 O12 1c **red, blue & black** .25 .25
FDC, Washington, DC 1.00
P# block of 4, UL or UR .25

O128 O12 4c **red, blue & black** .25 .25
FDC, Washington, DC 1.00
P# block of 4, LR only .40

O129 O12 13c **red, blue & black** .50 *15.00*
FDC, Washington, DC 1.00
P# block of 4, UR only 2.25

O129A O12 14c **red, blue & black**, *May 15, 1985* .45 .50
FDC, Washington, DC 1.00
Zip-copyright block of 6 2.90

O130 O12 17c **red, blue & black** .55 .40
FDC, Washington, DC 1.00
P# block of 4, LL only 2.50

O132 O12 $1 **red, blue & black** 2.25 1.00
FDC, Washington, DC 2.25
P# block of 4, UL only 10.00

O133 O12 $5 **red, blue & black** 9.50 *20.00*
FDC, Washington, DC 12.50
P# block of 4, LL only 45.00
Nos. O127-O133 (7) 13.75 37.40

No. O129A does not have a "c" after the "14."

COIL STAMPS

Perf. 10 Vert.

O135 O12 20c **red, blue & black** 1.75 2.00
FDC, Washington, DC 1.00
Pair 3.50 4.00
P# strip of 3, P# 1 7.00
P# strip of 5, P# 1 40.00
P# single, #1 — 12.50
a. Imperf., pair *1,000.*
b. Tagging omitted — —

O136 O12 22c **red, blue & blk, low gloss gum**, *May 15, 1985* 1.00 *2.00*
FDC, Washington, DC 1.00
Pair 2.00 *4.00*
Dull finish gum *65.00*
a. Tagging omitted —

Inscribed: Postal Card Rate D

1985, Feb. 4 ***Perf. 11***

O138 O12 (14c) **red, blue & black** 5.00 *15.00*
FDC, Washington, DC 1.00
P# block of 4, LR only 27.50 —

Frame line completely around blue design — O13

Inscribed: No. O139, Domestic Letter Rate D; No. O140, Domestic Mail E.

COIL STAMPS

1985-88 **Litho., Engr. (#O139)** ***Perf. 10 Vert.***

O138A O13 15c **red, blue & blk**, *June 11, 1988* .50 .50
FDC, Corpus Christi, TX 1.25
Pair 1.00 1.00

O138B O13 20c **red, blue & blk**, *May 19, 1988* .50 .30
FDC, Washington 1.25
Pair 1.00 .60

O139 O12 (22c) **red, blue & blk**, *Feb. 4* 5.25 *20.00*
FDC, Washington, DC 1.00
Pair 10.50 —
P# strip of 3, P# 1 15.00
P# strip of 5, P# 1 30.00
P# single, #1 — 27.50

O140 O13 (25c) **red, blue & black**, *Mar. 22, 1988* .75 *2.00*
FDC, Washington 1.25
Pair 1.50 —

O141 O13 25c **red, blue & blk**, *June 11, 1988* .65 .50
FDC, Corpus Christi, TX 1.25
Pair 1.30 1.00
a. Imperf., pair *800.00* —
Nos. O138A-O141 (5) 7.65 *23.30*

First day cancellation was applied to 137,721 covers bearing Nos. O138A and O141.

Plates of 400 in four panes of 100.

1989, July 5 **Litho.** ***Perf. 11***

O143 O13 1c **red, blue & black** .25 .25
FDC, Washington, DC 1.25

On No. O143, the denomination is shown as "1". See No. O154.

Type of 1985 and

O14

COIL STAMPS

1991 **Litho.** ***Perf. 10 Vert.***

O144 O14 (29c) **red, blue & blk**, *Jan. 22* .80 .50
FDC, Washington, DC 1.25
Pair 1.60 —

O145 O13 29c **red, blue & blk**, *May 24* .70 .30
FDC, Seattle, WA 1.25
Pair 1.40 .60

Plates of 400 in four panes of 100.

1991-93 **Litho.** ***Perf. 11***

O146 O13 4c **red, blue & blk**, *Apr. 6* .25 .30
FDC, Oklahoma City, OK 1.25

O146A O13 10c **red, blue & black**, *Oct. 19, 1993* .30 .30
FDC, Washington, DC 1.25

O147 O13 19c **red, blue & blk**, *May 24* .40 .50
FDC, Seattle, WA 1.25

O148 O13 23c **red, blue & blk**, *May 24* .50 .30
FDC, Seattle, WA 1.25
Horiz. pair with full vert. gutter between —
Vert. pair with full horiz. gutter between —

See No. O156 for 23c with microscopic text below eagle. Imperfs of No. O148 are printer's waste.

Perf. 11¼

O151 O13 $1 **red, blue & black**, *Sept. 1993* 5.00 .75
Nos. O146-O151 (5) 6.45 2.15

COIL STAMPS

Inscribed: No. O152, For U.S. addresses only G.

Perf. 9.8 Vert.

O152 O14 (32c) **red, blue & black**, *Dec. 13, 1994* .65 .50
FDC, Washington, DC 1.25
Pair 1.30 —

O153 O13 32c **red, blue & black**, *May 9, 1995* 1.50 .50
FDC, Washington, DC 1.25
Pair 3.00 —

Nos. O146A, O151, O153 have a line of microscopic text below the eagle.

1995, May 9 **Litho.** **Untagged** ***Perf. 11.2***

O154 O13 1c **red, blue & black** .25 .50
FDC, Washington, DC 1.25

Denomination on No. O154 has a cent sign. See No. O143.

O155 O13 20c **red, blue & black** .55 .50
FDC, Washington, DC 1.25

O156 O13 23c **red, blue & black** .60 .50
FDC, Washington, DC 1.25

COIL STAMP

1999, Oct. 8 Litho. *Perf. 9¾ Vert.*

O157 O13 33c **red, blue & black**	2.25	—
FDC, Washington, DC		1.25
Pair	4.50	—

Type of 1985
COIL STAMP

2001, Feb. 27 Litho. *Perf. 9¾ Vert.*

O158 O13 34c **red, blue & black**	2.25	.50
FDC, Washington, DC		1.25
Pair	4.50	—

Nos. O154-O158 have a line of microscopic text below the eagle.

Type of 1985
COIL STAMP

2002, Aug. 2 Photo. *Perf. 10 Vert.*

O159 O13 37c **red, blue & black**	.75	.50
First day cover, Washington, DC		1.25
First day cover, any other city		1.25
Pair	1.50	—
P# strip of 5, P#S111	8.00	—
P# single, same #	—	7.00

Type of 1985
COIL STAMP

2006, Mar. 8 Photo. *Perf. 10 Vert.*

O160 O13 39c **red, blue & black**	1.00	*1.00*
First day cover, Washington, DC		1.25
First day cover, any other city		1.25
Pair	1.60	—
P# strip of 5, #S111	9.00	—
P# single, #S111	—	6.00

Type of 1988

Designed by Bradbury Thompson.

Printed by Sterling Sommer for Ashton-Potter (USA) Ltd.

LITHOGRAPHED
Sheets of 240 in 12 panes of 20

2006, Sept. 29 *Perf. 11¼*

O161 O13 $1 **red, blue & black**	5.00	*1.25*
First day cover, Washington, DC		3.25
First day cover, any other city		3.25
Pane of 20	100.00	

No. O161 has a solid blue background. No. O151 has a background of crosshatched lines.

Type of 1985
COIL STAMP

2007, June 25 Litho. *Perf. 9¾*

O162 O13 41c **red, blue & black**	1.00	*1.00*
First day cover, Kansas City, MO		2.10
Pair	2.00	—
P# strip of 5, #S111	9.50	—
P# single, #S111	—	9.50

Nos. O159-O162 have solid blue backgrounds. Nos. O138A-O158 have a background of crosshatched lines.

Type of 1985

Designed by Bradbury Thompson. Printed by Banknote Corporation of America for Sennett Security Products.

Serpentine Die Cut 11½x10¾

2009, Feb. 24 Litho. Untagged
Self-Adhesive

O163 O13 1c **red, blue & black**	.25	*.40*
First day cover, Washington, DC		2.10
Pane of 20	1.00	

NEWSPAPER AND PERIODICAL STAMPS

First issued in September 1865 for prepayment of postage on bulk shipments of newspapers and periodicals. From 1875 on, the stamps were affixed to pages of receipt books, sometimes canceled, and retained by the post office.

Virtually all used stamps of Nos. PR1-PR4 are canceled by blue brush strokes and have faults such as tears, stains, creases, etc. All are rare. Most used stamps of Nos. PR9-PR32, PR57-PR79 and PR81-PR89 are pen canceled (or uncanceled), with many of Nos. PR9-PR32 also known canceled by a thick blue brush stroke or a handstamp cork or target cancellation. Used values for Nos. PR90-PR125 are for stamps with legible handstamp cancellations.

Discontinued on July 1, 1898.

Washington — N1

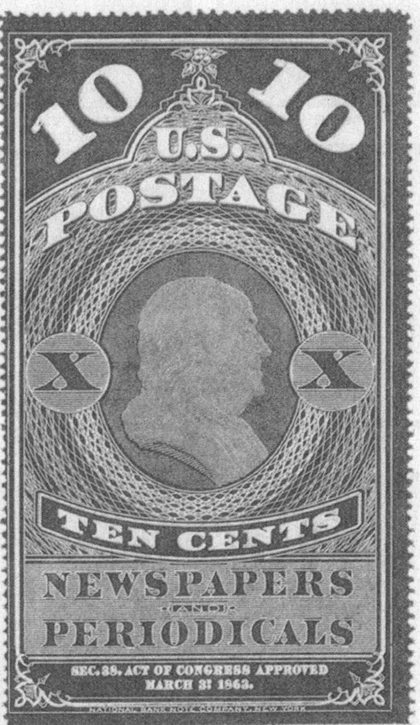

Franklin — N2

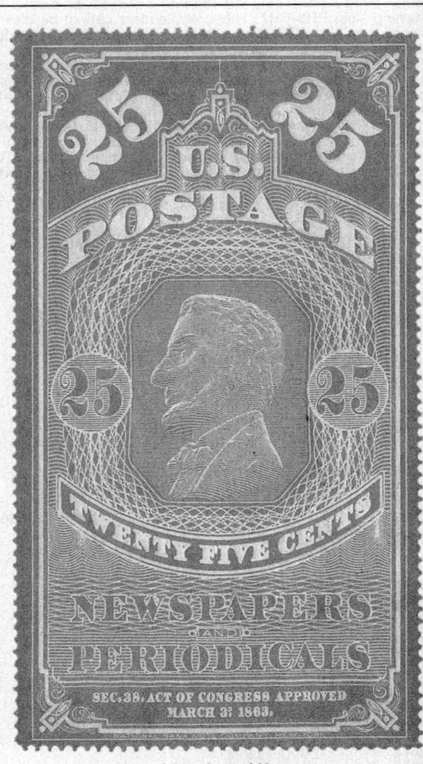

Lincoln — N3

Values for Nos. PR1-PR8 are for examples with perforations on all four sides. Examples with natural straight edges sell for somewhat less. Some panes were fully perforated, while others have natural straight edges either at top or bottom affecting five stamps in the pane of ten.

Printed by the National Bank Note Co.
Plates of 20 subjects in two panes of 10 each.
Thin hard paper, without gum
Size of design: 51x95mm

Typographed and Embossed

1865 Unwmk. *Perf. 12*

Colored Border

No.	Design	Description	Unused	Used
PR1	N1	5c **dark blue**	750.00	*2,000.*
		blue	750.00	*2,000.*
		Block of 4	3,750.	—
a.		5c **light blue**	1,350.	*4,250.*
PR2	N2	10c **blue green**	300.00	*2,000.*
a.		10c **green**	300.00	*2,000.*
		Block of 4	1,400.	—
b.		Pelure paper	400.00	*2,000.*
PR3	N3	25c **orange red**	400.00	*2,500.*
		Block of 4	1,700.	—
a.		25c **carmine red**	475.00	*2,500.*
		Block of 4	2,000.	—
b.		Pelure paper	500.00	

Nos. PR1-PR3 used are valued with faults.

White Border

Yellowish paper

No.	Design	Description	Unused	Used
PR4	N1	5c **light blue**	750.00	*5,000.*
		blue	750.00	—
		Block of 4	3,750.	
a.		5c **dark blue**	750.00	—
b.		Pelure paper	850.00	—

No. PR4 used is valued with faults.

REPRINTS of 1865 ISSUE

Printed by the Continental Bank Note Co. using the original National Bank Note Co. plates

1875 *Perf. 12*

Hard white paper, without gum

5c White Border, 10c and 25c Colored Border

No.	Design	Description	Value
PR5	N1	5c **dull blue** *(10,000)*	225.00
		dark blue	225.00
		Block of 4	1,000.
a.		Printed on both sides	*5,750.*
PR6	N2	10c **dark bluish green** *(7765)*	250.00
		deep green	250.00
		Block of 4	1,075.
a.		Printed on both sides	*4,250.*
PR7	N3	25c **dark carmine** *(6684)*	300.00
		dark carmine red	300.00
		Block of 4	1,350.
		Nos. PR5-PR7 (3)	775.00

750 examples of each value, which were remainders from the regular issue, were sold as reprints because of delays in obtaining Nos. PR5-PR7. These remainders cannot be distinguished from Nos. PR2-PR4, and are not included in the reprint quantities.

The Continental Bank Note Co. made another special printing from new plates, which did not have the colored border. These exist imperforate and perforated, but they were not regularly issued. Value, imperf. set $3,250.

On No. PR5, there is no thin line of color in the second white area on each side of the stamp. On No. PR8, there is often a thin line of color in this area, but not all examples of No. PR8 show this line (see illustration below). Expertization is based on color and paper.

#PR5 #PR8

Printed by the American Bank Note Co.

Soft porous paper, without gum

1881 White Border

No.	Design	Description	Value
PR8	N1	5c **dark blue** (5645)	650.00
		Block of 4	3,000.

Statue of Freedom on Capitol Dome, by Thomas Crawford — N4

"Justice" — N5

Ceres — N6

"Victory" — N7

Clio — N8

Minerva — N9

Vesta — N10

"Peace" — N11

"Commerce" — N12

Hebe — N13

Indian Maiden — N14

Values for used examples of Nos. PR9-PR113 are for fine-very fine examples for denominations to $3, and fine for denominations of $5 or higher. Used examples of some Scott numbers might not exist without faults.

Printed by the Continental Bank Note Co.

Plates of 100 subjects in two panes of 50 each

Thin hard paper

Size of design: 24x35mm

1875, Jan. 1 Engr. *Perf. 12*

No.	Design	Description	Unused	Used
PR9	N4	2c **black**	300.00	40.00
		gray black	300.00	40.00
		greenish black	300.00	40.00
		No gum	120.00	
		Handstamp or blue brush cancel		125.00
		Block of 4	1,350.	250.00
PR10	N4	3c **black**	300.00	45.00
		gray black	300.00	45.00
		No gum	120.00	
		Handstamp or blue brush cancel		125.00
		Block of 4	1,350.	225.00
PR11	N4	4c **black**	300.00	40.00
		gray black	300.00	40.00
		greenish black	300.00	40.00
		No gum	120.00	
		Handstamp or blue brush cancel		125.00
		Block of 4	1,350.	
PR12	N4	6c **black**	300.00	45.00
		gray black	300.00	45.00
		greenish black	300.00	45.00
		No gum	120.00	
		Handstamp or blue brush cancel		125.00
		Block of 4	1,350.	
PR13	N4	8c **black**	350.00	65.00
		gray black	350.00	65.00
		greenish black	350.00	65.00
		No gum	135.00	
		Handstamp or blue brush cancel		200.00
PR14	N4	9c **black**	600.00	125.00
		gray black	600.00	125.00
		No gum	225.00	
		Handstamp or blue brush cancel		400.00
		Double transfer at top	650.00	140.00
PR15	N4	10c **black**	375.00	60.00
		gray black	375.00	60.00
		greenish black	375.00	60.00
		No gum	135.00	
		Handstamp or blue brush cancel		150.00
		Block of 4	1,700.	
PR16	N5	12c **rose**	800.00	100.00
		pale rose	800.00	100.00
		No gum	325.00	
		Handstamp or blue brush cancel		325.00
PR17	N5	24c **rose**	850.00	125.00
		pale rose	850.00	125.00
		No gum	350.00	
		Handstamp or blue brush cancel		375.00
		Paper with silk fibers	*2,000.*	—
PR18	N5	36c **rose**	850.00	150.00
		pale rose	850.00	150.00
		No gum	350.00	
		Handstamp or blue brush cancel		300.00
PR19	N5	48c **rose**	1,250.	400.00
		pale rose	1,250.	400.00
		No gum	450.00	
		Handstamp or blue brush cancel		600.00
		Horiz. ribbed paper		—
PR20	N5	60c **rose**	1,250.	115.00
		pale rose	1,250.	115.00
		No gum	450.00	
		Handstamp or blue brush cancel		225.00
PR21	N5	72c **rose**	1,500.	375.00
		pale rose	1,500.	375.00
		No gum	550.00	
		Handstamp or blue brush cancel		800.00
PR22	N5	84c **rose**	1,850.	375.00
		pale rose	1,850.	375.00
		No gum	650.00	
		Handstamp or blue brush cancel		1,350.
PR23	N5	96c **rose**	2,000.	250.00
		pale rose	2,000.	250.00
		No gum	775.00	
		Handstamp or blue brush cancel		1,000.
PR24	N6	$1.92 **dark brown**	1,750.	250.00
		No gum	700.00	
		Handstamp or blue brush cancel		850.00
PR25	N7	$3 **vermilion**	2,500.	450.00
		No gum	975.00	
		Handstamp or blue brush cancel		1,250.
PR26	N8	$6 **ultramarine**	4,000.	550.00
		dull ultramarine	4,000.	550.00
		No gum	1,600.	
		Handstamp or blue brush cancel		2,000.
PR27	N9	$9 **yellow orange**	4,500.	*2,000.*
		No gum	1,750.	
		Handstamp or blue brush cancel		—
PR28	N10	$12 **blue green**	4,750.	*1,100.*
		No gum	1,850.	
		Handstamp or blue brush cancel		—
PR29	N11	$24 **dark gray violet**	4,750.	*1,200.*
		No gum	1,850.	
		Handstamp or blue brush cancel		—
PR30	N12	$36 **brown rose**	5,000.	*1,400.*
		No gum	2,000.	
		Handstamp or blue brush cancel		—
PR31	N13	$48 **red brown**	7,000.	*1,600.*
		No gum	2,600.	
		Handstamp or blue brush cancel		—
PR32	N14	$60 **violet**	6,500.	*1,750.*
		No gum	2,400.	
		Handstamp or blue brush cancel		—

SPECIAL PRINTING of 1875 ISSUE

Printed by the Continental Bank Note Co.

Hard white paper, without gum

1875 *Perf. 12*

No.	Design	Description	Value
PR33	N4	2c **gray black** *(5,000)*	700.00
		Block of 4	3,250.
a.		Horizontally ribbed paper (10,000)	500.00
PR34	N4	3c **gray black** *(5,000)*	700.00
		Block of 4	3,250.
a.		Horizontally ribbed paper (1,952)	550.00
PR35	N4	4c **gray black** *(4451)*	700.00
		Block of 4	3,250.
		Horizontally ribbed paper	1,000.

No.	Type	Description	Unused	Used
PR36	N4	6c **gray black** *(2348)*	900.00	
PR37	N4	8c **gray black** *(1930)*	975.00	
PR38	N4	9c **gray black** *(1795)*	1,050.	
PR39	N4	10c **gray black** *(1499)*	1,400.	
PR40	N5	12c **pale rose** *(1313)*	1,500.	
PR41	N5	24c **pale rose** *(411)*	2,100.	
PR42	N5	36c **pale rose** *(330)*	2,800.	
PR43	N5	48c **pale rose** *(268)*	3,750.	
PR44	N5	60c **pale rose** *(222)*	4,750.	
PR45	N5	72c **pale rose** *(174)*	4,500.	
PR46	N5	84c **pale rose** *(164)*	5,250.	
PR47	N5	96c **pale rose** *(141)*	*8,500.*	
PR48	N6	$1.92 **dark brown** *(41)*	*20,000.*	
PR49	N7	$3 **vermilion** *(20)*	*45,000.*	
PR50	N8	$6 **ultramarine** *(14)*	*80,000.*	
PR51	N9	$9 **yellow orange** *(4)*	*350,000.*	
PR52	N10	$12 **blue green** *(5)*	*175,000.*	
PR53	N11	$24 **dark gray violet** *(2)*	*500,000.*	
PR54	N12	$36 **brown rose** *(2)*	*400,000.*	
PR55	N13	$48 **red brown** *(1)*	—	
PR56	N14	$60 **violet** *(1)*	—	

Nos. PR50 and PR52 are valued in the grade of fine.

Although four examples of No. PR51 were sold, only one is currently documented.

Although two examples of No. PR53 were sold, only one is currently documented.

No. PR54 is valued in the grade of fine. Although two stamps were sold, only one is currently documented.

All values of this issue, Nos. PR33 to PR56, exist imperforate but were not regularly issued thus. Value, set $60,000.

Numbers in parentheses are quantities sold.

Printed by the American Bank Note Co.
Soft porous paper

1879 **Unwmk.** ***Perf. 12***

No.	Type	Description	Unused	Used
PR57	N4	2c **black**	75.00	15.00
		gray black	75.00	15.00
		greenish black	75.00	15.00
		No gum	30.00	
		Handstamp cancel		50.00
		Block of 4	350.00	
		Double transfer at top	85.00	22.50
		Cracked plate		—
PR58	N4	3c **black**	85.00	20.00
		gray black	85.00	20.00
		intense black	85.00	20.00
		No gum	35.00	
		Handstamp cancel		75.00
		Block of 4	350.00	
		Double transfer at top	95.00	27.50
PR59	N4	4c **black**	85.00	20.00
		gray black	85.00	20.00
		intense black	85.00	20.00
		greenish black	85.00	20.00
		No gum	35.00	
		Handstamp cancel		75.00
		Block of 4	350.00	
		Double transfer at top	95.00	27.50
a.		Double paper	—	
PR60	N4	6c **black**	125.00	35.00
		gray black	125.00	35.00
		intense black	125.00	35.00
		greenish black	125.00	35.00
		No gum	50.00	
		Handstamp cancel		150.00
		Block of 4	600.00	
		Double transfer at top	140.00	45.00
PR61	N4	8c **black**	135.00	35.00
		gray black	135.00	35.00
		greenish black	135.00	35.00
		No gum	55.00	
		Handstamp cancel		150.00
		Block of 4	625.00	
		Double transfer at top	150.00	42.50
PR62	N4	10c **black**	135.00	35.00
		gray black	135.00	35.00
		greenish black	135.00	35.00
		No gum	55.00	
		Handstamp cancel		150.00
		Block of 4	625.00	
		Double transfer at top	150.00	
PR63	N5	12c **red**	500.00	125.00
		No gum	210.00	
		Handstamp cancel		350.00
		Block of 4	2,250.	
PR64	N5	24c **red**	500.00	125.00
		No gum	210.00	
		Handstamp cancel		350.00
		Block of 4	2,250.	
PR65	N5	36c **red**	1,000.	325.00
		No gum	475.00	
		Handstamp cancel		750.00
		Block of 4	4,500.	
PR66	N5	48c **red**	1,000.	300.00
		No gum	450.00	
		Handstamp cancel		750.00
PR67	N5	60c **red**	1,250.	275.00
		No gum	550.00	
		Handstamp cancel		700.00
		Block of 4	4,500.	
a.		Imperf., pair	*4,000.*	
PR68	N5	72c **red**	1,500.	425.00
		No gum	700.00	
		Handstamp cancel		1,000.
PR69	N5	84c **red**	1,250.	350.00
		No gum	575.00	
		Handstamp cancel		850.00
		Block of 4	—	
PR70	N5	96c **red**	1,200.	275.00
		No gum	525.00	
		Handstamp cancel		700.00
		Block of 4	5,500.	
PR71	N6	$1.92 **pale brown**	550.00	175.00
		brown	550.00	175.00
		No gum	225.00	
		Handstamp cancel		500.00
		Block of 4	2,500.	
		Cracked plate	600.00	
PR72	N7	$3 **red vermilion**	625.00	200.00
		No gum	250.00	
		Handstamp cancel		550.00
		Block of 4	2,850.	
PR73	N8	$6 **blue**	1,050.	300.00
		ultramarine	1,100.	300.00
		No gum	400.00	
		Handstamp cancel		1,250.
PR74	N9	$9 **orange**	800.00	225.00
		No gum	325.00	
		Handstamp cancel		750.00
PR75	N10	$12 **yellow green**	850.00	250.00
		No gum	325.00	
		Handstamp cancel		*5,000.*
PR76	N11	$24 **dark violet**	800.00	300.00
		No gum	300.00	
		Handstamp cancel		1,000.
PR77	N12	$36 **Indian red**	850.00	350.00
		No gum	350.00	
		Handstamp cancel		1,250.
PR78	N13	$48 **yellow brown**	900.00	450.00
		No gum	350.00	
		Handstamp cancel		*3,000.*
PR79	N14	$60 **purple**	850.00	400.00
		bright purple	850.00	400.00
		No gum	350.00	
		Handstamp cancel		1,250.

See Die and Plate Proofs for other imperfs. on stamp paper.

SPECIAL PRINTING of 1879 ISSUE
Printed by the American Bank Note Co.
Without gum

1883

No.	Type	Description	Unused	Used
PR80	N4	2c **intense black** (4,514)	1,750.	
		Block of 4	7,500.	

REGULAR ISSUE
Printed by the American Bank Note Co.
With gum

1885 **Unwmk.** ***Perf. 12***

No.	Type	Description	Unused	Used
PR81	N4	1c **black,** *July 1, 1885*	95.00	12.50
		gray black	95.00	12.50
		intense black	95.00	12.50
		Never hinged	225.00	
		No gum	42.50	
		Handstamp cancel		35.00
		Block of 4	425.00	
		Block of 4, P#482, Impt.	650.00	
		Never hinged	1,000.	
		Double transfer at top	105.00	16.00
PR82	N5	12c **carmine**	200.00	30.00
		deep carmine	200.00	30.00
		rose carmine	200.00	30.00
		Never hinged	450.00	
		No gum	85.00	
		Handstamp cancel		105.00
		Block of 4	975.00	
		Plate crack (pos. 41)	*260.00*	
PR83	N5	24c **carmine**	225.00	32.50
		deep carmine	225.00	32.50
		rose carmine	225.00	32.50
		Never hinged	500.00	
		No gum	95.00	
		Handstamp cancel		200.00
		Block of 4	1,100.	
PR84	N5	36c **carmine**	350.00	57.50
		deep carmine	350.00	57.50
		rose carmine	350.00	57.50
		Never hinged	800.00	
		No gum	145.00	
		Handstamp cancel		250.00
		Block of 4	1,400.	
PR85	N5	48c **carmine**	425.00	75.00
		deep carmine	425.00	75.00
		Never hinged	975.00	
		No gum	180.00	
		Handstamp cancel		350.00
		Block of 4	1,850.	
PR86	N5	60c **carmine**	550.00	100.00
		deep carmine	550.00	100.00
		No gum	240.00	
		Handstamp cancel		*3,500.*
		Block of 4	2,500.	
PR87	N5	72c **carmine**	550.00	110.00
		deep carmine	550.00	110.00
		rose carmine	550.00	110.00
		No gum	240.00	
		Handstamp cancel		550.00
		Block of 4	2,500.	
PR88	N5	84c **carmine**	900.00	250.00
		rose carmine	900.00	250.00
		No gum	350.00	
		Handstamp cancel		850.00
		Block of 4	4,250.	
PR89	N5	96c **carmine**	750.00	190.00
		rose carmine	750.00	190.00
		Never hinged	1,750.	
		No gum	300.00	
		Handstamp cancel		800.00
		Block of 4	3,400.	

See Die and Plate Proofs for imperfs. on stamp paper.

Printed by the Bureau of Engraving and Printing

1894 **Unwmk.** ***Perf. 12***

Soft wove paper, with pale, whitish gum

No.	Type	Description	Unused	Used
PR90	N4	1c **intense black**	400.00	*5,000.*
		Never hinged	900.00	
		No gum	160.00	
		Block of 4	1,750.	
		Block of 4, P#482, Impt.	*3,000.*	
		Double transfer at top	425.00	
PR91	N4	2c **intense black**	450.00	—
		Never hinged	1,075.	
		No gum	190.00	
		Block of 4	2,000.	
		Double transfer at top	475.00	
PR92	N4	4c **intense black**	550.00	*13,500.*
		Never hinged	1,275.	
		No gum	210.00	
		Block of 4	2,450.	
PR93	N4	6c **intense black**	4,500.	
		Never hinged	*11,500.*	
		No gum	1,900.	
		Block of 4	—	
PR94	N4	10c **intense black**	1,300.	—
		Never hinged	*2,400.*	
		No gum	525.00	
		Block of 4	5,500.	
PR95	N5	12c **pink**	2,400.	*4,500.*
		Never hinged	*3,500.*	
		No gum	1,100.	
		Block of 4	12,000.	
PR96	N5	24c **pink**	3,750.	*8,000.*
		Never hinged	*7,500.*	
		No gum	1,850.	
		Block of 4	17,500.	
PR97	N5	36c **pink**	*50,000.*	
		Block of 4	—	
PR98	N5	60c **pink**	*40,000.*	*16,000.*
		Block of 4	—	
PR99	N5	96c **pink**	*50,000.*	—
PR100	N7	$3 **scarlet**	*50,000.*	
		Block of 4	—	
PR101	N8	$6 **pale blue**	*50,000.*	—
		No gum	*25,000.*	

Nos. PR90, PR95-PR98 used are valued with fine centering and small faults.

No. PR97 unused is valued in the grade of very good to fine. No. PR98 unused is valued in the grade of fine. Nos. PR99-PR100 unused are valued in the grade of fine-very fine.

Statue of Freedom — N15

N16

N17

N18

N19

N20

N21

N22

Size of designs: 1c-50c, 21x34mm; $2-$100, 24x35mm

1895, Feb. 1	**Unwmk.**		***Perf. 12***
PR102 N15	1c **black**	230.00	*125.00*
	Never hinged	500.00	
	No gum	90.00	
	Block of 4	1,050.	*600.00*
	P# strip of 3, Impt., T IV	*1,000.*	
	P# block of 6, Impt., T IV	*1,850.*	
PR103 N15	2c **black**	230.00	*125.00*
	gray black	230.00	*125.00*
	Never hinged	500.00	
	No gum	90.00	
	Block of 4	1,050.	—
	P# strip of 3, Impt., T IV	*1,000.*	
	P# block of 6, Impt., T IV	*1,850.*	
	Double transfer at top	250.00	—
PR104 N15	5c **black**	300.00	*300.00*
	gray black	300.00	*300.00*
	Never hinged	650.00	
	No gum	125.00	
	Block of 4	1,350.	
	P# strip of 3, Impt., T IV	*1,300.*	
	P# strip of 4, Impt., T IV	*1,750.*	
	P# block of 6, Impt., T IV	*2,500.*	
PR105 N15	10c **black**	600.00	*400.00*
	Never hinged	1,300.	
	No gum	240.00	
	Block of 4	3,000.	
	P# strip of 3, Impt., T IV	*2,500.*	
	P# block of 6, Impt., T IV	4,750.	
PR106 N16	25c **carmine**	750.00	*500.00*
	Never hinged	1,650.	
	No gum	300.00	
	Block of 4	3,500.	
	P# strip of 3, Impt., T IV	*3,250.*	
	P# block of 6, Impt., T IV	6,250.	
PR107 N16	50c **carmine**	*2,750.*	*800.00*
	Never hinged	*6,250.*	
	No gum	*875.00*	
	Block of 4	*12,000.*	
	P# strip of 3, Impt., T IV	*11,500.*	
PR108 N17	$2 **scarlet**	2,250.	*1,100.*
	Never hinged	*5,000.*	
	No gum	850.00	
	P# strip of 3, Impt., T IV	*14,000.*	
PR109 N18	$5 **ultra**	2,100.	*1,750.*
	No gum	800.00	
	P# strip of 3, Impt., T IV	*14,000.*	
PR110 N19	$10 **green**	2,500.	*2,000.*
	No gum	900.00	
PR111 N20	$20 **slate**	3,250.	*2,500.*
	No gum	1,200.	
PR112 N21	$50 **dull rose**	2,750.	*950.00*
	Never hinged	*6,250.*	
	No gum	1,050.	
	P# strip of 3, Impt., T IV	*20,000.*	
PR113 N22	$100 **purple**	3,500.	*7,000.*
	No gum	1,400.	

Nos. PR102-PR113 were printed from plates with arrows in the top, bottom and side margins, but no guidelines between the stamps.

1895-97	**Wmk. 191**		***Perf. 12***
PR114 N15	1c **black,** *Jan. 11, 1896*	8.00	*25.00*
	gray black	8.00	*25.00*
	Never hinged	20.00	
	No gum	2.75	
	Block of 4	35.00	—
	P# strip of 3, Impt., T IV	50.00	
	P# block of 6, Impt., T IV	175.00	
PR115 N15	2c **black,** *Nov. 21, 1895*	8.00	*25.00*
	gray black	8.00	*25.00*
	Never hinged	20.00	
	No gum	2.75	
	Block of 4	35.00	—
	P# strip of 3, Impt., T IV	50.00	
	P# block of 6, Impt., T IV	175.00	
PR116 N15	5c **black,** *Feb. 12, 1896*	13.00	*40.00*
	gray black	13.00	*40.00*
	Never hinged	27.50	
	No gum	4.25	
	Block of 4	57.50	—
	P# strip of 3, Impt., T IV	90.00	
	P# block of 6, Impt., T IV	300.00	
PR117 N15	10c **black,** *Sept. 13, 1895*	13.00	*25.00*
	gray black	13.00	*25.00*
	Never hinged	27.50	
	No gum	4.25	
	Block of 4	57.50	—
	P# strip of 3, Impt., T IV	90.00	
	P# block of 6, Impt., T IV	325.00	
	P# block of 8, Impt., T IV	650.00	
	Never hinged	1,300.	
PR118 N16	25c **carmine,** *Oct. 11, 1895*	20.00	*65.00*
	lilac rose	20.00	*65.00*
	Never hinged	45.00	
	No gum	7.00	
	Block of 4	87.50	—
	P# strip of 3, Impt., T IV	125.00	
	P# block of 6, Impt., T IV	400.00	
PR119 N16	50c **carmine,** *Sept. 19, 1895*	25.00	*75.00*
	rose carmine	25.00	*75.00*
	lilac rose	25.00	*75.00*
	Never hinged	55.00	
	No gum	8.50	
	Block of 4	110.00	—
	P# strip of 3, Impt., T IV	165.00	
	P# block of 6, Impt., T IV	500.00	
	P# block of 8, Impt., T IV	800.00	
PR120 N17	$2 **scarlet,** *Jan. 23, 1897*	30.00	*110.00*
	scarlet vermilion	30.00	*110.00*
	Never hinged	75.00	
	No gum	10.00	
	Block of 4	130.00	—
	P# strip of 3, Impt., T IV	200.00	
	P# block of 6, Impt., T IV	650.00	
PR121 N18	$5 **dark blue,** *Jan. 16, 1896*	40.00	*175.00*
	Never hinged	100.00	
	No gum	13.50	
	Block of 4	200.00	
	P# strip of 3, Impt., T IV	260.00	
	P# block of 6, Impt., T IV	750.00	
a.	$5 light blue	200.00	*500.00*
	Never hinged	500.00	
	No gum	67.50	
	Block of 4	*875.00*	*2,500.*
	P# strip of 3, Impt., T IV	900.00	
PR122 N19	$10 **green,** *Mar. 5, 1896*	42.50	*175.00*
	Never hinged	105.00	
	No gum	14.00	
	Block of 4	200.00	—
	P# strip of 3, Impt., T IV	275.00	
	P# block of 6, Impt., T IV	775.00	
	Never hinged	1,250.	
PR123 N20	$20 **slate,** *Jan. 27, 1896*	45.00	*200.00*
	Never hinged	110.00	
	No gum	15.00	
	Block of 4	210.00	—
	P# strip of 3, Impt., T IV	300.00	
	P# block of 6, Impt., T IV	800.00	
PR124 N21	$50 **dull rose,** *July 31, 1897*	75.00	*300.00*
	Never hinged	170.00	
	No gum	27.50	
	Block of 4	350.00	
	P# strip of 3, Impt., T IV	500.00	
	P# block of 6, Impt., T IV	1,250.	
	Never hinged	2,250.	
PR125 N22	$100 **purple,** *Jan. 23, 1896*	65.00	*275.00*
	Never hinged	150.00	
	No gum	22.50	
	Block of 4	300.00	
	P# strip of 3, Impt., T IV	450.00	
	P# block of 6, Impt., T IV	1,150.	
	Nos. PR114-PR125 (12)	384.50	*1,490.*
	Nos. PR114-PR125, never hinged	905.00	

Nos. PR114-PR125 were printed from the original plates with guide lines added in November 1895. Top and bottom plate strips and blocks of Nos. PR114-PR119 exist both with and without vertical guidelines. Those without guidelines sell for 4 to 5 time the values shown, which are for plate number strips and blocks with guidelines.

In 1899 the Government sold 26,989 sets of these stamps, but, as the stock of high values was not sufficient to make up the required number, an additional printing was made of the $5, $10, $20, $50 and $100. These are virtually indistinguishable from earlier printings.

POSTAL NOTE STAMPS

Postal note stamps were issued to supplement the regular money order service. They were a means of sending amounts under $1. One or two Postal note stamps, totaling 1c to 99c, were affixed to United States Postal Note cards that came in $0 to $10 denominations, and they were canceled by the clerk. The stamps were on the second of three parts, the one retained by the post office redeeming the Postal Note. They were discontinued March 31, 1951.

Catalogue Values for Unused Postal Note stamps are for Never Hinged items.

MO1

ROTARY PRESS PRINTING

1945, Feb. 1	**Unwmk.**	***Perf. 11x10½***	
PN1 MO1	1c **black** (155950-155951)	.35	.30
PN2 MO1	2c **black** (156003-156004)	.35	.30
PN3 MO1	3c **black** (156062-156063)	.35	.30
PN4 MO1	4c **black** (155943, 156942-156943)	.45	.30
PN5 MO1	5c **black** (156261-156262)	.45	.30
PN6 MO1	6c **black** (156064-156065)	.60	.30
PN7 MO1	7c **black** (156075-156076)	.60	.30
PN8 MO1	8c **black** (156077-156078)	1.00	.30
PN9 MO1	9c **black** (156251-156252)	1.00	.30
PN10 MO1	10c **black** (156274-156275)	1.20	.30
PN11 MO1	20c **black** (156276-156277)	2.00	.30
PN12 MO1	30c **black** (156303-156304)	2.50	.30
PN13 MO1	40c **black** (156283-156284)	4.00	.30
PN14 MO1	50c **black** (156322-156323)	4.00	.30
PN15 MO1	60c **black** (156324-156325)	4.50	.30
PN16 MO1	70c **black** (156344-156345)	7.00	.30
PN17 MO1	80c **black** (156326-156327)	8.25	.30
PN18 MO1	90c **black** (156352-156353)	10.00	.30
	Nos. PN1-PN18 (18)	48.60	5.40

Blocks of four are valued at four times the unused single value, and plate number blocks of four are valued at approximately four to five times the unused single value.

Postal note stamps exist on postal note cards with first day cancellation. Value, per card $25-$35. Value, cards with last day cancels, $35-$45. Value, single stamp on card canceled other than first day, $15-$25. For cards with multiple stamps, add $5-$10.

Numbers in parentheses are plate Nos.

PARCEL POST STAMPS

The Act of Congress approved Aug. 24, 1912, created postage rates on 4th class mail weighing 4 ounces or less at 1 cent per ounce or fraction. On mail over 4 ounces, the rate was by the pound. These rates were to be prepaid by distinctive postage stamps. Under this provision, the Post Office Department prepared 12 parcel post and 5 parcel post postage due stamps, usable only on parcel post packages starting Jan. 1, 1913. Other stamps were not usable on parcel post starting on that date.

Beginning on Nov. 27, 1912, the stamps were shipped to post offices offering parcel post service. Approximate shipping dates were: 1c, 2c, 5c, 25c, 1c due, 5c due, Nov. 27; 10c, 2c due, Dec. 9; 4c, 10c due, Dec. 12; 15c, 20c, 25c due, Dec. 16; 75c, Dec. 18. There was no prohibition on sale of the stamps prior to Jan. 1, 1913. Undoubtedly many were used on 4th class mail in Dec. 1912. Fourth class mail was expanded by adding former 2nd and 3rd class categories and was renamed "parcel post" effective Jan. 1, 1913. Normally 4th class (parcel post) mail did not receive a dated cancel unless a special service was involved. Small pieces, such as samples, are known with 1st class cancels.

With the approval of the Interstate Commerce Commission, the Postmaster General directed, in Order No. 7241 dated June 26, 1913, and effective July 1, 1913, that regular postage stamps should be valid on parcels. Parcel post stamps then became usable as regular stamps.

Parcel post and parcel post postage due stamps remained on sale, but no further printings were made. Remainders, consisting of 3,510,345 of the 75c, were destroyed in Sept. 1921.

The 20c was the first government-issued postage stamp of any country to show an airplane.

Post Office Clerk — PP1

City Carrier — PP2

Railway Postal Clerk — PP3

Rural Carrier — PP4

Mail Train and Mail Bag on Rack — PP5

Steamship "Kronprinz Wilhelm" and Mail Tender, New York — PP6

Automobile Service — PP7

Airplane Carrying Mail — PP8

Manufacturing (Steel Plant, South Chicago) — PP9

Dairying — PP10

Harvesting PP11

Fruit Growing (Florida Orange Grove) — PP12

Plate number and imprint consisting of value in words.

Marginal imprints, consisting of value in words, were added to the plates on January 27, 1913.

Designed by Clair Aubrey Huston.

Plates of 180 subjects in four panes of 45 each.

1913	**Wmk. 190**	**Engr.**	***Perf. 12***
Q1	PP1 1c **carmine rose** *(209,691,094)*	4.25	1.60
	carmine	4.25	1.60
	Never hinged	12.00	
	First day cover, *July 1, 1913*		*1,500.*
	On cover, 1913-25		6.00
	Block of 4	18.00	8.00
	P# block of 4, Impt.	40.00	
	P# block of 6, Impt.	100.00	
	P# block of 6	105.00	
	Never hinged	175.00	
	Double transfer	8.50	3.50
Q2	PP2 2c **carmine rose** *(206,417,253)*	5.00	1.25
	carmine	5.00	1.25
	Never hinged	12.50	
	First day cover, *July 1, 1913*		*1,750.*
	On cover, 1913-25		5.75
	Block of 4	24.00	6.50
	P# block of 4, Impt.	40.00	
	P# block of 6, Impt.	120.00	
	P# block of 6	140.00	
	Never hinged	230.00	
	Double transfer	—	—
a.	2c **lake**	*1,750.*	
b.	2c **carmine lake**	*350.00*	

No. Q2a is valued in the grade of fine to very fine.

Q3	PP3 3c **carmine,** *Apr. 5, 1913* *(29,027,433)*	9.00	6.00
	deep carmine	9.00	6.00
	Never hinged	24.00	
	First day cover, *July 1, 1913*		*3,500.*
	On cover, 1913-25		19.00
	Block of 4	40.00	35.00
	P# block of 4, Impt.	90.00	
	P# block of 6, Impt.	250.00	
	P# block of 6	225.00	
	Never hinged	375.00	
	P# block of 8, Impt. (side)	310.00	
	Never hinged	525.00	
	Retouched at lower right corner (No. 6257 LL 7)	25.00	14.50
	Double transfer (No. 6257 LL 6)	25.00	14.50
Q4	PP4 4c **carmine rose** *(76,743,813)*	27.50	3.00
	carmine	27.50	3.00
	Never hinged	77.50	
	First day cover, *July 1, 1913*		*3,500.*
	On cover, 1913-25		65.00
	Block of 4	120.00	17.50
	P# block of 4, Impt.	325.00	
	P# block of 6, Impt.	1,000.	
	Never hinged	1,650.	
	P# block of 6	975.00	
	Never hinged	1,600.	
	Double transfer	—	—
Q5	PP5 5c **carmine rose** *(108,153,993)*	22.50	2.25
	carmine	22.50	2.25
	Never hinged	62.50	
	First day cover, *July 1, 1913*		*3,500.*
	On cover, 1913-25		42.50
	Block of 4	100.00	14.00
	P# block of 4, Impt.	325.00	
	P# block of 6, Impt.	975.00	
	P# block of 6	950.00	
	Never hinged	1,550.	
	Double transfer	37.50	6.00
Q6	PP6 10c **carmine rose** *(56,896,653)*	40.00	3.00
	carmine	40.00	3.00
	Never hinged	90.00	
	First day cover, *July 1, 1913*		*12,500.*
	On cover, 1913-25		55.00
	Block of 4	190.00	25.00
	P# block of 4, Impt.	400.00	
	P# block of 6, Impt.	1,125.	
	P# block of 6	975.00	
	Never hinged	1,600.	
	Double transfer	—	—
Q7	PP7 15c **carmine rose** *(21,147,033)*	60.00	13.50
	carmine	60.00	13.50
	Never hinged	170.00	
	First day cover, *July 1, 1913*		—
	On cover, 1913-25		400.00
	Block of 4	280.00	90.00
	P# block of 4, Impt.	675.00	
	P# block of 6, Impt.	2,600.	
	P# block of 8, Impt.	3,100.	
	P# block of 6	2,300.	
	Never hinged	*3,700.*	

Q8 PP8 20c **carmine rose** *(17,142,393)*	110.00	25.00
carmine	110.00	25.00
Never hinged	260.00	
On cover, 1913-25		850.00
Block of 4	500.00	150.00
P# block of 4, Impt.	1,250.	
P# block of 6, Impt.	6,000.	
P# block of 8, Impt. (side)	6,500.	
P# block of 6	5,750.	
Never hinged	*9,000.*	
Q9 PP9 25c **carmine rose** *(21,940,653)*	52.50	8.00
carmine	52.50	8.00
Never hinged	145.00	
On cover, 1913-25		300.00
Block of 4	250.00	55.00
P# block of 6, Impt.	2,250.	
P# block of 8, Impt. (side)	3,250.	
P# block of 6	2,250.	
Never hinged	*3,500.*	
Q10 PP10 50c **carmine rose,** *Mar. 15, 1913 (2,117,793)*	200.00	45.00
carmine	200.00	45.00
Never hinged	500.00	
On cover, 1913-25		—
Block of 4	900.00	300.00
P# block of 4, Impt.	1,500.	
Never hinged	2,500.	
P# block of 6, Impt.	*17,500.*	
Never hinged	*24,000.*	
Q11 PP11 75c **carmine rose** *(2,772,615)*	80.00	35.00
carmine	80.00	35.00
Never hinged	180.00	
On cover, 1913-25		—
Block of 4	375.00	225.00
P# block of 6, Impt.	3,250.	
P# block of 8, Impt. (side)	3,250.	
Never hinged	*4,250.*	
P# block of 6	2,500.	
Never hinged	*3,750.*	
Q12 PP12 $1 **carmine rose,** *Jan. 3, 1913 (1,053,273)*	250.00	40.00
carmine	250.00	40.00
Never hinged	600.00	
On cover, 1913-25		1,250.
Block of 4	1,150.	225.00
P# block of 6, Impt.	*20,000.*	
Never hinged	*29,000.*	
P# block of 8, Impt. (side)	*21,000.*	
P# block of 6	*18,000.*	
Never hinged	*27,500.*	
Nos. Q1-Q12 (12)	860.75	183.60
Nos. Q1-Q12, never hinged	2,218.	

The 1c, 2c, 4c, 5c, and 10c are known in parcel post usage postmarked Jan. 1, 1913.

PARCEL POST POSTAGE DUE STAMPS

See notes preceding Scott No. Q1. Parcel Post Postage Due stamps were allowed to be used as regular postage due stamps from July 1, 1913.

PPD1

Designed by Clair Aubrey Huston.

Plates of 180 subjects in four panes of 45

1913 Wmk. 190 Engr. ***Perf. 12***

JQ1 PPD1 1c **dark green** (7,322,400)	8.00	4.00
yellowish green	8.00	4.00
Never hinged	22.50	
On cover, 1913-25		160.00
Block of 4	35.00	35.00
P# block of 6	450.00	
Never hinged	750.00	

Earliest documented use: Feb. 26, 1913.

JQ2 PPD1 2c **dark green** (3,132,000)	60.00	16.00
yellowish green	60.00	16.00
Never hinged	160.00	
On cover, 1913-25		225.00
Block of 4	260.00	140.00
P# block of 6	*3,000.*	
Never hinged	*4,850.*	

Earliest documented use: July 7, 1913.

JQ3 PPD1 5c **dark green** (5,840,100)	9.00	4.50
yellowish green	9.00	4.50
Never hinged	24.00	
On cover, 1913-25		200.00
Block of 4	40.00	35.00
P# block of 6	450.00	
Never hinged	775.00	

Earliest documented use: Jan. 15, 1913 (dated cancel on off-cover stamp).

JQ4 PPD1 10c **dark green** (2,124,540)	110.00	40.00
yellowish green	110.00	40.00
Never hinged	290.00	
On cover, 1913-25		650.00
Block of 4	500.00	375.00
P# block of 6	*7,500.*	
Never hinged	*10,500.*	

Earliest documented use: July 19, 1913.

JQ5 PPD1 25c **dark green** (2,117,700)	70.00	4.50
yellowish green	70.00	4.50
Never hinged	185.00	
On cover, 1913-25		—
Block of 4	325.00	35.00
P# block of 6	*3,500.*	
Never hinged	*6,000.*	

Earliest documented use: Aug. 30, 1913.

Nos. JQ1-JQ5 (5)	257.00	69.00
Nos. JQ1-JQ5, never hinged	642.50	

SPECIAL HANDLING STAMPS

The Postal Service Act, approved February 28, 1925, provided for a special handling stamp of the 25-cent denomination for use on fourth-class mail matter, which would secure for such mail matter the expeditious handling accorded to mail matter of the first class.

PP13

FLAT PLATE PRINTING

Plates of 200 subjects in four panes of 50

1925-55 Engr. Unwmk. ***Perf. 11***

QE1 PP13 10c **green,** wet printing, *1940*	2.00	1.00
Never hinged	4.25	
Block of 4	10.00	—
P# block of 6	25.00	
Never hinged	40.00	
First day cover		45.00
a. 10c **light green,** dry printing, *1955*	5.00	*150.00*
Never hinged	11.00	
Block of 4	25.00	
P# block of 6	75.00	
Never hinged	125.00	
b. 10c **yellow green,** printed on "special" booklet paper, *1928* (see note before #551)	2.00	1.00
Never hinged	4.25	
First day cover		45.00
Block of 4	10.00	
P# block of 6	25.00	
Never hinged	40.00	

Earliest documented use: No. QE1a, Feb. 26, 1958 (dated cancel on off-cover stamp).

QE2 PP13 15c **green,** wet printing, *1940*	2.25	.90
Never hinged	4.75	
Block of 4	11.00	—
P# block of 6	30.00	
Never hinged	47.50	
First day cover		45.00
a. 15c **light green,** dry printing, *1955*	5.00	*150.00*
Never hinged	10.00	
Block of 4	25.00	
P# block of 6	80.00	
Never hinged	135.00	
b. 15c **yellow green,** printed on "special" booklet paper, *1928* (see note before #551)	2.25	.90
Never hinged	4.75	
First day cover		45.00
Block of 4	11.00	
P# block of 6	30.00	
Never hinged	47.50	

Earliest documented use: No. QE2a, Aug. 1, 1957.

QE3 PP13 20c **green,** wet printing, *1940*	3.75	1.50
Never hinged	7.75	
Block of 4	17.50	—
P# block of 6	37.50	
Never hinged	60.00	
First day cover		45.00
First day cover, Nos. QE1-QE3		350.00
a. 20c **light green,** dry printing, *1955*	7.50	*150.00*
Never hinged	15.00	
Block of 4	37.50	
P# block of 6	85.00	
Never hinged	150.00	
b. 20c **yellow green,** printed on "special" booklet paper, *1928* (see note before #551)	3.75	1.50
Never hinged	7.75	
First day cover		45.00
Block of 4	17.50	
P# block of 6	37.50	
Never hinged	60.00	

"AT" joined at top

"TA" joined at top

Dot on second "T"

QE4 PP13 25c **deep green,** *April 11, 1925*	20.00	3.75
Never hinged	37.50	
Block of 4	115.00	24.00
P# block of 6	350.00	
Never hinged	525.00	
"A" and second "T" of "States" joined at top (Pl. 17103)	80.00	50.00
Never hinged	140.00	

	"A" and second "T" of "States" and "T" and "A" of "Postage" joined at top (Pl. 17103)	125.00	125.00
	Never hinged	210.00	
	Dot on second "T" of "States" (17103 UR 40)	*1,250.*	*375.00*
	First day cover		225.00
a.	25c **yellow green,** *1928*	16.50	*22.50*
	Never hinged	32.50	

Block of 4	90.00	*110.00*
P# block of 6	250.00	
Never hinged	360.00	

Earliest documented use: No. QE4a, May 1928 dated cancel on off-cover stamp; Jan. 30, 1934 (on cover).

Nos. QE1-QE4 (4)	28.00	7.15
Nos. QE1-QE4, never hinged	54.25	

See note on Wet and Dry Printings following No. 1029.

POSTAL INSURANCE STAMPS

Postal insurance stamps were issued to pay insurance on parcels for loss or damage. The stamps come in a booklet of one which also carries instructions for use and a receipt form for use if there is a claim. The booklets were sold by vending machine. Values in unused column are for complete booklets. Values in used column are for used stamps. Booklet cover illustrations are reduced.

QI1 — PPI1

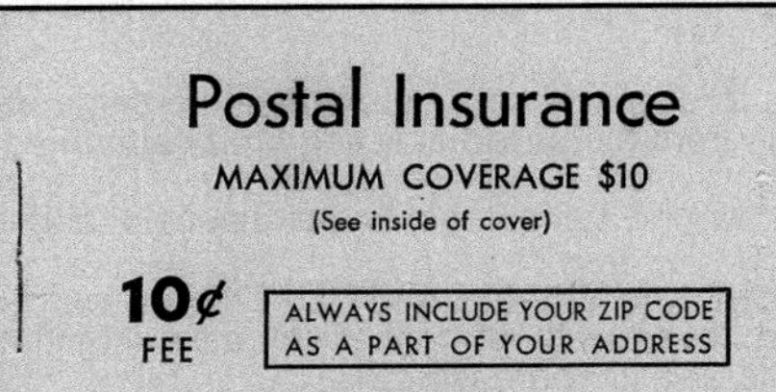

QI1 — PPIC1

1965, Aug. 19 **Typo.** ***Rouletted 9 at Top***

QI1 PPI1 (10c) **dark red** 140.00 —

No. QI1 paid insurance up to $10. It was sold at the Canoga Park, Calif., automatic post office, which opened Aug. 19, 1965. It was also sold at the Austin, Texas, post office beginning Oct. 28, 1965, and at the Wheaton, Maryland, post office beginning March 21, 1966. Sales of this booklet ceased on March 25, 1966. The "V" stands for "Vended."

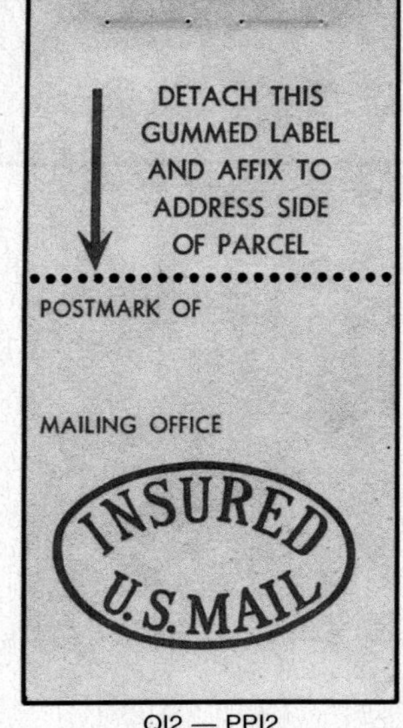

QI2 — PPI2

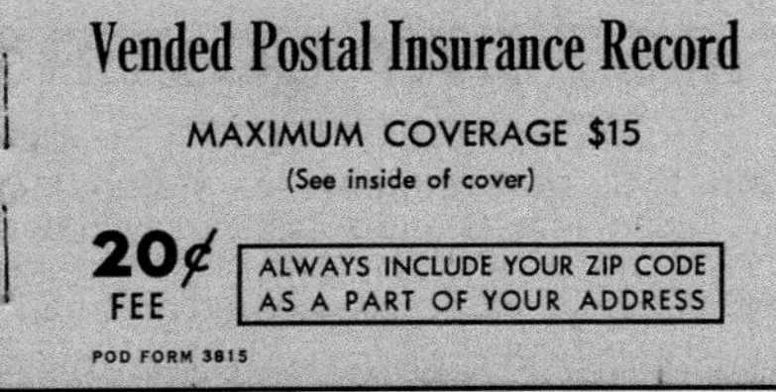

QI2 — PPIC2 Type I

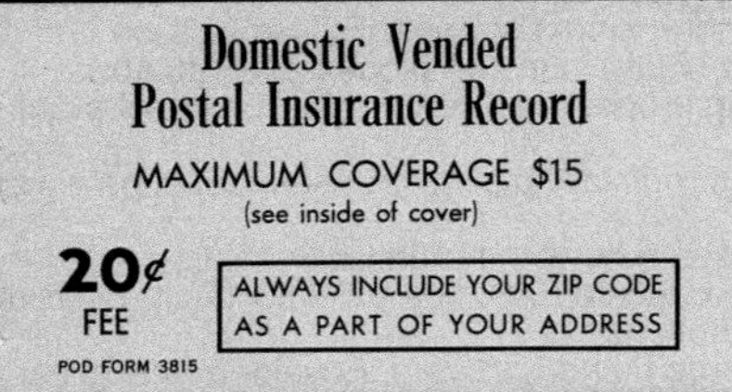

QI2 — PPIC2 Type II

1966, Mar. 26 **Litho.** ***Perf. 11 at Top***

QI2 PPI2 (20c) **red** 4.00 —

No. QI2 paid insurance up to $15. The rate increased from 20c to 25c on Apr. 18, 1976, and to 40c on July 18, 1976.

The QI2 booklet comes with two types of front covers, type I beginning "Vended..." and type II beginning "Domestic Vended...." There also are two types of back covers, the first with some white on black lettering, the second with all black on white lettering.

No 25c postal insurance stamps were printed. Existing examples of No. QI2 had 5c postage stamps added and the value on the cover was changed to 25c, usually by hand, but sometimes by handstamp or label. Twenty-cent stamps were added to make the 40c rate since new postal insurance stamps were not issued until 1977. Some 25c provisional booklets were further revalued to 40c by the addition of a 15c stamp. Each provisional booklet comes with both cover types.

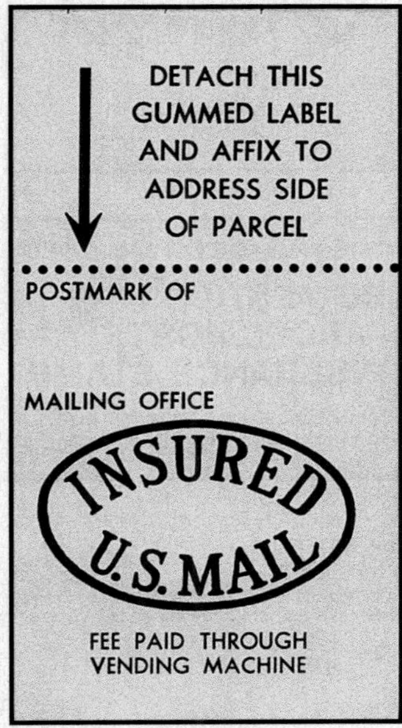

QI3 — PPI3

THIS PACKAGE CONTAINS ONE:
DOMESTIC PARCEL POST INSURANCE STAMP
($15 MAXIMUM COVERAGE PER PARCEL)
DEPOSIT 40¢ FEE TO PURCHASE

QI3 — PPIC3

"FEE PAID THROUGH VENDING MACHINE" Below "INSURED U.S. MAIL" Logo

1977, Aug. 28 **Litho.** ***Perf. 11 at Top***

QI3 PPI3 (40c) **black** 15.00 —

Available for use by Nov. 28, 1977 or earlier.

QI3 is often found misperfed with horizontal perforations running between "Postmark of" and "Mailing Office." This variety is relatively common and does not merit a large premium.

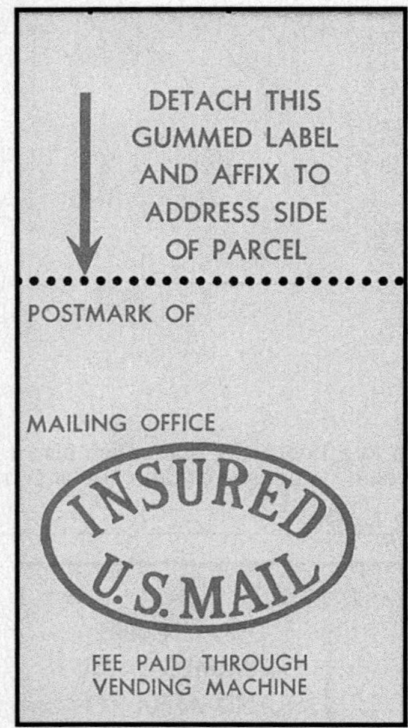

QI4 — PPI3

QI4 — PPIC4

1978, Nov. 20

QI4 PPI3 (50c) **green** 10.00 —

The rate increased to 50c on May 29, 1978. Examples of QI2 and QI3 exist revalued to 50c by the addition of stamps.

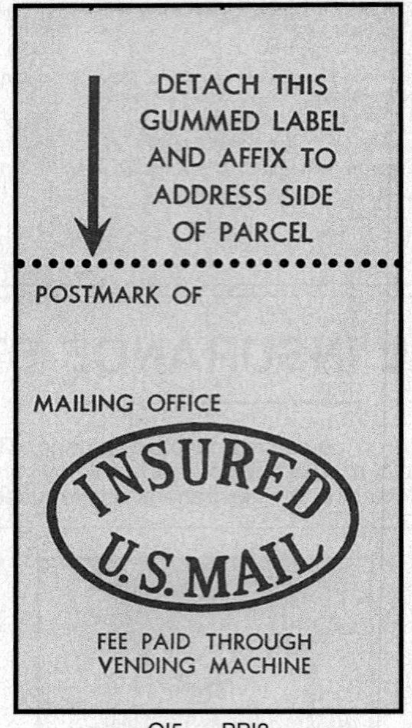

QI5 — PPI3

THIS PACKAGE CONTAINS ONE:
DOMESTIC
PARCEL POST
INSURANCE STAMP
($20 MAXIMUM COVERAGE PER PARCEL)
DEPOSIT 45c FEE TO PURCHASE

QI5 — PPIC5

1981, Sept. 1

QI5 PPI3 (45c) **red** 12.50 —

No. QI3 booklets exist revalued to 45c by the addition of a 5c stamp, and the QI4 booklet is known revalued to 45c on its cover.

FIRST DAY COVERS

All envelopes or cards are postmarked Washington, D.C., unless otherwise stated. Minors and sublistings without dates have the same date and city (if none is otherwise mentioned) as the previous listing. Minors and sublistings with dates differing from the previous listing are postmarked in Washington, D.C. unless otherwise stated.

Values are for first day covers in very fine condition, without tears, stains or smeared postmarks, and with sound stamps that have fresh color and are not badly off center.

Printed cachets on covers before Scott Nos. 772 and C20 sell at a substantial premium. Values for covers of Nos. 772-986 and C20-C45 are for those with the most common cachets and addressed. Unaddressed covers sell at a substantial premium and covers without cachet sell at a substantial discount. Values for covers from Scott 987 and C46 onward are for those with the most common cachets and unaddressed.

Values for 1st class rate stamps are for covers bearing single stamps. Blocks of 4 on first day covers usually sell for about 1½ times as much as singles; Plate number blocks of 4 at about 3 times; Plate number blocks of 6 at about 4 times; coil line pairs at about 3 times. Stamps with denominations less than the first class rate will have the proper multiple to make the rate if practical or additional postage. (See Nos. 899, 907-908, 930-931, etc.)

Dates given are those on which the stamps were first *officially* placed on sale. Many instances are known of stamps being sold in advance, contrary to regulations.

Numbers in parentheses are quantities stated to have received the first day cancel.

Listings from Scott Nos. 551 and C4 are for covers canceled at cities officially designated by the Post Office Department or Postal Service. Some tagged varieties and cities of special interest are exceptions.

Air post first day covers are listed following the Postage first day covers. Envelope, postal card and other first day covers are with the regular listings. Quantities given for se-tenant issues include the multiple and any single or combination of singles (see No. 2375a).

1851-57

5A 1c **blue, type Ib,** *July 1, 1851,* Boston, Mass. *150,000.*
7 1c **blue, type II,** *July 1, 1851* *25,000.*
Same on printed circular *4,000.*
10 3c **orange brown,** *July 1, 1851,* any city *12,500.*

The No. 5A cover is unique. Value is based on 1996 auction sale. The No. 7 cover also is unique.

1861

64 3c **pink,** *Aug. 17, 1861,* Baltimore, Md. *22,000.*
64b 3c **rose pink,** *Aug. 17, 1861,* Baltimore, Md. *23,000.*

The Nos. 64 and 64b covers are each unique.

1883

210 2c **red brown,** *Oct. 1,* any city *2,000.*
210, 211 2c, 4c **blue green,** *Oct. 1,* New York, N.Y. *50,000.*

The Nos. 210, 211 cover is unique.

1890

219D 2c **lake,** *Feb. 22,* any city *35,000.*

COLUMBIAN EXPOSITION ISSUE

1893

230 1c **deep blue,** *Jan. 1,* any city *20,000.*
Jan. 2, any city *5,000.*
231 2c **brown violet,** *Jan. 1,* any city *20,000.*
Jan. 2, any city *4,000.*
232 3c **green,** *Jan. 1,* any city *20,000.*
Jan. 2, any city *7,000.*
230, 232 on one cover, *Jan. 2,* Boston, Mass. *8,250.*
233 4c **ultramarine,** *Jan. 1,* any city *20,000.*
Jan. 2, any city *14,000.*
234 5c **chocolate,** *Jan. 1,* any city *27,500.*
Jan. 2, any city *17,500.*
235 6c **purple,** *Jan. 2,* any city *22,500.*
237 10c **black brown,** *Jan. 1,* any city *32,500.*
Jan. 2, any city *27,500.*
242 $2 **brown red,** *Jan. 2,* any city *65,000.*

As Jan. 1, 1893, was a Sunday, specialists recognize both Jan. 1 and 2 as "first day."

TRANS-MISSISSIPPI EXPOSITION ISSUE

1898

285 1c **green,** *June 17,* any city *12,500.*
286 2c **copper red,** *June 17,* any city *8,000.*
Pittsburgh, Pa *15,000.*
287 4c **orange,** *June 17* *27,500.*
288 5c **dull blue,** *June 17,* any city *16,000.*
285, 287-288 on one cover *75,000.*
285-288 on one cover *75,000.*
289 8c **violet brown,** *June 17,* any city *22,500.*
290 10c **gray violet,** *June 17* *27,500.*
285-290, all 6 on one cover, *June 17* *75,000.*
291 50c **sage green,** *June 17,* any city *90,000.*
292 $1 **black,** *June 17,* any city *172,500.*

PAN AMERICAN EXPOSITION ISSUE

1901

294 1c **green & black,** *May 1,* any city *4,500.*
295 2c **carmine & black,** *May 1,* any city *2,500.*
297 5c **ultra. & blk.,** *May 1,* any city *37,500.*
294, 295, 297 on one cover, *May 1,* Boston, Mass. *17,500.*
294, 296, 297 on one cover, *May 1,* Boston, Mass. *16,000.*
295, 298 on one cover, *May 1,* Washington, D.C. *33,500.*
296, 298 on one cover, *May 1,* Boston, Mass. *27,500.*
297, 298 on one cover, *May 1,* Philadelphia, Pa. *27,500.*
294-299, complete set of 6 on one cover *May 1,* any city *30,000.*

LOUISIANA PURCHASE EXPOSITION ISSUE

1904

323 1c **green,** *Apr. 30,* any city *7,500.*
324 2c **carmine,** *Apr. 30,* any city *5,000.*
325 3c **violet,** *Apr. 30,* any city *20,000.*
326 5c **dark blue,** *Apr. 30,* any city *22,500.*
327 10c **red brown,** *Apr. 30,* any city *24,000.*
323-327, all 5 on one cover, *Apr. 30,* New York *65,000.*

The Nos. 323-327 combination cover is unique.

1907

328 1c **Jamestown,** *Apr. 26,* any city *12,500.*
329 2c **Jamestown,** *Apr. 26,* any city *15,000.*

1908

331a 1c **green,** booklet single, *Dec. 2,* Washington, D.C. *28,500.*
332a 2c **carmine,** booklet single, *Nov. 16,* Washington, D.C. *28,500.*

1909

367 2c **Lincoln,** *Feb. 12,* any city 500.
On pictorial postcard, *Feb. 12,* Boston 600.

Imperf

368 2c **Lincoln,** *Feb. 12,* any city *12,000.*

ALASKA-YUKON ISSUE

1909

370 2c **carmine,** *June 1,* any city *3,000.*
On Expo-related picture postcard, *June 1* *5,000.*

HUDSON-FULTON ISSUE

1909

372 2c **carmine,** *Sept. 25,* any city 950.
On Expo-related picture postcard, *Sept. 25* 1,500.

Imperf

373 2c **carmine,** *Sept. 25,* any city *8,000.*

PANAMA-PACIFIC ISSUE

1913

397 1c **green,** *Jan. 1,* any city *8,000.*
399 5c **blue,** *Jan. 1* *31,000.*
400 10c **orange yellow,** *Jan. 1* *10,000.*
397, 399 & 400, all 3 on one cover, San Francisco, Cal. —

The editors would like to see expertization of the above 3-stamp cover.

1916-22 **COIL STAMP**

497 10c **orange yellow,** *Jan. 31, 1922,* any city *6,000.*

1918-20 **OFFSET PRINTING**

526 2c **carmine,** type IV, *Mar. 15, 1920* *850.*

1919

537 3c **Victory,** *Mar. 3,* any city *850.*

1919 ***Perf. 11x10***

541 3c **violet,** type II, *June 14, 1919,* any city *9,000.*

REGULAR ISSUE

1920 ***Perf. 10x11***

542 1c **green,** *May 26* *1,750.*

1920

548 1c **Pilgrim,** *Dec. 21,* any city, pair *1,000.*
Plymouth, Mass. *5,000.*
549 2c **Pilgrim,** *Dec. 21,* any city *700.*
Plymouth, Mass. *5,000.*
550 5c **Pilgrim,** *Dec. 21,* any city *2,500.*
548-550, complete set of 3 on one cover, *Dec. 21,* any city *2,250.*
Washington, D.C. *3,000.*

1922-26 ***Perf. 11***

551 ½c **Hale,** *Apr. 4, 1925,* block of 4 20.00
New Haven, Conn. *25.00*
551 & 576 on one cover, *Apr. 4, 1925,* New Haven, Conn. *165.00*
552 1c **Franklin,** *Jan. 17, 1923,* pair 27.50
Philadelphia, Pa. *47.50*
553 1½c **Harding,** *Mar. 19, 1925,* pair 52.50
553, 582, 598 on one cover, *Mar. 19, 1925* *190.00*
554 2c **Washington,** *Jan. 15, 1923* 42.50
555 3c **Lincoln,** *Feb. 12, 1923* 40.00
Hodgenville, Ky. *350.00*
556 4c **Martha Washington,** *Jan. 15, 1923* 65.00
557 5c **Roosevelt,** *Oct. 27, 1922* *135.00*
New York, N.Y. *190.00*
Oyster Bay, N.Y. *2,000.*
558 6c **Garfield,** *Nov. 20, 1922* 235.00
559 7c **McKinley,** *May 1, 1923* 185.00
Niles, O. *275.00*
560 8c **Grant,** *May 1, 1923* 190.00
561 9c **Jefferson,** *Jan. 15, 1923* 190.00
562 10c **Monroe,** *Jan. 15, 1923* 190.00
554, 556, 561 & 562, all 4 stamps issued *Jan. 15* on one cover *3,500.*
563 11c **Hayes,** *Oct. 4, 1922* 650.00
Fremont, O. *3,750.*
564 12c **Cleveland,** *Mar. 20, 1923* 185.00
Boston, Mass. (Philatelic Exhibition) *200.00*
Caldwell, N.J. *230.00*
565 14c **American Indian,** *May 1, 1923* 400.00
Muskogee, Okla. *1,250.*
566 15c **Statue of Liberty,** *Nov. 11, 1922* 575.00
567 20c **Golden Gate,** *May 1, 1923* *600.00*
San Francisco, Cal. *2,000.*
559, 560, 565 & 567, all 4 stamps issued *May 1* on one cover *10,000.*
568 25c **Niagara Falls,** *Nov. 11, 1922* *650.00*
569 30c **American Buffalo,** *Mar. 20, 1923* *800.00*
570 50c **Arlington,** *Nov. 11, 1922* *1,500.*
571 $1 **Lincoln Memorial,** *Feb. 12, 1923* *7,000.*
Springfield, Ill. *7,500.*
572 $2 **U.S. Capitol,** *Mar. 20, 1923* *17,500.*
573 $5 **America,** *Mar. 20, 1923* *30,000.*

Imperf

576 1½c **Harding,** *Apr. 4, 1925* 42.50

Perf. 10

581 1c **Franklin,** *Oct. 17, 1923,* not precanceled *6,000.*
582 1½c **Harding,** *Mar. 19, 1925* 40.00
583a 2c **Washington booklet pane of 6,** *Aug. 27, 1926* *1,500.*
584 3c **Lincoln,** *Aug. 1, 1925* 55.00
585 4c **Martha Washington,** *Apr. 4, 1925,* not precanceled 50.00
586 5c **Roosevelt,** *Apr. 4, 1925,* not precanceled 60.00
587 6c **Garfield,** *Apr. 4, 1925,* not precanceled 60.00
585-587, all 3 stamps issued *April 4* on one cover *1,000.*
588 7c **McKinley,** *May 29, 1926* 60.00
589 8c **Grant,** *May 29, 1926* 70.00
590 9c **Jefferson,** *May 29, 1926* 77.50
588-590, all 3 stamps issued *May 29* on one cover —
591 10c **Monroe,** *June 8, 1925* 95.00

Perf. 10 Vertically

597 1c **Franklin,** *July 18, 1923* *600.00*
598 1½c **Harding,** *Mar. 19, 1925* 65.00
599 2c **Washington,** *Jan. 15, 1923* *1,750.*
600 3c **Lincoln,** *May 10, 1924* 85.00
602 5c **Roosevelt,** *Mar. 5, 1924* 95.00
603 10c **Monroe,** *Dec. 1, 1924* 110.00

No. 599 is known used on Jan. 10, 11 and 13, 1923 (one each day). Jan. 15 was the first day of sale in Washington, D. C.

Perf. 10 Horizontally

604 1c **Franklin,** *July 19, 1924* 100.00
605 1½c **Harding,** *May 9, 1925* 80.00
606 2c **Washington,** *Dec. 31, 1923* 150.00

1923

610 2c **Harding,** perf. 11, *Sept. 1* 37.50
Marion, O. 22.50
611 2c **Harding,** imperf., *Nov. 15* 90.00
612 2c **Harding,** perf. 10, *Sept. 12* 100.00

1924

614 1c **Huguenot-Walloon,** *May 1,* pair 30.00
Albany, N.Y 30.00
Allentown, Pa. 30.00
Charleston, S.C. 30.00
Jacksonville, Fla. 30.00
Lancaster, Pa. 30.00
Mayport, Fla. 30.00
New Rochelle, N.Y. 30.00
New York, N.Y. 30.00
Philadelphia, Pa. 30.00
Reading, Pa. 30.00
615 2c **Huguenot-Walloon,** *May 1* 45.00
Albany, N.Y. 45.00
Allentown, Pa. 45.00
Charleston, S.C. 45.00
Jacksonville, Fla. 45.00
Lancaster, Pa. 45.00
Mayport, Fla. 45.00
New Rochelle, N.Y. 45.00
New York, N.Y. 45.00
Philadelphia, Pa. 45.00
Reading, Pa. 45.00
616 5c **Huguenot-Walloon,** *May 1* 70.00
Albany, N.Y. 70.00
Allentown, Pa. 70.00
Charleston, S.C. 70.00
Jacksonville, Fla. 70.00
Lancaster, Pa. 70.00
Mayport, Fla. 70.00
New Rochelle, N.Y. 70.00
New York, N.Y. 70.00
Philadelphia, Pa. 70.00
Reading, Pa. 70.00
614-616 on one cover, any city listed above 150.00
614-616 on one cover, any other city 400.00

1925

617 1c **Lexington-Concord,** *Apr. 4,* pair 30.00
Boston, Mass. 30.00
Cambridge, Mass. 30.00
Concord, Mass. 30.00
Concord Junction, Mass. 30.00
Lexington, Mass. 30.00
618 2c **Lexington-Concord,** *Apr. 4* 40.00
Boston, Mass. 40.00
Cambridge, Mass. 40.00
Concord, Mass 40.00
Concord Junction, Mass. 40.00
Lexington, Mass. 42.50
619 5c **Lexington-Concord,** *Apr. 4* 75.00
Boston, Mass. 75.00
Cambridge, Mass. 75.00
Concord, Mass. 75.00
Concord Junction, Mass. 75.00
Lexington, Mass. 75.00
617-619 on one cover, Concord Junction or Lexington 175.00
Set of 3 on one cover, any other city 150.00

1925

620 2c **Norse-American,** *May 18* 20.00
Algona, Iowa 20.00
Benson, Minn. 20.00
Decorah, Iowa 20.00
Minneapolis, Minn. 20.00
Northfield, Minn. 20.00
St. Paul, Minn. 20.00
621 5c **Norse-American,** *May 18* 25.00
Algona, Iowa 25.00
Benson, Minn. 25.00
Decorah, Iowa 25.00
Minneapolis, Minn. 25.00
Northfield, Minn. 25.00
St. Paul, Minn. 25.00
620-621 on one cover, any city 50.00

1925-26

622 13c **Harrison,** *Jan. 11, 1926* 25.00
Indianapolis, Ind. 40.00
North Bend, Ohio *(500)* 200.00
623 17c **Wilson,** *Dec. 28, 1925* 15.00
New York, N.Y. 15.00
Princeton, N.J. 15.00
Staunton, Va. 30.00

1926

627 2c **Sesquicentennial,** *May 10* 15.00
Boston, Mass. 15.00
Philadelphia, Pa. 15.00
628 5c **Ericsson,** *May 29* 40.00
Chicago, Ill. 40.00
Minneapolis, Minn. 40.00
New York, N.Y. 40.00
629 2c **White Plains,** New York, N.Y., *Oct. 18* 7.50
New York, N.Y., Inter-Philatelic Exhibition Agency cancellation 7.50
White Plains, N.Y. 7.50
Washington, D.C., *Oct. 28* 5.00
630 2c Sheet of 25, *Oct. 18* 1,800.
Sheet of 25, *Oct. 28* 1,000.

1926-34 ***Imperf.***

631 1½c **Harding,** *Aug. 27, 1926,* pair 35.00

Perf. 11x10½

632 1c **Franklin,** *June 10, 1927,* pair 45.00
632a Booklet pane of 6, *Nov. 2, 1927* *4,000.*
633 1½c **Harding,** *May 17, 1927,* pair 45.00
634 2c **Washington,** *Dec. 10, 1926* 50.00
635 3c **Lincoln,** *Feb. 3, 1927* 50.00
635a 3c **bright violet,** *Feb. 7, 1934* 30.00
636 4c **Martha Washington,** *May 17, 1927* 50.00
637 5c **Roosevelt,** *Mar. 24, 1927* 50.00
638 6c **Garfield,** *July 27, 1927* 60.00
639 7c **McKinley,** *Mar. 24, 1927* 60.00
637, 639, both stamps issued *Mar. 24* 500.00
640 8c **Grant,** *June 10, 1927* 70.00
632, 640, both stamps issued *June 10* 350.00
641 9c **Jefferson,** *May 17, 1927* 75.00
633, 636, 641 all three stamps issued *May 17* 550.00
642 10c **Monroe,** *Feb. 3, 1927* 100.00

1927

643 2c **Vermont,** *Aug. 3* 6.00
Bennington, Vt. 6.00
644 2c **Burgoyne,** *Aug. 3* 12.50
Albany, N.Y. 12.50
Rome, N.Y. 12.50
Syracuse, N.Y. 12.50
Utica, N.Y. 12.50

1928

645 2c **Valley Forge,** *May 26* 4.00
Cleveland, O. 67.50
Lancaster, Pa. 4.00
Norristown, Pa. 4.00
Philadelphia, Pa. 4.00
Valley Forge, Pa. 4.00
West Chester, Pa. 4.00
Cleveland, Midwestern Philatelic Sta. cancellation 4.00
646 2c **Molly Pitcher,** *Oct. 20* 15.00
Freehold, N.J. 15.00
Red Bank, N.J. 15.00

1928

647 2c **Hawaii,** *Aug. 13* 15.00
Honolulu, Hawaii 17.50
648 5c **Hawaii,** *Aug. 13* 22.50
Honolulu, Hawaii 25.00
647-648 on one cover 40.00
649 2c **Aero Conf.,** *Dec. 12* 7.00
650 5c **Aero Conf.,** *Dec. 12* 10.00
649-650 on one cover 15.00

1929

651 2c **Clark,** Vincennes, Indiana, *Feb. 25* 6.00
Washington, *Feb. 26,* first day of sale by Philatelic Agency 3.00

Perf. 11x10½

653 ½c **olive brown,** *May 25,* block of four 27.50
654 2c **Electric Light,** perf. 11, Menlo Park, N.J., *June 5* 10.00
Washington, D.C., *June 6,* first day of sale by Philatelic Agency 4.00
655 2c **Electric Light,** perf. 11x10½, *June 11* 80.00
656 2c **Electric Light,** perf. 10 vert., *June 11* 90.00
657 2c **Sullivan,** Auburn, N.Y., *June 17* 4.00
Binghamton, N.Y. 4.00
Canajoharie, N.Y. 4.00
Canandaigua, N.Y. 4.00
Elmira, N.Y. 4.00
Geneseo, N.Y. 4.00
Geneva, N.Y. 4.00
Horseheads, N.Y. 4.00
Owego, N.Y. 4.00
Penn Yan, N.Y 4.00
Perry, N.Y. 4.00
Seneca Falls, N.Y. 4.00
Waterloo, N.Y. 4.00
Watkins Glen, N.Y. 4.00
Waverly, N.Y. 4.00
Washington, D.C., *June 18* 2.00

1929

658 1c **Kansas,** *May 1,* pair 55.00
Newton, Kan., *Apr. 15* 325.00
659 1½c **Kansas,** *May 1,* pair 62.50
Colby, Kan., *Apr. 16* —
660 2c **Kansas,** *May 1* 62.50
Colby, Kan., *Apr. 16* —
661 3c **Kansas,** *May 1* 65.00
Colby, Kan., *Apr. 16* 450.00
662 4c **Kansas,** *May 1* 110.00
Colby, Kan., *Apr. 16* —
663 5c **Kansas,** *May 1* 110.00
Colby, Kan., *Apr. 16* —
664 6c **Kansas,** *May 1* 140.00
Newton, Kan., *Apr. 15* 900.00
665 7c **Kansas,** *May 1* 140.00
Colby, Kan., *Apr. 16* —
666 8c **Kansas,** *May 1* 140.00
Newton, Kan., *Apr. 15* 900.00
667 9c **Kansas,** *May 1* 165.00
Colby, Kan., *Apr. 16* —
668 10c **Kansas,** *May 1* 220.00
Colby, Kan., *Apr. 16* —
658-668 on 1 cover, Washington, D.C., *May 1* 1,500.
669 1c **Nebraska,** *May 1,* pair 55.00
Beatrice, Neb., *Apr. 15* 250.00
670 1½c **Nebraska,** *May 1,* pair 57.50
Hartington, Neb., *Apr. 15* 400.00
671 2c **Nebraska,** *May 1* 62.50
Auburn, Neb., *Apr. 15* 1,200.
Beatrice, Neb., *Apr. 15* —
Hartington, Neb., *Apr. 15* 300.00
672 3c **Nebraska,** *May 1* 65.00
Beatrice, Neb., *Apr. 15* 400.00
Hartington, Neb., *Apr. 15* 400.00
673 4c **Nebraska,** *May 1* 110.00
Beatrice, Neb., *Apr. 15* 400.00
Hartington, Neb., *Apr. 15* 400.00
674 5c **Nebraska,** *May 1* 110.00
Beatrice, Neb., *Apr. 15* 275.00
Hartington, Neb., *Apr. 15* 275.00
675 6c **Nebraska,** *May 1* 140.00
Auburn, Neb., *Apr. 17* 400.00
Ravenna, Neb., *Apr. 17* —
Wahoo, Neb., *Apr. 17* —
676 7c **Nebraska,** *May 1* 165.00
Auburn, Neb., *Apr. 17* 400.00
677 8c **Nebraska,** *May 1* 140.00
Humbolt, Neb., *Apr. 17* 250.00
Pawnee City, Neb., *Apr. 17* 400.00
678 9c **Nebraska,** *May 1* 165.00
Cambridge, Neb., *Apr. 17* 400.00
679 10c **Nebraska,** *May 1* 220.00
Tecumseh, Neb., *Apr. 18* —
669-679 on 1 cover, Washington, D.C., *May 1* *1,500.*
658-679 on 1 cover, Washington, D.C., *May 1* *5,000.*
680 2c **Fallen Timbers,** Erie, Pa., *Sept. 14* 3.50
Maumee, O. 3.50
Perrysburg, O. 3.50
Toledo, O. 3.50
Waterville, O. 3.50
Washington, D.C., *Sept. 16* 2.00
681 2c **Ohio River,** Cairo, Ill., *Oct. 19* 3.50
Cincinnati, O. 3.50
Evansville, Ind. 3.50
Homestead, Pa. 3.50
Louisville, Ky. 3.50
Pittsburgh, Pa. 3.50
Wheeling, W. Va. 3.50
Washington, D.C., *Oct. 21* 2.00

1930

682 2c **Massachusetts Bay Colony,** Boston, Mass. *Apr. 8 (60,000)* 3.50
Salem, Mass. 3.50
Washington, D.C., *Apr. 11* 2.00
683 2c **Carolina-Charleston,** Charleston, S.C. *Apr. 10* 3.50
Washington, D.C., *Apr. 11* 2.00

Perf. 11x10½

684 1½c **Harding,** Marion, O., *Dec. 1,* pair 4.50
Washington, D.C., *Dec. 2* 2.50
685 4c **Taft,** Cincinnati, O., *June 4* 6.00
Washington, D.C., *June 5* 3.00

Perf. 10 Vertically

686 1½c **Harding,** Marion, Ohio, *Dec. 1* 5.00
Washington, D.C., *Dec. 2* 3.00
687 4c **Taft,** *Sept. 18* 20.00

Perf. 11

688 2c **Braddock,** Braddock, Pa., *July 9* 4.00
Washington, D.C., *July 10* 2.00
689 2c **Von Steuben,** New York, N.Y., *Sept. 17* 4.00
Washington, D.C., *Sept. 18* 2.00

1931

690 2c **Pulaski,** Brooklyn, N.Y., *Jan. 16* 4.00
Buffalo, N.Y. 4.00
Chicago, Ill. 4.00
Cleveland, O. 4.00
Detroit, Mich. 4.00
Gary, Ind. 4.00
Milwaukee, Wis. 4.00
New York, N.Y. 4.00
Pittsburgh, Pa. 4.00
Savannah, Ga. 4.00
South Bend, Ind. 4.00
Toledo, O. 4.00
Washington, D.C., *Jan. 17* 2.00

1931 ***Perf. 11x10½, 10½x11***

692 11c **Hayes,** *Sept. 4* 100.
693 12c **Cleveland,** *Aug. 25* 100.
694 13c **Harrison,** *Sept. 4* 100.
695 14c **American Indian,** *Sept. 8* 100.
696 15c **Liberty,** *Aug. 27* 120.
697 17c **Wilson,** *July 25,* Brooklyn, N.Y. *2,750.*
Washington, D.C., *July 27* 400.
698 20c **Golden Gate,** *Sept. 8* 300.
699 25c **Niagara Falls,** *July 25,* Brooklyn, N.Y. *2,000.*
Washington, D.C., *July 27* 350.
697, 699 on one cover, Brooklyn, *July 25* *5,750.*
697, 699 on one cover, Washington, *July 27* *2,500.*
700 30c **American Buffalo,** *Sept. 8* 300.
701 50c **Arlington,** *Sept. 4* 400.
Woolrich, Pa., *Sept. 4* 625.

1931

702 2c **Red Cross,** *May 21* 3.50
Dansville, N.Y. 3.50
703 2c **Yorktown,** *Oct. 19,* Wethersfield, Conn. 3.50
Yorktown, Va. 3.50
Washington, D.C., *Oct. 20* 2.00

WASHINGTON BICENTENNIAL ISSUE

1932

704 ½c *Jan. 1,* block of 4 10.00
705 1c *Jan. 1,* pair 10.00
706 1½c *Jan. 1,* pair 10.00
707 2c *Jan. 1* 10.00
708 3c *Jan. 1* 10.00
709 4c *Jan. 1* 10.00
710 5c *Jan. 1* 10.00
711 6c *Jan. 1* 10.00
712 7c *Jan. 1* 10.00
713 8c *Jan. 1* 10.00
714 9c *Jan. 1* 10.00
715 10c *Jan. 1* 10.00
704-715, set of 12 on one cover, *Jan. 1* 110.00

1932

716 2c **Olympic Winter Games,** *Jan. 25,* Lake Placid, N.Y. 6.00
Washington, D.C., *Jan. 26* 1.50
717 2c **Arbor Day,** *Apr. 22,* Nebraska City, Neb. 4.00
Washington, D.C., *Apr. 23* 1.50
Adams, N.Y., *Apr. 23* 6.50
718 3c **Olympic Summer Games,** *June 15,* Los Angeles, Cal. 6.00
Washington, D.C., *June 16* 2.75
719 5c **Olympic Summer Games,** *June 15,* Los Angeles, Cal. 8.00
Washington, D.C., *June 16* 2.75
718, 719 on one cover, Los Angeles, Cal. 10.00
718, 719 on one cover, Washington, D.C. 4.50
720 3c **Washington,** *June 16* 7.50
720b Booklet pane of 6, *July 25* 100.00
721 3c **Washington Coil,** Sideways, *June 24* 15.00
722 3c **Washington Coil,** Endways, *Oct. 12* 15.00
723 6c **Garfield Coil,** Sideways, *Aug. 18,* Los Angeles, Cal. 15.00
Washington, D.C., *Aug. 19* 4.00
724 3c **William Penn,** *Oct. 24,* New Castle, Del. 3.25
Chester, Pa. 3.25
Philadelphia, Pa. 3.25
Washington, D.C., *Oct. 25* 1.25
725 3c **Daniel Webster,** *Oct. 24,* Franklin, N.H. 3.25
Exeter, N.H. 3.25
Hanover, N.H. 3.25
Washington, D.C., *Oct. 25* 1.25

1933

726 3c **Gen. Oglethorpe,** *Feb. 12,* Savannah, Ga., *(200,000)* 3.25
Washington, D.C., *Feb. 13* 1.50
727 3c **Peace Proclamation,** *Apr. 19,* Newburgh, N.Y. *(349,571)* 3.50
Washington, D.C., *Apr. 20* 1.25
728 1c **Century of Progress,** *May 25,* Chicago, Ill., strip of 3 3.00
Washington, D.C., *May 26* 1.00
729 3c **Century of Progress,** *May 25,* Chicago, Ill. 3.00
Washington, D.C., *May 26* 1.00
728, 729 on one cover 5.00

Covers mailed May 25, bearing Nos. 728 and 729 total 232,251.

730 1c **American Philatelic Society,** sheet of 25, *Aug. 25,* Chicago, Ill. 100.00
730a 1c **A.P.S.,** imperf., *Aug. 25,* Chicago, Ill., strip of 3 3.25
Washington, D.C., *Aug. 28* 1.25
731 3c **American Philatelic Society,** sheet of 25, *Aug. 25,* Chicago, Ill. 100.00
731a 3c **A.P.S.,** single, imperf., *Aug. 25,* Chicago, Ill. 3.25
Washington, D.C., *Aug. 28* 1.25
730a, 731a on one cover 5.50

Covers mailed Aug. 25 bearing Nos. 730, 730a, 731, 731a total 65,218.

732 3c **National Recovery Administration,** *Aug. 15,(65,000)* 3.25
Nira, Iowa, *Aug. 17* 2.50
733 3c **Byrd Antarctic,** *Oct. 9* 10.00
734 5c **Kosciuszko,** *Oct. 13,* Boston, Mass. *(23,025)* 4.50
Buffalo, N.Y. *(14,981)* 5.50
Chicago, Ill, *(26,306)* 4.50
Detroit, Mich. *(17,792)* 5.25
Pittsburgh, Pa. *(6,282)* 15.00
Kosciuszko, Miss. *(27,093)* 5.25
St. Louis, Mo. *(17,872)* 5.25
Washington, D.C., *Oct. 14* 1.60

1934

735 3c **National Exhibition,** sheet of 6, Byrd imperf., *Feb. 10,* New York, N.Y. 40.00
Washington, D.C., *Feb. 19* 27.50
735a 3c **National Exhibition,** single, imperf., New York, N.Y., *Feb. 10 (450,715)* 5.00
Washington, D.C., *Feb. 19* 2.75
736 3c **Maryland Tercentenary,** *Mar. 23* St. Mary's City, Md. *(148,785)* 1.60
Washington, D.C., *Mar. 24* 1.00
737 3c **Mothers of America,** perf. 11x10½, *May 2, any city* 1.60
738 3c **Mothers of America,** perf. 11, *May 2, any city* 1.60
737, 738 on one cover 4.00

Covers mailed at Washington, May 2 bearing Nos. 737 and 738 total 183,359.

739 3c **Wisconsin,** *July 7,* Green Bay, Wisc. *(130,000)* 1.10
Washington, D.C., *July 9* 1.00
740 1c **Parks, Yosemite,** *July 16* 2.25
Yosemite, Cal., *(60,000),* strip of 3 2.75
741 2c **Parks, Grand Canyon,** *July 24* 2.25
Grand Canyon, Ariz., *(75,000),* pair 2.75
742 3c **Parks, Mt. Rainier,** *Aug. 3* 2.50
Longmire, Wash., *(64,500)* 3.00
743 4c **Parks, Mesa Verde,** *Sept. 25* 2.25
Mesa Verde, Colo., *(51,882)* 2.75
744 5c **Parks, Yellowstone,** *July 30* 2.25
Yellowstone, Wyo., *(87,000)* 2.50
745 6c **Parks, Crater Lake,** *Sept. 5* 3.00
Crater Lake, Ore., *(45,282)* 3.25
746 7c **Parks, Arcadia,** *Oct. 2* 3.00
Bar Harbor, Maine *(51,312)* 3.25
747 8c **Parks, Zion,** *Sept. 18* 3.25
Zion, Utah, *(43,650)* 3.75
748 9c **Parks, Glacier Park,** *Aug. 27* 3.50
Glacier Park, Mont., *(52,626)* 3.75
749 10c **Parks, Smoky Mountains,** *Oct. 8* 6.00
Sevierville, Tenn., *(39,000)* 7.50

Imperf

750 3c **American Philatelic Society,** sheet of 6, *Aug. 28,* Atlantic City, N.J. 40.00
750a 3c **A.P.S.,** single, *Aug. 28,* Atlantic City, N.J. *(40,000)* 3.25
Washington, D.C., *Sept. 4* 2.00
751 1c **Trans-Mississippi Philatelic Expo.,** sheet of 6, *Oct. 10,* Omaha, Neb. 35.00
751a 1c **Trans-Miss. Phil. Expo.,** Omaha. Neb., *Oct. 10 (125,000),* strip of 3 3.25
Washington, D.C., Oct. 15 2.00

Nos. 752-771 issued Mar. 15

1935 **SPECIAL PRINTING**

752 3c **Peace Commemoration** 5.00
753 3c **Byrd** 6.00
754 3c **Mothers of America** 6.00
755 3c **Wisconsin Tercentenary** 6.00
756 1c **Parks, Yosemite,** strip of 3 6.00
757 2c **Parks, Grand Canyon,** pair 6.00
758 3c **Parks, Mount Rainier** 6.00

759 4c **Parks, Mesa Verde** 6.50
760 5c **Parks, Yellowstone** 6.50
761 6c **Parks, Crater Lake** 6.50
762 7c **Parks, Acadia** 6.50
763 8c **Parks, Zion** 7.50
764 9c **Parks, Glacier Park** 7.50
765 10c **Parks, Smoky Mountains** 7.50
766a 1c **Century of Progress,** strip of 3 5.50
Pane of 25 *250.00*
767a 3c **Century of Progress** 5.50
Pane of 25 *250.00*
768a 3c **Byrd** 6.50
Pane of 6 *250.00*
769a 1c **Parks, Yosemite,** strip of 3 4.00
Pane of 6 *250.00*
770a 3c **Parks, Mount Rainier** 5.00
Pane of 6 *250.00*
771 16c **Airmail Special Delivery** 12.50

Catalogue values from this point to No. 986 are for addressed covers with the most common cachets.

772 3c **Connecticut Tercentenary,** *Apr. 26,* Hartford, Conn. *(217,800)* 15.00
Washington, D.C., *Apr. 27* 2.25
773 3c **California Exposition,** *May 29,* San Diego, Cal. *(214,042)* 15.00
Washington, D.C., *May 31* 1.50
774 3c **Boulder Dam,** *Sept. 30,* Boulder City, Nev. *(166,180)* 15.00
Washington, D.C., *Oct. 1* 2.00
775 3c **Michigan Centenary,** *Nov. 1,* Lansing, Mich. *(176,962)* 15.00
Washington, D.C., *Nov. 2* 1.50

1936

776 3c **Texas Centennial,** *Mar. 2,* Gonzales, Texas *(319,150)* 20.00
Washington, D.C., *Mar. 3* 2.00
777 3c **Rhode Island Tercentenary,** *May 4,* Providence, R.I. *(245,400)* 14.00
Washington, D.C., *May 5* 2.25
778 **TIPEX** souvenir sheet, *May 9 (297,194) New York, N.Y.* (TIPEX cancellation) 14.00
Washington, D.C., *May 11* 3.50
782 3c **Arkansas Centennial,** *June 15,* Little Rock, Ark. *(376,693)* 13.00
Washington, D.C, *June 16* 1.25
783 3c **Oregon Territory Centennial,** *July 14,* Astoria, Ore. *(91,110)* 10.00
Daniel, Wyo., *(67,013)* 10.00
Lewiston, Ida., *(86,100)* 10.00
Missoula, Mont., *(59,883)* 11.00
Walla Walla, Wash., *(106,150)* 9.00
Washington, D.C., *July 15* 1.25
784 3c **Susan B. Anthony,** *Aug. 26 (178,500)* 15.00

1936-37

785 1c **Army,** *Dec. 15, 1936,* strip of 3 8.50
786 2c **Army,** *Jan. 15, 1937,* pair 8.50
787 3c **Army,** *Feb. 18, 1937* 8.50
788 4c **Army,** *Mar. 23, 1937* 8.50
789 5c **Army,** *May 26, 1937,* West Point, N.Y., *(160,000)* 8.50
Washington, D.C., *May 27* 4.50
790 1c **Navy,** *Dec. 15, 1936,* strip of 3 8.50
791 2c **Navy,** *Jan. 15, 1937,* pair 8.50
792 3c **Navy,** *Feb. 18, 1937* 8.50
793 4c **Navy,** *Mar. 23, 1937* 8.50
794 5c **Navy,** *May 26, 1937,* Annapolis, Md., *(202,806)* 8.50
Washington, D.C., *May 27* 4.50

Covers for #785 & 790 total 390,749; #786 & 791 total 292,570; #787 & 792 total 320,888; #788 & 793 total 331,000.

1937

795 3c **Ordinance of 1787,** *July 13* Marietta, Ohio *(130,531)* 9.00
New York, N.Y. *(125,134)* 9.00
Washington, D.C., *July 14* 1.25
796 5c **Virginia Dare,** *Aug. 18,* Manteo, N.C. *(226,730)* 11.00
797 10c **Souvenir Sheet,** *Aug. 26,* Asheville, N.C. *(164,215)* 11.00
798 3c **Constitution,** *Sept. 17,* Philadelphia, Pa. *(281,478)* 9.00
799 3c **Hawaii,** *Oct. 18,* Honolulu, Hawaii *(320,334)* 11.00
800 3c **Alaska,** *Nov. 12,* Juneau, Alaska *(230,370)* 10.00
801 3c **Puerto Rico,** *Nov. 25,* San Juan, P.R. *(244,054)* 10.00
802 3c **Virgin Islands,** *Dec. 15,* Charlotte Amalie, V.I. *(225,469)* 10.00

PRESIDENTIAL ISSUE

1938

803 ½c **Franklin,** *May 19,* Philadelphia, Pa. *(224,901),* block of 6 3.50
804 1c **G. Washington,** *Apr. 25 (124,037),* strip of 3 3.50
804b Booklet pane of 6, *Jan. 27, 1939* 12.50
805 1½c **M. Washington,** *May 5 (128,339),* pair 3.50
806 2c **J. Adams,** *June 3 (127,806),* pair 3.50
806b Booklet pane of 6, *Jan. 27, 1939* 15.00
807 3c **Jefferson,** *June 16 (118,097)* 3.50
807a Booklet pane of 6, *Jan. 27, 1939* 17.50
808 4c **Madison,** *July 1 (118,765)* 3.50
809 4½c **White House,** *July 11 (115,820)* 3.50
810 5c **Monroe,** *July 21 (98,282)* 3.50
811 6c **J.Q. Adams,** *July 28 (97,428)* 3.50
812 7c **Jackson,** *Aug. 4 (98,414)* 3.50
813 8c **Van Buren,** *Aug. 11 (94,857)* 3.50
814 9c **W.H. Harrison,** *Aug. 18 (91,229)* 3.50
815 10c **Tyler,** *Sept. 2 (83,707)* 3.50
816 11c **Polk,** *Sept. 8 (63,966)* 5.00
817 12c **Taylor,** *Sept. 14 (62,935)* 5.00
818 13c **Fillmore,** *Sept. 22 (58,965)* 5.00
819 14c **Pierce,** *Oct. 6 (49,819)* 5.00
820 15c **Buchanan,** *Oct. 13 (52,209)* 5.00
821 16c **Lincoln,** *Oct. 20 (59,566)* 7.50
822 17c **A. Johnson,** *Oct. 27 (55,024)* 6.00
823 18c **Grant,** *Nov. 3 (53,124)* 6.00
824 19c **Hayes,** *Nov. 10 (54,124)* 6.00
825 20c **Garfield,** *Nov. 10 (51,971)* 7.00
826 21c **Arthur,** *Nov. 22 (44,367)* 7.00
827 22c **Cleveland,** *Nov. 22 (44,358)* 8.00
828 24c **B. Harrison,** *Dec. 2 (46,592)* 8.00
829 25c **McKinley,** *Dec. 2 (45,691)* 8.00
830 30c **T. Roosevelt,** *Dec. 8 (43,528)* 9.00
831 50c **Taft,** *Dec. 8 (41,984)* 12.50
832 $1 **Wilson, purple & black,** *Aug. 29 (24,618)* 60.00
832c **red violet & black,** *Aug. 31, 1954 (20,202)* 30.00
833 $2 **Harding,** *Sept. 29 (19,895)* 120.00
834 $5 **Coolidge,** *Nov. 17 (15,615)* 200.00

1938

835 3c **Constitution,** *June 21,* Philadelphia, Pa. *(232,873)* 15.00
836 3c **Swedes and Finns,** *June 27,* Wilmington, Del. *(225,617)* 15.00
837 3c **Northwest Sesqui.,** *July 15,* Marietta, Ohio *(180,170)* 15.00
838 3c **Iowa,** *Aug. 24,* Des Moines, Iowa *(209,860)* 15.00

1939 COIL STAMPS ***Perf. 10 Vertically***

839 1c **G. Washington,** *Jan. 20,* strip of 3 5.00
840 1½c **M. Washington,** *Jan. 20,* pair 5.00
841 2c **J. Adams,** *Jan. 20,* pair 5.00
842 3c **Jefferson,** *Jan. 20* 5.00
843 4c **Madison,** *Jan. 20* 5.00
844 4½c **White House,** *Jan. 20* 5.00
845 5c **Monroe,** *Jan. 20* 5.00
846 6c **J.Q. Adams,** *Jan. 20* 6.50
847 10c **Tyler,** *Jan. 20* 9.00
839-847 on one cover, *Jan. 20* 45.00

Perf. 10 Horizontally

848 1c Strip of 3, *Jan. 27* 5.00
849 1½c Pair, *Jan. 27* 5.00
850 2c Pair, *Jan. 27* 5.00
851 3c *Jan. 27* 5.50
848-851 on one cover, *Jan. 27* 25.00

1939

852 3c **Golden Gate Expo,** *Feb. 18,* San Francisco, Cal. *(352,165)* 16.00
853 3c **N.Y. World's Fair,** *Apr. 1,* New York, N.Y. *(585,565)* 20.00
854 3c **Washington Inauguration,** *Apr. 30,* New York, N.Y. *(395,644)* 17.50
855 3c **Baseball Centennial,** *June 12,* Cooperstown, N.Y. *(398,199)* 40.00
856 3c **Panama Canal,** *Aug. 15,* U.S.S. Charleston, Canal Zone *(230,974)* 18.00
857 3c **Printing Tercentenary,** *Sept. 25,* New York, N.Y. *(295,270)* 15.00
858 3c **50th Statehood Anniversary,** Bismarck, N.D. *Nov. 2 (142,106)* 12.50
Pierre, S.D., *Nov. 2 (150,429)* 12.50
Helena, Mont., *Nov. 8 (130,273)* 12.50
Olympia, Wash., *Nov. 11 (150,429)* 12.50

FAMOUS AMERICAN ISSUE

1940

859 1c **Washington Irving,** *Jan. 29,* Tarrytown, N.Y. *(170,969),* strip of 3 4.50
860 2c **James Fenimore Cooper,** *Jan. 29,* Cooperstown, N.Y. *(154,836),* pair 3.00
861 3c **Ralph Waldo Emerson,** *Feb. 5,* Boston, Mass. *(185,148)* 3.00
862 5c **Louisa May Alcott,** *Feb. 5,* Concord, Mass. *(134,325)* 4.00
863 10c **Samuel L. Clemens,** *Feb. 13,* Hannibal, Mo. *(150,492)* 8.00
864 1c **Henry W. Longfellow,** *Feb. 16,* Portland, Me. *(160,508),* strip of 3 4.00
865 2c **John Greenleaf Whittier,** *Feb. 16,* Haverhill, Mass. *(148,423),* pair 3.00
866 3c **James Russell Lowell,** *Feb. 20,* Cambridge, Mass. *(148,735)* 3.00
867 5c **Walt Whitman,** *Feb. 20,* Camden, N.J. *(134,185)* 4.00
868 10c **James Whitcomb Riley,** *Feb. 24,* Greenfield, Ind. *(131,760)* 6.00
869 1c **Horace Mann,** *Mar. 14,* Boston, Mass. *(186,854),* strip of 3 3.00
870 2c **Mark Hopkins,** *Mar. 14,* Williamstown, Mass. *(140,286),* pair 3.00
871 3c **Charles W. Eliot,** *Mar. 28,* Cambridge, Mass. *(155,708)* 3.00
872 5c **Frances E. Willard,** *Mar. 28,* Evanston, Ill. *(140,483)* 4.00
873 10c **Booker T. Washington,** *Apr. 7,* Tuskegee Institute, Ala. *(163,507)* 10.00
874 1c **John James Audubon,** *Apr. 8,* St. Francisville, La. *(144,123),* strip of 3 4.00
875 2c **Dr. Crawford W. Long,** *Apr. 8,* Jefferson, Ga. *(158,128),* pair 3.00
876 3c **Luther Burbank,** *Apr. 17,* Santa Rosa, Cal. *(147,033)* 3.00
877 5c **Dr. Walter Reed,** *Apr. 17 (154,464)* 4.00
878 10c **Jane Addams,** *Apr. 26,* Chicago, Ill. *(132,375)* 6.00
879 1c **Stephen Collins Foster,** *May 3,* Bardstown, Ky. *(183,461),* strip of 3 3.00
880 2c **John Philip Sousa,** *May 3 (131,422),* pair 4.00
881 3c **Victor Herbert,** *May 13,* New York, N.Y. *(168,200)* 3.00
882 5c **Edward A. MacDowell,** *May 13,* Peterborough, N.H. *(135,155)* 4.00
883 10c **Ethelbert Nevin,** *June 10,* Pittsburgh, Pa. *(121,951)* 6.00
884 1c **Gilbert Stuart,** *Sept. 5,* Narragansett, R.I. *(131,965),* strip of 3 4.00
885 2c **James A. McNeill Whistler,** *Sept. 5,* Lowell, Mass. *(130,962),* pair 3.00
886 3c **Augustus Saint-Gaudens,** *Sept. 16,* New York, N.Y. *(138,200)* 3.00
887 5c **Daniel Chester French,** *Sept. 16,* Stockbridge, Mass. *(124,608)* 4.00
888 10c **Frederic Remington,** *Sept. 30,* Canton, N.Y. *(116,219)* 7.00
889 1c **Eli Whitney,** *Oct. 7,* Savannah, Ga. *(140,868),* strip of 3 4.00
890 2c **Samuel F.B. Morse,** *Oct. 7,* New York, N.Y. *(135,388),* pair 3.00
891 3c **Cyrus Hall McCormick,** *Oct. 14,* Lexington, Va. *(137,415)* 3.00
892 5c **Elias Howe,** *Oct. 14,* Spencer, Mass. *(126,334)* 4.00
893 10c **Alexander Graham Bell,** *Oct. 28,* Boston, Mass. *(125,372)* 10.00

1940

894 3c **Pony Express,** *Apr. 3,* St. Joseph, Mo. *(194,589)* 12.00
Sacramento, Cal. *(160,849)* 12.00
895 3c **Pan American Union,** *Apr. 14 (182,401)* 9.50
896 3c **Idaho Statehood,** *July 3,* Boise, Idaho *(156,429)* 9.50
897 3c **Wyoming Statehood,** *July 10* Cheyenne, Wyo. *(156,709)* 9.50
898 3c **Coronado Expedition,** *Sept. 7,* Albuquerque, N.M. *(161,012)* 9.50
899 1c **Defense,** *Oct. 16,* strip of 3 7.50
900 2c **Defense,** *Oct. 16,* pair 7.50
901 3c **Defense,** *Oct. 16* 7.50
899-901 on one cover 12.00

First day cancel was applied to 450,083 covers bearing one or more of Nos. 899-901.

902 3c **Thirteenth Amendment,** *Oct. 20,* World's Fair, N.Y. *(156,146)* 10.00

1941

903 3c **Vermont Statehood,** *Mar. 4,* Montpelier, Vt. *(182,423)* 10.00

MacArthur, W. Va.
Apr 15, 1942
First Day Cover

Covers exist with this cancellation. "First Day" refers to the first day of the new name of the town, previously known as Hollywood, W. Va.

1942

904 3c **Kentucky Statehood,** *June 1,* Frankfort, Ky. *(155,730)* 10.00
905 3c **"Win the War",** *July 4 (191,168)* 10.00
906 5c **Chinese Resistance,** *July 7,* Denver, Colo. *(168,746)* 20.00

1943-44

907 2c **Allied Nations,** *Jan. 14, 1943 (178,865),* pair 6.00
908 1c **Four Freedoms,** *Feb. 12, 1943 (193,800),* strip of 3 7.00
909 5c **Poland,** *June 22, 1943,* Chicago, Ill. *(88,170)* 10.00
Washington, D.C. *(136,002)* 5.00
910 5c **Czechoslovakia,** *July 12, 1943 (145,112)* 4.00
911 5c **Norway,** *July 27, 1943 (155,054)* 4.00
912 5c **Luxemborg,** *Aug. 10, 1943 (166,367)* 4.00
913 5c **Netherlands,** *Aug. 24, 1943 (148,763)* 4.00
914 5c **Belgium,** *Sept. 14, 1943 (154,220)* 4.00
915 5c **France,** *Sept. 28, 1943 (163,478)* 4.00
916 5c **Greece,** *Oct. 12, 1943 (166,553)* 4.00
917 5c **Yugoslavia,** *Oct. 26, 1943 (161,835)* 4.00
918 5c **Albania,** *Nov. 9, 1943 (162,275)* 4.00
919 5c **Austria,** *Nov. 23, 1943 (172,285)* 4.00
920 5c **Denmark,** *Dec. 7, 1943 (173,784)* 4.00
921 5c **Korea,** *Nov. 2, 1944 (192,860)* 5.00

1944

922 3c **Railroad,** *May 10,* Ogden, Utah *(151,324)* 10.00
Omaha, Neb. *(171,000)* 10.00
San Francisco, Cal. *(125,000)* 10.00
923 3c **Steamship,** *May 22,* Kings Point, N.Y. *(152,324)* 9.00
Savannah, Ga. *(181,472)* 9.00
924 3c **Telegraph,** *May 24 (141,907)* 9.00
Baltimore, Md. *(136,480)* 9.00
925 3c **Philippines,** *Sept. 27 (214,865)* 9.00
926 3c **Motion Picture,** *Oct. 31,* Hollywood, Cal. *(190,660)* 10.00
New York, N.Y. *(176,473)* 9.00

1945

927 3c **Florida,** *Mar. 3,* Tallahassee, Fla. *(228,435)* 9.00
928 5c **United Nations Conference,** *Apr. 25,* San Francisco, Cal. *(417,450)* 10.00
929 3c **Iwo Jima,** *July 11 (391,650)* 15.00

1945-46

930 1c **Roosevelt,** *July 26, 1945,* Hyde Park, N.Y. *(390,219),* strip of 3 5.00
931 2c **Roosevelt,** *Aug. 24, 1945,* Warm Springs, Ga. *(426,142),* pair 5.00
932 3c **Roosevelt,** *June 27, 1945 (391,650)* 5.00
933 5c **Roosevelt,** *Jan. 30, 1946 (466,766)* 5.00

1945

934 3c **Army**, *Sept. 28 (392,300)* 11.00
935 3c **Navy**, *Oct. 27*, Annapolis, Md. *(460,352)* 11.00
936 3c **Coast Guard**, *Nov. 10* New York, N.Y. *(405,280)* 11.00
937 3c **Alfred E. Smith**, *Nov. 26* New York, N.Y. *(424,950)* 3.00
938 3c **Texas**, *Dec. 29*, Austin, Tex. *(397,860)* 10.00

1946

939 3c **Merchant Marine**, *Feb. 26 (432,141)* 9.00
940 3c **Veterans of WWII**, *May 9 (492,786)* 11.00
941 3c **Tennessee**, *June 1, 1946*, Nashville, Tenn. *(463,512)* 4.00
942 3c **Iowa**, *Aug. 3*, Iowa City, Iowa *(517,505)* 4.00
943 3c **Smithsonian**, *Aug. 10 (402,448)* 4.00
944 3c **Kearny Expedition**, *Oct. 16*, Santa Fe, N.M. *(384,300)* 4.00

1947

945 3c **Thomas A. Edison**, *Feb. 11*, Milan, Ohio *(632,473)* 5.00
946 3c **Joseph Pulitzer**, *Apr. 10*, New York, N.Y. *(580,870)* 4.00
947 3c **Stamp Centenary**, *May 17*, New York, N.Y. *(712,873)* 4.00
948 5c and 10c **Centenary Exhibition Sheet**, *May 19*, New York, N.Y. *(502,175)* 4.50
949 3c **Doctors**, *June 9*, Atlantic City, N.J. *(508,016)* 10.00
950 3c **Utah**, *July 24*, Salt Lake City, Utah *(456,416)* 3.00
951 3c **"Constitution,"** *Oct. 21*, Boston, Mass. *(683,416)* 9.00
952 3c **Everglades Park**, *Dec. 5*, Florida City, Fla. *(466,647)* 3.00

1948

953 3c **Carver**, *Jan. 5*, Tuskegee Institute, Ala. *(402,179)* 3.00
954 3c **California Gold**, *Jan. 24*, Coloma, Calif. *(526,154)* 4.00
955 3c **Mississippi Territory**, *Apr. 7*, Natchez, Miss. *(434,804)* 2.00
956 3c **Four Chaplains**, *May 28 (459,070)* 10.00
957 3c **Wisconsin Centennial**, *May 29*, Madison, Wis. *(470,280)* 3.00
958 5c **Swedish Pioneers**, *June 4* Chicago, Ill. *(364,318)* 4.00
959 3c **Women's Progress**, *July 19*, Seneca Falls, N.Y. *(401,923)* 3.00
960 3c **William Allen White**, *July 31*, Emporia, Kans. *(385,648)* 2.50
961 3c **U.S.-Canada Friendship**, *Aug. 2*, Niagara Falls, N.Y. *(406,467)* 3.00
962 3c **Francis Scott Key**, *Aug. 9*, Frederick, Md. *(505,930)* 2.50
963 3c **Salute to Youth**, *Aug. 11 (347,070)* 2.50
964 3c **Oregon Territory Establishment**, *Aug. 14*, Oregon City, Ore. *(365,898)* 3.00
965 3c **Harlan Fiske Stone**, *Aug. 25*, Chesterfield, N.H. *(362,170)* 2.50
966 3c **Palomar Observatory**, *Aug. 30*, Palomar Mountain, Calif. *(401,365)* 5.00
967 3c **Clara Barton**, *Sept. 7*, Oxford, Mass. *(362,000)* 4.00
968 3c **Poultry Industry**, *Sept. 9*, New Haven, Conn. *(475,000)* 3.50
969 3c **Gold Star Mothers**, *Sept. 21 (386,064)* 2.00
970 3c **Fort Kearny**, *Sept. 22*, Minden, Neb. *(429,633)* 2.00
971 3c **Volunteer Firemen**, *Oct. 4*, Dover, Del. *(399,630)* 10.00
972 3c **Indian Centennial**, *Oct. 15*, Muskogee, Okla. *(459,528)* 3.50
973 3c **Rough Riders**, *Oct. 27*, Prescott, Ariz. *(399,198)* 2.50
974 3c **Juliette Low**, *Oct. 29*, Savannah, Ga. *(476,573)* 8.00
975 3c **Will Rogers**, *Nov. 4*, Claremore, Okla. *(450,350)* 3.00
976 3c **Fort Bliss**, *Nov. 5*, El Paso, Tex. *(421,000)* 5.00
977 3c **Moina Michael**, *Nov. 9*, Athens, Ga. *(374,090)* 2.50
978 3c **Gettysburg Address**, *Nov. 19*, Gettysburg, Pa. *(511,990)* 3.00
979 3c **American Turners Society**, *Nov. 20*, Cincinnati, Ohio *(434,090)* 2.00
980 3c **Joel Chandler Harris**, *Dec. 9*, Eatonton, Ga. *(426,199)* 2.25

1949

981 3c **Minnesota Territory**, *Mar. 3*, St. Paul, Minn. *(458,750)* 2.25
982 3c **Washington and Lee University**, *Apr. 12*, Lexington, Va. *(447,910)* 2.25
983 3c **Puerto Rico Election**, *Apr. 27*, San Juan, P.R. *(390,416)* 2.25
984 3c **Annapolis, Md.**, *May 23*, Annapolis, Md. *(441,802)* 3.00
985 3c **G.A.R.**, *Aug. 29*, Indianapolis, Ind. *(471,696)* 3.25
986 3c **Edgar Allan Poe**, *Oct. 7*, Richmond, Va. *(371,020)* 4.00

Catalogue values from this point to the end of the section are for unaddressed covers with the most common cachets.

1950

987 3c **American Bankers Assoc.**, *Jan. 3*, Saratoga Springs, N.Y. *(388,622)* 2.75
988 3c **Samuel Gompers**, *Jan. 27 (332,023)* 1.75

National Capital Sesquicentennial

989 3c **Freedom**, *Apr. 20 (371,743)* 1.50
990 3c **Executive**, *June 12 (376,789)* 1.50
991 3c **Judicial**, *Aug. 2 (324,007)* 1.50
992 3c **Legislative**, *Nov. 22 (352,215)* 1.50
993 3c **Railroad Engineers**, *Apr. 29*, Jackson, Tenn. *(420,830)* 4.00
994 3c **Kansas City Centenary**, *June 3*, Kansas City, Mo. *(405,390)* 1.50
995 3c **Boy Scouts**, *June 30*, Valley Forge, Pa. *(622,972)* 12.00
996 3c **Indiana Territory Sesquicentennial**, *July 4*, Vincennes, Ind. *(359,643)* 1.75
997 3c **California Statehood**, *Sept. 9*, Sacramento, Cal. *(391,919)* 2.50

1951

998 3c **United Confederate Veterans**, *May 30*, Norfolk, Va. *(374,235)* 3.00
999 3c **Nevada Centennial**, *July 14*, Genoa, Nev. *(336,890)* 1.50
1000 3c **Landing of Cadillac**, *July 24*, Detroit, Mich. *(323,094)* 1.50
1001 3c **Colorado Statehood**, *Aug. 1*, Minturn, Colo. *(311,568)* 1.50
1002 3c **American Chemical Society**, *Sept. 4*, New York, N.Y. *(436,419)* 1.75
1003 3c **Battle of Brooklyn**, *Dec. 10*, Brooklyn, N.Y. *(420,000)* 1.50

1952

1004 3c **Betsy Ross**, *Jan. 2*, Philadelphia, Pa. *(314,312)* 1.50
1005 3c **4-H Club**, *Jan. 15*, Springfield, Ohio *(383,290)* 3.25
1006 3c **B. & O. Railroad**, *Feb. 28*, Baltimore, Md. *(441,600)* 4.50
1007 3c **American Automobile Association**, *Mar. 4*, Chicago, Ill. *(520,123)* 1.75
1008 3c **NATO**, *Apr. 4 (313,518)* 1.50
1009 3c **Grand Coulee Dam**, *May 15*, Grand Coulee, Wash. *(341,680)* 1.50
1010 3c **Lafayette**, *June 13*, Georgetown, S.C. *(349,102)* 1.50
1011 3c **Mt. Rushmore Memorial**, *Aug. 11*, Keystone, S.D. *(337,027)* 1.50
1012 3c **Civil Engineers**, *Sept. 6*, Chicago, Ill. *(318,483)* 1.50
1013 3c **Service Women**, *Sept. 11 (308,062)* 2.00
1014 3c **Gutenberg Bible**, *Sept. 30 (387,078)* 1.50
1015 3c **Newspaper Boys**, *Oct. 4*, Philadelphia, Pa. *(626,000)* 1.50
1016 3c **Red Cross**, *Nov. 21*, New York, N.Y. *(439,252)* 2.50

1953

1017 3c **National Guard**, *Feb. 23 (387,618)* 2.00
1018 3c **Ohio Sesquicentennial**, *Mar. 2*, Chillicothe, Ohio *(407,983)* 1.50
1019 3c **Washington Territory**, *Mar. 2*, Olympia, Wash. *(344,047)* 1.50
1020 3c **Louisiana Purchase**, *Apr. 30*, St. Louis, Mo. *(425,600)* 1.50
1021 5c **Opening of Japan**, *July 14 (320,541)* 1.75
1022 3c **American Bar Association**, *Aug. 24*, Boston, Mass. *(410,036)* 8.00
1023 3c **Sagamore Hill**, *Sept. 14*, Oyster Bay, N.Y. *(379,750)* 1.50
1024 3c **Future Farmers**, *Oct. 13*, Kansas City, Mo. *(424,193)* 1.50
1025 3c **Trucking Industry**, *Oct. 27*, Los Angeles, Calif. *(875,021)* 1.50
1026 3c **Gen. G.S. Patton, Jr.**, *Nov. 11*, Fort Knox, Ky. *(342,600)* 5.00
1027 3c **New York City**, *Nov. 20*, New York, N.Y. *(387,914)* 1.50
1028 3c **Gadsden Purchase**, *Dec. 30*, Tucson, Ariz. *(363,250)* 1.50

1954

1029 3c **Columbia University**, *Jan. 4*, New York, N.Y. *(550,745)* 1.50

LIBERTY ISSUE

1954-67

1030 ½c **Franklin**, *Oct. 20, 1955 (223,122)*, block of 6 1.00
1031 1c **Washington**, *Aug. 26, 1954*, Chicago, Ill. *(272,581)*, strip of 3 1.00
1031A 1¼c **Palace of Governors**, *June 17, 1960*, Santa Fe, N.M., strip of 3 1.00
1031A and 1054A on one cover 1.50

First day cancel was applied to 501,848 covers bearing one or more of Nos. 1031A, 1054A.

1032 1½c **Mt. Vernon**, *Feb. 22, 1956*, Mount Vernon, Va. *(270,109)*, pair 1.00
1033 2c **Jefferson**, *Sept. 15, 1954*, San Francisco, Cal. *(307,300)*, pair 1.00
1033a 2c **Jefferson** on Silkote paper, *Dec. 17, 1954*, Westbrook, Maine *10,000.*
1034 2½c **Bunker Hill**, *June 17, 1959*, Boston, Mass. *(315,060)*, pair 1.00
1035 3c **Statue of Liberty**, *June 24, 1954*, Albany, N.Y. *(340,001)* 1.00
1035a Booklet pane of 6, *June 30, 1954* 3.50
1035e 3c Tagged, *July 6, 1966* 40.00
1036 4c **Lincoln**, *Nov. 19, 1954*, New York, N.Y. *(374,064)* 1.50
1036b Booklet pane of 6, *July 31, 1958*, Wheeling, W. Va. *(135,825)* 4.00
1036e 4c Tagged, *Nov. 2, 1963* 65.00

No. 1036e was supposed to have been issued at Dayton Nov. 2, but a mix-up delayed its issuance there until Nov. 4. About 510 Covers received the Nov. 2 cancellation.

1037 4½c **Hermitage**, *Mar. 16, 1959*, Hermitage, Tenn. *(320,000)* 1.00
1038 5c **Monroe**, *Dec. 2, 1954*, Fredericksburg, Va. *(255,650)* 1.00
1039 6c **T. Roosevelt**, *Nov. 18, 1955*, New York, N.Y. *(257,551)* 1.00
1040 7c **Wilson**, *Jan. 10, 1956*, Staunton, Va. *(200,111)* 1.00
1041 8c **Statue of Liberty** (flat plate), *Apr. 9, 1954* 1.00
1041B 8c **Statue of Liberty** (rotary press), *Apr. 9, 1954* 1.00

First day cancellation was applied to 340,077 covers bearing one or more of Nos. 1041-1041B.

1042 8c **Statue of Liberty** (Giori press), *Mar. 22, 1958*, Cleveland, O. *(223,899)* 1.00
1043 9c **Alamo**, *June 14, 1956*, San Antonio, Texas *(207,086)* 2.00
1044 10c **Independence Hall**, *July 4, 1956*, Philadelphia, Pa., *(220,930)* 1.00
1044d 10c Tagged, *July 6, 1966* 40.00
1044A 11c **Statue of Liberty**, *June 15, 1961 (238,905)* 1.25
1044Ac 11c Tagged, *Jan. 11, 1967* 40.00
1045 12c **B. Harrison**, *June 6, 1959*, Oxford, O. *(225,869)* 1.25
1045a 12c Tagged, *May 6, 1968* 40.00
1046 15c **Jay**, *Dec. 12, 1958 (205,680)* 1.25
1046a 15c Tagged, *July 6, 1966* 40.00
1047 20c **Monticello**, *Apr. 13, 1956*, Charlottesville, Va. *(147,860)* 1.25
1048 25c **Revere**, *Apr. 18, 1958*, Boston, Mass. *(196,530)* 1.25
1049 30c **Lee**, *Sept. 21, 1955*, Norfolk, Va. *(120,166)* 2.00
1050 40c **Marshall**, *Sept. 24, 1955*, Richmond, Va. *(113,972)* 2.00
1051 50c **Anthony**, *Aug. 25, 1955*, Louisville, Ky. *(110,220)* 6.00
1052 $1 **Henry**, *Oct. 7, 1955*, Joplin, Mo. *(80,191)* 15.00
1053 $5 **Hamilton**, *Mar. 19, 1956*, Paterson, N.J. *(34,272)* 50.00

1954-73 COIL STAMPS

1054 1c **Washington**, *Oct. 8, 1954*, Baltimore, Md. *(196,318)*, strip of 3 1.00
1054A 1¼c **Palace of Governors**, *June 17, 1960*, Santa Fe, N.M., strip of 3 1.00
1055 2c **Jefferson**, *Oct. 22, 1954*, St. Louis, Mo. *(162,050)*, pair 1.00
1055b 2c Tagged, *May 6, 1968*, pair, small holes 32.50
Large holes, pair or strip, *May 6, 1968* —
1056 2½c **Bunker Hill**, *Sept. 9, 1959*, Los Angeles, Calif. *(198,680)*, pair 2.00
1057 3c **Statue of Liberty**, *July 20, 1954 (137,139)* 1.00
1058 4c **Lincoln**, *July 31, 1958*, Mandan, N.D. *(184,079)* 1.50
1059 4½c **Hermitage**, *May 1, 1959*, Denver, Colo. *(202,454)* 1.75
1059A 25c **Revere**, *Feb. 25, 1965*, Wheaton, Md. *(184,954)* 1.25
1059Ab 25c Tagged, *Apr. 3, 1973*, New York, N.Y. 40.00

1954

1060 3c **Nebraska Territory**, *May 7*, Nebraska City, Neb. *(401,015)* 1.00
1061 3c **Kansas Territory**, *May 31*, Fort Leavenworth, Kans. *(349,145)* 1.00
1062 3c **George Eastman**, *July 12*, Rochester, N.Y. *(630,448)* 1.00
1063 3c **Lewis & Clark Expedition**, *July 28*, Sioux City, Iowa *(371,557)* 2.00

1955

1064 3c **Pennsylvania Academy of the Fine Arts**, *Jan. 15*, Philadelphia, Pa. *(307,040)* 1.00
1065 3c **Land Grant Colleges**, *Feb. 12*, East Lansing, Mich. *(419,241)* 1.25
1066 8c **Rotary International**, *Feb. 23*, Chicago, Ill. *(350,625)* 3.00
1067 3c **Armed Forces Reserve**, *May 21 (300,436)* 1.25
1068 3c **New Hampshire**, *June 21*, Franconia, N.H. *(330,630)* 2.00
1069 3c **Soo Locks**, *June 28*, Sault Sainte Marie, Mich. *(316,616)* 1.00
1070 3c **Atoms for Peace**, *July 28 (351,940)* 1.00
1071 3c **Fort Ticonderoga**, *Sept. 18*, Fort Ticonderoga, N.Y. *(342,946)* 1.50
1072 3c **Andrew W. Mellon**, *Dec. 20 (278,897)* 1.00

1956

1073 3c **Benjamin Franklin**, *Jan. 17*, Philadelphia, Pa. *(351,260)* 1.25
1074 3c **Booker T. Washington**, *Apr. 5*, Booker T. Washington Birthplace, Va. *(272,659)* 2.00
1075 11c **FIPEX Souvenir Sheet**, *Apr. 28*, New York, N.Y. *(429,327)* 5.00
1076 3c **FIPEX**, *Apr. 30*, New York, N.Y. *(526,090)* 1.00

1077 3c **Wildlife (Turkey),** *May 5,* Fond du Lac, Wis. *(292,121)* 1.75
1078 3c **Wildlife (Antelope),** *June 22,* Gunnison, Colo. *(294,731)* 1.75
1079 3c **Wildlife (Salmon),** *Nov. 9,* Seattle, Wash. *(346,800)* 1.75
1080 3c **Pure Food and Drug Laws,** *June 27,* Washington, D.C. *(411,761)* 1.00
1081 3c **Wheatland,** *Aug. 5,* Lancaster, Pa. *(340,142)* 1.00
1082 3c **Labor Day,** *Sept. 3,* Camden, N.J. *(338,450)* 1.00
1083 3c **Nassau Hall,** *Sept. 22,* Princeton, N.J. *(350,756)* 1.00
1084 3c **Devils Tower,** *Sept. 24,* Devils Tower, Wyo. *(285,090)* 1.25
1085 3c **Children,** *Dec. 15 (305,125)* 1.00

1957

1086 3c **Alexander Hamilton,** *Jan. 11,* New York, N.Y. *(305,117)* 1.00
1087 3c **Polio,** *Jan. 15 (307,630)* 1.50
1088 3c **Coast & Geodetic Survey,** *Feb. 11,* Seattle, Wash. *(309,931)* 1.00
1089 3c **Architects,** *Feb. 23,* New York, N.Y. *(368,840)* 1.25
1090 3c **Steel Industry,** *May 22,* New York, N.Y. *(473,284)* 1.00
1091 3c **Naval Review,** *June 10,* U.S.S. Saratoga, Norfolk, Va. *(365,933)* 1.25
1092 3c **Oklahoma Statehood,** *June 14,* Oklahoma City, Okla. *(327,172)* 1.00
1093 3c **School Teachers,** *July 1,* Philadelphia, Pa. *(357,986)* 2.00
(Spelling error) Philadelpia 8.00
1094 4c **Flag,** *July 4 (523,879)* 1.00
1095 3c **Shipbuilding,** *Aug. 15,* Bath, Maine *(347,432)* 1.25
1096 8c **Ramon Magsaysay,** *Aug. 31 (334,558)* 2.00
1097 3c **Lafayette Bicentenary,** *Sept. 6,* Easton, Pa. *(260,421)* 1.00
Fayetteville, N.C. *(230,000)* 1.00
Louisville, Ky. *(207,856)* 1.00
1098 3c **Wildlife** (Whooping Cranes), *Nov. 22,* New York, N.Y. *(342,970)* 1.25
New Orleans, La. *(154,327)* 1.25
Corpus Christi, Tex. *(280,990)* 1.25
1099 3c **Religious Freedom,** *Dec. 27,* Flushing, N.Y. *(357,770)* 1.00

1958

1100 3c **Gardening-Horticulture,** *Mar. 15,* Ithaca, N.Y. *(451,292)* 1.00
1104 3c **Brussels Exhibition,** *Apr. 17,* Detroit, Mich. *(428,073)* 1.00
1105 3c **James Monroe,** *Apr. 28,* Montross, Va. *(326,988)* 1.00
1106 3c **Minnesota Statehood,** *May 11,* Saint Paul, Minn. *(475,552)* 1.00
1107 3c **International Geophysical Year,** *May 31,* Chicago, Ill. *(397,000)* 1.00
1108 3c **Gunston Hall,** *June 12,* Lorton, Va. *(349,801)* 1.00
1109 3c **Mackinac Bridge,** *June 25,* Mackinac Bridge, Mich. *(445,605)* 1.75
1110 4c **Simon Bolivar,** *July 24* 2.00
1111 8c **Simon Bolivar,** *July 24* 2.50
1110-1111 on one cover 2.00

First day cancellation was applied to 708, 777 covers bearing one or more of Nos. 1110-1111.

1112 4c **Atlantic Cable,** *Aug. 15,* New York, N.Y. *(365,072)* 1.00

1958-59

1113 1c **Lincoln Sesquicentennial,** *Feb. 12, 1959,*
Hodgenville, Ky. *(379,862)* block of four 3.00
1114 3c **Lincoln Sesquicentennial,** *Feb. 27, 1959,* New York, N.Y. *(437,737)* 3.00
1115 4c **Lincoln-Douglas Debates,** *Aug. 27, 1958,* Freeport, Ill. *(373,063)* 3.00
1116 4c **Lincoln Sesquicentennial,** *May, 30, 1959 (894,887)* 3.00

1958

1117 4c **Lajos Kossuth,** *Sept. 19* 1.50
1118 8c **Lajos Kossuth,** *Sept. 19* 1.75
1117-1118 on one cover 3.00

First day cancellation was applied to 722,188 covers bearing one or more of Nos. 1117-1118.

1119 4c **Freedom of Press,** *Sept. 22,* Columbia, Mo. *(411,752)* 1.00
1120 4c **Overland Mail,** *Oct. 10,* San Francisco, Cal. *(352,760)* 1.00
1121 4c **Noah Webster,** *Oct. 16,* West Hartford, Conn. *(364,608)* 1.00
1122 4c **Forest Conservation,** *Oct. 27,* Tucson, Ariz. *(405,959)* 1.00
1123 4c **Fort Duquesne,** *Nov. 25,* Pittsburgh, Pa. *(421,764)* 1.00

1959

1124 4c **Oregon Statehood,** *Feb. 14,* Astoria, Ore. *(452,764)* 1.00
1125 4c **San Martin,** *Feb. 25* 1.75
1126 8c **San Martin,** *Feb. 25* 2.50
1125-1126 on one cover 3.00

First day cancellation was applied to 910,208 covers bearing one or more of No. 1125-1126.

1127 4c **NATO,** *Apr. 1 (361,040)* 1.25
1128 4c **Arctic Exploration,** *Apr. 6,* Cresson, Pa. *(397,770)* 1.00
1129 8c **World Trade,** *Apr. 20 (503,618)* 1.00
1130 4c **Silver Centennial,** *June 8,* Virginia City, Nev. *(337,233)* 1.00
1131 4c **St. Lawrence Seaway,** *June 26,* Massena, N.Y. *(543,211)* 1.25
1132 4c **Flag** (49 stars), *July 4,* Auburn, N.Y. *(523,773)* 1.00
1133 4c **Soil Conservation,** *Aug. 26,* Rapid City, S.D. *(400,613)* 1.00
1134 4c **Petroleum Industry,** *Aug. 27,* Titusville, Pa. *(801,859)* 1.50
1135 4c **Dental Health,** *Sept. 14,* New York, N.Y. *(649,813)* 3.50
1136 4c **Reuter,** *Sept. 29* 1.50
1137 8c **Reuter,** *Sept. 29* 1.75
1136-1137 on one cover 3.00

First day cancellation was applied to 1,207,933 covers bearing one or more of Nos. 1136-1137.

1138 4c **Dr. Ephraim McDowell,** *Dec. 3,* Danville, Ky. *(344,603)* 1.25

1960-61

1139 4c **Washington "Credo,"** *Jan. 20, 1960,* Mount Vernon, Va. *(438,335)* 1.25
1140 4c **Franklin "Credo,"** *Mar. 31, 1960,* Philadelphia, Pa. *(497,913)* 1.25
1141 4c **Jefferson "Credo,"** *May 18, 1960,* Charlottesville, Va. *(454,903)* 1.25
1142 4c **Francis Scott Key "Credo,"** *Sept. 14, 1960,* Baltimore, Md. *(501,129)* 1.25
1143 4c **Lincoln "Credo,"** *Nov. 19, 1960,* New York, N.Y. *(467,780)* 1.50
1144 4c **Patrick Henry "Credo,"** *Jan. 11, 1961,* Richmond, Va. *(415,252)* 1.25

1960

1145 4c **Boy Scouts,** *Feb. 8 (1,419,955)* 4.00
1146 4c **Olympic Winter Games,** *Feb. 18,* Olympic Valley, Calif, *(516,456)* 1.00
1147 4c **Masaryk,** *Mar. 7* 1.50
1148 8c **Masaryk,** *Mar. 7* 1.75
1147-1148 on one cover 3.00

First day cancellation was applied to 1,710,726 covers bearing one or more of Nos. 1147-1148.

1149 4c **World Refugee Year,** *Apr. 7 (413,298)* 1.00
1150 4c **Water Conservation,** *Apr. 18 (648,988)* 1.00
1151 4c **SEATO,** *May 31 (514,926)* 1.00
1152 4c **American Woman,** *June 2 (830,385)* 1.25
1153 4c **50-Star Flag,** *July 4,* Honolulu, Hawaii *(820,900)* 1.00
1154 4c **Pony Express Centennial,** *July 19,* Sacramento, Calif, *(520,223)* 1.75
1155 4c **Employ the Handicapped,** *Aug. 28,* New York, N.Y. *(439,638)* 1.50
1156 4c **World Forestry Congress,** *Aug. 29,* Seattle, Wash. *(350,848)* 1.00
1157 4c **Mexican Independence,** *Sept. 16,* Los Angeles, Calif, *(360,297)* 1.00
1158 4c **U.S.-Japan Treaty,** *Sept. 28 (545,150)* 2.00
1159 4c **Paderewski,** *Oct. 8* 1.50
1160 8c **Paderewski,** *Oct. 8* 1.75
1159-1160 on one cover 3.00

First day cancellation was applied to 1,057,438 covers bearing one or more of Nos. 1159-1160.

1161 4c **Robert A. Taft,** *Oct. 10,* Cincinnati, Ohio *(312,116)* 1.00
1162 4c **Wheels of Freedom,** *Oct. 15,* Detroit, Mich. *(380,551)* 1.00
1163 4c **Boys' Clubs,** *Oct. 18,* New York, N.Y. *(435,009)* 1.00
1164 4c **Automated P.O.,** *Oct. 20,* Providence, R.I. *(458,237)* 1.00
1165 4c **Mannerheim,** *Oct. 26* 1.25
1166 8c **Mannerheim,** *Oct. 26* 1.50
1165-1166 on one cover 3.00

First day cancellation was applied to 1,168,770 covers bearing one or more of Nos. 1165-1166.

1167 4c **Camp Fire Girls,** *Nov. 1,* New York, N.Y. *(324,944)* 3.00
1168 4c **Garibaldi,** *Nov. 2* 1.25
1169 8c **Garibaldi,** *Nov. 2* 1.50
1168-1169 on one cover 3.00

First day cancellation was applied to 1,001,490 covers bearing one or more of Nos. 1168-1169.

1170 4c **Senator George,** *Nov. 5,* Vienna, Ga. *(278,890)* 1.00
1171 4c **Andrew Carnegie,** *Nov. 25,* New York, N.Y. *(318,180)* 1.00
1172 4c **John Foster Dulles,** *Dec. 6 (400,055)* 1.00
1173 4c **Echo I,** *Dec. 15 (583,747)* 2.50

1961-65

1174 4c **Gandhi,** *Jan. 26, 1961* 1.50
1175 8c **Gandhi,** *Jan. 26, 1961* 2.00
1174-1175 on one cover 3.00

First day cancellation was applied to 1,013,515 covers bearing one or more of Nos. 1174-1175.

1176 4c **Range Conservation,** *Feb. 2, 1961,* Salt Lake City, Utah *(357,101)* 1.00
1177 4c **Horace Greeley,** *Feb. 3, 1961,* Chappaqua, N.Y. *(359,205)* 1.00
1178 4c **Fort Sumter,** *Apr. 12, 1961,* Charleston, S.C. *(602,599)* 4.00
1179 4c **Battle of Shiloh,** *Apr. 7, 1962,* Shiloh, Tenn. *(526,062)* 4.00
1180 5c **Battle of Gettysburg,** *July 1, 1963,* Gettysburg, Pa. *(600,205)* 4.00
1181 5c **Battle of Wilderness,** *May 5, 1964,* Fredericksburg, Va. *(450,904)* 4.00
1182 5c **Appomattox,** *Apr. 9, 1965,* Appomattox, Va. *(653,121)* 4.00

1961

1183 4c **Kansas Statehood,** *May 10,* Council Grove, Kansas *(480,561)* 1.00
1184 4c **Senator Norris,** *July 11 (482,875)* 1.00
1185 4c **Naval Aviation,** *Aug. 20,* San Diego, Calif. *(416,391)* 1.50
1186 4c **Workmen's Compensation,** *Sept. 4,* Milwaukee, Wis, *(410,236)* 1.00
1187 4c **Frederic Remington,** *Oct. 4 (723,443)* 1.25
1188 4c **China Republic,** *Oct. 10 (463,900)* 8.00
1189 4c **Naismith-Basketball,** *Nov. 6,* Springfield, Mass. *(479,917)* 7.50
1190 4c **Nursing,** *Dec. 28 (964,005)* 10.00

1962

1191 4c **New Mexico Statehood,** *Jan. 6,* Sante Fe, N.M. *(365,330)* 2.00
1192 4c **Arizona Statehood,** *Feb. 14,* Phoenix, Ariz. *(508,216)* 1.75
1193 4c **Project Mercury,** *Feb. 20,* Cape Canaveral, Fla. *(3,000,000)* 3.00
Any other city 5.00
1194 4c **Malaria Eradication,** *Mar. 30 (554,175)* 1.00
1195 4c **Charles Evans Hughes,** *Apr. 11 (544,424)* 1.00
1196 4c **Seattle World's Fair,** *Apr. 25,* Seattle, Wash. *(771,856)* 1.25
1197 4c **Louisiana Statehood,** *Apr. 30,* New Orleans, La. *(436,681)* 1.00
1198 4c **Homestead Act,** *May 20,* Beatrice, Nebr. *(487,450)* 1.00
1199 4c **Girl Scouts,** *July 24,* Burlington, Vt. *(634,347)* 5.00
1200 4c **Brien McMahon,** *July 28,* Norwalk, Conn. *(384,419)* 1.00
1201 4c **Apprenticeship,** *Aug. 31 (1,003,548)* 1.00
1202 4c **Sam Rayburn,** *Sept. 16,* Bonham, Texas *(401,042)* 1.50
1203 4c **Dag Hammarskjold,** *Oct. 23,* New York, N.Y. *(500,683)* 1.00
1203a 4c **Dag Hammarskjold,** original yellow inverted, *Oct. 23,* New York, N.Y. *2,500.*
1204 4c **Hammarskjold,** yellow inverted, *Nov. 16,* (about *75,000)* 5.00
1205 4c **Christmas,** *Nov. 1,* Pittsburgh, Pa. *(491,312)* 1.10
1206 4c **Higher Education,** *Nov. 14 (627,347)* 1.25
1207 4c **Winslow Homer,** *Dec. 15,* Gloucester, Mass. *(498,866)* 1.25

1963-66

1208 5c **Flag,** *Jan. 9, 1963 (696,185)* 1.00
1208a 5c Tagged, *Aug. 25, 1966* 30.00

REGULAR ISSUE

1962-66

1209 1c **Jackson,** *Mar. 22, 1963,* New York, N.Y. *(392,363),* block of 5 or 6 1.00
1209a 1c Tagged, *July 6, 1966,* block of 5 or 6 30.00
1213 5c **Washington,** *Nov. 23, 1962,* New York, N.Y. *(360,531)* 1.00
1213a Booklet pane of 5 + label, *Nov. 23, 1962,* New York, N.Y. *(111,452)* 4.00
1213b 5c Tagged, *Oct. 28, 1963,* Dayton, Ohio (about *15,000)* 30.00
1213c Booklet pane of 5 + label, tagged, *Oct. 28, 1963,* Dayton, Ohio 100.00
Washington, D.C. *(750)* 110.00
1214 8c **Pershing,** *Nov. 17, 1961,* New York, N.Y. *(321,031)* 1.25
1225 1c **Jackson,** Coil, *May 31, 1963,* Chicago, Ill. *(238,952),* pair and strip of 3 1.00
1225a 1c Coil, tagged, *July 6, 1966,* pair and strip of 3 30.00
1229 5c **Washington,** Coil, *Nov. 23, 1962,* New York, N.Y. *(184,627)* 1.00
1229a 5c Coil, tagged, *Oct. 28, 1963,* Dayton, Ohio (about *2,000)* 30.00

1963

1230 5c **Carolina Charter,** *Apr. 6,* Edenton, N.C. *(426,200)* 1.00
1231 5c **Food for Peace,** *June 4 (624,342)* 1.00
1232 5c **West Virginia Statehood,** *June 20,* Wheeling, W. Va. *(413,389)* 1.00
1233 5c **Emancipation Proclamation,** *Aug. 16,* Chicago, Ill, *(494,886)* 1.75
1234 5c **Alliance for Progress,** *Aug. 17 (528,095)* 1.00
1235 5c **Cordell Hull,** *Oct. 5* Carthage, Tenn. *(391,631)* 1.00
1236 5c **Eleanor Roosevelt,** *Oct. 11 (860,155)* 1.25
1237 5c **Science,** *Oct. 14 (504,503)* 1.25
1238 5c **City Mail Delivery,** *Oct. 26 (544,806)* 1.25
1239 5c **Red Cross,** *Oct. 29 (557,678)* 2.00
1240 5c **Christmas,** *Nov. 1,* Santa Claus, Ind. *(458,619)* 1.25
1240a 5c **Christmas,** tagged, *Nov. 2,* (about *500)* 60.00

Note below No. 1036b also applies to No. 1240a.

1241 5c **Audubon,** *Dec. 7,* Henderson, Ky. *(518,855)* 1.25

1964

1242 5c **Sam Houston,** *Jan. 10,* Houston, Tex. *(487,986)* 1.75
1243 5c **Charles Russell,** *Mar. 19,* Great Falls, Mont. *(658,745)* 1.25

1244 5c **N.Y. World's Fair,** *Apr. 22,* World's Fair, N.Y. *(1,656,346)* 3.00
1245 5c **John Muir,** *Apr. 29,* Martinez, Calif. *(446,925)* 1.50
1246 5c **John F. Kennedy,** *May 29,* Boston, Mass. *(2,003,096)* 3.00
Any other city 5.00
1247 5c **New Jersey Tercentenary,** *June 15,* Elizabeth, N.J. *(526,879)* 1.00
1248 5c **Nevada Statehood,** *July 22,* Carson City, Nev. *(584,973)* 1.00
1249 5c **Register & Vote,** *Aug. 1 (533,439)* 1.25
1250 5c **Shakespeare,** *Aug. 14,* Stratford, Conn. *(524,053)* 2.25
1251 5c **Drs. Mayo,** *Sept. 11,* Rochester, Minn. *(674,846)* 3.00
1252 5c **American Music,** *Oct. 15,* New York, N.Y. *(466,107)* 1.50
1253 5c **Homemakers,** *Oct. 26,* Honolulu, Hawaii *(435,392)* 1.00
1257b 5c **Christmas,** *Nov. 9,* Bethlehem, Pa. 3.00
1254-1257, any single 1.00
1257c 5c Tagged, *Nov. 10,* Dayton, O. 57.50
1254a-1257a, any single 30.00

First day cancellation was applied to 794,900 covers bearing Nos. 1254-1257 in singles or multiples and at Dayton to about 2,700 covers bearing Nos. 1254a-1257a in singles or multiples.

1258 5c **Verrazano-Narrows Bridge,** *Nov. 21,* Staten Island, N.Y. *(619,780)* 1.00
1259 5c **Fine Arts,** *Dec. 2 (558,046)* 1.00
1260 5c **Amateur Radio,** *Dec. 15,* Anchorage, Alaska *(452,255)* 5.00

1965

1261 5c **Battle of New Orleans,** *Jan. 8,* New Orleans, La. *(466,029)* 1.00
1262 5c **Physical Fitness-Sokol,** *Feb. 15 (864,848)* 1.25
1263 5c **Cancer Crusade,** *Apr. 1 (744,485)* 2.50
1264 5c **Churchill,** *May 13,* Fulton, Mo. *(773,580)* 3.00
1265 5c **Magna Carta,** *June 15,* Jamestown, Va. *(479,065)* 1.00
1266 5c **Intl. Cooperation Year,** *June 26,* San Francisco, Cal. *(402,925)* 1.00
1267 5c **Salvation Army,** *July 2,* New York, N.Y. *(634,228)* 3.00
1268 5c **Dante,** *July 17,* San Francisco, Cal. *(424,893)* 1.00
1269 5c **Herbert Hoover,** *Aug. 10,* West Branch, Iowa *(698,182)* 1.00
1270 5c **Robert Fulton,** *Aug. 19,* Clermont, N.Y. *(550,330)* 1.00
1271 5c **Florida Settlement,** *Aug. 28,* St. Augustine, Fla. *(465,000)* 1.00
1272 5c **Traffic Safety,** *Sept. 3,* Baltimore, Md. *(527,075)* 1.00
1273 5c **Copley,** *Sept. 17 (613,484)* 1.00
1274 11c **Intl. Telecommunication Union,** *Oct. 6 (332,818)* 1.10
1275 5c **Adlai Stevenson,** *Oct. 23,* Bloomington, Ill. *(755,656)* 1.00
1276 5c **Christmas,** *Nov. 2,* Silver Bell, Ariz. *(705,039)* 1.00
1276a 5c Tagged, *Nov. 15,* (about *300)* 50.00

PROMINENT AMERICANS ISSUE

1965-78

1278 1c **Jefferson,** *Jan. 12, 1968,* Jeffersonville, Ind., block of 5 or 6 1.00
1278a Booklet pane of 8, *Jan. 12, 1968,* Jeffersonville, Ind. 2.50
1278b Booklet pane of 4 + 2 labels, *May 10, 1971* 11.50

First day cancellation was applied to 655,680 covers bearing one or more of Nos. 1278, 1278a and 1299.

1279 1¼c **Gallatin,** *Jan. 30, 1967,* Gallatin, Mo. *(439,010)* 1.00
1280 2c **Wright,** *June 8, 1966,* Spring Green, Wis. *(460,427)* 1.00
1280a Booklet pane of 5 + label, *Jan. 8, 1968,* Buffalo, N.Y. *(147,244)* 3.50
1280c Booklet pane of 6, *May 7, 1971,* Spokane, Wash. 15.00
1281 3c **Parkman,** *Sept. 16, 1967,* Boston, Mass. *(518,355)* 1.00
1282 4c **Lincoln,** *Nov. 19, 1965,* New York, N.Y. *(445,629)* 1.50
1282a 4c Tagged, *Dec. 1, 1965,* Dayton, O. (about *2,000)* 32.50
Washington, D.C. *(1,200)* 32.50
1283 5c **Washington,** *Feb. 22, 1966 (525,372)* 1.00
1283a 5c Tagged, *Feb. 23, 1966,* (about *900)* 26.00
Dayton, Ohio (about *200)* 75.00
1283B 5c **Washington,** Redrawn, *Nov. 17, 1967,* New York, N.Y. *(328,983)* 1.00
1284 6c **Roosevelt,** *Jan. 29, 1966,* Hyde Park, N.Y. *(448,631)* 1.00
1284a 6c Tagged, *Dec. 29, 1966* 35.00
1284b Booklet pane of 8, *Dec. 28, 1967* 2.75
1284c Booklet pane of 5 + label, *Jan. 9, 1968* 100.00
1285 8c **Einstein,** *Mar. 14, 1966,* Princeton, N.J. *(366,803)* 3.00
1285a 8c Tagged, *July 6, 1966* 35.00
1286 10c **Jackson,** *Mar. 15, 1967,* Hermitage, Tenn. *(255,945)* 1.00
1286A 12c **Ford,** *July 30, 1968,* Greenfield Village, Mich. *(342,850)* 2.00
1287 13c **Kennedy,** *May 29, 1967,* Brookline, Mass. *(391,195)* 2.00
1288 15c **Holmes,** type I, *Mar. 8, 1968 (322,970)* 1.00
1288B 15c **Holmes,** from bklt., *June 14, 1978,* Boston, Mass. 1.00
1288Bc Booklet pane of 8 3.00

First day cancellation was applied to 387,119 covers bearing one or more of Nos. 1288B and 1305E.

1289 20c **Marshall,** *Oct. 24, 1967,* Lexington, Va. *(221,206)* 1.10
1289a 20c Tagged, *Apr. 3, 1973,* New York, N.Y. 35.00
1290 25c **Douglass,** *Feb. 14, 1967 (213,730)* 2.50
1290a 25c Tagged, *Apr. 3, 1973,* New York, N.Y. 40.00
1291 30c **Dewey,** *Oct. 21, 1968,* Burlington, Vt. *(162,790)* 1.75
1291a 30c Tagged, *Apr. 3, 1973,* New York, N.Y. 40.00
1292 40c **Paine,** *Jan. 29, 1968,* Philadelphia, Pa. *(157,947)* 1.75
1292a 40c Tagged, *Apr. 3, 1973,* New York, N.Y. 40.00
1293 50c **Stone,** *Aug. 13, 1968,* Dorchester, Mass. *(140,410)* 2.50
1293a 50c Tagged, *Apr. 3, 1973,* New York, N.Y. 40.00
1294 $1 **O'Neill,** *Oct. 16, 1967,* New London, Conn. *(103,102)* 6.00
1294a $1 Tagged, *Apr. 3, 1973,* New York, N.Y. 52.50
1295 $5 **Moore,** *Dec. 3, 1966,* Smyrna, Del. *(41,130)* 40.00
1295a $5 Tagged, *Apr. 3, 1973,* New York, N.Y. 100.00

First day cancellation was applied to 17,533 covers bearing one or more of Nos. 1059b, 1289a, 1290a, 1291a, 1292a, 1293a, 1294a and 1295a.

COIL STAMPS

1297 3c **Parkman,** *Nov. 4, 1975,* Pendleton, Ore. *(166,798)* 1.00
1298 6c **Roosevelt,** Perf. 10 Horiz., *Dec. 28, 1967* 1.00

First day cancellation was applied to 312,330 covers bearing one or more of Nos. 1298 and 1284b.

1299 1c **Jefferson,** *Jan. 12, 1968,* Jeffersonville, Ind., pair and strip of 3 1.00
1303 4c **Lincoln,** *May 28, 1966,* Springfield, Ill. *(322,563)* 1.50
1304 5c **Washington,** *Sept. 8, 1966,* Cincinnati, O. *(245,400)* 1.00
1305 6c **Roosevelt,** Perf. 10 vert., *Feb. 28, 1968 (317,199)* 1.00
1305E 15c **Holmes,** type I, *June 14, 1978,* Boston, Mass. 1.00
1305C $1 **O'Neill,** *Jan. 12, 1973,* Hempstead, N.Y. *(121,217)* 4.00

1966

1306 5c **Migratory Bird Treaty,** *Mar. 16,* Pittsburgh, Pa. *(555,485)* 1.75
1307 5c **Humane Treatment of Animals,** *Apr. 9,* New York, N.Y. *(524,420)* 1.25
1308 5c **Indiana Statehood,** *Apr. 16,* Corydon, Ind. *(575,557)* 1.00
1309 5c **Circus,** *May 2,* Delavan, Wis. *(754,076)* 2.00
1310 5c **SIPEX,** *May 21 (637,802)* 1.00
1311 5c **SIPEX, souvenir sheet,** *May 23 (700,882)* 1.10
1312 5c **Bill of Rights,** *July 1,* Miami Beach, Fla. *(562,920)* 1.75
1313 5c **Polish Millennium,** *July 30 (715,603)* 1.50
1314 5c **Natl. Park Service,** *Aug. 25,* Yellowstone National Park, Wyo. *(528,170)* 1.00
1314a 5c Tagged, *Aug. 26* 35.00
1315 5c **Marine Corps Reserve,** *Aug. 29 (585,923)* 1.50
1315a 5c Tagged, *Aug. 29* 35.00
1316 5c **Gen. Fed. of Women's Clubs,** *Sept. 12,* New York, N.Y. *(383,334)* 1.25
1316a 5c Tagged, *Sept. 13* 35.00
1317 5c **Johnny Appleseed,** *Sept. 24,* Leominster, Mass. *(794,610)* 1.50
1317a 5c Tagged, *Sept. 26* 35.00
1318 5c **Beautification of America,** *Oct. 5 (564,440)* 1.00
1318a 5c Tagged, *Oct. 5* 35.00
1319 5c **Great River Road,** *Oct. 21,* Baton Rouge, La. *(330,933)* 1.00
1319a 5c Tagged, *Oct. 22* 35.00
1320 5c **Savings Bond-Servicemen,** *Oct. 26,* Sioux City, Iowa *(444,421)* 1.00
1320a 5c Tagged, *Oct. 27* 35.00
1321 5c **Christmas,** *Nov. 1,* Christmas, Mich. *(537,650)* 1.00
1321a 5c Tagged, *Nov. 2* 35.00
1322 5c **Mary Cassatt,** *Nov. 17 (593,389)* 1.00
1322a 5c Tagged, *Nov. 17* 35.00

1967

1323 5c **National Grange,** *Apr. 17 (603,460)* 1.00
1324 5c **Canada Centenary,** *May 25,* Montreal, Canada *(711,795)* 1.00
1325 5c **Erie Canal,** *July 4,* Rome, N.Y. *(784,611)* 1.00
1326 5c **Search for Peace-Lions,** *July 5,* Chicago, Ill. *(393,197)* 1.00
1327 5c **Thoreau,** *July 12,* Concord, Mass. *(696,789)* 1.00
1328 5c **Nebraska Statehood,** *July 29,* Lincoln, Nebr. *(1,146,957)* 1.00
1329 5c **Voice of America,** *Aug. 1 (455,190)* 2.00
1330 5c **Davy Crockett,** *Aug. 17,* San Antonio, Tex. *(462,291)* 2.00
1332b 5c **Space Accomplishments,** *Sept. 29,* Kennedy Space Center, Fla. *(667,267)* 8.00
1331-1332, any single 3.25
1333 5c **Urban Planning,** *Oct. 2 (389,009)* 1.00
1334 5c **Finland Independence,** *Oct. 6,* Finland, Minn. *(408,532)* 1.00
1335 5c **Thomas Eakins,** *Nov. 2 (648,054)* 1.40
1336 5c **Christmas,** *Nov. 6,* Bethlehem, Ga. *(462,118)* 1.25
1337 5c **Mississippi Statehood,** *Dec. 11,* Natchez, Miss. *(379,612)* 1.00

1968-71

1338 6c **Flag** (Giori), *Jan. 24, 1968 (412,120)* 1.00
1338A 6c **Flag coil,** *May 30, 1969,* Chicago, Ill. *(248,434)* 1.00
1338D 6c **Flag** (Huck) *Aug. 7, 1970 (365,280)* 1.00
1338F 8c **Flag,** *May 10, 1971* 1.00
1338G 8c **Flag coil,** *May 10, 1971* 1.00

First day cancellation (May 10) was applied to 235,543 covers bearing one or more of Nos. 1338F-1338G.

1968

1339 6c **Illinois Statehood,** *Feb. 12,* Shawneetown, Ill. *(761,640)* 1.00
1340 6c **HemisFair'68,** *Mar. 30,* San Antonio, Tex. *(469,909)* 1.00
1341 $1 **Airlift,** *Apr. 4,* Seattle, Wash. *(105,088)* 7.00
1342 6c **Youth-Elks,** *May 1,* Chicago, Ill. *(354,711)* 1.00
1343 6c **Law and Order,** *May 17 (407,081)* 2.50
1344 6c **Register and Vote,** *June 27 (355,685)* 1.00
1354a 6c **Historic Flag series of 10,** *July 4,* Pittsburgh, Pa. *(2,924,962)* 15.00
1345-1354, any single 3.00
1355 6c **Disney,** *Sept. 11,* Marceline, Mo. *(499,505)* 25.00
1356 6c **Marquette,** *Sept. 20,* Sault Ste. Marie, Mich. *(379,710)* 2.00
1357 6c **Daniel Boone,** *Sept. 26,* Frankfort, Ky. *(333,440)* 1.25
1358 6c **Arkansas River,** *Oct. 1,* Little Rock, Ark. *(358,025)* 1.00
1359 6c **Leif Erikson,** *Oct. 9,* Seattle, Wash. *(376,565)* 1.00
1360 6c **Cherokee Strip,** *Oct. 15,* Ponca, Okla. *(339,330)* 1.00
1361 6c **John Trumbull,** *Oct. 18,* New Haven, Conn. *(378,285)* 2.00
1362 6c **Waterfowl Conservation,** *Oct. 24,* Cleveland, Ohio, *(349,719)* 1.25
1363 6c **Christmas,** tagged, *Nov. 1 (739,055)* 1.25
1363a 6c Untagged, *Nov. 2* 10.00
1364 6c **American Indian,** *Nov. 4 (415,964)* 1.25

1969

1368a 6c **Beautification of America,** *Jan. 16 (1,094,184)* 4.00
1365-1368, any single 1.00
1369 6c **American Legion,** *Mar. 15 (632,035)* 1.00
1370 6c **Grandma Moses,** *May 1 (367,880)* 1.50
1371 6c **Apollo 8,** *May 5,* Houston, Texas *(908,634)* 2.25
1372 6c **W.C. Handy,** *May 17,* Memphis, Tenn. *(398,216)* 2.25
1373 6c **California Bicentenary,** *July 16,* San Diego, Calif. *(530,210)* 1.00
1374 6c **J.W. Powell,** *Aug. 1,* Page, Ariz. *(434,433)* 1.00
1375 6c **Alabama Statehood,** *Aug. 2,* Huntsville, Ala. *(485,801)* 1.00
1379a 6c **Botanical Congress,** *Aug. 23,* Seattle, Wash. *(737,935)* 5.00
1376-1379, any single 1.50
1380 6c **Dartmouth Case,** *Sept. 22,* Hanover, N.H. *(416,327)* 1.00
1381 6c **Professional Baseball,** *Sept. 24,* Cincinnati, Ohio *(414,942)* 12.00
1382 6c **Intercollegiate Football,** *Sept. 26,* New Brunswick, N.J. *(414,860)* 6.50
1383 6c **Dwight D. Eisenhower,** *Oct. 14,*Abilene, Kans. *(1,009,560)* 1.00
1384 6c **Christmas,** *Nov. 3,* Christmas, Fla. *(555,500)* 1.25
1385 6c **Hope for Crippled,** *Nov. 20,* Columbus, Ohio *(342,676)* 1.25
1386 6c **William M. Harnett,** *Dec. 3,* Boston, Mass. *(408,860)* 1.00

1970-74

1390a 6c **Natural History,** *May 6, 1970,* New York, N.Y. *(834,260)* 4.00
1387-1390, any single 1.50
1391 6c **Maine Statehood,** *July 9, 1970,* Portland, Maine, *(472,165)* 2.75
1392 6c **Wildlife Conservation,** *July 20, 1970,* Custer, S.D. *(309,418)* 1.00
1393 6c **Eisenhower,** *Aug. 6, 1970* 1.00
1393a Booklet pane of 8 3.00
1393b Booklet pane of 5 + label 1.50

First day cancellations were applied to 823,540 covers bearing one or more of Nos. 1393 and 1401.

1393D 7c **Franklin,** *Oct. 20, 1972,* Philadelphia, Pa. *(309,276)* 1.00
1394 8c **Eisenhower** (multi), *May 10, 1971* 1.00
1395 8c **Eisenhower** (claret), *May 10, 1971* 1.00
1395a Booklet pane of 8 2.50
1395b Booklet pane of 6 2.50

1395c Booklet pane of 4 + 2 labels, *Jan. 28, 1972*, Casa Grande, Ariz. 2.25
1395d Booklet pane of 7 + label, *Jan. 28, 1972*, Casa Grande, Ariz. 2.25

First day cancellations were applied to 813,947 covers bearing one or more of Nos. 1394, 1395 and 1402. First day cancellations were applied to 181,601 covers bearing one or more of Nos. 1395c or 1395d.

1396 8c **Postal Service Emblem,** *July 1, 1971, any city (est. 16,300,000)* 1.00

First day cancels from over 16,000 different cities are known. Some are rare.

1397 14c **Fiorello H. LaGuardia,** *Apr. 24, 1972,* New York, N.Y. *(180,114)* 1.00
1398 16c **Ernie Pyle,** *May 7, 1971 (444,410)* 1.50
1399 18c **Elizabeth Blackwell,** *Jan. 23, 1974,* Geneva, N.Y. *(217,938)* 1.25
1400 21c **Amadeo Giannini,** *June 27, 1973,* San Mateo, Calif. *(282,520)* 1.50
1401 6c **Eisenhower coil,** *Aug. 6, 1970* 1.00
1402 8c **Eisenhower coil,** *May 10, 1971* 1.00

1970

1405 6c **Edgar Lee Masters,** *Aug. 22,* Petersburg Ill. *(372,804)* 1.00
1406 6c **Woman Suffrage,** *Aug. 26,* Adams, Mass. *(508,142)* 1.00
1407 6c **South Carolina Anniv.** *Sept. 12,* Charleston, S.C. *(533,000)* 1.00
1408 6c **Stone Mt. Memorial,** *Sept. 19,* Stone Mountain, Ga. *(558,546)* 1.00
1409 6c **Fort Snelling,** *Oct. 17,* Fort Snelling, Minn. *(497,611)* 1.00
1413a 6c **Anti-Pollution,** *Oct. 28,* San Clemente, Calif. *(1,033,147)* 4.00
1410-1413, any single 1.25
1414 6c **Christmas (Nativity),** *Nov. 5* 1.25
1414a 6c Precanceled, *Nov. 5* 7.50
1418b 6c **Christmas,** *Nov. 5* 5.50
1415-1418, any single 1.50
1414-1418 on one cover 8.50
1418c 6c Precanceled, *Nov. 5* 15.00
1415a-1418a, any single 5.00
1414a-1418a on one cover 30.00

First day cancellation was applied to 2,014,450 covers bearing one or more of Nos. 1414-1418 or 1414a-1418a.

1419 6c **United Nations,** *Nov. 20,* New York, N.Y. *(474,070)* 1.50
1420 6c **Pilgrims' Landing,** *Nov. 21,* Plymouth, Mass. *(629,850)* 1.00
1421 6c **Disabled Veterans,** *Nov. 24,* Cincinnati, Ohio, or Montgomery, Ala. 2.25
1422 6c **U.S. Servicemen,** *Nov. 24,* Cincinnati, Ohio, or Montgomery, Ala. 2.25
1422a 3.00

First day cancellation was applied to 476,610 covers at Cincinnati and 336,417 at Montgomery, each cover bearing one or more of Nos. 1421-1422.

1971

1423 6c **Wool Industry,** *Jan. 19,* Las Vegas, Nev. *(379,911)* 1.00
1424 6c **MacArthur,** *Jan. 26,* Norfolk, Va. *(720,035)* 2.50
1425 6c **Blood Donor,** *Mar. 12,* New York, N.Y. (644,497) 1.25
1426 8c **Missouri Sesquicentennial,** *May 8,* Independence, Mo. *(551,000)* 1.00
1430a 8c **Wildlife Conservation,** *June 12,* Avery Island, La. *(679,483)* 3.00
1427-1430, any single 1.25
1431 8c **Antarctic Treaty,** *June 23 (419,200)* 1.00
1432 8c **American Revolution Bicentennial,** *July 4 (434,930)* 1.00
1433 8c **John Sloan,** *Aug. 2,* Lock Haven, Pa. *(482,265)* 1.00
1435b 8c **Space Achievement Decade,** *Aug. 2,* Kennedy Space Center, Fla. *(1,403,644)* 2.50
Houston, Texas *(811,560)* 2.50
Huntsville, Ala. *(524,000)* 2.50
1434-1435, any single 1.25
1436 8c **Emily Dickinson,** *Aug. 28,* Amherst, Mass. *(498,180)* 1.00
1437 8c **San Juan,** *Sept. 12,* San Juan, P.R. *(501,668)* 1.00
1438 8c **Drug Abuse,** *Oct. 4,* Dallas, Texas *(425,330)* 1.25
1439 8c **CARE,** *Oct. 27,* New York, N.Y. *(402,121)* 1.00
1443a 8c **Historic Preservation,** *Oct. 29,* San Diego, Calif. *(783,242)* 3.00
1440-1443, any single 1.25
1444 8c **Christmas (religious),** *Nov. 10* 1.25
1445 8c **Christmas (secular),** *Nov. 10* 1.25
1444-1445 on one cover 1.50

First day cancellation was applied to 348,038 covers with No. 1444 and 580,062 with No. 1445.

1972

1446 8c **Sidney Lanier,** *Feb. 3,* Macon Ga. *(394,800)* 1.00
1447 8c **Peace Corps,** *Feb. 11 (453,660)* 1.00
1451a 2c **National Parks Centennial,** *Apr. 5,* Hatteras, N.C., block of 4 *(505,697)* 3.00
1448-1451, any single 1.00
1452 6c **National Parks,** *June 26,* Vienna, Va. *(403,396)* 1.00
1453 8c **National Parks,** *Mar. 1,* Yellowstone National Park, Wyo. 1.00
Washington, D.C. *(847,500)* 1.00
1454 15c **National Parks,** *July 28,* Mt. McKinley National Park, Alaska *(491,456)* 1.00
1455 8c **Family Planning,** *Mar. 18,* New York, N.Y. *(691,385)* 1.00
1459a 8c **Colonial Craftsmen** (Rev. Bicentennial), *July 4,* Williamsburg, Va. *(1,914,976)* 2.50
1456-1459, any single 1.00
1460 6c **Olympics,** *Aug. 17* 1.00
1461 8c **Winter Olympics,** *Aug. 17* 1.00
1462 15c **Olympics,** *Aug. 17* 1.00
1460-1462 and C85 on one cover 2.00

First day cancellation was applied to 971,536 covers bearing one or more of Nos. 1460-1462 and C85.

1463 8c **P.T.A.,** *Sept. 15,* San Francisco, Cal. *(523,454)* 1.00
1467a 8c **Wildlife,** *Sept. 20,* Warm Springs, Ore. *(733,778)* 3.00
1464-1467, any single 1.50
1468 8c **Mail Order,** *Sept. 27,* Chicago, Ill. *(759,666)* 1.50
1469 8c **Osteopathy,** *Oct. 9,* Miami, Fla. *(607,160)* 2.00
1470 8c **Tom Sawyer,** *Oct. 13,* Hannibal, Mo. *(459,013)* 2.50
1471 8c **Christmas (religious),** *Nov. 9* 1.00
1472 8c **Christmas (secular),** *Nov. 9* 1.00
1471-1472 on one cover 2.00

First day cancellation was applied to 713,821 covers bearing one or more of Nos. 1471-1472.

1473 8c **Pharmacy,** *Nov. 10,* Cincinnati, Ohio *(804,320)* 10.00
1474 8c **Stamp Collecting,** *Nov. 17,* New York, N.Y. *(434,680)* 1.25

1973

1475 8c **Love,** *Jan. 26,* Philadelphia, Pa. *(422,492)* 2.00
1476 8c **Pamphleteer** (Rev. Bicentennial), *Feb. 16,* Portland, Ore. *(431,784)* 1.00
1477 8c **Broadside** (Rev. Bicentennial), *Apr. 13,* Atlantic City, N.J. *(423,437)* 1.00
1478 8c **Post Rider** (Rev. Bicentennial), *June 22,* Rochester, N.Y. *(586,850)* 1.00
1479 8c **Drummer** (Rev. Bicentennial), *Sept. 28,* New Orleans, La. *(522,427)* 1.00
1483a 8c **Boston Tea Party** (Rev. Bicentennial), *July 4,* Boston, Mass. *(897,870)* 3.00
1480-1483, any single 1.00
1484 8c **George Gershwin,** *Feb. 28,* Beverly Hills, Calif. *(448,814)* 1.00
1485 8c **Robinson Jeffers,** *Aug. 13,* Carmel, Calif. *(394,261)* 1.00
1486 8c **Henry O. Tanner,** *Sept. 10,* Pittsburgh, Pa. *(424,065)* 2.50
1487 8c **Willa Cather,** *Sept. 20,* Red Cloud, Nebr. *(435,784)* 1.00
1488 8c **Nicolaus Copernicus,** *Apr. 23 (734,190)* 1.50
1498a 8c **Postal People,** *Apr. 30, any city* 5.00
1489-1498, any single 1.00

First day cancellation was applied at Boston to 1,205,212 covers bearing one or more of Nos. 1489-1498. Cancellations at other cities unrecorded.

1499 8c **Harry S Truman,** *May 8,* Independence, Mo. *(938,636)* 1.75
1500 6c **Electronics,** *July 10,* New York, N.Y. 1.00
1501 8c **Electronics,** *July 10,* New York, N.Y. 1.00
1502 15c **Electronics,** *July 10,* New York, N.Y. 1.00
1500-1502 and C86 on one cover 4.00

First day cancellation was applied to 1,197,700 covers bearing one or more of Nos. 1500-1502 and C86.

1503 8c **Lyndon B. Johnson,** *Aug. 27,* Austin, Texas *(701,490)* 1.00

1973-74

1504 8c **Angus Cattle,** *Oct. 5, 1973,* St. Joseph, Mo. *(521,427)* 1.00
1505 10c **Chautauqua,** *Aug. 6, 1974,* Chautauqua, N.Y. *(411,105)* 1.00
1506 10c **Wheat,** *Aug. 16, 1974,* Hillsboro, Kans. *(468,280)* 1.00
1507 8c **Christmas (religious),** *Nov. 7, 1973* 1.00
1508 8c **Christmas (secular),** *Nov. 7, 1973* 1.00
1507-1508 on one cover 1.10

First day cancellation was applied to 807,468 covers bearing one or both of Nos. 1507-1508.

1509 10c **Crossed Flags,** *Dec. 8, 1973,* San Francisco, Calif. 1.00

First day cancellation was applied to 341,528 covers bearing one or more of Nos. 1509 and 1519.

1510 10c **Jefferson Memorial,** *Dec. 14, 1973* 1.00
1510b Booklet pane of 5 + label 2.25
1510c Booklet pane of 8 2.50
1510d Booklet pane of 6, *Aug. 5, 1974,* Oakland, Calif. 3.00

First day cancellation was applied to 686,300 covers bearing one or more of Nos. 1510, 1510b, 1510c, 1520.

1511 10c **Zip Code,** *Jan. 4, 1974 (335,220)* 1.00
1518 6.3c **Bell Coil,** *Oct. 1, 1974 (221,141)* 1.00
1519 10c **Crossed Flags coil,** *Dec. 8, 1973,* San Francisco, Calif. 1.00
1520 10c **Jefferson Memorial coil,** *Dec. 14, 1973* 1.00

1974

1525 10c **Veterans of Foreign Wars,** *Mar. 11 (543,598)* 1.50
1526 10c **Robert Frost,** *Mar. 26,* Derry, N.H. *(500,425)* 1.00
1527 10c **EXPO '74,** *Apr. 18,* Spokane, Wash. *(565,548)* 1.00
1528 10c **Horse Racing,** *May 4,* Louisville, Ky. *(623,983)* 3.00
1529 10c **Skylab,** *May 14,* Houston, Tex. *(972,326)* 1.50
1537a 10c **UPU Centenary,** *June 6 (1,374,765)* 4.00
1530-1537, any single 1.00
1541a 10c **Mineral Heritage,** *June 13,* Lincoln, Neb. *(865,368)* 2.75
1538-1541, any single 1.00
1542 10c **Kentucky Settlement,** *June 15,* Harrodsburg, Ky. *(478,239)* 1.00
1546a 10c **Continental Congress** (Rev. Bicentennial), *July 4,* Philadelphia, Pa. *(2,124,957)* 2.75
1543-1546, any single 1.00
1547 10c **Energy Conservation,** *Sept. 23,* Detroit, Mich. *(587,210)* 1.00
1548 10c **Sleepy Hollow,** *Oct. 10,* North Tarrytown, N.Y. *(514,836)* 3.50
1549 10c **Retarded Children,** *Oct. 12,* Arlington Tex. *(412,882)* 1.00
1550 10c **Christmas (Religious),** *Oct. 23,* New York, N.Y. *(634,990)* 1.00
1551 10c **Christmas (Currier & Ives),** *Oct. 23,* New York, N.Y. *(634,990)* 1.00
1550-1551 on one cover 1.10
1552 10c **Christmas (Dove),** *Nov. 15,* New York, N.Y. *(477,410)* 1.50

1975

1553 10c **Benjamin West,** *Feb. 10,* Swarthmore, Pa. *(465,017)* 1.00
1554 10c **Paul L. Dunbar,** *May 1,* Dayton, Ohio *(397,347)* 1.50
1555 10c **D.W. Griffith,** *May 27,* Beverly Hills, Calif. *(424,167)* 1.00
1556 10c **Pioneer-Jupiter,** *Feb. 28,* Mountain View, Calif. *(594,896)* 1.25
1557 10c **Mariner 10,** *Apr. 4,* Pasadena, Calif. *(563,636)* 1.25
1558 10c **Collective Bargaining,** *Mar. 13 (412,329)* 1.00
1559 8c **Sybil Ludington** (Rev. Bicentennial), *Mar. 25,* Carmel, N.Y. *(394,550)* 1.00
1560 10c **Salem Poor** (Rev. Bicentennial, *Mar. 25,* Cambridge, Mass. *(415,565)* 1.50
1561 10c **Haym Salomon** (Rev. Bicentennial), *Mar. 25,* Chicago, Ill. *(442,630)* 1.00
1562 18c **Peter Francisco** (Rev. Bicentennial), *Mar. 25,* Greensboro, N.C. *(415,000)* 1.00
1563 10c **Lexington-Concord** (Rev. Bicentennial), *Apr. 19,* Lexington, Mass., or Concord, Mass, *(975,020)* 1.00
1564 10c **Bunker Hill** (Rev. Bicentennial), *June 17,* Charlestown, Mass. *(557,130)* 1.00
1568a 10c **Military Services** (Rev. Bicentennial), *July 4 (1,134,831)* 2.50
1565-1568, any single 1.00
1570a 10c **Apollo-Soyuz,** *July 15,* Kennedy Space Center, Fla. *(1,427,046)* 5.00
1569-1570, any single 3.00
1571 10c **International Women's Year,** *Aug. 26,* Seneca Falls, N.Y. *(476,769)* 1.00
1575a 10c **Postal Service Bicentenary,** *Sept. 3,* Philadelphia, Pa. *(969,999)* 2.50
1572-1575, any single 1.00
1576 10c **World Peace through Law,** *Sept. 29 (386,736)* 1.50
1578a 10c **Banking-Commerce,** *Oct. 6,* New York, N.Y. *(555,580)* 1.75
1577-1578, any single 1.00
1579 (10c) **Christmas (religious),** *Oct. 14* 1.00
1580 (10c) **Christmas (secular),** *Oct. 14* 1.00
1579-1580 on one cover 2.00

First day cancellation was applied to 730,079 covers bearing one or more of Nos. 1579-1580.

AMERICANA ISSUE

1975-79

1581 1c **Inkwell,** *Dec. 8, 1977,* St. Louis, Mo., multiple for 1st class rate 1.00
1582 2c **Speaker's Stand,** *Dec. 8, 1977,* St. Louis, Mo., multiple for 1st class rate 1.00
1584 3c **Ballot Box,** *Dec. 8, 1977,* St. Louis, Mo., multiple for 1st class rate 1.00
1585 4c **Books and Eyeglasses,** *Dec. 8, 1977,* St. Louis, Mo., multiple for 1st class rate 1.00

First day cancellation was applied to 530,033 covers bearing one or more of Nos. 1581-1582, 1584-1585.

1590 9c **Capitol Dome,** from bklt.,*Mar. 11, 1977,* New York, N.Y., plus postage for 1st class rate 1.00
1591 9c **Capitol Dome,** *Nov. 24, 1975 (190,117),* multiple for 1st class rate 1.00
1592 10c **Justice,** *Nov. 17, 1977,* New York, N.Y. *(359,050),* multiple for 1st class rate 1.00
1593 11c **Printing Press,** *Nov. 13, 1975,* Philadelphia, Pa. *(217,755),* multiple for 1st class rate 1.00
1594 12c **Torch,** *Apr. 8, 1981,* Dallas, TX, multiple for 1st class rate 1.00

First day cancellation was applied to 280,930 covers bearing one or more of Nos. 1594 and 1816.

1595 13c **Liberty Bell,** *Oct. 31, 1975,* Cleveland, Ohio *(256,734)* 1.00
1595a Booklet pane of 6 2.00
1595b Booklet pane of 7 + label 2.75
1595c Booklet pane of 8 2.50

1595d Booklet pane of 5 + label, *Apr. 2, 1976,* Liberty, Mo. 2.25

1596 13c **Eagle and Shield,** *Dec. 1, 1975,* Juneau, Alaska *(418,272)* 1.00

1597 15c **Flag,** *June 30, 1978,* Baltimore, Md. 1.00

1598 15c **Flag,** from bklt., *June 30, 1978,* Baltimore, Md. 1.00

1598a Booklet pane of 8 2.50

First day cancellation was applied to 315,359 covers bearing one or more of Nos. 1597, 1598, and 1618C.

1599 16c **Statue of Liberty,** *Mar. 31, 1978,* New York, N.Y. 1.00

1603 24c **Old North Church,** *Nov. 14, 1975,* Boston, Mass. *(208,973)* 1.00

1604 28c **Fort Nisqually,** *Aug. 11, 1978,* Tacoma, Wash. *(159,639)* 1.00

1605 29c **Sandy Hook Lighthouse,** *Apr. 14, 1978,* Atlantic City, N.J. *(193,476)* 1.50

1606 30c **Schoolhouse,** *Aug. 27, 1979,* Devils Lake, N.D. *(186,882)* 1.25

1608 50c **Betty Lamp,** *Sept. 11, 1979,* San Juan, P.R. *(159,540)* 1.50

1610 $1 **Rush Lamp,** *July 2, 1979,* San Francisco, Calif. *(255,575)* 3.00

1611 $2 **Kerosene Lamp,** *Nov. 16, 1978,* New York, N.Y. *(173,596)* 5.00

1612 $5 **Railroad Lantern,** *Aug. 23, 1979,* Boston, Mass. *(129,192)* 12.50

COIL STAMPS

1613 3.1c **Guitar,** *Oct. 25, 1979,* Shreveport, La. *(230,403)* 1.00

1614 7.7c **Saxhorns,** *Nov. 20, 1976,* New York, N.Y. *(285,290)* 1.00

1615 7.9c **Drum,** *Apr. 23, 1976,* Miami, Fla. *(193,270)* 1.00

1615C 8.4c **Piano,** *July 13, 1978,* Interlochen, Mich. *(200,392)* 1.00

1616 9c **Capitol Dome,** *Mar. 5, 1976,* Milwaukee, Wis. *(128,171)* 1.00

1617 10c **Justice,** *Nov. 4, 1977,* Tampa, Fla. *(184,954)* 1.00

1618 13c **Liberty Bell,** *Nov. 25, 1975,* Allentown, Pa. *(320,387)* 1.00

1618C 15c **Flag,** *June 30, 1978,* Baltimore, Md. 1.00

1619 16c **Statue of Liberty,** *Mar. 31, 1978,* New York, N.Y. 1.00

First day cancellation was applied to 376,338 covers bearing one or more of Nos. 1599 and 1619.

1975

1622 13c **13-Star Flag,** *Nov. 15,* Philadelphia, Pa. 1.00

1623 13c **Flag over Capitol,** *Mar. 11,* New York, N.Y. 1.50

1623a Booklet pane of 8, perf 11 (1 #1590 +7 #1623) 25.00

1623Bc Booklet pane of 8, perf. 10x9¾ (1 #1590A + 7 #1623B) 15.00

First day cancellation was applied to 242,208 covers bearing Nos. 1623, 1623a, 1623B or 1623Bc.

1625 13c **13-Star Flag coil,** *Nov. 15,* Philadelphia, PA 1.00

First day cancellation was applied to 362,959 covers bearing one or more of Nos. 1622 and 1625.

1976

1631a 13c **Spirit of '76,** *Jan. 1,* Pasadena, CA *(1,013,067)* 2.00

1629-1631, any single 1.25

1632 13c **Interphil '76,** *Jan. 17,* Philadelphia, Pa. *(519,902)* 1.00

1682a 13c **State Flags,** *Feb. 23* 27.50

1633-1682, any single 1.50

1683 13c **Telephone,** *Mar. 10,* Boston, Mass. *(662,515)* 1.00

1684 13c **Commercial Aviation,** *Mar. 19,* Chicago Ill. *(631,555)* 1.50

1685 13c **Chemistry,** *Apr. 6,* New York, N.Y. *(557,600)* 1.50

Bicentennial Souvenir Sheets of 5

1686 13c **Surrender of Cornwallis,** *May 29,* Philadelphia, Pa. 7.50

1687 18c **Declaration of Independence,** *May 29,* Philadelphia, Pa. 7.50

1688 24c **Declaration of Independence,** *May 29,* Philadelphia, Pa. 7.50

1689 31c **Washington at Valley Forge,** *May 29,* Philadelphia, Pa. 7.50

First day cancellation was applied to 879,890 covers bearing singles, multiples or complete sheets of Nos. 1686-1689.

1690 13c **Franklin,** *June 1,* Philadelphia, Pa. *(588,740)* 1.00

1694a 13c **Declaration of Independence,** *July 4,* Philadelphia, Pa. *(2,093,880)* 2.00

1691-1694, any single 1.00

1698a 13c **Olympic Games,** *July 16,* Lake Placid, N.Y. *(1,140,189)* 2.00

1695-1698, any single 1.00

1699 13c **Clara Maass,** *Aug. 18,* Belleville, N.J. *(646,506)* 2.50

1700 13c **Adolph S. Ochs,** *Sept. 18,* New York, N.Y. *(582,580)* 1.00

1701 13c **Christmas (religious),** *Oct. 27,* Boston, Mass. (540,050) 1.00

1702 13c **Christmas (secular),** *Oct. 27,* Boston, Mass. (181,410) 1.00

1703 13c **Christmas (secular),** block tagged, *Oct. 27,* Boston, Mass. (330,450) 1.00

1701 and 1702 or 1703 on one cover 1.25

1977

1704 13c **Washington at Princeton,** *Jan. 3,* Princeton, N.J. *(695,335)* 1.00

1705 13c **Sound Recording,** *Mar. 23 (632,216)* 1.25

1709a 13c **Pueblo Art,** *Apr. 13,* Santa Fe, N.M. *(1,194,554)* 2.00

1706-1709, any single 1.00

1710 13c **Lindbergh Flight,** *May 20,* Roosevelt Sta., N.Y. *(3,985,989)* 4.00

1711 13c **Colorado Statehood,** *May 21,* Denver, Colo. *(510,880)* 1.00

1715a 13c **Butterflies,** *June 6,* Indianapolis, Ind. *(1,218,278)* 2.00

1712-1715, any single 2.00

1716 13c **Lafayette's Landing,** *June 13,* Charleston, S.C. *(514,506)* 1.00

1720a 13c **Skilled Hands,** *July 4,* Cincinnati, Ohio *(1,263,568)* 2.00

1717-1720, any single 1.00

1721 13c **Peace Bridge,** *Aug. 4,* Buffalo, N.Y. *(512,995)* 1.00

1722 13c **Battle of Oriskany,** *Aug. 6,* Herkimer, N.Y. *(605,906)* 1.00

1724a 13c **Energy Conservation,** *Oct. 20 (410,299)* 1.50

1723-1724, any single 1.25

1725 13c **Alta California,** *Sept. 9,* San Jose, Calif. *(709,457)* 1.00

1726 13c **Articles of Confederation,** *Sept. 30,* York, Pa. *(605,455)* 1.00

1727 13c **Talking Pictures,** *Oct. 6,* Hollywood, Calif. *(570,195)* 1.50

1728 13c **Surrender at Saratoga** *Oct. 7,* Schuylerville, N.Y. *(557,529)* 1.00

1729 13c **Christmas (Valley Forge),** *Oct. 21,* Valley Forge, Pa. *(583,139)* 1.00

1730 13c **Christmas (mailbox),** *Oct. 21,* Omaha, Nebr. *(675,786)* 1.00

1978

1731 13c **Carl Sandburg,** *Jan. 6,* Galesburg, Ill. *(493,826)* 1.00

1733b 13c **Captain Cook,** *Jan. 20,* Honolulu, Hawaii, or Anchorage, Alaska 2.00

1732-1733, any single 1.50

First day cancellation was applied to 823,855 covers at Honolulu, and 672,804 at Anchorage, each cover bearing one or both of Nos. 1732-1733.

1734 13c **Indian Head Penny,** *Jan. 11,* Kansas City, Mo. *(512,426)* 1.50

REGULAR ISSUE

1978-80

1735 (15c) **"A" Eagle,** *May 22,* Memphis, Tenn. 1.00

1736 (15c) **"A" Eagle,** bklt. single *May 22,* Memphis, Tenn. 1.00

1736a Booklet pane of 8 2.50

1737 15c **Roses,** *July 11,* Shreveport, La. *(445,003)* 1.00

1737a Booklet pane of 8 2.50

1742a 15c **Windmills Booklet pane of 10,** *Feb. 7, 1980,* Lubbock, TX 3.50

1738-1742, any single 1.00

1743 15c **"A" Eagle coil,** *May 22,* Memphis, Tenn. 1.00

First day cancellation was applied to 689,049 covers bearing one or more of Nos. 1735, 1736 and 1743. First day cancellation was applied to 708,411 covers bearing one or more of Nos. 1738-1742a.

1978

1744 13c **Harriet Tubman,** *Feb. 1 (493,495)* 1.75

1748a 13c **American Quilts,** *Mar. 8,* Charleston, W.Va. 2.00

1745-1748, any single 1.00

First day cancellation was applied to 1,081,827 covers bearing one or more of Nos. 1745-1748.

1752a 13c **American Dance,** *Apr. 26,* New York, N.Y. *(1,626,493)* 2.00

1749-1752, any single 1.00

1753 13c **French Alliance,** *May 4,* York, Pa. *(705,240)* 1.00

1754 13c **Papanicolaou,** *May 18 (535,584)* 1.00

1755 13c **Jimmie Rodgers,** *May 24,* Meridian, Miss. *(599,287)* 1.00

1756 15c **George M. Cohan,** *July 3,* Providence, R.I. *(740,750)* 1.25

1757 **CAPEX** souv. sheet, *June 10,* Toronto, Canada *(1,994,067)* 2.75

1758 15c **Photography,** *June 26,* Las Vegas, Nev. *(684,987)* 1.00

1759 15c **Viking Missions,** *July 20,* Hampton, Va. *(805,051)* 1.00

1763a 15c **American Owls,** *Aug. 26,* Fairbanks, Alas. *(1,690,474)* 2.00

1760-1763, any single 1.25

1767a 15c **American Trees,** *Oct. 9,* Hot Springs National Park, Ark. *(1,139,100)* 2.00

1764-1767, any single 1.25

1768 15c **Christmas (Madonna),** *Oct. 18 (553,064)* 1.00

1769 15c **Christmas (Hobby Horse),** *Oct. 18,* Holly, Mich. *(603,008)* 1.00

1979-80

1770 15c **Robert Kennedy,** *Jan. 12 (624,582)* 2.00

1771 15c **Martin L. King,** *Jan. 13,* Atlanta, Ga. *(726,149)* 2.00

1772 15c **Year of Child,** *Feb. 15,* Philadelphia, Pa. *(716,782)* 1.00

1773 15c **John Steinbeck,** *Feb. 27,* Salinas, Calif. *(709,073)* 1.00

1774 15c **Albert Einstein,** *Mar. 4,* Princeton, N.J. *(641,423)* 3.50

1778a 15c **Toleware,** *Apr. 19,* Lancaster, Pa. *(1,581,962)* 2.00

1775-1778, any single 1.00

1782a 15c **American Architecture,** *June 4,* Kansas City, Mo. *(1,219,258)* 2.00

1779-1782, any single 1.00

1786a 15c **Endangered Flora,** *June 7,* Milwaukee, Wis. *(1,436,268)* 2.00

1783-1786, any single 1.00

1787 15c **Guide Dogs,** *June 15,* Morristown, N.J. *(588,826)* 1.25

1788 15c **Special Olympics,** *Aug. 9,* Brockport, N.Y. *(651,344)* 1.25

1789 15c **John Paul Jones,** *Sept. 23,* Annapolis, Md. 1.50

1789A 15c **John Paul Jones,** *Sept. 23,* Annapolis, Md. 1.50

Total for 1789 and 1789A is 587,018.

1790 10c **Olympic Javelin,** *Sept. 5,* Olympia, Wash. *(305,122)* 1.00

1794a 15c **Olympics 1980,** *Sept. 28,* Los Angeles, Calif. *(1,561,366)* 2.00

1791-1794, any single 1.25

1798b 15c **Winter Olympics,** *Feb. 1, 1980,* Lake Placid, N.Y. *(1,166,302)* 2.00

1795-1798, any single 1.25

1979

1799 15c **Christmas (Madonna),** *Oct. 18 (686,990)* 1.25

1800 15c **Christmas (Santa Claus),** *Oct. 18,* North Pole, Alaska *(511,829)* 1.25

1799-1800, both stamps issued *Oct. 18* 2.00

1801 15c **Will Rogers,** *Nov. 4,* Claremore, Okla. *(1,643,151)* 1.50

1802 15c **Viet Nam Veterans,** *Nov. 11,* Arlington, VA *(445,934)* 5.00

1980

1803 15c **W.C. Fields,** *Jan. 29,* Beverly Hills, CA *(633,303)* 2.00

1804 15c **Benjamin Banneker,** *Feb. 15,* Annapolis, MD *(647,126)* 2.00

1810a 15c **Letter Writing,** *Feb. 25 (1,083,360)* 2.50

1805-1810, any single 1.00

1980-81 DEFINITIVES

1811 1c **Quill Pen,** coil, *Mar. 6, 1980,* New York, NY *(262,921)* 1.00

1813 3.5c **Violins,** coil, *June 23, 1980,* Williamsburg, PA 1.00

FD cancel was applied to 716,988 covers bearing Nos. 1813 or U590.

1816 12c **Torch,** coil, *Apr. 8, 1981,* Dallas, TX 1.00

1818 (18c) **"B" Eagle,** *Mar. 15, 1981,* San Francisco, CA 1.25

FD cancel was applied to 511,688 covers bearing one or more of Nos. 1818-1820, U592 or UX88.

1819 (18c) **"B" Eagle,** bklt. single, *Mar. 15, 1981,* San Francisco, CA 1.00

1819a Booklet pane of 8 3.00

1820 (18c) **"B" Eagle,** coil, *Mar. 15, 1981,* San Francisco, CA 1.00

1980

1821 15c **Frances Perkins,** *Apr. 10 (678,966)* 1.00

1822 15c **Dolley Madison,** *May 20 (331,048)* 1.00

1823 15c **Emily Bissell,** *May 31,* Wilmington, DE *(649,509)* 1.00

1824 15c **Helen Keller, Anne Sullivan,** *June 27,* Tuscumbia, AL *(713,061)* 1.25

1825 15c **Veterans Administration,** *July 21 (634,101)* 1.50

1826 15c **Bernardo de Galvez,** *July 23,* New Orleans, LA *(658,061)* 1.00

1830a 15c **Coral Reefs,** *Aug. 26,* Charlotte Amalie, VI *(1,195,126)* 2.00

1827-1830, any single 1.00

1831 15c **Organized Labor,** *Sept. 1 (759,973)* 1.00

1832 15c **Edith Wharton,** *Sept. 5,* New Haven, CT *(633,917)* 1.00

1833 15c **Education,** *Sept. 12,*Franklin, MA *(672,592)* 1.50

1837a 15c **Indian Masks,** *Sept. 25,* Spokane, WA *(2,195,136)* 2.00

1834-1837, any single 1.00

1841a 15c **Architecture,** *Oct. 9,* New York, NY *(2,164,721)* 1.75

1838-1841, any single 1.00

1842 15c **Christmas (Madonna),** *Oct. 31 (718,614)* 1.25

1843 15c **Christmas (Toys),** *Oct. 31,* Christmas, MI *(755,108)* 1.25

GREAT AMERICANS ISSUE

1980-85

1844 1c **Dorothea Dix,** *Sept. 23, 1983,* Hampden, ME *(164,140)* 1.00

1845 2c **Igor Stravinsky,** *Nov. 18, 1982,* New York, NY *(501,719)* 1.00

1846 3c **Henry Clay,** *July 13, 1983 (204,320)* 1.00

1847 4c **Carl Schurz,** *June 3, 1983,* Watertown, WI *(165,010)* 1.00

1848 5c **Pearl Buck,** *June 25, 1983,* Hillsboro, WV *(231,852)* 1.00

1849 6c **Walter Lippman,** *Sept. 19, 1985,* Minneapolis, MN *(371,990)* 1.00

1850 7c **Abraham Baldwin,** *Jan. 25, 1985,* Athens, GA *(402,285)* 1.25

1851 8c **Henry Knox,** *July 25, 1985,* Thomaston, ME *(315,937)* 1.00
1852 9c **Sylvanus Thayer,** *June 7, 1985,* Braintree, MA *(345,649)* 1.25
1853 10c **Richard Russell,** *May 31, 1984,* Winder, GA *(183,581)* 1.00
1854 11c **Alden Partridge,** *Feb. 12, 1985,* Northfield, VT *(442,311)* 1.25
1855 13c **Crazy Horse,** *Jan. 15, 1982,* Crazy Horse, SD 2.00
1856 14c **Sinclair Lewis,** *Mar. 21, 1985,* Sauk Centre, MN *(308,612)* 1.00
1857 17c **Rachel Carson,** *May 28, 1981,* Springdale, PA *(273,686)* 1.00
1858 18c **George Mason,** *May 7, 1981,* Gunston Hall, VA *(461,937)* 1.00
1859 19c **Sequoyah,** *Dec. 27, 1980,* Tahlequah, OK *(241,325)* 1.50
1860 20c **Ralph Bunche,** *Jan. 12, 1982,* New York, NY 1.75
1861 20c **Thomas H. Gallaudet,** *June 10, 1983,* West Hartford, CT *(261,336)* 1.25
1862 20c **Harry S Truman,** *Jan. 26, 1984* *(267,631)* 1.50
1863 22c **John J. Audubon,** *Apr. 23, 1985,* New York, NY *(516,249)* 1.25
1864 30c **Frank Laubach,** *Sept. 2, 1984,* Benton, PA *(118,974)* 1.25
1865 35c **Charles Drew,** *June 3, 1981* *(383,882)* 1.75
1866 37c **Robert Millikan,** *Jan. 26, 1982,* Pasadena, CA 1.25
1867 39c **Grenville Clark,** *Mar. 20, 1985,* Hanover, NH *(297,797)* 1.25
1868 40c **Lillian Gilbreth,** *Feb. 24, 1984,* Montclair, NJ *(110,588)* 1.50
1869 50c **Chester W. Nimitz,** *Feb. 22, 1985,* Fredericksburg, TX *(376,166)* 2.00

1981

1874 15c **Everett Dirksen,** *Jan. 4,* Pekin, IL *(665,755)* 1.00
1875 15c **Whitney M. Young,** *Jan. 30,* New York, NY *(963,870)* 1.75
1879a 18c **Flowers,** *Apr. 23,* Fort Valley, GA *(1,966,599)* 2.50
1876-1879, any single 1.00

DEFINITIVES

1889a 18c **Animals Booklet pane of 10,** *May 14,* Boise, ID 5.00
1880-1889, any single 1.00
1890 18c **Flag-Anthem (grain),** *Apr. 24,* Portland, ME 1.00
1891 18c **Flag-Anthem (sea),** *Apr. 24,* Portland, ME 1.50
1892 6c **Star Circle,** *Apr. 24,* Portland, ME 1.00
1893 18c **Flag-Anthem (mountain),** *Apr. 24,* Portland, ME 1.00
1893a Booklet pane of 8 (2 #1892, 6 #1893) 2.50

FDC cancel was applied to 691,526 covers bearing one or more of Nos. 1890-1893 & 1893a.

1894 20c **Flag-Court,** *Dec. 17* 1.00
1895 20c **Flag-Court,** coil, *Dec. 17* 1.00
1896 20c **Flag-Court,** perf. 11x10½, *Dec. 17* *(185,543)* 1.00
1896a Booklet pane of 6 6.00
1896b Booklet pane of 10, *June 1, 1982* *10.00*

First day cancellations were applied to 598,169 covers bearing one or more of Nos. 1894-1896.

TRANSPORTATION ISSUE

1981-84

1897 1c **Omnibus,** *Aug. 19, 1983,* Arlington, VA *(109,463)* 1.00
1897A 2c **Locomotive,** *May 20, 1982,* Chicago, IL *(290,020)* 1.50
1898 3c **Handcar,** *Mar. 25, 1983,* Rochester, NY *(77,900)* 1.00
1898A 4c **Stagecoach,** *Aug. 19, 1982,* Milwaukee, WI *(152,940)* 1.00
1899 5c **Motorcycle,** *Oct. 10, 1983,* San Francisco, CA *(188,240)* 2.00
1900 5.2c **Sleigh,** *Mar. 21, 1983,* Memphis, TN *(141,979)* 1.00
1901 5.9c **Bicycle,** *Feb. 17, 1982,* Wheeling, WV *(814,419)* 1.75
1902 7.4c **Baby Buggy,** *Apr. 7, 1984,* San Diego, CA 1.00
1903 9.3c **Mail Wagon,** *Dec. 15, 1981,* Shreveport, LA *(199,645)* 1.00
1904 10.9c **Hansom,** *Mar. 26, 1982,* Chattanooga, TN 1.00
1905 11c **Railroad Caboose,** *Feb. 3, 1984,* Chicago, IL *(172,753)* 1.50
1906 17c **Electric Auto,** *June 25, 1982,* Greenfield Village, MI *(239,458)* 1.00
1907 18c **Surrey,** *May 18, 1981,* Notch, MO *(207,801)* 1.00
1908 20c **Fire Pumper,** *Dec. 10, 1981,* Alexandria, VA *(304,668)* 2.50
1909 $9.35 **Eagle,** *Aug. 12, 1983,* Kennedy Space Center, FL *(77,858)* 50.00
1909a Booklet pane of 3 *150.00*

1981

1910 18c **Red Cross,** *May 1 (874,972)* 2.00
1911 18c **Savings & Loan,** *May 8,* Chicago, IL *(740,910)* 1.00
1919a 18c **Space Achievement,** *May 21,* Kennedy Space Center, FL *(7,027,549)* 3.00
1912-1919, any single 1.00
1920 18c **Professional Management,** *June 18,* Philadelphia, PA *(713,096)* 1.00
1924a 18c **Wildlife Habitats,** *June 26,* Reno, NV *(2,327,609)* 2.50
1921-1924, any single 1.00
1925 18c **Year of Disabled,** *June 29,* Milford, MI *(714,244)* 1.00
1926 18c **Edna St. V. Millay,** *July 10,* Austerlitz, NY *(725,978)* 1.00
1927 18c **Alcoholism,** *Aug. 19 (874,972)* 3.00
1931a 18c **Architecture,** *Aug. 28,* New York, NY *(1,998,208)* 2.50
1928-1931, any single 1.00
1932 18c **Babe Zaharias,** *Sept. 22,* Pinehurst, NC 6.50
1933 18c **Bobby Jones,** *Sept. 22,* Pinehurst, NC 10.00
1932-1933, both stamps issued *Sept. 22,* Pinehurst, NC 12.50

First day cancel was applied to 1,231,543 covers bearing one or more of Nos. 1932-1933.

1934 18c **Frederic Remington,** *Oct. 9,* Oklahoma City, OK *(1,367,099)* 1.25
1935 18c **James Hoban,** *Oct. 13* 1.00
1936 20c **James Hoban,** *Oct. 13* 1.00
1935-1936, both stamps issued *Oct. 13* 3.00

FD cancel was applied to 635,012 covers bearing Nos. 1935-1936.

1938a 18c **Yorktown-Va. Capes Battle,** *Oct. 16,* Yorktown, VA *(1,098,278)* 1.50
1937-1938, any single 1.00
1939 (20c) **Christmas (Madonna),** *Oct. 28,* Chicago, IL *(481,395)* 1.00
1940 (20c) **Christmas (Teddy Bear),** *Oct. 28,* Christmas Valley, OR *(517,898)* 1.00
1941 20c **John Hanson,** *Nov. 5,* Frederick, MD *(605,616)* 1.00
1945a 20c **Desert Plants,** *Dec. 11,* Tucson, AZ *(1,770,187)* 2.50
1942-1945, any single 1.00

REGULAR ISSUE

1946 (20c) **"C" Eagle,** *Oct. 11,* Memphis, TN 1.00
1947 (20c) **"C" Eagle,** coil, *Oct. 11,* Memphis, TN 1.00
1948 (20c) **"C" Eagle,** bklt. single, *Oct. 11,* Memphis, TN 1.00
1948a Booklet pane of 10 *3.50*

First day cancellations were applied to 304,404 covers bearing one or more of Nos. 1946-1948.

1982

1949 20c **Bighorn,** *Jan. 8,* Bighorn, MT 1.25
1949a Booklet pane of 10 *6.00*
1950 20c **F.D. Roosevelt,** *Jan. 30,* Hyde Park, NY 1.00
1951 20c **Love,** *Feb. 1,* Boston, MA *(325,727)* 1.00
1952 20c **Washington,** *Feb. 22,* Mt. Vernon, VA 1.25
2002b 20c **Birds-Flowers,** perf 10½x11¼ *Apr. 14,* Washington, DC, or State Capital 30.00
1953-2002, any single 1.25
2002Ac 20c **Birds-Flowers,** perf 11¼x11 *Apr. 14,* Washington, DC, or State Capital —
1953A-2002A, any single —
2003 20c **U.S.-Netherlands,** *Apr. 20* 1.00
2004 20c **Library of Congress,** *Apr. 21* 1.00
2005 20c **Consumer Education,** *Apr. 27* 1.00
2009a 20c **Knoxville Fair,** *Apr. 29,* Knoxville, TN 2.50
2006-2009, any single 1.00
2010 20c **Horatio Alger,** *Apr. 30,* Willow Grove, PA 1.00
2011 20c **Aging,** *May 21,* Sun City, AZ *(510,677)* 1.00
2012 20c **Barrymores,** *June 8,* New York, NY 1.25
2013 20c **Dr. Mary Walker,** *June 10,* Oswego, NY 1.00
2014 20c **Peace Garden,** *June 30,* Dunseith, ND 1.00
2015 20c **America's Libraries,** *July 13,* Philadelphia, PA 1.00
2016 20c **Jackie Robinson,** *Aug. 2,* Cooperstown, NY 6.50
2017 20c **Touro Synagogue,** *Aug. 22,* Newport, RI *(517,264)* 2.00
2018 20c **Wolf Trap Farm Park,** *Sept. 1,* Vienna, VA *(704,361)* 1.00
2022a 20c **Architecture,** *Sept. 30 (1,552,567)* 2.50
2019-2022, any single 1.00
2023 20c **St. Francis,** *Oct. 7,* San Francisco, CA *(530,275)* 1.50
2024 20c **Ponce de Leon,** *Oct. 12,* San Juan, PR *(530,275)* 1.00
2025 13c **Puppy, Kitten,** *Nov. 3,* Danvers, MA *(239,219)* 1.25
2026 20c **Christmas (Madonna),** *Oct. 28* *(462,982)* 1.00
2030a 20c **Christmas (Children),** *Oct. 28,* Snow, OK *(676,950)* 2.50
2027-2030, any single 1.00

1983

2031 20c **Science & Industry,** *Jan. 19,* Chicago, IL *(526,693)* 1.00
2035a 20c **Balloons,** *Mar. 31,* Albuquerque, NM or Washington, DC *(989,305)* 2.50
2032-2035, any single 1.00
2036 20c **U.S.-Sweden,** *Mar. 24,* Philadelphia, PA *(526,373)* 1.00
2037 20c **Civilian Conservation Corps.,** *Apr. 5,* Luray, VA *(483,824)* 1.00
2038 20c **Joseph Priestley,** *Apr. 13,* Northumberland, PA *(673,266)* 1.00
2039 20c **Voluntarism,** *Apr. 20 (574,708)* 1.00
2040 20c **U.S.-Germany,** *Apr. 29,* Germantown, PA *(611,109)* 1.00
2041 20c **Brooklyn Bridge,** *May 17,* Brooklyn, NY *(815,085)* 1.75
2042 20c **TVA,** *May 18,* Knoxville, TN *(837,588)* 1.00
2043 20c **Physical Fitness,** *May 14,* Houston, TX *(501,336)* 1.25
2044 20c **Scott Joplin,** *June 9,* Sedalia, MO *(472,667)* 1.75
2045 20c **Medal of Honor,** *June 7 (1,623,995)* 6.00
2046 20c **Babe Ruth,** *July 6,* Chicago, IL *(1,277,907)* 5.00
2047 20c **Nathaniel Hawthorne,** *July 8,* Salem, MA *(442,793)* 1.00
2051a 13c **Summer Olympics,** *July 28,* South Bend, IN *(909,332)* 2.50
2048-2051, any single 1.25
2052 20c **Treaty of Paris,** *Sept. 2 (651,208)* 1.00
2053 20c **Civil Service,** *Sept. 9 (422,206)* 1.00
2054 20c **Metropolitan Opera,** *Sept. 14,* New York, NY *(807,609)* 1.50
2058a 20c **American Inventors,** *Sept. 21* *(1,006,516)* 2.50
2055-2058, any single 1.00
2062a 20c **Streetcars,** *Oct. 8,* Kennebunkport, ME *(1,116,909)* 2.50
2059-2062, any single 1.00
2063 20c **Christmas (Madonna),** *Oct. 28* *(361,874)* 1.00
2064 20c **Christmas (Santa),** *Oct. 28,* Santa Claus, IN *(388,749)* 1.00
2065 20c **Martin Luther,** *Nov. 11 (463,777)* 1.50

1984

2066 20c **Alaska Statehood,** *Jan. 3,* Fairbanks, AK *(816,591)* 1.00
2070a 20c **Winter Olympics,** *Jan. 6,* Lake Placid, NY *(1,245,807)* 2.50
2067-2070, any single 1.00
2071 20c **Federal Deposit Ins. Corp.,** *Jan. 12* *(536,329)* 1.00
2072 20c **Love,** *Jan. 31 (327,727)* 1.00
2073 20c **Carter Woodson,** *Feb. 1 (387,583)* 1.75
2074 20c **Soil & Water Conservation,** *Feb. 6,* Denver, CO *(426,101)* 1.00
2075 20c **Credit Union Act,** *Feb. 10,* Salem, MA *(523,583)* 1.00
2079a 20c **Orchids,** *Mar. 5,* Miami, FL *(1,063,237)* 2.50
2076-2079, any single 1.00
2080 20c **Hawaii Statehood,** *Mar. 12,* Honolulu, HI *(546,930)* 1.00
2081 20c **National Archives,** *Apr. 16 (414,415)* 1.00
2085a 20c **Olympics 1984,** *May 4,* Los Angeles, CA *(1,172,313)* 2.50
2082-2085, any single 1.25
2086 20c **Louisiana Exposition,** *May 11,* New Orleans, LA *(467,408)* 1.00
2087 20c **Health Research,** *May 17,* New York, NY *(845,007)* 1.00
2088 20c **Douglas Fairbanks,** *May 23,* Denver CO *(547,134)* 1.50
2089 20c **Jim Thorpe,** *May 24,* Shawnee, OK *(568,544)* 3.00
2090 20c **John McCormack,** *June 6,* Boston, MA *(464,117)* 1.00
2091 20c **St. Lawrence Seaway,** *June 26,* Massena, NY *(550,173)* 1.00
2092 20c **Waterfowl Preservation Act,** *July 2,* Des Moines, IA *(549,388)* 1.00
2093 20c **Roanoke Voyages,** *July 13,* Manteo, NC *(443,725)* 1.00
2094 20c **Herman Melville,** *Aug. 1,* New Bedford, MA *(378,293)* 1.75
2095 20c **Horace A. Moses,** *Aug. 6,* Bloomington, IN *(459,386)* 1.00
2096 20c **Smokey Bear,** *Aug. 13,* Capitan, NM *(506,833)* 5.00
2097 20c **Roberto Clemente,** *Aug. 17,* Carolina, PR *(547,387)* 9.00
2101a 20c **Dogs,** *Sept. 7,* New York, NY *(1,157,373)* 3.00
2098-2101, any single 1.50
2102 20c **Crime Prevention,** *Sept. 26* *(427,564)* 1.25
2103 20c **Hispanic Americans,** *Oct. 31* *(416,796)* 1.75
2104 20c **Family Unity,** *Oct. 1,* Shaker Heights, OH *(400,659)* 1.00
2105 20c **Eleanor Roosevelt,** *Oct. 11,* Hyde Park, NY *(479,919)* 1.25
2106 20c **Nation of Readers,** *Oct. 16* *(437,559)* 1.00
2107 20c **Christmas (Madonna),** *Oct. 30* *(386,385)* 1.00
2108 20c **Christmas (Santa),** *Oct. 30,* Jamaica, NY *(430,843)* 1.00
2109 20c **Vietnam Veterans' Memorial,** *Nov. 10 (434,489)* 5.00

1985

2110 22c **Jerome Kern,** *Jan. 23,* New York, NY (503,855) 1.00

REGULAR ISSUE

2111 (22c) **"D" Eagle,** *Feb. 1,* Los Angeles, CA 1.00
2112 (22c) **"D" Eagle, coil,** *Feb. 1,* Los Angeles, CA 1.00

2113 (22c) **"D" Eagle, bklt. single,** *Feb. 1,* Los Angeles, CA 1.00
2113a Booklet pane of 10 *7.50*

First Day cancel was applied to 513,027 covers bearing one or more of Nos. 2111-2113.

2114 22c **Flag over Capitol Dome,** *Mar. 29* 1.00
2115 22c **Flag over Capitol Dome,** coil, *Mar. 29* 1.00
2115c Inscribed "T" at bottom, *May 23, 1987,* Secaucus, NJ *1.00*

First Day Cancel was applied to 268,161 covers bearing one or more of Nos. 2114-2115.

2116 22c **Flag Over Capitol Dome,** bklt. single, *Mar. 29,* Waubeka, WI *(234,318)* 1.00
2116a Booklet pane of 5 3.50
2121a 22c **Seashells Booklet pane of 10,** *Apr. 4,* Boston, MA *(426,290)* *7.50*
2117-2121, any single 1.00
2122 $10.75 **Eagle and Half Moon,** type I, *Apr. 29,* San Francisco, CA *(93,154)* 50.00
2122a Booklet pane of 3 *125.00*
2122b Type II, *June 19, 1989* *350.00*
2122c Booklet pane of 3, type II *700.00*

TRANSPORTATION ISSUE

1985-87

2123 3.4c **School Bus,** *June 8, 1985,* Arlington, VA *(131,480)* 1.00
2124 4.9c **Buckboard,** *June 21, 1985,* Reno, NV 1.00
2125 5.5c **Star Route Truck,** *Nov. 1, 1986,* Fort Worth, TX *(136,021)* 1.00
2125a 5.5c **Star Route Truck,** untagged (Bureau precanceled), *Nov. 1, 1986,* Washington, DC 5.00
2126 6c **Tricycle,** *May 6, 1985,* Childs, MD *(151,494)* 1.25
2127 7.1c **Tractor,** *Feb. 6, 1987,* Sarasota, FL *(167,555)* 1.00
2127a 7.1c **Tractor,** "Non-profit Org." precancel in black, *Feb. 6, 1987,* Sarasota, FL 5.00
2127b 7.1c **Tractor,** "Non-profit 5-Digit Zip+4" precancel in black, untagged, *May 26, 1989,* Rosemont, IL *(202,804)* 1.00
2128 8.3c **Ambulance,** *June 21, 1986,* Reno, NV 1.00

First day cancel was applied to 338,765 covers bearing one or more of Nos. 2124 and 2128.

2129 8.5c **Tow Truck,** *Jan. 24, 1987,* Tucson, AZ *(224,285)* 1.25
2129a 8.5c **Tow Truck,** untagged (Bureau precancel) *Jan. 24, 1987,* Washington, DC 5.00
2130 10.1c **Oil Wagon,** *Apr. 18, 1985,* Oil Center, NM 1.25
2130a 10.1c "Bulk Rate Carrier Route Sort" precancel, *June 27, 1988 (136,428)* 1.25
2131 11c **Stutz Bearcat,** *June 11, 1985,* Baton Rouge, LA *(135,037)* 1.25
2132 12c **Stanley Steamer,** *Apr. 2, 1985,* Kingfield, ME *(173,998)* 1.25
2133 12.5c **Pushcart,** *Apr. 18, 1985,* Oil Center, NM 1.25

First day cancel was applied to 319,953 covers bearing one or more of Nos. 2130 and 2133.

2134 14c **Ice Boat,** *Mar. 23, 1985,* Rochester, NY *(324,710)* 1.25
2135 17c **Dog Sled,** *Aug. 20, 1986,* Anchorage, AK 1.75
2136 25c **Bread Wagon,** *Nov. 22, 1986,* Virginia Beach, VA *(151,950)* 1.25

1985

2137 22c **Mary McLeod Bethune,** *Mar. 5 (413,244)* 1.50
2141a 22c **Duck Decoys,** *Mar. 22,* Shelburne, VT *(932,249)* 2.50
2138-2141, any single 1.00
2142 22c **Winter Special Olympics,** *Mar. 25,* Park City, UT *(253,074)* 1.00
2143 22c **Love,** *Apr. 17,* Hollywood, CA *(283,072)* 1.00
2144 22c **Rural Electrification Administration,** *May 11,* Madison, SD *(472,895)* 1.00
2145 22c **AMERIPEX '86,** *May 25,* Rosemont, IL *(457,038)* 1.00
2146 22c **Abigail Adams,** *June 14,* Quincy, MA *(491,026)* 1.00
2147 22c **Frederic Auguste Bartholdi,** *July 18,* New York, NY *(594,896)* 1.00
2149 18c **George Washington, Washington Monument,** *Nov. 6 (376,238)* 1.00
2150 21.1c **Envelopes,** *Oct. 22 (119,941)* 1.00
2152 22c **Korean War Veterans,** *July 26 (391,754)* 3.00
2153 22c **Social Security Act,** *Aug. 14,* Baltimore, MD *(265,143)* 1.00
2154 22c **World War I Veterans,** *Aug. 26,* Milwaukee, WI 1.75
2158a 22c **Horses,** *Sept. 25,* Lexington, KY *(1,135,368)* 2.50
2155-2158, any single 1.50
2159 22c **Public Education in America,** *Oct. 1,* Boston, MA *(356,030)* 1.00
2163a 22c **International Youth Year,** *Oct. 7,* Chicago, IL *(1,202,541)* 2.50
2160, 2162-2163, any single 1.00
2161 2.00

2164 22c **Help End Hunger,** *Oct. 15 (299,485)* 1.00
2165 22c **Christmas (Madonna & Child),** *Oct. 30,* Detroit, MI 1.00
2166 22c **Christmas (Poinsettia),** *Oct. 30,* Nazareth, MI *(524,929)* 1.00

1986

2167 22c **Arkansas Statehood,** *Jan. 3,* Little Rock, AR *(364,729)* 1.00

GREAT AMERICANS ISSUE

1986-94

2168 1c **Margaret Mitchell,** *June 30, 1986,* Atlanta, GA *(316,764)* 2.00
2169 2c **Mary Lyon,** *Feb. 28, 1987,* South Hadley, MA *(349,831)* 1.00
2170 3c **Dr. Paul Dudley White,** *Sept. 15, 1986* 1.00
2171 4c **Father Flanagan,** *July 14, 1986,* Boys Town, NE *(367,883)* 1.25
2172 5c **Hugo Black,** *Feb. 27, 1986 (303,012)* 1.00
2173 5c **Luis Munoz Marin,** *Feb. 18, 1990,* San Juan, PR *(269,618)* 1.00
2175 10c **Red Cloud,** *Aug. 15, 1987,* Red Cloud, NE *(300,472)* 1.75
2176 14c **Julia Ward Howe,** *Feb. 12, 1987,* Boston, MA *(454,829)* 1.00
2177 15c **Buffalo Bill Cody,** *June 6, 1988* Cody, WY *(356,395)* 2.00
2178 17c **Belva Ann Lockwood,** *June 18, 1986,* Middleport, NY *(249,215)* 1.00
2179 20c **Virginia Apgar,** *Oct. 24, 1994,* Dallas, TX *(28,461)* 1.00
2180 21c **Chester Carlson,** *Oct. 21, 1988,* Rochester, NY *(288,073)* 1.00
2181 23c **Mary Cassatt,** *Nov. 4, 1988,* Philadelphia, PA *(322,537)* 1.00
2182 25c **Jack London,** *Jan. 11, 1986,* Glen Ellen, CA *(358,686)* 1.50
2182a Booklet pane of 10, *May 3, 1988,* San Francisco, CA 6.00
2183 28c **Sitting Bull,** *Sept. 14, 1989,* Rapid City, SD *(126,777)* 2.00
2184 29c **Earl Warren,** *Mar. 9, 1992 (175,517)* 1.25
2185 29c **Thomas Jefferson,** *Apr. 13, 1993,* Charlottesville, VA *(202,962)* 1.25
2186 35c **Dennis Chavez,** *Apr. 3, 1991,* Albuquerque, NM *(285,570)* 1.25
2187 40c **Claire Chennault,** *Sept. 6, 1990,* Monroe, LA *(186,761)* 2.00
2188 45c **Harvey Cushing,** *June 17, 1988,* Cleveland, OH *(135,140)* 1.25
2189 52c **Hubert Humphrey,** *June 3, 1991,* Minneapolis, MN *(93,391)* 1.40
2190 56c **John Harvard,** *Sept. 3, 1986,* Cambridge, MA 2.50
2191 65c **Hap Arnold,** *Nov. 5, 1988,* Gladwyne, PA *(129,829)* 2.50
2192 75c **Wendell Willkie,** *Feb. 18, 1992,* Bloomington, IN *(47,086)* 2.50
2193 $1 **Dr. Bernard Revel,** *Sept. 23, 1986,* New York, NY 5.00
2194 $1 **Johns Hopkins,** *June 7, 1989,* Baltimore, MD *(159,049)* 3.00
2195 $2 **William Jennings Bryan,** *Mar. 19, 1986,* Salem, IL *(123,430)* 6.00
2196 $5 **Bret Harte,** *Aug. 25, 1987,* Twain Harte, CA *(111,431)* 15.00
2197 25c **Jack London,** bklt. single, *May 3, 1988,* San Francisco, CA 1.00
2197a Booklet pane of 6 4.00

First day cancel was applied to 94,655 covers bearing one or more of Nos. 2183a, 2197, and 2197a.

1986

2201a 22c **Stamp Collecting Booklet pane of 4,** *Jan. 23,* State College, PA 4.00
2198-2201, any single 1.00

First day cancellation was applied to 675,924 covers bearing one or more of Nos. 2198-2201a.

2202 22c **Love,** *Jan. 30,* New York, NY 1.00
2203 22c **Sojourner Truth,** *Feb. 4,* New Paltz, NY *(342,985)* 1.75
2204 22c **Republic of Texas,** *Mar. 2,* San Antonio, TX *(380,450)* 1.75
2209a 22c **Fish Booklet pane of 5,** *Mar. 21,* Seattle, WA 5.00
2205-2209, any single 1.25

First day cancellation was applied to 988,184 covers bearing one or more of Nos. 2205-2209a.

2210 22c **Public Hospitals,** *Apr. 11,* New York, NY *(403,665)* 1.00
2211 22c **Duke Ellington,** *Apr. 29,* New York, NY *(397,894)* 2.25
2216 22c **Presidents Souvenir Sheet of 9 (Washington-Harrison),** *May 22,* Chicago, IL 4.50
2217 22c **Presidents Souvenir Sheet of 9 (Tyler-Grant),** *May 22,* Chicago, IL 4.50
2218 22c **Presidents Souvenir Sheet of 9 (Hayes-Wilson),** *May 22,* Chicago, IL 4.50
2219 22c **Presidents Souvenir Sheet of 9 (Harding-Johnson),** *May 22,* Chicago, IL 4.50
2216a-2219g, 2219i, any single 1.50
2219h 2.50

First day cancellation was applied to 9,009,599 covers bearing one or more of Nos. 2216-2219, 2216a-2219i.

2223a 22c **Polar Explorers,** *May 28,* North Pole, AK *(760,999)* 3.75
2220-2223, any single 1.25
2224 22c **Statue of Liberty,** *July 4,* New York, NY *(1,540,308)* 1.25

TRANSPORTATION ISSUE

1986-87

2225 1c **Omnibus,** *Nov. 26, 1986 (57,845)* 1.00
2226 2c **Locomotive,** *Mar. 6, 1987,* Milwaukee, WI *(169,484)* 1.50

1986

2238a 22c **Navajo Art,** *Sept. 4,* Window Rock, AZ *(1,102,520)* 2.00
2235-2238, any single 1.00
2239 22c **T.S. Eliot,** *Sept. 26,* St. Louis, MO *(304,764)* 1.00
2243a 22c **Woodcarved Figurines,** *Oct. 1 (629,399)* 2.00
2240-2243, any single 1.00
2244 22c **Christmas (Madonna),** *Oct. 24 (467,999)* 1.00
2245 22c **Christmas (Winter Village),** *Oct. 24,* Snow Hill, MD *(504,851)* 1.00

1987

2246 22c **Michigan Statehood Sesquicent.,** *Jan. 26,* Lansing, MI *(379,117)* 1.00
2247 22c **Pan American Games,** *Jan. 29,* Indianapolis, IN *(344,731)* 1.00
2248 22c **Love,** *Jan. 30,* San Francisco, CA *(333,329)* 1.00
2249 22c **Pointe du Sable,** *Feb. 20,* Chicago, IL *(313,054)* 1.50
2250 22c **Enrico Caruso,** *Feb. 27,* New York, NY *(389,834)* 1.25
2251 22c **Girl Scouts of America,** *Mar. 12 (556,391)* 2.50

TRANSPORTATION ISSUE

1987-88

2252 3c **Conestoga Wagon,** *Feb. 29, 1988,* Conestoga, PA *(155,203)* 1.00
2253 5c **Milk Wagon,** *Sept. 25, 1987,* Indianapolis, IN 1.00

First day cancel was applied to 162,571 covers bearing one or more of Nos. 2253 and 2262.

2254 5.3c **Elevator,** *Sept. 16, 1988,* New York, NY *(142,705)* 1.00
2255 7.6c **Carretta,** *Aug. 30, 1988,* San Jose, CA *(140,024)* 1.00
2256 8.4c **Wheelchair,** *Aug. 12, 1988,* Tucson, AZ *(136,337)* 1.00
2257 10c **Canal Boat,** *Apr. 11, 1987,* Buffalo, NY *(171,952)* 1.00
2258 13c **Police Patrol Wagon,** *Oct. 29, 1988,* Anaheim, CA *(132,928)* 1.50
2259 13.2c **Railway Coal Car,** *July 19, 1988,* Pittsburgh, PA *(123,965)* 1.00
2260 15c **Tugboat,** *July 12, 1988,* Long Beach, CA *(134,926)* 1.00
2261 16.7c **Popcorn Wagon,** *July 7, 1988,* Chicago, IL *(117,908)* 1.00
2262 17.5c **Racing Car,** *Sept. 25, 1987,* Indianapolis, IN 1.25
2263 20c **Cable Car,** *Oct. 28, 1988,* San Francisco, CA *(150,068)* 1.00
2264 20.5c **Fire Engine,** *Sept. 28, 1988,* San Angelo, TX *(123,043)* 1.75
2265 21c **Railway Mail Car,** *Aug. 16, 1988,* Santa Fe, NM *(124,430)* 1.00
2266 24.1c **Tandem Bicycle,** *Oct. 26, 1988,* Redmond, WA *(138,593)* 1.75

1987

2274a 22c **Special Occasions Booklet pane of 10,** *Apr. 20,* Atlanta, GA 5.00
2267-2274, any single 1.00

First day cancellation was applied to 1,588,129 covers bearing one or more of Nos. 2267-2274a.

2275 22c **United Way,** *Apr. 28 (556,391)* 1.00

1987-89

2276 22c **Flag and Fireworks,** *May 9, 1987* Denver, CO *(398,855)* 1.00
2276a Booklet pane of 20, *Nov. 30, 1987* 8.00
2277 (25c) **"E" Earth,** *Mar. 22, 1988* 1.25
2278 25c **Flag and Clouds,** *May 6, 1988,* Boxborough, MA *(131,265)* 1.25
2279 (25c) **"E" Earth,** coil, *Mar. 22, 1988* 1.25
2280 25c **Flag over Yosemite,** large block tagging, *May 20, 1988,* Yosemite, CA *(144,339)* 1.25
2280a 25c Prephosphored paper, *Feb. 14, 1989,* Yosemite, CA *(118,874)* 1.25
2281 25c **Honey Bee,** *Sept. 2, 1988,* Omaha, NE *(122,853)* 1.25
2282 (25c) **"E" Earth,** bklt. single, *Mar. 22, 1988* 1.25
2282a Booklet pane of 10 6.00

First day cancel was applied to 363,639 covers bearing one or more of Nos. 2277, 2279 and 2282.

2283 25c **Pheasant,** *Apr. 29, 1988,* Rapid City, SD *(167,053)* 1.25
2283a Booklet pane of 10 6.00

2285b 25c **Grosbeak & Owl, booklet pane of 10** *May 28, 1988,* Arlington, VA 6.00
2284-2285, any single 1.25

First day cancel was applied to 272,359 covers bearing one or more of Nos. 2284 and 2285.

2285A 25c **Flag and Clouds,** bklt. single, *July 5, 1988 (117,303)* 1.00
2285Ac Booklet pane of 6 4.00
2335a 22c **American Wildlife,** *June 13, 1987,* Toronto, Canada 50.00
2286-2335, any single 1.50

RATIFICATION OF THE CONSTITUTION

1987-90

2336 22c **Delaware,** *July 4, 1987,* Dover, DE *(505,770)* 1.50
2337 22c **Pennsylvania,** *Aug. 26, 1987,* Harrisburg, PA *(367,184)* 1.50
2338 22c **New Jersey,** *Sept. 11, 1987,* Trenton, NJ *(432,899)* 1.50
2339 22c **Georgia,** *Jan. 6, 1988,* Atlanta, GA *(467,804)* 1.50
2340 22c **Connecticut,** *Jan. 9, 1988,* Hartford, CT *(379,706)* 1.50
2341 22c **Massachusetts,** *Feb. 6, 1988,* Boston, MA *(412,616)* 1.50
2342 22c **Maryland,** *Feb. 15, 1988,* Annapolis, MD *(376,403)* 1.50
2343 25c **South Carolina,** *May 23, 1988,* Columbia, SC *(322,938)* 1.50
2344 25c **New Hampshire,** *June 21, 1988,* Concord, NH *(374,402)* 1.50
2345 25c **Virginia,** *June 25, 1988,* Williamsburg, VA *(474,079)* 1.50
2346 25c **New York,** *July 26, 1988,* Albany, NY *(385,793)* 1.50
2347 25c **North Carolina,** *Aug. 22, 1989,* Fayetteville, NC *(392,953)* 1.50
2348 25c **Rhode Island,** *May 29, 1990,* Pawtucket, RI *(305,566)* 1.50

1987

2349 22c **U.S.-Morocco Diplomatic Relations Bicent.,** *July 17 (372,814)* 1.00
2350 22c **William Faulkner,** *Aug. 3,* Oxford, MS *(480,024)* 1.00
2354a 22c **Lacemaking,** *Aug. 14,* Ypsilanti, MI 2.50
2351-2354, any single 1.00
2359a 22c **Drafting of Constitution Bicent. Booklet pane of 5,** *Aug. 28* 4.00
2355-2359, any single 1.25

First day cancellation was applied to 1,008,799 covers bearing one or more of Nos. 2355-2359a.

2360 22c **Signing of Constitution Bicent.,** *Sept. 17,* Philadelphia, PA *(719,975)* 1.25
2361 22c **Certified Public Accounting,** *Sept. 21,* New York, NY *(362,099)* 7.50
2366a 22c **Locomotives booklet pane of 5,** *Oct. 1,* Baltimore, MD 3.00
2362-2366, any single 1.25

First day cancellation was applied to 976,694 covers bearing one or more of Nos. 2362-2366a.

2367 22c **Christmas (Madonna),** *Oct. 23 (320,406)* 1.25
2368 22c **Christmas (Ornaments),** *Oct. 23,* Holiday-Anaheim, CA *(375,858)* 1.25

1988

2369 22c **Winter Olympics, Calgary,** *Jan. 10,* Anchorage, AK *(395,198)* 1.00
2370 22c **Australia Bicentennial,** *Jan. 26 (523,465)* 1.75
2371 22c **James Weldon Johnson,** *Feb. 2,* Nashville, TN *(465,282)* 1.75
2375a 22c **Cats,** *Feb. 5,* New York, NY *(872,734)* 4.50
2372-2375, any single 2.00
2376 22c **Knute Rockne,** *Mar. 9,* Notre Dame, IN *(404,311)* 4.00
2377 25c **Francis Ouimet,** *June 13,* Brookline, MA *(383,168)* 4.50
2378 25c **Love,** *July 4,* Pasadena, CA *(399,038)* 1.00
2379 45c **Love,** *Aug. 8,* Shreveport, LA *(121,808)* 1.25
2380 25c **Summer Olympics, Seoul,** *Aug. 19,* Colorado Springs, CO *(402,616)* 1.25
2385a 25c **Automobiles booklet pane of 5,** *Aug. 25,* Detroit, MI 4.00
2381-2385, any single 1.25

First day cancel was applied to 875,801 covers bearing one or more of Nos. 2381-2385a.

2389a 25c **Antarctic Explorers,** *Sept. 14 (720,537)* 3.00
2386-2389, any single 1.25
2393a 25c **Carousel Animals,** *Oct. 1,* Sandusky, OH *(856,380)* 4.00
2390-2393, any single 1.50
2394 $8.75 **Express Mail,** *Oct. 4,* Terre Haute, IN *(66,558)* 27.50
2396a 25c **Special Occasions (Happy Birthday, Best Wishes),** *Oct. 22,* King of Prussia, PA 4.00
2395-2396, any single 1.25
2398a 25c **Special Occasions (Thinking of You, Love You),** *Oct. 22,* King of Prussia, PA 4.00
2397-2398, any single 1.25

First day cancel was applied to 126,767 covers bearing one or more of Nos. 2395-2398, 2396a, 2398a.

2399 25c **Christmas (Madonna),** *Oct. 20 (247,291)* 1.25
2400 25c **Christmas (Contemporary),** *Oct. 20,* Berlin, NH *(412,213)* 1.25

1989

2401 25c **Montana,** *Jan. 15,* Helena, MT *(353,319)* 1.25
2402 25c **A. Philip Randolph,** *Feb. 3,* New York, NY *(363,174)* 1.75
2403 25c **North Dakota,** *Feb. 21,* Bismarck, ND *(306,003)* 1.00
2404 25c **Washington Statehood,** *Feb. 22,* Olympia, WA *(445,174)* 1.00
2409a 25c **Steamboats Booklet pane of 5,** *Mar. 3,* New Orleans, LA 3.00
2405-2409, any single 1.25

First day cancel was applied to 981,674 covers bearing one or more of Nos. 2405-2409a.

2410 25c **World Stamp Expo,** *Mar. 16,* New York, NY *(296,310)* 1.00
2411 25c **Arturo Toscanini,** *Mar. 25,* New York, NY *(309,441)* 1.00

BRANCHES OF GOVERNMENT

1989-90

2412 25c **House of Representatives,** *Apr. 4, 1989 (327,755)* 1.50
2413 25c **Senate,** *Apr. 6, 1989 (341,288)* 1.50
2414 25c **Executive Branch,** *Apr. 16, 1989* Mount Vernon, VA *(387,644)* 1.50
2415 25c **Supreme Court,** *Feb. 2, 1990 (233,056)* 1.50

1989

2416 25c **South Dakota,** *May 3,* Pierre, SD *(348,370)* 1.00
2417 25c **Lou Gehrig,** *June 10,* Cooperstown, NY *(694,227)* 4.00
2418 25c **Ernest Hemingway,** *July 17,* Key West, FL *(345,436)* 1.50
2419 $2.40 **Moon Landing,** *July 20 (208,982)* 7.50
2420 25c **Letter Carriers,** *Aug. 30,* Milwaukee, WI *(372,241)* 1.25
2421 25c **Bill of Rights,** *Sept. 25,* Philadelphia, PA *(900,384)* 1.00
2425a 25c **Dinosaurs,** *Oct. 1,* Orlando, FL *(871,634)* 3.00
2422-2425, any single 1.50
2426 25c **Southwest Carved Figure,** *Oct. 12,* San Juan, PR *(215,285)* 1.00
2427 25c **Christmas (Madonna),** *Oct. 19 (395,321)* 1.00
2427a Booklet pane of 10 6.00
2428 25c **Christmas (Sleigh with Presents),** *Oct. 19,* Westport, CT 1.00
2429 25c **Christmas (Sleigh with Presents) from bklt.,** *Oct. 19,* Westport, CT 1.00
2429a Booklet pane of 10 6.00

First day cancel was applied to 345,931 covers bearing one or more of Nos. 2428-2429a.

2431 25c **Eagle and Shield,** *Nov. 10,* Virginia Beach, VA 1.25
2433 90c **World Stamp Expo '89 Souvenir Sheet,** *Nov. 17 (281,725)* 7.00
2437a 25c **Classic Mail Transportation,** *Nov. 19 (916,389)* 2.50
2434-2437, any single 1.25
2438 25c **Classic Mail Transportation Souvenir Sheet,** *Nov. 28 (241,634)* 3.00

1990

2439 25c **Idaho Statehood,** *Jan. 6,* Boise, ID *(252,493)* 1.25
2440 25c **Love,** *Jan. 18,* Romance, AR 1.25
2441 25c **Love, from bklt.,** *Jan. 18,* Romance, AR 1.00
2441a Booklet pane of 10 6.00

First day cancel was applied to 257,788 covers bearing one or more of Nos. 2440-2441a.

2442 25c **Ida B. Wells,** *Feb. 1,* Chicago, IL *(229,226)* 2.00
2443 15c **Beach Umbrella,** *Feb. 3,* Sarasota, FL 1.25
2443a Booklet pane of 10 4.25

First day cancel was applied to 72,286 covers bearing one or more of Nos. 2443-2443a.

2444 25c **Wyoming Statehood,** *Feb. 23,* Cheyenne, WY *(317,654)* 1.00
2448a 25c **Classic Films,** *Mar. 23,* Hollywood, CA *(863,079)* 5.00
2445-2448, any single 2.50
2449 25c **Marianne Moore,** *Apr. 18,* Brooklyn, NY *(390,535)* 1.25

1990-95 TRANSPORTATION COILS

2451 4c **Steam Carriage,** *Jan. 25, 1991,* Tucson, AZ *(100,393)* 1.25
2452 5c **Circus Wagon,** engraved, *Aug. 31, 1990,* Syracuse, NY *(71,806)* 1.50
2452B 5c **Circus Wagon,** photogravure, *Dec. 8, 1992,* Cincinnati, OH 1.50
2452D 5c **Circus Wagon,** with cent sign, photogravure, *Mar. 20, 1995,* Kansas City MO *(20,835)* 2.00
2453 5c **Canoe,** engraved, *May 25, 1991,* Secaucus, NJ *(108,634)* 1.25
2454 5c **Canoe,** photogravure, *Oct. 22, 1991,* Secaucus, NJ 1.25
2457 10c **Tractor Trailer,** engr., *May 25, 1991,* Secaucus, NJ *(84,717)* 1.25
2458 10c **Tractor Trailer,** photo., *May 25, 1994,* Secaucus, NJ *(15,431)* 1.25
2463 20c **Cog Railway,** *June 9, 1995,* Dallas, TX *(28,883)* 1.25
2464 23c **Lunch Wagon,** *Apr. 12, 1991,* Columbus, OH *(115,830)* 1.25
2466 32c **Ferry Boat,** *June 2, 1995,* McLean VA 1.25

First day cancellation was applied to 59,100 covers bearing one or more of Nos. 2466, 2492.

2468 $1 **Seaplane,** *Apr. 20, 1990* Phoenix, AZ *(244,775)* 3.00

1990

2474a 25c **Lighthouses booklet pane of 5,** *Apr. 26* 5.00
2470-2474, any single 1.50

First day cancel was applied to 805,133 covers bearing one or more of Nos. 2470-2474a.

2475 25c **Flag,** *May 18,* Seattle, WA *(97,567)* 1.00

FLORA AND FAUNA ISSUE

1990-95

2476 1c **Kestrel,** *June 22,* Aurora, CO *(77,781)* 1.00
2477 1c **Kestrel, with cent sign,** *May 10, 1995* Aurora, CO *(21,767)* 1.00
2478 3c **Eastern Bluebird,** *June 22,* Aurora, CO *(76,149)* 1.00
2479 19c **Fawn,** *Mar. 11 (100,212)* 1.00
2480 30c **Cardinal,** *June 22,* Aurora, CO *(101,290)* 1.25
2481 45c **Pumpkinseed Sunfish,** *Dec. 2, 1992 (38,696)* 1.75
2482 $2 **Bobcat,** *June 1,* Arlington, VA *(49,660)* 5.00
2483 20c **Blue Jay,** booklet single, *June 15, 1995,* Kansas City MO 1.25

First day cancellation was applied to 16,847 covers bearing one or more of Nos. 2483, 2483a.

2484 29c **Wood Duck,** black denomination bklt. single, *Apr. 12,* Columbus, OH 1.00
2484a Booklet pane of 10 4.00
2485 29c **Wood Duck,** red denomination bklt. single, *Apr. 12,* Columbus, OH 1.00
2485a Booklet pane of 10 4.00

First day cancel was applied to 205,305 covers bearing one or more of Nos. 2484-2485, 2484a-2485a.

2486 29c **African Violet,** *Oct. 8, 1993,* Beaumont, TX 1.00
2486a Booklet pane of 10 4.00

First day cancellation was applied to 40,167 covers bearing one or more of Nos. 2486-2486a.

2487 32c **Peach,** booklet single, *July 8, 1995,* Reno NV 1.50
2488 32c **Pear,** booklet single, *July 8, 1995,* Reno NV 1.50

First day cancellation was applied to 71,086 covers bearing one or more of Nos. 2487-2488, 2488a, 2493-2495A.

2488a Booklet pane, 5 each #2488-2489 7.50
2489 29c **Red Squirrel,** self-adhesive, *June 25, 1993* Milwaukee, WI *(48,564)* 1.25
2490 29c **Red Rose,** self-adhesive, *Aug. 19, 1993* Houston, TX *(37,916)* 1.25
2491 29c **Pine Cone,** self-adhesive, *Nov. 5, 1993* Kansas City, MO *(110,924)* 1.25
2492 32c **Pink Rose,** self-adhesive, *June 2, 1995,* McLean VA 1.25

First day cancellation was applied to 59,100 covers bearing one or more of Nos. 2466, 2492.

2493 32c **Peach,** self-adhesive, *July 8, 1995,* Reno NV 1.25
2494 32c **Pear,** self-adhesive, *July 8, 1995,* Reno NV 1.25
2495 32c **Peach,** self-adhesive, serpentine die cut vert., *July 8, 1995,* Reno NV 1.25
2495A 32c **Pear,** self-adhesive, serpentine die cut vert., *July 8, 1995,* Reno NV 1.25

First day cancellation was applied to 71,086 covers bearing one or more of Nos. 2487-2488, 2488a, 2493-2495A.

1990

2500a 25c **Olympians,** *July 6,* Minneapolis, MN *(1,143,404)* 4.00
2496-2500, any single 1.25
2505a 25c **Indian Headdresses, booklet pane of 10** *Aug. 17,* Cody, WY 6.00
2501-2505, any single 1.25

First day cancel was applied to 979,580 covers bearing one or more of Nos. 2501-2505a.

2507a 25c **Micronesia, Marshall Islands,** *Sept. 28 (343,816)* 2.00
2506-2507, any single 1.25
2511a 25c **Sea Creatures,** *Oct. 3,* Baltimore, MD *(706,047)* 3.00
2508-2511, any single 1.25
2512 25c **Grand Canyon,** *Oct. 12,* Grand Canyon, AZ *(164,190)* 2.25
2513 25c **Dwight D. Eisenhower,** *Oct. 13,* Abilene, KS *(487,988)* 1.50
2514 25c **Christmas (traditional),** *Oct. 18* 1.25
2514b Booklet pane of 10 6.00

First day cancel was applied to 378,383 covers bearing one or more of Nos. 2514-2514a.

2515 25c **Christmas (secular),** *Oct. 18,* Evergreen, CO 1.25
2516 25c **Christmas (secular),** *Oct. 18,* Evergreen, CO 1.00
2516a Booklet pane of 10 6.00

First day cancel was applied to 230,586 covers bearing one or more of Nos. 2515-2516a.

1991-94

2517 (29c) **"F" Flower,** *Jan. 22, 1991 (106,698)* 1.25
2518 (29c) **"F" Flower,** coil, *Jan. 22, 1991 (39,311)* 1.25
2519 (29c) **"F" Flower,** bklt. single (bullseye perf. 11.2), *Jan. 22, 1991* 1.00
2519a Booklet pane of 10 7.25
2520 (29c) **"F" Flower,** bklt. single (perf. 11), *Jan. 22, 1991* 1.25
2520a Booklet pane of 10 8.00

First day cancel was applied to 32,971 covers bearing one or more of Nos. 2519-2520, 2519a-2520a.

2521 (4c) **Makeup Stamp,** *Jan. 22, 1991 (51,987)* 1.25
2522 (29c) **"F" Flag,** *Jan. 22, 1991 (48,821)* 1.25
2523 29c **Flag over Mt. Rushmore,** engraved, *Mar. 29, 1991* Mt. Rushmore, SD *(233,793)* 1.25
2523A 29c **Flag over Mt. Rushmore,** photogravure, *July 4, 1991* Mt. Rushmore, SD *(80,662)* 1.25
2524 29c **Flower,** *Apr. 5, 1991,* Rochester, NY *(132,233)* 1.00
2525 29c **Flower,** roulette 10 coil, *Aug. 16, 1991,* Rochester, NY *(144,750)* 1.00
2526 29c **Flower,** perf. 10 coil, *Mar. 3, 1992,* Rochester, NY *(35,877)* 1.00
2527 29c **Flower,** bklt. single, *Apr. 5, 1991,* Rochester, NY 1.00
2527a Booklet pane of 10 4.00

First day cancel was applied to 16,975 covers bearing one or more of Nos. 2527-2527a.

2528 29c **Flag and Olympic Rings,** bklt. single, *Apr. 21, 1991,* Atlanta, GA 1.25
2528a Booklet pane of 10 5.00

First day cancel was applied to 319,488 covers bearing one or more of Nos. 2528-2528a.

2529 19c **Fishing Boat,** two loops, *Aug. 8, 1991 (82,698)* 1.50
2529C 19c **Fishing Boat,** one loop, *June 25, 1994,* Arlington, VA *(14,538)* 1.50
2530 19c **Balloon,** *May 17, 1991,* Denver, CO 1.25
2530a Booklet pane of 10 5.00

First day cancel was applied to 96,351 covers bearing one or more of Nos. 2530-2530a.

2531 29c **Flags on Parade,** *May 30, 1991,* Waterloo, NY *(104,046)* 1.00
2531A 29c **Liberty Torch,** *June 25, 1991,* New York, NY *(68,456)* 1.25

1991-95

2532 50c **Switzerland,** *Feb. 22,* Washington, DC *(316,047)* 1.40
2533 29c **Vermont,** *Mar. 1,* Bennington, VT *(308,105)* 1.50
2534 29c **Savings Bonds,** *Apr. 30,* Washington, DC *(341,955)* 1.25
2535 29c **Love,** *May 9,* Honolulu, HI *(336,132)* 1.25
2536 29c **Love,** bklt. single, *May 9,* Honolulu, HI 1.25
2536a Booklet pane of 10 5.00

First day cancel was applied to 43,336 covers bearing one or more of Nos. 2536-2536a.

2537 52c **Love,** *May 9,* Honolulu, HI *(90,438)* 1.25
2538 29c **William Saroyan,** *May 22,* Fresno, CA *(334,373)* 1.50
2539 $1 **Eagle & Olympic Rings,** *Sept. 29,* Orlando, FL *(69,241)* 2.25
2540 $2.90 **Eagle & Olympic Rings,** *July 7,* San Diego, CA *(79,555)* 5.50
2541 $9.95 **Eagle & Olympic Rings,** *June 16,* Sacramento, CA *(68,657)* 15.00
2542 $14 **Eagle,** *Aug. 31,* Hunt Valley, MD *(54,727)* 27.50
2543 $2.90 **Futuristic Space Shuttle,** *June 3, 1993,* Kennedy Space Center, FL *(36,359)* 6.00
2544 $3 **Space Shuttle Challenger,** *June 22, 1995* Anaheim CA *(16,502)* 6.00
2544A $10.75 **Space Shuttle Endeavour,** *Aug. 4, 1995* Irvine CA *(10,534)* 15.00

1991

2549a 29c **Fishing Flies booklet pane of 5,** *May 31,* Cuddebackville, NY *(1,045,726)* 3.00
2545-2549, any single 1.25
2550 29c **Cole Porter,** *June 8,* Peru, IN *(304,363)* 1.25
2551 29c **Desert Storm/ Desert Shield,** *July 2* 2.50
2552 29c **Desert Storm/ Desert Shield,** bklt. single, *July 2* 2.50
2552a Booklet pane of 5 5.00

First day cancel was applied to 860,455 covers bearing one or more of Nos. 2551-2552, 2552a.

2557a 29c **Summer Olympics,** *July 12,* Los Angeles, CA *(886,984)* 3.00
2553-2557, any single 1.25
2558 29c **Numismatics,** *Aug. 13,* Chicago, IL *(288,519)* 1.25
2559 29c **World War II block of 10,** *Sept. 3,* Phoenix, AZ *(1,832,967)* 7.00
2559a-2559j, any single 2.50
2560 29c **Basketball,** *Aug. 28,* Springfield, MA *(295,471)* 2.25
2561 29c **District of Columbia,** *Sept. 7 (299,989)* 1.25
2566a 29c **Comedians booklet pane of 10,** *Aug. 29,* Hollywood, CA 3.00
2562-2566, any single 1.25

First day cancel was applied to 954,293 covers bearing one or more of Nos. 2562-2566a.

2567 29c **Jan Matzeliger,** *Sept. 15,* Lynn, MA *(289,034)* 1.75
2577a 29c **Space Exploration booklet pane of 10,** *Oct. 1,* Pasadena, CA 5.00
2568-2577, any single 1.25

First day cancel was applied to 1,465,111 covers bearing one or more of Nos. 2568-2577a.

2578 (29c) **Christmas (religious),** *Oct. 17,* Houston, TX 1.25
2579 (29c) **Christmas (secular),** *Oct. 17,* Santa, ID *(169,750)* 1.25
2581b (29c) **Christmas booklet pane of 4,** *Oct. 17,* Santa, ID 2.50
2580-2581, any single 1.25
2582 (29c) **Christmas,** bklt. single, *Oct. 17,* Santa, ID 1.25
2582a Booklet pane of 4 2.50
2583 (29c) **Christmas,** bklt. single, *Oct. 17,* Santa, ID 1.25
2583a Booklet pane of 4 2.50
2584 (29c) **Christmas,** bklt. single, *Oct. 17,* Santa, ID 1.25
2584a Booklet pane of 4 2.50
2585 (29c) **Christmas,** bklt. single, *Oct. 17,* Santa, ID 1.25
2585a Booklet pane of 4 2.50

First day cancel was applied to 168,794 covers bearing one or more of Nos. 2580-2585, 2581b, 2582a, 2583a, 2584a and 2585a.

1991-95

2587 32c **James K. Polk,** *Nov. 2, 1995,* Columbia TN *(189,429)* 1.25
2590 $1 **Surrender of Gen. John Burgoyne,** *May 5, 1994,* New York, NY *(379,629)* 2.50
2592 $5 **Washington & Jackson,** *Aug. 19, 1994,* Pittsburgh, PA *(16,303)* 12.50
2593 29c **Pledge of Allegiance,** black denomination, *Sept. 8, 1992,* Rome, NY 1.25
2593a Booklet pane of 10 5.00

First day cancel was applied to 61,464 covers bearing one or more of Nos. 2593-2593a.

2595 29c **Eagle & Shield,** brown denomination, *Sept. 25, 1992,* Dayton, OH 1.50
2596 29c **Eagle & Shield,** green denomination, *Sept. 25, 1992,* Dayton, OH 1.50
2597 29c **Eagle & Shield,** red denomination, *Sept. 25, 1992,* Dayton, OH 1.50

First day cancel was applied to 65,822 covers bearing one or more of Nos. 2595-2597.

2598 29c **Eagle,** *Feb. 4, 1994,* Sarasota, FL *(67,300)* 1.25
2599 29c **Statue of Liberty,** *June 24, 1994,* Haines City, FL *(39,810)* 1.25
2602 (10c) **Eagle & Shield,** Bulk Rate USA, *Dec. 13, 1991,* Kansas City, MO *(21,176)* 1.25
2603 (10c) **Eagle & Shield,** USA Bulk Rate, *May 29, 1993,* Secaucus, NJ 1.25
2604 (10c) **Eagle & Shield,** gold eagle, *May 29, 1993,* Secaucus, NJ 1.25

First day cancellation was applied to 36,444 covers bearing one or more of Nos. 2603-2604.

2605 23c **Flag,** *Sept. 27, 1991* 1.25
2606 23c **Reflected Flag,** *July 21, 1992,* Kansas City, MO *(35,673)* 1.25
2607 23c **Reflected Flag,** 7mm "23," *Oct. 9, 1992,* Kansas City, MO 1.25
2608 23c **Reflected Flag,** 8 ½mm "First Class" *May 14, 1993,* Denver, CO *(15,548)* 1.25
2609 29c **Flag over White House,** *Apr. 23, 1992 (56,505)* 1.25

1992

2615a 29c **Winter Olympics,** *Jan. 11,* Orlando, FL *(1,062,048)* 3.50
2611-2615, any single 1.25
2616 29c **World Columbian Stamp Expo,** *Jan. 24,* Rosemont, IL *(309,729)* 1.25
2617 29c **W.E.B. Du Bois,** *Jan. 31,* Atlanta, GA *(196,219)* 1.75
2618 29c **Love,** *Feb. 6,* Loveland, CO *(218,043)* 1.25
2619 29c **Olympic Baseball,** *Apr. 3,* Atlanta, GA *(105,996)* 2.00
2623a 29c **Voyages of Columbus,** *Apr. 24,* Christiansted, VI 2.75
2620-2623, any single 1.25

First day cancellation was applied to 509,270 covers bearing one or more of Nos. 2620-2623a.

2624 **First Sighting of Land Souvenir Sheet of 3,** *May 22,* Chicago, IL 3.50
2624a 1c 1.50
2624b 4c 1.50
2624c $1 2.50
2625 **Claiming a New World Souvenir Sheet of 3,** *May 22,* Chicago, IL 9.00
2625a 2c 1.50
2625b 3c 1.50
2625c $4 8.00
2626 **Seeking Royal Support Souvenir Sheet of 3,** *May 22,* Chicago, IL 3.00
2626a 5c 1.50
2626b 30c 1.50
2626c 50c 2.00
2627 **Royal Favor Restored Souvenir Sheet of 3,** *May 22,* Chicago, IL 7.50
2627a 6c 1.50
2627b 8c 1.50
2627c $3 7.50
2628 **Reporting Discoveries Souvenir Sheet of 3,** *May 22,* Chicago, IL 8.50
2628a 10c 1.50
2628b 15c 1.50
2628c $2 5.00
2629 $5 **Christopher Columbus Souvenir Sheet,** *May 22,* Chicago, IL 12.50

First day cancel was applied to 211,142 covers bearing one or more of Nos. 2624-2629.

2630 29c **New York Stock Exchange,** *May 17,* New York, NY *(261,897)* 2.50
2634a 29c **Space Accomplishments,** *May 29,* Chicago, IL 2.75
2631-2634, any single 1.50

First day cancel was applied to 277,853 covers bearing one or more of Nos. 2631-2634a.

2635 29c **Alaska Highway,** *May 30,* Fairbanks, AK *(186,791)* 1.25
2636 29c **Kentucky,** *June 1,* Danville, KY *(251,153)* 1.25
2641a 29c **Summer Olympics,** *June 11,* Baltimore, MD *(713,942)* 3.00
2637-2641, any single 1.25
2646a 29c **Hummingbirds booklet pane of 5,** *June 15* 3.00
2642-2646, any single 1.25

First day cancel was applied to 995,278 covers bearing one or more of Nos. 2642-2646a.

2696a 29c **Wildflowers,** *July 24,* Columbus, OH 30.00
2647-2696, any single 1.25

First day cancellation was applied to 3,693,972 covers bearing one or more of Nos. 2647-2696a.

2697 29c **World War II block of 10,** *Aug. 17,* Indianapolis, IN *(1,734,880)* 7.00
2697a-2697j, any single 2.50

First day cancellation was applied to 1,734,880 covers bearing one or more of Nos. 2697, 2697a-2697j.

2698 29c **Dorothy Parker,** *Aug. 22,* West End, NJ *(266,323)* 1.50
2699 29c **Theodore von Karman,** *Aug. 31 (256,986)* 1.50
2703a 29c **Minerals,** *Sept. 17* 2.75
2700-2703, any single 1.25

First day cancellation was applied to 681,416 covers bearing one or more of Nos. 2700-2703.

2704 29c **Juan Rodriguez Cabrillo,** *Sept. 28,* San Diego, CA *(290,720)* 1.25
2709a 29c **Wild Animals booklet pane of 5,** *Oct. 1,* New Orleans, LA 3.25
Any other city 4.00
2705-2709, any single 1.25

First day cancel was applied to 604,205 New Orleans covers bearing one or more of Nos. 2705-2709a.

2710 29c **Christmas (religious),** *Oct. 22* 1.25
2710a Booklet pane of 10 7.25

First day cancel was applied to 201,576 covers bearing one or more of Nos. 2710-2710a.

2714a 29c **Christmas (secular),** *Oct. 22,* Kansas City, MO 2.75
2711-2714, any single 1.25
2718a 29c **Christmas (secular) booklet pane of 4,** *Oct. 22,* Kansas City, MO 2.75
2715-2718, any single 1.25

First day cancel was applied to 461,937 covers bearing one or more of Nos. 2711-2714, 2715-2718 and 2718a.

2719 29c **Christmas (secular),** self-adhesive, *Oct. 28,* New York, NY *(48,873)* 1.25
2720 29c **Chinese New Year,** *Dec. 30,* San Francisco, CA *(138,238)* 2.25

1993

2721 29c **Elvis (Presley),** *Jan. 8,* Memphis, TN, AM cancellation, *(4,452,815)* 2.00
Any city, PM cancellation 3.00
2722 29c **Oklahoma!,** *Mar. 30,* Oklahoma City, OK *(283,837)* 1.25
2723 29c **Hank Williams,** perf 10, *June 9,* Nashville, TN 1.25
2723A 29c **Hank Williams,** perf 11.2x11.5, *June 9,* Nashville, TN —

First day cancel was applied to 311,106 covers bearing one or more of Nos. 2723-2723A.

2730a 29c **Rock & Roll/Rhythm & Blues Musicians,** *June 16,* Cleveland OH or Santa Monica CA 5.00
Any other city 5.00
2724-2730, any single 1.25
Any single, any other city 1.25

Value for No. 2730a is also for any se-tenant configuration of seven different stamps.
First day cancel was applied to 540,809 covers bearing one or more of Nos. 2724-2730a, 2731-2737b.

2737a 29c **Rock & Roll/Rhythm & Blues Musicians booklet pane of 8,** *June 16,* Cleveland, OH or Santa Monica CA 5.25
Any other city 5.25
2731-2737, any single 1.25
Any single, any other city 1.25
2737b 29c **Rock & Roll/Rhythm & Blues Musicians booklet pane of 4,** *June 16,* Cleveland, OH or Santa Monica CA 2.75
Any other city 2.75

For first day cancellation quantities, see No. 2730a.

2745a 29c **Space Fantasy booklet pane of 5,** *Jan. 25,* Huntsville, AL 3.25
2741-2745, any single 1.25

First day cancel was applied to 631,203 covers bearing one or more of Nos. 2741-2745a.

2746 29c **Percy Lavon Julian,** *Jan. 29,* Chicago, IL *(120,877)* 1.75
2747 29c **Oregon Trail,** *Feb. 12,* Salem, OR *(436,550)* 1.25

No. 2747 was also available on the first day of issue in 36 cities along the route of the Oregon Trail.

2748 29c **World University Games,** *Feb. 25,* Buffalo, NY *(157,563)* 1.50
2749 29c **Grace Kelly,** *Mar. 24,* Beverly Hills, CA *(263,913)* 3.50
2753a 29c **Circus,** *Apr. 6* 3.00
2750-2753, any single 1.50

First day cancel was applied to 676,927 covers bearing one or more of Nos. 2750-2753a.

2754 29c **Cherokee Strip Land Run,** *Apr. 17,* Enid, OK *(260,118)* 1.25
2755 29c **Dean Acheson,** *Apr. 21, (158,783)* 1.25
2759a 29c **Sporting Horses,** *May 1,* Louisville, KY 4.00
2756-2759, any single 2.00

First day cancel was applied to 448,059 covers bearing one or more of Nos. 2756-2759a.

2764a 29c **Garden Flowers booklet pane of 5,** *May 15,* Spokane, WA 3.00
2760-2764, any single 1.50

First day cancel was applied to 492,578 covers bearing one or more of Nos. 2760-2764a.

2765 29c **World War II block of 10,** *May 31,* 7.00
2765a-2765j, any single 2.50

First day cancel was applied to 543,511 covers bearing one or more of Nos. 2765, 2765a-2765j.

2766 29c **Joe Louis,** *June 22,* Detroit, MI *(229,272)* 3.00
2770a 29c **Broadway Musicals booklet pane of 4,** *July 14,* New York, NY 3.50
2767-2770, any single 1.25

First day cancel was applied to 308,231 covers bearing one or more of Nos. 2767-2770a.

2774a 29c **Country Music,** *Sept. 25,* Nashville, TN 3.00
2771-2774, any single 1.25
2778a 29c **Country Music booklet pane of 4,** *Sept. 25,* Nashville, TN 3.00
2775-2778, any single 1.25

First day cancel was applied to 362,904 covers bearing one or more of Nos. 2771-2774a, 2775-2778a.

2782a 29c **National Postal Museum,** *July 30* 2.75
2779-2782, any single 1.25

First day cancel was applied to 371,115 covers bearing one or more of Nos. 2779-2782a.

2784a 29c **Deafness/Sign Language,** *Sept. 20,* Burbank, CA 2.50
2783-2784, any single 1.50

First day cancel was applied to 112,350 covers bearing one or more of Nos. 2783-2784a.

2788a 29c **Classic Books,** *Oct. 23,* Louisville, KY 2.75
2785-2788, any single 1.25

First day cancel was applied to 269,457 covers bearing one or more of Nos. 2785-2788a.

2789 29c **Christmas (religious),** *Oct. 21,* Raleigh, NC 1.25
2790 29c **Christmas (religious),** booklet single, *Oct. 21,* Raleigh, NC 1.25
2790a Booklet pane of 4 2.50

First day cancellation was applied to 155,192 covers bearing one or more of Nos. 2789-2790a.

2794a 29c **Christmas (secular),** sheet stamps, *Oct. 21,* New York, NY 2.75
2791-2794, any single 1.25
2798a 29c **Christmas (secular) booklet pane of 10,** *Oct. 21,* New York, NY 6.50
2798b 29c **Christmas (secular) booklet pane of 10,** *Oct. 21,* New York, NY 6.50
2795-2798, any single 1.25
2799 29c **Christmas (snowman),** large self-adhesive, *Oct. 28,* New York, NY 1.25
2800 29c **Christmas (soldier),** self-adhesive, *Oct. 28,* New York, NY 1.25
2801 29c **Christmas (jack-in-the-box),** self-adhesive, *Oct. 28,* New York, NY 1.25
2802 29c **Christmas (reindeer),** self-adhesive, *Oct. 28,* New York, NY 1.25
2799-2802 on one cover 2.50
2803 29c **Christmas (snowman),** small self-adhesive, *Oct. 28,* New York, NY 1.25

First day cancel was applied to 384,262 covers bearing one or more of Nos. 2791-2794a, 2795-2798b, 2799-2803.

2804 29c **Mariana Islands,** *Nov. 4,* Saipan, MP *(157,410)* 1.25
2805 29c **Columbus' Landing in Puerto Rico,** *Nov. 19,* San Juan, PR *(222,845)* 1.25
2806 29c **AIDS Awareness,** *Dec. 1,* New York, NY 2.00
2806a Booklet single, perf. 11 vert. 2.00
2806b Booklet pane of 5 4.00

First day cancellation was applied to 209,200 covers bearing one or more of Nos. 2806-2806b.

1994

2811a 29c **Winter Olympics,** *Jan. 6,* Salt Lake City, UT 3.00
2807-2811, any single 1.25

First day cancellation was applied to 645,636 covers bearing one or more of Nos. 2807-2811a.

2812 29c **Edward R. Murrow,** *Jan. 21,* Pullman, WA *(154,638)* 1.25
2813 29c **Love,** self-adhesive, *Jan. 27,* Loveland, OH *(125,146)* 1.25
2814 29c **Love,** booklet single, *Feb. 14,* Niagara Falls, NY 1.25
2814a Booklet pane of 10 6.50
2814C 29c **Love,** *June 11,* Niagara Falls, NY *(42,109)* 1.25
2815 52c **Love,** *Feb. 14,* Niagara Falls, NY 1.50
2816 29c **Dr. Allison Davis,** *Feb. 1,* Williamstown, MA *(162,404)* 2.00
2817 29c **Chinese New Year,** *Feb. 5,* Pomona, CA *(148,492)* 2.00
2818 29c **Buffalo Soldiers,** *Apr. 22,* Dallas, TX *(107,223)* 3.00

No. 2818 was also available on the first day of issue in forts in Kansas, Texas and Arizona.

2828a 29c **Silent Screen Stars,** *Apr. 27,* San Francisco, CA 6.50
2819-2828, any single 2.00

First day cancellation was applied to 591,251 covers bearing one or more of Nos. 2819-2828a.

2833a 29c **Garden Flowers booklet pane of 5,** *Apr. 28,* Cincinnati, OH 3.25
2829-2833, any single 1.25

First day cancellation was applied to 153,069 covers bearing one or more of Nos. 2829-2833a.

2834 29c **World Cup Soccer,** *May 26,* New York, NY 2.00
2835 40c **World Cup Soccer,** *May 26,* New York, NY 2.00
2836 50c **World Cup Soccer,** *May 26,* New York, NY 2.00

First day cancellation was applied to 443,768 covers bearing one or more of Nos. 2834-2836.

2837 **World Cup Soccer souvenir sheet of 3,** *May 26,* New York, NY *(59,503)* 4.00
2838 29c **World War II block of 10,** *June 6,* USS Normandy 7.00
2838a-2838j, any single 2.50

No. 2838 was also available on the first day of issue in 13 other locations.
First day cancellation was applied to 744,267 covers bearing one or more of Nos. 2838, 2838a-2838j.

2839 29c **Norman Rockwell,** *July 1,* Stockbridge, MA *(232,076)* 1.50
2840 50c **Norman Rockwell Souvenir Sheet of 4,** *July 1,* Stockbridge, MA 4.00
2840a-2840d, any single 2.00

First day cancellation was applied to 19,734 covers bearing one or more of Nos. 2840-2840d.

2841 29c **Moon Landing Sheet of 12,** *July 20,* Washington, DC 6.50
2841a, single stamp 2.00

First day cancellation was applied to 303,707 covers bearing one or more of Nos. 2841-2841a.

2842 $9.95 **Moon Landing,** *July 20,* Washington, DC *(11,463)* 25.00
2847a 29c **Locomotives booklet pane of 5,** *July 28,* Chama, NM 5.00
2843-2847, any single 1.75

First day cancellation was applied to 169,016 covers bearing one or more of Nos. 2843-2847a.

2848 29c **George Meany,** *Aug. 16 (172,418)* 1.25
2853a 29c **American Music Series,** *Sept. 1,* New York, NY 4.50
2849-2853, any single 1.50

First day cancellation was applied to 156,049 covers bearing one or more of Nos. 2849-2853a.

2861a 29c **American Music Series,** *Sept. 17,* Greenville MS 6.00
2854-2861, any single 1.25

First day cancellation was applied to 483,737 covers bearing one or more of Nos. 2854-2861a.
Nos. 2854-2861 were available on the first day in 9 other cities.

2862 29c **James Thurber,** *Sept. 10,* Columbus OH *(39,064)* 1.25
2866a 29c **Wonders of the Sea,** *Oct. 3,* Honolulu HI 2.75
2863-2866, any single 1.25

First day cancellation was applied to 284,678 covers bearing one or more of Nos. 2863-2866a.

2868a 29c **Cranes,** *Oct. 9* 2.50
2867-2868, any single 1.25

First day cancellation was applied to 202,955 covers bearing one or more of Nos. 2867-2868a, 24,942 with the People's Republic of China stamps.

2869 29c **Legends of the West Pane of 20,** *Oct. 18,* Laramie WY *(429,680)* 15.00
Tucson, AZ *(220,417)* 15.00
Lawton, OK *(191,393)* 15.00
2869a-2869t, any single, any city 2.50

First day cancellation was applied to covers bearing one or more of Nos. 2869-2869t.

2871 29c **Christmas (religious),** perf 11¼, *Oct. 20 (155,192)* 1.25
2871A 29c **Christmas (religious),** perf 9¾x11, *Oct. 20 (155,192)* 1.25
2872 29c **Christmas (stocking),** *Oct. 20,* Harmony MN 1.25
2873 29c **Christmas (Santa Claus),** self-adhesive, *Oct. 20,* Harmony MN 1.25
2874 29c **Christmas (cardinal),** small self-adhesive, *Oct. 20,* Harmony MN 1.25

First day cancellation was applied to 132,005 covers bearing one or more of Nos. 2872, 2872a, 2873, 2874.

2875 $2 **Bureau of Printing and Engraving Souvenir sheet,** *Nov. 3,* New York, NY *(13,126)* 25.00
2875a $2 Single stamp 7.00
2876 29c **Chinese New Year (Boar),** *Dec. 30,* Sacramento CA 1.75
2877 (3c) **Dove, bright blue,** *Dec. 13* 1.25
2878 (3c) **Dove, dark blue,** *Dec. 13* 1.25
2879 (20c) **G, black,** *Dec. 13* 1.25
2880 (20c) **G, red,** *Dec. 13* 1.25
2881 (32c) **G, black,** *Dec. 13* 1.25
2881a Booklet pane of 10 6.75
2882 (32c) **G, red,** *Dec. 13* 1.25
2883 (32c) **G, black,** *Dec. 13* 1.25
2883a Booklet pane of 10 6.75
2884 (32c) **G, black,** *Dec. 13* 1.25
2884a Booklet pane of 10 6.75
2885 (32c) **G, red,** *Dec. 13* 1.25
2885a Booklet pane of 10 6.75
2886 (32c) **G, gray, blue, light blue, red & black,** self-adhesive, *Dec. 13* 1.25
2887 (32c) **G, black, blue & red,** self-adhesive, *Dec. 13* 1.25
2888 (25c) **G, black,** coil, *Dec. 13* 1.25
2889 (32c) **G, black,** coil, *Dec. 13* 1.25
2890 (32c) **G, blue,** coil, *Dec. 13* 1.25
2891 (32c) **G, red,** coil, *Dec. 13* 1.25
2892 (32c) **G, red,** rouletted coil, *Dec. 13* 1.25

Originally, No. 2893 (the 5c green Non-profit Presort G rate stamp) was only available through the Philatelic Fullfillment Center after their announcement 1/12/95. Requests for first day cancels received a 12/13/94 cancel, even though they were not available on that date. Value, $1.25.
First day cancellation was applied to 338,107 covers bearing one or more of Nos. 2877-2893(?), and U633-U634.

2897 32c **Flag Over Porch,** *May 19,* Denver CO 1.25

First day cancellation was applied to 66,609 covers bearing one or more of Nos. 2897, 2913-2914, 2916 and possibly, 2920.

1995-98

2902 (5c) **Butte,** coil, *Mar. 10,* State College PA 1.25

First day cancellation was applied to 80,003 covers bearing one or more of Nos. 2902, 2905, and U635-U636.

2902B (5c) **Butte,** self-adhesive coil, *June 15, 1996,* San Antonio TX 1.25

First day cancellation was applied to 87,400 covers bearing one or more of Nos. 2902B, 2904A, 2906, 2910, 2912A, 2915B.

2903 (5c) **Mountain,** purple & multi coil, *Mar. 16, 1996* San Jose CA 1.25
2904 (5c) **Mountain,** blue & multi coil, *Mar. 16,1996* San Jose CA 1.25

First day cancellation was applied to 28,064 covers bearing one or more of Nos. 2903-2904.

2904A (5c) **Mountain,** purple & multi self-adhesive coil, *June 15, 1996,* San Antonio TX 1.25

First day cancellation was applied to 87,400 covers bearing one or more of Nos. 2902B, 2904A, 2906, 2910, 2912A, 2915B.

2904B (5c) **Mountain,** purple & multi self-adhesive coil, inscription outlined, *Jan. 24, 1997,* Tucson, AZ 1.25
2905 (10c) **Auto,** coil, *Mar. 10,* State College PA 1.25
2906 (10c) **Auto,** self-adhesive coil, *June 15, 1996* San Antonio TX 1.25

First day cancellation was applied to 87,400 covers bearing one or more of Nos. 2902B, 2904A, 2906, 2910, 2912A, 2915B.

2907 (10c) **Eagle & Shield,** USA Bulk Rate self-adhesive coil, *May 21, 1996* 1.25

First day cancellation was applied to 54,102 covers bearing one or more of Nos. 2907, 2915A, 2915C, 2921.

2908 (15c) **Auto tail fin (dark orange yellow),** coil, *Mar. 17,* New York NY 1.25
2909 (15c) **Auto tail fin (buff),** coil, *Mar. 17,* New York, NY 1.25

First day cancellation was applied to 93,770 covers bearing one or more of Nos. 2908-2909, 2911-2912, 2919.

2910 (15c) **Auto tail fin (buff),** self-adhesive coil, *June 15, 1996,* San Antonio TX 1.25

First day cancellation was applied to 87,400 covers bearing one or more of Nos. 2902B, 2904A, 2906, 2910, 2915B.

2911 (25c) **Juke box,** coil, *Mar. 17,* New York NY 1.25
2912 (25c) **Juke box,** coil, *Mar. 17,* New York NY 1.25

First day cancellation was applied to 93,770 covers bearing one or more of Nos. 2908-2909, 2911-2912, 2919.

2912A (25c) **Juke box,** self-adhesive coil, bright orange red & multi, microperfs, *June 15, 1996,* New York NY 1.25

First day cancellation was applied to 87,400 covers bearing one or more of Nos. 2902B, 2904A, 2906, 2910, 2912A, 2915B.

2912B (25c) **Juke box,** self-adhesive coil, dark red & multi, *Jan. 24, 1997,* Tucson, AZ 1.25
2913 32c **Flag Over Porch,** coil, *May 19,* Denver CO 1.25
2914 32c **Flag Over Porch,** coil, *May 19,* Denver CO 1.25
2915 32c **Flag Over Porch,** self-adhesive, die cut 8.7 vert., *Apr. 18* 1.25
2915A 32c **Flag Over Porch,** self-adhesive, die cut 9.8 vert., 11 teeth, *May 21, 1996* 1.25
2915B 32c **Flag Over Porch,** self-adhesive die cut 11.5 vert., *June 15, 1996,* San Antonio TX 1.25

First day cancellation was applied to 87,400 covers bearing one or more of Nos. 2902B, 2904A, 2906, 2910, 2912A, 2915B.

2915C 32c **Flag Over Porch,** self-adhesive, die cut 10.9, *May 21, 1996* 2.00
2915D 32c **Flag Over Porch,** self-adhesive coil, self-adhesive die cut 9.8 vert., 9 teeth, *Jan. 24, 1997,* Tucson, AZ 1.25

First day cancellation was applied to 56,774 covers bearing one or more of Nos. 2904B, 2912B, 2915D and 2921b.

2916 32c **Flag Over Porch,** booklet single, *May 19,* Denver CO 1.25
2916a Booklet pane of 10 7.50
2919 32c **Flag Over Field,** self-adhesive, *Mar. 17,* New York NY 1.25

First day cancellation was applied to 93,770 covers bearing one or more of Nos. 2908-2909, 2911-2912, 2919.

2920 32c **Flag Over Porch,** self-adhesive, *Apr. 18* 1.25

First day cancellation was applied to 66,609 covers bearing one or more of Nos. 2897, 2913-2914, 2916 and possibly, 2920.
First day cancellation was applied to 57,639 covers bearing one or more of Nos. 2920d, 3030, 3044.

2921 32c **Flag Over Porch,** self-adhesive, booklet stamp, die cut 9.8 on 2 or 3 sides, *May 21, 1996* 1.25

First day cancellation was applied to 54,102 covers bearing one or more of Nos. 2907, 2915A, 2915C, 2921.

GREAT AMERICANS ISSUE

2933 32c **Milton Hershey,** *Sept. 13,* Hershey PA *(121,228)* 1.25
2934 32c **Cal Farley,** *Apr. 26, 1996,* Amarillo TX *(109,440)* 1.25
2935 32c **Henry Luce,** *Apr. 3, 1998,* New York NY *(76,982)* 1.25
2936 32c **Wallace,** *July 16, 1998,* Pleasantville NY *(72,183)* 1.25
2938 46c **Ruth Benedict,** *Oct. 20,* Virginia Beach VA *(24,793)* 1.40
2940 55c **Alice Hamilton,** *July 11,* Boston MA *(24,225)* 1.40
2941 55c **Justin Morrill,** *July 17, 1999* Strafford VT *(19,699)* 1.40
2942 77c **Mary Breckinridge,** *Nov. 9, 1998* Troy, NY 1.75

First day cancellation was applied to 121,662 covers bearing one or more of Nos. 2942, 3257-3261, 3263-3269.

2943 78c **Alice Paul,** *Aug. 18,* Mount Laurel NJ *(25,071)* 1.75

1995

2948 (32c) **Love,** *Feb. 1,* Valentines VA 1.50
2949 (32c) **Love,** self-adhesive, *Feb. 1,* Valentines VA 1.50

First day cancellation was applied to 70,778 covers bearing one or more of Nos. 2948, 2949.

2950 32c **Florida Statehood,** *Mar. 3,* Tallahassee FL *(167,499)* 1.25
2954a 32c **Earth Day,** *Apr. 20* 2.75
2951-2954, any single 1.25

First day cancellation was applied to 328,893 covers bearing one or more of Nos. 2951-2954, 2954a.

2955 32c **Richard Nixon,** *Apr. 26,* Yorba Linda CA *(377,605)* 1.25
2956 32c **Bessie Coleman,** *Apr. 27,* Chicago IL *(299,834)* 1.75
2957 32c **Love,** *May 12,* Lakeville PA 1.25
2958 55c **Love,** *May 12,* Lakeville PA 1.25
2959 32c **Love,** booklet single, *May 12,* Lakeville PA 1.25
2959a Booklet pane of 10 7.50
2960 55c **Love,** self-adhesive, *May 12,* Lakeville PA 1.40

First day cancellation was applied to 273,350 covers bearing one or more of Nos. 2957-2959, 2959a, and U637.

2965a 32c **Recreational Sports,** *May 20,* Jupiter FL 3.25
2961-2965, any single 1.50

First day cancellation was applied to 909,807 covers bearing one or more of Nos. 2961-2965, 2965a.

2966 32c **Prisoners of War & Missing in Action,** *May 29 (231,857)* 3.00
2967 32c **Marilyn Monroe,** *June 1,* Universal City CA *(703,219)* 3.25
Any other city 2.00
2968 32c **Texas Statehood,** *June 16,* Austin TX *(177,550)* 1.75
2973a 32c **Great Lakes Lighthouses booklet pane of 5,** *June 17,* Cheboygan MI 5.00
2969-2973, any single 2.00

First day cancellation was applied to 626,055 covers bearing one or more of Nos. 2969-2973, 2973a.

2974 32c **UN, 50th Anniv.,** *June 26,* San Francisco CA *(160,383)* 1.50
2975 32c **Civil War pane of 20,** *June 29,* Gettysburg PA 16.00
Any other city 16.00
2975a-2975t, any single, Gettysburg PA 2.50
Any other city 2.00

First day cancellation was applied to 1,950,134 covers bearing one or more of Nos. 2975, 2975a-2975t, and UX200-UX219.

2979a 32c **Carousel Horses,** *July 21,* Lahaska PA 3.25
2976-2979, any single 1.25

First day cancellation was applied to 479,038 covers bearing one or more of Nos. 2976-2979, 2979a.

2980 32c **Woman Suffrage,** *Aug. 26 (196,581)* 1.25
2981 32c **World War II block of 10,** *Sept. 2,* Honolulu HI 7.00
2981a-2981j, any single 2.50

First day cancellation was applied to 1,562,094 covers bearing one or more of Nos. 2981, 2981a-2981j.

2982 32c **American Music Series,** *Sept. 1,* New Orleans LA *(258,996)* 1.75
2992a 32c **American Music Series,** *Sept. 16,* Monterey CA 6.50
2983-2992, any single 1.50

First day cancellation was applied to 629,956 covers bearing one or more of Nos. 2983-2992, 2992a.

2997a 32c **Garden Flowers booklet pane of 5,** *Sept. 19,* Encinitas CA 4.00
2993-2997, any single 1.25

First day cancellation was applied to 564,905 covers bearing one or more of Nos. 2993-2997, 2997a.

2998 60c **Eddie Rickenbacker,** *Sept. 25,* Columbus OH *(24,283)* 1.75
2999 32c **Republic of Palau,** *Sept. 29,* Agana GU *(157,377)* 1.25
3000 32c **Comic Strips Pane of 20,** *Oct. 1,* Boca Raton FL 13.00
3000a-3000t, any single 2.00

First day cancellation was applied to 1,362,990 covers bearing one or more of Nos. 3000, 3000a-3000t.

3001 32c **US Naval Academy,** *Oct. 10,* Annapolis, MD *(222,183)* 2.00
3002 32c **Tennessee Williams,** *Oct. 13,* Clarksdale MS *(209,812)* 1.25
3003 32c **Christmas, Madonna,** perf 11.2, *Oct. 19* 1.25
3003A 32c **Christmas, Madonna,** perf
3003Ab Booklet pane of 10 7.25

First day cancellation was applied to 223,301 covers bearing one or more of Nos. 3003, 3003A-3003Ab.

3007a 32c **Christmas (secular) sheet,** *Sept. 30,* North Pole NY 3.25
3004-3007, any single 1.25
3007b 32c Booklet pane of 10, 3 #3004, etc. 7.25
3007c 32c Booklet pane of 10, 2 #3004, etc. 7.25

First day cancellation was applied to 487,816 covers bearing one or more of Nos. 3004-3007, 3007a.

3008-3011 32c **Christmas (secular) self-adhesive booklet stamps,** *Sept. 30,* North Pole NY 3.25
3008-3011, any single 1.25
3012 32c **Angel,** *Oct. 19,* Christmas FL 1.25
3013 32c **Children sledding,** *Oct. 19,* Christmas FL 1.25

First day cancellation was applied to 77,675 covers bearing one or more of Nos. 3012, 3013, 3018.

3014-3017 32c **Self-adhesive coils,** *Sept. 30,* North Pole NY 2.50
3014-3017, any single 1.25
3018 32c **Self-adhesive coil,** *Oct. 19,* Christmas FL 1.25

First day cancellation was applied to 77,675 covers bearing one or more of Nos. 3012, 3013, 3018.

3023a 32c **Antique Automobiles,** *Nov. 3,* New York NY 3.00
3019-3023, any single 1.25

First day cancellation was applied to 757,003 covers bearing one or more of Nos. 3019-3023, 3023a.

1996

3024 32c **Utah Statehood Cent.,** *Jan. 4,* Salt Lake City UT *(207,089)* 1.25
3029a 32c **Garden Flowers booklet pane,** *Jan. 19,* Kennett Square PA 3.50
3025-3029, any single 1.25

First day cancellation was applied to 876,176 covers bearing one or more of Nos. 3025-3029, 3029a.

3030 32c **Love self-adhesive,** *Jan. 20,* New York NY 1.25

First day cancellation was applied to 57,639 covers bearing one or more of Nos. 2920d, 3030, 3044.

FLORA AND FAUNA ISSUE

1996-2000

3031 1c **Kestrel,** *Nov. 19, 1999,* New York, NY *(14,431)* 1.50
3032 2c **Red-headed woodpecker,** *Feb. 2,* Sarasota FL *(37,319)* 1.25
3033 3c **Eastern Bluebird,** *Apr. 3 (23,405)* 1.25
3036 $1 **Red Fox,** *Aug. 14, 1998* 3.50

First day cancellation was applied to 46,557 covers bearing one or more of Nos. 3228-3229, 3036.

3044 1c **American Kestrel, coil,** *Jan. 20,* New York NY 1.25

First day cancellation was applied to 57,639 covers bearing one or more of Nos. 2920d, 3030, 3044.

3045 2c **Red-Headed Woodpecker,** *June 22, 1999 (14,377)* 1.25
3048 20c **Blue Jay, booklet stamp, self-adhesive,** *Aug. 2,* St. Louis MO 1.25

First day cancellation was applied to 32,633 covers bearing one or more of Nos. 3048, 3053.

3049 32c **Yellow Rose, booklet stamp, self-adhesive,** *Oct. 24,* Pasadena, CA *(7,849)* 1.25
3050 20c **Ring-necked Pheasant, booklet stamp, self-adhesive,** *July 31, 1998* Somerset NJ 1.25

First day cancellation was applied to 32,220 covers bearing one or more of Nos. 3050, 3055.

3052 33c **Coral Pink Rose,** serpentine die cut 11½x11¼, *Aug. 13, 1999,* Indianapolis, IN 1.25
3052E 33c **Coral Pink Rose,** serpentine die cut 10¾x10½, *Apr. 7, 2000,* New York, NY *(18,199)* 1.25
3053 20c **Blue Jay, coil, self-adhesive,** *Aug. 2,* St. Louis MO 1.25
3054 32c **Yellow Rose, self-adhesive,** *Aug. 1, 1997,* Falls Church VA *(20,029)* 1.25
3055 20c **Ring-necked Pheasant,coil, self-adhesive,** *July 31, 1998* Somerset NJ 1.25

First day cancellation was applied to 32,220 covers bearing one or more of Nos. 3050, 3055.

1996

3058 32c **Ernest E. Just,** *Feb. 1 (191,360)* 1.75
3059 32c **Smithsonian, 150th anniv.,** *Feb. 7, (221,399)* 1.25
3060 32c **Chinese New Year,** *Feb. 8,* San Francisco CA *(237,451)* 1.75
3064a 32c **Pioneers of Communication,** *Feb. 22,* New York NY 2.50
3061-3064, any single 1.25

First day cancellation was applied to 567,205 covers bearing one or more of Nos. 3061-3064, 3064a.

3065 32c **Fulbright Scholarships,** *Feb. 28,* Fayetteville AR *(227,330)* 1.25
3066 50c **Jacqueline Cochran,** *Mar. 9,* Indio CA *(30,628)* 1.75
3067 32c **Marathon,** *Apr. 11,* Boston MA *(177,050)* 2.00
3068 32c **Olympics, pane of 20,** *May 2* 13.00
3068a-3068t, any single 1.25
Atlanta, GA —

Washington DC first day cancellation was applied to 1,807,316 covers bearing one or more of Nos. 3068, 3068a-3068t. Atlanta was also an official first day city, and covers postmarked there are scarce.

3069 32c **Georgia O'Keeffe,** *May 23,* Santa Fe NM *(200,522)* 1.50
3070 32c **Tennessee Statehood, Bicen.,** *May 31,* Knoxville, Memphis or Nashville TN 1.25
3071 32c **Tennessee, self-adhesive,** *May 31,* Knoxville, Memphis or Nashville TN 1.25

First day cancellation was applied to 217,281 covers bearing one or more of Nos. 3070-3071.

3076a 32c **American Indian Dances, strip of 5,** *June 7,* Oklahoma City OK 2.75
3072-3076, any single 1.25

First day cancellation was applied to 653,057 covers bearing one or more of Nos. 3072-3076, 3076a.

3080a 32c **Prehistoric Animals,** *June 8,* Toronto, Canada 2.75
3077-3080, any single 1.50

First day cancellation was applied to 485,929 covers bearing one or more of Nos. 3077-3080, 3080a.

3081 32c **Breast Cancer Awareness,** *June 15 (183,896)* 1.25
Any other city 1.25

3082 32c **James Dean,** *June 24,* Burbank CA *(263,593)* 2.50

3086a 32c **Folk Heroes,** *July 11,* Anaheim CA 2.75
3083-3086, any single 1.25

First day cancellation was applied to 739,706 covers bearing one or more of Nos. 3083-3086, 3086a.

3087 32c **Centennial Olympic Games,** *July 19,* Atlanta GA *(269,056)* 1.25

3088 32c **Iowa Statehood, 150th Anniv.,** *Aug. 1,* Dubuque IA 1.25

3089 32c **Iowa Statehood, self-adhesive** *Aug. 1,* Dubuque IA 1.25
3088, 3089, both stamps issued *Aug. 1,* Dubuque, IA 1.75

First day cancellation was applied to 215,181 covers bearing one or more of Nos. 3088-3089.

3090 32c **Rural Free Delivery,** *Aug. 7,* Charleston WV *(192,070)* 1.25

3091-3095 32c **Riverboats,** *Aug. 22,* Orlando FL 3.50
3091-3095, any single 1.25

3095b 32c **Riverboats, special die cutting,** *Aug. 22,* Orlando FL 3.50

First day cancellation was applied to 770,384 covers bearing one or more of Nos. 3091-3095, 3095b.

3099a 32c **Big Band Leaders,** *Sept. 11,* New York NY 3.25
3096-3099, any single 1.25

First day cancellation was applied to 1,235,166 covers bearing one or more of Nos. 3096-3103, 3099a, 3103a.

3103a 32c **Songwriters,** *Sept. 11,* New York NY 3.25
3100-3103, any single 1.25

First day cancellation was applied to 1,235,166 covers bearing one or more of Nos. 3096-3103, 3099a, 3103a.

3104 23c **F. Scott Fitzgerald,** *Sept. 27,* St. Paul MN *(150,783)* 1.25

3105 32c **Endangered Species,** *Oct. 2,* San Diego CA 7.50
3105a-3105o, any single 1.25

First day cancellation was applied to 941,442 covers bearing one or more of Nos. 3105, 3105a-3105o.

3106 32c **Computer Technology,** *Oct. 8,* Aberdeen Proving Ground MD *(153,688)* 1.75

3107 32c **Christmas Madonna,** *Nov. 1,* Richmond VA 1.25

First day cancellation was applied to 164,447 covers bearing one or more of Nos. 3107, 3112.

3111a 32c **Christmas (secular),** *Oct. 8,* North Pole AK 2.75
3108-3111, any single 1.25

First day cancellation was applied to 884,339 covers bearing one or more of Nos. 3108-3111, 3111a, 3113-3117.

3112 32c **As No. 3107, self-adhesive,** *Nov. 1,* Richmond VA 1.25

3113-3116 32c **Christmas (secular), self-adhesive,** *Oct. 8,* North Pole AK 3.25
3113-3116, any single 1.25

3117 32c **Skaters, self-adhesive,** *Oct. 8,* North Pole AK 1.25

First day cancellation was applied to 884,339 covers bearing one or more of Nos. 3108-3111, 3111a, 3113-3117.

3118 32c **Hanukkah,** *Oct. 22 (179,355)* 1.75

3119 50c **Cycling,** *Nov. 1,* New York NY 4.00
3119a-3119b, any single 2.00

First day cancellation was applied to 290,091 covers bearing one or more of Nos. 3119, 3119a-3119b.

1997

3120 32c **Chinese New Year,** *Jan. 5,* Honolulu *(233,638)* 2.00

3121 32c **Benjamin O. Davis, Sr.,** *Jan. 28 (166,527)* 1.75

3122 32c **Statue of Liberty, self-adhesive,** *Feb. 1,* San Diego CA *(40,003)* 1.25

3123 32c **Love, Swans, self-adhesive,** *Feb. 4,* Los Angeles CA 1.25

3124 55c **Love, Swans, self-adhesive,** *Feb. 4,* Los Angeles CA 1.50

First day cancellation was applied to 257,380 covers bearing one or more of Nos. 3123-3124.

3125 32c **Helping Children Learn, self-adhesive** *Feb. 18 (175,410)* 1.50

3126 32c **Merian Botanical Prints, Citron, etc., self-adhesive, die cut 10.9x10.2,** *Mar. 3* 1.25

3127 32c **Merian Botanical Prints, Pineapple, etc., self-adhesive, die cut 10.9x10.2,** *Mar. 3* 1.25

3128 32c **Merian Botanical Prints, Citron, etc., self-adhesive, die cut 11.2x10.8,** *Mar. 3* 1.25

3128a 32c **Merian Botanical Prints, Citron, etc., self-adhesive, die cut mixed perf,** *Mar. 3* 1.25

3129 32c **Merian Botanical Prints, Pineapple, etc., self-adhesive, die cut 11.2x10.8,** *Mar. 3* 1.25

3129a 32c **Merian Botanical Prints, Pineapple, etc., self-adhesive, die cut mixed perf,** *Mar. 3* 1.25

First day cancellation was applied to 336,897 covers bearing one or more of Nos. 3126-3129, 3128a-3129a.

3131a 32c **Pacific 97,** *Mar. 13,* New York NY 2.00
3130-3131, any single 1.50

First day cancellation was applied to 371,908 covers bearing one or more of Nos. 3130-3131, 3131a.

3132 (25c) **Juke Box, self-adhesive** *Mar. 14,* New York NY 1.25

3133 32c **Flag over Porch, Self-adhesive** *Mar. 14,* New York NY 1.25

First day cancellation was applied to 26,0820 covers bearing one or more of Nos. 3132-3133.

3134 32c **Thornton Wilder,** *Apr. 17,* Hamden CT *(157,299)* 1.25

3135 32c **Raoul Wallenberg,** *Apr. 24 (168,668)* 2.00

3136 32c **Dinosaurs, pane of 15** *May 1,* Grand Junction CO 7.50
3136a-3136o, any single 1.25

First day cancellation was applied to 1,782,1221 covers bearing one or more of Nos. 3136, 3136a-3136o.

3137a 32c **Bugs Bunny,** *May 22,* Burbank CA *(378,142)* 2.00

3139 50c **Pacific 97, Franklin, pane of 12** *May 29,* San Francisco CA 12.00
3139a, single 2.00

3140 60c **Pacific 97,, pane of 12,** *May 30,* San Francisco CA 12.00
3140a, single 2.00

First day cancellation was applied to 328,401 covers bearing one or more of Nos. 3139-3140, 3139a-3140b.

3141 32c **Marshall Plan,** *June 4,* Cambridge MA *(157,622)* 1.50

3142 32c **Classic American Aircraft,** *July 19,* Dayton OH 10.00
3142a-3142t, any single 1.25

First day cancellation was applied to 1,413,833 covers bearing one or more of Nos. 3142, 3142a-3142t.

3146a 32c **Football Coaches** *July 25,* Canton OH 3.00
3143-3146, any single 1.75

First day cancellation was applied to 586,946 covers bearing one or more of Nos. 3143-3146.

3147 32c **Bear Bryant,** *Aug. 5,* Tuscaloosa AL *(119,428)* 1.75

3148 32c **Pop Warner,** *Aug. 7,* Philadelphia PA *(23,858)* 1.75

3149 32c **Vince Lombardi,** *Aug. 8,* Green Bay WI *(37,839)* 2.00

3150 32c **George Halas,** *Aug. 16,* Chicago IL *(26,760)* 1.75

3151 32c **American Dolls,** *July 28,* Anaheim CA 8.00
3151a-3151o, any single 1.25

First day cancellation was applied to 831,359 covers bearing one or more of Nos. 3151, 3151a-3151o.

3152 32c **Humphrey Bogart,** *July 31,* Los Angeles CA *(220,254)* 2.50

3153 32c **"The Star and Stripes Forever,"** *Aug. 21,* Milwaukee WI *(36,666)* 1.25

3157a 32c **Opera Singers,** *Sept. 10,* New York NY 2.75
3154-3157, any single 1.25

First day cancellation was applied to 386,689 covers bearing one or more of Nos. 3154-3157.

3165a 32c **Classical Composers and Conductors,** *Sept. 12,* Cincinnati OH 5.25
3158-3165, any single 1.25

First day cancellation was applied to 424,344 covers bearing one or more of Nos. 3158-3165.

3166 32c **Padre Felix Varela,** *Sept. 15,* Miami FL *(120,079)* 1.25

3167 32c **Department of the Air Force,** *Sept. 18 (178,519)* 1.50

3172a 32c **Classic Movie Monsters,** *Sept. 30,* Universal City CA 3.75
3168-3172, any single 1.50

First day cancellation was applied to 476,993 covers bearing one or more of Nos. 3168-3172.

3173 32c **First Supersonic Flight,** *Oct. 14,* Edwards AFB CA *(173,778)* 1.50

3174 32c **Women in Military Service,** *Oct. 18 (106,121)* 2.00

3175 32c **Kwanzaa,** *Oct. 22,* Los Angeles CA *(92,489)* 1.75

3176 32c **Christmas Madonna,** *Oct. 27 (35,809)* 1.25

3177 32c **Holly,** *Oct. 30,* New York NY *(87,332)* 1.25

3178 $3 **Mars Pathfinder,** *Dec. 10* Pasadena CA *(11,699)* 9.00

1998

3179 32c **Chinese New Year,** *Jan. 5,* Seattle WA *(234,269)* 2.00

3180 32c **Alpine Skiing,** *Jan. 22,* Salt Lake City UT *(196,504)* 1.25

3181 32c **Madam C. J. Walker,** *Jan. 28,* Indianapolis IN *(146,348)* 1.75

CELEBRATE THE CENTURY ISSUE

1998-2000

3182 32c **1900s,** *Feb. 3 (11,699),* Washington DC 8.50
3182a-3182o, any single 1.50

3183 32c **1910s,** *Feb. 3,* Washington DC 8.50
3183a-3183o, any single 1.50

First day cancellation was applied to 3,896,387 covers bearing one or more of Nos. 3182-3182o, 3183-3183o.

3184 32c **1920s,** *May 28,* Chicago IL 8.50
3184a-3184o, any single 1.75

First day cancellation was applied to 1,057,909 covers bearing one or more of Nos. 3184-3184o.

3185 32c **1930s,** *Sept. 10,* Cleveland OH 8.50
3185a-3185o, any single 1.75

First day cancellation was applied to 999,017 covers bearing one or more of Nos. 3185-3185o.

3186 33c **1940s,** *Feb. 18, 1999,* Dobbins AFB GA 8.50
3186a-3186o, any single 1.75

First day cancellation was applied to 1,459,138 covers bearing one or more of Nos. 3186-3186o.

3187 33c **1950s,** *May 26, 1999,* Springfield MA 8.50
3187a-3187o, any single 1.75

First day cancellation was applied to 1,454,906 covers bearing one or more of Nos. 3187-3187o.

3188 33c **1960s,** *Sept. 17, 1999,* Green Bay, WI 8.50
3188a-3188o, any single 1.75

First day cancellation was applied to 1,252,243 covers bearing one or more of Nos. 3188-3188o.

3189 33c **1970s,** *Nov. 18, 1999,* New York, NY 8.50
3189a-3189o, any single 1.75

First day cancellation was applied to 894,084 covers bearing one or more of Nos. 3189-3189o.

3190 33c **1980s,** *Jan. 12, 2000,* Kennedy Space Center, Titusville FL 8.50
3190a-3190o, any single 1.75

3191 33c **1990s,** *May 2, 2000,* Escondido, CA 8.50
3191a-3191o, any single 1.75

First day cancellation was applied to 1,172,962 covers bearing one or more of Nos. 3191-3191o.

1998

3192 32c **"Remember the Maine,"** *Feb. 15,* Key West FL *(161,657)* 1.75

3193-3197 32c **Flowering Trees,** *Mar. 19,* New York NY 3.75
3193-3197, any single 1.50

First day cancellation was applied to 666,199 covers bearing one or more of Nos. 3193-3197.

3202a 32c **Alexander Calder,** *Mar. 25* 3.75
3198-3202, any single 1.50

First day cancellation was applied to 588,887 covers bearing one or more of Nos. 3198-3202, 3202a.

3203 32c **Cinco de Mayo,** *Apr. 16,* San Antonio TX *(144,443)* 1.25

3204a 32c **Sylvester & Tweety,** *Apr. 27,* New York NY *(213,839)* 1.25

3206 32c **Wisconsin Statehood,** *May 29,* Madison WI *(130,810)* 1.25

1998-99

3207 (5c) **Wetlands,** *June 5,* McLean VA 1.25

3207A (5c) **Wetlands, Serpentine die cut,** *Dec. 14* 1.25

3208 (25c) **Diner,** *June 5,* McLean VA 1.25

First day cancellation was applied to 35,333 covers bearing one or more of Nos. 3207, 3208; 13,378 covers bearing one of more of Nos. 3207A, 3270-3271.

3208A (25c) **Diner, Serpentine die cut,** *June 5 (13,984)* 1.25

1898 TRANS-MISSISSIPPI STAMPS, CENT. ISSUE

1998

3209 **Sheet of 9,** *June 18,* Anaheim CA 6.50
3209a 1c 1.50
3209b 2c 1.50
3209c 4c 1.50
3209d 5c 1.50
3209e 8c 1.50
3209f 10c 1.50
3209g 50c 2.00
3209h $1 2.50
3209i $2 4.50
3210 $1 **Sheet of 9,** *June 18,* Anaheim CA 15.00

First day cancellation was applied to 203,649 covers bearing one or more of Nos. 3209-3210, 3209a-3209i.

1998

3211 32c **Berlin Airlift,** *June 26,* Berlin, Germany *(137,894)* 1.50

3215a 32c **Folk Musicians,** *June 26* 3.25
3212-3215, any single 1.25

First day cancellation was applied to 341,015 covers bearing one or more of Nos. 3212-3215, 3215a.

3219a 32c **Gospel Music,** *July 15,* New Orleans LA 3.25
3216-3219, any single 1.25

First day cancellation was applied to 330,533 covers bearing one or more of Nos. 3216-3219, 3219a.

3220 32c **Spanish Settlement of the Southwest,** *July 11,* Española NM *(122,182)* 1.25
3221 32c **Stephen Vincent Benét,** *July 22,* Harpers Ferry WV *(107,412)* 1.25
3225a 32c **Tropical Birds,** *July 29,* Ponce PR 3.00
3222-3225, any single 1.25

First day cancellation was applied to 371,354 covers bearing one or more of Nos. 3222-3225, 3225a.

3226 32c **Alfred Hitchcock,** *Aug. 3,* Los Angeles CA *(140,628)* 2.00
3227 32c **Organ & Tissue Donation,** *Aug. 5,* Columbus OH *(110,601)* 1.25
3228 (10c) **Modern Bicycle, Serpentine die cut,** *Aug. 14* 1.25
3229 (10c) **Modern Bicycle,** *Aug. 14* 1.25

First day cancellation was applied to 46,557 covers bearing one or more of Nos. 3228-3229, 3036.

3230-3234 32c **Bright Eyes,** *Aug. 20,* Boston MA 3.25
3230-3234, any single 1.75

First day cancellation was applied to 394,280 covers bearing one or more of Nos. 3230-3234.

3235 32c **Klondike Gold Rush Cent.,** *Aug. 21,* Nome or Skagway AK *(123,559)* 1.50
3236 32c **American Art, pane of 20,** *Aug. 27,* Santa Clara CA 9.00
3236a-3236t, any single 1.25

First day cancellation was applied to 924,031 covers bearing one or more of Nos. 3236, 3236a-3236t.

3237 32c **American Ballet,** *Sept. 16,* New York NY *(133,034)* 1.25
3242a 32c **Space Discovery,** *Oct. 1,* Kennedy Space Center FL 3.75
3238-3242, any single 1.25

First day cancellation was applied to 399,807 covers bearing one or more of Nos. 3238-3242, 3242a.

3243 32c **Giving & Sharing,** *Oct. 7,* Atlanta GA *(124,051)* 1.25
3244 32c **Christmas, Madonna,** *Oct. 15 (105,835)* 1.25
3245-3248 32c **Christmas, Secular,** *Oct. 15,* Christmas MI 3.25
3245-3248, any single 1.25
3249-3252 32c **Christmas, Secular, size: 23x30mm,** *Oct. 15,* Christmas MI 3.00
3249-3252, any single 1.25

First day cancellation was applied to 328,199 covers bearing one or more of Nos. 3245-3252.

3257 (1c) **Weather Vane, white USA,** *Nov. 9,* Troy NY 1.25
3258 (1c) **Weather Vane, pale blue USA,** *Nov. 9,* Troy NY 1.25
3259 22c **Uncle Sam,** *Nov. 9,* Troy NY 1.25
3260 (33c) **Uncle Sam's Hat,** *Nov. 9,* Troy NY 1.25
3261 $3.20 **Space Shuttle Landing,** *Nov. 9,* 5.00
3262 $11.75 **Piggyback Space Shuttle,** *Nov. 19,* New York NY *(3,703)* 25.00
3263 22c **Uncle Sam, coil,** *Nov. 9,* Troy NY 1.25
3264 (33c) **Uncle Sam's Hat, coil,** *Nov. 9,* Troy NY 1.25
3265 (33c) **Uncle Sam's Hat, self-adhesive coil, die cut 9.9, round corners,** *Nov. 9,* Troy NY 1.25
3266 (33c) **Uncle Sam's Hat, self-adhesive coil, die cut 9.9, square corners,** *Nov. 9,* Troy NY 1.50
3267 (33c) **Uncle Sam's Hat, self-adhesive booklet single, die cut 9.9** *Nov. 9,* Troy NY 1.25
3268 (33c) **Uncle Sam's Hat, self-adhesive booklet single, die cut 11.2x11.1** *Nov. 9,* Troy NY 1.25
3269 (33c) **Uncle Sam's Hat, self-adhesive booklet single, die cut 8** *Nov. 9,* Troy NY 1.25

First day cancellation was applied to 121,662 covers bearing one or more of Nos. 2942, 3257-3261, 3263-3269.

3270 (10c) **Eagle & Shield, Presorted Std.,** *Dec. 14* 1.25
3271 (10c) **Eagle & Shield, Presorted Std., self-adhesive, Serpentine die cut,** *Dec. 14* 1.25

First day cancellation was applied to 13,378 covers bearing one of more of Nos. 3207A, 3270-3271.

1999

3272 33c **Chinese New Year,** *Jan. 5,* Los Angeles CA *(151,436)* 2.00
3273 33c **Malcolm X,** *Jan. 20,* New York NY *(107,226)* 2.00
3274 33c **Love,** *Jan. 28,* Loveland CO 1.25
3275 55c **Love,** *Jan. 28,* Loveland CO 1.50

First day cancellation was applied to 189,331 covers bearing one of more of Nos. 3274, 3275, UX300.

3276 33c **Hospice Care,** *Feb. 9,* Largo FL *(136,976)* 1.25
3277 33c **Flag & City,** *Feb. 25,* Orlando FL 1.25
3278 33c **Flag & City, self-adhesive, die cut 11.1** *Feb. 25,* Orlando FL 1.25
3279 33c **Flag & City, self-adhesive, die cut 9.8** *Feb. 25,* Orlando FL 1.25
3280 33c **Flag & City, coil, perf. 9.9 vert.** *Feb. 25,* Orlando FL 1.25
3281 33c **Flag & City, self-adhesive coil, die cut 9.8 vert, square corners,** *Feb. 25,* Orlando FL 1.25
3282 33c **Flag & City, self-adhesive coil, die cut 9.8 vert., round corners,** *Feb. 25,* Orlando FL 1.25

First day cancellation was applied to 88,569 covers bearing one of more of Nos. 3277-3282.

3283 33c **Flag & Blackboard, self-adhesive, die cut 7.9,** *Mar. 13 (26,067)* 1.25
3286 33c **Irish Immigration,** *Feb. 26,* Boston MA *(127,213)* 1.50
3287 33c **Lunt & Fontanne,** *Mar. 2,* New York NY *(120,423)* 1.25
3292a 33c **Arctic Animals,** *Mar. 12,* Barrow AK 3.25
3288-3292, any single 1.25

First day cancellation was applied to 476,863 covers bearing one of more of Nos. 3288-3292, 3292a.

3293 33c **Sonoran Desert, Pane of 10,** *Apr. 6,* Tucson AZ 6.75
3293a-3293j, any single 1.25

First day cancellation was applied to 410,985 covers bearing one of more of Nos. 3293-3293j.

3294-3297 33c **Christmas Berries, die cut 11.2x11.7** *Apr. 10,* Ponchatoula LA 3.25
3294-3297, any single 1.25
3297e, dated 2000, *Mar. 15, 2000,* Ponchatoula LA 3.25
3294a-3296a, 3297c, any single 1.25
3298-3301 33c **Christmas Berries, die cut 9.5x10** *Apr. 10,* Ponchatoula LA 3.25
3298-3301, any single 1.25
3302-3305 33c **Christmas Berries, die cut 8.5 vert.** *Apr. 10,* Ponchatoula LA 3.25
3302-3305, any single 1.25

First day cancellation was applied to 101,344 covers bearing one of more of Nos. 3294-3305.

3306a 33c **Daffy Duck,** *Apr. 16,* Los Angeles CA 1.50

First day cancellation was applied to 177,988 covers bearing one of more of Nos. 3306-3307c, UX304.

3308 33c **Ayn Rand,** *Apr. 22,* New York NY *(123,660)* 2.50
3309 33c **Cinco de Mayo,** *Apr. 27,* San Antonio TX *(20,904)* 1.25
3310-3313 33c **Tropical Flowers,** *May 1,* Honolulu HI 3.25
3310-3313, any single 1.25

First day cancellation was applied to 311,495 covers bearing one of more of Nos. 3310-3313, 3313a, 3313b.

3314 33c **Bartram,** *May 18,* Philadelphia PA *(110,381)* 1.25
3315 33c **Prostate Cancer Awareness,** *July 22,* Austin TX *(113,299)* 1.25
3316 33c **California Gold Rush,** *June 18,* Sacramento CA *(123,648)* 1.25
3317-3320 33c **Aquarium Fish,** *June 24,* Anaheim CA 3.25
3317-3320, any single 1.25

First day cancellation was applied to 301,719 covers bearing one of more of Nos. 3317-3320, 3320a-3320c.

3321-3324 33c **Extreme Sports,** *June 25,* San Francisco CA 3.00
3321-3324, any single 1.25

First day cancellation was applied to 278,068 covers bearing one of more of Nos. 3321-3324, 3324a.

3328a 33c **American Glass,** *June 29,* Corning NY 3.00
3325-3328, any single 1.25

First day cancellation was applied to 272,792 covers bearing one of more of Nos. 3325-3328, 3328a.

3329 33c **James Cagney,** *July 22,* Burbank CA *(135,867)* 2.50
3330 55c **"Billy" Mitchell,** *July 30,* Milwaukee WI 1.50

First day cancellation was applied to 42,144 covers bearing one of more of Nos. 3330, C134.

3331 33c **Honoring Those Who Served,** *Aug. 16,* Kansas City MO *(130,306)* 2.00
3332 45c **Universal Postal Union,** *Aug. 25,* Beijing, China (20,371) 1.25
3337a 33c **Famous Trains,** *Aug. 26,* Cleveland, OH 3.75
Any other city 3.75
#3333-3337, any single, Cleveland, OH 1.50
#3333-3337, any single, any other city 1.50

First day cancellation was applied to 518,446 covers bearing one of more of Nos. 3333-3337, 3337a, UX307-UX311a.

3338 33c **Frederick Law Olmsted,** *Sept. 12,* Boston, MA (109,735) 1.25
3344a 33c **Hollywood Composers,** *Sept. 16,* Los Angeles, CA 3.75
#3339-3344, any single, Los Angeles, CA 1.25

First day cancellation was applied to 287,407 covers bearing one of more of Nos. 3339-3344, 3344a.

3350a 33c **Broadway Songwriters,** *Sept. 21,* New York, NY 3.75
#3345-3350, any single, New York, NY 1.25

First day cancellation was applied to 284,840 covers bearing one of more of Nos. 3345-3350, 3350a.

3351 33c **Insects & Spiders,** *Oct. 1,* Indianapolis, IN 10.00
#3351a-3351t, any single 1.25

First day cancellation was applied to 773,590 covers bearing one of more of Nos. 3351-3351t.

3352 33c **Hanukkah,** *Oct. 8,* Washington, DC 1.50
3353 22c **Uncle Sam perforated coil,** *Oct. 8,* Washington, DC 1.25

First day cancellation was applied to 44,534 covers bearing one of more of Nos. 3352-3353, O157.

3354 33c **NATO,** *Oct. 13,* Brussels, Belgium *(110,415)* 1.50
3355 33c **Christmas Madonna,** *Oct. 20,* Washington, DC *(110,460)* 1.25
3356-3359 33c **Christmas Deer, narrow frame (sheet),** *Oct. 20,* Rudolph, WI 3.00
3356-3359, any single 1.25
3360-3363 33c **Christmas Deer, thick frame (booklet),** *Oct. 20,* Rudolph, WI 3.00
3360-3363, any single 1.25
3364-3367 33c **Christmas Deer, smaller size (booklet),** *Oct. 20,* Rudolph, WI 3.00
3364-3367, any single 1.25

First day cancellation was applied to 239,350 covers bearing one of more of Nos. 3356-3367, 3359a, 3363a, 3367a-3367c.

3368 33c **Kwanzaa,** *Oct. 29,* Los Angeles, CA *(20,493)* 1.75
3369 33c **Year 2000,** *Dec. 27,* Washington, DC *(145,928)* 1.25

2000

3370 33c **Chinese New Year,** *Jan. 6,* San Francisco, CA *(155,586)* 2.00
3371 33c **Patricia Roberts Harris,** *Jan. 27,* Washington, DC *(82,211)* 1.75
3372 33c **Los Angeles Class Submarine,** with microprinting, *Mar. 27,* Groton, CT 1.50
3373 22c **S Class Submarine,** *Mar. 27,* Groton, CT 1.50
3374 33c **Los Angeles Class Submarine,** no microprinting, *Mar. 27,* Groton, CT 1.50
3375 55c **Ohio Class Submarine,** *Mar. 27,* Groton, CT 1.75
3376 60c **USS Holland,** *Mar. 27,* Groton, CT 1.75
3377 $3.20 **Gato Class Submarine,** *Mar. 27,* Groton, CT 6.00
3377a, Booklet pane of 5, #3373-3377, either selvage 11.00

First day cancellation was applied to 265,226 covers bearing one of more of Nos. 3372-3377, 3377a.

3378 33c **Pacific Coast Rain Forest Pane of 10,** *Mar. 29,* Seattle, WA 6.75
3378a-3378j, any single 1.25

First day cancellation was applied to 435,549 covers bearing one of more of Nos. 3378-3378j.

3383a 33c **Louise Nevelson,** *Apr. 6,* New York, NY 3.25
3379-3383, any single 1.25

First day cancellation was applied to 389,200 covers bearing one of more of Nos. 3379-3383, 3383a.

3388a 33c **Hubble Space Telescope,** *Apr. 10,* Greenbelt, MD 3.25
3384-3388, any single 1.25

First day cancellation was applied to 411,449 covers bearing one of more of Nos. 3384-3388, 3388a.

3389 33c **American Samoa,** *Apr. 17,* Pago Pago, AS *(107,346_* 1.25
3390 33c **Library of Congress,** *Apr. 24,* Washington, DC *(115,679)* 1.50
3391a 33c **Road Runner & Wile E. Coyote,** *Apr. 26,* Phoenix, AZ 1.50

First day cancellation was applied to 154,903 covers bearing one of more of Nos. 3391-3392, 3391a-3391c, 3392a-3392c.

3396a 33c **Distinguished Soldiers,** *May 3,* Washington, DC 3.25
Any other city 3.25
3393-3396, any single, Washington, DC 1.75
Any other city 1.50

First day cancellation was applied to 322,278 covers bearing one of more of Nos. 3393-3396, 3396a.

3397 33c **Summer Sports,** *May 5,* Spokane, WA *(110,768)* 1.25
3398 33c **Adoption,** *May 10,* Beverly Hills, CA 1.25

First day cancellation was applied to 137,903 covers bearing one of more of Nos. 3398, UX315.

3402a 33c **Youth Team Sports,** *May 27,* Lake Buena Vista, FL 3.25
3399-3402, any single 1.25

First day cancellation was applied to 309,349 covers bearing one of more of Nos. 3399-3402, 3402a.

3403 33c **The Stars and Stripes, pane of 20,** *June 14,* Baltimore, MD 10.00
3403a-3403t, any single 1.25

First day cancellation was applied to 1,121,071 covers bearing one of more of Nos. 3403-3403t.

3404-3407 33c **Berries,** die cut 8½ horiz., *June 16,* Buffalo, NY 3.25
3404-3407, any single 1.25

First day cancellation was applied to 35,671 covers bearing one of more of Nos. 3404-3407, 3407a.

3408 33c **Legends of Baseball, pane of 20,** *July 6,* Atlanta, GA 10.00
3408a-3708t, any single 1.75

First day cancellation was applied to 1,214,413 covers bearing one of more of Nos. 3408-3408t.

3409 60c **Probing the Vastness of Space,** *July 10,* Anaheim, CA 6.00
3409a-3409f, any single 1.50

First day cancellation was applied to 296,252 covers bearing one of more of Nos. 3409-3409f.

3410 $1 **Exploring the Solar System,** *July 11,* Anaheim, CA 9.00
3410a-3410e, any single 2.00

First day cancellation was applied to 49,500 covers bearing one of more of Nos. 3410-3410e.

3411 $3.20 **Escaping the Gravity of Earth,** *July 9,* Anaheim, CA 9.50
3411a-3411b, any single 3.75

First day cancellation was applied to 22,321 covers bearing one of more of Nos. 3411-3411b.

3412 $11.75 **Space Achievement and Exploration,** *July 7,* Anaheim, CA *(12,070)* 17.50

3413 $11.75 **Landing on the Moon,** *July 8,* Anaheim, CA *(11,639)* 17.50

3414-3417 33c **Stampin' The Future,** *July 13,* Anaheim, CA 3.25
3414-3417, any single 1.25

First day cancellation was applied to 294,434 covers bearing one of more of Nos. 3414-3417, 3417a.

DISTINGUISHED AMERICANS ISSUE 2000-2009

3420 10c **Joseph W. Stilwell,** *Aug. 24,* Providence, RI *(21,669)* 1.50

3422 23c **Wilma Rudolph, litho. & engr.** *July 14, 2004,* Sacramento, CA 1.25

3426 33c **Claude Pepper,** *Sept. 7,* Washington, DC *(60,689)* 1.25

3427 58c **Margaret Chase Smith,** *June 13, 2007,* Washington, DC 2.40

3427A 59c **James A. Michener,** *May 12, 2008,* Washington, DC 2.40

3428 63c **Dr. Jonas Salk,** *Mar. 8,* Washington, DC 2.50
Any other city 2.50

3430 75c **Harriet Beecher Stowe,** *June 13, 2007* Washington, DC 2.75

3431 76c **Hattie Caraway,** *Feb. 21, 2001,* Little Rock, AR 1.75

3432A 76c **Edward Trudeau,** *May 12, 2008,* Washington, DC 2.75

3432B 78c **Mary Lasker,** *May 15, 2009,* Washington, DC 2.75

3433 83c **Edna Ferber,** *July 29, 2002,* Appleton, WI 1.75

3435 87c **Dr. Albert Sabin,** *Mar. 8,* Washington, DC 3.00
Any other city 3.00

3436 23c **Wilma Rudolph, litho. booklet stamp** *July 14, 2004,* Sacramento, CA 1.25

3438 33c **California Statehood,** *Sept. 8,* Sacramento, CA *(119,729)* 1.25

3443a 33c **Deep Sea Creatures,** *Oct. 2,* Monterey, CA 3.75
#3439-3443, any single 1.25

First day cancellation was applied to 385,406 covers bearing one of more of Nos. 3439-3443, 3443a.

3444 33c **Thomas Wolfe,** *Oct. 3,* Asheville, NC *(112,293)* 1.25

3445 33c **White House,** *Oct. 18,* Washington, DC *(135,844)* 1.25

3446 33c **Edward G. Robinson,** *Oct. 24,* Los Angeles, CA *(120,125)* 2.00

3447 (10c) **New York Public Library Lion,** *Nov. 9,* New York, NY *(18,477)* 1.25

3448 (34c) **Flag Over Farm, perf,** *Dec. 15,* Washington, DC 1.25

3449 (34c) **Flag Over Farm, litho. self-adhesive,** *Dec. 15,* Washington, DC 1.25

3450 (34c) **Flag Over Farm, photo. self-adhesive,** *Dec. 15,* Washington, DC 1.25

3451 (34c) **Statue of Liberty, booklet stamp,** *Dec. 15,* Washington, DC 1.25

3452 (34c) **Statue of Liberty perforated coil,** *Dec. 15,* Washington, DC 1.25

3453 (34c) **Statue of Liberty self-adhesive coil,** *Dec. 15,* Washington, DC 1.25

3454-3457 (34c) **Flowers, booklet stamps die cut 10¼x10¾,** *Dec. 15,* Washington, DC 3.25
3454-3457, any single 1.25

3458-3461 (34c) **Flowers, booklet stamps die cut 11½x11¾,** *Dec. 15,* Washington, DC 3.25
3458-3461, any single 1.25

3462-3465 (34c) **Flowers, coil stamps,** *Dec. 15,* Washington, DC 3.25
3462-3465, any single 1.25

First day cancellation was applied to 178,635 covers bearing one of more of Nos. 3448-3465, 3450a, 3451a-3451d, 3457a-3457e, 3461a-3461c, 3465a.

2001

3466 34c **Statue of Liberty coil (rounded corners),** *Jan. 7,* Washington, DC 1.25

3467 21c **American Buffalo, perforated sheet stamp,** *Sept. 20,* Washington, DC 1.25

3468 21c **American Buffalo, perforated sheet stamp,** *Feb. 22,* Wall, SD 1.25

3468A 23c **George Washington, sheet stamp,** *Sept. 20,* Washington, DC 1.25

3469 34c **Flag Over Farm, perforated sheet stamp,** *Feb. 7,* New York, NY 1.25

3470 34c **Flag Over Farm, self-adhesive sheet stamp,** *Mar. 6,* Lincoln, NE 1.25

3471 55c **Eagle,** *Feb. 22,* Wall, SD 1.50

3471A 57c **Eagle,** *Sept. 20,* Washington, DC 1.50

3472 $3.50 **Capitol Dome,** *Jan. 29,* Washington, DC 6.25

3473 $12.25 **Washington Monument,** *Jan. 29,* Washington, DC 15.00

3475 21c **American Buffalo coil stamp,** *Feb. 22,* Wall, SD 1.25

3475A 23c **George Washington, coil stamp,** *Sept. 20,* Washington, DC 1.25

3476 34c **Statue of Liberty, perforated coil stamp,** *Feb. 7,* New York, NY 1.25

3477 34c **Statue of Liberty coil stamp (right angle corners),** *Feb. 7,* New York, NY 1.25

3478-3481 34c **Flower coil stamps,** *Feb. 7,* New York, NY 3.25
3478-3481, any single 1.25

Serpentine Die Cut 11¼

3482 20c **George Washington booklet stamp,** *Feb. 22,* Wall, SD 1.25

Serpentine Die Cut 10½x11¼

3483 21c **George Washington booklet stamp,** *Feb. 22,* Wall, SD 1.25

3484 21c **American Buffalo, booklet stamp, serp. die cut 11¼,** *Sept. 20,* Washington, DC 1.25

3484A 21c **American Buffalo, booklet stamp, serp. die cut 10½x11¼,** *Sept. 20,* Washington, DC *1.25*

3485 34c **Statue of Liberty booklet stamp,** *Feb. 7,* New York, NY 1.25

3487-3490 34c **Flower booklet stamps,** *Feb. 7,* New York, NY 3.25
3487-3490, any single 1.25

3491-3492 34c **Apple & Orange booklet stamps,** *Feb. 7,* Lincoln, NE 2.25
3491-3492, any single 1.25

3495 34c **Flag Over Farm, booklet stamp,** *Dec. 17,* Washington, DC 1.25

3496 (34c) **Love Letter,** *Jan. 19,* Tucson, AZ 1.25

3497 34c **Love Letters,** *Feb. 14,* Lovejoy, GA 1.25

Serpentine Die Cut 11½x10¾

3498 34c **Love Letters, die cut 11½x10¾,** *Feb. 14,* Lovejoy, GA 1.25

3499 55c **Love Letter,** *Feb. 14,* Lovejoy, GA 1.50

3500 34c **Chinese New Year,** *Jan. 20,* Oakland, CA 1.75

3501 34c **Roy Wilkins,** *Jan. 24,* Minneapolis, MN 1.25

3502 34c **American Illustrators pane of 20,** *Feb. 1,* New York, NY 9.50
3502a-3502t, any single 1.25

3503 34c **Diabetes Awareness,** *Mar. 16,* Boston, MA 1.25

3504 34c **Nobel Prize Centenary,** *Mar. 22,* Washington, DC 1.50

3505 **Pan-American Inverts Pane,** *Mar. 29,* New York, NY 6.00

3505a 1c 1.25

3505b 2c 1.25

3505c 4c 1.25

3505d 80c 1.75

3506 34c **Great Plains Prairie Pane of 10,** *Apr. 19,* Lincoln, NE 7.00

3507 34c **Peanuts,** *May 17,* Santa Rosa, CA 1.50

3508 34c **Honoring Veterans,** *May 23,* Washington, DC 2.00
Any other city 1.25

3509 34c **Frida Kahlo,** *June 21,* Phoenix, AZ 1.25

3519a 34c **Legendary Playing Fields,** *June 27,* New York, NY, Boston, MA, Chicago, IL or Detroit, MI 6.50
3510-3519, any single, New York, NY, Boston, MA, Chicago, IL or Detroit, MI 1.50

3520 (10c) **Atlas Statue,** *June 29,* New York, NY 1.25

3521 34c **Leonard Bernstein,** *July 10,* New York, NY 1.25

3522 (15c) **Woody Wagon,** *Aug. 3,* Denver, CO 1.25

3523 34c **Lucille Ball,** *Aug. 6,* Los Angeles, CA 2.50

3527a 34c **Amish Quilts,** *Aug. 9,* Nappanee, IN 3.25
3524-3527, any single 1.25

3531a 34c **Carniverous Plants,** *Aug. 23,* Des Plaines, IL 3.25
3528-3531, any single 1.25

3532 34c **Eid** *Sept. 1,* Des Plaines, IL 1.25

3533 34c **Enrico Fermi,** *Sept. 29,* Chicago, IL 1.25

3534a 34c **That's All Folks!,** *Oct. 1,* Beverly Hills, CA 1.25

First day cancellation was applied to 151,009 covers bearing one or more of Nos. 3534-3535, 3534a-3534c, 3535a-3535c.

3536 34c **Christmas, Madonna,** *Oct. 10,* Philadelphia, PA 1.25

3537-3540 34c **Christmas, Santas, black inscriptions, large date** *Oct. 10,* Santa Claus, IN 3.25
3537-3540, any single 1.25
3537a-3540a, small date (from booklet) 3.25
3537a-3540a, any single 1.25

3541-3544 34c **Christmas, Santas, green and red inscriptions,** *Oct. 10,* Santa Claus, IN 3.25
3541-3544, any single 1.25

3545 34c **James Madison,** *Oct. 18,* New York, NY 1.25

3546 34c **Thanksgiving,** *Oct. 19,* Dallas, TX 1.25

3547 34c **Hanukkah,** *Oct. 21,* New York, NY 1.25

3548 34c **Kwanzaa,** *Oct. 21,* New York, NY 1.25

3549 34c **United We Stand,** *Oct. 24,* Washington, DC 1.50

First day cancellation was applied to 451,053 covers bearing one or more of Nos. 3549, 3550, 3550A.

3549B 34c **United We Stand,** serpentine die cut 10½x10¾ booklet stamp *Oct. 24,* Washington, DC 1.50

Though No. 3549B was issued in Jan. 2002, first day covers received the Oct. 24, 2001 cancel.

Any other city in NY, NJ, CT, PA or DC metropolitan area 1.50

3550 34c **United We Stand coil, right angle corners,** *Oct. 24,* Washington, DC 1.50
Any other city in NY, NJ, CT, PA or DC metropolitan area 1.50

3550A 34c **United We Stand coil,** rounded corners, *Oct. 24,* Washington, DC 1.50
Any other city in NY, NJ, CT, PA or DC metropolitan area 1.25

3551 57c **Love Letters,** *Nov. 19,* Washington, DC 1.50

2002

3552-3555 34c **Winter Sports,** *Jan. 8,* Park City, UT 3.25
3552-3555, any single 1.25

3556 34c **Mentoring a Child,** *Jan. 10,* Annapolis, MD 1.25

3557 34c **Langston Hughes,** *Feb. 1,* New York, NY 1.25

3558 34c **Happy Birthday,** *Feb. 8,* Riverside, CA 1.25

3559 34c **Chinese New Year,** *Feb. 11,* New York, NY 1.50

3560 34c **U.S. Military Academy Bicent.,** *Mar. 16,* West Point, NY 2.00

3610a 34c **Greetings from America Pane,** *Apr. 4,* New York, NY 32.50
3561-3610, any single, New York, NY 1.25
3610a, Any other city 32.50
3561-3610, Any single, any other city 1.50
3561-3610, any state capital 2.50

3611 34c **Longleaf Pine Forest Pane of 10,** *Apr. 26,* Tallahassee, FL 7.00
3611a-3611j, any single 1.25

3612 5c **Toleware Coffeepot,** *May 31,* McLean, VA 1.25

3613 3c **Litho. Star sheet stamp,** *June 7,* Washington, DC 1.25
Any other city 1.25

3614 3c **Photo. Star sheet stamp,** *June 7,* Washington, DC 1.25
Any other city 1.25

3615 3c **Star coil stamp,** *June 7,* Washington, DC 1.25

3616 23c **George Washington,** water-activated gum sheet stamp, *June 7,* Washington, DC 1.00
3617 23c **George Washington,** gray green coil stamp, *June 7,* Washington, DC 1.00
3618 23c **George Washington,** booklet stamp, serp. die cut 11¼ on 3 sides, *June 7,* Washington, DC 1.00
3620 (37c) **Flag,** water-activated gum sheet stamp, *June 7,* Washington, DC 1.25
Any other city 1.25
3621 (37c) **Flag,** self-adhesive sheet stamp, serp. die cut 11¼x11, *June 7,* Washington, DC 1.25
Any other city 1.25
3622 (37c) **Flag,** coil stamp, *June 7,* Washington, DC 1.25
Any other city 1.25
3623 (37c) **Flag,** booklet stamp, serp. die cut 11¼ on 2, 3 or 4 sides, *June 7,* Washington, DC 1.25
Any other city 1.25
3624 (37c) **Flag,** booklet stamp, serp. die cut 10½x10¾ on 2 or 3 sides, *June 7,* Washington, DC 1.25
Any other city 1.25
3625 (37c) **Flag,** booklet stamp, serp. die cut 8 on 2, 3 or 4 sides, *June 7,* Washington, DC 1.25
Any other city 1.25
3626-3629 (37c) **Antique Toys,** booklet stamps, *June 7,* Washington, DC 3.25
Any other city 3.25
3626-3629, any single 1.25
3626-3629, any single, any other city 1.25
3629F 37c **Flag,** perf. 11¼, *Nov. 24,* Washington, DC 1.25
3630 37c **Flag,** self-adhesive sheet stamp, serp. die cut 11¼x11, *June 7,* Washington, DC 1.25
Any other city 1.25
3631 37c **Flag,** water-activated gum coil stamp, *June 7,* Washington, DC 1.25
3632 37c **Flag,** self-adhesive coil stamp, serp. die cut 10 vert., *June 7,* Washington, DC 1.25
3632A 37c **Flag coil, lacking star points at top** *Aug. 7, 2003* Columbus, OH —
3633 37c **Flag,** self-adhesive coil stamp, serp. die cut 8½ vert., *June 7,* Washington, DC 1.25
3634 37c **Flag,** self-adhesive booklet stamps, serp. die cut 11 on 3 sides, *June 7,* Washington, DC 1.25
3635 37c **Flag,** booklet stamp, serp. die cut 11¼ on 2, 3 or 4 sides, *June 7,* Washington, DC 1.25
3636 37c **Flag,** booklet stamp, serp. die cut 10½x10¾ on 2 or 3 sides, *June 7,* Washington, DC 1.25
3637 37c **Flag,** booklet stamp, serp. die cut 8 on 2, 3 or 4 sides, *Feb. 4, 2003* Washington, DC 1.25
3638-3641 37c **Antique Toys coil stamps,** *July 26,* Rochester, NY 5.00
3638-3641, any single 1.25
3642-3645 37c **Antique Toys booklet stamps,** *July 26,* Rochester, NY 3.25
3642-3645, any single 1.25

2003

3642a-3645f 37c **Antique Toys,** booklet stamps, serp. die cut 11x11¼ on 2 or 3 sides, *Sept. 3,* Washington, DC 3.25
3642a-3645f, any single 1.25

2002

3646 60c **Coverlet Eagle,** *July 12,* Oak Brook, IL 1.50
3647 $3.85 **Jefferson Memorial,** *July 30,* Washington, DC 7.00
Any other city 7.00
3648 $13.65 **Capitol Dome,** *July 30,* Washington, DC 25.00
Any other city 25.00
3649 37c **Masters of American Photography,** *June 13,* San Diego, CA 10.00
3649a-3649t, any single 1.25
3650 37c **John James Audubon,** *June 27,* Santa Clara, CA 1.25
3651 37c **Harry Houdini,** *July 3,* New York, NY 1.75
3652 37c **Andy Warhol,** *Aug. 9,* Pittsburgh, PA 1.75
3653-3656 37c **Teddy Bears,** *Aug. 15,* Atlantic City, NJ 4.00
3653-3656, any single 1.25
3657 37c **Love,** *Aug. 16,* Atlantic City, NJ 1.25
3658 60c **Love,** *Aug. 16,* Atlantic City, NJ 1.50
3659 37c **Ogden Nash,** *Aug. 19,* Baltimore, MD 1.25
3660 37c **Duke Kahanamoku,** *Aug. 24,* Honolulu, HI 1.25
3661-3664 37c **American Bats,** *Sept. 13,* Austin, TX 3.25
3661-3664, any single 1.25
3665-3668 37c **Women in Journalism,** *Sept. 14,* Fort Worth, TX 3.25
3665-3668, any single 1.25
3669 37c **Irving Berlin,** *Sept. 15,* New York, NY 1.25
3670-3671 37c **Neuter and Spay,** *Sept. 20,* Washington, DC 2.25
Any other city 2.25
3670-3671, either single, Washington, DC 1.25
3670-3671, either single, any other city 1.25
3672 37c **Hanukkah,** *Oct. 10,* Washington, DC 1.25
3673 37c **Kwanzaa,** *Oct. 10,* Washington, DC 1.25
3674 37c **Eid,** *Oct. 10,* Washington, DC 1.25
3675 37c **Christmas Madonna,** design size 19x27mm, *Oct. 10,* Chicago, IL 1.25
3676-3679 37c **Christmas Snowmen,** serp. die cut 11 (sheet stamps), *Oct. 28,* Houghton, MI 3.25
3676-3679, any single 1.25
3680-3683 37c **Christmas Snowmen,** serp. die cut 8½ vert. (coil stamps), *Oct. 28,* Houghton, MI 3.25
3680-3683, any single 1.25
3684-3687 37c **Christmas Snowmen,** serp. die cut 10¾x11 on 2 or 3 sides (large booklet stamps), *Oct. 28,* Houghton, MI 3.25
3684-3687, any single 1.25
3688-3691 37c **Christmas Snowmen,** serp. die cut 11 on 2 or 3 sides (small booklet stamps), *Oct. 28,* Houghton, MI 3.25
3688-3691, any single 1.25
3692 37c **Cary Grant,** *Oct. 15,* Los Angeles, CA 2.00
3693 (5c) **Sea Coast,** *Oct. 21,* Washington, DC 1.25
3694 37c **Hawaiian Missionary Stamps sheet,** *Oct. 24,* New York, NY 4.00
3694a-3694d, any single 1.25
3695 37c **Happy Birthday,** *Oct. 25,* New York, NY 1.25
3745a 37c **Greetings From America,** *Oct. 25,* New York, NY 35.00
3696-3745, any single 1.25
3696-3745, any state capital 1.50

2003

3746 37c **Thurgood Marshall,** *Jan. 7,* Washington, DC 1.25
3747 37c **Chinese New Year,** *Jan. 15,* Chicago, IL 1.50
3748 37c **Zora Neale Hurston,** *Jan. 24,* Eatonville, FL 1.25

American Design Series 2003-14

3749 1c **Tiffany Lamp,** *Mar. 16, 2007,* New York, NY 2.00
3749A 1c **Tiffany Lamp,** *Mar. 7, 2008,* New York, NY 2.00
3750 2c **Navajo Necklace,** *Aug. 20, 2004,* Indianapolis, IN 1.25
3751 2c **Navajo Necklace,** photo., serpentine die cut 11¼x11½, *Dec. 8, 2005,* Washington, DC 2.00
Any other city 2.00
3752 2c **Navajo Necklace,** litho., serpentine die cut 11¼x11, *Dec. 8, 2005,* Washington, DC 2.00
Any other city 2.00
3753 2c **Navajo Necklace,** litho., serpentine die cut 11¼x10¾, microprinting at left, *May 12, 2007,* Washington, DC 2.00
3754 3c **Silver Coffeepot,** *Mar. 16, 2007,* New York, NY 2.00
3755 4c **Chippendale Chair,** *Mar. 5, 2004,* New York, NY 1.25
3756 5c **Toleware, serpentine die cut 11¼x11¾,** *June 25, 2004,* Santa Clara, CA 1.25
3757 10c **American Clock,** *Jan. 24, 2003,* Tucson, AZ 1.25
3758 1c **Tiffany Lamp Coil,** *Mar. 1, 2003,* Biloxi, MS 1.25
3758A 1c **Tiffany Lamp,** litho. coil stamp, *June 7, 2008,* McLean, VA 2.10
3758B 2c **Navajo Necklace coil,** *Feb. 12, 2011,* Charleston, SC 2.10
3759 3c **Silver Coffeepot Coil,** *Sept. 16, 2005,* Milwaukee, WI 2.00
3761 4c **Chippendale Chair coil,** *July 19, 2007,* Washington, DC 2.00
3761A 4c **Chippendale Chair coil,** dated "2013" at UL, *Jan. 2,* Kansas City, MO 2.25
3762 10c **American Clock Coil,** *Aug. 4, 2006,* Independence, OH 2.00
3763 10c **American Clock coil,** litho., *July 15, 2008,* Washington, DC 2.00

American Culture Series

3766 $1 **Wisdom,** *Feb. 28,* Biloxi, MS 2.50
3769 (10c) **New York Public Library Lion,** perf. 10 vert., *Feb. 4,* Washington, DC 1.25
3771 80c **Special Olympics,** *Feb. 13,* Chicago, IL 1.75
3772 37c **American Filmmaking: Behind the Scenes Pane of 10,** *Feb. 25,* Beverly Hills, CA 7.25
3772a-3772j, any single 1.25
3773 37c **Ohio Statehood Bicentennial,** *Mar. 1,* Chillicothe, OH 1.25
3774 37c **Pelican Island National Wildlife Refuge, Cent.,** *Mar. 14,* Sebastian, FL 1.25
3775 (5c) **Sea Coast,** perf. 9¾ vert. *Mar. 19,* Washington, DC 1.25
3776-3780 37c **Old Glory,** *Apr. 3,* New York, NY 4.00
3776-3780, any single 1.25
3781 37c **Cesar E. Chavez,** *Apr. 23,* Los Angeles, CA 1.25
3782 37c **Louisiana Purchase, Bicent.,** *Apr. 30,* New Orleans, LA 1.25
3783 37c **First Flight,** *May 22,* Dayton, OH or Kill Devil Hills, NC 1.25
3784 37c **Purple Heart,** *May 30,* Mount Vernon, VA 1.50
3784A 37c **Purple Heart, serpentine die cut 10¾x10¼,** *Aug. 1,* Somerset, NJ —
3786 37c **Audrey Hepburn,** *June 11,* Los Angeles, CA 2.00
3787-3791 37c **Southeastern Lighthouses,** *June 13,* Tybee Island, GA 4.00
3767, 3788a, 3789-3791, Tybee Island, GA 4.00
3787-3791, 3788a, any single 1.50
3792-3801 (25c) **Eagle coils,** *June 26,* Santa Clara, CA 6.00
3792-3801, any single 1.25
3792a-3801b (25c) **Eagle coil dated "2005",** *Aug. 5,* Grand Rapids, MI 6.00
3792a-3801b, any single 1.25
3802 37c **Arctic Tundra,** *July 2,* Fairbanks, AK 7.50
3802a-3802j, any single 1.25
3803 37c **Korean War Veterans Memorial,** *July 27,* Washington, DC 2.50
3804-3807 37c **Mary Cassatt booklet stamps,** *Aug. 7,* Columbus, OH 3.25
3804-3807, any single 1.25
3808-3811 37c **Early Football Heroes,** *Aug. 8,* South Bend, IN 3.25
3808-3811, any single 1.25
3812 37c **Roy Acuff,** *Sept. 13,* Nashville, TN 1.25
3813 37c **District of Columbia,** *Sept. 23,* Washington, DC 1.25
3814-3818 37c **Reptiles and Amphibians,** *Oct. 7,* San Diego, CA 4.00
3814-3818, any single, San Diego, CA 1.25
3820 37c **Christmas Madonna,** design size 19½x28mm, *Oct. 23,* New York, NY 1.25
3821-3824 37c **Christmas Music Makers (sheet stamps),** serp. die cut 11x11¼, *Oct. 23,* New York, NY 3.25
3821-3824, any single 1.25
3825-3828 37c **Christmas Music Makers (vending machine booklet stamps),** serp. die cut 11¾x11 on 3 sides, *Oct. 23,* New York, NY 3.25
3825-3828, any single 1.25
3829 37c **Snowy Egret coil,** *Oct. 24,* New York, NY 1.25

2004

3830 37c **Snowy Egret booklet stamp,** *Jan. 30,* Norfolk, VA 1.25
3831 37c **Pacific Coral Reef,** *Jan. 2,* Honolulu, HI 7.50
3831a-3831j, any single 1.25
3832 37c **Chinese New Year,** *Jan. 13,* San Francisco, CA 1.50
3833 37c **Love Candy Hearts,** *Jan. 14,* Revere, MA 1.25
3834 37c **Paul Robeson,** *Jan. 20,* Princeton, NJ 1.25
3835 37c **Theodor Seuss Geisel (Dr. Seuss),** *Mar. 2,* La Jolla, CA 1.25
3836 37c **Flowers,** *Mar. 4,* New York, NY 1.25
3837 60c **Flowers,** *Mar. 4,* New York, NY 1.50
3838 37c **U.S. Air Force Academy,** *Apr. 1,* Colorado Springs, CO 2.00
3839 37c **Henry Mancini,** *Apr. 13,* Los Angeles, CA 1.25
3840-3843 37c **American Choreographers,** *May 4,* Newark, NJ 3.25
3840-3843, any single 1.25
3844-3853 (25c) **Eagle coils,** perf. 9¾ vert. *May 12,* Washington, DC 6.00
3844-3853, any single 1.25
3854 37c **Lewis & Clark,** *May 14,* Astoria, OR 1.75
Atchison, KS 1.75
Great Falls, MT 1.75
Hartford, IL 1.75
Ilwaco, WA 1.75
Orofino, ID 1.75
Omaha, NE 1.75
Pierre, SD 1.75
Sioux City, IA 1.75
St. Charles, MO 1.75
Washburn, ND 1.75

3855-3856 37c **Lewis & Clark booklet stamps,** *May 14,* Astoria, OR 2.75
Atchison, KS 2.75
Great Falls, MT 2.75
Hartford, IL 2.75
Ilwaco, WA 2.75
Orofino, ID 2.75
Omaha, NE 2.75
Pierre, SD 2.75
Sioux City, IA 2.75
St. Charles, MO 2.75
Washburn, ND 2.75
3855-3856, any single, any of the aforementioned 11 cities 1.40
3857-3861 37c **Isamu Noguchi,** *May 18,* Long Island City, NY 4.00
3857-3861, any single 1.25
3862 37c **National World War II Memorial,** *May 29,* Washington, DC 2.00
Any other city 2.00
3863 37c **Summer Olympics,** *June 9,* Philadelphia, PA 1.25
3864 (5c) **Sea Coast coil with black 2004 date,** *June 11,* Washington, DC 1.25
3865-3868 37c **Disney Characters,** *June 23,* Anaheim, CA 3.25
3865-3868, any single 1.25
3869 37c **U.S.S. Constellation,** *June 30,* Baltimore, MD 1.25
3870 37c **R. Buckminster Fuller,** *July 12,* Stanford, CA 1.25
3871 37c **James Baldwin,** *July 23,* New York, NY 1.25
3872 37c **Martin Johnson Heade,** *Aug. 12,* Sacramento, CA 1.25
3873 37c **Art of the American Indian pane of 10,** *Aug. 21,* Santa Fe, NM 7.00
3873a-3873j, any single, Santa Fe, NM 1.25
3876 37c **John Wayne,** *Sept. 9,* Los Angeles, CA 2.50
3877 37c **Sickle Cell Disease,** *Sept. 29,* Atlanta, GA 1.25
3878 37c **Cloudscapes,** *Oct. 4,* Milton, MA 9.00
3878a-3878o any single 1.25
3879 37c **Christmas Madonna,** *Oct. 14,* New York, NY 1.25
3880 37c **Hanukkah,** *Oct. 15,* New York, NY 1.25
3881 37c **Kwanzaa,** *Oct. 16,* Chicago, IL 1.25
3882 37c **Moss Hart,** *Oct. 25,* New York, NY 1.25
3883-3886 37c **Christmas Santa Ornaments,** serpentine die cut 11½x11, *Nov. 16,* New York, NY 3.25
3883-3886, any single 1.25
3887-3890 37c **Christmas Santa Ornaments,** serpentine die cut 10¼x10¾ on 2 or 3 sides, *Nov. 16,* New York, NY 3.25
3887-3890, any single 1.25
3891-3894 37c **Christmas Santa Ornaments,** serpentine die cut 8 on 2, 3 or 4 sides, *Nov. 16,* New York, NY 3.25
3891-3894, any single 1.25

2005

3895 37c **Chinese New Year double-sided pane,** *Jan. 6,* Honolulu, HI 20.00
3895a-3895l, any single 1.25
3896 37c **Marian Anderson,** *Jan. 27,* Washington, DC 1.25
3897 37c **Ronald Reagan,** *Feb. 9,* Simi Valley, CA 2.00
Any other city 1.50
3898 37c **Love,** *Feb. 18,* Atlanta, GA 1.25
3899 37c **Northeast Deciduous Forest,** *Mar. 3,* New York, NY 7.50
3899a-3899j, any single 1.25
3900-3903 37c **Spring Flowers,** *Mar. 15,* Chicago, IL 3.25
3900-3903, any single 1.25
3904 37c **Robert Penn Warren,** *Apr. 22,* Guthrie, KY 1.25
3905 37c **Yip Harburg,** *Apr. 28,* New York, NY 1.25
3906-3909 37c **American Scientists,** *May 4,* New Haven, CT 3.25
3906-3909, any single 1.25
3910 37c **Modern American Architecture,** *May 19,* Las Vegas NV 9.00
Any other city 9.00
3910a-3910l, any single, Las Vegas, NV 1.25
3910a-3910l, any single, any other city 1.25
3911 37c **Henry Fonda,** *May 20,* Los Angeles, CA 1.50
3912-3915 37c **Disney Characters,** *June 30,* Anaheim, CA 3.25
3912-3915, any single 1.50
3916-3925 37c **Advances in Aviation,** *July 29,* Oshkosh, WI 7.50
3916-3925, Vienna, VA 7.50
3916-3925, any single, Oshkosh, WI 1.50
3916-3925, any single, Vienna, VA 1.50
3926-3929 37c **Rio Grande Blankets,** *July 30,* Santa Fe, NM 3.25
3926-3929, any single 1.25
3930 37c **Presidential Libraries Act, 50th Anniv.,** *Aug. 4,* Grand Rapids, MI 1.25
Abilene, KS 1.50
Ann Arbor, MI 1.25
Atlanta, GA 1.25
Austin, TX 1.25
Boston, MA 1.50
College Station, TX 1.25
Hyde Park, NY 1.25
Independence, MO 1.50
Little Rock, AR 1.25
Simi Valley, CA 1.50
West Branch, IA 1.25
Yorba Linda, CA 1.25
3931-3935 37c **Sporty Cars of the 1950s,** *Aug. 20,* Detroit, MI 6.00
3931-3935, any single 2.00
3936 37c **Arthur Ashe,** *Aug. 27,* Flushing, NY 2.00
3937 37c **To Form a More Perfect Union pane of 10,** *Aug. 30,* Washington, DC 8.75
Greensboro, NC 8.75
Jackson, MS 8.75
Little Rock, AR 8.75
Memphis, TN 8.75
Montgomery, AL 8.75
Selma, AL 8.75
Topeka, KS 8.75
Any other city 8.75
3937a-3937j, any single, Washington, DC 2.00
3937a-3937j, any single, Greensboro, NC 2.00
3937a-3937j, any single, Jackson, MS 2.00
3937a-3937j, any single, Little Rock, AR 2.00
3937a-3937j, any single, Memphis, TN 2.00
3937a-3937j, any single, Montgomery, AL 2.00
3937a-3937j, any single, Selma, AL 2.00
3937a-3937j, any single, Topeka, KS 2.00
3937a-3937j, any single, any other city 2.00
3938 37c **Child Health,** *Sept. 7,* Philadelphia, PA 2.00
Any other city 2.00
3939-3942 37c **Let's Dance,** *Sept. 17,* New York, NY 4.25
Miami, FL 4.25
3939-3942, any single, New York, NY 2.00
3939-3942, any single, Miami, FL 2.00
3943 37c **Greta Garbo,** *Sept. 23,* New York, NY 2.25
3944 37c **Jim Henson and the Muppets,** *Sept. 28,* North Hollywood, CA 9.25
3944a-3944k, any single 2.00
3945-3948 37c **Constellations,** *Oct. 3,* Bloomfield Hills, MI 4.25
3945-3948, any single 2.00
3949-3952 37c **Christmas Cookies,** serpentine die cut 10¾x11, *Oct. 20,* New York, NY 4.25
Minneapolis, MN 4.25
3949-3952, any single, New York, NY 2.00
3949-3952, any single, Minneapolis, MN 5.00
3953-3956 37c **Christmas Cookies,** convertible booklet stamps, serpentine die cut 10¾x11 on 2 or 3 sides, *Oct. 20,* New York, NY 4.25
Minneapolis, MN 4.25
3953-3956, any single, New York, NY 2.00
3953-3956, any single, Minneapolis, MN 2.00
3957-3960 37c **Christmas Cookies,** vending machine booklet stamps, serpentine die cut 10½x10¾, *Oct. 20,* New York, NY 4.25
Minneapolis, MN 4.25
3957-3960, any single, New York, NY 2.00
3957-3960, any single, Minneapolis, MN 2.00
3961-3964 37c **Distinguished Marines,** *Nov. 10,* Washington, DC 4.25
Oceanside, CA 4.25
Any other city 4.25
3961-3964, any single, Washington, DC 2.50
3961-3964, any single, Oceanside, CA 2.50
3961-3964, any single, any other city 2.00
3965 (39c) **Flag and Statue of Liberty,** perf. 11¼, *Dec. 8,* Washington, DC 2.00
Any other city 2.00
3966 (39c) **Flag and Statue of Liberty,** self-adhesive, serpentine die cut 11¼x11, *Dec. 8,* Washington, DC 2.00
Any other city 2.00
3967 (39c) **Flag and Statue of Liberty,** coil stamp, perf. 9¾ vert., *Dec. 8,* Washington, DC 2.00
Any other city 2.00
3968 (39c) **Flag and Statue of Liberty,** self-adhesive coil stamp, photo., serpentine die cut 8½ vert., *Dec. 8,* Washington, DC 2.00
Any other city 2.00
3969 (39c) **Flag and Statue of Liberty,** self-adhesive coil stamp, photo., serpentine die cut 10¼ vert., *Dec. 8,* Washington, DC 2.00
Any other city 2.00
3970 (39c) **Flag and Statue of Liberty,** self-adhesive coil stamp, litho., serpentine die cut 9½ vert., *Dec. 8,* Washington, DC 2.00
3972 (39c) **Flag and Statue of Liberty,** self-adhesive booklet stamp with bright blue spot over date, photo., serpentine die cut 11¼x10¾ on 2 or 3 sides, *Dec. 8,* Washington, DC 2.00
Any other city 2.00
3973 (39c) **Flag and Statue of Liberty,** self-adhesive booklet stamp, serpentine die cut 10¼x10¾, *Dec. 8,* Washington, DC 2.00
Any other city 2.00

Although No. 3973 has an issue date of Dec. 8, it was not known to have been available until January 2006.

3974 (39c) **Flag and Statue of Liberty,** self-adhesive booklet stamp with dark blue spot over date, litho., serpentine die cut 11¼x11 on 2 or 3 sides, *Dec. 8,* Washington, DC 2.00
Any other city 2.00
3975 (39c) **Flag and Statue of Liberty,** self-adhesive booklet stamp, photo., serpentine die cut 8 on 2, 3 or 4 sides, *Dec. 8,* Washington, DC 2.00
Any other city 2.00

2006

3976 (39c) **Birds,** self-adhesive booklet stamp, *Jan. 3,* Washington, DC 2.00
Any other city 2.00
3978 39c **Flag and Statue of Liberty,** self-adhesive, *Apr. 8,* Washington, DC 2.00
Any other city 2.00
3979 39c **Flag and Statue of Liberty,** coil stamp, perf. 10 vert. *Mar. 8,* Washington, DC 2.00
Any other city 2.00
3980 39c **Flag and Statue of Liberty,** self-adhesive coil stamp, serpentine die cut 11 vert. with rounded corners, *Jan. 9,* Washington, DC 2.00
Any other city 2.00
3981 39c **Flag and Statue of Liberty,** self-adhesive coil stamp, serpentine die cut 9½ vert., *Apr. 8,* Washington, DC 2.00
Any other city 2.00
3985b 39c **Flag and Statue of Liberty,** photo., serpentine die cut 11.1 on 2 or 3 sides, *Nov. 8,* Washington, DC 2.00
3987-3994 39c **Children's Book Animals,** *Jan. 10,* Findlay, OH 7.50
3987-3994, any single 2.00
3995 39c **2006 Winter Olympics,** *Jan. 11,* Colorado Springs, CO 2.00
3996 39c **Hattie McDaniel,** *Jan. 25,* Beverly Hills, CA 2.00
3997 39c **Chinese New Year pane,** *Jan. 29,* Washington, DC 10.50
3997a-3997l, any single 2.00
3998 39c **Wedding Dove,** *Mar. 1,* New York, NY 2.00
3999 63c **Wedding Dove,** *Mar. 1,* New York, NY 2.50
4000 24c **Common Buckeye Butterfly,** perf. 11¼, *Mar. 8,* Washington, DC 2.00
Any other city 2.00
4001 24c **Common Buckeye Butterfly,** self-adhesive, serpentine die cut 11, *Mar. 8,* Washington, DC 2.00
Any other city 2.00
4001a 24c **Common Buckeye Butterfly,** self-adhesive booklet pane stamp, serpentine die cut 10¾x11¼, *Mar. 8,* Washington, DC 2.00
Any other city 2.00
4002 24c **Common Buckeye Butterfly,** self-adhesive coil stamp, serpentine die cut 8½ horiz., *Mar. 8,* Washington, DC 2.00
Any other city 2.00
4003-4007 39c **Crops of the Americas,** self-adhesive coil stamps, *Mar. 16,* New York, NY 5.25
4003-4007, any single 2.00
4008-4012 39c **Crops of the Americas,** self-adhesive booklet stamps, serpentine die cut 10¾x10½ on 2 or 3 sides, *Mar. 16,* New York, NY 5.25
4008-4012, any single 2.00
4013-4017 39c **Crops of the Americas,** self-adhesive booklet stamps, serpentine die cut 10¾x11¼ on 2 or 3 sides, *Mar. 16,* New York, NY 5.25
4013-4017, any single 2.00
4018 $4.05 **X-Plane,** *Mar. 17,* New York, NY 8.00
Any other city 8.00
4019 $14.40 **X-Plane,** *Mar. 17,* New York, NY 27.50
Any other city 27.50
4020 39c **Sugar Ray Robinson,** *Apr. 7,* New York, NY 2.00
4021-4024 39c **Benjamin Franklin,** *Apr. 7,* Philadelphia, PA 4.50
4021-4024, any single 2.00

4025-4028	39c **Disney Characters,** *Apr. 21,* Orlando, FL	4.50
	4025-4028, any single	2.00
4029	39c **Birds,** self-adhesive booklet stamp, *May 1,* Washington, DC	2.00
4030	39c **Katherine Anne Porter,** *May 15,* Kyle, TX	2.00
4031	39c **Amber Alert,** *May 25,* Arlington, TX	2.00
	Washington, DC	2.00
4032	39c **Purple Heart,** *May 26,* Washington, DC	2.00
4072a	39c **Wonders of America,** *May 27,* Washington, DC	32.50
	4033-4072, any single, Washington, DC	2.00
	4072a, any other city	32.50
	4033-4072, any single, any other city	2.75
4073	39c **Samuel de Champlain,** self-adhesive stamp, *May 28,* Washington, DC	2.00
	Ticonderoga, NY	2.00
	Annapolis Royal, Nova Scotia, Canada	2.00
4074	**Samuel de Champlain,** souvenir sheet, *May 28,* Washington, DC	4.75
	Ticonderoga, NY	4.75
	Annapolis Royal, Nova Scotia, Canada	4.75
4075	**Washington 2006 World Philatelic Exhibition,** souvenir sheet, *May 29,* Washington, DC	16.00
4075a	$1	3.25
4075b	$2	5.25
4075c	$5	10.00
4076	39c **Distinguished American Diplomats,** souvenir sheet, *May 30,* Washington, DC	6.00
	4076a-4076f, any single	2.00
4077	39c **Judy Garland,** *June 10,* New York, NY	2.50
4078	39c **Ronald Reagan,** *June 14,* Simi Valley, CA	2.00
4079	39c **Happy Birthday,** *June 23,* Santa Clara, CA	2.00
4080-4083	39c **Baseball Sluggers,** *July 15,* Bronx, NY	4.50
	4080-4083, any single	2.50
4084	39c **DC Comics Superheroes,** *July 20,* San Diego, CA	16.00
	4084a-4084t, any single	2.00
4085-4088	39c **Motorcycles,** *Aug. 7,* Sturgis, SD	4.50
	4085-4088, any single, Sturgis, SD	2.00
4089-4098	39c **Quilts of Gee's Bend,** *Aug. 24,* Chicago, IL	8.00
	4089-4098, any single, Chicago, IL	2.00
4099	39c **Southern Florida Wetland,** *Oct. 4,* Naples, FL	9.00
	4099a-4099j, any single	2.00
4100	39c **Christmas Madonna,** *Oct. 17,* Denver, CO	2.00
4101-4104	39c **Christmas Snowflakes,** denominations higher than year date, serpentine die cut 11¼x11, *Oct. 5,* New York, NY	4.50
	4101-4104, any single	2.00
4105-4108	39c **Christmas Snowflakes,** denominations even with year date, serpentine die cut 11¼x11½ on 2 or 3 sides, *Oct. 5,* New York, NY	4.50
	4105-4108, any single	2.00
4109-4112	39c **Christmas Snowflakes,** denominations even with year date, serpentine die cut 11¼x11 on 2 or 3 sides, *Oct. 5,* New York, NY	4.50
	4109-4112, any single	2.00
4113-4116	39c **Christmas Snowflakes,** denominations even with year date, serpentine die cut 8 on 2, 3 or 4 sides, *Oct. 5,* New York, NY	4.50
	4113-4116, any single	2.00
4117	39c **Eid,** *Oct. 6,* New York, NY	2.00
4118	39c **Hanukkah,** *Oct. 6,* New York, NY	2.00
4119	39c **Kwanzaa,** *Oct. 6,* New York, NY	2.00

2007-09

4120	39c **Ella Fitzgerald,** *Jan. 10,* New York, NY	2.00
4121	39c **Oklahoma Statehood,** *Jan. 11,* Oklahoma City, OK	2.00
4122	39c **Love,** self-adhesive booklet stamp, *Jan. 13,* Hershey, PA	2.00
4123	84c **International Polar Year,** *Feb. 21,* Fairbanks, AK	4.75
	4123a-4123b, either single	3.00
4124	39c **Henry Wadsworth Longfellow,** *Mar. 15,* New York, NY	2.00
4125	(41c) **Liberty Bell,** self-adhesive booklet stamp, large microprinting, 16mm bell, serpentine die cut 11¼x10¾, *Apr. 12,* Philadelphia, PA	2.10
4125b	(42c) **Forever,** dated "2008," *Aug. 22, 2008,* Falls Church, VA	2.10
4125d	(44c) **Forever,** dated "2009," *Aug. 7,* Pittsburgh, PA	2.10
4126	(41c) **Liberty Bell,** self-adhesive booklet stamp, small microprinting, 16mm bell, serpentine die cut 11¼x10¾, *Apr. 12,* Philadelphia, PA	2.10
4126b	(42c) **Forever,** dated "2008," *Aug. 22, 2008,* Falls Church, VA	2.10
4126d	(44c) **Forever,** dated "2009" in copper *Aug. 7,* Pittsburgh, PA	2.10
4127	(41c) **Liberty Bell,** self-adhesive booklet stamp, medium microprinting, 15mm bell, serpentine die cut 11¼x10¾, *Apr. 12,* Philadelphia, PA	2.10
4127d	(42c) **Forever,** dated "2008," *May 12, 2008* Washington, DC	2.10
4127f	(42c) **Forever,** small "2008" date, *Oct. 25, 2008,* New York, NY	2.10
4127i	(44c) **Forever,** dated "2009" in copper, *May 15, 2009,* Washington, DC	2.10
4128	(41c) **Liberty Bell,** self-adhesive booklet stamp, large microprinting, 16mm bell, serpentine die cut 8, *Apr. 12,* Philadelphia, PA	2.10
4128b	(42c) **Forever,** dated "2009," *Feb. 24,* Washington, DC	2.10
4129	(41c) **Flag,** perf. 11¼, *Apr. 12,* Washington, DC	2.10
4130	(41c) **Flag,** self-adhesive, serpentine die cut 11¼x10¾, *Apr. 12,* Washington, DC	2.10
4131	(41c) **Flag,** coil stamp, perf. 9¾ vert., *Apr. 12,* Washington, DC	2.10
4132	(41c) **Flag,** self-adhesive coil stamp, serpentine die cut 9½ vert., *Apr. 12,* Washington, DC	2.10
4133	(41c) **Flag,** self-adhesive coil stamp, serpentine die cut 11 vert., perpendicular corners, *Apr. 12,* Washington, DC	2.10
4134	(41c) **Flag,** self-adhesive coil stamp, serpentine die cut 8½ vert., *Apr. 12,* Washington, DC	2.10
4135	(41c) **Flag,** self-adhesive coil stamp, serpentine die cut 11 vert., rounded corners, *Apr. 12,* Washington, DC	2.10
4136	41c **Settlement of Jamestown,** *May 11,* Jamestown, VA	2.10
4137	26c **Florida Panther,** perf. 11¼x11 *May 12,* Washington, DC	2.10
4138	17c **Bighorn Sheep,** self-adhesive, serpentine die cut 11, *May 14,* Washington, DC	2.10
4139	26c **Florida Panther,** self-adhesive, serpentine die cut 11¼x11, *May 12,* Washington, DC	2.10
4140	17c **Bighorn Sheep,** self-adhesive coil, serpentine die cut 11 vert., *May 21,* Washington, DC	2.10
4141	26c **Florida Panther,** self-adhesive coil, serpentine die cut 11 vert., *May 12,* Washington, DC	2.10
4142	26c **Florida Panther,** self-adhesive booklet stamp, serpentine die cut 11¼x11 on 3 sides, *May 12,* Washington, DC	2.10
4143	39c **Star Wars,** *May 25,* Los Angeles, CA	12.50
	4143a-4143o, any single	2.10
4144	$4.60 **Air Force One,** *June 13,* Washington, DC	10.00
4145	$16.25 **Marine One,** *June 13,* Washington, DC	32.50
4146-4150	41c **Pacific Lighthouses,** *June 21,* Westport, WA	5.50
	4146-4150, any single	2.10
4151	41c **Wedding Heart,** *June 27,* Washington, DC	2.10
4152	58c **Wedding Heart,** *June 27,* Washington, DC	2.40
4153-4156	41c **Pollination,** type I, *June 29,* Washington, DC	4.50
	4153-4156, type I, any single	2.10
	4153a-4156a, type II	4.50
	4153a-4156a, type II, any single	2.10
4157	(10c) **Patriotic Banner coil,** serpentine die cut 11 vert., *July 4,* Washington, DC	2.00
4158	(10c) **Patriotic Banner coil,** serpentine die cut 11½ vert., *July 4,* Washington, DC	2.00
4159	41c **Marvel Comics Superheroes,** *July 26,* San Diego, CA	17.00
	4159a-4159t, any single	2.10
4160-4163	41c **Vintage Mahogany Speedboats,** *Aug. 4,* Clayton, NY	4.50
	4160-4163, any single	2.50
4164	41c **Purple Heart,** *Aug. 7,* Washington, DC	2.10
4165	41c **Louis Comfort Tiffany,** *Aug. 9,* Portland, OR	2.10
4166-4175	41c **Flowers,** self-adhesive coil stamps, *Aug. 10,* Portland, OR	8.25
	4166-4175, any single	2.10
4176-4185	41c **Flowers,** self-adhesive booklet stamps, *Aug. 10,* Portland, OR	8.25
	4176-4185, any single	2.10
4186	41c **Flag,** self-adhesive coil stamp with microprinting on right side of flagpole, serpentine die cut 9½ vert., *Aug. 15,* Washington, DC	2.10
4187	41c **Flag,** self-adhesive coil stamp with microprinting on left side of flagpole, serpentine die cut 9½ vert., *Aug. 15,* Washington, DC	2.10
4188	41c **Flag,** self-adhesive coil stamp with perpendicular corners, serpentine die cut 8½ vert., *Aug. 15,* Washington, DC	2.10
4189	41c **Flag,** self-adhesive coil stamp with rounded corners, serpentine die cut 11 vert., *Aug. 15,* Washington, DC	2.10
4190	41c **Flag,** self-adhesive booklet stamp with microprinting on right side of flagpole, *Aug. 15,* Washington, DC	2.10
4191	41c **Flag,** self-adhesive booklet stamp with microprinting on left side of flagpole, *Aug. 15,* Washington, DC	2.10
4192-4195	41c **Disney Characters,** *Aug. 16,* Orlando, FL	4.50
	4192-4195, any single	2.10
4196	41c **Celebrate,** *Aug. 17,* Stamford, CT	2.10
4197	41c **James Stewart,** *Aug. 17,* Universal City, CA	2.50
4198	41c **Alpine Tundra,** *Aug. 28,* Estes Park, CO	8.25
	4198a-4198j, any single	2.10
4199	41c **Gerald R. Ford,** *Aug. 31,* Grand Rapids, MI	2.10
	Rancho Mirage, CA	2.10
4200	41c **Jury Duty,** *Sept. 12,* New York, NY	2.10
4201	41c **Mendez v. Westminster,** *Sept. 14,* Santa Ana, CA	2.10
4202	41c **Eid,** *Sept. 28,* Washington, DC	2.10
4203-4204	41c **Auroras,** *Oct. 1,* Washington, DC	3.00
	4203-4204, any single	2.10
4205	41c **Yoda,** *Oct. 25,* New York, NY	2.10
4206	41c **Christmas Madonna,** *Oct. 25,* New York, NY	2.10
4207-4210	41c **Christmas Knits,** serpentine die cut 10¾, *Oct. 25,* New York, NY	4.50
	4207-4210, any single	2.10
4211-4214	41c **Christmas Knits,** serpentine die cut 11¼x11 on 2 or 3 sides, *Oct. 25,* New York, NY	4.50
	4211-4214, any single	2.10
4215-4218	41c **Christmas Knits,** serpentine die cut 8 on 2, 3 or 4 sides, *Oct. 25,* New York, NY	4.50
	4215-4218, any single	2.10
4219	41c **Hanukkah,** *Oct. 26,* New York, NY	2.10
4220	41c **Kwanzaa,** *Oct. 26,* New York, NY	2.10

2008

4221	41c **Chinese New Year,** *Jan. 9,* San Francisco, CA	2.50
4222	41c **Charles W. Chesnutt,** *Jan. 31,* Cleveland, OH	2.10
4223	41c **Marjorie Kinnan Rawlings,** *Feb. 21,* Hawthorne, FL	2.10
4224-4227	41c **American Scientists,** *Mar. 6,* New York, NY	4.50
	4224-4227, any single	2.10
4228-4231	42c **Flags,** coil stamps, perf. 10 vert., *Apr. 18,* Washington, DC	4.75
	4228-4231, any single	2.10
4232-4235	42c **Flags,** self-adhesive coil stamps, serpentine die cut 9½ vert., *Apr. 18,* Washington, DC	4.75
	4232-4235, any single	2.10
4236-4239	42c **Flags,** self-adhesive coil stamps, serpentine die cut 11 vert. with perpendicular corners, *Apr. 18,* Washington, DC	4.75
	4236-4239, any single	2.10
4240-4243	42c **Flags,** self-adhesive coil stamps, serpentine die cut 8½ vert., *Apr. 18,* Washington, DC	4.75
	4240-4243, any single	2.10
4244-4247	42c **Flags,** self-adhesive coil stamps, serpentine die cut 11 vert. with rounded corners, *Apr. 18,* Washington, DC	4.75
	4244-42471, any single	2.10
4248-4252	42c **American Journalists,** *Apr. 22,* Washington, DC	5.50
	4248-4252, any single	2.10

4253-4257 27c **Tropical Fruit,** serpentine die cut 11¼x10¾, *Apr. 25,* Burlingame, CA 4.00
4253-4257, any single 1.75
4258-4262 27c **Tropical Fruit,** self-adhesive coil stamps, serpentine die cut 8½ vert., *Apr. 25,* Burlingame, CA 4.00
4258-4262, any single 1.75
4263 42c **Purple Heart,** perf. 11¼, *Apr. 30,* Washington, DC 2.10
4264 42c **Purple Heart,** self-adhesive, serpentine die cut 11¼x10¾, *Apr. 30,* Washington, DC 2.10
4265 42c **Frank Sinatra,** *May 13,* New York, NY 3.00
Las Vegas, NV 3.00
4266 42c **Minnesota Statehood, 150th Anniv.,** *May 17,* St. Paul, MN 2.10
4267 62c **Dragonfly,** *May 19,* Washington, DC 2.50
4268 $4.80 **Mount Rushmore,** *June 6,* McLean, VA 9.75
4269 $16.50 **Hoover Dam,** *June 20,* Washington, DC 33.00
4270 42c **Love,** *June 10,* Washington, DC 2.10
4271 42c **Wedding Heart,** *June 10,* Washington, DC 2.10
4272 59c **Wedding Heart,** *June 10,* Washington, DC 2.40
4273-4282 42c **Flags of Our Nation,** *June 14,* Washington, DC 8.50
4273-4282, any single 2.10
4283-4292 42c **Flags of Our Nation,** *Sept. 2,* Washington, DC 8.50
4283-4292, any single 2.10
4293-4302 44c **Flags of Our Nation,** *Aug. 6, 2009* Pittsburgh, PA 9.00
4293-4302, any single 2.10
4303-4312 44c **Flags of Our Nation,** *Apr. 16, 2010* New York, NY 9.00
#4303-4312, any single 2.10
4313-4322 (44c) **Flags of Our Nation,** *Aug. 11, 2011* Columbus, OH 9.00
4313-4322, any single 2.10
4323-4332 (45c) **Flags of Our Nation,** *Aug. 16, 2012* Sacramento, CA 9.00
4323-4332, any single 2.10
4333 42c **Charles and Ray Eames,** *June 17,* Santa Monica, CA 13.50
4333a-4333p, any single 2.10
4334 42c **Summer Olympics,** *June 19,* Philadelphia, PA 2.10
4335 42c **Celebrate,** *July 10,* Washington, DC 2.10
4336-4340 42c **Vintage Black Cinema,** *July 16,* Newark, NJ 5.50
4336-4340, any single 2.10
4341 42c **Take Me Out to the Ballgame, Cent.,** *July 16,* Washington, DC 2.50
4342-4345 42c **Disney Characters,** *Aug. 7,* Anaheim, CA 4.75
4342-4345, any single 2.10
4346 42c **Albert Bierstadt,** *Aug. 14,* Hartford, CT 2.10
4347 42c **Sunflower,** *Aug. 15,* Hartford, CT 2.10
4348 (5c) **Sea Coast coil with 2008 date,** litho., *Sept. 5,* Washington, DC 2.10
4349 42c **Latin Jazz,** *Sept. 8,* Washington, DC 2.10
4350 42c **Bette Davis,** *Sept. 18,* Boston, MA 2.50
4351 42c **Eid,** *Sept. 23,* Washington, DC 2.10
4352 42c **Great Lakes Dunes,** *Oct. 2,* Empire, MI 8.50
4352a-4352j, any single 2.10
4353-4357 42c **Automobiles of the 1950s,** *Oct. 3,* Carlisle, PA 5.50
4353-4357, any single 2.10
4358 42c **Alzheimer's Disease Awareness,** *Oct. 17,* Morgantown, WV 2.10
4359 42c **Christmas Madonna,** *Oct. 23,* New York, NY 2.10
4360-4363 42c **Christmas Nutcrackers,** serpentine die cut 10¾x11 on 2 or 3 sides, *Oct. 23,* New York, NY 4.75
4360-4363, any single 2.10
4364-4367 42c **Christmas Nutcrackers,** serpentine die cut 11¼x11 on 2 or 3 sides, *Oct. 23,* New York, NY 4.75
4364-4367, any single 2.10
4368-4371 42c **Christmas Nutcrackers,** serpentine die cut 8 on 2, 3 or 4 sides, *Oct. 23,* New York, NY 4.75
4368-4371, any single 2.10
4372 42c **Hanukkah,** *Oct. 24,* New York, NY 2.10
4373 42c **Kwanzaa,** *Oct. 24,* New York, NY 2.10

2009

4374 42c **Alaska Statehood,** *Jan. 3,* Anchorage, AK 2.10
4375 42c **Chinese New Year,** *Jan. 8,* New York, NY 2.50
4376 42c **Oregon Statehood,** *Jan. 14,* Portland, OR 2.10
4377 42c **Edgar Allan Poe,** *Jan. 16,* Richmond, VA 2.50
4378 $4.95 **Redwood Forest,** *Jan. 16,* San Diego, CA 10.00
4379 $17.50 **Old Faithful,** *Jan. 16,* San Diego, CA 35.00
4380-4383 42c **Abraham Lincoln,** *Feb. 9,* Springfield, IL 5.00
4380-4383, any single 2.50
4384 42c **Civil Rights Pioneers,** *Feb. 21,* New York, NY 6.25
4384a-4384f, any single 2.10
4385 (10c) **Patriotic Banner coil,** perf. 9¾ vert., *Feb. 24,* Washington, DC 2.10
4386 61c **Richard Wright,** *Apr. 9,* Chicago, IL 2.50
4387 28c **Polar Bear,** serpentine die cut 11¼x11, *Apr. 16,* New York, NY 2.10
4388 64c **Dolphin,** *June 12,* Washington, DC 2.50
4389 28c **Polar Bear coil,** serpentine die cut 8½ vert., *Apr. 16,* New York, NY 2.10
4390 44c **Purple Heart,** *Apr. 28,* Washington, DC 2.10
4391 44c **Flag,** coil stamp, perf. 9¾ vert., *May 1,* Washington, DC 2.10
4392 44c **Flag,** litho. self-adhesive coil stamp, serpentine die cut 11 vert. with perpendicular corners, *May 8,* Washington, DC 2.10
4393 44c **Flag,** litho. self-adhesive coil stamp, serpentine die cut 9½ vert., *May 8,* Washington, DC 2.10
4394 44c **Flag,** photo. self-adhesive coil stamp, serpentine die cut 8½ vert., *May 8,* Washington, DC 2.10
4395 44c **Flag,** photo. self-adhesive coil stamp, serpentine die cut 11 vert. with rounded corners, *May 1,* Washington, DC 2.10
4396 44c **Flag,** self-adhesive booklet stamp, serpentine die cut 11¼x10¾ on 3 sides, *June 5,* McLean, VA 2.10
4397 44c **Wedding Rings,** *May 1,* Washington, DC 2.10
4398 61c **Wedding Cake,** *May 1,* Washington, DC 2.50
4399-4403 44c **The Simpsons,** *May 7,* Los Angeles, CA 5.75
4399-4403, any single 2.10
4404-4405 44c **Love (King and Queen of Hearts),** *May 8,* Washington, DC 3.00
4404-4405, either single 2.10
4406 44c **Bob Hope,** *May 29,* San Diego, CA 2.75
4407 44c **Celebrate,** *June 10,* Washington, DC 2.10
4408 44c **Anna Julia Cooper,** *June 11,* Washington, DC 2.10
4409-4413 44c **Gulf Coast Lighthouses,** *July 23,* Biloxi, MS 5.75
4409-4413, any single 2.10
4414 44c **Early TV Memories,** *Aug. 11,* North Hollywood, CA 18.00
4414a-4414t, any single 2.10
4415 44c **Hawaii Statehood,** *Aug. 21,* Honolulu, HI 2.10
4416 44c **Eid,** *Sept. 3,* Washington, DC 2.10
4417-4420 44c **Thanksgiving Day Parade,** *Sept. 9,* New York, NY 4.75
4417-4420, any single 2.10
4421 44c **Gary Cooper,** *Sept. 10,* Los Angeles, CA 2.50
4422 44c **Supreme Court Justices,** *Sept. 22,* Washington, DC 4.75
4422a-4422d, any single 2.10
4423 44c **Kelp Forest,** *Oct. 1,* Monterey, CA 9.00
4423a-4423j, any single 2.10
4424 44c **Christmas Madonna,** *Oct. 20,* San Simeon, CA 2.10
4425-4428 44c **Christmas Winter Holidays,** serpentine die cut 10¾x11 on 2 or 3 sides, *Oct. 8,* New York, NY 4.75
4425-4428, any single 2.10
4429-4432 44c **Christmas Winter Holidays,** serpentine die cut 8 on 2, 3 or 4 sides, *Oct. 8,* New York, NY 4.75
4429-4432, any single 2.10
4433 44c **Hanukkah,** *Oct. 9,* New York, NY 2.10
4434 44c **Kwanzaa,** *Oct. 9,* New York, NY 2.10

2010

4435 44c **Chinese New Year,** *Jan. 14,* Los Angeles, CA 2.50
4436 44c **2010 Winter Olympics,** *Jan. 22,* Park City, UT 2.10
4437 (44c) **Forever,** serpentine die cut 11¼x10¾ on 2, 3, or 4 sides, medium microprinting, bell 16mm wide, dated "2009" in copper, *Feb. 3,* Washington, DC 2.10
4438 $4.90 **Mackinac Bridge,** *Feb. 3,* Mackinaw City, MI 10.00
4439 $18.30 **Bixby Creek Bridge,** *Feb. 3,* Washington, DC 37.50
4440-4443 44c **Distinguished Sailors,** *Feb. 4,* Washington, DC 4.75
4440-4443, any single 2.10
4444 44c **Abstract Impressionists,** *Mar. 11,* Buffalo, NY 9.00
4444a-4444j, any single 2.10
4445 44c **Bill Mauldin,** *Mar. 31,* Santa Fe, NM 3.00
4446-4449 44c **Cowboys of the Silver Screen,** *Apr. 17,* Oklahoma City, OK 4.75
#4446-4449, any single 2.10
4450 44c **Love,** *Apr. 22,* Kansas City, MO 2.10
4451-4460 44c **Animal Rescue,** *Apr. 30,* North Hollywood, CA 9.00
#4451-4460, any single 2.10
4461 44c **Katharine Hepburn,** *May 12,* Old Saybrook, CT 2.50
4462 64c **Monarch Butterfly,** *May 17,* New York, NY 2.50
4463 44c **Kate Smith,** *May 27,* Washington, DC 2.10
4464 44c **Oscar Micheaux,** *June 22,* New York, NY 2.10
4465-4466 44c **Negro Leagues Baseball,** *July 15,* Kansas City, MO 3.00
4465-4466, either single 2.10
4467-4471 44c **Sunday Funnies,** *July 16,* Columbus, OH 5.75
4467-4471, any single 2.10
4472 44c **Scouting,** *July 27,* Fort A.P. Hill, VA 2.10
4473 44c **Winslow Homer,** *Aug. 12,* Richmond, VA 2.10
4474 44c **Hawaiian Rain Forest,** *Sept. 1,* Hawaii National Park, HI 9.00
4474a-4474j, any single 2.10
4475 44c **Mother Teresa,** *Sept. 5,* Washington, DC 2.50
4476 44c **Julia de Burgos,** *Sept. 14,* San Juan, PR 2.10
4477 44c **Christmas Angel With Lute,** *Oct. 21,* New York, NY 2.10
4478-4481 (44c) **Christmas Evergreens,** serpentine die cut 11 on 2 or 3 sides, *Oct. 21,* New York, NY 4.75
4478-4481, any single 2.10
4482-4485 (44c) **Christmas Evergreens,** serpentine die cut 11¼x10¾ on 2, 3 or 4 sides, *Oct. 21,* New York, NY 4.75
4482-4485, any single 2.10
4486 (44c) **Statue of Liberty,** coil stamp, serpentine die cut 9½ vert., *Dec. 1,* Washington, DC 2.10
4487 (44c) **Flag,** coil stamp, serpentine die cut 9½ vert., *Dec. 1,* Washington, DC 2.10
4487a, pair 3.00
4488 (44c) **Statue of Liberty,** coil stamp, serpentine die cut 11 vert., *Dec. 1,* Washington, DC 2.10
4489 (44c) **Flag,** coil stamp, serpentine die cut 11 vert., *Dec. 1,* Washington, DC 2.10
4489a, pair 3.00
4490 (44c) **Statue of Liberty,** coil stamp, serpentine die cut 8½ vert., *Dec. 1,* Washington, DC 2.10
4491 (44c) **Flag,** coil stamp, serpentine die cut 8½ vert., *Dec. 1,* Washington, DC 2.10
4491a, pair 3.00

2011

4492 (44c) **Chinese New Year,** *Jan. 22,* Morrow, GA 2.50
4493 (44c) **Kansas Statehood,** *Jan. 27,* Topeka, KS 2.10
4494 (44c) **Pres. Ronald Reagan,** *Feb. 10,* Simi Valley, CA 2.10
4495 (5c) **Art Deco Bird coil,** *Feb. 11,* Charleston, SC 2.10
4496 44c **Quill and Inkwell coil,** *Feb. 14,* Kansas City, MO 2.10
4497-4501 (44c) **Latin Music Legends,** *Mar. 16,* Austin, TX 5.75
4497-4501, any single 2.10
4502 (44c) **Celebrate,**photo., *Mar. 25,* Cleveland, OH 2.10
4503 (44c) **Jazz,** *Mar. 26,* New Orleans, LA 2.10
4504 20c **George Washington,** *Apr. 11,* Washington, DC 2.10
4505-4509 29c **Herbs,** *Apr. 7,* New York, NY 4.25
4505-4509, any single 2.10
4510 84c **Oveta Culp Hobby,** *Apr. 15,* Houston, TX 3.00
4511 $4.95 **New River Gorge Bridge,** *Apr. 11,* Fayetteville, WV 10.00
4512 20c **George Washington coil stamp,** *Apr. 11,* Washington, DC 2.10
4513-4517 29c **Herbs coil stamps,** *Apr. 7,* New York, NY 4.25
4513-4517, any single 2.10
4518 (44c) **Statue of Liberty booklet stamp,** serpentine die cut 11¼x 11 on 2, 3 or 4 sides, *Apr. 8,* New York, NY 2.10
4519 (44c) **Flag booklet stamp,** serpentine die cut 11¼x 11 on 2, 3 or 4 sides, *Apr. 8,* New York, NY 2.10
4519a, pair 3.00
4520 (44c) **Wedding Roses,** *Apr. 21,* Washington, DC 2.10

4521 64c **Wedding Cake,** *Apr. 11,* Washington, DC 2.50
4522-4523 (44c) **Civil War Sesquicentennial,** *Apr. 12,* Charleston, SC 3.00
4522-4523, any single 2.10
4524 (44c) **Go Green,** *Apr. 14,* Washington, DC 14.50
4524a-4524p, any single 2.10
4525 (44c) **Helen Hayes,** *Apr. 25,* Washington, DC 2.10
4526 (44c) **Gregory Peck,** *Apr. 28,* Beverly Hills, CA 2.10
4527-4528 (44c) **Space Firsts,** *May 4,* Kennedy Space Center, FL 3.00
4527-4528, either single 2.10
4529 (44c) **Purple Heart,** *May 5,* San Diego, CA 2.10
4530 (44c) **Indianapolis 500,** *May 20,* Indianapolis, IN 2.10
4531-4540 (44c) **Garden of Love,** *May 23,* Crestwood, KY 9.00
4531-4540, any single 2.10
4541-4544 (44c) **American Scientists,** *June 16,* St. Paul, MN 4.75
4541-4544, any single 2.10
4545 (44c) **Mark Twain,** *June 25,* Hannibal, MO 2.10
4546 (44c) **Pioneers of American Industrial Design,** *June 29,* New York, NY 12.00
4546a-4546l, any single 2.10
4547 (44c) **Owney, the Postal Dog,** *July 27,* Washington, DC 2.10
4548-4551 (44c) **U.S. Merchant Marine,** *July 28,* Great Neck, NY 4.75
4548-4551, any single 2.10
4552 (44c) **Eid,** *Aug. 12,* Columbus, OH 2.10
4553-4557 (44c) **Characters from Disney-Pixar Films (Send a Hello),** *Aug. 19,* Anaheim, CA 5.75
4553-4557, any single 2.10
4558 (44c) **Edward Hopper,** *Aug. 24,* Provincetown, MA 2.10
4559 (44c) **Statue of Liberty booklet stamp,** (Ashton-Potter printing), serpentine die cut 11¼x11 on 2 or 3 sides, microprinted "4evR," *Sept. 14,* Washington, DC 2.10
4560 (44c) **Flag booklet stamp,** (Ashton-Potter printing), serpentine die cut 11¼x11 on 2 or 3 sides, microprinted "4evR," *Sept. 14,* Washington, DC 2.10
4560a, pair 3.00
4561 (44c) **Statue of Liberty booklet stamp,** (Sennett printing), serpentine die cut 11¼x11 on 2 or 3 sides, microprinted "4evr," *Sept. 14,* Washington, DC 2.10
4562 (44c) **Flag booklet stamp,** (Sennett printing), serpentine die cut 11¼x11 on 2 or 3 sides, microprinted "4evr," *Sept. 14,* Washington, DC 2.10
4562a, pair 3.00
4563 (44c) **Statue of Liberty booklet stamp,** (Avery printing), serpentine die cut 11¼x11½ on 2 or 3 sides, microprinted "4EVR," *Sept. 14,* Washington, DC 2.10
4564 (44c) **Flag booklet stamp,** (Avery printing), serpentine die cut 11¼x11½ on 2 or 3 sides, microprinted "4EVR," *Sept. 14,* Washington, DC 2.10
4564a, pair 3.00
4565 (44c) **Barbara Jordan,** *Sept. 16,* Houston, TX 2.10
4566-4569 (44c) **Art of Romare Bearden,** *Sept. 28,* New York, NY 4.75
4566-4569, any single 2.10
4570 (44c) **Christmas Madonna,** *Oct. 13,* New York, NY 2.10
4571-4574 (44c) **Christmas Ornaments,** (Ashton-Potter printing), microprinted "USPS" on ornament collar, *Oct. 13,* New York, NY 4.75
4571-4574, any single 2.10
4575-4578 (44c) **Christmas Ornaments,** (Sennett double-sided booklet printing), microprinted "USPS" in various places, *Oct. 13,* New York, NY 4.75
4575-4578, any single 2.10
4579-4582 (44c) **Christmas Ornaments,** (Sennett ATM booklet printing), serpentine die cut 11¼x11 on 2, 3 or 4 sides, *Oct. 13,* New York, NY 4.75
4579-4582, any single 2.10
4583 (44c) **Hanukkah,** *Oct. 14,* New York, NY 2.10
4584 (44c) **Kwanzaa,** *Oct. 14,* New York, NY 2.10

2012

4585-4590 (25c) **Eagle coil stamps,** *Jan. 3,* Liberty, MO 4.25
4585-4590, any single 2.10
4591 (44c) **New Mexico Statehood,** *Jan. 6,* Santa Fe, NM 2.10
4592-4596 32c **Aloha Shirts,** serpentine die cut 11, *Jan. 19,* Honolulu, HI 4.50
4592-4596, any single 2.10
4597-4601 32c **Aloha Shirts coil stamps,** serpentine die cut 11 vert., *Jan. 19,* Honolulu, HI 4.50
4597-4601, any single 2.10
4602 65c **Wedding Cake,** *Jan. 20,* Alexandria, VA 2.50
4603 65c **Baltimore Checkerspot Butterfly,** *Jan. 20,* Baltimore, MD 2.50
4604-4607 65c **Dogs at Work,** *Jan. 20,* Merrifield, VA 6.50
4604-4607, any single 2.50
4608-4612 85c **Birds of Prey,** *Jan. 20,* Washington, DC 9.75
4608-4612, any single 3.00
4613-4617 45c **Weather Vane coil stamps,** *Jan. 20,* Shelburne, VT 5.75
4613-4617, any single 2.10
4618-4622 (45c) **Bonsai booklet stamps,** *Jan. 23,* Sacramento, CA 5.75
4618-4622, any single 2.10
4623 (45c) **Chinese New Year,** *Jan. 23,* San Francisco, CA 2.10
4624 (45c) **John H. Johnson,** *Jan. 31,* Chicago, IL 2.10
4625 (45c) **Heart Health,** *Feb. 9,* Washington, DC 2.10
4626 (45c) **Love,** *Feb. 14,* Colorado Springs, CO 2.10
Any other city, *Feb. 2* —

Postal Service officials declared on Feb. 2 that No. 4626 could be sold in post offices as of that date to make the stamp available to customers before St. Valentine's Day, but the first day ceremony for the stamp would still be held Feb. 14 in Colorado Springs, CO.

4627 (45c) **Arizona Statehood,** *Feb. 14,* Phoenix, AZ 2.10
4628 (45c) **Danny Thomas,** *Feb. 16,* Memphis, TN 2.10
4629-4632 (45c) **Flags coil stamps,** serpentine die cut 8½ vert., *Feb. 22,* Washington, DC 5.00
4629-4632, any single 2.10
4633-4636 (45c) **Flags coil stamps,** serpentine die cut 9½ vert., *Feb. 22,* Washington, DC 5.00
4633-4636, any single 2.10
4637-4640 (45c) **Flags coil stamps,** serpentine die cut 11 vert., *Feb. 22,* Washington, DC 5.00
4637-4640, any single 2.10
4641-4644 (45c) **Flags booklet stamps,** 18½mm from lower left to lower right corner of flag, *Feb. 22,* Washington, DC 5.00
4641-4644, any single 2.10
4645-4648 (45c) **Flags booklet stamps,** 19mm from lower left to lower right corner of flag, *Feb. 22,* Washington, DC 5.00
4645-4648, any single 2.10
4649 $5.15 **Sunshine Skyway Bridge,** *Feb. 28,* St. Petersburg, FL 10.50
4650 $18.95 **Carmel Mission,** *Feb. 28,* Carmel, CA 38.00
4651-4652 (45c) **Cherry Blossom Centennial,** *Mar. 24,* Washington, DC 3.00
4651-4652, any single 2.10
4653 (45c) **William H. Johnson,** *Apr. 11,* Baltimore, MD 2.10
4654-4663 (45c) **Twentieth Century Poets,** *Apr. 21,* Los Angeles, CA 9.00
4654-4663, any single 2.10
4664-4665 (45c) **Civil War Sesquicentennial,** *Apr. 24,* New Orleans, LA 3.00
4664-4665, any single 2.10
4666 (45c) **José Ferrer,** *Apr. 26,* New York, NY 2.10
4667 (45c) **Louisiana Statehood Bicentennial,** *Apr. 30,* Baton Rouge, LA 2.10
4668-4671 (45c) **Great Film Directors,** *May 23,* Silver Spring, MD 5.00
4668-4671, any single 2.10
4672 1c **Bobcat coil stamp,** *June 1,* San Marcos, TX 2.10
4672a 1c **Bobcat coil stamp,** dated "2015," *Feb. 21, 2015,* Mesa, AZ 2.25
4673-4676 (45c) **Flags booklet stamps,** photogravure, 19¼mm from lower left to lower right corner of flag, *June 1,* McLean, VA 5.00
4673-4676, any single 2.10
4677-4681 (45c) **Characters from Disney-Pixar Films (Mail a Smile),** *June 1,* Orlando, FL 5.75
4677-4681, any single 2.10
4682-4686 (32c) **Aloha Shirts booklet stamps,** *June 2,* McLean, VA 4.50
4682-4686, any single 2.10
4687-4690 (45c) **Bicycling,** *June 7,* Minneapolis, MN 5.00
4687-4690, any single 2.10
4691 (45c) **Girl Scouts of America,** *June 9,* Washington, DC 2.10
4692-4693 (45c) **Musicians (Edith Piaf and Miles Davis),** *June 12,* New York, NY 3.00
4692-4693, either single 2.10
4694-4697 (45c) **Major League Baseball All-Stars,** *July 20,* Cooperstown, NY 5.00
4694-4697, any single 2.10
4698-4701 (45c) **Innovative Choreographers,** *July 28,* Los Angeles, CA 5.00
4698-4701, any single 2.10
4702 (45c) **Edgar Rice Burroughs,** *Aug. 17,* Tarzana, CA 2.10
4703 (45c) **U.S.S. Constitution,** *Aug. 18,* Boston, MA 2.10
4704 (45c) **Purple Heart,** *Sept. 4,* Washington, DC 2.10
4704b (49c) **Purple Heart,** dated "2014," *Oct. 11,* Dover, DE 2.25
4705 (45c) **O. Henry,** *Sept. 11,* Greensboro, NC 2.10
4706-4709 (45c) **Flags ATM booklet stamps,** thin paper, *Sept. 22,* Humble, TX 5.00
4706-4709, any single 2.10
4710 (45c) **Earthscapes,** *Oct. 1,* Greenbelt, MD 13.50
4710a-4710o, any single 2.10
4711 (45c) **Christmas Holy Family,** *Oct. 10,* Washington, DC 2.10
4712-4715 (45c) **Christmas Santa and Sleigh,** *Oct. 13,* New York, NY 5.00
4712-4715, any single 2.10
4716 (45c) **Lady Bird Johnson,** *Nov. 30,* Austin, TX 6.75
4716a-4716f, any single 2.10
4717 $1 **Waves of Color,** *Dec. 1,* Orlando, FL 3.25
4718 $2 **Waves of Color,** *Dec. 1,* Orlando, FL 5.25
4719 $5 **Waves of Color,** *Dec. 1,* Orlando, FL 10.00
4720 $10 **Waves of Color,** *Dec. 1,* Orlando, FL 20.00

2013

4721 (45c) **Emancipation Proclamation, 150th Anniv.,** *Jan. 1,* Washington, DC 2.10
4722-4725 46c **Kaleidoscope Flowers,** *Jan. 14,* Kansas City, MO 5.00
4722-4725, any single 2.25
4726 (45c) **Chinese New Year,** *Jan. 16,* San Francisco, CA 2.10
4727-4730 33c **Apples,** serpentine die cut 11¼x10¾, *Jan. 17,* Yakima, WA 4.00
4727-4730, any single 2.10
4731-4734 33c **Apples coil stamps,** serpentine die cut 11 vert., *Jan. 17,* Yakima, WA 4.00
4731-4734, any single 2.10
4735 66c **Wedding Cake,** *Jan. 18,* Louisville, KY 2.60
4736 66c **Spicebush Swallowtail Butterfly,** *Jan. 23,* Pine Mountain, GA 2.60
4737 86c **Tufted Puffins,** *Jan. 23,* Seward, AK 3.00
4738 $5.60 **Arlington Green Bridge,** *Jan. 25,* Norcross, GA 11.50
4739 $19.95 **Grand Central Terminal,** *Feb. 1,* New York, NY 40.00
4740 ($1.10) **Earth (Global Forever),** *Jan. 28,* New York, NY 3.50
4741 (46c) **Love,** *Jan. 30,* Loveland, CO 2.25
4742 (46c) **Rosa Parks,** *Feb. 4,* Detroit or Dearborn, MI 2.25
4743-4747 (46c) **Muscle Cars,** *Feb. 22,* Daytona Beach, FL 6.00
4743-4747, any single 2.25
4748 (46c) **Modern Art in America,** *Mar. 7,* New York, NY 11.50
4748a-4748l, any single 2.25
4749 46c **Patriotic Star,** *Mar. 19,* San Francisco, CA 2.25
4750-4753 (46c) **La Florida,** *Apr. 3,* St. Augustine, FL 5.00
4750-4753, any single 2.25
4754-4763 (46c) **Vintage Seed Packets,** *Apr. 5,* Oaks, PA 9.25
4754-4763, any single 2.25
4764 (46c) **Flowers,** *Apr. 11,* New York, NY 2.25
4764a (49c) **Wedding Flowers, dated "2014,"** *May 2, 2014* Acton, MA 2.25
4765 66c **Flowers and "Yes I Do,"** *Apr. 11,* New York, NY 2.60
4766-4769 (46c) **Flags coil stamps,** serpentine die cut 8½ vert., *May 3,* Weston, MA 5.00
4766-4769, any single 2.25
4770-4773 (46c) **Flags coil stamps,** serpentine die cut 9½ vert., *May 3,* Weston, MA 5.00
4770-4773, any single 2.25
4774-4777 (46c) **Flags coil stamps,** serpentine die cut 11 vert., *May 3,* Weston, MA 5.00
4774-4777, any single 2.25
4778-4781 (46c) **Flags booklet stamps,** microprinting at lower left corner of flag, *May 17,* Rochester, NY 5.00
4778-4781, any single 2.25
4782-4785 (46c) **Flags booklet stamps,** microprinting at top of pole or lower left corner, *May 17,* Rochester, NY 5.00
4782-4785, any single 2.25
4782a-4785a **Flags booklet stamps,** overall tagging, *Aug. 16,* Independence, OH 5.25
4782a-4785a, any single 2.25
4782b-4785b **Flags booklet stamps,** dated "2014," *Mar. 17, 2014,* Liberty, MO 5.25
4782b-4785b, any single 2.25

4786 (46c) **Lydia Mendoza,** *May 15,* San Antonio, TX 2.25
4787-4788 (46c) **Civil War Sesquicentennial,** *May 23,* Vicksburg, MS or Gettysburg, PA 3.25
4787-4788, any single 2.25
4789 (46c) **Johnny Cash,** *June 5,* Nashville, TN 2.25
4790 (46c) **West Virginia Statehood,** *June 20,* Charleston, WV 2.25
4791-4795 (46c) **New England Coastal Lighthouses,** *July 13,* Portland, ME; New Castle, NH; Boston, MA; Narragansett, RI; and New London, CT 6.00
4791-4795, any single 2.25
4796-4799 (46c) **Flags booklet stamps,** serpentine die cut 11¼x11½ on 2 or 3 sides, *Aug. 8,* Milwaukee, WI 5.00
4796-4799, any single 2.25
4800 (46c) **Eid,** *Aug. 8,* Milwaukee, WI 2.25
4801 (46c) **Building a Nation,** *Aug. 8,* Washington, DC 11.00
4801a-4801l, any single 2.25
4802 1c **Bobcat coil stamp,** perf. 9¾ vert., *Aug. 9,* Milwaukee, WI 2.25
4803 (46c) **Althea Gibson,** *Aug. 23,* Flushing, NY 2.25
4804 (46c) **March on Washington, 50th Anniv.,** *Aug. 23,* Washington, DC 2.25
4805 (46c) **Battle of Lake Erie,** *Sept. 10,* Put-in-Bay, OH 2.25
4806 $2 **Inverted Jenny Pane of 6,** *Sept. 22,* Washington, DC 24.00
4806a, single stamp 5.25
4807 (46c) **Ray Charles,** *Sept. 23,* Atlanta, GA and Los Angeles, CA 2.25
4808-4812 (10c) **Snowflakes,** *Oct. 1,* Weston, MO 2.25
4808-4812, any single 2.25
4813 (46c) **Christmas - Holy Family,** *Oct. 11,* New York, NY 2.25
4814 ($1.10) **Christmas - Wreath,** *Oct. 24,* New York, NY 3.75
4815 (46c) **Christmas - Virgin and Child,** *Oct. 11,* New York, NY 2.25
4816 (46c) **Christmas - Poinsettia,** serpentine die cut 11 on 2 or 3 sides, *Oct. 10,* New York, NY 2.25
4816b (49c) **Poinsettia,** dated "2014," *Aug. 21, 2014* Hartford, CT 2.25
4817-4820 (46c) **Christmas - Gingerbread Houses,** *Nov. 6,* New York, NY 5.00
4817-4820, any single 2.25
4821 (46c) **Christmas - Poinsettia,** serpentine die cut 8 on 2, 3 or 4 sides, *Oct. 10,* New York, NY 2.75
4822-4823 (46c) **Medals of Honor,** *Nov. 11,* Washington, DC 4.00
4822-4823, any single 2.75
4823d (49c) **Medal of Honor,** dated "2014," *July 26,* Washington, DC 4.00
4822a-4823a, any single 2.75
4822b (49c) **Navy Medal of Honor,** dated "2015," *May 25,* Washington, DC 2.75
4823b (49c) **Army Medal of Honor,** dated "2015," *May 25,* Washington, DC 2.75
4824 (46c) **Hanukkah,** *Nov. 19,* New York, NY 2.75

Postal Service officials declared on Nov. 8 that No. 4824 could be sold in post offices on Nov. 9, but the first day ceremony was held on Nov. 19 in New York, NY. Official first day covers have that date and city.

4825-4844 (46c) **Harry Potter,** *Nov. 19,* Orlando, FL 18.50
4825-4844, any single 2.25
4845 (46c) **Kwanzaa,** *Nov. 26,* Philadelphia, PA 2.25

2014

4846 (46c) **Chinese New Year,** *Jan. 15,* San Francisco, CA 2.50
4847 (46c) **Love,** *Jan. 21,* New York, NY 2.25
4848-4852 49c **Ferns,** *Jan. 27,* Kansas City, MO 6.25
4848-4852, any single 2.25
4853 (49c) **Fort McHenry Flag and Fireworks coil stamp,** serpentine die cut 8½ vert., *Jan. 28,* Independence, MO 2.25
4854 (49c) **Fort McHenry Flag and Fireworks coil stamp,** serpentine die cut 9½ vert., *Jan. 28,* Independence, MO 2.25
4855 (49c) **Fort McHenry Flag and Fireworks booklet stamp,** serpentine die cut 11¼x10¾ on 2 or 3 sides, *Jan. 28,* Independence, MO 2.25
4856 (49c) **Shirley Chisholm,** *Jan. 31,* Brooklyn, NY 2.25
4857 34c **Hummingbird,** serpentine die cut 11¼x10¾, *Feb. 7,* Kansas City, MO 2.25
4858 34c **Hummingbird coil,** serpentine die cut 9½ vert., *Feb. 7,* Kansas City, MO 2.25
4859 70c **Great Spangled Fritillary Butterfly,** *Feb. 10,* Kansas City, MO 2.60
4860 21c **Abraham Lincoln,** serpentine die cut 11, *Feb. 12,* Springfield, IL 2.25
4861 21c **Abraham Lincoln coil,** serpentine die cut 8½ vert., *Feb. 12,* Springfield, IL 2.25
4862-4865 (49c) **Winter Flowers,** *Feb. 14,* Little Rock, AR 5.25
4862-4865, any single 2.25
4866 91c **Ralph Ellison,** *Feb. 18,* Kansas City, MO 3.00
4867 70c **Wedding Cake,** *Feb. 22,* Mesa, AZ 2.60
4868 (49c) **Fort McHenry Flag and Fireworks coil stamp,** serpentine die cut 11 vert., *Mar. 3,* Washington, DC 2.25
4869 (49c) **Fort McHenry Flag and Fireworks booklet stamp,** photo., serpentine die cut 11¼x11½ on 2 or 3 sides, without microprinted "USPS," *Mar. 3,* Washington, DC 2.25
4870 (49c) **Fort McHenry Flag and Fireworks booklet stamp,** litho., serpentine die cut 11¼x10¾ on 2 or 3 sides, microprinted "USPS" in fireworks, *Mar. 3,* Washington, DC 2.25
4871 (49c) **Fort McHenry Flag and Fireworks ATM booklet stamp,** litho., thin paper, serpentine die cut 11¼x11 on 2, 3 or 4 sides, microprinted "USPS" in fireworks, *Mar. 3,* Washington, DC 2.25
4872 $5.60 **Verrazano-Narrows Bridge,** *Mar. 4,* Brooklyn, NY 11.50
4873 $19.99 **USS Arizona Memorial,** *Mar. 13,* Honolulu, HI 40.00
4874-4878 (49c) **Ferns,** *Mar. 6,* Kansas City, MO 6.25
4874-4878, any single 2.25
4879 70c **C. Alfred "Chief" Anderson,** *Mar. 13,* Bryn Mawr, PA 2.60
4880 (49c) **Jimi Hendrix,** *Mar. 13,* Austin, TX 2.25
4881 70c **Flowers and "Yes I Do,"** *Mar. 21,* St. Louis, MO 2.60
4882-4891 (49c) **Songbirds,** *Apr. 5,* Dallas, TX 10.00
4882-4891, any single 2.25
4892 (49c) **Charlton Heston,** *Apr. 11,* Los Angeles, CA 2.25
4893 ($1.15) **Map of Sea Surface Temperatures,** *Apr. 22,* Washington, DC 3.50
4894-4897 (49c) **Flags,** *Apr. 25,* San Francisco, CA 5.25
4894-4897, any single 2.25
4898-4905 (49c) **Circus Posters,** *May 5,* Sarasota, FL 9.25
4898-4905, any single 2.25
4905c **Circus souvenir sheet,** *Dec. 10,* Baraboo, WI 4.50
4906 (49c) **Harvey Milk,** *May 22,* Washington, DC 2.25
4907 (49c) **Nevada Statehood, 150th Anniv.,** *May 29,* Las Vegas, NV 2.25
4908-4909 (49c) **Hot Rods,** *June 6,* York, PA 3.25
4908-4909, any single 2.25
4910-4911 (49c) **Civil War Sesquicentennial,** *July 30,* Petersburg, VA or Mobile, AL 3.25
4910-4911, any single 2.25
4912-4915 (49c) **Farmers Markets,** *Aug. 7,* Washington, DC 5.25
4912-4915, any single 2.25
4916 (49c) **Janis Joplin,** *Aug. 8,* San Francisco, CA 2.25
4917-4920 (49c) **Hudson River School Paintings,** *Aug. 21,* Hartford, CT 5.25
4917-4920, any single 2.25
4921 (49c) **Bombardment of Fort McHenry,** *Sept. 13,* Baltimore, MD 2.25
4922-4926 (49c) **Celebrity Chefs,** *Sept. 26,* Chicago, IL 6.25
4922-4926, any single 2.25
4927 $5.75 **Glade Creek Grist Mill,** *Sept. 29,* Danese, WV 11.50
4928-4935 (49c) **Batman,** *Oct. 9,* New York, NY 9.25
4928-4935, any single 2.25
4936 ($1.15) **Silver Bells Wreath,** *Oct. 23,* New York, NY 3.50
4937-4940 (49c) **Winter Fun,** serpentine die cut 10¾x11 on 2 or 3 sides, *Oct. 23,* New York, NY 5.25
4937-4940, any single 2.25
4941-4944 (49c) **Winter Fun,** serpentine die cut 11¼x11 on 2, 3 or 4 sides, *Oct. 23,* New York, NY 5.25
4941-4944, any single 2.25
4945 (49c) **Christmas - Magi,** *Nov. 19,* Washington, DC 2.25
4946-4949 (49c) **Christmas - Rudolph, the Red-Nosed Reindeer,** *Nov. 6,* Washington, DC 5.25
4946-4949, any single 2.25
4950-4951 (49c) **Wilt Chamberlain,** *Dec. 5,* Philadelphia, PA 3.25
4950-4951, any single 2.25

2015

4952 (49c) **Battle of New Orleans,** *Jan. 8,* Chalmette, LA 2.25
4953 $1 **Patriotic Waves,** *Jan. 12,* Kansas City, KS 3.25
4954 $2 **Patriotic Waves,** *Jan. 30,* Norcross, GA 5.25
4955-4956 (49c) **Love,** *Jan. 22,* Richmond, VA 3.25
4955-4956, any single 2.25
4957 (49c) **Chinese New Year,** *Feb. 7,* San Francisco, CA 2.25
4958 (49c) **Robert Robinson Taylor,** *Feb. 12,* Washington, DC 2.25
4959 (49c) **Rose and Heart,** *Feb. 14,* Riverside, CA 2.25
4960 70c **Tulip and Heart,** *Feb. 14,* Riverside, CA 2.60
4961-4963 (10c) **Flags,** *Feb. 27,* Grapevine, TX 2.25
4961-4963, any single 2.25
4964-4967 (49c) **Water Lilies,** *Mar. 20,* Cleveland, OH 5.25
4964-4967, any single 2.25
4968-4972 (49c) **Martín Ramírez,** *Mar. 26,* New York, NY 6.25
4968-4972, any single 2.25
4973-4977 (49c) **Ferns,** lithogruaphed coil stamps with microprinting dated 2014, *Mar. 27,* Kansas City, MO 6.25
4973-4977, any single 2.25
4973a-4977a (49c) **Ferns,** lithographed coil stamps with microprinting, dated "2015," *Mar. 27,* Kansas City, MO 6.25
4973a-4977a, any single 2.25
4978 (49c) **From Me to You,** *Apr. 1,* Washington, DC 2.25
4979 (49c) **Maya Angelou,** *Apr. 7,* Washington, DC 2.25
4980-4981 (49c) **Civil War Sesquicentennial,** *Apr. 9,* Appomattox, VA 3.25
4980-4981, any single 2.25
4982-4985 (49c) **Gifts of Friendship,** *Apr. 10,* Washington, DC 5.25
4982-4985, any single 2.25
4986 (49c) **Special Olympics World Games,** *May 9,* Irvine, CA 2.25
4987 (49c) **Help Find Missing Children,** *May 18,* Anaheim, CA 2.25
4988 (49c) **Air Force Medal of Honor,** *May 25,* Washington, DC 2.50
4988a, strip of 3 4.25
4989 (22c) **Emperor Penguins,** serpentine die cut 11¼x11, *June 1,* Kansas City, MO 2.25
4990 (22c) **Emperor Penguins coil,** serpentine die cut 11 vert., *June 1,* Kansas City, MO 2.25
4991-4994 (35c) **Coastal Birds,** serpentine die cut 11¼x11, *June 1,* Kansas City, MO 4.00
4991-4994, any single 2.25
4995-4998 (35c) **Coastal Birds coils,** serpentine die cut 9½ vert., *June 1,* Kansas City, MO 4.00
4995-4998, any single 2.25
4999 (71c) **Eastern Tiger Swallowtail Butterfly,** *June 1,* Kansas City, MO 2.75
5000 (71c) **Wedding Cake,** *June 1,* Kansas City, MO 2.75
5001 (71c) **Flowers and "Yes, I Do,"** *June 1,* Kansas City, MO 2.75
5002 (71c) **Tulip and Heart,** *June 1,* Kansas City, MO 2.75
5003 (93c) **Flannery O'Connor,** *June 5,* McLean, VA 3.25
5004-5007 (49c) **Summer Harvest,** *July 11,* Sacramento, CA 5.25
5004-5007, any single 2.25
5008 (49c) **Coast Guard,** *Aug. 4,* Washington, DC 2.25
5009 (49c) **Elvis Presley,** *Aug. 12,* Memphis, TN 2.25
5010-5011 (49c) **2016 World Stamp Show,** *Aug. 20,* Grand Rapids, MI 3.25
5010-5011, any single 2.25
5012 (49c) **Ingrid Bergman,** *Aug. 20,* Los Angeles, CA 2.25
5013-5018 (25c) **Eagle coil stamps,** serpentine die cut 10¼ vert., *Sept. 2,* Eagleville, MO 4.25
5013-5018, any single 2.25
5019 (49c) **Celebrate,** litho., *Sept. 9,* Kansas City, MO 2.25
5020 (49c) **Paul Newman,** *Sept. 18,* Cleveland, OH 2.25
5021-5030 (49c) **Christmas - A Charlie Brown Christmas,** *Oct. 1,* Santa Rosa, CA 10.00
5021-5030, any single 2.25
5031-5034 (49c) **Geometric Snowflakes,** *Oct. 23,* New York, NY 5.25
5031-5034, any single 2.25

2016

5036 (49c) **Love,** *Jan. 12,* Dallas, TX 2.25
5037 1c **Albemarle Pippin Apples,** *Aug. 12,* Kansas City, MO 2.25

5038 5c **Pinot Noir Grapes,** *Feb. 19,* Kansas City, MO 2.25
5039 10c **Red Pears,** *Jan. 17,* Washington, DC 2.25
5040 $6.45 **La Cueva del Indio,** *Jan. 17,* Washington, DC 13.00
5041 $22.95 **Columbia River Gorge,** *Jan. 17,* Washington, DC 46.00
5042-5051 (49c) **Botanical Art,** *Jan. 29,* Atlanta, GA 10.00
5042-5051, any single 2.25
5052 (49c) **Flag coil,** serpentine die cut 11 vert., *Jan. 29,* Washington, DC 2.25
5053 (49c) **Flag coil,** serpentine die cut 9½ vert., *Jan. 29,* Washington, DC 2.25
5054 (49c) **Flag booklet stamp,** microprinted "USPS" below flag, *Jan. 29,* Washington, DC 2.25
5055 (49c) **Flag booklet stamp,** microprinted "USPS" on second white stripe, *Jan. 29,* Washington, DC 2.25
5056 (49c) **Richard Allen,** *Feb. 2,* Philadelphia, PA 2.25
5057 (49c) **Chinese New Year,** *Feb. 5,* Jamaica, NY 2.25
5058 ($1.20) **Moon,** *Feb. 22,* Washington, DC 3.75
5059 (49c) **Sarah Vaughan,** *Mar. 29,* Newark, NJ 2.25
5060 (47c) **Shirley Temple,** *Apr. 18,* Los Angeles, CA 2.25
5061 (5c) **"USA" and Star,** *Apr. 28,* Dulles, VA 2.25
5062-5063 (47c) **2016 World Stamp Show,** *May 28* New York, NY 3.25
5062-5063, any single 2.25
5064 (47c) **Repeal of the Stamp Act,** *May 29,* New York, NY 2.25
5065-5068 (47c) **Service Cross Medals,** *May 30,* New York, NY 5.00
5065-5068, any single 2.25
5069-5076 (47c) **Views of Our Planets,** *May 31,* New York, NY 8.75
5069-5076, any single 2.25
5077-5078 (47c) **Pluto Explored,** *May 31,* New York, NY 3.25
5077-5078, any single 2.25
5079 (47c) **Classics Forever,** *June 1,* New York, NY 7.00
5079a-5079f, any single 2.25
5080 (47c) **National Parks Service, Cent.,** *June 2,* New York, NY 15.00
5080a-5080p, any single 2.25
5081-5090 (47c) **Colorful Celebrations,** *June 3,* New York, NY 9.50
5081-5090, any single 2.25
5091 (47c) **Indiana Statehood,** *June 7,* Indianapolis, IN 2.25
5092 (47c) **Eid,** *June 10,* Dearborn, MI 2.25
5093-5097 (47c) **Soda Fountain Favorites,** *June 30,* Nashville, TN 6.00
5093-5097, 5095a, any single 2.25
5098-5099 (25c) **Star Quilts,** *July 6,* Washington, DC 2.25
5098-5099, any single 2.25
5100 (47c) **Jaime Escalante,** *July 13,* Washington, DC 2.25
5101-5104 (47c) **Pickup Trucks,** *July 15,* Syracuse, NY 5.00
5101-5104, any single 2.25
5105 (89c) **Henry James,** *July 31,* Dulles, VA 3.00
Cancel dated "Jul 31 31016" 3.00
5106-5125 (47c) **Pets,** *Aug. 2,* Las Vegas, NV 19.00
5106-5125, any single 2.25
5126-5129 (47c) **Songbirds in Snow,** *Aug. 4,* Portland, OR 5.00
5126-5129, any single 2.25
5130 (47c) **Patriotic Spiral coil stamp,** *Aug. 19,* Kansas City, MO 2.25
5131 (47c) **Patriotic Spiral booklet stamp,** *Aug. 19,* Kansas City, MO 2.25
5132-5135 (47c) **Star Trek,** *Sept. 2,* New York, NY 5.00
5132-5135, any single 2.25
5136 (68c) **Eastern Tailed-Blue Butterfly,** *Sept. 24,* Kansas City, MO 2.60
5137-5140 (47c) **Jack-o'-lanterns,** *Sept. 29,* Anoka, MN 5.00
5137-5140, any single 2.25
5141 (47c) **Kwanzaa,** *Oct. 1,* Charleston, SC 2.25
5142 (47c) **Diwali,** *Oct. 5,* New York, NY 2.25
5143 (47c) **Christmas - Madonna and Child,** *Oct. 18,* Washington, DC 2.25
5144 (47c) **Christmas - Nativity,** *Nov. 3,* Washington, DC 2.25
5145-5148 (47c) **Christmas - Holiday Windows,** *Oct. 6,* New York, NY 5.00
5145-5148, any single 2.25
5149-5152 (47c) **Wonder Woman,** *Oct. 7,* New York, NY 5.00
5149-5152, any single 2.25
5153 (47c) **Hanukkah,** *Nov. 1,* Boca Raton, FL 2.25

2017

5154 (47c) **Chinese New Year,** *Jan. 5,* Seattle, WA 2.25
5155 (47c) **Love,** *Jan. 7,* Chino, CA 2.25
5156 $6.65 **Lili'uokalani Gardens,** *Jan. 22,* Kansas City, MO 13.50
5157 $23.75 **Gateway Arch,** *Jan. 22,* Kansas City, MO 47.50
5158 (49c) **Flag coil,** serpentine die cut 11 vert., *Jan. 27,* Norcross, GA 2.25
5159 (49c) **Flag coil,** serpentine die cut 9½ vert., *Jan. 27,* Norcross, GA 2.25
5160 (49c) **Flag booklet stamp,** microprinted "USPS" on fourth red stripe, *Jan. 27,* Norcross, GA 2.25
5161 (49c) **Flag booklet stamp,** microprinted "USPS" at right of second white stripe, *Jan. 27,* Norcross, GA 2.25
5162 (49c) **Flag booklet stamp,** microprinted "USPS" at left of second white stripe, *Jan. 27,* Norcross, GA 2.25
5163-5166 (34c) **Shells,** serpentine die cut 11¼x10¾, *Jan. 28,* San Diego, CA 4.00
5163-5166, any single 2.25
5167-5170 (34c) **Shells coil stamps,** serpentine die cut 9¾ vert., *Jan. 28,* San Diego, CA 4.00
5167-5170, any single 2.25
5171 (49c) **Dorothy Height,** *Feb. 1,* Washington, DC 2.25
5172 (5c) **"USA" and Star With Blue Frame,** *Feb. 10,* Fort Lauderdale, FL 2.25
5173 (49c) **Oscar de la Renta,** *Feb. 16,* New York, NY 11.00
5173a-5173k, any single 2.25
5174 (21c) **People Wearing Uncle Sam Hats,** *Feb. 18,* Mesa, AZ 2.25
5175 (49c) **Pres. John F. Kennedy,** *Feb. 20,* Boston, MA 2.25
5177 5c **Pinot Noir Grapes,** serpentine die cut 11¼x11, *Feb. 24,* Grapevine, TX 2.25
5178 10c **Red Pears,** serpentine die cut 11¼x11, *Mar. 23,* Cleveland, OH 2.25
5179 (49c) **Nebraska Statehood,** *Mar. 1,* Lincoln, NE 2.25
5180-5189 (49c) **WPA Posters,** *Mar. 7,* Hyde Park, NY 10.00
5180-5189, any single 2.25
5190 (49c) **Mississippi Statehood,** *Mar. 31,* Gulfport, MS 2.25
5191 (70c) **Robert Panara,** *Apr.11,* Rochester, NY 2.60
5192-5197 (49c) **Delicioso (Latin American Dishes),** *Apr. 20,* Albuquerque, NM 7.25
5192-5197, any single 2.25
5198 ($1.15) **Echeveria,** *Apr. 28,* San Francisco, CA 3.50
5199 (49c) **Boutonniere,** *May 2,* St. Louis, MO 2.25
5200 (70c) **Corsage,** *May 2,* St. Louis, MO 2.60
5201 3c **Strawberries,** coil stamp, *May 5,* Acton, MA 2.25
5202 (49c) **Henry David Thoreau,** *May 23,* Concord, MA 2.25
5203-5210 (49c) **Sports Balls,** *June 14,* Hartford, WI 9.25
5203-5210, any single 2.25
5211 (49c) **Total Solar Eclipse,** *June 20,* Laramie, WY 2.25
5212 (49c) **Paintings by Andrew Wyeth,** *July 12,* Chadds Ford, PA 12.00
5212a-5212l, any single 2.25
5213-5222 (49c) **Disney Villains,** *July 15,* Anaheim, CA 10.00
5213-5222, any single 2.25
5223-5227 (49c) **Sharks,** *July 26,* Newport, KY 6.25
5223-5227, any single 2.25
5228-5232 (49c) **Protect Pollinators,** *Aug. 3,* Richmond, VA 6.25
5228-5232, any single 2.25
5233-5236 (49c) **Flowers from the Garden,** coil stamps, *Aug. 16,* Sioux Falls, SD 5.25
5233-5236, any single 2.25
5237-5240 (49c) **Flowers from the Garden,** booklet stamps, *Aug. 16,* Sioux Falls, SD 5.25
5237-5240, any single 2.25
5241 (49c) **Father Ted Hesburgh,** serpentine die cut 11, *Sept. 1,* Notre Dame, IN 2.25
5242 (49c) **Father Ted Hesburgh,** serpentine die cut 9½ horiz., *Sept. 1,* Notre Dame, IN 2.25
5243-5246 (49c) **"The Snowy Day,"** *Oct. 4,* Brooklyn, NY 5.25
5243-5246, any single 2.25
5247-5250 (49c) **Christmas Carols,** *Oct. 5,* New York, NY 5.25
5247-5250, any single 2.25
5251 (49c) **National Museum of African American History and Culture,** *Oct. 13,* Washington, DC 2.25
5252-5253 (49c) **History of Ice Hockey,** *Oct. 20,* Detroit, MI 3.25
5252-5253, any single 2.25
5253c Souvenir sheet of 2, #5252a-5253a 3.25

2018

5254 (49c) **Chinese New Year,** *Jan. 11,* Honolulu, HI 2.25
5255 (49c) **Love,** *Jan. 18,* Phoenix, AZ 2.25
5256 2c **Meyer Lemons,** coil stamp, *Jan. 19,* Kenner, LA 2.25
5257 $6.70 **Byodo-In Temple,** *Jan. 21,* Kansas City, MO 13.50
5258 $24.70 **Sleeping Bear Dunes,** *Jan. 21,* Kansas City, MO 50.00
5259 (50c) **Lena Horne,** *Jan. 30,* New York, NY 2.25
5260 (50c) **Flag coil,** serpentine die cut 9½ vert., *Feb. 9,* Fort Lauderdale, FL 2.25
5261 (50c) **Flag coil,** serpentine die cut 11 vert., *Feb. 9,* Fort Lauderdale, FL 2.25
5262 (50c) **Flag booklet stamp,** microprinted "USPS" at left of flag fold on fourth red stripe, *Feb. 9,* Fort Lauderdale, FL 2.25
5263 (50c) **Flag booklet stamp,** microprinted "USPS" at right of flag fold on fifth white stripe, *Feb. 9,* Fort Lauderdale, FL 2.25
5264-5273 (50c) **Bioluminescent Life,** *Feb. 22,* Fort Pierce, FL 10.00
5264-5273, any single 2.25
5274 (50c) **Illinois Statehood,** *Mar. 5,* Springfield, IL 2.25
5275 (50c) **Mister Rogers,** *Mar. 23,* Pittsburgh, PA 2.25
5276-5279 (50c) **STEM Education,** *Apr. 6,* Washington, DC 5.25
5276-5279, any single 2.25
5280 (50c) **Peace Rose,** *Apr. 21,* Shreveport, LA 2.25
5281 (50c) **Air Mail Centenary,** blue, *May 1,* Washington, DC 2.25
5282 (50c) **Air Mail Centenary,** carmine lake, *Aug. 11,* College Park, MD 2.25
5283 (50c) **Sally Ride,** *May 23,* La Jolla, CA 2.25
5284 (50c) **Flag Act of 1818, Bicent.,** *June 9,* Appleton, WI 2.25
5285-5294 (50c) **Frozen Treats,** *June 20,* Austin, TX 10.00
5285-5294, any single 2.25
5295 $1 **Statue of Freedom,** *June 27,* Bellefonte, PA 3.25
5296 $2 **Statue of Freedom,** *June 27,* Bellefonte, PA 9.25
5297 $5 **Statue of Freedom,** *June 27,* Bellefonte, PA 10.00
5298 (50c) **O Beautiful,** *July 4,* Colorado Springs, CO 20.00
5298a-5298t, any single 2.25
5299 (50c) **Scooby-Doo,** *July 14,* Bloomington, MN 2.25
5300 (50c) **World War I, Cent.,** *July 27,* Kansas City, MO 2.25
5301-5305 (50c) **The Art of Magic,** *Aug. 7,* Las Vegas, NV 6.25
5301-5305, any single 2.25
5306 (50c) **The Art of Magic,** sheet of 3, lenticular stamps, *Aug. 7,* Las Vegas, NV 4.25
5306a, single stamp 2.25
5307-5310 (50c) **Dragons,** *Aug. 9,* Columbus, OH 5.25
5307-5310, any single 2.25
5311 ($1.15) **Poinsettia,** *Aug. 26,* Kansas City, MO 3.50
5312-5315 (50c) **John Lennon,** *Sept. 7,* New York, NY 5.25
5312-5315, any single 2.25
5316 (50c) **First Responders,** *Sept. 13,* Missoula, MT 2.25
5317-5320 (50c) **Birds in Winter,** *Sept. 22,* Quechee, VT 5.25
5317-5320, any single 2.25
5321-5330 (50c) **Hot Wheels, 50th Anniv.,** *Sept. 29,* Fort Worth, TX 10.00
5321-5330, any single 2.25
5331 (50c) **Christmas - Madonna and Child,** *Oct. 3,* Santa Fe, NM 2.25
5332-5335 (50c) **Christmas - Santa Claus,** booklet pane stamps, *Oct. 11,* Pigeon Forge, TN 5.25
5332-5335, any single 2.25
5336 (50c) **Christmas - Santa Claus,** souvenir sheet, *Oct. 11,* Pigeon Forge, TN 2.25
5337 (50c) **Kwanzaa,** *Oct. 10,* Raleigh, NC 2.25
5338 (50c) **Hanukkah,** *Oct. 16,* Newport, RI 2.25

2019

5339 (50c) **Love,** *Jan. 10,* San Juan, PR 2.25

2019

5340 (50c) **Chinese New Year,** *Jan. 17,* Houston, TX 2.25
5341 (15c) **People Wearing Uncle Sam's Hats coil,** serpentine die cut 11 vert., *Jan. 27,* Kansas City, MO 2.25
5342 (55c) **Flag coil,** serpentine die cut 11 horiz., *Jan. 27,* Kansas City, MO 2.40
5343 (55c) **Flag coil,** serpentine die cut 9½ horiz., *Jan. 27,* Kansas City, MO 2.40
5344 (55c) **Flag booklet stamp,** microprinted "USPS" at upper left corner of flag, *Jan. 27,* Kansas City, MO 2.40
5345 (55c) **Flag booklet stamp,** microprinted "USPS" to right of sixth red flag stripe, *Jan. 27,* Kansas City, MO 2.40
5346 (70c) **California Dogface Butterfly,** *Jan. 27,* Kansas City, MO 2.60
5347 $7.35 **Joshua Tree,** *Jan. 27,* Kansas City, MO 15.00

5348 $25.50 **Bethesda Fountain,** *Jan. 27,* Kansas City, MO 51.00
5349 (55c) **Gregory Hines,** *Jan. 28,* New York, NY 2.40
5350-5359 (55c) **Cactus Flowers,** *Feb. 15,* Mesa, AZ 11.00
5350-5359, any single 2.40
5360 (55c) **Alabama Statehood,** *Feb. 23,* Huntsville, AL 2.40
5361 (55c) **Star Ribbon,** serpentine die cut 11¼x10¾, *Mar. 22,* Oakbrook Terrace, IL 2.40
5362 (55c) **Star Ribbon coil stamp,** serpentine die cut 10¾ vert., *Mar. 22,* Oakbrook Terrace, IL 2.40
5363-5366 (35c) **Coral Reefs,** serpentine die cut 11¼x10¾, *Mar. 29,* St. Louis, MO 4.00
5363-5366, any single 2.40
5367-5370 (35c) **Coral Reefs coil stamps,** serpentine die cut 9½ vert., *Mar. 29,* St. Louis, MO 4.00
5367-5370, any single 2.40
5371 (55c) **Marvin Gaye,** *Apr. 2,* Los Angeles, CA 2.40
5372-5376 (55c) **Post Office Murals,** *Apr. 10,* Piggott, AR 6.75
5372-5376, any single 2.40
5377 (55c) **Maureen "Little Mo" Connolly Brinker,** *Apr. 23,* Dallas, TX 2.40
5378-5380 (55c) **Transcontinental Railroad, 150th Anniv.,** *May 10,* Promontory Summit, UT 4.50
5378-5380, any single 2.40
5381 (55c) **Wild and Scenic Rivers,** *May 21,* Bend, OR 13.50
5381a-5381l, any single 2.40
5382-5391 (55c) **Art of Ellsworth Kelly,** *May 31,* Spencertown, NY 12.50
5382-5391, any single 2.40
5392 (55c) **U.S.S. Missouri,** *June 11,* Honolulu, HI 2.40
5393 (55c) **Pres. George Herbert Walker Bush,** *June 12,* College Station, TX 2.40
5394 (55c) **Sesame Street, 50th Anniv.,** *June 22,* Detroit, MI 18.00
5394a-5394p, any single 2.40
5395-5398 (55c) **Frogs,** *July 9,* Boise, ID 5.75
5395-5398, any single 2.40

SEMI-POSTAL FIRST DAY COVERS

1998
B1 32c +8c **Breast Cancer,** *July 29,* Washington, DC (51,775) 2.00

2002
B2 (34c+11c) **Heroes of 2001,** *June 7,* New York, NY 3.50
Any other city 3.00

2003
B3 (37c+8c) **Stop Family Violence,** *Oct. 8,* Washington, DC 1.60
Any other city 1.60

2011
B4 (44c+11c) **Save Vanishing Wildlife,** *Sept. 20,* Washington, DC 2.40

2014
B5 (49c+11c) **Breast Cancer Awareness,** litho., *Sept. 30,* Sacramento, CA 2.40

2017
B6 (49c+11c) **Alzheimer's Disease Awareness,** *Nov. 30,* Baltimore, MD 2.40

AIR POST FIRST DAY COVERS

1918
C1 6c **orange,** *Dec. 10* *40,000.*
C2 16c **green,** *July 11* —
C3 24c **carmine rose & blue,** *May 13* —

Specialists question the existence of genuine first day covers of Nos. C2 and C3. The editors would like to see recent authenticated proof of the existence of these first day covers.

1923
C4 8c **dark green,** *Aug. 15* 400.00
C5 16c **dark blue,** *Aug. 17* 600.00
C6 24c **carmine,** *Aug. 21* 750.00

1926-27
C7 10c **dark blue,** *Feb. 13, 1926* 70.00
Chicago, Ill. 85.00
Detroit, Mich. 85.00
Cleveland, Ohio 130.00
Dearborn, Mich. 130.00
C8 15c **olive brown,** *Sept. 18, 1926* 85.00
C9 20c **yellow green,** *Jan. 25, 1927* 100.00
New York, N.Y. 125.00
C10 10c **dark blue,** *June 18, 1927* 25.00
St. Louis, Mo. 25.00
Little Falls, Minn. 35.00
Detroit, Mich. 35.00
C10a Booklet pane of 3, *May 26, 1928* 875.00
Cleveland Midwestern Philatelic Sta. cancel 800.00
C10a & 645 on one cover, Washington, D.C. 1,000.

1928-30
C11 5c **carmine & blue,** *July 25, 1928,* pair 50.00
C12 5c **violet,** *Feb. 10, 1930* 14.00
C13 65c **green,** *Apr. 19, 1930* 1,000.
C14 $1.30 **brown,** *Apr. 19, 1930* 900.00
C15 $2.60 **blue,** *Apr. 19, 1930* 1,000.
C13-C15 on one cover 10,000.

Values are for first day covers flown on Zeppelin flights with appropriate markings. Non-flown covers sell for less.

1931-33
C16 5c **violet,** *Aug. 19, 1931* 175.00
C17 8c **olive bister,** *Sept. 26, 1932* 15.00
C18 50c **green,** *Oct. 2, 1933,* New York, N.Y. *(3,500)* 200.00
Akron, Ohio, *Oct. 4* 300.00
Washington, D.C., *Oct. 5* 275.00
Miami, Fla., *Oct. 6* 150.00
Chicago, Ill., *Oct. 7* 250.00

1934-37
C19 6c **dull orange,** *June 30, 1934,* Baltimore, Md. *200.00*
New York, N.Y. *1,000.*
Brooklyn, N.Y. 1,500.
San Francisco, Calif. 1,500.
Washington, D.C., *July 1* 10.00

Catalogue values for Nos. C20-C45 are for addressed covers with the most common cachets.

C20 25c **blue,** *Nov. 22, 1935 (10,910)* 40.00
San Francisco, Cal. *(15,000)* 35.00
C21 20c **green,** *Feb. 15, 1937* 45.00
C22 50c **carmine,** *Feb. 15, 1937* 50.00
C21-C22 on one cover 100.00

First day covers of Nos. C21 and C22 total 40,000.

1938-39
C23 6c **dark blue & carmine,** *May 14, 1938,* Dayton, Ohio *(116,443)* 17.50
St. Petersburg, Fla. *(95,121)* 17.50
Washington, D.C., *May 15* 4.00
C24 30c **dull blue,** *May 16, 1939,* New York, N.Y. *(68,634)* 50.00

1941-44
C25 6c **carmine,** *June 25, 1941 (99,986)* 4.00
C25a Booklet pane of 3, *Mar. 18, 1943* 22.50
C26 8c **olive green,** *Mar. 21, 1944 (147,484)* 4.00
C27 10c **violet,** *Aug. 15, 1941,* Atlantic City, N.J. *(87,712)* 6.00
C28 15c **brown carmine,** *Aug. 19, 1941,* Baltimore, Md. *(74,000)* 8.00
C29 20c **bright green,** *Aug. 27, 1941,* Philadelphia, Pa. *(66,225)* 10.00
C30 30c **blue,** *Sept. 25, 1941,* Kansas City, Mo. *(57,175)* 17.50
C31 50c **orange,** *Oct. 29, 1941,* St. Louis, Mo. *(54,580)* 35.00

1946-48
C32 5c **carmine,** *Sept. 25, 1946* 2.00

First day covers of Nos. C32 & UC14 total 396,669.

C33 5c **carmine,** *Mar. 26, 1947 (342,634)* 2.00
C34 10c **black,** *Aug. 30, 1947 (265,773)* 2.00
C35 15c **bright blue green,** *Aug. 20, 1947,* New York, N.Y. *(230,338)* 1.75
C36 25c **blue,** *July 30, 1947,* San Francisco, Cal. *(201,762)* 2.25
C37 5c **carmine, coil,** *Jan. 15, 1948 (192,084)* 1.75
C38 5c **New York City,** *July 31, 1948,* New York, N.Y. *(371,265)* 1.75

1949
C39 6c **carmine,** *Jan. 18 (266,790)* 1.50
C39a Booklet pane of 6, *Nov. 18, 1949,* New York, N.Y. 8.00
C40 6c **Alexandria Bicentennial,** *May 11,* Alexandria, Va. *(386,717)* 1.50
C41 6c **carmine coil,** *Aug. 25 (240,386)* 1.25
C42 10c **U.P.U.,** *Nov. 18,* New Orleans, La. *(270,000)* 1.75
C43 15c **U.P.U.,** *Oct. 7,* Chicago, Ill. *(246,833)* 2.75
C44 25c **U.P.U.,** *Nov. 30,* Seattle, Wash. *(220,215)* 3.75
C45 6c **Wright Brothers,** *Dec. 17,* Kitty Hawk, N.C. *(378,585)* 2.75

Catalogue values from this point to the end of the section are for unaddressed covers with the most common cachets.

1952-59
C46 80c **Hawaii,** *Mar. 26, 1952,* Honolulu, Hawaii, *(89,864)* 22.50
C47 6c **Powered Flight,** *May 29, 1953,* Dayton, Ohio *(359,050)* 1.50
C48 4c **bright blue,** *Sept. 3, 1954,* Philadelphia, Pa. *(295,720)* 1.00
C49 6c **Air Force,** *Aug. 1, 1957 (356,683)* 3.00
C50 5c **red,** *July 31, 1958,* Colorado Springs, Colo. *(207,954)* 1.00
C51 7c **blue,** *July 31, 1958,* Philadelphia, Pa. *(204,401)* 1.00
C51a Booklet pane of 6, San Antonio, Tex. *(119,769)* 9.00
C52 7c **blue coil,** *July 31, 1958,* Miami, Fla. *(181,603)* 1.00
C53 7c **Alaska Statehood,** *Jan. 3, 1959,* Juneau, Alaska *(489,752)* 2.00
C54 7c **Balloon Jupiter,** *Aug. 17, 1959,* Lafayette, Ind.*(383,556)* 1.75
C55 7c **Hawaii Statehood,** *Aug. 21, 1959,* Honolulu, Hawaii *(533,464)* 2.00
C56 10c **Pan American Games,** *Aug. 27, 1959,* Chicago, Ill. *(302,306)* 1.00

1959-66
C57 10c **Liberty Bell,** *June 10, 1960,* Miami, Fla. *(246,509)* 1.50
C58 15c **Statue of Liberty,** *Nov. 20, 1959,* New York, N.Y. *(259,412)* 2.00
C59 25c **Abraham Lincoln,** *Apr. 22, 1960,* San Francisco, Cal. *(211,235)* 1.75
C59a 25c Tagged, *Dec. 29, 1966 (about 3,000)* 50.00
C60 7c **carmine,** *Aug. 12, 1960,* Arlington, Va. *(247,190)* 1.00
C60a Booklet pane of 6, *Aug. 19, 1960,* St. Louis, Mo. *(143,363)* 8.00
C61 7c **carmine coil,** *Oct. 22, 1960,* Atlantic City, N.J. *(197,995)* 1.00

1961-67
C62 13c **Liberty Bell,** *June 28, 1961,* New York, N.Y. *(316,166)* 1.00
C62a 13c Tagged, *Feb. 15, 1967* 50.00
C63 15c **Redrawn Statue of Liberty,** *Jan. 13, 1961,* Buffalo, N.Y. *(192,976)* 1.00
C63a 15c Tagged, *Jan. 11, 1967* 50.00
C64 8c **carmine,** *Dec. 5, 1962 (288,355)* 1.00
C64b Booklet pane of 5 + label *(146,835)* 3.50
C64a 8c Tagged, *Aug. 1, 1963,* Dayton, Ohio *(262,720)* 2.50
C65 8c **carmine coil,** *Dec. 5, 1962 (220,173)* 1.00

1963-69
C66 15c **Montgomery Blair,** *May 3, 1963,* Silver Spring, Md. *(260,031)* 2.00
C67 6c **Bald Eagle,** *July 12, 1963,* Boston, Mass. *(268,265)* 1.00
C67a 6c Tagged, *Feb. 15, 1967* 50.00
C68 8c **Amelia Earhart,** *July 24, 1963,* Atchison, Kan. *(437,996)* 5.00
C69 8c **Robert H. Goddard,** *Oct. 5, 1964,* Roswell, N.M. *(421,020)* 3.00
C70 8c **Alaska Purchase,** *Mar. 30, 1967,* Sitka, Alaska *(554,784)* 1.50
C71 20c **Audubon,** *Apr. 26, 1967,* Audubon (Station of N.Y.C.), N.Y. *(227,930)* 2.00
C72 10c **carmine,** *Jan. 5, 1968,* San Francisco, Cal. 1.00
C72b Booklet pane of 8 3.75
C72c Booklet pane of 5 + label, slogan 4 *Jan. 6, 1968* 125.00
With slogan 5 110.00
C73 10c **carmine coil,** *Jan. 5, 1968,* San Francisco, Cal. 1.00
C74 10c **Air Mail Service,** *May 15, 1968* *(521,084)* 1.50

C75 20c **USA and Jet,** *Nov. 22, 1968,* New York, N.Y. *(276,244)* 1.25
C76 10c **Moon Landing,** *Sept. 9, 1969 (8,743,070)* 6.00

1971-73

C77 9c **red,** *May 15, 1971,* Kitty Hawk, N.C. 1.00

First day cancellation was applied to 379,442 covers of Nos. C77 and UXC10.

C78 11c **carmine,** *May 7, 1971,* Spokane, Wash. 1.00
C78a Booklet pane of 4 + 2 labels 3.00
C79 13c **carmine,** *Nov. 16, 1973,* New York, N.Y. *(282,550)* 1.00
C79a Booklet pane of 5 + label, *Dec. 27, 1973,* Chicago, Ill. 3.00

First day cancellation was applied to 464,750 covers of Nos. C78, C78a and C82, and to 204,756 covers of Nos. C79a and C83.

C80 17c **Statue of Liberty,** *July 13, 1971,* Lakehurst, N.J. *(172,269)* 1.50
C81 21c **USA and Jet,** *May 21, 1971 (293,140)* 1.00
C82 11c **carmine coil,** *May 7, 1971,* Spokane, Wash. 1.00
C83 13c **carmine coil,** *Dec. 27, 1973,* Chicago, Ill. 1.00
C84 11c **National Parks Centennial,** *May 3, 1972,* Honaunau, Hawaii *(364,816)* 1.00
C85 11c **Olympics,** *Aug. 17, 1972* 1.00

First day cancellation was applied to 971,536 covers of Nos. 1460-1462 and C85.

C86 11c **Electronics,** *July 10, 1973,* New York, N.Y. 1.00

First day cancellation was applied to 1,197,700 covers of Nos. 1500-1502 and C86.

1974-79

C87 18c **Statue of Liberty,** *Jan. 11, 1974,* Hempstead, N.Y. *(216,902)* 1.25
C88 26c **Mt. Rushmore,** *Jan. 2, 1974,* Rapid City, S.D. *(210,470)* 2.00
C89 25c **Plane and Globes,** *Jan. 2, 1976,* Honolulu, Hawaii 1.00
C90 31c **Plane, Globes and Flag,** *Jan. 2, 1976,* Honolulu, Hawaii 1.25
C92a 31c **Wright Brothers,** *Sept. 23, 1978,* Dayton, Ohio 4.00
C91-C92, any single 3.00
C94a 21c **Octave Chanute,** *Mar. 29, 1979,* Chanute, Kan. *(459,235)* 4.00
C93-C94, any single 3.00
C96a 25c **Wiley Post,** *Nov. 20, 1979,* Oklahoma City, Okla. 4.00
C95-C96, any single 3.00
C97 31c **Olympics,** *Nov. 1, 1979,* Colorado Springs, CO 1.50

1980

C98 40c **Philip Mazzei,** *Oct. 13* 1.50
C99 28c **Blanche Stuart Scott,** *Dec. 30,* Hammondsport, NY *(238,502)* 2.00
C100 35c **Glenn Curtiss,** *Dec. 30,* Hammondsport, NY *(208,502)* 1.50

1983

C104a 28c **Olympics,** *June 17,* San Antonio, TX *(901,028)* 3.75
C101-C104, any single 1.75
C108a 40c **Olympics,** *Apr. 8,* Los Angeles, CA *(1,001,657)* 5.00
C105-C108, any single 1.75
C112a 35c **Olympics,** *Nov. 4,* Colorado Springs, CO*(897,729)* 4.50
C109-C112, any single 1.75

1985

C113 33c **Alfred V. Verville,** *Feb. 13,* Garden City, NY 1.50
C114 39c **Lawrence & Elmer Sperry,** *Feb. 13,* Garden City, NY 1.50

First day cancel was applied to 429,290 covers bearing one more of Nos. C113-C114.

C115 44c **Transpacific Air Mail,** *Feb. 15,* San Francisco, CA *(269,229)* 1.75

A total of 269,229 first day cancels were applied for Nos. C115 and UXC22.

C116 44c **Junipero Serra,** *Aug. 22,* San Diego, CA *(254,977)* 2.00

1988

C117 44c **Settling of New Sweden,** *Mar. 29,* Wilmington, DE *(213,445)* 1.50
C118 45c **Samuel P. Langley,** *May 14,* San Diego, CA 1.50
C119 36c **Igor Sikorsky,** *June 23,* Stratford, CT *(162,986)* 3.00

1989

C120 45c **French Revolution,** *July 14 (309,975)* 1.50
C121 45c **Southeast Carved Figure,** *Oct. 12,* San Juan, PR *(93,569)* 1.50
C125a 45c **Future Mail Transportation,** *Nov. 27 (765,479)* 6.50
C122-C125, any single 2.00
C126 45c **Future Mail Transportation Souvenir Sheet,** *Nov. 24 (257,826)* 6.50

1990

C127 45c **Tropical Coast,** *Oct. 12,* Grand Canyon, AZ *(137,068)* 1.50

1991

C128 50c **Harriet Quimby,** *Apr. 27,* Plymouth, MI 2.00
C129 40c **William T. Piper,** *May 17,* Denver, CO 2.00
C130 50c **Antarctic Treaty,** *June 21* 2.00
C131 50c **Bering Land Bridge,** *Oct. 12,* Anchorage, AK 2.00

1999

C133 48c **Niagara Falls,** *May 12,* Niagara Falls, NY *(20,878)* 2.50
C134 40c **Rio Grande,** *July 30,* Milwaukee, WI 2.50
any other city 2.50

First day cancel was applied to 42,144 covers bearing one more of Nos. 3330, C134.

2000

C135 60c **Grand Canyon,** *Jan. 20,* Grand Canyon, AZ *(64,282)* 3.00

2001

C136 70c **Nine-mile Prairie,** *Mar. 6,* Lincoln, NE 2.50
C137 80c **Mt. McKinley,** *Apr. 17,* Fairbanks, AK 3.00
C138 60c **Acadia National Park,** *May 30,* Bar Harbor, ME 3.00

2006

C139 63c **Bryce Canyon National Park,** *Feb. 24,* St. Louis, MO 3.00
Any other city 3.00
C140 75c **Great Smoky Mountains National Park,** *Feb. 24,* St. Louis, MO 3.00
Any other city 3.00
C141 84c **Yosemite National Park,** *Feb. 24,* St. Louis, MO 3.00
Any other city 3.00

2007

C142 69c **Okefenokee Swamp,** *June 1,* McLean, VA 3.00
C143 90c **Hagatña Bay,** *June 1,* Barrigada, GU 3.00

2008

C144 72c **13-Mile Woods, New Hampshire,** *May 16,* Rochester, NY 3.00
C145 94c **Trunk Bay, St. John, Virgin Islands,** *May 16,* Rochester, NY 3.50
St. John, VI 3.50

2009

C146 79c **Zion National Park,** *June 28,* Washington, DC 3.50
C147 98c **Grand Teton National Park,** *June 28,* Washington, DC 3.50

2011

C148 80c **Voyageurs National Park,** *Apr. 11,* Washington, DC 3.00

2012

C149 85c **Glacier National Park,** *Jan. 19,* Kalispell, MT 3.00
C150 $1.05 **Amish Buggy, Lancaster County, Pennsylvania,** *Jan. 20,* Lancaster, PA 3.50

U.S. Scott Mount Set for 2018 Supplements!

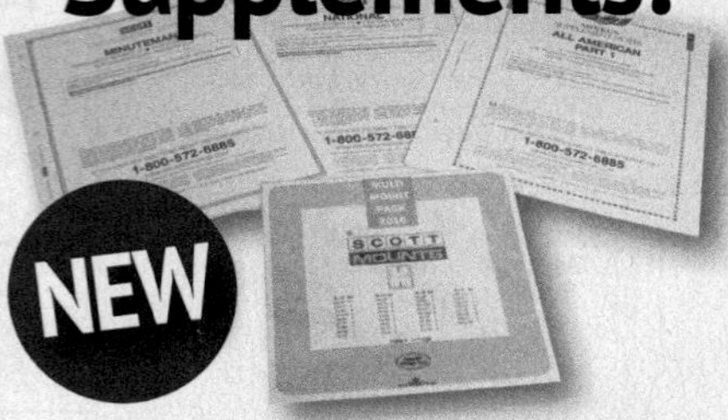

NEW

Take the work out of collecting with our NEWEST Scott U.S. Mount Set. The Scott U.S. Mount Set comes with customized, pre-cut mounts that fit all stamps displayed in the 2018 National, Minuteman, or All-American Pt. 1 supplements. Our high-quality mounts are center-cut to ensure secure storage and protection.

PURCHASE A MOUNT SET AND 2018 SUPPLEMENT TOGETHER AND SAVE OVER 15%!

U.S. MOUNT SET (MOUNTS ONLY)

Item#	Description	Retail	AA*
2018 B	2018 U.S. Mount Set, Black	$49.99	$39.99
2018 C	2018 U.S. Mount Set, Clear	$49.99	$39.99

SALE! 2018 NATIONAL SUPPLEMENT SET

Item#	Description	Retail	AA*	SALE
100S018BB	2018 National Supplement + Black Mount Set	$69.98	~~$56.98~~	$47.98
100S018BC	2018 National Supplement + Clear Mount Set	$69.98	~~$58.98~~	$47.98

SALE! 2018 MINUTEMAN SUPPLEMENT SET

Item#	Description	Retail	AA*	SALE
180S018BB	2018 U.S. Minuteman Supplement + Black Mount Set	$69.98	$56.98	$47.98
180S018BC	2018 U.S. Minuteman Supplement + Clear Mount Set	$69.98	$56.98	$47.98

SALE! 2018 ALL-AMERICAN PT. 1 SUPPLEMENT SET

Item#	Description	Retail	AA*	SALE
MAA118BB	2018 All-American Pt. 1 Supplement + Black Mount Set	$69.98	~~$56.98~~	$47.98
MAA118BC	2018 All-American Pt. 1 Supplement + Clear Mount Set	$69.98	$56.98	$47.98

www.AmosAdvantage.com

Call **800-572-6885**

Outside U.S. & Canada call: **(937) 498-0800**

Ordering Information: *AA prices apply to paid subscribers of Amos Media titles, or orders placed online. Prices, terms and product availability subject to change. Shipping and handling rates will apply. Taxes apply in CA, OH & IL.
Shipping & Handling: United States: Order total $0-$10.00charged $3.99 shipping. Order total $10.01-$79.99 charged $7.99 shipping. Order total $80.00 or more charged 10% of order total for shipping. Maximum Freight Charge $45.00. Canada: 20% of order total. Minimum charge $19.99 Maximum charge $200.00. Foreign: Orders are shipped via FedExl Intl. or USPS and billed actual freight.

BOOKLETS: PANES & COVERS

Most booklet panes issued before 1962 consist of a vertical block of 6 stamps perforated vertically through the center. The panes are perforated horizontally on all but the bottom edge and the top of the selvage tab. The selvage top, the two sides and the bottom are straight edged. Exceptions for panes issued before 1962 are the 1917 American Expeditionary Forces panes (30 stamps); Lindbergh and 6¢ 1943 air mails (3), and the Savings Stamps (10). Since 1962, panes have been issued with 3 to 20 stamps and various configurations. They have included one or more labels and two or more stamps se-tenant.

Flat plate booklet panes, with the exceptions noted above, were made from specially designed plates of 180 or 360 subjects. They are collected in plate positions. There are nine collectible positions on the 180-subject plate and 12 on the 360-subject plate.

Rotary booklet panes issued from 1926 to May 1978 (except for Nos. 1623a and 1623Bc) were made from specially designed plates of 180, 320, 360, and 400 subjects. They also are collected in plate positions. There are five collectible positions on the 360-subject plates which were printed before electric eye plates came into use, and 18 collectible positions on the Type II "new design" 360-subject rotary plates. There are 17 collectible positions in the rotary air mail 180-subject plate, and 21 collectible positions in the Type IV "modified design" 360-subject plate. There are 13 collectible positions on the 320-subject plates and 24 on the 400 subject plates. There are five collectible positions on Defense and War Savings 300-subject plates.

The generally accepted methods of designating pane positions as illustrated and explained hereafter are those suggested by George H. Beans in the May 1913 issue of "Everybody's Philatelist" and by B. H. Mosher in his monograph "Discovering U.S. Rotary Pane Varieties 1926-78." Some collectors seek all varieties possible, but the majority collect unused (A) panes and plate number (D) panes from flat plate issues, and plain panes and panes with electric eye bars and electric eye dashes, where available, from rotary plates.

Starting in 1977, BEP made two major changes in booklet production. Printing of panes was gradually moved from rotary plates to sleeves for modern high speed presses. Also, booklet production was transferred to Goebel booklet-forming machines. These changes virtually eliminated collectible pane positions for several years. However, beginning with No. BK156 (No. 2276a), BEP and other printers began placing printing process control marks in pane tabs. As a result, specialist booklet pane collectors actively resumed collecting pane positions. Collectible positions on these issues are not shown in this catalogue but can be found in the United States Stamp Society's Research Paper No. 2 "Folded Style Checklist," Michael O. Perry, editor. Also, because of the requirements of the Goebel machine, the subject size of printing plates or sleeves varied widely. For these reasons, plate layouts are not shown for each issue. The plate layout for No. 1288c and the sleeve layout for No. 1623a are shown as typical.

The following panes, issued after Mar. 11, 1977, were printed from pairs of rotary plates and assembled into booklets on the Goebel machine: Nos. 1288c, 1742a, 1819a, 1889a, and 1949a. One pane in 12 of those issues may have a join line along either long side of the pane, creating three collectible positions: no join line, join line top (or right) and join line bottom (or left). Except for Nos. 1736a and 2276a, all other booklet panes issued from Mar. 11, 1977 on were printed from intaglio sleeves, gravure cylinders, and/or offset plates.

At least one pane in every booklet produced on the BEP's Goebel machines contains two register marks in the tab: a cross register line (CRL) 1.5mm wide which runs across the width of the tab and a length register mark (LRM), typically 1.5x5mm, usually placed above the right hand (or top) stamp of the pane. Nos. 1623a and 1623Bc were regularly issued with the LRM over either stamp. Some examples of Nos. 1893a, 2121a and 3003Ab were issued with the LRM over the left stamp.

Starting with No. 1889a (except for No. 1948a), plate numbers (1 to 5 digits) were placed in the tab, normally over the left stamp. On booklets containing Nos. 1889a, 1949a and 2113a, the plate number is supposed to be on the top pane, the second pane not having a number. All subsequent multi-pane booklets have the plate number on each pane. Some multi-pane booklets contain panes with different plate numbers. The booklet value is determined by the top pane.

Most recent booklets have been printed by contractors other than the BEP so markings may differ or be absent.

Panes in all booklets assembled on the Goebel machine will be folded at least once. **Repeated handling of booklets with folded panes may cause the panes to fall apart.**

Booklet panes with tabs attached to the cover by adhesive instead of staples are valued on the basis of the tab intact. Minor damage on the back of the tab due to removal from the booklet does not affect the value. Some of these panes were furnished to first day cover processors unfolded and not pasted into covers. Around 1989, these panes were available to collectors through the Philatelic Agency.

All panes from 1967 to date are tagged, unless otherwise stated.

Dr. William R. Bush, Morton Dean Joyce, Robert E. Kitson, Richard F. Larkin, Dr. Robert Marks, Bruce H. Mosher, Michael O. Perry, the United States Stamp Society (formerly the Bureau Issues Association), and the Booklet Collectors Club helped the editors extensively in compiling the listings and preparing the illustrations of booklets, covers and plate layouts.

All illustrations in this section are reduced in size to a greater or lesser extent.

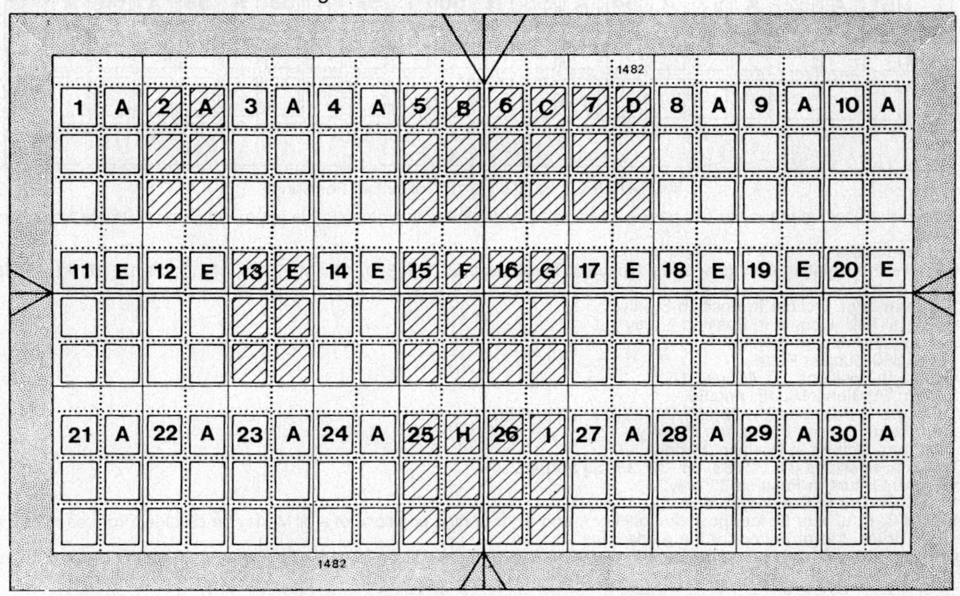

180-SUBJECT PLATE — 9 Collectible Positions

Beginning at upper left and reading from left to right, the panes are designated from 1 to 30. All positions not otherwise identifiable are designated by the letter A: Pane 1A, 2A, 3A, 4A, etc.

The identifiable positions are as follows:

A — The ordinary booklet pane without distinguishing features. Occurs in Position 1, 2, 3, 4, 8, 9, 10, 21, 22, 23, 24, 27, 28, 29, 30.
B — Split arrow and guide line at right. Occurs in Position 5 only.
C — Split arrow and guide line at left. Occurs in Position 6 only.
D — Plate number pane. Occurs in Position 7 only.
E — Guide line pane showing horizontal guide line between stamps 1-2 and 3-4 of the pane. Occurs in Positions 11, 12, 13, 14, 17, 18, 19, and 20.
F — Guide line through pane and at right. Occurs in Position 15 only.

G — Guide line through pane and at left. Occurs in Position 16 only.
H — Guide line at right. Occurs in Position 25 only.
I — Guide line at left. Occurs in Position 26 only.
Only positions B, F and H or C, G and I may be obtained from the same sheet, depending on whether the knife which separated the panes fell to right or left of the line. Side arrows, bottom arrows, or bottom plate numbers are seldom found because the margin of the sheets is usually cut off, as are the sides and bottom of each pane. In the illustrations, the dotted lines represent the rows of perforations, the unbroken lines represents the knife cut.

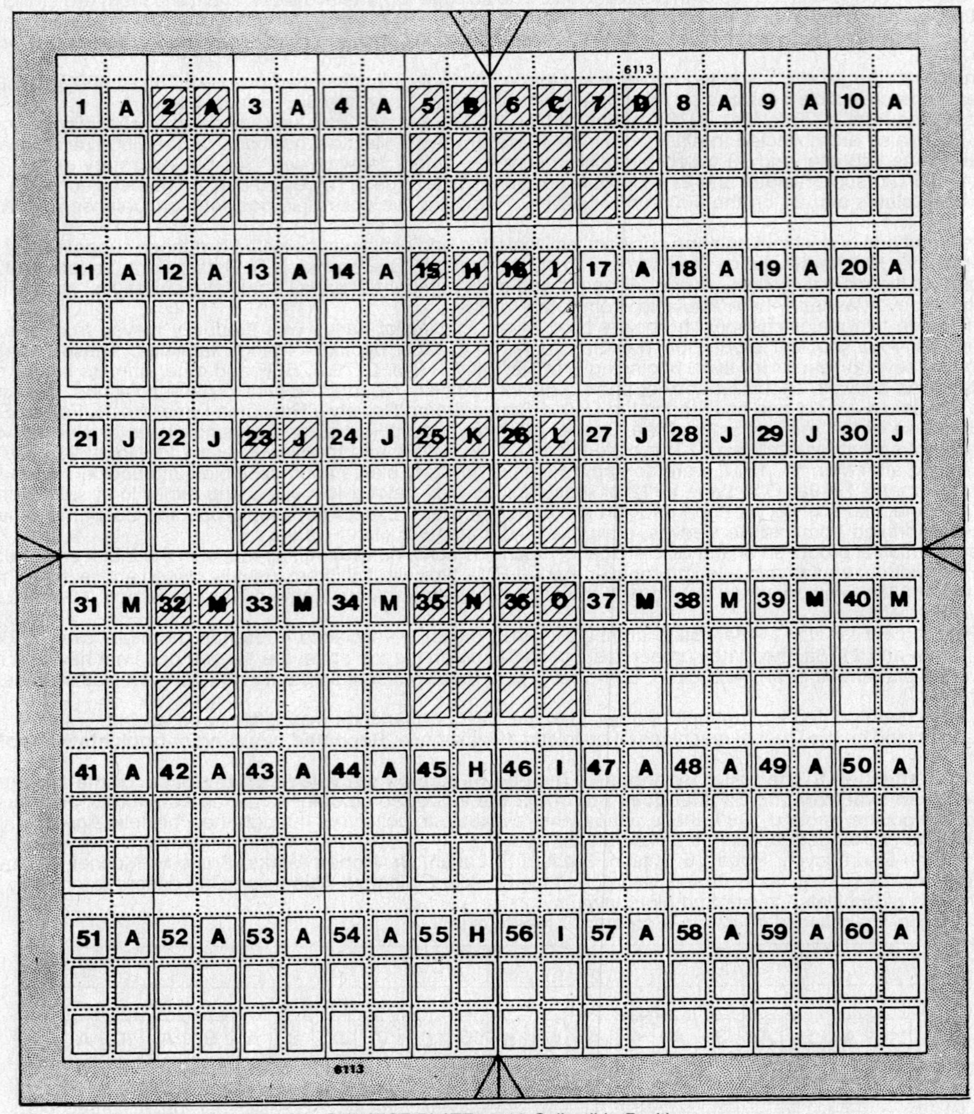

360-SUBJECT PLATE — 12 Collectible Positions

As with the 180-Subject Sheets, the position of the various panes is indicated by numbers beginning in the upper left corner with the No. 1 and reading from left to right to No. 60.
The identifiable positions are as follows:
A — The ordinary booklet pane without distinguishing features. Occurs in Positions 1, 2, 3, 4, 8, 9, 10, 11, 12, 13, 14, 17, 18, 19, 20, 41, 42, 43, 44, 47, 48, 49, 50, 51, 52, 53, 54, 57, 58, 59, and 60.
B — Split arrow and guide line at right. Occurs in Position 5 only.
C — Split arrow and guide line at left. Occurs in Position 6 only.
D — Plate number pane. Occurs in Position 7 only.
E, F, G — Do not occur in the 360-Subject Plate.
H — Guide line at right. Occurs in Positions 15, 45, and 55.
I — Guide line at left. Occurs in Positions 16, 46, and 56.
J — Guide line at bottom. Occurs in Positions 21, 22, 23, 24, 27, 28, 29 and 30.
K — Guide line at right and bottom. Occurs in Position 25 only.
L — Guide line at left and bottom. Occurs in Position 26 only.
M — Guide line at top. Occurs in Positions 31, 32, 33, 34, 37, 38, 39 and 40.
N — Guide line at top and right. Occurs in Position 35 only.
O — Guide line at top and left. Occurs in Position 36 only.
Only one each of Positions B or C, K, L, N or O; four positions of H or I, and eight or nine positions of J or M may be obtained from each 360 subject sheet, depending on whether the knife fell to the right or left, top or bottom of the guide lines.
Because the horizontal guide line appears so close to the bottom row of stamps on panes Nos. 21 to 30, Positions M, N, and O occur with great deal less frequency than Positions J, K and L.

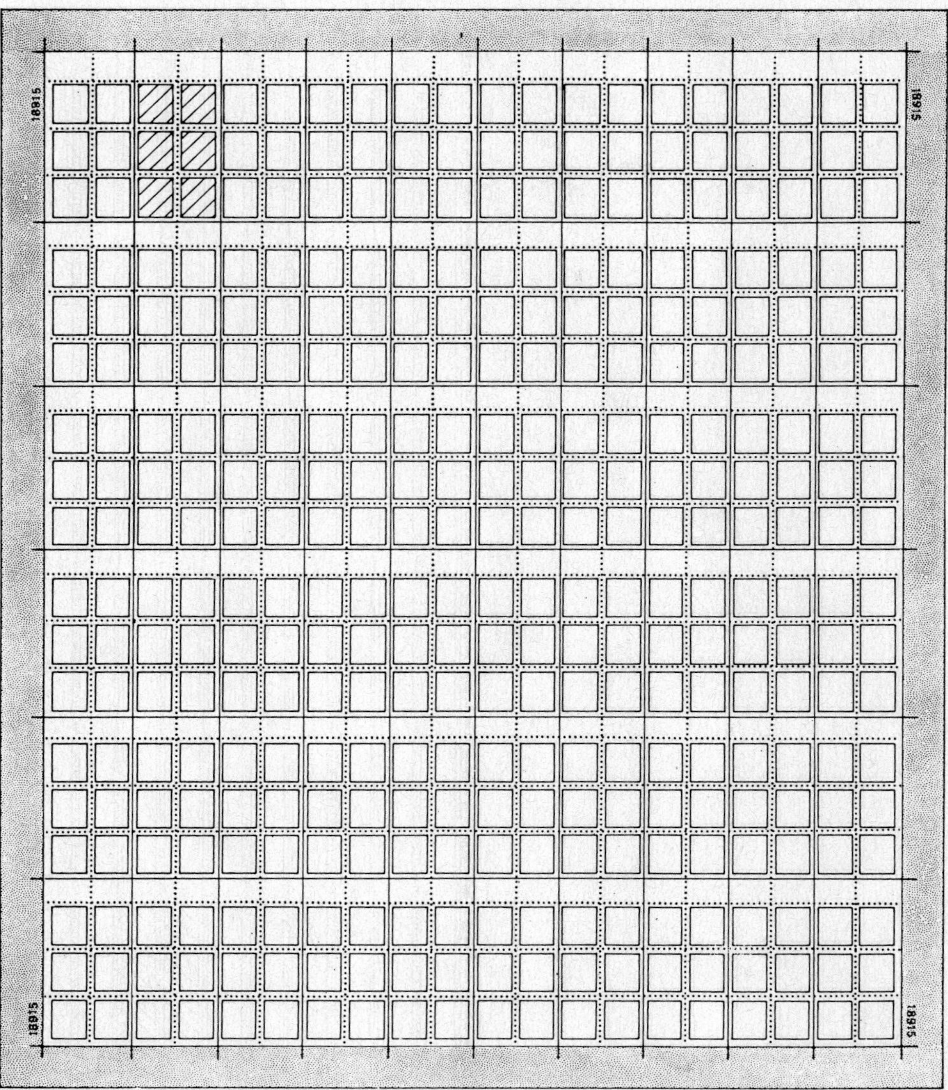

The 360-Subject Rotary Press Plate (before Electric Eye) Position A only

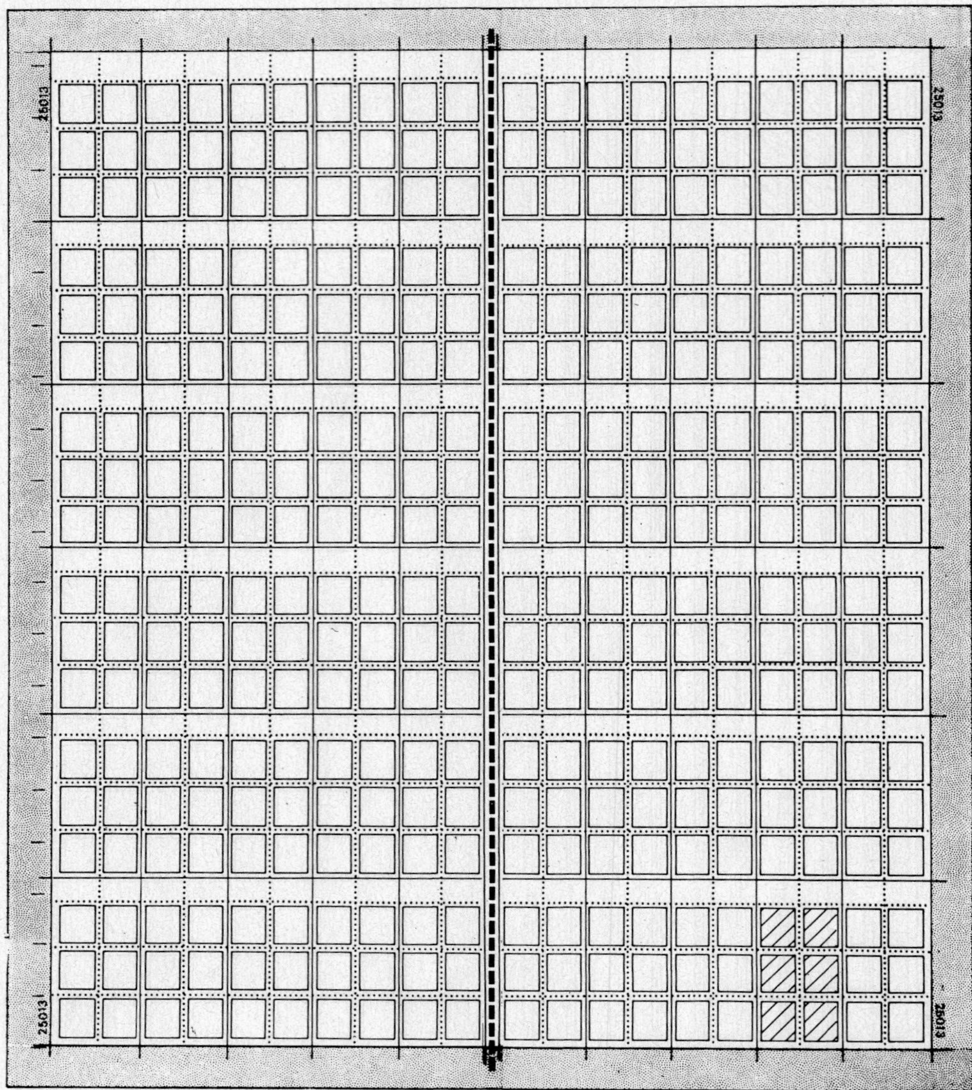

The 360-Subject Rotary Press Plate — Electric Eye

A modified design was put into use in 1956. The new plates have 20 frame bars instead of 17.

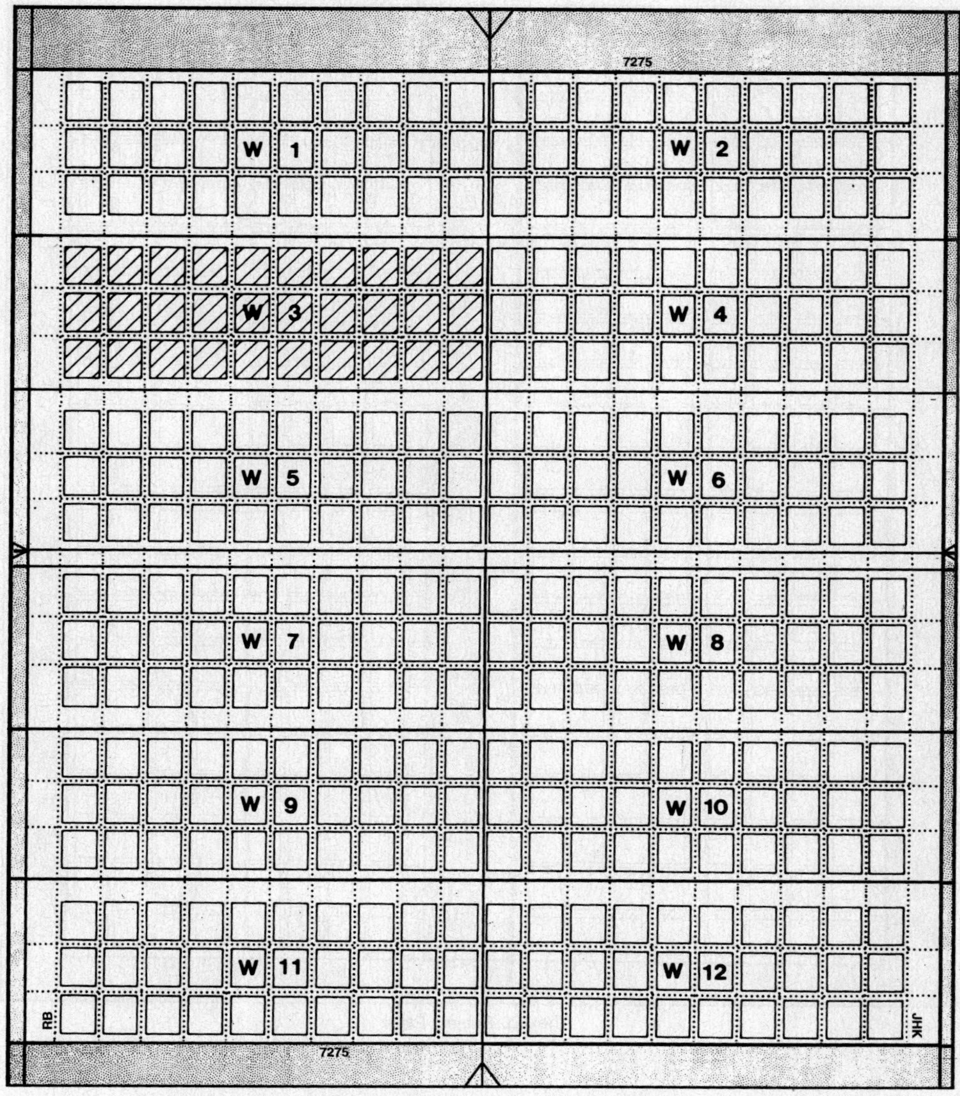

The A.E.F. Plate — 360-Subject Flat Plate — 8 Collectible Positions (See listings)

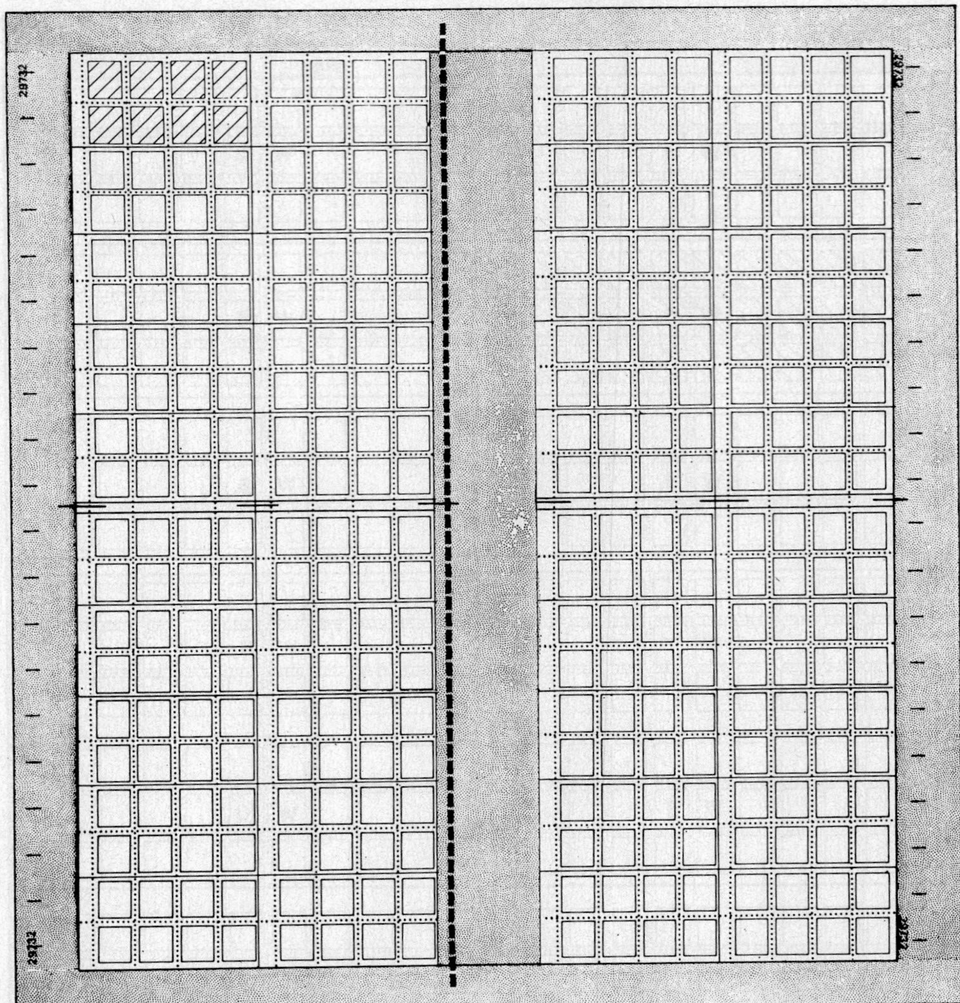

The 320-Subject Plate

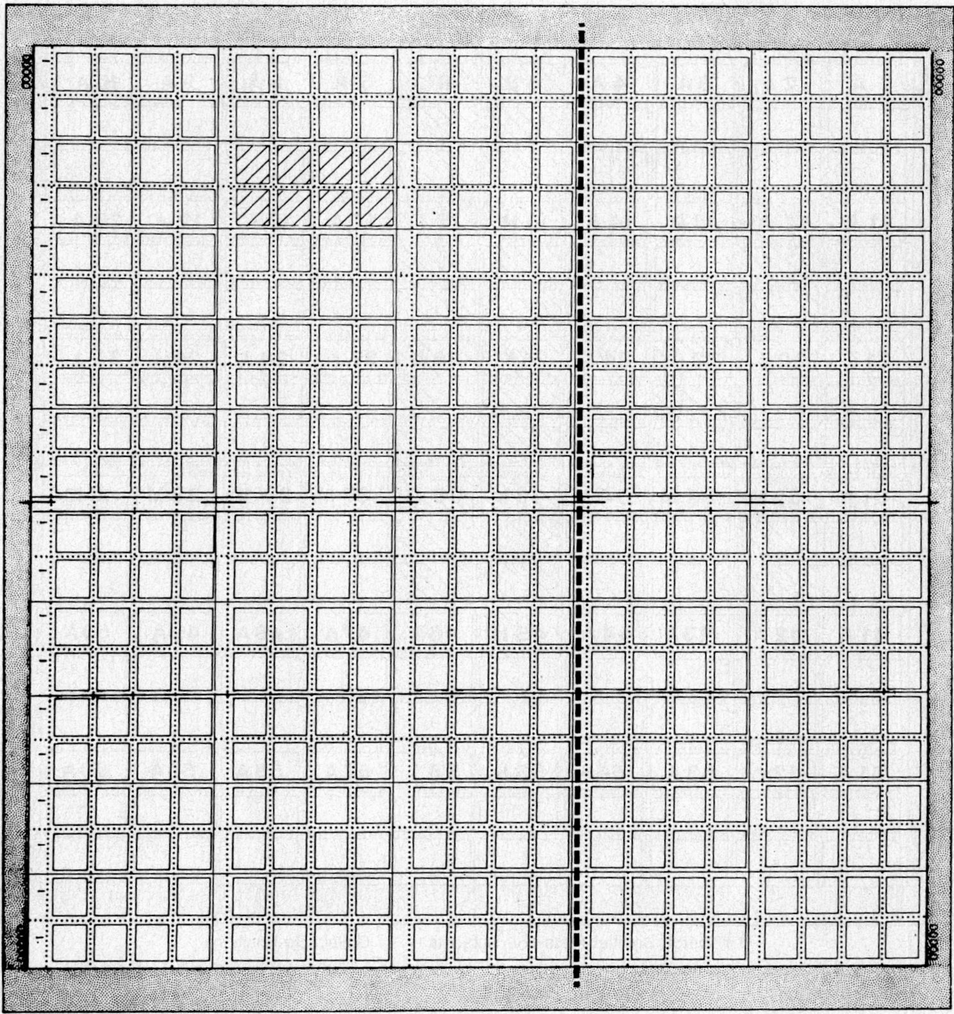

400-Subject Plate — The 300-Subject plate with double labels has the same layout.

1 A	2 A	3 A	4 A	5 B	6 C	7 A	8 A	9 A	10 A
11 A	12 A	13 A	14 A	15 H	16 I	17 A	18 A	19 A	20 A
21 J	22 J	23 J	24 J	25 K	26 L	27 J	28 J	29 J	30 J
31 M	32 M	33 M	34 M	35 N	36 O	37 M	38 M	39 M	40 M
41 A	42 A	43 A	44 A	45 H	46 I	47 A	48 A	49 A	50 A
51 A	52 A	53 A	54 A	55 H	56 I	57 A	58 A	59 A	60 A

19425 19425 19425 19425

Lindbergh Booklet Plate-180 Subjects — 11 Collectible Positions

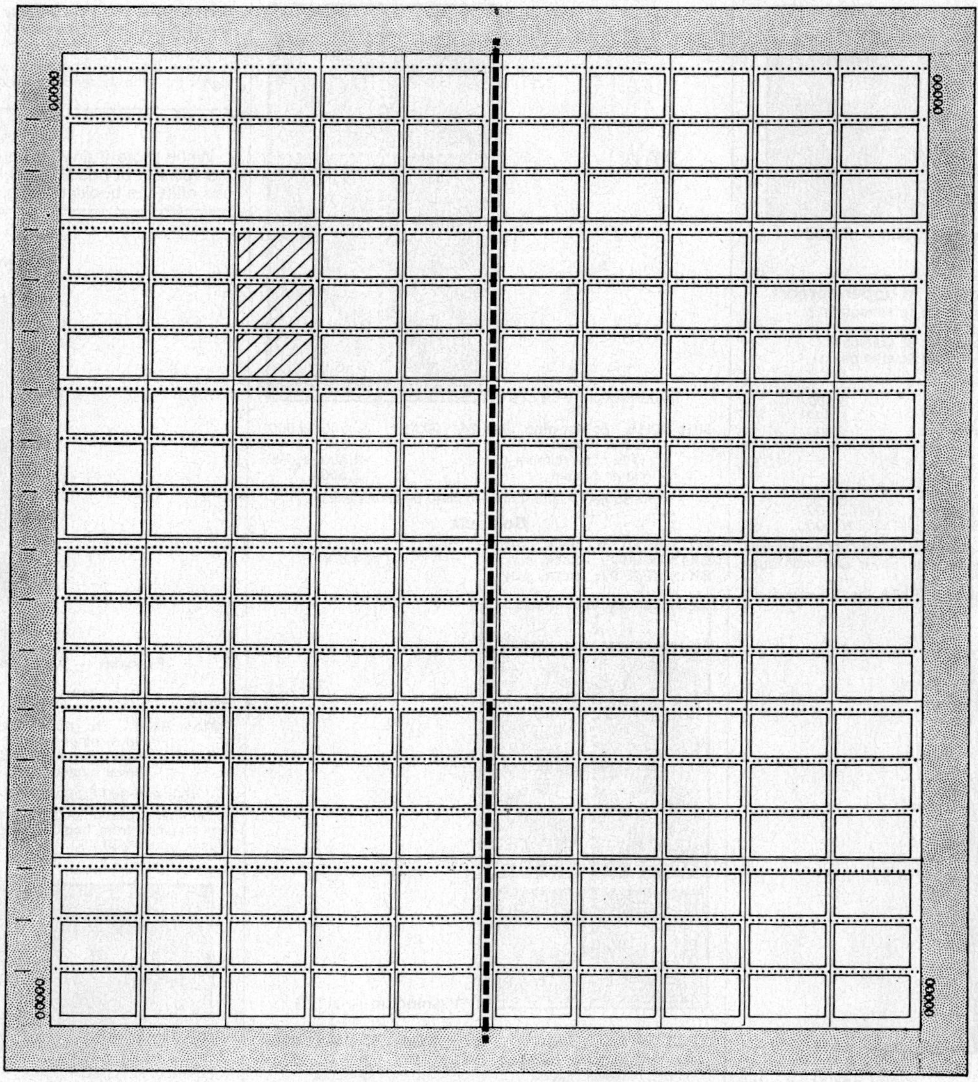

Airmail 180-Subject Rotary Press Plate — Electric Eye

Plate Sizes: No. 1288Bc to date.

Since 1978 numerous plate sizes from 78 to 1080 subjects have been used. Because plate size is not relevant to collecting these panes, we are not including this information in the catalogue.

BOOKLET PANES

Values for both unused and used booklet panes are for complete panes with selvage, and for panes of six unless otherwise stated. Panes in booklets are Never Hinged. Values for stapled booklets are for those with creasing along the lines of the staples. Values for booklets which were glued shut are for opened booklets without significant damage to the cover.

See other notes in the introduction to this section.

BOOKLET COVERS

Front covers of booklets of postage and airmail issues are illustrated and numbered.

Included are the Booklet Cover number (BC2A); and the catalogue numbers of the Booklet Panes (300b, 331a). The text of the inside and or back covers changes. Some modern issues have minor changes on the front covers also. When more than one combination of covers exists, the number of possible booklets is noted in parentheses after the booklet listing. Booklet covers that have no card stock color given are white.

USED BOOKLET PANES

Many early booklet panes are scarce to rare in used condition, and they are valued higher to much higher than the corresponding panes in unused condition. Such used panes are valued with contemporaneous cancellations, and it is strongly recommended that such panes be expertized by one of the competent expertizing bodies.

Washington — A88

Wmk. 191 Horizontally or Vertically

1900-03 *Perf. 12*

279Bj	A88 2c **red,** horizontal wmk., *Apr. 18*	500.	*3,000.*
	light red	500.	3,000.
	orange red, *1902*	500.	3,000.
	Never hinged	1,000.	
	With plate number (D)	1,350.	*6,000.*
	Never hinged	2,150.	

279Bk	A88 2c **red,** vertical watermark	500.	—
	orange red	750.	—
	Never hinged	1,000.	
	With plate number (D)	1,350.	*8,000.*
	Never hinged	2,150.	

360- (horiz. wmk.) and 180- (vert. wmk.) subject plates. All plate positions exist, except J, K, and L, due to the horizontal guide line being placed too far below stamps to appear on the upper panes.

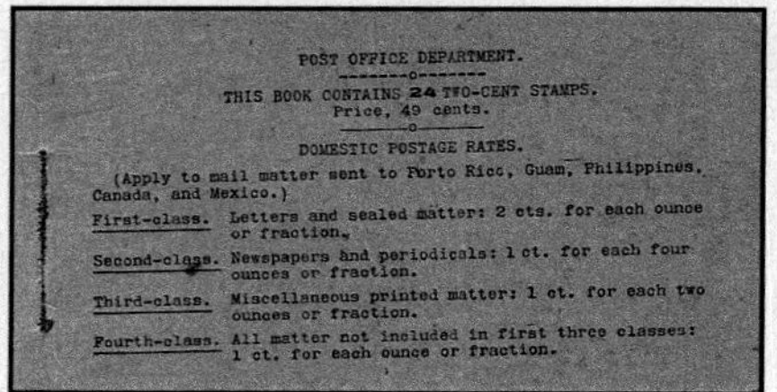
POST OFFICE DEPARTMENT.

THIS BOOK CONTAINS 24 TWO-CENT STAMPS.
Price, 49 cents.

DOMESTIC POSTAGE RATES.

(Apply to mail matter sent to Porto Rico, Guam, Philippines, Canada, and Mexico.)

First-class. Letters and sealed matter: 2 cts. for each ounce or fraction.

Second-class. Newspapers and periodicals: 1 ct. for each four ounces or fraction.

Third-class. Miscellaneous printed matter: 1 ct. for each two ounces or fraction.

Fourth-class. All matter not included in first three classes: 1 ct. for each ounce or fraction.

279Bj-279Bk — BC1

1900-03 **Text only cover**

25c booklet contains 2 panes of six 2c stamps.
49c booklet contains 4 panes of six 2c stamps.
97c booklet contains 8 panes of six 2c stamps.

Booklets sold for 1c more than the face value of the stamps.

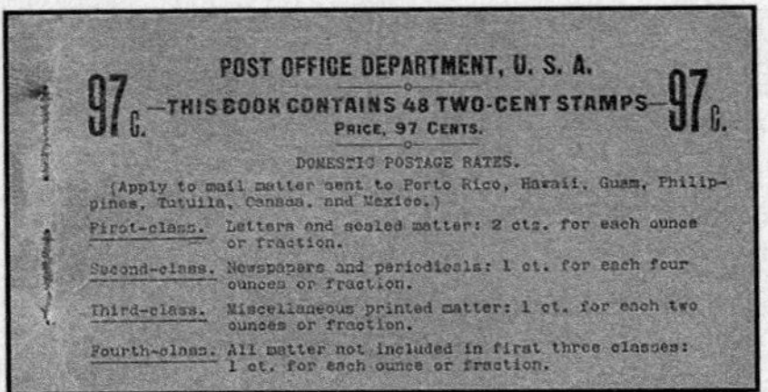

279Bj, 279Bk, 301c, 319, 332a — BC2B

1900-08

Text cover with price added in upper corners

25c booklets contain 4 panes of six 1c stamps or 2 panes of six 2c stamps.
49c booklet contains 4 panes of six 2c stamps.
97c booklet contains 8 panes of six 2c stamps.

Booklets

BK1	BC1	25c **black,** *cream*	*5,500.*
BK2	BC1	25c **black,** *buff*	*5,000.*
BK3	BC1	49c **green,** *cream*	*9,000.*
BK4	BC1	49c **black,** *buff*	—
BK5	BC1	97c **red,** *cream*	—
BK6	BC1	97c **black,** *gray*	—
BK7	BC2B	25c **black,** *cream* (3)	*6,000.*
BK8	BC2B	49c **black,** *buff* (3)	*5,000.*
BK9	BC2B	97c **black,** *gray* (3)	*12,500.*

Nos. BK1-BK6 and one type each of Nos. BK7-BK9 exist with specimen overprints handstamped on cover and individual stamps.

All covers of BK7-BK9 exist with "Philippines" overprint in 50mm or 48mm.

Franklin — A115

1903-07 **Wmk. 191 Vertically**

300b	A115	1c **blue green,** *Mar. 6, 1907*	600.	*11,500.*
		Never hinged	1,150.	
		With plate number (D)	1,200.	
		Never hinged	*2,250.*	
		With plate number 3472 over left stamp (D)	*8,750.*	
		Watermark horizontal	*2,000.*	

180-Subject Plates only. All plate positions exist.

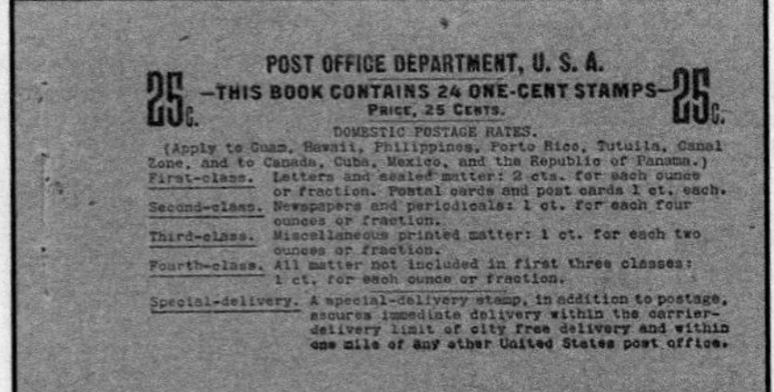

300b, 331a, 332a — BC2A

1900-08

Text cover with price added in upper corners

25c booklets contain 4 panes of six 1c stamps or 2 panes of six 2c stamps.
49c booklet contains 4 panes of six 2c stamps.

Booklet

BK10	BC2A	25c **black,** *green* (6)	*6,000.*

Washington — A116

301c	A116	2c **carmine,** *Jan. 24, 1903*	500.	*6,000.*
		Never hinged	950.	
		With plate number (D)	1,500.	*8,000.*
		Never hinged	*2,500.*	

180-Subject Plates only. All plate positions exist.

Booklets

BK11	BC2B	25c **black,** *cream*	*3,000.*
BK12	BC2B	49c **black,** *buff*	*4,000.*
BK13	BC2B	97c **black,** *gray*	—

Washington — A129

1903 **Type I** **Wmk. 191 Vertically**

319g	A129	2c **carmine,** *Dec. 3, 1903*	125.00	*450.00*
		Never hinged	240.00	
		With plate number (D)	275.00	*750.00*
		Never hinged	500.00	
		With round marker (B)	*7,000.*	
		Wmk. horizontal	*3,000.*	
		Never hinged	*5,000.*	
		With Plate number (D)	*7,000.*	
319n	A129	2c **carmine rose**	275.00	*700.00*
		Never hinged	500.00	
		With plate number (D)	425.00	*1,000.*
		Never hinged	725.00	
319p	A129	2c **scarlet**	185.00	*625.00*
		Never hinged	350.00	
		With plate number (D)	350.00	*900.00*
		Never hinged	625.00	

Booklets (Carmine type I shades)

BK14	BC2B	25c **black,** *cream* (11)	850.00
BK15	BC2A	49c **black,** *buff* (11)	*1,150.*
BK16	BC2A	49c **black,** *pink*	*2,500.*
BK17	BC2B	97c **black,** *gray* (11)	*2,750.*

Type II

319Fh	A129	2c **carmine,** *1907*	900.00	—
		Never hinged	1,500.	
		With plate number (D)	1,500.	
		Never hinged	2,500.	
319Fl	A129	2c **scarlet**	—	
319Fq	A129	2c **lake**	300.00	*800.00*
		Never hinged	575.00	
		With plate number (D)	550.00	
		Never hinged	900.00	

180-Subject Plates only. All plate positions exist.

Booklets (Lake type II shades)

BK14A	BC2B	25c **black,** *cream*	*1,350.*
BK15A	BC2A	49c **black,** *buff*	*2,500.*
BK16A	BC2A	49c **black,** *pink*	*4,000.*
BK17A	BC2B	97c **black,** *gray*	*5,750.*
BK17b	BC2B	97c **black,** *gray,* carmine type II panes	*15,000.*

Values for type II booklets with carmine panes are much higher than the values for booklets with the lake shade panes.

Booklet Covers

When more than one combination of covers exists, the number of possible booklets is noted in parentheses after the booklet listing.

Franklin — A138

1908 **Wmk. 191 Vertically**

331a	A138	1c **green,** *Dec. 1908*	150.00	*700.00*
		Never hinged	300.00	
		With plate number (D)	225.00	
		Never hinged	450.00	

180- and 360-Subject Plates. All plate positions exist.

No. 331 exists in horizontal pair, imperforate between, a variety resulting from booklet experiments. Not regularly issued. Value, unused $3,750.

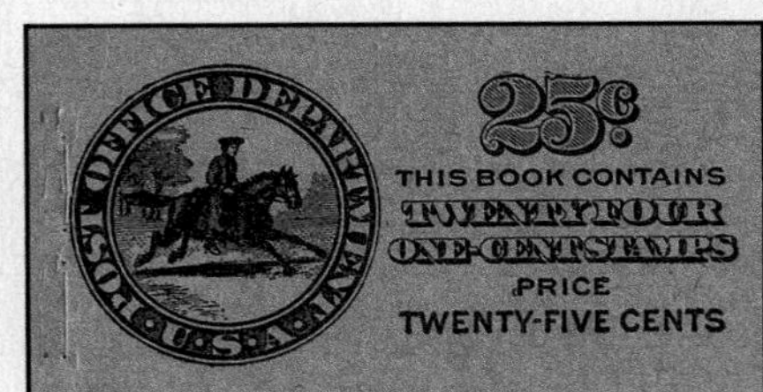

331a, 332a, 374a, 375a, 405b, 406a — BC3

1908-12 **Postrider**

25c booklet contains 4 panes of six 1c stamps.
25c booklet contains 2 panes of six 2c stamps.
49c booklet contains 4 panes of six 2c stamps.
97c booklet contains 8 panes of six 2c stamps.

Booklets

BK18	BC2A	25c **black,** *green* (3)	*1,800.*
BK19	BC3	25c **black,** *green*	*2,000.*

Washington — A139

332a	A139	2c **carmine,** *Nov. 16, 1908*	135.00	*500.00*
		Never hinged	240.00	
		With plate number (D)	175.00	
		Never hinged	310.00	

180- and 360-Subject Plates. All plate positions exist.

Booklets

BK20 BC2A 25c **black,** *cream* (2) *1,250.*
BK21 BC2A 49c **black,** *buff* (2) *2,750.*
BK22 BC2A 49c **black,** *pink* *3,250.*
BK23 BC2B 97c **black,** *gray* (3) *3,000.*
BK24 BC3 25c **black,** *cream* *1,250.*
BK25 BC3 49c **black,** *pink* *2,500.*
BK26 BC3 97c **black,** *gray* *3,500.*

1910 **Wmk. 190 Vertically** ***Perf. 12***

374a A138 1c **green,** *Oct. 7, 1910* 225.00 *400.00*
Never hinged 375.00
With plate number (D) 300.00
Never hinged 475.00

360-Subject Plates only. All plate positions exist.

Booklet

BK27 BC3 25c **black,** *green* (2) *2,000.*

375a A139 2c **carmine,** *Nov. 30, 1910* 125.00 *300.00*
Never hinged 200.00
With plate number (D) 170.00
Never hinged 290.00

360-Subject Plates only. All plate positions exist.

Booklets

BK28 BC3 25c **black,** *cream* (2) *900.00*
BK29 BC3 49c **black,** *pink* (2) *2,500.*
BK30 BC3 97c **black,** *gray* (2) *3,000.*

375c A139 2c **lake,** with plate number (D) *10,000.*

Only one example of No. 375c is recorded, and it is position D with #5450 on upper right tab.

Washington — A140

1912 **Wmk. 190 Vertically**

405b A140 1c **green,** *Feb. 8, 1912* 65.00 *75.00*
Never hinged 110.00
With plate number (D) 80.00
Never hinged 140.00

360-Subject Plates only. All plate positions exist.

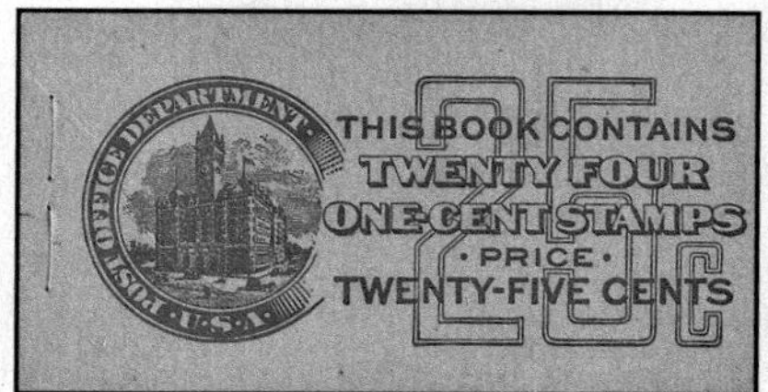

405b, 424d, 462a, 498e, 632a, 804b — BC4A

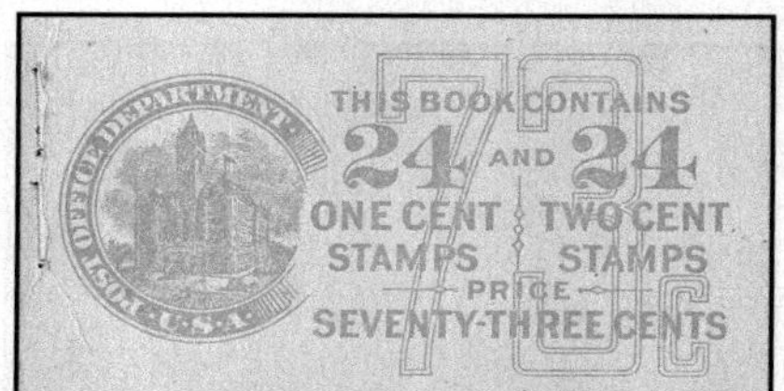

405b, 424d, 462a, 498e, 552a, 632a — BC4B

1912-39 **Washington P.O.**

Price of booklet in large numerals behind contents information

25c booklet contains 4 panes of six 1c stamps.
73c booklet contains 4 panes of six 1c stamps and 4 panes of six 2c stamps.
97c booklet contains 16 panes of six 1c stamps.

Ordinary Booklets

BK31 BC3 25c **black,** *green* (2) *1,000.*
BK32 BC4A 25c **green,** *green* (3) *1,250.*
BK33 BC4A 97c **green,** *lavender* *1,750.*

Combination Booklet

BK34 BC4B 73c **red,** 4 #405b + 4 #406a *3,000.*

Washington — A140

406a A140 2c **carmine,** *Feb. 8, 1912* 65.00 *90.00*
Never hinged 110.00
With plate number (D) 80.00 —
Never hinged 140.00

360-Subject Plates only. All plate positions exist.

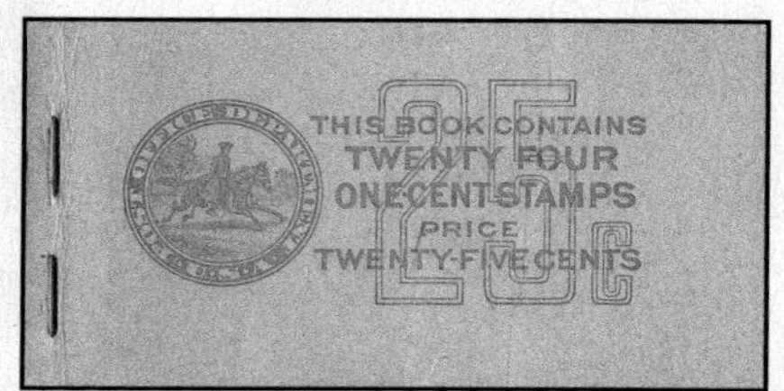

406a, 425e, 463a, 499e, 554c, 583a, 632a, 634d, 804b, 806b — BC5A

1912-39 **Small Postrider**

Large background numerals

25c booklets contain 4 panes of six 1c stamps or 2 panes of six 2c stamps.
49c booklet contains 4 panes of six 2c stamps.
97c booklets contain 16 panes of six 1c stamps or 8 panes of six 2c stamps.

Ordinary Booklets

BK35 BC3 25c **black,** *cream* (2) *825.00*
BK36 BC3 49c **black,** *pink* (2) *1,500.*
BK37 BC3 97c **black,** *gray* (2) 2,000.
BK38 BC5A 25c **red,** *buff* (3) *1,000.*
BK39 BC5A 49c **red,** *pink* (3) 1,750.
BK40 BC5A 97c **red,** *blue,* (3) 3,250.

Combination Booklet

See No. BK34.

Variety

BK35a As No. BK35, with 2 No. 406a and 3 Washburn Patent interleaving paper (embossed "Pat. Sept. 20, 1904" and with a washboard pattern throughout) 2,500.

1914 **Wmk. 190 Vertically** ***Perf. 10***

424d A140 1c **green** 5.25 *7.50*
Never hinged 8.75
Double transfer, Plate 6363 — —
With plate number (D) 14.00
Never hinged 22.50
Cracked plate —
e. As "d," imperf. *1,350.*
With plate number (D) *7,500.*

360-Subject Plates only. All plate positions exist.

All known examples of No. 424e are without gum. No. 424e with plate number (position D) is unique.

Research has proven beyond doubt that all examples of the previously listed No. 424e, booklet pane of 6, imperforate and without gum, are unissued fabrications made from an ungummed press sheet on stamp paper once undoubtedly housed in the Smithsonian philatelic collection.

Ordinary Booklets

BK41 BC4A 25c **green,** *green* (3) 300.00
BK42 BC4A 97c **green,** *lavender* (2) 140.00

Combination Booklet

BK43 BC4B 73c **red,** 4 #424d + 4 #425e (3) 300.00

425e A140 2c **carmine,** *Jan. 6, 1914* 17.50 *25.00*
Never hinged 30.00
With plate number (D) 42.50
Never hinged 70.00

360-Subject Plates only. All plate positions exist.

Ordinary Booklets

BK44 BC5A 25c **red,** *buff* (3) 500.00
BK45 BC5A 49c **red,** *pink* (3) 1,000.
BK46 BC5A 97c **red,** *blue* (3) 1,250.

Combination Booklet

See No. BK43.

1916 **Unwmk.** ***Perf. 10***

462a A140 1c **green,** *Oct. 15, 1916* 9.50 *12.50*
Never hinged 16.00
Cracked plate at right 250.00 —
Never hinged 350.00
Cracked plate at left 310.00
Never hinged 425.00
With plate number (D) 25.00
Never hinged 37.50

360-Subject Plates only. All plate positions exist.

Ordinary Booklets

BK47 BC4A 25c **green,** *green* 650.00
BK48 BC4A 97c **green,** *lavender* 500.00

Combination Booklets

BK49 BC4B 73c **red,** 4 #462a + 4 #463a (2) 900.00

463a A140 2c **carmine,** *Oct. 8, 1916* 110.00 *110.00*
Never hinged 180.00
With plate number (D) 150.00
Never hinged 240.00

360-Subject Plates only. All plate positions exist.

Ordinary Booklets

BK50 BC5A 25c **red,** *buff* *950.00*
BK51 BC5A 49c **red,** *pink* *1,500.*
BK52 BC5A 97c **red,** *blue* *2,750.*

Combination Booklets

See No. BK49.

BUYING & SELLING
U.S. COMPLETE BOOKLETS AND PANES
WITH A SPECIALTY IN EARLY BOOKLETS & PANES, REGULAR POSTAGE, AIRMAILS, BOB, ERRORS, BOOKLETS by USSS#s (BIA), PANES-POSITIONS AND PLATE NUMBERS.
PRICE LIST $2.00. (Free on Web)
WANT LISTS SOLICITED.
IF SELLING, WRITE WITH INVENTORY.
MOUNTAINSIDE STAMPS
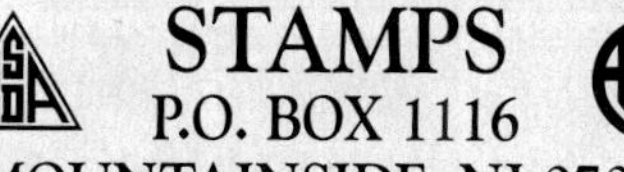
P.O. BOX 1116
MOUNTAINSIDE, NJ 07092
TEL: 908-419-9751
www.mountainsidestamps.com
E-mail:TJacks@verizon.net

1917-18 **Unwmk.** ***Perf. 11***

498e	A140 1c **green,** *Apr. 6, 1917*	2.50	*2.00*
	Never hinged	4.25	
	Double transfer	—	—
	With plate number (D)	6.00	*2.00*
	Never hinged	9.00	

360-Subject Plates only. All plate positions exist.

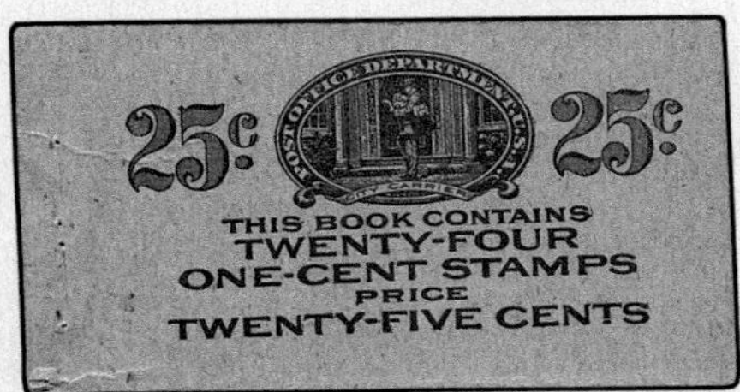

498e, 552a — BC6A

1917-23 **Oval designs**

25c booklet contains 4 panes of six 1c stamps.

Ordinary Booklets

BK53	BC4A 25c **green,** *green* (2)	300.00
BK54	BC4A 97c **green,** *lavender* (4)	85.00
BK55	BC6A 25c **green,** *green* (5)	110.00

Combination Booklets

BK56	BC4B 73c **red,** 4 #498e + 4 #499e (4)	75.00
BK57	BC4B 73c **red,** 4 #498e + 4 #554c (3)	100.00

Washington — A140

A.E.F. Panes of 30

1917, Aug.

498f	A140 1c **green** (pane of 30)	*1,050.*	*12,500.*
	Never hinged	*1,700.*	

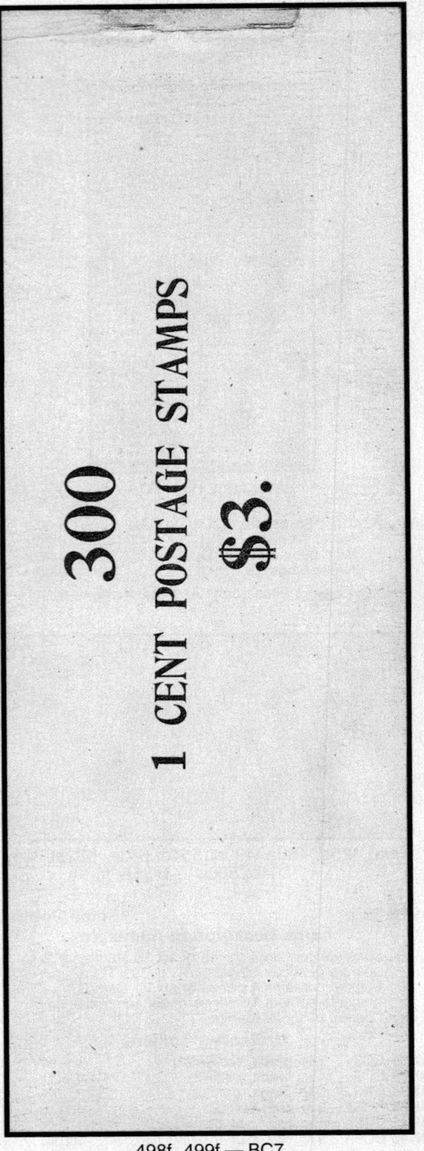

498f, 499f — BC7

A.E.F.

1917

$3 booklet contains 10 panes of thirty 1c stamps.
$6 booklet contains 10 panes of thirty 2c stamps.

Booklets sold for face value.

Booklet

BK64	BC7 $3 **black,** *green*	*22,500.*

499e	A140 2c **rose,** type I, *Mar. 31, 1917*	4.00	*2.50*
	Never hinged	6.75	
	With plate number (D)	7.00	*2.25*
	Never hinged	10.00	

360-Subject Plates only. All plate positions exist.

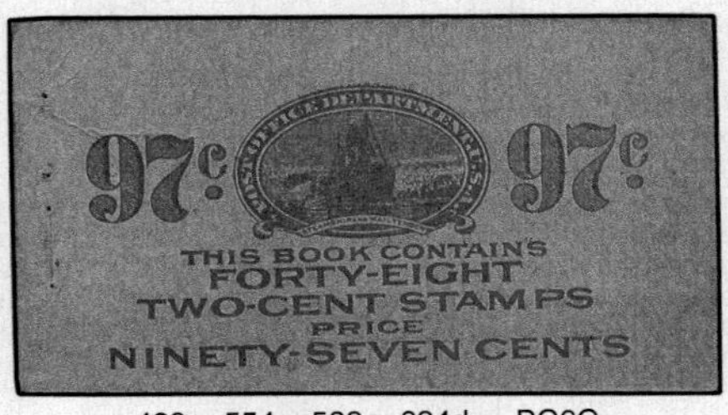

499e, 554c, 583a, 634d — BC6C

1917-27 **Oval designs**

97c booklet contains 8 panes of six 2c stamps.

Ordinary Booklets

BK58	BC5A 25c **red,** *buff* (5)	250.00
BK59	BC5A 49c **red,** *pink* (4)	400.00
BK60	BC5A 97c **red,** *blue* (3)	1,000.
BK61	BC6C 97c **red,** *blue* (2)	1,250.

Combination Booklets

See No. BK56.

499f	A140 2c **rose,** (pane of 30) type I	*20,000.*	—
	Never hinged	*29,000.*	

Booklet

BK65 BC7 $6 **black,** *pink*

No examples of No. BK65 are known. The number and description are provided only for specialist reference.

Nos. 498f and 499f were for use of the American Expeditionary Force in France.

They were printed from the ordinary 360-Subject Plates, the sheet being cut into 12 leaves of 30 stamps each in place of 60 leaves of 6 stamps each, and, of course, the lines of perforations changed accordingly.

The same system as used for designating plate positions on the ordinary booklet panes is used for designating the war booklet, only each war booklet pane is composed of 5 ordinary panes. Thus, No. W1 booklet pane would be composed of positions 1, 2, 3, 4, and 5 of an ordinary pane, etc.

The A. E. F. booklet panes were bound at side margins which accounts for side arrows sometimes being found on positions W5 and W6. As the top and bottom arrows were always removed when the sheets were cut, positions W1 and W2 cannot be distinguished from W7 and W8. Cutting may remove guidelines on these, but identification is possible by wide bottom margins. Positions W3 and W4 cannot be distinguished from W9 and W10.

There are thus just 8 collectible positions from the sheet as follows:

W1 or W7 Narrow top and wide bottom margins. Guide line at right.

W2 or W8 As W1, but guide line at left.

W3 or W9 Approximately equal top and bottom margins. Guide line at right.

W4 or W10 As W3, but guide line at left.

W5 Narrow bottom margin showing guideline very close to stamps. Wide top margin. Guide line at right. Pane with extra long tab may show part of split arrow at left.

W6 As W5, but guide line at left, split arrow at right. Guide line at left and at bottom. Arrow at lower right may or may not show.

W11 Narrow bottom and wide top margins. Guide line at right. Siderographer initials on left tab.

W12 Narrow bottom and wide top margins. Guide line at left. Finisher initials on right tab.

Washington — A140

501b	A140 3c **violet,** type I, *Oct. 17, 1917*	75.00	*80.00*
	Never hinged	125.00	
	With plate number (D)	105.00	
	Never hinged	160.00	

360-Subject Plates only. All plate positions exist.

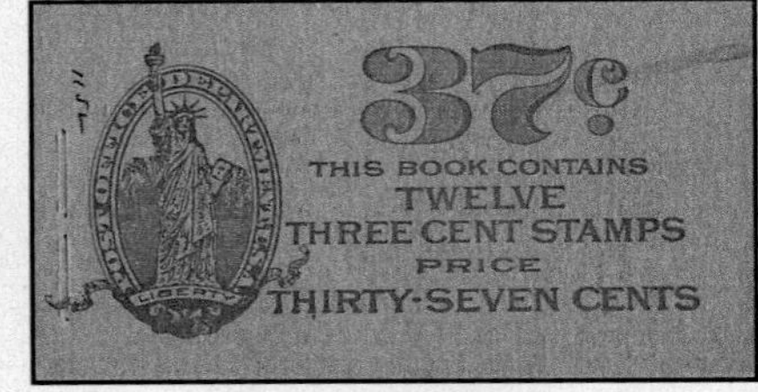

501b, 502b — BC6B

1917-18 **Oval designs**

37c booklet contains 2 panes of six 3c stamps.

Booklet

BK62 BC6B 37c **violet,** *sage* 500.00

502b A140 3c **violet,** type II, *Mar. 1918* 60.00 *75.00*
Never hinged 100.00
With plate number (D) 77.50
Never hinged 120.00

360-Subject Plates only. All plate positions exist.

Booklet

BK63 BC6B 37c **violet,** *sage* 225.00

Franklin — A155

1923 **Unwmk.** ***Perf. 11***

552a A155 1c **deep green,** *Aug. 1923* 7.50 *4.00*
Never hinged 12.50
With plate number (D) 13.00
Never hinged 21.00

360-Subject Plates only. All plate positions exist.

Ordinary Booklets

BK66 BC6A 25c **green,** *green* (2) 75.00
BK67 BC4A 97c **green,** *lavender* (3) *650.00*

Combination Booklet

BK68 BC4B 73c **red,** *buff,* 4 #552a + 4 #554c (3) 100.00

Washington — A157

554c A157 2c **carmine** 7.00 *3.00*
Never hinged 12.00
With plate number (D) 12.00
Never hinged 20.00

360-Subject Plates only. All plate positions exist.

Ordinary Booklets

BK69 BC5A 25c **red,** *buff* (3) *400.00*
BK70 BC5A 49c **red,** *pink* (3) 950.00
BK71 BC6C 97c **red,** *blue* (3) 1,500.

Combination Booklets

See Nos. BK57 and BK68.

ROTARY PRESS PRINTINGS

Two experimental plates were used to print No. 583a. At least one guide line pane (H) is known from these plates. The rest of rotary press booklet panes were printed from specially prepared plates of 360-subjects in arrangement as before, but without the guide lines and the plate numbers are at the sides instead of at the top as on the flat plates.

The only varieties possible are the ordinary pane (A) and partial plate numbers appearing at the right or left of the upper or lower stamps of a booklet pane when the trimming of the sheets is off center. The note applies to Nos. 583a, 632a, 634d, 720b, 804b, 806b and 807a, before Electric Eyes.

1926 ***Perf. 10***

583a A157 2c **carmine,** *Aug. 1926* 110.00 *150.00*
Never hinged 200.00
With guide line at right (H) *8,500.*

Only one example of No. 583a with guide line at right is recorded. Only the first two rotary plates laid out for booklets had guide lines.

Ordinary Booklets

BK72 BC5A 25c **red,** *buff* (3) *725.00*
BK73 BC5A 49c **red,** *pink* *1,000.*
BK74 BC6C 97c **red,** *blue* *2,250.*

1927 ***Perf. 11x10½***

632a A155 1c **green,** *Nov. 2, 1927* 5.00 *4.00*
Never hinged 8.00

Ordinary Booklets

BK75 BC5A 25c **green,** *green* (3) 65.00
BK76 BC4A 97c **green,** *lavender* 600.00
BK77 BC5A 97c **green,** *lavender* *2,750.*

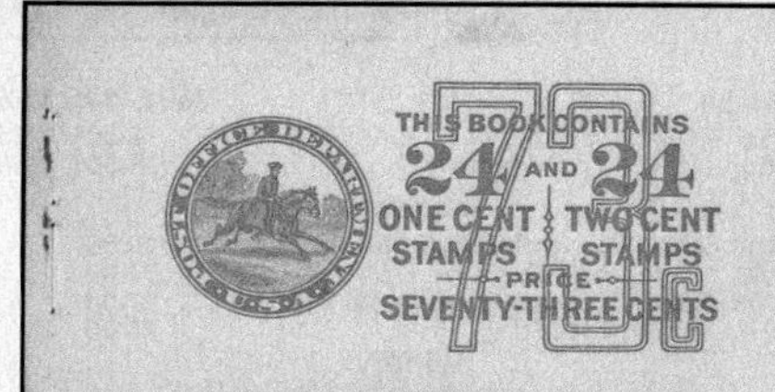

632a, 804b — BC5D

1927-39 **Small Postrider**

Large background numerals

73c booklet contains 4 panes of six 1c stamps and 4 panes of six 2c stamps.

Combination Booklets

BK78 BC4B 73c **red,** 4 #632a + 4 #634d —
BK79 BC5D 73c **red,** 4 #632a + 4 #634d (3) 85.00

634d A157 2c **carmine,** type I, *Feb. 25, 1927* 1.50 *1.50*
Never hinged 2.50

Ordinary Booklets

BK80 BC5A 25c **red,** *buff* (2) 10.00
a. With experimental cellophane interleaving *2,500.*
BK81 BC5A 49c **red,** *pink* (2) 14.00
BK82 BC5A 97c **red,** *blue* (3) 45.00
BK83 BC6C 97c **red,** *blue* 900.00

Combination Booklets

See Nos. BK78 and BK79.

56,000 booklets of BK80a were produced in 1928 using .00125 inch thick cellophane interleaving. Scarce, as few were saved.

Varieties

634e A157 2c **carmine lake,** type I *400.00* *1,000.*
Never hinged *750.00*

Booklet

BK82a BC5A As #BK82, with 8 panes of #634e *7,500.*

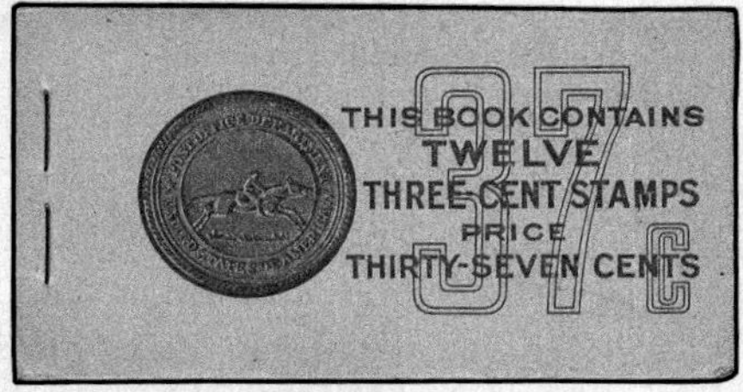

720b, 806b, 807a, 1035a — BC9A

1932-54 **Post Office Seal**

Large background numerals

25c booklet contains 2 panes of six 2c stamps.
37c booklet contains 2 panes of six 3c stamps.
49c booklet contains 4 panes of six 2c stamps.
73c booklets contain 4 panes of six 3c stamps or 4 panes of six 1c stamps and 4 panes of six 2c stamps.

Ordinary Booklets

BK84 BC9A 37c **violet,** *buff* (2) 125.00
a. With experimental cellophane interleaving *3,000.*
BK85 BC9A 73c **violet,** *pink* (2) 350.00

30,000 booklets of No. BK84a were made with .001 inch thick cellophane interleaving, similar to but thinner than the experimental interleaving used for No. BK80a. Poor handling qualities during booklet assembly plus higher cost prevented wider use. Placed on sale in Wash. D.C. post office in Sept., 1936. Extremely scarce, as few were saved.

Catalogue values for unused panes in this section, from this point to the end, are for Never Hinged items.

Washington — A276

In 1942 plates were changed to the Type II "new design" and the E. E. marks may appear at the right or left margins of panes of Nos. 804b, 806b and 807a. Panes printed from E. E. plates have 2½mm vertical gutter; those from pre-E. E. plates have 3mm vertical gutter.

1939-42 ***Perf. 11x10½***

804b A276 1c 3mm vert. gutter, *Jan. 27, 1939* 4.00 *.85*

Ordinary Booklets

BK86 BC5A 25c **green,** *green* 70.00
BK87 BC5A 97c **green,** *lavender* *450.00*
BK88 BC4A 97c **green,** *lavender* —

Combination Booklet

BK89 BC5D 73c **red,** 4 #804b + 4 #806b 125.00

804b A276 1c 2½mm vert. gutter, *Apr. 14, 1942* 2.00 *.50*

Ordinary Booklets

BK90 BC5A 25c **green,** *green* 8.25
BK91 BC5A 97c **green,** *lavender* 450.00

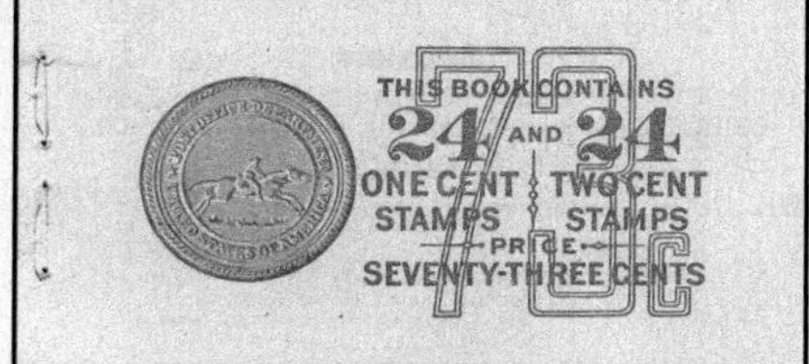

804b, 806b — BC9E

Washington — A226

1932

720b A226 3c **deep violet,** *July 25, 1932* 35.00 *12.50*
Never hinged 60.00

1939 **Post Office Seal**

Large background numerals

73c booklets contain 4 panes of six 3c stamps or 4 panes of six 1c stamps and 4 panes of six 2c stamps.

Combination Booklets

BK92	BC5D	73c **red,** 4 #804b + 4 #806b	32.50
BK93	BC9E	73c **red,** 4 #804b + 4 #806b	37.50

Adams — A278

806b	A278	2c 3mm vert. gutter, *Jan. 27, 1939*	22.50	*2.50*

Ordinary Booklets

BK94	BC5A	97c **red,** *blue*	*350.00*

Combination Booklet

See No. BK89.

806b	A278	2c 2½mm vert. gutter, *Apr. 25, 1942*	5.50	*1.00*

Ordinary Booklets

BK95	BC5A	97c **red,** *blue*	1,250.
BK96	BC5A	25c **red,** *buff*	17.50
BK97	BC9A	25c **red,** *buff*	80.00
BK98	BC5A	49c **red,** *pink*	45.00
BK99	BC9A	49c **red,** *pink*	70.00

Combination Booklets

See Nos. BK92 and BK93.

Jefferson — A279

807a	A279	3c 3mm vert. gutter, *Jan. 27, 1939*	30.00	*3.25*

Booklets

BK100	BC9A	37c **violet,** *buff*	85.00
BK101	BC9A	73c **violet,** *pink*	*700.00*

807a	A279	3c 2½mm vert. gutter, *Mar. 6, 1942*	8.50	*2.00*

Booklets

BK102	BC9A	37c **violet,** *buff* (3)	20.00
BK103	BC9A	73c **violet,** *pink* (3)	45.00

Variety

807d	A279	As "a," imperf between vert.	—

Statue of Liberty — A482

1954-58 ***Perf. 11x10½***

1035a	A482	3c pane of 6, *June 30, 1954*	3.50	*1.25*
1035d		Dry printing	4.50	*1.50*

Booklets

BK104	BC9A	37c **violet,** *buff,* with #1035a	19.00
a.		With #1035d	24.00
BK105	BC9A	73c **violet,** *pink,* with #1035a	21.00
a.		With #1035d	26.00

Variety

1035b	Horiz. pairs, imperf. btwn in #1035a with foldover (two pairs recorded in two full panes) or miscut (all three pairs in one full pane)	*5,000.*

Lincoln — A483

1036b	A483	4c pane of 6, *July 31, 1958*	2.75	*1.25*

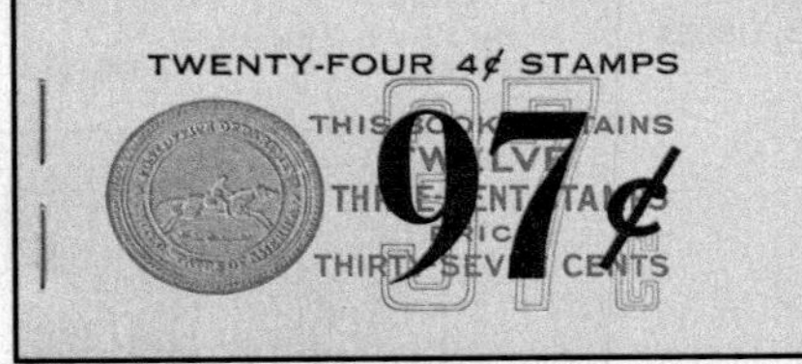

1036b — BC9F

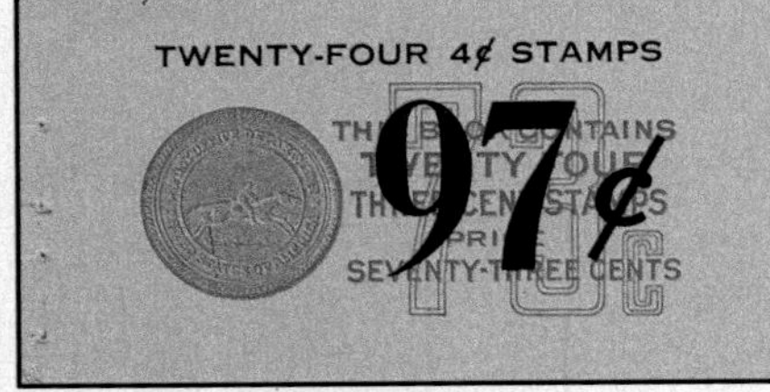

1036b — BC9G

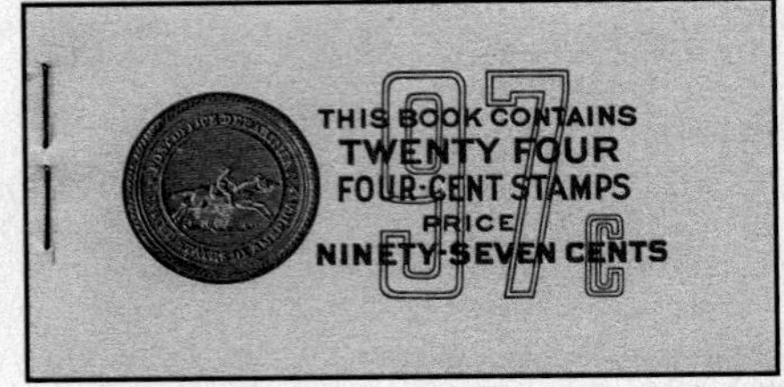

1036b — BC9H

1958

97c booklet contains 4 panes of six 4c stamps.

Booklets

BK106	BC9F	97c on 37c **violet,** *buff*	60.00
BK107	BC9G	97c on 73c **violet,** *pink*	30.00
BK108	BC9H	97c **blue,** *yellow*	150.00
BK109	BC9H	97c **blue,** *pink* (3)	17.50
a.		With experimental silicone interleaving	*150.00*

Variety

1036c	A483	As "b," imperf. horiz.	*10,000.*

Washington (Slogan 1) — A650

Slogan 2

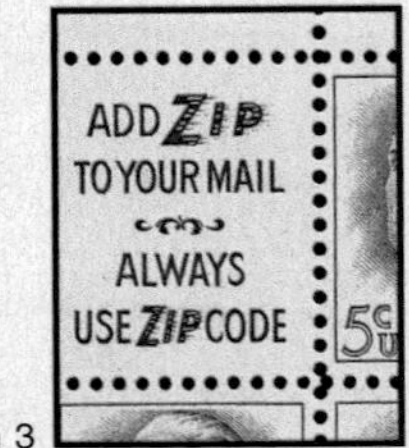

Slogan 3

1962-64 ***Perf. 11x10½***

Plate of 300 stamps, 60 labels

1213a	A650	5c pane of 5+label, slogan 1, *Nov. 23, 1962*	6.00	4.00
		With slogan 2, *1963*	16.00	7.00
		With slogan 3, *1964*	2.00	2.00

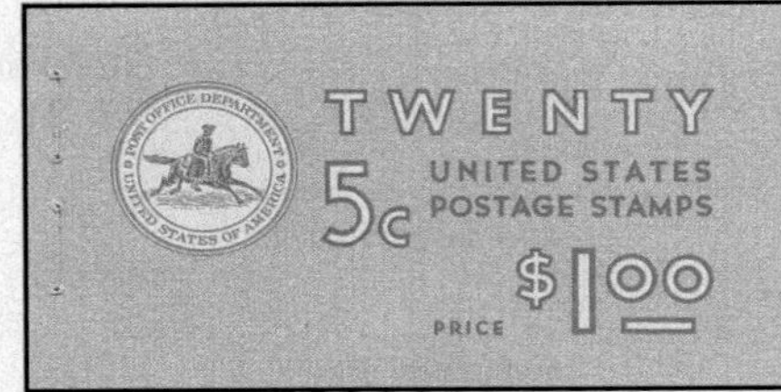

1213a — BC12A

1962-63 **Small Postrider**

$1 booklet contains 4 panes of five 5c stamps.

1213a, 1213c — BC13A

1963-64 **Mr. Zip**

$1 booklet contains 4 panes of five 5c stamps.

Booklets

BK110	BC12A	$1 **blue,** slogan 1	27.50
BK111	BC12A	$1 **blue,** slogan 2	110.00
BK112	BC13A	$1 **blue,** slogan 2	90.00
BK113	BC13A	$1 **blue,** slogan 3 (3)	13.50

1213c A650 As No. 1213a, tagged, slogan 2, *Oct. 28, 1963* 60.00 *10.00*
With slogan 3, *1964* 2.00 *1.50*

Booklets

BK114	BC13A	$1 **blue,** slogan 2	240.00
BK115	BC13A	$1 **blue,** slogan 3 (4)	8.00

Variety

1213d A650 Horiz. pair, imperf. btwn., in #1213a with foldover or miscut 1,750.

Jefferson — A710

1967-78 ***Perf. 11x10½***

1278a A710 1c pane of 8, shiny gum, *Jan. 12, 1968* 1.00 .75
Dull gum 1.75

Combination Booklets

See Nos. BK116, BK117B, BK118 and BK119.

Variety

1278e A710 As "a," dull gum, tagging omitted *85.00*

An experimental moisture-resistant gum was used on 1,000,000 panes of No. 1278a and 4,000,000 of No. 1393a released in March, 1971. This dull finish gum shows no breaker ridges. The booklets lack interleaving. This gum was also used for Nos. 1395c, 1395d, 1288c and all engraved panes from No. 1510b on unless noted.

Jefferson — A710

1278b A710 1c pane of 4+2 labels, slogans 5 & 4, *May 10, 1971* .75 .60

Combination Booklet

See No. BK122.

Wright — A712

Slogan 4

Slogan 5

1280a A712 2c pane of 5+label, slogan 4, *Jan. 8, 1968* 1.25 .80
With slogan 5 1.25 .80

Combination Booklets

See Nos. BK117 and BK120.

1280c A712 2c pane of 6, shiny gum, *May 7, 1971* 1.00 .75
Dull gum 1.10

Combination Booklets

See Nos. BK127 and BKC22.

The 1c and 6c panes of 8, Nos. 1278a and 1284b, were printed from 320-subject plates and from 400-subject plates, both with electric eye markings. The 2c and 6c panes of 5 stamps plus label, Nos. 1280a and 1284c, were printed from 360-subject plates.

Roosevelt — A716

Perf. 10½x11

1284b A716 6c pane of 8, *Dec. 28, 1967* 1.50 1.00

1278a, 1284b, 1393a — BC14A

1967-70

$2 booklet contains 4 panes of eight 6c stamps and 1 pane of eight 1c stamps.

Combination Booklet

BK116 BC14A $2 **brown,** 4 #1284b (6c)+1 #1278a(1c)(2) 7.00

Variety

1284e A716 6c As "b," tagging omitted *90.00* —

Combination Booklet

BK116a BC14A As #BK116, with 4 #1284e (6c) + 1 #1278a (1c) *250.00*

Roosevelt — A716

1284c A716 6c pane of 5+label, slogan 4, *Jan. 9, 1968* 1.40 1.00
With slogan 5 1.40 1.00

1278a, 1280a, 1284c, 1393b, 1395b — BC15

1968-71

$1 booklets contain 2 panes of six 8c stamps and 1 pane of four 1c stamps, or 3 panes of five 6c stamps and 1 pane of five 2c stamps.

Combination Booklet

BK117 BC15 $1 **brown,** 3 #1284c (6c) + 1 #1280a (2c) (2) 6.50

No. BK117 contains panes with slogan 4, slogan 5 or combinations of 4 and 5.

Oliver Wendell Holmes — A720

1288Bc A720 15c pane of 8, *June 14, 1978* 2.80 1.75

1288Bc — BC23

1978
$3.60 booklet contains 3 panes of eight 15c stamps.

Booklet

BK117A BC23 $3.60 **red & light blue,** no P# 8.00

Varieties

1288Be A720 As "c," vert. imperf. btwn. *1,500.*
1288Bi A720 As "c," tagging omitted *80.00 50.00*

Eisenhower — A815

Plate of 400 subjects for No. 1393a.

1970 Tagged ***Perf. 11x10½***

1393a A815 6c pane of 8, shiny gum, *Aug. 6* 2.00 2.00
Dull gum 2.25

1278a, 1393a, 1395a — BC16

1970-71 **Eisenhower**
$2 booklet contains 4 panes of eight 6c stamps and 1 pane of eight 1c stamps.
$1.92 booklet contains 3 panes of eight 8c stamps.

Combination Booklets

BK117B BC14A $2 **blue,** 4 #1393a (6c) + 1 #1278a (1c) 11.00
BK118 BC16 $2 **blue,** 4 #1393a (6c) + 1 #1278a (1c) (2) 9.00
BK119 BC16 $2 **blue,** dull gum, 4 #1393a (6c) + 1 #1278a (1c) (2) 9.00

Varieties

1393h A815 6c As "a," tagging omitted, shiny gum *250.00* —
Dull gum 325.00

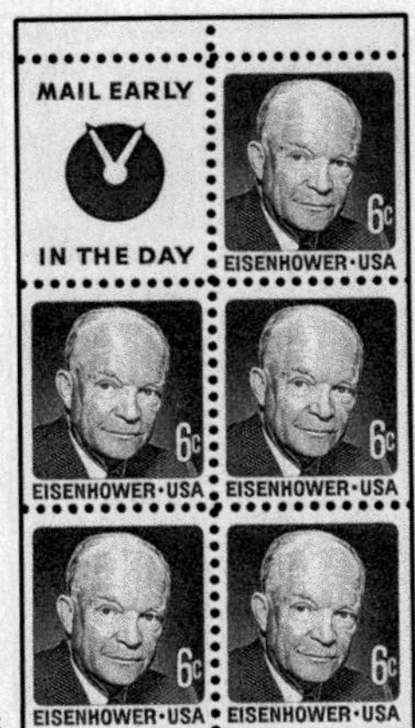

Eisenhower — A815

Plate of 300 stamps and 60 labels for No. 1393b.

1393b A815 6c pane of 5+label, slogan 4, *Aug. 6* 1.40 1.40
With slogan 5 1.40 1.40

Combination Booklet

BK120 BC15 $1 **blue,** 3 #1393b (6c) + 1 #1280a (2c) 5.50
BK120a BC15 $1 As #BK120, missing #1280a pane and with 4 panes of #1393b (error) —

No. BK120 contains panes with slogan 4, slogan 5 or combinations of 4 and 5.

Eisenhower — A815a

1971-72 **Shiny Gum** ***Perf. 11x10½***

1395a A815a 8c **deep claret,** pane of 8, *May 10, 1971* 2.00 2.00

Booklet

BK121 BC16 $1.92 **claret** (2) 6.00

Varieties

1395e A815a Vert. pair, imperf. btwn., in #1395a or #1395d with foldover *750.00*
1395f A815a As "a," tagging omitted — —

Eisenhower — A815a

1395b A815a 8c pane of 6, *May 10, 1971* 1.50 1.50

Combination Booklet

BK122 BC15 $1 **claret,** 2 #1395b (8c) + 1 #1278b (1c) (2) 4.00

Variety

1395g As "b," tagging omitted *80.00* —

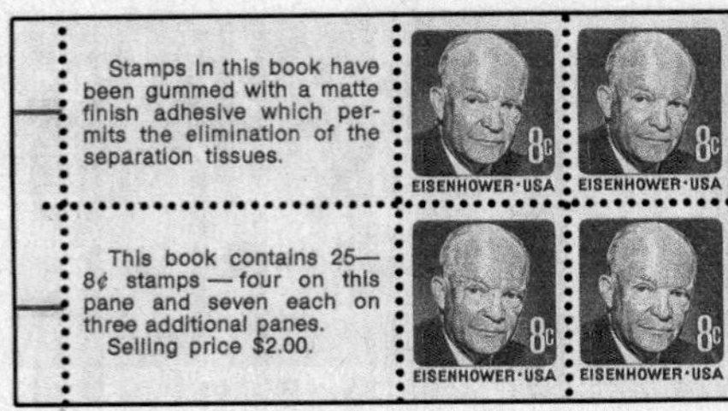

Stamps in this book have been gummed with a matte finish adhesive which permits the elimination of the separation tissues.
This book contains 25— 8¢ stamps — four on this pane and seven each on three additional panes. Selling price $2.00.
EISENHOWER·USA

Slogans 6 and 7

Eisenhower — A815a

Dull Gum

1395c A815a 8c pane of 4 + 2 labels, slogans 6 and 7, *Jan. 28, 1972* 1.65 1.10
1395d A815a 8c pane of 7 + label, slogan 4, *Jan. 28, 1972* 1.90 1.90
With slogan 5 1.90 1.90

1395c, 1395d — BC17A

1972 **Postal Service Emblem**
$2 booklet contains 3 panes of seven 8c stamps and 1 pane of four 8c stamps.

Combination Booklet

BK123 BC17A $2 **claret,** *yellow,* 3 #1395d + 1 #1395c 7.00

No. BK123 exists with covers printed on both thin and thick card stock.

Varieties

1395h As "c," tagging omitted *55.00* —
1395i As "d," tagging omitted —

Plate of 400 subjects for No. 1395a. Plate of 360 subjects for No. 1395b. Plate of 300 subjects (200 stamps and 100 double-size labels) for No. 1395c. Plate of 400 subjects (350 stamps and 50 labels) for No. 1395d.

A pane of No. 1395d is known with a foldover resulting in a vertical pair of stamp and label, imperf between.

Booklet Covers

When more than one combination of covers exists, the number of possible booklets is noted in parentheses after the booklet listing.

Jefferson Memorial (Slogan 8) — A924

1973-74 *Perf. 11x10½*

1510b A924 10c pane of 5 + label, slogan 8, *Dec. 14, 1973* 1.65 1.25

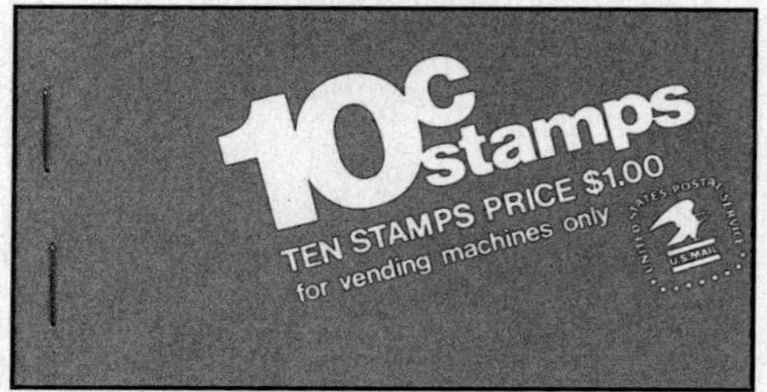

1510b — BC17B

1973 **Postal Service Emblem**

$1 booklet contains 2 panes of five 10c stamps.

Booklet

BK124 BC17B $1 **blue** 3.50

Jefferson Memorial — A924

1510c A924 10c pane of 8, *Dec. 14, 1973* 2.00 2.00

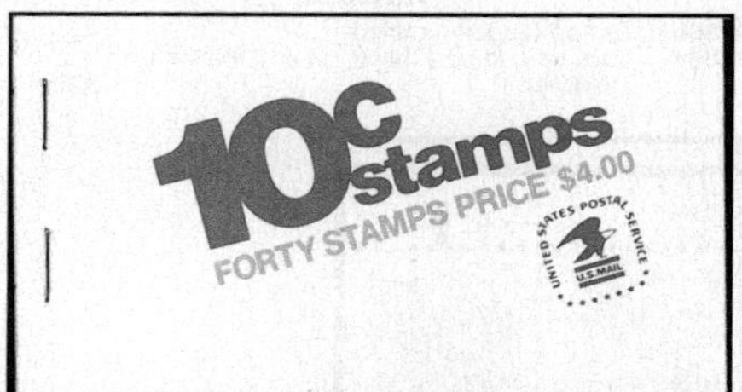

1510c — BC17C

1973 **Postal Service Emblem**

$4 booklet contains 5 panes of eight 10c stamps.

Booklet

BK125 BC17C $4 **red & blue** 10.00

No. BK125 exists with covers printed on both thin and thick card stock.

Jefferson Memorial — A924

1510d A924 10c pane of 6, *Aug. 5, 1974* 5.00 1.75
1510j As "d," tagging omitted —

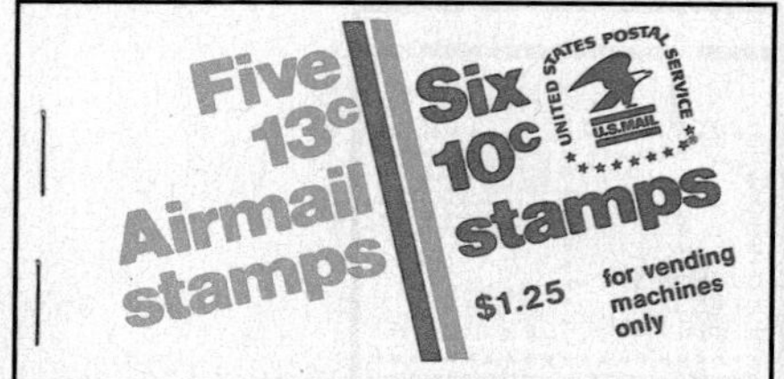

1510d, C79a — BC17D

1974 **Postal Service Emblem**

$1.25 booklet contains 1 pane of five 13c stamps and 1 pane of six 10c stamps.

Combination Booklet

BK126 BC17D $1.25 **red & blue,** 1 #1510d (10c) + 1 #C79a (13c) 6.50

Varieties

1510f Vert. pair, imperf. btwn., in #1510c miscut or with foldover 475.00
1510h As "c," tagging omitted — —
1510i As "b," double booklet pane of 10 + stamps with 2 horiz. pairs imperf. btwn. + stamp and label imperf. btwn. (FO) *1,750.*

Liberty Bell — A998

1975-78 *Perf. 11¼x10½*

1595a A998 13c pane of 6, *Oct. 31, 1975* 2.25 1.50

1595a, 1280c — BC19A

1975

90c booklet contains 1 pane of six 13c stamps and 1 pane of six 2c stamps.

Combination Booklet

BK127 BC19A 90c **red & blue,** 1 #1595a (13c) + 1 #1280c (2c) (2) 3.25

Variety

1595h As "a," miscut and inserted upside down into booklet cover, perfed below bottom stamps and with short "tab" at bottom —

Liberty Bell — A998

1595b A998 13c pane of 7 + label, slogan 8, *Oct. 31, 1975* 2.25 1.50
1595c A998 13c pane of 8, *Oct. 31, 1975* 2.25 1.50
1595i As "b," tagging omitted —
1595j As "c," tagging omitted —

1595b, 1595c — BC19B

1975

$2.99 booklet contains 2 panes of eight 13c stamps and 1 pane of seven 13c stamps.

Combination Booklet

BK128 BC19B $2.99 **red & blue,** 2 #1595c (13c) + 1 #1595b (13c) (2) 7.50

No. BK128 exists with covers printed on both thin and thick card stock.

Variety

1595e Vert. pair, imperf. btwn., in #1595c with foldover *1,100.*

Liberty Bell (Slogan 9) — A998

1595d A998 13c pane of 5 + label, slogan 9, *Apr. 2, 1976* 1.75 1.25

1595d — BC19C

1976

$1.30 booklet contains 2 panes of five 13c stamps.

Booklet

BK129 BC19C $1.30 **red & blue** 3.75

Variety

1595g Horiz. pair, imperf. btwn., in #1595d with foldover —

Fort McHenry Flag (15 Stars) — A1001

1977-78 ***Perf. 11x10½***

1598a A1001 15c pane of 8, *June 30, 1978* 3.75 1.50

1598a — BC21

1978

$1.20 booklet contains 1 pane of eight 15c stamps.

Booklet

BK130 BC21 $1.20 **red & light blue,** no P# 3.75

1623a — A994, A1018a

The LRM can either above the 9c stamp, as shown, or above the 13c stamp.

1623a A1018a Pane of 8 (1 #1590 + 7 #1623), *Mar. 11, 1977* 2.25 2.00

1623a — BC20

1977

$1 booklet contains 1 pane of one 9c stamp and seven 13c stamps.

Booklet

BK131 BC20 $1 **red & light blue,** no P# (3) 2.50

Variety

1623g As "a," tagging omitted —

Booklet

BK131a BC20 As #BK131, with #1623g —

Perf. 10x9¾

1623Bc A1018a Pane of 8 (1 #1590A + 7 #1623B), *Mar. 11, 1977* 15.00 15.00

Folded btwn. 2nd & 3rd rows *100.00* —

Normally produced panes were folded between the 1st and 2nd rows. The listed variety is from a special printing made to service first-day covers, and these were sold mint to collectors at the first-day site, and some were later sold at the Philatelic Agency.

Booklet

BK132 BC20 $1 **red & light blue,** no P# (2) 21.00

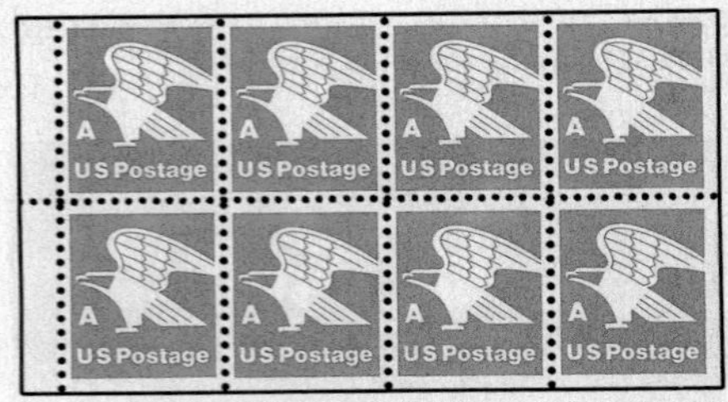

1736a — A1124

1978 **Tagged** ***Perf. 11x10½***

1736a A1124 A pane of 8, *May 22* 2.50 1.50

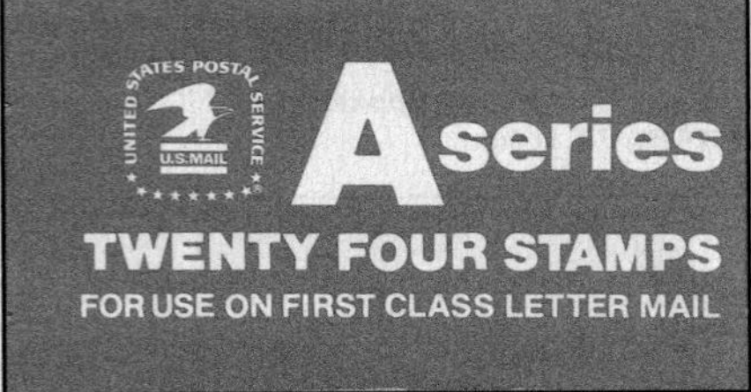

1736a — BC24

1978

$3.60 booklet contains 3 panes of eight A (15c) stamps.

Booklet

BK133 BC24 $3.60 **deep orange** 7.75

No. BK133 exists with covers printed on both thin and thick card stock.

Varieties

1736b As "a," tagging omitted —

1736c Vert. pair, imperf. btwn., in #1736a with foldover *1,000.*

1737a — A1126

Perf. 10

1737a A1126 15c pane of 8, *July 11* 2.50 2.00

1737a — BC22

1978
$2.40 booklet contains 2 panes of eight 15c stamps.

Booklet

BK134 BC22 $2.40 **rose red & yel grn,** no P# 5.25

Varieties

1737c As "a," imperf. *2,250.*
1737d As "a," tagging omitted *60.00*

Booklet

BK134a As #BK134, with 2 #1737c *4,000.*

Windmills — A1127-A1131

1980 ***Perf. 11***
1742a A1127 15c pane of 10, *Feb. 7* 3.50 3.00

1742a — BC25

1980
$3 booklet contains 2 panes of ten 15c stamps.

Booklet

BK135 BC25 $3 **light blue & dark blue,** *blue,* no P# 7.50

1819a — A1207

1981
1819a A1207 B pane of 8, *Mar. 15* 3.50 2.25

1819a — BC26

1981
$4.32 booklet contains 3 panes of eight B (18c) stamps.

Booklet

BK136 BC26 $4.32 **dull violet,** no P# 10.50

1889a — A1267-A1276

1889a A1267 18c pane of 10, *May 14* 5.00 5.00

1889a — BC28

1981
$3.60 booklet contains 2 panes of ten 18c stamps.

Booklet

BK137 BC28 $3.60 **gray & olive,** P#1-10 10.00
P#11-13 13.00
P#14-16 14.00

1893a — A1279-A1280

1893a A1279 Pane of 8 (2 #1892, 6 #1893), *Apr. 24* 3.00 2.50

1893a — BC27

1981

$1.20 booklet contains 1 pane of two 6c and six 18c stamps.

Booklet

BK138 BC27 $1.20 **blue & red,** P#1 3.25

Varieties

1893b As "a," vert. imperf. btwn. 60.00
1893d As "a," tagging omitted *675.00*

Booklets

BK138a BC27 As #BK138, with #1893b 60.00
BK138b BC27 As #BK138, with #1893d *300.00*

1896a — A1281

1981-83

1896a A1281 20c pane of 6, small block tagging, *Dec. 17, 1981* 3.00 2.25
Scored perforations 3.00 2.25

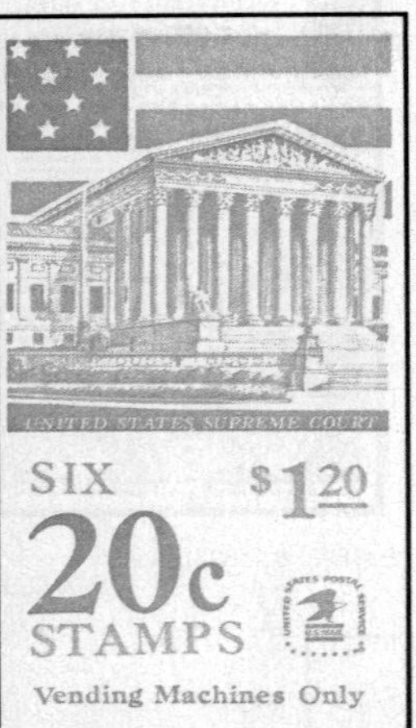

1896a — BC29

1982

$1.20 booklet contains 1 pane of six 20c stamps.

Booklet

BK139 BC29 $1.20 **blue & red,** P#1 (2) 3.25

1896b — A1281

1896b A1281 20c pane of 10, *June 1, 1982* 5.25 3.25
Scored perforations 7.50 5.00

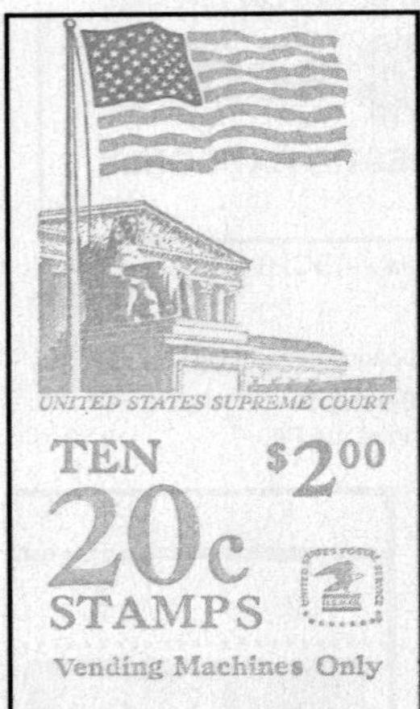

1896b — BC29A

1982

$2 booklet contains 1 pane of ten 20c stamps.

Booklet

BK140 BC29A $2 **blue & red,** P#1 (4) 5.50
P#4 47.50

Varieties

1896c As "b," tagging omitted — —
1896e A1281 20c pane of 10, large block tagging, *Nov. 17, 1983* 5.25 3.25
Scored perforations 5.25 3.25

1896b — BC29B

1983

$4 booklet contains 2 panes of ten 20c stamps.

Booklet

BK140A BC29B $4 **blue & red,** *Nov. 17, 1983,* P#2 11.00
P#3 17.50
P#4 *260.00*

Variety

1896f As "a," tagging omitted — —

The small block tagging is 16x18mm (Nos. 1896a-1896b). The large block tagging is 18x21mm (No. 1896e).

Booklet Covers

When more than one combination of covers exists, the number of possible booklets is noted in parentheses after the booklet listing.

1909a — A1296

1983

1909a A1296 $9.35 pane of 3, *Aug. 12* 57.50 —

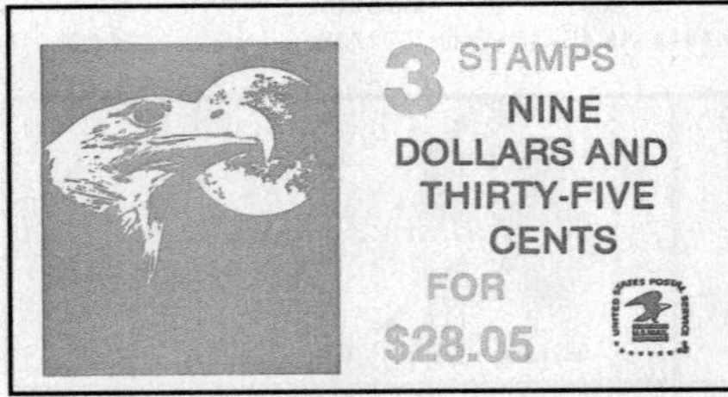

1909a — BC31

1983

$28.05 booklet contains 1 pane of three $9.35 stamps.

Booklet

BK140B BC31 28.05 **blue & red,** P#1111 57.50

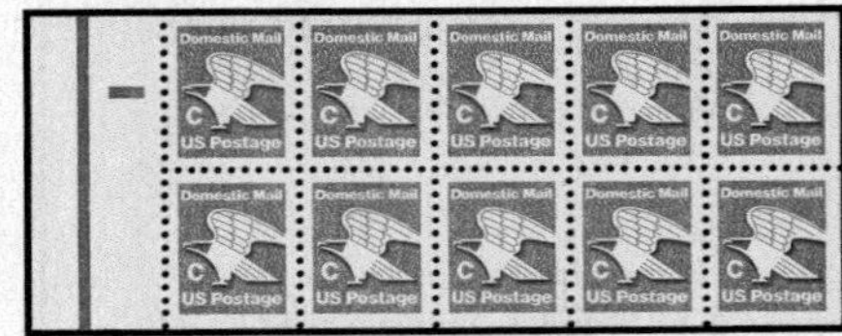

1948a — A1333

1981

1948a A1333 C pane of 10, *Oct. 11* 4.50 3.25

1948a — BC26A

1981

$4 booklet contains 2 panes of ten C (20c) stamps.

Booklet

BK141 BC26A $4 **brown,** *blue,* no P# 9.50

1949a — A1334

1982

1949a A1334 20c pane of 10, type I, *Jan. 8* 5.00 2.50
1949d As "a," type II 14.00 —

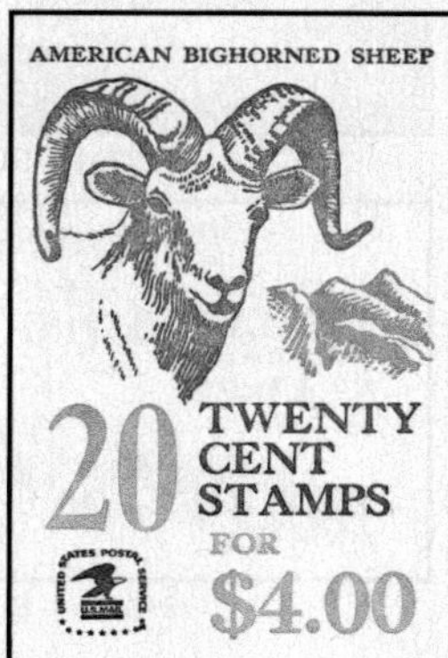

1949a — BC30

1982

$4 booklet contains 2 panes of ten 20c stamps.

Booklets

BK142	BC30 $4 **blue & yellow green,** P#1-6, 9-10	10.00
	P#11, 12, 15	35.00
	P#14	30.00
	P#16	65.00
	P#17-19	45.00
	P#20, 22-23	80.00
	P#24	67.50
	P#21, 28, 29	*350.00*
	P#25-26	*120.00*
a.	Type II, P#34	30.00

Varieties

1949b As "a," imperf. vert. *90.00*
1949f As "a," tagging omitted *55.00* —

Booklets

BK142b As #BK142, with 2 #1949b *180.00*
BK142c As #BK142, with 2 #1949f, P#4, 5, 6, 19 *100.00*

Stamps in No. 1949a are 18¾mm wide and have overall tagging. Stamps in No. 1949d are 18½mm wide and have block tagging.

Plate number does not always appear on top pane in Nos. BK142, BK142a. These booklets sell for more, except P#14 and 15.

Booklet cover BC30 comes in blue & yellow green and in blue & olive green. Both are equally common.

2113a — A1497

1985 ***Perf. 11***

2113a A1497 D pane of 10 *Feb. 1* 7.00 3.00

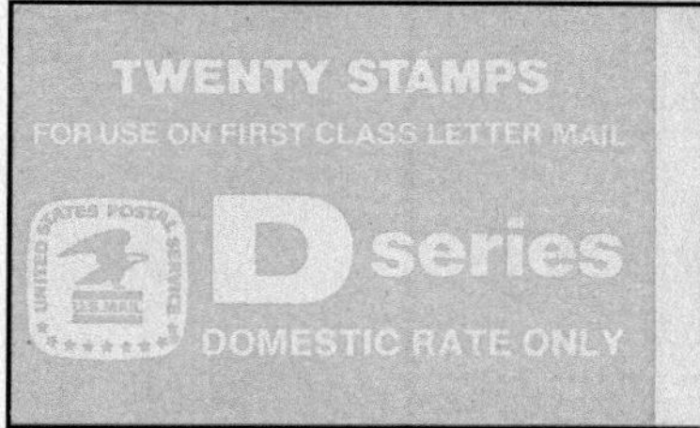

2113a BC26B

1985

$4.40 booklet contains 2 panes of ten D (22c) stamps.

Booklet

BK143 BC26B $4.40 **green,** P#1, 3, 4 14.00
P#2 *350.00*

Varieties

2113b As "a," horiz. imperf. btwn. *1,850.*
BK143a As #BK143, both panes #2113b *3,750.*

No. BK143 is known with no plate number on top pane and plate number 1, 2, 3 or 4 on bottom pane. These booklets sell for more except P#4. No. BK143 with P#1 or P#2 on bottom is rare; value, P#1 on bottom $1,000, P#2 on bottom $2,100.

2116a — A1499

Perf. 10 Horiz.

2116a A1499 22c pane of 5, *Mar. 29* 2.50 1.25
Scored perforations 2.50 —

2116a — BC33C

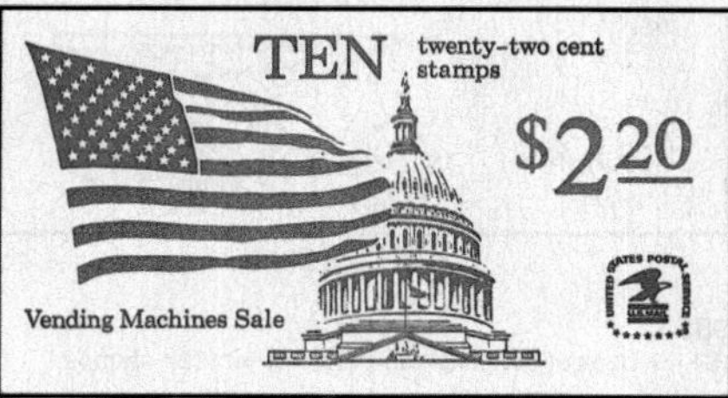

2116a — BC32

1985

$1.10 booklet contains one pane of five 22c stamps.
$2.20 booklet contains two panes of five 22c stamps.

Booklets

BK144	BC33C	$1.10 **blue & red,** P#1, 3 (2)	2.75
BK145	BC32	$2.20 **blue & red,** P#1, 3 (2)	5.25

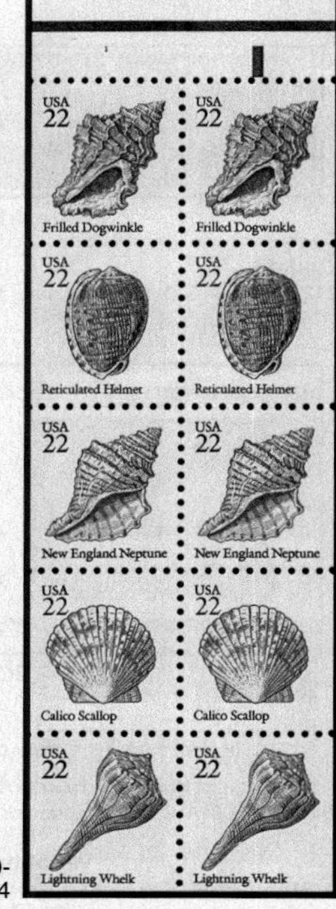

2121a — A1500-A1504

Perf. 10

2121a A1500 22c pane of 10, *Apr. 4* 4.50 3.00

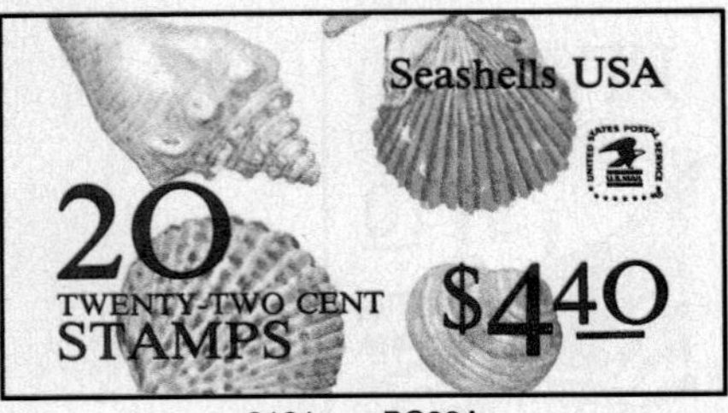

2121a — BC33A

Many different seashell configurations are possible on BC33A. Seven adjacent covers are necessary to show all 25 shells.

2121a — BC33B

1985

$4.40 booklet contains two panes of ten 22c stamps.

Booklets

BK146 BC33A $4.40 **multicolored,** P#1, 3 9.00
P#2 10.00
BK147 BC33B $4.40 **brown & blue,** P#1, 3, 5, 7, 10 9.00
P#6 17.50
P#8 10.00

Varieties

2121b As "a," violet omitted on both Nos. 2120 *400.00*
2121c As "a," vert. imperf. btwn. *350.00*
2121d As "a," imperf. —

2122a — A1505

1985-89 ***Perf. 10 Vert.***

2122a A1505 $10.75 type I, pane of 3, *Apr. 29, 1985* 60.00 —

2122a — BC31A

1985

$32.25 booklet contains 1 pane of three $10.75 stamps.

Booklet

BK148 BC31A $32.25 **multicolored,** P#11111 65.00

Varieties

2122c A1505 $10.75 type II, pane of 3, *June 19, 1989* 60.00 —

2122c — BC31B

1989

$32.25 booklet contains 1 pane of three $10.75 stamps.

Booklet

BK149 BC31B 32.25 **blue & red,** P#22222 (2) 65.00

2182a — A1564

1988 ***Perf. 11***

2182a A1564 25c pane of 10, *May 3* 5.00 3.75

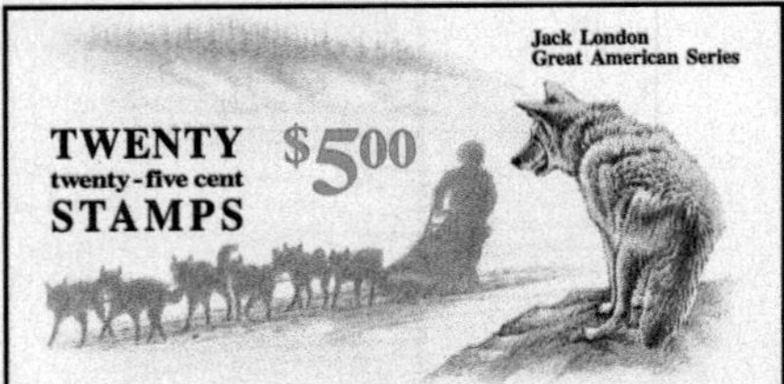

2182a — BC43

1988

$5 booklet contains two panes of ten 25c stamps.

Booklet

BK150 BC43 $5 **multicolored,** P#1-2 10.50

Varieties

2182c As "a," tagging omitted —
2182e As "a," all color omitted on right stamps *1,250.*
2182g As "a," tagging omitted on two stamps —

Booklets

BK150a BC43 As #BK150, both panes #2182c —
BK150b BC43 As #BK150, one pane #2182a, one pane #2182g —
BK150c BC43 As #BK150, both panes #2182g —

2197a — A1564

Perf. 10 on 2 or 3 Sides

2197a A1564 25c pane of 6, *May 3* 3.30 2.50

2197a — BC43A

2197a — BC43B

1988

$1.50 booklet contains one pane of six 25c stamps.
$3 booklet contains two panes of six 25c stamps.

Booklets

BK151 BC43A $1.50 **blue & brown,** P#1 3.30
BK152 BC43B $3 **brown & blue,** P#1 6.60

BK151 and BK152 exist with covers printed on both thin and thick card stock.

Variety

2197c A1564 25c As "a," tagging omitted 150.00

Booklet

BK151a BC43A As #BK151, with #2197c 160.00

2201a — A1581-A1584

1986

2201a A1581 22c pane of 4, *Jan. 23* 2.00 1.75

STAMP COLLECTING USA • AMERIPEX 86

The International Stamp Show at Chicago May 22 – June 1, 1986, will admit the bearer of this booklet cover free of charge.

Eight 22 cent stamps — $1.76

2201a — BC34

1986

$1.76 booklet contains 2 panes of four 22c stamps.

Booklet

BK153	BC34 $1.76 **purple & black,** P#1	4.00	

Varieties

2201b	As "a," black omitted on Nos. 2198, 2201	50.00	—
2201c	As "a," blue (litho.) omitted on Nos. 2198-2200	*1,500.*	
2201d	As "a," buff (litho.) omitted	—	
2201e	As "a," tagging omitted	—	

Booklets

BK153a	BC34 As #BK153, with 2 #2201b	100.00
BK153b	BC34 As #BK153, with 2 #2201c	*3,250.*

2209a — A1588-A1592

2209a	A1588 22c pane of 5, *Mar. 21*	5.00	2.75

2209a — BC35

1986

$2.20 booklet contains 2 panes of five 22c stamps.

Booklet

BK154	BC35 $2.20 **blue green and red,** P#11111, 22222	10.00

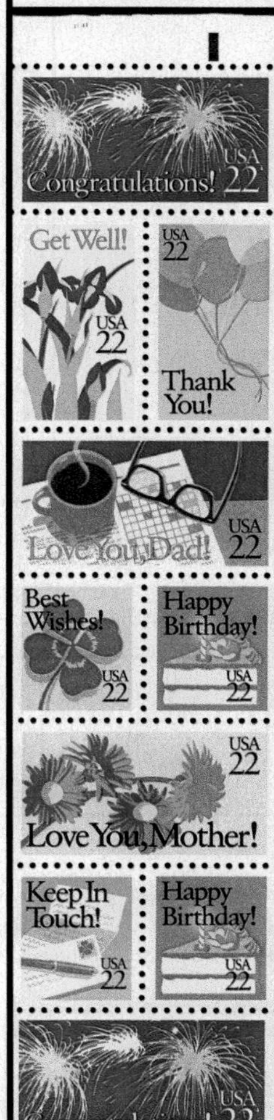

2274a — A1637-A1644

1987

2274a	A1637 22c pane of 10, *Apr. 20*	9.00	5.00

FOR 22 CENTS, YOU CAN ADD ONE OF THESE GREETINGS TO A LETTER TO ANYONE IN THE UNITED STATES, CANADA OR MEXICO.

Get Well!
Thank You!
Best Wishes!
Keep in Touch!
Love You, Dad!
Happy Birthday!
Congratulations!
Love You, Mother!

10 TWENTY-TWO CENT U.S. POSTAGE STAMPS 2.20

2274a — BC36

1987

$2.20 booklet contains 1 pane of ten 22c stamps.

Booklet

BK155	BC36 $2.20 **blue & red,** P#111111, 222222	10.00

2276a — A1646

Perf. 11

2276a	A1646 22c pane of 20, *Nov. 30*	9.00	—

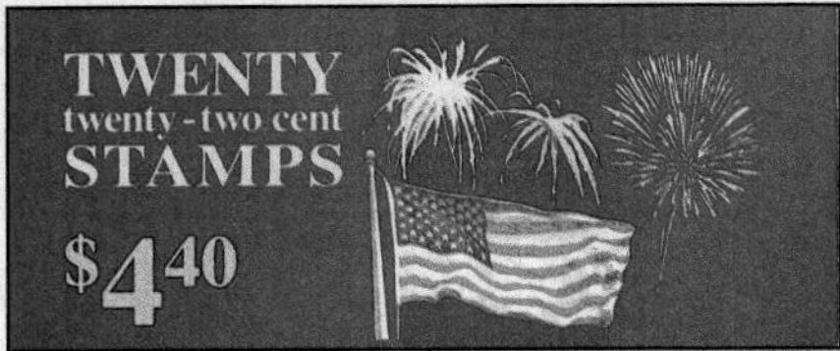

2276a — BC39

1987

$4.40 booklet contains one pane of twenty 22c stamps.

Booklet

BK156	BC39 $4.40 **multicolored,** no P#	9.00
	P#1111, 2222	11.00
	P#2122	17.50

Varieties

2276b	As "a," vert. pair, imperf. between	*1,450.*	
2276c	As "a," miscut and inserted upside down into booklet cover, imperf. between stamps and right selvage.		—

No. 2276a was made from sheets of No. 2276 which had alternating rows of perforations removed and the right sheet margins trimmed off.

2282a — A1647

1988 ***Perf. 10***

2282a A1647 E pane of 10, *Mar. 22*	6.50	3.50
Scored perforations	6.50	—

2282a — BC40

1988

$5 booklet contains two panes of ten E stamps.

Booklet

BK157 BC40 $5 **blue,** P#1111, 2222	13.00
P#2122	16.00

2283a — A1649a

Perf. 11

2283a A1649a 25c pane of 10, *Apr. 29*	6.00	3.50

2283a, 2283c — BC41

1988

$5 booklet contains two panes of ten 25c stamps.

Booklet

BK158 BC41 $5 **multicolored,** P#A1111	12.00

2283c — A1649a

Color Change

2283c A1649a 25c red removed from sky, pane of 10	45.00	—

Booklet

BK159 BC41 $5 **multicolored,** P#A3111, A3222	90.00

2285b — A1649b-A1649c

Perf. 10

2285b A1649b25c pane of 10, *May 28*	5.00	3.50

2285b — BC45

1988

$5 booklet contains two panes of ten 25c stamps.

Booklet

BK160 BC45 $5 **red & black,** P#1111, 1112, 1211, 1433, 1434, 1734, 2121, 2321, 3333, 5955 (2)	11.00
P#1133, 2111, 2122, 2221, 2222, 3133, 3233, 3412, 3413, 3422, 3521, 4642, 4644, 4911, 4941 (2)	17.50
P#1414	95.00
P#1634, 3512	50.00
P#3822	40.00
P#5453	165.00

No. BK160 exists with two cover types: one with one leaf at end of flowering branch, and one (shown) with two leaves. Two-leaf cover only contains panes with P# 1111, 1211, 2122 or 2222. One-leaf cover contains panes with all listed plate numbers.

Variety

2285f As "b," tagging omitted	*85.00*

Booklet

BK160a As #BK160, with 2 #2285f	*190.00*

2285Ac — A1648

2285Ac A1648 25c pane of 6, *July 5*	3.00	2.00

2285Ac — BC46

1988

$3 booklet contains two panes of six 25c stamps.

Booklet

BK161 BC46 $3 **blue & red,** P#1111	6.00

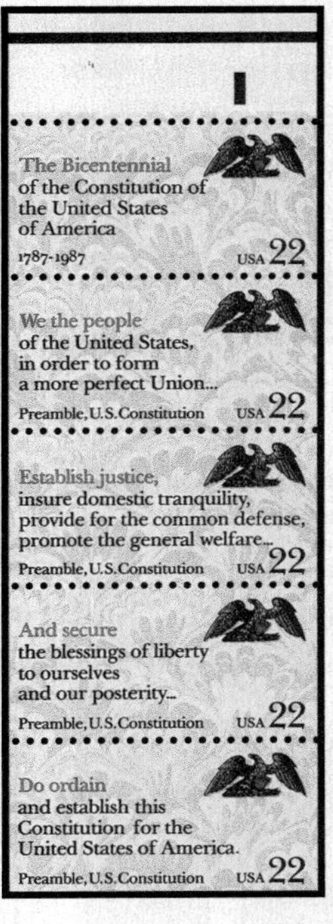
2359a — A1719-A1723

1987
2359a A1719 22c pane of 5, *Aug. 28* 3.75 2.25

2359a — BC37

1987
$4.40 booklet contains four panes of five 22c stamps.

Booklet
BK162 BC37 $4.40 **red & blue,** P#1111, 1112 15.00

2366a — A1726-A1730

2366a A1726 22c pane of 5, *Oct. 1* 2.50 2.00

2366a — BC38

1987
$4.40 booklet contains four panes of five 22c stamps.

Booklet
BK163 BC38 $4.40 **black & yellow,** P#1, 2 10.00

2385a — A1745-A1749

1988
2385a A1745 25c pane of 5, *Aug. 25* 3.25 2.50

2385a — BC47

1988
$5 booklet contains four panes of five 25c stamps.

Booklet
BK164 BC47 $5 **black & red,** P#1 13.00

2396a — A1759-A1760

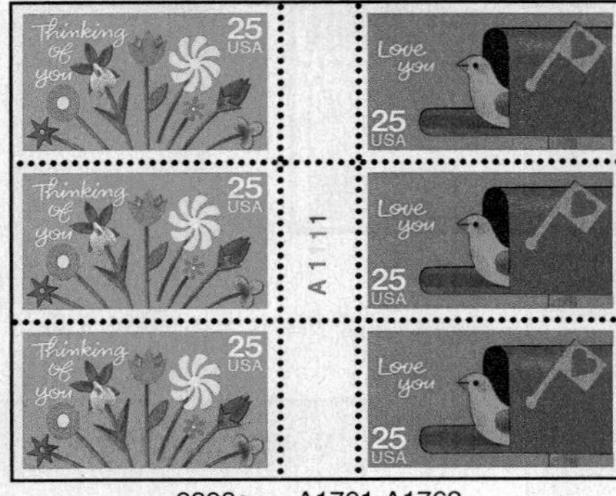
2398a — A1761-A1762

Perf. 11
2396a A1759 25c pane of 6, *Oct. 22* 3.50 3.25
2398a A1761 25c pane of 6, *Oct. 22* 3.50 3.25

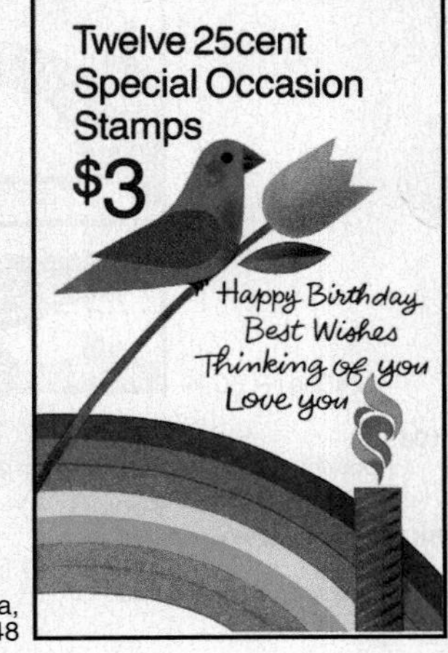
2396a, 2398a — BC48

1988
$3 booklet contains two panes of six 25c stamps.

Combination Booklet
BK165 BC48 $3 **multicolored,** 1 #2396a, 1 #2398a, P#A1111 (2) 7.00

Varieties
2398b As "a," imperf. horiz. 2,250.
2398c As "a," imperf —

One example of a mint, never-hinged and never-folded pane of No. 2396a is recorded. A second example of a never-folded pane of No. 2396a exists uncancelled, affixed to a USPS souvenir page. Examples of No. 2398a in mint, never-hinged, never-folded condition also are recorded (very scarce).

2409a — A1769-A1773

1989 ***Perf. 10***

2409a A1769 25c pane of 5, *Mar. 3* 3.00 1.75
Never folded pane, P#1 8.00
P#2 20.00

2409a — BC49

1989

$5 booklet contains four panes of five 25c stamps.

Booklet

BK166 BC49 $5 **blue & black,** P#1, 2 12.00

Variety

2409b As "a," tagging omitted — —

2427a — A1791

Perf. 11¼

2427a A1791 25c pane of 10, *Oct. 19* 5.00 3.50
Never folded pane, P#1 8.00

2427a — BC50

1989

$5 booklet contains two panes of ten 25c stamps.

Booklet

BK167 BC50 $5 **multicolored,** P#1 10.00

Variety

2427c As "a," imperf —

2429a — A1792

Perf. 11½

2429a A1792 25c pane of 10, *Oct. 19* 5.00 3.50
Never folded pane, P#1111 12.50

2429a — BC51

1989

$5 booklet contains two panes of ten 25c stamps.

Booklet

BK168 BC51 $5 **multicolored,** P#1111, 2111 10.00

Varieties

2429c As "a," horiz. imperf. between *2,250.*
2429d As "a," red omitted *3,250.*

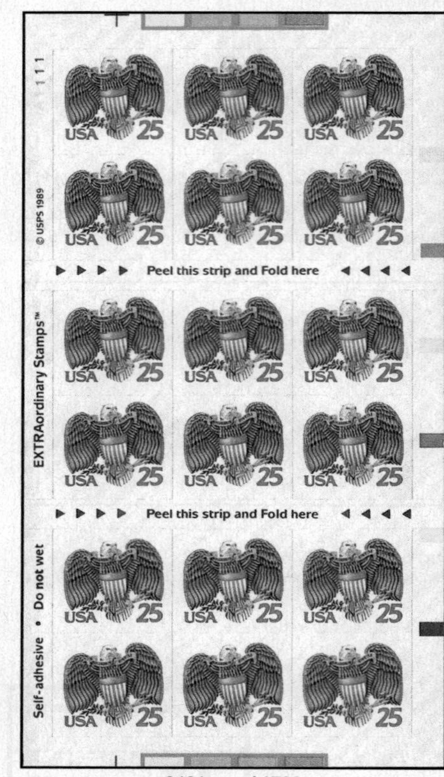

2431a — A1793

2431a — BC52

1989

$5 fold-it-yourself booklet contains eighteen self-adhesive 25c stamps.

Self-adhesive *Die cut*

2431a A1793 25c pane of 18, *Nov. 10,* P#A1111 10.00

By its nature, No. 2431a constitutes a complete booklet. Blue & red peelable paper backing is booklet cover (BC52). Sold for $5.

2441a — A1800

1990 ***Perf. 11½***

2441a A1800 25c pane of 10, *Jan. 18* 5.00 3.50
Never folded pane, P#1211 20.00
2441d As "a," tagging omitted —

2441a — BC53

1990

$5 booklet contains two panes of ten 25c stamps.

Booklet

BK169 BC53 $5 **multicolored,** P#1211 10.50
P#2111 20.00
P#2211 27.50
P#2222 17.50

Variety

2441c As "a," bright pink omitted *950.00*

Panes exist containing both normal and bright pink omitted stamps. Value is less than that of No. 2441c.

2443a — A1802

Perf. 11

2443a A1802 15c pane of 10, *Feb. 3* 3.00 2.50
Never folded pane, P#111111 7.00

2443a — BC54

1990

$3 booklet contains two panes of ten 15c stamps.

Booklet

BK170 BC54 $3 **multi,** P#111111 6.00
P#221111 9.00

Variety

2443c As "a," blue omitted *900.00*

2474a — A1829-A1833

Perf. 10

2474a A1829 25c pane of 5, *Apr. 26* 7.50 2.00
Never folded pane, P#1, 3, 5 9.50
P#2 11.50
P#4 52.50

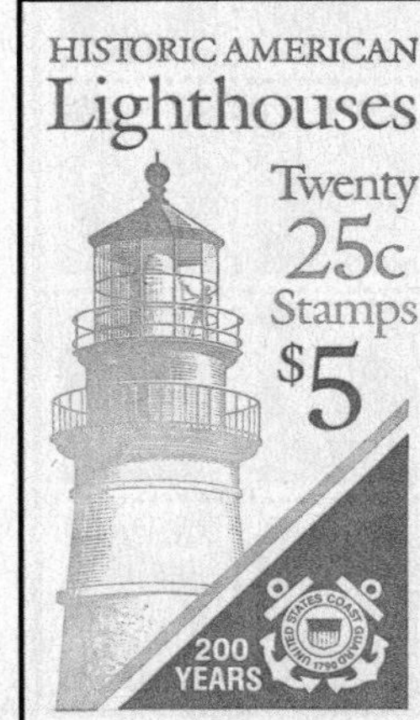

2474a — BC55

1990

$5 booklet contains four panes of five 25c stamps.

Booklet

BK171 BC55 $5 **blue & red,** P#1-5 (2) 30.00

Variety

2474b As "a," white omitted 85.00 —

Booklet

BK171a As #BK171, with 4 #2474b 350.00

Although often collected as a booklet pane, the 25¢ Flag ATM pane of 12 is not listed here because it does not have a removable selvage strip that allows it to be folded into a booklet. This pane is listed in the Postage section as No. 2475a.

2483a — A1847

1991-95

2483a A1847 20c **multicolored,** pane of 10, *June 15, 1995* 5.25 2.50
Never folded pane, P#S1111 6.25

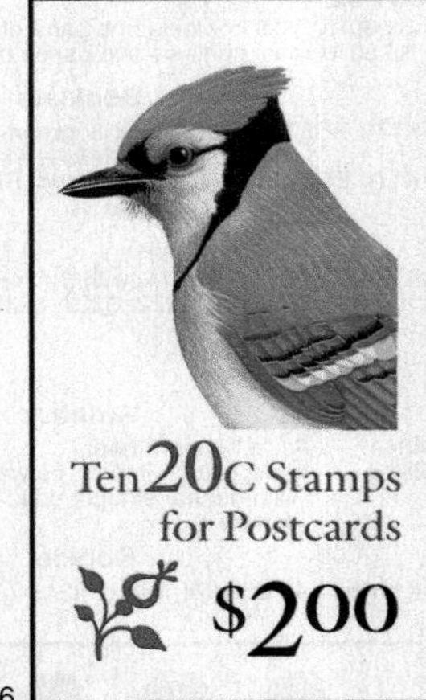

2483a — BC56

1995

$2 booklet contains one pane of 10 20c stamps.

Booklet

BK172 BC56 $2 **multicolored,** P#S1111 5.25

Variety

2483b As "a," imperf —

2484a — A1848

2484a A1848 29c **black & multi,** overall tagging, pane of 10, *Apr. 12, 1991* 6.00 3.75
Never folded pane, P#1111 9.00
2484e A1848 29c **black & multi,** prephosphored coated paper with surface tagging showing a solid appearance, pane of 10, *1992* 6.00 3.75

2484e — BC57

2484a, 2484e — BC57A

2485a — BC57B

1991-92

$2.90 booklet contains one pane of 10 29c stamps.
$5.80 booklet contains two panes of 10 29c stamps.

Booklets

BK173 BC57 $2.90 **black & green,** with No. 2484e, P#4444 6.25

BK174 BC57A $5.80 **black & red,** P#1111, 2222 12.00

P#1211 125.00

P#3222, 3333 18.00

BK174a As No. BK174, with 2 #2484e, P#2122, 2222, 3222, 3333 17.50

P#3221 95.00

P#3331 —

P#4444 15.00

Varieties

2484c As "a," imperf. horiz. *875.00*

2484g As "a," horiz. imperf. between and with natural straight edge at top or bottom *875.00*

Booklet

BK174b As #BK174, with 2 #2484g *1,750.*

2485a — A1848

2485a A1848 29c **red & multi,** pane of 10, *Apr. 12, 1991* 6.00 4.00

Never folded pane, P#K11111 11.00

Booklet

BK175 BC57B $5.80 **black & multi,** P#K11111 13.00

2486a — A1849

2486a A1849 29c pane of 10, *Oct. 8, 1993* 6.00 4.00

Never folded pane, P#K1111 6.50

2486a — BC58

2486a — BC58A

1993

$2.90 booklet contains one pane of 10 29c stamps.
$5.80 booklet contains two panes of 10 29c stamps.

Booklets

BK176 BC58 $2.90 **multicolored,** P#K1111 6.25

BK177 BC58A $5.80 **multicolored,** P#K1111 12.50

2488a — A1850-A1851

2488a A1850 32c **multicolored,** pane of 10, *July 8, 1995* 6.50 4.25

Never folded pane, P# 11111 7.25

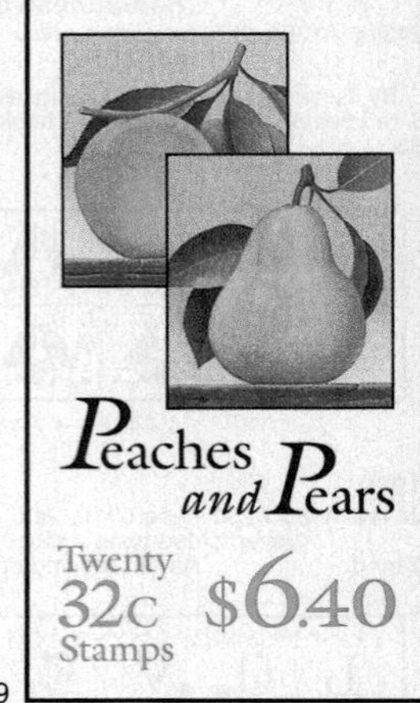

2488a — BC59

1995

$6.40 booklet contains two panes of 10 32c stamps.

Booklet

BK178 BC59 $6.40 **multicolored,** P#11111 13.00

2489a — A1852

Self-adhesive Stamps

Eighteen Stamps $5.22

2489a BC60

1993

$5.22 fold-it-yourself booklet contains 18 self-adhesive 29c stamps.

Self-Adhesive ***Die Cut***

2489a A1852 29c pane of 18, *June 25, 1993,* P#D11111, D22211, D22221, D22222, D23133 11.00

By its nature, No. 2489a constitutes a complete booklet (BC60). The peelable backing serves as a booklet cover.

Variety

2489b As "a," die cutting omitted —

USA29 USA29 USA29
USA29 USA29 USA29
USA29 USA29 USA29
S111 • Peel here to fold • Self-adhesive stamps • DO NOT WET
USA29 USA29 USA29
USA29 USA29 USA29
USA29 USA29 USA29

2490a — A1853

Self-adhesive Stamps
USA 29
Eighteen
29c Stamps $5.22

2490a BC61

1993

$5.22 fold-it-yourself booklet contains 18 self-adhesive 29c stamps.

Self-Adhesive ***Die Cut***

2490a A1853 29c pane of 18, *Aug. 19, 1993,* P#S111 11.00

By its nature, No. 2490a constitutes a complete booklet (BC61). The peelable backing, of which two types are known, serves as a booklet cover.

2491a — A1854

2491a — BC61A

1993

$5.22 fold-it-yourself booklet contains 18 self-adhesive stamps.

Self-Adhesive ***Die Cut***

2491a A1854 29c pane of 18, *Nov. 5, 1993,*

P#B3-11, 13-15	11.00
P#B1	16.00
P#B2, 12, 16	13.00

By its nature, No. 2491a constitutes a complete booklet (BC61A). The peelable backing serves as a booklet cover.

2492a — A1853

2492a — BC61B

1995

$6.40 fold-it-yourself booklet contains 20 self-adhesive 32c stamps.

Serpentine Die Cut 11.3x11.7 on 2, 3 or 4 Sides

Self-Adhesive

2492a A1853 32c pane of 20 + label, *June 2, 1995,* P#S111, S112, S333, S444, S555 — 13.00
2492b A1853 32c pane of 15 + label, *1996* — 9.75
2492e A1853 32c pane of 14, *1996* — 20.00
2492f A1853 32c pane of 16, *1996* — 20.00

By its nature, No. 2492a is a complete booklet (BC61B). The peelable backing serves as a booklet cover.

Nos. 2492a and 2492b exist on two types of surface-tagged paper that exhibit either a solid or grainy solid appearance. Values are the same. Nos. 2492e and 2492f have only tagging with a solid appearance.

Nos. 2492a and 2492b come either with no die cutting on the label or with die cutting.

No. 2492e contains blocks of 4, 6 and 4 stamps. No. 2492f contains blocks of 6, 6 and 4 stamps. The blocks are on rouletted backing paper. The peel-a-way strips that were between the blocks have been removed to fold the pane.

Booklets

See note before No. BK243. For illustration of booklet cover BC126, see before No. BK243.

BK178A BC126 $4.80 **blue,** No. 2492b (5) — 10.00
BK178B BC126 $4.80 **blue,** No. 2492f with bottom right stamp removed — 37.50
BK178C BC126 $9.60 **blue,** 2 #2492b, No P# (3) (grainy solid tagging only) — 20.00
BK178D BC126 $9.60 **blue,** 2 panes of #2492f ea with a stamp removed from either the top or bottom row, No P# (3) — 42.50

Combination Booklets

See note before No. BK243.

BK178E BC126 $9.60 **blue,** 1 ea #2492e, 2492f, no P# (3) — 45.00
BK178F BC126 $9.60 **blue,** #2492b, 2492f with bottom right stamp removed, no P# — *225.00*

No. BK178A was issued wrapped in cellophane and not wrapped in cellophane. The two cellophane-wrapped versions are scarcer.

No. BK178E was sold wrapped in cellophane with the contents of the booklet listed on a label. Three versions exist. No. 2492f is affixed to the booklet cover, and No. 2492e is loose.

The panes of #2492f with one stamp removed that are contained in Nos. BK178B, BK178D and BK178F cannot be made from No. 2492b, a pane of 15 + label. The label is located in the sixth or seventh row of the pane and is sometimes die cut. The panes with one stamp removed all have the stamp removed from the top or bottom row of the pane.

Nos. 2492a and 2492b exist on two types of surface-tagged paper that exhibit either a solid or grainy solid appearance. Values are the same. Nos. 2492e and 2492f have tagging with a solid appearance.

Varieties

2492d As "a," 2 stamps and parts of 7 others printed on backing liner — —
2492i As "a," 6 pairs plus stamp and label die cutting omitted vert. btwn. (due to miscutting) — *800.00*
2492j As "f," with 2 vert. pairs at bottom die cutting omitted horiz., in full bklt. #BK178D — —

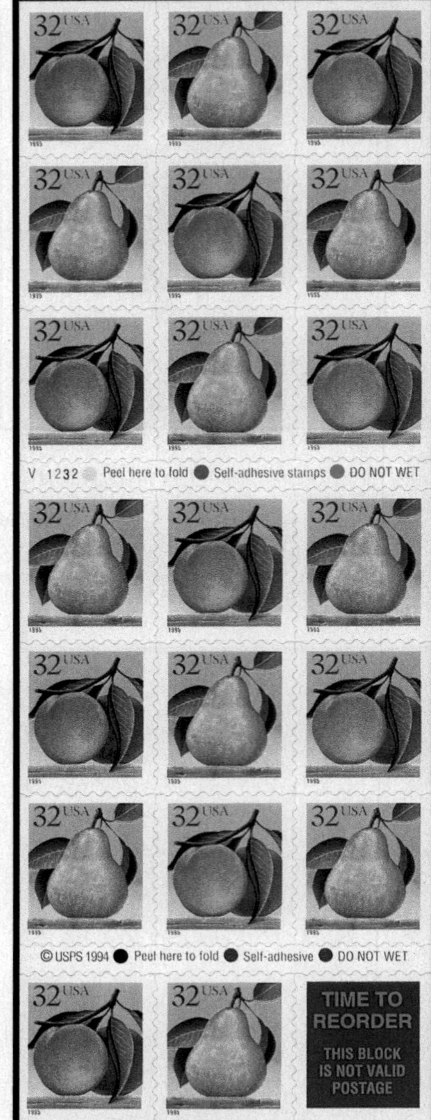

2494a — A1850-A1851

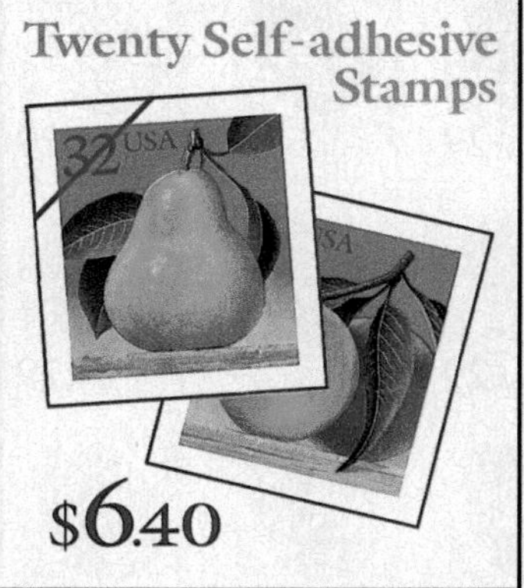

2494a BC61C

1995

$6.40 fold-it-yourself booklet contains 20 self-adhesive 32c stamps.

Serpentine Die Cut 8.8

2494a A1850 32c pane of 20+label, *July 8, 1995,* P# list 1 — 13.00
P# list 2 — 18.00
P#V33323 — 25.00
P#V11232 — —

By its nature, No. 2494a is a complete booklet (BC61C). The peelable backing serves as a booklet cover. It comes either with no die cutting on the label or with die cutting.

List 1 — P#V11111, V11122, V11132, V12132, V12211, V12221, V22212, V22222, V33142, V33243, V33333, V33343, V33353, V33363, V44424, V44434, V44454, V45434, V45464, V54365, V54565, V55365, V55565.
List 2 — P#V11131, V12131, V12232, V22221, V33143, V33453.

2505a — A1860-A1864

1990 ***Perf. 11***

2505a A1860 25c pane of 10, *Aug. 17* — 8.00 6.00
Never folded pane, P#1-2 — 15.00

2505a — BC62

1990

$5 booklet contains two panes of 10 25c stamps.

Booklet

BK179 BC62 $5 **multicolored,** P#1, 2 — 18.00

Varieties

2505b As "a," black (engr.) omitted — *2,500.*
2505d As "a," horiz. imperf. between — *2,250.*

The one example of No. 2505d that has been reported is actually split at the booklet fold and is a block of 4 and a block of 6.

2514b — A1873

1990 ***Perf. 11½***

2514b A1873 25c pane of 10, *Oct. 18* 5.00 3.25
Never folded pane, P#1 11.00

2514a — BC63

1990

$5 booklet contains two panes of 10 25c stamps.

Booklet

BK180 BC63 $5 **multicolored,** P#1 10.00

2516a — A1874

1990 ***Perf. 11½x11***

2516a A1874 25c pane of 10, *Oct. 18* 6.00 3.25
Never folded pane, P#1211 10.00

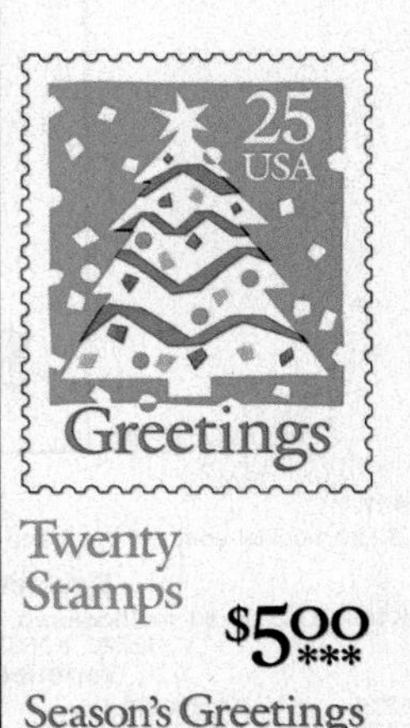

2516a — BC64

1990

$5 booklet contains two panes of 10 25c stamps.

Booklet

BK181 BC64 $5 **multicolored,** P#1211 12.00
P#1111 —

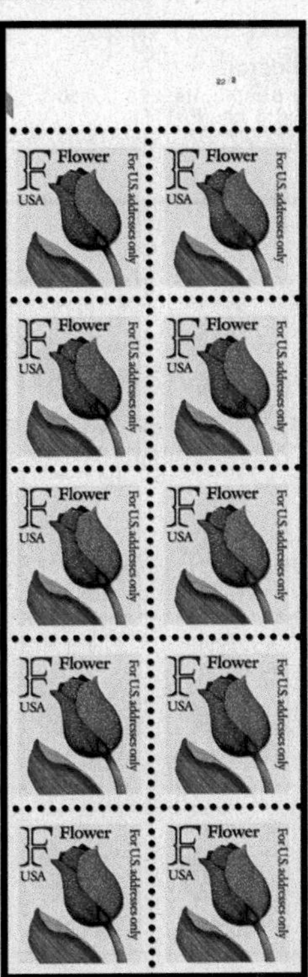

2519a — A1875

1991 ***Perf. 11.2 Bullseye***

2519a A1875 F pane of 10, *Jan. 22* 6.50 4.50

2519a, 2520a — BC65

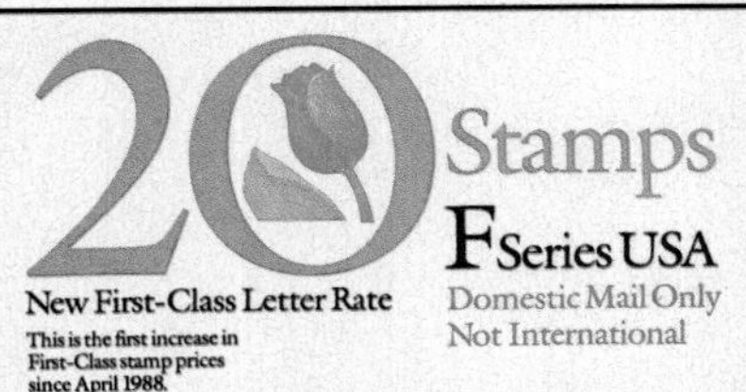

2519a, 2520a — BC65A

1991

$2.90 booklet contains one pane of 10 F stamps.

$5.80 booklet contains two panes of 10 F stamps.

Booklets

BK182 BC65 ($2.90) **yellow & multi,** P#2222 6.50
BK183 BC65A ($5.80) **grn, red & blk,** P#1111, 2121, 2222 13.00
P#1222, 2111, 2212 22.50

2520a — A1875

2520a A1875 F pane of 10, *Jan. 22* 15.00 4.50
Never folded pane, P#K1111 —

Booklet

BK184 BC65 ($2.90) like #BK182, **grn, red & blk,** P#K1111 15.00

Varieties

2520b As "a," imperf. horiz. —
2520c Horiz. pair, imperf between, in error booklet pane of 12 stamps *450.00*

No. 2520c is from a paper foldover before perforating.

Although often collected as a booklet pane, the nondenominated (29¢) F-rate Flag ATM pane of 12 is not listed here because it does not have a removable selvage strip that allows it to be folded into a booklet. This pane is listed in the Postage section as No. 2522a.

2527a — A1879

Perf. 11

2527a A1879 29c pane of 10, *Apr. 5* 6.00 3.50
Never folded pane, P#K1111 8.00

2527a — BC66

1991

$2.90 booklet contains one pane of 10 29c stamps.

Booklet

BK185 BC66 $5.80 **multicolored,** P#K1111, K2222, K3333 12.00

Varieties

2527d As "a," imperf horiz. *750.00*
2527e As "a," imperf vert. *500.00*

2528a — A1880

Perf. 11

2528a A1880 29c pane of 10, *Apr. 21* 6.00 3.50
Never folded pane 7.00

2528a — BC67

2528a — BC67A

1991

$2.90 booklet contains one pane of 10 29c stamps.

Booklets

BK186 BC67 $2.90 **black & multicolored,** P#K11111 6.00
BK186A BC67A $2.90 **red & multicolored,** P#K11111 (2) 6.75

Varieties

2528b As "a," imperf. horiz. *2,750.*
2528f As "d," two pairs, in #2528a with foldover —

Booklet Covers

When more than one combination of covers exists, the number of possible booklets is noted in parentheses after the booklet listing.

2530a — A1882

1991 *Perf. 10*

2530a A1882 19c pane of 10, *May 17* 4.00 2.75
Never folded pane, P#1111 5.00

2530a — BC68

1991

$3.80 booklet contains two panes of 10 19c stamps.

Booklet

BK187 BC68 $3.80 **black & blue,** P#1111, 2222 — 8.00
P#1222 — 32.50

2531Ab — A1884

2531Ab — BC68A

Self-adhesive Stamps
29 USA
Convenient: No Licking!
Strong Adhesive: Stays on Envelopes!
Easy to Use: No Tearing!
Eighteen Stamps

2531Ae — BC68B

1991-92

$5.22 fold-it-yourself booklet contains 18 self-adhesive 29c stamps.

Self-Adhesive — ***Die Cut***

2531Ab A1884 29c pane of 18, prephosphored coated paper with surface tagging showing a solid appearance, *June 25,* no P# — 11.00

By its nature, No. 2531Ab constitutes a complete booklet (BC68A). The peelable backing serves as a booklet cover.

Variety

2531Ae As "b," overall tagging (BC68B), *1992* — 11.00

2536a — A1890

1991 — ***Perf. 11***

2536a A1890 29c pane of 10, *May 9* — 6.00 3.50
Never folded pane, P#1111, 1112 — 7.00

2536a — BC69

1991

$5.80 booklet contains two panes of 10 29c stamps.

Booklet

BK188 BC69 $5.80 **multicolored,** P#1111, 1112 — 12.00
P#1113, 1123, 2223 — 16.00
P#1212 — 42.50

2549a — A1899-A1903

Perf. 11

2549a A1899 29c pane of 5, *May 31* — 5.50 3.00
Never folded pane, P#A23133, A23213 — 8.25
P#A11111, A22122, A22132, A33213 — —
P#A23124 — 25.00
P#A32225, A33233 — 15.00

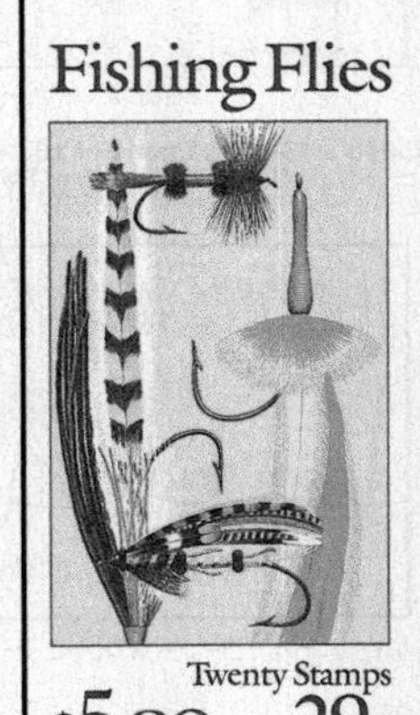

2549a — BC70

1991

$5.80 booklet contains four panes of 5 29c stamps.

Booklet

BK189 BC70 $5.80 **multicolored,** P#A22122, A23123, A23124, A33235, A44446, A45546, A45547 — 22.00
P#A11111, A22133, A23133, A23213 — 30.00
P#A22132, A32224, A32225, A33233 — 30.00
P#A31224 — 45.00

No. BK189 exists assembled from panes with different plate numbers.

P#33213 has yet to be found as top pane in booklets.

Variety

2545b Horiz. pair, imperf. between, in #2549a with foldover — *2,400.*

2552a — A1905

2552a A1905 29c pane of 5, *July 2* 3.00 2.25
Never folded pane, P#A11121111 4.00

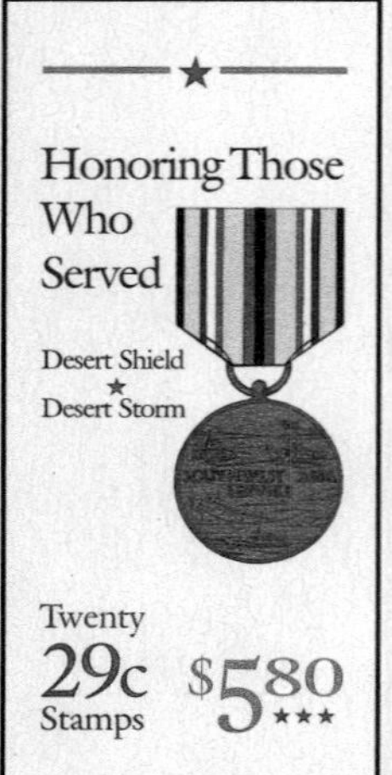

2552a — BC71

1991

$5.80 booklet contains four panes of 5 29c stamps.

Booklet

BK190 BC71 $5.80 **multicolored,** P#A11111111, A11121111 12.00

2566b — A1916-A1920

2566b A1916 29c pane of 10, *Aug. 29* 10.00 5.00
Never folded pane, P#1 12.00

2566a — BC72

1991

$5.80 booklet contains two panes of ten 29c stamps.

Booklet

BK191 BC72 $5.80 **scar, blk & brt vio,** P#1, 2 20.00

Varieties

2566c As "b," scar & brt violet (engr.) omitted *350.00*

2577a — A1922-A1931

2577a A1922 29c pane of 10, *Oct. 1* 9.00 4.50
Never folded pane, P#111111 11.00

2577a — BC73

1991

$5.80 booklet contains two panes of 10 29c stamps.

Booklet

BK192 BC73 $5.80 **blue, black & red,** P#111111 18.00
P#111112 22.00

2578a — A1933

Perf. 11¼

2578a A1933 (29c) pane of 10, *Oct. 17* 6.00 3.25
Never folded pane, P#1 9.50

2578a — BC74

1991

($5.80) booklet contains two panes of 10 (29c) stamps.

Booklet

BK193 BC74 ($5.80) **multicolored,** P#1 12.00

2581b — A1934

2582a — A1935

2584a — A1937

2583a — A1936

2585a — A1938

2581b A1934 (29c) pane, 2 each, #2580, 2581, *Oct. 17* 8.00 1.25
Never bound pane, P#A11111 10.00
2582a A1935 (29c) pane of 4, *Oct. 17* 2.40 1.25
Never bound pane, P#A11111 4.00
2583a A1936 (29c) pane of 4, *Oct. 17* 2.40 1.25
Never bound pane, P#A11111 4.00
2584a A1937 (29c) pane of 4, *Oct. 17* 2.40 1.25
Never bound pane, P#A11111 4.00
2585a A1938 (29c) pane of 4, *Oct. 17* 2.40 1.25
Never bound pane, P#A11111 4.00

2581b, 2582a-2585a — BC75

1991

($5.80) booklet contains five panes of 4 (29c) stamps.

Combination Booklet

BK194 BC75 ($5.80) **multicolored,** 1 each #2581b, 2582a-2585a, P#A11111, A12111 16.00

Nos. 2581b-2585a are unfolded panes.
Imperf examples of Nos. 2582a-2585a are printer's waste.

2593a — A1946

1992-94 *Perf. 10*

2593a A1946 29c **black & multi,** pane of 10, *Sept. 8* 6.00 4.25
Never folded pane, P#1111 7.00

2593a — BC76

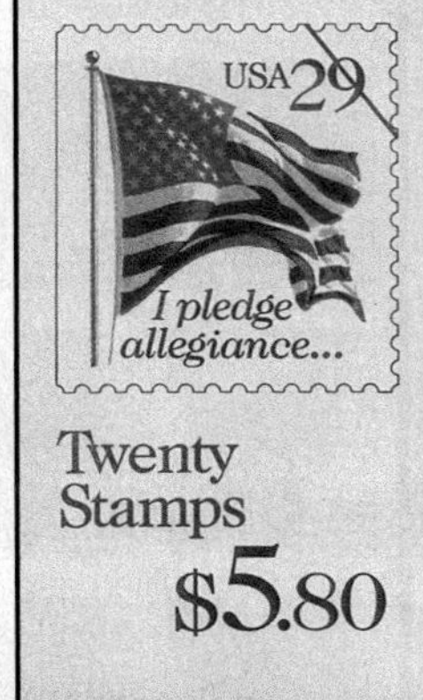

2593a — BC76A

1992

$2.90 booklet contains one pane of 10 29c stamps.
$5.80 booklet contains two panes of 10 29c stamps.

Booklets

BK195 BC76 $2.90 **blue & red,** P#1111 6.00
P#2222 11.00
BK196 BC76A $5.80 **blue & red,** P#1111 12.00
P#2222 20.00
P#1211, 2122 —

Perf. 11x10

2593Bc A1946 29c **black & multi,** pane of 10, shiny gum, *1993* 35.00 7.50
Low gloss gum 40.00

Booklet

BK197 BC76A $5.80 **blue & red,** shiny gum, P#1111, 1211, 2122, 2222, 2232, 3333 50.00
P#2232, low gloss gum 80.00
P#2333, low gloss gum —
P#2333, shiny gum —
P#3333, low gloss gum 175.00
P#4444, low gloss gum 140.00

2594a — A1946

2594a A1946 29c **red & multi,** pane of 10, *1993* 6.50 4.25
Never folded pane, P# K1111 7.50

2594a — BC76B

2594a — BC76C

1993-94

$2.90 booklet contains one pane of 10 29c stamps.
$5.80 booklet contains two panes of 10 29c stamps.

Booklet

BK198 BC76B $2.90 **black, red & blue,** P#K1111 6.00
BK199 BC76C $5.80 **multicolored,** *1994,* P#K1111 13.50

2595a — A1947

2595a — BC77

1992

$5 fold-it-yourself booklet contains 17 self-adhesive 29c stamps.

No. BC77 for Nos. 2595a, 2596a and 2597a differs in size and style of type as well as location of UPC labels.

Self-adhesive

Die Cut

2595a A1947 29c **brown & multi**, pane of 17 + label, *Sept. 25,* P#B1111-1, B1111-2, B2222-1, B2222-2, B3333-1, B3333-3, B3434-1, B3434-3, B4444-1 — 12.75
P#B4344-1, B4444-3 — 15.00
P#B4344-3 — *150.00*

Variety

2595d As "a," die cutting omitted — *725.00*

2596a A1947 29c **green & multi,** pane of 17 + label, *Sept. 25, 1992,* P#D11111, D21221, D22322, D32322, D32332, D43352, D43452, D43453, D54563, D54573, D65784 — 12.75
P#D54571, D54673, D61384 — 15.00
P#D32342, D42342 — 35.00
P#D54561 — 25.00

2597a A1947 29c **red & multi,** pane of 17 + label, *Sept. 25,* P#S1111 — 12.75

By their nature, Nos. 2595a-2597a constitute complete booklets (BC77). A peelable paper backing serves as a booklet cover for each. No. 2595a has a black and multicolored backing with serifed type. No. 2596a has a blue and multicolored backing, No. 2597a has a black and multicolored backing with unserifed type.

2598a — A1950

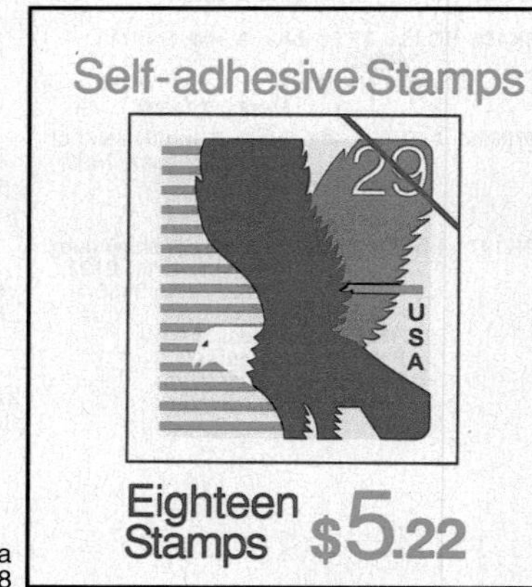

2598a BC78

1994

$5.22 fold-it-yourself booklet contains 18 self-adhesive 29c stamps.

Self-Adhesive *Die Cut*

2598a A1950 29c pane of 18, *Feb. 4, 1994,* P#M111, M112 — 11.00

By its nature, No. 2598a constitutes a complete booklet (BC78). The peelable backing serves as a booklet cover.

2599a — A1951

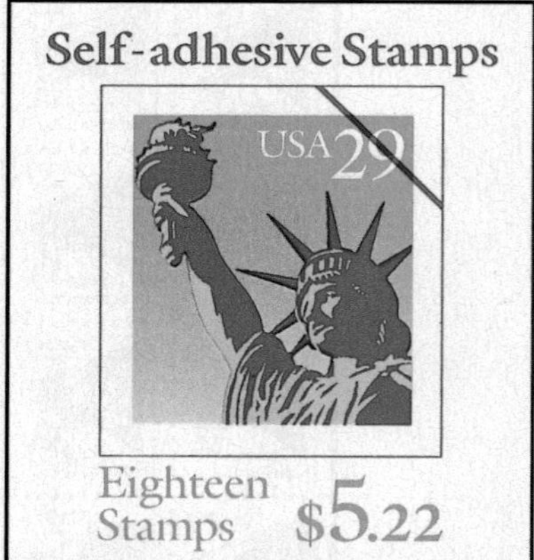

2599a — BC79

1994

$5.22 fold-it-yourself booklet contains 18 self-adhesive 29c stamps.

Self-Adhesive *Die Cut*

2599a A1951 29c pane of 18, *June 24, 1994,* P#D1111, D1212 — 11.00

By its nature, No. 2599a constitutes a complete booklet (BC79). The peelable backing serves as a booklet cover.

2646a — A1994-A1998

1992

2646a A1994 29c pane of 5, *June 15* 3.00 2.50
Never folded pane, P#A2212112,
A2212122, A2222222 4.00
P#A1111111, A2212222 10.00

Imperforate panes are proofs.

2646a — BC80

1992

$5.80 booklet contains four panes of 5 29c stamps.

Booklet

BK201 BC80 $5.80 **multicolored,** P#A1111111,
A2212112, A2212222,
A2222222 12.00
P#A2212122 18.00

No. BK201 exists assembled from panes with different plate numbers.

2709a — A2057-A2061

2709a A2057 29c pane of 5, *Oct. 1* 3.25 2.25
Never folded pane, P#K1111 4.25

2709a — BC83

1992

$5.80 booklet contains four panes of 5 29c stamps.

Booklet

BK202 BC83 $5.80 **multicolored,** P#K1111 13.00

Variety

2709b As "a," imperf. *2,000.*

2710a — A2062

Perf. 11¼

2710a A2062 29c pane of 10, *Oct. 22* 6.00 3.50
Never folded pane, P#1 7.00

2710a — BC83A

1992

$5.80 booklet contains two panes of 10 29c stamps.

Booklet

BK202A BC83A $5.80 **multicolored,** P#1 12.00

2718a — A2063-A2066

2718a A2063 29c pane of 4, *Oct. 22* 3.60 1.25
Never bound pane, P#A111111,
A222222 4.50
P#A112211 —

2718a — BC84

1992

$5.80 booklet contains five panes of 4 29c stamps.

Booklet

BK203 BC84 $5.80 **multi,** P#A111111, A112211,
A222222 18.00

Imperfs and part-perfs of No. 2718a are proofs.

2719a — A2064

2719a
BC85

1992

$5.22 fold-it-yourself booklet contains 18 self-adhesive 29c stamps.

Self-Adhesive

Die Cut

2719a A2064 29c **multicolored,** pane of 18, *Oct. 29,* P#V11111 12.00

By its nature, No. 2719a constitutes a complete booklet (BC85). The peelable paper backing serves as a booklet cover.

2737a — A2071, A2075-A2077

Tab format on No. 2737a is similar to that shown for No. 2737b.

1993

2737a A2071 29c pane of 8, 2 #2731, 1 each #2732-2737, *June 16* 5.25 2.25
Never folded pane, P#A22222 8.00
P#A13113 —

2737b A2071 29c pane of 4, #2731, 2735-2737 + tab, *June 16* 2.60 1.50
Never folded pane, P#A22222 3.50
P#A13113 5.00

2737a, 2737b — BC86

1993

$5.80 booklet contains one pane of four 29c stamps and two panes of eight 29c stamps.

Combination Booklet

BK204 BC86 $5.80 **multicolored,** 2 #2737a + 1 #2737b, P#A11111, A22222 13.25
P#A13113, A44444 15.00

No. 2737b without tab is indistinguishable from broken No. 2737a.

Never folded panes of No. 2737a with P#A11111 or P#A22222 exist missing the bottom stamp (found in some USPS mint sets). This was the only source for the never folded pane with P#A11111, and such panes are scarce.

No. BK204 exists assembled from panes with different plate numbers.

Imperforate panes of Nos. 2737a and 2737b are proofs.

2745a — A2086-A2090

2745a A2086 29c pane of 5, *Jan. 25* 3.00 2.25
Never folded pane, P#1111, 1211 4.00
P#2222 6.50

Half of the printing of No. 2745a shows a part of No. 2745 on the left side of the selvage tab. Values, same.

2745a — BC89

1993

$5.80 booklet contains four panes of 5 29c stamps.

Booklet

BK207 BC89 $5.80 **multi,** P#1111, 1211, 2222 12.00

2764a — A2105-A2109

2764a A2105 29c pane of 5, *May 15* 3.00 2.25
Never folded pane, P#1 4.00

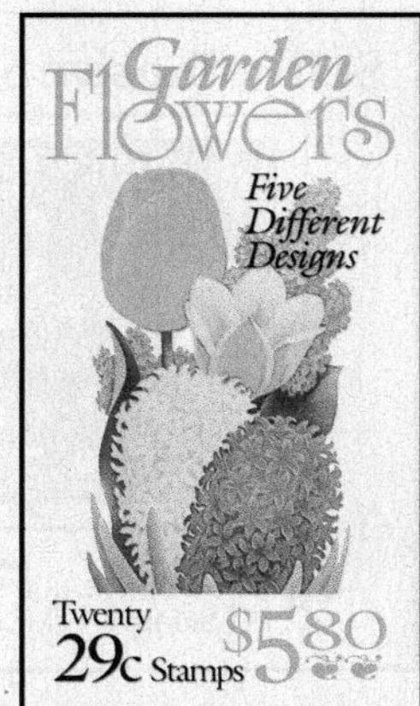

2764a — BC90

1993

$5.80 booklet contains four panes of 5 29c stamps.

Booklet

BK208 BC90 $5.80 **multicolored,** P#1, 2 12.00

Varieties

2764b As "a," black (engr.) omitted *135.00*
2764c As "a," imperf. *700.00*
2764d As "a," tagging omitted *650.00*

Booklet

BK208a As #BK208, with 4 #2764b *575.00*

2770a — A2069, A2112-A2114

2770a A2069 29c pane of 4, *July 14* 2.75 2.25
Never folded pane, P#A11111, A11121, A22222 3.75

Imperforate panes are proofs.

2770a — BC91

1993

$5.80 booklet contains five panes of 4 29c stamps.

Booklet

BK209 BC91 $5.80 **multicolored,** P#A11111, A11121, A22222, A23232, A23233 12.00

2778a — A2070, A2115-A2117

2778a A2070 29c pane of 4, *Sept. 25, 1993* 2.50 2.00
Never folded pane, P#A222222 3.50

Imperforate panes are proofs.

2778a — BC92

1993

$5.80 booklet contains five panes of 4 29c stamps.

Booklet

BK210 BC92 $5.80 **multicolored,** P#A111111, A222222, A333333, A422222 12.50
P#A333323 —

2790a — A2128

2790a A2128 29c pane of 4, *Oct. 21, 1993* 2.40 1.75
Never bound pane, P#K111111, K133333, K144444 3.50
P#K255555 *85.00*

2790a — BC93

1993

$5.80 booklet contains five panes of 4 29c stamps.

Booklet

BK211 BC93 $5.80 **multicolored,** P#K111111, K133333, K144444, K255555, K266666 12.00
P#K222222 35.00

No. BK211 exists assembled from panes with different plate numbers.

Variety

2790c As "a," imperf. —

2798a — A2129-A2132

2798a A2129 29c pane of 10, 3 each #2795-2796, 2 each #2797-2798, *Oct. 21, 1993* 8.50 4.00
Never folded pane, P#111111 10.00

2798b A2129 29c pane of 10, 3 each #2797-2798, 2 each #2795-2796, *Oct. 21, 1993* 8.50 4.00
Never folded pane, P#111111 10.00

2798a — BC94

1993

$5.80 booklet contains two panes of 10 29c stamps.

Combination Booklet

BK212 BC94 $5.80 **multicolored,** 1 each #2798a, 2798b, P#111111, 222222 19.00

On No. 2798b the plate number appears close to the top row of perfs. Different selvage markings can be found there.

2802a — A2129-A2132

2802a — BC95

1993

$3.48 fold-it-yourself booklet contains 12 self-adhesive 29c stamps.

Self-Adhesive

Die Cut

2802a A2129 29c pane of 12, 3 each #2799-2802, *Oct. 28, 1993,* P#V1111111, V2221222, V2222112, V2222122, V2222221, V2222222 9.00
P#V3333333 10.50

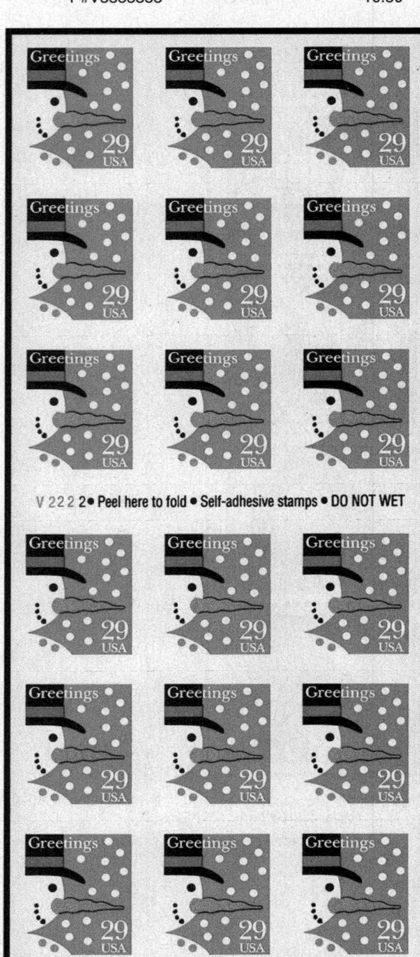

2803a — A2131

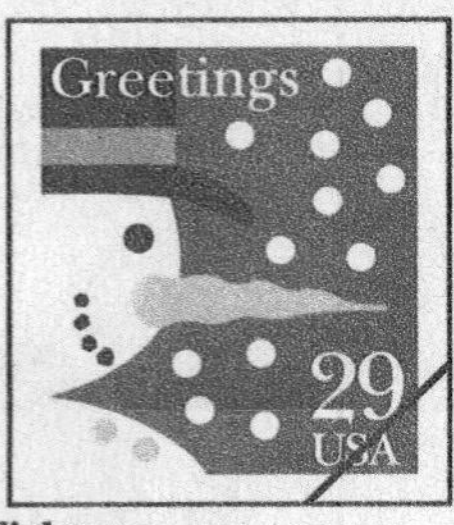

2803a
BC96

1993

$5.22 fold-it-yourself booklet contains 18 self-adhesive 29c stamps.

2803a A2131 29c pane of 18, *Oct. 28, 1993,* P#V1111 11.00
P# V2222 13.00

By their nature, Nos. 2802a-2803a constitute complete booklets (BC95-BC96). The peelable backing serves as a booklet cover.

2806b — A2135

2806b A2135 29c pane of 5, *Dec. 1, 1993* 3.50 2.00
Never folded pane, P#K111 4.50

2806b — BC97

1993

$2.90 booklet contains two panes of 5 29c stamps.

Booklet

BK213 BC97 $2.90 **black & red,** P#K111 7.00

2813a — A2142

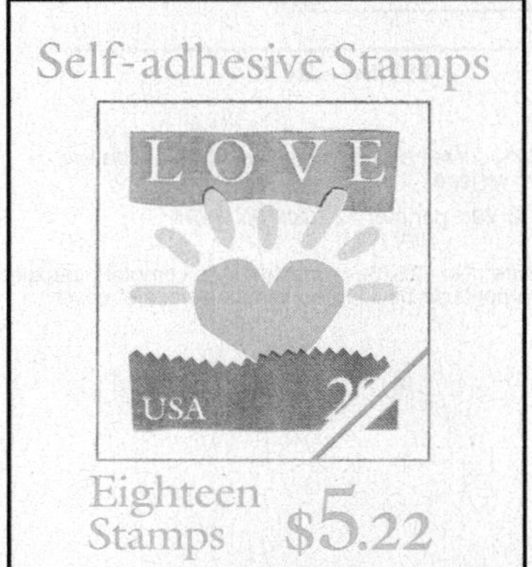

2813a BC98

1994

$5.22 fold-it-yourself booklet contains 18 self-adhesive 29c stamps.

Self-Adhesive *Die Cut*

2813a	A2142 29c pane of 18, *Jan. 27,* P#, see list	11.00
	P#B111-5, B333-14	*70.00*
	P#B444-7, B444-8, B444-9	14.00
	P#B333-5, B333-7, B333-8	20.00
	P#B334-11	*750.00*
	P#B344-11	50.00
	P#B434-10	100.00

By its nature, No. 2813a constitutes a complete booklet (BC98). The peelable backing serves as a booklet cover.

List — #B111-1, B111-2, B111-3, B111-4, B121-5, B221-5, B222-4, B222-5, B222-6, B333-9, B333-10, B333-11, B333-12, B333-17, B344-12, B344-13, B444-10, B444-13, B444-14, B444-15, B444-16, B444-17, B444-18, B444-19, B555-20, B555-21

2814a — A2143

2814a	A2143 29c pane of 10, *Feb. 14, 1994*	6.00	3.50
	Never folded pane, P#A11111	7.50	

Variety

2814d	As "a," imperf.	—

2814a — BC99

1994

$5.80 booklet contains two panes of 10 29c stamps.

Booklet

BK214	BC99 $5.80 **multicolored,** P#A11111, A11311, A12112, A21222, A22122, A22322	12.00
	P#A12111, A12211, A12212, A21311	25.00
	P#A22222	16.00

2833a — A2158-A2162

2833a	A2158 29c pane of 5, *Apr. 28, 1994*	3.00	2.25
	Never folded pane, P#2	3.50	

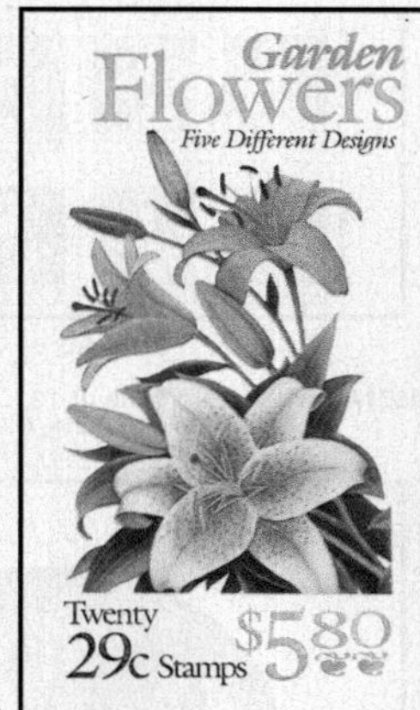

2833a — BC100

1994

$5.80 booklet contains four panes of 5 29c stamps.

Booklet

BK215	BC100 $5.80 **multicolored,** P#1, 2	12.00

Varieties

2833b	As "a," imperf	*400.00*
2833c	As "a," black (engr.) omitted	*125.00*
2833d	As "a," tagging omitted	—

Booklets

BK215a	As #BK215, with 4 #2833c	*525.00*
BK215b	As #BK215, with 3 #2833a, 1 #2833c	—

2847a — A2171-A2175

2847a	A2171 29c pane of 5, *July 28, 1994*	3.75	2.00
	Never folded pane, P#S11111	4.50	

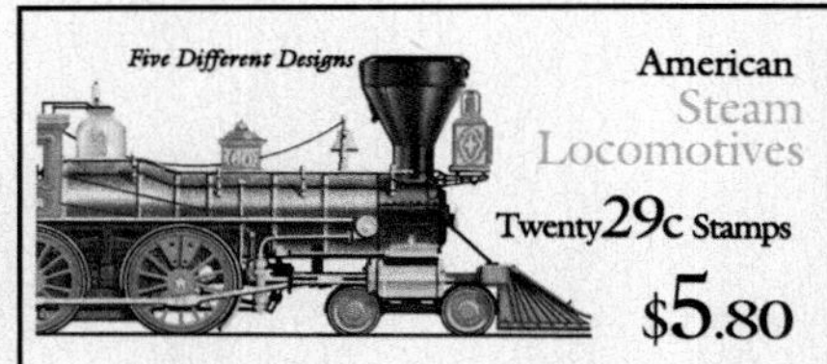

2847a — BC101

1994

$5.80 booklet contains four panes of 5 29c stamps.

Booklet

BK216	BC101 $5.80 **multicolored,** P#S11111	15.00

Variety

2847b	As "a," imperf	*2,500.*

2871Ab — A2200

2871Ab A2200 29c pane of 10, *Oct. 20, 1994* 6.25 3.50
Never folded pane, P#1, 2 7.00

2871Ab — BC102

1994

$5.80 booklet contains two panes of 10 29c stamps.

Booklet

BK217 BC102 $5.80 **multicolored,** P#1, 2 12.50

2872a — A2201

2872a A2201 29c pane of 20, *Oct. 20, 1994* 12.50 6.00
Never folded pane, P#P11111, P22222, P44444 14.00
P#P33333 —

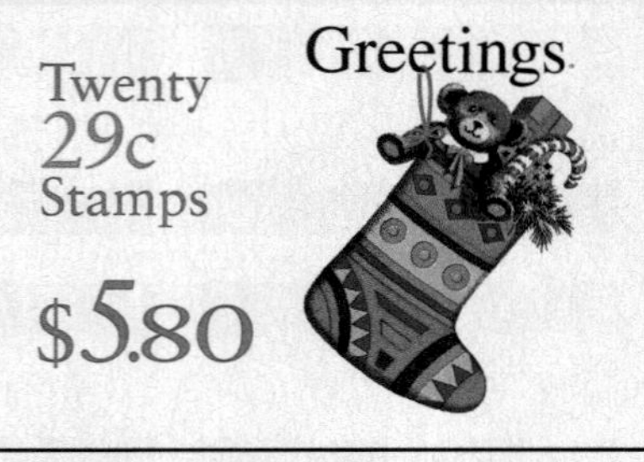

2872a — BC103

1994

$5.80 booklet contains one pane of 20 29c stamps.

Booklet

BK218 BC103 $5.80 **multicolored,** P#P11111, P22222, P33333, P44444 12.50

Variety

2872f As "a," imperf. —

2873a — A2202

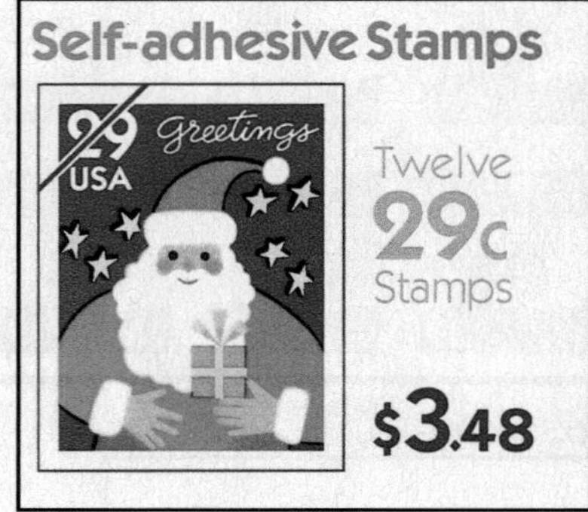

2873a — BC104

1994

$3.48 fold-it-yourself booklet contains 12 self-adhesive 29c stamps.

2873a A2202 29c pane of 12, *Oct. 20, 1994,* P#V1111 8.50

By its nature, No. 2873a constitutes a complete booklet (BC104). The peelable backing serves as a booklet cover.

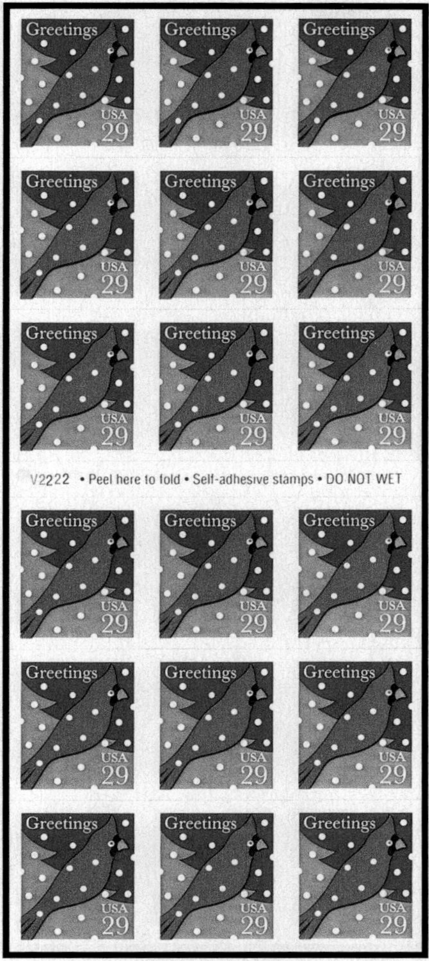

2874a — A2203

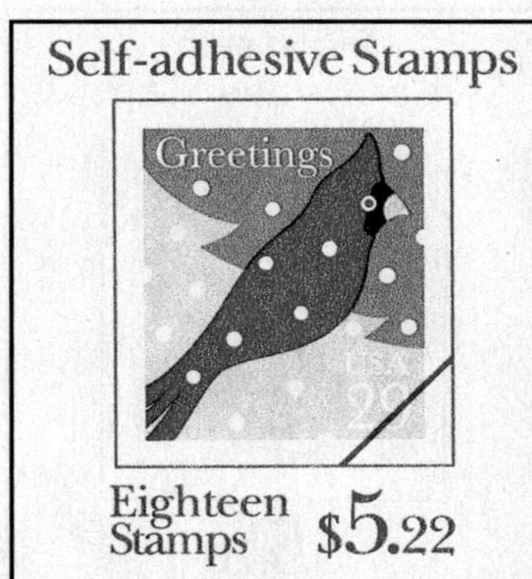

2874a BC105

1994

$5.22 fold-it-yourself booklet contains 18 self-adhesive 29c stamps.

2874a A2203 29c pane of 18, *Oct. 20, 1994,* P#V1111, V2222 11.00

By its nature, No. 2874a constitutes a complete booklet (BC105). The peelable backing serves as a booklet cover.

2881a — A2208

1994 ***Perf. 11.2x11.1***

2881a A2208 (32c) **black "G" & multi,** pane of 10, *Dec. 13, 1994* 12.50 5.00

2881a, 2883a — BC106

2883a — BC106A

2884a — BC106B

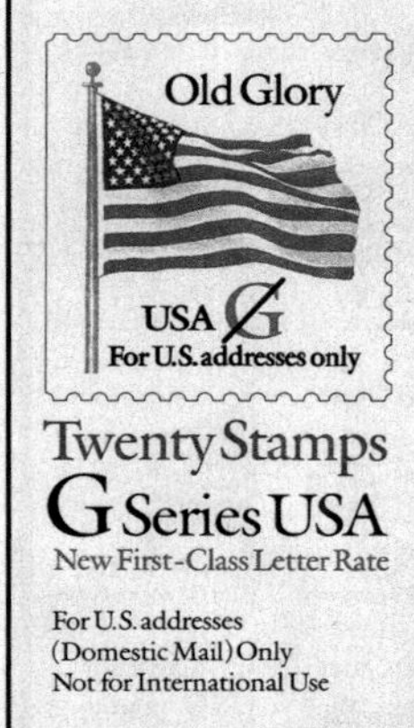

2885a — BC106C

1994

($3.20) booklet contains one pane of 10 G stamps.
($6.40) booklet contains two panes of 10 G stamps.

No. BC106 was printed on both coated (BK219) and uncoated (BK220) paper. The coated paper has a shiny, uniform appearance, while the uncoated paper appears faded and washed out.

Booklet

BK219 BC106 ($3.20) **pale blue & red,** P#1111 12.50

Perf. 10x9.9

2883a A2208 (32c) **black "G" & multi,** pane of 10, *Dec. 13, 1994* 6.50 3.75

Booklets

BK220 BC106 ($3.20) **pale blue & red,** P#1111, 2222 6.50

BK221 BC106A ($6.40) **blue & red,** P#1111, 2222 13.00

Perf. 10.9

2884a A2208 (32c) **blue "G" & multi,** pane of 10, *Dec. 13, 1994* 6.50 3.75

Booklet

BK222 BC106B ($6.40) **blue "G" & multi,** P#A1111, A1211, A2222, A3333, A4444 13.00

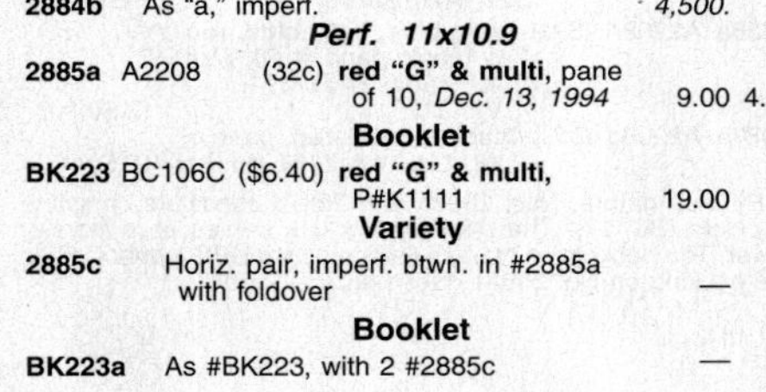

No. BK222 exists with panes that have different plate numbers.

Variety

2884b As "a," imperf. 4,500.

Perf. 11x10.9

2885a A2208 (32c) **red "G" & multi,** pane of 10, *Dec. 13, 1994* 9.00 4.50

Booklet

BK223 BC106C ($6.40) **red "G" & multi,** P#K1111 19.00

Variety

2885c Horiz. pair, imperf. btwn. in #2885a with foldover —

Booklet

BK223a As #BK223, with 2 #2885c —

2886a — A2208b

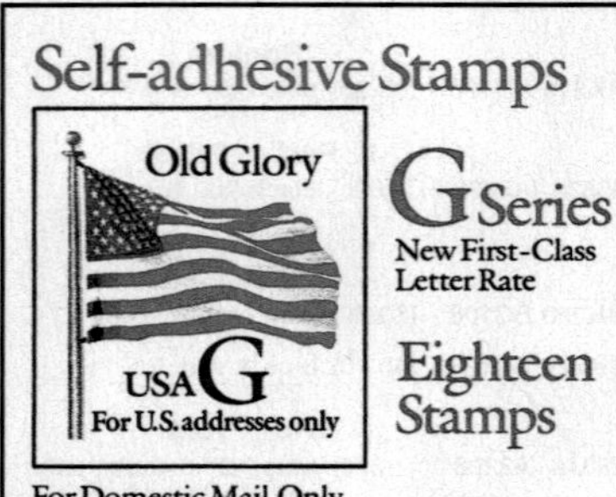

2886a, 2887a BC107

1994

($5.76) fold-it-yourself booklet contains 18 self-adhesive G stamps.

Self-Adhesive ***Die Cut***

2886a A2208b (32c) **gray, blue, light blue, red & black,** pane of 18, *Dec. 13, 1994,* P#V11111, V22222 12.50

2887a A2208c (32c) **black, blue & red,** pane of 18, *Dec. 13, 1994,* no P# 12.50

By their nature, Nos. 2886a and 2887a constitute complete booklets (BC107). The peelable backing serves as a booklet cover. The backing on No. 2886a contains a UPC symbol, while the backing on No. 2887a does not.

2916a — A2212

Perf. 10.8x9.8

2916a A2212 32c **blue, tan, brown, red & light blue,** pane of 10, *May 19, 1995* 6.50 3.25

Never folded pane, P#11111 7.25

2916a — BC108

1995

$3.20 booklet contains one pane of 10 32c stamps.
$6.40 booklet contains two panes of 10 32c stamps.

Booklets

BK225 BC108 $3.20 **blue & red,** P#11111, 22222, 33332 6.50
P#23222, 44444 —

BK226 BC108 $6.40 **multicolored,** P#11111, 22222, 33332, 44444 13.00
P#23222 17.50

Variety

2916b As "a," imperf. —

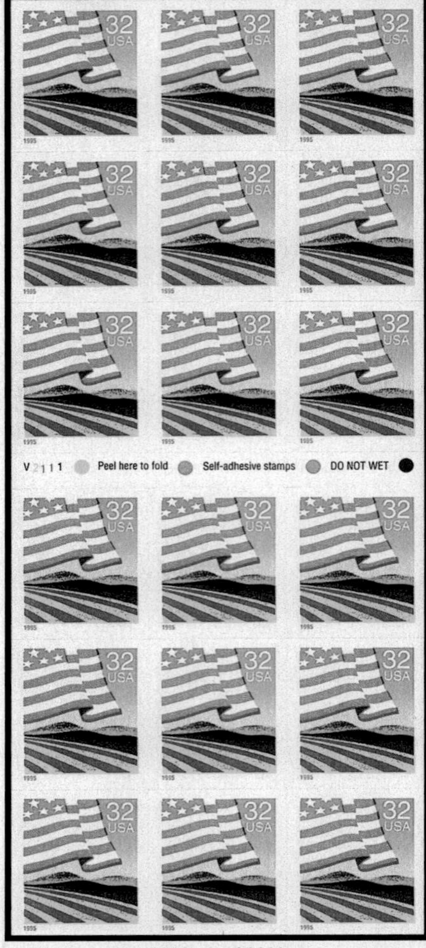

2919a — A2230

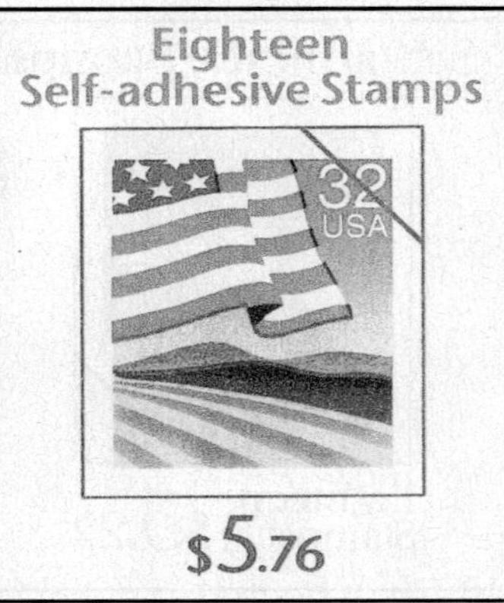

2919a BC113

1995

$5.76 fold-it-yourself booklet contains 18 self-adhesive 32c stamps.

Self-Adhesive ***Die Cut***

2919a A2230 32c pane of 18, *Mar. 17, 1995,* P#V1111 12.00
P#V1311 25.00
P#V1433, V2222, V2322 20.00
P#V2111 50.00

By its nature No. 2919a is a complete booklet (BC113). The peelable backing serves as a booklet cover.

2920a — A2212

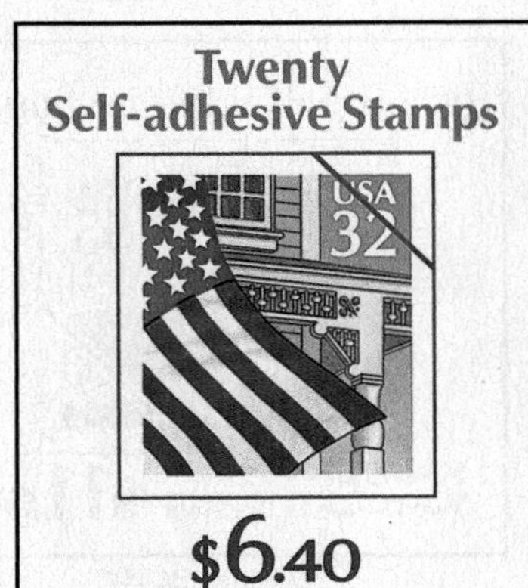

2920a
BC114

1995

$6.40 fold-it-yourself booklet contains 20 self-adhesive 32c stamps.

Serpentine Die Cut 8.7 on 2 or 3 Sides

Self-Adhesive

2920a A2212 32c pane of 20 + label, large date, *Apr. 18, 1995* (see List 1) 13.00
P#V23422 25.00
P#V23522 40.00
P#V57663 125.00

2920c A2212 32c pane of 20 + label, small date, *Apr. 18, 1995,* P#V11111 110.00

Varieties

2920g As "a," partial pane of 10, 3 stamps and parts of 7 stamps printed on backing liner —

2920k Vert. pair, die cutting missing btwn., three examples in No. 2920a with shift in die cutting (PS) —

By their nature Nos. 2920a, 2920c are complete booklets (BC114). The rouletted peelable backing, of which two versions are known on No. 2920a, serves as a booklet cover.

Date on No. 2920a is nearly twice as large as date on No. 2920c.

No. 2920a comes either with no die cutting on the label or with die cutting.

List 1 — P#V12211, V12212, V12312, V12321, V12322, V12331, V13322, V13831, V13834, V13836, V22211, V23322, V23432, V34743, V34745, V36743, V42556, V45554, V56663, V56665, V56763, V65976, V78989.

2920f — A2212

Serpentine Die Cut 8.7

Self-Adhesive

2920f	A2212	32c pane of 15 + label	9.75
2920h	A2212	32c pane of 15, see note, *1996*	*47.50*

Booklets

BK226A	BC126	$4.80 **blue,** 1 #2920f, no P# (4)	10.00
BK226B	BC126	$4.80 **blue,** 1 #2920h, no P# (3)	*67.50*
BK227	BC126	$9.60 **blue,** 2 #2920f (3)	20.00

No. 2920h is a pane of 16 with one stamp removed. The missing stamp is the lower right stamp in the pane or (more rarely) the upper left stamp. No. 2920h cannot be made from No. 2920f, a pane of 15 + label. The label is located in the sixth or seventh row of the pane and is die cut. If the label is removed, an impression of the die cutting appears on the backing paper.

Nos. BK226A-B and BK227 are makeshift vending machine booklets. See note before No. BK243.

For illustration of booklet cover BC126, see before No. BK243.

2920De — A2212

2920De — BC114a

Serpentine Die Cut 11.3

Self-Adhesive

2920De A2212 32c pane of 10, *Jan. 20, 1996* 8.00

By its nature No. 2920De is a complete booklet (BC114a). The rouletted peelable backing serves as a booklet cover.

Below is a list of known plate numbers. Some numbers are scarcer than the value indicated in the listing.

No. 2920De — P#V11111, V12111, V23222, V31121, V32111, V32121, V44322, V44333, V44444, V55555, V66666, V66886, V67886, V68886, V68896, V76989, V77666, V77668, V77766, V77776, V78698, V78886, V78896, V78898, V78986, V78989, V89999.

2921a — A2212

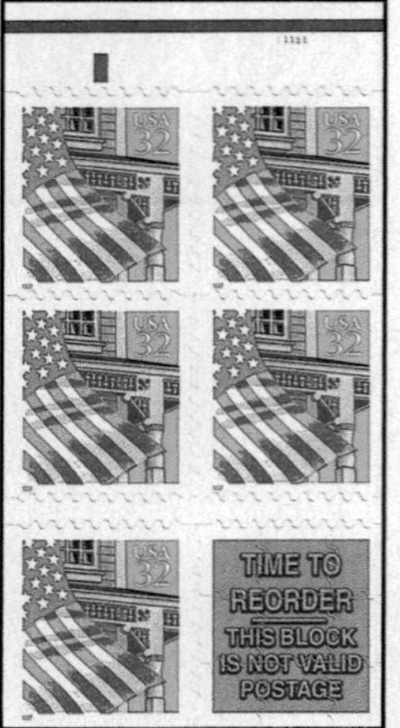

2921d — A2212

Serpentine Die Cut 9.8

Self-Adhesive

2921a A2212 32c pane of 10, dated red "1996," *May 21, 1996* 9.00
Never folded pane, P#21221, 22221, 22222 10.50
2921c A2212 32c pane of 10, dated red "1997," *Jan. 24, 1997* 12.00
Never folded pane, P#11111 14.00
2921d A2212 32c pane of 5 + label, dated red "1997," *Jan. 24, 1997* 8.00
Never folded pane, P#11111 9.50

Combination Booklet

BK227A BC108 $4.80 **multicolored,** 1 ea #2921c-2921d P#11111 20.00

No. BK227A is only source of No. 2921c with P# above right column of stamps and no length register marks or cross register lines on selvage tab. Some of the panes have color registration markings on the selvage tab. No. 2921d has no control markings - just the P# over the right column of stamps.

Booklets

BK228 BC108 $6.40 **blue, red & black,** 2 #2921a (5) 18.00

Known numbers for BK228: P#11111, 13111, 21221, 22221, 22222, 44434, 44444, 55555, 55556, 66666, 77777, 88788, 88888, 99999. Some numbers are scarcer than the value indicated in the listing.

No. BK228 is only source of No. 2921a, which has P# above left column of stamps and no length register marks or cross register lines in selvage tab.

BK228A BC108 $9.60 **multicolored,** 3 #2921c, P#11111 50.00

No. BK228A is only source of No. 2921c with P# above left column of stamps and length register marks and cross register lines on selvage tab.

Variety

2921e As "a," die cutting omitted *200.00*

Booklet

BK228b As #BK228, with 2 #2921e, P#11111, 13111 *400.00*

2949a — A2264

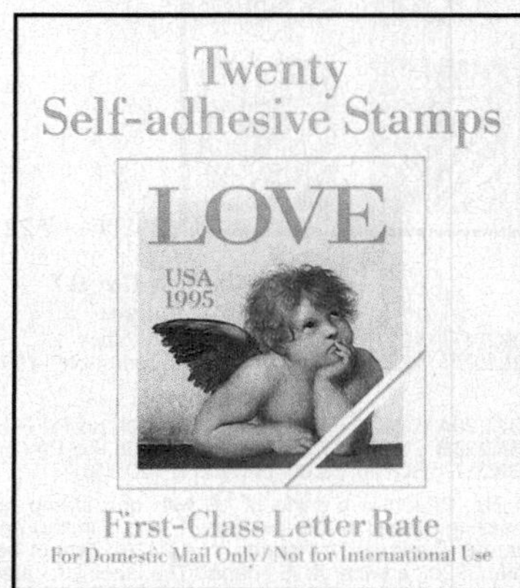

2949a
BC115

1995

($6.40) fold-it-yourself booklet contains 20 self-adhesive non-denominated 32c stamps.

Self-Adhesive ***Die Cut***

2949a A2264 (32c) pane of 20 + label, *Feb. 1, 1995,* P#B1111-1, B2222-1, B2222-2, B3333-2 13.00

By its nature, No. 2949a is a complete booklet (BC115). The peelable backing serves as a booklet cover.

Variety

2949c As "a," red (engr.) omitted *2,000.*

2959a — A2272

Perf. 9.8x10.8

2959a A2272 32c pane of 10, *May 12, 1995* 6.50 3.25
Never folded pane, P#1 6.75

2959a — BC116

1995

$6.40 booklet contains two panes of 10 32c stamps.

Booklet

BK229 BC116 $6.40 **multicolored,** P#1 13.00

Variety

2959c As "a," imperf. *500.00*

Booklet

BK229a As #BK229, with 2 #2959c *1,000.*

2960a — A2274

2960a — BC117

1995

$11 fold-it-yourself booklet contains 20 self-adhesive 55c stamps.

Self-Adhesive ***Die Cut***

2960a A2274 55c pane of 20 + label, *May 12, 1995,* P#B1111-1, B2222-1 22.50

By its nature, No. 2960a is a complete booklet (BC117). The peelable backing serves as a booklet cover. It comes either with no die cutting on the label or with die cutting.

2973a — A2283-A2287

2973a A2283 32c pane of 5, *June 17, 1995* 4.50 2.50
Never folded pane, P#S11111 5.00

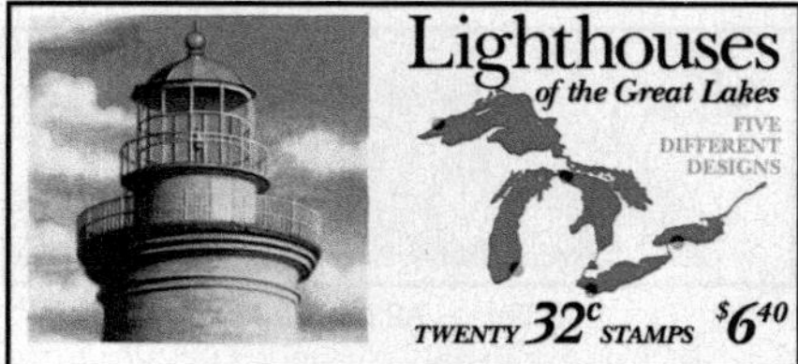

2973a — BC118

1995

$6.40 booklet contains four panes of 5 32c stamps.

Booklet

BK230 BC118 $6.40 **multicolored,** P#S11111 18.00

Variety

2973b As "a," 2 vert. pairs imperf. horiz. of #2972 and 2973, in pane of 7+ stamps in cplt. bklt. #BK230 (due to foldover) —

2997a — A2306-A2310

2997a A2306 32c pane of 5, *Sept. 19, 1995* 3.25 2.25
Never folded pane, P#2 4.25

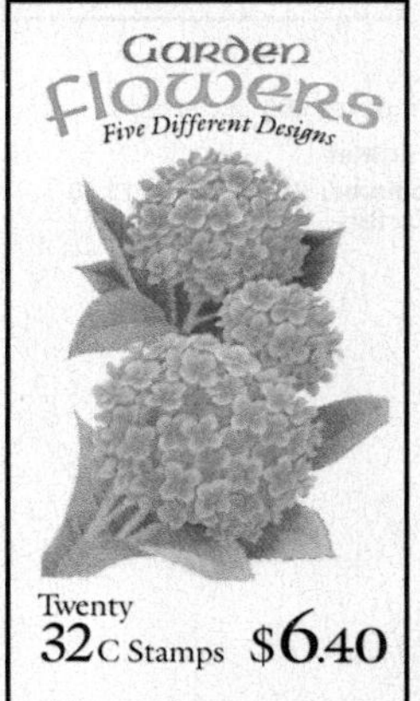

2997a — BC119

1995

$6.40 booklet contains four panes of 5 32c stamps.

Booklet

BK231 BC119 $6.40 **multicolored,** P#2 13.00

Variety

2997b As "a," imperf. *2,250.*

3003Ab — A2316

3003Ab A2316 32c pane of 10, *Oct. 19, 1995* 6.50 4.00
Never folded pane, P#1 7.50

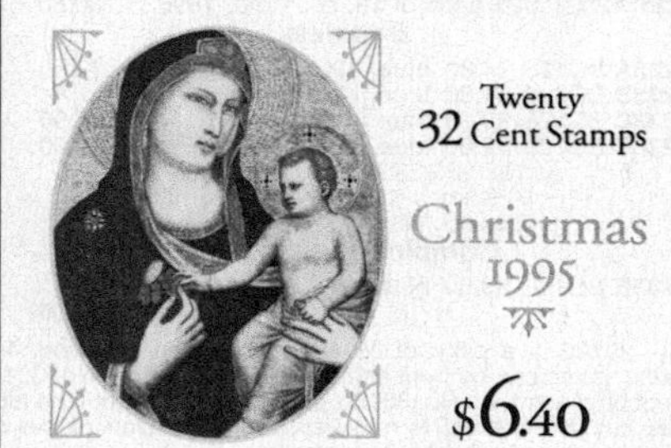

3003b — BC120

1995

$6.40 booklet contains two panes of 10 32c stamps.

Booklet

BK232 BC120 $6.40 **multicolored,** P#1 13.00

3007b — A2317-A2320

3007b A2317 32c pane of 10, 3 each #3004-3005, 2 each #3006-3007, *Sept. 30, 1995* 8.00 4.00
Never folded pane, P#P1111 9.00

3007c A2317 32c pane of 10, 2 each #3004-3005, 3 each #3006-3007, *Sept. 30, 1995* 8.00 4.00
Never folded pane, P#P1111 9.00

Variety

3007e As "b," miscut and inserted upside down into booklet cover, with full bottom selvage —

3007b-3007c — BC121

1995

$6.40 booklet contains two panes of 10 32c stamps

Combination Booklet

BK233 BC121 $6.40 **multicolored,** 1 each #3007b, 3007c, P#P1111, P2222 16.00
Tab at bottom (#3007e), in complete booklet with #3007c —

No. BK233 also is known with 2 panes of No. 3007b or 2 panes of No. 3007c.

3011a — A2317-A2320

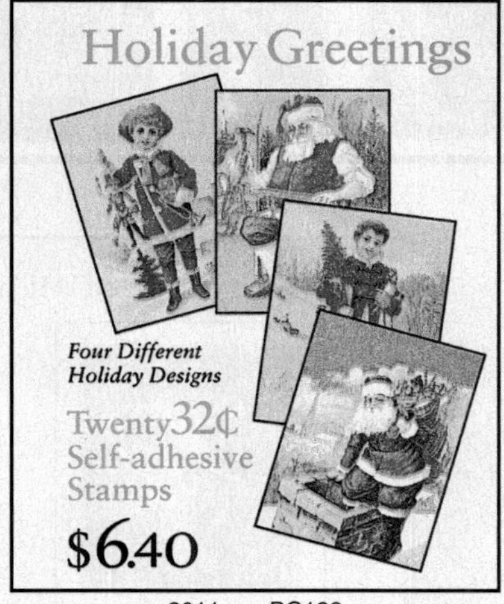

3011a — BC122

1995

$6.40 fold-it-yourself booklet contains 20 self-adhesive 32c stamps

Serpentine Die Cut

3011a A2317 32c pane of 20 +label, *Sept. 30, 1995,* P#V1111, V1211, V3233, V3333, V4444 19.00
P#V1212 26.00

By its nature, No. 3011a is a complete booklet (BC122). The peelable backing serves as a booklet cover.

3012a — A2321

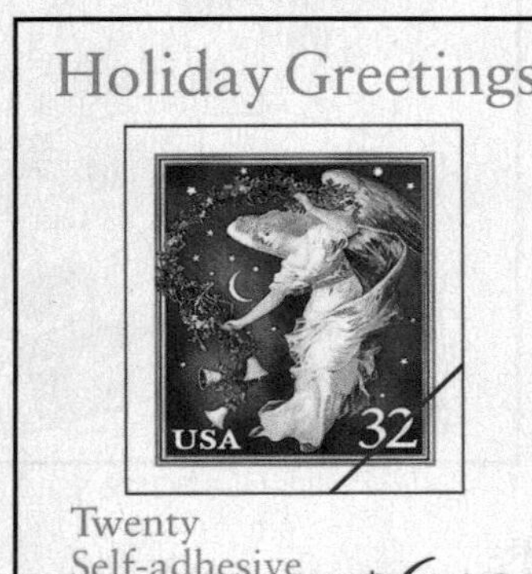

3012a
BC123

1995

$6.40 fold-it-yourself booklet contains 20 self-adhesive 32c stamps

Serpentine Die Cut

3012a A2321 32c pane of 20 + label, *Oct. 19, 1995,* P#B1111, B2222, B3333 13.00

By its nature, No. 3012a is a complete booklet (BC123). The peelable backing serves as a booklet cover.

No. 3012a comes either with no die cutting on the label (1995 printing) or with die cutting from the 1996 printing.

3012c A2321 32c pane of 15 + label, *1996,* no P# 12.00

3012d A2321 32c pane of 15, see note, *1996* 30.00

Booklets

BK233A BC126 $4.80 **blue,** #3012c (2) 12.50
BK233B BC126 $4.80 **blue,** #3012d —
BK233C BC126 $9.60 **blue** 2 #3012c (3) 25.00
BK233D BC126 $9.60 **blue,** 2 #3012d, no P# (3) 70.00
f. As No. BK233D, but one pane is of 16 stamps (thus 31 stamps in the booklet) (error) —

Combination Booklet

BK233E BC126 $9.60 **blue,** 1 ea #3012c, 3012d (2) 75.00

No. 3012d is a pane of 16 with one stamp removed. The missing stamp can be from either row 1, 2, 3, 7 or 8. No. 3012d cannot be made from No. 3012c, a pane of 15 + label. The label is die cut. If the label is removed, an impression of the die cutting appears on the backing paper.

Nos. BK233A-E are makeshift vending machine booklets. See note before No. BK243.

For illustration of booklet cover BC126, see before No. BK243.

3013a — A2322

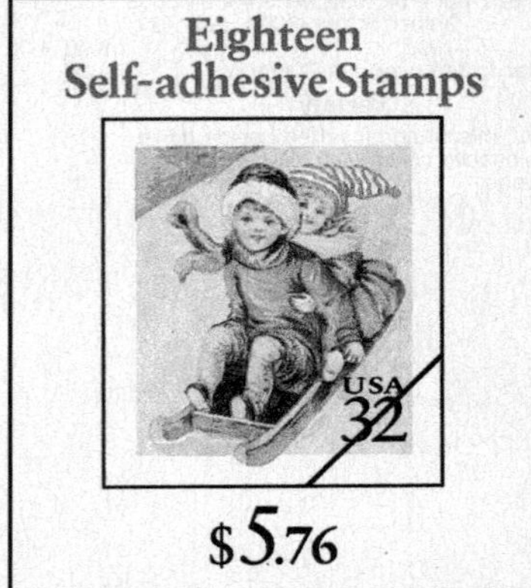

3013a
BC124

1995

$5.76 fold-it-yourself booklet contains 18 self-adhesive 32c stamps

Die Cut

3013a A2322 32c Pane of 18, *Oct. 19, 1995,* P#V1111 12.00

Variety

3013b As "a," tagging omitted —

By its nature, No. 3013a is a complete booklet (BC124). The peelable backing serves as a booklet cover.

3029a — A2329-A2333

3029a A2329 32c pane of 5, *Jan. 19, 1996* 3.25 2.50
Never folded pane, P#P1 3.75

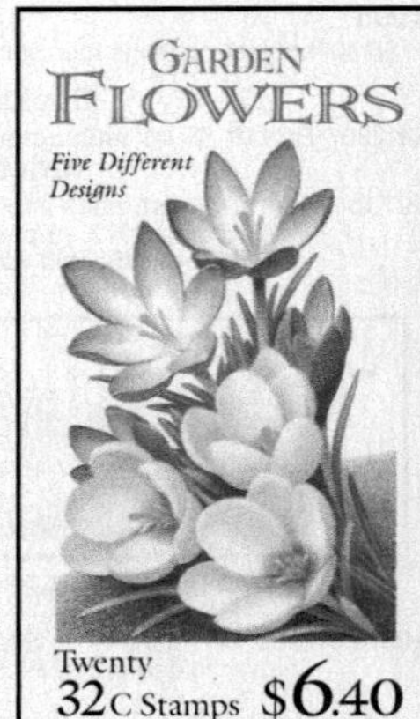

3029a — BC125

1996

$6.40 booklet contains four panes of 5 32c stamps

Booklet

BK234 BC125 $6.40 **multicolored,** P#1 13.00

Variety

3029b As "a," imperf. —

3030a — A2334

Serpentine Die Cut 11.3x11.7

3030a A2334 32c pane of 20+label, *Jan. 20, 1996* 13.00

By its nature, No. 3030a is a complete booklet (BC115). The peelable backing serves as a booklet cover.
P#B1111-1, B1111-2, B2222-1, B2222-2.

3030b A2334 32c pane of 15 + label, *1996* 9.75

Booklets

For illustration of booklet cover BC126, see before No. BK243.

BK235 BC126 $4.80 **blue,** #3030b (4) 10.00
BK236 BC126 $9.60 **blue,** 2 #3030b (3) 20.00

Varieties

3030g As "a," stamps 1-5 with double impression of red (engr. "LOVE") 1,000.
3030h As "a," red (engr. "LOVE") omitted 1,200.
3030i As "a," die cutting omitted —
3030j As "e," two examples in booklet pane of 20 (No. 3030a) *1,000.*

3048a — A1847

Ten Self-adhesive Stamps for Postcards
USA 20
$2.00

3048a-3048c — BC128

1996

$2.00 fold-it-yourself booklet contains 10 self-adhesive 20c stamps
$2.00 booklet contains 10 self-adhesive 20c stamps

Serpentine Die Cut 10.4x10.8

3048a A1847 20c pane of 10, *Aug. 2, 1996,* P#S1111, S2222 4.00

By is nature, No. 3048a is a complete booklet (BC128). The peelable backing serves as a booklet cover.

3048b, 3048c — A1847

3048b A1847 20c Booklet pane of 4 70.00
3048c A1847 20c Booklet pane of 6 100.00

No. 3048a exists on two types of surface-tagged paper that exhibit either a solid appearance (P# S1111) or a grainy solid appearance (P# S1111 and S2222).

Nos. 3048b-3048c are from the vending machine booklet No. BK237 that has a glue strip at the top edge of the top pane, the peelable strip removed and the rouletting line 2mm lower than on No. 3048a on some booklets, when the panes are compared with bottoms aligned. Vending booklets with plate #S2222 always have gauge 8½ rouletting on booklet covers. Convertible booklets (No. 3048a) with plate #S2222 always have gauge 12½ rouletting on booklet covers. Vending booklets with plate #S1111 can have either 8½ or 12½ gauge rouletting on booklet cover, and it may be impossible to tell a vending booklet with 12½ gauge rouletting and plate #S1111 from a convertible booklet with peelable strip removed.

Combination Booklet

BK237 BC128 $2 **multicolored,** 1 ea #3048b, 3048c, P#S1111, S2222 175.00

3049a — A1853

Serpentine Die Cut 11.3x11.7

3049a A1853 32c pane of 20 + label, *Oct. 24, 1996,* P#S1111, S2222 13.00

By its nature, No. 3049a is a complete booklet (BC61B). The peelable backing, of which three types are known, serves as a booklet cover.

3049b, 3049c, 3049d — A1853

3049b A1853 32c pane of 4, *Dec. 1996,* no P# 2.60
3049c A1853 32c pane of 5 + label, *Dec. 1996,* P#S1111 3.50
3049d A1853 32c pane of 6, *Dec. 1996,* without P# 4.00

Fifteen Self-adhesive Stamps
USA32
$4.80
UNITED STATES POSTAL SERVICE
We Deliver For You.

3049b, 3049c, 3049d — BC129

1996

$4.80 booklet contains 15 self-adhesive 32c stamps
$9.60 booklet contains 30 self-adhesive 32c stamps

Combination Booklet

BK241 BC129 $4.80 **multicolored,** 1 ea #3049b-3049d, P#S1111 10.25

Booklet

BK242 BC129 $9.60 **multicolored,** 5 #3049d, P#S1111 20.00

The backing on Nos. BK241-BK242 is roulетted between each pane.

The plate # single in No. 3049c from No. BK241 is on the lower left stamp. In No. 3049d from BK242, P# single is the lower right stamp on the bottom pane of the booklet.

Variety

3049d Pane of 6 containing P# single 6.00

3050a, 3050c — A2350

3050a, 3050c, 3051Ab-3051Ac BC130

1998

$2.00 fold-it-yourself booklet contains 10 self-adhesive 20c stamps
$2.00 booklet contains 10 self-adhesive 20c stamps

1998 ***Serpentine Die Cut 11.2***

3050a A2350 20c pane of 10, *July 31, 1998,* P#V1111, V2222, V2232, V3233 — 6.50
P#V2342, V2343, V3232 — 75.00

Serpentine Die Cut 11

3050c A2350 20c pane of 10, *July 31, 1998,* P#V2333, V2342, V2343, V3232, V3243, V3333 — 35.00
P#V2232, V2332 — 70.00

By their nature Nos. 3050a and 3050c are complete booklets (BC130). The peelable backing serves as a booklet cover. All stamps in Nos. 3050a and 3050c are upright.

3051Ab, 3051Ac — A2350

Serpentine Die Cut 10½x11 on 3 Sides (#3051), 10.6x10.4 on 3 sides (#3051A)

1999 **Self-Adhesive**

3051Ab A2350 20c pane, 4 #3051, 1 #3051A turned sideways at top, *July 1999* — 10.00

3051Ac A2350 20c pane, 4 #3051, 1 #3051A turned sideways at bottom, *July 1999* — 10.00

Booklet

BK242A BC130 $2.00 **multicolored,** #3051Ab, 3051Ac, P#V1111, *July 1999* — 20.00

3052a-3052c — A2351

Serpentine Die Cut 11½x11¼

3052a	A2351	33c pane of 4, no P#	3.60
3052b	A2351	33c pane of 5 + label, no P#	4.50
3052c	A2351	33c pane of 6, P#S111	5.50

3052a-3052c — BC131A

1999

$4.95 booklet contains 15 self-adhesive 33c stamps + label

Combination Booklet

BK242B BC131A $4.95 **multicolored,** 1 each #3052a-3052c, P#S111, *Aug. 13, 1999* — 13.75

No. BK242B has a self-adhesive strip on #3052b that adheres to the plastic-coated peelable backing of #3052a when the booklet is closed. When the booklet is opened, this strip is sticky and may adhere firmly to mounts, album pages, etc. Removal of this strip will damage the backing paper of #3052b.

Plate number for No. BK242B is on backing paper below bar code on No. 3052c.

3052d — A2351

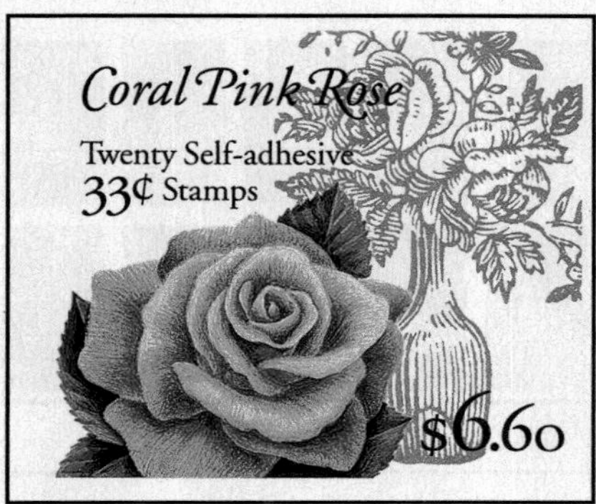

3052d — BC131

1999

$6.60 fold-it-yourself booklet contains 20 self-adhesive 33c stamps + label

3052d A2351 33c pane of 20 + label, P#S111, S222 — 17.50

No. 3052d is a complete booklet (BC131). The peelable backing serves as a booklet cover.

Variety

3052k As "d," die cutting omitted — *5,500.*

3052Ef — A2351

Serpentine Die Cut 10¾x10½ on 2 or 3 Sides

2000

3052Ef A2351 33c pane of 20, *Apr. 7, 2000,* P#S111, S222, S333 — 15.00

By its nature, No. 3052Ef is a complete booklet. Eight stamps and the booklet cover (similar to BC131) are printed on one side of the peelable backing and twelve stamps plus P# appear on the other side of the backing.

Varieties

3052Eh As "f," all 12 stamps on one side with black ("33 USA," etc.) omitted — —

3052Ej As "f," vert. die cutting missing between (PS) — —

3071a — A2370

3071a — BC127

1996

$6.40 fold-it-yourself booklet contains 20 self-adhesive 32c stamps

Serpentine Die Cut 9.9x10.8

3071a A2370 32c pane of 20, *May 31, 1996,* P#S11111 13.00

By its nature, No. 3071a is a complete booklet (BC127). The peelable backing serves as a booklet cover.

3089a — A2387

3089a — BC133

1996

$6.40 fold-it-yourself booklet contains 20 self-adhesive 32c stamps

Serpentine Die Cut 11.6x11.4

3089a A2387 32c pane of 20, *Aug. 1, 1996,* P#B1111 13.00

By its nature, No. 3089a is a complete booklet (BC133). The peelable backing serves as a booklet cover.

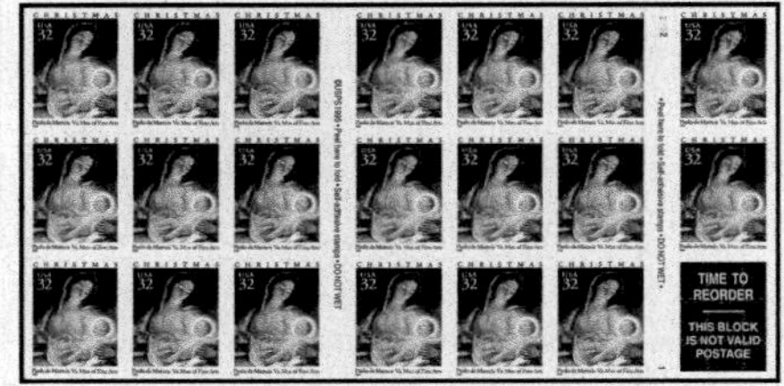
3112a — A2405

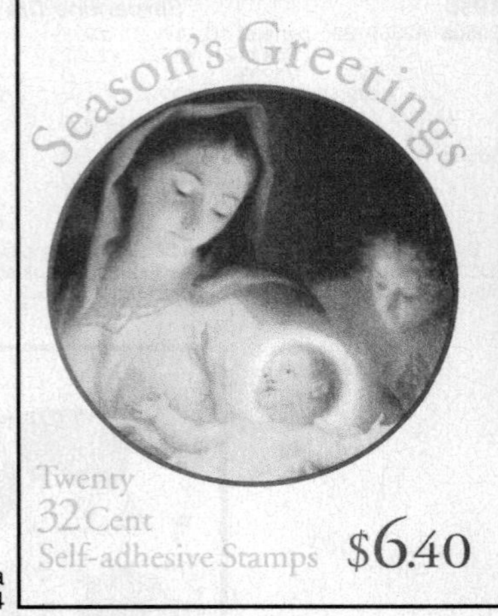

3112a
BC134

1996

$6.40 fold-it-yourself booklet contains 20 self-adhesive 32c stamps

Serpentine Die Cut 10 on 2, 3 or 4 Sides

3112a A2405 32c pane of 20 + label, *Nov. 1, 1996* 15.00

Variety

3112c As "a," die cutting omitted *400.00*
3112d As "a," top seven stamps with black (engr.) missing (PS) —

By its nature No. 3112a is a complete booklet (BC134). The peelable backing serves as a booklet cover.

No. 3112d is missing the black lettering at bottom due to a small upward shift of the horizontal perforations. This lettering is the only engraved black on the stamp.

Below is a list of known plate numbers. Some numbers may be scarcer than the value indicated in the listing.

P#1111-1, 1211-1, 2212-1, 2222-1, 2323-1, 3323-1, 3333-1, 3334-1, 4444-1, 5544-1, 5555-1, 5556-1, 5556-2, 5656-2, 6656-2, 6666-1, 6666-2, 6766-1, 7887-1, 7887-2, 7888-2, 7988-2.

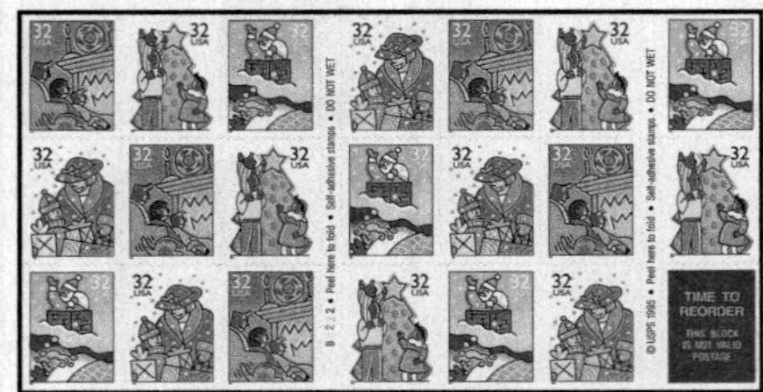
3116a — A2406-2409

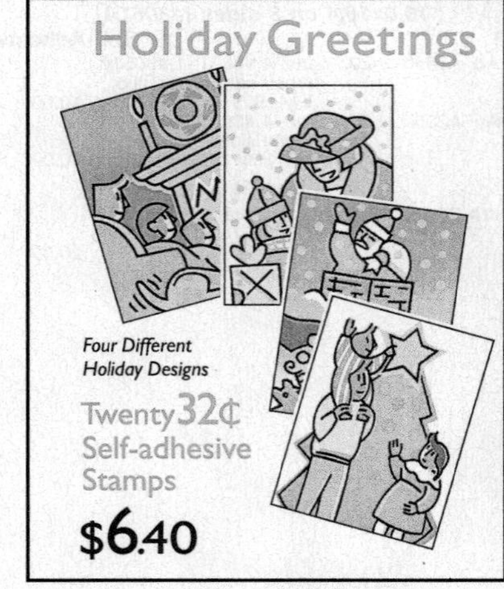

3116a — BC135

1996

$6.40 fold-it-yourself booklet contains 20 self-adhesive 32c stamps

Serpentine Die Cut 11.8x11.5 on 2, 3 or 4 Sides

3116a A2406 32c pane of 20 + label, *Oct. 8, 1996*, P#B1111, B2222, B3333 — 13.00

Variety

3116c As "a," die cutting omitted — *1,250.*

By its nature No. 3116a is a complete booklet (BC135). The peelable backing serves as a booklet cover.

3117a — A2410

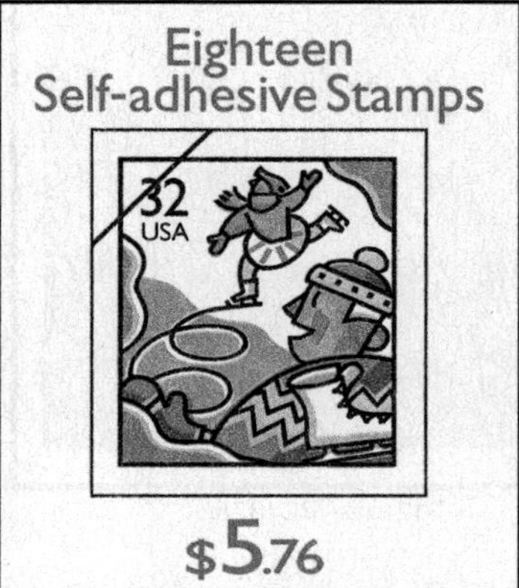

3117a
BC136

1996

$5.76 fold-it-yourself booklet contains 18 self-adhesive 32c stamps

Die Cut

3117a A2410 32c pane of 18, *Oct. 8, 1996*, P#V1111, V2111 — 12.00

By its nature No. 3117a is a complete booklet (BC136). The peelable backing serves as a booklet cover.

MAKESHIFT VENDING MACHINE BOOKLETS

The booklets listed below were released in 1996 to meet the need for $4.80 and $9.60 vending machine booklets. The booklets consist of blocks of sheet stamps folded and affixed to a standard cover (BC126) with a spot of glue.

The cover varies from issue to issue in the line of text on the front that indicates the number of stamps contained in the booklet and in the four lines of text on the back that describe the contents of the booklet and list the booklet's item number. Due to the folding required to make stamps fit within the covers, the stamp blocks may easily fall apart when booklets are opened. Stamps may also easily detach from booklet cover.

Front

Back — BC126

1996

$4.80 booklet contains 15 32c stamps
$9.60 booklet contains 30 32c stamps

A number of different stamps have been sold in BC126. The text on the front and back changes to describe the contents of the booklet. The enclosed stamps are affixed to the cover with a spot of glue.

Booklets

BK243	BC126	$4.80	**blue,** 15 #2897 (32c Flag Over Porch)	11.50
BK244	BC126	$4.80	**blue,** 15 #2957 (32c Cherub/Love)	11.50
BK245	BC126	$4.80	**blue,** 15 #3024 (32c Utah)	13.00
BK246	BC126	$4.80	**blue,** 15 #3065 (32c Fulbright Scholarships)	11.50
BK247	BC126	$4.80	**blue,** 15 #3069 (32c Georgia O'Keeffe)	11.25
BK248	BC126	$4.80	**blue,** 15 #3070 (32c Tennessee)	11.50
BK249	BC126	$4.80	**blue,** 3 #3076a (32c Indian Dances)	12.00
BK250	BC126	$4.80	**blue,** 15 #3082 (32c James Dean)	13.50
BK251	BC126	$4.80	**blue,** 15 (#3083-3086) (32c Folk Heroes)	11.00
BK252	BC126	$4.80	**blue,** 15 #3087 (32c Olympic Centennial)	12.50
BK253	BC126	$4.80	**blue,** 15 #3088 (32c Iowa)	12.00
BK254	BC126	$9.60	**blue,** 30 #3090 (32c Rural Free Delivery)	25.00
BK255	BC126	$4.80	**blue,** 3 #3095a (32c Riverboats)	13.00
BK256	BC126	$4.80	**blue,** #3105a-3105o (32c Endangered Species)	12.00
BK257	BC126	$4.80	**blue,** 15 #3107 (32c Madonna Christmas)	11.00
BK258	BC126	$4.80	**blue,** 15 #3118 (32c Hanukkah)	11.00

The contents of #BK251 may vary.

See Nos. BK178A-BK178F, BK226A-BK226B, BK227, BK233A-BK233E, BK235-BK236, BK266-BK269, BK272-BK274, BK277-BK278.

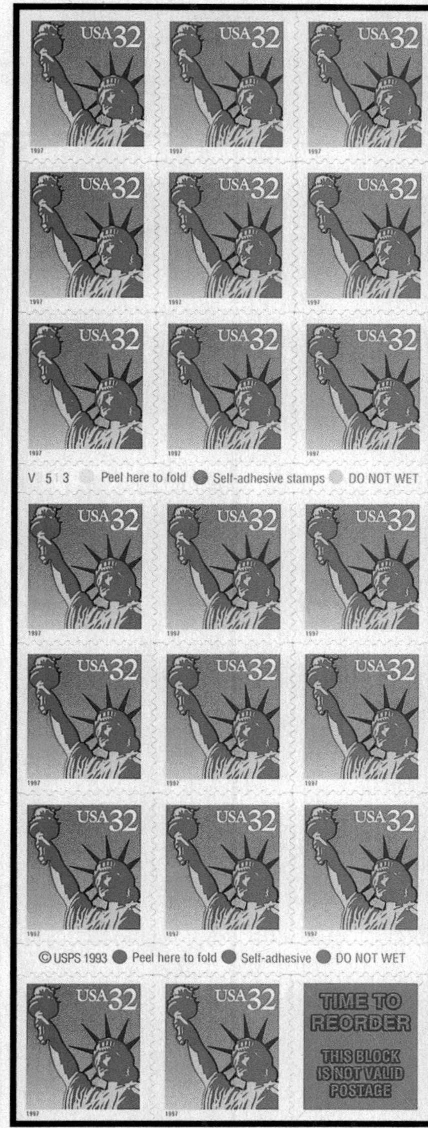

3122a — A1951

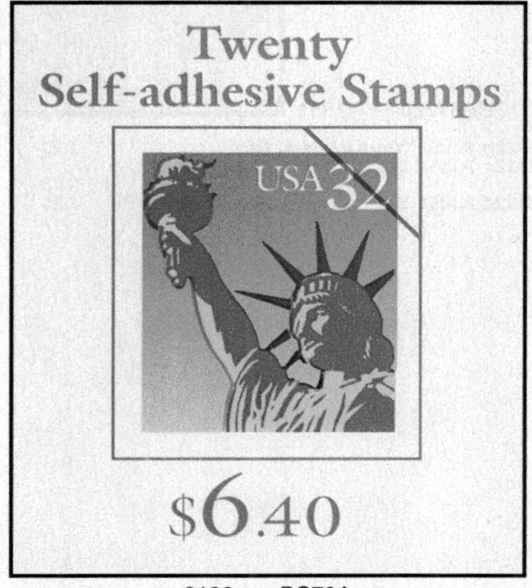

3122a — BC79A

1997

$6.40 fold-it-yourself booklet contains 20 self-adhesive 32c stamps

Serpentine Die Cut 11

3122a A1951 32c pane of 20 + label, *Feb. 1,* P#V1111, V1211, V1311, V2122, V2222, V2311, V2331, V3233, V3333, V3513, V4532 14.00

Variety

3122h As "a," die cutting omitted —

By its nature, No. 3122a is a complete booklet (BC79A). The peelable backing, of which two versions are known, serves as a booklet cover.

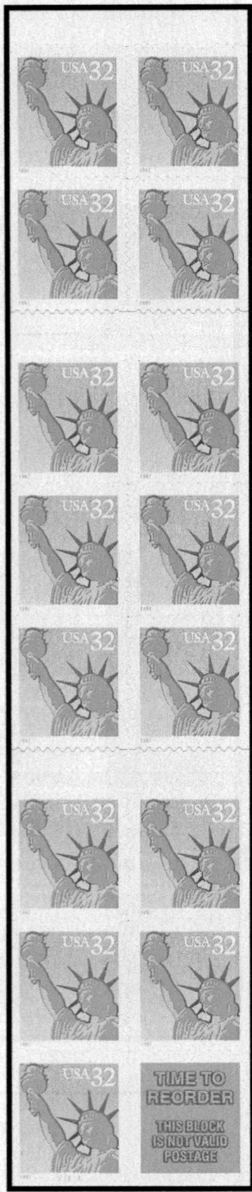

3122b-3122d — A1951

3122b A1951 32c pane of 4, *Feb. 1,* no P# 2.80
3122c A1951 32c pane of 5 + label, *Feb. 1,* P#V1111 3.75
3122d A1951 32c pane of 6, *Feb. 1,* without P# 4.25

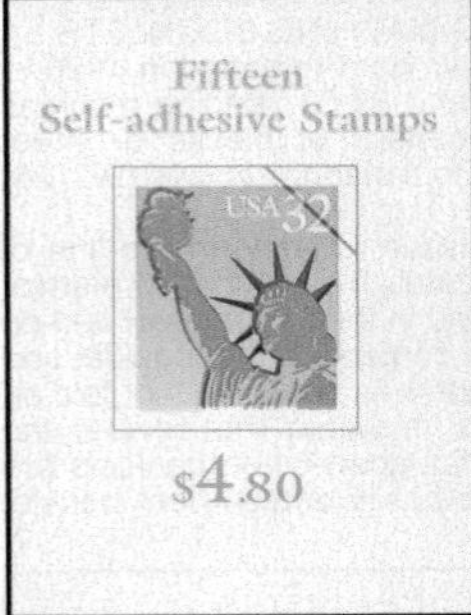

3122b-3122d — BC79B

1997

$4.80 fold-it-yourself booklet contains 15 self-adhesive 32c stamps
$9.60 fold-it-yourself booklet contains 30 self-adhesive 32c stamps

Combination Booklet

BK259 BC79B $4.80 **multicolored,** 1 ea #3122b-3122d, P#V1111 11.00

Booklet

BK260 BC79B $9.60 **multicolored,** 5 #3122d, P#V1111 23.00

The backing on Nos. BK259-BK260 is roulletted between each pane.

Variety

3122d pane of 6 containing P# single 6.00

The plate # single in No. 3122c is the lower left stamp and should be collected unused with the reorder label to its right to differentiate it from the plate # single in No. 3122d which is the lower left stamp in the bottom pane of the booklet and should be collected with a normal stamp adjoining it at right. In used condition, these plate # singles are indistinguishable.

Serpentine Die Cut 11.5x11.8 on 2, 3 or 4 Sides

3122Ef A1951 32c pane of 20 + label, P#V1211, V2122, V2222 40.00
P#V1111 60.00

By its nature, No. 3122Ef is a complete booklet (BC79A). The peelable backing, of which two versions are known, serves as a booklet cover.

3122Eg A1951 32c pane of 6, *1997,* without plate # single 9.00

Booklet

BK260A BC79B $9.60 **multicolored,** 5 #3122Eg, P#V1111 50.00

Variety

3122Eg pane of 6 containing P# single 13.50

The plate # single in No. 3122Eg from No. BK260A is the lower left stamp in the bottom pane of the booklet.

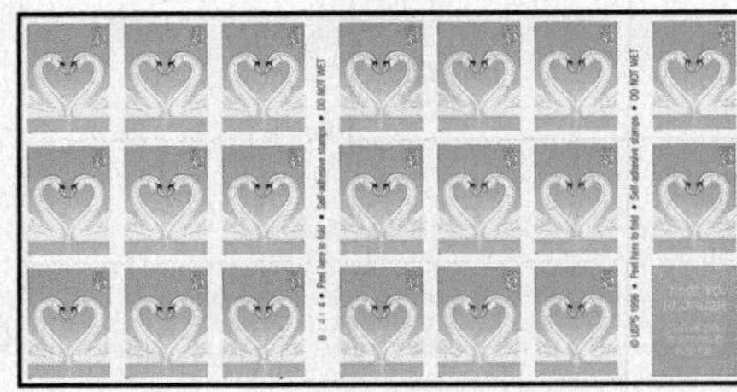

3123a — A2415

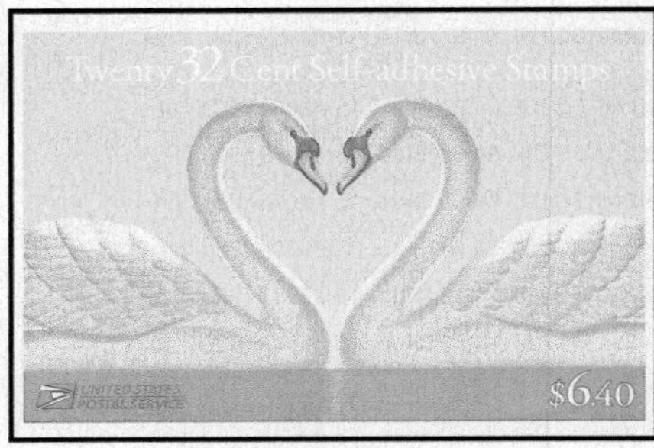

3123a — BC137

1997

$6.40 fold-it-yourself booklet contains 20 self-adhesive 32c stamps

Serpentine Die Cut 11.8x11.6 on 2, 3 or 4 Sides

3123a A2415 32c pane of 20 + label, *Feb. 4,* P#B1111, B2222, B3333, B4444, B5555, B6666, B7777 13.00

Varieties

3123c As "a," die cutting omitted *1,000.*
3123d As "a," black omitted —

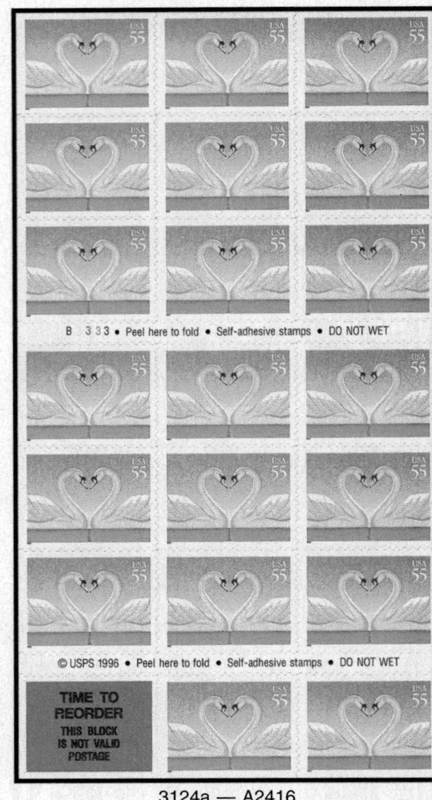

3124a — A2416

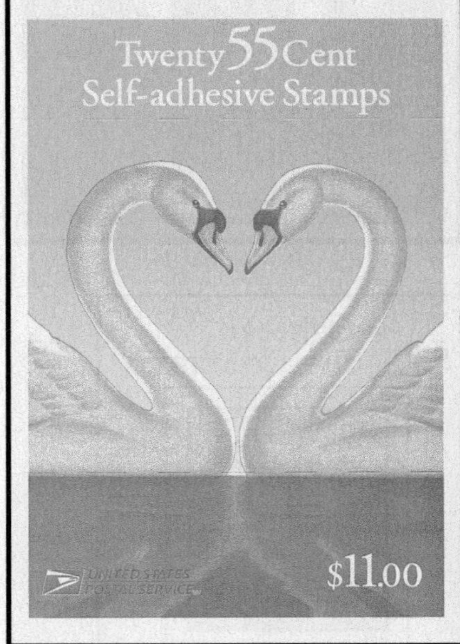

3124a — BC137A

1997

$11 fold-it-yourself booklet contains 20 self-adhesive 55c stamps

Serpentine Die Cut 11.6x11.8 on 2, 3 or 4 Sides

3124a A2416 55c pane of 20 + label, *Feb. 4,* P#B1111, B2222, B3333, B4444 22.00

By their nature, Nos. 3123a-3124a are complete booklets (BC137 and BC137A). The peelable backing serves as a booklet cover.

3127a — A2418-A2419

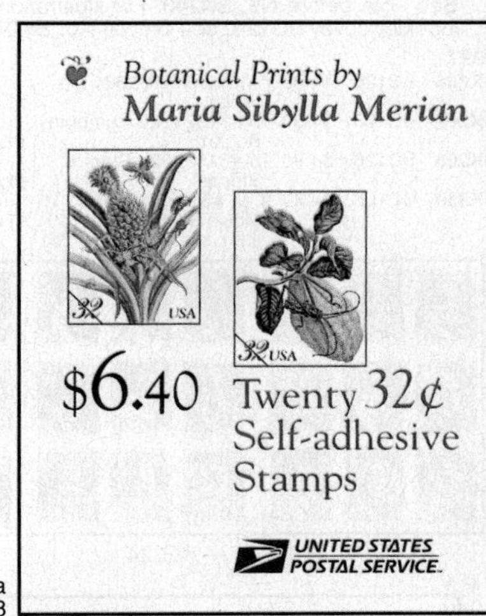

3127a
BC138

1997

$6.40 fold-it-yourself booklet contains 20 32c stamps

Serpentine Die Cut 10.9x10.2 on 2, 3 or 4 Sides

3127a A2418 32c pane of 20 + label, 10 ea #3126-3127, *Mar. 3,* P#S11111, S22222, S33333 13.00

By its nature, No. 3127a is a complete booklet (BC138). The peelable backing serves as a booklet cover.

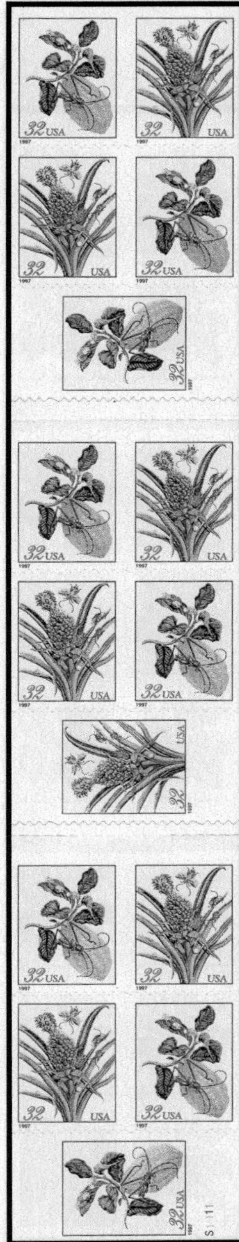
3128b, 3129b — A2418-A2419

3128b A2418 32c pane of 5, 2 ea #3128-3129, 1 #3128a, *Mar. 3,* no P# or P#S11111 6.50

3129b A2419 32c pane of 5, 2 ea #3128-3129, 1 #3129a, *Mar. 3,* no P# 8.50

3128b, 3129b — BC138A

1997

$4.80 booklet contains 15 32c stamps

Combination Booklet

BK261 BC138A $4.80 2 #3128b, 1 #3129b, P#S11111 21.50

In No. BK261, No. 3128b at top has no plate #, while the No. 3128b at bottom has a plate # in the selvage.

3176a — A2459

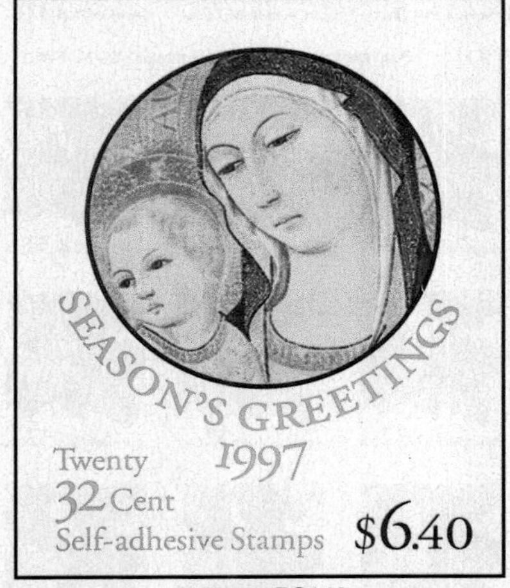

3176a — BC140

1997

$6.40 fold-it-yourself booklet contains 20 self-adhesive 32c stamps

Serpentine Die Cut 9.9 on 2, 3 or 4 Sides

1997, Oct. 27 **Tagged**

3176a A2459 32c pane of 20 + label, P#1111, 2222, 3333 13.00

By its nature, No. 3176a is a complete booklet (BC140). The peelable backing serves as a booklet cover.

3177a — A2460

3177a BC141

1997

$6.40 fold-it-yourself booklet contains 20 self-adhesive 32c stamps

Serpentine Die Cut 11.2x11.6 on 2, 3 or 4 Sides

1997, Oct. 30 **Tagged**

Self-Adhesive

3177a A2460 32c pane of 20 + label, P#B1111, B2222, B3333 13.00

By its nature No. 3177a is a complete booklet (BC141). The peelable backing serves as a booklet cover.

3177b-3177d — A2460

3177b	A2460	32c	Booklet pane of 4, no P#	2.60
3177c	A2460	32c	Booklet pane of 5 + label, no P#	3.25
3177d	A2460	32c	Booklet pane of 6, no P# or P#B1111	3.90

3177b-3177d — BC141A

1997

$4.80 booklet contains 15 self-adhesive 32c stamps

$9.60 booklet contains 30 self-adhesive 32c stamps

Combination Booklet

BK264 BC141A $4.80 **black & green,** 1 ea #3177b-3177d, P#B1111 9.75

Booklet

BK265 BC141A $9.60 **black & green,** 5 #3177d, P#B1111 20.00

Panes in Nos. BK264-BK265 are separated by rouletting between each pane.

MAKESHIFT VENDING MACHINE BOOKLETS

See note before No. BK243. For illustration of booklet cover BC126, see before No. BK243.

1997

BK266	BC126	$4.80	#3151a-3151o (32c Dolls)	11.00
BK267	BC126	$4.80	15 #3152 (32c Humphrey Bogart)	11.00
BK268	BC126	$4.80	15 #3153 (32c Stars & Stripes)	11.00
BK269	BC126	$4.80	3 ea #3168-3172 (32c Movie Monsters)	11.00

3244a — A2524

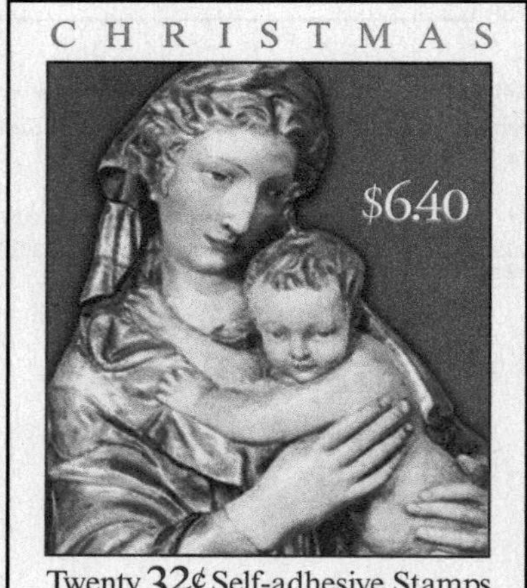

3244a — BC142

1998

$6.40 fold-it-yourself booklet contains 20 self-adhesive 32c stamps

Serpentine Die Cut 10.1x9.9 on 2, 3 or 4 Sides

1998, Oct. 15 **Tagged**

3244a A2524 32c pane of 20 + label, P#11111, 22222, 33333 13.00

No. 3244a is a complete booklet (BC142). The peelable backing serves as a booklet cover.

3248a-3248c — A2525-A2528

Serpentine Die Cut 11.3x11.6 on 2, or 3 Sides

1998, Oct. 15 **Tagged**

3248a	A2525	32c pane of 4, #3245-3248, no P#	13.00
3248b	A2525	32c pane of 5, #3245-3246, 3248, 2 #3247 + label, no P#	16.25
3248c	A2525	32c pane of 6, #3247-3248, 2 each #3245-3246, P#B111111	19.50

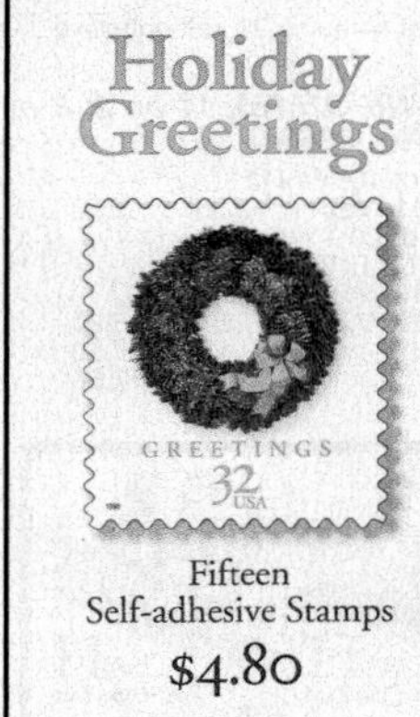

Holiday Greetings
GREETINGS
32 USA
Fifteen
Self-adhesive Stamps
$4.80

3248a-3248c — BC143

1998

$4.80 booklet contains 15 self-adhesive 32c stamps

Combination Booklet

BK270	BC143	$4.80 **multi**, 1 each #3248a-3248c, P#B111111	*50.00*

Varieties

3248d	A2525	32c As "a," die cutting omitted	—
3248e	A2525	32c As "b," die cutting omitted	—
3248f	A2525	32c As "c," die cutting omitted	—

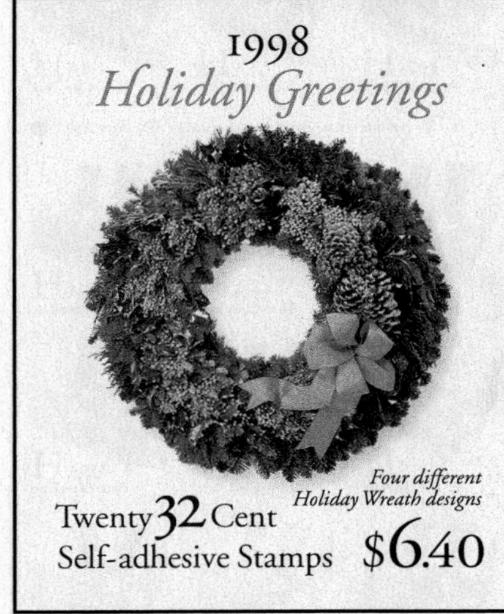

3252c, 3252e — BC143A

1998

$6.40 fold-it-yourself booklet contains 20 self-adhesive 32c stamps

Serpentine Die Cut 11.4x11.5 on 2, 3 or 4 Sides

3252c	A2525	32c pane of 20, 5 each #3249-3252 + label, P#B333333, B444444, B555555	27.00
		P#B222222	37.00

Serpentine Die Cut 11.7x11.6 on 2, 3 or 4 Sides

3252e	A2525	32c pane of 20, 5 each #3249a-3252a + label, P#B111111, B222222	35.00

Nos. 3252c and 3252e are complete booklets (BC143A). The peelable backing serves as a booklet cover.

Variety

3252i	As "c," die cutting omitted	*4,500.*

3267a — A2531

Serpentine Die Cut 9.9 on 2 or 3 Sides

1998, Nov. 9

3267a	A2531	(33c) pane of 10	7.50

3267a, 3268a — BC144

1998

($6.60) booklet contains 20 self-adhesive (33c) stamps
($3.30) fold-it-yourself booklet (#3268a) contains 10 self-adhesive (33c) stamps

Booklet

BK271	BC144	($6.60) **multi**, 2 #3267a, P#1111, 2222, 3333	15.00

3268c — A2531

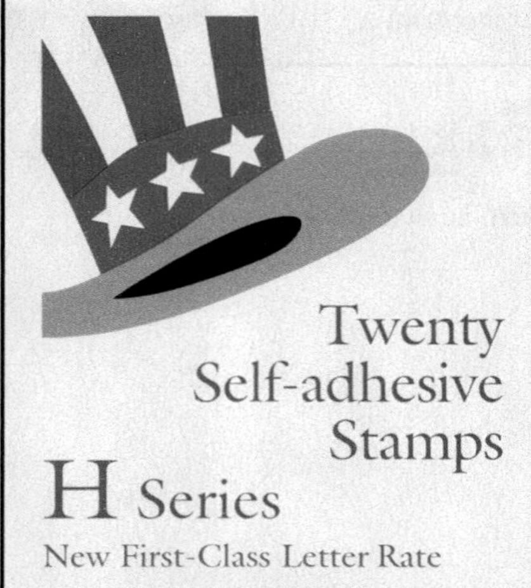

3268c — BC144A

1998
($6.60) fold-it-yourself booklet contains 20 self-adhesive (33c) stamps

Die cut 11¼ on 3 sides (No. 3268a), 11 on 2, 3 or 4 Sides (No. 3268c)

3268a	A2531	(33c) pane of 10, P#V1111, V1211, V2211, V2222	7.50
3268c	A2531	(33c) pane of 20 + label, P#V1111, V1112, V1113, V1213, V2113, V2122, V2213, V2223	15.00
		P# V1122	22.50
		P# V1222, V2222	17.50

3269a — A2531

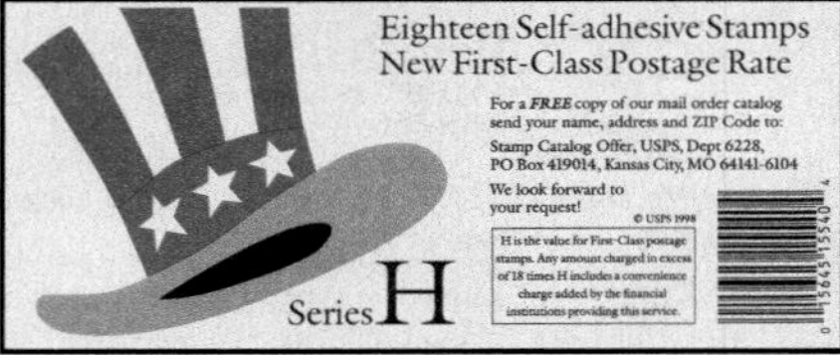

3269a — BC144B

1998
($5.94) fold-it-yourself booklet contains 18 self-adhesive (33c) stamps

Die Cut 8

3269a	A2531	(33c) pane of 18, P#V1111	12.00

Nos. 3268a, 3268c, 3269a are complete booklets (BC144, BC144A, BC144B). The peelable backing serves as a booket cover.

MAKESHIFT VENDING MACHINE BOOKLETS

See note before No. BK243. For illustration of booklet cover BC126, see before No. BK243.

1998

BK272	BC126	$4.80	15 (#3222-3225) (32c Tropical Birds)	11.00
BK273	BC126	$4.80	15 #3237 (32c Ballet)	11.00
BK274	BC126	$4.80	3 #3242a (32c Space Discovery)	11.50

Configuration of stamps in #BK272 may vary.

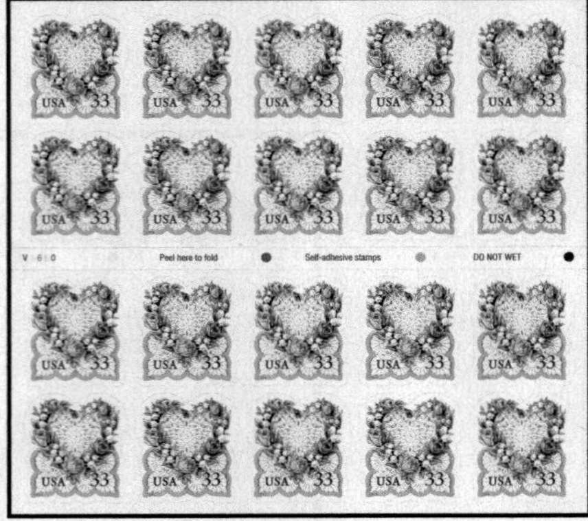
3274a — A2537

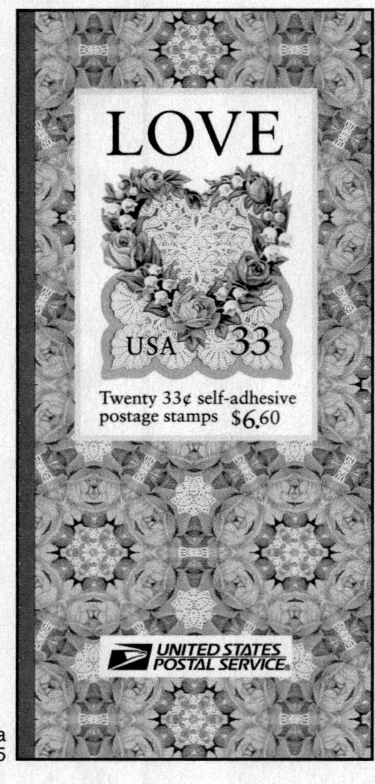

3274a
BC145

1999
$6.60 Fold-it-yourself booklet contains 20 self-adhesive 33c stamps

Tagged ***Die Cut***

3274a	A2537	33c pane of 20, *Jan. 28, 1999*	13.00

No. 3274a is a complete booklet (BC145). The peelable backing serves as a booklet cover.

Below is a list of known plate numbers. Some numbers are scarcer than the value indicated in the listing.

P#V1111, V1112, V1117, V1118, V1211, V1212, V1213, V1233, V1313, V1314, V1333, V1334, V1335, V2123, V2221, V2222, V2223, V2424, V2425, V2426, V2324, V3123, V3124, V3125, V3133, V3134, V3323, V3327, V3333, V3334, V3336, V4549, V5650.

Variety

3274c	As "a," die cutting omitted	*1,000.*

3278a-3278c — A2540

Serpentine Die Cut 11 on 2, 3 or 4 Sides

1999 **Tagged**

Self-Adhesive

3278a A2540 33c pane of 4, no P# 2.60
3278b A2540 33c pane of 5 + label, P#V1111, V1112, V1121, V1122, V1212, V2212 3.25
3278c A2540 33c pane of 6, no P# 3.90

3278a-3278c — BC146

1999

$4.95 booklet contains 15 self-adhesive 33c stamps

COMBINATION BOOKLET

BK275 BC146 $4.95 **multi,** 1 each #3278a-3278c, P#V1111, V1112, V1121, V1122, V1212, V2212 10.00

The plate # single in No. 3278b from No. BK275 is the lower left stamp in the bottom pane of the booklet.

3278d, 3278j — A2540

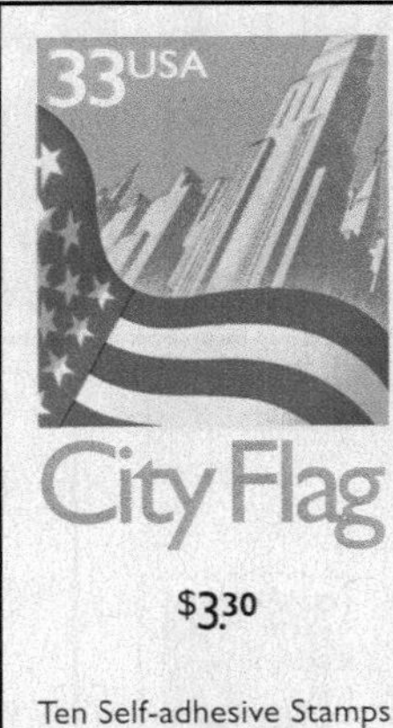

3278d — BC146A

1999

$3.30 Fold-it-yourself booklet contains 10 self-adhesive 33c stamps

3278d	A2540	33c pane of 10, P#V1113, V2322, V2324, V3433, V3434, V3545	13.00
		P#V1111	—
		P#V1112	35.00
		P#V2323	—

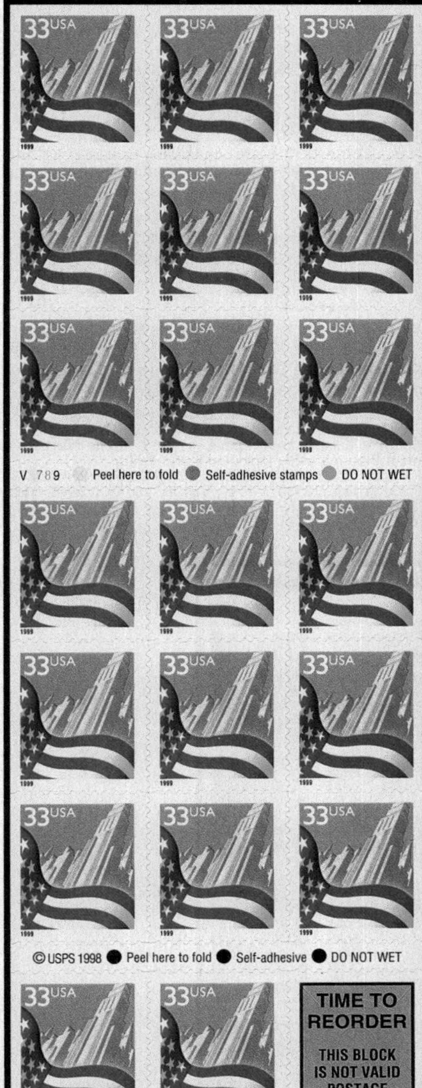

3278e, 3278Fg — A2540

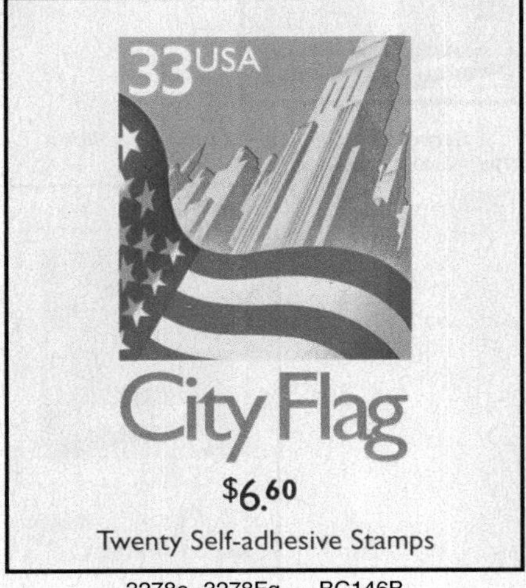

3278e, 3278Fg — BC146B

1999

$6.60 Fold-it-yourself booklet contains 20 self-adhesive 33c stamps

3278e A2540 33c pane of 20 + label, P#V1111, V1211, V2122, V2222, V2223, V3333, V4444 17.00
P#V8789 —

Nos. 3278d-3278e are complete booklets (BC146A, BC146B). The peelable backing serves as a booklet cover.

Variety

3278h As "e," die cutting omitted —

Serpentine Die Cut 11¼

3278j A2540 33c pane of 10, P#V2222 9.00
P#V1111, V1112 15.00
P#V1113, V2322 45.00
P#V3434 —

By its nature No. 3278j is a complete booklet. The peelable backing serves as a booklet cover and is similar to BC146A.

Serpentine Die Cut 11½x11¾ on 2, 3 or 4 Sides

3278Fg A2540 33c pane of 20 + label 28.00

No. 3278Fg is a complete booklet. The peelable backing serves as a booklet cover and is similar to BC146B.

Below is a list of known plate numbers. Some numbers are scarcer than the value indicated in the listing.

P# V1111, V1131, V2222, V2223, V2227, V2243, V2323, V2423, V2443, V3333, V4444, V5428, V5445, V5446, V5576, V5578, V6423, V6456, V6546, V6556, V6575, V6576, V7567, V7663, V7667, V7676, V8789.

3279a — A2540

Serpentine Die Cut 9.8 on 2 or 3 Sides

3279a A2540 33c pane of 10 8.50

3279a — BC146C

1999

$6.60 Booklet contains 20 self-adhesive 33c stamps

BOOKLET

BK276 BC146C $6.60 **multi,** 2 #3279a, P#1111, 1121 17.00

3283a — A2541

3283a — BC147

1999

$5.94 fold-it-yourself booklet contains 18 self-adhesive 33c stamps

Serpentine Die Cut 7.9 on 2, 3 or 4 Sides

Tagged

3283a A2541 33c pane of 18, P#V1111 12.00

No. 3283a is a complete booklet (BC147). The peelable backing serves as a booklet cover.

3297b — A2550-A2553

3297b BC148

1999

$6.60 fold-it-yourself booklet contains 20 self-adhesive 33c stamps + label

Serpentine Die Cut 11¼x11½ on 2, 3 or 4 Sides

1999-2000 **Tagged**

Self-Adhesive

3297b A2550 33c pane of 20, 5 ea #3294-3297 + label 17.50

No. 3297b is a complete booklet (BC148). The peelable backing serves as a booklet cover.

P#B1111, B1112, B2211, B2222, B3331, B3332, B3333, B4444, B5555.

3297d, BC148A — A2550-A2553

Serpentine Die Cut 11¼x11½ on 2 or 3 Sides

3297d A2550 33c pane of 20, 5 #3297e + label, *Mar. 15, 2000,* P#B1111 25.00

By its nature, No. 3297d is a double-sided complete booklet. Eight stamps and the booklet cover (BC148A) plus P# are printed on one side of the peelable backing and 12 stamps are printed on the other side of the backing.

3301a-3301c — A2550-A2553

Serpentine Die Cut 9½x10 on 2 or 3 sides

3301a	A2550	33c pane of 4, no P#	4.00
3301b	A2550	33c pane of 5 + label, no P#	5.00
3301c	A2550	33c pane of 6, P#B1111, B1112, B2212, B2222	6.00
		P#B2221	—

3301a-3301c — BC148B

1999

$4.95 booklet contains 15 self-adhesive 33c stamps + label

COMBINATION BOOKLET

BK276A BC148B $4.95 **multicolored,** 1 each #3301a-3301c, P# see 3301c 17.00

3313b, BC149 — A2556-A2559

Serpentine Die Cut 10.9 on 2 or 3 Sides

1999 **Tagged**

3313b A2556 33c pane of 20, all P# (see below) except P#S22444 13.00
P#S22444 *2,500.*

By its nature, No. 3313b is a complete booklet. Eight stamps and the booklet cover (BC149) plus P# are printed on one side of the peelable backing and 12 stamps are printed on the other side of the backing.

P#S11111, S22222, S22244, S22344, S22444, S22452, S22462, S23222, S24222, S24224, S24242, S24244, S24422, S24442, S24444, S26462, S32323, S32333, S32444, S33333, S44444, S45552, S46654, S55452, S55552, S56462, S62544, S62562, S64452, S64544, S65544, S65552, S66462, S66544, S66552, S66562, S66652.

3355a, BC150 — A2599

1999, Oct. 20 ***Serpentine Die Cut 11¼***

Self-Adhesive

3355a A2599 33c pane of 20, P#B1111, B2222, B3333 18.00

No. 3355a is a complete booklet. Eight stamps and the booklet cover (BC150) plus P# are printed on one side of the peelable backing and 12 stamps are printed on the other side of the backing.

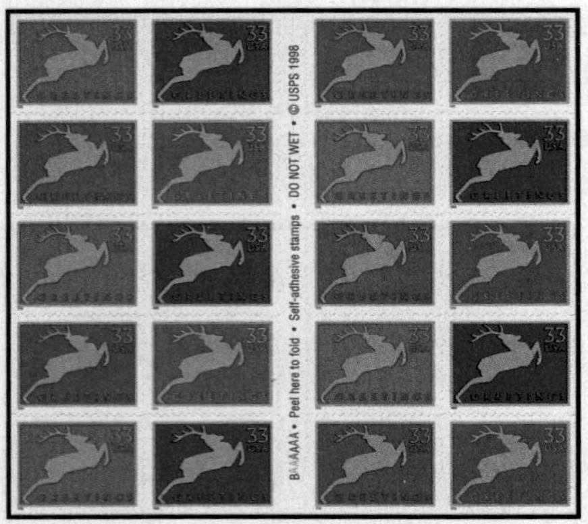

3363a — A2600

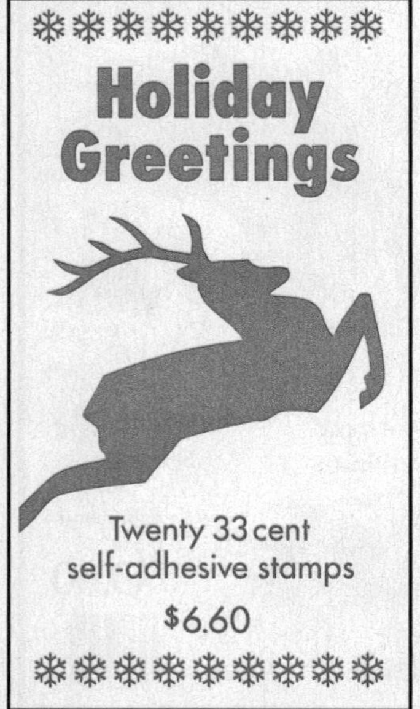

3363a
BC151

1999

$6.60 fold-it-yourself booklet contains 20 self-adhesive 33c stamps

1999, Oct. 20 ***Serpentine Die Cut 11¼***

Self-Adhesive

3363a A2600 33c pane of 20, P#B111111, B222222, B333333, B444444, B555555, B666666, B777777, B888888, B999999, B000000, BAAAAAA, BBBBBBB 22.50

No. 3363a is a complete booklet (BC151). The peelable backing serves as a booklet cover.

Variety

3363d As "a," die cutting omitted *500.00*

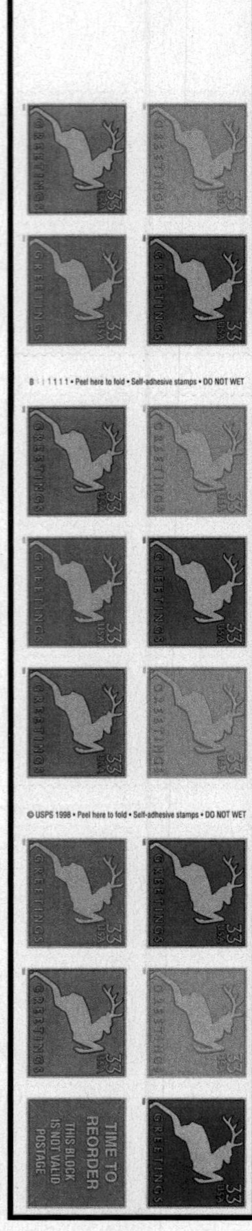

3367a-3367c — A2600

Serpentine Die Cut 11½x11¼ on 2 or 3 sides

Stamp Size: 21x19mm

3367a A2600 33c pane of 4, no P# 5.50
3367b A2600 33c pane of 5 + label, no P# 7.00
3367c A2600 33c pane of 6, P#B111111, B222222 8.00

3367a-3367c — BC152

1999

$4.95 fold-it-yourself booklet contains 15 self-adhesive 33c stamps

COMBINATION BOOKLET

BK276B BC152 $4.95 **green & gold,** 1 each #3367a-3367c, P# see 3367c 21.00

MAKESHIFT VENDING MACHINE BOOKLETS

See note before No. BK243. For illustration of booklet cover BC126, see before No. BK243.

1999

BK277 BC126 $4.95 4 each #3325, 3327-3328, 3 #3326 (33c American Glass) 11.00
BK278 BC126 $4.95 3 each #3333-3337 (33c Famous Trains) 11.00

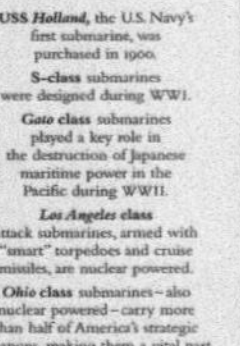

3377a — A2604-A2608

THE DOLPHIN PIN

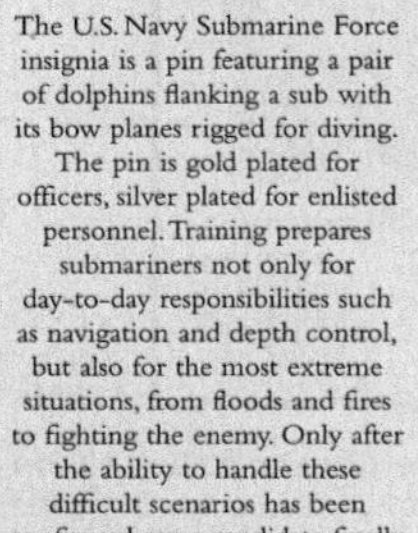

The U.S. Navy Submarine Force insignia is a pin featuring a pair of dolphins flanking a sub with its bow planes rigged for diving. The pin is gold plated for officers, silver plated for enlisted personnel. Training prepares submariners not only for day-to-day responsibilities such as navigation and depth control, but also for the most extreme situations, from floods and fires to fighting the enemy. Only after the ability to handle these difficult scenarios has been confirmed can a candidate finally wear the coveted "dolphins."

Selvage 1

THE SUBMARINE STAMPS
U.S. Navy Submarines
A Century of Service to America

USS ***Holland,*** the U.S. Navy's first submarine, was purchased in 1900.

S-class submarines were designed during WWI.

Gato **class** submarines played a key role in the destruction of Japanese maritime power in the Pacific during WWII.

Los Angeles **class** attack submarines, armed with "smart" torpedoes and cruise missiles, are nuclear powered.

Ohio **class** submarines—also nuclear powered—carry more than half of America's strategic weapons, making them a vital part of America's nuclear deterrence.

Selvage 2

2000, Mar. 27 ***Perf. 11***

3377a pane of 5 with selvage 1 15.00 —
With selvage 2 15.00 —

3377a — BC153

2000

$9.80 booklet contains 2 panes of one 22c, 33c, 55c, 60c and $3.20 stamps and 6 leaves of text.

Booklet

BK279 BC153 $9.80 **multicolored,** no P# 30.00

No. BK279 contains one pane with selvage 1 and one pane with selvage 2.

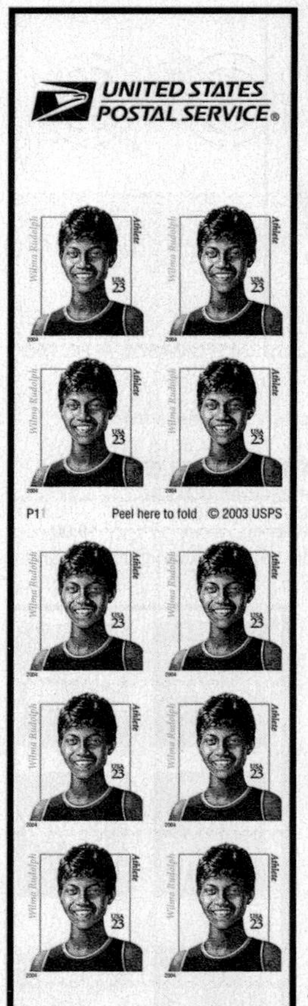

3436a, 3436b, 3436c — A2652

Serpentine Die Cut 11¼x10¾ on 3 Sides

2004, July 14 Self-Adhesive Litho.

3436a A2652 23c pane of 4, no P# 1.80
3436b A2652 23c pane of 6, no P# 2.70
3436c A2652 23c As "a" & "b" in cplt booklet of 10 (No. BK279A), die cutting omitted and peel strip intact, P#P44 —
3436d A2652 23c pane of 10, P#P11, P22 4.50

3436a, 3436b, 3436d — BC153A

2004

$2.30 booklet contains 10 self-adhesive 23c stamps

$2.30 fold-it-yourself booklet contains 10 self-adhesive 23c stamps

COMBINATION BOOKLET

BK279A BC153A $2.30 **multi,** #3436a-3436b, no P# 4.50

By its nature, No. 3436d is a complete booklet (BC153A). The peelable backing serves as a booklet cover. No. BK279A lacks the self-adhesive panel that covers the rouletting. The backing on No. 3436b has a different product code (672900) than that found on the lower portion of No. 3436c (673000).

Variety

3436e A2652 As "d," die cutting omitted —

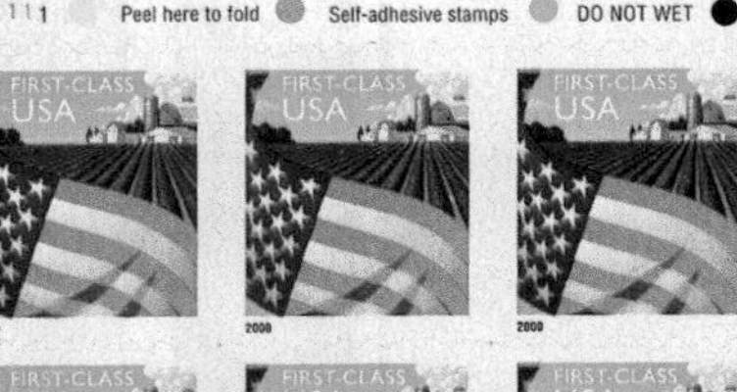

3450a — A2678

3450a BC154

2000

$6.12 fold-it-yourself booklet contains 18 self-adhesive (34c) stamps

2000 ***Serpentine Die Cut 8 on 2, 3 or 4 Sides***

Self-Adhesive

3450a A2678 (34c) pane of 18, P#V1111, *Dec. 15* 16.00

No. 3450a is a complete booklet (BC154). The peelable backing serves as a booklet cover.

3451a — A2679

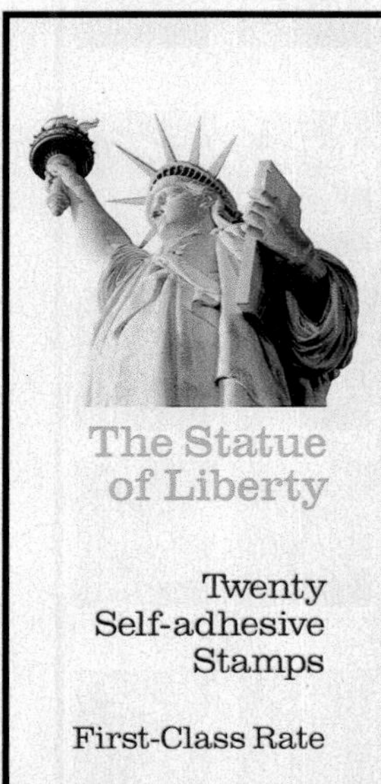

3451a — BC155

2000

$6.80 fold-it-yourself booklet contains 20 self-adhesive (34c) stamps

Serpentine Die Cut 11 on 2, 3 or 4 Sides

2000, Dec. 15 Self-Adhesive

3451a A2679 (34c) pane of 20, P#V1111, V2222 14.00

No. 3451a is a complete booklet (BC155). The peelable backing serves as a booklet cover.

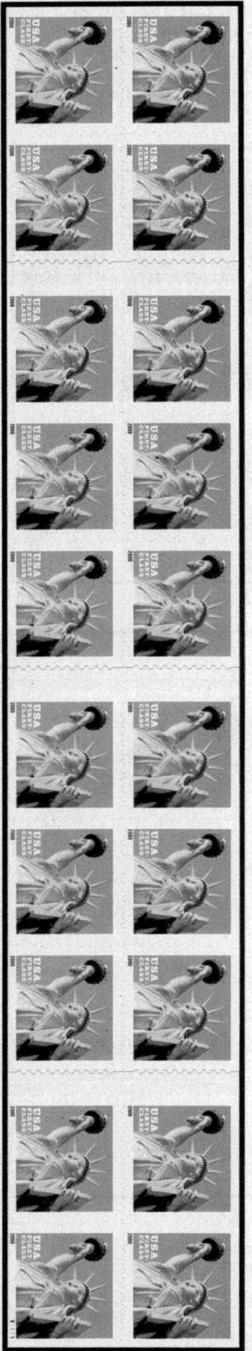
3451b-3451c — A2679

3451b A2679 (34c) pane of 4, without plate # 3.00
3451c A2679 (34c) pane of 6, no P# 5.75

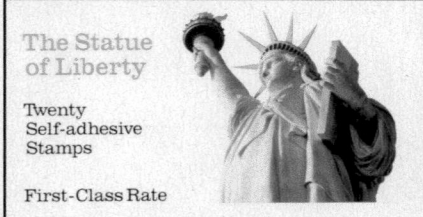

3451b, 3451c — BC156

2000

$6.80 booklet contains 20 self-adhesive (34c) stamps

COMBINATION BOOKLET

BK280 BC156 ($6.80) **multicolored,** 1 #3451b without P#, 1 #3451b with P#V1111 or V2222, 2 #3451c 20.00

The plate # on No. 3451b from No. BK280 is on the lower right stamp of the right pane of 4 of the booklet.

Varieties

3451b pane of 4, containing P# single 4.50
3451d As "a," die cutting omitted —

3457b-3457d — A2681-A2684

Serpentine Die Cut 10½x10¾ on 2 or 3 Sides (#3454-3457), 11½x11¾ on 2 or 3 sides (#3458-3461)

2000 **Self-Adhesive**

3457b A2681 (34c) pane of 4, #3454-3457, *Dec. 15* 4.25
3457c A2681 (34c) pane of 6, #3456, 3457, 2 each #3454-3455, no P#, *Dec. 15* 7.00
3457d A2681 (34c) pane of 6, #3454, 3455, 2 each #3456-3457, no P#, *Dec. 15* 7.00

3457b-3457d — BC158

2000

$6.80 booklet contains 20 self-adhesive (34c) stamps

COMBINATION BOOKLET

BK281 BC158 ($6.80) **multicolored,** #3457c, 3457d, 2 #3457b, P#S1111 19.00

P# on No. BK281 is on the backing paper of the top pane of No. 3457b.

3457e, BC157 — A2681-A2684

3457e A2681 (34c) pane of 20, 5 each # 3454-3457, P#S1111, *Dec. 15* 22.50

No. 3457e is a complete booklet. Eight stamps and the booklet cover (BC157) are printed on one side of the peelable backing and 12 stamps plus P# are printed on the other side of the backing.

3461b A2681 pane of 20, 2 each #3461a, 3 each #3457a, #S1111, *Dec. 15* 55.00
3461c A2681 pane of 20, 2 each #3457a, 3 each #3461a, #S1111, *Dec. 15* 90.00

Nos. 3461b and 3461c are complete booklets. Two blocks of four with the same gauge die cutting and the booklet cover (BC157) are printed on one side of the peelable backing and three blocks of four with the other gauge die cutting plus P# are printed on the other side of the backing.

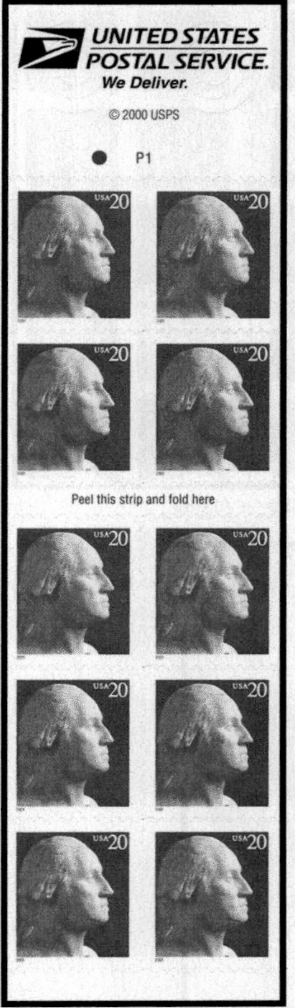

3482a, 3483c, 3483f — A2686

3482a, 3483c, 3483f — BC159

2001

$2 fold-it-yourself booklet contains 10 self-adhesive 20c stamps
$2 booklet contains 10 self-adhesive 20c stamps

Serpentine Die Cut 11¼x11 on 3 Sides

2001, Feb. 22 **Self-Adhesive**

3482a A2686 20c pane of 10, P#P1, P2, P3 5.50

3482b, 3483c — A2686

3482b A2686 20c pane of 4, P#P1, P2, P3 2.20
3482c A2686 20c pane of 6, no P# 3.30

COMBINATION BOOKLET

BK281A BC159 $2 **multicolored,** #3482b-3482c, P#P1, P2 5.50
P#P3 10.00

No. BK281A has slightly smaller cover (BC159) than No. 3482a and lacks self-adhesive panel that covers the rouletting.

3483a A2686 20c pane of 4, 2 #3482 at L, 2 #3483 at R, P#P1, P2, P3 12.50
3483b A2686 20c pane of 6, 3 #3482 at L, 3 #3483 at R, no P# 20.00
3483c A2686 20c pane of 10, 5 #3482 at L, 5 #3483 at R, P#P1, P2 30.00
P#P3 45.00
3483d A2686 20c pane of 4, 2 #3483 at L, 2 #3282 at R, P#P1, P2, P3 12.50
3483e A2686 20c pane of 6, 3 #3483 at L, 3 #3282 at R, no P# 20.00
3483f A2686 20c pane of 10, 5 #3483 at L, 5 #3282 at R, P#P1, P2 30.00
P#P3 45.00

Nos. 3482a, 3483c and 3483f are complete booklets (BC159) and include a self-adhesive panel that covers the rouletting. The peelable backing, which is slightly longer than that on Nos. BK282 and BK282A, serves as a booklet cover.

COMBINATION BOOKLETS

BK282 BC159 $2 **multicolored,** #3483a-3483b, P#P1, P2 32.50
P#P3 *55.00*
BK282A BC159 $2 **multicolored,** #3483d-3483e, P#P1, P2 32.50
P#P3 *55.00*

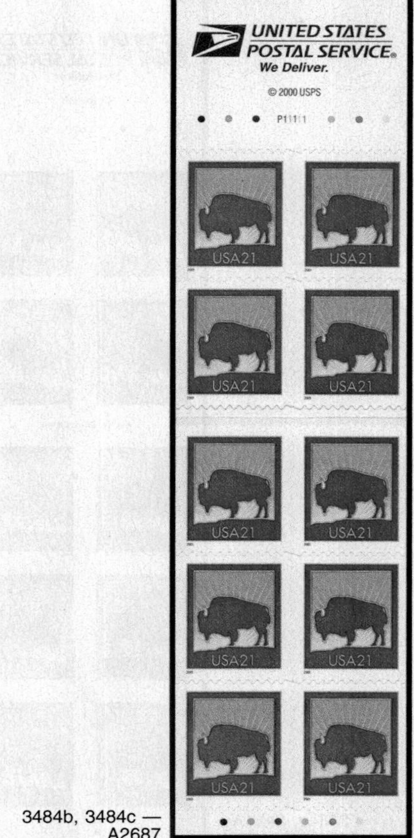

3484b, 3484c — A2687

BISON
Ten 21 cent
Self - adhesive
Stamps
$2.10

3484d, 3484Ag, 3484Aj — BC159A

2001

$2.10 fold-it-yourself booklet contains 10 self-adhesive 21c stamps
$2.10 booklet contains 10 self-adhesive 21c stamps

Serpentine Die Cut 11¼ on 3 Sides

2001, Sept. 20 **Self-Adhesive**

3484b A2687 21c pane of 4, P#P111111, P333333, P444444 2.40
3484c A2687 21c pane of 6, no P# 3.60

COMBINATION BOOKLET

BK282B BC159A $2.10 **multi,** #3484b-3484c, P#P111111, P333333, P444444 6.00

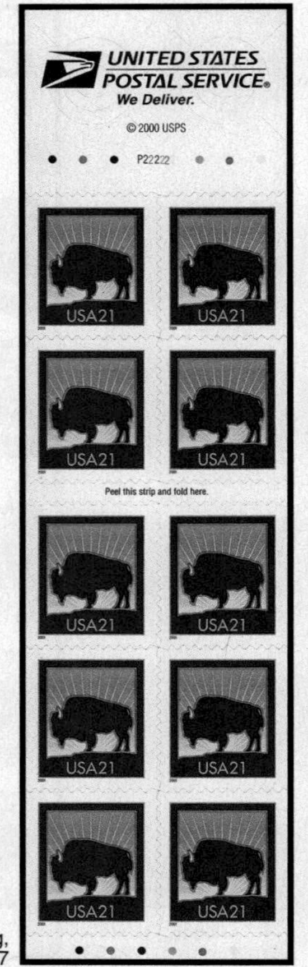

3484d, 3484Ag,
3484Aj — A2687

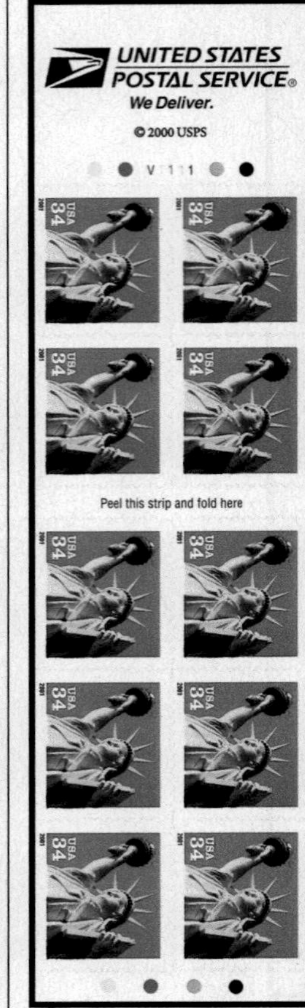

3485a — A2689

3484d A2687 21c pane of 10, P#P111111, P222222, P333333, P444444, P555555 6.00

Serpentine Die Cut 10½x11¼ on 3 Sides

3484Ae A2687 21c pane of 4, 2 #3484 at L, 2# 3484A at R, P#P111111, P333333, P444444 12.50
3484Af A2687 21c pane of 6, 3 #3484 at L, 3# 3484A at R, no P# 20.00
3484Ag A2687 21c pane of 10, 5 #3484 at L, 5# 3484A at R, P#P111111, P222222, P333333, P444444 30.00
P#P555555 45.00
3484Ah A2687 21c pane of 4, 2 #3484A at L, 2# 3484 at R, P#P111111, P333333, P444444 12.50
3484Ai A2687 21c pane of 6, 3 #3484A at L, 3# 3484 at R, no P# 20.00
3484Aj A2687 21c pane of 10, 5 #3484A at L, 5# 3484 at R, P#P111111, P222222, P333333, P444444 30.00
P#P555555 45.00

COMBINATION BOOKLETS

BK282C BC159A $2.10 **multi,** #3484Ae-3484Af, P#P111111, P333333, P444444 32.50
BK282D BC159A $2.10 **multi,** #3484Ah-3484Ai, P#P111111, P333333, P444444 32.50

Nos. 3484d, 3484Ag and 3484Aj are complete booklets (BC159A). The peelable backing serves as a booklet cover. Nos. BK282B-BK282D lack self-adhesive panel that covers the rouletting. Nos. BK282B-BK282D have a small 662900 UPC code on cover back, while Nos. 3484d, 3484Ag and 3484Aj have a large 662800 UPC code on cover back.

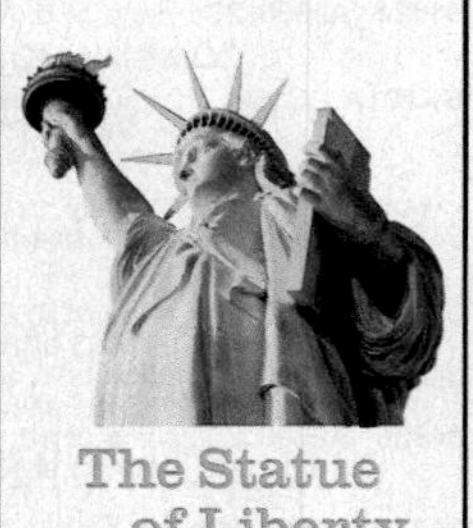

3485a — BC160

2001

$3.40 fold-it-yourself booklet contains 10 self-adhesive 34c stamps

2001, Feb. 7 ***Serpentine Die Cut 11 on 3 Sides***

Self-Adhesive

3485a A2689 34c pane of 10, P#V1111, V1221 7.00

3485b — A2689

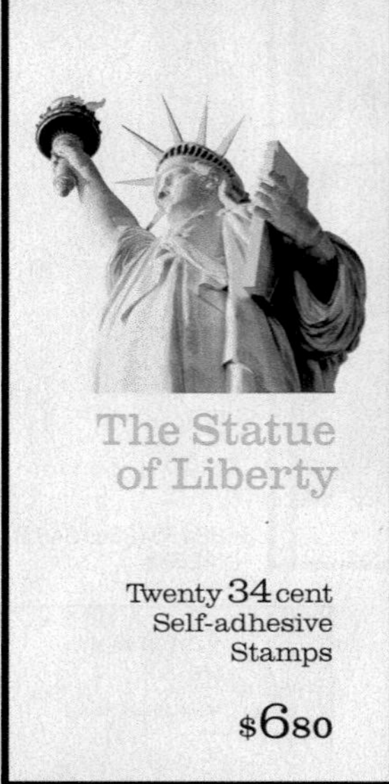

3485b — BC160B

2001

$6.80 fold-it-yourself booklet contains 20 self-adhesive 34c stamps

3485b A2689 34c pane of 20, P#V1111, V1211, V1221, V2111, V2112, V2121, V2122, V2212, V2222 14.00

Nos. 3485a-3485b are complete booklets (BC160 and BC160B). The peelable backing serves as a booklet cover.

Variety

3485f As "b," die cutting omitted —

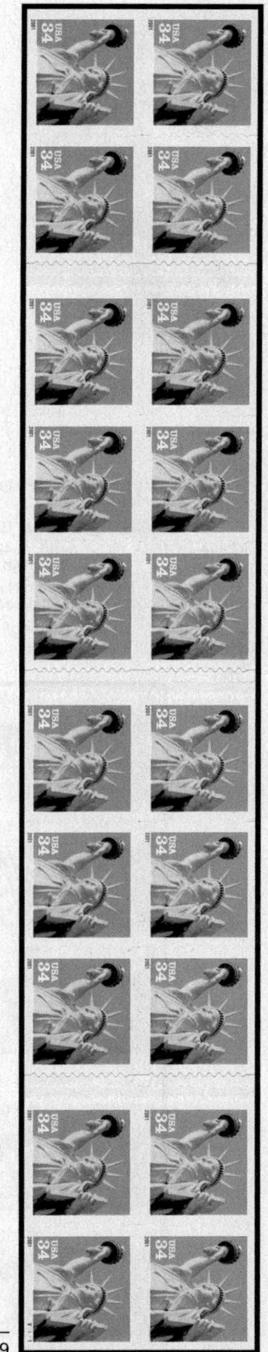

3485c, 3485d — A2689

3485c	A2689	34c pane of 4, without P#	3.00
3485d	A2689	34c pane of 6, no P#	4.50

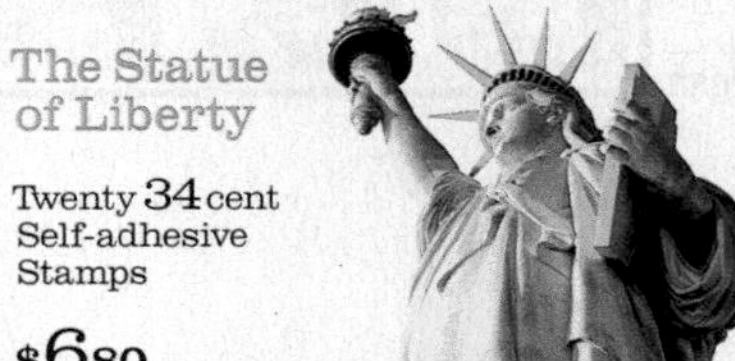

3485c, 3485d — BC160A

2001

$6.80 booklet contains 20 self-adhesive 34c stamps

COMBINATION BOOKLET

BK283 BC160A $6.80 **multicolored,** 1 #3485c with P#, 1 #3485c without P#, 2 3485d, P#V1111, V2212, V2222 16.00
P#V1112, V1121, V1122 —

The plate # on No. 3485c from No. BK283 is on the lower right stamp of the right pane of 4 of the booklet.

Variety

3485c Pane of 4 containing P#V1111, V1122, V2212, V2222 4.00
Pane of 4 containing P#V1112, V1121 —

3490b, 3490c, 3490d — A2690-A2693

Serpentine Die Cut 10½x 10¾ on 2 or 3 Sides

2001, Feb. 7 **Self-Adhesive**

3490b	34c pane of 4	3.50
3490c	34c pane of 6, #3489-3490, 2 each #3487-3488	5.00
3490d	34c pane of 6, #3487-3488, 2 each #3489-3490	5.00

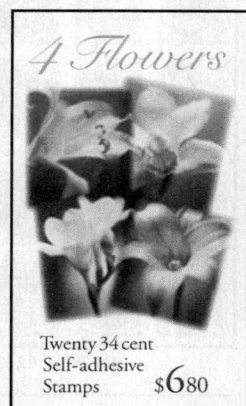

3490b, 3490c, 3490d — BC162

2001

$6.80 booklet contains 20 self-adhesive 34c stamps

COMBINATION BOOKLET

BK284 BC162 $6.80 **multicolored,** #3490c-3490d, 2 #3490b, P#S1111 17.50

P# on No. BK284 is on the backing paper of the bottom pane of No. 3490b.

3490e, BC161 — A2690-A2693

3490e 34c pane of 20, 5 #3490a, P#S1111, S2222 20.00

No. 3490e is a complete booklet with 12 stamps plus P# on one side and eight stamps plus booklet cover (BC161) on the other side. The peelable backing serves as a booklet cover.

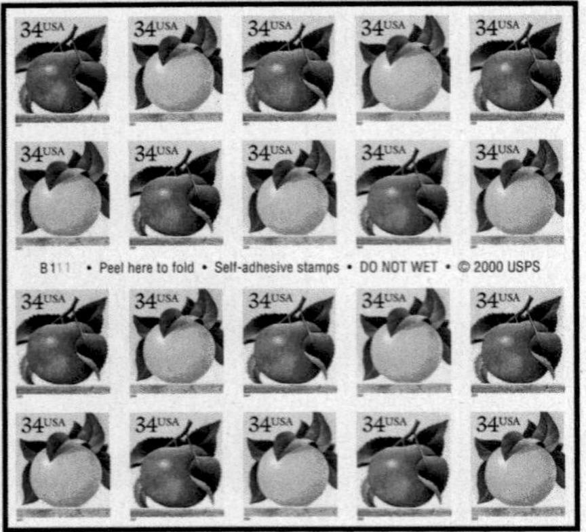

3492b — A2694-A2695

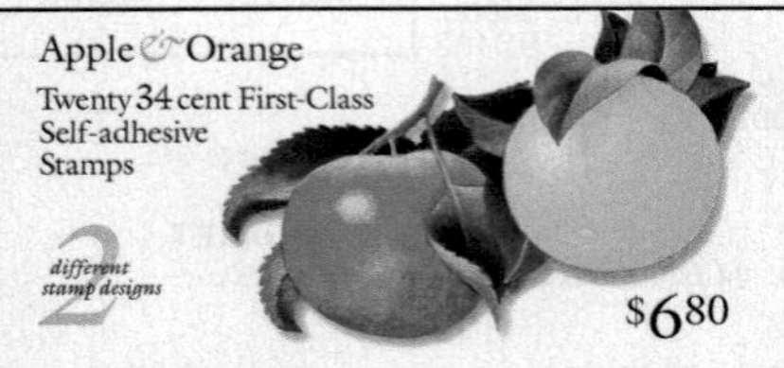

3492b — BC163

2001

$6.80 fold-it-yourself booklet contains 20 self-adhesive 34c stamps

Serpentine Die Cut 11¼ on 2, 3 or 4 sides

2001, Mar. 6 **Self-Adhesive**

3492b 34c pane of 20, 10 each #3491-3492, P# B1111, B2222, B3333, B4444, B5555, B6666, B7777 14.00

No. 3492b is a complete booklet (BC163). The peelable backing serves as a booklet cover.

Varieties

3492e As "b," die cutting omitted *5,500.*
3492f As "b," right four stamps yellow omitted *3,500.*

3494b, 3494c, 3494d — A2694-A2695

2001, May ***Serpentine Die Cut 11½x10¾***

Self-Adhesive

3494b 34c pane of 4, 2 each #3493-3494, without P# 4.20
3494c 34c pane of 6, 3 each #3493-3494, #3493 at UL, no P# 6.30
3494d 34c pane of 6, 3 each #3493-3494, #3494 at UL, no P# 6.30

3494b, 3494c, 3494d — BC163A

2001

$6.80 booklet contains 20 self-adhesive 34c stamps

COMBINATION BOOKLET

BK284A BC163A $6.80 **multi,** #3494c, 3494d, 2 #3494b, P#B1111 22.50

The plate # on No. 3494b from No. BK284A is on bottom left stamp in the bottom pane of the booklet.

Variety

3494b Pane of 4 with P#B1111 5.50

3495a — A2688

3495a — BC163B

2001

$6.12 booklet contains 18 self-adhesive 34c stamps

Serpentine Die Cut 8 on 2, 3 or 4 Sides

2001, Dec. 17 **Self-Adhesive**

3495a 34c pane of 18, #V1111 18.00

Nos. 3495a is a complete booklet (BC163B). The peelable backing serves as a booklet cover.

3496a — A2699

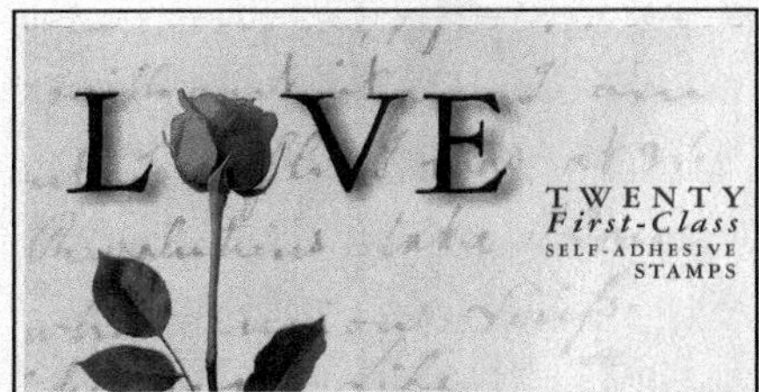

3496a — BC164

2001

$6.80 fold-it-yourself booklet contains 20 self-adhesive (34c) stamps

2001 ***Serpentine Die Cut 11¼ on 2, 3, or 4 Sides***
Self-Adhesive

3496a A2699 (34c) pane of 20, P#B1111, B2222, *Jan. 19* 18.00

No. 3496a is a complete booklet (BC164). The peelable backing serves as a booklet cover.

3497a — A2700

3497a — BC165

2001

$6.80 fold-it-yourself booklet contains 20 self-adhesive 34c stamps

2001 ***Serpentine Die Cut 11¼ on 2, 3 or 4 Sides***
Self-Adhesive

3497a A2700 34c pane of 20, P#B1111, B2222, B3333, B4444, B5555, *Feb. 14* 18.00

No. 3497a is a complete booklet (BC165). The peelable backing serves as a booklet cover.

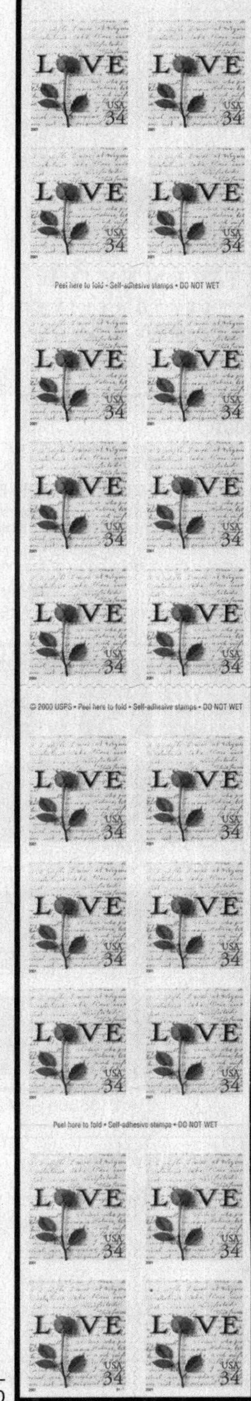

3498a, 3498b — A2700

Size: 18x21mm

Serpentine Die Cut 11½x10¾

3498a A2700 34c pane of 4, without P#, *Feb. 14* 3.50

3498b A2700 34c pane of 6, no P#, *Feb. 14* 5.10

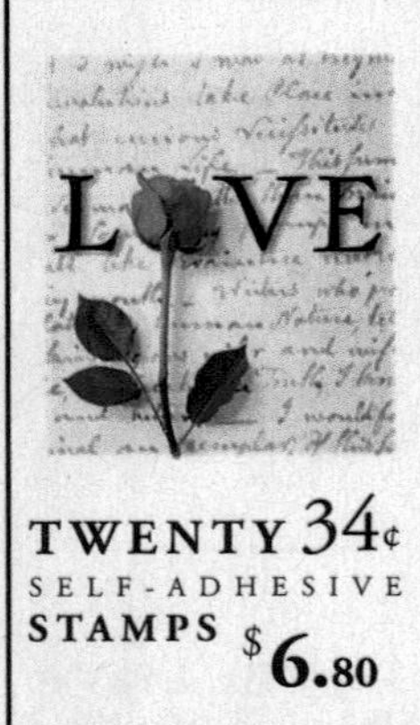

3498a, 3498b — BC166

2001

$6.80 booklet contains 20 self-adhesive 34c stamps

COMBINATION BOOKLET

BK285 BC166 $6.80 **multicolored,** 2 each #3498a-3498b, P#B1111 21.00

The plate # on No. 3498a from No. BK285 is on bottom left stamp in the bottom pane of the booklet.

Variety

3498a pane of 4, containing P#B1111 5.50

3536a — A2737

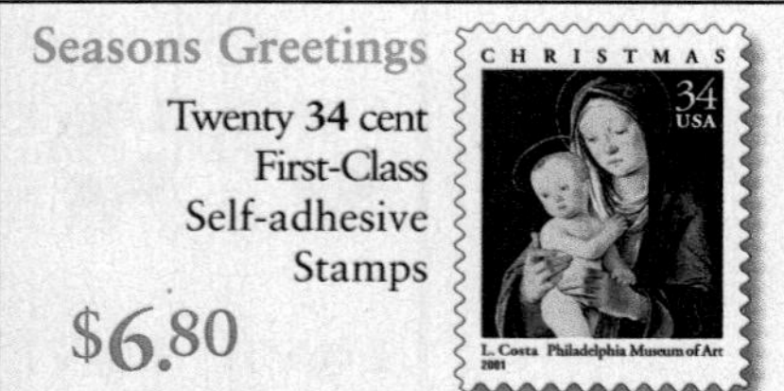

3536a — BC167

2001

$6.80 fold-it-yourself booklet contains 20 self-adhesive 34c stamps

Serpentine Die Cut 11½ on 2, 3 or 4 Sides

2001, Oct. 10 **Self-Adhesive**

3536a A2737 34c pane of 20, P#B1111 15.00

No. 3536a is a complete booklet (BC167). The peelable backing serves as a booklet cover.

3540d, 3540g, BC168 — A2738-A2741

Serpentine Die Cut 10¾x11 on 2 or 3 Sides

3540d A2738 34c pane of 20, small date, 5 #3540c + label, P#S1111 18.00

3540g A2738 34c pane of 20, large date, 5 #3540f + label, P#S3333, S4444 40.00

Nos. 3540d and 3540g are complete booklets with 12 stamps plus P# on one side and eight stamps plus booklet cover (BC168) on the other side. The peelable backing serves as a booklet cover.

3544b, 3544c, 3544d — A2738-A2741

Green Denomination

Stamp Size: 21x18½mm

Serpentine Die Cut 11 on 2 or 3 sides

3544b A2738 34c pane of 4, #3541-3544 3.60

3544c A2738 34c pane of 6, #3543-3544, 2 #3541-3542 5.40

3544d A2738 34c pane of 6, #3541-3542, 2 #3543-3544 5.40

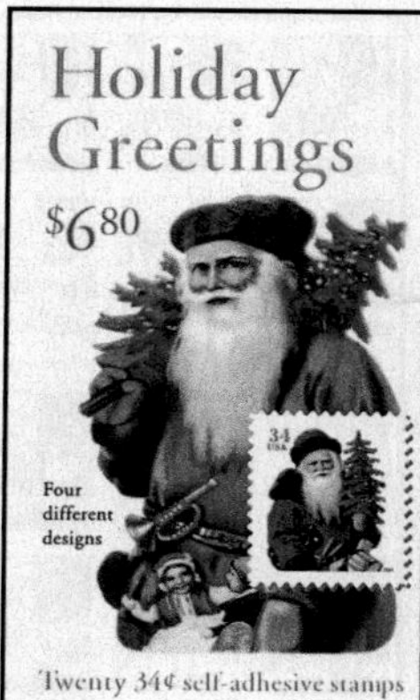

3544b, 3544c,
3544d — BC169

2001

$6.80 booklet contains 20 self-adhesive 34c stamps

COMBINATION BOOKLET

BK286 BC169 $6.80 **multi,** #3544c-3544d, 2 #3544b, P#V1111 18.00

P# on No. BK286 is on the backing paper of the bottom pane of No. 3544b.

3549a — A2744

3549a — BC170

2001

$6.80 booklet contains 20 self-adhesive 34c stamps

Serpentine Die Cut 11¼ on 2, 3 or 4 Sides

2001, Oct. 24 **Self-Adhesive**

3549a A2744 34c Pane of 20, P#B1111, B2222, B3333, B4444 15.00

No. 3549a is a complete booklet (BC170). The peelable backing serves as a booklet cover.

3549Bc, 3549Bd — A2744

Serpentine Die Cut 10½x10¾ on 2 or 3 Sides

2002, Jan. **Self-Adhesive**

3549Bc A2744 34c pane of 4 3.40
3549Bd A2744 34c pane of 6 5.10

3549Bc,
3549Bd — BC171

2002

$6.80 booklet contains 20 self-adhesive 34c stamps

COMBINATION BOOKLET

BK287 BC171 $6.80 **multi,** 2 each #3549Bc, 3549Bd, P#S1111 17.00

P# on No. BK287 is on the backing paper of the lower example of No. 3549Bd.

3549Be, BC172 — A2744

3549Be A2744 34c pane of 20, P#S1111 18.00

No. 3549Be is a complete booklet with 12 stamps plus P# on one side and eight stamps plus booklet cover (BC172) on the other side. The peelable backing serves as a booklet cover.

Washington Type of 2002

3618a, 3618b — A2686

Serpentine Die Cut 11¼x11 on 3 Sides

2002, June 7 **Self-Adhesive**

3618a A2686 23c pane of 4, P#P1, P2, P3 2.00
3618b A2686 23c pane of 6, no P# 3.00

3618c, 3619e, 3619f — BC173

2002

$2.30 booklet contains 10 self-adhesive 23c stamps

COMBINATION BOOKLET

BK288 BC173 $2.30 **multi,** #3618a-3618b, P#P1, P2, P4 5.00

No. BK288 has a 671800 UPC code on cover back, while No. 3618c has a 671000 UPC code on cover back.

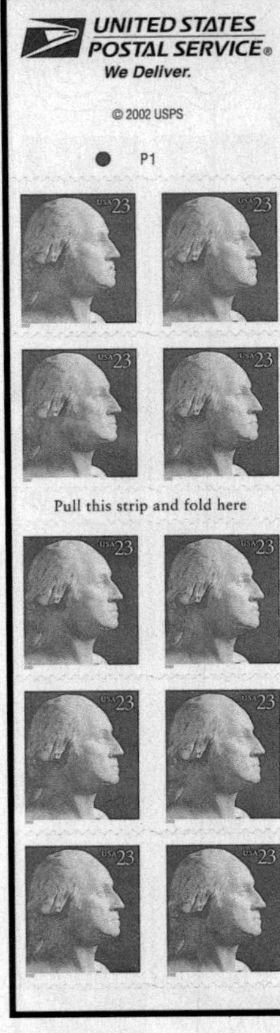

3618c — A2686

3618c A2686 23c pane of 10, P#P1, P2, P3 5.00

No. 3618c is a complete booklet and includes a self-adhesive panel that covers the rouletting. The peelable backing (BC173), which is slightly longer than on No. BK288, serves as a booklet cover.

Washington Type of 2002

Serpentine Die Cut 10½x11 on 3 Sides

2002, June 7 **Self-Adhesive**

3619a A2686 23c pane of 4, 2 #3619 at L, 2 #3618 at R, P#P1, P2, P3 10.00
3619b A2686 23c pane of 6, 3 #3619 at L, 3 #3618 at R, no P# 15.00
3619c A2686 23c pane of 4, 2 #3618 at L, 2 #3619 at R, P#P1, P2, P4 10.00
3619d A2686 23c pane of 6, 3 #3618 at L, 3 #3619 at R, no P# 15.00

COMBINATION BOOKLETS

BK289 BC173 $2.30 **multi,** #3619a-3619b, P#P1, P2, P4 25.00
BK289A BC173 $2.30 **multi,** #3619c-3619d, P#P1, P2, P4 25.00

Serpentine Die Cut 10½x11 on 3 Sides

Self-Adhesive

3619e A2686 23c pane of 10, 5 #3619 at L, 5 #3618 at R, P#P1, P2, P3 27.50
3619f A2686 23c pane of 10, 5 #3618 at L, 5 #3619 at R, P#P1, P2, P3 27.50

Nos. 3619e and 3619f are complete booklets and include a self-adhesive panel that covers the rouletting. The peelable backing (BC173), which is slightly longer than those on Nos. BK289 and BK289A, serves as a booklet cover.

Variety

3619i Nos. 3619c and 3619d in bklt. of 10 (#BK289A), imperf. vert. btwn. on both panes —

3623a — A2807

3623a — BC174

2002

$7.40 fold-it-yourself booklet contains 20 self-adhesive (37c) stamps

Serpentine Die Cut 11¼ on 2, 3 or 4 Sides

2002, June 7 **Self-Adhesive** **Litho.**

3623a A2807 (37c) pane of 20, P#B1111, B2222, B3333 15.00

No. 3623a is a complete booklet (BC174). The peelable backing serves as a booklet cover.

3624a, 3624b — A2807

Serpentine Die Cut 10½x10¾ on 2 or 3 Sides

2002, June 7 Self-Adhesive Photo.

3624a A2807 (37c) pane of 4, no P# 3.60
3624b A2807 (37c) pane of 6 5.40

3624a, 3624b — BC175

2002

$7.40 booklet contains 20 self-adhesive (37c) stamps

COMBINATION BOOKLET

BK290 BC175 ($7.40) **multi,** 2 each #3624a, 3624b, P#S11111 18.00

Plate number on No. BK290 is on the backing paper of the lower example of No. 3624b.

3624c, BC176 — A2807

Serpentine Die Cut 10½x10¾ on 2 or 3 Sides

3624c A2807 (37c) pane of 20, P#S1111 18.00

No. 3624c is a complete booklet with 12 stamps plus P# on one side and eight stamps plus booklet cover (BC176) on the other side. The peelable backing serves as a booklet cover.

3625a — A2807

3625a BC177

2002

$6.66 fold-it-yourself booklet contains 18 self-adhesive (37c) stamps

Serpentine Die Cut 8 on 2, 3 or 4 Sides

2002, June 7 Self-Adhesive Photo.

3625a A2807 (37c) pane of 18, P#V1111 16.50

No. 3625a is a complete booklet (BC177). The peelable backing serves as a booklet cover.

3629b, 3629c, 3629d — A2808-A2811

Serpentine Die Cut 11 on 2 or 3 Sides

2002, June 7 **Self-Adhesive** **Photo.**

3629b A2808 (37c) pane of 4, #3626-3629, no P# 3.00
3629c A2808 (37c) pane of 6, #3627, 3629, 2 each #3626, 3628, no P# 4.50
3629d A2808 (37c) pane of 6, #3626, 3628, 2 each #3627, 3629, no P# 4.50

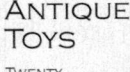

3629b, 3629c, 3629d — BC178

2002

$7.40 booklet contains 20 self-adhesive (37c) stamps

COMBINATION BOOKLET

BK291 BC178 ($7.40) **multi,** #3629c-3629d, 2 #3629b, no P# 15.00

3629e — A2808-A2811

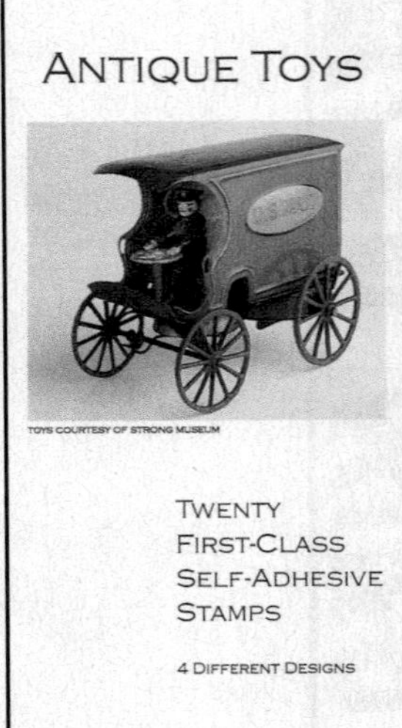

3629e — BC179

2002

$7.40 fold-it-yourself booklet contains 20 self-adhesive (37c) stamps

Serpentine Die Cut 11 on 2, 3 or 4 Sides

3629e A2808 (37c) pane of 20, 5 each #3626-3629, P#V1111, V1112, V2222 15.00

No. 3629e is a complete booklet (BC179). The peelable backing serves as a booklet cover.

3634a — A2812

3634a — BC180

2002

$3.70 fold-it-yourself booklet contains 10 self-adhesive 37c stamps

Serpentine Die Cut 11.1 on 3 Sides

2002, June 7 **Self-Adhesive** **Photo.**

3634a A2812 37c pane of 10, P#V1111 7.50

No. 3634a is a complete booklet (BC180). The peelable backing serves as a booklet cover.

3634c, 3634d — A2812

Serpentine Die Cut 11 on 2 or 3 Sides

2003, Nov. Self-Adhesive Photo.

3634c A2812 37c pane of 4 #3634b, no P# 3.00
3634d A2812 37c pane of 6 #3634b 4.50

3634c, 3634d — BC180A

2002

$7.40 booklet contains 20 self-adhesive 37c stamps

COMBINATION BOOKLET

BK291A BC180A $7.40 **multi,** 2 each #3634c, 3634d, P#V1111 15.00

Plate number on No. BK291A is on the backing paper of the lower example of No. 3634d.

Serpentine Die Cut 11.3 on 3 Sides

2002(?) Self-Adhesive Photo.

3634f A2812 37c pane of 10, P#V1111 10.00

No. 3634f is a complete booklet (BC180). The peelable backing serves as a booklet cover.

3635a — A2812

3635a — BC181

2002

$7.40 fold-it-yourself booklet contains 20 self-adhesive 37c stamps

Serpentine Die Cut 11¼ on 2, 3 or 4 Sides

2002, June 7 Self-Adhesive Litho.

3635a A2812 37c pane of 20, P#B1111, B2222, B3333, B4444, B5555, B6666, B7777 15.00

No. 3635a is a complete booklet (BC181). The peelable backing serves as a booklet cover.

3636a, 3636b — A2812

Serpentine Die Cut 10½x10¾ on 2 or 3 Sides

2002, June 7 Self-Adhesive Photo.

3636a A2812 37c pane of 4, no P# 3.00
3636b A2812 37c pane of 6 4.50

3636a, 3636b — BC182

2002

$7.40 fold-it-yourself booklet contains 20 self-adhesive 37c stamps

COMBINATION BOOKLET

BK291B BC182 $7.40 **multi,** 2 each #3636a, 3636b, P#S11111 15.00

Plate number on No. BK291B is on the backing paper of the lower example of No. 3636b.

3636c, BC183 — A2812

Serpentine Die Cut 10½x10¾ on 2 or 3 Sides

2002, June 7 **Self-Adhesive** **Photo.**

3636c A2812 37c pane of 20, P#S1111, S2222, S3333, S4444, S5555, S6666 15.00

No. 3636c is a complete booklet with 12 stamps plus P# on one side and eight stamps plus booklet cover (BC183) on the other side. The peelable backing serves as a booklet cover.

Variety

3636f As "c," 11 stamps and part of 12th stamp on reverse printed on backing liner, the 8 stamps on front side imperf —

Serpentine Die Cut 11¼x11 on 2 or 3 Sides

2004, July **Self-Adhesive** **Photo.**

3636De A2812 37c pane of 20, P#V1111, V1112, V2222 25.00

No. 3636De is a complete booklet with 12 stamps plus P# on one side and eight stamps plus booklet cover (BC183) on the other side. The peelable backing serves as a booklet cover.

3637a — A2812

3637a—BC184

2003

$6.66 fold-it-yourself booklet contains 18 self-adhesive 37c stamps

Serpentine Die Cut 8 on 2, 3 or 4 Sides

2003, Feb. 4 **Self-Adhesive** **Photo.**

3637a A2812 37c pane of 18, #V1111 13.50

No. 3637a is a complete booklet (BC184). The peelable backing serves as a booklet cover.

3645b, 3645c, 3645d — A2813-A2816

Serpentine Die Cut 11 on 2 or 3 Sides

2002, July 26 **Self-Adhesive** **Photo.**

3645b A2813 37c pane of 4, #3642-3645, no P# 3.00

3645c A2813 37c pane of 6, #3643, 3645, 2 each #3642, 3644, no P# 4.50

3645d A2813 37c pane of 6, #3642, 3644, 2 each #3643, 3645, P#V1111 4.50

ANTIQUE
TOYS
TWENTY 37¢
SELF-ADHESIVE
STAMPS
$7.40
4 DIFFERENT DESIGNS

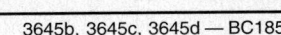

3645b, 3645c, 3645d — BC185

2002

$7.40 booklet contains 20 self-adhesive 37c stamps

COMBINATION BOOKLET

BK292 BC185 $7.40 **multi,** #3645c-3645d, 2 #3645b, P#V1111 15.00

Plate number on No. BK292 is on the backing paper of No. 3645d.

3645e — A2813-A2816

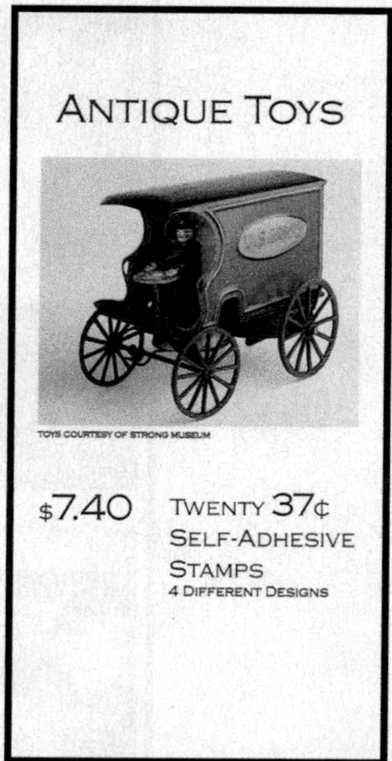

3645e — BC186

2002

$7.40 fold-it-yourself booklet contains 20 self-adhesive 37c stamps

Serpentine Die Cut 11 on 2, 3 or 4 Sides

3645e A2813 37c pane of 20, 5 each #3642-3645, P#V1111, V1112, V2221, V2222 15.00

No. 3645e is a complete booklet (BC186). The peelable backing serves as a booklet cover.

3645h, BC179A — A2813-A2816

Serpentine Die Cut 11x11¼ on 2 or 3 Sides

2003, Sept. 3 Self-Adhesive Photo.

3645h A2813 37c pane of 20, P#V1111, V1112, V2221, V2222 15.00

No. 3645h is a complete double-sided booklet. Eight stamps and the booklet cover (BC179A) are printed on one side of the peelable backing paper, and 12 stamps plus P# appear on the other side of the backing paper.

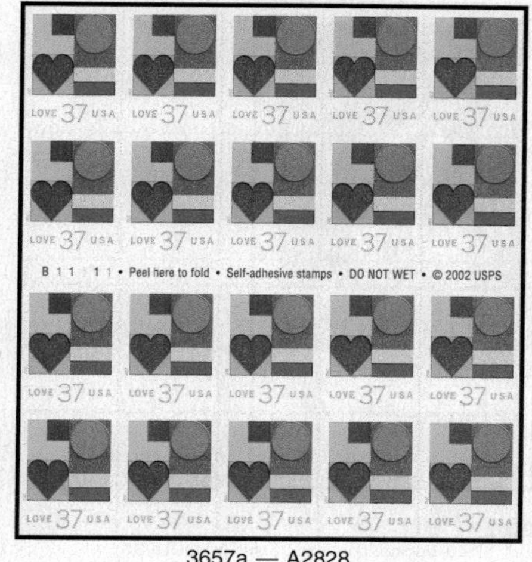

3657a — A2828

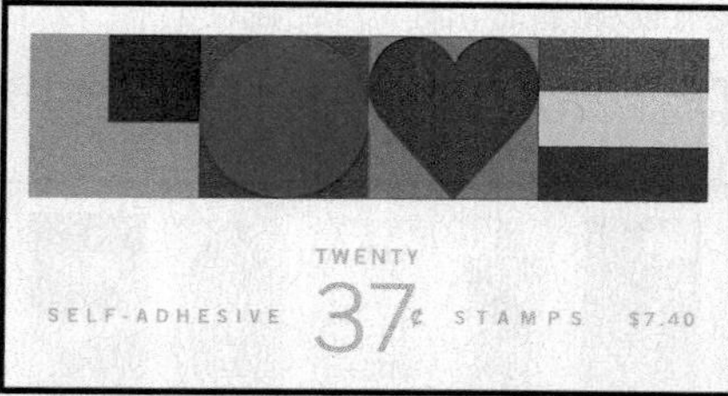

3657a — BC187

2002

$7.40 fold-it-yourself booklet contains 20 self-adhesive 37c stamps

Serpentine Die Cut 11 on 2, 3 or 4 Sides

2002, Aug. 16 Self-Adhesive Litho.

3657a A2828 37c pane of 20, P#B11111, B22222, B33333, B44444, B55555, B66666, B77777 15.00

No. 3657a is a complete booklet (BC187). The peelable backing serves as a booklet cover.

Variety

3657b As "a," silver ("Love 37 USA") missing on top five stamps (CM) *750.00*

3675a — A2843

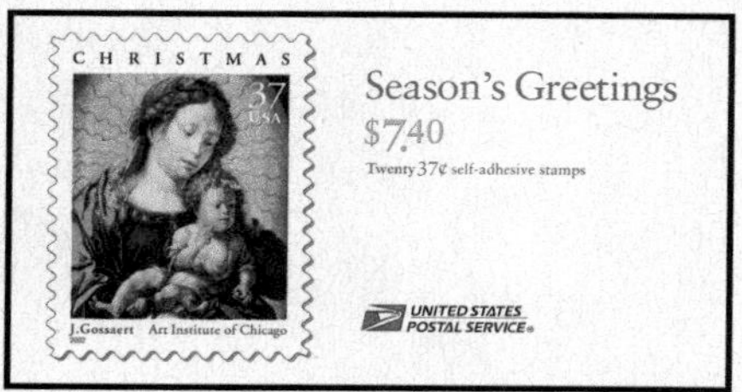

3675a — BC188

2002

$7.40 fold-it-yourself booklet contains 20 self-adhesive 37c stamps

Serpentine Die Cut 11x11¼ on 2, 3 or 4 Sides

2002, Oct. 10 Self-Adhesive

3675a A2843 37c pane of 20, P#B1111, B2222 15.00

No. 3675a is a complete booklet (BC188). The peelable backing serves as a booklet cover.

3687b, BC189 — A2844-A2847

Serpentine Die Cut 10¾ on 2 or 3 Sides

2002, Oct. 28 Self-Adhesive

3687b A2844 37c Pane of 20, P#S1111, S1113, S2222, S4444 25.00

No. 3687b is a complete booklet with 12 stamps plus P# on one side and eight stamps plus booklet cover (BC189) on the other side. The peelable backing serves as a booklet cover.

3691b, 3691c, 3691d — A2848-A2851

Serpentine Die Cut 11 on 2 or 3 Sides

3691b A2848 37c Pane of 4, #3688-3691 4.60
3691c A2848 37c Pane of 6, #3690-3691, 2 each #3688-3689, no P# 7.00
3691d A2848 37c Pane of 6, #3688-3689, 2 each #3690-3691 7.00

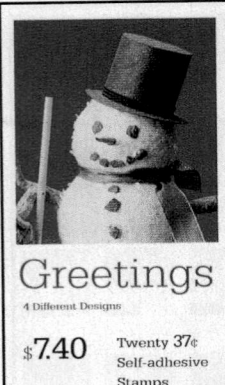

Greetings
4 Different Designs
$7.40 Twenty 37¢ Self-adhesive Stamps

3691b, 3691c, 3691d — BC190

2002

$7.40 booklet contains 20 self-adhesive 37c stamps

COMBINATION BOOKLET

BK293 BC190 $7.40 **multi,** #3691c, 3691d, 2 #3691b, P#V1111 23.00

Plate number on No. BK293 is on the backing paper of the upper example of No. 3691b.

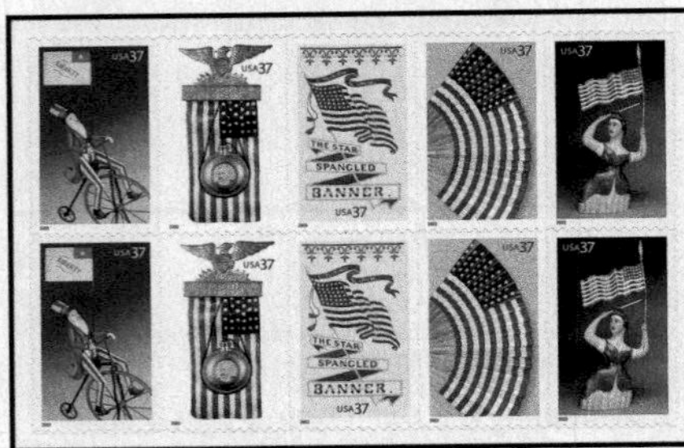

3780b — A2883-A2887

Backing 1

Backing 2

2003, Apr. 3 Litho. *Serpentine Die Cut 10x9¾*

Self-Adhesive

3780b A2883 37c Pane of 2 #3780a with backing 1 7.50
With backing 2 7.50

3780b — BC191

2003

$7.40 booklet contains 20 self-adhesive stamps

Booklet

BK294 BC191 $7.40 **multi,** no P# 15.00

No. BK294 contains one No. 3780b with backing 1 and one No. 3780b with backing 2.

3807b, BC193 — A2902-A2905

Serpentine Die Cut 10¾ on 2 or 3 Sides

2003, Aug. 7 Self-Adhesive Photo.

3807b A2902 37c pane of 20, 5 #3807a, P#S11111 15.00

No. 3807b is a complete double-sided booklet. Eight stamps and the booklet cover (BC193) are printed on one side of the peelable backing paper and 12 stamps plus P# are printed on the other side of the backing paper.

3820a, BC194 — A2843

Serpentine Die Cut 11x11¼ on 2 or 3 Sides

2003, Oct. 23 Self-Adhesive

Size: 28x19½mm

3820a A2843 37c pane of 20, P#P1111, P2222, P3333, P4444 15.00

No. 3820a is a complete double-sided booklet. Eight stamps, P# and the booklet cover (BC194) are printed on one side of the peelable backing paper, and 12 stamps plus P# are printed on the other side of the backing paper.

On one version of this pane (shown), an incorrect bar code was printed over with white ink, mostly covering the incorrect code, and the correct bar code was then added. This version is much scarcer; value $30.

3824b, BC195 — A2917-A2920

Serpentine Die Cut 11¾x11 on 2 or 3 Sides

2003, Oct. 23 Self-Adhesive

3824b A2917 37c Pane of 20, 5 each #3821-3824, P#S1111, S2222 20.00

No. 3824b is a complete double-sided booklet. Eight stamps plus P# and the booklet cover (BC195) are printed on one side of the peelable backing paper, and 12 stamps plus P# are printed on the other side of the backing paper.

3828b, 3828c, 3828d — A2921-A2924

Serpentine Die Cut 10½x10¾ on 2 or 3 Sides

3828b A2921 37c Pane of 4, #3825-3828, no P# 4.00

3828c A2921 37c Pane of 6, #3827-3828, 2 each #3825-3828, no P# 6.00

3828d A2921 37c Pane of 6, #3825-3826, 2 each #3827-3828, P#S111111 6.00

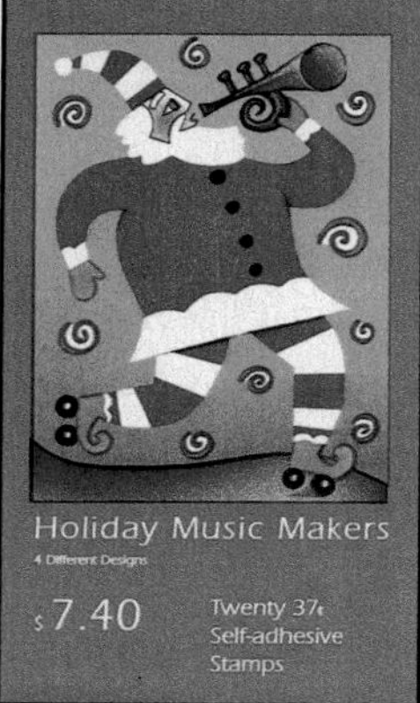

3828b, 3828c, 3828d — BC196

2003

$7.40 booklet contains 20 self-adhesive 37c stamps

COMBINATION BOOKLET

BK296 BC196 $7.40 **multi,** #3828c, 3828d, 2 each #3828b, P#S11111 21.00

Plate number on No. BK296 is printed on the backing paper of No. 3828d.

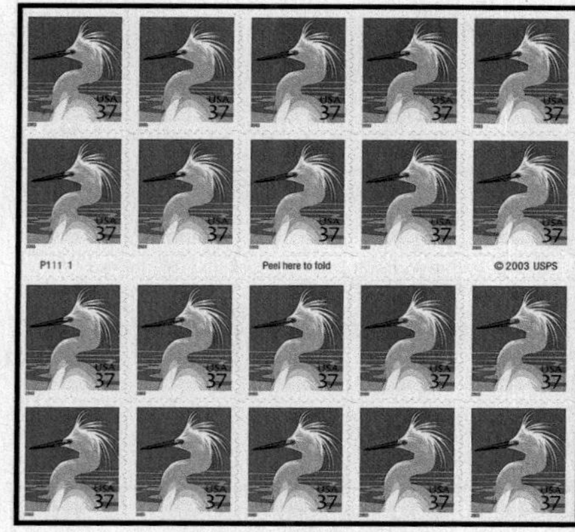

3830a — A2925

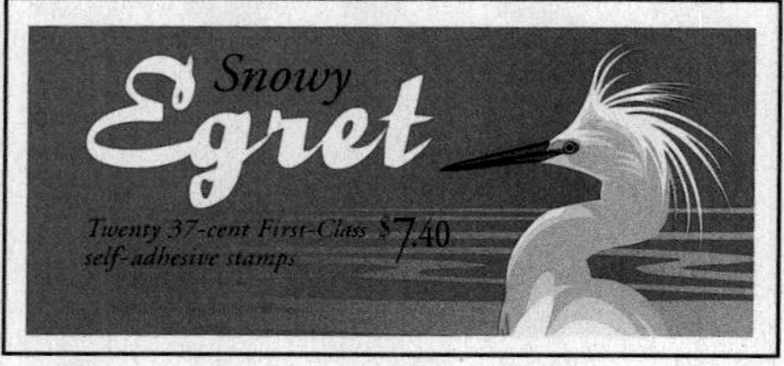

3830a — BC197

2004

$7.40 fold-it-yourself booklet contains 20 self-adhesive 37c stamps

Serpentine Die Cut 11½x11 on 2, 3 or 4 Sides

2004, Jan. 30 Self-Adhesive Litho.

3830a A2925 37c pane of 20, P#P11111, P22222 15.00

No. 3830a is a complete booklet (BC197). The peelable backing serves as a booklet cover.

Variety

3830b As "a," die cutting omitted —

Serpentine Die Cut 11½x11 on 2, 3 or 4 Sides

2005? Self-Adhesive Photo.

With "USPS" Microprinted on Bird's Breast

3830De A2925 37c pane of 20, P#P33333, P44444 *110.00*, P#P55555 —

No. 3830De is a complete booklet (BC197). The peelable backing serves as a booklet cover.

Variety

3830Dg As "e," die cutting omitted *1,200.*

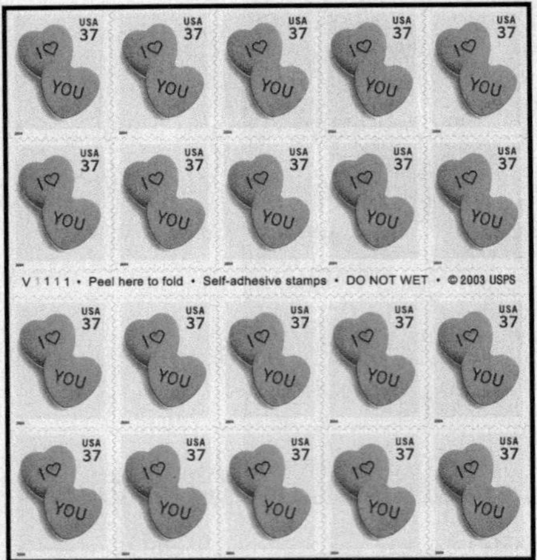

3833a — A2928

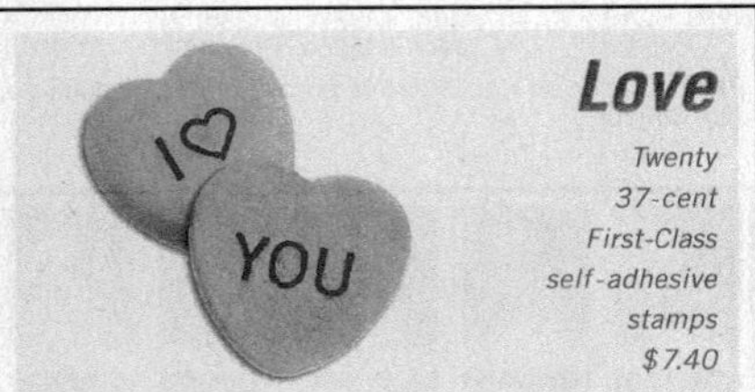

3833a — BC198

2004

$7.40 fold-it-yourself booklet contains 20 self-adhesive 37c stamps

Serpentine Die Cut 10¾ on 2, 3 or 4 Sides

2004, Jan. 14 Self-Adhesive Photo.

3833a A2928 37c pane of 20, P#V1111 15.00

No. 3833a is a complete booklet (BC198). The peelable backing serves as a booklet cover.

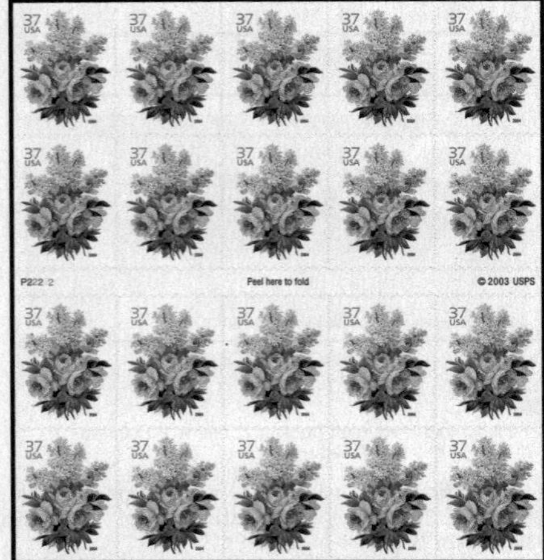

3836a — A2931

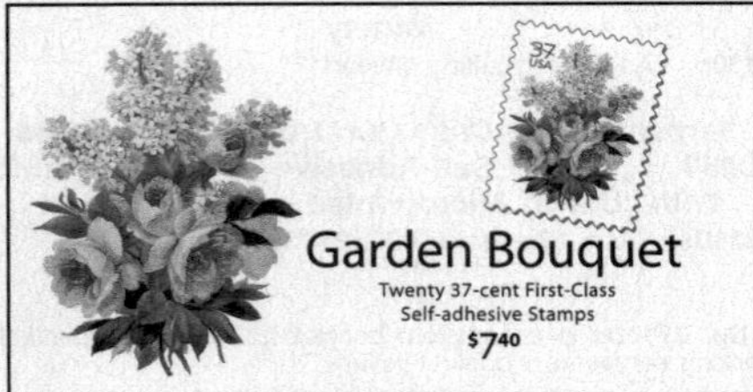

3836a — BC199

2004

$7.40 booklet contains 20 self-adhesive stamps

Serpentine Die Cut 10¾ on 2, 3 or 4 Sides

2004, Mar. 4 Self-Adhesive Litho.

3836a A2931 37c pane of 20, P#P11111, P22222, P33333, P44444, P55555, P66666, P77777, P88888 15.00

No. 3836a is a complete booklet (BC199). The peelable backing serves as a booklet cover.

3856b — A2940-A2941

Backing 1

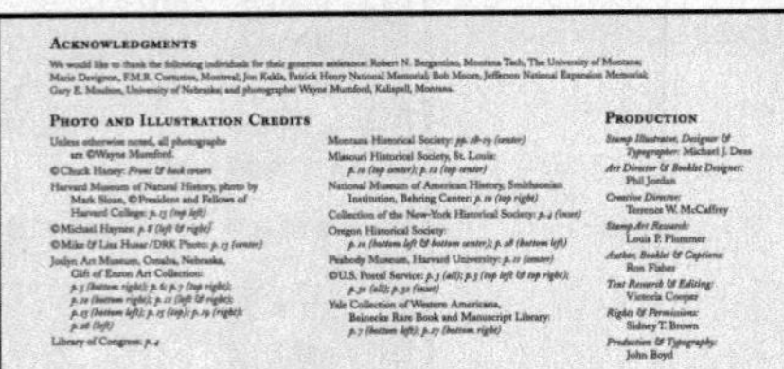

Backing 2

Serpentine Die Cut 10½x10¾

2004, May 14 Self-Adhesive Litho. & Engr.

3856b A2940 37c Pane, 5 each #3855-3856 with backing 1 9.00

With backing 2 9.00

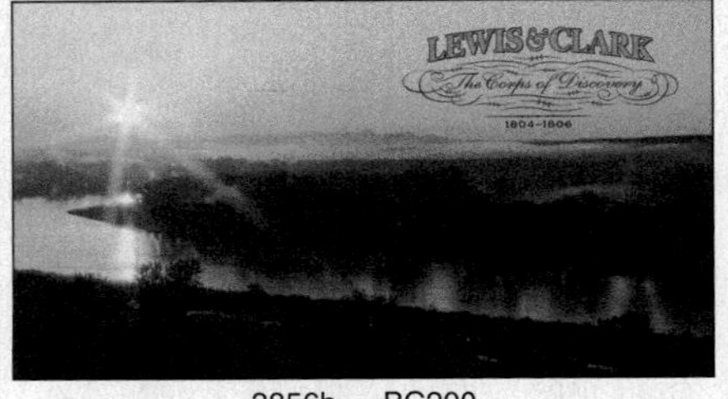

3856b — BC200

2004

$8.95 booklet contains 20 self-adhesive stamps

Booklet

BK297 BC200 $8.95 **multi,** no P# 18.00

No. BK297 contains one No. 3856b with backing 1 and one No. 3856b with backing 2.

3872a, BC201 — A2956

Serpentine Die Cut 10¾ on 2 or 3 Sides

2004, Aug. 12 Self-Adhesive Photo.

3872a A2956 37c pane of 20, P#S1111 15.00

No. 3872a is a complete booklet with 12 stamps plus P# on one side and eight stamps plus booklet cover (BC201) on the other side. The peelable backing serves as a booklet cover.

Variety

3872b Die cutting omitted, pair, in #3872a with foldover —

3879a, BC202 — A2961

Serpentine Die Cut 10¾x11 on 2 or 3 Sides

2004, Oct. 14 Self-Adhesive Litho.

3879a A2961 37c pane of 20, P#P1111 15.00

No. 3879a is a complete booklet with 12 stamps plus P# on one side and eight stamps plus P# and a label that serves as a booklet cover (BC202) on the other side.

Variety

3879b As "a," die cutting omitted —

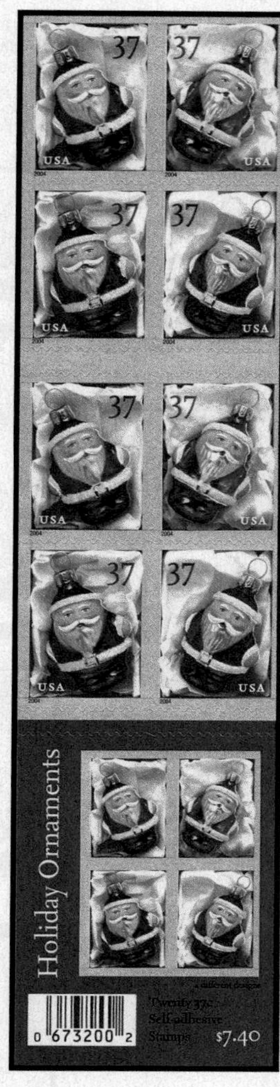

3886b, BC203
—A2965-A2968

Serpentine Die Cut 11½x11 on 2 or 3 Sides

2004, Nov. 16 Self-Adhesive Photo.

3886b A2965 37c pane of 20, 5 #3886a, P#S1111, S2222 20.00

No. 3886b is a complete double-sided booklet. Eight stamps and the booklet cover (BC203) are on one side of the peelable backing paper and 12 stamps plus P# are on the other side of the backing paper.

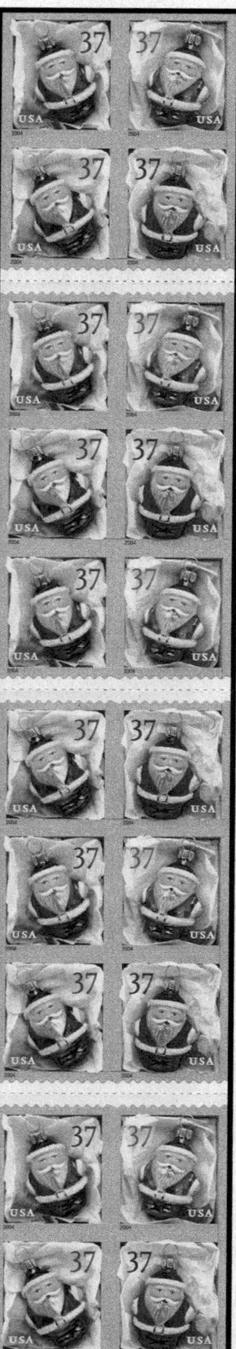

3890b, 3890c, 3890d
— A2969-A2972

Serpentine Die Cut 10¼x10¾ on 2 or 3 Sides

3890b A2969 37c pane of 4 #3887-3890, no P# 3.60
3890c A2969 37c pane of 6 #3889-3890, 2 each #3887-3888, no P# 5.50
3890d A2969 37c pane of 6 #3887-3888, 2 each #3889-3890, P#S11111 5.50

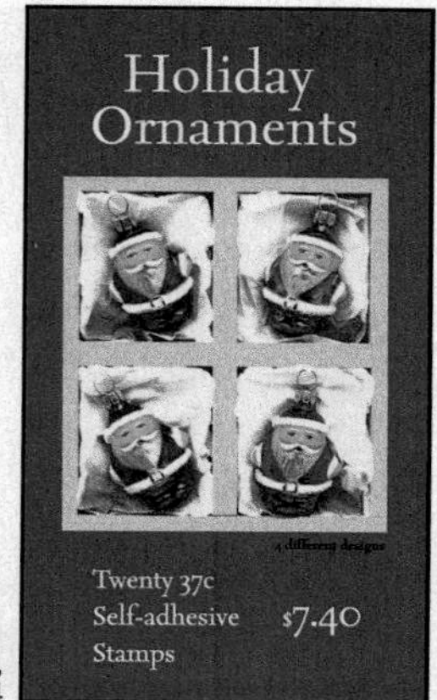

3890b, 3890c,
3890d — BC204

2004

$7.40 booklet contains 20 self-adhesive 37c stamps

COMBINATION BOOKLET

BK298 BC204 $7.40 **multi,** #3890c, 3890d, 2 #3890b, P#S11111 20.00

Plate number on No. BK298 is printed on the backing paper of No. 3890d.

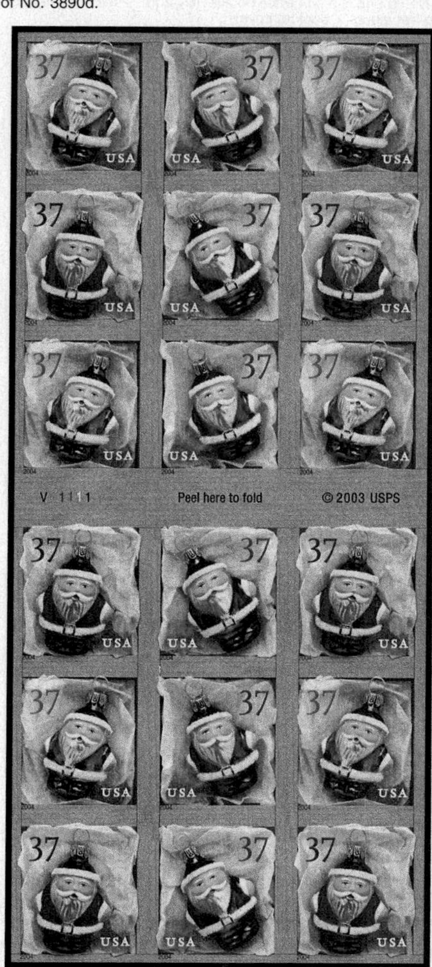

3894b — A2969-A2972

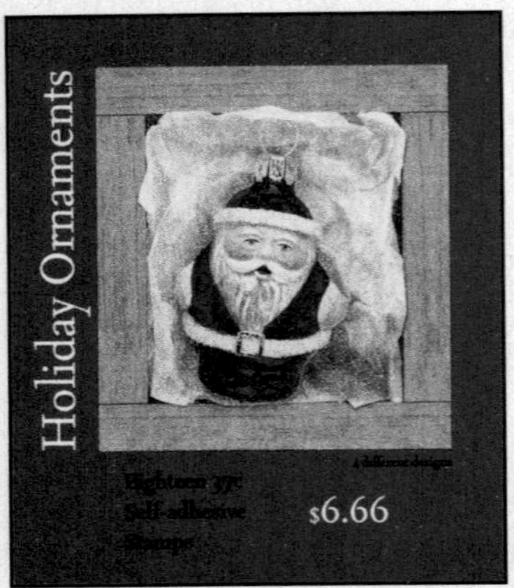

3894b
BC205

2004

$6.66 fold-it-yourself booklet contains 18 self-adhesive 37c stamps

Serpentine Die Cut 8 on 2, 3 or 4 Sides

3894b A2969 37c pane of 18, 6 each #3891, 3893, 3 each #3892, 3894, P#V11111 36.00

No. 3894b is a complete booklet (BC205). The peelable backing serves as a booklet cover.

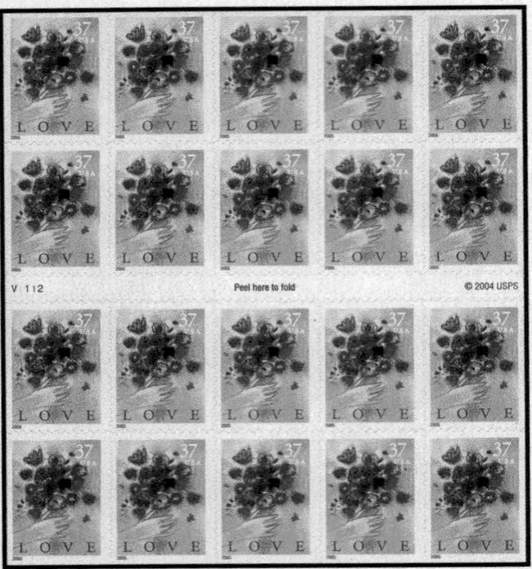

3898a — A2975

3898a — BC206

2005

$7.40 booklet contains 20 self-adhesive stamps

Serpentine Die Cut 10¾x11 on 2, 3 or 4 Sides

2005, Feb. 18 Self-Adhesive Photo.

3898a A2975 37c pane of 20, #V1111, V1112 15.00

No. 3898a is a complete booklet (BC206). The peelable backing serves as a booklet cover.

3903b, BC207 — A2977-A2980

Serpentine Die Cut 10¾ on 2 or 3 Sides

2005, Mar. 15 Self-Adhesive Litho.

3903b A2977 37c pane of 20, P#P1111 17.00
P#P2222 20.00

Variety

3903c As "b," die cutting omitted on side with eight stamps —

No. 3903b is a complete booklet with 12 stamps plus P# on one side and eight stamps plus P# and a label that serves as a booklet cover (BC207) on the other side.

3929b, BC208 — A3003-A3006

Serpentine Die Cut 10¾ on 2 or 3 Sides

2005, July 30 Self-Adhesive Litho.

3929b A3003 37c pane of 20, P#P1111 15.00

No. 3929b is a complete booklet with 12 stamps plus two P# on one side and eight stamps plus a label that serves as a booklet cover (BC208) on the other side.

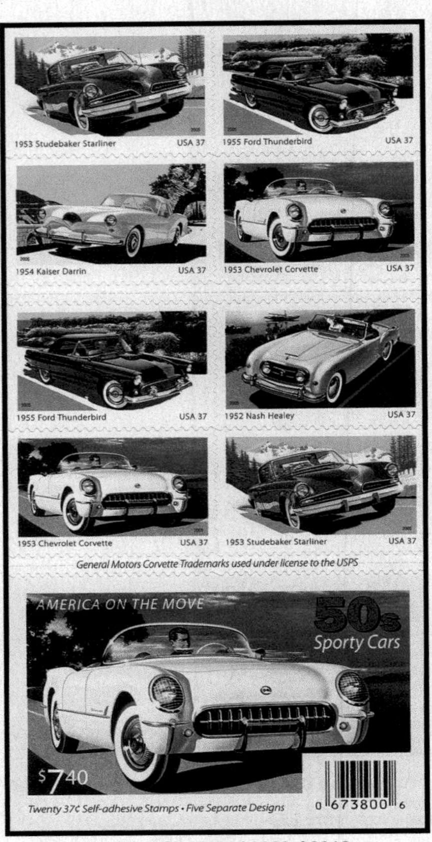

3935b, BC209 — A3008-A3012

Serpentine Die Cut 10¾ on 2 or 3 Sides

2005, Aug. 20 Self-Adhesive Litho.

3935b A3008 37c pane of 20, P#P1111 32.00

No. 3935b is a complete booklet with 12 stamps (2 each #3931, 3933, 3935, and 3 each #3932, 3934) plus P# on one side and eight stamps (1 each #3932, 3934, and 2 each #3931, 3933, 3935) plus a label that serves as the booklet cover (BC209) on the other side.

3956b, BC210 — A3026-A3029

Serpentine Die Cut 10¾x11 on 2 or 3 Sides

2005, Oct. 20 Self-Adhesive Photo.

3956b A3026 37c pane of 20 #3956a, P#S1111 20.00

No. 3956b is a complete double-sided booklet. Eight stamps and the booklet cover (BC210) are on one side of the peelable backing paper and 12 stamps plus P# are on the other side of the backing.

3960b, 3960c, 3960d — A3030-A3033

Serpentine Die Cut 10½x10¾ on 2 or 3 Sides

3960b A3030 37c pane of 4 #3957-3960 4.50
3960c A3030 37c pane of 6 #3959-3960, 2 each #3957-3958, no P# 7.00
3960d A3030 37c pane of 6 #3957-3958, 2 each #3959-3960, no P# 7.00

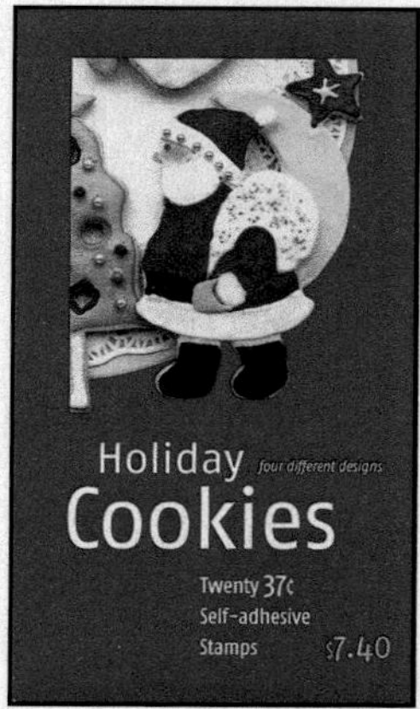

Holiday four different designs
Cookies
Twenty 37c
Self-adhesive
Stamps $7.40

3960b, 3960c, 3960d — BC211

2005

$7.40 booklet contains 20 self-adhesive 37c stamps

COMBINATION BOOKLET

BK299 BC211 $7.40 **multi,** #3960c, 3960d, 2 #3960b, P#S1111 23.00

Plate number on No. BK299 is printed on the backing paper of the lower example of No. 3960b.

3966a, 3972a, 3973a, BC212 — A3038

Serpentine Die Cut 11¼x10¾ on 2 or 3 Sides

2005, Dec. 8 **Self-Adhesive** **Litho.**

3966a A3038 (39c) pane of 20, P#P1111 16.00

Variety

3966b As "a," die cutting omitted —

Photo.

Serpentine Die Cut 11¼x10¾ on 2 or 3 Sides

3972a A3038 (39c) pane of 20, P#V1111 16.00

Serpentine Die Cut 10½x10¾ on 2 or 3 Sides

3973a A3038 (39c) pane of 20, P#S1111 16.00

Nos. 3966a, 3972a and 3973a are complete double-sided booklets. Eight stamps and the booklet cover (BC212) are on one side of the peelable backing paper and 12 stamps plus P# are on the other side of the backing paper. On No. 3966a, the stamps on one side are upside-down with relation to the stamps on the other side. On Nos. 3972a and 3973a the stamps are all aligned the same on both sides.

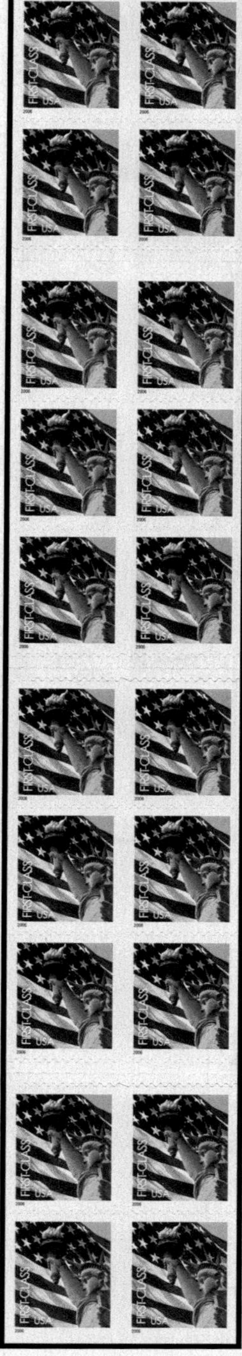

3974a, 3974b — A3038

Serpentine Die Cut 11¼x11 on 2 or 3 Sides

Litho.

3974a A3038 (39c) pane of 4 3.20

3974b A3038 (39c) pane of 6, no P# 4.80

3974a, 3974b — BC213

2005

($7.80) booklet contains 20 self-adhesive (39c) stamps

COMBINATION BOOKLET

BK300 BC213 ($7.80) **multi,** 2 each #3974a, 3974b, P#S1111 16.00

Plate number on No. BK300 is printed on the backing paper of the upper example of No. 3974a.

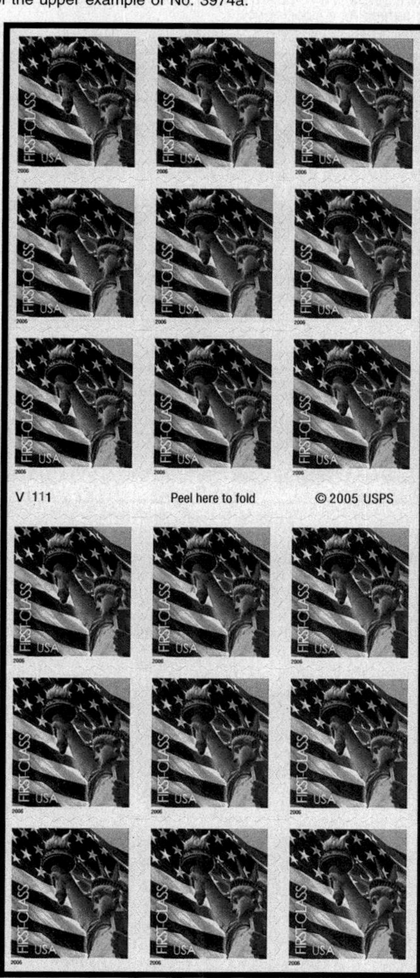

3975a — A3038

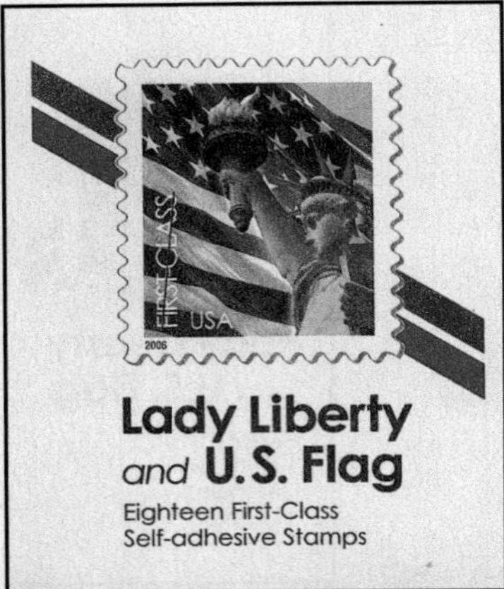

Lady Liberty
and U.S. Flag
Eighteen First-Class
Self-adhesive Stamps

3975a
BC214

2005

($7.02) fold-it-yourself booklet contains 18 self-adhesive (39c) stamps

Serpentine Die Cut 8 on 2, 3 or 4 Sides

Photo.

3975a A3038 (39c) pane of 18, P#V1111 14.50

No. 3975a is a complete booklet (BC214). The peelable backing serves as a booklet cover.

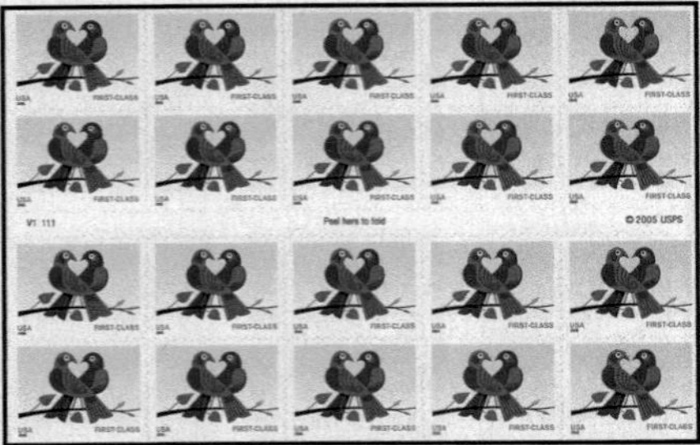

3976a — A3039

3976a — BC215

2006

($7.80) fold-it-yourself booklet contains 20 self-adhesive (39c) stamps

Serpentine Die Cut 11 on 2, 3 or 4 Sides

2006, Jan. 3 Self-Adhesive Photo.

3976a A3039 (39c) pane of 20, P#V11111 20.00

No. 3976a is a complete booklet (BC215). The peelable backing serves as a booklet cover.

3978a — A3040

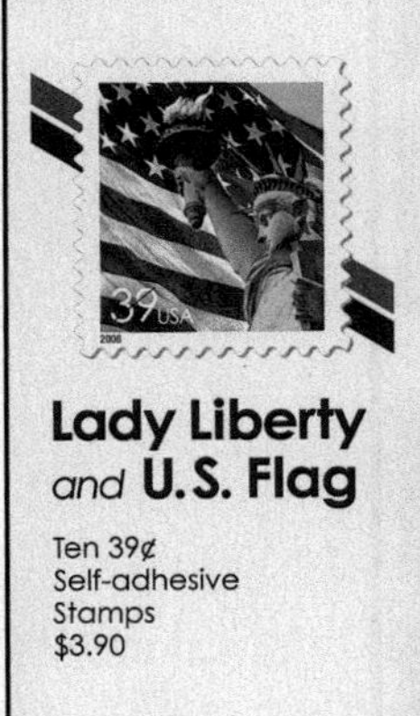

3978a — BC216

2006

$3.90 fold-it-yourself booklet contains 10 self-adhesive 39c stamps

Serpentine Die Cut 11¼x10¾ on 3 Sides

2006, Apr. 8 Self-Adhesive Litho.

3978a A3040 39c pane of 10, P#P1111, P2222 8.50

No. 3978a is a complete booklet (BC216). The peelable backing serves as a booklet cover.

3978b, 3985a, BC217
— A3040

Serpentine Die Cut 11¼x10¾ on 2 or 3 Sides

2006, Apr. 8 Self-Adhesive Litho.

3978b A3040 39c pane of 20, P#P1111 17.00

Variety

3978c As "b," die cutting omitted on the side with eight stamps —

No. 3978b is a complete booklet with 12 stamps plus P# on one side and eight stamps plus a label that serves as the booklet cover (BC217) on the other side.

Flag and Statue of Liberty (No. 3978b) Type of 2006

Serpentine Die Cut 11¼x10¾ on 2 or 3 Sides

2006, Apr. 8 Self-Adhesive Photo.

Without Microprinting

3985a A3040 39c pane of 20, #V1111 16.00

No. 3985a is a complete booklet with 12 stamps plus P# on one side and eight stamps plus a label that serves as the booklet cover (BC217) on the other side. The fonts of the UPC code on the booklet cover for No. 3985a differ from those used on No. 3978b.

3985c, 3985d — A3040

Serpentine Die Cut 11.1 on 2 or 3 Sides

2006, Nov. 8 Self-Adhesive Photo.

3985c A3040 39c pane of 4 3.20
3985d A3040 39c pane of 6, no P# 4.80

3985c,
3985d — BC216A

2006

$7.80 fold-it-yourself booklet contains 20 self-adhesive 39c stamps

COMBINATION BOOKLET

BK300A BC216A $7.80 **multi,** 2 each #3985c, 3985d P#V11111 16.00

Plate number on No. BK300A is printed on the backing paper of the lower example of No. 3985c.

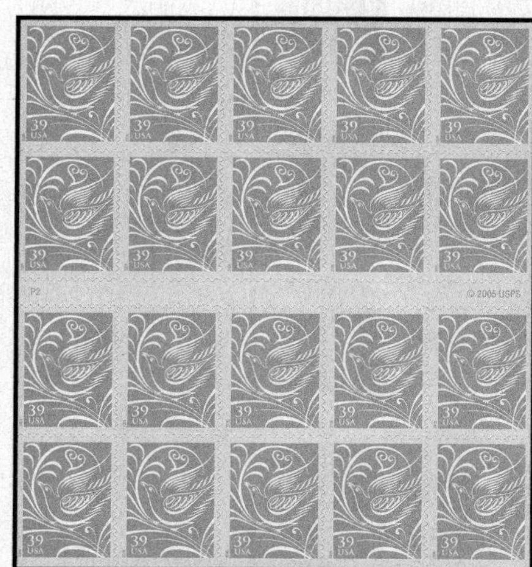

3998a — A3051

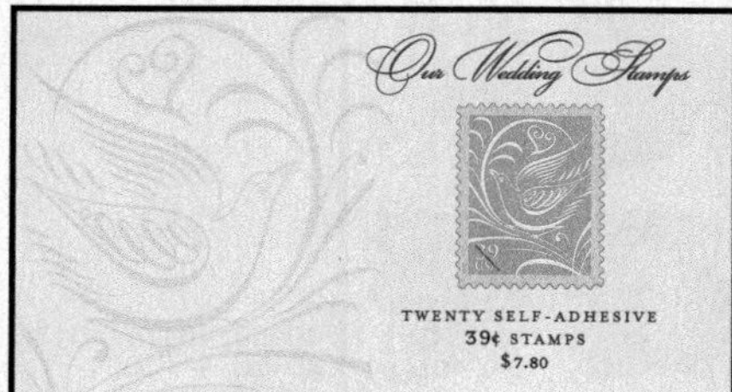

Our Wedding Stamps
TWENTY SELF-ADHESIVE
39¢ STAMPS
$7.80

3998a — BC218

2006

$7.80 booklet contains 20 self-adhesive 39c stamps

Serpentine Die Cut 10¾x11 on 2, 3 or 4 Sides

2006, Mar. 1 Self-Adhesive Litho.

3998a A3051 39c pane of 20, #P1, P2 16.00

Variety

3998b As "a," die cutting omitted —

No. 3998a is a complete booklet (BC218). The peelable backing serves as a booklet cover.

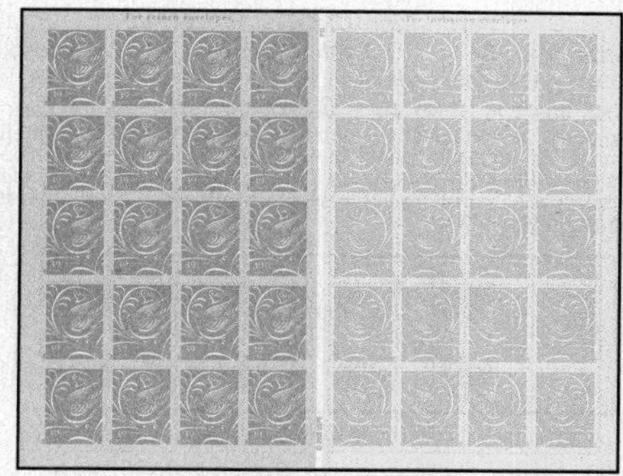

3999a — A3051-A3052

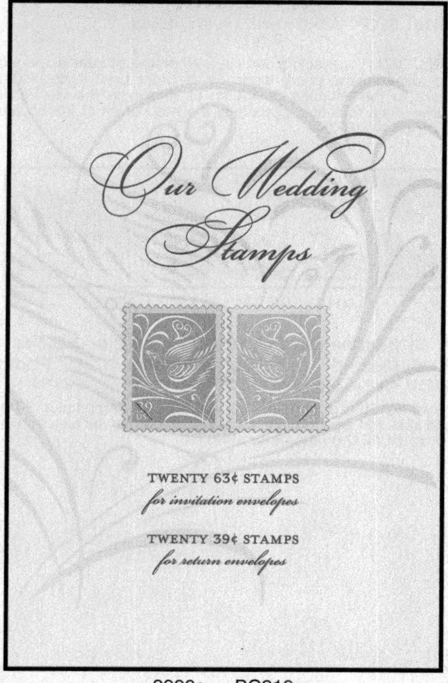

3999a — BC219

2006

$20.40 booklet contains 20 self-adhesive 39c stamps and 20 self-adhesive 63c stamps

Serpentine Die Cut 10¾x11

3999a Pane of 40 (20 each #3998-3999), #P11 45.00

No. 3999a is a complete booklet (BC219). The peelable backing serves as a booklet cover.

4001b — A3053

4001b — BC220

2006

$2.40 fold-it-yourself booklet contains 10 self-adhesive 24c stamps

Serpentine Die Cut 10¾x11¼

2006, Mar. 8 Self-Adhesive Photo.

4001b A3053 24c pane of 10 #4001a, P#V1111 5.00

No. 4001b is a complete booklet (BC220). The peelable backing paper serves as a booklet cover. No. 4001b was sold flat. It has a self-adhesive panel that covers the rouletting on the inside of the booklet cover that is not found in BK301. Three large cuts of rouletting separate the two halves of the booklet cover on No. 4001b.

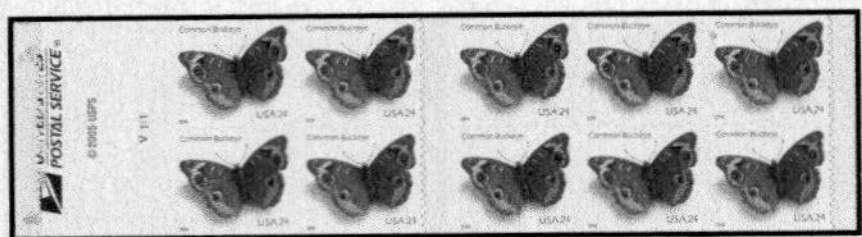

4001c, 4001d — A3053

4001c A3053 24c pane of 4 #4001a, P#V1111 2.00
4001d A3053 24c pane of 6 #4001a, no P# 3.00

COMBINATION BOOKLET

BK301 BC220 $2.40 **multi,** #4001c, 4001d, P#V1111 5.00

No. BK301 was sold glued shut. When the booklet is opened, the self-adhesive panel found on the right side of No. 4001d sticks to the left side of 4001c, as shown in the illustration above. Fine rouletting separates the two halves of the booklet cover on No. BK301.

4012b, BC221 — A3054-A3058

Serpentine Die Cut 10¾x10½ on 2 or 3 Sides

2006, Mar. 16 Self-Adhesive Photo.

4012b A3054 39c pane of 20, P#S1111 25.00

No. 4012b is a complete booklet with 12 stamps plus P# on one side and eight stamps plus a label that serves as a booklet cover (BC221) on the other side.

4016a, 4017b, 4017c, 4017d — A3054-A3058

Serpentine Die Cut 10¾x11¼ on 2 or 3 Sides

Litho.

4016a A3054 39c pane of 4, #4013-4016, no P# 4.50
4017b A3054 39c pane of 4, #4013-4015, 4017, no P# 4.50
4017c A3054 39c pane of 6, #4013-4016, 2 #4017, no P# 6.75
4017d A3054 39c pane of 6, #4013-4015, 4017, 2 #4016, no P# 6.75

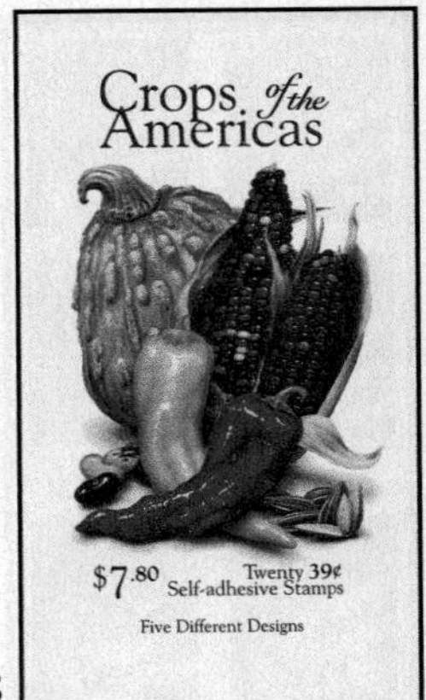

4016a, 4017b, 4017c, 4017d — BC222

2006

$7.80 booklet contains 20 self-adhesive 39c stamps

COMBINATION BOOKLET

BK302 BC222 $7.80 **multi,** #4016a, 4017b, 4017c, 4017d, no P# 22.50

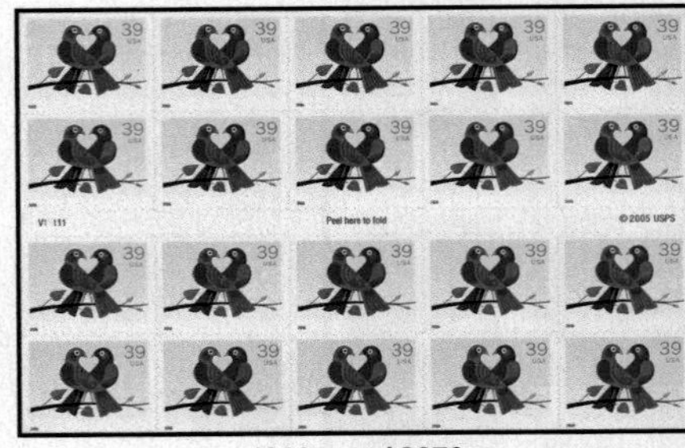

4029a — A3070

4029a — BC223

2006

$7.80 fold-it-yourself booklet contains 20 self-adhesive 39c stamps

Serpentine Die Cut 11 on 2, 3 or 4 Sides

2006, May 1 Self-Adhesive Photo.

4029a A3070 39c pane of 20, P#V11111 19.00

No. 4029a is a complete booklet (BC223). The peelable backing serves as a booklet cover.

4098b, BC224 — A3127-A3136

Serpentine Die Cut 10¾ on 2 or 3 Sides

2006, Aug. 24 Self-Adhesive Photo.

4098b A3127 39c pane of 20, P#S11111 22.50

No. 4098b is a complete booklet with 12 stamps (1 each #4090-4093, 4095-4098, and 2 each #4089, 4094) plus P# on one side and eight stamps (1 each #4090-4093, 4095-4098) plus a label that serves as the booklet cover (BC224) on the other side.

4100a, BC225 — A3138

Serpentine Die Cut 10¾x11 on 2 or 3 Sides

2006 Self-Adhesive Litho.

4100a A3138 39c pane of 20, P#P1111, *Oct. 17* 16.00

No. 4100a is a complete double-sided booklet with 12 stamps plus P# on one side of the peelable backing and eight stamps plus P# and the label that serves as a booklet cover (BC225) on the other side of the backing.

4108b, BC226 — A3139-A3142

Serpentine Die Cut 11¼x11½ on 2 or 3 Sides

4108b A3139 39c pane of 20, P#S1111, *Oct. 5* 18.00

No. 4108b is a complete double-sided booklet. Eight stamps and the label that serves as a booklet cover (BC226) are on one side of the peelable backing and 12 stamps plus P# are on the other side of the backing.

4112b, 4112c, 4112d — A3139-A3142

Serpentine Die Cut 11¼x10¾ on 2 or 3 Sides

4112b A3139 39c pane of 4, #4109-4112*Oct. 5* 4.00
4112c A3139 39c pane of 6, #4111-4112, 2 each #4109-4110, no P#, *Oct. 5* 6.00
4112d A3139 39c pane of 6, #4109-4110, 2 each #4111-4112, *Oct. 5* 6.00

4112b, 4112c, 4112d — BC227

2006

$7.80 booklet contains 20 self-adhesive 39c stamps

COMBINATION BOOKLET

BK303 BC227 $7.80 **multi,** #4112c, 4112d, 2 #4112b, P#S1111 20.00

Plate number on No. BK303 is printed on the backing paper of No. 4112d.

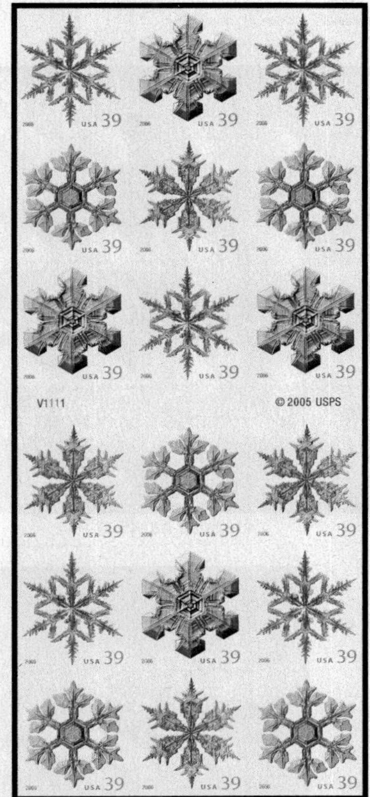

4116b — A3139-A3142

Snowflakes
Four different designs
Eighteen
39¢
Self-adhesive Stamps
$7.02

4116b
BC228

2006

$7.02 fold-it-yourself booklet contains 18 self-adhesive 39c stamps

Serpentine Die Cut 8 on 2, 3 or 4 Sides

Photo.

4116b A3139 39c pane of 18, 4 each #4114, 4116, 5 each #4113, 4115, P#V1111, *Oct. 5* 27.00

No. 4116b is a complete booklet (BC228). The peelable backing serves as a booklet cover.

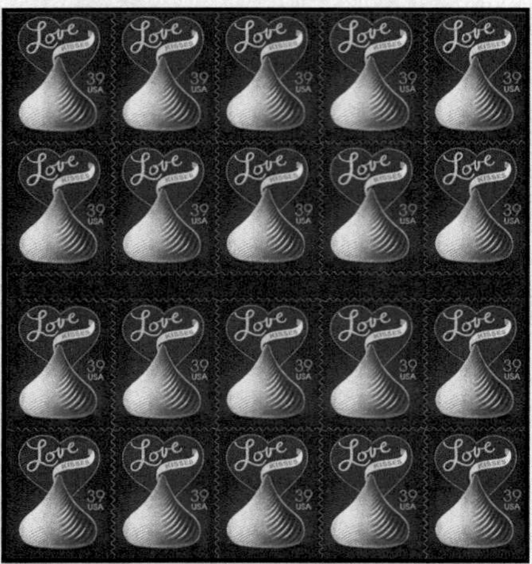

4122a — A3145

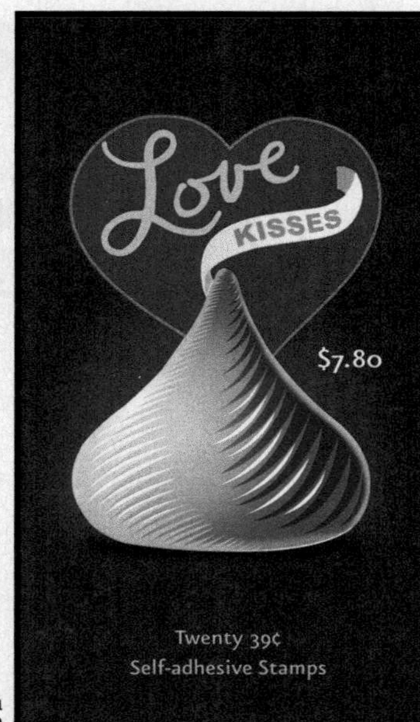

4122a
BC229

2007

$7.80 fold-it-yourself booklet contains 20 self-adhesive 39c stamps

Serpentine Die Cut 10¾x11 on 2, 3 or 4 Sides

2007, Jan. 13 Self-Adhesive Photo.

4122a A3145 39c pane of 20 16.00

No. 4122a is a complete booklet (BC229). The peelable backing serves as a booklet cover. The plate number (V1111) is printed on the rear cover of the booklet.

4125a, 4125c, 4126a, 4126c, 4127a, 4127e, 4127j, BC230 — A3148

No. BC230 was printed by three different manufacturers with differences in the fonts used in the UPC code.

Serpentine Die Cut 11¼x10¾ on 2 or 3 Sides

2007, Apr. 12 Self-Adhesive Photo.

Large Microprinting, Bell 16mm Wide

4125a A3148 (41c) pane of 20, "2007" year date, P#V11111 22.00

4125c A3148 (42c) pane of 20 #4125b, "2008" year date, P#V11111 22.00

4125g A3148 (44c) pane of 20 #4125f, "2009" year date, P#V11111 22.00

Litho.

Small Microprinting, Bell 16mm Wide

4126a A3148 (41c) pane of 20, "2007" year date, P#P11111 22.00

4126c A3148 (42c) pane of 20 #4126b, "2008" year date, P#P11111 22.00

4126e A3148 (44c) pane of 20 #4126d, "2009" year date in copper, P#P11111 22.00

Medium Microprinting, Bell 15mm Wide

4127a A3148 (41c) pane of 20, P#S11111, "2007" year date 22.00

4127e A3148 (42c) pane of 20, P#S11111, "2008" year date 22.00

4127j A3148 (44c) pane of 20, P#S11111, "2009" year date in copper 22.00

Varieties

4125d As "c," copper ("FOREVER") omitted *1,000.*

4125e As "c," copper ("FOREVER") omitted on side with 12 stamps, copper splatters on side with 8 stamps —

4126g As "c," die cutting omitted —

4127m As "e," die cutting omitted *500.00*

Nos. 4125a, 4125c, 4125g, 4126a, 4126c, 4126e, 4127a, 4127e, and 4127j are complete double-sided booklets with 12 stamps plus P# on one side of the peelable backing and eight stamps and a label that serves as a booklet cover (BC230) on the other side of the backing. On Nos. 4125c and 4126c, the bar code number found on the booklet cover was changed to "06777005." On Nos. 4125g and 4126e, the bar code number found on the booket cover was changed to "0678900."

No. 4127a and its varieties exist on two types of surface-tagged paper that exhibit either an uneven or solid appearance, as follows: tagging on No. 4127a appears uneven on both sides (most common), solid on both sides (value, $80), uneven on eight-stamp side and solid on 12-stamp side (extremely scarce); tagging on No. 4127e appears solid on both sides, or solid on eight-stamp side and uneven on 12-stamp side (value, $25); tagging on No. 4127j appears solid.

Issued: Nos. 4125f, 4126e, Aug. 7, 2009.

4127b, 4127c — A3148

Medium Microprinting, Bell 15mm Wide

4127b A3148 (41c) pane of 4 #4127 4.40

4127c A3148 (41c) pane of 6 #4127, no P# 6.60

4127g A3148 (42c) pane of 4 #4127f 4.40

4127h A3148 (42c) pane of 6 #4127f, no P# 6.60

Nos. 4127g and 4127h have a smaller "2008" date. The "2008" date on No. 4127e is the same size as the "2007" date on No. 4127a.

4127b, 4127c, 4127g, 4127h — BC231

2007

$8.20 booklet contains 20 self-adhesive (41c) stamps

COMBINATION BOOKLETS

BK304 BC231 ($8.20) **multi,** 2 each #4127b, 4127c, P#S11111 22.00

BK304a BC231 ($8.40) **multi,** 2 each #4127g, 4127h, P#S11111 22.00

Plate number on No. BK304 is printed on the backing of the lower example of No. 4127b. On No. BK304a, plate number appears on the backing of the lower example of No. 4127g.

Nos. 4127b and 4127c exist with rouletting on backing paper of either gauge 9½ or 13.

4128a — A3148

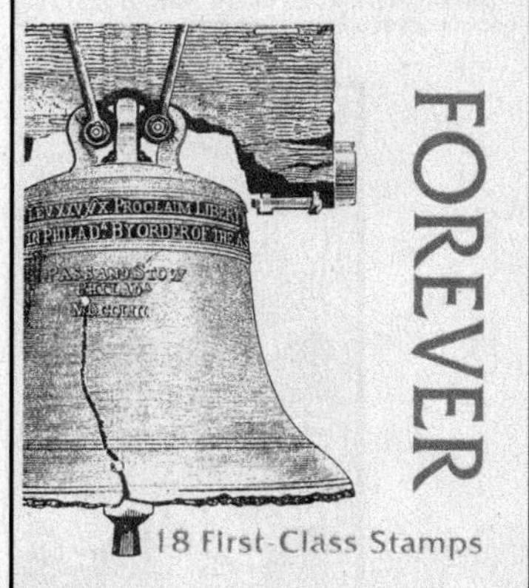

4128a BC232

2007

$7.38 fold-it-yourself booklet contains 18 self-adhesive (41c) stamps

Serpentine Die Cut 8 on 2, 3 or 4 Sides

Large Microprinting, Bell 16mm Wide

Photo.

4128a A3148 (41c) pane of 18, "2007" year date ('07) 20.00

4128c A3148 (42c) pane of 18 #4128b, "2009" year date in black, P#V11111 ('09) 20.00

Nos. 4128a and 4128c are complete booklets (BC232). The peelable backing serves as a booklet cover.

Two versions of No. 4128a exist. The original issue has P#V11 on the backing paper, while a second printing has P#V22222 on the peelable strip on the front.

On No. 4128a, the bar code number on the booklet cover is "0-569900-1." On No. 4128c, the bar code number on the booklet cover was changed to "0-573300-2."

See No. 4437a.

4142a — A3152

4142a — BC233

2007

$2.60 fold-it-yourself booklet contains 10 self-adhesive 26c stamps

Serpentine Die Cut 11¼x11 on 3 Sides

2007, May 12 **Self-Adhesive** **Photo.**

4142a A3152 26c pane of 10, P#V11111 5.50

No. 4142a is a complete booklet (BC233). The peelable backing serves as a booklet cover.

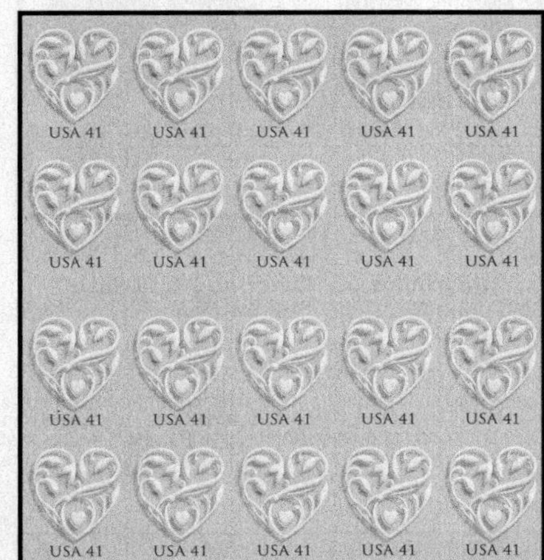

4151a — A3161

4151a — BC234

2007

$8.20 fold-it-yourself booklet contains 20 self-adhesive 41c stamps

Serpentine Die Cut 10¾ on 2, 3 or 4 Sides

2007, June 27 **Self-Adhesive** **Litho.**

4151a A3161 41c pane of 20 20.00

No. 4151a is a complete booklet (BC234). The peelable backing, which has a plate number (P11111), serves as a booklet cover.

4156d, BC235 — A3163-A3166

Serpentine Die Cut 11 on 2 or 3 Sides

2007, June 29 — Self-Adhesive — Litho.

4156d A3163 41c pane of 20, 3 each #4153-4156, 2 each #4153a-4156a, P#P1111 17.00

No. 4156d is a complete double-sided booklet with 12 stamps (2 each #4153-4156, 1 each 4153a-4156a) on one side of the peelable backing and eight stamps plus P# and the label that serves as a booklet cover (BC235) on the other side of the backing.

4165a, BC236 — A3173

Serpentine Die Cut 10¾ on 2 or 3 Sides

2007, Aug. 9 — Self-Adhesive — Litho.

4165a A3173 41c pane of 20, #P11111 17.00

No. 4165a is a complete double-sided booklet with 12 stamps on one side and eight stamps plus P# and a label that serves as the booklet cover (BC236) on the other side.

4185a, BC237 — A3174-A3183

Serpentine Die Cut 11¼x11½ on 2 or 3 Sides

2007, Aug. 10 — Self-Adhesive — Photo.

4185a 41c pane of 20, 2 each #4176-4185, P#V1111 25.00

Variety

4185b As "a," die cutting missing on Nos. 4178 and 4183 on side with eight stamps (PS) *1,000.*

No. 4185a is a complete double-sided booklet with 12 stamps (2 each #4176-4177, and 1 each #4178-4185) plus P# on one side and eight stamps (#4178-4185) plus a label (BC237) that serves as the booklet cover on the other side.

4190a—A3184

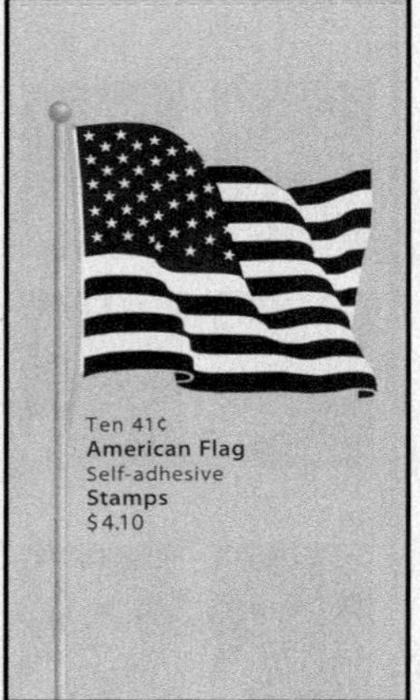

4190a — BC238

2007

$4.10 fold-it-yourself booklet contains 10 self-adhesive 41c stamps

Serpentine Die Cut 11¼x10¾ on 3 Sides

2007, Aug. 15 — Self-Adhesive — Litho.

With "USPS" Microprinted on Right Side of Flagpole

4190a 41c pane of 10, P#P11111 8.50

By its nature, No. 4190a is a complete booklet (BC238). The peelable backing serves as a booklet cover.

4191a, BC239 — A3184

Serpentine Die Cut 11¼x10¾ on 2 or 3 Sides

With "USPS" Microprinted on Left Side of Flagpole

4191a 41c pane of 20, P#S11111 17.00

No. 4191a is a complete double-sided booklet with 12 stamps plus P# on one side of the peelable backing and eight stamps plus a label (BC239) that serves as the booklet cover on the other side.

4206a, BC240 — A3198

Serpentine Die Cut 10¾x11 on 2 or 3 Sides

2007, Oct. 25 — Self-Adhesive — Litho.

4206a A3198 41c pane of 20, P#P1111 17.00

No. 4206a is a complete double-sided booklet with 12 stamps on one side of the peelable backing and eight stamps plus P# and the label that serves as a booklet cover (BC240) on the other side of the backing.

4210d, BC241 — A3199-A3202

Serpentine Die Cut 10¾ on 2 or 3 Sides

4210d 41c pane of 20, P#S1111 17.00

No. 4210d is a complete double-sided booklet. Eight stamps (two each #4207-4210) plus P# and the label that serves as a booklet cover (BC241) are on one side of the peelable backing and 12 stamps (three each #4207-4210) are on the other side of the backing.

4214b, 4214c, 4214d — A3203-A3206

Serpentine Die Cut 11¼x11 on 2 or 3 Sides

4214b 41c pane of 4, #4211-4214 5.00
4214c 41c pane of 6, #4213-4214, 2 each #4211-4212, no P# 7.50
4214d 41c pane of 6, #4211-4212, 2 each #42131-4214, no P# 7.50

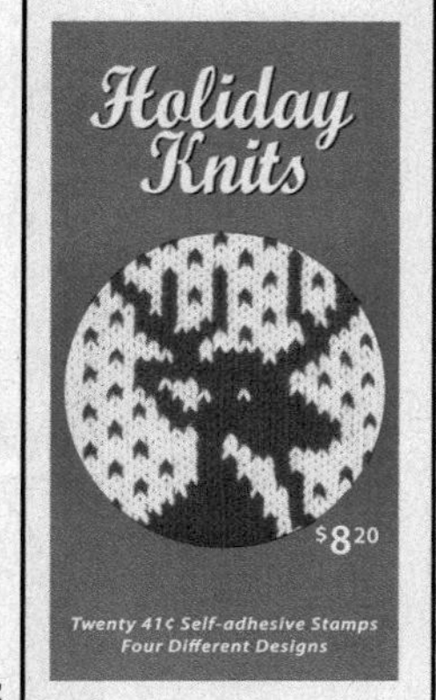

4214b, 4214c, 4214d — BC242

2007

$8.20 booklet contains 20 self-adhesive 41c stamps

COMBINATION BOOKLET

BK305 BC242 $8.20 **multi,** #4214c, 4214d, 2 #4214b, P#S1111 27.50

On No. BK305, plate number appears on the backing of the lower example of No. 4214b.

4218b — A3203-A3206

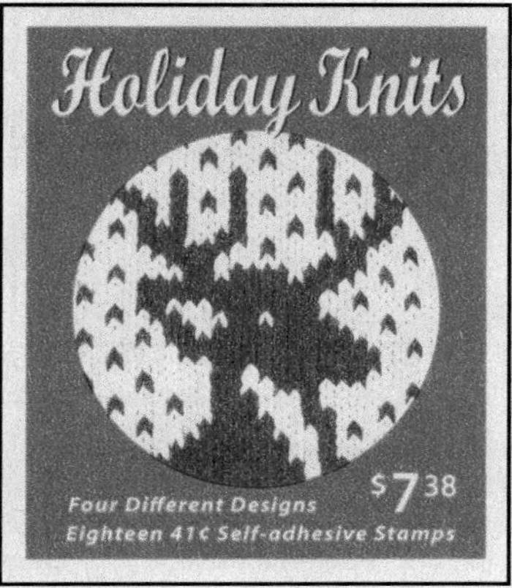

4218b BC243

2007

$7.38 fold-it-yourself booklet contains 18 self-adhesive 41c stamps

Serpentine Die Cut 8 on 2, 3 or 4 Sides

Photo.

4218b 41c pane of 18, 4 each #4215, 4218, 5 each #4216, 4217, P#V1111 23.50

No. 4218b is a complete booklet (BC243). The peelable backing serves as a booklet cover.

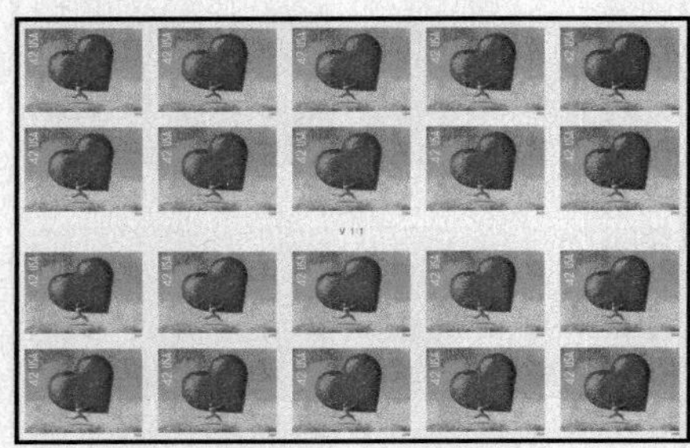
4270a — A3233

4270a — BC244

2008

$8.40 fold-it-yourself booklet contains 20 self-adhesive 42c stamps

Serpentine Die Cut 10¾ on 2, 3 or 4 Sides

2008, June 10 **Self-Adhesive** **Photo.**

4270a A3233 42c pane of 20, P#V1111 19.00

No. 4270a is a complete booklet (BC244). The peelable backing serves as a booklet cover.

4271a — A3234

4271a — BC245

2008

$8.40 fold-it-yourself booklet contains 20 self-adhesive 42c stamps

Serpentine Die Cut 10¾ on 2, 3 or 4 Sides

2008, June 10 Self-Adhesive Litho.

4271a A3234 42c pane of 20 18.00

No. 4271a is a complete booklet (BC245). The peelable backing, which has a plate number (P1111), serves as a booklet cover.

4346a, BC246 — A3308

Serpentine Die Cut 11 on 2 or 3 Sides

2008, Aug. 14 Self-Adhesive Litho.

4346a A3308 42c pane of 20, P#S1111 17.00

No. 4346a is a complete booklet with 12 stamps plus P# on one side and eight stamps plus booklet cover (BC246) on the other side. The peelable backing serves as a booklet cover.

4347a, BC247 — A3309

Serpentine Die Cut 11¼x10¾ on 2 or 3 Sides

2008, Aug. 15 Self-Adhesive Litho.

4347a A3309 42c pane of 20, P#P1111 17.00

No. 4347a is a complete booklet with 12 stamps plus P# on one side and eight stamps plus booklet cover (BC247) on the other side. The peelable backing serves as a booklet cover.

4359a, BC248 — A3319

Serpentine Die Cut 10¾x11 on 2 or 3 Sides

2008, Oct. 23 Self-Adhesive Litho.

4359a A3319 42c pane of 20, P#P11111 17.00

No. 4359a is a complete double-sided booklet with 12 stamps on one side of the peelable backing and eight stamps plus P# and the label that serves as a booklet cover (BC248) on the other side of the backing.

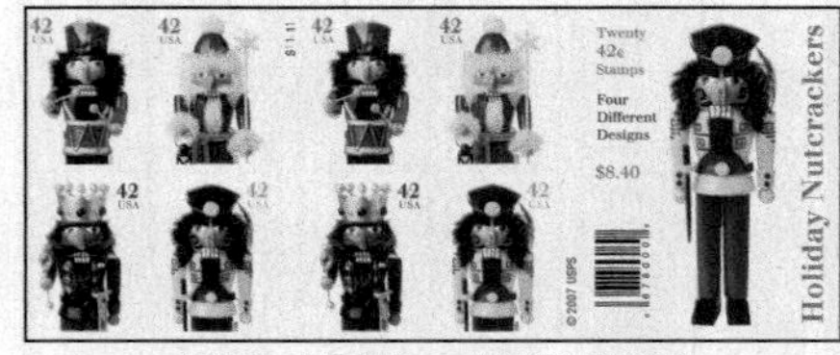

4363b, BC249 — A3320-A3323

Serpentine Die Cut 10¾x11 on 2 or 3 Sides

2008, Oct. 23 Self-Adhesive

4363b 42c pane of 20, P#S11111 20.00

No. 4363b is a complete double-sided booklet. Eight stamps (two each #4360-4363) plus P# and the label that serves as a booklet cover (BC249) are on one side of the peelable backing and 12 stamps (three each #4360-4363) are on the other side of the backing.

4367b, 4367c, 4367d — A3324-A3327

Serpentine Die Cut 11¼x11 on 2 or 3 Sides

2008, Oct. 23 Self-Adhesive

4367b 42c pane of 4, #4364-4367 5.00

4367c 42c pane of 6, #4366-4367, 2 each #4364-4365, no P# 7.50

4367d 42c pane of 6, #4364-4365, 2 each #4366-4367, no P# 7.50

4367b, 4367c, 4367d — BC250

$8.40 booklet contains 20 self-adhesive 42c stamps

COMBINATION BOOKLET

BK306 BC250 $8.40 **multi,** #4367c, 4367d, 2 #4367b, P#S11111 25.00

On No. BK306, plate number appears on the backing of the lower example of No. 4367b.

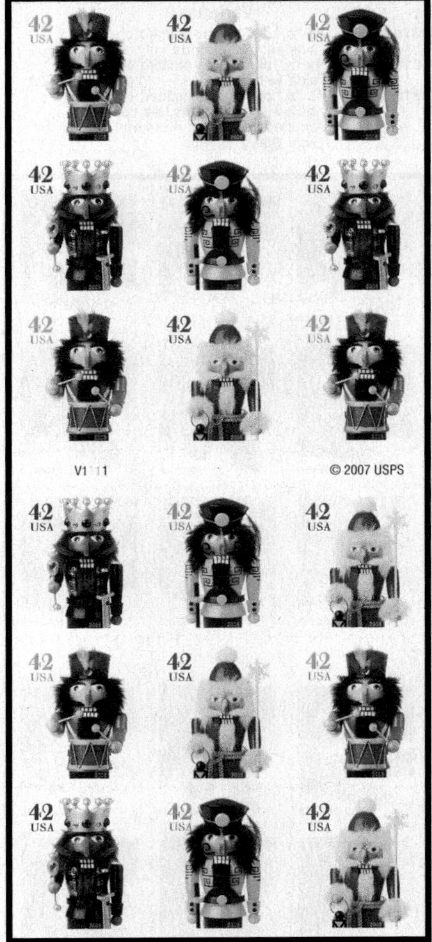

4371b — A3324-A3327

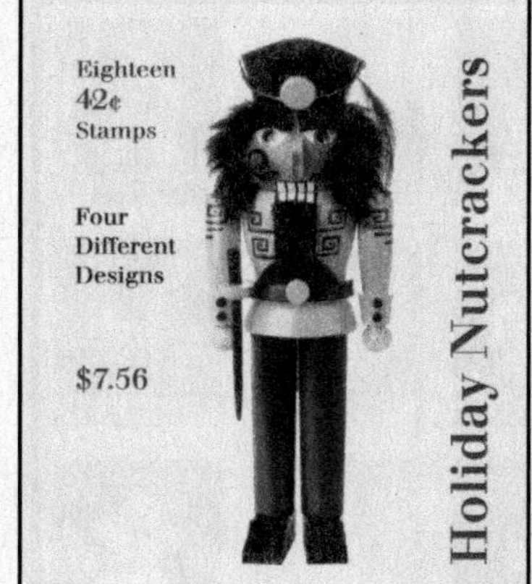

4371b BC251

2008

$7.56 fold-it-yourself booklet contains 18 self-adhesive 42c stamps

Serpentine Die Cut 8 on 2, 3 or 4 Sides

Photo.

4371b 42c pane of 18, 5 each #4368-4369, 4 each #4370-4371, P#V1111 22.50

No. 4371b is a complete booklet (BC251). The peelable backing serves as a booklet cover.

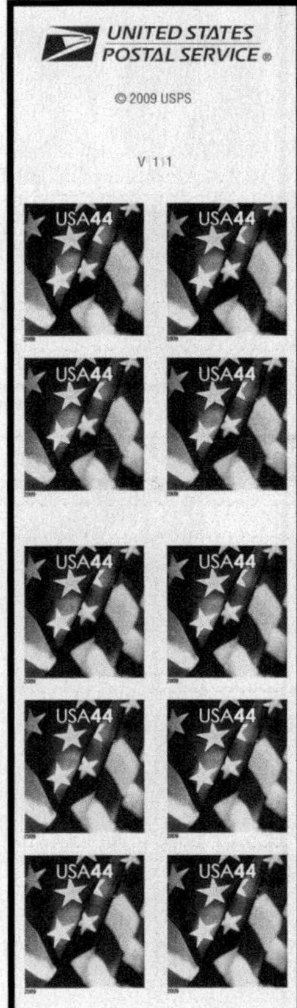

4396a—A3342

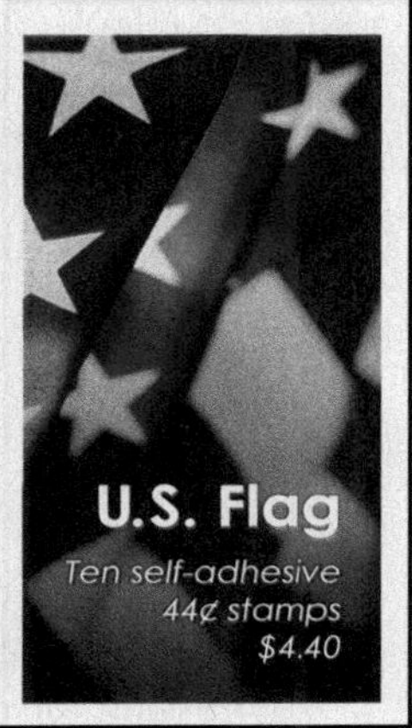

4396a — BC252

2009

$4.40 fold-it-yourself booklet contains 10 self-adhesive 44c stamps

Serpentine Die Cut 11¼x10¾ on 3 Sides

2009, June 5 Self-Adhesive Photo.

4396a A3342 44c pane of 10, #V1111 9.00

By its nature, No. 4396a is a complete booklet (BC252). The peelable backing serves as a booklet cover.

4403b — A3345-A3349

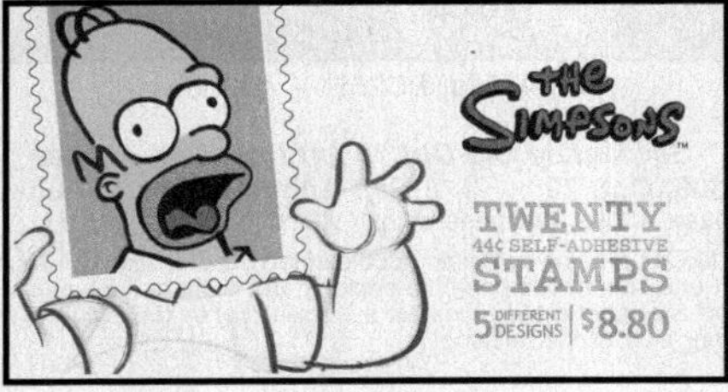

4403b — BC253

2009

$8.80 fold-it-yourself booklet contains 20 self-adhesive 44c stamps

Serpentine Die Cut 10¾ on 2, 3 or 4 Sides

2009, May 7 Litho.

4403b 44c pane of 20, 4 each #4399-4403, no P# (4) 23.00

No. 4403b is a complete booklet (BC253). The peelable backing, which has a plate number (S11111), serves as a booklet cover. The four different booklet covers show #4399 (shown above), #4400 and 4403, #4401, and #4402.

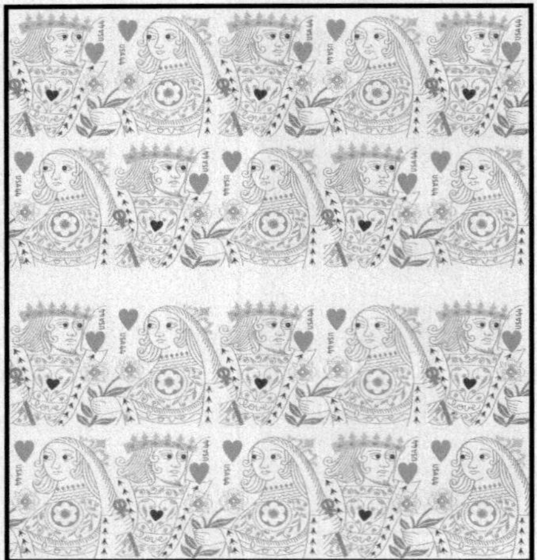

4405b — A3350-A3351

4405b — BC254

2009

$8.80 fold-it-yourself booklet contains 20 self-adhesive 44c stamps

Serpentine Die Cut 10¾ on 2, 3 or 4 Sides

2009, May 8 **Litho.**

4405b 44c pane of 20, 10 each #4404-4405 23.00

No. 4405b is a complete booklet (BC254). The peelable backing, which has a plate number (V11111), serves as a booklet cover.

4424a, BC255 — A3368

Serpentine Die Cut 10¾x11 on 2 or 3 Sides

2009, Oct. 20 **Self-Adhesive** **Litho.**

4424a A3368 44c pane of 20, P#P11111 18.00

No. 4424a is a complete double-sided booklet with 12 stamps on one side of the peelable backing and eight stamps plus P# and the label that serves as a booklet cover (BC255) on the other side of the backing.

4428b, BC256 — A3369-A3372

Serpentine Die Cut 10¾x11 on 2 or 3 Sides

2009, Oct. 8 **Self-Adhesive** **Litho.**

4428b 44c pane of 20, P#S1111 22.00

No. 4428b is a complete double-sided booklet. Eight stamps (two each #4425-4428) plus P# and the label that serves as a booklet cover (BC256) are on one side of the peelable backing and 12 stamps (three each #4425-4428) are on the other side of the backing.

Varieties

4428c As "b," die cutting omitted on side with 12 stamps —

4428d As "b," die cutting omitted on side with 8 stamps —

4432b — A3373-A3376

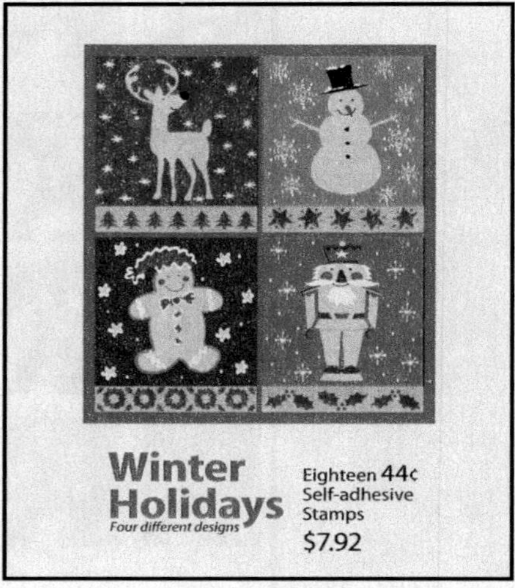

4432b — BC257

2009

$7.92 fold-it-yourself booklet contains 18 self-adhesive 44c stamps

Serpentine Die Cut 8 on 2, 3 or 4 Sides

2009, Oct. 8 **Photo.**

4432b 44c pane of 18, 5 each #4429, 4431, 4 each #4430, 4432, P#V1111 20.00

No. 4432b is a complete booklet (BC257). The peelable backing serves as a booklet cover.

"Forever" Liberty Bell Type of 2007
Serpentine Die Cut 11¼x10¾ on 2, 3 or 4 Sides

2010, Feb. 3 **Self-Adhesive** **Litho.**

Medium Microprinting, Bell 16mm Wide

Dated "2009" in Copper

4437a A3148 (44c) pane of 18 #4437, P#P11111 20.00

No. 4437a is a complete booklet (BC232). The peelable backing serves as a booklet cover. On No. 4437a, the bar code number found on the cover is "0-573300-2," the same as No. 4128c.

4481b, BC258 — A3421-A3424

Serpentine Die Cut 11 on 2 or 3 Sides

2010, Oct. 21 **Self-Adhesive** **Litho.**

4481b (44c) pane of 20, P#S11111 22.00

No. 4481b is a complete double-sided booklet. Eight stamps (two each #4478-4481) plus P# and the label that serves as a booklet cover (BC258) are on one side of the peelable backing and 12 stamps (three each #4478-4481) are on the other side of the backing.

Varieties

4481d As "b," die cutting omitted on side with 12 stamps *700.00*

4481e As "b," die cutting omitted on side with 8 stamps *700.00*

4481f As "b," die cutting omitted on side with 12 stamps, die cutting omitted on bottom 4 stamps on side with 8 stamps —

4485b — A3425-A3428

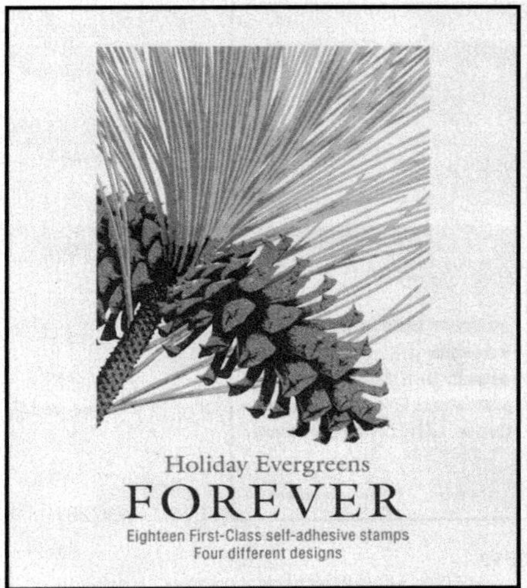

4485b — BC259

2010

($7.92) fold-it-yourself booklet contains 18 self-adhesive (44c) stamps

Serpentine Die Cut 11¼x10¾ on 2, 3 or 4 Sides

2010, Oct. 21 **Litho.**

4485b (44c) pane of 18, 5 each #4482, 4484, 4 each #4483, 4485 P#P11111 20.00

No. 4485b is a complete booklet (BC259). The peelable backing serves as a booklet cover.

4519b — A3429-A3430

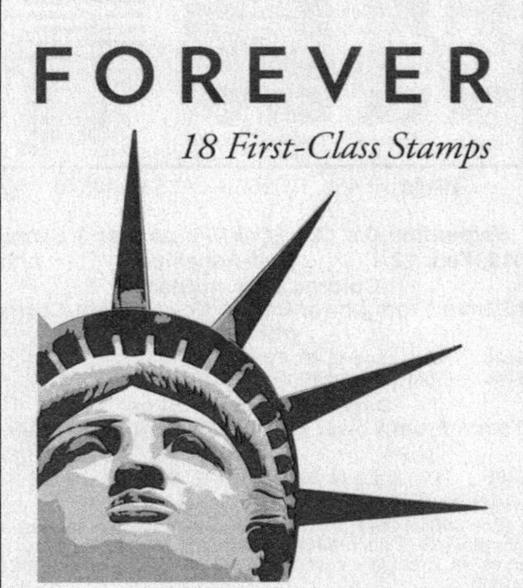

4519b — BC260

2011

($7.92) fold-it-yourself booklet contains 18 self-adhesive (44c) stamps

Serpentine Die Cut 11¼x10¾ on 2, 3 or 4 Sides

2011, Apr. 8 **Litho.**

4519b (44c) pane of 18, 9 each #4518-4519, P#S111111 20.00

No. 4519b is a complete booklet (BC260). The peelable backing serves as a booklet cover.

4560b, BC261 — A3429-A3430

Serpentine Die Cut 11¼x11 on 2 or 3 Sides

2011, Sept. 14 **Self-Adhesive** **Litho.**

Stamps With Microprinting "4evR"

4560b (44c) pane of 20, P#P11111 25.00

No. 4560b is a complete double-sided booklet. Eight stamps (two each #4559-4560) plus P# and the label that serves as a booklet cover (BC261, with bar code number having a closed "4" and a small "2") are on one side of the peelable backing and 12 stamps (three each #4559-4560) are on the other side of the backing.

Stamps With Microprinting "4evr"

4562b (44c) pane of 20, P#S111111 22.00

No. 4562b is a complete double-sided booklet. Eight stamps (two each #4561-4562) plus P# and the label that serves as a booklet cover (BC261, with bar code number having a open "4" and a small "2") are on one side of the peelable backing and 12 stamps (three each #4561-4562) are on the other side of the backing.

Photo.

Serpentine Die Cut 11¼x11½ on 2 or 3 Sides

Stamps With Microprinting "4EVR"

4564b (44c) pane of 20, P#V11111 22.00

No. 4564b is a complete double-sided booklet. Eight stamps (two each #4563-4564) plus P# and the label that serves as a booklet cover (BC261, with bar code number having a open "4" and a large "2") are on one side of the peelable backing and 12 stamps (three each #4563-4564) are on the other side of the backing.

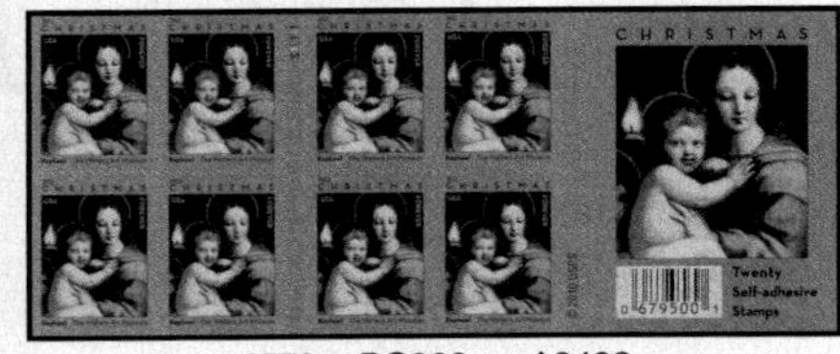

4570a, BC262 — A3493

Serpentine Die Cut 10¾x11 on 2 or 3 Sides

2011, Oct. 13 **Self-Adhesive** **Litho.**

4570a (44c) pane of 20, P#S11111 22.00

No. 4570a is a complete double-sided booklet. Eight stamps plus P# and the label that serves as a booklet cover (BC262) are on one side of the peelable backing and 12 stamps are on the other side of the backing.

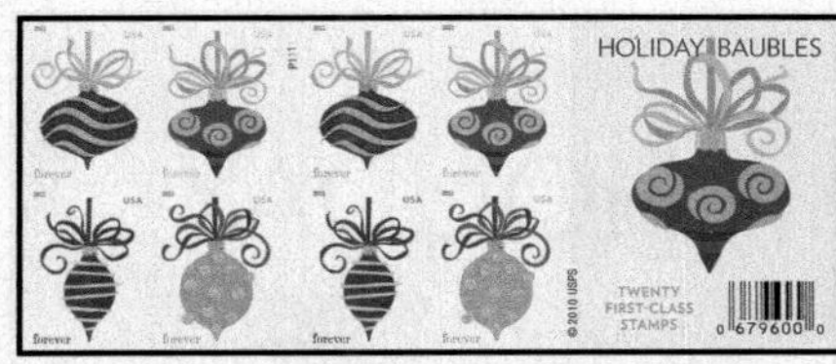

4574b, 4578b, BC263 — A3494-A3498

Serpentine Die Cut 10¾x11 on 2 or 3 Sides

2011, Oct. 13 **Self-Adhesive** **Litho.**

Stamps With Microprinted "USPS" on Ornament Collar

4574b (44c) pane of 20, P#P1111 22.00

Microprinted "USPS" in Places Other Than Collar of Ornament

4578b (44c) pane of 20, P#S11111 22.00

Nos. 4574b and 4578b are complete double-sided booklets. Eight stamps (two each types A3494-A3497) plus P# and the label that serves as a booklet cover (BC263) are on one side of the peelable backing and 12 stamps (three each types A3494-A3497) are on the other side of the backing.

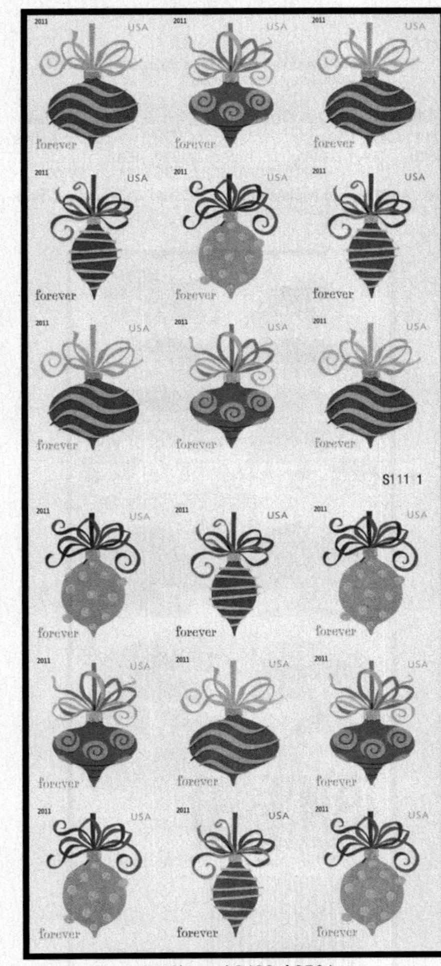

4582b — A3498-A3501

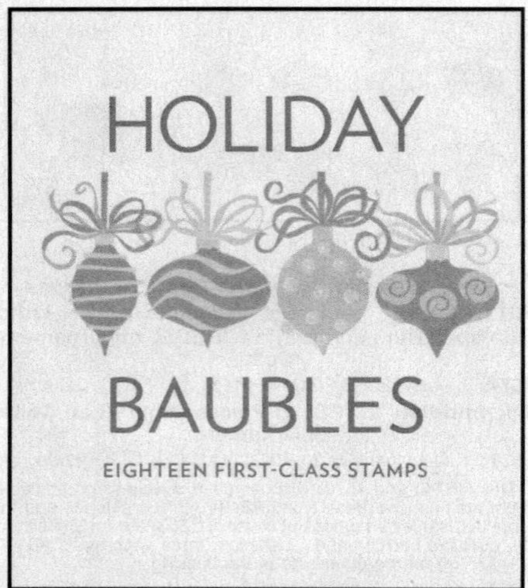

4582b — BC264

2011

($7.92) fold-it-yourself booklet contains 18 self-adhesive (44c) stamps

Serpentine Die Cut 11¼x11 on 2, 3 or 4 Sides

2011, Oct. 13 **Litho.**

4582b (44c) pane of 18, 5 each #4579, 4582, 4 each #4580-4581, P#S11111 20.00

No. 4582b is a complete booklet (BC264). The peelable backing serves as a booklet cover.

4622b, BC265 — A3526-A3530

Serpentine Die Cut 11x10¾ on 2 or 3 Sides

2012, Jan. 23 **Self-Adhesive** **Litho.**

4622b (45c) pane of 20, P#P11111 40.00

No. 4622b is a complete double-sided booklet with 12 stamps (3 each #4618, 4621, 2 each #4619, 4620, 4622) on one side of the peelable backing and eight stamps (#4618, 4621, 2 each #4619, 4620, 4622) plus P# and the label that serves as a booklet cover (BC265) on the other side of the backing.

4644c, 4648b, BC266 — A3537-A3540

Serpentine Die Cut 11¼x10¾ on 2 or 3 Sides

2012, Feb. 22 **Self-Adhesive** **Litho.**

Colored Dots in Stars

18½mm From Lower Left to Lower Right Corner of Flag

4644c (45c) pane of 20, P#P1111 25.00

4644e (45c) pane of 20, P#P2222 25.00

Dark Dots Only in Stars

19mm From Lower Left to Lower Right Corners of Flag

4648b (45c) pane of 20, P#S11111, S22222 30.00

No. 4644c is a complete double-sided booklet with 12 stamps (3 each #4641-4644) on one side of the peelable backing and eight stamps (2 each #4641-4644) plus P# and the label that serves as a booklet cover (BC266) on the other side of the backing.

No. 4644e is a complete double-sided booklet with 12 stamps (3 each #4641a-4644a) on one side of the peelable backing and eight stamps (2 each #4641a-4644a) plus P# and the label that serves as a booklet cover (BC266) on the other side of the backing.

No. 4648b is a complete double-sided booklet with 12 stamps (3 each #4645-4648) on one side of the peelable backing and eight stamps (2 each #4645-4648) plus P# and the label that serves as a booklet cover (BC266) on the other side of the backing.

4676b—A3537-A3540

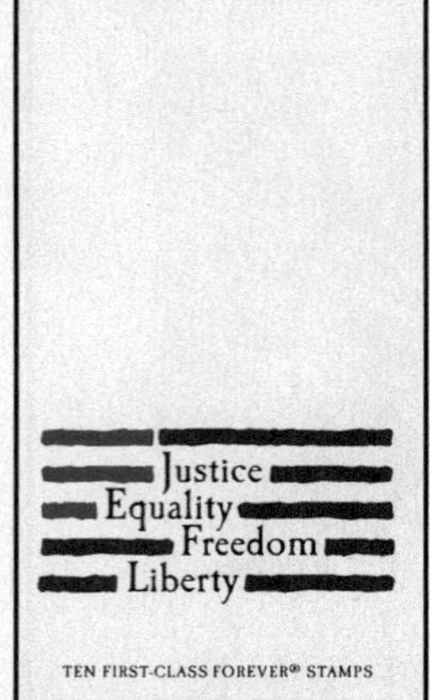

4676b — BC267

2012

$4.50 fold-it-yourself booklet contains 10 self-adhesive (45c) stamps

Serpentine Die Cut 11¼x10¾ on 3 Sides

2012, June 1 **Self-Adhesive** **Photo.**

Colored Dots in Stars

19¼mm From Lower Left to Lower Right Corners of Flag

4676b (45c) pane of 10, P#V1111 11.00

By its nature, No. 4676b is a complete booklet (BC267). The peelable backing serves as a booklet cover.

4686b—A3506-A3510

4686b — BC268

2012

$3.20 fold-it-yourself booklet contains 10 self-adhesive 32c stamps

Serpentine Die Cut 11¼x10¾ on 3 Sides

2012, June 2 Self-Adhesive Litho.

4686b 32c pane of 10, P#P11111 45.00

By its nature, No. 4686b is a complete booklet (BC268). The peelable backing serves as a booklet cover.

4709b — A3537-A3540

4709b — BC269

2012

($8.10) fold-it-yourself booklet contains 18 self-adhesive (45c) stamps

Serpentine Die Cut 11¼x10¾ on 2, 3 or 4 Sides

2012, Sept. 22 Litho.

4709b (45c) pane of 18, 5 each #4706-4707, 4 each #4708-4709, P#P1111 20.00

No. 4709b is a complete booklet (BC269). The peelable backing serves as a booklet cover.

4711a, BC270 — A3590

Serpentine Die Cut 11 on 2 or 3 Sides

2012, Oct. 10 Self-Adhesive Litho.

4711a A3590 (45c) pane of 20, P#S11111 22.00

4711c A3590 (45c) imperf. pane of 20, P#S11111 35.00

No. 4711a is a complete double-sided booklet. Eight stamps plus P# and the label that serves as a booklet cover (BC270) are on one side of the peelable backing and 12 stamps are on the other side of the backing.

4715b, BC271 — A3591-A3594

Serpentine Die Cut 11x10¾ on 2 or 3 Sides

2012, Oct. 13 Self-Adhesive Litho.

4715b (45c) pane of 20, P#P1111 22.00

4715d (45c) imperf. pane of 20, P#P1111 40.00

No. 4715b is a complete double-sided booklet. Eight stamps (two each of Nos. 4712-4715) plus P# and the label that serves as a booklet cover (BC271) are on one side of the peelable backing and 12 stamps (three each of Nos. 4712-4715) are on the other side of the backing.

4763b, BC272 — A3628-A3637

Serpentine Die Cut 10¾ on 2 or 3 Sides

2013, Apr. 5 Self-Adhesive Photo.

4763b (46c) pane of 20, P#V11111 50.00

No. 4763b is a complete double-sided booklet. Eight stamps (1 each #4755-4758, 4760-4763) plus P# and the label that serves as a booklet cover (BC272) are on one side of the peelable backing and 12 stamps (2 each #4754, 4759, 1 each #4755-4758, 4760-4763) are on the other side of the backing.

4781b, 4785d, 4799b, BC273 — A3640-A3643

Serpentine Die Cut 11¼x10¾ on 2 or 3 Sides
2013, May 17 Self-Adhesive Litho.
Microprinted "USPS" at Lower Left Corner of Flag

4781b (46c) pane of 20, P#P1111 30.00

With Microprinted "USPS" Near Top of Pole or at Lower Left Corner Near Rope (#4783)

4785d (46c) pane of 20, P#S1111 22.00

No. 4781b is a complete double-sided booklet with 12 stamps (3 each #4778-4781) on one side of the peelable backing and eight stamps (2 each #4778-4781) plus P# and the label that serves as a booklet cover (BC273) on the other side of the backing.

No. 4785d is a complete double-sided booklet with 12 stamps (3 each #4782-4785) on one side of the peelable backing and eight stamps (2 each #4782-4785) plus P# and the label that serves as a booklet cover (BC273) on the other side of the backing.

Two types of BC273 exist. On No. 4781b, the diagonal and vertical lines of the "4" in the bar code touch, while on No. 4785d, they do not touch.

4785f—A3640-A3543

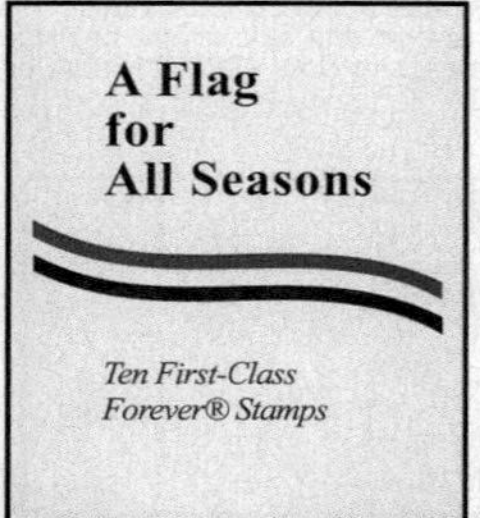

4785f — BC274

2013

$4.60 fold-it-yourself booklet contains 10 self-adhesive (46c) stamps

Serpentine Die Cut 11¼x10¾ on 3 Sides
2013, Aug. 16 Self-Adhesive Photo.
With Microprinted "USPS" Near Top of Pole or at Lower Left Corner Near Rope (#4783a)

4785f (46c) pane of 10, 3 each # 4782a, 4783a, 2 each #4784a, 4785a, P#S1111 11.00

By its nature, No. 4785f is a complete booklet (BC274). The peelable backing serves as a booklet cover.

Flags Type of 2013
Serpentine Die Cut 11¼x10¾ on 2 or 3 Sides
2014, Mar. 17 Litho.
With Microprinted "USPS" Near Top of Pole or at Lower Left Corner Near Rope (#4783)
Overall Tagging

4785h pane of 20, 5 each #4782b, 4783b, 4784b, 4785b (dated "2014"), P#S2222 22.00

4785i As "h," die cutting omitted on side with 8 stamps and 3 pairs on side with 12 stamps —

On day of issue, No. 4785h sold for $9.80, with individual stamps selling for 49c each.

Flags Type of 2013
Serpentine Die Cut 11¼x11½ on 2 or 3 Sides
2013, Aug. 8 Self-Adhesive Litho.
Microprinted "USPS" in Various Places

4799b (46c) pane of 20, P#V1111 25.00

No. 4799b is a complete double-sided booklet with 12 stamps (3 each #4796-4799) on one side of the peelable backing and eight stamps (2 each #4796-4799) plus P# and the label that serves as a booklet cover (BC273) on the other side of the backing.

BC273 on No. 4799b is like that found on No. 4785c.

4815a, BC275 — A3678

Serpentine Die Cut 11 on 2 or 3 Sides
2013, Oct. 11 Self-Adhesive Litho.

4815a A3678 (46c) pane of 20, P#S11111 22.00
4815c A3678 (46c) imperf. pane of 20, P#S11111 35.00

No. 4815a is a complete double-sided booklet. Eight stamps plus P# and the label that serves as a booklet cover (BC275) are on one side of the peelable backing and 12 stamps are on the other side of the backing.

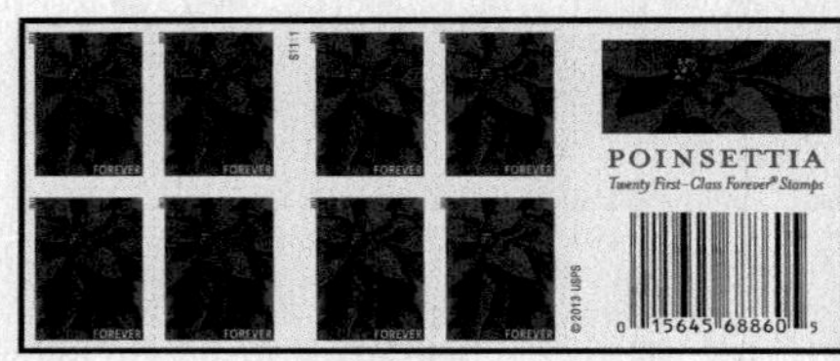

4816a, BC276 — A3679

Serpentine Die Cut 11 on 2 or 3 Sides
2013-14 Self-Adhesive Litho.

4816a A3679 (46c) pane of 20, P#S1111 22.00
4816c A3697 As #4816a, dated "2014," P#S2222 22.00
4816e A3697 As #4816a, imperf. 35.00

Issued: No. 4816a, 10/10/13; No. 4816c, 8/21/14.

No. 4816a and 4816c are complete double-sided booklets. Eight stamps plus P# and the label that serves as a booklet cover (BC276) are on one side of the peelable backing and 12 stamps are on the other side of the backing. The booklet cover on No. 4816c has a USPS emblem over a smaller bar code.

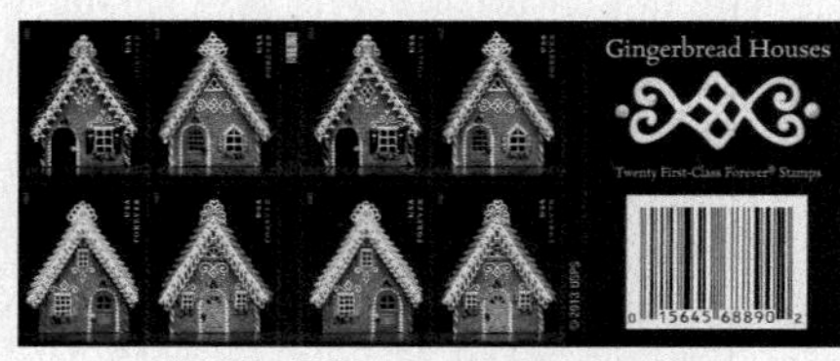

4820b, BC277 — A3680-A3683

Serpentine Die Cut 11 on 2 or 3 Sides
2013, Nov. 6 Self-Adhesive Litho.

4820c (46c) pane of 20, P#S1111 22.00
4820e (46c) pane of 20, P#S2222 22.00
4820g (46c) imperf. pane of 20, P#S1111 40.00

Nos. 4820c, 4820e and 4820g are complete double-sided booklets. Eight stamps plus P# and the label that serves as a booklet cover (BC277) are on one side of the peelable backing and 12 stamps are on the other side of the backing.

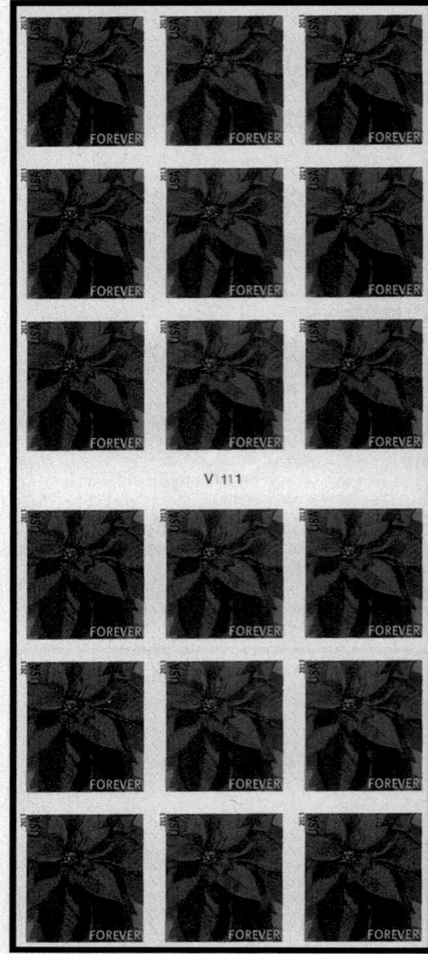

4821a — A3684

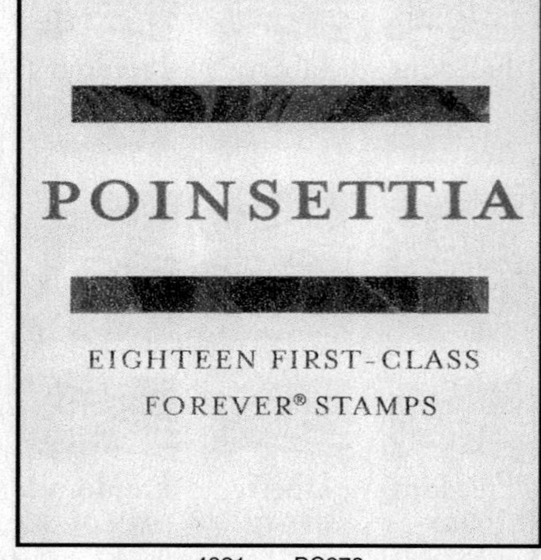

4821a — BC278

($8.28) fold-it-yourself booklet contains 18 self-adhesive (46c) stamps

Serpentine Die Cut 8 on 2, 3 or 4 Sides
2013, Oct. 10 Self-Adhesive Photo.

4821a A3684 (46c) pane of 18, P#V1111 18.00

No. 4821a is a complete booklet (BC278). The peelable backing serves as a booklet cover.

4828a — A3688-A3691

4832a — A3692-A3695

4836a — A3696-A3699

4840a — A3700-A3703

4844a — A3704-A3707

2013, Nov. 19 Litho. *Serpentine Die Cut 11*
Self-Adhesive

4828a	(46c) pane of 4, #4825-4828, + central label, no P#	4.40	
4828b	(46c) imperf. pane of 4	12.50	—
4832a	(46c) pane of 4, #4829-4832, + central label, no P#	4.40	
4832b	(46c) imperf. pane of 4	12.50	—
4836a	(46c) pane of 4, #4833-4836, + central label, no P#	4.40	
4836b	(46c) imperf. pane of 4	12.50	—
4840a	(46c) pane of 4, #4837-4840, + central label, no P#	4.40	
4840b	(46c) imperf. pane of 4	12.50	—
4844a	(46c) pane of 4, #4841-4844, + central label, no P#	4.40	
4844b	(46c) imperf. pane of 4	12.50	—

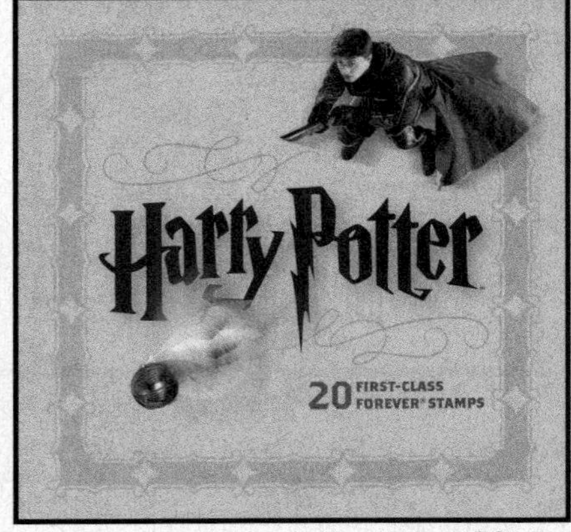

4828a, 4832a, 4836a, 4840a, 4844a — BC279

2013
$9.20 booklets contain 20 self-adhesive (46c) stamps

COMBINATION BOOKLETS

BK307	BC279	$9.20	**multi,** #4828a, 4832a, 4836a, 4840a, 4844a, no P#	22.00
BK307a	BC279	$9.20	**multi,** #4828b, 4832b, 4836b, 4840b, 4844b, no P#	62.50

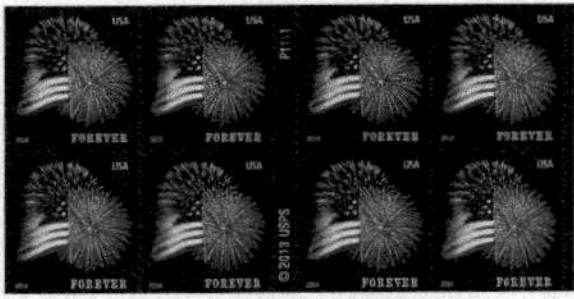

4855a, BC280 — A3716

Serpentine Die Cut 11¼x10¾ on 2 or 3 Sides
2014, Jan. 28 Self-Adhesive Litho.

4855a (49c) pane of 20, P#P1111, P2222 22.00

No. 4855a is a complete double-sided booklet with 12 stamps on one side of the peelable backing and eight stamps plus P# and the label that serves as a booklet cover (BC280) on the other side of the backing.

4865b, BC281 — A3721-A3724

Serpentine Die Cut 11 on 2 or 3 Sides
2014, Feb. 14 Self-Adhesive Litho.

4865b	(49c) pane of 20, 5 each #4862-4865, P#S11111	22.00
4865d	(49c) imperf. pane of 20	35.00

No. 4865b is a complete double-sided booklet. Eight stamps (2 each #4862-4865) plus P# and the label that serves as a booklet cover (BC281) are on one side of the peelable backing and 12 stamps (3 each #4862-4865) are on the other side of the backing.

Fort McHenry Flag and Fireworks Type of 2014 and

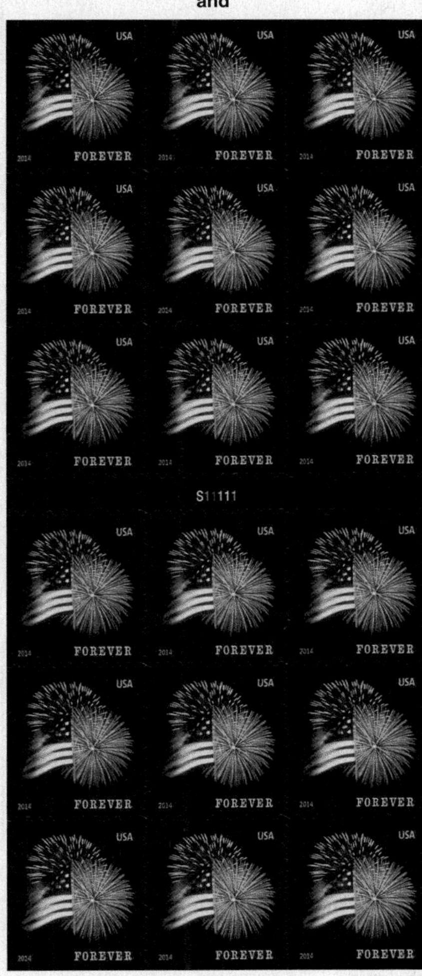

4871a — A3716

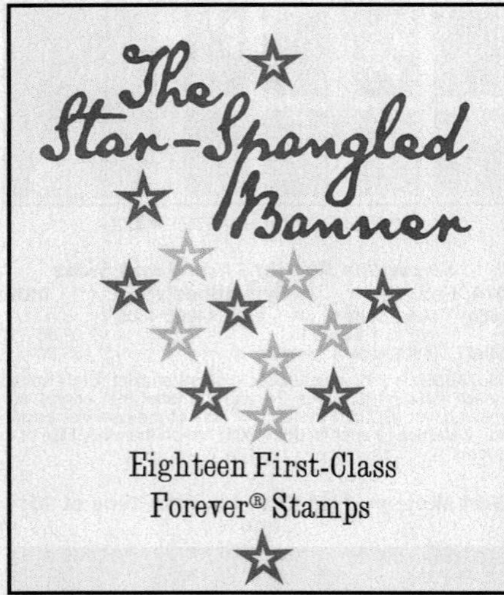

4871a — BC282

2014

($8.82) fold-it-yourself booklet contains 18 self-adhesive (49c) stamps

Serpentine Die Cut 11¼x11½ on 2 or 3 Sides

2014, Mar. 3 Self-Adhesive Photo.

Without "USPS" Microprinting

4869a (49c) pane of 20, P#C1111 22.00

Litho.

Serpentine Die Cut 11¼x10¾ on 2 or 3 Sides

With "USPS" Microprinted in Fireworks Above Flagpole

4870a (49c) pane of 20, P#S11111 22.00

The actual design images on Nos. 4855, 4869 and 4870 differ slightly in size. This is easiest seen by measuring the height of the flagpole: No. 4855 is 13mm, No. 4869 is 14mm, and No. 4870 is 12mm.

Thin Paper

Serpentine Die Cut 11¼x11 on 2, 3, or 4 Sides

4871a (49c) pane of 18, P#S11111 20.00

Nos. 4869a and 4870a are complete double-sided booklets with 12 stamps on one side of the peelable backing and eight stamps plus P# and the label that serves as a booklet cover (BC280) on the other side of the backing.

No. 4871a is a complete booklet (BC282). The peelable backing serves as a booklet cover.

4891b, BC283 — A3735-A3744

Serpentine Die Cut 10¾ on 2 or 3 Sides

2014, Apr. 5 Self-Adhesive Litho.

4891b (49c) pane of 20, P#P1111 22.00
4891d (49c) imperf. pane of 20, P#P1111 40.00

No. 4891b is a complete double-sided booklet. Eight stamps (1 each #4883-4886, 4888-4891) plus P# and the label that serves as a booklet cover (BC283) are on one side of the peelable backing and 12 stamps (2 each #4882, 4887, 1 each #4883-4886, 4888-4891) are on the other side of the backing.

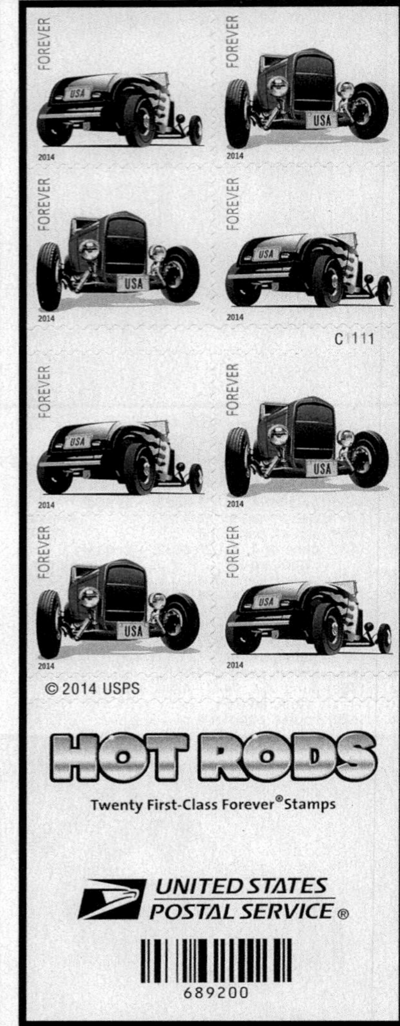

4909b, BC284 — A3761-A3762

Serpentine Die Cut 11¾x11¼ on 2 or 3 Sides

2014, June 6 Self-Adhesive Photo.

4909b (49c) pane of 20, P#C1111 22.00
4909d (49c) imperf. pane of 20, P#C1111 40.00

No. 4909b is a complete booklet with 12 stamps (6 each Nos. 4908-4909) on one side and 8 stamps (4 each Nos.4908-4909), plate number, and booklet cover (BC284) on the other side. The peelable backing serves as a booklet cover.

4920b, BC285 — A3770-A3773

Serpentine Die Cut 11¾ on 2 or 3 Sides

2014, Aug. 21 Self-Adhesive Photo.

4920b (49c) pane of 20, P#C1111 22.00
4920d (49c) imperf. pane of 20, P#C1111 40.00

No. 4920b is a complete booklet with 12 stamps (3 each Nos. 4917-4920) on one side and 8 stamps (2 each Nos. 4917-4920), plate number, and booklet cover (BC285) on the other side. The peelable backing serves as a booklet cover.

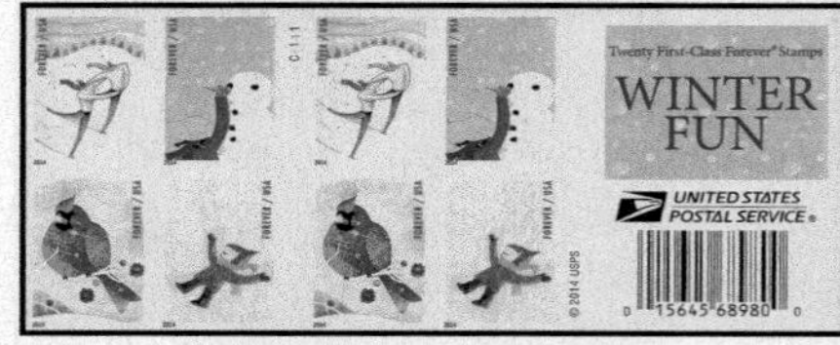

4940b, BC286 — A3790-A3793

Serpentine Die Cut 10¾x11 on 2 or 3 Sides

2014, Oct. 23 Self-Adhesive Photo.

4940b (49c) pane of 20, P#C1111 22.00
4940d (49c) imperf. pane of 20, P#C1111 35.00

No. 4940b is a complete double-sided booklet. Eight stamps (two each Nos. 4937-4940) plus P# and the label that serves as a booklet cover (BC286) are on one side of the peelable backing and 12 stamps (three each Nos. 4937-4940) are on the other side of the backing.

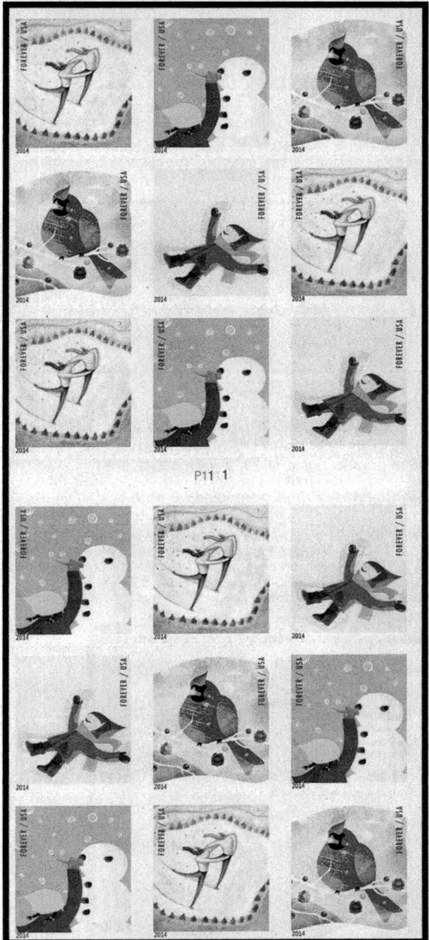
4944b — A3794-A3797

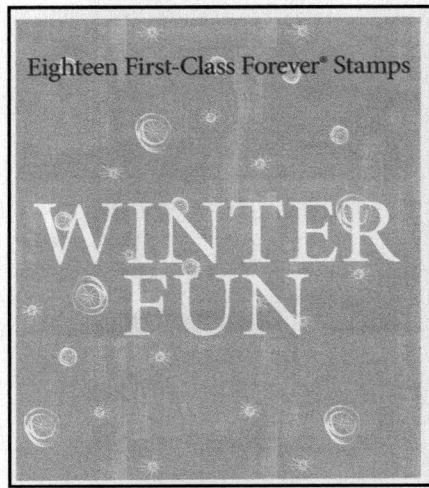

4944b — BC287

2014

($8.82) fold-it-yourself booklet contains 18 self-adhesive (49c) stamps

Serpentine Die Cut 11¼x11 on 2, 3 or 4 Sides

2014, Oct. 23 **Litho.**

4944b (49c) pane of 18, 5 each #4941-4942, 4 each #4943-4944, P#P1111 27.00

No. 4944b is a complete booklet (BC287). The peelable backing serves as a booklet cover.

4945a, BC288 — A3798

Serpentine Die Cut 10¾x11 on 2 or 3 Sides

2014, Nov. 19 **Self-Adhesive** **Litho.**

4945a A3798 (49c) pane of 20, P#S11111 22.00
4945c A3798 (49c) imperf. pane of 20, P#S11111 35.00

No. 4945a is a complete double-sided booklet. Eight stamps plus P# and the label that serves as a booklet cover (BC288) are on one side of the peelable backing and 12 stamps are on the other side of the backing.

4949b, BC289 — A3799-A3802

Serpentine Die Cut 11x10¾ on 2 or 3 Sides

2014, Nov. 6 **Self-Adhesive** **Photo.**

4949b (49c) pane of 20, P#C11111 24.00
4949d (49c) imperf. pane of 20, P#C11111 37.50

No. 4949b is a complete double-sided booklet. Eight stamps (two each of Nos. 4946-4949) plus P# and the label that serves as a booklet cover (BC289) are on one side of the peelable backing and 12 stamps (three each of Nos. 4946-4949) are on the other side of the backing.

4967b, BC290 — A3817-A3820

Serpentine Die Cut 11x11¼ on 2 or 3 Sides

2015, Mar. 20 **Self-Adhesive** **Litho.**

4967b (49c) pane of 20, 5 each #4964-4967, P#S1111 22.00
4967d (49c) imperf. pane of 20, P#S1111 35.00

No. 4967b is a complete double-sided booklet. Eight stamps (2 each #4964-4967) plus P# and the label that serves as a booklet cover (BC290) are on one side of the peelable backing and 12 stamps (3 each #4964-4967) are on the other side of the backing.

No. 4967b is known with the block of 4 at left on the 12-stamp side having no gum. Such booklets are rare and fragile.

5007b, BC291 — A3847-A3850

Serpentine Die Cut 11¼x10¾ on 2 or 3 Sides

2015, July 11 **Self-Adhesive** **Litho.**

5007b (49c) pane of 20, P#P1111 22.00
5007d (49c) imperf. pane of 20, P#P1111 35.00

No. 5007b is a complete double-sided booklet with 12 stamps on one side of the peelable backing and eight stamps plus P# and the label that serves as a booklet cover (BC291) on the other side of the backing.

5030b, BC292 — A3857-A3866

Serpentine Die Cut 10¾ on 2 or 3 Sides

2015, Oct. 1 Self-Adhesive Litho.

5030b	(49c)	pane of 20, P#S1111	24.00
5030d	(49c)	imperf. pane of 20, P#S1111	35.00

No. 5030b is a complete booklet with 12 stamps (Nos. 5023-5030, 2 each Nos. 5021-5022) on one side and 8 stamps (Nos.5023-5030), plate number, and booklet cover (BC292) on the other side. The peelable backing serves as a booklet cover.

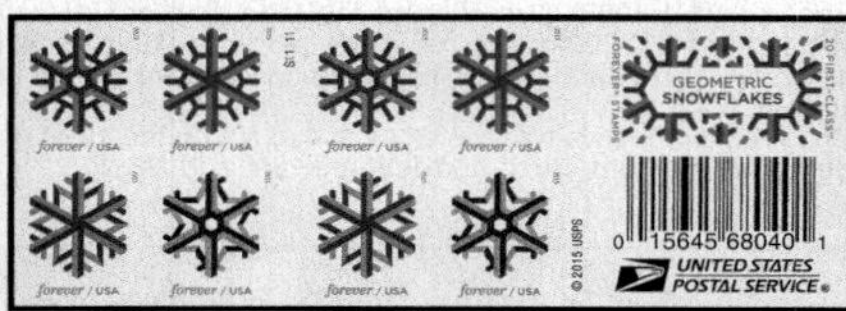

5034b, BC293 — A3867-A3870

Serpentine Die Cut 11¼x10¾ on 2 or 3 Sides

2015, Oct. 23 Self-Adhesive Litho.

5034b	(49c)	pane of 20, P#S11111	22.00
5034d	(49c)	imperf. pane of 20, P#S11111	35.00

No. 5034b is a complete booklet with 12 stamps (3 each Nos. 5031-5034) on one side and 8 stamps (2 each Nos.5031-5034), plate number, and booklet cover (BC293) on the other side. The peelable backing serves as a booklet cover.

5051b — A3877-A3886

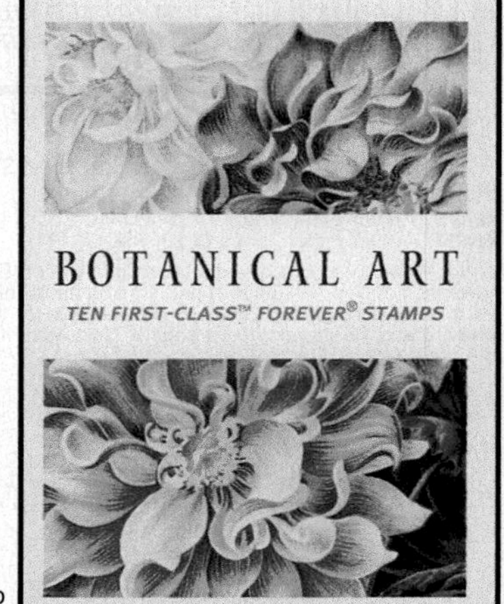

5051b
BC294

2016

$4.90 fold-it-yourself booklet contains 10 self-adhesive (49c) stamps

Serpentine Die Cut 10¾ on 2 or 3 Sides

2016, Jan. 29 Litho.

5051b	(49c)	pane of 10, #5042-5051, P#P1111	12.00

By its nature, No. 5051b is a complete booklet (BC294). The peelable backing serves as a booklet cover.

5051c, BC295 — A3877-A3886

Serpentine Die Cut 10¾ on 2 or 3 Sides

2016, Jan. 29 Self-Adhesive Litho.

5051c	(49c)	pane of 20, 2 each #5042-5051, P#P1111	24.00
5051e	(49c)	imperf. pane of 20, 2 each #5042-5051, P#P1111	150.00

No. 5051c is a complete double-sided booklet. Eight stamps (Nos. 5042-5049) plus P# and the label that serves as a booklet cover (BC295) are on one side of the peelable backing and 12 stamps (Nos. 5042-5049, 2 each Nos. 5050-5051) are on the other side of the backing.

5054a — A3887

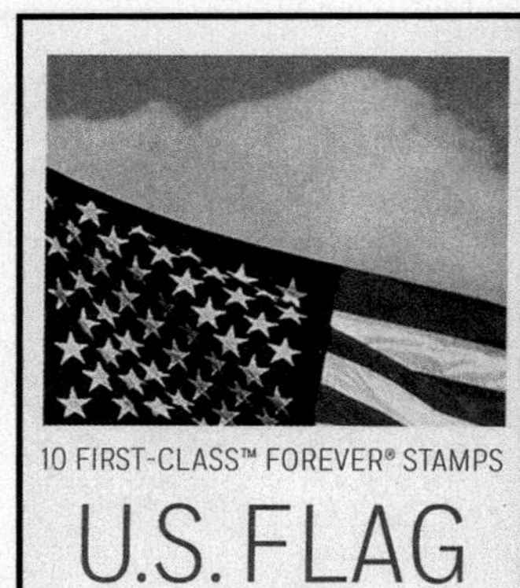

5054a
BC296

2016

$4.90 fold-it-yourself booklet contains 10 self-adhesive (49c) stamps

Serpentine Die Cut 11¼x10¾ on 2 or 3 Sides

2016, Jan. 29 **Litho.**

5054a A3887 (49c) pane of 10, P#S11111 11.00

By its nature, No. 5054a is a complete booklet (BC296). The peelable backing serves as a booklet cover.

5054b, 5055a, BC297 — A3887

Serpentine Die Cut 11¼x10¾ on 2 or 3 Sides

2016, Jan. 29 **Self-Adhesive** **Litho.**

With Microprinted "USPS" to Right of Flagpole Under Flag

5054b A3887 (49c) pane of 20, P#S11111 22.00

With Microprinted "USPS" on Second White Flag Stripe

5055a A3887 (49c) Pane of 20, P#P1111 22.00

Nos. 5054b and 5055a are complete double-sided booklets. Eight stamps plus P# and the label that serves as a booklet cover (BC297) are on one side of the peelable backing and 12 stamps are on the other side of the backing. The booklet covers for Nos. 5054b and 5055a have different fonts in the numbers in the bar code.

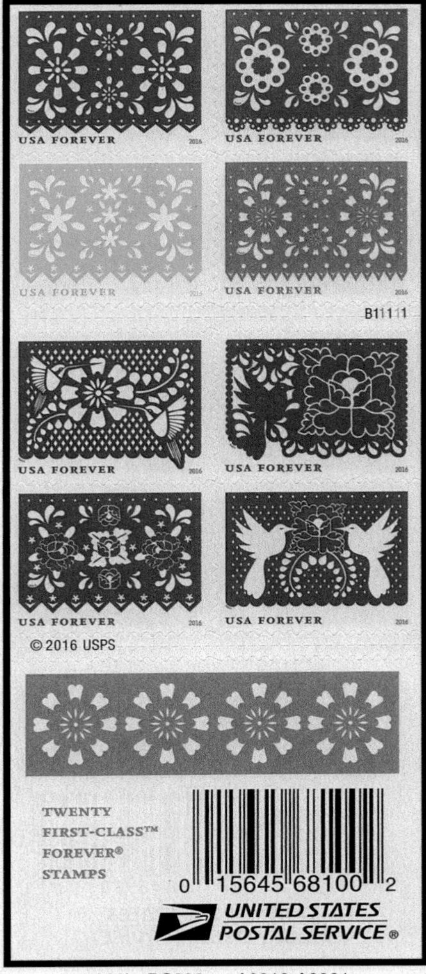

5090b, BC298 — A3912-A3921

Serpentine Die Cut 11 on 2 or 3 Sides

2016, June 3 **Self-Adhesive** **Litho.**

5090b (47c) Pane of 20, P#B11111 22.00

No. 5090b is a complete booklet with 12 stamps (Nos. 5083-5090, 2 each Nos. 5081-5082) on one side and 8 stamps (Nos. 5083-5090), plate number, and booklet cover (BC298) on the other side. The peelable backing serves as a booklet cover.

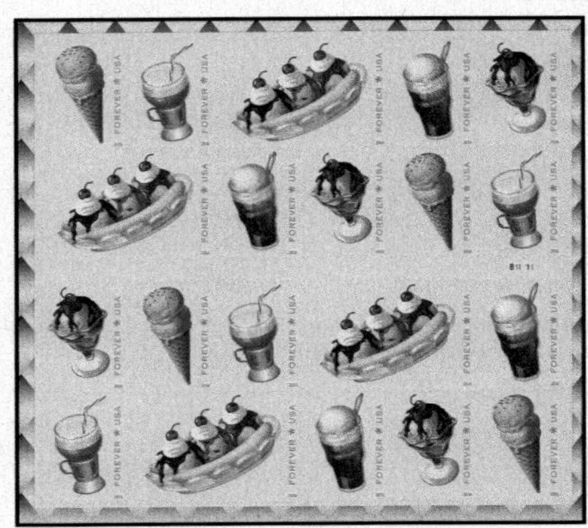

5097c — A3924-A3928

5097c — BC299

2016

$9.40 fold-it-yourself booklet contains 20 self-adhesive (47c) stamps

2016, June 30 **Litho.** ***Serpentine Die Cut 10¾***

5097c (47c) pane of 20, 4 each #5093-5094, 5096-5097, 2 each #5095, 5095a 22.00

No. 5097c is a complete booklet (BC299). The peelable backing, which has a plate number (B11111), serves as a booklet cover.

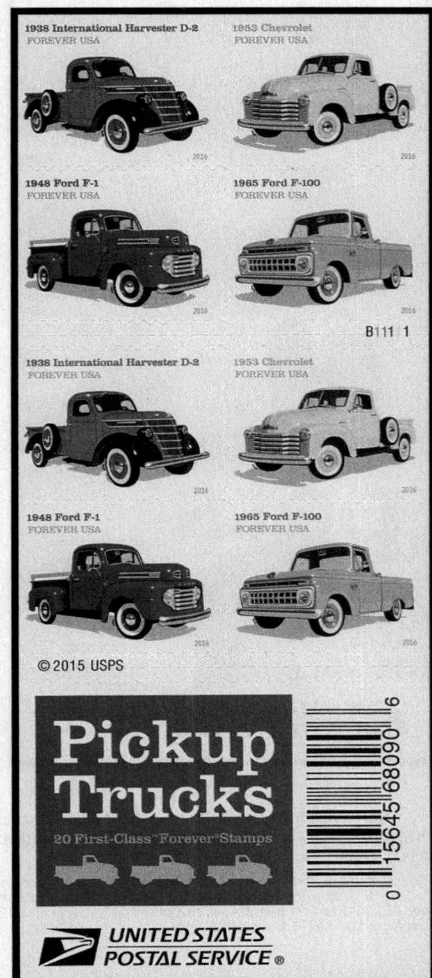

5104b, BC300 — A3932-A3935

Serpentine Die Cut 11 on 2 or 3 Sides

2016, July 15 **Litho.**

Self-Adhesive

5104b (47c) Pane of 20, P#B11111 22.00

No. 5104b is a complete booklet with 12 stamps (3 each Nos. 5101-5104) on one side and 8 stamps (2 each Nos. 5101-5104), plate number, and booklet cover (BC300) on the other side. The peelable backing serves as a booklet cover.

5125a, BC301 — A3937-A3956

Serpentine Die Cut 11 on 2 or 3 Sides

2016, Aug. 2 Self-Adhesive Litho.

5125a (47c) pane of 20, #5106-5125, P#P1111 22.00

No. 5125a is a complete double-sided booklet. Eight stamps (#5118-5125) plus P# and the label that serves as a booklet cover (BC301) are on one side of the peelable backing and 12 stamps (#5106-5117) are on the other side of the backing.

5129b, BC302 — A3957-A3960

Serpentine Die Cut 10¾ on 2 or 3 Sides

2016, Aug. 4 Self-Adhesive Litho.

5129b (47c) pane of 20, 5 each #5126-5129, P#P1111 22.00

No. 5129b is a complete double-sided booklet. Eight stamps (2 each #5126-5129) plus P# and the label that serves as a booklet cover (BC302) are on one side of the peelable backing and 12 stamps (3 each #5126-5129) are on the other side of the backing.

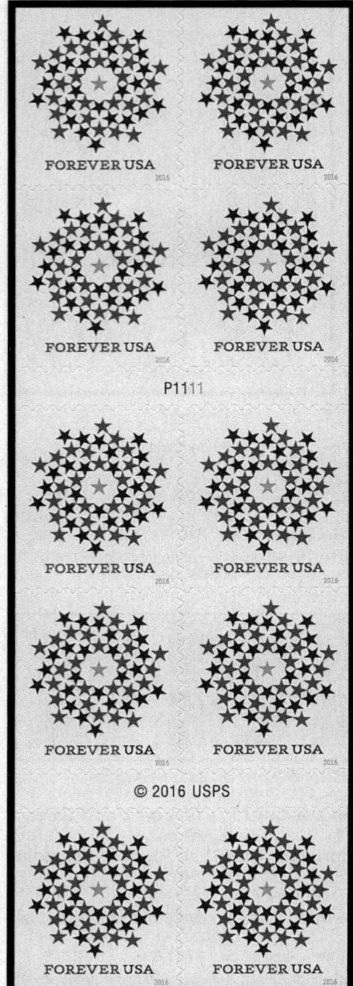

5131a — A3961

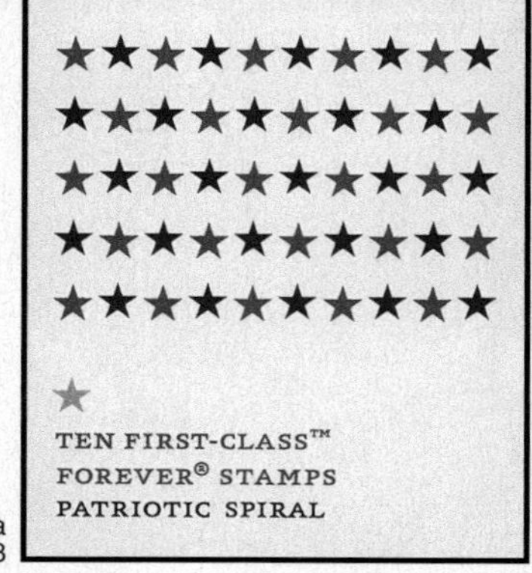

5131a BC303

2016

$4.70 fold-it-yourself booklet contains 10 self-adhesive (47c) stamps

Serpentine Die Cut 11 on 2 or 3 Sides

2016, Aug. 19 Litho.

5131a A3961 (47c) pane of 10, P#P1111 11.00

By its nature, No. 5131a is a complete booklet (BC303). The peelable backing serves as a booklet cover.

5140b, BC304 — A3967-A3970

Serpentine Die Cut 11x10¾ on 2 or 3 Sides

2016, Sept. 29 **Litho.**

Self-Adhesive

5140b (47c) pane of 20, 5 each #5137-5140, P#B11111 22.00

No. 5140b is a complete double-sided booklet. Eight stamps (2 each #5137-5140) plus P# and the label that serves as a booklet cover (BC304) are on one side of the peelable backing and 12 stamps (3 each #5137-5140) are on the other side of the backing.

5143a, BC305 — A3973

5144a, BC306 — A3974

5148b, BC307 — A3975-A3978

Serpentine Die Cut 10¾x11 on 2 or 3 Sides

2016 **Litho.**

Self-Adhesive

5143a A3973 (47c) pane of 20, P#P11111, *Oct. 18* 22.00

5144a A3974 (47c) pane of 20, P#P11111, *Nov. 3* 22.00

5148b (47c) pane of 20, 5 each #5145-5148, P#B1111, *Oct. 7* 22.00

No. 5143a is a complete double-sided booklet. Eight stamps plus P# and the label that serves as a booklet cover (BC305) are on one side of the peelable backing and 12 stamps are on the other side of the backing. No. 5144a is a complete double-sided booklet. Eight stamps plus P# and the label that serves as a booklet cover (BC306) are on one side of the peelable backing and 12 stamps are on the other side of the backing. No. 5148b is a complete double-sided booklet. Eight stamps (2 each #5145-5148) plus P# and the label that serves as a booklet cover (BC307) are on one side of the peelable backing and 12 stamps (3 each #5145-5148) are on the other side of the backing.

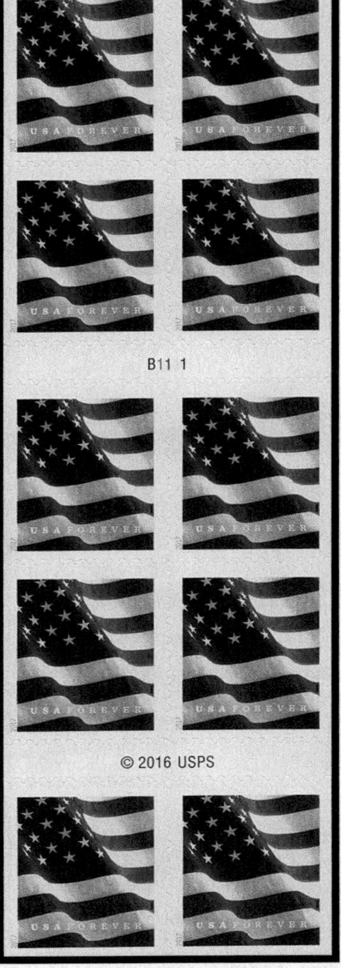

5160a — A3988

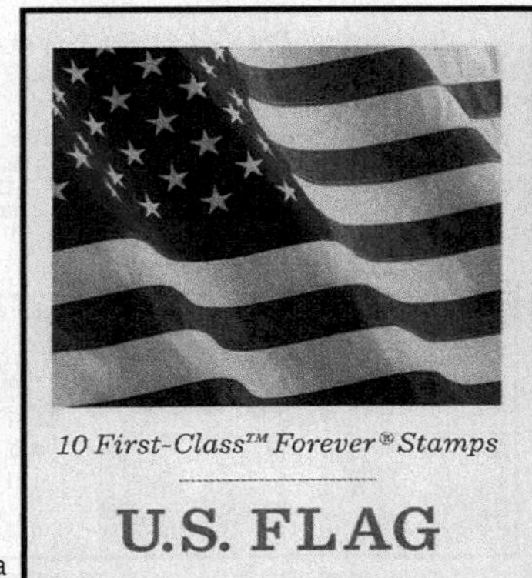

5160a BC308

2017

$4.90 fold-it-yourself booklet contains 10 self-adhesive (49c) stamps

Serpentine Die Cut 11¼x10¾ on 2 or 3 Sides

2017, Jan. 27 **Litho.**

Microprinted "USPS" at Right on Fourth Red Stripe

5160a A3988 (49c) pane of 10, P#B1111 11.00

By its nature, No. 5160a is a complete booklet (BC308). The peelable backing serves as a booklet cover.

5160b, 5161a, BC309 — A3988

Serpentine Die Cut 11¼x10¾ on 2 or 3 Sides

2017, Jan. 27 **Self-Adhesive** **Litho.**

With Microprinted "USPS" at Right of Fourth Red Stripe

5160b (49c) pane of 20, P#B1111 22.00

With Microprinted "USPS" at Right on Second White Stripe

5161a (49c) pane of 20, P#P1111 22.00

Nos. 5160b and 5161a are complete double-sided booklets. Eight stamps plus P# and the label that serves as a booklet cover (BC309) are on one side of the peelable backing and 12 stamps are on the other side of the backing. The booklet covers for Nos. 5160b and 5161a have different fonts in the numbers in the bar code.

5162a — A3988

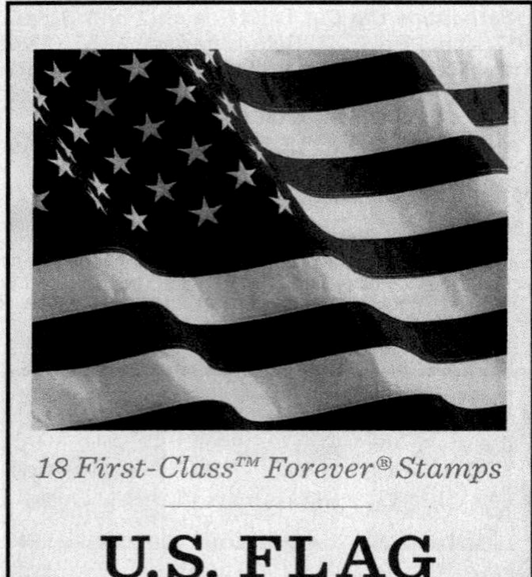

5162a — BC310

($8.82) fold-it-yourself booklet contains 18 self-adhesive (49c) stamps

Serpentine Die Cut 11¼x10¾ on 2, 3 or 4 Sides

2017, Jan. 27 Self-Adhesive Litho.

Microprinted "USPS" at Left on Second White Stripe

5162a A3988 (49c) pane of 18, P#P1111 50.00

No. 5162a is a complete booklet (BC310). The peelable backing serves as a booklet cover.

5189b, BC311 — A4009-A4018

Serpentine Die Cut 11 on 2 or 3 Sides

2017, Mar. 7 Self-Adhesive Litho.

5189b (49c) pane of 20, P#P1111 22.00

No. 5189b is a complete double-sided booklet. Eight stamps (1 each #5181-5184, 5186-5189) plus P# and the label that serves as a booklet cover (BC311) are on one side of the peelable backing and 12 stamps (2 each #5180, 5185, 1 each #5181-5184, 5186-5189) are on the other side of the backing.

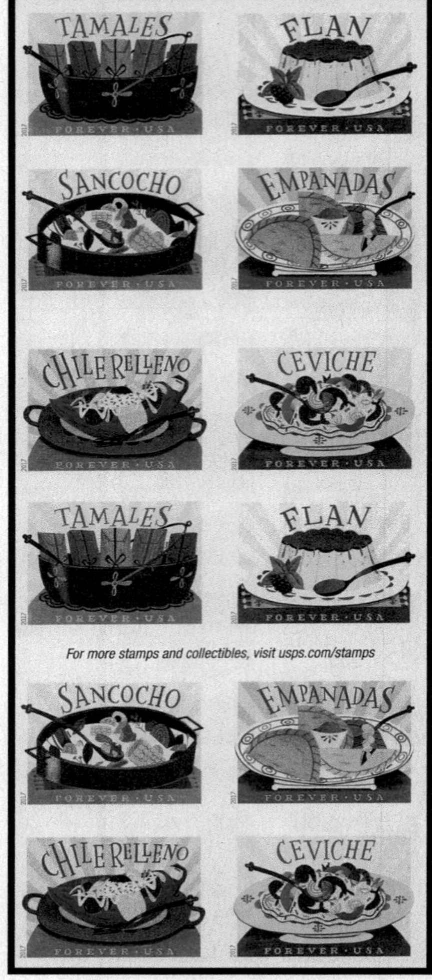

5197b, BC312 — A4021-A4026

Serpentine Die Cut 11 on 2 or 3 Sides

2017, Apr. 20 Self-Adhesive Litho.

5197b (49c) pane of 20, P#B11111 22.00

No. 5197b is a complete double-sided booklet. Eight stamps (1 each Nos. 5194-5197, 2 each Nos. 5192-5193) plus P# and the label that serves as a booklet cover (BC312) are on one side of the peelable backing and 12 stamps (2 each Nos. 5192-5197) are on the other side of the backing.

5240b, BC313 — A4077-A4080

Serpentine Die Cut 11 on 2 or 3 Sides

2017, Aug. 16 Self-Adhesive Litho.

5240b (49c) pane of 20, 5 each #5237-5240, P#B1111 22.00

No. 5240b is a complete double-sided booklet. Eight stamps (2 each Nos. 5237-5240) plus P# and the label that serves as a booklet cover (BC313) are on one side of the peelable backing and 12 stamps (3 each Nos. 5237-5240) are on the other side of the backing.

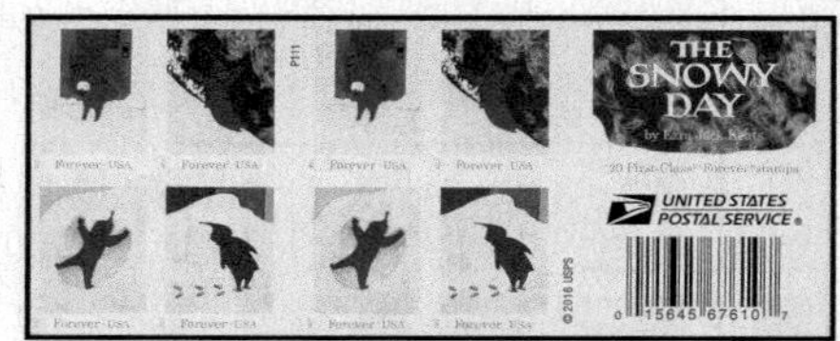

5246b, BC314 — A4082-A4085

Serpentine Die Cut 10¾ on 2 or 3 Sides

2017, Oct. 4 Self-Adhesive Litho.

5246b (49c) pane of 20, 5 each #5243-5246, P#P1111 22.00

No. 5246b is a complete double-sided booklet. Eight stamps (2 each Nos. 5243-5246) plus P# and the label that serves as a booklet cover (BC314) are on one side of the peelable backing and 12 stamps (3 each Nos. 5243-5246) are on the other side of the backing.

5250b, BC315 — A4086-A4089

Serpentine Die Cut 10¾ on 2 or 3 Sides

2017, Oct. 5 Self-Adhesive Litho.

5250b (49c) pane of 20, 5 each #5247-5250, P#B1111 22.00

No. 5250b is a complete double-sided booklet. Eight stamps (2 each Nos. 5247-5250) plus P# and the label that serves as a booklet cover (BC315) are on one side of the peelable backing and 12 stamps (3 each Nos. 5247-5250) are on the other side of the backing.

5262a, 5263a, BC316 — A4099

Serpentine Die Cut 11¼x10¾ on 2 or 3 Sides

2018, Feb. 9 Self-Adhesive Litho.

With Microprinted "USPS" at Left of Flag Fold on Fourth Red Stripe

5262a A4099 (50c) pane of 20, P#P111 22.00

With Microprinted "USPS" at Right of Flag Fold on Fifth White Stripe

5263a A4099 (50c) Pane of 20, P#B111 22.00

Nos. 5262a and 5263a are complete double-sided booklets. Eight stamps plus P# and the label that serves as a booklet cover (BC316) are on one side of the peelable backing and 12 stamps are on the other side of the backing. The booklet covers for Nos. 5262a and 5263a have different fonts in the numbers in the bar code.

5280a, BC317 — A4116

Serpentine Die Cut 11¼x10¾ on 2 or 3 Sides

2018, Apr. 21 Self-Adhesive Litho.

5280a A4116 (50c) Pane of 20, P#P1111 22.00

No. 5280a is a complete double-sided booklet. Eight stamps plus P# and the label that serves as a booklet cover (BC317) are on one side of the peelable backing and 12 stamps are on the other side of the backing.

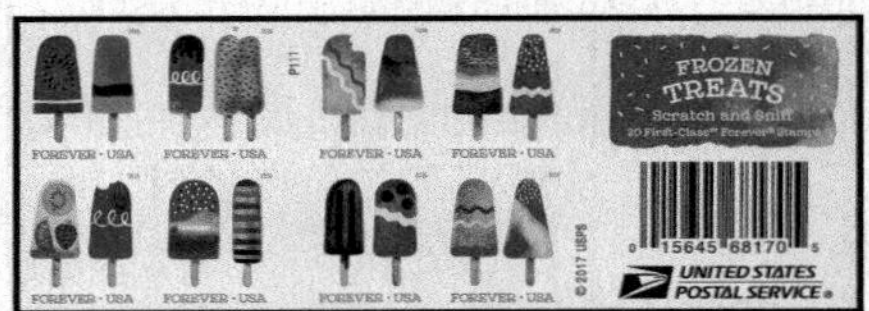

5294b, BC318 — A4120-A4129

Serpentine Die Cut 11¼x10¾ on 2 or 3 Sides

2018, June 20 Litho.

Self-Adhesive

5294b (50c) pane of 20, P#P1111 22.00

Nos. 5294b has a scratch-and-sniff coating with a fruity aroma, and is a double-sided booklet with 12 stamps on one side (Nos. 5286-5289, 5291-5294, 2 each Nos 5285, 5290), and eight stamps (Nos. 5286-5289, 5291-5294) plus a label that serves as the booklet cover (BC318) on the other side.

5320b, BC319 — A4165-A4168

Serpentine Die Cut 10¾ on 2 or 3 Sides

2018, Sept. 22 Self-Adhesive Litho.

5320b (50c) pane of 20, 5 each #5317-5320, P#B11111 22.00

No. 5320b is a complete double-sided booklet. Eight stamps (2 each Nos. 5317-5320) plus P# and the label that serves as a booklet cover (BC319) are on one side of the peelable backing and 12 stamps (3 each Nos. 5317-5320) are on the other side of the backing.

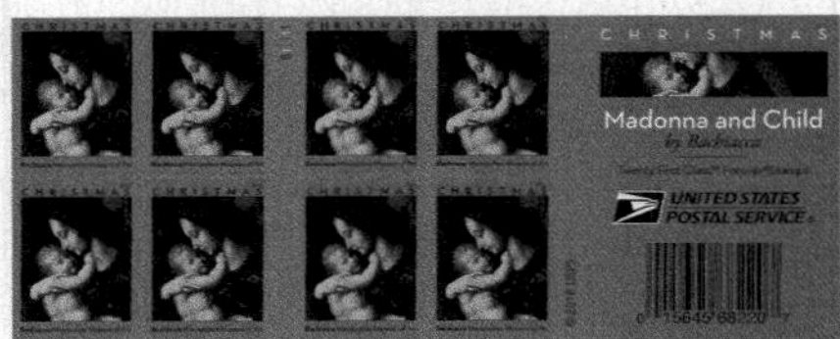

5331a, BC320 — A4179

5335b, BC321 — A4180-A4183

Serpentine Die Cut 10¾x11 on 2 or 3 Sides

2018 Litho.

Self-Adhesive

5331a A4179 (50c) pane of 20, P#B11111, *Oct. 3* 22.00

5335b (50c) pane of 20, 5 each #5332-5335, P#P11111, *Oct. 11* 22.00

No. 5331a is a complete double-sided booklet. Eight stamps plus P# and the label that serves as a booklet cover (BC320) are on one side of the peelable backing and 12 stamps are on the other side of the backing.

No. 5335b is a complete double-sided booklet. Eight stamps (2 each Nos. 5332-5335) plus P# and the label that serves as a booklet cover (BC321) are on one side of the peelable backing and 12 stamps (3 each Nos. 5332-5335) are on the other side of the backing.

5344a, 5345a, BC322 — A4189

Serpentine Die Cut 10¾x11¼ on 2 or 3 Sides

2019, Jan. 27 Litho.

Self-Adhesive

Microprinted "USPS" at Upper Left Corner of Flag

5344a A4189 (55c) pane of 20, P#P1111 22.00

Microprinted "USPS" to Right of Sixth Red Flag Stripe

5345a A4189 (55c) pane of 20, P#B1111 22.00

Nos. 5344a and 5345a are complete booklets with 12 stamps on one side and 8 stamps, plate number, and booklet cover (BC322) on the other side. The peelable backing serves as a booklet cover. The booklet covers for Nos. 5344a and 5345a have different fonts for the numbers in the bar code.

5359b, BC323 — A4194-A4203

Serpentine Die Cut 11 on 2 or 3 Sides

2019, Feb. 15 Litho.

Self-Adhesive

5359b (55c) pane of 20, 2 each #5350-5359, P#B11111 22.00

No. 5359b is a complete double-sided booklet. Eight stamps (Nos. 5352-5359) plus P# and the label that serves as a booklet cover (BC323) are on one side of the peelable backing and 12 stamps (Nos. 5352-5359, 2 each Nos. 5350-5351) are on the other side of the backing.

5398b, BC324 — A4234-A4237

Serpentine Die Cut 11x10¾ on 2 or 3 Sides

2019, July 9 **Litho.**

Self-Adhesive

5398b (55c) pane of 20, 5 each #5395-5398, P#B11111 22.00

No. 5398b is a complete double-sided booklet. Eight stamps (2 each Nos. 5395-5398) plus P# and the label that serves as a booklet cover (BC324) are on one side of the peelable backing and 12 stamps (3 each Nos. 5395-5398) are on the other side of the backing.

AIR POST BOOKLET PANES

C10a — AP6

FLAT PLATE PRINTING

1928 ***Perf. 11***

C10a AP6 10c **dark blue,** *May 26* 70.00 *65.00*
Never hinged 115.00
Tab at bottom, never hinged *9,000.*
Tab at bottom, hinged *7,500.*

No. C10a was printed from specially designed 180-subject plates arranged exactly as a 360-subject plate-each pane of three occupying the relative position of a pane of six in a 360-subject plate. Plate numbers appear at the sides, therefore Position D does not exist except partially on panes which have been trimmed off center. All other plate positions common to a 360-subject plate are known.

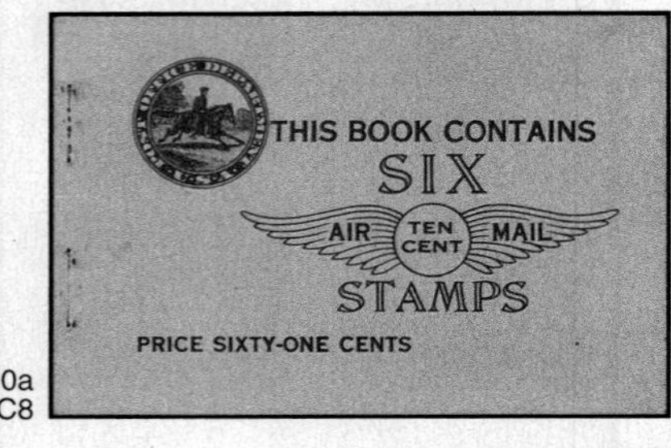

C10a BC8

1928 **Postrider and Wings**

61c booklet contains 2 panes of three 10c stamps.

Booklet

BKC1 BC8 61c **blue** 230.00
Tab at bottom, one pane in complete booklet *11,000.*

Catalogue values for unused panes in this section, from this point to the end, are for Never Hinged items.

C25a — AP17

ROTARY PRESS PRINTINGS

1943

C25a AP17 6c **carmine,** *Mar. 18* 3.50 1.50
180-Subject Plates Electric Eye Convertible.

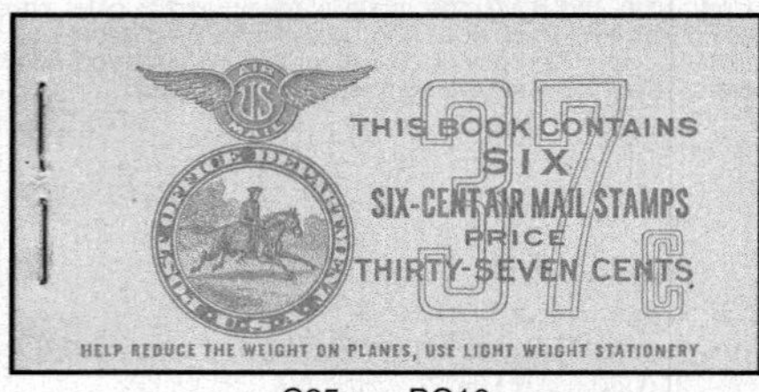

C25a — BC10

Large background numerals

1943 **Postrider and Wings**

37c booklet contains 2 panes of three 6c stamps.
73c booklet contains 4 panes of three 6c stamps.

Booklets

BKC2 BC10 37c **red** 8.00
BKC3 BC10 73c **red** 16.00

C39a — AP19

1949 ***Perf. 10½x11***

C39a AP19 6c **carmine,** *Nov. 18* 12.00 5.00
C39c Dry printing 25.00 —

C39a — BC11A

1949 **U.S. Airmail Wings**

The 73c and 85c booklets were the last sold for 1c over face value.

73c booklet contains 2 panes of six 6c stamps.

Booklets

BKC4 BC11A 73c **red,** with #C39a (3) 25.00
BKC4a BC11A 73c **red,** with #C39c 50.00

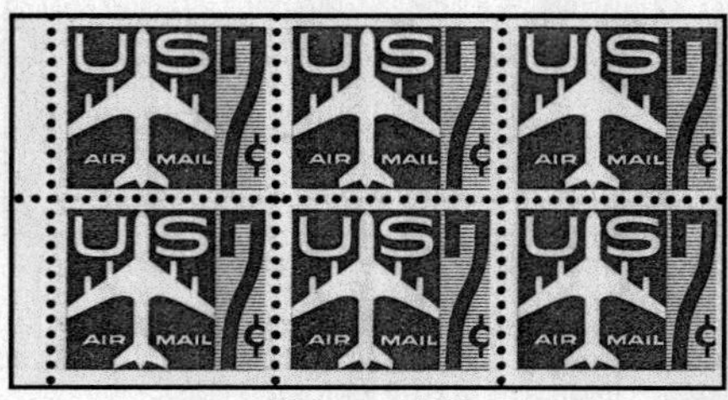
C51a — AP33

1958

C51a AP33 7c **blue,** *July 31* 6.50 5.00

C51a — BC11B

C51a, C60a — BC11C

1958-60 **U.S. Airmail Wings**

The 73c and 85c booklets were the last sold for 1c over face value.

85c booklet contains 2 panes of six 7c stamps.

Booklets

BKC5 BC11B 85c on 73c **red** 13.00
BKC6 BC11C 85c **blue** 13.00

1960

C60a AP33 7c **carmine,** *Aug. 19* 7.00 6.00

Booklets

BKC7	BC11C	85c **blue**	14.00
BKC8	BC11C	85c **red**	16.00

The different booklet slogan labels are illustrated with the regular-issue booklets in the Booklets section, beginning after No. 1036c.

C64b — AP42

1962-64

C64b AP42 8c **carmine,** pane of 5 + label, slogan 1, *Dec. 5, 1962* 6.00 3.00
With slogan 2, *1963* 45.00 5.00
With slogan 3, *1964* 12.00 2.50

For tagged variety, see No. C64c.

C64b, C64c — BC11D

C64b, C64c — BC11E

1962-64 **U.S. Airmail Wings**

80c booklet contains 2 panes of five 8c stamps.
$2 booklet contains 5 panes of five 8c stamps.

C64b, C64c — BC13B

1963-64 **Mr. Zip**

$2 booklet contains 5 panes of five 8c stamps.

Booklets (No. C64b)

BKC9	BC11D	80c **black,** *pink,* slogan 1	21.00
BKC10	BC11E	$2 **red,** *pink,* slogan 1	32.50
BKC11	BC11D	80c **black,** *pink,* slogan 3 (2)	30.00
BKC12	BC11E	$2 **red,** *pink,* slogan 2	275.00
BKC13	BC13B	$2 **red,** *pink,* slogan 2	300.00
BKC14	BC13B	$2 **red,** slogan 3	*3,500.*
BKC15	BC13B	$2 **red,** *pink,* slogan 3	100.00

Fake examples of No. BKC14, such as booklets containing panes with extra staple holes, having obvious signs of being restapled and/or containing panes from two or more booklets, are known in the marketplace. Expertization by competent authorities is strongly recommended.

C64c AP42 As No. C64b, tagged, slogan 3, *1964* 1.75 .75

Plate of 360 subjects (300 stamps, 60 labels).

Booklets (No. C64c)

BKC16	BC11D	80c **black** (2)	65.00
BKC17	BC11D	80c **black,** *pink*	*500.00*
BKC18	BC13B	$2 **red,** *pink*	*350.00*
BKC19	BC13B	$2 **red** (3)	11.50

C72b — AP49

1968-73 ***Perf. 11x10½***

C72b AP49 10c **carmine,** pane of 8, *Jan. 5, 1968* 2.25 2.00

C72b — BC14B

1968

$4 booklet contains 5 panes of eight 10c stamps.

Booklet

BKC20 BC14B $4 **red** (2) 12.00

Varieties

C72d Vert. pair, imperf. btwn., in #C72b with foldover *5,250.* —
C72f As "b," tagging omitted —

C72c — AP49

C72c AP49 10c **carmine,** pane of 5 + label, slogan 4, *Jan. 6, 1968* 3.50 1.25
With slogan 5 3.50 1.25
C72g As "c," tagging omitted, slogan 4 —
As "c," tagging omitted, slogan 5 —

C72c — BC15A

1968

$1 booklet contains 2 panes of five 10c stamps.

Booklet

BKC21 BC15A $1 **red** (2) 8.00

No. BKC21 normally is found with one pane each of slogans 4 and 5, and only very occasionally with two panes each of slogan 4 or slogan 5.

C78a — AP54

C78a AP54 11c **carmine,** pane of 4 + 2 labels, slogans 5 & 4, *May 7, 1971* 1.25 1.00
C78d As "a," tagging omitted —

C78a, 1280c — BC15B

1971

$1 booklet contains 2 panes of four 11c stamps and 1 pane of six 2c stamps.

Combination Booklet

BKC22 BC15B $1 **red,** 2 #C78a + 1 #1280c (2) 3.75

C79a — AP55

C79a AP55 13c **carmine,** pane of 5 + label, slogan 8, *Dec. 27, 1973* 1.50 1.00

C79a — BC18

1973

$1.30 booklet contains 2 panes of five 13c stamps.

Booklet

BKC23 BC18 $1.30 **blue & red** (2) 3.25

Combination Booklet

See No. BK126.

No. C72b, the 8-stamp pane, was printed from 320-subject plate and from 400-subject plate; No. C72c, C78a and C79a from 360-subject plates.

COMPUTER VENDED POSTAGE STAMPS

Unlike meters, except for the limits of the service requested, computer vended postage stamps are usable from any post office at any date.

Self-service user-interactive mailing system machines which vended computer-printed postage were in service and available to the general public at the Martin Luther King, Jr., Station of the Washington, DC, Post Office, and at the White Flint Mall in Kensington, MD, until May 7, 1990.

Machines were also available for use by delegates to the 20th Universal Postal Congress at the Washington Convention Center between Nov. 13 and Dec. 14, 1989. These machines, Washington Nos. 11 and 12, were not readily accessible by the general public.

A variety of services were available by using the machines, which could weigh items to be sent, determine postage rates through the connected computer, permit the customer to cancel the transaction or continue with it and generate a postage stamp, a label and a receipt. The stamps produced were valid only for domestic postage.

A tagged orange strip runs along the left side of the stamp. The requested mail service is in a double line box.

The denomination is in the upper box at right under "U.S. Postage." The date of the transaction is below the denomination. Next to the date is a number which indicates the item number within the transaction. The maximum number of items per transaction may be five.

Above the post office location is a box at right which gives the machine number, followed by the transaction or serial number. Stamps from the same transaction, which are generated and printed at the same time, will have the same transaction number, but different item numbers, even if different mail services are requested. Transaction numbers go back to 00001 every time the machine is reset. Below this is the weight of the item to be mailed.

Along with each stamp generated came an unattached label with one of three slogan types: "We Deliver. . .," used from September to November, "We Deliver. . . / United States Postal Service," used thereafter, and "Developed by / Technology Resource Department," used only on Machine 11 during its limited use.

Listings and values are for the basic denominations of the five postal services, though others are known or possible (45c, 65c, 85c for first class over 1 oz., $1.10 for certified first class, $3.25 for priority mail, $8.50 for express mail to post office boxes, parcel post weight and zone variations, etc.). Values for used copies are for those with a regular cancellation.

A total of 3,000 unused sets of five different service stamps and unused sets of two 25c (Nos. 02501-12500) first class stamps furnished to the Philatelic Agency have a first day date and serial numbers with the final three digits matching. First day dates Nos. 00101-02500 were sold over the counter at post offices.

Stamps were intended to be dispensed individually. The height of the stamps produced differs from machine to machine. Unsevered strips of stamps are known, as are unsevered strips of a slogan and one or more stamps. Printing varieties such as squeezes (more than one impression condensed on to one stamp) and stretches (impression stretched out so that a complete impression will not fit on the paper) also are known.

Issues starting with No. 31 will be explained with the listings.

CVP1

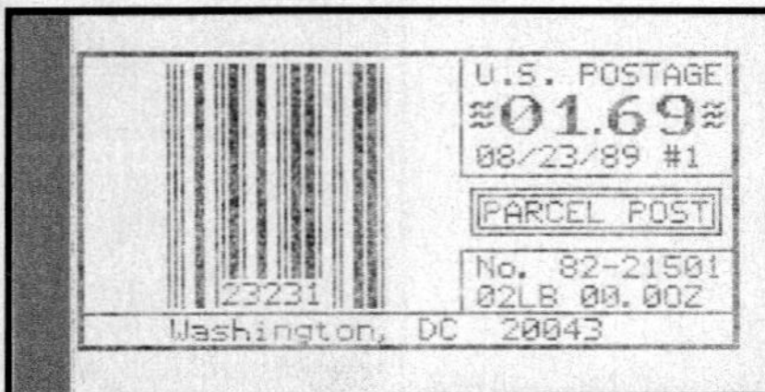

CVP2

1989, Aug. 23 **Tagged** ***Guillotined***

Self-Adhesive

Washington, DC, Machine 82

CVP1 CVP1 25c **First Class,** any date other than first day 6.00 —
a. First day dated, serial Nos. 12501-15500 5.00 —
b. First day dated, serial Nos. 00001-12500 5.00 —
On cover with first day cancel *150.00*
c. First day dated, over No. 27500 — —
On cover with first day cancel *150.00*

CVP2 CVP1 $1 **Third Class,** any date other than first day — —
a. First day dated, serial Nos. 24501-27500 — —
b. First day dated, over No. 27500 — —

CVP3 CVP2 $1.69 **Parcel Post,** any date other than first day — —
a. First day dated, serial Nos. 21501-24500 — —
b. First day dated, over No. 27500 — —

CVP4 CVP1 $2.40 **Priority Mail,** any date other than first day — —
a. First day dated, serial Nos. 18501-21500 — —
b. Priority Mail ($2.74), with bar code (CVP2) 100.00
c. First day dated, over No. 27500 — —
On cover with first day cancel or verifying receipt *500.00*

CVP5 CVP1 $8.75 **Express Mail,** any date other than first day — —
a. First day dated, serial Nos. 15501-18500 — —
b. First day dated, over No. 27500 — —
On cover with first day cancel or verifying receipt —
Nos. 1a-5a (5) 82.50 —

Washington, DC, Machine 83

CVP6 CVP1 25c **First Class,** any date other than first day 6.00 —
a. First day dated, serial Nos. 12501-15500 5.00 —
b. First day dated, serial Nos. 00001-12500 5.00 —
On cover with first day cancel *150.00*
c. First day dated, over No. 27500 — —
On cover with first day cancel *150.00*

Error dates 11/17/90 and 11/18/90 exist.

CVP7 CVP1 $1 **Third Class,** any date other than first day — —
a. First day dated, serial Nos. 24501-27500 — —
b. First day dated, over No. 27500 — —

CVP8 CVP2 $1.69 **Parcel Post,** any date other than first day — —
a. First day dated, serial Nos. 21501-24500 — —
b. First day dated, over No. 27500 — —

CVP9 CVP1 $2.40 **Priority Mail,** any date other than first day — —
a. First day dated, serial Nos. 18501-21500 — —
b. First day dated, over No. 27500 — —
On cover with first day cancel or verifying receipt *500.00*

A Priority Mail $3.25 value also exists unused. A Priority Mail stamp exists on cover with error date 11/17/90 exists, and an unused stamp with error date 11/18/90 exists.

c. Priority Mail ($2.74), with bar code (CVP2) 100.00

Error date 11/18/90 exists.

CVP10 CVP1 $8.75 **Express Mail,** any date other than first day — —
a. First day dated, serial Nos. 15501-18500 — —
b. First day dated, over No. 27500 — —
On cover with first day cancel or verifying receipt —
Nos. 6a-10a (5) 57.50 —

Error date 11/17/90 exists.

1989, Sept. 1

Kensington, MD, Machine 82

CVP11 CVP1 25c **First Class,** any date other than first day 6.00 —
a. First day dated, serial Nos. 12501-15500 5.00 —
b. First day dated, serial Nos. 00001-12500 5.00 —
On cover with first day cancel *100.00*
c. First day dated, over No. 27500 — —
On cover with first day cancel *100.00*

CVP12 CVP1 $1 **Third Class,** any date other than first day — —
a. First day dated, serial Nos. 24501-27500 — —
b. First day dated, over No. 27500 — —

CVP13 CVP2 $1.69 **Parcel Post,** any date other than first day — —
a. First day dated, serial Nos. 21501-24500 — —
b. First day dated, over No. 27500 — —

CVP14 CVP1 $2.40 **Priority Mail,** any date other than first day — —
a. First day dated, serial Nos. 18501-21500 — —
b. First day dated, over No. 27500 — —
c. Priority Mail ($2.74), with bar code (CVP2) 100.00

CVP15 CVP1 $8.75 **Express Mail,** any date other than first day — —
a. First day dated, serial Nos. 15501-18500 — —
b. First day dated, over No. 27500 — —
Nos. 11a-15a (5) 57.50 —
Nos. 1b, 11b (2) 10.00 —

Kensington, MD, Machine 83

CVP16 CVP1 25c **First Class,** any date other than first day 6.00 —
a. First day dated, serial Nos. 12501-15500 5.00 —
b. First day dated, serial Nos. 00001-12500 5.00 —
c. First day dated, over No. 27500 — —
On cover with first day cancel *100.00*

CVP17 CVP1 $1 **Third Class,** any date other than first day — —
a. First day dated, serial Nos. 24501-27500 — —
b. First day dated, over No. 27500 — —

CVP18 CVP2 $1.69 **Parcel Post,** any date other than first day — *12.50*
a. First day dated, serial Nos. 21501-24500 — —
b. First day dated, over No. 27500 — —

CVP19 CVP1 $2.40 **Priority Mail,** any date other than first day — —
a. First day dated, serial Nos. 18501-21500 — —

b. First day dated, over No. 27500 — —
c. Priority Mail ($2.74), with bar code (CVP2) 100.00

CVP20 CVP1 $8.75 **Express Mail,** any date other than first day — —
a. First day dated, serial Nos. 15501-18500 — —
b. First day dated, over No. 27500 — —
Nos. 16a-20a (5) 57.50 —
Nos. 6b, 16b (2) 10.00 —

Unsevered pairs and single with advertising label exist for most, if not all, of the machine vended items from Kensington machine #83. Other combinations also exist.

1989, Nov. Washington, DC, Machine 11

CVP21 CVP1 25c **First Class** *150.00*
a. First Class, with bar code (CVP2) —

Stamps in CVP1 design with $1.10 denominations exist (certified first class) dated 11/20/89. Value, unused, $650. A 45c denomination exists unused (dated 11/22/89) on cover to Europe and on Certificate of Mailing.

CVP22 CVP1 $1 **Third Class** *500.00*
CVP23 CVP2 $1.69 **Parcel Post** *500.00*
CVP24 CVP1 $2.40 **Priority Mail** *500.00*
a. Priority Mail ($2.74), with bar code (CVP2) —
CVP25 CVP1 $8.75 **Express Mail** *500.00*

No. CVP21 dated Nov. 30 known on cover, Nos. CVP24-CVP25 known dated Dec. 2.

Washington, DC, Machine 12

CVP26 CVP1 25c **First Class** *200.00*

No. CVP26, dated 12/13/89 is known on cover. $1.10 Certified First Class stamps dated 11/20/89 exist on covers.

CVP27 CVP1 $1 **Third Class** *600.00*

A $1.40 Third Class stamp of type CVP2, dated Dec. 1 is known on a Dec. 2 cover.

CVP28 CVP2 $1.65 **Parcel Post** *600.00*
CVP29 CVP1 $2.40 **Priority Mail** *600.00*
a. Priority Mail ($2.74), with bar code (CVP2) —
CVP30 CVP1 $8.75 **Express Mail** *600.00*

Nos. CVP29-CVP30 known dated Dec. 1. An $8.50 Express Mail stamp, dated Dec. 2, exists on cover.

CVP3 — Type I

CVP3 — Type II

Denomination printed by ECA GARD Postage and Mailing Center machines.

COIL STAMPS

1992, Aug. 20 Engr. Tagged *Perf. 10 Horiz.*

CVP31 CVP3 29c **red & blue,** type I, prephosphored paper (solid tagging), dull gum .75 .25
Pair 1.50
P# strip of 5, P#1 8.00
P# single, #1 5.50
a. 29c Type I, prephosphored paper (mottled tagging), shiny gum .75 .25
Pair 1.50 —
P# strip of 5, P#1 8.00 —
P# single, #1 5.50
First day cover, Oklahoma City, OK 1.25
b. 32c Type II, prephosphored paper (solid tagging), dull gum, *Nov. 1994* .90 .40
Pair 1.80
P# strip of 5, P#1 35.00
P# single, #1 *30.00*
c. 32c Type II, prephosphored paper (mottled tagging), shiny gum 1.25 .40
Pair 2.50
P# strip of 5, P#1 12.00
P# single, #1 *15.00*

Types I and II differ in style of asterisk, period between dollar and cent figures and font used for figures, as shown in illustrations.

No. CVP31 was available at test sites in Arlington and Crystal City, VA, and in the Southern Maryland, Miami, Oklahoma City, Detroit and Santa Ana, CA, divisions. They were produced for use in ECA GARD Postage and Mailing Center (PMC) machines which can produce denominations from 1c through $99.99.

For Nos. CVP31-CVP31a, the 29c value is listed because it was the current first class rate and was the only value available through the USPS Philatelic Sales Division. The most common denomination available other than 29c is 1c (value 25c) because these were made in quantity, by collectors and dealers, between plate number strips. Later the machines were adjusted to provide only 19c and higher value stamps.

For Nos. CVP31b-CVP31c, the 32c value is listed because it was the first class rate in effect for the majority of the period the stamps were in use.

CVP4

Denominations printed by Unisys PMC machines.

1994, Feb. 19 Photo. Tagged *Perf. 9.9 Vert.*

CVP32 CVP4 29c **dark red & dark blue** .75 .35
Pair 1.50 —
P# strip of 5, #A11 8.50 —
P# single, #A11 5.00
First day cover, Merrifield, VA *(26,390)* 1.25

No. CVP32 was available at six test sites in northern Virginia. It was produced for use in machines which can produce values from 19c to $99.99. See note following No. CVP31.

For No. CVP32, the 29c value has been listed because it was the first class rate in effect at the time the stamp was issued.

1996, Jan. 26 Photo. Tagged *Perf. 9.9 Vert.*

CVP33 CVP4 32c **bright red & blue,** "1996" below design .75 .25
Pair 1.50 —
P# strip of 5, same, #11 8.50 —
P# single, #11 6.50

Letters in "USA" on No. CVP33 are thicker than on No. CVP32. Numerous other design differences exist in the moire pattern and in the bunting. No. CVP33 has "1996" in the lower left corner; No. CVP32 has no date.

For No. CVP33, the 32c value has been listed because it was the first class rate in effect at the time the stamp was issued.

CVP5

Illustration reduced.

1999, June Tagged *Die Cut*
Self-Adhesive

CVP34 CVP5 33c **black** *50.00* —
On cover *75.00*
a. "Priority Mail" under encryption at LL — —
b. "Express Mail" under encryption at LL — —

No. CVP34 was available from 15 NCR Automated Postal Center machines located in central Florida. Machines could produce values in any denomination required. The backing paper is taller and wider than the stamp.

Sales of No. CVP34 were discontinued in 2000 or 2001.

CVP6

Illustration reduced.

1999, May 7 Tagged *Die Cut*
Self-Adhesive
Size: 77½x39mm
Microprinting Above Red Orange Line

CVP35 CVP6 33c **black & red orange,** control numbers only at LL, round corners 20.00 —
Square corners 220.00 —
a. "Priority Mail" at LL, square corners 150.00 —
Round corners — —
b. "Priority Mail AS" and text string at LL, square corners 150.00 —
Round corners — —

No Microprinting Above Red Orange Line

CVP36 CVP6 33c **black & red orange,** control numbers only at LL, round corners 9.00 —
Square corners 250.00 —
a. "Priority Mail" at LL, square corners 125.00 —
Round corners — —
b. "Priority Mail AS" and text string at LL, square corners 125.00 —
Round corners — —

Size: 73½x42mm

CVP37 CVP6 33c **black & pink,** control numbers only at LL 3.75 —
a. "Priority Mail" at LL 5.00 —
b. "Priority Mail AS" and text string at LL 5.00 —

Nos. CVP35-CVP37 were available from 18 IBM Neopost machines located in central Florida, and at least one machine in the Washington, DC area (Merrifield, VA Automated Postal Center). The backing paper is taller than the stamp. Any denomination could be printed up to $99.99.

Simplypostage.com — CVP8

Serpentine Die Cut 8 at Right
2001 Self-Adhesive
Eagle and Stars Background

CVP39 CVP8 34c **black, blue & orange,** *2001* — —
On cover 75.00
Pane of 4 —
CVP40 CVP8 34c **black, blue & orange,** with control number at UL, *2001* — —
On cover 75.00
Pane of 4 —

Flag Background

CVP41 CVP8 34c **black, blue & orange,** with control number at UL, *2001* — —
On cover 150.00
Pane of 4 —
CVP42 CVP8 34c **black, blue & orange,** with control number at LL, *2001* — 20.00
On cover 150.00
Pane of 4 —

Customers could print up to five panes of Nos. CVP39-CVP42 in each transaction. Panes were consecutively numbered identifying the total number of stamps and panes in each transaction.

Large Flag Design

The item shown was produced by Neopost. It was found that the large flag image hampered the barcode from being scanned. It is believed no examples were actually sold to the public. Five panes of four are believed to exist.

Neopostage.com — CVP9

Serpentine Die Cut 8¾ at Right
2002, June Self-Adhesive

CVP43 CVP9 21c **black, blue & orange,** —
a. Booklet pane of 10 —
CVP44 CVP9 23c **black, blue & orange,** — —
On cover —
a. Booklet pane of 10 90.00
CVP45 CVP9 34c **black, blue & orange,** — —
On cover —
a. Booklet pane of 10 — —
CVP46 CVP9 37c **black, blue & orange,** — —
On cover —
a. Booklet pane of 10 60.00
CVP47 CVP9 50c **black, blue & orange,** — —
On cover —
a. Booklet pane of 10 180.00
CVP47B CVP9 57c **black, blue & orange,** *June 24, 2002* —
a. Booklet pane of 10 —

CVP48	CVP9 60c **black, blue & orange,**		—	—
	On cover			—
a.	Booklet pane of 10	160.00		
CVP49	CVP9 70c **black, blue & orange,**		—	—
	On cover			—
a.	Booklet pane of 10	180.00		
CVP50	CVP9 80c **black, blue & orange,**		—	—
	On cover			—
a.	Booklet pane of 10	180.00		
CVP51	CVP9 $3.50 **black, blue & orange,**		—	—
a.	Booklet pane of 1		—	
b.	Booklet pane of 2		—	
c.	Booklet pane of 5		—	
d.	Booklet pane of 10		—	
CVP52	CVP9 $3.85 **black, blue & orange,**		—	
a.	Booklet pane of 1		—	
b.	Booklet pane of 2		—	
c.	Booklet pane of 5		—	
d.	Booklet pane of 10		—	
CVP52E	CVP9 $12.45 **black, orange & blue,** *June 30, 2002*		—	
a.	Booklet pane of 1		—	
CVP53	CVP9 $13.65 **black, blue & orange,**		—	—
	On cover			—
a.	Booklet pane of 1		—	
b.	Booklet pane of 2		—	
c.	Booklet pane of 5		—	
d.	Booklet pane of 10		—	

Nos. CVP43-CVP53 were printed only with the stated values.

Denominations of 34c, 57c, $3.50 and perhaps others exist with a ICNOVA kiosk location designation. These were produced during pre-issue testing at a location not publicly accessible and are not considered to be valid postage. Stamps from the ICNOVA location have much smaller 2-D bar code squares. The denominations listed above come from other publicly accessible kiosk locations from June 20, 2002, forward. Official sales of these stamps began on June 20, 2002, or later for some denominations.

The 21c, 34c, 57c, $3.50 and $12.45 denominations were only sold from June 21 to June 29, 2002. They are all scarce, and some are rare. The 37c, $3.85 and $13.65 denominations were not sold until June 30, 2002, when the rate change took effect.

While the name on Nos. CVP39-CVP42 reads simplypostage.com and the name on Nos. CVP43-CVP53 reads neopostage.com, both were products of Neopost.

Earliest documented use: Nos. CVP43, CVP47, CVP51-CVP52, not known used; Nos. CVP44, CVP46, CVP48-CVP49, CVP53, 6/30; No. CVP45, 6/21; No. CVP50, 7/3.

CVP10

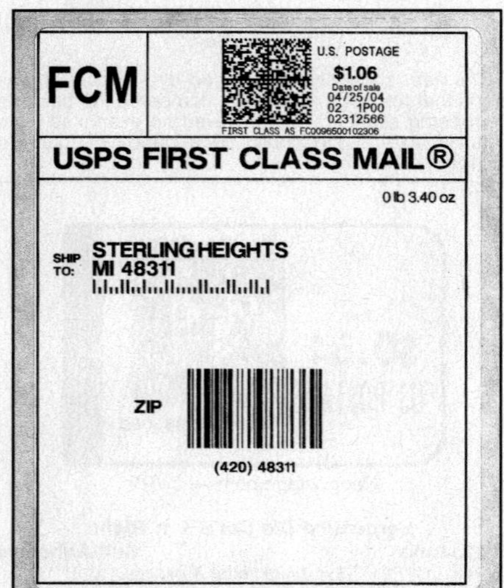

IBM Pitney Bowes — CVP11

Illustrations reduced.

2004, Apr. 14	**Self-Adhesive**		***Die Cut***
CVP54	CVP10 37c **black & pink**	5.00	—
a.	"First Class Mail" under encryption at LL	2.50	—
b.	"Priority Mail" under encryption at LL	2.50	—
c.	"Parcel Post" under encryption at LL	2.50	—
d.	"International" under encryption at LL	2.50	—

CVP55	CVP11 37c **black,** "US Postage" under encryption at LL	2.50	—
a.	"First Class Mail" under encryption at LL	—	—
b.	"Priority Mail" under encryption at LL	—	—
c.	"Parcel Post" under encryption at LL	—	—
d.	"International" under encryption at LL	—	—

Nos. CVP54-CVP55 could be printed in any denomination up to $99.99. Catalogue values for Nos. CVP54-CVP54d and CVP55 are for stamps with low denominations. Stamps with denominations appropriate to the service described are valued correspondingly higher.

CVP12

IBM Pitney Bowes — CVP13

Illustrations reduced.

2004, Nov. 19	**Self-Adhesive**		***Die Cut***
CVP56	CVP12 37c **black & pink**	2.50	.45
CVP57	CVP13 37c **black & pink**	1.25	.45

Nos. CVP56-CVP57 could be printed in any denomination. No. CVP56 could be printed with three different rate inscriptions under the denomination. No. CVP57 could be printed with 18 different rate inscriptions and/or service indicators under the denomination, and with at least 27 different rate inscriptions and or/service indicators under the denomination on stamps with a four-digit code after the zip code.

Blank Under Denomination

"IM" and Numbers Under Encryption

CVP58	CVP13 60c **black & pink**	3.00	.50
CVP59	CVP13 80c **black & pink**	3.75	.50

"PM" and Numbers Under Encryption

CVP60	CVP13 $3.85 **black & pink**	15.00	.50

"EM" and Numbers Under Encryption

CVP61	CVP13 $13.65 **black & pink**	42.50	1.00

"IB" and Numbers Under Encryption

CVP62	CVP13 $1 **black & pink**	4.00	.25

Nos. CVP58-CVP61 could only be printed in denominations listed. No. CVP62 could be printed in any denomination above 99c. As of May 12, 2008, it was possible to create stamps with "IB" and numbers under encryption in any denomination. The computer software was later changed to once again only permit stamps of certain denominations to be created with "IB" and numbers under the encryption.

IBM Pitney Bowes Type of 2004

2006	**Self-Adhesive**		***Die Cut***

Blank Under Denomination

"IM" and Numbers Under Encryption

CVP63	CVP13 48c **black & pink**	1.50	.40
CVP64	CVP13 63c **black & pink**	1.75	.50
CVP65	CVP13 84c **black & pink**	2.25	.50

"PM" and Numbers Under Encryption

CVP66	CVP13 $4.05 **black & pink**	11.00	.50
CVP66A	CVP13 $8.10 **black & pink**	30.00	1.00

"EM" and Numbers Under Encryption

CVP67	CVP13 $14.40 **black & pink**	32.50	1.00

Nos. CVP63-CVP67 could only be printed in denominations listed.

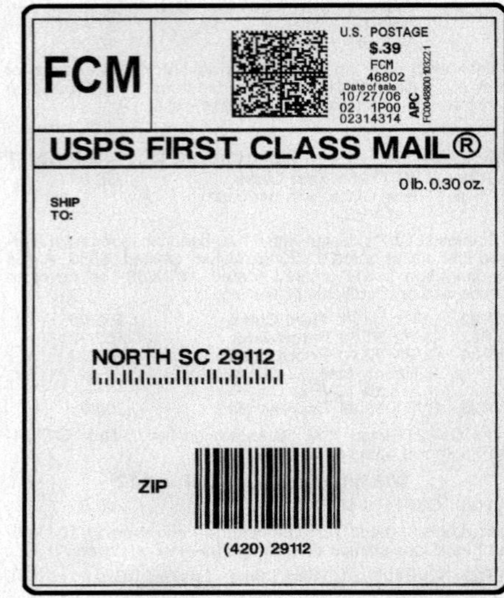

IBM Pitney Bowes — CVP14

Illustration reduced.

2006	**Self-Adhesive**		***Die Cut***

No Inscription Under Encryption

Serial Number to Right of "APC"

"Ship To:" Above Destination City

CVP69	CVP14 39c **black**	2.25	.25

Nos. CVP69 could be printed in any denomination, with 14 different rate inscriptions and/or service indicators under the denomination on stamps having "Ship To:" at the left and no code below the weight, and at least 29 different rate inscriptions and/or service indicators under the denomination on stamps having a four-digit code at the right that is even with the words "Ship To:" and below the weight.

IBM Pitney Bowes Type of 2004

2006(?)-07	**Self-Adhesive**		***Die Cut***

Blank Under Denomination

"IB" and Numbers Under Encryption

CVP70	CVP13 39c **black & pink**	1.00	.50
CVP71	CVP13 41c **black & pink**	1.75	.50
CVP72	CVP13 69c **black & pink**	2.50	.70

"IM" and Numbers Under Encryption

CVP73	CVP13 61c **black & pink**	2.25	.50
CVP74	CVP13 90c **black & pink**	3.50	.95

Nos. CVP70-CVP74 could only be printed in the denominations listed.

Nos. CVP71-CVP74 issued May, 2007. No. CVP70 was issued before the May rate change. As of May 12, 2008, it was possible to create stamps with "IB" and numbers under encryption in any denomination. The computer software was later changed to once again only permit stamps of certain denominations to be created with "IB" and numbers under the encryption. No. CVP70 was available for sale from Nov. 2006 to May 13, 2007. Nos. CVP71-CVP72 were available for sale from May 14, 2007 to May 11, 2008.

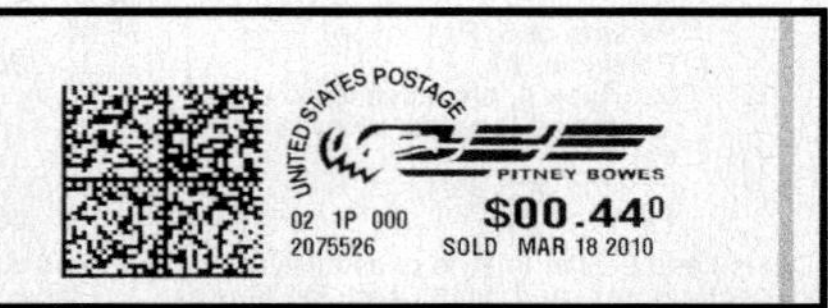

Pitney Bowes With Eagle at Right, One Code Number to Left of Sold Date — CVP15

Illustration reduced.

2006, Dec.	**Self-Adhesive**		***Die Cut***
CVP75	CVP15 41c **black & pink,** no inscription below sold date	—	—
a.	"Mailed From Zip Code ..." on bottom line	—	—
b.	"Postcard" on bottom line	—	—
c.	"First-Class Mail" on bottom line	—	—
d.	"First-Class Mail Intl" on bottom line	—	—
e.	"Priority" on bottom line	—	—
f.	"Priority Envelope" on bottom line	—	—
g.	"Priority Box" on bottom line	—	—
h.	"Express Mail" on bottom line	—	—
i.	"Express Envelope" on bottom line	—	—

j. "Parcel Post" on bottom line — —
k. "Priority Tube" on bottom line — —
l. "First Class" on bottom line — —

No. CVP75 was put into service at large companies and universities in Dec. 2006, with the majority of the machines not being available to the general public. Information about this stamp was not made available until 2007. Other rates and inscriptions might be available.

Nos. CVP75a could be printed in any denomination. Nos. CVP75b-CVP75f could be printed only in pre-programmed denominations based on the current rates for the service, or in any denominations at or above the minimum rates for the service. Values are for stamps with low denominations. A stamp with "Priority - Irregular Shape" on the bottom line has been reported to exist but has not been seen by the editors. Inscriptions generated by the software may vary from machine to machine depending on when the software was installed.

Two distinctly different colors of phosphor stripes on labels used in Mail & Go machines are known, with many Mail & Go adhesives appearing in both versions.

Private sector operators of Pitney Bowes "Mail & Go" machines are not bound to use only label paper supplied by Pitney Bowes. Competing label paper producers make and sell labels in the formats required for the machines that dispense Nos. CVP75 and CVP84. Thus, Nos. CVP75 and CVP84 without the Pitney Bowes logo on the reverse are not errors.

IBM Pitney Bowes Type of 2004

2008, May **Self-Adhesive** ***Die Cut***

Blank Under Denomination

"IM" and Numbers Under Encryption

CVP76 CVP13 94c **black & pink** 3.00 .60
CVP77 CVP13 $1.20 **black & pink** 3.75 1.25

Nos. CVP76-CVP77 could only be printed in the denominations listed.

IBM — CVP16

Illustration reduced.

Die Cut With Rounded Corners

2008, June 4 **Self-Adhesive**

CVP78 CVP16 42c **black & pink** 4.25 —
a. Without "date of sale" inscription, *2009* — —

Die Cut With Perpendicular Corners

CVP79 CVP16 42c **black & pink** 4.25 —
a. Without "date of sale" inscription, *2009* — —

Nos. CVP78-CVP79 were made available during a pilot study to evaluate a new IBM kiosk at Schaumburg, IL. No. CVP78 could be printed in any denomination from 1c to $25. Each kiosk transaction was limited to $100. Individual panes with 6, 7, 8, 9 or 10 stamps could be purchased as long as the total face value of the pane did not exceed $100. The pane of 10 exists with the vertical pink tagging stripe along the left side of the stamps. The pane of 10 could only be bought with stamps denominated from 1c to $10. Stamps denominated from $10.01 to $16.66 could only be purchased in panes containing fewer than 10 stamps. Stamps denominated from $16.67 to $25 could only be purchased as a single stamp.

IBM Pitney Bowes Type of 2004

2009 **Self-Adhesive** ***Die Cut***

Blank Under Denomination

"IM" and Numbers Under Encryption

CVP80 CVP13 98c **black & pink** 2.00 .60
CVP81 CVP13 $1.24 **black & pink** 2.50 1.25

Nos. CVP80-CVP81 could only be printed in denominations listed.

IBM (Statue of Liberty) — CVP17

Illustration reduced.

Die Cut With Rounded Corners

2009, June 5 **Self-Adhesive**

CVP82 CVP17 44c **black & pink** 7.50 —
a. Without "date of sale" inscription, *2009* — —

Die Cut With Perpendicular Corners

CVP83 CVP17 44c **black & pink** 7.50 —
a. Without "date of sale" inscription, *2009* — —

No. CVP82 could be printed in any denomination from 1c to $25. Nos. CVP82-CVP83 were made available during a pilot study to evaluate a new IBM kiosk at Schaumburg, IL. The machine study at Schaumburg was scheduled to end on July 31, 2009. No. CVP82 was created for purchases of one to five individual stamps or any extra stamps beyond multiples of 10 ending in numerals 1 to 5.

INVERTS

Labels used to produce stamps in the dimensions of many items of CVP54 and similar later issues in this format were packaged in a fanfolded strip two labels wide and packaged in boxes that are stored in the machines from which the labels are fed to printers as purchases occur. Nothing prevents the labels from being fed in reverse, which results in inverted paper "errors." Such "inverts" (with phosphor stripe appearing on the opposite edge of the stamp than the intended edge) can be deliberately produced, and therefore are not listed.

SERVICE-INSCRIBED STAMPS

Listings of small label stamps from CVP84 reveal that various service-related abbreviations appear under the denominations of some stamps. From CVP84 onward (including the FOLD HERE varieties), all denominated stamps may be purchased that include service-specific indicators under the denominations (e.g., EXPRESS for a clearly identifiable service as well as abbreviations that are less clear such as EM HFPU FRB). When a machine asks a mailer if any postage is already affixed to an item, the mailer can indicate that all postage but one cent or more is affixed. A customer stating that almost all required postage is already affixed will result in the stamp vending machine dispensing a stamp with a service-specific indicator that has a face value as low as one cent. For this reason, listings no longer include small format vended stamps with service-specific indicators beyond No. CVP84, because the stamps can be produced to show any face value, use not being restricted to the class indicated, and all types may be used on any mail matter.

Flag
CVP18

Serpentine Die Cut 13¼x12½

2011, Oct. 18 **Self-Adhesive**

CVP84 CVP18 44c **multicolored,** date sold only on bottom line — —
a. Date sold and "Postcard" on bottom line — —
b. Date sold and "First-Class" on bottom line — —

No. CVP84 was issued in panes of 10. It was made available at Mail & Go postal stations in Super Target stores in the Dallas, TX area. Panes could be printed in any denomination from 29c to $9.99. Serpentine die cut 9 examples of No. CVP84 with dates earlier than Oct. 18 were produced at Pitney Bowes facilities. This serpentine die cut 9 sticker stock is not known to have been sent out for use in machines that were available for use by the general public. No. CVP84 was made available in 2013 with dozens of images other than the flag shown. These optional images are for various holidays and events, as well as social causes, such as support for breast cancer, education and recycling. One image, for bridal showers, has been made available in two different types.

Pitney Bowes With Eagle at Left — CVP18a

Pitney Bowes Without Eagle — CVP18b

Die Cut With Perpendicular Corners

2011, Oct. 18 **Self-Adhesive**

CVP84C CVP18a 46c **black & pink,** no inscription below sold date 5.00 —
d. CVP18b 46c With eagle emblem omitted — —
e. "Mailed From Zip Code ..." on bottom line — —
f. "Postcard" on bottom line 7.50 —
g. "First-Class Mail" on bottom line 5.00 —
h. "First-Class Mail Intl" on bottom line — —
i. "Priority Mail" on bottom line — —
j. "Priority Envelope" on bottom line — —
k. "Priority Box" on bottom line — —
l. "Priority Tube" on bottom line — —
m. "Priority - Irregular Shape" on bottom line — —
n. "Express Mail" on bottom line — —

No. CVP84C was made available at Mail & Go postal stations in Super Target stores in the Dallas, TX area, and presumably could be printed in any denomination.

In 2013, twelve Mail & Go machines vending No. CVP84C and the holiday and social cause designs noted under No. CVP84 were installed and operated at thirteen Rite Aid drug stores in central California along the Highway 1 corridor. The machines were installed by the LePages Company (a USPS-licensed manufacturer and wholesaler of USPS-brand mailing supplies). They were placed under the jurisdiction of the Oakland, CA region of the USPS throughout most of 2014-15. Postmasters in the towns supported the machines officially with Priority Mail containers, postal labels and daily mail collection. The locations were listed by the USPS in its online Internet database of self-service post office locations. The machines appear to have been removed between Oct. 2015 and Jan. 2016.

The stamps vended by these machines were officially approved by the USPS and are no different than stamps sold from the same models of machines installed at colleges and universities across the nation. Locations of about 40 other privately supported Mail & Go machines have been recorded. These other machines are installed and operated by Pitney Bowes employees who manage mail rooms the company operates under contracts. At those locations, the mail room staff takes the daily mail to the local post officce, and there is no USPS logistical support.

The USPS regulations classify Mail & Go machines as "third party kiosks." No. CVP84Cd is an error that Pitney Bowes technicians could not explain. It appeared for a short time on a machine in Illinois and at the U.S. Department of Defense Medical HQ facility mailroom in Annandale, Va., and other unidentified locations.

Thermal prints generated by vending machines with too little electrically generated heat tend to fade very quickly.

APC With Vertical Coding at Right of Date CVP19

Die Cut With Rounded Corners

2012, Apr. 12 **Self-Adhesive**

CVP85 CVP19 **black & pink** 1.50 —
a. Die cut with perpendicular corners, colored bar at left, "Fold Here" at center, 100x38mm — —

No. CVP85 has "APC" reading upwards at right. No. CVP78 has "IBM" reading upwards at right. No. CVP85 was available during a nationwide test of machines, and could be printed in any denomination from 1c to $99.99.

No. CVP85a was produced on label stock normally used for No. CVP87 when machines ran out of label stock to produce orders for Nos. CVP85, CVP85B, and varieties of CVP86.

APC With Vertical Coding At Left of Date — CVP19a

Die Cut With Rounded Corners

2012 **Self-Adhesive**

CVP85B CVP19a **black & pink** 1.50 —
c. Die cut with perpendicular corners, colored bar at left, "FOLD HERE" at center, 100x38mm — —

No. CVP85Bc was produced on label stock normally used for No. CVP87 when machines ran out of stock to produce orders for Nos. CVP85, CVP85B, and varieties of CVP86.

APC Variable Vignette Stamp CVP20

Die Cut With Rounded Corners

2012, Apr. 12 **Self-Adhesive**

CVP86 CVP20 (45c) **black & pink** 2.00 —
a. Die cut with perpendicular corners, colored bar at left, "Fold Here" at center, 100x38mm 4.00 —

No. CVP86 was available during a nationwide test of machines, and could be printed only as "Forever" stamps. The vignette portion of the stamp at left could be chosen from a gallery of six images (Mr. Zip, Heart, Flowers, Flag, Eagle, and Balloons and "Celebrate!", which is depicted). Values are for any vignette, or for any other vignette that may be programmed into the machine at a later date. Each vignette design could be purchased in a quantities ranging from 1 stamp to 100 stamps, but because a $1 minimum purchase was required, at least three examples of the first stamp chosen had to be purchased. A maximum of ten stamps could be printed on a sheet. Sales of stamps that are not in multiples of 10 were printed in strips, smaller-sized sheets containing an even number of stamps, or in sheets having one label inscribed "This Block Is Not Valid Postage" when the sheet contained an odd number of stamps.

No. CVP86a was produced on wide-label stock normally used for No. CVP87 when the small-label printer was defective or the machine had run out of small-label stock.

Examples of No. CVP86 without a printed image at left are the result of machines having their image-printing capability shut off so pre-printed label stock for producing No. CVP88 could be substituted for the blank label stock used for Nos. CVP85 and CVP86. See footnote under No. CVP88 for information about examples of No. CVP86 with date of purchase inscriptions to right of "Forever."

APC With Vertical Coding to Right of Date — CVP21

Die Cut With Perpendicular Corners

2012, Apr. 12 **Self-Adhesive**

CVP87 CVP21 **black & pink** — —

No. CVP87 was available during a nationwide test of machines, and could be printed in any denomination from 1c to $99.99. Stamps can be inscribed with a variety of different service inscriptions.

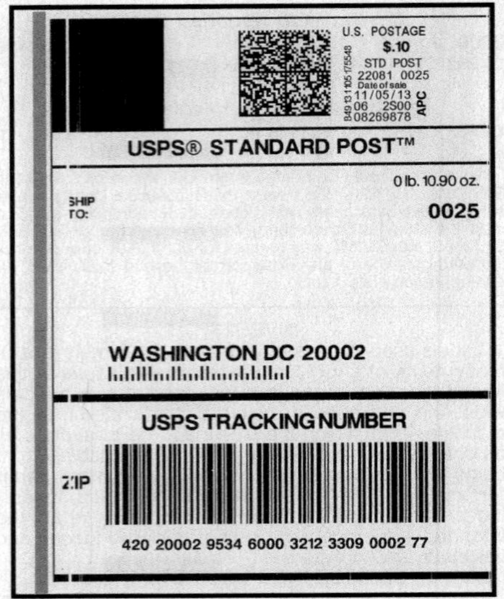

APC With Vertical Coding to Left of Date — CVP21a

Die Cut With Perpendicular Corners

2012 **Self-Adhesive**

CVP87A CVP21a **black & pink** — —

Labels of type CVP21a with postage indicia inscribed FCM LETTER below the denomination have only a bar code and the Zip code of the destination at the bottom third rather than a USPS TRACKING NUMBER. Labels for which a Certified Mail fee has been paid have a CERTIFIED MAIL bar code. Express Mail labels have POSTAL USE ONLY form at the bottom.

On Nov. 7, 2013, the USPS had distributed and had begun requiring the use of "signalling label" stock with a clear phosphor stripe. The clear stripe appears positioned vertically along the left margin of the labels. Labels with pink stripes along the right margin continued to be used until stocks were exhausted or labels with pre-printed vignettes were issued for use in some machines on Apr. 1, 2014 (CVP90-CVP91).

APC With Vertical Coding at Left of Date And Clear Phosphor Stripe Along Left Margin — CVP21b

Die Cut With Rounded Corners

2013, Nov. 7 **Self-Adhesive**

CVP87B CVP21b **black** 5.00 —
c. Die cut with perpendicular corners, colored bar at left, "Fold Here" at center, 100x38mm 8.50 —

The Scheduled Delivery and Expected Delivery inscriptions, date and times seen on Nos. CVP89B and CVP89C replaced "THIS BLOCK IS NOT VALID FOR POSTAGE" on labels normally found adjacent to Nos, CVP87B and CVP92A when sold for other than Priority Mail.

Mailbox CVP22

Die Cut With Rounded Corners

2012, Oct. 31 **Self-Adhesive**

CVP88 CVP22 (45c) **multicolored** 3.50 —

The mailbox vignette is preprinted on No. CVP88. This preprinted stock was placed in machines in November 2012 and was to be removed from machines on December 31, 2012. The earliest known date of sale is Nov. 10, 2012.

Examples of No. CVP88 with the mailbox design covered by images used for Nos. CVP85 and CVP86 were the result of machines having their blank label stock replaced with the preprinted label stock while the machine's image-printing capability was not shut off to accommodate the preprinted stock.

On No. CVP88, the number of the month and last two digits of the year in which the stamp was purchased, separated by an asterisk, appear to the right of "Forever." If the operator of the machine programmed it to sell No. CVP88 but failed to turn off the vignettes available as No. CVP86 and did not load the preprinted Christmas Mailbox label stock, the resulting vended product would be No. CVP86 with the month and year appearing to the right of "FOREVER."

Labels inscribed "This Block Is Not Valid For Postage" differ from similar labels created with No. CVP86. Various sizes of "Void" overprints on these labels exist.

USPS Emblem — CVP22a

Die Cut With Rounded Corners

2013, Oct. 31 **Self-Adhesive**

CVP88A CVP22a (46c) **black & pink** 3.00 —
b. Die cut with perpendicular corners, colored bar at left, "Fold Here" at center, 100x38mm 7.50 —

This design was first placed in a few machines in the Washington, DC and Merrifield, VA area on Oct. 31, 2013. Stamps vended with encoded dates prior to Nov. 7, 2013 were test stamps. On Nov. 6, 2013, the USPS declared the test to be successful and the image was released for general use as a fall-back design.

No. CVP88Ab was produced on wide-label stock normally used to produce No. CVP87 when the small-label printer was either defective or machines ran out of stock to produce orders for No. CVP88A. The earliest known sale date of No. CVP88Ab is Nov. 2, 2013.

Examples of CVP88A lacking the eagle vignette could be made if the machine had blank label stock in the feeder but was set to print on pre-printed labels such as No. CVP89. When the machine has pre-printed labels (starting with No. CVP89) in the feeder and is set to print on blank labels, the Eagle vignette will print on top of the preprinted image.

Reindeer — CVP23

Die Cut With Rounded Corners

2013, Nov. 7 **Self-Adhesive**

CVP89 CVP23 (46c) **multicolored** 3.50 2.00

The reindeer vignette is preprinted on No. CVP89. The issue date is the earliest documented sale date.

USPS Emblem With Clear Phosphor Stripe Along Left Margin — CVP23a

Die Cut With Rounded Corners

2014, Jan. 8 **Self-Adhesive**

CVP89A CVP23a (46c) **black** 3.00 —
d. (50c) Vertical serial number with no leading letter, *2018* — —

Examples of CVP89A lacking the eagle vignette could be made if the machine had blank label stock in the feeder but was set to print on pre-printed labels such as No. CVP89. When the machine has pre-printed labels (starting with No. CVP89) in the feeder and is set to print on blank labels, the Eagle vignette will print on top of the preprinted image. Examples known include 2018-generation stamps with serial number with no leading letter.

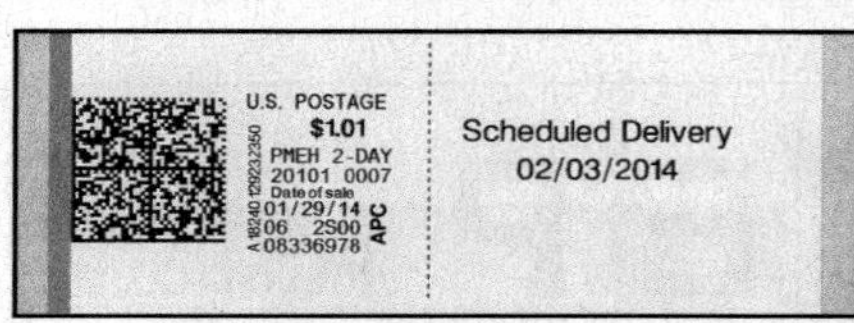

APC With Scheduled Delivery — CVP23b

Die Cut With Perpendicular Corners

2014, Jan. Self-Adhesive

CVP89B CVP23b **black & pink** — —

No. CVP89B is generated when the mailer answers a machine-system prompt with a "no" answer when asked if the full-length label (Type CVP21) will fit on the mailer's item. This is vended only when pre-printed labels are installed in the machine or the small-label printer is defective.

For selected mail service the USPS doesn't track, the field to the right of "FOLD HERE" remains blank (in effect creating No. CVP87Bc).

APC With Expected Delivery — CVP23c

Die Cut With Perpendicular Corners

2014, Jan. Self-Adhesive

CVP89C CVP23c **black & pink** — —

See note after No. CVP89B.

Spiderman — CVP24

Die Cut With Rounded Corners

2014, Apr. 1 Self-Adhesive

CVP90 CVP24 (49c) **multicolored** 2.50 2.00

The Spiderman vignette is preprinted on No. CVP90.

Flag CVP25

Die Cut With Rounded Corners

2014, Apr. 1 Self-Adhesive

CVP91 CVP25 (49c) **multicolored** 1.75 1.25

a. "FOREVER" (only) missing — —

b. (50c) With vertical serial number with no leading letter, *2018* — —

The flag vignette is preprinted on No. CVP91.

Examples of No. CVP91b exist with the USPS Eagle emblem (see illustration at design CVP23a) printed on top of the preprinted flag design label; value, $10. It is theoretically possible that blank labels without a preprinted flag or other preprinted design could be inserted in the new machine, and (likely) be printed without the operator having turned on the thermal-printed USPS logo that machines can produce on-site, leaving an indicia and value printed on a stamp without any pictorial element. Such varieties are products of local operator error that has occurred on all issues from No. CVP88 in 2013 and can be manufactured through illicit cooperation of postal officials.

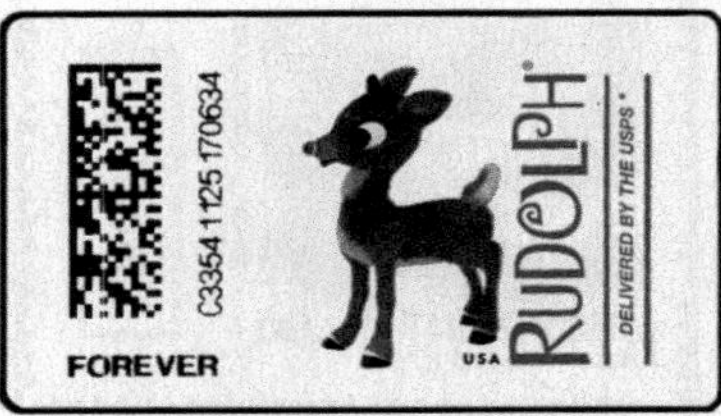

Rudolph, the Red-Nosed Reindeer — CVP26

Die Cut With Rounded Corners

2014, Nov. 6 Self-Adhesive

CVP92 CVP26 (49c) **multicolored** 2.50 1.75

The Rudolph vignette is preprinted on No. CVP92.

From Nov. 14, 2014, Automated Postal Centers (APC) vending machines were renamed by the USPS to be Self Service Kiosks (SSK), and the machines were changed to issue stamps inscribed "SSK" rather than "APC."

SSK With Vertical Coding at Left of Date CVP27

Die Cut With Rounded Corners

2014, Nov. 14 Self-Adhesive

CVP93 CVP27 **black & pink** — —

a. **Black**, with vertical transparent stripe at left 1.00 —

No. CVP93 was available at machines that had not yet retired the pink-striped labels.

It was not intended by the USPS that indicia inscribed with SSK would be printed on pink-striped labels. The design was shifted to appear farther to the right, to insure the bar code would remain uncompromised and at a safe distance from the clear phosphor stripe on the newer labels. Almost all examples of this issue will have SSK appearing within the pink stripe.

Value of No. CVP93a is for 49c denomination, current at the time. Other denominations pro-rata.

F
U.S. POSTAGE
$.15
FCM PARCEL
20120
12/06/14
06 2S00
08313738
SSK
USPS® FIRST-CLASS MAIL®
0 lb. 8.20 oz.
SHIP TO:
NIKISKI AK 99635
USPS TRACKING NUMBER
9574 2000 0060 4340 0004 84

SSK With Vertical Coding to Left of Date — CVP28

Die Cut With Perpendicular Corners

2014, Nov. 14 Self-Adhesive

CVP94 CVP28 **black & pink** — —

a. Indicia at upper right with no leading letter, various service level indicators, *2018* — —

Like No. CVP87A, No. CVP94 exists in other denominations inscribed with various mail service inscriptions or with blackened square in place of letters such as "F," above.

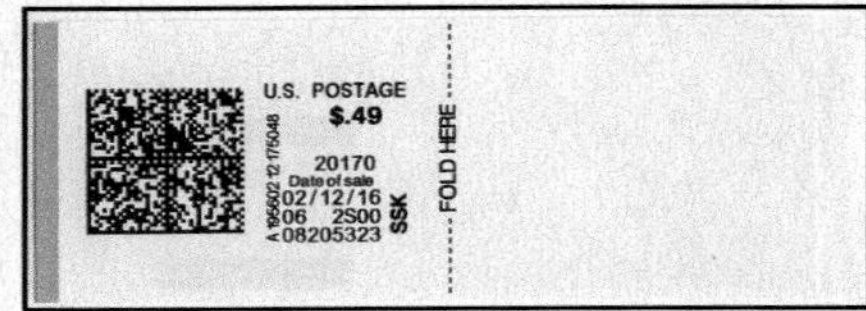

SSK With Blank Area at Right of "Fold Here" — CVP29

Die Cut With Perpendicular Corners

2014, Nov. 14 Self-Adhesive

CVP95 CVP29 **black & pink** — —

a. **black,** vertical serial number with no leading letter, clear phosphor stripe, *2018* — —

See note below No. CVP89B.

SSK With "Expected Delivery" at Right of Dotted Line — CVP30

Die Cut With Perpendicular Corners

2014, Nov. 14 Self-Adhesive

CVP96 CVP30 **black & pink** — —

a. **black,** vertical serial number with no leading letter, various service level indicators, clear phosphor stripe, *2018* — —

See note below No. CVP89B.

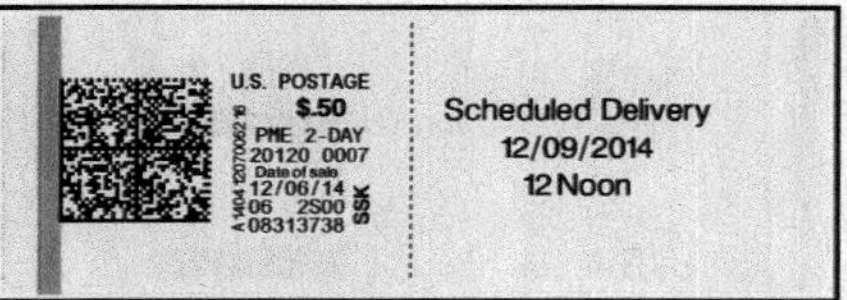

SSK With "Scheduled Delivery" at Right of Dotted Line — CVP31

Die Cut With Perpendicular Corners

2014, Nov. 14 Self-Adhesive

CVP97 CVP31 **black & pink** — —

a. **black,** vertical serial number with no leading letter, various service level indicators, clear phosphor stripe, *2018* — —

See note below No. CVP89B.

Charlie Brown Looking in Mailbox — CVP32

Die Cut With Rounded Corners

2015, Oct. 20 Self-Adhesive

CVP98 CVP32 (49c) **multicolored** 2.50 1.00

The Charlie Brown vignette is preprinted on No. CVP98. Issue date is earliest recorded sale date. Post offices were authorized to place the labels in machines at the close of business on Oct. 20, which many did prior to the SSK system-wide date change that occurs daily prior to midnight.

mPOS — CVP33

Die Cut With Rounded Corners

2015 Self-Adhesive

CVP99 CVP33 **black** — —

No. CVP99 is generated by a mobile hand-held point-of-sale vending machine with integrated thermal postage printer and embedded credit/debit card acceptance processor. Possible denominations are limited to the postage prices applicable to each available pre-printed type of Priority and Express Mail flat rate envelopes and packages (rate determined by scanning the bar code on the package the customer needs). While this indicia is intended to be affixed to mail matter at the time it is presented, postage can be generated and sold in quantities to take away for later use. Labels are generated from vertical coils with blank labels.

Wreath in Window CVP34

Die Cut With Rounded Corners

2016, Oct. 27 **Self-Adhesive**

CVP100 CVP34 (47c) **multicolored** 1.50 1.00

The wreath in window vignette is preprinted on No. CVP100. Issue date is earliest recorded sale date.

Christmas Cookies — CVP35

Die Cut With Rounded Corners

2017, Oct. 17 **Self-Adhesive**

CVP101 CVP35 (49c) **multicolored** 2.50 1.00

a. On 2018-generation stamp with serial number with no leading letter — —

The Christmas cookies vignette is preprinted on No. CVP101. Issue date is earliest recorded sale date.

Flag CVP36

Die Cut With Rounded Corners

2018, Aug. 23 **Self-Adhesive**

CVP108 CVP36 (50c) **multicolored** — —

The flag vignette is preprinted on No. CVP108. Issue date is earliest recorded sale date.

Santa Claus CVP37

Die Cut With Rounded Corners

2018, Oct. 21 **Self-Adhesive**

CVP109 CVP37 (50c) **multicolored** — —

The Santa Claus vignette is preprinted on No. CVP109. Issue date is earliest recorded sale date.

MACHINE SET-UP AND TEST LABELS

Test labels were generated when machines were activated. They were not intended for public distribution.

Other samples, advertizing labels, proofs, etc. exist.

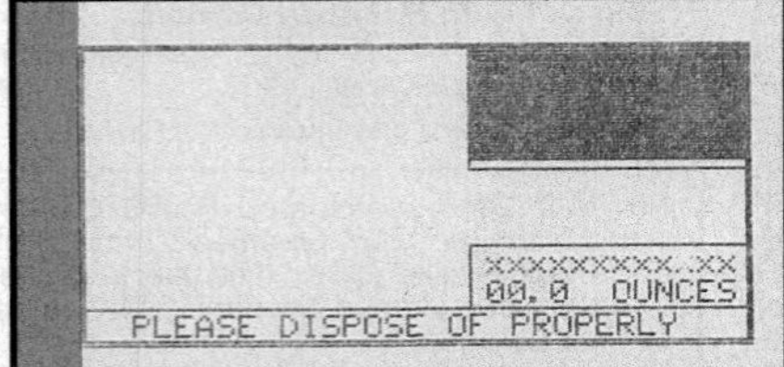

Autopost Test Label — CVPT1

Autopost Test Label with Bar Code — CVPT2

1989 **Self-Adhesive** *Guillotined*

Tagged

CVPT1 CVPT1 **black & orange** 100.00

CVPT2 CVPT2 **black & orange** —

APC Test Label — CVPT3

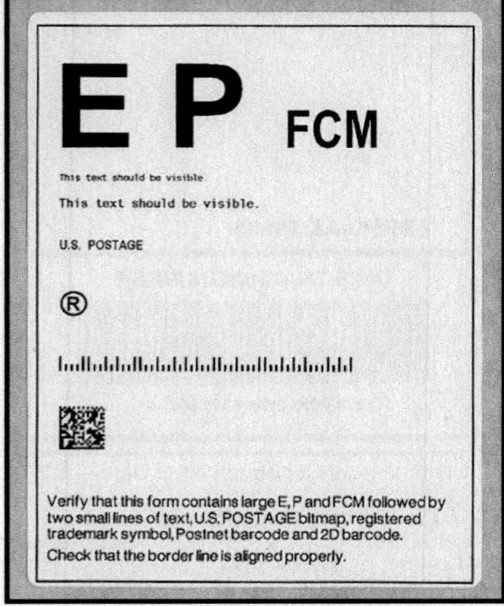

APC Test Label — CVPT4

2004, Apr. 14 **Self-Adhesive** *Die Cut*

CVPT3 CVPT3 **black & pink** —

CVPT4 CVPT4 **black** —

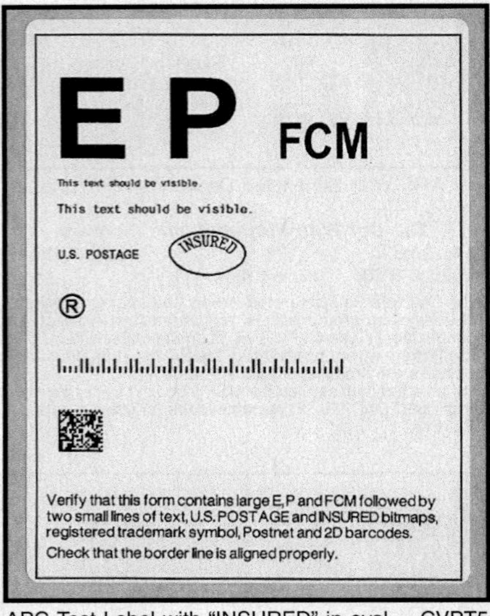

APC Test Label with "INSURED" in oval — CVPT5

APC Test Label with "APC" in Pink Bar — CVPT6

2004, Nov. 19 **Self-Adhesive** *Die Cut*

CVPT5 CVPT5 **black** —

CVPT6 CVPT6 **black & pink** 30.00

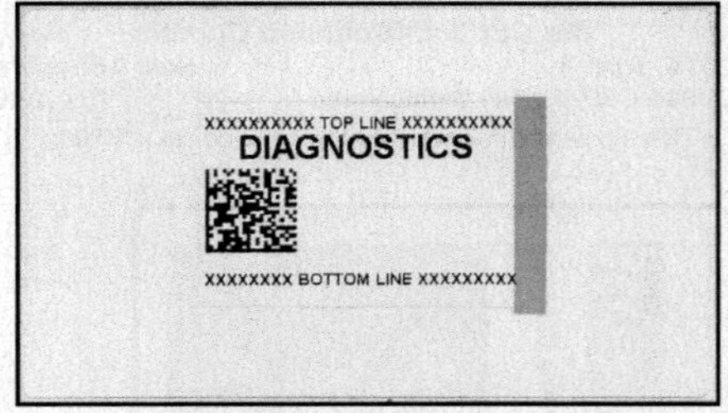

APC Diagnostics Test Label — CVPT7

2004, Nov. 19 **Self-Adhesive** *Die Cut*

CVPT7 CVPT7 **black & pink** —

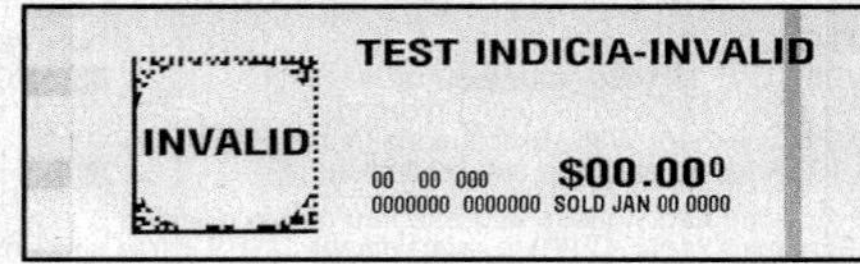

CVPT7A

Pitney Bowes "Mail & Go" Kiosks

Die Cut With Perpendicular Corners

2011, Oct. **Self-Adhesive**

CVPT7A CVPT7A **black & pink** — —

Flag — CVPT7B

Serpentine Die Cut 13¼x12½

2011, Oct. **Self-Adhesive**

CVPT7B CVPT7B **black & multicolored** — —

Theoretically, serpentine die cut 9 examples of No. CVPT7B could exist from set-up of machines used at the Pitney Bowes facilities in Connecticut, where die cut 9 paper labels are known to have been loaded. The editors have not seen an example of this label die cut 9.

APC Test Label With Vertical "VOID" at Right of Sale Date CVPT8

2012 ***Die Cut With Rounded Corners***
Self-Adhesive

CVPT8 CVPT8 **black & pink** 30.00

Compare with Nos. CVPT14 and CVPT20.

Mailbox — CVPT8A

2012, Nov. ***Die Cut With Rounded Corners***
Self-Adhesive

CVPT8A CVPT8A **black & multicolored** — —

APC Test Vend Label for Setup to Use Thermal Vignettes — CVPT9

2013 ***Die Cut With Rounded Corners***
Self-Adhesive

CVPT9 CVPT9 **black & pink** 12.00

APC Test Vend Label for Setup to Use No. CVP89 — CVPT10

2013 ***Die Cut With Rounded Corners***
Self-Adhesive

CVPT10 CVPT10 **black & multicolored** 12.00

APC Test Vend Label for Setup to Use No. CVP89 — CVPT11

2013 ***Die Cut With Rounded Corners***
Self-Adhesive

CVPT11 CVPT11 **black & multicolored** —

No. CVPT11 occasionally appears vertically se-tenant with No. CVPT10.

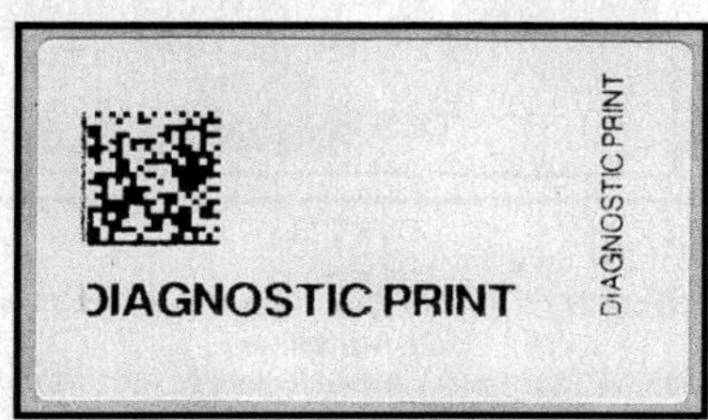

APC Diagnostics Test Label With Clear Phosphor Stripe Along Left Side for Setup to Use No. CVP89A — CVPT12

2013 ***Die Cut With Rounded Corners***
Self-Adhesive

CVPT12 CVPT12 **black** 10.00

APC Diagnostics Test Label For Pre-printed Label Setup — CVPT13

2013 ***Die Cut With Rounded Corners***
Self-Adhesive

CVPT13 CVPT13 **black & multicolored** —

APC Test Vend Label With Vertical "VOID VOID VOID" to Left of Sale Date — CVPT14

2014 ***Die Cut With Rounded Corners***
Self-Adhesive

CVPT14 CVPT14 **black & pink** —

Compare with Nos. CVPT8 and CVPT20.

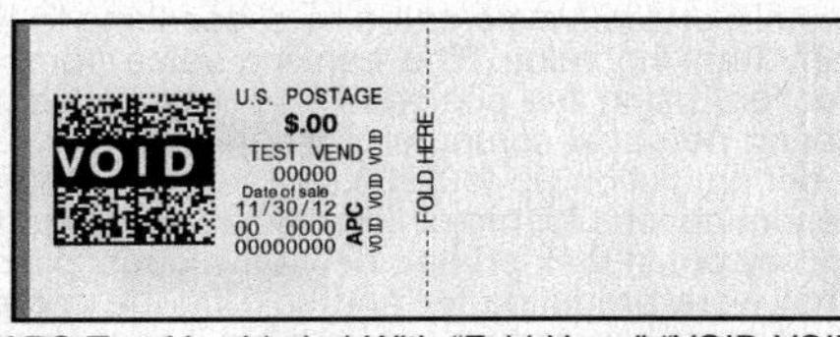

APC Test Vend Label With "Fold Here," "VOID VOID VOID" at Right of Date — CVPT15

2012-14 ***Die Cut With Perpendicular Corners***
Self-Adhesive

CVPT15 CVPT15 **black & pink** —
a. "VOID VOID VOID" vertically at left of date —

CVPT16

2014, Apr. 1 ***Die Cut With Rounded Corners***
Self-Adhesive

CVPT16 CVPT16 **black & multicolored** 12.00

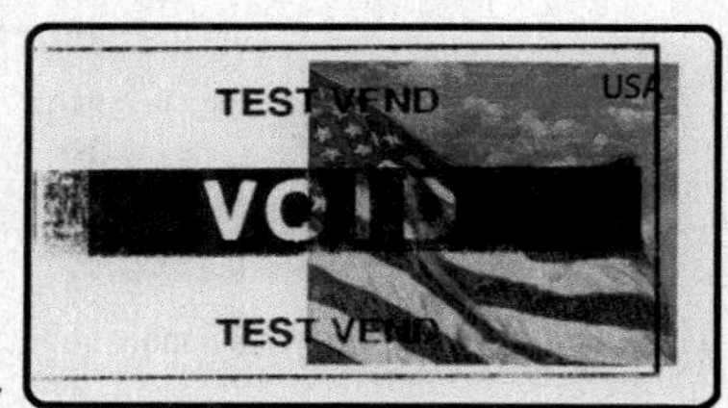

CVPT17

2014, Apr. 1 ***Die Cut With Rounded Corners***
Self-Adhesive

CVPT17 CVPT17 **black & multicolored** 12.00

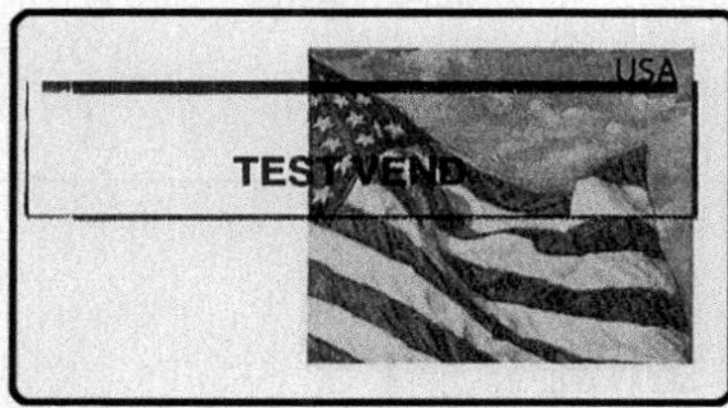

CVPT17A

2014 ***Die Cut With Rounded Corners***
Self-Adhesive

CVPT17A CVPT17A **black & multicolored** —

No. CVPT17A occasionally appears vertically se-tenant with No. CVPT17.

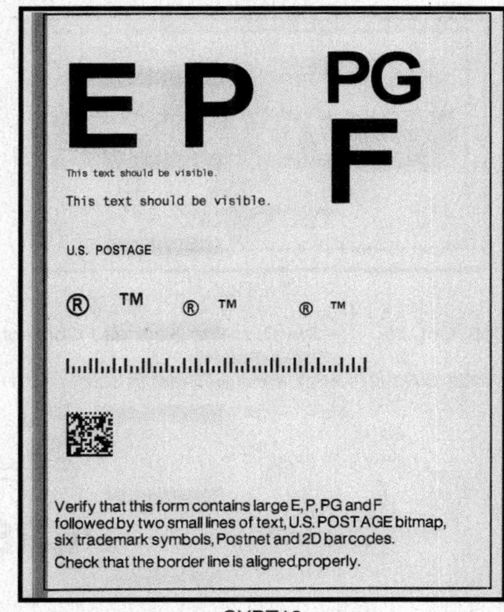

CVPT18

2014 ***Die Cut With Perpendicular Corners***
Self-Adhesive

CVPT18 CVPT18 **black & multicolored** —

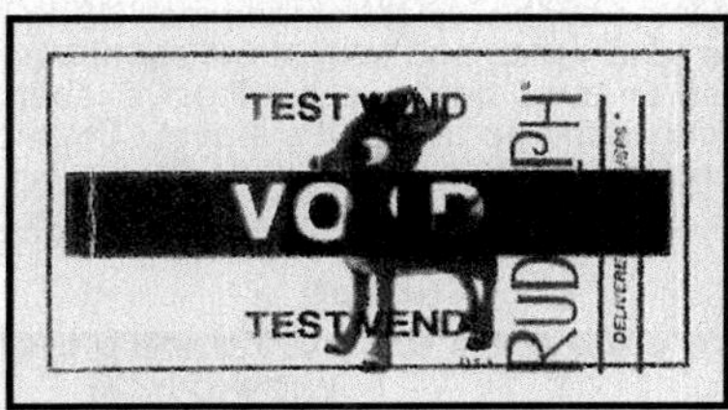

CVPT19

2014, Nov. 1 ***Die Cut With Rounded Corners***
Self-Adhesive

CVPT19 CVPT19 **black & multicolored** 15.00

SSK With "VOID VOID VOID" at Left of Sale Date — CVPT20

2014, Nov. ***Die Cut With Rounded Corners***
Self-Adhesive

CVPT20 CVPT20 **black** —

Compare with Nos. CVPT8 and CVPT14.

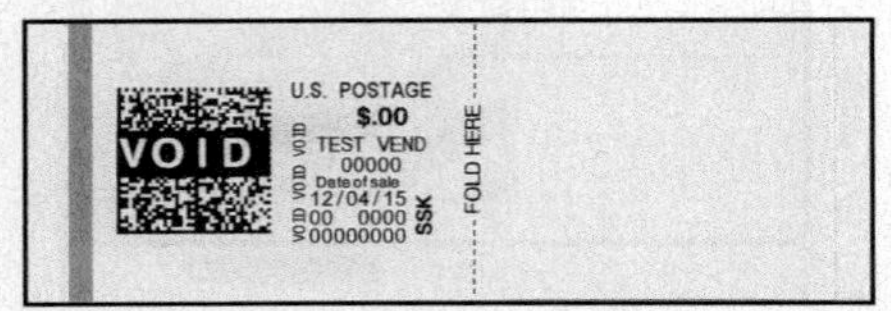

SSK Test Vend Label With "Fold Here," "VOID VOID VOID" at Left of Date — CVPT21

2014, Nov. ***Die Cut With Perpendicular Corners***
Self-Adhesive

CVPT21 CVPT21 **black & pink** 2.50

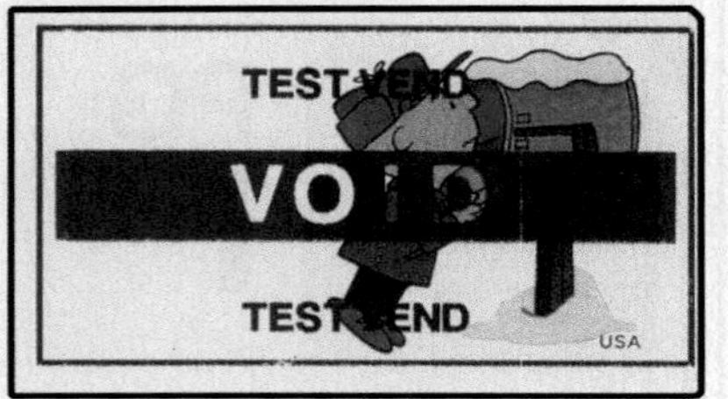

CVPT22

2015, Oct. 29 ***Die Cut With Rounded Corners***
Self-Adhesive

CVPT22 CVPT22 **black & multicolored** 10.00

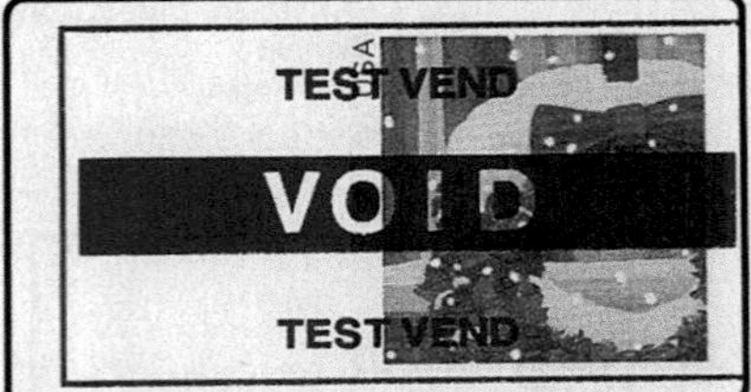

CVPT23

2016, Oct. 27 ***Die Cut With Rounded Corners***
Self-Adhesive

CVPT23 CVPT23 **black & multicolored** 5.00 —

POSTAL CARDS

On July 5, 1990 the first of a number of "Postal Buddy" machines was placed in service at the Merrifield, VA post office. The machine printed out numerous items such as address labels (including monogram if you wished), fax labels, "penalty" cards, denominated postal cards, etc. Certain services were free, such as the penalty card mailed to your post office for change of address. The 15-cent denominated card cost 33-cents each and could be used to notify others of address change, meeting notices, customized messages, etc. Borders, messages, backs are different. The cards also came in sheets of 4.

These machines were tested in at least 30 locations in Virginia, including 16 post offices.

Denominated Postal Cards

Number under design includes machine number, year, date (1 through 366) and transaction number.

1990, July 5

CVUX1 15c 6.00 *10.00*
First day cancel, Merrifield, VA *(6,500)* 5.00

1991, Feb. 3

CVUX2 19c 3.00 *8.00*
First day cancel, any location 35.00

Number under design includes ZIP Code of the originating machine (22203 in illustration), machine number (101), last digit of year, numbers of month and day (21203 for Dec. 3, 1992) and transaction number (041).

1992, Nov. 13

CVUX3 19c 6.00 *15.00*
First day dated, Reston or Chantilly, VA 25.00

A total of 171 machines were used, with 109 in the greater Washington, DC area (including locations in Virginia and Maryland), 59 in the greater San Diego area, and 3 in Denver. The machine numbers (011, 012, 021, 101, 111, 121, 131) when combined with the zip code created unique identification numbers for each machine.

No. 3 is known also on fluorescent paper. Two different designs on back known for each paper type.

The contract for Postal Buddy machines was canceled Sept. 16, 1993. After the contract was canceled, the Postal Buddy Corporation sold remaining stocks of card stock to the public with both reverse designs imprinted. By using this stock and a high quality copier, very dangerous counterfeits can be created. The duplication of numbers in the transaction line will be one indicator.

PERSONAL COMPUTER POSTAGE

Personal computer postage, approved by the US Postal Service, was created by subscribing to Stamps.com, an internet website. Customers ordered self-adhesive labels showing vignettes, but lacking any franking value. The franking value portion of the stamps could be printed at the customer's convenience at any computer with an internet connection, using the customer's access codes. Any postage printed would be charged against the customer's account. In 2005, Endicia.com began offering personal computer postage.

Stamps with major listings could be printed in any denomination up to $999.99. Stamps with minor listings could only be printed in denominations calculated by the weight of the piece being mailed. Denominations for minor listings can range from 23c to $133.20. Customers could print the franking value (encryption and text) of the stamps on whatever they put in their printer, be it envelopes, plain gummed labels or regular paper. These listings are limited to items on the self-adhesive labels shown that were produced for and sold by the companies that created the software that generates the franking value portion of the stamp. The labels of a particular company must have on it a franking value that is produced by that company's software that matches the label's dimensions.

Neopost

CVPA1

2000 ***Serpentine Die Cut 8***
Self-Adhesive

1CVP1 CVPA1 33c **black, yellow & pink** — —
On cover — —
Pane of 10 — —

Stamps.com

Flag and Star — CVPA1a

2002, July ***Serpentine Die Cut 5¾ at Left***
"Stamps.com" in Lower Case Letters
Identification Code Below Zip Code

1CVP2	CVPA1a 37c **black, blue & orange,** no mail class inscribed		7.00	3.00
	On cover			4.00
	Sheet of 25		175.00	

Identification Code Above Zip Code

1CVP2A	CVPA1a 37c **black, blue & orange**		4.00	3.00
	On cover			3.50
	Sheet of 25		100.00	
	a.	"First Class" below "US Postage"	2.75	2.00
	b.	"Priority" below "US Postage"	8.25	2.50
	c.	"Express" below "US Postage"	25.00	5.00
	d.	"Media Mail" below "US Postage"	7.75	2.50
	e.	"Parcel Post" below "US Postage"	7.75	2.50
	f.	"Bound Printed Matter" below "US Postage"	7.75	2.50
	g.	"BPM" below "US Postage"	7.75	2.50

See Nos. 1CVP9, 1CVP21.

No. 1CVP2 apparently could be printed in denominations up to and including 37c. The 37c denomination comes with "FIRST-CLASS" between the Zip code and the identification code.

Later versions of the Stamps.com software allow any denomination to be printed, as well as additional or different mail-class inscriptions, on any basic stamp except for No. 1CVP2.

Values for Nos. 1CVP2A and 1CVP3-1CVP42 are for items appropriate to the service described. Stamps with denominations far lower than those appropriate to the service are valued correspondingly lower.

The software changes allow Nos. 1CVP2A and 1CVP3-1CVP37 to be printed with the mail-class inscriptions described for Nos. 1CVP38f-1CVP38p.

Later software changes allow Nos. 1CVP2A, 1CVP3-1CVP42 and 1CVP51-1CVP58 to be printed with mail-class inscriptions "Library Mail," "Intl. First Class," "Intl Priority," "Intl Express," and "M-Bag" with any denomination.

Love — CVPA2

2002 ***Serpentine Die Cut 5¾ at Left***

1CVP3 CVPA2 37c **black, blue & orange**		4.00	4.00
	On cover		5.00
	Sheet of 25	100.00	
a.	"First Class" below "US Postage"	2.75	2.00
b.	"Priority" below "US Postage"	8.25	2.50
c.	"Express" below "US Postage"	25.00	5.00
d.	"Media Mail" below "US Postage"	7.75	2.50
e.	"Parcel Post" below "US Postage"	7.75	2.50
f.	"Bound Printed Matter" below "US Postage"	7.75	2.50
g.	"BPM" below "US Postage"	7.75	2.50

Statue of Liberty and Flag — CVPA3

Liberty Bell and Flag — CVPA4

Eagle and Flag — CVPA5

George Washington and Flag — CVPA6

Capitol Building and Flag — CVPA7

2003, June ***Serpentine Die Cut 5¾ at Left***

1CVP4 CVPA3 37c **black, blue & orange**		3.50	2.00
	On cover		3.00
a.	"First Class" below "US Postage"	3.25	2.00
b.	"Priority" below "US Postage"	8.00	1.00
c.	"Express" below "US Postage"	25.00	3.00
d.	"Media Mail" below "US Postage"	7.50	1.00
e.	"Parcel Post" below "US Postage"	7.50	1.00
f.	"Bound Printed Matter" below "US Postage"	7.50	1.00
g.	"BPM" below "US Postage"	7.50	1.00
1CVP5 CVPA4 37c **black, blue & orange**		3.50	2.00
	On cover		3.00
a.	"First Class" below "US Postage"	3.25	2.00
b.	"Priority" below "US Postage"	8.00	1.00
c.	"Express" below "US Postage"	25.00	3.00
d.	"Media Mail" below "US Postage"	7.50	1.00
e.	"Parcel Post" below "US Postage"	7.50	1.00
f.	"Bound Printed Matter" below "US Postage"	7.50	1.00
g.	"BPM" below "US Postage"	7.50	1.00
1CVP6 CVPA5 37c **black, blue & orange**		3.50	2.00
	On cover		3.00
a.	"First Class" below "US Postage"	3.25	2.00
b.	"Priority" below "US Postage"	8.00	1.00
c.	"Express" below "US Postage"	25.00	3.00
d.	"Media Mail" below "US Postage"	7.50	1.00
e.	"Parcel Post" below "US Postage"	7.50	1.00
f.	"Bound Printed Matter" below "US Postage"	7.50	1.00
g.	"BPM" below "US Postage"	7.50	1.00
1CVP7 CVPA6 37c **black, blue & orange**		3.50	2.00
	On cover		3.00
a.	"First Class" below "US Postage"	3.25	.25
b.	"Priority" below "US Postage"	8.00	1.00
c.	"Express" below "US Postage"	25.00	3.00
d.	"Media Mail" below "US Postage"	7.50	1.00
e.	"Parcel Post" below "US Postage"	7.50	1.00
f.	"Bound Printed Matter" below "US Postage"	7.50	1.00
g.	"BPM" below "US Postage"	7.50	1.00
1CVP8 CVPA7 37c **black, blue & orange**		3.50	2.00
	On cover		3.00
a.	"First Class" below "US Postage"	3.25	.45
b.	"Priority" below "US Postage"	8.00	1.00
c.	"Express" below "US Postage"	25.00	3.00
d.	"Media Mail" below "US Postage"	7.50	1.00
e.	"Parcel Post" below "US Postage"	7.50	1.00
f.	"Bound Printed Matter" below "US Postage"	7.50	1.00
g.	"BPM" below "US Postage"	7.50	1.00
h.	Strip of 5, #1CVP4-1CVP8	17.50	

Flag and Star Type of 2002 Redrawn With "Stamps.com" in Upper Case Letters

2003, June ***Serpentine Die Cut 5¾ at Left***

Identification Code Above Zip Code

1CVP9 CVPA1a 37c **black, blue & orange,** "US Postage" only		3.00	1.50
	On cover		2.50
	Sheet of 25	75.00	
a.	"First Class" below "US Postage"	2.00	.45
b.	"Priority" below "US Postage"	8.00	1.00
c.	"Express" below "US Postage"	25.00	3.00
d.	"Media Mail" below "US Postage"	7.50	1.00
e.	"Parcel Post" below "US Postage"	7.50	1.00
f.	"Bound Printed Matter" below "US Postage"	7.50	1.00
g.	"BPM" below "US Postage"	7.50	1.00

Snowman — CVPA8

Snowflakes CVPA9

Holly — CVPA10

Dove — CVPA11

Gingerbread Man and Candy — CVPA12

2003, Dec. ***Serpentine Die Cut 4½ at Left***

1CVP10	CVPA8 37c **black, blue & orange**	3.00	1.50
	On cover		2.50
a.	"First Class" below "US Postage"	2.00	1.00
b.	"Priority" below "US Postage"	8.00	1.00
c.	"Express" below "US Postage"	25.00	3.00
d.	"Media Mail" below "US Postage"	7.50	1.00
e.	"Parcel Post" below "US Postage"	7.50	1.00
f.	"Bound Printed Matter" below "US Postage"	7.50	1.00
g.	"BPM" below "US Postage"	7.50	1.00
1CVP11	CVPA9 37c **black, blue & orange**	3.00	1.50
	On cover		2.50
a.	"First Class" below "US Postage"	2.00	1.00
b.	"Priority" below "US Postage"	8.00	1.00
c.	"Express" below "US Postage"	25.00	3.00
d.	"Media Mail" below "US Postage"	7.50	1.00
e.	"Parcel Post" below "US Postage"	7.50	1.00
f.	"Bound Printed Matter" below "US Postage"	7.50	1.00
g.	"BPM" below "US Postage"	7.50	1.00
1CVP12	CVPA10 37c **black, blue & orange**	3.00	1.50
	On cover		2.50
a.	"First Class" below "US Postage"	2.00	1.00
b.	"Priority" below "US Postage"	8.00	1.00
c.	"Express" below "US Postage"	25.00	3.00
d.	"Media Mail" below "US Postage"	7.50	1.00
e.	"Parcel Post" below "US Postage"	7.50	1.00
f.	"Bound Printed Matter" below "US Postage"	7.50	1.00
g.	"BPM" below "US Postage"	7.50	1.00
1CVP13	CVPA11 37c **black, blue & orange**	3.00	1.50
	On cover		2.50
a.	"First Class" below "US Postage"	2.00	1.00
b.	"Priority" below "US Postage"	8.00	1.00
c.	"Express" below "US Postage"	25.00	3.00
d.	"Media Mail" below "US Postage"	7.50	1.00
e.	"Parcel Post" below "US Postage"	7.50	1.00
f.	"Bound Printed Matter" below "US Postage"	7.50	1.00
g.	"BPM" below "US Postage"	7.50	1.00
1CVP14	CVPA12 37c **black, blue & orange**	3.00	1.50
	On cover		2.50
a.	"First Class" below "US Postage"	2.00	1.00
b.	"Priority" below "US Postage"	8.00	1.00
c.	"Express" below "US Postage"	25.00	3.00
d.	"Media Mail" below "US Postage"	7.50	1.00
e.	"Parcel Post" below "US Postage"	7.50	1.00
f.	"Bound Printed Matter" below "US Postage"	7.50	1.00
g.	"BPM" below "US Postage"	7.50	1.00
h.	Strip of 5, #1CVP10-1CVP14	12.50	

Mailbox — CVPA13

2004, Mar. ***Serpentine Die Cut 6½ at Left***

1CVP15	CVPA13 37c **black, blue & orange**	25.00	15.00
	On cover		35.00
a.	"First Class" below "US Postage"	25.00	15.00
b.	"Priority" below "US Postage"	—	—
c.	"Express" below "US Postage"	—	—
d.	"Media Mail" below "US Postage"	—	—
e.	"Parcel Post" below "US Postage"	—	—
f.	"Bound Printed Matter" below "US Postage"	—	—
g.	"BPM" below "US Postage"	—	—

Blank sheets of No. 1CVP15 were sent free of charge to those who responded to special Stamps.com promotions which offered a fixed amount of free postage as an enticement to new subscribers. The franking portion of the stamps could only be applied after subscribing.

George Washington CVPA14

Thomas Jefferson — CVPA15

Abraham Lincoln — CVPA16

Theodore Roosevelt — CVPA17

John F. Kennedy — CVPA18

2004, Apr. ***Serpentine Die Cut 6½ at Left***

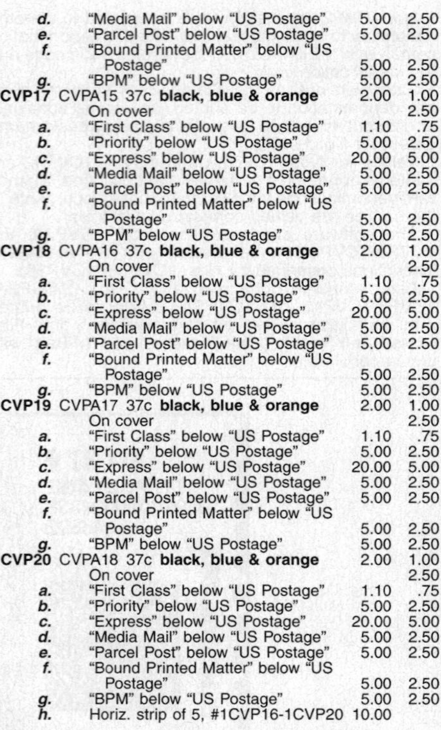

1CVP16	CVPA14 37c **black, blue & orange**	2.00	1.00
	On cover		2.50
a.	"First Class" below "US Postage"	1.10	.75
b.	"Priority" below "US Postage"	5.00	2.50
c.	"Express" below "US Postage"	20.00	5.00
d.	"Media Mail" below "US Postage"	5.00	2.50
e.	"Parcel Post" below "US Postage"	5.00	2.50
f.	"Bound Printed Matter" below "US Postage"	5.00	2.50
g.	"BPM" below "US Postage"	5.00	2.50
1CVP17	CVPA15 37c **black, blue & orange**	2.00	1.00
	On cover		2.50
a.	"First Class" below "US Postage"	1.10	.75
b.	"Priority" below "US Postage"	5.00	2.50
c.	"Express" below "US Postage"	20.00	5.00
d.	"Media Mail" below "US Postage"	5.00	2.50
e.	"Parcel Post" below "US Postage"	5.00	2.50
f.	"Bound Printed Matter" below "US Postage"	5.00	2.50
g.	"BPM" below "US Postage"	5.00	2.50
1CVP18	CVPA16 37c **black, blue & orange**	2.00	1.00
	On cover		2.50
a.	"First Class" below "US Postage"	1.10	.75
b.	"Priority" below "US Postage"	5.00	2.50
c.	"Express" below "US Postage"	20.00	5.00
d.	"Media Mail" below "US Postage"	5.00	2.50
e.	"Parcel Post" below "US Postage"	5.00	2.50
f.	"Bound Printed Matter" below "US Postage"	5.00	2.50
g.	"BPM" below "US Postage"	5.00	2.50
1CVP19	CVPA17 37c **black, blue & orange**	2.00	1.00
	On cover		2.50
a.	"First Class" below "US Postage"	1.10	.75
b.	"Priority" below "US Postage"	5.00	2.50
c.	"Express" below "US Postage"	20.00	5.00
d.	"Media Mail" below "US Postage"	5.00	2.50
e.	"Parcel Post" below "US Postage"	5.00	2.50
f.	"Bound Printed Matter" below "US Postage"	5.00	2.50
g.	"BPM" below "US Postage"	5.00	2.50
1CVP20	CVPA18 37c **black, blue & orange**	2.00	1.00
	On cover		2.50
a.	"First Class" below "US Postage"	1.10	.75
b.	"Priority" below "US Postage"	5.00	2.50
c.	"Express" below "US Postage"	20.00	5.00
d.	"Media Mail" below "US Postage"	5.00	2.50
e.	"Parcel Post" below "US Postage"	5.00	2.50
f.	"Bound Printed Matter" below "US Postage"	5.00	2.50
g.	"BPM" below "US Postage"	5.00	2.50
h.	Horiz. strip of 5, #1CVP16-1CVP20	10.00	

Flag and Star Type of 2002 Redrawn With Orange Stars and Text at Left

2004, Apr. ***Serpentine Die Cut 6½ at Left***

"Stamps.com" in Upper Case Letters

Identification Code Above Zip Code

1CVP21	CVPA1a 37c **black, blue & orange**	2.00	1.00
	On cover		2.50
	Sheet of 25	50.00	
a.	"First Class" below "US Postage"	1.35	.75
b.	"Priority" below "US Postage"	6.00	2.50
c.	"Express" below "US Postage"	22.50	5.00
d.	"Media Mail" below "US Postage"	6.00	2.50
e.	"Parcel Post" below "US Postage"	6.00	2.50
f.	"Bound Printed Matter" below "US Postage"	6.00	2.50
g.	"BPM" below "US Postage"	6.00	2.50

Bicycling — CVPA19

Running — CVPA20

Swimming CVPA21

Boxing — CVPA22

Equestrian CVPA23

Basketball CVPA24

Judo — CVPA25

Soccer — CVPA26

Gymnastics CVPA27

Tennis — CVPA28

2004, Apr. ***Serpentine Die Cut 6½ at Left***

1CVP22	CVPA19 37c **black, blue & orange**	3.00	2.00
	On cover		3.00
a.	"First Class" below "US Postage"	2.50	1.50
b.	"Priority" below "US Postage"	8.00	1.00
c.	"Express" below "US Postage"	25.00	3.00
d.	"Media Mail" below "US Postage"	7.50	1.00
e.	"Parcel Post" below "US Postage"	7.50	1.00
f.	"Bound Printed Matter" below "US Postage"	7.50	1.00
g.	"BPM" below "US Postage"	7.50	1.00
1CVP23	CVPA20 37c **black, blue & orange**	3.00	2.00
	On cover		3.00
a.	"First Class" below "US Postage"	2.50	1.50
b.	"Priority" below "US Postage"	8.00	1.00
c.	"Express" below "US Postage"	25.00	3.00
d.	"Media Mail" below "US Postage"	7.50	1.00
e.	"Parcel Post" below "US Postage"	7.50	1.00
f.	"Bound Printed Matter" below "US Postage"	7.50	1.00
g.	"BPM" below "US Postage"	7.50	1.00
1CVP24	CVPA21 37c **black, blue & orange**	3.00	2.00
	On cover		3.00
a.	"First Class" below "US Postage"	2.50	1.50
b.	"Priority" below "US Postage"	8.00	1.00
c.	"Express" below "US Postage"	25.00	3.00
d.	"Media Mail" below "US Postage"	7.50	1.00
e.	"Parcel Post" below "US Postage"	7.50	1.00
f.	"Bound Printed Matter" below "US Postage"	7.50	1.00
g.	"BPM" below "US Postage"	7.50	1.00
1CVP25	CVPA22 37c **black, blue & orange**	3.00	2.00
	On cover		3.00
a.	"First Class" below "US Postage"	2.50	1.50
b.	"Priority" below "US Postage"	8.00	1.00
c.	"Express" below "US Postage"	25.00	3.00
d.	"Media Mail" below "US Postage"	7.50	1.00
e.	"Parcel Post" below "US Postage"	7.50	1.00
f.	"Bound Printed Matter" below "US Postage"	7.50	1.00
g.	"BPM" below "US Postage"	7.50	1.00
1CVP26	CVPA23 37c **black, blue & orange**	3.00	2.00
	On cover		3.00
a.	"First Class" below "US Postage"	2.50	1.50
b.	"Priority" below "US Postage"	8.00	1.00
c.	"Express" below "US Postage"	25.00	3.00
d.	"Media Mail" below "US Postage"	7.50	1.00
e.	"Parcel Post" below "US Postage"	7.50	1.00
f.	"Bound Printed Matter" below "US Postage"	7.50	1.00

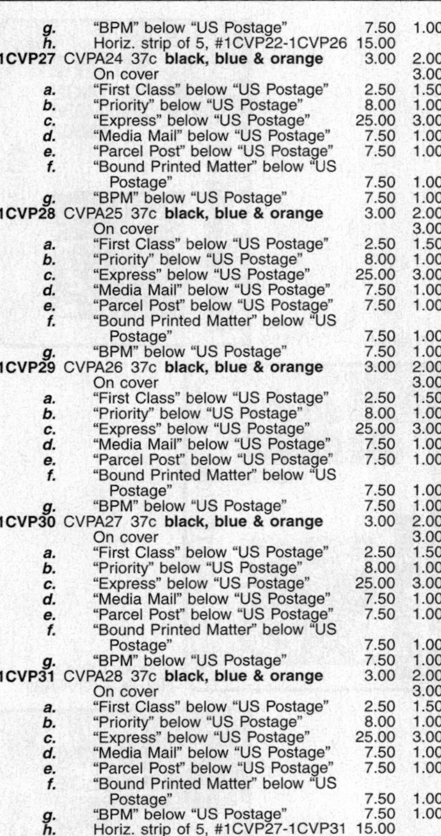

g.	"BPM" below "US Postage"	7.50	1.00
h.	Horiz. strip of 5, #1CVP22-1CVP26	15.00	
1CVP27	CVPA24 37c **black, blue & orange**	3.00	2.00
	On cover		3.00
a.	"First Class" below "US Postage"	2.50	1.50
b.	"Priority" below "US Postage"	8.00	1.00
c.	"Express" below "US Postage"	25.00	3.00
d.	"Media Mail" below "US Postage"	7.50	1.00
e.	"Parcel Post" below "US Postage"	7.50	1.00
f.	"Bound Printed Matter" below "US Postage"	7.50	1.00
g.	"BPM" below "US Postage"	7.50	1.00
1CVP28	CVPA25 37c **black, blue & orange**	3.00	2.00
	On cover		3.00
a.	"First Class" below "US Postage"	2.50	1.50
b.	"Priority" below "US Postage"	8.00	1.00
c.	"Express" below "US Postage"	25.00	3.00
d.	"Media Mail" below "US Postage"	7.50	1.00
e.	"Parcel Post" below "US Postage"	7.50	1.00
f.	"Bound Printed Matter" below "US Postage"	7.50	1.00
g.	"BPM" below "US Postage"	7.50	1.00
1CVP29	CVPA26 37c **black, blue & orange**	3.00	2.00
	On cover		3.00
a.	"First Class" below "US Postage"	2.50	1.50
b.	"Priority" below "US Postage"	8.00	1.00
c.	"Express" below "US Postage"	25.00	3.00
d.	"Media Mail" below "US Postage"	7.50	1.00
e.	"Parcel Post" below "US Postage"	7.50	1.00
f.	"Bound Printed Matter" below "US Postage"	7.50	1.00
g.	"BPM" below "US Postage"	7.50	1.00
1CVP30	CVPA27 37c **black, blue & orange**	3.00	2.00
	On cover		3.00
a.	"First Class" below "US Postage"	2.50	1.50
b.	"Priority" below "US Postage"	8.00	1.00
c.	"Express" below "US Postage"	25.00	3.00
d.	"Media Mail" below "US Postage"	7.50	1.00
e.	"Parcel Post" below "US Postage"	7.50	1.00
f.	"Bound Printed Matter" below "US Postage"	7.50	1.00
g.	"BPM" below "US Postage"	7.50	1.00
1CVP31	CVPA28 37c **black, blue & orange**	3.00	2.00
	On cover		3.00
a.	"First Class" below "US Postage"	2.50	1.50
b.	"Priority" below "US Postage"	8.00	1.00
c.	"Express" below "US Postage"	25.00	3.00
d.	"Media Mail" below "US Postage"	7.50	1.00
e.	"Parcel Post" below "US Postage"	7.50	1.00
f.	"Bound Printed Matter" below "US Postage"	7.50	1.00
g.	"BPM" below "US Postage"	7.50	1.00
h.	Horiz. strip of 5, #1CVP27-1CVP31	15.00	

The item pictured above was produced by Stamps.com for a special promotional mailing of its own and was not made available unused to customers.

Leaning Tower of Pisa — CVPA29

Sphinx and Pyramids — CVPA30

Sydney Opera House — CVPA31

Mayan Pyramid — CVPA32

Asian Temple — CVPA33

2004, July ***Serpentine Die Cut 6½ at Left***

1CVP32	CVPA29 37c **black, blue & orange**	3.00	2.00
	On cover		3.00
a.	"First Class" below "US Postage"	2.30	1.50
b.	"Priority" below "US Postage"	8.00	1.00
c.	"Express" below "US Postage"	25.00	3.00
d.	"Media Mail" below "US Postage"	7.50	1.00
e.	"Parcel Post" below "US Postage"	7.50	1.00
f.	"Bound Printed Matter" below "US Postage"	7.50	1.00
g.	"BPM" below "US Postage"	7.50	1.00
1CVP33	CVPA30 37c **black, blue & orange**	3.00	2.00
	On cover		3.00
a.	"First Class" below "US Postage"	2.30	1.50
b.	"Priority" below "US Postage"	8.00	1.00
c.	"Express" below "US Postage"	25.00	3.00
d.	"Media Mail" below "US Postage"	7.50	1.00
e.	"Parcel Post" below "US Postage"	7.50	1.00
f.	"Bound Printed Matter" below "US Postage"	7.50	1.00
g.	"BPM" below "US Postage"	7.50	1.00
1CVP34	CVPA31 37c **black, blue & orange**	3.00	2.00
	On cover		3.00
a.	"First Class" below "US Postage"	2.30	1.50
b.	"Priority" below "US Postage"	8.00	1.00
c.	"Express" below "US Postage"	25.00	3.00
d.	"Media Mail" below "US Postage"	7.50	1.00
e.	"Parcel Post" below "US Postage"	7.50	1.00
f.	"Bound Printed Matter" below "US Postage"	7.50	1.00
g.	"BPM" below "US Postage"	7.50	1.00
1CVP35	CVPA32 37c **black, blue & orange**	3.00	2.00
	On cover		3.00
a.	"First Class" below "US Postage"	2.30	1.50
b.	"Priority" below "US Postage"	8.00	1.00
c.	"Express" below "US Postage"	25.00	3.00
d.	"Media Mail" below "US Postage"	7.50	1.00
e.	"Parcel Post" below "US Postage"	7.50	1.00
f.	"Bound Printed Matter" below "US Postage"	7.50	1.00
g.	"BPM" below "US Postage"	7.50	1.00
1CVP36	CVPA33 37c **black, blue & orange**	3.00	2.00
	On cover		3.00
a.	"First Class" below "US Postage"	2.30	1.50
b.	"Priority" below "US Postage"	8.00	1.00
c.	"Express" below "US Postage"	25.00	3.00
d.	"Media Mail" below "US Postage"	7.50	1.00
e.	"Parcel Post" below "US Postage"	7.50	1.00
f.	"Bound Printed Matter" below "US Postage"	7.50	1.00
g.	"BPM" below "US Postage"	7.50	1.00
h.	Strip of 5, #1CVP32-1CVP36	15.00	

Computer and Letters — CVPA34

2005, Mar. ***Serpentine Die Cut 6½ at Left***

1CVP37	CVPA34 37c **black, blue & orange**	25.00	15.00
	On cover		75.00
a.	"First Class" below "US Postage"	25.00	15.00
b.	"Priority" below "US Postage"	—	—
c.	"Express" below "US Postage"	—	—
d.	"Media Mail" below "US Postage"	—	—
e.	"Parcel Post" below "US Postage"	—	—
f.	"Bound Printed Matter" below "US Postage"	—	—
g.	"BPM" below "US Postage"	—	—

Blank sheets of No. 1CVP37 were sent free of charge to those who responded to special Stamps.com promotions which offered a fixed amount of free postage as an enticement to new subscribers. The franking portion of the stamps could only be applied after subscribing.

Logo — CVPA35

2005, Aug. ***Die Cut Perf. 6½ at Left***

1CVP38	CVPA35 37c **black, blue & orange**	1.00	.45
	On cover		2.50
a.	"Priority" below "US Postage"	8.00	1.00
b.	"Express" below "US Postage"	25.00	3.00
c.	"Media Mail" below "US Postage"	7.50	1.00
d.	"Parcel Post" below "US Postage"	7.50	1.00
e.	"BPM" below "US Postage"	7.50	1.00
f.	"Aerogramme" below "US Postage"	1.40	1.00
g.	"Intl Air Letter" below "US Postage"	1.25	1.00
h.	"Intl Eco Letter" (Economy Letter Mail) below "US Postage"	5.50	1.00
i.	"GXG" (Global Express Guaranteed) below "US Postage"	50.00	6.00
j.	"EMS" (Global Express Mail) below "US Postage"	32.50	4.00
k.	"GPM" (Global Priority Mail) below "US Postage"	8.00	1.00
l.	"Intl Air Parcel" (Air Parcel Post) below "US Postage"	26.00	3.00
m.	"Intl Eco Parcel" (Economy Parcel Post) below "US Postage"	32.50	4.00
n.	"M-Bag (Air)" below "US Postage"	35.00	5.00
o.	"M-Bag (Economy)" below "US Postage"	18.00	3.00
p.	"Mat for Blind" below "US Postage"	1.25	—
q.	"Library Mail"	5.00	1.00

Values for lettered varieties on Nos. 1CVP38 are based on the prices set as the minimum values for each service classification in the software available at the time the stamps were issued. In mid-December 2005, the software was changed to allow for a 1c minimum value for any of these lettered varieties.

In 2006, No. 1CVP38 was made available on a coil roll. Value, $1.40.

Snowman — CVPA36

Candy Cane — CVPA37

Dove — CVPA38

Stylized Christmas Tree and Window — CVPA39

2005, Nov. ***Die Cut Perf. 6 at Right***

1CVP39	CVPA36 37c **multicolored**	1.60	.45
	On cover		2.50
a.	"Priority" below "US Postage"	8.00	1.00
b.	"Express" below "US Postage"	25.00	3.00
c.	"Media Mail" below "US Postage"	7.50	1.00
d.	"Parcel Post" below "US Postage"	7.50	1.00
e.	"BPM" below "US Postage"	7.50	1.00
f.	"Aerogramme" below "US Postage"	1.40	1.00
g.	"Intl Air Letter" below "US Postage"	1.25	1.00
h.	"Intl Eco Letter" (Economy Letter Mail) below "US Postage"	5.50	1.00
i.	"GXG" (Global Express Guaranteed) below "US Postage"	50.00	6.00
j.	"EMS" (Global Express Mail) below "US Postage"	32.50	4.00
k.	"GPM" (Global Priority Mail) below "US Postage"	8.00	1.00
l.	"Intl Air Parcel" (Air Parcel Post) below "US Postage"	26.00	3.00
m.	"Intl Eco Parcel" (Economy Parcel Post) below "US Postage"	32.50	4.00
n.	"M-Bag (Air)" below "US Postage"	35.00	5.00
o.	"M-Bag (Economy)" below "US Postage"	18.00	3.00
p.	"Mat for Blind" below "US Postage"	.25	—
1CVP40	CVPA37 37c **multicolored**	1.60	.45
	On cover		2.50
a.	"Priority" below "US Postage"	8.00	1.00
b.	"Express" below "US Postage"	25.00	3.00
c.	"Media Mail" below "US Postage"	7.50	1.00
d.	"Parcel Post" below "US Postage"	7.50	1.00
e.	"BPM" below "US Postage"	7.50	1.00
f.	"Aerogramme" below "US Postage"	1.40	1.00
g.	"Intl Air Letter" below "US Postage"	1.25	1.00
h.	"Intl Eco Letter" (Economy Letter Mail) below "US Postage"	5.50	1.00
i.	"GXG" (Global Express Guaranteed) below "US Postage"	50.00	6.00
j.	"EMS" (Global Express Mail) below "US Postage"	32.50	4.00
k.	"GPM" (Global Priority Mail) below "US Postage"	8.00	1.00
l.	"Intl Air Parcel" (Air Parcel Post) below "US Postage"	26.00	3.00
m.	"Intl Eco Parcel" (Economy Parcel Post) below "US Postage"	32.50	4.00
n.	"M-Bag (Air)" below "US Postage"	35.00	5.00

o. "M-Bag (Economy)" below "US Postage" 18.00 3.00
p. "Mat for Blind" below "US Postage" .45 —

1CVP41 CVPA38 37c **multicolored** 1.60 .45
On cover 2.50
a. "Priority" below "US Postage" 8.00 1.00
b. "Express" below "US Postage" 25.00 3.00
c. "Media Mail" below "US Postage" 7.50 1.00
d. "Parcel Post" below "US Postage" 7.50 1.00
e. "BPM" below "US Postage" 7.50 1.00
f. "Aerogramme" below "US Postage" 1.40 1.00
g. "Intl Air Letter" below "US Postage" 1.25 1.00
h. "Intl Eco Letter" (Economy Letter Mail) below "US Postage" 5.50 1.00
i. "GXG" (Global Express Guaranteed) below "US Postage" 50.00 6.00
j. "EMS" (Global Express Mail) below "US Postage" 32.50 4.00
k. "GPM" (Global Priority Mail) below "US Postage" 8.00 1.00
l. "Intl Air Parcel" (Air Parcel Post) below "US Postage" 26.00 3.00
m. "Intl Eco Parcel" (Economy Parcel Post) below "US Postage" 32.50 4.00
n. "M-Bag (Air)" below "US Postage" 35.00 5.00
o. "M-Bag (Economy)" below "US Postage" 18.00 3.00
p. "Mat for Blind" below "US Postage" .45 —

1CVP42 CVPA39 37c **multicolored** 1.60 .45
On cover 2.50
a. "Priority" below "US Postage" 8.00 1.00
b. "Express" below "US Postage" 25.00 3.00
c. "Media Mail" below "US Postage" 7.50 1.00
d. "Parcel Post" below "US Postage" 7.50 1.00
e. "BPM" below "US Postage" 7.50 1.00
f. "Aerogramme" below "US Postage" 1.40 1.00
g. "Intl Air Letter" below "US Postage" 1.25 1.00
h. "Intl Eco Letter" (Economy Letter Mail) below "US Postage" 5.50 1.00
i. "GXG" (Global Express Guaranteed) below "US Postage" 50.00 6.00
j. "EMS" (Global Express Mail) below "US Postage" 32.50 4.00
k. "GPM" (Global Priority Mail) below "US Postage" 8.00 1.00
l. "Intl Air Parcel" (Air Parcel Post) below "US Postage" 26.00 3.00
m. "Intl Eco Parcel" (Economy Parcel Post) below "US Postage" 32.50 4.00
n. "M-Bag (Air)" below "US Postage" 35.00 5.00
o. "M-Bag (Economy)" below "US Postage" 18.00 3.00
p. "Mat for Blind" below "US Postage" .45 —
q. Vert. strip, 2 each #1CVP39-1CVP42 6.00

Values for lettered varieties on Nos. 1CVP39-1CVP42 are based on the prices set as the minimum values for each service classification in the software available at the time the stamps were issued. In mid-December 2005, the software was changed to allow for a 1c minimum value for any of these lettered varieties.

Endicia.com

CVPA40

CVPA41

2005-06 *Serpentine Die Cut 10¼*

1CVP43 CVPA40 24c **black & bright rose** 10.00 4.00
a. 39c "First Class" under "US Postage" 2.00 .50
b. 63c "Intl. Mail" under "US Postage" 3.25 2.50
c. $4.05 "Priority Mail" under "US Postage" 12.00 2.50

Coil Stamps
Serpentine Die Cut 10½x10¼ on 2 Sides

1CVP44 CVPA41 24c **black & pink** 11.00 4.00
a. 39c "First Class" under "US Postage" 2.25 .50
b. 63c "Intl. Mail" under "US Postage" 3.50 2.50
c. $4.05 "Priority Mail" under "US Postage" 12.50 2.50

Issued: Nos. 1CVP43, Nov. 2005; Nos. 1CVP44, Jan. 2006.

Originally, face values of 2c, 52c, 63c, 87c, $1.11, $1.35, $1.59, $1.83, $2.07, $2.31, $2.55, $2.79, $3.03, and $3.27 could also be printed on stamps with the "First class" inscription. Additionally, an 84c face value could be printed on stamps with the "Intl. Mail" inscription, and a $8.10 face value could be printed on stamps with the "Priority Mail" inscription. Values for Nos. 1CVP43-1CVP44 are for stamps with the listed face values and mail-class inscription. Values for stamps with lower or higher face values are correspondingly lower or higher.

In 2007, software changes permitted Nos. 1CVP43 and 1CVP44 to be printed with mail class inscriptions "Media Mail," "BPM," "Parcel Post," "Library Mail," and "Express Mail," as well as any face value for any mail-class inscription.

Nos. 1CVP43 and 1CVP44 printed after the software changes are inscribed "First Class" under "US Postage" and sell for considerably less than the values shown. Stamps printed before the software changes are inscribed "Postcard" under "US Postage," as shown in the illustrations.

Stamps.com

Flag and Mount Rushmore — CVPA42

Flag and Eagle — CVPA43

Flag and Statue of Liberty — CVPA44

Flag and Liberty Bell — CVPA45

2006, Mar. *Die Cut Perf. 6 at Right*

1CVP51 CVPA42 39c **multicolored** .80 .45
On cover 2.50
1CVP52 CVPA43 39c **multicolored** .80 .45
On cover 2.50
1CVP53 CVPA44 39c **multicolored** .80 .45
On cover 2.50
1CVP54 CVPA45 39c **multicolored** .80 .45
On cover 2.50
a. Vert. strip of 8, 2 each #1CVP51-1CVP54 8.00

Other service inscriptions with any possible face value can be printed on Nos. 1CVP51-1CVP54.

Stamps.com

Leaning Tower of Pisa — CVPA46

Taj Mahal — CVPA47

Eiffel Tower — CVPA48

Parthenon — CVPA49

2006 *Die Cut Perf 6 at Right*

1CVP55 CVPA46 39c **multicolored** .80 .45
On cover 2.50

Serial Number Under Encryption
APC

1CVP56 CVPA47 39c **multicolored** .80 .45
On cover 2.50
1CVP57 CVPA48 39c **multicolored** .80 .45
On cover 2.50
1CVP58 CVPA49 39c **multicolored** .80 .45
On cover 2.50
a. Vert. strip, 2 each #1CVP55-1CVP58 8.00

With the introduction of the new software in December 2005, any stamp could have any denomination 1c and above, and any service classification.

Pitney Bowes Stamp Expressions

CVPA50

Illustration reduced.

2006 *Die Cut Perf. 6 Horiz.*

Inscribed "pitneybowes.com/se" at Right

1CVP59 CVPA50 39c **black** + label 1.35 .80
On cover 4.00

The stamp and label are separated by vertical roulettes. Users could create their own label images on the Pitney Bowes Stamp Expressions website (which required approval of the image from Pitney Bowes before it could be used), or download various pre-approved label images from the website into their personal computers. Stamps could be printed without label images. Stamps were printed on rolls of tagged thermal paper from a device that could be operated without a direct connection to the personal computer. See No. 1CVT1.

Stamps.com

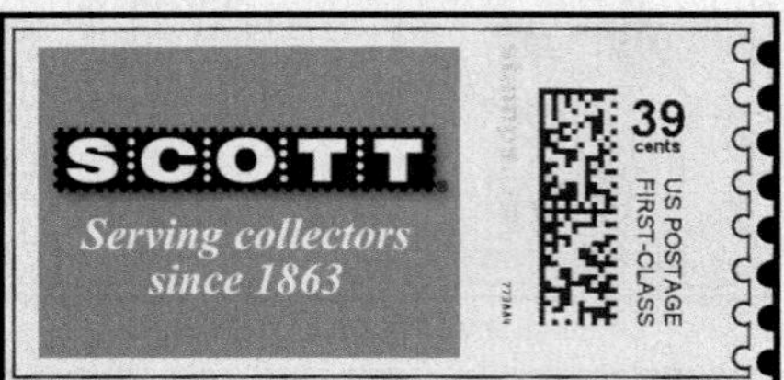

CVPA51

Personalizable Images — CVPA52

Illustration CVPA51 is reduced.

2006, Sept. ***Die Cut Perf. 6 at Right***

1CVP60 CVPA51 39c **multicolored** 1.50 .95
On cover 4.50
a. Numerals in denomination 2½mm high, thicker text 1.50 .95
On cover 4.50

Perf. Die Cut Perf. 6 at Top

1CVP61 CVPA52 39c **multicolored** 1.50 .95
On cover 4.50
a. Numerals in denomination 2½mm high, thicker text 1.50 .95
On cover 4.50

Users could requisition sheets of Nos. 1CVP60 and 1CVP61 with images of their choice from Stamps.com at $4.99 per sheet of 24. Priority and Express service classifications could also be printed on Nos. 1CVP60-1CVP61 with any denomination. Stamps exist with slightly larger die cutting (60x30mm and 30x60mm) in both squared and rounded corners. The denomination type shown on Nos. 1CVP60-1CVP61 can be placed on label types CVPA36-CVPA39, CVPA42-CVPA49, CVPA53-CVPA60 and any later stamps.com labels of this size.

Numerals in denomination are 3mm tall on Nos. 1CVP60-1CVP61. Serial numbers on Nos. 1CPVP60-1CVP61 lack periods and have small bank-check style numerals.

Autumn Leaves — CVPA53

Pumpkins — CVPA54

Basket of Apples, Sheaf of Wheat, Falling Leaves and Pumpkins — CVPA55

Leaves and Carved Pumpkin — CVPA56

2006 ***Die Cut Perf. 6 at Right***

1CVP62 CVPA53 39c **multicolored** 1.25 .45
On cover 2.50
1CVP63 CVPA54 39c **multicolored** 1.25 .45
On cover 2.50
1CVP64 CVPA55 39c **multicolored** 1.25 .45
On cover 2.50
1CVP65 CVPA56 39c **multicolored** 1.25 .45
On cover 2.50
a. Vert. strip, 2 each #1CVP62-1CVP65 10.00

See note after No. 1CVP58.

"Season's Greetings" — CVPA57

Christmas Trees — CVPA58

Snowman — CVPA59

Dove — CVPA60

2006 ***Die Cut Perf. 6 at Right***

1CVP66 CVPA57 39c **multicolored** 1.25 .45
On cover 2.50
1CVP67 CVPA58 39c **multicolored** 1.25 .45
On cover 2.50
1CVP68 CVPA59 39c **multicolored** 1.25 .45
On cover 2.50
1CVP69 CVPA60 39c **multicolored** 1.25 .45
On cover 2.50
a. Vert. strip, 2 each #1CVP66-1CVP69 10.00

See note after No. 1CVP58.

Flag — CVPA61

Statue of Liberty and Flag — CVPA62

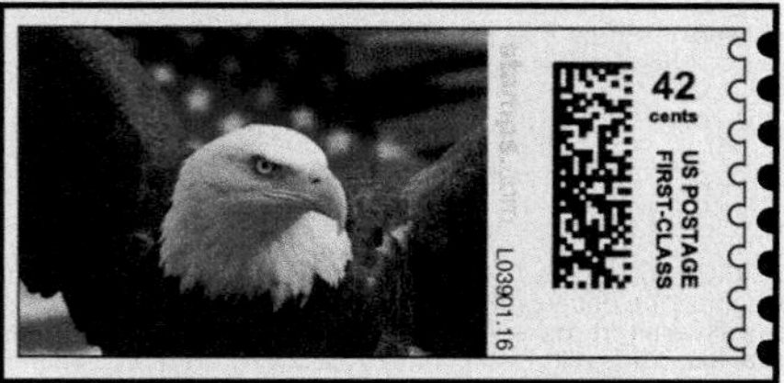

Bald Eagle and Flag — CVPA63

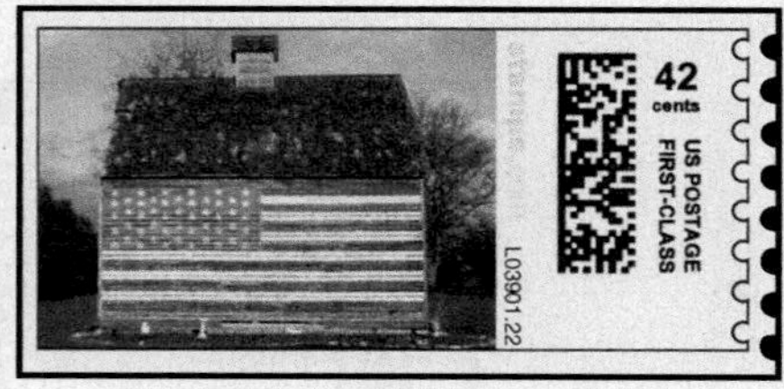

Flag Painted on Building — CVPA64

2008 ***Die Cut Perf. 5½ at Right***

Serial Number With Period, Large Letters and Numerals

1CVP70 CVPA61 42c **multicolored** 1.25 .45
On cover 2.50
1CVP71 CVPA62 42c **multicolored** 1.25 .45
On cover 2.50
1CVP72 CVPA63 42c **multicolored** 1.25 .45
On cover 2.50
1CVP73 CVPA64 42c **multicolored** 1.25 .45
On cover 2.50

On Nos. 1CVP70-1CVP105, and perhaps on other stamps, placement of the stamp serial number and the stamps.com logo might differ on various printings of the label stock. Descriptive text outside the frame might also vary or not be present on these various printings.

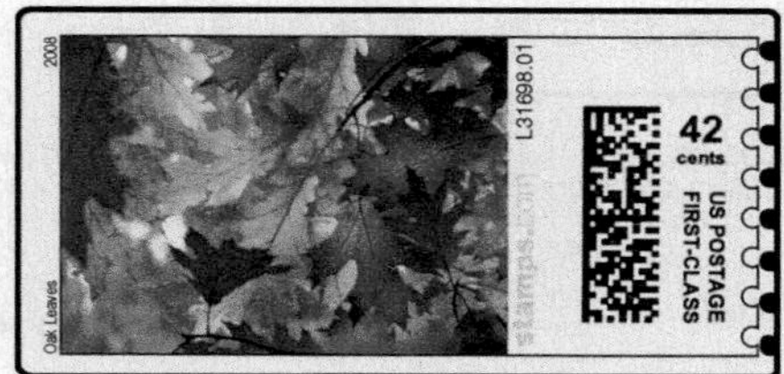

Autumn — CVPA65

Designs: No. 1CVP74, Oak leaves. No. 1CVP75, Pumpkin patch. No. 1CVP76, Autumn reflection. No. 1CVP77, Pumpkins and gourds.

2008 ***Die Cut Perf. 5½ at Right***

Serial Number With Period, Large Letters and Numerals

1CVP74	CVPA65 42c **multicolored**	1.25	.45
	On cover		2.50
1CVP75	CVPA65 42c **multicolored**	1.25	.45
	On cover		2.50
1CVP76	CVPA65 42c **multicolored**	1.25	.45
	On cover		2.50
1CVP77	CVPA65 42c **multicolored**	1.25	.45
	On cover		2.50

Flowers — CVPA66

Designs: No. 1CVP78, Sunflowers. No. 1CVP79, Daisies. No. 1CVP80, Sunflower sky. No. 1CVP81, Treasure flowers.

2008 ***Die Cut Perf. 5½ at Right***

Serial Number With Period, Large Letters and Numerals

1CVP78	CVPA66 42c **multicolored**	1.25	.45
	On cover		2.50
1CVP79	CVPA66 42c **multicolored**	1.25	.45
	On cover		2.50
1CVP80	CVPA66 42c **multicolored**	1.25	.45
	On cover		2.50
1CVP81	CVPA66 42c **multicolored**	1.25	.45
	On cover		2.50

Endangered Animals — CVPA67

Designs: No. 1CVP82, Bengal tiger. No. 1CVP83, Hawksbill turtle. No. 1CVP84, Panda. No. 1CVP85, African rhino.

2008 ***Die Cut Perf. 5½ at Right***

Serial Number With Period, Large Letters and Numerals

1CVP82	CVPA67 42c **multicolored**	1.25	.45
	On cover		2.50
1CVP83	CVPA67 42c **multicolored**	1.25	.45
	On cover		2.50
1CVP84	CVPA67 42c **multicolored**	1.25	.45
	On cover		2.50
1CVP85	CVPA67 42c **multicolored**	1.25	.45
	On cover		2.50

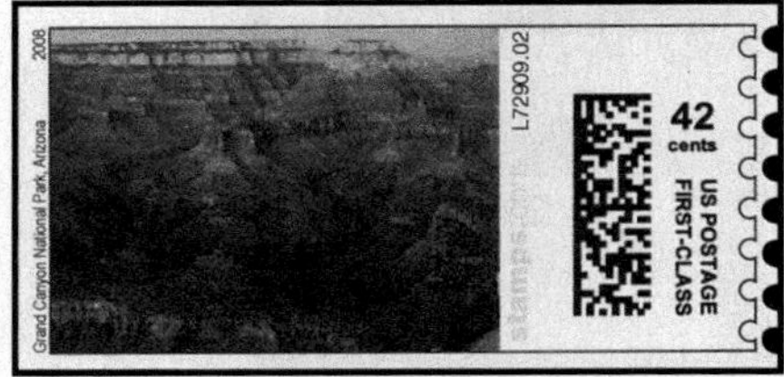

Parks — CVPA68

Designs: No. 1CVP86, Grand Canyon National Park, Arizona. No. 1CVP87, Yosemite National Park, California. No. 1CVP88, Niagara Falls. No. 1CVP89, Arches National Park, Utah.

2008 ***Die Cut Perf. 5½ at Right***

Serial Number With Period, Large Letters and Numerals

1CVP86	CVPA68 42c **multicolored**	1.25	.45
	On cover		2.50
1CVP87	CVPA68 42c **multicolored**	1.25	.45
	On cover		2.50
1CVP88	CVPA68 42c **multicolored**	1.25	.45
	On cover		2.50
1CVP89	CVPA68 42c **multicolored**	1.25	.45
	On cover		2.50

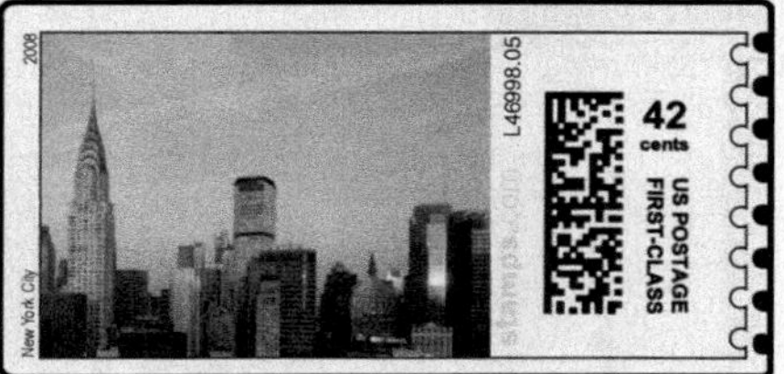

City Skylines — CVPA69

Designs: No. 1CVP90, New York City. No. 1CVP91, St. Louis. No. 1CVP92, Chicago. No. 1CVP93, San Francisco.

2008 ***Die Cut Perf. 5½ at Right***

Serial Number With Period, Large Letters and Numerals

1CVP90	CVPA69 42c **multicolored**	1.25	.45
	On cover		2.50
1CVP91	CVPA69 42c **multicolored**	1.25	.45
	On cover		2.50
1CVP92	CVPA69 42c **multicolored**	1.25	.45
	On cover		2.50
1CVP93	CVPA69 42c **multicolored**	1.25	.45
	On cover		2.50

Presidential Memorials — CVPA70

Designs: No. 1CVP94, Washington Monument. No. 1CVP95, Lincoln Memorial. No. 1CVP96, Jefferson Memorial. No. 1CVP97, Mount Rushmore.

2008 ***Die Cut Perf. 5½ at Right***

Serial Number With Period, Large Letters and Numerals

1CVP94	CVPA70 42c **multicolored**	1.25	.45
	On cover		2.50
1CVP95	CVPA70 42c **multicolored**	1.25	.45
	On cover		2.50
1CVP96	CVPA70 42c **multicolored**	1.25	.45
	On cover		2.50
1CVP97	CVPA70 42c **multicolored**	1.25	.45
	On cover		2.50

Christmas — CVPA71

Designs: No. 1CVP98, Ornament, "Happy Holidays." No. 1CVP99, Gingerbread men, "Season's Greetings." No. 1CVP100, Snowflake, "Happy Holidays." No. 1CVP101, Christmas tree, "Season's Greetings."

2008 ***Die Cut Perf. 5½ at Right***

Serial Number With Period, Large Letters and Numerals

Without Year or Text at Left

1CVP98	CVPA71 42c **multicolored**	1.25	.45
	On cover		2.50
1CVP99	CVPA71 42c **multicolored**	1.25	.45
	On cover		2.50
1CVP100	CVPA71 42c **multicolored**	1.25	.45
	On cover		2.50
1CVP101	CVPA71 42c **multicolored**	1.25	.45
	On cover		2.50

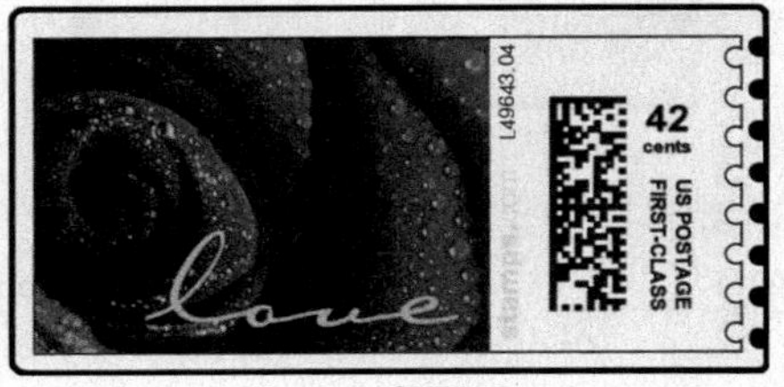

Love — CVPA72

"Love" and: No. 1CVP102, Rose. No. 1CVP103, Small hearts. No. 1CVP104, Large heart. No. 1CVP105, Hearts on curtain.

2009 ***Die Cut Perf. 5½ at Right***

Serial Number With Period, Large Letters and Numerals

Without Year or Text at Left

1CVP102	CVPA72 42c **multicolored**	1.25	.45
	On cover		2.50
1CVP103	CVPA72 42c **multicolored**	1.25	.45
	On cover		2.50
1CVP104	CVPA72 42c **multicolored**	1.25	.45
	On cover		2.50
1CVP105	CVPA72 42c **multicolored**	1.25	.45
	On cover		2.50

Wavy Lines — CVPA73

2009 ***Die Cut Perf 6½ at Right***

1CVP106	CVPA73 44c **multicolored**	1.25	.45
	On cover		2.50

Software allowed for other inscriptions below "US Postage," including "Library Mail."

Endicia.com

CVPA74

Globe — CVPA74a

2009 ***Serpentine Die Cut 10¼x10½***

1CVP107	CVPA74 44c **orange & black,** with space between denomination and "US POSTAGE"	1.25	.45
	On cover		2.50
1CVP107A	CVPA74a 45c **orange & black,** with no space between denomination and "US POSTAGE"	—	—

Software allowed for six other inscriptions below "US Postage" (Priority Mail, Media Mail, Parcel Post, Library Mail, Express Mail and Intl Mail) and any face value for any mail-class inscription.

Stamps.com

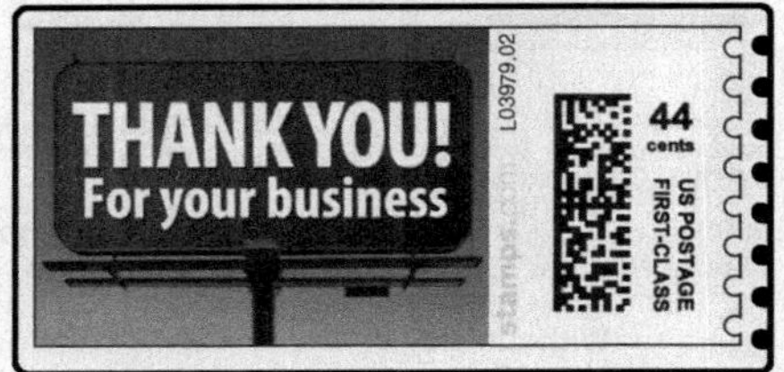

Thank You For Your Business — CVPA75

Text: No. 1CVP108, On billboard. No. 1CVP109, And building. No. 1CVP110, On red background. No. 1CVP111, And two people shaking hands.

2009 ***Die Cut Perf. 5½ at Right***

Serial Number With Period, Large Letters and Numerals

Without Year or Text at Left

1CVP108 CVPA75 44c **multicolored** 1.25 .45
On cover 2.50
1CVP109 CVPA75 44c **multicolored** 1.25 .45
On cover 2.50
1CVP110 CVPA75 44c **multicolored** 1.25 .45
On cover 2.50
1CVP111 CVPA75 44c **multicolored** 1.25 .45
On cover 2.50

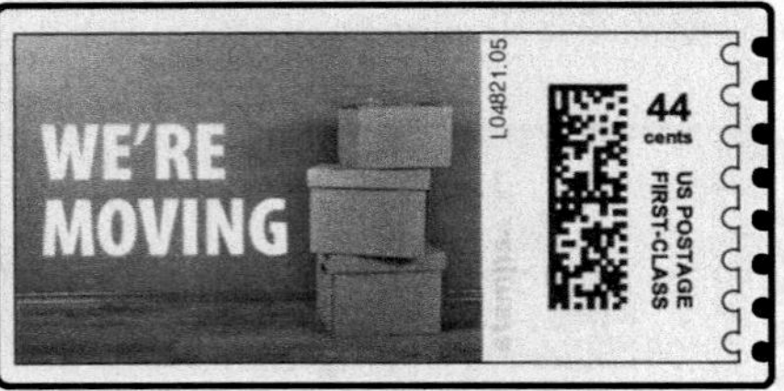

We're Moving — CVPA76

Text: No. 1CVP112, Stack of three boxes, green background. No. 1CVP113, Eleven boxes, orange background. No. 1CVP114, Four boxes, green background. No. 1CVP115, Four boxes, red background.

2009 ***Die Cut Perf. 5½ at Right***

Serial Number With Period, Large Letters and Numerals

Without Year or Text at Left

1CVP112 CVPA76 44c **multicolored** 1.25 .45
On cover 2.50
1CVP113 CVPA76 44c **multicolored** 1.25 .45
On cover 2.50
1CVP114 CVPA76 44c **multicolored** 1.25 .45
On cover 2.50
1CVP115 CVPA76 44c **multicolored** 1.25 .45
On cover 2.50

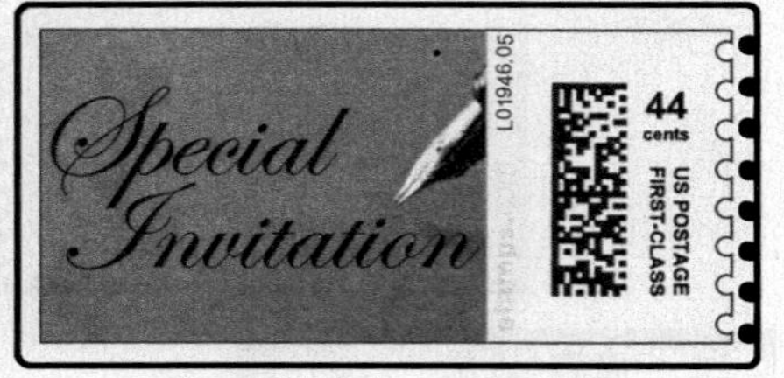

Special Invitation — CVPA77

Text: No. 1CVP116, And pen nib. No. 1CVP117, And circled "15" on calendar. No. 1CVP118, On card on envelope. No. 1CVP119, On wax seal.

2009 ***Die Cut Perf. 5½ at Right***

Serial Number With Period, Large Letters and Numerals

Without Year or Text at Left

1CVP116 CVPA77 44c **multicolored** 1.25 .45
On cover 2.50
1CVP117 CVPA77 44c **multicolored** 1.25 .45
On cover 2.50
1CVP118 CVPA77 44c **multicolored** 1.25 .45
On cover 2.50
1CVP119 CVPA77 44c **multicolored** 1.25 .45
On cover 2.50

US Flag — CVPA78

Flag: No. 1CVP120, On flagpole. No. 1CVP121, Behind Statue of Liberty. No. 1CVP122, Behind bald eagle. No. 1CVP123, On United States map.

2009 ***Die Cut Perf. 5½ at Right***

Serial Number With Period, Large Letters and Numerals

Without Year or Text at Left

1CVP120 CVPA78 44c **multicolored** 1.25 .45
On cover 2.50
1CVP121 CVPA78 44c **multicolored** 1.25 .45
On cover 2.50
1CVP122 CVPA78 44c **multicolored** 1.25 .45
On cover 2.50
1CVP123 CVPA78 44c **multicolored** 1.25 .45
On cover 2.50

Patriotic Symbols CVPA79

Designs: No. 1CVP124, Statue of Liberty. No. 1CVP125, Flag. No. 1CVP126, Bald eagle.

2010 ***Die Cut Perf. 5½ Vert.***

1CVP124 CVPA79 44c **multicolored** 1.25 .45
On cover 2.50
1CVP125 CVPA79 44c **multicolored** 1.25 .45
On cover 2.50
1CVP126 CVPA79 44c **multicolored** 1.25 .45
On cover 2.50

Jewish Symbols CVPA80

Designs: No. 1CVP127, Menorah. No. 1CVP125, Dreidel. No. 1CVP126, Star of David.

2010 ***Die Cut Perf. 5½ Vert.***

1CVP127 CVPA80 44c **multicolored** 1.25 .45
On cover 2.50
1CVP128 CVPA80 44c **multicolored** 1.25 .45
On cover 2.50
1CVP129 CVPA80 44c **multicolored** 1.25 .45
On cover 2.50

Christmas CVPA81

Designs: No. 1CVP130, Christmas stocking. No. 1CVP131, Christmas tree. No. 1CVP132, Santa Claus.

2010 ***Die Cut Perf. 5½ Vert.***

1CVP130 CVPA81 44c **multicolored** 1.25 .45
On cover 2.50
1CVP131 CVPA81 44c **multicolored** 1.25 .45
On cover 2.50
1CVP132 CVPA81 44c **multicolored** 1.25 .45
On cover 2.50

Valentine's Day — CVPA82

Designs: No. 1CVP133, Hearts. No. 1CVP134, Rose. No. 1CVP135, Candy hearts.

2011 ***Die Cut Perf. 5½ Vert.***

1CVP133 CVPA82 44c **multicolored** 1.25 .45
On cover 2.50
1CVP134 CVPA82 44c **multicolored** 1.25 .45
On cover 2.50
1CVP135 CVPA82 44c **multicolored** 1.25 .45
On cover 2.50

Christian Symbols CVPA83

Designs: No. 1CVP136, Cross. No. 1CVP137, Fish. No. 1CVP138, Rosary beads.

2011 ***Die Cut Perf. 5½ Vert.***

1CVP136 CVPA83 44c **multicolored** 1.25 .45
On cover 2.50
1CVP137 CVPA83 44c **multicolored** 1.25 .45
On cover 2.50
1CVP138 CVPA83 44c **multicolored** 1.25 .45
On cover 2.50

OFFICAL STAMPS PRINTED TO ORDER

1CVPO1

1CVPO2

2002-06 ***Serpentine Die Cut 10.6***

Self-Adhesive

1CVPO1 1CVPO1 37c **blk, red & bluish gray**, no denomination below vignette — —
On cover —
1CVPO2 1CVPO2 37c **blk, red & blue**, denomination below vignette — —
On cover —
1CVPO3 1CVPO2 39c **blk, red & blue**, denomination below vignette — —
On cover —
1CVPO5 1CVPO2 $4.05 **blk, red & blue**, denomination below vignette — —
On cover —

Endicia filled federal agency orders for stamps to be limited for use by government officials. Nos. 1CVPO1 and 1CVPO2 were printed in sheets of 10. 39c and 41c denominations are thought to exist.

COMPUTER VENDED POSTAGE TEST STAMPS
Pitney Bowes Stamp Expressions

CVT1

Illustration reduced.

2006 ***Die Cut Perf. 6 Horiz.***

Inscribed "pbstampexpressions.com" at Right

1CVT1	CVT1 39c **black** + label	5.00	—
	On cover		—

No. 1CVT1 were produced only by beta testers of the Pitney Bowes Stamp Expressions system, and as such were not available to normal subscribers to the system. Examples are known to have passed through the mail. Notes concerning No. 1CVP59 apply to No. 1CVT1.

NON-PERSONALIZABLE POSTAGE

These stamps, approved by the USPS, were non-personalizable stamps that could be purchased directly from private manufacturers, which shipped them to the customer. Other non-personalizable stamps have been created by a variety of companies, all sold at excessive amounts over face value as "collectibles". Such items are not listed here. Most items created that sold for excessive amounts over face value have vignettes that are licensed images, usually depicting sport team emblems or other sports-related themes, or celebrities.

Personalized postage stamps, first available in 2004, created by a variety of different companies, and heretofore listed with Scott numbers having a "2CVP" prefix, are no longer listed. Personalized stamps, though valid for postage, are not sold at any U.S. Postal Service post office. They are available only by on-line ordering through the company's website. Stamps are only available from the companies in full panes of 20. Each pane is sold at a significant premium above the stated face value to cover the costs of personalization, shipping and handling.

In recent years, there has been a steadily increasing number of private companies, either directly licensed by the USPS or created as spinoff companies of these licensees, creating distinctly different personalized stamps. None of the companies has issued fewer than seven stamps for each rate change, with one issuing as many as 42 different stamps. Because mailing rates set by the USPS are expected to change yearly, the collective output of distinctly different, rate-based stamps from these various companies likely will increase. There are no restrictions in place to prevent more firms from bringing personalized stamps to the marketplace, or to keep stamp producers from offering even more customer options. Some personalized stamps do not differ in any appreciable manner from some of the non-personalizable stamps sold as collectibles and not listed here.

NON-PERSONALIZABLE POSTAGE

Stamps.com

CVPC1

CVPC2

2007, May ***Die Cut***

Self-Adhesive

3CVP1	CVPC1 2c **black & gray green**	.25	.25
a.	Inscribed "US Postag"	—	—

Die Cut Perf. 5¼ at Right

3CVP2	CVPC2 2c **multicolored**	.25	.25
a.	Tagged	*1.40*	*1.40*

2008 ***Die Cut***

Self-Adhesive

3CVP3	CVPC1 1c **black & gray**	.25	.25

No. 3CVP1 was printed in sheets of 40 stamps. Stamps with serial numbers ending in "06" are No. 3CVP1a. Sheets were sold for face value plus a shipping charge and were obtainable through the stamps.com website.

No. 3CVP2 was printed in sheets of 20. Full sheets were given free of charge to first-time stamps.com customers, but the full sheets were available for sale to other customers at face value plus a shipping charge through the stamps.com website.

Stamps.com Type of 2007

2019 ***Die Cut***

Self-Adhesive

3CVP4	CVPC1 5c **black & gray**	.25	.25

No. 3CVP4 was printed in sheets of 40 stamps that were sold for face value plus a shipping charge and were obtainable through the stamps.com website.

VENDING & AFFIXING MACHINE PERFORATIONS

Imperforate sheets of 400 were first issued in 1906 at the request of several makers of vending and affixing machines. The machine manufacturers made coils from the imperforate sheets and applied various perforations to suit the particular needs of their machines. These privately applied perforations were used for many years and form a chapter of postal history.

The Post Office Department had different arrangements with the various manufacturers of vending and affixing machines. Schermack and Mailometer coils were perforated in each city where those firms had customers. United States Automatic Vending Company perforated and coiled stamps for its machines under POD supervision in New York City, which were then returned for sale at any post office that had customers for them; in that respect, USAV coils can be regarded as semi-official. Farwell coils were perforated for the firm's use only on its Mailometer equipment, to avoid paying the coiling fee charged by Mailometer. Attleboro perforations were simply unusual separations punched into imperforate stamps by a philatelic publisher to create unusual perforation varieties for its customers. Covel perforations were applied to imperforate coil stamps supplied by the firm's purchasing agent, Alvin Filstrup (a stamp collector), as a convenience to use those stamps on mail from the company's sales staff, and on pre-stamped payment envelopes from customers, to its headquarters.

In 1927, the Post Office Department ceased supplying unfinished imperforate sheets to private firms, and required all users of proprietary perforations to configure their equipment to accept government coil stamps.

Unused values are for pairs, used values for singles. Used multiples are highly valued, with prices often equalling or exceeding those for unused pairs or strips. "On cover" values are for single stamps used commercially in the proper period when known that way. Several, primarily the Alaska-Yukon and Hudson-Fulton commemoratives, are known almost exclusively on covers from contemporaneous stamp collectors and stamp dealers. Virtually all are rare and highly prized by specialists.

The 2mm and 3mm spacings refer only to the 1908-10 issues. (See note following No. 330 in the Postage section.) Values for intermediate spacings would roughly correspond to the lower-valued of the two listed spacings. Guide line pairs of 1906-10 issues have 2mm spacing except the Alaska-Yukon and Hudson-Fulton issues, which have 3mm spacing. Scott Nos. 408-611 have 3mm spacing, except the "A" plates which have 2¾mm spacing and Scott No. 577, which has both 2¾mm and 3mm spacing. (All spacing measurements are approximate.)

Spacing on paste-up pairs is not a factor in valuing them. Because they were joined together by hand, many different spacings can occur, from less than 2mm to more than 3mm.

Perfins listed here are punched into the stamp just before being affixed to an envelope. The most common pattern consisted of a 7mm square made up of nine holes. Pins would be removed to create special perfins for each company using the machines. The catalogue value is for the most common perfin pattern on each stamp.

* — Many varieties are suspected or known to have been perforated for philatelic purposes and not actually used in machines. These are indicated by an asterisk before the number. Several of these privately applied perforation varieties exist in blocks, which were not produced in the regular course of business. They are valued at a premium over the multiple of the coil pairs contained, with an additional premium for plate numbers attached.

Counterfeits are prevalent, especially of items having a basic imperf. variety valued far lower than the vending machine coil.

The Vending and Affixing Machine Perforations Committee of the Bureau Issues Association (now the United States Stamp Society), William R. Weiss, Jr., Richard Champagne and Melvin Getlan compiled these listings.

The Attleboro Stamp Co.

See following U.S. Automatic Vending Company.

THE BRINKERHOFF COMPANY

Sedalia, Mo., Clinton, Iowa
Manufacturers of Vending Machines

Perforations Type I

Stamps were cut into strips and joined before being perforated.

Left Column = Unused Pair
Right Column = Used Single

On Issue of 1906-1908

314	1c **blue green**	220.00	35.00
	Guide line pair	400.00	
	Strip of 4	450.00	*150.00*
	Center line block of 4	*4,000.*	
320	2c **carmine**	250.00	35.00
	Guide line pair	475.00	
	Pasteup pair	360.00	
	Strip of 4	500.00	
* 320A	2c **lake**	180.00	30.00
	Guide line pair	360.00	
	Pasteup pair	260.00	
	Guide line strip of 4	750.00	

On Issue of 1908-09

* 343	1c **green**	135.00	25.00
	Guide line pair	325.00	
	Pasteup pair	250.00	
	Pasteup strip of 4	500.00	
* 344	2c **carmine**	115.00	25.00
	On cover		*1,750.*
	Guide line pair	225.00	
	Pasteup pair	200.00	
	Strip of 4	275.00	
	Guide line strip of 4	500.00	
* 345	3c **deep violet**	150.00	—
	Guide line pair	300.00	
	Strip of 4	400.00	
	Guide line strip of 4	600.00	
* 346	4c **orange brown**	175.00	140.00
	Guide line pair	310.00	
	Pasteup pair	225.00	
	Pasteup strip of 4	600.00	
* 347	5c **blue**	400.00	90.00
	On cover		*5,000.*
	Guide line pair	625.00	

On Lincoln Issue of 1909

* 368	2c **carmine,** coiled endwise	185.00	*190.00*
	Guide line pair	350.00	
	Strip of 4	500.00	
	Guide line strip of 4	700.00	

On Alaska-Yukon Issue of 1909

* 371	2c **carmine,** coiled sideways	*625.00*	—
	Guide line pair	*1,150.*	

On Issue of 1910

* 383	1c **green**	*550.00*	
	Guide line pair	—	

On Issue of 1912

* 408	1c **green**	35.00	17.50
	On cover		*1,400.*
	Guide line pair	70.00	
	Pasteup pair	57.50	
	Strip of 4	100.00	
	Strip of 4, middle column with perforations omitted	150.00	
	Guide line strip of 4	200.00	
	Pasteup strip of 4	175.00	
* 409	2c **carmine**	35.00	17.50
	On cover		*4,000.*
	Guide line pair	70.00	
	Pasteup pair	57.50	
	Strip of 4	100.00	*100.00*
	Guide line strip of 4	200.00	
	Pasteup strip of 4	100.00	

Type IIa — One Knife Cut

Type IIb — Two Knife Cuts

Perforations Type II, 2 Holes

The Type II items listed below are without knife cuts and did not pass through the vending machine. Types IIa and IIb (illustrated above) have knife cuts, applied by the vending machine, to help separate the stamps.

Left Column = Unused Pair
Right Column = Used Single

On Issue of 1906-08

314	1c **blue green**		
	* Type II	100.00	14.00
	On cover		*925.00*
	Type IIa	90.00	14.00
	Guide line pair	175.00	
	* Type IIb	475.00	—
	Pasteup pair	800.00	
320	2c **carmine**		
	* Type II	220.00	*70.00*
	On cover		*750.00*
	Guideline pair	350.00	
	Pasteup pair	325.00	
	Type IIa	45.00	14.00
	On cover		*600.00*
	Guide line pair	150.00	
320A	2c **lake**		
	* Type II	230.00	*70.00*
	On cover		*600.00*
	Strip of 4	450.00	
	Guide line strip of 4	600.00	
	Pasteup strip of 4	550.00	
	Type IIa	95.00	14.50
	On cover		*600.00*
	Guide line pair	185.00	
	Pasteup pair	105.00	
	Strip of 4	450.00	
	Guide line strip of 4	600.00	

No.	Description	Unused	Used
	* Type IIb	380.00	80.00

On Issue of 1908-09

No.	Description	Unused	Used
343	1c **green**		
	* Type II	70.00	
	On cover		750.00
	Guide line pair	120.00	
	Type IIa	21.00	3.75
	On cover		750.00
	Pasteup pair	35.00	
	Type IIb	37.50	
	On cover		2,500.
	Pasteup pair	65.00	
	Pasteup strip of 4	250.00	
344	2c **carmine**		
	* Type II	80.00	
	On cover, pair		750.00
	Guide line pair	175.00	
	Pasteup pair	140.00	
	Strip of 4	200.00	
	Guide line strip of 4	400.00	
	Pasteup strip of 4	300.00	
	Type IIa	26.00	3.75
	On cover		850.00
	Guide line pair	40.00	
	Strip of 4	200.00	
	Type IIb	30.00	7.00
	Guide line pair	80.00	
	Pasteup pair	65.00	
345	3c **deep violet**		
	* Type II	115.00	14.00
	Guide line pair	290.00	
	Pasteup pair	250.00	
	* Type IIa	95.00	14.00
	On cover		1,750.
	Guide line pair	190.00	
	Strip of 4	225.00	
	* Type IIb	340.00	
346	4c **orange brown**		
	* Type II	175.00	
	Guide line pair	300.00	
	Strip of 4	325.00	
	Guide line strip of 4	500.00	
	* Type IIa	160.00	55.00
	On cover		1,450.
	Guide line pair	260.00	
	Pasteup pair	220.00	
	Strip of 4	225.00	
	* Type IIb	175.00	55.00
	On cover		1,750.
	Strip of 4	275.00	
347	5c **blue**		
	* Type II	260.00	260.00
	Guide line pair	450.00	
	Strip of 4	500.00	
	Guide line strip of 4	900.00	
	* Type IIa	170.00	110.00
	On cover		3,500.
	Pasteup pair	240.00	
	Strip of 4	250.00	
	* Type IIb	250.00	
	Pasteup pair	425.00	
	Strip of 4	325.00	

On Lincoln Issue of 1909

No.	Description	Unused	Used
368	2c **carmine**		
	* Type II	85.00	—
	On cover		1,250.
	Guide line pair	175.00	
	Strip of 4	250.00	100.00
	Guide line strip of 4	400.00	
	Type IIa	80.00	16.00
	On cover		1,500.
	Guide line pair	325.00	
	Pasteup pair	275.00	
	Strip of 4	200.00	
	Guide line strip of 4	500.00	
	Pasteup strip of 4	400.00	
	Type IIb	240.00	25.00
	On cover		3,750.
	Guide line pair	800.00	
	Strip of 4	650.00	

On Alaska-Yukon Issue of 1909

No.	Description	Unused	Used
371	2c **carmine**		
	* Type II, coiled sideways	190.00	110.00
	On cover		1,250.
	Guide line pair	400.00	
	Pasteup pair	400.00	
	Strip of 4	375.00	
	Guide line strip of 4	800.00	
	Type IIa, coiled sideways	190.00	50.00
	On cover		900.00
	Guide line pair	360.00	
	Pasteup pair	290.00	
	Guide line strip of 4	700.00	
371	2c **carmine**		
	Type II, coiled endwise	975.00	
	Guide line pair	1,750.	

On Hudson-Fulton Issue of 1909

No.	Description	Unused	Used
373	2c **carmine**		
	* Type II, coiled sideways	300.00	
	Guide line pair	650.00	
	Pasteup pair	650.00	
	Pasteup strip of 4	900.00	

On Issue of 1910

No.	Description	Unused	Used
383	1c **green**		
	* Type II	40.00	
	Guide line pair	80.00	
	Strip of 4	100.00	50.00
	Guide line strip of 4	200.00	
	Type IIa	50.00	10.00
	On cover		1,000.
	Type IIb	100.00	55.00
	On cover		1,250.
	Guide line pair	190.00	
	Pasteup pair	175.00	
384	2c **carmine**		
	* Type II	42.50	
	On cover		950.00
	Guide line pair	75.00	
	Pasteup pair	75.00	
	Guide line strip of 4	175.00	
	Pasteup strip of 4	170.00	
	Type IIa	130.00	
	On cover		1,250.
	Pasteup pair	200.00	
	Type IIb	70.00	10.00
	On cover		1,800.
	Guide line pair	200.00	
	Pasteup pair	145.00	
	Strip of 4	200.00	
	Pasteup strip of 4	300.00	
408	1c **green**		
	* Type II	105.00	—
	On cover		1,650.
	Guide line pair	175.00	
	Pasteup pair	130.00	
	Strip of 4	250.00	
	* Type IIa	130.00	
	Guide line pair	230.00	
	Strip of 4	300.00	
	Guide line strip of 4	500.00	
	Type IIb	27.50	6.00
	On cover		3,750.
	Guide line pair	52.50	
	Pasteup strip of 4	125.00	
409	2c **carmine**		
	* Type II	75.00	
	On cover		1,000.
	Guide line pair	160.00	
	Pasteup pair	145.00	
	Guide line strip of 4	350.00	
	Pasteup strip of 4	300.00	
	* Type IIa	300.00	—
	On cover		1,000.
	Guide line pair	525.00	
	Type IIb	35.00	6.00
	On cover		750.00
	Guide line pair	65.00	
	Strip of 4	100.00	
	Guide line strip of 4	200.00	

Covel Manufacturing Co.

See following the Attleboro Stamp Company.

THE FARWELL COMPANY

Chicago, Ill.

A wholesale dry goods firm using Schermack (Mailometer) affixing machines. In 1911 the Farwell Company began to make and perforate their own coils. These were sometimes wrongly called "Chambers" perforations.

Type A

Type B

Stamps were perforated in sheets, then cut into strips and coiled. Blocks exist.

The following listings are grouped according to the number of holes, further divided into two types of spacing, narrow and wide.

The type symbols (3A2) indicate 3 holes over 2 holes with narrow, type A, spacing between groups.

Types A and B occurred in different rows on the same sheet. Left margin or pasteup stamps sometimes show different perforation type on the two sides.

Commercial usages of Farwell perforations are generally, but not always, on printed Farwell Co. corner card covers.

Left Column=Unused Pair
Right Column=Used Single

Group 1, no spacing

On Issue of 1910

No.	Description	Unused	Used
384	2c **carmine,** 7 holes		1,050.
	On cover		5,000.
	Unused pair, 2mm spacing	3,250.	
	Unused pair, 3mm spacing	3,250.	
384	2c **carmine,** 6 holes		3,250.
	On cover		5,000.
	Unused pair, 2mm spacing	5,000.	
	Unused pair, 3mm spacing	5,000.	

Group 2, two and three holes

On Issue of 1910

No.	Description	Unused	Used
383	1c **green**		
	2B3 Unused pair, 2mm spacing	1,500.	250.00
	2B3 Unused pair, 3mm spacing	1,750.	
	3A2 Unused pair, 2mm spacing	1,500.	
	3A2 Strip of 4, 3mm spacing	3,500.	
	On cover		—
	Guide line pair	1,900.	
	3A2 Unused pair, 3mm spacing	1,750.	
384	2c **carmine**		
	2A3 Unused pair, 2mm spacing	340.00	250.00
	On cover		1,300.
	Guide line pair	1,250.	
	2A3 Unused pair, 3mm spacing	600.00	
	Guide line pair	1,250.	
	Pasteup pair	1,000.	
	2B3 Unused pair, 2mm spacing	1,050.	275.00
	On cover		—
	2B3 Unused pair, 3mm spacing	1,250.	
	Pasteup pair	1,550.	
	3A2 Unused pair, 2mm spacing	550.00	250.00
	On cover		1,850.
	Guide line pair	925.00	
	Strip of 4	2,000.	
	3A2 Unused pair, 3mm spacing	600.00	
	3B2 Unused pair, 2mm spacing	475.00	375.00
	Guide line pair	1,750.	
	Strip of 4	1,250.	
	Guide line strip of 4	2,500.	
	3B2 Unused pair, 3mm spacing	475.00	
	3B2 Used pair, 3mm spacing		500.00

Group 3, three and four holes

On Issue of 1910

No.	Description	Unused	Used
383	1c **green**		
	3B4 Unused pair, 2mm spacing	380.00	250.00
	Pasteup pair	800.00	
	Strip of 4	1,500.	
	3B4 Unused pair, 3mm spacing	380.00	
	4B3 Unused pair, 2mm spacing	550.00	250.00
	4A3 Used single		375.00
	4B3 Unused pair, 3mm spacing	550.00	
384	2c **carmine**		
	3B4 Unused pair, 2mm spacing	925.00	290.00
	On cover		—
	Guide line pair	1,350.	
	3B4 Unused pair, 3mm spacing	925.00	
	4B3 Unused pair, 2mm spacing	1,000.	450.00
	On cover		875.00
	Guide line pair	2,000.	
	Guide line strip of 4	3,000.	
	4B3 Unused pair, 3mm spacing	1,000.	
	4A3 On cover		—

Group 4, four and four holes

On Issue of 1908-09

No.	Description	Unused	Used
343	1c **green**		
	* A Unused pair, 2mm spacing	400.00	
	* B Unused pair, 2mm spacing	400.00	
	On cover		675.00
344	2c **carmine**		
	* A Unused pair, 2mm spacing	360.00	
	* A Unused pair, 3mm spacing	550.00	
	* B Unused pair, 2mm spacing	275.00	125.00
	* B Unused pair, 3mm spacing	275.00	

On Lincoln Issue of 1909

No.	Description	Unused	Used
368	2c **carmine**		
	* A Unused pair, 2mm spacing	1,050.	
	* A Unused pair, 3mm spacing	1,050.	
	* B Unused pair, 2mm spacing	1,050.	
	* B Unused pair, 3mm spacing	1,050.	

On Issue of 1910

No.	Description	Unused	Used
383	1c **green**		
	A Unused pair, 2mm spacing	85.00	75.00
	Guide line pair	190.00	
	Strip of 4	350.00	
	Guide line strip of 4	500.00	
	Strip of 4, both A and B spacings	1,500.	
	Block of 4, both A and B spacings	1,250.	
	A Unused pair, 3mm spacing	80.00	
	B Unused pair, 2mm spacing	85.00	—
	On cover		360.00
	Guide line pair	175.00	
	Strip of 4	400.00	
	Guide line strip of 4	600.00	
	B Unused pair, 3mm spacing	70.00	—
384	2c **carmine**		
	A Unused pair, 2mm spacing	95.00	30.00
	Guide line pair	190.00	
	Guide line strip of 4	450.00	
	Block of 4, both A and B spacings	500.00	
	A Unused pair, 3mm spacing	80.00	
	Block of 4, both A and B spacings	500.00	
	B Unused pair, 2mm spacing	90.00	22.50
	On cover		525.00
	Guide line pair	180.00	
	Pasteup pair	200.00	
	Guide line strip of 4	400.00	
	B Unused pair, 3mm spacing	85.00	
	Strip of 4	200.00	
	Block of 4, both A and B spacings	500.00	

On Issue of 1912

No.	Description	Unused	Used
408	1c **green**		
	A Unused pair	47.50	3.25
	On cover		500.00
	Guide line pair	85.00	
	Strip of 4	150.00	
	Margin block of 4, arrow	600.00	
	Margin block of 4, arrow, both A and B spacings	700.00	
	B Unused pair	47.50	3.25
	On cover		300.00
	Guide line pair	80.00	

	Strip of 4	200.00	
	Guide line strip of 4	300.00	
409	2c **carmine**		
	A Unused pair	47.50	3.25
	On cover		50.00
	Guide line pair	175.00	
	Guide line strip of 4	250.00	
	Strip of 4, both A and B spacings	*400.00*	
	Block of 4	*300.00*	
	Margin block of 4, arrow, both A and B spacings	*700.00*	
	B Unused pair	47.50	3.25
	On cover		50.00
	Guide line pair	80.00	
	Strip of 4	200.00	
	Guide line strip of 4	300.00	

On Issue of 1916-17

482	2c **carmine**		
	A Unused pair	*725.00*	*75.00*
	On cover		*1,250.*
	Guide line pair	*1,100.*	
	Pasteup pair	*1,000.*	
	B Unused pair	*575.00*	*80.00*
	On cover		*1,500.*
	Guide line pair	*1,050.*	
	Guide line strip of 4	*2,500.*	

Group 5, four and five holes

On Issue of 1910

383	1c **green**		
	4A5 Unused pair, 2mm spacing	*1,150.*	—
	Guide line pair	*1,750.*	
	Strip of 4	*3,000.*	
	Block of 4	*1,300.*	
	4A5 Unused pair, 3mm spacing	1,100.	
384	2c **carmine**		
	4A5 Unused pair, 2mm spacing	*925.00*	—
	Guide line pair	*1,750.*	
	Guide line strip of 4	*5,000.*	
	4A5 Unused pair, 3mm spacing	875.00	
	Pasteup pair	1,750.	
	Strip of 4	*2,500.*	
	Pasteup strip of 4	*3,500.*	

On Issue of 1912

408	1c **green**		
	4A5 Unused pair	1,250.	
	Guide line pair	*2,250.*	
	Guide line strip of 4	*6,000.*	
	* 5A4 Unused pair	1,250.	
	Guide line pair	*2,250.*	
409	2c **carmine**		
	* 4A5 Unused pair	1,250.	*450.00*
	Guide line or pasteup pair	*2,250.*	
	Guide line strip of 4	*6,000.*	
	* 5A4 Unused pair	1,900.	
	Guide line pair	*3,000.*	

INTERNATIONAL VENDING MACHINE CO.

Baltimore, Md.

Similar to the Government coin stamp #322, but approximately perf. 12½ with somewhat inconsistent spacing.

On Issue of 1906-08

320	2c **carmine,** unused pair	*2,750.*
320b	2c **scarlet,** unused pair	*2,250.*

On Issue of 1908-09

343	1c **green,** unused pair	*3,150.*
344	2c **carmine,** unused pair	*1,250.*
345	3c **dp violet,** unused pair	*1,250.*
346	4c **org brown,** unused pair	—
347	5c **blue,** unused pair	*6,500.*

THE MAILOMETER COMPANY

Detroit, Mich.

Formerly the Schermack Mailing Machine Co., then Mail-om-eter Co., and later the Mail-O-Meter Co. Their round-hole perforations were developed in an attempt to get the Bureau of Engraving and Printing to adopt a larger perforation for coil stamps.

Perforations Type I

Used experimentally in Detroit and Chicago in August, 1909. Later used regularly in the St. Louis branch.

Two varieties exist: six holes 1.95mm in diameter spaced an average 1.2mm apart with an overall length of 17.7mm, and six holes 1.95mm in diameter spaced an average 1.15mm apart with an overall length of 17.45mm.

The 17.7mm length perfs are much scarcer than the 17.45mm length perfs and merit a 20% premium over the values shown.

To date, the vast majority of commercial covers are franked with the 17.7mm length perf. stamps.

Left Column=Unused Pair
Right Column=Used Single

On Issue of 1906-08

* 320	2c **carmine,** unused pair	450.00	
	Strip of 4	1,000.	
* 320b	2c **scarlet,** unused pair	390.00	
	Strip of 4	800.00	
* 320A	2c **lake,** unused pair	330.00	
	Guide line pair	925.00	
	Strip of 4	700.00	
	Guide line strip of 4	*2,000.*	

On Issue of 1908-09

343	1c **green**		
	Unused pair, 2mm spacing	52.50	27.50
	On cover		*775.00*
	Guide line pair	80.00	
	Strip of 4	150.00	
	Guide line strip of 4	200.00	
	Unused pair, 3mm spacing	57.50	
344	2c **carmine**		
	Unused pair, 2mm spacing	47.50	5.50
	On cover, St. Louis		*87.50*
	On cover, Detroit or Chicago		*1,550.*
	On cover, Washington, D.C.		*2,200.*
	Guide line pair	100.00	
	With perforated control mark, single		*110.00*
	Same, on cover		*500.00*
	Strip of 4	150.00	
	Guide line strip of 4	210.00	
	Unused pair, 3mm spacing	52.50	
345	3c **deep violet**		
	Unused pair, 2mm spacing	75.00	22.50
	Guide line pair	150.00	
	Strip of 4	200.00	*75.00*
	Guide line strip of 4	325.00	
	Unused pair, 3mm spacing	75.00	
346	4c **org brown**		
	Unused pair, 2mm spacing	150.00	45.00
	Guide line pair	290.00	
	Strip of 4	250.00	
	Guide line strip of 4	650.00	
	Unused pair, 3mm spacing	105.00	
347	5c **blue**		
	Unused pair, 2mm spacing	165.00	45.00
	Guide line pair	290.00	
	Guide line strip of 4	650.00	
	B margin strip of 4, P# & Impt. T V	*1,500.*	

On Lincoln Issue of 1909

* 368	2c **carmine**		
	Unused pair, 2mm spacing	210.00	*120.00*
	Guide line pair	425.00	
	Guide line strip of 4	800.00	
	Strip of 4, 2mm and 3mm spacings	500.00	
	Unused pair, 3mm spacing	150.00	
	Used pair		100.00
	Strip of 4	500.00	

On Alaska-Yukon Issue of 1909

* 371	2c **carmine**		
	Unused pair	260.00	*120.00*
	Guide line pair	475.00	
	Guide line strip of 4	900.00	

On Hudson-Fulton Issue of 1909

* 373	2c **carmine**		
	Unused pair	240.00	*110.00*
	Guide line pair	475.00	
	Pasteup pair	425.00	
	Pasteup strip of 4	800.00	

On Issue of 1910

383	1c **green**		
	Unused pair, 2mm spacing	50.00	3.75
	On cover		—
	Guide line pair	90.00	
	Strip of 4	150.00	*75.00*
	Guide line strip of 4	300.00	
	Unused pair, 3mm spacing	45.00	

The recorded No. 383 2mm used strip of 4 is precanceled St. Louis.

384	2c **carmine**		
	Unused pair, 2mm spacing	65.00	5.50
	On cover		85.00
	Guide line pair	115.00	
	Strip of 4	200.00	
	Guide line strip of 4	325.00	
	Unused pair, 3mm spacing	52.50	
	Block of 4	300.00	
	P# block of 6, Impt.	*875.00*	

On Issue of 1912

* 408	1c **green**		
	Unused pair	29.00	5.00
	Guide line pair	55.00	
	Strip of 4	100.00	
* 409	2c **carmine**		
	Unused pair	29.00	5.00
	On cover		*525.00*
	Guide line pair	55.00	
	Strip of 4	125.00	
	Guide line strip of 4		*500.00*

Perforations Type II

Used experimentally: Chicago, 1909; Detroit, 1911. Perforation holes are 1.95mm in diameter, spacing between perforation holes is 1.15mm, length of seven perforation holes is 20.6mm.

On Issue of 1906-08

* 320	2c **carmine,** unused pair	775.00	
* 320b	2c **scarlet,** unused pair	875.00	
	Guide line pair	1,650.	

On Issue of 1908-09

343	1c **green**		
	Unused pair, 2mm spacing	80.00	16.50
	Guide line pair	165.00	
	Strip of 4	200.00	
	Unused pair, 3mm spacing	80.00	
344	2c **carmine**		
	Unused pair, 2mm spacing	95.00	16.50
	On cover		*5,750.*
	Guide line pair	190.00	
	Strip of 4	250.00	
	Unused pair, 3mm spacing	95.00	
* 345	3c **deep violet**		
	Unused pair, 2mm spacing	350.00	*75.00*
	Pasteup pair	525.00	
	Strip of 4	750.00	
* 346	4c **org brown**		
	Unused pair, 2mm spacing	525.00	
	Unused pair, 3mm spacing	550.00	
	Strip of 4, 2mm and 3mm spacings	*1,000.*	
* 347	5c **blue,** unused pair, 2mm spacing	950.00	

On Lincoln Issue of 1909

* 368	2c **carmine**		
	Unused pair, 2mm spacing	800.00	
	Unused pair, 3mm spacing	750.00	

On Alaska-Yukon Issue of 1909

* 371	2c **carmine,** unused pair	825.00	

On Hudson-Fulton Issue of 1909

* 373	2c **carmine**		
	Unused pair	600.00	
	Guide line pair	950.00	
	Pasteup pair	875.00	
	Strip of 4	*1,250.*	

On Issue of 1910

383	1c **green**		
	Unused pair, 2mm spacing	190.00	32.50
	Guide line pair	390.00	
	Pasteup pair	375.00	
	Unused pair, 3mm spacing	190.00	
	Strip of 4	500.00	
384	2c **carmine**		
	Unused pair, 2mm spacing	200.00	*65.00*
	On cover		*5,000.*
	Unused pair, 3mm spacing	190.00	

Perforations Type III

Used experimentally in Detroit in 1910. Perforation holes are 1.5mm in diameter, spacing between holes is 1.5mm.

On Issue of 1906-08

* 320	2c **carmine,** unused pair	1,000.	
* 320b	2c **scarlet,** unused pair	1,000.	

On Issue of 1908-09

343	1c **green**		
	Unused pair	220.00	
	Guide line pair	450.00	
	Strip of 4	450.00	
	Unused pair, 3mm spacing	220.00	
344	2c **carmine**		
	Unused pair	250.00	
	Guide line pair	575.00	
	Strip of 4	500.00	
	Unused pair, 3mm spacing	275.00	
	Pasteup pair	*525.00*	
	Pasteup strip of 4	*1,000.*	
* 345	3c **deep violet**		
	Unused pair	390.00	
	Guide line pair	700.00	
	Pasteup pair	1,500.	
* 346	4c **org brown**		
	Unused pair	550.00	
	Pasteup pair	800.00	
	Unused pair, 3mm spacing	475.00	
* 347	5c **blue,** unused pair	*900.00*	
	Pasteup pair	*1,450.*	

On Lincoln Issue of 1909

* 368	2c **carmine**		
	Unused pair, 2mm spacing	350.00	*110.00*
	Unused pair, 3mm spacing	300.00	

Pasteup pair 500.00

On Alaska-Yukon Issue of 1909

* 371 2c **carmine,** unused pair 925.00

On Hudson-Fulton Issue of 1909

* 373 2c **carmine**
Unused pair 875.00
Guide line pair *1,650.*
Pasteup pair —

Perforations Type IV

Used in St. Louis branch office.

Left Column = Unused Pair
Right Column = Used Single

On Issue of 1906-08

* 320 2c **carmine,** unused pair 275.00 *85.00*
Guide line pair 550.00
Pasteup pair 500.00
* 320b 2c **scarlet,** unused pair 190.00 *70.00*
Guide line pair 575.00

On Issue of 1908-09

343 1c **green**
Unused pair, 2mm spacing 75.00 10.00
Guide line pair 145.00
Pasteup pair 140.00
Pasteup strip of 4 325.00
Strip of 4, 2mm and 3mm spacings 200.00
Unused pair, 3mm spacing 65.00
344 2c **carmine**
Unused pair, 2mm spacing 80.00 10.00
On cover —
Guide line pair 140.00
Pasteup pair 130.00
Guide line strip of 4 350.00
Pasteup strip of 4 300.00
Strip of 4, 2mm and 3mm spacings 200.00
Block of 4 *400.00*
Unused pair, 3mm spacing 70.00
345 3c **deep violet**
Unused pair, 2mm spacing 175.00
Guide line pair 325.00
Pasteup pair 300.00
Strip of 4 *100.00*
Guide line strip of 4 700.00
Center line block of 4 *1,500.*
346 4c **org brown**
Unused pair, 2mm spacing 275.00
Guide line pair 525.00
Unused pair, 3mm spacing 220.00
347 5c **blue**
Unused pair, 2mm spacing 360.00 *60.00*
Guide line pair 600.00
Strip of 4 725.00
Block of 4 *800.00*
P# block of 6, Impt. *1,500.*

On Lincoln Issue of 1909

* 368 2c **carmine**
Unused pair, 2mm spacing 120.00 30.00
Guide line pair 230.00
Pasteup pair 210.00
Strip of 4 300.00
Pasteup strip of 4 500.00
Unused pair, 3mm spacing 120.00
Block of 4 *1,200.*

On Alaska-Yukon Issue of 1909

* 371 2c **carmine**
Unused pair 400.00
Guide line pair 700.00
Pasteup pair 700.00
Block of 4 —

On Hudson-Fulton Issue of 1909

* 373 2c **carmine**
Unused pair 400.00
On cover —
Guide line pair 650.00
Margin block of 4, arrow *900.00*

On Issue of 1910

383 1c **green**
Unused pair, 2mm spacing 16.50 2.50
On cover *250.00*
Guide line pair 26.00
Pasteup pair 25.00
Strip of 4 100.00 *350.00*
Guide line strip of 4 325.00
Pasteup strip of 4 250.00
Margin block of 4, arrow *500.00* *1,500.*
Unused pair, 3mm spacing 11.50
Strip of 4 *100.00*

The recorded No. 383 3mm used strip of 4 is precanceled 2 lines and has some perforations omitted.

384 2c **carmine**
Unused pair, 2mm spacing 29.00 1.40
On cover *100.00*
Guide line pair 47.50
Pasteup pair 45.00
Guide line strip of 4 350.00
Pasteup strip of 4 325.00
Strip of 4, 2mm and 3mm spacings 150.00
Unused pair, 3mm spacing 27.50

Strip of 4 125.00
Block of 4 *300.00* *200.00*

On Issue of 1912

408 1c **green**
Unused pair 8.25 1.40
On cover 70.00
Guide line pair 12.50
Pasteup pair 11.00
Strip of 4 40.00
Guide line strip of 4 200.00
Pasteup strip of 4 150.00
Block of 4 *250.00*
409 2c **carmine**
Unused pair 9.25 .80
On cover 40.00
Guide line pair 16.50
Pasteup pair 15.50
Strip of 4 40.00
Guide line strip of 4 200.00
Pasteup strip of 4 150.00
Margin block of 4, arrow *250.00*

On Issue of 1916-17

481 1c **green** *650.00*
Precanceled (St. Louis), 2 types *850.00*
482 2c **carmine**
Unused pair *140.00* *75.00*
On cover *350.00*
Guide line pair *250.00*
Pasteup pair *290.00*
Strip of 4 325.00
Guide line strip of 4 650.00
Pasteup strip of 4 550.00
Block of 4 *300.00*
483 3c **violet,** type I
Unused pair *190.00* *225.00*
On cover *575.00*
Guide line pair *390.00*
Pasteup pair *290.00*

Perforations Type V

Perforation holes are 1.8 mm in diameter, spacing between perforation holes is 1.35mm, length of seven perforation holes is 20.7mm.

1911

On Issue of 1910

383 1c **green**
Single on cover —
Unused pair 100.00
Guide line pair 300.00
Strip of 4 600.00
Guide line strip of 4 900.00
384 2c **carmine**
Single on cover *3,000.*
Unused pair —
Strip of 4 —
With perforated control mark, single —

THE SCHERMACK COMPANY

Detroit, Mich.

These perforations were developed by the Schermack Mailing Machine Co. before it became the Mailometer Co. The Type III perforation was used in the company's affixing machines from 1908 through 1927 or 1928.

Perforations Type I. Eight Holes

Perforated in sheets, then cut into strips and coiled.

Left Column = Unused Pair
Right Column = Used Single

On Issue of 1906-08

314 1c **blue green**
Eight holes, unused pair 175.00 *110.00*
Guide line pair 350.00
Strip of 4 500.00
Block of 4 *800.00*
* Seven holes, unused pair 1,550.
Pasteup pair *1,900.*
* Six holes, unused pair 1,050.
Guide line pair 2,650.
320 2c **carmine**
Eight holes, unused pair 150.00 *60.00*
On cover *2,500.*
Guide line pair 375.00
Pasteup pair 350.00

Strip of 4 400.00
Guide line strip of 4 750.00
Pasteup strip of 4 600.00
Block of 4 *500.00* *200.00*
Seven holes, unused pair 1,400. *325.00*
On cover *8,750.*
Guide line pair 2,200.
Pasteup pair 1,800.
Strip of 4 *3,000.*
* Six holes, unused pair 1,250.
Guide line pair *2,600.*
* 320b 2c **scarlet**
* Six holes, guide line pair *1,750.*
* 320A 2c **lake**
* Eight holes, unused pair 400.00 *120.00*
Block of 4 *1,500.*
* Seven holes, unused pair 1,000.
Guide line pair *2,500.*
* Six holes, unused pair *3,250.*
Guide line pair *1,550.*
* 315 5c **blue**
* Eight holes, unused pair —

On Issue of 1908-09

* 343 1c **green**
Unused pair, 2mm spacing 300.00 85.00
Guide line pair 550.00
Guide line strip of 4 700.00
Unused pair, 3mm spacing —
* 344 2c **carmine**
Unused pair, 2mm spacing *1,650.*
Guide line pair *2,750.*
Unused pair, 3mm spacing —
* 345 3c **deep violet**
Unused pair, 2mm spacing *1,900.*
Guide line pair *3,000.*
* 346 4c **org brown**
Unused pair, 2mm spacing 825.00
Guide line pair 1,550.
Unused pair, 3mm spacing —
* 347 5c **blue**
Unused pair, 2mm spacing 825.00
Guide line pair *1,550.*

On Lincoln Issue of 1909

* 368 2c **carmine**
* Eight holes, unused pair, 2mm spacing 230.00 *85.00*
Guide line pair 425.00
Strip of 4 600.00
Guide line strip of 4 *1,000.*
* Eight holes, unused pair, 3mm spacing 260.00 *125.00*
Block of 4 *1,000.*
* Seven holes, unused pair, 2mm spacing *1,350.*
Guide line pair *2,750.*
* Seven holes, unused pair, 3mm spacing —
* Six holes, unused pair, 2mm spacing 1,150.
Guide line pair *2,500.*
* Six holes, unused pair, 3mm spacing —
Guide line pair *1,750.*

Perforations Type II

Cut into strips and joined before being perforated.

Left Column = Unused Pair
Right Column = Used Single

On Issue of 1906-08

314 1c **blue green**
* Unused pair 350.00 *85.00*
On cover *2,250.*
Guide line pair 575.00
Strip of 4 700.00
Guide line strip of 4 *1,200.*
320 2c **carmine**
* Unused pair 175.00 *60.00*
Guide line pair 320.00
Guide line strip of 4 750.00
*320A 2c **lake**
* Unused pair 300.00 *110.00*
Guide line pair 525.00
Strip of 4 700.00
*315 5c **blue**
* Unused pair *9,000.* *1,900.*
Guide line pair —

On Issue of 1908-09

* 343 1c **green**
Unused pair, 2mm spacing *825.00*
Guide line pair *1,500.*
Unused pair, 3mm spacing *875.00*
* 344 2c **carmine**
Unused pair, 2mm spacing *825.00*
Guide line pair *1,500.*
Unused pair, 3mm spacing *1,100.*
* 345 3c **deep violet**
Unused pair, 2mm spacing *875.00*
Guide line pair *1,650.*
* 346 4c **org brown**
Unused pair, 2mm spacing *1,500.*
Guide line pair *2,250.*
Unused pair, 3mm spacing —

No.	Description	Unused	Used
* 347	5c **blue**		
	Unused pair, 2mm spacing	1,150.	
	Guide line pair	2,000.	

On Lincoln Issue of 1909

No.	Description	Unused	Used
* 368	2c **carmine**		
	Unused pair, 2mm spacing	175.00	70.00
	Guide line pair	325.00	
	Strip of 4	450.00	
	Guide line strip of 4	750.00	
	Unused pair, 3mm spacing	155.00	

On Issue of 1910

No.	Description	Unused	Used
* 383	1c **green**		
	Guide line or pasteup pair, 2mm spacing	250.00	
	Unused pair, 3mm spacing	250.00	
* 384	2c **carmine**		
	Unused pair, 2mm spacing	—	
	Unused pair, 3mm spacing	—	

The existence of genuine examples of Nos. 383-384 has been questioned.

Perforations Type III

Left Column = Unused Pair
Right Column = Used Single

On Issue of 1906-08

No.	Description	Unused	Used
314	1c **blue green**		
	* Unused pair	12.50	2.50
	On cover		140.00
	Guide line pair	27.50	
	Pasteup pair	22.50	
	Strip of 4	50.00	100.00
	Guide line strip of 4	100.00	
	Pasteup strip of 4	75.00	
	With both type I (eight holes) and Type III perfs		—
	Block of 4	800.00	
	With perforated control mark, on postcard		100.00
320	2c **carmine,** Type I		
	* Unused pair	19.00	6.00
	On cover		85.00
	Guide line pair	35.00	
	Pasteup pair	32.50	
	Strip of 4	50.00	100.00
	Guide line strip of 4	150.00	
	Pasteup strip of 4	75.00	
	Block of 4	950.00	
	With both type I (eight holes) and Type III perfs		—
* 320b	2c **scarlet,** Type I		
	* Unused pair	27.50	6.00
	On cover		—
	Guide line pair	47.50	
	Strip of 4	75.00	
	Guide line strip of 4	175.00	
320c	2c **carmine rose,** Type I, unused pair, 2mm spacing	65.00	
* 320A	2c **lake,** Type II		
	* Unused pair	27.50	3.00
	On cover		65.00
	Guide line pair	52.50	500.00
	Pasteup pair	47.50	
	Strip of 4	75.00	125.00
	Guide line strip of 4	175.00	
	Pasteup strip of 4	100.00	
	With perforated control mark, single		3,500.
	With both type I (eight holes) and Type III perfs		—
	Block of 4	350.00	
320Ad	2c **carmine,** Type II, single	135.00	—
	On cover		2,500.
	Pair	290.00	
	Guide line pair	500.00	6,000.
	Strip of 4	750.00	
	Guide line strip of 4	2,000.	
	Pasteup strip of 4	1,250.	
314A	4c **brown,** single	100,000.	50,000.
	On cover		140,000.
	Pair	250,000.	
	Strip of 3	300,000.	
	Guide line pair	375,000.	
315	5c **blue**		
	* Unused pair	7,000.	
	Strip of 4	17,000.	
	Block of 4	15,000.	

On Issue of 1908-09

No.	Description	Unused	Used
343	1c **green**		
	Unused pair, 2mm spacing	6.25	1.40
	On cover		30.00
	Guide line pair	11.50	
	Pasteup pair	10.00	
	Strip of 4	25.00	
	Guide line strip of 4	50.00	
	Pasteup strip of 4	40.00	
	Block of 4	300.00	
	Unused pair, 3mm spacing	7.50	
	With perforated control mark, single		45.00
	Same, on cover		500.00
344	2c **carmine**		
	Unused pair, 2mm spacing	6.50	1.40
	On cover		22.50
	Guide line pair	11.50	
	Pasteup pair	10.00	
	Strip of 4	25.00	
	Guide line strip of 4	50.00	
	Pasteup strip of 4	40.00	
	Block of 4		50.00
	Unused pair, 3mm spacing	7.50	
	With perforated control mark, single		45.00
	Same, on cover		500.00
	Block of 4	300.00	
345	3c **deep violet**		
	Unused pair, 2mm spacing	27.50	14.00
	On cover		—
	Guide line pair	57.50	
	Pasteup pair	52.50	
	Strip of 4	75.00	
	Pasteup strip of 4	175.00	
	Margin block of 4, arrow	300.00	
	Unused pair, 3mm spacing	175.00	
	With perforated control mark, single		1,500.
	Same, on cover		8,000.
346	4c **org brown**		
	Unused pair, 2mm spacing	40.00	19.00
	On cover		3,000.
	Guide line pair	62.50	
	Strip of 4	100.00	
	Guide line strip of 4	200.00	
	Margin block of 4, arrow	500.00	
	Unused pair, 3mm spacing	25.00	
	With perforated control mark, single		1,650.
	Same, on cover		10,000.
347	5c **blue**		
	Unused pair, 2mm spacing	62.50	19.00
	On cover		2,750.
	Guide line pair	115.00	
	Strip of 4	200.00	
	Guide line strip of 4	400.00	
	Margin block of 4, arrow	500.00	

On Lincoln Issue of 1909

No.	Description	Unused	Used
368	2c **carmine**		
	Unused pair, 2mm spacing	75.00	14.00
	On cover		210.00
	Guide line pair	150.00	250.00
	Pasteup pair	135.00	
	Guide line strip of 4	350.00	
	Pasteup strip of 4	300.00	
	Block of 4	200.00	
	Strip of 4, 2mm and 3mm spacings	225.00	100.00
	Unused pair, 3mm spacing	57.50	
	Block of 4	300.00	

On Alaska-Yukon Issue of 1909

No.	Description	Unused	Used
* 371	2c **carmine**		
	Unused pair	100.00	
	On cover		4,500.
	Guide line pair	190.00	
	Pasteup pair	175.00	
	Strip of 4	225.00	
	Guide line strip of 4	475.00	
	Pasteup strip of 4	450.00	

On Hudson-Fulton Issue of 1909

No.	Description	Unused	Used
* 373	2c **carmine**		
	Unused pair	130.00	
	Guide line pair	230.00	
	Pasteup pair	210.00	
	Strip of 4	350.00	

On Issue of 1910

No.	Description	Unused	Used
383	1c **green**		
	Unused pair, 2mm spacing	5.25	1.40
	On cover		25.00
	Guide line pair	10.00	
	Pasteup pair	9.00	
	Guide line strip of 4	65.00	
	Pasteup strip of 4	60.00	
	Unused pair, 3mm spacing	3.75	
	With perforated control mark, single		45.00
	Same, on cover		450.00
	Strip of 4	25.00	

Earliest documented use: Feb. 8, 1911.

No.	Description	Unused	Used
384	2c **carmine**		
	Unused pair, 2mm spacing	11.50	1.40
	On cover		25.00
	Guide line pair	19.00	
	Strip of 4	30.00	
	Guide line strip of 4	75.00	
	Unused pair, 3mm spacing	9.00	
	With perforated control mark, single		45.00
	Same, on cover		450.00
	Strip of 4		50.00
	Block of 4	300.00	

On Issue of 1912

No.	Description	Unused	Used
408	1c **green**		
	Unused pair	2.60	.70
	On cover		25.00
	Guide line pair	5.25	
	Pasteup pair	5.00	
	Strip of 4	30.00	
	Guide line strip of 4	75.00	
	Pasteup strip of 4	60.00	100.00
	Block of 4	150.00	
	With perforated control mark, single		52.50
	Same, on cover		380.00
409	2c **carmine**		
	Unused pair	2.60	.55
	On cover		25.00
	Guide line pair	5.25	
	Pasteup pair	5.00	
	Strip of 4	25.00	200.00
	Guide line strip of 4	75.00	
	Pasteup strip of 4	60.00	
	Block of 4	150.00	
	Aniline ink ("pink back")		—
	With perforated control mark, single		52.50
	Same, on cover		380.00
	Single stamp in pasteup with strip of three No. TD14a test stamps	6,000.	

Earliest documented use: Mar. 13, 1912.

On Issue of 1916-17

No.	Description	Unused	Used
481	1c **green**		
	Unused pair	3.75	.45
	On cover		25.00
	Guide line pair	7.50	
	Pasteup pair	7.00	
	Strip of 4	30.00	
	Guide line strip of 4	75.00	
	Pasteup strip of 4	60.00	
	Margin block of 4, arrow		50.00
	Center line block of 4	100.00	
482	2c **carmine,** Type I		
	Unused pair	4.75	.65
	On cover		22.50
	Guide line pair	10.00	
	Pasteup pair	9.00	
	Strip of 4	25.00	90.00
	Guide line strip of 4	75.00	50.00
	Pasteup strip of 4	60.00	
	Aniline ink ("pink back")	—	

Earliest documented use: Dec. 16, 1916.

No.	Description	Unused	Used
482A	2c **deep rose,** Type Ia, single	—	65,000.
	On cover		70,000.
	Pair		140,000.
483	3c **violet,** type I		
	Unused pair	12.50	3.00
	On cover		110.00
	Guide line pair	22.50	
	Pasteup pair	20.00	
	Strip of 4	40.00	
	Guide line strip of 4	100.00	
	Pasteup strip of 4	75.00	
	Block of 4	290.00	
	With perforated control mark, single		500.00
	On cover		3,000.

Earliest documented use: Nov. 2, 1917.

No.	Description	Unused	Used
484	3c **violet,** type II		
	Unused pair	19.00	5.00
	On cover		110.00
	Guide line pair	35.00	
	Pasteup pair	30.00	
	Strip of 4	40.00	
	Guide line strip of 4	100.00	
	Pasteup strip of 4	75.00	
	With perforated control mark, single		500.00
	On cover		4,000.

Earliest documented use: Apr. 5, 1918.

On Issue of 1918-20

No.	Description	Unused	Used
531	1c **green**		
	Unused pair	17.50	5.00
	On cover		120.00
	Guide line pair	35.00	
	Pasteup pair	30.00	
	Strip of 4	40.00	50.00
	Guide line strip of 4	100.00	
	Pasteup strip of 4	75.00	
532	2c **carmine,** Type IV		
	Unused pair	47.50	3.75
	On cover		85.00
	Guide line pair	90.00	
	Pasteup pair	85.00	
	Strip of 4	75.00	100.00
	Guide line strip of 4	250.00	
	Pasteup strip of 4	200.00	
	Pasteup strip of 4, left pair No. 532, right pair No. 482	2,250.	

Earliest documented use: Apr. 28, 1920.

No.	Description	Unused	Used
533	2c **carmine,** Type V		
	Unused pair	425.00	50.00
	On cover		300.00
	Guide line pair	1,000.	
	Pasteup pair	950.00	
	Guide line strip of 4	2,500.	
	Pasteup strip of 4	2,000.	
534	2c **carmine,** Type Va		
	Unused pair	30.00	2.50
	On cover		110.00
	Guide line pair	62.50	
	Pasteup pair	57.50	
	Strip of 4	100.00	100.00
	Guide line strip of 4	200.00	
	Pasteup strip of 4	150.00	
534A	2c **carmine,** Type VI		
	Unused pair	52.50	5.00
	On cover		85.00
	Guide line pair	105.00	
	Pasteup pair	95.00	
	Strip of 4	150.00	80.00
	Guide line strip of 4	350.00	
	Pasteup strip of 4	250.00	

Earliest documented use: Aug. 31, 1920.

No.	Description	Unused	Used
534B	2c **carmine,** Type VII		
	Unused pair	1,400.	200.00
	On cover		450.00
	Guide line pair	2,300.	

No.	Description		
	Pasteup pair	2,150.	
	Strip of 4	3,000.	
535	3c **violet,** Type IV		
	Unused pair	22.50	4.00
	On cover		85.00
	Guide line pair	47.50	
	Pasteup pair	42.50	
	Strip of 4	60.00	100.00
	Guide line strip of 4	200.00	275.00
	Pasteup strip of 4	150.00	
	Block of 4	150.00	

On Issue of 1923-26

No.	Description		
575	1c **green,** unused single	27.50	
	Unused pair	230.00	7.50
	On cover		450.00
	Guide line pair	450.00	
	Pasteup pair	425.00	
	Guide line strip of 4	1,000.	
	Pasteup strip of 4	900.00	
	Margin block of 4, arrow	300.00	
	Precanceled	5.25	1.40
	On cover, precanceled		130.00
	Strip of 4		50.00

The recorded No. 575 used strip of 4 is precanceled.

No.	Description		
576	1½c **yellow brown**		
	Unused pair	27.50	5.00
	On cover		250.00
	Guide line pair	47.50	
	Pasteup pair	42.50	
	Strip of 4	75.00	
	Guide line strip of 4	125.00	
	Pasteup strip of 4	90.00	
	Block of 4	300.00	
	Precanceled	5.25	1.10
	On cover, precanceled		90.00
577	2c **carmine**		
	Unused pair	32.50	1.40
	On cover		25.00
	Guide line pair	47.50	
	Pasteup pair	42.50	
	Strip of 4	65.00	100.00
	Guide line strip of 4	175.00	
	Pasteup strip of 4	150.00	
	Block of 4	300.00	

On Harding Issue of 1923

No.	Description		
611	2c **black**		
	Unused pair	110.00	19.00
	On cover		6,000.
	Guide line pair	190.00	
	Pasteup pair	175.00	
	Strip of 4	225.00	
	Guide line strip of 4	450.00	
	Pasteup strip of 4	400.00	
	Block of 4	250.00	150.00
	Margin block of 4, arrow	350.00	
	Center line block of 4	1,750.	

U.S. AUTOMATIC VENDING COMPANY

New York, N.Y.

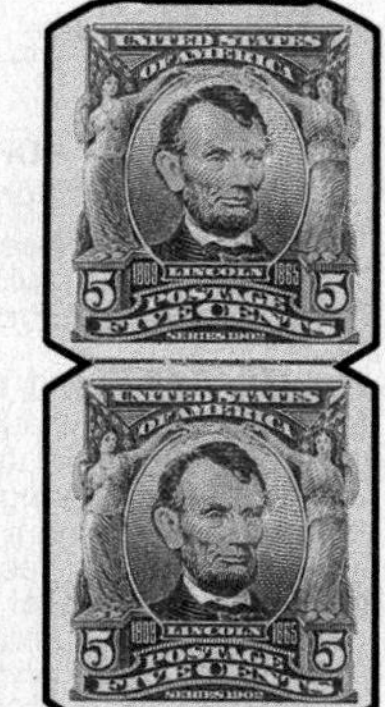

Separations Type I

Cut into strips and joined before being perforated.

Two varieties exist: 15½ and 16mm between notches of the perforations.

Left Column = Unused Pair
Right Column = Used Single
On Issue of 1906-08
Coiled Endwise

No.	Description		
314	1c **blue green**	57.50	14.00
	On cover		3,000.
	Guide line pair	110.00	
	Pasteup pair	100.00	
	Strip of 4	150.00	
	Guide line strip of 4	450.00	
320	2c **carmine**	52.50	10.00
	On cover		4,250.
	Guide line pair	105.00	
	Pasteup pair	92.50	
	Strip of 4	150.00	
320b	2c **scarlet**	62.50	8.75
	On cover		4,250.
	Guide line pair	125.00	
* 320A	2c **lake**	105.00	10.00
	Guide line pair	230.00	
	Pasteup pair	210.00	
	Strip of 4	425.00	
	Guide line strip of 4	600.00	
	Pasteup strip of 4	500.00	
315	5c **blue**	1,100.	2,250.
	On cover		12,500.
	Guide line pair	2,250.	
	Pasteup pair	1,900.	
	Strip of 4	2,500.	
	Guide line strip of 4	5,000.	

On Issue of 1906-08
Coiled Endwise

No.	Description		
343	1c **green**	14.00	2.00
	On cover		130.00
	On postcard		60.00
	Guide line pair	27.50	
	Pasteup pair	25.00	
	Strip of 4	100.00	100.00
	Guide line strip of 4	125.00	

Earliest documented use: Jan. 4, 1909.

No.	Description		
344	2c **carmine**	11.50	2.00
	On cover		130.00
	Guide line pair	22.50	
	Pasteup pair	20.00	
	Strip of 4	50.00	50.00
	Guide line strip of 4	125.00	
	Pasteup strip of 4	100.00	
* 345	3c **deep violet**	40.00	11.00
	On cover		675.00
	Guide line pair	80.00	
	Pasteup pair	75.00	
	Strip of 4	100.00	
	Guide line strip of 4	200.00	
* 346	4c **orange brown**	62.50	12.00
	Guide line pair	135.00	
	Pasteup pair	120.00	
	Strip of 4	150.00	
	Guide line strip of 4	300.00	
347	5c **blue**	115.00	55.00
	On cover		2,250.
	On cover (pair) with No. 373 USAV Type II pair		7,500.
	Guide line pair	220.00	
	Pasteup pair	200.00	
	Strip of 4	250.00	
	Guide line strip of 4	500.00	
	Pasteup strip of 4	400.00	

On Lincoln Issue of 1909

No.	Description		
368	2c **carmine,** coiled endwise	47.50	8.75
	On cover		2,250.
	First day cover, *Feb. 12, 1909*		14,500.
	Guide line pair	90.00	325.00
	Pasteup pair	85.00	
	Strip of 4	150.00	
	Guide line strip of 4	300.00	
	Pasteup strip of 4	250.00	

On Alaska-Yukon Issue of 1909

No.	Description		
* 371	2c **carmine,** coiled sideways	100.00	16.00
	On cover		675.00
	Guide line pair	190.00	
	Strip of 4	225.00	
	Guide line strip of 4	500.00	
	Pasteup strip of 4	400.00	
	Type 1a, No T. and B. margins	175.00	21.00
	Type 1a, Guide line pair	290.00	
	Type 1a, Pasteup pair	275.00	

Type Ia stamps are a deep shade and have a misplaced position dot in the "S" of "Postage." Beware of trimmed copies of No. 371 type I.

On Issue of 1910

No.	Description		
383	1c **green**	7.50	3.00
	On cover		120.00
	On postcard		45.00
	Guide line pair	12.50	
	Pasteup pair	11.00	
	Strip of 4	50.00	
	Guide line strip of 4	125.00	
* 384	2c **carmine**	27.50	5.50
	Guide line pair	47.50	
	Pasteup pair	42.50	
	Guide line strip of 4	250.00	

On Issue of 1912

No.	Description		
* 408	1c **green**	12.50	2.50
	Guide line pair	22.50	
	Guide line strip of 4	75.00	
	Pasteup strip of 4	200.00	
* 409	2c **carmine**	16.50	5.00
	Guide line pair	27.50	
	Pasteup pair	25.00	
	Guide line strip of 4	175.00	
	Pasteup strip of 4	150.00	

Separations Type II

Similar to Type I but with notches farther apart and a longer slit. Cut into strips and joined before being perforated.

Left Column = Unused Pair
Right Column = Used Single
On Issue of 1906-08
Coiled Sideways

No.	Description		
* 314	1c **blue green**		
	* Unused pair	57.50	10.00
	On cover		—
	Guide line pair	95.00	
	Pasteup pair	90.00	
	Strip of 4	300.00	
	Guide line strip of 4	800.00	
* 320	2c **carmine**		
	* Unused pair	100.00	
	Guide line pair	145.00	
	Strip of 4	300.00	
* 320b	2c **scarlet**		
	* Unused pair	70.00	6.00
	Guide line pair	115.00	
	Strip of 4	350.00	
	Guide line strip of 4	500.00	
* 315	5c **blue**		
	* Unused pair	1,100.	
	Guide line pair	2,500.	

On Issue of 1908-09

No.	Description		
343	1c **green**		
	Unused pair, 2mm spacing	16.50	4.00
	On cover		1,250.
	Guide line pair	26.00	
	Pasteup pair	24.00	
344	2c **carmine**		
	Unused pair, 2mm spacing	19.00	
	On cover		3,000.
	Guide line pair	30.00	
	Strip of 4	100.00	
* 345	3c **deep violet**		
	Unused pair, 2mm spacing	72.50	
	Guide line pair	125.00	
	Unused pair, 3mm spacing	—	
* 346	4c **org brown**		
	Unused pair, 2mm spacing	110.00	
	Guide line pair	190.00	
	Unused pair, 3mm spacing	95.00	
* 347	5c **blue**		
	Unused pair, 2mm spacing	220.00	
	Guide line pair	350.00	

On Lincoln Issue of 1909

No.	Description		
368	2c **carmine**		
	Unused pair, 2mm spacing	120.00	27.50
	Guide line pair	220.00	
	Guide line strip of 4	400.00	
	Strip of 4, 2mm and 3mm spacings	250.00	
	Unused pair, 3mm spacing	110.00	

On Alaska-Yukon Issue of 1909

No.	Description		
* 371	2c **carmine**		
	Unused pair	95.00	50.00
	On cover		650.00
	Guide line pair	165.00	
	Pasteup pair	150.00	
	Guide line strip of 4	350.00	
	Pasteup strip of 4	300.00	

On Hudson-Fulton Issue of 1909

No.	Description		
* 373	2c **carmine**		
	Unused pair	100.00	22.50
	On cover		2,750.
	Guide line pair	190.00	
	Pasteup pair	175.00	
	Strip of 4	400.00	
	Guide line strip of 4	500.00	
	Pasteup strip of 4	450.00	

See No. 347 USAV type I for combination cover.

On Issue of 1910

No.	Description		
383	1c **green**		
	Unused pair, 2mm spacing	19.00	
	On cover		1,100.
	Guide line pair	32.50	
	Unused pair, 3mm spacing	14.50	
384	2c **carmine**		
	Unused pair, 2mm spacing	27.50	
	On cover		3,000.
	Guide line pair	47.50	
	Guide line strip of 4	175.00	
	Unused pair, 3mm spacing	19.00	

On Issue of 1912

No.	Description		
408	1c **green**		
	Unused pair	12.50	2.50
	On cover		1,650.
	Guide line pair	22.00	
	Strip of 4	50.00	
409	2c **carmine**		
	Unused pair	19.00	5.00
	Guide line pair	30.00	

Perforations Type III

Cut into strips and joined before being perforated.

Left Column = Unused Pair
Right Column = Used Single

On Issue of 1906-08

No.	Description	Unused Pair	Used Single
* 314	1c **blue green**		
	* Unused pair	62.50	14.00
	Guide line pair	115.00	
* 320	2c **carmine**		
	* Unused pair	115.00	
* 320b	2c **scarlet**		
	* Unused pair	75.00	14.00
	Guide line pair	125.00	
	Strip of 4	150.00	
	Guide line strip of 4	300.00	
* 315	5c **blue**		
	* Unused pair	1,100.	
	Guide line or pasteup pair	*2,250.*	

On Issue of 1908-09

No.	Description	Unused Pair	Used Single
343	1c **green**		
	Unused pair, 2mm spacing	35.00	6.50
	Guide line pair	57.50	
	Pasteup pair	52.50	
	Strip of 4	150.00	
	Pasteup strip of 4	225.00	
	Unused pair, 3mm spacing	32.50	
344	2c **carmine**		
	Unused pair, 2mm spacing	35.00	6.50
	Guide line pair	57.50	
	Unused pair, 3mm spacing	47.50	
* 345	3c **deep violet**		
	Unused pair, 2mm spacing	140.00	
	Guide line pair	240.00	
* 346	4c **org brown**		
	Unused pair, 2mm spacing	140.00	17.50
	Guide line pair	240.00	
	Strip of 4	300.00	
	Unused pair, 3mm spacing	125.00	
* 347	5c **blue**		
	Unused pair, 2mm spacing	180.00	
	Guide line pair	325.00	
	Strip of 4	350.00	

On Lincoln Issue of 1909

No.	Description	Unused Pair	Used Single
* 368	2c **carmine**		
	Unused pair, 2mm spacing	80.00	21.00
	Guide line pair	145.00	
	Strip of 4	225.00	
	Guide line strip of 4	325.00	
	Unused pair, 3mm spacing	62.50	
	Experimental perf. 11.75	*3,500.*	
	Guide line pair	*7,500.*	

On Alaska-Yukon Issue of 1909

No.	Description	Unused Pair	Used Single
* 371	2c **carmine**		
	Unused pair	115.00	22.50
	On cover		—
	Guide line pair	180.00	
	Pasteup pair	165.00	
	Guide line strip of 4	350.00	

On Hudson-Fulton Issue of 1909

No.	Description	Unused Pair	Used Single
* 373	2c **carmine**		
	Unused pair	125.00	22.50
	On cover		—
	Guide line pair	180.00	
	Pasteup pair	165.00	
	Strip of 4	225.00	
	Guide line strip of 4	350.00	

On Issue of 1910

No.	Description	Unused Pair	Used Single
383	1c **green**		
	Unused pair, 2mm spacing	17.50	3.00
	Guide line pair	29.00	
	Pasteup pair	30.00	
	Strip of 4	100.00	*50.00*
	Pasteup strip of 4	175.00	
	Unused pair, 3mm spacing	15.00	
384	2c **carmine**		
	Unused pair, 2mm spacing	21.00	3.00
	Guide line pair	32.50	
	Strip of 4	100.00	
	Unused pair, 3mm spacing	17.50	

On Issue of 1912

No.	Description	Unused Pair	Used Single
408	1c **green**		
	Unused pair	11.50	
	Guide line pair	19.00	
	Pasteup pair	20.00	
	Strip of 4	100.00	
	Guide line strip of 4	150.00	
	Pasteup strip of 4	125.00	
409	2c **carmine**		
	Unused pair	21.00	
	Guide line pair	29.00	
	Pasteup pair	27.50	
	Strip of 4	125.00	
	Guide line strip of 4	175.00	
	Pasteup strip of 4	175.00	

On 1914 Rotary Press Coil

No.	Description	Unused Pair	Used Single
459	2c **carmine**		
	Unused pair	*22,500.*	*15,000.*

This firm also produced coil strips of manila paper, folded so as to form small "pockets", each "pocket" containing one 1c stamp and two 2c stamps, usually imperforate but occasionally with either government or U.S.A.V. private perforations. The manila "pockets" were perforated type II, coiled sideways. They fit U.S.A.V. ticket vending machines. Multiples exist.

Values are for "pockets" with known combinations of stamps, listed by basic Scott Number. Other combinations exist, but are not listed due to the fact that the stamps may have been added at a later date.

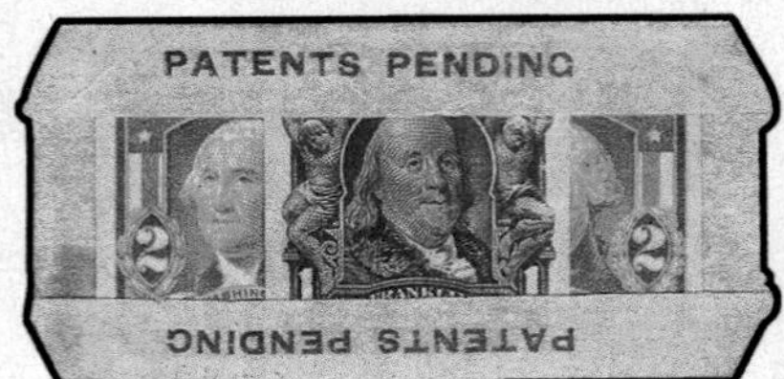

314 + 320b

Pocket Type 1 (1908)
("Patents Pending" on front in green at top and bottom, 3 serial numbers in red on reverse on the left)

Type 1-1	314 + 320	*3,000.*
Type 1-2	314 + 320b	*3,000.*

343 + 371

Pocket Type 2 (1909)
("Patent Applied For" handstamped in greenish blue at top of the pocket, 3 serial numbers in red on reverse on the left)

Type 2-1	343 + 371	1,250.
Type 2-2	343 + 372	750.
Type 2-3	343 (USAV type I) + 371	1,500.
Type 2-4	343 + 375	750.

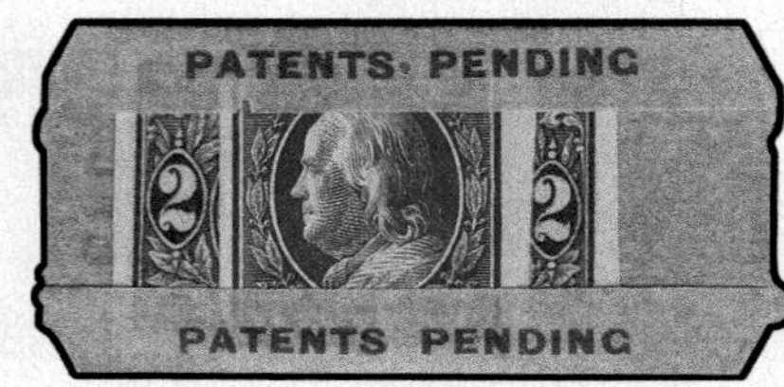

347 + 371

Pocket Type 3 (1909)
("Patents Pending" printed in red at top and bottom, 3 serial numbers printed in red on reverse on the right)

Type 3-1	343 + 371	750.
Type 3-1A	343 + 372	750.
Type 3-2	343 + 373	750.
Type 3-3	343 + 375	650.
Type 3-4	383 + 406	650.

343 + 344

Pocket Type 4 (1909)
(No printing on front, 3 serial numbers printed in red on reverse on the left)

Type 4-1	343 + 344	325.
Type 4-2	343 + 368	350.
Type 4-3	343 + 371	350.
Type 4-4	383 + 344	325.
Type 4-5	383 (USAV Type II) + 344	325.
Type 4-6	383 + 384	325.
Type 4-7	383 + 406	325.

THE ATTLEBORO STAMP COMPANY

Attleboro, Mass.

This Company used an affixing machine to stamp its newsletters during the summer and fall of 1909.

Nos. 343-344

No. 371

Right Column = Used Single
Left Column = Unused Pair

On Issue of 1908-09

No.	Description	Unused Pair	Used Single
343	1c **green**	*1,650.*	1,000.
	On Attleboro Philatelist wrapper		*5,500.*
	On cover		*12,500.*
	Guide line pair	*2,750.*	
	Pasteup pair	*2,500.*	—
	Strip of 4		
344	2c **carmine**	*45,000.*	
	Pair, on Attleboro wrapper		*20,000.*

Both the unused and the used No. 344 pairs are unique.

On Alaska-Yukon Issue of 1909

No.	Description	Unused Pair	Used Single
371	2c **carmine,** coiled sidewise	*3,250.*	*1,350.*
	On wrapper or cover		*10,000.*
	Guide line pair	*7,500.*	—
	Pasteup pair	*7,000.*	
	Strip of 4	*7,000.*	

COVEL MANUFACTURING COMPANY

Benton Harbor, Mich.

For the convenience of collectors, we list here the Covel coils that are avidly collected by specialists even though they were not dispensed by a vending or affixing machine.

From 1913 to 1920, this firm used a Rosback stroke perforator to apply gauge 11.75 perforations to imperforate coil stamps for use on company mail. The perforations resemble gauge 12 government perforations, so exact measurement (12-67 on a United States Specialist Gauge) is necessary, and expert certification is advisable (required for unused examples).

Stamps known to have Covel/Rosback perforations:

No. 314, vert. and horiz., used and on cover (unused pair value, $200; on cover value, $250); also known on cover in combination with No. 314 with Schermack Type III perfs. (value, $500).

No. 320, perf. horiz., used and on cover; perf. vert., unused (value of unused single with certification, $400).

No. 345, perf. vert., on cover (value, $1,000).

No. 408, perf. vert., unused, used, on cover (value, $300).

No. 481, on cover (value, $1,000).

No. 483, on cover (value, $500).

IMPERFORATE FLAT PLATE COIL STAMPS

The United States Post Office Department began issuing stamps finished and wound into coiled rolls in 1908, to firms that participated in a postage vending machine competition sponsored by Postmaster General George von L. Meyer. Entrants had the option of ordering the stamps coiled "sidewise" (wound horizontally) or "endwise" (wound vertically), with or without perforations, in rolls of 500 or 1,000 stamps. (Firms that preferred to manufacture their own coils by proprietary methods are listed in the Vending and Affixing Machine Perforations section of the catalogue.)

Except for being perforated or imperforate, all coil stamps manufactured by the Bureau of Engraving and Printing in 1908 and 1909 were produced by stripping printed sheets into ribbons 10- or 20-subjects long and manually pasting the strips together end to end, with a manila leader and trailer strip to form an outer wrapper and inner core for each roll. The 1908 orders were provided only to eight firms that participated in the original tests. In 1909, postmasters were authorized to accept orders for coil stamps from businesses. The forms for these special orders offered the choices of roll length, horizontal or vertical format, and perforated or imperforate. Buyers paid a premium above the face value of the stamps, 3¢ per roll of 500 and 6¢ per roll of 1,000, as a coiling fee.

By 1910, demand for coil stamps had grown to such an extent that the BEP installed a mechanized system called "Auto Wound," which pasted together sheets of stamps 10 subjects across, then slit and coiled them simultaneously. Perforated Auto-Wound coils required a coarser gauge than the 12-gauge sheet- and booklet-stamp standard, so a new gauge 8½ spacing became standard for perforated coils, while imperforate coils remained unchanged. Thus the coils listed in this section are counterparts to both versions of perforated coils, but for reasons of historical convenience, they have been numbered to match their imperforate sheet stamp counterparts, but with suffixes H or V to indicate horizontal and vertical formats, respectively.

In 1914, the BEP further streamlined coil stamp production with the web-fed Stickney rotary presses. The first rotary press stamp was an imperforate 2¢ George Washington coil stamp, Scott 459. The shift to rotary presses ended all flat-plate coil stamp production, both perforated and imperforate.

Imperforate coil stamps are often difficult or impossible to differentiate from sheet stamps, but many can be authenticated, especially as pairs or strips, and some bear authenticating marks of contemporaneous experts.

The numbers assigned below are those of the regularly issued imperforate sheet stamps to which "H" or "V" has been added to indicate that the stamps are coiled horizontally (side by side), or vertically (top to bottom).

Values for stamps on cover are for single stamps.

FLAT PLATE PRINTING

1908 **Wmk. 191** ***Imperf.***

314V A115 1c **blue green,** pair, never hinged *18,500.* —
Strip of 4 — —
Guide line pair —
Guide line strip of 4 —

The Philatelic Foundation has certified one unused No. 314V pair (with coil leader strip attached). The existence of any of the other listed items has been questioned by specialists. The editors would like to see certified evidence of the other listings.

314H A115 1c **blue green,** pair *2,100.* —
Never hinged *3,750.*
On cover *1,300.*
Pair on cover *2,000.*
Strip of 4 — —
Never hinged *8,000.*
Guide line pair *5,000.*
Guide line strip of 4 8,000.
Pasteup pair *3,500.*
Never hinged *5,500.*
Pasteup strip of 4 *5,000.*
Never hinged *8,000.*

Earliest documented use: Mar. 9, 1908.

320V A129 2c **carmine,** pair *1,650.* —
On cover *3,000.*
Strip of 4 — —
Guide line pair —
Guide line strip of 4 —

Earliest documented use: Apr. 9, 1908.

320H A129 2c **carmine,** pair 550.00 —
Strip of 4 — —
Guide line pair —
Guide line strip of 4 —

Earliest documented use: June 4, 1908.

1908-10 ***Imperf.***

343V A138 1c **green,** pair 25.00 15.00
Never hinged 40.00
On cover 20.00
Strip of 4 60.00 —
Never hinged 110.00
Guide line pair 60.00 150.00
Never hinged 110.00
Guide line strip of 4 110.00
Never hinged 220.00
Pasteup pair 50.00
Never hinged 90.00

Earliest documented use: Nov. 18, 1909.

343H A138 1c **green,** pair 50.00 30.00
Never hinged 80.00
Strip of 4 120.00 —
Never hinged 200.00
Guide line pair 100.00 100.00
Never hinged 180.00
Guide line strip of 4 220.00
Never hinged 400.00
Pasteup pair 80.00
Never hinged 150.00
Pasteup strip of 4 150.00
Never hinged 280.00

344V A139 2c **carmine,** pair 30.00 30.00
Never hinged 50.00
On cover 25.00
Strip of 4 70.00 —
Never hinged 130.00
Guide line pair 60.00 —
Never hinged 110.00
Guide line strip of 4 110.00
Never hinged 200.00
Pasteup pair 50.00
Never hinged 90.00
Pasteup strip of 4 80.00
Never hinged 150.00
Foreign entry, design of 1c *2,500.* *3,250.*
Never hinged *4,500.*

Earliest documented use: Oct. 13, 1909.

344H A139 2c **carmine,** pair (2mm spacing) 35.00 30.00
Never hinged 60.00
On cover *600.00*
Strip of 4 90.00
Never hinged 160.00
Guide line pair 90.00
Never hinged 160.00
Guide line strip of 4 150.00
Never hinged 280.00
Pasteup pair 75.00
Never hinged 130.00
Pair (3mm spacing) 40.00 —
Never hinged 70.00
Strip of 4 100.00
Never hinged 180.00
Guide line pair 90.00 150.00
Never hinged 160.00
Guide line strip of 4 160.00
Never hinged 280.00

Earliest documented use: March 23, 1909.

345H A140 3c **deep violet,** type I, pair 6,250.

No. 345H was printed from star plates with 3mm spacing between stamps on the six outer rows at the left and right sides of each 400-subject press sheet, and 2mm spacing between stamps on the inner four rows on each side of the center guide lines. Earlier imperforate 3¢ stamps were issued only as uncut sheets, not as coils, and were printed from plates with 2mm horizontal spacing only. Stamps with 3mm spacing are coil stamps; stamps with 2mm spacing are either coil stamps or imperforate sheet stamps.

346V A140 4c **orange brown,** pair 170.00
Never hinged 300.00
On cover —
Strip of 4 375.00 —
Never hinged 650.00
Guide line pair 325.00 125.00
Never hinged 600.00
Guide line strip of 4 550.00
Never hinged 1,000.
Pasteup pair 250.00
Never hinged 400.00
Pasteup strip of 4 450.00
Never hinged 800.00

Earliest documented use: Feb. 18, 1911.

347V A140 5c **blue,** pair 175.00 —
Never hinged 300.00
On cover —
Strip of 4 425.00 300.00
Never hinged 725.00
Guide line pair 350.00 —
Never hinged 600.00
Guide line strip of 4 600.00
Never hinged 1,000.
Pasteup pair 275.00
Never hinged 450.00
Pasteup strip of 4 500.00
Never hinged 900.00

Earliest documented use: April 17, 1909.

1909 ***Imperf.***

368V A141 2c **carmine,** *Lincoln,* pair 180.00 —
Never hinged 280.00
On cover —
Strip of 4 450.00 —
Never hinged 750.00
Guide line pair 360.00 —
Never hinged 650.00
Guide line strip of 4 625.00 —
Never hinged 1,100.
Pasteup pair 300.00
Never hinged 500.00
Pasteup strip of 4 450.00
Never hinged 750.00

Earliest documented use: Feb. 12, 1909.

368H A141 2c **carmine,** *Lincoln,* pair 250.00 —
Never hinged 425.00
On cover —
Strip of 4 600.00
Never hinged 950.00
Guide line pair 500.00
Never hinged 800.00
Guide line strip of 4 850.00
Never hinged 1,300.
Pasteup pair 400.00
Never hinged 650.00
Pasteup strip of 4 600.00
Never hinged 900.00

Earliest documented use: Dec. 9, 1909.

1910 **Wmk. 190** ***Imperf.***

383V A138 1c **green,** pair 12.00 —
Never hinged 20.00
On cover 10.00
Strip of 4 27.50 —
Never hinged 45.00
Guide line pair 25.00 —
Never hinged 40.00
Guide line strip of 4 60.00 —
Never hinged 105.00
Pasteup pair 20.00
Never hinged 35.00
Pasteup strip of 4 35.00
Never hinged 60.00
Double transfer — —

Earliest documented use: Mar. 24, 1911.

383H A138 1c **green,** pair (2mm spacing) 17.50 —
Never hinged 30.00
Strip of 4 42.50 —
Never hinged 70.00
Guide line pair 35.00 —
Never hinged 65.00
Guide line strip of 4 65.00 —
Never hinged 115.00
Pasteup pair 30.00
Never hinged 50.00
Pair (3mm spacing) 17.50 —
Never hinged 28.00
Strip of 4 42.50 —
Never hinged 70.00
Guide line pair 35.00 —
Never hinged 65.00
Guide line strip of 4 65.00 —
Never hinged 115.00

384V A139 2c **carmine,** pair 14.00 —
Never hinged 25.00
On cover 10.00
Strip of 4 30.00 —
Never hinged 50.00
Guide line pair 30.00 —
Never hinged 55.00
Guide line strip of 4 55.00 —
Never hinged 90.00
Pasteup pair 24.00
Never hinged 40.00
Pasteup strip of 4 35.00
Never hinged 60.00
Foreign entry, design of 1c *1,500.* —
Never hinged 2,500.

Earliest documented use: Oct. 21, 1910.

384H A139 2c **carmine,** pair (2mm spacing) 27.50 —
Never hinged 45.00
Strip of 4 70.00
Never hinged 115.00
Guide line pair 60.00 —
Guide line strip of 4 105.00 —
Pasteup pair 50.00
Never hinged 90.00
Pasteup strip of 4 80.00

Never hinged	130.00	
Pair (3mm spacing)	25.00	—
Never hinged	40.00	
Strip of 4	70.00	—
Never hinged	110.00	
Guide line pair	55.00	—
Never hinged	90.00	
Guide line strip of 4	100.00	—
Never hinged	180.00	

Earliest documented use: Mar. 9, 1912.

1912 **Wmk. 190** ***Imperf.***

408V A140 1c **green,** pair	4.00	
Never hinged	7.00	
On cover		—
Strip of 4	9.00	
Never hinged	15.00	
Guide line pair	9.00	
Never hinged	15.00	
Guide line strip of 4	14.00	
Never hinged	25.00	
Pasteup pair	7.00	

Never hinged	12.00
Pasteup strip of 4	11.00
Never hinged	20.00

Earliest documented use: May 17, 1912.

408H A140 1c **green,** pair	5.00
Never hinged	8.00
Strip of 4	12.00
Never hinged	20.00
Guide line pair	10.00
Never hinged	17.50
Guide line strip of 4	17.50
Never hinged	25.00
Pasteup pair	8.00
Never hinged	14.00
Pasteup strip of 4	—

409V A140 2c **carmine,** pair	4.00
Never hinged	7.00
Strip of 4	9.00
Never hinged	15.00
Guide line pair	8.00
Never hinged	15.00
Guide line strip of 4	14.00
Never hinged	26.00
Pasteup pair	7.00

Never hinged	11.00
Pasteup strip of 4	11.00
Never hinged	20.00

Earliest documented use: May 29, 1912.

409H A140 2c **carmine,** pair	6.00	
Never hinged	10.00	
On cover		—
Strip of 4	14.00	
Never hinged	22.50	
Guide line pair	9.00	
Never hinged	16.00	
Guide line strip of 4	15.00	
Never hinged	26.00	
Pasteup pair	7.00	
Never hinged	12.00	
Pasteup strip of 4	12.00	
Never hinged	22.00	
Double transfer	7.00	

Earliest documented use: Dec. 17, 1914.

COMMEMORATIVE STAMPS, QUANTITIES ISSUED

Quantities issued fall into four categories. First are stamps where reasonably accurate counts are made of the number of stamps sold. Second are stamps where the counts are approximations of the number sold.

Third are stamps where the count is of quantities shipped to post offices and philatelic sales units, but no adjustments are made for returned or destroyed stamps.

Fourth are stamps for which the quantity printed is furnished but no other adjustments are made.

Occasionally more accurate figures are determined. In these cases the quantities here will be adjusted. For example, it is now known that while 2,000,000 sets of the Voyages of Columbus souvenir sheets were printed, the number sold was 1,185,170 sets.

Scott No.		Quantity
230		449,195,550
231		1,464,588,750
232		11,501,250
233		19,181,550
234		35,248,250
235		4,707,550
236		10,656,550
237		16,516,950
238		1,576,950
239		617,250
240		243,750
241		55,050
242		45,550
243		27,650
244		26,350
245		27,350
285		70,993,400
286		159,720,800
287		4,924,500
288		7,694,180
289		2,927,200
290		4,629,760
291		530,400
292		56,900
293		56,200
294		91,401,500
295		209,759,700
296		5,737,100
297		7,201,300
298		4,921,700
299		5,043,700
323		79,779,200
324		192,732,400
325		4,542,600
326		6,926,700
327		4,011,200
328		77,728,794
329		149,497,994
330		7,980,594
367		148,387,191
368		1,273,900
369		637,000
370		152,887,311
371		525,400
372		72,634,631
373		216,480
397 & 401		334,796,926
398 & 402		503,713,086
399 & 403		29,088,726
400 & 404		16,968,365
537		99,585,200
548		137,978,207
549		196,037,327
550		11,321,607
610		1,459,487,085
611		770,000
612		99,950,300
614		51,378,023
615		77,753,423
616		5,659,023
617		15,615,000
618		26,596,600
619		5,348,800
620		9,104,983
621		1,900,983
627		307,731,900
628		20,280,500
629		40,639,485
630	(sheet of 25)	107,398
643		39,974,900
644		25,628,450
645		101,330,328
646		9,779,896
647		5,519,897
648		1,459,897
649		51,342,273
650		10,319,700
651		16,684,674
654		31,679,200
655		210,119,474
656		133,530,000
657		51,451,880
658		13,390,000
659		8,240,000
660		87,410,000
661		2,540,000
662		2,290,000
663		2,700,000
664		1,450,000
665		1,320,000
666		1,530,000
667		1,130,000
668		2,860,000
669		8,220,000
670		8,990,000
671		73,220,000
672		2,110,000
673		1,600,000
674		1,860,000
675		980,000
676		850,000
677		1,480,000
678		530,000
679		1,890,000
680		29,338,274
681		32,680,900
682		74,000,774
683		25,215,574
688		25,609,470
689		66,487,000
690		96,559,400
702		99,074,600
703		25,006,400
704		87,969,700
705		1,265,555,100
706		304,926,800
707		4,222,198,300
708		456,198,500
709		151,201,300
710		170,565,100
711		111,739,400
712		83,257,400
713		96,506,100
714		75,709,200
715		147,216,000
716		51,102,800
717		100,869,300
718		168,885,300
719		52,376,100
724		49,949,000
725		49,538,500
726		61,719,200
727		73,382,400
728		348,266,800
729		480,239,300
730	(sheet of 25)	456,704
730a		11,417,600
731	(sheet of 25)	441,172
731a		11,029,300
732		1,978,707,300
733		5,735,944
734		45,137,700
735	(sheet of 6)	811,404
735a		4,868,424
736		46,258,300
737		193,239,100
738		15,432,200
739		64,525,400
740		84,896,350
741		74,400,200
742		95,089,000
743		19,178,650
744		30,980,100
745		16,923,350
746		15,988,250
747		15,288,700
748		17,472,600
749		18,874,300
750	(sheet of 6)	511,391
750a		3,068,346
751	(sheet of 6)	793,551
751a		4,761,306
752		3,274,556
753		2,040,760
754		2,389,288
755		2,294,948
756		3,217,636
757		2,746,640
758		2,168,088
759		1,822,684
760		1,724,576
761		1,647,696
762		1,682,948
763		1,638,644
764		1,625,244
765		1,644,900
766	(pane of 25)	98,712
766a		2,467,800
767	(pane of 25)	85,914
767a		2,147,850
768	(pane of 6)	267,200
768a		1,603,200
769	(pane of 6)	279,960
769a		1,679,760
770	(pane of 6)	215,920
770a		1,295,520
771		1,370,560
772		70,726,800
773		100,839,600
774		73,610,650
775		75,823,900
776		124,324,500
777		67,127,650
778	(sheet of 4)	2,809,039
778a		2,809,039
778b		2,809,039
778c		2,809,039
778d		2,809,039
782		72,992,650
783		74,407,450
784		269,522,200
785		105,196,150
786		93,848,500
787		87,741,150
788		35,794,150
789		36,839,250
790		104,773,450
791		92,054,550
792		93,291,650
793		34,552,950
794		36,819,050
795		84,825,250
796		25,040,400
797		5,277,445
798		99,882,300

799	78,454,450	967	57,823,000	1119	118,390,200
800	77,004,200	968	52,975,000	1120	125,770,200
801	81,292,450	969	77,149,000	1121	114,114,280
802	76,474,550	970	58,332,000	1122	156,600,200
835	73,043,650	971	56,228,000	1123	124,200,200
836	58,654,368	972	57,832,000	1124	120,740,200
837	65,939,500	973	53,875,000	1125	133,623,280
838	47,064,300	974	63,834,000	1126	45,569,088
852	114,439,600	975	67,162,200	1127	122,493,280
853	101,699,550	976	64,561,000	1128	131,260,200
854	72,764,550	977	64,079,500	1129	47,125,200
855	81,369,600	978	63,388,000	1130	123,105,000
856	67,813,350	979	62,285,000	1131	126,105,050
857	71,394,750	980	57,492,610	1132	209,170,000
858	66,835,000	981	99,190,000	1133	120,835,000
859	56,348,320	982	104,790,000	1134	115,715,000
860	53,177,110	983	108,805,000	1135	118,445,000
861	53,260,270	984	107,340,000	1136	111,685,000
862	22,104,950	985	117,020,000	1137	43,099,200
863	13,201,270	986	122,633,000	1138	115,444,000
864	51,603,580	987	130,960,000	1139	126,470,000
865	52,100,510	988	128,478,000	1140	124,560,000
866	51,666,580	989	132,090,000	1141	115,455,000
867	22,207,780	990	130,050,000	1142	122,060,000
868	11,835,530	991	131,350,000	1143	120,540,000
869	52,471,160	992	129,980,000	1144	113,075,000
870	52,366,440	993	122,315,000	1145	139,325,000
871	51,636,270	994	122,170,000	1146	124,445,000
872	20,729,030	995	131,635,000	1147	113,792,000
873	14,125,580	996	121,860,000	1148	44,215,200
874	59,409,000	997	121,120,000	1149	113,195,000
875	57,888,600	998	119,120,000	1150	121,805,000
876	58,273,180	999	112,125,000	1151	115,353,000
877	23,779,000	1000	114,140,000	1152	111,080,000
878	15,112,580	1001	114,490,000	1153	153,025,000
879	57,322,790	1002	117,200,000	1154	119,665,000
880	58,281,580	1003	116,130,000	1155	117,855,000
881	56,398,790	1004	116,175,000	1156	118,185,000
882	21,147,000	1005	115,945,000	1157	112,260,000
883	13,328,000	1006	112,540,000	1158	125,010,000
884	54,389,510	1007	117,415,000	1159	119,798,000
885	53,636,580	1008	2,899,580,000	1160	42,696,000
886	55,313,230	1009	114,540,000	1161	106,610,000
887	21,720,580	1010	113,135,000	1162	109,695,000
888	13,600,580	1011	116,255,000	1163	123,690,000
889	47,599,580	1012	113,860,000	1164	123,970,000
890	53,766,510	1013	124,260,000	1165	124,796,000
891	54,193,580	1014	115,735,000	1166	42,076,800
892	20,264,580	1015	115,430,000	1167	116,210,000
893	13,726,580	1016	136,220,000	1168	126,252,000
894	46,497,400	1017	114,894,600	1169	42,746,400
895	47,700,000	1018	118,706,000	1170	124,117,000
896	50,618,150	1019	114,190,000	1171	119,840,000
897	50,034,400	1020	113,990,000	1172	117,187,000
898	60,943,700	1021	89,289,600	1173	124,390,000
902	44,389,550	1022	114,865,000	1174	112,966,000
903	54,574,550	1023	115,780,000	1175	41,644,200
904	63,558,400	1024	115,244,600	1176	110,850,000
906	21,272,800	1025	123,709,600	1177	98,616,000
907	1,671,564,200	1026	114,789,600	1178	101,125,000
908	1,227,334,200	1027	115,759,600	1179	124,865,000
909	19,999,646	1028	116,134,600	1180	79,905,000
910	19,999,646	1029	118,540,000	1181	125,410,000
911	19,999,646	1060	115,810,000	1182	112,845,000
912	19,999,646	1061	113,603,700	1183	106,210,000
913	19,999,646	1062	128,002,000	1184	110,810,000
914	19,999,646	1063	116,078,150	1185	116,995,000
915	19,999,646	1064	116,139,800	1186	121,015,000
916	14,999,646	1065	120,484,800	1187	111,600,000
917	14,999,646	1066	53,854,750	1188	110,620,000
918	14,999,646	1067	176,075,000	1189	109,110,000
919	14,999,646	1068	125,944,400	1190	145,350,000
920	14,999,646	1069	122,284,600	1191	112,870,000
921	14,999,646	1070	133,638,850	1192	121,820,000
922	61,303,000	1071	118,664,600	1193	289,240,000
923	61,001,450	1072	112,434,000	1194	120,155,000
924	60,605,000	1073	129,384,550	1195	124,595,000
925	50,129,350	1074	121,184,600	1196	147,310,000
926	53,479,400	1075	2,900,731	1197	118,690,000
927	61,617,350	1076	119,784,200	1198	122,730,000
928	75,500,000	1077	123,159,400	1199	126,515,000
929	137,321,000	1078	123,138,800	1200	130,960,000
930	128,140,000	1079	109,275,000	1201	120,055,000
931	67,255,000	1080	112,932,200	1202	120,715,000
932	133,870,000	1081	125,475,000	1203	121,440,000
933	76,455,400	1082	117,855,000	1204	40,270,000
934	128,357,750	1083	122,100,000	1205	861,970,000
935	138,863,000	1084	118,180,000	1206	120,035,000
936	111,616,700	1085	100,975,000	1207	117,870,000
937	308,587,700	1086	115,299,450	1230	129,945,000
938	170,640,000	1087	186,949,627	1231	135,620,000
939	135,927,000	1088	115,235,000	1232	137,540,000
940	260,339,100	1089	106,647,500	1233	132,435,000
941	132,274,500	1090	112,010,000	1234	135,520,000
942	132,430,000	1091	118,470,000	1235	131,420,000
943	139,209,500	1092	102,230,000	1236	133,170,000
944	114,684,450	1093	102,410,000	1237	130,195,000
945	156,540,510	1094	84,054,400	1238	128,450,000
946	120,450,600	1095	126,266,000	1239	118,665,000
947	127,104,300	1096	39,489,600	1240	1,291,250,000
948	10,299,600	1097	122,990,000	1241	175,175,000
949	132,902,000	1098	174,372,800	1242	125,995,000
950	131,968,000	1099	114,365,000	1243	128,025,000
951	131,488,000	1100	122,765,200	1244	145,700,000
952	122,362,000	1104	113,660,200	1245	120,310,000
953	121,548,000	1105	120,196,580	1246	511,750,000
954	131,109,500	1106	120,805,200	1247	123,845,000
955	122,650,500	1107	128,815,200	1248	122,825,000
956	121,953,500	1108	108,415,200	1249	453,090,000
957	115,250,000	1109	107,195,200	1250	123,245,000
958	64,198,500	1110	115,745,280	1251	123,355,000
959	117,642,500	1111	39,743,640	1252	126,970,000
960	77,649,600	1112	114,570,200	1253	121,250,000
961	113,474,500	1113	120,400,200	1254-1257	1,407,760,000
962	120,868,500	1114	91,160,200	1258	120,005,000
963	77,800,500	1115	114,860,200	1259	125,800,000
964	52,214,000	1116	126,500,000	1260	122,230,000
965	53,959,100	1117	120,581,280	1261	115,695,000
966	61,120,010	1118	44,064,576	1262	115,095,000

Scott No.	Quantity
1263	119,580,000
1264	125,180,000
1265	120,135,000
1266	115,405,000
1267	115,855,000
1268	115,340,000
1269	114,840,000
1270	116,140,000
1271	116,900,000
1272	114,085,000
1273	114,880,000
1274	26,995,000
1275	128,495,000
1276	1,139,930,000
1306	116,835,000
1307	117,470,000
1308	123,770,000
1309	131,270,000
1310	122,285,000
1311	14,680,000
1312	114,160,000
1313	128,475,000
1314	119,535,000
1315	125,110,000
1316	114,853,200
1317	124,290,000
1318	128,460,000
1319	127,585,000
1320	115,875,000
1321	1,173,547,420
1322	114,015,000
1323	121,105,000
1324	132,045,000
1325	118,780,000
1326	121,985,000
1327	111,850,000
1328	117,225,000
1329	111,515,000
1330	114,270,000
1331-1332	120,865,000
1333	110,675,000
1334	110,670,000
1335	113,825,000
1336	1,208,700,000
1337	113,330,000
1339	141,350,000
1340	144,345,000
1342	147,120,000
1343	130,125,000
1344	158,700,000
1345-1354	228,040,000
1355	153,015,000
1356	132,560,000
1357	130,385,000
1358	132,265,000
1359	128,710,000
1360	124,775,000
1361	128,295,000
1362	142,245,000
1363	1,410,580,000
1364	125,100,000
1365-1368	192,570,000
1369	145,770,000
1370	139,475,000
1371	187,165,000
1372	125,555,000
1373	144,425,000
1374	135,875,000
1375	151,110,000
1376-1379	159,195,000
1380	129,540,000
1381	130,925,000
1382	139,055,000
1383	150,611,200
1384	1,709,795,000
1385	127,545,000
1386	145,788,800
1387-1390	201,794,200
1391	171,850,000
1392	142,205,000
1405	137,660,000
1406	135,125,000
1407	135,895,000
1408	132,675,000
1409	134,795,000
1410-1413	161,600,000
1414-1414a	683,730,000
1415-1418,1415a-1418a	489,255,000
1419	127,610,000
1420	129,785,000
1421-1422	134,380,000
1423	136,305,000
1424	134,840,000
1425	130,975,000
1426	161,235,000
1427-1430	175,679,600
1431	138,700,000
1432	138,165,000
1433	152,125,000
1434-1435	176,295,000
1436	142,845,000
1437	148,755,000
1438	139,080,000
1439	130,755,000
1440-1443	170,208,000
1444	1,074,350,000
1445	979,540,000
1446	137,355,000
1447	150,400,000
1448-1451	172,730,000
1452	104,090,000
1453	164,096,000
1454	53,920,000
1455	153,025,000
1456-1459	201,890,000
1460	67,335,000
1461	179,675,000
1462	46,340,000
1463	180,155,000
1464-1467	198,364,800
1468	185,490,000
1469	162,335,000
1470	162,789,950
1471	1,003,475,000
1472	1,017,025,000
1473	165,895,000
1474	166,508,000
1475	320,055,000
1476	166,005,000
1477	163,050,000
1478	159,005,000
1479	147,295,000
1480-1483	196,275,000
1484	139,152,000
1485	128,048,000
1486	148,008,000
1487	139,608,000
1488	159,475,000
1489-1498	486,020,000
1499	157,052,800
1500	53,005,000
1501	159,775,000
1502	39,005,000
1503	152,624,000
1504	145,840,000
1505	151,335,000
1506	141,085,000
1507	885,160,000
1508	939,835,000
1525	143,930,000
1526	145,235,000
1527	135,052,000
1528	156,750,000
1529	164,670,000
1530-1537	190,156,800
1538-1541	167,212,800
1542	156,265,000
1543-1546	195,585,000
1547	148,850,000
1548	157,270,000
1549	150,245,000
1550	835,180,000
1551	882,520,000
1552	213,155,000
1553	159,995,000
1554	146,365,000
1555	148,805,000
1556	173,685,000
1557	158,600,000
1558	153,355,000
1559	63,205,000
1560	157,865,000
1561	166,810,000
1562	44,825,000
1563	144,028,000
1564	139,928,000
1565-1568	179,855,000
1569-1570	161,863,200
1571	145,640,000
1572-1575	168,655,000
1576	146,615,000
1577-1578	146,195,000
1579	739,430,000
1580	878,690,000
1629-1631	219,455,000
1632	157,825,000
1633-1682	436,005,000
1683	159,915,000
1684	159,060,000
1685	158,470,000
1686	1,990,000
1687	1,983,000
1688	1,953,000
1689	1,903,000
1690	164,890,000
1691-1694	208,035,000
1695-1698	185,715,000
1699	130,592,000
1700	158,322,800
1701	809,955,000
1702-1703	963,370,000
1704	150,328,000
1705	176,830,000
1706-1709	195,976,000
1710	208,820,000
1711	192,250,000
1712-1715	219,830,000
1716	159,852,000
1717-1720	188,310,000
1721	163,625,000
1722	156,296,000
1723-1724	158,678,000
1725	154,495,000
1726	168,050,000
1727	158,810,000
1728	153,736,000
1729	882,260,000
1730	921,530,000
1731	156,560,000
1732-1733	202,155,000
1744	156,525,000
1745-1748	165,182,400
1749-1752	157,598,400
1753	102,856,000
1754	152,270,000
1755	94,600,000
1756	151,570,000
1757	15,170,400
1758	161,228,000
1759	158,880,000
1760-1763	186,550,000
1764-1767	168,136,000
1768	963,120,000
1769	916,800,000
1770	159,297,600
1771	166,435,000
1772	162,535,000
1773	155,000,000
1774	157,310,000
1775-1778	174,096,000
1779-1782	164,793,600
1783-1786	163,055,000
1787	161,860,000
1788	165,775,000
1789	160,000,000
1790	67,195,000
1791-1794	186,905,000
1795-1798	208,295,000
1799	873,710,000
1800	931,880,000
1801	161,290,000
1802	172,740,000
1803	168,995,000
1804	160,000,000
1805-1810	232,134,000
1821	163,510,000
1822	256,620,000
1823	95,695,000
1824	153,975,000
1825	160,000,000
1826	103,850,000
1827-1830	204,715,000
1831	166,545,000
1832	163,310,000
1833	160,000,000
1834-1837	152,404,000
1838-1841	152,420,000
1842	692,500,000
1843	718,715,000
1874	160,155,000
1875	159,505,000
1876-1879	210,633,000
1910	165,175,000
1911	107,240,000
1912-1919	337,819,000
1920	99,420,000
1921-1924	178,930,000
1925	100,265,000
1926	99,615,000
1927	97,535,000
1928-1931	167,308,000
1932	101,625,000
1933	99,170,000
1934	101,155,000
1935	101,200,000
1936	167,360,000
1937-1938	162,420,000
1939	597,720,000
1940	792,600,000
1941	167,130,000
1942-1945	191,560,000
1950	163,939,200
1952	180,700,000
1953-2002	666,950,000
2003	109,245,000
2004	112,535,000
2006-2009	126,640,000
2010	107,605,000
2011	173,160,000
2012	107,285,000
2013	109,040,000
2014	183,270,000
2015	169,495,000
2016	164,235,000
2017	110,130,000
2018	110,995,000
2019-2022	165,340,000
2023	174,180,000
2024	110,261,000
2026	703,295,000
2027-2030	788,880,000
2031	118,555,000
2032-2035	226,128,000
2036	118,225,000
2037	114,290,000
2038	165,000,000
2039	120,430,000
2040	117,025,000
2041	181,700,000
2042	114,250,000
2043	111,775,000
2044	115,200,000
2045	108,820,000
2046	184,950,000
2047	110,925,000
2048-2051	395,424,000
2052	104,340,000
2053	114,725,000
2054	112,525,000
2055-2058	193,055,000
2059-2062	207,725,000
2063	715,975,000
2064	848,525,000
2065	165,000,000
2066	120,000,000
2067-2070	319,675,000
2071	103,975,000
2072	554,675,000
2073	120,000,000
2074	106,975,000
2075	107,325,000
2076-2079	306,912,000
2080	120,000,000
2081	108,000,000
2082-2085	313,350,000
2086	130,320,000
2087	120,000,000
2088	117,050,000
2089	115,725,000
2090	116,600,000
2091	120,000,000
2092	123,575,000
2093	120,000,000
2094	117,125,000
2095	117,225,000
2096	95,525,000
2097	119,125,000

2098-2101	216,260,000
2102	120,000,000
2103	108,140,000
2104	117,625,000
2105	112,896,000
2106	116,500,000
2107	751,300,000
2108	786,225,000
2109	105,300,000
2110	124,500,000
2137	120,000,000
2138-2141	300,000,000
2142	120,580,000
2143	729,700,000
2144	124,750,000
2145	203,496,000
2146	126,325,000
2147	130,000,000
2152	119,975,000
2153	120,000,000
2154	119,975,000
2155-2158	147,940,000
2159	120,000,000
2160-2163	130,000,000
2164	120,000,000
2165	759,200,000
2166	757,600,000
2198-2201	67,996,800
2202	947,450,000
2203	130,000,000
2204	136,500,000
2205-2209	219,990,000
2210	130,000,000
2211	130,000,000
2216	5,825,050
2217	5,825,050
2218	5,825,050
2219	5,825,050
2220-2223	130,000,000
2224	220,725,000
2235-2238	240,525,000
2239	131,700,000
2240-2243	240,000,000
2244	690,100,000
2245	882,150,000
2246	167,430,000
2247	166,555,000
2248	811,560,000
2249	142,905,000
2250	130,000,000
2251	149,980,000
2267-2274	610,425,000
2275	156,995,000
2286-2335	645,975,000
2336	166,725,000
2337	186,575,000
2338	184,325,000
2339	165,845,000
2340	155,170,000
2341	102,100,000
2342	103,325,000
2343	162,045,000
2344	153,925,000
2345	160,425,000
2346	183,290,000
2347	179,800,000
2348	164,130,000
2349	157,475,000
2350	156,225,000
2351-2354	163,980,000
2355-2359	584,340,000
2360	168,995,000
2361	163,120,000
2362-2366	394,776,000
2367	528,790,000
2368	978,340,000
2369	158,870,000
2370	145,560,000
2371	97,300,000
2372-2375	158,556,000
2376	97,300,000
2377	153,045,000
2378	841,240,000
2379	169,765,000
2380	157,215,000
2381-2385	635,238,000
2386-2389	162,142,500
2390-2393	305,015,000
2395-2398	480,000,000
2399	821,285,000
2400	1,030,850,000
2401	165,495,000
2402	151,675,000
2403	163,000,000
2404	264,625,000
2405-2409	204,984,000
2410	103,835,000
2411	152,250,000
2412	138,760,000
2413	137,985,000
2414	138,850,000
2415	150,545,000
2416	164,680,000
2417	262,755,000
2418	191,755,000
2420	188,400,000
2421	191,860,000
2422-2425	406,988,000
2426	137,410,000
2427	913,335,000
2428	900,000,000
2429	399,243,000
2433	2,017,225
2434-2437	163,824,000
2438	2,047,200
2439	173,000,000
2440	886,220,000
2441	995,178,000
2442	153,125,000

2444	169,495,000
2445-2448	176,808,000
2449	150,000,000
2470-2474	733,608,000
2496-2500	178,587,500
2501-2505	619,128,000
2506-2507	151,430,000
2508-2511	278,264,000
2512	143,995,000
2513	142,692,000
2517	728,919,000
2515	599,400,000
2516	320,304,000
2532	103,648,000
2533	179,990,000
2534	150,560,000
2538	161,498,000
2545-2549	744,918,000
2550	149,848,000
2551	200,003,000
2552	200,000,000
2553-2557	170,025,600
2558	150,310,000
2559	15,218,000
2560	149,810,000
2561	149,260,000
2562-2566	699,978,000
2567	148,973,000
2577a	33,394,800
2615a	32,000,000
2616	148,665,000
2617	149,990,000
2618	835,000,000
2619	160,000,000
2623a	40,005,000
2624	1,185,170
2625	1,185,170
2626	1,185,170
2627	1,185,170
2628	1,185,170
2629	1,185,170
2630	148,000,000
2634a	37,315,000
2635	146,610,000
2636	160,000,000
2641a	32,000,000
2646a	87,728,000
2696a	11,000,000
2697	12,000,000
2698	105,000,000
2699	142,500,000
2703a	36,831,000
2704	85,000,000
2709a	80,000,000
2720	105,000,000
2721	517,000,000
2722	150,000,000
2723	152,000,000
2730a	14,285,715
2731	98,841,000
2732	32,947,000
2733	32,947,000
2734	32,947,000
2735	65,894,000
3736	65,894,000
2737	65,894,000
2745a	140,000,000
2746	105,000,000
2747	110,000,000
2748	110,000,000
2749	172,870,000
2753a	65,625,000
2754	110,000,000
2755	115,870,000
2759a	40,000,000
2764a	199,784,500
2765	12,000,000
2766	160,000,000
2770a	128,735,000
2774a	25,000,000
2778a	170,000,000
2782a	37,500,000
2784a	41,840,000
2788a	37,550,000
2804	88,300,000
2805	105,000,000
2806	100,000,000
2806a	250,000,000
2811a	35,800,000
2812	150,500,000
2813	357,949,584
2814	830,000,000
2814C	300,000,000
2815	274,800,000
2816	155,500,000
2817	105,000,000
2818	185,500,000
2828a	18,600,000
2833a	166,000,000
2834	201,000,000
2835	300,000,000
2836	269,370,000
2837	60,000,000
2838	12,060,000
2839	209,000,000
2840	20,000,000
2841	12,958,000
2842	100,500,000
2847a	159,200,000
2848	150,500,000
2853a	34,436,000
2854	24,986,000
2855	24,986,000
2856	24,986,000
2857	19,988,800
2858	19,988,800
2859	19,988,800
2860	19,988,800
2861	19,988,800

2862	150,750,000
2866a	56,475,000
2868a	77,748,000
2869	20,000,000
2870	150,186
2871	518,500,000
2872	602,500,000
2873	236,997,600
2874	45,000,000
2875	5,000,000
2876	80,000,000
2948	214,700,000
2949	1,220,970,000
2950	94,500,000
2954a	50,000,000
2955	80,000,000
2956	97,000,000
2957	315,000,000
2958	300,000,000
2965a	30,000,000
2966	125,000,000
2967	400,000,000
2968	92,424,000
2973a	120,200,000
2974	60,000,000
2975	300,000,000
2979a	62,500,000
2980	105,000,000
2981	10,000,000
2982	150,000,000
2983-2992	15,000,000
2992	15,000,000
2997a	200,000,000
2998	300,000,000
2999	85,000,000
3000	300,000,000
3001	80,000,000
3002	80,000,000
3003	300,000,000
3007a	75,000,000
3008	350,495,000
3009	350,495,000
3010	350,495,000
3011	350,495,000
3013	90,000,000
3023a	30,000,000
3024	120,000,000
3029a	160,000,000
3030	2,550,000,000
3058	92,100,000
3059	115,600,000
3060	93,150,000
3064a	23,292,500
3065	111,000,000
3066	314,175,000
3067	209,450,000
3068	16,207,500
3069	153,300,000
3070	100,000,000
3071	60,120,000
3076a	27,850,000
3080a	22,218,000
3081	95,600,000
3082	300,000,000
3086a	23,681,250
3087	133,613,000
3088	103,400,000
3089	60,000,000
3090	134,000,000
3095a	32,000,000
3099a	23,025,000
3103a	23,025,000
3104	300,000,000
3105	14,910,000
3106	93,612,000
3107	243,575,000
3111a	56,479,000
3112	847,750,000
3116a	451,312,500
3117	495,504,000
3118	103,520,000
3120	106,000,000
3121	112,000,000
3123	1,660,000,000
3124	814,000,000
3125	122,000,000
3131a	65,000,000
3134	97,500,000
3135	96,000,000
3136	14,600,000
3137	37,800,000
3138	118,000
3139	593,775
3140	592,849
3141	42,250,000
3142	8,050,000
3146a	22,500,000
3147	20,000,000
3148	20,000,000
3149	10,000,000
3150	10,000,000
3151	7,000,000
3152	195,000,000
3153	323,000,000
3157a	21,500,000
3158-3161	12,900,000
3162-3165	8,600,000
3166	22,250,000
3167	45,250,000
3172a	36,250,000
3173	173,000,000
3174	37,000,000
3175	133,000,000
3176	882,500,000
3177	1,621,465,000
3178	15,000,000
3179	51,000,000
3180	80,000,000
3181	45,000,000

3182	12,533,000
3183	12,533,000
3184	12,533,000
3185	12,533,000
3186	12,533,000
3187	12,533,000
3188	8,000,000
3189	6,000,000
3190	6,000,000
3191	8,250,000
3192	30,000,000
3193-3197	250,000,000
3198-3202	80,000,000
3203	85,000,000
3204	39,600,000
3205	650,000
3206	32,000,000
3209	2,200,000
3210	2,200,000
3211	30,000,000
3212-3215	45,000,000
3216-3219	45,000,000
3220	46,300,000
3221	30,000,000
3222-3225	70,000,000
3226	65,000,000
3227	50,000,000
3230-3234	180,000,000
3235	28,000,000
3236	4.000.000
3237	130,750,000
3238-3242	185,000,000
3243	50,000,000
3244	925,200,000
3245-3248	116,760,000
3249-3252	991,750,000
3272	51,000,000
3273	100,000,000
3274	1,000,000,000
3275	
3276	100,000,000
3286	40,400,000
3287	42,500,000
3288-3292	73,155,000
3293	10,000,000
3306	42,700,000
3307	500,000
3308	42,500,000
3309	105,000,000
3310-3313	1,500,000,000
3314	145,375,000
3315	78,100,000
3316	89,270,000
3317-3320	141,175,000
3321-3324	151,976,000
3325-3328	116,038,500
3329	75,500,000
3330	100,750,000
3331	101,800,000
3332	43,150,000
3333-3337	120,000,000
3338	42,500,000
3339-3344	42,500,000
3345-3350	42,500,000
3351	4,235,000
3352	65,000,000
3354	44,600,000
3355	1,555,560,000
3356-3359	116,500,000
3360-3363	1,785,060,000
3364-3367	118,125,000
3368	95,000,000
3369	120,000,000

Quantities for Nos. 3370-on, and for Nos. 3190, 3191 and 3236, are for quantities ordered.

3370	56,000,000
3371	150,000,000
3372	65,150,000
3373-3377	15,000,000
3378	10,000,000
3379-3383	55,000,000
3384-3388	105,350,000
3389	16,000,000
3390	55,000,000
3391	30,000,000
3392	236,000
3393-3396	55,000,000
3397	90,600,000
3398	200,000,000
3399-3402	88,000,000
3403	4,000,000
3408	11,250,000
3409	1,695,000
3410	1,695,000
3411	1,695,000
3412	1,695,000
3413	1,695,000
3413-3417	100,000,000
3438	53,000,000
3439-3443	85,000,000
3444	53,000,000
3445	125,000,000
3446	52,000,000
3496	500,000,000
3497	1,500,000,000
3498	80,000,000
3499	180,000,000
3500	55,000,000
3501	200,000,000
3502	125,000,000
3503	100,000,000
3504	35,000,000
3505	1,598,000
3506	8,960,000
3507	125,000,000
3508	200,000,000
3509	55,000,000
3510-3519	125,000,000
3521	55,000,000
3523	110,000,000
3524-3527	96,000,000
3528-3531	100,000,000
3532	75,000,000
3533	30,000,000
3534a	275,000,000
3535	236,000
3536	800,000,000
3537-3540	125,000,000
3537a-3540a	1,500,000,000
3541-3544	201,000,000
3545	32,000,000
3546	69,000,000
3547	49,000,000
3548	40,000,000
3551	100,000,000
3552-3555	80,000,000
3556	125,000,000
3557	120,000,000
3558	75,000,000
3559	70,000,000
3560	55,000,000
3561-3610	200,000,000
3611	7,000,000
3649	3,000,000
3650	70,000,000
3651	61,000,000
3652	61,000,000
3653-3656	200,000,000
3657	1,500,000,000
3658	150,000,000
3659	75,000,000
3660	62,800,000
3661-3664	111,000,000
3665-3668	61,000,000
3669	61,000,000
3670-3671	200,000,000
3672	35,000,000
3673	40,000,000
3674	35,000,000
3675	739,200,000
3676-3679	125,000,000
3680-3683	300,000,000
3684-3687	1,705,000,000
3688-3691	200,000,000
3692	80,000,000
3694	1,610,000
3695	50,000,000
3696-3745	200,000,000
3746	150,000,000
3747	70,000,000
3748	70,000,000
3771	60,000,000
3772	7,000,000
3773	50,000,000
3774	55,000,000
3776-3780	60,000,000
3781	75,000,000
3782	54,000,000
3783	85,000,000
3786	80,000,000
3787-3791	125,000,000
3802	6,000,000
3803	86,800,000
3804-3807	778,800,000
3808-3811	70,000,000
3812	52,000,000
3813	72,000,000
3814-3818	80,000,000
3820	700,000,000
3821-3824	1,875,000,000
3825-3828	200,990,000
3831	7,600,000
3832	80,000,000
3833	750,000,000
3834	130,000,000
3835	172,000,000
3836	750,000,000
3837	150,000,000
3838	60,000,000
3839	80,000,000
3840-3843	57,000,000
3854	62,200,000
3855-3856	20,000,000
3857-3861	57,000,000
3862	96,400,000
3863	71,800,000
3865-3868	284,000,000
3869	45,800,000
3870	60,000,000
3871	50,000,000
3872	794,000,000
3873	8,700,000
3876	100,000,000
3877	96,400,000
3878	8,336,000
3879	776,400,000
3881	60,000,000
3882	45,000,000
3883-3886	125,000,000
3887-3890	200,990,000
3891-3894	270,000,000
3895	4,500,000
3896	150,000,000
3897	170,000,000
3898	1,500,000,000
3899	5,600,000
3900-3903	790,000,000
3904	45,000,000
3905	40,000,000
3906-3909	50,000,000
3910	5,000,000
3911	65,000,000
3912-3915	215,000,000
3916-3925	110,000,000
3926-3929	420,000,000
3930	40,000,000
3931-3935	640,000,000
3936	75,000,000
3937	5,000,000
3938	65,000,000
3939-3942	70,000,000
3943	40,000,000
3944	21,000,000
3945-3948	70,000,000
3949-3952	200,000,000
3953-3956	800,000,000
3957-3960	100,000,000
3961-3964	60,000,000
3976	600,000,000
3987-3994	192,000,000
3995	60,000,000
3996	150,000,000
3997	5,000,000
3998-3999	200,000,000
4020	100,000,000
4021-4024	40,000,000
4025-4028	175,000,000
4029	400,000,000
4030	30,000,000
4031	80,000,000
4032	50,000,000
4033-4072	204,000,000
4073	40,000,000
4074	1,000,000
4075	3,000,000
4076	3,000,000
4077	75,000,000
4078	50,000,000
4079	60,000,000
4080-4083	200,000,000
4084	12,500,000
4085-4088	85,000,000
4089-4098	500,000,000
4099	5,000,000
4100	700,000,000
4101-4104	200,000,000
4105-4108	1,515,000,000
4109-4112	100,000,000
4113-4116	54,000,000
4117	35,000,000
4118	40,000,000
4119	40,000,000
4120	150,000,000
4121	25,000,000
4122	300,000,000
4123	2,000,000
4124	30,000,000
4136	60,000,000
4143	30,000,000
4146-4150	175,000,000
4151	500,000,000
4152	200,000,000
4153-4156	420,000,000
4153a-4156a	280,000,000
4159	12,500,000
4160-4163	36,000,000
4165	500,000,000
4192-4195	200,000,000
4196	60,000,000
4197	55,000,000
4198	5,000,000
4199	80,000,000
4200	40,000,000
4201	40,000,000
4202	40,000,000
4203-4204	80,000,000
4205	100,000,000
4206	700,000,000
4207-4210	1,700,000,000
4211-4214	80,900,000
4215-4218	88,200,000
4219	50,000,000
4220	50,000,000
4221	72,000,000
4222	125,000,000
4223	30,000,000
4224-4227	28,000,000
4228-4252	30,000,000
4265	120,000,000
4266	60,000,000
4270	750,000,000
4271	500,000,000
4272	100,000,000
4273-4282	500,000,000
4283-4292	500,000,000
4293-4302	500,000,000
4303-4312	500,000,000
4333-4322	250,000,000
4333	24,000,000
4334	40,000,000
4335	75,000,000
4336-4340	40,000,000
4341	75,000,000
4342-4345	125,000,000
4346	300,000,000
4349	30,000,000
4350	60,000,000
4351	25,000,000
4352	35,000,000
4353-4357	50,000,000
4358	65,000,000
4359	600,000,000
4360-4363	1,300,000,000
4368-4371	126,324,000
4372	40,000,000
4373	35,000,000
4374	30,000,000
4375	60,000,000
4376	30,000,000
4377	30,000,000
4380-4383	50,000,000
4384	24,000,000
4386	100,000,000
4397	300,000,000
4399-4403	1,000,000,000

Scott No.	Quantity
4404-4405	500,000,000
4406	100,000,000
4407	100,000,000
4408	125,000,000
4409-4413	100,000,000
4414	50,000,000
4415	40,000,000
4416	20,000,000
4417-4420	40,000,000
4421	40,000,000
4422	8,000,000
4423	25,000,000
4424	600,000,000
4425-4428	1,300,000,000
4433	35,000,000
4434	30,000,000
4435	40,000,000
4436	45,000,000
4440-4443	25,000,000
4444	3,000,000
4445	20,000,000
4446-4449	40,000,000
4450	300,000,000
4451-4460	391,400,000
4461	50,000,000
4463	40,000,000
4464	80,000,000
4465-4466	80,000,000
4467-4471	85,000,000
4472	40,000,000
4473	40,000,000
4474	25,000,000
4475	60,000,000
4476	30,000,000
4477	300,000,000
4478-4481	2,000,000,000
4482-4485	157,080,000
4492	80,640,000
4493	50,000,000
4494	100,000,000
4497-4501	60,000,000
4502	100,000,000
4503	50,000,000
4520	300,000,000
4521	75,000,000
4522-4523	60,000,000
4524	160,000,000
4525	40,000,000
4526	40,000,000
4527-4528	60,000,000
4530	50,000,000
4531-4540	300,000,000
4541-4544	30,000,000
4545	50,000,000
4546	36,000,000
4547	60,000,000
4548-4551	60,000,000
4552	20,000,000
4553-4557	200,000,000
4558	60,000,000
4565	100,000,000
4566-4569	40,000,000
4570	600,000,000
4571-4574	600,000,000
4575-4578	900,000,000
4579-4582	252,000,000
4583	25,000,000
4584	35,000,000
4591	50,000,000
4618-4622	400,000,000
4623	72,000,000
4624	80,000,000
4625	50,000,000
4626	300,000,000
4627	40,000,000
4651-4652	150,000,000
4653	70,000,000
4654-4662	20,000,000
4664-4665	30,000,000
4666	20,000,000
4667	40,000,000
4668-4671	25,000,000
4677-4681	125,000,000
4687-4690	40,000,000
4691	40,000,000
4692-4693	30,000,000
4694-4697	80,000,000
4694	3,000,000
4695	3,000,000
4696	3,000,000
4697	3,000,000
4698-4701	25,000,000
4702	20,000,000
4703	25,000,000
4705	20,000,000
4710	39,999,990
4716	12,000,000
4721	55,000,000
4726	31,200,000
4741	311,000,000
4742	83,000,000
4743-4747	95,000,000
4748	23,400,000
4750-4753	92,000,000
4754-4763	400,000,000
4786	30,000,000
4787-4788	10,800,000
4789	60,000,000
4790	30,000,000
4791-4795	81,000,000
4801	30,000,000
4803	40,000,000
4804	59,000,000
4805	26,000,000
4806	13,200,000
4807	60,000,000
4822-4823	81,000,000
4825-4844	100,000,000
4846	17,600,400
4847	50,000,000
4856	33,500,000
4862-4865	500,000,000
4866	30,000,000
4880	60,000,000
4882-4891	400,000,000
4892	20,000,000
4898-4905	60,000,000
4905b	900,000
4906	30,000,000
4907	35,000,000
4908-4909	100,000,000
4910-4911	10,800,000
4912-4915	100,000,000
4916	50,000,000
4917-4920	100,000,000
4921	30,000,000
4922-4926	20,000,000
4928-4935	80,000,000
4950-4951	50,000,000
4952	30,000,000
4955-4956	200,000,000
4957	17,600,400
4958	30,000,000
4968-4972	20,000,000
4978	45,000,000
4979	80,000,004
4980-4981	10,800,000
4982-4985	80,000,004
4986	50,000,000
4987	60,000,000
4988	30,000,000

Figure for No. 4988 includes Nos. 4822b and 4822c.

Scott No.	Quantity
5003	20,000,000
5008	15,000,000
5009	100,000,000
5010-5011	12,000,000
5012	20,000,000
5019	60,000,000
5020	12,000,000
5036	150,000,000
5056	30,000,000
5057	15,000,000
5059	25,000,000
5060	22,000,000
5062-5063	9,600,000
5064	12,000,000
5065-5068	20,400,000
5069-5076	40,000,000
5077-5078	15,000,000
5079	18,000,000
5080	100,000,000
5091	30,000,000
5092	15,000,000
5093-5097	50,000,000
5100	12,000,000
5105	20,000,000
5132-5135	80,000,000
5141	15,000,000
5142	30,000,000
5149-5152	60,000,000
5153	15,000,000
5154	15,000,000
5155	250,000,000
5171	35,000,000
5173	17,600,000
5175	84,000,000
5179	20,000,000
5180-5189	100,000,000
5190	25,000,000
5192-5197	200,000,000
5199	500,000,000
5200	50,000,000
5202	12,000,000
5203-5210	80,000,000
5211	60,000,000
5212	2,100,000
5213-5222	60,000,000
5223-5227	40,000,000
5228-5232	60,000,000
5241	15,000,000
5242	2,000,000
5251	15,000,000
5252-5253	15,000,000
5253c	500,000
5254	15,000,000
5259	35,000,000
5264-5273	40,000,000
5274	25,000,000
5275	12,000,000
5276-5279	15,000,000
5281	7,500,000
5282	20,000,000
5283	20,000,000
5284	20,000,000
5298	3,000,000
5299	252,000,000
5300	20,000,000
5301-5305	20,000,000
5306	1,500,000
5307-5310	30,000,000
5312-5315	40,000,000
5316	60,000,000
5321-5330	100,000,000
5340	20,100,000
5349	40,000,000
5360	25,000,000
5371	40,000,000
5372-5376	30,000,000
5377	20,000,000
5378-5380	50,400,000
5381	60,000,000
5382-5391	20,000,000
5392	20,000,000
5393	40,000,000
5394	3,875,000
5395-5398	200,000,000

AIR POST STAMPS

Scott No.	Quantity
C1	3,395,854
C2	3,793,887
C3	2,134,888
C4	6,414,576
C5	5,309,275
C6	5,285,775
C7	42,092,800
C8	15,597,307
C9	17,616,350
C10	20,379,179
C11	106,887,675
C12	97,641,200
C13	93,536
C14	72,428
C15	61,296
C16	57,340,050
C17	76,648,803
C18	324,070
C19	302,205,100
C20	10,205,400
C21	12,794,600
C22	9,285,300
C23	349,946,500
C24	19,768,150
C25	4,746,527,700
C26	1,744,878,650
C27	67,117,400
C28	78,434,800
C29	42,359,850
C30	59,880,850
C31	11,160,600
C32	864,753,100
C33	971,903,700
C34	207,976,550
C35	756,186,350
C36	132,956,100
C37	33,244,500
C38	38,449,100
C39	5,070,095,200
C40	75,085,000
C41	260,307,500
C42	21,061,300
C43	36,613,100
C44	16,217,100
C45	80,405,000
C46	18,876,800
C47	78,415,000
C48	50,483,977
C49	63,185,000
C50	72,480,00
C51	1,326,960,000
C52	157,035,000
C53	90,055,200
C54	79,290,000
C55	84,815,000
C56	38,770,000
C57	39,960,000
C58	98,160,000
C59	
C60	1,289,460,000
C61	87,140,000
C62	
C63	
C64	
C65	
C66	42,245,000
C67	
C68	63,890,000
C69	62,255,000
C70	55,710,000
C71	50,000,000
C72	
C73	
C74	60,000,000
C75	
C76	152,364,800
C77	
C78	
C79	
C80	
C81	
C82	
C83	
C84	78,210,000
C85	96,240,000
C86	58,705,000
C87	
C88	
C89	
C90	
C91-C92	
C93-C94	
C95-C96	
C97	
C101-C104	165,000,000
C105-C108	165,000,000
C109-C112	175,000,000
C113	98,600,000
C114	110,475,000
C115	167,625,000
C116	45,700,000
C117	22,975,000
C118	201,150,000
C119	111,550,000
C120	38,532,000
C121	39,325,000
C122-C125	106,360,000

C126	1,944,000
C127	48,000,000
C128	250,000,000
C129	182,400,000
C130	113,000,000
C131	15,260,000
C132	100,000,000
C133	100,750,000
C134	100,750,000
C135	100,800,00
C136	85,000,000
C137	85,000,000
C138	100,000,000
C139	145,000,000
C140	100,000,000
C141	100,000,000
C142	100,000,000
C143	100,000,000
C144	70,000,000
C145	100,000,000
C146	40,000,000
C147	100,000,000
C148	40,000,000
C149	30,000,000
C150	60,000,000

CARRIERS' STAMPS

The term "Carriers' Stamps" is applied to certain stamps of the United States used to defray delivery to a post office on letters going to another post office, and for collection and delivery in the same city (local letters handled only by the carrier department). A less common usage was for a collection fee from the addressee at the post office ("drop letters"). During the period when these were in use, the ordinary postage fee defrayed the carriage of mail matter from post office to post office only.

In many of the larger cities the private ("Local") posts delivered mail to the post office or to an addressee in the city direct for a fee of 1 or 2 cents (seldom more), and adhesive stamps were often employed to indicate payment. (See introduction to "Local Stamps" section.)

Carrier service dates back at least to 1689 when the postmaster of Boston was instructed "to receive all letters and deliver them at 1d." In 1794, the law allowed a penny post to collect 2 cents for the delivery of a letter. As these early fees were paid in cash, little evidence survives.

In 1851 the Federal Government, under the acts of 1825 and 1836, began to deliver letters in many cities and so issued Carriers' stamps for local delivery service. This Act of Congress of March 3, 1851, effective July 1, 1851 (succeeding Act of 1836), provided for the collecting and delivering of letters to the post office by carriers, "for which not exceeding 1 or 2 cents shall be charged."

Carriers' stamps were issued under the authority of, or derived from, the postmaster general. The "General Issues" (Nos. LO1-LO2) were general issues of which No. LO2 was valid for postage at face value, and No. LO1 at the value set upon sale, in any post office. They were issued under the direct authority of the postmaster general. The "City Carrier Department" were valid in the city in which they were issued either directly by or sanctioned by the local postmaster under authority derived from the postmaster general.

These "General" and "City Carrier Department" Carriers' stamps prepaid the fees of official letter carriers who were appointed by the postmaster general and were under heavy bond to the United States for the faithful performance of their duties. Some of the letter carriers received fixed salaries from the government. Others were paid from the fees received for the delivery and collection of letters carried by them. After discontinuance of carrier fees on June 30, 1863, all carriers of the United States Post Office were government employees, paid by salary at a yearly rate.

Some Carriers' stamps are often found on cover with the regular government stamps and have the official post office cancellation applied to them as well. Honour's City Express and the other Charleston, S.C., Carrier stamps almost always have the stamp uncanceled or canceled with pen, or less frequently pencil.

Unless indicated otherwise, values for Carriers' stamps on cover are for covers having the stamp tied by a handstamped cancellation. Carriers' stamps, either uncanceled or pen-canceled, **on covers to which they apparently belong**, also are valued where possible. For covers with stamps canceled by pen or pencil with initials or name of carrier, as sometimes seen on No. LO2 from Washington, and on Baltimore carrier stamps, the premium is 75% of the on-cover value.

All Carriers' stamps are imperforate and on wove paper, either white or colored through, unless otherwise stated.

Counterfeits exist of many Carriers' stamps.

GENERAL ISSUE CARRIER STAMPS

Franklin — OC1

Engraved and printed by Toppan, Carpenter, Casilear & Co.
Plate of 200 subjects divided into two panes of 100 each, one left, one right

1851, Sept. Engr. Unwmk. *Imperf.*

LO1 OC1 (1c) **dull blue** (shades), *rose*	*7,000.*	*8,000.*
On cover from Philadelphia		*17,500.*
On cover from New York		*30,000.*
On cover from New Orleans with 3c #10 (a 2nd #LO1 removed)		*30,000.*
Pair	*18,000.*	*18,000.*
Strip of 3	*26,500.*	*26,000.*
Major plate crack	—	
Major plate crack, on cover		*50,000.*
Corner plate cracks (91L)	—	—
Double transfer	—	—
Double transfer, on cover		*30,000.*

Earliest documented use: Oct. 28, 1851.

Cancellations

Red star (Philadelphia)	*8,000.*
Blue town (Philadelphia)	+1,000.
Red town (New York)	+1,000.
Black town (New York), unique	+4,000.
Blue grid (New York)	—
Black grid (New York)	—
Black grid (New Orleans)	+6,000.
Green grid (New Orleans)	—

Of the entire issue of 310,000 stamps, 250,000 were sent to New York, 50,000 to New Orleans, 10,000 to Philadelphia. However, the quantity sent to each city is not indicative of proportionate use. More appear to have been used in Philadelphia than in the other two cities. The use in all three cities was notably limited.

No. LO1, major plate crack on cover, is unique. The double transfer on cover also is unique, as is the unused pair.

U.S.P.O. Despatch

Eagle — OC2

Engraved and printed by Toppan, Carpenter, Casilear & Co.
Plate of 200 subjects divided into two panes of 100 each, one upper, one lower

1851, Nov. 17 Unwmk. *Imperf.*

LO2 OC2 1c **blue** (shades)	50.00	*80.00*
On cover, used alone		500.00
On cover, precanceled		600.00
On cover, pair or 2 singles		*1,500.*
On cover with 1c #9		*8,500.*
On cover with three 1c #9		*4,500.*
On cover with 3c #11		400.
On cover with 3c #25		—
On cover with 3c #26		*600.*
On cover with strip of 3, 3c #26		—
On cover with 5c #30A and 10c #32		*33,000.*
On cover, tied by town handstamp, with 3c #65 (Washington, D.C.)		*4,500.*
On 3c envelope #U1, #LO2 pen canceled		—
On 3c envelope #U2, tied by handstamp		—
On 3c envelope #U2, #LO2 pen canceled		—
On 3c envelope #U10, not canceled, with certicate		*500.00*
Pair	110.00	*400.00*
Pair on cover (Cincinnati)		*1,250.*
Block of 4	300.00	
Margin block of 8, imprint	*850.00*	
Double transfer	—	—
Double transfer on cover		—

Earliest documented use: Jan. 3, 1852.

Cancellations

Red star	*80.*
Philadelphia	+50.
Cincinnati	+200.
Black grid	—
Blue grid	+300.
Red grid	+300.
Black town	+5.
Blue town	+100.
Red town	+300.
Kensington, Pa. (red)	—
Kensington, Pa. red "3c"	—
Washington, D.C.	+1,000.
Blue squared target	—
Red squared target	—
Railroad	—
Black carrier (Type C32)	—
Red carrier (Type C32)	—
Carrier's initial, manuscript	—

Used principally in Philadelphia, Cincinnati, Washington, D.C., and Kensington, Pa.

GOVERNMENT REPRINTS

Printed by the Continental Bank Note Co. (first and second printings) and American Bank Note Co. (third printing).

First reprinting-10,000 stamps of each design, on May 19, 1875 (all sold).

Second reprinting-10,000 stamps of each design, on Dec. 22, 1875 (all sold).

Third reprinting of Franklin stamp - 1881 (2,110 sold).

Third reprinting of Eagle stamp - 1881 (9,680 sold).

The first reprinting of the Franklin stamp was on the rose paper of the original, obtained from Toppan, Carpenter, Casilear & Co. Two batches of ink were used, both darker than the original. The second reprinting was on rose paper using ink that fluoresces green. The third reprinting was on much thicker, paler paper in an indigo color. All of these differ under ultraviolet light. The design of the reprints is not as distinct as the original design and may appear a bit "muddy" in the lathework above the vignette.

The first two reprintings of 10,000 each of the Eagle stamp are on the same hard white paper used for special printings of the postage issue. Stamps from the second reprinting were printed with ink that fluoresces green. Stamps from the third reprinting are on thick wove paper using ink that does not fluoresce. Reprints may be differentiated from the originals under ultraviolet light by the whiteness of the paper. Nos. LO3-LO6 are ungummed, Nos. LO1-LO2 have brown gum. No. LO1 was printed on a somewhat yellowish paper.

Franklin Reprints

1875 *Imperf.*

LO3 OC1 (1c) **blue,** *rose*	50.
indigo, *rose*	70.
Block of 4	225.
Margin block of 4, imprint	—
Corner plate cracks (91L)	100.

Short transfer —

Perf. 12

LO4 OC1 (1c) **blue** *16,000.*
Pair *35,000.*

No. LO4 is valued in the grade of average to fine.

Eagle Reprints

Imperf.

LO5 OC2 1c **blue** 25.
Block of 4 125.
Margin block of 8, imprint & Pl.# —

Perf. 12

LO6 OC2 1c **blue** 175.
Block of 4 1,000.
Margin block of 8, imprint & Pl.# *12,500.*

No. LO6 is valued with the perfs cutting slightly into the design.

CITY CARRIER DEPARTMENT STAMPS

All are imperforate.

Baltimore, Md.

C1

1850-55 Typo. Settings of 10 (2x5) varieties

1LB1 C1 1c **red** (shades), *bluish* 180. 160.
On cover, tied by handstamp *1,000.*
On cover with 1c #9 —
On cover (tied) with 3c #11 *500.*
On cover (tied) with 3c #11A *500.*
1LB2 C1 1c **blue** (shades), *bluish* 200. 150.
On cover, tied *1,000.*
On cover (tied) with 3c #11 *500.*
On cover, uncanceled, with 3c #11A *225.*
a. Bluish laid paper — —
1LB3 C1 1c **blue** (shades) 160. 100.
On cover, tied by handstamp *1,500.*
On cover, tied by ms. *250.*
Block of 4 *1,000.*
a. Laid paper 200. 150.
On cover, tied by handstamp *1,000.*
b. Block of 14 containing three tete-beche gutter pairs (unique) *6,250.*
1LB4 C1 1c **green** — 1,000.
On cover, tied by handstamp *5,000.*
On cover, not tied *1,200.*
On cover with 1c #7, tied by handstamp *2,250.*
On cover, not tied, with 3c #10A *2,000.*
On cover with 3c #11, ms. tied —
On 3c envelope #U10 *3,500.*
Pair *5,000.*
1LB5 C1 1c **red** 2,250. 1,750.
On cover, tied by handstamp *4,500.*
On cover, not tied *3,000.*
On cover (tied) with 3c #10 or 10A *5,000.*

The No. 1LB4 pair is the unique multiple of this stamp.

Cancellations on Nos. 1LB1-1LB5:

Black grid —
Blue grid —
Black cross —
Black town —
Blue town +100.
Black numeral —
Blue numeral —
Black pen —

C2

1856 Typo.

1LB6 C2 1c **blue** (shades) 130. 90.
On cover 400.
On cover with 3c #11 or 11A *1,000.*
On cover with 3c #25 (both tied) *1,350.*
On cover with 3c #26 *1,250.*
On cover with 3c #26A —
1LB7 C2 1c **red** (shades) 130. 90.
On cover *300.*
On cover (tied) with 3c #25 *350.*
On cover (tied) with 3c #26 *350.*
On 3c envelope #U9, tied *300.*
On 3c envelope #U10, tied *350.*
Block of 4 *850.*

C3

The sheet consisted of at least four panes of 10 placed horizontally, the two center panes tete beche. This makes possible five horizontal tete beche gutter pairs.

Plate of 10 (2x5); 10 Varieties

1857 Typo.

1LB8 C3 1c **black** (shades) 65. 50.
On cover, tied by handstamp *125.*
On cover, tied by handstamp, to Germany *3,750.*
On cover (tied) with 3c #26 225.
On 3c envelope #U9, tied *225.*
On 3c envelope #U10 *225.*
On 3c envelope #U27, tied *250.*
Strip of 3 (not tied), on cover *4,000.*
Block of 4 275.
Pane of 10 *1,000.*
Tete beche gutter pair *650.*
a. "SENT," Pos. 7 100. 75.
On cover, tied by handstamp *175.*
On cover (tied) with 3c #26 *250.*
On 3c envelope #U9, tied *250.*
On 3c envelope #U10, tied *250.*
b. Short rays, Pos. 2 100. 75.
On cover (tied) with 3c #26 *600.*
c. "ONS," Pos. 5 — —
d. "ONS" and "SENTS," late state Pos. 7, on cover —

Cancellations

Black pen (or pencil) 20.00
Blue town +2.50
Black town +2.50
Black Steamship —

1LB9 C3 1c **red** (shades) 100. 90.
On cover *175.*
On cover (tied) with 3c #26 *300.*
On 3c envelope #U9 *325.*
On 3c envelope #U10 *325.*
Block of 6 *2,750.*
a. "SENT," Pos. 7 140. 110.
On cover (tied) with 3c #26 *500.*
b. Short rays, Pos. 2 140. 110.
c. As "b," double impression *800.*

The block of 6 of No. 1LB9 is the only recorded multiple of this stamp.

Cancellations on Nos. 1LB6-1LB7, 1LB9:

Black town —
Blue town —
Blue numeral —
Black pen —
Carrier's initial, manuscript +25.

Boston, Mass.

C6

Several Varieties

1849-50 Pelure Paper Typeset

3LB1 C6 1c **blue** 375. 180.
On cover, tied by handstamp 300.
On cover, uncanceled 150.
On cover with 5c #1 *4,500.*
On cover with two 5c #1 *8,750.*
On cover with 3c #10 *450.*
a. Wrong ornament at left *400.*
On cover, not tied, with certificate —

Cancellations

Red town —
Red grid —
Black ornate double oval —
Black "Penny Post Paid" in 3-bar circle —

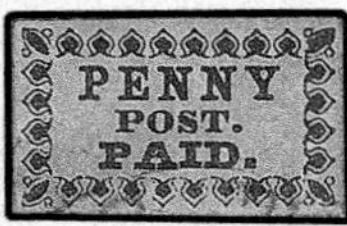

C7

Several Varieties

1851 Wove Paper Colored Through Typeset

3LB2 C7 1c **blue** (shades), *slate* 190. 100.
On cover 220.
On cover with 5c #1 *12,500.*
On cover with 3c #10 500.
On cover with 3c #11A 325.
On 3c envelope #U2, #U5 or #U9 350.
Tete beche gutter pair *600.*

Cancellations on Nos. 3LB2:

Black small fancy circle —
Black diamond grid +100.
Red town —
Black grid —
Black PAID —
Black crayon —
Red small fancy circle +50.
Red diamond grid +100.
Black railroad —
Black hollow star —
Black pencil —
Red crayon —
Black "Penny Post Paid" in 3-bar circle —
Red "Penny Post Paid" in 3-bar circle —

Charleston, S. C.

John H. Honour was appointed a letter carrier at Charleston, in 1849, and engaged his brother-in-law, E. J. Kingman, to assist him. They separated in 1851, dividing the carrier business of the city between them. At the same time Kingman was appointed a letter carrier. In March, 1858, Kingman retired, being replaced by Joseph G. Martin. In the summer of 1858, John F. Steinmeyer, Jr., was added to the carrier force. When Honour retired in 1860, John C. Beckman was appointed in his place.

Each of these carriers had stamps prepared. These stamps were sold by the carriers. The Federal Government apparently encouraged their use.

Honour's City Express

C8

1849 Typo. Wove Paper Colored Through

4LB1 C8 2c **black**, *brown rose* *10,000.*
Cut to shape *4,000.* *4,000.*
On cover, not canceled, with certificate *17,000.*
On cover, cut to shape, tied, with 10c #2 *40,000.*
4LB2 C8 2c **black**, *yellow*, cut to shape —
On cover, not tied, with certificate *12,500.*
On cover, cut to shape, uncanceled —
On cover, rectangular-cut, tied, with 10c #2 —

Cancellations on Nos. 4LB1-4LB2: Red grid, red town, red crayon.

No. 4LB1 unused is a unique uncanceled stamp on piece. The used cut-to-shape stamp is also unique. Additionally, each of the listed covers bearing No. 4LB1 is unique.

Four examples of No. 4LB2 are recorded, each listing above being unique.

4LB2A C8 2c **black**, *bluish gray*, on cover, cut to shape —

No. 4LB2A is unique.

C10

1854 Wove Paper Typeset

4LB3 C10 2c **black** *1,500.*
On cover, tied by pen cancel *3,000.*
On cover with 3c #11 or 11A, tied *4,000.*
On cover with 3c #11 or 11A, not tied *3,250.*

Cancellations

Black town —
Blue town —
Black pen —
Black pencil —
Brown "PAID" —
Initial "H" —

C11

Several Varieties

1849-50 Typeset

Wove Paper Colored Through

4LB5 C11 2c **black**, *bluish*, pelure *750.* *500.*
On cover (not tied) *3,250.*
On cover with pair 5c #1b —
On cover with two 5c #1b —
On cover (tied) with 3c #11 or 11A *4,500.*
a. "Ceuts" *5,750.*

4LB7 C11 2c **black**, *yellow* 750. 1,000.
On cover, tied by handstamp 9,000.
On cover, not canceled 2,000.
a. "Ccnts," ms. tied on cover 14,500.

No. 4LB5a is unique. It is without gum and is valued thus. No. 4LB7a also is unique.

The varieties of type C11 on bluish wove (thicker) paper and pink, pelure paper are not believed genuine.

Cancellation Nos. 4LB5, 4LB7:

Red town —
Black pen —
Red pen —
Red crayon —

C13

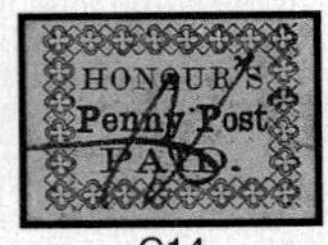
C14

C15

Several varieties of each type

1851-58 **Typeset**

Wove Paper Colored Through

4LB8 C13 2c **black**, *bluish* 350. 175.
On cover, tied by handstamp 700.
On cover, not tied 300.
On cover with 10c #2 5,500.
On cover, tied, with 3c #10 1,500.
On cover, tied, with 3c #11 or 11A 1,500.
On cover, tied, with 3c #26 1,500.
Pair 1,500.
a. Period after "PAID" 500. 250.
On cover 650.
On cover, ms. tied, with 5c #1, tied 19,000.
On cover, ms. tied, with 3c #11 or 11A 750.
b. "Cens" 700. 900.
On cover, ms. tied, with 3c #11 or 11A 3,250.
c. "Conours" and "Bents" —

The No. 4LB8 with No. 2 combination cover is unique. It is a cover front only and is valued thus.

No. 4LB8a on cover with 5c No. 1 is unique.

4LB9 C13 2c **black**, *bluish*, pelure 850. 950.
4LB10 C13 2c **black**, *pink*, pelure, on cover 7,000.
4LB11 C14 (2c) **black**, *bluish* — 375.
On cover, tied by handstamp, with 3c #11 or 11A 12,500.
On cover, ms. tied, with 3c #11 or 11A 3,000.
On 3c envelope #U10, tied 1,500.
On cover, tied, to foreign destination (Ireland), unique 25,000.
4LB12 C14 (2c) **black**, *bluish*, pelure —
4LB13 C15 (2c) **black**, *bluish* ('58) 750. 400.
On cover with 3c #11A, Aiken, S.C. postmark, tied by handstamp (unique) 6,000.
On cover with 3c #26, tied by pen cancel 4,500.
On cover with 3c #26, tied by handstamp cancel 3,750.
Horiz. pair 3,500.
a. Comma after "PAID" 1,100.
b. No period after "Post" 1,400.

The pair of No. 4LB13 is the unique multiple of this stamp.

A 2c of design C13 exists on pink pelure paper. It is believed not to have been issued by the post, but to have been created later and perhaps accidentally.

Cancellations on Nos. 4LB8-4LB13

Black town —
Blue town —
Red town —
Black pen —
Black pencil —
Red crayon —
Brown cork initial "H"

Kingman's City Post

C16

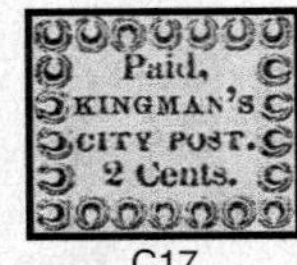
C17

Several varieties of each

Wove Paper Colored Through

1851(?)-58(?) **Typeset**

4LB14 C16 2c **black**, *bluish* 1,400. 900.
Vert. pair, ms. tied, on Valentine cover 6,000.
On cover with 3c #11 7,000.
On cover with 3c #26 6,000.
a. "Kingman's" erased 5,000.

4LB15 C17 2c **black**, *bluish* 800. 800.
On cover —
Vertical pair —
Horiz. pair, not tied, on Valentine cover 8,750.
Vertical strip of 3 uncanceled, on cover 22,500.
a. "Kingman's" erased, on cover with 3c #11, tied by pen cancel (unique) 4,500.

The No. 4LB14 pair on cover is the only recorded multiple of this stamp.

The 4LB15 pair and strip of 3 actually are uncanceled on covers and are valued thus. The horiz. pair on cover is ms. canceled.

Cancellations on Nos. 4LB14-4LB15: Black town, black pen.

Martin's City Post

C18

Several Varieties

1858 **Wove Paper Colored Through** **Typeset**

4LB16 C18 2c **black**, *bluish* 8,000.

Beckman's City Post

Same as C19, but inscribed: "Beckmann's City Post."

1860

4LB17 C19 2c **black**, on cover —

No. 4LB17 is unique. It is on cover with 3c No. 26, both tied by black circle townmark: "CHARLESTON, S.C. JUN 18, 1860".

Steinmeyer's City Post

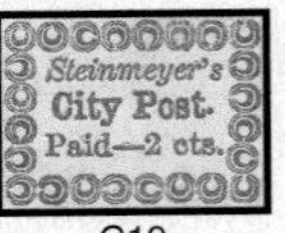
C19

C20

Several varieties of Type C19

Type C20 printed from plate of 10 (2x5) varieties

1859 **Wove Paper Colored Through** **Typeset**

4LB18 C19 2c **black**, *bluish* 21,000.
On cover, uncanceled —
4LB19 C20 2c **black**, *bluish* 4,500. —
4LB20 C20 2c **black**, *pink* 200.
Block of 4 850.
Sheet of 10 2,250.
4LB21 C20 2c **black**, *yellow* 200.
Block of 4 850.
Sheet of 10 2,250.

Sheets of 10 of Nos. 4LB20-4LB21 exist signed by J.F. Steinmeyer Jr. These sell for about 50% more than the unsigned sheets.

Two examples of No. 4LB18 are known on cover, both uncanceled.

Cancellation on Nos. 4LB19-4LB21: Black pen.

Cincinnati, Ohio

Williams' City Post

Organized by C. C. Williams, who was appointed and commissioned by the Postmaster General.

C20a

1854 **Wove Paper** **Litho.**

9LB1 C20a 2c **brown** — 4,000.
On cover, tied by handstamp —
On cover, tied by pen cancel 4,500.
On cover with 1c #9 7,500.
Pair 7,500.

Cancellations

Red squared target —
Black pen —
Blue company circle —

Frazer & Co.

Local stamps of designs L146-L147 were carrier stamps when used on cover between Feb. 3, 1848 and June 30, 1849.

Cleveland, Ohio

Bishop's City Post

Organized by Henry S. Bishop, "Penny Postman" who was appointed and commissioned by the Postmaster General.

C20b

C20c

1854 **Wove Paper** **Litho.**

10LB1 C20b **blue** 5,000. 4,000.
On cover, tied by handstamp 15,000.
Pair on cover, canceled by pencil, with 3c #11, with certificate 17,000.

Vertically Laid Paper

10LB2 C20c 2c **black**, *bluish* 4,000. 6,000.
On cover —
Pair —
Pair on cover, canceled by pencil, with 3c #11 14,000.

Cancellations on #10LB1-10LB2

Red town —
Red boxed numeral —
Black pencil —
Black pen —

No. 10LB2 unused is unique. It is cut in at bottom and without gum, and is valued thus.

Louisville, Ky.

Wharton's U.S.P.O. Despatch

Carrier Service was first established by the Louisville Post Office about 1854, with one carrier. David B. Wharton, appointed a carrier in 1856, issued an adhesive stamp in 1857, but as he was soon thereafter replaced in the service, it is believed that few, if any, of these stamps were used. Brown & McGill, carriers who succeeded Wharton, issued stamps in April, 1858.

C21

Sheet of 50 subjects in two panes of 25 (5x5) each, one upper, one lower

1857 **Lithographed by Robyn & Co.**

5LB1 C21 (2c) **bluish green** (shades) 125.
Block of 4 650.
Pane of 25 3,250.
Sheet of 50 7,000.

Brown & McGill's U. S. P. O. Despatch

C22

1858, Nov.-1860 **Litho. by Hart & Maypother**

5LB2 C22 (2c) **blue** (shades) 250. 750.
On cover, not tied, with 3c #26 750.
On cover with 3c #26, tied by handstamp 6,250.
Block of 4 1,250.

1858, Feb.-Aug.

5LB3 C22 (2c) **black** 4,500. 15,000.
On cover, not tied, with 3c #26 17,500.

The value for No. 5LB3 used refers to the finer of the two known used (canceled) examples; it is extremely fine and on a piece with a 3c #26.

Cancellations on Nos. 5LB2-5LB3: Blue town, black pencil.

New York, N. Y.

United States City Despatch Post

By an order made on August 1, 1842, the Postmaster General established a carrier service in New York known as the "United States City Despatch Post." Local delivery service had been authorized by the Act of Congress of July 2, 1836.

Greig's City Despatch Post was sold to the U. S. P. O. Department and on August 16, 1842, began operation as the "United States City Despatch Post" under the superintendence of Alexander M. Greig who was appointed a U. S. letter carrier for that purpose.

The Greig circular introducing this service stated that letter boxes had been placed throughout the city, that letters might be sent prepaid or collect, and that registry service was available for an extra 3 cents.

The City Despatch Post stamps were accepted for the service of the United States City Despatch Post. The stamps thus used bear the cancellation of the New York Post Office, usually "U.S." in an octagon which served to indicate that the carrier service was now a government operation (no longer a private local post) as well as a cancellation.

C23

Engraved and printed by Rawdon, Wright & Hatch.

Plate of 42 (6x7) subjects
Wove Paper Colored Through

1842 **Engr.**

6LB1 C23 3c **black**, *grayish* 2,000.
On cover, tied by handstamp 12,000.
On cover, not tied 10,000.
On cover, not tied, with Aug. 16 (1842) cancel, First day of government carrier service 100,000.

Cancellations

Red "U.S" in octagon 2,000.
Red circle "U.S. City Despatch Post" —
Red town —

Used examples that do not bear the official cancellation of the New York Post Office and unused examples are classed as Local stamps. See No. 40L1.

Some examples are canceled by a circular date stamp reading "U.S. CITY DESPATCH POST" or, infrequently, a New York town postmark. When canceled "FREE" in frame they were used as local stamps. See No. 40L1 in Locals section.

No. 6LB3 was the first stamp issued by authority of the U.S.P.O. Department. The 3c denomination included 1 cent in lieu of drop letter postage until June 30, 1845, and the maximum legal carrier fee of 2 cents. Service was discontinued late in November, 1846.

C24

Wove Paper (unsurfaced) Colored Through
Engraved plate of 50 in two panes of 25

1842-45

6LB2 C24 3c **black**, *rosy buff* 5,000.
6LB3 C24 3c **black**, *light blue* 1,500. 750.
On cover, tied by handstamp 2,500.
On cover, not tied 1,000.
Pair 5,000.
Double transfer 1,000.
6LB4 C24 3c **black**, *green* 11,500.
a. 3c **black**, *apple green* —

Some authorities consider No. 6LB2 to be an essay, and No. 6LB4 a color changeling. No. 6LB2 unused is valued without gum.

Glazed Paper, Surface Colored

6LB5 C24 3c **black**, *blue green* (shades) 200. 175.
On cover, tied by handstamp 600.
Five on cover 20,000.
Pair — 400.
Strip of 3 650.
Strip of 4 800.
Strip of 5 —
Ribbed paper — —
Double transfer —
a. Double impression 1,500.
b. 3c **black**, *blue* 650. 300.
On cover 750.
Strip of 3 + single on cover 14,000.
Strip of 3 2,500. —
Block of 12 40,000. —
Ribbed paper —
c. As "b," double impression 1,000.
d. 3c **black**, *green* 1,250. 750.
black, *apple green* 2,000.
Pair 2,750.
On cover 1,250.
Five examples on cover 45,000.
e. As "d," double impression — —
On cover —

Cancellations

Red curved PAID —
Red "U.S City Despatch Post" —
Red "U.S" in octagon —
Red New York —
Red double line circle "U.S. City Despatch Post" —

No. 6LB5 has been noted on cover with the 5c New York signed "R.H.M.," No. 9X1d.

6LB6 C24 3c **black**, *pink*, on cover front 14,500.

No. 6LB6 is unique.

No. 6LB5 Surcharged in Red

1846

6LB7 C24 2c on 3c **black**, *bluish green* 14,000.
On cover, not tied, with certificate 70,000.

The City Dispatch 2c red formerly listed as No. 6LB8 is now listed under Local Stamps as No. 160L1.

U.S. MAIL

C27

Issued by the Postmaster at New York, N.Y.

1849 **Wove Paper, Colored Through** **Typo.**

6LB9 C27 1c **black**, *rose* 100. 100.
On cover, tied by handstamp 350.
On cover with 5c #1 2,000.
Pair 250.
Block of 4 600.

1849-50 **Glazed Surface Paper**

6LB10 C27 1c **black**, *yellow* 100. 100.
On cover, tied by handstamp 350.
On cover with 5c #1 1,500.
Pair 250.
Block of 4 600.
6LB11 C27 1c **black**, *buff* 100. 100.
On cover 250.
On cover, not tied, with 5c #1, with certificate 3,000.
a. Pair, one stamp sideways 2,850.

Cancellations on #6LB9-6LB11

Red town —
Red grid —
Red "PAID" +50.
Black numeral in circle —
Red "N.Y. U.S. CITY MAIL" in circle +150.
Black pen —
Black pencil —

Philadelphia, Pa.

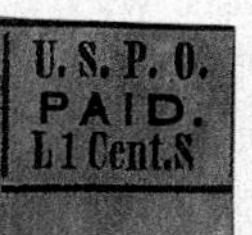

C28

Several Varieties
Thick Wove Paper Colored Through

1849-50 **Typeset**

7LB1 C28 1c **black**, *rose* (with "L P") 450.
On cover, tied by handstamp 3,000.
On cover, not canceled 2,000.
On cover with 5c #1 or 1a 6,000.
7LB2 C28 1c **black**, *rose* (with "S") 3,000.
On cover, not canceled 4,500.
7LB3 C28 1c **black**, *rose* (with "H") 275.
On cover, tied by handstamp 3,750.
On cover, not canceled 1,000.
On cover with 5c #1 3,500.
7LB4 C28 1c **black**, *rose* (with "L S") 400. 500.
On cover, not canceled 3,000.
7LB5 C28 1c **black**, *rose* (with "J J") 7,500.
On cover with 5c #1, uncanceled 70,000.

The unique used No. 7LB5 is an uncanceled stamp on a cover front.

C29

Several Varieties

7LB6 C29 1c **black**, *rose* 300. 250.
On cover, tied by handstamp 2,500.
On cover, uncanceled 500.
7LB7 C29 1c **black**, *blue*, glazed 1,000.
On cover, tied by handstamp 6,500.
On cover, uncanceled 1,250.
On cover with 5c #1 3,500.
7LB8 C29 1c **black**, *vermilion*, glazed 700.
On cover, tied by handstamp 1,500.
On cover, uncanceled 900.
On cover with 5c dark brown #1a, uncanceled 12,500.
On cover with 5c orange brown #1b, uncanceled 21,000.
7LB9 C29 1c **black**, *yellow*, glazed 2,750. 2,250.
On cover, not canceled 4,000.
On cover with 3c #10, uncanceled 2,000.

Cancellations on Nos. 7LB1-7LB9: Normally these stamps were left uncanceled on the letter, but occasionally were accidentally tied by the Philadelphia town postmark which was normally struck in blue ink.

A 1c black on buff (unglazed) of type C29 is believed to be a color changeling.

C30

Settings of 25 (5x5) varieties (Five basic types)

1850-52 **Litho.**

7LB11 C30 1c **gold**, *black*, glazed 175. 110.
On cover, tied by handstamp 600.
On cover, uncanceled 325.
On cover (tied) with 5c #1 3,500.
On cover (tied) with 3c #10 800.
On cover (uncanceled) with 3c #10 250.
Block of 19 8,250.
7LB12 C30 1c **blue** 400. 275.
On cover, tied by handstamp 1,250.
On cover, not tied 400.
On cover (tied) with 3c #10 1,750.
On cover (tied) with 3c #11 1,250.
Pair 1,600.
7LB13 C30 1c **black** 750. 550.
On cover, tied by handstamp 2,500.
On cover, uncanceled 1,250.
On cover (tied) with 3c #10 —
On cover (not tied) with 3c #11 3,250.

Cancellations on #7LB11-7LB13

Red star —
Red town —
Blue town —

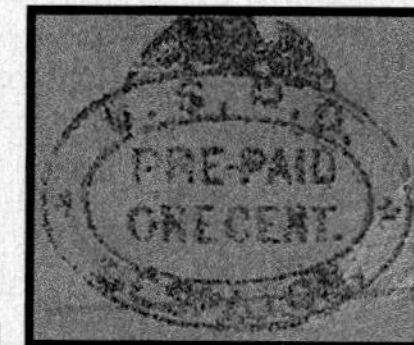

C31

Handstamped

7LB14 C31 1c **blue**, *buff* 3,250.

No. 7LB14 was handstamped on coarse dark buff paper on which rectangles in the approximate size of the type C31 handstamp had been ruled in pencil. The stamps so produced were later cut out and show traces of the adjoining handstamp markings as well as parts of the penciled rectangle. Some uncanceled examples exist on covers.

1855(?)

7LB16 C31 1c **black** 5,000.
On cover with strip of 3, 1c #9 —
On cover with 3c 1851 stamp removed, tied by handstamp 7,000.

C32

1856(?) **Handstamped**

7LB18 C32 1c **black**	*1,250.*	*2,000.*
Paper showing blue plate imprint		*4,000.*
On cover (cut diamond-shaped) with pair 1c #7 and single 1c #9		—
On cover with strip of 3, 1c #7		*17,000.*
On cover with 3c #11		*9,500.*
On 3c envelope #U5		—
On 3c envelope #U10, not canceled		*9,000.*

Cancellations on #7LB16, 7LB18

Black circled grid —
Black town —

Nos. 7LB16 and 7LB18 were handstamped on the sheet margins of U.S. 1851 1c stamps, cut out and used as adhesives. The paper therefore has some surface bluing, and some stamps show parts of the plate imprint.

Values are for stamps cut square unless otherwise mentioned.

ENVELOPES

Handstamps of types C31 and C32 were also used to make stamped envelopes and letter sheets or circulars. These same types were also used as postmarks or cancellations in the same period.

A handstamp similar to C32, but with "U.S.P. DESPATCH" in serif capitals, is believed to have been used only as a postmark.

Type C31 exists struck in blue or red, type C32 in blue, black or red. When found on cover, on various papers, struck alone, they are probably postmarks and not prepaid stamped envelopes. As such, these entire covers, depending upon the clarity of the handstamp and the general attractiveness of the letter are valued between $400 and $800.

When found on envelopes with the Carrier stamp canceled by a handstamp (such as type C31 struck in blue on a buff envelope canceled by the red solid star cancellation) they can be regarded as probably having been sold as prepaid envelopes. Value approximately $3,000.

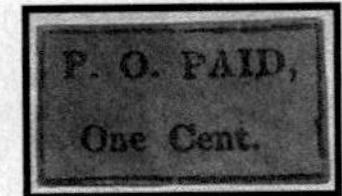

Labels of these designs are believed by most specialists not to be carrier stamps. Those seen are uncanceled, either off cover or affixed to stampless covers of the early 1850s. Some students believe they should be given carrier status.

St. Louis, Mo.

C36

C37

Illustrations enlarged to show details of the two types (note upper corners especially). Sizes of actual designs are 17 1/2x22mm.

1849 **White Wove Paper** **Litho.**
Two Types

8LB1 C36 2c **black**	*7,000.*	*3,000.*
8LB2 C37 2c **black**	*6,000.*	—

Cancellation on Nos. 8LB1-8LB2: Black town.

C38

1857 **Litho.**

8LB3 C38 2c **blue**	*22,500.*
On cover, tied by handstamp	*55,000.*
On Valentine cover, ms. cancel, not tied	*35,000.*

The used example off cover is unique. Five covers are recorded.

Cancellations on No. 8LB3: Black boxed "1ct," "Paid" in arc, black pen.

LOCAL STAMPS

This listing of Local stamps includes stamps issued by Local Posts (city delivery), Independent Mail Routes and Services, Express Companies and other private posts which competed with, or supplemented, official services.

The Independent Mail Routes began using stamps early in 1844 and were put out of business by an Act of March, 1845, which became effective July 1, 1845. By this Act, the Government reduced the zones to two, reduced the rates to 5c and 10c and applied them to weight instead of the number of sheets of paper which composed a letter.

Most of the Local Posts still in business were forced to discontinue service by an Act of 1861, except Boyd's and Hussey's which were able to continue about 20 years longer because of the particular nature of their business. Other posts appeared illegally and sporadically after 1861 and were quickly suppressed.

City posts generally charged 1c to deliver a letter to the Post Office (usually the letter bore a government stamp as well) and 2c for intracity delivery (such letters naturally bore only local stamps). These usages are not catalogued separately because the value of a cover is determined as much by its attractiveness as its franking, rarity being the basic criterion.

Only a few Local Posts used special handstamps for canceling. The stamps frequently were left uncanceled, were canceled by pen, or less often by pencil. **Unless indicated otherwise, values for stamps on cover are for covers having the stamp tied by a handstamped cancellation, either private or governmental.** Local stamps, either uncanceled or pen canceled, **on covers to which they apparently belong**, also are valued where possible.

The absence of any specific cancellation listed indicates that no company handstamp is known so used, and that the canceling, if any, was done by pen, pencil or government handstamp. Local stamps used on letters directed out of town (and consequently bearing government stamps) sometimes, because of their position, are tied together with the government stamp by the cancellation used to cancel the latter.

Values for envelopes are for entires unless specifically mentioned.

All Local stamps are imperforate and on wove paper, either white or colored through, unless otherwise stated.

Counterfeits exist of many Local stamps, but most of these are crude reproductions and would deceive only the novice.

Adams & Co.'s Express, California

This post started in September, 1849, operating only on the Pacific Coast.

D. H. Haskell, Manager
L1 L2

Nos. 1L2-1L5 Printed in Sheets of 40 (8x5)

1854 **Litho.**

1L1 L1 25c **black,** *blue*	*2,750.*	—
On cover		—
1L2 L2 25c **black** (initials in black)	75.00	—
Block of 4	375.00	
Sheet of 40	—	
a. Initials in red		—
b. Without initials		—

Cancellation (1L1-1L2): Black Express Co.

Nos. 1L1-1L2 were the earliest adhesive franks issued west of the Mississippi River.

No. 1L2 usually bear manuscript control markings "LR" for Louis Reed or less commonly "ICW" for Isaiah C. Wood.

Glazed Surface Cardboard

1L3 L2 25c **black,** *pink*	30.00
Block of 4	160.00
Sheet of 40	2,000.
Retouched flaw above LR "25"	100.00

No. 1L3 was probably never placed in use as a postage stamp.

Overprinted in red "Over our California lines only"

1L4 L2 25c **black** (with initials "LR" or "ICW")	750.00	—

L4

L5

1L5 L4 25c **black** (black surcharge) *4,000.* —
1L6 L5 25c **black** *3,000.*
Pair *7,500.*

The pair of No. 1L6 is unique.

NEWSPAPER STAMP

L6

1LP1 L6 **black,** *claret* — *2,000.*

Cancellation: Blue company oval.

ENVELOPES

L6a

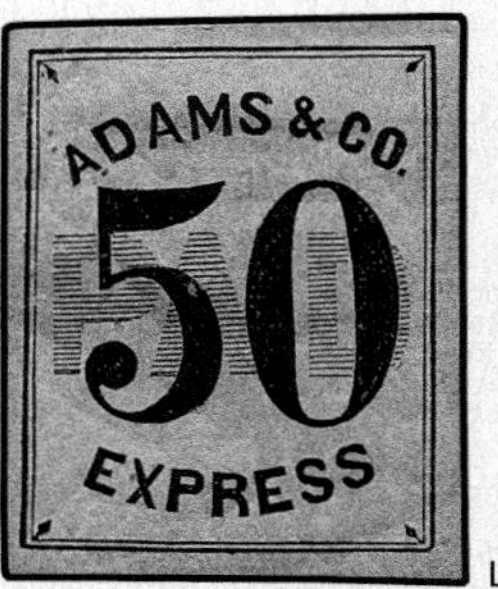

L6b

Typo.

1LU1 L6a 25c **blue** (cut square) *15,000.*
1LU2 L6a 25c **black,** on U.S. #U9 — —
1LU3 L6b 50c **black,** on U.S. #U9 *2,500.* *2,500.*
1LU4 L6b 50c **black,** *buff* *15,000.*

Nos. 1LU2 and 1LU3 exist cut out and apparently used as adhesives.
Cancellation: Blue company oval.

Adams' City Express Post, New York, N.Y.

L7

L7a

L8

1850-51 **Typo.**

2L2 L7 2c **black,** *buff* *5,000.* *2,250.*
On cover, canceled, not tied, with certificate *10,000.*
2L3 L7a 1c **black,** *gray,* pelure paper — —
2L4 L8 2c **black,** *gray* *450.00* *450.00*
On cover, tied by handstamp *5,500.*
2L5 L8 2c **blue,** —
On cover, pen cancel *7,500.*

Nos. 2L3-2L4 were reprinted in black on white wove paper. Some students claim that a 1c in blue on white wove paper exists as originals.

Allen's City Dispatch, Chicago, Ill.

Established by Edwin Allen for intracity delivery of letters and circulars. The price of the stamps is believed to have been determined on a quantity basis. Uncanceled and canceled remainders were sold to collectors after suppression of the post in February, 1883.

L9

Sheet of 100 (10x10)

1882 **Typo.** ***Perf. 10***

3L1 L9 **pink** 7.50 *25.00*
On cover *900.00*
Block of 4 *40.00*
a. Horizontal pair, imperf. between —
3L2 L9 **black** 12.50 *100.00*
On cover, tied by handstamp *1,500.*
Block of 4 55.00
a. Horizontal pair, imperf. between —
3L3 L9 **red,** *yellow* .75 *20.00*
On cover, tied by handstamp *900.00*
Block of 4 *3.25*
a. Imperf., pair *150.00*
b. Horizontal pair, imperf. between —
3L4 L9 **blackish purple** 120.00

Cancellations: Violet company oval, violet "eagle."

American Express Co., New York, N.Y.

Believed by some researchers to have been established by Smith & Dobson in 1856, and short-lived.

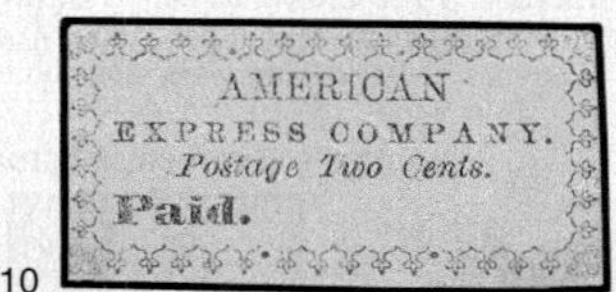

L10

Typeset
Glazed Surface Paper

4L1 L10 2c **black,** *green* *9,000.*

American Letter Mail Co.

Lysander Spooner established this independent mail line operating to and from New York, Philadelphia and Boston.

L12

L13

1844 **Sheet of 20 (5x4)** **Engr.**

5L1 L12 5c **black,** thin paper (2nd printing) 7.50 *35.00*
Thick paper (1st printing) 35.00 *50.00*
On cover, tied *750.00*
On cover, not tied *450.00*
Pair on cover *1,000.*
Pair on cover, tied by handstamp, with # 96L3a, ms. tied *10,000.*
Block of 4, thin paper 40.00
Sheet of 20, thin paper 225.00

No. 5L1 has been extensively reprinted in several colors, distinguishable by the rust marks on the plate, which were mostly removed from the margins and gutters between stamps but remain within the stamp designs. Cancellations: Red dotted star (2 types). Red "PAID," black brush, red brush.

Engr.

5L2 L13 **black,** *gray* 150.00 *250.00*
On cover, tied by handstamp *1,000.*
On cover, ms. tied *500.00*
On cover, not tied *350.00*
Pair on cover, tied by ms. 1,200.
Vertical strip of 4 *3,000.*
Block of 4 *4,000.*
5L3 L13 **blue,** *gray* *2,000.* *1,750.*
On cover, uncanceled, with certificate *11,000.*
On cover, not tied, with certificate *5,000.*
On cover, tied by ms. *10,000.*

Cancellations: Red "PAID," red company oval.

A. W. Auner's Despatch Post, Philadelphia, Pa.

L13a

1851 **Cut to shape** **Typeset**

154L1 L13a **black,** *grayish* *9,000.*
On cover, not tied, with certificate *16,500.*

Nos. 154L1 unused and on cover are each unique.

Baker's City Express Post, Cincinnati, Ohio

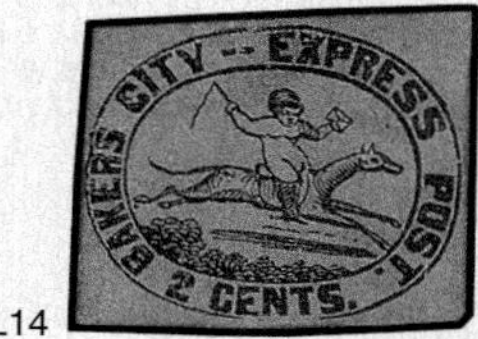

L14

1849

6L1 L14 2c **black,** *pink* *2,250.*
On cover, uncanceled, with certificate *12,500.*

Bank & Insurance Delivery Office or City Post

See Hussey's Post.

Barnard's Cariboo Express, British Columbia

The adhesives were used on British Columbia mail and the post did not operate in the United States, so the formerly listed PAID and COLLECT types are omitted. This company had an arrangement with Wells, Fargo & Co. to exchange mail at San Francisco.

Barnard's City Letter Express, Boston, Mass.

Established by Moses Barnard

L19

1845

7L1 L19 **black,** *yellow,* glazed paper *1,250.* *1,000.*
On cover, not canceled *3,000.*
7L2 L19 **red** *1,000.*
On cover, ms. cancel, not tied, with certificate *5,000.*

No. 7L2 unused and on cover are each unique.

Barr's Penny Dispatch, Lancaster, Pa.

Established by Elias Barr.

L19a

L20

1855 **Five varieties of each** **Typeset**

8L1 L19a **red** 1,000. 1,000.
On cover, ms. tied *5,000.*
On cover, ms. cancel, not tied, with certificate *2,000.*
8L2 L20 **black,** *green* 300. 250.
On cover, uncanceled *900.*
On cover with 3c #11 —
Pair *750.*

Bayonne City Dispatch, Bayonne City, N.J.

Organized April 1, 1883, to carry mail, with three daily deliveries. Stamps sold at 80 cents per 100.

L21

1883 **Sheet of 10** **Electrotyped**
9L1 L21 1c **black** 200. 275.
On cover, tied by handstamp *750.*
On cover with 1c #183 & 2c #206 *2,750.*
On cover with 3c #207 *1,600.*

Cancellation: Purple concentric circles.

ENVELOPE

1883, May 15 **Handstamped**
9LU1 L21 1c **purple,** *amber* 175. *1,000.*

Bentley's Dispatch, New York, N.Y.

Established by H. W. Bentley, who acquired Cornwell's Madison Square Post Office, operating until 1856, when the business was sold to Lockwood. Bentley's postmark was double circle handstamp.

L22

L22a

1856(?) **Glazed Surface Paper**
10L1 L22 **gold** *9,000. 9,000.*
10L2 L22a **gold** *7,500.*
Pair *10,000.*

Two unused examples of No. 10L1 are known, while the used example is unique.

Cancellation: Black "PAID."

Berford & Co.'s Express, New York, N.Y.

Organized by Richard G. Berford and Loring L. Lombard. Carried letters, newspapers and packages by steamer to Panama and points on the West Coast, North and South America. Agencies in West Indies, West Coast of South America, Panama, Hawaii, etc.

L23

1851
11L1 L23 3c **black** *5,000. 7,000.*
On cover, not canceled —
11L2 L23 6c **green** — —
On cover, tied *5,000.*
11L3 L23 10c **violet** *5,000.*
On cover, not canceled *5,000.*
Four cut to shape on cover *15,000.*
Pair —
a. Horiz. tete beche pair
On cover with normal pair *50,000.*
Two tete beche pair on cover *75,000.*
11L4 L23 25c **red** *17,000.*
On cover with #11L1 & 2 #11L2 *60,000.*

Values of cut to shape stamps are about half of those quoted.
No. 11L4 unused and on cover are each unique.
Cancellation: Red "B & Co. Paid" (sometimes impressed without ink). Dangerous counterfeits exist of Nos. 11L1-11L4.

Bicycle Mail Route, California

During the American Railway Union strike, Arthur C. Banta, Fresno agent for Victor bicycles, established this post to carry mail from Fresno to San Francisco and return, employing messengers on bicycles. The first trip was made from Fresno on July 6, 1894. Service was discontinued on July 18 when the strike ended. In all, 380 letters were carried. Stamps were used on covers with U.S. Government adhesive stamps and on stamped envelopes.

L24

Printed from single die. Sheet of six.
Error of spelling "SAN FRANSISCO"

1894 **Typo.** ***Rouletted 10***
12L1 L24 25c **green** 150. *200.*
On cover 2,750.
Block of 4 700.
Pane of 6 *1,750.*

L25

Retouched die. Spelling error corrected.
12L2 L25 25c **green** 30. 75.
On cover 1,500.
On cover with No. 220, both tied *2,000.*
Block of 4 125.
Pane of 6 250.
a. "Horiz." pair, imperf. "vert" 75.
As "a," pane of 6 —

ENVELOPES

12LU1 L25 25c **brown,** on 2c No. U311 200. *1,750.*
12LU2 L25 25c **brown,** on 2c No. U312 200. *1,750.*

Cancellation: Two black parallel bars 2mm apart.
Stamps and envelopes were reprinted from the defaced die.

Bigelow's Express, Boston, Mass.

Authorities consider items of this design to be express company labels rather than stamps.

Bishop's City Post, Cleveland, Ohio

See Carriers' Stamps, Nos. 10LB1-10LB2.

Blizzard Mail

Organized March, 1888, to carry mail to New York City during the interruption of U.S. mail by the Blizzard of 1888. Used March 12-16.

L27

1888, Mar. 12 **Quadrille Paper** **Typo.**
163L1 L27 5c **black** *3,750.*
a. "CETNS" instead of "CENTS" —
b. Tete beche pair —

D.O. Blood & Co., Philadelphia, Pa.
I. Philadelphia Despatch Post

Operated by Robertson & Co., predecessor of D.O. Blood & Co.

L28

Initialed "R & Co."

1843 **Cut to Shape** **Handstamped**
15L1 L28 3c **red,** *bluish* *1,500.*
On cover, not tied *8,500.*

1842
15L2 L28 3c **black** *1,500.*
On cover, not tied, with certificate *15,000.*

Cancellations on Nos. 15L1-15L2: Red "3," red pattern of segments.

L29

Initialed "R & Co"
With or without shading in background

1843 **Litho.**
15L3 L29 (3c) **black,** *grayish* 750.
On cover, tied by handstamp *12,500.*
On cover, tied by ms. cancel *5,000.*
On cover, not tied, with certificate *3,500.*
a. Double impression —

Cancellation on No. 15L3: Red "3"
The design shows a messenger stepping over the Merchants' Exchange Building, which then housed the Government Post Office, implying that the private post gave faster service.
See illustration L161 for similar design.

II. D.O. Blood & Co.

Formed by Daniel Otis Blood and Walter H. Blood in 1845. Successor to Philadelphia Despatch Post which issued Nos. 15L1-15L3.

L30

Initialed "Dob & Cos" or "D.O.B. & Co."

1845 **Shading in background**
15L4 L30 (3c) **black,** *grayish* 600.
On cover, tied by handstamp *7,000.*
On cover, not tied *1,500.*

L31

1845

15L5 L31 (2c) **black**	125.	*250.*
On cover		—
On cover, not tied, with certificate		*800.*
Block of 4	*475.*	
Pane of 12	*5,500.*	

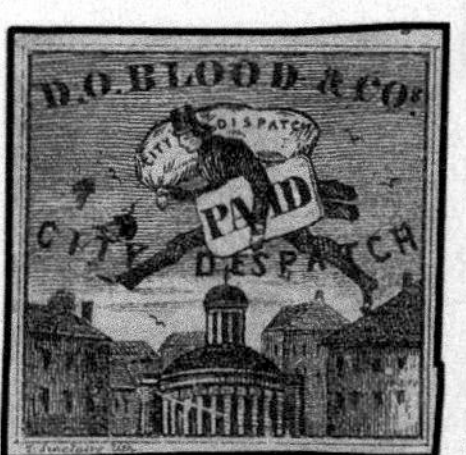

L32

1847

15L6 L32 (2c) **black**	—	200.
On cover		—
On cover, not tied, with certificate		*1,250.*
On cover, not tied, with 5c #1		—

Cancellations on Nos. 15L4-15L6: Black dot pattern, black cross, red "PAID."

Dangerous counterfeits exist of Nos. 15L3-15L6.

L33

L34

L35

1846-47

15L7 L33 (2c) **black**	175.00	350.00
On cover, tied by handstamp		*1,750.*
On cover, cut to shape, tied by handstamp		*1,100.*
On cover, not tied		*750.00*
15L8 L34 (2c) **black**	110.00	75.00
On cover, tied by handstamp		*950.00*
On cover, uncanceled		*500.00*
On cover, uncanceled, with 5c #1		*2,000.*
On cover, tied by handstamp, with two 5c #1, tied by handstamps		*25,000.*
On cover, tied by handstamp, with 3c #26A		500.00
15L9 L35 (2c) **black**	100.00	60.00
On cover, tied by handstamp		*1,500.*
On cover with 5c #1 or 1a		*1,750.*
On cover, not tied		*500.00*
Block of 4		—

Values for Nos. 15L7-15L9 cut to shape are half of those quoted.

"On cover" listings of Nos. 15L7-15L9 are for stamps tied by government town postmarks, either Philadelphia, or rarely Baltimore.

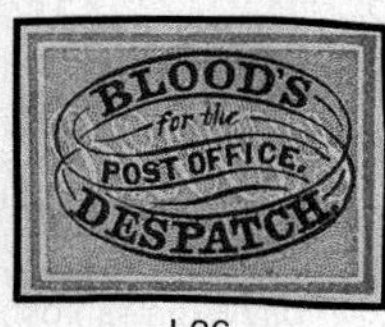

L36

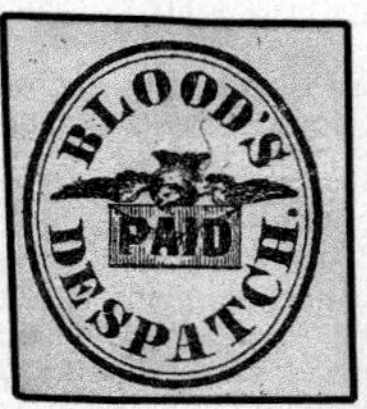

L37

1848

15L10 L36 (2c) **black & blue**	350.00	*500.00*
On cover, tied by handstamp		*2,250.*
On cover, not tied		*1,750.*
On cover, not canceled		*1,000.*
On cover, with 5c #1		—
Pair	*1,300.*	
On cover, with 10c #2		*1,500.*
15L11 L37 (2c) **black,** *pale green*	325.00	325.00
On cover, tied by handstamp		*2,000.*
On cover, not tied		*1,500.*

Cancellation: Black grid.

L38

L39

L40

L41

1848-54

15L12 L38 (2c) **gold,** *black,* glazed	*110.00*	100.00
On cover, tied by handstamp		*500.00*
On cover, acid tied		200.00
On cover, uncanceled, with 5c #1		*2,000.*
15L13 L39 1c **bronze,** *black,* glazed ('50)	25.00	12.50
On cover, tied by handstamp		*225.00*
On cover, acid tied		75.00
On cover, acid tied, with 5c #1 or 1b		*2,000.*
On cover, acid tied, with pair of 5c #1b		—
On cover, acid tied, with 10c #2		—
On cover with 10c #2, both tied		*9,000.*
On cover, acid tied, with three 1c #7		*1,100.*
On cover, acid tied, with 3c #10		*1,000.*
On cover, acid tied, with 3c #10A		*1,000.*
On cover, acid tied, with 3c #11		*1,000.*
Block of 4	150.00	
Pane of 24	*1,250.*	
15L14 L40 (1c) **bronze,** *lilac* ('54)	4.25	2.50
On cover, tied by handstamp		*200.00*
On cover, acid tied		30.00
On cover, acid tied, with 1c #9		*300.00*
On cover with 3c #11		*375.00*
On cover, acid tied, with 10c #14		*1,500.*
On cover, tied by handstamp, with 1c #24 and three 3c #26		*1,150.*
On cover, tied by handstamp, with 3c #26		*200.00*
On cover, acid tied, with 10c #32		—
On cover, acid tied, with 3c #64b		*250.00*
On cover, acid tied, with 3c #65		*225.00*
Block of 4	50.00	
Pane of 25	*750.00*	
a. Laid paper	—	—
b. Tete beche pair	—	
15L15 L40 (1c) **blue & pink,** *bluish* ('53)	22.50	12.50
On cover, tied by handstamp		*200.00*
On cover, acid tied		50.00
On cover, acid tied, with 1c #7 and three 3c #11		*1,000.*
Block of 4	80.00	
Pane of 25	*1,250.*	
a. Laid paper	35.00	—
Block of 4	150.00	
15L16 L40 (1c) **bronze,** *black,* glazed ('54)	30.00	25.00
On cover, tied by handstamp		*225.00*
On cover, acid tied		75.00
On cover, tied by handstamp, with 3c #11		*275.00*
15L17 L41 (2c) **bronze,** *black,* glazed	35.00	20.00
On cover, tied by handstamp		*225.00*
On cover, acid tied		75.00
On cover, acid or handstamp tied, with 5c #1		*1,250.*
On cover, not tied, with 5c #1		*750.*
On cover, handstamp tied, with pair of 5c #1 or 1a		*11,000.*
On cover, acid or handstamp tied, with 10c #2		*5,000.*

D.O. Blood & Co. reduced the cost for mailing letters from 2c to 1c as of Jan. 8, 1849, in anticipation of the government carrier rate reduction. As a result, Nos. 15L12 and 15L17 could be purchased for 1c after this date.

Cancellations: Black grid (No. 15L12, 15L17). Nos. 15L13-15L16 were almost always canceled with an acid which discolored both stamp and cover.

III. Blood's Penny Post

Blood's Penny Post was acquired by the general manager, Charles Kochersperger, in 1855, when Daniel O. Blood died.

Henry Clay — L42

1855 **Engr. by Draper, Welsh & Co.**

15L18 L42 (1c) **black**	35.00	10.00
On cover		150.00
On cover, tied by handstamp, with 3c #11		*400.00*
On cover, not tied, with 1c #24		*900.00*
On cover, tied by handstamp, with 1c #24 and 3c #26		*2,000.*
On cover, tied by handstamp, with 3c #26		*350.00*
On 3c entire #U9		300.00
Block of 4	175.00	

Cancellations: Black or red circular "Blood's Penny Post," black "1" in frame, red "1" in frame.

ENVELOPES

L42A

L43

L44

1848-60 **Embossed**

15LU1 L42A **albino embossing,** *white*		—
15LU1A L42A **albino embossing,** *buff*	—	4,000.
15LU1B L43 **red,** *white*	75.00	*100.00*
a. **Pink,** *white*		*100.00*
15LU2 L43 **red,** *buff*	—	150.00
15LU3 L44 **red,** *white*	75.00	160.00
15LU4 L44 **red,** *buff*	75.00	125.00

One example of No. 15LU1 is recorded, uncanceled, with the embossed stamp cut out and reattached. Two examples of No. 15LU1A are recorded, canceled by the "Blood's Despatch/28 So. Sixth" handstamp.

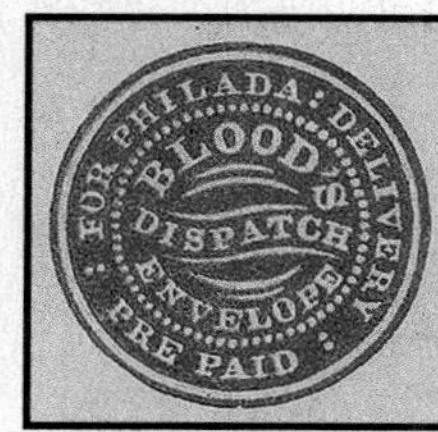

L45

15LU5 L45 **red,** *white*	35.00	75.00
Used with 3c #11		350.00
Used with 3c #26		*350.00*
15LU6 L45 **red,** *amber*	35.00	100.00
15LU6A L45 **red,** *buff*		*350.00*
Used with 10c #2		—
Used with three 1c #9		—
Used with 3c #11		—

Laid Paper

15LU7 L45 **red,** *white*	35.00	125.00
Used with acid tied #15L14		*200.00*
a. Impressed on US env. #U9		300.00
b. Impressed on US env. #U2		—
c. Impressed on US env. #U1		—
d. Impressed on US env. #U3		*500.00*
15LU8 L45 **red,** *amber*	35.00	125.00
Used with 3c No. 25		200.00

15LU9 L45 **red,** *buff* 35.00 250.00
Used with 3c No. 26A —
15LU10 L45 **red,** *blue* *6,500.*

Nos. 15LU1-15LU9 exist in several envelope sizes. No. 15LU6A exists in many shades, from buff to brown, as a result of various printings and changes over time.

Cancellations: Black grid (Nos. 15LU1-15LU4), black company circle (2 sizes and types). When on government envelope, the Blood stamp was often left uncanceled.

Bouton's Post, New York, N.Y.
I. Franklin City Despatch Post

Organized by John R. Bouton

L46

1847	Glazed Surface Paper	Typo.	
16L1 L46 (2c) **black,** *green*		*7,500.*	
a. "Bouton" in blk. ms. vert. at side		*7,000.*	
On cover			*14,000.*

II. Bouton's Manhattan Express

Acquired from William V. Barr

L47

1847		Typo.
17L1 L47 2c **black,** *pink*	*4,000.*	
Cut to shape	*900.*	
On cover, uncanceled		*4,500.*

III. Bouton's City Dispatch Post

(Sold to Swarts' in 1849.)

Corner Leaves — L48

Corner Dots — L49

Design: Zachary Taylor

1848		Litho.
18L1 L48 2c **black**	—	600.
On cover		*10,000.*
On cover with 5c #1		*27,500.*
On cover with 10c #2		*50,000.*
18L2 L49 2c **black,** *gray blue*	—	250.
On cover, tied by handstamp		750.
On cover tied by Swarts' handstamp		*1,000.*
On cover, tied by handstamp, with 5c #1, tied by red grid handstamp		*20,000.*
On cover with 10c #2		*5,000.*

Cancellations on Nos. 18L1-18L2: Red "PAID BOUTON."

The No. 18L2 with No. 2 combination cover is unique. It is a cover front only and is valued thus.

Boyce's City Express Post, New York, N.Y.

L50

Center background has 17 parallel lines

1852	Glazed Surface Paper	Typo.	
19L1 L50 2c **black,** *green*		*1,500.*	*1,000.*
Cut to shape		*850.00*	
On cover, tied by manuscript cancel			*4,000.*
On cover, uncanceled			*1,500.*

Boyd's City Express, New York, N.Y.

Boyd's City Express, as a post, was established by John T. Boyd, on June 17, 1844. In 1860 the post was briefly operated by John T. Boyd, Jr., under whose management No. 20L15 was issued.

For about six months in 1860 the post was suspended. It was then sold to William and Mary Blackham who resumed operation on Dec. 24, 1860.

The Blackham issues began with No. 20L16. Boyd's had arrangements to handle local delivery mail for Pomeroy, Letter Express, Brooklyn City Express Post, Staten Island Express Post and possibly others.

L51

Designs L51-L56, L59-L60 have a rectangular frame of fine lines surrounding the design.

1844	Glazed Surface Paper	Litho.
20L1 L51 2c **black,** *green*		*1,000.*
On cover		*4,000.*
On cover, not tied, with #117L4		*7,000.*

Cancellation: Red "FREE."

L52

Plain background. Map on globe.

1844	Litho.
20L2 L52 2c **black,** *yellow green*	175.00
On cover	*450.00*

Cancellation: Red "FREE."

L53

Plain background. Only globe shaded.

1845		Engr.
20L3 L53 2c **black,** *bluish green*	—	250.00
On cover		*500.00*

Cancellation: Red "FREE."

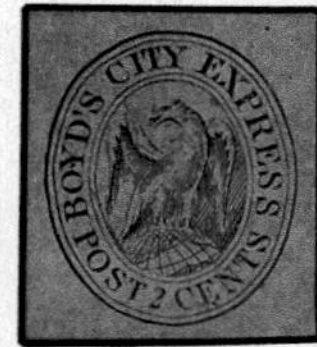

L54

Inner oval frame of two thin lines. Netted background, showing but faintly on late impressions.

1845		Engr.
20L4 L54 2c **black,** *green*	—	15.00
On cover, tied by handstamp		250.00
On cover, not tied		75.00
On cover, tied, with 5c U.S. Postmaster Provisional #9X1		*30,000.*
On cover, tied, with 5c #1		*5,000.*
On cover, not tied, with 5c #1		*1,500.*
On cover, not tied, with two 5c #1		*12,500.*
Double transfer		35.00
a. Diagonal half used as 1c on cover		*2,300.*

Cancellations: Red "FREE." Black grid.

The 20L4 and 9X1 on cover is the only recorded usage of a local stamp and a Postmaster Provisional on full cover. Nos. 20L4 and 9X1 also are recorded on a rebacked cover front.

1848		
20L5 L54 2c **gold,** *cream*	*600.00*	*600.00*
On cover, not tied		*1,750.*
On cover, cut to shape, not tied		*750.00*

Designs L54-L59 (except No. 20L23) were also obtainable die cut. An extra charge was made for such stamps. In general, genuine Boyd die-cuts sell for 75% of rectangular cut stamps. Stamps hand cut to shape are worth much less.

L55

No period after "CENTS." Inner oval frame has heavy inner line.

1848		Engr.
20L7 L55 2c **black,** *green* (glazed)	10.00	15.00
On cover, tied by handstamp		175.00
On cover, tied by handstamp, with 5c #1		*2,750.*
On cover with 3c #10		—
On cover, tied, with 3c #11		*275.00*
On cover, with 2c #28L5		—
Block of 4	40.00	
Partially erased transfer	—	
On cover		—
a. 2c **black,** *yellow green*		15.00
On cover		135.00

Cancellation: Black grid.

No. 20L7a is on unglazed surface-colored paper.

L56

Period after "CENTS." Inner frame as in L55.

1852		Litho.
20L8 L56 2c **black,** *green*	—	35.00
On cover		*150.00*
Vert. strip of 3 on cover		*300.00*
On cover, tied by handstamp, with partial 3c #11A		—
20L9 L56 2c **gold,**	12.50	80.00
On cover, tied by handstamp		*750.00*
On cover with 3c #11		—
Block of 4	80.00	

Cancellations on Nos. 20L8-20L9: Black cork. Black "PAID J.T.B."

No. 20L8 was reprinted in 1862 on unglazed paper, and about 1880 on glazed paper without rectangular frame.

The existence of No. 20L8, vert. strip of 3, on cover has been questioned by specialists. The editors would like to see authenticated evidence of its existence.

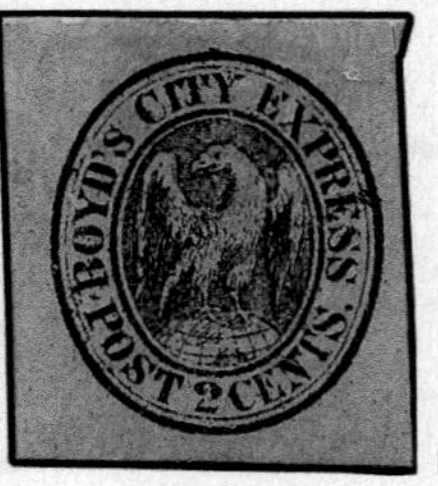

L57

Period after "CENTS." Inner oval frame has heavy outer line. Eagle's tail pointed. Upper part of "2" open, with heavy downstroke at left shorter than one at right. "2C" closer than "T2."

1854		
20L10 L57 2c **black,** *green*	32.50	25.00
On cover, tied by handstamp		200.00

Cancellation: Black "PAID J.T.B."

L58

Outer oval frame of three lines, outermost heavy. Solid background.

1855 Unglazed Paper Colored Through Typo.

20L11 L58 2c **black,** *olive green* *65.00* 90.00
On cover, tied by handstamp *350.00*

1856

20L12 L58 2c **brick red,** *white* 50.00 45.00
On cover, tied by handstamp *500.00*
20L13 L58 2c **dull orange,** *white* 50.00 45.00
On cover *400.00*
a. Printed on both sides —

Cancellation on Nos. 20L11-20L13: Black "PAID J.T.B."

Nos. 20L11-20L13 were reprinted in the 1880's for sale to collectors. They were printed from a new small plate of 25 on lighter weight paper and in colors of ink and paper lighter than the originals.

L59

Similar to No. 20L10, but eagle's tail square. Upper part of "2" closed (in well printed specimens) forming a symmetrical "o" with downstrokes equal. "T2" closer than "2C."

1857 Glazed Surface Paper Litho.

20L14 L59 2c **black,** *green* 12.50 *25.00*
On cover 90.00
On cover, tied by handstamp, with 3c #11 —
On cover, tied by handstamp, with 3c #11A —
On cover, tied by handstamp, with 3c #26 125.00
Pair on cover —
Block of 4 65.00
a. Serrate perf. —

The serrate perf. is probably of private origin.

No. 20L15 was made by altering the stone of No. 20L14, and many traces of the "S" of "CENTS" remain.

1860

20L15 L59 1c **black,** *green* 1.00 *50.00*
On cover, tied by handstamp *400.00*
Block of 4 7.50
a. "CENTS" instead of "CENT" — —
On cover *450.00*

Cancellation on Nos. 20L14-20L15: Black "PAID J.T.B."

L60

Center dots before "POST" and after "CENTS."

1861

20L16 L60 2c **black,** *red* 7.50 20.00
On cover, tied by handstamp 225.00
Block of 4 37.50
a. Tete beche pair 45.00
20L17 L60 1c **black,** *lilac* 12.50 17.50
On cover, tied by handstamp 250.00
On cover, tied by handstamp, with 3c #26 *200.00*
On cover, tied by handstamp, with 3c #65 *500.00*
Block of 4 50.00
a. "CENTS" instead of "CENT" 50.00 *75.00*
Two on cover (No. 20L17a) —
b. "1" inverted —
20L18 L60 1c **black,** *blue gray* 22.50 35.00
On cover, tied by handstamp *250.00*
On cover, tied by handstamp, with 3c #26 *225.00*
On cover, tied by handstamp, with 3c #65 *225.00*
Block of 4 90.00
a. "CENTS" instead of "CENT" 75.00 90.00
On cover 250.00
On cover, tied by handstamp, with 1c #24 and three 3c #26 *2,000.*
b. "1" inverted —

Cancellations on Nos. 20L16-20L18: Black or blue company oval, black company circle, black or blue "PAID" in circle.

1861

20L19 L60 2c **gold,** *250.00*
Block of 4 —
a. Tete beche pair —
20L20 L60 2c **gold,** *green* 20.00
Block of 4 —
a. Tete beche pair —
20L21 L60 2c **gold,** *dark blue* 12.50
On cover, tied by handstamp *150.00*
Block of 4 —
a. Tete beche pair *300.00*
20L22 L60 2c **gold,** *crimson* 25.00
Block of 4 —
a. Tete beche pair —

1866 Typo.

20L23 L58 2c **black,** *red* 7.50 25.00
On cover, tied by handstamp 250.00
Block of 4 37.50
a. Tete beche pair 55.00

Cancellations: Black company, black "PAID" in circle.

No. 20L23 was reprinted from a new stone on paper of normal color. See note after No. 20L13.

L61

No period or center dots.

1866 Typo.

20L24 L61 1c **black,** *lilac* *30.00* *65.00*
On cover, tied by handstamp *500.00*
Block of 4 —
20L25 L61 1c **black,** *blue* 6.00 *50.00*
On cover, tied by handstamp *500.00*
Block of 4 30.00

Cancellation on Nos. 20L24-20L25: Black company.

Reprints exist of Nos. 20L24 and 20L25. Originals of No. 20L24 are grayish black on glazed paper, while the reprints are deep black on unglazed paper. Reprints of No. 20L25 are identical to the originals, and it is customary to regard stamps with original gum as originals and those without gum as reprints.

Boyd's City Dispatch

(Change in Name)

L62

1874 Glazed Surface Paper Litho.

20L26 L62 2c **light blue** 35.00 40.00
On cover —
Block of 4 —

A unique sheet of 100 exists. It demonstrates 10 transfer types (2x5) repeated ten times to produce the printing stone. The same stone was modified to produce Nos. 20L30-20L36.

The 2c black on wove paper, type L62, is a cut-out from the Bank Notices Nos. 20LUX1, 20LUX2, or 20LUX3.

Surface Colored Paper

20L28 L62 2c **black,** *red* —
20L29 L62 2c **blue,** *red* *1,500.*

The adhesives of type L62 were made from the third state of the envelope die.

Nos. 20L28 and 20L29 are color trials, possibly used postally.

L63

1877 Litho.

20L30 L63 2c **lilac,** *roseate* —

Laid Paper

20L31 L63 2c **lilac,** *roseate* —

Wove Paper

Perf. 12½

20L32 L63 2c **lilac,** *roseate* 27.50 25.00
On cover *200.00*
a. 2c **lilac,** *grayish* 27.50 25.00

Laid Paper

20L33 L63 2c **lilac,** *roseate* 25.00
a. 2c **lilac,** *grayish* —

Glazed Surface Paper

20L34 L63 2c **brown,** *yellow* 35.00 35.00
On cover, tied by handstamp —
a. Imperf. horizontally —

L64

1877 Laid Paper *Perf. 11, 12, 12½*

20L35 L64 (1c) **violet,** *lilac* 15.00 17.50
On cover, tied by handstamp *450.00*
a. (1c) **red lilac,** *lilac* 27.50 27.50
b. (1c) **gray lilac,** *lilac* 17.50 17.50
c. Vert. pair, imperf. horiz. *400.00*
20L36 L64 (1c) **gray,** *roseate* 15.00 15.00
On cover, tied by handstamp *325.00*
a. (1c) **gray,** *grayish* 15.00

Cancellations on Nos. 20L30-20L36: Black "PAID" in circle. Purple company oval.

Boyd's Dispatch

(Change in Name)

Mercury Series — Type I — L65

Printed in sheets of 100.
Inner frame line at bottom broken below foot of Mercury.
Printed by C.O. Jones.

1878 Litho. Wove Paper *Imperf.*

20L37 L65 **black,** *pink* 400.00 300.00

Surface Colored Wove Paper

20L38 L65 **black,** *orange red* *750.00* *500.00*
20L39 L65 **black,** *crimson* *450.00* *300.00*

Laid Paper

20L40 L65 **black,** *salmon* *450.00*
20L41 L65 **black,** *lemon* *450.00* *400.00*
20L42 L65 **black,** *lilac pink* *450.00*

Nos. 20L37-20L42 are color trials, some of which may have been used postally.

Surface Colored Paper

Perf. 12

20L43 L65 **black,** *crimson* 60.00 50.00
On cover, tied by handstamp *300.00*
a. **black,** *dull brown red* 40.00 40.00
On cover, tied by handstamp *300.00*
20L43A L65 **black,** *orange red* 150.00 150.00
On cover, tied by handstamp *1,000.*

Cancellations on Nos. 20L37-20L43A: Black "PAID" in circle. Purple company oval.

Wove Paper

Perf. 11, 11½, 12, 12½ and Compound

20L44 L65 (1c) **black,** *pink* 1.50 2.50
On cover *200.00*
a. Horizontal pair, imperf. between — —

1879 ***Perf. 11, 11½, 12***

20L45 L65 (1c) **black,** *blue* 10.00 15.00
On cover, tied by handstamp 200.00

20L46 L65 (1c) **blue,** *blue* 27.50 32.50
On cover, tied by handstamp *400.00*

1880 ***Perf. 11, 12, 13½***

20L47 L65 (1c) **black,** *lavender* 8.00 20.00
On cover, tied by handstamp *300.00*
Block of 4 50.00
a. Horizontal pair, imperf. between *400.00*

20L48 L65 (1c) **blue,** *lavender* — —

1881 **Laid Paper** ***Perf. 12, 12½, 14***

20L49 L65 (1c) **black,** *pink* *350.00*
On cover, tied by handstamp *600.00*

1880

20L50 L65 (1c) **black,** *lilac pink* 7.00 25.00
On cover, tied by handstamp *325.00*

Mercury Series — Type II — L65a — 20L51

Printed by J. Gibson

No break in frame, the great toe raised, other toes touching line

1881 **Wove Paper** ***Perf. 12, 16 & Compound.***

20L51 L65a (1c) **black,** *blue* 35.00 30.00

20L52 L65a (1c) **black,** *pink* 75.00 75.00
On cover, tied by handstamp *400.00*

Laid Paper

20L53 L65a (1c) **black,** *pink* 7.50 7.50
On cover, tied by handstamp 125.00

20L54 L65a (1c) **black,** *lilac pink* 12.50 10.00
On cover *200.00*

Mercury Series — Type III — L65b — 20L55

Printed by the "Evening Post"

No break in frame, the great toe touching

Perf. 10, 11½, 12, 16 & Compound

1882 **Wove Paper**

20L55 L65b (1c) **black,** *blue* 4.00 10.00
On cover, tied by handstamp *225.00*
Pair on cover 225.00

20L56 L65b (1c) **black,** *pink* .40 *1.50*
On cover, tied by handstamp 100.00
Block of 4 2.00

Cancellations on Nos. 20L44-20L56: black or purple company ovals of various types, purple company circle, purple "SPECIAL," purple Maltese cross.

ENVELOPES

Boyd's City Post

Boyd's envelopes and cards (LU and LUX numbers) are valued as entires, cut squares are worth much less.

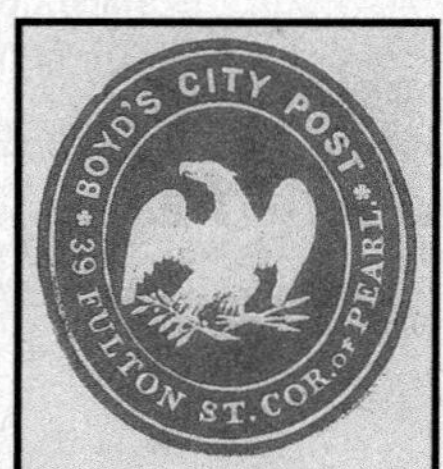

L66

Imprinted in upper right corner.
Used envelopes show Boyd's handstamps.

1864 **Diagonally Laid Paper** **Embossed**

20LU1 L66 **red** *175.00*
20LU2 L66 **red,** *amber* *90.00*
20LU3 L66 **red,** *yellow* — —
20LU4 L66 **blue** *175.00* —
20LU5 L66 **blue,** *amber* *175.00*
20LU6 L66 **blue,** *yellow* — —
20LU6A L66 **blue,** *blue* —

Several shades of red and blue.
No. 20LU6A is an indicium cut to shape. It is unique.

20LU7 L66 **deep blue,** *orange,* cut square *600.00*
Entire *5,500.*

Reprinted on pieces of white, fawn and oriental buff papers, vertically, horizontally or diagonally laid.

Wove Paper

20LU8 L66 **red,** *cream* *175.00*
20LU9 L66 **red,** *orange* — *2,500.*
20LU10 L66 **blue,** *cream* —
20LU11 L66 **blue,** *orange* —
Impression at upper left *4,000.*
20LU11A L66 **blue,** *amber* — —

Boyd's City Dispatch

L67a

L67b

L67a. Lines and letters sharp and clear. Trefoils at sides pointed and blotchy, middle leaf at right long and thick at end.
L67b. Lines and letters thick and rough. Lobes of trefoils rounded and definitely outlined. Stamp impressed normally in upper right corner of envelope; L67b rarely in upper left.

1867 **Diagonally Laid Paper** **Typo.**

20LU12 L67 2c **red** (a) (b) — *800.00*
20LU13 L67 2c **red,** *amber* (b) — *300.00*
20LU14 L67 2c **red,** *cream* (b) — *300.00*
a. On horiz. laid paper —
b. Double impression, second impression in black, cut to shape —
20LU15 L67 2c **red,** *yellow* (a) (b) — *300.00*
20LU16 L67 2c **red,** *orange* (b) — *300.00*
a. Stamp impressed at upper left —

Wove Paper

20LU17 L67 2c **red** (a) (b) — *300.00*
20LU18 L67 2c **red,** *cream* (a) (b) — *300.00*
20LU19 L67 2c **red,** *yellow* (a) — —
20LU20 L67 2c **red,** *orange* (a) (b) — —
20LU21 L67 2c **red,** *blue* (a) (b) 500.00 *400.00*

Design as Type L62

First state of die, showing traces of old address

1874 **Diagonally Laid Paper**

20LU22 L62 2c **red,** *amber* *200.00*
20LU23 L62 2c **red,** *cream* — *200.00*

Wove Paper

20LU24 L62 2c **red,** *amber* *200.00*
20LU25 L62 2c **red,** *yellow* *200.00*

Second state of die, no traces of address

1875 **Diagonally Laid Paper**

20LU26 L62 2c **red,** *amber* *1,250.*
20LU27 L62 2c **red,** *cream* — *375.00*

Wove Paper

20LU28 L62 2c **red,** *amber* *450.00*

L68

1877 **Laid Paper**

20LU29 L68 2c **red,** *amber* *800.00*

Stamp usually impressed in upper left corner of envelope.

L69

1878 **Diagonally Laid Paper**

20LU30 L69 (1c) **red,** *amber* — *650.00*

Wove Paper

20LU31 L69 (1c) **red,** *cream* —
20LU32 L69 (1c) **red,** *yellow* —

Boyd's Dispatch

Mercury Series — Type IV — L70

Mercury Series-Type IV

Shading omitted in banner. No period after "Dispatch." Short line extends to left from great toe.

1878 **Diagonally Laid Paper**

20LU33 L70 **black** 40.00 *100.00*
20LU34 L70 **black,** *amber* *80.00*
20LU35 L70 **black,** *cream* 50.00 *100.00*
20LU36 L70 **red** *50.00*
20LU37 L70 **red,** *amber* 35.00 *45.00*
20LU38 L70 **red,** *cream* 35.00 *80.00*
20LU39 L70 **red,** *yellow green* —
20LU40 L70 **red,** *orange* *350.00*
20LU41 L70 **red,** *fawn* —

Wove Paper

20LU42 L70 **red** — *800.00*

Mercury Series — Type V — L71

Mercury Series-Type V

Colorless crosshatching lines in frame work. Very little shading on arms and legs.

1878 **Diagonally Laid Paper**

20LU43 L71 **red** — *450.00*
20LU44 L71 **red,** *cream* 25.00 *50.00*

Wove Paper

20LU44A L71 **red** *1,000.*

Boyd's Bank Notices

IMPORTERS' AND TRADERS' NATIONAL BANK OF NEW YORK

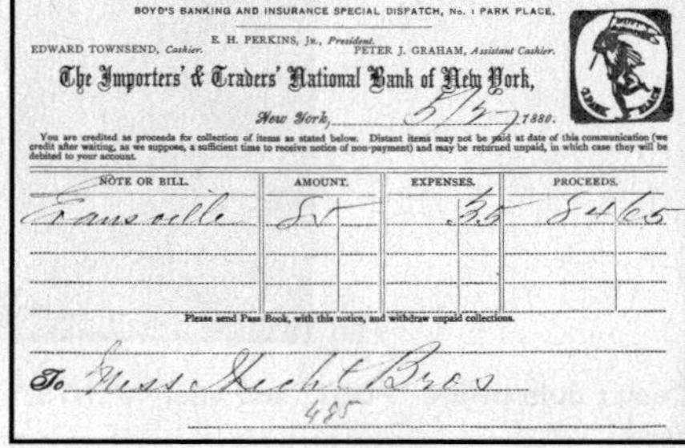

BOYD'S BANKING AND INSURANCE SPECIAL DISPATCH, No. 1 PARK PLACE.

E. H. PERKINS, Jr., *President.*
EDWARD TOWNSEND, *Cashier.* PETER J. GRAHAM, *Assistant Cashier.*

The Importers' & Traders' National Bank of New York,

New York, ... 1880.

You are credited as proceeds for collection of items as stated below. Distant items may not be paid at date of this communication (we credit after waiting, as we suppose, a sufficient time to receive notice of non-payment) and may be returned unpaid, in which case they will be debited to your account.

NOTE OR BILL.	AMOUNT.	EXPENSES.	PROCEEDS.

Please send Pass Book, with this notice, and withdraw unpaid collections.

To ....

No. 20LUX9a

1874-83

Incomplete Year Date ("187 "), Card Stock

20LUX1 L62 (2c) **black,** 155x100mm *250.00*

Complete Year Date, Medium Wove Paper

20LUX2 L62 2c **black,** 157x104mm (1875) —
20LUX3 L62 2c **black,** 152x104mm (1876) *250.00*
20LUX4 L68 2c **black,** 154x105mm (1876) —
20LUX5 L68 2c **black,** 156x108mm (1877) *400.00*

20LUX6 L69 (1c) **black,** 156x108mm (1878) —
a. Four officers in masthead instead of three —
20LUX7 L70 (1c) **black,** 158x110mm (1879) *250.00*
20LUX8 L70 (1c) **black,** large year date and city, 158x110mm (1879) *250.00*
20LUX9 L70 (1c) **black,** 149x102mm (1880) *75.00* —
a. Three officers in masthead instead of four, 156x112mm *400.00*
20LUX10 L70 (1c) **black,** 149x102mm (1881) —
a. Four officers in masthead instead of three —
20LUX11 L71 (1c) **black,** 152x106mm (1883) —

Sizes of these cards may vary by up to two millimeters in either dimension from the measurements shown.

Nos. 20LUX5 and 20LUX9 exist on paper with a papermaker's watermark. Nos. 20LUX6, 20LUX9 and 20LUX10 may be found with either three or four bank officers listed in the masthead. The major number is the card that was issued first. No. 20LUX11 is known only unused, and may be a remainder that was printed but not used.

Values for Nos. 20LUX1-20LUX13 are for full covers. Cut squares sell for much less.

NATIONAL PARK BANK

1881 (?) **Medium Wove Paper**
20LUX12 L71 (1c) **black,** 122x63mm ('83) *300.00*

No postmarks or cancellations were used on Bank Notices. Boyd's sometimes added the recipient's address in pencil.

FLEISCHMANN'S MODEL BAKERY

1879 **Card Stock**
20LUX13 L69 (1c) **black,** 130x75mm *3,000.*

This card is imprinted "Fleischmann's Model Bakery."

Bradway's Despatch, Millville, N.J.

Operated by Isaac Bradway

L72

1857 **Typo.**
21L1 L72 **gold,** *lilac,* on cover, not tied, with certificate *9,250.*
On cover, not tied, with 3c #11, with certificate *12,000.*

Brady & Co., New York, N.Y.

Operated by Abner S. Brady at 97 Duane St. Successor to Clark & Co.

L73

1857 **Typo.**
22L1 L73 1c **red,** *yellow* 1,000. 1,000.
On cover, tied by company handstamp *22,000.*
On cover, tied by "PAID" handstamp *10,000.*

Cancellations: Blue boxed "PAID," blue company oval.
Reprints exist.

No. 22L1 tied on corner by company handstamp is unique. Three covers recorded with stamp tied by "PAID."

Brady & Co.'s Penny Post, Chicago, Ill.

L74

1860(?) **Litho.**
23L1 L74 1c **violet** *650.00* —

The authenticity of this stamp has not been fully established.

Brainard & Co.

Established by Charles H. Brainard in 1844, operating between New York, Albany and Troy, Exchanged mail with Hale & Co. by whom Brainard had been employed.

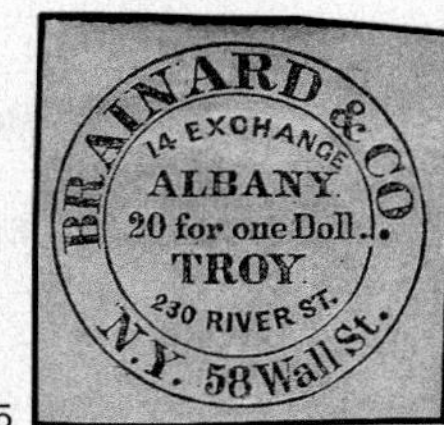

L75

1844 **Typo.**
24L1 L75 **black** *1,000. 1,250.*
On cover, two stamps tied —
On cover, tied by pen cancel *2,500.*
On cover, not tied *2,000.*
On cover, cut to shape, not tied *1,750.*
24L2 L75 **blue** *1,000. 1,250.*
On cover, not tied *4,500.*

Nos. 21L1-24L2 cut to shape are one half of values quoted.

Brigg's Despatch, Philadelphia, Pa.

Established by George W. Briggs

L76

1847
25L1 L76 (2c) **black,** *yellow buff* *1,000.*
On cover, not tied, with certificate *11,500.*
25L2 L76 (2c) **black,** *blue,* cut to shape *7,500.*

No. 25L2 is unique. It is on cover, manuscript "X" cancel, genuine, but Philatelic Foundation has declined to give an opinion as to whether the stamp originated on the cover.

L77

1848
25L4 L77 (2c) **gold,** *yellow,* glazed *5,500.*
On cover, not tied —
25L5 L77 (2c) **gold,** *black,* glazed *4,000.*
On cover —
25L6 L77 (2c) **gold,** *pink* —

No. 25L4 used and on cover are each unique.

Handstamps formerly illustrated as types L78 and L79 are included in the section "Local Handstamped Covers" at the end of the Local Stamp listings. They were used as postmarks and there is no evidence that any prepaid handstamped envelopes or letter sheets were ever sold.

Broadway Post Office, New York, N.Y.

Started by James C. Harriott in 1848. Sold to Dunham & Lockwood in 1855.

L80

1849(?) **Typo.**
26L1 L80 (1c) **gold,** *black,* glazed *1,000. 1,250.*
Cut to shape 250.
On cover —
Pair (tied) on cover —

1851(?)
26L2 L80 (1c) **black** 250. 400.
On cover *1,500.*
On cover, cut to shape, tied by handstamp *1,000.*
On cover with 3c #11 *2,750.*
Pair *1,000. 1,000.*
Pair on part of cover *1,500.*
Block of 4 *2,250.*

Cancellation: Black oval "Broadway City Express Post-Office 2 Cts." Also know with red "Paid" cancel.

Bronson & Forbes' City Express Post, Chicago, Ill.

Operated by W.H. Bronson and G.F. Forbes.

L81

1856 **Typo.**
27L1 L81 **black,** *green* 600. *2,000.*
On cover —
On cover, tied by handstamp, with 3c #11 *14,000.*
27L2 L81 **black,** *lilac* *3,500.*

Cancellation: Black circle "Bronson & Forbes' City Express Post" (2 types).

No. 27L2 is unique.

Brooklyn City Express Post, Brooklyn, N.Y.

According to the foremost students of local stamps, when this concern was organized its main asset was the business of Kidder's City Express Post, of which Isaac C. Snedeker was the proprietor.

L82

L83

1855-64 **Glazed Surface Paper** **Typo.**
28L1 L82 1c **black,** *blue* (shades) 25.00 *80.00*
On cover, tied by handstamp *400.00*
Block of 4 125.00
a. Tete beche pair *80.00*
28L2 L82 1c **black,** *green* 20.00 50.00
On cover, tied by handstamp *350.00*
On cover, tied by handstamp, with 3c #65 *1,250.*
Block of 4 100.00
a. Tete beche pair *125.00*
28L3 L83 2c **black,** *crimson* 60.00 70.00
On cover, tied by handstamp *400.00*
Block of 4 *300.00*
28L4 L83 2c **black,** *pink* 17.50 *100.00*
On cover, tied by handstamp *550.00*
On cover, tied by handstamp, with 3c #65 *1,750.*
Block of 4 100.00
a. Tete beche pair 60.00
28L5 L83 2c **black,** *dark blue* 50.00 *90.00*
On cover, tied by handstamp *500.00*
On cover, tied by handstamp, with 3c #11 *500.00*
Block of 4 *250.00*

No. 28L5 has frame (dividing) lines around design.

28L6 L83 2c **black,** *orange* — —
On cover —
a. Tete beche pair —

Unsurfaced Paper Colored Through
28L7 L83 2c **black,** *pink* 300.00 750.00

Cancellations: Black ring, red "PAID."
Reprints exist of Nos. 28L1-28L4, 28L6.

Browne & Co.'s City Post Office, Cincinnati, Ohio

Operated by John W.S. Browne

L84

L85

1852-55 **Litho.**
29L1 L84 1c **black** (Brown & Co.) 175. 150.
On cover, tied by handstamp *1,000.*
On cover with 3c #11 *2,750.*
Pair *450.*
29L2 L85 2c **black** (Browne & Co.) 175. 175.
On cover, tied by handstamp *5,750.*
On cover with 3c #11A *4,500.*
Pair *575.*

Cancellations: Black, blue or red circle "City Post"," red, bright blue or dull blue circle "Browne & Co. City Post Paid."

Browne's Easton Despatch, Easton, Pa.

Established by William J. Browne

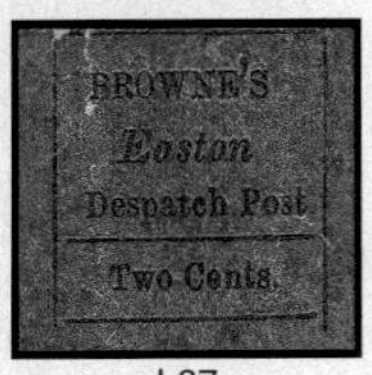

L87

L88

1857 **Glazed Surface Paper** **Typeset**

30L1	L87	2c **black,** *red*	—	*5,000.*
30L2	L88	2c **black,** *red*	—	—

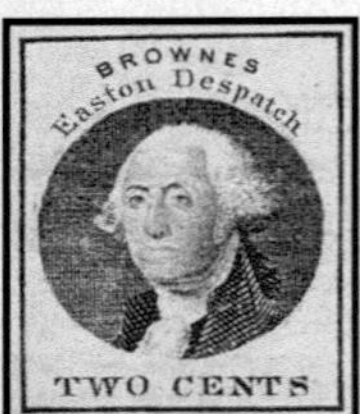

George Washington — L89

Wove Paper **Engr.**

30L3	L89	2c **black**	750.	*1,000.*
		Pair	*1,600.*	
		Block of 6	*5,750.*	

The No. 30L3 block of 6 is the only reported block of this stamp. Three pairs are reported.

The used value of No. 30L3 is for an example with pen cancel. There is one stamp with a handstamp cancel; value, $4,750.

Cancellation on No. 30L3: Black oval "Browne's Despatch Easton Pa."

Brown's City Post, New York, N.Y.

Established by stamp dealer William P. Brown for philatelic purposes.

L86

1877 **Glazed Surface Paper** **Typo.**

31L1	L86	1c **black,** *bright red*	200.00	*275.00*
		On cover, tied by handstamp		*2,250.*
31L2	L86	1c **black,** *yellow*	200.00	*275.00*
		On cover, tied by handstamp		*1,000.*
31L3	L86	1c **black,** *green*	200.00	*275.00*
		On cover, tied by handstamp		*1,000.*
31L4	L86	1c **black,** *violet*	200.00	*275.00*
		On cover, tied by handstamp		*2,250.*
31L5	L86	1c **black,** *vermilion*	200.00	*275.00*
		On cover, tied by handstamp		*500.00*

Cancellation: Black and purple circle "Brown's Despatch Paid."

Bury's City Post, New York, N.Y.

L90

No. 32L1

L91

1857 **Embossed without color**

32L1	L90	1c *blue*	*8,000.*	

Handstamped

32L2	L91	**black,** *blue*	—	

Bush's Brooklyn City Express, Brooklyn, N.Y.

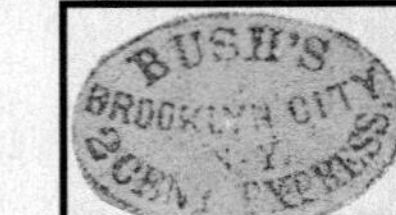

L91a

1848(?) **Cut to shape** **Handstamped**

157L1	L91a	2c **red,** *green,* glazed	*27,500.*	

No. 157L1 is unique. It is uncanceled on a large piece.

See Bush handstamp in Local Handstamped Covers section.

California City Letter Express Co., San Francisco, Calif.

Organized by J.W. Hoag, proprietor of the Contra-Costa Express, for local delivery. Known also as the California Letter Express Co.

L92

L93

L93a

1862-66 **Typeset**

33L1	L92	10c **red**	*3,000.*	—
		On cover, not tied		*7,500.*
		On cover, not tied, with 10c #68, with certificate		*23,000.*
33L2	L92	10c **blue**		—
		On cover, not tied, with certificate		*16,500.*
33L3	L92	10c **green**	5,500.	
		On cover, uncanceled, with certificate		*18,000.*
33L4	L93	10c **red**	—	—
33L5	L93	10c **blue**		*14,000.*
33L6	L93	10c **green**	*19,000.*	
		On cover, not tied, with certificate		*31,000.*

No side ornaments, "Hoogs & Madison's" in one line

33L7	L93a	10c **red**		*1,200.*
		On cover, not tied, with certificate		*19,000.*
33L8	L93a	10c **blue**	*4,000.*	
		On cover, not tied, with 10c #68, with certificate		*50,000.*

Nos. 33L1 unused, 33L1 on cover with #68, 33L3 used, 33L3 on cover, 33L6 unused, 33L6 on (patriotic) cover, 33L7 used, 33L7 on cover, 33L8 unused and 33L8 on cover with #68 each are unique. The other varieties of Nos. 33L1-33L8 are all rare.

California Penny Post Co.

Established in 1855 by H. L. Goodwin and partners. At first confined its operations to San Francisco, Sacramento, Stockton and Marysville, but branches were soon established at Benicia, Coloma, Nevada, Grass Valley and Mokelumne Hill. Operation was principally that of a city delivery post, as it transported mail to the General Post Office and received mail for local delivery. Most of the business of this post was done by means of prepaid envelopes.

L94

L94b

L94a

L95

L95a

1855 **Litho.**

34L1	L94	2c **blue**	700.	*750.*
		On cover		*20,000.*
		Pair	*3,000.*	
34L1B	L94b	2c **blue**		—
34L1A	L94a	3c **blue**	*850.*	
34L2	L95	5c **blue**	*250.*	*425.*
		On cover		*1,250.*
		Block of 4	750.	
34L3	L95a	10c **blue**	475.	—
		On cover		*3,000.*
		Pair	*1,000.*	

Cancellation: Blue circle "Penny Post Co."

Only one example of No. 34L1 on cover is recorded. The stamp is tied by manuscript cancel. Three examples of No. 34L1A are recorded, each uncanceled on cover.

L96

34L4	L96	5c **blue**	*600.*	*1,750.*
		On cover		*3,000.*
		On cover, uncanceled, with 10c #14		*55,000.*
		Strip of 3	*3,500.*	

The strip of 3 of No. 34L4 has faults but is unique. Value is for strip in faulty condition.

ENVELOPES

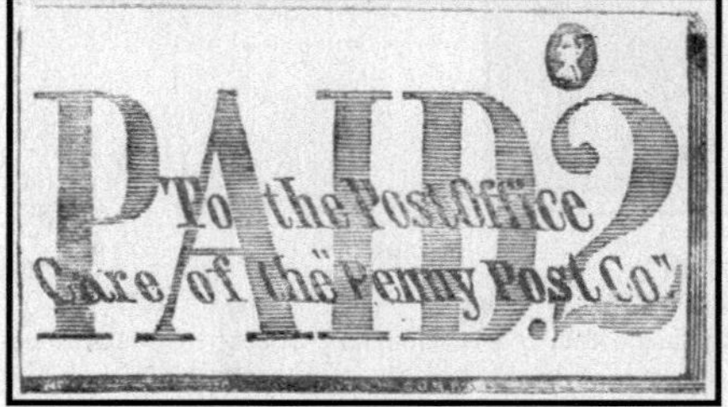

L97

1855-59

34LU1	L97	2c **black,** *white*	200.	*900.*
		With 1c #9		—
		With 3c #11		*9,000.*
		With 10c #14		*11,000.*
a.		Impressed on 3c US env. #U10	250.	*1,000.*

34LU2 L97 5c **blue,** *blue* 200. *900.*
34LU3 L97 5c **black,** *buff* 200. *900.*
a. Impressed on 3c US env. #U10 *1,500.*
34LU4 L97 7c **black,** *orange buff* —
a. Impressed on 3c US env. #U10 —

L98

34LU6 L98 7c **vermilion** on 3c US env. #U9 200.00 *1,000.*
34LU7 L98 7c **vermilion** on 3c US env. #U10 225.00 *1,750.*

L98A

34LU8 L98A 5c **black,** *white* 150. *1,200.*
34LU9 L98A 5c **black,** *buff* 150. *1,200.*
On cover, with 3c #11 *3,500.*
a. Impressed on 3c US env. #U10 *1,250.*
34LU10 L98A 7c **black,** *white* 150. *1,000.*
On cover, with 3c #11 —
a. Impressed on 3c US env. #U9 *1,750.*
34LU11 L98A 7c **black,** *buff* 150.00 *1,100.*
a. Impressed on 3c US env. #U10 *1,500.*
34LU11C L98A **black,** *buff,* "Collect Penny Postage" (no denomination) 250. *1,500.*
On cover, with 3c #11 —

L98B

34LU11B L98B 7c **black** on 3c US env. #U10 250. *1,400.*
34LU12 L98B 7c **black** on 3c US env. #U9 250. *4,500.*

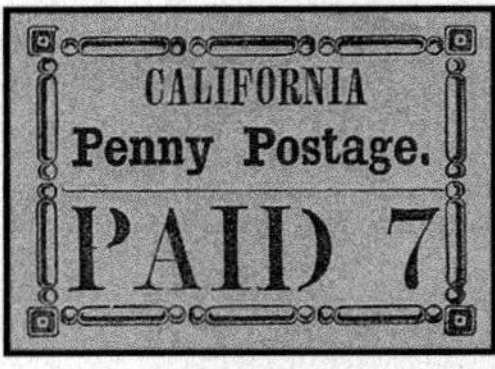

L98C

34LU13 L98C 5c **black,** *buff* — —

L98D

34LU13A L98D 5c **black,** *buff* —
34LU14 L98D 7c **black,** *buff* 300. *3,000.*
With 3c #11 *5,000.*
34LU15 L98D 7c **black** on 3c US env. #U9 350. *2,500.*
34LU16 L98D 7c **black** on 3c US env. #U10 — —

The non-government envelopes of types L97, L98A, L98C and L98D bear either 1c No. 9 or 3c No. 11 adhesives. These adhesives are normally canceled with the government postmark of the town of original mailing. Values are for covers of this kind. The U.S. adhesives are seldom canceled with the Penny Post cancellation. When they are, the cover sells for more.

At least eight different varieties of the 34LU14 are known with different printed instructions/addresses, some with room to add U.S. postage.

Carnes' City Letter Express, San Francisco, Calif.

Established by George A. Carnes, former P.O. clerk.

L99

1864 **Typo.**
35L1 L99 (5c) **rose** 175. 300.
On cover, tied *15,000.*
Block of 4 *750.*

Cancellations: Black dots. Blue dots. Blue "Paid." Blue oval "Wm. A. Frey."
See illustration L206

Overprinted in Blue

35L2 L99 10c **rose** 200.00

L100

1864 **Litho.**
35L3 L100 5c **bronze** 125.00
a. Tete beche pair 300.00
35L4 L100 5c **gold** 125.00
a. Tete beche pair 300.00
35L5 L100 5c **silver** 125.00
a. Tete beche pair 300.00
35L6 L100 5c **black** 125.00
a. Tete beche pair 300.00
35L7 L100 5c **blue** 100.00
a. Tete beche pair 250.00
35L8 L100 5c **red** 125.00
a. Tete beche pair 300.00

Printed in panes of 18 (3x6) from three settings of 6 (3x2), with the bottom setting inverted, creating three tete-beche pairs.

G. Carter's Despatch, Philadelphia, Pa.

Operated by George Carter

L101

1849-51
36L1 L101 2c **black** — 100.00
On cover, tied by pen cancel *225.00*
On cover, with 5c #1 —
On cover, with 5c #1, tied by handstamp *5,500.*
a. Vertically ribbed paper — 140.00
On cover, tied by pen cancel *300.00*

No. 36L1 exists on paper with a blue, red or maroon wash. The origin and status are unclear.
Cancellation: Black circle "Carter's Despatch."

ENVELOPE

L102

36LU1 L102 **blue,** *buff* *1,000.*
Cut to shape *150.*
On cover with 3c No. 10 *3,250.*
On cover with 3c No. 11 *1,750.*

Cheever & Towle, Boston, Mass.

Sold to George H. Barker in 1851

L104

1849(?)
37L1 L104 2c **blue** *600.* *350.*
Cut to shape 125.
On cover, tied by handstamp *7,000.*
On cover, not tied *1,500.*
On cover, not tied, cut to shape *500.*

Cancellation: Red oval "Towle's City Despatch Post 7 State Street."

Chestnut Street Line, Philadelphia, Pa.

The portrait almost certainly pictures Stephen Girard, a wealthy Philadelphian who died in 1836 and left his $6 million fortune to the city.

L104a

1856
169L1 L104a 1c **black,** *pink glazed* *17,500.*
On cover, with 3c #11 *25,000.*
169L2 L104a 1c **black,** *yellow glazed,* on cover, with 3c #11 *40,000.*

Only one each recorded of Nos. 169L1 used, 169L1 on cover, and 169L2 on cover.

Chicago Penny Post, Chicago, Ill.

L105

1862 **Typo.**
38L1 L105 (1c) **orange brown** 800. 1,250.
On cover, serrated perforations *5,000.*

Reprints exist.

Cancellation: Black circle "Chicago Penny Post A. E. Cooke Sup't."

Cincinnati City Delivery, Cincinnati, Ohio

Operated by J. Staley, who also conducted the St. Louis City Delivery Co. He established the Cincinnati post in January, 1883. The government suppressed both posts after a few weeks. Of the 25,000 Cincinnati City Delivery stamps printed, about 5,000 were sold for postal use. The remainders, both canceled and uncanceled, were sold to collectors.

L106

1883 **Typo.** ***Perf. 11***
39L1 L106 (1c) **carmine** 2.50 *12.50*
On cover *300.00*
a. Imperf., pair — —

Cancellation: Purple target.

City Despatch Post, New York, N.Y.

The City Despatch Post was started Feb. 1, 1842, by Alexander M. Greig and Henry T. Windsor. Greig's Post extended to 23rd St. Its operations were explained in a circular which throws light on the operations of all Local Posts:

New York City Despatch Post, Principal Office, 46 William Street.

"The necessity of a medium of communication by letter from one part of the city to another being universally admitted, and the Penny Post, lately existing having been relinquished, the opportunity has been embraced to reorganize it under an entirely new proprietary and management, and upon a much more comprehensive basis, by which Despatch, Punctuality and Security-those essential elements of success-may at once be attained, and the inconvenience now experienced be entirely removed."

"*** Branch Offices-Letter boxes are placed throughout every part of the city in conspicuous places; and all letters deposited therein not exceeding two ounces in weight, will be punctually delivered three times a day *** at three cents each."

"*** Post-Paid Letters.-Letters which the writers desire to send free, must have a free stamp affixed to them. An ornamental stamp has been prepared for this purpose *** 36 cents per dozen or 2 dolls. 50c per hundred. ***"

"No money must be put in boxes. All letters intended to be sent forward to the General Post Office for the inland mails must have a free stamp affixed to them."

"Unpaid Letters.-Letters not having a free stamp will be charged three cents, payable by the party to whom they are addressed, on delivery."

"Registry and Despatch.-A Registry will be kept for letters which it may be wished to place under special charge. Free stamps must be affixed for such letters for the ordinary postage, and three cents additional be paid (or an additional fee stamp be affixed), for the Registration."

NOTE: The word "Free," as used in this circular, should be read as "Prepaid." Likewise, the octagonal "FREE" cancellation should be taken to mean "Prepaid" (that is, "Free" of further charge).

The City Despatch Post was purchased by the United States Government and ceased to operate as a private carrier on August 15, 1842. It was replaced by the "United States City Despatch Post" which began operation on August 16, 1842, as a Government carrier.

No. 40L1 was issued by Alexander M. Greig; No. 40L2 and possibly No. 40L3 by Abraham Mead; Nos. 40L4-40L8 probably by Charles Cole.

L106a

FREE

Cancellation

This was the first adhesive stamp used in the United States. This stamp was also used as a carrier stamp. See No. 6LB1.

Plate of 42 (6x7) subjects

1842, Feb. 1

40L1 L106a 3c **black,** *grayish* 375. 350.
On cover, tied by handstamp *2,500.*
On cover, not tied *1,100.*
First day cover *25,000.*
Pair 850.
Block of 4 2,000.
Sheet of 42 *32,500.*

No. 40L1 was used until Aug. 16, 1842, the first day of operation of the U.S. City Despatch Post. The latest recorded No. 40L1 cover is dated Aug. 13, 1842.

Cancellations: Red framed "FREE" (see illustration above), red circle "City Despatch Post" (2 types).

Die reprints of No. 40L1 were made in 1892 on grayish white, orange, red and green surface-colored papers. It is believed that only four sets were made. Value, each reprint $500.

1846 **Glazed Surface Paper**

40L2 L106a 2c **black,** *green* *200.00* 150.00
On cover, tied by handstamp *750.00*
On cover, not tied *400.00*
a. With ms. "Cummings & Wright" overprint *3,000.*
On cover ("C&W" overprint) —

1847

40L3 L106a 2c **black,** *pink* *2,500.*
On cover, not tied, with certificate *9,000.*

Cancellations: Red framed "FREE," black framed "FREE," red circle "City Despatch Post."

L107

Similar to L106a with "CC" at sides.

1847-52

40L4 L107 2c **black,** *green glazed* *1,500.* 200.
On cover, tied by handstamp *1,500.*
On cover, not tied *600.*
Retouched plate ("Big Pupil" of right eye (Pos. 5 and 6)) —
On cover —
a. "C" at right inverted *4,000.*
b. "C" at left sideways —
On cover, tied by handstamp *1,000.*
c. "C" at right only —

Some students think No. 40L4c may have just a badly worn sideways "C" at left.

40L5 L107 2c **black,** *grayish* 900.
On cover, tied by handstamp *3,000.*
On cover, not tied *2,000.*
a. "C" at right inverted —
b. "C" at left sideways —
On cover, tied *4,250.*
On cover, uncanceled *1,250.*
c. "C" in ms. between "Two" and "Cents" *1,500.* *1,000.*
On cover, tied by handstamp *3,000.*
On cover, not tied *1,500.*
d. "C" at left sideways plus "C" in ms. between "Two" and "Cents" *4,000.*

40L6 L107 2c **black,** *vermilion glazed* 450. 400.
On cover, tied by handstamp *1,500.*
On cover, not tied *600.*
a. "C" at right inverted —
b. "C" at left sideways *4,500.*
On cover, tied by handstamp 5,250.
On cover, not tied *4,750.*

40L8 L107 2c **black,** *yellowish buff* ('52) — —
On cover, not tied, with certificate *15,000.*
a. "C" at right inverted *9,000.*
b. "C" at left sideways *9,000.*

Each of the No. 40L6b covers are unique as listed.

An uncanceled example of No. 40L8 exists on cover.

Cancellations: Red framed "FREE," black framed "FREE," black "PAID," red "PAID," red circle company, black grid of 4 short parallel bars.

City Dispatch, New York, N.Y.

L107a

1846 **Typo.**

160L1 L107a 2c **red** *3,000.* *4,500.*
On cover —
Vertical pair *19,000.*

The unique vertical pair is the only reported multiple of No. 160L1.

Cancellations: Red "PAID"; blue manuscript.

City Dispatch, Philadelphia, Pa.

Justice — L108

1860 **Thick to Thin Wove Paper** **Litho.**

41L1 L108 1c **black** 7.50 50.00
On cover, tied by handstamp *500.00*
Block of 4 55.00

Cancellations: Black circle "Penny Post Philada.," black circled grid of X's.

City Dispatch, St. Louis, Mo.

L109

Initials in black ms.

1851 **Litho.**

42L1 L109 2c **black,** *blue* *40,000.*

No. 42L1 used is unique. A second example, on cover, is recorded.

City Dispatch Post Office, New Orleans, La.

Stamps sold at 5c each, or 30 for $1.

L110

1847 **Glazed Surface Paper** **Typeset**

43L1 L110 (5c) **black,** *green* *6,000.*
On cover —

43L2 L110 (5c) **black,** *pink* *6,000.*
On cover, not canceled —

City Express Post, Philadelphia, Pa.

L111

L112

184-(?) **Typeset**

44L1 L111 2c **black,** on cover, uncanceled, with certificate *11,000.*

44L2 L112 (2c) **black,** *pink* *10,000.*
On cover, uncanceled, with certificate *20,000.*

44L3 L112 (2c) **red,** *yellow,* on cover, uncanceled *30,000.*

One example recorded of Nos. 44L1 and 44L3. Six No. 44L2 recorded, five of these uncanceled on covers.

See illustration L8.

City Letter Express Mail, Newark, N.J.

Began business under the management of Augustus Peck at a time when there was no free city delivery in Newark.

L113

1856 **Litho.**

45L1 L113 1c **red** *350.00* *500.00*
Cut to shape 100.00
On cover —
On cover, cut to shape, tied by handstamp, with 3c #11 *17,000.*

45L2 L113 2c **red,** on cover, cut to shape, uncanceled, with certificate *11,000.*

On No. 45L2, the inscription reads "City Letter/Express/City Delivery" in three lines across the top. The example on cover is unique.

City Mail Co., New York, N.Y.

There is evidence that Overton & Co. owned this post.

L114

1845

46L1 L114 (2c) **black,** *grayish* *1,500.* *1,500.*
On cover, not tied, with certificate *8,000.*

Cancellation: Red "PAID."

City One Cent Dispatch, Baltimore, Md.

L115

1851

47L1 L115 1c **black,** *pink* (on cover) —

Clark & Co., New York, N.Y.

(See Brady & Co.)

L116

1857 **Typo.**

48L1 L116 1c **red,** *yellow* 600. *900.*
On cover *2,500.*

Cancellation: Blue boxed "PAID."

Clark & Hall, St. Louis, Mo.

Established by William J. Clark and Charles F. Hall.

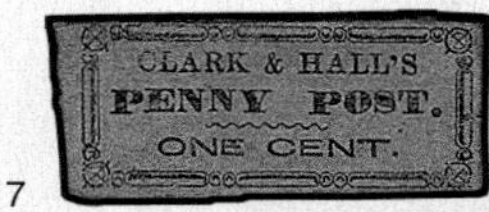

L117

1851 **Several varieties** **Typeset**

49L1 L117 1c **black,** *pink,* on cover, uncanceled, with certificate 19,000.

Clarke's Circular Express, New York, N.Y.

Established by Marion M. Clarke

George Washington — L118

Impression handstamped through inked ribbon
Cut squares from envelopes or wrappers

1865-68(?)

50LU1 L118 **blue,** wove paper 6,250.
a. Diagonally laid paper *4,500.*
50LU2 L118 **black,** diag. laid paper *5,750.*

No. 50LU1 unused is unique.

Cancellation: Blue dated company circle.

Clinton's Penny Post, Philadelphia, Pa.

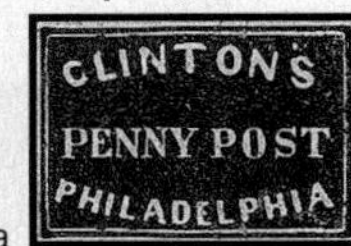

L118a

Typo.

161L1 L118a (1c) **black** *22,500.*

Cook's Dispatch, Baltimore, Md.

Established by Isaac Cook

L119

1853

51L1 L119 (1c) **green,** *white* *4,000.* *3,000.*
Cut to shape *1,500.*
On cover —

Cancellation: Red straight-line "I cook."

Cornwell's Madison Square Post Office, New York, N.Y.

Established by Daniel H. Cornwell. Sold to H.W. Bentley.

L120

1856 **Typo.**

52L1 L120 (1c) **red,** *blue* *1,500.* —
On cover, tied by handstamp *10,000.*
52L2 L120 (1c) **reddish brown** 250. *600.*
brownish red 250. *600.*
On cover, tied by handstamp *10,000.*
Strip of 3 —

Five Types identified of Nos. 52L1 and 52L2.

Cancellation: Black oval "Cornwall's Madison Square Post Office." Covers also bear black boxed "Paid Swarts." The covers of Nos. 52L1 and 52L2 are each unique.

Cressman & Co.'s Penny Post, Philadelphia, Pa.

L121

1856 **Glazed Surface Paper**

53L1 L121 (1c) **gold,** *black* *350.* *350.*
On cover, tied *1,500.*
Pair *1,200.*
53L2 L121 (1c) **gold,** *lilac,* on cover, acid tied *25,000.*

The vertical pair of No. 53L1 is unique. No. 53L2 also is unique.

Cancellation: Acid. (See D.O. Blood & Co. Nos. 15L13-15L16.)

Crosby's City Post, New York, N.Y.

Established by Oliver H. Crosby. Stamps printed by J.W. Scott & Co.

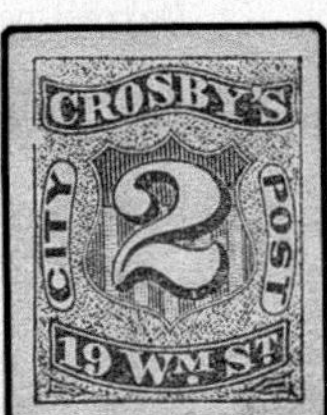

L123

Printed in sheets 25 (5x5), imprint at left.

1870 **Typo.**

54L1 L123 2c **carmine** (shades) 1.00 *50.00*
On cover, tied by handstamp *750.00*
Pair —
Sheet of 25 50.00

Cancellation: Black oval "Crosby's City Post."

Cummings' City Post, New York, N.Y.

Established by A. H. Cummings.

L124

1844 **Glazed Surface Paper** **Typo.**

55L1 L124 2c **black,** *rose* *1,000.*
On cover, tied, with certificate *5,000.*
On cover, not tied, with certificate —
55L2 L124 2c **black,** *green* *650.*
On cover *2,500.*
55L3 L124 2c **black,** *yellow* *750.*
On cover, tied by handstamp *2,000.*
On cover, not tied, with certificate *1,500.*

Cancellations: Red boxed "FREE," red boxed "PAID AHC," black cork (3 types).

L125

55L4 L125 2c **black,** *green* *750.00* *750.00*
55L5 L125 2c **black,** *olive* *750.00* *750.00*

L126

55L7 L126 2c **black,** *vermilion* *8,250.*
On cover, uncanceled, with certificate *22,000.*

As L124, but "Cummings" erased on cliche

55L8 L124 2c **black,** *vermilion* —

Nos. 55L7 on cover and 55L8 each are unique.

Cutting's Despatch Post, Buffalo, N.Y.

Established by Thomas S. Cutting

L127

Cut to shape

1847 **Glazed Surface Paper**

56L1 L127 2c **black,** *vermilion* —
On cover, cut to shape, uncanceled, with certificate *22,000.*

Davis's Penny Post, Baltimore, Md.

Established by William D. Davis and brother.

L128

1856 **Several varieties** **Typeset**

57L1 L128 (1c) **black,** *lilac* *2,750.*
On cover, tied by handstamp *12,500.*
a. "Pennq," pos. 2 *8,250.* *8,250.*

Cancellation: Red company circle.

Deming's Penny Post, Frankford, Pa.

Established by Sidney Deming

L129

1854 **Litho.**

58L1 L129 (1c) **black,** *grayish* *6,000.*
On cover, with 3c #11 *18,000.*

Douglas' City Despatch, New York, N.Y.

Established by George H. Douglas

L130

L131

Printed in sheets of 25

1879 **Typo.** ***Perf. 11***

59L1 L130 (1c) **pink** 10.00 *15.00*
On cover *300.00*
a. Imperf. 30.00 —

59L2 L130 (2c) **blue** 10.00 *15.00*
On cover, tied by handstamp *500.00*
a. Imperf. 50.00 —
b. Printed on both sides, imperf. —

Printed in sheets of 50 (10x5).

Perf. 11, 12 & Compound

59L3 L131 1c **vermilion** 15.00 *35.00*
On cover *325.00*
a. Imperf. 1.00 —
59L4 L131 1c **orange** 25.00 *50.00*
On cover, tied by handstamp *600.00*
59L5 L131 1c **blue** 30.00 *50.00*
On cover *300.00*
a. Imperf. 1.00 —
59L6 L131 1c **slate blue** 20.00 25.00
a. Imperf. 7.50 —

Cancellations on Nos. 59L1-59L6: Ornate purple design, purple circular design composed of bars and wedges.

Imperforates are believed to be remainders sold by the printer.

Dupuy & Schenck, New York, N.Y.

Established by Henry J. Dupuy and Jacob H. Schenck, formerly carriers for City Despatch Post and U. S. City Despatch Post.

Beehive — L132

1846-47 **Engr.**

60L1 L132 (1c) **black,** glazed paper 175. *300.*
On cover, tied by handstamp *1,750.*
On cover, tied by ms. *1,250.*
60L2 L132 (1c) **black,** *gray* 175. *300.*
On cover, tied by handstamp *1,500.*
On cover, tied by pen cancel *1,000.*
On cover, not tied *450.*

Cancellation: Red "PAID."

Eagle City Post, Philadelphia, Pa.

Established by W. Stait, an employee of Adams' Express Co.

L133

Black manuscript "WS" on used examples

1847 **Pelure Paper** **Typeset**

61L1 L133 (2c) **black,** *grayish* *14,000.* *10,000.*
Cut to shape, on cover —

No. 61L1 unused is unique. Value reflects a 1997 auction sale.

L134

Two types: 39 and 46 points around circle.

1846 **Litho.**

61L2 L134 (2c) **black** 125.00 *250.00*
On cover, tied by handstamp *1,500.*
On cover, not tied *1,000.*
Block of 4 600.00
a. Tete beche pair 500.00
Block of 18, containing 4 tete beche pairs *4,000.*
On cover, manuscript tied, with 5c #1 *17,500.*

Paper varies in thickness.
Five types identified of Nos. 61L3-61L4.
The No. 61L2 with No. 1 combination cover is unique.

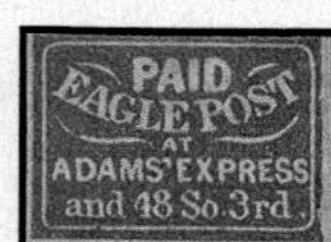

L135

1850

61L3 L135 (1c) **red,** *bluish* 225.00 225.00
On cover, not tied, with certificate *1,750.*
Cracked plate *350.00*
On cover with 5c #1 —
61L4 L135 (1c) **blue,** *bluish* 175.00 250.00
On cover, tied by handstamp *6,500.*
On cover, not tied *400.00*
Block of 4 *1,150.*
Cracked plate *350.00*

Cancellations on Nos. 61L2-61L4: Red "PAID" in large box, red circular "Stait's at Adams Express."

East River Post Office, New York, N. Y.

Established by Jacob D. Clark and Henry Wilson in 1850, and sold to Sigmund Adler in 1852.

L136

1852 **Typo.**

62L1 L136 (1c) **black,** *rose* (on cover) —

L137

1852-54 **Litho.**

62L3 L137 (1c) **black,** *green,* glazed *1,000.* —
On cover, not tied —

L138

1855

62L4 L138 (1c) **black,** *green,* glazed 250.00 250.00
On cover *800.00*
On cover, not tied *400.00*
Vertical pair *4,250.*

The unique No. 62L4 pair is the only recorded multiple of any of the East River Post Office stamps.

Eighth Avenue Post Office, New York, N.Y.

L139

1852 **Typo.**

63L1 L139 **red,** on cover *19,000.*

One example known, uncanceled on cover.

Empire City Dispatch, New York, N.Y.

Established by J. Bevan & Son and almost immediately suppressed by the Government.

L140

1881 **Typo.** **Laid Paper** ***Perf. 12***

64L1 L140 **black,** *green* 2.00
Block of 4 10.00
a. Imperf., pair 35.00
Block of 4 100.00
b. Horiz. pair, imperf. btwn. 60.00
c. Vert. pair, imperf. btwn. 40.00

No. 64L1 issued in panes of 100 (10x10) without marginal markings.

Essex Letter Express, New York, N.Y.

L141

1856 **Glazed Surface Paper** **Typo.**

65L1 L141 2c **black,** *red* *1,250.*

Though uncanceled examples exist affixed to covers, some authorities doubt that No. 65L1 was placed in use.

Faunce's Penny Post, Atlantic City, N.J.

Established in 1884 by Ancil Faunce to provide local delivery of letters to and from the post office. Discontinued in 1887.

L141a

1885 **Die cut**

152L1 L141a (1c) **black,** *red* 325. 350.
On cover *1,500.*

Jabez Fearey & Co.'s Mustang Express, Newark, N.J.

Established by Jabez Fearey, Local Agent of the Pacific & Atlantic Telegraph Co.

L142

1887 (?) **Glazed Surface Paper** **Typeset**

66L1 L142 **black,** *red* *400.00*
On cover —

Some authorities consider this item to be an express company label rather than a stamp.

Fiske & Rice

Authorities consider items of this design to be express company labels rather than stamps.

Floyd's Penny Post, Chicago, Ill.

Established by John R. Floyd early in 1860, operated by him until June 20, 1861, then continued by Charles W. Mappa.

John R. Floyd — L144

1860 **Typo.**

68L1 L144 (1c) **blue** (shades) — 125.
On cover, tied by handstamp *1,000.*
On cover with 3c #26 *2,750.*
On cover with 3c #65 *1,500.*
Pair 275.
Strip of 4 *1,250.*
68L2 L144 (1c) **brown** *500.* *1,000.*
On cover *4,250.*

68L3 L144 (1c) **green** *4,500.* *3,250.*
On cover —
On 3c pink entire *20,000.*

Cancellations: Black circle "Floyd's Penny Post Chicago," black circle "Floyd's Penny Post" and sunburst, black or blue oval "Floyd's Penny Post Chicago."

Franklin City Despatch Post, N.Y.

(See Bouton's Manhattan Express.)

Frazer & Co., Cincinnati, Ohio.

Established by Hiram Frazer. Stamps used while he was a Cincinnati letter carrier. Stamps of designs L146 and L147 were carrier stamps when used on cover betweeen Feb, 3, 1848 and June 30, 1849.

L145

Cut to shape

1845 **Glazed Surface Paper**
69L1 L145 2c **black,** *green,* on cover —

L146

1845-51 **Wove Paper** **Litho.**
69L2 L146 2c **black,** *pink* — *3,500.*
On cover, ms. tied *6,750.*
69L3 L146 2c **black,** *green* *2,500.* *2,750.*
On 1847 cover, tied by handstamp *11,000.*
On cover, not tied *3,500.*
69L4 L146 2c **black,** *yellow* *2,500.* *2,500.*
On cover, tied by handstamp *7,000.*
69L5 L146 2c **black,** *grayish* *2,500.* *2,500.*
On cover, tied by handstamp *7,000.*

Two stamps of type L146 show manual ms. erasure of "& Co."

L147

1848-51
69L6 L147 2c **black,** *rose* *2,750.*
On 1848 cover, not tied, with certificate *6,500.*
69L7 L147 2c **black,** *blue* (shades) *3,500.* *2,000.*
69L8 L147 2c **black,** *yellow* *2,750.*
On 1848 part-printed notice *7,500.*

Hiram Frazer was a government letter carrier until June 5, 1849. Therefore, any usage before that date is a government-carrier usage, not a local-post usage.

Freeman & Co.'s Express, New York, N.Y.

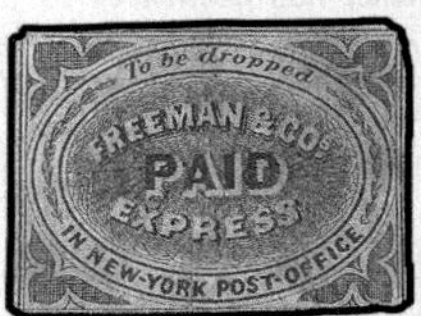

L147a

1855 (?) **Litho.**
164L1 L147a (25c) **blue** *3,500.*
On cover, not tied, with certificate —

Friend's Boarding School, Barnesville, Ohio.

(Barclay W. Stratton, Supt.)

On Nov. 6, 1877 the school committee decided to charge the students one cent for each letter carried to or from the post office, one and a half miles away. Adhesive labels were prepared and sold for one cent each. Their sale and use continued until 1884.

Type I

Type II

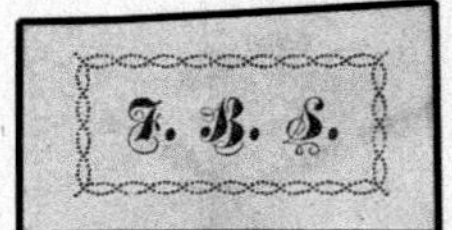

Type III

Three main types and sizes of frame

1877 **Typo.**
151L1 L147b (1c) **black** *175.00* —
On cover, uncanceled, affixed to backflap *400.00*
On cover, tied by handstamp, with 3c #158 *2,400.*
On cover, tied by handstamp, with 2c #210 *2,500.*

No. 151L1 was usually affixed to the back of the envelope and left uncanceled.

Gahagan & Howe City Express, San Francisco, Calif.

Established by Dennis Gahagan and C. E. B. Howe, as successors to John C. Robinson, proprietor of the San Francisco Letter Express. Sold in 1865 to William E. Loomis, who later purchased the G. A. Carnes business. Loomis used the adhesive stamps and handstamps of these posts, changing the Carnes stamp by erasing his name.

L148

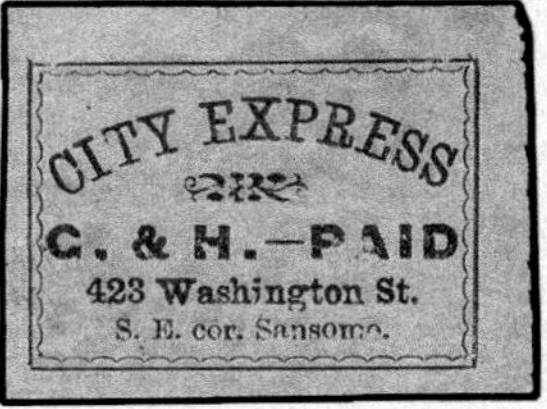

L149

1849-70 **Typeset**
70L1 L148 5c **light blue** 1,200. *800.*
70L2 L149 (5c) **blue** 150. 400.
a. Tete beche pair *450.*
Sheet of 20, with 4 tete beche pairs —

Sheets of No. 70L2 contain five vertical rows of 4, the first two rows being reversed against the others, making horizontal tete beche pairs with wide margins between. The pairs were not evenly locked up in the form. There are five different types of No. 70L2.

L150

70L3 L150 (5c) **black** 40.00 45.00
Pair 100.00
Strip of 3 175.00

No. 70L3 Overprinted

70L4 L150 10c **black** *1,500.*

Cancellations: Blue or black oval "Gahagan & Howe," blue or black oval "San Francisco Letter Express" and horseman (Robinson), blue or black oval "PAID" (Loomis).

Glen Haven Daily Mail, Glen Haven, N.Y.

Glen Haven was located at the head of Skaneateles Lake, Cayuga County, N.Y., until 1910 when the City of Syracuse, having purchased the land for reservoir purposes, razed all the buildings.

Glen Haven, by 1848, had become a famous Water Cure resort, with many sanitariums conducted there. The hamlet had a large summer colony interested in dress reform under the leadership of Amelia Jenks Bloomer; also antislavery, and other reform movements.

A local post was established by the hotel and sanitarium managements for their guests' convenience to deliver mail to the U.S. post offices at Homer or Scott, N.Y. The local stamps were occasionally pen canceled. They are known tied to cover with the Homer or Scott town postmark when the local stamp was placed adjacent to the government stamp and received the cancellation accidentally. The local stamps are only known used in conjunction with government stamps.

L151

L152

1854-58 **Several varieties of each** **Typeset**
71L1 L151 1c **black,** *dark green* 1,000.
a. "Gien" instead of "Glen" *3,500.*
On cover, uncanceled, with 3c #26, with certificate *6,250.*

No. 71L1a unused (actually uncanceled on piece) and on cover with #26 each are unique.

Glazed Surface Paper

71L2 L152 1c **black,** *green* *500.* *500.*
On cover *2,000.*
On cover, tied by handstamp. with 3c #11 *3,750.*

Links at corners — L153

Varying ornaments at corners — L153a

Several varieties of each
Glazed Surface Paper

71L3 L153 1c **black,** *green* 200. *225.*
On cover *2,000.*
On cover, tied by handstamp, with 3c #11 *1,750.*
On cover, not tied, with 3c #11 *500.*
Pair 700.
71L4 L153a 1c **black,** *green* 300. 350.
On cover *1,000.*
On 3c entire #U9, tied by handstamp *1,000.*
On cover, tied by handstamp, with three 1c #7 *1,100.*
"Block" of 3 *900.00*

The strip of 3 of No. 71L4 is the only known multiple of any Glen Haven stamp. It has faults and is valued thus.

Gordon's City Express, New York, N. Y.

Established by Samuel B. Gordon

L154

1848-52 Typo. Surface Colored Paper

72L1	L154 2c **black,** *vermilion*		*7,000.*	
	On cover, uncanceled, with certificate			*15,000.*
72L2	L154 2c **black,** *green*		150.	*175.*
	On cover, tied by handstamp			950.

Glazed Surface Paper

72L3	L154 2c **black,** *green*	125.	*200.*
	On cover, not tied		650.

Cancellation: Small black or red "PAID."

Grafflin's Baltimore Despatch, Baltimore, Md.

Established by Joseph Grafflin; operated from Apr. 1, 1855, until June 30, 1863.

L155

Printed in sheets of 49

1856 Litho.

73L1	L155 1c **black**	200.	*350.*
	On cover, tied by handstamp		*4,000.*
	On cover, tied by handstamp, with 3c #11		*4,500.*
	Block of 4	*1,050.*	

Originals show traces of a fine horizontal line through tops of most of the letters in "BALTIMORE."

Guy's City Despatch, Philadelphia, Pa.

Established by F. A. Guy, who employed 8 carriers.

L156

Sheets of 25 (5x5)

1879 Typo. *Perf. 11, 12, 12½*

74L1	L156 (1c) **pink**	30.00	35.00
	On cover, tied by handstamp		800.00
	Block of 4	150.00	
a.	Imperf., pair	—	
74L2	L156 (1c) **blue**	45.00	60.00
	On cover, tied by handstamp		1,500.
	Block of 4	225.00	
a.	Imperf., pair	—	
b.	(1c) **Ultramarine**	*75.00*	*100.00*

Cancellation: Purple company oval.

Guy's City Despatch was in operation from April to June, 1879. When Guy's was suppressed, the remainders were sold to a New York stamp dealer.

Hackney & Bolte Penny Post, Atlantic City, N.J.

Established in 1886 by Evan Hackney and Charles Bolte to provide delivery of mail to and from the post office. Discontinued in 1887.

L156a

Die cut

153L1	L156a (1c) **black,** *red*	250.	375.
	On cover		*1,500.*
	On cover, tied by handstamp, with 2c #210		*4,500.*

Hale & Co.

Established by James W. Hale at New York, N.Y., to carry mail to points in New England, New York State, Philadelphia and Baltimore. Stamps sold at 6 cents each or "20 for $1.00."

L157

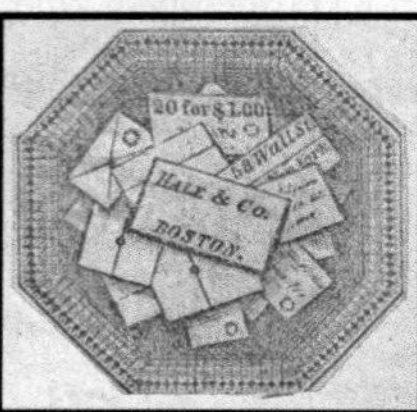

L158

Pelure paper was used for initial printings, with medium wove paper used subsequently.

Printed in sheets of 20 (5x4)

1844 Typo.

75L1	L157 (6c) **light blue** (shades)	65.00	40.00
	Cut to shape		17.50
	On cover, tied by handstamp		500.00
	Cut to shape on cover, tied by handstamp		200.00
	Pair on cover, not tied		*800.00*
	Strip of 3 on cover, tied by handstamp		*7,000.*
	Strip of 3 on cover, not tied		*2,750.*
a.	Pelure paper		—
75L2	L157 (6c) **red,** *bluish*	*300.00*	300.00
	Cut to shape		75.00
	On cover, tied by handstamp		*2,500.*
	On cover, tied by pencil cancel		*1,500.*
	On cover, not tied		*500.00*
	Cut to shape on cover, tied by handstamp		*1,000.*
	Pair on cover		—
	Ms. "23 State," cut to shape		*1,900.*
	On cover		*4,500.*
a.	Pelure paper		—

Two covers recorded showing the manuscript change of address.

Same Handstamped in Black or Red, "City Despatch Office, 23 State St."

75L3	L157 (6c) **red,** *bluish* (Bk), cut to shape	*2,000.*
	Pair, partly cut to shape	*44,000.*
75L4	L157 (6c) **blue** (R), cut to shape	*2,000.*

No. 75L3 single and pair each are unique.

No. 75L3 and 75L4 represent the first handstamped overprints in philately.

Same as Type L157 but street address omitted

75L5	L158 (6c) **blue** (shades)	40.00	20.00
	Cut to shape		5.00
	On cover, tied by handstamp		450.00
	On cover, not tied		300.00
	Cut to shape on cover, tied by handstamp		300.00
	Pair on cover, tied by handstamp		900.00
	Strip of 3 on cover, not tied		—
	Pair	*500.00*	
	Block of 9	—	
	Block of 15	*9,500.*	
	Sheet of 20 (5x4)	*17,000.*	
	Ms. "23 State St.," on cover, tied by handstamp		*7,500.*

Cancellations on Nos. 75L1-75L5: Large red "PAID," red, black or blue oval "Hale & Co." (several types and cities), small red ornamental framed box (several types), red negative monogram "WE," magenta ms. "NB" (New Bedford).

The No. 75L5 sheet of 20 is unique.

Same as Type L158 Handstamped in Red "Office / 23 State St"

75L6	L158 (6c) **blue,** on cover	—

No. 75L6 is unique.

Hall & Mills' Despatch Post, New York, N.Y.

Established by Gustavus A. Mills and A. C. Hall.

L159

Several Varieties

1847 Glazed Surface Paper Typeset

76L1	L159 (2c) **black,** *green*	300.	300.
	On cover, tied by handstamp		*2,500.*
	On cover with 5c #1		*2,500.*

T.A. Hampton City Despatch, Philadelphia, Pa.

L159a

L159b

Several varieties of L159a.

1847 Cut to shape Typeset

77L1	L159a (2c) **black**	*1,500.*	
	On cover, tied by handstamp		*14,000.*
	On cover, uncanceled, with certificate		*5,000.*
77L2	L159b **black**	*4,000.*	
	On cover		*13,000.*

Only one cover known with No. 77L1 tied by handstamp. Five or six covers are known with stamp uncanceled.

Two covers known with No. 77L2, each with stamp canceled, not tied. May 23 cover with certificate is valued above. Second cover is undated Valentine cover. The unused No. 77L2 is unique.

A handstamp similar to type L159b with denomination "2cts" or "3c" instead of "PAID." in center has been used as a postmark.

Hanford's Pony Express, New York, N.Y.

Established by John W. Hanford.

L160

1845 Glazed Surface Paper Typo.

78L1	L160 2c **black,** *orange yellow* (shades)	400.	400.
	Cut to shape		60.
	On cover, tied by handstamp		*2,250.*
	On cover, not tied		*1,250.*

Cancellation: Small red "PAID."

The handstamp in black or red formerly listed as Nos. 78LU1-78LU6 is illustrated in the Local Handstamped Covers section. It was used as a postmark and there is no evidence that any prepaid handstamped envelopes or lettersheets were ever sold.

George S. Harris City Despatch Post, Philadelphia, Pa.

L160a

L160b

1847 (?) **Litho. or Typo.**

79L1 L160a (2c) **black,** on cover —

Litho. or Typo.

79L2 L160b **black,** on cover 30,000.

One example each known of Nos. 79L1-79L2, each uncanceled on cover, No. 79L2 with certificate.

Hartford, Conn. Mail Route

L161

Plate of 12 (6x2) varieties

1844 **Glazed Surface Paper** **Engr.**

80L1 L161 (5c) **black,** *yellow* 1,250. 2,000.
On cover, not canceled 11,000.
On cover, not tied 11,000.
Pair 5,000.
Pair on cover, not canceled 32,500.

80L3 L161 **black,** *pink* 3,500.

Chemically affected examples of No. 80L1 appear as buff, and of No. 80L3 as salmon.

Cancellations are usually initials or words ("S," "W," "South," etc.) in black ms. This may indicate destination or routing.

Hill's Post, Boston, Mass.

Established by Oliver B. Hill

L162

1849 **Typo.**

81L1 L162 1c **black,** *rose,* on cover, tied by handstamp 7,500.
On cover, canceled but not tied, with certificate 6,500.

Only one No. 81L1 tied to cover recorded. Six covers recorded bearing No. 80L1 not tied, all but one of those also uncanceled.

A. M. Hinkley's Express Co., New York, N.Y.

Organized by Abraham M. Hinkley, Hiram Dixon and Hiram M. Dixon, in 1855, and business transferred to the Metropolitan Errand & Carrier Express Co. in same year.

L163

Sheets of 64 (8x8)

1855 **Litho.**

82L1 L163 1c **red,** *bluish* 650.00
Block of 4 —
a. Tete-beche pair —

It is doubtful that No. 82L1 was ever placed in use.

Only one example of No. 82L1a is recorded. It is contained in a block of 16 of No. 82L1.

Reprints exist on white paper somewhat thicker than the originals.

Homan's Empire Express, New York, N.Y.

Established by Richard S. Homan

L164

1852 **Several varieties** **Typeset**

83L1 L164 **black,** *yellow* — —
a. "1" for "I" in "PAID" 9,750.

No. 83L1a is unique. It is affixed to a cover front, uncanceled, with certificate.

Hopedale Penny Post, Milford, Mass.

Hopedale was a large farm community southwest of Milford, Mass. The community meeting of Feb. 2, 1849, voted to arrange for regular transportation of mail to the nearest post office, which was at Milford, a mile and a half distant, at a charge of 1c a letter. A complete history of this community may be found in "The Hopedale Community," published in 1897.

Rayed asterisks in corners — L165

Plain asterisks in corners — L166

Several varieties of Types L165-L166.

1849 **Glazed Surface Paper** **Typeset**

84L1 L165 (1c) **black,** *pink* 800.00 800.00
On cover with 3c #11, handstamp tied 3,750.
On cover with 3c #11A, not canceled 1,000.

84L2 L166 (1c) **black,** *pink* 1,000. 1,000.

Types L165 and L166 probably were printed together in a single small plate.

L167

Wove Paper **Typo.**

84L3 L167 (1c) **black,** *yellow* — 2,400.
Cut to shape 900.
On cover —

84L4 L167 (1c) **black,** *pink* 600. 600.
Pair 4,500.

The No. 84L4 pair is unique, defective at top. It is the only recorded multiple of any Hopedale Penny Post issue.

J. A. Howell's City Despatch, Philadelphia, Pa.

L167a

184? **Typo.**

165L1 L167a **black** —

Hoyt's Letter Express, Rochester, N.Y.

David Hoyt, agent at Rochester for the express company of Livingston, Wells & Pomeroy, operated a letter and package express by boats on the Genesee Canal between Dansville, N.Y., and Rochester, where connection was also made with Pomeroy's Letter Express.

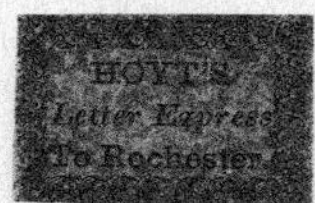

L168

Several Varieties

1844 **Glazed Surface Paper** **Typeset**

85L1 L168 (5c) **black,** *vermilion* 4,000. —
a. "Lettcr" instead of "Letter" —
Pair, #85L1, 85L1a, on cover front —

Humboldt Express, Nevada

A branch of Langton's Pioneer Express, connecting with the main line of Pioneer Express at Carson City, Nevada, and making tri-weekly trips to adjacent points.

L169

1863 **Litho.**

86L1 L169 25c **brown** 1,750. 1,250.
Pair 2,750.
On cover (U.S. Envelopes Nos. U34 or U35) 40,000.
On cover with 3c #65 —

Cancellations: Blue oval "Langton's Pioneer Express Unionville." Red "Langton & Co."

Hussey's Post, New York, N.Y.

Established by George Hussey.

Reprints available for postage are so described.

L170

1856 **Litho.**

87L1 L170 (1c) **blue** 500. 500.
On cover, tied by handstamp 2,750.
On cover, with U.S. 3c (#11) —

L171

1857

87L2 L171 (1c) **black** 300. 200.
On cover, tied by handstamp 1,850.

87L3 L171 (1c) **red** 200.
On cover, tied by handstamp 750.

Cancellation on Nos. 87L1-87L3: Black "FREE."

L172

1858

87L4 L172 1c **brown red** 45. 125.
On cover, tied by handstamp 450.
Pair on cover 1,000.

87L5 L172 1c **black** *175.* —
On cover —
Block of 4 —
Strip of 7 —

Cancellation on Nos. 87L4-87L5: Black circle "1ct PAID HUSSEY 50 Wm. ST," date in center.

The No. 87L5 block of 4 and strip of 7 are unique.

L173

1858

87L6 L173 (1c) **black** 5.00 —
On cover —
87L7 L173 (1c) **rose red** 5.00 —
On cover —
Sheet of 46 *350.00*
87L8 L173 (1c) **red** 60.00 —
On cover —
Sheet of 46 —

Type L173 was printed in sheets of 46: 5 horizontal rows of 8, one row of 6 sideways at botton. Type L173 saw little, if any, commercial use and was probably issued mainly for collectors. Covers exist, many with apparently contemporaneous corner cards. On-cover stamps bear a black HUSSEY'S POST handstamp, but most if not all of Nos. 87L6-87L8 were canceled after the post ceased to operate.

L174

1858 **Typo.**

87L9 L174 (1c) **blue** 5.00

L175

1859 **Litho.**

87L10 L175 1c **rose red** 15.00 *40.00*
On cover, tied by handstamp *400.00*

No. 87L10 in orange red is not known to have been placed in use.

Cancellations: Black "FREE," black company circle "1 CT PAID HUSSEY 50 WM ST.," no date in center (smaller than cancel on Nos. 87L4-87L5).

87L11 L175 1c **lake** —
87L12 L175 1c **black** —

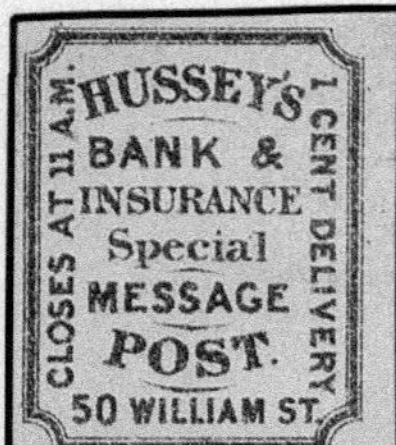

L176

1862

87L13 L176 1c **black** 25.00
87L14 L176 1c **blue** 15.00 *25.00*
On cover, tied by handstamp *600.00*
87L15 L176 1c **green** 20.00
On cover *450.00*
87L16 L176 1c **red** 30.00
87L17 L176 1c **red brown** 30.00
87L18 L176 1c **brown** 30.00
87L19 L176 1c **lake** —
87L20 L176 1c **purple** 30.00
87L21 L176 1c **yellow** 30.00

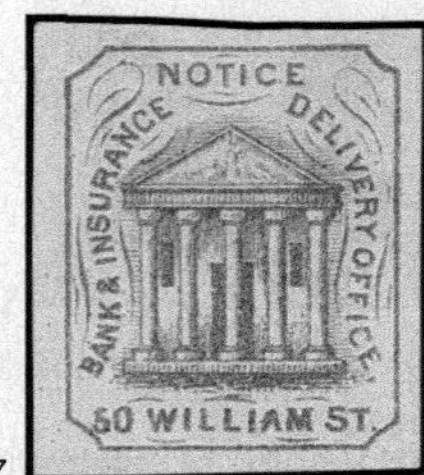

L177

Similar to L174 but has condensed "50" and shows a short flourish line over the "I" of "DELIVERY."

Printed in sheets of 49

1862

87L22 L177 (1c) **blue** 3.00 *25.00*
On cover —

L178

Similar to L171, but no dots in corners — L179

Printed in sheets of 30

1863

87L23 L178 (1c) **blue** 7.50
87L24 L179 (1c) **black** 5.00
Sheet of 30 225.00
87L25 L179 (1c) **red** 6.50
Sheet of 30 250.00
On cover with 6c #115 *12,500.*

See No. 87L52.

L180

87L26 L180 1c **brown red** 5.00 *25.00*
Block of 4 25.00
On cover, tied by handstamp *450.00*

A so-called "reprint" of No. 87L26, made for J. W. Scott, has a colored flaw extending diagonally upward from the "I" in "CITY."

Reprints of types L173, L174, L178, L179 and L180 were made in 1875-76 on thicker paper in approximately normal colors and were available for postage.

See No. 87L52

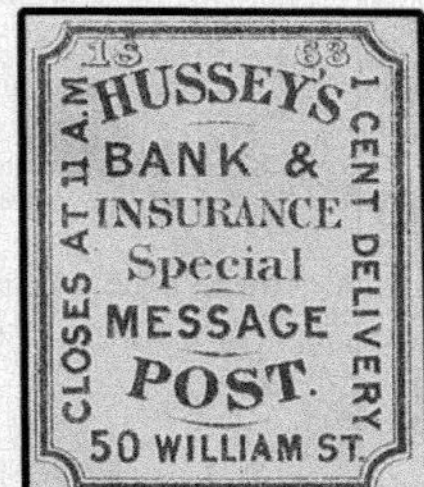

L182

1863

87L27 L182 1c **blue** 20.00
Cut to shape 12.50
On cover, tied by handstamp *500.00*
87L28 L182 1c **green** 27.50 —
Cut to shape 14.00
On cover, tied by handstamp *550.00*
87L29 L182 1c **yellow** 25.00 —
Cut to shape 12.50
On cover, tied by handstamp *500.00*
87L30 L182 1c **brown** 27.50
Cut to shape 14.00
87L31 L182 1c **red brown** 30.00
Cut to shape 15.00
87L32 L182 1c **red** 27.50
Cut to shape 14.00
87L33 L182 1c **black** 40.00
Cut to shape 20.00
87L34 L182 1c **violet** 40.00
Cut to shape 20.00
87L35 L182 2c **brown** 40.00 *75.00*
Cut to shape 20.00
On cover, tied by handstamp *650.00*

The 2c blue dated 1863 exists only as a counterfeit.

1865

87L38 L182 2c **blue** 35.00 *45.00*
On cover, tied by handstamp *475.00*

1867

87L39 L182 2c **blue** 45.00 40.00
On cover, tied by handstamp *450.00*

1868

87L40 L182 2c **blue** 40.00 *65.00*
On cover, tied by handstamp *500.00*

1869

87L41 L182 2c **blue** 45.00 *70.00*
On cover, tied by handstamp *500.00*

1871

87L42 L182 2c **blue** 40.00 *65.00*
On cover, tied by handstamp *750.00*

L183

1872 **Wove Paper**

87L43 L183 **black** 5.00 *20.00*
On cover, tied by handstamp *300.00*
Pair on cover, tied by handstamp *1,500.*
87L44 L183 **red lilac** 9.00 *40.00*
On cover, tied by handstamp *300.00*
87L45 L183 **blue** 6.00 *40.00*
On cover, tied by handstamp *300.00*
Pair on cover, tied by handstamp *750.00*
87L46 L183 **green** 10.00 *45.00*
On cover, tied by handstamp *300.00*

Sheets contain four panes of 28 each. Double periods after "A.M." on two stamps in two panes, and on four stamps in the other two panes.

Covers show postmark reading: "HUSSEY'S SPECIAL-MESSENGER EXPRESS-PAID-54 PINE ST."

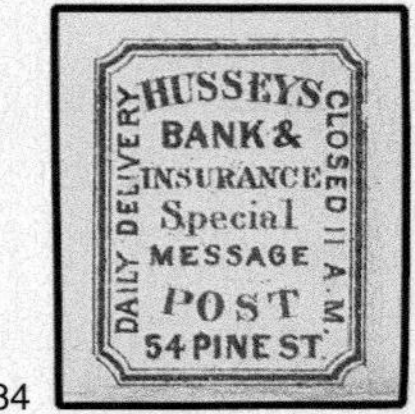

L184

1872 **Thick Laid paper**

87L47 L184 **black** 10.00 *35.00*
On cover —
Block of 4 45.00
87L48 L184 **yellow** 17.50 *65.00*
87L49 L184 **red brown** 17.50 *50.00*
On cover *200.00*
87L50 L184 **red** 17.50 *40.00*
On cover —

L185

1873 **Thin Wove Paper**

87L51 L185 2c **black** 75.00 *150.00*
On cover, tied by handstamp *500.00*

A reprint of No. 87L51, believed to have been made for J. W. Scott, shows a 4mm break in the bottom frameline under "54."

Type of 1863

1875 **Thick Wove Paper**

87L52 L179 (1c) **blue** *750.00*

L186

L186 in imitation of L180, but no corner dots, "S" for "$," etc.

1875

87L53 L186 1c **black** 2.00

Some authorities believe Nos. 87L52-87L53 are imitations made from new stones. Attributed to J. W. Scott.

"Copyright 1877" — L188

L188a

1877 **Thick Wove Paper**

87L55 L188 **black** 175.00 —
On cover *600.00*

Error of design, used provisionally. Stamp was never copyrighted. Printed singly.

87L56 L188a **black** 350.00

Thin Wove Paper

87L57 L188a **blue** 45.00
87L58 L188a **rose** 30.00
On cover —

Perf. 12½

87L59 L188a **blue** 3.00 *10.00*
On cover *250.00*
a. Imperf. horizontally, pair —
87L60 L188a **rose** 3.00 *10.00*
On cover *250.00*

"TRADE MARK" small — L189

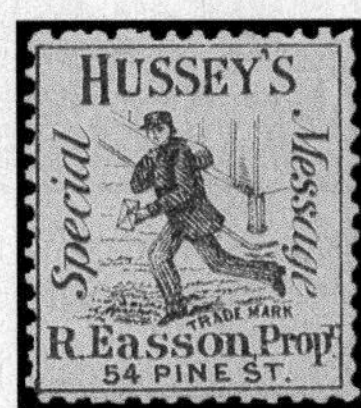

"TRADE MARK" medium — L190

1878 **Wove Paper** ***Perf. 11, 11½, 11x12, 12***

87L61 L189 **blue** 15.00 *50.00*
On cover, tied by handstamp *150.00*
87L62 L189 **carmine** 12.50 *40.00*
On cover, tied by handstamp *200.00*
87L63 L189 **black** 100.00

Nos. 87L61-87L63 exist imperforate.

Perf. 11, 12, 12½, 14, 16 and Compound

87L64 L190 **blue** 5.00 *17.50*
On cover, tied by handstamp *200.00*
87L65 L190 **red** 5.00 *10.00*
On cover, tied by handstamp *150.00*
87L66 L190 **black** —

The existence of No. 87L66 either perforated or as an imperf reprint has been questioned by specialists. The editors would like to see authenticated evidence of its existence.

Nos. 87L64-87L65 imperf. are reprints.

"TRADE MARK" larger, touching "s" of "Easson." — L191

1879 ***Perf. 11, 12, and Compound***

87L67 L191 **blue** 3.00 *10.00*
On cover, tied by handstamp *300.00*

1880 ***Imperf.***

87L70 L191 **blue** 4.00 *50.00*
On cover, tied by handstamp *450.00*
87L71 L191 **red** 5.00 *75.00*
87L72 L191 **black** 4.00

The authenticity of Nos. 87L70-87L72 has not been fully established.

L192

Two types of L192:
I. Imprint "N. F. Seebeck, 97 Wall St. N. Y." is in lower tablet below "R Easson, etc."
II. Imprint in margin below stamp.

1880 **Glazed Surface Wove Paper** ***Perf. 12***

87L73 L192 **brown,** type I 10.00 *20.00*
On cover, tied by handstamp *250.00*
Block of 4 —
a. Type II 3.00 *5.00*
On cover, tied by handstamp *250.00*
b. Horiz. pair, imperf. between 50.00
c. Imperf., pair, type I 50.00
87L74 L192 **ultramarine,** type I 12.50 *25.00*
On cover, tied by handstamp *350.00*
a. Imperf., pair —
Imperf (single) on cover *135.00*
b. Deep blue, type II 40.00
87L75 L192 **red,** type II 1.50 *3.50*
On cover, tied by handstamp *175.00*
Block of 4 6.50
a. Imperf, single on cover *150.00*
b. Horiz. pair, imperf between —

1882 ***Perf. 16, 12x16***

87L76 L192 **brown,** type I 12.50 *30.00*
On cover, tied by handstamp *125.00*
87L77 L192 **ultramarine,** type I 10.00 *20.00*
On cover, tied by handstamp *125.00*

Cancellations: Violet 3-ring target, violet ornamental "T." Imperf. impressions of Type I in various colors, on horizontally laid paper, ungummed, are color trials.

SPECIAL DELIVERY STAMPS

L181

Typographed; Numerals Inserted Separately

1863 **Glazed Surface Paper**

87LE1 L181 5c **black,** *vermilion* 2.00 *17.50*
On cover, tied by handstamp *325.00*
87LE2 L181 10c **gold,** *green* 2.50 *20.00*
On cover, tied by handstamp *325.00*
87LE3 L181 15c **gold,** *black* 3.50 *27.50*
On cover, tied by handstamp *325.00*
On cover with 1c #87L10, tied by handstamps —
87LE4 L181 20c **black** 2.00 *17.50*
On cover, tied by handstamp *325.00*
87LE5 L181 25c **gold,** *blue* 4.00 *40.00*
On cover, tied by handstamp *325.00*
87LE6 L181 30c **black,** *vermilion* —
87LE7 L181 50c **black,** *green* —

Nos. 87LE1-87LE7 on cover show Hussey handstamp cancellations in various types.

Nos. 87LE4 and 87LE5 are on unglazed paper, the latter surface colored. Ten minor varieties of each value, except the 30c and 50c, which have the figures in manuscript. Printed in two panes of 10, certain values exist in horizontal cross-gutter tete beche pairs.

Originals of the 5c to 20c have large figures of value. The 25c has condensed figures with decimal point. Reprints exist with both large and condensed figures. Reprints of the 25c also exist with serifs on large figures.

Most of the Hussey adhesives are known on cover, tied with Hussey Express postmarks. Many of these were canceled after the post ceased to operate as a mail carrier. "On cover" values are for original stamps used while the post was operating.

LETTERSHEETS AND WRAPPERS (No. 87LUP2)

L192a

1856 **Handstamped** **Inscribed: "82 Broadway"**

87LUP1 L192a **black** — *500.*

L192b

1858 **Inscribed: "50 William St. Basement"**

87LUP2 L192b **black,** *manila* — *600.*
With 1c #87L3, tied by handstamp *1,250.*
87LUP3 L192b **black** — *650.*
With 1c #87L2, tied by handstamp *2,750.*
With 1c #87L3, tied by handstamp *1,750.*

Nos. 87LUP1 and 87LUP3 appear on papers of various colors.

Jefferson Market P. O., New York, N. Y.

Established by Godfrey Schmidt

L193

1850 **Glazed Surface Paper** **Litho.**

88L1 L193 (2c) **black,** *pink* *9,750.*
88L2 L193 (2c) **black,** *blue* —
On cover, tied by handstamp —
On cover, not tied *3,500.*

Four examples recorded of No. 88L1, all unused. Five No. 88L2 recorded, all on covers (two with stamp tied by handstamp).

Jenkins' Camden Dispatch, Camden, N. J.

Established by Samuel H. Jenkins and continued by William H. Jenkins.

George Washington — L194

There are two types of design L194.

1853-54 **Litho.**
89L1 L194 **black** (fine impression) (1854) 350. 450.
Block of 9 7,500.
On cover, not tied 900.
On cover, tied by ms., with certificate 3,000.

George Washington — L194a

Typo. from Woodcut

89L2 L194a **black,** *yellow* (coarse impression) (1853) 3,000.
On cover, tied by ms., with certificate 6,500.

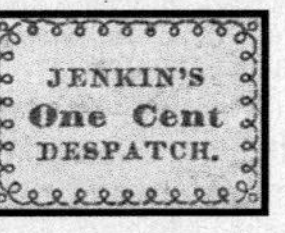

L195

Typeset

89L3 L195 1c **black,** *grayish* (1853) —
On cover, tied by ms. 17,500.

No. 89L3 was probably the first stamp issued by Jenkins. Each of the four known examples is of a different type. One exampled is unused; three are recorded on cover (one of which is uncanceled).

Johnson & Co.'s City Despatch Post, Baltimore, Md.

Operated by Ezekiel C. Johnson, letter carrier

L196

1848 **Typeset**
90L1 L196 2c **black,** *lavender*, on cover, uncanceled 22,500.

Two recorded examples of No. 90L1, each uncanceled on cover.

Jones' City Express, Brooklyn, N. Y.

George Washington — L197

1845 **Glazed Surface Paper** **Engr.**
91L1 L197 2c **black,** *pink* 1,000. 1,500.
On cover, not tied, with certificate 3,000.

Cancellation: Red oval "Boyd's City Express Post."

Kellogg's Penny Post & City Despatch, Cleveland, Ohio

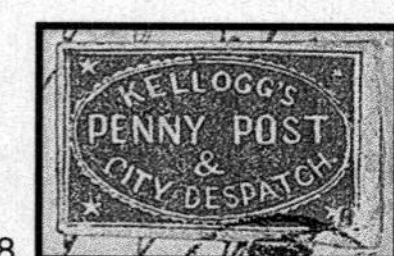

L198

1853 **Typo.**
92L1 L198 (1c) **vermilion** 1,750.
On cover, tied by handstamp —
On cover, tied by handstamp, with 3c #11, with certificate 42,500.
On cover, not tied, with 3c #11, with certificate 15,000.
On 3c entire #U2, tied by handstamp 9,000.

Cancellation: Black grid.

Kidder's City Express Post, Brooklyn, N.Y.

In 1847, Henry A. Kidder took over the post of Walton & Co., and with the brothers Isaac C. Snedeker and George H. Snedeker increased its scope. In 1851, the business was sold to the Snedekers. It was operated under the old name until 1853 when the Brooklyn City Express Post was founded.

L199

Stamps bear black manuscript "I S" control in two styles.

1847 **Glazed Surface Paper** **Typo.**
93L1 L199 2c **black,** *blue* (shades) 750. 500.
On cover, tied by handstamp 6,000.
On cover, not tied 4,500.
Block of 4 3,500.

Cancellation: Red "PAID."

Reprinted on green paper.

Kurtz Union Despatch Post, New York, N.Y.

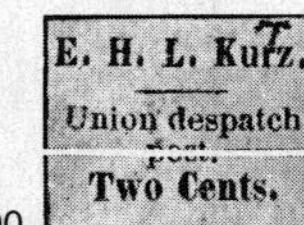

L200

Typeset; "T" in Black Ms.

1853 **Glazed Surface Paper**
94L1 L200 2c **black,** *green* 3,500.

Langton & Co.

(See Humboldt Express.)

Ledger Dispatch, Brooklyn, N.Y.

Established by Edwin Pidgeon. Stamps reported to have been sold at 80 cents per 100. Suppressed after a few months.

L201

1882 **Typo.** ***Rouletted 12 in color***
95L1 L201 **rose** (shades) 300. 600.
Block of 4 1,500.

Letter Express

Established by Henry Wells. Carried mail for points in Western New York, Chicago, Detroit and Duluth.

L202

L203

1844 **Glazed Surface Paper** **Typo.**
96L1 L202 5c **black,** *pink* 300.00 200.00
On cover, tied by ms. cancel 1,000.
On cover, not tied 500.00
Pair on cover, tied by handstamp 3,500.
Pair on cover, tied by ms. cancel 2,000.
Pair on cover, not tied 1,000.
Pair 700.00 450.00
Block of 10 28,500.
96L2 L202 5c **black,** *green* — 500.00
On cover, tied by ms. cancel 5,000.
On cover, not tied 3,500.
Pair 1,500.
96L3 L203 10c **black,** *pink* — 500.00
On cover, tied by ms. cancel 2,000.
On cover, not tied 1,500.
On cover, not tied, with #117L1, not tied, with certificate 2,000.
Pair 1,500. 1,500.
Pair on cover, uncanceled 5,000.
Strip of 3 9,250.
a. Bisect on cover, tied by ms. cancel —
Bisect on cover, uncanceled 2,000.

No. 96L3a was sold as a horizontal or vertical bisect. It is known used singly for 5c (rare), or as two bisects for 10c (extremely rare). Stamps are known almost exclusively tied with black ms. "X" covering the cut, and can be authenticated by experts.

The block of 10 of No. 96L1 is the only block recorded of any Letter Express issue. Value represents actual auction sale price in 1999.

L204

96L4 L204 10c **black,** *scarlet* — 2,500.
On cover, tied by ms. cancel, with certificate 9,250.
a. Tete beche pair, one stamp a horiz. bisect, on piece 8,750.

Cancellations: Red large partly boxed "PAID," red boxed "Boyd's City Express Post."

Locomotive Express Post

L205

1847 (?) **Handstamped**
97L1 L205 **black,** uncancelled, on cover —

No. 97L1 is unique.

Wm. E. Loomis Letter Express, San Francisco, Calif.

William E. Loomis established this post as the successor to the Gahagan & Howe City Express, which he bought in 1865. He continued to use the Gahagan & Howe stamps unchanged. Later Loomis bought Carnes' City Letter Express. He altered the Carnes stamp by erasing "CARNES" from the plate and adding the address below the oval: "S.E. cor. Sans'e & Wash'n."

L206

1868 **Typo.**
98L1 L206 (5c) **rose** 300.00 650.00
On cover, tied by ms. 4,250.

Cancellation: Blue "PAID."

McGreely's Express, Alaska

Established in 1898 by S. C. Marcuse to carry letters and packages by motorboat between Dyea and Skagway, Alaska.

L208

1898 **Typo.** ***Perf. 14***
155L1 L208 25c **blue** 50.00
Block of 4 250.00

The status of No. 155L1 is questioned.

McIntire's City Express Post, New York, N.Y.

Established by William H. McIntire

Mercury — L207

1859 **Litho.**

99L1 L207 2c **pink**	10.00	*100.00*
Block of 4	75.00	
On cover, tied by handstamp		*3,250.*
a. Period after CENTS omitted	—	

Cancellation: Black oval "McIntire's City Express Post Paid."

McMillan's City Dispatch Post, Chicago, Ill.

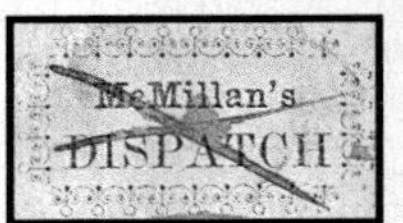

L208a

1855 **Typeset**

100L1 L208a **black,** *rose* — *25,000.*

No. 100L1 is unique.

Mac & Co's Dispatch, Fallsington-Morrisville, Pa.

L208b

Typo.

166L1 L208b 1c **black,** on 3c entire #U1, uncanceled, with certificate — *17,500.*

No. 166L1 is unique.

Magic Letter Express, Richmond, Va.

Established by Evans, Porter & Co.

L209

L209a

1865 **Typo.**

101L1 L209 1c **black,** on cover, not tied by cancel		*40,000.*
101L2 L209a 2c **black,** *brown*		*14,000.*
101L3 L209a 5c **black,** *brown*	—	*8,000.*
On cover		*24,000.*

Nos. 101L1-101L2 each are unique.

Mason's New Orleans City Express, New Orleans, La.

J. Mason, proprietor

L210

1850-51 **Typeset**

102L1 L210 ½c **black,** *blue* (value changed to "1" in black ms.)		*12,500.*
On cover, tied		—
102L2 L210 2c **black,** *yellow*	—	*3,000.*
On cover, tied by handstamp		*10,000.*

Cancellations: Red grid, small red circle "Mason's City Express."

Mearis' City Despatch Post, Baltimore, Md.

Established by Malcom W. Mearis

L211

L212

Black ms. initials "M W M" control on all stamps

1850-51 **Typeset**

103L1 L211 1c **black,** *gray*	—	—
On cover, tied by handstamp		*22,000.*
103L2 L212 1c **black,** *gray*	—	
103L3 L212 2c **black,** *gray*	—	
On cover, uncancelled, with certificate		*15,000.*
a. Horiz. pair, #103L2-103L3	—	

Two types of No. 103L3.

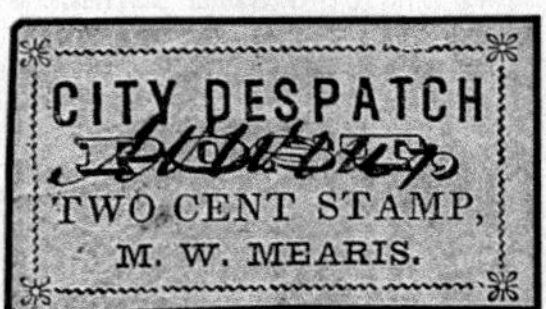

L213

Two types of each.

103L4 L213 1c **black,** *gray*	—
103L5 L213 2c **black,** *gray*	—
a. Horiz. pair, #103L4-103L5	—

L214

103L6 L214 1c **black,** *gray* — *11,000.*

No. 103L6 is unique; tied on small piece by handstamp.

Corner ornaments of Nos. 103L1-103L6 differ on each stamp. All varieties of Nos. 103L1-103L6 contained in one plate.

Menant & Co.'s Express, New Orleans, La.

L215

1853 (?) **Typo.**

104L1 L215 2c **dark red** — *15,000.*

Only four examples are known. Two have Philatelic Foundation Certificates. All four have faults, and the stamp is valued thus.

Reprints are fairly common and are orange red, not dark red.

Mercantile Library Association, New York, N.Y.

Stamps paid for special delivery service of books ordered from the library, and of forms especially provided to subscribers. The forms bore a government stamp on the outside, a library stamp inside.

L216

1870-75 **Litho.**

105L1 L216 5c **black,** *maroon*	*250.*	*350.*
105L2 L216 5c **black,** *yellow*	*350.*	*500.*
a. With delivery check attached at right	*1,150.*	
b. With order number on tab below stamp		—
105L3 L216 5c **blue**	*350.*	*500.*
Pair, on postal card		*1,400.*
105L5 L216 6c **black,** *maroon*	*2,250.*	—
105L6 L216 10c **black,** *yellow*	*500.*	*750.*

No. 105L5 is slightly larger than the 5c and 10c stamps.

The stamps "on cover" are affixed to cutouts from order blanks showing order number, title of book desired, and subscriber's name and address. When canceled, the stamps and order blanks show a dull blue double-lined oval inscribed "MERCANTILE LIBRARY ASSOCIATION" and date in center. The stamps are really more a form of receipt for a prepaid parcel delivery service than postage stamps.

POSTAL CARD

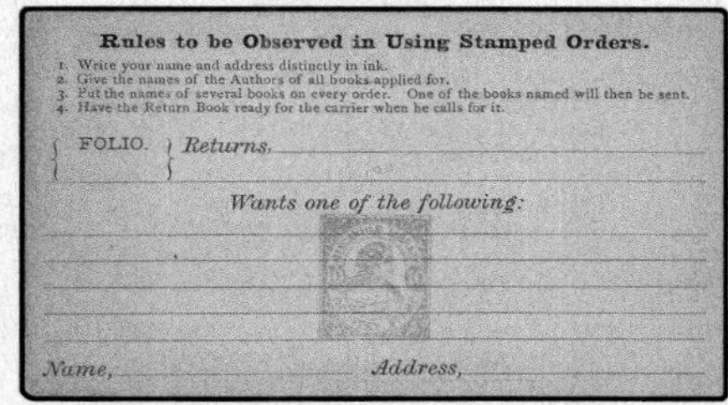
Rules to be Observed in Using Stamped Orders.

1. Write your name and address distinctly in ink.
2. Give the names of the Authors of all books applied for.
3. Put the names of several books on every order. One of the books named will then be sent.
4. Have the Return Book ready for the carrier when he calls for it.

FOLIO. | *Returns.*

Wants one of the following:

Name, *Address,*

Printed on U.S. Postal Card, First Issue

105LUX1 L216a 10c **yellow** — *2,500.*

No. 105LUX1 is unique.

Messenkope's Union Square Post Office, New York, N.Y.

Established by Charles F. Messenkope in 1849 and sold to Joseph E. Dunham in 1850.

L217

1849 **Glazed Surface Paper** **Litho.**

106L1 L217 (1c) **black,** *green*	90.	90.
On cover, tied by handstamp		*500.*
Two singles on cover (2c rate), tied by handstamp		*3,000.*
Pair on cover (2c rate), tied by handstamp		*3,000.*
On cover with 5c #1		*3,000.*
On cover, tied by handstamp, with 3c #10		*1,500.*
On cover, tied by handstamp, with 3c #11		*2,000.*
On cover with 3c #26		*1,000.*
Strip of 3	*400.*	
106L2 L217 (2c) **black,** *pink*	—	—
On cover		—

Some examples of No. 106L1 are found with "MESSENKOPES" crossed through in black ms. in an apparent attempt (by Dunham?) to obliterate it.

Cancellations: Red "PAID," red oval "DUNHAMS UNION SQUARE POST OFFICE," red grid of dots.

Metropolitan Errand and Carrier Express Co., New York, N.Y.

Organized Aug. 1, 1855, by Abraham M. Hinkley, Hiram Dixon, and others.

L218

L219

Printed in sheets of 100 (10x10), each stamp separated by thin ruled lines.

1855 Thin to Medium Wove Paper Engr.

107L1 L218 1c **red orange** (shades) 20.00 *25.00*
Cut to shape 5.00 *4.00*
On cover, tied by handstamp *600.00*
On cover, cut to shape, tied by handstamp *150.00*
On cover, cut to shape, tied by handstamp, with 3c #11 *900.00*
Pair 35.00
Pair on cover, tied by handstamp —
Pair on cover, uncanceled *1,000.*
Block of 4 *90.00*
107L2 L218 5c **red orange** 225.00
Cut to shape 60.00
107L3 L218 10c **red orange** 300.00
Cut to shape 60.00
107L4 L218 20c **red orange** 325.00
Cut to shape 60.00

Cancellations: Black, blue or green boxed "PAID."
The imprint "Baldwin, Bald & Cousland New York" appears in the bottom margin of the two stamps at the bottom right of the sheets.
Nos. 107L1-107L4 have been extensively reprinted in brown and in blue on paper much thicker than the originals.

ENVELOPE
Embossed
Wide Diagonally Laid Paper

107LU1 L219 2c **red,** *amber,* entire *125.00* —

No. 107LU1 has been reprinted on amber wove, diagonally laid or horizontally laid paper with narrow lines. The embossing is sharper than on the original.

Metropolitan Post Office, New York, N.Y.

Established by Lemuel Williams who later took William H. Laws as a partner.

L220

L221

L222

L223

Nos. 108L1-108L5 were issued die cut

1852-53 Glazed Surface Paper Embossed

108L1 L220 (2c) **red** (L. Williams) *550.* *550.*
On cover, tied by pencil, with certificate —
On cover, tied by blue ms., with two 3c #11 and strip of 3 12c #17 —
108L2 L221 (2c) **red** (address and name erased) *1,000.* *1,000.*
On cover, uncanceled, with certificate *5,500.*
108L3 L222 (2c) **red** *275.* *350.*
On cover, tied by handstamp *3,500.*
108L3A L222 (2c) **blue** *600.* *700.*
On cover, tied by handstamp *7,500.*
On cover, tied by handstamp, with 3c #11 *8,250.*

Wove Paper

108L4 L223 1c **red** 75. *90.*
On cover 300.
On cover, tied by handstamp, with 3c #11 *1,500.*
On cover, cut to shape, not tied, with 3c #11A *500.*
108L5 L223 1c **blue** 600. *100.*
Cut to shape 400.
On cover 350.
On cover, cut to shape, tied by handstamp, with 3c #11 *300.*
On cover, tied by handstamp, with 3c #26 *700.*

Cancellations: Black circle "METROPOLITAN P. O.," black boxed "PAID W. H. LAWS," black smudge.

G. A. Mills' Despatch Post, New York, N.Y.

Established by Gustavus A. Mills at 6 Wall St., succeeding Hall & Mills.

L224

Several Varieties

1847 Glazed Surface Paper Typeset

109L1 L224 (2c) **black,** *green* *500.* 500.
On cover, uncanceled *1,400.*
On cover, not tied, with 5c #1 *7,500.*
On cover with 10c #2 —

Moody's Penny Dispatch, Chicago, Ill.

Robert J. Moody, proprietor

"CHICAGO" 8mm — L225

Several Varieties

1856 Glazed Surface Paper Typeset

110L1 L225 (1c) **black,** *red,* *1,750.* *1,750.*
On cover, tied by handstamp, with 3c #11 *16,000.*
On cover with three 1c #9 *70,000.*
Vert. strip of 3 showing 3 varieties: period, colon, comma after "Dispatch" *18,000.* 6,000.
a. "CHICAGO" sans serif and 12½mm *2,750.*
b. "Henny" instead of "Penny," on cover, tied by handstamp, with 3c #11 *45,000.*

Cancellations: Blue circle "Moody's Despatch."
The vertical strip of 3, the cover with the three 1c stamps and No. 110L1b, are each unique.

Morton's Post, Philadelphia, Pa.

L225a

167L1 L225a 2c **black,** *grayish,* on cover, uncanceled, with certiifi-cate *14,000.*

No. 167L1 is unique.

New York City Express Post, New York, N.Y.

L226

Several varieties

1847 Glazed Surface Paper Engr.

111L1 L226 2c **black,** *green* *1,200.* *1,500.*
Cut to shape 400. *450.*
On cover, not tied *1,750.*
On cover, tied by handstamp *4,000.*
On cover, cut to shape, tied by handstamp *2,000.*

Wove Paper

111L2 L226 2c **orange** — —
On cover *8,000.*

One Cent Despatch, Baltimore, Md., Washington, D.C.

Established by J.H. Wiley to deliver mail in Washington, Georgetown and Baltimore. Made as many as five deliveries daily at 1 cent if prepaid, or 2 cents payable on delivery.

Washington, D.C. — L227

Two types:
I. Courier's letter points to "O" of "ONE."
II. Letter points to "N" of "ONE."

Inscribed at bottom "Washington City"

1856 Litho.

112L1 L227 1c **violet** *225.* 150.
On cover, tied by handstamp *750.*
On cover, tied by handstamp, with 3c #11 *1,500.*
On cover, tied, with 10c #15 *5,500.*
On 3c entire #U1, tied by handstamp *750.*
Horiz. pair, types I & II *1,250.*

Baltimore, Maryland — L228

No name at bottom

112L2 L228 1c **red** 450. 250.
On cover, tied by handstamp *1,750.*
On cover with 3c #11 *2,250.*

The No. 112L1 pair is the unique multiple of either One Cent Despatch stamp.
Cancellation on Nos. 112L1-112L2: Black circle "City Despatch."

Overton & Co.

Carried mail principally between New York and Boston; also to Albany. Stamps sold for 6c each, 20 for $1.

L229

1844

113L1 L229 (6c) **black,** *greenish* *400.* *400.*
On cover, tied by ms. *5,000.*
On cover, not tied *2,250.*
Pair *850.*
a. "FREE" printed below design *1,750.*
On cover *4,000.*
Pair on cover, not tied, with certificate *18,500.*

Cancellation: Black "PAID." Red "Cd."

Penny Express Co.

Little information is available on this post, but a sheet is known carrying the ms. initials of Henry Reed of the Holladay staff. The post was part of the Holladay Overland Mail and Express Co. system.

In 1866 in the West the "short-bit" or 10 cents was the smallest currency generally used. The word "penny" is believed to refer to the "half-bit" or 5 cents (nickel).

L230

Printed in sheets of 32 (8x4)

1866 **Litho.**
114L1 L230 5c **black** 400.00
Pair *850.00*
a. Sheet of 32 initialed "HR," black ms., original gum *7,000.*
114L2 L230 5c **blue** 15.00
Block of 4 65.00
Sheet of 32, no gum 650.00
114L3 L230 5c **red** 15.00
Block of 4 65.00
Sheet of 32, no gum 650.00

Nos. 114L1-114L3 lack gum and probably were never placed in use.

Philadelphia Despatch Post, Philadelphia, Pa.

(See D.O. Blood & Co.)

Pinkney's Express Post, New York, N.Y.

L231

1851 **Glazed Surface Paper** **Typo.**
115L1 L231 2c **black,** *green* *1,400.*
Cut to shape *800.*
On cover, tied by ms., with certificate *4,500.*
On cover, uncanceled, with certificate *9,000.*
On cover, uncanceled, cut to shape, with certificate *3,500.*

On the cover with No. 115L1 tied, the stamp is faulty. It is valued thus.

Pips Daily Mail, Brooklyn, N.Y.

L232

1862 (?) **Litho.**
116L2 L232 1c **black,** *buff* 375. *2,250.*
116L3 L232 1c **black,** *yellow* 600.
116L4 L232 1c **black,** *dark blue* 800.

Two types of Nos. 116L2-116L4: Type I, period after "Avenue;" Type II, comma after "Avenue."
No. 116L2 used is unique.

Pomeroy's Letter Express.

Established in 1844 by George E. Pomeroy. Carried mail principally to points in New York State. Connected with Letter Express for Western points.

L233

Engraved by John E. Gavit, Albany, N.Y.
(Seen as "GAVIT" in bottom part of stamp). Sheets of 40 (8x5).

Value Complete ("20 for $1")

1844 **Surface Colored Wove Paper**
117L1 L233 5c **black,** *greenish yellow, dull yellow* — *100.00*
On cover, tied by ms. *1,000.*
On cover, handstamp cancel *1,000.*
Pair *375.00*
Pair on cover *3,500.*
Block of 4 —

Value Incomplete ("20 for $-")

117L2 L233 **black,** *greenish yellow, dull yellow* — *1,500.*
On cover, tied by ms. *5,000.*
On cover, handstamp cancel, not tied *4,500.*
On cover, ms. cancel, not tied *3,500.*
On cover, with No. 117L1 —

Value Complete ("20 for $1")

Thick Wove Paper

117L2A L233 5c **black,** *buff,* without gum —
117L2B L233 5c **black,** *yellow, buff tint on back,* without gum 5.00
Sheet of 40 300.00
117L2C L233 5c **black,** *yellow (colored through),* without gum 5.00
a. 5c **black,** orange yellow (colored through), with gum 10.00

No. 117L2A may be a proof impression. Nos. 117L2B-117L2Ca may be remainders or reprints.

Thin Bond Paper

117L3 L233 5c **blue (shades)** 150.00 *500.00*
On cover, not tied *2,000.*
On cover, tied by pen cancel *2,500.*
Pair on cover, not tied *6,000.*
Block of 4 —
117L4 L233 5c **black** 5.00 *150.00*
On cover *1,500.*
Pair on cover, red "Paid" cancel *7,500.*
Strip of 4 on cover *5,000.*
Block of 4 30.00
Sheet of 40, without gum 350.00
117L5 L233 5c **red (shades)** 5.00 *300.00*
On cover, not tied *3,500.*
Strip of 3 on cover *8,500.*
Block of 4 25.00
Sheet of 40 300.00
117L6 L233 5c **lake** — *750.00*
On cover, tied by ms. *1,500.*
Pair on cover —
On cover, handstamp cancel *6,000.*
Block of 4 —

Cancellations: Large red partly boxed "PAID" (Nos. 117L1, 117L6), red "Cd" (Nos. 117L1-117L2, 117L4); stamps are considered "tied to cover" by this "Cd" when the impression shows through the letter paper.

Reprints/remainders of Nos. 117L1, 117L3, 117L4 and 117L5 are plentiful in unused condition, including multiples and sheets. They differ slightly from the original issue Nos. 117L1 and 117L2. Authentication of Nos. 117L1 and 117L2 unused is recommended. A 5c chocolate brown and a 5c bright yellow were prepared but not issued. No. 117L2 was never remaindered.

Thin Pelure Paper

117L7 L233 5c **deep blue (shades)** — —
Pair on cover, not tied *2,500.*
117L8 L233 5c **black** — —
Pair — —
117L9 L233 5c **chocolate brown** — —

5c stamps on a medium, fibrous paper in orange, deep blue, black, red and brown exist. It is believed that stamps on this paper come from remainders of a printing that was prepared but never issued. They may also be reprints.

P. O. Paid, Philadelphia, Pa.

See note in Carriers' Stamps Section.

Price's City Express, New York, N.Y.

L235

1857-58 **Glazed Surface Paper** **Litho.**
119L1 L235 2c **black,** *vermilion* 275.
On cover, tied by handstamp *5,000.*
On cover, ms. tied *900.*
On cover, not tied, with certificate *750.*
On cover, tied by handstamp, with 3c #26 —
119L2 L235 2c **black,** *green* 250.
Cut to shape 85.

L236

1858 **Sheets of 108 (12x9)**
119L3 L236 2c **black,** *green* 5.00 *150.00*
On cover —
Block of 4 27.50

Cancellation on #119L3: red oval "Price's/City Letter Exp/3 Everett House/Paid."

Price's Eighth Avenue Post Office, New York, N.Y.

Established by James Price at 350 Eighth Avenue, in 1854, and sold to Russell in the same year.

L237

1854 **Litho.**
120L1 L237 (2c) **red,** *bluish* 600.00
On cover, uncanceled, with certificate *7,500.*

Priest's Despatch, Philadelphia, Pa.

Established by Solomon Priest

L238

L239

1851 **Glazed Surface Paper** **Typo.**
121L1 L238 (2c) **silver,** *vermilion* *2,250.* —
121L2 L238 (2c) **gold,** *dark blue* *500.*

Wove Paper

121L2A L238 (2c) **bronze,** *bluish* *500.* *1,000.*
121L3 L238 (2c) **black,** *yellow* *500.*
On cover, uncanceled, with 3c #11, with certificate *5,500.*
121L4 L238 (2c) **black,** *rose* *500.*
On cover, uncanceled, with certificate *2,000.*
121L5 L238 (2c) **black,** *blue* *1,000.*
121L6 L239 (2c) **black,** *yellow* *500.*
On cover, uncanceled, with certificate *1,500.*
On cover, uncanceled, with 3c #11, with certificate *4,500.*
121L7 L239 (2c) **black,** *blue* *750.*
On cover, uncanceled, with certificate *3,250.*
121L8 L239 (2c) **black,** *rose* *500.*
121L9 L239 (2c) **black,** *emerald,* uncanceled, on cover *6,500.*

No. 121L9 is believed to be unique.

Prince's Letter Dispatch, Portland, Maine

Established by J. H. Prince of Portland. Mail carried nightly by messenger travelling by steamer to Boston. Stamp engraved by Lowell of Lowell & Brett, Boston, his name appearing in the design below the steamship.

L240

Printed in sheets of 40 (5x8)

1861 **Litho.**
122L1 L240 **black** 7.50 *125.00*
On cover, tied by handstamp *5,000.*
On cover, uncanceled, with certificate —
On cover, tied by handstamp, with 3c #65 *8,000.*
On cover, tied by handstamp, with 3c #94 *5,000.*
Block of 4 40.00
Sheet of 40 550.00

Cancellations: Black, blue or red Boston datestamps, blue company serrated oval, black "Boston & Portland/Express/11 State Street, Boston/34 Exchange Street, Portland" framed ribbon-marker handstamp.

Private Post Office, San Francisco, Calif.
ENVELOPES

L241

Impressed on U.S. Envelopes, 1863-64 Issue

1864 **Typo.**

123LU1 L241 15c **blue,** *orange* (on US #U56) *600.00*
123LU2 L241 15c **blue,** *buff* (on US #U54) *600.00*
a. 15c **blue** (on US #U58) *700.00* *4,750.*
b. 15c **blue,** *buff* (on US #U59) *600.00*
123LU3 L241 25c **blue,** *buff* (on US #U54) *600.00*

Providence Despatch, Providence, R.I.

L242

1849 **Typeset**

124L1 L242 **black** *2,000.*

Public Letter Office, San Francisco, Calif.
ENVELOPES

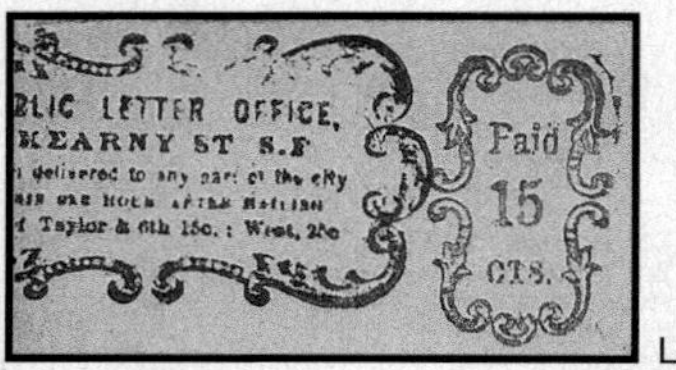

L243

Impressed on U.S. Envelopes, 1863-64 Issue

1864 **Typeset**

125LU1 L243 **black** *400.00*
125LU2 L243 **blue** *400.00*
125LU3 L243 15c **blue** *450.00* *5,000.*
125LU4 L243 25c **blue** *450.00*

The Private Post Office of San Francisco changed its name to Public Post Office sometime in 1864. The office address was the same for both, 5 Kearny St.

Reed's City Despatch Post, San Francisco, Calif.

Pioneer San Francisco private post. Also serving Adams & Co. for city delivery.

L244

1853-54 **Glazed Surface Paper** **Litho.**

126L1 L244 **black,** *green,* on cover, tied by handstamp —
126L2 L244 **black,** *blue,* on cover, uncanceled *27,500.*

No. 126L1 is unique. Two No. 126L2 recorded, each uncanceled on cover.

Cancellation: Blue double-circle "Adams & Co. San Francisco."

Ricketts & Hall, Baltimore, Md.

L244a

1857 **Cut to shape** **Typo.**

127L1 L244a 1c **red,** *bluish* — *9,000.*
On cover —

Of the seven recorded examples of No. 127L1, three have been cut to shape removing the outer address circle, including the unique unused stamp. One of the three examples on cover has had the outer address circle removed.

Robison & Co., Brooklyn, N.Y.

L245

1855-56 **Typo.**

128L1 L245 1c **black,** *blue* *4,750.* *4,750.*
On cover, tied *7,000.*

Cancellation: Blue "PAID."

Roche's City Dispatch, Wilmington, Del.

L246

1850 **Glazed Surface Paper** **Typo.**

129L1 L246 (2c) **black,** *green* *2,250.*
Cut to shape *1,750.*
On cover, uncanceled, with certificate *8,250.*
On cover, cut to shape, uncanceled, with certificate *3,500.*

A black negative handstamp similar to type L246 served solely as a postmark and no evidence exists that any prepaid handstamped envelopes or lettersheets were ever sold.

Rogers' Penny Post, Newark, N.J.

Established by Alfred H. Rogers, bookseller, at 194 Broad St., Newark, N.J.

L246a

Cut to shape

1856 **Glazed Surface Paper** **Handstamped**

162L1 L246a (1c) **black,** *green* *30,000.*

No. 162L1 is unique. It is on a tiny piece. Value represents 2000 auction sale price.

See Rogers' handstamp in Local Handstamp Covers section.

Russell 8th Ave. Post Office, New York, N.Y.

(See Price's Eighth Avenue Post Office.)

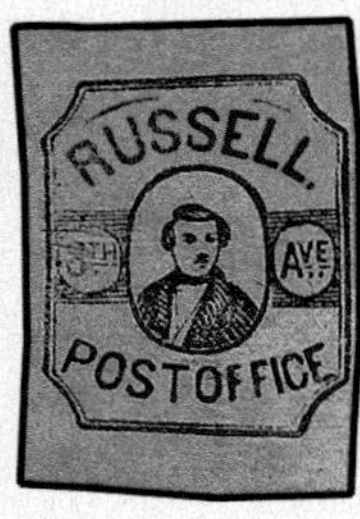

L247

1854-58 **Wood Engraving**

130L1 L247 (2c) **blue,** *rose* *600.* *500.*
On cover, uncanceled, with certificate —
On cover, tied by handstamp *27,500.*
On cover, tied with 3c #11 —
130L2 L247 (2c) **black,** *yellow* *750.* *650.*
On cover, tied *5,000.*
On cover, uncanceled, with 3c #11, with certificate *9,250.*
130L3 L247 (2c) **red,** *bluish* *900.* *750.*
On cover, tied by handstamp *8,250.*
On cover, not tied, with 3c #11, with certificate *5,750.*
130L4 L247 (2c) **blue green,** *green* *3,000.*

No. 130L4 used is unique. It is damaged and is valued thus.

St. Louis City Delivery Company, St. Louis, Mo.

(See Cincinnati City Delivery.)

L249

1883 **Typo.** ***Perf. 12***

131L1 L249 (1c) **red** 4.00 7.50
Block of 4 17.50
On cover, tied by handstamp *2,750.*
a. Imperf., pair —
b. Horiz. pair, imperf between *350.00*

Cancellation: Purple target.

Smith & Stephens' City Delivery, St. Louis, Mo.

L284

Typeset

158L1 L284 1c **black,** *pale rose,* on cover, tied by ms. cancel 25,000.

No. 158L1 is unique.

Smith's City Express Post, New York, N.Y.

Successor to the American Express Co.

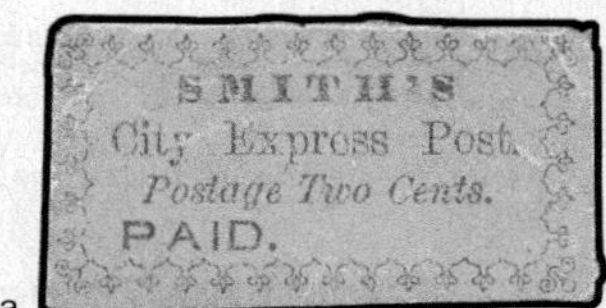

L284a

Typeset
Glazed Surface Paper

168L1 L284a 2c **black,** *green* —

Spaulding's Penny Post, Buffalo, N.Y.

L283

L283a

1848-49

156L1 L283 2c **vermilion** *40,000.*
156L2 L283a 2c **carmine** *40,000.*
On cover —

Nos. 156L1 unused, 156L2 unused and 156L2 on cover each are unique.

A No. 156L1 on cover, uncanceled, was reported but has not been seen.

Spence & Brown Express Post, Philadelphia, Pa.

L285

1847 (?) **Typeset**

159L1 L285 2c **black,** *bluish* *10,000.* *11,500.*

One each recorded of No. 159L1 unused and used.

L286

1848 **Litho.**

159L2 L286 (2c) **black** *2,500.* —
On cover, tied by ms. *33,000.*
Block of 4 —

No. 159L2 on cover is unique.

Squier & Co. City Letter Dispatch, St. Louis, Mo. (Jordan & Co.)

This post began to operate as a local carrier on July 6, 1859 and was discontinued in the early part of 1860. Squier & Co. used imperforate stamps; their successors (Jordan & Co.) about Jan. 1 1860, used the roulettes.

L248

1859 **Litho.** ***Imperf.***

132L1 L248 1c **green** *150.* *175.*
On cover *1,500.*
On cover, tied by handstamp, with 3c #26 *4,000.*
On cover, tied by ms., with 3c #26 *1,000.*
On cover, uncanceled, with 3c #26 *600.*
Block of 4 *750.*

1860 ***Rouletted 19***

132L2 L248 1c **rose brown** *280.* *280.*
On cover *1,000.*
On cover, with 3c #26, each tied by handstamps (unique) *11,500.*
132L3 L248 1c **brownish purple** *280.* *280.*
On cover *1,000.*
132L4 L248 1c **green** *280.* *350.*
On cover *1,000.*
On cover, tied by handstamp, with 3c #26 *5,000.*

Cancellation: Black circle "Jordan's Penny Post Saint Louis."

Staten Island Express Post, Staten Island, N. Y.

Established by Hagadorn & Co., with office at Stapleton, Staten Island. Connected with Boyd for delivery in New York City.

L250

1849 **Typo.**

133L1 L250 3c **vermilion** *1,400.* *1,100.*
On cover, tied by ms. *4,750.*
On cover, not tied *3,500.*
On cover, uncanceled, with certificate *3,250.*
133L2 L250 6c **vermilion,** on cover —

Stringer & Morton's City Despatch, Baltimore, Md.

According to an advertisement in the Baltimore newspapers, dated October 19, 1850, this post aimed to emulate the successful posts of other cities, and divided the city into six districts, with a carrier in each district. Stamps were made available throughout the city.

L251

1850 **Glazed Surface Paper**

134L1 L251 (1c) **gold,** *black* *500.* —
On cover, uncanceled *650.*
On cover with pair if 5c #1 *7,500.*

Cancellation: Black circle "Baltimore City Despatch & Express Paid."

Sullivan's Dispatch Post, Cincinnati, Ohio

L252

1853 **Glazed Surface Paper** **Litho.**

135L1 L252 (2c) **black,** *green,* uncanceled, on cover —

Wove Paper

135L2 L252 (2c) **bluish black,** uncanceled, on magazine, with certificate *40,000.*
135L3 L252 (2c) **green** *60,000.*
On cover —

Nos. 135L1-135L2 are either die cut octagonally or cut round. They do not exist cut square.

Each listed Sullivan Post item is unique. Additionally, a second No. 135L2 on magazine is in the Smithsonian Institution collection.

Swarts' City Dispatch Post, New York, N.Y.

Established by Aaron Swarts, at Chatham Square, in 1847, becoming one of the largest local posts in the city.

The postmarks of Swarts' Post Office are often found on stampless covers, as this post carried large quantities of mail without using adhesive stamps.

Zachary Taylor
L253

George Washington
L254

1849-53 **Glazed Surface Paper** **Litho.**

136L1 L253 (2c) **black,** *light green* — *175.00*
On cover, tied by handstamp *450.00*
On cover, not tied *300.00*
On cover, tied, with 5c #1 *45,000.*
On cover with 3c #10 *450.00*
136L2 L253 (2c) **black,** *dark green* — 135.00
On cover, tied by handstamp *375.00*

Wove Paper

136L3 L253 (2c) **pink** — 35.00
On cover, tied by handstamp *500.00*
On cover with 5c #1 —
136L4 L253 (2c) **red** (shades) 20.00 20.00
On cover, tied by handstamp *600.00*
On cover, not tied *450.00*
On cover with 5c #1 *5,000.*
On cover, tied by handstamp cancel, with 1c #7 *8,500.*
On cover, tied by handstamp, with 3c #11 *650.00*
Block of 4 85.00
Sheet of 25 *600.00*

The 136L4 with No. 7 combination cover is unique.

136L5 L253 (2c) **pink,** *blue* 60.00
On cover, tied by handstamp *375.00*
136L6 L253 (2c) **red,** *blue* 60.00
On cover, tied by handstamp *400.00*
136L7 L253 (2c) **black,** *blue gray* 200.00 150.00
On cover, tied by handstamp *400.00*
On cover, uncanceled *225.00*
On cover, tied by "PAID" handstamp, with 10c #2, tied by grid *35,000.*
136L8 L253 (2c) **blue** 200.00
On cover, tied by handstamp *1,250.*
136L9 L254 (1c) **red** — 40.00
On cover, tied by handstamp *350.00*
On cover, tied by handstamp, with 3c #11 450.00
On cover, tied by handstamp, with 3c #11A 450.00
136L10 L254 (1c) **pink** — 30.00
On cover, tied by handstamp *250.00*
On cover, tied by handstamp, with 3c #11 *800.00*
On cover, tied by handstamp, with 3c #26 *350.00*
136L11 L254 (1c) **red,** *bluish* — 100.00
On cover *500.00*
136L12 L254 (1c) **pink,** *bluish* — 100.00
On cover *450.00*

Bouton's Stamp with Red ms. "Swarts" at Top

136L13 L49 2c **black,** *gray blue* *500.00* *550.00*
On cover, tied by handstamp *1,500.*
On cover, not tied *600.00*

L255

Five minor varieties, the stamps in each vertical row being identical.

Printed in sheets of 25 (5x5)

136L14 L255 1c **blue** 15. 60.
On cover, tied by handstamp 175.
On cover, tied by handstamp, with 3c #11A *225.*
Block of 4 *65.*
a. Thin paper 8.00
Block of 4 35.
Sheet of 25 *225.00*
136L15 L255 1c **red** — *500.*
On cover, tied by handstamp *1,000.*
On cover, not tied, with 10c #2 *2,250.*
On cover with 3c #10 *1,650.*
On cover, tied by handstamp, with 3c #11A *4,000.*
136L16 L255 1c **red,** *bluish* — 135.
On cover, tied by handstamp *1,000.*
136L17 L255 1c **black,** on cover, tied by handstamp *17,500.*

Nos. 136L3-136L4, 136L9-136L10, 136L14-136L15 have been reprinted.

Cancellations: Red boxed "PAID" (mostly on Nos. 136L1-136L8, 136L13), black boxed "PAID SWARTS" (mostly on Nos. 136L9-136L12), black oval "Swarts Post Office Chatham Square" (Nos. 136L9-136L12), black oval "Swarts B Post Chatham Square," black grids (5-bar rectangle, 6-bar circle, solid star, hollow star, star in circle, etc). Other handstamp postmarks of the post have been found as cancellations. Government town postmarks exist on almost all Swarts stamps.

Teese & Co. Penny Post, Philadelphia, Pa.

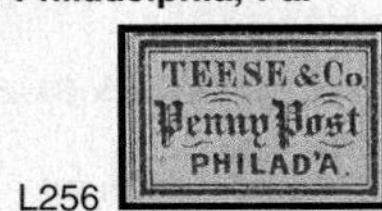

L256

Printed in sheet of 200 divided into two panes of 100. Each pane includes setting of 20, repeated 5 times. Vertical or horizontal tete-beche pairs appear twice in each setting. Twenty varieties.

1852 **Wove Paper** **Litho.**

137L1 L256 (1c) **blue,** *bluish* 20.00 125.00
On cover, tied by handstamp *3,000.*
On cover, tied by handstamp, with 3c #11A *2,250.*
Block of 4 90.00
a. Tete beche pair 100.00

Telegraph Despatch P. O., Philadelphia, Pa.

L257

L257a

1848

138L1 L257 1c **black,** *yellowish* *2,750.*
On cover, tied by ms., with certificate *15,000.*
On cover, not tied, with certificate *5,500.*
138L2 L257a 2c **black,** *yellowish,* on cover with 5c #1b *21,000.*

One example known of No. 138L2.

Third Avenue Post Office, New York, N.Y.

Established by S. Rothenheim, a former carrier for Boyd's City Express. All stamps were cut to shape by hand before being sold and exist only in that form.

L258

1855 Glazed Surface Paper Handstamped

139L1 L258 2c **black,** *green* 500. 500.
On cover, uncanceled 1,250.
On cover, uncanceled, with 3c #11, with certificate 1,600.
139L1A L258 2c **blue,** *green,* on cover, uncanceled, with certificate 2,250.
139L2 L258 2c **black,** *maroon* 3,250. 2,250.

Unsurfaced Paper colored through

139L3 L258 2c **black,** *yellow* 2,250.
On cover, uncanceled, with 3c #11, with certificate 3,000.
139L4 L258 2c **black,** *blue* —
On cover, uncanceled, with 3c #11, with certificate 11,000.
139L5 L258 2c **black,** *brown* 2,250.
139L6 L258 2c **black,** *buff* 2,500.
139L7 L258 2c **black,** *pink* 5,250.
On cover, uncanceled, with 3c #11 6,500.
139L8 L258 2c **black,** *green* 4,150. 2,200.

Nos. 139L1A, 139L2, 139L4 on cover, 139L7-139L8 unused and 139L8 used are each unique.

Cancellation on No. 139L1: Black "PAID."

Union Despatch, Chicago, Ill.

Established by William Stiles and his son, Edmund.

L258a

L258c

1855 ***Irregular Rough Perf. 12½ to 15***

170L1 L258a 5c **brownish red** — —
170L3 L258c 20c **grayish green** — —

Union Post, New York, N.Y.

UNION
POST
HRS

L259

Thick Glazed Surface Paper

1846 Handstamped

140L3 L259 **blue,** *green* ("UNOIN") 3,000.
a. "UNION" spelled correctly, on cover —

The unique example of No. 140L3a is badly damaged, with only half the stamp still on the cover.

140L4 L259 **red,** *blue* ("UNION") 2,000.
On cover —

Type L259 was used also as a postmark, usually struck in blue.

Union Square Post Office, New York, N.Y.

Established by Joseph E. Dunham about 1850. In 1851 Dunham acquired Messenkope's Union Square Post Office, operating the combined posts until 1854 or 1855. The business was sold in 1855 to Phineas C. Godfrey.

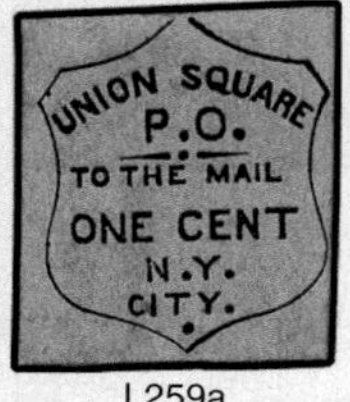

L259a

L260

Printed in sheets of 120 (6x20)

1852 Typo.

141L1 L259a 1c **black,** *dark green* 9.00 45.00
On cover, tied by handstamp 900.00
On cover, tied by handstamp, with 3c #11A 1,250.
On cover, not tied, with 3c #11A 750.00
Block of 4 45.00
141L2 L259a 1c **black,** *light apple green* 40.00 75.00
On cover, tied by handstamp 700.00
On cover, tied by handstamp, with 3c #11 1,500.
On cover, cut to shape, tied by handstamp, with 3c #11 200.00
141L3 L260 2c **black,** *rose* 3.50 3,000.
On cover 3,500.
Block of 4 17.50

Used stamps must bear handstamp cancels.

Walton & Co.'s City Express, Brooklyn, N.Y.

Operated by Wellington Walton.

L261

1846 Glazed Surface Paper Litho.

142L1 L261 2c **black,** *pink* 700. 900.
On cover, tied by ms. —
On cover, ms. cancel, not tied, with certificate 16,000.
On cover, handstamp cancel, not tied —
On cover, cut to shape, tied by handstamp, with certificate 4,500.
On cover, cut to shape, handstamp cancel, not tied, with certificate 6,000.

Cancellations: Black "PAID / W. W." Black oblong quad (ties stamp "through" to cover).

Wells, Fargo and Co.

Wells, Fargo & Company entered the Western field about July 1, 1852, to engage in business on the Pacific Coast, and soon began to acquire other express businesses, eventually becoming the most important express company in its territory.

The Central Overland, California and Pikes Peak Express Company, inaugurated in 1860, was the pioneer Pony Express system and was developed to bring about quicker communication between the extreme portions of the United States. Via water the time was 28 to 30 days, with two monthly sailings, and by the overland route the time was 28 days. In 1860 the pioneer Pony Express carried letters only, reducing the time for the 2,100 miles (St. Joseph to San Francisco) to about 12 days. The postage rate was originally $5 the half-ounce.

About April 1, 1861, Wells, Fargo & Company became agents for the Central Overland, California and Pikes Peak Express Company and issued $2 red and $4 green stamps.

During the July 1 to Oct. 24, 1861, period of use of Nos. 143L3-143L6, Wells, Fargo & Co. was under contract with the U.S. government, so stamps used during this period are technically official issues authorized by Congress.

The rates were cut in half about July 1, 1861, and new stamps were issued: the $1 red, $2 green and $4 black, and the $1 garter design.

The revival of the Pony Express in 1862, known as the "Virginia City Pony" resulted in the appearance of the "cents" values, first rate.

Advertisement in the Placerville newspaper, Aug. 7, 1862: "Wells, Fargo & Co.'s Pony Express. On and after Monday, the 11th inst., we will run a Pony Express Daily between Sacramento and Virginia City, carrying letters and exchange papers, through from San Francisco in 24 hours, Sacramento in 15 hours and Placerville in 10 hours. Rates: All letters to be enclosed in our franks, and TEN CENTS PREPAID, in addition, for each letter weighing half an ounce or less, and ten cents for each additional half-ounce."

Wells, Fargo & Company used various handstamps to indicate mail transit. These are illustrated and described in the handbook, "Wells, Fargo & Co.'s Handstamps and Franks" by V. M. Berthold, published by Scott Stamp & Coin Co., Ltd. (out of print). The history of the Pony Express, a study of the stamps and reprints, and a survey of existing covers are covered in "The Pony Express," by M. C. Nathan and Winthrop S. Boggs, published by the Collectors Club, 22 E. 35th., New York, N.Y. 10016.

Wells Fargo stamps of types L262 and L264 were lithographed by Britton & Rey, San Francisco. Type L263 was printed by George F. Nesbitt, New York.

L262

Front hoof missing

The $2 and $4 stamps were printed from plates of 20 (5x4), while the $1 was printed from a plate of 40 (8x5), and divided into two panes of 20 (4x5) each.

1861 (April to July 1) Litho.

143L1 L262 $2 **red** 190. 800.
On US envelope #U10 —
On US envelope #U16 12,500.
On US envelope #U17 12,500.
On US envelope #U18 12,500.
On US envelope #U32 15,000.
On US envelope #U32 (patriotic cover) 100,000.
On US envelope #U33 32,500.
On US envelope #U65 —
On cover, tied by "Running Pony" handstamp, with 5c #30A and 10c #35, to Prince Edward Island (unique) 350,000.
143L2 L262 $4 **green** 500. 6,000.
Block of 4 9,000.
On US envelope #U33 —

The No. 143L2 block is the only recorded $4 block.

1861 (July 1 to Nov.)

143L3 L262 $1 **red** 100. 900.
Block of 4 750.
Sheet of 40 10,000.
On US envelope #U11 —
On US envelope #U15 9,000.
On US envelope #U17 9,000.
On US envelope #U32 10,000.
On US envelope #U33 12,500.
On US envelope #U35 9,000.
On US envelope #U40 10,000.
On US envelope #U41 9,000.
Front hoof missing (9R) 1,750. 6,000.
143L4 L262 $2 **green** 300. 4,500.
Block of 4 1,500.
On US envelope #U41 50,000.
143L5 L262 $4 **black** 190. 7,500.
Block of 4 —
On cover to Wash., D.C., tied by handstamp 350,000.

Cancellations: Blue, black or magenta express company.

Nos. 143L1-143L5 and 143L7-143L9 were reprinted in 1897. The reprints are retouched. Shades vary from originals. Originals and reprints are fully described in "The Pony Express," by M. C. Nathan and W. S. Boggs (Collectors Club).

L263

Printed in sheets of 20 (5x4). One example recorded with Nesbitt imprint (pos. 18).

1861 Thin Wove Paper

143L6 L263 $1 **blue** 800. 1,250.
Strip of 3 —
On 10c US env. #U40 75,000.
On 10c US env. #U40 with 10c #35, tied 185,000.

No. 143L6 used only from east to west.

Most counterfeits have a horizontal line bisecting the shield. Some genuine stamps have a similar line drawn in with blue or red ink. Value for genuine with line, $300.

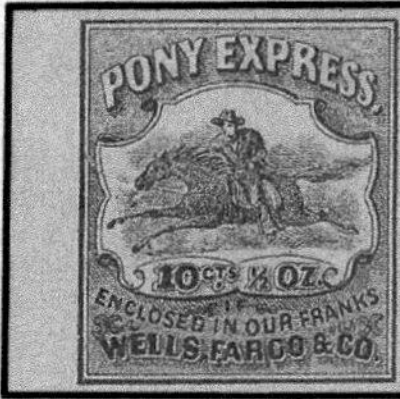

L264

Printed in sheets of 40 (8x5), four panes of 10, each pane 2x5.

1862-64

143L7 L264 10c **brown** (shades) 50. 175.
Pair 125. 500.
Block of 4 500.
On US envelope #U26 6,500.
On US envelope #U32 4,000.
On US envelope #U34 6,000.

On US envelope #U35 — 5,500.
On cover with 3c #65 — —

143L8 L264 25c **blue** 75. *175.*
Pair 175.
Block of 4 500.
On plain cover *2,250.*
Strip of 3 on cover —
On US envelope #U10 —
On US envelope #U26 *2,000.*
On US envelope #U34 *4,750.*
On US envelope #U35 *4,500.*

143L9 L264 25c **red** 30. *100.*
Pair 80.
Block of 4 225.
Sheet of 40 *4,500.*
On US envelope #U9 —
On US envelope #U10 *8,000.*
On US envelope #U34 *8,000.*
On US envelope #U34 with 3c #65 *13,500.*
On US envelope #U35 *8,000.*
Pair on US envelope #U35 *9,000.*
On US envelope #U59 *3,750.*

Cancellations on Nos. 143L7-143L9: Blue or black express company, black town.

STEAMSHIP EXPRESS STAMP

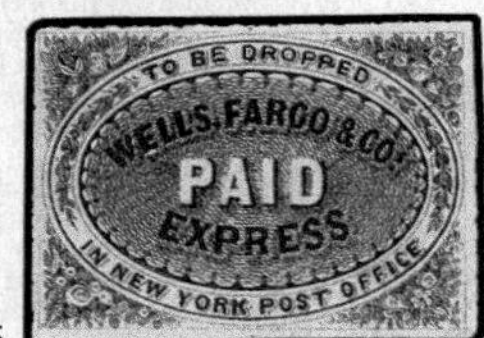

L265

1860

143LP1 L265 **black** *1,250.* —
On cover, uncanceled, with certificate *6,000.*

No. 143LP1 was issued to pay the steamship express fee, plus the drop-rate fee for delivery at the New York City Post Office. The use on cover is unique.

NEWSPAPER STAMPS

L266

L267

L268

L269

L270

1861-70

143LP2 L266 **blue** *1,250.*
143LP3 L267 **blue** 20.00 *75.00*
Pair 100.00
Block of 4 —
Sheet of 50 —
a. Thin paper 40.00 *100.00*

143LP4 L268 **blue** 50.00

Roulletted 10

143LP5 L267 **blue** 25.00 *125.00*
On wrapper *1,500.*
Pair 55.00
Block of 4 125.00
a. Thin paper —

143LP6 L268 **blue** 22.50
a. Tete beche pair 350.00

Design L267 was printed in sheets of 50 (5x10).

1883-88 ***Perf. 11, 12, 12½***

143LP7 L268 **blue** 12.50 *25.00*
143LP8 L269 **blue** 25.00 *35.00*
143LP9 L270 **blue** 3.50 *5.00*
Double transfer —
On wrapper *2,400.*
Strip of 3 on wrapper —
a. Vertical pair, imperf. between 125.00
b. Horiz. strip of 3, imperf. vert. between all stamps, natural straight edge at right *350.00*

FOR PUBLISHERS' USE

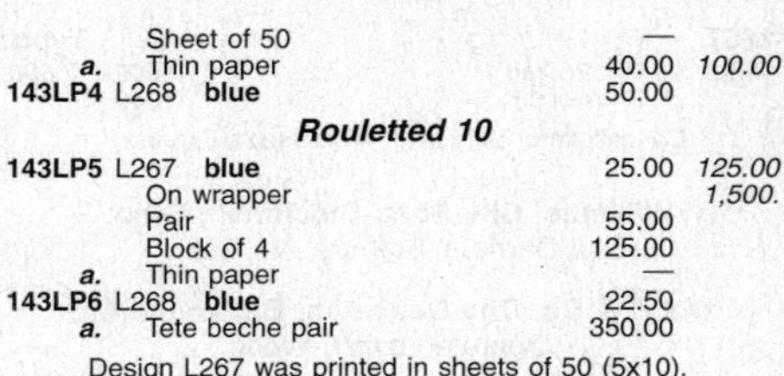

L271

1876 **Typo.**

143LP10 L271 **blue** 8.50 *25.00*
Pair 17.50 *60.00*
Block of 4 45.00
Sheet of 50 —
On wrapper *1,750.*
On wrapper with #143LP9 —

Cancellation: Blue company.

ENVELOPES

1862

143LU1 L264 10c **red** — *1,250.*
On US envelope #U34 *3,000.*
143LU2 L264 10c **blue** — —
On US envelope #U34 *9,500.*
143LU3 L264 25c **red** 700.00
On "Gould & Curry" overall advertising env. 700.00
On US envelope #U34 950.00

Westervelt's Post, Chester, N.Y.

Operated by Charles H. Westervelt. Rate was 1 cent for letters and 2 cents for packages carried to the post office. Local and government postage required prepayment.

L273

1863 (?) **Several varieties** **Typeset**

144L1 L273 (1c) **black,** *buff* 35.00 *100.00*
On cover *1,000.*
On cover, tied by handstamp, with 3c #65 *1,400.*
Sheet of 6 *675.00*
144L2 L273 **black,** *lavender* 40.00 75.00
On cover 2,000.

Indian Chief — L274

1864 (?) **Six varieties** **Typeset**

144L9 L274 (1c) **red,** *pink* 75.00 75.00
On cover *1,250.*
On cover, tied by handstamp, with 3c #65 *3,000.*

General U. S. Grant — L275

1865 **Six varieties** **Typo.**

144L29 L275 2c **black,** *yellow* 50.00 —
144L30 L275 2c **black,** *gray green* 50.00 —
144L40 L275 2c **red,** *pink* 50.00 —

All of the Westervelt stamps are believed to have a philatelic flavor, although it is possible that Nos. 144L1-144L2 were originally issued primarily for postal purposes. It is possible that Nos. 144L9, 144L29-144L30 and 144L40 were used in the regular course of business, particularly No. 144L9.

However, the large number of varieties on various colors of paper, which exist both as originals as well as contemporaneous and near-contemporaneous reprints, are believed to have been produced solely for sale to collectors. Design L275 was certainly issued primarily for sale to collectors. Many of the unlisted colors in all three types exist only as reprints. Forgeries of all three designs also exist.

L276

ENVELOPES

Impressed at top left

1865 **Typo.**

144LU1 L276 **red,** *white* —
144LU2 L276 **red brown,** *orange* — *300.00*
144LU3 L276 **black,** *bluish* 175.00
144LU4 L276 **black,** *buff* —
144LU5 L276 **black,** *white* —

It is possible that Nos. 114LU1-144LU5 were corner cards and had no franking value.

Westtown, Westtown, Pa.

The Westtown School at Westtown, Pa., is the oldest of the secondary schools in America, managed by the Society of Friends. It was established in 1799. In 1853 the school authorities decided that all outgoing letters carried by stage should pay a fee of 2 cents. Prepaid stamps were placed on sale at the school. Stamps were usually affixed to the reverse of the letter sheets or envelopes.

At first, letters were usually mailed at West Chester, Pa. After March 4, 1859, letters were sent from Street Road Post Office, located at the railroad station. Later this became the Westtown Post Office. The larger stamp was the first used. The smaller stamp came into use about 1867.

L277 - Type I

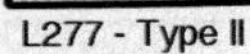
L277 - Type II

L277 - Type III

L277 - Type IV

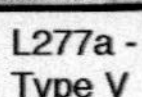

L277a - Type V

L277a - Type VI

L277a - Type VIII

1853-67(?) **Litho.**

145L1 L277 (2c) **gold** 45. —
- On front of cover, tied with 3c #11 — *4,500.*
- On front of cover, uncanceled, with 1c #9 — *1,000.*
- On front of cover, uncanceled, with 3c #11 — *150.*
- On front of cover, uncanceled, with 3c #26a — *200.*

145L2 L277a (2c) **gold** 30. —
- On cover — *400.*
- On cover, tied by handstamp, with 3c #158 — *1,750.*
- Block of 4 — *400.*
- Block of 6 — *1,000.*
- *a.* Tete beche pair — *300.*

No. 145L1 in red brown is a fake.

Whittelsey's Express, Chicago, Ill.

Operated by Edmund A. and Samuel M. Whittelsey

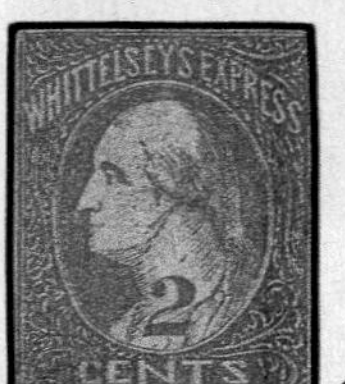

George Washington — L278

1857 **Typo.**

146L1 L278 2c **red** *2,000.* *6,500.*
- Block of 11 — *20,000.*

Cancellation: Blue oval "Whittelsey's Express."

Williams' City Post, Cincinnati, Ohio.

(See Carriers' Stamps, No. 9LB1.)

Wood & Co. City Despatch, Baltimore, Md.

Operated by W. Wood

L280

1856 **Typeset**

148L1 L280 (1c) **black,** *yellow*, on cover, ms. cancel, not tied, with certificate — *13,000.*
- On printed matter, tied by ms. — *7,500.*
- On 3c red entire #U10, tied by ms., with certificate — *14,500.*

W. Wyman, Boston, Mass.

Established to carry mail between Boston and New York

L281

1844 **Litho.**

149L1 L281 5c **black** — *750.00*
- On cover, tied by ms., Wyman handstamp — *3,250.*
- On cover, tied by ms., Overton handtsamp — *10,000.*
- On cover, not tied — *1,750.*

No. 149L1 may have been sold singly at 6 cents each.

Zieber's One Cent Dispatch, Pittsburgh, Pa.

L282

1851 **Typeset**

150L1 L282 1c **black,** *gray blue* *20,000.*
- On cover, acid cancel, with 3c #10 — —

No. 150L1 used and on cover are each unique.

Cancellation: Acid

For Local #151L1 see **Friend's Boarding School.**
For Local #152L1 see **Faunce's Penny Post.**
For Local #153L1 see **Hackney & Bolte Penny Post.**
For Local #154L1 see **A. W. Auner's Despatch Post.**
For Local #155L1 see **McGreely's Express.**
For Local #156L1-156L2 see **Spaulding's Penny Post.**
For Local #157L1 see **Bush's Brooklyn City Express.**
For Local #158L1 see **Smith & Stephens City Delivery.**
For Local #159L1-159L2 see **Spence & Brown Express Post.**
For Local #160L1 see **City Dispatch, New York City.**
For Local #161L1 see **Clinton's Penny Post.**
For Local #162L1 see **Rogers' Penny Post.**
For Local #163L1 see **Blizzard Mail.**
For Local #164L1 see **Freeman & Co.'s Express, New York City.**
For Local #165L1 see **J. A. Howell's City Despatch.**
For Local #166L1 see **Mac & Co's Dispatch.**
For Local #167L1 see **Morton's Post.**
For Local #168L1 see **Smith's City Express Post.**
For Local #169L1-169L2 see **Chestnut Street Line.**
For Local #170L1, 170L3 see **Union Despatch.**

LOCAL HANDSTAMPED COVERS

In 1835-1860 when private companies carried mail, many of them used handstamps on the covers they carried. Examples of these handstamps are shown on this and following pages.

Accessory Transit Co. of Nicaragua

Blue or Black

Red, Black or Blue

A sub-variety shows "Leland" below "MAILS" in lower right corner.

Red or Blue

1853

Barker's City Post, Boston, Mass.

Black

Also known with "34" instead of "10" Court Square.

1855-59

E. N. Barry's Despatch Post, New York, N.Y.

Black or Red

1852

Bates & Co., New Bedford, Mass.

(Agent for Hale & Co. at New Bedford)

Red or Black

1845

Branch Post Office, New York, N. Y.
(Swarts' Chatham Square Post Office)

Red

1847

Brigg's Despatch, Philadelphia, Pa.

Black

1848

Bush's Brooklyn City Express, Brooklyn, N. Y.

Red

1848

Cover shows red PAID.

Central Post Office, New York, N.Y.

Black

1856

Cover shows black PAID.

City Despatch Post, New York, N. Y.
(Used by Mead, successor to United States City Despatch Post.)

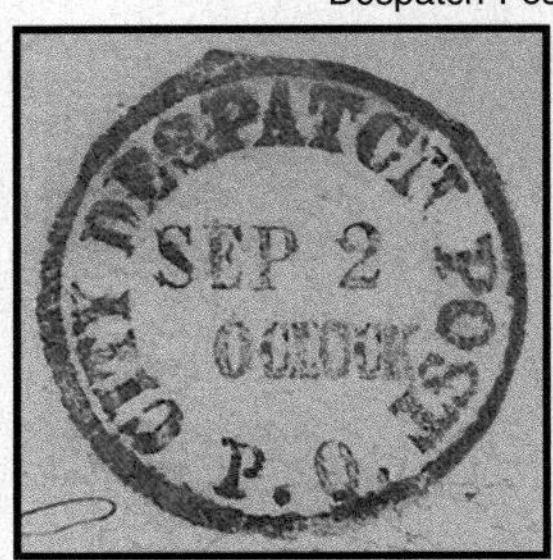

Black

1848

City Despatch Post, Baltimore, Md.

Red

1846-47

City Despatch & Express, Baltimore, Md.

Black

1850

Cole's City Despatch P. O., New York, N. Y.
(Used by Cole with some of the City Despatch Post stamps.)

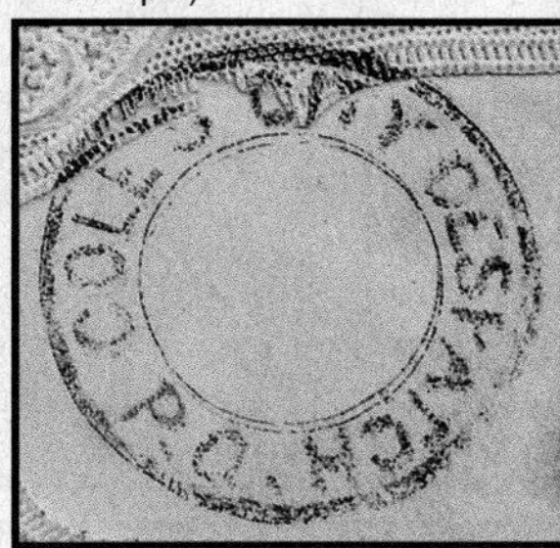

Black or Red

1848-50

Cumming's Express, New York, N.Y.

Red

1846

Dunhams Post Office, New York, N. Y.
(See Union Square Post Office).

Red

1848-52

Freeman & Cos Express, Marysville, Calif.

Greenish Blue

1851

Gay, Kinsley & Co., Boston, Mass.
(A package express)

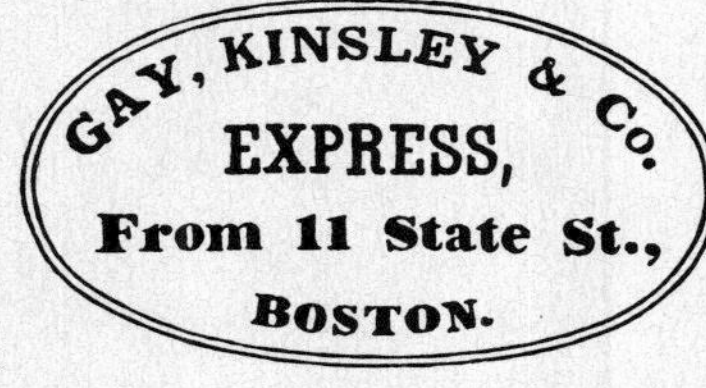

Red

Hanford's Pony Express Post, New York, N.Y.

Black or Red

1845-51

Hartford Penny Post, Hartford, Conn.

Black

1852-61

Hudson Street Post Office, New York, N. Y.

Red

1850

Cover shows red PAID.

Jones & Russell's Pikes Peak Express Co.,
Denver, Colo.

Black

1859-60

Kenyon's Letter Office, 91 Wall St., New York City

Red

1846-60

Langton & Bros. Express, French Corral

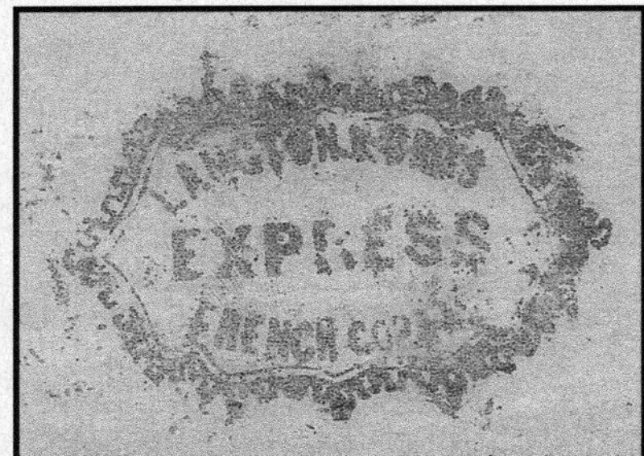

Blue

1849-53

Letter Express, San Francisco, Cal.
(See Gahagan & Howe, San Francisco, Cal.)

Blue

1865-66

Libbey & Co.'s City Post, Boston, Mass.

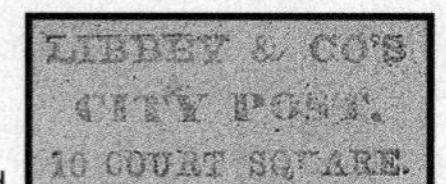

Black or Red

1852

Cover has 3c 1851 postmarked Boston, Mass.

Manhattan Express, New York, N. Y.
(W. V. Barr. See Bouton's Manhattan Express.)

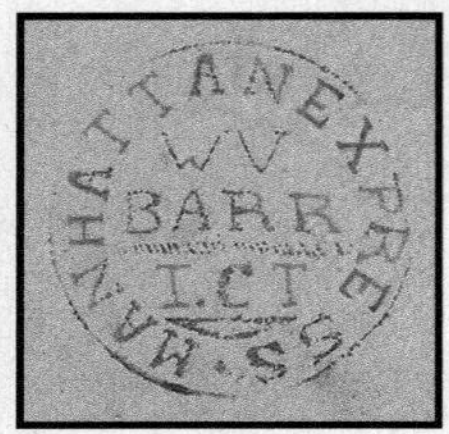

Red

1847

New York Penny Post,
New York, N. Y.

Black or Red

1840-41

Also known with hour indicated.

Noisy Carriers, San Francisco, Cal.

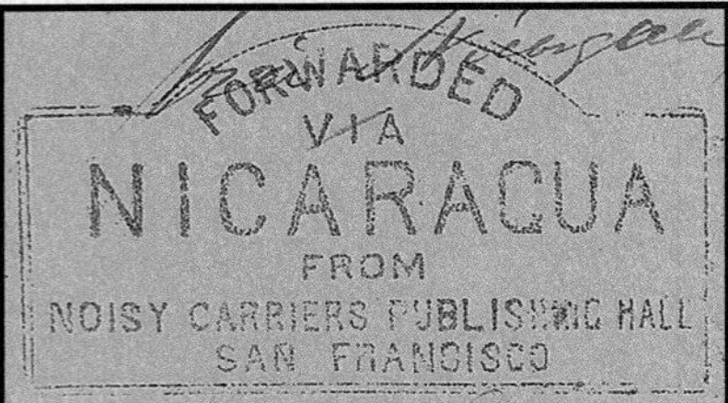

Blue or Green

Blue

Black or Red

Black, Blue or Green

Black

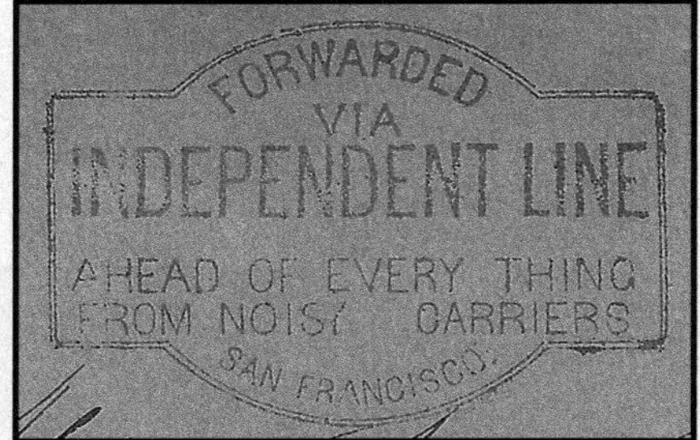

Black or Blue

1853-56

Northern Liberties News Rooms, Philadelphia, Pa.
(Actually a carrier marking mechanically applied.)

Black

Black

1835-36

Overton & Co.'s City Mail,
New York, N. Y.

Red

1844-45

Pony Express

Blue or Red

1860

Blue (Enlarged)

1861

Black or Carmine

1860-61

Blue or Red

1853-56

from

St. Joseph, Mo.	Black or Green
Denver City, K. T.	Black
Leavenworth City, K. T.	Black
San Francisco, Cal.	Blue

Black or Green

1860-61

Red

Blue

1860

Rogers' Penny Post, Newark, N. J.

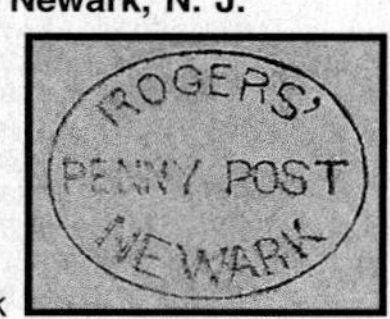

Black

1856

Spark's Post Office, New York, N. Y.

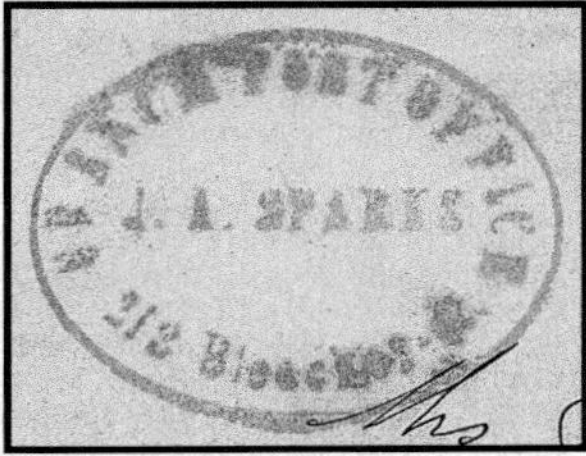

Red, Green, Blue or Black

1848

Spaulding's Penny Post, Buffalo, N. Y.

Black

1848

Spence & Brown Express Post, Philadelphia, Pa.

Black

1848

Stait's Despatch Post, Philadelphia, Pa.
(Eagle City Post)

Red or Black

1850-51

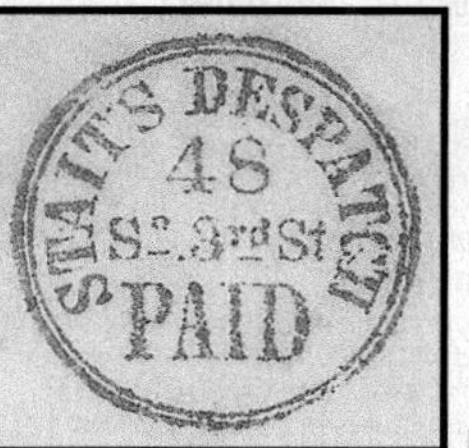

Red

1850-55

Stone's City Post, New York, N. Y.

Red

1858-59

J. W. Sullivan's Newspaper Office, San Francisco, Cal.

Black or Red

1854-55

Towle & Co. Letter Delivery, Boston, Mass.

Red

1847

Towle's City Dispatch Post, Boston, Mass.

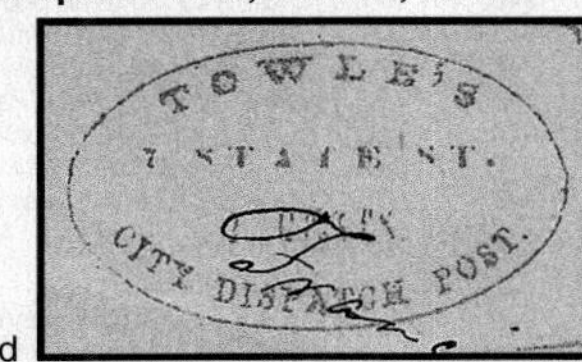

Red

1849

Towle's City Post, Boston, Mass.

(Also 10 Court Sq.) Red

1849-50

Cover shows PAID.

Sign-up now to get weekly email exclusive online deals and the latest product updates. Visit AmosAdvantage.com/Newsletter and register today.

ITEM	W x H (mm)	DESCRIPTION	MOUNTS	RETAIL	AA*
PRE-CUT SINGLE MOUNTS					
901	40 x 25	U.S. Standard Comm. Hor. Water Activated	40	$3.50	**$2.39**
902	25 x 40	U.S. Standard Comm. Vert. Water Activated	40	$3.50	**$2.39**
903	25 x 22	U.S. Regular Issue – Hor. Water Activated	40	$3.50	**$2.39**
904	22 x 25	U.S. Regular Issue – Vert. Water Activated	40	$3.50	**$2.39**
905	41 x 31	U.S. Semi-Jumbo – Horizontal	40	$3.50	**$2.39**
906	31 x 41	U.S. Semi-Jumbo – Vertical	40	$3.50	**$2.39**
907	50 x 31	U.S. Jumbo – Horizontal	40	$3.50	**$2.39**
908	31 x 50	U.S. Jumbo – Vertical	40	$3.50	**$2.39**
909	25 x 27	U.S. Famous Americans/Champions Of Liberty	40	$3.50	**$2.39**
910	33 x 27	United Nations	40	$3.50	**$2.39**
911	40 x 27	United Nations	40	$3.50	**$2.39**
976	67 x 25	Plate Number Coils, Strips of Three	40	$6.25	**$3.99**
984	67 x 34	Pacific '97 Triangle	10	$3.50	**$2.39**
985	111 x 25	Plate Number Coils, Strips of Five	25	$6.25	**$3.99**
986	51 x 36	U.S. Hunting Permit/Express Mail	40	$6.25	**$3.99**
1045	40 x 26	U.S. Standard Comm. Hor. Self-Adhesive	40	$3.50	**$2.39**
1046	25 x 41	U.S. Standard Comm. Vert. Self-Adhesive	40	$3.50	**$2.39**
1047	22 x 26	U.S. Definitives Vert. Self Adhesive	40	$3.50	**$2.39**
966	Value Pack	(Assortment pre-cut sizes)	320	$23.25	**$15.25**
975	Best Pack	(Assortment pre-cut sizes - Black Only)	160	$14.75	**$9.99**
PRE-CUT PLATE BLOCK, FDC, POSTAL CARD MOUNTS					
912	57 x 55	Regular Issue Plate Block	25	$6.25	**$3.99**
913	73 x 63	Champions of Liberty	25	$6.25	**$3.99**
914	106 x 55	Rotary Press Standard Commemorative	20	$6.25	**$3.99**
915	105 x 57	Giori Press Standard Commemorative	20	$6.25	**$3.99**
916	127 x 70	Giori Press Jumbo Commemorative	10	$6.25	**$3.99**
917	165 x 94	First Day Cover	10	$6.25	**$3.99**
918	140 x 90	Postal Card Size/Submarine Booklet Pane	10	$6.25	**$3.99**
1048	152 x 107	Large Postal Cards	8	$10.25	**$6.99**
STRIPS 215MM LONG					
919	20	U.S. 19th Century, Horizontal Coil	22	$7.99	**$5.25**
920	22	U.S. Early Air Mail	22	$7.99	**$5.25**
921	24	U.S., Vertical Coils, Christmas (#2400, #2428 etc.)	22	$7.99	**$5.25**
922	25	U.S. Commemorative and Regular	22	$7.99	**$5.25**
1049	26	U.S. Commemorative and Regular	22	$7.99	**$5.25**
923	27	U.S. Famous Americans	22	$7.99	**$5.25**
924	28	U.S. 19th Century, Liechtenstein	22	$7.99	**$5.25**
1050	29	Virginia Dare, British Empire, etc.	22	$7.99	**$5.25**
925	30	U.S. 19th Century; Jamestown, etc; Foreign	22	$7.99	**$5.25**
926	31	U.S. Horizontal Jumbo and Semi-Jumbo	22	$7.99	**$5.25**
927	33	U.S. Stampin' Future, UN	22	$7.99	**$5.25**
1054	34	U.S. American Landmarks, Eclipse	22	$7.99	**$5.25**
928	36	U.S. Hunting Permit, Canada	15	$7.99	**$5.25**
1051	37	U.S., British Colonies	22	$7.99	**$5.25**
929	39	U.S. Early 20th Century	15	$7.99	**$5.25**
930	41	U.S. Vert. Semi-Jumbo ('77 Lafayette, Pottery, etc.)	15	$7.99	**$5.25**
931		Multiple Assortment: One strip of each size 22-41 above (SMKB) (2 x 25mm strips)	12	$7.99	**$5.25**
1052	42	U.S., British Colonies	22	$7.99	**$5.25**
1053	43	U.S., British Colonies	22	$7.99	**$5.25**
932	44	U.S. Vertical Coil Pair Garden Flowers Booklet Pane	15	$7.99	**$5.25**
933	48	U.S. Farley, Gutter Pair	15	$7.99	**$5.25**
934	50	U.S. Jumbo (Lyndon Johnson, '74 U.P.U., etc.)	15	$7.99	**$5.25**
935	52	U.S. Standard Commemorative Block (Butterflies)	15	$7.99	**$5.25**
936	55	U.S. Standard Plate Block - normal margins	15	$7.99	**$5.25**
937	57	U.S. Standard Plate Block - wider margins	15	$7.99	**$5.25**
938	61	U.S. Blocks, Israel Tabs, '99 Christmas Madonna Pane	15	$7.99	**$5.25**
STRIPS 240MM LONG					
939	63	U.S. Jumbo Commemorative Horizontal Block	10	$9.25	**$5.99**
940	66	U.S. CIPEX Souvenir Sheet, Self-Adhesive Booklet Pane (#2803a, 3012a)	10	$9.25	**$5.99**
941	68	U.S. ATM Booklet Pane, Farley Gutter Pair & Souvenir Sheet	10	$9.25	**$5.99**
942	74	U.S. TIPEX Souvenir Sheet	10	$9.25	**$5.99**
943	80	U.S. Standard Commemorative Vertical Block	10	$9.25	**$5.99**
944	82	U.S. Blocks of Four, U.N. Chagall	10	$9.25	**$5.99**
945	84	Israel Tab Block, Mars Pathfinder Sheetlet	10	$9.25	**$5.99**
946	89	Submarine Booklet, Souvenir Sheet World Cup, Rockwell	10	$9.25	**$5.99**
947	100	U.S. '74 U.P.U. Block, U.N. Margin Inscribed Block	7	$9.25	**$5.99**
948	120	Various Souvenir Sheets and Blocks	7	$9.25	**$5.99**
STRIPS 265MM LONG					
1035	25	U.S. Coils Strips of 11	12	$9.25	**$5.99**
949	40	U.S. Postal People Standard Standard & Semi-Jumbo Commemorative Strip	10	$9.25	**$5.99**
981	44	U.S. Long self-adhesive booklet panes	10	$9.25	**$5.99**
1030	45	Various (Canada Scott #1725-1734)	10	$9.25	**$5.99**
1036	46	U.S. Long self adhesive booklet panes of 15	10	$9.25	**$5.99**
950	55	U.S. Regular Plate Block or Strip of 20	10	$9.25	**$5.99**
951	59	U.S. Double Issue Strip	10	$9.25	**$5.99**
952	70	U.S. Jumbo Commemorative Plate Block	10	$12.50	**$8.50**
1031	72	Various (Canada Scott #1305a-1804a)	10	$12.50	**$8.50**
1032	75	Plate Blocks: Lance Armstrong, Prehistoric Animals, etc.	10	$12.50	**$8.50**
1060	76	U.S. 1994 Stamp Printing Centennial Souvenir Sheet, etc.	10	$12.50	**$8.50**
953	91	U.S. Self-Adhesive Booklet Pane '98 Wreath, '95 Santa	10	$12.50	**$8.50**
1033	95	Mini-Sheet Plate Blocks w/top header	10	$12.50	**$8.50**
1061	96	U.S., Foreign	10	$12.50	**$8.50**
954	105	U.S. Standard Semi-Jumbo Commemorative Plate Number Strip	10	$12.50	**$8.50**
955	107	Same as above–wide margin	10	$12.50	**$8.50**
956	111	U.S. Gravure-Intaglio Plate Number Strip	10	$14.75	**$9.99**
1062	115	Foreign Small Sheets	10	$17.50	**$11.99**
957	127	U.S. 2000 Space S/S, World War II S/S	10	$17.50	**$11.99**
1063	131	Looney Tunes sheets; World War II Souvenir Sheet Plate Block	10	$17.50	**$11.99**
1064	135	U.S., Japan Gifts of Friendship sheet	10	$17.50	**$11.99**
958	137	Great Britain Coronation	10	$17.50	**$11.99**
1065	139	Sheets: Soda Fountain, Lady Bird Johnson, Earthscapes, etc.	10	$17.50	**$11.99**
1066	143	Sheets: Merchant Marine Ships, 2013 Hanukkah, etc.	10	$17.50	**$11.99**
1067	147	Sheets: Pickup Trucks, Animal Rescue, Washington D.C., etc.	10	$17.50	**$11.99**
1068	151	Sheets: Go Green, Bicycling, Happy New Year, Ben Franklin, etc.	10	$17.50	**$11.99**
STRIPS 265MM LONG, continued					
959	158	American Glass, U.S. Football Coaches Sheets	10	$17.99	**$12.50**
1077	160	Sheets: Pacific '97 Triangle Mini, Trans-Mississippi	5	$12.50	**$8.50**
1069	163	Sheets: Modern Architecture, UN Human Rights, etc.	5	$12.50	**$8.50**
1070	167	Sheets: John F. Kennedy, Classics Forever, Made in America, etc.	5	$12.50	**$8.50**
1071	171	Film Directors, Foreign Souvenir Sheets	5	$12.50	**$8.50**
960	175	Large Block, Souvenir Sheet	5	$12.50	**$8.50**
1072	181	Sheets: Jimi Hendrix, Johnny Cash, American Photography, etc.	5	$17.50	**$11.99**
1073	185	Frank Sinatra, Ronald Reagan, Arthur Ashe, Creast Cancer, etc.	5	$17.50	**$11.99**
1074	188	Sheets: Yoda, 9/11 Heroes, Andy Warhol, Frida Kahlo, etc	5	$17.50	**$11.99**
1078	192	Olympic, etc.	5	$17.50	**$11.99**
1075	198	Sheets: Modern American Art, Super Heroes, Baseball Sluggers, etc.	5	$17.50	**$11.99**
1076	215	Celebrity Chefs sheets; Foreign sheets	5	$17.50	**$11.99**
961	231	U.S. Full Post Office Pane Regular and Commemorative	5	$17.99	**$12.50**
SOUVENIR SHEETS/SMALL PANES					
962	204 x 153	New Year 2000, U.S. Bicentennial S/S	4	$9.25	**$5.99**
963	187 x 144	55¢ Victorian Love Pane, U.N. Flag Sheet	9	$15.50	**$10.25**
964	160 x 200	U.N., Israel Sheet	10	$15.50	**$10.25**
965	120 x 207	U.S. AMERIPEX Presidential Sheet	4	$6.25	**$3.99**
968	229 x 131	World War II S/S Plate Block Only	5	$9.25	**$5.99**
970	111 x 91	Columbian Souvenir Sheet	6	$6.25	**$4.75**
972	148 x 196	Apollo Moon Landing/Carnivorous Plants	4	$7.99	**$5.25**
989	129 x 122	U.S. Definitive Sheet: Harte, Hopkins, etc.	8	$10.25	**$6.99**
991	150 x 185	Breast Cancer/Fermi/Soccer/'96 Folk Heroes	5	$10.25	**$6.99**
996	188 x 197	Illustrators, '98 Music: Folk, Gospel; Country/Western	4	$10.25	**$6.99**
997	151 x 192	Olympic	5	$10.25	**$6.99**
998	174 x 185	Buffalo Soldiers	5	$10.25	**$6.99**
999	130 x 198	Silent Screen Stars	5	$10.25	**$6.99**
1000	190 x 199	Stars Stripes/Baseball/Insects & Spiders/Legends West/ Aircraft, Comics, '96 Olympics, Civil War	4	$10.25	**$6.99**
1001	178 x 181	Cranes	4	$10.25	**$6.99**
1002	183 x 212	Wonders of the Sea, We the People	3	$10.25	**$6.99**
1003	156 x 264	$14 Eagle	4	$10.25	**$6.99**
1004	159 x 270	$9.95 Moon Landing	4	$10.25	**$6.99**
1005	159 x 259	$2.90 Priority/$9.95 Express Mail	4	$10.25	**$6.99**
1006	223 x 187	Hubble, Hollywood Legends, O'Keefe Sheets	3	$10.25	**$6.99**
1007	185 x 181	Deep Sea Creatures, Olmsted Sheets	4	$10.25	**$6.99**
1008	152 x 228	Indian Dances/Antique Autos	5	$10.25	**$6.99**
1009	165 x 150	River Boat/Hanukkah	6	$10.25	**$6.99**
1010	275 x 200	Dinosaurs/Large Gutter Blocks	2	$10.25	**$6.99**
1011	161 x 160	Pacific '97 Triangle Mini Sheets	6	$10.25	**$6.99**
1012	174 x 130	Road Runner, Daffy, Bugs, Sylvester & Tweety	6	$10.25	**$6.99**
1013	196 x 158	Football Coaches	4	$10.25	**$6.99**
1014	184 x 184	American Dolls, Flowering Trees Sheets	4	$10.25	**$6.99**
1015	186 x 230	Classic Movie Monsters	3	$10.25	**$6.99**
1016	187 x 160	Trans-Mississippi Sheet	4	$10.25	**$6.99**
1017	192 x 230	Celebrate The Century	3	$10.25	**$6.99**
1018	156 x 204	Space Discovery	5	$10.25	**$6.99**
1019	182 x 209	American Ballet	5	$10.25	**$6.99**
1020	139 x 151	Christmas Wreaths	5	$10.25	**$6.99**
1021	129 x 126	Justin Morrill, Henry Luce	8	$10.25	**$6.99**
1022	184 x 165	Baseball Fields, Bright Eyes	4	$10.25	**$6.99**
1023	185 x 172	Shuttle Landing Pan Am Invert Sheets	4	$10.25	**$6.99**
1024	172 x 233	Sonoran Desert	3	$10.25	**$6.99**
1025	150 x 166	Prostate Cancer	5	$10.25	**$6.99**
1026	201 x 176	Famous Trains	4	$10.25	**$6.99**
1027	176 x 124	Canada - Historic Vehicles	5	$10.25	**$6.99**
1028	245 x 114	Canada - Provincial Leaders	5	$10.25	**$6.99**
1029	177 x 133	Canada - Year of the Family	5	$10.25	**$6.99**
1034	181 x 213	Arctic Animals	3	$10.25	**$6.99**
1037	179 x 242	Louise Nevelson	3	$10.25	**$6.99**
1038	179 x 217	Library Of Congress	3	$10.25	**$6.99**
1039	182 x 232	Youth Team Sports	3	$10.25	**$6.99**
1040	183 x 216	Lucille Ball Scott #3523	3	$10.25	**$6.99**
1041	182 x 244	American Photographers	3	$10.25	**$6.99**
1042	185 x 255	Andy Warhol	3	$10.25	**$6.99**
1043	165 x 190	American Film Making	4	$10.25	**$6.99**
1044	28 x 290	American Eagle PNC Strips of 11	12	$9.25	**$5.99**

Available in clear or black backgrounds. Please specify color choice when ordering.

2018 NATIONAL, MINUTEMAN OR ALL-AMERICAN SUPPLEMENT MOUNT PACKS

ITEM	DESCRIPTION	RETAIL	AA*
2018 B	2017 National, Minuteman or All-American Supplement Mount Pack - BLACK	$49.99	**$39.99**
2018 C	2017 National, Minuteman or All-American Supplement Mount Pack - CLEAR	$49.99	**$39.99**

www.AmosAdvantage.com

Call 1-800-572-6885

Outside U.S. & Canada 937-498-0800

Mail to: P.O. Box 4129, Sidney OH 45365

ORDERING INFORMATION: *AA prices apply to paid subscribers of Amos Media titles, or orders placed online. Prices, terms and product availability subject to change. Taxes will apply in CA, OH, & IL. Shipping and handling rates will apply.
SHIPPING & HANDLING: United States: Order total $0-$10.00 charged $3.99 shipping; Order total $10.01-$79.99 charged $7.99 shipping; Order total $80.00 or more charged 10% of order total for shipping. Maximum Freight Charge $45.00. **Canada:** 20% of order total. Minimum charge $19.99; maximum charge $200.00. **Foreign:** Orders are shipped via FedEx Int'l. or USPS and billed actual freight.

STAMPED ENVELOPES AND WRAPPERS

Fine-Very Fine

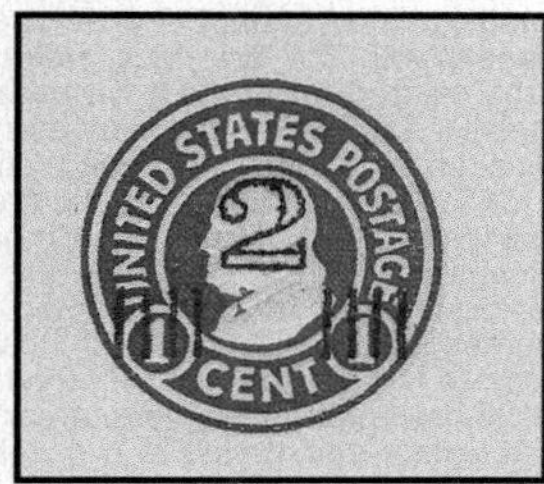

THE SCOTT CATALOGUE VALUES CUT SQUARES IN THIS GRADE

Very Fine

Extremely Fine

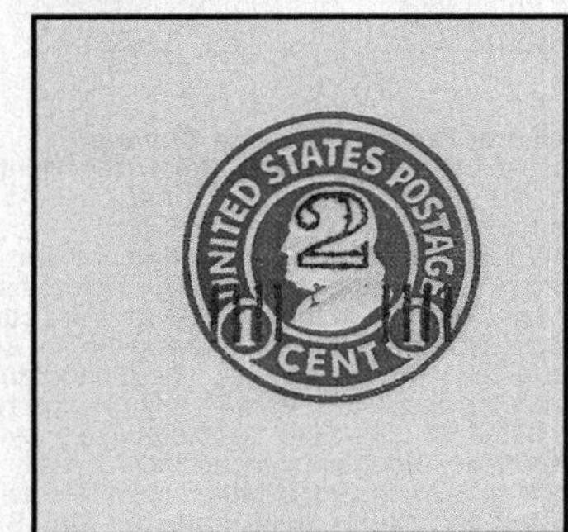

VALUES

Values for used envelopes are for examples used within the period of issue. Envelopes used much later sell at substantially reduced prices.

Unless otherwise noted, values for cut squares and most entires are for examples in the grade of very fine. Very fine cut squares will have the design well centered within moderately large margins. The margins on 20th century cut squares should be at least ¼ inch on the cut sides unless indicated otherwise. Cut squares of modern issues should show full tagging bars when they exist. An illustrated grading guide is shown above. These examples are computer-manipulated images made from single digitized master illustrations. Selected issues from both the 19th and 20th centuries are shown in the grades of fine-very fine, very fine and extremely fine. In addition to margin size, collectors are reminded that very fine cut squares (and entires) also will possess a fresh appearance and be free from defects.

Precanceled cut squares must include the entire precancellation. Values for unused entires are for those without printed or manuscript address, and for the most popular sizes. In a number of cases the larger envelopes are less expensive than the values shown here, for example, Nos. U348-U351. Values for letter sheets and wrappers are for folded entires. Unfolded examples sell for more.

"Full corner" cut squares include both back and side flaps. These items generally command a premium of 25% or more above the cut square values shown here, which are not for "full corners."

A plus sign (+) before a Catalogue number indicates that the item was not regularly issued and is not known used.

Envelopes are not available before the First day of issue so most cachets are applied after the envelope has been canceled. First day covers are valued uncacheted. First day covers prior to Nos. U532, UC18 and UO73 are addressed. Minimum values are $1 through 1986, and $1.25 after.

PRECANCELED CUT SQUARES

Precanceled envelopes do not normally receive another cancellation. Since the lack of a cancellation makes it impossible to distinguish between cut squares from used and unused envelopes, they are valued here as used only. Precanceled entires are valued mint and used since entires will show evidence of usage.

HISTORY

STAMPED ENVELOPES were first issued on July 1, 1853. They have always been made by private contractors, after public bidding, usually at four-year intervals. They have always been sold to the public at postage value plus cost of manufacture. They have appeared in many sizes and shapes, made of a variety of papers, with a number of modifications.

George F. Nesbitt & Co. made the government envelopes during the 1853-70 period. The Nesbitt seal or crest on the tip of the top flap was officially ordered discontinued July 7, 1853.

Watermarks in envelope paper, illustrated in this introduction, were mandatory from their first appearance in 1853. One important exception started in 1919 and lasted until the manila newspaper wrappers were discontinued in October 1934. The envelope contractor, due to inability to obtain watermarked Manila paper, was permitted to buy unwatermarked stock in the open market, a procedure that accounts for the wide range of shades and weights in this paper, including glazed and unglazed brown (kraft) paper. No. U615, and other unwatermarked envelopes that follow will be so noted in the listings. Diagonally laid paper has been used for some envelopes beginning with Scott U571.

A few stamped envelopes, in addition to the Manila items noted above, have been found without watermarks or with unauthorized watermarks. Such unusual watermarks or lack of watermarks are errors, bidders' samples or "specimen" envelopes, and most of them are quite rare.

Watermarks usually have been changed with every four-year contract, and thus serve to identify the envelope contractor, and since 1911, the manufacturer of the paper.

Envelope paper watermarks can be seen by spreading the envelope open and holding it against the light.

COLORS IN ENVELOPE PAPER

Stamped envelopes usually have been supplied in several colors and qualities of paper, some of which blend into each other and require study for identification. The following are the principal colors and their approximate years of use for stamped envelopes and wrappers:

Amber: 1870-1920 and 1929-1943; in two qualities; a pale yellow color; its intentional use in the Nesbitt series is doubtful.

Amber-Manila: 1886-98; same as Manila-amber.

Blue: 1874-1943; usually in two qualities; light and dark shades.

Buff: 1853-70; called cream, 1870-78; and oriental buff, 1886-1920; varies widely in shades.

Canary: 1873-78; another designation given to lemon.

Cream: 1870-78; see buff; second quality in 1c and 2c envelopes.

Fawn: 1874-86; very dark buff, almost light chocolate.

Lemon: 1873-78; Post Office official envelopes only, same as canary.

Manila: 1861-1934; second quality envelopes 1886-1928, and most wrappers; light and dark shades 1920-34; also kraft colored paper in later years.

Manila-Amber: 1886-98; amber shade of Manila quality.

Orange: 1861-83; second and third qualities only.

Oriental Buff: 1886-1920; see buff.

White: 1853-date; two qualities 1915-53; three qualities 1915-25; many shades including ivory, light gray, and bluish; far more common than any other color of paper. Envelopes that have no paper color given are white.

Laid paper was used almost exclusively from 1853 to 1915, but there were a few exceptions, mostly in the Manila papers. Wove paper has been the rule since 1915.

EMBOSSING AND PRINTING DIES

Until the modern era, stamped envelopes were always embossed, with the colorless areas slightly raised above the colored (or printed) flat background. While this process was not made mandatory in the original act, custom and tradition firmly established this policy. In 1977, No. U584 became the first envelope to have no embossing. Since 1977, most envelopes are not embossed. Embossing is an unusual procedure, seldom seen in other printed matter. Embossed impressions without color and those where lines are raised are not unusual. The method of making envelope embossings has few counterparts in the typographic industries, and hence is not well understood, even by stamp collectors.

Three types of dies are used, closely interrelated in their derivation, MASTER dies, HUB dies and WORKING (or PRINTING) dies. These types and the ways in which they are made, have undergone many changes with the years, and some of the earlier techniques are unrecorded and rather vague. No attempt will be made to describe other than the present day-methods. As an aid to clarity, the design illustrated herewith is the interlocked monogram "US," within a single circular border. Dies with curved faces for rotary printing are used extensively, as well as with straight faces for flat printing; only the latter will be described, since the basic principles are the same for both.

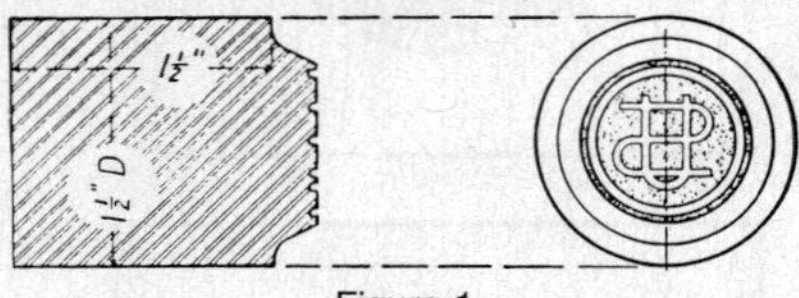

Figure 1

Master Die for Envelope Stamps

Colorless Lines are Recessed Below the Printing Surface.

It Reads Backward.

The MASTER die (Figure 1) is engraved on the squared end of a small soft steel cylinder, before hardening. The lines that are to remain colorless are cut or engraved into the face of this die, leaving the flat area of the face to carry the printing ink. The monogram is reversed, reading backward, as with any printing type or plate. Instead of engraving, a master die may be made by transfer under heavy pressure, usually for some modification in design, in which case it is called a sub-master or supplementary-master die. Submaster dies are sometimes made without figures of value, when the balance of the design is as desired, and only the figures of value engraved by hand. Various other combinations of transfer and engraving are known, always resulting in a reversed design, with recessed lines and figures, from which proofs can be pulled, and which accurately represents the printing surface that is desired in the eventual working die. The soft steel of a master die, after engraving and transferring is completed, is hardened by heat treatments before it can be used for making hubs.

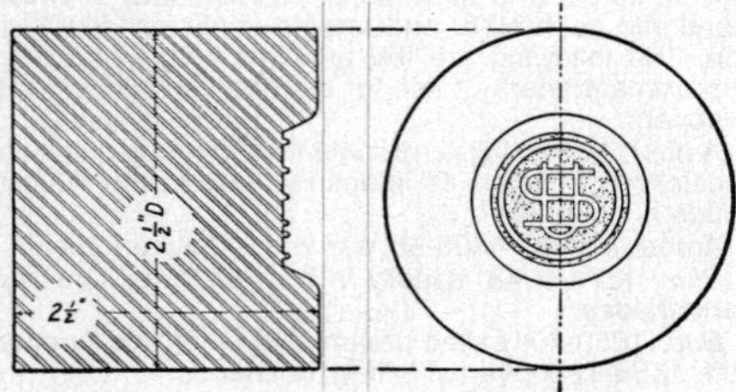

Figure 2

Hub Die for Envelope Stamps

Colorless Lines Protrude above the Surface.

The Monogram Reads Forward.

The HUB die (Figure 2), also called HOB die, is made from soft steel by transfer under pressure from the hardened master or sub-master die, which serves as a matrix or pattern. Since it is a transfer from the master die, the colorless lines protrude from the surface and it reads forward. This transfer impression of the hub die is made in a depression at the end of a sturdy cylinder, as it is subject to extremely hard service in making many working dies.

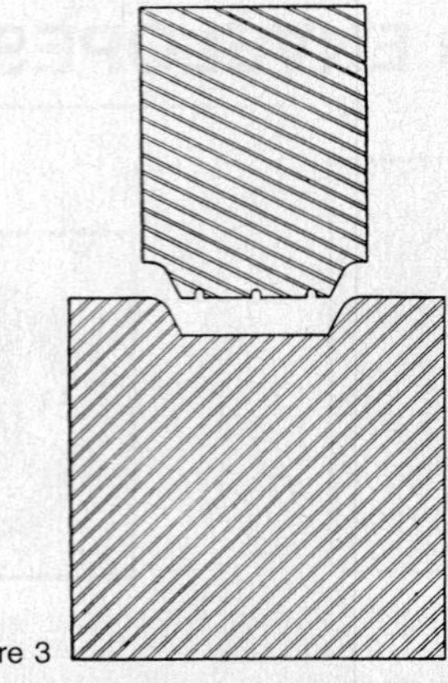

Figure 3

Pressure Transfer From Master Die to Hub Die

Above, Hardened Steel Master Die with Recessed Monogram.

Below, Soft Steel Hub Die Blank.

Figure 3 shows the relative position of the hardened steel master die as it enters the depression in the soft steel hub die blank. Some surplus metal may be squeezed out as the master die is forced into the hub blank, and require removal, leading to possible minor differences between the hub and master dies. At the completion of the pressure transfer the engraver may need to touch up the protruding surfaces to eliminate imperfections, to make letters and figures more symmetrical, and to improve the facial lines of the bust.

A hub die may be made by normal transfer, as above, the figures of value then ground off, and thus be ready for use in making a sub-master die without figures of value, and in which the figures of value may be engraved or punched. Since a hub die may be used to make a hundred or more working dies, it must be exceedingly sturdy and withstand terrific punishment without damage. Duplicate hub dies are frequently made from master dies, as stand-bys or reserves. After completion, hub dies are hardened. Hub dies cannot be engraved, nor can proof impressions be taken from them.

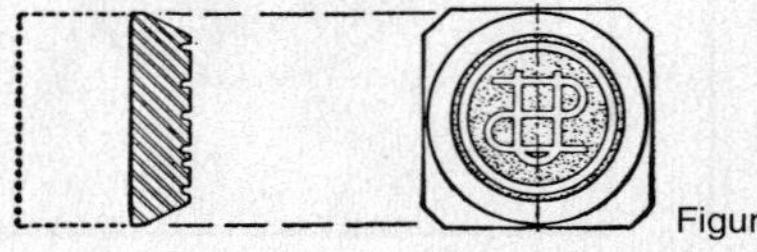

Figure 4

Working or Printing Die for Envelope Stamps

An exact Replica of the Master Die, except for size and shape of shank, which is designed for Printers} lock-up.

It Reads Backward.

The WORKING, or PRINTING, die (Figure 4) is like the type or plate that printers use, and may be thin to clamp to a base block, or type-high with square sides to lock in a printer's form. Its face reads backward, i.e., in reverse, and it is an exact replica of the master die as well as an exact matrix of the hub die.

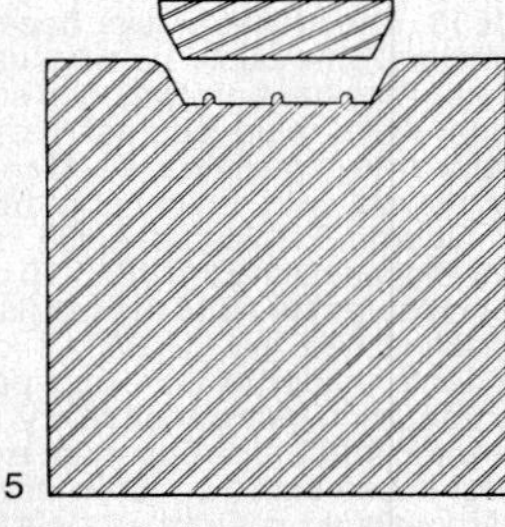

Figure 5

Pressure Transfer from Hub to Working Die

Above, Soft Steel Blank for Working Die.

Below, Hardened Steel Hub Die with Protruding Lines.

The process of pressure transfer is shown in Figure 5. where the soft steel blank of the working die is entering the depression on the top end of the hardened hub die, In fact the pressure transfer of working dies from hub dies closely resembles that of minting coins, and many of these envelope stamp dies are made at the United States Mint in Philadelphia.

In some cases even working dies may be made without figures of value, and the figures of value individually engraved thereon. This is known to be the case in Die B of the 6c orange airmail stamped envelope die, where the size and position of the "6" has eleven variations.

There are some known instances, as in the case of the 4c and 5c envelopes dies of 1903 and 1907, where the engraved master dies were used as printing dies, since the anticipated demand did not justify the expense of making hub dies.

While working envelope dies are heat treated to the hardest temper known, they do wear down eventually to a point where impressions deteriorate and are unsatisfactory, due to shallow recesses or to broken areas, and such dies are destroyed. In many cases these printing dies can be reworked, or deepened, by annealing the steel, touching up the lines or busts by hand engraving to restore the letters or renew the facial contour lines, and then rehardened for subsequent use. This recutting is the principal cause for minor die varieties in envelope stamps. When working dies are no longer useful, they are mutilated and eventually melted down into scrap metal.

The average "life" (in number of good impressions obtained) of a hardened steel working die, as used in envelope printing and embossing machines is around 30,000,000 on flat bed presses, and 43,000,000 on rotary presses. With a production of stamped envelopes of approximately 2 billion annually, 60 to 75 working dies are worn out each year, and require replacement with new dies or a reworking of old dies. Some 200 to 250 working dies can be in constant use, since most envelope printing presses are set up for a special size, type or value, and few can be operated continuously at maximum capacity.

Master and hub dies of obsolete envelope issues are kept in the vaults of the Bureau of Engraving and printing in Washington, as are the original dies of adhesive stamps, revenue paper, government securities and paper currency.

PRINTING ENVELOPE STAMPS

Embossed envelope stamps are not printed against a rigid flat platen, as is the normal printed page, but against a somewhat flexible or resilient platen or make-ready (Figure 6). This resilient platen is hard enough to produce a clear full impression from the ink on the face of the working die, and soft enough to push the paper into the uninked recesses that correspond to the engraved lines cut into the master die. The normal result is raised lines or embossments without ink or color, standing out in relief against an inked or colored background. The method differs from the usual embossing technique, where rigid dies are used on both sides of the paper, as in notarial seals. The use of the resilient platen in envelope embossing permits far higher operating speeds than can be obtained with rigid embossing dies, without the need of such accurate register between the printing surface and the platen.

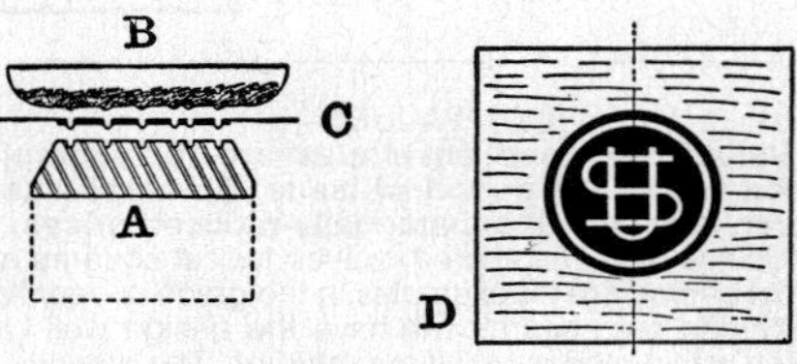

Figure 6

Printing Process for Embossed

A. Working Die, Carrying ink on its surface.

B. Resilient Platen, or Make-ready, Pushing Paper into uninked recesses, so that lines of Embossed Monogram receive no color.

C. Paper of Envelope Blank, after Printing and Embossing. Heavy line shows deposit of ink on surface of paper, but Embossed Lines are not inked.

D. Front view of Embossed impression.

When these recessed lines in a working die become filled with ink or other foreign material, the paper is not pushed in, the plugged area receives ink, and the corresponding colorless line does not appear on the stamp. This accounts for missing letters, lines or figures, and is a printing error, not a die variety.

An ALBINO impression is where two or more envelope blanks are fed into the printing press. The one adjacent to the printing die receives the color and the embossing, while the others are embossed only. Albinos are printing errors and are sometimes worth more than normal, inked impressions. Because of the nature of the printing process, many albinos were produced, and most collectors will not pay much, or any, premium for most of them. Albinos of earlier issues, canceled while current, are scarce.

Before January 1, 1965, stamped envelopes were printed by two processes: (1.) The rotary, with curved dies, on Huckins and Harris presses. (2.) The flat process, with straight dies, as illustrated, on the O'Connell-type press, which is a redesigned Hartford press. The flat bed presses include a gumming and folding attachment, while the rotary presses, running at higher speeds, require separate folding machines.

Different master dies in every denomination are required for Huckins, Harris and flat bed presses. This difference gives rise to most of the major die varieties in envelope stamps.

Web-fed equipment which converts paper from a roll into finished envelopes in a continuous operation has produced envelopes starting with Nos. U547 and UC37. Albino impressions do not occur on envelopes produced by web-fed equipment.

Some authorities claim that Scott U37, U48, U49, U110, U124, U125, U130, U133A, U137A, U137B, U137C, W138, U140A, U145, U162, U178A, U185, U220, U285, U286, U298, U299, UO3, UO32, UO38, UO45 and UO45A (with plus sign + before number), were not regularly issued and are not known to have been used.

Wrappers are listed with envelopes of corresponding design, and are numbered with the prefix "W" instead of "U."

ENVELOPE WATERMARKS

Watermark Illustrations 5, 6, 17 and 18 are condensed. Watermark 4 was intended for Official (Post Office Dept.) envelopes, but some leftover paper was also used for regular envelopes. Watermarks 9 and 10 (penalty) paper was never intended for public sale, but some manila/amber manila paper envelopes were released due to factory paper mixups. Watermarks 17-18 were the last laid paper watermarks; watermarks 19-21 the first wove paper watermarks. Beginning with No. U615, unwatermarked paper was used for some issues. Beginning with No. U625, unwatermarked paper was used for all issues.

Wmks. 1 (1853-70) & 2 (1870-78)

Wmk. 3 (1876)

Wmk. 4 (1877-82)

Wmk. 5 (1878-82)

Wmk. 6 (1882-86)

Wmks. 7 (1886-90) & 8 (1890-94)

Wmks. 9 (1886-87) & 10 (1886-99)

Wmk. 11 (1893)

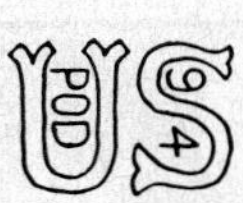

Wmks. 12 (1894-98) & 13 (1899-1902)

Wmks. 14 (1903-07) & 15 (1907-11)

Wmks. 15A (1907-11) & 16 (1911-15)

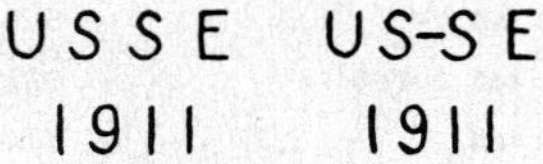

USSE US-SE
1911 1911

Wmks. 17 & 18 (1911-15)

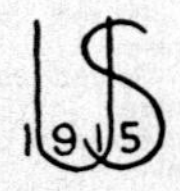

Wmk. 19, 20 & 21 (1915-19)

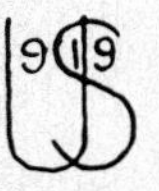

Wmks. 22 & 23 (1919-20)

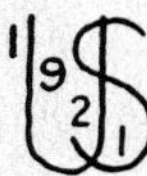

Wmks. 24 & 25 (1921-24)

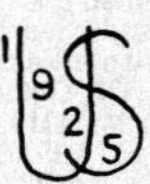

Wmks. 26 & 27 (1925-28)

Wmks. 28 & 28A (1929-32)

Wmks. 29, 30 & 30A (1929-32)

Wmks. 31, 32, 33 (1933-36)

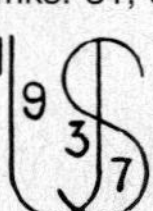

Wmks. 35 & 36 (1937-40)

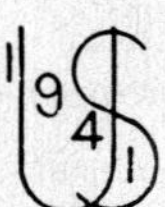

Wmks. 38 & 39 (1941-44)

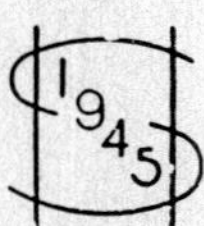
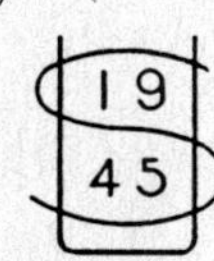

Wmks. 40 & 41 (1945-48)

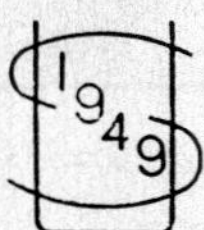
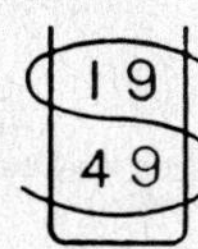

Wmks. 42 & 43 (1949-52)

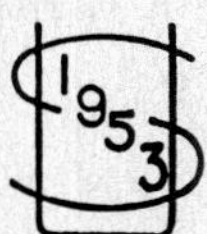
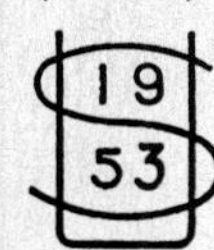

Wmks. 44 & 45 (1953-56)

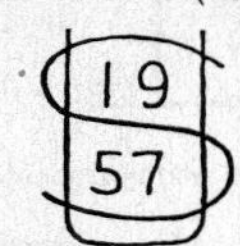

Wmk. 46 (1957-60)

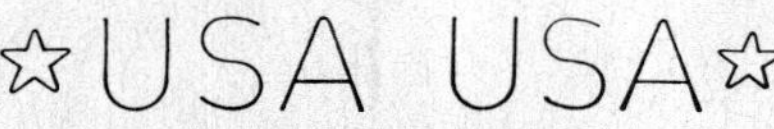

Wmks. 47 & 48 (1961-88)

Wmks. 49 & 50 (1965-92)

Letter Sheet (1886-94)

Official Envelopes (1991)

Washington — U1

"THREE" in short label with curved ends; 13mm wide at top. Twelve varieties.

U2

"THREE" in short label with straight ends; 15½mm wide at top. Three varieties.

U3

"THREE" in short label with octagonal ends. Two varieties.

U4

"THREE" in wide label with straight ends; 20mm wide at top.

U5

"THREE" in medium wide label with curved ends; 14½mm wide at top. Ten varieties. A sub-variety shows curved lines at either end of label omitted; both T's have longer cross stroke; R is smaller (20 varieties).

U6

Four varieties.

U7

"TEN" in short label; 15½mm wide at top.

U8

"TEN" in wide label; 20mm wide at top.

Printed by George F. Nesbitt & Co., New York, N.Y.

1853-55

On Diagonally Laid Paper (Early printings of No. U1 on Horizontally Laid Paper)

U1	U1	3c	**red**	350.00	35.00
			Entire	1,800.	60.00
U2	U1	3c	**red,** *buff*	90.00	30.00
			Entire	850.00	40.00
U3	U2	3c	**red**	950.00	50.00
			Entire	3,500.	120.00
U4	U2	3c	**red,** *buff*	425.00	45.00
			Entire	4,500.	80.00
U5	U3	3c	**red** ('54)	5,750.	500.00
			Entire	*26,000.*	800.00
U6	U3	3c	**red,** *buff* ('54)	3,750.	100.00
			Entire	—	150.00
U7	U4	3c	**red**	5,000.	150.00
			Entire	—	325.00
U8	U4	3c	**red,** *buff*	*8,250.*	175.00
			Entire	—	325.00
U9	U5	3c	**red** ('54)	40.00	4.00
			Entire	140.00	8.00
U10	U5	3c	**red,** *buff* ('54)	20.00	4.00
			Entire	70.00	6.00
U11	U6	6c	**red**	275.00	90.00
			Entire	350.00	175.00
U12	U6	6c	**red,** *buff*	145.00	90.00
			Entire	350.00	200.00
U13	U6	6c	**green**	260.00	150.00
			Entire	575.00	400.00
U14	U6	6c	**green,** *buff*	200.00	125.00
			Entire	450.00	225.00
U15	U7	10c	**green** ('55)	400.00	100.00
			Entire	675.00	175.00
U16	U7	10c	**green,** *buff* ('55)	175.00	90.00
			Entire	425.00	175.00
a.		10c	**pale green,** *buff*	135.00	70.00
			Entire	375.00	125.00
U17	U8	10c	**green** ('55)	375.00	140.00
			Entire	675.00	225.00
a.		10c	**pale green**	275.00	125.00
			Entire	675.00	200.00
U18	U8	10c	**green,** *buff* ('55)	375.00	100.00
			Entire	625.00	190.00
a.		10c	**pale green,** *buff*	350.00	100.00
			Entire	600.00	190.00

Earliest documented uses: No. U1, July 6, 1853; No. U2, July 12, 1853 (Nesbitt seal); No. U3, July 7, 1853 (Nesbitt seal); No. U4, July 7, 1853 (flap missing); No. U5, Feb. 18, 1854; No. U6, Feb. 24, 1854; No. U7, Oct. 6, 1853; No. U8, Nov. 9, 1853; No. U9, May 30, 1854; No. U10, Mar. 24, 1854; No. U11, Mar. 25, 1855; No. U12, Feb. 22, 1855; No. U13, Nov. 29, 1853; No. U14, Nov. 10, 1853; No. U15, Oct. 15, 1856; No. U16, May 15, 1857 (cut square), June 15, 1857 (entire); No. U16a, Dec. 19, 1856 (cut square), June 4, 1857 (entire); No. U17, no dates documented; No. U17a, Nov. 14, 1855; No. U18, June 1, 1855; No. U18a, Sept. 4, 1855.

Nos. U9, U10, U11, U12, U13, U14, U17, and U18 have been reprinted on white and buff papers, wove or vertically laid, and are not known entire. The originals are on diagonally laid paper. Value, set of 8 reprints on laid, $225. Reprints on wove sell for more.

The first printings of Nos. U1, U2, U3, U4 and U7 have G.F. Nesbitt crests printed on the envelope flaps. These sell for a premium. Such examples of Nos. U1-U4 with 1853 year-dated cancels sell for a very large premium.

No. U1 with watermark having a space between lines and on horizontally laid paper sells for a substantial premium.

Franklin — U9

Period after "POSTAGE." (Eleven varieties.)

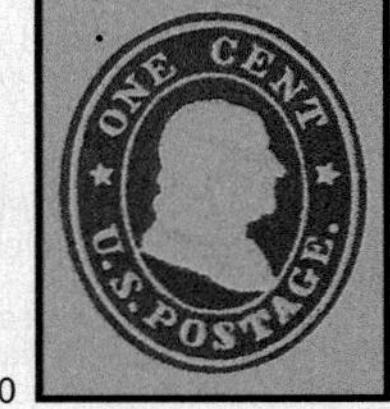

Franklin — U10

Bust touches inner frame-line at front and back.

Franklin — U11

No period after "POSTAGE." (Two varieties.)

Washington — U12

Nine varieties of type U12.

Envelopes are on diagonally laid paper. Wrappers on vertically or horizontally laid paper, or on unwatermarked wove paper (Nos. U21A, W22, W25)

Wrappers of the 1 cent denomination were authorized by an Act of Congress, February 27, 1861, and were issued in October, 1861. These were suspended in 1863, and their use resumed in June, 1864.

1860-61

W18B	U9	1c	**blue** ('61)	*5,500.*	
			Entire	—	
U19	U9	1c	**blue,** *buff*	35.00	12.50
			Entire	85.00	30.00
W20	U9	1c	**blue,** *buff* ('61)	65.00	50.00
			Entire	120.00	75.00
W21	U9	1c	**blue,** *manila* ('61)	55.00	45.00
			Entire	125.00	75.00
U21A	U9	1c	**blue,** *orange*	*950.00*	*325.00*
			Entire	*1,800.*	
W22	U9	1c	**blue,** *orange* ('61)	*3,000.*	
			Entire	*5,500.*	
U23	U10	1c	**blue,** *orange*	500.00	350.00
			Entire	800.00	600.00
U24	U11	1c	**blue,** *amber*	350.00	110.00
			Entire	675.00	300.00
W25	U11	1c	**blue,** *manila* ('61)	*6,750.*	*1,500.*
			Entire	*17,500.*	*5,500.*
U26	U12	3c	**red**	25.00	17.50
			Entire	55.00	32.50
U27	U12	3c	**red,** *buff*	22.50	12.50
			Entire	45.00	22.50
U28	U12+U9	3c + 1c	**red & blue**	250.00	225.00
			Entire	500.00	400.00
U29	U12+U9	3c + 1c	**red & blue,** *buff*	250.00	250.00
			Entire	500.00	450.00
U30	U12	6c	**red**	1,800.	1,500.
			Entire	*3,250.*	
U31	U12	6c	**red,** *buff*	3,500.	1,450.
			Entire	*5,000.*	*15,000.*
U32	U12	10c	**green**	1,250.	450.00
			Entire	*10,000.*	700.00
U33	U12	10c	**green,** *buff*	1,250.	400.00
			Entire	*3,250.*	600.00

Nos. U26, U27, U30 to U33 have been reprinted on the same vertically laid paper as the reprints of the 1853-55 issue, and are not known entire. Value, Nos. U26-U27, $75 each; Nos. U30-U33, $75 each.

Washington — U13

17 varieties for Nos. U34-U35; 2 varieties for No. U36.

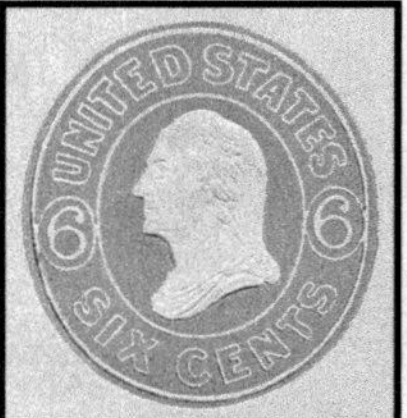

Washington — U14

Washington — U15

Washington — U16

Envelopes are on diagonally laid paper.

U36 and U45 come on vertically or horizontally laid paper. U36 appeared in August, 1861, and was withdrawn in 1864. Total issue 211,800.

1861

U34	U13	3c **pink**	27.50	5.00
		Entire	60.00	12.50
U35	U13	3c **pink,** *buff*	32.50	6.00
		Entire	62.50	12.00
U36	U13	3c **pink,** *blue* (Letter Sheet)	65.00	65.00
		Entire	230.00	*250.00*
+U37	U13	3c **pink,** *orange*	*2,750.*	
		Entire	*5,000.*	
U38	U14	6c **pink**	100.00	80.00
		Entire	200.00	190.00
U39	U14	6c **pink,** *buff*	60.00	60.00
		Entire	150.00	160.00
U40	U15	10c **yellow green**	40.00	30.00
		Entire	77.50	60.00
a.		10c **blue green**	40.00	30.00
		Entire	77.50	60.00
U41	U15	10c **yellow green,** *buff*	40.00	30.00
		Entire	77.50	70.00
a.		10c **blue green,** *buff*	40.00	30.00
		Entire	77.50	52.50
U42	U16	12c **red & brown,** *buff*	180.00	180.00
		Entire	475.00	*650.00*
a.		12c **lake & brown,** *buff*	*1,250.*	
U43	U16	20c **red & blue,** *buff*	250.00	225.00
		Entire	450.00	*1,250.*
U44	U16	24c **red & green,** *buff*	225.00	210.00
		Entire	625.00	*2,000.*
a.		24c **lake & green,** *salmon*	275.00	225.00
		Entire	750.00	*2,400.*
U45	U16	40c **black & red,** *buff*	325.00	400.00
		Entire	700.00	*4,500.*

Nos. U38 and U39 have been reprinted on the same papers as the reprints of the 1853-55 issue, and are not known entire. Value, set of 2 reprints, $60.

Jackson — U17

"U.S. POSTAGE" above. Downstroke and tail of "2" unite near the point (seven varieties).

Jackson — U18

"U.S. POSTAGE" above. The downstroke and tail of the "2" touch but do not merge.

Jackson — U19

"U.S. POST" above. Stamp 24-25mm wide (Sixteen varieties).

Jackson — U20

"U.S. POST" above. Stamp 25½-26¼mm wide. (Twenty-five varieties.)

Envelopes are on diagonally laid paper.
Wrappers on vertically or horizontally laid paper.

1863-64

U46	U17	2c **black,** *buff*	50.00	24.00
		Entire	80.00	37.50
W47	U17	2c **black,** *dark manila*	75.00	65.00
		Entire	120.00	90.00
+U48	U18	2c **black,** *buff*	*2,250.*	
		Entire	*4,500.*	
+U49	U18	2c **black,** *orange*	1,750.	
		Entire	4,000.	
U50	U19	2c **black,** *buff* ('64)	17.50	11.00
		Entire	40.00	21.00
W51	U19	2c **black,** *buff* ('64)	425.00	275.00
		Entire	650.00	600.00
U52	U19	2c **black,** *orange* ('64)	20.00	11.00
		Entire	37.50	18.00
W53	U19	2c **black,** *dark manila* ('64)	42.50	40.00
		Entire	175.00	140.00
U54	U20	2c **black,** *buff* ('64)	17.50	9.50
		Entire	37.50	16.00
W55	U20	2c **black,** *buff* ('64)	95.00	65.00
		Entire	160.00	120.00
U56	U20	2c **black,** *orange* ('64)	17.50	10.00
		Entire	32.50	16.00
W57	U20	2c **black,** *light manila* ('64)	22.50	14.00
		Entire	37.50	30.00

Washington — U21

79 varieties for Nos. U58-U61; 2 varieties for Nos. U63-U65.

Washington — U22

1864-65

U58	U21	3c **pink**	8.00	1.60
		Entire	20.00	3.25
U59	U21	3c **pink,** *buff*	7.50	1.25
		Entire	20.00	3.00
U60	U21	3c **brown** ('65)	60.00	40.00
		Entire	125.00	125.00
U61	U21	3c **brown,** *buff* ('65)	50.00	30.00
		Entire	115.00	95.00
U62	U21	6c **pink**	75.00	29.00
		Entire	160.00	85.00
U63	U21	6c **pink,** *buff*	35.00	27.50
		Entire	90.00	60.00
U64	U21	6c **purple** ('65)	50.00	26.00
		Entire	80.00	80.00
U65	U21	6c **purple,** *buff* ('65)	40.00	20.00
		Entire	70.00	80.00
U66	U22	9c **lemon,** *buff* ('65)	375.00	250.00
		Entire	575.00	*1,500.*
U67	U22	9c **orange,** *buff* ('65)	125.00	90.00
		Entire	210.00	300.00
a.		9c **orange yellow,** *buff*	150.00	90.00
		Entire	225.00	300.00
U68	U22	12c **brown,** *buff* ('65)	275.00	275.00
		Entire	600.00	*1,200.*
U69	U22	12c **red brown,** *buff* ('65)	125.00	55.00
		Entire	180.00	450.00
U70	U22	18c **red,** *buff* ('65)	70.00	95.00
		Entire	180.00	*800.00*
U71	U22	24c **blue,** *buff* ('65)	70.00	95.00
		Entire	200.00	*1,000.*
U72	U22	30c **green,** *buff* ('65)	80.00	80.00
		Entire	200.00	*2,200.*
a.		30c **yellow green,** *buff*	75.00	75.00
		Entire	200.00	*2,000.*
U73	U22	40c **rose,** *buff* ('65)	80.00	*250.00*
		Entire	340.00	*2,000.*

Nos. U60 and U61 issued on legal-size covers only.

Printed by George H. Reay, Brooklyn, N. Y.

The engravings in this issue are finely executed.

Franklin — U23

Bust points to the end of the "N" of "ONE."

Jackson — U24

Bust narrow at back. Small, thick figures of value.

UNITED POSTAL STATIONERY SOCIETY

$3 or $6000?
With UPSS
you'd know!
Specialized
catalogs from the
World's Largest Postal
Stationery Society
Bimonthly Journal
Auctions
404 Sundown Road
Knoxville, TN 37934
WWW.UPSS.ORG

Washington — U25

Queue projects below bust.

Lincoln — U26

Neck very long at the back.

Stanton — U27

Bust pointed at the back; figures "7" are normal.

Jefferson — U28

Queue forms straight line with the bust.

Clay — U29

Ear partly concealed by hair, mouth large, chin prominent.

Webster — U30

Has side whiskers.

Scott — U31

Straggling locks of hair at top of head; ornaments around the inner oval end in squares.

Hamilton — U32

Back of bust very narrow, chin almost straight; labels containing figures of value are exactly parallel.

Perry — U33

Front of bust very narrow and pointed; inner lines of shields project very slightly beyond the oval.

1870-71

U74	U23	1c **blue**	32.50	30.00
		Entire	75.00	45.00
	a.	1c **ultramarine**	60.00	35.00
		Entire	130.00	60.00
U75	U23	1c **blue,** *amber*	25.00	27.50
		Entire	55.00	40.00
	a.	1c **ultramarine,** *amber*	55.00	30.00
		Entire	95.00	55.00
U76	U23	1c **blue,** *orange*	17.00	15.00
		Entire	35.00	22.50
W77	U23	1c **blue,** *manila*	35.00	35.00
		Entire	85.00	75.00
U78	U24	2c **brown**	35.00	16.00
		Entire	57.50	22.50
U79	U24	2c **brown,** *amber*	14.00	10.00
		Entire	40.00	17.50
U80	U24	2c **brown,** *orange*	8.00	6.50
		Entire	15.00	11.00
W81	U24	2c **brown,** *manila*	25.00	20.00
		Entire	60.00	57.50
U82	U25	3c **green**	7.00	1.00
		Entire	16.00	4.00
	a.	3c **brown** (error), entire	*9,000.*	
U83	U25	3c **green,** *amber*	6.00	2.00
		Entire	17.50	5.00
U84	U25	3c **green,** *cream*	8.00	4.50
		Entire	16.00	10.00
U85	U26	6c **dark red**	17.50	16.00
		Entire	47.50	21.00
	a.	6c **vermilion**	17.50	16.00
		Entire	50.00	20.00
U86	U26	6c **dark red,** *amber*	30.00	20.00
		Entire	55.00	40.00
	a.	6c **vermilion,** *amber*	30.00	20.00
		Entire	75.00	30.00
U87	U26	6c **dark red,** *cream*	30.00	25.00
		Entire	70.00	40.00
	a.	6c **vermilion,** *cream*	25.00	20.00
		Entire	70.00	40.00
U88	U27	7c **vermilion,** *amber* ('71)	55.00	175.00
		Entire	80.00	*900.00*
U89	U28	10c **olive black**	650.00	900.00
		Entire	900.00	1,200.
U90	U28	10c **olive black,** *amber*	625.00	800.00
		Entire	1,000.	1,400.
U91	U28	10c **brown**	82.50	70.00
		Entire	130.00	150.00
U92	U28	10c **brown,** *amber*	85.00	52.50
		Entire	120.00	200.00
	a.	10c **dark brown,** *amber*	85.00	75.00
		Entire	120.00	125.00
U93	U29	12c **plum**	100.00	82.50
		Entire	225.00	*500.00*
U94	U29	12c **plum,** *amber*	110.00	100.00
		Entire	225.00	*750.00*
U95	U29	12c **plum,** *cream*	225.00	200.00
		Entire	300.00	

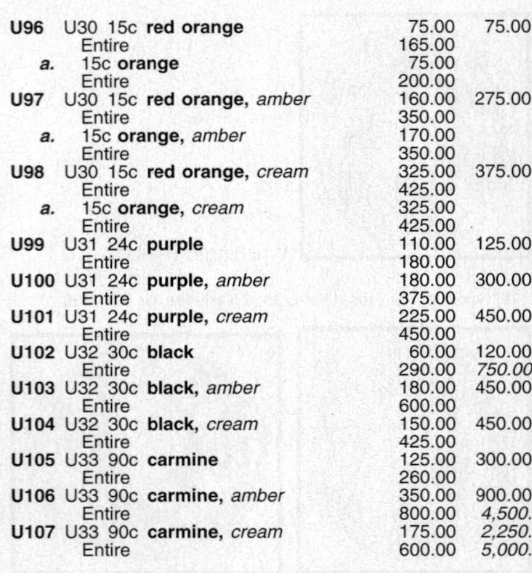

U96	U30	15c **red orange**	75.00	75.00
		Entire	165.00	
	a.	15c **orange**	75.00	
		Entire	200.00	
U97	U30	15c **red orange,** *amber*	160.00	275.00
		Entire	350.00	
	a.	15c **orange,** *amber*	170.00	
		Entire	350.00	
U98	U30	15c **red orange,** *cream*	325.00	375.00
		Entire	425.00	
	a.	15c **orange,** *cream*	325.00	
		Entire	425.00	
U99	U31	24c **purple**	110.00	125.00
		Entire	180.00	
U100	U31	24c **purple,** *amber*	180.00	300.00
		Entire	375.00	
U101	U31	24c **purple,** *cream*	225.00	450.00
		Entire	450.00	
U102	U32	30c **black**	60.00	120.00
		Entire	290.00	*750.00*
U103	U32	30c **black,** *amber*	180.00	450.00
		Entire	600.00	
U104	U32	30c **black,** *cream*	150.00	450.00
		Entire	425.00	
U105	U33	90c **carmine**	125.00	300.00
		Entire	260.00	
U106	U33	90c **carmine,** *amber*	350.00	900.00
		Entire	800.00	*4,500.*
U107	U33	90c **carmine,** *cream*	175.00	*2,250.*
		Entire	600.00	*5,000.*

Printed by Plimpton Manufacturing Co.

U34

Bust forms an angle at the back near the frame. Lettering poorly executed. Distinct circle in "O" of "Postage."

U35

Lower part of bust points to the end of the "E" in "ONE." Head inclined downward.

U36

Bust narrow at back. Thin numerals. Head of "P" narrow. Bust broad at front, ending in sharp corners.

U37

Bust broad. Figures of value in long ovals.

U38

Similar to U37 but the figure "2" at the left touches the oval.

U39

Similar to U37 but the "O" of "TWO" has the center netted instead of plain and the "G" of "POSTAGE" and the "C" of "CENTS" have diagonal crossline.

U40

Bust broad: numerals in ovals short and thick.

U41

Similar to U40 but the ovals containing the numerals are much heavier. A diagonal line runs from the upper part of the "U" to the white frame-line.

U42

Similar to U40 but the middle stroke of "N" in "CENTS" is as thin as the vertical strokes.

U43

Bottom of bust cut almost semi-circularly.

U44

Thin lettering, long thin figures of value.

U45

Thick lettering, well-formed figures of value, queue does not project below bust.

U46

Top of head egg-shaped; knot of queue well marked and projects triangularly.

Taylor — U47

Die 1- Figures of value with thick, curved tops

Die 2- Figures of value with long, thin tops

U48

Neck short at back.

U49

Figures of value turned up at the ends.

U50

Very large head.

U51

Knot of queue stands out prominently.

U52

Ear prominent, chin receding.

U53

No side whiskers, forelock projects above head.

U54

Hair does not project; ornaments around the inner oval end in points.

U55

Back of bust rather broad, chin slopes considerably; labels containing figures of value are not exactly parallel.

U56

Front of bust sloping; inner lines of shields project considerably into the inner oval.

1874-86

No.	Die	Description	Unused	Used
U108	U34	1c **dark blue**	175.00	60.00
		Entire	250.00	125.00
a.		1c **light blue**	175.00	60.00
		Entire	250.00	150.00
U109	U34	1c **dark blue,** *amber*	150.00	75.00
		Entire	200.00	140.00
+U110	U34	1c **dark blue,** *cream*	1,000.	
U111	U34	1c **dark blue,** *orange*	15.00	15.00
		Entire	40.00	25.00
a.		1c **light blue,** *orange*	12.50	12.50
		Entire	30.00	25.00
W112	U34	1c **dark blue,** *manila*	62.50	40.00
		Entire	105.00	90.00
U113	U35	1c **light blue**	2.25	1.00
		Entire	4.00	2.00
a.		1c **dark blue**	6.50	6.50
		Entire	27.50	20.00
U114	U35	1c **light blue,** *amber*	3.25	3.25
		Entire	8.25	6.00
a.		1c **dark blue,** *amber*	17.50	10.00
		Entire	30.00	20.00
U115	U35	1c **blue,** *cream*	4.25	4.25
		Entire	10.00	6.50
a.		1c **dark blue,** *cream*	17.50	8.50
		Entire	32.50	20.00
U116	U35	1c **light blue,** *orange*	.75	.40
		Entire	1.25	1.00
a.		1c **dark blue,** *orange*	4.00	2.50
		Entire	16.00	8.00
U117	U35	1c **light blue,** *blue* ('80)	6.50	5.00
		Entire	15.00	9.00
U118	U35	1c **light blue,** *fawn* ('79)	7.00	5.00
		Entire	17.00	12.00
U119	U35	1c **light blue,** *manila* ('86)	8.00	3.25
		Entire	17.00	5.00
W120	U35	1c **light blue,** *manila*	1.25	1.10
		Entire	2.75	1.75
a.		1c **dark blue,** *manila*	8.00	7.00
		Entire	16.00	15.00
U121	U35	1c **light blue,** *amber manila* ('86)	17.50	10.00
		Entire	29.00	25.00
U122	U36	2c **brown**	140.00	65.00
		Entire	175.00	100.00
U123	U36	2c **brown,** *amber*	67.50	40.00
		Entire	125.00	85.00
+U124	U36	2c **brown,** *cream*	1,000.	
+U125	U36	2c **brown,** *orange*	*18,000.*	
		Entire	*35,000.*	
W126	U36	2c **brown,** *manila*	125.00	85.00
		Entire	325.00	160.00
W127	U36	2c **vermilion,** *manila*	2,500.	500.00
		Entire	3,250.	*5,000.*
U128	U37	2c **brown**	60.00	35.00
		Entire	110.00	85.00
U129	U37	2c **brown,** *amber*	80.00	45.00
		Entire	125.00	77.50
+U130	U37	2c **brown,** *cream*	*35,000.*	
W131	U37	2c **brown,** *manila*	17.50	15.00
		Entire	29.00	26.00
U132	U38	2c **brown**	70.00	27.50
		Entire	120.00	80.00
U133	U38	2c **brown,** *amber*	325.00	70.00
		Entire	550.00	175.00
+U133A	U38	2c **brown,** *cream*	*70,000.*	
U134	U39	2c **brown**	800.00	160.00
		Entire	1,400.	300.00
U135	U39	2c **brown,** *amber*	425.00	150.00
		Entire	650.00	180.00
U136	U39	2c **brown,** *orange*	50.00	27.50
		Entire	80.00	37.50
W137	U39	2c **brown,** *manila*	75.00	40.00
		Entire	125.00	55.00
+U137A	U39	2c **vermilion**	*32,500.*	
+U137B	U39	2c **vermilion,** *amber*	*30,000.*	
		Entire	—	
+U137C	U39	2c **vermilion,** *orange*	*70,000.*	
+W138	U39	2c **vermilion,** *manila*	*25,000.*	
U139	U40	2c **brown** ('75)	57.50	37.50
		Entire	85.00	55.00
U140	U40	2c **brown,** *amber* ('75)	85.00	62.50
		Entire	130.00	85.00
+U140A	U40	2c **reddish brown,** *orange* ('75)	*17,500.*	
		Entire	*32,500.*	
W141	U40	2c **brown,** *manila* ('75)	32.50	25.00
		Entire	45.00	40.00
U142	U40	2c **vermilion** ('75)	8.00	5.00
		Entire	12.00	6.00
a.		2c **pink**	8.00	5.00
		Entire	16.00	9.00
U143	U40	2c **vermilion,** *amber* ('75)	9.00	5.00
		Entire	12.00	6.50
U144	U40	2c **vermilion,** *cream* ('75)	17.50	7.00
		Entire	25.00	12.50
+U145	U40	2c **vermilion,** *orange* ('75)	*35,000.*	
U146	U40	2c **vermilion,** *blue* ('80)	110.00	40.00
		Entire	*200.00*	140.00
U147	U40	2c **vermilion,** *fawn* ('75)	7.00	5.00
		Entire	15.00	7.00
W148	U40	2c **vermilion,** *manila* ('75)	4.00	3.50
		Entire	9.00	6.50
U149	U41	2c **vermilion** ('78)	45.00	25.00
		Entire	90.00	40.00
a.		2c **pink**	52.50	27.00
		Entire	90.00	42.50
U150	U41	2c **vermilion,** *amber* ('78)	45.00	15.00
		Entire	75.00	25.00
U151	U41	2c **vermilion,** *blue* ('80)	10.00	8.00
		Entire	25.00	25.00
a.		2c **pink,** *blue*	11.00	8.00
		Entire	17.50	12.50
U152	U41	2c **vermilion,** *fawn* ('78)	10.00	4.00
		Entire	17.50	9.00
U153	U42	2c **vermilion** ('76)	75.00	30.00
		Entire	115.00	45.00
U154	U42	2c **vermilion,** *amber* ('76)	300.00	90.00
		Entire	450.00	200.00
W155	U42	2c **vermilion,** *manila* ('76)	20.00	10.00
		Entire	45.00	20.00
U156	U43	2c **vermilion** ('81)	1,250.	175.00
		Entire	2,000.	*500.00*
U157	U43	2c **vermilion,** *amber* ('81)	*42,500.*	*27,500.*
		Entire	*60,000.*	
W158	U43	2c **vermilion,** *manila* ('81)	90.00	55.00
		Entire	200.00	200.00
U159	U44	3c **green**	35.00	10.00
		Entire	60.00	17.50
U160	U44	3c **green,** *amber*	35.00	10.00
		Entire	70.00	20.00
U161	U44	3c **green,** *cream*	35.00	12.00
		Entire	65.00	30.00
+U162	U44	3c **green,** *blue*	*75,000.*	
U163	U45	3c **green**	1.40	.30
		Entire	4.25	2.25
U164	U45	3c **green,** *amber*	1.50	.70
		Entire	4.25	2.00
U165	U45	3c **green,** *cream*	8.50	6.50
		Entire	19.00	11.00
U166	U45	3c **green,** *blue*	7.50	6.00
		Entire	17.00	11.00
U167	U45	3c **green,** *fawn* ('75)	4.75	3.50
		Entire	9.25	5.00
U168	U46	3c **green** ('81)	1,000.	80.00
		Entire	3,500.	275.00
U169	U46	3c **green,** *amber*	450.00	140.00
		Entire	700.00	300.00
U170	U46	3c **green,** *blue* ('81)	*11,500.*	*2,750.*
		Entire	*20,000.*	*4,250.*
U171	U46	3c **green,** *fawn* ('81)	*40,000.*	*2,750.*
		Entire		*14,000.*
U172	U47	5c **blue,** die 1 ('75)	10.00	10.00
		Entire	20.00	16.00
U173	U47	5c **blue,** die 1, *amber* ('75)	12.50	11.00
		Entire	21.00	17.00
U174	U47	5c **blue,** die 1, *cream* ('75)	95.00	45.00
		Entire	190.00	150.00
U175	U47	5c **blue,** die 1, *blue* ('75)	22.50	17.50
		Entire	40.00	35.00
U176	U47	5c **blue,** die 1, *fawn* ('75)	150.00	65.00
		Entire	325.00	
U177	U47	5c **blue,** die 2 ('75)	11.00	9.00
		Entire	18.00	18.00
U178	U47	5c **blue,** die 2, *amber* ('75)	8.00	8.00
		Entire	18.00	19.00
+U178A	U47	5c **blue,** die 2, *cream* ('76)	*10,000.*	
		Entire	*17,500.*	
U179	U47	5c **blue,** die 2, *blue* ('75)	20.00	12.50
		Entire	50.00	50.00
U180	U47	5c **blue,** die 2, *fawn* ('75)	125.00	50.00
		Entire	225.00	225.00
U181	U48	6c **red**	8.00	6.50
		Entire	15.00	12.50
a.		6c **vermilion**	8.00	6.50
		Entire	15.00	12.50
U182	U48	6c **red,** *amber*	12.50	6.50
		Entire	24.00	15.00
a.		6c **vermilion,** *amber*	12.50	6.50
		Entire	24.00	15.00
U183	U48	6c **red,** *cream*	50.00	17.50
		Entire	100.00	100.00
a.		6c **vermilion,** *cream*	45.00	15.00
		Entire	82.50	40.00
U184	U48	6c **red,** *fawn* ('75)	17.50	12.50
		Entire	32.50	50.00
+U185	U49	7c **vermilion**	*1,200.*	
U186	U49	7c **vermilion,** *amber*	125.00	75.00
		Entire	225.00	
U187	U50	10c **brown**	40.00	20.00
		Entire	65.00	
U188	U50	10c **brown,** *amber*	75.00	35.00
		Entire	170.00	
U189	U51	10c **chocolate** ('75)	6.00	4.00
		Entire	12.00	9.25
a.		10c **bister brown**	7.00	5.00
		Entire	12.50	10.50
b.		10c **yellow ocher**	*3,000.*	
		Entire	*5,250.*	
U190	U51	10c **chocolate,** *amber* ('75)	7.00	6.00
		Entire	13.00	14.00
a.		10c **bister brown,** *amber*	7.00	6.00
		Entire	13.00	14.00
b.		10c **yellow ocher,** *amber*	*3,000.*	
		Entire	*5,250.*	
U191	U51	10c **brown,** *oriental buff* ('86)	12.50	8.75
		Entire	20.00	15.00
U192	U51	10c **brown,** *blue* ('86)	12.50	8.00
		Entire	20.00	20.00
a.		10c **gray black,** *blue*	12.50	7.50
		Entire	30.00	20.00
b.		10c **red brown,** *blue*	12.50	7.50
		Entire	20.00	20.00
U193	U51	10c **brown,** *manila* ('86)	12.50	10.00
		Entire	22.50	25.00
a.		10c **red brown,** *manila*	12.50	10.00
		Entire	22.50	25.00
U194	U51	10c **brown,** *amber manila* ('86)	17.50	9.00
		Entire	30.00	30.00
a.		10c **red brown,** *amber manila*	17.50	9.00
		Entire	40.00	30.00
U195	U52	12c **plum**	250.00	100.00
		Entire	575.00	*1,000.*
U196	U52	12c **plum,** *amber*	200.00	160.00
		Entire	350.00	*1,000.*
U197	U52	12c **plum,** *cream*	200.00	130.00
		Entire	850.00	*2,200.*
U198	U53	15c **orange**	50.00	35.00
		Entire	100.00	100.00
U199	U53	15c **orange,** *amber*	140.00	130.00
		Entire	300.00	*2,000.*
U200	U53	15c **orange,** *cream*	450.00	300.00
		Entire	800.00	*2,000.*
U201	U54	24c **purple**	175.00	150.00
		Entire	260.00	*1,500.*
a.		Printed on both sides, one inverted and overlapping, cut to shape	450.00	
U202	U54	24c **purple,** *amber*	180.00	100.00
		Entire	375.00	*2,500.*
U203	U54	24c **purple,** *cream*	200.00	100.00
		Entire	750.00	
U204	U55	30c **black**	55.00	25.00
		Entire	90.00	200.00
U205	U55	30c **black,** *amber*	70.00	60.00
		Entire	130.00	*250.00*
U206	U55	30c **black,** *cream* ('75)	300.00	325.00
		Entire	600.00	
U207	U55	30c **black,** *oriental buff* ('81)	90.00	80.00
		Entire	160.00	
U208	U55	30c **black,** *blue* ('81)	90.00	80.00
		Entire	170.00	
U209	U55	30c **black,** *manila* ('81)	80.00	70.00
		Entire	190.00	
U210	U55	30c **black,** *amber manila* ('86)	190.00	100.00
		Entire	260.00	
U211	U56	90c **carmine** ('75)	80.00	75.00
		Entire	130.00	*500.00*
U212	U56	90c **carmine,** *amber* ('75)	175.00	250.00
		Entire	250.00	
U213	U56	90c **carmine,** *cream* ('75)	1,000.	
		Entire	2,000.	
U214	U56	90c **carmine,** *oriental buff* ('86)	140.00	250.00
		Entire	300.00	400.00
U215	U56	90c **carmine,** *blue* ('86)	160.00	250.00
		Entire	250.00	325.00
U216	U56	90c **carmine,** *manila* ('86)	120.00	225.00
		Entire	240.00	*700.00*
U217	U56	90c **carmine,** *amber manila* ('86)	140.00	200.00
		Entire	300.00	*700.00*

Note: No. U206 has watermark #2; No. U207 watermark #6 or #7. No U213 has watermark #2; No. U214 watermark #7. These envelopes cannot be positively identified except by the watermark.

U57

Single line under "POSTAGE."

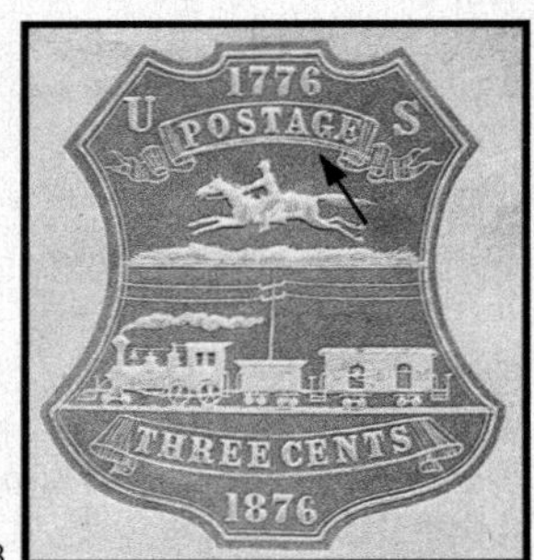

U58

Double line under "POSTAGE."

1876 Printed by Plimpton Manufacturing Co.

U218	U57 3c **red**	30.00	25.00
	Entire	70.00	50.00
U219	U57 3c **green**	30.00	17.50
	Entire	60.00	40.00
+U220	U58 3c **red**	*27,500.*	
	Entire	*42,500.*	
U221	U58 3c **green**	30.00	25.00
	Entire	75.00	50.00

Used examples of Nos. U218-U221 with exposition cancels and/or typed addresses sell for a premium.

Garfield — U59

Printed by Plimpton Manufacturing Co. and Morgan Envelope Co.

1882-86

U222	U59 5c **brown**	5.00	3.00
	Entire	10.00	7.50
U223	U59 5c **brown,** *amber*	5.25	3.50
	Entire	11.00	10.00
+U224	U59 5c **brown,** *oriental buff* ('86)	130.00	
	Entire	200.00	
+U225	U59 5c **brown,** *blue*	75.00	
	Entire	120.00	
U226	U59 5c **brown,** *fawn*	300.00	
	Entire	800.00	

Washington — U60

1883, October

U227	U60 2c **red**	5.50	2.25
	Entire	11.00	4.00
a.	2c **brown** (error), entire	*3,000.*	
U228	U60 2c **red,** *amber*	6.50	2.75
	Entire	12.00	6.00
U229	U60 2c **red,** *blue*	8.00	5.00
	Entire	12.50	8.00
U230	U60 2c **red,** *fawn*	9.00	5.25
	Entire	14.00	7.00

Washington — U61

Wavy lines fine and clear.

1883, November Four Wavy Lines in Oval

U231	U61 2c **red**	5.00	2.50
	Entire	9.50	4.00
U232	U61 2c **red,** *amber*	6.00	3.75
	Entire	11.00	5.75
U233	U61 2c **red,** *blue*	10.00	7.50
	Entire	12.00	10.00
U234	U61 2c **red,** *fawn*	7.50	4.75
	Entire	11.00	6.00
W235	U61 2c **red,** *manila*	18.00	6.25
	Entire	30.00	20.00

U62

Retouched die. Wavy lines thick and blurred.

1884, June

U236	U62 2c **red**	15.00	4.00
	Entire	20.00	7.75
U237	U62 2c **red,** *amber*	20.00	10.00
	Entire	30.00	11.00
U238	U62 2c **red,** *blue*	29.00	12.00
	Entire	40.00	15.00
U239	U62 2c **red,** *fawn*	20.00	11.00
	Entire	22.50	12.50

U63

3½ links over left "2."

U240	U63 2c **red**	90.00	45.00
	Entire	150.00	72.50
U241	U63 2c **red,** *amber*	550.00	300.00
	Entire	1,500.	750.00
U242	U63 2c **red,** *fawn*	*25,000.*	
	Entire	*47,500.*	

U64

2 links below right "2."

U243	U64 2c **red**	110.00	75.00
	Entire	140.00	100.00
U244	U64 2c **red,** *amber*	250.00	100.00
	Entire	400.00	125.00
U245	U64 2c **red,** *blue*	275.00	125.00
	Entire	500.00	150.00
U246	U64 2c **red,** *fawn*	275.00	175.00
	Entire	525.00	200.00

U65

Round "O" in "TWO." White lines above "WO" of "TWO" joined to form thick white dash.

U247	U65 2c **red**	1,500.	400.00
	Entire	2,500.	*800.00*
U248	U65 2c **red,** *amber*	2,500.	750.00
	Entire	5,000.	*2,500.*
U249	U65 2c **red,** *fawn*	750.	500.00
	Entire	1,250.	*750.00*

Jackson, Die 1 — U66

Die 1- Numeral at left is 2 ¾ mm wide

Die 2- Numeral at left is 3 ¼ mm wide

1883-86

U250	U66 4c **green,** die 1	4.00	3.50
	Entire	6.50	6.00
U251	U66 4c **green,** die 1, *amber*	5.00	3.50
	Entire	7.50	8.00
U252	U66 4c **green,** die 1, *oriental buff* ('86)	13.00	9.00
	Entire	20.00	20.00
U253	U66 4c **green,** die 1, *blue* ('86)	11.00	6.50
	Entire	20.00	20.00
U254	U66 4c **green,** die 1, *manila* ('86)	16.00	7.50
	Entire	25.00	25.00
U255	U66 4c **green,** die 1, *amber manila* ('86)	22.50	10.00
	Entire	32.50	30.00
U256	U66 4c **green,** die 2	8.00	5.00
	Entire	17.50	10.00
U257	U66 4c **green,** die 2, *amber*	12.50	7.00
	Entire	22.50	20.00
U258	U66 4c **green,** die 2, *manila* ('86)	12.50	7.50
	Entire	22.50	18.00
U259	U66 4c **green,** die 2, *amber manila* ('86)	12.50	7.50
	Entire	22.50	18.00

1884, May

U260	U61 2c **brown**	17.50	5.75
	Entire	20.00	9.00
U261	U61 2c **brown,** *amber*	17.50	6.50
	Entire	20.00	10.00
U262	U61 2c **brown,** *blue*	17.50	10.00
	Entire	26.00	14.00
U263	U61 2c **brown,** *fawn*	15.00	9.25
	Entire	20.00	12.50
W264	U61 2c **brown,** *manila*	15.00	11.50
	Entire	30.00	30.00

1884, June

Retouched Die

U265	U62 2c **brown**	15.00	6.50
	Entire	25.00	12.00
U266	U62 2c **brown,** *amber*	60.00	40.00
	Entire	90.00	50.00
U267	U62 2c **brown,** *blue*	22.50	9.00
	Entire	30.00	15.00
U268	U62 2c **brown,** *fawn*	15.00	11.00
	Entire	21.00	15.00
W269	U62 2c **brown,** *manila*	25.00	15.00
	Entire	32.50	24.00

2 Links Below Right "2"

U270	U64 2c **brown**	115.00	50.00
	Entire	150.00	110.00
U271	U64 2c **brown,** *amber*	425.00	125.00
	Entire	575.00	350.00

U272	U64 2c **brown,** *fawn*	*7,000.*	*2,000.*
	Entire	*8,500.*	*4,000.*

Round "O" in "Two"

U273	U65 2c **brown**	225.00	100.00
	Entire	375.00	190.00
U274	U65 2c **brown,** *amber*	225.00	100.00
	Entire	375.00	225.00
U275	U65 2c **brown,** *blue*		*10,000.*
	Entire		*47,500.*
U276	U65 2c **brown,** *fawn*	700.00	750.00
	Entire	1,200.	*1,200.*

Washington — U67

Extremity of bust below the queue forms a point.

U68

Extremity of bust is rounded. Similar to U61. Two wavy lines in oval.

1884-86

U277	U67 2c **brown**	.50	.25
	Entire	1.00	.40
a.	2c **brown lake,** die 1	22.50	21.00
	Entire	27.50	26.00
U278	U67 2c **brown,** *amber*	.65	.50
	Entire	1.75	1.00
a.	2c **brown lake,** *amber*	35.00	25.00
	Entire	42.50	32.50
U279	U67 2c **brown,** *oriental buff* ('86)	6.00	2.10
	Entire	9.00	9.00
U280	U67 2c **brown,** *blue*	3.00	2.10
	Entire	4.50	4.50
U281	U67 2c **brown,** *fawn*	3.75	2.40
	Entire	5.50	4.00
U282	U67 2c **brown,** *manila* ('86)	12.00	4.00
	Entire	17.50	12.00
W283	U67 2c **brown,** *manila*	8.00	5.00
	Entire	11.00	11.00
U284	U67 2c **brown,** *amber manila* ('86)	7.00	5.75
	Entire	15.00	12.00
+U285	U67 2c **red**	600.00	
	Entire	1,200.	
+U286	U67 2c **red,** *blue*	225.00	
	Entire	350.00	
W287	U67 2c **red,** *manila*	150.00	
	Entire	190.00	
U288	U68 2c **brown**	325.00	50.00
	Entire	700.00	150.00
U289	U68 2c **brown,** *amber*	20.00	13.00
	Entire	25.00	25.00
U290	U68 2c **brown,** *blue*	850.00	325.00
	Entire	1,600.	450.00
U291	U68 2c **brown,** *fawn*	25.00	25.00
	Entire	50.00	50.00
W292	U68 2c **brown,** *manila*	30.00	19.00
	Entire	35.00	30.00

Gen. U.S. Grant — US1

Printed by American Bank Note Co.
Issued August 23, 1886. Withdrawn June 30, 1894.
Letter Sheet, 160x271mm

1886 **Creamy White Paper**

Stamp in upper right corner

U293	US1 2c **green,** entire	30.00	20.00

Perforation varieties:

83 perforations at top	30.00	20.00
42 perforations at top	150.00	100.00
33 perforations at top	45.00	20.00

All with 41 perforations at top

Inscribed: Series 1	30.00	20.00
Inscribed: Series 2	30.00	20.00
Inscribed: Series 3	30.00	20.00
Inscribed: Series 4	30.00	20.00
Inscribed: Series 5	30.00	20.00
Inscribed: Series 6	30.00	20.00
Inscribed: Series 7	30.00	20.00
No inscription, continuous side perforations	30.00	20.00
No inscription, interrupted side perforations	30.00	20.00

Earliest documented use: Aug. 23, 1886 (FDC).

Franklin — U69

Washington — U70

Bust points between third and fourth notches of inner oval "G" of "POSTAGE" has no bar.

U71

Bust points between second and third notches of inner oval; "G" of "POSTAGE" has a bar; ear is indicated by one heavy line; one vertical line at corner of mouth.

U72

Frame same as U71; upper part of head more rounded; ear indicated by two curved lines with two locks of hair in front; two vertical lines at corner of mouth.

Jackson — U73

Grant — U74

There is a space between the beard and the collar of the coat. A button is on the collar.

U75

The collar touches the beard and there is no button.

Printed by Plimpton Manufacturing Co. and Morgan Envelope Co., Hartford, Conn.; James Purcell, Holyoke, Mass.

1887-94

U294	U69 1c **blue**	.55	.25
	Entire	1.00	.50
U295	U69 1c **dark blue** ('94)	6.50	2.50
	Entire	11.50	7.50
U296	U69 1c **blue,** *amber*	3.25	1.25
	Entire	5.50	3.50
U297	U69 1c **dark blue,** *amber* ('94)	40.00	22.50
	Entire	60.00	27.50
+U298	U69 1c **blue,** *oriental buff*	*7,000.*	—
	Entire	*12,000.*	
+U299	U69 1c **blue,** *blue*	*10,000.*	
	Entire	*18,000.*	
U300	U69 1c **blue,** *manila*	.65	.35
	Entire	1.25	.75
W301	U69 1c **blue,** *manila*	.45	.30
	Entire	1.25	.60
U302	U69 1c **dark blue,** *manila* ('94)	27.50	12.50
	Entire	35.00	20.00
W303	U69 1c **dark blue,** *manila* ('94)	12.50	10.00
	Entire	20.00	15.00
U304	U69 1c **blue,** *amber manila*	12.50	5.00
	Entire	17.50	10.00
U305	U70 2c **green**	15.00	10.00
	Entire	32.50	15.00
U306	U70 2c **green,** *amber*	40.00	17.50
	Entire	55.00	25.00
U307	U70 2c **green,** *oriental buff*	80.00	40.00
	Entire	120.00	70.00
U308	U70 2c **green,** *blue*	*12,500.*	4,250.
	Entire		*22,000.*
U309	U70 2c **green,** *manila*	*10,000.*	1,000.
	Entire	*22,500.*	1,200.
U310	U70 2c **green,** *amber manila*	*28,000.*	*4,000.*
	Entire	—	*3,250.*
U311	U71 2c **green**	.30	.25
	Entire	.70	.25
a.	2c **dark green** ('94)	.45	.30
	Entire	1.00	.85
b.	Double impression, entire	375.00	
U312	U71 2c **green,** *amber*	.40	.25
	Entire	.75	.30
a.	Double impression	90.00	
b.	2c **dark green,** *amber* ('94)	.55	.35
	Entire	1.50	1.20
U313	U71 2c **green,** *oriental buff*	.55	.25
	Entire	1.10	.40
a.	2c **dark green,** *oriental buff* ('94)	2.00	1.00
	Entire	4.00	4.00
b.	Double impression	150.00	
U314	U71 2c **green,** *blue*	.60	.30
	Entire	1.20	.40
a.	2c **dark green** *blue* ('94)	.80	.40
	Entire	3.00	2.25
U315	U71 2c **green,** *manila*	2.00	.50
	Entire	3.00	1.00
a.	2c **dark green** *manila* ('94)	2.75	.75
	Entire	3.25	2.00
W316	U71 2c **green,** *manila*	3.50	2.50
	Entire	10.00	7.00
U317	U71 2c **green,** *amber manila*	2.50	1.90
	Entire	5.50	3.00
a.	2c **dark green,** *amber manila* ('94)	3.50	3.00
	Entire	7.00	4.00
U318	U72 2c **green**	110.00	12.50
	Entire	190.00	50.00
U319	U72 2c **green,** *amber*	160.00	27.50
	Entire	200.00	50.00
U320	U72 2c **green,** *oriental buff*	125.00	40.00
	Entire	240.00	70.00
U321	U72 2c **green,** *blue*	150.00	70.00
	Entire	250.00	90.00
U322	U72 2c **green,** *manila*	225.00	70.00
	Entire	300.00	110.00
U323	U72 2c **green,** *amber manila*	400.00	100.00
	Entire	700.00	300.00
U324	U73 4c **carmine**	3.25	2.00
	Entire	6.00	5.50
a.	4c **lake**	3.50	2.00
	Entire	7.00	3.75
b.	4c **scarlet** ('94)	3.50	2.00
	Entire	7.00	3.75
U325	U73 4c **carmine,** *amber*	3.50	3.50
	Entire	7.00	4.00
a.	4c **lake,** *amber*	3.50	3.50
	Entire	10.00	10.00
b.	4c **scarlet,** *amber* ('94)	4.00	3.75
	Entire	11.00	7.00
U326	U73 4c **carmine,** *oriental buff*	6.00	3.50
	Entire	14.00	14.00
a.	4c **lake,** *oriental buff*	7.00	3.50
	Entire	15.00	15.00

U327	U73	4c **carmine,** *blue*	5.50	4.00
		Entire	15.00	15.00
a.		4c **lake,** *blue*	6.00	4.00
		Entire	16.00	16.00
U328	U73	4c **carmine,** *manila*	8.00	7.00
		Entire	15.00	15.00
a.		4c **lake,** *manila*	8.00	6.00
		Entire	20.00	20.00
b.		4c **pink,** *manila*	15.00	10.00
		Entire	21.00	12.50
U329	U73	4c **carmine,** *amber manila*	6.00	3.25
		Entire	14.00	15.00
a.		4c **lake,** *amber manila*	6.00	3.25
		Entire	20.00	20.00
b.		4c **pink,** *amber manila*	15.00	10.00
		Entire	21.00	12.50
U330	U74	5c **blue**	3.75	4.00
		Entire	7.50	8.00
U331	U74	5c **blue,** *amber*	6.00	2.50
		Entire	11.00	14.00
a.		Double impression, entire	—	
U332	U74	5c **blue,** *oriental buff*	6.50	4.00
		Entire	16.00	18.00
U333	U74	5c **blue,** *blue*	7.00	6.00
		Entire	17.00	20.00
U334	U75	5c **blue** ('94)	20.00	12.50
		Entire	50.00	50.00
U335	U75	5c **blue,** *amber* ('94)	11.00	7.50
		Entire	22.00	40.00
U336	U55	30c **red brown**	40.00	45.00
		Entire	60.00	*600.00*
a.		30c **yellow brown**	40.00	45.00
		Entire	60.00	*600.00*
b.		30c **chocolate**	40.00	45.00
		Entire	60.00	*600.00*
U337	U55	30c **red brown,** *amber*	40.00	45.00
		Entire	60.00	*600.00*
a.		30c **yellow brown,** *amber*	40.00	45.00
		Entire	60.00	*600.00*
b.		30c **chocolate,** *amber*	40.00	45.00
		Entire	60.00	*600.00*
U338	U55	30c **red brown,** *oriental buff*	40.00	45.00
		Entire	60.00	*600.00*
a.		30c **yellow brown,** *oriental buff*	40.00	45.00
		Entire	60.00	*600.00*
U339	U55	30c **red brown,** *blue*	40.00	45.00
		Entire	60.00	*600.00*
a.		30c **yellow brown,** *blue*	40.00	45.00
		Entire	60.00	*600.00*
U340	U55	30c **red brown,** *manila*	40.00	45.00
		Entire	60.00	*600.00*
a.		30c **brown,** *manila*	40.00	45.00
		Entire	60.00	*600.00*
U341	U55	30c **red brown,** *amber manila*	40.00	45.00
		Entire	75.00	*600.00*
a.		30c **yellow brown,** *amber manila*	40.00	45.00
		Entire	75.00	*600.00*
U342	U56	90c **purple**	55.00	85.00
		Entire	100.00	*1,500.*
U343	U56	90c **purple,** *amber*	70.00	85.00
		Entire	120.00	*1,500.*
U344	U56	90c **purple,** *oriental buff*	75.00	85.00
		Entire	140.00	*1,500.*
U345	U56	90c **purple,** *blue*	75.00	85.00
		Entire	140.00	*1,500.*
U346	U56	90c **purple,** *manila*	80.00	85.00
		Entire	150.00	*1,500.*
U347	U56	90c **purple,** *amber manila*	80.00	85.00
		Entire	150.00	*1,500.*

Columbus and Liberty — U76

Four dies were used for the 1c, 2c and 5c:
1 — Meridian behind Columbus' head. Period after "CENTS" and "AMERICA" appears on 1c, 2c and 5c.
2 — No meridian. With periods. Appears on 1c, 2c and 5c.
3 — With meridian. No periods. Appears on 1c, 2c and 10c.
4 — No meridian. No periods. Appears on 2c.

1893

U348	U76	1c **deep blue**	2.00	1.25
		Entire	3.00	2.00
		Entire, Expo. station machine cancel		100.00
		Entire, Expo. station duplex hand-stamp cancel		250.00
U349	U76	2c **violet**	1.50	.50
		Entire	3.50	1.50
		Entire, Expo. station machine cancel		40.00
		Entire, Expo. station duplex hand-stamp cancel		85.00
a.		2c **dark slate** (error)	*1,500.*	
		Entire	*4,000.*	
U350	U76	5c **chocolate**	6.50	7.00
		Entire	15.00	12.00
		Entire, Expo. station machine cancel		150.00
		Entire, Expo. station duplex hand-stamp cancel		250.00
a.		5c **slate brown** (error)	*700.00*	*1,400.*
		Entire	*1,100.*	*1,500.*
U351	U76	10c **slate brown**	25.00	27.50
		Entire	75.00	75.00
		Entire, Expo. station machine cancel		250.00
		Entire, Expo. station duplex hand-stamp cancel		450.00

Franklin — U77

Bust points to fourth notch of inner circle.

Washington — U78

Bust points to first notch of inner oval and is only slightly concave below.

U79

Bust points to middle of second notch of inner oval and is quite hollow below. Queue has ribbon around it.

U80

Same as die 2, but hair flowing. No ribbon on queue.

Lincoln — U81

Bust pointed but not draped.

U82

Bust broad and draped.

U83

Head larger, inner oval has no notches.

Grant — U84

Similar to design of 1887-95 but smaller.

1899

U352	U77	1c **green**	2.75	.25
		Entire	4.75	.50
U353	U77	1c **green,** *amber*	5.00	1.50
		Entire	8.50	2.75
U354	U77	1c **green,** *oriental buff*	10.00	2.75
		Entire	20.00	5.00
U355	U77	1c **green,** *blue*	10.00	7.50
		Entire	19.00	12.50
U356	U77	1c **green,** *manila*	2.50	.95
		Entire	6.50	2.00
W357	U77	1c **green,** *manila*	2.75	1.10
		Entire	9.00	4.00
U358	U78	2c **carmine**	3.00	1.75
		Entire	8.00	5.00
U359	U78	2c **carmine,** *amber*	15.00	12.50
		Entire	27.50	21.00
U360	U78	2c **carmine,** *oriental buff*	17.50	11.00
		Entire	30.00	25.00
U361	U78	2c **carmine,** *blue*	55.00	35.00
		Entire	75.00	52.50
U362	U79	2c **carmine**	.35	.25
		Entire	.65	.30
a.		2c **dark lake**	30.00	30.00
		Entire	37.50	35.00
U363	U79	2c **carmine,** *amber*	1.75	.25
		Entire	2.75	.60
U364	U79	2c **carmine,** *oriental buff*	1.20	.25
		Entire	3.00	.60
U365	U79	2c **carmine,** *blue*	1.50	.55
		Entire	3.50	2.00
W366	U79	2c **carmine,** *manila*	9.00	3.25
		Entire	15.00	12.00
U367	U80	2c **carmine**	5.00	2.75
		Entire	10.00	6.75
U368	U80	2c **carmine,** *amber*	8.00	6.50
		Entire	16.00	15.00
U369	U80	2c **carmine,** *oriental buff*	17.50	12.50
		Entire	35.00	25.00
U370	U80	2c **carmine,** *blue*	11.00	10.00
		Entire	25.00	18.00
U371	U81	4c **brown**	15.00	12.50
		Entire	27.50	18.00
U372	U81	4c **brown,** *amber*	15.00	12.50
		Entire	30.00	24.00
U373	U82	4c **brown**	*6,500.*	1,000.
		Entire	*9,000.*	
U374	U83	4c **brown**	10.00	8.00
		Entire	26.00	15.00
U375	U83	4c **brown,** *amber*	60.00	25.00
		Entire	90.00	45.00
W376	U83	4c **brown,** *manila*	12.50	12.50
		Entire	35.00	45.00
U377	U84	5c **blue**	9.00	9.00
		Entire	16.00	16.00
U378	U84	5c **blue,** *amber*	10.00	10.00
		Entire	25.00	20.00

Franklin — U85

Washington — U86

"D" of "UNITED" contains vertical line at right that parallels the left vertical line. One short and two long vertical lines at the right of "CENTS."

Grant — U87

Lincoln — U88

Printed by Hartford Manufacturing Co., Hartford, Conn.

1903

U379	U85 1c **green**	.75	.25
	Entire	1.20	.35
U380	U85 1c **green,** *amber*	10.00	2.00
	Entire	20.00	7.00
U381	U85 1c **green,** *oriental buff*	12.50	2.50
	Entire	22.50	3.00
U382	U85 1c **green,** *blue*	15.00	2.50
	Entire	30.00	3.00
U383	U85 1c **green,** *manila*	3.50	.90
	Entire	5.00	1.25
W384	U85 1c **green,** *manila*	2.50	.40
	Entire	4.50	.80
a.	Double impression, entire letter sheet	*275.00*	
U385	U86 2c **carmine**	.40	.25
	Entire	.85	.35
a.	2c **pink**	2.00	1.50
	Entire	3.00	2.00
b.	2c **red**	2.00	1.50
	Entire	3.00	2.00
U386	U86 2c **carmine,** *amber*	2.00	.50
	Entire	3.50	.80
a.	2c **pink,** *amber*	5.50	3.00
	Entire	7.50	4.00
b.	2c **red,** *amber*	12.50	7.00
	Entire	20.00	10.00
U387	U86 2c **carmine,** *oriental buff*	2.00	.30
	Entire	3.25	.35
a.	2c **pink,** *oriental buff*	3.50	2.00
	Entire	5.00	3.00
b.	2c **red,** *oriental buff*	4.00	2.25
	Entire	5.50	3.25
U388	U86 2c **carmine,** *blue*	1.75	.50
	Entire	2.75	.60
a.	2c **pink,** *blue*	17.50	14.00
	Entire	30.00	18.00
b.	2c **red,** *blue*	17.50	14.00
	Entire	30.00	18.00
W389	U86 2c **carmine,** *manila*	15.00	9.00
	Entire	25.00	14.00
U390	U87 4c **chocolate**	17.50	11.00
	Entire	30.00	14.00
U391	U87 4c **chocolate,** *amber*	17.50	11.00
	Entire	32.50	14.00
W392	U87 4c **chocolate,** *manila*	20.00	12.50
	Entire	45.00	35.00
U393	U88 5c **blue**	15.00	11.00
	Entire	30.00	16.00
U394	U88 5c **blue,** *amber*	15.00	11.00
	Entire	30.00	18.00

U89

Re-cut die — "D" of "UNITED" is well rounded at right. The three lines at the right of "CENTS" and at the left of "TWO" are usually all short; the lettering is heavier and the ends of the ribbons slightly changed.

1904 **Re-cut Die**

U395	U89 2c **carmine**	.75	.25
	Entire	1.75	.45
a.	2c pink	5.00	2.50
U396	U89 2c **carmine,** *amber*	7.50	1.00
	Entire	12.50	2.00
a.	2c pink, *amber*	8.50	3.00
U397	U89 2c **carmine,** *oriental buff*	5.00	1.10
	Entire	8.00	1.50
a.	2c pink, *oriental buff*	6.50	2.75
U398	U89 2c **carmine,** *blue*	3.75	.90
	Entire	5.50	1.40
a.	2c pink, *blue*	5.00	2.50
W399	U89 2c **carmine,** *manila*	12.50	8.00
	Entire	30.00	24.00
a.	2c pink, *manila*	25.00	17.50
	Entire	70.00	85.00
b.	Double impression, entire	*375.00*	

Franklin — U90

Die 1

Die 2

Die 3

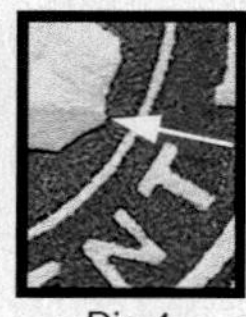

Die 4

Die 1 — Wide "D" in "UNITED."
Die 2 — Narrow "D" in "UNITED."
Die 3 — Wide "S-S" in "STATES" (1910).
Die 4 — Sharp angle at back of bust, "N" and "E" of "ONE" are parallel (1912).

Printed by Mercantile Corp. and Middle West Supply Co., Dayton, Ohio

1907-16

U400	U90 1c **green,** die 1, laid paper	.35	.25
	Entire	1.00	.75
	Wove paper	.35	.25
	Entire	2.00	2.00
a.	Die 2, laid paper	.85	.25
	Entire	1.50	.75
	Wove paper	.85	.25
	Entire	1.50	.75
b.	Die 3, laid paper	.85	.55
	Entire	1.50	1.50
	Wove paper	2.00	2.00
	Entire	6.50	8.00
c.	Die 4, laid paper	.85	.25
	Entire	1.50	1.00
	Wove paper	.85	.25
	Entire	1.50	1.00
U401	U90 1c **green,** *amber,* die 1, laid paper	2.00	.40
	Entire	3.00	2.50
	Wove paper	2.00	.40
	Entire	3.50	1.50
a.	Die 2, laid paper	2.50	1.00
	Entire	4.00	3.00
	Wove paper	3.00	2.50
	Entire	5.00	5.00
b.	Die 3, laid paper	3.25	3.00
	Entire	4.00	5.00
	Wove paper	75.00	50.00
	Entire	100.00	75.00
c.	Die 4, laid paper	2.00	1.00
	Entire	4.00	3.00
	Wove paper	2.00	.65
	Entire	3.00	2.50
U402	U90 1c **green,** *oriental buff,* die 1, laid paper	9.00	.75
	Entire	12.50	2.50
	Wove paper	9.00	.75
	Entire	12.50	2.50
a.	Die 2	12.50	1.50
	Entire	18.50	1.75
b.	Die 3, laid paper	14.00	1.50
	Entire	20.00	2.50
	Wove paper	1.00	.75
	Entire	2.50	3.00
c.	Die 4	3.50	.75
	Entire	4.50	2.50
U403	U90 1c **green,** *blue,* die 1, laid paper	9.00	.75
	Entire	12.50	2.25
	Wove paper	9.00	1.00
	Entire	12.50	4.00
a.	Die 2	12.50	3.00
	Entire	16.50	4.00
b.	Die 3	11.50	3.00
	Entire	17.50	7.00
c.	Die 4, laid paper	.75	.65
	Entire	1.00	1.50
	Wove paper	1.00	.75
	Entire	2.50	3.50
U404	U90 1c **green,** *manila,* die 1, laid paper	2.00	1.90
	Entire	3.75	4.50
	Wove paper	.75	1.00
	Entire	2.00	5.25
a.	Die 3	4.50	3.00
	Entire	7.00	4.50
W405	U90 1c **green,** *manila,* die 1, laid paper	.65	.25
	Entire	1.00	2.00
	Wove paper	1.00	1.00
	Entire	3.25	10.00
a.	Die 2	60.00	25.00
	Entire	90.00	30.00
b.	Die 3	11.00	4.00
	Entire	36.00	25.00
d.	Double impression, entire	*175.00*	

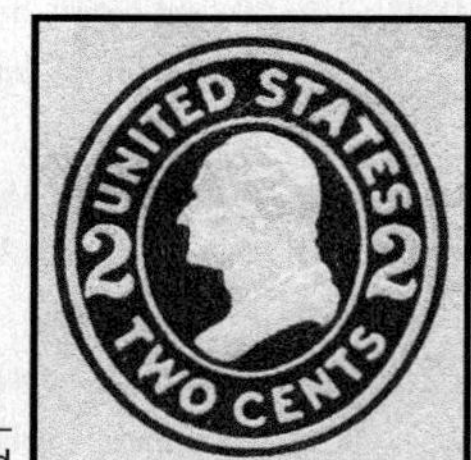

Washington — U91 — brown red

U91 Die 1 — carmine

U91 Die 2

U91 Die 3 — brown red

U91 Die 4

U91 Die 5

U91 Die 6

U91 Die 7

U91 Die 8

Die 1 — Oval “O” in “TWO” and “C” in “CENTS.” Front of bust broad.

Die 2 — Similar to 1 but hair re-cut in two distinct locks at top of head.

Die 3 — Round “O” in “TWO” and “C” in “CENTS,” coarse lettering.

Die 4 — Similar to 3 but lettering fine and clear, hair lines clearly embossed. Inner oval thin and clear.

Die 5 — All “S's” wide (1910).

Die 6 — Similar to 1 but front of bust narrow (1913).

Die 7 — Similar to 6 but upper corner of front of bust cut away (1916).

Die 8 — Similar to 7 but lower stroke of “S” in “CENTS” is a straight line. Hair as in Die 2 (1916).

U406	U91 2c **brown red,** die 1	.90	.25
	Entire	2.60	.30
a.	Die 2	40.00	7.00
	Entire	95.00	50.00
b.	Die 3	.80	.25
	Entire	2.50	1.00
U407	U91 2c **brown red,** *amber,* die 1	6.50	2.00
	Entire	9.00	6.00
a.	Die 2	350.00	65.00
	Entire	700.00	200.00
b.	Die 3	4.50	1.25
	Entire	7.00	6.00
U408	U91 2c **brown red,** *oriental buff,* die 1	8.75	1.50
	Entire	12.00	3.75
a.	Die 2	275.00	125.00
	Entire	500.00	300.00
b.	Die 3	7.50	2.50
	Entire	11.00	5.00
U409	U91 2c **brown red,** *blue,* die 1	5.75	2.00
	Entire	8.00	3.75
a.	Die 2	375.00	200.00
	Entire	550.00	500.00
b.	Die 3	5.75	1.75
	Entire	8.00	3.50
W410	U91 2c **brown red,** *manila,* die 1	35.00	35.00
	Entire	52.50	45.00
U411	U91 2c **carmine,** die 1, laid paper	.35	.25
	Entire	1.00	.75
	Wove paper	.55	.45
	Entire	1.50	1.00
a.	Die 2, laid paper	.75	.25
	Entire	2.00	1.50
	Wove paper	1.00	.55
	Entire	2.00	.50
b.	Die 3, laid paper	.75	.25
	Entire	2.00	1.00
	Wove paper	1.20	1.50
	Entire	4.00	7.00
c.	Die 4, laid paper	.65	.25
	Entire	1.00	.75
	Wove paper	.75	.25
	Entire	1.50	1.00
d.	Die 5, laid paper	.65	.30
	Entire	1.50	1.00
	Wove paper	1.00	1.00
	Entire	2.00	5.00
e.	Die 6, laid paper	.60	.25
	Entire	1.50	.75
	Wove paper	.60	.25
	Entire	1.00	.75
f.	Die 7, wove paper	3.00	3.00
	Entire	12.00	10.00
	Laid paper	75.00	25.00
	Entire	125.00	100.00
g.	Die 8	37.50	25.00
	Entire	52.50	30.00
h.	#U411 with added impression of #U400, entire	475.00	
i.	#U411 with added impression of #U416a, entire	475.00	
k.	As No. U411, double impression, entire	175.00	
U412	U91 2c **carmine,** *amber,* die 1, laid paper	.50	.25
	Entire	1.50	.75
	Wove paper	.50	.25
	Entire	1.50	.75
a.	Die 2, laid paper	1.00	.25
	Entire	3.50	4.00
	Wove paper	1.00	1.00
	Entire	2.50	15.00
b.	Die 3, laid paper	2.25	2.00
	Entire	3.00	5.00
	Wove paper	45.00	25.00
	Entire	75.00	60.00
c.	Die 4, laid paper	.55	.25
	Entire	1.50	.75
	Wove paper	1.00	1.00
	Entire	5.00	7.50
d.	Die 5	.90	.35
	Entire	1.50	.55
e.	Die 6, laid paper	.70	.25
	Entire	1.50	.75
	Wove paper	.60	.25
	Entire	1.00	.75
f.	Die 7, wove paper	35.00	25.00
	Entire	50.00	32.50
	Laid paper	125.00	100.00
	Entire	250.00	250.00
U413	U91 2c **carmine,** *oriental buff,* die 1, laid paper	.55	.25
	Entire	1.00	.75
	Wove paper	1.00	.25
	Entire	2.00	.75
a.	Die 2, laid paper	2.00	.45
	Entire	5.00	3.00
	Wove paper	7.00	10.00
	Entire	15.00	50.00
b.	Die 3	9.00	3.00
	Entire	15.00	5.50
c.	Die 4, laid paper	.55	1.00
	Entire	1.25	4.00
	Wove paper	1.00	1.00
	Entire	2.50	5.00
d.	Die 5	3.50	1.25
	Entire	5.00	3.25
e.	Die 6, laid paper	1.00	.70
	Entire	2.00	1.25
	Wove paper	1.20	1.00
	Entire	3.00	2.00
f.	Die 7	100.00	45.00
	Entire	135.00	62.50
g.	Die 8	25.00	17.50
	Entire	40.00	22.50
U414	U91 2c **carmine,** *blue,* die 1, laid paper	.55	.25
	Entire	1.30	.75
	Wove paper	.60	.25
	Entire	1.50	.75
a.	Die 2, laid paper	1.00	1.00
	Entire	5.00	2.50
	Wove paper	1.50	8.00
	Entire	6.50	30.00
b.	Die 3, laid paper	2.75	2.00
	Entire	4.00	6.50
	Wove paper	50.00	30.00
	Entire	75.00	50.00
c.	Die 4, laid paper	.50	.50
	Entire	1.00	3.50
	Wove paper	1.00	1.00
	Entire	2.50	10.00
d.	Die 5, laid paper	1.00	.45
	Entire	3.00	1.00
	Wove paper	70.00	40.00
	Entire	100.00	75.00
e.	Die 6, laid paper	.65	.30
	Entire	1.10	.75
	Wove paper	.55	.30
	Entire	1.50	.75
f.	Die 7	37.50	25.00
	Entire	50.00	35.00
g.	Die 8	37.50	25.00
	Entire	50.00	35.00
W415	U91 2c **carmine,** *manila,* die 1, laid paper	5.00	2.00
	Entire	8.00	*12.00*
	Wove paper	50.00	15.00
	Entire	70.00	75.00
a.	Die 2	5.50	1.25
	Entire	8.00	*20.00*
b.	Die 5	5.50	2.50
	Entire	8.00	*18.00*
c.	Die 7	120.00	97.50
	Entire	175.00	125.00

U90 4c Die 1

U90 4c Die 2

Die 1 — “F” close to (1mm) left “4.”
Die 2 — “F” far from (1¾mm) left “4.”

U416	U90 4c **black,** die 2, laid paper	2.00	1.50
	Entire	4.00	6.50
	Wove paper	30.00	20.00
	Entire	50.00	65.00
a.	Die 1, wove paper	1.50	2.00
	Entire	5.00	10.00
	Laid paper	7.50	4.00
	Entire	15.00	10.00
U417	U90 4c **black,** *amber,* die 2	7.50	2.50
	Entire	12.00	4.00
a.	Die 1, laid paper	.75	2.00
	Entire	1.50	20.00
	Wove paper	1.00	2.00
	Entire	2.50	10.00

Die 1 — Tall “F” in “FIVE”

Die 2 — Short “F” in “FIVE”

Die 1 — Tall “F” in “FIVE.”
Die 2 — Short “F” in “FIVE.”

U418	U91 5c **blue,** die 2, laid paper	1.50	1.50
	Entire	5.00	6.00
	Wove paper	.75	1.00
	Entire	2.00	5.00
a.	Die 1	7.00	2.25
	Entire	13.50	6.50
b.	5c **blue,** *buff,* die 2 (error)	*3,250.*	
c.	5c **blue,** *blue,* die 2 (error)	*3,000.*	
d.	As “c,” die 1 (error), entire	*6,250.*	
U419	U91 5c **blue,** *amber,* die 2, laid paper	1.00	.75
	Entire	5.00	5.00
	Wove paper	3.00	1.50
	Entire	10.00	10.00
a.	Die 1	15.00	12.00
	Entire	25.00	14.00

On July 1, 1915 the use of laid paper was discontinued and wove paper was substituted. Nos. U400 to W405 and U411 to U419 exist on both papers: U406 to W410 come on laid only. Nos. U429 and U430 exist on laid paper.

Franklin — U92

Die 1

Die 2

Die 3

Die 4

Die 5

(The 1c and 4c dies are the same except for figures of value.)
Die 1 — UNITED nearer inner circle than outer circle.
Die 2 — Large U; large NT closely spaced.
Die 3 — Knob of hair at back of neck. Large NT widely spaced.
Die 4 — UNITED nearer outer circle than inner circle.
Die 5 — Narrow oval C, (also O and G).

Printed by Middle West Supply Co. and International Envelope Corp., Dayton, Ohio.

1915-32

U420	U92 1c **green,** die 1 ('17)	.25	.25
	Entire	.40	.25
a.	Die 2	100.00	55.00
	Entire, size 8	200.00	70.00
b.	Die 3	.35	.25
	Entire	.50	.25
c.	Die 4	.55	.40
	Entire	.80	.50
d.	Die 5	.45	.35
	Entire	.75	.45
U421	U92 1c **green,** *amber,*die 1 ('17)	.55	.30
	Entire	.80	.45
a.	Die 2	400.00	175.00
	Entire, size 8	750.00	300.00
b.	Die 3	1.40	.65
	Entire	2.00	.95
c.	Die 4	1.90	.85
	Entire	2.50	1.25
d.	Die 5	1.10	.55
	Entire	1.75	.80
U422	U92 1c **green,** *oriental buff,* die 1 ('17)	2.40	.90
	Entire	3.25	1.40
a.	Die 4	5.50	1.25
	Entire	8.00	2.75
U423	U92 1c **green,** *blue,* die 1 ('17)	.50	.35
	Entire	1.00	.50
a.	Die 3	.80	.45
	Entire	1.25	.70
b.	Die 4	1.40	.65
	Entire	2.50	.95
c.	Die 5	.85	.35
	Entire	1.60	.65
U424	U92 1c **grn,** *manila* (unglazed), die 1 ('16)	6.50	4.00
	Entire	8.00	5.00
W425	U92 1c **grn,** *manila* (unglazed), die 1 ('16)	.30	.25
	Entire	1.00	.25
a.	Die 3	175.00	125.00
	Entire	250.00	200.00
U426	U92 1c **green,** *brown* (glazed) , die 1 ('20)	45.00	16.00
	Entire	57.50	27.50
W427	U92 1c **green,** *brown* (glazed), die 1 ('20)	65.00	35.00
	Entire	80.00	*60.00*
a.	Printed on unglazed side	*400.00*	
	Entire	*750.00*	
b.	Unglazed on both sides		*150.00*
U428	U92 1c **green,** *brown* (unglazed), die 1 ('20)	12.50	7.50
	Entire	22.50	24.00
W428A	U92 1c **green,** *brown* (unglazed), die 1 ('20), entire		*3,000.*

All manila envelopes of circular dies are unwatermarked. Manila paper, including that of Nos. U424 and W425, exists in many shades.

Washington — U93

Die 1

Die 2

Die 3

Die 4

Die 5

Die 6

Die 7

Die 8

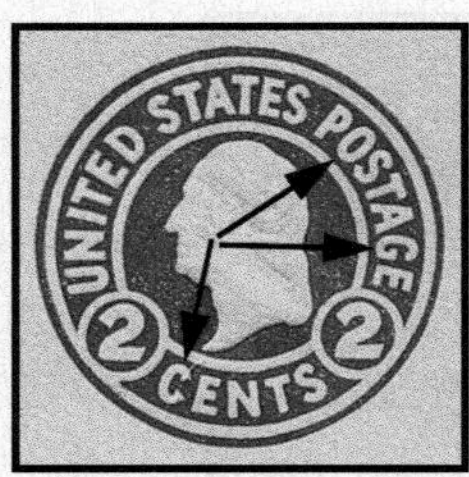

Die 9

(The 1½c, 2c, 3c, 5c, and 6c dies are the same except for figures of value.)
Die 1 — Letters broad. Numerals vertical. Large head (9¼mm). from tip of nose to back of neck. E closer to inner circle than N of cents.
Die 2 — Similar to 1; but U far from left circle.
Die 3 — Similar to 2; but all inner circles very thin (Rejected die).
Die 4 — Large head as in Die 1. C of CENTS close to circle. Baseline of right numeral "2" slants downward to right. Left numeral "2" is larger.
Die 5 — Small head (8¾mm) from tip of nose to back of neck. T and S of CENTS close at bottom.
Die 6 — Similar to 5; but T and S of CENTS far apart at bottom. Left numeral slopes to right.
Die 7 — Large head. Both numerals slope to right. Clean cut lettering. All letters T have short top strokes.
Die 8 — Similar to 7; but all letters T have long top strokes.
Die 9 — Narrow oval C (also O and G).

U429	U93 2c **carmine,** die 1, *Dec. 20, 1915*	.25	.25
	Entire	.40	.25
a.	Die 2	15.00	7.00
	Entire	25.00	10.00
b.	Die 3	40.00	50.00
	Entire	80.00	*200.00*
c.	Die 4	25.00	15.00
	Entire	40.00	20.00
d.	Die 5	.55	.35
	Entire	1.00	.45
e.	Die 6	.65	.30
	Entire	1.25	.60
f.	Die 7	.70	.25
	Entire	1.25	.75
g.	Die 8	.50	.25
	Entire	1.00	.50
h.	Die 9	.50	.25
	Entire	1.00	.45
i.	2c **green** (error), die 1, entire	*12,500.*	
j.	#U429 with added impression of #U420	600.00	
	Entire	1,000.	
k.	#U429 with added impression of #U416a, entire	*3,500.*	
l.	#U429 with added impression of #U400, entire	950.00	
m.	#U429, double impression, entire	1,500.	
n.	As "f," double impression, entire	*750.00*	
o.	As "e," triple impression	—	
p.	As "m," second impression on side flap, entire		*250.00*

Earliest documented use: Feb. 20, 1916.

U430	U93 2c **carmine,** *amber,* die 1 ('16)	.30	.25
	Entire	.50	.25
a.	Die 2	20.00	12.50
	Entire	30.00	15.00
b.	Die 4	50.00	25.00
	Entire	70.00	30.00
c.	Die 5	1.60	.35
	Entire	2.25	.60
d.	Die 6	1.25	.40
	Entire	2.25	.75
e.	Die 7	.75	.35
	Entire	1.75	.95
f.	Die 8	.70	.30
	Entire	1.10	.45
g.	Die 9	.65	.25
	Entire	1.10	.35
h.	As No. U430, with added impression of 4c black (#U416a), entire	*600.00*	
i.	As "g," with added impression of 2c car. die 1 on side flap, entire	—	
U431	U93 2c **carmine,** *oriental buff,* die 1 ('16)	2.25	.65
	Entire	4.75	1.40
a.	Die 2	180.00	75.00
	Entire	260.00	*250.00*
b.	Die 4	75.00	60.00
	Entire	100.00	75.00
c.	Die 5	3.50	2.00
	Entire	6.00	2.75

d.	Die 6	3.50	2.00
	Entire	7.00	2.75
e.	Die 7	3.50	2.00
	Entire	6.00	3.25
U432	U93 2c **carmine,** *blue,* die 1 ('16)	.30	.25
	Entire	.60	.25
b.	Die 2	35.00	25.00
	Entire	50.00	35.00
c.	Die 3	130.00	90.00
	Entire	180.00	*400.00*
d.	Die 4	60.00	50.00
	Entire	90.00	55.00
e.	Die 5	1.10	.30
	Entire	2.00	.75
f.	Die 6	1.10	.40
	Entire	2.00	.60
g.	Die 7	.85	.35
	Entire	1.75	.65
h.	Die 8	.65	.25
	Entire	1.50	.50
i.	Die 9	1.00	.30
	Entire	2.75	.55
j.	2c purple (error), die 9	—	
k.	Double impression	650.00	
U432A	U93 2c **car,** *manila,* die 7, unwatermarked, entire	*50,000.*	
W433	U93 2c **carmine,** *manila,* die 1 ('16)	.25	.25
	Entire	.50	.30
W434	U93 2c **carmine,** *brown* (glazed) ('20), die 1	70.00	45.00
	Entire	95.00	55.00
W435	U93 2c **carmine,** *brown* (unglazed), die 1 ('20)	90.00	60.00
	Entire	115.00	*150.00*
U436	U93 3c **purple,** die 1 ('32)	.30	.25
	Entire	.55	.25
a.	3c **dark violet,** die 1 ('17)	.60	.25
	Entire	1.00	.25
b.	3c **dark violet,** die 5 ('17)	1.75	.75
	Entire	3.25	.90
c.	3c **dark violet,** die 6 ('17)	2.10	1.40
	Entire	3.25	1.50
d.	3c **dark violet,** die 7 ('17)	1.50	.95
	Entire	3.00	1.00
e.	3c **purple,** die 7 ('32)	.70	.30
	Entire	1.75	.75
f.	3c **purple,** die 9 ('32)	.45	.25
	Entire	.60	.30
g.	3c **carmine** (error), die 1	35.00	35.00
	Entire	60.00	*70.00*
h.	3c **carmine** (error), die 5	27.50	—
	Entire	50.00	—
i.	#U436 with added impression of #U420, entire	900.00	
j.	#U436 with added impression of #U429, entire	900.00	950.00
k.	As "f," double impression, preprinted, entire	*600.00*	
U437	U93 3c **purple,** *amber,* die 1 ('32)	.35	.25
	Entire	.60	.35
a.	3c **dark violet,** die 1 ('17)	5.50	1.25
	Entire	9.00	2.25
b.	3c **dark violet,** die 5 ('17)	8.50	2.50
	Entire	12.00	3.00
c.	3c **dark violet,** die 6 ('17)	8.50	2.50
	Entire	12.00	3.00
d.	3c **dark violet,** die 7 ('17)	8.50	2.25
	Entire	12.00	2.50
e.	3c **purple,** die 7 ('32)	.75	.25
	Entire	1.25	.50
f.	3c **purple,** die 9 ('32)	.55	.25
	Entire	1.00	.30
g.	3c **carmine** (error), die 5	375.00	400.00
	Entire	475.00	*750.00*
h.	3c **black** (error), die 1	190.00	—
	Entire	300.00	*375.00*
U438	U93 3c **dark violet,** *oriental buff,* die 1 ('17)	22.50	5.50
	Entire	32.50	21.00
a.	Die 5	22.50	5.50
	Entire	32.50	27.50
b.	Die 6	30.00	8.00
	Entire	45.00	35.00
c.	Die 7	30.00	10.00
	Entire	45.00	45.00

Earliest documented use: Nov. 2, 1917.

U439	U93 3c **purple,** *blue,* die 1 ('32)	.35	.25
	Entire	.75	.25
a.	3c **dark violet,** die 1 ('17)	7.00	2.00
	Entire	14.00	6.00
b.	3c **dark violet,** die 5 ('17)	7.50	6.00
	Entire	15.00	7.50
c.	3c **dark violet,** die 6 ('17)	7.50	6.00
	Entire	15.00	7.50
d.	3c **dark violet,** die 7 ('17)	10.00	6.00
	Entire	17.50	7.50
e.	3c **purple,** die 7 ('32)	.75	.25
	Entire	1.50	.50
f.	3c **purple,** die 9 ('32)	.60	.25
	Entire	1.50	.45
g.	3c **carmine** (error), die 5	225.00	300.00
	Entire	400.00	*725.00*
U440	U92 4c **black,** die 1 ('18)	1.75	.60
	Entire	3.25	2.00
a.	With added impression of 2c carmine (#U429), die 1, entire	450.00	
U441	U92 4c **black,** *amber,* die 1 ('18)	3.00	.85
	Entire	5.00	2.00
a.	4c black, *amb,* with added impression of 2c car (#U429), die 1	175.00	
U442	U92 4c **black,** *blue,* die 1 ('21)	3.25	.85
	Entire	5.75	1.75
U443	U93 5c **blue,** die 1 ('18)	3.25	2.75
	Entire	5.75	3.25

Earliest documented use: Oct. 29, 1919.

U444	U93 5c **blue,** *amber,* die 1 ('18)	4.00	1.60
	Entire	6.50	3.50
U445	U93 5c **blue,** *blue,* die 1 ('21)	3.25	3.25
	Entire	7.50	4.25

The following envelopes were officially issued June 16, 1932, in Washington, DC, and first day uses are known to exist: Nos. U436, U436e, U436f, U437 and U439. Nos. U437e, U437f, U439e and U439f presumably were issued at the same time, but first day uses have not yet been reported.

For 1½c and 6c see Nos. U481-W485, U529-U531.

Surcharged Envelopes

The provisional 2c surcharges of 1920-21 were made at central post offices with canceling machines using slugs provided by the Post Office Department.

Double or triple surcharge listings of 1920-25 are for examples with surcharge directly or partly upon the stamp.

Surcharged on 1874-1920 Envelopes indicated by Numbers in Parentheses

Type 1

1920-21 **Surcharged in Black**

U446	U93 2c on 3c **dark vio** (U436a, die 1)	11.00	10.00
	Entire	22.50	12.50
a.	On No. U436b (die 5)	11.00	10.00
	Entire	22.50	12.50
b.	As U446, double surcharge	140.00	
	Entire	425.00	

Surcharged

Type 2

Rose Surcharge

U447	U93 2c on 3c **dark vio** (U436a, die 1)	8.00	7.50
	Entire	16.00	10.00
b.	On No. U436c (die 6)	10.00	8.50
	Entire	25.00	10.00

Black Surcharge

U447A	U92 2c on 1c **green** (U420, die 1)		
	Entire	*3,000.*	
U447C	U93 2c on 2c **carmine** (U429, die 1)	—	
U447D	U93 2c on 2c **carmine,** *amber* (U430, die 1)	12,000.	
U448	U93 2c on 3c **dark vio** (U436a, die 1)	2.75	2.00
	Entire	4.00	2.50
a.	On No. U436b (die 5)	2.75	2.00
	Entire	4.00	2.50
b.	On No. U436c (die 6)	3.50	2.00
	Entire	5.00	2.50
c.	On No. U436d (die 7)	2.75	2.00
	Entire	4.00	2.50
U449	U93 2c on 3c **dark violet,** *amber* (U437a, die 1)	6.50	6.00
	Entire	9.00	7.50
a.	On No. U437b (die 5)	13.00	7.50
	Entire	17.50	10.00
b.	On No. U437c (die 6)	9.50	6.00
	Entire	13.50	7.50
c.	On No. U437d (die 7)	8.50	6.50
	Entire	12.00	8.00
U450	U93 2c on 3c **dark violet,** *oriental buff* (U438, die 1)	12.50	15.00
	Entire	20.00	18.00
a.	On No. U438a (die 5)	15.00	15.00
	Entire	22.50	18.00
b.	On No. U438b (die 6)	15.00	15.00
	Entire	22.50	18.00
c.	On No. U438c (die 7)	130.00	90.00
	Entire	160.00	125.00
U451	U93 2c on 3c **dark violet,** *blue* (U439a, die 1)	11.00	10.50
	Entire	18.00	11.50
b.	On No. U439b (die 5)	11.00	10.50
	Entire	18.00	11.50
c.	On No. U439c (die 6)	11.00	10.50
	Entire	18.00	11.50
d.	On No. U439d (die 7)	22.50	22.50
	Entire	37.50	27.50

Type 2 exists in three city sub-types.

Surcharged

Type 3

Bars 2mm apart, 25 to 26mm in length from outer edges of end bars

U451A	U90 2c on 1c **green** (U400, die 1)	*25,000.*	
	Entire	—	
U452	U92 2c on 1c **green** (U420, die 1)	1,750.	
	Entire	3,250.	
a.	On No. U420b (die 3)	3,000.	
	Entire	4,000.	
b.	As No. U452, double surcharge	3,750.	
	Entire	4,500.	
U453	U91 2c on 2c **car** (U411b, die 3)	3,500.	
	Entire	6,000.	
a.	On No. U411 (die 1)	3,250.	
	Entire	5,500.	
U453B	U91 2c on 2c **carmine,** *blue* (U414e, die 6)	1,250.	750.00
	Entire	2,250.	
U453C	U91 2c on 2c **carmine,** *oriental buff* (U413e, die 6)	1,400.	*750.00*
	Entire	2,000.	
d.	On No. U413 (die 1)	1,400.	
	Entire	2,000.	
U454	U93 2c on 2c **car** (U429e, die 6)	125.00	
	Entire	225.00	
a.	On No. U429 (die 1)	300.00	
	Entire	375.00	
b.	On No. U429d (die 5)	500.00	
	Entire	650.00	
c.	On No. U429f (die 7)	125.00	
	Entire	200.00	
U455	U93 2c on 2c **carmine,** *amber* (U430, die 1)	1,250.	
	Entire	3,000.	
a.	On No. U430d (die 6)	1,500.	
	Entire	3,000.	
b.	On No. U430e (die 7)	1,500.	
	Entire	3,000.	
U456	U93 2c on 2c **carmine,** *oriental buff* (U431a, die 2)	225.00	
	Entire	375.00	
a.	On No. U431c (die 5)	225.00	
	Entire	550.00	
b.	On No. U431e (die 7)	800.00	
	Entire	950.00	
c.	As No. U456, double surcharge	700.00	
U457	U93 2c on 2c **carmine,** *blue* (U432f, die 6)	325.00	
	Entire	400.00	
a.	On No. U432e (die 5)	275.00	
	Entire	475.00	
b.	On No. U432g (die 7)	650.00	
	Entire	800.00	
U458	U93 2c on 3c **dark vio** (U436a, die 1)	.50	.35
	Entire	.75	.45
a.	On No. U436b (die 5)	.50	.40
	Entire	.75	.50
b.	On No. U436c (die 6)	.50	.35
	Entire	.75	.45
c.	On No. U436d (die 7)	.50	.35
	Entire	.75	.45
d.	As #U458, double surcharge	25.00	7.50
	Entire	35.00	10.00
e.	As #U458, triple surcharge	90.00	
	Entire	150.00	
f.	As #U458, dbl. surch., 1 in **magenta**	90.00	
	Entire	150.00	
g.	As #U458, dbl. surch., types 2 & 3	140.00	
	Entire	190.00	
h.	As "a," double surcharge	27.50	15.00
	Entire	37.50	20.00
i.	As "a," triple surcharge	110.00	
	Entire	160.00	
j.	As "a," double surch., both **magenta**	110.00	
	Entire	150.00	
k.	As "b," double surcharge	25.00	8.00
	Entire	35.00	11.00
l.	As "c," double surcharge	25.00	8.00
	Entire	35.00	11.00
m.	As "c," triple surcharge	110.00	
	Entire	150.00	
n.	Double impression of indicia, single surcharge, entire	450.00	
U459	U93 2c on 3c **dark violet,** *amber* (U437c, die 6)	3.00	1.00
	Entire	4.50	1.75
a.	On No. U437a (die 1)	4.00	1.00
	Entire	5.50	1.75
b.	On No. U437b (die 5)	4.00	1.00
	Entire	5.50	1.75
c.	On No. U437d (die 7)	3.00	1.00
	Entire	5.50	1.75
d.	As #U459, double surcharge	35.00	
	Entire	50.00	
e.	As "a," double surcharge	35.00	
	Entire	50.00	
f.	As "b," double surcharge	35.00	
	Entire	50.00	
g.	As "b," double surcharge, types 2 & 3	125.00	
	Entire	175.00	

h. As "c," double surcharge 35.00
Entire 50.00
U460 U93 2c on 3c **dark violet,** *oriental buff* (U438a, die 5) 3.50 2.00
Entire 4.50 2.50
a. On No. U438 (die 1) 3.50 2.00
Entire 4.50 2.50
b. On No. U438b (die 6) 4.00 2.00
Entire 5.50 2.50
c. As #U460, double surcharge 20.00
Entire 30.00
d. As "a," double surcharge 20.00
Entire 30.00
e. As "b," double surcharge 20.00
Entire 30.00
f. As "b," triple surcharge 150.00
Entire 250.00
U461 U93 2c on 3c **dark violet,** *blue* (U439a, die 1) 6.00 1.00
Entire 8.25 1.50
a. On No. U439b (die 5) 6.00 1.00
Entire 8.25 1.50
b. On No. U439c (die 6) 6.00 2.50
Entire 8.25 3.50
c. On No. U439d (die 7) 12.50 7.50
Entire 17.50 15.00
d. As #U461, double surcharge 17.50
Entire 40.00 30.00
e. As "a," double surcharge 17.50
Entire 40.00 30.00
f. As "b," double surcharge 17.50
Entire 40.00 30.00
g. As "c," double surcharge 17.50
Entire 50.00 40.00
U462 U87 2c on 4c **chocolate** (U390) 475.00 260.00
Entire 800.00 500.00
U463 U87 2c on 4c **chocolate,** *amber* (U391) 750.00 350.00
Entire 1,200. 500.00
U463A U90 2c on 4c **black** (U416, die 2) 800.00 400.00
Entire 1,500.
U464 U93 2c on 5c **blue** (U443) 850.00
Entire 1,600.

Type 3 exists in 11 city sub-types.

Surcharged

Type 4

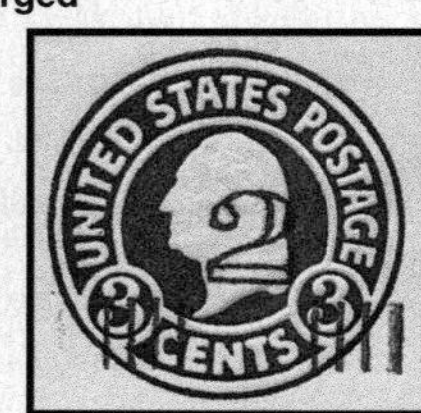

Bars 1 mm apart, 21 to 23 mm in length from outer edges of end bars

U465 U92 2c on 1c **green** (U420, die 1) 900.00
Entire 1,900.
a. On No. U420b (die 3) 1,100.
Entire 2,400.
U466 U91 2c on 2c **car** (U411e, die 6), entire 22,500.
U466A U93 2c on 2c **carmine** (U429, die 1) 700.00
Entire 1,150.
c. On No. U429d (die 5) 900.00
Entire 1,350.
d. On No. U429e (die 6) 900.00
Entire 1,350.
e. On No. U429f (die 7) 750.00
Entire 1,200.
U466B U93 2c on 2c **carmine,** *amber* (U430c) *15,000.*
Entire *22,500.*
U466C U93 2c on 2c **carmine,** *oriental buff* (U431), entire *15,000.*
U466D U25 2c on 3c **green,** die 2 (U82) *7,500.*
U467 U45 2c on 3c **green,** die 2 (U163) 325.00
Entire 525.00
U468 U93 2c on 3c **dark vio** (U436a, die 1) .70 .45
Entire 1.00 .75
a. On No. U436b (die 5) .70 .50
Entire 1.00 .75
b. On No. U436c (die 6) .70 .50
Entire 1.00 .75
c. On No. U436d (die 7) .70 .50
Entire 1.00 .75
d. As #U468, double surcharge 20.00
Entire 30.00
e. As #U468, triple surcharge 90.00
Entire 140.00
f. As #U468, dbl. surch., types 2 & 4 125.00
Entire 175.00
g. As "a," double surcharge 20.00
Entire 30.00
h. As "b," double surcharge 20.00
Entire 30.00
i. As "c," double surcharge 20.00
Entire 30.00
j. As "c," triple surcharge 100.00
Entire 150.00
k. As "c," inverted surcharge 75.00
Entire 125.00
l. 2c on 3c **carmine** (error), (U436h) 600.00
Entire 1,400.
m. As #U468, triple surcharge, one inverted, entire *700.00*
U469 U93 2c on 3c **dark violet,** *amber* (U437a, die 1) 3.75 2.25
Entire 5.00 2.75
a. On No. U437b (die 5) 3.75 2.25
Entire 5.00 2.75
b. On No. U437c (die 6) 3.75 2.25
Entire 5.00 2.75
c. On No. U437d (die 7) 3.75 2.25
Entire 5.00 2.75
d. As #U469, double surcharge 30.00
Entire 40.00
e. As "a," double surcharge 30.00
Entire 40.00
f. As "a," double surcharge, types 2 & 4 100.00
Entire 150.00
g. As "b," double surcharge 30.00
Entire 40.00
h. As "c," double surcharge 30.00
Entire 40.00
U470 U93 2c on 3c **dark violet,** *oriental buff* (U438, die 1) 6.00 2.50
Entire 10.00 5.00
a. On No. U438a (die 5) 6.00 2.50
Entire 10.00 6.00
b. On No. U438b (die 6) 6.00 2.50
Entire 10.00 6.00
c. On No. U438c (die 7) 42.50 32.50
Entire 70.00 70.00
d. As #U470, double surcharge 25.00
Entire 35.00
e. As #U470, double surch., types 2 & 4 80.00
Entire 130.00
f. As "a," double surcharge 25.00
Entire 35.00
g. As "b," double surcharge 25.00
Entire 35.00
U471 U93 2c on 3c **dark violet,** *blue* (U439a, die 1) 6.00 1.75
Entire 12.50 3.50
a. On No. U439b (die 5) 7.00 1.75
Entire 13.00 6.00
b. On No. U439c (die 6) 7.00 1.75
Entire 13.00 3.50
c. On No. U439d (die 7) 10.00 10.00
Entire 35.00 30.00
d. As #U471, double surcharge 25.00
Entire 40.00
e. As #U471, double surch., types 2 & 4 160.00
Entire 275.00
f. As "a," double surcharge 25.00
Entire 40.00
g. As "b," double surcharge 25.00
Entire 40.00
U471A U83 2c on 4c **brown,** (U374), entire 625.00
U472 U87 2c on 4c **chocolate** (U390) 11.00 11.00
Entire 25.00 16.00
a. Double surcharge 150.00
U473 U87 2c on 4c **chocolate,** *amber* (U391) 17.00 10.00
Entire 27.50 13.50

Type 4 exists in 30 city sub-types.

Surcharged

Double Surcharge, Type 4 and 1c as above

U474 U93 2c on 1c on 3c **dark violet** (U436a, die 1) 175. *500.*
Entire 325.
a. On No. U436b (die 5) 200.
Entire 500.
b. On No. U436d (die 7) 850.
Entire 1,050.
U475 U93 2c on 1c on 3c **dark violet,** *amber* (U437a, die 1) 150.
Entire 350.

Surcharged

U476 U93 2c on 3c **dark violet,** *amber* (U437a, die 1) 200.
Entire 475. 450.
a. On No. U437c (die 6) 700.
Entire 1,000.
b. As #U476, double surcharge —

Surcharged at Duncan, OK.

Surcharged Type 6

U477 U93 2c on 3c **dark vio** (U436a, die 1) 120.
Entire 175.
a. On No. U436b (die 5) 250.
Entire 300.
b. On No. U436c (die 6) 250.
Entire 300.
c. On No. U436d (die 7) 250.
Entire 300.
U478 U93 2c on 3c **dark violet,** *amber* (U437a, die 1) 250.
Entire 375.

Surcharged at Frederick, OK, and other Oklahoma towns.

Handstamped Surcharged in Black or Violet

U479 U93 2c on 3c **dark violet** (Bk) (U436a, die 1) 240. —
Entire 525.
a. On No. U436b (die 5) 625.
Entire 950.
b. On No. U436d (die 7) 425.
Entire 525.
U480 U93 2c on 3c **dark violet** (V) (U436d, die 7) *4,500.*
Entire *6,500.*
a. Double overprint —

Expertization by competent authorities is required for Nos. U476-U480.

Surcharged at Daytona, FL (#U479) and Orlando Beach, FL (#U480).

Type of 1916-32 Issue

1925

U481 U93 1½c **brown,** die 1, *Mar. 19* .25 .25
Entire .60 .25
Entire, 1st day cancel 60.00
a. Die 8 .70 .25
Entire 1.00 .50
b. 1½c purple, die 1 (error) ('34) 55.00
Entire 100.00 —
U482 U93 1½c **brown,** die 1, *amber* .90 .40
Entire 1.50 .60
a. Die 8 1.75 .75
Entire 2.25 .80
U483 U93 1½c **brown,** die 1, *blue* 1.60 .95
Entire 2.50 1.25
a. Die 8 2.40 1.25
Entire 3.25 1.40
U484 U93 1½c **brown,** die 1, *manila* 5.00 3.00
Entire 12.00 6.00
W485 U93 1½c **brown,** die 1, *manila* .85 .25
Entire 2.00 .45
a. With added impression of #W433 120.00 —

The manufacture of newspaper wrappers was discontinued in 1934.

New rates on printed matter effective Apr. 15, 1925, resulted in revaluing some of the current envelopes.

Under the caption "Revaluation of Surplus Stocks of the 1 cent envelopes," W. Irving Glover, Third Assistant Postmaster-General, distributed through the Postal Bulletin a notice to postmasters authorizing the surcharging of envelopes under stipulated conditions.

Surcharging was permitted "at certain offices where the excessive quantities of 1 cent stamped envelopes remained in stock on April 15, 1925."

Envelopes were revalued by means of post office canceling machines equipped with special dies designed to imprint "1 ½" in the center of the embossed stamp and four vertical bars over the original numerals "1" in the lower corners.

Postmasters were notified that the revaluing dies would be available for use only in the International and "Universal" Model G machines and that the overprinting of surplus envelopes would be restricted to post offices having such canceling equipment available.

Envelopes of Preceding Issues Surcharged

Provisional surcharges exist for California cities Santa Rosa and Santa Ana. These were unauthorized but served postal duty. All are scarce. Expertization recommended.

1925 — **On Envelopes of 1887**

U486 U71 1½c on 2c **green** (U311) 500.00
Entire 1,150.
U487 U71 1½c on 2c **green,** *amber* (U312) 900.00
Entire 1,500.

On Envelopes of 1899

U488 U77 1½c on 1c **green** (U352) 500.00
Entire 850.00
U489 U77 1½c on 1c **green,** *amber* (U353) 110.00 60.
Entire 200.00 90.

On Envelopes of 1907-16

U490 U90 1½c on 1c **green** (U400, die 1) 6.25 3.50
Entire 10.00 5.50
a. On No. U400a (die 2) 15.00 9.00
Entire 20.00 12.00
b. On No. U400b (die 3) 35.00 17.50
Entire 50.00 22.50
c. On No. U400c (die 4) 9.00 2.50
Entire 13.00 4.00
U491 U90 1½c on 1c **green,** *amber* (U401c, die 4) 7.00 3.00
Entire 12.00 8.50
a. On No. U401 (die 1) 12.50 3.50
Entire 17.50 8.50
b. On No. U401a (die 2) 110.00 70.00
Entire 140.00 140.00
c. On No. U401b (die 3) 60.00 50.00
Entire 100.00 100.00
U492 U90 1½c on 1c **green,** *oriental buff* (U402a, die 2) 500.00 150.00
Entire 800.00 175.00
a. On No. U402c (die 4) 700.00 250.00
Entire 1,400. 300.00
U493 U90 1½c on 1c **grn,** *blue* (U403c, die 4) 100.00 65.00
Entire 140.00 70.00
a. On No. U403a (die 2) 100.00 67.50
Entire 140.00 90.00
U494 U90 1½c on 1c **grn,** *manila* (U404, die 1) 250.00 100.00
Entire 500.00 150.00
a. On No. U404a (die 3) 950.00
Entire 1,250.

On Envelopes of 1916-20

U495 U92 1½c on 1c **green** (U420, die 1) .80 .25
Entire 1.10 .45
a. On No. U420a (die 2) 80.00 52.50
Entire 120.00 90.00
b. On No. U420b (die 3) 2.10 .70
Entire 3.00 .85
c. On No. U420c (die 4) 2.10 .85
Entire 3.00 1.15
d. As #U495, double surcharge 10.00 3.00
Entire 15.00 5.00
e. As "b," double surcharge 10.00 3.00
Entire 15.00 5.00
f. As "c," double surcharge 10.00 3.00
Entire 15.00 5.00
U496 U92 1½c on 1c **grn,** *amber* (U421, die 1) 15.00 12.50
Entire 27.50 15.00
a. On No. U421b (die 3) 725.00
Entire 1,500.
b. On No. U421c (die 4) 15.00 12.50
Entire 27.50 15.00
U497 U92 1½c on 1c **green,** *oriental buff* (U422, die 1) 3.75 1.90
Entire 7.00 2.25
a. On No. U422b (die 4) 67.50
Entire 100.00
U498 U92 1½c on 1c **grn,** *blue* (U423c, die 4) 1.40 .75
Entire 2.25 1.00
a. On No. U423 (die 1) 2.40 1.50
Entire 4.25 2.00
b. On No. U423b (die 3) 1.75 1.50
Entire 3.25 2.00
U499 U92 1½c on 1c **green,** *manila* (U424) 8.00 6.00
Entire 16.00 7.00
U500 U92 1½c on 1c **green,** *brown* (unglazed) (U428) 60.00 30.00
Entire 85.00 35.00
U501 U92 1½c on 1c **green,** *brown* (glazed) (U426) 65.00 30.00
Entire 90.00 35.00
U502 U93 1½c on 2c **carmine** (U429, die 1) 200.00 —
Entire 450.00 —
a. On No. U429d (die 5) 250.00
Entire 500.00
b. On No. U429f (die 7) 250.00
Entire 500.00
c. On No. U429e (die 6) 325.00
Entire —
d. On No. U429g (die 8) 450.00
U503 U93 1½c on 2c **carmine,** *oriental buff* (U431c, die 5) 200.00 —
Entire 500.00 —
a. Double surcharge —
b. Double surcharge, one inverted *700.00*
U504 U93 1½c on 2c **car,** *blue* (U432, die 1) 300.00 —
Entire 450.00 —
a. On No. U432g (die 7) 300.00
Entire 450.00
b. As "a," double surcharge, entire *350.00*
c. On No. U432f (die 6), entire *400.00*

On Envelopes of 1925

U505 U93 1½c on 1½c **brown** (U481, die 1) 300.00
Entire 550.00
a. On No. U481a (die 8) 300.00
Entire 500.00
b. As No. U505, double surcharge, entire *2,000.*
U506 U93 1½c on 1½c **brown,** *blue* (U483a, die 8) 200.00
Entire 550.00
a. On No. U483 (die 1) 300.00

The paper of No. U500 is not glazed and appears to be the same as that used for the wrappers of 1920.
Type 8 exists in 20 city sub-types.

Surcharged

Black Surcharge

On Envelopes of 1887

U507 U69 1½c on 1c **blue** (U294) 1,750.
Entire 2,400.
U507B U69 1½c on 1c **blue,** *manila* (U300) 4,750.
Entire 5,500.

On Envelope of 1899

U508 U77 1½c on 1c **green,** *amber* (U353) 55.00
Entire 90.00

On Envelopes of 1903

U508A U85 1½c on 1c **green** (U379) 2,750.
Entire 5,000.
U509 U85 1½c on 1c **green,** *amber* (U380) 12.50 10.00
Entire 27.50 *35.00*
a. Double surcharge 75.00
Entire 100.00
U509B U85 1½c on 1c **green,** *oriental buff* (U381) 40.00 40.00
Entire 60.00 50.00

On Envelopes of 1907-16

U510 U90 1½c on 1c **green** (U400, die 1) 2.75 1.25
Entire 4.75 1.50
b. On No. U400a (die 2) 9.00 4.00
Entire 13.50 6.00
c. On No. U400b (die 3) 37.50 8.00
Entire 50.00 11.00
d. On No. U400c (die 4) 3.50 1.25
Entire 7.50 2.00
e. As No. U510, double surcharge 25.00
Entire 50.00
U511 U90 1½c on 1c **green,** *amber* (U401, die 1) 200.00 100.00
Entire 325.00 150.00
U512 U90 1½c on 1c **green,** *oriental buff* (U402, die 1) 7.00 4.00
Entire 14.00 6.50
a. On No. U402c (die 4) 21.00 14.00
Entire 30.00 17.00
U513 U90 1½c on 1c **grn,** *blue* (U403, die 1) 6.00 4.00
Entire 9.50 5.00
a. On No. U403c (die 4) 6.00 4.00
Entire 9.50 5.00
U514 U90 1½c on 1c **green,** *manila* (U404, die 1) 30.00 9.00
Entire 45.00 22.50
a. On No. U404a (die 3) 77.50 40.00
Entire 100.00 95.00

On Envelopes of 1916-20

U515 U92 1½c on 1c **green** (U420, die 1) .40 .25
Entire .75 .30
a. On No. U420a (die 2) 15.00 15.00
Entire 30.00 20.00
b. On No. U420b (die 3) .40 .25
Entire .75 .30
c. On No. U420c (die 4) .40 .25
Entire .75 .30
d. As #U515, double surcharge 10.00
Entire 15.00
e. As #U515, inverted surcharge 15.00
Entire 30.00
f. As #U515, triple surcharge 15.00
Entire 30.00
g. As #U515, dbl. surch., one invtd., entire —
h. As "b," double surcharge 10.00
Entire 15.00
i. As "b," inverted surcharge 15.00
Entire 30.00
j. As "b," triple surcharge 25.00
Entire 40.00
k. As "c," double surcharge 10.00
Entire 15.00
l. As "c," inverted surcharge 15.00
Entire 30.00
U516 U92 1½c on 1c **green,** *amber* (U421c, die 4) 50.00 27.50
Entire 65.00 37.50
a. On No. U421 (die 1) 55.00 32.50
Entire 70.00 42.50
U517 U92 1½c on 1c **green,** *oriental buff* (U422, die 1) 6.25 1.25
Entire 9.00 1.50
a. On No. U422a (die 4) 7.25 1.50
Entire 10.00 2.00
U518 U92 1½c on 1c **green,** *blue* (U423b, die 4) 5.00 1.50
Entire 7.50 5.00
a. On No. U423 (die 1) 8.25 4.50
Entire 27.50 18.00
b. On No. U423a (die 3) 27.50 7.50
Entire 40.00 9.00
c. As "a," double surcharge 30.00
Entire 42.50
U519 U92 1½c on 1c **green,** *manila* (U424, die 1) 25.00 12.00
Entire 42.50 15.00
a. Double surcharge 100.00
U520 U93 1½c on 2c **car** (U429, die 1) 300.00 —
Entire 475.00 —
a. On No. U429d (die 5) 275.00
Entire 450.00
b. On No. U429e (die 6) 275.00
Entire 475.00
c. On No. U429f (die 7) 275.00
Entire 600.00
U520D U93 1½c on 2c **car,** *amber* (U430c, die 5), entire —
U520E U92 1½c on 4c **black** (U440, die 1), entire —

Magenta Surcharge

U521 U92 1½c on 1c **green** (U420b, die 3), *Oct. 22, 1925* 4.25 3.50
Entire 6.50 5.50
Entire, 1st day cancel, Washington, D.C. 100.00
a. Double surcharge 75.00
Entire 125.00

Sesquicentennial Exposition Issue

150th anniversary of the Declaration of Independence.

Liberty Bell — U94

Die 1. The center bar of "E" of "postage" is shorter than top bar.
Die 2. The center bar of "E" of "postage" is of same length as top bar.

1926, July 27

U522 U94 2c **carmine,** die 1 1.00 .50
Entire 1.50 .95
a. Die 2 5.50 3.75
Entire 10.00 5.50
Entire, die 2, 1st day cancel, Washington, D.C. 32.50
Entire, die 2, 1st day cancel, Philadelphia 27.50

Washington Bicentennial Issue

200th anniversary of the birth of George Washington.

Mount Vernon — U95

2c Die 1 — "S" of "Postage" normal.
2c Die 2 — "S" of "Postage" raised.

1932

U523	U95	1c **olive green,** *Jan. 1*	1.00	.80
		Entire	1.50	1.75
		Entire, 1st day cancel		18.00
U524	U95	1½c **chocolate,** *Jan. 1*	2.00	1.50
		Entire	2.75	2.50
		Entire, 1st day cancel		18.00
U525	U95	2c **carmine,** die 1,*Jan. 1*	.40	.25
		Entire	.50	.25
		Entire, 1st day cancel		16.00
a.		2c **carmine,** die 2	60.00	20.00
		Entire	80.00	27.50
b.		2c **carmine,** *blue,* die 1 (error) entire	*30,000.*	
U526	U95	3c **violet,** *June 16*	1.75	.35
		Entire	2.25	.40
		Entire, 1st day cancel		18.00
U527	U95	4c **black,** *Jan. 1*	15.00	17.50
		Entire	20.00	*35.00*
		Entire, 1st day cancel		30.00
U528	U95	5c **dark blue,** *Jan. 1*	3.50	3.50
		Entire	4.25	*20.00*
		Entire, 1st day cancel		20.00
		Nos. U523-U528 (6)	23.65	23.90

Type of 1916-32 Issue

1932, Aug. 18

U529	U93	6c **orange,** die 7	6.00	4.00
		Entire	9.50	7.50
		Entire, 1st day cancel, Los Angeles		20.00
U530	U93	6c **orange,** *amber,* die 7	10.00	10.00
		Entire	15.00	12.50
		Entire, 1st day cancel, Los Angeles		20.00
U531	U93	6c **orange,** *blue,* die 7	10.00	10.00
		Entire	15.00	12.50
		Entire, 1st day cancel		20.00

Franklin — U96

Die 1

Die 2

Die 3

Die 1 — Short (3½mm) and thick "I" in thick circle.
Die 2 — Tall (4½mm) and thin "1" in thin circle; upper and lower bars of E in ONE long and 1mm from circle.
Die 3 — As in Die 2, but E normal and 1½mm from circle.

Printed by International Envelope Corp.

1950

U532	U96	1c **green,** die 1, *Nov. 16*	5.00	1.75
		Entire	8.00	2.25
		Entire, 1st day cancel, NY, NY		1.00
a.		Die 2	6.50	3.00
		Entire	11.00	3.75
b.		Die 3	6.50	3.00
		Entire	11.00	3.75
		Precanceled, die 3		1.25
		Entire, precanceled, die 3	2.50	1.50

Washington — U97

Die 1

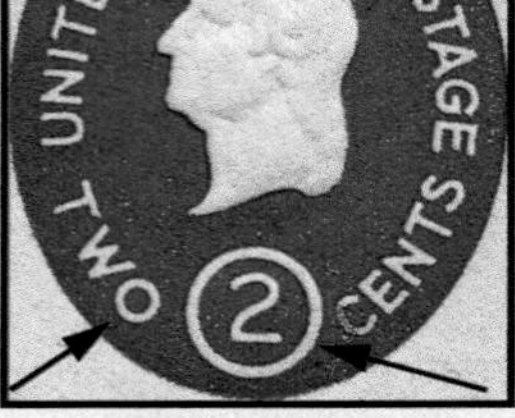
Die 2

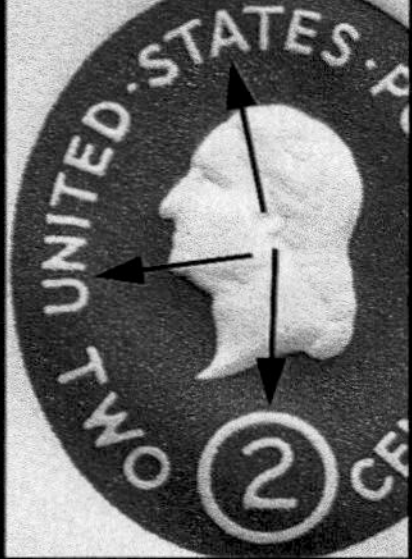
Die 3

Die 4

Die 1 — Thick "2" in thick circle; toe of "2" is acute angle.
Die 2 — Thin "2" in thin circle; toe of "2" is almost right angle; line through left stand of "N" in UNITED and stand of "E" in POSTAGE goes considerably below tip of chin; "N" of UNITED is tall; "O" of TWO is high.
Die 3 — Figure "2" as in Die 2. Short UN in UNITED thin crossbar in A of STATES.
Die 4 — Tall UN in UNITED; thick crossbar in A of STATES; otherwise like Die 3.

U533	U97	2c **carmine, die 3**	.70	.25
		Entire	1.20	.35
		Entire, precanceled, die 3	.30	.25
a.		Die 1, *Nov. 17*	.80	.30
		Entire	1.40	.45
		Entire, 1st day cancel, NY, NY		1.00
b.		Die 2	1.40	.85
		Entire	1.80	.95
c.		Die 4	1.30	.60
		Entire	1.50	.65
		Entire, precanceled	.40	.25

Die 1

Die 2

Die 3

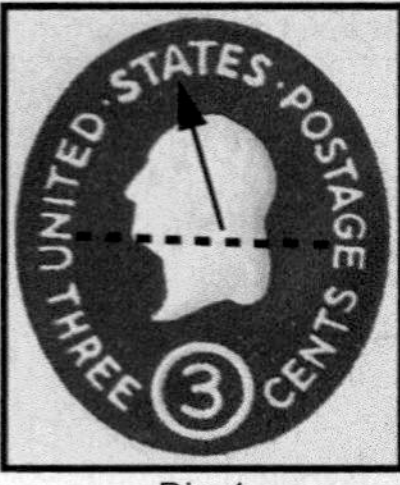

Die 4

Die 5

Die 1 — Thick and tall (4½mm) "3" in thick circle; long top bars and short stems in T's of STATES.
Die 2 — Thin and tall (4½mm) "3" in medium circle; short top bars and long stems in T's of STATES.
Die 3 — Thin and short (4mm) "3" in thin circle; lettering wider than Dies 1 and 2; line from left stand of N to stand of E is distinctly below tip of chin.
Die 4 — Figure and letters as in Die 3. Line hits tip of chin; short N in UNITED and thin crossbar in A of STATES.
Die 5 — Figure, letter and chin line as in Die 4; but tall N in UNITED and thick crossbar in A of STATES.

U534	U97	3c **dark violet,** die 4	.35	.25
		Entire	.45	.25
a.		Die 1, *Nov. 18*	1.90	.70
		Entire	2.40	1.20
		Entire, 1st day cancel, NY, NY		1.00
b.		Die 2, *Nov. 19*	.75	.50
		Entire	1.50	.55
		Entire, 1st day cancel, NY, NY		4.00
c.		Die 3	.55	.25
		Entire	1.00	.45
d.		Die 5	.75	.45
		Entire	1.20	.65
e.		As "c," double impression	*300.00*	

Washington — U98

1952

U535	U98	1½c **brown**	4.50	3.50
		Entire	5.50	4.25
		Precanceled		1.25
		Entire, precanceled	1.50	1.50

Die 1

Die 2

Die 3

Die 1 — Head high in oval (2mm below T of STATES). Circle near (1mm) bottom of colored oval.
Die 2 — Head low in oval (3mm). Circle 1½mm from edge of oval. Right leg of A in POSTAGE shorter than left. Short leg on P.
Die 3 — Head centered in oval (2½mm). Circle as in Die 2. Legs of A of POSTAGE about equal. Long leg on P.

1958

U536	U96	4c **red violet,** die 1, *July 31*	.75	.25
		Entire	.95	.25
		Entire, 1st day cancel, Montpelier, Vt. *(163,746)*		1.00
a.		Die 2	.90	.25

	Entire	1.20	.25
b.	Die 3	.90	.25
	Entire	1.20	.25

Nos. U429, U429f, U429h, U533, U533a-U533c Surcharged in Red at Left of Stamp

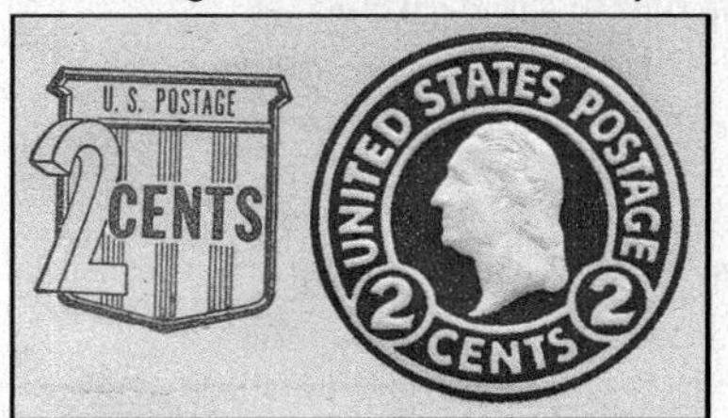

1958

U537	U93 2c + 2c **carmine,** die 1	3.25	1.50
	Entire	4.25	*15.00*
a.	Die 7	10.00	7.00
	Entire	14.00	*15.00*
b.	Die 9	4.75	5.00
	Entire	7.00	15.00
U538	U97 2c + 2c **carmine,** die 1	.70	.80
	Entire	1.10	*1.25*
a.	Die 2	.90	1.00
	Entire	2.80	3.00
b.	Die 3	.70	.70
	Entire	1.90	*2.00*
c.	Die 4	.70	1.00
	Entire	1.40	*1.50*

Nos. U436a, U436e-U436f, U534, U534b-U534d Surcharged in Green at Left of Stamp

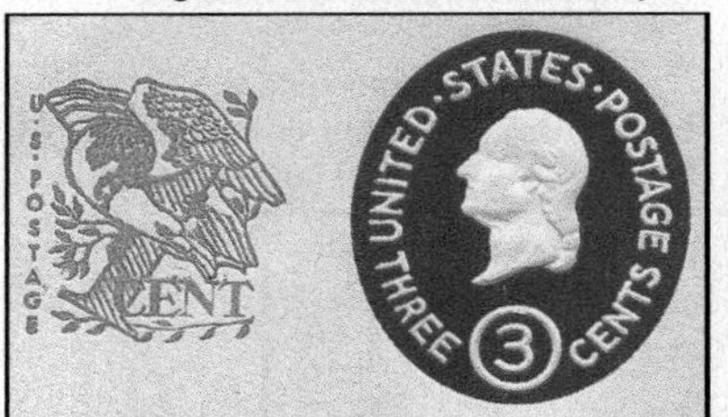

U539	U93 3c + 1c **purple,** die 1	12.50	9.00
	Entire	16.50	17.50
a.	Die 7	11.00	7.50
	Entire	14.00	17.50
b.	Die 9	17.50	15.00
	Entire	27.50	27.50
U540	U97 3c + 1c **dark violet,** die 3	.40	1.00
	Entire	.50	2.00
a.	Die 2	—	—
	Entire	*3,500.*	—
b.	Die 4	.65	1.00
	Entire	.80	*2.00*
c.	Die 5	.70	1.00
	Entire	.95	2.00

Earliest documented uses: Nos. U540b and U540c, both Aug. 1, 1958 (first day of new 4¢ letter rate).

Benjamin Franklin — U99

George Washington — U100

Die 1

Die 2

Dies of 1¼c

Die 1 — The "4" is 3mm high. Upper leaf in left cluster is 2mm from "U."

Die 2 — The "4" is 3½mm high. Leaf clusters are larger. Upper leaf at left is 1mm from "U."

1960

U541	U99 1¼c **turquoise,** die 1, *June 25, 1960*	.65	.50
	Entire	.80	.55
	Entire, 1st day cancel, Birmingham, Ala. *(211,500)*		1.00
	Precanceled		.25
	Entire, precanceled	.45	.45
a.	Die 2, precanceled		1.25
	Entire, precanceled	1.75	1.75
U542	U100 2½c **dull blue,** *May 28, 1960*	.80	.50
	Entire	.90	.60
	Entire, 1st day cancel, Chicago, Ill. *(196,977)*		1.00
	Precanceled		.25
	Entire, precanceled	.75	.55

Precanceled cut squares

Precanceled envelopes do not normally receive another cancellation. Since the lack of a cancellation makes it impossible to distinguish between cut squares from used and unused envelopes, they are valued here as used only.

Pony Express Centennial Issue

Pony Express Rider — U101

Envelope White Outside, Blue Inside.

1960

U543	U101 4c **brown,** *July 19, 1960*	.55	.30
	Entire	.70	.40
	Entire, 1st day cancel, St. Joseph, Mo. *(407,160)*		1.00

Abraham Lincoln — U102

Die 1

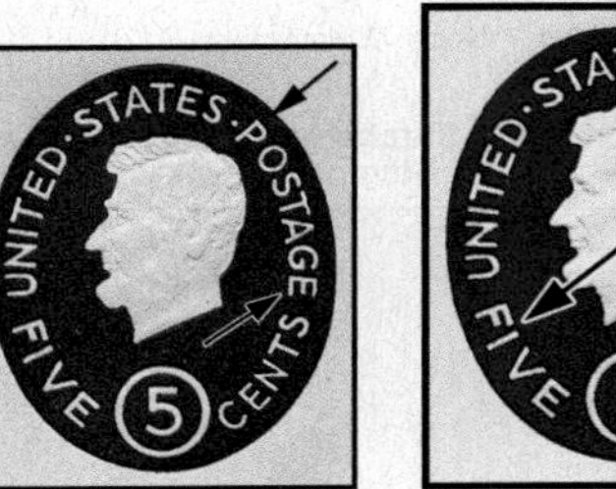

Die 2 Die 3

Die 1 — Center bar of E of POSTAGE is above the middle. Center bar of E of STATES slants slightly upward. Nose sharper, more pointed. No offset ink specks inside envelope on back of die impression.

Die 2 — Center bar of E of POSTAGE in middle. P of POSTAGE has short stem. Ink specks on back of die impression.

Die 3 — FI of FIVE closer than Die 1 or 2. Second T of STATES seems taller than ES. Ink specks on back of die impression.

1962

U544	U102 5c **dark blue,** die 2, *Nov. 19, 1962*	.80	.25
	Entire	1.10	.30
	Entire, 1st day cancel, Springfield, Ill. *(163,258)*		1.50
a.	Die 1	.80	.25
	Entire	1.10	.30
b.	Die 3	.85	.35
	Entire	1.20	.40
c.	Die 2 with albino impression of 4c (#U536)	50.00	—
	Entire	120.00	
d.	Die 3 with albino impression of 4c (#U536), entire	*125.00*	—
e.	Die 3 on complete impression of 4c (#U536), cut square	*125.00*	

No. U536 Surcharged in Green at left of Stamp

Two types of surcharge:

Type I — "U.S. POSTAGE" 18½mm high. Serifs on cross of T both diagonal. Two lines of shading in C of CENT.

Type II — "U.S. POSTAGE" 17½mm high. Right serif on cross of T is vertical. Three shading lines in C.

1962

U545	U96 4c + 1c **red vio,** die 1, type I, *Nov. 1962*	1.25	1.10
	Entire	1.50	2.50
a.	Type II	1.25	1.10
	Entire	1.50	2.50

Values for used envelopes are for examples used within the period of issue. Envelopes used much later sell at substantially reduced prices.

New York World's Fair Issue

Issued to publicize the New York World's Fair, 1964-65.

Globe with Satellite Orbit — U103

1964

U546	U103 5c **maroon,** *Apr. 22, 1964*	.55	.40
	Entire	.70	2.00
	Entire, 1st day cancel World's Fair, N.Y. *(466,422)*		1.00

Liberty Bell — U104

Old Ironsides — U105

Eagle — U106

Head of Statue of Liberty — U107

Printed by the United States Envelope Company, Williamsburg, Pa. Designed (6c) by Howard C. Mildner and (others) by Robert J. Jones.

1965-69

U547 U104 1¼c **brown,** *Jan. 6, 1965* .50
Entire .90 2.00
Entire, 1st day cancel, Washington, D.C. 1.00
U548 U104 1 4/10c **brown,** *Mar. 26, 1968* .50
Entire 1.00 2.00
Entire, 1st day cancel, Springfield, Mass. *(134,832)* 1.00
U548A U104 1 6/10c **orange,** *June 16, 1969* .50
Entire 1.00 2.00
Entire, 1st day cancel, Washington, D.C. 1.00
b. 1 6/10c **brown (error), entire** *5,000.*
U549 U105 4c **bright blue,** *Jan. 6, 1965* .90 .25
Entire 1.00 .25
Entire, 1st day cancel, Washington, D.C. 1.00
U550 U106 5c **bright purple,** *Jan. 5, 1965* .75 .25
Entire .85 1.00
Entire, 1st day cancel, Williamsburg, Pa. *(246,496)* 1.00
a. Bar tagged, *Aug. 15, 1967* 3.00 1.00
Entire 5.00 5.00
Entire, tagged, 1st day cancel 3.50
b. orange-red (air post) instead of yellow-green tagging, entire *350.00*

Tagged

U551 U107 6c **light green,** *Jan. 4, 1968* .70 .25
Entire .80 .25
Entire, 1st day cancel, New York, N.Y. *(184,784)* 1.25
a. 6c **dark gray green,** entire 200.00 —

First day covers of the 1¼c and 4c total 451,960.

Nos. U549-U550 Surcharged in Red or Green at Left of Stamp

1968, Feb. 5

U552 U105 4c + 2c **bright blue** (R) 3.25 2.00
Entire 3.75 2.50
Entire, 1st day cancel 6.00
U553 U106 5c + 1c **bright purple** (G) 3.00 2.75
Entire 3.50 3.25
Entire, 1st day cancel 6.00
a. Tagged 3.00 2.75
Entire 4.00 3.25
Entire, 1st day cancel 6.00
b. With 2c surcharge type "b" (error) 400.00

Tagged
Envelopes from No. U554 onward are tagged, except for bulk-rate and non-profit envelopes, which are untagged. The tagging element is in the ink through No. 608 unless otherwise noted. From No. 611 on, envelopes have bar or block tagging unless otherwise noted.

Herman Melville Issue

Issued to honor Herman Melville (1819-1891), writer, and the whaling industry.

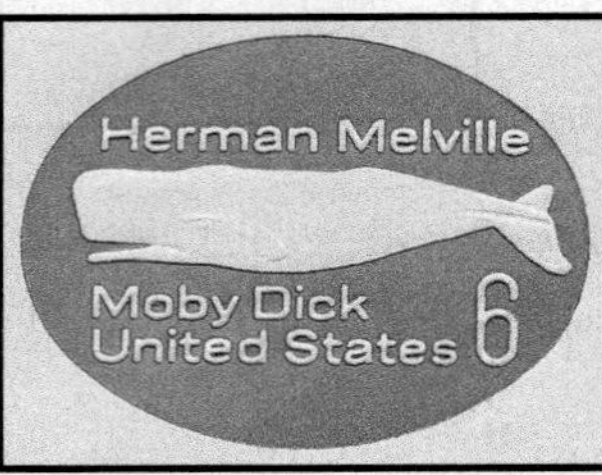

Moby Dick — U108

1970, Mar. 7

U554 U108 6c **blue** .50 .25
Entire .60 2.00
Entire, 1st day cancel, New Bedford, Mass. *(433,777)* 1.50

Youth Conference Issue

Issued to publicize the White House Conference on Youth, Estes Park, Colo., Apr. 18-22.

Conference Emblem Symbolic of Man's Expectant Soul and of Universal Brotherhood U109

Printed by United States Envelope Company, Williamsburg, Pa. Designed by Chermayeff and Geismar Associates.

1971, Feb. 24

U555 U109 6c **light blue** .70 1.00
Entire .80 3.00
Entire, 1st day cancel, Washington, D.C. *(264,559)* 1.00

Liberty Bell Type of 1965 and

Eagle — U110

Printed by the United States Envelope Co., Williamsburg, Pa. Designed (8c) by Bradbury Thompson.

1971

U556 U104 1 7/10c **deep lilac,** untagged, *May 10* .35
Entire .35 1.50
Entire, 1st day cancel, Baltimore, Md. *(150,767)* 1.00
U557 U110 8c **ultramarine,** *May 6* .40 .25
Entire .60 .40
Entire, 1st day cancel, Williamsburg, Pa. *(193,000)* 1.00

Nos. U551 and U555 Surcharged in Green at Left of Stamp

c

1971, May 16

U561 U107 6c + (2c) **light green** .90 1.25
Entire 1.00 2.50
Entire, 1st day cancel, Washington, D.C. 2.50
a. Inverted surcharge, entire *225.00*
U562 U109 6c + (2c) **light blue** 2.00 2.50
Entire 2.50 3.00
Entire, 1st day cancel, Washington, D.C. 3.00
a. Inverted surcharge printed on reverse, entire —

Bowling Issue

Issued as a salute to bowling and in connection with the 7th World Tournament of the International Bowling Federation, Milwaukee, Wis.

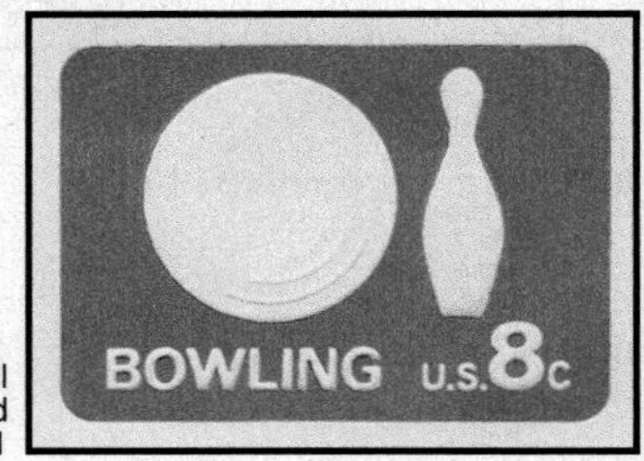

Bowling Ball and Pin — U111

Designed by George Giusti.

1971, Aug. 21

U563 U111 8c **rose red** .60 .25
Entire .70 2.00
Entire, 1st day cancel, Milwaukee, Wis. *(281,242)* 1.00

Aging Conference Issue

White House Conference on Aging, Washington, D.C., Nov. 28-Dec. 2, 1971.

Conference Symbol — U112

Designed by Thomas H. Geismar.

1971, Nov. 15

U564 U112 8c **light blue** .50 .25
Entire .75 3.00
Entire, 1st day cancel, Washington, D.C. *(125,000)* 1.00

International Transportation Exhibition Issue

U.S. International Transportation Exhibition, Dulles International Airport, Washington, D.C., May 27-June 4.

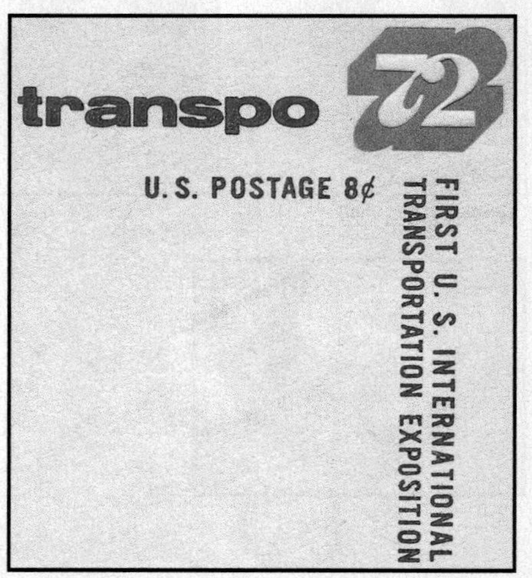

Transportation Exhibition Emblem — U113

Emblem designed by Toshihiki Sakow.

1972, May 2

U565 U113 8c **ultramarine & rose red** .50 .25
Entire .75 .60
Entire, 1st day cancel, Washington, D.C. 1.00

No. U557 Surcharged in Ultramarine at Left of Stamp

1973, Dec. 1

U566 U110 8c + 2c **brt. ultramarine** .40 1.25
Entire .75 2.50
Entire, 1st day cancel, Washington, D.C. 1.50

Liberty Bell — U114

1973, Dec. 5

U567 U114 10c **emerald** .40 .25
Entire .70 .35
Entire, 1st day cancel, Philadelphia, Pa. *(142,141)* 1.00

"Volunteer Yourself" — U115

Designed by Norman Ives.

1974, Aug. 23

Untagged

U568 U115 1 8/10c **blue green** .25
Entire 1.00 2.00
Entire, 1st day cancel, Cincinnati, Ohio 1.00

Tennis Centenary Issue

Centenary of tennis in the United States.

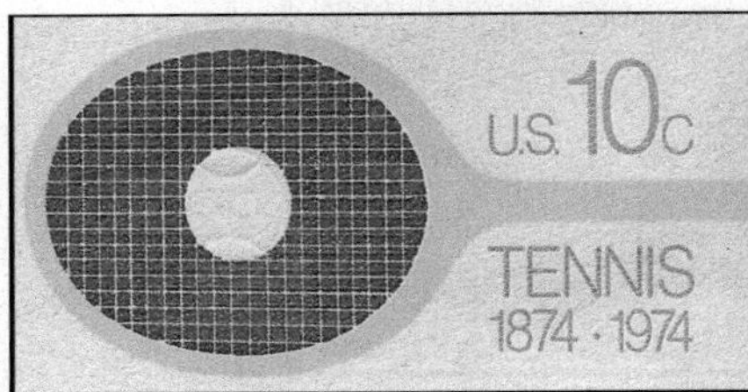

Tennis Racquet — U116

Designed by Donald Moss.

1974, Aug. 31 **Block Tagged**

U569 U116 10c **yellow, brt. blue & light green** .55 .25
Entire .80 2.00
Entire, 1st day cancel, Forest Hills, N.Y. *(245,000)* 1.25

Bicentennial Era Issue

The Seafaring Tradition — Compass Rose U118

The American Homemaker — Quilt Pattern — U119

The American Farmer — Sheaf of Wheat — U120

The American Doctor — Mortar — U121

The American Craftsman — Tools, c. 1750 — U122

Designs (in brown on left side of envelope): 10c, Norwegian sloop Restaurationen. No. U572, Spinning wheel. No. U573, Plow. No. U574, Colonial era medical instruments and bottle. No. U575, Shaker rocking chair.
Designed by Arthur Congdon.

1975-76 **Embossed** **Diagonally Laid Paper**

U571 U118 10c **brown & blue,** *light brown, Oct. 13, 1975* .30 .25
Entire .45 2.00
Entire, 1st day cancel, Minneapolis, Minn. *(255,304)* 1.00
a. Brown ("10c/USA," etc.) omitted, entire *125.00*

U572 U119 13c **brown & blue green,** *light brown, Feb. 2, 1976* .35 .25
Entire .55 2.00
Entire, 1st day cancel, Biloxi, Miss. *(196,647)* 1.00
a. Brown ("13c/USA," etc.) omitted, entire *125.00*

U573 U120 13c **brown & bright green,** *light brown, Mar. 15, 1976* .35 .25
Entire .55 2.00
Entire, 1st day cancel, New Orleans, La. *(214,563)* 1.00
a. Brown ("13c/USA," etc.) omitted, entire *125.00*

U574 U121 13c **brown & orange,** *light brown, June 30, 1976* .35 .25
Entire .55 2.00
Entire, 1st day cancel, Dallas, Texas 1.50
a. Brown ("13c/USA," etc.) omitted, entire *125.00*

U575 U122 13c **brown & carmine,** *lt. brown, Aug. 6, 1976* .35 .25
Entire .55 2.00
Entire, 1st day cancel, Hancock, Mass. 1.00
a. Brown ("13c/USA," etc.) omitted, entire *125.00*
Nos. U571-U575 (5) 1.70 1.25

Liberty Tree, Boston, 1646 U123

Designed by Leonard Everett Fisher.

1975, Nov. 8 **Embossed**

U576 U123 13c **orange brown** .30 .25
Entire .40 2.00
Entire, 1st day cancel, Memphis, Tenn. *(226,824)* 1.00

Star and Pinwheel — U124

U125

U126

Eagle — U127

Uncle Sam — U128

Designers: 2c, Rudolph de Harak. 2.1c, Norman Ives. 2.7c, Ann Sforza Clementino. 15c, George Mercer.

1976-78 **Embossed**

U577 U124 2c **red,** untagged, *Sept. 10, 1976* .25
Entire .70 1.50
Entire, 1st day cancel, Hempstead, N.Y. *(81,388)* 1.00

U578 U125 2.1c **green,** untagged, *June 3, 1977* .25
Entire .90 2.00
Entire, 1st day cancel, Houston, Tex. *(120,280)* 1.00

U579 U126 2.7c **green,** untagged, *July 5, 1978* .25
Entire 1.00 1.50
Entire, 1st day cancel, Raleigh, N.C. *(92,687)* 1.00

U580 U127 (15c) **orange,** *May 22, 1978* .40 .25
Entire .55 .75
Entire, 1st day cancel, Memphis, Tenn. 1.00

U581 U128 15c **red,** ink tagged, *June 3, 1978* .40 .25
Entire .55 .60
Entire, 1st day cancel, Williamsburg, Pa. *(176,000)* 1.00
a. Bar tagged *7.00 7.00*

For No. U581 with surcharge, see No. U586b.

Bicentennial Issue

Centennial Envelope, 1876 — U129

1976, Oct. 15 **Embossed**

U582 U129 13c **emerald** .35 .25
Entire .70 .40
Entire, 1st day cancel, Los Angeles, Cal. *(277,222)* 1.00

Golf Issue

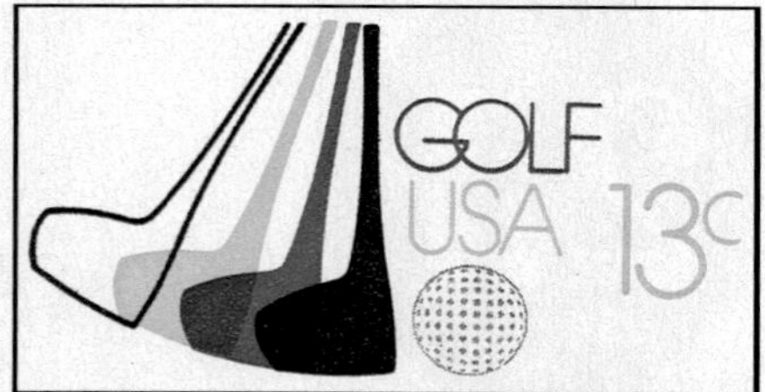

Golf Club in Motion and Golf Ball — U130

Designed by Guy Salvato.

1977, Apr. 7 **Photogravure and Embossed**

U583 U130 13c **black, blue & yellow green** .65 .25
Entire .75 3.00
Entire, 1st day cancel, Augusta, Ga. *(252,000)* 1.50
a. Black omitted, entire *500.00*
b. Black & blue omitted, entire *500.00*
c. Black, blue & yellow green omitted, entire *500.00*

On No. U583c, the embossing is present.

Energy Issue

Conservation and development of national resources.

"Conservation" U131

"Development" U132

Designed by Terrance W. McCaffrey.

1977, Oct. 20 **Photo.**

Bar Tagged

U584 U131 13c **black, red & yellow** .45 .25
Entire .55 2.00
Entire, 1st day cancel, Ridley Park, Pa. 1.00
a. Red, yellow & tagging omitted, entire *190.00*
b. Yellow & tagging omitted, entire *150.00*
c. Black omitted, entire *135.00*
d. Black & red omitted, entire *350.00*

U585 U132 13c **black, red & yellow** .45 .25
Entire .55 .25
Entire, 1st day cancel, Ridley Park, Pa. 1.00

First day cancellation applied to 353,515 of Nos. U584 and U585.

Olive Branch and Star — U133

Designed by George Mercer.

1978, July 28 **Embossed**

Black Surcharge

U586 U133 15c on 16c **blue** .40 .25
Entire .55 1.00
Entire, 1st day cancel, Williamsburg, Pa. *(193,153)* 1.00
a. Surcharge omitted, entire 225.00 1,000.
b. Surcharge on No. U581, entire 260.00
c. As "a," with surcharge printed on envelope flap 175.00 —
d. Surcharge inverted (in lower left corner), entire 200.00 —

Auto Racing Issue

Indianapolis 500 Racing Car — U134

Designed by Robert Peak.

1978, Sept. 2 **Embossed**

U587 U134 15c **red, blue & black** .45 .25
Entire .60 3.00
Entire, 1st day cancel, Ontario, Cal. *(209,147)* 1.75
a. Black omitted, entire 100.00
b. Black & blue omitted, entire *170.00*
c. Red & tagging omitted, entire 100.00
d. Red, blue & tagging omitted, entire *170.00*
e. Tagging bar inverted at LL, entire 100.00
f. Tagging bar on reverse, entire —

No. U576 Surcharged

1978, Nov. 28 **Embossed**

U588 U123 15c on 13c **orange brown** .40 .25
Entire .55 1.00
Entire, 1st day cancel, Williamsburg, Pa. *(137,500)* 1.00
a. Surcharge inverted (in lower left corner), entire —

U135

1979, May 18 **Untagged** **Embossed**

U589 U135 3.1c **ultramarine** .35
Entire .55 2.50
Entire, 1st day cancel, Denver, Colo. *(117,575)* 1.00

Weaver Violins — U136

1980, June 23 **Untagged** **Embossed**

U590 U136 3.5c **purple** .35
Entire .35 1.50
Entire, 1st day cancel, Williamsburg, Pa. 1.00
a. 3.5c **violet**, tagged (in ink), error of color and tagging using ink intended for No. U592, entire *300.00 500.00*

U137

1982, Feb. 17 **Untagged** **Embossed**

U591 U137 5.9c **brown** .35
Entire .35 2.50
Entire, 1st day cancel, Wheeling, WV 1.00

Eagle — U138

1981, Mar. 15 **Embossed**

U592 U138 (18c) **violet** .45 .25
Entire .55 1.00
Entire, 1st day cancel, Memphis, TN *(179,171)* 1.00

U139

1981, Apr. 2 **Embossed**
U593 U139 18c **dark blue** .45 .25
Entire .55 4.00
Entire, 1st day cancel, Star City, IN *(160,439)* 1.00

Eagle — U140

1981, Oct. 11 **Embossed**
U594 U140 (20c) **brown** .45 .25
Entire .55 .60
Entire, 1st day cancel, Memphis, TN *(304,404)* 2.00

Veterinary Medicine Issue

Seal of Veterinarians U141

Design at left side of envelope shows 5 animals and bird in brown, "Veterinary Medicine" in gray.
Designed by Guy Salvato.

1979, July 24 **Embossed**
U595 U141 15c **brown & gray** .50 .25
Entire .90 3.00
Entire, 1st day cancel, Seattle, WA *(209,658)* 1.00
a. Gray omitted, entire *425.00*
b. Brown omitted, entire *500.00*
c. Gray & brown omitted, tagging omitted, entire *325.00*

On No. U595c, the embossing of the seal is present.

Olympic Games Issue

22nd Olympic Games, Moscow, July 19-Aug. 3, 1980.

U142

Design (multicolored on left side of envelope) shows two soccer players with ball.
Designed by Robert M. Cunningham.

1979, Dec. 10 **Embossed**
U596 U142 15c **red, green & black** .60 .25
Entire .70 2.00
Entire, 1st day cancel, East Rutherford, NJ *(179,336)* 1.00
a. Red & green omitted, tagging omitted, entire *150.00*
b. Black omitted, tagging omitted, entire *150.00*
c. Black & green omitted, entire *150.00*
d. Red omitted, tagging omitted, entire *325.00*
e. All colors omitted *250.00*
f. Tagging omitted, entire 125.00
g. Black omitted, tagged, entire —

No. U596c exists with a portion of the green present in the Olympics 1980 design at the lower left corner of the envelope.
On No. U596e, the blind embossing of "USA 15c" remains.

Highwheeler Bicycle — U143

Design (blue on left side of envelope) shows racing bicycle.
Designed by Robert Hallock.

1980, May 16 **Embossed**
U597 U143 15c **blue & rose claret** .40 .25
Entire .55 2.00
Entire, 1st day cancel, Baltimore, MD *(173,978)* 1.25
a. Blue ("15c USA") omitted, entire 100.00
b. As "a," tagging omitted 100.00

Yacht — U144

Designed by Cal Sachs.

1980, Sept. 15 **Embossed**
U598 U144 15c **blue & red** .40 .25
Entire .65 2.00
Entire, 1st day cancel, Newport, RI *(192,220)* 1.00

Italian Honeybee and Orange Blossoms U145

Bee and petals colorless embossed.
Designed by Jerry Pinkney.

1980, Oct. 10 **Photogravure and Embossed**
U599 U145 15c **brown, green & yellow** .35 .25
Entire .50 2.00
Entire, 1st day cancel, Paris, IL *(202,050)* 1.00
a. Brown ("USA 15c") omitted, entire *100.00*
b. Green omitted, entire *100.00*

No. U599b also has almost all of the brown color missing.

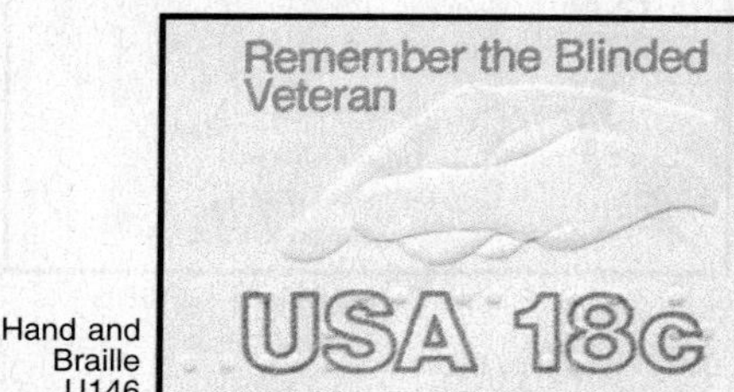

Hand and Braille U146

Hand and braille colorless embossed.
Designed by John Boyd.

1981, Aug. 13 **Embossed**
U600 U146 18c **blue & red** .45 .25
Entire .55 3.00
Entire, 1st day cancel, Arlington, VA *(175,966)* 1.00
a. Blue omitted, entire *300.00*
b. Red omitted, entire *210.00*

Capitol Dome — U147

1981, Nov. 13 **Embossed**
U601 U147 20c **deep magenta, ink** tagged .45 .25
Entire .55 .25
Entire, 1st day cancel, Los Angeles, CA 1.00
a. Bar tagged 4.50 1.50

U148

Designed by Bradbury Thompson.

1982, June 15 **Embossed**
U602 U148 20c **dark blue, black & magenta** .45 .25
Entire .55 2.00
Entire, 1st day cancel, Washington, DC *(163,905)* 1.00
a. Dark blue omitted, entire *175.00*
b. Dark blue & magenta omitted, entire *175.00*
c. All colors omitted, entire *175.00*

On No. 602c, the colorless embossed impression of the Great Seal is present.

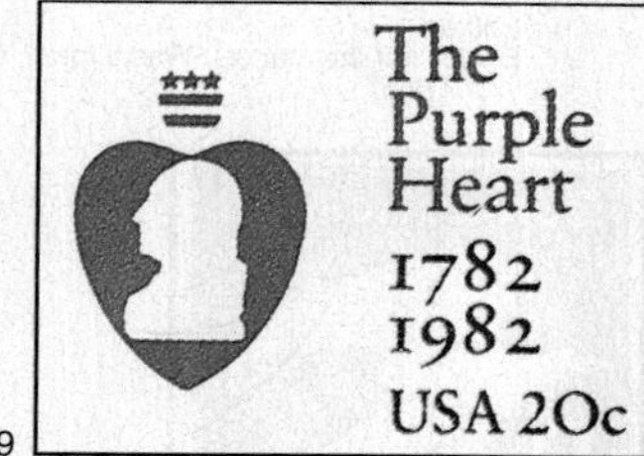

U149

Designed by John Boyd.

1982, Aug. 6 **Embossed**
U603 U149 20c **purple & black** .75 .25
Entire 1.00 3.00
Entire, 1st day cancel, Washington, DC *(110,679)* 1.25
a. Black omitted, entire *80.00*
b. Purple omitted, entire *200.00*

U150

1983, Mar. 21 **Untagged** **Embossed**
U604 U150 5.2c **orange** .90
Entire .75 1.00
Entire, 1st day cancel, Memphis, TN *(141,979)* 1.00

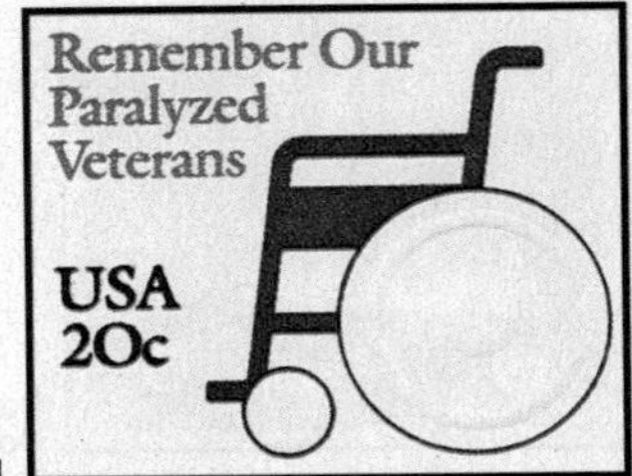

U151

1983, Aug. 3 **Embossed**

U605 U151 20c **red, blue & black** .45 .25
Entire .55 2.00
Entire, 1st day cancel, Portland, OR *(21,500)* 1.00
- *a.* Red omitted, entire *260.00*
- *b.* Blue omitted, entire *260.00*
- *c.* Red & black omitted, entire *125.00*
- *d.* Blue & black omitted, entire *125.00*
- *e.* Black omitted, entire *230.00*

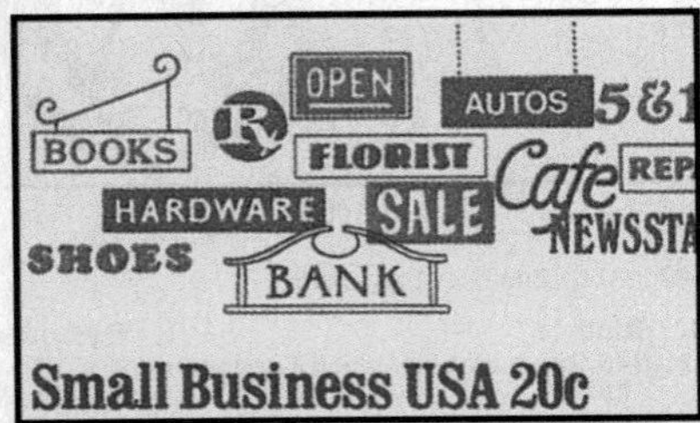

U152

Designed by Peter Spier and Pat Taylor.
Design shows storefronts at lower left. Stamp and design continue on back of envelope.

1984, May 7 **Photo.**

U606 U152 20c **multi** .50 .25
Entire .60 2.00
Entire, 1st day cancel, Washington, DC *(77,665)* 1.00

U153

Designed by Bradbury Thompson.

1985, Feb. 1 **Embossed**

U607 U153 (22c) **deep green** .55 .30
Entire .65 .40
Entire, 1st day cancel, Los Angeles, CA 1.00

American Buffalo U154

Designed by George Mercer.

1985, Feb. 25 **Embossed**

U608 U154 22c **violet brown**, ink tagged .55 .25
Entire .65 .25
Entire, 1st day cancel, Bison, SD *(105,271)* 1.00
- *a.* Untagged, 3 precancel lines, unwatermarked, *Nov. 1, 1986* .25
  Entire .60 .25
- *b.* Bar tagged 2.00 1.00
  Entire 10.00 1.25
- *c.* As "b," tagging omitted — —

Original printings of No. U608 were printed with luminescent ink. later printings have a luminescent vertical bar to the left of the stamp.

Frigate U.S.S. Constitution — U155

Designed by Cal Sacks.

1985, May 3 **Untagged** **Embossed**

U609 U155 6c **green blue** .35
Entire .35 3.00
Entire, 1st day cancel, Boston, MA *(170,425)* 1.25

The Mayflower — U156

Designed by Robert Brangwynne.

1986, Dec. 4 **Untagged Precanceled** **Embossed**

U610 U156 8.5c **black & gray** .65
Entire .75 3.00
Entire, 1st day cancel, Plymouth, MA *(105,164)* 1.00

Stars U157

Designed by Joe Brockert.

1988, Mar. 26 **Typo. & Embossed**

U611 U157 25c **dark red & deep blue,** small block tagging .60 .25
Entire .70 .25
Entire, 1st day cancel, Star, MS *(29,393)* 1.25
- *a.* Dark red (25) omitted, tagging omitted 50.00 —
  Entire 60.00 —
- *b.* Tagging omitted, entire 14.00
- *c.* Dark red (25) omitted, tagging not omitted *60.00*
- *d.* Large block tagging .60 .25
  Entire .70 .25

The tagging bar on No. U611 is 8x10mm. The tagging bar on No. U611d is 16x15mm.

U.S. Frigate Constellation — U158

Designed by Jerry Dadds.

1988, Apr. 12 **Untagged Precanceled** **Typo. & Embossed**

U612 U158 8.4c **black & bright blue** .65
Entire .75 4.00
Entire, 1st day cancel, Baltimore, MD *(41,420)* 1.25
- *a.* Black omitted, entire *500.00*

Snowflake — U159

Designed by Randall McDougall. "Holiday Greetings!" inscribed in lower left.

1988, Sept. 8 **Typo.**

U613 U159 25c **dark red & green** 1.25 *20.00*
Entire 1.50 *40.00*
Entire, 1st day cancel, Snowflake, AZ *(32,601)* 1.25

Stars U160

Designed by Joe Brockert. "Philatelic Mail" and asterisks in dark red below vignette; continuous across envelope face and partly on reverse.

1989, Mar. 10 **Typo.**

U614 U160 25c **dark red & deep blue** .50 .25
Entire .60 .30
Entire, 1st day cancel, Cleveland, OH 1.25
- *a.* Tagging omitted, entire —
- *b.* Red omitted, entire 125.00

No. U614 was issued only in No. 9 size.

Stars — U161

Designed by Joe Brockert.

1989, July 10 **Typo.** **Unwmk.**

U615 U161 25c **dark red & deep blue** .50 .25
Entire .60 .30
Entire, 1st day cancel, Washington, DC *(33,461)* 1.25
- *a.* Dark red omitted, entire *425.00*

Lined with a blue design to provide security for enclosures. Issued only in No. 9 size.

Love! U162

Designed by Tim Girvin.

1989, Sept. 22 **Litho. & Typo.** **Unwmk.**

U616 U162 25c **dark red & bright blue** .50 .75
Entire .60 2.00
Entire, 1st day cancel, McLean, VA *(69,498)* 1.25
- *a.* Dark red and bright blue omitted, entire 150.00
- *b.* Bright blue omitted, entire 150.00

No. U616 has light blue lines printed diagonally over the entire surface of the envelope. Issued only in No. 9 size.

Shuttle Docking at Space Station — U163

Designed by Richard Sheaff.

1989, Dec. 3 Typo. Unwmk.
Die Cut

U617 U163 25c **ultramarine** .90 .60
Entire 1.00 2.00
Entire, 1st day cancel, Washington, DC 1.25
a. Ultramarine omitted, entire *400.00*

A hologram, visible through the die cut window to the right of "USA 25," is affixed to the inside of the envelope.
Available only in No. 9 size.
See Nos. U625, U639.

Vince Lombardi Trophy, Football Players — U164

Designed by Bruce Harman.

1990, Sept. 9 Typo. Unwmk. *Die Cut*

U618 U164 25c **vermilion** .90 .60
Entire 1.00 2.00
Entire, 1st day cancel, Green Bay, WI *(54,589)* 1.25

A hologram, visible through the die cut window to the right of "USA 25," is affixed to the inside of the envelope.
Issued only in No. 10 size.

Star — U165

Designed by Richard Sheaff.

1991, Jan. 24 Typo. & Embossed Wmk.

U619 U165 29c **ultramarine & rose** .60 .30
Entire .70 .35
Entire, unwatermarked, *May 1, 1992* .70 .35
Entire, 1st day cancel, Washington, DC *(33,025)* 1.25
a. Ultramarine omitted, entire *300.00*
b. Rose omitted, tagged, entire *250.00*
c. Rose omitted, tagging omitted, entire *275.00*
d. Tagging omitted, entire —

Unwatermarked envelopes are on recycled paper, were issued May 1, 1992, and have a "recycled" imprint under the flap.
See No. U623.

Birds — U166

Designed by Richard Sheaff
Stamp and design continue on back of envelope. Illustration reduced.

1991, May 3 Typo. Wmk.
Untagged, Precanceled

U620 U166 11.1c **blue & red** .90
Entire .55 2.00
Entire, 1st day cancel, Boxborough, MA *(20,720)* 1.25
Entire, unwatermarked, *May 1, 1992* .60 .25
a. Blue omitted, entire —

Unwatermarked envelopes are on recycled paper, were issued May 1, 1992, and have a "recycled" imprint under the flap.

Love — U167

Designed by Salahattin Kanidinc.

1991, May 9 Litho. Unwmk.

U621 U167 29c **light blue, purple & bright rose** .60 .60
Entire .70 .70
Entire, 1st day cancel, Honolulu, HI *(40,110)* 1.25
a. Bright rose omitted, entire *200.00*
b. Purple omitted, entire *400.00*

Envelopes on recycled paper were issued May 1, 1992, and have a "recycled" imprint under the flap. Envelopes on recycled paper show more gray in the paper, and "29/USA" is in a lighter shade of purple.

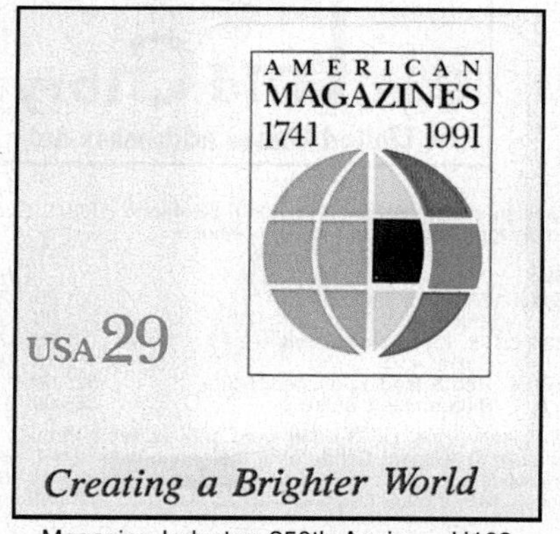

Magazine Industry, 250th Anniv. — U168

Designed by Bradbury Thompson.

1991, Oct. 7 Photo. & Typo. Unwmk.

U622 U168 29c **multicolored** .70 1.00
Entire .80 2.50
Entire, 1st day cancel, Naples, FL *(26,020)* 1.25

The photogravure vignette, visible through the die cut window to the right of "USA 29", is affixed to the inside of the envelope. Issued only in No. 10 size.

Star U169

Designed by Richard Sheaff.
Stamp and design continue on back of envelope.

1991, July 20 Typo. Unwmk.

U623 U169 29c **ultra & rose** .60 .30
Entire .70 1.00
Entire, 1st day cancel, Washington, DC *(16,038)* 1.25
a. Ultra omitted, entire *350.00*
b. Rose omitted, entire *200.00*

Lined with a blue design to provide security for enclosures. Envelopes on recycled paper were issued May 1, 1992, and have a "recycled" imprint under the flap. Issued only in No. 9 size. Value $1.50.

Country Geese U170

Designed by Marc Zaref.

1991, Nov. 8 Litho. & Typo. Wmk.

U624 U170 29c **blue gray & yellow** .60 .60
Entire .70 3.00
Entire, 1st day cancel, Virginia Beach, VA *(21,031)* 1.25
Entire, unwatermarked, *May 1, 1992* 1.00 .70

Unwatermarked envelopes are on recycled paper were issued May 1, 1992, and have a "recycled" imprint under the flap.

Space Shuttle Type of 1989

Designed by Richard Sheaff.

1992, Jan. 21 Typo. Unwmk. *Die Cut*

U625 U163 29c **yellow green** .80 .50
Entire 1.00 2.00
Entire, 1st day cancel, Virginia Beach, VA *(37,646)* 1.25

A hologram, visible through the die cut window to the right of "USA 29," is affixed to the inside of the envelope. Examples on recycled paper were issued May 1, 1992 and have a "recycled" imprint under the flap. Issued only in No. 10 size. Value $1.25.

U171

Designed by Harry Zelenko.

1992, Apr. 10 Typo. & Litho. *Die Cut*

U626 U171 29c **multicolored** .60 1.00
Entire .70 3.00
Entire, 1st day cancel, Dodge City, KS *(34,258)* 1.25

The lithographed vignette, visible through the die cut window to the right of "USA 29," is affixed to the inside of the envelope. Issued only in the No. 10 size.

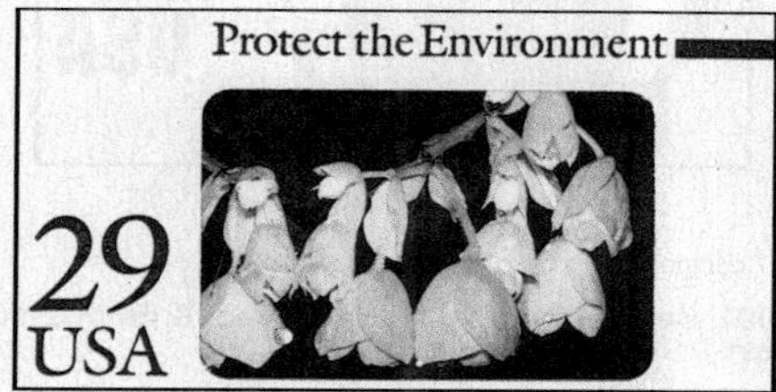

Hillebrandia — U172

Designed by Joseph Brockert. Illustration reduced.

1992, Apr. 22

U627 U172 29c **multicolored** .65 1.00
Entire .75 3.00
Entire, 1st day cancel, Chicago, IL *(29,432)* 1.25

The lithographed vignette, visible through the die cut window to the right of "29 USA," is affixed to the inside of the envelope.

Inscribed "Save the Rain Forests" in the lower left. Issued only in the No. 10 size.

Star — U173

Designed by Joseph Brockert.

1992, May 19 Typo. & Embossed Precanceled
Untagged

U628 U173 19.8c **red & blue** .40
Entire .60 *10.00*
Entire, 1st day cancel, Las Vegas, NV *(18,478)* 1.25

Issued only in No. 10 size.

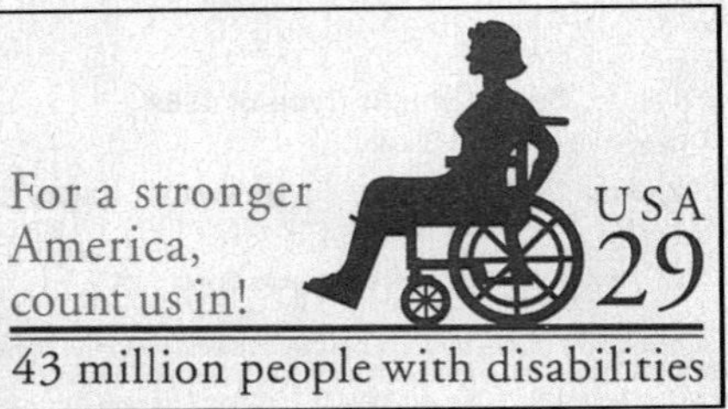

U174

Designed by Richard Sheaff. Illustration reduced.

1992, July 22 Typo.

U629 U174 29c **red & blue** .60 .30
Entire .70 2.00
Entire, 1st day cancel, Washington, DC *(28,218)* 1.25

U175

Designed by Nancy Krause. Illustration reduced.

1993, Oct. 2 Typo. & Litho. *Die Cut*

U630 U175 29c **multicolored** 1.10 1.10
Entire 1.25 3.00
Entire, 1st day cancel, King of Prussia, PA *(6,511)* 1.25

The lithographed vignette, visible through the die cut window to the right of "USA 29," is affixed to the inside of the envelope. Issued only in the No. 10 size.

U176

Designed by Richard Sheaff.

1994, Sept. 17 Typo. & Embossed

U631 U176 29c **brown & black** .70 1.25
Entire .80 3.00
Entire, 1st day cancel, Canton, OH *(28,977)* 1.25
a. Black ("29/USA") omitted, entire *325.00*

Issued only in No. 10 size.

Liberty Bell — U177

Designed by Richard Sheaff.

1995, Jan. 3 Typo. & Embossed

U632 U177 32c **greenish blue & blue** .65 .30
Entire .75 .40
Entire, 1st day cancel, Williamsburg, PA 1.25
a. Greenish blue omitted *100.00*
Entire *400.00*
b. Blue ("USA 32") omitted 90.00
Entire 200.00
c. All colors omitted, entire —

First day cancellation was applied to 54,102 of Nos. U632, UX198.

A colorless embossed design is present on No. U632c.

See No. U638.

Design sizes: 49x38mm (#U633), 53x44mm (U634). Stamp and design continue on back of envelope.

1995 Typo.

U633 U178 (32c) **blue & red** 1.25 2.00
Entire, #6¾ 1.75 3.00
U634 U178 (32c) **blue & red** 1.25 2.00
Entire, #10 1.75 3.00
a. Red & tagging omitted, entire *325.00*
b. Blue omitted, entire *325.00*

Originally, Nos. U633-U634 were only available through the Philatelic Fulfillment Center after their announcement 1/12/95. Envelopes submitted for first day cancels received a 12/13/94 cancel, even though they were not available on that date.

U179

Design size: 58x25mm. Stamp and design continue on back of envelope.

Designed by Douglas Smith.

1995, Mar. 10 Typo.
Precanceled, Untagged

U635 U179 (5c) **green & red brown** .40
Entire .55 1.00
Entire, 1st day cancel, State College, PA 1.25

Graphic Eagle — U180

Designed by Uldis Purins.

1995, Mar. 10 Typo.
Precanceled, Untagged

U636 U180 (10c) **dark carmine & blue** 1.50
Entire .40 *10.00*
Entire, 1st day cancel, State College, PA 1.25

Issued only in No. 10 size.

Spiral Heart — U181

Designed by Uldis Purins.

1995, May 12 Typo.

U637 U181 32c **red,** *light blue* .65 .30
Entire .75 2.00
Entire, 1st day cancel, Lakeville, PA 1.25
a. Red omitted, entire *200.00*

On No. U637a, the red "RECYCLED" and recycling symbol appear on the bottom backflap.

Liberty Bell Type

1995, May 16 Typo.

U638 U177 32c **greenish blue & blue** .70 .30
Entire .80 .35
Entire, 1st day cancel, Washington, DC 1.25
a. Greenish blue omitted, entire *175.00*

No. U638 was printed on security paper and was issued only in No. 9 size.

Space Shuttle Type of 1989

Designed by Richard Sheaff.

1995, Sept. 22 Typo. *Die Cut*

U639 U163 32c **carmine rose** .75 .35
Entire .85 2.00
Entire, 1st day cancel, Milwaukee, WI 1.25

A hologram, visible through the die cut window to the right of "USA 32," is affixed to the inside of the envelope. No. U639 was issued only in No. 10 size.

U182

Designed by Richard Sheaff.

1996, Apr. 20 Typo. & Litho. *Die Cut*

U640 U182 32c **multicolored** .70 .30
Entire .80 2.00
Entire, 1st day cancel, Chicago, IL *(9,921)* 1.25

The lithographed vignette, visible through the die cut window to the right of "USA 32c," is affixed to the inside of the envelope. Issued only in the No. 10 size.

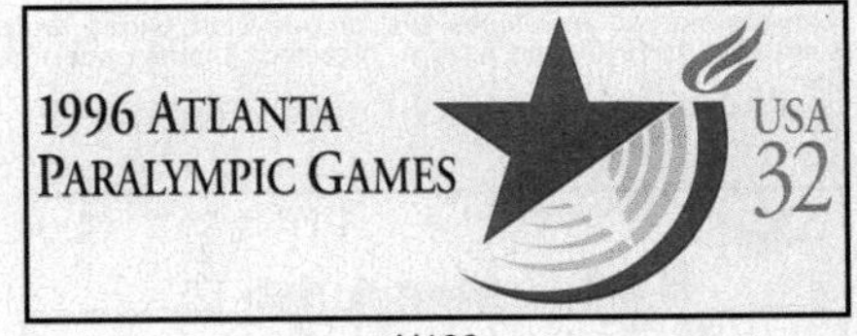

U183

Designed by Brad Copeland. Illustration reduced.

1996, May 2

U641 U183 32c **multicolored** .70 .30
Entire .80 3.00
Entire, 1st day cancel, Washington, DC 1.25
a. Blue & red omitted, entire *260.00*
b. Blue & gold omitted, entire *550.00*

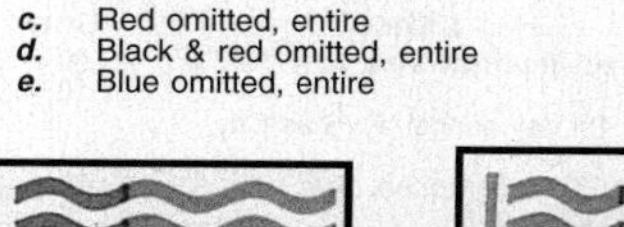

c.	Red omitted, entire	*260.00*
d.	Black & red omitted, entire	*450.00*
e.	Blue omitted, entire	*300.00*

U184

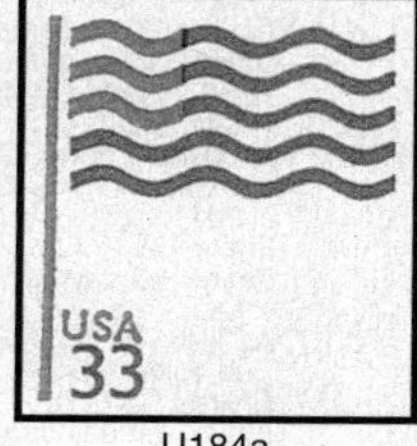

U184a

Designed by Richard Sheaff.

1999, Jan. 11 **Typo. & Embossed**

U642	U184 33c **yellow, blue & red**, tagging bar to left of design	1.00	.30
	Entire	1.50	.40
	Entire, 1st day cancel, Washington, DC		1.25
a.	Tagging bar to right of design	7.50	3.00
	Entire	10.00	5.00
b.	As "a," blue omitted, entire		*200.00*
c.	As "a," yellow omitted, entire	*175.00*	
d.	As "a," yellow and blue omitted, entire	*175.00*	
e.	As "a," blue and red omitted, entire	*175.00*	
f.	As "a," all colors omitted, entire	*175.00*	
g.	As No. U642, red omitted, entire	*450.00*	
h.	As No. U642, yellow and red omitted, entire	—	
i.	As No. U642, blue and red omitted, entire	—	
j.	Tagging omitted	—	

Earliest documented use of No. U642a, 10/12/99.

On No. U642f, the distinctive tagging bar is present. Expertization is required.

1999, Jan. 11 **Typo.**

U643	U184a 33c **blue & red**	1.00	.30
	Entire	1.50	.40
	Entire, 1st day cancel, Washington, DC		1.25
a.	Tagging bar to right of design	10.00	5.00
	Entire	9.00	3.50

Issued only in No. 9 size.

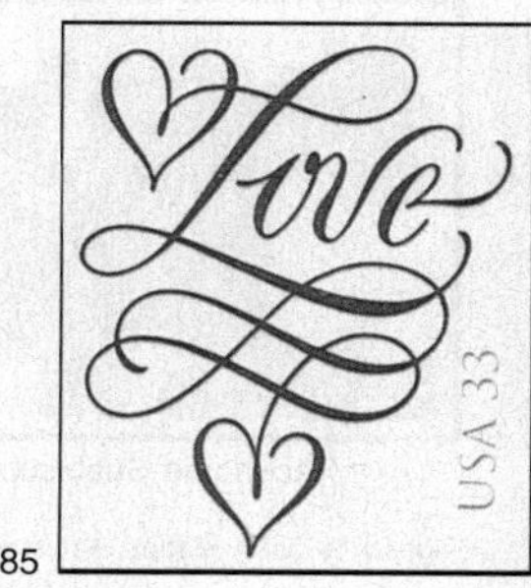

U185

Designed by Julian Waters.

1999, Jan. 28 **Litho.**

U644	U185 33c **violet**	.65	.30
	Entire	.80	2.00
	Entire, 1st day cancel, Loveland, CO		1.25
a.	Tagging bar to right of design	.65	.30
	Entire	.80	.40

Lincoln — U186

Designed by Richard Sheaff.

1999, June 5 **Typo. & Litho.**

U645	U186 33c **blue & black**	.65	.30
	Entire	.80	.40
	Entire, 1st day cancel, Springfield, IL		1.25

Eagle — U187

Designed by Michael Doret.

2001, Jan. 7 **Typo.**

U646	U187 34c **blue gray & gray**	.70	.30
	Entire	.85	.40
	Entire, 1st day cancel, Washington, DC		1.25
a.	Blue gray omitted	175.00	
	Entire	225.00	
b.	Gray omitted	—	

Many color shades known.

All No. U646 were printed on recycled paper. It was also produced using a different blue-gray recycled paper starting in 2002, and valued much higher thus by specialists.

Lovebirds U188

Designed by Robert Brangwynne.

2001, Feb. 14 **Litho.**

U647	U188 34c **rose & dull violet**	.70	.30
	Entire	.85	2.00
	Entire, 1st day cancel, Lovejoy, GA		1.25

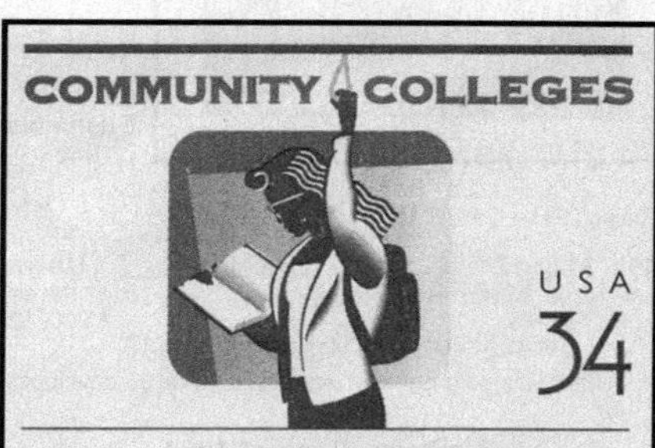

Community Colleges, Cent. — U189

Designed by Howard Paine.

2001, Feb. 20 **Typo.**

U648	U189 34c **dark blue & orange brown**	.70	.30
	Entire	.85	2.00
	Entire, 1st day cancel, Joliet, IL		1.25

Ribbon Star — U190

Designed by Terrence W. McCaffrey.

2002, June 7 **Typo.**

U649	U190 37c **red, blue & gray**	.75	.35
	Entire	.90	.45
	Entire, 1st day cancel, Washington, DC		1.25
	Entire, 1st day cancel, any other city		1.25
a.	Gray omitted, entire		—
b.	Blue and gray omitted, entire		—

All No. U649 were printed on recycled paper. It was also produced using a different blue-gray recycled paper starting in 2002.

Type of 1995 Inscribed "USA / Presorted / Standard"

Designed by Uldis Purins.

2002, Aug. 8 **Typo.** **Untagged**

Precanceled

U650	U180 (10c) **dark carmine & blue**		.25
	Entire	1.25	*30.00*
	Entire, 1st day cancel, Washington, DC		1.25

Issued only in No. 10 size.

Nurturing Love — U191

Designed by Craig Frazier.

2003, Jan. 25 **Typo.**

U651	U191 37c **olive green & yellow orange**	.80	.35
	Entire	.95	3.00
	Entire, 1st day cancel, Tucson, AZ		1.25
a.	Tagging omitted, entire	60.00	

Jefferson Memorial Type

Designed by Derry Noyes.

2003, Dec. 29 **Typo.**

U652	A2818 $3.85 **multicolored**	12.50	6.25
	Entire	17.00	9.00
	Entire, 1st day cancel, Washington, DC		5.75

On No. U652, the stamp indicia is printed on the flap of the envelope.

Disney Type of 2004

Designed by David Pacheco.

2004, June 23 **Letter Sheet** **Litho.**

U653	A2949 37c **multicolored**	2.50	2.25
	Entire	2.50	2.50
	Entire, 1st day cancel, Anaheim, CA		2.50
U654	A2950 37c **multicolored**	2.50	2.25
	Entire	2.50	2.50
	Entire, 1st day cancel, Anaheim, CA		2.50
U655	A2951 37c **multicolored**	2.50	2.25
	Entire	2.50	2.50
	Entire, 1st day cancel, Anaheim, CA		2.50
a.	All color missing on reverse, entire		—
U656	A2952 37c **multicolored**	2.50	2.25
	Entire	2.50	2.50
	Entire, 1st day cancel, Anaheim, CA		2.50
a.	Booklet of 12 letter sheets, 3 each #U653-U656	30.00	

No. U656a sold for $14.95.

White Lilacs and Pink Roses Type of 2004

Designed by Richard Sheaff.

2005, Mar. 3 **Letter Sheet** **Litho.**

U657	A2931 37c **multicolored**	3.00	2.50
	First day cancel, New York, NY		2.50

No. U657 was sold in pads of 12 for $14.95.

Computer-generated Study of an X-Plane — U192

2006, Jan. 5 **Typo.** **Unwmk.**

U658	U192 $4.05 **multicolored**	10.00	9.00
	Entire	12.00	10.00
	Entire, 1st day cancel, Kansas City, MO		6.50

Benjamin Franklin — U193

Designed by Richard Sheaff.

2006, Jan. 9 **Typo.** **Unwmk.**

U659 U193 39c **blue green & black** .80 .40
Entire 1.00 .50
Entire, 1st day cancel, Washington, DC 1.25
Entire, 1st day cancel, any other city 1.25
a. All color omitted, entire —
b. Tagging omitted, entire 45.00

On No. 659a, the tagging bar and the blue green printing on the reverse are present.

Air Force One — U194

Designed by Phil Jordan.

2007, May 6 **Typo.** **Unwmk.**

U660 U194 $4.60 **multicolored** 12.50 10.00
Entire 15.00 12.50
Entire, 1st day cancel, Kansas City, MO 9.25

No. U660 was sold only in packs of 5, 10 or 25 envelopes.

Marine One — U195

Designed by Phil Jordan.

2007, May 6 **Typo.** **Unwmk.**

U661 U195 $16.25 **multicolored** 35.00 20.00
Entire 40.00 30.00
Entire, 1st day cancel, Kansas City, MO 33.00

No. U661 was sold only in packs of three envelopes, with each envelope having a different Star Wars character (Darth Vader, Yoda, or Obi-wan Kenobi) on the back of the envelope. Values for entires are for any envelope back.

Horses — U196

Illustration reduced. Designed by Tom Engeman.

2007, May 12 **Typo.** **Unwmk.**

U662 U196 41c **reddish brown & black** .85 .40
Entire 1.00 2.00
Entire, 1st day cancel, Washington, DC 2.10

Elk U197

Designed by Carl T. Herrman.

2008, May 2 **Typo.** **Unwmk.**

U663 U197 42c **green & black**, tagging bar 20mm tall, Ashton-Potter printing .85 .40
Entire, Ashton-Potter printing 1.00 2.00
Entire, 1st day cancel, Washington, DC 2.10
a. Tagging bar 26mm tall, Westvaco printing .85 .40
Entire, Westvaco printing 1.00 .50
Entire, 1st day cancel, Washington, DC 2.10
b. Tagging bar 19mm tall, *Aug. 16* .85 .40
Entire, Ashton-Potter litho. printing 1.00 .50
Entire, Ashton-Potter litho. printing, 1st day cancel, Hartford, CT 2.10

No. U663 was printed by National Envelope for Ashton-Potter (USA) Ltd. No. U663a was printed by Westvaco. Envelopes printed by Westvaco have copyright and recycled content text, found on the envelope's back, in black. These features are in green on Ashton-Potter envelopes. All Westvaco envelopes have pointed flaps, while the Ashton-Potter envelopes have flaps with curved ends.

No. U663b was printed by Ashton-Potter (USA) Ltd. The lithographed impressions of No. U663b are slightly sharper (some tree branches are slightly thinner and more distinct) than the typographed impressions on Nos. U663 and U663a, but because of the nature of the design are nonetheless difficult to distinguish without measuring the tagging bar. Entires of No. U663b have the recycling emblem on the back of the envelope at the right side of the paper content statement. On No. U663 the recycling emblem is in the lower left corner.

Mount Rushmore U198

Designed by Carl T. Herrman.

2008, May 12 **Typo.** **Unwmk.**

U664 U198 $4.80 **multicolored** 12.50 10.00
Entire 15.00 12.50
Entire, 1st day cancel, Kansas City, MO 9.75

No. U664 was sold only in packs of 5, 10 or 25 envelopes.

Sunflower Type of 2008

Designed by Derry Noyes.

Letter Sheet

2008, Aug. 15 **Litho.** **Unwmk.**

U665 A3309 42c **multicolored** 4.00 3.00
Entire, 1st day cancel, Hartford, CT 4.25

No. U665 was sold in packs of 10 for $14.95.

Redwood Forest Type of 2009

Designed by Carl T. Herrman.

2009, Jan. 16 **Typo.** **Unwmk.**

U666 A3332 $4.95 **multicolored** 10.00 7.50
Entire 10.00 7.50
Entire, 1st day cancel, Kansas City, MO 10.00

No. U666 was sold only in packs of 5.

Liberty Bell U199

Designed by Terrence W. McCaffrey.

2009-11 **Litho.** **Unwmk.**

U667 U199 (44c) **multicolored,** *May 11* .90 .90
Entire 1.10 2.00
Entire, 1st day cancel, Kansas City, MO 2.40
a. As #U667, typographed, *Aug. 18* .90 .45
Typographed, entire 1.10 .55
#U667a, entire, 1st day cancel, Kansas City, MO 2.40
b. As #U667, dated "2011," "FOREVER" multicolored (with color dots), *Jan. 3, 2011* .90 .90
Entire 1.10 1.10
Entire, 1st day cancel, Kansas City, MO 2.40
c. As #U667b, "FOREVER" in brown (solid color), *Jan. 3, 2011* .90 .90
Entire 1.10 1.10
Entire, 1st day cancel, Kansas City, MO 2.40

No. U667 had a franking value of 44c on the day of issue and will be valid for the one ounce first class postage rate after any new rates go into effect. The envelope was created primarily for customers desiring a printed return address on the envelope, and was not sold individually. Water-activated gum envelopes sold in boxes of 50 for $26.80 and boxes of 500 for $247. Self-adhesive envelopes sold in boxes of 50 for $31.80 and boxes of 500 for $262. A pack of 18 envelopes containing one example of each of the twelve different envelope styles of No. U667 and the six different self-adhesive envelope styles of No. U668 was sold for the convenience of collectors for $10.92. A similar package was sold in 2010, having examples of Nos. U667 and U668 with a "Cradle to Cradle" recycling emblem added on the backs fo the envelopes.

No. U667a was printed by National Envelope. The size of black dots on No. U667a are much larger than on No. U667, which is most noticeable on the bell fastenings. This also makes the appearance of the bell on No. U667a far grainier than No. U667. The text on the bell, particularly the Roman numeral date, is indistinct and difficult to read even under magnification on No. U667a, but sharper and easier to read on No. U667. The horizontal wood grain lines are distinct on the bell stock on No. U667, but No. U667a has no fine detail of the grain lines.

The typographed version (No. U667a) can also be distinguished from No. U667 by the position of the recycle logo on the back. On the litho. version it is to the right of the recycle text; on the typo. version it is to the left of the text.

Nos. U667 and U667a are dated "2009." The year date is found on the crown of the bell between the fastenings. No. U667b is available in No. 10 window and both regular and window No. 9 (security) and No. 6¾ envelope sizes. No. U667c is only found in the No. 10 regular envelope size only.

Nos. U667b and U667c were reprinted in June 2012 in the No. 10 size without the 'Cradle to Cradle' recycling logo on the back.

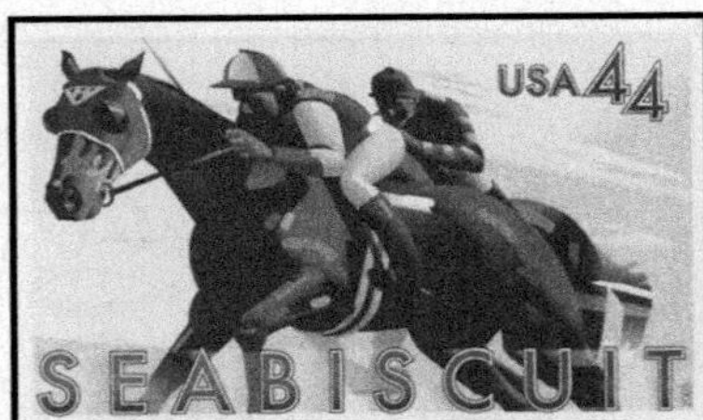

Racehorse Seabiscuit — U200

Designed by John Mattos. Printed by Ashton-Potter (USA) Ltd.

2009, May 11 **Litho.** **Unwmk.**

U668 U200 44c **multicolored** .90 .45
Entire 1.10 1.50
Entire, 1st day cancel, Kansas City, MO 2.40
a. As No. U668, typographed, *June 1* .90 .45
Typographed, entire 1.10 .55
Entire, 1st day cancel, Kansas City, MO 2.40
b. As No. U668, triple impression of black, entire —

No. U668 self-adhesive flap envelopes were not sold individually, but were sold in boxes and packs like No. U667.

No. U668a was printed by National Envelope. The screened blue dots cover the entire area between the "S" and the "C" on No. U668, but appear more random on No. U668a. The pattern of blue dots running towards the shoulder under the head and neck of the horse is long and distinct on No. U668, but barely noticeable, with only a few dots showing, on No. U668a.

See note under No. U667. The third paragraph of that note also applies to Nos. U668 and U668a.

Gulf Coast Lighthouses Type of 2009

Designed by Howard E. Paine.

2009, July 23 **Litho.**

U669 A3354 44c **multicolored** 3.25 3.00
Entire 3.25 3.25
Entire, 1st day cancel, Biloxi, MS 4.25
U670 A3355 44c **multicolored** 3.25 3.00
Entire 3.25 3.25
Entire, 1st day cancel, Biloxi, MS 4.25
U671 A3356 44c **multicolored** 3.25 3.00
Entire 3.25 3.25
Entire, 1st day cancel, Biloxi, MS 4.25
U672 A3357 44c **multicolored** 3.25 3.00
Entire 3.25 3.25
Entire, 1st day cancel, Biloxi, MS 4.25

U673 A3358 44c **multicolored** 3.25 3.00
Entire 3.25 3.25
Entire, 1st day cancel, Biloxi, MS 4.25
Nos. U669-U673 (5) 16.25 15.00

Pack of ten, containing two of each letter sheet, sold for $15.95.

Mackinac Bridge U201

Designed by Carl T. Herrman.

2010, Jan. 4 Typo. Unwmk.
U674 U201 $4.90 **multicolored** 12.50 10.00
Entire 15.00 12.50
Entire, first day cancel, Kansas City, MO 10.00

No. U674 was sold only in packs of 5.

New River Gorge Bridge, West Virginia U202

Designed by Carl T. Herrman.

2011, Jan. 3 Typo. Unwmk.
U675 U202 $4.95 **multicolored** 12.50 10.00
Entire 15.00 12.50
Entire, first day cancel, Kansas City, MO 10.00

No. U675 was sold only in packs of 5.

Sunshine Skyway Bridge, Florida U203

Designed by Carl T. Hermann.

2012, Jan. 3 Typo. Unwmk.
U676 U203 $5.15 **multicolored** 12.50 10.00
Entire 15.00 12.50
Entire, first day cancel, Liberty, MO 10.50

No. U676 was sold only in packs of 5.

Purple Martin U204

Designed by William J. Gicker.

2012, Jan. 23 Litho. Unwmk.

Design Size: 48x33mm

U677 U204 (45c) **multicolored** .95 .50
Entire 1.10 .55
Entire, first day cancel, Mulberry, FL 2.40

Design Size: 50x35mm

U678 U204 (45c) **multicolored** .95 .50
Entire 1.10 .55
Entire, first day cancel, Mulberry, FL 2.40

No. U677 was from No. 6¾ size envelopes only. No. U678 was from No. 9 and No. 10 size envelopes.

No. U678 was reprinted in June 2012 without the 'Cradle to Cradle' recycling logo on the back.

Arlington Green Bridge Type of 2013

Designed by Derry Noyes.

2013, Jan. 25 Typo. Unwmk.
U679 A3612 $5.60 **multicolored** 11.00 8.00
Entire 11.00 7.50
Entire, first day cancel, Norcross, GA 11.00

No. U679 was sold only in packs of 5.

Bank Swallows U205

Designed by William J. Gicker.

2013, Mar. 1 Litho. Unwmk.

Design Size: 38x35mm

U680 U205 (46c) **multicolored** .95 .50
Entire 1.25 2.00
Entire, first day cancel, Sacramento, CA 2.40

Design Size: 41x38mm

U681 U205 (46c) **multicolored** .95 .50
Entire 1.25 .60
Entire, first day cancel, Sacramento, CA 2.40

No. U680 is from No. 6¾ size envelopes only. No. U681 is from No. 9 and No. 10 size envelopes.

Eagle, Shield and Flags — U206

Designed by Richard Sheaff.

2013, Aug. 9 Litho. Unwmk.
U682 U206 (46c) **multicolored** .95 .50
Entire 1.25 2.00
Entire, first day cancel, Milwaukee, WI 2.40
a. Double impression of magenta, entire —
b. Triple impression of light blue, entire —

Verrazano-Narrows Bridge Type of 2014

Designed by Phil Jordan.

2014, Mar. 4 Typo. Unwmk.
U683 A3726 $5.60 **multicolored** 12.50 8.00
Entire 15.00 8.00
Entire, first day cancel, Brooklyn, NY 11.00

No. U683 was sold only in packs of 5, 10 or 25.

Poinsettia — U207

Snowflake — U208

Snowflake — U209

Cardinal — U210

Child Making Snowman — U211

Designed by Ethel Kessler (Nos. U684, U687, U688), Jennifer Arnold (Nos. U685, U686).

2014, Oct. 1 Litho. Unwmk.
U684 U207 (49c) **multicolored** 2.00 1.50
Entire 2.00 1.50
Entire, first day cancel, Washington, DC 2.25
U685 U208 (49c) **multicolored** 2.00 1.50
Entire 2.00 1.50
Entire, first day cancel, Washington, DC 2.25
U686 U209 (49c) **multicolored** 2.00 1.50
Entire 2.00 1.50
Entire, first day cancel, Washington, DC 2.25
U687 U210 (49c) **multicolored** 2.00 1.50
Entire 2.00 1.50
Entire, first day cancel, Washington, DC 2.25
U688 U211 (49c) **multicolored** 2.00 1.50
Entire 2.00 1.50
Entire, first day cancel, Washington, DC 2.25
Nos. U684-U688 (5) 10.00 7.50

Packs of 10 No. U684 and 10 self-adhesive stickers sold for $9.95. Packs containing 5 each of Nos. U685 and U686 and 10 self-adhesive stickers sold for $9.95. Packs containing 5 each of Nos. U687 and U688 and 10 self-adhesive stickers sold for $9.95. Nos. U684-U688 were available only as No. 10 size envelopes.

Glade Creek Grist Mill Type of 2014

Designed by Derry Noyes.

2015, Jan. 12 **Typo.** **Unwmk.**

U689	A3780 $5.75 **multicolored**	11.50	8.25
	Entire	11.50	8.25
	Entire, first day cancel, Kansas City, MO		11.50

No. U689 was sold only in packs of 5.

Red Water Lily — U212

White Water Lily — U213

Designed by Phil Jordan.

2015, Apr. 17 **Litho.** **Unwmk.**

U690	U212 (49c) **multicolored**	2.00	1.75
	Entire	2.00	2.00
	Entire, first day cancel, New York, NY		3.25
U691	U213 (49c) **multicolored**	2.00	1.75
	Entire	2.00	2.00
	Entire, first day cancel, New York, NY		3.25

Nos. U690 and U691 were only sold in packets of 10 containing five of each envelope and 10 stickers for $9.95. Nos. U690 and U691 were only available in #10 size with self-adhesive flap.

Forget-me-nots — U214

Designed by Ethel Kessler.

2015, May 18 **Litho.** **Unwmk.**

U692	U214 (49c) **multicolored**	2.00	1.75
	Entire	2.00	2.00
	Entire, first day cancel, Anaheim, CA		3.25

No. U692 was sold only in packets of 10 + 10 stickers for $9.95. It was only available in #10 size with self-adhesive flap.

La Cueva del Indio Type of 2016

Designed by Greg Breeding.

2016, Jan. 17 **Typo.** **Unwmk.**

U693	A3875 $6.45 **multicolored**	13.00	9.50
	Entire	13.00	9.50
	Entire, first day cancel, Washington, DC		13.00

No. U693 was sold only in packs of 5.

Northern Cardinal U215

Designed by Derry Noyes.

2016, Nov. 3 **Litho.** **Unwmk.**

U694	U215 (47c) **multicolored**	1.75	1.75
	Entire	2.00	2.00

No. U694 was sold only in packets of 12 + 12 stickers for $9.95. It was only available in #10 size with self-adhesive flap. Packets of No. U694 were sold in post offices in Ohio and Puerto Rico (and perhaps elsewhere) in late December, prior to the acknowledgment of the existence of the envelope by USPS Stamp Services. The packets were not offered for sale by USPS Stamp Fulfillment Services until Jan. 4, 2017. In late January, the packet was made available for direct order on the USPS Stamp Fulfillment Services website, which then noted that the day of issue was Jan. 8, 2017, even though the packets could be ordered on Jan. 4. The official first day of issue was announced as Nov. 3, 2016 in the Feb. 16, 2017 *Postal Bulletin,* but no indication was given that any first day cancels would be made available for this issue. The earliest documented use is postmarked Jan. 3, 2017.

Lili'uokalani Gardens Type of 2017

Designed by Greg Breeding.

2017, Jan. 22 **Typo.** **Unwmk.**

U695	A3986 $6.65 **multicolored**	13.50	9.75
	Entire	13.50	9.75
	Entire, first day cancel, Kansas City, MO		13.50

No. U695 was sold only in packs of 5.

Barn Swallows — U216

Designed by William J. Gicker.

2017, Mar. 3 **Litho.** **Unwmk.**

U696	U216 (49c) **multicolored**	1.25	.50
	Entire	1.25	.60
	Entire, first day cancel, Reno, NV		2.50

Byodo-In Temple Type of 2018

Designed by Greg Breeding.

2018, Jan. 21 **Typo.** **Unwmk.**

U697	A4096 $6.70 **multicolored**	13.50	9.75
	Entire	13.50	9.75
	Entire, first day cancel, Kansas City, MO		13.50

No. U697 was sold only in packs of 5.

Joshua Tree Type of 2019

Designed by Greg Breeding.

2019, Jan. 27 **Typo.** **Unwmk.**

U698	A4191 $7.35 **multicolored**	15.00	10.00
	Entire	15.00	10.00
	Entire, first day cancel, Kansas City, MO		15.00

No. U698 was sold only in packs of 5 or 10.

AIR POST STAMPED ENVELOPES AND AIR LETTER SHEETS

All envelopes have carmine and blue borders, unless noted. There are seven types of borders:

Carmine Diamond in Upper Right Corner.

a — Diamonds measure 9 to 10mm paralled to edge of envelope and 11 to 12mm along oblique side (with top flap open). Sizes 5 and 13 only.

b — Like "a" except diamonds measure 7 to 8mm along oblique side (with top flap open). Sizes 5 and 13 only.

c — Diamonds measure 11 to 12mm parallel to edge of envelope. Size 8 only.

Blue Diamond in Upper Right Corner.

d — Lower points of top row of diamonds point to left. Size 8 only.

e — Lower points of top row of diamonds point to right. Size 8 only.

Diamonds Omitted in Upper Right Corner (1965 Onward)

f — Blue diamond above at left of stamp.

g — Red diamond above at left of stamp.

UC1

5c — Vertical rudder is not semi-circular but slopes down to the left. The tail of the plane projects into the G of POSTAGE. Border types a, b, c, d and e.

UC2

Die 2 (5c and 8c): Vertical rudder is semi-circular. The tail of the plane touches but does not project into the G of POSTAGE. Border types b, d, and e for the 5c; b and d for the 8c.

Die 2 (6c) — Same as UC2 except three types of numeral.

2a — The numeral "6" is 6½mm wide.

2b — The numeral "6" is 6mm wide.

2c — The numeral "6" is 5½mm wide.

Eleven working dies were used in printing the 6c. On each, the numeral "6" was engraved by hand, producing several variations in position, size and thickness.

Nos. UC1 and UC2 occur with varying size blue blobs, caused by a shallow printing die. They are not constant.

Border types b and d for dies 2a and 2b; also without border (June 1944 to Sept. 1945) for dies 2a, 2b and 2c.

Die 3 (6c): Vertical rudder leans forward. S closer to O than to T of POSTAGE. E of POSTAGE has short center bar. Border types b and d, also without border.

No. UC1 with 1933 and 1937 watermarks and No. UC2 with 1933 watermark were issued in Puerto Rico.

No. UC1 in blue black, with 1925 watermark #26 and border type a, is a proof.

1929-44

UC1	UC1 5c **blue,** *Jan. 12, 1929*	3.00	2.00
	Entire, border a or b	4.50	2.25
	Entire, border c, d or e	8.25	5.75
	First day cancel, border a, entire		40.00
	1933 wmk. #33, border d, entire	*750.00*	*750.00*
	1933 wmk. #33, border b, entire	—	—
	1937 wmk. #36, border d, entire	—	*2,500.*
	1937 wmk. #36, border b, entire	—	—
	Bicolored border omitted, entire	1,200.	
a.	Orange and blue border, type b	375.00	*450.00*
UC2	UC2 5c **blue,** die 2	9.00	5.00
	Entire, border b	12.00	6.50
	Entire, border e	18.00	12.50
	1929 wmk. #28, border d, entire	—	*1,500.*
	1933 wmk. #33, border b, entire	*650.00*	—
	1933 wmk. #33, border d, entire	325.00	—
UC3	UC2 6c **orange,** die 2a, *July 1, 1934*	1.25	.40
	Entire, bicolored border	1.50	.60
	Entire, without border	2.25	1.25
	Entire, 1st day cancel		14.00
a.	With added impression of 3c purple (#U436a), entire without border	*4,000.*	
b.	Double impression of indicium, entire, with bicolored border	—	
UC4	UC2 6c **orange,** die 2b ('42)	3.00	2.00
	Entire, without border	4.50	2.50
	Entire, bicolored border, 1941 wmk. #39	60.00	22.00
UC5	UC2 6c **orange,** die 2c ('44)	.70	.30
	Entire, without border	.95	.45
UC6	UC2 6c **orange,** die 3 ('42)	1.00	.35
	Entire, bicolored border	1.50	.75
	Entire, without border	2.50	.90
	Entire, carmine of border omitted	*4,000.*	
a.	6c orange, *blue,* die 3 (error) Entire, without border	*15,000.*	*10,000.*
b.	Double impression, entire	*400.00*	
UC7	UC2 8c **olive green,** die 2, *Sept. 26, 1932*	10.00	3.50
	Entire, bicolored border	15.00	15.00
	Entire, 1st day cancel		11.00

Surcharged in Black on Envelopes Indicated by Number in Parenthesis

1945

UC8	U93 6c on 2c **carmine** (U429, die 1)	1.25	.65
	Entire	1.60	1.00
a.	On U429f, die 7	2.25	1.50
	Entire	3.00	2.00
b.	On U429g, die 8	1.90	1.10
	Entire	3.00	1.75
c.	On U429h, die 9	8.00	7.50
	Entire	15.00	11.00
d.	6c on 1c green (error) (U420)	*1,750.*	
	Entire	*2,500.*	
e.	6c on 3c dk violet (error) (U436a)	*2,000.*	
	Entire	*4,000.*	
f.	6c on 3c dk violet (error), *amber* (U437a)	*3,000.*	
	Entire	*3,500.*	
g.	6c on 3c violet (error) (U526)	*3,000.*	
	Entire	*6,500.*	
UC9	U95 6c on 2c **carmine** (U525)	40.00	35.00
	Entire	80.00	45.00

Ten surcharge varieties are found on Nos. UC8-UC9.

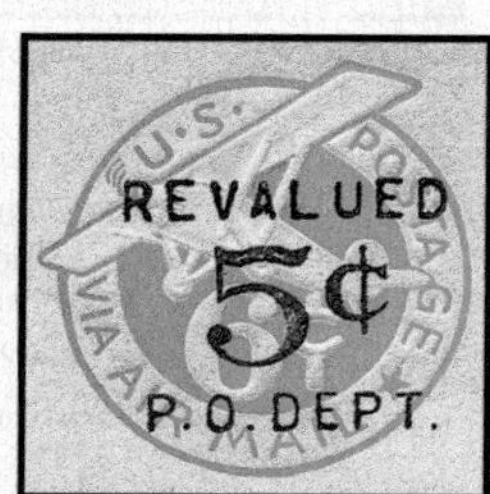

Surcharged in Black on 6c Air Post Envelopes without borders

1946

UC10	UC2 5c on 6c **orange,** die 2a	2.75	1.50
	Entire	5.50	2.50
	First day of rate, *Oct. 1, 1946,* entire		100.00
a.	Double surcharge	75.00	
UC11	UC2 5c on 6c **orange,** die 2b	8.00	5.50
	Entire	11.00	7.00
	First day of rate, *Oct. 1, 1946,* entire		150.00
UC12	UC2 5c on 6c **orange,** die 2c	.75	.50
	Entire	1.25	.60
	First day of rate, *Oct. 1, 1946,* entire		75.00
a.	Double surcharge	75.00	*900.00*
UC13	UC2 5c on 6c **orange,** die 3	.70	.60
	Entire	.90	.75
	First day of rate, *Oct. 1, 1946,* entire		75.00
a.	Double surcharge	75.00	50.00
c.	Double surcharge, one on reverse	—	
UC13B	U93 5c on 6c (UC8a), entire	—	
	First day of rate, *Oct. 1, 1946,* entire		—

The 6c borderless envelopes and the revalued envelopes were issued primarily for use to and from members of the armed forces. The 5c rate came into effect Oct. 1, 1946.

Ten surcharge varieties are found on Nos. UC10-UC13.

DC-4 Skymaster UC3

Envelopes with borders types b and d.

Die 1 — The end of the wing at the right is a smooth curve. The juncture of the front end of the plane and the engine forms an acute angle. The first T of STATES and the E's of UNITED STATES lean to the left.

Die 2 — The end of the wing at the right is a straight line. The juncture of the front end of the plane and the engine is wide open. The first T of STATES and the E's of UNITED STATES lean to the right.

1946

UC14	UC3 5c **carmine,** die 1, *Sept. 25, 1946*	.75	.25
	Entire, bicolored border	1.00	.40
	Entire, 1st day cancel		1.50
	Entire, bicolored border omitted	*2,500.*	
UC15	UC3 5c **carmine,** die 2	.75	.25
	Entire, bicolored border	1.00	.40

No. UC14, printed on flat bed press, measures 21½mm high. No. UC15, printed on rotary press, measures 22mm high. See No. UC18.

DC-4 Skymaster — UC4

1947-55 **Typographed, Without Embossing**

Letter Sheets for Foreign Postage

UC16	UC4 10c **bright red,** *pale blue,* "Air Letter" on face, 2-line inscription on back, entire	8.50	7.00
	Entire, 1st day cancel, *Apr. 29, 1947*		2.00
	Die cutting reversed, unfolded entire	150.00	
e.	Blue omitted, entire	400.00	
f.	Overlay omitted front & back, entire	*100.00*	
g.	Overlay omitted from front only, entire	*500.00*	
UC16a	UC4 10c **bright red,** *pale blue, Sept. 1951,* "Air Letter" on face, 4-line inscription on back, entire	17.50	10.00
	Die cutting reversed, entire	400.00	
b.	10c **chocolate,** *pale blue,* entire	450.00	
UC16c	UC4 10c **bright red,** *pale blue, Nov. 1953,* "Air Letter" and "Aerogramme" on face, 4-line inscription on back, entire	45.00	12.50
	Die cutting reversed, entire	150.00	
UC16d	UC4 10c **bright red,** *pale blue, 1955,* "Air Letter" and "Aerogramme" on face, 3-line inscription on back, entire	9.00	8.00
	Die cutting reversed, entire	100.00	
	Dark blue (inscriptions & border diamonds) omitted	*2,000.*	
	Die cutting omitted, folded entire	*90.00*	

Printed on protective tinted paper containing colorless inscription.

UNITED STATES FOREIGN AIR MAIL multiple, repeated in parallel vertical or horizontal lines.

Postage Stamp Centenary Issue

Centenary of the first postage stamps issued by the United States Government.

Washington and Franklin, Early and Modern Mail-carrying Methods — UC5

Two dies: Rotary, design measures 22¼mm high; and flat bed press, design 21¾mm high.

1947, May 21 **Embossed**

For Domestic Postage

UC17	UC5 5c **carmine** (rotary)	.50	.30
	Entire, bicolored border b	.60	.40
	Entire, 1st day cancel, NY, NY		1.75
a.	Flat plate printing	.50	.30
	Entire	.60	.40
	Entire, 1st day cancel, NY, NY		1.25

Type of 1946

Type I: 6's lean to right.
Type II: 6's upright.

1950 , Sept. 22

UC18	UC3 6c **carmine,** type I	.75	.25
	Entire, bicolored border	.85	.30
	Entire, 1st day cancel, Philadelphia		1.00
a.	Type II	.90	.25
	Entire	1.20	.30

Several other types differ slightly from the two listed.

Nos. UC14, UC15, UC18 Surcharged in Red Left of Stamp

1951

UC19	UC3 6c on 5c **carmine,** die 1	.85	1.50
	Entire	1.25	*1.75*
a.	Surcharge inverted at lower left, entire		—
UC20	UC3 6c on 5c **carmine,** die 2	.85	1.50
	Entire	1.25	1.75
a.	6c on 6c **carmine** (error) entire	*1,500.*	
b.	Double surcharge	*975.00*	—

To qualify as No. UC20b, both surcharges must be to the left of the indicia.

Nos. UC14-UC15 Surcharged in Red at Left of Stamp

1952

UC21	UC3 6c on 5c **carmine,** die 1	25.00	20.00
	Entire	35.00	25.00
a.	Double surcharge, entire	*600.00*	
UC22	UC3 6c on 5c **carmine,** die 2, *Aug. 29, 1952*	3.75	2.50
	Entire	9.00	4.25
	Entire, 1st day cancel, Norfolk, Va.		25.00
a.	Double surcharge	250.00	
b.	Triple surcharge, entire	275.00	

To qualify as Nos. UC22a or UC22b, all surcharges must be to the left of the indicia.

No. UC17 Surcharged in Red

UC23	UC5 6c on 5c **carmine**	*850.*	
	Entire	*1,250.*	

The 6c on 4c black (No. U440) is believed to be a favor printing.

Fifth International Philatelic Exhibition Issue

FIPEX, the Fifth International Philatelic Exhibition, New York, N.Y., Apr. 28-May 6, 1956.

Eagle in Flight — UC6

1956, May 2

UC25	UC6 6c **red**	.75	.50
	Entire	1.00	.80
	Entire, 1st day cancel, New York, N.Y. *(363,239)*		1.25

Two types exist, differing slightly in the clouds at top.

Skymaster Type of 1946

1958, July 31

UC26	UC3 7c **blue**	.65	.50
	Entire	1.00	.55
	Entire, 1st day cancel, Dayton, O. *(143,428)*		1.00

Nos. UC3-UC5, UC18 and UC25 Surcharged in Green at Left of Stamp

1958

UC27 UC2 6c + 1c **orange,** die 2a 250.00 *300.00*
Entire, without border 350.00 *600.00*
Entire, with border 8,000.
UC28 UC2 6c + 1c **orange,** die 2b 65.00 80.00
Entire, without border 100.00 *250.00*
UC29 UC2 6c + 1c **orange,** die 2c 30.00 55.00
Entire 45.00 *110.00*
UC30 UC3 6c + 1c **carmine,** type I 1.00 .50
Entire 1.25 .65
a. Type II 1.00 .50
Entire 1.25 .65
UC31 UC6 6c + 1c **red** 1.00 .50
Entire 1.40 .85

Jet Airliner — UC7

Type I: Back inscription in 3 lines.
Type II: Back inscription in 2 lines.

Letter Sheet for Foreign Postage

1958-59 Typographed, Without Embossing

UC32 UC7 10c **blue & red,** *blue,* II, *May, 1959,* entire 6.00 5.00
b. Red omitted, II, entire *625.00*
c. Blue omitted, II, entire *600.00*
UC32a UC7 10c **blue & red,** *blue,* I, *Sept. 12, 1958,* entire 10.00 5.00
Entire, 1st day cancel, St. Louis, Mo. *(92,400)* 1.25
Die cutting reversed, entire 75.00
d. Red omitted, I, entire *700.00*

Silhouette of Jet Airliner — UC8

1958, Nov. 21 Embossed

UC33 UC8 7c **blue** .60 .25
Entire .70 .30
Entire, 1st day cancel, New York, N.Y. *(208,980)* 1.00

1960, Aug. 18

UC34 UC8 7c **carmine** .60 .25
Entire .70 .30
Entire, 1st day cancel, Portland, Ore. *(196,851)* 1.00

Jet Airliner and Globe — UC9

Letter Sheet for Foreign Postage

Typographed, Without Embossing

1961, June 16

UC35 UC9 11c **red & blue,** *blue,* entire 3.00 3.50
Entire, 1st day cancel, Johnstown, Pa. *(163,460)* 1.00
Die cutting reversed, entire 35.00
a. Red omitted, entire *750.00*
b. Blue omitted, entire *950.00*

Jet Airliner — UC10

1962, Nov. 17 Embossed

UC36 UC10 8c **red** .55 .25
Entire .75 .30
Entire, 1st day cancel, Chantilly, Va. *(194,810)* 1.00

Jet Airliner — UC11

1965-67

UC37 UC11 8c **red,** *Jan. 7* .45 .25
Entire, border "f" .60 .30
Entire, border "g" *22.50*
Entire, 1st day cancel, Chicago, Ill. *(226,178)* 1.00
a. Tagged, *Aug. 15, 1967* 3.50 .30
Entire 6.00 .75
Tagged, 1st day cancel 3.50

No. UC37a has a 8x24mm panel at left of stamp that glows orange red under ultraviolet light.

Pres. John F. Kennedy and Jet Plane UC12

Letter Sheets for Foreign Postage

Typographed, Without Embossing

1965, May 29

UC38 UC12 11c **red & dark blue,** *blue,* entire 3.75 4.00
Entire, 1st day cancel, Boston, Mass. *(337,422)* 1.50
Die cutting reversed, entire 40.00

1967, May 29

UC39 UC12 13c **red & dark blue,** *blue,* entire 3.25 4.00
Entire, 1st day cancel, Chicago, Ill. *(211,387)* 1.50
Die cutting reversed, entire *100.00*
a. Red omitted, entire *600.00*
b. Dark blue omitted, entire *500.00*

Jet Liner — UC13

Designed by Robert J. Jones.

1968, Jan. 8 Tagged Embossed

UC40 UC13 10c **red** .50 .25
Entire .80 .25
Entire, 1st day cancel, Chicago, Ill. *(157,553)* 1.00

No. UC37 Surcharged in Red at Left of Stamp

1968, Feb. 5

UC41 UC11 8c + 2c **red** .65 .25
Entire 1.00 .50
Entire, 1st day cancel, Washington, D.C. 8.00

Tagging

Envelopes and Letter Sheets from No. UC42 onward are tagged unless otherwise noted.

Human Rights Year Issue

Issued for International Human Rights Year, and to commemorate the 20th anniversary of the United Nations' Declaration of Human Rights.

Globes and Flock of Birds — UC14

Printed by Acrovure Division of Union-Camp Corporation, Englewood, N.J. Designed by Antonio Frasconi.

Letter Sheet for Foreign Postage

1968, Dec. 3 Tagged Photo.

UC42 UC14 13c **gray, brown, orange & black,** *blue,* entire 8.00 7.50
Entire, 1st day cancel, Washington, D.C. *(145,898)* 1.25
Die cutting reversed, entire 75.00
a. Orange omitted, entire *800.00*
b. Brown omitted, entire *375.00*
c. Black omitted, entire *700.00*
d. Gray and black omitted, entire —
e. Tagging omitted, entire 50.00

No. UC42 has a luminescent panel ⅜x1 inch on the right globe. The panel glows orange red under ultraviolet light.

Jet Plane — UC15

Printed by United States Envelope Co., Williamsburg, Pa. Designed by Robert Geissmann.

1971, May 6 Embossed (Plane)

Center Circle Luminescent

UC43 UC15 11c **red & blue** .50 *1.75*
Entire .75 *2.00*
Entire, 1st day cancel, Williamsburg, Pa. *(187,000)* 1.00

Birds in Flight — UC16

Printed by Bureau of Engraving and Printing. Designed by Soren Noring.

Letter Sheet for Foreign Postage

1971 Tagged Photo.

UC44 UC16 15c **gray, red, white & blue,** *blue,* entire, *May 28* 1.50 *7.50*
Entire, 1st day cancel, Chicago, Ill. *(130,669)* 1.25
Die cutting reversed, entire 30.00
a. "AEROGRAMME" added to inscription, entire, *Dec. 13* 1.50 *7.50*
Entire, 1st day cancel, Philadelphia, Pa. 1.25

Die cutting reversed, entire 30.00
b. As #UC44, red omitted, entire *300.00*
c. As "a," red omitted, entire —

Folding instructions (2 steps) in capitals on No. C44; (4 steps) in upper and lower case on No. UC44a.
On Nos. UC44-UC44a the white rhomboid background of "USA postage 15c" is luminescent. No. UC44 is inscribed: "VIA AIR MAIL-PAR AVION". "postage 15c" is in gray. See No. UC46.

No. UC40 Surcharged in Green at Left of Stamp

1971, June 28 **Embossed**
UC45 UC13 10c + (1c) **red** 1.50 .75
Entire 2.50 *5.00*
Entire, 1st day cancel, Washington, D.C. 8.00

HOT AIR BALLOONING CHAMPIONSHIPS ISSUE

Hot Air Ballooning World Championships, Albuquerque, N.M., Feb. 10-17, 1973.

"usa" Type of 1971

Design: Three balloons and cloud at left in address section; no birds beside stamp. Inscribed "INTERNATIONAL HOT AIR BALLOONING." "postage 15c" in blue.
Printed by Bureau of Engraving and Printing. Designed by Soren Noring (vignette) and Esther Porter (balloons).

Letter Sheet for Foreign Postage

1973, Feb. 10 **Tagged** **Photo.**
UC46 UC16 15c **red, white & blue,** *blue,* entire 1.00 *7.50*
Entire, 1st day cancel, Albuquerque, N.M. *(210,000)* 1.00

Folding instructions as on No. UC44a. See notes after No. UC44.

Bird in Flight — UC17

1973, Dec. 1 **Luminescent Ink**
UC47 UC17 13c **rose red** .30 .25
Entire .40 .25
Entire, 1st day cancel, Memphis, Tenn. *(132,658)* 1.00

Beginning with No. UC48, all listings are letter sheets for foreign postage.

UC18

Printed by the Bureau of Engraving and Printing. Designed by Bill Hyde.

Letter Sheet for Foreign Postage.

1974, Jan. 4 **Tagged** **Photo.**
UC48 UC18 18c **red & blue,** *blue,* entire 1.00 *6.00*
Entire, 1st day cancel, Atlanta, Ga. *(119,615)* 1.00
Die cutting reversed, entire *40.00*
a. Red omitted, entire *200.00*

25TH ANNIVERSARY OF NATO ISSUE

UC19

Design: "NATO" and NATO emblem at left in address section.
Printed by Bureau of Engraving and Printing. Designed by Soren Noring.

Letter Sheet for Foreign Postage

1974, Apr. 4 **Tagged** **Photo.**
UC49 UC19 18c **red & blue,** *blue,* entire 1.00 *6.00*
Entire, 1st day cancel, Washington, D.C. 1.00
Die cutting reversed, entire *100.00*

UC20

Printed by Bureau of Engraving and Printing. Designed by Robert Geissmann.

Letter Sheet for Foreign Postage

1976, Jan. 16 **Tagged** **Photo.**
UC50 UC20 22c **red & blue,** *blue,* entire 1.00 *6.00*
Entire, 1st day cancel, Tempe, Ariz. *(118,303)* 1.00
Die cutting reversed, entire 17.50
a. Red color missing due to foldover and die cutting —

"USA" — UC21

Printed by Bureau of Engraving and Printing. Designed by Soren Noring.

Letter Sheet for Foreign Postage

1978, Nov. 3 **Tagged** **Photo.**
UC51 UC21 22c **blue,** *blue,* entire 1.00 *3.00*
Entire, 1st day cancel, St. Petersburg, Fla. *(86,099)* 1.00
Die cutting reversed, entire 25.00

22nd OLYMPIC GAMES, MOSCOW, JULY 19-AUG. 3, 1980.

UC22

Design (multicolored in bottom left corner) shows discus thrower.
Printed by Bureau of Engraving and Printing. Designed by Robert M. Cunningham.

Letter Sheet for Foreign Postage

1979, Dec. 5 **Tagged** **Photo.**
UC52 UC22 22c **red, black & green,** *bluish,* entire 1.50 *6.00*
Entire, 1st day cancel, Bay Shore, N.Y. 1.00

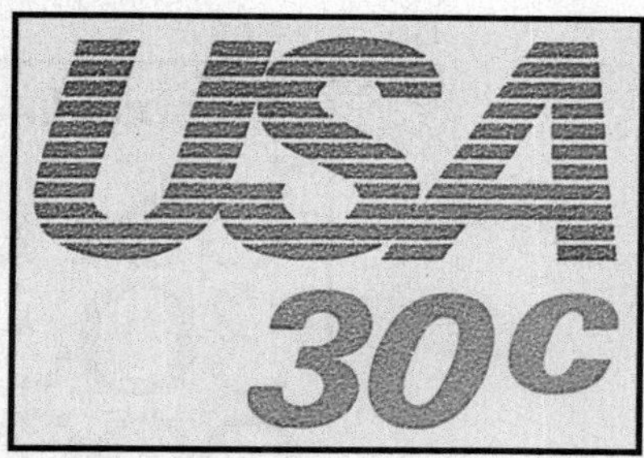

"USA" — UC23

Design (brown on No. UC53, green and brown on No. UC54): lower left, Statue of Liberty. Inscribed "Tour the United States." Folding area shows tourist attractions.
Printed by Bureau of Engraving and Printing.
Designed by Frank J. Waslick.

Letter Sheet for Foreign Postage

1980, Dec. 29 **Tagged** **Photo.**
UC53 UC23 30c **blue, red & brown,** *blue,* entire .85 *6.00*
Entire, 1st day cancel, San Francisco, CA 1.25
Die cutting reversed, entire 20.00
a. Red (30) omitted, entire 70.00

1981, Sept. 21 **Tagged** **Photo.**
UC54 UC23 30c **yellow, magenta, blue & black,** *blue,* entire .65 *6.00*
Entire, 1st day cancel, Honolulu, HI 1.25
Die cutting reversed, entire 20.00

UC24

Design: "Made in USA . . . world's best buys!" on flap, ship, tractor in lower left. Reverse folding area shows chemicals, jet silhouette, wheat, typewriter and computer tape disks. Printed by Bureau of Engraving and Printing.
Designed by Frank J. Waslick.

Letter Sheet for Foreign Postage

1982, Sept. 16 **Tagged** **Photo.**
UC55 UC24 30c **multi,** *blue,* entire .80 *6.00*
Entire, 1st day cancel, Seattle, WA 1.25
Die cutting reversed, entire —

WORLD COMMUNICATIONS YEAR

World Map Showing Locations of Satellite Tracking Stations — UC25

Design: Reverse folding area shows satellite, tracking station.
Printed by Bureau of Engraving and Printing.
Designed by Esther Porter.

Letter Sheet for Foreign Postage

1983, Jan. 7 **Tagged** **Photo.**
UC56 UC25 30c **multi,** *blue,* entire .90 *8.00*
Entire, 1st day cancel, Anaheim, CA 1.25
Die cutting reversed, entire 25.00

1984 OLYMPICS

UC26

Indicia in black, multicolor design of woman equestrian at lower left with montage of competitive events on reverse folding area.

Printed by the Bureau of Engraving & Printing.

Designed by Bob Peak.

Letter Sheet for Foreign Postage

1983, Oct. 14 **Tagged** **Photo.**

UC57	UC26 30c **black & multi,** *light blue,* entire	.85	*8.00*
	Entire, 1st day cancel, Los Angeles, CA		1.25
	Die cutting reversed, entire	*45.00*	

WEATHER SATELLITES, 25TH ANNIV.

Landsat Infrared and Thermal Mapping Bands UC27

Design: Landsat orbiting the earth at lower left with three Landsat photographs on reverse folding area. Inscribed: "Landsat views the Earth."

Printed by the Bureau of Engraving & Printing.

Designed by Esther Porter.

Letter Sheet for Foreign Postage

1985, Feb. 14 **Tagged** **Photo.**

UC58	UC27 36c **multi,** *blue,* entire	1.25	*12.50*
	Entire, 1st day cancel, Goddard Flight Center, MD		1.40
	Die cutting reversed, entire	30.00	

NATIONAL TOURISM WEEK

Urban Skyline — UC28

Design: Inscribed "Celebrate America" at lower left and "Travel. . . the perfect freedom" on folding area. Skier, Indian chief, cowboy, jazz trumpeter and pilgrims on reverse folding area.

Printed by the Bureau of Engraving & Printing.

Designed by Dennis Luzak.

Letter Sheet for Foreign Postage

1985, May 21 **Tagged** **Photo.**

UC59	UC28 36c **multi,** *blue,* entire	1.25	*12.50*
	Entire, 1st day cancel, Washington, DC		1.40
	Die cutting reversed, entire	25.00	
a.	Black omitted, entire	*600.00*	—

MARK TWAIN AND HALLEY'S COMET

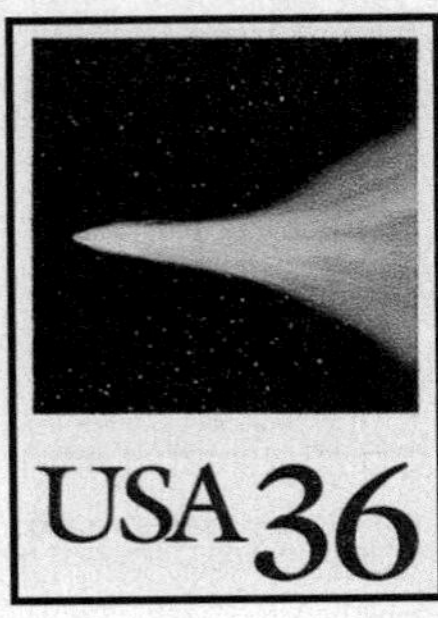

Comet Tail Viewed from Space — UC29

Design: Portrait of Twain at lower left and inscribed "I came in with Halley's Comet in 1835. It is coming again next year, and I expect to go out with it. It will be the greatest disappointment of my life if I don't go out with Halley's Comet." "1835 . Mark Twain . 1910 . Halley's Comet . 1985" and Twain, Huckleberry Finn, steamboat and comet on reverse folding areas.

Printed by the Bureau of Engraving & Printing.

Designed by Dennis Luzak.

Letter Sheet for Foreign Postage

1985, Dec. 4 **Tagged** **Photo.**

UC60	UC29 36c **multi,** entire	2.00	*12.50*
	Entire, 1st day cancel, Hannibal, MO		2.00
	Die cutting reversed, entire	25.00	

UC30

Printed by the Bureau of Engraving & Printing.

Letter Sheet for Foreign Postage

1988, May 9 **Litho.** **Tagged**

UC61	UC30 39c **multi,** entire	1.25	*12.50*
	Entire, 1st day cancel, Miami, FL *(27,446)*		1.60
a.	Tagging bar to left of design ('89)	1.25	*1.50*

On No. UC61, the tagging bar is between "USA" and "39."

MONTGOMERY BLAIR, POSTMASTER GENERAL 1861-64

Blair and Pres. Abraham Lincoln — UC31

Design: Mail bags and "Free city delivery," "Railway mail service" and "Money order system" at lower left. Globe, locomotive, bust of Blair, UPU emblem and "The Paris conference of 1863, initiated by Postmaster General Blair, led, in 1874, to the founding of the Universal Postal Union" contained on reverse folding area.

Printed by the Bureau of Engraving & Printing.

Designed by Ned Seidler.

Letter Sheet for Foreign Postage

1989, Nov. 20 **Litho.** **Tagged**

UC62	UC31 39c **multicolored,** entire	1.40	*16.00*
	Entire, 1st day cancel, Washington, DC		1.75
a.	Double impression		—
b.	Triple impression		—
c.	Quadruple impression		—

UC32

Designed by Bradbury Thompson.

Printed by the Bureau of Engraving and Printing.

Letter Sheet for Foreign Postage

1991, May 17 **Litho.** **Tagged**

UC63	UC32 45c **gray, red & blue,** *blue,* entire	1.40	*16.00*
a.	White paper	1.00	*16.00*
	Entire, 1st day cancel, Denver, CO *(19,941)*		1.40

Thaddeus Lowe (1832-1913), Balloonist — UC33

Designed by Davis Meltzer.

Printed by the Bureau of Engraving & Printing.

Letter Sheet for Foreign Postage

1995, Sept. 23 **Litho.** **Tagged**

UC64	UC33 50c **multicolored,** *blue,* entire	1.50	*20.00*
	Entire, 1st day cancel, Tampa, FL		1.25

Voyageurs Natl. Park, Minnesota UC34

Designed by Phil Jordan.

Printed by Bureau of Engraving & Printing.

Letter Sheet for Foreign Postage

1999, May 15 **Litho.** **Tagged**

UC65	UC34 60c **multicolored,** *blue,* entire	1.75	*12.50*
	Entire, 1st day cancel, Denver, CO		1.50

No. UC65 used is often found with additional postage affixed.

OFFICIAL ENVELOPES & WRAPPERS

By the Act of Congress, January 31, 1873, the franking privilege of officials was abolished as of July 1, 1873 and the Postmaster General was authorized to prepare official envelopes. At the same time official stamps were prepared for all Departments. Department envelopes became obsolete July 5, 1884. After that, government offices began to use franked envelopes of varied design. These indicate no denomination and lie beyond the scope of this Catalogue.

Post Office Department

UO1

Numeral 9mm high.

UO2

Numeral 9mm high.

UO3

Numeral 9½mm high.

Printed by George H. Reay, Brooklyn, N.Y.

1873

UO1	UO1	2c	**black,** *lemon*	22.50	10.00
			Entire	40.00	15.00
UO2	UO2	3c	**black,** *lemon*	12.50	6.50
			Entire	35.00	11.00
+UO3	UO2	3c	**black**	*17,500.*	
			Entire	*45,000.*	
UO4	UO3	6c	**black,** *lemon*	25.00	17.50
			Entire	40.00	25.00

The No. UO3 entire is unique. It has a tear through the stamp that has been professionally repaired. Value based on auction sale in 1999.

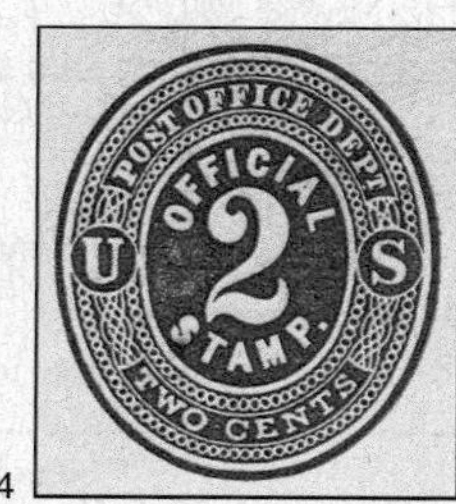

UO4

Numeral 9¼mm high.

UO5

Numeral 9¼mm high.

UO6

Numeral 10½mm high.

Printed by Plimpton Manufacturing Co., Hartford, Conn.

1874-79

UO5	UO4	2c	**black,** *lemon*	8.00	4.25
			Entire	17.50	7.00
UO6	UO4	2c	**black**	120.00	37.50
			Entire	175.00	57.50
UO7	UO5	3c	**black,** *lemon*	2.75	.85
			Entire	4.25	1.50
UO8	UO5	3c	**black**	1,750.	1,200.
			Entire	4,250.	
UO9	UO5	3c	**black,** *amber*	120.00	37.50
			Entire	175.00	60.00
UO10	UO5	3c	**black,** *blue*	—	
			Entire	*42,500.*	
UO11	UO5	3c	**blue,** *blue* ('75)	*20,000.*	
			Entire	*32,500.*	
UO12	UO6	6c	**black,** *lemon*	12.50	6.50
			Entire	26.00	12.50
UO13	UO6	6c	**black**	1,250.	1,750.
			Entire	3,750.	

Fakes exist of Nos. UO3, UO8 and UO13.

Postal Service

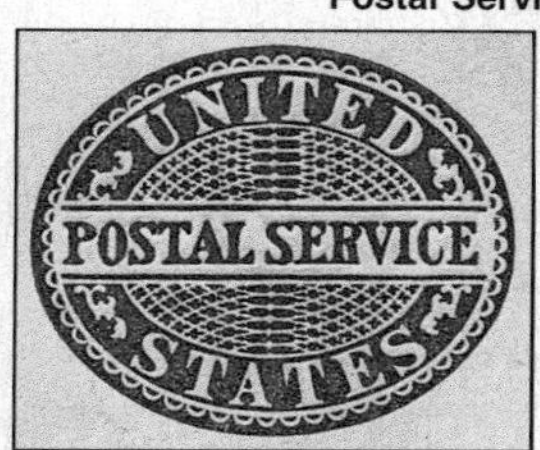

UO7

1877

UO14	UO7	**black**	6.00	4.50
		Entire	11.00	6.00
UO15	UO7	**black,** *amber*	125.00	42.50
		Entire	575.00	65.00
UO16	UO7	**blue,** *amber*	125.00	40.00
		Entire	575.00	65.00
UO17	UO7	**blue,** *blue*	7.50	6.75
		Entire	12.00	10.50

War Department

Franklin — UO8

Bust points to the end of "N" of "ONE".

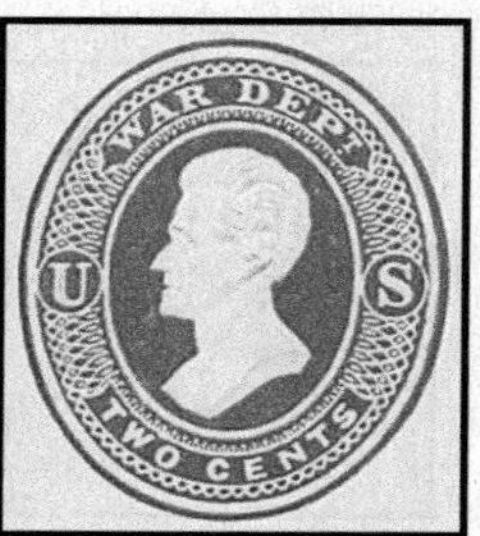

Jackson — UO9

Bust narrow at the back.

Washington — UO10

Queue projects below the bust.

Lincoln — UO11

Neck very long at the back.

Jefferson — UO12

Queue forms straight line with bust.

Clay — UO13

Ear partly concealed by hair, mouth large, chin prominent.

Webster — UO14

Has side whiskers.

Scott — UO15

Hamilton — UO16

Back of bust very narrow; chin almost straight; the labels containing the letters "U S" are exactly parallel.

Printed by George H. Reay.

1873

UO18	UO8	1c	**dark red**	350.00	200.00
	Entire			900.00	325.00
WO18A	UO8	1c	**dark red**, *manila*, entire		—
UO19	UO9	2c	**dark red**	1,000.	—
	Entire			2,250.	*5,000.*
UO20	UO10	3c	**dark red**	12.50	30.00
	Entire			17.50	70.00
UO21	UO10	3c	**dark red**, *amber*	*27,500.*	
	Entire			*42,500.*	
UO22	UO10	3c	**dark red**, *cream*	500.00	250.00
	Entire			850.00	350.00
UO23	UO11	6c	**dark red**	250.00	100.00
	Entire			475.00	250.00
UO24	UO11	6c	**dark red**, *cream*	4,000.	425.00
	Entire			6,500.	*3,500.*
UO25	UO12	10c	**dark red**	*7,500.*	2,250.
	Entire			*22,500.*	*4,000.*
UO26	UO13	12c	**dark red**	90.00	50.00
	Entire			175.00	—
UO27	UO14	15c	**dark red**	125.00	55.00
	Entire			210.00	*375.00*
UO28	UO15	24c	**dark red**	100.00	40.00
	Entire			200.00	*1,500.*
UO29	UO16	30c	**dark red**	250.00	150.00
	Entire			500.00	725.00

1873

UO30	UO8	1c	**vermilion**	200.00	
	Entire			375.00	
WO31	UO8	1c	**vermilion**, *manila*	17.50	14.00
	Entire			35.00	25.00
+UO32	UO9	2c	**vermilion**	400.00	
	Entire			*22,500.*	
WO33	UO9	2c	**vermilion**, *manila*	250.00	
	Entire			700.00	*1,000.*
UO34	UO10	3c	**vermilion**	75.00	40.00
	Entire			150.00	125.00
UO35	UO10	3c	**vermilion**, *amber*	85.00	40.00
	Entire			325.00	*400.00*
UO36	UO10	3c	**vermilion**, *cream*	12.50	12.50
	Entire			37.50	26.00
UO37	UO11	6c	**vermilion**	75.00	
	Entire			160.00	
+UO38	UO11	6c	**vermilion**, *cream*	400.00	
	Entire			*22,500.*	
UO39	UO12	10c	**vermilion**	300.00	
	Entire			650.00	
UO40	UO13	12c	**vermilion**	130.00	
	Entire			200.00	
UO41	UO14	15c	**vermilion**	200.00	
	Entire			4,000.	
UO42	UO15	24c	**vermilion**	300.00	
	Entire			550.00	
UO43	UO16	30c	**vermilion**	250.00	
	Entire			425.00	

UO17

Bottom serif on "S" is thick and short; bust at bottom below hair forms a sharp point.

UO18

Bottom serif on "S" is thick and short; front part of bust is rounded.

UO19

Bottom serif on "S" is short; queue does not project below bust.

UO20

Neck very short at the back.

UO21

Knot of queue stands out prominently.

UO22

Ear prominent, chin receding.

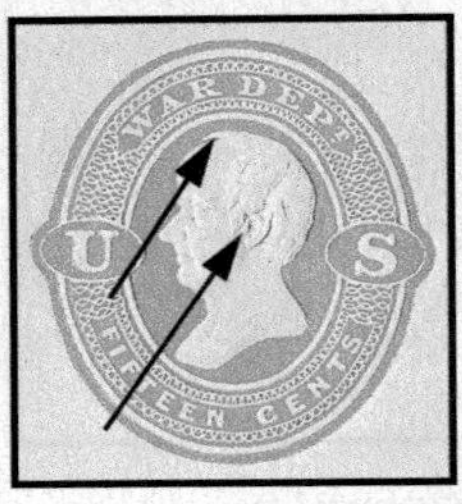

UO23

Has no side whiskers; forelock projects above head.

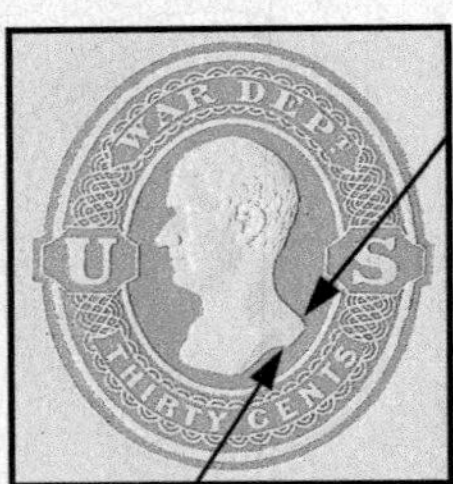

UO24

Back of bust rather broad; chin slopes considerably; the label containing letters "U S" are not exactly parallel.

Printed by Plimpton Manufacturing Co.

1875

UO44	UO17	1c	**red**	175.00	85.00
	Entire			240.00	250.00
+UO45	UO17	1c	**red**, *amber*	600.00	
+UO45A	UO17	1c	**red**, *orange*	*32,500.*	
WO46	UO17	1c	**red**, *manila*	4.50	2.75
	Entire			9.50	6.50
UO47	UO18	2c	**red**	90.00	—
	Entire			150.00	
UO48	UO18	2c	**red**, *amber*	12.50	17.50
	Entire			22.50	27.50
UO49	UO18	2c	**red**, *orange*	12.50	17.50
	Entire			15.00	30.00
WO50	UO18	2c	**red**, *manila*	90.00	40.00
	Entire			200.00	—
UO51	UO19	3c	**red**	11.00	10.00
	Entire			20.00	17.50
UO52	UO19	3c	**red**, *amber*	12.50	10.00
	Entire			22.50	16.00
UO53	UO19	3c	**red**, *cream*	5.00	3.75
	Entire			9.00	6.50
UO54	UO19	3c	**red**, *blue*	3.00	2.00
	Entire			4.00	4.50
UO55	UO19	3c	**red**, *fawn*	6.00	2.75
	Entire			11.00	4.00
UO56	UO20	6c	**red**	45.00	30.00
	Entire			85.00	—
UO57	UO20	6c	**red**, *amber*	65.00	40.00
	Entire			110.00	—
UO58	UO20	6c	**red**, *cream*	175.00	85.00
	Entire			450.00	
UO59	UO21	10c	**red**	180.00	80.00
	Entire			225.00	—
UO60	UO21	10c	**red**, *amber*	650.00	
	Entire			1,150.	
UO61	UO22	12c	**red**	25.00	25.00
	Entire			140.00	*250.00*
UO62	UO22	12c	**red**, *amber*	400.00	
	Entire			650.00	
UO63	UO22	12c	**red**, *cream*	450.00	
	Entire			700.00	
UO64	UO23	15c	**red**	200.00	125.00
	Entire			300.00	—
UO65	UO23	15c	**red**, *amber*	650.00	
	Entire			1,000.	
UO66	UO23	15c	**red**, *cream*	525.00	
	Entire			850.00	
UO67	UO24	30c	**red**	150.00	140.00
	Entire			210.00	—
UO68	UO24	30c	**red**, *amber*	550.00	
	Entire			1,700.	
UO69	UO24	30c	**red**, *cream*	675.00	
	Entire			1,100.	

POSTAL SAVINGS ENVELOPES

Issued under the Act of Congress, approved June 25, 1910, in lieu of penalty or franked envelopes. Unused remainders, after mid-October 1914, were overprinted with the Penalty Clause. Regular stamped envelopes, redeemed by the Government, were also overprinted for official use.

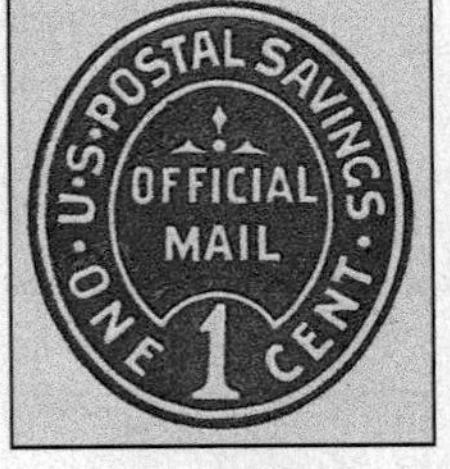

UO25

1911

UO70	UO25	1c	**green**	75.00	25.00
	Entire			110.00	42.50
UO71	UO25	1c	**green**, *oriental buff*	175.00	85.00
	Entire			275.00	100.00
UO72	UO25	2c	**carmine**	12.50	4.00
	Entire			21.00	12.00
a.		2c	**carmine**, *manila* (error)	*1,200.*	*1,000.*
	Entire			*1,800.*	*1,400.*

Tagged

Envelopes from No. UO73 onward are tagged unless otherwise noted.

OFFICIAL MAIL

Great Seal — UO26

1983, Jan. 12 **Typo. & Embossed**

UO73	UO26	20c	**blue**, entire	1.00	*10.00*
	First day cancel, Washington, DC				1.00

UO27

1985, Feb. 26 **Typo. & Embossed**

UO74 UO27 22c **blue,** entire .90 *5.00*
First day cancel, Washington, DC 1.00

UO28

1987, Mar. 2 **Typo.**

UO75 UO28 22c **blue,** entire 1.50 *25.00*
First day cancel, Washington, DC 1.00
a. Tagging omitted —

Used exclusively to mail U.S. Savings Bonds.

UO29

1988, Mar. 22 **Typo.**

UO76 UO29 (25c) **black & blue,** entire 1.25 *10.00*
First day cancel, Washington, DC 1.25

Used exclusively to mail U.S. Savings Bonds.

UO30

UO31

1988, Apr. 11 **Typo. & Embossed**

UO77 UO30 25c **black & blue,** entire .85 *6.00*
First day cancel, Washington, DC 1.25
a. Denomination & lettering as on No. UO78, entire *5.00* *6.00*

Nos. UO77 and UO77a used to mail U.S. Savings Bonds and also occasionally used by the director of admissions at the U.S. Air Force Academy and by Air Force recruiting stations for intra-agency correspondence.

Typo.

UO78 UO31 25c **black & blue,** entire 1.00 *35.00*
First day cancel, Washington, DC *(12,017)* 1.25
a. Denomination & lettering as on No. UO77, entire 1.00 *35.00*

No. UO78 used to mail U.S. Savings Bonds. Also used by the Department of Agriculture.

First day cancellations applied to 12,017 of Nos. UO77, UO78.

Used Values

Postally used examples of Nos. UO79-UO94 seldom appear in the marketplace and thus cannot be valued with as much certainty as the editors would like. They must show evidence of postal usage. Clear cancels are valued even higher. The editors would like to have records of sales of examples of these used envelopes. If a value exists, it is based on a known transaction(s) or consultation with experts.

1990, Mar. 17 **Typo.**

Stars and "E Pluribus Unum" illegible. "Official" is 13mm, "USA" is 16mm long.

UO79 UO31 45c **black & blue,** entire 1.25 *80.00*
First day cancel, Springfield, VA *(5,956)* 1.50
UO80 UO31 65c **black & blue,** entire 1.75 *100.00*
First day cancel, Springfield, VA *(6,922)* 2.25

Used exclusively to mail U.S. passports.

UO32

Stars and "E Pluribus Unum" clear and sharply printed. "Official" is 14½mm, "USA" is 17mm long.

1990, Aug. 10 **Litho.**

UO81 UO32 45c **black & blue,** entire 1.25 *80.00*
First day cancel, Washington, DC *(7,160)* 1.50
UO82 UO32 65c **black & blue,** entire 1.75 *50.00*
First day cancel, Washington, DC *(6,759)* 2.25

Used exclusively to mail U.S. passports.

UO33

1991, Jan. 22 **Typo.** **Wmk.**

UO83 UO33 (29c) **black & blue,** entire 1.00 *20.00*
First day cancel, Washington, DC *(30,549)* 1.25

Used exclusively to mail U.S. Savings Bonds.

UO34

1991, Apr. 6 **Wmk.** **Litho. & Embossed**

UO84 UO34 29c **black & blue,** entire .70 *5.00*
First day cancel, Oklahoma City, OK *(27,841)* 1.25
a. Unwatermarked paper, entire *May 1, 1992* 7.50 *4.00*

No. UO84a has a "recycled" imprint under the flap.

UO35

1991, Apr. 17 **Typo.** **Wmk.**

UO85 UO35 29c **black & blue,** entire .70 *20.00*
First day cancel, Washington, DC *(25,563)* 1.25
Entire, unwatermarked, *May 1, 1992* 75.00 *20.00*

Used exclusively to mail U.S. Savings Bonds. Unwatermarked envelopes on recycled paper were issued May 1, 1992, and have a "recycled" imprint under the flap. Value, unused $3., used $35.

Consular Service, Bicent. — UO36

Designed by Zebulon Rogers. Quotation from O. Henry on flap.

1992, July 10 **Litho.** **Unwmk.**

UO86 UO36 52c **blue & red,** entire 6.00 *20.00*
First day cancel, Washington, DC *(30,374)* 2.25
a. 52c blue & red, *blue-white,* entire 1.50 *20.00*
UO87 UO36 75c **blue & red,** entire 11.00 *30.00*
First day cancel, Washington, DC *(25,995)* 3.25
a. 75c blue & red, *blue-white,* entire 2.50 *30.00*

Used exclusively to mail U.S. passports.

Available only in 4⅜ inch x 8⅞ inch size with self-adhesive flap.

Original issues have "USPS copyright" on left under flap. Reissues (Nos. UO86a and UO87a) have it at right.

UO37

1995-99 **Typo. & Embossed** **Unwmk.**

UO88 UO37 32c **blue & red,** entire, *May 9, 1995* .90 *7.00*
First day cancel, Washington, DC 1.25
UO89 UO37 33c **blue & red,** entire, *Feb. 22, 1999* .90 *8.00*
First day cancel, Washington, DC 1.25

Type of 1995

2001, Feb. 27 **Typo. & Embossed** **Unwmk.**

UO90 UO37 34c **blue & red,** entire 1.00 *10.00*
First day cancel, Washington, DC 1.25

Type of 1995

2002, Aug. 2 **Typo. & Embossed** **Unwmk.**

UO91 UO37 37c **blue & red,** type I, entire 1.00 *15.00*
First day cancel, Washington, DC 1.25
First day cancel, any other city 1.25
a. Type II, entire, *Aug. 2, 2002* 1.00 *35.00*

Type I has 29x28mm blue panel, top of "USA" even with the bottom of the eagle's neck and is made with "100% recycled paper" as noted on reverse. Type II has a 27½x27½mm blue panel, top of "USA" even with the highest arrow, and has no mention of "100% recycled paper" on reverse.

Type of 1995

2006, Jan. 9 Typo. & Embossed Unwmk.

UO92 UO37 39c **blue & red, entire**	2.00	*10.00*
Entire, 1st day cancel, Washington, DC		1.25
Entire, 1st day cancel, any other city		1.25

Type of 1995

2007, May 12 Typo. & Embossed Unwmk.

UO93 UO37 41c **blue & red,** entire	2.00	*15.00*
Entire, 1st day cancel, Washington, DC		2.10

Type of 1995

2008, June 20 Typo. Unwmk.

UO94 UO37 42c **blue & red,** entire	2.00	*15.00*
Entire, 1st day cancel, Washington, DC		2.10

POSTAL CARDS

Values are for unused cards as sold by the Post Office, without printed or written address or message, and used cards with Post Office cancellation, when current. Used cards with postage added to meet higher rates sell for less. Used cards for international rates are for proper usage. Those used domestically sell for less.

The "Preprinted" values are for unused cards with printed or written address or message.

Starting with No. UX21, the Government Printing Office began printing the postal cards. Many outside firms produced cards starting October 1994 with Nos. UX178-UX197. The last GPO-produced cards were Nos. UX449 and UY45, January 9, 2006.

Nos. UX1-UX48 are typographed; others are lithographed (offset) unless otherwise stated.

Numerous printing varieties exist. Varieties of surcharged cards include (a) inverted surcharge at lower left, (b) double surcharge, one inverted at lower left, (c) surcharge in other abnormal positions, including back of card. Such surcharge varieties command a premium.

Colored cancellations sell for more than black in some instances. **All values are for entire cards.**

As of Jan. 1, 1999, postal cards were sold individually for 1c over face value. Currently, they are sold for 2c over face value.

See Computer Vended Postage section for "Postal Buddy" cards.

Since 1875 it has been possible to purchase some postal cards in sheets for multiple printing, hence pairs, strips and blocks are available. Some sheets have been cut up so that cards exist with stamp inverted, in center of card, two on one card, in another corner, etc. These are only curiosities and of minimal value.

Liberty — PC1

Wmk. Large "U S P O D" in Monogram, (90x60mm)

1873, May 12 Size: 130x76mm

UX1 PC1 1c **brown,** *buff*	375.00	25.00
Preprinted	70.00	
First day of use cover, May 12, 1873, Springfield MA		*12,500.*

The U.S. Postal Card Agency in Springfield, Mass. began distributing postal cards to post offices on May 12, 1873. The Springfield post office received its shipment that same day and immediately placed them on sale, so the one postal card postmarked May 12, 1873, from Springfield is the legitimate earliest documented use supported by Post Office Dept. records. Other cities began receiving the cards by train on May 13.

Wmk. Small "U S P O D" in Monogram, (53x36mm)

1873, July 6

UX3 PC1 1c **brown,** *buff*	75.00	3.50
Preprinted	22.50	
a. Without watermark		775.00

The watermarks on Nos. UX1, UX3 and UX4 are found in normal position, inverted, reversed, and inverted and reversed. They are often dim, especially on No. UX4. Values listed are for clear watermarks.

No. UX3a is not known unused. Cards offered as such are either unwatermarked proofs, or have partial or vague watermarks. See No. UX65.

Liberty — PC2

Inscribed

WRITE THE ADDRESS ON THIS SIDE—THE MESSAGE ON THE OTHER

1875 Wmk. Small "U S P O D" in Monogram

UX4 PC2 1c **black,** *buff, Sept. 28*	3,500.	350.
Preprinted	700.	

Unwmk.

UX5 PC2 1c **black,** *buff, Sept. 30*	75.00	.45
Preprinted	7.00	

For other postal card of type PC2 see No. UX7.

Liberty — PC3

For International Use

1879, Dec. 1

UX6 PC3 2c **blue,** *buff*	35.00	25.00
Preprinted	11.50	
a. 2c **dark blue,** *buff*	35.00	25.00
Preprinted	11.50	

See Nos. UX13 and UX16.

Type of PC2, Inscribed

NOTHING BUT THE ADDRESS CAN BE PLACED ON THIS SIDE.

1881, Oct. 17 (?)

UX7 PC2 1c **black,** *buff*	70.00	.40
Preprinted	6.50	
a. 23 teeth below "ONE CENT"	1,750.	65.00
Preprinted	225.00	
b. Printed on both sides	*1,200.*	*750.00*

Jefferson — PC4

1885, Aug. 24

UX8 PC4 1c **brown,** *buff*	55.00	1.25
Preprinted	10.00	
c. 1c **dark chocolate,** *buff*	450.00	65.00
Preprinted	75.00	
d. Double impression	*5,500.*	*7,500.*
e. Double impression, one inverted	*9,500.*	
f. Printed on both sides	—	
g. "M" in double frame above "O" of "POSTAL"		*1,250.*

Card was printed in many shades of brown ink. Earliest documented use: Aug. 29, 1885.

PC5

Head of Jefferson facing right, centered on card.

1886, Dec 1

UX9 PC5 1c **black,** *buff*	25.00	.55
Preprinted	1.75	
a. 1c **black,** *dark buff*	75.00	5.00
Preprinted	20.00	
b. Double impression	*4,000.*	*1,500.*
c. Double impression, one inverted	*10,000.*	
d. **1c black,** *salmon pink*	*1,500.*	*3,250.*
e. Triple impression	*4,500.*	

No. UX9d was printed on spacer paper used for counting.

Grant — PC6

1891, Dec. 16 **Size: 155x95mm**

UX10 PC6 1c **black,** *buff* 47.50 1.75
Preprinted 7.50
a. Double impression, one inverted *3,500.*
Double impression, second impression inverted and quadruple split *3,250.*
b. Double impression *1,750.*
c. Triple impression, one inverted *7,000.*
d. Quintuple impression, three inverted *6,500.*

Two types exist of No. UX10.
Earliest documented use: Dec. 23, 1891.

Size: 117x75mm

UX11 PC6 1c **blue,** *grayish white* 22.50 3.00
Preprinted 5.00
b. Double impression, one inverted *8,000.*

Cards printed in black instead of blue are invariably proofs.
Earliest documented use: Dec. 21, 1891.

PC7

Head of Jefferson facing left.
Small wreath and name below.

1894, Jan. 2 **Size: 140x89mm**

UX12 PC7 1c **black,** *buff* 45.00 .65
Preprinted 2.25
a. Double impression —

Two types exist of No. UX12: flat bed printing and rotary press printing.

For International Use
Type of PC3

1897, Jan. 25 **Size: 140x89mm**

UX13 PC3 2c **blue,** *cream* 250.00 85.00
Preprinted 85.00

Earliest documented use: Apr. 17, 1897.

PC8

Head same as PC7. Large wreath and name below.

1897, Dec. 1 **Size: 139x82mm**

UX14 PC8 1c **black,** *buff* 40.00 .45
Preprinted 2.75
a. Double impression, one inverted *7,000.* *7,000.*
Preprinted —
b. Printed both sides —
Preprinted *3,000.*
c. Double impression — —
Preprinted —
d. **Black,** *salmon pink,* preprinted 1,500.

No. UX14d was printed on spacer paper used for counting.

John Adams — PC9

1898 **Size: 126x74mm**

UX15 PC9 1c **black,** *buff, Mar. 31* 47.50 15.00
Preprinted 12.50

For International Use
Design same as PC3, without frame around card.
Size: 140x82mm

UX16 PC3 2c **black,** *buff* 15.00 *17.00*
Preprinted 5.00

McKinley — PC10

1902

UX17 PC10 1c **black,** *buff* *14,000.*
Preprinted *2,500.* *3,750.*

Earliest documented use; May 27, 1902.

McKinley — PC11

1902

UX18 PC11 1c **black,** *buff* 17.50 .35
Preprinted 1.75
a. Double impression *7,500.*

Earliest documented use; July 14, 1902.
Two types exist of Nos. UX18-UX20.

McKinley — PC12

1907

UX19 PC12 1c **black,** *buff* 45.00 .50
Preprinted 2.25

Earliest documented use: June 28, 1907.

Same design, correspondence space at left

1908, Jan. 2

UX20 PC12 1c **black,** *buff* 57.50 4.50
Preprinted 8.50

PC13

McKinley, background shaded.

1910

UX21 PC13 1c **blue,** *bluish* 105.00 13.00
Preprinted 17.50
a. 1c **bronze blue,** *bluish* 400.00 100.00
Preprinted 150.00
b. Double impression *1,600.*
Preprinted 650.00
c. Triple impression *3,000.*
Preprinted *1,500.*
d. Double impression, one inverted —
e. Four arcs above and below "IS" of inscription to left of stamp impression are pointed *2,100.* *600.00*
Preprinted *900.00*

Earliest documented use: Feb. 13, 1910.
A No. UX21 card exists with Philippines No. UX11 printed on the back.

PC14

Same design, white background.

1910, Apr. 13

UX22 PC14 1c **blue,** *bluish* 22.50 .45
Preprinted 2.00
a. Double impression *850.00*
b. Triple impression *3,500.* *3,250.*
c. Triple impression, one inverted —
d. Quintuple impression *6,000.*

See No. UX24.

PC15

Head of Lincoln, solid background.

1911, Jan. 21 **Size: 127x76mm**

UX23 PC15 1c **red,** *cream* 11.00 5.50
Preprinted 3.50
a. Triple impression —
b. Double impression *7,000.*

See No. UX26.

Design same as PC14

1911, Aug. 10 **Size: 140x82mm**

UX24 PC14 1c **red,** *cream* 12.00 .35
Preprinted 1.25
a. Double impression *3,250.*
b. Triple impression —

Cards with 1920 2-line surcharge are considered favor items.

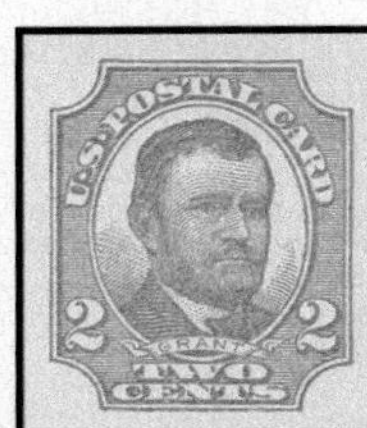

Grant — PC16

For International Use

1911, Oct. 27 **Size: 140x82mm**

UX25 PC16 2c **red,** *cream* 1.50 *20.00*
Preprinted .65
a. Double impression *10,000.*

For surcharge see No. UX36.

Design same as PC15

1913, July 29 **Size: 127x76mm**

UX26 PC15 1c **green,** *cream* 13.00 7.50
Preprinted 2.50

Jefferson — PC17

Die I — End of queue small, sloping sharply downward to right.

Die II (re-cut) — End of queue large and rounded.

1914-16 **Size: 140x82mm**

UX27	PC17 1c **green,** *buff,* die I, *June 4*	.25	.25
	Preprinted	.25	
a.	1c **green,** *cream*	5.00	.65
	Preprinted	1.25	
b.	Double impression	*2,500.*	*2,750.*
e.	Triple impression	*6,000.*	
f.	Quadruple impression	*6,500.*	

On gray, rough surfaced card

UX27C	PC17 1c **green,** die I, *Dec. 22, 1916*	*3,250.*	250.00
	Preprinted	*625.00*	
UX27D	PC17 1c **dark green,** die II, *1916*	*20,000.*	175.00
	Preprinted	550.00	

For surcharges see Nos. UX39 and UX41.

Lincoln — PC19

1917, Mar. 14 **Size: 127x76mm**

UX28	PC19 1c **green,** *cream*	.60	.30
	Preprinted	.30	
a.	1c **green,** *dark buff*	1.50	.60
	Preprinted	.50	
b.	Double impression	*3,500.*	—
	Preprinted	*2,500.*	

No. UX28 was printed also on light buff and canary. See No. UX43. For surcharges see Nos. UX40 and UX42.

Jefferson — PC20

Die I — Rough, coarse impression. End of queue slopes sharply downward to right. Left basal ends of "2" form sharp points.

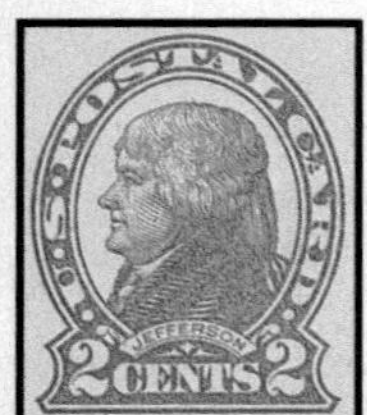

Jefferson — PC20a

Die II — Fine, clear impression. End of queue is almost horizontal at right. Left basal ends of "2" form balls.

1917-18 **Size: 140x82mm**

UX29	PC20 2c **red,** *buff,* die I, *Oct. 22*	42.50	2.10
	Preprinted	6.50	
a.	2c **lake,** *cream,* die I	50.00	4.00
	Preprinted	9.00	
c.	2c **vermilion,** *buff,* die I	850.00	165.00
	Preprinted	70.00	
UX30	PC20a 2c **red,** *cream,* die II, *Jan. 23, 1918*	30.00	1.60
	Preprinted	4.50	

2c Postal Cards of 1917-18 Revalued

Surcharged in one line by canceling machine at Washington, DC

1920, Apr.

UX31	PC20a 1c on 2c **red,** *cream,* die II	*3,000.*	*4,000.*
	Preprinted	*2,250.*	

Surcharged in two lines by canceling machine (46 Types)

UX32	PC20 1c on 2c **red,** *buff,* die I	52.50	12.50
	Preprinted	15.00	
a.	1c on 2c **vermilion,** *buff*	150.00	60.00
	Preprinted	60.00	
b.	Double surcharge	150.00	100.00
	Preprinted	100.00	—
c.	Double surcharge, one inverted, both in normal position on stamp	—	—
	Preprinted	—	
d.	Double surcharge, one inverted at lower left	65.00	30.00
	Preprinted	30.00	
e.	Triple surcharge	—	—
	Preprinted	—	
f.	Inverted surcharge at lower left	65.00	30.00
	Preprinted	30.00	
UX33	PC20a 1c on 2c **red,** *cream,* die II	13.00	2.00
	Preprinted	2.50	
a.	Inverted surcharge, on stamp	150.00	*200.00*
	Preprinted	—	—
b.	Double surcharge	150.00	*175.00*
	Preprinted	50.00	
c.	Double surcharge, one inverted, both in normal position on stamp	350.00	
	Preprinted	—	
d.	Triple surcharge	375.00	
e.	Double surcharge, one inverted at lower left	30.00	25.00
	Preprinted	20.00	
f.	Inverted surcharge at lower left	30.00	30.00
	Preprinted	20.00	
g.	Triple surcharge, one inverted at lower left	—	—
	Preprinted	—	
h.	Double surcharge, one inverted on back		—

Double and triple surcharges on Nos. UX32 and UX33 generally sell for less than above values if one or more of the surcharges is not on the stamp.

Surcharged in Two Lines by Press Printing

1920

UX34	PC20 1c on 2c **red,** *buff,* die I	700.00	52.50
	Preprinted	125.00	
a.	Double surcharge	1,000.	
UX35	PC20a 1c 2c **red,** *cream,* die II	225.00	37.50
	Preprinted	55.00	
a.	Double surcharge, one inverted at lower left		—

Surcharges were prepared from (a) special dies fitting International and Universal post office canceling machines (Nos. UX31-UX33), and (b) printing press dies (Nos. UX34-UX35). There are 38 canceling machine types on Die I, and 44 on Die II. There are two printing press types of each die.

UX36	PC16 1c on 2c **red,** *cream* (#UX25)		*95,000.*

Unused examples of No. UX36 (New York surcharge) were probably made by favor. Used examples of No. UX36 (Los Angeles surcharge, three to four examples used in Long Beach are recorded) are unquestionably authentic. Surcharges on other numbers exist, but their validity is doubtful.

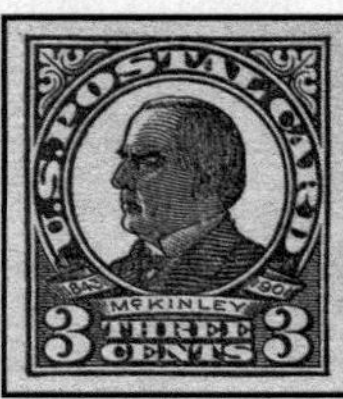

McKinley — PC21

For International Use

1926, Feb. 1

UX37	PC21 3c **red,** *buff*	4.50	*22.50*
	Preprinted	1.75	
	First day cancel, Washington, DC		200.00
a.	3c **red,** *yellow*	6.00	*22.50*
	Preprinted	1.75	
b.	Double impression	*5,000.*	
	Preprinted	*4,250.*	

Franklin — PC22

1951, Nov. 16

UX38	PC22 2c **carmine rose,** *buff*	.35	.25
	Preprinted	.25	
	First day cancel		1.00
a.	Double impression	500.00	
b.	2c **carmine rose,** *dark buff,* (error)	700.00	
c.	2c **lake,** *buff,*	35.00	25.00
d.	Indicia omitted (inscriptions normal or partial)	*1,000.*	

No. UX38b was printed on spacer paper used for counting. For surcharge see No. UX47.

Nos. UX27 and UX28 Surcharged by Canceling Machine at Left of Stamp in Light Green

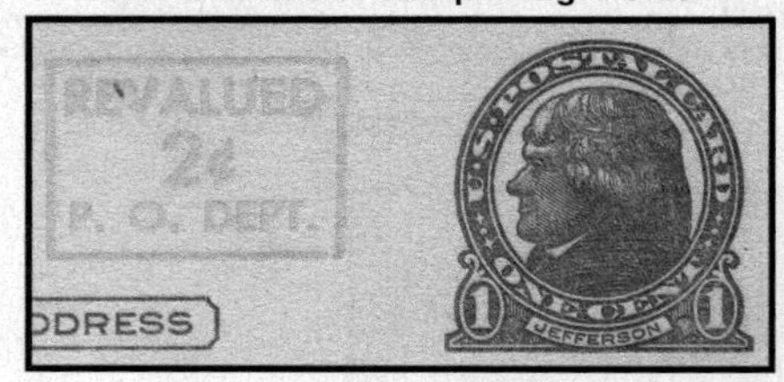

1952

UX39	PC17 2c on 1c **green,** *buff, Jan. 1*	.50	.35
	Preprinted	.25	
	First day cancel, any city		12.00
a.	Surcharged vertically, reading down	8.00	*10.00*
	Preprinted	3.00	
b.	Double surcharge	20.00	*25.00*
c.	Double surcharge, one inverted at lower left	20.00	25.00
d.	Inverted surcharge at lower left	12.00	12.00
e.	Triple surcharge	—	—
f.	Triple surcharge, one inverted at lower left	—	—
g.	Surcharge black (error)	*3,750.*	
h.	As "a," surcharge reading up	—	
UX40	PC19 2c on 1c **green,** *cream, Mar. 22*	.65	.45
	Preprinted	.40	
	First day cancel, Washington, D.C.		22.50
a.	Surcharged vertically, reading down	7.00	5.50
	Preprinted	4.00	
b.	Double surcharge	240.00	
c.	Double surcharge, one inverted at lower left	280.00	
d.	Inverted surcharge at lower left	180.00	

Nos. UX27 and UX28 With Similar Surcharge Typographed at Left of Stamp in Dark Green

1952

UX41	PC17 2c on 1c **green,** *buff*	5.00	2.00
	Preprinted	1.75	
a.	Inverted surcharge at lower left	85.00	125.00
	Preprinted	45.00	
b.	Double surcharge	—	—
	Preprinted	700.00	
c.	Vert. pair of cards, one with surcharge omitted	275.00	
UX42	PC19 2c on 1c **green,** *cream*	5.00	2.50
	Preprinted	3.00	
a.	Surcharged by offset lithography	5.00	2.50
b.	Surcharged on back	250.00	
c.	Double surcharge	—	

Type of 1917

1952, July 31 **Size: 127x76mm**

UX43 PC19 2c **carmine,** *buff* .30 *1.00*
Preprinted .25
First day cancel 1.00

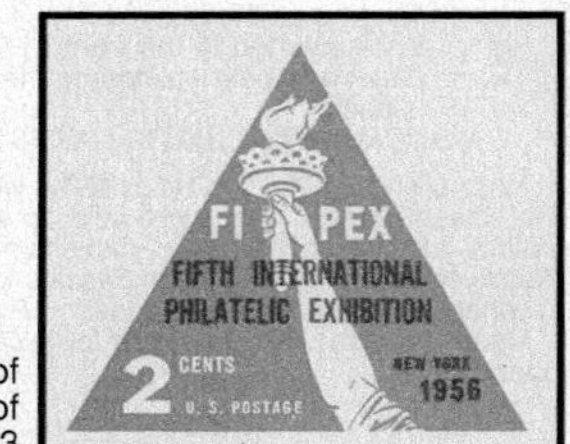

Torch and Arm of Statue of Liberty — PC23

Fifth International Philatelic Exhibition (FIPEX), New York City, Apr. 28-May 6, 1956.

1956, May 4

UX44 PC23 2c **deep carmine & dark violet blue,** *buff* .25 *1.00*
First day cancel, New York, NY *(537,474)* 1.00
a. Dark violet blue omitted 525.00 *600.00*
b. Double impression of dark violet blue 40.00 —
c. Double impression of deep carmine 40.00 30.00
d. Double impression of deep carmine & dark violet blue *550.00*
e. Double impression of deep carmine, dark violet blue omitted *500.00*
f. 2c **rose pink & dark violet blue,** *buff* 100.00 75.00
g. As "f," dark violet blue omitted *750.00*
h. 2c **pink & dark violet blue,** *buff* *1,500.* *750.00*
i. As "h," double impression of dark violet blue *1,500.*

Statue of Liberty — PC24

For International Use

1956, Nov. 16

UX45 PC24 4c **deep red & ultramarine,** *buff* 1.50 *110.00*
First day cancel, New York, NY *(129,841)* 1.00

See No. UY16.

Statue of Liberty — PC25

1958, Aug. 1

UX46 PC25 3c **purple,** *buff* .50 .25
First day cancel, Philadelphia, Pa. *(180,610)* 1.00
a. "N GOD WE TRUST" 12.00 *25.00*
First day cancel, Philadelphia, Pa. *175.00*
b. Double impression *1,000.*
c. Double impression one inverted *4,500.*
d. Precanceled with 3 printed purple lines, *1961* 4.25 2.50
e. Indicia omitted (inscription normal) *750.00*
f. 3c **purple,** *dark buff* (error) *900.00*

On No. UX46d, the precanceling lines are incorporated with the design. The earliest documented postmark on this experimental card is Oct. 31, 1961. UX46f was printed on spacer paper used for counting.

See No. UY17.

No. UX38 Surcharged by Canceling Machine at Left of Stamp in Black

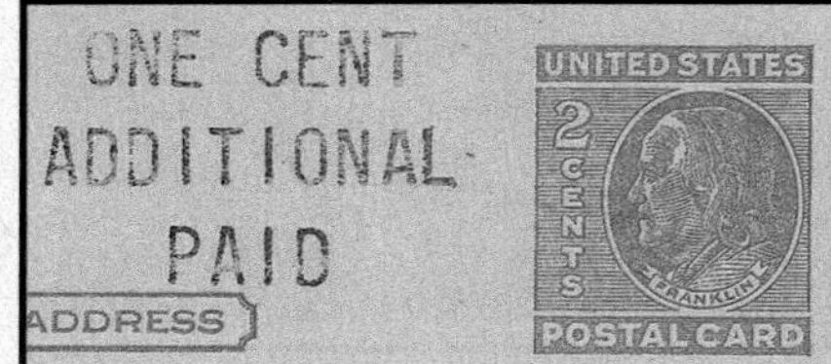

1958

UX47 PC22 2c + 1c **carmine rose,** *buff* 225.00 *800.00*
a. Surcharge inverted at lower left 500.00

The surcharge was applied to 750,000 cards for the use of the General Electric Co., Owensboro, Ky. A variety of the surcharge shows the D of PAID beneath the N of ADDITIONAL. All known examples of No. UX47 have a printed advertisement on the back and a small punch hole near lower left corner.

Used value is for commercially used card.

Lincoln PC26

Precanceled with 3 printed red violet lines

1962, Nov. 19

UX48 PC26 4c **red violet** .50 .25
First day cancel, Springfield, IL *(162,939)* 1.25
a. Tagged, *June 25, 1966* .60 .25
b. Inscription omitted *750.00*
First day cancel, Bellevue, OH 30.00

No. UX48a was printed with luminescent ink.

See note on Luminescence in "Information for Collectors."

See No. UY18.

Used values are for contemporaneous usage without additional postage applied. Used values for international-rate cards are for proper usage.

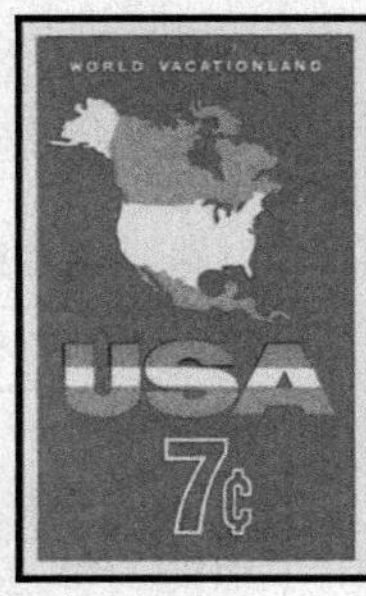

Map of Continental United States — PC27

Designed by Suren H. Ermoyan

For International Use

1963, Aug. 30

UX49 PC27 7c **blue & red** 4.00 *80.00*
First day cancel, New York, NY 1.00
a. Blue omitted *7,500.*

First day cancellation was applied to 270,464 of Nos. UX49 and UY19. See Nos. UX54, UX59, UY19-UY20.

Flags and Map of U.S. PC28

175th anniv. of the U.S. Customs Service.

Designed by Gerald N. Kurtz

Precanceled with 3 printed blue lines

1964, Feb. 22

UX50 PC28 4c **red & blue** .50 *1.00*
First day cancel, Washington, DC *(313,275)* 1.00
a. Blue omitted 550.00
b. Red omitted —
c. Double impression of red —

No. UX50c is unique and is a miscut foldunder card.

Americans "Moving Forward" (Street Scene) — PC29

Issued to publicize the need to strengthen the US Social Security system. Released in connection with the 15th conf. of the Intl. Social Security Association at Washington, DC.

Designed by Gerald N. Kurtz

Precanceled with a blue and 2 red printed lines

1964, Sept. 26

UX51 PC29 4c **dull blue & red** .40 *1.00*
First day cancel, Washington, D.C. *(293,650)* 1.00
a. Red omitted —
b. Dull blue omitted *625.00 625.00*

Coast Guard Flag — PC30

175th anniv. of the U.S. Coast Guard.

Designed by Muriel R. Chamberlain

Precanceled with 3 printed red lines

1965, Aug. 4

UX52 PC30 4c **blue & red** .30 *1.00*
First day cancel, Newburyport, Mass. *(338,225)* 1.25
a. Blue omitted *4,000.*

Crowd and Census Bureau Punch Card — PC31

Designed by Emilio Grossi

Precanceled with 3 bright blue printed lines

1965, Oct. 21

UX53 PC31 4c **bright blue & black** .30 *1.00*
First day cancel, Philadelphia, Pa. *(275,100)* 1.00

Map Type of 1963
For International Use

1967, Dec. 4

UX54 PC27 8c **blue & red** 4.50 *80.00*
First day cancel, Washington, DC 1.00

First day cancellation was applied to 268,077 of Nos. UX54 and UY20.

Lincoln PC33

Designed by Robert J. Jones

Precanceled with 3 printed green lines

1968, Jan. 4 — **Luminescent Ink**

UX55 PC33 5c **emerald** .30 *.60*
First day cancel, Hodgenville, Ky. 1.25
a. Double impression —

First day cancellation was applied to 274,000 of Nos. UX55 and UY21.

Experts have questioned the existence of No. UX55a. The editors would like to see a certified example of this error.

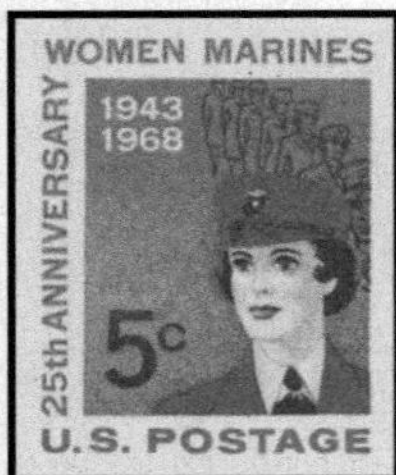

Woman Marine, 1968, and Marines of Earlier Wars — PC34

25th anniv. of the Women Marines.

Designed by Muriel R. Chamberlain

1968, July 26

UX56 PC34 5c **rose red & green** .35 *1.00*
First day cancel, San Francisco, Cal. *(203,714)* 1.25

Tagged

Postal cards from No. UX57 onward are either tagged or printed with luminescent ink unless otherwise noted.

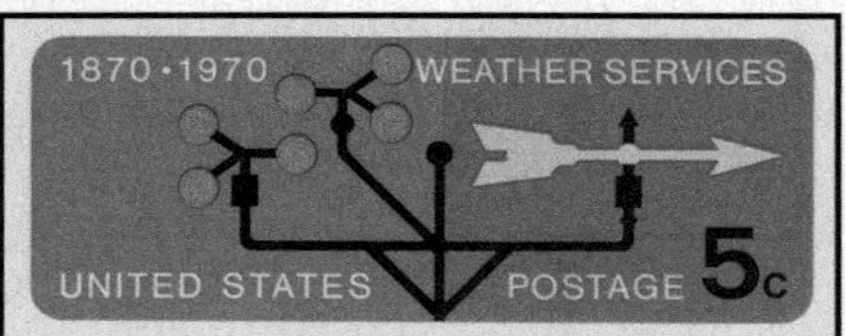

Weather Vane — PC35

Centenary of the Army's Signal Service, the Weather Services (Weather Bureau).

Designed by Robert Geissmann

1970, Sept. 1

UX57 PC35 5c **blue, yellow, red & black** .30 *1.00*
First day cancel, Fort Myer, Va. *(285,800)* 1.00
a. Yellow & black omitted *1,250.* *750.00*
Preprinted 300.00
b. Blue omitted *750.00* *5,000.*
c. Black omitted *1,250.* *850.00*
Preprinted 300.00

Paul Revere — PC36

Issued to honor Paul Revere, Revolutionary War patriot.

Designed by Howard C. Mildner after statue near Old North Church, Boston

Precanceled with 3 printed brown lines

1971, May 15

UX58 PC36 6c **brown** .30 *1.00*
First day cancel, Boston, Mass. 1.00
a. Double impression *3,250.*

First day cancellation was applied to 340,000 of Nos. UX58 and UY22.

Map Type of 1963
For International Use

1971, June 10

UX59 PC27 10c **blue & red** 4.50 *80.00*
First day cancel, New York, NY 1.00

First day cancellation was applied to 297,000 of Nos. UX59 and UXC11.

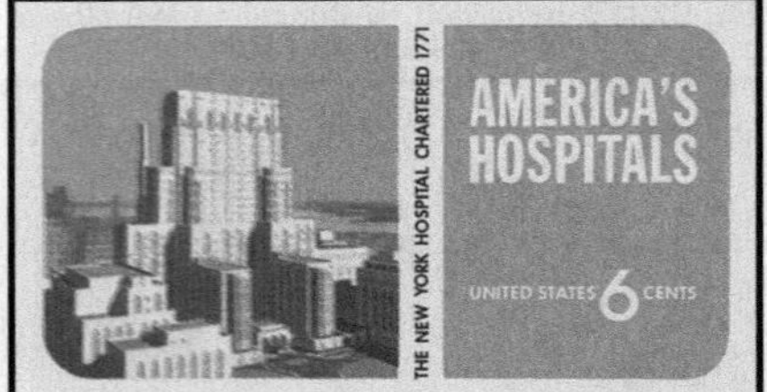

New York Hospital, New York City — PC37

Issued as a tribute to America's hospitals in connection with the 200th anniversary of New York Hospital.

Designed by Dean Ellis

1971, Sept. 16

UX60 PC37 6c **blue & multicolored** .30 *1.00*
First day cancel, New York, NY *(218,200)* 1.00
a. Blue & yellow omitted *1,000.*
b. Yellow omitted *500.00*
c. Red & black omitted —
d. Red omitted —
e. Tagging omitted 150.00
f. Black omitted *3,500.*

No. UX60f is significantly miscut, with only a small portion of the indicia present at the center top. The black vertical inscription line at the center is missing.

U.S.F. Constellation — PC38

Monument Valley — PC39

Gloucester, Mass. — PC40

Tourism Year of the Americas.

Designed by Melbourne Brindle

1972, June 29 — **Size: 152½x108½mm**

UX61 PC38 6c **black,** U.S.F. Constellation, *buff* (Yosemite, Mt. Rushmore, Niagara Falls, Williamsburg on back) 1.00 *10.00*
First day cancel, any city 1.25
a. Address side blank *300.00*
b. Reverse blank *650.00* *750.00*
c. Tagging omitted 200.00

UX62 PC39 6c **black,** Monument Valley, *buff* (Monterey, Redwoods, Gloucester, U.S.F. Constellation on back) .50 *10.00*
First day cancel, any city 1.25
a. Black omitted on back *575.00*
b. Orange omitted on back —
c. Reverse blank 475.00
d. Tagging omitted 200.00

UX63 PC40 6c **black,** Gloucester, *buff* (Rodeo, Mississippi Riverboat, Grand Canyon, Monument Valley on back) .50 *6.00*
First day cancel, any city 1.25
a. Black inverted *1,500.*
b. Reverse blank 450.00
c. Tagging omitted 200.00
d. Back inverted to the front 800.00
e. Black and pale salmon omitted on back —
Nos. UX61-UX63,UXC12-UXC13 (4) 2.45 *26.50*

Nos. UX61-UX63, UXC12-UXC13 went on sale throughout the United States. They were sold as souvenirs without postal validity at Belgica Philatelic Exhibition in Brussels and were displayed at the American Embassies in Paris and Rome. This is reflected in the first day cancel.

Used value for No. UX61b is for a card that is canceled but unaddressed.

John Hanson — PC41

Designed by Thomas Kronen after statue by Richard Edwin Brooks in Maryland Capitol

Precanceled with 3 printed blue lines.

1972, Sept. 1

UX64 PC41 6c **blue** .50 *1.00*
First day cancel, Baltimore, MD 1.00
a. Coarse paper .75 *1.25*

Liberty Type of 1873

Centenary of first U.S. postal card.

1973, Sept. 14

UX65 PC1 6c **magenta** .25 *1.00*
First day cancel, Washington, D.C. *(289,950)* 1.00
a. Tagging omitted *500.00*
b. Tagging inverted at lower left *500.00*

Samuel Adams — PC42

Designed by Howard C. Mildner

Precanceled with 3 printed orange lines

1973, Dec. 16

UX66 PC42 8c **orange** .50 *1.00*
First day cancel, Boston, Mass. *(147,522)* 1.00
a. Coarse paper .75 *1.00*
b. Double impression *1,000.*
c. As "a," double impression *1,750.*

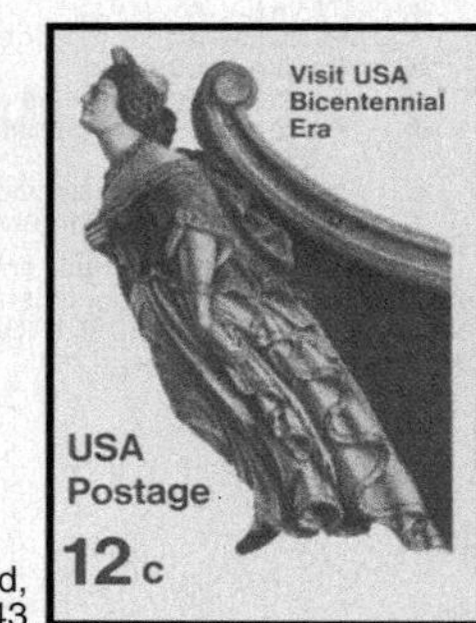

Ship's Figurehead, 1883 — PC43

Design is after a watercolor by Elizabeth Moutal of the oak figurehead by John Rogerson from the barque Edinburgh.

For International Use

1974, Jan. 4

UX67 PC43 12c **multicolored** .35 *50.00*
First day cancel, Miami, Fla. *(138,500)* 1.00
a. Yellow omitted *1,000.*
b. Tagging omitted *300.00*

Charles Thomson — PC44

John Witherspoon — PC45

Caesar Rodney — PC46

Designed by Howard C. Mildner

Precanceled with 3 printed emerald lines

1975-76

UX68 PC44 7c **emerald,** *Sept. 14, 1975* .30 *10.00*
First day cancel, Bryn Mawr, Pa. 1.00

Precanceled with 3 printed brown lines

UX69 PC45 9c **yellow brown,** *Nov. 10, 1975* .30 *1.00*
First day cancel, Princeton, N.J. 1.00

Precanceled with 3 printed blue lines

UX70 PC46 9c **blue,** *July 1, 1976* .30 *1.00*
First day cancel, Dover, Del. 1.00
a. Double impression *4,500.*

First day cancellation applied to 231,919 of Nos. UX68 and UY25; 254,239 of Nos. UX69 and UY26; 304,061 of Nos. UX70 and UY27.

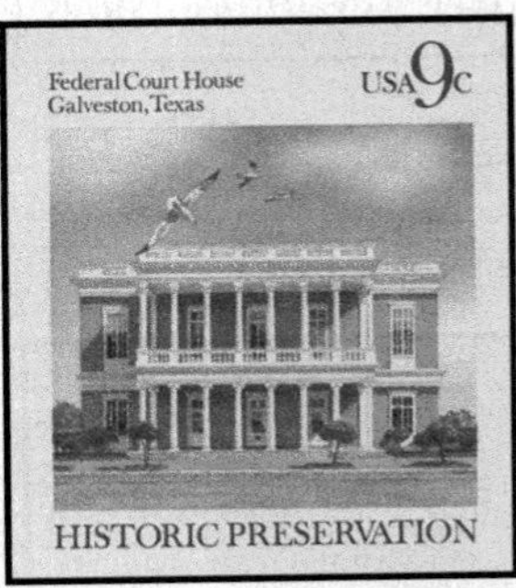

Federal Court House, Galveston, Texas — PC47

The Court House, completed in 1861, is on the National Register of Historic Places.

Designed by Donald Moss

1977, July 20

UX71 PC47 9c **multicolored** .25 *1.00*
First day cancel, Galveston, Tex. *(245,535)* 1.00
a. Black Omitted *6,000.*
b. Tagging omitted 150.00

Nathan Hale — PC48

Designed by Howard C. Mildner

Precanceled with 3 printed green lines

1977, Oct. 14

UX72 PC48 9c **green** .25 *1.00*
First day cancel, Coventry, Conn. 1.00
a. Cent sign missing after "9" 125.00
b. Double impression *1,400.*

First day cancellation applied to 304,592 of Nos. UX72 and UY28.

Approximately 400 examples are recorded of No. UX72a. The variety also exists on fluorescent stock (18 recorded). Value thus is 7 times the listed value.

Cincinnati Music Hall — PC49

Centenary of Cincinnati Music Hall, Cincinnati, Ohio.

Designed by Clinton Orlemann

1978, May 12

UX73 PC49 10c **multicolored** .30 *1.00*
First day cancel, Cincinnati, O. *(300,000)* 1.75

John Hancock — PC50

Designed by Howard Behrens

Precanceled with 3 printed brown orange lines.

1978

UX74 PC50 (10c) **brown orange,** *May 19* .30 *1.00*
First day cancel, Quincy, Mass. *(299,623)* 1.00

Inscribed "U.S. Postage 10¢"

UX75 PC50 10c **brown orange,** *June 20* .30 1.00
First day cancel, Quincy, Mass. *(187,120)* 1.00

Coast Guard Cutter Eagle — PC51

Designed by Carl G. Evers

For International Use

1978, Aug. 4

UX76 PC51 14c **multicolored** .40 *40.00*
First day cancel, Seattle, Wash. *(196,400)* 1.00

Molly Pitcher Firing Cannon at Monmouth — PC52

Bicentennial of Battle of Monmouth, June 28, 1778, and to honor Molly Pitcher (Mary Ludwig Hays).

Designed by David Blossom

1978, Sept. 8 **Litho.**

UX77 PC52 10c **multicolored** .30 *1.60*
First day cancel, Freehold, N.J. *(180,280)* 1.00

Clark and his Frontiersmen Approaching Fort Sackville — PC53

Bicentenary of capture of Fort Sackville from the British by George Rogers Clark.

Designed by David Blossom

1979, Feb. 23 **Litho.**

UX78 PC53 10c **multicolored** .30 *1.50*
First day cancel, Vincennes, Ind. 1.00
a. Yellow omitted —

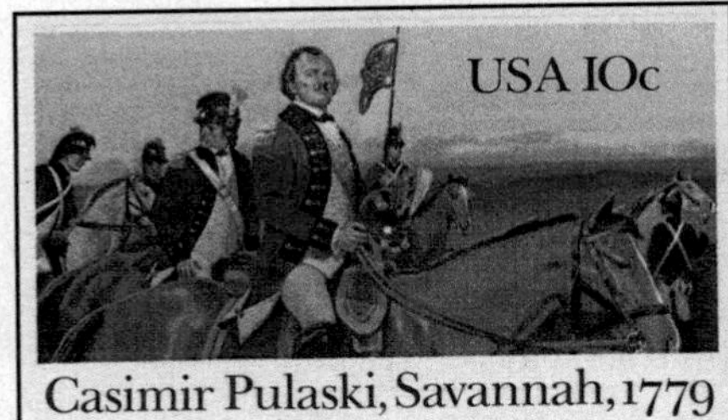

Gen. Casimir Pulaski — PC54

Bicentenary of the death of Gen. Casimir Pulaski (1748-1779), Polish nobleman who served in American Revolutionary Army.

1979, Oct. 11 **Litho.**

UX79 PC54 10c **multicolored** .30 *1.50*
First day cancel, Savannah. GA *(210,000)* 1.00

Olympic Games Issue

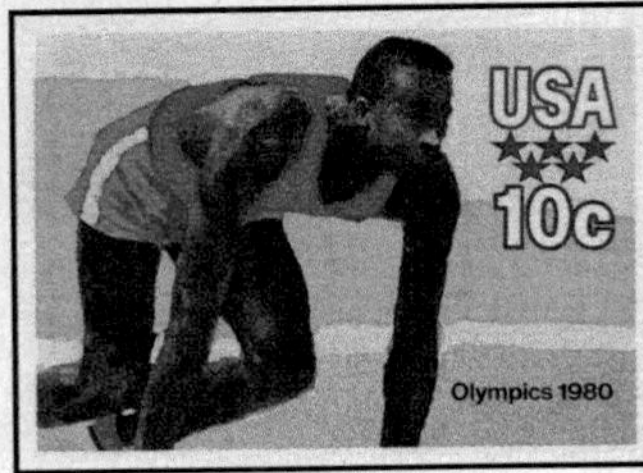

Sprinter PC55

22nd Olympic Games, Moscow, July 19-Aug. 3, 1980.

Designed by Robert M. Cunningham

1979, Sept. 17 **Litho.**

UX80 PC55 10c **multicolored** .60 *1.50*
First day cancel, Eugene, Ore. 1.00
a. Tagging omitted 200.00 *300.00*

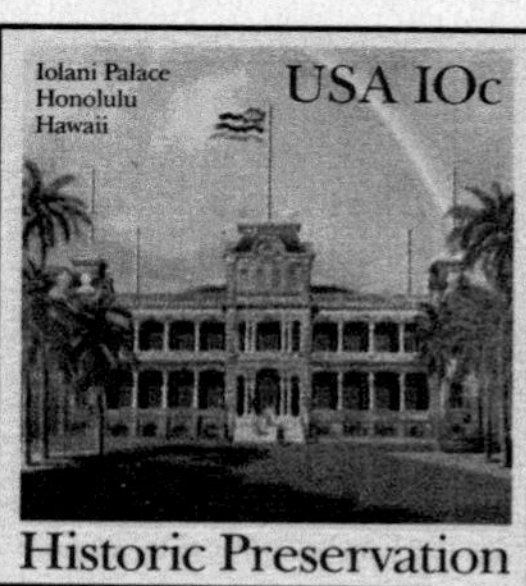

Iolani Palace, Honolulu — PC56

1979, Oct. 1 **Litho.**

UX81 PC56 10c **multicolored** .30 *1.50*
First day cancel, Honolulu, HI *(242,804)* 1.00
a. Tagging omitted — —

Women's Figure Skating PC57

13th Winter Olympic Games, Lake Placid, N.Y., Feb. 12-24.

Designed by Robert M. Cunningham

For International Use

1980, Jan. 15 **Litho.**

UX82 PC57 14c **multicolored** .60 *35.00*
a. Double impression of tagging bar, one at left *400.00*
First day cancel, Atlanta, GA *(160,977)* 1.00

Salt Lake Temple, Salt Lake City — PC58

1980, Apr. 5 **Litho.**

UX83 PC58 10c **multicolored** .25 *1.50*
First day cancel, Salt Lake City, UT *(325,260)* 1.00
a. Tagging omitted 300.00

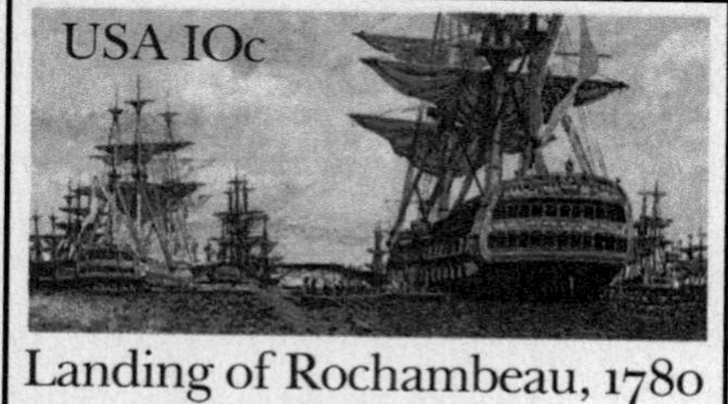

Rochambeau's Fleet — PC59

Count Jean-Baptiste de Rochambeau's landing at Newport, R.I. (American Revolution) bicentenary.

Designed by David Blossom

1980, July 11 **Litho.**

UX84 PC59 10c **multicolored** .25 *1.50*
First day cancel, Newport, R.I. *(180,567)* 1.00
a. Front normal, black & yellow on back *4,000.*
b. Magenta & blue omitted *3,000.*
Preprinting on reverse *1,500.*

Whig Infantrymen — PC60

Bicentenary of the Battle of Kings Mountain (American Revolution).

Designed by David Blossom

1980, Oct. 7 **Litho.**

UX85 PC60 10c **multicolored** .25 *1.50*
First day cancel, Kings Mountain, NC *(136,130)* 1.00

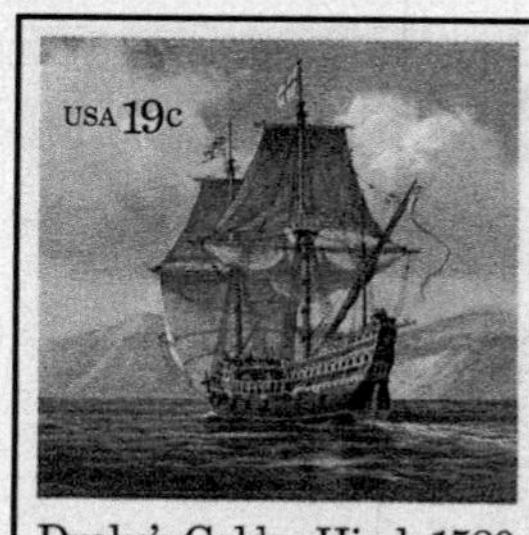

Golden Hinde — PC61

300th anniv. of Sir Francis Drake's circumnavigation (1578-1580).

Designed by Charles J. Lundgren

For International Use

1980, Nov. 21

UX86 PC61 19c **multicolored** .75 *50.00*
First day cancel, San Rafael, CA *(290,547)* 1.00

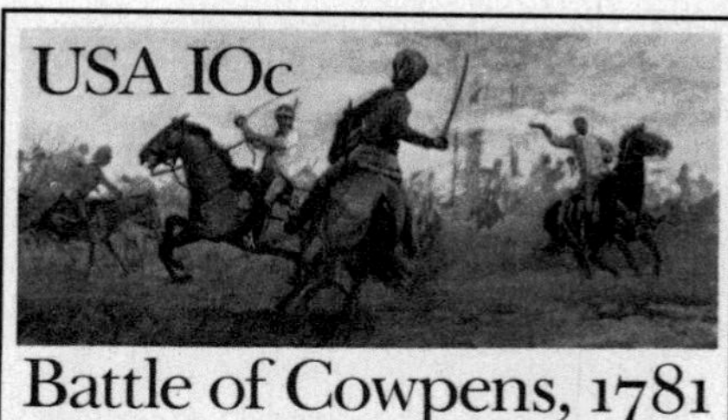

Cols. Washington and Tarleton — PC62

Bicentenary of the Battle of Cowpens (American Revolution).

Designed by David Blossom

1981, Jan. 17

UX87 PC62 10c **multicolored** .25 *25.00*
First day cancel, Cowpens, SC *(160,000)* 1.00

Eagle — PC63

Precanceled with 3 printed violet lines

1981, Mar. 15

UX88 PC63 (12c) **violet** .35 *.65*
First day cancel, Memphis, TN 1.00

See No. 1818, FDC section.

Isaiah Thomas — PC64

Designed by Chet Jezierski

1981, May 5 **Precanceled with 3 printed lines**

UX89 PC64 12c **light blue** .30 *.75*
First day cancel, Worcester, MA *(185,610)* 1.00

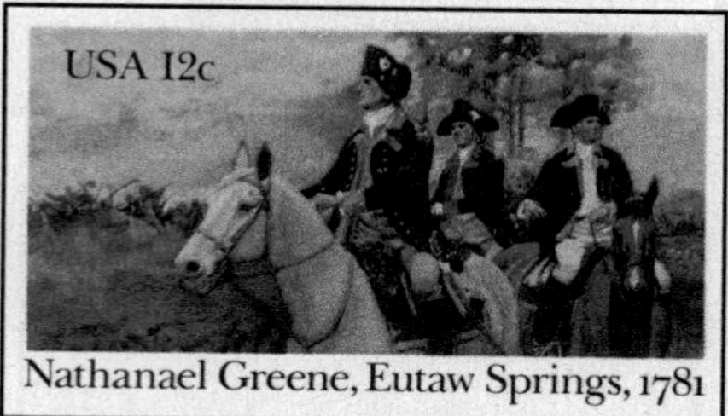

PC65

Bicentenary of the Battle at Eutaw Springs (American Revolution)

Designed by David Blossom

1981, Sept. 8 **Litho.**

UX90 PC65 12c **multicolored** .30 *25.00*
First day cancel, Eutaw Springs, SC *(115,755)* 1.00
a. Red & yellow omitted *2,900.*

PC66

Designed by David Blossom

1981, Sept. 23

UX91 PC66 12c **multicolored** .30 *30.00*
First day cancel, Saint Louis, MO 1.00

Robert Morris — PC67

1981 **Precanceled with 3 printed lines**

UX92 PC67 (13c) **buff**, *Oct. 11* .30 *.60*
First day cancel, Memphis, TN 1.00

See No. 1946, FDC section.

Inscribed: U.S. Postage 13¢

UX93 PC67 13c **buff**, *Nov. 10* .30 *.60*
First day cancel, Philadelphia, PA 1.00
a. Buff omitted 500.00

On No. UX93a, the copyright symbol and "1981" in buff is present at the lower left corner of the card.

General Francis Marion (1732?-1795) — PC68

Designed by David Blossom

1982, Apr. 3 **Litho.**

UX94 PC68 13c **multicolored** .30 *1.00*
First day cancel, Marion, SC *(141,162)* 1.00

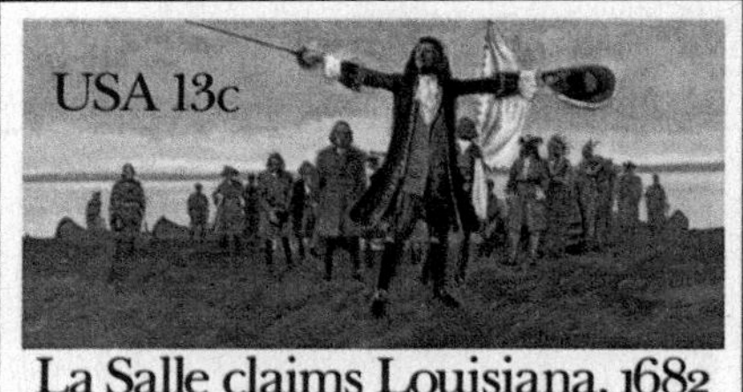

Rene Robert Cavelier, Sieur de la Salle (1643-1687) — PC69

Designed by David Blossom

1982, Apr. 7 **Litho.**

UX95 PC69 13c **multicolored** .30 *1.00*
First day cancel, New Orleans, LA 1.00

PC70

Designed by Melbourne Brindle

1982, June 18 **Litho.**

UX96 PC70 13c brown, red & cream, *buff* .30 *1.00*
First day cancel, Philadelphia, PA 1.00
a. Brown & cream omitted *1,000.*

PC71

Designed by Clint Orlemann

1982, Oct. 14 **Litho.**

UX97 PC71 13c **multicolored** .30 *1.00*
First day cancel, St. Louis, MO 1.00

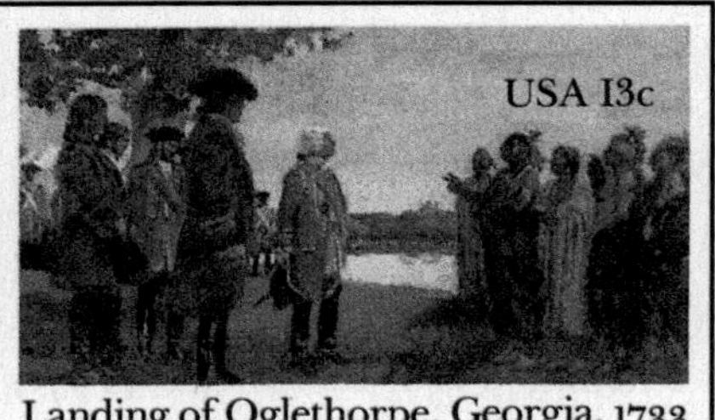

Gen. Oglethorpe Meeting Chief Tomo-Chi-Chi of the Yamacraw — PC72

Designed by David Blossom

1983, Feb. 12 **Litho.**

UX98 PC72 13c **multicolored** .30 *1.00*
First day cancel, Savannah, GA *(165,750)* 1.00

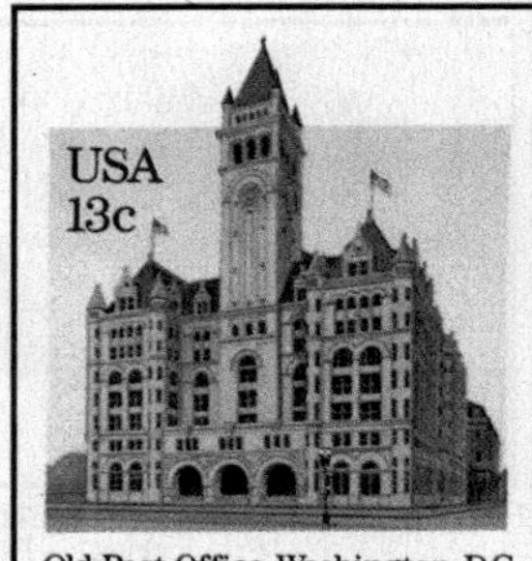

PC73

Designed by Walter Brooks

1983, Apr. 19 **Litho.**

UX99 PC73 13c **multicolored** .30 *1.00*
First day cancel, Washington, DC *(125,056)* 1.00

Olympics 84, Yachting — PC74

Designed by Bob Peak

1983, Aug. 5 **Litho.**

UX100 PC74 13c **multicolored** .30 *1.00*
First day cancel, Long Beach, CA *(132,232)* 1.00
a. Yellow & red omitted *5,500.* —
Preprinted *5,000.*

The Ark and the Dove — PC75

Designed by David Blossom

1984, Mar. 25 **Litho.**

UX101 PC75 13c **multicolored** .30 *1.00*
First day cancel, St. Clement's Island, MD *(131,222)* 1.00

Runner Carrying Olympic Torch — PC76

Designed by Robert Peak

1984, Apr. 30 **Litho.**

UX102 PC76 13c **multicolored** .30 *1.25*
First day cancel, Los Angeles, CA *(110,627)* 1.00
a. Black & yellow inverted 7,000.
b. Tagging omitted 350.00

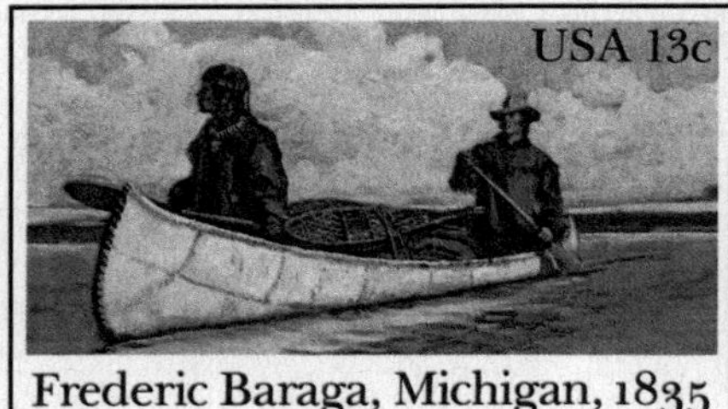

Father Baraga and Indian Guide in Canoe — PC77

Designed by David Blossom

1984, June 29 **Litho.**

UX103 PC77 13c **multicolored** .30 *1.00*
First day cancel, Marquette, MI *(100,156)* 1.00

Dominguez Adobe at Rancho San Pedro — PC78

Designed by Earl Thollander

1984, Sept. 16 **Litho.**

UX104 PC78 13c **multicolored** .30 *1.00*
First day cancel, Compton, CA *(100,545)* 1.00
a. Black & blue omitted *1,500.*
b. Tagging omitted —

Charles Carroll (1737-1832) — PC79

Designed by Richard Sparks

1985 **Precanceled with 3 printed lines**

UX105 PC79 (14c) **pale green,** *Feb. 1* .45 *.65*
First day cancel, New Carrollton, MD *(135,642)* 1.00

Inscribed: USA 14

UX106 PC79 14c **pale green,** *Mar. 6* .45 *.55*
First day cancel, Annapolis, MD *(111,122)* 1.00

Clipper Flying Cloud — PC80

Designed by Richard Schlecht

For International Use

1985, Feb. 27 **Litho.**
UX107 PC80 25c **multicolored** .70 *35.00*
First day cancel, Salem, MA *(95,559)* 1.25

No. UX107 was sold by the USPS at CUP-PEX 87, Perth, Western Australia, with a cachet honoring CUP-PEX 87 and the America's Cup race. Value $2.

George Wythe (1726-1806) — PC81

Designed by Chet Jezierski from a portrait by John Fergusson.

Precanceled with 3 printed lines

1985, June 20
UX108 PC81 14c **bright apple green** .30 *.75*
First day cancel, Williamsburg, VA *(133,334)* 1.00
a. Indicia missing —

On No. UX108a, the left precancel, "George Wythe" and the copyright symbol are normal.

Arrival of Thomas Hooker and Hartford Congregation — PC82

Settlement of Connecticut, 350th Anniv.

Designed by David Blossom

1986, Apr. 18 **Litho.**
UX109 PC82 14c **multicolored** .30 *1.50*
First day cancel, Hartford, CT *(76,875)* 1.00

Stamp Collecting — PC83

Designed by Ray Ameijide

1986, May 23 **Litho.**
UX110 PC83 14c **multicolored** .30 *1.25*
First day cancel, Chicago, IL *(75,548)* 1.00

No. UX110 was sold by the USPS at "Najubria 86," in Germany, with a show cachet. Value: unused, $6; used, $20.

Francis Vigo (1747-1836) — PC84

Designed by David Blossom

1986, May 24 **Litho.**
UX111 PC84 14c **multicolored** .30 *1.25*
First day cancel, Vincennes, IN *(100,141)* 1.00

No. UX111 is a joint issue with an Italy 450-lira postal card of the same design.

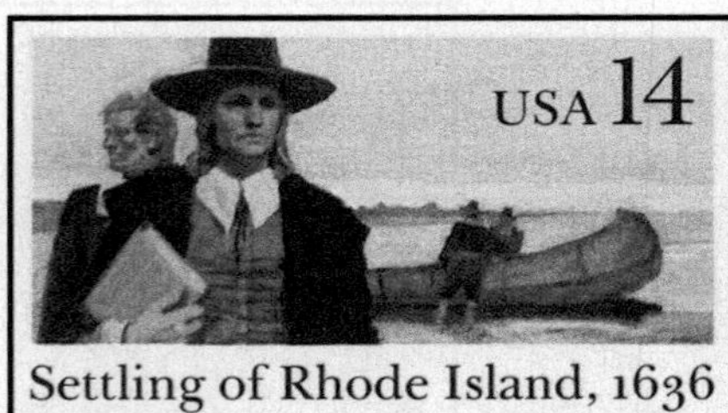

Roger Williams (1603-1683), Clergyman, Landing at Providence — PC85

Settling of Rhode Island, 350th Anniv.

Designed by David Blossom

1986, June 26 **Litho.**
UX112 PC85 14c **multicolored** .30 *1.50*
First day cancel, Providence, RI *(54,559)* 1.00

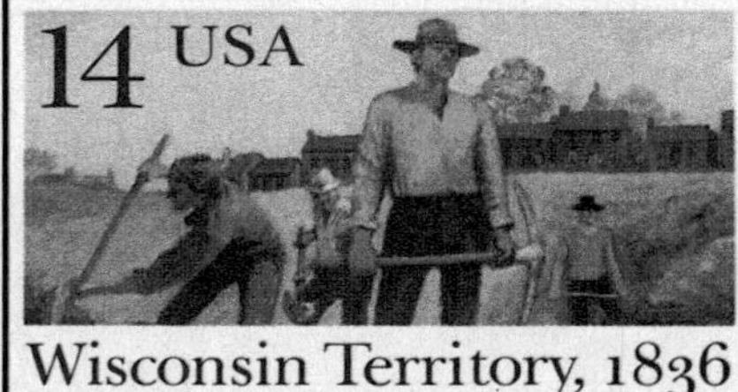

Miners, Shake Rag Street Housing — PC86

Wisconsin Territory Sesquicentennial.

Designed by David Blossom

1986, July 3 **Litho.**
UX113 PC86 14c **multicolored** .30 *1.00*
First day cancel, Mineral Point, WI *(41,224)* 1.00
a. Tagging omitted 200.00

The First Muster, by Don Troiani — PC87

Designed by Bradbury Thompson

1986, Dec. 12 **Litho.**
UX114 PC87 14c **multicolored** .30 *1.25*
First day cancel, Boston, MA *(72,316)* 1.00
a. Tagging omitted —

PC88

The self-scouring steel plow invented by blacksmith John Deere in 1837 pictured at lower left.

Designed by William H. Bond

1987, May 22 **Litho.**
UX115 PC88 14c **multicolored** .30 *1.25*
First day cancel, Moline, IL *(160,009)* 1.00

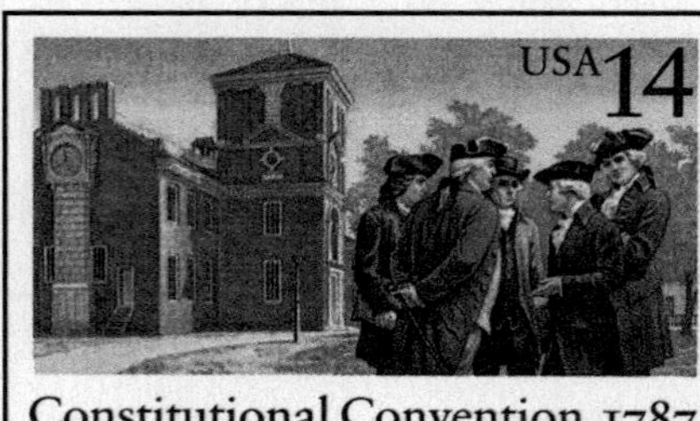

Convening of the Constitutional Convention, 1787 — PC89

George Mason, Gouverneur Morris, James Madison, Alexander Hamilton and Charles C. Pinckney are listed in the lower left corner of the card.

Designed by David K. Stone

1987, May 25 **Litho.**
UX116 PC89 14c **multicolored** .30 *1.00*
First day cancel, Philadelphia, PA *(138,207)* 1.00
a. Double black and blue, with first day cancel *650.00*

Stars and Stripes — PC90

Designed by Steven Dohanos

1987, June 14 **Litho.**
UX117 PC90 14c **black, blue & red** .30 *1.00*
First day cancel, Baltimore, MD 1.00
a. Double impression of tagging bar *175.00*

No. UX117 was sold by the USPS at Cologne, Germany, with a cachet for Philatelia '87. Value $2.

Take Pride in America — PC91

Designed by Lou Nolan

1987, Sept. 22 **Litho.**
UX118 PC91 14c **multicolored** .30 *1.25*
First day cancel, Jackson, WY *(47,281)* 1.00

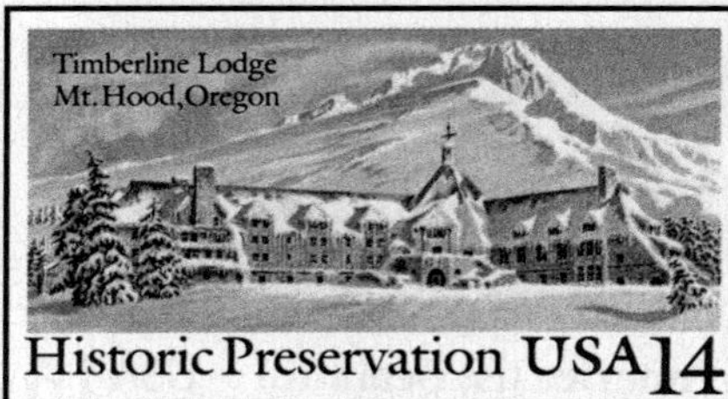

Timberline Lodge, 50th Anniversary — PC92

Designed by Walter DuBois Richards

1987, Sept. 28 **Litho.**

UX119 PC92 14c **multicolored** .30 *1.25*
First day cancel, Timberline, OR *(63,595)* 1.25

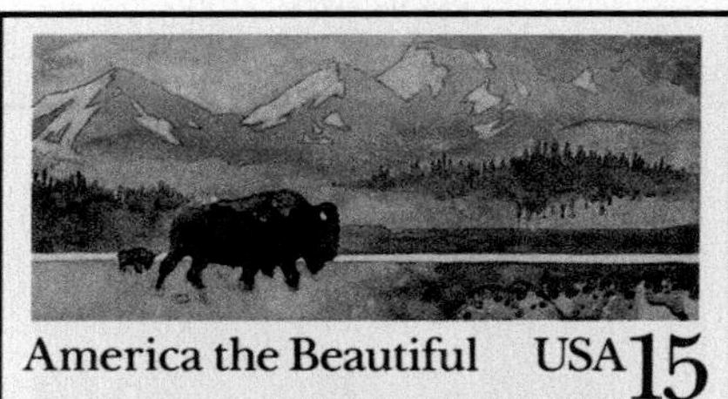

American Buffalo and Prairie — PC93

Designed by Bart Forbes

1988, Mar. 28 **Litho.**

UX120 PC93 15c **multicolored** .30 *.60*
First day cancel, Buffalo, WY *(52,075)* 1.00

- *a.* Black and tagging omitted 1,750.
- *b.* Printed on both sides *350.00*
- *c.* Front normal, blue & black on back *500.00*
- *d.* Black & magenta and tagging omitted *1,000.*
- *e.* Black, yellow, blue & tagging omitted *1,250.*
- *f.* Black, blue & tagging omitted *1,750.*
- *g.* Black, magenta, yellow & tagging omitted *1,750.*
- *h.* Double black impression —
- *i.* Triple black impression —
- *j.* Double black and blue impression —
- *k.* Double magenta & blue, and triple black impression —
- *l.* Magenta and tagging omitted —

Tagged

Postal cards from No. UX57 onward are either tagged or printed with luminescent ink unless otherwise noted.

PC94

Designed by Pierre Mion

1988, May 4 **Litho.**

UX121 PC94 15c **multicolored** .30 *1.00*
First day cancel, Washington, DC *(52,188)* 1.00

Yorkshire, Squarerigged Packet — PC95

Inscribed: Yorkshire, Black Ball Line, Packet Ship, circa 1850 at lower left.

Designed by Richard Schlect

For International Use

1988, June 29 **Litho.**

UX122 PC95 28c **multicolored** .60 *30.00*
First day cancel, Mystic, CT *(46,505)* 1.00

- *a.* Black & blue omitted *850.00*
- *b.* Black, blue, yellow & tagging omitted *1,250.*
- *c.* Black, magenta & tagging omitted *1,000.*
- *d.* Black, magenta, yellow & tagging omitted *1,000.*
- *e.* Black & tagging omitted *2,000.*

Harvesting Corn Fields — PC96

Iowa Territory Sesquicentennial.

Designed by Greg Hargreaves

1988, July 2 **Litho.**

UX123 PC96 15c **multicolored** .30 *1.00*
First day cancel, Burlington, IA *(45,565)* 1.00

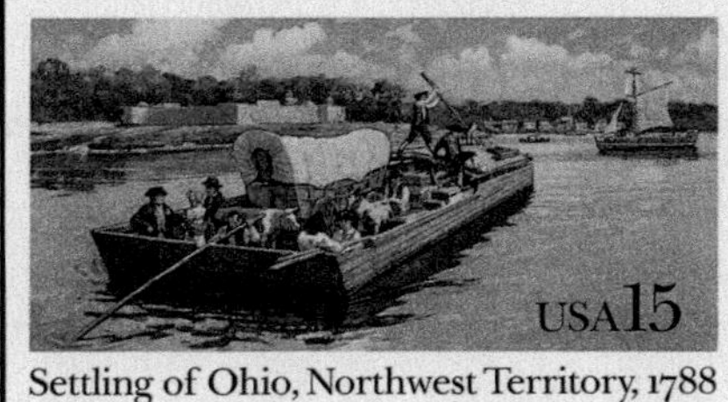

Flatboat Ferry Transporting Settlers Down the Ohio River — PC97

Bicentenary of the settlement of Ohio, the Northwest Territory. Design at lower left shows map of the eastern United States with Northwest Territory highlighted.

Designed by James M. Gurney and Susan Sanford

1988, July 15 **Litho.**

UX124 PC97 15c **multicolored** .30 *1.00*
First day cancel, Marietta, OH *(28,778)* 1.00

- *a.* Black, blue, yellow & tagging omitted *1,150.*
- *b.* Black, magenta & tagging omitted *750.00*
- *c.* Blue, black & tagging omitted *900.00*
- *d.* Black & tagging omitted *2,000.*
- *e.* Black, magenta, yellow & tagging omitted *1,500.*

PC98

Designed by Robert Reynolds

1988, Sept. 20 **Litho.**

UX125 PC98 15c **multicolored** .30 *1.00*
First day cancel, San Simeon, CA *(84,786)* 1.00

- *a.* Black, magenta & tagging omitted *750.00*
- *b.* Black, blue, yellow & tagging omitted *2,000.*
- *c.* Black, magenta, yellow & tagging omitted *1,000.*
- *d.* Black & tagging omitted *2,000.*
- *e.* Black, blue & tagging omitted *1,000.*

Pressman, New Yorker Reading Newspaper, 1787 — PC99

Designed by Roy Andersen

1988, Oct. 27 **Litho.**

UX126 PC99 15c **multicolored** .30 *1.00*
First day cancel, New York, NY *(37,661)* 1.00

Red-tailed Hawk and Sonora Desert at Sunset — PC100

Designed by Bart Forbes

1989, Jan. 13 **Litho.**

UX127 PC100 15c **multicolored** .30 *1.00*
First day cancel, Tucson, AZ *(51,891)* 1.00

Healy Hall, Georgetown University — PC101

Designed by John Morrell. Inscription at lower left: "Healy Hall / Georgetown / Washington, DC / HISTORIC PRESERVATION."

1989, Jan. 23 **Litho.**

UX128 PC101 15c **multicolored** .30 *1.00*
First day cancel, Washington, DC *(54,897)* 1.00

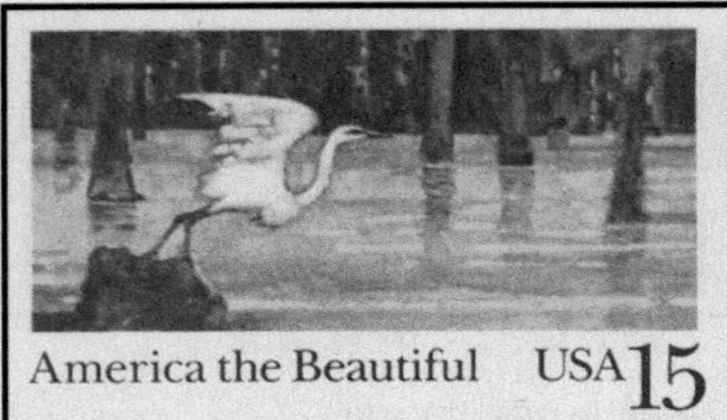

Great Blue Heron, Marsh — PC102

Designed by Bart Forbes

1989, Mar. 17 **Litho.**
UX129 PC102 15c **multicolored** .30 *1.00*
First day cancel, Okefenokee, GA *(58,208)* 1.25

Settling of Oklahoma — PC103

Designed by Bradbury Thompson

1989, Apr. 22 **Litho.**
UX130 PC103 15c **multicolored** .30 *1.00*
First day cancel, Guthrie, OK *(68,689)* 1.00

Used values are for contemporaneous usage without additional postage applied. Used values for international-rate cards are for proper usage.

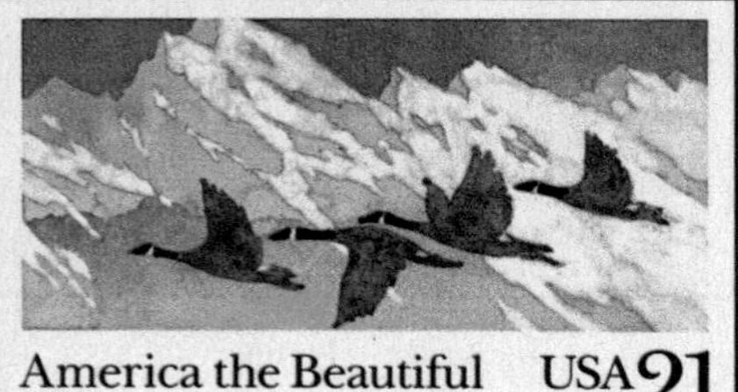

Canada Geese and Mountains — PC104

Designed by Bart Forbes

1989, May 5 **Litho.** **For Use to Canada**
UX131 PC104 21c **multicolored** .50 *35.00*
First day cancel, Denver, CO *(59,303)* 1.25

Seashore — PC105

Designed by Bart Forbes

1989, June 17 **Litho.**
UX132 PC105 15c **multicolored** .30 *1.25*
First day cancel, Cape Hatteras, NC *(67,073)* 1.25

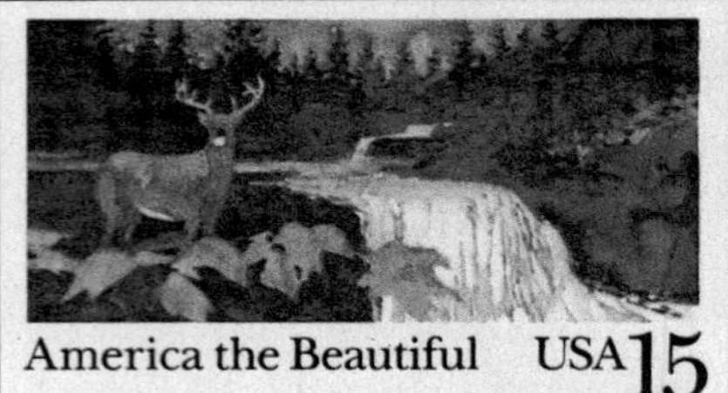

PC106

Designed by Bart Forbes

1989, Aug. 26 **Litho.**
UX133 PC106 15c **multicolored** .30 *1.25*
First day cancel, Cherokee, NC *(67,878)* 1.25

Jane Addams' Hull House Community Center 1889, Chicago — PC107

Designed by Michael Hagel

1989, Sept. 16 **Litho.**
UX134 PC107 15c **multicolored** .30 *1.25*
First day cancel, Chicago, IL *(53,773)* 1.00

Aerial View of Independence Hall, Philadelphia — PC108

Designed by Bart Forbes

1989, Sept. 25 **Litho.**
UX135 PC108 15c **multicolored** .30 *1.25*
First day cancel, Philadelphia, PA *(61,659)* 1.00

See No. UX139.

Inner Harbor, Baltimore — PC109

Designed by Bart Forbes

1989, Oct. 7 **Litho.**
UX136 PC109 15c **multicolored** .30 *1.25*
First day cancel, Baltimore, MD *(58,746)* 1.00

See No. UX140.

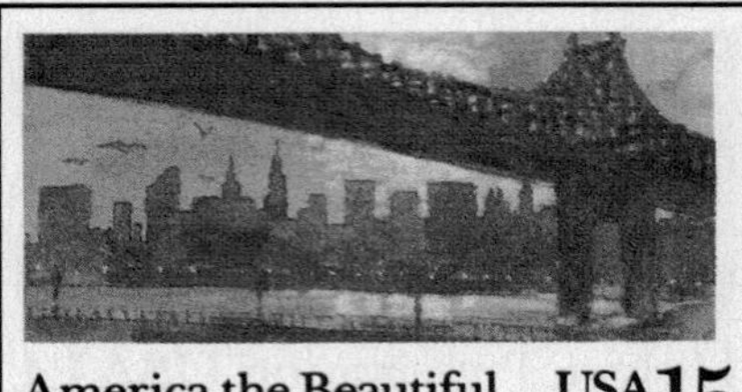

59th Street Bridge, New York City — PC110

Designed by Bart Forbes

1989, Nov. 8 **Litho.**
UX137 PC110 15c **multicolored** .30 *1.25*
First day cancel, New York, NY *(48,044)* 1.00

See No. UX141.

West Face of the Capitol, Washington D.C. — PC111

Designed by Bart Forbes

1989, Nov. 26 **Litho.**
UX138 PC111 15c **multicolored** .30 *1.25*
First day cancel, Washington, DC 1.00

See No. UX142.

1989, Dec. 1 **Litho.**

Designed by Bart Forbes. Issued in sheets of 4 + 2 inscribed labels picturing 20th UPU Congress or World Stamp Expo '89 emblems, and rouletted 9½ on 2 or 3 sides.

UX139 PC108 15c **multicolored** 3.50 *5.00*
First day cancel, Washington, DC 1.00
UX140 PC109 15c **multicolored** 3.50 *5.00*
First day cancel, Washington, DC 1.00
UX141 PC110 15c **multicolored** 3.50 *5.00*
First day cancel, Washington, DC 1.00
UX142 PC111 15c **multicolored** 3.50 *5.00*
First day cancel, Washington, DC 1.00
a. Sheet of 4, #UX139-UX142 15.00
b. As "a," inverted rouletting —
Nos. UX139-UX142 (4) 14.00 20.00

Unlike Nos. UX135-UX138, Nos. UX139-UX142 do not contain inscription and copyright symbol at lower left. Order on sheet is Nos. UX140, UX139, UX142, UX141.

Most examples of No. UX142a and UX139 are bent at the upper right corner.

The White House — PC112

Jefferson Memorial — PC113

Designed by Pierre Mion. Space for message at left.

1989 **Litho.**

UX143 PC112 15c **multicolored**, *Nov. 30* 1.50 *12.00*
First day cancel, Washington, DC 2.00

UX144 PC113 15c **multicolored**, *Dec. 2* 1.50 *12.00*
First day cancel, Washington, DC 2.00

Nos. UX143-UX144 sold for 50c each. Illustrations of the buildings without denominations are shown on the back of the card.

Rittenhouse Paper Mill, Germantown, PA — PC114

Designed by Harry Devlin.

1990, Mar. 13 **Litho.**

UX145 PC114 15c **multicolored** .30 *1.50*
First day cancel, New York, NY *(9,866)* 1.00

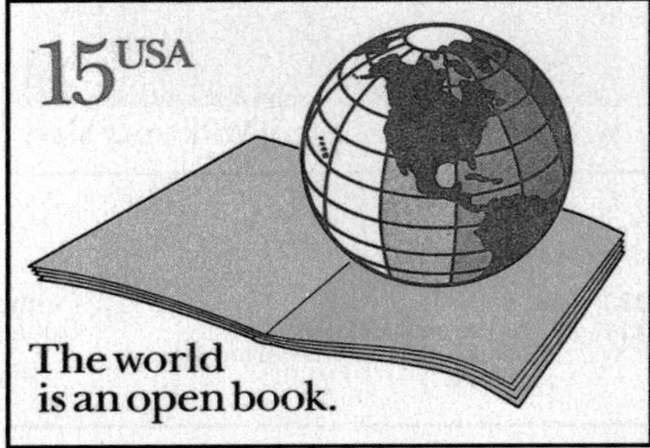

World Literacy Year — PC115

Designed by Joe Brockert.

1990, Mar. 22 **Litho.**

UX146 PC115 15c **multicolored** .30 *1.00*
First day cancel, Washington, DC *(11,163)* 1.00

PC116

Designed by Bradbury Thompson. Inscription in upper left corner: "Fur Traders Descending the Missouri / George Caleb Bingham, 1845 / Metropolitan Museum of Art".

1990, May 4 **Litho.**

UX147 PC116 15c **multicolored** 1.50 *12.00*
First day cancel, St. Louis, MO *(13,632)* 2.00

No. UX147 sold for 50c and shows more of the painting without the denomination on the back.

PC117

Designed by Frank Constantino. Inscription at lower left: "HISTORIC PRESERVATION SERIES / Isaac Royall House, 1700s / Medford, Massachusetts / National Historic Landmark".

1990, June 16 **Litho.**

UX148 PC117 15c **multicolored** .30 *1.50*
First day cancel, Medford, MA *(21,708)* 1.00

Quadrangle, Stanford University — PC119

Designed by Jim M'Guinness.

1990, Sept. 30 **Litho.**

UX150 PC119 15c **multicolored** .30 *1.50*
First day cancel, Stanford, CA *(28,430)* 1.00

Constitution Hall, Washington, DC — PC120

Designed by Pierre Mion. Inscription at upper left: "Washington: Constitution Hall (at right)/ Memorial Continental Hall (reverse side) / Centennial, Daughters of the American Revolution".

1990, Oct. 11 **Litho.**

UX151 PC120 15c **multicolored** 1.50 *12.00*
First day cancel, Washington, DC *(33,254)* 2.00

No. UX151 sold for 50c.

Chicago Orchestra Hall — PC121

Designed by Michael Hagel. Inscription at lower left: "Chicago: Orchestra Hall / HISTORIC PRESERVATION / Chicago Symphony Orchestra / Centennial, 1891-1991".

1990, Oct. 19 **Litho.**

UX152 PC121 15c **multicolored** .30 *1.50*
First day cancel, Chicago, IL *(28,546)* 1.00

PC122

Designed by Richard Sheaff.

1991, Jan. 24 **Litho.**

UX153 PC122 19c **rose, ultramarine & black** .40 *1.00*
First day cancel, Washington, DC *(26,690)* 1.00

PC123

Designed by Howard Koslow.

1991, Apr. 1 **Litho.**

UX154 PC123 19c **multicolored** .40 *1.50*
First day cancel, New York, NY *(27,063)* 1.00

Old Red, University of Texas Medical Branch, Galveston, Cent. — PC124

Designed by Don Adair.

1991, June 14 **Litho.**

UX155 PC124 19c **multicolored** .40 *1.50*
First day cancel, Galveston, TX *(24,308)* 1.00

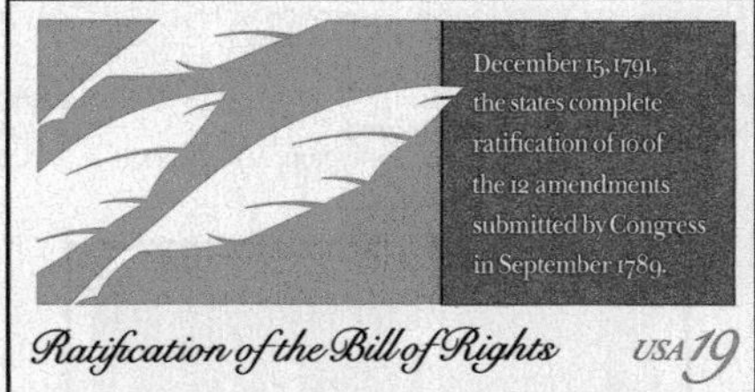

Ratification of the Bill of Rights, Bicent. — PC125

Designed by Mark Zaref.

1991, Sept. 25 **Litho.**

UX156 PC125 19c **red, blue & black** .40 *1.50*
First day cancel, Richmond, VA *(27,457)* 1.00

Main Building, University of Notre Dame PC126

Designed by Frank Costantino. Inscription at lower left: Notre Dame / Sesquicentennial / 1842-1992.

1991, Oct. 15 **Litho.**

UX157 PC126 19c **multicolored** .40 *1.50*
First day cancel, Notre Dame, IN *(34,325)* 1.00

Niagara Falls — PC127

Designed by Wendell Minor.

For Use to Canada & Mexico

1991, Aug. 21 **Litho.**
UX158 PC127 30c **multicolored** .75 *20.00*
First day cover, Niagara Falls, NY *(29,762)* 1.25

Tagged

Postal cards from No. UX57 onward are either tagged or printed with luminescent ink unless otherwise noted.

The Old Mill — PC128

Designed by Harry Devlin. Inscription at lower left: The Old Mill / University of Vermont / Bicentennial.

1991, Oct. 29 **Litho.**
UX159 PC128 19c **multicolored** .40 *1.50*
First day cancel, Burlington, VT *(23,965)* 1.00

Wadsworth Atheneum, Hartford, CT — PC129

Designed by Frank Costantino. Inscription at lower left: Wadsworth Atheneum / Hartford, Connecticut / 150th Anniversary / 1842-1992.

1992, Jan. 16 **Litho.**
UX160 PC129 19c **multicolored** .40 *1.50*
First day cancel, Hartford, CT *(41,499)* 1.00

Cobb Hall, University of Chicago — PC130

Designed by Michael P. Hagel. Inscription at lower left: Cobb Hall / The University of Chicago / Centennial Year, 1991-1992.

1992, Jan. 23 **Litho.**
UX161 PC130 19c **multicolored** .40 *1.50*
First day cancel, Chicago, IL *(27,150)* 1.00

Waller Hall, Willamette University — PC131

Designed by Bradbury Thompson. Inscription at lower left: Waller Hall / Salem, Oregon / Willamette University / Sesquicentennial / 1842-1992.

1992, Feb. 1 **Litho.**
UX162 PC131 19c **multicolored** .40 *1.50*
First day cancel, Salem, OR *(28,463)* 1.00

PC132

Designed by Dennis Simon. Space for message at left. Inscription at upper left: "At right: The Reliance, USA 1903 / Reverse: The Ranger, USA 1937."

1992, May 6 **Litho.**
UX163 PC132 19c **multicolored** 1.75 *12.00*
First day cancel, San Diego, CA *(19,944)* 2.00

No. UX163 sold for 50 cents.

PC133

Designed by Ken Hodges.

1992, May 9 **Litho.**
UX164 PC133 19c **multicolored** .40 *2.00*
First day cancel, Stevenson, WA *(32,344)* 1.00

Ellis Island Immigration Museum — PC134

Designed by Howard Koslow. Inscription at lower left: "Ellis Island / Centennial 1992."

1992, May 11 **Litho.**
UX165 PC134 19c **multicolored** .40 *1.50*
First day cancel, Ellis Island, NY *(38,482)* 1.00

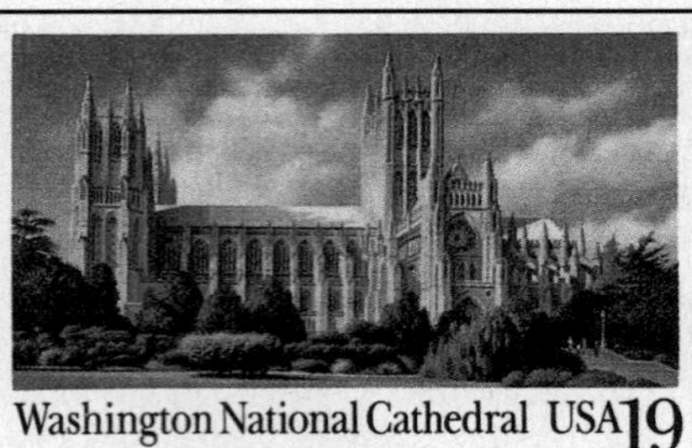

PC135

Designed by Howard Koslow.

1993, Jan. 6 **Litho.**
UX166 PC135 19c **multicolored** .40 *1.50*
First day cancel, Washington, DC *(8,315)* 1.00

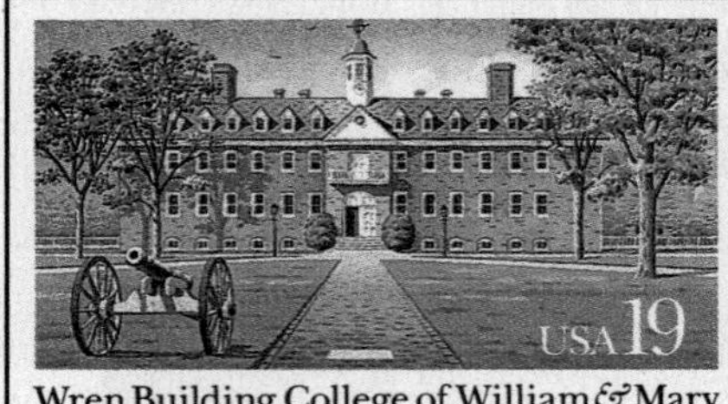

PC136

Designed by Pierre Mion.

1993, Feb. 8 **Litho.**
UX167 PC136 19c **multicolored** .40 *1.50*
First day cancel, Williamsburg, VA *(9,758)* 1.00

Opening of Holocaust Memorial Museum — PC137

Designed by Tom Engeman. Space for message at left. Inscription at upper left: "Washington, DC: / United States / Holocaust Memorial Museum."

1993, Mar. 23 **Litho.**
UX168 PC137 19c **multicolored** 1.75 *3.00*
First day cancel, Washington, DC *(8,234)* 2.00

No. UX168 sold for 50c, and shows aerial view of museum on the back.

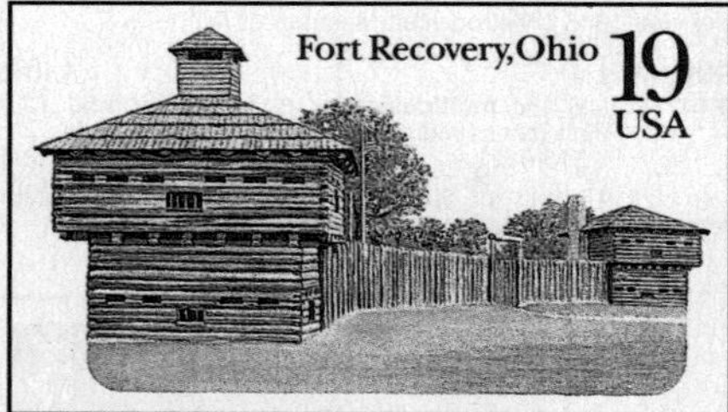

PC138

Designed by Michael Hagel.

1993, June 13 **Litho.**
UX169 PC138 19c **multicolored** .40 *1.25*
First day cancel, Fort Recovery, OH *(8,254)* 1.00

PC139

Designed by Robert Timberlake.

1993, Sept. 14 **Litho.**
UX170 PC139 19c **multicolored** .40 *1.25*
First day cancel, Chapel Hill, NC *(7,796)* 1.00

PC140

Designed by Frank Constantino.

1993, Sept. 17 **Litho.**
UX171 PC140 19c **multicolored** .40 *1.25*
First day cancel, Worcester, MA *(4,680)* 1.00

PC141

Designed by Michael Hagel.

1993, Oct. 9 **Litho.**
UX172 PC141 19c **multicolored** .40 *1.50*
First day cancel, Jacksonville, IL *(5,269)* 1.00

PC142

Designed by Harry Devlin.

1993, Oct. 14 **Litho.**
UX173 PC142 19c **multicolored** .40 *1.25*
First day cancel, Brunswick, ME *(33,750 est.)* 1.00

PC143

Designed by Michael Hagel.

1994, Feb. 12 **Litho.**
UX174 PC143 19c **multicolored** .40 *1.25*
First day cancel, Springfield, IL *(26,164)* 1.00

PC144

Designed by Michael Hagel.

1994, Mar. 11 **Litho.**
UX175 PC144 19c **multicolored** .40 *1.25*
First day cancel, Springfield, OH *(20,230)* 1.00

PC145

Designed by William Matthews.

1994, Aug. 11 **Litho.**
UX176 PC145 19c **multicolored** .40 *1.25*
First day cancel, Chinle, AZ *(19,826)* 1.00

St. Louis Union Station — PC146

Designed by Harry Devlin.

1994, Sept. 3 **Litho.**
UX177 PC146 19c **multicolored** .40 *1.25*
First day cancel, St. Louis, MO *(38,881)* 1.00

Legends of the West Type

Designed by Mark Hess.

1994, Oct. 18 **Litho.**
UX178 A2197 19c Home on the Range 1.10 *3.00*
UX179 A2197 19c Buffalo Bill 1.10 *3.00*
UX180 A2197 19c Jim Bridger 1.10 *3.00*
UX181 A2197 19c Annie Oakley 1.10 *3.00*
UX182 A2197 19c Native American Culture 1.10 *3.00*
UX183 A2197 19c Chief Joseph 1.10 *3.00*
UX184 A2197 19c Bill Pickett (revised) 1.10 *3.00*

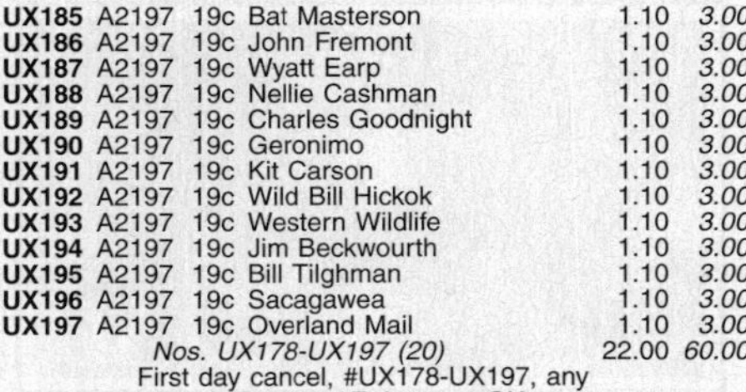

UX185 A2197 19c Bat Masterson 1.10 *3.00*
UX186 A2197 19c John Fremont 1.10 *3.00*
UX187 A2197 19c Wyatt Earp 1.10 *3.00*
UX188 A2197 19c Nellie Cashman 1.10 *3.00*
UX189 A2197 19c Charles Goodnight 1.10 *3.00*
UX190 A2197 19c Geronimo 1.10 *3.00*
UX191 A2197 19c Kit Carson 1.10 *3.00*
UX192 A2197 19c Wild Bill Hickok 1.10 *3.00*
UX193 A2197 19c Western Wildlife 1.10 *3.00*
UX194 A2197 19c Jim Beckwourth 1.10 *3.00*
UX195 A2197 19c Bill Tilghman 1.10 *3.00*
UX196 A2197 19c Sacagawea 1.10 *3.00*
UX197 A2197 19c Overland Mail 1.10 *3.00*
Nos. UX178-UX197 (20) 22.00 *60.00*
First day cancel, #UX178-UX197, any card, Tucson, AZ, Lawton, OK or Laramie, WY *(10,000 USPS est.)* 1.50

Nos. UX178-UX197 sold in packages of 20 different for $7.95.

Red Barn — PC147

Designed by Wendell Minor.

1995, Jan. 3 **Litho.**
UX198 PC147 20c **multicolored** .40 *.75*
First day cancel, Williamsburg, PA 1.00

First day cancellation was applied to 54,102 of Nos. U632, UX198.

PC148

1995 **Litho.**
UX199 PC148 (20c) **black, blue & red** 3.00 *6.00*

No. UX199 was only available through the Philatelic Fullfillment Center after its announcement 1/12/95. Cards submitted for first day cancels received a 12/13/94 cancel, even though they were not available on that date. Value $1.00.

Civil War Types

Designed by Mark Hess.

1995, June 29 **Litho.**
UX200 A2289 20c Monitor & Virginia 1.75 *3.00*
UX201 A2289 20c Robert E. Lee 1.75 *3.00*
UX202 A2289 20c Clara Barton 1.75 *3.00*
UX203 A2289 20c Ulysses S. Grant 1.75 *3.00*
UX204 A2289 20c Battle of Shiloh 1.75 *3.00*
UX205 A2289 20c Jefferson Davis 1.75 *3.00*
UX206 A2289 20c David Farragut 1.75 *3.00*
UX207 A2289 20c Frederick Douglass 1.75 *3.00*
UX208 A2289 20c Raphael Semmes 1.75 *3.00*
UX209 A2289 20c Abraham Lincoln 1.75 *3.00*
UX210 A2289 20c Harriet Tubman 1.75 *3.00*
UX211 A2289 20c Stand Watie 1.75 *3.00*
UX212 A2289 20c Joseph E. Johnston 1.75 *3.00*
UX213 A2289 20c Winfield Hancock 1.75 *3.00*
UX214 A2289 20c Mary Chesnut 1.75 *3.00*
UX215 A2289 20c Battle of Chancellorsville 1.75 *3.00*
UX216 A2289 20c William T. Sherman 1.75 *3.00*
UX217 A2289 20c Phoebe Pember 1.75 *3.00*
UX218 A2289 20c Stonewall Jackson 1.75 *3.00*
UX219 A2289 20c Battle of Gettysburg 1.75 *3.00*
Nos. UX200-UX219 (20) 35.00 *60.00*
First day cancel, any card, Gettysburg, PA 1.50
First day cancel, any card, any other city 1.50

Nos. UX200-UX219 sold in packages of 20 different for $7.95.

PC148a

For International Use

1995, Aug. 24 **Litho.**

UX219A PC148a 50c **multicolored**	1.25	*9.00*
First day cancel, St. Louis, MO *(6,008)*		1.25

PC149

Designed by Richard Sheaff.

1995, Sept. 3 **Litho.**

UX220 PC149 20c **multicolored**	.40	*1.00*
First day cancel, Hunt Valley, MD *(5,281)*		1.00

Comic Strip Types

Designed by Carl Herrman.

1995, Oct. 1 **Litho.**

UX221 A2313 20c The Yellow Kid	2.50	*3.00*
UX222 A2313 20c Katzenjammer Kids	2.50	*3.00*
UX223 A2313 20c Little Nemo in Slumberland	2.50	*3.00*
UX224 A2313 20c Bringing Up Father	2.50	*3.00*
UX225 A2313 20c Krazy Kat	2.50	*3.00*
UX226 A2313 20c Rube Goldberg's Inventions	2.50	*3.00*
UX227 A2313 20c Toonerville Folks	2.50	*3.00*
UX228 A2313 20c Gasoline Alley	2.50	*3.00*
UX229 A2313 20c Barney Google	2.50	*3.00*
UX230 A2313 20c Little Orphan Annie	2.50	*3.00*
UX231 A2313 20c Popeye	2.50	*3.00*
UX232 A2313 20c Blondie	2.50	*3.00*
UX233 A2313 20c Dick Tracy	2.50	*3.00*
UX234 A2313 20c Alley Oop	2.50	*3.00*
UX235 A2313 20c Nancy	2.50	*3.00*
UX236 A2313 20c Flash Gordon	2.50	*3.00*
UX237 A2313 20c Li'l Abner	2.50	*3.00*
UX238 A2313 20c Terry and the Pirates	2.50	*3.00*
UX239 A2313 20c Prince Valiant	2.50	*3.00*
UX240 A2313 20c Brenda Starr Reporter	2.50	*3.00*
Nos. UX221-UX240 (20)	50.00	60.00
First day cancel, any card, Boca Raton, FL		1.50

Nos. UX221-UX240 sold in packages of 20 different for $7.95.

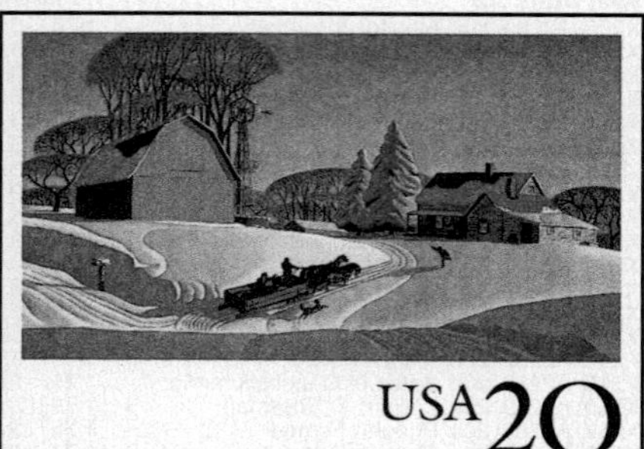

Winter Scene — PC150

1996, Feb. 23 **Litho.**

UX241 PC150 20c **multicolored**	.45	*1.00*
First day cancel, Watertown, NY *(11,764)*		1.00

Summer Olympics Type

Designed by Richard Waldrep.

1996, May 2 **Size: 150x108mm** **Litho.**

UX242 A2368 20c Men's cycling	2.75	*3.00*
UX243 A2368 20c Women's diving	2.75	*3.00*
UX244 A2368 20c Women's running	2.75	*3.00*
UX245 A2368 20c Men's canoeing	2.75	*3.00*
a. Tagging omitted	—	
UX246 A2368 20c Decathlon (javelin)	2.75	*3.00*
a. Inverted impression of entire address side, men's cycling picture on reverse	*350.00*	
UX247 A2368 20c Women's soccer	2.75	*3.00*
UX248 A2368 20c Men's shot put	2.75	*3.00*
UX249 A2368 20c Women's sailboarding	2.75	*3.00*
UX250 A2368 20c Women's gymnastics	2.75	*3.00*
UX251 A2368 20c Freestyle wrestling	2.75	*3.00*
UX252 A2368 20c Women's softball	2.75	*3.00*
UX253 A2368 20c Women's swimming	2.75	*3.00*
UX254 A2368 20c Men's sprints	2.75	*3.00*
UX255 A2368 20c Men's rowing	2.75	*3.00*
UX256 A2368 20c Beach volleyball	2.75	*3.00*
UX257 A2368 20c Men's basketball	2.75	*3.00*
UX258 A2368 20c Equestrian	2.75	*3.00*
UX259 A2368 20c Men's gymnastics	2.75	*3.00*
UX260 A2368 20c Men's swimming	2.75	*3.00*
UX261 A2368 20c Men's hurdles	2.75	*3.00*
a. Booklet of 20 postal cards, #UX242-UX261	55.00	
First day cancel, any card, Washington, DC		1.50

First day cancels of Nos. UX242-UX261 were available as sets from the US Postal Service. Unused sets of Nos. UX242-UX261 were not available from the US Philatelic Fullfillment Center for several months after the "official" first day. No. UX261a sold for $12.95.

PC151

Designed by Harry Devlin.

1996, June 1 **Litho.**

UX262 PC151 20c **multicolored**	.50	*1.00*
First day cancel, Annapolis, MD *(8,793)*		1.00

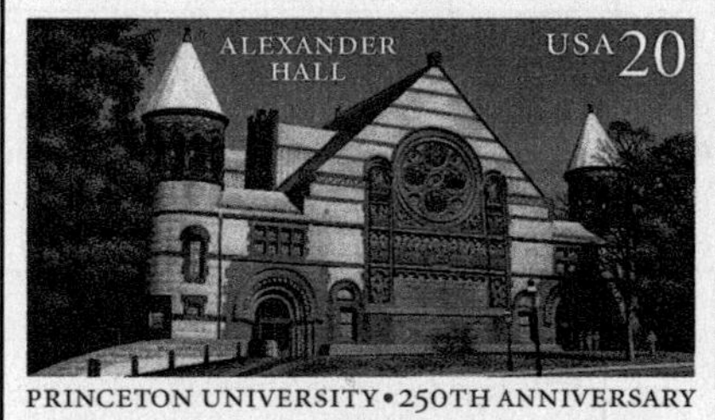

PC152

Designed by Howard Koslow.

1996, Sept. 20 **Litho.**

UX263 PC152 20c **multicolored**	.50	*1.00*
First day cancel, Princeton, NJ *(11,621)*		1.00

Endangered Species Type

Designed by James Balog.

1996, Oct. 2 **Litho.**

UX264 A2403 20c Florida panther	3.75	3.00
UX265 A2403 20c Black-footed ferret	3.75	3.00
UX266 A2403 20c American crocodile	3.75	3.00
UX267 A2403 20c Piping plover	3.75	3.00
UX268 A2403 20c Gila trout	3.75	3.00
UX269 A2403 20c Florida manatee	3.75	3.00
UX270 A2403 20c Schaus swallowtail butterfly	3.75	3.00
UX271 A2403 20c Woodland caribou	3.75	3.00
UX272 A2403 20c Thick-billed parrot	3.75	3.00
UX273 A2403 20c San Francisco garter snake	3.75	3.00
UX274 A2403 20c Ocelot	3.75	3.00
UX275 A2403 20c Wyoming toad	3.75	3.00
UX276 A2403 20c California condor	3.75	3.00
UX277 A2403 20c Hawaiian monk seal	3.75	3.00
UX278 A2403 20c Brown pelican	3.75	3.00
a. Booklet of 15 cards, #UX264-UX278	57.50	
First day cancel, #UX264-UX278, any card, San Diego, CA *(5,000)*		1.75

Nos. UX264-UX278 were issued bound three-to-a-page in a souvenir booklet that was sold for $11.95.

Love (Swans) Type

Designed by Supon Design.

1997, Feb. 4 **Litho.**

UX279 A2415 20c multicolored	.80	*2.50*

Stamp Designs Depicted on Reverse of Card

Scott 2814	2.50	2.50
Scott 2815	2.50	2.50
Scott 3123	2.50	2.50
Scott 3124	2.50	2.50
Sheet of 4, #2814-2815, 3123-3124	10.00	
Scott 2202	7.50	3.50
Scott 2248	7.50	3.50
Scott 2440	7.50	3.50
Scott 2813	7.50	3.50
Sheet of 4, #2202, 2248, 2440, 2813	30.00	

No. UX279 was sold in sets of 3 sheets of 4 picture postal cards with 8 different designs for $6.95 (two sheets of #2814-2815, 3123-3124 and one sheet of #2202, 2248, 2440, 2813). The cards are separated by microperfs. The picture side of each card depicted a previously released Love stamp design without the inscriptions and value.

First day cancels were not available on Feb. 4. It was announced after Feb. 4 that collectors could purchase the cards and send them to the U.S.P.S. for First Day cancels. Value $1.50 each.

PC153

Designed by Howard Koslow.

1997, May 7 **Litho.**

UX280 PC153 20c **multicolored**	.50	*1.00*
First day cancel, New York, NY *(9,576)*		1.00

Bugs Bunny Type

Designed by Warner Bros.

1997, May 22 **Litho.**

UX281 A2425 20c **multicolored**	1.25	*2.00*
First day cancel, Burbank, CA		1.75
a. Booklet of 10 cards	12.50	

No. UX281a sold for $5.95.

First day cancellations applied to 378,142 of Nos. UX281 and 3138.

Golden Gate in Daylight — PC154

Golden Gate at Sunset — PC155

Designed by Carol Simowitz.

1997, June 2 **Litho.**

UX282 PC154 20c **multicolored,** *June 2* .40 *1.00*
First day cancel, San Francisco, CA 1.25

For International Use

UX283 PC155 50c **multicolored,** *June 3* 1.10 *12.00*
First day cancel, San Francisco, CA 2.00

First day cancellation was applied to 21,189 of Nos. UX282-UX283.

PC156

Designed by Richard Sheaff.

1997, Sept. 7 **Litho.**

UX284 PC156 20c **multicolored** .40 *1.00*
First day cancel, Baltimore, MD *(9,611)* 1.00

Similar to Classic Movie Monsters with 20c Denomination

Designed by Derry Noyes.

1997, Sept. 30 **Litho.**

UX285 A2451 20c Phantom of the Opera 1.60 *2.00*
UX286 A2452 20c Dracula 1.60 *2.00*
UX287 A2453 20c Frankenstein's Monster 1.60 *2.00*
UX288 A2454 20c The Mummy 1.60 *2.00*
UX289 A2455 20c The Wolf Man 1.60 *2.00*
a. Booklet of 20 cards, 4 each #UX285-UX289 32.00
First day cancel, #UX285-UX289, any card, Universal City, CA 1.75

Nos. UX285-UX289 were issued bound in a booklet of 20 cards containing four of each card. Booklet was sold in package for $5.95.

PC157

Designed by Howard Paine.

1998, Apr. 20 **Litho.**

UX290 PC157 20c **multicolored** .50 *1.00*
First day cancel, University, MS *(22,276)* 1.00

Similar to Sylvester & Tweety with 20c Denomination

Designed by Brenda Guttman.

1998, Apr. 27 **Litho.**

UX291 A2487 20c **multicolored** 1.40 *2.00*
First day cancel, New York, NY 1.75
a. Booklet of 10 cards 14.00

No. UX291a sold for $5.95.

First day cancellations applied to 231,839 of Nos. UX291, 3204 and 3205.

PC158

Designed by Phil Jordan.

1998, May 1 **Litho.**

UX292 PC158 20c **multicolored** .50 *1.00*
First day cancel, Philadelphia, PA *(13,853)* 1.00

Similar to Tropical Birds with 20c Denomination and No Inscription

Designed by Phil Jordan.

1998, July 29 **Litho.**

UX293 A2503 20c Antillean euphonia 1.25 *1.75*
UX294 A2504 20c Green-throated carib 1.25 *1.75*
UX295 A2505 20c Crested honeycreeper 1.25 *1.75*
UX296 A2506 20c Cardinal honeyeater 1.25 *1.75*
a. Booklet of 20 cards, 5 ea #UX293-UX296 25.00
First day cancel, #UX293-UX296, any card, Ponce PR 1.75

Nos. UX293-UX296 were issued bound in a booklet of 20 cards containing five of each card. Illustration of the stamp without denomination is shown on the back of each card. Booklet was sold in packages for $6.95.

American Ballet Type

Designed by Derry Noyes.

1998, Sept. 16 **Litho.**

UX297 A2517 20c **multicolored** 1.25 *1.50*
a. Booklet of 10 cards 12.50
First day cancel, New York, NY 1.75

No. UX297a was sold for $5.95.

PC159

Designed by Richard Sheaff.

1998, Oct. 3 **Litho.**

UX298 PC159 20c **multicolored** .50 *1.00*
First day cancel, Boston, MA *(14,812)* 1.00

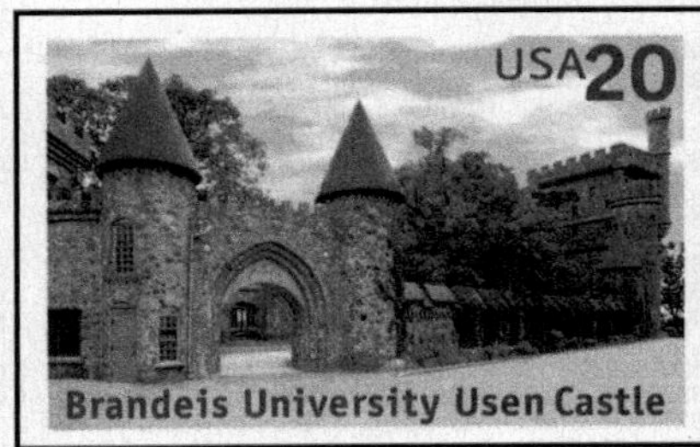

PC160

Designed by Richard Sheaff.

1998, Oct. 17 **Litho.**

UX299 PC160 20c **multicolored** .50 *1.00*
First day cancel, Waltham, MA *(14,137)* 1.00

Victorian Love Type

Designed by John Grossman, Holly Sudduth

1999, Jan. 28 **Litho.**

UX300 A2537 20c **multicolored** 1.25 *1.50*
First day cancel, Loveland, CO 1.00

No. UX300 was sold in packs containing 5 sheets of 4 cards for $6.95.

PC161

Designed by Carl Herrman.

1999, Feb. 5 **Litho.**

UX301 PC161 20c **multicolored** .50 *1.00*
First day cancel, Madison, WI *(12,582)* 1.00

PC162

Designed by Derry Noyes.

1999, Feb. 11

UX302 PC162 20c **multicolored** .50 *1.00*
First day cancel, Lexington, VA *(17,556)* 1.00

PC163

UNITED POSTAL STATIONERY SOCIETY

$30 $900?
With UPSS
you'd know!
Specialized catalogs from the
World's Largest Postal Stationery Society
Bimonthly Journal
Auctions
404 Sundown Road
Knoxville, TN 37934
WWW.UPSS.ORG

Designed by Richard Sheaff.

1999, Mar. 11

UX303 PC163 20c **red & black** .50 *1.00*
First day cancel, Newport, RI *(13,649)* 1.00

Daffy Duck Type

Designed by Ed Wieczyk.

1999, Apr. 16 **Litho.**

UX304 A2554 20c **multicolored** 1.30 1.30
First day cancel, Los Angeles, CA 1.30
a. Booklet of 10 cards 13.00

No. UX304a sold for $6.95.

First day cancellation was applied to 177,988 of UX304, 3306 and 3307.

PC164

Designed by Richard Sheaff.

1999, May 14 **Litho.**

UX305 PC164 20c **multicolored** .50 *1.00*
First day cancel, Mount Vernon, VA *(14,642)* 1.00

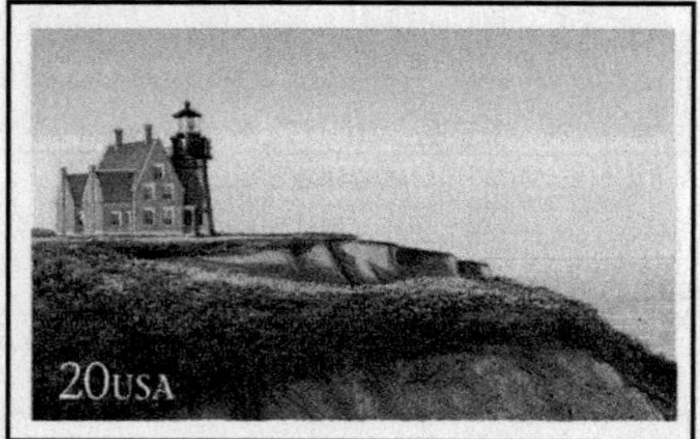

Block Island Lighthouse — PC165

Designed by Derry Noyes.

1999, July 24 **Litho.**

UX306 PC165 20c **multicolored** .40 *1.00*
First day cancel, Block Island, RI *(12,694)* 1.25

Famous Trains Type

Designed by Howard Paine.

1999, Aug. 26 **Litho.**

UX307 A2583 20c Super Chief 1.50 *2.00*
UX308 A2582 20c Hiawatha 1.50 *2.00*
UX309 A2579 20c Daylight 1.50 *2.00*
UX310 A2580 20c Congressional 1.50 *2.00*
UX311 A2581 20c 20th Century Limited 1.50 *2.00*
a. Booklet of 20 cards, 4 ea #UX307-UX311 32.50
First day cancel, #UX307-UX311, any card, Cleveland, OH 1.75
First day cancel, #UX307-UX311, any card, any other city 1.75

Nos. UX307-UX311 were issued bound in a booklet of 20 cards containing four of each card. Booklet sold for $6.95.

PC166

Designed by Ethel Kessler.

2000, Feb. 28 **Litho.**

UX312 PC166 20c **multicolored** .40 *1.00*
First day cancel, Salt Lake City, UT *(14,230)* 1.00

PC167

Designed by Richard Sheaff.

2000, Mar. 18 **Litho.**

UX313 PC167 20c **multicolored** .40 *1.00*
First day cancel, Nashville, TN *(12,690)* 1.00

Road Runner & Wile E. Coyote Type

Designed by Ed Wleczyk, Warner Bros.

2000, Apr. 26 **Litho.**

UX314 A2622 20c **multicolored** 1.40 1.40
First day cancel, Phoenix, AZ 1.40
a. Booklet of 10 cards 14.00

No. UX314a sold for $6.95.

First day cancellation was applied to 154,903 of UX314 and 3391.

Adoption Type

Designed by Greg Berger.

2000, May 10 **Litho.**

UX315 A2628 20c **multicolored** 1.40 *1.50*
First day cancel, Beverly Hills, CA 1.40
a. Booklet of 10 cards 14.00

No. UX315a sold for $6.95. The design, without denominations, is shown on the back of the card.

First day cancellation was applied to 137,903 of UX315 and 3398.

PC168

Designed by Howard Paine.

2000, May 19 **Litho.**

UX316 PC168 20c **multicolored** .40 *1.00*
First day cancel, Middlebury, VT *(13,586)* 1.00

Stars and Stripes Type

Designed by Richard Sheaff.

2000, June 14 **Litho.**

UX317 A2633 20c Sons of Liberty Flag, 1775 2.00 2.00
UX318 A2633 20c New England Flag, 1775 2.00 2.00
UX319 A2633 20c Forster Flag, 1775 2.00 2.00
UX320 A2633 20c Continental Colors, 1776 2.00 2.00
a. Sheet of 4 cards, #UX317-UX320 8.00
UX321 A2633 20c Francis Hopkinson Flag, 1777 2.00 2.00
UX322 A2633 20c Brandywine Flag, 1777 2.00 2.00
UX323 A2633 20c John Paul Jones Flag, 1779 2.00 2.00
UX324 A2633 20c Pierre L'Enfant Flag, 1783 2.00 2.00
a. Sheet of 4 cards, #UX321-UX324 8.00
UX325 A2633 20c Indian Peace Flag, 1803 2.00 2.00
UX326 A2633 20c Easton Flag, 1814 2.00 2.00
UX327 A2633 20c Star-Spangled Banner, 1814 2.00 2.00
UX328 A2633 20c Bennington Flag, c. 1820 2.00 2.00
a. Sheet of 4 cards, #UX325-UX328 8.00
UX329 A2633 20c Great Star Flag, 1837 2.00 2.00
UX330 A2633 20c 29-Star Flag, 1847 2.00 2.00
UX331 A2633 20c Fort Sumter Flag, 1861 2.00 2.00
UX332 A2633 20c Centennial Flag, 1876 2.00 2.00
a. Sheet of 4 cards, #UX329-UX332 8.00
UX333 A2633 20c 38-Star Flag, 1877 2.00 2.00
UX334 A2633 20c Peace Flag, 1891 2.00 2.00
UX335 A2633 20c 48-Star Flag, 1912 2.00 2.00
UX336 A2633 20c 50-Star Flag, 1960 2.00 2.00
a. Sheet of 4 cards, #UX333-UX336 8.00
First day cancel, any card, Baltimore, MD .90

Nos. UX320a, UX324a, UX328a, UX332a and UX336a were sold together in a package for $8.95. Microperforations are between individual cards on each sheet. Illustrations of the flags, without denominations, are shown on the back of the cards.

Legends of Baseball Type

Designed by Phil Jordan.

2000, July 6 **Litho.**

UX337 A2638 20c Jackie Robinson 1.50 1.50
UX338 A2638 20c Eddie Collins 1.50 1.50
UX339 A2638 20c Christy Mathewson 1.50 1.50
UX340 A2638 20c Ty Cobb 1.50 1.50
UX341 A2638 20c George Sisler 1.50 1.50
UX342 A2638 20c Rogers Hornsby 1.50 1.50
UX343 A2638 20c Mickey Cochrane 1.50 1.50
UX344 A2638 20c Babe Ruth 1.50 1.50
UX345 A2638 20c Walter Johnson 1.50 1.50
UX346 A2638 20c Roberto Clemente 1.50 1.50
UX347 A2638 20c Lefty Grove 1.50 1.50
UX348 A2638 20c Tris Speaker 1.50 1.50
UX349 A2638 20c Cy Young 1.50 1.50
UX350 A2638 20c Jimmie Foxx 1.50 1.50
UX351 A2638 20c Pie Traynor 1.50 1.50
UX352 A2638 20c Satchel Paige 1.50 1.50
UX353 A2638 20c Honus Wagner 1.50 1.50
UX354 A2638 20c Josh Gibson 1.50 1.50
UX355 A2638 20c Dizzy Dean 1.50 1.50
UX356 A2638 20c Lou Gehrig 1.50 1.50
a. Booklet of 20 cards, #UX337-UX356 30.00
First day cancel, any card, Atlanta, GA .90

No. UX356a sold for $8.95.

Christmas Deer Type of 1999

Designed by Tom Nikosey.

2000, Oct. 12 **Litho.** ***Rouletted on 2 sides***

UX357 A2600 20c **gold & blue** 1.25 1.25
UX358 A2600 20c **gold & red** 1.25 1.25
UX359 A2600 20c **gold & purple** 1.25 1.25
UX360 A2600 20c **gold & green** 1.25 1.25
a. Sheet of 4, #UX357-UX360 5.00
First day cancel, any card, Rudolph, WI 1.75

Nos. UX357-UX360 were sold in packs containing five No. UX360a for $8.95.

PC169

Designed by Derry Noyes.

2001, Mar. 30 **Litho.**

UX361 PC169 20c **multicolored** .40 *1.00*
First day cancel, New Haven, CT 1.00

PC170

Designed by Ethel Kessler.

2001, Apr. 26 **Litho.**

UX362 PC170 20c **multicolored** .40 *1.00*
First day cancel, Columbia, SC 1.00

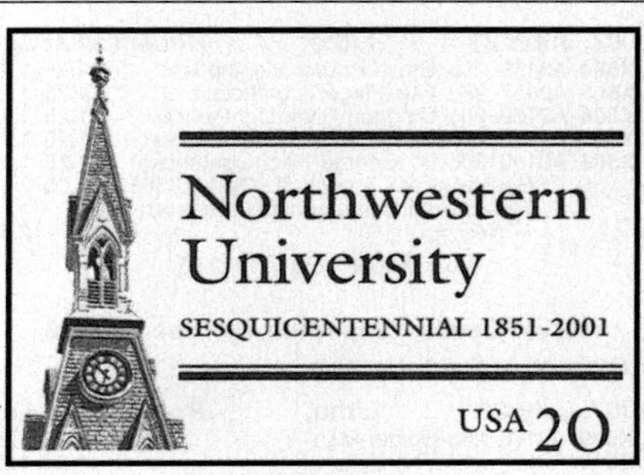

PC171

Designed by Howard Paine.

2001, Apr. 28 **Litho.**
UX363 PC171 20c **multicolored** .40 *1.00*
First day cancel, Evanston, IL 1.00

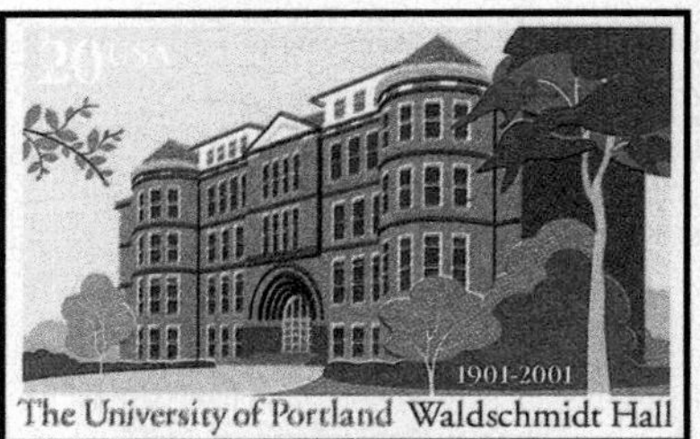

PC172

Designed by Richard Sheaff.

2001, May 1 **Litho.**
UX364 PC172 20c **multicolored** .40 *1.00*
First day cancel, Portland, OR 1.00

Legendary Playing Fields Type with 21c Denomination

Designed by Phil Jordan.

2001, June 27 **Litho.**
UX365 A2712 21c Ebbets Field 2.00 2.00
UX366 A2713 21c Tiger Stadium 2.00 2.00
UX367 A2714 21c Crosley Field 2.00 2.00
UX368 A2715 21c Yankee Stadium 2.00 2.00
UX369 A2716 21c Polo Grounds 2.00 2.00
UX370 A2717 21c Forbes Field 2.00 2.00
UX371 A2718 21c Fenway Park 2.00 2.00
UX372 A2719 21c Comiskey Park 2.00 2.00
UX373 A2720 21c Shibe Park 2.00 2.00
UX374 A2721 21c Wrigley Field 2.00 2.00
a. Booklet of 10 cards, #UX365-UX374 22.50
First day cancel, any card, New York, NY, Boston, MA, Chicago, IL, or Detroit MI 1.00
No. UX374a sold for $6.95.

White Barn — PC173

Designed by Derry Noyes.

2001, Sept. 20 **Litho.**
UX375 PC173 21c **multicolored** .45 *1.00*
First day cancel, Washington, DC 1.00

That's All Folks! Type

Designed by Ed Wleczyk, Warner Bros.

2001, Oct. 1 **Litho.**
UX376 A2736 21c **multicolored** 1.50 1.50
First day cancel, Beverly Hills, CA 1.50
a. Booklet of 10 cards 15.00
No. UX376a sold for $7.25.

Christmas Santas Type

Designed by Richard Sheaff.

2001, Oct. 10 **Litho.** ***Rouletted on 2 Sides***
UX377 A2740 21c **multicolored** 1.25 1.25
UX378 A2741 21c **multicolored** 1.25 1.25
UX379 A2738 21c **multicolored** 1.25 1.25
UX380 A2739 21c **multicolored** 1.25 1.25
a. Sheet of 4, #UX377-UX380 5.50
First day cancel, any card, Santa Claus, IN 1.25
Packages of 5 No. UX380a sold for $9.25.

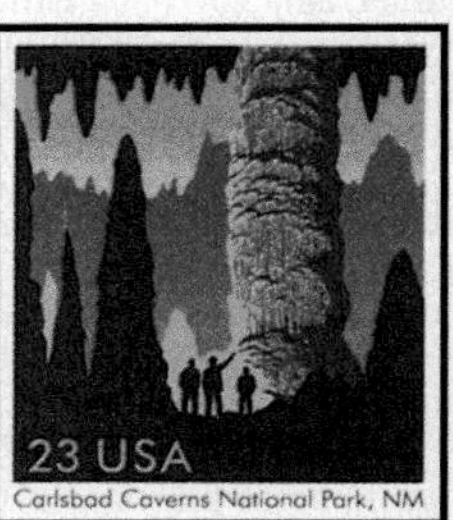

Carlsbad Caverns National Park — PC174

Designed by Carl Herrman.

2002, June 7 **Litho.**
UX381 PC174 23c **multicolored** .50 *.75*
First day cancel, Carlsbad, NM 1.00
First day cancel, any other city 1.00

Teddy Bears Type

Designed by Margaret Bauer.

2002, Aug. 15 **Litho.** ***Rouletted on 2 Sides***
UX382 A2827 23c Ideal Bear, c. 1905 1.25 1.25
UX383 A2826 23c Gund Bear, c. 1948 1.25 1.25
UX384 A2824 23c Bruin Bear, c. 1907 1.25 1.25
UX385 A2825 23c "Stick" Bear, 1920s 1.25 1.25
a. Sheet of 4, #UX382-UX385 5.50
First day cancel, any card, Atlantic City, NJ 1.25
Packages of 5 No. UX385a sold for $9.25.

Christmas Snowmen Type

Designed by Derry Noyes.

2002, Oct. 28 **Litho.** ***Rouletted on 2 Sides***
Design Size: 28x38mm
UX386 A2844 23c **multicolored** 1.25 1.25
UX387 A2845 23c **multicolored** 1.25 1.25
UX388 A2846 23c **multicolored** 1.25 1.25
UX389 A2847 23c **multicolored** 1.25 1.25
a. Sheet of 4, #UX386-UX389 5.50
First day cancel, any card, Houghton, MI 1.00
Packages of 5 #UX389a sold for $9.75.

Old Glory Type

Designed by Richard Sheaff.

2003, Apr. 3 **Litho.** ***Rouletted on 1 Side***
UX390 A2883 23c **multicolored** 1.25 1.25
UX391 A2884 23c **multicolored** 1.25 1.25
UX392 A2885 23c **multicolored** 1.25 1.25
UX393 A2886 23c **multicolored** 1.25 1.25
UX394 A2887 23c **multicolored** 1.25 1.25
a. Booklet of 20 cards, 4 each #UX390-UX394 25.00
First day cancel, any card, New York, NY 1.00
No. UX394a sold for $9.75.

Southeastern Lighthouses Type

Designed by Howard E. Paine.

2003, June 13 **Litho.** ***Rouletted on 1 Side***
UX395 A2893 23c **multicolored** 1.25 1.25
UX396 A2894 23c **multicolored** 1.25 1.25
UX397 A2895 23c **multicolored** 1.25 1.25
UX398 A2896 23c **multicolored** 1.25 1.25
UX399 A2897 23c **multicolored** 1.25 1.25
a. Booklet of 20 cards, 4 each #UX395-UX399 25.00
First day cancel, any card, Tybee Island, GA 1.00
No. UX399a sold for $9.75.

Ohio University, 200th Anniv. — PC175

Designed by Tom Engemann.

2003, Oct. 10 **Litho.**
UX400 PC175 23c **multicolored** .50 *1.00*
First day cancel, Athens, OH 1.00

Christmas Music Makers Type

Designed by Ethel Kessler.

2003, Oct. 23 **Litho.** ***Rouletted on 2 Sides***
UX401 A2917 23c **multicolored** 1.10 1.10
UX402 A2918 23c **multicolored** 1.10 1.10
UX403 A2919 23c **multicolored** 1.10 1.10
UX404 A2920 23c **multicolored** 1.10 1.10
a. Sheet of 4, #UX401-UX404 4.50
First day cancel, any card, New York, NY 1.00
Packages of 5 #UX404a sold for $9.75.

Columbia University, 250th Anniv. — PC176

Designed by Tom Engeman.

2004, Mar. 25 **Litho.**
UX405 PC176 23c **multicolored** .50 *1.00*
First day cancel, New York, NY 1.00

Harriton House, Bryn Mawr, PA, Bicent. PC177

Designed by Carl T. Herrman.

2004, June 10 **Litho.**
UX406 PC177 23c **multicolored** .50 *1.00*
First day cancel, Bryn Mawr, PA 1.00

Disney: Friendship Type of 2004

Designed by David Pacheco.

2004, June 23 **Litho.**
UX407 A2950 23c **multicolored** 1.50 1.25
UX408 A2951 23c **multicolored** 1.50 1.25
UX409 A2949 23c **multicolored** 1.50 1.25
UX410 A2952 23c **multicolored** 1.50 1.25
a. Booklet of 20 cards, 5 each #UX407-UX410 30.00
First day cancel, any card, Anaheim, CA 1.00
No. UX410a sold for $9.75.

Art of the American Indian Type of 2003

Designed by Richard Sheaff.

2004, Aug. 21 **Litho.** ***Rouletted on 1 Side***
UX411 A2957 23c Mimbres bowl 1.25 1.25
UX412 A2957 23c Kutenai parfleche 1.25 1.25
UX413 A2957 23c Tlingit sculptures 1.25 1.25
UX414 A2957 23c Ho-Chunk bag 1.25 1.25
UX415 A2957 23c Seminole doll 1.25 1.25
UX416 A2957 23c Mississippian effigy 1.25 1.25
UX417 A2957 23c Acoma pot 1.25 1.25
UX418 A2957 23c Navajo weaving 1.25 1.25
UX419 A2957 23c Seneca carving 1.25 1.25
UX420 A2957 23c Luiseño basket 1.25 1.25
a. Booklet of 20 cards, 2 each #UX411-UX420 25.00
First day cancel, any card, Santa Fe, NM 1.00
No. UX420a sold for $9.75.

Cloudscapes Type

Designed by Howard E. Paine.

2004, Oct. 4 **Litho.** ***Rouletted at Left***
UX421 A2960 23c Cirrus radiatus 1.60 *2.50*
UX422 A2960 23c Cirrostratus fibratus 1.60 *2.50*
UX423 A2960 23c Cirrocumulus undulatus 1.10 *1.50*

UX424 A2960 23c Cumulonimbus mammatus 1.10 *1.50*
UX425 A2960 23c Cumulonimbus incus 1.60 *2.50*
UX426 A2960 23c Altocumulus stratiformis 1.10 *1.50*
UX427 A2960 23c Altostratus translucidus 1.60 *2.50*
UX428 A2960 23c Altocumulus undulatus 1.10 *1.50*
UX429 A2960 23c Altocumulus castellanus 1.60 *2.50*
UX430 A2960 23c Altocumulus lenticularis 1.10 *1.50*
UX431 A2960 23c Stratocumulus undulatus 1.60 *2.50*
UX432 A2960 23c Stratus opacus 1.60 *2.50*
UX433 A2960 23c Cumulus humilis 1.60 *2.50*
UX434 A2960 23c Cumulus congestus 1.60 *2.50*
UX435 A2960 23c Cumulonimbus with tornado 1.60 *2.50*
a. Booklet of 20, #UX421-UX422, UX425, UX427, UX429, UX431-UX435, 2 each #UX423-UX424, UX426, UX428, UX430 27.00
First day cancel, any card, Milton, MA 1.00

No. UX435a sold for $9.75.

Disney: Celebration Type of 2005

Designed by David Pacheco.

2005, June 30 **Litho.**
UX436 A2989 23c **multicolored** 1.25 1.10
UX437 A2990 23c **multicolored** 1.25 1.10
UX438 A2991 23c **multicolored** 1.25 1.10
UX439 A2992 23c **multicolored** 1.25 1.10
a. Booklet of 20 cards, 5 each #UX436-UX439 25.00
First day cancel, any card, Anaheim, CA 1.00

No. UX439a sold for $9.75.

Sporty Cars Type of 2005

Designed by Art M. Fitzpatrick.

2005, Aug. 20 **Litho.** ***Rouletted at Left***
UX440 A3012 23c 1955 Ford Thunderbird 1.25 1.00
UX441 A3011 23c 1952 Nash Healey 1.25 1.00
UX442 A3010 23c 1953 Chevrolet Corvette 1.25 1.00
UX443 A3008 23c 1953 Studebaker Starliner 1.25 1.00
UX444 A3009 23c 1954 Kaiser Darrin 1.25 1.00
a. Booklet of 20 cards, 4 each #UX440-UX444 25.00
First day cancel, any card, Detroit, MI 1.75

No. UX444a sold for $9.75.

Let's Dance Type

Designed by Ethel Kessler.

2005, Sept. 17 **Litho.** ***Rouletted at Left***
UX445 A3018 23c Cha cha cha 1.25 1.00
UX446 A3019 23c Mambo 1.25 1.00
UX447 A3017 23c Salsa 1.25 1.00
UX448 A3016 23c Merengue 1.25 1.00
a. Booklet of 20, 5 each #UX445-UX448 25.00
First day cancel, any card, New York, NY 1.75
First day cancel, any card, Miami, FL 1.75

No. UX448a sold for $9.75.

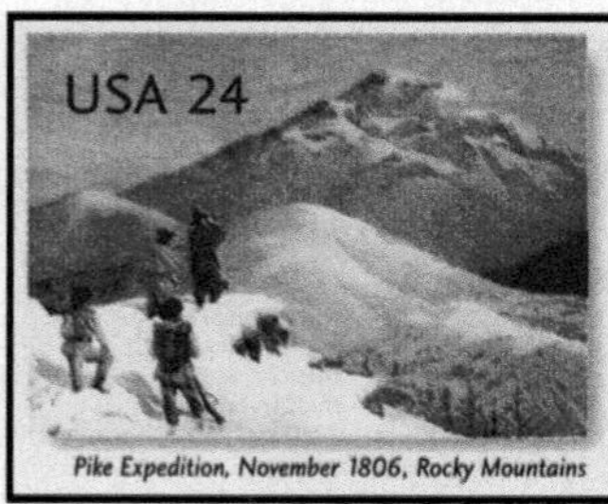

Zebulon Pike Expedition at Pikes Peak, Bicent. PC178

Designed by Carl Herrman.

2006, Jan. 9 **Litho.**
UX449 PC178 24c **multicolored** .55 *1.00*
First day cancel, Washington, DC 1.75
First day cancel, any other city 1.75

Disney: Romance Type of 2006

Designed by David Pacheco.

2006, Apr. 21 **Litho.** ***Rouletted at Left***
UX450 A3066 24c **multicolored** 1.25 1.00
UX451 A3067 24c **multicolored** 1.25 1.00
UX452 A3069 24c **multicolored** 1.25 1.00
UX453 A3068 24c **multicolored** 1.25 1.00
a. Booklet of 20, 5 each #UX450-UX4538 25.00
First day cancel, any card, Orlando, FL 1.75

No. UX453a sold for $9.75.

Baseball Sluggers Type of 2006

Designed by Phil Jordan.

2006, July 15 **Litho.** ***Rouletted at Left***
UX454 A3121 24c Mickey Mantle 1.25 1.25
UX455 A3118 24c Roy Campanella 1.25 1.25
UX456 A3119 24c Hank Greenberg 1.25 1.25
UX457 A3120 24c Mel Ott 1.25 1.25
a. Booklet of 20 cards, 5 each #UX454-UX457 25.00
First day cancel, any card, Bronx, NY 1.75

No. UX457a sold for $9.95.

DC Comics Superheroes Type of 2006

Designed by Carl T. Herrman.

2006, July 20 **Litho.** ***Rouletted at Left***
UX458 A3122 24c Superman cover 1.50 1.50
UX459 A3122 24c Superman 1.50 1.50
UX460 A3122 24c Batman cover 1.50 1.50
UX461 A3122 24c Batman 1.50 1.50
UX462 A3122 24c Wonder Woman cover 1.50 1.50
UX463 A3122 24c Wonder Woman 1.50 1.50
UX464 A3122 24c Green Lantern cover 1.50 1.50
UX465 A3122 24c Green Lantern 1.50 1.50
UX466 A3122 24c Green Arrow cover 1.50 1.50
UX467 A3122 24c Green Arrow 1.50 1.50
UX468 A3122 24c The Flash cover 1.50 1.50
UX469 A3122 24c The Flash 1.50 1.50
UX470 A3122 24c Plastic Man cover 1.50 1.50
UX471 A3122 24c Plastic Man 1.50 1.50
UX472 A3122 24c Aquaman cover 1.50 1.50
UX473 A3122 24c Aquaman 1.50 1.50
UX474 A3122 24c Supergirl cover 1.50 1.50
UX475 A3122 24c Supergirl 1.50 1.50
UX476 A3122 24c Hawkman cover 1.50 1.50
UX477 A3122 24c Hawkman 1.50 1.50
a. Booklet of 20 cards, #UX458-UX477 30.00
First day cancel, any card, San Diego, CA 1.75

No. UX477a sold for $9.95.

Southern Florida Wetland Type of 2006

Designed by Ethel Kessler.

2006, Oct. 4 **Litho.** ***Rouletted on 1 Side***
UX478 A3137 39c Snail kite 4.50 4.00
UX479 A3137 39c Cape Sable seaside sparrow 4.50 4.00
a. Sheet of 2, #UX478-UX479 9.00
UX480 A3137 39c Wood storks 4.50 4.00
UX481 A3137 39c Florida panther 4.50 4.00
a. Sheet of 2, #UX480-UX481 9.00
UX482 A3137 39c Bald eagle 4.50 4.00
UX483 A3137 39c White ibis 4.50 4.00
a. Sheet of 2, #UX482-UX483 9.00
UX484 A3137 39c American crocodile 4.50 4.00
UX485 A3137 39c Everglades mink 4.50 4.00
a. Sheet of 2, #UX484-UX485 9.00
UX486 A3137 39c Roseate spoonbills 4.50 4.00
UX487 A3137 39c American alligator 4.50 4.00
a. Sheet of 2, #UX486-UX487 9.00
First day cancel, any card, Naples, FL 2.00
Nos. UX478-UX487 (10) 45.00 40.00

Packet of 10 cards sold for $7.95.

Pineapple — PC179

Designed by Ethel Kessler.

2007, May 12 **Litho.**
UX488 PC179 26c **multicolored** .60 *1.00*
First day cancel, Washington, DC 1.75

Star Wars Type of 2007

Designed by Terrence McCaffrey and William J. Gicker, Jr.

2007, May 27 **Litho.** ***Rouletted at Left***
UX489 A3153 26c Darth Vader 1.75 1.75
UX490 A3153 26c Luke Skywalker 1.75 1.75
UX491 A3153 26c C-3PO 1.75 1.75
UX492 A3153 26c Queen Padmé Amidala 1.75 1.75
UX493 A3153 26c Millennium Falcon 1.75 1.75
UX494 A3153 26c Emperor Palpatine 1.75 1.75
UX495 A3153 26c Anakin Skywalker and Obi-Wan Kenobi 1.75 1.75
UX496 A3153 26c Obi-Wan Kenobi 1.75 1.75
UX497 A3153 26c Boba Fett 1.75 1.75
UX498 A3153 26c Darth Maul 1.75 1.75
UX499 A3153 26c Yoda 1.75 1.75
UX500 A3153 26c Princess Leia and R2-D2 1.75 1.75
UX501 A3153 26c Chewbacca and Han Solo 1.75 1.75
UX502 A3153 26c X-wing Starfighter 1.75 1.75
UX503 A3153 26c Stormtroopers 1.75 1.75
a. Booklet of 15, #UX489-UX503 26.00
First day cancel, any card, Los Angeles, CA 3.00

No. UX503a sold for $12.95.

Pacific Lighthouses Type of 2007

Designed by Howard E. Paine.

2007, June 21 **Litho.** ***Rouletted at Left***
UX504 A3158 26c Grays Harbor Lighthouse 1.25 1.25
UX505 A3157 26c Five Finger Lighthouse 1.25 1.25
UX506 A3159 26c Umpqua River Lighthouse 1.25 1.25
UX507 A3156 26c Diamond Head Lighthouse 1.25 1.25
UX508 A3160 26c St. George Reef Lighthouse 1.25 1.25
a. Booklet of 20, 4 each #UX504-UX508 26.00
First day cancel, any card, Westport, WA 2.50

No. UX503a sold for $12.95.

Marvel Comics Superheroes Type of 2006

Designed by Carl T. Herrman.

2007, July 26 **Litho.** ***Rouletted at Left***
UX509 A3168 26c Spider-Man 1.25 1.25
UX510 A3168 26c The Hulk 1.25 1.25
UX511 A3168 26c Sub-Mariner 1.25 1.25
UX512 A3168 26c The Thing 1.25 1.25
UX513 A3168 26c Captain America 1.25 1.25
UX514 A3168 26c Silver Surfer 1.25 1.25
UX515 A3168 26c Spider-Woman 1.25 1.25
UX516 A3168 26c Iron Man 1.25 1.25
UX517 A3168 26c Elektra 1.25 1.25
UX518 A3168 26c Wolverine 1.25 1.25
UX519 A3168 26c Spider-Man cover 1.25 1.25
UX520 A3168 26c Incredible Hulk cover 1.25 1.25
UX521 A3168 26c Sub-Mariner cover 1.25 1.25
UX522 A3168 26c Fantastic Four cover 1.25 1.25
UX523 A3168 26c Captain America cover 1.25 1.25
UX524 A3168 26c Silver Surfer cover 1.25 1.25
UX525 A3168 26c Spider-Woman cover 1.25 1.25
UX526 A3168 26c Iron Man cover 1.25 1.25
UX527 A3168 26c Elektra cover 1.25 1.25
UX528 A3168 26c X-Men cover 1.25 1.25
a. Booklet of 20 cards, #UX509-UX528 26.00
First day cancel, any card, San Diego, CA 1.75

No. UX528a sold for $12.95.

Disney: Magic Type of 2007

Designed by David Pacheco.

2007, Aug. 16 **Litho.** ***Rouletted at Left***
UX529 A3185 26c Mickey Mouse 1.25 1.25
UX530 A3186 26c Peter Pan and Tinker Bell 1.25 1.25
UX531 A3187 26c Dumbo and Timothy Mouse 1.25 1.25
UX532 A3188 26c Aladdin and Genie 1.25 1.25
a. Booklet of 20, 5 each #UX529-UX532 26.00
First day cancel, any card, Orlando, FL 2.50

No. UX503a sold for $12.95.

Mount St. Mary's University, Bicent. PC180

Designed by Richard Sheaff.

2008, Apr. 26 **Litho.**
UX533 PC180 27c **multicolored** .60 *1.00*
First day cancel, Emmitsburg, MD 1.75

Corinthian Column From Capitol Building — PC181

Designed by Gerald Gallo.

2008, May 12 **Litho.**
UX534 PC181 27c **multicolored** .60 *1.00*
First day cancel, Washington, DC 1.75

Disney: Imagination Type of 2008

Designed by David Pacheco.

2008, Aug. 7 **Litho.** ***Rouletted at Left***
UX535 A3305 27c Steamboat Willie 1.40 1.40
UX536 A3304 27c Pongo and Pup 1.40 1.40
UX537 A3306 27c Princess Aurora, Flora, Fauna, Merryweather 1.40 1.40

UX538 A3307 27c Mowgli and Baloo 1.40 1.40
a. Booklet of 20, 5 each #UX535-UX538 28.00
First day cancel, any card, Anaheim, CA 2.60

No. UX538a sold for $13.95.

Great Lakes Dunes Type of 2008

Designed by Ethel Kessler.

2008, Oct. 2 Litho. *Rouletted on 1 Side*

UX539 A3312 42c Vesper sparrow 1.90 1.90
UX540 A3312 42c Piping plover 1.90 1.90
a. Sheet of 2, #UX539-UX540 4.00
UX541 A3312 42c Eastern hognose snake 1.90 1.90
UX542 A3312 42c Common mergansers 1.90 1.90
a. Sheet of 2, #UX541-UX542 4.00
UX543 A3312 42c Piping plover nestlings 1.90 1.90
UX544 A3312 42c Red fox 1.90 1.90
a. Sheet of 2, #UX543-UX544 4.00
UX545 A3312 42c Tiger beetle 1.90 1.90
UX546 A3312 42c White-footed mouse 1.90 1.90
a. Sheet of 2, #UX545-UX546 4.00
UX547 A3312 42c Spotted sandpiper 1.90 1.90
UX548 A3312 42c Red admiral butterfly 1.90 1.90
a. Sheet of 2, #UX547-UX548 4.00
First day cancel, any card, Empire, MI 3.00
Nos. UX539-UX548 (10) 19.00 19.00

Packet of 10 cards sold for $8.95.

Automobiles of the 1950s Type of 2008

Designed by Carl T. Herrman.

2008, Oct. 3 Litho. *Rouletted at Left*

UX549 A3316 27c 1957 Lincoln Premiere 1.40 1.40
UX550 A3317 27c 1957 Chrysler 300C 1.40 1.40
UX551 A3313 27c 1959 Cadillac Eldorado 1.40 1.40
UX552 A3314 27c 1957 Studebaker Golden Hawk 1.40 1.40
UX553 A3315 27c 1957 Pontiac Safari 1.40 1.40
a. Booklet of 20, 4 each #UX549-UX553 28.00
First day cancel, any card, Carlisle, PA 2.60

No. UX553a sold for $13.95.

Miami University (Oxford, Ohio), Bicent. PC182

Designed by Howard E. Paine

2009, Feb. 17 Litho.

UX554 PC182 27c **multicolored** .60 *1.00*
First day cancel, Oxford, OH 1.75

White, Orange and White Koi — PC183

Black, Red and White Koi — PC184

Designed by Ethel Kessler.

2009, Apr. 17 Litho.

UX555 PC183 28c **multicolored** .65 *1.00*
First day cancel, New York, NY 1.90
UX556 PC184 28c **multicolored** .65 *1.00*
First day cancel, New York, NY 1.90
a. Pair, #UX555-UX556 1.50

Nos. UX555 and UX556 were also printed in uncut sheets of 40 cards (20 of each) on a rougher stock and having a background dot pattern that differs from the cut cards. Nos. UX555 and UX556 were sold in 2010 with a "Cradle to Cradle" recycling emblem added to the front of the card.

The Simpsons Type of 2009

Designed by Matt Groening.

2009, May 7 Litho. *Rouletted at Left*

UX557 A3345 28c Homer Simpson 1.50 1.50
UX558 A3346 28c Marge Simpson 1.50 1.50
UX559 A3347 28c Bart Simpson 1.50 1.50
UX560 A3348 28c Lisa Simpson 1.50 1.50
UX561 A3349 28c Maggie Simpson 1.50 1.50
a. Booklet of 20, 4 each #UX557-UX561 30.00
First day cancel, any card, Los Angeles, CA 2.75

No. UX561a sold for $14.95.

Gulf Coast Lighthouses Type of 2009

Designed by Howard E. Paine.

2009, July 23 Litho. *Rouletted at Left*

UX562 A3354 28c Matagorda Island Lighthouse 1.50 1.50
UX563 A3355 28c Sabine Pass Lighthouse 1.50 1.50
UX564 A3356 28c Biloxi Lighthouse 1.50 1.50
UX565 A3357 28c Sand Island Lighthouse 1.50 1.50
UX566 A3358 28c Fort Jefferson Lighthouse 1.50 1.50
a. Booklet of 20, 4 each #UX562-UX566 30.00
First day cancel, any card, Biloxi, MS 2.75

No. UX566a sold for $14.95.

Early TV Memories Type of 2009

Designed by Carl T. Herrman.

2009, Aug. 11 Litho. *Rouletted at Left*

UX567 A3359 28c Alfred Hitchcock Presents 1.50 1.50
UX568 A3359 28c Burns and Allen 1.50 1.50
UX569 A3359 28c The Dinah Shore Show 1.50 1.50
UX570 A3359 28c Dragnet 1.50 1.50
UX571 A3359 28c The Ed Sullivan Show 1.50 1.50
UX572 A3359 28c The Honeymooners 1.50 1.50
UX573 A3359 28c Hopalong Cassidy 1.50 1.50
UX574 A3359 28c Howdy Doody 1.50 1.50
UX575 A3359 28c I Love Lucy 1.50 1.50
UX576 A3359 28c Kukla, Fran and Ollie 1.50 1.50
a. With Dragnet picture on back *550.00*
UX577 A3359 28c Lassie 1.50 1.50
a. With Ed Sullivan picture on back —
UX578 A3359 28c The Lone Ranger 1.50 1.50
UX579 A3359 28c Ozzie and Harriet 1.50 1.50
UX580 A3359 28c Perry Mason 1.50 1.50
UX581 A3359 28c The Phil Silvers Show 1.50 1.50
UX582 A3359 28c The Red Skelton Show 1.50 1.50
UX583 A3359 28c Texaco Star Theater 1.50 1.50
UX584 A3359 28c The Tonight Show 1.50 1.50
UX585 A3359 28c The Twilight Zone 1.50 1.50
UX586 A3359 28c You Bet Your Life 1.50 1.50
a. Booklet of 20, #UX567-UX586 30.00
First day cancel, any card, North Hollywood, CA 2.75

No. UX586a sold for $14.95.

Kelp Forest Type of 2009

Designed by Ethel Kessler.

2009, Oct. 1 Litho. *Rouletted on 1 Side*

UX587 A3367 44c Western gull, southern sea otters, red sea urchin 1.90 1.90
UX588 A3367 44c Lion's mane nudibranch 1.90 1.90
a. Sheet of 2, #UX587-UX588 4.00
UX589 A3367 44c Northern kelp crab 1.90 1.90
UX590 A3367 44c Vermilion rockfish 1.90 1.90
a. Sheet of 2, #UX589-UX590 4.00
UX591 A3367 44c Yellowtail rockfish, white-spotted rose anemone 1.90 1.90
UX592 A3367 44c Pacific rock crab, jeweled top snail 1.90 1.90
a. Sheet of 2, #UX591-UX592 4.00
UX593 A3367 44c Harbor seal 1.90 1.90
UX594 A3367 44c Brown pelican 1.90 1.90
a. Sheet of 2, #UX593-UX594 4.00
UX595 A3367 44c Treefish, Monterey turban snail, brooding sea anemones 1.90 1.90
UX596 A3367 44c Copper rockfish 1.90 1.90
a. Sheet of 2, #UX595-UX596 4.00
First day cancel, any card, Monterey, CA 3.00

Packet of 10 cards sold for $8.95.

Cowboys of the Silver Screen Type of 2010

Designed by Carl T. Herrman.

2010, Apr. 17 Litho.

UX597 A3389 28c Roy Rogers 1.50 1.50
UX598 A3390 28c Tom Mix 1.50 1.50
UX599 A3391 28c William S. Hart 1.50 1.50
UX600 A3392 28c Gene Autry 1.50 1.50
a. Booklet of 20, 5 each #UX597-UX600 30.00
First day cancel, any card, Oklahoma City, OK 2.75

No. UX600a sold for $14.95.

National Parks Types of Air Post and Air Post Postal Cards of 1999-2009

Designed by Journey Group, Inc.

2010, Apr. 20 Litho.

UX601 AP109 28c Acadia 1.50 1.50
UX602 APC23 28c Badlands 1.50 1.50
UX603 AP110 28c Bryce Canyon 1.50 1.50
UX604 AP106 28c Grand Canyon 1.50 1.50
UX605 AP111 28c Great Smoky Mountains 1.50 1.50
UX606 AP108 28c Mount McKinley 1.50 1.50
UX607 APC22 28c Mount Rainier 1.50 1.50
UX608 AP116 28c St. John, Virgin Islands 1.50 1.50
UX609 AP112 28c Yosemite 1.50 1.50
UX610 AP117 28c Zion 1.50 1.50
a. Booklet of 20, 2 each #UX601-UX610 30.00
First day cancel, any card, Washington, DC 2.75

No. UX610a sold for $14.95.

Hawaiian Rain Forest Type of 2010

Designed by Ethel Kessler.

2010, Sept. 1 Litho. *Rouletted on 1 Side*

UX611 A3417 44c 'Apapane, Hawaiian mint 1.90 1.90
UX612 A3417 44c Pulelehua butterfly, kolea lau nui, 'ilihia 1.90 1.90
a. Sheet of 2, #UX611-UX612 4.00
UX613 A3417 44c Hawaii 'amakihi, Hawaii 'elepaio, ohi'a lehua 1.90 1.90
UX614 A3417 44c Happyface spider, 'ala'ala wai nui 1.90 1.90
a. Sheet of 2, #UX613-UX614 4.00
UX615 A3417 44c 'I'iwi, haha 1.90 1.90
UX616 A3417 44c 'Akepa, 'ope'ape'a 1.90 1.90
a. Sheet of 2, #UX615-UX616 4.00
UX617 A3417 44c Koele Mountain damselfly, 'akala 1.90 1.90
UX618 A3417 44c Jewel orchid 1.90 1.90
a. Sheet of 2, #UX617-UX618 4.00
UX619 A3417 44c 'Oma'o, 'ohelo kau la'au 1.90 1.90
UX620 A3417 44c 'Oha 1.90 1.90
a. Sheet of 2, #UX619-UX620 4.00
First day cancel, any card, Hawaii National Park, HI 3.00
Nos. UX611-UX620 (10) 19.00 19.00

Packet of 10 cards sold for $8.95.

Common Terns — PC185

Designed by Chuck Ripper.

2011, Apr. 7 Litho.

UX621 PC185 29c **multicolored** .65 *1.00*
First day cancel, New York, NY 1.90

Characters From Disney-Pixar Films (Send a Hello) Type of 2011

Designed by Terrence W. McCaffrey and William J. Gicker.

2011, Aug. 19 Litho. *Rouletted at Left*

UX622 A3484 29c Toy Story 1.50 1.50
UX623 A3482 29c Cars 1.50 1.50
UX624 A3485 29c Up 1.50 1.50
UX625 A3483 29c Ratatouille 1.50 1.50
UX626 A3486 29c WALL-E 1.50 1.50
a. Booklet of 20, 4 each #UX622-UX626 30.00
First day cancel, any card, Anaheim, CA 2.75

No. UX626a sold for $14.95.

Sailboat — PC186

Designed by Derry Noyes.

2012, Jan. 22 Litho.

UX627 PC186 (32c) **multicolored** .70 .70
First day cancel, Oyster Bay, NY 1.90

Characters From Disney-Pixar Films (Mail a Smile) Type of 2012

Designed by William J. Gicker.

2012, June 1 **Litho.** ***Rouletted at Left***

UX628 A3565 (45c) A Bug's Life 1.60 1.60
UX629 A3567 (45c) Finding Nemo 1.60 1.60
UX630 A3566 (45c) The Incredibles 1.60 1.60
UX631 A3569 (45c) Monsters, Inc. 1.60 1.60
UX632 A3568 (45c) Toy Story 2 1.60 1.60
a. Booklet of 20, 4 each #UX628-UX632 32.00
First day cancel, any card, Orlando, FL 3.00

No. UX632a sold for $15.95.

Sailboat Type of 2012

Designed by Derry Noyes.

2012, June 22 Litho. ***Microperforated on 2 Sides***
Size of Card:140x108mm

UX633 PC186 (32c) **multicolored** .75 .75
a. Sheet of 4 3.00
First day cancel, Lancaster, PA 1.90

No. UX633 was sold only in packages of 10 sheets that sold for $14.10.

Scenic American Landscapes Types of Air Post of 1999-2012 Inscribed "Forever"

Designed by Journey Group, Inc.

2012, June 23 **Litho.** ***Rouletted at Left***

UX634 AP115 (32c) 13-Mile Woods, NH 1.60 1.60
UX635 AP120 (32c) Glacier National Park, MT 1.60 1.60
UX636 AP117 (32c) Grand Teton National Park, WY 1.60 1.60
UX637 AP114 (32c) Hagatña Bay, Guam 1.60 1.60
UX638 AP121 (32c) Lancaster County, PA 1.60 1.60
UX639 AP104 (32c) Niagara Falls, NY 1.60 1.60
UX640 AP107 (32c) Nine-Mile Prairie, NE 1.60 1.60
UX641 AP113 (32c) Okefenokee Swamp, GA and FL 1.60 1.60
UX642 AP105 (32c) Rio Grande, TX 1.60 1.60
UX643 AP119 (32c) Voyageurs National Park, MN 1.60 1.60
a. Booklet of 20, 2 each #UX634-UX643 32.00
First day cancel, any card, Lancaster, PA 3.00

No. UX643a sold for $15.95.

Deer — PC187

Designed by Ethel Kessler.

2013, Mar. 8 **Litho.**

UX644 PC187 (33c) **multicolored** .75 .75
First day cancel, Middleburg, VA 2.00

Tree — PC188

Designed by Ethel Kessler.

2014, Mar. 28 **Litho.**

UX645 PC188 (34c) **multicolored** .80 .80
First day cancel, New York, NY 2.00

Flowers and Bee — PC189

Designed by Ethel Kessler.

2015, July 31 **Litho.**

UX646 PC189 (35c) **multicolored** .80 .80
First day cancel, Clackamas, OR 2.00

Tecophilaea Cyanocrocus (Azulillo) — PC190

Designed by Ethel Kessler.

2017, Aug. 11 **Litho.**

UX647 PC190 (34c) **multicolored** .80 .80
First day cancel, Independence, OH 2.00

PAID REPLY POSTAL CARDS

These are sold to the public as two unsevered cards, one for message and one for reply. These are listed first as unsevered cards and then as severed cards. Values are for:

Unused cards (both unsevered and severed) without printed or written address or message.

Unsevered cards sell for a premium if never folded.

Used unsevered cards, Message Card with Post Office cancellation and Reply Card uncanceled (from 1968 value is for a single used severed card); and used severed cards with cancellation when current.

Used values for International Paid Reply Cards are for proper usage. Those domestically used or with postage added sell for less than the unused value.

"Preprinted," unused cards (both unsevered and severed) with printed or written address or message. Used value applies after 1952.

First day cancel values are for cards without cachets.

PM1

Head of Grant, card framed.
PR1 inscribed "REPLY CARD."

1892, Oct. 25 **Size: 140x89mm**

UY1 PM1+PR1 1c +1c **black,** *buff,* unsevered 40.00 9.00
Preprinted 15.00
a. Message card printed on both sides, reply card blank 250.00 *750.00*
b. Message card blank, reply card printed on both sides 300.00
c. Cards joined at bottom 200.00 100.00
Preprinted 100.00
m. PM1 Message card detached 6.00 1.75
Preprinted 3.00
r. PR1 Reply card detached 6.00 1.75
Preprinted 3.00

For other postal cards of types PM1 and PR1 see No. UY3.

Liberty — PM2

PR2 inscribed "REPLY CARD."

1893, Mar. 1 **For International Use**

UY2 PM2+PR2 2c +2c **blue,** *grayish white,* unsevered 22.50 20.00
Preprinted 12.50
a. 2c+2c **dark blue,** *grayish white,* unsevered 22.50 20.00
Preprinted 12.50
b. Message card printed on both sides, reply card blank 500.00
c. Message card blank, reply card printed on both sides —
d. Message card normal, reply card blank 300.00
m. PM2 Message card detached 5.00 *6.00*
Preprinted 2.50
r. PR2 Reply card detached 5.00 *6.00*
Preprinted 2.50

For other postal cards of types PM2 and PR2 see No. UY11.

Design same as PM1 and PR1, without frame around card

1898, Sept.

Size: 140x82mm

UY3 PM1+PR1 1c +1c **black,** *buff,* unsevered 67.50 12.50
Preprinted 12.50
a. Message card normal, reply card blank 400.00
b. Message card printed on both sides, reply card blank 450.00
c. Message card blank, reply card printed on both sides 450.00
d. Message card without "Detach annexed card/for answer" 250.00 150.00
Preprinted —
e. Message card blank, reply card normal 250.00
f. Message card normal, reply card double impression, preprinted *825.00*
m. PM1 Message card detached 12.50 2.50
Preprinted 6.00
r. PR1 Reply card detached 12.50 2.50
Preprinted 6.00
s. As "m," solid black bar under left star —

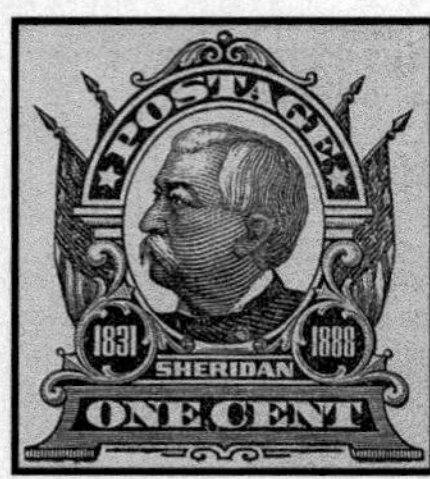

PR3

PM3 pictures Sherman.

1904, Mar, 31

UY4 PM3+PR3 1c +1c **black,** *buff,* unsevered 57.50 6.50
Preprinted 10.00
a. Message card normal, reply card blank 275.00
b. Message card printed on both sides, reply card blank *950.00*
c. Message card blank, reply card normal 275.00
d. Message card blank, reply card printed on both sides *750.00* 175.00
Preprinted 200.00
m. PM3 Message card detached 9.00 1.10
Preprinted 4.00
r. PR3 Reply card detached 9.00 1.10
Preprinted 4.00

PM4

PR4 pictures Martha Washington.

Double frame line around instructions

1910, Sept. 14

UY5 PM4+PR4 1c +1c **blue,** *bluish,* unsevered 175.00 25.00
Preprinted 40.00
a. Message card normal, reply card blank *425.00* *750.00*
m. PM4 Message card detached 15.00 3.75
Preprinted 9.00
r. PR4 Reply card detached 15.00 3.75
Preprinted 9.00

1911, Oct. 27

UY6 PM4+PR4 1c +1c **green,** *cream,* unsevered 175.00 25.00
Preprinted 60.00
a. Message card normal, reply card blank *1,500.*
m. PM4 Message card detached 22.50 6.50
Preprinted 12.50
r. PR4 Reply card detached 22.50 6.50
Preprinted 12.50

Single frame line around instructions

1915, Sept. 18

UY7 PM4+PR4 1c +1c **green,** *cream,* unsevered 1.50 .50
Preprinted .60
a. 1c+1c **dark green,** *buff,* unsevered 1.50 .50
Preprinted .60
b. Message card normal, reply card blank *1,500.*
m. PM4 Message card detached .30 .25
Preprinted .20
r. PR4 Reply card detached .30 .25
Preprinted .20
s. As "a," missing Reply indicia *2,000.*

See No. UY13.

PR5

PM5 pictures George Washington.

1918, Aug. 2

UY8 PM5+PR5 2c +2c **red,** *buff,* unsevered 90.00 40.00
Preprinted 30.00
m. PM5 Message card detached 20.00 7.50
Preprinted 10.00
r. PR5 Reply card detached 20.00 7.50
Preprinted 10.00

Same Surcharged

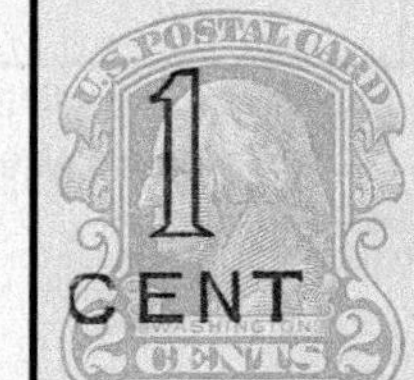

Fifteen canceling machine types

1920, Apr.

UY9 PM5+PR5 1c on 2c+1c on 2c **red,** *buff,* unsevered 20.00 11.00
Preprinted 10.00
a. Message card normal, reply card no surcharge 85.00 —
Preprinted —
b. Message card normal, reply card double surcharge 85.00 —
Preprinted —
c. Message card double surcharge, reply card normal 85.00 —
Preprinted —
d. Message card no surcharge, reply card normal 85.00 —
Preprinted —
e. Message card no surcharge, reply card double surcharge 85.00
m. PM5 Message card detached 5.00 4.00
Preprinted 3.00
r. PR5 Reply card detached 5.00 4.00
Preprinted 3.00
s. As "r," double surcharge *350.00*

One press printed type

UY10 PM5+PR5 1c on 2c+1c on 2c **red,** *buff,* unsevered 450.00 200.00
Preprinted 150.00
a. Message card no surcharge, reply card normal *1,100.* —
Preprinted —
b. Surcharge double on message card, reply card normal *950.00*
m. PM5 Message card detached 75.00 45.00
Preprinted 40.00
r. PR5 Reply card detached 75.00 45.00
Preprinted 40.00

Designs same as PM2 and PR2

1924, Mar. 18 **For International Use**

Size: 139x89mm

UY11 PM2+PR2 2c +2c **red,** *cream,* unsevered 2.50 *50.00*
Preprinted 1.50
m. PM2 Message card detached .50 *14.00*
Preprinted .40
r. PR2 Reply card detached .50 *20.00*
Preprinted .40

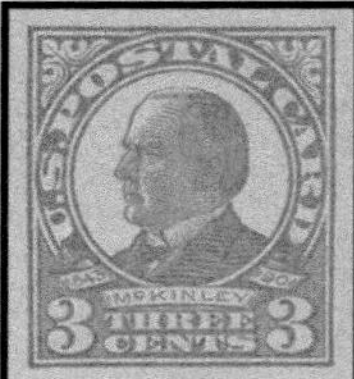

PM6

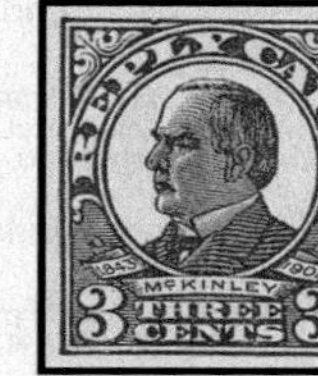

PR6

PR6 inscribed "REPLY CARD."

For International Use

1926, Feb. 1

UY12 PM6+PR6 3c +3c **red,** *buff,* unsevered 12.00 *27.50*
Preprinted 6.00
a. 3c +3c **red,** *yellow,* unsevered 12.00 *27.50*
Preprinted 6.00
First day cancel —
m. PM6 Message card detached 3.00 *7.50*
Preprinted 1.50
r. PR6 Reply card detached 3.00 *10.00*
Preprinted 1.50

Type of 1910

Single frame line around instructions

1951, Dec. 29

UY13 PM4+PR4 2c +2c **carmine,** *buff,* unsevered 1.40 *2.25*
Preprinted .65
First day cancel, Washington, D.C. 1.25
m. PM4 Message card detached .35 *1.00*
Preprinted .25
r. PR4 Reply card detached .35 *1.00*
Preprinted .25

No. UY7a Surcharged Below Stamp in Green by Canceling Machine

1952, Jan. 1

UY14 PM4+PR4 2c on 1c+2c on 1c **green,** *buff,* unsevered 1.25 *2.25*
Preprinted .50
a. Surcharge vertical at left of stamps 14.00 7.50
Preprinted 7.50
b. Surcharge horizontal at left of stamps 15.00 12.50
Preprinted 8.50
c. Inverted surcharge horizontal at left of stamps 140.00 90.00
Preprinted 75.00
d. Message card normal, reply card no surcharge 40.00 40.00
Preprinted —
e. Message card normal, reply card double surcharge 40.00 40.00
Preprinted —
f. Message card no surcharge, reply card normal 40.00 40.00
Preprinted —
g. Message card double surcharge, reply card normal 40.00 40.00
Preprinted —
h. Both cards, dbl. surch. 50.00 50.00
Preprinted —
i. As No. UY14, reply card surcharge missing, message card with second surcharge on reverse 70.00
m. PM4 Message card detached .40 *1.00*
Preprinted .30
r. PR4 Reply card detached .40 *1.00*
Preprinted .30

No. UY7a with Similar Surcharge (horizontal) Typographed at Left of Stamp in Dark Green

1952

UY15 PM4+PR4 2c on 1c+2c on 1c **green,** *buff,* unsevered 115.00 45.00
Preprinted 35.00
a. Surcharge on message card only 175.00
b. Message side normal, reply side no surcharge —
m. PM4 Message card detached 17.50 10.00
Preprinted 9.00
r. PR4 Reply card detached 17.50 10.00
Preprinted 9.00

On No. UY15a, the surcharge also appears on blank side of card.

Liberty Type

For International Use

1956, Nov. 16

UY16 PC24 4c +4c **carmine & dark violet blue,** *buff,* unsevered 1.25 *90.00*
First day cancel, New York, N. Y. *(127,874)* 1.00
a. Message card printed on both halves 125.00 —
b. Reply card printed on both halves 125.00 —
c. Double scarlet on reply side 200.00 —
First day cancel 350.00
d. Double scarlet on message side 200.00 —
e. Double violet blue on message side —
f. Double violet blue on both sides —
g. Message side blank, reply side normal —
m. Message card detached .40 *40.00*
r. Reply card detached .40 *40.00*

Liberty Type of 1956

1958, July 31

UY17 PC25 3c +3c **purple,** *buff,* unsevered 3.50 *2.00*
First day cancel, Boise, Idaho *(136,768)* 1.00
a. One card blank 750.00
Preprinted 500.00
b. Double impression on one card, preprinted *1,000.*

Both halves of No. UY17 are identical, inscribed as No. UX46, "This side of card is for address."

Lincoln Type

1962, Nov. 19

Precanceled with 3 printed red violet lines

UY18 PC26 4c +4c **red violet,** unsevered 3.50 *2.50*
First day cancel, Springfield, Ill. *(107,746)* 1.00
a. Tagged, *Mar. 7, 1967* 6.50 3.00
First day cancel, Dayton, OH 30.00

Both halves of No. UY18 are identical, inscribed as No. UX48, "This side of card is for address."

No. UY18a was printed with luminescent ink.

Map Type

1963, Aug. 30 **For International Use**

UY19 PC27 7c +7c **blue & red,** unsevered 2.50 *80.00*
First day cancel, New York 1.00
a. Message card normal, reply card blank 400.00 100.00
b. Message card blank, reply card normal 400.00 —
c. Additional message card printed on back of reply card *750.00*
d. Double red on message side —
e. Double red & blue on message side *500.00*
m. Message card detached .85 *35.00*
r. Reply card detached .85 *35.00*
s. Double impression of blue on message side 350.00
t. Double impression of blue on reply side *500.00*

Message card inscribed "Postal Card With Paid Reply" in English and French. Reply card inscribed "Reply Postal Card Carte Postale Résponse."

Map Type of 1963

1967, Dec. 4 **For International Use**

UY20 PC27 8c +8c **blue & red,** unsevered 2.50 *80.00*
First day cancel, Washington, D.C. 1.00
m. Message card detached .85 *35.00*
r. Reply card detached .85 *35.00*
s. Message card normal, reply card blank *750.00*

Message card inscribed "Postal Card With Paid Reply" in English and French. Reply card inscribed "Reply Postal Card Carte Postale Résponse."

Tagged

Paid Reply Postal cards from No. UY21 onward are either tagged or printed with luminescent ink unless otherwise noted.

Lincoln Type

1968, Jan. 4

UY21 PC33 5c +5c **emerald,** unsevered 1.25 *2.00*
First day cancel, Hodgenville, Ky. 1.50
a. Printed on one side only *800.00*

Paul Revere Type

1971, May 15

Precanceled with 3 printed brown lines.

UY22 PC36 6c +6c **brown,** unsevered .85 *2.00*
First day cancel, Boston, Mass. 1.00

John Hanson Type

1972, Sept. 1

Precanceled with 3 printed blue lines.

UY23 PC41 6c +6c **blue,** unsevered 1.00 *2.00*
First day cancel, Baltimore, Md. 1.00

Samuel Adams Type

1973, Dec. 16

Precanceled with 3 printed orange lines

UY24 PC42 8c +8c **orange,** unsevered .75 *2.00*
First day cancel, Boston, Mass. *(105,369)* 1.00
a. Coarse paper 1.25 *2.00*
b. Printed on one side only *800.00*
Preprinted 700.00
c. As "a," printed on one side only 500.00

Thomson, Witherspoon, Rodney, Hale & Hancock Types

1975-78

Precanceled with 3 printed emerald lines

UY25 PC44 7c +7c **emerald,** unsevered, *Sept. 14, 1975* .75 *8.00*
First day cancel, Bryn Mawr, Pa. 1.00

Precanceled with 3 printed yellow brown lines

UY26 PC45 9c +9c **yellow brown,** unsevered, *Nov. 10, 1975* .75 *2.00*
First day cancel, Princeton, N.J. 1.00

Precanceled with 3 printed blue lines

UY27 PC46 9c +9c **blue,** unsevered, *July 1, 1976* 1.00 *2.00*
First day cancel, Dover, Del. 1.00

Precanceled with 3 printed green lines

UY28 PC48 9c +9c **green,** unsevered, *Oct. 14, 1977* 1.00 *2.00*
First day cancel, Coventry, Conn. 1.00

Inscribed "U.S. Domestic Rate"

Precanceled with 3 printed brown orange lines

UY29 PC50 (10c +10c) **brown orange,** unsevered, *May 19, 1978* 7.50 *9.00*
First day cancel, Quincy, Mass. 1.75

Precanceled with 3 printed brown orange lines

UY30 PC50 10c +10c **brown orange,** unsevered, *June 20, 1978* 1.00 *2.00*
First day cancel, Quincy, Mass. 1.00
a. One card "Domestic Rate," other "Postage 10¢" —
b. Printed on one side only *700.00*
Nos. UY25-UY30 (6) 12.00

Eagle Type

Inscribed "U. S. Domestic Rate"

1981, Mar. 15

Precanceled with 3 printed violet lines

UY31 PC63 (12c +12) **violet,** unsevered 1.00 *2.00*
First day cancel, Memphis, TN 1.00

Isaiah Thomas Type

1981, May 5 **Precanceled with 3 printed lines**

UY32 PC64 12c +12c **light blue,** unsevered 5.00 *2.00*
First day cancel, Worcester, MA 1.00
a. Small die on one side 3.00 —

Morris Type

Inscribed "U.S. Domestic Rate"

1981 **Precanceled with 3 printed lines**

UY33 PC67 (13c +13c) **buff,** *Oct. 11,* unsevered 1.50 *2.00*
First day cancel, Memphis, TN 1.25

Inscribed "U.S. Postage 13¢"

UY34 PC67 13c +13c **buff,** *Nov. 10,* unsevered .85 .25
First day cancel, Philadelphia, PA 1.25
a. Message card normal, reply card blank 350.00
b. Extra copyright symbol and "USPS 1981" on back of reply card 45.00

Charles Carroll Type

Inscribed: U.S. Domestic Rate

1985 **Precanceled with 3 printed lines**

UY35 PC79 (14c +14c) **pale green,** *Feb. 1,* unsevered 3.00 *2.00*
First day cancel, New Carrollton, MD 1.25

Inscribed: USA

UY36 PC79 14c +14c **pale green,** *Mar. 6,* unsevered 1.00 *2.00*
First day cancel, Annapolis, MD 1.25
a. One card blank *5,000.*

George Wythe Type

Precanceled with 3 printed lines

1985, June 20

UY37 PC81 14c +14c **bright apple green,** unsevered .75 *2.00*
First day cancel, Williamsburg, VA 1.25
a. One card blank, preprinted 275.00

Flag Type

1987, Sept. 1

UY38 PC90 14c +14c **black, blue & red,** unsevered .75 2.00
First day cancel, Washington, DC *(22,314)* 1.25

America the Beautiful Type

1988, July 11

UY39 PC93 15c +15c **multicolored,** unsevered .75 *1.50*
First day cancel, Buffalo, WY *(24,338)* 1.25

Flag Type

1991, Mar. 27

UY40 PC122 19c +19c **rose, ultramarine & black,** unsevered .80 *1.50*
First day cancel, Washington, DC *(25,562)* 1.25
a. One card blank *650.00*

Red Barn Type

1995, Feb. 1 **Litho.**

UY41 PC147 20c +20c **multi,** unsevered .80 *1.50*
First day cancel, Williamsburg, PA 1.50
a. One card blank —

Block Island Lighthouse Type

1999, Nov. 10 **Litho.**

UY42 PC165 20c +20c **multi,** unsevered .85 *1.50*
First day cancel, Block Island, RI 1.75

White Barn Type

2001, Sept. 20 **Litho.**

UY43 PC173 21c +21c **multi,** unsevered .90 *1.50*
First day cancel, Washington, DC 1.50

Carlsbad Caverns Type

2002, June 7 **Litho.**

UY44 PC174 23c+23c **multi,** unsevered 1.00 *1.25*
First day cancel, Carlsbad, NM 1.50
First day cancel, any other city 1.50

Pikes Peak Type of 2006

2006, Jan. 9 **Litho.**

UY45 PC178 24c+24c **multicolored,** unsevered 1.10 *1.25*
First day cancel, Washington, DC 1.50
First day cancel, any other city 1.50

Pineapple Type of 2007

2007, May 12 **Litho.**

UY46 PC179 26c+26c **multicolored,** unsevered 1.25 *1.40*
First day cancel, Washington, DC 2.40

Corinthian Column Type of 2008

2008, May 12 **Litho.**

UY47 PC181 27c+27c **multicolored,** unsevered 1.25 *1.40*
First day cancel, Washington, DC 2.40

Koi Types of 2009

2009, Apr. 17 **Litho.**

UY48 PC183+PC184 28c+28c **multicolored,** unsevered 1.25 *1.40*
First day cancel, New York, NY 2.40
m. PC183 Card detached .60 .60
r. PC184 Card detached .60 .60

Common Terns Type of 2011

2011, Apr. 7 **Litho.**

UY49 PC185 29c+29c **multicolored,** unsevered 1.40 *1.60*
First day cancel, New York, NY 4.00

Sailboat Type of 2012

2012, Jan. 22 **Litho.**

UY50 PC186 (32c)+(32c) **multicolored,** unsevered 1.40 *1.60*
First day cancel, Oyster Bay, NY 4.00

Deer Type of 2013

2013, Mar. 8 **Litho.**

UY51 PC187 (33c)+(33c) **multicolored,** unsevered 1.50 *1.75*
First day cancel, Middleburg, VA 4.00

Tree Type of 2014

2014, Mar. 28 **Litho.**

UY52 PC188 (34c)+(34c) **multicolored,** unsevered 1.60 *1.90*
First day cancel, New York, NY 4.00

Flowers and Bee Type of 2015

2015, July 31 **Litho.**

UY53 PC189 (35c)+(35c) **multicolored,** unsevered 1.60 *1.90*
First day cancel, Clackamas, OR 4.00

Tecophilaea Cyanocrocus (Azulillo) Type of 2017

2017, Aug.11 **Litho.**

UY54 PC190 (34c)+(34c) **multicolored,** unsevered 1.60 *1.90*
First day cancel, Independence, OH 4.00

AIR POST POSTAL CARDS

Eagle in Flight — APC1

1949, Jan.10 **Typo.**

UXC1 APC1 4c **red orange,** *buff* .60 *.75*
Preprinted .35
First day cancel, Washington, D.C. *(236,620)* 3.00
a. 4c **deep red,** *buff* *475.00 450.00*
First day cancel, Washington, D.C. *250.00*

Expertization is recommended for No. UXC1a.

Type of Air Post Stamp, 1954

1958, July 31

UXC2 AP31 5c **red,** *buff* 2.00 .75
First day cancel, Wichita, Kans. *(156,474)* 1.00

Type of 1958 Redrawn

1960, June 18 **Lithographed (Offset)**

UXC3 AP31 5c **red,** *buff,* bicolored border 6.50 4.50
First day cancel, Minneapolis, Minn. *(228,500)* 1.50
a. Red omitted —
b. Two lozenges at left double printed, red over blue 200.00

Size of stamp of No. UXC3: 18½x21mm; on No. UXC2: 19x22mm. White cloud around eagle enlarged and finer detail of design on No. UXC3. Inscription "AIR MAIL-POSTAL CARD" has been omitted and blue and red border added on No. UXC3.

Bald Eagle — APC2

Precanceled with 3 printed red lines

1963, Feb. 15

UXC4 APC2 6c **red,** bicolored border 1.10 *2.50*
First day cancel, Maitland, Fla. *(216,203)* 1.50

Emblem of Commerce Department's Travel Service — APC3

Issued at the Sixth International Philatelic Exhibition (SIPEX), Washington, D.C., May 21-30.

1966, May 27 **For International Use**

UXC5 APC3 11c **blue & red** .65 *40.00*
First day cancel, Washington, D.C. *(272,813)* 1.00

Four photographs at left on address side show: Mt. Rainier, New York skyline, Indian on horseback and Miami Beach. The card has blue and red border.

See Nos. UXC8, UXC11.

Virgin Islands and Territorial Flag — APC4

50th anniv. of the purchase of the Virgin Islands.

Designed by Burt Pringle

1967, Mar. 31 **Litho.**

UXC6 APC4 6c **multicolored** .75 *12.50*
First day cancel, Charlotte Amalie, V. I. *(346,906)* 1.00
a. Red & yellow omitted *1,700.*
b. Orange red (instead of red) 6.00

The orange red in No. UXC6b is most easily seen in the two lines at the bottom of the card.

Borah Peak, Lost River Range, Idaho, and Scout Emblem — APC5

12th Boy Scout World Jamboree, Farragut State Park, Idaho, Aug. 1-9.

Designed by Stevan Dohanos

1967, Aug. 4 **Litho.**

UXC7 APC5 6c **blue, yellow, black & red** .75 *15.00*
First day cancel, Farragut State Park, ID *(471,585)* 1.00
a. Blue omitted —
b. Blue & black omitted *7,500.*
c. Red & yellow omitted *11,000.*

Travel Service Type of 1966

Issued in connection with the American Air Mail Society Convention, Detroit, Mich.

1967, Sept. 8 **For International Use**

UXC8 APC3 13c **blue & red** 1.50 *45.00*
First day cancel, Detroit, Mich. *(178,189)* 1.00

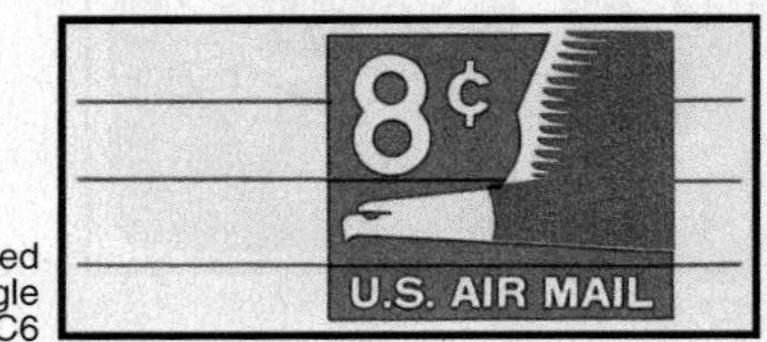

Stylized Eagle APC6

Designed by Muriel R. Chamberlain

Precanceled with 3 printed red lines

1968, Mar. 1

UXC9 APC6 8c **blue & red** .75 *2.50*
First day cancel, New York, N.Y. *(179,923)* 1.00
a. Tagged, *Mar. 19, 1969* 2.50 3.00
Tagged, first day cancel 15.00
b. **Blue & pale pink**, tagged *1,250.*

No. UXC9a is known with tagging omitted. It can be distinguished from No. UXC9, as No. UXC9a was printed on fluorescent stock. Believed to be unique. Value $2,500.

Tagged

Air Post Postal Cards from No. UXC10 onward are either tagged or printed with luminescent ink unless otherwise noted.

Precanceled with 3 printed blue lines

1971, May 15

UXC10 APC6 9c **red & blue** .50 *1.25*
First day cancel, Kitty Hawk, N.C. 1.00

Travel Service Type of 1966
For International Use

1971, June 10

UXC11 APC3 15c **blue & red** 1.75 *55.00*
First day cancel, New York, N.Y. 1.00

Grand Canyon APC7

Niagara Falls APC8

Tourism Year of the Americas 1972.

Designed by Melbourne Brindle

1972, June 29 **Size: 152½x108½mm** **Litho.**

UXC12 APC7 9c **black,** Grand Canyon, *buff* (Statue of Liberty, Hawaii, Alaska, San Francisco on back) .75 *75.00*
First day cancel, any city 1.50
a. Red and blue lozenges omitted *3,500.*
b. Red lozenges omitted —
c. Tagging omitted 2,250.

For International Use

UXC13 APC8 15c **black,** Niagara Falls, *buff* (Mt. Vernon, Washington, D.C., Lincoln, Liberty Bell on back) .75 *75.00*
First day cancel, any city 1.50
a. Address side blank *1,500.*
b. Double blue lozenges *6,000.*
c. Tagging omitted *2,250.*
d. Red and blue lozenges omitted —

See note after No. UX63.

Stylized Eagle — APC9

Eagle Weather Vane — APC10

Designed by David G. Foote (11c) & Stevan Dohanos (18c)

1974, Jan. 4 **Litho.**

UXC14 APC9 11c **ultramarine & red** 1.10 *25.00*
First day cancel, State College, Pa. *(160,500)* 1.00
a. Double tagging *500.00*
b. Tagging omitted *500.00*
c. Tagging inverted *400.00*

For International Use

UXC15 APC10 18c **multicolored** 1.10 *32.50*
First day cancel, Miami, Fla. *(132,114)* 1.00
a. Tagging omitted 350.00
b. Black and yellow omitted *7,500.*

All following issues are for international use.

Angel Gabriel Weather Vane — APC11

Designed by Stevan Dohanos

1975, Dec. 17 **Litho.**

UXC16 APC11 21c **multicolored** .85 *40.00*
First day cancel, Kitty Hawk, N.C. 1.00
a. Blue & red omitted *7,500.*
b. Tagging omitted 250.00 —

Curtiss (JN4H) Jenny — APC12

Designed by Keith Ferris

1978, Sept. 16 **Litho.**

UXC17 APC12 21c **multicolored** 1.00 *40.00*
First day cancel, San Diego, Cal. *(174,886)* 1.25

Gymnast APC13

22nd Olympic Games, Moscow, July 19-Aug. 3, 1980.

Designed by Robert M. Cunningham

1979, Dec. 1 **Litho.**

UXC18 APC13 21c **multicolored** 1.25 *40.00*
First day cancel, Fort Worth, Tex. 1.00

Pangborn, Herndon and Miss Veedol — APC14

First non-stop transpacific flight by Clyde Pangborn and Hugh Herndon, Jr., 50th anniv.

Designed by Ken Dallison

1981, Jan. 2 **Litho.**

UXC19 APC14 28c **multicolored** 1.00 *30.00*
First day cancel, Wenatchee, WA 1.25
a. Tagging omitted —

Gliders — APC15

Designed by Robert E. Cunningham

1982, Mar. 5 **Litho.**
UXC20 APC15 28c **magenta, yellow, blue & black** 1.00 *35.00*
First day cancel, Houston, TX *(106,932)* 1.25

Speedskater — APC16

Designed by Robert Peak

1983, Dec. 29 **Litho.**
UXC21 APC16 28c **multicolored** 1.00 *30.00*
First day cancel, Milwaukee, WI *(108,397)* 1.25
a. Red, pink, magenta, yellow, double impression, one inverted *4,250.*

No. UXC21a also exhibits a dramatic color shift.

Martin M-130 China Clipper Seaplane — APC17

Designed by Chuck Hodgson

1985, Feb. 15 **Litho.**
UXC22 APC17 33c **multicolored** 1.00 *30.00*
First day cancel, San Francisco, CA 1.50

First day cancellation was applied to 269,229 of Nos. UXC22 and C115.

Chicago Skyline — APC18

AMERIPEX '86, Chicago, May 22-June 1.

Designed by Ray Ameijide

1986, Feb. 1 **Litho.**
UXC23 APC18 33c **multicolored** 1.00 *30.00*
First day cancel, Chicago, IL *(84,480)* 1.25

No. UXC23 was sold at Sudposta '87 by the U.S.P.S. with a show cachet.

DC-3 — APC19

Designed by Chuck Hodgson

1988, May 14 **Litho.**
UXC24 APC19 36c **multicolored** .85 *30.00*
First day cancel, San Diego, CA 1.25

No. UXC24 was sold at SYDPEX '88 by the USPS with a cachet for Australia's bicentennial and SYDPEX '88.

First day cancellations applied to 167,575 of Nos. UXC24 and C118.

Yankee Clipper — APC20

Designed by Chuck Hodgson.

1991, June 28 **Litho.**
UXC25 APC20 40c **multicolored** .90 *30.00*
First day cancel, Flushing, NY *(24,865)* 1.50

Mt. Rainier — APC22

Designed by Ethel Kessler.

1999, May 15 **Litho.**
UXC27 APC22 55c **multicolored** 1.25 *30.00*
First day cancel, Denver, CO 1.50

First day cancellation was applied to 19,658 of Nos. UXC27 and UC65.
See note before No. C133.

Badlands Natl. Park, South Dakota — APC23

Designed by Ethel Kessler.

2001, Feb. 22 **Litho.**
UXC28 APC23 70c **multicolored** 1.40 *20.00*
First day cancel, Wall, SD 1.50

OFFICIAL POSTAL CARDS

PO1

1913, July **Size: 126x76mm**
UZ1 PO1 1c **black** 700.00 500.00

All No. UZ1 cards have printed address and printed form on message side.

Used values are for contemporaneous usage without additional postage applied.

Great Seal — PO2

1983-85
UZ2 PO2 13c **blue,** *Jan. 12* .75 *100.00*
First day cancel, Washington, DC 1.00
UZ3 PO2 14c **blue,** *Feb. 26, 1985* .80 *90.00*
First day cancel, Washington, DC *(62,396)* 1.25

Official postal cards from No. UZ4 onward are tagged unless otherwise noted.

PO3

Designed by Bradbury Thompson

1988, June 10 **Litho.**
UZ4 PO3 15c **multicolored** .80 *75.00*
First day cancel, New York *(133,498)* 1.25

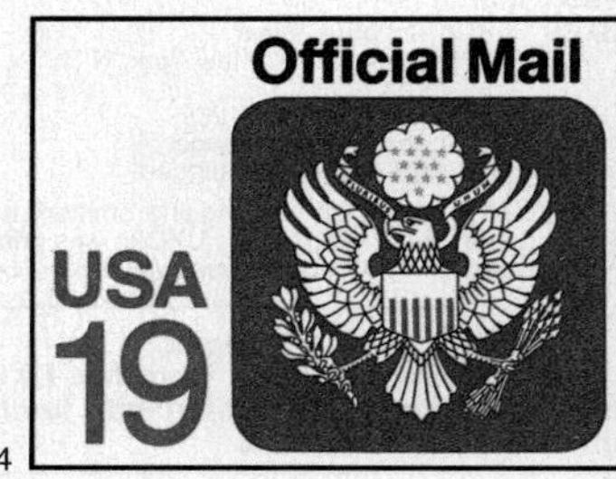

PO4

Designed by Bradbury Thompson

1991, May 24 **Litho.**
UZ5 PO4 19c **multicolored** .80 *75.00*
First day cancel, Seattle, WA *(23,097)* 1.25

PO5

1995, May 9 **Litho.**
UZ6 PO5 20c **multicolored** .90 *75.00*
First day cancel, Washington, DC 1.25

REVENUE STAMPS

The Commissioner of Internal Revenue advertised for bids for revenue stamps in August 1862, and the contract was awarded to Butler & Carpenter of Philadelphia.

Nos. R1-R102 were used to pay taxes on documents and proprietary articles including playing cards. Until December 25, 1862, the law stated that a stamp could be used only for payment of the tax upon the particular instrument or article specified on its face. After that date, stamps, except the Proprietary, could be used indiscriminately.

Most stamps of the first issue appeared in the latter part of 1862 or early in 1863. The 5c and 10c Proprietary were issued in the fall of 1864, and the 6c Proprietary on April 13, 1871.

Plate numbers and imprints are usually found at the bottom of the plate on all denominations except 25c and $1 to $3.50. On these it is nearly always at the left of the plate. The imprint reads "Engraved by Butler & Carpenter, Philadelphia" or "Jos. R. Carpenter."

Plates were of various sizes: 1c and 2c, 210 subjects (14x15); 3c to 20c, 170 subjects (17x10); 25c to 30c, 102 subjects (17x6); 50c to 70c, 85 subjects (17x5); $1 to $1.90, 90 subjects (15x6); $2 to $10, 72 subjects (12x6); $15 to $50, 54 subjects (9x6); $200, 8 subjects (2x4). No. R132, one subject.

The paper varies, the first employed being thin, hard and brittle until September, 1869, from which time it acquired a softer texture and varied from medium to very thick. Early printings of some revenue stamps occur on paper which appears to have laid lines. Some are found on experimental silk paper, first employed about August, 1870.

Some of the stamps were in use eight years and were printed several times. Many color variations occurred, particularly if unstable pigments were used and the color was intended to be purple or violet, such as the 4c Proprietary, 30c and $2.50 stamps. Before 1868 dull colors predominate on these and the early red stamps. In later printings of the 4c Proprietary, 30c and $2.50 stamps, red predominates in the mixture and on the dollar values of red is brighter. The early $1.90 stamp is dull purple, imperforate or perforated. In a later printing, perforated only, the purple is darker.

In the first issue, canceling usually was done with pen and ink and all values quoted are for stamps canceled in that way. Handstamped cancellations as a rule sell for more than pen. Printed and stencil cancellations are scarce and command much higher prices. Herringbone, punched or other types of cancellation which break the surface of the paper adversely affect prices.

Many, but not all, of the pre-1898 revenue stamps exist unused with original gum. These are not valued in the listings, but they sell for more than used examples in the marketplace. Uncanceled first through third revenue stamps without gum are generally not considered unused by the marketplace because the vast majority have been soaked or sweated from documents.

1862-72 revenue stamps from the first three issues were often used on large folded documents. As a result, multiples (blocks and strips of four or more) are not often found in sound condition. In addition, part perforate pairs of all but the most common varieties generally are off center. Catalogue values of the noted multiples are for items in fine condition or for very fine appearing examples with small faults. Examples of such multiples in a true very fine grade without any faults are scarce to rare and will sell for substantially more than catalogue value.

Where a stamp is known in a given form or variety but insufficient information is available on which to base a value, its existence is indicated by a dash.

Part perforate stamps are understood to be imperforate horizontally unless otherwise stated.

Part perforate stamps with an asterisk (*) after the value exist imperforate horizontally or vertically. As a general rule, part perforate first issue revenues that are imperforate vertically are considerably scarcer than their imperforate horizontally counterparts.

Part perforate PAIRS should be imperforate between the stamps as well as imperforate at opposite ends. See illustration **Type A** under "Information For Collectors-Perforations."

All imperforate or part perforate stamps listed are known in pairs or larger multiples. Certain unlisted varieties of this nature exist as singles and specialists believe them genuine. Exceptions are Nos. R11a, R13a, R22a, R51b, R60b, R80a, R112b, and R115b, which have not been reported in multiples but are regarded as legitimate by most students. Authenticated imperforate errors from later issues that exist only as singles include No. R728.

With respect to plate varieties (double transfers, cracked plates, scratched plates, etc.), there can be numerous types of each for a given stamp, ranging from minute to extremely dramatic, and with great differences in scarcity and value. Unless specifically named (e.g., T5, T7, T13) or described (e.g., complete double transfer, doubling of shields at top), the values given are generally for the most common type.

Documentary revenue stamps were no longer required after December 31, 1967.

First Issue

R1

George Washington — R2

Old Paper

1862-71 Engr. *Perf. 12*

R1		R1 1c **Express, red**	
	a.	Imperf.	100.00
		Pair	250.00
		Block of 4	700.00
		Short transfer, No. 156	—
	b.	Part perf.	55.00*
		Pair	200.00
		Block of 4	750.00
		Short transfer, No. 156	—
	c.	Perf.	1.50
		Pair	3.25
		Block of 4	12.50
		Double transfer	45.00
		Short transfer, No. 156	85.00
		Foreign entry of 2c, pos. 66	—
	d.	As No. R1c, silk paper	*350.00*
	e.	As No. R1c, vertical pair, imperf. between	*200.00*
	f.	As "c," foreign entry of 2c, pos. 210	—
R2		R1 1c **Playing Cards, red**	
	a.	Imperf.	4,000.
		Pair	*8,500.*
		Cracked plate	—
	b.	Part perf.	2,250.
		Pair	*4,750.*
	c.	Perf.	210.00
		Pair	450.00
		Block of 4	950.00
		Cracked plate	350.00
		Scratched plate	—
	d.	As No. R2c, silk paper	1,000.
R3		R1 1c **Proprietary, red**	
	a.	Imperf.	1,250.
		Pair	*2,600.*
	b.	Part perf.	300.00*
		Pair	750.00
		Block of 4	*3,000.*
	c.	Perf.	.50
		Pair	1.25
		Block of 4	3.25
	d.	As No. R3c, silk paper	60.00
		Pair	145.00
		Block of 4	*375.00*
R4		R1 1c **Telegraph, red**	
	a.	Imperf.	850.00
		Pair	2,750.
	c.	Perf.	20.00
		Pair	45.00
		Block of 4	110.00
		Scratched plate	50.00
		Double transfer in bottom scroll	—

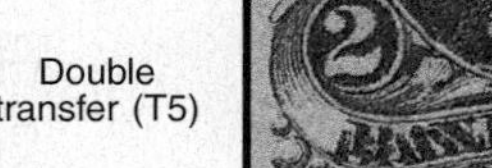

Double transfer (T5)

R5		R2 2c **Bank Check, blue**	
	a.	Imperf.	1.50
		Pair	19.00
		Block of 4	190.00
		Major double transfer (T5)	100.00
		Minor double transfer (T5)	20.00
		Privately rouletted	—
	b.	Part perf.	5.50*
		Pair	17.00
		Block of 4	140.00
		Major double transfer (T5)	300.00
		Cracked plate	22.50
	c.	Perf.	.50
		Pair	2.00
		Block of 4	8.00
		Major double transfer (T5)	75.00
		Minor double transfer (T5)	10.00
		Scratched plate	15.00
	e.	As No. R5c, Double impression	*1,000.*
	f.	As No. R5c, pair imperf between	500.00
R6		R2 2c **Bank Check, orange**	
	b.	Part perf.	60.00*
		Pair	—
	c.	Perf.	.45
		Pair	.90
		Block of 4	2.50
		Major double transfer (T5)	350.00
		Minor double transfer (T5)	8.00
	d.	As No. R6c, silk paper	275.00
	e.	As No. R6c, **orange**, *green*	900.00
	f.	As No. R6c, half used as 1c on document	250.00

Double transfer (T7)

R7		R2 2c **Certificate, blue**	
	a.	Imperf.	17.50
		Pair	45.00
		Block of 4	200.00
		Major double transfer (T7)	500.00
		Scratched plate	30.00
		Foreign entry, top numerals (1¢)	—
	c.	Perf.	32.50
		Pair	75.00
		Block of 4	300.00
		Major double transfer (T7)	750.00
		Cracked plate	37.50
		Foreign entry, top numerals (1¢)	100.00
R8		R2 2c **Certificate, orange**	
	c.	Perf.	45.00
		Pair	200.00
		Block of 4	*850.00*
		Major double transfer (T7)	800.00
R9		R2 2c **Express, blue**	
	a.	Imperf.	15.00
		Pair	50.00
		Block of 4	160.00
		Double transfer	60.00
	b.	Part perf.	35.00*
		Pair	140.00
		Block of 4	350.00
		Double transfer at bottom, pos.47	75.00
	c.	Perf.	.40
		Pair	1.25
		Block of 4	6.50
		Double transfer	17.50
		Cracked plate, pos. 62	20.00
		Foreign entry of 1c, pos. 68	—

R10 R2 2c **Express, orange**
b. Part perf. *3,250.*
c. Perf. 14.00
Pair 30.00
Block of 4 62.50
Double transfer 24.00
Cracked plate, pos. 62 —
Foreign entry of 1c, pos. 68 —
d. As No. R10c, silk paper 200.00

R11 R2 2c **Playing Cards, blue**
a. Imperf. *1,750.*
b. Part perf. 325.00
Pair 750.00
c. Perf. 4.50
Pair 13.00
Block of 4 50.00
Scratched plate, position 210 30.00

R12 R2 2c **Playing Cards, org**
c. Perf. 55.00
Pair *500.00*

Double transfer (T13)

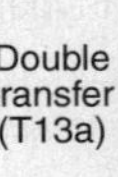

Double transfer (T13a)

R13 R2 2c **Proprietary, blue**
a. Imperf. 1,350.
b. Part perf. 300.
Pair 700.
Block of 4 *2,000.*
c. Perf. .40
Pair .90
Block of 4 5.00
Double transfer (T13) 150.00
T13a double transfer, pos. 147: top and bottom elements 250.00
T13a double transfer, pos. 133: bottom elements only 100.00
T13a double transfer, pos. 161: top elements only 100.00
Double transfer covering entire stamp 750.00
Short transfer at upper right —
Cracked plate 25.00

What can't you live without?
REVENUES
Among the largest stocks in the U.S.A.
Request Revenue price list or shop online at:
www.astampdealer4u.com
FRANK BACHENHEIMER
6547 Midnight Pass Rd. #89,
Sarasota, FL 34242
Ph. 941-349-0222
Email: frankb@astampdealer4u.com

d. As No. R13c, silk paper 250.00
Double transfer (T13a) 350.00
e. **ultramarine** 350.00
Pair 750.00
Block of 4 —
Double transfer (T13) —
Complete double transfer (T13a) *1,050.*
f. As No. R13c, horiz. half used as 1c on document —

R14 R2 2c **Proprietary, orange**
c. Perf. 65.00
Pair 350.00
Block of 4 —
Double transfer (T13) 350.00
Complete double transfer (T13a) 700.00

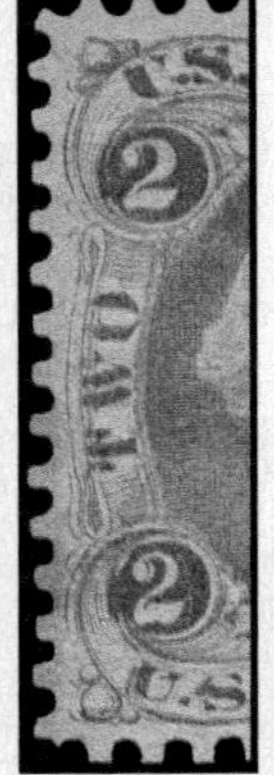
Double transfer (T15)

Double transfer (T15a)

R15 R2 2c **U.S. Internal Revenue, orange** ('64)
a. Imperf —
Pair —
b. Part perf. —
Pair —
c. Perf. .25
Pair .60
Block of 4 2.00
Double transfer (T15) 65.00
Complete double transfer (T15a) 50.00
Complete double transfer, pos. 145 150.00
Double transfer 12.00
Triple transfer 40.00
Cracked plate 10.00
d. As No. R15c, silk paper 1.00
Pair 2.25
e. As No. R15c, **orange**, *green* *2,250.*
f. As No. R15c, half used as 1c on document *250.00*

The existence of Nos. R15a and R15b has been questioned by specialists. The editors would like to see authenticated evidence of the existence of these varieties. A horizontal pair, imperforate horizontally, has been certified but that certification is very old, and the item requires a reconsideration and a modern authentication if found to be genuine. This item probably is a perforation error.

R3

R16 R3 3c **Foreign Exchange, green**
b. Part perf. 1,100.
Pair *2,750.*
c. Perf. 5.00
Pair 12.00
Block of 4 75.00
Double transfer at top, position 11 —
Gouged plate ("bruised chin"), positions 18, 19, 20, 21 —
d. As No. R16c, silk paper 200.00

R17 R3 3c **Playing Cards, green** ('63)
a. Imperf. *40,000.*
Pair *90,000.*
c. Perf. 200.00
Pair 450.00
Block of 4 *1,000.*

R18 R3 3c **Proprietary, green**
b. Part perf. 1,250.
Pair *3,000.*
Block of 4 —
c. Perf. 9.00
Pair 20.00
Block of 4 45.00
Double transfer in numerals 12.50
Double transfer, 4 value ovals shifted north 175.00
Double transfer, 4 value ovals shifted west 125.00
Cracked plate 20.00
d. As No. R18c, silk paper 150.00
Pair 400.00
e. As No. R18c, double impression *1,500.*
f. As No. R18c, printed on both sides *4,000.*

R19 R3 3c **Telegraph, green**
a. Imperf. 100.00
Pair 500.00
Block of 4 1,200.
Privately perforated, sewing machine perf. *700.00*
b. Part perf. 30.00
Pair 82.50
Block of 4 350.00
c. Perf. 3.00
Pair 8.75
Block of 4 80.00

R20 R3 4c **Inland Exchange, brown** ('63)
c. Perf. 2.25
Pair 5.25
Block of 4 22.50
Double transfer at top, position 78 15.00
d. As No. R20c, silk paper 190.00

R21 R3 4c **Playing Cards, slate** ('63)
c. Perf. 750.00
Pair *1,600.*
Block of 4 *3,500.*

R22 R3 4c **Proprietary, purple**
a. Imperf. —
b. Part perf. 600.00
Pair 1,400.
Block of 4 2,750.
c. Perf. 8.50
Pair 20.00
Block of 4 55.00
Double transfer at top 19.00
Double transfer at bottom 13.50
Plate gash in lower left numeral, position 88 —
d. As No. R22c, silk paper 250.00
Pair *600.00*
Block of 4 —

There are shade and color variations of Nos. R21-R22. See foreword of "Revenue Stamps" section.

R23 R3 5c **Agreement, red**
c. Perf. .50
Pair 1.00
Block of 4 2.10
Double transfer in numerals 25.00
Double transfer across top, pos. 160, late state 75.00
d. As No. R23c, silk paper 4.50
Pair 8.00
Block of 4 22.50
e. As No. R23c, half used as 2c on document *2,500.*

R24 R3 5c **Certificate, red**
a. Imperf. 4.00
Pair 35.00
Block of 4 250.00
b. Part perf. 15.00
Pair 150.00
Block of 4 400.00
c. Perf. .50
Pair 1.25
Block of 4 3.00
Double transfer in upper label 10.00
Double transfer throughout 200.00
Triple transfer, position 121 35.00
Scratched plate, position 170 —
d. As No. R24c, silk paper 1.10
Pair 2.50
Block of 4 10.00
Complete double transfer —
e. As No. R24c, half used as 2c on document —
f. As No. R24d, impression of No. R3 on back *3,000.*

R25 R3 5c **Express, red**
a. Imperf. 8.00
Pair 30.00
Block of 4 210.00
b. Part perf. 8.00*
Pair 100.00
Block of 4 300.00
c. Perf. .40
Pair .90
Block of 4 2.25
Double transfer, position 75 15.00

R26 R3 5c **Foreign Exchange, red**
b. Part perf. *2,000.*
Pair —
c. Perf. .50
Pair 1.25
Block of 4 15.00
Double transfer at top 20.00
Double transfer at bottom 10.00
d. As No. R26c, silk paper 750.00

R27 R3 5c **Inland Exchange, red**
a. Imperf. 10.00
Pair 37.50
Block of 4 120.00
Double transfer at top 77.50
Cracked plate 95.00
b. Part perf. 6.75
Pair 42.50
Block of 4 110.00
Double transfer at top 47.50
Cracked plate 90.00
c. Perf. .60
Pair 1.30
Block of 4 3.00
Double transfer at top 27.50
Double transfer at bottom —
Double transfer at left and right 60.00
Cracked plate 32.50
d. As No. R27c, silk paper 17.50
Pair 50.00
e. As No. R27c, double impression *3,500.*

R28 R3 5c **Playing Cards, red** ('63)
c. Perf. 40.00
Pair 90.00
Block of 4 200.00

d. As No. R28c, silk paper *1,000.*
e. Double impression *1,400.*
R29 R3 5c **Proprietary, red** ('64)
c. Perf. 30.00
Pair 70.00
Block of 4 200.00
Scratched plate 45.00
d. As No. R29c, silk paper 375.00
R30 R3 6c **Inland Exchange, orange** ('63)
c. Perf. 2.25
Pair 18.50
Block of 4 100.00
Scratched plate, position 19 15.00
Double transfer at top —
d. As No. R30c, silk paper 290.00
R31 R3 6c **Proprietary, orange** ('71)
c. Perf. *1,600.*

Nearly all examples of No. R31 are faulty or repaired and poorly centered. The catalogue value is for a fine centered stamp with minor faults which do not detract from its appearance.

R32 R3 10c **Bill of Lading, blue**
a. Imperf. 70.00
Pair 300.00
Block of 4 800.00
b. Part perf. 600.00
Pair 1,750.
c. Perf. 1.75
Pair 4.00
Block of 4 10.00
Double transfer, positions 33 and 143 —
Tool gouge, position 151 —
e. As No. R32c, half used as 5c on document *300.00*
R33 R3 10c **Certificate, blue**
a. Imperf. 400.00
Pair 850.00
Block of 4 *2,500.*
Cracked plate —
b. Part perf. 850.00*
Pair 2,500.
Block of 4 —
c. Perf. .35
Pair .75
Block of 4 2.25
Double transfer at right, position 93 15.00
Cracked plate 15.00
Scratched plate —
d. As No. R33c, silk paper 6.00
Pair 17.50
Block of 4 90.00
e. As No. R33c, half used as 5c on document *300.00*
R34 R3 10c **Contract, blue**
b. Part perf. 625.00
Pair 1,600.
Block of 4 —
be. As No. R34b, **ultramarine** 1,000.
c. Perf. .50
Pair 1.25
Block of 4 4.75
Complete double transfer 70.00
ce. As No. R34c, **ultramarine** 1.00
Pair 2.50
Block of 4 17.50
d. As No. R34c, silk paper 4.25
Pair 11.00
Block of 4 70.00
f. As No. R34c, half used as 5c on document *300.00*
R35 R3 10c **Foreign Exchange, blue**
c. Perf. 14.00
Pair 30.00
Block of 4 92.50
d. As No. R35c, silk paper —
e. As No. R35c, **ultramarine** 20.00
Pair 60.00
Block of 4 180.00
R36 R3 10c **Inland Exchange, blue**
a. Imperf. 500.00
Pair 1,750.
Block of 4 *4,000.*
b. Part perf. 4.50*
Pair 15.00
Block of 4 80.00
c. Perf. .30
Pair .60
Block of 4 1.75
Double transfer at right —
Scratched plate —
d. As No. R36c, silk paper 125.00
Pair 275.00
Block of 4 —
e. As No. R36c, half used as 5c on document *300.00*
R37 R3 10c **Power of Attorney, blue**
a. Imperf. 1,000.
Pair 2,500.
Block of 4 *6,250.*
b. Part perf. 30.00
Pair 100.00
Block of 4 300.00
c. Perf. 1.00
Pair 2.25
Block of 4 8.00
Scrathed plate —
e. As No. R37c, half used as 5c on document *300.00*
R38 R3 10c **Proprietary, blue** ('64)
c. Perf. 19.00
Pair 45.00
Block of 4 110.00
R39 R3 15c **Foreign Exchange, brown** ('63)
c. Perf. 17.00
Pair 50.00
Block of 4 250.00
e. Double impression *1,500.*
R40 R3 15c **Inland Exchange, brown**
a. Imperf. 45.00
Pair 250.00
Block of 4 900.00
Cracked plate 60.00
Double transfer at top, pos. 68 100.00
b. Part perf. 14.00
Pair 50.00
Block of 4 450.00
Cracked plate 37.50
c. Perf. 2.00
Pair 5.00
Block of 4 12.00
Double transfer at top, position 68 20.00
Cracked plate, position 11 14.00
e. As No. R40b, double impression *2,250.*
f. As No. R40c, double impression *950.00*
R41 R3 20c **Foreign Exchange, red**
a. Imperf. 95.00
Pair 400.00
Block of 4 1,000.
c. Perf. 80.00
Pair 200.00
Block of 4 450.00
d. As No. R41c, silk paper 500.00
Double transfer —
R42 R3 20c **Inland Exchange, red**
a. Imperf. 17.00
Pair 50.00
Block of 4 400.00
b. Part perf. 22.50
Pair 60.00
Block of 4 300.00
c. Perf. .45
Pair 1.00
Block of 4 14.00
d. As No. R42c, silk paper —
e. As No. R42c, half used as 5c on document *300.00*

R4

R5

R43 R4 25c **Bond, red**
a. Imperf. 300.00
Pair 750.00
Block of 4 *5,000.*
b. Part perf. 6.75
Pair 60.00
Block of 4 400.00
c. Perf. 3.75
Pair 8.00
Block of 4 60.00
R44 R4 25c **Certificate, red**
a. Imperf. 11.00
Pair 50.00
Block of 4 500.00
b. Part perf. 6.75*
Pair 40.00
Block of 4 250.00
c. Perf. .50
Pair 1.10
Block of 4 8.00
Double transfer, top or bottom 2.00
Triple transfer —
Scratched plate, position 57 —
d. As No. R44c, silk paper 2.75
Pair 8.25
Block of 4 27.50
e. As No. R44c, printed on both sides *3,500.*
f. As No. R44c, impression of No. R48 on back *6,000.*

U.S.
REVENUES
We maintain a huge selection of
quality material. We stock literature
and album pages for revenue stamps.
• All Scott-listed revenue stamps
• Revenue Proofs and Essays
• Taxpaid Revenues
• Revenue Stamped & Embossed Paper
• Revenue Stamps used on Document
• Telegraph Stamps
• Weekly Special Offers in Linn's Stamp News
WE WELCOME YOUR WANT LIST!
VIEW OUR COMPLETE UP-TO-DATE ONLINE PRICE LIST ON OUR WEBSITE.
RICHARD FRIEDBERG
310 Chestnut Street • Meadville, PA 16335
(814) 724-5824 • Fax (814) 337-8940
Email: richard@friedbergstamps.com
www.friedbergstamps.com

No.	Description	Value
R45	R4 25c **Entry of Goods, red**	
a.	Imperf.	75.00
	Pair	180.00
	Block of 4	500.00
	Top frame line double, pos. 23	100.00
b.	Part perf.	400.00
	Pair	*950.00*
	Top frame line double, pos. 23	675.00
c.	Perf.	1.50
	Pair	50.00
	Block of 4	140.00
	Top frame line double, pos. 23	11.00
d.	As No. R45c, silk paper	150.00
R46	R4 25c **Insurance, red**	
a.	Imperf.	12.50
	Pair	42.50
	Block of 4	*750.00*
b.	Part perf.	19.00
	Pair	40.00
	Block of 4	250.00
c.	Perf.	.30
	Pair	.75
	Block of 4	5.50
	Cracked plate	17.50
d.	As No. R46c, silk paper	7.00
	Pair	13.00
e.	As No. R46c, double impression	*750.00*
R47	R4 25c **Life Insurance, red**	
a.	Imperf.	50.00
	Pair	150.00
	Block of 4	650.00
b.	Part perf.	1,250.
	Pair	3,000.
c.	Perf.	11.00
	Pair	50.00
	Block of 4	240.00
R48	R4 25c **Power of Attorney, red**	
a.	Imperf.	10.00
	Pair	50.00
	Block of 4	500.00
b.	Part perf.	45.00
	Pair	125.00
	Block of 4	*600.00*
c.	Perf.	1.00
	Pair	2.25
	Block of 4	12.50
	Double transfer	1.10
	Bottom frame line double	5.50
d.	As No. R48c, silk paper	*1,750.*
R49	R4 25c **Protest, red**	
a.	Imperf.	35.00
	Pair	200.00
	Block of 4	850.00
b.	Part perf.	1,000.
	Pair	2,250.
c.	Perf.	10.00
	Pair	29.00
	Block of 4	115.00
R50	R4 25c **Warehouse Receipt, red**	
a.	Imperf.	55.00
	Pair	250.00
	Block of 4	*1,200.*
b.	Part perf.	1,300.
	Pair	2,900.
c.	Perf.	45.00
	Pair	100.00
	Block of 4	325.00
R51	R4 30c **Foreign Exchange, lilac**	
a.	Imperf.	200.00
	Pair	650.00
	Block of 4	*3,500.*
b.	Part perf.	*11,000.*
c.	Perf.	60.00
	Pair	225.00
	Block of 4	—
	Double transfer	100.00
	Top frame line double	85.00
d.	As No. R51c, silk paper	*675.00*
R52	R4 30c **Inland Exchange, lilac**	
a.	Imperf.	72.50
	Pair	350.00
	Block of 4	1,000.
b.	Part perf.	90.00
	Pair	425.00
	Block of 4	—
c.	Perf.	8.50
	Pair	40.00
	Block of 4	140.00
	Double transfer	30.00
d.	As No. R52c, silk paper	*1,500.*

There are shade and color variations of Nos. R51-R52. See foreword of "Revenue Stamps" section.

No.	Description	Value
R53	R4 40c **Inland Exchange, brown**	
a.	Imperf.	*2,500.*
	Pair	*5,750.*
b.	Part perf.	9.00
	Pair	50.00
	Block of 4	210.00
	Double transfer	50.00
c.	Perf.	8.00
	Pair	18.00
	Block of 4	275.00
	Double transfer	30.00
d.	As No. R53c, silk paper	425.00
f.	As No. R53c, double impression	—
R54	R5 50c **Conveyance, blue**	
a.	Imperf.	20.00
	Pair	100.00
	Block of 4	600.00
b.	Part perf.	3.50
	Pair	45.00
	Block of 4	160.00
c.	Perf.	.35
	Pair	.70
	Block of 4	2.50
	Double transfer	6.00
	Cracked plate	15.00
	Scratched plate at bottom, pos. 52	15.00
ce.	As No. R54c, **ultramarine**	.50
	Pair	1.25
	Block of 4	10.00
d.	As No. R54c, silk paper, **blue**	3.00
	Pair	6.50
	Powder blue	10.00
de.	As No. R54d, **ultramarine**	—
R55	R5 50c **Entry of Goods, blue**	
b.	Part perf.	17.50
	Pair	300.00
	Block of 4	650.00
c.	Perf.	.60
	Pair	2.00
	Block of 4	25.00
	Double transfer, position 20	14.00
	Scratched plate, position 76	20.00
d.	As No. R55c, silk paper	150.00
	Pair	275.00
R56	R5 50c **Foreign Exchange, blue**	
a.	Imperf.	75.00
	Pair	200.00
b.	Part perf.	125.00
	Pair	550.00
c.	Perf.	7.50
	Pair	42.50
	Block of 4	140.00
	Double transfer at left	11.00
e.	As No. R56c, double impression	*750.00*
f.	As No. R56c, half used as 25c on document	*350.00*
R57	R5 50c **Lease, blue**	
a.	Imperf.	35.00
	Pair	200.00
	Block of 4	*1,000.*
b.	Part perf.	250.00
	Pair	600.00
	Block of 4	1,400.
c.	Perf.	10.00
	Pair	67.50
	Block of 4	225.00
R58	R5 50c **Life Insurance, blue**	
a.	Imperf.	45.00
	Pair	160.00
	Block of 4	950.00
	Double transfer	47.50
b.	Part perf.	200.00
c.	Perf.	1.75
	Pair	10.00
	Block of 4	50.00
	Double transfer at top, position 10 and 13	20.00
e.	As No. R58c, double impression	*1,100.*

Cracked Plate (C59)

No.	Description	Value
R59	R5 50c **Mortgage, blue**	
a.	Imperf.	22.50
	Pair	100.00
	Block of 4	500.00
	Scratched plate, diagonal, positions 26, 42, 43	35.00
b.	Part perf.	5.00
	Pair	225.00
	Block of 4	500.00
	Cracked plate, positions 64 and 81	37.50
	Scratched plate, diagonal, positions 26, 42, 43	25.00
c.	Perf.	.70
	Pair	2.00
	Block of 4	7.50
	Cracked plate, positions 64 and 81	12.50
	Scratched plate, diagonal, positions 26, 42, 43	12.50
	Double transfer	3.50
	Tool gouge, position 63	40.00
d.	As No. R59c, silk paper	—
e.	As No. R59a, double impression	—
f.	As No. R59c, double impression	—

The plate crack listed for Nos. R59b and R59c crosses positions 64 and 81. The illustrated crack (C59) is position 64. Value is for a single. The scratch listed for Nos. R59a, R59b and R59c crosses positions 26, 42 and 43. Value is for a single.

No.	Description	Value
R60	R5 50c **Original Process, blue**	
a.	Imperf.	5.50
	Pair	77.50
	Block of 4	*1,000.*
b.	Part perf.	*4,000.*
c.	Perf.	1.00
	Pair	2.75
	Block of 4	7.50
	Double transfer at top and left, position 28	12.00
	Double transfer at bottom	8.00
	Scratched plate	10.00
d.	As No. R60c, silk paper	7.50
	Pair	22.50
	Block of 4	150.00
e.	As No. R60c, half used as 25c on document	—
R61	R5 50c **Passage Ticket, blue**	
a.	Imperf.	140.00
	Pair	375.00
	Block of 4	*1,250.*
b.	Part perf.	575.00
	Pair	1,650.
c.	Perf.	2.25
	Pair	12.50
	Block of 4	225.00
	Scratched plate, position 9	25.00
R62	R5 50c **Probate of Will, blue**	
a.	Imperf.	55.00
	Pair	250.00
	Block of 4	950.00
b.	Part perf.	250.00
	Pair	825.00
	Block of 4	1,650.
	Scratched plate	300.00
c.	Perf.	22.50
	Pair	50.00
	Block of 4	350.00
R63	R5 50c **Surety Bond, blue**	
a.	Imperf.	400.00
	Pair	*1,200.*
b.	Part perf.	2.75
	Pair	15.00
	Block of 4	100.00
c.	Perf.	.30
	Pair	1.75
	Block of 4	10.00
e.	As No. R63c, **ultramarine**	.75
	Pair	5.50
	Block of 4	55.00
R64	R5 60c **Inland Exchange, orange**	
a.	Imperf.	110.00
	Pair	400.00
	Block of 4	*800.00*
b.	Part perf.	82.50
	Pair	225.00
	Block of 4	550.00
c.	Perf.	9.00
	Pair	20.00
	Block of 4	100.00
d.	As No. R64c, silk paper	85.00
	Pair	190.00
R65	R5 70c **Foreign Exchange, green**	
a.	Imperf.	650.00
	Pair	2,750.
b.	Part perf.	200.00
	Pair	950.00
	Block of 4	*2,000.*
	Scratched plate at bottom, pos. 52	250.00
c.	Perf.	14.00
	Pair	40.00
	Block of 4	250.00
	Scratched plate at bottom, pos. 52	30.00
	Double transfer at top	—
d.	As No. R65c, silk paper	75.00
	Pair	175.00

Pairs and blocks of No. R65b are valued in the grade of fine.

R6

R7

No.	Description	Value
R66	R6 $1 **Conveyance, red**	
a.	Imperf.	27.50
	Pair	90.00
	Block of 4	700.00
	Double transfer	35.00
	Right frame line double	90.00
	Top frame line double	125.00
b.	Part perf.	*5,500.*
	Pair	*7,000.*
c.	Perf.	27.50
	Pair	75.00
	Block of 4	160.00
	Double transfer	37.50
	Right frame line double, position 60	77.50
	Top frame line double, position 6	60.00
d.	As No. R66c, silk paper	200.00
R67	R6 $1 **Entry of Goods, red**	
a.	Imperf.	50.00
	Pair	150.00
	Block of 4	750.00
c.	Perf.	2.75
	Pair	6.50
	Block of 4	55.00
	Scratched plate, position 43	15.00
d.	As No. R67c, silk paper	180.00
R68	R6 $1 **Foreign Exchange, red**	
a.	Imperf.	90.00
	Pair	250.00
	Block of 4	*1,475.*
	Left frame line double, pos. 80	180.00
c.	Perf.	.75
	Pair	1.75
	Block of 4	11.00

	Double transfer, pos. 79	20.00
	Recut frame lines at upper left	6.00
	Left frame line double, pos. 80	19.00
	Recut shield at upper left	40.00
d.	As No. R68c, silk paper	150.00
e.	As No. R68d, half used as 50c on document	*300.00*
R69	R6 $1 **Inland Exchange, red**	
a.	Imperf.	17.00
	Pair	75.00
	Block of 4	850.00
	Double transfer of top shields, position 29	110.00
b.	Part perf.	*6,000.**
	Pair	*12,500.*
c.	Perf.	.70
	Pair	2.00
	Block of 4	9.50
	Double transfer at bottom	4.25
	Double transfer of top shields, position 29	21.00
d.	As No. R69c, silk paper	6.00
	Pair	9.00
	Block of 4	35.00
e.	As No. R69c, horiz. pair, imperf. vert.	—
f.	As No. R69c, half used as 50c on document	*300.00*

No. R69e is an error from a pane of stamps that was intended to be issued fully perforated. It can be differentiated from No. R69b by the color, paper and date of cancel. Expertization is strongly recommended.

R70	R6 $1 **Lease, red**	
a.	Imperf.	50.00
	Pair	150.00
	Block of 4	600.00
	Double transfer at bottom	80.00
	Double transfer at top, pos. 17	—
c.	Perf.	4.50
	Pair	12.00
	Block of 4	80.00
	Double transfer at bottom	11.00
	Cracked plate	26.00
	Double transfer at top, pos. 17	—
e.	As No. R70c, half used as 50c on document	*500.00*
R71	R6 $1 **Life Insurance, red**	
a.	Imperf.	300.00
	Pair	650.00
	Block of 4	*1,400.*
	Right frame line double	500.00
c.	Perf.	10.00
	Pair	25.00
	Block of 4	60.00
	Right frame line double, pos. 46	50.00
d.	As No. R71c, silk paper	*750.00*
e.	As No. R71c, half used as 50c on document	*1,000.*
R72	R6 $1 **Manifest, red**	
a.	Imperf.	47.50
	Pair	120.00
	Block of 4	700.00
c.	Perf.	40.00
	Pair	85.00
	Block of 4	210.00
e.	As No. R72c, half used as 50c on document	*300.00*
R73	R6 $1 **Mortgage, red**	
a.	Imperf.	27.50
	Pair	85.00
	Block of 4	650.00
	Double transfer at left	45.00
	Bottom frame line double, position 13	60.00
c.	Perf.	300.00
	Pair	650.00
	Block of 4	1,400.
	Double transfer at left	350.00
	Bottom frame line double, position 13	450.00
R74	R6 $1 **Passage Ticket, red**	
a.	Imperf.	350.00
	Pair	750.00
	Block of 4	*1,600.*
c.	Perf.	350.00
	Pair	750.00
	Block of 4	1,750.
R75	R6 $1 **Power of Attorney, red**	
a.	Imperf.	100.00
	Pair	250.00
	Block of 4	700.00
c.	Perf.	2.75
	Pair	6.00
	Block of 4	26.00
	Double transfer	9.50
	Recut	11.50
e.	As No. R75c, half used as 50c on document	—
R76	R6 $1 **Probate of Will, red**	
a.	Imperf.	100.00
	Pair	300.00
	Block of 4	*800.00*
	Right frame line double	160.00
	Double transfer at top	225.00
c.	Perf.	55.00
	Pair	125.00
	Block of 4	325.00
	Right frame line double	75.00
R77	R7 $1.30 **Foreign Exchange, orange** ('63)	
a.	Imperf.	*11,000.*
c.	Perf.	120.00
	Pair	300.00
	Block of 4	—
	Double transfer	—

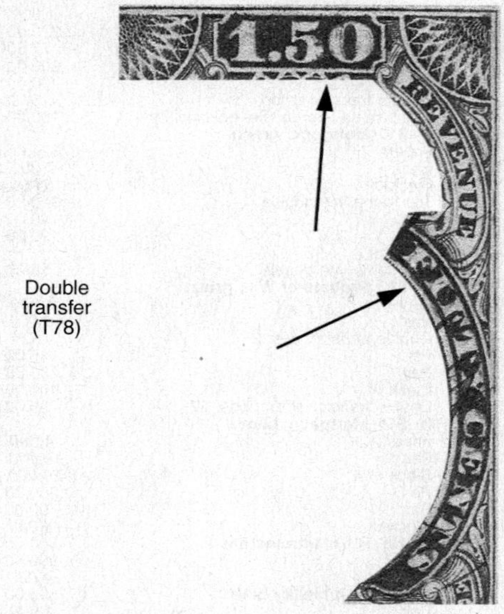

Double transfer (T78)

R78	R7 $1.50 **Inland Exchange, blue**	
a.	Imperf.	32.50
	Pair	140.00
	Block of 4	600.00
	Bottom frame line double	—
c.	Perf.	7.00
	Pair	75.00
	Block of 4	400.00
	Double transfer (T78)	13.50
	Top and bottom frame lines doubled	—
	Cracked plate	—
R79	R7 $1.60 **Foreign Exchange, green** ('63)	
a.	Imperf.	1,400.
	Pair	*5,000.*
c.	Perf.	180.00
	Pair	500.00
R80	R7 $1.90 **Foreign Exchange, purple** ('63)	
a.	Imperf.	*12,500.*
c.	Perf.	200.00
	Pair	500.00
	Block of 4	1,200.
d.	As No. R80c, silk paper	450.00

There are many shade and color variations of No. R80. See foreword of "Revenue Stamps" section.

R8

R81	R8 $2 **Conveyance, red**	
a.	Imperf.	250.00
	Pair	600.00
	Block of 4	1,400.
b.	Part perf.	3,250.
	Pair	*8,500.*
c.	Perf.	4.00
	Pair	10.00
	Block of 4	65.00
	Cracked plate, position 17	32.50
	Scratched plate, position 9	—
d.	As No. R81c, silk paper	40.00
	Pair	90.00
	Block of 4	200.00
e.	As No. R81c, half used as $1 on document	*600.00*
R82	R8 $2 **Mortgage, red**	
a.	Imperf.	150.00
	Pair	350.00
	Block of 4	950.00
c.	Perf.	7.00
	Pair	16.00
	Block of 4	60.00
	Double transfer at upper left, pos. 27	25.00
	Cracked plate, position 8	—
	Scratched plate, position 2	—
	Plate erosion, pos. 43	20.00
d.	As No. R82c, silk paper	60.00
	Pair	125.00
e.	As No. R82c, half used as $1 on document	*900.00*
R83	R8 $2 **Probate of Will, red** ('63)	
a.	Imperf.	*7,000.*
	Pair	*16,000.*
c.	Perf.	90.00
	Pair	200.00
	Block of 4	425.00
	Double transfer	90.00
e.	As No. R83c, half used as $1 on document	*750.00*
R84	R8 $2.50 **Inland Exchange, purple** ('63)	
a.	Imperf.	*12,000.*
	Pair	*40,000.*
c.	Perf.	22.50
	Pair	50.00
	Block of 4	325.00
d.	As No. R84c, silk paper	40.00
	Pair	90.00
	Block of 4	425.00
e.	As No. R84c, double impression	*2,000.*

There are many shade and color variations of Nos. R84c and R84d. See foreword of "Revenues Stamps" section.

R85	R8 $3 **Charter Party, green**	
a.	Imperf.	200.00
	Pair	450.00
	Block of 4	2,750.
c.	Perf.	11.00
	Pair	65.00
	Block of 4	300.00
	Double transfer at top	25.00
	Double transfer at bottom	12.00
	Scratched plate, position 44	—
d.	As No. R85c, silk paper	175.00
	Pair	275.00
e.	As No. R85c, printed on both sides	*7,000.*
f.	As No. R85c, half used as $1.50 on document	—
g.	As No. R85c, impression of No. RS208 on back	*17,000.*
R86	R8 $3 **Manifest, green**	
a.	Imperf.	200.00
	Pair	450.00
	Block of 4	*3,500.*
c.	Perf.	55.00
	Pair	125.00
	Block of 4	300.00
	Double transfer	210.00
R87	R8 $3.50 **Inland Exchange, blue** ('63)	
a.	Imperf.	*10,000.*
	Pair	*37,500.*
c.	Perf.	70.00
	Pair	180.00
	Block of 4	450.00
e.	As No. R87c, printed on both sides	*4,000.*

The $3.50 has stars in upper corners.

AUCTIONS
WITH A DIFFERENCE
Specializing in revenues & back of book. Including...
• Scott listed revenues
• Checks & documents
• Taxpaid revenues
• Covers & postal history
• Stock & bond certificates
• WRITE FOR NEXT CATALOG •
H.J.W. DAUGHERTY
P.O. Box 1146S, Eastham, Mass. 02642
Phone 508-255-7488
Email: hjwdonline@gmail.com
Web: www.hjwdonline.com

R9

R10

R88	R9	$5 **Charter Party, red**	
a.		Imperf.	300.00
		Pair	650.00
		Block of 4	*1,500.*
		Right frame line double	425.00
		Top frame line double	425.00
c.		Perf.	10.00
		Pair	65.00
		Block of 4	200.00
		Right frame line double	70.00
		Top frame line double	60.00
d.		As No. R88c, silk paper	170.00
R89	R9	$5 **Conveyance, red**	
a.		Imperf.	50.00
		Pair	200.00
		Block of 4	*900.00*
c.		Perf.	11.00
		Pair	24.00
		Block of 4	110.00
d.		As No. R89c, silk paper	160.00
		Pair	350.00
R90	R9	$5 **Manifest, red**	
a.		Imperf.	250.00
		Pair	600.00
		Block of 4	*1,300.*
		Left frame line double	325.00
c.		Perf.	120.00
		Pair	300.00
		Block of 4	650.00
		Left frame line double	175.00
R91	R9	$5 **Mortgage, red**	
a.		Imperf.	200.00
		Pair	800.00
		Block of 4	—
c.		Perf.	25.00
		Pair	87.50
		Block of 4	1,200.
R92	R9	$5 **Probate of Will, red**	
a.		Imperf.	700.00
		Pair	1,600.
		Block of 4	*3,600.*
c.		Perf.	27.50
		Pair	100.00
		Block of 4	375.00
R93	R9	$10 **Charter Party, green**	
a.		Imperf.	900.00
		Pair	*1,900.*
		Block of 4	—
c.		Perf.	37.50
		Pair	100.00
		Block of 4	450.00
		Double transfer	85.00
R94	R9	$10 **Conveyance, green**	
a.		Imperf.	175.00
		Pair	350.00
		Block of 4	1,000.
		Double transfer at top	225.00
c.		Perf.	77.50
		Pair	200.00
		Block of 4	700.00
		Double transfer at top	125.00
		Right frame line double, position 71	150.00
R95	R9	$10 **Mortgage, green**	
a.		Imperf.	825.00
		Pair	2,250.
		Block of 4	*6,000.*
		Top frame line double	900.00
c.		Perf.	40.00
		Pair	120.00
		Block of 4	—
		Top frame line double	55.00
R96	R9	$10 **Probate of Will, green**	
a.		Imperf.	4,000.
		Pair	*9,000.*
		Double transfer, pos. 27	—
c.		Perf.	45.00
		Pair	100.00
		Block of 4	400.00
		Double transfer at top, pos. 27	90.00
R97	R10	$15 **Mortgage, blue**	
a.		Imperf.	4,500.
		Pair	*10,000.*
		Block of 4	*20,000.*
c.		Perf.	300.00
		Pair	700.00
		Block of 4	*4,000.*
e.		As No. R97c, **ultramarine**	500.00
		Pair	900.00
		Block of 4	*4,000.*
f.		As No. R97c, **milky blue**	525.00
		Pair	1,900.
R98	R10	$20 **Conveyance, orange**	
a.		Imperf.	175.00
		Pair	450.00
		Block of 4	2,000.
c.		Perf.	125.00
		Pair	300.00
		Block of 4	800.00
d.		As No. R98c, silk paper	175.00
		Pair	350.00
R99	R10	$20 **Probate of Will, orange**	
a.		Imperf.	3,500.
		Pair	*8,000.*
		Block of 4	*18,000.*
c.		Perf.	3,000.
		Pair	*6,500.*
		Block of 4	*14,000.*
R100	R10	$25 **Mortgage, red** ('63)	
a.		Imperf.	3,250.
		Pair	*7,000.*
		Block of 4	*18,000.*
c.		Perf.	250.00
		Pair	600.00
		Block of 4	*1,300.*
		Scratched plate	—
d.		As No. R100c, silk paper	300.00
e.		As No. R100c, horiz. pair, imperf. between	*3,500.*
R101	R10	$50 **U.S. Internal Revenue, green** ('63)	
a.		Imperf.	325.00
		Pair	750.00
		Block of 4	2,500.
c.		Perf.	210.00
		Pair	450.00
		Block of 4	950.00
		Cracked plate	250.00

R11

Illustration reduced.

R102	R11	$200 **U.S. Int. Rev., green & red** ('64)	
a.		Imperf.	2,500.
		Pair	*5,500.*
		Block of 4	*15,000.*
c.		Perf.	850.00
		Pair	2,250.
		Block of 4	*4,500.*

DOCUMENTARY STAMPS
Second Issue

After release of the First Issue revenue stamps, the Bureau of Internal Revenue received many reports of fraudulent cleaning and re-use. The Bureau ordered a Second Issue with new designs and colors, using a patented "chameleon" paper which is usually violet or pinkish, with silk fibers.

While designs are different from those of the first issue, stamp sizes and make up of the plates are the same as for corresponding denominations.

R12

R12a

George Washington

Engraved and printed by Jos. R. Carpenter, Philadelphia.

Various Frames and Numeral Arrangements

1871 ***Perf. 12***

R103	R12	1c **blue & black**	100.00
		Cut cancel	40.00
		Pair	220.00
		Block of 4	475.00
a.		Inverted center	*1,600.*
		Cut cancel	*750.00*
		Pair	*3,500.*
		Block of 4	—
R104	R12	2c **blue & black**	2.75
		Cut cancel	.30
		Pair	6.25
		Block of 4	40.00
a.		Inverted center	*5,000.*
		Cut cancel	*3,500.*
R105	R12a	3c **blue & black**	75.00
		Cut cancel	30.00
		Pair	160.00
		Block of 4	350.00
R106	R12a	4c **blue & black**	160.00
		Cut cancel	65.00
		Pair	340.00
		Block of 4	725.00
a.		Half used as 2c on document	*1,000.*
R107	R12a	5c **blue & black**	2.00
		Cut cancel	.50
		Pair	6.00
		Block of 4	22.50
a.		Inverted center	*4,000.*
		Cut cancel	*2,500.*
b.		Half used as 2c on document	*1,000.*
R108	R12a	6c **blue & black**	300.00
		Cut cancel	100.00
		Pair	625.00
		Block of 4	1,400.
R109	R12a	10c **blue & black**	1.50
		Cut cancel	.30
		Pair	9.50
		Block of 4	25.00
		Double transfer	—
a.		Inverted center	*2,000.*
		Cut cancel	*1,250.*
		Pair	*5,250.*
b.		Double impression of center	—
c.		Half used as 5c on document	*300.00*

No. R109a is valued in the grade of fine.

R110	R12a	15c **blue & black**	100.00
		Cut cancel	35.00
		Pair	210.00
		Block of 4	450.00
R111	R12a	20c **blue & black**	10.00
		Cut cancel	4.00
		Pair	22.50
		Block of 4	87.50
a.		Inverted center	*8,000.*
		Cut cancel	*3,000.*
		Pair	*17,000.*

No. R111a is valued in the grade of fine and with small faults, as almost all examples have faults.

R13

R13a

R112	R13	25c **blue & black**	1.50
		Cut cancel	.30
		Pair	3.25
		Block of 4	11.00

	Double transfer, position 57	50.00
a.	Inverted center	*13,000.*
	Cut cancel	*6,500.*
b.	Imperf.	—
c.	Privately rouletted, sewing machine perfs	160.00
	Cut cancel	80.00
	Pair	375.00
	Block of 4	1,750.
d.	Privately perforated 8	600.00
R113	R13 30c **blue & black**	175.00
	Cut cancel	70.00
	Pair	370.00
	Block of 4	825.00
R114	R13 40c **blue & black**	150.00
	Cut cancel	50.00
	Pair	325.00
R115	R13a 50c **blue & black**	1.40
	Cut cancel	.35
	Pair	3.00
	Block of 4	9.25
	Double transfer	20.00
a.	Inverted center	1,050.
	Cut cancel	650.00
	Pair	*2,750.*
	Punch cancel	275.00
	Pair	575.00
b.	Imperf.	*800.00*
c.	Privately perforated, sewing machine perfs	500.00
	Pair	1,200.
	Block of 4	*2,250.*
d.	Privately perforated 8-9	—
R116	R13a 60c **blue & black**	250.00
	Cut cancel	80.00
	Pair	550.00
	Foreign entry, design of 70c	500.00
R117	R13a 70c **blue & black**	100.00
	Cut cancel	35.00
	Pair	210.00
a.	Inverted center	*4,000.*
	Cut cancel	*1,250.*

R13b

R118	R13b $1 **blue & black**	10.00
	Cut cancel	2.25
	Pair	22.50
	Block of 4	55.00
a.	Inverted center	*6,000.*
	Cut cancel	*1,500.*
	Punch cancel	*1,000.*
b.	Half used as 50c on document	*1,000.*
R119	R13b $1.30 **blue & black**	750.00
	Cut cancel	175.00
	Pair	1,650.
R120	R13b $1.50 **blue & black**	22.50
	Cut cancel	9.00
	Pair	65.00
	Block of 4	—
	Foreign entry, design of $1	600.00
a.	Privately perforated sewing machine perfs	*3,500.*
	Cut cancel	*2,500.*
	Pair	—
R121	R13b $1.60 **blue & black**	750.00
	Cut cancel	325.00
	Pair	1,650.
R122	R13b $1.90 **blue & black**	500.00
	Cut cancel	150.00
	Pair	1,100.
	Block of 4	—

R13c

R123	R13c $2 **blue & black**	25.00
	Cut cancel	10.00
	Pair	55.00
	Block of 4	350.00
	Double transfer at top	45.00
R124	R13c $2.50 **blue & black**	60.00
	Cut cancel	30.00
	Pair	130.00
	Block of 4	750.00
R125	R13c $3 **blue & black**	75.00
	Cut cancel	35.00
	Pair	170.00
	Block of 4	600.00
	Double transfer	—
R126	R13c $3.50 **blue & black**	500.00
	Cut cancel	250.00
	Pair	1,100.

R13d

R127	R13d $5 **blue & black**	40.00
	Cut cancel	15.00
	Pair	110.00
	Block of 4	500.00
a.	Inverted center	*3,000.*
	Cut cancel	*1,500.*
	Punch cancel	*1,100.*
R128	R13d $10 **blue & black**	260.00
	Cut cancel	90.00
	Pair	550.00
	Block of 4	*1,200.*

R13e

R129	R13e $20 **blue & black**	900.00
	Cut cancel	275.00
	Pair	2,000.
	Block of 4	*9,000.*
R130	R13e $25 **blue & black**	850.00
	Cut cancel	275.00
	Pair	2,000.
R131	R13e $50 **blue & black**	1,050.
	Cut cancel	325.00
	Pair	2,400.

R13f

R132	R13f $200 **red, blue & black**	*8,500.*
	Cut cancel	*3,250.*

Printed in sheets of one.

R13g

R133	R13g $500 **red orange, green & black**	*16,500.*

Printed in sheets of one.

Value for No. R133 is for a very fine appearing example with a light circular cut cancel or with minor flaws.

Inverted Centers: Fraudulently produced inverted centers exist, some excellently made.

Confusion resulting from the fact that all 1c through $50 denominations of the Second Issue were uniform in color, caused the ordering of a new printing with values in distinctive colors.

Plates used were those of the preceding issue.

Third Issue

Engraved and printed by Jos. R. Carpenter, Philadelphia.
Various Frames and Numeral Arrangements.
Violet "Chameleon" Paper with Silk Fibers.

1871-72 ***Perf. 12***

R134 R12 1c **claret & black** ('72) 65.00
Cut cancel 30.00
Pair 140.00
Block of 4 425.00
R135 R12 2c **orange & black** .40
Cut cancel .25
Pair .80
Block of 4 1.75
Double transfer —
a. 2c vermilion & black (error) *900.00*
b. Inverted center 425.00
Cut cancel 300.00
Pair *1,850.*
Block of 4 4,250.
c. Imperf., pair —
Block of 4 —
d. As No. R135, double impression of frame *1,750.*
e. As No. R135, frame printed on both sides *1,800.*
f. As No. R135, double impression of center *150.00*
R136 R12a 4c **brown & black** ('72) 110.00
Cut cancel 45.00
Pair 250.00
R137 R12a 5c **orange & black** .35
Cut cancel .25
Pair .75
Block of 4 1.60
Scratched plate —
a. Inverted center *5,000.*
Cut cancel *3,750.*
"Block" of 3 *15,000.*
b. Half used as 2c on document *1,000.*

No. R137a is valued in the grade of fine.

R138 R12a 6c **orange & black** ('72) 125.00
Cut cancel 50.00
Pair 275.00
Block of 4 1,100.
R139 R12a 15c **brown & black** ('72) 27.50
Cut cancel 10.00
Pair 65.00
Block of 4 200.00
a. Inverted center *16,000.*
Cut cancel *9,000.*
Pair 15,000.

The used pair of No. R139a is unique. It has average centering and has manuscript and waffle-iron grid cancels. Value reflects 2011 auction sale price.

R140 R13 30c **orange & black** ('72) 50.00
Cut cancel 15.00
Pair 110.00
Block of 4 350.00
Double transfer —
a. Inverted center *3,500.*
Cut cancel *1,750.*
R141 R13 40c **brown & black** ('72) 110.00
Cut cancel 35.00
Pair 240.00
Block of 4 525.00
R142 R13a 60c **orange & black** ('72) 140.00
Cut cancel 55.00
Pair 350.00
Block of 4 750.00
Foreign entry, design of 70c 200.00
R143 R13a 70c **green & black** ('72) 90.00
Cut cancel 30.00
Pair 220.00
Block of 4 500.00
R144 R13b $1 **green & black** ('72) 3.00
Cut cancel .80
Pair 10.00
Block of 4 80.00
a. Inverted center *12,500.*
Cut cancel *10,000.*
Block of 4, on document *85,000.*

No. R144a is valued in the grade of fine.

R145 R13c $2 **vermilion & black** ('72) 55.00
Cut cancel 25.00
Pair 120.00
Block of 4 375.00
Double transfer at top 70.00
R146 R13c $2.50 **claret & black** ('72) 110.00
Cut cancel 35.00
Pair 240.00
Block of 4 525.00
a. Inverted center *25,000.*
Cut cancel *17,000.*
R147 R13c $3 **green & black** ('72) 110.00
Cut cancel 35.00
Pair 240.00
Block of 4 525.00
Double transfer —
R148 R13d $5 **vermilion & black** ('72) 50.00
Cut cancel 20.00
Pair 110.00
Block of 4 240.00
R149 R13d $10 **green & black** ('72) 400.00
Cut cancel 85.00
Pair 900.00
Block of 4 2,100.
R150 R13e $20 **orange & black** ('72) 900.00
Cut cancel 350.00
Pair 1,800.
Block of 4 *5,000.*
a. $20 vermilion & black (error) 1,250.
Cut cancel 700.00

See note on Inverted Centers after No. R133.

1874 ***Perf. 12***

R151 R12 2c **orange & black,** *green* .25
Cut cancel .25
Pair .50
Block of 4 1.00
a. Inverted center 800.00
Cut cancel 375.00
Pair 1,750.

Liberty — R14

1875-78 ***Perf. 12***

R152 R14 2c **blue,** *blue*
a. silk paper 3.00 .45
Pair 6.00 .90
Block of 4 14.00 1.90
Double transfer — 5.50
b. Wmk. 191R ('78) 2.00 .35
Pair 4.00 .70
Block of 4 12.00 2.10
Double transfer — 5.50
c. Wmk. 191R, rouletted 6 90.00 32.50
Pair 200.00 125.00
"L" shaped strip of 3 600.00
d. As "a," vert. pair, imperf. horiz. 525.00
e. As "b," imperf., pair *350.00*
f. As "b," vert. pair, imperf. horiz. 350.00

The watermarked paper came into use in 1878. The rouletted stamps probably were introduced in 1881.

Nos. 279, 267a, 267, 279Bg, 279B, 272-274 Overprinted in Red or Blue

a — Rectangular Periods

a — Square Periods

b

b — Small Period after "I"

Overprint "a" exists in two (or possibly more) settings, with upright rectangular periods or with altered right leg of "R" and square periods (pos. 10, 20, 30, 40, 50, 60, 70, 80, 90, 100), both illustrated. Overprint "b" has 4 stamps with small period following the "I" in each pane of 100 (pos. 41, 46, 91 & 96).

1898 **Wmk. 191** ***Perf. 12***

For Nos. R153-R160, values in the first column are for unused examples, values in the second column are for used.

R153 A87(a) 1c **deep grn,** red overprint 5.00 2.75
Block of 4 29.00 12.00
P# strip of 3, Impt. 35.00
P# block of 6, Impt. 110.00
R154 A87(b) 1c **green,** red overprint .35 .35
Block of 4 1.50 1.50
P# strip of 3, Impt. 10.50
P# block of 6, Impt. 57.50
a. Overprint inverted 35.00 22.50
Block of 4 175.00 —
P# strip of 3, Impt. 190.00
P# block of 6, Impt. 450.00
b. Overprint on back instead of face, inverted *4,000.*
c. Pair, one without overprint *10,000.*
Vert. strip of 3 containing No. R154c at top and No. R154b at bottom —
d. Half used as ½c on document *750.00*
R155 A88(b) 2c **pink,** type III, blue overprint, *July 1, 1898* .30 .25
Block of 4 1.25 1.10
P# strip of 3, Impt. 11.50
P# block of 6, Impt. 55.00
Dot in "S" of "CENTS" 1.10
P# strip of 3, Impt. 18.00
b. 2c **carmine,** type III, blue overprint, *July 1, 1898* .35 .25
Block of 4 1.40 1.10
P# strip of 3, Impt. 13.00
P# block of 6, Impt. 57.50
Dot in "S" of "CENTS" 1.40
P# strip of 3, Impt. 24.00
c. As No. R155, overprint inverted, *July 1898* 6.50 4.50
Block of 4 27.50 20.00
P# strip of 3, Impt. 65.00
P# block of 6, Impt. 160.00
d. Vertical pair, one without overprint *1,750.*
e. Horiz. pair, one without overprint —
f. As No. R155, overprint on back instead of face, inverted 350.00
i. Double ovt., one split *850.00*

NOTE: Old No. R155 is now Nos. R155b, R155Ag; old No. R155a is Nos. R155c, R155Ah; old No. R155b is Nos. R155d, R155e; old No. R155c is No. R155f.

R155A A88(b) 2c **pink,** type IV, blue overprint *July 1, 1898* .25 .25
Block of 4 1.25 1.10
P# strip of 3, Impt. 10.50
P# block of 6, Impt. 52.50
g. 2c **carmine,** type IV, blue overprint, *July 1, 1898* .25 .25
Block of 4 1.40 1.10
P# strip of 3, Impt. 11.50
P# block of 6, Impt. 55.00
h. As No. R155A, overprint inverted, *July 1898* 2.75 2.00
Block of 4 13.00 9.25
P# strip of 3, Impt. 32.50
P# block of 6, Impt. 77.50

Handstamped Type "b" or Type "c" in Magenta

c

R156 A93(b) 8c **violet brown** *5,250.*
R157 A94(b) 10c **dark green** *4,000.*
Block of 6 —
a. As No. R157, handstamped type "c" — —
R158 A95(b) 15c **dark blue** *6,250.*
Pair —

Nos. R156-R158 were emergency provisionals, privately prepared, not officially issued.

Privately Prepared Provisionals

No. 285 Overprinted in Red

1898 **Wmk. 191** ***Perf. 12***

R158A A100 1c **dark yellow green** *15,000.* *12,500.*

No. R158A is valued in sound condition and in the grade of fine to very fine. Most examples have faults, and such examples sell for less.

No. 285 Ovptd. "I.R./P.I.D. & Son" in Red

R158B A100 1c **dark yellow green** *25,000.* *30,000.*

No. R158B is valued with small faults as each of the four recorded examples have faults.

Nos. R158A-R158B were overprinted with federal government permission by the Purvis Printing Co. upon order of Capt. L. H. Chapman of the Chapman Steamboat Line. Both the Chapman Line and P. I. Daprix & Son operated freight-carrying steamboats on the Erie Canal. The Chapman Line touched at Syracuse, Utica, Little Falls and Fort Plain; the Daprix boat ran between Utica and Rome. Overprintings of 250 of each stamp were made.

Dr. Kilmer & Co. provisional overprints and St. Louis provisional proprietary stamps are listed under "Private Die Medicine Stamps," Nos. RS307-RS315 and RS320-395.

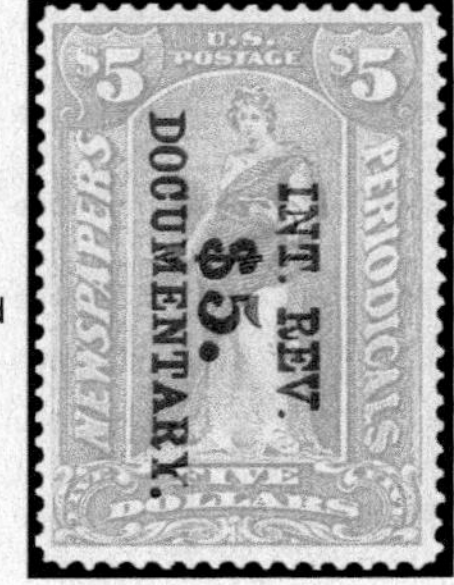

Newspaper Stamp No. PR121 Surcharged in Red

1898 *Perf. 12*

R159	N18 $5 **dark blue,** surcharge reading down	550.00	325.00
	Block of 4	2,300.	1,400.
	P# strip of 3, Impt.	*2,400.*	
R160	N18 $5 **dark blue,** surcharge reading up	150.00	140.00
	Block of 4	625.00	*750.00*
	P# strip of 3, Impt.	2,000.	*750.00*

Battleship—R15

There are two styles of rouletting for the proprietary and documentary stamps of the 1898 issue, an ordinary rouletting 5½ and one by which small rectangles of the paper are cut out, usually called hyphen-hole perforation 7. Several stamps are known with an apparent roulette 14 caused by slippage of a hyphen-hole 7 rouletting wheel.

1898 **Wmk. 191R** *Rouletted 5½*

R161	R15 ½c **orange**	5.00	*25.00*
	Block of 4	22.50	*160.00*
	P# block of 6	300.00	
R162	R15 ½c **dark gray**	.30	.25
	Block of 4	1.60	1.10
	P# block of 6	225.00	
	Double transfer		7.75
a.	Vert. pair, imperf. horiz.	125.00	
R163	R15 1c **pale blue**	.25	.25
	Block of 4	1.00	1.00
	P# block of 6	40.00	
	Double transfer	10.00	
a.	Vert. pair, imperf. horiz.	8.00	
b.	Imperf., pair	*600.00*	
R164	R15 2c **car rose**	.30	.30
	Block of 4	1.50	1.50
	P# block of 6	50.00	
	Double transfer	1.10	.30
a.	Vert. pair, imperf. horiz.	125.00	
b.	Imperf., pair	400.00	
c.	Horiz. pair, imperf. vert.	375.00	
R165	R15 3c **dark blue**	3.50	.35
	Block of 4	14.00	1.40
	P# block of 6	425.00	
	Double transfer	—	
R166	R15 4c **pale rose**	2.50	.35
	Block of 4	11.50	1.40
	P# block of 6	425.00	
a.	Vert. pair, imperf. horiz.	250.00	
R167	R15 5c **lilac**	.65	.35
	Block of 4	3.25	1.25
	P# block of 6	275.00	
a.	Pair, imperf. horiz. or vert.	350.00	175.00
b.	Horiz. pair, imperf. btwn.		*650.00*
R168	R15 10c **dark brown**	2.00	.25
	Block of 4	12.00	1.25
	P# block of 6	350.00	
a.	Vert. pair, imperf. horiz.	40.00	35.00
b.	Horiz. pair, imperf. vert.	—	
R169	R15 25c **pur brown**	7.50	.50
	Block of 4	32.50	2.25
	P# block of 6	750.00	
	Double transfer	—	
R170	R15 40c **blue lilac**	125.00	1.50
	Block of 4	600.00	52.50
	P# block of 6	—	
	Cut cancel		.35
R171	R15 50c **slate violet**	35.00	.25
	Block of 4	150.00	2.25
	P# block of 6	850.00	
a.	Imperf., pair	*450.00*	
b.	Horiz. pair, imperf. btwn.		*550.00*
R172	R15 80c **bister**	125.00	.50
	Block of 4	600.00	32.50
	P# block of 6	—	
	Cut cancel		.25

Numerous double transfers exist on this issue.

Hyphen Hole Perf. 7

R163p	1c	.30	.25
	Block of 4	1.60	1.50
	P# block of 6	50.00	
R164p	2c	.35	.25
	Block of 4	2.75	1.10
	P# block of 6	60.00	
R165p	3c	40.00	1.40
	Block of 4	170.00	6.25
	P# block of 6	750.00	
R166p	4c	17.50	1.60
	Block of 4	75.00	7.75
	P# block of 6	—	
R167p	5c	17.50	.35
	Block of 4	75.00	1.60
	P# block of 6	450.00	
R168p	10c	10.00	.25
	Block of 4	42.50	1.25
	P# block of 6	450.00	
R169p	25c	20.00	.50
	Block of 4	85.00	1.75
	P# block of 6	—	
R170p	40c	210.00	35.00
	Block of 4	1,000.	225.00
	P# block of 6	—	
	Cut cancel		12.50
R171p	50c	75.00	1.00
	Block of 4	350.00	6.75
	P# block of 6	—	
b.	Horiz. pair, imperf. btwn.	—	*250.00*
R172p	80c	250.00	60.00
	Block of 4	1,250.	240.00
	P# block of 6	—	
	Cut cancellation		20.00

Commerce — R16

1898 *Rouletted 5½*

R173	R16 $1 **dark green**	30.00	.25
	Block of 4	140.00	1.00
	Cut cancel		.25
a.	Vert. pair, imperf. horiz.	800.00	
b.	Horiz. pair, imperf. vert.	—	325.00
p.	Hyphen hole perf. 7	37.50	2.00
	Block of 4		10.00
	Cut cancel		.75
R174	R16 $3 **dark brown**	55.00	1.25
	Block of 4	—	6.00
	Cut cancel		.30
a.	Horiz. pair, imperf. vert.		500.00
p.	Hyphen hole perf. 7	110.00	3.50
	Block of 4		15.00
	Cut cancel		.40
R175	R16 $5 **orange red**	100.00	2.00
	Block of 4	—	10.00
	Cut cancel		.30
R176	R16 $10 **black**	175.00	3.50
	Block of 4		17.00
	Cut cancel		.65
a.	Horiz. pair, imperf. vert.		—
R177	R16 $30 **red**	600.00	175.00
	Block of 4		700.00
	Cut cancel		47.50
R178	R16 $50 **gray brown**	350.00	7.00
	Block of 4		32.50
	Cut cancel		2.50

See Nos. R182-R183.

John Marshall — R17

Alexander Hamilton — R18

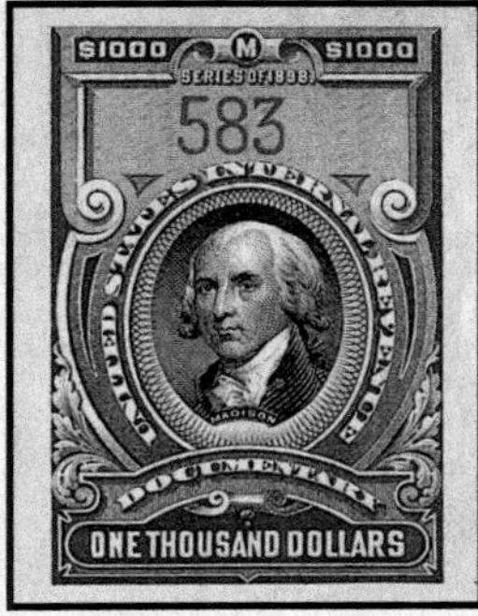

James Madison — R19

Various Portraits in Various Frames, Each Inscribed "Series of 1898"

1899 *Imperf.*

Without Gum

R179	R17 $100 **yellow brown & black**	350.00	40.00
	Cut cancel		22.50
	Vertical strip of 4	—	190.00
	Vertical strip of 4, cut cancel		95.00
R180	R18 $500 **carmine lake & black**	2,500.	800.00
	Cut cancel		350.00
	Vertical strip of 4	—	3,500.
	Vertical strip of 4, cut cancel		1,500.
R181	R19 $1000 **green & black**	1,750.	350.00
	Cut cancel		150.00
	Vertical strip of 4	—	1,650.
	Vertical strip of 4, cut cancel		600.00

1900 *Hyphen-hole perf. 7*

Allegorical Figure of Commerce

R182	R16 $1 **carmine**	55.00	.55
	Cut cancel		.30
	Block of 4	230.00	2.50
	Block of 4, cut cancel		1.25
R183	R16 $3 **lake** (fugitive ink)	350.00	60.00
	Cut cancel		10.00
	Block of 4	1,500.	290.00
	Block of 4, cut cancel		45.00

Warning: The ink on No. R183 will run in water.

Surcharged in Black with Open Numerals of Value

R184	R16 $1 **gray**	45.00	.40
	Cut cancel		.30
	Block of 4	—	1.75
	Block of 4, cut cancel		1.25
a.	Horiz. pair, imperf. vert		—
b.	Surcharge omitted	140.00	
	Surcharge omitted, cut cancel		82.50
R185	R16 $2 **gray**	45.00	.40
	Cut cancel		.25
	Block of 4	190.00	1.60
	Block of 4, cut cancel		1.10
R186	R16 $3 **gray**	190.00	15.00
	Cut cancel		6.00
	Block of 4	—	67.50
	Block of 4, cut cancel		25.00
R187	R16 $5 **gray**	100.00	11.00
	Cut cancel		1.60
	Block of 4	—	47.50
	Block of 4, cut cancel		8.00

R188	R16 $10 **gray**	250.00	25.00
	Cut cancel		4.50
	Block of 4	—	110.00
	Block of 4, cut cancel		19.00
R189	R16 $50 **gray**	2,250.	575.00
	Cut cancel		140.00
	Block of 4		2,750.
	Block of 4, cut cancel		625.00

Surcharged in Black with Ornamental Numerals of Value

Warning: If Nos. R190-R194 are soaked, the center part of the surcharged numeral may wash off. Before the surcharging, a square of soluble varnish was applied to the middle of some stamps.

1902

R190	R16 $1 **green**	60.00	3.50
	Cut cancel		.30
	Block of 4	—	15.00
	Block of 4, cut cancel		1.25
a.	Inverted surcharge		*190.00*
R191	R16 $2 **green**	60.00	2.50
	Cut cancel		.45
	Block of 4	—	11.00
	Block of 4, cut cancel		1.90
a.	Surcharged as No. R185	150.00	90.00
b.	Surcharged as No. R185, in violet	*2,000.*	—
c.	As "a," double surcharge	*150.00*	
d.	As "a," triple surcharge	*2,500.*	
e.	Pair, Nos. R191c and R191d	*5,000.*	
R192	R16 $5 **green**	275.00	42.50
	Cut cancel		5.00
	Block of 4	—	175.00
	Block of 4, cut cancel		25.00
a.	Surcharge omitted	300.00	
b.	Pair, one without surcharge	*600.00*	
R193	R16 $10 **green**	525.00	225.00
	Cut cancel		80.00
	Block of 4		950.00
	Block of 4, cut cancel		350.00
R194	R16 $50 **green**	3,000.	1,250.
	Cut cancel		350.00
	Block of 4	—	—
	Block of 4, cut cancel		1,500.

R20

Inscribed "Series of 1914"

1914 Wmk. 190 Offset Printing *Perf. 10*

R195	R20 ½c **rose**	16.00	5.00
	Block of 4	67.50	21.00
R196	R20 1c **rose**	3.50	.30
	Block of 4	15.00	1.25
R197	R20 2c **rose**	5.00	.30
	Block of 4	21.50	1.25
	Double impression	—	
R198	R20 3c **rose**	125.00	40.00
	Block of 4	525.00	175.00
R199	R20 4c **rose**	35.00	2.50
	Block of 4	150.00	11.50
	Recut U. L. corner	*325.00*	
R200	R20 5c **rose**	12.00	.40
	Block of 4	50.00	1.75
R201	R20 10c **rose**	10.00	.25
	Block of 4	42.50	1.25
R202	R20 25c **rose**	60.00	.60
	Block of 4	260.00	2.50
R203	R20 40c **rose**	40.00	3.00
	Block of 4	175.00	13.00
R204	R20 50c **rose**	15.00	.35
	Block of 4	62.50	1.50
R205	R20 80c **rose**	250.00	17.00
	Block of 4	1,050.	72.50
	Nos. R195-R205 (11)	571.50	69.70

Wmk. 191R

R206	R20 ½c **rose**	1.60	.50
	Block of 4	7.00	2.50
R207	R20 1c **rose**	.25	.25
	Block of 4	1.00	1.00
	Double impression	*300.00*	—
R208	R20 2c **rose**	.30	.25
	Block of 4	1.25	1.10
R209	R20 3c **rose**	1.50	.25
	Block of 4	6.50	1.10
R210	R20 4c **rose**	4.50	.50
	Block of 4	21.00	2.25
R211	R20 5c **rose**	2.00	.35
	Block of 4	9.00	1.50
R212	R20 10c **rose**	.80	.25
	Block of 4	3.75	1.00
R213	R20 25c **rose**	10.00	1.50
	Block of 4	42.50	7.00
R214	R20 40c **rose**	150.00	15.00
	Cut cancel		.50
	Block of 4	700.00	65.00
R215	R20 50c **rose**	35.00	.40
	Cut cancel		.25
	Block of 4	160.00	1.75
R216	R20 80c **rose**	225.00	35.00
	Cut cancel		1.25
	Block of 4	950.00	250.00
	Nos. R206-R216 (11)	430.95	54.25

Liberty — R21

Inscribed "Series 1914"

Engr.

R217	R21 $1 **green**	85.00	.55
	Cut cancel		.25
	Block of 4	—	3.00
	Block of 4, cut cancel		1.10
a.	$1 **yellow green**	85.00	.25
R218	R21 $2 **carmine**	150.00	1.00
	Cut cancel		.25
	Block of 4	625.00	4.50
	Block of 4, cut cancel		1.00
R219	R21 $3 **purple**	175.00	5.00
	Cut cancel		.80
	Block of 4	800.00	27.50
	Block of 4, cut cancel		3.25
R220	R21 $5 **blue**	120.00	4.50
	Cut cancel		.65
	Block of 4	500.00	19.00
	Block of 4, cut cancel		3.25
R221	R21 $10 **yellow orange**	375.00	7.50
	Cut cancel		1.10
	Block of 4	—	35.00
	Block of 4, cut cancel		5.00
R222	R21 $30 **vermilion**	900.00	21.00
	Cut cancel		2.25
	Block of 4	—	90.00
	Block of 4, cut cancel		11.50
R223	R21 $50 **violet**	2,000.	1,000.
	Cut cancel		450.00
	Block of 4		*5,000.*

Portrait Types of 1899 Inscribed "Series of 1915" (#R224), or "Series of 1914"

1914-15 Without Gum *Perf. 12*

R224	R19 $60 **brown** *(Lincoln)*	250.00	150.00
	Vertical strip of 4		800.00
	Cut cancel		70.00
	Vertical strip of 4, cut cancel		325.00
R225	R17 $100 **green** *(Washington)*	77.50	45.00
	Vertical strip of 4		190.00
	Cut cancel		16.00
	Vertical strip of 4, cut cancel		70.00
R226	R18 $500 **blue** *(Hamilton)*	—	650.00
	Cut cancel		275.00
	Vertical strip of 4, cut cancel		1,150.
R227	R19 $1000 **orange** *(Madison)*	—	750.00
	Cut cancel		325.00
	Vert. strip of 4, cut cancel		1,400.

The stamps of types R17, R18 and R19 in this and subsequent issues were issued in vertical strips of 4 which are imperforate at the top, bottom and right side; therefore, single stamps are always imperforate on one or two sides.

R22

Two types of design R22 are known.

Type I — With dot in centers of periods before and after "CENTS."

Type II — Without such dots.

First printings were done by commercial companies, later printings by the Bureau of Engraving and Printing.

1917 Offset Printing Wmk. 191R *Perf. 11*

R228	R22 1c **carmine rose**	.35	.25
	Block of 4	1.50	1.00
	Double impression	20.00	4.00
R229	R22 2c **carmine rose**	.25	.25
	Block of 4	1.10	1.00
	Double impression	20.00	5.00
R230	R22 3c **carmine rose**	1.75	.40
	Block of 4	7.25	1.75
	Double impression	—	—
R231	R22 4c **carmine rose**	.75	.25
	Block of 4	3.50	1.10
	Double impression	—	—
R232	R22 5c **carmine rose**	.30	.25
	Block of 4	1.25	1.00
R233	R22 8c **carmine rose**	3.00	.35
	Block of 4	13.50	1.60
R234	R22 10c **carmine rose**	.40	.25
	Block of 4	1.90	1.00
	Double impression		5.25
R235	R22 20c **carmine rose**	.75	.25
	Block of 4	3.50	1.10
	Double impression		—
R236	R22 25c **carmine rose**	1.75	.25
	Block of 4	7.50	1.10
	Double impression		—
R237	R22 40c **carmine rose**	2.25	.50
	Block of 4	10.50	2.25
	Double impression	8.00	5.00
R238	R22 50c **carmine rose**	2.50	.25
	Block of 4	10.50	1.00
	Double impression	—	—
R239	R22 80c **carmine rose**	9.00	.35
	Block of 4	40.00	1.50
	Double impression	42.50	—
	Nos. R228-R239 (12)	23.05	3.60

No. R234 is known used provisionally as a playing card revenue stamp in August 1932 with a "P.J.W.Co." (P.J. Wenger Co) and date cancellation. Value for this use, authenticated, $400.

Liberty Type of 1914 without "Series 1914"

1917-33 Engr.

R240	R21 $1 **yellow green**	12.50	.30
	Block of 4	55.00	1.25
a.	$1 green	9.50	.25
R241	R21 $2 **rose**	20.00	.25
	Block of 4	85.00	1.10
R242	R21 $3 **violet**	75.00	1.50
	Cut cancel		.30
	Block of 4	—	6.50
R243	R21 $4 **yellow brown** ('33)	50.00	2.00
	Cut cancel		.30
	Block of 4	—	10.00
	Block of 4, cut cancel		1.40
R244	R21 $5 **dark blue**	35.00	.35
	Cut cancel		.25
	Block of 4	—	1.50
R245	R21 $10 **orange**	75.00	1.40
	Cut cancel		.30
	Block of 4	—	7.00
	Block of 4, cut cancel		1.25

Portrait Types of 1899 without "Series of" and Date

1917 Without Gum *Perf. 12*

R246	R17 $30 **deep orange, green numerals** *(Grant)*	55.00	13.00
	Cut cancel		2.25
	Vertical strip of 4		—
	Vert. strip of 4, cut cancel		3.50
a.	As "b," imperf. pair		*1,000.*
b.	Numerals in blue	125.00	3.50
	Cut cancel		1.50
R247	R19 $60 **brown** *(Lincoln)*	65.00	8.00
	Cut cancel		.85
	Vertical strip of 4		—
	Vert. strip of 4, cut cancel		5.00
R248	R17 $100 **green** *(Washington)*	45.00	2.00
	Cut cancel		.50
	Vertical strip of 4		—
	Vert. strip of 4, cut cancel		3.00
R249	R18 $500 **blue, red numerals** *(Hamilton)*	350.00	50.00
	Cut cancel		15.00
	Vertical strip of 4		*250.00*
	Vert. strip of 4, cut cancel		70.00
	Double transfer	—	85.00
a.	Numerals in orange	425.00	65.00
	Cut cancel		20.00
	Vert. strip of 4		—
	Vert. strip of 4, cut cancel		—
	Double transfer	—	—
	Vert. strip of 4, bottom stamp double transfer	—	—
R250	R19 $1000 **orange** *(Madison)*	175.00	20.00
	Cut cancel		7.50
	Vertical strip of 4		100.00
	Vert. strip of 4, cut cancel		35.00
a.	Imperf., pair		*2,000.*

See note after No. R227.

1928-29 Offset Printing *Perf. 10*

R251	R22 1c **carmine rose**	2.10	1.60
	Block of 4	9.50	7.50
R252	R22 2c **carmine rose**	.60	.30
	Block of 4	3.00	1.50
R253	R22 4c **carmine rose**	7.00	4.00
	Block of 4	32.50	19.00
R254	R22 5c **carmine rose**	1.75	.55
	Block of 4	8.50	2.50
R255	R22 10c **carmine rose**	2.75	1.25
	Block of 4	13.00	5.50
R256	R22 20c **carmine rose**	6.00	4.50
	Block of 4	27.50	20.00
	Double impression		—

Engr.

R257	R21 $1 **green**	200.00	45.00
	Block of 4	—	—
	Cut cancel		5.00
R258	R21 $2 **rose**	90.00	5.00
	Block of 4	—	20.00
R259	R21 $10 **orange**	325.00	75.00
	Block of 4	—	—
	Cut cancel		30.00

1929 Offset Printing *Perf. 11x10*

R260	R22 2c **carmine rose** ('30)	3.00	2.75
	Block of 4	13.00	12.00
	Double impression	—	—
R261	R22 5c **carmine rose** ('30)	2.00	1.90
	Block of 4	10.00	8.75
R262	R22 10c **carmine rose**	9.25	6.75
	Block of 4	45.00	32.50
R263	R22 20c **carmine rose**	15.00	8.25
	Block of 4	70.00	42.50

Types of 1917-33 Overprinted in Black

SERIES 1940

1940 Wmk. 191R Offset Printing *Perf. 11*

R264	R22 1c **rose pink**	3.75	2.40
	Cut cancel		.35
	Perf. initial		.25
R265	R22 2c **rose pink**	5.00	2.25
	Cut cancel		.45
	Perf. initial		.35
R266	R22 3c **rose pink**	11.00	5.00
	Cut cancel		.90
	Perf. initial		.55
R267	R22 4c **rose pink**	5.00	.80
	Cut cancel		.30
	Perf. initial		.25
R268	R22 5c **rose pink**	5.00	1.25
	Cut cancel		.35
	Perf. initial		.25
R269	R22 8c **rose pink**	22.50	17.00
	Cut cancel		3.50
	Perf. initial		2.50
R270	R22 10c **rose pink**	2.50	.65
	Cut cancel		.25
	Perf. initial		.25
R271	R22 20c **rose pink**	3.25	.80
	Cut cancel		.30
	Perf. initial		.25
R272	R22 25c **rose pink**	8.00	1.50
	Cut cancel		.30
	Perf. initial		.25
R273	R22 40c **rose pink**	6.75	.90
	Cut cancel		.25
	Perf. initial		.25
R274	R22 50c **rose pink**	11.00	.55
	Cut cancel		.25
	Perf. initial		.25
R275	R22 80c **rose pink**	14.00	1.75
	Cut cancel		.35
	Perf. initial		.25

Engr.

R276	R21 $1 **green**	80.00	1.25
	Cut cancel		.35
	Perf. initial		.25
R277	R21 $2 **rose**	80.00	2.00
	Cut cancel		.35
	Perf. initial		.25
R278	R21 $3 **violet**	115.00	37.50
	Cut cancel		4.25
	Perf. initial		2.00
b.	Vert. pair, imperf. horiz.		*750.00*

Only one example of No. R278b is recorded. It is thinned and is valued thus.

R279	R21 $4 **yellow brown**	210.00	35.00
	Cut cancel		5.50
	Perf. initial		2.10
R280	R21 $5 **dark blue**	100.00	20.00
	Cut cancel		1.60
	Perf. initial		.75
R281	R21 $10 **orange**	275.00	50.00
	Cut cancel		4.25
	Perf. initial		.75

Types of 1917 Handstamped "Series 1940" like R264-R281 in Blue (Nos. R282-R284, R286), Green (Nos. R282-R283, R286) or Violet (No. R285)

1940 Wmk. 191R *Perf. 12*
Without Gum

R282	R17 $30 **vermilion**		1,250.
	Cut cancel		500.
	Perf. initial		350.
a.	With black 2-line handstamp in larger type		*25,000.*
b.	Green handstamp, 3-hole punch cancel		—
R283	R19 $60 **brown**		2,400.
	Cut cancel		1,000.
	Perf. initial		800.
a.	As #R282a, cut cancel		*12,500.*
b.	Green handstamp, 3-hole punch cancel		—
R284	R17 $100 **green**		4,500.
	Cut cancel		2,200.
	Perf. initial		1,500.
R285	R18 $500 **blue**		3,000.
	Cut cancel		1,400.
	Perf. initial		1,000.
	Double transfer		—
a.	As #R282a	*3,250.*	*4,000.*
	Cut cancel		*2,650.*
	Double transfer	—	—
b.	Blue handstamp, double transfer	—	
R286	R19 $1000 **orange**		1,250.
	Cut cancel		500.
	Perf. initial		400.
b.	Double overprint, cut cancel		—

Types of 1917 Handstamped with black 2-line "Series 1941" in larger type.

1941

R287	R17 $30 vermilion		—
R287A	R19 $60 brown		—

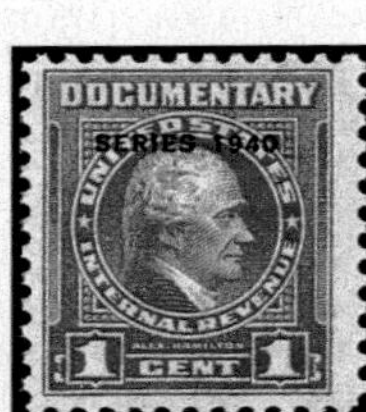

Alexander Hamilton — R23

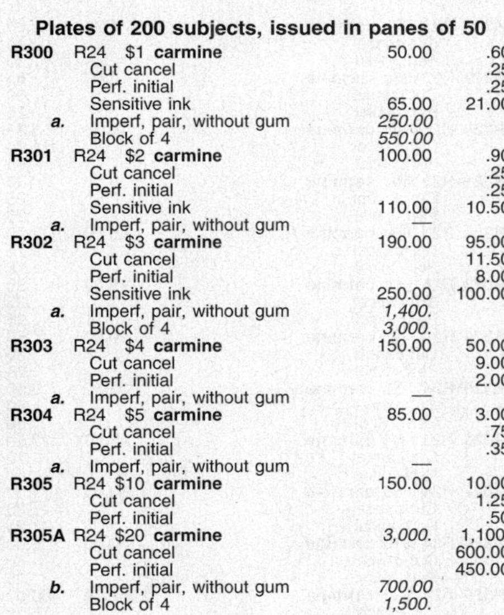

Levi Woodbury — R24

Overprinted in Black

Various Portraits: 2c, Oliver Wolcott, Jr. 3c, Samuel Dexter. 4c, Albert Gallatin. 5c. G. W. Campbell. 8c, Alexander Dallas. 10c, William H. Crawford. 20c, Richard Rush. 25c, S. D. Ingham. 40c. Louis McLane. 50c, William J. Duane. 80c, Roger B. Taney. $2, Thomas Ewing. $3, Walter Forward. $4, J. C. Spencer. $5, G. M. Bibb. $10, R. J. Walker. $20, William M. Meredith.

The "sensitive ink" varieties are in a bluish-purple overprint showing minute flecks of gold.

1940 Engr. Wmk. 191R *Perf. 11*
Plates of 400 subjects, issued in panes of 100

R288	R23 1c **carmine**	5.75	4.50
	Cut cancel		1.75
	Perf. initial		.90
	Sensitive ink	9.00	4.25
a.	Imperf, pair, without gum	*250.00*	
	Block of 4	*500.00*	
R289	R23 2c **carmine**	8.50	4.00
	Cut cancel		1.75
	Perf. initial		1.00
	Sensitive ink	9.00	4.25
a.	Imperf, pair, without gum	*250.00*	
	Block of 4	*500.00*	
R290	R23 3c **carmine**	30.00	12.00
	Cut cancel		4.00
	Perf. initial		2.75
	Sensitive ink	32.50	9.25
a.	Imperf, pair, without gum	*250.00*	
	Block of 4	*500.00*	
R291	R23 4c **carmine**	62.50	27.50
	Cut cancel		5.25
	Perf. initial		4.25
a.	Imperf, pair, without gum	*250.00*	
	Block of 4	*500.00*	
R292	R23 5c **carmine**	4.75	.80
	Cut cancel		.35
	Perf. initial		.30
a.	Imperf, pair, without gum	*250.00*	
	Block of 4	*500.00*	
R293	R23 8c **carmine**	85.00	60.00
	Cut cancel		18.00
	Perf. initial		13.00
a.	Imperf, pair, without gum	*250.00*	
	Block of 4	*500.00*	
R294	R23 10c **carmine**	4.25	.60
	Cut cancel		.30
	Perf. initial		.25
a.	Imperf, pair, without gum	*250.00*	
	Block of 4	*500.00*	
R295	R23 20c **carmine**	5.50	4.25
	Cut cancel		1.25
	Perf. initial		.85
a.	Imperf, pair, without gum	*250.00*	
	Block of 4	*500.00*	
R296	R23 25c **carmine**	5.00	.75
	Cut cancel		.35
	Perf. initial		.25
a.	Imperf, pair, without gum	*250.00*	
	Block of 4	*500.00*	
R297	R23 40c **carmine**	75.00	30.00
	Cut cancel		6.50
	Perf. initial		2.75
a.	Imperf, pair, without gum	*250.00*	
	Block of 4	*500.00*	
R298	R23 50c **carmine**	8.00	.60
	Cut cancel		.30
	Perf. initial		.25
a.	Imperf, pair, without gum	*250.00*	
	Block of 4	*500.00*	
R299	R23 80c **carmine**	200.00	110.00
	Cut cancel		29.00
	Perf. initial		20.00
a.	Imperf, pair, without gum	*475.00*	
	Block of 4	*1,400.*	

Plates of 200 subjects, issued in panes of 50

R300	R24 $1 **carmine**	50.00	.60
	Cut cancel		.25
	Perf. initial		.25
	Sensitive ink	65.00	21.00
a.	Imperf, pair, without gum	*250.00*	
	Block of 4	*550.00*	
R301	R24 $2 **carmine**	100.00	.90
	Cut cancel		.25
	Perf. initial		.25
	Sensitive ink	110.00	10.50
a.	Imperf, pair, without gum	—	
R302	R24 $3 **carmine**	190.00	95.00
	Cut cancel		11.50
	Perf. initial		8.00
	Sensitive ink	250.00	100.00
a.	Imperf, pair, without gum	*1,400.*	
	Block of 4	*3,000.*	
R303	R24 $4 **carmine**	150.00	50.00
	Cut cancel		9.00
	Perf. initial		2.00
a.	Imperf, pair, without gum	—	
R304	R24 $5 **carmine**	85.00	3.00
	Cut cancel		.75
	Perf. initial		.35
a.	Imperf, pair, without gum	—	
R305	R24 $10 **carmine**	150.00	10.00
	Cut cancel		1.25
	Perf. initial		.50
R305A	R24 $20 **carmine**	*3,000.*	1,100.
	Cut cancel		600.00
	Perf. initial		450.00
b.	Imperf, pair, without gum	*700.00*	
	Block of 4	*1,500.*	

Thomas Corwin — R25

Various Frames and Portraits: $50, James Guthrie. $60, Howell Cobb. $100, P. F. Thomas. $500, J. A. Dix, $1,000, S. P. Chase.

Plates of 16 subjects, issued in strips of 4
Without Gum *Perf. 12*

R306	R25 $30 **carmine**	230.00	75.00
	Cut cancel		20.00
	Perf. initial		13.50
R306A	R25 $50 **carmine**	—	*8,500.*
	Cut cancel		2,250.
	Perf. initial		900.00
R307	R25 $60 **carmine**	450.00	80.00
	Cut cancel		45.00
	Perf. initial		22.50
a.	Vert. pair, imperf. btwn.	*2,750.*	*1,500.*
R308	R25 $100 **carmine**	375.00	100.00
	Cut cancel		45.00
	Perf. initial		15.00
R309	R25 $500 **carmine**	—	5,000.
	Cut cancel		2,250.
	Perf. initial		800.00
R310	R25 $1000 **carmine**	—	650.00
	Cut cancel		300.00
	Perf. initial		200.00

The $30 to $1,000 denominations in this and following similar issues, and the $2,500, $5,000 and $10,000 stamps of 1952-58 have straight edges on one or two sides. They were issued without gum through No. R723.

Nos. R288-R310 Overprinted

SERIES 1941

1941 Wmk. 191R *Perf. 11*

R311	R23 1c **carmine**	5.00	2.75
	Cut cancel		.85
	Perf. initial		.75
R312	R23 2c **carmine**	5.25	1.10
	Cut cancel		.55
	Perf. initial		.45
R313	R23 3c **carmine**	10.00	4.25
	Cut cancel		1.75
	Perf. initial		1.10
R314	R23 4c **carmine**	7.50	1.75
	Cut cancel		.40
	Perf. initial		.25
R315	R23 5c **carmine**	1.50	.40
	Cut cancel		.30
	Perf. initial		.30
R316	R23 8c **carmine**	21.00	8.50
	Cut cancel		3.75
	Perf. initial		2.75
R317	R23 10c **carmine**	2.00	.35
	Cut cancel		.30
	Perf. initial		.25

No.	Description	Unused	Used
R318	R23 20c **carmine**	4.75	.65
	Cut cancel		.40
	Perf. initial		.30
R319	R23 25c **carmine**	2.40	.65
	Cut cancel		.30
	Perf. initial		.25
R320	R23 40c **carmine**	16.00	3.25
	Cut cancel		1.10
	Perf. initial		.65
R321	R23 50c **carmine**	3.50	.30
	Cut cancel		.25
	Perf. initial		.25
R322	R23 80c **carmine**	65.00	12.00
	Cut cancel		3.75
	Perf. initial		2.75
R323	R24 $1 **carmine**	15.00	.30
	Cut cancel		.25
	Perf. initial		.25
R324	R24 $2 **carmine**	20.00	.50
	Cut cancel		.30
	Perf. initial		.25
R325	R24 $3 **carmine**	32.50	3.50
	Cut cancel		.40
	Perf. initial		.30
R326	R24 $4 **carmine**	47.50	27.50
	Cut cancel		1.10
	Perf. initial		.80
R327	R24 $5 **carmine**	60.00	1.10
	Cut cancel		.30
	Perf. initial		.25
R328	R24 $10 **carmine**	100.00	6.00
	Cut cancel		.30
	Perf. initial		.25
R329	R24 $20 **carmine**	850.00	400.00
	Cut cancel		75.00
	Perf. initial		50.00

Without Gum *Perf. 12*

No.	Description	Unused	Used
R330	R25 $30 **carmine**	275.00	55.00
	Cut cancel		17.50
	Perf. initial		11.50
R331	R25 $50 **carmine**	1,500.	1,000.
	Cut cancel		400.00
	Perf. initial		250.00
R332	R25 $60 **carmine**	275.00	87.50
	Cut cancel		27.50
	Perf. initial		13.50
R333	R25 $100 **carmine**	140.00	37.50
	Cut cancel		7.75
	Perf. initial		5.00
R334	R25 $500 **carmine**	—	375.00
	Cut cancel		200.00
	Perf. initial		75.00
R335	R25 $1000 **carmine**	1,500.	225.00
	Cut cancel		60.00
	Perf. initial		30.00

Nos. R288-R310 Overprinted

SERIES 1942

1942 **Wmk. 191R** *Perf. 11*

No.	Description	Unused	Used
R336	R23 1c **carmine**	.65	.60
	Cut cancel		.30
	Perf. initial		.25
R337	R23 2c **carmine**	.60	.60
	Cut cancel		.30
	Perf. initial		.25
R338	R23 3c **carmine**	.90	.80
	Cut cancel		.35
	Perf. initial		.25
R339	R23 4c **carmine**	1.75	1.10
	Cut cancel		.30
	Perf. initial		.25
R340	R23 5c **carmine**	.60	.35
	Cut cancel		.25
	Perf. initial		.25
R341	R23 8c **carmine**	9.50	4.75
	Cut cancel		1.40
	Perf. initial		1.10
R342	R23 10c **carmine**	1.75	.35
	Cut cancel		.25
	Perf. initial		.25
R343	R23 20c **carmine**	1.75	.60
	Cut cancel		.30
	Perf. initial		.25
R344	R23 25c **carmine**	3.00	.55
	Cut cancel		.30
	Perf. initial		.25
R345	R23 40c **carmine**	6.50	1.75
	Cut cancel		.55
	Perf. initial		.35
R346	R23 50c **carmine**	4.00	.35
	Cut cancel		.25
	Perf. initial		.25
R347	R23 80c **carmine**	27.50	13.00
	Cut cancel		3.00
	Perf. initial		2.00
R348	R24 $1 **carmine**	12.50	.25
	Cut cancel		.25
	Perf. initial		.25
R349	R24 $2 **carmine**	15.00	.30
	Cut cancel		.25
	Perf. initial		.25
R350	R24 $3 **carmine**	27.50	3.25
	Cut cancel		.45
	Perf. initial		.25
R351	R24 $4 **carmine**	35.00	7.50
	Cut cancel		.55
	Perf. initial		.30
R352	R24 $5 **carmine**	37.50	1.50
	Cut cancel		.25
	Perf. initial		.25
R353	R24 $10 **carmine**	85.00	3.75
	Cut cancel		.40
	Perf. initial		.25
R354	R24 $20 **carmine**	300.00	45.00
	Cut cancel		20.00
	Perf. initial		11.50
a.	Imperf., perf. initials		—

Without Gum *Perf. 12*

No.	Description	Unused	Used
R355	R25 $30 **carmine**	125.00	42.50
	Cut cancel		15.00
	Perf. initial		7.00
R356	R25 $50 **carmine**	2,250.	1,400.
	Cut cancel		375.00
	Perf. initial		190.00
R357	R25 $60 **carmine**	*5,000.*	1,500.
	Cut cancel		450.00
	Perf. initial		190.00
R358	R25 $100 **carmine**	325.00	175.00
	Cut cancel		100.00
	Perf. initial		75.00
R359	R25 $500 **carmine**	*2,000.*	275.00
	Cut cancel		160.00
	Perf. initial		87.50
R360	R25 $1000 **carmine**	6,500.	175.00
	Cut cancel		70.00
	Perf. initial		55.00

Nos. R288-R310 Overprinted

SERIES 1943

1943 **Wmk. 191R** *Perf. 11*

No.	Description	Unused	Used
R361	R23 1c **carmine**	.80	.65
	Cut cancel		.30
	Perf. initial		.25
R362	R23 2c **carmine**	.65	.55
	Cut cancel		.30
	Perf. initial		.25
R363	R23 3c **carmine**	3.75	3.50
	Cut cancel		.70
	Perf. initial		.40
R364	R23 4c **carmine**	1.60	1.50
	Cut cancel		.40
	Perf. initial		.35
R365	R23 5c **carmine**	.70	.45
	Cut cancel		.30
	Perf. initial		.25
R366	R23 8c **carmine**	6.00	4.00
	Cut cancel		1.90
	Perf. initial		1.25
R367	R23 10c **carmine**	.85	.30
	Cut cancel		.25
	Perf. initial		.25
R368	R23 20c **carmine**	2.50	.80
	Cut cancel		.40
	Perf. initial		.35
R369	R23 25c **carmine**	2.75	.50
	Cut cancel		.30
	Perf. initial		.30
R370	R23 40c **carmine**	7.50	4.00
	Cut cancel		1.75
	Perf. initial		.90
R371	R23 50c **carmine**	2.00	.30
	Cut cancel		.25
	Perf. initial		.25
R372	R23 80c **carmine**	27.50	8.00
	Cut cancel		3.00
	Perf. initial		1.50
R373	R24 $1 **carmine**	9.00	.35
	Cut cancel		.25
	Perf. initial		.25
R374	R24 $2 **carmine**	18.00	.35
	Cut cancel		.25
	Perf. initial		.25
R375	R24 $3 **carmine**	30.00	3.00
	Cut cancel		.45
	Perf. initial		.30
R376	R24 $4 **carmine**	55.00	10.00
	Cut cancel		1.50
	Perf. initial		1.00
R377	R24 $5 **carmine**	52.50	.75
	Cut cancel		.40
	Perf. initial		.25
R378	R24 $10 **carmine**	85.00	5.00
	Cut cancel		1.75
	Perf. initial		.70
R379	R24 $20 **carmine**	275.00	60.00
	Cut cancel		10.00
	Perf. initial		5.50

Without Gum *Perf. 12*

No.	Description	Unused	Used
R380	R25 $30 **carmine**	150.00	25.00
	Cut cancel		7.50
	Perf. initial		6.00
R381	R25 $50 **carmine**	250.00	75.00
	Cut cancel		15.00
	Perf. initial		6.00
R382	R25 $60 **carmine**	375.00	125.00
	Cut cancel		42.50
	Perf. initial		14.00
R383	R25 $100 **carmine**	50.00	22.50
	Cut cancel		6.75
	Perf. initial		4.25
R384	R25 $500 **carmine**	*800.00*	325.00
	Cut cancel		125.00
	Perf. initial		87.50
R385	R25 $1000 **carmine**	*800.00*	200.00
	Cut cancel		60.00
	Perf. initial		40.00

Nos. R288-R310 Overprinted

Series 1944

1944 **Wmk. 191R** *Perf. 11*

No.	Description	Unused	Used
R386	R23 1c **carmine**	.50	.45
	Cut cancel		.25
	Perf. initial		.25
R387	R23 2c **carmine**	.65	.55
	Cut cancel		.30
	Perf. initial		.25
R388	R23 3c **carmine**	.65	.40
	Cut cancel		.30
	Perf. initial		.25
R389	R23 4c **carmine**	.75	.65
	Cut cancel		.30
	Perf. initial		.25
R390	R23 5c **carmine**	.40	.25
	Cut cancel		.25
	Perf. initial		.25
R391	R23 8c **carmine**	2.25	1.75
	Cut cancel		.50
	Perf. initial		.45
R392	R23 10c **carmine**	.50	.25
	Cut cancel		.25
	Perf. initial		.25
R393	R23 20c **carmine**	1.10	.35
	Cut cancel		.25
	Perf. initial		.25
R394	R23 25c **carmine**	2.00	.30
	Cut cancel		.25
	Perf. initial		.25
R395	R23 40c **carmine**	3.75	.80
	Cut cancel		.40
	Perf. initial		.30
R396	R23 50c **carmine**	4.00	.35
	Cut cancel		.30
	Perf. initial		.30
R397	R23 80c **carmine**	21.00	5.50
	Cut cancel		1.75
	Perf. initial		.90
R398	R24 $1 **carmine**	10.00	.30
	Cut cancel		.25
	Perf. initial		.25
R399	R24 $2 **carmine**	15.00	.45
	Cut cancel		.35
	Perf. initial		.25
R400	R24 $3 **carmine**	25.00	2.40
	Cut cancel		.55
	Perf. initial		.25
R401	R24 $4 **carmine**	32.50	11.50
	Cut cancel		1.40
	Perf. initial		1.10
R402	R24 $5 **carmine**	32.50	.50
	Cut cancel		.35
	Perf. initial		.30
R403	R24 $10 **carmine**	65.00	1.60
	Cut cancel		.40
	Perf. initial		.30
R404	R24 $20 **carmine**	275.00	19.00
	Cut cancel		4.00
	Perf. initial		2.50

Without Gum *Perf. 12*

No.	Description	Unused	Used
R405	R25 $30 **carmine**	110.00	35.00
	Cut cancel		9.00
	Perf. initial		7.00
R406	R25 $50 **carmine**	50.00	22.50
	Cut cancel		7.00
	Perf. initial		4.75
R407	R25 $60 **carmine**	350.00	75.00
	Cut cancel		29.00
	Perf. initial		10.50
R408	R25 $100 **carmine**	70.00	12.50
	Cut cancel		5.25
	Perf. initial		3.25
R409	R25 $500 **carmine**	—	*3,250.*
	Cut cancel		1,750.
	Perf. initial		1,250.
R410	R25 $1000 **carmine**	*4,000.*	500.00
	Cut cancel		200.00
	Perf. initial		125.00

Nos. R288-R310 Overprinted

Series 1945

1945 **Wmk. 191R** *Perf. 11*

No.	Description	Unused	Used
R411	R23 1c **carmine**	.40	.30
	Cut cancel		.25
	Perf. initial		.25
R412	R23 2c **carmine**	.40	.30
	Cut cancel		.25
	Perf. initial		.25
R413	R23 3c **carmine**	.75	.50
	Cut cancel		.30
	Perf. initial		.25
R414	R23 4c **carmine**	.45	.35
	Cut cancel		.30
	Perf. initial		.25
R415	R23 5c **carmine**	.45	.30
	Cut cancel		.25
	Perf. initial		.25
R416	R23 8c **carmine**	6.25	2.75
	Cut cancel		.75
	Perf. initial		.40
R417	R23 10c **carmine**	1.25	.25
	Cut cancel		.25
	Perf. initial		.25
R418	R23 20c **carmine**	8.00	1.50
	Cut cancel		.60
	Perf. initial		.35
R419	R23 25c **carmine**	1.75	.30
	Cut cancel		.25
	Perf. initial		.25
R420	R23 40c **carmine**	9.00	1.25
	Cut cancel		.55
	Perf. initial		.40

R421 R23 50c **carmine** 4.00 .25
Cut cancel .25
Perf. initial .25
R422 R23 80c **carmine** 26.00 14.00
Cut cancel 4.00
Perf. initial 2.75
R423 R24 $1 **carmine** 13.50 .30
Cut cancel .25
Perf. initial .25
R424 R24 $2 **carmine** 13.50 .40
Cut cancel .25
Perf. initial .25
R425 R24 $3 **carmine** 27.50 3.00
Cut cancel 1.00
Perf. initial .75
R426 R24 $4 **carmine** 35.00 4.25
Cut cancel .70
Perf. initial .45
R427 R24 $5 **carmine** 35.00 .50
Cut cancel .30
Perf. initial .25
R428 R24 $10 **carmine** 65.00 2.50
Cut cancel .40
Perf. initial .30
R429 R24 $20 **carmine** 200.00 16.00
Cut cancel 3.75
Perf. initial 3.00

Without Gum ***Perf. 12***

R430 R25 $30 **carmine** 200.00 40.00
Cut cancel 10.00
Perf. initial 5.75
R431 R25 $50 **carmine** 230.00 45.00
Cut cancel 20.00
Perf. initial 12.00
R432 R25 $60 **carmine** 450.00 80.00
Cut cancel 32.50
Perf. initial 14.00
R433 R25 $100 **carmine** 50.00 20.00
Cut cancel 9.00
Perf. initial 5.50
R434 R25 $500 **carmine** 750.00 325.00
Cut cancel 125.00
Perf. initial 75.00
R435 R25 $1000 **carmine** 500.00 125.00
Cut cancel 45.00
Perf. initial 25.00

Nos. R288-R310 Overprinted

Series 1946

1946 **Wmk. 191R** ***Perf. 11***

R436 R23 1c **carmine** .30 .30
Cut cancel .25
Perf. initial .25
R437 R23 2c **carmine** .45 .35
Cut cancel .25
Perf. initial .25
R438 R23 3c **carmine** .55 .40
Cut cancel .30
Perf. initial .25
R439 R23 4c **carmine** .80 .65
Cut cancel .30
Perf. initial .25
R440 R23 5c **carmine** .45 .30
Cut cancel .25
Perf. initial .25
R441 R23 8c **carmine** 2.50 2.00
Cut cancel .40
Perf. initial .35
R442 R23 10c **carmine** 1.10 .30
Cut cancel .25
Perf. initial .25
R443 R23 20c **carmine** 1.75 .50
Cut cancel .30
Perf. initial .25
R444 R23 25c **carmine** 6.00 .35
Cut cancel .25
Perf. initial .25
R445 R23 40c **carmine** 4.50 .85
Cut cancel .40
Perf. initial .25
R446 R23 50c **carmine** 6.00 .30
Cut cancel .25
Perf. initial .25
R447 R23 80c **carmine** 17.50 5.00
Cut cancel .75
Perf. initial .50
R448 R24 $1 **carmine** 16.00 .30
Cut cancel .25
Perf. initial .25
R449 R24 $2 **carmine** 19.00 .30
Cut cancel .25
Perf. initial .25
R450 R24 $3 **carmine** 27.50 5.00
Cut cancel .90
Perf. initial .40
R451 R24 $4 **carmine** 60.00 20.00
Cut cancel 3.75
Perf. initial 2.00
R452 R24 $5 **carmine** 40.00 .50
Cut cancel .30
Perf. initial .25
R453 R24 $10 **carmine** 72.50 1.75
Cut cancel .40
Perf. initial .30
R454 R24 $20 **carmine** 200.00 16.00
Cut cancel 3.50
Perf. initial 1.60

Without Gum ***Perf. 12***

R455 R25 $30 **carmine** 75.00 17.50
Cut cancel 5.25
Perf. initial 3.25
R456 R25 $50 **carmine** 65.00 12.50
Cut cancel 5.00
Perf. initial 2.75
R457 R25 $60 **carmine** 110.00 22.50
Cut cancel 14.00
Perf. initial 7.75
R458 R25 $100 **carmine** 90.00 12.50
Cut cancel 4.25
Perf. initial 3.00
R459 R25 $500 **carmine** *1,750.* 150.00
Cut cancel 47.50
Perf. initial 26.00
R460 R25 $1000 **carmine** *750.00* 160.00
Cut cancel 37.50
Perf. initial 18.00

Nos. R288-R310 Overprinted

Series 1947

1947 **Wmk. 191R** ***Perf. 11***

R461 R23 1c **carmine** .85 .55
Cut cancel .30
Perf. initial .25
R462 R23 2c **carmine** .75 .55
Cut cancel .30
Perf. initial .25
R463 R23 3c **carmine** .85 .55
Cut cancel .30
Perf. initial .25
R464 R23 4c **carmine** .90 .75
Cut cancel .30
Perf. initial .25
R465 R23 5c **carmine** .55 .40
Cut cancel .30
Perf. initial .25
R466 R23 8c **carmine** 1.75 .80
Cut cancel .30
Perf. initial .25
R467 R23 10c **carmine** 1.40 .30
Cut cancel .25
Perf. initial .25
R468 R23 20c **carmine** 2.25 .55
Cut cancel .30
Perf. initial .25
R469 R23 25c **carmine** 3.00 .70
Cut cancel .30
Perf. initial .25
R470 R23 40c **carmine** 5.50 1.10
Cut cancel .35
Perf. initial .25
R471 R23 50c **carmine** 3.75 .40
Cut cancel .30
Perf. initial .25
R472 R23 80c **carmine** 12.00 8.00
Cut cancel .85
Perf. initial .35
R473 R24 $1 **carmine** 8.25 .35
Cut cancel .30
Perf. initial .25
R474 R24 $2 **carmine** 14.00 .65
Cut cancel .30
Perf. initial .25
R475 R24 $3 **carmine** 17.50 6.00
Cut cancel 1.25
Perf. initial .90
R476 R24 $4 **carmine** 19.00 5.00
Cut cancel .55
Perf. initial .40
R477 R24 $5 **carmine** 27.50 .60
Cut cancel .30
Perf. initial .25
R478 R24 $10 **carmine** 67.50 3.00
Cut cancel .80
Perf. initial .30
R479 R24 $20 **carmine** 110.00 14.00
Cut cancel 1.40
Perf. initial .90

Without Gum ***Perf. 12***

R480 R25 $30 **carmine** 180.00 27.50
Cut cancel 6.00
Perf. initial 2.75
R481 R25 $50 **carmine** 90.00 17.50
Cut cancel 5.50
Perf. initial 3.25
R482 R25 $60 **carmine** 210.00 60.00
Cut cancel 25.00
Perf. initial 9.25
R483 R25 $100 **carmine** 85.00 15.00
Cut cancel 6.00
Perf. initial 2.10
R484 R25 $500 **carmine** *900.00* 250.00
Cut cancel 67.50
Perf. initial 50.00
R485 R25 $1000 **carmine** *550.00* 100.00
Cut cancel 40.00
Perf. initial 24.00

Nos. R288-R310 Overprinted

Series 1948

1948 **Wmk. 191R** ***Perf. 11***

R486 R23 1c **carmine** .35 .30
Cut cancel .25
Perf. initial .25
R487 R23 2c **carmine** .50 .45
Cut cancel .30
Perf. initial .25
R488 R23 3c **carmine** .60 .40
Cut cancel .30
Perf. initial .25
R489 R23 4c **carmine** .55 .40
Cut cancel .30
Perf. initial .25
R490 R23 5c **carmine** .50 .25
Cut cancel .25
Perf. initial .25
R491 R23 8c **carmine** 1.00 .50
Cut cancel .30
Perf. initial .30
R492 R23 10c **carmine** 1.00 .25
Cut cancel .25
Perf. initial .25
R493 R23 20c **carmine** 2.50 .40
Cut cancel .30
Perf. initial .25
R494 R23 25c **carmine** 2.25 .30
Cut cancel .25
Perf. initial .25
R495 R23 40c **carmine** 7.00 1.75
Cut cancel .35
Perf. initial .25
R496 R23 50c **carmine** 2.50 .30
Cut cancel .25
Perf. initial .25
R497 R23 80c **carmine** 12.00 8.00
Cut cancel 3.25
Perf. initial .80
R498 R24 $1 **carmine** 10.50 .30
Cut cancel .25
Perf. initial .25
R499 R24 $2 **carmine** 18.00 .40
Cut cancel .30
Perf. initial .25
R500 R24 $3 **carmine** 24.00 3.50
Cut cancel .60
Perf. initial .40
R501 R24 $4 **carmine** 35.00 4.00
Cut cancel 1.00
Perf. initial .70
R502 R24 $5 **carmine** 30.00 .50
Cut cancel .35
Perf. initial .25
R503 R24 $10 **carmine** 70.00 1.50
Cut cancel .40
Perf. initial .30
a. Pair, one dated "1946" —
R504 R24 $20 **carmine** 400.00 18.00
Cut cancel 5.00
Perf. initial 2.25

Without Gum ***Perf. 12***

R505 R25 $30 **carmine** 150.00 35.00
Cut cancel 7.00
Perf. initial 4.00
R506 R25 $50 **carmine** 180.00 27.50
Cut cancel 12.00
Perf. initial 3.75
a. Vert. pair, imperf. btwn. *2,500.*
R507 R25 $60 **carmine** 300.00 75.00
Cut cancel 25.00
Perf. initial 8.00
a. Vert. pair, imperf. btwn. *2,500.*
R508 R25 $100 **carmine** 140.00 20.00
Cut cancel 6.00
Perf. initial 4.00
a. Vert. pair, imperf. btwn. *2,000.*

No. R508a is known as four used singles, all four positions from a single pane of four, clearly imperf. horiz. before being separated.

R509 R25 $500 **carmine** 1,500. 200.00
Cut cancel 75.00
Perf. initial 45.00
R510 R25 $1000 **carmine** 450.00 125.00
Cut cancel 50.00
Perf. initial 25.00

Nos. R288-R310 Overprinted

Series 1949

1949 **Wmk. 191R** ***Perf. 11***

R511 R23 1c **carmine** .40 .35
Cut cancel .30
Perf. initial .25
R512 R23 2c **carmine** .75 .45
Cut cancel .30
Perf. initial .25
R513 R23 3c **carmine** .60 .50
Cut cancel .30
Perf. initial .25
R514 R23 4c **carmine** .80 .60
Cut cancel .30
Perf. initial .25
R515 R23 5c **carmine** .55 .30
Cut cancel .25
Perf. initial .25
R516 R23 8c **carmine** 1.00 .70
Cut cancel .30
Perf. initial .25
R517 R23 10c **carmine** .60 .35
Cut cancel .30
Perf. initial .25
R518 R23 20c **carmine** 1.75 .75
Cut cancel .40
Perf. initial .30
R519 R23 25c **carmine** 2.25 .85
Cut cancel .35
Perf. initial .30
R520 R23 40c **carmine** 6.50 2.75
Cut cancel .55
Perf. initial .40
R521 R23 50c **carmine** 5.00 .40
Cut cancel .30
Perf. initial .25

No.	Type	Description	Unused	Used
R522	R23	80c **carmine**	15.00	7.50
		Cut cancel		2.00
		Perf. initial		.90
R523	R24	$1 **carmine**	13.50	.85
		Cut cancel		.40
		Perf. initial		.30
R524	R24	$2 **carmine**	17.00	2.50
		Cut cancel		.50
		Perf. initial		.35
R525	R24	$3 **carmine**	27.50	8.00
		Cut cancel		3.00
		Perf. initial		1.10
R526	R24	$4 **carmine**	30.00	8.00
		Cut cancel		3.50
		Perf. initial		1.90
R527	R24	$5 **carmine**	32.50	4.25
		Cut cancel		.75
		Perf. initial		.50
R528	R24	$10 **carmine**	72.50	5.25
		Cut cancel		1.10
		Perf. initial		.90
R529	R24	$20 **carmine**	150.00	15.00
		Cut cancel		2.50
		Perf. initial		1.60

Without Gum *Perf. 12*

No.	Type	Description	Unused	Used
R530	R25	$30 **carmine**	200.00	35.00
		Cut cancel		8.00
		Perf. initial		4.25
R531	R25	$50 **carmine**	210.00	60.00
		Cut cancel		16.00
		Perf. initial		7.50
R532	R25	$60 **carmine**	350.00	70.00
		Cut cancel		27.50
		Perf. initial		11.50
R533	R25	$100 **carmine**	100.00	21.00
		Cut cancel		4.50
		Perf. initial		2.75
R534	R25	$500 **carmine**	*1,250.*	260.00
		Cut cancel		125.00
		Perf. initial		57.50
R535	R25	$1000 **carmine**	*1,000.*	160.00
		Cut cancel		47.50
		Perf. initial		22.50

Nos. R288-R310 Overprinted

Series 1950

1950 **Wmk. 191R** *Perf. 11*

No.	Type	Description	Unused	Used
R536	R23	1c **carmine**	.40	.25
		Cut cancel		.25
		Perf. initial		.25
R537	R23	2c **carmine**	.40	.35
		Cut cancel		.30
		Perf. initial		.25
R538	R23	3c **carmine**	.50	.40
		Cut cancel		.30
		Perf. initial		.25
R539	R23	4c **carmine**	.70	.50
		Cut cancel		.30
		Perf. initial		.25
R540	R23	5c **carmine**	.45	.35
		Cut cancel		.30
		Perf. initial		.25
R541	R23	8c **carmine**	1.75	.80
		Cut cancel		.30
		Perf. initial		.25
R542	R23	10c **carmine**	.80	.30
		Cut cancel		.25
		Perf. initial		.25
R543	R23	20c **carmine**	1.40	.45
		Cut cancel		.35
		Perf. initial		.30
R544	R23	25c **carmine**	2.00	.45
		Cut cancel		.35
		Perf. initial		.30
R545	R23	40c **carmine**	6.00	2.10
		Cut cancel		.50
		Perf. initial		.30
R546	R23	50c **carmine**	8.00	.35
		Cut cancel		.30
		Perf. initial		.25
R547	R23	80c **carmine**	15.00	8.50
		Cut cancel		1.00
		Perf. initial		.60
R548	R24	$1 **carmine**	15.00	.40
		Cut cancel		.30
		Perf. initial		.25
R549	R24	$2 **carmine**	17.50	2.75
		Cut cancel		.45
		Perf. initial		.25
R550	R24	$3 **carmine**	20.00	6.00
		Cut cancel		1.40
		Perf. initial		.80
R551	R24	$4 **carmine**	27.50	7.50
		Cut cancel		2.75
		Perf. initial		1.40
R552	R24	$5 **carmine**	35.00	1.00
		Cut cancel		.35
		Perf. initial		.25
R553	R24	$10 **carmine**	70.00	10.00
		Cut cancel		1.00
		Perf. initial		.65
R554	R24	$20 **carmine**	150.00	15.00
		Cut cancel		3.50
		Perf. initial		2.10

Without Gum *Perf. 12*

No.	Type	Description	Unused	Used
R555	R25	$30 **carmine**	150.00	70.00
		Cut cancel		17.50
		Perf. initial		10.50
R556	R25	$50 **carmine**	125.00	22.50
		Cut cancel		11.00
		Perf. initial		6.50
a.		Vert. pair, imperf. horiz.		—
R557	R25	$60 **carmine**	260.00	75.00
		Cut cancel		25.00
		Perf. initial		9.75
R558	R25	$100 **carmine**	100.00	22.50
		Cut cancel		6.00
		Perf. initial		3.25
R559	R25	$500 **carmine**	*1,250.*	125.00
		Cut cancel		55.00
		Perf. initial		32.50
R560	R25	$1000 **carmine**	*900.00*	95.00
		Cut cancel		30.00
		Perf. initial		19.00

Nos. R288-R310 Overprinted

Series 1951

1951 **Wmk. 191R** *Perf. 11*

No.	Type	Description	Unused	Used
R561	R23	1c **carmine**	.30	.25
		Cut cancel		.25
		Perf. initial		.25
R562	R23	2c **carmine**	.30	.35
		Cut cancel		.25
		Perf. initial		.25
R563	R23	3c **carmine**	.30	.35
		Cut cancel		.25
		Perf. initial		.25
R564	R23	4c **carmine**	.30	.35
		Cut cancel		.25
		Perf. initial		.25
R565	R23	5c **carmine**	.30	.35
		Cut cancel		.25
		Perf. initial		.25
R566	R23	8c **carmine**	1.25	.45
		Cut cancel		.25
		Perf. initial		.25
R567	R23	10c **carmine**	.30	.35
		Cut cancel		.25
		Perf. initial		.25
R568	R23	20c **carmine**	.30	.55
		Cut cancel		.30
		Perf. initial		.25
R569	R23	25c **carmine**	.30	.50
		Cut cancel		.30
		Perf. initial		.25
R570	R23	40c **carmine**	3.75	1.60
		Cut cancel		.55
		Perf. initial		.35
R571	R23	50c **carmine**	3.00	.60
		Cut cancel		.30
		Perf. initial		.25
R572	R23	80c **carmine**	10.00	3.25
		Cut cancel		2.00
		Perf. initial		1.00
R573	R24	$1 **carmine**	16.00	.30
		Cut cancel		.25
		Perf. initial		.25
R574	R24	$2 **carmine**	21.00	.55
		Cut cancel		.35
		Perf. initial		.30
R575	R24	$3 **carmine**	16.00	4.00
		Cut cancel		2.10
		Perf. initial		1.25
R576	R24	$4 **carmine**	20.00	12.50
		Cut cancel		4.00
		Perf. initial		2.25
R577	R24	$5 **carmine**	10.00	.70
		Cut cancel		.35
		Perf. initial		.25
R578	R24	$10 **carmine**	18.00	2.50
		Cut cancel		1.25
		Perf. initial		.90
R579	R24	$20 **carmine**	55.00	16.00
		Cut cancel		5.00
		Perf. initial		3.25

Without Gum *Perf. 12*

No.	Type	Description	Unused	Used
R580	R25	$30 **carmine**	150.00	25.00
		Cut cancel		7.50
		Perf. initial		5.00
a.		Imperf., pair	*2,500.*	*2,000.*
R581	R25	$50 **carmine**	250.00	45.00
		Cut cancel		12.50
		Perf. initial		7.50
R582	R25	$60 **carmine**	275.00	75.00
		Cut cancel		25.00
		Perf. initial		16.00
R583	R25	$100 **carmine**	90.00	25.00
		Cut cancel		7.50
		Perf. initial		5.00
R584	R25	$500 **carmine**	*900.00*	175.00
		Cut cancel		75.00
		Perf. initial		35.00
R585	R25	$1000 **carmine**	*750.00*	150.00
		Cut cancel		55.00
		Perf. initial		40.00

No. R583 is known imperf horizontally. It exists as a reconstructed used vertical strip of 4 that was separated into single stamps.

Documentary Stamps and Types of 1940 Overprinted in Black

Series 1952

Designs: 55c, $1.10, $1.65, $2.20, $2.75, $3.30, L. J. Gage; $2500, William Windom; $5000, C. J. Folger; $10,000, W. Q. Gresham.

1952 **Wmk. 191R** *Perf. 11*

No.	Type	Description	Unused	Used
R586	R23	1c **carmine**	.35	.30
		Cut cancel		.25
		Perf. initial		.25
R587	R23	2c **carmine**	.50	.35
		Cut cancel		.25
		Perf. initial		.25
R588	R23	3c **carmine**	.40	.35
		Cut cancel		.30
		Perf. initial		.25
R589	R23	4c **carmine**	.45	.30
		Cut cancel		.25
		Perf. initial		.25
R590	R23	5c **carmine**	.35	.30
		Cut cancel		.25
		Perf. initial		.25
R591	R23	8c **carmine**	.90	.60
		Cut cancel		.30
		Perf. initial		.25
R592	R23	10c **carmine**	.50	.30
		Cut cancel		.25
		Perf. initial		.25
R593	R23	20c **carmine**	1.25	.40
		Cut cancel		.30
		Perf. initial		.25
R594	R23	25c **carmine**	2.50	.45
		Cut cancel		.30
		Perf. initial		.30
R595	R23	40c **carmine**	6.00	1.75
		Cut cancel		.55
		Perf. initial		.45
R596	R23	50c **carmine**	3.50	.30
		Cut cancel		.25
		Perf. initial		.25
R597	R23	55c **carmine**	.60	15.00
		Cut cancel		2.00
		Perf. initial		1.10
R598	R23	80c **carmine**	19.00	4.00
		Cut cancel		.80
		Perf. initial		.75
R599	R24	$1 **carmine**	7.00	1.50
		Cut cancel		.75
		Perf. initial		.40
R600	R24	$1.10 **carmine**	25.00	30.00
		Cut cancel		14.00
		Perf. initial		6.25
R601	R24	$1.65 **carmine**	175.00	62.50
		Cut cancel		37.50
		Perf. initial		21.00
R602	R24	$2 **carmine**	17.00	.90
		Cut cancel		.30
		Perf. initial		.25
R603	R24	$2.20 **carmine**	160.00	70.00
		Cut cancel		35.00
		Perf. initial		16.00
R604	R24	$2.75 **carmine**	190.00	70.00
		Cut cancel		35.00
		Perf. initial		16.00
R605	R24	$3 **carmine**	32.50	6.00
		Cut cancel		1.60
		Perf. initial		1.40
a.		Horiz. pair, imperf. btwn.	*1,300.*	
R606	R24	$3.30 **carmine**	225.00	90.00
		Cut cancel		50.00
		Perf. initial		25.00
R607	R24	$4 **carmine**	37.50	6.00
		Cut cancel		2.10
		Perf. initial		1.60
R608	R24	$5 **carmine**	32.50	1.25
		Cut cancel		.50
		Perf. initial		.40
R609	R24	$10 **carmine**	60.00	1.25
		Cut cancel		.50
		Perf. initial		.35
R610	R24	$20 **carmine**	92.50	16.00
		Cut cancel		4.50
		Perf. initial		3.00

Without Gum *Perf. 12*

No.	Type	Description	Unused	Used
R611	R25	$30 **carmine**	90.00	27.50
		Cut cancel		6.00
		Perf. initial		4.25
R612	R25	$50 **carmine**	95.00	35.00
		Cut cancel		9.00
		Perf. initial		5.50
R613	R25	$60 **carmine**	600.00	70.00
		Cut cancel		19.00
		Perf. initial		10.50
R614	R25	$100 **carmine**	110.00	10.00
		Cut cancel		4.00
		Perf. initial		2.10
R615	R25	$500 **carmine**	*750.00*	160.00
		Cut cancel		100.00
		Perf. initial		40.00
R616	R25	$1000 **carmine**	*325.00*	75.00
		Cut cancel		20.00
		Perf. initial		12.50
R617	R25	$2500 **carmine**	*1,250.*	275.00
		Cut cancel		175.00
		Perf. initial		125.00
R618	R25	$5000 **carmine**	—	*5,000.*
		Cut cancel		1,900.
		Perf. initial		1,500.
R619	R25	$10,000 **carmine**	*1,750.*	*1,400.*
		Cut cancel		1,200.
		Perf. initial		1,100.

Documentary Stamps and Types of 1940 Overprinted in Black

Series 1953

1953 **Wmk. 191R** *Perf. 11*

No.	Type	Description	Unused	Used
R620	R23	1c **carmine**	.40	.35
		Cut cancel		.25
		Perf. initial		.25

No.	Description	Unused	Used
R621	R23 2c **carmine**	.40	.30
	Cut cancel		.25
	Perf. initial		.25
R622	R23 3c **carmine**	.45	.35
	Cut cancel		.25
	Perf. initial		.25
R623	R23 4c **carmine**	.60	.45
	Cut cancel		.30
	Perf. initial		.25
R624	R23 5c **carmine**	.50	.30
	Cut cancel		.25
	Perf. initial		.25
a.	Vert. pair, imperf. horiz.		*1,150.*
R625	R23 8c **carmine**	1.10	.85
	Cut cancel		.30
	Perf. initial		.25
R626	R23 10c **carmine**	.65	.35
	Cut cancel		.25
	Perf. initial		.25
R627	R23 20c **carmine**	1.50	.50
	Cut cancel		.30
	Perf. initial		.25
R628	R23 25c **carmine**	1.75	.65
	Cut cancel		.35
	Perf. initial		.25
R629	R23 40c **carmine**	2.50	.90
	Cut cancel		.50
	Perf. initial		.35
R630	R23 50c **carmine**	3.00	.35
	Cut cancel		.25
	Perf. initial		.25
R631	R23 55c **carmine**	7.00	2.00
	Cut cancel		.80
	Perf. initial		.55
a.	Horiz. pair, imperf. vert.	*550.00*	
R632	R23 80c **carmine**	10.00	2.10
	Cut cancel		1.50
	Perf. initial		1.40
R633	R24 $1 **carmine**	5.25	.35
	Cut cancel		.25
	Perf. initial		.25
R634	R24 $1.10 **carmine**	12.00	2.50
	Cut cancel		2.10
	Perf. initial		1.60
a.	Horiz. pair, imperf. vert.	*700.00*	
b.	Imperf. pair	*850.00*	
R635	R24 $1.65 **carmine**	12.00	4.50
	Cut cancel		3.25
	Perf. initial		2.10
R636	R24 $2 **carmine**	9.00	.75
	Cut cancel		.35
	Perf. initial		.25
R637	R24 $2.20 **carmine**	20.00	6.00
	Cut cancel		2.75
	Perf. initial		2.10
R638	R24 $2.75 **carmine**	1.75	7.00
	Cut cancel		3.75
	Perf. initial		2.75
R639	R24 $3 **carmine**	17.00	4.00
	Cut cancel		1.75
	Perf. initial		1.40
R640	R24 $3.30 **carmine**	50.00	17.50
	Cut cancel		10.00
	Perf. initial		5.00
R641	R24 $4 **carmine**	40.00	15.00
	Cut cancel		4.00
	Perf. initial		3.25
R642	R24 $5 **carmine**	27.50	1.25
	Cut cancel		.55
	Perf. initial		.35
R643	R24 $10 **carmine**	60.00	2.25
	Cut cancel		1.10
	Perf. initial		.90
R644	R24 $20 **carmine**	140.00	22.50
	Cut cancel		4.50
	Perf. initial		2.40

Without Gum ***Perf. 12***

No.	Description	Unused	Used
R645	R25 $30 **carmine**	125.00	20.00
	Cut cancel		8.00
	Perf. initial		4.25
R646	R25 $50 **carmine**	175.00	42.50
	Cut cancel		15.00
	Perf. initial		6.25
R647	R25 $60 **carmine**	1,000.	425.00
	Cut cancel		170.00
	Perf. initial		75.00
	With complete receipt tab	*2,000.*	
R648	R25 $100 **carmine**	70.00	15.00
	Cut cancel		5.75
	Perf. initial		3.75
R649	R25 $500 **carmine**	*3,500.*	175.00
	Cut cancel		70.00
	Perf. initial		29.00
R650	R25 $1000 **carmine**	800.00	80.00
	Cut cancel		27.50
	Perf. initial		16.00
R651	R25 $2500 **carmine**	2,000.	1,750.
	Cut cancel		575.00
	Perf. initial		375.00
R652	R25 $5000 **carmine**	—	*7,500.*
	Cut cancel		*3,750.*
	Perf. initial		2,000.
R653	R25 $10,000 **carmine**	—	*4,250.*
	Cut cancel		1,250.
	Perf. initial		750.00

In 1955, the BEP began printing flat plate documentary stamps Nos. R654-R681 using the dry-printing method. This method used paper with a 5-10% moisture content versus the 15-35% moisture content for the wet printing. The dry-printed stamps from the same plates are .25-.75mm larger than the wet-printed examples. Four sub-varieties are known: (1) wet printing with ridged yellow gum, (2) wet printing with smooth yellow gum, (3) dry printing with smooth white gum, and (4) dry printing with smooth white gum.

Types of 1940
Without Overprint

1954 **Wmk. 191R** ***Perf. 11***

No.	Description	Unused	Used
R654	R23 1c **carmine**	.25	.25
	Cut cancel		.25
	Perf. initial		.25
a.	Horiz. pair, imperf. vert.	*1,500.*	
R655	R23 2c **carmine**	.25	.30
	Cut cancel		.25
	Perf. initial		.25
R656	R23 3c **carmine**	.25	.30
	Cut cancel		.25
	Perf. initial		.25
R657	R23 4c **carmine**	.25	.30
	Cut cancel		.25
	Perf. initial		.25
R658	R23 5c **carmine**	.25	.25
	Cut cancel		.25
	Perf. initial		.25
a.	Vert. pair, imperf. horiz.	—	
R659	R23 8c **carmine**	.25	.25
	Cut cancel		.25
	Perf. initial		.25
R660	R23 10c **carmine**	.25	.25
	Cut cancel		.25
	Perf. initial		.25
R661	R23 20c **carmine**	.30	.40
	Cut cancel		.30
	Perf. initial		.25
R662	R23 25c **carmine**	.35	.45
	Cut cancel		.30
	Perf. initial		.25
R663	R23 40c **carmine**	.75	.60
	Cut cancel		.45
	Perf. initial		.35
R664	R23 50c **carmine**	1.00	.25
	Cut cancel		.25
	Perf. initial		.25
a.	Horiz. pair, imperf. vert.	900.00	
R665	R23 55c **carmine**	.90	1.25
	Cut cancel		.55
	Perf. initial		.45
R666	R23 80c **carmine**	1.50	1.90
	Cut cancel		1.25
	Perf. initial		1.10
R667	R24 $1 **carmine**	.90	.35
	Cut cancel		.30
	Perf. initial		.25
R668	R24 $1.10 **carmine**	2.00	2.50
	Cut cancel		1.60
	Perf. initial		1.10
R669	R24 $1.65 **carmine**	25.00	7.50
	Cut cancel		3.75
	Perf. initial		.75
R670	R24 $2 **carmine**	1.00	.45
	Cut cancel		.25
	Perf. initial		.25
R671	R24 $2.20 **carmine**	2.25	3.75
	Cut cancel		2.75
	Perf. initial		1.60
R672	R24 $2.75 **carmine**	25.00	55.00
	Cut cancel		30.00
	Perf. initial		17.50
R673	R24 $3 **carmine**	2.00	2.00
	Cut cancel		.90
	Perf. initial		.55
R674	R24 $3.30 **carmine**	3.50	5.00
	Cut cancel		3.25
	Perf. initial		2.10
R675	R24 $4 **carmine**	2.75	4.00
	Cut cancel		2.10
	Perf. initial		1.60
R676	R24 $5 **carmine**	3.25	.50
	Cut cancel		.35
	Perf. initial		.25
R677	R24 $10 **carmine**	5.00	1.50
	Cut cancel		.85
	Perf. initial		.70
R678	R24 $20 **carmine**	10.00	6.50
	Cut cancel		3.25
	Perf. initial		1.90

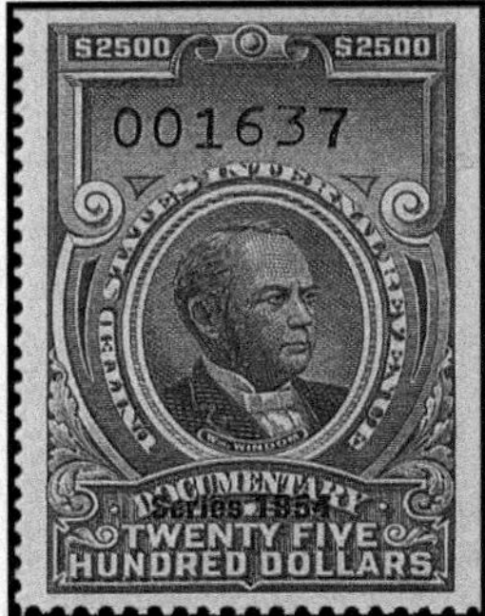

Documentary Stamps & Type of 1940 Ovptd. in Black

1954 **Wmk. 191R** ***Perf. 12***
Without Gum

No.	Description	Unused	Used
R679	R25 $30 **carmine**	55.00	17.50
	Cut cancel		5.25
	Perf. initial		3.50
	With complete receipt tab	55.00	
a.	Booklet pane of 4	*225.00*	
	Complete booklet, 10 #R679a	*2,250.*	
R680	R25 $50 **carmine**	55.00	29.00
	Cut cancel		10.00
	Perf. initial		6.25
	With complete receipt tab	55.00	
a.	Booklet pane of 4	*225.00*	
	Complete booklet, 10 #R680a	*2,250.*	
R681	R25 $60 **carmine**	55.00	30.00
	Cut cancel		13.00
	Perf. initial		9.25
	With complete receipt tab	55.00	
a.	Booklet pane of 4	*225.00*	
	Complete booklet, 10 #R681a	*2,250.*	
R682	R25 $100 **carmine**	55.00	7.50
	Cut cancel		5.25
	Perf. initial		4.00
	With complete receipt tab	55.00	
a.	Booklet pane of 4	*225.00*	
	Complete booklet, 10 #R682a	*2,250.*	
R683	R25 $500 **carmine**	*150.00*	87.50
	Cut cancel		30.00
	Perf. initial		25.00
	With complete receipt tab	150.00	
a.	Booklet pane of 4	*600.00*	
	Complete booklet, 2 #R683a	*1,200.*	
R684	R25 $1000 **carmine**	300.00	90.00
	Cut cancel		21.00
	Perf. initial		17.00
	With complete receipt tab	*300.00*	
a.	Booklet pane of 4	*1,200.*	
	Complete booklet, 1 #R684a	*1,200.*	
R685	R25 $2500 **carmine**	*350.00*	350.00
	Cut cancel		100.00
	Perf. initial		65.00
	With complete receipt tab	*350.00*	
a.	Booklet pane of 4	*1,400.*	
	Complete booklet, 10 #R685a	*14,000.*	
R686	R25 $5000 **carmine**	*1,750.*	1,500.
	Cut cancel		625.00
	Perf. initial		550.00
	With complete receipt tab	*1,750.*	
a.	Booklet pane of 4	*7,000.*	
R687	R25 $10,000 **carmine**	*1,750.*	*2,250.*
	Cut cancel		1,000.
	Perf. initial		400.00
	With complete receipt tab	*1,750.*	
a.	Booklet pane of 4	*7,000.*	

Documentary Stamps and Type of 1940 Overprinted in Black
Series 1955

1955 **Wmk. 191R** ***Perf. 12***
Without Gum

No.	Description	Unused	Used
R688	R25 $30 **carmine**	110.00	17.50
	Cut cancel		7.00
	Perf. initial		3.75
R689	R25 $50 **carmine**	125.00	30.00
	Cut cancel		11.00
	Perf. initial		7.00
R690	R25 $60 **carmine**	200.00	45.00
	Cut cancel		17.50
	Perf. initial		5.25
R691	R25 $100 **carmine**	160.00	20.00
	Cut cancel		6.00
	Perf. initial		4.00
R692	R25 $500 **carmine**	1,250.	200.00
	Cut cancel		75.00
	Perf. initial		35.00
R693	R25 $1000 **carmine**	*1,500.*	80.00
	Cut cancel		22.50
	Perf. initial		15.00
R694	R25 $2500 **carmine**	*1,250.*	275.00
	Cut cancel		125.00
	Perf. initial		75.00
R695	R25 $5000 **carmine**	*4,000.*	*2,000.*
	Cut cancel		800.00
	Perf. initial		550.00
R696	R25 $10,000 **carmine**	—	1,250.
	Cut cancel		750.00
	Perf. initial		275.00

Documentary Stamps and Type of 1940 Overprinted "Series 1956"

1956 **Wmk. 191R** **Without Gum** ***Perf. 12***

No.	Description	Unused	Used
R697	R25 $30 **carmine**	180.00	20.00
	Cut cancel		10.00
	Perf. initial		4.75
R698	R25 $50 **carmine**	300.00	27.50
	Cut cancel		15.00
	Perf. initial		6.50
R699	R25 $60 **carmine**	250.00	60.00
	Cut cancel		20.00
	Perf. initial		7.50
R700	R25 $100 **carmine**	125.00	15.00
	Cut cancel		6.00
	Perf. initial		5.00
R701	R25 $500 **carmine**	*1,500.*	150.00
	Cut cancel		35.00
	Perf. initial		22.50
R702	R25 $1000 **carmine**	*1,750.*	100.00
	Cut cancel		25.00
	Perf. initial		13.00
R703	R25 $2500 **carmine**	—	750.00
	Cut cancel		290.00
	Perf. initial		170.00
R704	R25 $5000 **carmine**	—	1,700.
	Cut cancel		800.00
	Perf. initial		500.00
R705	R25 $10,000 **carmine**	—	750.00
	Cut cancel		240.00
	Perf. initial		150.00

Documentary Stamps and Type of 1940 Overprinted "Series 1957"

1957 **Wmk. 191R** ***Perf. 12***
Without Gum

R706 R25 $30 **carmine** 275.00 60.00
Cut cancel 15.00
Perf. initial 6.75
R707 R25 $50 **carmine** 160.00 47.50
Cut cancel 14.00
Perf. initial 5.75
R708 R25 $60 **carmine** *1,500.* 400.00
Cut cancel 140.00
Perf. initial 57.50
R709 R25 $100 **carmine** 140.00 20.00
Cut cancel 9.00
Perf. initial 4.50
R710 R25 $500 **carmine** 900.00 200.00
Cut cancel 70.00
Perf. initial 37.50
R711 R25 $1000 **carmine** *1,750.* 100.00
Cut cancel 35.00
Perf. initial 21.00
R712 R25 $2500 **carmine** — 1,200.
Cut cancel 450.00
Perf. initial 300.00
R713 R25 $5000 **carmine** *4,250.* 1,800.
Cut cancel 1,000.
Perf. initial 450.00
R714 R25 $10,000 **carmine** — 650.00
Cut cancel 225.00
Perf. initial 175.00

Documentary Stamps and Type of 1940 Overprinted in Black "Series 1958"

1958 **Wmk. 191R** ***Perf. 12***
Without Gum

R715 R25 $30 **carmine** 140.00 27.50
Cut cancel 17.50
Perf. initial 8.25
R716 R25 $50 **carmine** 190.00 35.00
Cut cancel 17.00
Perf. initial 6.75
R717 R25 $60 **carmine** 210.00 42.50
Cut cancel 20.00
Perf. initial 10.50
R718 R25 $100 **carmine** 225.00 15.00
Cut cancel 6.50
Perf. initial 2.10
R719 R25 $500 **carmine** 600.00 125.00
Cut cancel 50.00
Perf. initial 25.00
R720 R25 $1000 **carmine** *2,750.* 90.00
Cut cancel 45.00
Perf. initial 35.00
R721 R25 $2500 **carmine** — 1,500.
Cut cancel 775.00
Perf. initial 500.00
R722 R25 $5000 **carmine** — *4,250.*
Cut cancel 2,700.
Perf. initial 2,250.
R723 R25 $10,000 **carmine** — 2,750.
Cut cancel 1,900.
Perf. initial 1,000.

Documentary Stamps and Type of 1940 Without Overprint

1958 **Wmk. 191R** ***Perf. 12***
With Gum

R724 R25 $30 **carmine** 11.00 7.00
Cut cancel 6.00
Perf. initial 4.25
With complete receipt tab 14.00
a. Booklet pane of 4 *57.50*
Complete booklet, 10 #R724a *575.00*
b. Vert. pair, imperf. horiz. *3,000.*
R725 R25 $50 **carmine** 12.00 7.00
Cut cancel 4.00
Perf. initial 3.25
With complete receipt tab 15.00
a. Booklet pane of 4 *60.00*
Complete booklet, 10 #R725a *600.00*
b. Vert. pair, imperf. horiz. *3,500.*
R726 R25 $60 **carmine** 17.50 21.00
Cut cancel 11.00
Perf. initial 5.50
With complete receipt tab 22.00
a. Booklet pane of 4 *90.00*
Complete booklet, 10 #R726a *900.00*
R727 R25 $100 **carmine** 13.00 4.75
Cut cancel 3.25
Perf. initial 2.00
With complete receipt tab 16.00
a. Booklet pane of 4 *65.00*
Complete booklet, 10 #R727a *650.00*
R728 R25 $500 **carmine** 17.50 26.00
Cut cancel 10.50
Perf. initial 7.75
With complete receipt tab 22.00
a. Booklet pane of 4 *90.00*
Complete booklet, 10 #R728a *900.00*
R729 R25 $1000 **carmine** 16.00 21.00
Cut cancel 10.50
Perf. initial 7.75
With complete receipt tab 20.00
a. Booklet pane of 4 *80.00*
Complete booklet, 10 #R729a *800.00*
b. Vert. pair, imperf. horiz. *1,750.*
c. Vert. pair, imperf. btwn. *1,500.*
R730 R25 $2500 **carmine** *175.00* 175.00
Cut cancel 90.00
Perf. initial 55.00
With complete receipt tab —
a. Booklet pane of 4 *800.00*
Complete booklet, 10 #R730a —
R731 R25 $5000 **carmine** 275.00 175.00
Cut cancel 90.00
Perf. initial 65.00
With complete receipt tab —
a. Booklet pane of 4 *1,200.*
Complete booklet, 10 #R731a —
R732 R25 $10,000 **carmine** *275.00* 140.00
Cut cancel 55.00
Perf. initial 25.00
With complete receipt tab —
a. Booklet pane of 4 *1,200.*
Complete booklet, 10 #R732a —

Internal Revenue Building, Washington, D.C. — R26

Centenary of the Internal Revenue Service.

Giori Press Printing

1962, July 2 **Unwmk.** ***Perf. 11***

R733 R26 10c **violet blue & bright green** 1.00 .40
Never hinged 1.25
Cut cancel .25
Perf. initial .25
P# block of 4 15.00
Cross gutter block of 4 *2,500.*
Horiz. pair with vert. gutter *200.00*
Vert. pair with horiz. gutter *400.00*

1963 **"Established 1862" Removed**

R734 R26 10c **violet blue & bright green** 3.00 .70
Never hinged 5.00
Cut cancel .25
Perf. initial .25
P# block of 4 30.00

Documentary revenue stamps were no longer required after Dec. 31, 1967.

PROPRIETARY STAMPS

Stamps for use on proprietary articles were included in the first general issue of 1862-71. They are R3, R13, R14, R18, R22, R29, R31 and R38.

Several varieties of "violet" paper were used in printing Nos. RB1-RB10. One is grayish with a slight greenish tinge, called "intermediate" paper by specialists. It should not be confused with the "green" paper, which is truly green.

All values prior to 1898 are for used examples. Printed cancellations on proprietary stamps command sizable premiums.

George Washington — RB1

RB1a

Engraved and printed by Jos. R. Carpenter, Philadelphia.
Various Frame Designs

1871-74 **Engr.** ***Perf. 12***

RB1 RB1 1c **green & black**
a. Violet paper ('71) 8.00
Pair 17.00
Block of 4 37.50
b. Green paper ('74) 14.00
Pair 35.00
Block of 4 85.00
c. As "a," Imperf. 80.00
Imperf., pair 175.00
Imperf., block of 4 475.00
d. As "a." Inverted center *5,250.*
RB2 RB1 2c **green & black**
a. Violet paper ('71) 8.75
Pair 19.00
Block of 4 42.50
Double transfer 30.00
b. Green paper ('74) 30.00
Pair 67.50
Block of 4 160.00
Double transfer 90.00
c. As "a," Invtd. center *40,000.*
d. As "b," Invtd. center *8,000.*
e. As "b," vert. half used as 1c on document —

Only three examples recorded of the inverted center on violet paper, No. RB2c. Value is for example with very good to fine centering and very small faults.

RB2d is valued with fine centering and small faults.

RB3 RB1a 3c **green & black**
a. Violet paper ('71) 32.50
Pair 75.00
Block of 4 160.00
Double transfer —
b. Green paper ('74) 67.50
Pair 150.00
Block of 4 325.00
c. As "a," privately perforated, sewing machine perfs 800.00
d. As "a," inverted center *14,000.*

No. RB3d is valued with small faults because all of the 8 recorded examples have faults.

RB4 RB1a 4c **green & black**
a. Violet paper ('71) 16.00
Pair 37.50
Block of 4 100.00
Double transfer —
b. Green paper ('74) 25.00
Pair 60.00
Block of 4 130.00
c. As "a," inverted center *15,000.*
d. As "b," vert. half used as 2c on document —

No. RB4c is valued with small faults as all seven of the recorded examples have faults.

RB5 RB1a 5c **green & black**
a. Violet paper ('71) 175.00
Pair 360.00
Block of 4 750.00
b. Green paper ('74) 250.00
Pair 525.00
Block of 4 1,075.
c. As "a," inverted center *155,000.*

No. RB5c is unique. Value represents price realized in 2000 auction sale.

RB6 RB1a 6c **green & black**
a. Violet paper ('71) 57.50
Pair 125.00
Block of 4 350.00
Double transfer —
b. Green paper ('74) 140.00
Pair 325.00
Block of 4 725.00
RB7 RB1a 10c **green & black** ('73)
a. Violet paper ('71) 300.00
Pair 700.00
Block of 4 —
Double transfer —
b. Green paper ('74) 65.00
Pair 150.00
Block of 4 350.00

See note on Inverted Centers after No. R133.

RB1b

RB8	RB1b 50c **green & black ('73)**		
a.	Violet paper ('71)	1,000.	
	Pair	*2,250.*	
b.	Green paper ('74)	850.00	
RB9	RB1b $1 **green & black** ('73)		
a.	Violet paper ('71)	*3,500.*	
	Pair	—	
b.	Green paper ('74)	*12,500.*	

RB1c

RB10	RB1c $5 **green & black** ('73)		
a.	Violet paper ('71)	*11,000.*	
	Pair	*26,000.*	
b.	Green paper ('74)	*75,000.*	

No. RB10b is valued with small faults.

When the Carpenter contract expired Aug. 31, 1875, the proprietary stamps remaining unissued were delivered to the Bureau of Internal Revenue. Until the taxes expired, June 30, 1883, the B.I.R. issued 34,315 of the 50c, 6,585 of the $1 and 2,109 of the $5, Nos. RB8-RB10. No. RB19, the 10c blue, replaced No. RB7b, the 10c on green paper, after 336,000 stamps were issued, exhausting the supply in 1881.

George Washington — RB2

RB2a

Plates prepared and printed by both the National Bank Note Co. and the Bureau of Engraving and Printing. No. RB11, and possibly others, also printed by the American Bank Note Co. All silk paper printings were by National, plus early printings of Nos. RB11b-RB14b, RB16b, RB17b. All rouletted stamps printed by the BEP plus Nos. RB15b, RB18b, RB19b. Otherwise, which company printed the stamps can be told only by guide lines (BEP) or full marginal inscriptions. ABN used National plates with A.B. Co. added on the second stamp to the left of the National inscription.

1875-81 ***Perf.***

RB11	RB2 1c **green**	
a.	Silk paper	2.25
	Pair	5.00
	Block of 4	12.50
	Double transfer	—
b.	Wmk 191R	.50
	Pair	1.25
	Block of 4	3.00
c.	Rouletted 6	175.00
	Pair	400.00
	Block of 4	925.00
d.	As No. RB11b, vert. pair, imperf btwn.	*400.00*
RB12	RB2 2c **brown**	
a.	Silk paper	3.25
	Pair	7.00
	Block of 4	65.00
b.	Wmk 191R	2.00
	Pair	4.50
	Block of 4	11.00
c.	Rouletted 6	190.00
	Pair	400.00
	Block of 4	950.00
RB13	RB2a 3c **orange**	
a.	Silk paper	14.00
	Pair	30.00
	Block of 4	70.00
b.	Wmk 191R	4.00
	Pair	9.00
	Block of 4	21.00
c.	Rouletted 6	160.00
	Pair	350.00
	Block of 4	800.00
d.	As No. RB13c, horiz. pair, imperf. between	*2,500.*
e.	As No. RB13c, vert. pair, imperf. between	*2,500.*
f.	Privately perforated, sewing machine perfs	—
RB14	RB2a 4c **red brown**	
a.	Silk paper	10.00
	Pair	25.00
	Block of 4	55.00
b.	Wmk 191R	9.00
	Pair	21.00
	Block of 4	45.00
c.	Rouletted 6	*22,000.*
RB15	RB2a 4c **red**	
b.	Wmk 191R	6.00
	Pair	15.00
	Block of 4	35.00
c.	Rouletted 6	450.00
	Pair	1,000.
RB16	RB2a 5c **black**	
a.	Silk paper	200.00
	Pair	425.00
	Block of 4	—
b.	Wmk 191R	125.00
	Pair	275.00
	Block of 4	—
c.	Rouletted 6	*1,850.*
	Pair	—
	Block of 4	—
RB17	RB2a 6c **violet blue**	
a.	Silk paper	35.00
	Pair	75.00
	Block of 4	200.00
b.	Wmk 191R	25.00
	Pair	60.00
	Block of 4	150.00
c.	Rouletted 6	*1,100.*
RB18	RB2a 6c **violet**	
b.	Wmk 191R	35.00
	Pair	85.00
	Block of 4	225.00
c.	Rouletted 6	*2,500.*
RB19	RB2a 10c **blue** ('81)	
b.	Wmk 191R	400.00
	Pair	850.00
	Block of 4	—

Many fraudulent roulettes exist.

Battleship — RB3

Inscribed "Series of 1898." and "Proprietary."

See note on rouletting preceding No. R161.

1898 Wmk. 191R Engr. ***Rouletted 5½***

RB20	RB3 ⅛c **yellow green**	.25	.25
	Block of 4	1.00	1.00
	P# block of 6	125.00	
	Double transfer	—	
a.	Vert. pair, imperf. horiz.	—	
b.	Vert. pair, imperf. btwn.	*1,100.*	
RB21	RB3 ¼c **brown**	.25	.25
a.	¼c **red brown**	.25	.25
b.	¼c **yellow brown**	.25	.25
c.	¼c **orange brown**	.25	.25
d.	¼c **bister**	.25	.25
	Block of 4	1.00	1.00
	P# block of 6	110.00	
	Double transfer	—	—
e.	Vert. pair, imperf. horiz.	—	—
f.	Printed on both sides	—	
RB22	RB3 ⅜c **deep orange**	.30	.30
	Block of 4	1.40	1.90
	P# block of 6	200.00	
a.	Horiz. pair, imperf. vert.	12.50	
b.	Vert. pair, imperf. horiz.	—	
RB23	RB3 ⅝c **deep ultra**	.25	.25
	Block of 4	1.25	1.10
	P# block of 6	75.00	
	Double transfer	1.50	
a.	Vert. pair, imperf. horiz.	85.00	—
b.	Horiz. pair, imperf. btwn.	*450.00*	*400.00*
RB24	RB3 1c **dark green**	2.25	.50
	Block of 4	11.00	2.25
	P# block of 6	250.00	
a.	Vert. pair, imperf. horiz.	*600.00*	
RB25	RB3 1¼c **violet**	.35	.25
	Block of 4	1.50	1.00
	P# block of 6	200.00	
a.	1¼c **brown violet**	.25	.25
b.	Vert. pair, imperf. btwn.	—	
RB26	RB3 1⅞c **dull blue**	15.00	2.00
	Block of 4	65.00	—
	P# block of 6	800.00	
	Double transfer	—	
RB27	RB3 2c **violet brown**	1.40	.35
	Block of 4	6.75	—
	P# block of 6	450.00	
	Double transfer		—
a.	Horiz. pair, imperf. vert.	60.00	
RB28	RB3 2½c **lake**	5.00	.35
	Block of 4	25.00	1.50
	P# block of 6	250.00	
a.	Vert. pair, imperf. horiz.	400.00	
RB29	RB3 3¾c **olive gray**	42.50	15.00
	Block of 4	210.00	—
	P# block of 6	—	
RB30	RB3 4c **purple**	16.00	1.50
	Block of 4	75.00	7.50
	P# block of 6	—	
	Double transfer	—	
RB31	RB3 5c **brown orange**	15.00	1.50
	Block of 4	70.00	7.00
	P# block of 6	*1,500.*	
a.	Vert. pair, imperf. horiz.	—	*400.00*
b.	Horiz. pair, imperf. vert.	—	*750.00*
	Nos. RB20-RB31 (12)	98.55	22.50

Hyphen Hole Perf. 7

RB20p	⅛c	.30	.25
	Block of 4	1.00	1.00
	P# block of 6	125.00	
RB21p	¼c	.25	.25
b.	¼c **yellow brown**	.25	.25
c.	¼c **orange brown**	.25	.25
	Block of 4	.55	1.00
d.	¼c **bister**	.25	.25
	P# block of 6	125.00	
RB22p	⅜c	.50	.35
	Block of 4	2.25	—
	P# block of 6	200.00	
RB23p	⅝c	.30	.25
	Block of 4	1.50	1.25
	P# block of 6	100.00	
RB24p	1c	30.00	15.00
	Block of 4	140.00	67.50
	P# block of 6	550.00	
RB25p	1¼c	.30	.30
	Block of 4	1.40	1.25
	P# block of 6	250.00	
a.	1¼c brown violet	.25	.25
RB26p	1⅞c	40.00	9.00
	Block of 4	200.00	—
	P# block of 6	1,250.	
RB27p	2c	10.00	1.00
	Block of 4	45.00	—
	P# block of 6	*550.00*	
RB28p	2½c	7.50	.40
	Block of 4	40.00	—
	P# block of 6	375.00	
RB29p	3¾c	100.00	27.50
	Block of 4	500.00	140.00
	P# block of 6	—	
RB30p	4c	70.00	22.50
	Block of 4	350.00	100.00
	P# block of 6	—	

No.	Description	Unused	Used
RB31p	5c	85.00	25.00
	Block of 4	425.00	190.00
	P# block of 6	*1,500.*	

See note after No. RS315 regarding St. Louis Provisional Labels of 1898.

RB4

Inscribed "Series of 1914"

1914 Offset Printing Wmk. 190 *Perf. 10*

No.	Description	Unused	Used
RB32	RB4 ⅛c **black**	.25	.35
	Block of 4	1.25	1.60
RB33	RB4 ¼c **black**	4.00	1.50
	Block of 4	18.00	
RB34	RB4 ⅜c **black**	.35	.35
	Block of 4	1.50	1.50
RB35	RB4 ⅝c **black**	10.00	3.00
	Block of 4	45.00	
RB36	RB4 1¼c **black**	7.50	1.75
	Block of 4	35.00	
RB37	RB4 1⅞c **black**	80.00	22.50
	Block of 4	350.00	
RB38	RB4 2½c **black**	19.00	3.50
	Block of 4	80.00	15.00
RB39	RB4 3⅛c **black**	230.00	67.50
	Block of 4	950.00	
RB40	RB4 3¾c **black**	75.00	27.50
	Block of 4	400.00	
RB41	RB4 4c **black**	110.00	45.00
	Block of 4	550.00	
RB42	RB4 4⅜c **black**	*3,000.*	—
	Block of 4	*13,000.*	
RB43	RB4 5c **black**	200.00	110.00
	Block of 4	—	
	Nos. RB32-RB41,RB43 (11)	736.10	282.95

Wmk. 191R

No.	Description	Unused	Used
RB44	RB4 ⅛c **black**	.35	.30
	Block of 4	1.50	1.50
RB45	RB4 ¼c **black**	.25	.25
	Block of 4	1.25	1.10
	Double impression	30.00	
RB46	RB4 ⅜c **black**	.75	.45
	Block of 4	3.50	2.00
RB47	RB4 ½c **black**	4.25	3.75
	Block of 4	17.50	
RB48	RB4 ⅝c **black**	.30	.25
	Block of 4	1.50	1.10
RB49	RB4 1c **black**	5.50	5.50
	Block of 4	25.00	25.00
RB50	RB4 1¼c **black**	.65	.40
	Block of 4	3.00	1.75
RB51	RB4 1½c **black**	4.25	3.00
	Block of 4	17.50	14.00
RB52	RB4 1⅞c **black**	1.35	.90
	Block of 4	6.00	4.00
RB53	RB4 2c **black**	7.50	6.00
	Block of 4	32.50	
RB54	RB4 2½c **black**	2.00	1.40
	Block of 4	9.00	7.50
RB55	RB4 3c **black**	6.00	4.00
	Block of 4	27.50	
RB56	RB4 3⅛c **black**	10.00	5.00
	Block of 4	42.50	
RB57	RB4 3¾c **black**	22.50	11.00
	Block of 4	92.50	
RB58	RB4 4c **black**	.50	.30
	Block of 4	2.25	1.50
RB59	RB4 4⅜c **black**	22.50	11.00
	Block of 4	92.50	
RB60	RB4 5c **black**	6.00	3.75
	Block of 4	26.00	
RB61	RB4 6c **black**	90.00	52.50
	Block of 4	425.00	
RB62	RB4 8c **black**	30.00	16.00
	Block of 4	130.00	
RB63	RB4 10c **black**	20.00	11.00
	Block of 4	97.50	
RB64	RB4 20c **black**	40.00	24.00
	Block of 4	175.00	
	Nos. RB44-RB64 (21)	274.65	160.75

RB5

1919 Offset Printing *Perf. 11*

No.	Description	Unused	Used
RB65	RB5 1c **dark blue**	.25	.25
	Block of 4	1.25	1.10
	Double impression	30.00	20.00
RB66	RB5 2c **dark blue**	.35	.25
	Block of 4	1.50	1.10
	Double impression	70.00	
RB67	RB5 3c **dark blue**	1.50	.75
	Block of 4	6.00	3.50
	Double impression	70.00	
RB68	RB5 4c **dark blue**	2.25	.75
	Block of 4	10.00	
RB69	RB5 5c **dark blue**	3.00	1.25
	Block of 4	13.50	5.75
RB70	RB5 8c **dark blue**	27.50	20.00
	Block of 4	120.00	
RB71	RB5 10c **dark blue**	12.50	5.00
	Block of 4	57.50	25.00
RB72	RB5 20c **dark blue**	20.00	7.50
	Block of 4	100.00	
RB73	RB5 40c **dark blue**	75.00	25.00
	Block of 4	350.00	
	Nos. RB65-RB73 (9)	142.35	60.75

FUTURE DELIVERY STAMPS

Issued to facilitate the collection of a tax upon each sale, agreement of sale or agreement to sell any products or merchandise at any exchange or board of trade, or other similar place for future delivery.

Documentary Stamps of 1917 Overprinted in Black or Red

Type I

1918-34 Wmk. 191R Offset Printing *Perf. 11*

Overprint Horizontal (Lines 8mm apart)

Left Value — Unused With Gum

Right Value — Used

No.	Description	Unused	Used
RC1	R22 2c **carmine rose**	8.75	.25
	Block of 4	37.50	1.10
RC2	R22 3c **carmine rose** ('34)	47.50	37.50
	Cut cancel		20.00
RC3	R22 4c **carmine rose**	17.50	.25
	Cut cancel		.25
	Block of 4	80.00	1.10
b.	Double impression of stamp		10.00
RC3A	R22 5c **carmine rose** ('33)	100.00	7.50
	Block of 4	—	37.50
RC4	R22 10c **carmine rose**	24.00	.35
	Block of 4	110.00	1.50
a.	Double overprint	—	5.25
b.	"FUTURE" omitted	—	*500.00*
c.	"DELIVERY FUTURE"		37.50
RC5	R22 20c **carmine rose**	40.00	.25
	Cut cancel		.25
	Block of 4	200.00	1.10
a.	Double overprint		21.00
RC6	R22 25c **carmine rose**	85.00	.60
	Cut cancel		.30
	Block of 4	390.00	3.00
	Block of 4, cut cancel		1.50
RC7	R22 40c **carmine rose**	110.00	1.25
	Cut cancel		.35
	Block of 4	480.00	5.75
	Block of 4, cut cancel		1.50
RC8	R22 50c **carmine rose**	27.50	.35
	Cut cancel		.25
	Block of 4	130.00	1.50
a.	"DELIVERY" omitted	—	*110.00*
RC9	R22 80c **carmine rose**	190.00	15.00
	Cut cancel		4.00
	Block of 4	900.00	70.00
	Block of 4, cut cancel		16.00
a.	Double overprint		37.50
	Double overprint, cut cancel		6.25

Engr.

Overprint Vertical, Reading Up (Lines 2mm apart)

No.	Description	Unused	Used
RC10	R21 $1 **green** (R)	75.00	.35
	Cut cancel		.25
	Block of 4	320.00	1.60
a.	Overprint reading down		*450.00*
b.	Black overprint		—
	Cut cancel		125.00
RC11	R21 $2 **rose**	85.00	.45
	Cut cancel		.25
	Block of 4	390.00	2.00
RC12	R21 $3 **violet** (R)	270.00	3.50
	Cut cancel		.30
	Block of 4	—	16.00
	Block of 4, cut cancel		1.50
a.	Overprint reading down	—	52.50
RC13	R21 $5 **dark blue** (R)	150.00	.60
	Cut cancel		.25
	Block of 4	—	2.75
	Block of 4, cut cancel		1.10
RC14	R21 $10 **orange**	180.00	1.35
	Cut cancel		.30
	Block of 4	800.00	5.00
	Block of 4, cut cancel		1.40
a.	"DELIVERY FUTURE"		*110.00*
RC15	R21 $20 **olive bister**	450.00	9.00
	Cut cancel		.80
	Perf initial		.35
	Block of 4		47.50
	Block of 4, cut cancel		3.50

Overprint Horizontal (Lines 11⅔mm apart)

Perf. 12

Without Gum

No.	Description	Unused	Used
RC16	R17 $30 **vermilion,** green numerals	150.00	5.50
	Cut cancel		1.75
	Perf initial		1.25
	Vertical strip of 4		30.00
	Vertical strip of 4, cut cancel		8.25
a.	Numerals in blue	160.00	4.75
	Cut cancel		2.00
	Perf initial		1.50
b.	Imperf., blue numerals		*150.00*
RC17	R19 $50 **olive green** *(Cleveland)*	125.00	3.00
	Cut cancel		.90
	Vertical strip of 4		15.00
	Vertical strip of 4, cut cancel		3.50
a.	$50 olive bister	125.00	2.75
	Cut cancel		.25
	Perf initial		.50
RC18	R19 $60 **brown**	160.00	9.00
	Cut cancel		1.20
	Perf initial		.80
	Vertical strip of 4		40.00
	Vertical strip of 4, cut cancel		5.75
a.	Vert. pair, imperf. horiz.		*950.00*
RC19	R17 $100 **yellow green** ('34)	260.00	37.50
	Cut cancel		9.00
	Perf initial		7.00
	Vertical strip of 4	—	*200.00*
	Vertical strip of 4, cut cancel		37.50
RC20	R18 $500 **blue,** red numerals (R)	325.00	25.00
	Cut cancel		9.00
	Perf initial		7.50
	Vertical strip of 4		125.00
	Vertical strip of 4, cut cancel		45.00
	Double transfer		40.00
	Vert. strip of 4, bottom stamp double transfer	—	150.00
a.	Numerals in orange	—	70.00
	Cut cancel		20.00
	Perf initial		15.00
	Vert. strip of 4		300.00
	Vert. strip of 4, cut cancel		100.00
	Double transfer	—	100.00
	Vert. strip of 4, bottom stamp double transfer	—	350.00
RC21	R19 $1000 **orange**	230.00	7.50
	Cut cancel		2.00
	Perf initial		1.50
	Vertical strip of 4		32.50
	Vertical strip of 4, cut cancel		9.00
a.	Vert. pair, imperf. horiz.		*1,350.*

See note after No. R227.

1923-24 Offset Printing *Perf. 11*

Overprint Horizontal (Lines 2mm apart)

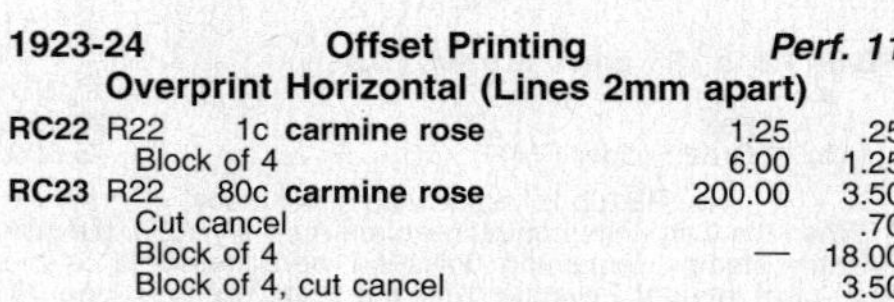

No.	Description	Unused	Used
RC22	R22 1c **carmine rose**	1.25	.25
	Block of 4	6.00	1.25
RC23	R22 80c **carmine rose**	200.00	3.50
	Cut cancel		.70
	Block of 4	—	18.00
	Block of 4, cut cancel		3.50

Type II

1925-34 **Engr.**

No.	Type	Description	Unused	Used
RC25	R21	$1 **green** (R)	100.00	2.00
		Cut cancel		.45
		Block of 4	—	8.00
		Block of 4, cut cancel		1.50
RC26	R21	$10 **orange** (Bk) ('34)	260.00	29.00
		Cut cancel		18.00
		Perf initial		11.50

Overprint Type I

1928-29 **Offset Printing** ***Perf. 10***

No.	Type	Description	Unused	Used
RC27	R22	10c **carmine rose**		*5,000.*
RC28	R22	20c **carmine rose**		*5,000.*

Some specialists have questioned the status of No. RC28, believing known examples to be either fraudulently reperforated examples of No. RC5, or examples of No. R256 with fake overprints applied. The editors would like to see authenticated evidence of the existence of No. RC28.

STOCK TRANSFER STAMPS

Issued to facilitate the collection of a tax on all sales or agreements to sell, or memoranda of sales or delivery of, or transfers of legal title to shares or certificates of stock.

Documentary Stamps of 1917 Overprinted in Black or Red

1918-22 **Offset Printing** **Wmk. 191R** ***Perf. 11***

Overprint Horizontal (Lines 8mm apart)

No.	Type	Description	Unused	Used
RD1	R22	1c **carmine rose**	1.00	.25
		Block of 4	4.25	1.10
a.		Double overprint	—	—
RD2	R22	2c **carmine rose**	.25	.25
		Block of 4	1.10	1.10
a.		Double overprint	—	15.00
		Double overprint, cut cancel		7.50
		Double impression of stamp		—
RD3	R22	4c **carmine rose**	.25	.25
		Block of 4	1.25	1.10
a.		Double overprint	—	4.25
		Double overprint, cut cancel		2.10
b.		"STOCK" omitted		10.50
d.		Ovpt. lines 10mm apart		—
		Double impression of stamp		6.00
RD4	R22	5c **carmine rose**	.30	.25
		Block of 4	1.40	1.10
a.		Ovpt. lines 7mm apart		—
RD5	R22	10c **carmine rose**	.30	.25
		Block of 4	1.40	1.10
a.		Double overprint	—	5.25
		Double overprint, cut cancel		2.75
b.		"STOCK" omitted		—
		Double impression of stamp		—
RD6	R22	20c **carmine rose**	.55	.25
		Perf initial		.25
		Block of 4	2.25	1.10
a.		Double overprint		6.25
b.		"STOCK" double		—
		Double impression of stamp		6.00
RD7	R22	25c **carmine rose**	2.25	.30
		Cut cancel		.25
		Block of 4	10.50	1.30
RD8	R22	40c **carmine rose** ('22)	2.25	.25
		Block of 4	10.50	1.10
RD9	R22	50c **carmine rose**	.80	.25
		Block of 4	3.75	1.10
a.		Double overprint		—
		Double impression of stamp		—
RD10	R22	80c **carmine rose**	10.00	.45
		Cut cancel		.25
		Block of 4	45.00	2.00

Engr.

Overprint Vertical, Reading Up (Lines 2mm apart)

No.	Type	Description	Unused	Used
RD11	R21	$1 **green** (R)	225.00	40.00
		Cut cancel		10.00
		Block of 4	—	—
		Block of 4, cut cancel		15.00
a.		Overprint reading down	300.00	60.00
		Overprint reading down, cut cancel		20.00
RD12	R21	$1 **green** (Bk)	3.00	.30
		Block of 4	13.00	1.40
a.		Pair, one without overprint	—	*180.00*
b.		Overprinted on back instead of face, inverted	—	*150.00*
c.		Overprint reading down	—	7.50
d.		$1 yellow green	3.00	.25
RD13	R21	$2 **rose**	3.00	.25
		Perf initial		.25
		Block of 4	13.00	1.10
a.		Overprint reading down		11.50
		Overprint reading down, cut cancel		1.50
b.		Vert. pair, imperf. horiz.	*800.00*	
RD14	R21	$3 **violet** (R)	35.00	6.00
		Cut cancel		.30
		Perf initial		.25
		Block of 4	160.00	—
		Block of 4, cut cancel		1.50
RD15	R21	$4 **yellow brown**	15.00	.30
		Cut cancel		.25
		Block of 4	65.00	1.30
RD16	R21	$5 **dark blue** (R)	10.00	.30
		Cut cancel		.25
		Block of 4	42.50	1.30
		Block of 4, cut cancel		.25
a.		Overprint reading down	42.50	1.35
		Overprint reading down, cut cancel		.25
RD17	R21	$10 **orange**	37.50	.45
		Cut cancel		.25
		Block of 4	150.00	2.00
		Block of 4, cut cancel		.40
RD18	R21	$20 **olive bister** ('21)	150.00	18.00
		Cut cancel		4.50
		Perf initial		2.25
		Block of 4	650.00	82.50
		Block of 4, cut cancel		25.00
a.		Overprint reading down		—

Shifted overprints on the $2, and $10 result in "TRANSFER STOCK," "TRANSFER" omitted, and possibly other varieties.

Overprint Horizontal (Lines 11½mm apart)

1918 **Without Gum** ***Perf. 12***

No.	Type	Description	Unused	Used
RD19	R17	$30 **vermilion,** green numerals	55.00	6.50
		Cut cancel		2.25
		Perf initial		1.25
		Vertical strip of 4		29.00
		Vertical strip of 4, cut cancel		10.00
a.		Numerals in blue	200.00	75.00
RD20	R19	$50 **olive green** *(Cleveland)*	160.00	70.00
		Cut cancel		27.50
		Perf initial		25.00
		Vertical strip of 4		300.00
		Vertical strip of 4, cut cancel		120.00
RD21	R19	$60 **brown**	350.00	30.00
		Cut cancel		12.00
		Perf initial		7.25
		Vertical strip of 4		100.00
		Vertical strip of 4, cut cancel		47.50
RD22	R17	$100 **green**	50.00	7.50
		Cut cancel		3.00
		Perf initial		2.25
		Vertical strip of 4		32.50
		Vertical strip of 4, cut cancel		13.00
RD23	R18	$500 **blue** (R)	550.00	160.00
		Cut cancel		75.00
		Perf initial		55.00
		Vertical strip of 4		—
		Vertical strip of 4, cut cancel		325.00
		Double transfer	*900.00*	250.00
a.		Numerals in orange		175.00
		Numerals in orange, double transfer		300.00
RD24	R19	$1,000 **orange**	425.00	110.00
		Cut cancel		35.00
		Perf initial		22.50
		Vertical strip of 4		400.00
		Vertical strip of 4, cut cancel		160.00

See note after No. R227.

1928 **Offset Printing** ***Perf. 10***

Overprint Horizontal (Lines 8mm apart)

No.	Type	Description	Unused	Used
RD25	R22	2c **carmine rose**	5.50	.30
		Block of 4	24.00	1.40
RD26	R22	4c **carmine rose**	5.50	.30
		Block of 4	24.00	1.40
RD27	R22	10c **carmine rose**	5.50	.30
		Block of 4	24.00	1.40
a.		Inverted overprint		*1,400.*
b.		Ovpt. lines 9½mm apart		—
RD28	R22	20c **carmine rose**	6.50	.35
		Perf initial		.25
		Block of 4	29.00	1.50
		Double impression of stamp		—
RD29	R22	50c **carmine rose**	10.00	.50
		Block of 4	47.50	2.25

Engr.

Overprint Vertical, Reading Up (Lines 2mm apart)

No.	Type	Description	Unused	Used
RD30	R21	$1 **green**	60.00	.35
		Cut cancel		.25
		Block of 4	—	1.60
a.		$1 yellow green	60.00	.50
RD31	R21	$2 **carmine rose**	55.00	.35
		Perf initial		.25
		Block of 4	—	1.50
a.		Pair, one without overprint	*225.00*	*190.00*
RD32	R21	$10 **orange**	60.00	.50
		Cut cancel		.25
		Perf initial		.25
		Block of 4	—	2.25
		Perf. 11 at top or bottom		—

Overprinted Horizontally in Black

1920 **Offset Printing** ***Perf. 11***

No.	Type	Description	Unused	Used
RD33	R22	2c **carmine rose**	12.50	1.00
		Block of 4	60.00	4.25
RD34	R22	10c **carmine rose**	3.00	.35
		Block of 4	14.00	1.50
b.		Inverted overprint	*2,250.*	*1,250.*
RD35	R22	20c **carmine rose**	5.75	.25
		Block of 4	26.00	1.10
a.		Horiz. pair, one without overprint	210.00	
d.		Inverted overprint (perf. initials)		—
RD36	R22	50c **carmine rose**	5.00	.30
		Block of 4	24.00	1.25

Shifted overprints on the 10c, 20c and 50c result in "TRANSFER STOCK," "TRANFSER" omitted, "STOCK" omitted, pairs, and other varieties.

Engr.

No.	Type	Description	Unused	Used
RD37	R21	$1 **green**	85.00	17.50
		Cut cancel		3.25
		Block of 4	375.00	80.00
		Block of 4, cut cancel		15.00
RD38	R21	$2 **rose**	100.00	17.50
		Cut cancel		3.25
		Block of 4	425.00	80.00
		Block of 4, cut cancel		15.00

Offset Printing

Perf. 10

No.	Type	Description	Unused	Used
RD39	R22	2c **carmine rose**	13.00	1.10
		Block of 4	67.50	5.00
		Double impression of stamp	—	
RD40	R22	10c **carmine rose**	5.25	.55
		Block of 4	26.00	2.50
RD41	R22	20c **carmine rose**	6.00	.25
		Cut cancel		.25
		Block of 4	30.00	1.10

Documentary Stamps of 1917-33 Overprinted in Black

1940 **Offset Printing** **Wmk. 191R** ***Perf. 11***

No.	Type	Description	Unused	Used
RD42	R22	1c **rose pink**	4.50	.65
		Cut cancel		.25
		Perf. initial		.25
a.		"Series 1940" inverted (pos. 31LR)	*1,000.*	600.00
		Pair, one normal, one inverted		900.00
		Cut cancel		125.00

No. RD42a always comes with a natural straight edge at left.

No.	Type	Description	Unused	Used
RD43	R22	2c **rose pink**	6.00	.65
		Cut cancel		.25
		Perf. initial		.25

RD45 R22 4c **rose pink** 7.50 .35
Cut cancel .25
Perf. initial .25
RD46 R22 5c **rose pink** 8.00 .25
Cut cancel .25
Perf. initial .25
RD48 R22 10c **rose pink** 14.00 .35
Cut cancel .25
Perf. initial .25
RD49 R22 20c **rose pink** 17.00 .35
Cut cancel .25
Perf. initial .25
RD50 R22 25c **rose pink** 17.00 1.10
Cut cancel .35
Perf. initial .25
RD51 R22 40c **rose pink** 11.00 1.00
Cut cancel .35
Perf. initial .25
RD52 R22 50c **rose pink** 12.50 .35
Cut cancel .25
Perf. initial .25
RD53 R22 80c **rose pink** 280.00 110.00
Cut cancel 60.00
Perf. initial 30.00

Engr.

RD54 R21 $1 **green** 50.00 .60
Cut cancel .35
Perf. initial .25
RD55 R21 $2 **rose** 55.00 1.00
Cut cancel .40
Perf. initial .25
RD56 R21 $3 **violet** 350.00 18.00
Cut cancel .75
Perf. initial .50
RD57 R21 $4 **yellow brown** 125.00 1.60
Cut cancel .50
Perf. initial .30
RD58 R21 $5 **dark blue** 100.00 2.00
Cut cancel .55
Perf. initial .35
RD59 R21 $10 **orange** 275.00 10.00
Cut cancel 1.10
Perf. initial .75
RD60 R21 $20 **olive bister** 500.00 150.00
Cut cancel 25.00
Perf. initial 11.50

Nos. RD19-RD24 Handstamped in Blue "Series 1940"

1940 Wmk. 191R *Perf. 12*
Without Gum

RD61 R17 $30 **vermilion** *2,000.* 1,500.
Cut cancel 650.
Perf. initial 400.
RD62 R19 $50 **olive green** *2,500.* *2,500.*
Cut cancel 1,250.
Perf. initial 400.
a. Double ovpt., perf. initial *1,400.*
RD63 R19 $60 **brown** *5,500.* *3,000.*
Cut cancel 1,000.
Perf. initial 500.
RD64 R17 $100 **green** *5,000.* 850.00
Cut cancel 350.
Perf. initial 110.
RD65 R18 $500 **blue** 4,250.
Cut cancel 1,600.
Perf. initial 950.
Double transfer *3,750.*
RD66 R19 $1,000 **orange**
Cut cancel *5,000.*
Perf. initial 3,000.

Alexander Hamilton — ST1

Levi Woodbury — ST2

Overprinted in Black
SERIES 1940

Same Portraits as Nos. R288-R310.

1940 Engr. Wmk. 191R *Perf. 11*

RD67 ST1 1c **bright green** 17.50 3.25
Cut cancel .65
Perf. initial .40
a. Imperf, pair, without gum *250.00*
RD68 ST1 2c **bright green** 10.00 1.75
Cut cancel .30
Perf. initial .30
a. Imperf, pair, without gum *250.00*
RD70 ST1 4c **bright green** 19.00 4.50
Cut cancel .65
Perf. initial .35
a. Imperf, pair, without gum *250.00*
RD71 ST1 5c **bright green** 12.00 1.75
Cut cancel .25
Perf. initial .25
a. Imperf, pair, without gum *250.00*
b. Without overprint, cut cancel *850.00*
RD73 ST1 10c **bright green** 16.00 2.10
Cut cancel .25
Perf. initial .25
a. Imperf, pair, without gum *250.00*
RD74 ST1 20c **bright green** 19.00 2.40
Cut cancel .25
Perf. initial .25
a. Imperf, pair, without gum *250.00*
RD75 ST1 25c **bright green** 60.00 10.50
Cut cancel .90
Perf. initial .45
a. Imperf, pair, without gum *250.00*
RD76 ST1 40c **bright green** 125.00 50.00
Cut cancel 3.50
Perf. initial 1.25
a. Imperf, pair, without gum *250.00*
RD77 ST1 50c **bright green** 16.00 2.10
Cut cancel .45
Perf. initial .30
a. Imperf, pair, without gum *250.00*
RD78 ST1 80c **bright green** 180.00 75.00
Cut cancel 27.50
Perf. initial 3.50
a. Imperf, pair, without gum *250.00*
RD79 ST2 $1 **bright green** 75.00 4.25
Cut cancel .55
Perf. initial .30
a. Without overprint, perf. initial *750.00*
RD80 ST2 $2 **bright green** 75.00 12.00
Cut cancel .75
Perf. initial .30
a. Imperf, pair, without gum *250.00*
RD81 ST2 $3 **bright green** 110.00 15.00
Cut cancel .90
Perf. initial .25
a. Imperf, pair, without gum *250.00*
RD82 ST2 $4 **bright green** 800.00 300.00
Cut cancel 110.00
Perf. initial 50.00
a. Imperf, pair, without gum *250.00*
RD83 ST2 $5 **bright green** 110.00 16.00
Cut cancel 2.00
Perf. initial .30
a. Imperf, pair, without gum *250.00*
RD84 ST2 $10 **bright green** 250.00 60.00
Cut cancel 6.50
Perf. initial 3.25
a. Imperf, pair, without gum *250.00*
RD85 ST2 $20 **bright green** 1,250. 125.00
Cut cancel 15.00
Perf. initial 5.75
a. Imperf, pair, without gum *250.00*

Nos. RD67-RD85 exist imperforate, without overprint. Value, set of pairs, $750.

Thomas Corwin — ST3

Overprinted "SERIES 1940"

Various frames and portraits as Nos. R306-R310.

Without Gum *Perf. 12*

RD86 ST3 $30 **bright green** *6,000.* 200.00
Cut cancel 100.00
Perf. initial 37.50
RD87 ST3 $50 **bright green** 3,250. 900.00
Cut cancel 275.00
Perf. initial 92.50
RD88 ST3 $60 **bright green** *5,000.* *2,250.*
Cut cancel 850.00
Perf. initial 160.00
RD89 ST3 $100 **bright green** *3,000.* 450.00
Cut cancel 150.00
Perf. initial 67.50
RD90 ST3 $500 **bright green** —
Cut cancel 2,400.
Perf. initial 1,400.
RD91 ST3 $1,000 **bright green** *4,000.*
Cut cancel 2,650.
Perf. initial 1,500.

Nos. RD86-RD91 exist as unfinished imperforates with complete receipt tabs, without overprints or serial numbers. Known in singles, pairs (Nos. RD86-RD88 and Nos. RD90-RD91, value $300 per pair; No. RD89, value $150 per pair), panes of four with plate number, uncut sheets of four panes (with two plate numbers), cross gutter blocks of eight, and blocks of four with vertical gutter between and plate number.

Stock Transfer Stamps and Type of 1940 Overprinted in Black

SERIES 1941

1941 Wmk. 191R *Perf. 11*

RD92 ST1 1c **bright green** .80 .55
Cut cancel .25
Perf. initial .25
RD93 ST1 2c **bright green** .60 .30
Cut cancel .25
Perf. initial .25
RD95 ST1 4c **bright green** .65 .25
Cut cancel .25
Perf. initial .25
RD96 ST1 5c **bright green** .60 .25
Cut cancel .25
Perf. initial .25
RD98 ST1 10c **bright green** 1.10 .25
Cut cancel .25
Perf. initial .25
RD99 ST1 20c **bright green** 2.40 .30
Cut cancel .25
Perf. initial .25
RD100 ST1 25c **bright green** 2.40 .45
Cut cancel .30
Perf. initial .30
RD101 ST1 40c **bright green** 3.75 .75
Cut cancel .30
Perf. initial .25
RD102 ST1 50c **bright green** 5.00 .35
Cut cancel .25
Perf. initial .25
RD103 ST1 80c **bright green** 35.00 10.00
Cut cancel .80
Perf. initial .60
RD104 ST2 $1 **bright green** 25.00 .25
Cut cancel .25
Perf. initial .25
RD105 ST2 $2 **bright green** 27.50 .30
Cut cancel .25
Perf. initial .25
RD106 ST2 $3 **bright green** 40.00 1.50
Cut cancel .35
Perf. initial .25
RD107 ST2 $4 **bright green** 65.00 8.50
Cut cancel .60
Perf. initial .30
RD108 ST2 $5 **bright green** 65.00 .65
Cut cancel .30
Perf. initial .25
RD109 ST2 $10 **bright green** 140.00 5.50
Cut cancel 1.00
Perf. initial .25
RD110 ST2 $20 **bright green** 500.00 110.00
Cut cancel 25.00
Perf. initial 5.00

Perf. 12
Without Gum

RD111 ST3 $30 **bright green** 2,250. 500.00
Cut cancel 110.00
Perf. initial 40.00
RD112 ST3 $50 **bright green** 1,250. 750.00
Cut cancel 175.00
Perf. initial 70.00
RD113 ST3 $60 **bright green** *2,500.* 1,000.
Cut cancel 275.00
Perf. initial 175.00
RD114 ST3 $100 **bright green** 500.00 210.00
Cut cancel 65.00
Perf. initial 45.00
RD115 ST3 $500 **bright green** 4,000. *3,500.*
Cut cancel 2,500.
Perf. initial 1,200.
RD116 ST3 $1,000 **bright green** — *4,000.*
Cut cancel 1,500.
Perf. initial 1,000.

Stock Transfer Stamps and Type of 1940 Overprinted in Black

SERIES 1942

1942 Wmk. 191R *Perf. 11*

RD117 ST1 1c **bright green** .75 .30
Cut cancel .25
Perf. initial .25
RD118 ST1 2c **bright green** .65 .35
Cut cancel .25
Perf. initial .25
RD119 ST1 4c **bright green** 3.50 1.10
Cut cancel .55
Perf. initial .45
RD120 ST1 5c **bright green** .70 .25
Cut cancel .25
Perf. initial .25
a. Overprint inverted *1,000.*
Cut cancel *700.00*
Perf. initial *350.00*
RD121 ST1 10c **bright green** 2.25 .25
Cut cancel .25
Perf. initial .25
RD122 ST1 20c **bright green** 2.75 .25
Cut cancel .25
Perf. initial .25
RD123 ST1 25c **bright green** 2.50 .25
Cut cancel .25
Perf. initial .25
RD124 ST1 40c **bright green** 5.75 .40
Cut cancel .25
Perf. initial .25
RD125 ST1 50c **bright green** 6.50 .25
Cut cancel .25
Perf. initial .25

RD126 ST1 80c **bright green** 30.00 6.00
Cut cancel 1.50
Perf. initial .35

RD127 ST2 $1 **bright green** 27.50 .40
Cut cancel .25
Perf. initial .25

RD128 ST2 $2 **bright green** 45.00 .40
Cut cancel .25
Perf. initial .25

RD129 ST2 $3 **bright green** 50.00 1.10
Cut cancel .30
Perf. initial .25

RD130 ST2 $4 **bright green** 65.00 24.00
Cut cancel .65
Perf. initial .25

RD131 ST2 $5 **bright green** 60.00 .40
Cut cancel .25
Perf. initial .25
a. Double overprint, perf. initial *2,500.*

RD132 ST2 $10 **bright green** 125.00 9.50
Cut cancel 2.00
Perf. initial 1.10

RD133 ST2 $20 **bright green** 350.00 65.00
Cut cancel 15.00
Perf. initial 5.00

Perf. 12
Without Gum

RD134 ST3 $30 **bright green** 900.00 100.00
Cut cancel 40.00
Perf. initial 30.00

RD135 ST3 $50 **bright green** 950.00 200.00
Cut cancel 55.00
Perf. initial 27.50

RD136 ST3 $60 **bright green** 2,500. 275.00
Cut cancel 110.00
Perf. initial 62.50

RD137 ST3 $100 **bright green** *900.00* 110.00
Cut cancel 35.00
Perf. initial 21.00

RD138 ST3 $500 **bright green** *15,000.*
Cut cancel *10,000.*
Perf. initial *8,500.*

RD139 ST3 $1,000 **bright green** — 2,750.
Cut cancel 850.00
Perf. initial 300.00

Stock Transfer Stamps and Type of 1940 Overprinted in Black

SERIES 1943

1943 Wmk. 191R *Perf. 11*

RD140 ST1 1c **bright green** .55 .30
Cut cancel .25
Perf. initial .25

RD141 ST1 2c **bright green** .60 .40
Cut cancel .25
Perf. initial .25

RD142 ST1 4c **bright green** 2.10 .25
Cut cancel .25
Perf. initial .25

RD143 ST1 5c **bright green** .60 .25
Cut cancel .25
Perf. initial .25

RD144 ST1 10c **bright green** 1.50 .25
Cut cancel .25
Perf. initial .25

RD145 ST1 20c **bright green** 2.25 .25
Cut cancel .25
Perf. initial .25

RD146 ST1 25c **bright green** 6.75 .35
Cut cancel .25
Perf. initial .25

RD147 ST1 40c **bright green** 6.25 .30
Cut cancel .25
Perf. initial .25

RD148 ST1 50c **bright green** 5.75 .30
Cut cancel .25
Perf. initial .25

RD149 ST1 80c **bright green** 35.00 7.50
Cut cancel 2.50
Perf. initial 1.25

RD150 ST2 $1 **bright green** 27.50 .25
Cut cancel .25
Perf. initial .25

RD151 ST2 $2 **bright green** 30.00 .50
Cut cancel .25
Perf. initial .25

RD152 ST2 $3 **bright green** 35.00 2.50
Cut cancel .45
Perf. initial .30

RD153 ST2 $4 **bright green** 85.00 30.00
Cut cancel 5.00
Perf. initial 3.00

RD154 ST2 $5 **bright green** 90.00 .60
Cut cancel .30
Perf. initial .25

RD155 ST2 $10 **bright green** 140.00 7.50
Cut cancel 1.50
Perf. initial .45

RD156 ST2 $20 **bright green** 450.00 90.00
Cut cancel 45.00
Perf. initial 10.00

Perf. 12
Without Gum

RD157 ST3 $30 **bright green** 2,500. 750.00
Cut cancel 100.00
Perf. initial 32.50

RD158 ST3 $50 **bright green** 2,500. 250.00
Cut cancel 50.00
Perf. initial 20.00

RD159 ST3 $60 **bright green** *4,000.* *2,750.*
Cut cancel 850.00
Perf. initial 200.00

RD160 ST3 $100 **bright green** 225.00 90.00
Cut cancel 30.00
Perf. initial 20.00

RD161 ST3 $500 **bright green** — 2,250.
Cut cancel 1,100.
Perf. initial 450.00

RD162 ST3 $1,000 **bright green** 2,500. 2,000.
Cut cancel 500.00
Perf. initial 200.00

Stock Transfer Stamps and Type of 1940 Overprinted in Black

Series 1944

1944 Wmk. 191R *Perf. 11*

RD163 ST1 1c **bright green** .90 .75
Cut cancel .35
Perf. initial .25

RD164 ST1 2c **bright green** .70 .25
Cut cancel .25
Perf. initial .25

RD165 ST1 4c **bright green** .70 .35
Cut cancel .25
Perf. initial .25

RD166 ST1 5c **bright green** .65 .25
Cut cancel .25
Perf. initial .25

RD167 ST1 10c **bright green** 1.00 .30
Cut cancel .25
Perf. initial .25

RD168 ST1 20c **bright green** 2.25 .25
Cut cancel .25
Perf. initial .25

RD169 ST1 25c **bright green** 3.25 .90
Cut cancel .25
Perf. initial .25

RD170 ST1 40c **bright green** 17.50 8.00
Cut cancel 3.25
Perf. initial 1.75

RD171 ST1 50c **bright green** 5.50 .30
Cut cancel .25
Perf. initial .25

RD172 ST1 80c **bright green** 17.50 6.25
Cut cancel 2.75
Perf. initial 1.75

RD173 ST2 $1 **bright green** 17.50 .50
Cut cancel .30
Perf. initial .25

RD174 ST2 $2 **bright green** 60.00 .75
Cut cancel .35
Perf. initial .25

RD175 ST2 $3 **bright green** 55.00 2.00
Cut cancel .35
Perf. initial .25

RD176 ST2 $4 **bright green** 95.00 17.50
Cut cancel 1.75
Perf. initial .75

RD177 ST2 $5 **bright green** 65.00 3.50
Cut cancel .40
Perf. initial .25

RD178 ST2 $10 **bright green** 150.00 7.25
Cut cancel 1.00
Perf. initial .45

RD179 ST2 $20 **bright green** 350.00 25.00
Cut cancel 9.00
Perf. initial 5.50

Perf. 12
Without Gum

Designs: $2,500, William Windom. $5,000, C. J. Folger. $10,000, W. Q. Gresham.

RD180 ST3 $30 **bright green** 850.00 125.00
Cut cancel 50.00
Perf. initial 22.50

RD181 ST3 $50 **bright green** 1,000. 150.00
Cut cancel 30.00
Perf. initial 17.50

RD182 ST3 $60 **bright green** *4,750.* 750.00
Cut cancel 125.00
Perf. initial 70.00

RD183 ST3 $100 **bright green** 3,250. 100.00
Cut cancel 35.00
Perf. initial 17.50

RD184 ST3 $500 **bright green** *2,500.* *2,250.*
Cut cancel 1,750.
Perf. initial 650.00

RD185 ST3 $1,000 **bright green** *3,000.* 2,500.
Cut cancel 1,500.
Perf. initial 400.00

RD185A ST3 $2,500 **bright green** —

RD185B ST3 $5,000 **bright green**, perf. initial *65,000.*

RD185C ST3 $10,000 **bright green**, cut cancel *45,000.*
Perf. initial *35,000.*

Nos. RD185A-R185C exist as unfinished imperforates with complete receipt tabs, without overprints or serial numbers. Known in singles, pairs, panes of four with plate number, uncut sheets of four panes (with two plate numbers), cross gutter blocks of eight, and blocks of four with vertical gutter between and plate number. Value, pairs $450 each.

Stock Transfer Stamps and Type of 1940 Overprinted in Black

Series 1945

1945 Wmk. 191R *Perf. 11*

RD186 ST1 1c **bright green** .45 .25
Cut cancel .25
Perf. initial .25

RD187 ST1 2c **bright green** .45 .35
Cut cancel .25
Perf. initial .25

RD188 ST1 4c **bright green** .50 .35
Cut cancel .25
Perf. initial .25

RD189 ST1 5c **bright green** .45 .25
Cut cancel .25
Perf. initial .25

RD190 ST1 10c **bright green** 1.25 .35
Cut cancel .25
Perf. initial .25

RD191 ST1 20c **bright green** 2.25 .45
Cut cancel .25
Perf. initial .25

RD192 ST1 25c **bright green** 3.50 .40
Cut cancel .30
Perf. initial .25

RD193 ST1 40c **bright green** 5.00 .25
Cut cancel .25
Perf. initial .25

RD194 ST1 50c **bright green** 11.00 .45
Cut cancel .30
Perf. initial .25

RD195 ST1 80c **bright green** 17.50 4.75
Cut cancel 1.00
Perf. initial .70

RD196 ST2 $1 **bright green** 20.00 .30
Cut cancel .25
Perf. initial .25

RD197 ST2 $2 **bright green** 37.50 .90
Cut cancel .30
Perf. initial .25

RD198 ST2 $3 **bright green** 65.00 1.75
Cut cancel .50
Perf. initial .25

RD199 ST2 $4 **bright green** 65.00 4.25
Cut cancel 1.10
Perf. initial .65

RD200 ST2 $5 **bright green** 40.00 1.00
Cut cancel .30
Perf. initial .25

RD201 ST2 $10 **bright green** 95.00 12.00
Cut cancel 1.50
Perf. initial 1.00

RD202 ST2 $20 **bright green** 375.00 25.00
Cut cancel 5.00
Perf. initial 1.40

Perf. 12
Without Gum

RD203 ST3 $30 **bright green** 300.00 90.00
Cut cancel 40.00
Perf. initial 22.50

RD204 ST3 $50 **bright green** 275.00 70.00
Cut cancel 12.50
Perf. initial 8.00

RD205 ST3 $60 **bright green** 1,750. 500.00
Cut cancel 200.00
Perf. initial 55.00

RD206 ST3 $100 **bright green** 600.00 75.00
Cut cancel 20.00
Perf. initial 10.50

RD207 ST3 $500 **bright green** — 1,400.
Cut cancel 800.00
Perf. initial 450.00

RD208 ST3 $1,000 **bright green** *3,250.* 2,250.
Cut cancel 1,050.
Perf. initial 500.00

RD208A ST3 $2,500 **bright green**
Cut cancel *25,000.*
Perf. initial *17,500.*

RD208B ST3 $5,000 **bright green**
Cut cancel *45,000.*

RD208C ST3 $10,000 **bright green**
Cut cancel *45,000.*

Stock Transfer Stamps and Type of 1940 Overprinted in Black

Series 1946

1946 Wmk. 191R *Perf. 11*

RD209 ST1 1c **bright green** .50 .35
Cut cancel .25
Perf. initial .25
a. Pair, one dated "1945" *850.00*

RD210 ST1 2c **bright green** .50 .25
Cut cancel .25
Perf. initial .25

RD211 ST1 4c **bright green** .50 .25
Cut cancel .25
Perf. initial .25

RD212 ST1 5c **bright green** .55 .25
Cut cancel .25
Perf. initial .25

RD213 ST1 10c **bright green** 1.25 .25
Cut cancel .25
Perf. initial .25

RD214 ST1 20c **bright green** 2.50 .30
Cut cancel .25
Perf. initial .25

RD215 ST1 25c **bright green** 3.00 .40
Cut cancel .30
Perf. initial .25

RD216 ST1 40c **bright green** 6.50 1.25
Cut cancel .40
Perf. initial .25

RD217 ST1 50c **bright green** 6.75 .25
Cut cancel .25
Perf. initial .25

RD218 ST1 80c **bright green** 24.00 9.50
Cut cancel 3.25
Perf. initial 1.60

RD219 ST2 $1 **bright green** 17.50 .90
Cut cancel .35
Perf. initial .25

No.	Type	Denom.	Color	Unused	Used
RD220	ST2	$2	**bright green**	19.00	1.00
		Cut cancel			.40
		Perf. initial			.25
RD221	ST2	$3	**bright green**	35.00	2.25
		Cut cancel			.45
		Perf. initial			.25
RD222	ST2	$4	**bright green**	35.00	9.00
		Cut cancel			3.50
		Perf. initial			1.25
RD223	ST2	$5	**bright green**	60.00	2.25
		Cut cancel			.35
		Perf. initial			.25
RD224	ST2	$10	**bright green**	100.00	4.25
		Cut cancel			1.25
		Perf. initial			.35
RD225	ST2	$20	**bright green**	550.00	75.00
		Cut cancel			16.00
		Perf. initial			8.75

Without Gum — ***Perf. 12***

No.	Type	Denom.	Color	Unused	Used
RD226	ST3	$30	**bright green**	350.00	62.50
		Cut cancel			25.00
		Perf. initial			18.00
RD227	ST3	$50	**bright green**	450.00	75.00
		Cut cancel			27.50
		Perf. initial			15.00
RD228	ST3	$60	**bright green**	1,250.	250.00
		Cut cancel			60.00
		Perf. initial			20.00
RD229	ST3	$100	**bright green**	225.00	90.00
		Cut cancel			27.50
		Perf. initial			17.00
RD230	ST3	$500	**bright green**	*2,500.*	350.00
		Cut cancel			125.00
		Perf. initial			90.00
RD231	ST3	$1,000	**bright green**	2,000.	300.00
		Cut cancel			200.00
		Perf. initial			95.00
RD232	ST3	$2,500	**bright green**		*25,000.*
		Cut cancel			*15,000.*
		Perf. initial			*12,500.*
RD233	ST3	$5,000	**bright green**		
		Cut cancel			*17,500.*
		Perf. initial			*7,500.*
RD234	ST3	$10,000	**bright green**		
		Cut cancel			*22,500.*

Stock Transfer Stamps and Type of 1940 Overprinted in Black

Series 1947

1947 — **Wmk. 191R** — ***Perf. 11***

No.	Type	Denom.	Color	Unused	Used
RD235	ST1	1c	**bright green**	2.75	.90
		Cut cancel			.35
		Perf. initial			.25
RD236	ST1	2c	**bright green**	2.75	.90
		Cut cancel			.35
		Perf. initial			.25
RD237	ST1	4c	**bright green**	2.00	.70
		Cut cancel			.35
		Perf. initial			.25
RD238	ST1	5c	**bright green**	2.00	.60
		Cut cancel			.35
		Perf. initial			.25
RD239	ST1	10c	**bright green**	2.00	.90
		Cut cancel			.35
		Perf. initial			.25
RD240	ST1	20c	**bright green**	3.75	.90
		Cut cancel			.30
		Perf. initial			.25
RD241	ST1	25c	**bright green**	6.00	.90
		Cut cancel			.35
		Perf. initial			.25
RD242	ST1	40c	**bright green**	6.00	1.40
		Cut cancel			.35
		Perf. initial			.25
RD243	ST1	50c	**bright green**	7.50	.35
		Cut cancel			.25
		Perf. initial			.25
RD244	ST1	80c	**bright green**	32.50	14.00
		Cut cancel			5.50
		Perf. initial			3.75
RD245	ST2	$1	**bright green**	25.00	1.00
		Cut cancel			.35
		Perf. initial			.25
RD246	ST2	$2	**bright green**	35.00	1.25
		Cut cancel			.35
		Perf. initial			.25
RD247	ST2	$3	**bright green**	50.00	2.50
		Cut cancel			.60
		Perf. initial			.35
RD248	ST2	$4	**bright green**	70.00	9.50
		Cut cancel			1.60
		Perf. initial			.90
RD249	ST2	$5	**bright green**	50.00	3.25
		Cut cancel			.65
		Perf. initial			.35
RD250	ST2	$10	**bright green**	225.00	11.00
		Cut cancel			3.25
		Perf. initial			2.25
RD251	ST2	$20	**bright green**	300.00	50.00
		Cut cancel			12.50
		Perf. initial			6.75

Without Gum — ***Perf. 12***

No.	Type	Denom.	Color	Unused	Used
RD252	ST3	$30	**bright green**	2,000.	85.00
		Cut cancel			25.00
		Perf. initial			13.00
RD253	ST3	$50	**bright green**	1,500.	275.00
		Cut cancel			65.00
		Perf. initial			25.00
RD254	ST3	$60	**bright green**	2,750.	250.00
		Cut cancel			80.00
		Perf. initial			50.00
RD255	ST3	$100	**bright green**	175.00	70.00
		Cut cancel			22.50
		Perf. initial			17.00
RD256	ST3	$500	**bright green**	2,500.	850.00
		Cut cancel			400.00
		Perf. initial			175.00
RD257	ST3	$1,000	**bright green**	2,500.	140.00
		Cut cancel			75.00
		Perf. initial			40.00
RD258	ST3	$2,500	**bright green**	*3,000.*	
		Cut cancel			400.00
		Perf. initial			350.00
RD259	ST3	$5,000	**bright green**	2,500.	
		Cut cancel			600.00
		Perf. initial			500.00
RD260	ST3	$10,000	**bright green**	—	
		Cut cancel			75.00
		Perf. initial			—
a.		Vert. pair, imperf. horiz., cut cancel			—

Stock Transfer Stamps and Type of 1940 Overprinted in Black

Series 1948

1948 — **Wmk. 191R** — ***Perf. 11***

No.	Type	Denom.	Color	Unused	Used
RD261	ST1	1c	**bright green**	.45	.35
		Cut cancel			.25
		Perf. initial			.25
RD262	ST1	2c	**bright green**	.45	.35
		Cut cancel			.25
		Perf. initial			.25
RD263	ST1	4c	**bright green**	.80	.45
		Cut cancel			.30
		Perf. initial			.25
RD264	ST1	5c	**bright green**	.45	.25
		Cut cancel			.25
		Perf. initial			.25
RD265	ST1	10c	**bright green**	.55	.35
		Cut cancel			.25
		Perf. initial			.25
RD266	ST1	20c	**bright green**	1.60	.40
		Cut cancel			.25
		Perf. initial			.25
RD267	ST1	25c	**bright green**	1.90	.55
		Cut cancel			.30
		Perf. initial			.25
RD268	ST1	40c	**bright green**	5.00	1.00
		Cut cancel			.35
		Perf. initial			.25
RD269	ST1	50c	**bright green**	7.00	.45
		Cut cancel			.25
		Perf. initial			.25
RD270	ST1	80c	**bright green**	30.00	9.50
		Cut cancel			3.50
		Perf. initial			2.25
RD271	ST2	$1	**bright green**	17.50	.50
		Cut cancel			.30
		Perf. initial			.20
RD272	ST2	$2	**bright green**	35.00	1.00
		Cut cancel			.30
		Perf. initial			.25
RD273	ST2	$3	**bright green**	60.00	10.00
		Cut cancel			3.00
		Perf. initial			1.60
RD274	ST2	$4	**bright green**	70.00	20.00
		Cut cancel			3.75
		Perf. initial			2.25
RD275	ST2	$5	**bright green**	80.00	5.00
		Cut cancel			.50
		Perf. initial			.25
RD276	ST2	$10	**bright green**	90.00	7.25
		Cut cancel			1.00
		Perf. initial			.75
RD277	ST2	$20	**bright green**	275.00	30.00
		Cut cancel			10.00
		Perf. initial			4.75

Perf. 12

Without Gum

No.	Type	Denom.	Color	Unused	Used
RD278	ST3	$30	**bright green**	350.00	100.00
		Cut cancel			35.00
		Perf. initial			18.00
RD279	ST3	$50	**bright green**	225.00	95.00
		Cut cancel			32.50
		Perf. initial			16.00
RD280	ST3	$60	**bright green**	2,000.	250.00
		Cut cancel			75.00
		Perf. initial			27.50
RD281	ST3	$100	**bright green**	175.00	30.00
		Cut cancel			10.00
		Perf. initial			7.00
RD282	ST3	$500	**bright green**	2,500.	375.00
		Cut cancel			200.00
		Perf. initial			52.50
RD283	ST3	$1,000	**bright green**	2,500.	125.00
		Cut cancel			80.00
		Perf. initial			40.00
RD284	ST3	$2,500	**bright green**	2,500.	1,750.
		Cut cancel			600.00
		Perf. initial			225.00
RD285	ST3	$5,000	**bright green**	2,500.	1,750.
		Cut cancel			600.00
		Perf. initial			225.00
RD286	ST3	$10,000	**bright green**		
		Cut cancel			75.00
		Perf. initial			—

Stock Transfer Stamps and Type of 1940 Overprinted in Black

Series 1949

1949 — **Wmk. 191R** — ***Perf. 11***

No.	Type	Denom.	Color	Unused	Used
RD287	ST1	1c	**bright green**	2.25	.70
		Cut cancel			.35
		Perf. initial			.25
RD288	ST1	2c	**bright green**	2.25	.75
		Cut cancel			.35
		Perf. initial			.25
RD289	ST1	4c	**bright green**	2.50	.75
		Cut cancel			.35
		Perf. initial			.25
RD290	ST1	5c	**bright green**	3.00	.75
		Cut cancel			.35
		Perf. initial			.25
RD291	ST1	10c	**bright green**	7.50	1.00
		Cut cancel			.35
		Perf. initial			.25
RD292	ST1	20c	**bright green**	12.00	1.00
		Cut cancel			.35
		Perf. initial			.25
RD293	ST1	25c	**bright green**	13.00	1.25
		Cut cancel			.40
		Perf. initial			.25
RD294	ST1	40c	**bright green**	30.00	3.25
		Cut cancel			.50
		Perf. initial			.30
RD295	ST1	50c	**bright green**	35.00	.45
		Cut cancel			.35
		Perf. initial			.25
RD296	ST1	80c	**bright green**	45.00	10.00
		Cut cancel			4.25
		Perf. initial			3.00
RD297	ST2	$1	**bright green**	32.50	1.00
		Cut cancel			.35
		Perf. initial			.25
RD298	ST2	$2	**bright green**	60.00	1.75
		Cut cancel			.50
		Perf. initial			.30
RD299	ST2	$3	**bright green**	110.00	10.00
		Cut cancel			2.25
		Perf. initial			1.10
RD300	ST2	$4	**bright green**	110.00	20.00
		Cut cancel			3.00
		Perf. initial			1.75
RD301	ST2	$5	**bright green**	85.00	3.00
		Cut cancel			.30
		Perf. initial			.25
RD302	ST2	$10	**bright green**	150.00	12.50
		Cut cancel			3.75
		Perf. initial			2.00
RD303	ST2	$20	**bright green**	325.00	22.50
		Cut cancel			10.00
		Perf. initial			6.25

Perf. 12

Without Gum

No.	Type	Denom.	Color	Unused	Used
RD304	ST3	$30	**bright green**	2,000.	150.00
		Cut cancel			45.00
		Perf. initial			18.00
RD305	ST3	$50	**bright green**	2,250.	300.00
		Cut cancel			75.00
		Perf. initial			27.50
RD306	ST3	$60	**bright green**	2,500.	400.00
		Cut cancel			175.00
		Perf. initial			75.00
RD307	ST3	$100	**bright green**	225.00	70.00
		Cut cancel			35.00
		Perf. initial			18.00
RD308	ST3	$500	**bright green**	*1,500.*	300.00
		Cut cancel			65.00
		Perf. initial			35.00
RD309	ST3	$1,000	**bright green**	*1,500.*	85.00
		Cut cancel			52.50
		Perf. initial			32.50
RD310	ST3	$2,500	**bright green**		
		Cut cancel			*750.00*
		Perf. initial			600.00
RD311	ST3	$5,000	**bright green**		
		Cut cancel			*675.00*
		Perf. initial			*600.00*
RD312	ST3	$10,000	**bright green**		475.00
		Cut cancel			45.00
		Perf. initial			—
a.		Pair, one without ovpt., cut cancel			*8,000.*

No. RD312a is unique.

Stock Transfer Stamps and Type of 1940 Overprinted in Black

Series 1950

1950 — **Wmk. 191R** — ***Perf. 11***

No.	Type	Denom.	Color	Unused	Used
RD313	ST1	1c	**bright green**	.80	.40
		Cut cancel			.30
		Perf. initial			.25
RD314	ST1	2c	**bright green**	.70	.35
		Cut cancel			.25
		Perf. initial			.25
RD315	ST1	4c	**bright green**	.65	.40
		Cut cancel			.25
		Perf. initial			.25
RD316	ST1	5c	**bright green**	.75	.25
		Cut cancel			.25
		Perf. initial			.25
RD317	ST1	10c	**bright green**	3.25	.30
		Cut cancel			.25
		Perf. initial			.25
RD318	ST1	20c	**bright green**	5.00	.80
		Cut cancel			.35
		Perf. initial			.25
RD319	ST1	25c	**bright green**	10.00	1.00
		Cut cancel			.25
		Perf. initial			.25
RD320	ST1	40c	**bright green**	15.00	1.50
		Cut cancel			.35
		Perf. initial			.25

No.	Type	Denom.	Color	Unused	Used
RD321	ST1	50c	**bright green**	19.00	.50
		Cut cancel			.30
		Perf. initial			.25
RD322	ST1	80c	**bright green**	27.50	7.25
		Cut cancel			2.40
		Perf. initial			1.50
RD323	ST2	$1	**bright green**	27.50	.55
		Cut cancel			.25
		Perf. initial			.25
RD324	ST2	$2	**bright green**	40.00	1.25
		Cut cancel			.35
		Perf. initial			.25
RD325	ST2	$3	**bright green**	70.00	8.50
		Cut cancel			1.25
		Perf. initial			1.00
RD326	ST2	$4	**bright green**	85.00	20.00
		Cut cancel			7.50
		Perf. initial			5.00
RD327	ST2	$5	**bright green**	70.00	3.25
		Cut cancel			.45
		Perf. initial			.25
RD328	ST2	$10	**bright green**	210.00	12.50
		Cut cancel			2.25
		Perf. initial			1.00
RD329	ST2	$20	**bright green**	250.00	60.00
		Cut cancel			40.00
		Perf. initial			10.00

Perf. 12

Without Gum

No.	Type	Denom.	Color	Unused	Used
RD330	ST3	$30	**bright green**	350.00	190.00
		Cut cancel			75.00
		Perf. initial			22.50
a.		Booklet pane of 4		*3,300.*	
RD331	ST3	$50	**bright green**	750.00	225.00
		Cut cancel			85.00
		Perf. initial			35.00
a.		Booklet pane of 4		*3,300.*	
RD332	ST3	$60	**bright green**	1,000.	250.00
		Cut cancel			125.00
		Perf. initial			60.00
a.		Booklet pane of 4		*4,750.*	
RD333	ST3	$100	**bright green**	150.00	55.00
		Cut cancel			30.00
		Perf. initial			15.00
a.		Vert. pair, imperf. btwn.		2,000.	*1,750.*
RD334	ST3	$500	**bright green**	*2,500.*	350.00
		Cut cancel			160.00
		Perf. initial			95.00
RD335	ST3	$1,000	**bright green**	275.00	85.00
		Cut cancel			35.00
		Perf. initial			22.50
RD336	ST3	$2,500	**bright green**	2,500.	2,500.
		Cut cancel			1,250.
		Perf. initial			900.00
a.		Booklet pane of 4		*10,000.*	
RD337	ST3	$5,000	**bright green**	2,500.	2,500.
		Cut cancel			900.00
		Perf. initial			750.00
a.		Booklet pane of 4		*10,000.*	
RD338	ST3	$10,000	**bright green**	2,500.	1,500.
		Cut cancel			125.00
		Perf. initial			100.00
a.		Booklet pane of 4		*10,000.*	

Stock Transfer Stamps and Type of 1940 Overprinted in Black

Series 1951

1951		**Wmk. 191R**			***Perf. 11***
RD339	ST1	1c	**bright green**	3.00	.75
		Cut cancel			.40
		Perf. initial			.25
RD340	ST1	2c	**bright green**	2.50	.50
		Cut cancel			.30
		Perf. initial			.25
RD341	ST1	4c	**bright green**	3.00	.75
		Cut cancel			.35
		Perf. initial			.25
RD342	ST1	5c	**bright green**	2.25	.55
		Cut cancel			.25
		Perf. initial			.25
RD343	ST1	10c	**bright green**	3.00	.35
		Cut cancel			.25
		Perf. initial			.25
RD344	ST1	20c	**bright green**	10.00	1.25
		Cut cancel			.35
		Perf. initial			.25
RD345	ST1	25c	**bright green**	12.00	1.50
		Cut cancel			.35
		Perf. initial			.25
RD346	ST1	40c	**bright green**	50.00	12.50
		Cut cancel			4.00
		Perf. initial			2.00
RD347	ST1	50c	**bright green**	20.00	1.50
		Cut cancel			.30
		Perf. initial			.25
RD348	ST1	80c	**bright green**	40.00	14.00
		Cut cancel			5.25
		Perf. initial			2.25
RD349	ST2	$1	**bright green**	40.00	1.25
		Cut cancel			.35
		Perf. initial			.25
RD350	ST2	$2	**bright green**	55.00	1.75
		Cut cancel			.35
		Perf. initial			.25
RD351	ST2	$3	**bright green**	70.00	14.00
		Cut cancel			4.50
		Perf. initial			2.00
RD352	ST2	$4	**bright green**	350.00	25.00
		Cut cancel			10.00
		Perf. initial			2.25
RD353	ST2	$5	**bright green**	90.00	4.00
		Cut cancel			.35
		Perf. initial			.25
RD354	ST2	$10	**bright green**	170.00	11.00
		Cut cancel			3.00
		Perf. initial			1.75
RD355	ST2	$20	**bright green**	300.00	35.00
		Cut cancel			10.00
		Perf. initial			5.75

Perf. 12

Without Gum

No.	Type	Denom.	Color	Unused	Used
RD356	ST3	$30	**bright green**	*2,500.*	200.00
		Cut cancel			55.00
		Perf. initial			25.00
RD357	ST3	$50	**bright green**	*2,500.*	125.00
		Cut cancel			32.50
		Perf. initial			20.00
RD358	ST3	$60	**bright green**	*2,500.*	*1,600.*
		Cut cancel			800.00
		Perf. initial			450.00
RD359	ST3	$100	**bright green**	250.00	100.00
		Cut cancel			35.00
		Perf. initial			15.00
RD360	ST3	$500	**bright green**	*2,500.*	550.00
		Cut cancel			210.00
		Perf. initial			125.00
RD361	ST3	$1,000	**bright green**	275.00	125.00
		Cut cancel			80.00
		Perf. initial			57.50
RD362	ST3	$2,500	**bright green**		*4,250.*
		Cut cancel			2,500.
		Perf. initial			2,000.
RD363	ST3	$5,000	**bright green**	—	*3,250.*
		Cut cancel			1,250.
		Perf. initial			1,000.
RD364	ST3	$10,000	**bright green**	*2,000.*	250.00
		Cut cancel			150.00
		Perf. initial			75.00

Stock Transfer Stamps and Type of 1940 Overprinted in Black

Series 1952

1952		**Wmk. 191R**			***Perf. 11***
RD365	ST1	1c	**bright green**	42.50	27.50
		Cut cancel			7.00
		Perf. initial			3.00
RD366	ST1	10c	**bright green**	45.00	27.50
		Cut cancel			7.00
		Perf. initial			3.00
RD367	ST1	20c	**bright green**	400.00	—
		Cut cancel			—
		Perf. initial			—
RD368	ST1	25c	**bright green**	550.00	—
		Cut cancel			—
		Perf. initial			—
RD369	ST1	40c	**bright green**	140.00	55.00
		Cut cancel			18.00
		Perf. initial			12.00
RD370	ST2	$4	**bright green**	*1,500.*	1,250.
		Perf. initial			—
RD371	ST2	$10	**bright green**	*3,500.*	—
		Cut cancel			—
		Perf. initial			—
RD372	ST2	$20	**bright green**	*6,000.*	—
		Cut cancel			—
		Perf. initial			—

Stock Transfer Stamps were discontinued in 1952.

CORDIALS, WINES, ETC. STAMPS

RE1

Inscribed "Series of 1914"

1914	**Wmk. 190**	**Offset Printing**		***Perf. 10***
RE1	RE1	¼c **green**	1.25	.60
RE2	RE1	½c **green**	.60	.55
RE3	RE1	1c **green**	.65	.35
RE4	RE1	1 ½c **green**	3.25	1.90
RE5	RE1	2c **green**	5.25	4.25
RE6	RE1	3c **green**	4.25	1.60
RE7	RE1	4c **green**	3.25	1.90
RE8	RE1	5c **green**	1.75	1.00
RE9	RE1	6c **green**	9.50	4.00
a.		Double impression		—
RE10	RE1	8c **green**	7.25	1.90
RE11	RE1	10c **green**	4.50	3.75
RE12	RE1	20c **green**	6.00	2.40
RE13	RE1	24c **green**	19.00	10.00
RE14	RE1	40c **green**	4.50	.90

RE1a

		Without Gum		***Imperf.***
RE15	RE1a	$2 **green**	12.50	.25
a.		Double impression		125.00

1914		**Wmk. 191R**		***Perf. 10***
RE16	RE1	¼c **green**	8.50	6.50
RE17	RE1	½c **green**	7.50	4.00
RE18	RE1	1c **green**	.30	.25
RE19	RE1	1 ½c **green**	110.00	60.00
RE20	RE1	2c **green**	.30	.25
a.		Double impression		—
RE21	RE1	3c **green**	3.75	2.50
RE22	RE1	4c **green**	1.25	1.10
RE23	RE1	5c **green**	20.00	13.00
a.		Double impression		—
RE24	RE1	6c **green**	.90	.40
RE25	RE1	8c **green**	2.75	.65
RE26	RE1	10c **green**	.90	.35
RE27	RE1	20c **green**	1.10	.55
RE28	RE1	24c **green**	17.50	1.00
RE29	RE1	40c **green**	45.00	14.00

Imperf

Without Gum

RE30	RE1a	$2 **green**	65.00	3.75

Perf. 11

RE31	RE1	2c **green**	160.00	140.00

WINE STAMPS

Issued Without Gum

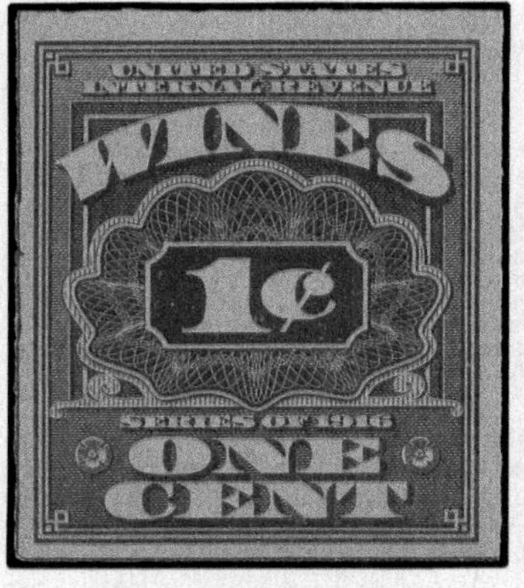

RE2

Inscribed: "Series of 1916"

1916 Wmk. 191R Offset Printing *Rouletted 3½*

Plates of 100 subjects

No.	Type	Denom.	Color	Unused	Used
RE32	RE2	1c	**green**	.50	.45
a.	Double impression			200.00	
RE33	RE2	3c	**green**	6.50	5.25
RE34	RE2	4c	**green**	.40	.50
a.	Double impression				—
RE35	RE2	6c	**green**	2.75	1.10
RE36	RE2	7½c	**green**	7.75	4.25
RE37	RE2	10c	**green**	1.50	.45
RE38	RE2	12c	**green**	5.25	4.75
RE39	RE2	15c	**green**	1.75	1.90
RE40	RE2	18c	**green**	30.00	32.50
RE41	RE2	20c	**green**	.35	.30
RE42	RE2	24c	**green**	6.00	4.00
a.	Double impression			200.00	
RE43	RE2	30c	**green**	3.50	3.75
a.	Double impression				—
RE44	RE2	36c	**green**	30.00	18.00
RE45	RE2	50c	**green**	1.00	.50
RE46	RE2	60c	**green**	7.00	3.00
RE47	RE2	72c	**green**	40.00	37.50
RE48	RE2	80c	**green**	1.50	.90
RE49	RE2	$1.20	**green**	9.00	7.25
RE50	RE2	$1.44	**green**	13.00	3.75
RE51	RE2	$1.60	**green**	35.00	30.00
RE52	RE2	$2	**green**	1.75	1.60

For rouletted 7 see Nos. RE60-RE80, RE102-RE105.

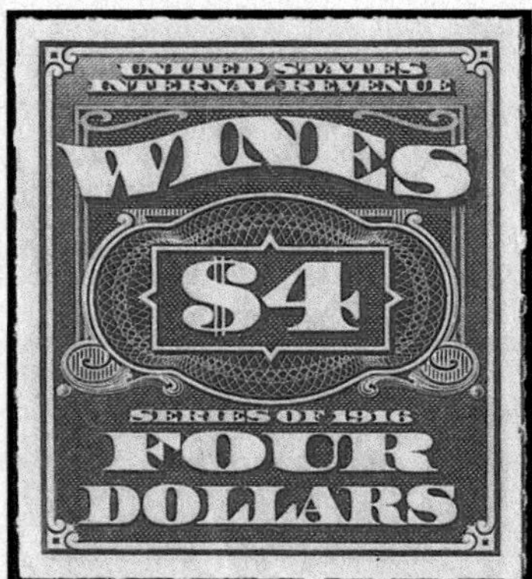

RE3

Engr.

Plates of 50 subjects

No.	Type	Denom.	Color	Unused	Used
RE53	RE3	$4	**green**	1.10	.30
RE54	RE3	$4.80	**green**	4.50	4.00
RE55	RE3	$9.60	**green**	1.60	.45

Nos. RE32-RE55 exist in many shades. Size variations of 1c-$2 are believed due to offset printing. For rouletted 7 see Nos. RE81-RE83, RE106-RE107.

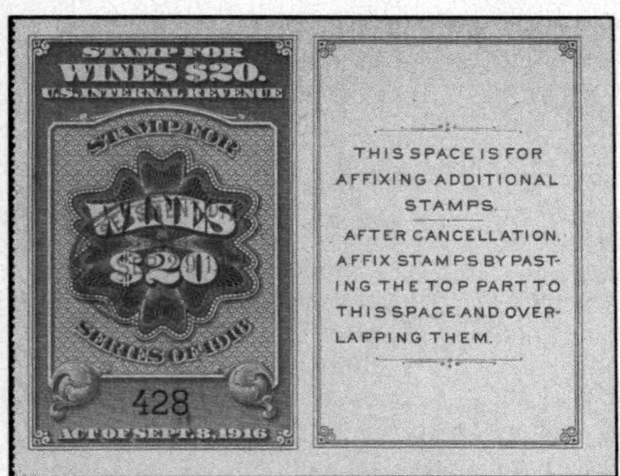

RE4

Illustration reduced.

Plates of 6 subjects

Perf. 12 at left

No.	Type	Denom.	Color	Unused	Used
RE56	RE4	$20	**green**	125.00	60.00
RE57	RE4	$40	**green**	275.00	70.00
RE58	RE4	$50	**green**	90.00	57.50
RE59	RE4	$100	**green**	350.00	225.00

Stamps of design RE4 have an adjoining tablet at right for affixing additional stamps. Values are for examples with the tablets attached. Examples with the tablets removed sell for much less. Used stamps with additional stamps tied on the tablet with cancels sell for about five times the values given. See Nos. RE107A-RE107D.

Same designs as Issue of 1916

1933 Wmk. 191R Offset Printing *Rouletted 7*

No.	Type	Denom.	Color	Unused	Used
RE60	RE2	1c	**light green**	3.25	.50
a.	Double impression				—
RE61	RE2	3c	**light green**	7.50	2.75
RE62	RE2	4c	**light green**	2.25	.55
RE63	RE2	6c	**light green**	13.00	7.50
RE64	RE2	7½c	**light green**	6.75	1.40
RE65	RE2	10c	**light green**	2.75	.25
a.	Double impression				—
RE66	RE2	12c	**light green**	13.00	6.00
RE67	RE2	15c	**light green**	5.00	.40
RE69	RE2	20c	**light green**	7.50	.25
a.	Double impression			—	—
RE70	RE2	24c	**light green**	5.75	.25
a.	Double impression			—	*160.00*
RE71	RE2	30c	**light green**	6.00	.25
a.	Double impression				—
RE72	RE2	36c	**light green**	14.00	1.25
RE73	RE2	50c	**light green**	4.75	.30
RE74	RE2	60c	**light green**	10.00	.25
RE75	RE2	72c	**light green**	17.50	.40
RE76	RE2	80c	**light green**	17.50	.40
RE77	RE2	$1.20	**light green**	17.00	1.75
RE78	RE2	$1.44	**light green**	35.00	5.25
RE79	RE2	$1.60	**light green**	750.00	275.00
RE80	RE2	$2	**light green**	40.00	4.50

Engr.

No.	Type	Denom.	Color	Unused	Used
RE81	RE3	$4	**light green**	50.00	8.75
RE82	RE3	$4.80	**light green**	55.00	17.50
RE83	RE3	$9.60	**light green**	210.00	100.00

RE5

Inscribed: "Series of 1934"

Plates of 200 and 224 subjects

Offset Printing

1934-40 Wmk. 191R *Rouletted 7*

Issued With and Without Gum

No.	Type	Denom.	Color	Unused	Used
RE83A	RE5	⅕c	**green** ('40)	.75	.25
RE84	RE5	½c	**green**	.55	.65
RE85	RE5	1c	**green**	.70	.25
RE86	RE5	1¼c	**green**	1.10	1.00
RE87	RE5	1½c	**green**	7.50	*8.75*
RE88	RE5	2c	**green**	2.25	1.00
RE89	RE5	2½c	**green**	2.00	.70
RE90	RE5	3c	**green**	5.25	4.25
RE91	RE5	4c	**green**	3.00	.30
RE92	RE5	5c	**green**	.70	.25
RE93	RE5	6c	**green**	2.00	.60
RE94	RE5	7½c	**green**	3.25	.25
RE95	RE5	10c	**green**	.50	.70
RE96	RE5	12c	**green**	2.10	.25
RE96A	RE5	14⅖c	**green** ('40)	230.00	3.50
b.	Imperf, pair, without gum			*5,000.*	
RE97	RE5	15c	**green**	.90	.25
RE98	RE5	18c	**green**	1.75	.25
RE99	RE5	20c	**green**	1.40	.25
RE100	RE5	24c	**green**	2.75	.25
RE101	RE5	30c	**green**	2.00	.25

Nos. RE83A-RE101 unused are valued without gum. Examples with gum sell for substantially more.

Nos. RE83A, RE86, RE96A were printed from plates of 200 only and all were issued without gum.

No. RE96Ab was printed but not delivered to the Internal Revenue Service for use.

Plates of 100 subjects

Issued Without Gum

No.	Type	Denom.	Color	Unused	Used
RE102	RE2	40c	**green**	4.75	.25
RE102A	RE2	43⅕c	**green** ('40)	35.00	2.75
RE103	RE2	48c	**green**	45.00	4.00
RE104	RE2	$1	**green**	29.00	11.50
RE105	RE2	$1.50	**green**	45.00	17.00
	Perforated initials				5.75

Engr.

Plates of 50 subjects.

No.	Type	Denom.	Color	Unused	Used
RE106	RE3	$2.50	**green**	52.50	18.00
	Perforated initials				9.00
RE107	RE3	$5	**green**	45.00	7.50
	Perforated initials				3.25

Stamps of types RE5 and RE2 overprinted "Rectified Spirits / Puerto Rico" are listed under Puerto Rico.

Nos. RE102-RE204 issued without gum.

Inscribed: "Series of 1916"

Plates of 6 subjects

1934 *Perf. 12 at left*

No.	Type	Denom.	Color	Unused	Used
RE107A	RE4	$20	**yellow green**		2,500.
RE107B	RE4	$40	**yellow green**		*12,000.*

Perf. 12 At Left

No.	Type	Denom.	Color	Unused	Used
RE107C	RE4	$50	**yellow green**		*10,000.*
RE107D	RE4	$100	**yellow green**	*3,500.*	*1,000.*

Perf. 12½ At Left

No.	Type	Denom.	Color	Unused	Used
RE107E	RE4	$50	**yellow green**	—	*5,000.*
RE107F	RE4	$100	**yellow green**	*1,750.*	500.00

The serial numbers of Nos. RE107A-RE107F are much thinner than on Nos. RE56-RE59. See valuing note after No. RE59.

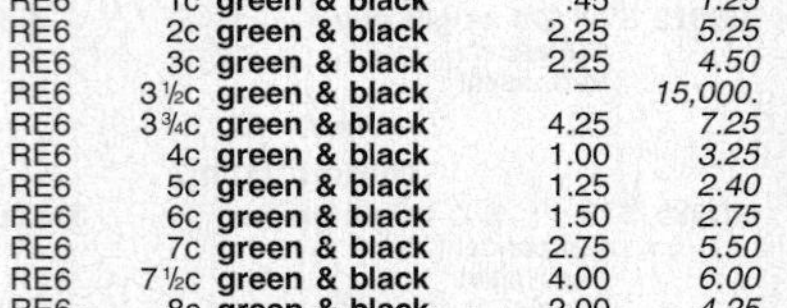

RE6

Offset Printing

Inscribed "Series of 1941"

1942 Wmk. 191R *Rouletted 7*

No.	Type	Denom.	Color	Unused	Used
RE108	RE6	⅕c	**green & black**	.35	*.55*
RE109	RE6	¼c	**green & black**	.90	*2.50*
RE110	RE6	½c	**green & black**	1.10	*2.10*
a.	Horiz. pair, imperf. vertically			200.00	
RE111	RE6	1c	**green & black**	.45	*1.25*
RE112	RE6	2c	**green & black**	2.25	*5.25*
RE113	RE6	3c	**green & black**	2.25	*4.50*
RE114	RE6	3½c	**green & black**	—	*15,000.*
RE115	RE6	3¾c	**green & black**	4.25	*7.25*
RE116	RE6	4c	**green & black**	1.00	*3.25*
RE117	RE6	5c	**green & black**	1.25	*2.40*
RE118	RE6	6c	**green & black**	1.50	*2.75*
RE119	RE6	7c	**green & black**	2.75	*5.50*
RE120	RE6	7½c	**green & black**	4.00	*6.00*
RE121	RE6	8c	**green & black**	2.00	*4.25*
RE122	RE6	9c	**green & black**	6.00	*9.50*
RE123	RE6	10c	**green & black**	2.00	1.10
RE124	RE6	11¼c	**green & black**	2.25	*6.00*
RE125	RE6	12c	**green & black**	3.00	*6.00*
RE126	RE6	14c	**green & black**	15.00	*26.00*
RE127	RE6	15c	**green & black**	2.25	*3.00*
a.	Horiz. pair, imperf. vertically				*1,500.*
RE128	RE6	16c	**green & black**	5.00	*9.00*
RE129	RE6	19⅕c	**green & black**	250.00	7.75
RE130	RE6	20c	**green & black**	2.75	2.10
RE131	RE6	24c	**green & black**	2.00	.25
RE132	RE6	28c	**green & black**	*5,000.*	*2,500.*
RE133	RE6	30c	**green & black**	.55	.25
RE134	RE6	32c	**green & black**	210.00	7.50
RE135	RE6	36c	**green & black**	1.25	.25
RE136	RE6	40c	**green & black**	1.00	.25
RE137	RE6	45c	**green & black**	3.25	.25
RE138	RE6	48c	**green & black**	8.00	9.25
RE139	RE6	50c	**green & black**	3.50	7.50
RE140	RE6	60c	**green & black**	1.60	.25
RE141	RE6	72c	**green & black**	4.75	1.50
RE142	RE6	80c	**green & black**	*400.00*	10.50
RE143	RE6	84c	**green & black**	—	90.00
RE144	RE6	90c	**green & black**	9.00	.25
RE145	RE6	96c	**green & black**	5.50	.30

See Nos. RE182D-RE194.

Denomination Spelled Out in Two Lines — RE7

1942 Engraved, Offset (denominations)

No.	Type	Denom.	Color	Unused	Used
RE146	RE7	$1.20	**yel grn & blk**	3.50	.25
RE147	RE7	$1.44	**yel grn & blk**	.70	.30
a.	Denomination missing (FO)			*2,750.*	*2,750.*
	Pair, one with denomination missing (FO)			—	—
b.	First line small letters, second line larger letters			3,000.	*4,500.*
RE148	RE7	$1.50	**yel grn & blk**	150.00	67.50
RE149	RE7	$1.60	**yel grn & blk**	3.50	1.40
RE150	RE7	$1.68	**yel grn & blk**	120.00	50.00
	Perforated initials				35.00
RE151	RE7	$1.80	**yel grn & blk**	1.00	.25
a.	Pair, one with denomination missing (FO)			*5,000.*	

No. RE151a may be collected as a vertical pair or a horizontal pair.

No.	Type	Denom.	Color	Unused	Used
RE152	RE7	$1.92	**yel grn & blk**	35.00	*72.50*
RE153	RE7	$2.40	**yel grn & blk**	4.75	1.25
RE154	RE7	$3	**yel grn & blk**	35.00	*42.50*
RE155	RE7	$3.36	**yel grn & blk**	92.50	29.00
RE156	RE7	$3.60	**yel grn & blk**	*200.00*	10.00
RE157	RE7	$4	**yel grn & blk**	32.50	5.25
RE158	RE7	$4.80	**yel grn & blk**	*175.00*	3.75
RE159	RE7	$5	**yel grn & blk**	17.50	10.50
RE159A	RE7	$7.14	**yel grn & blk**	*150.00*	
RE160	RE7	$7.20	**yel grn & blk**	7.00	.50
RE161	RE7	$10	**yel grn & blk**	240.00	200.00

RE162	RE7	$20 **yel grn & blk**		130.00	77.50
RE163	RE7	$50 **yel grn & blk**		125.00	77.50
		Perforated initials			21.00
RE164	RE7	$100 **yel grn & blk**		375.00	30.00
		Perforated initials			21.00
RE165	RE7	$200 **yel grn & blk**		190.00	24.00
		Perforated initials			8.75
RE165A	RE7	$300 **yel grn & blk**		*150.00*	
RE165B	RE7	$400 **yel grn & blk**		*8,000.*	*16,000.*
RE166	RE7	$500 **yel grn & blk**		*250.00*	150.00
		Perforated initials			35.00
RE167	RE7	$600 **yel grn & blk**		*200.00*	125.00
RE167A	RE7	$700 **yel grn & blk**		*150.00*	
RE167B	RE7	$800 **yel grn & blk**		*150.00*	
RE168	RE7	$900 **yel grn & blk**		*2,500.*	*4,000.*
		Perforated initials			*1,500.*
RE169	RE7	$1,000 **yel grn & blk**		*250.00*	250.00
RE170	RE7	$2,000 **yel grn & blk**		*3,000.*	*3,000.*
RE171	RE7	$3,000 **yel grn & blk**		200.00	*225.00*
RE172	RE7	$4,000 **yel grn & blk**		*1,000.*	1,000.

Denomination Repeated, Spelled Out in One Line

1949

RE173	RE7	$1 **yellow green & black**		1.75	1.60
RE174	RE7	$2 **yellow green & black**		3.75	2.10
RE175	RE7	$4 **yellow green & black**		1,000.	600.00
		Perforated initials			175.00
RE176	RE7	$5 **yellow green & black**		*100.00*	82.50
RE177	RE7	$6 **yellow green & black**		700.00	700.00
RE178	RE7	$7 **yellow green & black**		*100.00*	47.50
RE179	RE7	$8 **yellow green & black**		1,250.	600.00
		Perforated initials			85.00
RE179A	RE7	$9 **yel grn & blk**		*150.00*	
RE180	RE7	$10 **yellow green & black**		4.00	*5.25*
		Perforated initials			2.10
RE180A	RE7	$12 **yel grn & blk**		*150.00*	
RE181	RE7	$20 **yellow green & black**		25.00	5.25
		Perforated initials			1.90
RE182	RE7	$30 **yellow green & black**		*2,000.*	1,250.
RE182A	RE7	$40 **yel grn & blk**		*150.00*	
RE182B	RE7	$60 **yel grn & blk**		*150.00*	
RE182C	RE7	$70 **yel grn & blk**		*150.00*	
RE182D	RE7	$80 **yel grn & blk**		*150.00*	
RE182E	RE7	$90 **yel grn & blk**		*150.00*	

The $90 denomination, No. RE182E, was printed but was not delivered to the Internal Revenue Service for use.

Types of 1942-49

1951-54 — **Offset Printing**

RE182F	RE6	1 7/10c **green & black**		*22,500.*	*25,000.*
RE183	RE6	3⅖c **green & black**		20.00	*52.50*
RE183A	RE6	6 7/10c **green & black**		*150.00*	
RE184	RE6	8½c **green & black**		6.00	*20.00*
RE184A	RE6	10⅕c **green & black**		*150.00*	
RE185	RE6	13⅖c **green & black**		27.50	*82.50*
RE186	RE6	17c **green & black**		6.00	*15.00*
RE187	RE6	20⅖c **green & black**		110.00	62.50
RE188	RE6	33½c **green & black**		35.00	*92.50*
RE189	RE6	38¼c **green & black**		150.00	90.00
RE190	RE6	40⅘c **green & black**		1.40	.80
RE191	RE6	51c **green & black**		1.50	1.40
RE192	RE6	67c **green & black**		4.75	4.25
RE193	RE6	68c **green & black**		1.00	.70
RE194	RE6	80⅖c **green & black**		175.00	110.00

The 6 7/10c and 10⅕c denominations, Nos. RE183A and RE184A, were printed but were not delivered to the Internal Revenue Service for use.

Engr.

Denomination Spelled Out in Two Lines in Small Letters

Two types of $1.60⅘:

I — The "4" slants sharply. Loop of "5" almost closes to form oval. Each numeral 2mm high.

II — The "4" is less slanted. Loop of "5" more open and nearly circular. Each numeral 2½mm high.

RE195	RE7	$1.50¾ **yel grn & blk**		17.50	*47.50*
RE196	RE7	$1.60⅘ **yel grn & blk** (I)		1.60	1.00
	a.	"DOLLLAR"		75.00	25.00
		Perforated initials			20.00
	b.	As "a," horiz. pair, one with denomination missing		*6,250.*	
	c.	Type II		1,000.	250.00
	d.	First line larger letters, second line small letters		*15,000.*	*5,000.*
RE197	RE7	$1.88 3/10 **yel grn & blk**		240.00	85.00
		Perforated initials			35.00

Denomination Spelled Out in Two Lines in Slightly Larger Letters Same as Nos. RE146-RE172

RE198	RE7	$1.60⅘ **yel grn & blk** (II)		35.00	6.25
	b.	Type I ('53)		75.00	25.00
RE199	RE7	$2.01 **yel grn & blk**		1.25	1.00
RE200	RE7	$2.68 **yel grn & blk**		1.25	1.40
RE201	RE7	$4.08 **yel grn & blk**		50.00	35.00
RE202	RE7	$5.76 **yel grn & blk**		275.00	225.00
RE203	RE7	$8.16 **yel grn & blk**		6.50	7.00
RE204	RE7	$9.60 **yel grn & blk**		*4,500.*	*7,500.*

No. RE196d unused is unique.

Wine stamps were discontinued on Dec. 31, 1954.

BEER STAMPS

Basic stamps were printed by the Bureau of Engraving and Printing, unless otherwise noted.

All stamps are imperforate, unless otherwise noted.

Values for Nos. REA1-REA13 are for stamps with small faults, due to the fragile nature of the thin paper. Used values for Nos. REA14-REA199 are for canceled stamps with small faults.

All examples of Nos. REA1-REA13 contain a circular pattern of 31 perforations in the design, 27 or 28½mm in diameter, often poorly punched.

Values for cut squares of Nos. REA1-REA13 are for margins clear of the design. Die cut and cut to shape stamps are valued for margins clear to slightly cutting into the design.

Eric Jackson, Michael Aldrich, Henry Tolman II and Thomas W. Priester helped the editors extensively in compiling the listings.

An excellent study of beer stamps by Frank Applegate appeared in *Weekly Philatelic Gossip* from Oct. 1-Nov. 26, 1927.

A List of the Beer Stamps of the United States of America by Ernest R. Vanderhoof appeared in the *American Philatelist* in June 1934. This was reprinted in pamphlet form.

United States Beer Stamps by Thomas W. Priester, published in 1979, comprised an illustrated and priced catalogue, illustrations of all known provisional surcharges, background notes on the stamps and tax laws, and a census of over 27,500 stamps. The catalogue and census sections were updated in the 1990 edition.

Printed by the Treasury Department. Tax rate $1 per barrel (bbl.).

12½c = ⅛ barrel	$1 = 1 barrel
16⅔c = ⅙ barrel	$2 = 1 hogshead
25c = ¼ barrel	$5 = 5 barrels
33⅓c = ⅓ barrel	$10 = 10 barrels
50c = ½ barrel	$25 = 25 barrels

1866 — **Engr.**

REA1	12½c **orange**	450.	750.
	Cut to shape		125.
a.	Die cut	500.	325.
b.	Silk paper		*2,250.*
REA2	16⅔c **dark green**	200.	450.
	Cut to shape		30.
a.	Die cut		85.
REA3	25c **blue**	75.	150.
	Cut to shape		25.
a.	Die cut		50.
b.	Silk paper		*4,500.*
	Double transfer		—
REA4	50c **orange brown**	35.	50.
	Printed cancellation, "A.S. 1869"		200.
	Cut to shape		10.
a.	Die cut		200.
REA5	$1 **black**	500.	275.
	Cut to shape		75.
a.	Die cut		225.
REA6	$2 **red**	1,500.	1,600.
	Cut to shape		200.
a.	Die cut		1,000.

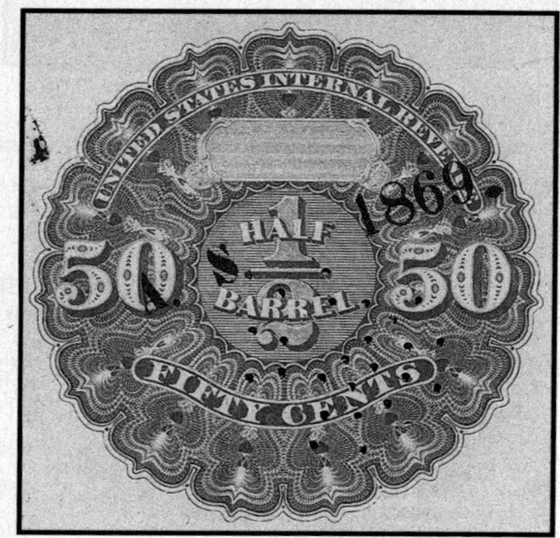

Printed by the Treasury Department. See individual rates before No. REA1.

1867 — **Engr.**

REA7	12½c **orange**	*3,250.*	2,000.
	Cut to shape		1,000.
a.	Die cut	1,000.	1,500.
REA8	16⅔c **dark green**	*3,500.*	*2,600.*
	Cut to shape		550.
a.	Die cut		*2,000.*
REA9	25c **blue**	250.	300.
	Cut to shape		50.
a.	Die cut		450.
REA10	33⅓c **violet brown**		*5,500.*
	Cut to shape		*2,750.*
b.	Silk paper		*3,500.*
c.	33⅓c **ocher red,** cut to shape		*3,500.*
d.	33⅓c **ocher red,** die cut		*14,500.*
REA11	50c **orange brown**	75.	125.
	Printed cancellation, "A.S. 1869"		425.
	Cut to shape		35.
a.	Die cut		150.
REA12	$1 **black**		2,500.
	Cut to shape		400.
a.	Die cut		1,250.
REA13	$2 **red**	*4,000.*	*1,350.*
	Cut to shape	1,250.	500.
a.	Die cut		*1,500.*

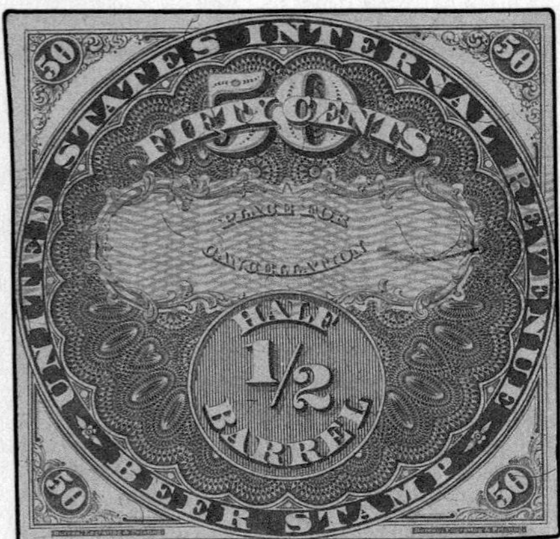

See individual rates before No. REA1.

Silk Paper

1870 Engr. Lilac Security Lines

REA14 12½c **brown** *1,000.* 350.
a. Yellow security lines 2,500. 2,000.
REA15 16⅔c **yellow orange** 300.
a. Yellow security lines *1,100.*
b. Gray-green and yellow security lines *2,500.*
c. 16⅔c **yellow ocher,** lilac security lines 2,000.
REA16 25c **green** 125.
a. Yellow security lines 225.
b. Gray-green & yellow security lines *2,500.*
REA17 50c **red** 400. 125.
a. Yellow security lines 2,500. 1,250.
b. Gray-green and yellow security lines 2,250. 2,000.
c. 50c **brick red,** lilac security lines 1,500.
d. 50c **brick red,** yellow security lines *3,250.*
REA18 $1 **blue** *3,000. 1,500.*
a. Yellow security lines *1,500.* 500.
b. Gray-green and yellow security lines *2,500.*
REA19 $2 **black** *2,000.* 950.
a. Yellow security lines *4,500.*
b. Gray-green and yellow security lines *5,000.*

The security lines were printed across the center of the stamp where the cancel was to be placed.

Andrew Jackson

Designs: 16⅔c, Abraham Lincoln. 25c, Daniel Webster. 33⅓c, David G. Farragut. 50c, William T. Sherman. $1, Hugh McCulloch. $2, Alexander Hamilton.

Centers printed by the Bureau of Engraving and Printing. Frames printed by the National Bank Co.

See individual rates before No. REA1.

1871 Engr.

Centers, Plate Letters and Position Numbers in Black

REA20 12½c **blue,** white silk paper 125.
a. Pinkish gray silk paper 200.
b. Gray silk paper 65.
c. Green silk paper 200.
REA21 16⅔c **vermilion,** white silk paper 400.
a. Pinkish gray silk paper 500.
b. Gray silk paper 425.
c. Green silk paper 425.
REA22 25c **green,** white silk paper 25.
a. Pinkish gray silk paper 125.
b. Gray silk paper 50.
c. Green silk paper 30.
REA23 33⅓c **orange,** green silk paper *4,500.*
b. Gray silk paper *11,000.*
REA24 33⅓c **violet brown,** white silk paper 12,500.

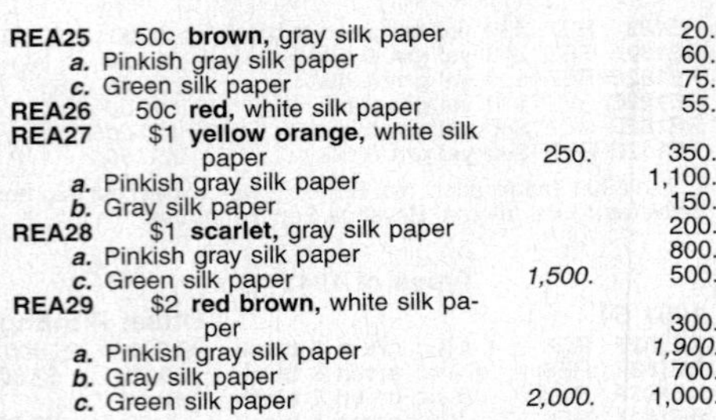

REA25 50c **brown,** gray silk paper 20.
a. Pinkish gray silk paper 60.
c. Green silk paper 75.
REA26 50c **red,** white silk paper 55.
REA27 $1 **yellow orange,** white silk paper 250. 350.
a. Pinkish gray silk paper 1,100.
b. Gray silk paper 150.
REA28 $1 **scarlet,** gray silk paper 200.
a. Pinkish gray silk paper 800.
c. Green silk paper *1,500.* 500.
REA29 $2 **red brown,** white silk paper 300.
a. Pinkish gray silk paper *1,900.*
b. Gray silk paper 700.
c. Green silk paper *2,000.* 1,000.

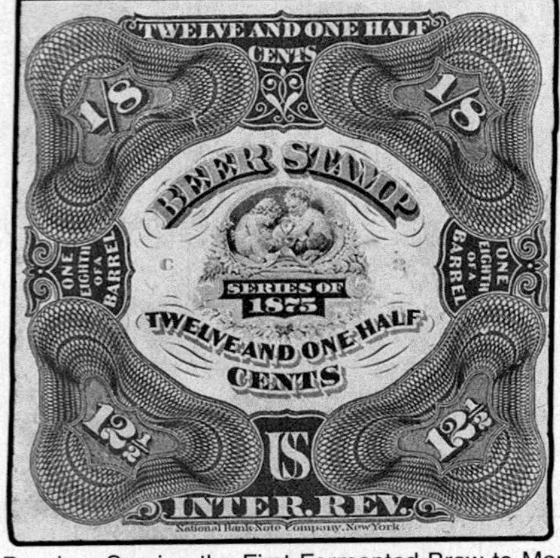

Bacchus Serving the First Fermented Brew to Man

Printed by the National Bank Note Co. See individual rates before No. REA1.

1875 Typo. & Engr.

Center in Black

REA30 12½c **blue** 25.00
REA31 16⅔c **red brown** 150.00
REA32 25c **green** 40.00
a. Inverted center *55,000.*
REA33 33⅓c **violet** *3,000.* 1,250.
REA34 50c **orange** 100.00 100.00
REA35 $1 **red** 225.00 225.00
REA36 $2 **brown** 650.00
a. Inverted center *1,500. 55,000.*

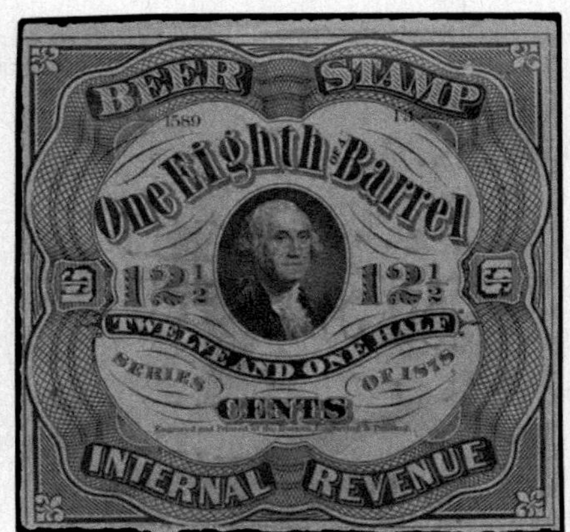

Designs: 12½c, Washington. 16⅔c, Corwin. 25c, Benton. 33⅓c, Thomas. 50c, Jefferson. $1, Johnson. $2, Wright.

Stamps on pale green paper have short greenish blue fibers. Plate designations for center consist of plate letter or number at left and position number at right.

See individual rates before No. REA1.

1878 Typo. & Engr. Wmk. USIR

Center, Plate Letters and Position Numbers in Black

REA37 12½c **blue,** *green* 7.50
b. Green silk paper, unwmkd. 1,250.
c. Pale green paper 200.00
With plate number and position number *1,250.*
d. Light blue paper, with plate number (and position number) 35.00
e. Blue paper, no plate letter or number or position number 30.00
f. Dark blue paper, no plate letter or number or position number 50.00
REA38 16⅔c **light brown,** *green* 7.50
One line under Cents 75.00
b. Green silk paper, unwmkd., one line under Cents 250.00 140.00

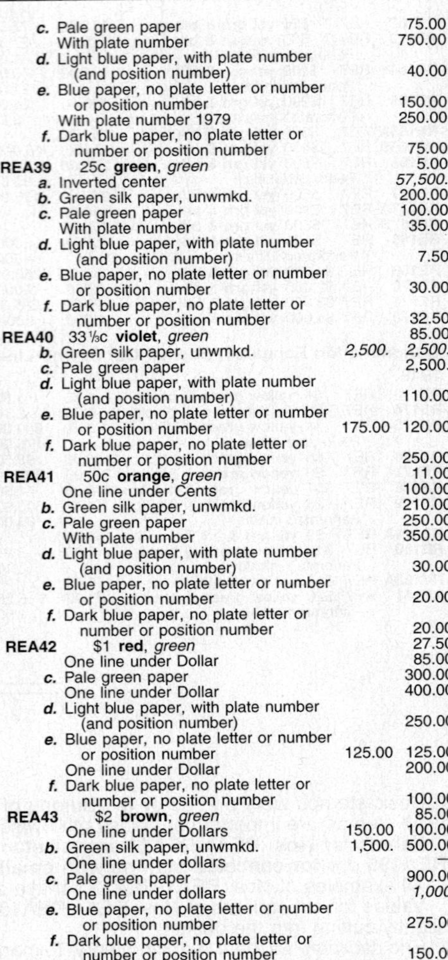

c. Pale green paper 75.00
With plate number 750.00
d. Light blue paper, with plate number (and position number) 40.00
e. Blue paper, no plate letter or number or position number 150.00
With plate number 1979 250.00
f. Dark blue paper, no plate letter or number or position number 75.00
REA39 25c **green,** *green* 5.00
a. Inverted center *57,500.*
b. Green silk paper, unwmkd. 200.00
c. Pale green paper 100.00
With plate number 35.00
d. Light blue paper, with plate number (and position number) 7.50
e. Blue paper, no plate letter or number or position number 30.00
f. Dark blue paper, no plate letter or number or position number 32.50
REA40 33⅓c **violet,** *green* 85.00
b. Green silk paper, unwmkd. *2,500. 2,500.*
c. Pale green paper 2,500.
d. Light blue paper, with plate number (and position number) 110.00
e. Blue paper, no plate letter or number or position number 175.00 120.00
f. Dark blue paper, no plate letter or number or position number 250.00
REA41 50c **orange,** *green* 11.00
One line under Cents 100.00
b. Green silk paper, unwmkd. 210.00
c. Pale green paper 250.00
With plate number 350.00
d. Light blue paper, with plate number (and position number) 30.00
e. Blue paper, no plate letter or number or position number 20.00
f. Dark blue paper, no plate letter or number or position number 20.00
REA42 $1 **red,** *green* 27.50
One line under Dollar 85.00
c. Pale green paper 300.00
One line under Dollar 400.00
d. Light blue paper, with plate number (and position number) 250.00
e. Blue paper, no plate letter or number or position number 125.00 125.00
One line under Dollar 200.00
f. Dark blue paper, no plate letter or number or position number 100.00
REA43 $2 **brown,** *green* 85.00
One line under Dollars 150.00 100.00
b. Green silk paper, unwmkd. 1,500. 500.00
One line under dollars —
c. Pale green paper 900.00
One line under dollars *1,000.*
e. Blue paper, no plate letter or number or position number 275.00
f. Dark blue paper, no plate letter or number or position number 150.00

See Nos. REA58-REA64, REA65-REA71, REA75-REA81.

Stamps of 1878 Surcharged in Various Ways

Type B

Four general surcharge types:

A — Bureau of Engraving and Printing surcharge "TAX $2 PER BBL./SERIES OF 1898" printed diagonally in red, letters 4¼mm high.

B — same, but letters 5½mm high.

C — handstamped provisional surcharge with similiar wording in 1-3 lines, more than 30 styles.

D — printed provisional 2-line surcharges, horizontal in various colors.

Tax rate $2 per bbl.

25c = ⅛ barrel	$1 = ½ barrel
33⅓c = ⅙ barrel	$2 = 1 barrel
50c = ¼ barrel	$4 = 1 hogshead
66⅔c = ⅓ barrel	

1898 Type A

REA44 (25c) on 12½c #REA37f 400.00
a. Type C surcharge 325.00
b. Type D surcharge *1,500.*
REA45 (33⅓c) on 16⅔c #REA38e 100.00
a. on #REA38f 200.00
b. As "a," type C surcharge 350.00

c.	As "a," type D surcharge	750.00	500.00
d.	on #REA38d		800.00
e.	As "c," double impression of surcharge		—
REA46	(50c) on 25c #REA39f		90.00
a.	Type C surcharge		150.00
b.	Type D surcharge		2,250.
c.	on #REA39e		*1,750.*
d.	on #REA39, type C surcharge		*5,750.*
REA47	(66⅔c) on 33⅓c #REA40, plate B		1,500.
REA48	($1) on 50c #REA41f		35.00
a.	Type C surcharge		375.00
b.	Type D surcharge		750.00
REA49	($2) on $1 #REA42f		125.00
a.	Type C surcharge		*1,500.*
b.	Type D surcharge		*1,750.*
c.	on #REA42e, type C surcharge		*2,250.*
REA50	($4) on $2 #REA43f	*1,500.*	500.00
a.	Type C surcharge		700.00
b.	Type D surcharge		*3,000.*
c.	on #REA43e, type C surcharge		*4,000.*

Type B

REA51	(25c) on 12½c #REA37f		95.00
a.	on #REA37e	225.00	225.00
b.	As "a," type C surcharge		*7,250.*
REA52	(33⅓c) on 16⅔c #REA38d	2,000.	1,250.
a.	on #REA38f	*1,100.*	*1,500.*
b.	on #REA38e	*1,100.*	*1,500.*
REA53	(50c) on 25c #REA39f		25.00
a.	on #REA39e		25.00
REA54	(66⅔c) on 33⅓c #REA40f		*9,500.*
a.	Type D surcharge		*9,000.*
b.	On #REA40, plate B, dark blue paper		*6,000.*
REA55	($1) on 50c #REA41f		12.50
REA56	($2) on $1 #REA42f		50.00
REA57	($4) on $2 #REA43f	1,000.	500.00

Counterfeit type C and D overprints exist.

Designs: 25c, Washington. 33⅓c, Corwin. 50c, Benton. 66⅔c, Thomas. $1, Jefferson. $2, Johnson. $4, Wright.
See individual rates before No. REA44.

1898 — Typo. & Engr. — Wmk. USIR

Center in Black, Dark Blue Paper

REA58	25c **blue**	110.
REA59	33⅓c **brown**	85.
REA60	50c **green**	25.
REA61	66⅔c **violet**	*12,500.*
REA62	$1 **yellow**	20.
REA63	$2 **red**	25.
REA64	$4 **dark brown**	225.

Used values for 1901-51 issues are for stamps canceled by perforated company name (or abbreviation) and date.

Designs: 20c, Washington. 26⅔c, Corwin. 40c, Benton. 53⅓c, Thomas. 80c, Jefferson. $1.60, Johnson. $3.20, Wright.
Tax rate $1.60 per bbl.

20c = ⅛ barrel
26⅔c = ⅙ barrel
40c = ¼ barrel
53⅓c = ⅓ barrel
80c = ½ barrel
$1.60 = 1 barrel
$3.20 = 1 hogshead

Engr. (center) & Typo. (frame)

1901 — Wmk. USIR

Dark Blue Paper

REA65	20c **blue**		75.
REA66	26⅔c **yellow orange**		75.
REA67	40c **green**		17.50
REA68	53⅓c **violet**	*8,500.*	*7,000.*
REA69	80c **brown**		17.50
REA70	$1.60 **red**		75.
REA71	$3.20 **dark brown**		1,250.

Stamps of 1901 Provisionally Surcharged by Bureau of Engraving & Printing Diagonally in Red "TAX $1 PER BBL./SERIES OF 1902"

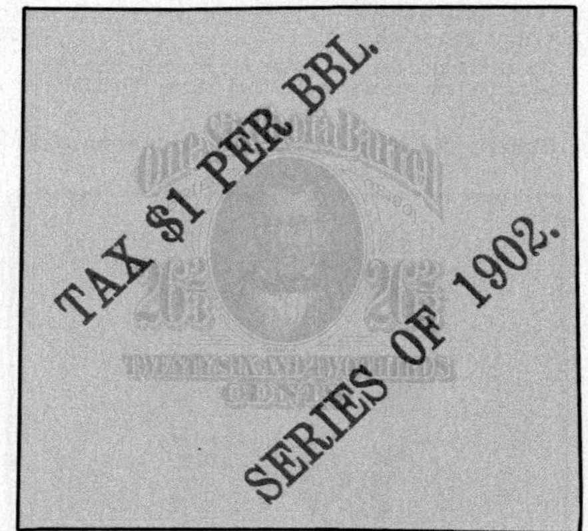

1902

REA72	(16⅔c) on 26⅔c #REA66		150.
REA73	(33⅓c) on 53⅓c #REA68		*5,250.*
REA74	($2) on $3.20 #REA71	*1,500.*	1,000.

Designs: 12½c, Washington. 16⅔c, Corwin. 25c, Benton. 33⅓c, Thomas. 50c, Jefferson. $1, Johnson. $2, Wright.
Stamps on pale green paper have short greenish blue fibers.
See individual rates before No. REA1.

1902 — Typo. & Engr. — Wmk. USIR

Center in Black

REA75	12½c **blue**		
a.	Dark blue paper		75.00
b.	Pale green paper		350.00
c.	Light blue paper		110.00
d.	Bright blue paper		50.00
REA76	16⅔c **yellow orange**		
a.	Dark blue paper		250.00
b.	Pale green paper		350.00
c.	Light blue paper	225.00	225.00
d.	Bright blue paper		400.00
REA77	25c **green**		
a.	Dark blue paper		25.00
b.	Pale green paper		85.00
c.	Light blue paper		25.00
d.	Bright blue paper		30.00
REA78	33⅓c **violet**		
a.	Dark blue paper		275.00
c.	Light blue paper		750.00
d.	Bright blue paper		1,000.
REA79	50c **brown**		
a.	Dark blue paper		20.00
b.	Pale green paper		30.00
c.	Light blue paper		25.00
d.	Bright blue paper		20.00
REA80	$1 **red**		
a.	Dark blue paper		125.00
b.	Pale green paper	400.00	325.00
c.	Light blue paper		75.00
d.	Bright blue paper		75.00
REA81	$2 **dark brown**		
a.	Dark blue paper		1,250.
b.	Pale green paper		900.00
c.	Light blue paper		575.00
d.	Bright blue paper		725.00

For surcharges see Nos. REA99A, REA100A, REA100Ab, REA141.

In the 1911-33 issues, the 5-25 barrel sizes were generally available only as center cutouts of the stamp. Values for these are for cutout portions that show enough of the denomination (or surcharge) to identify the item.

See individual rates before No. REA1.

1909-11 — Engr. — Wmk. USIR

Paper of Various Shades of Blue

REA82	12½c **black**		500.00
REA83	16⅔c **black**	200.00	90.00
REA84	25c **black**	550.00	450.00
REA85	33⅓c **black**		*20,000.*
REA86	50c **black**	55.00	6.00
REA87	$1 **black**	1,000.	750.00
REA88	$2 **black**	*10,000.*	*8,000.*

Center Cutout Only

REA89	$5 **black,** *1911*	*150.00*
REA90	$10 **black,** *1911*	*250.00*
REA91	$25 **black,** *1911*	*250.00*

For surcharges see Nos. REA97, REA99-REA100, REA103-REA105, REA128.

1910 — Engr. — Wmk. USIR

Paper of Various Shades of Blue

REA92	12½c **red brown**	75.00
REA93	25c **green**	10.00
REA94	$1 **carmine**	110.00
REA95	$2 **orange**	125.00

For surcharges see Nos. REA96, REA98, REA101-REA102, REA126.

1914 Provisional Issue

Stamps of of 1902-11 With Printed Provisional BEP Diagonal Surcharge "EMERGENCY/TAX/UNDER ACT OF 1914" in Red, Black or Yellow, or Handstamped Surcharge of Value Spelled Out in Full and Separate "Roscoe Irwin" Handstamped Facsimile Signature

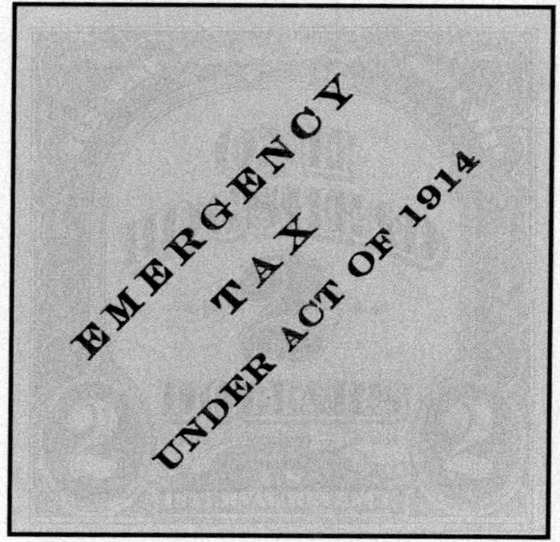

Tax rate $1.50 per bbl.

18¾c = ⅛ barrel	$1.50 = 1 barrel
25c = ⅙ barrel	$3 = 1 hogshead
37½c = ¼ barrel	$7.5 = 5 barrels
50c = ⅓ barrel	$15 = 10 barrels
75c = ½ barrel	$37.50 = 25 barrels

1914 **Entire Stamps**

No.	Description		
REA96	(18¾c) on 12½ #REA92		65.00
REA97	(25c) on 16⅔c #REA83		60.00
REA98	(37½c) on 25c #REA93		7.50
	a. 37½c handstamped; 50mm signature		750.00
REA99	(50c) on 33⅓c #REA85		225.00
REA99A	(50c) on 33⅓c #REA78d	*1,750.*	900.00
REA100	(75c) on 50c #REA86		7.50
	c. 75c handstamped on #REA86; 50mm signature		175.00
	d. As "c," 65mm signature		350.00
REA100A	(75c) On 50c #REA79c		1,000.
	b. (75c) On 50c #REA79b		*11,500.*
REA101	($1.50) on $1 #REA94		50.00
	a. $1.50 handstamped; 50mm signature		*2,000.*
	b. As "a," 65mm signature		*9,000.*
REA102	($3.00) on $2 #REA95		75.00
	a. $3 handstamped; 76mm signature		*2,750.*

Center Cutout Only

No.	Description		
REA103	($7.50) on $5 #REA89		17.50
REA104	($15) on $10 #REA90		160.00
REA105	($37.50) on $25 #REA91		225.00

For surcharges see Nos. REA119, REA123, REA133, REA140, REA140A.

See individual rates before No. REA96.

1914 **Engr.** **Wmk. USIR**

Paper of Various Shades of Blue

Entire Stamp

No.	Description		
REA106	18¾c **red brown**		85.00
REA107	25c **black**		175.00
	a. 25c **violet blue**	*3,500.*	*2,500.*
REA108	37½c **green**		17.50
	a. 37½c **black**		*32,500.*
REA108B	50c **black**		—
REA109	75c **black**		6.00
REA110	$1.50 **red orange**		30.00
REA111	$3 **orange**		200.00

Center Cutout Only

No.	Description		
REA112	$7.50 **black**		10.00
REA113	$15 **black**		15.00
REA114	$37.50 **black**		7.50

For surcharges see Nos. REA118, REA120, REA120a, REA121, REA124-REA125, REA127, REA129-REA131, REA134, REA134a, REA137, REA144, REA146-REA149.

See individual rates before No. REA96.

1916 **Engr.** **Wmk. USIR**

Paper of Various Shades of Greenish Blue

Entire Stamp

No.	Description		
REA115	37½c **green**		110.00
REA116	75c **black**		45.00

For surcharges see Nos. REA122, REA124, REA138. Surcharge also exists in manuscript on No. REA115.

Stamps of 1914-16 Provisionally Surcharged Types A, B & C

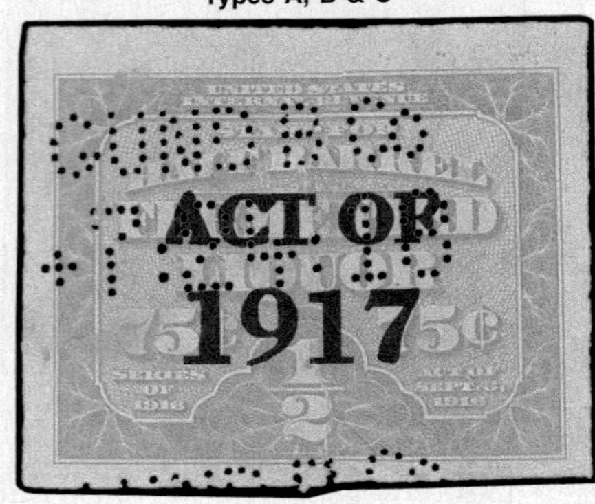

Type C

Surcharge types:

A — "ACT OF 1917" handstamped in 1-3 lines in more than 30 styles.

B — "ACT OF 1917" locally printed horizontally in black or red.

C — "ACT OF 1917" printed in black or red by BEP, horizontally on ⅛ bbl-1 hhd and reading down on 5-25 bbl.

Surcharge also exists in manuscript on some values. Tax rate $3 per bbl.

37½c = ⅛ barrel	$3 = 1 barrel
50c = ⅙ barrel	$6 = 1 hogshead
75c = ¼ barrel	$15 = 5 barrels
$1 = ⅓ barrel	$30 = 10 barrels
$1.50 = ½ barrel	$75 = 25 barrels

1917 **Type A Surcharge**

Entire Stamp

No.	Description		
REA117	(37½c) on #REA96		*27,500.*
REA118	(37½c) on #REA106		325.00
	b. Type B surcharge		*15,000.*
	c. Type C surcharge	500.00	500.00
	d. As No. REA118, double surcharge		—
REA119	(50c) on #REA97		150.00
REA120	(50c) on #REA107a	1,000.	600.00
	a. On #REA107	500.00	500.00
REA120B	(75c) on #REA98		*25,000.*
REA121	(75c) on #REA108		140.00
REA122	(75c) on #REA115		60.00
	b. Type B surcharge		10,000.
	c. Type C surcharge		100.00
REA123	($1) on #REA99		175.00
REA124	($1.50) on #REA116		75.00
	b. Type B surcharge		*10,000.*
	c. Type C surcharge	45.00	7.50
	d. As "c," inverted surcharge	1,750.	
	e. As No. REA124, double surcharge		—

$1.50 surcharge exists in manuscript on No. REA109. Value, $1,250.

No.	Description		
REA125	($3) on #REA110	100.00	100.00
	c. Type C surcharge		40.00
REA126	($6) on #REA102		*5,000.*
REA127	($6) on #REA111	1,000.	500.00

Center Cutout Only

No.	Description		
REA128	($15) on #REA103		500.00
REA129	($15) on #REA112, entire stamp, type C surcharge	6,000.	
REA130	($30) on #REA113		100.00
	c. Type C surcharge		45.00
REA131	($75) on #REA114		225.00
	c. Type C surcharge		12.50

For surcharges see Nos. REA132, REA132a, REA135-REA136, REA139-REA139b, REA142-REA143, REA145, REA150-REA151.

Stamps of 1914-17 Provisionally Surcharged "ACT OF 1918" or "Revenue Act of 1918" With Rubber Stamp in Various Colors in More Than 20 Styles

A subtype has the incorrect date of 1919 due to the effective date of the act (at least five styles).

Tax rate $6 per bbl.

75c = ⅛ barrel	$6 = 1 barrel
$1 = ⅙ barrel	$12 = 1 hogshead
$1.50 = ¼ barrel	$30 = 5 barrels
$2 = ⅓ barrel	$60 = 10 barrels
$3 = ½ barrel	$150 = 25 barrels

1918 **Entire Stamp**

No.	Description		
REA132	(75c) on #REA118	900.	600.
	a. On #REA118c	1,000.	1,750.
REA133	($1) on #REA97	*3,500.*	*3,000.*
REA134	($1) on #REA107	2,500.	
	a. On #REA107a	10,000.	

Exists with additional overprint "Non-Intoxicating, containing not to/exceed 2¾% of Alcohol by weight." Value, *$1,750.*

No.	Description		
REA135	($1) on #REA119	8,000.	
REA136	($1) on #REA120		*2,500.*
REA137	($1.50) on #REA108	*2,000.*	1,100.
	a. Surcharge dated "1919"		3,500.
REA138	($1.50) on #REA115	*3,000.*	1,250.
REA139	($1.50) on #REA122c		75.
	a. Surcharge dated "1919"	350.	60.
	b. On #REA122	1,600.	1,600.
REA140	($2) on #REA99	2,000.	1,250.
REA140A	($2) on #REA99A	1,500.	
REA141	($2) on #REA99A	*5,000.*	*5,000.*

No. REA141 bears additional 1917 provisional surcharge, as well as the 1914 surcharge, but was not issued in that form without 1918 surcharge.

No.	Description		
REA142	($2) on #REA123	*27,500.*	
REA143	($3) on #REA124c	175.	75.
	a. Surcharge dated "1919"	750.	600.
REA144	($6) on #REA110	*2,000.*	1,000.
REA145	($6) on #REA125c		50.
	a. Surcharge dated "1919"	750.	500.
REA146	($12) on #REA111	*2,000.*	1,000.
REA147	($12) on #REA111		75.

No. REA147 bears additional 1917 Type C provisional surcharge but was not issued in that form without 1918 surcharge.

Center Cutout Only

No.	Description		
REA148	($30) on #REA112		85.
REA149	($60) on #REA113		85.
REA150	($60) on #REA130c		350.
	a. Entire stamp	5,000.	
REA151	($150) on #REA131c		45.
	a. Entire stamp	8,000.	

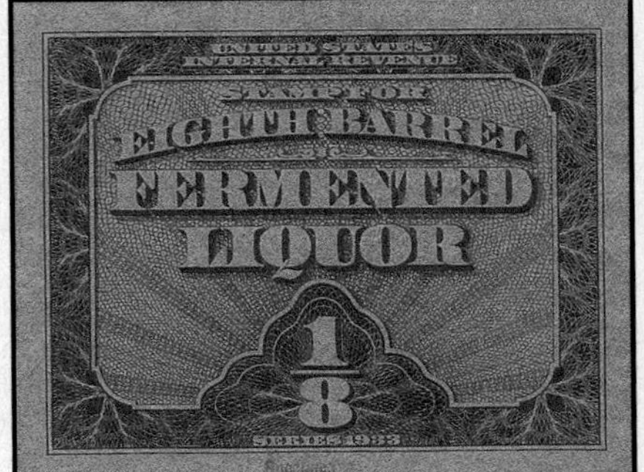

REA152-REA158

REA159-REA161

Tax rate $5 per barrel through Jan. 11, 1934. $6 rate also effective Dec. 5, 1933. Provisional handstamp "Surcharged $6.00 Rate" in 1-3 lines (seven styles).

1933 Engr. Wmk. USIR

Paper of Various Shades of Greenish Blue to Blue

Type A

Entire Stamp

REA152	⅛ bbl., **violet red**		17.50
a.	Provisional surcharge, $6 rate		4,500.
REA153	⅙ bbl., **purple**		700.00
REA154	¼ bbl., **green**		8.00
a.	Provisional surcharge, $6 rate		—
REA155	⅓ bbl., **brown orange**		2,750.
REA156	½ bbl., **orange**	70.00	5.00
a.	Provisional surcharge, $6 rate		*1,750.*
REA157	1 bbl., **blue**		25.00
a.	Provisional surcharge, $6 rate		*3,000.*
REA158	1 hhd., **black**		*9,000.*
REA159	5 bbl., **black,** center cut-out only		250.00
REA160	10 bbl., **black,** with cut-out center, rouletted 7 at left		*7,500.*
a.	Center cutout only		250.00
REA161	25 bbl., **black,** with cut-out center, rouletted 7 at left		7,500.
a.	Center cutout only		250.00

Center cutout portions of Nos. REA159-REA161 are on greenish blue paper. See Nos. REA177-REA178A for examples on bright blue paper.

Nos. REA152-REA159, REA161 Surcharged in Black

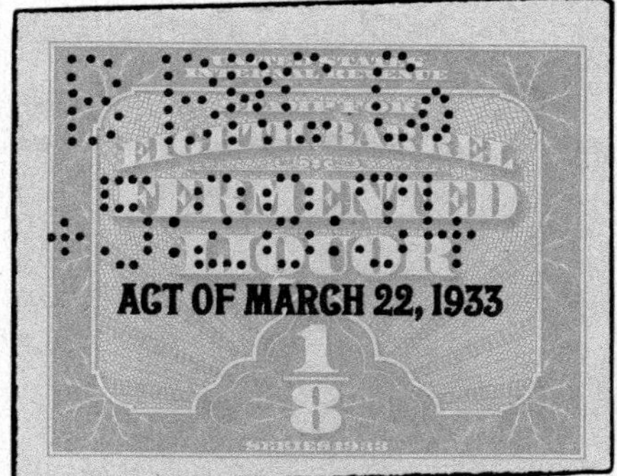

Type B

A — additional provisional handstamped surcharge.
B — additional manuscript and handstamped surcharges.
Tax rate same as Nos. REA152-REA161.

1933 Engr. Wmk. USIR

Entire Stamp

REA162	⅛ bbl., **violet red**		10.00
REA163	⅙ bbl., **purple**		175.00
REA164	¼ bbl., **green**		15.00
a.	With 1918 provisional handstamped surcharge, $6 rate		*2,250.*
b.	Type A surcharge, $6 rate		*4,500.*
REA165	⅓ bbl., **brown orange**		*6,000.*
REA166	½ bbl., **orange**		15.00
a.	Type A surcharge, $6 rate		*3,250.*
b.	Type B surcharge, $6 rate		*5,000.*
REA167	1 bbl., **blue**		25.00
REA168	1 hhd., **black**		*11,000.*
REA169	5 bbl., **black**		*4,500.*
a.	Center cutout only		500.00
REA170	25 bbl., **black,** center cutout only		450.00

REA171-REA176

REA177-REA178A

Tax rate same as previous issue. Provisional handstamp reads "SOLD AT $5.00 RATE" or "$5.00 RATE."

1933 Engr. Wmk. USIR

Entire Stamp

REA171	⅛ bbl., **violet red**		35.00
REA172	⅙ bbl., **purple**		500.00
REA173	¼ bbl., **green**	75.00	8.00
a.	Provisional surcharge, $5 rate		*17,500.*
REA174	½ bbl., **brown orange**	100.00	5.00
a.	Provisional surcharge, $5 rate		*1,500.*
REA175	1 bbl., **blue**		110.00
REA176	1 hhd., **black**		*9,000.*

Bright Blue Paper

REA177	5 bbl., **black**		*2,000.*
a.	Entire stamp with cut-out center		7.50
b.	Center cutout only		1.00
REA178	10 bbl., **black**	800.00	500.00
b.	Entire stamp with cut-out center		10.00
c.	Center cutout only		1.00
REA178A	25 bbl., **black**		500.00
b.	Entire stamp with cut-out center		4.50
c.	Center cutout only		1.00
d.	Rouletted 7 at left		—

For surcharge see Nos. REA180B, REA199.

Nos. REA173-REA174 with BEP Printed Surcharge, "Act of March 22, 1933"

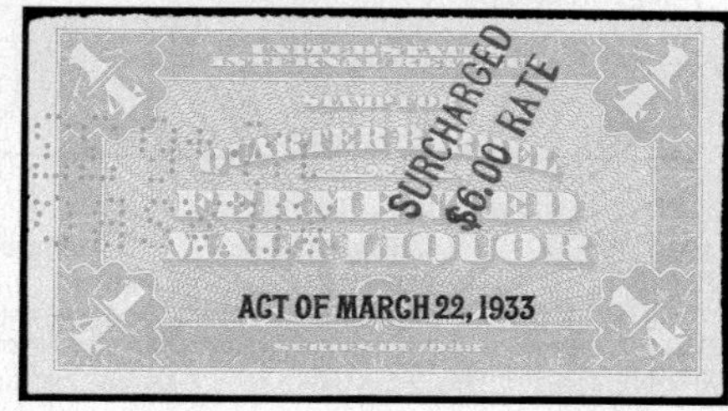

Additional provisional handstamped surcharge, $6 rate as previous issue.

1933-40 Entire Stamp

REA179	¼ bbl., **green**		27.50
a.	Handstamped "Surcharged $6 rate," *1940*		2,750.
REA180	½ bbl., **brown orange**		12.50
a.	Handstamped "Surcharged $6 rate," *1940*		3,250.

No. REA178 with handstamp surcharge, "Value increased under Revenue Act of 1940."

1940 Entire Stamp

REA180B	10 bbl., **black**		—

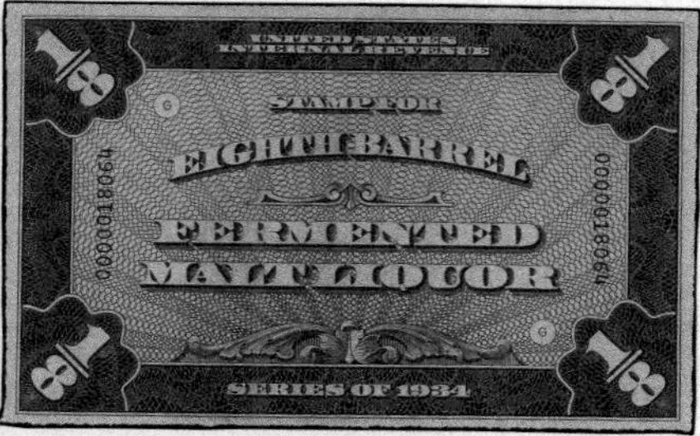

REA181-REA187

REA188-REA189

Tax rates $5 per bbl; $6 from July 1, 1940; $7 from Nov. 1, 1942; $8 from Apr. 1, 1944.

1934-45 Engr. Wmk. USIR

With Black Control Numbers

REA181	⅛ bbl., **violet red**	140.00	7.50
a.	With cutout center		2.00
b.	Ovptd. "NOT LESS THAN 3⅝ GALLONS," uncut		—
REA182	⅙ bbl., **purple**		150.00
a.	With cutout center		100.00
b.	Ovptd. "NOT LESS THAN 4⅚ GALLONS," uncut		—
REA183	¼ bbl., **green**		4.00
a.	With cutout center		2.50
b.	Ovptd. "NOT LESS THAN 7¼ GALLONS," uncut		—
REA184	⅓ bbl., **brown orange**	—	*25,000.*
REA185	½ bbl., **orange**		3.00
a.	With cutout center		2.00
REA186	1 bbl., **blue**		7.50
a.	With cutout center		7.50
REA187	1 hhd., **black**, with cutout center	—	500.00
REA188	100 bbl., **carmine,** *1942*		200.00
a.	With cutout center		10.00
REA189	500 bbl., **dark brown,** with cut-out center, *1945*		500.00

Most values also exist as center cutout portions only.

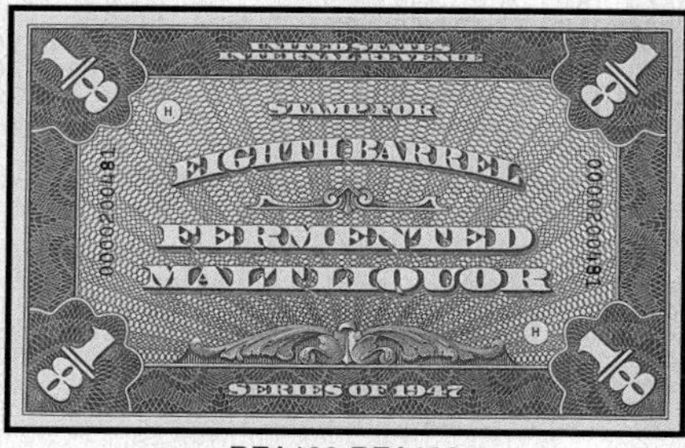

REA190-REA193

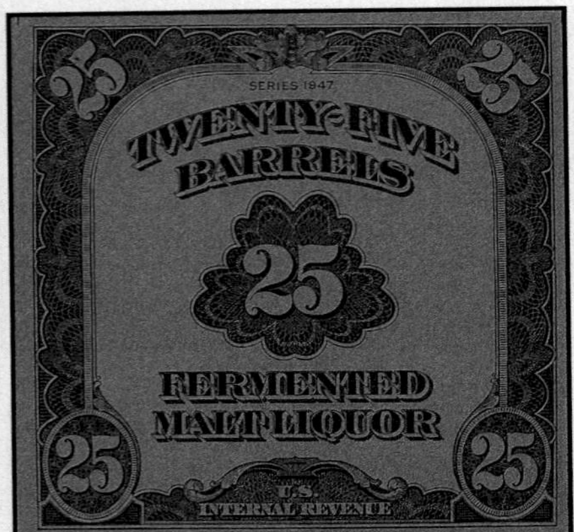

REA194-REA198

Tax rates $8 per bbl, $9 from Nov. 1, 1951.

1947	**Black Control Numbers**		**Litho.**
REA190	⅛ bbl., **carmine**	125.00	60.00
a.	With cutout center		15.00
REA190B	⅛ bbl., **purple**	225.00	
REA191	¼ bbl., **green**	100.00	20.00
a.	With cutout center		22.50
REA192	½ bbl., **orange**	30.00	10.00
a.	With cutout center		12.50
REA193	1 bbl., **blue**	100.00	150.00
a.	With cutout center		15.00
	Blue Paper		
REA194	5 bbl., **black**	80.00	200.00
a.	With cutout center		12.50
REA195	10 bbl., **black**	125.00	300.00
a.	With cutout center		27.50
REA196	25 bbl., **black**	*1,100.*	*3,200.*
a.	With cutout center		*3,000.*
	White Paper		
REA197	100 bbl., **carmine**	125.00	250.00
a.	With cutout center		10.00
REA198	500 bbl., **dark brown**	550.00	600.00
a.	With cutout center		60.00

All values except No. REA190B also exist as center cutouts only.

No. REA190B was not officially issued.

No. REA178A Provisionally Handstamp Surcharged in Black or Purple

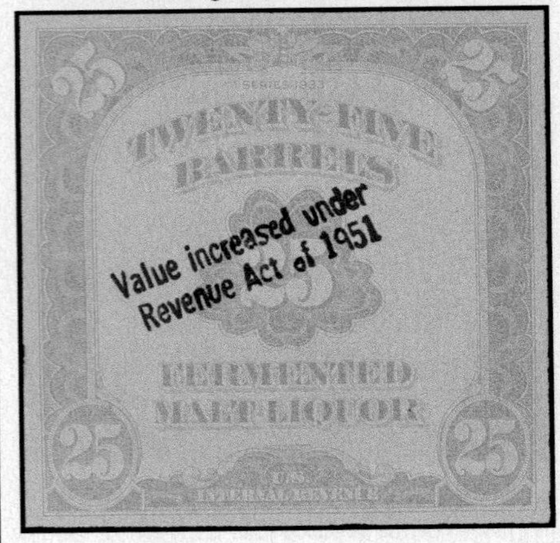

Tax rate $9 per bbl.

1951		
REA199	($225) on 25 bbl., #REA178A, uncut	*25,000.*

Also exists as center cutout only, showing portion of handstamped surcharge. Value, $150.

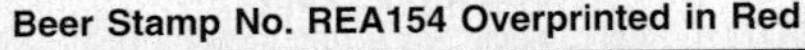

FERMENTED FRUIT JUICE STAMPS

Fermented fruit juice stamps were issued pending the ratification of the Repeal Amendment (Dec. 5, 1933) that made full-strength beer and wine legal again.

Congress, as a temporary measure, redefined intoxicating beverages by changing the legal definition from .5% to 3.2%, thus permitting the sale of 3.2 beer and wine beginning in early May 1933.

Regular wine stamps were available to pay the Internal Revenue taxes. However, these Fermented Fruit Juice stamps were authorized for placement on individual bottles or containers of fermented fruit juice. Use was discontinued Dec. 4, 1933.

Stamps are valued in the grade of very fine. Most stamps are found in average to fine condition. Unused stamps are valued with original gum.

REF1

Plates of 220 subjects in two panes of 110.

1933	**Wmk. USIR**		**Engr.**	***Perf. 11***
REF1	REF1	4 oz **gray**		175.00
REF3	REF1	8 oz **light green**	150.00	150.00
REF4	REF1	12 oz **light blue**	25.00	11.00
REF5	REF1	13 oz **olive green**		100.00
REF6	REF1	16 oz **lavender**	700.00	350.00
REF7	REF1	24 oz **orange**		350.00
REF8	REF1	29 oz **brown**	400.00	360.00
REF9	REF1	32 oz **red**	160.00	160.00

A dark blue 7-ounce stamp was issued, but the only recorded examples currently are in the National Postal Museum collection.

No. REF4 stamps normally are canceled "H. B. Co." (Hoffman Beverage Company) or "M. D. C." (Mission Dry Corporation). Specialists collect them by date (H. B. Co. and M. D. C.) and control number (M. D. C.). Identifiable cancels from other companies are scarce and sell for premiums from 50% to 250% more than the used value shown for No. REF4.

Earliest documented use: May 27, 1933 (No. REF4).

Beer Stamp No. REA154 Overprinted in Red

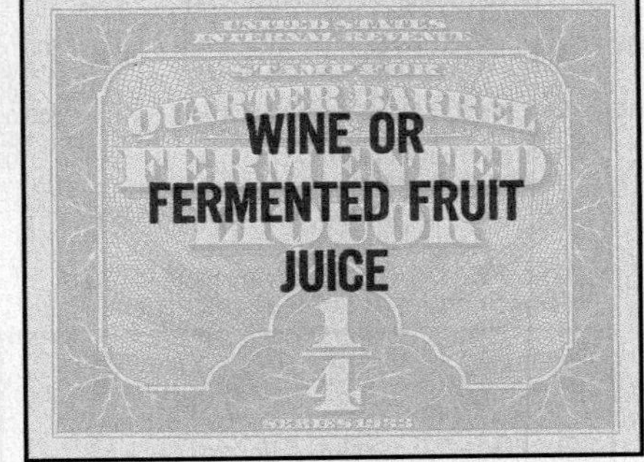

1933	**Engr.**	***Imperf.***
REF10	¼ bbl., **green**, *blue*	*37,500.*

The ½ barrel and 1 barrel beer stamps, Nos. REA156-REA157, also were issued with this overprint, but no examples are currently recorded.

PLAYING CARDS

Stamps for use on packs of playing cards were included in the first general issue of 1862-71. They are Nos. R2, R11, R12, R17, R21 and R28. The tax on playing cards was repealed effective June 22, 1965.

"ON HAND . . ." — RF1

"ACT OF . . ." — RF2

1894 Engr. Unwmk. *Rouletted 5½*

RF1	RF1	2c **lake**	1.50	1.00
		P# block of 6, Impt. T I	200.00	
	a.	Horizontal pair, imperf. between	*600.00*	*500.00*
	b.	Horiz. pair, imperf. vert.	—	
RF2	RF2	2c **ultramarine**	30.00	3.00
		P# block of 6, Impt. T I	350.00	
	a.	2c **blue**	35.00	4.00
		P# block of 6, Impt. T I	450.00	
	b.	Imperf., pair	600.00	
	c.	Imperf. horizontally	160.00	160.00
	d.	Rouletted 12½	100.00	100.00
	e.	Imperf. horizontally, rouletted 12½ vertically, pair	225.00	225.00

No vertical pairs of No. RF2e are known. Pairs will be horizontal. Singles are valued at 50% of the pair value.

Rouletted 5½, 7; Hyphen Hole 7

1896-99 Wmk. 191R

RF3	RF2	2c **blue**	15.00	.65
	a.	2c **ultramarine** ('99)	15.00	2.00
	b.	Imperf., pair	125.00	

No. RF3 surcharged " VIRGIN / ISLANDS / 4 CTS" are listed under Danish West Indies.

1902 *Perf. 12*

RF4	RF2	2c **deep blue**	—	65.00

No. RF4 is known with cancel date "1899" but that is due to the use of an old canceling plate. The stamp was first used in 1902.

Stamp of 1899 Surcharged in Rose

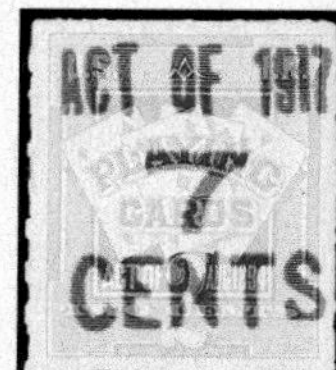

1917 Wmk. 191R *Rouletted 7*

RF5	RF2	7c on 2c **ultramarine**	*750.00*	700.00
	a.	Inverted surcharge	*2,000.*	

The surcharge on No. RF5 was handstamped at the Internal Revenue Office in New York City. Different handstamps were used at other Internal Revenue Offices as well, values $400 to $750.

Surcharged in Black

1917

RF6	RF2	(7c) on 2c **blue**		65.00
	a.	Inverted surcharge		65.00

The "17" indicated that the 7 cent tax had been paid according to the Act of 1917.

Used by N. Y. Consolidated Card Co.

Cancellations are in red.

Surcharged in Black

RF7	RF2	7c on 2c **blue**	1,100.	
	a.	Inverted surcharge	550.00	

Used by Standard Playing Card Co.

The surcharges on Nos. RF7-RF10, RF13, RF15, RF18 were applied by the manufacturers, together with their initials, dates, etc., thus forming a combination of surcharge and precancellation. The surcharge on No. RF16 was made by the Bureau of Engraving and Printing. After it appeared the use of some combinations was continued but only as cancellations.

Surcharged Vertically Reading Up in Red or Violet

RF8	RF2	7c on 2c **blue**	1,750.
	a.	Double surcharge	3,000.
	b.	Reading down	2,750.

Used by Russell Playing Card Co. (red surcharge/cancellation) and Standard Playing Card Co. of Chicago (violet surcharge/cancellation).

Surcharged Vertically, Reading Up in Black, Violet or Red

RF9	RF2	7c on 2c **blue**	10.00
	a.	Double surcharge (violet)	100.00
	b.	Numeral omitted (black)	90.00
	c.	Surcharge reading down	15.00
	d.	As "c," numeral omitted (black)	77.50
	e.	As "c," double surcharge (violet)	*300.00*
	f.	Double surcharge, one down (red)	*325.00*
	g.	Surcharge and "A.D." in violet	*400.00*
	h.	Surcharge and "A.D." in red, "U.S.P.C. Co." in black	*1,500.*
	i.	Surcharge and "A.D." in red reading up, "U.S.P.C. Co." in black reading down	*2,500.*
	j.	As "g," reading down	*2,500.*
	k.	Double surcharge (black)	*1,100.*
	l.	Double surcharge (red)	*2,500.*
	m.	Double surcharge and "A.D.," both reading down (red)	—
	n.	Double surcharge and "U.S. P.C. Co.," both reading down (black)	*2,750.*
	o.	Violet surcharge reading down on #RF4 (perf. 12)	*4,500.*

"A.D." (Andrew Dougherty Co.) printed in red, "S. P. C. Co." (Standard Playing Card Co.) printed in violet, "U.S.P.C. Co." printed in black. The first two became divisions of United States Playing Card Co.

See No. RF13.

Surcharged in Carmine

RF10	RF2	7c on 2c **blue**	85.00
	a.	Inverted surcharge	60.00
	b.	Double surcharge	1,250.
	c.	Double surcharge, inverted	550.00
	d.	Triple surcharge	*3,000.*

Used by Russell Playing Card Co.

RF3

1918 Size: 21x40mm *Imperf.*

RF11	RF3	**blue**	50.00	32.50
		Block of 4	190.00	150.00

Private Roulette 14

RF12	RF3	**blue**	400.
	a.	Rouletted 13 in red	*2,250.*
	b.	Rouletted 6½	750.
	c.	Perf. 12 horiz., imperf. vert.	300.
	d.	Perf. 12 on 4 sides	*1,250.*

Nos. RF11-RF12 served as 7c stamps when used before April 1, 1919, and as 8c stamps when used after that date.

No. RF11 is known handstamped "7" or "8," or both "7" and "8," as well as "Act of 1918" in black or magenta, either by the user to indicate the value when applied to the pack or by the IRS district offices at the time of sale.

No. RF12 was used by N. Y. Consolidated Card Co., Nos. RF12a, RF12b were used by Russell Playing Card Co., Nos. RF12, RF12c, RF12d were used by Logan Printing House.

Surcharged like No. RF9 (but somewhat smaller) in Violet, Red or Black

Private Roulette 9½

RF13	RF3	7c **blue**	55.00
	a.	Inverted surcharge	60.00
	b.	Double surcharge	*1,750.*
	c.	Double surcharge, inverted	*1,750.*
	d.	Surcharge omitted	—

No. RF13b is a red surcharge, and it was used only by Andrew Dougherty Co. No. RF13c is a black surcharge, and it was used only by U.S. Playing Card Co.

See No. RF9.

Stamp of 1899 Surcharged in Magenta or Rose

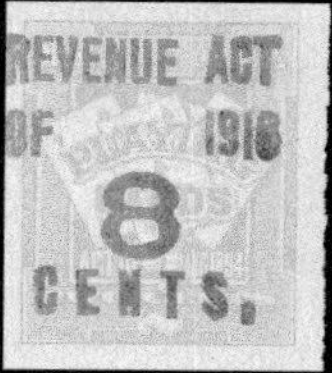

No. RF14

Black Handstamp, See Footnote

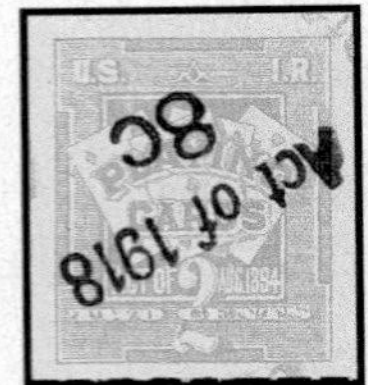

1919 ***Rouletted 7***

RF14 RF2 8c on 2c **ultramarine** 150.00
 a. Double surcharge 1,100.
 b. Inverted surcharge 2,750.

The surcharge on No. RF14 was handstamped at the Internal Revenue Office in New York City. A handstamp in black is known, and it often was applied inverted (see illustration). Value, $1,000.

Exists in pair, one double surcharge, also in pair, one with inverted surcharge.

Inverted Surcharge in Carmine

RF15 RF2 8c on 2c **blue** 650.00
 a. Double surcharge *2,000.*

No. RF15 is surcharged only with large "8c" inverted, and overprinted with date and initials (also inverted). No. RF16 is often found with additional impression of large "8c," as on No. RF15, but in this usage the large "8c" is a cancellation.

Used by Russell Playing Card Co.

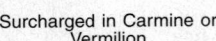

Surcharged in Carmine or Vermilion

RF16 RF2 8c on 2c **blue** 250.00 1.50
 a. Inverted surcharge *3,000.*

See note after No. RF15.

RF4

1922 **Size: 19x22mm** ***Rouletted 7***

RF17 RF4 (8c) **blue** 30.00 1.50
 Block of 4 140.00 —

No. RF17, rouletted 7 and perforated 11, surcharged " VIRGIN / ISLANDS / 4 cts." are listed under Danish West Indies.

Surcharged in Carmine, Blue or Black

RF18 RF4 8c on (8c) **blue** 100.00
 a. Inverted surcharge 100.00

Used by Pyramid Playing Card Co.

RF5

1924 ***Rouletted 7***

RF19 RF5 10c **blue** 25.00 .50
 Block of 4 110.00

ROTARY PRESS COIL STAMP

1926 ***Perf. 10 Vertically***

RF20 RF5 10c **blue** .30
 Pair 3.25
 Joint line pair 6.50

No. RF20 exists only precanceled. **Bureau precancels:** 11 different.

FLAT PLATE PRINTING

1927 ***Perf. 11***

RF21 RF5 10c **blue** 40.00 7.00
 Block of 4 175.00

1929 ***Perf. 10***

RF22 RF5 10c **blue** 30.00 5.50
 Block of 4 125.00 —

RF6

ROTARY PRESS COIL STAMP

1929 ***Perf. 10 Horizontally***

RF23 RF6 10c **light blue** .25
 Pair 2.50
 Joint line pair 5.00

No. RF23 exists only precanceled. **Bureau precancels:** 16 different.

FLAT PLATE PRINTING

1930 ***Perf. 10***

RF24 RF6 10c **blue** 25.00 2.00
 Block of 4 110.00 11.00
 a. Horiz. pair, imperf. vert. 175.00

1931 ***Perf. 11***

RF25 RF6 10c **blue** 25.00 1.50
 Block of 4 110.00 —

No. R234 is known used provisionally as a playing card revenue stamp August 6 and 8, 1932. Value for this use, authenticated, $400.

RF7

ROTARY PRESS COIL STAMP

1940 **Wmk. 191R** ***Perf. 10 Vertically***

RF26 RF7 **blue,** wet printing — .45
 Pair 2.25
 Joint line pair 4.50

Unwmk.

RF26A RF7 **blue,** dry printing 27.50 .40

See note after No. 1029.

Bureau precancels: 11 different.

RF8

ROTARY PRESS COIL STAMP

1940 **Wmk. 191R** ***Perf. 10 Horizontally***

RF27 RF8 **blue,** wet printing 3.00 .25
 Pair 7.50
 Joint line pair 12.50

Unwmk.

RF27A RF8 **blue,** dry printing 3.25

Bureau precancels: 10 different.

FLAT PLATE PRINTING

Wmk. 191R ***Perf. 11***

RF28 RF8 **blue,** wet printing 5.25 .80
 Block of 4 26.00 —
 a. Dry printing 5.25 4.25

ROTARY PRESS PRINTING

Unwmk.

RF28B RF8 **blue,** dry printing 5.25
 Block of 4 —

Wmk. 191R ***Perf. 10x11***

RF29 RF8 **blue** 200.00 92.50
 Block of 4 900.00 —
 a. Imperforate (P.C. Co.) *2,000.*

SILVER TAX STAMPS

The Silver Purchase Act of 1934 imposed a 50 per cent tax on the net profit realized on a transfer of silver bullion occurring after May 15, 1934. The tax was paid by affixing stamps to the transfer memorandum. Congress authorized the Silver Tax stamps on June 19, 1934. They were discontinued after June 4, 1963.

Documentary Stamps of 1917 Overprinted

1934 Offset Printing Wmk. 191R *Perf. 11*

No.	Type	Description	Unused	Used
RG1	R22	1c **carmine rose**	2.00	.95
RG2	R22	2c **carmine rose**	2.10	.65
		Double impression of stamp	—	
RG3	R22	3c **carmine rose**	2.40	.80
RG4	R22	4c **carmine rose**	2.50	1.60
RG5	R22	5c **carmine rose**	4.00	1.40
RG6	R22	8c **carmine rose**	5.50	3.25
RG7	R22	10c **carmine rose**	5.75	3.00
RG8	R22	20c **carmine rose**	8.25	3.75
RG9	R22	25c **carmine rose**	7.50	4.25
RG10	R22	40c **carmine rose**	8.75	6.00
RG11	R22	50c **carmine rose**	12.00	7.50
RG12	R22	80c **carmine rose**	22.50	12.00

Engr.

No.	Type	Description	Unused	Used
RG13	R21	$1 **green**	45.00	16.00
RG14	R21	$2 **rose**	52.50	25.00
RG15	R21	$3 **violet**	95.00	35.00
RG16	R21	$4 **yellow brown**	100.00	40.00
RG17	R21	$5 **dark blue**	85.00	25.00
RG18	R21	$10 **orange**	100.00	27.50

Perf. 12

Without Gum

No.	Type	Description	Unused	Used
RG19	R17	$30 **vermilion**	1,100.	75.00
		Cut cancel		20.00
RG20	R19	$60 **brown**	1,250.	90.00
		Cut cancel		27.50
		Vertical strip of 4		400.00
RG21	R17	$100 **green**	900.00	50.00
		Vertical strip of 4		210.00
RG22	R18	$500 **blue**	1,000.	400.00
		Cut cancel		125.00
		Vertical strip of 4		—
RG23	R19	$1000 **orange**	—	125.00
		Cut cancel		60.00
		Vertical strip of 4		—

See note after No. R227.

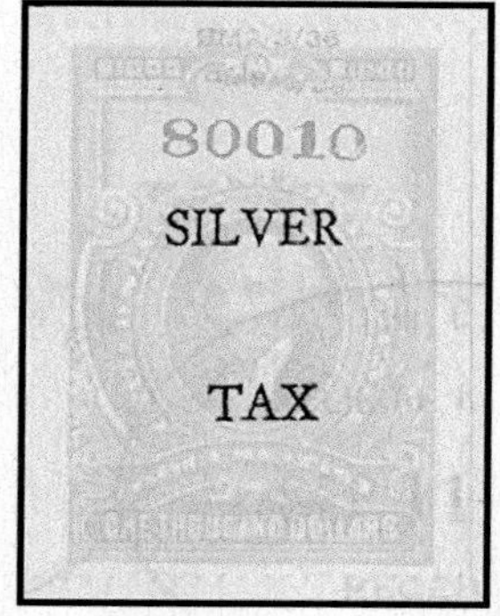

Same Overprint, spacing 11mm between words

1936 Without Gum *Perf. 12*

No.	Type	Description	Unused	Used
RG26	R17	$100 **green**	1,250.	125.00
		Vertical strip of 4		—
RG27	R19	$1000 **orange**		2,250.

Documentary Stamps of 1917 Handstamped "SILVER TAX" in Violet, Large Block Letters, in Two Lines

1939 Wmk. 191R Offset Printing *Perf. 10*

No.	Type	Description	Unused	Used
RG28	R22	1c **rose pink**		*17,500.*

Perf. 11

No.	Type	Description	Unused	Used
RG29	R22	3c **rose pink**		*17,500.*
RG30	R22	5c **rose pink**		*17,500.*
RG31	R22	10c **rose pink**		*17,500.*
RG32	R22	80c **rose pink**		*17,500.*

Other handstamps exist on various values. One has letters 4mm high, 2mm wide with "SILVER" and "TAX" applied in separate operations. Denominations with this overprint are the 1c, 2c, 5c, 10c, $2 and $5. Another has "Silver Tax" in two lines in a box, but it is believed this handstamp was privately applied. Denominations with this overprint are the 5c, 40c, $4 and $10.

Overprint Typewritten in Black ($2, $3) or Red ($5)

1934-35 Engr. *Perf. 11*

No.	Type	Description	Unused	Used
RG34	R21	$2 **carmine**		*10,000.*
RG35	R21	$3 **violet**		*10,000.*
RG36	R21	$5 **dark blue**		*10,000.*

Nos. RG35 and RG36 are unique.
Typewritten overprints also exist on 2c, 3c, 4c, 20c and 50c.

Type of Documentary Stamps 1917, Overprinted in Black

1940 Offset Printing *Perf. 11*

No.	Type	Description	Unused	Used
RG37	R22	1c **rose pink**	30.00	—
RG38	R22	2c **rose pink**	30.00	—
RG39	R22	3c **rose pink**	30.00	—
RG40	R22	4c **rose pink**	35.00	—
RG41	R22	5c **rose pink**	22.50	—
RG42	R22	8c **rose pink**	35.00	—
RG43	R22	10c **rose pink**	30.00	—
RG44	R22	20c **rose pink**	35.00	—
RG45	R22	25c **rose pink**	30.00	—
RG46	R22	40c **rose pink**	52.50	—
RG47	R22	50c **rose pink**	52.50	—
RG48	R22	80c **rose pink**	52.50	—

Engr.

No.	Type	Description	Unused	Used
RG49	R21	$1 **green**	350.00	—
RG50	R21	$2 **rose**	500.00	—
RG51	R21	$3 **violet**	600.00	—
RG52	R21	$4 **yellow brown**	900.00	—
RG53	R21	$5 **dark blue**	1,100.	—
RG54	R21	$10 **orange**	1,500.	—

Nos. RG19-RG20, RG26 Handstamped in Blue

1940 Without Gum *Perf. 12*

No.	Type	Description	Unused	Used
RG55	R17	$30 **vermilion**	—	*7,000.*
a.		Double "Series 1940" overprint		—
RG56	R19	$60 **brown**	—	*24,000.*
RG57	R17	$100 **green**	—	*6,000.*

Nos. R274, R278, R280, R281, R308 Handstamped in Black "Silver Tax"

1940 *Perf. 11*

No.	Type	Description	Unused	Used
RG57A	R22	50c **rose pink**		*3,600.*
RG57B	R21	$3 **violet**		*3,600.*
RG57C	R21	$5 **dark blue**		*3,600.*
RG57D	R21	$10 **orange**		*2,450.*
RG57E	R17	$100 **carmine**		*3,600.*

Additional denominations bearing the provisional "Silver Tax" handstamp might exist.

Alexander Hamilton — RG1

Levi Woodbury — RG2

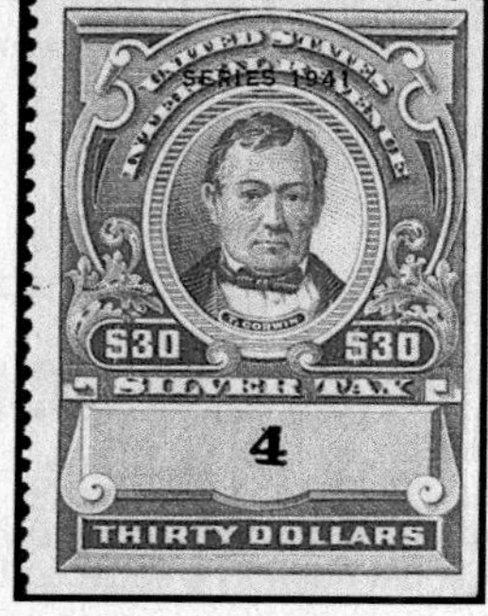

Thomas Corwin — RG3

Overprinted in Black **SERIES 1941**

1941 Wmk. 191R Engr. *Perf. 11*

No.	Type	Description	Unused	Used
RG58	RG1	1c **gray**	10.00	2.40
a.		Imperf, pair, without gum	*75.00*	
RG59	RG1	2c **gray** *(Oliver Wolcott, Jr.)*	10.00	3.00
a.		Imperf, pair, without gum	*75.00*	
RG60	RG1	3c **gray** *(Samuel Dexter)*	10.00	3.00
a.		Imperf, pair, without gum	*75.00*	
RG61	RG1	4c **gray** *(Albert Gallatin)*	10.00	5.25
a.		Imperf, pair, without gum	*75.00*	
RG62	RG1	5c **gray** *(G.W. Campbell)*	15.00	9.25
a.		Imperf, pair, without gum	*75.00*	
RG63	RG1	8c **gray** *(A.J. Dallas)*	15.00	—
a.		Imperf, pair, without gum	*75.00*	
RG64	RG1	10c **gray** *(Wm. H. Crawford)*	17.50	8.50
a.		Imperf, pair, without gum	*75.00*	
RG65	RG1	20c **gray** *(Richard Rush)*	30.00	7.75
a.		Imperf, pair, without gum	*75.00*	
RG66	RG1	25c **gray** *(S.D. Ingham)*	35.00	—
a.		Imperf, pair, without gum	*75.00*	
RG67	RG1	40c **gray** *(Louis McLane)*	60.00	37.50
a.		Imperf, pair, without gum	*75.00*	
RG68	RG1	50c **gray** *(Wm. J. Duane)*	60.00	32.50
a.		Imperf, pair, without gum	*75.00*	
RG69	RG1	80c **gray** *(Roger B. Taney)*	100.00	32.50
a.		Imperf, pair, without gum	*125.00*	
RG70	RG2	$1 **gray**	150.00	50.00
a.		Imperf, pair, without gum	*600.00*	
RG71	RG2	$2 **gray** *(Thomas Ewing)*	350.00	75.00
a.		Imperf, pair, without gum	*600.00*	
RG72	RG2	$3 **gray** *(Walter Forward)*	375.00	100.00
a.		Imperf, pair, without gum	*600.00*	
RG73	RG2	$4 **gray** *(J.C. Spencer)*	425.00	95.00
a.		Imperf, pair, without gum	*600.00*	
RG74	RG2	$5 **gray** *(G.M. Bibb)*	325.00	100.00
a.		Imperf, pair, without gum	*600.00*	
RG75	RG2	$10 **gray** *(R.J. Walker)*	750.00	125.00
a.		Imperf, pair, without gum	*650.00*	
RG76	RG2	$20 **gray** *(Wm. M. Meredith)*	1,250.	300.00
a.		Imperf, pair, without gum	*2,000.*	

Perf. 12

Without Gum

No.	Type	Description	Unused	Used
RG77	RG3	$30 **gray**	*3,500.*	750.
		Cut cancel		175.
RG78	RG3	$50 **gray** *(James Guthrie)*	*3,500.*	*4,250.*
RG79	RG3	$60 **gray** *(Howell Cobb)*	*3,500.*	750.
		Cut cancel		175.
RG80	RG3	$100 **gray** *(P.F. Thomas)*	*7,500.*	700.
		Cut cancel		175.
		Vertical strip of 4		—
RG81	RG3	$500 **gray** *(J.A. Dix)*		*32,500.*
RG82	RG3	$1000 **gray** *(S.P. Chase)*	*5,000.*	*2,750.*
		Cut cancel		*1,750.*

Nos. RG58-RG82 Overprinted Instead:

1942 **Wmk. 191R** ***Perf. 11***

No.	Type	Denom.	Color	Unused	Used
RG83	RG1	1c	**gray**	3.25	—
RG84	RG1	2c	**gray**	3.25	—
RG85	RG1	3c	**gray**	3.25	—
RG86	RG1	4c	**gray**	3.25	—
RG87	RG1	5c	**gray**	3.25	—
RG88	RG1	8c	**gray**	8.00	—
RG89	RG1	10c	**gray**	8.00	—
RG90	RG1	20c	**gray**	15.00	—
RG91	RG1	25c	**gray**	26.00	—
RG92	RG1	40c	**gray**	35.00	—
RG93	RG1	50c	**gray**	40.00	—
RG94	RG1	80c	**gray**	100.00	—
RG95	RG2	$1	**gray**	150.00	72.50
a.	Overprint "SERIES 5942"			*2,000.*	
RG96	RG2	$2	**gray**	160.00	72.50
a.	Overprint "SERIES 5942"			1,350.	
	Block of 4, one stamp ovptd. "SERIES 5942"			*2,000.*	
RG97	RG2	$3	**gray**	300.00	140.00
a.	Overprint "SERIES 5942"			1,450.	
RG98	RG2	$4	**gray**	350.00	140.00
a.	Overprint "SERIES 5942"			*2,500.*	
RG99	RG2	$5	**gray**	300.00	175.00
a.	Overprint "SERIES 5942"			*2,000.*	
RG100	RG2	$10	**gray**	725.00	700.00
RG101	RG2	$20	**gray**	1,250.	
a.	Overprint "SERIES 5942"			*10,000.*	

Perf. 12
Without Gum

No.	Type	Denom.	Color	Unused	Used
RG102	RG3	$30	**gray**	*7,500.*	*4,500.*
	Cut cancel				*3,500.*
RG103	RG3	$50	**gray**	*40,000.*	—
RG104	RG3	$60	**gray**	*7,500.*	*2,250.*
	Cut cancel				750.
RG105	RG3	$100	**gray**		3,500.
	Cut cancel				950.
RG106	RG3	$500	**gray**		*6,000.*
	Cut cancel				*4,000.*
RG107	RG3	$1000	**gray**	*15,000.*	*8,500.*
	Cut cancel				*4,500.*

Silver Purchase Stamps of 1941 without Overprint

1944 **Wmk. 191R** ***Perf. 11***

No.	Type	Denom.	Color	Unused	Used
RG108	RG1	1c	**gray**	1.00	.30
RG109	RG1	2c	**gray**	1.00	.65
RG110	RG1	3c	**gray**	1.40	1.00
RG111	RG1	4c	**gray**	1.60	1.25
RG112	RG1	5c	**gray**	3.25	2.75
RG113	RG1	8c	**gray**	5.00	2.75
RG114	RG1	10c	**gray**	6.50	3.25
RG115	RG1	20c	**gray**	10.00	5.50
RG116	RG1	25c	**gray**	16.00	6.00
RG117	RG1	40c	**gray**	24.00	11.50
RG118	RG1	50c	**gray**	25.00	14.00
RG119	RG1	80c	**gray**	32.50	20.00
RG120	RG2	$1	**gray**	67.50	21.00
RG121	RG2	$2	**gray**	95.00	47.50
RG122	RG2	$3	**gray**	125.00	37.50
RG123	RG2	$4	**gray**	150.00	85.00
RG124	RG2	$5	**gray**	150.00	47.50
RG125	RG2	$10	**gray**	225.00	35.00
	Cut cancel				19.00
RG126	RG2	$20	**gray**	900.00	550.00
	Cut cancel				275.00

Perf. 12
Without Gum

No.	Type	Denom.	Color	Unused	Used
RG127	RG3	$30	**gray**	750.00	175.00
	Cut cancel				80.00
	Vertical strip of 4				—
a.	Booklet pane of 4			*7,250.*	
RG128	RG3	$50	**gray**	1,500.	700.00
	Cut cancel				350.00
	Vertical strip of 4				—
a.	Booklet pane of 4			*9,500.*	
RG129	RG3	$60	**gray**	*2,500.*	575.00
	Cut cancel				275.00
a.	Booklet pane of 4			*10,000.*	
RG130	RG3	$100	**gray**	*2,000.*	35.00
	Cut cancel				15.00
	Vertical strip of 4				—
RG131	RG3	$500	**gray**	1,200.	500.00
	Cut cancel				250.00
	With complete receipt tab			*1,500.*	
a.	Booklet pane of 4			*6,500.*	
	Complete booklet, 2 #RG131a			*13,500.*	
RG132	RG3	$1000	**gray**	900.00	160.00
	Cut cancel				80.00
	Vertical strip of 4				—
	With complete receipt tab			1,000.	
a.	Booklet pane of 4			—	
	Complete booklet, 1 #RG132a			*5,000.*	

CIGARETTE TUBES STAMPS

These stamps were for a tax on the hollow tubes of cigarette paper, with or without thin cardboard mouthpieces attached. They were sold in packages so buyers could add loose tobacco to make cigarettes.

Documentary Stamp of 1917 Overprinted

1919 **Offset Printing** **Wmk. 191R** ***Perf. 11***

No.	Type	Denom.	Color	Unused	Used
RH1	R22	1c	**carmine rose**	1.25	.75
	Block of 4			5.50	3.00
	On package				60.00
	Pair on package				75.00
	P# block of 8			175.00	
a.	Without period			22.50	10.00
	On package				—
	Block of 4, one stamp #RH1a			70.00	

1929 ***Perf. 10***

No.	Type	Denom.	Color	Unused	Used
RH2	R22	1c	**carmine rose**	60.00	11.00
	On package				—

RH1

1933 **Without Gum** **Wmk. 191R** ***Perf. 11***

No.	Type	Denom.	Color	Unused	Used
RH3	RH1	1c	**rose** (shades)	5.00	2.50
	Block of 4			22.50	12.50
	On package				45.00
RH4	RH1	2c	**rose** (shades)	20.00	7.50
	Pair				17.50
	Block of 4				50.00
	On package				110.00

Cigarette tube on-package values for Nos. RH1 and RH3 are for fine undamaged stamps affixed to a full package of Himyar Tobacco cigarette tubes manufactured by the Axton-Fisher Tobacco Co. Opened packages containing no cigarette tubes sell for 50 to 100 percent less. No. RH1 pairs are unseparated stamps. The listing for No. RH1 pair on package is not on a Himyar package.

Specialists have questioned whether No. RH1a is known on packages. The editors would like to see evidence of the existence of these listings.

RH2

1945 **Wmk. 191R** ***Perf. 11***

No.	Type	Denom.	Color	Unused	Used
RH5	RH2	10c	**rose**		—

POTATO TAX STAMPS

These stamps were required by the Potato Act of 1935, an amendment to the Agricultural Adjustment Act that became effective Dec. 1, 1935.

Potato growers were given allotments for which they were provided Tax Exempt Potato stamps. Growers exceeding their allotments would have paid for the excess with Tax Paid Potato stamps at the rate of ¾ cent per pound.

On Jan. 6, 1936, the U. S. Supreme Court declared the Agricultural Adjustment Act unconstitutional. Officially the Potato Act was in effect until Feb. 10, 1936, when it was repealed by Congress but, in essence, the law was ignored once the Supreme Court ruling was issued.

Because of the Act's short life, Tax Paid stamps were never used.

Young Woman from *The Bouquet* — RI1

Tax Paid Potatoes

1935	**Engr.**	**Unwmk.**	***Perf. 11***
RI1	RI1	¾c **carmine rose**	1.00
RI2	RI1	1½c **black brown**	1.00
RI3	RI1	2¼c **yellow green**	1.00
RI4	RI1	3c **light violet**	1.00
RI5	RI1	3¾c **olive bister**	1.25
RI6	RI1	7½c **orange brown**	4.00
RI7	RI1	11¼c **deep orange**	5.00
RI8	RI1	18¾c **violet brown**	12.50
RI9	RI1	37½c **red orange**	15.00
RI10	RI1	75c **blue**	17.50
RI11	RI1	93¾c **rose lake**	20.00
RI12	RI1	$1.12½ **green**	40.00
RI13	RI1	$1.50 **yellow brown**	40.00
		Nos. RI1-RI13 (13)	159.25

RI2

Tax Exempt Potatoes

1935	**Engr.**	**Unwmk.**	***Perf. 11x10½***	
RI14	RI2	2 lb **black brown**	2.00	*37.50*
a.		Booklet pane of 12	16.00	*375.00*
		Provisional booklet of 24, purple on pink cover	35.00	
		Provisional booklet of 96, purple on buff cover	100.00	
		Provisional booklet of 192, purple on white cover	250.00	
		Definitive booklet of 96, black on buff cover	100.00	
		Definitive booklet of 192, black on white cover	200.00	
RI15	RI2	5 lb **black brown**	25.00	
a.		Booklet pane of 12	*750.00*	
		Provisional booklet of 192, purple on white cover	*5,000.*	
		Provisional booklet of 24, purple on pink cover	*1,000.*	
RI16	RI2	10 lb **black brown**	35.00	
a.		Booklet pane of 12	*550.00*	
		Provisional booklet of 192, purple on white cover	*5,000.*	
RI17	RI2	25 lb **black brown**	*550.00*	
		No gum	150.00	
a.		Booklet pane of 12	*5,000.*	
		No gum	2,500.	
		Provisional booklet of 24, purple on pink cover, with stamps stuck down, badly disturbed gum	*5,500.*	
RI18	RI2	50 lb **black brown**	1.50	*50.00*
a.		Booklet pane of 12	30.00	
		Provisional booklet of 24, purple on pink cover	50.00	
		Provisional booklet of 96, purple on buff cover	150.00	
		Provisional booklet of 192, purple on white cover	300.00	
		Definitive booklet of 96, black on buff cover	100.00	
		Definitive booklet of 192, black on white cover	150.00	
		Nos. RI14-RI16,RI18 (4)	*63.50*	

The booklet panes are arranged 4x3 with a tab at top. Edges are imperforate at left, right and bottom, yielding four stamps fully perforated, six stamps imperf. on one side and two stamps imperf. on two sides per pane. Values for single stamps are for examples perforated on all four sides. Stamps with straight edges generally sell for less.

These stamps were printed from 360-subject rotary booklet plates and cut into 30 panes of 12. The panes were stapled into booklets of 24 (2 panes, pink covers), 96 (8 panes, buff covers) and 196 (16 panes, white covers), with handstamped covers (provisionals) and later with covers printed with the Dept. of Agriculture seal in the center (definitives). Both types of cover were prepared by the Bureau of Engraving and Printing.

Values for booklets are for examples containing panes that have very good to fine centering, because the overwhelming majority of booklets are in this grade. It should be noted that Scott values for individual panes (listed above) are for very fine panes. For this reason, individual panes are valued higher than the per-pane value of panes in booklets. For example, a pane of No. RI14a is valued at $14, but the No. RI14 definitive booklet of 96 (8 panes) is valued at $100, or $12.50 per pane, which is a little more than what a collector would pay for an individual very good to fine pane. Booklets containing very fine panes will command a premium over the values given.

One No. RI17 192-stamp booklet exists, from which some panes have been removed, but no complete 192-stamp booklet is known to exist.

A 100 lb Tax Exempt stamp was printed, but all are believed to have been destroyed.

TOBACCO SALE TAX STAMPS

These stamps were required to pay the tax on the sale of tobacco in excess of quotas set by the Secretary of Agriculture. The tax was 25 per cent of the price for which the excess tobacco was sold. It was intended to affect tobacco harvested after June 28, 1934 and sold before May 1, 1936. The tax was stopped when the Agricultural Adjustment Act was declared unconstitutional by the Supreme Court on Dec. 1, 1935.

Values for unused stamps are for examples with original gum.

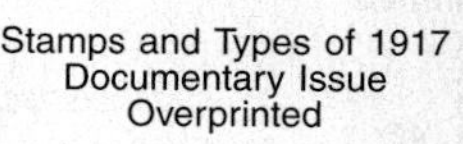

Stamps and Types of 1917 Documentary Issue Overprinted

1934	**Offset Printing**	**Wmk. 191R**	***Perf. 11***	
RJ1	R22	1c **carmine rose**	.30	.25
RJ2	R22	2c **carmine rose**	.40	.25
RJ3	R22	5c **carmine rose**	1.25	.50
RJ4	R22	10c **carmine rose**	1.60	.45
a.		Inverted overprint	15.00	*22.50*
RJ5	R22	25c **carmine rose**	4.75	2.00
RJ6	R22	50c **carmine rose**	7.50	2.00
		Engr.		
RJ7	R21	$1 **green**	15.00	2.00
RJ8	R21	$2 **rose**	35.00	2.25
RJ9	R21	$5 **dark blue**	40.00	4.25
RJ10	R21	$10 **orange**	50.00	10.00
RJ11	R21	$20 **olive bister**	110.00	12.50
		Nos. RJ1-RJ11 (11)	265.80	36.45

On No. RJ11 the overprint is vertical, reading up.

The right serif on the "T" of "TOBACCO" exists both normal and split. Both varieties exist within the same sheet, and the quantities of each type are approximately equal.

No. RJ2 is known with a counterfeit inverted overprint.

NARCOTIC TAX STAMPS

The Revenue Act of 1918 imposed a tax of 1 cent per ounce or fraction thereof on opium, coca leaves and their derivatives. The tax was paid by affixing Narcotic stamps to the drug containers. The tax lasted from Feb. 25, 1919, through Apr. 30, 1971.

Members of the American Revenue Association helped compile the listings in this section.

Documentary Stamps of 1917 Handstamped "NARCOTIC," "Narcotic," "NARCOTICS" or "ACT/NARCOTIC/1918" in Magenta, Black, Blue, Violet or Red

RJA22

RJA25

1919 Wmk. 191R Offset Printing ***Perf. 11***

No.	Design	Value	Color	Unused	Used
RJA9	R22	1c	**carmine rose**	3.00	1.90
RJA10	R22	2c	**carmine rose**	6.00	4.00
RJA11	R22	3c	**carmine rose**	35.00	37.50
RJA12	R22	4c	**carmine rose**	13.00	10.00
RJA13	R22	5c	**carmine rose**	20.00	16.00
RJA14	R22	8c	**carmine rose**	16.00	12.50
RJA15	R22	10c	**carmine rose**	52.50	20.00
RJA17	R22	25c	**carmine rose**	47.50	32.50
RJA18	R22	40c	**carmine rose**	*150.00*	*150.00*
RJA19	R22	50c	**carmine rose**	—	*22.50*
RJA20	R22	80c	**carmine rose**	*150.00*	*150.00*

Engr.

No.	Design	Value	Color	Unused	Used
RJA21	R21	$1	**green**	200.00	125.00
RJA22	R21	$2	**rose**		*2,000.*
RJA23	R21	$3	**violet**		*2,500.*
RJA24	R21	$5	**dark blue**		*1,750.*
RJA25	R21	$10	**orange**		*1,500.*

Drug manufacturer cancels have enabled experts to identify conclusively the origin of only six of the handstamped overprints. Four of these read simply "Narcotic." A 3-line handstamp, "Act / Narcotic / 1918," was used in Seattle; "Narcotics" in Kansas City, Missouri. Perhaps as many as 20 other styles and sizes have been recorded, although these occur only on mint stamps.

Many fake overprints exist.

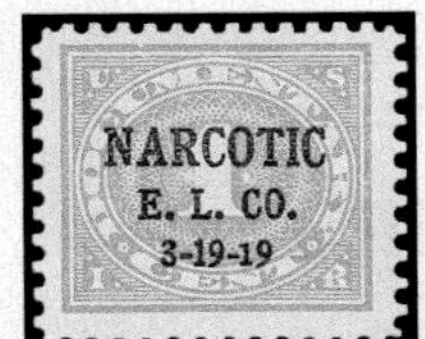

No. R228 Overprinted in Black

1919 Wmk. 191R ***Perf. 11***

"NARCOTIC" 14½mm wide

No.	Design	Value	Color	Unused	Used
RJA26	R22	1c	**carmine rose**		*3,750.*

Overprinted by Eli Lilly Co., Indianapolis, for that firm's use.

No. R228 Overprinted in Black: "J W & B / NARCOTIC"

1919 Wmk. 191R ***Perf. 11***

"NARCOTIC" 14½mm wide

No.	Design	Value	Color	Unused	Used
RJA27	R22	1c	**carmine rose**		*6,500.*
RJA27A	R22	2c	**carmine rose**		*7,500.*

Overprinted by John Wyeth & Brother, Philadelphia, for that firm's use.

The overprints on Nos. RJA27 and RJA27A are often mistaken for a cancellation used on the government-issued stamps Nos. RJA33-RJA40, with the latter having the "NARCOTICS" overprint measuring 17.5mm.

Nos. R228, R231-R232 Handstamped in Blue

1919 Wmk. 191R ***Perf. 11***

No.	Design	Value	Color	Unused	Used
RJA28	R22	1c	**carmine rose**		*1,250.*
RJA28A	R22	4c	**carmine rose**		*1,500.*
RJA29	R22	5c	**carmine rose**		—
RJA29A	R22	25c	**carmine rose**		—
RJA29B	R21	$1	**green** (violet handstamp)		—

The handstamp was applied by the Powers-Weightmann-Rosengarten Co., Philadelphia, for that firm's use.

Proprietary Stamps of 1919 Handstamped "NARCOTIC" in Blue

1919 Wmk. 191R Offset Printing ***Perf. 11***

No.	Design	Value	Color	Unused	Used
RJA30	RB5	1c	**dark blue**	—	—
RJA31	RB5	2c	**dark blue**	—	
RJA32	RB5	4c	**dark blue**	—	

No. RB65 is known with "Narcotic" applied in red ms.

The editors would like to see authenticated evidence of the existence of Nos. RJA30-RJA32.

Documentary Stamps of 1917 Overprinted in Black, "Narcotic" 17½mm wide

1919 Wmk. 191R Offset Printing ***Perf. 11***

No.	Design	Value	Color	Unused	Used
RJA33	R22	1c	**carmine rose** *(6,900,000)*	1.25	.80
RJA34	R22	2c	**carmine rose** *(3,650,000)*	2.50	1.10
RJA35	R22	3c	**carmine rose** *(388,400)*	40.00	21.00
RJA36	R22	4c	**carmine rose** *(2,400,000)*	6.00	4.75
RJA37	R22	5c	**carmine rose** *(2,400,000)*	15.00	10.50
RJA38	R22	8c	**carmine rose** *(1,200,000)*	25.00	18.00
RJA39	R22	10c	**carmine rose** *(3,400,000)*	3.75	2.75
RJA40	R22	25c	**carmine rose** *(700,000)*	25.00	16.00

Overprint Reading Up

Engr.

No.	Design	Value	Color	Unused	Used
RJA41	R21	$1	**green** *(270,000)*	47.50	20.00

The overprint on Nos. RJA33-RJA41 was produced by the Bureau of Engraving & Printing. Fake overprints exist on Nos. RJA33-RJA41. In the genuine the C's are not slanted.

NT1

NT2

1919-64 Offset Printing Wmk. 191R ***Imperf.***

No.	Design	Value	Color	Unused	Used
RJA42a	NT1	1c	**violet**		5.25
RJA43a	NT2	1c	**violet**		.55
RJA44a	NT2	2c	**violet**		1.40

Rouletted 7

No.	Design	Value	Color	Unused	Used
RJA42b	NT1	1c	**violet**	1.25	.30
d.		1c	**purple**		7.50
RJA43b	NT2	1c	**violet**		.30
d.		1c	**purple**		5.25
RJA44b	NT2	2c	**violet**		.55
d.		2c	**purple**		5.25
RJA45b	NT2	3c	**violet**		175.00

The purple shade, Nos. RJA42d, RJA43d and RJA44d, is a distinctive shade with a decidedly reddish cast to it that arose because of the unavailability during WWII of inks previously used. All authenticated purple stamps were used from 1944 to 1947.

NT3

NT4

Imperf

No.	Design	Value	Color	Unused	Used
RJA46a	NT3	1c	**violet**		2.75
RJA47a	NT3	2c	**violet**		1.60
RJA48a	NT3	3c	**violet**	*750.00*	*750.00*
RJA49a	NT3	4c	**violet** ('42)		—
RJA50a	NT3	5c	**violet**		42.50
RJA52a	NT3	8c	**violet**		75.00
RJA53a	NT3	9c	**violet** ('53)		67.50
RJA54a	NT3	10c	**violet**		32.50
RJA55a	NT3	16c	**violet**		52.50
RJA56a	NT3	18c	**violet** ('61)		110.00
RJA57a	NT3	19c	**violet** ('61)		125.00
RJA58a	NT3	20c	**violet**		375.00

Nos. RJA47a-RJA58a have "CENTS" below the value.

Rouletted 7

No.	Design	Value	Color	Unused	Used
RJA46b	NT3	1c	**violet**		.75
d.		1c	**purple**		9.00
RJA47b	NT3	2c	**violet**		.75
d.		2c	**purple**		8.25
RJA49b	NT3	4c	**violet**		11.00
d.		4c	**purple**		30.00
RJA50b	NT3	5c	**violet**	10.00	4.00
d.		5c	**purple**		13.00
RJA51b	NT3	6c	**violet**		1.00
d.		6c	**purple**		9.25
RJA52b	NT3	8c	**violet**		4.25
d.		8c	**purple**		26.00
RJA53b	NT3	9c	**violet**		21.00
RJA54b	NT3	10c	**violet**		.55
d.		10c	**purple**		7.00

No.	Type	Denom.	Color	Unused	Used
RJA55b	NT3	16c	**violet**	10.00	4.00
d.		16c	**purple**		14.50
RJA56b	NT3	18c	**violet**		12.50
RJA57b	NT3	19c	**violet**	50.00	26.00
RJA58b	NT3	20c	**violet**	250.00	350.00

Nos. RJA47b-RJA58b have "CENTS" below the value.

Imperf

No.	Type	Denom.	Color	Unused	Used
RJA59a	NT4	1c	**violet**		47.50
RJA60a	NT4	2c	**violet**		50.00
RJA61a	NT4	3c	**violet**	55.00	52.50
RJA63a	NT4	6c	**violet**		62.50
RJA65a	NT4	9c	**violet** ('61)		35.00
RJA66a	NT4	10c	**violet**		17.50
RJA67a	NT4	16c	**violet**		16.00
RJA68a	NT4	18c	**violet** ('61)	*250.00*	250.00
RJA69a	NT4	19c	**violet**		16.00
RJA70a	NT4	20c	**violet**	*300.00*	275.00
RJA71a	NT4	25c	**violet**		—
RJA72a	NT4	40c	**violet**		1,000.
RJA74a	NT4	$1.28	**green**		32.50
c.	As "a," measuring ¾ inch by 8 inches with wide side margins				*200.00*

On Nos. RJA60a-RJA74a the value tablet is solid.

Rouletted 7

No.	Type	Denom.	Color	Unused	Used
RJA59b	NT4	1c	**violet**		10.50
c.	Rouletted 3½			10.00	5.00
RJA60b	NT4	2c	**violet**	27.50	20.00
RJA61b	NT4	3c	**violet**	350.00	350.00
RJA62b	NT4	5c	**violet**	35.00	26.00
RJA63b	NT4	6c	**violet**	30.00	25.00
RJA64b	NT4	8c	**violet**	65.00	50.00
RJA65b	NT4	9c	**violet**		21.00
RJA66b	NT4	10c	**violet**		17.50
RJA67b	NT4	16c	**violet**	27.50	20.00
RJA68b	NT4	18c	**violet**		425.00
RJA69b	NT4	19c	**violet**		190.00
RJA70b	NT4	20c	**violet**		240.00
RJA71b	NT4	25c	**violet**		21.00
c.	Rouletted 3½				4.25
d.		25c	**purple**		—
RJA72b	NT4	40c	**violet**	*3,500.*	*4,000.*
c.	Rouletted 3½			80.00	67.50
RJA73b	NT4	$1	**green**		1.60
d.		$1	**violet** (error)		*2,000.*
RJA74b	NT4	$1.28	**green**		10.50
d.	As "b," measuring ¾ inch by 8 inches with wide side margins				*100.00*

On Nos. RJA60b-RJA74b the value tablet is solid.

1963(?)-70 Offset Printing *Imperf.*
Unwatermarked

No.	Type	Denom.	Color	Unused	Used
RJA75a	NT1	1c	**violet**		7.75
RJA76a	NT2	1c	**violet**		1.10
RJA77a	NT2	2c	**violet**		5.25
RJA79a	NT3	1c	**violet**		5.25
RJA80a	NT3	2c	**violet**	175.00	
RJA82a	NT3	5c	**violet**		72.50
RJA83a	NT3	6c	**violet**		—
RJA85a	NT3	9c	**violet**		—
RJA86a	NT3	10c	**violet**		—
RJA87a	NT3	16c	**violet**		150.00
RJA88a	NT3	18c	**violet**		—

Nos. RJA80a-RJA89a have "CENTS" below the value.

Rouletted 7

No.	Type	Denom.	Color	Unused	Used
RJA75b	NT1	1c	**violet**	2.10	
RJA76b	NT2	1c	**violet**		1.10
RJA77b	NT2	2c	**violet**	2.10	
RJA78b	NT2	3c	**violet**	*100.00*	175.00
RJA79b	NT3	1c	**violet**		2.10
RJA80b	NT3	2c	**violet**	3.00	2.00
RJA81b	NT3	4c	**violet**		10.00
RJA83b	NT3	6c	**violet**	22.50	
RJA84b	NT3	8c	**violet**		5.25
RJA85b	NT3	9c	**violet**	60.00	50.00
RJA86b	NT3	10c	**violet**	22.50	
RJA87b	NT3	16c	**violet**		4.25
RJA88b	NT3	18c	**violet**	52.50	
RJA89b	NT3	20c	**violet**	325.00	

Nos. RJA80-RJA89 have "CENTS" below the value.

Imperf

No.	Type	Denom.	Color	Unused	Used
RJA91a	NT4	1c	**violet**		67.50
RJA93a	NT4	3c	**violet**		85.00
RJA94a	NT4	6c	**violet**		100.00
RJA96a	NT4	10c	**violet**		*1,500.*
RJA97a	NT4	16c	**violet**		40.00
RJA98a	NT4	19c	**violet**		26.00
RJA99a	NT4	20c	**violet**		*2,500.*
RJA101a	NT4	40c	**violet**		*1,000.*
RJA104a	NT4	$4	**green** ('70)	*1,000.*	*1,000.*

On Nos. RJA92a-RJA104a the value tablet is solid.

Rouletted 7

No.	Type	Denom.	Color	Unused	Used
RJA91b	NT4	1c	**violet**		15.00
RJA92b	NT4	2c	**violet**	80.00	
RJA93b	NT4	3c	**violet**	120.00	*160.00*
RJA94b	NT4	6c	**violet**	80.00	
RJA94Cb	NT4	8c	**violet**	175.00	
RJA95b	NT4	9c	**violet**	130.00	
RJA96b	NT4	10c	**violet**	70.00	
RJA97b	NT4	16c	**violet**		21.00
RJA98b	NT4	19c	**violet**	*350.00*	400.00
RJA99b	NT4	20c	**violet**	*425.00*	
RJA100b	NT4	25c	**violet**	200.00	250.00
RJA102b	NT4	$1	**green**	37.50	
RJA103b	NT4	$1.28	**green**	60.00	
d.	As "b," measuring ¾ inch by 8 inches with wide side margins			125.00	

On Nos. RJA92b-RJA103b the value tablet is solid.

NT5

Denomination added in black by rubber plate in an operation similar to precanceling.

1963 Engr. Unwmk. *Imperf.*

No.	Type	Denom.	Color	Unused	Used
RJA105	NT5	1c	**violet,** type 2	90.00	85.00
a.	Type 1			*140.00*	*140.00*
b.	Type 3			*50.00*	

Printed in sheets of 144 in six columns of 24 stamps. The majority of the stamps have block markings in all four corners of the margin (type 1), and many fewer have block margins only in the two left corners (type 2). A third scarcer type has dashes in the left two corners (Type 3). Despite the printing totals, type 2 is the most common of the three varieties and, therefore, is listed as the major number.

Nos. RJA105, RJA105a, and RJA105b were issued in vertical coil strips.

Denomination on Stamp Plate
1964 Offset Printing *Imperf.*

No.	Type	Denom.	Color	Unused	Used
RJA106	NT5	1c	**violet**	90.00	5.25

RJA106 was issued in sheet of 80 stamps.

MARIHUANA TAX STAMPS

Act of Congress, 1937, to enforce uniform regulation of cannabis.

Nos. R240, R244, R245 Overprinted

Issued with gum. Unused values are for stamps that are never hinged.

1937 Engr. *Perf. 11*

No.	Type	Denom.	Color	Unused	Used
RJM1	R21	$1	**yellow green**	400.	*15,000.*
	On document				—
	P# block of 6			*3,000.*	
a.	Imperf, pair			*900.*	
RJM2	R21	$5	**blue**	*475.*	
	P# block of 6			*4,000.*	
a.	Imperf, pair			*900.*	
RJM3	R21	$10	**yellow orange**	*425.*	
	P# block of 6			*3,750.*	
a.	Imperf, pair			*900.*	

Same overprint on No. R248

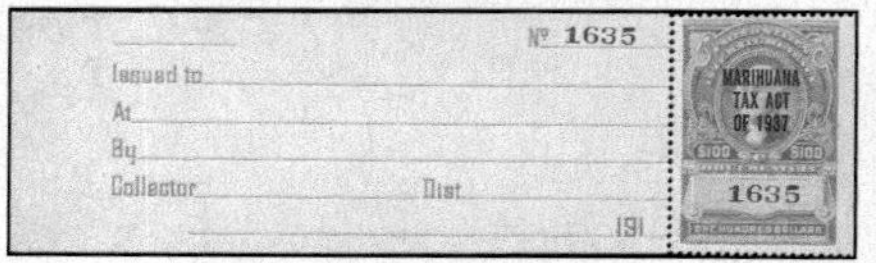

Illustration reduced.

Without Gum *Perf. 12*
Control Number in Red

No.	Type	Denom.	Color	Unused	Used
RJM4	R17	$100	**green,** with complete receipt tab	*750.*	
a.	Booklet pane of 4			*3,500.*	
	Complete booklet, 4 #RJM4a			*15,000.*	

Nos. R300, R304, R305 Without Date Inscription Overprinted

1962 *Perf. 11*

No.	Type	Denom.	Color	Unused	Used
RJM5	R24	$1	**carmine**	*425.*	
RJM6	R24	$5	**carmine**	*425.*	
RJM7	R24	$10	**carmine**	*425.*	

No. R306A Without Date Inscription Overprinted

Illustration reduced.

No.	Type	Denom.	Color	Unused	Used
RJM8	R25	$50	**carmine,** with complete receipt tab, no serial #	*1,400.*	
a.	Booklet pane of 4			*5,750.*	

CONSULAR SERVICE FEE STAMPS

Act of Congress, April 5, 1906, effective June 1, 1906, provided that every consular officer should be provided with special adhesive stamps printed in denominations determined by the Department of State.

Every document for which a fee was prescribed had to have attached a stamp or stamps representing the amount collected, and such stamps were used to show payment of these prescribed fees.

These stamps were usually affixed close to the signature, or at the lower left corner of the document. If no document was issued, the stamp or stamps were attached to a receipt for the amount of the fee and canceled either with pen and ink or rubber stamp showing the date of cancellation and bearing the initials of the canceling officer or name of the Consular Office. Stamps with embossed cancels sell for somewhat less. These stamps were not sold to the public uncanceled. Their use was discontinued Sept. 30, 1955.

Bisect uses may be on full documents or partial documents, which sell for only slightly less. Some bisects may only be found on partial documents.

CSF1

1906 Unwmk. Engr. *Perf. 12*

RK1	CSF1	25c **dark green**	120.00
RK2	CSF1	50c **carmine**	150.00
RK3	CSF1	$1 **dark violet**	12.50
a.		Diagonal half used as 50c with 2 #RK3, paying $2.50 fee, on document	*325.00*
RK4	CSF1	$2 **brown**	6.75
RK5	CSF1	$2.50 **dark blue**	2.00
RK6	CSF1	$5 **brown red**	42.50
a.		Horizontal or diagonal half used as $2.50, on document	*250.00*
RK7	CSF1	$10 **orange**	140.00
a.		Diagonal half used as $5, on partial document	—

Perf. 10

RK8	CSF1	25c **dark green**	120.00
RK9	CSF1	50c **carmine**	150.00
RK10	CSF1	$1 **dark violet**	750.00
RK11	CSF1	$2 **brown**	175.00
a.		Diagonal half used as $1, on document	—
RK12	CSF1	$2.50 **dark blue**	32.50
RK13	CSF1	$5 **brown red**	500.00

Perf. 11

RK14	CSF1	25c **dark green**	140.00
RK15	CSF1	50c **carmine**	225.00
RK16	CSF1	$1 **dark violet**	2.25
		reddish violet	*2.25*
a.		Diagonal half used as 50c, on document	*425.00*
RK17	CSF1	$2 **brown**	2.50
RK18	CSF1	$2.50 **dark blue**	1.10
RK19	CSF1	$5 **brown red**	5.00
a.		Diagonal half used as $2.50, on document	50.00
RK20	CSF1	$9 **gray**	35.00
RK21	CSF1	$10 **orange**	65.00
a.		Diagonal half used as $5, on document	110.00

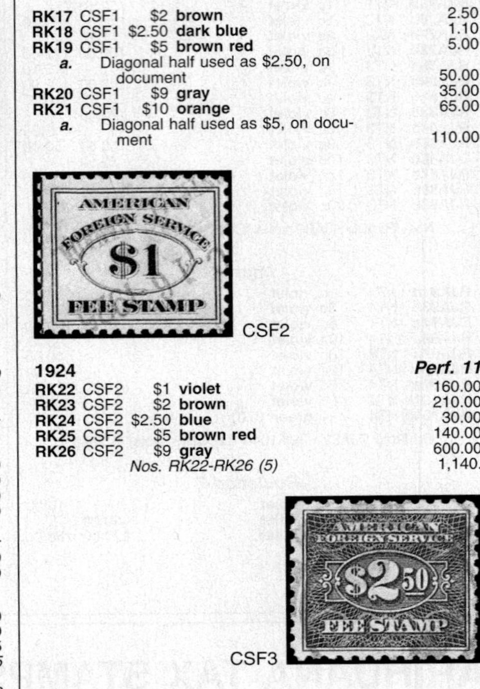

CSF2

1924 *Perf. 11*

RK22	CSF2	$1 **violet**	160.00
RK23	CSF2	$2 **brown**	210.00
RK24	CSF2	$2.50 **blue**	30.00
RK25	CSF2	$5 **brown red**	140.00
RK26	CSF2	$9 **gray**	600.00
		Nos. RK22-RK26 (5)	1,140.

CSF3

1925-52 *Perf. 10*

RK27	CSF3	$1 **violet**	47.50
RK28	CSF3	$2 **brown**	125.00
RK29	CSF3	$2.50 **ultramarine**	3.00
RK30	CSF3	$5 **carmine**	27.50
RK31	CSF3	$9 **gray**	75.00

Perf. 11

RK32	CSF3	25c **green** ('37)	160.00
RK33	CSF3	50c **orange** ('34)	160.00
RK34	CSF3	$1 **deep violet**	4.00
		violet	4.00
		lilac	4.00
a.		Diagonal half used as 50c, on document	—
RK35	CSF3	$2 **brown**	5.75
RK36	CSF3	$2.50 **blue**	.60
a.		$2.50 ultramarine	.55
RK37	CSF3	$5 **carmine**	3.50
RK38	CSF3	$9 **gray**	35.00
RK39	CSF3	$10 **blue gray** ('37)	175.00
RK40	CSF3	$20 **violet** ('52)	210.00
		Nos. RK27-RK40 (14)	1,032.

Consular Fee

The "Consular Fee stamp" on revenue stamped paper (previously listed as No. RN-Y1 but since deleted) was found to be nothing more than an illustration. Two identical examples are known.

CUSTOMS FEE STAMPS

New York Custom House

Issued to indicate the collection of miscellaneous customs fees. Use was discontinued on February 28, 1918. The stamps were not utilized in the collection of customs duties.

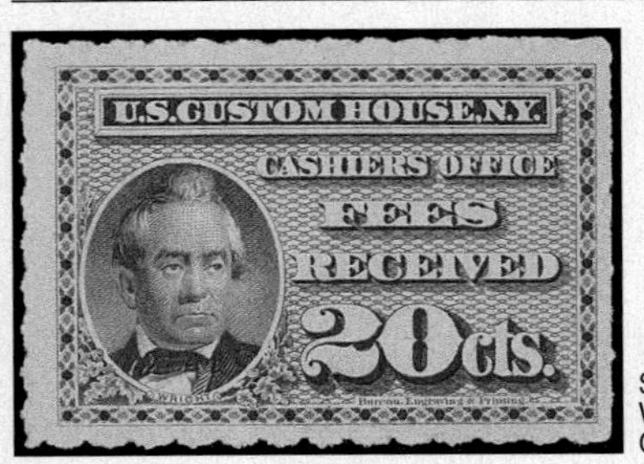

Silas Wright
CF1

Size: 48x34mm

1887 Engr. *Rouletted 5½*

RL1	CF1 20c **dull rose**	135.00	1.00
a.	20c **red**, perf. 10		*7,500.*
b.	Vert. half used as 10c, on document		*250.00*
c.	20c **red**, rouletted 7		*600.00*
RL2	CF1 30c **orange**	190.00	2.50
RL3	CF1 40c **green**	210.00	4.25
RL4	CF1 50c **dark blue**	210.00	6.00
RL5	CF1 60c **red violet**	160.00	2.50
RL6	CF1 70c **brown violet**	170.00	35.00
RL7	CF1 80c **brown**	240.00	85.00
RL8	CF1 90c **black**	290.00	100.00
	Nos. RL1-RL8 (8)	1,605.	236.25

Each of these stamps has its own distinctive background.

EMBOSSED REVENUE STAMPED PAPER

Some of the American colonies of Great Britain used embossed stamps in raising revenue, as Britain had done from 1694. The British government also imposed stamp taxes on the colonies, and in the early 19th century the U.S. government and some of the states enacted similar taxes.

Under one statute or another, these stamps were required on such documents as promissory notes, bills of exchange, insurance policies, bills of lading, bonds, protests, powers of attorney, stock certificates, letters patent, writs, conveyances, leases, mortgages, charter parties, commissions and liquor licenses.

A few of these stamps were printed, but most were colorless impressions resembling a notary public's seal.

The scant literature of these stamps includes E.B. Sterling's revenue catalogue of 1888, *The Stamps that Caused the American Revolution: The Stamps of the British Stamp Act for America,* by Adolph Koeppel, published in 1976 by the Town of North Hempstead (New York) American Revolution Bicentennial Commission, *New Discovery from British Archives on the 1765 Tax Stamps for America,* edited by Adolph Koeppel and published in 1962 by the American Revenue Association, *First Federal Issue 1798-1801 U.S. Embossed Revenue Stamped Paper,* by W.V. Combs, published in 1979 by the American Philatelic Society, *Second Federal Issue, 1801-1802,* by W.V. Combs, published in 1988 by the American Revenue Association, and *Third Federal Issue, 1814-1817,* by W.V. Combs, published in 1993 by the American Revenue Association.

Values are for stamps of clear impression on entire documents of the most common usage in good condition. The document may be folded. Unusual or rare usages may sell for much more. Parts of documents, cut squares or poor impressions sell for much less.

Colin MacR. Makepeace originally compiled the listings in this section.

INCLUDING COLONIAL EMBOSSED REVENUES

I. COLONIAL ISSUES

A. MASSACHUSETTS

Act of January 8, 1755

In effect May 1, 1755-April 30, 1757

ERP1

ERP2

ERP3

ERP4

Die 2 — ERP2

Typo.

RM1 ERP1 ½p **red** 2,500.

Embossed

RM2 ERP2 2p 400.
RM3 ERP3 3p 160.
RM4 ERP4 4p 700.

A second die of ERP2 with no fin on the under side of the codfish has been seen. There were at least two dies of the ½p.

B. NEW YORK

Act of December 1, 1756

In effect January 1, 1757-December 31, 1760

ERP9

Typo.

RM9 ERP9 ½p **red** *1,600.*

Embossed

RM10 ERP9 1p 1,750.
RM11 ERP9 2p 450.
RM12 ERP9 3p 550.
RM13 ERP9 4p 550.

II. BRITISH REVENUES FOR USE IN AMERICA

Act of March 22, 1765

In effect November 1, 1765-May 1, 1766.

A. ALMANAC STAMPS

ERP15

Engr.

RM15 ERP15 2p **red**
RM16 ERP15 4p **red** —
RM17 ERP15 8p **red**

Proofs of all of these stamps printed in the issued color are known. Full size facsimile reproductions in the color of the originals were made about 1876 of the proof sheets of the 8p stamp, Plates 1 and 2, Dies 1 to 50 inclusive.

B. PAMPHLETS AND NEWSPAPER STAMPS

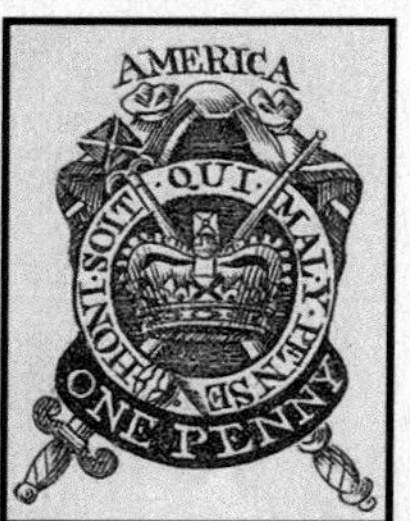

ERP18

Engr.

RM18 ERP18 ½p **red,** on newspaper *2,000.*
RM19 ERP18 1p **red** —
RM20 ERP18 2p **red**

Proofs of all of these stamps printed in the issued color are known. Full size facsimile reproductions in the color of the originals were made about 1876 of the proof sheets of the 1p stamp, Plates 3 and 4, Dies 51 to 100 inclusive.

C. GENERAL ISSUE

ERP24

ERP25

ERP26

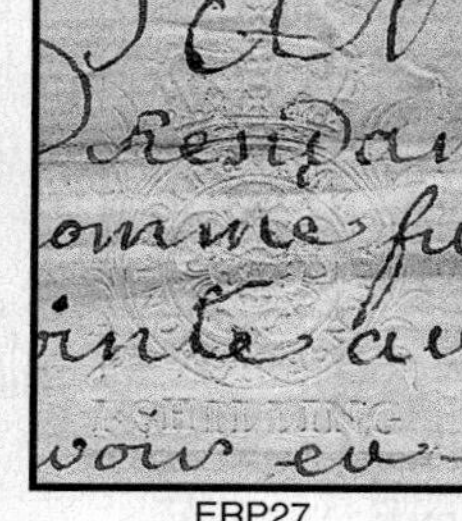

ERP27

ERP28

ERP29

ERP30

ERP31

ERP33

ERP34

ERP35

Embossed

RM24	ERP24	3p	*4,500.*
RM25	ERP25	4p	*4,500.*
RM26	ERP26	6p	*4,500.*
RM27	ERP27	1sh	*2,500.*
RM28	ERP28	1sh6p	*1,750.*
RM29	ERP29	2sh	*4,500.*
RM30	ERP30	2sh3p	*3,250.*
RM31	ERP31	2sh6p	*4,000.*
a.	Not on document		450.
RM33	ERP33	4sh	*2,500.*
RM34	ERP34	5sh	*3,750.*
RM35	ERP35	10sh	*4,750.*

Proofs exist of similar 1sh, 1sh6p and 2sh6p stamps inscribed "AMERICA CONT.& c."

Various Similar Designs

RM36	£1	
RM37	£2	—
RM38	£3	—
RM39	£4	
RM40	£6	—
RM41	£10	—

The £1 to £10 denominations probably exist only as proofs.

D. PLAYING CARDS STAMP

Type similar to EP29, with Arms of George III Encircled by Garter.

RM42	1sh	—

All of these were embossed without color and most of them were embossed directly on the document except the 2sh 6p which was general embossed on a rectangular piece of bluish or brownish stiff paper or cardboard only slightly larger than the stamp which was attached to the document by a small piece of metal. Three dies exist of the 3p; two of the 4p, 6p, 1sh, 1sh 6p, 2sh and 2sh 3p.

All of these stamps have the word "America" somewhere in the design and this is the feature which distinguishes them from the other British revenues. The stamps of the general issue are occasionally found with a design of a British revenue stamp struck over the American design, as a number of them were afterwards re-struck and used elsewhere as British revenues.

These stamps are sometimes called the "Teaparty" or "Tax on Tea" stamps. This, however, is a misnomer, as the act under which these stamps were issued laid no tax on tea. The tax on tea was levied by an act passed two years later, and the duties imposed by that act were not collected by stamps.

It must be remembered that these stamps were issued under an act applicable to all of the British colonies in America which included many which are not now part of the United States. Examples have been seen which were used in Quebec, Nova Scotia and in the West Indies. So great was the popular clamor against taxation by a body in which the colonists had no representation that ships bringing the stamps from England were not allowed to land them in some of the colonies, the stamps were destroyed in others, and in practically all of those which are now a part of the United States the "Stamp Masters" who were to administer the act were forced to resign and to take oath that they would never carry out the duties of the offices. Notwithstanding the very general feeling about these stamps there is evidence that a very small number of them were actually used on ships' documents for one vessel clearing from New York and for a very small number of vessels clearing from the Savannah River. Florida was at this time under British authority and the only known examples of these stamps used in what is now the United States, a 4p (#RM25), a 1sh (#RM27), and two examples of the 5sh (#RM34) were used there.

III. ISSUES OF THE UNITED STATES

A. FIRST FEDERAL ISSUE

Act of July 6, 1797

In effect July 1, 1798-February 28, 1801

RM142

RM228

The distinguishing feature of the stamps of this issue is the name of a state in the design. These stamps were issued by the Federal Government, however, and not by the states. The design, with the exception of the name of the state, was the same for each denomination; but different denominations had the shield and the eagle in different positions. The design of only one denomination of these stamps is illustrated.

In addition to the eagle and shield design on the values from four cents to ten dollars there are two other stamps for each state, similar in design to one another, one of which is illustrated above at right. All of these stamps are embossed without color.

Values are for clearly impressed examples.

RM45	4c	Connecticut	45.00
RM46	10c	Connecticut	125.00
RM47	20c	Connecticut	300.00
RM48	25c	Connecticut	45.00
RM49	30c	Connecticut	*2,750.*
RM50	50c	Connecticut	135.00
RM51	75c	Connecticut	—
RM52	$1	Connecticut	*1,500.*
RM53	$2	Connecticut	—
RM54	$4	Connecticut	*1,250.*
RM58	4c	Delaware	350.00
RM59	10c	Delaware	350.00
RM60	20c	Delaware	650.00
RM61	25c	Delaware	450.00
RM62	30c	Delaware	—
RM63	50c	Delaware	700.00
RM64	75c	Delaware	900.00
RM65	$1	Delaware	—
RM71	4c	Georgia	250.00
RM72	10c	Georgia	250.00
RM73	20c	Georgia	—
RM74	25c	Georgia	250.00
RM75	30c	Georgia	*3,000.*
RM76	50c	Georgia	1,250.
RM77	75c	Georgia	*2,250.*
RM78	$1	Georgia	—
RM84	4c	Kentucky	20.00
RM85	10c	Kentucky	100.00
RM86	20c	Kentucky	250.00
RM87	25c	Kentucky	40.00
RM88	30c	Kentucky	300.00
RM89	50c	Kentucky	60.00
RM90	75c	Kentucky	125.00
RM91	$1	Kentucky	*7,500.*
RM97	4c	Maryland	75.00
RM98	10c	Maryland	50.00
RM99	20c	Maryland	800.00
RM100	25c	Maryland	75.00
RM101	30c	Maryland	600.00
RM102	50c	Maryland	125.00
RM103	75c	Maryland	100.00
RM104	$1	Maryland	—
RM106	$4	Maryland	—
RM110	4c	Massachusetts	20.00
RM111	10c	Massachusetts	40.00
RM112	20c	Massachusetts	85.00
RM113	25c	Massachusetts	50.00
RM114	30c	Massachusetts	850.00
RM115	50c	Massachusetts	100.00
RM116	75c	Massachusetts	900.00
RM117	$1	Massachusetts	350.00
RM123	4c	New Hampshire	30.00
RM124	10c	New Hampshire	30.00
RM125	20c	New Hampshire	750.00
RM126	25c	New Hampshire	70.00
RM127	30c	New Hampshire	425.00
RM128	50c	New Hampshire	80.00
RM129	75c	New Hampshire	80.00
RM130	$1	New Hampshire	*3,500.*
RM136	4c	New Jersey	450.00
RM137	10c	New Jersey	150.00
RM138	20c	New Jersey	—
RM139	25c	New Jersey	110.00
RM140	30c	New Jersey	750.00
RM141	50c	New Jersey	175.00
RM142	75c	New Jersey	*1,500.*
RM143	$1	New Jersey	—
RM147	$10	New Jersey	*4,750.*
RM149	4c	New York	35.00
RM150	10c	New York	20.00
RM151	20c	New York	60.00
RM152	25c	New York	50.00
RM153	30c	New York	25.00
RM154	50c	New York	30.00
RM155	75c	New York	50.00
RM156	$1	New York	250.00
RM157	$2	New York	—
RM159	$5	New York	—
RM160	$10	New York	—
RM162	4c	North Carolina	50.00
RM163	10c	North Carolina	50.00
RM164	20c	North Carolina	950.00
RM165	25c	North Carolina	55.00
RM166	30c	North Carolina	3,500.
RM167	50c	North Carolina	175.00
RM168	75c	North Carolina	450.00
RM169	$1	North Carolina	*3,750.*
RM175	4c	Pennsylvania	27.50
RM176	10c	Pennsylvania	17.50
RM177	20c	Pennsylvania	25.00
RM178	25c	Pennsylvania	15.00
RM179	30c	Pennsylvania	27.50
RM180	50c	Pennsylvania	22.50
RM181	75c	Pennsylvania	70.00
RM182	$1	Pennsylvania	350.00
RM184	$4	Pennsylvania	13,000.
RM187		Pennsylvania, "Ten cents per centum"	—
RM188	4c	Rhode Island	35.00
RM189	10c	Rhode Island	50.00
RM190	20c	Rhode Island	200.00
RM191	25c	Rhode Island	65.00
RM192	30c	Rhode Island	2,250.
RM193	50c	Rhode Island	150.00
RM194	75c	Rhode Island	*1,500.*
RM195	$1	Rhode Island	*1,250.*
RM201	4c	South Carolina	65.00
RM202	10c	South Carolina	130.00
RM203	20c	South Carolina	350.00
RM204	25c	South Carolina	125.00
RM205	30c	South Carolina	—
RM206	50c	South Carolina	140.00
RM207	75c	South Carolina	*4,000.*
RM208	$1	South Carolina	*7,500.*
RM211	$5	South Carolina	—
RM214	4c	Tennessee	500.00
RM215	10c	Tennessee	240.00
RM216	20c	Tennessee	—
RM217	25c	Tennessee	300.00
RM218	30c	Tennessee	—
RM219	50c	Tennessee	*1,250.*
RM220	75c	Tennessee	—
RM221	$1	Tennessee	—
RM227	4c	Vermont	75.00
RM228	10c	Vermont	35.00
RM229	20c	Vermont	350.00
RM230	25c	Vermont	100.00
RM231	30c	Vermont	*1,350.*
RM232	50c	Vermont	130.00
RM233	75c	Vermont	*3,500.*
RM234	$1	Vermont	—
RM238	$10	Vermont	—
RM240	4c	Virginia	15.00
RM241	10c	Virginia	15.00
RM242	20c	Virginia	125.00
RM243	25c	Virginia	20.00
RM244	30c	Virginia	500.00
RM245	50c	Virginia	25.00
RM246	75c	Virginia	50.00
RM247	$1	Virginia	*1,000.*

The Act called for a $2, $4, $5 and $10 stamp for each state; only the listed ones have been seen.

The Act also called for a "Ten cents per centum" and a "Six mills per dollar" stamp for each state, none of which has been seen except No. RM187.

A press and a set of dies, one die for each denomination, were prepared and sent to each state where it was the duty of the Supervisors of the Revenue to stamp all documents presented to them upon payment of the proper tax. The Supervisors were also to have on hand for sale blank paper stamped with the different rates of duty to be sold to the public upon which the purchaser would later write or print the proper type of instrument corresponding with the value of the stamp impressed thereon. So far as is now known there was no distinctive watermark for the paper sold by the government. The Vermont set of dies is in the Vermont Historical Society at Montpelier.

B. SECOND FEDERAL ISSUE

Act of April 23, 1800

In effect March 1, 1801-June 30, 1802

No. RM266 Counter Stamp

No. RM266

Government watermark in italics; laid paper

RM260a 4c 15.00
RM261a 10c 20.00
RM262a 20c 65.00
RM263a 25c 15.00
RM264a 30c 75.00
RM265a 50c 65.00
RM266a 75c 30.00
RM267a $1 250.00

Government watermark in roman; wove paper

RM260b 4c 15.00
RM261b 10c 20.00
RM262b 20c 75.00
RM263b 25c 15.00
RM264b 30c 75.00
RM265b 50c 45.00
RM266b 75c 50.00
RM267b $1 225.00
RM271b $10 *3,250.*

No Government watermark

RM260c 4c 50.00
RM261c 10c 50.00
RM262c 20c 85.00
RM263c 25c 17.50
RM264c 30c 400.00
RM265c 50c 85.00
RM266c 75c 100.00
RM267c $1 200.00
RM269c $4 *500.00*

The distinguishing feature of the stamps of this issue is the counter stamp, the left stamp shown in the illustration, which usually appears on a document below the other stamp. In the right stamp the design of the eagle and the shield are similar to their design in the same denomination of the First Federal Issue but the name of the state is omitted and the denomination appears below instead of above the eagle and the shield. All of these stamps were embossed without color.

All the paper which was furnished by the government contained the watermark vertically along the edge of the sheet, "GEN STAMP OFFICE," either in Roman capitals on wove paper or in italic capitals on laid paper. The wove paper also had in the center of each half sheet either the watermark "W. Y. & Co." or "Delaware." William Young & Co. who owned the Delaware Mills made the government paper. The laid paper omitted the watermark "Delaware." The two stamps were separately impressed. The design of the eagle and shield differed in each value.

All the stamping was done in Washington, the right stamp being put on in the General Stamp Office and the left one or counter stamp in the office of the Commissioner of the Revenue as a check on the stamping done in the General Stamp Office. The "Com. Rev. C. S." in the design of the counter stamp stands for "Commissioner of the Revenue, Counter Stamp."

The Second Federal issue was intended to include $2 and $5 stamps, but these denominations have not been seen.

C. THIRD FEDERAL ISSUE

Act of August 2, 1813
In effect January 1, 1814-December 31, 1817

No. RM286

Watermarked

RM275a 5c 10.00
RM276a 10c 10.00
RM277a 25c 15.00
RM278a 50c 10.00
RM279a 75c 13.00
RM280a $1 14.50
RM281a $1.50 22.50
RM282a $2 45.00
RM283a $2.50 40.00
RM284a $3.50 240.00
RM286a $5 250.00

Unwmk.

RM275b 5c 15.00
RM276b 10c 10.00
RM277b 25c 15.00
RM278b 50c 10.00
RM279b 75c 17.50
RM280b $1 30.00
RM281b $1.50 100.00
RM282b $2 100.00
RM283b $2.50 160.00
RM284b $3.50 150.00
RM285b $4 *550.00*
RM286b $5 *250.00*

The distinguishing features of the stamps of this issue are the absence of the name of a state in the design and the absence of the counter stamp. Different values show different positions of the eagle.

All stamps of this issue were embossed without color at Washington. The paper with the watermark "Stamp U. S." was sold by the government. Unwatermarked paper may be either wove or laid.

IV. ISSUES BY VARIOUS STATES

DELAWARE

Act of June 19, 1793
In effect October 1, 1793-February 7, 1794

ERP50

ERP51

ERP53

RM291 ERP50 5c *6,500.*
RM292 ERP51 20c *5,000.*
RM293 ERP53 50c —

In some cases a reddish ink was used in impressing the stamp and in other cases the impressions are colorless.

Besides the denominations listed, 3c, 33c, and $1 stamps were called for by the taxing act. Stamps of these denominations have not been seen.

VIRGINIA

Act of February 20, 1813
In effect May 1, 1813-April 30, 1815
Act of December 21, 1814
In effect May 1, 1815-February 27, 1816

ERP60

ERP61

RM305 ERP61 4c
a. Die cut 17.50
b. On document 100.00
RM306 ERP60 6c
a. Die cut 17.50
b. On document 300.00
RM307 ERP61 10c
b. On document 500.00
RM308 ERP60 12c
a. Die cut 25.00
b. On document 300.00
RM309 ERP61 20c
a. Die cut 60.00
b. On document 500.00
RM310 ERP61 25c
a. Die cut 17.50
b. On document 275.00
RM311 ERP61 37c
a. Die cut 17.50
b. On document *1,000.*
RM312 ERP61 45c
a. Die cut 60.00
b. On document *1,250.*
RM313 ERP61 50c
a. Die cut 17.50
b. On document 500.00
RM314 ERP61 70c
a. Die cut 40.00
b. On document *1,000.*
RM315 ERP61 75c
a. Die cut 17.50
b. On document *750.00*
RM316 ERP61 95c
a. Die cut 40.00
b. On document *1,000.*
RM317 ERP61 100c
a. Die cut 60.00
b. On document *750.00*
RM318 ERP61 120c
b. On document *1,000.*
RM319 ERP61 125c
a. Die cut 125.00
b. On document *1,000.*
RM323 ERP60 175c
a. Die cut 17.50
RM325 ERP61 200c
a. Die cut 17.50
b. On document 475.00

All of these stamps are colorless impressions and with some exceptions as noted below those issued under the 1813 Act cannot be distinguished from those issued under the 1814 Act. The 10c, 20c, 45c, 70c, 95c, 120c, 145c, 150c, 170c and 190c were issued only under the 1813 Act, the 6c, 12c, and 37c only under the 1814 Act.

No. RM311 has the large lettering of EP60 but the 37 is to the left and the XXXVII to the right as in EP61. The design of the dogwood branch and berries is similar but not identical in all values.

When the tax on the document exceeded "two hundred cents," two or more stamps were impressed or attached to the document. For instance a document has been seen with 45c and 200c to make up the $2.45 rate, and another with 75c and 200c.

Since both the Virginia and the Third Federal Acts to some extent taxed the same kind of document, and since during the period from Jan. 1, 1814 to Feb. 27, 1816, both Acts were in effect in Virginia, some instruments have both stamps on them.

The circular die cut Virginia stamps about 29mm in diameter were cut out of previously stamped paper which after the Act was repealed, was presented for redemption at the office of the Auditor of Public Accounts. They were threaded on fine twine and until about 1940 preserved in his office as required by law. Watermarked die cut Virginia stamps are all cut out of Third Federal watermarked paper.

Not seen yet, the 145c, 150c, and 170c stamps were called for by the 1813 Act, and 195c by both the 1813 and 1814 Acts.

MARYLAND

1. Act of February 11, 1818
In effect May 1, 1818-March 7, 1819

ERP70

RM362 ERP70 30c **red,** printed 400.
Sheet of 4 2,500.
RM363 ERP70 50c **red,** printed —

The Act called for five other denominations, none of which has been seen. The Act imposing this tax was held unconstitutional by the United States Supreme Court in the case of McCulloch vs. Maryland.

2. Act of March 10, 1845
In effect May 10, 1845-March 10, 1856

ERP71

RM370 ERP71 10c 15.00
RM371 ERP71 15c 14.00
RM372 ERP71 25c 14.00
RM373 ERP71 50c 16.00
RM374 ERP71 75c 40.00
RM375 ERP71 $1 16.00
RM376 ERP71 $1.50 35.00

RM377	ERP71	$2	60.00
RM378	ERP71	$2.50	20.00
RM379	ERP71	$3.50	60.00
RM380	ERP71	$4	100.00
RM381	ERP71	$5.50	60.00
RM382	ERP71	$6	75.00

Nos. RM370-RM382 are embossed without color with a similar design for each value. They vary in size from 20mm in diameter for the 10c to 33mm for the $6.

V. FEDERAL LICENSES TO SELL LIQUOR, ETC.

1. Act of June 5, 1794
In effect September 30, 1794-June 30, 1802

ERP80

RM400	ERP80	$5	550.00

Provisionals are in existence using the second issue Connecticut Supervisors' stamp with the words "Five Dollars" written or printed over it or the second issue of the New Hampshire Supervisors' stamp without the words "Five Dollars."

2. Act of August 2, 1813
In effect January 1, 1814-December 31, 1817

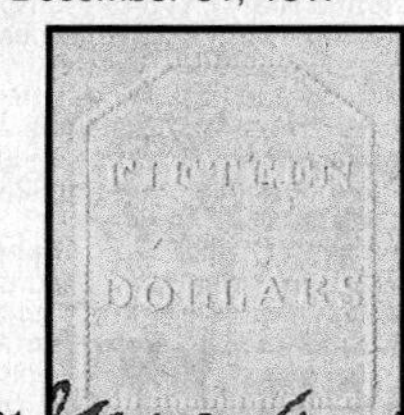

ERP81

RM451	ERP81	$10	725.00
RM452	ERP81	$12	750.00
RM453	ERP81	$15	425.00
RM454	ERP81	$18	900.00
RM455	ERP81	$20	*1,400.*
RM456	ERP81	$22.50	650.00
RM457	ERP81	$25	550.00
RM458	ERP81	$30	*1,500.*
RM459	ERP81	$37.50	550.00

The Act of December 23, 1814, increased the basic rates of $10, $12, $15, $20 and $25 by 50 per cent, effective February 1, 1815. This increase applied to the unexpired portions of the year so far as licenses then in effect were concerned and these licenses were required to be brought in and to have the payment of the additional tax endorsed on them.

VI. FEDERAL LICENSES TO WORK A STILL

Act of July 24, 1813
In effect January 1, 1814-December 31, 1817

(Embossed) — ERP82

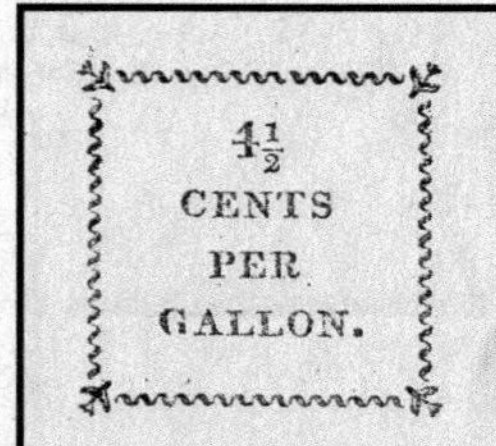

(Printed) — ERP83

RM466	4½c		
b.	ERP83	Printed	*2,000.*
RM468	9c		
a.	ERP82	Embossed	*1,500.*
b.	ERP83	Printed	*1,800.*
RM471	18c		
a.	ERP82	Embossed	—
b.	ERP83	Printed	*1,400.*
RM472	21c		
a.	ERP82	Embossed	—
RM475	32c		
a.	ERP82	Embossed	—
RM477	36c		
b.	ERP83	Printed	*2,100.*
RM478	42c		
b.	ERP83	Printed	*2,000.*
RM480	52c		
a.	ERP82	Embossed	*2,000.*
RM484	70c		
a.	ERP82	Embossed	*2,100.*
RM488	$1.08		
a.	ERP82	Embossed	*2,000.*

The statute under which these were issued provided for additional rates of 2½c, 5c, 10c, 16c, 25c, 26c, 35c, 42c, 50c, 54c, 60c, 64c, 84c, $1.04, $1.05, $1.20, $1.35, $1.40, $2.10, $2.16 and $2.70 per gallon of the capacity of the still. Stamps of these denominations have not been seen.

VII. SUPERVISORS' AND CUSTOM HOUSE SEALS

1. Seals came into use on required certificates, as follows: April 1, 1791, domestic and imported distilled spirits; July 1, 1792, imported wine.

Check Letter Shown in Left Field — ERP90

RM501	ERP90	B	South Carolina	40.00
RM503	ERP90	D	Virginia	*1,350.*
RM505	ERP90	F	Delaware	—
RM506	ERP90	G	Pennsylvania	90.00
RM508	ERP90	I	New York	22.50
RM509	ERP90	K	Connecticut	30.00
RM510	ERP90	L	Rhode Island	90.00
RM511	ERP90	M	Massachusetts	22.50
RM512	ERP90	N	New Hampshire	700.00
RM514	ERP90	P	Kentucky	—

Use of RM501-RM514 on certificates for domestic distilled spirits shows payment of the tax that was being resisted in the Whiskey Rebellion. All such reported uses are from the New England states. Nos. RM501-RM514 were removed from service in late 1799. In Connecticut and Massachusetts, they were returned to service after July 1, 1802.

2. Use from October 2, 1799

ERP91

RM552	ERP91	North Carolina	500.00
RM553	ERP91	Virginia	—
RM554	ERP91	Maryland	200.00
RM556	ERP91	Pennsylvania	250.00
RM558	ERP91	New York	15.00
RM559	ERP91	Connecticut	30.00
RM560	ERP91	Rhode Island	35.00
RM561	ERP91	Massachusetts	25.00
RM562	ERP91	New Hampshire	90.00

Nos. RM552-RM562 were necessitated by excessive wear on Nos. RM501-RM514.

3. Custom House Seals

ERP92

RM575	ERP92	Custom House, Philadelphia	50.00
RM576	ERP92	Custom House, Perth Amboy, N.J.	50.00

The Philadelphia Customs House Seal came into use in 1802 and was used on import documents for distilled spirits, tea and wine. It functioned in the way that the Supervisor's Seals functioned in other states. When the Perth Amboy Customs House Seal came into use is not known, but there are recorded examples from the 1820's.

The editors would like to hear from those having other Customs House Seals used on import documents.

REVENUE STAMPED PAPER

These stamps were printed in various denominations and designs on a variety of financial documents, including checks, drafts, receipts, specie clerk statements, insurance policies, bonds and stock certificates.

They were authorized by Act of Congress of July 1, 1862, effective October 1, 1862, although regular delivery of stamped paper did not begin until July 1, 1865. The 2-cent tax on receipts ended Oct. 1, 1870. The 2-cent tax on checks and sight drafts ended July 1, 1883. All other taxes ended Oct. 1, 1872. The use of stamped paper was revived by the War Revenue Act of 1898, approved June 13, 1898. Type X was used July 1, 1898 through June 30, 1902.

Most of these stamps were typographed; some, types H, I and J, were engraved. They were printed by private firms under supervision of government representatives from dies loaned by the Bureau of Internal Revenue. Types A-F, P-W were printed by the American Phototype Co., New York (1865-75); type G, Graphic Co., New York (1875-83); types H-L, Joseph R. Carpenter, Philadelphia (1866-75); types M-N, A. Trochsler, Boston (1873-75); type O, Morey and Sherwood, Chicago (1874). Type X was printed by numerous regional printers under contract with the government.

Samples of these stamps are known for types B-G, P and Q with a section of the design removed and replaced by the word "Sample." Types G, P-Q, U-W exist with a redemption clause added by typography or rubber stamp. Redeemed type X's have a 5mm punched hole.

Multiples or single impressions on various plain papers are usually considered proofs or printers' waste.

For further information see "Handbook for United States Revenue Stamped Paper," published (1979) by the American Revenue Association.

Illustration size varies, with actual size quoted for each type.

Values for types A-O are for clear impressions on plain entire checks and receipts. Attractive documents with vignettes sell for more. The value of individual examples is also affected by the place of use. For example, territorial usage generally sells for more than a similar item from New York City.

Values for types P-W are for stamps on documents with attractive engravings, usually stock certificates, bonds and insurance policies.

Examples on plain documents and cut squares sell for less.

Type A

Size: 22x25mm

RN-A1	2c **black**	90.	75.
	a. Printed on both sides		30.
RN-A2	2c **orange**		160.
RN-A3	2c **gray**		*2,000.*
RN-A4	2c **blue**		*8,000.*
RN-A5	2c **brown**		*5,000.*
RN-A8	2c **purple**		*2,000.*
RN-A9	2c **green**		*1,350.*
	a. Inverted		—

No. RN-A4 is unique. The unique example of No. RN-A9a is on a partial document. The catalogue value for RN-A8 is for an impression on William Moller & Son stationery; a second more violet shade is on Carter, Kirkland & Co. receipts. Value of latter is $3,250.

Same Type with 1 Entire and 53 or 56 Partial Impressions in Vertical Format ("Tapeworm")
Left Col. — Full Document
Right Col. — Strip with Bank Names

RN-A10	2c **orange**, 1 full plus 56 partial impressions	675.	100.
	Cut square (full strip without bank names)		45.
RN-A11	2c **orange**, 1 full plus 53 partial impressions	*1,100.*	250.

Nos. RN-A10 and RN-A11 were used by the Mechanics' National Bank of New York on a bank specie clerk's statement. It was designed so that the full stamp or one of the repeated bottom segments fell on each line opposite the name of a bank.

The three additional banks were added at the bottom of the form. No. RN-A11 must show white space below the "First National Bank" line.

Eagle Type B

Size: 31x48mm

RN-B1	2c **orange**	5.00	3.00
	yellow orange	5.00	3.00
	deep orange	5.00	3.00
	a. Printed on both sides	200.00	20.00
	b. Double impression	350.00	
	c. Printed on back		—
	d. With 10 centimes blue French handstamp, right	400.00	
	e. Inverted		*600.00*

The unique example of No. RN-B1e is on a partial document.

All examples of the previously-listed "yellow" have some red in them.

RN-B2	2c **black**		40.00
RN-B3	2c **blue**		40.00
	light blue		40.00
RN-B4	2c **brown**	125.00	40.00
RN-B5	2c **bronze**		40.00
RN-B6	2c **green** (shades)	110.00	15.00
RN-B10	2c **red** (shades)	200.00	22.50
RN-B11	2c **purple**		125.00
RN-B13	2c **violet** (shades)	125.00	40.00
	a. 2c **violet brown**		45.00

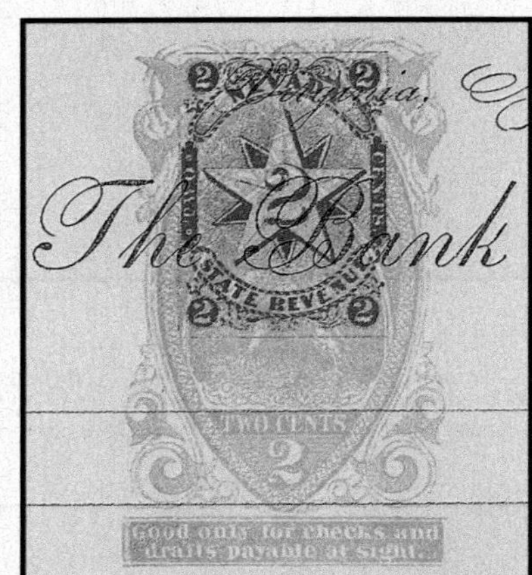

"Good only for checks and drafts payable at sight." in Rectangular Tablet at Base

RN-B16	2c **orange**	45.00	12.50
	a. With 2c orange red Nevada	325.00	250.00

"Good only for checks and drafts payable at sight." in Octagonal Tablet at Base

RN-B17	2c **orange**	42.50	10.00
	a. Tablet inverted		1,750.
	b. With 2c orange red Nevada		35.00
	c. With 2c green Nevada		35.00
	d. With 2c dull violet Nevada		*1,500.*
	e. With 2c brownish violet Nevada		*2,500.*

"Good when issued for the payment of money." in Octagonal Tablet at Base

RN-B20	2c **orange**	70.00	15.00
	a. Printed on both sides	30.00	10.00
	b. As "a," one stamp inverted		*1,500.*
	c. Tablet inverted		*4,000.*

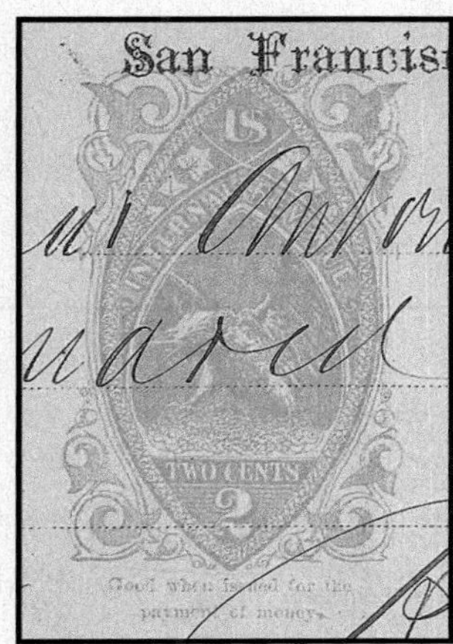

"Good when issued for the payment of money" in two lines at base in orange

RN-B23	2c **orange**		900.00

"Good when the amount does not exceed $100." in Octagonal Tablet at Base

RN-B24	2c **orange**	200.00	50.00

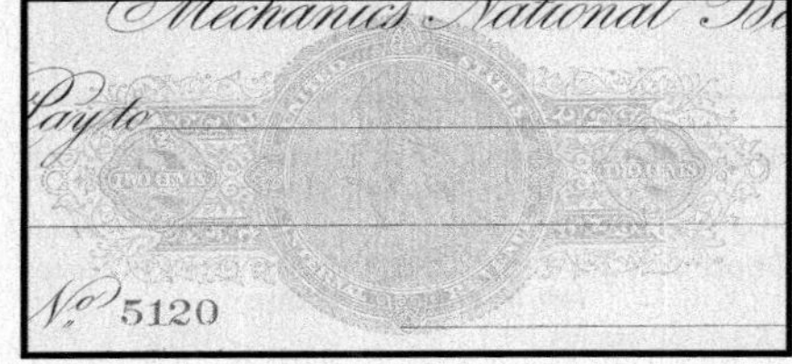

Washington Type C

Size: 108x49mm

RN-C1	2c **orange**	7.00	4.00
	red orange	7.00	4.00
	yellow orange	7.00	4.00
	salmon	8.00	4.00
	brown orange	8.00	4.00
	a. "Good when used..." vert. at left black		*2,250.*

All examples of the previously-listed "yellow" have some red in them.

RN-C2	2c **brown**	30.00	12.00
	a. 2c **buff**	30.00	12.00
RN-C5	2c **pale red** (shades)	50.00	25.00
RN-C8	2c **green**		—

"Good only for Sight Draft" in two lines in color of stamp

RN-C9	2c **orange,** legend at lower right	85.00	50.00
RN-C11	2c **brown,** legend at lower left		110.00
RN-C13	2c **orange,** legend at lower left	45.00	20.00

"Good only for Receipt for Money Paid" in two lines in color of stamp

RN-C15	2c **orange,** legend at lower right	*2,500.*	*1,750.*
RN-C16	2c **orange,** legend at lower left		350.00

"Good when issued for the payment of money" in one line at base in color of stamp

RN-C17	2c **orange** (shades)		575.00

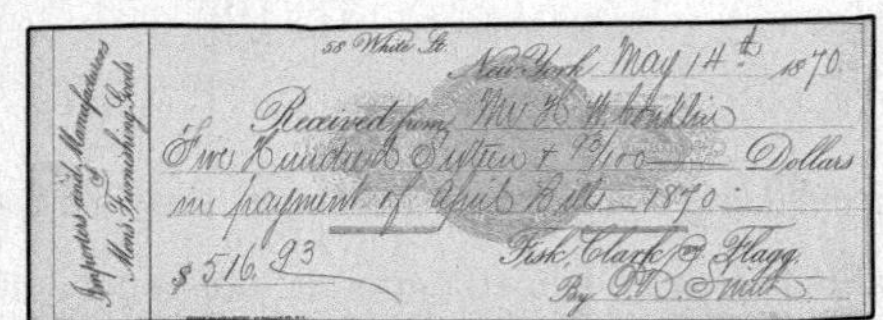

"Good when issued for the/Payment of Money" in two tablets at lower left and right

RN-C19 2c **orange** 550.00
a. Printed on both sides 35.00

"Good/only for Bank/Check" in 3-part Band

RN-C21 2c **orange** 60.00 12.50
salmon 12.50
yellow orange 20.00
a. Inverted 750.00
b. With 2c red orange Nevada 140.00 65.00
c. Printed on back *2,900.*
RN-C22 2c **brown** 300.00 25.00
a. Printed on back 1,800.

"Good when the amount does not exceed $100" in tablet at lower right

RN-C26 2c **orange** 200.00

Franklin Type D

Size: 80x43mm

RN-D1 2c **orange** (shades) 10.00 4.00
a. Double impression —
b. Printed on back 700.00 400.00
c. Inverted 475.00

All examples of the previously-listed "yellow" have some red in them and are included in the "shades."

RN-D3 2c **brown** *3,000.* *500.00*
RN-D4 2c **buff** (shades) 9.00 5.00
RN-D5 2c **red** *2,000.*

"Good only for/Bank Check" in panels within circles at left and right

RN-D7 2c **orange** 25.00 10.00
a. Printed on back 2,100.

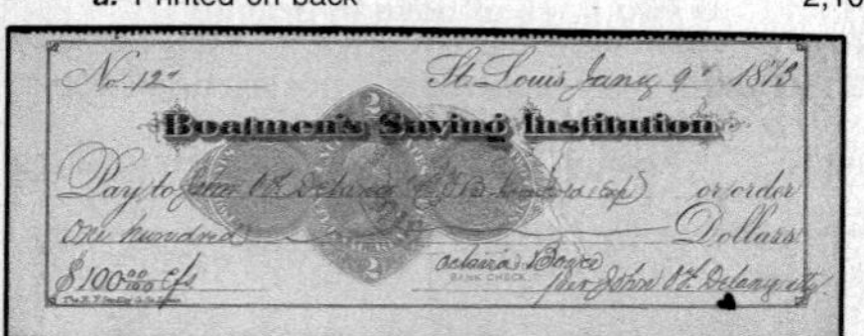

"Good only for/Bank Check" in two lines at lower right in color of stamp

RN-D8 2c **orange** 850.00

"Good only for Sight Draft" in two lines at lower left in color of stamp

RN-D9 2c **orange** 175.00 75.00

Franklin Type E

Size: 28x50mm

RN-E2 2c **brown** *1,200.*
RN-E4 2c **orange** 12.50 5.00
Broken die, lower right or left 40.00 20.00
a. Double impression *925.00*

"Good only for sight draft" in two lines at base in orange

RN-E5 2c **orange** 75.00 37.50

"Good only for Bank / Check" in two lines at base in orange

RN-E6 2c **orange** —

"Good only for / Bank Check" in colorless letters in two lines above and below portrait

RN-E7 2c **orange** 75.00 17.50
a. Double impression —

Franklin Type F

Size: 56x34mm

RN-F1 2c **orange** 10.00 5.00
a. Inverted —

All examples of the previously-listed "yellow" have some red in them

Liberty Type G

Size: 80x48mm

RN-G1 2c **orange** 6.00 4.00
a. Printed on back 65.00 40.00
b. Printed on back, inverted 125.00 50.00

All examples of the previously-listed "yellow" have some red in them.

Imprint: "Graphic Co., New York" at left and right in minute type

RN-G3 2c **orange** 100.00 100.00

Eagle Type H

Size: 32x50mm

RN-H3 2c **orange** 15.00 5.00
a. Inverted —
b. Double impression 600.00
c. "Good when used for payment of money," black *750.00*
d. "Good when used as a receipt for payment of money," black *750.00*
e. As "d," upward at left *1,600.*
f. As "d," legend in red *1,500.*
g. "Good when used as a receipt for the payment of money," black *400.00*
h. As "g," inverted legend *7,500.*
i. As "g," legend in two lines *700.00*
j. As "g," legend in violet *700.00*
k. As "g," legend in yellow *2,000.*
l. "Good only when used as a receipt for the payment of moneys," black *750.00*

"Good for check or sight draft only" at left and right in color of stamp

RN-H5 2c **orange**

Experts claim that No. RN-H5 exists only as a proof.

"Good for bank check or sight draft only" in black

RN-H6 2c **orange** 150.00

Type I
Design R2 of 1862-72 adhesive revenues
"BANK CHECK"
Size: 20x23mm

RN-I1 2c **orange** 225.00

"U.S. INTER. REV."

RN-I2 2c **orange** 650.00 350.00

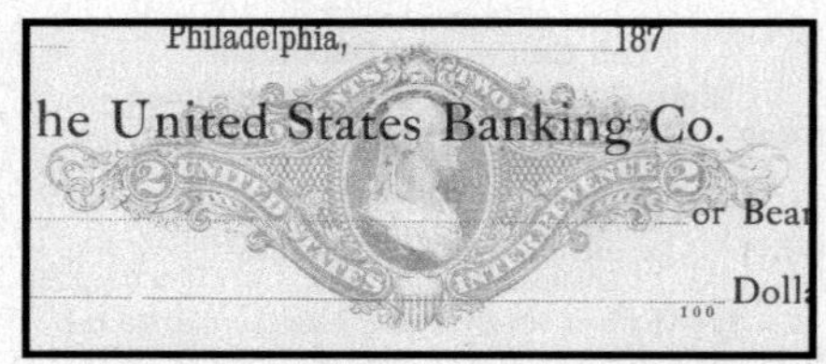

Washington Type J

Size: 105x40mm
Background of medallion crosshatched, filling oval except for bust

RN-J4 2c **orange** 20.00 10.00
pale orange 20.00 10.00
deep orange 50.00 12.50
a. Double impression *500.00*
b. "Good only for . . ." added vertically at left in red orange 750.00
RN-J5 2c **red** 50.00 13.00
a. Double impression —

"Good for check or sight draft only" curved, below

RN-J9 2c **red** — *2,000.*

Background shaded below bust and at left.

RN-J11 2c **orange** 60.00 15.00

Washington Type K

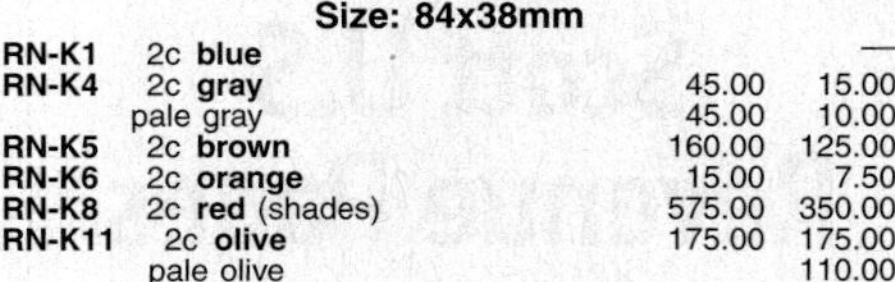

Size: 84x38mm

RN-K1	2c **blue**		—
RN-K4	2c **gray**	45.00	15.00
	pale gray	45.00	10.00
RN-K5	2c **brown**	160.00	125.00
RN-K6	2c **orange**	15.00	7.50
RN-K8	2c **red** (shades)	575.00	350.00
RN-K11	2c **olive**	175.00	175.00
	pale olive		110.00

Washington Type L

Size: 50x33mm

RN-L1	2c **blue** (shades)	175.00	—
RN-L2	2c **turquoise**	250.00	200.00
RN-L3	2c **gray**	35.00	20.00
	pale gray	35.00	20.00
RN-L4	2c **green**	900.00	600.00
	light green	600.00	400.00
RN-L5	2c **orange**	15.00	10.00
RN-L6	2c **olive**		55.00
	gray olive		30.00
RN-L10	2c **red**	15.00	10.00
	a. 2c **violet red**	15.00	10.00
RN-L13	2c **brown**	—	275.00

Washington Type M

Size: 68x37mm

RN-M2	2c **orange**	50.00	10.00
	a. Printed on back, inverted		*1,600.*

All examples of the previously-listed "yellow" have some red in them.

RN-M3	2c **green**		475.00
RN-M4	2c **gray**		1,250.

Eagle, Numeral and Monitor Type N

Size: 107x48mm

RN-N3	2c **orange**	60.00	15.00
	a. Printed on back	300.00	225.00
	b. Inverted		900.00
RN-N4	2c **light brown**		150.00

Liberty Type O

Size: 75x35mm

RN-O2	2c **orange**	1,750.	600.

Values for types P-W

are for stamps on documents with attractive engravings, usually stock certificates, bonds and insurance policies. Examples on plain documents sell for less.

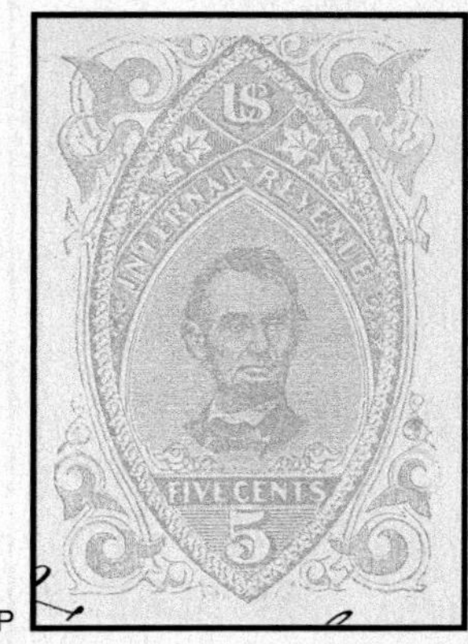

Lincoln Type P

Size: 32x49mm

RN-P2	5c **brown**		350.00
	Cut square		90.00
RN-P3	5c **green**		—
RN-P4	5c **pink**		—
RN-P5	5c **orange**	50.00	45.00
	Cut square		8.00

All examples of the previously listed "yellow" have some orange in them.

RN-P6	5c **red** (shades)	—	210.00
	Cut square		40.00

No. RN-P3 only exists in combination with a 25c green or 50c green. No. RN-P4 is unique and only exists in combination with a $1 pink. See Nos. RN-T2, RN-V1, RN-W6.

Madison Type Q (See note before No. RN-P2)

Size: 28x56mm

RN-Q1	5c **orange**	175.	150.
	Cut square		20.
	brownish orange	175.	150.
RN-Q2	5c **brown**		*2,750.*
	Cut square		500.

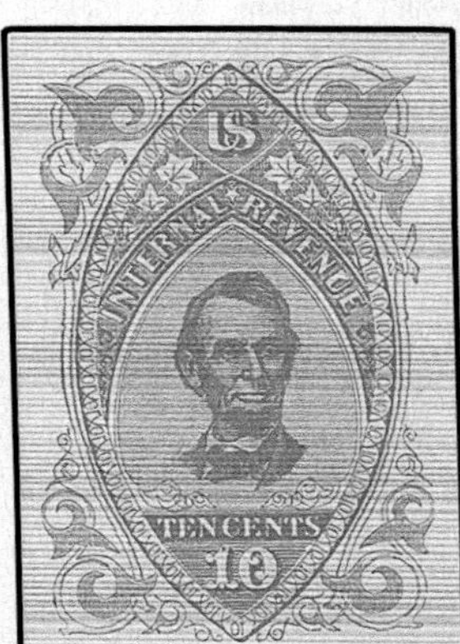

Type R, Frame as Type B, Lincoln in Center

Size: 32x49mm

RN-R1	10c **brown**		*2,500.*
RN-R2	10c **pale red**	—	675.
	Cut square		100.
RN-R3	10c **orange**		500.
	Cut square		50.

"Good when the premium does not exceed $10" in tablet at base

RN-R6	10c **orange**	—	400.
	Cut square		50.

Motto Without Tablet

RN-R7	10c **orange**		
	Cut square		500.

Washington Type S (See note before No. RN-P2)

Size: 33x54mm

RN-S1	10c **orange**		*3,750.*

"Good when the premium does not exceed $10" in tablet at base

RN-S2	10c **orange**		*4,750.*
	Cut square		500.

Eagle Type T (See note before No. RN-P2)

For type T design with Lincoln in center see type V, Nos. RN-V1 to RN-V10.

Size: 33x40mm

RN-T1	25c **black**	—	
	Cut square		—
RN-T2	25c **green**		*7,500.*
RN-T3	25c **red**	175.00	*100.00*
	Cut square		9.00
RN-T4	25c **orange**	150.00	75.00
	Cut square		7.50
	light orange	150.00	75.00
	light orange, cut square		7.50
	brown orange		75.00
	brown orange, cut square		8.00

No. RN-T2 includes No. RN-P3, and a 25c green, type T, obliterating a No. RN-V4.

"Good when the premium does not exceed $50" in tablet at base

RN-T6	25c **orange**	450.	350.
	Cut square		50.
RN-T7	25c **orange,** motto without tablet		1,500.
	Cut square		400.

"Good when the amount insured shall not exceed $1000" in tablet at base

RN-T8	25c **deep orange**	800.	700.
	Cut square		75.
RN-T9	25c **orange,** motto without tablet		
	Cut square		600.

Franklin Type U (See note before No. RN-P2)

Size: 126x65mm

RN-U1	25c **orange**	35.00	35.00
	Cut square		5.00
RN-U2	25c **brown**	45.00	35.00
	Cut square		5.00

"Good when the premium does not exceed $50" in tablet at lower right

RN-U3	25c **red**		*8,000.*
RN-U4	25c **orange**		*2,500.*
	Cut square		400.

Tablet at lower left

RN-U5	25c **red**	800.	
	Cut square		250.
RN-U6	25c **orange**	500.	450.
	Cut square		65.

All examples of the previously-listed "yellow" have some red in them.

Tablet at base

RN-U7	25c **brown**		*1,750.*
	Cut square		300.
RN-U9	25c **orange**		*1,000.*
	Cut square		400.

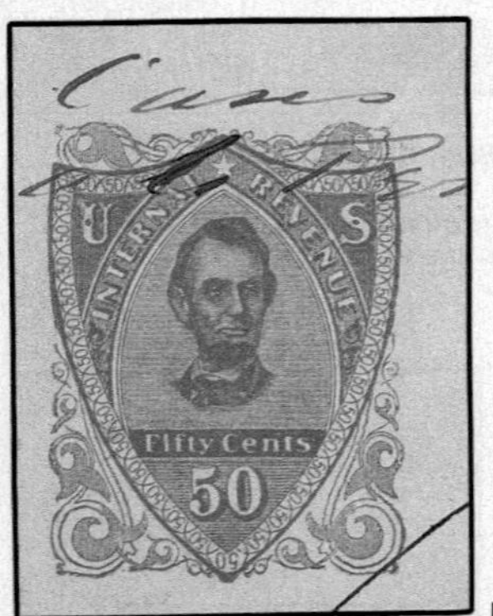

Lincoln Type V

Size: 32x41mm

RN-V1	50c **green**		175.00
	Cut square		52.50
RN-V2	50c **brown**	—	400.00
	Cut square		125.00
RN-V4	50c **orange**	175.00	90.00
	Cut square		17.50
	deep orange	175.00	90.00
	deep orange, cut square		17.50
RN-V5	50c **red**	700.00	
	Cut square		250.00

No. RN-V1 includes a 50c green, type V, and a No. RN-P3, obliterating a No. RN-W2.

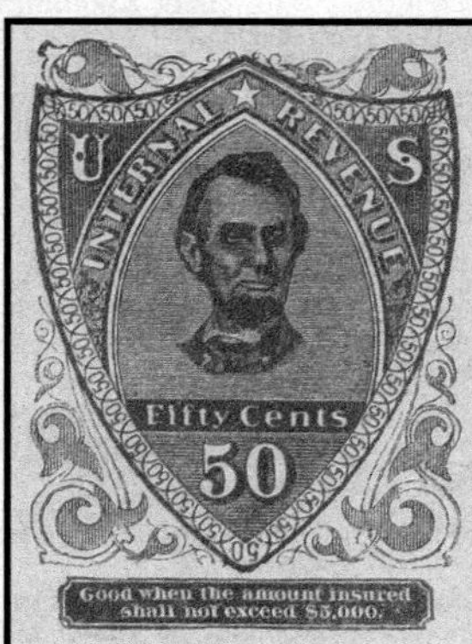

"Good when the amount insured shall not exceed $5000" in tablet at base

RN-V6	50c **orange**	450.00	400.00
	Cut square		65.00
RN-V9	50c **red**		—
	Cut square		550.00

Motto Without Tablet

RN-V10	50c **orange**		
	Cut square		600.00

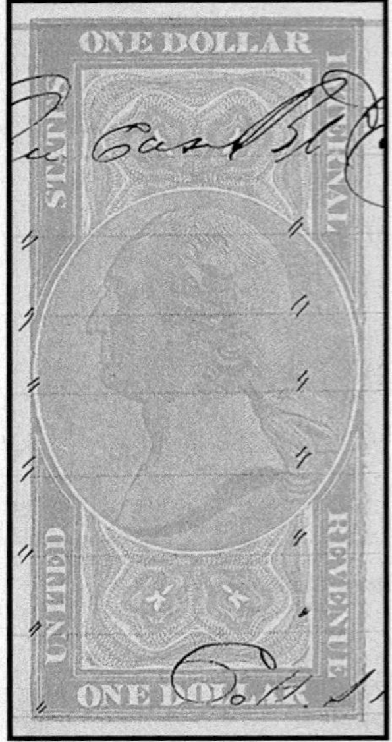

Washington Type W (See note before No. RN-P2)

Size: 34x73mm

RN-W2	$1 **orange** (shades)	150.00	85.00
	Cut square		15.00
RN-W5	$1 **brown**		*4,500.*
RN-W6	$1 **pink**		*3,750.*

The former light brown is now included with the orange shades.

No. RN-W6 used with No. RN-P4 is unique. Two examples of No. RN-W6 exist used alone.

SPANISH-AMERICAN WAR SERIES

Many of these stamps were used for parlor car tax and often were torn in two or more parts.

Liberty Type X

1898 **Size: 68x38mm**

RN-X1	1c **rose**	800.00	—
	Partial		65.00
	dark red, partial		65.00
RN-X4	1c **orange**	165.00	
a.	On pullman ticket	600.00	—
	Partial		25.00
b.	As "a," printed on back		
	As "a," printed on back, partial		65.00
RN-X5	1c **green**	65.00	30.00
	Partial		25.00
a.	On parlor car ticket	65.00	15.00
b.	On pullman ticket	500.00	
	On pullman ticket, partial		15.00
RN-X6	2c **yellow**	2.00	1.00
	pale olive		*900.00*
RN-X7	2c **orange**	3.00	2.00
	pale orange	3.00	2.00
a.	Printed on back only	500.00	500.00
c.	Printed on front and back	—	*2,500.*
d.	Vertical		85.00
e.	Double impression		—
f.	On pullman ticket	1,000.	200.00
g.	Inverted		750.00

No. RN-X1 exists only as a four-part unused pullman ticket, used as an unsevered auditor's and passenger's parts of the four-part ticket, or partial as a used half of a two-part ticket. Nos. RN-X4a and RN-X5b exist as unused two-part tickets and as used half portions. No. RN-X7f exists as an unused four-part ticket and as a used two-piece portion with nearly complete stamp design.

Scott U.S Revenue Pages

The Scott U.S. Revenue Pages have been completely revised and updated! Page layouts have been updated to eliminate connected boxes and all boxes have been sized to accommodate stamp mounts.

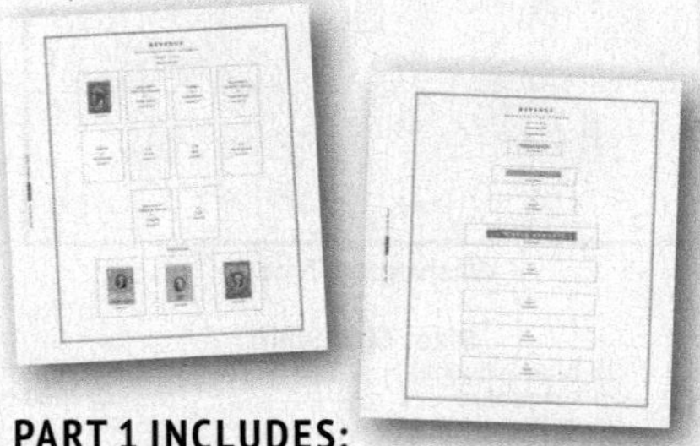

PART 1 INCLUDES:

- ☐ Documentary (R)
- ☐ Proprietary (RB)
- ☐ Future Delivery (RC)
- ☐ Stock Transfer (RD)

Item	Retail	AA
160RVN1	$72.99	**$62.04**

PART 2 INCLUDES:

- ☐ Cordials & Wines (RE)
- ☐ Fermented Fruit Juice (REF)
- ☐ Playing Cards (RF)
- ☐ Silver Tax (RG)
- ☐ Cigarette Tubes (RH)
- ☐ Potato Tax (RI)
- ☐ Tobacco Sales Tax (RJ)
- ☐ Narcotic Tax (RJA).
- ☐ Consular Service Fee (RK)
- ☐ Customs Fee (RL)
- ☐ Motor Vehicle Use (RV)
- ☐ Boating (RVB)
- ☐ Camp (RVC)
- ☐ Trailer Permit (RVT)
- ☐ Distilled Spirits Excise Tax (RX)
- ☐ Firearms Transfer Tax (RY)
- ☐ Rectification Tx (RZ)
- ☐ Postal Note (PN)
- ☐ Postal Savings (PS)
- ☐ Savings (S)
- ☐ War Savings (WS)
- ☐ Treasury Savings (TS)

Item	Retail	AA
160RVN2	$69.99	**$59.49**

Visit **www.AmosAdvantage.com**

Call **800-572-6885**

Outside U.S. & Canada call: **(937) 498-0800**

Ordering Information: *AA prices apply to paid subscribers of Amos Media titles, or orders placed online. Prices, terms and product availability subject to change. Shipping and handling rates will apply. Taxes apply in CA, OH & IL.
Shipping & Handling: United States: Order total $0-$10.00charged $3.99 shipping. Order total $10.01-$79.99 charged $7.99 shipping. Order total $80.00 or more charged 10% of order total for shipping. Maximum Freight Charge $45.00. Canada: 20% of order total. Minimum charge $19.99 Maximum charge $200.00. Foreign: Orders are shipped via FedExl Intl. or USPS and billed actual freight.

PRIVATE DIE PROPRIETARY STAMPS

The extraordinary demands of the Civil War upon the Federal Treasury resulted in Congress devising and passing the Revenue Act of 1862. The Government provided revenue stamps to be affixed to boxes or packages of matches, and to proprietary medicines, perfumery, playing cards — as well as to documents, etc.

But manufacturers were permitted, at their expense, to have dies engraved and plates made for their exclusive use. Many were only too willing to do this because a discount or premium of from 5% to 10% was allowed on orders from the die which often made it possible for them to undersell their competitors. Also, the considerable advertising value of the stamps could not be overlooked. These are now known as Private Die Proprietary stamps.

The face value of the stamp used on matches was determined by the number, i.e., 1c for each 100 matches or fraction thereof. Medicines and perfumery were taxed at the rate of 1c for each 25 cents of the retail value or fraction thereof up to $1 and 2c for each 50 cents or fraction above that amount. Playing cards were first taxed at the same rate but subsequently the tax was 5c for a deck of 52 cards and 10c for a greater number of cards or double decks.

The stamp tax was repealed on March 3, 1883, effective July 1, 1883.

The various papers were:

a. Old paper, 1862-71. First Issue. Hard and brittle varying from thick to thin.
b. Silk paper, 1871-77. Second Issue. Soft and porous with threads of silk, mostly red, blue and black, up to ¼inch in length.
c. Pink paper, 1877-78. Third Issue. Soft paper colored pink ranging from pale to deep shades.
d. Watermarked paper, 1878-83. Fourth Issue. Soft porous paper showing part of "USIR." Roulettes on watermarked paper are rouletted 6.
e. Experimental silk paper. Medium smooth paper, containing minute fragments of silk threads either blue alone or blue and red (infrequent), widely scattered, sometimes but a single fiber on a stamp.

Early printings of some private die revenue stamps are on paper which appears to have laid lines.

These stamps were usually torn in opening the box or container. **Values quoted are for fine-veryfine examples that may be somewhat faulty but reasonably attractive, with the faults usually not readily apparent on the face.** Nos. RS278-RS306 are valued in the grade of very fine. Sound examples of these stamps (other than Nos. RS278-RS306) at a grade of fine-very fine can sell for 50% to 300% more than catalogue value. Outstanding examples of stamps in this section with a lower catalogue value can bring many multiples of catalogue value.

PRIVATE DIE MATCH STAMPS

A

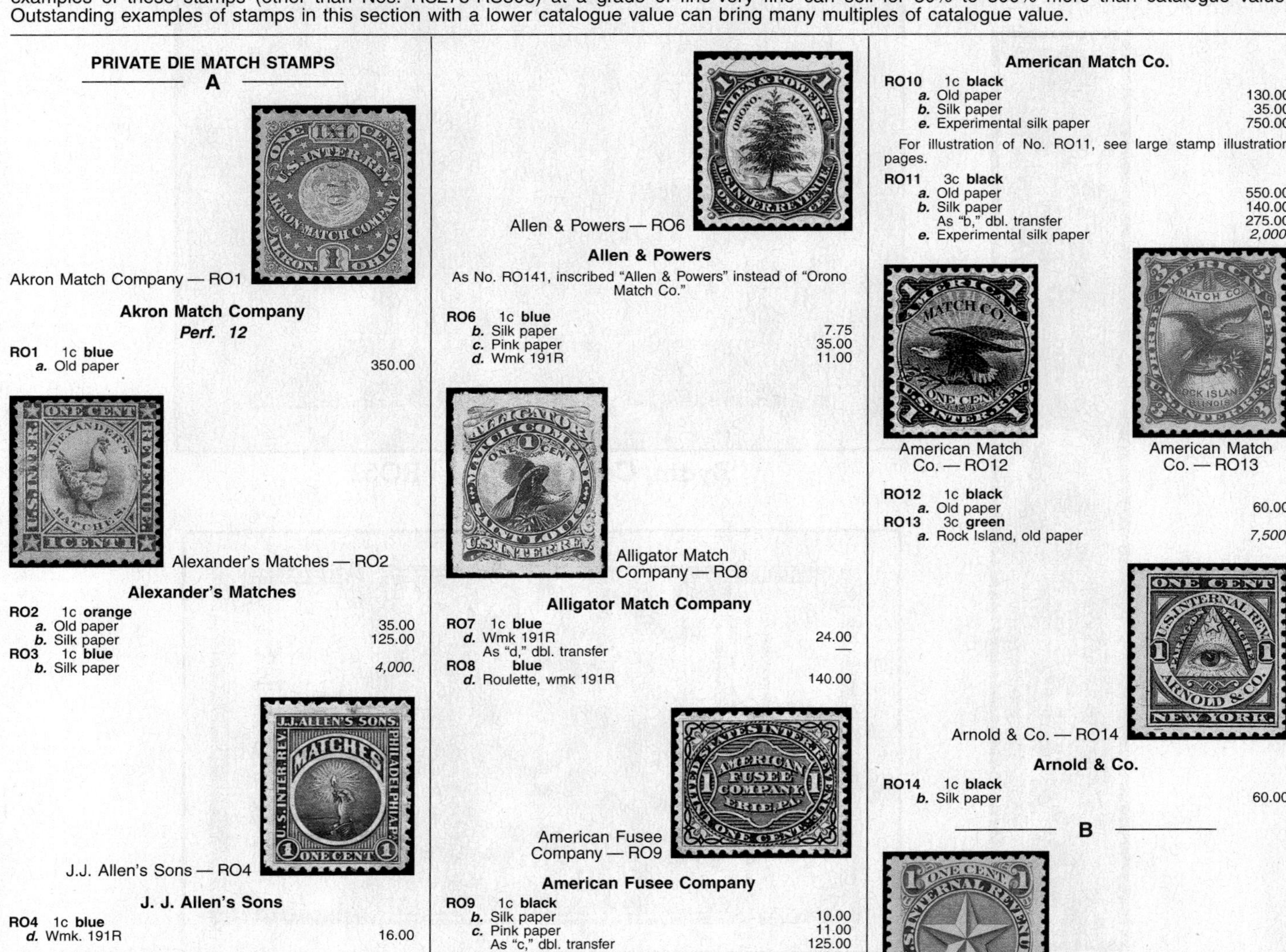

Akron Match Company — RO1

Akron Match Company

Perf. 12

RO1 1c **blue**
a. Old paper 350.00

Alexander's Matches — RO2

Alexander's Matches

RO2 1c **orange**
a. Old paper 35.00
b. Silk paper 125.00
RO3 1c **blue**
b. Silk paper *4,000.*

J.J. Allen's Sons — RO4

J. J. Allen's Sons

RO4 1c **blue**
d. Wmk. 191R 16.00

Thos. Allen — RO5

Thos. Allen

RO5 1c **green**
a. Old paper 175.00

Allen & Powers — RO6

Allen & Powers

As No. RO141, inscribed "Allen & Powers" instead of "Orono Match Co."

RO6 1c **blue**
b. Silk paper 7.75
c. Pink paper 35.00
d. Wmk 191R 11.00

Alligator Match Company — RO8

Alligator Match Company

RO7 1c **blue**
d. Wmk 191R 24.00
As "d," dbl. transfer —
RO8 **blue**
d. Roulette, wmk 191R 140.00

American Fusee Company — RO9

American Fusee Company

RO9 1c **black**
b. Silk paper 10.00
c. Pink paper 11.00
As "c," dbl. transfer 125.00
d. Wmk 191R 10.00
As "d," dbl. transfer —

American Match Company — RO10

American Match Co.

RO10 1c **black**
a. Old paper 130.00
b. Silk paper 35.00
e. Experimental silk paper 750.00

For illustration of No. RO11, see large stamp illustration pages.

RO11 3c **black**
a. Old paper 550.00
b. Silk paper 140.00
As "b," dbl. transfer 275.00
e. Experimental silk paper *2,000.*

American Match Co. — RO12

American Match Co. — RO13

RO12 1c **black**
a. Old paper 60.00
RO13 3c **green**
a. Rock Island, old paper *7,500.*

Arnold & Co. — RO14

Arnold & Co.

RO14 1c **black**
b. Silk paper 60.00

B

Bagley & Dunham — RO15

Bagley & Dunham

RO15 **green**
d. Wmk 191R 32.50

Barber & Peckham – RO21

Bousfield & Poole – RO37

American Match Co. RO11

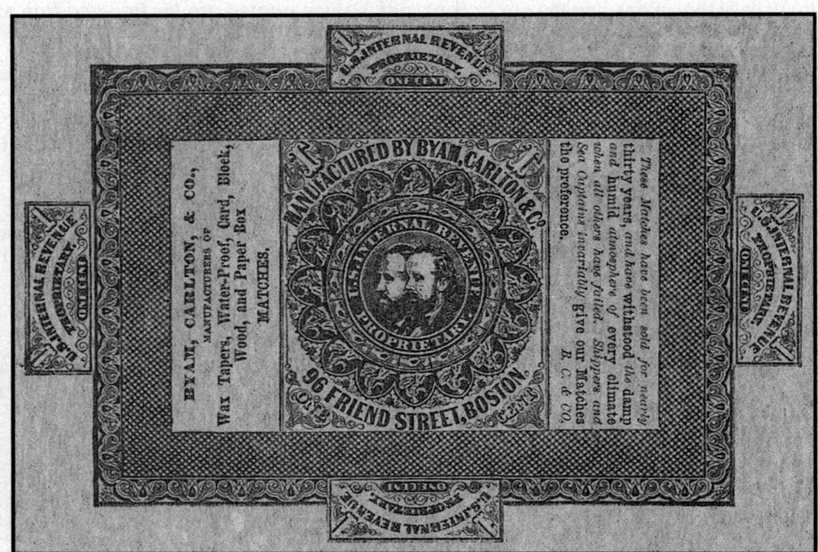

Byam, Carlton & Co. – RO51

Byam, Carlton & Co. – RO52

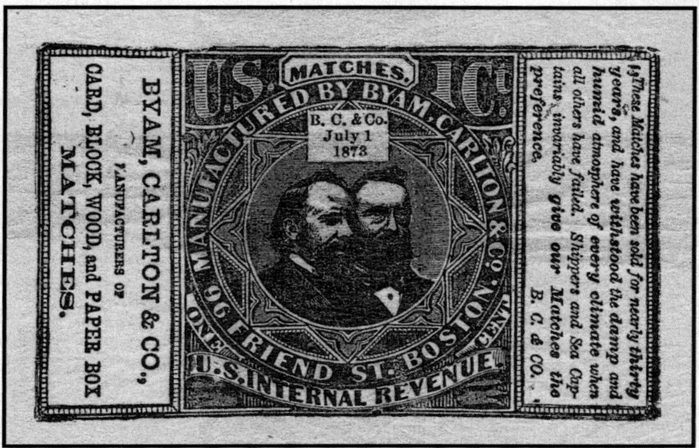

Byam, Carlton & Co. – RO54

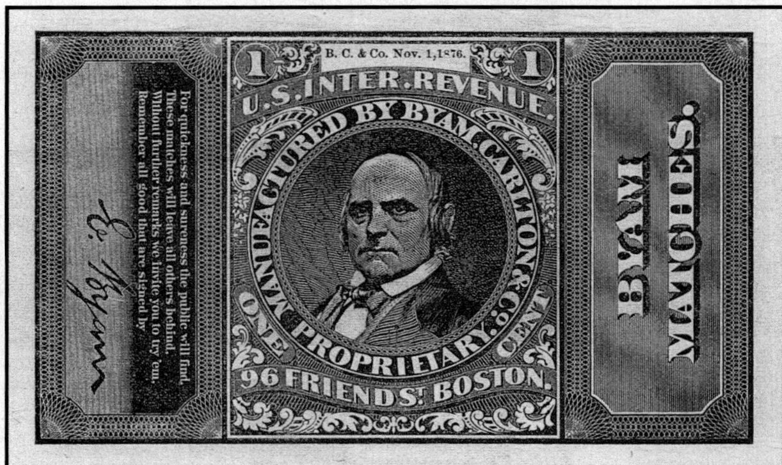

Byam, Carlton & Co. – RO55

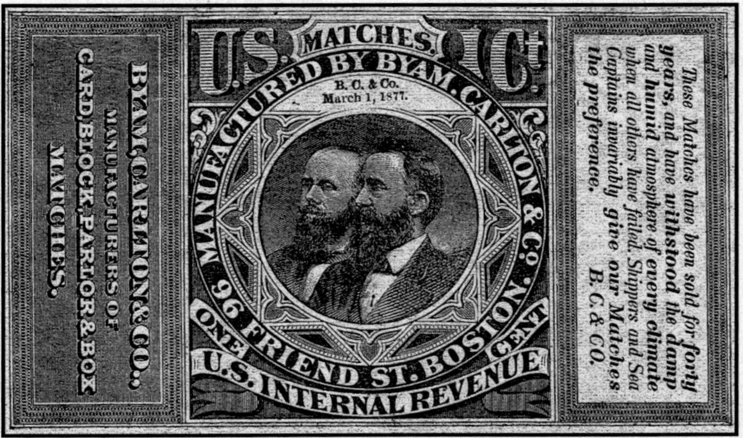

Byam, Carlton & Co. – RO56

Wm. Gates – RO90

Geo. & O. C. Barber — RO16

Geo. & O. C. Barber

As No. RO17, inscribed "Geo. & O. C. Barber" instead of "Barber Match Co."

RO16	**blue**	
	a. Old paper	72.50
	d. Roulette, wmk. 191R	—

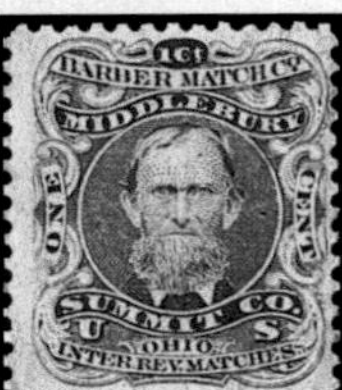

Barber Match Co. — RO17

Barber Match Co.

RO17	1c **blue**	
	a. Old paper	25.00
	As "a," dbl. transfer	85.00
	b. Silk paper	1.25
	As "b," dbl. transfer	37.50
	c. Pink paper	20.00
	As "b," dbl. transfer	85.00
	d. Wmk 191R	1.75
	As "d," dbl. transfer	35.00
	e. Experimental silk paper	150.00
	u. **Ultra,** old paper	550.00
RO18	1c **blue**	
	d. Roulette, wmk 191R	5,000.
RO19	3c **black**	
	a. Old paper	200.00
	b. Silk paper	140.00
	e. Experimental silk paper	*1,000.*

Barber & Peckham — RO20

Barber & Peckham

RO20	1c **blue**	
	a. Old paper	67.50

For illustration of No. RO21, see large stamp illustration pages.

RO21	3c **black**	
	a. Old paper	300.00

Bauer & Beudel — RO22

Bauer & Beudel

RO22	1c **blue**	
	a. Old paper	72.50
	b. Silk paper	160.00
	u. **Ultra,** old paper	275.00

A.B. & S. (A. Beecher & Son) — RO23

A. B. & S. (A. Beecher & Son)

As No. RO175, inscribed "A. B. & S." instead of "C. B. C. S." in the four corners.

RO23	1c **orange**	
	a. Old paper	17.00
	As "a," dbl. transfer	—
	b. Silk paper	67.50
	As "b," dbl. transfer	—
	e. Experimental silk paper	175.00
	As "e," dbl. transfer	225.00

RO24

B. Bendel & Co. — RO25

Illustration reduced.

B. Bendel & Co.

RO24	1c **brown**	
	b. Silk paper	2.75
	As "b," dbl. transfer	—
	d. Wmk. 191R	650.00
RO25	12c **brown**	
	b. Silk paper	500.00

H. Bendel — RO26

H. Bendel

Nos. RO26-RO27 are RO24-RO25 altered to read "H. Bendel doing business as B. Bendel & Co."

RO26	1c **brown**	
	b. Silk paper	5.00
	c. Pink paper	2.50
	d. Wmk. 191R	2.00
RO27	12c **brown**	
	b. Silk paper	550.00

H. & M. Bentz — RO28

H. & M. Bentz

RO28	1c **blue**	
	a. Old paper	42.50

Bent & Lea — RO29

Bent & Lea

RO29	1c **black**	
	a. Old paper	40.00
	As "a," dbl. transfer at left	125.00
	e. Experimental silk paper	50.00
	As "e," dbl. transfer	600.00

B. J. & Co. — RO30

B. J. & Co. (Barber, Jones & Co.)

As No. RO100 with "B. J. & Co." added above eagle.

RO30	1c **green**	
	b. Silk paper	140.00
	As "b," dbl. transfer	175.00

Bock, Schneider & Co. — RO31

Bock, Schneider & Co.

RO31	1c **black**	
	b. Silk paper	20.00

Wm. Bond & Co. — RO32/RO33

Wm. Bond & Co.

RO32	4c **black**	
	b. Silk paper	275.00
RO33	4c **green**	
	b. Silk paper	175.00
	c. Pink paper	200.00
	d. Wmk. 191R	18.00

Bousfield & Poole — RO34/RO35

Bousfield & Poole

RO34	1c **lilac**	
	a. Old paper	275.00
	As "a," dbl. transfer	300.00
RO35	1c **black**	
	a. Old paper	18.00
	As "a," dbl. transfer	70.00
	b. Silk paper	15.00
	As "b," dbl. transfer	90.00
	e. Experimental silk paper	90.00

For illustration of Nos. RO36-RO37, see large stamp illustration pages.

RO36	3c **lilac**	
	a. Old paper	3,000.
RO37	3c **black**	
	a. Old paper	200.00
	b. Silk paper	150.00
	As "b," dbl. transfer	175.00
	e. Experimental silk paper	2,000.

Boutell & Maynard — RO38

Boutell & Maynard

RO38 1c **black**
b. Silk paper 300.00

Bowers & Dunham — RO39

Bowers & Dunham

As No. RO15, inscribed "Bowers & Dunham" instead of "Bagley & Dunham."

RO39 1c **green**
d. Wmk 191R 275.00
RO40 1c **blue**
d. Wmk 191R 95.00

B. & N. (Brocket & Newton) — RO41

B. & N. (Brocket & Newton)

RO41 1c **lake**
b. Die I, silk paper 45.00
RO42 1c **lake**
b. Die II, silk paper 8.25

The initials "B. & N." measure 5¼mm across the top on Die I, and 4¾mm on Die II.

RO43

Brown & Durling

RO43 1c **black**
a. Old paper 2,500.
RO44 1c **green**
a. Old paper 82.50

L. W. Buck & Co. — RO45

L. W. Buck & Co.

RO45 1c **black**
a. Old paper *3,000.*
e. Experimental silk paper 2,000.

D. Burhans & Co. — RO46

D. Burhans & Co.

RO46 1c **black**
a. Old paper 200.00
As "a," dbl. transfer 275.00
b. Silk paper *10,000.*
e. Experimental silk paper 1,100.

Charles Busch — RO47

Charles Busch

RO47 1c **black**
d. Wmk 191R 35.00

Byam, Carlton & Co. — RO48

Byam, Carlton & Co.

RO48 1c **black**
a. Imperf., old paper *6,500.*

2 heads to left, 41x75mm.

Byam, Carlton & Co. — RO49

RO49 1c **black,** 19x23mm
a. Old paper 27.50
b. Silk paper 7.75
d. Wmk 191R 2.00
As "d," dbl. transfer 140.00
e. Experimental silk paper 140.00
i. As "d," Vert. pair, imperf. horiz. 140.00
RO50 1c **black**
a. Old paper 2,000.

2 heads to left, buff wrapper, 131x99mm.

For illustrations of Nos. RO51, RO52, RO54, RO55 and RO56, see large stamp illustration pages.

RO51 1c **black**
a. Old paper 275.00

As #RO50, 131x89mm.

RO52 1c **black**
a. Old paper 70.00

1 head to right, white wrapper, 94x54mm.

RO53 1c **black**
a. Old paper 175.00

As #RO52, buff wrapper.

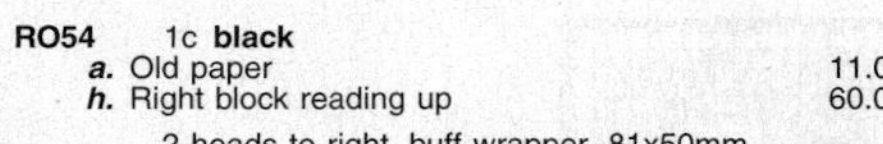

RO54 1c **black**
a. Old paper 11.00
h. Right block reading up 60.00

2 heads to right, buff wrapper, 81x50mm

RO55 1c **black**
a. Old paper 35.00

1 head to left, white wrapper, 94x56mm.

RO56 1c **black**
a. Old paper 10.00

As #RO50, 95x57mm.

C

Cannon Match Co. — RO57

Cannon Match Co.

As No. RO68, "Cannon Match Co." instead of "W. D. Curtis."

RO57 1c **green**
c. Pink paper 55.00

Cardinal Match Co. — RO58

Cardinal Match Co.

RO58 1c **lake**
d. Wmk 191R 32.50

As No. RO41, "F.E.C." instead of "B. & N." — RO59

F. E. C. (Frank E. Clark)

RO59 1c **lake**
a. Old paper 110.00
b. Silk paper 110.00
e. Experimental silk paper 150.00

Chicago Match Co. — RO60

Chicago Match Co.

RO60 3c **black**
a. Old paper 1,000.

Henry A. Clark — RO61

Henry A. Clark

RO61 1c **green**
b. Silk paper 110.00

Jas. L. Clark — RO62/RO63

Jas. L. Clark

RO62	1c **green**	
	b. Silk paper	2.75
	c. Pink paper	27.50
	d. Wmk 191R	1.75
	As "d," dbl. transfer	67.50
RO63	1c **green**	
	d. Rouletted, wmk 191R	1,400.

Clark Match Co. — RO64

The Clark Match Co.

RO64	1c **lake**	
	b. Silk paper	10.00

Cramer & Kemp — RO65/RO66

Cramer & Kemp

RO65	1c **black**	
	a. Old paper	72.50
RO66	1c **blue**	
	a. Old paper	125.00
	b. Silk paper	7.75
	e. Experimental silk paper	*1,500.*
	u. **Ultra,** old paper	750.00

Crown Match Co. — RO67

Crown Match Co.

RO67	1c **black**	
	b. Silk paper	25.00

W. D. Curtis Matches — RO68

W. D. Curtis Matches

RO68	1c **green**	
	a. Old paper	160.00
	b. Silk paper	140.00
	e. Experimental silk paper	1,000.

D

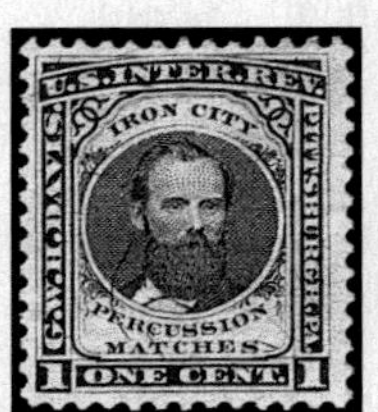
G. W. H. Davis — RO69/RO70

G. W. H. Davis

RO69	1c **black**	
	b. Silk paper	52.50
RO70	1c **carmine**	
	d. Wmk 191R	125.00

W.E. Doolittle — RO71

W. E. Doolittle

RO71	1c **blue**	
	a. Old paper	550.00

E. P. Dunham — RO72

E. P. Dunham

RO72	1c **green**	
	d. Wmk 191R	90.00

E

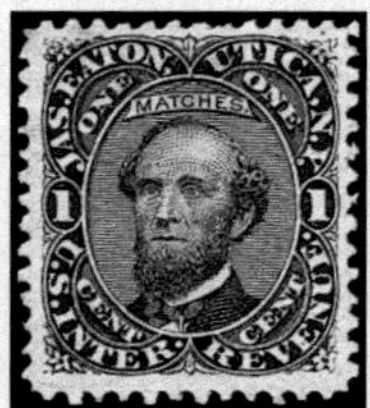
Jas. Eaton — RO73

Jas. Eaton — RO74

Jas. Eaton

RO73	1c **black**	
	a. Old paper	55.00
	b. Silk paper	1.50
	c. Pink paper	20.00
	d. Wmk 191R	1.75
	e. Experimental silk paper	225.00
RO74	1c **black**	
	d. Wmk 191R, rouletted	72.50

E.B. Eddy — RO75

E.B. Eddy — RO75A

E. B. Eddy

RO75	1c **carmine**	
	d. Wmk 191R, Die I	25.00
RO75A	1c **carmine**	
	d. Wmk 191R, Die II	40.00

Die II shows eagle strongly recut; ribbon across bottom is narrower; color is deeper.

Aug. Eichele — RO76

Aug. Eichele

RO76	1c **black**	
	a. Old paper	160.00

P. Eichele & Co. — RO77

P. Eichele & Co.

As No. RO78, "P. Eichele & Co." at top.

RO77	1c **blue**	
	a. Old paper	67.50
	b. Silk paper	8.25
	e. Experimental silk paper	225.00
	u. **Ultra,** old paper	1,750.

Eichele & Co. — RO78/RO79

Eichele & Co.

RO78	1c **blue**	
	b. Silk paper	5.00
	c. Pink paper	20.00
	d. Wmk 191R	4.50
RO79	1c **blue**	
	d. Wmk 191R, rouletted	500.00

J.W. Eisenhart's — RO80

J. W. Eisenhart's Matches

RO80	1c **blue**	
	b. Silk paper	55.00
	c. Pink paper	125.00
	d. Wmk 191R	42.50

Excelsior Match Co.—RO81/RO82

Excelsior Match Co.

RO81	1c **black**	
	b. Silk paper, Watertown, NY	110.00
RO82	1c **black**	
	b. Silk paper, Syracuse, NY	10.00
	c. Pink paper	20.00
	d. Wmk 191R	10.00
	As "d," dbl. transfer	52.50

Excelsior Match, Baltimore — RO83

Excelsior Match, Baltimore, Md.

RO83 1c **blue**	
a. Old paper	95.00
b. Silk paper	125.00
u. **Ultra,** old paper	1,250.

F

G. Farr & Co. — RO84

G. Farr & Co.

RO84 1c **black**	
a. Old paper	140.00

L. Frank — RO85

L. Frank

RO85 1c **brown**	
b. Silk paper	110.00

G

Gardner, Beer & Co. — RO86

Gardner, Beer & Co.

RO86 1c **black**	
c. Pink paper	300.00

Wm. Gates — RO88

Wm. Gates

RO87 1c **black**	
a. Old paper, Die I	9.00
b. Silk paper, Die I	6.00
RO88 1c **black**	
a. Old paper, Die II	50.00
b. Silk paper, Die II	5.50
As "b," dbl. transfer	35.00
e. Experimental silk paper	1,250.

The shirt collar is colorless in Die I and shaded in Die II. The colorless circle surrounding the portrait appears about twice as wide on Die I as it does on Die II.

RO89 3c **black**	
a. Old paper	60.00
As "a," dbl. transfer	92.50
b. Silk paper	52.50
As "b," dbl. transfer	90.00
d. Wmk 191R	
As "d," dbl. transfer	—
e. Experimental silk paper	225.00

For illustration of Nos. RO90-RO91, see large stamp illustration pages.

RO90 6c **black**	
a. Old paper	200.00
RO91 3c **black**	
b. Silk paper, 3 1c stamps	160.00

William Gates' Sons — RO92

William Gates' Sons

The 1c is as No. RO87, 3c as No. RO91, "William Gates' Sons" replaces "Wm. Gates."

For illustration of No. RO94, see large stamp illustration pages.

RO92 1c **black**	
b. Silk paper	35.00
c. Pink paper	11.00
d. Wmk 191R	2.25
RO93 1c **black**	
d. Wmk 191R, rouletted	*3,250.*
RO94 3c **black**	
b. Silk paper, 3 1c stamps	140.00
c. Pink paper	200.00
d. Wmk 191R	95.00

A. Goldback & Co. — RO95

A. Goldback & Co.

RO95 1c **green**	
b. Silk paper	55.00

A. Goldback — RO96

A. Goldback

As No. RO95, "A. Goldback" instead of "A. Goldback & Co."

RO96 1c **green**	
b. Silk paper	200.00
c. Pink paper	15,000.

T. Gorman & Bro. — RO97

T. Gorman & Bro.

As No. RO99, "T. Gorman & Bro." instead of "Thomas Gorman."

RO97 1c **black**	
a. Old paper	900.00
As "a," dbl. transfer	—
RO98 1c **green**	
a. Old paper	35.00
As "a," dbl. transfer	—
b. Silk paper	40.00

Thomas Gorman

RO99 1c **green**	
b. Silk paper	4.50
c. Pink paper	40.00
d. Wmk 191R	82.50

Greenleaf & Co. — RO100

Greenleaf & Co. — RO101/RO102

Greenleaf & Co.

RO100 1c **green**	
a. Old paper	100.00
b. Silk paper	125.00
e. Experimental silk paper	1,500.
RO101 3c **carmine**	95.00
a. Old paper	95.00
b. Silk paper	175.00
e. Experimental silk paper	1,250.
RO102 5c **orange**	
a. Old paper	175.00
b. Silk paper	4,500.
e. Experimental silk paper	1,250.

Griggs & Goodwill — RO103/RO104

Griggs & Goodwill

RO103 1c **black**	
b. Silk paper	60.00
RO104 1c **green**	
b. Silk paper	35.00
As "b," dbl. transfer	160.00

As No. RO69, inscribed "Griggs & Scott" instead of "G. W. H. Davis." — RO105

Griggs & Scott

RO105 1c **black**	
a. Old paper	12.00
b. Silk paper	42.50
e. Experimental silk paper	80.00

H

Charles S. Hale — RO106

Charles S. Hale

RO106 1c **green**	
c. Pink paper	300.00

Henning & Bonhack — RO107

Henning & Bonhack

RO107 1c **blue**	
a. Old paper	350.00

W. E. Henry & Co. — RO108

W. E. Henry & Co.

RO108 1c **red**
d. Wmk 191R 35.00
RO109 1c **black**
d. Wmk 191R 17.00

J. G. Hotchkiss — RO110

The J. G. Hotchkiss Match Co.

RO110 1c **green**
b. Silk paper 17.00
c. Pink paper 50.00
d. Wmk 191R 12.00

B. & H. D. Howard

RO111 1c **lake**
a. Old paper 125.00
RO112 1c **blue**
a. Old paper 12.00
u. **Ultra,** old paper 1,000.

L. G. Hunt — RO113

L. G. Hunt

RO113 1c **black**
a. Old paper 850.00
b. Silk paper 1,650.
e. Experimental silk paper 750.00

D. F. Hutchinson Jr. — RO114

D. F. Hutchinson Jr.

RO114 1c **lake**
d. Wmk 191R 22.50

I

As No. RO116, "Ives Matches" instead of "P. T. Ives." — RO115

Ives Matches

RO115 1c **blue**
a. Old paper 7.75
As "a," dbl. transfer —
b. Silk paper 6.75
u. **Ultra,** old paper 950.00

P. T. Ives — RO116/RO117

P. T. Ives

For illustration of No. RO118, see large stamp illustration pages.

RO116 1c **blue**
b. Silk paper 7.75
c. Pink paper 45.00
d. Wmk 191R 5.00
RO117 1c **blue**
d. Wmk 191R, rouletted 650.00
RO118 8c **blue**
a. Old paper 240.00
e. Experimental silk paper *2,500.*
u. **Ultra,** old paper *3,250.*

Ives & Judd — RO119

Ives & Judd

RO119 1c **green**
b. Silk paper 27.50
c. Pink paper 60.00
d. Wmk 191R 160.00

Ives & Judd Match Co. — RO120

The Ives & Judd Match Co.

RO120 1c **green**
d. Wmk 191R 140.00
As "d," dbl. transfer 325.00

J

Jock & Wildner — RO120A

Jock & Wildner

RO120A 1c **red brown**
a. Old paper, imperf. *9,000.*

Some specialists believe No. RO120A was not officially issued. Three examples are recorded.

K

Kirby & Sons — RO121

Kirby & Sons

RO121 1c **green**
b. Silk paper 77.50

W. S. Kyle — RO122

W. S. Kyle

RO122 1c **black**
a. Old paper 22.50
As "d," dbl. transfer 82.50
b. Silk paper 17.00
e. Experimental silk paper *2,500.*

L

Lacour's Matches — RO123

Lacour's Matches

RO123 1c **black**
a. Old paper 20.00
As "a,"dbl. transfer 110.00
b. Silk paper 60.00
e. Experimental silk paper 140.00

Leeds, Robinson & Co. — RO124

Leeds, Robinson & Co.

RO124 1c **green**
d. Wmk 191R 82.50

H. Leigh — RO125

H. Leigh

RO125 1c **blue**
d. Wmk 191R 11.00

Leigh & Palmer — RO126

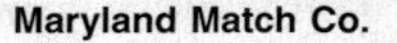

Leigh & Palmer

As No. RO125, "Leigh & Palmer" replaces "H. Leigh."

RO126 1c **black**
b. Silk paper 25.00
c. Pink paper 77.50
d. Wmk 191R 47.50

John Loehr — RO127

John Loehr

RO127 1c **blue**
b. Silk paper 27.50

As No. RO127, "Joseph" replaces "John." — RO128

Joseph Loehr

RO128 1c **blue**
b. Silk paper 3.50
c. Pink paper 22.50
d. Wmk 191R 5.50

M

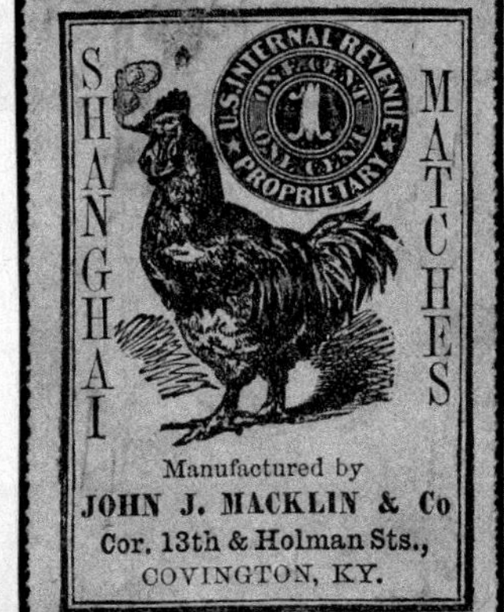

John J. Macklin & Co. — RO129

John J. Macklin & Co.

RO129 1c **black**
a. Old paper, rouletted *10,000.*
f. Thin buff paper, rouletted *20,000.*

F. Mansfield & Co. — RO130

F. Mansfield & Co.

RO130 1c **blue**
b. Silk paper 7.25
c. Pink paper 15.00
d. Wmk 191R 14.00

Maryland Match Co. — RO131

Maryland Match Co.

RO131 1c **blue**
b. Silk paper 140.00
d. Wmk 191R *42,500.*

"Matches" — RO132

"Matches"

RO132 1c **blue**
a. Old paper 7.75
As "a," dbl. transfer 110.00
b. Silk paper 5.50
e. Experimental silk paper 160.00
u. **Ultra,** old paper *2,000.*

See Nos. RO168-RO169.

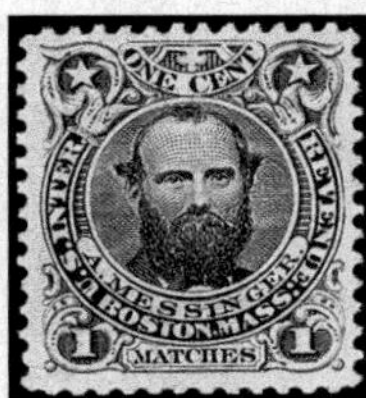

A. Messinger — RO133

A. Messinger

RO133 1c **black**
b. Silk paper 4.50
c. Pink paper 20.00
d. Wmk 191R 4.00

N

National Match Co. — RO134

National Match Co.

RO134 1c **blue**
d. Wmk 191R 77.50

Newbauer & Co. (N. & C.) follows No. RO139.

National Union Match Co. items are bogus.

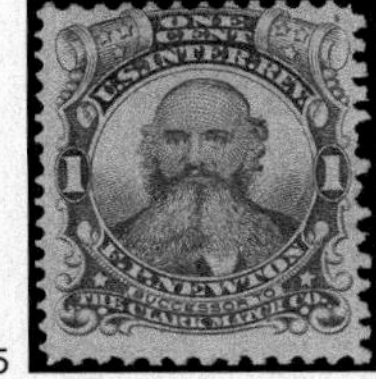

F. P. Newton — RO135

F. P. Newton

RO135 1c **lake**
b. Silk paper 3.50
c. Pink paper 17.50
d. Wmk 191R 4.50

See No. RO64 for another "The Clark Match Co." design.

New York Match Co. — RO136

New York Match Co. — RO137

New York Match Co.

No. RO136 is as No. RO22, "New York Match Co." instead of "Bauer & Beudel."

RO136 1c **blue**
a. Old paper, Shield 1,000.
b. Silk paper 9.00

No. RO137 is as No. RO111, "New York Match Co." instead of "B. & H. D. Howard."

RO137 1c **vermilion**
a. Old paper, Eagle 100.00
b. Silk paper 11,000.
e. Experimental silk paper 500.00
As "e," dbl. transfer 625.00

New York Match Co. — RO139

RO138 1c **green,** 22x60mm
a. Old paper 60.00
b. Silk paper 11.00
e. Experimental silk paper 110.00

RO139 5c **blue,** 22x60mm
b. Silk paper 1,000.

N. & C. — RO140

N. & C. (Newbauer & Co.)

RO140 4c **green**
b. Silk paper 5.50
c. Pink paper 140.00
d. Wmk 191R 6.75
i. As "b," imperf., pair, unused *1,000.*

O

Orono Match Co. — RO141

Orono Match Co.

RO141 1c **blue**
a. Old paper 40.00
b. Silk paper 40.00
e. Experimental silk paper 1,750.
u. **Ultra,** old paper 1,500.

P

Park City Match Co. — RO142

Wm. Gates – RO91

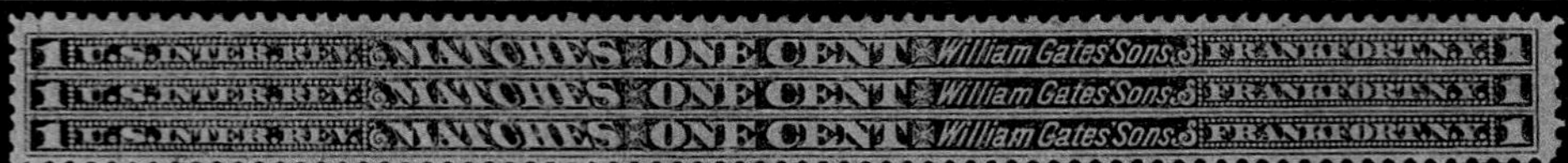

William Gates' Sons – RO94

P.T. Ives – RO118

J.C. Ayer & Co. – RS4

Barham Pile Cure Co. – RS14

D.S. Barnes
RS15

D.S. Barnes
RS16

D.S. Barnes
RS17

Demas
Barnes RS23

T.H. Barr & Co. – RS27

Demas Barnes & Co. – RS24

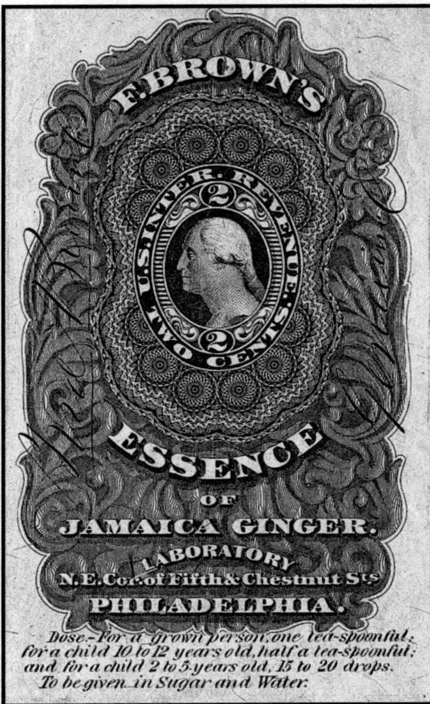

Fred Brown Co. – RS37

John I. Brown & Son – RS39

J.W. Campion & Co. – RS47

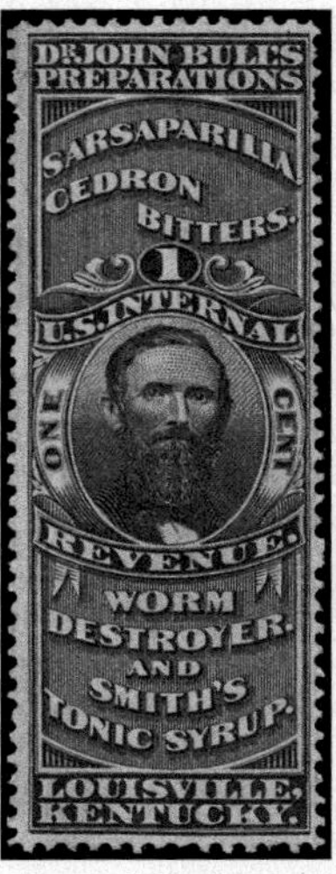

Dr.
John Bull
RS42

Dr. A.W. Chase, Son & Co. – RS55

Cannon & Co. – RS49

Cook & Bernheimer – RS61

Oliver Crook & Co. – RS65

Jeremiah Curtis & Son – RS67

Curtis & Brown – RS72

Dalley's Magical Pain Extractor – RS74

Dalley's Galvanic Horse Salve – RS73

Park City Match Co.

RO142 1c **green**
a. Old paper 55.00
b. Silk paper 52.50
e. Experimental silk paper 2,500.
RO143 3c **orange**
a. Old paper 60.00
e. Experimental silk paper —

Penn Match Co. Limited — RO144

Penn Match Co. Limited

RO144 1c **blue**
d. Wmk 191R 50.00

Pierce Match Co. — RO145

Pierce Match Co.

RO145 1c **green**
a. Old paper 4,000.

P. M. Co. (Portland M. Co.) — RO146

P. M. Co. (Portland M. Co.)

RO146 1c **black**
a. Old paper 27.50

Portland Match Co.

RO147 1c **black**
a. Old paper, wrapper 110.00

The value of No. RO147 applies to the most common date (Dec. 1866); all others are much rarer.

V.R. Powell — RO148

V.R. Powell—RO149-RO151

V. R. Powell

RO148 1c **blue**
a. Old paper 10.00
As "a," dbl. transfer 110.00
b. Silk paper 12.00

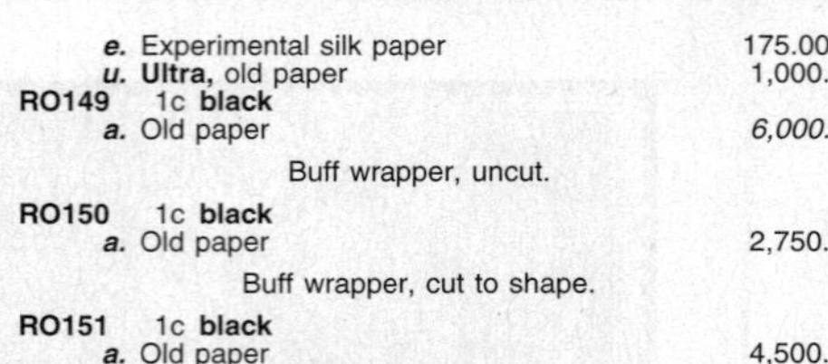

e. Experimental silk paper 175.00
u. **Ultra,** old paper 1,000.
RO149 1c **black**
a. Old paper *6,000.*

Buff wrapper, uncut.

RO150 1c **black**
a. Old paper 2,750.

Buff wrapper, cut to shape.

RO151 1c **black**
a. Old paper 4,500.

White wrapper, cut to shape.

R

Reading Match Company

RO152 1c **black**
d. Wmk 191R 10.00

Reed & Thompson — RO153

Reed & Thompson

RO153 1c **black**
d. Wmk 191R 22.50

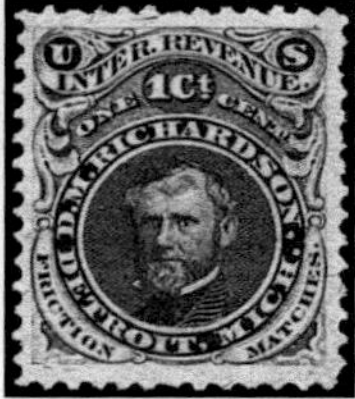

D.M. Richardson RO155

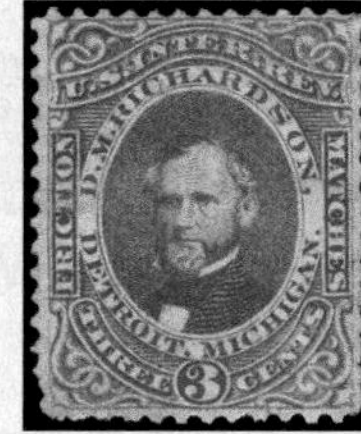

D.M. Richardson RO156

D. M. Richardson

RO154 1c **red**
a. Old paper 175.00
RO155 1c **black**
a. Old paper 4.00
b. Silk paper 3.25
As "b," dbl. transfer 80.00
e. Experimental silk paper 75.00
RO156 3c **vermilion**
a. Old paper 190.00
RO157 3c **blue**
a. Old paper 7.75
b. Silk paper 5.00
As "b," dbl. transfer 30.00
e. Experimental silk paper 92.50

RO158

The Richardson Match Co. — RO159

The Richardson Match Co.

The 1c is as No. RO154, 3c as No. RO156, inscribed "The Richardson Match Co." instead of "D. M. Richardson."

RO158 1c **black**
b. Silk paper 2.25
c. Pink paper 6.75
d. Wmk 191R 9.00
RO159 3c **blue**
b. Silk paper 95.00

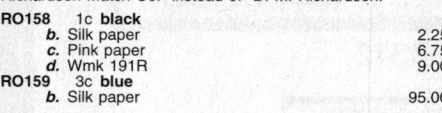

H. & W. Roeber — RO160

H. & W. Roeber

RO160 1c **blue**
a. Old paper 8.00
As "a," dbl. transfer 200.00
b. Silk paper 3.00
e. Experimental silk paper *1,750.*
u. **Ultra,** old paper *1,500.*

William Roeber — RO161

William Roeber

As No. RO160, "William Roeber" instead of "H. & W. Roeber."

RO161 1c **blue**
b. Silk paper 2.75
c. Pink paper 9.00
d. Wmk 191R 4.00
RO162 1c **blue**
d. Wmk 191R, rouletted 125.00

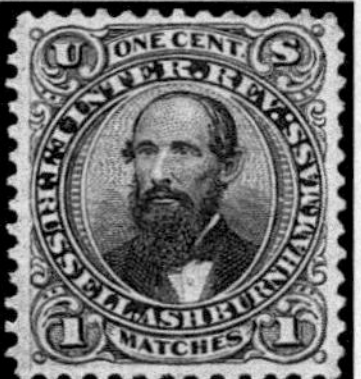

E. T. Russell — RO163

E. T. Russell

RO163 1c **black**
a. Old paper 10.00
b. Silk paper 20.00
e. Experimental silk paper *70.00*

R. C. & W. (Ryder, Crouse & Welch) — RO164

R. C. & W. (Ryder, Crouse & Welch)

RO164 1c **lake**
d. Wmk 191R 110.00

S

San Francisco Match Co. — RO165

Illustration reduced.

San Francisco Match Company

RO165 12c **blue**
b. Silk paper 550.00

Schmitt & Schmittdiel — RO166/RO167

Schmitt & Schmittdiel

RO166 1c **vermilion**
b. Silk paper 5.50
c. Pink paper 100.00
d. Wmk 191R 5.50
RO167 3c **blue**
b. Silk paper 67.50

E. K. Smith — RO168/RO169

E. K. Smith

RO168 1c **blue**
b. Silk paper 14.00
c. Pink paper 55.00
d. Wmk 191R 20.00
RO169 1c **blue**
d. Wmk 191R, rouletted *7,000.*

See No. RO132.

Standard Match Co. — RO170

The Standard Match Company

RO170 1c **black**
d. Wmk 191R 35.00

H. Stanton — RO171

H. Stanton

RO171 1c **black**
a. Old paper 17.00
b. Silk paper 11.00
c. Pink paper 22.50
d. Wmk 191R 10.00
e. Experimental silk paper 125.00

Star Match — RO172

Star Match

RO172 1c **black**
a. Old paper 5.50
b. Silk paper 1.10
As "b," dbl. transfer —
c. Pink paper 2.00
d. Wmk 191R 1.25
As "d," dbl. transfer 20.00
e. Experimental silk paper 85.00

Swift & Courtney — RO173

Swift & Courtney

As No. RO174, "Swift & Courtney" in one line.

RO173 1c **blue**
a. Old paper 3.50
b. Silk paper 3.50
As "b," dbl. transfer —
e. Experimental silk paper 47.50
u. **Ultra,** old paper 110.00

Swift & Courtney & Beecher Co.— RO174

Swift & Courtney & Beecher — RO175

Swift & Courtney & Beecher Co.

RO174 1c **blue**
b. Silk paper 3.50
c. Pink paper 5.50
d. Wmk 191R 2.25
As "d," dbl. transfer —
RO175 1c **black**
d. Wmk 191R 110.00

T

Trenton Match Co. — RO176

Trenton Match Co.

RO176 1c **blue**
d. Wmk 191R 12.00

E. R. T. (E. R. Tyler) — RO177

E. R. T. (E. R. Tyler)

As No. RO119, inscribed "E. R. T." instead of "Ives & Judd."

RO177 1c **green**
a. Old paper 17.00
b. Silk paper 4.50
As "b," dbl. transfer —
e. Experimental silk paper 125.00

U

Alex Underwood & Co. — RO178

Alex. Underwood & Co.

RO178 1c **green**
a. Old paper 110.00
b. Silk paper 160.00
e. Experimental silk paper *2,250.*

Union Match Co. — RO179

Union Match Co.

RO179 1c **black**
d. Wmk 191R 55.00

U.S.M. Co. — RO180

U. S. M. Co. (Universal Safety Match Co.)

RO180 1c **black**
a. Old paper 4.50
b. Silk paper 30.00
e. Experimental silk paper 110.00

W

Washington Match Co. — RO181

Washington Match Co.

RO181 1c **black**
b. Silk paper 50.00

Wilmington Parlor Match Co. — RO182

Wilmington Parlor Match Co.

RO182 1c **black**
a. Old paper 175.00
b. Silk paper *11,500.*
e. Experimental silk paper 500.00

Wise & Co. — RO183

Wise & Co.

RO183 1c **black**
a. Old paper 2,000.

Z

F. Zaiss & Co. — RO184

F. Zaiss & Co.

RO184 1c **black**
b. Silk paper 2.25
c. Pink paper 9.00
d. Wmk 191R 2.75

L. Pills – RS90

Reuben P. Hall & Co. – RS94

(Dr.) S.B. Hartman & Co.
RS99

The Father Mathew Temperance & Manufacturing Company – RS85

(Dr.) S.B. Hartman & Co. – RS100

John F. Henry
RS114

Hiscox & Co.
RS123

Herrick's Pills
RS117

The Home Bitters Co. – RS128

Hostetter & Smith – RS132

S.D. Howe – RS134

S.D. Howe – RS137

T.J. Husband – RS140

James A. Jackson & Co. – RS143

Dr. D. Jayne & Son – RS149

Lyon Manufg. Co. – RS167

Dr. Jas. C. Kerr – RS159

Jacob Lippman & Bro. – RS163

T.W. Marsden – RS175

T.W. Marsden – RS176

Mercado & Seully – RS177

Mette & Kanne – RS180

J.B. Kelly & Co.
RS153

Zisemann, Griesheim & Co. — RO185

RO185 1c **green**
a. Old paper 3,000.
RO186 1c **blue**
a. Old paper 160.00
b. Silk paper 25.00
u. **Ultra,** old paper 3,000.

PRIVATE DIE CANNED FRUIT STAMP

T. Kensett & Co. — RP1

T. Kensett & Co.

RP1 1c **green**
a. Old paper 2,500.

Virtually all examples of No. RP1a are faulty to some degree, with many being extremely faulty.

PRIVATE DIE MEDICINE STAMPS

A

Anglo American Drug Co. — RS1

Anglo American Drug Co.

RS1 1c **black**
d. Wmk 191R 75.00

J. C. Ayer & Co.

For illustration of No. RS4, see large stamp illustration pages.

RS2 1c **brn car**
a. Old paper, imperf. *22,500.*
RS3 1c **green**
a. Old paper, imperf. *25,000.*
RS4 1c **black,** imperf.
a. Old paper, Type I 275.00
b. Silk paper, Type I 250.00
d. Wmk 191R, Type I 95.00
e. Experimental silk paper, Type I —
f. Old paper, Type 2 225.00
g. Silk paper, Type 2 200.00
As "g", dbl. transfer —
h. Pink paper, Type 2 *2,250.*
i. Wmk 191R, Type 2 77.50

Type I: long, full-pointed "y" in "Ayers"; Type 2: short, truncated "y" in "Ayers".

RS5 1c **blue**
a. Old paper, imperf. *22,500.*
RS6 1c **orange**
a. Old paper, imperf. *22,500.*
RS6F 1c **red**
a. Old paper, imperf. *22,500.*
RS7 1c **gray lilac**
a. Old paper, imperf. *22,500.*

J.C. Ayer & Co. — RS8, RS9, RS11/RS13

J.C. Ayer & Co. RS10

RS8 4c **red**
a. Old paper, die cut *12,500.*
RS9 4c **blue**
a. Old paper, die cut 10.50
b. Silk paper 10.50
d. Wmk 191R 10.50
e. Experimental silk paper *2,000.*
u. **Ultra,** old paper *1,500.*
RS10 4c **blue**
a. Old paper, imperf. 450.00
b. Silk paper 450.00
d. Wmk 191R 350.00
RS11 4c **purple**
a. Old paper, die cut *22,500.*
RS12 4c **green**
a. Old paper, die cut *17,500.*
RS13 4c **vermilion**
a. Old paper, die cut *17,500.*

The 4c in black was printed and sent to Ayer & Co. It may exist but has not been seen by collectors.

B

Barham Pile Cure Co.

For illustration of No. RS14, see large stamp illustration pages.

RS14 4c **green**
d. Wmk lozenges 90.00

D. S. Barnes

The 1c, 2c and 4c are about 184mm, 242mm and 304mm tall. The products mentioned differ. "D. S. Barnes" is in manscript.

For illustration of No. RS16 and RS17, see large stamp illustration pages.

RS15 1c **vermilion**
a. Old paper 750.00
RS16 2c **vermilion**
a. Old paper 675.00
RS17 4c **vermilion**
a. Old paper 1,400.
RS18 1c **black**
a. Old paper 30.00
RS19 2c **black**
a. Old paper 60.00
RS20 4c **black**
a. Old paper 82.50

RS22 Foreign entry

Demas Barnes

Same as above but with "Demas Barnes" in serifed letters.

For illustration of No. RS23, see large stamp illustration pages.

RS21 1c **black**
a. Old paper 27.50
RS22 2c **black**
a. Old paper 75.00
As "a," foreign entry of 1c (No. RS15 or RS21), old paper *2,750.*
RS23 4c **black**
a. Old paper 35.00

Demas Barnes & Co.

For illustration of No. RS24, see large stamp illustration pages.

RS24 1c **black**
a. Old paper 20.00
b. Silk paper 675.00
e. Experimental silk paper *5,000.*
RS25 2c **black**
a. Old paper 20.00
b. Silk paper 500.00
e. Experimental silk paper 1,250.
RS26 4c **black**
a. Old paper 20.00

T. H. Barr & Co.

For illustration of No. RS27, see large stamp illustration pages.

RS27 4c **black**
a. Old paper 30.00
As "a," dbl. transfer 225.00
e. Experimental silk paper 450.00

Barry's — RS28/RS29

Barry's

RS28 2c **green**
a. Old paper, Tricopherous 12.00
b. Silk paper 22.50
RS29 2c **green**
b. Silk paper, Proprietary 6.75
As "b," dbl. transfer *1,000.*
c. Pink paper 275.00
d. Wmk 191R 6.00

D. M. Bennett — RS30

D. M. Bennett

RS30 1c **lake**
a. Old paper 20.00
e. Experimental silk paper 4,000.

W. T. Blow — RS31

W. T. Blow

RS31 1c **green**
a. Old paper 325.00
b. Silk paper 77.50
c. Pink paper 450.00
d. Wmk 191R 95.00
e. Experimental silk paper 1,900.

B. Brandreth — RS33

R. Brandreth — RS35

B. Brandreth

RS32 1c **black**
a. Old paper, perf. 1,750.
b. Silk paper 1,750.
RS33 1c **black**
a. Old paper, imperf. 2.75
b. Silk paper 1.75
e. Experimental silk paper 42.50

Nos. RS32-RS33 inscribed "United States Certificate of Genuineness" around vignette.

RS34 1c **black,** 41x50mm
b. Silk paper, imperf. 300.00

RS35 1c **black,** 24x30mm
b. Silk paper, imperf. 2.00
c. Pink paper 11.00
d. Wmk 191R 2.25
p. Wmk 191R, perf. *2,000.*

Dr. C.F. Brown — RS36

Dr. C. F. Brown

RS36 1c **greenish blue**
a. Old paper 650.00
b. Silk paper 87.50
d. Wmk 191R 100.00

Fred Brown Co.

For illustration of No. RS37, see large stamp illustration pages.

RS37 2c **black**
a. Old paper, imperf., Die I 140.00
b. Silk paper 47.50
c. Pink paper 3,750.
d. Wmk 191R 40.00
e. Experimental silk paper *1,500.*
RS38 2c **black**
b. Silk paper, imperf., Die II 82.50

Die I has "E" of "Fred" incomplete. Die II shows recutting in the "E" of "Fred" and "Genuine."

John I. Brown & Son.

For illustration of No. RS39, see large stamp illustration pages.

RS39 1c **black**
a. Old paper 11.00
b. Silk paper 45.00
d. Wmk 191R 10.00
RS40 2c **green**
a. Old paper 11.00
As "a," dbl. transfer —
b. Silk paper 20.00
c. Pink paper 400.00
d. Wmk 191R 400.00
e. Experimental silk paper *1,650.*
RS41 4c **brown**
a. Old paper 550.00
b. Silk paper 140.00
d. Wmk 191R 2,000.

Dr. John Bull

For illustration of No. RS42, see large stamp illustration pages.

RS42 1c **black**
a. Old paper 210.00
b. Silk paper 22.50
c. Pink paper 825.00
d. Wmk 191R 22.50
e. Experimental silk paper 1,100.
RS43 4c **blue**
a. Old paper 225.00
b. Silk paper 13.50
c. Pink paper 600.00
d. Wmk 191R 12.00
e. Experimental silk paper *1,750.*
u. **Ultra,** old paper *2,750.*

J. S. Burdsal & Co.

"J. S. Burdsal & Co./Sole Proprietors" added under United States Proprietary Medicine Co. design, as on Nos. RS245-RS247.

RS44 1c **black**
b. White silk paper, wrapper 60.00
d. Wmk 191R, white paper, wrapper 40.00
RS45 1c **black**
b. Orange silk paper, wrapper *12,500.*
d. Wmk 191R, orange paper, wrapper 4,000.
RS45A 1c **black**
b. Yellow silk paper, wrapper 7,500.

Joseph Burnett & Co. — RS46

Joseph Burnett & Co.

RS46 4c **black**
a. Old paper 125.00
b. Silk paper 16.00
c. Pink paper 550.00
d. Wmk 191R 7.75

C

J. W. Campion & Co.

For illustration of No. RS47, see large stamp illustration pages.

RS47 4c **black,** imperf.
b. Silk paper 550.00
d. Wmk 191R 425.00
p. As "d," pair, perf. horiz. 2,750.
RS48 4c **black**
b. Die cut, silk paper 160.00
c. Pink paper 550.00
d. Wmk 191R 125.00

Cannon & Co.

For illustration of No. RS49, see large stamp illustration pages.

RS49 4c **green**
b. Silk paper 150.00
c. Pink paper 325.00
d. Wmk 191R 90.00

The Centaur Co. — RS50/RS52

The Centaur Co.

RS50 1c **vermilion**
c. Pink paper 72.50
d. Wmk 191R 11.00
RS51 2c **black**
c. Pink paper 16.00
d. Wmk 191R 4.00
RS52 4c **black**
d. Wmk 191R 67.50

Dr. A. W. Chase, Son & Co.

For illustration of No. RS55, see large stamp illustration pages.

RS53 1c **black**
b. Silk paper 160.00
d. Wmk 191R 10,000.
RS54 2c **black**
b. Silk paper 160.00
RS55 4c **black**
b. Silk paper 300.00

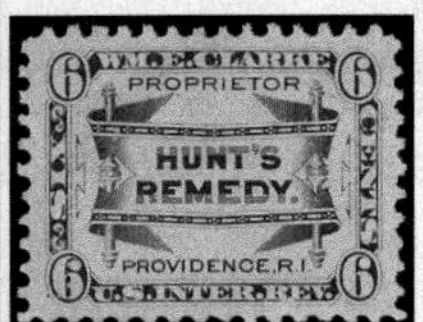

Wm. E. Clarke
RS56 RS57

Wm. E Clarke

RS56 3c **blue**
d. Wmk 191R 350.00
RS57 6c **black**
d. Wmk 191R 100.00

R. C. & C. S. Clark — RS58

R. C. & C. S. Clark

RS58 4c **black**
b. Silk paper 20.00
d. Wmk 191R 27.50

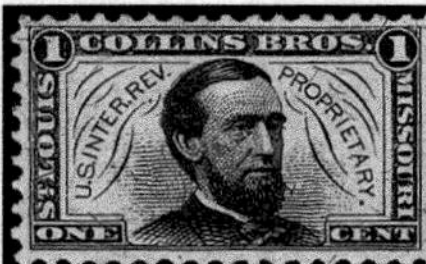

Collins Bros. — RS59

Collins Bros.

RS59 1c **black**
a. Old paper 29.00
b. Silk paper 1,000.
e. Experimental silk paper *2,500.*

W. H. Comstock — RS60

W. H. Comstock

RS60 1c **black**
d. Wmk 191R 5.50

Cook & Bernheimer

For illustration of No. RS61, see large stamp illustration pages.

RS61 4c **blue**
d. Wmk 191R 140.00

Charles N. Crittenton — RS62/RS64

Charles N. Crittenton

RS62 1c **black**
b. Silk paper 11.00
RS63 1c **blue**
c. Pink paper 14.00
d. Wmk 191R 7.25
RS64 2c **black**
b. Silk paper 95.00
c. Pink paper 55.00
d. Wmk 191R 5.50

Oliver Crook & Co.

For illustration of No. RS65, see large stamp illustration pages.

RS65 4c **black**
a. Old paper 750.00
b. Silk paper 27.50
e. Experimental silk paper 150.00

Jeremiah Curtis & Son

For illustration of No. RS67, see large stamp illustration pages.

RS66 1c **black**
a. Old paper, die I, small "1s." 140.00
RS67 1c **black**
d. Wmk 191R, die II, large "1s." 125.00
RS68 2c **black**
a. Old paper 11.00
b. Silk paper 11.00
As "b," dbl. transfer —
c. Pink paper 175.00
d. Wmk 191R 400.00

Die II numerals nearly fill the circles.

Curtis & Brown RS69

Mishler Herb Bitters Co. – RS181

Moody, Michel & Co. – RS182

Morehead's – RS186

New York Pharmacal Association
RS187

Dr. M. Perl & Co. – RS188

Bennett Pieters & Co. – RS191

Bennett Pieters & Co. – RS192

R. V.
Pierce
RS190

Radway & Co. – RS193

M., P.J. & H.M. Sands – RS209

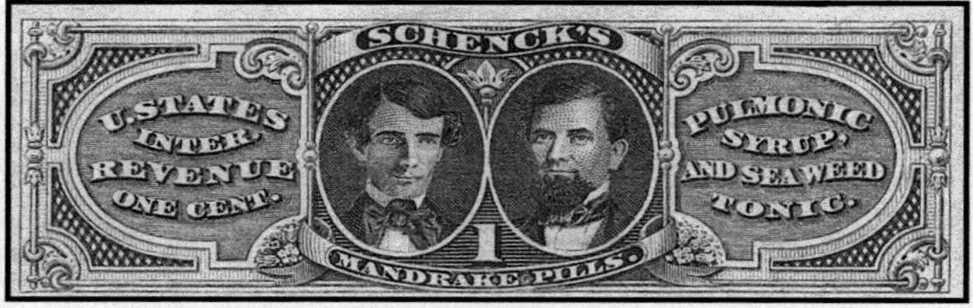

Scheetz's Celebrated Bitter Cordial – RS210

Schenck's Mandrake Pills – RS212

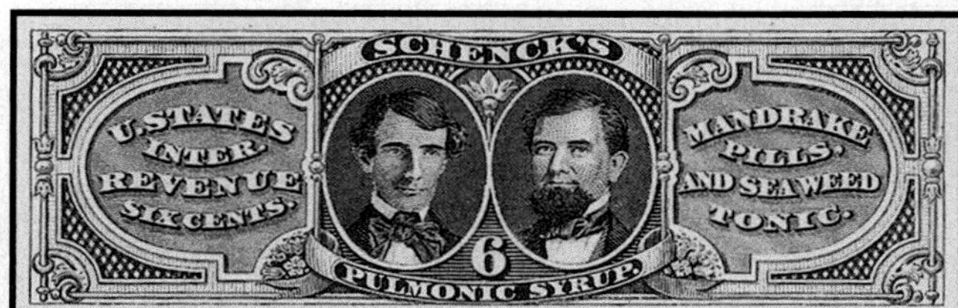

Schenck's Pulmonic Syrup – RS213

J.E. Schwartz & Co. – RS215

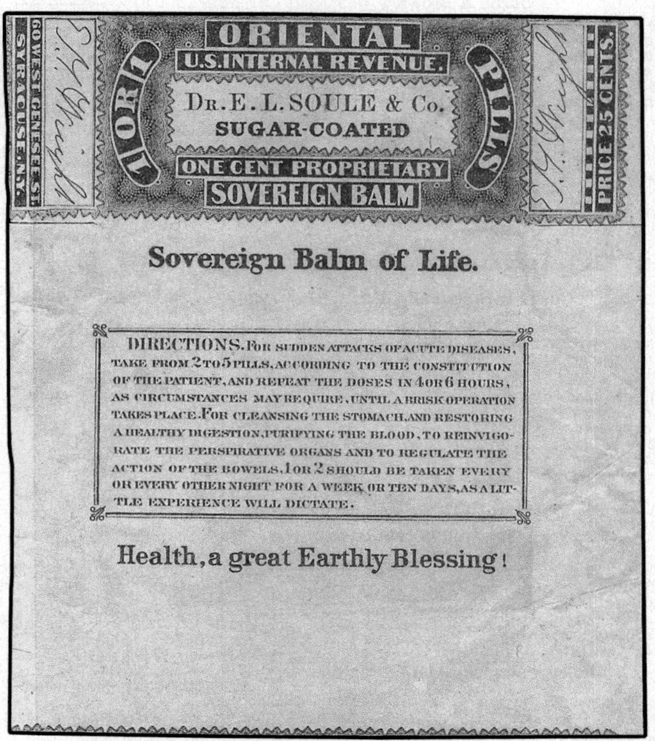

Dr. D.H. Seelye & Co. – RS222

Dr. E.L. Soule & Co. – RS227

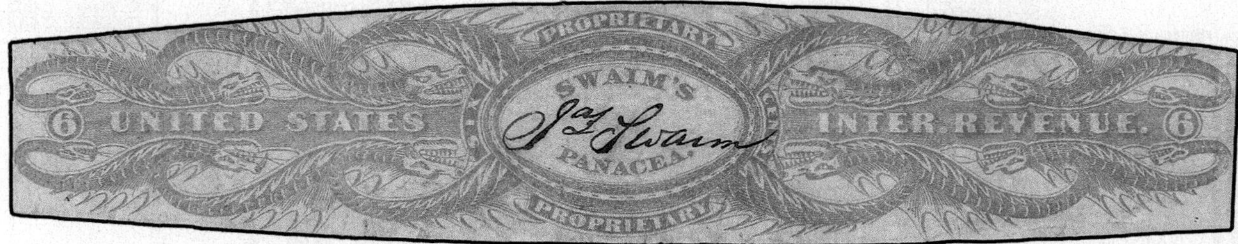

Jas. Swaim RS231

Wm. Swaim RS234

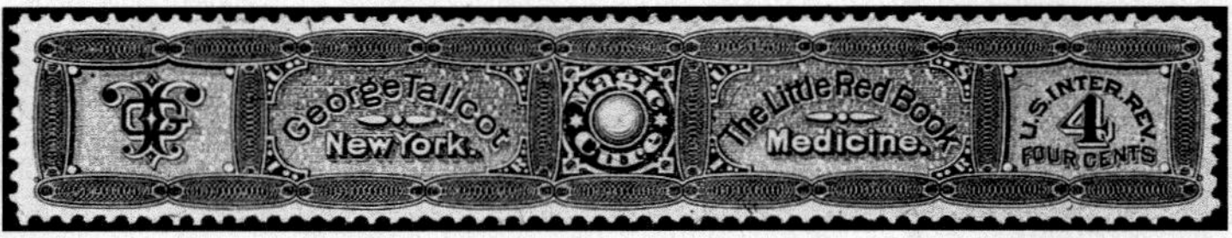

George Tallcot RS240

United States Proprietary Medicine Co. – RS243

S.R. Van Duzer – RS249

Curtis & Brown

RS69 1c **black**
a. Old paper 6.25
b. Silk paper 4.50
e. Experimental silk paper *6,000.*
RS70 2c **black**
b. Silk paper 200.00

Curtis & Brown Mfg. Co. RS71

Curtis & Brown Mfg. Co.

These are identical to RS69-RS70 with "Mfg. Co. Limtd." instead of the right hand "TWO CENTS."

For illustration of No. RS72, see large stamp illustration pages.

RS71 1c **black**
c. Pink paper 275.00
d. Wmk 191R 10.00
RS72 2c **black**
b. Silk paper 2,450.
d. Wmk 191R *1,750.*

D

Dalley's Galvanic Horse Salve

For illustration of No. RS73, see large stamp illustration pages.

RS73 2c **green**
a. Old paper 250.00
b. Silk paper 275.00
d. Wmk 191R 325.00

Dalley's Magical Pain Extractor

For illustration of No. RS74, see large stamp illustration pages.

RS74 1c **black**
a. Old paper 16.00
b. Silk paper 12.00
d. Wmk 191R 9.25
ah. As "a," $100 500.00
dh. As "d," $100 20.00

Denomination on Nos. RS74ah and RS74dh reads "$100" in error, instead of "$1.00."

Perry Davis & Son — RS75/RS81

Perry Davis & Son

RS75 1c **blue**
a. Old paper 10.00
b. Silk paper 4.00
c. Pink paper 400.00
d. Wmk 191R 3.00
e. Experimental silk paper 210.00
u. **Ultra,** old paper *1,750.*
RS76 2c **brown red**
a. Old paper 300.00
RS77 2c **black**
a. Old paper 90.00
RS78 2c **dull purple**
b. Silk paper 11.00
RS78A 2c **slate**
b. Silk paper 14.00
d. Wmk 191R 7.25
RS79 2c **dull red**
b. Silk paper 100.00
RS80 2c **brown**
b. Silk paper *10,500.*
RS81 4c **brown**
a. Old paper 14.50
b. Silk paper 4.50
d. Wmk 191R 3.25

P.H. Drake & Co. — RS82/RS83

Illustration reduced.

P. H. Drake & Co.

RS82 2c **black**
a. Old paper *4,500.*
RS83 4c **black**
a. Old paper 67.50
b. Silk paper 77.50
e. Experimental silk paper 275.00

F

B. A. Fahnestock — RS84

Illustration reduced.

B. A. Fahnestock

RS84 1c **lake,** imperf.
a. Old paper 175.00
b. Silk paper 140.00

The Father Mathew Temperance & Manufacturing Company

For illustration of No. RS85, see large stamp illustration pages.

RS85 4c **black**
d. Wmk 191R 17.50

A. H. Flanders, M.D. — RS87

A. H. Flanders, M. D.

RS86 1c **green,** perf.
b. Silk paper 16.00
d. Wmk 191R 14.50
RS87 1c **green,** part perf.
a. Old paper 27.50
b. Silk paper 2.25
c. Pink paper 45.00
d. Wmk 191R 3.25

Fleming Bros. — RS88/RS90

Fleming Bros.
Vermifuge

RS88 1c **black,** imperf.
a. Old paper 16.00
b. Silk paper 25.00
d. Wmk 191R 70.00
e. Experimental silk paper 140.00

L. Pills

For illustration of No. RS90, see large stamp illustration pages.

RS89 1c **black,** imperf.
a. Old paper *7,000.*
RS90 1c **blue,** imperf.
a. Old paper 7.75
b. Silk paper 9.00
As "b," dbl. transfer 77.50
d. Wmk 191R 11.00
As "d," dbl. transfer 77.50
e. Experimental silk paper *2,000.*
u. **Ultra,** old paper 3,500.

Seth W. Fowle & Son — RS91

Seth W. Fowle & Son, J. P. Dinsmore

RS91 4c **black**
a. Old paper 22.50
b. Silk paper 3.25
d. Wmk 191R 3.25

G

G. G. Green — RS92/RS93

G. G. Green

RS92 3c **black**
d. Wmk 191R 7.75
h. As "d," tete beche pair *2,500.*
RS93 3c **black,** rouletted
d. Wmk 191R 250.00

H

Reuben P. Hall & Co.

For illustration of No. RS94, see large stamp illustration pages.

RS94 4c **black**
a. Old paper 22.50
b. Silk paper 22.50
d. Wmk 191R 25.00
e. Experimental silk paper *2,500.*

Hall & Ruckel — RS95

Hall & Ruckel — RS96

Hall & Ruckel as agents for Xavier Bazin — RS95h/RS96h

Hall & Ruckel

RS95 1c **green**
a. Old paper 2.00
b. Silk paper 2.00
c. Pink paper 35.00
d. Wmk 191R 2.00
e. Experimental silk paper 35.00
h. Handstamped "X.B." (Xavier Bazin) and obliteration, wmk 191R 30.00
RS96 3c **black**
a. Old paper 3.50
b. Silk paper 3.25
c. Pink paper 67.50
d. Wmk 191R 3.25
h. Handstamped "X.B." (Xavier Bazin) and obliteration, wmk 191R 60.00

Dr. Harter & Co. — RS97

Dr. Harter & Co.

RS97 1c **black**
a. Old paper 27.50
b. Silk paper 18.00
e. Experimental silk paper *3,500.*

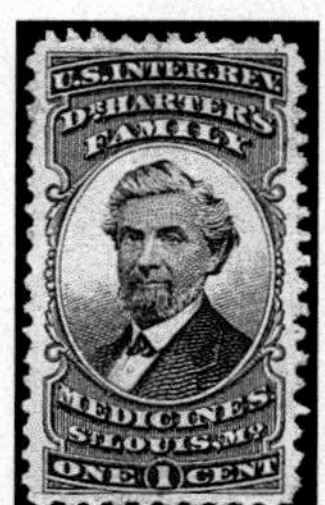

Dr. Harter — RS98

Dr. Harter's

As No. RS97, inscribed "Dr. Harter" instead of "Dr. Harter & Co."

RS98 1c **black**
b. Silk paper 4.50
c. Pink paper 17.50
d. Wmk 191R 5.50
f. Dbl. impression, silk paper *4,500.*

(Dr.) S. B. Hartman & Co.

For illustrations of Nos. RS99 and RS100, see large stamp illustration pages.

RS99 4c **black**
a. Old paper 2,500.
b. Silk paper 87.50
c. Pink paper 1,750.
d. Wmk 191R 1,750.
RS100 6c **black**
a. Old paper 1,000.
b. Silk paper 400.00

E. T. Hazeltine — RS101/RS103

E. T. Hazeltine

RS101 1c **black**
d. Wmk 191R 21.00
RS102 2c **blue**
b. Silk paper 42.50
RS103 4c **black**
a. Old paper 1,000.
b. Silk paper 27.50
d. Wmk 191R 20.00
e. Experimental silk paper 3,750.
i. Imperf, pair, old paper *3,000.*

E. H. (Edward Heaton) — RS105

E. H. (Edward Heaton)

RS104 3c **black**
d. Wmk 191R 55.00
RS105 3c **brown**
d. Wmk 191R 20.00

Helmbold's — RS106/RS109

Helmbold's

RS106 2c **blue**
a. Old paper 2.00
As "a," dbl. transfer —
b. Silk paper 400.00
RS107 3c **green**
a. Old paper 55.00
b. Silk paper 40.00
RS108 4c **black**
a. Old paper 5.00
As "a," dbl. transfer 175.00
b. Silk paper 225.00
e. Experimental silk paper *2,500.*

RS109 6c **black**
a. Old paper 2.25
b. Silk paper 4.00
e. Experimental silk paper 57.50

A.L. Helmbold's — RS110

A. L. Helmbold's

Same as "Helmbold's" but inscribed "A. L. Helmbold's."

RS110 2c **blue**
b. Silk paper 140.00
c. Pink paper 500.00
d. Wmk 191R 110.00
RS111 4c **black**
b. Silk paper 30.00
c. Pink paper 300.00
d. Wmk 191R 11.00

John F. Henry — RS112

Illustration reduced.

John F. Henry

RS112 2c **violet**
a. Old paper 900.00
RS113 4c **bister**
a. Old paper 2,100.

For illustration of No. RS114, see large stamp illustration pages.

RS114 1c **black**
a. Old paper 67.50
b. Silk paper 1.10
c. Pink paper 15.00
d. Wmk 191R 1.75
e. Experimental silk paper 250.00

Horiz. pairs imperf between were issued of No. RS114d. All known pairs were originally separated, and some have been matched and rejoined. Three rejoined pairs are reported.

RS115 2c **blue**
a. Old paper 40.00
b. Silk paper 7.25
c. Pink paper 160.00
d. Wmk 191R 6.75
u. **Ultra,** old paper *2,000.*
RS116 4c **red**
a. Old paper 200.00
b. Silk paper 1.75
c. Pink paper 40.00
d. Wmk 191R 2.75
e. Experimental silk paper 225.00

Herrick's Pills

For illustration of No. RS117, see large stamp illustration pages.

RS117 1c **black**
a. Old paper 100.00
b. Silk paper 45.00
c. Pink paper 160.00
d. Wmk 191R 50.00
e. Experimental silk paper 250.00
i. Imperf, pair, old paper *3,000.*

No. RS117i is valued in sound condition. Most pairs are faulty and sell for much less.

Herrick's Pills & Plasters — RS118

Herrick's Pills & Plasters

RS118 1c **red**
a. Old paper 2.75
b. Silk paper 5.50
c. Pink paper 82.50
d. Wmk 191R 2.75
e. Experimental silk paper 3,000.

J.E. Hetherington — RS120

J. E. Hetherington

RS119 1c **black**
d. Wmk 191R 20.00
RS120 2c **black**
d. Wmk 191R 725.00
RS121 3c **black**
d. Wmk 191R 25.00
i. Imperf, pair 2,250.

Hiscox & Co.

For illustration of No. RS123, see large stamp illustration pages.

RS122 2c **black**
d. Wmk 191R 17.00
RS123 4c **black**
b. Silk paper 125.00
c. Pink paper 525.00
d. Wmk 191R 1,750.

Holloway's Pills and Ointment — RS124/RS125

Holloway's Pills and Ointment

RS124 1c **blue**
a. Old paper, perf. 11.00
RS125 1c **blue**
a. Old paper, imperf. 750.00

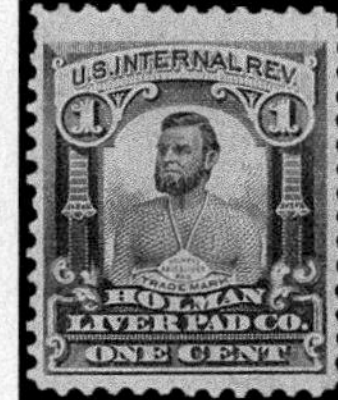

Holman Liver Pad Co. — RS126/RS127

Holman Liver Pad Co.

RS126 1c **green**
d. Wmk 191R 22.50
RS127 4c **green**
d. Wmk 191R 11.00

The Home Bitters Co.

For illustration of No. RS128, see large stamp illustration pages.

RS128 2c **blue**
d. Wmk 191R 250.00
As "d," dbl. transfer —
RS129 3c **green**
b. Silk paper 125.00
c. Pink paper 175.00
d. Wmk 191R 110.00
RS130 4c **green**
b. Silk paper 250.00
d. Wmk 191R 400.00

Hop Bitters Co. — RS131

Hop Bitters Co.

RS131 4c **black**
d. Wmk 191R 7.75

Hostetter & Smith

For illustration of No. RS132, see large stamp illustration pages.

RS132 4c **black**
a. Old paper, imperf. 82.50
As "a," dbl. transfer —
b. Silk paper 45.00
As "b," dbl. transfer 55.00
c. Pink paper 110.00
As "c," dbl. transfer 125.00
d. Wmk 191R 35.00
As "d," dbl. transfer 42.50
e. Experimental silk paper 3,000.
RS133 6c **black**
a. Old paper, imperf. 100.00
e. Experimental silk paper 1,500.

S. D. Howe

For illustration of No. RS137, see large stamp illustration pages.

RS134 4c **black,** Duponco's Pills
a. Old paper 140.00
b. Silk paper 500.00
RS135 4c **red,** Duponco's Pills
b. Silk paper 475.00
RS136 4c **green,** Duponco's Pills
b. Silk paper 475.00

Nos. RS135b and RS136b were never used.

RS137 4c **blue,** Arabian Milk
b. Silk paper 10.00
d. Wmk 191R 175.00

C.E. Hull & Co. — RS138

C. E. Hull & Co.

RS138 1c **black**
a. Old paper 325.00
b. Silk paper 6.25
c. Pink paper 60.00
d. Wmk 191R 6.25

T. J. Husband

For illustration of No. RS140, see large stamp illustration pages.

RS139 2c **violet**
a. Old paper, imperf. 2,500.
RS140 2c **vermilion**
a. Old paper, imperf. 17.00
b. Silk paper 11.00
d. Wmk 191R 10.00

Hutchings & Hillyer — RS141

Hutchings & Hillyer

RS141 4c **green**
a. Old paper, imperf. 22.50
b. Silk paper 35.00
e. Experimental silk paper 250.00

I

H. A. Ingham & Co. — RS142

H. A. Ingham & Co.

RS142 1c **black**
d. Wmk 191R 60.00

J

James A. Jackson & Co.

For illustration of No. RS143, see large stamp illustration pages.

RS143 4c **green**
a. Old paper 2,250.
b. Silk paper 400.00
As "b," dbl. transfer —

Dr. D. Jayne & Son

For illustration of No. RS149, see large stamp illustration pages.

RS144 1c **blue,** imperf.
a. Old paper 20,000.
ap. As "a," perf 1,500.
b. Silk paper 3,500.
bp. As "b," perf. *3,500.*
d. Wmk 191R 600.00
dp. As "d," perf *6,500.*
RS145 2c **black,** imperf.
a. Old paper *10,000.*
ap. As "a," perf *4,000.*
b. Silk paper 2,250.
d. Wmk 191R 1,400.
dp. As "d," perf —
RS146 4c **green,** imperf.
a. Old paper *5,500.*
ap. As "a," perf *6,000.*
b. Silk paper 2,250.
c. Pink paper 1,500.
d. Wmk 191R 650.00
dp. As "d," perf —
RS146F 4c **red,** imperf.
a. Old paper *7,000.*
RS146G 4c **orange,** imperf.
a. Old paper *15,000.*
ap. As "a," perf. and die cut *10,000.*
h. As "a," die cut *16,000.*
RS147 1c **blue,** die cut
a. Old paper 6.75
ap. As "a," perf & die cut *160.00*
As No. RS147ap, horiz. laid paper 62.50
b. Silk paper 5.50
bp. As "b," perf & die cut *275.00*
c. Pink paper 250.00
cp. As "c," perf & die cut *275.00*
d. Wmk 191R 5.50
dp. As "d," perf & die cut *1,500.*
e. Experimental silk paper *2,000.*
RS148 2c **black,** die cut
a. Old paper 11.00
As "a," dbl. transfer 60.00
ap. As "a," perf & die cut *45.00*
b. Silk paper 9.00
As "b," dbl. transfer 60.00
bp. As "b," perf & die cut *250.00*
c. Pink paper 110.00
As "c," dbl. transfer 125.00
cp. As "c," perf & die cut *900.00*
d. Wmk 191R 5.50
As "d," dbl. transfer 100.00
e. Experimental silk paper 210.00
RS149 4c **green,** die cut
a. Old paper 7.75
ap. As "a," perf & die cut 50.00
Vert. laid paper 40.00
b. Silk paper 5.50
As "b," dbl. transfer —
bp. As "b," perf & die cut *240.00*
c. Pink paper 100.00
d. Wmk 191R 9.25
dp. As "d," perf & die cut *1,750.*
e. Experimental silk paper 190.00

I. S. Johnson & Co. — RS150

I. S. Johnson & Co.

RS150 1c **vermilion**
b. Silk paper 1.50
As "b," dbl. transfer 22.50
c. Pink paper 16.00
As "c," dbl. transfer 60.00
d. Wmk 191R 1.00
As "d," dbl. transfer 27.50

Johnston Holloway & Co. — RS151/RS152

Johnston Holloway & Co.

RS151 1c **black**
b. Silk paper 4.00
d. Wmk 191R 3.00
RS152 2c **green**
b. Silk paper 4.00
d. Wmk 191R 3.25

K

J. B. Kelly & Co.

For illustration of No. RS153, see large stamp illustration pages.

RS153 4c **black,** imperf.
a. Old paper 2,250.
e. Experimental silk paper 2,500.

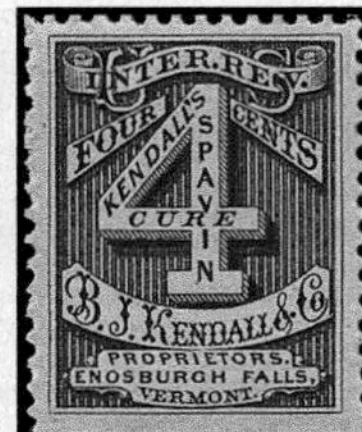

B. J. Kendall & Co. — RS154

B. J. Kendall & Co.

RS154 4c **blue**
d. Wmk 191R 35.00

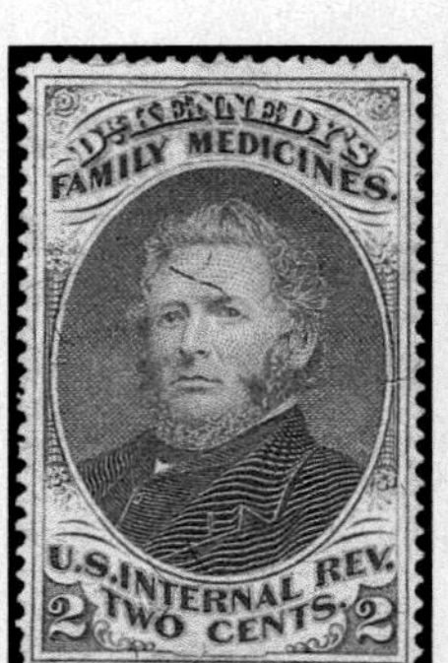

Dr. Kennedy — RS155

Dr. Kennedy — RS156

Dr. Kennedy

RS155 2c **green**
a. Old paper 60.00
b. Silk paper 9.00
c. Pink paper 40.00
d. Wmk 191R 6.75
As "d," dbl. transfer —
e. Experimental silk paper *3,500.*
RS156 6c **black**
b. Silk paper 9.00
c. Pink paper 82.50
d. Wmk 191R 9.00

Kennedy & Co. RS157

United States Proprietary Medicine Co. – RS247

World's Dispensary Medical Association RS272

World's Dispensary Medical Association RS273

Dr. J. Walker – RS253

West India Manufacturing Co. – RS264

Hostetter Co. – RS285

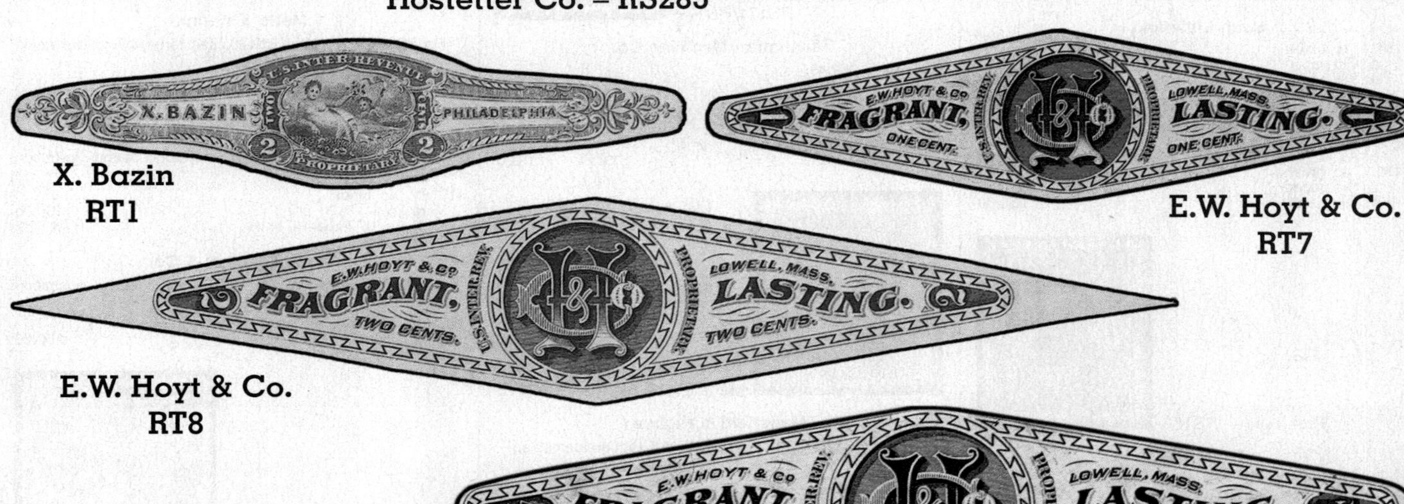

X. Bazin RT1

E.W. Hoyt & Co. RT7

E.W. Hoyt & Co. RT8

E.W. Hoyt & Co. – RT11

Kennedy & Co.

RS157 2c **black**
b. Silk paper 7.75
c. Pink paper 110.00
d. Wmk 191R 9.25

K & Co. (Kennedy & Co.)

RS158 1c **green**
d. Wmk 191R 8.25

Dr. Jas. C. Kerr

For illustration of No. RS159, see large stamp illustration pages.

RS159 4c **blue**
a. Old paper *8,750.*
b. Silk paper 350.00
d. Wmk 191R 200.00

RS160 6c **black**
a. Old paper 1,000.

L

Lawrence & Martin

RS161 4c **black**
d. Wmk 191R 50.00

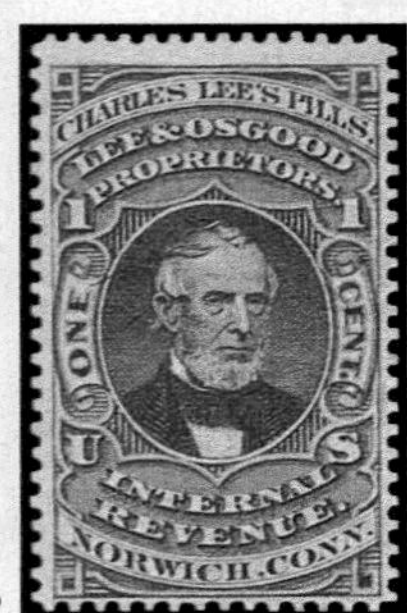

Lee & Osgood — RS162

Lee & Osgood

RS162 1c **blue**
a. Old paper 16.00
b. Silk paper 22.50
d. Wmk 191R 17.00

Jacob Lippman & Bro.

For illustration of No. RS163, see large stamp illustration pages.

RS163 4c **blue**
a. Old paper 2,000.
b. Silk paper 2,500.
e. Experimental silk paper 3,750.

Alvah Littlefield — RS165

Alvah Littlefield

RS164 1c **black**
a. Old paper 2.25
b. Silk paper 1.25
As "b," dbl. transfer 82.50
d. Wmk 191R 22.50
e. Experimental silk paper 200.00
As "e," horiz. laid paper *1,500.*
As "e," dbl. transfer 250.00

RS165 4c **green**
a. Old paper 2,000.
b. Silk paper 250.00

Prof. Low — RS166

Prof. Low

RS166 1c **black**
b. Silk paper 3.50
As "b," dbl. transfer —
c. Pink paper 20.00
As "c," dbl. transfer 60.00
d. Wmk 191R 3.50
As "d," dbl. transfer 45.00

Lyon Manufg. Co.

As No. RS24, inscribed "Lyon Manufg. Co." instead of "Demas Barnes & Co."

For illustration of No. RS167, see large stamp illustration pages.

RS167 1c **black**
b. Silk paper 22.50
c. Pink paper 400.00
d. Wmk 191R 16.00

RS168 2c **black**
b. Silk paper 10.00
c. Pink paper 200.00
d. Wmk 191R 10.00
i. Vert. pair, imperf btwn., wmk 191R 2,250.

M

J. McCullough

As No. RS134, inscribed "J. McCullough" instead of "S. D. Howe."

RS169 4c **black**
b. Silk paper 140.00
d. Wmk 191R 125.00

J. H. McLean — RS170

Dr. J. H. McLean

RS170 1c **black**
a. Old paper 2.75
As "a," dbl. transfer 55.00
b. Silk paper 1.75
As "b," dbl. transfer 72.50
c. Pink paper 17.00
As "c," dbl. transfer —
d. Wmk 191R 1.75
As "d," dbl. transfer 40.00
e. Experimental silk paper 140.00
i. As "a," vert. pair, imperf horiz. —

Manhattan Medicine Co. — RS171/RS172

Manhattan Medicine Co.

RS171 1c **violet**
d. Wmk 191R 42.50
u. As "d," **purple** 67.50

RS172 2c **black**
b. Silk paper 30.00
c. Pink paper 42.50
d. Wmk 191R 16.00

Mansfield & Higbee — RS173

Mansfield & Higbee

As No. RS174, inscribed "Mansfield & Higbee Memphis, Tenn."

RS173 1c **blue**
b. Silk paper 18.00
i. As "b," pair, imperf btwn. 250.00
j. As "b," block of 4, imperf btwn. 275.00

S. Mansfield & Co. — RS174

S. Mansfield & Co.

RS174 1c **blue**
b. Silk paper 30.00
bi. As "b," pair, imperf. btwn. 300.00
bj. As "b," block of 4, imperf. within 500.00
c. Pink paper 250.00
ci. As "c," pair, imperf. btwn. 750.00
cj. As "c," block of 4, imperf. within 1,000.
d. Wmk 191R 17.00
di. As "d," pair, imperf. btwn. 400.00
dj. As "d," block of 4, imperf. within 275.00

Nos. RS173-RS174 are perf on 4 sides. The "i." and "j." varieties served as 2c or 4c stamps. Straight-edged stamps from severed pairs or blocks are worth much less.

T. W. Marsden

For illustrations of Nos. RS175-RS176, see large stamp illustration pages.

RS175 2c **blue**
a. Old paper *11,500.*

RS176 4c **black**
a. Old paper 525.00

Mercado & Seully

For illustration of No. RS177, see large stamp illustration pages.

RS177 2c **black,** imprf.
a. Old paper *7,500.*

Merchant's Gargling Oil — RS178/RS179

Merchant's Gargling Oil

RS178 1c **black**
a. Old paper 275.00
b. Silk paper 45.00
c. Pink paper 1,750.
d. Wmk 191R 35.00
e. Experimental silk paper *3,250.*

RS179 2c **green**
a. Old paper 275.00
b. Silk paper 35.00
As "b," foreign entry *3,250.*
c. Pink paper 1,500.
d. Wmk 191R 27.50
As "d," foreign entry *3,750.*
e. Experimental silk paper 3,250.

Foreign entry is over design of No. RO11.

Mette & Kanne

For illustration of No. RS180, see large stamp illustration pages.

RS180 3c **black**
d. Wmk 191R 400.00

Mishler Herb Bitters Co.

For illustration of No. RS181, see large stamp illustration pages.

RS181 4c **black**
d. Wmk 191R 150.00
p. As "d," imperf at ends 1,500.

Moody, Michel & Co.

For illustration of No. RS182, see large stamp illustration pages.

RS182 4c **black,** imperf.
b. Silk paper 200.00

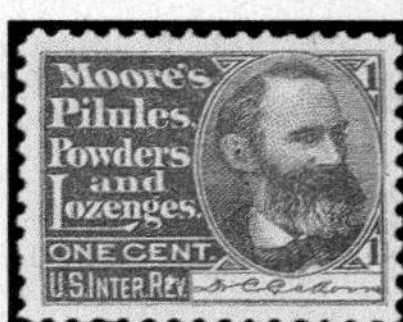

Dr. C. C. Moore — RS183

Dr. C. C. Moore

RS183 1c **vermilion,** Pilules
d. Wmk 191R 6.75

RS184 2c **black,** Sure Cure
b. Silk paper 82.50
c. Pink paper *17,500.*

d. Wmk 191R 30.00

Morehead's

For illustration of No. RS186, see large stamp illustration pages.

RS185 1c **black,** Magnetic Plaster
a. Old paper 30.00
e. Experimental silk paper *2,500.*
RS186 4c **black,** Neurodyne
a. Old paper *4,500.*

N

New York Pharmacal Association

For illustration of No. RS187, see large stamp illustration pages.

RS187 4c **black**
b. Silk paper 17.00
c. Pink paper 40.00
d. Wmk 191R 11.00

P

Dr. M. Perl & Co.

For illustration of No. RS188, see large stamp illustration pages.

RS188 6c **black,** cut to shape
a. Old paper 1,650.

All known examples of No. RS188a are faulty or defective.

R. V. Pierce — RS189/RS190

R. V. Pierce

For illustration of No. RS190, see large stamp illustration pages.

RS189 1c **green**
b. Silk paper 25.00
c. Pink paper 200.00
d. Wmk 191R 27.50
RS190 2c **black**
a. Old paper 30.00
b. Silk paper 8.25
As "b," dbl. transfer —
c. Pink paper 35.00
d. Wmk 191R 7.75
e. Experimental silk paper 160.00

Bennett Pieters & Co.

For illustration of No. RS191, see large stamp illustration pages.

RS191 4c **black**
a. Old paper 650.00
b. Silk paper *4,000.*
e. Experimental silk paper *5,000.*
RS192 6c **black**
a. Old paper 1,600.
i. As "a," imperf *3,000.*

R

Radway & Co.

For illustration of No. RS193, see large stamp illustration pages.

RS193 2c **black**
a. Old paper 5.00
b. Silk paper 3.25
As "b," dbl. transfer 72.50
c. Pink paper 12.00
As "c," dbl. transfer 110.00
d. Wmk 191R 5.50
As "d," dbl. transfer 82.50
e. Experimental silk paper 90.00

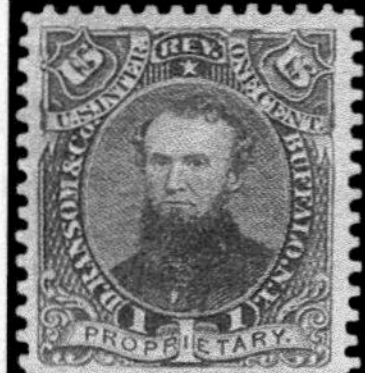

D. Ransom & Co. — RS194

D. Ransom & Co.

RS194 1c **blue**
a. Old paper 5.00
b. Silk paper 3.00
As "b," dbl. transfer —
e. Experimental silk paper 175.00
RS195 2c **black**
a. Old paper 27.50
b. Silk paper 35.00
e. Experimental silk paper 175.00

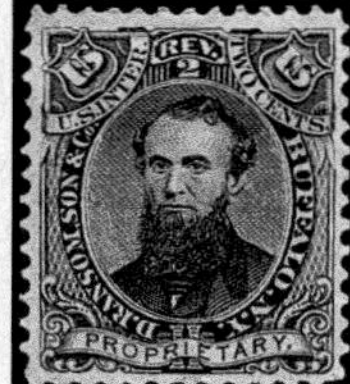

D. Ransom, Son & Co. — RS197

D. Ransom, Son & Co.

As Nos. RS194-RS195 with "Son" added.

RS196 1c **blue**
b. Silk paper 4.50
As "b," dbl. transfer —
c. Pink paper 17.00
d. Wmk 191R 6.75
RS197 2c **black**
b. Silk paper 18.00
c. Pink paper 82.50
d. Wmk 191R 11.00

Redding's Russia Salve — RS198

Redding's Russia Salve

RS198 1c **black**
b. Silk paper 9.00
As "b," dbl. transfer 150.00
d. Wmk 191R 9.00

Ring's Vegetable Ambrosia — RS199/RS200

Ring's Vegetable Ambrosia

RS199 2c **blue**
b. Silk paper, imperf. 3,750.
p. As "b," perf. *14,500.*
RS200 4c **black,** imperf.
a. Old paper 5,500.
b. Silk paper 5,500.

No. RS199p is unique.

Ring's Vegetable Ambrosia — RS201/RS202

Ring's Vegetable Ambrosia — RS203

RS201 2c **blue,** die cut
b. Silk paper 25.00
RS202 4c **black,** die cut
a. Old paper 17.00
b. Silk paper 17.00
d. Wmk 191R 25.00
e. Experimental silk paper 175.00
RS203 4c **black,** perf.
b. Silk paper 2,000.
bk. As "b," perf & die cut *4,500.*
bp. As "b," part perf. 3,750.
d. Wmk 191R 2,750.
dk. As "d," perf & die cut *5,000.*
dp. As "d," part perf. —

J. B. Rose & Co. — RS204/RS205

J. B. Rose & Co.

RS204 2c **black**
b. Silk paper 6.75
As "b," dbl. transfer 160.00
c. Pink paper 35.00
As "c," dbl. transfer 225.00
RS205 4c **black**
a. Old paper *8,500.*
b. Silk paper 160.00
As "b," dbl. transfer 230.00

Rumford Chemical Works

RS206 2c **green**
d. Wmk 191R 5.00
RS207 2c **green,** imperf.
d. Wmk 191R 27.50

S

A. B. & D. Sands

RS208 1c **green**
a. Old paper 11.00
b. Silk paper 22.50
e. Experimental silk paper 110.00

M., P. J. & H. M. Sands

The #RS208 die was altered to make #RS209.
For illustration of No. RS209, see large stamp illustration pages.

RS209 2c **green**
b. Silk paper 20.00
c. Pink paper 125.00
d. Wmk 191R 17.00

Scheetz's Celebrated Bitter Cordial

For illustration of No. RS210, see large stamp illustration pages.

RS210 4c **black,** perf.
b. Silk paper 1,000.
RS211 4c **black,** imperf.
b. Silk paper *8,000.*

Schenck's Mandrake Pills

For illustration of No. RS212, see large stamp illustration pages.

RS212 1c **green,** imperf.
a. Old paper 5.50
b. Silk paper 11.00
As "b," dbl. transfer 50.00
c. Pink paper 125.00
d. Wmk 191R 5.50
As "d," dbl. transfer —
p. As "d," perf. *4,000.*
e. Experimental silk paper *1,750.*

Schenck's Pulmonic Syrup

For illustration of No. RS213, see large stamp illustration pages.

RS213 6c **black,** imperf.
a. Old paper 8.25
p. As "a," perf. 240.00
b. Silk paper 5.50
As "b," dbl. transfer 62.50
c. Pink paper 110.00
d. Wmk 191R 200.00
As "d," dbl. transfer —
e. Experimental silk paper 250.00

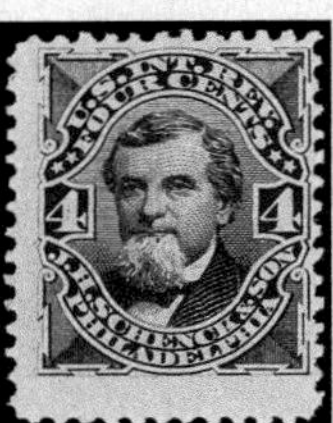

J. H. Schenck & Son — RS214

J. H. Schenck & Son

RS214 4c **black**
d. Wmk 191R 11.00

J. E. Schwartz & Co.

As No. RS84, inscribed "J. E. Schwartz & Co." instead of "B. A. Fahnestock."
For illustration of No. RS215, see large stamp illustration pages.

RS215 1c **lake,** imperf.
b. Silk paper 160.00
c. Pink paper 1,100.
d. Wmk 191R 125.00

"A. L. Scovill" follows No. RS219.

Seabury & Johnson — RS216

Seabury & Johnson — RS218

Illustration reduced.

Seabury & Johnson

RS216 1c **black**
d. Wmk 191R 82.50
RS217 1c **black**
d. Wmk 191R, printed obliteration over "porous" 5.50
h. "Porous" obliterated by pen 5.50
RS218 1c **lake**
d. Wmk 191R *3,250.*

"Dr. D. H. Seelye & Co." follows No. RS221

Dr. S. Brown Sigesmond — RS219

Dr. S. Brown Sigesmond

RS219 4c **blue**
d. Wmk 191R 125.00

A. L. Scovill & Co. — RS220/RS221

A. L. Scovill & Co.

RS220 1c **black**
a. Old paper 2.00
As "a," dbl. transfer —
b. Silk paper 2.75
As "b," dbl. transfer —
e. Experimental silk paper 77.50
r. As "b," printed on both sides *2,500.*
RS221 4c **green**
a. Old paper 2.25
b. Silk paper 5.50
e. Experimental silk paper 190.00

Dr. D. H. Seelye & Co.

For illustration of No. RS222, see large stamp illustration pages.

RS222 8c **black,** imperf.
a. Old paper 27.50

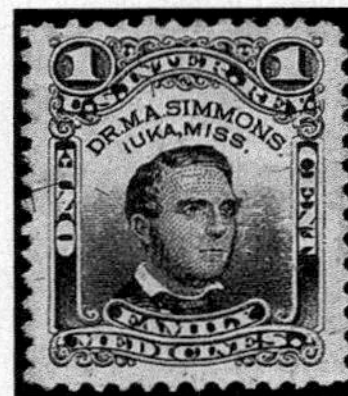

Dr. M. A. Simmons — RS223

Dr. M. A. Simmons

RS223 1c **black,** Iuka, Miss.
b. Silk paper 125.00
d. Wmk 191R *14,000.*
RS224 1c **black,** St. Louis, Mo.
d. Wmk 191R 125.00

S. N. Smith & Co.

As No. RS65, inscribed "S. N. Smith & Co." instead of "Oliver Crook & Co."
For illustration of No. RS225, see large stamp illustration pages.

RS225 4c **black**
b. Silk paper 55.00
d. Wmk 191R 55.00

Dr. E. L. Soule & Co.

For illustration of No. RS227, see large stamp illustration pages.

N.Y. Wrapper

RS226 1c **blue**
a. Old paper 82.50
As "a," foreign entry *1,750.*

Syracuse Wrapper

RS227 1c **blue**
a. Old paper 82.50
As "a," foreign entry *2,000.*
b. Silk paper 40.00
As "b," foreign entry *1,500.*
e. Experimental silk paper *3,000.*
u. **Ultra,** old paper 975.00
As "u," foreign entry —

For Nos. RS226, RS227, the foreign entry is the design of No. RT1 (pos. 1).

H. R. Stevens — RS228/RS229

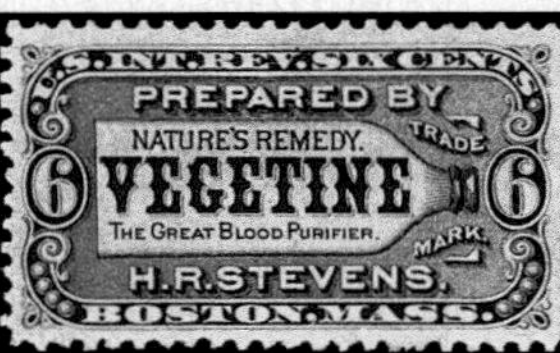

H.R. Stevens RS230

H. R. Stevens

RS228 1c **brown**
d. Wmk 191R 18.00
RS229 2c **chocolate**
d. Wmk 191R 6.75
RS230 6c **black**
c. Pink paper 125.00
d. Wmk 191R 6.75

Jas. Swaim

For illustration of No. RS231, see large stamp illustration pages.

RS231 6c **orange,** die cut
a. Old paper *6,500.*
f. As "a," without signature *20,000.*

Manuscript signature.

RS232 8c **orange,** imperf.
a. Old paper *3,000.*
ah. As "a," manuscript signature *10,000.*
bh. Manuscript signature, silk paper *10,000.*
RS233 8c **orange,** die cut
a. Old paper 400.00
ah. As "a," manuscript signature 4,500.
bh. Manuscript signature, silk paper *7,500.*
e. Experimental silk paper *3,000.*

Wm. Swaim

For illustration of No. RS234, see large stamp illustration pages.

RS234 8c **orange,** imperf.
a. Old paper *20,000.*
ak. As "a," without signature *20,000.*
b. Silk paper *6,000.*
bk. As "b," without signature *20,000.*
d. Wmk 191R 2,600.

No. RS234d is found with signature "Suaim" or "Swaim." Also, No. RS234b is found with a period under the raised "m" of "Wm" and the right leg of "w" of "Swaim" retouched, both by pen.

RS235 8c **orange,** die cut
a. Old paper *2,500.*
b. Silk paper 210.00
bh. As "b," manuscript signature *25,000.*
bk. As "b," inverted signature *18,000.*
d. Wmk 191R 250.00

No. RS235bh is unique.

Dr. G. W. Swett — RS237

Illustration reduced.

Dr. G. W. Swett

RS236 4c **black,** die cut
a. Old paper 18.00
RS237 4c **green,** perf.
b. Silk paper 250.00
d. Wmk 191R *2,750.*
RS238 4c **green,** perf. & cie cut
b. Silk paper 450.00
d. Wmk 191R *3,250.*

T

George Tallcot

For illustration of No. RS240, see large stamp illustration pages.

RS239 2c **vermilion**
d. Wmk 191R 17.00
RS240 4c **black**
b. Silk paper 95.00
c. Pink paper *12,000.*
d. Wmk 191R 22.50

Tarrant & Co. — RS241

Tarrant & Company

RS241 4c **red**
b. Silk paper 3.25
c. Pink paper 100.00
d. Wmk 191R 2.25

John L. Thompson — RS242

John L. Thompson

RS242 1c **black**
- *a.* Old paper 6.75
  - As "a," dbl. transfer —
- *b.* Silk paper 8.25
- *d.* Wmk 191R 6.75
- *e.* Experimental silk paper 160.00

U

United States Proprietary Medicine Co.

For illustration of No. RS243, see large stamp illustration pages.

RS243 4c **black**
- *a.* Old paper 50.00
- *b.* Silk paper 125.00
- *e.* Experimental silk paper 350.00

RS244 6c **black**
- *a.* Old paper *2,500.*
- *e.* Experimental silk paper *24,000.*

No. RS244e is unique.

U. S. Proprietary Medicine Co. Wrappers

For illustration of No. RS247, see large stamp illustration pages.

RS245 1c **black,** *white*
- *a.* Old paper 50.00
- *b.* Silk paper 50.00
- *e.* Experimental silk paper *1,250.*

RS246 1c **black,** *yel*
- *a.* Old paper 140.00
- *b.* Silk paper 250.00

RS247 1c **black,** *org*
- *a.* Old paper 1,500.
- *b.* Silk paper *7,000.*

RS248 1c **black,** *org red*
- *a.* Old paper *3,500.*
- *b.* Silk paper *10,000.*

V

S. R. Van Duzer

For illustration of No. RS249, see large stamp illustration pages.

RS249 4c **black**
- *a.* Old paper 45.00
- *b.* Silk paper 40.00
- *d.* Wmk 191R 210.00

RS250 6c **black**
- *d.* Wmk 191R 82.50

A. Vogeler & Co. — RS251

A. Vogeler & Co.

RS251 1c **black**
- *b.* Silk paper 1.75
- *d.* Wmk 191R 2.25

Vogeler, Meyer & Co. — RS252

Vogeler, Meyer & Co.

RS252 1c **vermilion**
- *c.* Pink paper 4.50
- *d.* Wmk 191R 1.50

W

Dr. J. Walker

For illustration of No. RS253, see large stamp illustration pages.

RS253 4c **black**
- *a.* Old paper 45.00
- *b.* Silk paper 25.00
  - As "b," dbl. transfer 55.00
- *d.* Wmk 191R 22.50
  - As "d," dbl. transfer 45.00
- *e.* Experimental silk paper *1,500.*

H. H. Warner & Co. — RS254/RS255

H. H. W. & Co. (H. H. Warner & Co.)

RS254 1c **brown**
- *d.* Wmk 191R 6.75

RS255 6c **brown,** 19x26mm
- *d.* Wmk 191R 90.00

RS256 2c **brown,** 88x11mm
- *d.* Wmk 191R 35.00

RS257 4c **brown,** 95x18mm
- *d.* Wmk 191R 35.00

RS258 6c **brown**
- *d.* Wmk 191R 8.25
  - As "d," dbl. transfer 55.00

Weeks & Potter — RS259

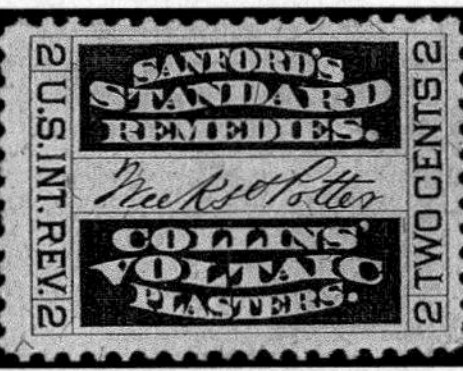

Weeks & Potter—RS260/RS261

Weeks & Potter—RS262

Weeks & Potter

RS259 1c **black**
- *b.* Silk paper 7.75
- *d.* Wmk 191R 6.00

RS260 2c **black**
- *b.* Silk paper 110.00

RS261 4c **black**
- *b.* Silk paper 30.00
- *c.* Pink paper 30.00
- *d.* Wmk 191R 7.75

RS262 2c **red**
- *c.* Pink paper 40.00
- *d.* Wmk 191R 7.75

Wells, Richardson & Co. — RS263

Wells, Richardson & Co.

RS263 4c **black**
- *d.* Wmk 191R 30.00

West India Manufacturing Co.

For illustration of No. RS264, see large stamp illustration pages.

RS264 4c **black,** die I
- *b.* Silk paper 300.00
- *c.* Pink paper 400.00
- *d.* Wmk 191R 750.00

RS264A 4c **black,** die II
- *d.* Wmk 191R 675.00

Die II shows evidence of retouching, particularly in the central disk.

Edward Wilder — RS265/RS269

Edward Wilder

RS265 1c **green,** imperf.
- *a.* Old paper *1,750.*
- *b.* Silk paper 325.00
- *d.* Wmk 191R 325.00
- *e.* Experimental silk paper *7,500.*

RS266 1c **green,** die cut
- *a.* Old paper 55.00
- *b.* Silk paper 50.00
- *d.* Wmk 191R 25.00
- *e.* Experimental silk paper 900.00

RS266A 4c **vermilion,** imperf
- *e.* Experimental silk paper *16,000.*

RS267 4c **vermilion,** die cut
- *a.* Old paper 200.00
- *b.* Silk paper *2,250.*
- *e.* Experimental silk paper 300.00

RS268 4c **lake,** imperf.
- *b.* Silk paper 275.00
- *d.* Wmk 191R 2,250.

RS269 4c **lake,** die cut
- *a.* Old paper *2,500.*
- *b.* Silk paper 14.00
- *d.* Wmk 191R 14.00

No. RS266Ae is unique.

Rev. E.A. Wilson — RS270

Rev. E. A. Wilson

RS270 12c **blue**
- *b.* Silk paper 80.00
- *d.* Wmk 191R 550.00

Thos. E. Wilson, M.D. — RS271

Thos. E. Wilson, M. D.

RS271 4c **black**
- *a.* Old paper *25,000.*

No. RS271a is unique.

World's Dispensary Medical Assocn.

For illustration of No. RS273, see large stamp illustration pages.

RS272 1c **green**
- *d.* Wmk 191R 27.50

RS273 2c **black,** 56x25mm
- *d.* Wmk 191R 9.00

Wright's Indian Vegetable Pills — RS274

Wright's Indian Vegetable Pills

RS274	1c **green**	
	a. Old paper	2.25
	b. Silk paper	1.75
	c. Pink paper	40.00
	d. Wmk 191R	3.50
	As "d," dbl. transfer	—
	e. Experimental silk paper	150.00

Z

J.H. Zeilin & Co. — RS275/RS277

J.H. Zeilin & Co.

RS275	2c **red**	
	b. Silk paper	1,100.
RS276	2c **green**	
	b. Silk paper, perf.	45.00
	d. Wmk 191R	—
RS277	2c **green**	
	a. Old paper, imperf.	300.00
	b. Silk paper	8.25
	c. Pink paper	140.00
	d. Wmk 191R	5.50

1898-1900

See rouletting note preceding No. R161.

Left value = Unused

Right value = Used

The Antikamnia Chemical Co. — RS278

The Antikamnia Chemical Co.

RS278	2½c **carmine**		
	p. Hyphen hole perf. 7	4.00	4.00

Fernet Branca (Branca Bros.) — RS279

Fernet Branca (Branca Bros.)

RS279	4c **black**		
	r. Rouletted 5½	9.50	9.50
	p. Hyphen hole perf. 7	9.50	9.50

Emerson Drug Co. — RS281

Emerson Drug Co.

RS280	¼c **carmine**		
	p. Hyphen hole perf. 7	7.00	3.00
RS281	⅝c **green**		
	p. Hyphen hole perf. 7	7.00	3.50
RS282	1¼c **violet brown**		
	p. Hyphen hole perf. 7	9.00	7.00
RS283	2½c **brown orange**		
	p. Hyphen hole perf. 7	8.50	5.00

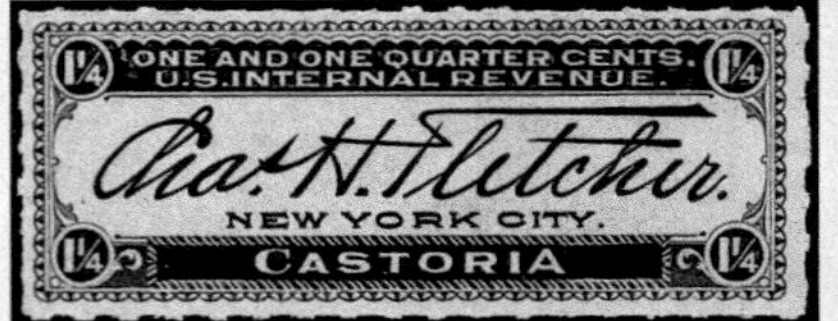

Chas. H. Fletcher — RS284

Chas. H. Fletcher

RS284	1¼c **black**		
	r. Rouletted 5½	.60	.60
	p. Hyphen hole perf. 7	.60	.60

Hostetter Co.

For illustration of No. RS285, see large stamp illustration pages.

RS285	2½c **black,** imperf	.60	.60

Johnson & Johnson — RS286

Johnson & Johnson

RS286	⅝c **carmine**		
	r. Rouletted 5½	.50	.50
	p. Hyphen hole perf. 7	.50	.50

Lanman & Kemp — RS287

Lanman & Kemp

RS287	⅝c **green**		
	r. Rouletted 5½	8.50	6.00
	p. Hyphen hole perf. 7	11.00	4.50
RS288	1¼c **brown**		
	r. Rouletted 5½	11.00	6.50
	p. Hyphen hole perf. 7	16.00	12.00
RS289	1⅞c **blue**		
	r. Rouletted 5½	11.00	8.00
	p. Hyphen hole perf. 7	21.00	11.00

J. Ellwood Lee Co. — RS290

J. Ellwood Lee Co.

RS290	⅛c **dk blue**		
	p. Hyphen hole perf. 7	3.25	3.00
RS291	⅝c **carmine**		
	p. Hyphen hole perf. 7	2.75	2.00
RS292	1¼c **dk green**		
	p. Hyphen hole perf. 7	2.25	2.00
RS293	2½c **orange**		
	p. Hyphen hole perf. 7	2.75	2.50
RS294	5c **chocolate**		
	p. Hyphen hole perf. 7	3.00	2.75

Charles Marchand — RS295

Charles Marchand

RS295	⅝c **black**		
	r. Rouletted 5½	8.50	8.50
	p. Hyphen hole perf. 7	9.00	9.00

RS296	1¼c **black**		
	r. Rouletted 5½	1.75	1.75
	p. Hyphen hole perf. 7	1.75	1.75
RS297	1⅞c **black**		
	r. Rouletted 5½	2.50	2.50
	p. Hyphen hole perf. 7	3.00	3.00
RS298	2½c **black**		
	r. Rouletted 5½	3.00	3.00
	p. Hyphen hole perf. 7	3.00	3.00
RS299	3⅛c **black**		
	r. Rouletted 5½	8.50	8.50
	p. Hyphen hole perf. 7	8.50	8.50
RS300	4⅜c **black**		
	r. Rouletted 5½	16.00	16.00
	p. Hyphen hole perf. 7	16.00	16.00
RS301	7½c **black**		
	r. Rouletted 5½	11.00	11.00
	p. Hyphen hole perf. 7	11.00	11.00

Od Chem. Co. — RS302

Od Chem. Co.

RS302	2½c **carmine**		
	p. Hyphen hole perf. 7	—	2.50

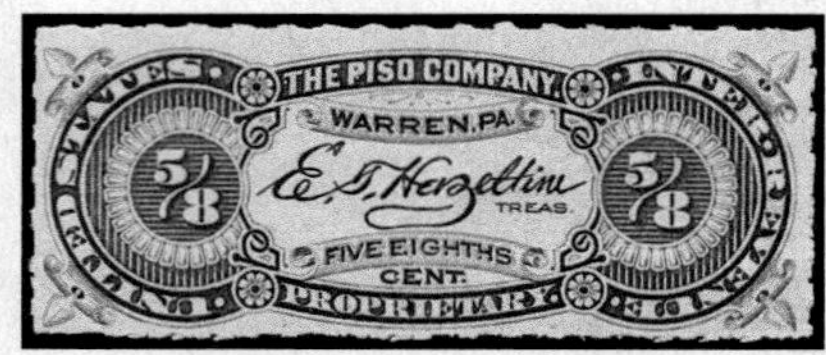

The Piso Company — RS303

The Piso Company (E. T. Hazeltine)

RS303	⅝c **blue**		
	r. Rouletted 5½	.50	.50
	p. Hyphen hole perf. 7	.50	.50

Radway & Co. — RS304

Radway & Co.

RS304	⅝c **blue**		
	r. Rouletted 5½	1.25	1.25
	p. Hyphen hole perf. 7	1.25	1.25

Warner's Safe Cure Co. — RS305

Warner's Safe Cure Co.

RS305	3⅛c **brown**		
	r. Rouletted 5½	1.25	1.25
	p. Hyphen hole perf. 7	1.25	1.25

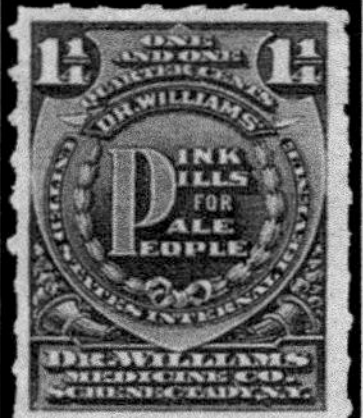

Dr. Williams Medicine Co. — RS306

Dr. Williams Medicine Co.

RS306	1¼c **pink**		
	p. Hyphen hole perf. 7	3.50	3.50

DR. KILMER & CO., PROVISIONAL PROPRIETARY STAMPS

Postage Stamps of 1895, 1897-1903, Nos. 267a, 279, 279Bg and 268, Precancel Overprinted in Black:

Dr. K. & Co.
I. R.
7-5-'98.

a

Overprint "a," Large "I.R." Dated July 5, 1898.

1898		Wmk. 191	*Perf. 12*
RS307	A87	1c **deep green**	175.00
a.		Red (trial) plus black ovpts.	*2,500.*
RS308	A88	2c **pink,** type III	160.00
RS308A	A88	2c **pink,** type IV	175.00
b.		Dark blue (trial) ovpt.	*2,500.*
RS309	A89	3c **purple**	160.00
a.		Red (trial) ovpt.	—
b.		Inverted ovpt.	*1,500.*

The trial overprint in dark blue on the 2c stamp is known used on July 5.

b

Overprint "b," Small "I.R.," "Dr. K. & Co." with Serifs Dated July 6, 7, 9, 11 to 14, 1898

RS310	A87	1c **deep green**	140.00
RS311	A88	2c **pink,** type III	150.00
RS311A	A88	2c **pink,** type IV	77.50
RS312	A89	3c **purple**	67.50
a.		Inverted ovpt.	*1,500.*

Dr. K. & Co.
I. R.
Binghamton,
N. Y.
7-13-'98

c

Overprint "c," Small "I.R.," "Dr. K. & Co." without Serifs Dated July 7, 9, 11 to 14, 1898

RS313	A87	1c **deep green**	150.00
RS314	A88	2c **pink,** type III	150.00
RS314A	A88	2c **pink,** type IV	100.00
RS315	A89	3c **purple**	125.00
a.		Inverted ovpt.	*2,500.*

Nos. RS307a, RS308Ab and RS309a were all overprinted on July 5, the first day of overprinting. Though called "trials," there is every reason to believe they were used in the regular course of business, as they represented money spent by Dr. Kilmer & Co. and there was no reason not to use them. Four examples are recorded of No. RS307a, three of No. RS308Ab and one of No. RS309a. For the inverted overprints, four examples are recorded of No. RS309b, 16 of No. RS312a and three of No. RS315a. Forgeries exist of No. RS312a, all dated July 6. The height of "I.R." is shorter on the forgeries, and the periods after these letters are circular rather than diamond shaped. Many varieties of the Kilmer overprints exist. For the complete listing see "The Case of Dr. Kilmer's," by Morton Dean Joyce, 1954 (also serialized in "The Bureau Specialist," Mar.-Nov. 1957).

ST. LOUIS PROVISIONAL PROPRIETARY STAMPS

U.S. "Battleship" revenue stamps (Nos. RB20-RB31) not being available to meet the July 1, 1898, effective date of new taxes on proprietary medicines, eleven proprietary drug companies (10 in St. Louis, Missouri, and one in Macon, Georgia) struck agreements with local collectors of internal revenue to print their own revenue stamps for temporary use and pay their taxes by sworn returns until the government-issued stamps were available. Even though one company that used such stamps was from Macon, Georgia, these stamps are commonly referred to as the St. Louis Provisionals.

The Antikamnia Chemical Co. — RS320/RS321

The Antikamnia Chemical Co. — RS323

1898			*Imperf.*

Antikamnia Chemical Co., St. Louis

RS320	⅛c	**black,** *yellow*	2,750.
RS321	2½c	**black**	500.00
RS323	no value	**black,** *yellow*	750.00

No. RS323 was for use on free samples not subject to tax.

Fairchild Chemical Laboratory Co. — RS325

Fairchild Chemical Laboratory Co., St. Louis

Imperf

RS325	⅝c	**black**	*25,000.*

INTERNAL REVENUE TAX.
2 1-2 CENTS.
Stamps not being obtainable at time of sale and shipment of this package, the tax will be paid on sworn returns thereof to Collector of Internal Revenue, Macon, Ga.
W. R. HOLMES, Macon, Ga.

W.R. Holmes — RS330

W.R. Holmes, Macon, Georgia

Rouletted 9½ Horiz. in Green, Imperf Vert.

RS330	2½c	**green**	*25,000.*

Lambert Pharmacal Co. — RS335

Lambert Pharmacal Co., St. Louis

Imperf

RS335	2½c	**red**	1,000.

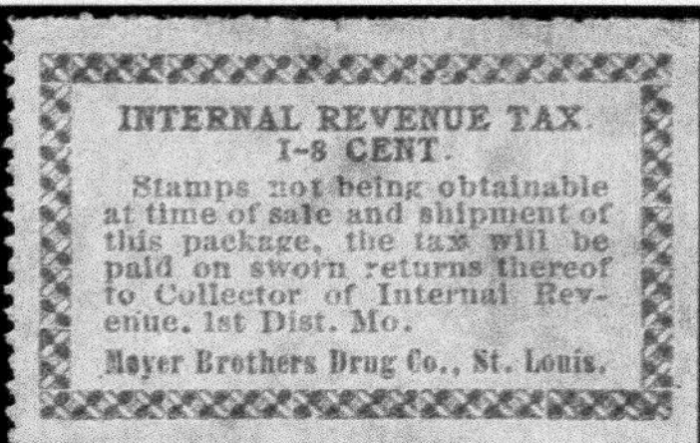
INTERNAL REVENUE TAX.
1-8 CENT.
Stamps not being obtainable at time of sale and shipment of this package, the tax will be paid on sworn returns thereof to Collector of Internal Revenue. 1st Dist. Mo.
Meyer Brothers Drug Co., St. Louis.

Meyer Brothers Drug Co. — RS340/RS350

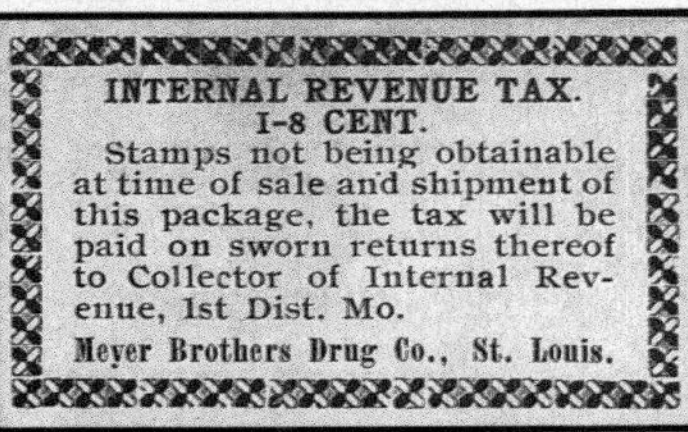
INTERNAL REVENUE TAX.
1-8 CENT.
Stamps not being obtainable at time of sale and shipment of this package, the tax will be paid on sworn returns thereof to Collector of Internal Revenue, 1st Dist. Mo.
Meyer Brothers Drug Co., St. Louis.

Meyer Brothers Drug Co. — RS351/RS361

Meyer Brothers Drug Co., St. Louis

These stamps were printed on at least three distinct papers: white, buff and rough manila.

Rouletted 9½ Horiz. in Green, Perf 12 and/or Imperf Vert.

RS340a	⅛c	**green,** white paper	*17,500.*
RS343b	⅝c	**green,** buff paper	*17,500.*
RS345c	1¼c	**green,** rough manila paper	*25,000.*
RS348c	5c	**green,** rough manila paper	*25,000.*
RS349a	7⅞c	**green,** white paper	*25,000.*
RS350b	11¼c	**green,** buff paper	*25,000.*

Imperf

RS351a	⅛c	**black,** white paper	125.00
RS352a	¼c	**black,** white paper	125.00
RS353a	⅜c	**black,** white paper	125.00
RS354a	⅝c	**black,** white paper	125.00
RS355a	1c	**black,** white paper	125.00
RS357a	2c	**black,** white paper	125.00
RS358a	3c	**black,** white paper	125.00
RS359a	4c	**black,** white paper	125.00
RS360a	5c	**black,** white paper	125.00
RS361a	11¼c	**black,** white paper	125.00

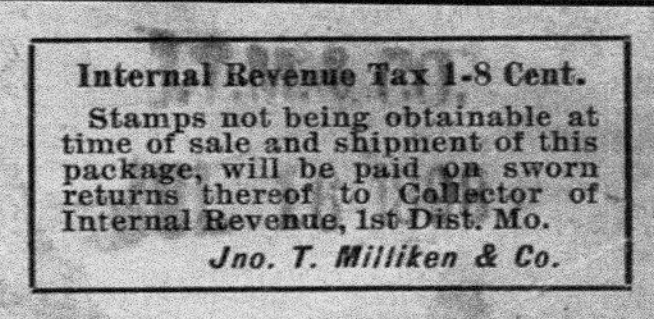
Internal Revenue Tax 1-8 Cent.
Stamps not being obtainable at time of sale and shipment of this package, will be paid on sworn returns thereof to Collector of Internal Revenue, 1st Dist. Mo.
Jno. T. Milliken & Co.

John T. Milliken & Co. — RS365/RS366

John T. Milliken & Co., St. Louis

Imperf

RS365	⅛c	**black**	1,250.
RS366	⅝c	**black**	1,250.

Phenique Chemical Co. — RS370/RS377

Phenique Chemical Co., St. Louis

These stamps were printed on two distinct papers: yellow and buff.

Imperf

RS370b	⅛c	**black,** buff paper	*25,000.*
RS371a	¼c	**black,** yellow paper	*17,500.*
RS372a	⅝c	**black,** yellow paper	*12,500.*
RS372b	⅝c	**black,** buff paper	*25,000.*
RS374a	1⅞c	**black,** yellow paper	*25,000.*
RS375a	2½c	**black,** yellow paper	*25,000.*
RS376b	3⅛c	**black,** buff paper	*25,000.*
RS377b	3¾c	**black,** buff paper	*25,000.*

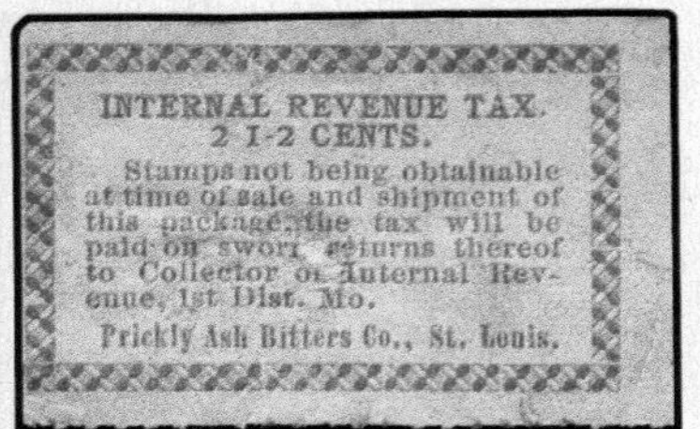

Prickly Ash Bitters Co. — RS381

Prickly Ash Bitters Co., St. Louis

Rouletted 9½ Horiz. in Green, Imperf Vert.

RS381	2½c **green**	*12,500.*

T.M. Sayman — RS385/RS387

T.M. Sayman, St. Louis

Imperf

RS385	¼c **dark blue**	*25,000.*
RS386	⅝c **dark blue**	*17,500.*
RS387	1¼c **dark blue**	*25,000.*

Van Dyke Bitters Co. — RS390

Van Dyke Bitters Co., St. Louis

Imperf

RS390	2½ **blue,** *bluish glazed*	5,500.

Walker Pharmacal Co. — RS395

Walker Pharmacal Co., St. Louis

Imperf

RS395	2½ **black**	*25,000.*

PRIVATE DIE PERFUMERY STAMPS

X. Bazin

For illustration of No. RT1, see large stamp illustration pages.

RT1	2c **blue,** die cut	
a.	Old paper	1,400.

This stamp was never placed in use.

RT2

Corning & Tappan — RT3/RT4

Corning & Tappan

RT2	1c **black,** imperf.	
d.	Wmk 191R	2,250.
h.	Die cut, 19mm diameter	125.00
k.	Die cut, 21mm diameter	175.00
RT3	1c **black,** perf.	
d.	Wmk 191R	800.00
RT4	1c **blue,** perf.	
d.	Wmk 191R	4.50

Fetridge & Co. — RT5

Illustration reduced.

Fetridge & Co.

RT5	2c **vermilion,** cut to shape	
a.	Old paper	150.00

E. W. Hoyt & Co.

For illustrations of Nos. RT7, RT8 and RT11, see large stamp illustration pages.

RT6	1c **black,** imperf.	
b.	Silk paper	*4,000.*
c.	Pink paper	3,500.
d.	Wmk 191R	160.00
RT7	1c **black,** die cut	
b.	Silk paper	37.50
c.	Pink paper	37.50
d.	Wmk 191R	18.00
RT8	2c **black,** imperf.	
d.	Wmk 191R	900.00
RT9	2c **black,** die cut	
d.	Wmk 191R	100.00
RT10	4c **black,** imperf.	
b.	Silk paper	2,250.
c.	Pink paper	300.00
d.	Wmk 191R	1,750.
RT11	4c **black,** die cut	
b.	Silk paper	125.00
c.	Pink paper	80.00
d.	Wmk 191R	80.00

The 2c is larger than the 1c, 4c larger than the 2c.

Kidder & Laird — RT12

Kidder & Laird

RT12	1c **vermilion**	
d.	Wmk 191R	17.00
RT13	2c **vermilion**	
d.	Wmk 191R	17.00

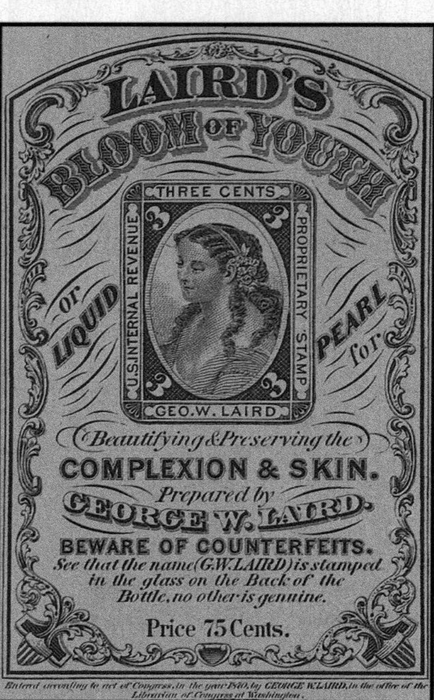

George W. Laird — RT14/RT15

George W. Laird

RT14	3c **black,** imperf.	
b.	Silk paper	800.00
	As "b," dbl. transfer	1,750.
c.	Pink paper	1,000.
	As "c," dbl. transfer	2,250.
d.	Wmk 191R	800.00
	As "d," dbl. transfer	2,500.
ap.	Perf, old paper	*3,250.*
	As "ap," Dbl. transfer	*5,500.*
bp.	Perf, silk paper	*9,000.*
RT15	3c **black,** die cut	
a.	Old paper, die cut	3,000.
ap.	As "a," perf & die cut	1,250.
b.	Silk paper	110.00
	As "b," dbl. transfer	250.00
bp.	As "b," perf & die cut	*1,500.*
c.	Pink paper	3,250.
	As "c," dbl. transfer	6,500.
d.	Wmk 191R	110.00
	As "d," dbl. transfer	325.00
e.	Experimental silk paper	*3,000.*
	Double transfer	*3,500.*

Lanman & Kemp — RT16/RT18

Lanman & Kemp

RT16	1c **black**	
b.	Silk paper	8.25
	As "b," dbl. transfer	—
c.	Pink paper	950.00
d.	Wmk 191R	8.25
RT17	2c **brown**	
b.	Silk paper	35.00
d.	Wmk 191R	11.00
RT18	3c **green**	
b.	Silk paper	9.00
	As "b," dbl. transfer	175.00
d.	Wmk 191R	9.00
	As "d," dbl. transfer	77.50

Tetlow's Perfumery — RT19

Tetlow's Perfumery

RT19	1c **vermilion**	
d.	Wmk 191R	3.75

C. B. Woodworth & Son — RT20/RT21

C. B. Woodworth & Son

RT20	1c **green**	
b.	Silk paper	6.00
	As "b," dbl. transfer	67.50
c.	Pink paper	20.00
	As "c," dbl. transfer	82.50
d.	Wmk 191R	7.75
	As "d," dbl. transfer	67.50
RT21	2c **blue**	
b.	Silk paper	180.00
c.	Pink paper	*4,000.*
d.	Wmk 191R	10.00

R. & G. A. Wright — RT22/RT25

R. & G. A. Wright

RT22	1c **blue**	
a.	Old paper	6.75
b.	Silk paper	9.00
d.	Wmk 191R	67.50
e.	Experimental silk paper	125.00

RT23 2c **black**
a. Old paper 13.00
b. Silk paper 25.00
d. Wmk 191R 600.00
RT24 3c **lake**
a. Old paper 35.00
b. Silk paper 125.00
d. Wmk 191R 525.00
RT25 4c **green**
a. Old paper 110.00
b. Silk paper 160.00
d. Wmk 191R 750.00

Young, Ladd & Coffin — RT26/RT33

Young, Ladd & Coffin

RT26 1c **green**, imperf.
b. Silk paper 110.00
c. Pink paper 100.00
d. Wmk 191R 110.00
RT27 1c **green**, perf.
b. Silk paper 25.00
c. Pink paper 17.00
d. Wmk 191R 17.00
RT28 2c **blue**, imperf.
b. Silk paper 150.00
c. Pink paper 130.00
d. Wmk 191R 90.00
RT29 2c **blue**, perf.
b. Silk paper 60.00
c. Pink paper 110.00
d. Wmk 191R 17.00
RT30 3c **vermilion**, imperf.
b. Silk paper 130.00
c. Pink paper 150.00
d. Wmk 191R 95.00
RT31 3c **vermilion**, perf.
b. Silk paper 40.00
c. Pink paper 8.25
d. Wmk 191R 7.75
RT32 4c **brown**, imperf.
b. Silk paper *9,500.*
c. Pink paper 160.00
d. Wmk 191R 110.00
RT33 4c **brown**, perf.
b. Silk paper 45.00
c. Pink paper 14.00
d. Wmk 191R 5.50

PRIVATE DIE PLAYING CARD STAMPS

RU1

Caterson Brotz & Co.

RU1 5c **brown**
d. Wmk 191R *12,000.*

This stamp was never placed in use. Value is for an unused stamp with perfs trimmed off. Three examples are recorded: one fully perfed, two with perfs trimmed off.

A. Dougherty — RU2/RU6

A. Dougherty — RU5

A. Dougherty

RU2 2c **orange**
a. Old paper 175.00
RU3 4c **black**
a. Old paper 75.00
RU4 5c **blue,** 20x26mm
a. Old paper 4.00
b. Silk paper 7.00
As "b," dbl. transfer —
c. Pink paper 14.00
e. Experimental silk paper *1,500.*
As "e," inverted dbl. transfer —
u. **Ultra,** old paper *1,750.*
RU5 5c **blue,** 18x23mm
d. Wmk 191R 7.50
RU6 10c **blue**
a. Old paper 60.00

The 2c, 4c and 5c have numerals in all four corners.

Eagle Card Co. — RU7

Eagle Card Co.

RU7 5c **black**
d. Wmk 191R 150.00

Goodall — RU8

Goodall (London, New York)

As No. RU13, "London Goodall New York" replaces both "American Playing Cards" and "Victor E. Mauger and Petrie New York."

RU8 5c **black**
a. Old paper 175.00
b. Silk paper 10.00
e. Experimental silk paper 2,750.

Samuel Hart & Co. — RU9

Samuel Hart & Co.

RU9 5c **black**
a. Old paper 9.00
b. Silk paper 9.00
e. Experimental silk paper 2,750.

Lawrence & Cohen — RU10/RU11

Lawrence & Cohen

RU10 2c **blue**
a. Old paper 150.00
RU11 5c **green**
a. Old paper 10.00
b. Silk paper 12.50
e. Experimental silk paper 165.00

Jn. J. Levy — RU12

Jn. J. Levy

RU12 5c **black**
a. Old paper 35.00
b. Silk paper 40.00
e. Experimental silk paper 140.00

Victor E. Mauger & Petrie — RU13

Victor E. Mauger and Petrie

RU13 5c **blue**
b. Silk paper 6.00
c. Pink paper 7.00
d. Wmk 191R 5.00

New York Consolidated Card Co. — RU14

New York Consolidated Card Co.

RU14 5c **black**
b. Silk paper 7.50
c. Pink paper 22.50
d. Wmk 191R 7.00

Paper Fabrique — RU15

Paper Fabrique Company

RU15 5c **black**
b. Silk paper 15.00
c. Pink paper 30.00
d. Wmk 191R 12.50

Russell, Morgan & Co. — RU16

Russell, Morgan & Co.

RU16 5c **black**
d. Wmk 191R 30.00

MOTOR VEHICLE USE REVENUE STAMPS

When affixed to a motor vehicle, the stamp permitted use of that vehicle for a stated period. The purchase month is shown in parentheses, and the denomination corresponds to the month in which the stamp is purchased, in relation to when the stamp expired. Thus, a stamp purchased in June expired that month, and the denomination is the lowest of the all the denominations in that year's set. A stamp purchased in July was good through the following June, and thus has the highest denomination in its set, and so on. Sales of motor vehicle use stamps ceased in June 1946.

Unused stamps are valued with gum on the face. Stamps without gum sell for reduced prices. Stamps with car details on the reverse are used, whether they have gum on the face or not.

RV1

1942 Wmk. 191R OFFSET PRINTING *Perf. 11*

With Gum on Back

RV1	RV1	$2.09	**light green** *(February)*	1.75	.50

With Gum on Face

Inscriptions on Back

RV2	RV1	$1.67	**light green** *(March)*	32.50	8.50
RV3	RV1	$1.25	**light green** *(April)*	25.00	7.50
RV4	RV1	84c	**light green** *(May)*	27.50	7.25
RV5	RV1	42c	**light green** *(June)*	27.50	7.25

With Gum and Control Number on Face

Inscriptions on Back

RV6	RV1	$5	**rose red** *(July)*	3.25	1.50
RV7	RV1	$4.59	**rose red** *(August)*	60.00	13.00
RV8	RV1	$4.17	**rose red** *(September)*	65.00	16.00
RV9	RV1	$3.75	**rose red** *(October)*	60.00	12.50
RV10	RV1	$3.34	**rose red** *(November)*	60.00	12.50
RV11	RV1	$2.92	**rose red** *(December)*	60.00	12.50
			Nos. RV1-RV11 (11)	422.50	99.00

1943

RV12	RV1	$2.50	**rose red** *(January)*	67.50	16.00
RV13	RV1	$2.09	**rose red** *(February)*	45.00	11.00
RV14	RV1	$1.67	**rose red** *(March)*	40.00	12.50
RV15	RV1	$1.25	**rose red** *(April)*	40.00	9.00
RV16	RV1	84c	**rose red** *(May)*	40.00	9.00
RV17	RV1	42c	**rose red** *(June)*	40.00	10.00
RV18	RV1	$5	**yellow** *(July)*	3.75	1.00
RV19	RV1	$4.59	**yellow** *(August)*	70.00	17.00
RV20	RV1	$4.17	**yellow** *(September)*	87.50	21.00
RV21	RV1	$3.75	**yellow** *(October)*	87.50	21.00
RV22	RV1	$3.34	**yellow** *(November)*	100.00	22.00
RV23	RV1	$2.92	**yellow** *(December)*	120.00	25.00
			Nos. RV12-RV23 (12)	741.25	174.50

1944

RV24	RV1	$2.50	**yellow** *(January)*	140.00	25.00
RV25	RV1	$2.09	**yellow** *(February)*	80.00	19.00
RV26	RV1	$1.67	**yellow** *(March)*	67.50	16.00
RV27	RV1	$1.25	**yellow** *(April)*	67.50	17.00
RV28	RV1	84c	**yellow** *(May)*	60.00	16.00
RV29	RV1	42c	**yellow** *(June)*	60.00	16.00

Gum on Face

Control Number and Inscriptions on Back

RV30	RV1	$5	**violet** *(July)*	2.40	1.75
RV31	RV1	$4.59	**violet** *(August)*	100.00	21.00
RV32	RV1	$4.17	**violet** *(September)*	75.00	19.00
RV33	RV1	$3.75	**violet** *(October)*	75.00	19.00
RV34	RV1	$3.34	**violet** *(November)*	67.50	12.50
RV35	RV1	$2.92	**violet** *(December)*	67.50	12.50
			Nos. RV24-RV35 (12)	862.40	194.75

1945

RV36	RV1	$2.50	**violet** *(January)*	60.00	12.00
RV37	RV1	$2.09	**violet** *(February)*	52.50	12.00
RV38	RV1	$1.67	**violet** *(March)*	52.50	10.50
RV39	RV1	$1.25	**violet** *(April)*	52.50	10.50
RV40	RV1	84c	**violet** *(May)*	42.50	9.00
RV41	RV1	42c	**violet** *(June)*	30.00	7.25

Daniel Manning — RV2

Gum on Face

Control Number and Inscriptions on Back

1945 Wmk. 191R Offset Printing *Perf. 11*

Bright Blue Green & Yellow Green

RV42	RV2	$5	*(July)*	3.25	1.00
RV43	RV2	$4.59	*(August)*	75.00	19.00
RV44	RV2	$4.17	*(Sept.)*	75.00	19.50
RV45	RV2	$3.75	*(October)*	67.50	12.50
RV46	RV2	$3.34	*(November)*	55.00	12.00
RV47	RV2	$2.92	*(December)*	50.00	9.00
			Nos. RV36-RV47 (12)	615.75	134.25

1946

Bright Blue Green & Yellow Green

RV48	RV2	$2.50	*(January)*	52.50	12.50
RV49	RV2	$2.09	*(February)*	52.50	12.00
RV50	RV2	$1.67	*(March)*	42.50	9.00
RV51	RV2	$1.25	*(April)*	32.50	9.00
RV52	RV2	84c	*(May)*	32.50	9.00
RV53	RV2	42c	*(June)*	25.00	1.20
			Nos. RV48-RV53 (6)	237.50	52.70

BOATING STAMPS

Required on applications for the certificate of number for motorboats of more than 10 horsepower, starting April 1, 1960. The pictorial upper part of the $3 stamp was attached to the temporary certificate and kept by the boat owner. The lower part (stub), showing number only, was affixed to the application and sent by the post office to the U.S. Coast Guard, which issued permanent certificates. The $3 fee was for three years. The $1 stamp covered charges for reissue of a lost or destroyed certificate of number. These stamps were used in the 12 states and the District of Columbia that had not passed laws in conformity with the Boating Act of 1958.

Catalogue value for unused stamps in this section are for Never Hinged items.

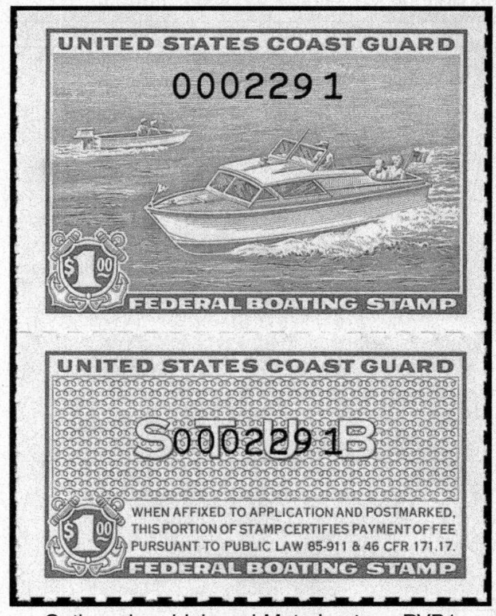

Outboard and Inboard Motorboats — RVB1

Offset Printing, Number Typographed

1960, Apr. 1 **Unwmk.** ***Rouletted***

RVB1	RVB1 $1 **rose red, black number**	37.50	*750.00*
	P# block of 4	160.00	
	On license		—
RVB2	RVB1 $3 **blue, red number**	45.00	30.00
	P# block of 4	190.00	
	On license		55.00
	First day license		*550.00*

Nos. RVB1 and RVB2 unused stamp values are for MNH complete two-part stamps. Used values are for stamps, without the stubs, bearing a complete cancel dated between April 1, 1960, and January 31, 1964. On-license values are for clean licenses with undamaged stamps and a complete cancel. A license fold can be expected. Mute oval cancels are usually favor cancels.

CAMP STAMPS

The Camp Stamp program of the Department of Agriculture's National Forest Service was introduced in 1985. The public was offered the option of prepaying their recreation fees through the purchase of camp stamps. The fees varied but were typically $3 to $4.

The stamps were supplied in rolls with the backing rouletted 9 horizontally. The letter preceding the serial number indicated the face value and printer (A-D, Denver; E-J, Washington). The stamps were designed so that any attempt to remove them from the fee envelope would cause them to come apart.

The program ended in the summer of 1988. The envelopes containing the stamps were destroyed by the National Forerst Service after use. No used examples have been reported.

Catalogue value for unused stamps in this section are for Never Hinged items.

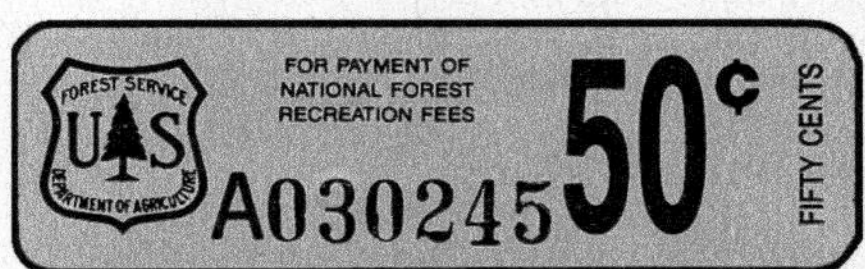

National Forest Service Logo — RVC1

Printed in Denver, CO.

1985 **Typo.** ***Die Cut***

Self-Adhesive, Coated Paper

RVC1	RVC1	50c **black,** *pink,* "A"	*200.00*
a.		Serifed letter "A," serial number with comma	*400.00*
RVC2	RVC1	$1 **black,** *red,* "B"	*200.00*
a.		Serifed letter "B," serial number with comma	*400.00*
RVC3	RVC1	$2 **black,** *yellow,* "C"	*200.00*
a.		Serifed letter "C," serial number with comma	*400.00*
RVC4	RVC1	$3 **black,** *green,* "D"	*200.00*
a.		Serifed letter "D," serial number with comma	*400.00*

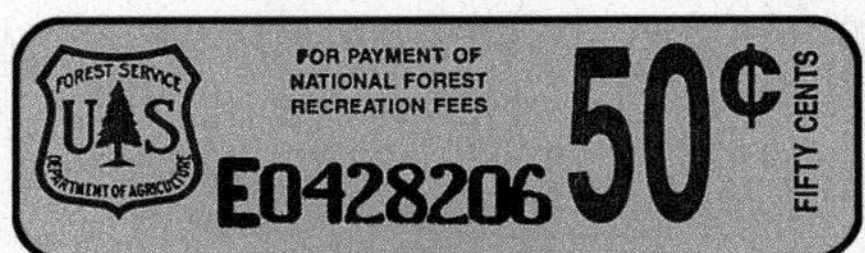

RVC2

Printed by the Government Printing Office, Washington, DC (?).

1986 **Typo.** ***Die Cut***

Self-Adhesive, Coated Paper

RVC5	RVC2	50c **black,** *pink,* "E"	500.00
RVC6	RVC2	$1 **black,** *red,* "F"	500.00
RVC7	RVC2	$2 **black,** *yellow,* "G"	500.00
RVC8	RVC2	$3 **black,** *green,* "H"	550.00
a.		Serial number omitted	—
RVC9	RVC2	$5 **black,** *silver,* "I"	1,000.
RVC10	RVC2	$10 **black,** *bronze,* "J"	*1,500.*

NATIONAL PARK SERVICE GOLDEN EAGLE PASS STAMP

Issued by the National Park Service of the Department of the Interior for use as a $25 annual Golden Eagle Pass for entry to national parks nationwide. The pass was valid January 1 through December 31, 1988. Printed as a perforated souvenir sheet of seven, only the two right stamps were applied to the license. The Golden Eagle Pass stamp is usually collected as a complete souvenir sheet that bears a serial number at the top. The mint souvenir sheet was tipped into the National Park Service license brochure that included the souvenir sheet and the pass to which the stamps were to be affixed. Most dealers sell the mint stamp in this original issue configuration. Six different first day covers, one with each artist's stamp design and bearing a complete souvenir sheet (without selvage), canceled at the post office serving the park shown on the cachet and stamp, were produced. Each is signed by the artist. Problems with the issue format caused the stamp program to be terminated after 1988. National Park stamps, in a similar format but with a $10 face value, were issued for nine more years from 1989 to 1997 as part of the National Park Foundation's Arts for the Parks program. While all ten stamps often are collected as a series, the $10 stamps are not federal revenue stamps.

No. RVP1 is tipped onto the brochure; thus there will be some gum disturbance in the top selvage. Stamps are values as never hinged.

RVP1

1987, Dec. 10 **Unwmk.** ***Perf. 12½***

RVP1 RVP1 $25 **multicolored,** souvenir sheet of 7 — 65.00 25.00
On license — 50.00
First day cover — 100.00

a. Tipped into issue brochure with license — 75.00
b. Specimen (marked "sample") — 150.00

TRAILER PERMIT STAMPS

Issued by the National Park Service of the Department of the Interior. Required to be affixed to "License to Operate Motor Vehicle" starting July 1, 1939, when a house trailer was attached to a motor vehicle entering a national park or national monument.

Issued to rangers in booklets of 50 (five 2x5 panes).

Use was continued at least until 1952.

Unused stamps may have a ranger's handwritten control number. Stamps on license have been found only used for the large parks in the western United States.

Trailer and Automobile
RVT1

1939 **Unwmk.** **Offset Printing** ***Perf. 11***

RVT1 RVT1 50c **bright blue** — *2,500.* —
On license — *4,500.*
RVT2 RVT1 $1 **carmine** — *1,500.* 600.00
On license — *800.00*

Earliest documented use: May 14,1939 (No. RVT2).

DISTILLED SPIRITS EXCISE TAX STAMPS

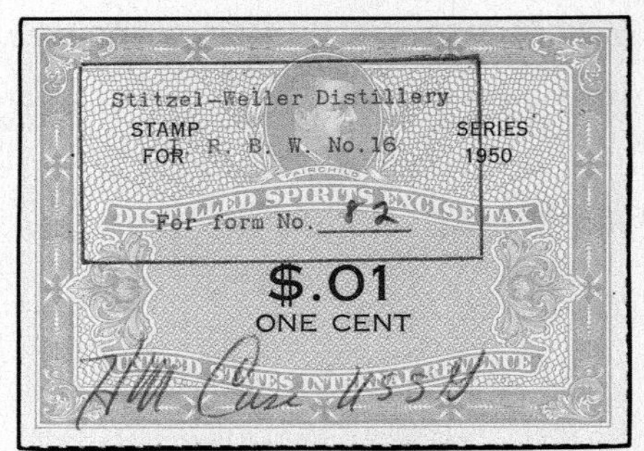

Charles S. Fairchild, Secretary of Treasury 1887-89 — DS1

Actual size: 89½x63½mm

Inscribed "STAMP FOR SERIES 1950"

1950 Wmk. 191R Offset Printing *Rouletted 7*

Left Value — Unused
Right Value — Used

No.	Design	Denomination	Unused	Used
RX1	DS1	1c **yellow green & black**	50.00	27.50
		Punched cancel		21.00
RX2	DS1	3c **yellow green & black**	140.00	100.00
		Punched cancel		92.50
RX3	DS1	5c **yellow green & black**	27.50	20.00
		Punched cancel		17.50
RX4	DS1	10c **yellow green & black**	25.00	17.50
		Punched cancel		15.00
RX5	DS1	25c **yellow green & black**	40.00	11.00
		Punched cancel		9.00
RX6	DS1	50c **yellow green & black**	25.00	11.00
		Punched cancel		8.00
RX7	DS1	$1 **yellow green & black**	30.00	3.00
		Punched cancel		1.75
RX8	DS1	$3 **yellow green & black**	40.00	20.00
		Punched cancel		15.00
RX9	DS1	$5 **yellow green & black**	30.00	6.50
		Punched cancel		4.50
RX10	DS1	$10 **yellow green & black**	15.00	3.00
		Punched cancel		1.75
RX11	DS1	$25 **yellow green & black**	25.00	12.50
		Punched cancel		9.25
RX12	DS1	$50 **yellow green & black**	25.00	8.75
		Punched cancel		5.00
RX13	DS1	$100 **yellow green & black**	15.00	4.00
		Punched cancel		3.00
RX14	DS1	$300 **yellow green & black**	45.00	25.00
		Punched cancel		21.00
RX15	DS1	$500 **yellow green & black**	30.00	15.00
		Punched cancel		10.00
RX16	DS1	$1,000 **yellow green & black**	25.00	11.00
		Punched cancel		8.00
RX17	DS1	$1,500 **yellow green & black**	70.00	50.00
		Punched cancel		40.00
RX18	DS1	$2,000 **yellow green & black**	12.50	5.00
		Punched cancel		4.00
RX19	DS1	$3,000 **yellow green & black**	35.00	25.00
		Punched cancel		15.00
RX20	DS1	$5,000 **yellow green & black**	35.00	25.00
		Punched cancel		17.50
RX21	DS1	$10,000 **yellow green & black**	45.00	27.50
		Punched cancel		22.50
RX22	DS1	$20,000 **yellow green & black**	55.00	35.00
		Punched cancel		30.00
RX23	DS1	$30,000 **yellow green & black**	90.00	70.00
		Punched cancel		50.00
RX24	DS1	$40,000 **yellow green & black**	750.00	950.00
		Punched cancel		600.00
RX25	DS1	$50,000 **yellow green & black**	200.00	95.00
		Punched cancel		75.00

Inscription "STAMP FOR SERIES 1950" Omitted

1952

Left Value — Unused
Right Value — Used

No.	Design	Denomination	Unused	Used
RX27	DS1	3c **yellow green & black**	*900.00*	
RX28	DS1	5c **yellow green & black**	300.00	
		Punched cancel		40.00
RX29	DS1	10c **yellow green & black**	35.00	90.00
		Punched cancel		5.00
RX30	DS1	25c **yellow green & black**	45.00	90.00
		Punched cancel		15.00
RX31	DS1	50c **yellow green & black**	45.00	90.00
		Punched cancel		15.00
RX32	DS1	$1 **yellow green & black**	30.00	90.00
		Punched cancel		2.50
RX33	DS1	$3 **yellow green & black**	55.00	90.00
		Punched cancel		22.50
RX34	DS1	$5 **yellow green & black**	55.00	90.00
		Punched cancel		25.00
RX35	DS1	$10 **yellow green & black**	30.00	90.00
		Punched cancel		2.50
RX36	DS1	$25 **yellow green & black**	40.00	90.00
		Punched cancel		10.00
RX37	DS1	$50 **yellow green & black**	90.00	90.00
		Punched cancel		25.00
RX38	DS1	$100 **yellow green & black**	30.00	90.00
		Punched cancel		2.50
RX39	DS1	$300 **yellow green & black**	40.00	90.00
		Punched cancel		7.50
RX40	DS1	$500 **yellow green & black**	450.00	
		Punched cancel		30.00
RX41	DS1	$1,000 **yellow green & black**	140.00	75.00
		Punched cancel		6.00
RX42	DS1	$1,500 **yellow green & black**	*900.00*	
RX43	DS1	$2,000 **yellow green & black**	700.00	
		Punched cancel		75.00
RX44	DS1	$3,000 **yellow green & black**	750.00	
		Punched cancel		700.00
RX45	DS1	$5,000 **yellow green & black**	600.00	
		Punched cancel		50.00
RX46	DS1	$10,000 **yellow green & black**	700.00	
		Punched cancel		90.00

Five other denominations with "Stamp for Series 1950" omitted were prepared but are not known to have been put into use: 1c, $20,000, $30,000, $40,000 and $50,000.

Stamps listed as used have staple holes.

Distilled Spirits Excise Tax stamps were discontinued in 1959.

FIREARMS TRANSFER TAX STAMPS

Used on transfer tax documents for tax paid transfers of National Firearms Act weapons. Prior to 1968, transfers of NFA weapons were processed by the Alcohol, Tobacco and Firearms division of the Internal Revenue Service. Current examples of firearms transfer stamps are not available for sale to collectors because of the possibility of fraudulent misuse.

Documentary Stamp of 1917 Overprinted Vertically in Black. Reading Up

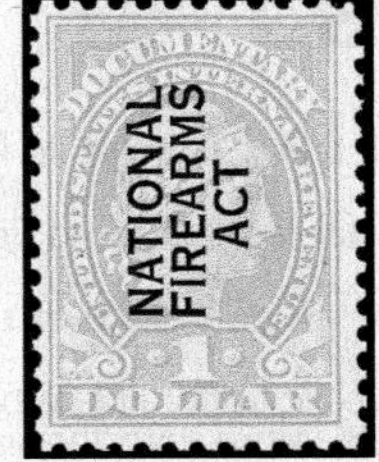

1938 Engr. Wmk. 191R *Perf. 11*

Without Gum

No.	Design	Denomination	Unused	Used
RY1	R21	$1 **green**	600.00	—
		On license		

RY1

Eagle, Shield and Stars from U.S. Seal

Two types of $200:

I — Serial number with serifs, not preceded by zeros. Tips of 6 lines project into left margin.

II — Gothic serial number preceded by zeros. Five line tips in left margin.

Size: 28x42mm

Without Gum

1934 Wmk. 191R *Perf. 12*

No.	Design	Denomination	Unused	Used
RY2	RY1	$200 **dark blue & red,** type I, #1-1600	2,000.	1,500.
		On license		*1,750.*

Issued in vertical strips of 4 which are imperforate at top, bottom and right side.

See Nos. RY4, RY6-RY8.

RY2

1939 Size: 28x33½mm *Perf. 11*

No.	Design	Denomination	Unused	Used
RY3	RY2	$1 **green**	85.00	35.00
		On license		—

See No. RY5.

1966 Wmk. 191R *Perf. 12*

Size: 29x43mm

No.	Design	Denomination	Unused	Used
RY4	RY1	$200 **dull blue & red,** type II, #1601(?) - #3000(?)	750.00	700.00
		On license		750.00

No. RY4 has a clear impression and is printed on white paper. No. RY2 has a "muddy" impression in much darker blue ink and is printed on off-white paper.

1960, July 1 Size: 29x34mm *Perf. 11*

No.	Design	Denomination	Unused	Used
RY5	RY2	$5 **red**	85.00	45.00
		On license		200.00

No. RY5 was issued in sheets of 50 (10x5) with straight edge on four sides of sheet.

The watermark is hard to see on many examples of #RY4-RY5.

Gothis Serial Numbers

1974(?) **Unwmk.** ***Perf. 12***
Size: 29x43mm

RY6	RY1 $200 **dull blue & red**, type II, #3001-up	275.00	110.00
	On license		125.00
a.	Booklet pane of 4	*1,100.*	

Panes of 32

1990(?) **Litho.** **Without Gum** ***Imperf.***

RY7	RY1 $200 **dull blue**	*900.00*	
	On license	*1,150.*	

1990 ***Perf. 12½***

RY8	RY1 $200 **dull blue**	350.00	80.00
	On license		150.00
RY9	RY2 $5 **red,** *1994*	450.00	150.00
	On license		200.00

Nos. RY7 and RY8 do not have a printed serial number or the tabs at left. Because the stamps do not have a serial number mint stamps were not sold to the public.

WARNING: Nos. RY7-RY9 are usually taped or glued to the transfer of title documents. The glue used is NOT water soluble. Attempts to soak the stamps may result in damage.

2001(?) ***Serpentine Die Cut 11.5***
Self-Adhesive

RY10	RY2 $5 **dull red**	125.00	
	On license	*250.00*	

RY3

2012(?) **Litho.** ***Serpentine Die Cut 11***
Self-Adhesive

RY11	RY3 $200 **dull blue**	—	175.00
	On license		225.00

2014 **Photo.** ***Serpentine Die Cut 6.3***
Self-Adhesive

RY12	RY3 $200 **dull blue**		150.00
	On license		200.00

RECTIFICATION TAX STAMPS

Used to indicate payment of the tax on distilled spirits that were condensed and purified for additional blending through repeated distillations.

RZ1

Actual size: 89½x64mm

1946 **Offset Printing** **Wmk. 191R** ***Rouletted 7***

RZ1	RZ1	1c **blue & black**	6.75	4.00
		Punched cancel		2.00
RZ2	RZ1	3c **blue & black**	22.50	8.00
		Punched cancel		7.50
RZ3	RZ1	5c **blue & black**	12.50	2.50
		Punched cancel		1.25
RZ4	RZ1	10c **blue & black**	12.50	3.00
		Punched cancel		1.25
RZ5	RZ1	25c **blue & black**	12.50	3.00
		Punched cancel		2.00
RZ6	RZ1	50c **blue & black**	17.50	5.00
		Punched cancel		3.50
RZ7	RZ1	$1 **blue & black**	17.50	4.00
		Punched cancel		2.50
RZ8	RZ1	$3 **blue & black**	90.00	18.00
		Punched cancel		9.00
RZ9	RZ1	$5 **blue & black**	30.00	10.00
		Punched cancel		6.00
RZ10	RZ1	$10 **blue & black**	22.50	3.00
		Punched cancel		1.25
RZ11	RZ1	$25 **blue & black**	90.00	10.00
		Punched cancel		3.00
RZ12	RZ1	$50 **blue & black**	90.00	7.50
		Punched cancel		3.00
RZ13	RZ1	$100 **blue & black**	*175.00*	9.50
		Punched cancel		3.50
RZ14	RZ1	$300 **blue & black**	*220.00*	10.00
		Punched cancel		7.50
RZ15	RZ1	$500 **blue & black**	*240.00*	10.00
		Punched cancel		7.00
RZ16	RZ1	$1000 **blue & black**	*240.00*	18.00
		Punched cancel		15.00
RZ17	RZ1	$1500 **blue & black**	*260.00*	60.00
		Punched cancel		45.00
RZ18	RZ1	$2000 **blue & black**	*260.00*	80.00
		Punched cancel		60.00

Stamps listed as used have staple holes.

HUNTING PERMIT STAMPS

Authorized by an Act of Congress, approved March 16, 1934, to license hunters. Receipts go to maintain waterfowl life in the United States. Sales to collectors were made legal June 15, 1935.

No. RW1 used is valued with handstamp or manuscript cancel, though technically it was against postal regulations to deface the stamp or to apply a postal cancellation. Beginning with No. RW2, the used values are for stamps with signatures.

Nos. RW1-RW12 were issued in panes of 28, of which 10 stamps have a straight edge on one or two sides. Such examples sell for 20%-30% less than the values shown.

Plate number blocks of six have selvage on two sides. Values for plate blocks of Nos. RW1-RW25 are for bottom plate blocks or top plate blocks with narrow selvage. Top margin plate blocks with wide untrimmed selvage sell for approximately 20%-25% more than the values shown.

Hunting permit stamps are valid from July 1 - June 30. Stamps have been made available prior to the date of validity, and stamps are sold through the philatelic agency after the period of validity has passed.

All hunting permit stamps through No. RW68A were printed by the Bureau of Engraving & Printing.

Catalogue values for all unused stamps in this section are for stamps with never-hinged original gum. Minor natural gum skips and bends are normal on Nos. RW1-RW20. No-gum stamps are without signature or other cancel.

Catalogue values for all unused stamps in this section are for stamps with never-hinged original gum. Minor natural gum skips and bends are normal on Nos. RW1-RW20. No-gum stamps are without signature or other cancel.

Nos. RW1-RW12 were issued in panes of 28, of which 10 stamps have a straight edge on one or two sides. Such examples sell for 20%-30% less than the values shown.

Department of Agriculture
Various Designs Inscribed
"U. S. Department of Agriculture"

Mallards Alighting — HP1

Engraved: Flat Plate Printing
Issued in panes of 28 subjects.

1934 **Unwmk.** ***Perf. 11***
Inscribed "Void after June 30, 1935"

RW1	HP1 $1 **blue**	750.	175.
	Hinged	300.	
	No gum	175.	
	P# block of 6	16,500.	

Used value is for stamp with handstamp or manuscript cancel.

It is almost certain that examples of No. RW1 offered as imperforate vertical pairs or as vertical pairs imperforate horizontally are from printer's waste. Additionally, it is almost certain that all imperforate vertical pairs are pairs imperforate horizontally that have had the vertical perforations trimmed off. No horizontal imperforate pairs are known. All recorded pairs are vertical, with narrow side margins. Most examples exist without gum and with faults. Some pairs have gum on the front (which in some cases appears to have been removed).

The stamps imperforate horizontally are recorded as a unique vertical block of eight, with the other recorded varieties being the manufactured imperforate vertical pairs.

Canvasbacks Taking to Flight — HP2

1935 Inscribed "Void after June 30, 1936"

RW2	HP2 $1 **rose lake**	750.	160.
	deep rose lake	—	
	Hinged	375.	
	No gum	175.	
	P# block of 6	12,500.	
	deep rose lake	—	

Canada Geese in Flight — HP3

1936 Inscribed "Void after June 30, 1937"

RW3	HP3 $1 **brown black**	325.	100.
	Hinged	150.	
	No gum	90.	
	P# block of 6	3,500.	

Scaup Ducks Taking to Flight — HP4

1937 Inscribed "Void after June 30, 1938"

RW4	HP4 $1 **light green**	300.	65.
	Hinged	140.	
	No gum	85.	
	P# block of 6	3,250.	

Pintail Drake and Hen Alighting — HP5

1938 Inscribed "Void after June 30, 1939"

RW5	HP5 $1 **light violet**	425.	75.
	Hinged	200.	
	No gum	85.	
	P# block of 6	4,500.	

Department of the Interior
Various Designs Inscribed
"U. S. Department of the Interior"

Green-winged Teal — HP6

1939 Inscribed "Void after June 30, 1940"

RW6	HP6 $1 **chocolate**	250.	50.
	Hinged	115.	
	No gum	60.	
	P# block of 6	2,500.	

Black Mallards — HP7

1940 Inscribed "Void after June 30, 1941"

RW7	HP7 $1 **sepia**	250.	50.
	Hinged	115.	
	No gum	60.	
	P# block of 6	2,500.	

Family of Ruddy Ducks — HP8

1941 Inscribed "Void after June 30, 1942"

RW8	HP8 $1 **brown carmine**	225.	50.
	Hinged	95.	
	No gum	45.	
	P# block of 6	2,500.	

Baldpates — HP9

1942 Inscribed "Void after June 30, 1943"

RW9	HP9 $1 **violet brown**	225.	45.
	Hinged	95.	
	No gum	45.	
	P# block of 6	2,500.	

Wood Ducks — HP10

1943 Inscribed "Void After June 30, 1944"

RW10	HP10 $1 **deep rose**	120.	35.
	Hinged	55.	
	No gum	35.	
	P# block of 6	700.	

White-fronted Geese — HP11

1944 Inscribed "Void after June 30, 1945"

RW11	HP11 $1 **red orange**	125.	35.
	Hinged	45.	
	No gum	35.	
	P# block of 6	750.	

DUCKS
shduck.com
• Federal
• State
• Prints
• Errors
• Auctions
with easy on line bidding
• Conservation
Duck Catalog FREE!
72 color pages!
281.493.6386
Sam Houston Duck Co.
P.O. Box 8200087, Houston, TX 77282 ASDA • APS Life

Shoveller Ducks in Flight — HP12

1945 **Inscribed "Void after June 30, 1946"**

RW12	HP12 $1 **black**	100.	25.
	Hinged	45.	
	No gum	35.	
	P# block of 6	600.	

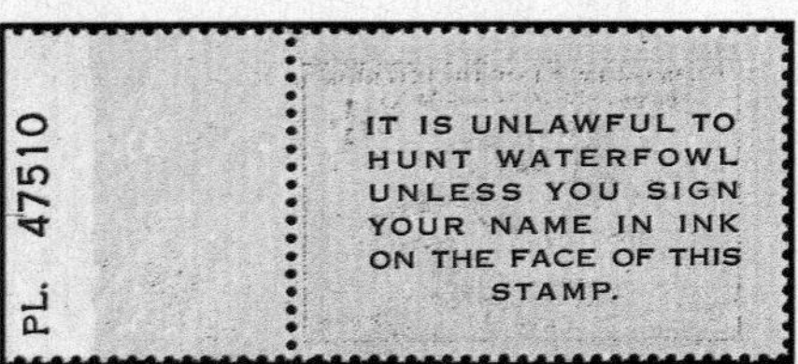

Beginning with No. RW13, there is a message printed on the back of the sheet stamps telling hunters to sign their names on the face of the stamp. On Nos. RW13-RW17, offset plate no. 47510 for the printing on the backs of the stamps appears on the back of the selvage opposite the stamp in position 24 on the upper right panes. These are collected as plate blocks of six with side and bottom selvage bearing the plate number on the back of the selvage opposite the center margin stamp. Value, mint never hinged $550 each for Nos. RW13-RW16, $2,500 for No. RW17.

QUACK!
QUACK!

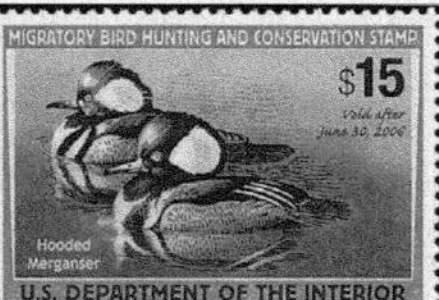

If you are interested in...

STATE DUCK STAMPS

And Are Serious About Completing Your Collection... Michael Jaffe Stamps Can Be Your Complete Duck Dealer!

Over 99% of all pictorial duck stamps always in stock at very competitive & attractive prices! Send $5.00 refundable for your Complete Duck Catalog which lists all pictorial Duck Stamps including listings of over 600 Indian Reservation stamps!

NEW ISSUE SERVICE!

Receive all the new State Duck Stamps without the hassle of trying to order them yourself. Automatically charged to your charge card as they come out. Only $1.75 over agency cost per stamp.

ALSO IN STOCK... ★ DUCK PRINTS ★ DUCK SOUVENIR CARDS ★ DUCK ALBUMS ★ FEDERAL DUCK STAMPS, MINT, USED & UNUSED FOR FRAMING ★ DUCK FIRST DAY COVERS ★ SATISFACTION GUARANTEED ON EVERYTHING SOLD

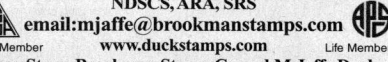

MICHAEL JAFFE STAMPS INC.
P.O. Box 61484, Vancouver, WA 98666
Phone 360-695-6161 • FAX 360-695-1616
TOLL-FREE ORDER NUMBER 800-782-6770
NDSCS, ARA, SRS
email:mjaffe@brookmanstamps.com
Life Member www.duckstamps.com Life Member
Ebay Store: Brookman Stamp Co and M Jaffe Ducks

Redhead Ducks — HP13

1946 **Inscribed "Void after June 30, 1947"**

RW13	HP13 $1 **red brown**	50.00	12.50
	No gum	15.00	
	P# block of 6	310.00	

The previously listed No. RW13a in a bright rose pink shade has been determined to be a chemically induced changeling.

Snow Geese — HP14

1947 **Inscribed "Void after June 30, 1948"**

RW14	HP14 $1 **black**	55.00	15.00
	No gum	18.00	
	P# block of 6	340.00	

Buffleheads in Flight — HP15

1948 **Inscribed "Void after June 30, 1949"**

RW15	HP15 $1 **bright blue**	60.00	12.00
	No gum	15.00	
	P# block of 6	400.00	

Goldeneye Ducks — HP16

1949 **Inscribed "Void after June 30, 1950"**

RW16	HP16 $2 **bright green**	70.00	15.00
	No gum	20.00	
	P# block of 6	425.00	

Trumpeter Swans in Flight — HP17

1950 **Inscribed "Void after June 30, 1951"**

RW17	HP17 $2 **violet**	90.00	15.00
	No gum	20.00	
	P# block of 6	550.00	

Gadwall Ducks — HP18

1951 **Inscribed "Void after June 30, 1952"**

RW18	HP18 $2 **gray black**	90.00	15.00
	No gum	20.00	
	P# block of 6	550.00	

Harlequin Ducks — HP19

1952 **Inscribed "Void after June 30, 1953"**

RW19	HP19 $2 **deep ultramarine**	90.00	15.00
	No gum	20.00	
	P# block of 6	550.00	

Blue-winged Teal — HP20

1953 **Inscribed "Void after June 30, 1954"**

RW20	HP20 $2 **deep brown rose**	90.00	15.00
	No gum	20.00	
	P# block of 6	550.00	

No. RW21 and following issues are printed on dry, pregummed paper and the back inscription is printed on top of the gum, except for the self-adhesive stamp issues starting in 1998.

Ring-necked Ducks — HP21

1954 Inscribed "Void after June 30, 1955"

RW21 HP21 $2 **black** 85.00 15.00
No gum 20.00
P# block of 6 550.00

Blue Geese — HP22

1955 Inscribed "Void after June 30, 1956"

RW22 HP22 $2 **dark blue** 85.00 12.50
No gum 20.00
P# block of 6 575.00
a. Back inscription inverted *5,500. 4,500.*

American Merganser — HP23

1956 Inscribed "Void after June 30, 1957"

RW23 HP23 $2 **black** 85.00 12.50
No gum 20.00
P# block of 6 575.00

American Eiders — HP24

1957 Inscribed "Void after June 30, 1958"

RW24 HP24 $2 **emerald** 85.00 12.50
No gum 20.00
P# block of 6 575.00
a. Back inscription inverted *5,000.*

Canada Geese — HP25

1958 Inscribed "Void after June 30, 1959"

RW25 HP25 $2 **black** 85.00 12.50
No gum 20.00
P# block of 6 575.00
a. Back inscription inverted —

Labrador Retriever Carrying Mallard Drake — HP26

Giori Press Printing
Issued in panes of 30 subjects

1959 Inscribed "Void after June 30, 1960"

RW26 HP26 $3 **multicolored** 130. 12.50
No gum 45.00
P# block of 4 550.00
a. Back inscription inverted *25,000. 15,000.*

Redhead Ducks — HP27

1960 Inscribed "Void after June 30, 1961"

RW27 HP27 $3 **multicolored** 95.00 12.50
No gum 30.00
P# block of 4 425.00

Mallard Hen and Ducklings — HP28

1961 Inscribed "Void after June 30, 1962"

RW28 HP28 $3 **multicolored** 95.00 12.50
No gum 30.00
P# block of 4 450.00

Pintail Drakes Coming in for Landing — HP29

1962 Inscribed "Void after June 30, 1963"

RW29 HP29 $3 **multicolored** 110.00 12.50
No gum 35.00
P# block of 4 500.00
a. Back inscription omitted —

Pair of Brant Landing — HP30

1963 Inscribed "Void after June 30, 1964"

RW30 HP30 $3 **multicolored** 100.00 12.50
No gum 35.00
P# block of 4 450.00

Hawaiian Nene Geese — HP31

1964 Inscribed "Void after June 30, 1965"

RW31 HP31 $3 **multicolored** 100.00 12.50
No gum 35.00
P# block of 6 1,950.

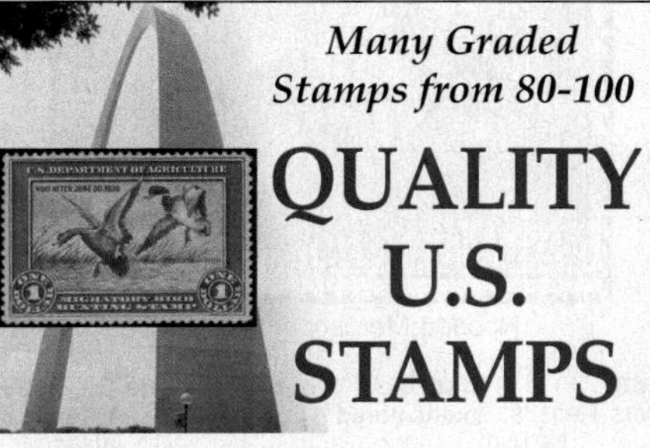

Many Graded
Stamps from 80-100
QUALITY
U.S.
STAMPS

HB Philatelics
Proofs & Essays
Federal & State Hunting Permits
Guy Gasser
P.O. Box 2320 • Florissant, MO 63032
Phone 314-330-8684
E-mail: guy@hbphilatelics.com
www.hbphilatelics.com
Official APS Web Sponsor

Three Canvasback Drakes — HP32

1965 **Inscribed "Void after June 30, 1966"**

RW32 HP32 $3 **multicolored** 100.00 12.50
No gum 40.00
P# block of 4 450.00

Whistling Swans — HP33

1966 **Inscribed "Void after June 30, 1967"**

RW33 HP33 $3 **multicolored** 100.00 12.50
No gum 40.00
P# block of 4 500.00

Old Squaw Ducks — HP34

1967 **Inscribed "Void after June 30, 1968"**

RW34 HP34 $3 **multicolored** 100.00 12.50
No gum 40.00
P# block of 4 550.00

Hooded Mergansers — HP35

1968 **Inscribed "Void after June 30, 1969"**

RW35 HP35 $3 **multicolored** 65.00 12.50
No gum 20.00
P# block of 4 300.00
a. Back inscription omitted —

White-winged Scoters — HP36

1969 **Inscribed "Void after June 30, 1970"**

RW36 HP36 $3 **multicolored** 65.00 8.00
No gum 20.00
P# block of 4 275.00

Ross's Geese — HP37

1970 **Engraved & Lithographed**
Inscribed "Void after June 30, 1971"

RW37 HP37 $3 **multicolored** 65.00 8.00
No gum 20.00
P# block of 4 280.00

Three Cinnamon Teal — HP38

1971 **Inscribed "Void after June 30, 1972"**

RW38 HP38 $3 **multicolored** 42.50 8.00
No gum 15.00
P# block of 4 180.00

Emperor Geese — HP39

1972 **Inscribed "Void after June 30, 1973"**

RW39 HP39 $5 **multicolored** 30.00 6.00
No gum 8.00
P# block of 4 125.00

Steller's Eiders — HP40

1973 **Inscribed "Void after June 30, 1974"**

RW40 HP40 $5 **multicolored** 18.00 6.00
No gum 7.00
P# block of 4 75.00

Wood Ducks — HP41

RW41a

1974 **Inscribed "Void after June 30, 1975"**

RW41 HP41 $5 **multicolored** 18.00 5.00
No gum 6.00
P# block of 4 72.50
a. Back inscription missing, but printed vertically on face of stamp and selvage, from foldover *4,750.*

Canvasback Ducks and Decoy — HP42

1975 **Inscribed "Void after June 30, 1976"**

RW42 HP42 $5 **multicolored** 15.00 5.00
No gum 7.00
P# block of 4 65.00

Family of Canada Geese — HP43

1976 **Engr.**
Inscribed "Void after June 30, 1977"

RW43 HP43 $5 **green & black** 10.00 5.00
No gum 7.00
P# block of 4 50.00

Pair of Ross's Geese — HP44

1977 **Litho. & Engr.**

Inscribed "Void after June 30, 1978"

RW44 HP44 $5 **multicolored** 10.00 5.00
No gum 7.00
P# block of 4 50.00

Hooded Merganser Drake — HP45

1978 **Inscribed "Void after June 30, 1979"**

RW45 HP45 $5 **multicolored** 10.00 5.00
No gum 7.00
P# block of 4 40.00

Green-winged Teal — HP46

1979 **Inscribed "Void after June 30, 1980"**

RW46 HP46 $7.50 **multicolored** 12.50 6.00
No gum 8.00
P# block of 4 50.00

Mallards — HP47

1980 **Inscribed "Void after June 30, 1981"**

RW47 HP47 $7.50 **multicolored** 12.50 6.00
No gum 8.00
P# block of 4 55.00

Ruddy Ducks — HP48

1981 **Inscribed "Void after June 30, 1982"**

RW48 HP48 $7.50 **multicolored** 12.50 6.00
No gum 8.00
P# block of 4 50.00

Canvasbacks — HP49

1982 **Inscribed "Void after June 30, 1983"**

RW49 HP49 $7.50 **multicolored** 15.00 7.00
No gum 9.00
P# block of 4 60.00
a. Orange and violet omitted *10,000.*

A certificate from a recognized expertization committee is required for No. RW49a.

Pintails — HP50

1983 **Inscribed "Void after June 30, 1984"**

RW50 HP50 $7.50 **multicolored** 15.00 7.00
No gum 7.00
P# block of 4 60.00

Widgeons — HP51

1984 **Inscribed "Void after June 30, 1985"**

RW51 HP51 $7.50 **multicolored** 12.50 7.00
No gum 7.00
P# block of 4 50.00

See Special Printings section that follows.

Cinnamon Teal — HP52

1985 **Inscribed "Void after June 30, 1986"**

RW52 HP52 $7.50 **multicolored** 15.00 8.00
No gum 7.00
P# block of 4 60.00
a. Light blue (litho.) omitted *20,000.*

The omitted color on No. RW52a coincides with a double paper splice affecting the top row of five stamps from the sheet and top ⅓ of stamps in the second row. There is also a color changeling of the brownish red ducks and their reflections in the water to yellow and yellow orange, respectively, on the error stamps. This error currently exists as three vertical strips of 6 (top stamp the error) and a plate number block of 12 (2x6, top two stamps the error).

Fulvous Whistling Duck — HP53

1986 **Inscribed "Void after June 30, 1987"**

RW53 HP53 $7.50 **multicolored** 15.00 8.00
No gum 9.00
P# block of 4 60.00
a. Black omitted *1,900.*

Redheads — HP54

1987 ***Perf. 11½x11***

Inscribed "Void after June 30, 1988"

RW54 HP54 $10 **multicolored** 17.50 8.00
No gum 8.00
P# block of 4 70.00

Snow Goose — HP55

1988 **Inscribed "Void after June 30, 1989"**

RW55 HP55 $10 **multicolored** 17.50 8.00
No gum 8.00
P# block of 4 70.00

Lesser Scaup — HP56

1989 **Inscribed "Void after June 30, 1990"**

RW56 HP56 $12.50 **multicolored** 21.50 8.00
No gum 9.00
P# block of 4 85.00

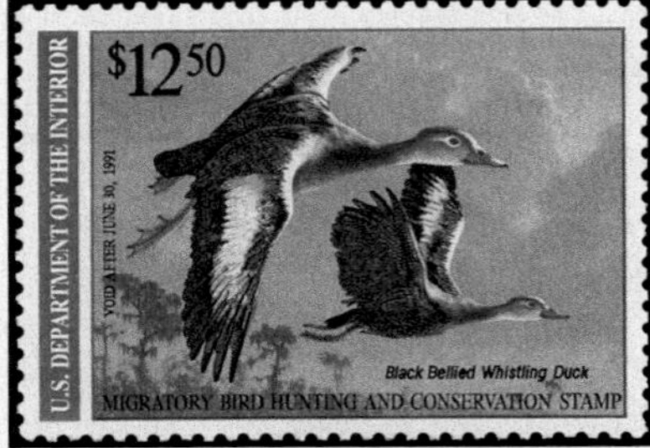
Black Bellied Whistling Duck — HP57

1990 **Inscribed "Void after June 30, 1991"**

RW57 HP57 $12.50 **multicolored** 20.00 8.00
No gum 9.00
P# block of 4 85.00
a. Back inscription omitted *300.00*
b. Black inscription printed on the stamp paper rather than the gum —
No gum —

The back inscription is normally on top of the gum so beware of examples with gum removed offered as No. RW57a. Full original gum must be intact on No. RW57a. Used examples of No. RW57a cannot exist.

Some philatelic researchers have questioned the existence of No. RW57b as a genuine error. There appears to be evidence that the inscriptions printed on the gum on the back can leach through to the paper on one of the types of gums used on these stamps. Further research is ongoing.

King Eiders HP58

1991 **Inscribed "Void after June 30, 1992"**

RW58 HP58 $15 **multicolored** 30.00 8.00
No gum 15.00
P# block of 4 120.00
a. Black (engr.) omitted *20,000.*

Spectacled Eider — HP59

1992 **Inscribed "Void after June 30, 1993"**

RW59 HP59 $15 **multicolored** 30.00 10.00
No gum 15.00
P# block of 4 125.00

Canvasbacks — HP60

1993 **Inscribed "Void after June 30, 1994"**

RW60 HP60 $15 **multicolored** 27.50 9.00
No gum 15.00
P# block of 4 125.00
a. Black (engr.) omitted *2,100. 1,500.*

Red-breasted Mergansers — HP61

1994 ***Perf. 11¼x11***

Inscribed "Void after June 30, 1995"

RW61 HP61 $15 **multicolored** 27.50 10.00
No gum 15.00
P# block of 4 125.00

Mallards — HP62

1995 **Inscribed "Void after June 30, 1996"**

RW62 HP62 $15 **multicolored** 32.50 12.00
No gum 15.00
P# block of 4 135.00

Surf Scoters — HP63

1996 **Inscribed "Void after June 30, 1997"**

RW63 HP63 $15 **multicolored** 32.50 12.00
No gum 12.50
P# block of 4 130.00

Canada Goose — HP64

"Long breast feather" plate flaw

"Short breast feather" plate flaw

1997 **Inscribed "Void after June 30, 1998"**

RW64 HP64 $15 **multicolored** 27.50 12.00
No gum 15.00
P# block of 4 120.00
"Long breast feather" plate flaw, pos. 28 85.00 —
In pair with normal stamp 175.00
"Short breast feather" plate flaw, pos. 28 65.00 —
In pair with normal stamp 110.00

Barrow's Goldeneye — HP65

1998 ***Perf. 11¼***

Inscribed "Void after June 30, 1999"

RW65 HP65 $15 **multicolored** 42.50 22.50
No gum 22.50
P# block of 4 200.00

Self-Adhesive

Die Cut Perf. 10

RW65A HP65 $15 *Barrow's Goldeneye* 35.00 17.50
No gum 15.00

Nos. RW65 and later issues were sold in panes of 30 (RW65 and RW66) or 20 (RW67 and later issues), with four plate numbers per pane. The self-adhesives starting with No. RW65A were sold in panes of 1. The self-adhesives are valued unused as complete panes and used as single stamps.

Greater Scaup — HP66

1999 ***Perf. 11¼***

Inscribed "Void after June 30, 2000"

RW66 HP66 $15 **multicolored** 40.00 20.00
No gum 22.50
P# block of 4 170.00

Self-Adhesive

Die Cut Perf. 10

RW66A HP66 $15 **multicolored** 25.00 12.00
No gum 15.00

Mottled Duck — HP67

2000 ***Perf. 11¼***

Inscribed "Void after June 30, 2001"

RW67 HP67 $15 **multicolored** 32.50 15.00
No gum 17.50
P# block of 4 135.00

Self-Adhesive

Die Cut Perf. 10

RW67A HP67 $15 **multicolored** 25.00 14.00
No gum 17.50

Northern Pintail — HP68

2001 ***Perf. 11¼***

Inscribed "Void after June 30, 2002"

RW68 HP68 $15 **multicolored** 30.00 18.00
No gum 17.50
P# block of 4 140.00

Self-Adhesive

Die Cut Perf. 10

RW68A HP68 $15 **multicolored** 25.00 14.00
No gum 15.00

Black Scoters — HP69

Printed by Banknote Corporation of America.

2002 ***Perf. 11¼***

Inscribed "Void after June 30, 2003"

RW69 HP69 $15 **multicolored** 30.00 16.00
No gum 17.50
P# block of 4 125.00

Self-Adhesive

Serpentine Die Cut 11x10¾

RW69A HP69 $15 **multicolored** 25.00 12.00
No gum 15.00

Snow Geese — HP70

Printed by Ashton-Potter (USA) Ltd.

2003 ***Perf. 11***

Inscribed "Void after June 30, 2004"

RW70 HP70 $15 **multicolored** 30.00 16.00
No gum 17.50
P# block of 4 125.00
b. Imperf, pair *5,000.*
c. Back inscription omitted *4,500.*

Self-Adhesive

Serpentine Die Cut 11x10¾

RW70A HP70 $15 **multicolored** 25.00 12.00
No gum 15.00

Redheads — HP71

Printed by Banknote Corporation of America for Sennett Security Products.

2004 ***Perf. 11***

Inscribed "Void after June 30, 2005"

RW71 HP71 $15 **multicolored** 30.00 16.00
No gum 17.00
P# block of 4 125.00

Self-Adhesive

Serpentine Die Cut 11x10¾

RW71A HP71 $15 **multicolored** 25.00 12.00
No gum 15.00

Hooded Mergansers — HP72

Printed by Banknote Corporation of America for Sennett Security Products.

Two types of RW72: I, No framelines at top, right or bottom (from left two panes of the press sheet); II, Gray framelines at top, right and bottom (from right two panes of the press sheet).

2005 **Litho. & Engr.** ***Perf. 11***

Inscribed "Void after June 30, 2006"

RW72 HP72 $15 **multicolored,** type I 25.00 16.00
No gum 16.00
P# block of 4 120.00
b. Souvenir sheet of 1 1,750.
c. Type II 22.50 16.00
No gum 16.00
P# block of 4 100.00
d. As "b," without artist's signature (error) *3,250.*

No. RW72b sold for $20. 1,000 No. RW72b were issued. Approximately 750 were signed by the artist in black, value $1,750 as shown. Approximately 150 were signed in blue ink, value $2,500. Approximately 100 were signed in gold ink, value $3,000. Most examples of No. RW72b are in the grade of F-VF. Catalogue values are for Very Fine examples.

The Duck Stamp Office never announced the existence of No. RW72b to the public through a press release or a website announcement during the time the sheet was on sale, apparently because it was not clear beforehand that the souvenir sheet could be produced successfully and on time. No. RW72b sold out before a public announcement of the item's existence could be made.

Self-Adhesive

Litho. & Debossed

Serpentine Die Cut 11x10¾

RW72A HP72 $15 **multicolored** 22.50 11.00
No gum 15.00

One hundred press sheets containing four panes of 20 of No. RW72 and one hundred press sheets containing 18 of No. RW72A were offered for sale by the U.S. Fish and Wildlife Service at a premium above face value.

Ross's Goose — HP73

Printed by Banknote Corporation of America for Sennett Security Products

2006 **Litho. & Engr.** ***Perf. 11***

Inscribed "Void after June 30, 2007"

RW73 HP73 $15 **multicolored** 22.50 11.00
No gum 15.00
P# block of 4 110.00
b. Souvenir sheet of 1 120.00 —
c. As "b," without artist's signature (error) *2,500.*

No. RW73b sold for $25. All examples of No. RW73b have a black signature of the artist on a designated line in the sheet margin. Ten thousand were issued.

The sheet margin has a line designated for the signature of the engraver, Piotr Naszarkowski, but no sheets were sold with his signature. Naszarkowski signed approximately 2,500 sheets during three days at the Washington 2006 World Philatelic Exhibition, and he signed another 2,500 or more after the conclusion of the exhibition. Value $150.

Self-Adhesive

Serpentine Die Cut 11x10¾

RW73A HP73 $15 **multicolored** 22.50 11.00
No gum 15.00

Two hundred fifty press sheets containing four panes of 20 of No. RW73 and two hundred fifty press sheets containing 18 of No. RW73A were offered for sale by the U.S. Fish and Wildlife Service.

Ring-necked Ducks — HP74

Printed by Banknote Corporation of America for Sennett Security Products.

2007 **Litho.** ***Perf. 11***

Inscribed "Void after June 30, 2008"

RW74 HP74 $15 **multicolored** 27.50 11.00
No gum 16.00
P# block of 4 115.00

b.	Souvenir sheet of 1	125.00	
c.	As "b", without artist's signature (error)	*2,750.*	

No. RW74b sold for $25 plus a shipping fee. The artist signed No. RW74b on a designated line in the sheet margin. Ten thousand were issued. There is no back inscription on No. RW74b.

Self-Adhesive

Serpentine Die Cut 11x10¾

RW74A	HP74 $15 **multicolored**	22.50	11.00
	No gum	15.00	

Five hundred press sheets containing four panes of 20 of No. RW74 and 500 press sheets containing 18 of No. RW74A were offered for sale by the Fish and Wildlife Service.

Northern Pintails — HP75

Printed by Ashton-Potter (USA) Ltd.

2008 **Litho.** ***Perf. 13¼***

Inscribed "Void after June 30, 2009"

RW75	HP75 $15 **multicolored**	27.50	11.00
	No gum	16.00	
	Inscription block of 4	115.00	
b.	Souvenir sheet of 1	70.00	—
c.	As "b," without artist's signature (error)	*500.00*	

A sheet commemorating the 75th anniversary of Hunting Permit stamps containing one example of No. RW75 and a label with the vignette of No. RW1 sold for $50. Value, $90.

No. RW75b sold for $30 plus a shipping fee. The artist signed No. RW75b on a designated line in the sheet margin. Ten thousand were prepared.

Self-Adhesive

Serpentine Die Cut 10¾

RW75A	HP75 $15 **multicolored**	32.50	11.00
	No gum	25.00	

Long-tailed Duck and Decoy — HP76

Printed by Ashton-Potter (USA) Ltd.

2009 **Litho.** ***Perf. 13¼***

Inscribed "Void after June 30, 2010"

RW76	HP76 $15 **multicolored**	27.50	11.00
	No gum	16.00	
	P# block of 4	115.00	
b.	Souvenir sheet of 1	60.00	
c.	As "b," without artist's signature (error)	*400.00*	

No. RW76b sold for $30 plus a shipping fee. The artist signed No. RW76b on a designated line in the sheet margin. Ten thousand were prepared.

Self-Adhesive

Serpentine Die Cut 11x10¾

RW76A	HP76 $15 **multicolored**	22.50	11.00
	No gum	20.00	

American Wigeon — HP77

Printed by Banknote Corporation of America for Sennett Security Products.

2010 **Litho.** ***Perf. 11¼x11***

Inscribed "Void after June 30, 2011"

RW77	HP77 $15 **multicolored**	27.50	11.00
	No gum	16.00	
	P# block of 4	110.00	
b.	Souvenir sheet of 1, perf. 13¼	50.00	
c.	As "b," without artist's signature (error)	*225.00*	

No. RW77b was sold for $30 plus a shipping fee. The artist signed No. RW77b on a designated line in the sheet margin. Ten thousand were prepared. There is no back inscription on No. RW77b, and the stamp on the sheet is tagged.

Self-Adhesive

Serpentine Die Cut 11x10¾

RW77A	HP77 $15 **multicolored**	25.00	11.00
	No gum	20.00	

White-fronted Geese — HP78

Printed by Ashton-Potter (USA) Ltd.

2011 **Litho.** ***Perf. 13¼***

Inscribed "Void after June 30, 2012"

RW78	HP78 $15 **multicolored**	27.50	11.00
	No gum	16.00	
	P# block of 4	110.00	
b.	Souvenir sheet of 1	60.00	
c.	As "b," without artist's signature (error)	*175.00*	

No. RW78b was sold for $25 plus a shipping fee. The artist signed No. RW78b on a designated line in the sheet margin. Ten thousand were prepared.

Self-Adhesive

Serpentine Die Cut 11x10¾

RW78A	HP78 $15 **multicolored**	25.00	11.00
	No gum	20.00	

Wood Duck — HP79

Printed by Ashton-Potter (USA) Ltd.

2012 **Litho.** ***Perf. 13¼***

Inscribed "Void after June 30, 2013"

RW79	HP79 $15 **multicolored**	27.50	11.00
	No gum	16.00	
	P# block of 4	110.00	
b.	Souvenir sheet of 1	60.00	
c.	As "b," without artist's signature (error)	*1,750.*	

No. RW79b was sold for $25 plus a shipping fee. The artist signed No. RW79b on a designated line in the sheet margin. There is a back inscription on No. RW79b. Five thousand were prepared.

One No. RW79b was signed in red ink as a "surprise" for a random buyer. This was not authorized.

Self-Adhesive

Serpentine Die Cut 11x10¾

RW79A	HP79 $15 **multicolored**	25.00	11.00
	No gum	20.00	

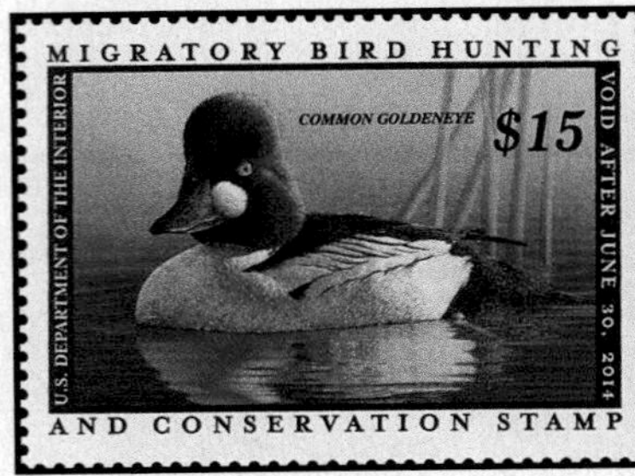

Common Goldeneye — HP80

Printed by Ashton-Potter (USA) Ltd.

2013 **Litho.** ***Perf. 13¼***

Inscribed "Void after June 30, 2014"

RW80	HP80 $15 **multicolored**	27.50	11.00
	No gum	16.00	
	P# block of 4	110.00	
b.	Souvenir sheet of 1	60.00	
c.	As "b," without artist's signature (error)	*1,250.*	

No. RW80b was sold for $25 plus a shipping fee. The artist signed No. RW80b on a designated line in the sheet margin. There is a back inscription on No. RW80b. Five thousand were prepared.

Self-Adhesive

Serpentine Die Cut 11x10¾

RW80A	HP80 $15 **multicolored**	25.00	11.00
	No gum	20.00	

Canvasbacks — HP81

Printed by Ashton-Potter (USA) Ltd.

2014 **Litho.** ***Perf. 13¼***

Inscribed "Void after June 30, 2015"

RW81	HP81 $15 **multicolored**	27.50	11.00
	No gum	16.00	
	P# block of 4	110.00	

Self-Adhesive

Serpentine Die Cut 11x10¾

RW81A	HP81 $15 **multicolored**	25.00	12.50
	No gum	20.00	

Ruddy Ducks — HP82

Printed by Ashton-Potter (USA) Ltd.

2015 **Litho.** ***Perf. 13¼***

Inscribed "Void after June 30, 2016"

RW82	HP82 $25 **multicolored**	37.50	12.00
	No gum	25.00	
	P# block of 4	160.00	

Self-Adhesive

Serpentine Die Cut 11x10¾

RW82A HP82 $25 **multicolored** 37.50 12.50
No gum 32.50

Trumpeter Swans — HP83

Printed by Ashton-Potter (USA) Ltd.

2016 Litho. *Perf. 13¼*

Inscribed "Void after June 30, 2017"

RW83 HP83 $25 **multicolored** 55.00 15.00
No gum 35.00
P# block of 4 225.00

Self-Adhesive

Serpentine Die Cut 11x10¾

RW83A HP83 $25 **multicolored** 37.50 12.50
No gum 32.50

Canada Geese — HP84

Printed by Ashton-Potter (USA) Ltd.

2017 Litho. *Perf. 13¼*

Inscribed "Void after June 30, 2018"

RW84 HP84 $25 **multicolored** 37.50 12.50
No gum 25.00
P# block of 4 160.00

Self-Adhesive

Serpentine Die Cut 11x10¾

RW84A HP84 $25 **multicolored** 37.50 12.50
No gum 32.50

Mallards — HP85

Printed by Ashton-Potter (USA) Ltd.

2018 Litho. *Serpentine Die Cut 11x10¾*

Inscribed "Void after June 30, 2019"

Self-Adhesive

RW85 HP85 $25 **multicolored** 37.50 12.50
No gum 25.00
P# block of 4 160.00
b. Souvenir sheet of 4 160.00

Sheet of 1

RW85A HP85 $25 **multicolored** 37.50

Inscriptions on the backing paper differ for Nos. RW85, RW85A, and RW85b. Once removed from the backing paper, used examples are considered to be No. RW85.

Wood Duck and Decoy — HP86

Printed by Ashton-Potter (USA) Ltd.

2019 Litho. *Serpentine Die Cut 11x10¾*

Inscribed "Void after June 30, 2020"

Self-Adhesive

RW86 HP86 $25 **multicolored** 37.50 12.50
No gum 25.00
P# block of 4 160.00

Sheet of 1

RW86A HP86 $25 **multicolored** 37.50

Inscriptions on the backing paper differ for Nos. RW86 and RW86A. Once removed from the backing paper, used examples are considered to be No. RW86.

SPECIAL PRINTING

After No. RW51 became void, fifteen uncut sheets of 120 (4 panes of 30 separated by gutters) were overprinted "1934-84" and "50th ANNIVERSARY" in the margins and auctioned by the U.S. Fish and Wildlife Service.

Bids were accepted from September 1 through November 1, 1985. Minimum bid for each sheet was $2,000. The face value of each sheet, had they still been valid, was $900. Each sheet also had the sheet number and pane position printed in the corner of each pane ("01 of 15-1," "01 of 15-2," etc.). Fourteen of the sheets were sold at this and one subsequent auction and one was donated to the Smithsonian.

An individual sheet could be broken up to create these identifiable collectibles: 4 margin overprint blocks of 10; cross gutter block of 4; 6 horizontal pairs with gutter between; 8 vertical pairs with gutter between.

Single stamps from the sheet cannot be distinguished from No. RW51. No used examples can exist.

RW51x $7.50 *Widgeons*

DESIGNERS

1934	*RW1*	*J.N. Darling*
1935	*RW2*	*Frank W. Benson*
1936	*RW3*	*Richard E. Bishop*
1937	*RW4*	*J.D. Knap*
1938	*RW5*	*Roland Clark*
1939	*RW6*	*Lynn Bogue Hunt*
1940	*RW7*	*Francis L. Jaques*
1941	*RW8*	*E.R. Kalmbach*
1942	*RW9*	*A. Lassell Ripley*
1943	*RW10*	*Walter E. Bohl*
1944	*RW11*	*Walter A. Weber*
1945	*RW12*	*Owen J. Bromme*
1946	*RW13*	*Robert W. Hines*
1947	*RW14*	*Jack Murray*
1948	*RW15*	*Maynard Reece*
1949	*RW16*	*"Roge" E. Preuss*
1950	*RW17*	*Walter A. Weber*
1951	*RW18*	*Maynard Reece*
1952	*RW19*	*John H. Dick*
1953	*RW20*	*Clayton B. Seagears*
1954	*RW21*	*Harvey D. Sandstrom*
1955	*RW22*	*Stanley Stearns*
1956	*RW23*	*Edward J. Bierly*
1957	*RW24*	*Jackson Miles Abbott*
1958	*RW25*	*Leslie C. Kouba*
1959	*RW26*	*Maynard Reece*
1960	*RW27*	*John A. Ruthven*
1961	*RW28*	*Edward A. Morris*
1962	*RW29*	*Edward A. Morris*
1963	*RW30*	*Edward J. Bierly*
1964	*RW31*	*Stanley Stearns*
1965	*RW32*	*Ron Jenkins*
1966	*RW33*	*Stanley Stearns*
1967	*RW34*	*Leslie C. Kouba*
1968	*RW35*	*C.G. Pritchard*
1969	*RW36*	*Maynard Reece*
1970	*RW37*	*Edward J. Bierly*
1971	*RW38*	*Maynard Reece*
1972	*RW39*	*Arthur M. Cook*
1973	*RW40*	*Lee LeBlanc*
1974	*RW41*	*David A. Maass*
1975	*RW42*	*James P. Fisher*
1976	*RW43*	*Alderson Magee*
1977	*RW44*	*Martin R. Murk*
1978	*RW45*	*Albert Earl Gilbert*
1979	*RW46*	*Kenneth L. Michaelsen*
1980	*RW47*	*Richard W. Plasschaert*
1981	*RW48*	*John S. Wilson*
1982	*RW49*	*David A. Maass*
1983	*RW50*	*Phil Scholer*
1984	*RW51*	*William C. Morris*
1985	*RW52*	*Gerald Mobley*
1986	*RW53*	*Burton E. Moore, Jr.*
1987	*RW54*	*Arthur G. Anderson*
1988	*RW55*	*Daniel Smith*
1989	*RW56*	*Neal R. Anderson*
1990	*RW57*	*Jim Hautman*
1991	*RW58*	*Nancy Howe*
1992	*RW59*	*Joe Hautman*
1993	*RW60*	*Bruce Miller*
1994	*RW61*	*Neal R. Anderson*
1995	*RW62*	*Jim Hautman*
1996	*RW63*	*Wilhelm Goebel*
1997	*RW64*	*Robert Hautman*
1998	*RW65*	*Robert Steiner*
1999	*RW66*	*Jim Hautman*
2000	*RW67*	*Adam Grimm*
2001	*RW68*	*Robert Hautman*
2002	*RW69*	*Joe Hautman*
2003	*RW70*	*Ron Louque*
2004	*RW71*	*Scot Storm*
2005	*RW72*	*Mark Anderson*
2006	*RW73*	*Sherrie Russell Meline*
2007	*RW74*	*Richard Clifton*
2008	*RW75*	*Joe Hautman*
2009	*RW76*	*Joshua Spies*
2010	*RW77*	*Robert Bealle*
2011	*RW78*	*James Hautman*
2012	*RW79*	*Joe Hautman*
2013	*RW80*	*Robert Steiner*
2014	*RW81*	*Adam Grimm*
2015	*RW82*	*Jennifer Miller*
2016	*RW83*	*Joe Hautman*
2017	*RW84*	*James Hautman*
2018	*RW85*	*Robert Hautman*
2019	*RW86*	*Scot Storm*

QUANTITIES SOLD

(Quantities from No. RW65 on are quantities ordered. Quantities sold of these numbers were much less.)

RW1	**635,001**	*RW43*	**2,170,194**
RW2	**448,204**	*RW44*	**2,196,774**
RW3	**603,623**	*RW45*	**2,216,621**
RW4	**783,039**	*RW46*	**2,090,155**
RW5	**1,002,715**	*RW47*	**2,045,114**
RW6	**1,111,561**	*RW48*	**1,907,120**
RW7	**1,260,810**	*RW49*	**1,926,253**
RW8	**1,439,967**	*RW50*	**1,867,998**
RW9	**1,383,629**	*RW51*	**1,913,861**
RW10	**1,169,352**	*RW52*	**1,780,636**
RW11	**1,487,029**	*RW53*	**1,794,484**
RW12	**1,725,505**	*RW54*	**1,663,270**
RW13	**2,016,841**	*RW55*	**1,402,096**
RW14	**1,722,677**	*RW56*	**1,415,882**
RW15	**2,127,603**	*RW57*	**1,408,373**
RW16	**1,954,734**	*RW58*	**1,423,374**
RW17	**1,903,644**	*RW59*	**1,347,393**
RW18	**2,167,767**	*RW60*	**1,402,569**
RW19	**2,296,628**	*RW61*	**1,471,751**
RW20	**2,268,446**	*RW62*	**1,539,622**
RW21	**2,184,550**	*RW63*	**1,560,123**
RW22	**2,369,940**	*RW64*	**1,697,590**
RW23	**2,332,014**	*RW65*	**1,195,000**
RW24	**2,355,190**	*RW65A*	**2,805,000**
RW25	**2,176,425**	*RW66*	**1,194,000**
RW26	**1,626,115**	*RW66A*	**2,799,600**
RW27	**1,725,634**	*RW67*	**1,200,000**
RW28	**1,344,236**	*RW67A*	**2,800,000**
RW29	**1,147,212**	*RW68*	**1,194,000**
RW30	**1,448,191**	*RW68A*	**2,806,000**
RW31	**1,573,155**	*RW69*	**1,194,000**
RW32	**1,558,197**	*RW69A*	**2,806,000**
RW33	**1,805,341**	*RW70*	**1,000,000**
RW34	**1,934,697**	*RW70A*	**3,000,000**
RW35	**1,837,139**	*RW71*	**1,000,000**
RW36	**2,072,108**	*RW71A*	**3,000,000**
RW37	**2,420,244**	*RW85*	**200,000**
RW38	**2,445,977**	*RW85b*	**12,600**
RW39	**2,184,343**	*RW85A*	**2,155,000**
RW40	**2,094,414**	*RW86*	**65,000**
RW41	**2,214,056**	*RW86A*	**2,365,000**
RW42	**2,237,126**		

JUNIOR DUCK STAMPS

As a courtesy to Duck stamp collectors, we list here the Duck stamps issued under the Federal Junior Duck Stamp program, run by the U.S. Fish and Wildlife Service branch of the Department of the Interior and the Federal Duck Stamp Office. The purpose of this program is to teach youth through the medium of art the importance of conserving wetlands and migratory birds.

Students in kindergarden to 12th grade from all 50 states, the District of Columbia, American Samoa and the U.S. Virgin Islands are invited to participate in an annual art competition. The winning entry from each state, district or territory competes for the national championship. The national winner's art appears on that year's Junior Duck stamp, which is sold to raise funds to support the Junior Duck Stamp art and educational program. The United States Postal Service, through its Stamp Fulfillment Services unit, acts as a sales agent for these stamps.

These stamps are not valid for hunting, nor is it required that hunters buy the stamps in order to hunt.

A precursor sheet of nine stamps was released in 1992 as a part of a pilot program instituted before the formal, annual Junior Duck Stamp art competition was begun. The sheet shows stamps from Arkansas, California (2), Florida (2), Illinois (2), Kansas and Vermont. Value, $30.

All issues were printed in panes of 30 with four control/plate numbers. Imperforate examples of Nos. JDS1, JDS2 and JDS3 exist and are believed to be printer's waste.

Catalogue values for all stamps in this section are for stamps with never-hinged original gum.

JD1

1993 **Artist: Jason Parsons (IL)**
JDS1 JD1 $5 *Redhead* 100.00

1994 **Artist: Clark Weaver (PA)**
JDS2 JD1 $5 *Hooded mergansers* 135.00

1995 **Artist: Jie Huang (MT)**
JDS3 JD1 $5 *Pintail* 425.00

1996 **Artist: Clark Weaver (PA)**
JDS4 JD1 $5 *Canvasbacks* 500.00

1997 **Artist: Scott Russell (CA)**
JDS5 JD1 $5 *Canada geese* 475.00

1998 **Artist: Eric Peterson (MI)**
JDS6 JD1 $5 *Black ducks* 475.00

1999 **Artist: Ryan Kirby (IL)**
JDS7 JD1 $5 *Wood ducks* 475.00

2000 **Artist: Bonnie Latham (MN)**
JDS8 JD1 $5 *Pintails* 325.00

2001 **Artist: Aremy McCann (MN)**
JDS9 JD1 $5 *Trumpeter swan* 60.00

2002 **Artist: Nathan Closson (MT)**
JDS10 JD1 $5 *Mallards* 40.00

2003 **Artist: Nathan Bauman (PA)**
JDS11 JD1 $5 *Green-winged teal* 25.00

2004 **Artist: Adam Nisbett (MO)**
JDS12 JD1 $5 *Fulvous whistling ducks* 20.00

2005 **Artist: Kerissa Nelson (WI)**
JDS13 JD1 $5 *Ring-necked ducks* 17.50

2006 **Artist: Rebekah Nastav (MO)**
JDS14 JD1 $5 *Redhead* 12.50

2007 **Artist: Paul Willey (AR)**
JDS15 JD1 $5 *Wigeons* 10.00

2008 **Artist: Seokkyun Hong (TX)**
JDS16 JD1 $5 *Hawaiian Nene Geese* 10.00

2009 **Artist: Lily Spang (OH)**
JDS17 JD1 $5 *Wood duck* 10.00

2010 **Artist: Rui Huang (OH)**
JDS18 JD1 $5 *Hooded merganser* 10.00

2011 **Artist: Abraham Hunter (IL)**
JDS19 JD1 $5 *Ring-necked ducks* 10.00

2012 **Artist: Christine Clayton (OH)**
JDS20 JD1 $5 *Northern pintail* 10.00

2013 **Artist: Madison Grimm (SD)**
JDS21 JD1 $5 *Canvasback* 10.00

Type of 1993

2014 **Artist: Si Youn Kim (NJ)**
JDS22 JD1 $5 *King eider* 10.00

Type of 1993

2015 **Artist: Andrew Kneeland (WY)**
JDS23 JD1 $5 *Wood ducks* 10.00

Type of 1993

2016 **Artist: Stacy Shen (CA)**
JDS24 JD1 $5 *Ross's geese* 10.00

Type of 1993

2017 **Artist: Isaac Schreiber (VA)**
JDS25 JD1 $5 *Trumpeter swans* 10.00

Type of 1993

2018 **Artist: Rayen Kang (GA)**
JDS26 JD1 $5 *Emperor goose* 10.00

Type of 1993

2019 **Artist: Nicole Jeon (NY)**
JDS27 JD1 $5 *Harlequin duck* 10.00

STATE HUNTING PERMIT STAMPS

These stamps are used on licenses for hunting waterfowl (ducks, geese, swans) by states and Indian reservations. Stamps which include waterfowl along with a variety of other animals are listed here. Stamps for hunting birds that exclude waterfowl are not listed.

A number of states print stamps in sheets as well as in booklets. The booklets are sent to agents for issuing to hunters. Both varieties are listed. The major listing is given to the sheet stamp since it generally is available in larger quantities and has been the more popularly collected item. In some cases the stamp removed from a booklet, with no tabs or selvage, is identical to a single sheet stamp (see Rhode Island). In these cases the identifiable booklet stamp with tabs and selvage receives an unlettered listing. If the single booklet stamp can be identified by type of perforation or the existence of one or more straight edges, the item receives a lettered listing (see Oregon).

Governor's editions are sold at a premium over the license fee with proceeds intended to help waterfowl habitats. Only those which differ from the regular stamp are listed.

After the period of validity, a number of these stamps were sold at less than face value. This explains the low values on stamps such as Montana Nos. 30, 33, and Flathead Indian Reservation Nos. 2-10.

When used, most stamps are affixed to licenses and signed by the hunter. Values for used stamps are for examples off licenses and without tabs. Although used examples may be extremely scarce, they will always sell for somewhat less than unused examples (two-thirds of the unused value would be the upper limit).

ALABAMA

Printed in sheets of 10.
Stamps are numbered serially.

Catalogue values for all unused stamps in this section are for Never Hinged items.

Artists: Barbara Keel, #1; Wayne Spradley, #2; Jack Deloney, #3; Joe Michelet, #4; John Lee, #5, 25; William Morris, #6, 14; Larry Martin, #7; Danny W. Dorning, #8; Robert C. Knutson, #9, 16, 20; John Warr, #10; Elaine Byrd, #11; Steven Garst, #12; Larry Chandler, #13, 24; James Brantley, #15; Neil Blackwell, #17; Judith Huey, #18; E. Hatcher, #19; Eddie LeRoy, #21, 37; David Sellers, #22, 26, 27; H. Andrew McNeely, #23. Clarence Stewart, #28, #32; David Nix, #29, 33, 39; Jim Denney, #30, 34; John Denney, #31; Steve Burney #35; John Denney, #36 38, 40.

1979-2018

1	$5 Wood ducks, rouletted	12.00	3.00
2	$5 Mallards, *1980*	12.00	3.00
3	$5 Canada geese, *1981*	12.00	3.00
4	$5 Green-winged teal, *1982*	12.00	3.00
5	$5 Widgeons, *1983*	12.00	3.00
6	$5 Buffleheads, *1984*	12.00	3.00
7	$5 Wood ducks, *1985*	12.00	3.00
8	$5 Canada geese, *1986*	12.00	3.00
9	$5 Pintails, *1987*	14.00	3.00
10	$5 Canvasbacks, *1988*	10.00	3.00
11	$5 Hooded mergansers, *1989*	10.00	3.00
12	$5 Aleutian Canada goose, *1990*	10.00	2.50
13	$5 Redheads, *1991*	10.00	2.50
14	$5 Cinnamon teal, *1992*	10.00	2.50
15	$5 Green-winged teal, *1993*	10.00	2.50
16	$5 Canvasbacks, *1994*	10.00	2.50
17	$5 Canada geese, *1995*	10.00	2.50
18	$5 Wood ducks, *1996*	12.00	2.50
19	$5 Snow goose, *1997*	10.00	2.50
20	$5 Barrow's goldeneye, *1998*	10.00	2.50
21	$5 Redheads, *1999*	10.00	2.50
22	$5 Buffleheads, *2000*	10.00	2.50
23	$5 Ruddy duck, *2001*	10.00	2.50
24	$5 Pintail, *2002*	10.00	2.50
25	$5 Wood ducks, *2003*	10.00	2.50
26	$5 Ring-necked ducks, *2004*	10.00	2.50
27	$5 Canada geese, *2005*	10.00	2.50
28	$5 Canvasback, *2006*	10.00	2.50
29	$5 Blue-winged teal, *2007*	10.00	2.50
30	$5 Hooded mergansers, *2008*	10.00	2.50
31	$5 Wood ducks, *2009*	10.00	2.50
32	$5 Pintail, *2010*	10.00	2.50
33	$5 Wigeon, *2011*	10.00	2.50
34	$5 Ring-necked ducks, *2012*	10.00	2.50
35	$5 Canvasbacks, *2013*	10.00	2.50
36	$5 Pintails, *2014*	10.00	2.50
37	$5 Mallards, *2015*	10.00	2.50
38	$10 Wigeons, *2016*	16.00	3.50
39	$10 Canada geese, *2017*	16.00	3.50
40	$10 Blue-winged teal, *2018*	16.00	3.50

ALASKA

Printed in sheets of 30.
Stamps are numbered serially on reverse. Booklet pane stamps printed in panes of 5.

Catalogue values for all unused stamps in this section are for Never Hinged items.

1986 Alaska Waterfowl Stamp

Artist: Daniel Smith, #1; James Meger, #2; Carl Branson, #3; Jim Beaudoin, #4; Richard Timm, #5; Louis Frisino, #6; Ronald Louque, #7; Fred Thomas, #8; Ed Tussey, #9; George Lockwood, #10, 13, 23; Cynthia Fisher, #11, 20; Wilhelm Goebel, #12; Robert Steiner, #14, 18, 22, 25; Sherrie Russell Meline, #15; Adam Grimm, #16, 19; Greg Alexander, #17; Don Moore, #21, 24; Sue Steinacher, #26-27; Donna Dewhurst, #28-29; Milo Burcham, #30-33; Declan Troy, #34.

1985-2018

1	$5 Emperor geese	10.00	3.00
2	$5 Steller's eiders, *1986*	10.00	3.00
3	$5 Spectacled eiders, perforated, *1987*	10.00	
a.	Bklt. single, rouletted, with tab	10.00	2.50
4	$5 Trumpeter swans, perforated, *1988*	10.00	
a.	Bklt. single, rouletted, with tab	10.00	2.50
5	$5 Barrow's goldeneyes, perforated, *1989*	10.00	
a.	Bklt. single, rouletted, with tab	10.00	2.50
b.	Governor's edition	*100.00*	

No. 5b was sold in full panes through a sealed bid auction.

6	$5 Old squaws, perforated, *1990*	10.00	
a.	Bklt. single, rouletted, with tab	10.00	2.50
7	$5 Snow geese, perforated, *1991*	10.00	
a.	Bklt. single, rouletted, with tab	10.00	2.50
8	$5 Canvasbacks, perforated, *1992*	10.00	
a.	Bklt. single, rouletted, with tab	10.00	2.50
9	$5 Tule white front geese, perforated, *1993*	14.00	
a.	Bklt. single, rouletted, with tab	14.00	2.50
10	$5 Harlequin ducks, perforated, *1994*	20.00	
a.	Bklt. single, rouletted, with tab	15.00	2.50
b.	Governor's edition	*75.00*	
11	$5 Pacific brant, perforated, *1995*	20.00	
a.	Bklt. single, rouletted, with tab	18.00	2.50
12	$5 Canada geese, *1996*	25.00	
a.	Bklt. single, rouletted, with tab	20.00	2.50
13	$5 King eiders, *1997*	16.00	
a.	Bklt. single, rouletted, with tab	16.00	2.50
14	$5 Barrow's goldeneye, *1998*	12.00	
a.	Bklt. single, with tab	12.00	2.50
15	$5 Pintail, *1999*	12.00	
a.	Bklt. single, with tab	12.00	2.50
16	$5 Common eider, *2000*	18.00	
a.	Bklt. single, with tab	10.00	2.50
17	$5 American wigeon, *2001*	12.50	
a.	Bklt. single, with tab	12.50	2.50
18	$5 Black scoters, *2002*	10.00	
a.	Bklt. single, with tab	10.00	2.50
19	$5 Lesser Canada geese, *2003*	12.00	
a.	Bklt. single, with tab	12.00	2.50
20	$5 Lesser scaup, *2004*	10.00	
a.	Bklt. single, with tab	10.00	2.50
21	$5 Hooded merganser, *2005*	10.00	
a.	Bklt. single, with tab	10.00	2.50
22	$5 Pintails, mallard, green-winged teal, *2006*	10.00	
a.	Bklt. single, with tab	10.00	2.50
23	$5 Northern shovelers, *2007*	10.00	
a.	Bklt. single, with tab	10.00	2.50
24	$5 Northern pintails, *2008*	10.00	
a.	Bklt. single, with tab	10.00	2.50
25	$5 Mallards, *2009*	10.00	
a.	Bklt. single, with tab	10.00	2.50
26	$5 Pintails, *2010*	17.50	
a.	Bklt. single, with tab	12.00	2.50
27	$5 Canada goose, *2011*	10.00	
a.	Bklt. single, with tab	10.00	2.50
28	$5 Harlequin ducks, *2012*	10.00	
a.	Bklt. single, with tab	10.00	2.50
29	$5 White-fronted geese, *2013*	10.00	
a.	Bklt. single, with tab	10.00	2.50
30	$5 White-fronted scoter, *2014*	10.00	
a.	Bklt. single, with tab	10.00	2.50
31	$5 Northern pintail, *2015*	10.00	
a.	Bklt. single, with tab	10.00	2.50
32	$5 Brant, *2016*	10.00	
a.	Bklt. single, with tab	10.00	2.50
33	$10 Wigeon, *2017*	16.00	
a.	Bklt. single, with tab	16.00	3.50
34	$10 Bufflehead, *2018*	16.00	
a.	Bklt. single, with tab	16.00	3.50

David R. Torre

• COLLECTOR
• DEALER

buying and selling

U.S. FISH AND GAME STAMPS

Specializing in exceptional single stamps, rare multiples and examples on original licenses showing their usage.

waterfowlstampsandmore.com

P.O. BOX 4298
SANTA ROSA, CA 95402
707-525-8785
email:dektorre@comcast.net

ARIZONA

Printed in booklet panes of 5 with tab and in sheets of 30.

Stamps are numbered serially.

Catalogue values for all unused stamps in this section are for Never Hinged items.

Artists: Daniel Smith, #1; Sherrie Russell Meline, #2, 6-7, 9, 11-18, 21-27; Robert Steiner, #3; Ted Blaylock, #4; Brian Jarvi, #5; Harry Adamson, #8, Larry Hayden, #10; Tom Finley, #19, 20.

1987-2013

No.		Unused	Used
1	$5.50 Pintails, perf. 4 sides	11.00	
a.	Bklt. single, perf. 3 sides, with tab	11.00	3.00
2	$5.50 Green-winged teal, perf. 4 sides, *1988*	12.00	
a.	Bklt. single, perf. 3 sides, with tab	12.00	3.00
3	$5.50 Cinnamon teal, perf. 4 sides, *1989*	11.00	
a.	Bklt. single, perf. 3 sides, with tab	11.00	2.50
b.	$5.50 +$50 Governor's edition	75.00	
4	$5.50 Canada geese, perf. 4 sides, *1990*	12.00	
a.	Bklt. single, perf. 3 sides, with tab	12.00	2.50
b.	$5.50 +$50 Governor's edition	75.00	
5	$5.50 Blue-winged teal, perf. 4 sides, *1991*	10.00	
a.	Bklt. single, perf. 3 sides, with tab	11.00	2.50
b.	$55.50 Governor's edition	75.00	
6	$5.50 Buffleheads, perf. 4 sides, *1992*	10.00	
a.	Bklt. single, perf. 3 sides, with tab	11.00	2.50
b.	$55.50 Governor's edition	75.00	
7	$5.50 Mexican ducks, perf. 4 sides, *1993*	12.00	
a.	Bklt. single, perf. 3 sides, with tab	12.00	2.50
b.	$55.50 Governor's edition	75.00	
8	$5.50 Mallards, perf. 4 sides, *1994*	12.00	
a.	Bklt. single, perf. 3 sides, with tab	12.00	2.50
b.	$55.50 Governor's edition	75.00	
9	$5.50 Widgeon, perf. 4 sides, *1995*	12.00	
a.	Bklt. single, perf. 3 sides, with tab	12.00	2.50
b.	$55.50 Governor's edition	75.00	
10	$5.50 Canvasbacks, perf. 4 sides, *1996*	11.00	
a.	Bklt. single, perf 3 sides, with tab	11.00	2.50
b.	$55.50 Governor's edition	75.00	
11	$5.50 Gadwalls, *1997*	12.00	
a.	Bklt. single, perf 3 sides, with tab	12.00	2.50
b.	$55.50 Governor's edition	75.00	
12	$5.50 Wood duck, *1998*	12.00	
a.	Bklt. single, perf 3 sides, with tab	12.00	2.50
b.	$55.50 Governor's edition	—	
13	$5.50 Snow goose, *1999*	12.00	
a.	Bklt. single, perf. 3 sides, with tab	12.00	2.50
b.	$55.50 Governor's edition	75.00	
14	$7.50 Ruddy duck, *2000*	14.00	
a.	Bklt. single, perf. 3 sides, with tab	14.00	2.50
b.	$55.50 Governor's edition	75.00	
15	$7.50 Redheads, *2001*	14.00	
a.	Bklt. single, perf. 3 sides, with tab	14.00	2.50
b.	$55.50 Governor's edition	75.00	
16	$7.50 Ring-necked ducks, *2002*	14.00	
a.	Bklt. single, perf. 2 sides, with tabs	14.00	2.50
b.	$55.50 Governor's edition	75.00	
17	$7.50 Northern shovelers, *2003*	14.00	
a.	Bklt. single, perf. 2 sides, with tabs	14.00	2.50
b.	$55.50 Governor's edition	75.00	
18	$7.50 Lesser scaup, *2004*	12.00	
a.	Bklt. single, perf. 2 sides, with tabs	12.00	2.50
b.	$55.50 Governor's edition	75.00	—
19	$7.50 Pintails, *2005*	9.50	
a.	Bklt. single, perf. 3 sides, with tabs	10.50	2.50
20	$7.50 Canada geese, *2006*	9.50	
a.	Bklt. single, perf. 3 sides, with tabs	10.50	2.50
b.	$55 Governor's edition	75.00	
21	$8.75 Wood ducks, *2007*	11.00	
a.	Bklt. single, perf. 2 or 3 sides, with tabs	12.00	2.50
b.	$55 Governor's edition	75.00	
22	$8.75 Canvasbacks, *2008*	11.00	
a.	Bklt. single, perf. 2 or 3 sides, with tabs	12.00	2.50
23	$8.75 Hooded mergansers, *2009*	11.00	
a.	Bklt. single, perf. 2 or 3 sides, with tabs	12.00	2.50
24	$8.75 Green-winged teal, *2010*	11.00	
a.	Bklt. single, perf. 2 or 3 sides, with tabs	12.00	2.50
25	$8.75 Bufflehead, *2011*	11.00	
a.	Bklt. single, perf. on 2 or 3 sides, with tabs	12.00	2.50
26	$8.75 Wigeons, *2012*	11.00	
a.	Bklt. single, perf. on 2 or 3 sides, with tabs	12.00	2.50
27	$8.75 Pintail, *2013*	8.00	2.50
a.	Bklt. single, perf. on 2 or 3 sides, with tabs	12.00	2.50

The stamp pictured above, depicting a child's drawing of wigeons in flight, was printed in 2009 in a limited edition of 500 stamps. It was valid for hunting. Value, $175.

The stamp pictured above, depicting a child's drawing of green-winged teal, was printed in 2010 in a limited edition. It was valid for hunting. Value, $135.

The stamp pictured above, depicting a child's drawing of a wood duck, was printed in 2011 in a limited edition. It was valid for hunting. Value, $55.

The stamp pictured above, depicting a child's drawing of a mallard, was printed in a limited edition. It was valid for hunting. Value, $14.

The stamp pictured above, depicting a child's drawing of a fulvous whistling duck, was printed in a limited edition. It was valid for hunting. Value, $12.

ARKANSAS

Imperforate varieties of these stamps exist in large quantities. Imperforate examples of Nos. 1 and 2 were sold by the state for $1 each.

No. 1 printed in sheets and booklet panes of 30, others in sheets and booklet panes of 10.

Stamps are numbered serially on reverse.

Catalogue values for all unused stamps in this section are for Never Hinged items.

Artists: Lee LeBlanc, #1; Maynard Reece, #2, 8, 43-44; David Maass, #3, 10, 21; Larry Hayden, #4, 15; Ken Carlson, #5, 13; John P. Cowan, #6; Robert Bateman. #7; Phillip Crowe, #9, 16, 22, 27-27A, 30-30A; Daniel Smith, #11, 14; Jim Hautman, #12, 19, 31-31A, 34-34A, 38-38A; L. Chandler, #17, 20, 25-25A; John Dearman, #18; Zettie Jones, #23; Ralph McDonald, #24-24A. Scot Storm, #26-26A, 32-32B, 36-36A; Cynthie Fisher, #28-28A; Joe Hautman, #29-29A; Milo Burcham, #35-35A; Robert Hautman, #37-37A.

1981-2018

No.		Unused	Used
1	$5.50 Mallards	45.00	12.00
a.	Booklet pane of 30	—	
	Booklet single with top tab, Nos. 110,001-200,000 on back	50.00	
2	$5.50 Wood ducks, *1982*	40.00	9.00
3	$5.50 Green-winged teal, *1983*	50.00	12.00
4	$5.50 Pintails, *1984*	22.50	5.00
5	$5.50 Mallards, *1985*	13.00	4.00
6	$5.50 Black swamp mallards, *1986*	11.00	4.00
7	$7 Wood ducks, *1987*	12.00	4.00

Stamps like Nos. 7 and 8 with $5.50 face values were sold following an order of the state Supreme Court restoring the fee level of 1986. The stamps were sold after the 1988 season had ended. Value, $11 each.

No.		Unused	Used
8	$7 Pintails, *1988*	12.00	4.00

See footnote following No. 7.

No.		Unused	Used
9	$7 Mallards, *1989*	12.00	4.00
10	$7 Black ducks & mallards, *1990*	12.00	4.00
11	$7 Sulphur river widgeons, *1991*	12.00	4.00
12	$7 Shirey Bay shovelers, *1992*	12.00	4.00
13	$7 Grand prairie mallards, *1993*	12.00	4.00
14	$7 Canada goose, *1994*	16.00	4.00
15	$7 White River mallards, *1995*	14.00	4.00
16	$7 Mallards, black labrador, *1996*	14.00	4.00
17	$7 Labrador retriever, mallards, *1997*	15.00	4.00
18	$7 Labrador retriever, mallards, *1998*	12.00	4.00
19	$7 Wood duck, *1999*	12.00	4.00
20	$7 Mallards and golden retriever, *2000*	11.00	4.00
21	$7 Canvasbacks, *2001*	11.00	4.00
22	$7 Mallards, *2002*	11.00	4.00
23	$7 Mallards & Chesapeake retriever, *2003*	14.00	4.00
24	$7 Mallards, *2004*	11.00	4.00
24A	$20 Mallards, *2004*	30.00	4.00
25	$7 Mallards, Labrador retriever *2005*	12.00	4.00
25A	$20 Mallards, Labrador retriever *2005*	30.00	4.00
26	$7 Mallards, *2006*	12.00	4.00
26A	$20 Mallards, *2006*	30.00	4.00
27	$7 Mallards, Labrador retriever *2007*	12.00	4.00
27A	$20 Mallards, Labrador retriever *2007*	28.00	4.00
28	$7 Mallards, Labrador retriever, *2008*	12.00	4.00

No.	Description	Unused	Used
28A	$20 Mallards, Labrador retriever, *2008*	28.00	4.00
29	$7 Hooded mergansers, *2009*	12.00	4.00
29A	$20 Hooded mergansers, *2009*	28.00	4.00
30	$7 Mallards and Black Labrador retriever, *2010*	12.00	4.00
30A	$20 Mallards and Black Labrador retriever, *2010*	35.00	4.00
31	$7 Mallards, *2011*	12.00	4.00
31A	$20 Mallards, *2011*	35.00	4.00

Resident and non-resident fees begin in 2004.

No.	Description	Unused	Used
32	$7 Green-winged teal, *2012*	12.00	4.00
32A	$20 Green-winged teal, *2012*	35.00	4.00
32B	$35 Green-winged teal, *2012 revalued*	55.00	—
33	$7 Mallards, *2013*	12.00	4.00
33A	$35 Mallards, *2013*	45.00	10.00
34	$7 Mallards, *2014*	12.00	4.00
34A	$35 Mallards, *2014*	45.00	10.00
35	$7 Snow geese, *2015*	12.00	4.00
35A	$35 Snow geese, *2015*	45.00	10.00
36	$7 Mallards, *2016*	12.00	4.00
36A	$35 Mallards, *2016*	45.00	10.00
37	$7 Mallards and yellow labrador retriever, *2017*	12.00	4.00
37A	$35 Mallards and yellow labrador retriever, *2017*	45.00	10.00
38	$7 Ring-necked ducks, *2018*	10.00	2.00
38A	$35 Ring-necked ducks, *2018*	39.00	2.00

CALIFORNIA

Honey Lake Waterfowl Stamps

Fee $5.00 457
STATE OF CALIFORNIA
DEPARTMENT OF FISH AND GAME
SEASONAL PERMIT for
HONEY LAKE
Valid during 1959-60 Waterfowl Season
Stamp must be pasted on back of 1959-60 Hunting License. Owner must validate by signing name across face of stamp. 1284 7-59 500 SPO

Required to hunt waterfowl at Honey Lake. Valid for a full season. Stamps are rouletted. Used values are for signed copies. Unsigned stamps without gum probably were used. Values for these stamps are higher than used values, but lower than values shown for gummed unused stamps.

1956-86

No.	Description	Unused	Used
A1	$5 black, *1956-1957*		—
A2	$5 black, *blue green, 1957-1958*		—
A3	$5 black, *dark yellow, 1958-1959*		—
A4	$5 black, *dark yellow, 1959-1960*	850.00	500.00
A5	$5 black, *1960-1961*		1,200.
A6	$5 black, *bluish green, 1961-1962*	—	1,200.
A7	$5 black, *dark yellow, 1962-1963*		900.00
A8	$5 black, *1963-1964*		400.00
A9	$6.50 black, *pink, 1964-1965*	900.00	400.00
A10	$6.50 black, *1965-1966*		350.00
A11	$6.50 black, *yellow*, Nos. 1-700, printer's information at bottom right, *1966-1967*		375.00
a.	Serial Nos. 701-1050, no printer's information		18,500.
A12	$10 black, *pink, 1967-1968*	—	350.00
A13	$10 black, *blue, 1968-1969*	—	450.00
A14	$10 black, *green, 1969-1970*	—	500.00
A15	$15 black, *dark yellow, 1970-1971*	—	750.00
A16	$15 black, *pink, 1971-1972*		1,950.
A17	$15 black, *blue, 1972-1973*		3,750.
A18	$15 black, *blue, 1973-1974*	—	—
A19	$15 black, *pink, 1974-1975*	40.00	25.00
A20	$15 black, *green, 1975-1976*	125.00	35.00
A21	$15 black, *light yellow, 1976-1977*	125.00	35.00
A22	$20 black, *blue, 1977-1978*	125.00	35.00
A23	$20 blk, *light yel brown, 1978-1979*	125.00	35.00
A24	$20 black, *light yellow, 1979-1980*	125.00	35.00
A25	$15 black, *light blue, 1980-1981*	100.00	30.00
A26	$20 black, *light yellow, 1981-1982*		—
A27	$20 black, *pink, 1982-1983*	90.00	30.00
A28	$20 black, *light green, 1983-1984*	45.00	25.00
A29	$20 black, *dark yellow, 1984-1985*	42.50	25.00
A30	$20 black, *light blue, 1985-1986*	37.50	20.00

Eighteen $5 black on dark yellow permit stamps were sold for hunting at the state-owned and operated Madeline Plains waterfowl management area for the 1956-57 season. No examples have been recorded.

Statewide Hunting License Validation Stamps

Fees are for resident, junior and non-resident hunters. "No fee" stamps were for disabled veterans. Stamps with special serial numbers for state officials are known for some years. Nos. 2A1-2A3 imperf on 3 sides, roulетted at top. Others die cut.
Stamps are numbered serially.
Used values are for written-upon stamps. Starting with No. 2A4, unused values are for stamps on backing paper.

Remove stamp with this tab. Affix it to application. Tear off tab.
CALIFORNIA HUNTING LICENSE
H 20910-14
(Print this number on tags)
Resident $4.00
Expires June 30, 1963
Date License Issued
Deer Tag No.
Bear Tag No.
Pheasant Tag No.

1962-1963

No.	Description	Unused	Used
2A1	$4 black	375.00	7.00
a.	Ovptd. "NO FEE"	275.00	250.00
2A2	$1 black, *yellow*	1,500.	75.00
2A3	$25 black, *green*	3,500.	150.00

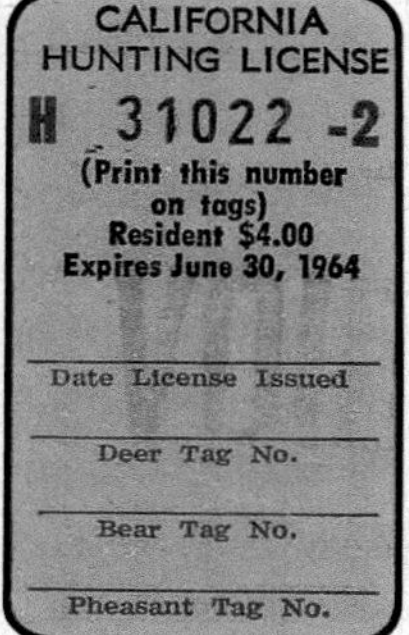

No. 2A4

1963-1964

No.	Description	Unused	Used
2A4	$4 black, *green*		3.00
a.	Ovptd. "NO FEE"	—	—
2A5	$1 black, *gray*	—	20.00
2A6	$25 black, *yellow orange*		550.00

1964-1965

No.	Description	Unused	Used
2A7	$4 black, *pink*	30.00	1.00
a.	Ovptd. "NO FEE"	300.00	200.00
2A8	$1 black, *yellow brown*	225.00	25.00
2A9	$25 black, *dark gray*		70.00

1965-1966

No.	Description	Unused	Used
2A10	$4 black, *gray*	25.00	1.00
a.	Ovptd. "NO FEE"		—
2A11	$1 black, *yellow gray*		25.00
2A12	$25 black, *ivory*		75.00

1966-1967

No.	Description	Unused	Used
2A13	$4 black, *salmon*	25.00	1.00
a.	Ovptd. "NO FEE"		375.00
2A14	$1 black, *lt blue*	75.00	10.00
2A15	$25 black, *burgundy*		65.00

1967-1968

No.	Description	Unused	Used
2A16	$4 black, *yellow*	20.00	1.00
a.	Ovptd. "NO FEE"		350.00
2A17	$1 black, *green*	45.00	5.00
a.	black, *yellow gray*		—
2A18	$25 black, *brown*	75.00	25.00

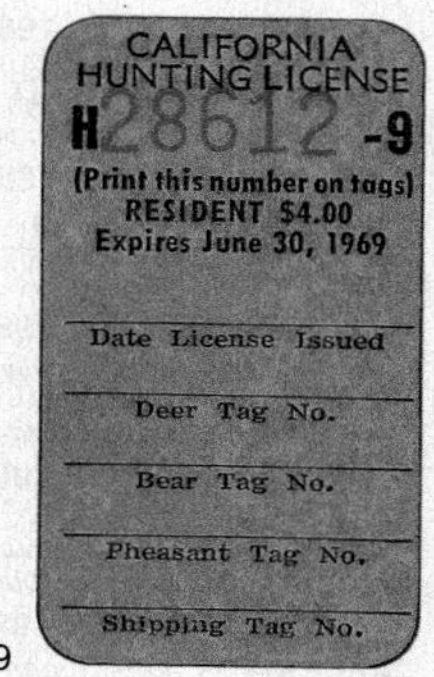

No. 2A19

1968-1969

No.	Description	Unused	Used
2A19	$4 black, *pink*	55.00	1.00
a.	Ovptd. "NO FEE"		350.00
2A20	$1 black, *blue gray*	175.00	20.00
2A21	$25 black, *light orange*		85.00

1969-1970

No.	Description	Unused	Used
2A22	$4 black	55.00	1.00
a.	Ovptd. "NO FEE"		350.00
2A23	$1 black, *dark pink*	175.00	20.00
2A24	$25 black, *light yellow*	70.00	25.00

1970-1971

No.	Description	Unused	Used
2A25	$4 black, *manila*	70.00	2.00
a.	Ovptd. "NO FEE"	1,500.	750.00
2A26	$1 black, *blue gray*	75.00	10.00
2A27	$25 black, *gray brown*	100.00	25.00

1971-1972

No.	Description	Unused	Used
2A28	$4 black, *green*	45.00	1.00
a.	Ovptd. "NO FEE"		350.00
b.	Ovptd. "DISABLED VETERANS/NO FEE"		450.00
2A29	$1 black, *lavender*		20.00
2A30	$25 black, *peach*	275.00	35.00

1972-1973

No.	Description	Unused	Used
2A31	$6 black, *pink*		1.00
a.	Ovptd. "DISABLED VETERANS/NO FEE"		450.00
2A32	$2 black, *light yellow*		30.00
2A33	$35 black, *lavender*	225.00	

1973-1974

No.	Description	Unused	Used
2A34	$6 black, *blue*		1.00
a.	Ovptd. "DISABLED VETERANS/NO FEE"		450.00
2A35	$2 black, *lavender*	175.00	20.00
2A36	$35 black, *gray*	275.00	35.00

1974-1975

No.	Description	Unused	Used
2A37	$6 black, *green*	35.00	1.00
a.	Ovptd. "DISABLED VETERANS/NO FEE"		475.00
2A38	$2 black, *orange*		20.00
2A39	$35 black, *reddish purple*	175.00	25.00

1975-1976

No.	Description	Unused	Used
2A40	$10 red brown, *brown*	40.00	1.00
a.	Ovptd. "DISABLED VETERANS/NO FEE"	—	500.00
2A41	$2 black, *dark red*	80.00	20.00
2A42	$35 black, *yellow*	85.00	25.00

1976-1977

No.	Description	Unused	Used
2A43	$10 black, *blue*	30.00	1.00
a.	Ovptd. "DISABLED VETERANS/NO FEE"		800.00
2A44	$2 black, *gray violet*	100.00	20.00
a.	Inscibed "Deer Tag No." instead of "Bear Tag No."	—	
2A45	$35 black, *lavender*	85.00	25.00

1977-1978

No.	Description	Unused	Used
2A46	$10 black, *red orange*	30.00	1.00
a.	Ovptd. "DISABLED VETERANS/NO FEE"		450.00
2A47	$2 black, *yellow green*	95.00	25.00
2A48	$35 black, *pink*	95.00	

1978-1979

No.	Description	Unused	Used
2A49	$10 black, *yellow*	40.00	1.50
a.	Ovptd. "DISABLED VETERANS/NO FEE"		400.00
2A50	$2 black, *red*	80.00	20.00
2A51	$35 black, *light brown*	85.00	

1979-1980

No.	Description	Unused	Used
2A52	$10 black, *red*	30.00	1.00
a.	Ovptd. "DISABLED VETERANS/NO FEE"		400.00
2A53	$2 black, *yellow green*	80.00	20.00
2A54	$35 black, *dark blue*	85.00	

1980-1981

No.	Description	Unused	Used
2A55	$10.25 black, *blue*	30.00	1.00
a.	Ovptd. "DISABLED VETERANS/NO FEE"		1,000.
2A56	$2 black, *light brown*	75.00	15.00
2A57	$36.25 black, *tan*	75.00	25.00

1981-1982

No.	Description	Unused	Used
2A58	$11.50 black, *dark green*	30.00	1.00
2A59	$2.25 black, *blue*	75.00	20.00
2A60	$40 black, *gray*	200.00	

No.	Description	Unused	Used
	1982-1983		
2A61	$12.50 black, *pink*	30.00	1.00
2A62	$2.50 black, *brown*	75.00	20.00
2A63	$43.50 black, *orange*	*140.00*	
	1983-1984		
2A64	$13.25 black, *blue*	50.00	1.00
2A65	$2.75 black, *purple*	*150.00*	20.00
2A66	$46.50 black, *green*	*175.00*	
	1984-1985		
2A67	$13.25 black, *yellow*	*50.00*	1.00
2A68	$2.75 black, *green*	*150.00*	20.00
2A69	$49.25 black, *brown*	*175.00*	
	1985-1986		
2A70	$14 black, *blue*	*50.00*	1.00
2A71	$3.50 black, *yellow*	*150.00*	20.00
2A72	$51.75 black, *purple*	*175.00*	
	1986-1987		
2A73	$18.50 black, *green*		1.00
2A74	$4.50 black, *dark blue*		*15.00*
	1987-1988		
2A76	$17.50 black, *dark blue*		1.00
2A77	$4.50 black, *purple*		*15.00*
	1988-1989		
2A79	$19.25 black, *tan*		1.00
2A80	$5 black, *yellow*		*15.00*
	1989-1990		
2A82	$19.75 black, *blue gray*		1.00
2A83	$5 black, *dark green*		*15.00*
	1990-1991		
2A85	$21.50 black, *reddish gray*		1.00
2A86	$5.50 black, *yellow*		*15.00*
2A87	$73 black, *pink*		*25.00*
	1991-1992		
2A88	$23.10 black, *lime green*		1.00
2A89	$5.50 black, *bluish purple*		*15.00*
2A90	$79.80 black, *brown*		*25.00*
	1992-1993		
2A91	$24.15 black, *yellow*	—	1.00
2A92	$5.80 black, *greenish gold*		*15.00*
2A93	$83.75 black, *mauve*	—	*25.00*

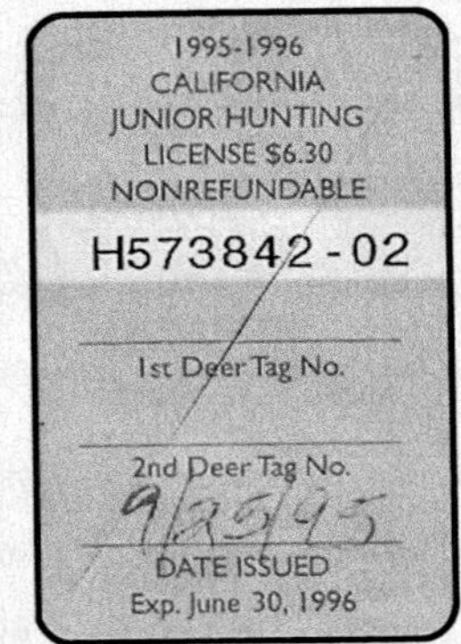

No.	Description	Unused	Used
	1993-1994		
2A94	$24.40 black & white, *green*		1.00
2A95	$5.80 black & white, *light blue*		*15.00*
	1994-1995		
2A97	$24.95 black & white, *pale yellow*		1.00
2A98	$6.05 black & white, *lavender*		*15.00*
2A99	$86.90 black & white, *gray*		*25.00*
	1996-1997		
2A100	$25.45 black, *gray brown*		1.00
2A101	$6.30 black, *pink*		*15.00*
2A102	$88.70 black, *pale blue*		*25.00*

Statewide Waterfowl Issues

Nos. 1-24 printed in booklet panes of five, No. 25 in pane of 4.

Issues through 1978 are die cut and self-adhesive. Starting with the 1979 issue, stamps are rouletted. Stamps are numbered serially.

Catalogue values for all unused stamps in this section are for Never Hinged items.

Artists: Paul Johnson, #1-8, 38; Ken Michaelson, #9; Walter Wolfe, #10-11; Robert Steiner, #12, 18-20, 26-35; Robert Richert, #13; Charles Allen, #14; Robert Montanucci, #15; Richard Wilson, #16; Sherrie Russell Meline, #17, 23, 37; Ronald Louque, #21; Larry Hayden, #22; Richard Clifton, #24-25, 43, 44; Richard Radigonda, #36; Harry Adamson, #39; Jeffrey Klinefelter, #40; Tim Taylor, #41; Shari Erickson, #42; John Nelson Harris, #45, 48; Chuck Black, #46; Guy Crittenden, #47.

Stamps valued with original backing paper. Caution should be used when buying especially Nos. 1 and 2. Both these issues have wider rouletting on the backing paper than Nos. 3-9.

1971-2017

No.	Description	Unused	Used
1	$1 Pintails	350.00	65.00
2	$1 Canvasbacks, *1972*	1,100.	150.00
3	$1 Mallards, *1973*	12.50	2.50
4	$1 White-fronted geese, *1974*	3.00	2.50
5	$1 Green-winged teal, backing paper with red wavy lines, *1975*	40.00	8.00
	Waxy backing paper without lines	140.00	

The gum bleeds through the stamp with red wavy lines resulting in a spotted or blotchy effect. Little or no gum bleeds through on stamps with waxy backing paper.

No.	Description	Unused	Used
6	$1 Widgeons, *1976*	22.50	2.50
7	$1 Cinnamon teal, *1977*	40.00	9.00
8	$5 Cinnamon teal, *1978*	12.50	2.50
9	$5 Hooded mergansers, *1978*	80.00	15.00
10	$5 Wood ducks, *1979*	9.00	2.50
11	$5 Pintails, *1980*	9.00	2.50
12	$5 Canvasbacks, *1981*	9.00	2.50
13	$5 Widgeons, *1982*	9.00	2.50
14	$5 Green-winged teal, *1983*	12.00	2.50
15	$7.50 Mallard decoy, *1984*	11.00	2.50
16	$7.50 Ring-necked ducks, *1985*	11.00	2.50
17	$7.50 Canada goose, *1986*	11.00	3.00
18	$7.50 Redheads, *1987*	11.00	3.00
19	$7.50 Mallards, *1988*	11.00	3.00
20	$7.50 Cinnamon teal, *1989*	11.00	3.00
21	$7.50 Canada goose, *1990*	11.00	3.00
22	$7.50 Gadwalls, *1991*	11.00	3.00
23	$7.90 White-fronted goose, *1992*	13.00	3.00
24	$10.50 Pintails, *1993*	16.00	4.00

Rouletted Horiz.

No.	Description	Unused	Used
25	$10.50 Wood duck, *1994*	15.00	4.00

Perf. Vertically

Birds in flight, denomination at: b, UL. c, UR. d, LL. e, LR.

No.	Description	Unused	Used
26	$10.50 Snow geese, booklet pane of 4, #b.-e., *1995*	65.00	
a.	Souvenir sheet of 4, #b.-e. (decorative border)	*125.00*	
b.-e.	Booklet single, each	15.00	4.00

Stamps in No. 26a are perfed on all four sides. No. 26a exists imperf. Value, $300.

Perf. Horizontally

No.	Description	Unused	Used
27	$10.50 Mallards, *1996*	16.00	2.50

Issued in panes of 4.

No.	Description	Unused	Used
28	$10.50 Pintails, *1997*	16.00	2.50
29	$10.50 Green-winged teal, pair, *1998*	32.50	
a.-b.	a, Female, b, Male, each	15.00	2.50

No. 29 issued in strips of 4 stamps.

No.	Description	Unused	Used
30	$10.50 Wood duck, pair, *1999*	40.00	
a.-b.	a, Male, b, Male and female, each	14.00	2.50

No. 30 issued in strips of 2 pairs.

No.	Description	Unused	Used
31	$10.50 Canada geese, mallard, widgeon *2000*	16.00	2.50
32	$10.50 Canvasbacks, *2001*	16.00	2.50
33	$10.50 Pintails, *2002*	16.00	2.50
34	$10.50 Mallards, *2003*	20.00	2.50
35	$13.90 Cinnamon teal, *2004*	17.00	2.50

Perf. Vertically

No.	Description	Unused	Used
36	$14.20 Pintails, *2005*	17.50	2.50
37	$14.95 White-fronted goose, *2006*	18.50	2.50
38	$16 Pintails, *2007*	30.00	2.50

Perf. Horizontally

No.	Description	Unused	Used
39	$16.80 Mallards, *2008*	24.00	2.50

Rouletted at Top

No.	Description	Unused	Used
40	$17.85 Shovelers, *2009*	24.00	2.50

Rouletted Horiz.

No.	Description	Unused	Used
41	$18.10 Redheads, *2010*	35.00	2.50
42	$18.93 Barrow's goldeneyes, *2011*	35.00	2.50
43	$19.44 Canada geese, *2012*	30.00	2.50
44	$20.01 Wigeons, *2013*	30.00	2.50
45	$20.26 Lesser scaup, *2014*	25.00	2.50
46	$20.52 Green-winged teal, *2015*	25.00	2.50
47	$20.52 Lesser snow geese, *2016*	25.00	2.50
48	$20.52 Ruddy duck, *2017*	25.00	2.50

COLORADO

North Central Goose Stamp

Used in an area extending from Ft. Collins to approximately 50 miles east of the city.

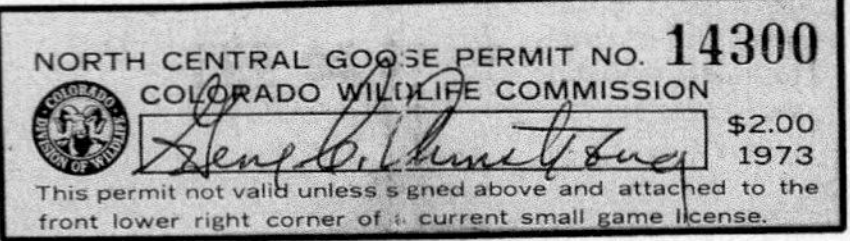

Illustration reduced.

1973

No.	Description	Unused	Used
A1	$2 black	—	—

No. A1 is die cut and self-adhesive. Unused stamps have glassine backing.

Statewide Issues

Printed in booklet panes of 5 and panes of 30. Stamps are numbered serially. Imperforate varieties of these stamps are printer's proofs.

Catalogue values for all unused stamps in this section are for Never Hinged items.

Artists: Robert Steiner, #1-2; Charles Allen, #3; Dan Andrews, #4, 29; Sarah Woods, #5; Cynthie Fisher, #6, 9-14; Bill Border, #7; Gerald G. Putt, #8; Jeffrey Klinefelter, #15-16, 18-19. Michael Ashman, #17; Craig Fairbert #20; Richard Clifton, #21-23, 25-26, 28; Charles Black, #24; Guy Crittenden, #27.

1990-2018

No.	Description	Unused	Used
1	$5 Canada geese	12.00	
	Bklt. single, with tab, Nos. 80,001-150,000	12.50	3.00
a.	$5 +$50 Governor's edition	60.00	
2	$5 Mallards, *1991*	17.50	
	Bklt. single, with tab, Nos. 80,001-150,000	16.00	3.00
a.	$5 +$50 Governor's edition	60.00	
3	$5 Pintails, *1992*	10.00	
	Bklt. single, with tab, Nos. 80,001-150,000	10.00	3.00
a.	$5 +$50 Governor's edition	60.00	
4	$5 Green-winged teal, *1993*	12.00	
	Bklt. single, with tab, Nos. 80,001-150,000	12.00	3.00
a.	$5 +$50 Governor's edition	60.00	
5	$5 Wood ducks, *1994*	12.00	
	Bklt. single, with tab	12.00	2.50
6	$5 Buffleheads, *1995*	12.00	
	Bklt. single, with tab	12.00	2.50
7	$5 Cinnamon teal, *1996*	12.00	
	Bklt. single, with tab and top selvage	12.00	2.50
8	$5 Widgeons, gold text, *1997*	10.00	
a.	Bklt. single, with tab and top selvage, text in black & white	12.00	2.50
9	$5 Redheads, *1998*	10.00	
a.	Bklt. single, with tab and side selvage	10.00	2.50
10	$5 Blue-winged teal, *1999*	10.00	
a.	Blkt. single, with tab and side selvage	10.00	2.50
11	$5 Gadwalls, *2000*	10.00	
a.	Bklt. single, with tab and side selvage	10.00	2.50
12	$5 Ruddy ducks, *2001*	10.00	2.50
a.	Bklt. single, with tab	*2,000.*	
13	$5 Common goldeneyes, *2002*	10.00	2.50
a.	Bklt. single, with tab	*700.00*	
14	$5 Canvasbacks, *2003*	10.00	2.50
15	$5 Snow geese, *2004*	10.00	2.50
16	$5 Shovelers, *2005*	10.00	2.50
17	$5 Ring-necked ducks, *2006*	10.00	2.50
18	$5 Hooded mergansers, *2007*	10.00	2.50
19	$5 Lesser scaup, *2008*	10.00	2.50
20	$5 Barrow's goldeneye, *2009*	10.00	2.50
21	$5 Pintails, *2010*	10.00	2.50
22	$5 Green-winged teal, *2011*	10.00	2.50
23	$5 Ross's geese, *2012*	10.00	2.50
24	$5 Greater scaups, *2013*	9.00	2.50
25	$5 Canada geese, *2014*	9.00	2.50
26	($7.50) Wood ducks, *2015*	10.00	2.50

27	($10) Mallards, *2016*	15.00	2.50
28	($10) Redheads, *2017*	15.00	2.50
29	($10) Ring-necked ducks, *2018*	7.50	2.50

CONNECTICUT

Printed in booklet panes of 10 and sheets of 30.
Stamps are numbered serially.
Imperforate varieties are proofs.

Catalogue values for all unused stamps in this section are for Never Hinged items.

Artists: Thomas Hirata, #1; Robert Leslie, #2, 9; Phillip Crowe, #3; Keith Mueller, #4, 7, 15; Robert Steiner, #5; Joe Hautman, #6; George Lockwood, #8; Robert Richert, #10; Paul Fusco, #11-14; Burt Schuman, #16; Clint Herdman, #17-19; Richard Clifton, #20, John Brennan, #21; Guy Crittenden, #22; Jeffrey Klinefelter, #23; Mark Throne, #24-25.

1993-2018

1	$5 Black ducks	12.00	3.00
	Booklet pane pair with L & R selvage, Nos. 51,001-81,000	24.00	
a.	Sheet of 4	85.00	
b.	$5 +$50 Governor's edition	70.00	
2	$5 Canvasbacks, *1994*	11.00	3.00
	Booklet pair with L & R selvage, Nos. 53,000-up	22.50	
a.	Sheet of 4	55.00	
3	$5 Mallards, *1995*	15.00	3.00
	Booklet pair with L & R selvage	30.00	
4	$5 Oldsquaw ducks, *1996*	16.00	3.00
	Booklet pair with L & R selvage	32.50	
5	$5 Green-winged teal, *1997*	11.00	3.00
a.	$5 +$50 Governor's edition	*150.00*	
6	$5 Mallards, *1998*	10.00	3.00
7	$5 Canada geese, *1999*	15.00	3.00
a.	$5 +$50 Governor's edition	*450.00*	
8	$5 Wood duck, *2000*	10.00	3.00
a.	$5 +$50 Governor's edition	*425.00*	
9	$5 Buffleheads, *2001*	9.00	3.00
a.	$5 +$50 Governor's edition	*425.00*	
10	$5 Greater scaups, *2002*	12.00	3.00
a.	$5 +$50 Governor's edition	*450.00*	

11	$5 Black Duck, *2003*	10.00	3.00
12	$5 Wood duck, *2004*	25.00	3.00
13	$10 Mallards, *2005*	14.00	3.00
14	$10 Buffleheads, *2006*	25.00	3.00
15	$10 Black duck decoy, *2007*	14.00	3.00
16	$10 Common goldeneyes, *2008*	14.00	3.00

17	$10 Black duck, *2009*	16.00	3.00

18	$13 Common goldeneyes, *2010*	25.00	3.00
19	$13 Pintail, *2012*	21.00	3.00
20	$13 Wood ducks, *2013*	21.00	3.00
21	$13 Hooded mergansers, *2014*	21.00	3.00
22	$13 Shovelers, *2015*	21.00	3.00
23	$13 Atlantic brant, *2016*	21.00	3.00
24	$17 Canvasbacks and lighthouse, *2017*	27.50	4.00

Self-Adhesive

25	$17 Surf scoters and lighthouse, *2018*	27.50	4.00

DELAWARE

Printed in sheets of 10.
Starting in 1991, a portion of the printing is numbered serially on the reverse.

Catalogue values for all unused stamps in this section are for Never Hinged items.

Artists: Ned Mayne, #1; Charles Rowe, #2; Lois Butler, #3; John Green, #4; Nolan Haan, #5; Don Breyfogle, #6; Robert Leslie, #7, 10; Bruce Langton, #8; Jim Hautman, #9; Francis Sweet, #11; Ronald Louque, #12; Richard Clifton, #13, 17, 19, 26, 30, 34, 36; Robert Metropulos, #14; Louis Frisino, #15; Michael Ashman, #16, 21; Jeffrey Klinefelter, #18, 24, 35; Russ Duerksen, #20; Brian Blight, #22; George Lockwood, #23, 28; Bonnie Field, #25; Joanna Rivera, #26; John Stewart, #29; Steve Oliver, #31; George LaVanish, #32; Tom Morgan Crain, #33; Dee Dee Murry, #37; Catherine Temple, #38; Daniel Allard, #39.

1980-2018

1	$5 Black ducks	65.00	20.00
2	$5 Snow geese, *1981*	50.00	20.00
3	$5 Canada geese, *1982*	50.00	20.00
4	$5 Canvasbacks, *1983*	35.00	10.00
5	$5 Mallards, *1984*	15.00	5.00
6	$5 Pintail, *1985*	12.00	3.00
7	$5 Widgeons, *1986*	11.00	3.00
8	$5 Redheads, *1987*	11.00	3.00
9	$5 Wood ducks, *1988*	9.00	3.00
10	$5 Buffleheads, *1989*	9.00	3.00
11	$5 Green-winged teal, *1990*	10.00	3.00
a.	$5 +$50 Governor's edition	85.00	
12	$5 Hooded merganser, no serial number on reverse, *1991*	10.00	
	With serial number on reverse	11.00	3.00
13	$5 Blue-winged teal, no serial number on reverse, *1992*	10.00	
	With serial number on reverse	10.00	2.50
14	$5 Goldeneye, no serial number on reverse, *1993*	10.00	
	With serial number on reverse	10.00	2.50
15	$5 Blue goose, no serial number on reverse, *1994*	12.00	
	With serial number on reverse	12.00	2.50
16	($6) Scaup, no serial number on reverse, *1995*	11.00	
	With serial number on reverse	11.00	2.50
17	$6 Gadwall, no serial number on reverse, *1996*	12.00	
	With serial number on reverse	12.00	2.50
18	$6 White-winged scoter, no serial number on reverse, *1997*	12.00	
	With serial number on reverse	12.00	2.50
19	$6 Blue-winged teal, *1998*	11.00	2.50
20	$6 Tundra swan, *1999*	11.00	
21	$6 American brant, *2000*	12.00	2.50
22	$6 Oldsquaw, *2001*	11.00	2.50
23	$6 Ruddy ducks, *2002*	11.00	2.50
24	$9 Ring-necked ducks, *2003*	12.00	3.00
25	$9 Black scoters and lighthouse, *2004*	12.00	3.00
a.	$9 +$50 Governor's edition	95.00	
26	$9 Common mergansers and lighthouse, *2005*	12.00	3.00
a.	$9 +$50 Governor's edition	75.00	
27	$9 Red-breasted mergansers, *2006*	12.00	3.00
28	$9 Surf scoters, lighthouse *2007*	12.00	3.00
29	$9 Greater scaup, lighthouse, *2008*	12.00	3.00
30	$9 Black ducks, *2009*	12.00	3.00
31	$9 Canvasback, *2010*	12.00	3.00
32	$9 Hooded mergansers, *2011*	12.00	3.00
33	$9 Lesser scaup, *2012*	12.00	3.00
34	$9 Wigeon, *2013*	12.00	3.00
35	$9 Blue-winged teal, *2014*	12.00	3.00
a.	$9 +$50 Governor's edition	85.00	
36	$9 Black ducks, *2015*	13.00	3.00
37	$9 Green-winged teal, yellow Labrador retriever, *2016*	13.00	3.00
38	$15 Canvasbacks, Chesapeake retriever, *2017*	24.00	4.00
39	$15 Pintails, Golden retriever, *2018*	20.00	4.00

FLORIDA

#1-7 issued in booklet panes of 5. Nos. 8-19 in sheets of 10. No. 20 in sheet of 12.
Stamps are numbered serially and rouletted. Serial numbers for stamps with survey tabs attached end in -04.

Catalogue values for all unused stamps in this section are for Never Hinged items.

Illustration reduced.

Artists: Bob Binks, #1, 7; Ernest Simmons, #2; Clark Sullivan, #3; Lee Cable, #4; Heiner Hertling, #5; John Taylor, #6; Robert Steiner, #8; Ronald Louque, #9-10; J. Byron Test, #11; Ben Test, #12; Richard Hansen, #13; Richard Clifton, #14; John Mogus, #15; Antonie Rossini, #16; Kenneth Nanney, #17; Wally Makuchal, #18; M. Frase, #19; Brian Blight, #20; John Harris, #21, 23; Jeffrey Klinefelter, #22; John Nelson Harris, #24.

1979-2003

1	$3.25 Green-winged teal	140.00	20.00
	With tab	175.00	
2	$3.25 Pintails, *1980*	15.00	5.00
	With tab	20.00	

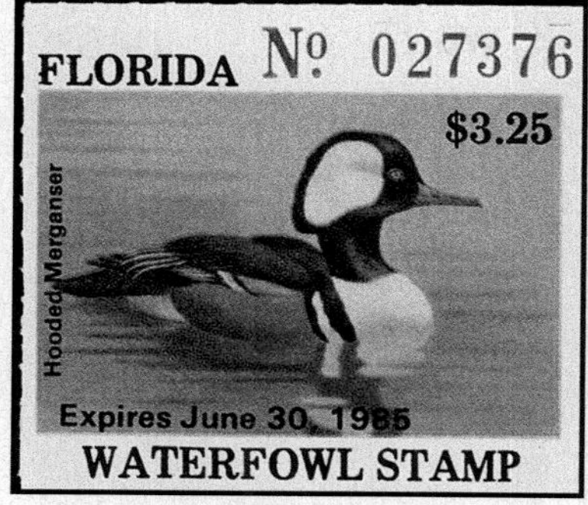

3	$3.25 Widgeon, *1981*	15.00	5.00
	With tab	40.00	
4	$3.25 Ring-necked ducks, *1982*	22.50	5.00
	With tab	30.00	
5	$3.25 Buffleheads, *1983*	45.00	5.00
	With tab	60.00	
6	$3.25 Hooded merganser, *1984*	11.00	3.50
	With tab	35.00	
7	$3.25 Wood ducks, *1985*	11.00	3.50
	With tab	30.00	
8	$3 Canvasbacks, *1986*	11.00	3.50
	With small tab at top	11.00	
	With larger survey tab at side and small tab at top	25.00	
9	$3.50 Mallards, *1987*	9.00	3.50
	With small tab at top	9.00	
	With larger survey tab at side and small tab at top	25.00	

10 $3.50 Redheads, *1988* 8.00 2.50
With small tab at top 8.00
With larger survey tab at side and small tab at top 20.00
11 $3.50 Blue-winged teal, *1989* 8.00 2.50
With small tab at top 8.00
With larger survey tab at side and small tab at top 35.00
12 $3.50 Wood ducks, *1990* 8.00 2.50
With small tab at top 8.00
With larger survey tab at side and small tab at top 35.00
13 $3.50 Northern Pintails, *1991* 9.00 2.50
With small tab at top 9.00
With larger survey tab at side and small tab at top 30.00
14 $3.50 Ruddy duck, *1992* 8.00 2.50
With small tab at top 7.00
With larger survey tab at side and small tab at top 12.00
15 $3.50 American widgeon, *1993* 8.00 2.50
With small tab at top 8.00
With larger survey tab at side and small tab at top 27.50
16 $3.50 Mottled duck, *1994* 9.00 2.50
With small tab at top 9.00
With larger survey tab at side and small tab at top 27.50
17 $3.50 Fulvous whistling duck, *1995* 9.00 2.50
With small tab at top 9.00
With larger survey tab at side and small tab at top 27.50
18 $3.50 Goldeneyes, *1996* 15.00 2.50
With small tab at top 15.00
With larger survey tab at side and small tab at top 27.50
19 ($3.00) Hooded merganser, *1997* 11.00 2.50
With small tab at top 11.00
With larger survey tab at side and small tab at top 27.50

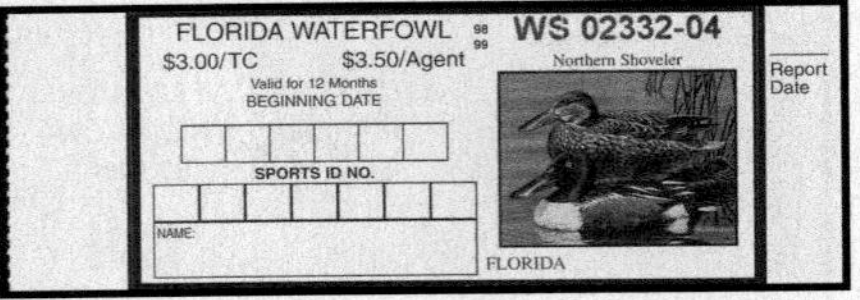

Self-Adhesive

20 $3 Shoveler, *1998* 35.00 2.50

Sold for $3.50 through agents.

21 $3 Pintail, *1999* 12.00 2.50

Sold for $3.50 through agents.

22 $3 Ring-necked duck, *2000* 10.00 2.50

Sold for $3.50 through agents.

23 $3 Canvasback, *2001* 10.00 2.50

Sold for $3.50 through agents.

24 $3 Mottled duck, *2002* 20.00 2.50

Sold for $3.50 through agents. No. 24 with rouletting and with duck facing right come from a special limited reprinting demanded by the artist to correct the appearance of his work. Value, $95.

The 2003 stamp was sold by Florida officials only to the stamp's artist. Values: $125; with small tab at top, $165.

GEORGIA

Not required to hunt waterfowl until 1989.
Nos. 1-4 printed in sheets of 30, others in sheets of 20.
Starting with No 5, stamps are numbered serially.

Catalogue values for all unused stamps in this section are for Never Hinged items.

Artists: Daniel Smith, #1; Jim Killen, #2, 14; James Partee, Jr., #3; Paul Bridgeford, #4; Ralph J. McDonald, #5; Guy Coheleach, #6; Phillip Crowe, #7-8, 11; Jerry Raedeke, #9, 13, 15; Herb Booth, #10; David Lanier, #12.

1985-99

1 $5.50 Wood ducks 15.00
2 $5.50 Mallards, *1986* 9.00
3 $5.50 Canada geese, *1987* 9.00
4 $5.50 Ring-necked ducks, *1988* 9.00
5 $5.50 Duckling & golden retriever puppy, *1989* 14.00 2.50
6 $5.50 Wood ducks, *1990* 9.00 2.50
7 $5.50 Green-winged teal, *1991* 9.50 2.50
8 $5.50 Buffleheads, *1992* 15.00 2.50
9 $5.50 Mallards, *1993* 15.00 2.50
10 $5.50 Ring-necked ducks, *1994* 15.00 2.50
11 $5.50 Widgeons, Labrador retriever, *1995* 32.50 2.50
12 $5.50 Black ducks, *1996* 25.00 2.50
13 $5.50 Lesser scaup, Cockspur Island lighthouse, *1997* 40.00 2.50
14 $5.50 Labrador retriever, ring-necked ducks, *1998* 27.50 2.50
15 $5.50 Pintails, *1999* 22.50 2.50

HAWAII

Required for the hunting of small game. Hunting birds was illegal in Hawaii until 2003. Game bird hunting was permitted beginning July 1, 2003. Game birds that can be hunted include pheasants, francolins, partridges, quail, sand grouses, doves and wild turkeys.

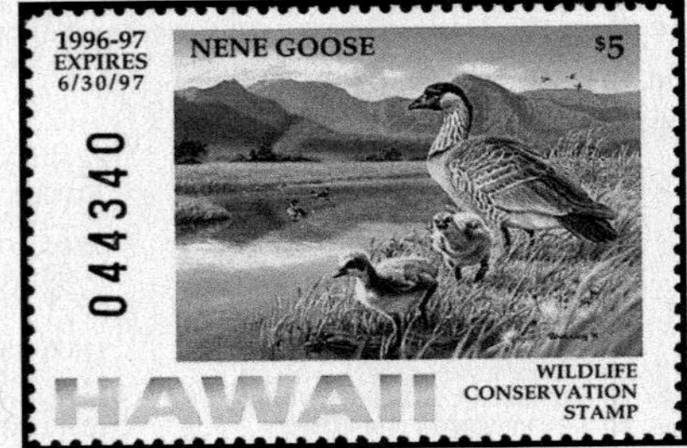

Artists: Patrick Ching, #1, D. Van Zyle, #2; Michael Furuya, #3, 16; Norman Nagai, #4, 7, 10, 13, 14; Marion Berger, #5; Daniel Wang, #6, 15; Joy Keown, #8, 9. Shane Hamamoto, #11. Dan Hoyes, #12; Carol Tredway, #17-18, 20; David Hayes, #19; James Basham, #21.

1996-2018

1 $5 Nene goose 9.00
With tab 9.00
a. $5 +$50 Governor's edition 75.00
b. As No. 1, sheet of 4 125.00

No. 1b exists imperf. Value, $175.

2 $5 Hawaiian duck, *1997* 9.00
With tab 12.00
a. As No. 2, sheet of 4 45.00

No. 2a exists imperf. Value, $195.

3 $5 Wild turkey, *1998* 10.00
With tab 12.00
4 $5 Ring-necked pheasant, *1999* 10.00
With tab 12.00
5 $5 Erckel's francolin, *2000* 10.00
With tab 12.00
6 $5 Green pheasant, *2001* 10.00
With tab 12.00
7 $10 Chukar partridge, *2002* 15.00
8 $10 Nene geese, *2003* 15.00
9 $10 Nene geese, *2004* 15.00
10 $10 California quail, *2005* 15.00
11 $10 Black francolin, *2006* 15.00
12 $10 Gray francolin, *2007* 15.00
13 $10 Chukar partridge, *2008* 15.00
14 $10 California quail, *2009* 15.00
15 $10 Green pheasant, *2011* 15.00
16 $10 Wild turkey, *2011* 15.00
17 $10 Mouflon sheep, *2012* 15.00
18 $10 Mouflon sheep, *2015* 16.00
19 $10 Axis deer, *2016* 16.00
20 $10 Pheasant, wild sheep, *2017* 16.00
21 $10 Boar, *2018* 16.00

IDAHO

Printed in booklet panes of 5 and sheets of 30, except No. 5, which was issued in booklets of 10. Numbered serially except for No. 11.

Catalogue values for all unused stamps in this section are for Never Hinged items.

Artists: Robert Leslie, #1; Jim Killen, #2; Daniel Smith, #3; Francis E. Sweet, #4, Richard Clifton, #6, 11; Richard Plasschaert, #7; Sherrie Russell Meline, #8; Bill Moore, #9; David Gressard, #10; T. Smith, #12; Maynard Reece, #13.

1987-98

1 $5.50 Cinnamon teal, perforated 15.00
a. Bklt. single, rouletted, with 2-part tab 12.00 3.00
2 $5.50 Green-winged teal, perforated, *1988* 13.00
a. Bklt. single, rouletted, with 2-part tab 13.00 3.00
3 $6 Blue-winged teal, perforated, *1989* 10.00
a. Bklt. single, rouletted, with 2-part tab 11.00 3.00
4 $6 Trumpeter swans, perforated, *1990* 21.00
a. Bklt. single, rouletted, with 2-part tab 21.00 3.00

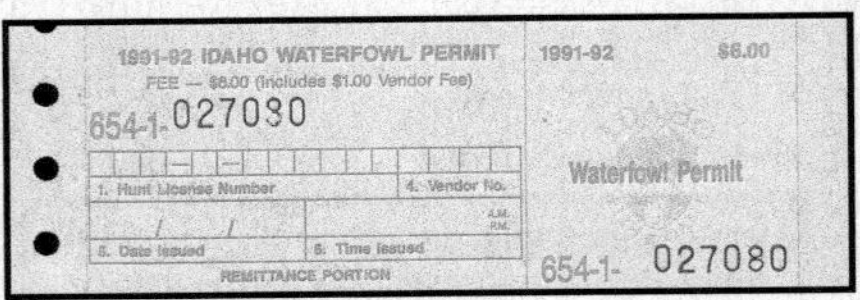

Die cut self-adhesive

5 $6 green, *1991* 175.00 *35.00*

No. 5 was used provisionally in 1991 when the regular stamps were delayed. Unused value is for stamp, remittance tab and selvage pieces on backing paper.

Designs like No. 1

6 $6 Widgeons, perforated, *1991* 10.00
a. Bklt. single, rouletted, with 2-part tab 10.00 2.50
7 $6 Canada geese, perforated, *1992* 10.00
a. Bklt. single, rouletted, with 2-part tab 10.00 2.50
8 $6.00 Common goldeneye, perforated, *1993* 12.00
a. Bklt. single, rouletted, with 2-part tab 12.00 2.50
9 $6 Harlequin ducks, perforated, *1994* 12.00
a. Bklt. single, rouletted, with 2-part tab 12.00 2.50
10 $6 Wood ducks, perforated, *1995* 12.00
a. Bklt. single, rouletted, with 2-part tab 12.00 2.50
11 $6.50 Mallard, *1996* 16.00 2.50
12 $6.50 Shovelers, *1997* 22.50 2.50
13 $6.50 Canada geese, *1998* 15.00 2.50

ILLINOIS

Daily Usage Stamps for State-operated Waterfowl Areas.

Date and fee overprinted in black. $2 and $3 stamps were for hunting ducks, $5 stamps for hunting geese and pheasants. 1953-58 had separate pheasant stamps. No duck stamp was printed in 1971.

Some unused stamps have dry gum.

Used stamps have no gum or have staple holes.

Black printing.

Stamps are numbered serially.

1951-1972

No.	Description	Unused	Used
A1	$2 yellow, *manila*, imperf., 1951	—	
A2	$2 green, *manila, 1952*	—	
A3	$2 orange, *blue, 1953*	—	—
A4	$2 green, *manila, 1956*	—	—
A5	$2 orange, *light blue green, 1957*	*550.*	*300.*
A6	$2 green, *manila, 1958*	*450.*	*300.*
A7	$3 green, *manila, 1959*	*375.*	*250.*
A8	$5 red brown, *light blue green, 1959*	*375.*	*250.*
A9	$3 red brown, *light blue green, 1960*	*375.*	*250.*
A10	$5 green, *manila, 1960*	*375.*	*250.*
A11	$3 green, *manila, 1961*	*375.*	*250.*
A12	$5 red brown, *light blue green, 1961*	*375.*	*250.*
A13	$3 green, *manila, 1962*	*375.*	*250.*
A14	$5 red brown, *light blue green, 1962*	*375.*	*250.*
A15	$3 orange, *light blue green, 1963*	*375.*	*250.*
A16	$5 green, *manila, 1963*	*375.*	*250.*
A17	$3 green, *manila, 1964*	*375.*	*250.*
A18	$5 red, *light blue green, 1964*	*375.*	*250.*
A19	$3 orange, *light blue green, 1965*	*375.*	*250.*
A20	$5 green, *manila, 1965*	*375.*	*250.*
A21	$3 green, *manila, 1966*	*375.*	*250.*
A22	$5 orange, *light blue green, 1966*	*375.*	*250.*
A23	$3 orange, *light blue green, 1967*	*375.*	*250.*
A24	$5 green, *yellow, 1967*	*375.*	*250.*
A25	$3 green, *yellow, 1968*	*375.*	*250.*
A26	$5 orange, *light blue, 1968*	*375.*	*250.*
A27	$3 orange, *light blue, 1969*	*375.*	*250.*
A28	$5 green, *manila, 1969*	*375.*	*250.*
A29	$3 green, *manila, 1970*	*1,500.*	*900.*
A30	$5 orange, *light blue, 1970*	*1,750.*	*900.*
A31	$5 green, *manila, 1971*	*1,950.*	*1,000.*
A32	$3 orange, *light blue green, 1972*	*9,500.*	
A33	$5 orange, *light blue green, 1972*	*8,500.*	*2,500.*

Catalogue values for unused stamps in this section, from this point to the end, are for Never Hinged items.

No. A34

No. A35

1977-91(?)

No.	Description	Unused	Used
A34	black, *light blue*, duck, *1991*	—	—
A35	black, *manila*, goose	—	—

Nos. A34-A35 do not show year or denomination and were used until 1994. No. A34 used before 1991 should exist but has not been reported yet. Separate pheasant and controlled quail and pheasant stamps of a similar design have also been used.

No. A36

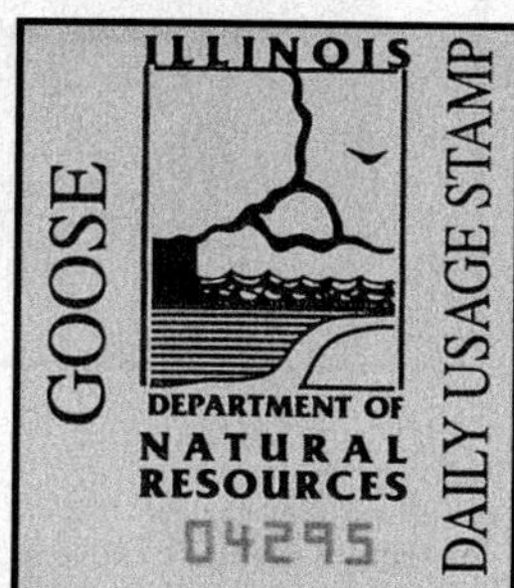

No. A37

1996

No.	Description	Unused	Used
A36	black, *light blue*, duck	—	—
A37	black, *manila*, goose	—	—

Nos. A36-A37 do not show year or denomination.

Statewide Issues

Nos. 1-10 in sheets of 10. Starting with No. 11, in booklet panes of 5; starting with No. 22, in panes of 10.

Stamps are numbered serially and rouletted.

Catalogue values for all unused stamps in this section are for Never Hinged items.

Artists: Robert Eschenfeldt, #1; Robert G. Larson, #2; Richard Lynch, #3; Everett Staffeldt, #4; John Eggert, #5; Bart Kassabaum, #6, 9, 11, 13; Jim Trindel, #7; Arthur Sinden, #8, 12, 14; George Kieffer, #10; Charles McKay Freeman, #15; John Henson, #16; Phillip Crowe, #17-21; Thomas Hirata, #22-24; Jim Killen, #25-29; Gerald Putt, #30-32. Christina Van Dellen, #33; Karen Latham, #34; Abraham Hunter, #35-36.

1975-2010

No.	Description	Unused	Used
1	$5 Mallard	*325.00*	75.00
2	$5 Wood ducks, *1976*	*150.00*	50.00
3	$5 Canada goose, *1977*	100.00	35.00
4	$5 Canvasbacks, *1978*	100.00	22.50
5	$5 Pintail, *1979*	85.00	16.00
6	$5 Green-winged teal, *1980*	75.00	16.00
7	$5 Widgeons, *1981*	85.00	16.00
a.	"Green-winged teal"	*225.00*	
8	$5 Black ducks, *1982*	60.00	12.50
9	$5 Lesser scaup, *1983*	75.00	10.00
10	$5 Blue-winged teal, *1984*	60.00	10.00
11	$5 Redheads, *1985*	16.00	3.00
	With 2-part tab	22.50	
12	$5 Gadwalls, *1986*	12.00	3.00
	With 2-part tab	20.00	
13	$5 Buffleheads, *1987*	12.00	3.00
	With 2-part tab	15.00	
14	$5 Common goldeneyes, *1988*	12.00	2.50
	With 2-part tab	15.00	
15	$5 Ring-necked ducks, *1989*	10.00	2.50
	With 2-part tab	10.00	
16	$10 Lesser snow geese, *1990*	16.00	3.00
	With 2-part tab	17.00	
17	$10 Labrador retriever & Canada goose, *1991*	16.00	3.00
	With 2-part tab	16.00	
a.	Governor's edition with tab	*85.00*	
18	$10 Retriever & mallards, *1992*	25.00	3.00
	With 2-part tab	27.50	
19	$10 Pintail decoys and puppy, *1993*	32.50	3.00
	With 2-part tab	35.00	
20	$10 Canvasbacks & retrievers, *1994*	32.50	3.00
	With 2-part tab	35.00	
21	$10 Retriever, green-winged teal, decoys, *1995*	32.50	3.00
	With 2-part tab	35.00	
22	$10 Wood ducks, *1996*	20.00	2.50
23	$10 Canvasbacks, *1997*	17.50	2.50
24	$10 Canada geese, *1998*	17.50	2.50
25	$10 Canada geese, black Labrador retriever, *1999*	22.50	2.50
a.	Anniversary edition, perforated	*92.50*	
b.	Governor's edition, perforated	*92.50*	
c.	Silver edition, perforated	*92.50*	

Nos. 25a-25c were sold as a set of three.

No.	Description	Unused	Used
26	$10 Mallards, golden retriever, *2000*	22.50	2.50
27	$10 Pintails, yellow Labrador retriever, *2001*	22.50	2.50
28	$10 Canvasbacks, Chesapeake retriever, *2002*	22.50	2.50
29	$10 Green-winged teal, Labrador retriever, *2003*	17.50	2.50
30	$10 Wood ducks, *2004*	17.50	2.50
31	$10 Green-winged teals, *2005*	17.50	2.50
32	$10 Northern pintails, *2006*	17.50	2.50
33	$10 Bufflehead, *2007*	17.50	2.50
34	$10 Greater scaup, *2008*	40.00	2.50
35	$10 Common goldeneyes, *2009*	75.00	2.50
36	$15 Blue-winged teal, *2010*	40.00	2.50

INDIANA

Issued in booklet panes of 4 (Nos. 1-10) and booklet panes of 2, starting with No. 11.

Stamps are numbered serially and rouletted.

Catalogue values for all unused stamps in this section are for Never Hinged items.

Artists: Justin H. (Sonny) Bashore, #1-2; Carl (Spike) Knuth, #3; Daniel Renn Pierce, #4; Dean Barrick, #5; Rodney Crossman, #6; George Metz, #7; Kieth Freeman, #8; Lyn Briggs, #9; Rick Pas, #10; Ronald Louque, #11; Susan Hastings Bates, #12.

Bruce Langton, #13, 17; Ann Dahoney, #14; Ken Bucklew, #15, 20, 22, 24, 29, 32; Richard Hansen, #16; Jeffrey Klinefelter, #18, 26, 28, 30, 33, 34-38, 39; Jeffrey Mobley. #19; Charles Riggles, #21, 23, 31; George Lockwood, #25; Biran Blight, 27.

1976-2014

No.	Description	Unused	Used
1	$5 Green-winged teal, *1976*	12.00	2.50
2	$5 Pintail, *1977*	10.00	2.50
3	$5 Canada geese, *1978*	8.00	2.50
4	$5 Canvasbacks, *1979*	8.00	2.50
5	$5 Mallard ducklings, *1980*	8.00	2.50
6	$5 Hooded mergansers, *1981*	8.00	2.50
7	$5 Blue-winged teal, *1982*	8.00	2.50
8	$5 Snow geese, *1983*	8.00	2.50
9	$5 Redheads, *1984*	8.00	2.50
10	$5 Pintail, *1985*	10.00	2.50
	With tab	10.50	
11	$5 Wood duck, *1986*	8.00	2.50
	With tab	10.00	
12	$5 Canvasbacks, *1987*	8.00	2.50
	With tab	10.00	
13	$6.75 Redheads, *1988*	10.00	2.50
	With tab	10.50	
14	$6.75 Canada goose, *1989*	10.00	2.50
	With tab	10.50	
15	$6.75 Blue-winged teal, *1990*	10.00	2.50
	With tab	10.50	
16	$6.75 Mallards, *1991*	10.00	2.50
	With tab	10.50	
17	$6.75 Green-winged teal, *1992*	10.00	2.50
	With tab	10.50	
18	$6.75 Wood ducks, *1993*	10.00	2.50
	With tab	10.50	

19	$6.75 Pintail, *1994*	10.00	2.50
	With tab	10.50	
20	$6.75 Goldeneyes, *1995*	10.00	2.50
	With tab	10.50	
21	$6.75 Black ducks, *1996*	10.00	2.50
	With tab	10.50	
22	$6.75 Canada geese, *1997*	10.00	2.50
	With tab	10.50	
23	$6.75 Widgeon, *1998*	10.00	2.50
	With tab	10.50	
24	$6.75 Bluebills, *1999*	9.00	2.50
	With tab	10.00	
25	$6.75 Ring-necked duck, *2000*	9.00	2.50
	With tab	10.00	
26	$6.75 Hooded mergansers, *2001*	9.00	2.50
	With tab	10.00	
27	$6.75 Green-winged teal, *2002*	9.00	2.50
	With tab	10.00	
28	$6.75 Northern shovelers, *2003*	9.00	2.50
	With tab	10.00	
29	$6.75 Wood duck, *2004*	9.00	2.50
	With tab	10.00	
30	$6.75 Buffleheads, *2005*	9.00	2.50
	With tab	10.00	
31	$6.75 Gadwalls, *2006*	9.00	2.50
	With tab	10.00	
32	$6.75 Pintails, *2007*	9.00	2.50
	With tab	10.00	
33	$6.75 Shovelers, *2008*	9.00	2.50
	With tab	10.00	
34	$6.75 Snow geese, *2009*	9.00	2.50
	With tab	10.00	
35	$6.75 Black duck, *2010*	20.00	2.50
	With tab	25.00	
36	$6.75 Wigeon, *2011*	9.00	2.50
	With tab	10.00	
37	$6.75 Canada geese, *2012*	20.00	2.50
	With tab	25.00	
38	$6.75 Wood ducks, *2013*	9.00	2.50
	With tab	10.00	
39	$6.75 Blue-winged teal, *2014*	9.00	2.50
	With tab	10.00	

IOWA

Catalogue values for all unused stamps in this section are for Never Hinged items.

Issued in booklet pane of 5 (No. 1), 10 (others) and sheets of 10 (No. 19).

Artists: Maynard Reece, #1, 6, 22; Thomas Murphy, #2; James Landenberger, #3; Mark Reece, #4; Nick Klepinger, #5, 7; Andrew Peters, #8; Paul Brigford, #9, 12, 15; Brad Reece, #10; Tom Walker, #11; Larry Zach, #13. Jack C. Hahn, #14, 18; John Heidersbach, #16; Mark Cary, #17; Patrick Murillo, #19; Jerry Raedeke, #20; Charlotte Edwards, #21, 26; Dietmar Krumrey, #23, 25, 33; Cynthia Fisher, #24; Sherrie Russell Meline, #27, 29, 35; Mark Anderson, #28; Darren Maurer, #30, 31, 36, 40-41; Neal Anderson, #32, 34; Ronnie Hughes, #37; Mark Kness #38; Tomas Miller, #39; Jeffrey Klinefelter, #42; Jeffrey Hoff, #43; Mike Brown, #44.

1972-98

1	$1 Mallards	100.00	25.00
2	$1 Pintails, *1973*	35.00	7.50
3	$1 Gadwalls, rouletted, *1974*	85.00	7.00
4	$1 Canada geese, *1975*	95.00	9.00
5	$1 Canvasbacks, *1976*	25.00	2.50
6	$1 Lesser scaup, rouletted, *1977*	21.00	2.50
7	$1 Wood ducks, rouletted, *1978*	50.00	5.00
8	$5 Buffleheads, *1979*	250.00	25.00
9	$5 Redheads, *1980*	27.50	6.00
10	$5 Green-winged teal, rouletted, *1981*	27.50	4.00
11	$5 Snow geese, rouletted, *1982*	18.00	2.50
12	$5 Widgeons, *1983*	18.00	2.75
13	$5 Wood ducks, *1984*	35.00	3.00
14	$5 Mallard & mallard decoy, *1985*	20.00	2.50
15	$5 Blue-winged teal, *1986*	15.00	2.50
16	$5 Canada goose, *1987*	15.00	2.50
17	$5 Pintails, *1988*	15.00	2.50
18	$5 Blue-winged teal, *1989*	15.00	2.50
19	$5 Canvasbacks, *1990*	10.00	2.50
20	$5 Mallards, *1991*	10.00	2.50
21	$5 Labrador retriever & ducks, *1992*	10.00	2.50
22	$5 Mallards, *1993*	10.00	2.50
23	$5 Green-winged teal, *1994*	10.00	2.50
24	$5 Canada geese, *1995*	10.00	2.50
25	$5 Canvasbacks, *1996*	10.00	2.50
26	$5 Canada geese, *1997*	10.00	2.50
27	$5 Pintails, *1998*	12.00	2.50

1999

28	Trumpeter swan, *1999*	30.00	2.50

No. 28 not required for hunting. The Department of Natural Resources sent customers No. 28 upon receipt of a postcard given to the customer after paying license fee of $5.

2000

29	Hooded merganser, *2000*	15.00	2.50

No. 29 not required for hunting. The Department of Natural Resources sent customers No. 29 upon receipt of a postcard given to the customer after paying license fee of $5.

2001

30	Snow goose, *2001*	15.00	2.50

No. 30 not required for hunting. The Department of Natural Resources sent customers No. 30 upon receipt of a postcard given to the customer after paying license fee of $5.

2002-15

31	Shovelers, *2002*	17.50	4.00
32	Ruddy duck, *2003*	15.00	4.00
33	Wood ducks, *2004*	14.00	4.00
34	Green-winged teals, *2005*	14.00	4.00
35	Ring-necked duck, *2006*	27.50	4.00
36	Wigeon, *2007*	17.00	4.00
37	Wood duck, *2008*	17.00	4.00
38	Pintail, *2009*	30.00	4.00
39	Green-winged teal, *2010*	30.00	4.00
40	Hooded merganser, *2011*	17.50	4.00
41	Blue-winged teal, *2012*	17.50	4.00
42	Wood ducks, *2013*	17.50	4.00
43	Redhead, *2014*	17.50	4.00
44	Canada geese, *2015*	15.00	4.00

Nos. 31-44 not required for hunting.

The Department of Natural Resources sent customers Nos. 31-38 upon receipt of a postcard given to the customer after paying license fee of $8.50.

Nos. 39-44 were sent to customers upon receipt of a postcard given to the customer after paying license fee of $10.

KANSAS

Marion County Resident Duck Stamps

Wording, type face, border and perforation/roulette differs.

Used values are for stamps without gum.

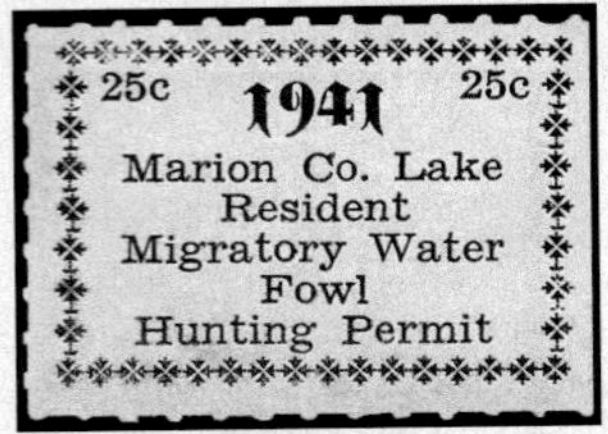

1941-42

A1	25c black	—
A2	25c black, *1942*	—

Remainders from 1941 were rubber stamped "1942" in purple and initialed "J.E.M." by the Park and Lake Supervisor.

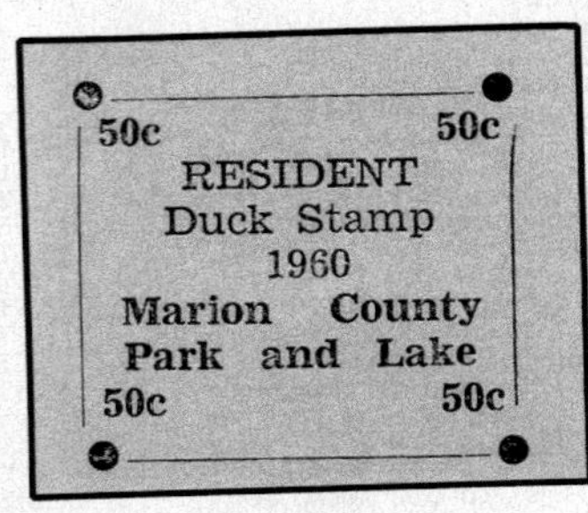

1943-73

A3	25c black, *pink*		—
A4	25c black, *green, 1944*		—
A5	25c green, *1945*		—
A6	25c black, *yellow, 1946*		*17,500.*
A7	25c black, *pink, 1947*		*6,500.*
A8	50c black, *blue, 1948*		*19,500.*
A9	50c black, *1949*		—
A10	50c black, *blue, 1950*		—
A11	50c black, *1951*		—
A12	50c black, *1952*		—
A13	50c black, *blue, 1953*		—
A14	50c black, *pink, 1954*	95.	*65.*
A15	50c black, *green, 1955*	95.	*65.*
A16	50c black, *1956*	110.	*100.*
A17	50c black, *blue, 1957*	85.	*65.*
a.	"1" instead of "I" in "RESIDENT," pos. 3	*1,500.*	*1,250.*
b.	1st 2 lines reversed, pos. 6	*2,250.*	*1,750.*
A18	50c black, *light yellow, 1958*	375.	*850.*
A19	50c black, *1959*	65.	*55.*
A20	50c black, *pink, 1960*	85.	*75.*
a.	Missing ornamental ball, pos. 9	*2,250.*	
A21	50c black, *1961*	125.	*100.*
A22	50c black, *1962*	200.	*150.*
A23	50c black, *pink, 1963*	550.	*400.*
A24	50c black, *pink, 1964*	550.	*400.*
a.	2nd & 3rd lines reversed, pos. 10	*16,500.*	
A25	50c black, *green, 1965*	400.	*300.*
A26	50c black, *yellow, 1966*	—	*19,500.*
A27	50c black, *green, 1967*	*6,500.*	*3,500.*
A28	50c black, *pink, 1968*	250.	*200.*
A29	50c black, *yellow, 1969*	250.	*200.*
a.	"Dusk" instead of "Duck," pos. 8	*17,500.*	
A30	50c black, *1970*	375.	*350.*
A31	50c black, *pink, 1971*	*4,500.*	*3,000.*
A32	50c black, *blue, 1972*	*4,500.*	*3,000.*
A33	50c black, *pink, 1973*	*14,000.*	*8,500.*

Statewide Issues

Issued in booklet panes of 10 (Nos. 1-5) and sheets of 30 (starting with No. 2). Starting with No. 11, issued in sheets of 10. No. 1 issued in booklets with one pane of 10 (serial number has prefix "DD") and booklets with two panes of 10 (serial number has prefix "SS").

Nos. 1-4 numbered serially.

Catalogue values for all unused stamps in this section are for Never Hinged items.

Artists: Guy Coheleach, #1; Ann Dahoney, #2, 8; Leon Parson, #3; Wes Dewey, #4; J. Byron Test, #5; Jerry Thomas, #6, 10; Jerry Roedeke, #7; Neal Anderson, #9; Dustin Teasley, #14-18.

1987-96

No.	Description	Unused	Used
1	$3 Green-winged teal	10.00	2.50
	Pair from booklet pane with L & R selvage	20.00	
2	$3 Canada geese, *1988*	8.00	2.50
	Pair from booklet pane with L & R selvage	16.00	
a.	Serial number missing	—	
3	$3 Mallards, *1989*	8.00	2.50
	Pair from booklet pane with L & R selvage	16.00	
4	$3 Wood ducks, *1990*	8.00	2.50
	Pair from booklet pane with L & R selvage	16.00	
5	$3 Pintail, rouletted, *1991*	8.00	2.50
	Pair from booklet pane with selvage at L & straight edge at R	16.00	
6	$3 Canvasbacks, *1992*	8.00	2.50
7	$3 Mallards, *1993*	9.00	2.50
8	$3 Blue-winged teal, *1994*	9.00	2.50
9	$3 Barrow's goldeneye, *1995*	9.00	2.50
10	$3 American widgeon, *1996*	10.00	2.50

No. 2a resulted from a drastic misregistration of the serial numbers during printing. Only one example is documented.

Artist: Dustin Teasley.

1997-2004 **Self-Adhesive** ***Die Cut***

No.	Description	Unused	Used
11	$3 blue	9.00	2.50
12	$3 green, *1998*	9.00	2.50
13	$3 red, *1999*	8.50	2.50
14	$3 red lilac, *2000*	8.50	2.50
15	$3 orange, *2001*	8.50	2.50
16	$3 blue, *2002*	20.00	2.50
17	$5 green, *2003*	9.50	2.50
18	$5 red, *2004*	9.50	2.50

KENTUCKY

Printed in booklet panes of 5, starting with No. 12 in panes of 30.

Stamps are numbered serially.

Catalogue values for all unused stamps in this section are for Never Hinged items.

Artists: Ray Harm, #1, 7; David Chapple, #2; Ralph J. McDonald, #3, 10; Lynn Kaatz, #4, 15; Phillip Crowe, #5, 9; Jim Oliver, #6; Phillip Powell, #8, 13; Jim Killen, #11; Laurie Parsons Yarnes, #12; Harold Roe, #14, 17; Tim Donovan, #16; Larry Chandler, #18; Ben Burney, #19; Chris Walden, #20-24; Rick Hill, #25.

1985-2009

No.	Description	Unused	Used
1	$5.25 Mallards, rouletted	15.00	3.00
	With tab	15.00	
2	$5.25 Wood ducks, rouletted, *1986*	10.00	2.50
	With tab	10.00	
3	$5.25 Black ducks, *1987*	9.00	2.50
	With tab	10.00	
4	$5.25 Canada geese, *1988*	9.00	2.50
	With tab	10.00	
5	$5.25 Retriever & canvasbacks, *1989*	15.00	2.50
	With tab	16.00	
6	$5.25 Widgeons, *1990*	9.00	2.50
	With tab	11.00	
7	$5.25 Pintails, *1991*	9.00	2.50
	With tab	11.00	
8	$5.25 Green-winged teal, *1992*	13.00	2.50
	With tab	15.00	
9	$5.25 Canvasback & decoy, *1993*	20.00	2.50
	With tab	22.50	
10	$5.25 Canada goose, *1994*	16.00	2.50
	With tab	19.00	
11	$7.50 Retriever, decoy, ringnecks, *1995*	25.00	3.00
	With tab	27.50	
12	$7.50 Blue-winged teal, *1996*	13.00	3.00
13	$7.50 Shovelers, *1997*	13.00	3.00
14	$7.50 Gadwalls, *1998*	15.00	3.00
15	$7.50 Common goldeneyes, *1999*	25.00	3.00
16	$7.50 Hooded mergansers, *2000*	19.00	3.00
17	$7.50 Mallards, *2001*	12.00	3.00
18	$7.50 Pintails, *2002*	12.00	3.00
19	$7.50 Snow geese, *2003*	12.00	3.00
20	$7.50 Black ducks, *2004*	17.50	3.00
21	$7.50 Canada geese, *2005*	19.00	3.00
22	$7.50 Mallards, *2006*	12.00	3.00
23	$7.50 Green-winged teal, *2007*	12.00	3.00
24	$7.50 Pintails, *2008*	12.00	3.00
25	$7.50 Snow geese, *2009*	12.00	3.00

Nos. 19-25 not required for hunting.

LOUISIANA

Printed in sheets of 30.

Stamps are numbered serially. Stamps without numbers are artist presentation examples.

Two fees: resident and non-resident.

Catalogue values for all unused stamps in this section are for Never Hinged items.

Artists: David Noll, #1-1A; Elton Louviere, #2-2A; Brett J. Smith, #3-3A; Bruce Heard, #4-4A; Ronald Louque, #5-5A, 8-8A, 11-11A, 25-25A; Don Edwards, #6-6A; John Bertrand, #7-7A; R. Hall, #9-9A; R. C. Davis, #10-10A; Jude Brunet, #12-12A; Edward Butler, #13-13A; Reggie McLeroy, #14-14A; Dale Pousson, #15-15A; Jeffrey Klinefelter, #16-16A, 20-20A, 24-24A; Ken Michaelsen, #17-17A. Edward Suthoff, #18-18A. Tony Bernard, #19-19A, 26-26A; Anthony Padgett, #21-21A; Richard Clifton #22-22A, 29-29A; Wes Dewey, #23-23A; Guy Crittenden, #27-27A; John Nelson Harris, #28-28A; Tim Taylor, #30-30A.

1989-2018

No.	Description	Unused	Used
1	$5 Blue-winged teal	12.00	2.50
b.	Governor's edition	*100.00*	
1A	$7.50 Blue-winged teal	14.00	2.50
b.	Governor's edition	*150.00*	

Nos. 1b and 2b were available only through a sealed bid auction where sheets of 30 of each denomination with matching serial numbers were sold as a unit.

No.	Description	Unused	Used
2	$5 Green-winged teal, *1990*	9.50	2.50
2A	$7.50 Green-winged teal, *1990*	12.00	2.50
3	$5 Wood ducks, *1991*	9.00	2.50
3A	$7.50 Wood ducks, *1991*	13.00	2.50
4	$5 Pintails, *1992*	9.00	2.50
4A	$7.50 Pintails, *1992*	13.00	2.50
5	$5 American widgeon, *1993*	12.00	2.50
5A	$7.50 American widgeon, *1993*	13.00	2.50
6	$5 Mottled duck, *1994*	12.00	2.50
6A	$7.50 Mottled duck, *1994*	13.00	2.50
7	$5 Speckle bellied goose, *1995*	12.00	2.50
7A	$7.50 Speckle bellied goose, *1995*	13.00	2.50
8	$5 Gadwall, *1996*	12.00	2.50
8A	$7.50 Gadwall, *1996*	13.00	2.50
9	$5 Ring-necked ducks, *1997*	10.00	2.50
9A	$13.50 Ring-necked ducks, *1997*	22.50	2.50
10	$5.50 Mallards, *1998*	11.00	2.50
b.	Governor's edition	*150.00*	
10A	$13.50 Mallards, *1998*	22.50	2.50
b.	Governor's edition	*200.00*	
11	$5.50 Snow geese, *1999*	11.00	2.50
11A	$13.50 Snow geese, *1999*	22.50	2.50
12	$5.50 Lesser scaup, *2000*	11.00	2.50
12A	$13.50 Lesser scaup, *2000*	40.00	2.50

No. 12A sold for $25 as stamps were printed before fee increase was finalized.

No.	Description	Unused	Used
13	$5.50 Shovelers, *2001*	11.00	2.50
13A	$25 Shovelers, *2001*	35.00	2.50
14	$5.50 Canvasbacks, *2002*	11.00	2.50
14A	$25 Canvasbacks, *2002*	35.00	2.50
15	$5.50 Redheads, *2003*	11.00	2.50
15A	$25 Redheads, *2003*	35.00	2.50
16	$5.50 Hooded mergansers, *2004*	10.00	2.50
16A	$25 Hooded mergansers, *2004*	35.00	2.50
17	$5.50 Pintails, Labrador retriever, *2005*	10.00	2.50
17A	$25 Pintails, Labrador retriever, *2005*	35.00	2.50
18	$5.50 Mallards, Labrador retriever, *2006*	10.00	2.50
18A	$25 Mallards, Labrador retriever, *2006*	35.00	2.50
19	$5.50 Mallards, Labrador retriever, *2007*	10.00	2.50
19A	$25 Mallards, Labrador retriever, *2007*	35.00	2.50
20	$5.50 Wood ducks, Golden retriever, *2008*	10.00	2.50
20A	$25 Wood ducks, Golden retriever, *2008*	35.00	2.50
21	$5.50 Ducks, Chesapeake Bay retriever, *2009*	10.00	2.50
21A	$25 Ducks, Chesapeake Bay retriever, *2009*	35.00	2.50
22	$5.50 Pintails, *2010*	10.00	2.50
22A	$25 Pintails, *2010*	35.00	2.50
23	$5.50 Wood ducks, *2011*	15.00	2.50
23A	$25 Wood ducks, *2011*	35.00	2.50
24	$5.50 Wigeons, *2012*	10.00	2.50
24A	$25 Wigeons, *2012*	35.00	2.50
25	$5.50 Mallards, *2013*	10.00	2.50
25A	$25 Mallards, *2013*	35.00	2.50
26	$5.50 White-fronted geese, *2014*	10.00	2.50
26A	$25 White-fronted geese, *2014*	35.00	2.50
27	$5.50 Blue-winged teal, *2015*	10.00	2.50
27A	$25 Blue-winged teal, *2015*	35.00	2.50
28	$5.50 Gadwalls, *2016*	15.00	2.50
28A	$25 Gadwalls, *2016*	35.00	2.50
29	$5.50 Green-winged teal, *2017*	10.00	2.50
29A	$25 Green-winged teal, *2017*	35.00	2.50
30	$5.50 Canvasbacks, *2018*	6.50	2.50
30A	$25 Canvasbacks, *2018*	30.00	2.50

Nos.15-30A not required for hunting.

MAINE

Printed in sheets of 10. Nos. 1-10 are numbered serially.

Catalogue values for all unused stamps in this section are for Never Hinged items.

Artists: David Maass, #1-3; Ron Van Gilder, #4; Rick Allen, #5; Jeannine Staples, #6, 10, 15, 18, 20, 23, 25; Thea Flanagan, #7; Patricia D. Carter, #8; Persis Weirs, #9; Susan Jordan, #11; Richard Alley, #12, 19, 16, 21, 24, 33; Paul Fillion, #13; T. Kemp, #14; Darby Mumford, #17; Daniel Cake, #22; Georgette Kanach, #26; Olga Wing, #27; Rebekah LaCourse, #28; Janine Folsom, #29; Richard Alley, Jr., #30; Rebekah Lowell, #31, 34; Michael Loring, #32; Joanna Huffman, #35.

1984-2018

No.	Description	Unused	Used
1	$2.50 Black ducks	20.00	5.00
2	$2.50 Common eiders, *1985*	25.00	5.00
3	$2.50 Wood ducks, *1986*	9.00	2.50
4	$2.50 Buffleheads, *1987*	8.00	2.50
5	$2.50 Green-winged teal, *1988*	8.00	2.50
6	$2.50 Common goldeneyes, *1989*	8.00	2.50
7	$2.50 Canada geese, *1990*	8.00	2.50
8	$2.50 Ring-necked duck, *1991*	8.00	2.50
9	$2.50 Old squaw, *1992*	8.00	2.50
10	$2.50 Hooded merganser, *1993*	8.00	2.50
11	$2.50 Mallards, *1994*	9.00	2.50
12	$2.50 White-winged scoters, *1995*	12.00	2.50
13	$2.50 Blue-winged teal, *1996*	12.00	2.50
14	$2.50 Greater scaup, *1997*	12.00	2.50
15	$2.50 Surf scoters, *1998*	8.00	2.50
16	$2.50 Black duck, *1999*	9.00	2.50
17	$2.50 Common eider, *2000*	8.00	2.50
18	$2.50 Wood duck, *2001*	8.00	2.50
19	$2.50 Buffleheads, *2002*	8.00	2.50
20	$5.50 Green-winged teal, *2003*	10.00	2.50
21	$8.50 Barrow's goldeneye, *2004*	12.50	2.50
22	$8.50 Canada goose, *2005*	12.50	2.50
23	$7.50 Ring-necked ducks, *2006*	11.50	2.50

24	$7.50	Long-tailed ducks, *2007*	11.50	2.50
25	$7.50	Hooded mergansers, *2008*	11.50	2.50
26	$7.50	Mallards, *2009*	11.50	2.50
27	$7.50	Harlequin ducks, *2010*	11.50	2.50
28	$7.50	Wood ducks, *2011*	11.50	2.50
29	$7.50	Ring-necked ducks, *2012*	11.50	2.50
30	$7.50	Greater scaup, *2013*	11.50	2.50
31	$7.50	Wigeon, *2014*	11.50	2.50
32	$7.50	Canvasbacks, *2015*	11.50	2.50
33	$7.50	Blue-winged teal, *2016*	11.50	2.50
34	$7.50	Common eiders, *2017*	11.50	2.50
35	$7.50	Pintails, *2018*	11.50	2.50

MARYLAND

Nos. 1-19 printed in sheets of 10. Starting with No. 20, printed in sheets of 5 with numbered tab at bottom and selvage at top.

Each stamp has tab. Unused value is for stamp with tab. Many used examples have tab attached.

Catalogue values for all unused stamps in this section are for Never Hinged items.

Artists: John Taylor, #1, 6, 24; Stanley Stearns, #2, 5; Louis Frisino, #3, 13, 20; Jack Schroeder, #4, 7; Arthur Eakin, #8; Roger Bucklin, #9; Roger Lent, #10, 16; Carla Huber, #11, 17; David Turnbaugh, #12, 18, 23, 27, 31, 37; Francis Sweet, #14; Christopher White, #15; Will Wilson, #19; Robert Bealle, #21, 30, 35; Charles Schauck, #22; Paul Makuchal, #25, 33, 40, 44; Wally Makuchal, #26, 36; Wilhelm Goebel, #28, 32, 39; James Kinnett, #29; Jim Taylor, #34, 38, 42; Stephen Perrine, #41; Richard Menard Jr., #43; Paul Bridgford, #45.

1974-2012

1	$1.10	Mallards	11.00	2.50
2	$1.10	Canada geese, rouletted, *1975*	10.00	2.50
3	$1.10	Canvasbacks, rouletted, *1976*	10.00	2.50
4	$1.10	Greater scaup, *1977*	10.00	2.50
5	$1.10	Redheads, *1978*	10.00	2.50
6	$1.10	Wood ducks, rouletted, *1979*	10.00	2.50
7	$1.10	Pintail decoy, rouletted, *1980*	10.00	2.50
8	$3	Widgeon, rouletted, *1981*	9.00	2.50
9	$3	Canvasback, *1982*	8.00	2.50
10	$3	Wood duck, *1983*	12.00	2.50
11	$6	Black ducks, *1984*	14.00	2.50
12	$6	Canada geese, *1985*	12.00	2.50
13	$6	Hooded mergansers, *1986*	12.00	2.50
14	$6	Redheads, *1987*	13.00	2.50
15	$6	Ruddy ducks, *1988*	12.00	2.50
16	$6	Blue-winged teal, *1989*	12.00	2.50
17	$6	Lesser scaup, *1990*	12.00	2.50
18	$6	Shovelers, *1991*	12.00	2.50
19	$6	Bufflehead, *1992*	12.00	2.50
20	$6	Canvasbacks, *1993*	17.50	2.50
21	$6	Redheads, *1994*	12.00	2.50
22	$6	Mallards, *1995*	35.00	2.50
23	$6	Canada geese, *1996*	37.50	2.50
24	$6	Canvasbacks, *1997*	15.00	2.50
25	$6	Pintails, *1998*	15.00	2.50
26	$6	Wood ducks, *1999*	15.00	2.50
27	$6	Old squaws, *2000*	20.00	2.50
28	$6	Wigeons, *2001*	11.00	2.50
29	$9	Black scoters, *2002*	15.00	2.50
30	$9	Lesser scaup, *2003*	15.00	2.50
31	$9	Pintails, *2004*	15.00	2.50
32	$9	Ruddy duck, *2005*	15.00	2.50
33	$9	Canada geese, *2006*	15.00	2.50
34	$9	Wood ducks, *2007*	15.00	2.50
35	$9	Canvasback, *2008*	15.00	2.50
36	$9	Blue-winged teal, *2009*	15.00	2.50
37	$9	Hooded merganser, *2010*	15.00	2.50
38	$9	Canada geese, *2011*	15.00	2.50
39	($9)	Wigeons, *2012*	15.00	2.50

MARYLAND DEPARTMENT OF NATURAL RESOURCES
2013-2014 Migratory Game Bird Stamp

Stamp revenue is deposited into the Wildlife Management & Protection Fund and used solely for migratory game bird projects, including habitat enhancement, research, management, and surveys.

Natural Resources Article, §10-308.1, Annotated Code of Maryland establishes the Maryland migratory game bird stamp, which is required for all migratory game bird hunters, including persons not required to have a hunting license and holders of senior hunting licenses. You are not required to affix this stamp to your hunting license, but the license with printed proof of purchase must be in your possession while hunting migratory game birds.

633397

2013-16 ***Die Cut***

Souvenir Sheet Self-Adhesive

40	($9)	Lesser scaup, *2013*	12.00	2.50
41	($9)	Ring-necked duck, *2014*	12.00	2.50
42	($9)	Canvasbacks, *2015*	12.00	2.50
43	($9)	Shovelers, *2016*	12.00	2.50
44	($9)	Black ducks, *2017*	12.00	2.50
45	($9)	Green-winged teal, *2018*	12.00	2.50

Public Lands Hunting Stamps

Required to hunt waterfowl in state-managed wildlife areas.

Issued in booklet panes of 10.

1975-79

A1	$2	purple	*2,950.*	95.
A2	$2	black, *pink, 1976*	*1,950.*	45.
A3	$2	black, *yellow, 1977*	*1,650.*	45.
A4	$2	black, *1978*	*4,500.*	135.
A5	$2	black, *yellow, 1979*	*1,500.*	35.

MASSACHUSETTS

Printed in sheets of 12.

Catalogue values for all unused stamps in this section are for Never Hinged items.

Artists: Milton Weiler, #1; Tom Hennessey, #2; William Tyner, #3-5; Randy Julius, #6, 8, 10, 12, 19, 27, 33, 38; John Eggert, #7, 9, 24; Joseph Cibula, #11; Robert Piscatori, #13, 15, 25, 30; Peter Baedita, #14, 29; Lou Barnicle, #16; Warren Racket Shreve, #17; Benjamin Smith, #18; Donald Little, #20, 32; Sergio Roffo, #21; David Brega, #22; Christine Wilkinson, #23; Stephen Badlam #26; Barry Julius, #28, 36; Larry Denton, #31. Matthew Schulz, #34; Gregg Coppolo, #35; Janice Sexton, #37.

1974-2011

1	$1.25	Wood duck decoy, rouletted	15.00	3.00
2	$1.25	Pintail decoy, *1975*	13.00	3.00
3	$1.25	Canada goose decoy, *1976*	13.00	3.00
4	$1.25	Goldeneye decoy, *1977*	13.00	3.00
5	$1.25	Black duck decoy, *1978*	13.00	3.00
6	$1.25	Ruddy turnstone duck decoy, *1979*	15.00	3.00
a.		Imperf, pair	160.00	
7	$1.25	Old squaw decoy, *1980*	15.00	3.00
8	$1.25	Red-breasted merganser decoy, *1981*	15.00	3.00
9	$1.25	Greater yellowlegs decoy, *1982*	15.00	3.00
10	$1.25	Redhead decoy, *1983*	15.00	3.00
11	$1.25	White-winged scoter decoy, *1984*	15.00	3.00
12	$1.25	Ruddy duck decoy, *1985*	12.00	3.00
13	$1.25	Preening bluebill decoy, *1986*	12.00	2.50
14	$1.25	American widgeon decoy, *1987*	12.00	2.50
15	$1.25	Mallard decoy, *1988*	12.00	2.50
16	$1.25	Brant decoy, *1989*	10.00	2.50
17	$1.25	Whistler hen decoy, *1990*	10.00	2.50
18	$5	Canvasback decoy, *1991*	10.00	2.50
19	$5	Black-bellied plover decoy, *1992*	10.00	2.50
20	$5	Red-breasted merganser decoy, *1993*	10.00	2.50
21	$5	White-winged scoter decoy, *1994*	10.00	2.50
22	$5	Female hooded merganser decoy, *1995*	10.00	2.50
23	$5	Eider decoy, *1996*	10.00	2.50
24	$5	Curlew decoy, *1997*	10.00	2.50
25	$5	Canada goose decoy, *1998*	10.00	2.50
26	$5	Old squaw decoy, *1999*	10.00	2.50
27	$5	Merganser hen decoy, *2000*	10.00	2.50
28	$5	Black duck decoy, *2001*	10.00	2.50
29	$5	Bufflehead decoy, *2002*	10.00	2.50
30	$5	Greenwing teal decoy, *2003*	10.00	2.50
31	$5	Wood duck drake decoy, *2004*	10.00	2.50
32	$5	Old squaw drake decoy, *2005*	10.00	2.50
33	$5	Long-billed curlew decoy, *2006*	18.00	2.50
34	$5	Goldeneye decoy, *2007*	10.00	2.50
35	$5	Black duck decoy, *2008*	10.00	2.50
36	$5	White-winged scoter decoy, *2009*	10.00	2.50
37	$5	Canada goose decoy, *2010*	10.00	2.50
38	$5	Brant decoy, *2011*	18.00	2.50

MICHIGAN

Nos. 1-5 printed in sheets of 10 with center gutter, rouletted. Printed in sheets of 10 die cut self-adhesives on backing paper (Nos. 6-19), or sheets of 15 (starting with No. 20).

Nos. 1, 3-19 are serially numbered.

Catalogue values for all unused stamps in this section are for Never Hinged items.

Artist: Oscar Warbach.

1976

1	$2.10	Wood duck	5.00	2.50

Artists: Larry Hayden, #2, 5, 12; Richard Timm, #3; Andrew Kurzmann, #4; Dietmar Krumrey, #6, 14, 23-24, 28, 33; Gjisbert van Frankenhuyzen, #7; Rod Lawrence, #8, 15, 20, 25, 27, 32; Larry Cory, #9, 16; Robert Steiner, #10; Russell Cobane, #11; John Martens, #13; Heiner Hertling, #17; Clark Sullivan, #18; David Bollman, #19; Rusty Fretner, #21; M. Monroe, #22; Kim Diment, #26; Tim McDonald, #29; Christopher Smith, #30, 39, 41, 43; Peter Mathios, #31; Lorna Poulos, #34; J.P. Edwards, #35; Richard Clifton, #36, 38; George Lockwood, #37; Guy Crittenden, #40, 42.

1977-2018

2	$2.10	Canvasbacks	225.00	35.00
		With numbered tab	275.00	
3	$2.10	Mallards, *1978*	20.00	5.00
		With tab	47.50	
4	$2.10	Canada geese, *1979*	60.00	5.00
		With tab	75.00	
5	$3.75	Lesser scaup, *1980*	17.50	4.00
		With tab	25.00	
6	$3.75	Buffleheads, *1981*	25.00	4.00
7	$3.75	Redheads, *1982*	25.00	4.00

Unused value is for stamp with sufficient margin to show printed spaces for date and time the stamp was sold.

8	$3.75	Wood ducks, *1983*	25.00	4.00
9	$3.75	on $3.25 Pintails, *1984*	25.00	3.00

No. 9 not issued without surcharge.

10	$3.75	Ring-necked ducks, *1985*	25.00	3.00
11	$3.75	Common goldeneyes, *1986*	22.00	2.50
12	$3.85	Green-winged teal, *1987*	11.00	2.50
13	$3.85	Canada geese, *1988*	10.00	2.50
14	$3.85	Widgeons, *1989*	10.00	2.50
15	$3.85	Wood ducks, *1990*	10.00	2.50
16	$3.85	Blue-winged teal, *1991*	9.00	2.50
17	$3.85	Red-breasted merganser, *1992*	9.00	2.50
18	$3.85	Hooded merganser, *1993*	9.00	2.50
19	$3.85	Black duck, *1994*	9.00	2.50

20	$4.35 Blue winged teal, *1995*	9.00	3.00
21	$4.35 Canada geese, *1996*	9.00	3.00
22	$5 Canvasbacks, *1997*	20.00	3.00
23	$5 Pintail, *1998*	9.00	3.00
24	$5 Shoveler, *1999*	9.00	3.00

Self-Adhesive Die Cut

25	$5 Mallards, *2000*	20.00	3.00
26	$5 Ruddy ducks, *2001*	10.00	3.00
27	$5 Wigeons, *2002*	9.00	3.00
28	$5 Redheads, *2003*	9.00	3.00

Rouletted

29	$5 Wood duck, *2004*	9.00	3.00
30	$5 Blue-winged teals, *2005*	9.00	3.00
31	$5 Widgeon, *2006*	9.00	3.00
32	$5 Pintails, *2007*	8.00	3.00
33	$5 Wood ducks, *2008*	8.00	3.00
34	$5 Canvasbacks, *2009*	10.00	3.00
35	$5 Buffleheads, *2010*	8.00	3.00
36	$5 Mallard, *2011*	8.00	3.00
37	$5 Ring-necked ducks, *2012*	8.00	3.00
38	$5 Black duck, *2013*	8.00	3.00
39	$5 Long-tailed ducks, *2014*	8.00	3.00
40	$6 Common goldeneyes, *2015*	10.00	3.00
41	$6 Green-winged teal, *2016*	10.00	3.00
42	$6 Shovelers, *2017*	10.00	3.00
43	$6 Wigeons and Black Labrador retriever, *2018*	9.00	3.00

Nos. 24-43 not required for hunting.

MINNESOTA

License Surcharge Stamps

No. A1 printed in sheets of 10. These stamps served as a $1 surcharge to cover the cost of a license increase.

Nos. A1-A2 issued to raise funds for acquisition and development of wildlife lands.

1957 *Perf. 12½*

A1	$1 Mallards & Pheasant	85.00	6.00

1971 MINNESOTA $1.00
Department of Natural Resources
Additional one dollar surcharge to be paid by sportsmen, pursuant to Laws 1971 Chapter 867, for the acquisition and development of wildlife lands.

1971 *Rouletted 9½*

A2	$1 black, *dark yellow*	—	20.00

Cancellation of No. A2 was not required. Value for used stamp is for an example without gum.

Regular Issues

Printed in sheets of 10.

Catalogue values for all unused stamps in this section are for Never Hinged items.

Artists: David Maass, #1, 3; Leslie Kouba, #2; James Meger, #4; Terry Redlin, #5, 9, Phil Scholer, #6, 17; Gary Moss, #7; Thomas Gross, #8; Brian Jarvi, #10; Ron Van Gilder, #11; Robert Hautman, #12, 16, 25; Jim Hautman, #13, 20; Kevin Daniel, #14, 21; Daniel Smith, #15; Edward DuRose, #18, 40; Bruce Miller, #19; Thomas Moen, #22, 31; John House, #23; Kim Norlien, #24; John Freiberg, #26; Mark Kness, #27, 34; Scot Storm, #28, 33, 39; David Chapman, #29, 37; Joe Hautman, #30; Sara Stack, #32; Kevin Nelson, #35; Stephen Hamrick, #36; Thomas Moen, #38; Timothy Turenne, #41; Mark Thone, #42.

1977-2018

1	$3 Mallards	15.00	2.50
2	$3 Lesser scaup, *1978*	12.00	2.50
3	$3 Pintails, *1979*	12.00	2.50
4	$3 Canvasbacks, *1980*	12.00	2.50
5	$3 Canada geese, *1981*	9.50	2.50
6	$3 Redheads, *1982*	12.00	2.50
7	$3 Blue geese & snow goose, *1983*	12.00	2.50
8	$3 Wood ducks, *1984*	12.00	2.50
9	$3 White-fronted geese, *1985*	9.00	2.50
10	$5 Lesser scaup, *1986*	10.00	2.50

Beginning with this issue, left side of sheet has an agent's tab, detachable from the numbered tab.

11	$5 Common goldeneyes, *1987*	11.00	2.50
	With numbered tab	11.00	
	With agent's and numbered tabs	16.00	
12	$5 Buffleheads, *1988*	11.00	2.50
	With numbered tab	11.00	
	With agent's and numbered tabs	17.50	
13	$5 Widgeons, *1989*	11.00	2.50
	With numbered tab	11.00	
	With agent's and numbered tabs	17.50	
14	$5 Hooded mergansers, *1990*	25.00	2.50
	With numbered tab	25.00	
	With agent's and numbered tabs	40.00	
15	$5 Ross's geese, *1991*	10.00	2.50
	With numbered tab	10.00	
	With agent's and numbered tabs	14.00	
16	$5 Barrow's goldeneyes, *1992*	10.00	2.50
	With numbered tab	10.00	
	With agent's and numbered tabs	14.00	
17	$5 Blue-winged teal, *1993*	10.00	2.50
	With numbered tab	10.00	
	With agent's and numbered tabs	14.00	
18	$5 Ringneck duck, *1994*	10.00	2.50
	With numbered tab	10.00	
	With agent's and numbered tabs	13.00	
19	$5 Gadwall, *1995*	10.00	2.50
	With numbered tab	10.00	
	With agent's and numbered tabs	13.00	
20	$5 Greater scaup, *1996*	12.00	2.50
	With numbered tab	12.00	
	With agent's and numbered tabs	18.00	
21	$5 Shovelers, *1997*	11.00	2.50
	With numbered tab	11.00	
	With agent's and numbered tabs	15.00	
22	$5 Harlequins, *1998*	13.00	2.50
	With numbered tab	13.00	
	With agent's and numbered tabs	19.00	
23	$5 Green-winged teal, *1999*	11.00	2.50
	With numbered tab	11.00	
	With agent's and numbered tabs	15.00	

Self- Adhesive Die Cut

24	$5 Red-breasted merganser, *2000*	20.00	2.50

No. 24 is on backing paper affixed to back of license form.

25	$5 Black duck, *2001*	30.00	2.50

No. 25 is on backing paper affixed to back of license form.

26	$5 Ruddy duck, *2002*	15.00	2.50
27	$5 Oldsquaws, *2003*	15.00	2.50
28	$7.50 Common mergansers, *2004*	15.00	2.50
29	$7.50 White-winged scoters, lighthouse, *2005*	15.00	2.50
30	$7.50 Mallard, *2006*	15.00	2.50
31	$7.50 Lesser scaups, *2007*	15.00	2.50
32	$7.50 Ross's geese, *2008*	15.00	2.50
33	$7.50 Common goldeneyes, *2009*	15.00	2.50
34	$7.50 Wood duck, *2010*	15.00	2.50
35	$7.50 Red-breasted merganser, *2011*	15.00	2.50
36	$7.50 Ruddy duck, *2012*	15.00	2.50
37	$7.50 Pintail, *2013*	15.00	2.50
38	$7.50 Canada geese, *2014*	15.00	2.50
39	$7.50 Harlequin duck, *2015*	30.00	2.50
40	$7.50 Wigeon, *2016*	15.00	2.50
41	$7.50 Redheads, *2017*	15.00	2.50
42	$7.50 White-winged scoters, *2018*	15.00	2.50

Nos. 26-42 are on backing paper affixed to mailing envelopes. Beginning with No. 32, stamps are not required for hunting.

MISSISSIPPI

Starting with No. 2, stamps are printed in sheets of 10. Nos. 2-14 are rouletted. All stamps are numbered serially.

Catalogue values for all unused stamps in this section are for Never Hinged items.

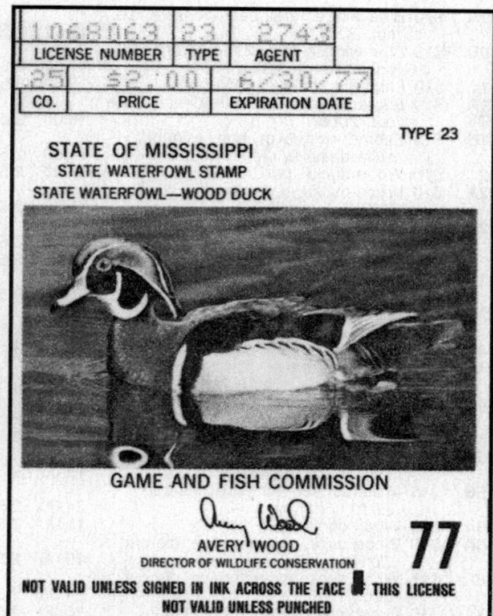

Artists: Carroll & Gwen Perkins, #1; Allen Hughes, #2; John C. A. Reimers, #3, 6; Carole Pigott Hardy, #4; Bob Tompkins, #5, 13; Jerry Johnson, #7; Jerrie Glasper, #8; Tommy Goodman, #9; Lottie Fulton, #10; Joe Lattl, #11, 17, 22-23; Robert Garner, #12; Debra Aven Swartzendruber, #14; Kathy Dickson, #15; Phillip Crowe, #16; Eddie Suthoff, #18; Emitt Thames, #19-20; James Josey, #21; John MacHudspeth, #24-33B, 36-38B; Joe MacHudspeth, Jr., #34-35B, 39-39B, 42-42B; Lauren Doherty, #40-40B; Paul Brown, #41-41B; Bill Stripling, #43-43B.

1976 **Without Gum**

1	$2 Wood duck	18.00	5.00
a.	Complete 2-part data processing card	25.00	

1977-2018

2	$2 Mallards	10.00	2.50
3	$2 Green-winged teal, *1978*	10.00	2.50
4	$2 Canvasbacks, *1979*	10.00	2.50
5	$2 Pintails, *1980*	10.00	2.50
6	$2 Redheads, *1981*	10.00	2.50
7	$2 Canada geese, *1982*	10.00	2.50
8	$2 Lesser scaup, *1983*	10.00	2.50
9	$2 Black ducks, *1984*	10.00	2.50
10	$2 Mallards, *1985*	10.00	2.50
a.	Vert. serial No., imperf btwn. serial No. and stamp	150.00	
b.	Horiz. serial No., no vert. silver bar	700.00	
11	$2 Widgeons, *1986*	10.00	2.50
12	$2 Ring-necked ducks, *1987*	10.00	2.50
13	$2 Snow geese, *1988*	10.00	2.50
14	$2 Wood ducks, *1989*	7.00	2.50
15	$2 Snow geese, *1990*	12.50	2.50
16	$2 Labrador retriever & canvasbacks, *1991*	7.50	2.50
17	$2 Green-winged teal, *1992*	7.50	2.50
18	$5 Mallards, *1993*	9.00	2.50
19	$5 Canvasbacks, *1994*	10.00	2.50
20	$5 Blue-winged teals, *1995*	15.00	2.50
21	$5 Hooded merganser, *1996*	17.00	2.50
22	$5 Pintail, *1997*	22.50	2.50
23	$5 Pintails, *1998*	13.00	2.50
24	$5 Ring-necked duck, *1999*	10.00	2.50
24A	$5 Ring-necked duck, self-adhesive, die cut, *1999*	10.00	2.50
25	$5 Mallards, *2000*	10.00	2.50
25A	$5 Mallards, self-adhesive, die cut, *2000*	*400.00*	
26	$5 Gadwall, *2001*	15.00	2.50
26A	$10 Gadwall, self-adhesive, die cut, *2001*	15.00	2.50
27	$10 Wood duck, *2002*	15.00	2.50
27A	$10 Wood duck, self-adhesive, die cut, *2002*	15.00	2.50
28	$10 Pintail, *2003*	15.00	2.50
28A	$10 Pintail, self-adhesive, die cut, *2003*	15.00	2.50
29	$10 Wood ducks, *2004*	15.00	2.50
29A	$10 Wood ducks, self-adhesive, die cut, *2004*	15.00	2.50
30	$10 Blue-winged teal, *2005*	15.00	2.50

No.	Description	Unused	Used
30A	$10 Blue-winged teal, self-adhesive, die cut, *2005*	15.00	2.50
30B	$15 Blue-winged teal, non-resident, self-adhesive, die cut, *2005*	24.00	2.50
31	$10 Labrador retriever, *2006*	15.00	2.50
31A	$10 Labrador retriever, self-adhesive, die cut, *2006*	15.00	2.50
31B	$15 Labrador retriever, non-resident, self-adhesive, die cut, *2006*	24.00	2.50
32	$10 Wood ducks, perf., *2007*	15.00	2.50
32A	$10 Wood ducks, self-adhesive, die cut, *2007*	15.00	2.50
32B	$15 Wood ducks, self-adhesive, die cut, *2007*	24.00	2.50
33	$10 Green-winged teal, perf., *2008*	15.00	2.50
33A	$10 Green-winged teal, self-adhesive, die cut, *2008*	15.00	2.50
33B	$15 Green-winged teal, self-adhesive, die cut, *2008*	24.00	2.50
34	$10 Blue-winged teal, perf., *2009*	15.00	2.50
34A	$10 Blue-winged teal, self-adhesive, die cut, *2009*	15.00	2.50
34B	$15 Blue-winged teal, self-adhesive, die cut, *2009*	24.00	2.50
35	$10 Mallards, perf., *2010*	15.00	2.50
35A	$10 Mallards, self-adhesive, die cut, *2010*	15.00	2.50
35B	$15 Mallards, self-adhesive, die cut, *2010*	24.00	2.50
36	$10 Wood duck, perf., *2011*	15.00	2.50
36A	$10 Wood duck, self-adhesive, die cut, *2011*	15.00	2.50
36B	$15 Wood duck, self-adhesive, die cut, *2011*	24.00	2.50
37	$10 Green-winged teal, perf., *2012*	15.00	2.50
37A	$10 Green-winged teal, self-adhesive, die cut, *2012*	15.00	2.50
37B	$15 Green-winged teal, self-adhesive, die cut, *2012*	24.00	2.50
38	$10 Mallard, perf., *2013*	15.00	2.50
38A	$10 Mallard, self-adhesive, die cut *2013*	15.00	2.50
38B	$15 Mallard, self-adhesive, die cut *2013*	24.00	2.50
39	$10 Wood ducks, perf., *2014*	16.00	2.50
39A	$10 Wood ducks, self-adhesive, die cut *2014*	16.00	2.50
39B	$15 Wood ducks, self-adhesive, die cut *2014*	24.00	2.50
40	$10 Pintail, perf., *2015*	16.00	2.50
40A	$10 Pintail, self-adhesive, die cut, *2015*	16.00	2.50
40B	$15 Pintail, self-adhesive, die cut, *2015*	24.00	2.50
41	$10 Pintail, perf., *2016*	16.00	2.50
41A	$10 Pintail, self-adhesive, die cut, *2016*	16.00	2.50
41B	$15 Pintail, self-adhesive, die cut, *2016*	24.00	2.50
42	$10 Gadwall, perf., *2017*	16.00	2.50
42A	$10 Gadwall, self-adhesive, die cut, *2017*	16.00	2.50
42B	$15 Gadwall, self-adhesive, die cut, *2017*	24.00	2.50
43	$10 Canvasback, perf., *2018*	16.00	2.50
43A	$10 Canvasback, self-adhesive, die cut, *2018*	16.00	2.50
43B	$15 Canvasback, self-adhesive, die cut, *2018*	21.00	2.50

MISSOURI

Issued in booklet panes of five with tab. Nos. 1-8 are rouletted. No. 18 issued in pane of 30.

Catalogue values for all unused stamps in this section are for Never Hinged items.

Artists: Charles Schwartz, #1; David Plank, #2; Tom Crain, #3, 8; Gary Lucy, #4; Doug Ross, #5; Glenn Chambers, #6; Ron Clayton, #7; Ron Ferkol, #9, 13, 18; Bruce Bollman, #10; Kathy Dickson, #11; Eileen Melton, #12; Kevin Guinn, #14; Thomas Bates, #15; Keith Alexander, #16; Ryan Peterson, #17.

1979-96

No.	Description	Unused	Used
1	$3.40 Canada geese	*325.00*	75.00
	With tab	*400.00*	
2	$3.40 Wood ducks, *1980*	*80.00*	18.00
	With tab	*95.00*	
3	$3 Lesser scaup, *1981*	50.00	9.00
	With tab	65.00	
4	$3 Buffleheads, *1982*	50.00	8.00
	With tab	65.00	
5	$3 Blue-winged teal, *1983*	45.00	8.00
	With tab	55.00	
6	$3 Mallards, *1984*	40.00	7.00
	With tab	50.00	
7	$3 American widgeons, *1985*	22.50	3.00
	With tab	25.00	
8	$3 Hooded mergansers, *1986*	12.00	3.00
	With tab	15.00	
9	$3 Pintails, *1987*	9.00	3.00
	With tab	13.00	
10	$3 Canvasback, *1988*	8.00	2.50
	With tab	11.00	
11	$3 Ring-necked ducks, *1989*	8.00	2.50
	With tab	9.25	

All examples of Nos. 12b, 13b, 14b, 15b, 16b, 17b are signed by the governor.

No.	Description	Unused	Used
12	$5 Redheads, *1990*	8.00	2.50
	With two part tab	10.00	
a.	$50 Governor's edition with tab	75.00	
b.	$100 Governor's edition with tab	300.00	
13	$5 Snow geese, *1991*	8.00	2.50
	With two part tab	9.00	
a.	$50 Governor's edition with tab	72.50	
b.	$100 Governor's edition with tab	300.00	
14	$5 Gadwalls, *1992*	8.00	2.50
	With tab	9.00	
a.	$50 Governor's edition with tab	75.00	
b.	$100 Governor's edition with tab	200.00	
15	$5 Green-winged teal, *1993*	8.00	2.50
	With tab	9.00	
a.	$50 Governor's edition with tab	75.00	
b.	$100 Governor's edition with tab	200.00	
16	$5 White-fronted goose, *1994*	8.00	2.50
	With 2-part tab	9.00	
a.	$50 Governor's edition with tab	75.00	
b.	$100 Governor's edition with tab	200.00	
17	$5 Goldeneyes, *1995*	8.00	2.50
	With 2-part tab	9.00	
a.	$50 Governor's edition with tab	75.00	
b.	$100 Governor's edition with tab	200.00	
18	$5 Black ducks, *1996*	8.00	2.50

MONTANA

Bird License Stamps

Required to hunt waterfowl.

Resident ($2, $4, $6), youth ($1, $2), and non-resident ($25, $30, $53) bird licenses. Licenses were no longer produced for youth, beginning in 1985, and non-resident, beginning in 1989.

Nos. 1-33 rouletted.

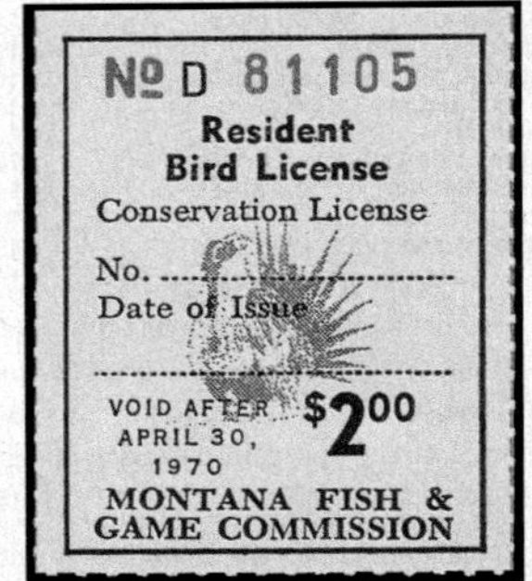

1969

No.	Description	Unused	Used
A1	$2 Sage grouse	450.00	15.00
A2	$1 Sage grouse	450.00	50.00
A3	$25 Sage grouse	450.00	75.00

1970

No.	Description	Unused	Used
A4	$2 Sage grouse	650.00	10.00
a.	Missing "1" in "1971," pos. 10		*650.00*
A5	$1 Sage grouse	*2,500.*	150.00
A6	$25 Sage grouse	—	*500.00*

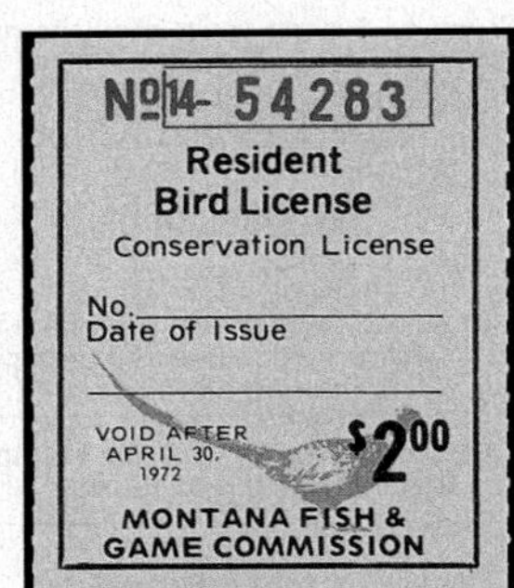

1971

No.	Description	Unused	Used
A7	$2 Pheasant	700.00	10.00
A8	$1 Pheasant	700.00	35.00
A9	$25 Pheasant	700.00	50.00

1972

No.	Description	Unused	Used
A10	$2 Pheasant	700.00	10.00
A11	$1 Pheasant	700.00	35.00
A12	$25 Pheasant	700.00	50.00

1973

No.	Description	Unused	Used
A13	$2 Pheasant	700.00	10.00
A14	$1 Pheasant	700.00	35.00
A15	$25 Pheasant	700.00	50.00

1974

No.	Description	Unused	Used
A16	$2 Pheasant	700.00	10.00
A17	$1 Pheasant	700.00	35.00
A18	$25 Pheasant	700.00	50.00

1975

No.	Description	Unused	Used
A19	$2 Pheasant	700.00	10.00
A20	$1 Pheasant	700.00	35.00
A21	$25 Pheasant	700.00	50.00

1976

No.	Description	Unused	Used
A22	$4 Pheasant	700.00	10.00
A23	$2 Pheasant	700.00	35.00
A24	$30 Pheasant	700.00	50.00

1977

No.	Description	Unused	Used
A25	$4 Pheasant	700.00	10.00
A26	$2 Pheasant	700.00	35.00
A27	$30 Pheasant	700.00	50.00

1978

No.	Description	Unused	Used
A28	$4 Sage grouse	8.00	2.00
A29	$2 Sage grouse	8.00	5.00
A30	$30 Sage grouse	8.00	5.50

1979

No.	Description	Unused	Used
A31	$4 Snow geese	8.00	2.00
A32	$2 Snow geese	8.00	5.00
A33	$30 Snow geese	8.00	5.50

EXPIRES APRIL 30, 1984 — 1983 RESIDENT BIRD LICENSE — MO. DAY — $4.00 — 14- 056809 — DATE OF ISSUE — CONSERVATION LICENSE — A-1 — MONTANA DEPARTMENT OF FISH, WILDLIFE AND PARKS

1980

No.	Description	Unused	Used
A36	$30 black, *gray green*	*50.00*	

1982

No.	Description	Unused	Used
A40	$4 black, *yellow*	5.00	

1983

No.	Description	Unused	Used
A43	$4 black, *yellow gray*	*2,250.*	5.00
A44	$2 black, *gray*	*2,250.*	
A45	$30 black, *light blue*	*2,250.*	

1984

No.	Description	Unused	Used
A46	$4 black, *light blue green*	*1,350.*	5.00
A47	$2 black, *light violet*	*1,500.*	
A48	$30 black, *gray*	*1,250.*	

1985

No.	Description	Unused	Used
A49	$4 black, *light blue*	*1,450.*	5.00
A50	$30 black, *lavender*	*1,250.*	

1986

No.	Description	Unused	Used
A51	$4 black, *orange*	*1,800.*	5.00
A52	$30 black, *light blue*	*1,800.*	

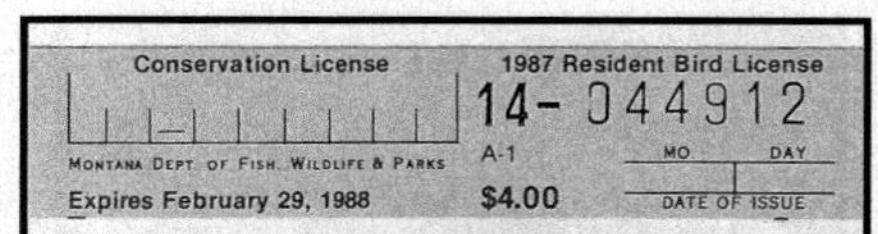

1987

A53	$4 black, *orange brown*	*750.00*	3.00
A54	$30 black, *tan*	*950.00*	

1988

A55	$6 black, *light blue*	*650.00*	3.00
A56	$53 black, *purple*	*850.00*	

1989-99

A57	$6 black, *rose*	175.00	2.00
A58	$6 black, *lavender, 1990*	150.00	2.00
A59	$6 black, *pale blue, 1991*	100.00	2.00
A60	$6 black, *brown, 1992*	70.00	2.00
A61	$6 black, *blue, 1993*	60.00	1.50
A62	$6 black, *red orange, 1994*	55.00	1.50
A63	$6 black, *blue, 1995*	42.50	1.50
A64	$6 black, *purple, 1996*	25.00	1.00
A65	$6 black, *mauve, 1997*	15.00	1.00
A66	$6 black, *gray, 1998*	13.00	1.00
A67	$6 black, *green, 1999*	13.00	1.00

Waterfowl Stamps

Issued in booklet panes of 10 and sheets of 30.
Stamps are numbered serially.
Stamps with serial numbers above 31,000 (1986) and above 21,000 (other years) are from booklet panes.

Catalogue values for all unused stamps in this section are for Never Hinged items.

Artist: Joe Thornbrugh, #34, 38, 39, 45, 46, 48; Roger Cruwys, #35, 37, 42; Dave Samuelson, #36; Craig Philips, #40; Darrell Davis, #41; Wayne Dowdy, #43; Jim Borgreen, #44, 50, 51; Cliff Rossberg, #47, 49.

1986-2003

34	$5 Canada geese	12.00	3.00
	Pair from booklet pane with L & R selvage	*1,750.*	
	Top pair from booklet pane with agent tabs and L & R selvage	—	
35	$5 Redheads, *1987*	15.00	3.00
	Pair from booklet pane with L & R selvage	30.00	
	Top pair from booklet pane with agent tabs and L & R selvage	55.00	
36	$5 Mallards, *1988*	7.00	3.00
	Pair from booklet pane with L & R selvage	25.00	
	Top pair from booklet pane with agent tabs and L & R selvage	40.00	
37	$5 Black Labrador retriever & pintail, *1989*	7.00	3.00
	Pair from booklet pane with L & R selvage	25.00	
	Top pair from booklet pane with agent tabs and L & R selvage	40.00	
a.	Governor's edition	*140.00*	

No. 37a was available only in full sheets only through a sealed bid auction.

38	$5 Blue-winged & cinnamon teal, *1990*	7.00	2.50
	Pair from booklet pane with L & R selvage	20.00	
	Top pair from booklet pane with agent tabs and L & R selvage	25.00	
39	$5 Snow geese, *1991*	7.00	2.50
	Pair from booklet pane with L & R selvage	20.00	
	Top pair from booklet pane with agent tabs and L & R selvage	25.00	
40	$5 Wood ducks, *1992*	7.00	2.50
	Pair from booklet pane with L & R selvage	20.00	
	Top pair from booklet pane with agent tabs and L & R selvage	25.00	
41	$5 Harlequin ducks, *1993*	7.00	2.50
	Pair from booklet pane with L & R selvage	22.00	
	Top pair from booklet pane with agent tabs and L & R selvage	25.00	
42	$5 Widgeons, *1994*	7.00	2.50
	Pair from booklet pane with L & R selvage	25.00	
	Top pair from booklet pane with agent tabs and L & R selvage	25.00	
43	$5 Tundra swans, *1995*	7.00	2.50
	Pair from booklet pane with L & R selvage	25.00	
	Top pair from booklet pane with agent tabs and L & R selvage	25.00	
44	$5 Canvasbacks, *1996*	7.00	2.50
	Pair from booklet pane with L & R selvage	25.00	
	Top pair from booklet pane with agent tabs and L & R selvage	30.00	
45	$5 Golden retriever, mallard, *1997*	7.00	2.50
	Pair from booklet pane with L & R selvage	25.00	
	Top pair from booklet pane with agent tabs and L & R selvage	30.00	
46	$5 Gadwalls, *1998*	7.00	2.50
	Pair from booklet pane with L & R selvage	25.00	
	Top pair from booklet pane with agent tabs and L & R selvage	30.00	
47	$5 Barrow's goldeneye, *1999*	7.00	2.50
	Pair from booklet pane with L & R selvage	25.00	
	Top pair from booklet pane with agent tabs and L & R selvage	30.00	
48	$5 Mallard decoy, Chesapeake retriever, *2000*	7.00	2.50
	Pair from booklet pane with L & R selvage	25.00	
	Top pair from booklet pane with agent tabs and L & R selvage	30.00	
49	$5 Canada geese, *2001*	7.00	2.50
	Pair from booklet pane with L & R selvage	25.00	
	Top pair from booklet pane with agent tabs and L & R selvage	30.00	
50	($5) Sandhill crane, *2002*	11.00	2.50
51	$5 Mallards, *2003*	75.00	2.50

No. 51 is not required for hunting.

NEBRASKA

Habitat Stamps

Required to hunt waterfowl.
Printed in sheets of 20.

Catalogue values for all unused stamps in this section are for Never Hinged items.

1977-98

A1	$7.50 Ring-necked pheasant	12.00	1.50
A2	$7.50 White-tailed deer, *1978*	12.00	1.50
A3	$7.50 Bobwhite quail, *1979*	12.00	1.50
A4	$7.50 Pheasant, *1980*	12.00	1.50
A5	$7.50 Cottontail rabbit, *1981*	12.00	1.50
A6	$7.50 Coyote, *1982*	12.00	1.50
A7	$7.50 Wild turkey, *1983*	12.00	1.50
A8	$7.50 Canada goose, *1984*	12.00	1.50
A9	$7.50 Cardinal, *1985*	12.00	1.50
A10	$7.50 Sharp-tailed grouse, *1986*	12.00	1.50
A11	$7.50 Sandhill crane, *1987*	12.00	1.50
A12	$7.50 Snow geese, *1988*	12.00	1.50
A13	$7.50 Mallards, *1989*	12.00	1.50
A14	$7.50 Pheasants, *1990*	12.00	1.50
A15	$7.50 Canada geese, *1991*	12.00	1.50
A16	$10.00 Raccoon, *1992*	15.00	1.50
A17	$10.00 Fox squirrel, *1993*	15.00	1.50
A18	$10.00 Hungarian partridge, *1994*	15.00	1.50
A19	$10.00 Prairie pronghorns, *1995*	15.00	1.50
A20	$10.00 Ring-necked pheasant, *1996*	15.00	1.50
A21	$10.00 White-tailed deer, *1997*	15.00	1.50
A22	$10.00 Mourning doves, *1998*	15.00	1.50

Pictorial Labels

These stamps are not valid for any hunting fees.
Printed in sheets of 10.
Stamps are numbered serially.

Catalogue values for all unused stamps in this section are for Never Hinged items.

Artist: Neal Anderson.

1991-95

1	$6 Canada geese	11.00
2	$6 Pintails, *1992*	11.00
3	$6 Canvasbacks, *1993*	11.00
4	$6 Mallards, *1994*	11.00
5	$6 Wood ducks, *1995*	11.00

Waterfowl Stamp

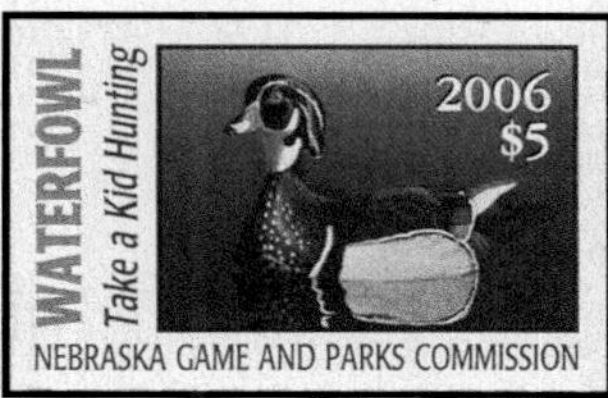

Artist: Brett Cooper

2006-08 ***Rouletted***

6	$5 Wood duck	10.00	2.50
7	$5 Canvasbacks, *2007*	10.00	2.50
8	$5 Trumpeter swans, *2008*	10.00	2.50

Nos. 6-8 are required for hunting.

Artist: Bethany Cooper

2009 ***Rouletted***

9	$5 Pintail, *2009*	10.00	2.50

No. 9 is required for hunting.

NEVADA

Printed in booklet panes of 4.
Stamps are rouletted and selvage is found above and below stamps on the pane. The tab portion of the panes in imperforate.
Starting with No. 4 stamps are numbered serially.

Catalogue values for all unused stamps in this section are for Never Hinged items.

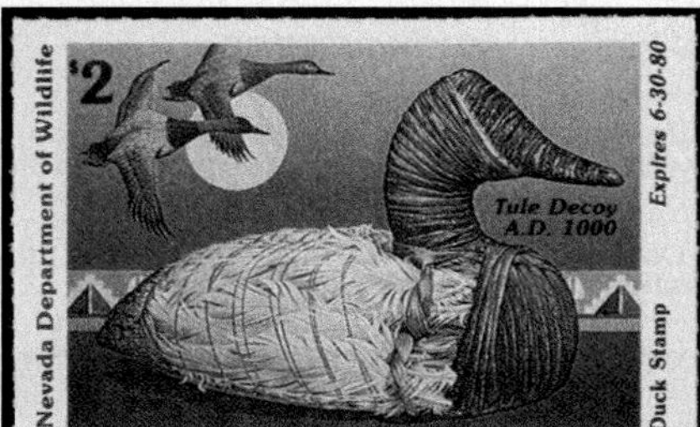

Artists: Larry Hayden, #1; Dick Mcrill, #2; Phil Scholer, #3; Richard Timm, #4; Charles Allen, #5; Robert Steiner, #6; Richard Wilson, #7; Nolan Haan. #8, 12; Sherrie Russell Meline, #9, 21, 31; Jim Hautman, #10; Robert Hautman, #11; Tak Nakamura, #13, 17; Richard Clifton, #14, 22; Steve Hopkins, #15; Mark Mueller, #16; Jeffrey Klinefelter, #18, 23, 28, 32, 37; B. Blight, #19; Janie Kreutzjans, #20; Jeff Hoff, #24; David Brevick, #25; Louis Frisino, #26; Adam Oswald, #27, 33. Ken Michaelsen, #29; James Edwards, #30; Gerald Putt, #34; Rebekah Nastav, #35; Jocelyn Beatty, #36; Mark Thorne, #38; Guy Crittenden, #39.

1979-2017

No.	Description	Unused	Used
1	$2 Canvasbacks and decoy	30.00	12.00
	With numbered tab	45.00	

Stamps with tabs without numbers are printer's waste.

No.	Description	Unused	Used
2	$2 Cinnamon teal, *1980*	8.00	3.00
	With tab	10.00	
3	$2 Whistling swans, *1981*	10.00	3.00
	With tab	12.00	
4	$2 Shovelers, *1982*	10.00	3.00
	With tab	12.00	
5	$2 Gadwalls, *1983*	10.50	3.00
	With tab	11.00	
6	$2 Pintails, *1984*	11.00	3.00
	With tab	12.00	
7	$2 Canada geese, *1985*	20.00	3.00
	With tab	25.00	
8	$2 Redheads, *1986*	17.50	2.50
	With tab	25.00	
9	$2 Buffleheads, *1987*	15.00	2.50
	With tab	20.00	
10	$2 Canvasbacks, *1988*	11.00	2.50
	With tab	13.00	
11	$2 Ross's geese, *1989*	12.00	2.50
	With tab	15.00	
12	$5 Green-winged teal, *1990*	11.00	2.50
	With tab	13.00	
13	$5 White-faced ibis, *1991*	11.00	2.50
	With tab	13.00	
14	$5 American widgeon, *1992*	10.00	2.50
	With tab	11.00	
15	$5 Common goldeneye, *1993*	10.00	2.50
	With tab	11.00	
16	$5 Mallards, *1994*	10.00	2.50
	With tab	11.00	
17	$5 Wood duck, *1995*	10.00	2.50
	With tab	11.00	
18	$5 Ring-necked ducks, *1996*	15.00	2.50
	With tab	20.00	
19	$5 Ruddy ducks, *1997*	11.00	2.50
	With tab	13.00	
20	$5 Hooded merganser, *1998*	12.00	2.50
	With tab	15.00	
21	$5 Canvasback decoy, *1999*	11.00	2.50
	With tab	13.00	
22	$5 Canvasbacks, *2000*	15.00	2.50
	With tab	18.00	
23	$5 Lesser Scaups, *2001*	12.00	2.50
	With tab	15.00	
24	$5 Cinnamon teal, *2002*	11.00	2.50
25	$5 Green-winged teal, *2003*	11.00	2.50
	With tab	11.00	
26	$10 Redheads, *2004*	25.00	2.50
	With tab	27.50	
27	$10 Gadwalls, *2005*	14.00	2.50
	With tab	16.00	
28	$10 Tundra swans, *2006*	14.00	2.50
	With tab	16.00	
29	$10 Wood ducks, *2007*	15.00	2.50
	With tab	16.00	
30	$10 Pintail, *2008*	15.00	2.50
	With tab	16.00	
31	$10 Canada goose, *2009*	15.00	2.50
	With tab	16.00	
32	$10 Shovelers, *2010*	15.00	2.50
	With tab	16.00	
33	$10 Green-winged teal, *2011*	15.00	2.50
	With tab	16.00	
34	$10 Wigeon, *2012*	15.00	2.50
	With tab	16.00	
35	$10 Snow goose, *2013*	15.00	2.50
	With tab	16.00	
36	$10 American coots, *2014*	15.00	2.50
	With tab	16.00	
37	$10 White-fronted geese, *2015*	15.00	2.50
	With tab	16.00	
38	$10 Buffleheads, *2016*	15.00	2.50
	With tab	16.00	
39	$10 Ruddy duck, *2017*	15.00	2.50
	With tab	16.00	

NEW HAMPSHIRE

Printed in booklet panes of 1 with 2-part tab and in sheets of 30. Sheet stamps are perf on four sides. Stamps are numbered serially.

Catalogue values for all unused stamps in this section are for Never Hinged items.

Artists: Richard Plasschaert, #1; Phillip Crowe, #2; Thomas Hirata, #3; Durrant Bell, #4; Robert Steiner, #5-9; Richard Clifton, #10-11, 15; Louis Frisino, #12; Matthew Scharle, #13; Jeffrey Klinefelter, #14; Jim Collins, #16, 20, 23, 24; Bruce Holloway, #17, 21; Susan Knowles Jordan, #18; Charles Freeman, #19; Lindsey Rothe, #22. Kate Kotulak, #25.

1983-2007

No.	Description	Unused	Used
1	$4 Wood ducks	110.00	
a.	Booklet single with 2-part tab	135.00	25.00
2	$4 Mallards, *1984*	75.00	
a.	Booklet single with 2-part tab	110.00	20.00
3	$4 Blue-winged teal, *1985*	75.00	
a.	Booklet single with 2-part tab	95.00	20.00
4	$4 Hooded mergansers, *1986*	20.00	
a.	Booklet single with 2-part tab	30.00	6.00
5	$4 Canada geese, *1987*	12.00	
a.	Booklet single with 2-part tab	14.00	4.00
b.	$50 Governor's edition	*200.00*	
6	$4 Buffleheads, *1988*	12.00	
a.	Booklet single with 2-part tab	14.00	3.00
b.	$4 +$46 Governor's edition	50.00	
7	$4 Black ducks, *1989*	11.00	
a.	Booklet single with 2-part tab	12.00	3.00
b.	$4 +$50 Governor's edition	67.50	
8	$4 Green-winged teal, *1990*	11.00	
a.	Booklet single with 2-part tab	12.00	3.00
b.	$4 +$50 Governor's edition	62.50	
9	$4 Golden retriever & mallards, *1991*	15.00	
a.	Booklet single with 2-part tab	17.00	3.00
b.	$4 +$50 Governor's edition	80.00	

Governor's Editions that follow are so inscribed.

No.	Description	Unused	Used
10	$4 Ring-necked ducks, *1992*	10.00	
a.	Booklet single with 2-part tab	12.00	3.00
b.	Governor's edition	*275.00*	
11	$4 Hooded mergansers, *1993*	10.00	
a.	Booklet single with 2-part tab	12.00	3.00
b.	Governor's edition	*275.00*	
12	$4 Common goldeneyes, *1994*	10.00	
a.	Bklt. single with 2-part tab	12.00	2.50
b.	Governor's edition	*125.00*	
13	$4 Northern pintails, *1995*	10.00	
a.	Bklt. single with 2-part tab	12.00	2.50
b.	Governor's edition	*100.00*	
14	$4 Surf scooters, *1996*	10.00	
a.	Bklt. single with 2-part tab	12.00	2.50
b.	Governor's edition	100.00	
15	$4 Wood ducks, *1997*	10.00	
a.	Bklt. single with 2-part tab	12.00	2.50
b.	Governor's edition	*125.00*	
16	$4 Canada geese, *1998*	10.00	
a.	Bklt. single with 2-part tab	12.00	2.50
b.	Governor's edition	*130.00*	
17	$4 Mallards, *1999*	11.00	
a.	Bklt. single with 2-part tab	12.00	2.50
b.	Governor's edition	*130.00*	
18	$4 Black ducks, *2000*	11.00	
a.	Bklt. single with 2-part tab	12.00	2.50
b.	Governor's edition	—	
19	$4 Blue-winged teal, *2001*	11.00	
a.	Bklt. single with 2-part tab	12.00	2.50
b.	Governor's edition	—	
20	$4 Pintails, *2002*	8.00	
a.	Bklt. single with 2-part tab	10.00	2.50
b.	Governor's edition	*150.00*	
21	$4 Wood ducks, *2003*	8.00	
a.	Bklt. single with 2-part tab	10.00	2.50
b.	Governor's edition	*125.00*	
22	$4 Wood duck, *2004*	8.00	
a.	Bklt. single with 2-part tab	10.00	2.50
b.	Governor's edition	*125.00*	
23	$4 Old squaws, lighthouse, *2005*	10.00	
a.	Bklt. single with 2-part tab	12.50	
b.	Governor's edition	*125.00*	
24	$4 Common eiders, *2006*	8.00	
a.	Bklt. single with 2-part tab	10.00	2.50
b.	Governor's edition	*125.00*	
25	$4 Black ducks, *2007*	8.00	
a.	Bklt. single with 2-part tab	8.00	2.50
b.	Governor's edition	*125.00*	

NEW JERSEY

Resident and non-resident fees.
Printed in sheets of 30 (starting with No. 1) and booklet panes of 10 (all but Nos. 1A, 2A, 3A, 8b, 8Ab). Sheet stamps are perforated on 4 sides.
Stamps are numbered serially.

Catalogue values for all unused stamps in this section are for Never Hinged items.

Artists: Thomas Hirata, #1-1A, 8-8A; David Maass, #2-2A; Ronald Louque, #3-3A; Louis Frisino, #4-4A; Robert Leslie, #5-5A, 9-9A, 14=14A, 25-25A; Daniel Smith, #6-6A; Richard Plasschaert, #7-7A; Bruce Miller, #10-10A; Wilhelm Goebel, #11-11A, 13-13A; Joe Hautman, #12-12A, 17-17A; Phillip Crowe, #15-15A, 21-21A; Richard Clifton, #16-16A; Bob Hautman, #18-18A, 19-19A; Jim Killen, #20-20A; Roger Cruwys, #23-24A.

1984-2008

No.	Description	Unused	Used
1	$2.50 Canvasbacks	35.00	
b.	Booklet single, #51,000-102,000	60.00	10.00
1A	$5 Canvasbacks	50.00	10.00
2	$2.50 Mallards, *1985*	15.00	
b.	Booklet single, #51,000-102,000	25.00	6.00
2A	$5 Mallards, *1985*	18.00	5.00
3	$2.50 Pintails, *1986*	15.00	
b.	Booklet single, #51,000-102,000	15.00	3.00
3A	$5 Pintails, *1986*	13.00	3.00
4	$2.50 Canada geese, *1987*	17.00	
b.	Booklet single, #51,000-102,000	17.00	3.00
4A	$5 Canada geese, *1987*	17.00	
c.	Booklet single, #45,001-60,000	17.00	3.00
5	$2.50 Green-winged teal, *1988*	12.00	
b.	Booklet single, #51,000-102,000	12.00	3.00
5A	$5 Green-winged teal, *1988*	12.00	
c.	Booklet single, #45,001-60,000	12.00	3.00
6	$2.50 Snow geese, *1989*	11.00	
b.	Booklet single, #45,001-60,000	11.00	3.00
c.	Governor's edition	*72.50*	
6A	$5 Snow geese, *1989*	11.00	
d.	Booklet single, #45,001-60,000	11.00	3.00
e.	Governor's edition	*140.00*	

Nos. 11b and 12b were available only in sets of sheets of 30 stamps with matching serial numbers through a sealed bid auction.

No.	Description	Unused	Used
7	$2.50 Wood ducks, *1990*	12.00	
b.	Booklet single, #45,001-60,000	12.00	3.00
7A	$5 Wood ducks, *1990*	12.00	
c.	Booklet single, #45,001-60,000	12.00	3.00
8	$2.50 Atlantic brant, *1991*	9.00	
b.	Booklet single, #45,001-60,000	9.00	3.00
c.	Atlantic "brandt"	32.50	
8A	$5 Atlantic brant, *1991*	12.00	
d.	Booklet single, #45,001-60,000	12.00	3.00
e.	Atlantic "brandt"	37.50	

Matching serial number sets of Nos. 8c and 8Ae were available for sale only with the purchase of matching serial number sets of Nos. 8 and 8A.

No.	Description	Unused	Used
9	$2.50 Bluebills, *1992*	10.00	
b.	Booklet single, #27,691-78,690	10.00	2.50
9A	$5 Bluebills, *1992*	10.00	
c.	Booklet single, #27,691-57,690	10.00	2.50
10	$2.50 Buffleheads, *1993*	10.00	
b.	Booklet single, #27,691-78,690	10.00	2.50
c.	Sheet of 4	*75.00*	
d.	Governor's edition, signed by Florio or Whitman	42.50	
10A	$5 Buffleheads, *1993*	10.00	
e.	Booklet single, #27,691-57,690	10.00	2.50
f.	Sheet of 4	*75.00*	
g.	Governor's edition, signed by Florio or Whitman	82.50	

Nos. 10c and 10Af were available only in sets of sheets with matching serial numbers. The set of sheets sold for $35.

Nos. 10d and 10Ag were available only in sets with matching serial numbers.

No.	Description	Unused	Used
11	$2.50 Black ducks, *1994*	12.00	
b.	Bklt. single, perf. 2 or 3 sides	12.00	2.50
11A	$5 Black ducks, *1994*	14.00	
c.	Bklt. single, perf. 2 or 3 sides	14.00	2.50
12	$2.50 Widgeons, lighthouse, *1995*	12.00	
b.	Bklt. single, perf. 3 sides	12.00	2.50
12A	$5 Widgeons, lighthouse, *1995*	14.00	
c.	Bklt. single, perf. 3 sides	14.00	2.50
13	$5 Goldeneyes, lighthouse, *1996*	14.00	
b.	Bklt. single, perf. 2 or 3 sides	14.00	2.50
13A	$10 Goldeneyes, lighthouse, *1996*	16.00	
c.	Bklt. single, perf. 2 or 3 sides	16.00	2.50

The $2.50 was printed but not used as the rate no longer existed. Later they were sold to collectors. Value, unused $10.

No.	Description	Unused	Used
14	$5 Old squaws, schooner, *1997*	12.00	
b.	Bklt. single, perf. 2 or 3 sides	12.00	2.50
14A	$10 Old squaws, schooner, *1997*	16.00	
c.	Bklt. single, perf. 2 or 3 sides	16.00	2.50
15	$5 Mallards, *1998*	12.00	
b.	Bklt. single, perf. 2 or 3 sides	12.00	2.50
15A	$10 Mallards, *1998*	15.00	
c.	Bklt. single, perf. 2 or 3 sides	15.00	2.50
16	$5 Redheads, perf. 4 sides, *1999*	12.00	
b.	Bklt. single, perf. 2 or 3 sides	12.00	2.50
16A	$10 Redheads, perf. 4 sides, *1999*	15.00	
c.	Bklt. single, perf. 2 or 3 sides	15.00	2.50
17	$5 Canvasbacks, perf. 4 sides, *2000*	13.00	
b.	Bklt. single, perf. 2 or 3 sides	13.00	2.50

17A $10 Canvasbacks, perf. 4 sides, *2000* 15.00
c. Bklt. single, perf. 2 or 3 sides 15.00 2.50
18 $5 Tundra swans, perf. 4 sides, *2001* 11.00
b. Bklt. single, perf. 2 or 3 sides 11.00 2.50
18A $10 Tundra swans, perf. 4 sides, *2001* 14.00
c. Bklt. single, perf. 2 or 3 sides 14.00 2.50
19 $5 Wood ducks, perf. 4 sides, *2002* 11.00
b. Bklt. single, perf. 2 or 3 sides 11.00 2.50
19A $10 Wood ducks, perf. 4 sides, *2002* 14.00
c. Bklt. single, perf. 2 or 3 sides 14.00 2.50
20 $5 Pintails, Labrador retriever perf. 4 sides, *2003* 15.00
b. Bklt. single, perf. 2 or 3 sides 17.50 2.50
20A $10 Pintails, Labrador retriever, perf. 4 sides, *2003* 15.00
c. Bklt. single, perf. 2 or 3 sides 17.50 2.50
21 $5 Hooded merganser decoy, Labrador retriever, perf. 4 sides, *2004* 10.00
b. Bklt. single, perf. 2 or 3 sides 10.00 2.50
21A $10 Hooded merganser decoy, Labrador retriever, perf. 4 sides, *2004* 15.00
c. Bklt. single, perf. 2 or 3 sides 30.00 2.50
22 $5 Canvasback decoys, Chesapeake Bay retriever, perf. 4 sides, *2005* 15.00
b. Bklt. single, perf. 2 or 3 sides 15.00 2.50
22A $10 Canvasback decoys, Chesapeake Bay retriever, perf. 4 sides, *2005* 17.50
c. Bklt. single, perf. 2 or 3 sides 17.50 2.50
23 $5 Wood duck decoy, Golden retriever, perf. 4 sides, *2006* 10.00
b. Bklt. single, perf. 2 or 3 sides 10.00 2.50
23A $10 Wood duck decoy, Golden retriever, perf. 4 sides, *2006* 14.00
c. Bklt. single, perf. 2 or 3 sides 14.00 2.50
24 $5 Green-winged teal, Labrador retriever, perf. 4 sides, *2007* 8.00
b. Bklt. single, perf. 2 or 3 sides 8.00 2.50
24A $10 Green-winged teal, Labrador retriever, perf. 4 sides, *2007* 14.00
c. Bklt. single, perf. 2 or 3 sides 14.00 2.50
25 $5 Canvasbacks, perf. 4 sides, *2008* 8.00
b. Bklt. single, perf. 2 or 3 sides 8.00 2.50
25A $10 Canvasbacks, perf. 4 sides, *2008* 14.00
c. Bklt. single, perf. 2 or 3 sides 14.00 2.50

NEW MEXICO

Printed in booklet panes of 5 and sheets of 30. Stamps are numbered serially.

Catalogue values for all unused stamps in this section are for Never Hinged items.

Artist: Robert Steiner.

1991-94
1 $7.50 Pintails 14.00
Booklet single, with large tab and selvage 14.00 5.00
a. $7.50 +$50 Governor's edition 72.50
2 $7.50 American widgeon, *1992* 14.00
Booklet single, with large tab and selvage 14.00 4.00
a. $7.50 +$50 Governor's edition 65.00
3 $7.50 Mallard, *1993* 14.00
Booklet single, with large tab and selvage 14.00 4.00
a. Sheet of 4 60.00
b. $7.50 +$50 Governor's edition 65.00

No. 3a exists imperf. Value, $100.

No. 4: b, Three birds in flight. c, Two birds in flight. d, Two birds flying over land. e, Bird's head close-up.

4 $7.50 Green-winged teal, sheet of 4, #b.-e., *1994* 85.00
a. Souvenir sheet of 4, #b.-e. (decorative border) 125.00
b.-e. Bklt. single with large tab and selvage, each 15.00 4.00
f. Bklt. pane of 4, #b.-e. 85.00

Stamps in Nos. 4-4a are printed with continuous design and have serial numbers reading down. Stamps in No. 4f have framelines around each design, inscriptions at the top and serial numbers reading up.

No. 4a exists imperf. Value, $225.

NEW YORK

Not required to hunt. Printed in sheets of 30.

Catalogue values for all unused stamps in this section are for Never Hinged items.

Artists: Larry Barton, #1; David Maass, #2; Lee LeBlanc, #3; Richard Plasschaert, #4; Robert Bateman, #5; John Seerey-Lester, #6; Terry Isaac, #7; Anton Ashak, #8; Ron Kleiber, #9; Jerome Hageman, #10; Frederick Szatkowski, #11; Len Rusin, #12; R. Easton, #13; Barbara Woods, #14; Richard Clifton, #15; Rob Leslie, #16; Bruce Miller, #17; Adam Grimm, #18.

1985-2002
1 $5.50 Canada geese 13.00
2 $5.50 Mallards, *1986* 9.00
3 $5.50 Wood ducks, *1987* 9.00
4 $5.50 Pintails, *1988* 9.00
5 $5.50 Greater scaup, *1989* 9.00
6 $5.50 Canvasbacks, *1990* 9.00
7 $5.50 Redheads, *1991* 11.00
8 $5.50 Wood ducks, *1992* 11.00
9 $5.50 Blue-winged teal, *1993* 10.00
10 $5.50 Canada geese, *1994* 12.00
11 $5.50 Common goldeneye, *1995* 12.00
12 $5.50 Common loon, *1996* 11.00
13 $5.50 Hooded merganser, *1997* 9.00
14 $5.50 Osprey, *1998* 9.00
15 $5.50 Buffleheads, *1999* 14.00
16 $5.50 Wood ducks, *2000* 17.00
17 $5.50 Pintails, *2001* 9.00
18 $5.50 Canvasbacks, *2002* 9.00 3.00

NORTH CAROLINA

Not required to hunt until 1988. Printed in sheets of 30. Starting with No. 6, stamps are numbered serially.

Catalogue values for all unused stamps in this section are for Never Hinged items.

Artists: Richard Plasschaert, #1, 10; Jim Killen, #2, 13; Thomas Hirata, #3-4, 16-16A; Larry Barton, #5; Ronald Louque, #6, 18-18A, 19-20A; Louis Frisino, #7; Robert Leslie, #8, 14; Phillip Crowe, #9, 12; Bruce Miller, #11; Wilhelm Goebel, #15-15A, 21-21A; Robert Flowers, #17-17A; Gerald Putt, #25-25A, 27-27A; Scot Storm, #26-26A, 28-28A, 32-32A; Richard Clifton, #29-30A, 35-35A; Jeffrey Klinefelter, #31-31A; Guy Crittenden, #33-33A; Garrett Jacobs, #34-34A, #36-36A.

1983-2018
1 $5.50 Mallards 50.00
2 $5.50 Wood ducks, *1984* 35.00
3 $5.50 Canvasbacks, *1985* 25.00
4 $5.50 Canada geese, *1986* 20.00
5 $5.50 Pintails, *1987* 15.00
6 $5 Green-winged teal, *1988* 10.00 3.00
7 $5 Snow geese, *1989* 16.00 3.00
8 $5 Redheads, *1990* 16.00 3.00
9 $5 Blue-winged teals, *1991* 16.00 3.00
10 $5 American widgeons, *1992* 16.00 3.00
11 $5 Tundra swans, *1993* 16.00 3.00
12 $5 Buffleheads, *1994* 16.00 3.00
13 $5 Brant, lighthouse, *1995* 16.00 3.00
14 $5 Pintails, *1996* 16.00 3.00
15 $5 Wood ducks, perf., *1997* 12.00 3.00
15A $5 Wood ducks, self-adhesive, die cut, *1997* 40.00
16 $5 Canada geese, perf., *1998* 12.00 3.00
16A $5 Canada geese, self-adhesive, die cut, *1998* 30.00
17 $5 Green-winged teal, perf., *1999* 12.00 3.00
17A $5 Green-winged teal, self-adhesive, die cut, *1999* 20.00
18 $10 Green-winged teals, perf., *2000* 25.00 3.00
18A $10 Green-winged teals, self-adhesive, die cut, *2000* 25.00
19 $10 Black duck, perf., *2001* 17.00 3.00
19A $10 Black duck, self-adhesive, die cut, *2001* 20.00
20 $10 Pintails, hunters, dog, perf., *2002* 17.00 3.00
20A $10 Pintails, hunters, dog, self-adhesive, die cut, *2002* 25.00
21 $10 Ring-necked ducks, hunters, dog, perf., *2003* 17.00 3.00
21A $10 Ring-necked ducks, hunters, dog, self-adhesive, die cut, *2003* 30.00
22 $10 Mallards, perf., *2004* 14.00 3.00
22A $10 Mallards, self-adhesive, die cut, *2004* 20.00
23 $10 Green-winged teals, perf., *2005* 14.00 3.00
23A $10 Green-winged teals, self-adhesive, die cut, *2005* 20.00
24 $10 Lesser scaups, perf., *2006* 14.00 3.00
24A $10 Lesser scaups, self-adhesive, die cut, *2006* 15.00
25 $10 Wood ducks, perf., *2007* 15.00 3.00
25A $10 Wood ducks, self-adhesive, die cut, *2007* 15.00
26 $10 Surf scoters, perf., *2008* 15.00 3.00
26A $10 Surf scoters, self-adhesive, die cut, *2008* 15.00
27 $10 Wigeons, perf., *2009* 15.00 3.00
27A $10 Wigeons, self-adhesive, die cut, *2009* 15.00
28 $10 Snow geese, perf., *2010* 15.00 3.00
28A $10 Snow geese, self-adhesive, die cut, *2010* 15.00
29 $10 Canada geese, perf., *2011* 15.00 3.00
29A $10 Canada geese, self-adhesive, die cut, *2011* 15.00
30 $10 Redheads, perf., *2012* 15.00 3.00
30A $10 Redheads, self-adhesive, die cut, *2012* 15.00
31 $10 Shovelers, perf., *2013* 15.00 3.00
31A $10 Shovelers, self-adhesive, die cut *2013* 15.00
32 $10 Hooded mergansers, perf., *2014* 15.00 3.00
32A $10 Hooded mergansers, self-adhesive, die cut *2014* 15.00
33 $10 Black ducks, perf., *2015* 15.00 3.00
33A $10 Black ducks, self-adhesive, die cut, *2015* 15.00
34 $13 Atlantic brant and lighthouse, perf., *2016* 20.00 3.00
34A $13 Atlantic brant and lighthouse, self-adhesive, die cut, *2016* 20.00
35 $13 Gadwalls, perf., *2017* 20.00 3.00
35A $13 Gadwalls, self-adhesive, die cut, *2017* 20.00
36 $13 Canvasbacks, perf., *2018* 16.50 2.50
36A $13 Canvasbacks, self-adhesive, die cut, *2018* 16.50

Nos. 21-36A not required for hunting.

NORTH DAKOTA

Small Game Hunting Stamps

Required to hunt small game and waterfowl statewide. Resident and non-resident fees.

Values for 1967-70 non-resident stamps are for examples with staple holes.

Used values are for signed stamps. Unused values for Nos. 12, 16, 18, 20, 22, 24, 26 and 28 are for stamps on backing.

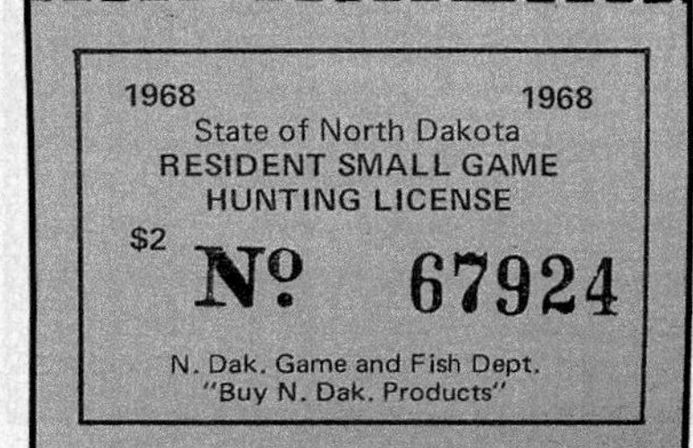

1967-80
1 $2 black, *green* *950.00* 60.00
2 $25 black, *green* *7,500.* *350.00*
3 $2 black, *pink, 1968* 200.00 20.00
4 $25 black, *yellow, 1968* *500.00*
5 $2 black, *green, 1969* 190.00 20.00
6 $35 black, *1969* *450.00*
7 $2 blue, *1970* 160.00 15.00
8 $35 black, *pink, 1970* *250.00* *50.00*
9 $2 black, *yellow, 1971* 125.00 10.00
10 $35 black, *1971* *275.00*
11 $3 black, *pink, 1972* 65.00 5.00
12 $35 red, *1972* *325.00* *75.00*
13 $3 black, *yellow, 1973* 65.00 5.00

14 $35 green, *1973* 2,950. 275.00
15 $3 black, *blue, 1974* 125.00 15.00
16 $35 red, *1974* *275.00* *50.00*
17 $3 black, *1975* 95.00 10.00
18 $35 green, *1975* *225.00* *40.00*
19 $3 black, *dark yellow, 1976* 55.00 5.00
20 $35 red, *1976* *125.00* 25.00
21 $3 black, *1977* 90.00 10.00
22 $35 red, *1977* *100.00* 25.00
23 $5 black, *1978* 45.00 5.00
24 $40 red, *1978* 85.00 20.00
25 $5 black, *1979* 35.00 5.00
26 $40 red, *1979* 45.00 15.00
27 $5 black, *1980* 35.00 5.00
28 $40 green, *1980* 45.00 15.00

Small Game and Habitat Stamps

Required to hunt small game and waterfowl statewide.

Resident ($9), youth ($6) and non-resident ($53) fees.

Resident stamps issued in booklet panes of 5 numbered 20,001-150,000 (1982-86 issues) or 20,001-140,000 (starting with 1987 issue) or sheets of 30 numbered 150,001 and up (1982-86 issues) or 140,001 and up (starting with 1987 issue).

Starting with 1984, resident booklet stamps have straight edges at sides.

Nos. 31, 34, 37, 40 are die cut self adhesives.

Unused values are for stamps on backing.

All youth stamps were issued in booklet panes of 5. Non-resident stamps for 1981, 1982, 1996 and following years were issued in booklet panes of 5.

The 1984-95 non-resident stamps were issued se-tenant with non-resident waterfowl and non-resident general game stamps (rouletted on three sides). The 1994 and 1995 non-resident stamps also were issued se-tenant with only the non-resident general game stamp (rouletted at sides), as well as in booklet panes of 5 (rouletted top and bottom).

Catalogue values for all unused stamps in this section, from this point to the end, are for Never Hinged items.

1981 1981
State of North Dakota
RESIDENT SMALL GAME LICENSE - $6.00
AND HABITAT LICENSE - $3.00
№ 973
N.D. Game and Fish Dept.
NON-TRANSFERABLE

A1

1981
29 A1 $9 black 35.00 3.00
30 A1 $6 black, *blue green* *175.00* 25.00
31 A1 $53 blue 110.00 20.00

A2

Artists: Richard Plaschaert, #32, 73; Terry Radlin, #35; David Maass, #38; Leslie Kouba, #41; Mario Fernandez, #44; Ronald Louque, #47, 75; Louis Frisino, #50; Robert Leslie, #53; Roger Cruwys, #56; Thomas Hirata, #59; Phillip Crowe, #62, 77, 81; Bruce Miller, #65; Darrell Davis, #67; Richard Clifton, #69; Wilhelm Goebel, #71; Jeffrey Klinefelter, #79.

1982
32 A2 $9 Canada geese 100.00
Booklet single with L & R selvage *450.00* 25.00

Serial numbers 1-20,000 are from sheets of 10. Stamps without selvage from booklets sell for considerably less.

33 A1 $6 black, *blue* *175.00* 25.00
34 A1 $53 black 35.00 15.00

1983
35 A2 $9 Mallards 65.00
Booklet single with L & R selvage *1,100.* 25.00

Serial numbers 1-20,000 are from sheets. Stamps without selvage from booklets sell for considerably less.

36 A1 $6 black, *orange* 25.00
37 A1 $53 black *40.00*

1984
38 A2 $9 Canvasbacks 40.00
a. Booklet single, perforated horiz. on 1 or 2 sides *1,350.* 25.00
39 A1 $6 black, *light blue* 25.00
40 A1 $53 black *40.00*

1985
41 A2 $9 Greater scaup 20.00
a. Booklet single, perforated horiz. on 1 or 2 sides *3,250.* 25.00
42 A1 $6 black, *light blue* 25.00
43 A1 $53 black *40.00*

1986
44 A2 $9 Pintails 20.00
a. Booklet single, perforated horiz. on 1 or 2 sides *190.00* 20.00
45 A1 $6 black, *light blue* 20.00
46 A1 $53 black *35.00*

1987
47 A2 $9 Snow geese 12.00
a. Booklet single, perforated horiz. on 1 or 2 sides *50.00* 18.00
48 A1 $6 black, *light blue* — 25.00
49 A1 $53 black *30.00*

1988
50 A2 $9 White-winged scoters 12.00
a. Booklet single, perforated horiz. on 1 or 2 sides 30.00 12.00
51 A1 $6 black, *light blue* — 25.00
52 A1 $53 black *30.00*

Stamps Inscribed "Small Game"

Resident ($6), youth ($3) and non-resident ($50, $75) fees.

1989
53 A2 $6 Redheads 8.00
a. Booklet single, perforated horiz. on 1 or 2 sides 15.00 8.00
54 A1 $3 black, *light blue* — 25.00
55 A1 $50 black 30.00

1990
56 A2 $6 Labrador retriever & mallard 8.00
a. Booklet single, perforated horiz. on 1 or 2 sides 15.00 8.00
57 A1 $3 black, *light blue* 200.00 25.00
58 A1 $50 black 25.00

1991
59 A2 $6 Green-winged teal 8.00
a. Booklet single, perforated horiz. on 1 or 2 sides 13.00 6.00
60 A1 $3 black, *light blue* 200.00 25.00
61 A1 $50 black *350.00* 25.00

1992
62 A2 $6 Blue-winged teal 8.00
a. Booklet single, perforated horiz. on 1 or 2 sides 13.00 6.00
63 A1 $3 black, *light blue* 325.00
64 A1 $50 black 25.00

When supplies of No. 64 ran out, No. 58 was used with the date changed by hand. Unused examples exist. Value, $300.

1993
65 A2 $6 Wood ducks 8.00
a. Booklet single, perforated horiz. on 1 or 2 sides 13.00 6.00
66 A1 $50 black *550.00* 25.00

1994
67 A2 $6 Canada geese 8.00
a. Booklet single, perforated horiz. on 1 or 2 sides 10.00 6.00
68 A1 $75 black, rouletted on 2 adjacent sides *400.00* 20.00
a. Booklet single, rouletted top and bottom —

1995
69 A2 $6 Widgeon 8.00
a. Booklet single, perforated horiz. on 1 or 2 sides 10.00 5.00
70 A1 $75 black, rouletted on 2 adjacent sides *350.00* 20.00
a. Booklet single, rouletted top and bottom —

1996
71 A2 $6 Mallards 8.00
a. Booklet single, perforated horiz. on 1 or 2 sides 10.00 2.50
72 A1 $75 black, rouletted at top and bottom —

1997
73 A2 $6 White-fronted geese 8.00
a. Booklet single, perforated horiz. on 1 or 2 sides 10.00 2.50
74 A1 $75 black, rouletted at top and bottom —

1998
75 A2 $6 Blue-winged teal 8.00
a. Bklt. single, perforated horiz. on 1 or 2 sides 10.00 2.50
76 A1 $75 black, rouletted at top and bottom —

1999
77 A2 $6 Gadwalls 8.00
a. Bklt. single, perforated horiz. on 1 or 2 sides 10.00 2.50
78 A1 $75 black, rouletted at top and bottom —

2000-01
79 $6 Pintails, *2000* 8.00
a. Bklt. single, perforated horiz. on 1 or 2 sides 10.00 2.50
81 A2 $6 Canada geese, *2001* 10.00
a. Bklt. single, perforated horiz. on 1 or 2 sides 10.00 2.50

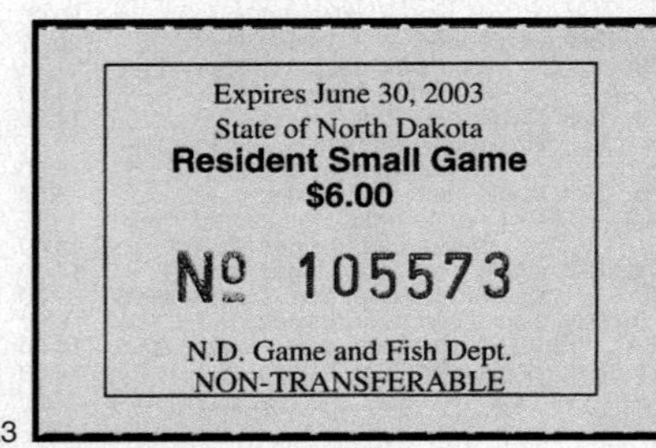

A3

2002-15
83 A3 $6 black, *green, 2002* 12.00
84 A3 $6 black, *green, 2003* 12.00
85 A3 $6 black, *green, 2004* 12.00
86 A3 $6 black, *green, 2005* 12.00
87 A3 $6 black, *green, 2006* 9.00
88 A3 $6 black, *green, 2007* 8.00
89 A3 $6 black, *green, 2008* 8.00
90 A3 $6 black, *green, 2009* 8.00
91 A3 $6 black, *green, 2010* 8.00
92 A3 $6 black, *green, 2011* 8.00
93 A3 $6 black, *green, 2012* 8.00
94 A3 $6 black, *green, 2013* 8.00
95 A3 $10 black, *green, 2014* 13.00
96 A3 $10 black, *green, 2015* 13.00

Non-Resident Waterfowl Stamps

Required by non-residents to hunt waterfowl only.

Unused examples of Nos. A1a, A13a-A19a have no serial number. Used stamps have number written in.

Nos. A1-A10 are self-adhesive, die cut. Others are rouletted.

Catalogue values for all unused stamps in this section are for Never Hinged items.

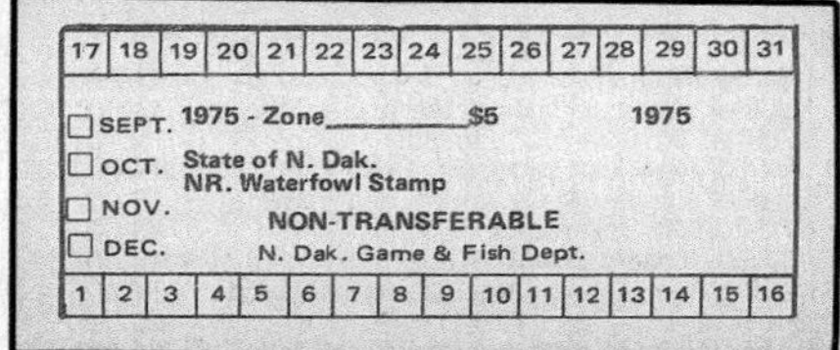

Illustration reduced.

1975-99
A1 $5 green *225.00*
a. No serial number 150.00 —
A2 $5 red, *1976* *425.00* *100.00*
A3 $5 red, *1977* 225.00 *75.00*
A4 $5 red, *1978* 110.00 25.00
A5 $5 red, *1979* 85.00 20.00
A6 $5 green, *1980* 90.00 20.00
A7 $8 blue, *1981* 200.00 25.00
A8 $8 black, *1982* 27.50 15.00
A9 $8 black, *1983* *55.00*
A10 $8 black, *1984* *50.00*
A11 $8 black, *1985* *45.00*
A12 $8 black, *1986* *45.00*
A13 $8 black, *1987* *40.00*
a. No serial number *550.00* *50.00*
A14 $8 black, *1988* 35.00
a. No serial number *450.00* *50.00*
A15 $8 black, *1989* 25.00
a. No serial number, light green paper *450.00* *50.00*
A16 $8 black, *1990* 25.00
a. No serial number *400.00* *50.00*

A17	$8 black, *1991*	*500.00*	25.00
a.	No serial number	375.00	*35.00*
A18	$8 black, *1992*		20.00
a.	No serial number	*300.00*	35.00

When supplies of No. A18 ran out, No. A16 was used with the date changed by hand. Values, unused $200, used $50.

A19	$10 black, *1993*	*375.00*	20.00
a.	No serial number	*275.00*	30.00
A20	$10 black, rouletted on 2 adjacent sides, *1994*	*375.00*	20.00
a.	No serial number, rouletted top and bottom	275.00	30.00
A21	$10 black, rouletted on 2 adjacent sides, *1995*	*350.00*	20.00
a.	No serial number, rouletted top and bottom	150.00	25.00
A22	$10 black, rouletted top and bottom, *1996*	*110.00*	20.00
A23	$10 black, rouletted top and bottom, *1997*	*95.00*	14.00
A24	$10 black, rouletted top and bottom, *1998*	*85.00*	12.00
A25	$10 black, rouletted top and bottom, *1999*	*75.00*	12.00

Resident Sportsmen's Stamps

Required to hunt a variety of game, including waterfowl.

Catalogue values for all unused stamps in this section are for Never Hinged items.

1992-93 Resident
ND Sportsmens License
$25.00
Fishing - Small Game
General Game & Habitat
Furbearer
№ 12968
NON-TRANSFERABLE

1992-98

2A1	$25 black & purple, *1992-1993*	*2,500.*	*95.00*
2A2	$25 black & purple, *1993-1994*	*1,500.*	*35.00*
2A3	$25 black & purple, *1994-1995*	*375.00*	*25.00*
2A4	$25 black & purple, *1995-1996*	*250.00*	*20.00*
2A5	$25 black & purple, *1996-1997*	*200.00*	*15.00*
2A6	$27 black & purple, *1997-1998*	*125.00*	*12.00*

OHIO

Pymatuning Lake Waterfowl Hunting Stamps

Pymatuning Hunting License
Valid when attached to Resident Hunters and Trappers License.
Authority H. B. 668.
YEAR
1938
$1.00
NO FEE

1938-45

A1	$1 black, *light yellow*	—
A2	$1 black, *gray, 1939*	—
A3	$1 black, *blue, 1940*	—
A4	$1 black, *pink, 1941*	—
A5	$1 black, *green, 1942*	—
A6	$1 black, *1943*	—
A7	$1 black, *manila, 1944*	—
A8	$1 black, *manila, 1945*	—

Statewide Issues

Nos. 1-18 printed in sheets of 16. Starting with No. 19, stamps are printed in souvenir sheets of 1.

Catalogue values for all unused stamps in this section are for Never Hinged items.

Artists: John Ruthven, #1; Harry Antis, #2; Harold Roe, #3, 6, 15, 17; Ronald Louque, #4; Lynn Kaatz, #5, 8; Cynthie Fisher, #7; Jon Henson, #9; Gregory Clair, #10, 25; Samuel Timm, #11; Kenneth Nanney, #12; Richard Clifton, #13, 26; Ron Kleiber, #14; D. J. Cleland-Hura, #16: Timothy Donovan, #18; Mark Anderson, #19; Brian Blight, #20, 22; Jeffrey Klinefelter, #21, 27, 32, 36; Robert Mertopulos, #23; Adam Grimm, #24, 33; Joel Rogers, #28, 30; Jeffrey Hoff, #29; Tom Morgan Crain, #31; Gunnar Hillard, #34; Christine Clayton, #35; Daniel Allard, #37.

1982-2018

1	$5.75 Wood ducks	50.00	10.00
2	$5.75 Mallards, *1983*	35.00	10.00
3	$5.75 Green-winged teal, *1984*	35.00	8.00
4	$5.75 Redheads, *1985*	25.00	6.00
5	$5.75 Canvasback, *1986*	25.00	5.00
6	$6 Blue-winged teal, *1987*	12.00	4.00
7	$6 Common goldeneyes, *1988*	12.00	4.00
8	$6 Canada geese, *1989*	12.00	3.00
9	$9 Black ducks, *1990*	16.00	3.00
10	$9 Lesser scaup, *1991*	16.00	3.00
11	$9 Wood duck, *1992*	16.00	3.00
12	$9 Buffleheads, *1993*	16.00	3.00
13	$11 Mallards, *1994*	21.00	2.50
14	$11 Pintails, *1995*	22.50	2.50
15	$11 Hooded mergansers, *1996*	24.00	2.50
16	$11 Wigeons, *1997*	20.00	2.50
17	$11 Gadwall, *1998*	20.00	2.50
18	$11 Mallard, *1999*	18.00	2.50

Souvenir Sheet

Rouletted

19	$11 Buffleheads, *2000*	18.00	2.50
20	$11 Canvasback, *2001*	18.00	2.50
21	$11 Ring-necked ducks, *2002*	17.00	2.50
22	$11 Hooded mergansers, *2003*	17.00	2.50
23	$15 Tundra swans, *2004*	20.00	2.50
24	$15 Wood duck, *2005*	20.00	2.50
25	$15 Pintail, *2006*	27.50	2.50
26	$15 Canada goose, *2007*	40.00	2.50
27	$15 Green-winged teal, *2008*	22.50	2.50
28	$15 Common goldeneye, *2009*	22.50	2.50
29	$15 Ruddy ducks, *2010*	22.50	2.50
30	$15 Red-breasted merganser, *2011*	40.00	2.50
31	$15 Mallards, *2012*	22.50	2.50
32	$15 Blue-winged teal, *2013*	22.50	2.50
33	$15 Pintail, *2014*	22.50	2.50
34	$15 Shovelers, *2015*	22.50	2.50
35	$15 Wood ducks, *2016*	22.50	2.50
36	$15 Wigeons, *2017*	22.50	2.50
37	$15 Ring-necked ducks, *2018*	19.00	2.50

Nos. 19-37 not required for hunting.

OKLAHOMA

Printed in booklet panes of 10 (Nos. 1-3) and booklet panes of 5 (Starting with No. 4). No. 10 was the first to be printed in a sheet of 30, No. 17 in a sheet of 24.

Catalogue values for all unused stamps in this section are for Never Hinged items.

Artists: Patrick Sawyer, #1; Hoyt Smith, #2, 5, 7, 20; Jeffrey Frey, #3; Gerald Mobley, #4, 6; Rayburn Foster, #8, 12; Jim Gaar, #9; Wanda Mumm, #10; Ronald Louque, #11; Jeffrey Mobley, #13; Jerome Hageman, #14; Richard Kirkman, #15; Richard Clifton, #16, 33; Greg Everhart, #17; Mark Anderson, #18, 24, 38; Jeffrey Klinefelter, #19, 26; Paul Makuchal, #21; Daniel Brevick, #22; Brian Blight, #23; Scot Storm, #25; James Hublick, #27. Jeffrey Hoff, #28; Russell Duerksen, #29; Timothy Turenne, #30; John Brennan, #31, 34; George Lockwood, #32; Shea Meyer, #35; Guy Crittenden, #36; Adam Oswald, #37; Paul Bridgford, #39.

1980-2018

1	$4 Pintails	30.00	10.00
2	$4 Canada goose, *1981*	17.50	8.00
3	$4 Green-winged teal, *1982*	10.00	4.00
4	$4 Wood ducks, *1983*	10.00	10.00
5	$4 Ring-necked ducks, *1984*	10.00	3.00
	With tab	10.00	
6	$4 Mallards, *1985*	8.00	3.00
	With tab	10.00	
7	$4 Snow geese, *1986*	10.00	3.00
	With tab	10.00	
8	$4 Canvasbacks, *1987*	8.00	3.00
	With tab	9.00	
9	$4 Widgeons, *1988*	8.00	3.00
	With tab	9.00	
10	$4 Redheads, *1989*	8.00	3.00
	Booklet single, with tab & selvage at L, selvage at R	9.00	
a.	Governor's edition	*125.00*	

No. 10a was available only in sheets of 30 through a sealed bid auction.

11	$4 Hooded merganser, *1990*	7.50	3.00
	Booklet single, with tab & selvage at L, selvage at R	8.50	
12	$4 Gadwalls, *1991*	7.50	3.00
	Booklet single, with tab & selvage at L, selvage at R	8.50	
13	$4 Lesser scaup, *1992*	7.50	3.00
	Booklet single, with tab & selvage at L, selvage at R	8.50	
14	$4 White-fronted geese, *1993*	7.50	3.00
	Booklet single, with tab & selvage at L, selvage at R	8.50	
15	$4 Blue-winged teal, *1994*	7.50	3.00
	Booklet single, with tab & selvage at L, selvage at R	8.50	
16	$4 Ruddy ducks, *1995*	7.50	3.00
	Booklet single, with tab & selvage at L, selvage at R	8.50	
17	$4 Bufflehead, *1996*	7.50	3.00
	Booklet single, with selvage at L & R	8.50	
18	$4 Goldeneyes, *1997*	7.50	3.00
	Bklt. single, with selvage at L & R	8.50	
19	$4 Shovelers, *1998*	7.50	3.00
	Bklt. single, with selvage at L & R	8.50	
20	$4 Canvasbacks, *1999*	15.00	3.00
21	$4 Pintails, *2000*	8.00	3.00
22	$4 Canada goose, *2001*	8.00	3.00
23	$4 Green-winged teal, *2002*	8.00	3.00
24	$10 Wood duck, *2003*	15.00	3.00
25	$10 Mallard, *2004*	15.00	3.00
26	$10 Snow geese, *2005*	15.00	3.00
27	$10 Widgeons, *2006*	15.00	3.00
28	$10 Redheads, *2007*	15.00	3.00
29	$10 Mallards, Labrador retriever, *2008*	15.00	3.00
30	$10 Gadwalls, *2009*	15.00	3.00
31	$10 Ring-necked duck, *2010*	15.00	3.00
32	$10 Blue-winged teal, *2011*	15.00	3.00
33	$10 White-fronted goose, *2012*	15.00	3.00
34	$10 Common goldeneye, *2013*	15.00	3.00
35	$10 Canvasback, *2014*	15.00	3.00
36	$10 Pintails, *2015*	15.00	3.00
37	$10 Mallard, *2016*	15.00	3.00
38	$10 Green-winged teal, *2017*	15.00	3.00
39	$10 Shovelers, *2018*	14.00	3.00

OREGON

Non-resident fees begin in 1994.

Issued in sheets of 30, except for No. 6. Nos. 2-4 also exist from booklet panes of 5.

Stamps are numbered serially. Nos. 11b, 11c have serial numbers on sheet selvage.

Nos. 10 and 11 were issued on computer form. Unused values are for stamps on form.

Catalogue values for all unused stamps in this section are for Never Hinged items.

Artists: Michael Sieve, #1-3; Dorothy M. Smith, #4; Darrell Davis, #5; Phillip Crowe, #7; Roger Cruwys, #8; Louis Frisino,

#9; Kip Richmond, #10; R. Bruce Horsfall, #11; Richard Plasschaert, #12-13; Robert Steiner, #14-37; Harold Cramer Smith, #38; Tim Turene, #39; Robert Andrea, #40; Richard Clifton, #41-42.

1984-88

1 $5 Canada geese 20.00 7.00
2 $5 Lesser snow goose, *1985* 25.00 10.00
Booklet single, with 3 tabs (2 at left) *350.00*
3 $5 Pacific brant, perf. 4 sides, *1986* 15.00
a. Booklet single, with 2-part tab 15.00 4.00
4 $5 White-fronted geese, perf. 4 sides, *1987* 15.00
a. Booklet single, with 2-part tab 15.00 3.00
5 $5 Great Basin Canada geese, *1988* 15.00 3.00
a. Booklet pane of 1 15.00

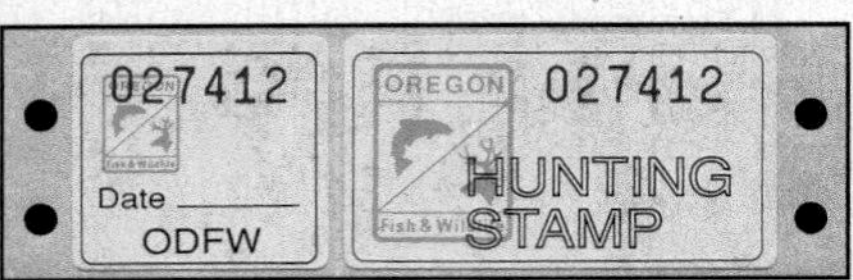

1989-2018 **Die cut self-adhesive**

6 ($5) Red Nos., 16,001 and up 15.00 *6.00*
a. Black Nos., 001-16,000 30.00 *12.50*

This provisional stamp was used in early 1989, when the regular stamps were delayed. Unused value is for stamp and adjacent label with serial number on backing paper.

Designs like No. 1

7 $5 Black Labrador retriever & pintails, *1989* 15.00 2.50
a. Booklet pane of 1 15.00
8 $5 Mallards & golden retriever, *1990* 15.00 2.50
a. Booklet pane of 1 15.00
9 $5 Buffleheads & Chesapeake Bay retriever, perf, *1991* 15.00
a. Rouletted at L 15.00 2.50

No. 9a is straight edged on 3 sides and stamp is attached to paper by selvage. Unused value is for stamp attached to paper.

10 $5 Green-winged teal, *1992* 15.00
a. Die cut, self-adhesive 15.00 2.50
11 $5 Mallards, vert., *1993* 15.00
a. Die cut self-adhesive 15.00 2.50
b. Sheet of 2 22.50
c. $50 Governor's edition sheet of 1 75.00

No. 11b contains No. 11 and the Oregon upland bird stamp. Nos. 11b, 11c exist imperf. Values: No. 11a imperf., $150; No. 11b imperf., $350.

12 $5 Pintails, perf. 4 sides, *1994* 15.00
a. Die cut self-adhesive 15.00 2.50
13 $25 Pintails, diff., die cut self-adhesive, *1994* 40.00 —
14 $5 Wood ducks, *1995* 15.00
a. Booklet pane of 1 15.00 2.50
15 $25 Columbian sharp-tailed grouse, bklt. pane of 1, *1995* 160.00 —
16 $5 Mallards, *1996* 20.00
a. Booklet pane of 1 15.00 2.50
17 $25 Common snipe, booklet pane of 1, *1996* 140.00 —
18 $5 Canvasbacks, *1997* 20.00
a. Booklet pane of 1 15.00 2.50
19 $25 Canvasbacks, booklet pane of 1, *1997* 140.00
20 $5 Pintails, *1998* 20.00
a. Booklet pane of 1 15.00 2.50
21 $25 Pintails, booklet pane of 1, *1998* 37.50
22 $5 Canada geese, *1999* 17.50
a. Booklet pane of 1 15.00 2.50
23 $25 Canada geese, booklet pane of 1, *1999* 65.00
24 $7.50 Canada geese, mallard, widgeon, *2000* 15.00 2.50
a. Booklet pane of 1, no cover 50.00
25 $7.50 Redheads, *2001* 15.00 2.50
a. Booklet pane of 1, no cover 20.00
26 $7.50 American wigeon, *2002* 14.00 2.50
a. Booklet pane of 1, no cover 14.00
27 $7.50 Wood duck, *2003* 14.00 2.50
a. Booklet pane of 1, no cover 14.00
28 $7.50 Ross's goose, *2004* 13.00 2.50
a. Booklet pane of 1, no cover 15.00
29 $7.50 Hooded merganser, *2005* 13.00 2.50
a. Booklet pane of 1, no cover 13.00
30 $7.50 Pintail, mallard, *2006* 12.00 2.50
a. Booklet pane of 1, no cover 12.00
31 $7.50 Wood ducks, *2007* 12.00 2.50
a. Booklet pane of 1, no cover 12.00
32 $7.50 Pintails, *2008* 12.00 2.50
a. Booklet pane of 1, no cover 12.00
33 $7.50 Mallards, *2009* 12.00 2.50
a. Booklet pane of 1, no cover 12.00
34 $9.50 Wood duck, *2010* 16.00 2.50
a. Booklet pane of 1, no cover 16.00
35 $9.50 Canvasback, *2011* 16.00 2.50
a. Booklet pane of 1, no cover 16.00
36 $9.50 Mallard, *2012* 16.00 2.50
a. Booklet pane of 1, no cover 16.00
37 $9.50 Wigeons, *2013* 16.00 2.50
a. Booklet pane of 1, no cover 16.00
38 $9.50 Canada geese, *2014* 16.00 2.50
a. Booklet pane of 1, no cover 16.00
39 $9.50 Pintail, *2015* 16.00 2.50
a. Booklet pane of 1, no cover 16.00
40 $10.50 Common mergansers, *2016* 18.00 2.50
a. Booklet pane of 1, no cover 18.00
41 $10.50 Gadwalls, *2017* 18.00 2.50
a. Booklet pane of 1, no cover 18.00
42 $11 Buffleheads, *2018* 17.00 2.50
a. Booklet pane of 1, no cover 17.00

Nos. 27-42 not required for hunting.

PENNSYLVANIA

Not required to hunt.
Printed in sheets of 10.

Catalogue values for all unused stamps in this section are for Never Hinged items.

Artists: Ned Smith, #1, 3; Jim Killen, #2; Robert Knutson, #4; Robert Leslie, #5; John Heldersbach, #6; Ronald Louque, #7; Thomas Hirata, #8, 12; Gerald W. Putt, #9, 14, 16, 18, 20, 23, 25, 27, 29, 31, 33, 36; Robert Sopchick, #10; Glen Reichard, #11; Mark Bray, #13; Clark Weaver, #15, 17, 19; Jocelyn Beatty, #21, 32; Carl Clark, #22; Kerry Holzman, #24; Scott Calpino, #26, 28, 30; Linda Hilgert, #34; Scott Calpino, #35.

1983-2018

1 $5.50 Wood ducks 10.00
2 $5.50 Canada geese, *1984* 8.00
3 $5.50 Mallards, *1985* 8.00
4 $5.50 Blue-winged teal, *1986* 8.00
5 $5.50 Pintails, *1987* 8.00
6 $5.50 Wood ducks, *1988* 8.00
7 $5.50 Hooded mergansers, *1989* 9.00
8 $5.50 Canvasbacks, *1990* 9.00
9 $5.50 Widgeons, *1991* 9.00
10 $5.50 Canada geese, *1992* 9.00
11 $5.50 Northern shovelers, *1993* 9.00
12 $5.50 Pintails, *1994* 9.00
13 $5.50 Buffleheads, *1995* 9.00
14 $5.50 Black ducks, *1996* 9.00
15 $5.50 Hooded merganser, *1997* 9.00
16 $5.50 Wood ducks, *1998* 9.00
17 $5.50 Ring-necked ducks, *1999* 9.00
18 $5.50 Green-winged teal, *2000* 9.00
19 ($5.50) Pintails, *2001* 9.00
20 $5.50 Snow geese, *2002* 9.00 2.50
21 $5.50 Canvasbacks, *2003* 9.00 2.50
22 $5.50 Hooded mergansers, *2004* 9.00 2.50
23 $5.50 Red-breasted mergansers, *2005* 8.00 2.50
24 $5.50 Pintails, *2006* 8.00 2.50
25 $5.50 Wood ducks, *2007* 8.00 2.50
26 $5.50 Redheads, *2008* 8.00 2.50
27 $5.50 Hooded mergansers, *2009* 8.00 2.50
28 $5.50 Canvasbacks, *2010* 8.00 2.50
29 $5.50 Wigeons, *2011* 8.00 2.50
30 $5.50 Ruddy ducks, *2012* 8.00 2.50
31 $5.50 Black ducks, *2013* 8.00 2.50
32 $5.50 Shoveler, *2014* 8.00 2.50
33 $5.50 Green-winged teal, *2015* 8.00 2.50
34 $5.50 Pintails, *2016* 8.00 2.50
35 $5.50 Buffleheads, *2017* 8.00 2.50
36 $5.50 Mallards, *2018* 8.00 2.50

RHODE ISLAND

Issued in booklet panes of 5 and sheets of 30. Starting with No. 8, the spacing of the reverse text of the booklet stamp differs from the sheet stamp. Stamps are numbered serially.

Catalogue values for all unused stamps in this section are for Never Hinged items.

Artists: Robert Steiner, #1-7, 9-10, 16; Charles Allen, #8; Keith Mueller, #11-15, 17-20; Miri Kim, #21-23; Jung Kim, #24; Lea Fabre, #25; Eleni Giannopoulos, #26; Joel Dunn, #27; Hope Anderson, #28; Amena Simone, #29, Kaia Bennett, #30.

1989-2018

1 $7.50 Canvasbacks 12.00 3.00
Booklet single, with tab 16.00
a. $7.50 +$50 Governor's edition 92.50

No. 1a exists without serial number.

2 $7.50 Canada geese, *1990* 12.00 3.00
Booklet single, with tab 15.00
a. $7.50 +$50 Governor's edition 72.50

No. 2a exists without serial number.

3 $7.50 Wood ducks & Labrador retriever, *1991* 20.00 3.00
Booklet single, with tab 22.50
a. $7.50 +$50 Governor's edition 60.00

No. 3a exists without serial number.

4 $7.50 Blue-winged teal, *1992* 15.00 3.00
Booklet single, with tab 15.00
a. $7.50 +$50 Governor's edition 60.00

No. 4a exists without serial number.

5 $7.50 Pintails, *1993* 13.00 3.00
Booklet single, with tab 13.00
a. Sheet of 4 65.00

No. 5a imperf. is printer's waste.

6 $7.50 Wood ducks, *1994* 17.00 2.50
Booklet single, with tab and selvage 17.00
7 $7.50 Hooded mergansers, *1995* 13.00 2.50
Booklet single, with tab and selvage 13.00
a. Governor's edition *110.00*

No. 7a inscribed "Governor's edition."

8 $7.50 Harlequin, *1996* 22.50 2.50
Booklet single, with tab and selvage 22.50
a. Governor's edition *125.00*

No. 8a inscribed "Governor's edition" and has serial number with "G" prefix.

9 $7.50 Greater scaup, *1997* 13.00 2.50
Booklet single, with tab and selvage 14.00
a. Governor's edition *110.00*

No. 9a inscribed "Governor's edition" and has serial number with "G" prefix.

10 $7.50 Black ducks, *1998* 13.00 2.50
Booklet single, with tab and selvage 14.00
a. Governor's edition *125.00*

No. 11-14 do not have a serial number.

Rouletted

11 $7.50 Common eiders, *1999* 17.00 2.50
Horiz. pair from booklet pane 60.00

Booklet pane contains 10 stamps.

12 $7.50 Canvasbacks, *2000* 16.00 2.50
a. Inscribed "Hunter" 18.00
a. Governor's edition —
13 $7.50 Mallard, black duck, *2001* 16.00 2.50
a. Inscribed "Hunter" 17.50
a. Governor's edition *125.00*
14 $7.50 White-winged scoter, lighthouse, *2002* 13.00 2.50
a. Inscribed "Hunter" 13.00
b. Governor's edition 130.00 —
15 $7.50 Old squaws, *2003* 12.00 2.50
a. Inscribed "Hunter" 13.00
b. Governor's edition 130.00 —
16 $7.50 Canvasbacks, *2004* 11.00 2.50
a. Inscribed "Hunter" 12.00
b. Governor's edition 130.00 —
17 $7.50 Black ducks, lighthouse, *2005* 11.00 2.50
a. Inscribed "Hunter" 11.00
18 $7.50 Canvasbacks, lighthouse, *2006* 11.00 2.50
a. Inscribed "Hunter" 11.00
b. Governor's edition *130.00* —
19 $7.50 Harlequin decoy, *2007* 11.00 2.50
a. Inscribed "Hunter" 11.00
b. Governor's edition *130.00* —
20 $7.50 Mallard decoys, *2008* 11.00 2.50
a. Inscribed "Hunter" 15.00
21 $7.50 Mallard decoys, *2009* 11.00 2.50
a. Inscribed "Hunter" 11.00
22 $7.50 Red-breasted merganser, *2010* 12.50 2.50
a. Inscribed "Hunter" 12.50
23 $7.50 Barrow's goldeneye, *2011* 12.50 2.50
a. Inscribed "Hunter" 12.50
24 $7.50 Mallard, *2012* 12.50 2.50
a. Inscribed "Hunter" 12.50

No.	Description	Unused	Used
25	$7.50 Canvasback, *2013*	12.50	2.50
a.	Inscribed "Hunter"	12.50	
26	$7.50 Canvasbacks, *2014*	12.50	2.50
a.	Inscribed "Hunter"	12.50	
27	$7.50 Mallard, *2015*	12.50	2.50
a.	Inscribed "Hunter"	12.50	
28	$7.50 Wood duck, *2016*	12.50	2.50
a.	Inscribed "Hunter"	12.50	
29	$7.50 Lesser scaup, *2017*	12.50	2.50
a.	Inscribed "Hunter"	12.50	

Self-Adhesive

No.	Description	Unused	Used
30	$7.50 Harlequin, *2018*	10.50	2.50
a.	Inscribed "Hunter"	10.50	

Nos. 15-30 have no serial number.

SOUTH CAROLINA

Issued in sheets of 30. Stamps with serial numbers were to be issued to hunters.

Catalogue values for all unused stamps in this section are for Never Hinged items.

Artists: Lee LeBlanc, #1; Bob Binks, #2; Jim Killen, #3, 8, 11, 27-33; Al Dornish, #4; Rosemary Millette, #5; Daniel Smith, #6; Steve Dillard, #7; Lee Cable, #9; John Wilson, #10; Russell Cobane, #12; Bob Bolin, #13; Joe Hautman, #14; Rodney Huckaby, #15, 17, 22, 25; D. J. Cleland-Hura, #16, 18; Denise Nelson, #19; Mark Constantine, #20; Jeffrey Klinefelter, #21; James Hublick, #23; Eddie LeRoy, #24; Richard D. Benson, #26; Donnie Hughes, #34; Richard Clifton, #35-36; Scott Storm, #37-38.

1981-2018

No.	Description	Unused	Used
1	$5.50 Wood ducks	60.00	15.00

No. 2-22 do not have a serial number.

No.	Description	Unused	Used
2	$5.50 Mallards, *1982*	95.00	
a.	Serial number on reverse	*400.00*	25.00
3	$5.50 Pintails, *1983*	95.00	
a.	Serial number on reverse	*350.00*	25.00
4	$5.50 Canada geese, *1984*	65.00	
a.	Serial number on reverse	*150.00*	15.00
5	$5.50 Green-winged teal, *1985*	60.00	
a.	Serial number on reverse	85.00	15.00
6	$5.50 Canvasbacks, *1986*	25.00	
a.	Serial number on reverse	42.50	10.00
7	$5.50 Black ducks, *1987*	20.00	
a.	Serial number on reverse	22.50	5.00
8	$5.50 Widgeon & spaniel, *1988*	20.00	
a.	Serial number on reverse	30.00	5.00
9	$5.50 Blue-winged teal, *1989*	11.00	
a.	Serial number on reverse	14.00	4.00
10	$5.50 Wood ducks, *1990*	10.00	
a.	Serial number on reverse	10.00	4.00
b.	$5.50 +$44.50 Governor's edition	82.50	
c.	$5.50 +$94.50 Governor's edition	190.00	

All examples of No. 10c are signed by the governor.

No.	Description	Unused	Used
11	$5.50 Labrador retriever, pintails & decoy, *1991*	11.00	
a.	Serial number on reverse	11.00	4.00
12	$5.50 Buffleheads, *1992*	15.00	
a.	Serial number on front	15.00	3.00
13	$5.50 Lesser scaups, *1993*	15.00	
a.	Serial number on front	15.00	3.00
14	$5.50 Canvasbacks, *1994*	15.00	
a.	Serial number on front	15.00	2.50
15	$5.50 Shovelers, lighthouse, *1995*	15.00	
a.	Serial number on front	15.00	2.50
16	$5.50 Redheads, lighthouse, *1996*	18.00	
a.	Serial number on front	18.00	2.50
17	$5.50 Old squaws, *1997*	18.00	
a.	Serial number on front	18.00	2.50
18	$5.50 Green-winged teals, *1998*	18.00	
a.	Serial number on front	18.00	2.50
19	$5.50 Barrow's goldeneyes, *1999*	18.00	
20	$5.50 Wood ducks, boykin spaniel, *2000*	15.00	2.50
21	$5.50 Mallard, decoy, yellow Labrador retriever, *2001*	15.00	2.50
22	$5.50 Wigeons, chocolate Labrador retriever, *2002*	15.00	2.50
23	$5.50 Green-winged teal, *2003*	15.00	2.50
24	$5.50 Pintails, Labrador retriever, *2004*	15.00	2.50
25	$5.50 Canvasbacks, *2005*	10.00	2.50
26	$5.50 Black ducks, *2006*	10.00	2.50
27	$5.50 Redheads, Golden retriever, *2007*	10.00	2.50
28	$5.50 Blue-winged teal, Labrador retriever, *2008*	10.00	2.50
29	$5.50 Ring-necked duck, Labrador retriever, *2009*	10.00	2.50
30	$5.50 Wood duck and Boykin spaniel, *2010*	10.00	2.50
31	$5.50 Blue-winged teal and Chocolate Labrador retriever, *2011*	10.00	2.50
32	$5.50 Green-winged teal and Golden retriever, *2012*	10.00	2.50
33	$5.50 Black duck and Boykin spaniel, *2013*	10.00	2.50
34	$5.50 Wood ducks, *2014*	10.00	2.50
35	$5.50 Hooded mergansers, *2015*	15.00	2.50
36	$5.50 Mottled ducks, *2016*	10.00	2.50
37	$5.50 Wigeons, *2017*	10.00	2.50
38	$5.50 Pintail, *2018*	10.00	2.50

Nos. 23-38 have no serial number.

SOUTH DAKOTA

Resident Waterfowl Stamps

Vertical safety paper (words read up)

1949-50

No.	Description	Unused	Used
1	$1 blk, *grn,* vert. safety paper	*1,750.*	85.00
a.	Horizontal safety paper	—	*150.00*
2	$1 blk, *lt brn,* vert. safety paper	*1,450.*	65.00
a.	Horizontal safety paper	—	*175.00*

Safety paper design of Nos. 1 and 2 washes out if stamp is soaked. Washed out examples sell for considerably less. Used values are for stamps showing safety paper design.

Printed in booklet panes of 5. Stamps are numbered serially.

Catalogue values for all unused stamps in this section, from this point to the end of the Resident Waterfowl stamps, are for Never Hinged items.

Artists: Robert Kusserow, #3; Don Steinbeck, #4; John Moisan, #5; John Wilson, #6, 12; Rosemary Millett, #7, 9; Marion Toillion, #8; John Green, #10, 17; Russell Duerksen, #11, 15-16, 19-20; Mark Anderson, #13, 18, 21, 22; Jeff Reuter, #14; Joshua Spies. #23.

1976-2003

No.	Description	Unused	Used
3	$1 Mallards	25.00	3.00
a.	Serial number 4mm high	65.00	10.00
4	$1 Pintails, *1977*	27.50	2.50
5	$1 Canvasbacks, *1978*	13.00	2.50
6	$2 Canada geese, *1986*	8.50	2.50
7	$2 Blue geese, *1987*	7.00	2.50
8	$2 White-fronted geese, *1988*	7.00	2.50
9	$2 Mallards, *1989*	7.00	2.50
10	$2 Blue-winged teal, *1990*	7.00	2.50
11	$2 Pintails, *1991*	7.00	2.50
12	$2 Canvasbacks, *1992*	7.00	2.50
13	$2 Lesser scaup, *1993*	7.00	2.50
14	$2 Redheads, *1994*	7.00	2.50
15	$2 Wood ducks, *1995*	7.00	2.50
16	$2 Canada geese, *1996*	7.00	2.50
17	$2 Widgeons, *1997*	7.00	2.50
18	$2 Green-winged teal, *1998*	7.00	2.50

Migratory Bird Certification Stamps

No.	Description	Unused	Used
19	$3 Tundra swan, *1999*	9.00	2.50
20	$3 Buffleheads, *2000*	9.00	2.50
21	$3 Mallards, *2001*	9.00	2.50
22	$3 Canvasbacks, *2002*	9.00	2.50
23	$3 Pintails, *2003*	9.00	2.50

2004-07

No.	Description	Unused	Used
24	$3 purple	9.00	2.50
25	$5 magenta, *2005*	9.00	2.50
26	$5 brown orange, *2006*	9.00	2.50
27	$5 brown, *2007*	9.00	2.50

Non-resident Waterfowl Stamps

Nos. A1-A7, A9 have serial No. in red. Nos. A1-A18 issued in booklet panes of 5. Type faces and designs of Nos. A1-A18 vary.

Unused values are for unpunched stamps. Used values are for signed and punched stamps.

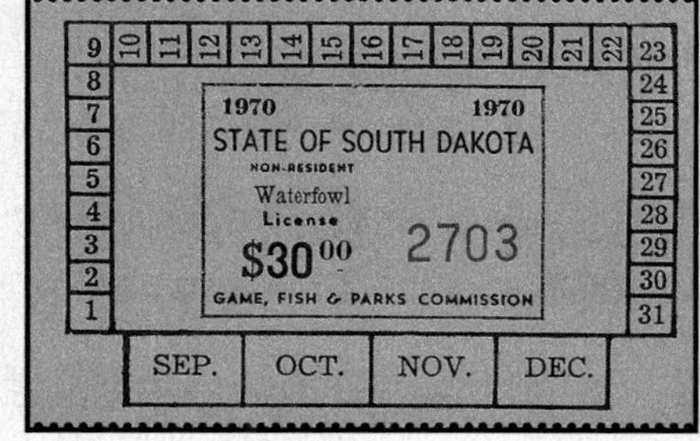

Illustration reduced.

1970-86

No.	Description	Unused	Used
A1	$30 black, *pink*	20.00	
a.	Missing serial number	*7,500.*	
A2	$30 black, *pink, 1971*	9.00	
a.	Overprinted "3"		*350.00*
A3	$30 black, *1972*	3.75	
a.	Overprinted "4"		—
A4	$30 black, *blue, 1973*	8.00	
a.	Overprinted "2"	*2,950.*	—
b.	Overprinted "4"		—
A5	$30 black, *green, 1974*	5.50	
a.	Overprinted "1"	*25.00*	
b.	Overprinted "2"	*30.00*	
c.	Overprinted "4"	*30.00*	
A6	$30 black, *yellow, 1975*	6.50	
a.	Overprinted "UNIT 1"	*45.00*	
b.	Overprinted "UNIT 4"	*35.00*	
c.	Overprinted "UNIT 3"		—
A7	$30 black, *yellow, 1976*	5.00	
a.	Overprinted "1"	18.00	
b.	Overprinted "2"	30.00	*20.00*
c.	Serial No. 4mm high	*18.00*	
d.	As "c," overprinted "1"	*35.00*	
e.	As "c," overprinted "2"	*85.00*	
A8	$30 black, *red, 1977*	7.00	
a.	Overprinted "1"	*20.00*	
b.	Overprinted "2"	*30.00*	
c.	Overprinted "3"	*35.00*	
d.	Overprinted "4"	*30.00*	
e.	Overprinted "5"	*200.00*	
A9	$30 black, *yellow, 1978*	7.00	
a.	Overprinted "1" and 3 strikes of "UNIT 2"	*150.00*	
b.	Overprinted "1"	*175.00*	

No.	Description	Unused	Used
A10	$30 black, *red, 1979*	2.50	
A11	$30 black, *light manila, 1980*	4.50	
a.	Overprinted "1"	6.00	
b.	Overprinted "2"	10.00	
A12	$30 black, *light yellow, 1981*	4.50	
a.	Overprinted "UNIT 1"	6.00	
b.	Overprinted "UNIT 2"	10.00	5.00
A13	$30 black, *blue, 1982*	6.50	
A14	$50 black, *dark yellow, 1982*	7.00	
a.	Overprinted "UNIT 2"		—
A15	$50 black, *red, 1983*	8.00	
a.	Overprinted "AREA 1"	*50.00*	
b.	Overprinted "AREA 2"	*65.00*	
c.	Serial No. with serifs	*500.00*	
A16	$50 black, *light manila, 1984*	16.00	
a.	Overprinted "A"	*325.00*	
b.	Overprinted "B"	*125.00*	
A17	$50 black, *red, 1985*	*3,500.*	*750.00*
A18	$50 black, *1986*	*9.00*	5.00

Bennett County Canada Goose Stamps

Type faces and designs vary. Nos. 2A1-2A2 imperf. Nos. 2A3-2A12 printed in booklet panes of 5, perforated horizontally. Some show vertical perforations.

Nos. 2A1-2A4 were free. No. 2A5 cost $5. Stamps were issued to hunters by means of a drawing.

Used values are for signed stamps.

Illustration reduced.

1974-78

No.	Description	Unused	Used
2A1	black	65.00	35.00
2A2	black, *pink, 1975*	*175.00*	

No.	Description	Unused	Used
2A3	black, *blue, 1976*	30.00	25.00
2A4	black, *yellow, 1977*	25.00	25.00
2A5	black, *greenish blue, 1978*	*800.00*	

West River Unit Canada Goose

Counties handstamped.

Used values are for signed stamps.

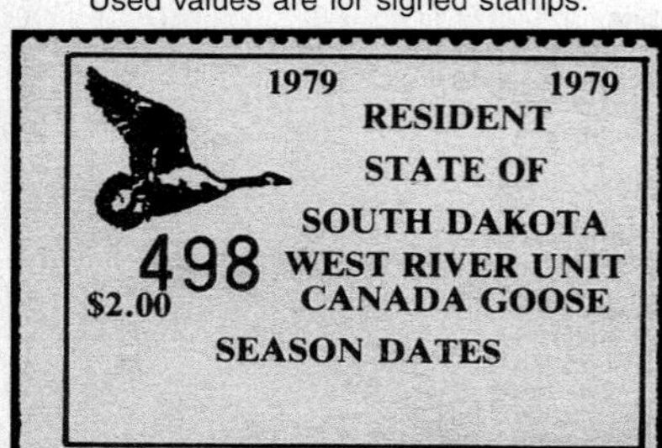

1979

No.	Description	Unused	Used
2A6	$2 black, *yellow*	*500.00*	
a.	Bennettt County	*750.00*	275.00
b.	Haakon County	*275.00*	
c.	Jackson County	*275.00*	
d.	Pennington County	*225.00*	100.00

Stamps overprinted for Perkins County exist but may not have been regularly issued.

1980

No.	Description	Unused	Used
2A7	$2 black, *blue*	75.00	
a.	Bennett County	225.00	*75.00*
b.	Haakon County	100.00	
c.	Jackson County	110.00	
d.	As "c," missing serial number	—	
e.	Pennington County	90.00	*45.00*
f.	Perkins County	110.00	

Prairie Canada Geese

Counties or Units handstamped.

Used values are for signed stamps.

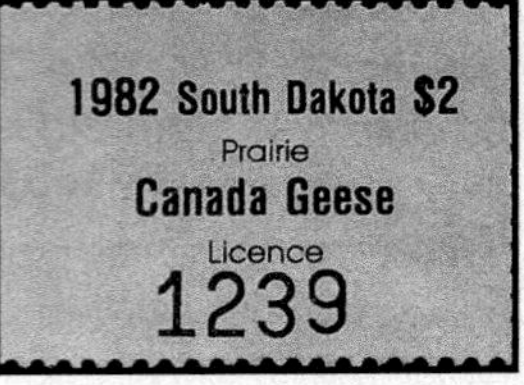

1981

Perf. 12

No.	Description	Unused	Used
2A8	$2 black, *red*	8.00	
a.	Bennett County	80.00	*35.00*
b.	Haakon County	60.00	*20.00*
c.	Jackson County	60.00	*20.00*
d.	Pennington County	60.00	
e.	Perkins County	60.00	

1982

No.	Description	Unused	Used
2A9	$2 black, *blue*	150.00	
a.	Bennett County	*1,250.*	*350.00*
b.	Haakon County	*850.00*	
c.	Jackson County	*850.00*	
d.	Pennington County	*850.00*	
e.	Perkins County	*850.00*	

1983

Perf. 12

No.	Description	Unused	Used
2A10	$2 black, *yellow*	60.00	
a.	UNIT 2A	70.00	
b.	UNIT 31	70.00	*35.00*
c.	UNIT 39	70.00	*35.00*
d.	UNIT 49	70.00	*35.00*
e.	UNIT 53	70.00	*35.00*
f.	UNIT 11, 3mm type	100.00	*50.00*
g.	UNIT 23	100.00	

Rouletted top and bottom

No.	Description	Unused	Used
2A11	$2 black, *yellow*	11.00	
a.	UNIT 2A	65.00	
b.	UNIT 6	45.00	
c.	UNIT 11, 3mm type	60.00	
d.	UNIT 11, 4½mm type	45.00	
e.	UNIT 23	45.00	
f.	UNIT 31	65.00	
g.	UNIT 32	45.00	
h.	UNIT 39	65.00	
i.	UNIT 42	45.00	
j.	UNIT 49	65.00	
k.	UNIT 53, 3mm type	45.00	
l.	UNIT 53, 4½mm type	50.00	

1984

Perf. 12

No.	Description	Unused	Used
2A12	$2 black, *green*	45.00	
a.	UNIT 6	75.00	
b.	UNIT 11, 3mm type	85.00	
c.	UNIT 11, 4½mm type	75.00	
d.	UNIT 23, 3mm type	85.00	
e.	UNIT 23, 4½mm type	75.00	*30.00*
f.	UNIT 32	85.00	
g.	UNIT 42	75.00	
h.	UNIT 47, 3mm type	85.00	
i.	UNIT 53, 3mm type	75.00	
j.	UNIT 47, 4½mm type		*65.00*
k.	UNIT 53, 4½mm type		*65.00*

1985

Rouletted two adjacent sides

No.	Description	Unused	Used
2A13	$2 black, *red*		
a.	UNIT 47		*100.00*
b.	UNIT 53		*100.00*
c.	UNIT 23		*125.00*
d.	UNIT 32		*175.00*
e.	UNIT 42		*125.00*
f.	UNIT 11		*175.00*

1986

No fee printed on stamp

Imperf. on 3 sides, rouletted at top

No.	Description	Unused	Used
2A14	black		
a.	UNIT 11		*110.00*
b.	UNIT 47		*110.00*
c.	UNIT 53		*110.00*
d.	UNIT 23		*150.00*

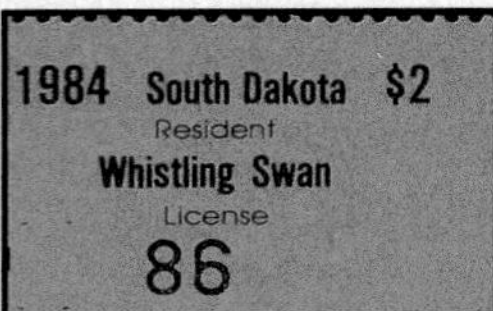

105 stamps for hunting whistling swans during the 1984 season exist. The season was canceled. Value, unused $275.

Pheasant Restoration Stamps

Required to hunt all small game, including waterfowl. Printed in booklet panes of 5. No. 3A4 rouletted, others perforated. Stamps are numbered serially.

Catalogue values for all unused stamps in this section, from this point to the end of the Wildlife Habitat stamps, are for Never Hinged items.

1977-88

No.	Description	Unused	Used
3A1	$5 Pheasants	13.00	2.50
a.	Rubber-stamped serial number		—
3A2	$5 Pheasants, *1978*	13.00	1.50
3A3	$5 Pheasants, *1979*	13.00	1.50
3A4	$5 Pheasants, *1980*	13.00	2.00
a.	Serial number omitted		—
3A5	$5 Pheasants, *1981*	13.00	1.50
3A6	$5 Pheasants, *1982*	13.00	1.50
a.	Pair, imperf. between		—
3A7	$5 Pheasant, *1983*	13.00	1.00
3A8	$5 Pheasant, *1984*	13.00	2.00
3A9	$5 Pheasant, *1985*	13.00	2.00
3A10	$5 Pheasants, *1986*	13.00	2.50
3A11	$5 Pheasants, *1987*	15.00	2.00
3A12	$5 Pheasants, *1988*	13.00	2.00

Wildlife Habitat Stamps

Required to hunt all small game, including waterfowl. Printed in booklet panes of 5. Starting with No. 3A18 stamps are rouletted, others are perforated. Stamps are numbered serially.

1989-99

No.	Description	Unused	Used
3A13	$8 Pheasants	13.00	2.00
3A14	$8 White-tailed deer, *1990*	13.00	2.00
3A15	$8 Greater prairie chicken, *1991*	13.00	2.00
3A16	$8 Mule Deer, *1992*	13.00	2.50
3A17	$8 Sharp-tailed grouse, *1993*	13.00	2.00
a.	Pair, imperf. between		—
3A18	$8 Turkey, *1994*	13.00	2.00
3A19	$8 Elk, *1995*	13.00	2.00
3A20	$8 Pheasants, *1996*	13.00	2.00
3A21	$8 Antelope, *1997*	13.00	2.00
3A22	$8 Buffalo, *1998*	13.00	2.00
3A23	$8 Buffalo, *1999*	13.00	2.00

Resident Small Game Stamps

Required by residents wishing to hunt small game, including waterfowl. Nos. 4A1, 4A2 issued panes of 10. Others issued in booklet panes of 5. Stamps are numbered serially in red from 1960 to 1967 and 1978. Non-resident small game stamps were not required for hunting.

Catalogue values for all unused stamps in this section are for Never Hinged items.

1960-79

4A1	$2 black, *pink*	15.00	2.00
4A2	$2 black, *blue, 1961*	30.00	3.00
4A3	$2 black, *dark yellow, 1962*	40.00	3.00
4A4	$2 black, *light yellow, 1963*	30.00	3.00
4A5	$2 black, *green, 1964*	30.00	3.00
4A6	$2 black, *1965*	30.00	3.00
4A7	$2 black, *yellow, 1966*	12.00	2.00
4A8	$2 black, *light green, 1967*	30.00	2.00
4A9	$2 black, *light yellow, 1968*	12.00	2.00
4A10	$3 black, *blue, 1969*	30.00	2.00
4A11	$3 black, *light yellow, 1970*	12.00	2.00
4A12	$3 black, *green, 1971*		3.00
4A13	$3 black, *light yellow, 1972*	12.00	2.00
4A14	$3 black, *light yellow, 1973*	10.00	2.00
4A15	$3 black, *1974*	12.00	2.00
4A16	$3 black, *pink, 1975*	10.00	2.00
4A17	$3 black, *gray, 1976*	8.00	1.00
4A18	$3 black, *red, 1977*	7.00	1.00
4A19	$3 black, *1978*	7.00	1.00
4A20	$3 black, *red, 1979*	8.00	1.00

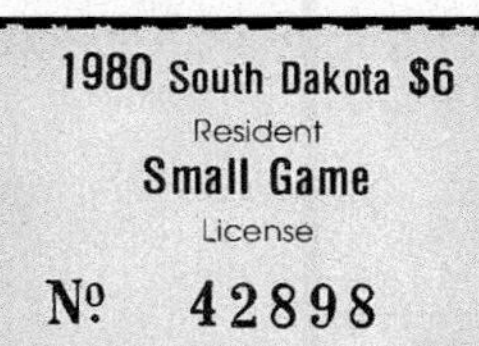

1980-98

4A21	$6 black	8.00	1.00
4A22	$6 black, *light yellow, 1981*	9.00	1.00
4A23	$6 black, *blue, 1982*	5.00	.50
4A24	$6 black, *green, 1983*	10.00	1.00
4A25	$6 black, *light blue, 1984*	*20.00*	1.00
4A26	$6 black, *light blue, 1985*	12.00	1.00
4A27	$6 black, *light blue green, 1986*		2.00
4A28	$6 black, *1987*		2.00
4A29	$6 black, *light green, 1988*	5.00	.50
4A30	$6 black, *1989*		1.00
4A31	$6 black, *light green, 1990*	8.00	.50
4A32	$6 black, *light blue green, 1991*	5.00	.50
4A33	$6 black, *light green, 1992*		1.00
4A34	$6 black, *light pink, 1993*	5.00	.50
4A35	$6 black, *light blue, 1994*	5.00	.50
4A36	$6 black, *yellow, 1995*		1.00
4A37	$6 black, *pink, 1996*	5.00	.50
4A38	$6 black, *light blue, 1997*		.50
4A39	$6 black, *pink, 1998*	8.00	.50

TENNESSEE

Stamps are die cut self-adhesives and are numbered serially.

Cards include both license cost and a fee of 30c (Nos. 1-5), 50c (Nos. 6-13) or $1 (starting with No. 14).

Nos. 3, 5, 7-15 come as 3-part card.

Starting with No. 12, cards come in four parts as well.

1979 and 1980 issues are for resident and non-resident fees.

Unused values are for stamps on original computer card stub.

Catalogue values for all unused stamps in this section are for Never Hinged items.

Artists: Dick Elliott, #1-2; Phillip Crowe, #3-4, 7, 17; Bob Gillespie, #5; Ken Schulz, #6; Allen Hughes, #8; Jimmy Stewart, #9; Ralph J. McDonald, #10, 18; Thomas Hirata, #11, 16; Jim Lamb, #12; Roger Cruwys, #13; Tom Freeman, #14; Richard Clifton, #15, 19; Bob Leslie, #20; Bethany Carter, #21; Beth Ann McMurray, #22; Nick Williamson, #23, 24.; J. Mefford, #25; Joshua Lester, #26-27; Lauren Pollard, #28; Kaydee Hankes, #29-30; Brandon Sharp, #31; Olivia Hughes, #32-33; Joanna Rush, #34, 36; Jet Smith, #35; McKenzie Covrig, #37; Sophie Perry, #38; Mary Alford, #39; Brienna Miller, #40.

1979-2018

1	$2 Mallards	75.00	25.00
2	$5 Mallards	*400.00*	*150.00*
3	$2 Canvasbacks, *1980*	45.00	15.00
	3-part card	725.00	
4	$5 Canvasbacks, *1980*	*150.00*	75.00
5	$2 Wood ducks, *1981*	45.00	10.00
	3-part card	—	
6	$6 Canada geese, *1982*	55.00	15.00
7	$6 Pintails, *1983*	50.00	15.00
	3-part card	65.00	
8	$6 Black ducks, *1984*	50.00	12.00
	3-part card	65.00	
9	$6 Blue-winged teal, *1985*	20.00	7.00
	3-part card	45.00	
10	$6 Mallard, *1986*	15.00	5.00
	3-part card	50.00	
11	$6 Canada geese, *1987*	12.00	5.00
	3-part card	25.00	

Card exists with 2/28/88 expiration date rather than correct 2/29 date.

12	$6 Canvasbacks, *1988*	12.00	4.00
	3-part card	20.00	
	4-part card	20.00	
13	$6 Green-winged teal, *1989*	12.00	4.00
	3-part card	20.00	
	4-part card	20.00	
14	$12 Redheads, *1990*	18.00	4.00
	3-part card	25.00	
	4-part card	25.00	
15	$12 Mergansers, *1991*	18.00	4.00
	3-part card	22.00	
	4-part card	22.00	
16	$13 Wood ducks, *1992*	18.00	4.00
	4-part card	22.00	
17	$13 Pintails & decoy, *1993*	20.00	4.00
	4-part card	25.00	
18	$15 Mallard, *1994*	25.00	5.00
	4-part card	30.00	
19	$16 Ring-necked duck, *1995*	30.00	5.00
	4-part card	35.00	
20	$17 Black ducks, *1996*	40.00	5.00
	4-part card	45.00	

Starting With No. 21 Stamps Are Perforated. Not Required For Hunting

21	$10 Mallard, *1999*	15.00	2.50
22	$10 Bufflehead, *2000*	15.00	2.50
23	$10 Wood ducks, *2001*	15.00	2.50
24	$10 Green-winged teal, *2002*	15.00	2.50
25	$10 Canada geese, *2003*	15.00	2.50
26	$10 Wood ducks, *2004*	15.00	2.50
27	$10 Mallards, *2005*	15.00	2.50
28	$10 Canada goose, *2006*	15.00	2.50
29	$10 Harlequin, *2007*	15.00	2.50
30	$10 Wood ducks, *2008*	15.00	2.50
31	$10 Mallards, *2009*	15.00	2.50
32	$10 Wood ducks, *2010*	15.00	2.50
33	$10 Wood ducks, *2011*	16.00	2.50
34	$10 Cinnamon teal, *2012*	16.00	2.50
35	$10 King eiders, *2013*	16.00	2.50
36	$10 Wood ducks, *2014*	16.00	2.50
37	$10 Green-winged teal, *2015*	16.00	2.50
38	$10 Northern shoveler, *2016*	16.00	2.50
39	$10 Cinnamon teal, *2017*	16.00	2.50
40	$10 Pintails, *2018*	13.50	2.50

TEXAS

Printed in sheets of 10.
Nos. 1-4 are rouletted.
Stamps are numbered serially.

Catalogue values for all unused stamps in this section are for Never Hinged items.

Artists: Larry Hayden, #1, 12; Ken Carlson, #2, 14; Maynard Reece, #3; David Maass, #4, 9, 15, 26; John Cowan, #5, 8; Herb Booth, #6, 25, 33; Gary Moss, #7, 32; Robert Bateman, #10; Daniel Smith, #11, 16; Jim Hautman, #13, 17, 22, 28; Phillip Crowe, #18; Robert Hautman, #19, 31; Sherrie Russell Meline, #20, 23; John Dearman, #21; Scott and Stuart Gentling, #24; Bruce Miller, #27, 35; Scot Storm, #29; Peter Mathios, #30; Calvin Carter, #34.

1981-2015

1	$5 Mallards	25.00	8.00
2	$5 Pintails, *1982*	20.00	5.00
3	$5 Widgeons, *1983*	85.00	18.00
4	$5 Wood ducks, *1984*	25.00	5.00
5	$5 Snow geese, *1985*	10.00	3.00
6	$5 Green-winged teal, *1986*	10.00	2.50
7	$5 White-fronted geese, *1987*	10.00	2.50
8	$5 Pintails, *1988*	10.00	2.50
9	$5 Mallards, *1989*	10.00	2.50
10	$5 American widgeons, *1990*	10.00	2.50
11	$7 Wood duck, *1991*	11.00	2.50
12	$7 Canada geese, *1992*	11.00	2.50
13	$7 Blue-winged teal, *1993*	11.00	2.50
14	$7 Shovelers, *1994*	11.00	2.50
15	$7 Buffleheads, *1995*	11.00	2.50

Beginning with No. 16, these stamps were sold only in booklets with other wildlife stamps and were not valid for hunting.

16	$3 Gadwalls, *1996*	75.00
17	$3 Cinnamon teal, *1997*	65.00
18	$3 Pintail, labrador retriever, *1998*	55.00
19	$3 Canvasbacks, *1999*	40.00
20	$3 Hooded merganser, *2000*	30.00
21	$3 Snow geese, *2001*	20.00
22	$3 Redheads, *2002*	20.00
23	$3 Mottled duck, *2003*	20.00
24	$3 American goldeneye, *2004*	15.00
25	$7 Mallards, *2005*	15.00
26	$7 Green-winged teals, *2006*	22.50
27	$7 Wood duck, *2007*	13.00
28	$7 Pintails, *2008*	13.00
29	$7 Blue-winged teal, *2009*	13.00
30	$7 Wigeons, *2010*	13.00
31	$7 White-fronted geese, *2011*	13.00
32	$7 Canada geese, *2012*	20.00
33	$7 Wood ducks, *2013*	13.00
34	$7 Cinnamon teal, *2014*	13.00
35	$7 Ring-necked duck, *2015*	20.00

No. 23 was issued in booklets with seven other wildlife stamps and was not valid for hunting.

Nos. 25-35 were issued in booklets with five other wildlife stamps and were not valid for hunting.

UTAH

Game Bird Stamps

For hunting game birds, including waterfowl. In 1951 No. A1 or No. 2A1 were required, in 1952 No. A3 or 2A2. No. A1 printed in booklet panes of 25, others in booklet panes of 10. Perforated.

A1

A2

1951

A1	A1	$3 brown, resident	*20.00*	*7.00*
A2	A1	$15 red, non-resident	*100.00*	50.00

1952

A3	A2	$3 red, resident	*75.00*	
A4	A2	$15 blue, non-resident	*225.00*	*50.00*

Resident Fishing and Hunting Stamps

For hunting game birds, including waterfowl. Printed in sheets of 40. No. 2A1 printed on linen.

Unused values are for stamps with deer tags attached at left.

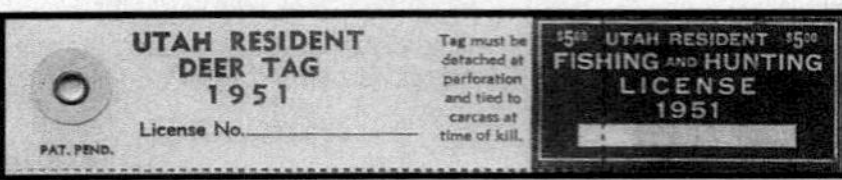
No. 2A1

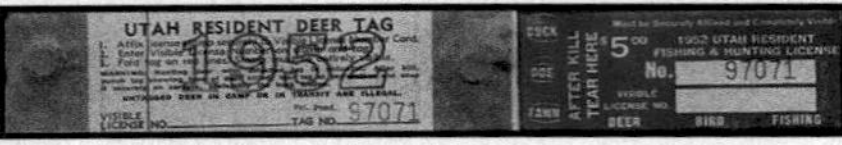
No. 2A2

1951-52

2A1	$5 blue	5.00	1.50
2A2	$5 green, *1952*	5.00	1.50

Waterfowl Issues

Printed in sheets of 30 or in booklet panes of 5 (starting in 1990). No. 11 issued in sheets of 9.

Stamps are numbered serially.

Catalogue values for all unused stamps in this section are for Never Hinged items.

Artists: Leon Parsons, #1; Arthur Anderson, #2; David Chapple, #3; Jim Morgan, #4; Daniel Smith, #5; Robert Steiner, #6-12.

1986-97

1	$3.30 Whistling swans	10.00	3.00
2	$3.30 Pintails, *1987*	8.00	3.00
3	$3.30 Mallards, *1988*	8.00	2.50
4	$3.30 Canada geese, *1989*	8.00	2.50
5	$3.30 Canvasbacks, perf. 4 sides, *1990*	8.00	
a.	Booklet single, with 2-part tab	8.00	2.50
6	$3.30 Tundra swans, perf. 4 sides, *1991*	12.00	
a.	Booklet single, with 2-part tab	12.00	2.50
7	$3.30 Pintails, perf. 4 sides, *1992*	10.00	
a.	Booklet single, with 2-part tab	10.00	2.50
8	$3.30 Canvasbacks, perf. 4 sides, *1993*	10.00	
a.	Booklet single, with 2-part tab	10.00	2.50
9	$3.30 Chesapeake Retriever and ducks, perf. 4 sides, *1994*	*85.00*	
a.	Booklet single, with 2-part tab	*85.00*	2.50
10	$3.30 Green-winged teal, *1995*	12.00	
a.	Booklet single, with 2-part tab	12.00	2.50
b.	Governor's edition	130.00	
11	$7.50 White-fronted goose, *1996*	15.00	2.50
a.	$97.50 Governor's edition	125.00	

Redheads: a, Male, serial # at UL. b, Female, serial # at LL.

12	Pair, *1997*	75.00	
a.-b.	$7.50 Any single	26.00	2.50
c.	$97.50 Governor's Edition	110.00	

No. 12c is No. 12 without the central perforations. The denomination appears only in the upper right corner. The bottom inscription has Governor's Edition plus a serial number.

VERMONT

Printed in sheets of 30.

Catalogue values for all unused stamps in this section are for Never Hinged items.

Artists: Jim Killen, #1-4; Richard Plasschaert, #5-8; Reed Prescott, #9, 11; Robert Mullen, #10; J. Collins, #12; George Lockwood, #13-17; Richard E. Bishop, #18-21; Heather Forcier, #22-25.

1986-2010

1	$5 Wood ducks	12.00	4.00
2	$5 Common goldeneyes, *1987*	12.00	3.00
3	$5 Black ducks, *1988*	12.00	2.50
4	$5 Canada geese, *1989*	12.00	2.50
5	$5 Green-winged teal, *1990*	12.00	2.50
6	$5 Hooded mergansers, *1991*	12.00	2.50
7	$5 Snow geese, *1992*	12.00	2.50
8	$5 Mallards, *1993*	12.00	2.50
9	$5 Ring-necked duck, *1994*	12.00	2.50
10	$5 Bufflehead, *1995*	12.00	2.50
11	$5 Lesser scaup, *1996*	12.00	2.50
12	$5 Pintails, *1997*	12.00	2.50
13	$5 Blue-winged teal, *1998*	12.00	2.50
14	$5 Canvasbacks, *1999*	12.00	2.50
15	$5 Widgeons, *2000*	10.00	2.50
16	$5 Old squaws, *2001*	10.00	2.50
17	$5 Greater scaups, *2002*	10.00	2.50
18	$5 Mallards, *2003*	10.00	2.50
19	$5 Pintails, *2004*	10.00	2.50
20	$5 Canvasbacks, *2005*	10.00	2.50
21	$5 Canada goose, *2006*	10.00	2.50
22	$5 Ring-necked duck, *2007*	12.00	2.50
23	$7.50 Harlequin, *2008*	12.00	2.50
24	$7.50 Harlequin, *2009*	12.00	2.50
25	$7.50 Wood duck, *2010*	12.00	2.50

No. 26

2011-13 ***Die Cut***

Self-Adhesive

26	$7.50 black + numbered sticker, *2011*	25.00	2.50
27	$7.50 black + numbered sticker, *2012*	13.00	2.50
28	$7.50 black + numbered sticker, *2013*	13.00	2.50

VIRGINIA

Printed in booklet panes of 10 and/or sheets of 30. Stamps are numbered serially.

Catalogue values for all unused stamps in this section are for Never Hinged items.

Artists: Ronald Louque, #1, 24-24A; Arthur LeMay, #2; Louis Frisino, #3; Robert Leslie, #4, 11; Carl Knuth, #5, 12, 17; Bruce Miller, #6; Francis Sweet, #7; Richard Clifton, #8; Wilhelm Goebel, #9; Roger Cruwys, #10; Tim Donovan, #13-14, 19-19A; Jim Wilson, #15-16; Guy Crittenden, #18-18B, 20-20A, 23-23A, 27-27A, 30-30A; Spike Knuth, #21-21A; John Obolewicz, #22-22A, 25-25A, 29-29A; Janet Hong, #26-26A; Brian Murillo, #31-31A.

1988-2018

No.	Description	Unused	Used
1	$5 Mallards, serial Nos. 1-40,000	13.00	2.50
	Booklet pair with L & R selvage, serial Nos. above 40,000	27.50	
2	$5 Canada geese, serial Nos. 1-40,000, *1989*	12.00	2.50
	Booklet pair with L & R selvage, serial Nos. above 40,000	25.00	
3	$5 Wood ducks, serial Nos. 1-20,000, *1990*	7.00	2.50
	Booklet pair with L & R selvage, serial Nos. above 20,000	24.00	
4	$5 Canvasbacks, serial Nos. 1-20,000, *1991*	7.00	2.50
	Booklet pair with L & R selvage, serial Nos. above 20,000	24.00	
5	$5 Buffleheads, serial Nos. 1-20,000, *1992*	7.00	2.50
	Booklet pair with L & R selvage, serial Nos. above 20,000	24.00	
6	$5 Black ducks, serial Nos. 1-20,000, *1993*	7.00	2.50
	Booklet pair with L & R selvage, serial Nos. above 20,000	24.00	
7	$5 Lesser scaup, *1994*	7.00	2.50
	Booklet pair with L & R selvage	24.00	
8	$5 Snow geese, *1995*	7.00	2.50
	Booklet pair with L & R selvage	24.00	
9	$5 Hooded mergansers, *1996*	12.00	2.50
10	($5) Pintail, Labrador retriever, *1997*	7.00	2.50
11	$5 Mallards, *1998*	12.00	2.50
12	$5 Green-winged teal, *1999*	12.00	2.50
13	$5 Mallards, *2000*	12.00	2.50
14	$5 Blue-winged teal, *2001*	10.00	2.50
15	$5 Canvasbacks, *2002*	10.00	2.50
16	$5 Tundra Swan, *2003*	10.00	2.50
17	$5 American goldeneye, *2004*	10.00	2.50
18	$9.75 Wood ducks, perf. *2005*	13.00	2.50
18A	$9.75 Wood ducks, self-adhesive, die cut *2005*	14.00	2.50
18B	$9.75 Wood ducks, rouletted, with tab *2005*	13.00	2.50
19	$10 Black ducks, perf. *2006*	13.00	2.50
19A	$10 Black ducks, self-adhesive, die cut *2006*	14.00	2.50
20	$10 Canada geese, perf. *2007*	13.50	2.50
20A	$10 Canada geese, self-adhesive, die cut *2007*	13.50	2.50
21	$10 Wigeons, perf., *2008*	13.50	2.50
21A	$10 Wigeons, self-adhesive, die cut, *2008*	13.50	2.50
22	$10 Ring-necked duck, perf., *2009*	13.50	2.50
22A	$10 Ring-necked duck, self-adhesive, die cut, *2009*	13.50	2.50
23	$10 Green-winged teal, perf., *2010*	13.50	2.50
23A	$10 Green-winged teal, self-adhesive, die cut, *2010*	16.00	2.50
24	$10 Redheads, perf., *2011*	16.00	2.50
24A	$10 Redheads, self-adhesive, die cut, *2011*	16.00	2.50
25	$10 Buffleheads, perf., *2012*	16.00	2.50
25A	$10 Buffleheads, self-adhesive, die cut, *2012*	16.00	2.50
26	$10 Hooded mergansers, perf. *2013*	16.00	2.50
26A	$10 Hooded mergansers, self-adhesive, die cut *2013*	16.00	2.50
27	$10 Canvasbacks, perf. *2014*	16.00	2.50
27A	$10 Canvasbacks, self-adhesive, die cut *2014*	16.00	2.50
28	$10 Tundra swans, perf. *2015*	16.00	2.50
28A	$10 Tundra swans, self-adhesive, die cut, *2015*	16.00	2.50
29	$10 Pintails, perf. *2016*	16.00	2.50
29A	$10 Pintails, self-adhesive, die cut, *2016*	16.00	2.50
30	$10 Ring-necked ducks, perf. *2017*	16.00	2.50
30A	$10 Ring-necked ducks, self-adhesive, die cut, *2017*	16.00	2.50
31	$10 Canada goose, perf. *2018*	13.50	2.50
31A	$10 Canada goose, self-adhesive, die cut, *2018*	13.50	2.50

Starting with 2005, Virginia stamps are mandatory for hunting.

WASHINGTON

Printed in booklet panes of 1 and sheets of 30. Stamps are numbered serially. Booklet panes starting with No. 7 without staple holes were sold to collectors.

Catalogue values for all unused stamps in this section are for Never Hinged items.

Artists: Keith Warrick, #1; Ray Nichol, #2; Robert Bateman, #3; Maynard Reece, #4; Thomas Quinn, #5; Ronald Louque, #6-7; Phillip Crowe, #8; Fred Thomas, #9, 28; David Hagenbaumer, #10; Cynthie Fisher, #11, 30; Greg Beecham, #12; A. Young, #13; Robert Steiner, #14-16, 22-27; Adam Grimm, #17; Don Nicholson Miller, #18-19; Dan Smith, #20-21; Bart Rulon, #29; Gunnar Hillard, #31; Doug Snyder, #32, Dee Dee Murry, #33; Donnie Hughes, #34.

1986-2018

No.	Description	Unused	Used
1	$5 Mallards, Nos. 1-60,000	9.00	
	Booklet pane of 1, Nos. 60,001-160,000	12.50	4.00
2	$5 Canvasbacks, Nos. 1-24,000, *1987*	12.00	
	Booklet pane of 1, Nos. 24,001-124,000	12.00	3.00
3	$5 Harlequin, Nos. 1-60,000, *1988*	9.00	
	Booklet pane of 1, Nos. 60,001-160,000	10.00	3.00
4	$5 American widgeons, Nos. 1-60,000, *1989*	9.00	
	Booklet pane of 1, Nos. 60,001-160,000	10.00	2.50
5	$5 Pintails, Nos. 1-60,000, *1990*	9.00	
	Booklet pane of 1, Nos. 60,001-160,000	10.00	2.50
6	$5 Wood duck, Nos. 1-30,000, *1991*	12.00	
	Booklet pane of 1, Nos. above 30,000	12.00	4.00
7	$6 Wood duck, Nos. 100,000-130,000, *1991*	10.00	
	Booklet pane of 1, Nos. above 130,000	10.00	2.50
8	$6 Labrador puppy & Canada geese, Nos. 1-30,000, *1992*	14.00	
	Booklet pane of 1, Nos. above 30,000	14.00	2.50
9	$6 Snow geese, Nos. 1-30,000, *1993*	10.00	
	Booklet pane of 1, Nos. above 30,000	10.00	2.50
10	$6 Black brant, Nos. 1-30,000, *1994*	14.00	
	Booklet pane of 1, Nos. above 30,000	14.00	2.50
11	$6 Mallards, Nos. 1-30,000, *1995*	12.00	
	Booklet pane of 1, Nos. above 30,000	12.00	2.50
12	$6 Redheads, Nos. 1-25,050, *1996*	22.50	
	Booklet pane of 1, Nos. above 25,050	22.50	2.50
13	$6 Canada geese, Nos. 9600001-9625050, *1997*	12.00	
	Bklt. pane of 1, Nos. above 9625050	12.00	2.50
14	$6 Barrow's goldeneye Nos. 1-25,050, *1998*	15.00	
	Bklt. pane of 1, Nos. 25,051-27,050	15.00	2.50
15	$6 Bufflehead, *1999*	15.00	
a.	Bklt. pane of 1	15.00	2.50
16	$6 Canada geese, mallard, widgeon, *2000*	25.00	
a.	Bklt. pane of 1	25.00	2.50
17	$6 Mallards, *2001*	17.50	
a.	Bklt. pane of 1	17.50	2.50
18	$10 Green-winged teal, *2002*	20.00	
a.	Souvenir sheet of 1	20.00	2.50
19	$10 Pintails, *2003*	20.00	
a.	Souvenir sheet of 1	22.50	2.50
20	$10 Canada goose, *2004*	17.50	
a.	Souvenir sheet of 1	17.50	2.50
21	$10 Barrow's goldeneyes, *2005*	17.50	
a.	Souvenir sheet of 1	17.50	2.50
22	$10 Widgeons, mallard, *2006*	15.00	
a.	Souvenir sheet of 1	15.00	2.50
23	$10 Ross's goose, *2007*	15.00	
a.	Souvenir sheet of 1	15.00	2.50
24	$10 Wood ducks, *2008*	15.00	
a.	Souvenir sheet of 1	15.00	2.50
25	$11 Canada goose, *2009*	15.00	
a.	Souvenir sheet of 1	16.00	2.50
26	$10 Pintail, *2010*	40.00	
a.	Souvenir sheet of 1	35.00	2.50
27	$10 Ruddy duck, *2011*	15.00	
a.	Souvenir sheet of 1	15.00	2.50
28	$15 Brant, *2012*	22.00	
a.	Souvenir sheet of 1	22.00	2.50
29	$15 Shovelers, *2013*	22.00	
a.	Souvenir sheet of 1	22.00	2.50
30	$15 Redheads, *2014*	22.00	
a.	Souvenir sheet of 1	22.00	2.50
31	$15 Canvasbacks, *2015*	22.00	
a.	Souvenir sheet of 1	22.00	2.50
32	$15 Hooded merganser, *2016*	22.00	
a.	Souvenir sheet of 1	22.00	2.50
33	$15 Cinnamon teal and yellow Labrador retriever, *2017*	22.00	
a.	Souvenir sheet of 1	22.00	2.50
34	$15 Wood ducks, *2018*	18.50	
a.	Souvenir sheet of 1	18.50	2.50

Nos. 19-34 not required for hunting.

WEST VIRGINIA

Printed in sheets of 30 and booklet panes of 5. All booklet stamps have straight edges at sides. Starting in 1990, booklet stamps are numbered serially. Some, but not all, of the 1988 booklet stamps are numbered serially. Stamps from sheets are not numbered serially.

Catalogue values for all unused stamps in this section are for Never Hinged items.

Artists: Daniel Smith, #1-2; Steven Dillard, #3-4; Ronald Louque, #5-6; Louis Frisino, #7-8; Robert Leslie, #9-10; Thomas Hirata, #11-12; Phillip Crowe, #13-14; Richard Clifton, #15-16; Fran Sweet, #17-18; Karl Badgley, #19-20.

1987-96

No.	Description	Unused	Used
1	$5 Canada geese, resident	17.50	8.00
	Booklet single with tab at top	65.00	
2	$5 Canada geese, non-resident	16.00	8.00
	Booklet single with tab at top	65.00	
3	$5 Wood ducks, resident, *1988*	10.00	4.00
	Booklet single with tab at top, no serial number	35.00	
a.	Booklet single with serial number on reverse	50.00	4.00
4	$5 Wood ducks, non-resident, *1988*	12.00	4.00
	Booklet single with tab at top, no serial number	35.00	
a.	Booklet single with serial number on reverse	50.00	4.00
5	$5 Decoys, resident, *1989*	13.00	3.00
	Booklet single with tab at top	35.00	
a.	Governor's edition	*65.00*	
6	$5 Decoys, non-resident, *1989*	18.00	3.00
	Booklet single with tab at top	35.00	
a.	Governor's edition	*65.00*	

Nos. 5a and 6a were available only in sheets of 30 through a sealed bid auction.

No.	Description	Unused	Used
7	$5 Labrador retriever & decoy, resident, *1990*	20.00	
a.	Booklet single	15.00	3.00
8	$5 Labrador retriever & decoy, non-resident, *1990*	22.00	
a.	Booklet single	15.00	3.00
9	$5 Mallards, resident, *1991*	12.00	
a.	Booklet single	12.00	2.50
10	$5 Mallards, non-resident, *1991*	12.00	
a.	Booklet single	12.00	2.50
b.	Sheet, 3 each #9-10	50.00	

No. 10b is numbered serially; exists imperf. without serial numbers.

No.	Description	Unused	Used
11	$5 Canada geese, resident, *1992*	12.00	
a.	Booklet single	12.00	2.50
12	$5 Canada geese, non-resident, *1992*	12.00	
a.	Booklet single	12.00	2.50
13	$5 Pintails, resident, *1993*	12.00	
a.	Booklet single	12.00	2.50
14	$5 Pintails, non-resident, *1993*	12.00	
a.	Booklet single	12.00	2.50
15	$5 Green-winged teal, resident, *1994*	12.00	
a.	Booklet single	12.00	2.50
16	$5 Green-winged teal, non-resident, *1994*	12.00	
a.	Booklet single	12.00	2.50
17	$5 Mallards, resident, *1995*	12.00	
a.	Booklet single	12.00	2.50
18	$5 Mallards, non-resident, *1995*	12.00	
a.	Booklet single	12.00	2.50
19	$5 Widgeons, resident, *1996*	12.00	
a.	Booklet single	12.00	2.50
20	$5 Widgeons, non-resident, *1996*	12.00	
a.	Booklet single	12.00	2.50

WISCONSIN

Printed in sheets of 10. Starting in 1980 the left side of the sheet has an agent tab and a numbered tab, the right side a numbered tab.

Catalogue values for all unused stamps in this section are for Never Hinged items.

Artists: Owen Gromme, #1; Rockne (Rocky) Knuth, #2, 6; Martin Murk, #3; Timothy Schultz, #4, 29; William Koelpin, #5; Michael James Riddet, #7, 15, 26; Greg Alexander, #8, 20; Don Moore, #9, 17, 23; Al Kraayvanger, #10; Richard Timm, #11; Rick Kelley, #12; Daniel Renn Pierce, #13; Terry Doughty, #14, 25, 28, 39; Frank Middlestadt, #16, 22; Les Didler, #18, 21, 24; Sam Timm, #19; Arthur Anderson, #27, 30; Brian Kuether, #31; Robert Leum, #32; Craig Fairgut, #33; James Pieper, #34, 38; John Rickaby, #35; William Millonig, #36; Caleb Metrich, #37, 41; Sara Stack, #40.

1978-2018

1	$3.25 Wood ducks	65.00	9.00
2	$3.25 Buffleheads, rouletted, *1979*	20.00	6.00
3	$3.25 Widgeons, *1980*	12.00	2.50
	With tab	15.00	
4	$3.25 Lesser Scaup, *1981*	10.00	2.50
	With tab	13.00	
5	$3.25 Pintails, *1982*	9.00	2.50
	With numbered tab	9.00	
	With agent's and numbered tab	10.00	
6	$3.25 Blue-winged teal, *1983*	9.00	2.50
	With numbered tab	9.00	
	With agent's and numbered tab	10.00	
7	$3.25 Hooded merganser, *1984*	9.00	2.50
	With numbered tab	9.00	
	With agent's and numbered tab	10.00	
8	$3.25 Lesser scaup, *1985*	12.00	2.50
	With numbered tab	12.00	
	With agent's and numbered tab	15.00	
9	$3.25 Canvasbacks, *1986*	15.00	2.50
	With numbered tab	15.00	
	With agent's and numbered tab	21.00	
10	$3.25 Canada geese, *1987*	9.00	2.50
	With numbered tab	9.00	
	With agent's and numbered tab	10.00	
11	$3.25 Hooded merganser, *1988*	9.00	2.50
	With numbered tab	9.00	
	With agent's and numbered tab	10.00	
12	$3.25 Common goldeneye, *1989*	9.00	2.50
	With numbered tab	9.00	
	With agent's and numbered tab	10.00	
13	$3.25 Redheads, *1990*	9.00	2.50
	With numbered tab	9.00	
	With agent's and numbered tab	10.00	
14	$5.25 Green-winged teal, *1991*	9.00	2.50
	With numbered tab	9.00	
	With agent's and numbered tab	10.00	
15	$5.25 Tundra swans, *1992*	10.00	2.50
	With numbered tab	10.00	
	With agent's and numbered tab	12.00	
16	$5.25 Wood ducks, *1993*	10.00	2.50
	With numbered tab	10.00	
	With agent's and numbered tab	12.00	
17	$5.25 Pintails, *1994*	10.00	2.50
	With numbered tab	10.00	
	With agent's and numbered tabs	12.00	
18	$5.25 Mallards, *1995*	10.00	2.50
	With numbered tab	10.00	
	With agent's and numbered tabs	12.00	
19	($5.25) Green-winged teal, *1996*	10.00	2.50
	With numbered tab	10.00	
	With agent's and numbered tabs	12.00	
20	($7) Canada geese, *1997*	15.00	2.50
	With numbered tab	15.00	
	With agent's and numbered tabs	17.00	
21	$7 Snow goose, *1998*	15.00	2.50
	With numbered tab	15.00	
	With agent's and numbered tabs	17.00	
22	$7 Greater scaups, *1999*	12.00	2.50
23	$7 Canvasbacks, *2000*	12.00	2.50
24	$7 Common goldeneyes, *2001*	14.00	2.50
25	$7 Shovelers, *2002*	11.00	2.50
26	$7 Ring-necked ducks, *2003*	11.00	2.50
27	$7 Pintail, *2004*	11.00	2.50
28	$7 Wood ducks, *2005*	12.50	2.50
29	$7 Green-winged teals, *2006*	12.00	2.50
30	$7 Redheads, *2007*	12.00	2.50
31	$7 Canvasbacks, *2008*	12.00	2.50
32	$7 Wigeons, *2009*	12.00	2.50
33	$7 Wood ducks, *2010*	12.00	2.50
34	$7 Shovelers, *2011*	12.00	2.50
35	$7 Redhead, *2012*	12.00	2.50
36	$7 Long-tailed ducks, *2013*	12.00	2.50
37	$7 Wood duck, *2014*	12.00	2.50
38	$7 Blue-winged teal, *2015*	12.00	2.50
39	$7 Ring-necked ducks, *2016*	12.00	2.50
40	$7 Canvasbacks and lighthouse, *2017*	12.00	2.50
41	$7 Canada geese, *2018*	10.00	2.50

Nos. 26-41 not required for hunting.

WYOMING

Issued in panes of 5. Required to fish as well as to hunt all small and big game, including waterfowl. Stamps are numbered serially.

Catalogue values for all unused stamps in this section are for Never Hinged items.

Artists: From photo by Luroy Parker, #1; Robert Kusserow, #2; Dan Andrews, #3, 33; Ted Feeley, #4; Clark Ostergaard, #5; Dave Wade, #6, 8, 10, 13, 17; Connie J. Robinson, #7; Sarah Rogers, #9; James Brooks, #11; Peter Eades, #12; D. Enright, #14; Garth Hegeson, #15; Nick Reitzel, #16; Brent Todd, #18; Paul Kay, #19; Rene Piskorski, #20, 29; Dustin Van Wechel, #21; Ron Staker, #22; Scott Greenig, #23; Art Biro, #24; Jenny Forge, #25; William Smith, #26; Kreig Jacque, #27; Amanda Morton, #28; Karla Mann, #30; Kim Diment, #31, Kip Richmond, #32; Andrew Kneeland, #34; Justin Hayward, #35.

No. 1 is in vertical format. All others are horizontal.

1984-2018

1	$5 Meadowlark	75.00	6.00
2	$5 Canada geese, *1985*	50.00	5.00
3	$5 Antelope, *1986*	90.00	8.00
4	$5 Grouse, *1987*	85.00	8.00
5	$5 Trout, *1988*	110.00	12.00
6	$5 Mule deer, *1989*	175.00	15.00
7	$5 Bear, *1990*	50.00	5.00
8	$5 Rams, *1991*	45.00	3.50
9	$5 Bald eagle, *1992*	35.00	3.50
10	$5 Elk, *1993*	25.00	3.50
11	$5 Bobcat, *1994*	25.00	3.50
12	$5 Moose, *1995*	22.00	3.50
13	$5 Turkey, *1996*	22.00	3.00
14	$5 Mountain goats, *1997*	22.00	3.00
15	$5 Trumpeter swan, *1998*	20.00	3.00
16	$5 Brown trout, *1999*	20.00	3.00
17	$5 Buffalo, *2000*	20.00	3.00
18	$10 White-tailed deer, *2001*	20.00	5.00
19	$10 River otters, *2002*	20.00	5.00
20	$10 Mountain bluebirds, *2003*	20.00	5.00
21	$10 Mountain lion, *2004*	20.00	5.00
22	$10.50 Burrowing owls, *2005*	20.00	5.00
23	$10.50 Cut-throat trout, *2006*	20.00	5.00
24	$10.50 Blue grouses, *2007*	20.00	5.00
25	$12.50 Black-footed ferret, *2008*	20.00	5.00
26	$12.50 Great gray owl, *2009*	20.00	5.00
27	$12.50 Cinnamon teal, *2010*	20.00	5.00
28	$12.50 Wolverine, *2011*	18.00	5.00
29	$12.50 Black bear, *2012*	18.00	5.00
30	$12.50 Greater short-horned lizard, *2013*	18.00	5.00
31	$12.50 Ruffed grouse, *2014*	18.00	5.00
32	$12.50 Sauger, *2015*	18.00	5.00
33	$12.50 Swift fox, *2016*	18.00	5.00
34	$12.50 Mallard, *2017*	18.00	5.00
35	$12.50 Mallard, *2017*	21.00	5.00

INDIAN RESERVATIONS

Stamps for other reservations exist and will be listed after more information is received about them.

CHEYENNE RIVER INDIAN RESERVATION

South Dakota
Birds and Small Game Stamps

A1

1984?-91 ***Rouletted 9.75***

A1 A1 black, *light yellow,* member	*5,500.*	*350.*
a. Rouletted 6.5	—	850.
A2 A1 black, *yellow,* non-member	*2,250.*	*150.*

Nos. A1-A2 issued in booklet panes of 6 with tab at left. No. A2 printed with diagonal lines on front.

Catalogue values for all unused stamps in this section, from this point to the end, are for Never Hinged items.

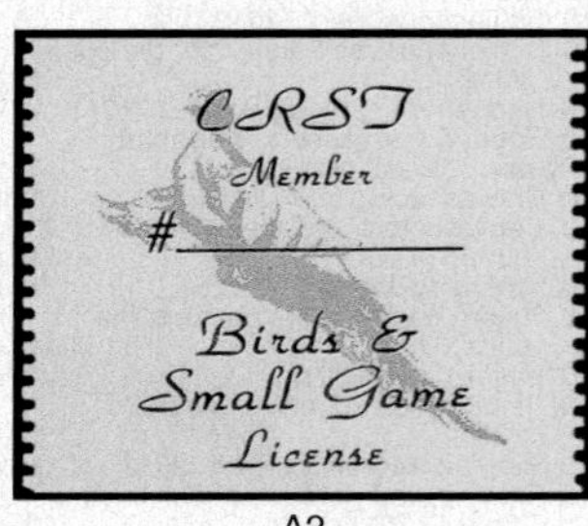

A2

1989-97 **Self-Adhesive** ***Perf. 12 Vert.***

A3 A2 black, *yellow,* member	25.00	10.00
A4 A2 black, *yellow,* non-member	45.00	15.00

With Water-Activated Gum

A5 A2 black, *light yellow,* member	13.00	5.00
A6 A2 black, *light yellow,* non-member	27.50	10.00

Rouletted

A7 A2 black, *yellow,* non-member	*150.00*	*45.00*

Nos. A3-A7 issued in booklet panes of 5.

Waterfowl Stamps

Catalogue values for all unused stamps in this section are for Never Hinged items.

1993		**_Perf. 12 Vert._**	
1	black, *light yellow,* member	15.00	5.00
2	black *light yellow,* non-member	27.50	10.00

Nos. 1-2 issued in panes of 5.

COLVILLE INDIAN RESERVATION

Washington Bird Stamps

Required by non-tribal members to hunt birds, including waterfowl.

Catalogue values for all unused stamps in this section are for Never Hinged items.

Tribal Bird Stamp

A1

1991 Tribal Bird Stamp Nº 0011 $20.00

A2

1990-91	**Self-Adhesive**	**_Die Cut_**	
1 A1	black, *yellow*	—	
	Numbered serially in red		
2 A2	$20 black, *yellow, 1992*	—	—

CROW INDIAN RESERVATION

Montana Waterfowl Stamps

Catalogue values for all unused stamps in this section are for Never Hinged items.

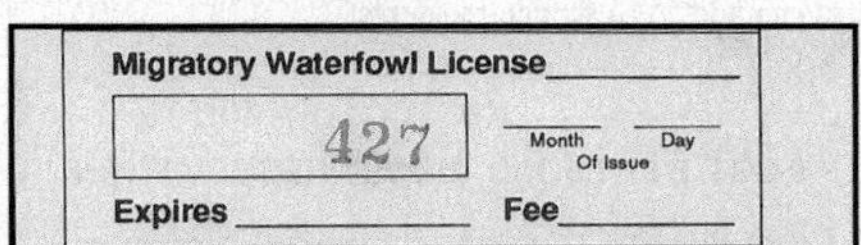

Numbered serially in red

1992	**Self-Adhesive**	**_Die Cut_**	
1	blue	*95.00*	*40.00*
a.	Inscribed "Apr. 30, 199_"	*250.00*	*75.00*

Issued in panes of 5 stamps (4 each No. 1, 1 No. 1a).

Stamps without serial numbers exist. Some may have been issue to hunters during an abbreviated 1993 season.

CROW CREEK SIOUX INDIAN RESERVATION

South Dakota Non-Indian Small Game Hunting Stamps

Issued 1961-64. The 1961 fee was $2.50. No example is recorded. The 1962 stamps were changed by hand for use in 1963 and 1964. No example of the 1964 stamp is recorded.

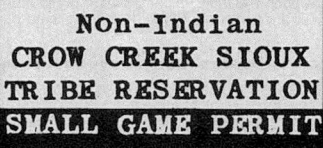

Non-Indian CROW CREEK SIOUX TRIBE RESERVATION SMALL GAME PERMIT 1962 169 1962

1962-63			
2	$5 black	*19,500.*	—
3	$5 black, *1963*	—	—

Waterfowl Stamps

Fees: $10, reservation resident, non-tribal member; $30, South Dakota resident; $65, non-South Dakota resident.

Catalogue values for all unused stamps in this section, from this point to the end, are for Never Hinged items.

1989-90		**_Perf. Horiz._**	
5	$10 black	250.	*150.*
6	$30 black	*7,500.*	*750.*
7	$65 black	*950.*	*350.*
	1990		
8	$10 black, *1990*	175.	*100.*
9	$30 black, *1990*	125.	
10	$65 black, *1990*	550.	*300.*

Fees: $5, tribal member; $15, affiliate, reservation resident; $30 ($35), South Dakota resident/non-resident daily use; $75 ($100), South Dakota resident/non-resident season.

1994 Tribal Member WATERFOWL $5 0205

1994		**_Rouletted Horiz._**	
11	$5 green	125.00	15.00
12	$15 blue	200.00	
13	$30 red	200.00	
a.	$25 red (error)	—	
14	$75 red	300.00	75.00

1995-99		**_Perf. Horiz._**	
15	$5 green & multi	95.00	10.00
16	$15 blue & multi	110.00	
17	$30 red & multi	135.00	
18	$75 red & multi	165.00	40.00
19	$5 green & multi, *1996*	27.50	10.00
20	$15 blue & multi, *1996*	45.00	
21	$35 red & multi, *1996*	75.00	
22	$100 red & multi, *1996*	125.00	35.00
23	$5 green & multi, *1997*	12.00	
24	$15 blue & multi, *1997*	35.00	
25	$35 red & multi, *1997*	85.00	
26	$75 red & multi, *1997*	190.00	

No. 25 is inscribed $75, but sold for $35.

27	$5 green & multi, *1998*	12.00	
28	$15 blue & multi, *1998*	35.00	
29	$35 red & multi, *1998*	85.00	
30	$75 red & multi, *1998*	190.00	
31	$5 green & multi, *1999*	12.00	
32	$15 blue & multi, *1999*	35.00	
33	$35 red & multi, *1999*	85.00	
34	$75 red & multi, *1999*	190.00	

Waterfowl Stamps

Fees: $5, tribal member; $15, $20, $30, affiliate; $35, $40, non-resident daily use; $75, $100, non-resident season.

2000-04			
35	$5 green & multi	*75.00*	—
36	$15 blue & multi	*75.00*	—
37	$35 red & multi	*75.00*	—
38	$75 red & multi	*75.00*	—
39	$5 green & multi, *2001*	*100.00*	—
40	$20 blue & multi, *2001*	*100.00*	—
41	$40 red & multi, *2001*	*100.00*	—
42	$100 red & multi, *2001*	*100.00*	—
43	$5 green & multi, *2002*	*125.00*	—
44	$20 blue & multi, *2002*	*125.00*	—
45	$40 red & multi, *2002*	*125.00*	—
46	$100 red & multi, *2002*	*125.00*	—
47	$5 green & multi, *2003*	—	—
48	$30 blue & multi, *2003*	—	—
49	$40 red & multi, *2003*	—	—
50	$100 red & multi, *2003*	—	—
51	$5 green & multi, *2004*		—
52	$30 blue & multi, *2004*	—	—
53	$40 red & multi, *2004*	—	—
54	$100 red & multi, *2004*	—	—

In 2001, $15 affiliate, $35 non-resident daily use and $75 non-resident season stamps were printed. It is not known whether these stamps with incorrect fees were sold. Value, set $200.

Twenty-five stamps for 2005 were printed; one example is recorded on license.

INDIAN RESERVATION STAMPS
• Largest and most comprehensive stock!
• Over 600 different stamps from over 18 different Reservations currently in stock.
• Many extremely scarce stamps available.
• Stamp album available which pictures all known Reservation stamps.
• Price list pictures and prices most available stamps. Send $5, refundable with the first order.
MICHAEL JAFFE STAMPS

P.O. Box 61484
Vancouver, WA 98666
(360)695-6161 • (800)782-6770
mjaffe@brookmanstamps.com
www.duckstamps.com
Ebay Store: Brookman Stamp Co and M Jaffe Ducks

Fees: $10, tribal member; $25, affiliate; $40, non-resident daily use; $100, non-resident season.

2006

59	$10 blue	—	—
60	$25 green	—	—
61	$40 red	—	—
62	$100 red	—	—

Sportsmen's Stamps

For hunting game including waterfowl.

Fees: $10, tribal member; $25, reservation resident, non-tribal member; $100, South Dakota resident; $250, non-South Dakota resident.

Used values are for signed stamps.

Catalogue values for all unused stamps in this section are for Never Hinged items.

1989-90

A1	$10 black	400.	*100.*
A2	$25 black	1,100.	*300.*
A3	$100 black	350.	*75.*
A4	$250 black	350.	*150.*
A5	$10 black, *1990*	450.	*100.*
A6	$25 black, *1990*	550.	*150.*
A7	$100 black, *1990*	225.	*125.*
A8	$250 black, *1990*	350.	*150.*

Goose Stamps

Fees: $5, tribal member; $10, $15, $20, affiliate; $50, non-resident.

1998-2004

2A1	$5 green	—	—
2A2	$10 blue	—	—
2A3	$50 red	—	—
2A4	$5 green & multi, *1999*	*100.00*	—
2A5	$10 blue & multi, *1999*	*100.00*	—
2A6	$50 red & multi, *1999*	*100.00*	—
2A7	$5 green & multi, *2000*	*60.00*	—
2A8	$10 blue & multi, *2000*	*60.00*	—
2A9	$50 red & multi, *2000*	*60.00*	—
2A10	$5 green & multi, *2001*	*60.00*	—
2A11	$10 blue & multi, *2001*	*60.00*	—
2A12	$50 red & multi, *2001*	*60.00*	—
2A13	$5 green & multi, *2002*	*150.00*	—
2A14	$15 blue & multi, *2002*	*150.00*	—
2A15	$50 red & multi, *2002*	*150.00*	—
2A16	$5 green & multi, *2003*	—	—
2A17	$20 blue & multi, *2003*	—	—
2A18	$50 red & multi, *2003*	—	—
2A21	$50 red & multi, *2004*	—	—

In 1997, $5 tribal member, $10 affiliate, and $50 non-resident stamps were printed, but the season was canceled. Value, set $400.

Tribal member and affiliate stamps were printed for 2004 but no examples are known. In 2005, 25 stamps were printed.

Fees: $10, tribal member; $25, affiliate; $75, non-resident.

2006

2A25	$10 blue	—	—
2A26	$25 green	—	—
2A27	$75 red	—	—

FLATHEAD INDIAN RESERVATION

Montana
Bird or Fish Stamps

Catalogue values for all unused stamps in this section are for Never Hinged items.

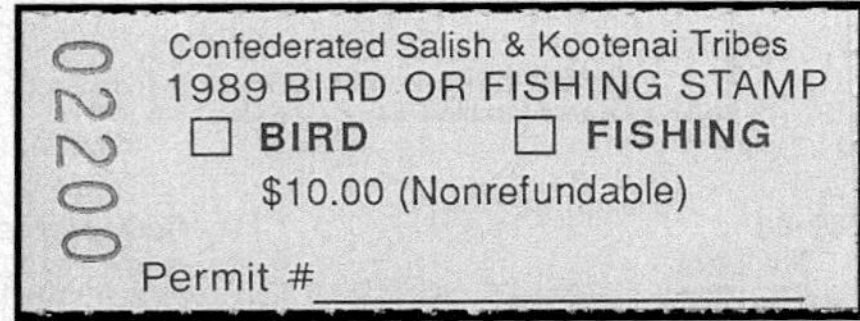

Numbered serially in Red

1987-90		*Imperf.*	
1	$10 black	*750.00*	*350.00*
	Rouletted 7		
1A	$10 black, *1988*, # ends in 0-5	*650.00*	*275.00*
b.	Rouletted 5.5, # ends in 8 or 9	*950.00*	*300.00*
c.	Rouletted 5.5x7, # ends in 6 or 7	*950.00*	*300.00*
	Rouletted 5.5x11		
2	$10 blue, *1989*	16.00	5.00
b.	Rouletted 6.5	30.00	10.00
	Rouletted 6.5		
	Self-Adhesive		
3	$10 blue, *1990*	16.00	5.00

No. 1A printed in booklet panes of 10. Nos. 2-3 printed in booklet panes of 5 stamps se-tenant with 5 stamps marked "Duplicate."

Joint Bird License Stamps

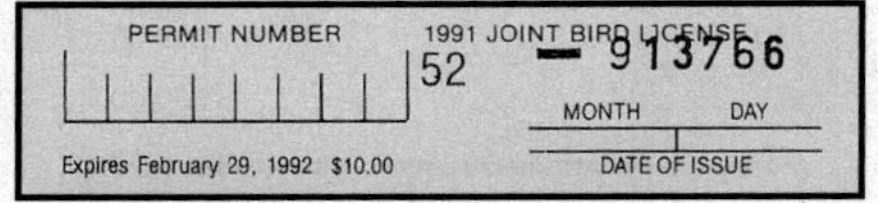

Numbered serially

1991	**Self-Adhesive**	***Die Cut***	
4	$10 black, *green*	10.50	5.00

Printed in booklet panes of 10.

Bird License Stamps

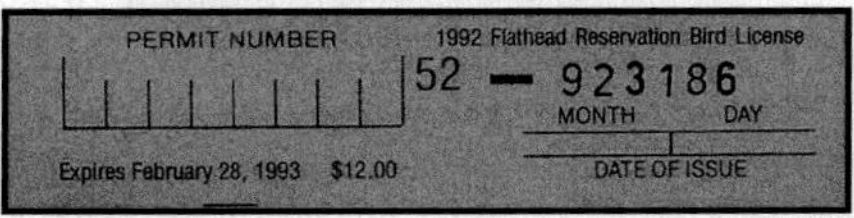

Numbered serially

1992-2000	**Self-Adhesive**	***Die Cut***	
5	$12 black, *rose*, season	10.50	5.00
6	$12 black, *salmon*, 3-day	9.50	5.00
7	$12 black, *dark green*, season, *1993*	8.00	4.00
8	$12 black, *dark blue*, 3-day, *1993*	7.50	4.00
9	$12 black, *blue*, season, *1994*	8.00	4.00
10	$12 black, *orange*, 3-day, *1994*	7.00	3.00
11	$12 black, *yellow*, resident, *1995*	8.00	3.00
12	$55 black, *pale blue green*, non-resident, *1995*	*17.50*	*9.00*
13	$12 black, *turquoise*, resident, *1996*	11.00	3.00
14	$55 black, *pale orange*, non-resident, *1996*	*18.00*	*15.00*
15	$12 black, *pale yellow*, resident, *1997*	10.00	3.00
16	$55 black, *pale blue green*, non-resident, *1997*	*11.00*	
17	$13 black, *turquoise*, resident, *1998*	12.00	3.00
18	$56 black, *blue*, non-resident, *1998*	*12.00*	*3.00*
19	$13 black, *orange*, resident, *1999*	10.00	3.00
20	$56 black, *red*, non-resident, *1999*	*10.00*	*3.00*
21	$13 black, *yellow*, reservation, *2000*	12.00	3.00
22	$14 black, *green*, resident, *2000*	12.00	3.00
23	$110 black, *pink*, out-of-state, *2000*	*12.00*	*3.00*

Printed in booklet panes of 10.

FORT BELKNAP INDIAN RESERVATION

Montana
Waterfowl Stamps

Catalogue values for all unused stamps in this section are for Never Hinged items.

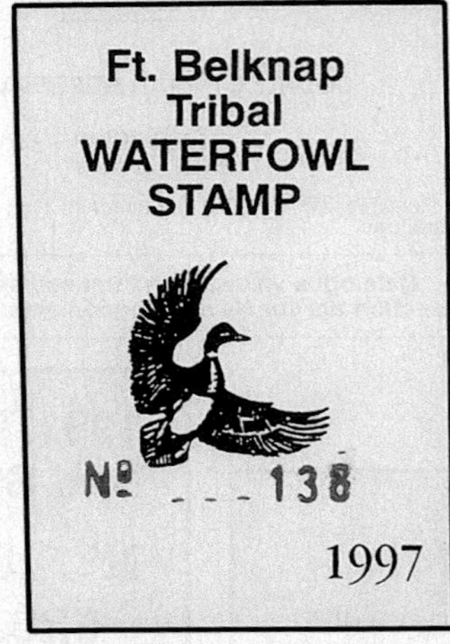

A1

1996-2010		**Self-Adhesive**	***Die Cut***
1	A1	black	37.50
		Serially Numbered in Red	
2	A1	black, *1997*	67.50
3	A1	green, *1998*	45.00
4	A1	red, *1999*	82.50
5	A1	red, *2000*	160.00
6	A1	dark green, *2001*	160.00
7	A1	maroon, *2003*	135.00
8	A1	blue, *2004*	135.00
9	A1	black, *2005*	135.00
10	A1	green, *2006*	135.00
11	A1	maroon, *yellow*, *2007*	135.00
12	A1	blue, *blue*, *2008*	135.00
13	A1	red, *yellow*, *2009*	135.00
14	A1	green, *2010*	135.00

No. 1 is undated. Nos. 2-14 are dated. No stamp was released in 2002.

Nos. 1-14 were required in addition to a Federal Hunting Permit Stamp.

Hunting licenses on Fort Belknap Reservation cost $10 for residents and $110 for non-residents.

FORT BERTHOLD INDIAN RESERVATION

North Dakota
Small Game Stamps

Stamps issued before 1990 may exist.

Issued in booklet panes of 6 stamps and 6 tabs. Required for hunting small game including waterfowl.

Values are for stamps with tabs. Fees varied, usually $6 for tribe members and $20-$30 for non-members.

Stamps are numbered serially.

Catalogue values for all unused stamps in this section are for Never Hinged items.

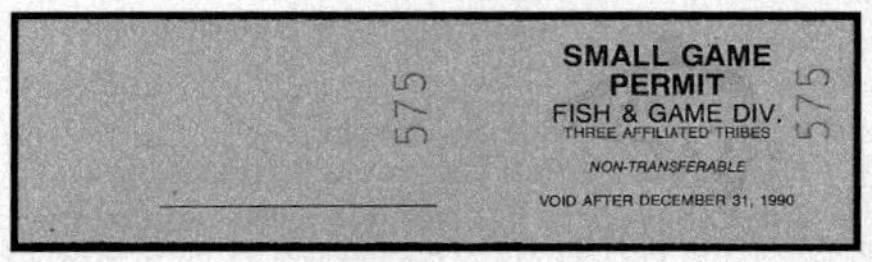

1990-98		*Rouletted*	
A6	black, *pink*	*85.00*	*25.00*
A7	black, *green, 1991*	*80.00*	
A8	black, *pink, 1992*	*80.00*	
A9	black, *blue, 1993*	*150.00*	
A10	black, *pink, 1994*	70.00	
A11	black, *pink, 1995*	*100.00*	*25.00*
A12	black, *green, 1996*	57.50	
A13	black, *light green, 1997*	50.00	*12.00*
A14	black, *green, 1998*	30.00	
A15	black, *green, 1999*	30.00	
A16	black, *orange, 2000*	25.00	
A17	black, *green, 2001*	27.50	
A18	black, *blue, 2002*	25.00	
A19	black, *pink, 2003*	25.00	
A20	black, *blue, 2004*	27.50	
A21	black, *orange, 2005*	27.50	
A22	black, *orange, 2006*	30.00	
A23	black, *yellow, 2007*	30.00	

Waterfowl Stamps

Stamps issued before 1990 may exist.
Issued in booklet panes of 6 stamps and 6 tabs.
Required for non-member waterfowl hunters only.
Values are for stamps with tabs.
Fees varied, usually $20-$30.
Stamps are numbered serially.

Catalogue values for all unused stamps in this section are for Never Hinged items.

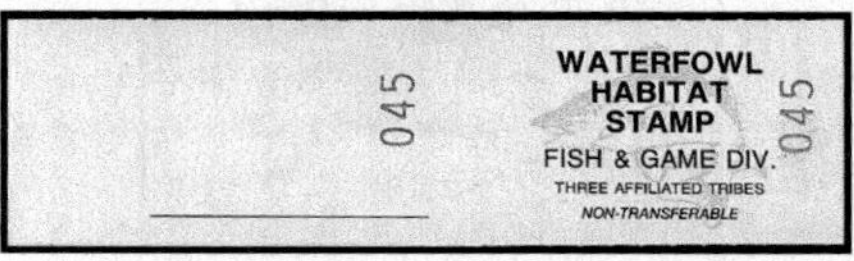

1990-2000		*Rouletted*	
2A6	black	*1,750.*	
2A7	black, *blue, 1991*	*500.*	
2A8	black, *yellow, #1-60, 1992*	*2,750.*	
2A9	black, *yellow, #61-120, 1993*	*400.*	
2A10	black, *green, #1-60, 1994*	*375.*	
2A11	black, *green, #61-120, 1995*	*200.*	*50.00*
2A12	black, *green, #121-198, 1996*	*175.*	
2A13	black, *light green, #199-276, 1997*	*200.*	
2A14	black, *light green, #277-334, 1998*	*200.*	
2A15	black, *light green, #335-432, 1999*	*225.*	
2A16	black, *light green, #433-588, 2000*	*175.*	
2A17	black, *yellow, #589-744, 2001*	*225.*	
2A18	black, *red, #745-900, 2002*	*250.*	
2A19	black, *orange, #901-1056, 2003*	*250.*	
2A20	black, *pink, #1057-1212, 2004*	*250.*	
2A21	black, *red, #1213-1368, 2005*	*250.*	
2A22	black, *blue, #1369-1524, 2006*	*200.*	
2A23	black, *pink, #1525-1680, 2007*	*200.*	

Sandhill Crane Stamps

Issued in booklet panes of 6 stamps and 6 tabs.
Required for non-member waterfowl hunters only.
Values are for stamps with tabs.
Fees varied, usually $20-$30.
Stamps are numbered serially.

Catalogue values for all unused stamps in this section are for Never Hinged items.

1997-99		*Rouletted*
3A1	black, *orange, #1-30*	*1,250.*
3A2	black, *orange, #31-60, 1998*	*1,250.*
3A3	black, *orange, #61-90, 1999*	*3,500.*

FORT PECK INDIAN RESERVATION

Montana

Stamps issued before 1975 may exist.

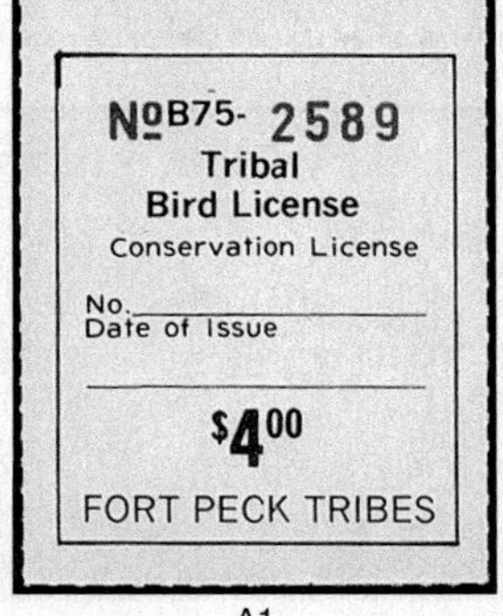

A1

1975-78		*Rouletted*
2	A1 $4 black	*1,250.*
3	A1 $4 black, *1976*	90.
a.	Double impression	*11,500.*
4	A1 $4 black, *1977*	*19,500.*
5	A1 $5 black, *orange, 1978*	225.

Waterfowl Stamp

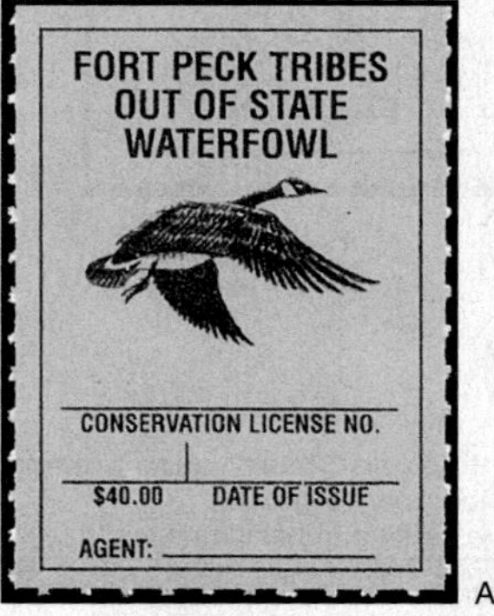

A2

1996		*Rouletted*
6	A2 $10 black, *orange,* resident	20.00
7	A2 $40 black, *green,* out-of-state	30.00

JICARILLA APACHE INDIAN RESERVATION

New Mexico Wildlife Stamp

Catalogue values for all unused stamps in this section are for Never Hinged items.

A1

A2

1988-96	Self-Adhesive	*Die Cut*
1	A1 $5 black & gold, *white*	110.00

Rouletted

Water-Activated Gum

2	A2 $5 black & gold, *blue*	12.00

Serial Number Greater than 9000

3	A2 $5 black & gold, *blue,*	80.00

No. 2 was issued in blocks of 4.

No. 2 measures 38.5mm x 64mm. No. 3 is 37mm x 61mm or 66mm.

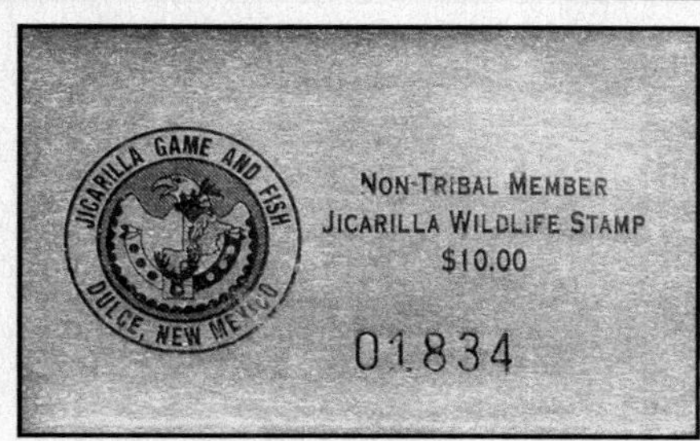

A3

1999-2000	Self-Adhesive	*Die Cut*
4	A3 $10 blue & black, *gold,* non-tribal	72.50
5	A3 $5 black, *gold,* tribal, *2000*	60.00
6	A3 $10 black, *gold,* non-tribal, *2000*	60.00

A4

2004	Self-Adhesive	*Die Cut*
7	A4 ($15) brown & multi, tribal	*225.00*
8	A4 ($15) blue gray & multi, non-tribal	*225.00*

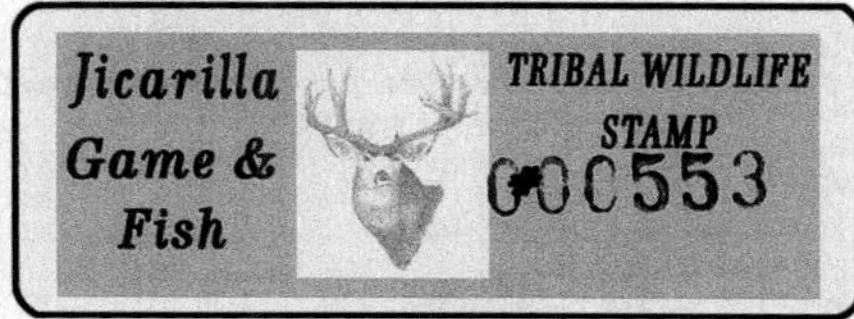

A5

2007	Self-Adhesive	*Die Cut*
9	A5 ($15) green & multi, tribal	*175.00*
10	A5 ($15) brown & multi, non-tribal	*175.00*

Type of 2004

2008-9	Self-Adhesive	*Die Cut*
11	A4 ($20) red & multi, tribal	*175.00*
12	A4 ($20) yellow & multi, non-tribal	*175.00*
13	A4 ($20) orange & multi, tribal, *2009*	*175.00*
14	A4 ($20) green & multi, non-tribal, *2009*	*175.00*

Nos. 10-11 have a star hand punched to the right of the serial number.

LAKE TRAVERSE (SISSETON-WAHPETON) INDIAN RESERVATION

South Dakota-North Dakota Waterfowl Stamps

No examples are recorded of stamps from 1987-1990. No. 1 is die cut. Nos. 6, 8-9 are die cut, self-adhesive. No. 7 issued in booklet panes of 5, rouletted, numbered serially in red.

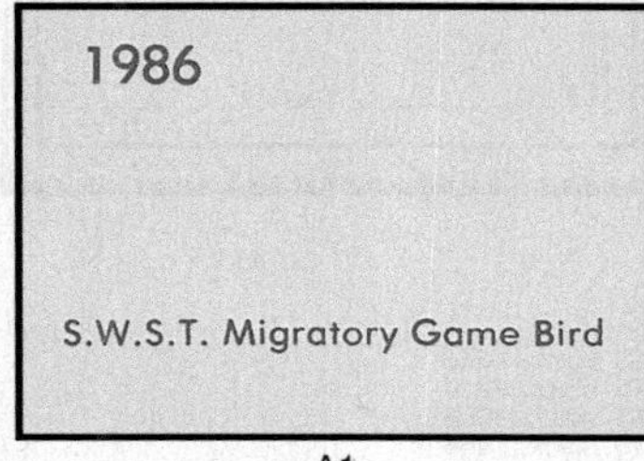

A1

A2

A3

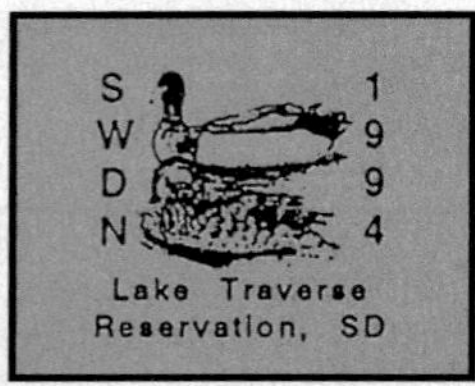

A4

1986-2004

1	A1	green	*225.00*	*75.00*

Catalogue values for all unused stamps in this section, from this point to the end, are for Never Hinged items.

6	A2	black, *bright green, 1991*	*125.00*	
7	A3	Wood duck, *1992*	15.00	
8	A2	black, *bright red, 1993*	25.00	
9	A4	black, *yellow orange, 1994*	7.50	4.00

Inscribed SWST

10	A4	black, *red orange, 1995*	12.00	4.00
11	A4	black, *blue, 1996*	10.00	4.00
12	A4	black, *bright green, 1997*	11.00	3.00
13	A4	black, *red, 1998*	40.00	
14	A4	black, *orange, 1999*	10.00	
15	A4	black, *yellow green, 2000*	35.00	
16	A4	black, *yellow, 2001*	8.00	
17	A4	black, *orange, 2002*	8.00	
18	A4	black, *blue, 2003*	30.00	
19	A4	black, *yellow, 2004*	25.00	

LOWER BRULE INDIAN RESERVATION

South Dakota Waterfowl Stamps

Serial Nos. are in red. Year and fee are written by hand or typewritten on each stamp. The $5 fee was for for non-members and non-Indians. There was a $2.50 fee for tribal members but no examples of these stamps are recorded.

Numbers have been reserved for the $2.50 stamps.

Since no year is on an unused stamp, they are listed under the first year only.

1962-70

2	$5 black	—
4	$5 black, *1963*	—
6	$5 black, *1964*	*4,750.*
8	$5 black, *1965*	*4,750.*
10	$5 black, *1966*	*4,250.*
12	$5 black, *1967*	*3,750.*
14	$5 black, *1968*	*3,500.*
18	$5 black, *1969*	*7,500.*

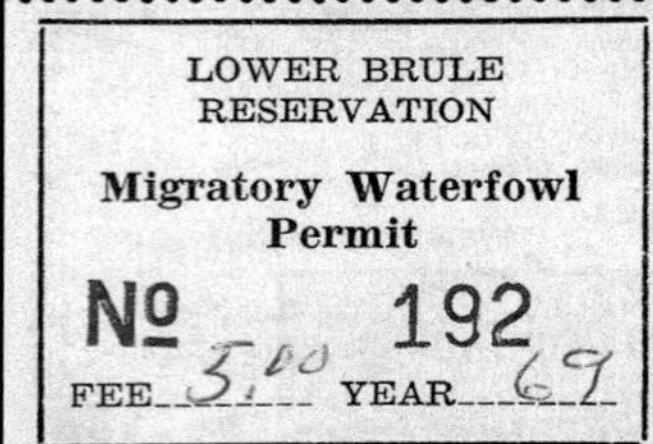

1969-71

20	$5 black	*9,000.*
22	$5 black, *1970*	—
24	$5 black, *1971*	—
26	$5 black, *1972*	—

Migratory Bird Hunting and Conservation Stamps

Issued in panes of 20.

All stamps have serial number on reverse.

Catalogue values for all unused stamps in this section, from this point to the end, are for Never Hinged items.

Designs: Nos. 27-31, Birds on the wing. Nos. 32-34, Bison, birds. Nos. 35-37, Deer, birds on the wing. Nos. 38-40, Birds landing, on the ground. Nos. 41-43, Canada geese. No. 44-46, Birds on the wing, diff. Nos. 47-49, Three birds. Nos. 50-51, Elk. Nos. 52-53, Birds on the wing, diff. Nos. 54-55, Canada geese, diff. Nos. 56-57, Eight birds on ground, three in air. Nos. 58-59, Mountains, ducks on water. Nos. 60-61, Goose. Nos. 62-63, Elk, diff.

1995-2008

27	$5	green, tribal member	10.00
28	$5	orange brown, resident deeded land owner / operator	10.00
29	$5	blue, resident government employee	10.00
30	$10	red, non-tribal S.D. resident	15.00
31	$10	purple, non-resident, out of state	15.00
32	$5	multi, tribal / resident, *1996*	10.00
33	$10	multi, non-tribal S.D. resident, *1996*	15.00
34	$10	multi, non-resident, out of state, *1996*	15.00
35	$5	multi, tribal / resident, *1997*	10.00
36	$10	multi, non-tribal S.D. resident, *1997*	15.00
37	$10	multi, non-resident, out of state, *1997*	15.00
38	$5	multi, tribal / resident, *1998*	10.00
39	$10	multi, non-tribal S.D. resident, *1998*	15.00
40	$10	multi, non-resident, out of state, *1998*	15.00
41	$5	multi, tribal / resident, *1999*	10.00
42	$10	multi, non-tribal S. D. resident, *1999*	15.00
43	$10	multi, non-resident, out of state, *1999*	15.00
44	$5	multi, tribal / resident, *2000*	25.00
45	$10	multi, non-tribal S. D. resident, *2000*	40.00
46	$10	multi, non-resident, out of state, *2000*	40.00
47	$5	multi, tribal / resident, *2001*	25.00
48	$10	multi, non-tribal S. D. resident, *2001*	45.00
49	$10	multi, non-resident, out of state, *2001*	45.00
50	$5	multi, tribal, *2002*	25.00
51	$10	multi, non-tribal, *2002*	45.00
52	$5	multi, tribal, *2003*	35.00
53	$10	multi, non-tribal, *2003*	55.00
54	$5	multi, tribal, *2004*	35.00
55	$10	multi, non-tribal, *2004*	55.00
56	$5	multi, tribal, *2005*	35.00
57	$10	multi, non-tribal, *2005*	55.00
58	$5	multi, tribal, *2006*	35.00
59	$10	multi, non-tribal, *2006*	55.00
60	$5	multi, tribal, *2007*	35.00
61	$10	multi, non-tribal, *2007*	55.00
62	$5	multi, tribal, *2008*	35.00
63	$10	multi, non-tribal, *2008*	55.00

PINE RIDGE (OGLALA SIOUX) INDIAN RESERVATION

South Dakota Waterfowl Stamps

Nos. 1-3 issued in booklet panes of 5, numbered serially in red.

No. 2 perforated, others rouletted.

A1

A2

A3

1	A1	$4 black	*250.00*	

Earliest known use of No. 1 is 1988.

Catalogue values for all unused stamps in this section, from this point to the end, are for Never Hinged items.

2	A2	$4 black, perforated	15.00
3	A3	$4 Canada geese, *1992*	11.00

$6 stamps picturing Canada geese were produced and sold for the 1993 season. The same stamp was rubber handstamped for the 1994 season. However, there was no hunting season those years. Value, each $15.

ROSEBUD INDIAN RESERVATION

South Dakota Tribal Game Bird Stamps

Nos. 1-4 have red serial number. Stamps for 1960, 1964-69 may exist.

Since no year is on an unused stamp, they are listed under the first year only.

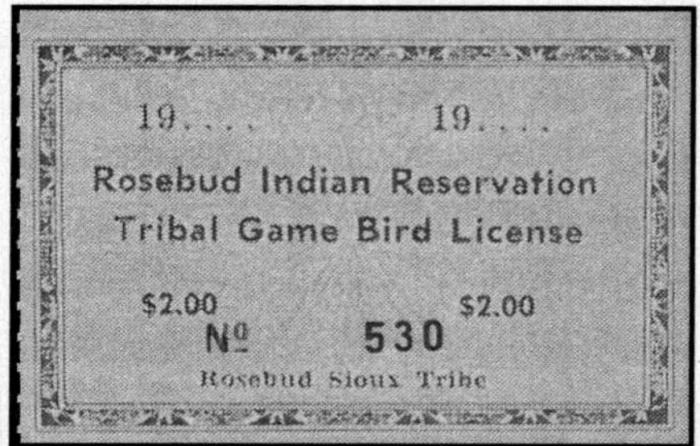

1959-63 *Rouletted*

1	$2 green, *light green*	—	
2	$2 green, *light green, 1961*	*9,000.*	
3	$2 green, *light green, 1962*	*10,500.*	
4	$2 green, *light green, 1963*	—	

The last two digits of the year date is filled in by hand on Nos. 1-4.

Small Game Stamps

Rosebud Reservation
SMALL GAME
Nº 2399

No. 12

Rosebud Reservation
SMALL GAME

No. 13

1979-80

12	black	*1,950.*	
13	black, *1980*	*135.00*	

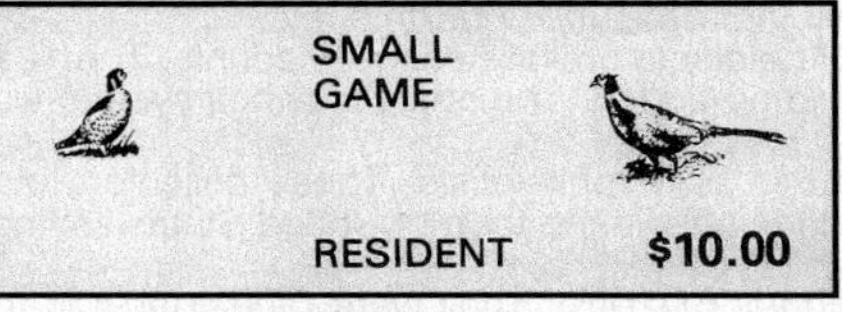

Nos. 14, 15

1988-93 *Imperf.*

14	$10 black, resident	25.00	*20.00*
15	$45 black, non-resident, *1989*	125.00	

Nos. 16, 17

1990-2000 **Self-Adhesive** *Die Cut*

16	$10 black, resident	125.00	*15.00*
a.	Overprinted "RESIDENT" over "Non-resident"	*7,500.*	*1,500.*
17	$45 black, non-resident	650.00	*75.00*
18	black, tribal, *1996*	27.50	12.50
a.	$10 Handwritten value	*900.00*	
19	black, resident, *1996*	77.50	27.50
a.	$50 Handwritten value		
20	black, non-resident, *1996*	225.00	*45.00*
21	$19 red, tribal, *2000*		*110.00*
22	$50 red, resident, *2000*	300.00	*110.00*
23	$85 red, non-resident, *2000*	100.00	*45.00*

Unused values for Nos. 16-17 are for never hinged stamps.
No 20 is valued with small faults, usually staple holes. Stamps without faults sell for more.

No. 24

2001 **Die cut, self-adhesive**

24	$40 black, red & blue, resident		
25	$40 black, red & blue, non-resident		

SAN CARLOS INDIAN RESERVATION

Arizona
Habitat Conservation Stamps

Catalogue values for all unused stamps in this section are for Never Hinged items.

A1

1997-2012 **Die cut, self-adhesive**

1	A1 $5 gold & black, no serial no.	650.00	
a.	With handwritten serial no.	650.00	

Serially Numbered in Gray

2	A1 $5 gold & black, *1998*	12.50	
a.	With purple year date handstamp, handwritten serial no.	650.00	
b.	With handwritten 2001 year date	67.50	
3	A1 $5 gold & black, *1999*	12.50	
a.	With handwritten 2001 year date	67.50	
4	A1 $5 gold & black, *2000*	12.50	
5	A1 $5 red, without serial no., *2001*	55.00	
6	A1 $5 blue, narrow date, without serial no., *2002*	22.50	
a.	Wide year date	32.50	
b.	With handwritten 2003 year date	32.50	

Serially Numbered in Black

7	A1 $5 green, *2003*	22.50	
8	A1 $5 brown, *2004*	22.50	
9	A1 $5 brown, wide serial no., *2005*	17.50	
a.	Narrow serial no.	85.00	
10	A1 $5 green, *2006*	45.00	
11	A1 $5 orange, *2007*	22.50	
12	A1 $5 purple, *2008*	22.50	
13	A1 $5 blue, *2009*	22.50	
14	A1 $5 green *2010*	22.50	
15	A1 $5 vio blue, *2011*	22.50	
16	A1 $5 red, *2012*	22.50	

SPIRIT LAKE INDIAN RESERVATION

South Dakota
Waterfowl Stamps

Catalogue values for all unused stamps in this section are for Never Hinged items.

A1

A2

1996-2008 **Die cut, self-adhesive**

1	A1 black	32.50	
2	A1 black, *1997*	45.00	
3	A1 black, *1998*	45.00	
4	A1 black, *1999*	17.50	
5	A1 black, *2000*	22.50	
6	A1 black, *2001*	22.50	
7	A2 multi, *2001*	12.50	
8	A2 multi, *2002*	12.50	
9	A2 multi, *2003*	12.50	
10	A2 multi, *2004*	12.50	
11	A2 multi, *2005*	12.50	
12	A2 multi, *2006*	9.00	
13	A2 multi, *2007*	9.00	
14	A2 multi, *2008*	9.00	

STANDING ROCK INDIAN RESERVATION

South Dakota-North Dakota
Waterfowl Stamps

Catalogue values for all unused stamps in this section are for Never Hinged items.

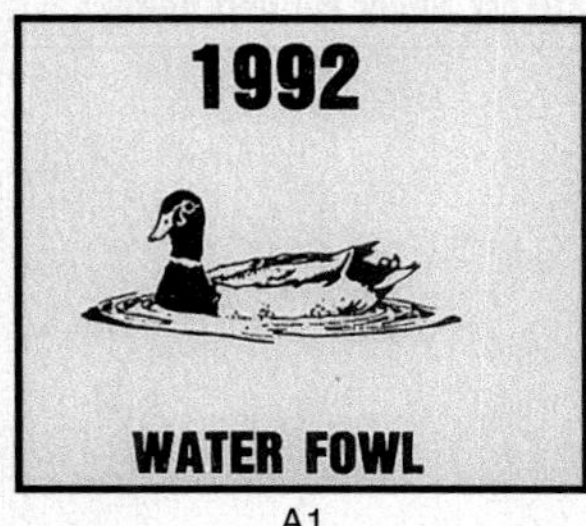

A1

1992-98 **Die cut, self-adhesive**

1	A1 black	16.00	5.00
2	A1 black, *1993*	10.00	4.00

Inscribed "SRST"

3	A1 black, *1994*	8.50	3.00
4	A1 black, *1995*	15.00	5.00
5	A1 black, *1996*	13.00	4.00
6	A1 black, *1997*	9.00	4.00
7	A1 black, *1998*	15.00	4.00

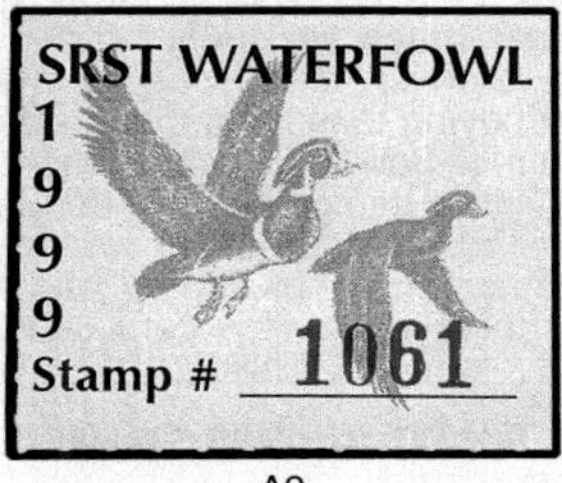

A2

Serially Numbered in Red

1999-2004 *Rouletted*

8	A2 black	10.00	5.00
9	A2 black, *2000*	9.00	6.00
10	A2 black, *2001*	9.00	6.00
11	A2 black, *yellow, 2002*	12.50	9.00
12	A2 black, *2003*	9.00	6.00
13	A2 yellow, *2004*	9.00	6.00

WINNEBAGO INDIAN RESERVATION

Nebraska
Migratory Bird Stamps

Catalogue values for all unused stamps in this section are for Never Hinged items.

A1

1997 **Die cut, self-adhesive**

1	A1	multicolored	9.00	4.50

ZUNI INDIAN RESERVATION

New Mexico
Habitat Stamps

Catalogue values for all unused stamps in this section are for Never Hinged items.

A1 A2 A3

Nos. 2-16 have various native designs. Each has a year date.

Serially Numbered in Red

1995-2010 **Die cut, self-adhesive**

1	A1	multicolored	17.50	9.00

Serially Numbered in Black

2	A2	multicolored, *1996*	20.00	10.00
3	A2	multicolored, *1997*	20.00	10.00
4	A2	multicolored, *1998*	32.50	12.50
5	A2	multicolored, *1999*	18.00	10.00
6	A2	multicolored, *2000*	18.00	10.00
7	A2	multicolored, *2001*	22.50	10.00
8	A2	multicolored, *2002*	22.50	10.00
9	A2	multicolored, *2003*	22.50	10.00
10	A2	multicolored, *2004*	22.50	10.00

Serially Numbered in Red

11	A2	multicolored, *2005*	22.50	10.00
12	A2	multicolored, *2006*	22.50	10.00
13	A2	multicolored, *2007*	22.50	10.00
a.		Plastic coated, no gum	*22.50*	

Plastic Coated Without Gum

14	A2	multicolored, *2008*	*22.50*	
15	A2	multicolored, *2009*	*22.50*	
16	A3	multicolored, *2010*	*22.50*	

SAVINGS STAMPS

"Savings Stamps" is a general philatelic category that includes four slightly different types of stamps issued at different times by either the U.S. Post Office Department or the U.S. Treasury Department. Their common feature was that they all effectively acted as a means for ordinary citizens to save and/or invest incrementally, a little bit at a time. At the same time, the investments effectively were loans to the federal government.

The four types of Savings Stamps are Postal Savings Stamps (issued from 1911-41) and Savings Stamps (1954-61), both issued by the Post Office Department; and War Savings Stamps (1917-45) and a Treasury Savings Stamp (1920), both issued by the Treasury Department.

Postal Savings Stamps were issued in 10c to $5.00 denominations and were redeemable in the form of credits to postal savings accounts. The 1911 10c stamps were available either as stamps or as a stamp imprint on a card to which other stamps could be added. The postal savings system was discontinued March 28, 1966.

Savings Stamps, also issued in 10c to $5.00 denominations, are the savings stamps most familiar to older philatelists. These collectors may remember buying these stamps at school and placing them in booklets. When full, the booklets were redeemable in the form of United States savings bonds. Sale of Savings Stamps was discontinued June 30, 1970.

War Savings Stamps were issued in 25c and $5 denominations (1917-20) and 10c to $5 denominations (1942-45). They were redeemable in the form of United States treasury war certificates, defense bonds or war bonds.

One Treasury Savings Stamp with a $1.00 denomination was issued in 1920. These stamps were redeemable in the form of either war savings stamps or treasury savings certificates.

POSTAL SAVINGS STAMPS

Values for unused Postal Savings stamps are for examples with full original gum. Values for used examples of Nos. PS1, PS4, PS6-PS10 are for stamps with cancels. Values for used examples of Nos. PS11-PS15 and S1-S7 are for stamps without gum.

PS1

Plates of 400 subjects in four panes of 100 each
FLAT PLATE PRINTING

1911, Jan. 3 **Wmk. 191** **Engr.** ***Perf. 12***

Size of design: 18x21½mm

PS1	PS1 10c **orange**	8.50	1.40
	Never hinged	17.50	
	Block of 4, 2mm spacing	37.50	
	Block of 4, 3mm spacing	40.00	
	P# strip of 3, Impt. open star	57.50	
	P# block of 6, Impt. open star	550.00	

Plate Nos. 5504-5507.

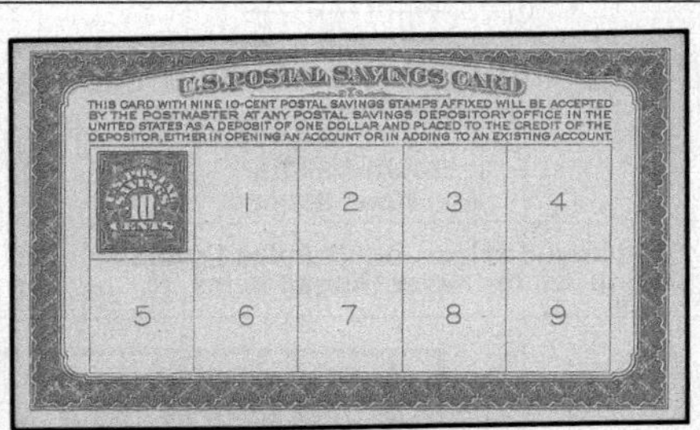

PS1a

Size of design: 137x79mm
Imprinted on Deposit Card

1911, Jan. 3 **Unwmk.**

PS2	PS1a 10c **orange**	300.00	65.00

A 10c deep blue with head of Washington in circle imprinted on deposit card (design 136x79mm) exists, but there is no evidence that it was ever placed in use.

1911, Aug. 14 **Wmk. 190** ***Perf. 12***

PS4	PS1 10c **deep blue**	5.00	1.00
	Never hinged	8.50	
	Block of 4, 2mm spacing	22.50	
	Block of 4, 3mm spacing	25.00	
	P# strip of 3, Impt. open star	30.00	
	P# block of 6, Impt. open star	200.00	
	Never hinged	400.00	

Plate Nos. 5504-5507.

Imprinted on Deposit Card

1911 **Size of design: 133x78mm** **Unwmk.**

PS5	PS1a 10c **deep blue**	*250.00*	40.00

1936 **Unwmk.** ***Perf. 11***

PS6	PS1 10c **deep blue**	3.00	1.25
	violet blue	3.00	1.25
	Never hinged	5.50	
	Block of 4	15.00	
	P# block of 6, Impt. solid star	85.00	
	Never hinged	150.00	

Plate Nos. 21485, 21486.

PS2

Plates of 400 subjects in four panes of 100 each
FLAT PLATE PRINTING

1940 **Unwmk.** **Engr.** ***Perf. 11***

Size of design: 19x22mm

PS7	PS2 10c **deep ultramarine,** *Apr. 3*	17.50	6.00
	Never hinged	32.00	
	Block of 4	75.00	
	P# block of 6	190.00	
	Never hinged	325.00	

Plate Nos. 22540, 22541.

PS8	PS2 25c **dark car rose,** *Apr. 1*	20.00	9.00
	Never hinged	36.00	
	Block of 4	85.00	
	P# block of 6	220.00	
	Never hinged	375.00	

Plate Nos. 22542, 22543.

PS9 PS2 50c **dark blue green,** *Apr. 1* 50.00 17.50
Never hinged 90.00
Block of 4 210.00
P# block of 6 700.00
Never hinged 1,200.

Plate No. 22544.

PS10 PS2 $1 **gray black,** *Apr. 1* 140.00 17.50
Never hinged 250.00
Block of 4 575.00
P# block of 6 1,500.
Never hinged 2,650.

Plate No. 22545.

Nos. PS11-PS15 redeemable in the form of United States Treasury Defense, War or Savings Bonds.

Catalogue values for unused stamps in this section, from this point to the end, are for Never Hinged items.

Minute Man — PS3

E.E. Plates of 400 subjects in four panes of 100 each
ROTARY PRESS PRINTING

1941, May 1 **Unwmk.** ***Perf. 11x10½***
Size of design: 19x22½mm

PS11 PS3 10c **rose red** .60 .25
a. 10c **carmine rose** .60
Block of 4 2.40
P# block of 4 7.25
b. Bklt. pane of 10, *July 30,* trimmed horizontal edges 50.00
As "b," with Electric Eye marks at left 55.00
c. Booklet pane of 10, perf. horizontal edges 100.00
As "c," with Electric Eye marks at left 115.00

Plate Nos., sheet stamps, 22714-22715, 22722-22723, 148245-148246.
Plate Nos., booklet panes, 147084, 147086, 148241-148242.

PS12 PS3 25c **blue green** 2.00 .25
Block of 4 8.25
P# block of 4 22.50
b. Bklt. pane of 10, *July 30* 60.00
Booklet pane with Electric Eye marks at left 65.00

Plate Nos., sheet stamps, 22716-22717, 22724-22725, 148247-148248.
Plate Nos., booklet panes, 147087-147088, 148243-148244.

PS13 PS3 50c **ultramarine** 7.50 1.00
Block of 4 32.50
P# block of 4 50.00

Plate Nos. 22718-22719, 22726-22727.

PS14 PS3 $1 **gray black** 12.50 2.50
Block of 4 52.50
P# block of 4 75.00

Plate Nos. 22720, 22728.

FLAT PLATE PRINTING
Plates of 100 subjects in four panes of 25 each

Size: 36x46mm ***Perf. 11***

PS15 PS3 $5 **sepia** 42.50 10.00
Block of 4 175.00
P# block of 6 at top or bottom 475.00

Plate Nos. 22730-22737, 22740.

SAVINGS STAMPS

Catalogue values for unused stamps in this section are for Never Hinged items.

Minute Man — S1

E.E. Plates of 400 subjects in four panes of 100 each
ROTARY PRESS PRINTING

1954-57 **Unwmk.** ***Perf. 11x10½***
Size of design: 19x22½mm

S1 S1 10c **rose red,** wet printing, *Nov. 30, 1954* .60 .25
Block of 4 2.40
P# block of 4 3.50
a. Booklet pane of 10, *Apr. 22, 1955* 150.00
Booklet pane with Electric Eye marks at left 165.00
b. Dry printing .40 .25
Block of 4 1.75
P# block of 4 3.00
c. As "b," booklet pane of 10 150.00
Booklet pane with Electric Eye marks at left 165.00

Plate Nos., sheet stamps, 164991-164992 (wet), 165917-165918, 166643-166644, 167089-167090, 168765-168766 (dry).
Plate Nos., booklet panes, 165218-165219 (wet), 165954-165955, 167001-167002 (dry).

S2 S1 25c **blue green,** wet printing, *Dec. 30, 1954* 7.50 1.00
Block of 4 30.00
P# block of 4 35.00
a. Booklet pane of 10, *Apr. 15, 1955* 850.00
Booklet pane with Electric Eye marks at left 875.00
Complete booklet, 4 #S2a *3,750.*
b. Dry printing 7.50 1.00
Block of 4 30.00
P# block of 4 35.00
c. As "b," booklet pane of 10 800.00
Booklet pane with Electric Eye marks at left 825.00

Plate Nos., sheet stamps, 165007-165008 (wet), 165919-165920 (dry), booklet panes, 165220-165221 (wet), 165956-165957 (dry).

S3 S1 50c **ultramarine,** wet printing, *Dec. 31, 1956* 9.00 1.50
Block of 4 37.50
P# block of 4 50.00
a. Dry printing 9.00 1.50
Block of 4 37.50
P# block of 4 50.00

Plate Nos. 165050-165051 (wet), 166741-166742, 166941-166942 (dry).

S4 S1 $1 **gray black,** *Mar. 13, 1957* 25.00 4.00
Block of 4 100.00
P# block of 4 120.00

Plate Nos. 166097-166098, 166683-166684.

FLAT PLATE PRINTING
Plates of 100 subjects in four panes of 25 each

Size: 36x46mm ***Perf. 11***

S5 S1 $5 **sepia,** *Nov. 30, 1956* 110.00 15.00
Block of 4 475.00
P# block of 6 at top or bottom 900.00

Plate No. 166068.

Minute Man and 48-Star Flag — S2

GIORI PRESS PRINTING
Plates of 400 subjects in four panes of 100 each

1958, Nov. 18 **Unwmk.** ***Perf. 11***

S6 S2 25c **dark blue & carmine** 2.00 .25
Block of 4 8.00
P# block of 4 10.00
a. Booklet pane of 10 75.00

Plate Nos.: sheet stamps, 166921, 166925, 166946; booklet panes, 166913, 166916.

Minute Man and 50-Star Flag — S3

Plates of 400 subjects in four panes of 100 each.

1961 **Unwmk.** ***Perf. 11***

S7 S3 25c **dark blue & carmine** 1.50 .25
Block of 4 6.00
P# block of 4 11.00
a. Booklet pane of 10 300.00

Plate Nos.: sheet stamps, 167473, 167476, 167486, 167489, 169089; booklet panes, 167495, 167502, 167508, 167516.

WAR SAVINGS STAMPS

Values for unused War Savings stamps and the Treasury Savings stamp are for examples with full original gum. Nos. WS2 and WS3 are known canceled, but other War Savings stamps were left uncanceled. Examples without gum generally were reomved from savings certificates or booklets. **Caution:** Beware of stamps without gum that have been regummed to appear unused with gum.

WS1

Plates of 300 subjects in six panes of 50 each
FLAT PLATE PRINTING

1917, Dec. 1 **Unwmk.** **Engr.** ***Perf. 11***
Size of design: 28x18½mm

WS1 WS1 25c **deep green** 16.00 2.25
Never hinged 30.00
On document (thrift card) 7.50
Block of 4 70.00
Margin strip of 3, P# 80.00
P# block of 6 1,200.

Plate Nos. 56800, 56810-56811, 56817, 57074-57077, 57149-57152, 57336, 57382, 57395-57396, 57399, 57443, 58801-58804, 59044-59045, 59156, 61207-61210.

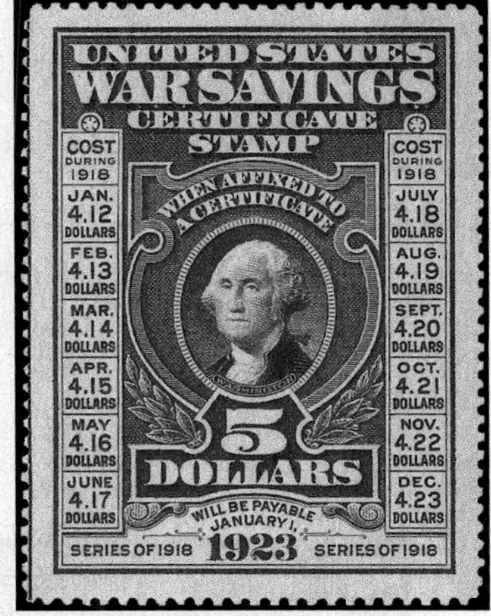

George Washington — WS2

Plates of 80 subjects in four panes of 20 each
FLAT PLATE PRINTING

1917 **Unwmk.** **Engr.** ***Perf. 11***
Size of design: 39x55mm

WS2 WS2 $5 **deep green,** *Nov. 17* 125.00 35.00
Never hinged 250.00
No gum 30.00
On document 45.00
Block of 4 450.00 —
Margin stamp with P# 150.00
P# block of 6 *1,650.*
b. Vert. pair, imperf. horiz. —

Plate Nos. 56914-56917, 57066-57073, 57145-57148, 57169-57176, 57333-57334, 57343-57348, 58431, 58433-58438, 58726-58729, 59071, 60257-60260, 60659-60662, 60665-60668, 60846-60852, 60899, 61203-61206, 61265-61268, 61360-61367, 61388, 61435, 61502.

Rouletted 7

WS3 WS2 $5 **deep green** 1,200. 650.
Never hinged *2,750.*
No gum 475.
On document 700.
Block of 4 5,000.
Margin copy with P# 2,000.

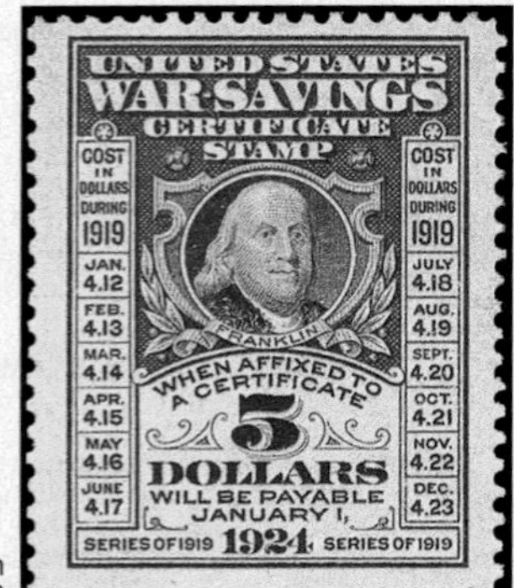

Benjamin Franklin — WS3

Plates of 150 subjects in six panes of 25 each
FLAT PLATE PRINTING

1919, July 3 **Unwmk.** **Engr.** ***Perf. 11***

Size of design: 27x36mm

WS4 WS3 $5 **deep blue** 325.
Never hinged 800.
No gum 160.
On document 275.
Block of 4 1,350.
Margin stamp with P# 500.
Margin stamp with inverted P# 600.

Plate Nos. 61882-61885, 61910-61913, 61970-61972, 61997-61998, 62007-62013.

George Washington WS4

Plates of 100 subjects in four panes of 25 each
FLAT PLATE PRINTING

1919, Dec. 11 **Unwmk.** **Engr.** ***Perf. 11***

Size of design: 36x41½mm

WS5 WS4 $5 **carmine** 800.
Never hinged 2,250.
No gum 350.
On document 500.
Block of 4 *3,500.*
Margin stamp with P# 1,100.

Plate Nos. 67545-67552, 69349-69352, 69673-69675, 69677-69680, 69829.

Abraham Lincoln WS5

Plates of 100 subjects in four panes of 25 each
FLAT PLATE PRINTING

1920, Dec. 21 **Unwmk.** **Engr.** ***Perf. 11***

Size of design: 39½x42mm

WS6 WS5 $5 **orange,** *green* 4,500.
Never hinged *12,000.*
No gum 1,250.
On document 1,500.
Block of 4 *6,500.*
Margin stamp with P# 5,000.

Plate Nos. 73129-73136.

Catalogue values for unused stamps in this section, from this point to the end, are for Never Hinged items.

Minute Man — WS6

Plates of 400 subjects in four panes of 100 each
ROTARY PRESS PRINTING

1942 **Unwmk.** ***Perf. 11x10½***

Size of design: 19x22½mm

WS7 WS6 10c **rose red,** *Oct. 29* .60 .25
a. 10c carmine rose .60
Block of 4 2.40
P# block of 4 6.00
b. Booklet pane of 10, *Oct. 27* 50.00
Booklet pane with Electric Eye marks at left 55.00

Plate Nos., sheet stamps, 149492-149495, 150206-150207, 150706-150707, 155311-155312.
Plate Nos., booklet panes, 149655-149657, 150664.

WS8 WS6 25c **dark blue green,** *Oct. 15* 1.10 .25
Block of 4 5.00
P# block of 4 8.25
b. Booklet pane of 10, *Nov. 6* 50.00
Booklet pane with Electric Eye marks at left 55.00

Plate Nos., sheet stamps, 149587-149590, 150320-150321, 150708-150709, 155313-155314, 155812-155813, 156517-156518, booklet panes, 149658-149660, 150666.

WS9 WS6 50c **deep ultra,** *Nov. 12* 4.00 1.25
Block of 4 16.00
P# block of 4 22.50

Plate Nos. 149591-149594.

WS10 WS6 $1 **gray black,** *Nov. 17* 12.50 3.50
Block of 4 52.50
P# block of 4 70.00

Plate Nos. 149595-149598.

Type of 1942
FLAT PLATE PRINTING
Plates of 100 subjects in four panes of 25 each

1945 **Unwmk.** **Size: 36x46mm** ***Perf. 11***

WS11 WS6 $5 **violet brown** 55.00 17.50
Block of 4 240.00
P# block of 6 at top or bottom 500.00

Plate Nos. 150131-150134, 150291.

Type of 1942
Coil Stamps

1943, Aug. 5 **Unwmk.** ***Perf. 10 Vertically***

WS12 WS6 10c **rose red** 2.75 .90
Pair 6.00
Line pair 10.50

Plate Nos. 153286-153287.

WS13 WS6 25c **dark blue green** 5.00 1.75
Pair 10.50
Line pair 22.50

Plate Nos. 153289-153290.

TREASURY SAVINGS STAMP

Alexander Hamilton TS1

FLAT PLATE PRINTING

1920, Dec. 21 **Unwmk.** **Engr.** ***Perf. 11***

Size of design: 33½x33½mm

TS1 TS1 $1 **red,** *green* 3,750.
Never hinged —
No gum 1,500.
On document 1,750.
Block of 4 *15,000.*
Margin stamp with P# *5,000.*

Plate Nos. 73196-73203.

No. TS1 was not canceled. Examples without gum are considered used, as these generally were removed from savings cards. **Caution:** Beware of stamps without gum that have been regummed to appear unused with gum.

TELEGRAPH STAMPS

These stamps were issued by the individual companies for use on their own telegrams, and can usually be divided into three classes: Free franking privileges issued to various railroad, newspaper and express company officials, etc., whose companies were large users of the lines; those issued at part cost to the lesser officials of the same type companies; and those bearing values which were usually sold to the general public. Occasionally, some of the companies granted the franking privilege to stockholders and minor State (not Federal) officials. Most Telegraph Stamps were issued in booklet form and will be found with one or more straight edges.

Serial numbers may show evidence of doubling, often of a different number. Such doubling is not scarce.

American Rapid Telegraph Company

Organized Feb. 21, 1879, in New York State. Its wires extended as far north as Boston, Mass., and west to Cleveland, Ohio. It was amalgamated with the Bankers and Merchants Telegraph Co., but when that company was unable to pay the fixed charges, the properties of the American Rapid Telegraph Company were sold on Mar. 11, 1891, to a purchasing committee comprised of James W. Converse and others. This purchasing committee deeded the property and franchise of the American Rapid Telegraph Company to the Western Union Telegraph Company on June 25, 1894. Issued three types of stamps: Telegram, Collect and Duplicate. Telegram stamps were issued in sheets of 100 and were used to prepay messages which could be dropped in convenient boxes for collection. Collect and duplicate stamps were issued in alternate rows on the same sheet of 100 subjects. Collect stamps were attached to telegrams sent collect, the receiver of which paid the amount shown by the stamps, while the Duplicate stamps were retained by the Company as vouchers. **Remainders with punched cancellations were bought up by a New York dealer.**

T1

T2

"Prepaid Telegram" Stamps

Engraved and Printed by the American Bank Note Co.

1881 *Perf. 12*

No.	Type	Description	Unused	Used
1T1	T1	1c **black**	20.00	4.75
		Punched		.25
		Block of 4	87.50	
		Punched		1.00
1T2	T1	3c **orange**	50.00	32.50
		Punched		1.50
		Block of 4, punched		10.00
1T3	T1	5c **bister brown**	4.75	1.25
		Punched		.25
		Block of 4	21.00	
		Punched		1.10
a.		5c **brown**	4.75	1.40
		Punched		.25
		Block of 4	21.00	
		Punched		1.00
1T4	T1	10c **purple**	20.00	5.75
		Punched		.25
		Block of 4	85.00	
		Punched		1.00
1T5	T1	15c **green**	8.75	2.50
		Punched		.25
		Block of 4	40.00	
		Punched		1.00
1T6	T1	20c **red**	8.75	2.50
		Punched		.25
		Block of 4, punched		.80
1T7	T1	25c **rose**	12.00	1.75
		Punched		.25
		Block of 4	52.50	
		Punched		1.00
1T8	T1	50c **blue**	32.50	12.50
		Punched		1.50
		Block of 4, punched		8.00

"Collect" Stamps

No.	Type	Description	Unused	Used
1T9	T2	1c **brown**	8.00	5.50
		Punched		.25
1T10	T1	5c **blue**	6.50	4.00
		Punched		.25
1T11	T2	15c **red brown**	6.75	3.25
		Punched		.25
1T12	T2	20c **olive green**	6.50	4.00
		Punched		.25

T3

"Office Coupon" Stamps

No.	Type	Description	Unused	Used
1T13	T3	1c **brown**	14.50	4.40
		Punched		.25
a.		Pair, #1T9, 1T13, punched		2.00
		As "a," block of 4, punched		4.50
1T14	T3	5c **blue**	12.00	5.25
		Punched		.25
a.		Pair, #1T10, 1T14	60.00	
		Punched		3.00
		As "a," block of 4	125.00	
		Punched		7.00
1T15	T3	15c **red brown**	21.00	4.75
		Punched		.25
a.		Pair, #1T11, 1T15	50.00	
		Punched		2.50
		As "a," block of 4	110.00	
		Punched		5.50
1T16	T3	20c **olive green**	21.00	4.75
		Punched		.25
a.		Pair, #1T12, 1T16, punched		2.75
		As "a," block of 4, punched		6.00

Atlantic Telegraph Company

Organized 1884 at Portland, Maine. Its lines extended from Portland, Me., to Boston, Mass., and terminated in the office of the Baltimore and Ohio Telegraph Company at Boston. Later bought out by the Baltimore and Ohio Telegraph Co. Stamps issued by the Atlantic Telegraph Company could also be used for messages destined to any point on the Baltimore and Ohio system. Stamps were printed in panes of six and a full book sold for $10. **Remainders of these stamps, without control numbers, were purchased by a Boston dealer and put on the market about 1932.**

T4

1888 *Perf. 13*

No.	Type	Description	Unused	Used
2T1	T4	1c **green**	6.00	—
		Remainders		2.25
		Pane of 6	—	
		Remainders		14.00
2T2	T4	5c **blue**	9.00	—
		Remainders		2.25
		Pane of 6	—	
		Remainders		14.00
a.		Horiz. pair, imperf. vert.	—	
b.		Vert. pair, imperf. horiz.	25.00	—
2T3	T4	10c **purple brown**	10.00	—
		Remainders		2.25
		Pane of 6	—	
		Remainders		14.00
a.		Horiz. pair, imperf. between	40.00	—
2T4	T4	25c **carmine**	7.50	—
		Remainders		2.25
		Pane of 6, remainders		16.00
a.		Vert. pair, imperf. horiz., remainders	—	

Baltimore & Ohio Telegraph Companies

"The Baltimore & Ohio Telegraph Co. of the State of New York" was incorporated May 17, 1882. Organization took place under similar charter in 26 other states. It absorbed the National Telegraph Co. and several others. Extended generally along the lines of the Baltimore & Ohio Railroad, but acquired interests in other states. Company absorbed in 1887 by the Western Union Telegraph Co. Stamps were issued in booklet form and sold for $5 and $10, containing all denominations.

T5

Engraved by the American Bank Note Co.

1885 *Perf. 12*

No.	Type	Description	Unused	Used
3T1	T5	1c **vermilion**	110.00	30.00
		Pane of 6	700.00	
3T2	T5	5c **blue**	110.00	40.00
3T3	T5	10c **red brown**	55.00	15.00
		Pane of 6	325.00	
3T4	T5	25c **orange**	95.00	30.00
3T5	T6	**brown**	1.75	
		Pane of 4	12.50	

T6

1886

No.	Type	Description	Unused	Used
3T6	T6	**black**	2.00	*25.00*
		Pane of 4	22.50	

Imprint of Kendall Bank Note Co.

1886 **Thin Paper** *Perf. 14*

No.	Type	Description	Unused	Used
3T7	T5	1c **green**	8.00	3.00
a.		Thick paper	15.00	.85
b.		Imperf., pair	90.00	
3T8	T5	5c **blue**	5.00	1.25
a.		Thick paper	11.00	4.00
b.		Imperf., pair		55.00
3T9	T5	10c **brown**	8.50	.75
a.		Thick paper	12.50	1.50
3T10	T5	25c **deep orange**	55.00	.75
a.		Thick paper	65.00	1.50

Used examples of Nos. 3T7-3T20 normally have heavy grid cancellations. Lightly canceled stamps command a premium.

Litho. by A. Hoen & Co.

1886 **Imprint of firm** *Perf. 12*

No.	Type	Description	Unused	Used
3T11	T5	1c **green**	3.00	.65
		Pane of 6	22.50	—
3T12	T5	5c **blue**	9.00	.65
		Pane of 6	60.00	—
a.		Imperf., pair	90.00	
3T13	T5	10c **dark brown**	9.00	.75
		Pane of 6	60.00	—
a.		Vert. pair, imperf. between	60.00	

Wmk. "A HOEN AND CO. BALTIMORE" in double lined capitals in sheet

Perf. 12

No.	Type	Description	Unused	Used
3T14	T5	1c **green**	17.50	1.25
		Pane of 6	115.00	—
3T15	T5	5c **blue**	30.00	1.50
		Pane of 6	190.00	—
a.		Imperf., pair	52.50	—
3T16	T5	10c **dark brown**	20.00	1.25
		Pane of 6	130.00	—

Lithographed by Forbes Co., Boston

1887 **Imprint of firm** *Perf. 12½*

No.	Type	Description	Unused	Used
3T17	T5	1c **green**	60.00	2.75
3T18	T5	5c **blue**	90.00	6.00
3T19	T5	10c **brown**	90.00	5.50
3T20	T5	25c **yellow**	90.00	8.25
a.		25c **orange**	90.00	5.50

Baltimore & Ohio-Connecticut River Telegraph Companies

The Connecticut River Telegraph Co. ran from New Haven to Hartford. An agreement was entered wherein the Baltimore & Ohio System had mutual use of their lines. This agreement terminated when the Baltimore & Ohio System was absorbed by the Western Union. The Connecticut River Telegraph Company then joined the United Lines. In 1885 stamps (black on yellow) were issued and sold in booklets for $10. In 1887 the Connecticut River Telegraph Co. had extended its lines to New Boston, Mass., and new books of stamps (black on blue) were issued for use on this extension. **Remainders were canceled with bars and sold to a New York dealer.**

T7

1885-87 *Perf. 11*

4T1	T7 1c **black,** *yellow*	7.50	6.00
	Remainders		1.25
	Pane of 10	77.50	
	Remainders		6.00
a.	Imperf., pair	40.00	
b.	Vert. pair, imperf. horiz., remainders		—
4T2	T7 5c **black,** *yellow*	5.00	10.00
	Remainders		1.00
	Pane of 10	52.50	
	Remainders		6.00
a.	Horizontal pair, imperf. horiz., remainders		—
b.	Vert. pair, imperf. between, remainders		35.00
c.	Imperf., pair, remainders		35.00
4T3	T7 1c **black,** *blue* ('87)	12.50	—
	Remainders		4.00
	Pane of 10	130.00	
	Remainders		35.00
4T4	T7 5c **black,** *blue* ('87)	15.00	9.00
	Remainders		4.00
	Pane of 10	160.00	
	Remainders		52.50

California State Telegraph Company

Incorporated June 17, 1854 as the California Telegraph Company and constructed a line from Nevada through Grass Valley to Auburn. Extended to run from San Francisco to Marysville via San Jose and Stockton. Later absorbed Northern Telegraph Co. and thus extended to Eureka. It was incorporated as the California State Telegraph Company on April 6, 1861. At the time of its lease to the Western Union on May 16, 1867 the California State consisted of the following companies which had been previously absorbed:

Alta California Telegraph Co., Atlantic and Pacific States Telegraph Co., National Telegraph Co., Northern California Telegraph Co., Overland Telegraph Co., Placerville and Humboldt Telegraph Co., Tuolumne Telegraph Co. Stamps were issued in booklets, six to a pane. **Remainders of Nos. 5T1 and 5T4 are without frank numbers.**

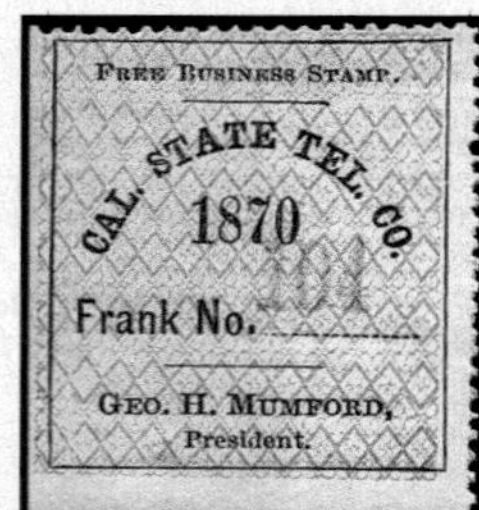

T8

1870 *Perf. 13½*

5T1	T8 **black & blue**	500.	—
	Pane of 6	3,250.	
	Without number	1,250.	

T9

1870 *Perf. 12, 13*

5T2	T9 **black & red,** without number	390.00	250.00

T10

1871 **Dated "1871"**

5T3	T9 **black & red,** without number	1,250.	
a.	Imperf.	*2,500.*	—
5T4	T10 **black & salmon,** blue number	750.	650.00
	Pane of 6	*4,750.*	
	Without number	1,000.	

1872

5T5	T10 **green & red,** red number (no year date)	400.00	
	Pane of 6	—	

1873 **Dated "1873"**

5T6	T10 **red & salmon,** blue number	500.00	

1874 **Dated "1874"**

5T7	T10 **blue & salmon,** black number	575.00	
	Pane of 6	—	

1875 **Dated "1875"**

5T8	T10 **brown & green,** black number	475.00	
	Pane of 6	—	

City & Suburban Telegraph Company (New York City and Suburban Printing Telegraph Company)

Organized 1855. Extended only through New York City and Brooklyn. Sold out to the American Telegraph Co. Stamps were sold to the public for prepayment of messages, which could be dropped in convenient boxes for collection. Stamps were issued in sheets of 60 having a face value of $1. These were arranged in six vertical rows of ten, the horizontal rows having the following denominations: 2c, 1c, 1c, 1c, 2c, 3c.

Counterfeits are known both in black and blue, mostly on pelure or hard white paper. Originals are on soft wove paper, somewhat yellowish. Scalloped edge is more sharply etched on the counterfeits.

T11

Typo. *Imperf.*

6T1	T11 1c **black**	650.	*750.*
	Pair	—	
	Block of 4	—	
6T2	T11 2c **black**	950.	950.
	Pair	—	
	Pair, 2c + 1c	1,750.	
6T3	T11 3c **black**	1,100.	1,000.
	Pair	—	
	Strip of 3, 1c, 2c & 3c		*7,500.*

Colusa, Lake & Mendocino Telegraph Company

Was organized in California early in 1873. First known as the Princeton, Colusa and Grand Island Telegraph Co. In May, 1873 they completed their line from Princeton through Colusa, at which point it was connected with the Western Union office, to Grand Island. On Feb. 10, 1875 it was incorporated as the Colusa, Lake & Mendocino Telegraph Co. Its lines were extended into the counties of Colusa, Lake, Mendocino and Napa. Eventually reached a length of 260 miles. Went out of business in 1892. Stamps were issued for prepayment of messages and were sold in books. When sold they were stamped "P.L.W." (the superintendent's initials) in blue. The 5c value was printed 10 to a pane, being two horizontal rows of five. Of the 10c and 25c nothing definite is known about the settings.

T11a

1876 *Perf. 12*

7T1	T11a 5c **black**	*1,100.*	—
	Block of 4	*5,000.*	
	Pane of 10	*14,000.*	
	Without "P.L.W."	*2,500.*	
7T2	T11a 10c **black**	*11,000.*	—
7T3	T11a 25c **red**	*12,000.*	—

Commercial Union Telegraph Company

Incorporated in New York State on March 31, 1886. Its lines ran from Albany through Troy to Berlin, N.Y., thence to North Adams, Mass. The lines of this Company, which was controlled by the Postal Telegraph Company, were later extended throughout Northern New York and the States of Massachusetts, Vermont, New Hampshire and Maine. Stamps issued in panes of four.

T12

T13

T14

1891 **Lithographed by A. C. Goodwin** *Perf. 12*

8T1	T12 25c **yellow**	35.00	—
	Pane of 4	150.00	
8T2	T13 25c **green**	35.00	10.00
	Pane of 4	150.00	
a.	Horiz. pair, imperf. vert.	90.00	
8T3	T14 **lilac rose**	75.00	—

Mutual Union Telegraph Company

Incorporated October 4, 1880. Extended over 22 states. Absorbed about 1883 by the Western Union Telegraph Co. Franks issued for use of stockholders, in books, four to a pane.

T15

Engr. by Van Campen Engraving Co., New York

1882-83 *Perf. 14*

9T1	T15 **blue**	50.00	20.00
	Pane of 4	225.00	
a.	Vert. pair, imperf. horizontal	140.00	—
b.	Imperf., pair	150.00	
9T2	T15 **carmine**	50.00	—
	Pane of 4	225.00	

North American Telegraph Company

Incorporated October 15, 1885 to run from Chicago to Minneapolis, later being extended into North and South Dakota. Absorbed in 1929 by the Postal System.

Apparently these stamps were not canceled when used. Issued in panes of four.

T15a

1899-1907 *Perf. 12*

10T1	T15a	**violet** (1899)	275.00	
		Pane of 4	1,100.	
10T2	T15a	**green** (1901)	950.00	
10T3	T15a	**dark brown** (1902)	750.00	
10T4	T15a	**blue** (1903)	500.00	
10T5	T15a	**violet** (1904)	350.00	
		Pane of 4	800.00	
a.		Horiz. pair, imperf. vertically	1,500.	
10T6	T15a	**red brown** (1905)	400.00	
a.		Imperf., pair	*2,000.*	—
10T7	T15a	**rose** (1906)	750.00	
10T8	T15a	**green** (1907)	2,250.	

Nos. 10T1 to 10T8 are known imperforate.

Northern Mutual Telegraph Company

Incorporated in New York State as the Northern Mutual Telegraph and Telephone Company on June 20, 1882. Its line, which consisted of a single wire, extended from Syracuse to Ogdensburg via Oswego, Watertown and Clayton, a distance of 170 miles. It was sold to the Bankers and Merchants Telegraph Company in 1883. Stamps were in use for a few days only in April, 1883. Issued in panes of 35 having a face value of $5. Seven horizontal rows of five covering all denominations as follows: 2 rows of 25c, 1 of 20c, 2 of 10c, 2 of 5c. **The remainders and plates were purchased by a New York dealer in 1887.**

T16

1883 *Perf. 14*

11T1	T16	5c **yellow brown**	6.50	—
		Block of 4	30.00	
11T2	T16	10c **yellow brown**	8.50	—
		Block of 4	37.50	
11T3	T16	20c **yellow brown**	20.00	—
		Horizontal pair	45.00	
11T4	T16	25c **yellow brown**	5.50	—
		Block of 4	30.00	
		Pane of 35	375.00	

The first reprints are lighter in color than the originals, perf. 14 and the gum is yellowish instead of white. The pane makeup differs in the reprints. The second reprints are darker than the original, perf. 12. Value $1 each.

Northern New York Telegraph Company

Organized about 1892. Extended from Malone, N.Y. to Massena, N.Y. Re-incorporated as the New York Union Telegraph Co. on April 2, 1896.

T16a

T16b

T16c

Typo. by Charles H. Smith, Brushton, N.Y.

1894-95 *Rouletted*

12T1	T16a	**green** (overprinted in red "Frank 1894")	45.	
		Pane of 6	290.	
a.		Imperf., pair	50.	
		Pane of 6	160.	
12T2	T16a	**red** (overprinted in black "Frank 1895")	160.	
		Pane of 6	1,500.	
a.		Imperf., pair	50.	
		Pane of 6	160.	
12T3	T16b	1c **yellow** (overprinted in black "One")	80.	
		Pane of 6	525.	
a.		Imperf., pair	50.	
		Pane of 6	160.	
12T4	T16c	10c **blue** (overprinted in red "10")	150.	
		Pane of 6	950.	
a.		Imperf., pair	50.	
		Pane of 6	160.	

Some specialists believe that Nos. 12T1-12T4 were not issued and probably are essays. However, one Northern New York stamp is recorded tied to a piece of a telegraph form by a punch cancel.

Pacific Mutual Telegraph Company

Incorporated in Missouri on June 21, 1883. Operated between St. Louis and Kansas City, Mo., during the years 1884 and 1885. It had 15 offices, 425 miles of poles and 850 miles of wire. The controlling interests were held by the Bankers and Merchants Telegraph Company. The name was changed on Sept. 10, 1910 to Postal Telegraph-Cable Company of Missouri. Stamps were issued in booklets having a face value of $10 and containing 131 stamps as follows: 50-1c, 20-5c, 45-10c, 16-25c. They are not known used.

T17

1883 *Perf. 12*

13T1	T17	1c **black**	40.00	
13T2	T17	1c **slate**	.35	
		Block of 4	1.50	
a.		1c gray	.35	
		Block of 4	1.50	
13T3	T17	5c **black,** *buff*	1.00	
		Block of 4	4.50	
13T4	T17	10c **black,** *green*	.35	
		Block of 4	1.75	
a.		Horiz. pair, imperf. between	—	
13T5	T17	25c **black,** *salmon buff*	1.00	
		Block of 4	4.50	

Pacific Postal Telegraph-Cable Company

The Pacific Postal Telegraph-Cable Company was the Pacific Coast Department of the Postal Telegraph-Cable Company, and was organized in 1886. Its first wire ran from San Francisco to New Westminster, B.C., where it touched the lines of the Canadian Pacific Railway Company, then the only connection between the Eastern and Western Postal systems. Later the Postal's own wires spanned the continent and the two companies were united.

Stamps issued in booklet form in vertical panes of five.

T17a

Perf. 12 Horiz.

14T1	T17a	10c **brown**	160.00	100.00
		Pane of 5	800.00	
14T2	T17a	15c **black**	160.00	100.00
		Pane of 5	800.00	
14T3	T17a	25c **rose red**	160.00	100.00
		Pane of 5	800.00	
14T4	T17a	40c **green**	160.00	100.00
		Pane of 5	800.00	
14T5	T17a	50c **blue**	190.00	100.00
		Pane of 5	950.00	

These stamps were issued with three sizes of frank numbers; large closely spaced, small closely spaced and small widely spaced figures. They also exist without frank numbers.

Postal Telegraph Company

Organized in New York in 1881. Reorganized in 1891 as the Postal Telegraph-Cable Co. The Postal Telegraph Co stamps of 1885 were issued in sheets of 100. **Some years after the reorganization a New York dealer purchased the remainders which were canceled with a purple star.** The Postal Telegraph-Cable Co. issued frank stamps in booklets, usually four stamps to a pane. This company was merged with the Western Union Telegraph Company in 1943.

T18

T19

T20

T21

Engraved by Hamilton Bank Note Co.

1885 *Perf. 14*

15T1	T18	10c **green**	4.00	—
		Remainders		.25
		Block of 4	17.50	
		Remainders		1.25
a.		Horiz. pair, imperf. btwn., remainders		20.00
b.		10c **deep green**	3.50	—
		Remainders		.25
		Block of 4	15.00	
		Remainders		1.25
15T2	T19	15c **orange red**	3.50	—
		Remainders		.60
		Block of 4	15.00	—
		Remainders		3.00
a.		Horizontal pair, imperf. between	37.50	
15T3	T20	25c **blue**	2.00	5.00
		Remainders		.25
		Block of 4	9.00	
		Remainders		.75
a.		Horizontal pair, imperf. between	37.50	
15T4	T21	50c **brown**	1.75	—
		Remainders		.60
		Block of 4	8.00	
		Remainders		3.00

The 25c in ultramarine and the 50c in black were printed and perforated 16 but are not known to have been issued. Value about $7.50 each.

T22

T22a

Typographed by Moss Engraving Co.

1892-1920 *Perf. 14*

Signature of A.B. Chandler

15T5	T22	**blue gray** (1892)	50.00	
a.		Imperf., pair	120.00	

Perf. 13 to 14½ and Compound

15T6	T22	**gray lilac** (1892)	55.00	
15T7	T22	**red** (1893)	20.00	10.00
		Pane of 4	85.00	
15T8	T22	**red brown** (1893)	6.00	4.00

Perf. 12

15T9	T22	**violet brown** (1894)	6.75	
15T10	T22	**gray green** (1894)	4.50	
a.		Imperf., pair	10.00	
		Pane of 4	25.00	
15T11	T22	**blue** (1895)	50.00	
15T12	T22	**rose** (1895)	500.00	

Nos. 15T11 and 15T12 are from a new die resembling T22 but without shading under "Postal Telegraph Co."

15T13	T22a	**slate green** (1896)	5.50	
		Pane of 4	25.00	
15T14	T22a	**brown** (1896)	450.00	

Signature of Albert B. Chandler

15T15	T22a	**lilac brown** (1897)	1.50	*10.00*
		Pane of 4	6.50	
15T16	T22a	**orange** (1897)	400.00	

Typographed by Knapp & Co.

15T17	T22a	**pale blue** (1898)	2.25	
		Pane of 4	10.00	

15T18	T22a	**rose** (1898)	500.00	

Typographed by Moss Engraving Co.

Perf. 12

15T19	T22a	**orange brown** (1899)	1.75	
		Pane of 4	8.25	

Perf. 11

15T20	T22a	**blue** (1900)	3.00	3.00
a.		"I" of "Complimentary" omitted	.75	1.00
		Pane of 4	3.25	

The variety 15T20a represents a different die with many variations in the design.

Perf. 14

15T21	T22a	**sea green** (1901)	.60	.60
		Pane of 4	2.50	
a.		Horiz. pair, imperf. between	—	

Signature of John W. Mackay

15T22	T22a	**chocolate** (1902)	1.25	.65
		Pane of 4	5.50	
a.		Horiz. pair, imperf. vert.	—	

Signature of Clarence H. Mackay

15T23	T22a	**blue** (1903)	2.75	2.50
		Pane of 4	12.50	

Perf. 12

15T24	T22a	**blue,** *blue* (1904)	4.00	3.00
		Pane of 4	17.50	
15T25	T22a	**blue,** *yellow* (1905)	5.00	
		Pane of 4	22.50	
15T26	T22a	**blue,** *light blue* (1906)	5.00	5.00
		Pane of 4	22.50	
a.		Horiz. pair, imperf. vert.	—	

T22b

Perf. 12

15T27	T22b	**black,** *yellow* (laid paper) (1907)	80.00	
		Pane of 4	350.00	
15T28	T22b	**blue,** *pink* (laid paper) (1907)	50.00	
		Pane of 4	225.00	

"One Telegram of 10 Words" — T22c

15T29	T22c	**blue** (1908)	65.00	
		Pane of 4	275.00	
15T30	T22c	**yellow** (1908)	550.00	
		Pane of 4	2,250.	
15T31	T22c	**black** (1908)	55.00	
		Pane of 4	225.00	
15T32	T22c	**brown** (1909)	45.00	
		Pane of 4	190.00	
a.		Date reads "1908"	*2,350.*	
		Pair, one #15T32a, one #15T32	*3,000.*	
15T33	T22c	**olive green** (1909)	25.00	
		Pane of 4	105.00	
15T34	T22c	**dark blue** (1910)	40.00	
15T35	T22c	**dark brown** (1910)	40.00	
		Pane of 4	170.00	
15T36	T22c	**violet** (1911)	550.00	
15T37	T22c	**blue** (1912)	850.00	
15T38	T22c	**violet** (1913)	1,250.	

Perf. 14

15T39	T22c	**violet** (not dated) (1914)	550.00	
a.		Red violet	600.00	
		Pane of 4	2,250.	

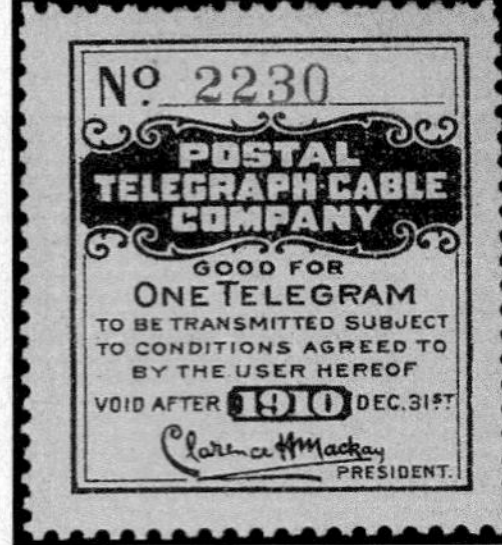

"One Telegram"

Perf. 12

15T40	T22c	**blue** (1908)	60.00	
		Pane of 4	260.00	
a.		Horiz. pair, imperf. between	300.00	
15T41	T22c	**lilac** (1909)	25.00	
		Pane of 4	110.00	
15T42	T22c	**black,** *yellow* (laid paper) (1910)	550.00	
a.		Date reads "1909"	*2,500.*	
15T43	T22c	**violet** (1910)	15.00	
a.		**Red violet**	15.00	
		Pane of 4	—	
		Pane of 8	140.00	
15T44	T22c	**dark blue** (1911)	60.00	
		Pane of 4	260.00	
a.		Vert. pair, imperf between	*1,500.*	
15T45	T22c	**light violet** (1912)	40.00	
		Pane of 4	180.00	

Perf. 14

15T46	T22c	**dark blue** (1913)	175.00	
		Pane of 8	1,500.	
a.		Imperf. vertically, pair	260.00	
b.		Perf. 12	100.00	
		Pane of 4	425.00	
c.		Horiz. pair, imperf. between	*500.00*	
15T47	T22c	**dark blue** (not dated) (1914) (no spurs)	.25	
		Pane of 4	2.50	
		Pane of 8	5.00	
a.		Dark blue (spurs)	.25	
		Pane of 4	2.50	

In panes of four the stamps are 4½mm apart horizontally, panes of eight 5½mm. There are two types of design T22c, one with and one without spurs on colored curved lines above "O" of "Postal" and below "M" of "Company". No. 15T47 comes in both types.

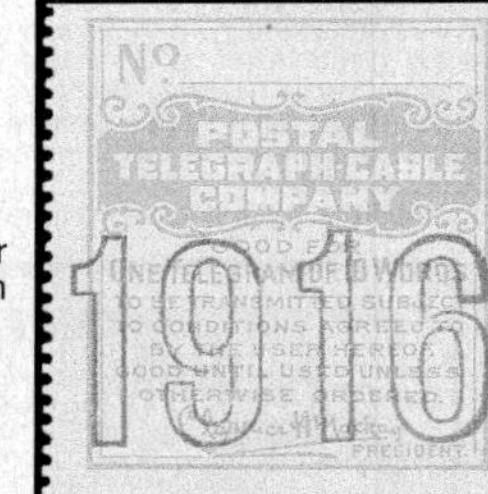

Nos. 15T39 & 15T47 Handstamped, All Four Numerals Complete on Each Stamp

15T47A	T22c	**violet** (1916)	*5,000.*	
15T48	T22c	**dark blue** (1917)	*2,500.*	
15T49	T22c	**dark blue** (1918)	*2,300.*	
15T49A	T22c	**dark blue** (1919)	110.	
		Pane of 8	975.	
15T49B	T22c	**dark blue** (1920)	90.	
		Pane of 8	825.	

No. 15T49B is handstamped "1920" in small single line numerals.

T22d

1907 ***Perf. 12***

15T50	T22d	1c **dark brown**	35.00	20.00
		Pane of 4	150.00	
15T51	T22d	2c **dull violet**	30.00	20.00
		Pane of 4	130.00	
15T52	T22d	5c **green**	35.00	22.50
		Pane of 4	150.00	
15T53	T22d	25c **light red**	37.50	20.00
		Pane of 4	160.00	

T22e

1931 ***Perf. 14***

15T54	T22e	25c **gray blue** (1931)	.25	
		Pane of 6	2.00	

No. 15T54 Overprinted "1932" and Control Number in Red

1932

15T55	T22e	25c **gray blue**	110.00	
		Pane of 6	700.00	

Many varieties between Nos. 15T5 and 15T55 are known without frank numbers.

OFFICIAL

Inscribed "Supts."

1900-14 ***Perf. 11, 12***

15TO1	T22a	**black,** *magenta*	2.00	2.00

"C. G. W." (Chicago, Great Western Railroad) at top

For Use of Railroad Superintendents

Perf. 12

15TO2	T22c	**carmine** (1908)	50.00	
		Pane of 4	240.00	
15TO3	T22c	**carmine** (1909)	600.00	
15TO4	T22c	**carmine** (1910)	750.00	
15TO5	T22c	**carmine** (1911)	600.00	
15TO6	T22c	**carmine** (1912)	190.00	

Perf. 14

15TO7	T22c	**carmine** (1913)	600.00	
a.		Perf. 12	*1,500.*	
15TO8	T22c	**dull red** (not dated) (1914)	.50	
		Pane of 8	5.00	

"E. P." (El Paso and Northeastern Railroad) at top

Perf. 12

15TO9	T22c	**orange** (1908)	450.00	

"I. C." (Illinois Central Railroad) at top

15TO10	T22c	**green** (1908)	80.00
		Pane of 4	330.00
15TO11	T22c	**yellow green** (1909)	15.00
		Pane of 4	—
		Pane of 8	130.00
15TO12	T22c	**dark green** (1910)	160.00
15TO13	T22c	**dark green** (1911)	110.00
		Pane of 4	475.00
		Pane of 8	950.00
15TO14	T22c	**dark green** (1912)	1,250.

Perf. 14

15TO15	T22c	**dark green** (1913)	1,500.
15TO16	T22c	**dark green** (not dated) (1914) (no spurs)	2.50
		Pane of 4	11.00
		Pane of 8	22.50
a.		**Green** (spurs)	1.25
		Pane of 4	7.50
b.		Line under "PRESIDENT" (no spurs)	1.00
		Pane of 8	12.50

(See note after No. 15T47.)

Both types of design T22c are known of 15TO16.

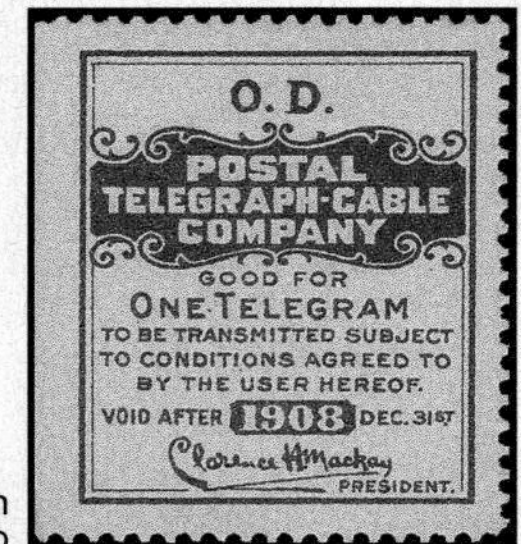

"O. D." (Old Dominion Steamship Co.) at top

Perf. 12

15TO17	T22c	**violet** (1908)	*4,000.*

"P. R." (Pennsylvania Railroad) at top

15TO18	T22c	**orange brown** (1908)	35.00
		Pane of 4	150.00
		Pane of 8	300.00
15TO19	T22c	**orange brown** (1909)	40.00
		Pane of 4	175.00
		Pane of 8	375.00
15TO20	T22c	**orange brown** (1910)	40.00
		Pane of 4	175.00
		Pane of 8	375.00
15TO21	T22c	**orange brown** (1911)	175.00
15TO22	T22c	**orange brown** (1912)	110.00
		Pane of 4	*700.00*

Perf. 14

15TO23	T22c	**orange brown** (1913)	40.00
		Pane of 8	350.00
a.		Perf. 12	150.00

"P. R. R." (Pennsylvania Rail Road) at top

15TO24	T22c	**orange** (not dated) (1914)	27.50
		Pane of 4	125.00
		Pane of 8	250.00

"S. W." (El Paso Southwestern Railroad) at top — 15TO26

Perf. 12

15TO25	T22c	**yellow** (1909)	850.00
15TO26	T22c	**yellow** (1910)	1,500.
15TO27	T22c	**yellow** (1911)	500.00
15TO28	T22c	**yellow** (1912)	500.00
		Pane of 4	2,250.

Nos. 15TO1-15TO17 and 15TO25-15TO28 are without frank numbers.

TO1

1942 — Litho. — Unwmk.

15TO29	TO1	5c **pink**	6.50	3.00
		Pane of 8	55.00	
15TO30	TO1	25c **pale blue**	7.75	4.00
		Pane of 8	65.00	

The stamps were issued in booklets to all Postal Telegraph employees in the Armed Forces for use in the United States. They were discontinued Oct. 8, 1943. Used stamps normally bear manuscript cancellations.

Western Union Telegraph Company

Organized by consolidation in 1856, eventually extending coverage throughout the United States. Frank stamps were issued regularly since 1871 in booklet form. The large size, early issues, were in panes of four, 1871-1913; the medium size, later issues, were in panes of six, 1914-32; and the final small size issues were in panes of nine, 1933 to 1946.

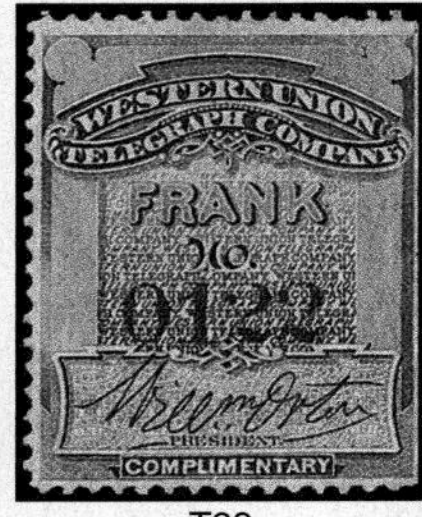

T23

T24

Engraved by the National Bank Note Co.

1871-94 — ***Perf. 12***

Signature of William Orton

16T1	T23	**green** (not dated) (1871)	35.00	22.50
16T2	T23	**red** (not dated) (1872)	40.00	20.00
		Pane of 4	175.00	
16T3	T23	**blue** (not dated) (1873)	45.00	22.50
		Pane of 4	200.00	
16T4	T23	**brown** (not dated) (1874)	35.00	22.50
		Pane of 4	160.00	
16T5	T24	**deep green** (1875)	37.50	21.00
16T6	T24	**red** (1876)	40.00	
		Pane of 4	180.00	
16T7	T24	**violet** (1877)	42.50	28.00
16T8	T24	**gray brown** (1878)	40.00	

Signature of Norvin Green

16T9	T24	**blue** (1879)	40.00	28.00
		Pane of 4	180.00	

Engraved by the American Bank Note Co.

16T10	T24	**lilac rose** (1880)	27.50	
		Pane of 4	120.00	
16T11	T24	**green** (1881)	25.00	
		Pane of 4	110.00	
16T12	T24	**blue** (1882)	15.00	
		Pane of 4	70.00	
16T13	T24	**yellow brown** (1883)	27.50	
		Pane of 4	120.00	
16T14	T24	**gray violet** (1884)	.60	.30
		Pane of 4	3.00	
16T15	T24	**green** (1885)	3.25	1.75
		Pane of 4	15.00	
16T16	T24	**brown violet** (1886)	3.25	2.00
		Pane of 4	15.00	
a.		Imperf pair, without frank numbers	—	
16T17	T24	**red brown** (1887)	4.50	
		Pane of 4	22.50	
16T18	T24	**blue** (1888)	3.25	
		Pane of 4	15.00	
16T19	T24	**olive green** (1889)	1.75	.80
		Pane of 4	8.00	
16T20	T24	**purple** (1890)	.75	.40
		Pane of 4	3.25	
16T21	T24	**brown** (1891)	1.50	
		Pane of 4	6.50	
16T22	T24	**vermilion** (1892)	1.75	
		Pane of 4	8.00	
16T23	T24	**blue** (1893)	1.40	.40
		Pane of 4	6.25	

Signature of Thos. T. Eckert

16T24	T24	**green** (1894)	.60	.40
		Pane of 4	3.00	

T25

Engraved by the International Bank Note Co.

1895-1913 — ***Perf. 14***

Signature of Thos. T. Eckert

16T25	T25	**dark brown** (1895)	.50	.40
		Pane of 4	2.50	
16T26	T25	**violet** (1896)	.50	.40
		Pane of 4	2.50	
16T27	T25	**rose red** (1897)	.50	.40
		Pane of 4	2.50	
16T28	T25	**yellow green** (1898)	.50	.40
		Pane of 4	2.50	
a.		Vertical pair, imperf. between	—	
16T29	T25	**olive green** (1899)	.50	.40
		Pane of 4	2.25	
16T30	T25	**red violet,** perf. 13 (1900)	.50	.45
		Pane of 4	3.00	
16T31	T25	**brown,** perf. 13 (1901)	.50	.40
		Pane of 4	2.50	
16T32	T25	**blue** (1902)	8.00	
		Pane of 4	40.00	

Signature of R.C. Clowry

16T33	T25	**blue** (1902)	8.00	
		Pane of 4	40.00	
16T34	T25	**green** (1903)	.60	.40
		Pane of 4	4.00	
16T35	T25	**red violet** (1904)	.60	
		Pane of 4	2.75	
16T36	T25	**carmine rose** (1905)	.60	.50
		Pane of 4	2.75	
16T37	T25	**blue** (1906)	.80	.40
		Pane of 4	4.00	
a.		Vertical pair, imperf. between	*200.00*	
16T38	T25	**orange brown** (1907)	1.75	.90
		Pane of 4	10.00	
16T39	T25	**violet** (1908)	2.00	1.00
		Pane of 4	9.00	
16T40	T25	**olive green** (1909)	2.00	
		Pane of 4	10.00	

Perf. 12

16T41	T25	**buff** (1910)	.75	.50
		Pane of 4	3.25	

Engraved by the American Bank Note Co.

Signature of Theo. N. Vail

16T42	T24	**green** (1911)	14.00	
		Pane of 4	65.00	
16T43	T24	**violet** (1912)	9.00	
		Pane of 4	42.50	

Imprint of Kihn Brothers Bank Note Company

Perf. 14

16T44	T24	**brown** (1913)	10.00	
		Pane of 4	50.00	
a.		Vert. pair, imperf. between	35.00	
b.		Horiz. pair, imperf. between	40.00	

T26

Engraved by the E.A. Wright Bank Note Co.

1914-15 — **Signature of Theo. N. Vail** — ***Perf. 12***

16T45	T26	5c **brown** (1914)	1.10	
		Pane of 6	8.00	
a.		Vert. pair, imperf. between	—	
b.		Horiz. pair, imperf. between	—	
16T46	T26	25c **slate** (1914)	7.00	5.00
		Pane of 6	45.00	

Signature of Newcomb Carlton

16T47	T26	5c **orange** (1915)	1.50	
		Pane of 6	10.00	
		orange yellow	5.00	
16T48	T26	25c **olive green** (1915)	4.00	
		Pane of 6	30.00	
a.		Vert. pair, imperf. horizontally	45.00	

T27

Engraved by the American Bank Note Co.

1916-32

16T49 T27 5c **light blue** (1916) 1.50
Pane of 6 11.00
16T50 T27 25c **carmine lake** (1916) 1.75
Pane of 6 11.00

Engraved by the Security Bank Note Co.

Perf. 11

16T51 T27 5c **yellow brown** (1917) 1.00
Pane of 6 7.50
16T52 T27 25c **deep green** (1917) 3.00
Pane of 6 20.00
16T53 T27 5c **olive green** (1918) .60
Pane of 6 4.50
16T54 T27 25c **dark violet** (1918) 1.75
Pane of 6 14.00
16T55 T27 5c **brown** (1919) 1.25
Pane of 6 9.00
16T56 T27 25c **blue** (1919) 3.25
Pane of 6 22.50

Engraved by the E.A. Wright Bank Note Co.

Perf. 12

16T57 T27 5c **dark green** (1920) .65
Pane of 6 4.25
a. Vert. pair, imperf. between *300.00*
16T58 T27 25c **olive green** (1920) .75
Pane of 6 5.00

Engraved by the Security Bank Note Co.

16T59 T27 5c **carmine rose** (1921) .55
Pane of 6 4.25
16T60 T27 25c **deep blue** (1921) 1.30
Pane of 6 8.50
16T61 T27 5c **yellow brown** (1922) .55
Pane of 6 3.75
a. Horizontal pair, imperf. between 16.00
16T62 T27 25c **claret** (1922) 1.65
Pane of 6 11.50
16T63 T27 5c **olive green** (1923) .65
Pane of 6 4.25
16T64 T27 25c **dull violet** (1923) 1.35
Pane of 6 9.00
16T65 T27 5c **brown** (1924) 1.75
Pane of 6 12.00
16T66 T27 25c **ultramarine** (1924) 4.00
Pane of 6 30.00
16T67 T27 5c **olive green** (1925) .65
Pane of 6 4.25
16T68 T27 25c **carmine rose** (1925) 1.10
Pane of 6 7.00
16T69 T27 5c **blue** (1926) 1.00
Pane of 6 6.50
16T70 T27 25c **light brown** (1926) 2.25
Pane of 6 14.00
16T71 T27 5c **carmine** (1927) .85
Pane of 6 5.75
16T72 T27 25c **green** (1927) 7.25
Pane of 6 47.50

Engraved by the E. A. Wright Bank Note Co.

Without Imprint

16T73 T27 5c **yellow brown** (1928) .75
Pane of 6 4.50
16T74 T27 25c **dark blue** (1928) 1.00
Pane of 6 6.25

Engraved by the Security Bank Note Co.

Without Imprint

16T75 T27 5c **dark green** (1929) .30 .25
Pane of 6 2.00
16T76 T27 25c **red violet** (1929) .85 .50
Pane of 6 5.50
16T77 T27 5c **olive green** (1930) .25 .25
Pane of 6 1.75
16T78 T27 25c **carmine** (1930) .25 .25
Pane of 6 2.00
a. Horiz. pair, imperf. vertically 35.00
16T79 T27 5c **brown** (1931) .25 .25
Pane of 6 1.60
16T80 T27 25c **blue** (1931) .25 .25
Pane of 6 1.60
16T81 T27 5c **green** (1932) .25 .25
Pane of 6 1.60
16T82 T27 25c **rose carmine** (1932) .25 .25
Pane of 6 1.60

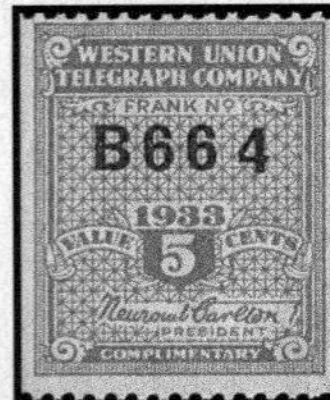

T28

Lithographed by Oberly & Newell Co.

1933-40 **Without Imprint** *Perf. 14x12½*

16T83 T28 5c **pale brown** (1933) .25
Pane of 9 3.25
16T84 T28 25c **green** (1933) .25
Pane of 9 3.25

Lithographed by Security Bank Note Co.

Without Imprint

Perf. 12, 12½

Signature of R. B. White

16T85 T28 5c **lake** (1934) .25
Pane of 9 2.50
16T86 T28 25c **dark blue** (1934) .25
Pane of 9 2.50
16T87 T28 5c **yellow brown** (1935) .25
Pane of 9 2.50
16T88 T28 25c **lake** (1935) .25
Pane of 9 2.50
16T89 T28 5c **blue** (1936) .25 .25
Pane of 9 2.75
16T90 T28 25c **apple green** (1936) .25 .25
Pane of 9 2.50
16T91 T28 5c **bister brown** (1937) .25
Pane of 9 2.50
16T92 T28 25c **carmine rose** (1937) .25
Pane of 9 2.50
16T93 T28 5c **green** (1938) .25 .25
Pane of 9 3.00
16T94 T28 25c **blue** (1938) .30 .25
Pane of 9 3.50
16T95 T28 5c **dull vermilion** (1939) 1.00
Pane of 9 11.50
a. Horiz. pair, imperf. between —
16T96 T28 25c **bright violet** (1939) .50
Pane of 9 6.00
16T97 T28 5c **light blue** (1940) .55
Pane of 9 5.75
16T98 T28 25c **bright green** (1940) .50
Pane of 9 5.50

Samuel F. B. Morse
T29

Plates of 90 stamps.
Stamp designed by Nathaniel Yontiff.
Unlike the frank stamps, Nos. 16T99 to 16T103 were sold to the public in booklet form for use in prepayment of telegraph services.

Engraved by Security Bank Note Co. of Philadelphia

1940 **Unwmk.** *Perf. 12, 12½x12, 12x12½*

16T99 T29 1c **yellow green** 1.25
Pane of 5 6.50
a. Imperf., pair 50.00
16T100 T29 2c **chestnut** 1.75 1.00
Pane of 5 15.00
a. Imperf., pair 50.00
16T101 T29 5c **deep blue** 3.00
Pane of 5 18.00
a. Vert. pair, imperf. btwn. 65.00
b. Imperf., pair 50.00
16T102 T29 10c **orange** 5.00
Pane of 5 27.50
a. Imperf., pair 50.00
16T103 T29 25c **bright carmine** 4.00
Pane of 5 24.00
a. Imperf., pair 50.00

Type of 1933-40

1941 **Litho.** *Perf. 12½*

Without Imprint

Signature of R.B. White

16T104 T28 5c **dull rose lilac** .25
Pane of 9 2.50
16T105 T28 25c **vermilion** .60
Pane of 9 6.00

1942 **Signature of A.N. Williams**

16T106 T28 5c **brown** .30
Pane of 9 3.50
16T107 T28 25c **ultramarine** .30
Pane of 9 3.50

1943

16T108 T28 5c **salmon** .30
Pane of 9 3.50
16T109 T28 25c **red violet** .30
Pane of 9 3.50

1944

16T110 T28 5c **light green** .65
Pane of 9 7.25
16T111 T28 25c **buff** .35
Pane of 9 3.75

1945

16T112 T28 5c **light blue** .40
Pane of 9 5.00
a. Pair, imperf. between —
16T113 T28 25c **light green** .35
Pane of 9 3.75

1946

16T114 T28 5c **light bister brown** 1.25
Pane of 9 15.00
16T115 T28 25c **rose pink** 1.00
Pane of 9 12.00

Many of the stamps between 16T1 and 16T98 and 16T104 to 16T115 are known without frank numbers. Several of them are also known with more than one color used in the frank number and with handstamped and manuscript numbers. The numbers are also found in combination with various letters: O, A, B, C, D, etc.

Western Union discontinued the use of Telegraph stamps with the 1946 issue.

United States
Telegraph-Cable-Radio Carriers

Booklets issued to accredited representatives to the World Telecommunications Conferences, Atlantic City, New Jersey, 1947. Valid for messages to points outside the United States. Issued by All America Cables & Radio, Inc., The Commercial Cable Company, Globe Wireless, Limited, Mackay Radio and Telegraph Company, Inc., R C A Communications, Inc., Tropical Radio Telegraph Company and The Western Union Telegraph Company.

TX1

1947 **Litho.** **Unwmk.** *Perf. 12½*

17T1 TX1 5c **olive bister** 7.00
Pane of 9 70.00
Pane of 9, 8 5c + 1 10c *900.00*
17T2 TX1 10c **olive bister** 750.00
17T3 TX1 50c **olive bister** 9.00
Pane of 9 90.00

UNLISTED ISSUES

Several telegraph or wireless companies other than those listed above have issued stamps or franks, but as evidence of actual use is lacking, they are not listed. Among these are:

American District Telegraph Co.
American Telegraph Typewriter Co.
Continental Telegraph Co.
Los Angeles and San Gabriel Valley Railroad
Marconi Wireless Telegraph Co.
Mercantile Telegraph Co.
Telepost Co.
Tropical Radio Telegraph Co.
United Fruit Co. Wireless Service.
United Wireless Telegraph Co.

ESSAYS

An essay is a proposed design that differs in some way from the issued stamp.

During approximately 1845-1890, when private banknote engravers competed for contracts to print U.S. postage stamps, essays were produced primarily as examples of the quality of the firms' work and as suggestions as to what their finished product would look like. In most cases, dies were prepared, often with stock vignettes used in making banknotes. These dies were used to print essays for the Post Office Department. Rarely did the competitors go so far as to have essay plates made.

From 1894 onward, virtually all stamps were engraved and printed by the Bureau of Engraving and Printing (BEP). This usually required two types of essays. The first was a model design which was approved — or disapproved — by the Postmaster General. Sometimes preliminary drawings were made by the BEP designers, often in an enlarged size, subsequently photographically reduced to stamp size. An accepted stamp design usually became the engraver's model.

Occasionally during the course of engraving the die, a "progressive proof" was pulled to check the progress of the engraver's work. Because these were produced from an incompletely engraved die, they differ from the final design and are listed here as essays.

During approximately 1867-1870, various experiments were conducted to prevent the reuse of postage stamps. These included experimental grill types, safety papers, water-sensitive papers and inks, coupon essays, and others. These also differed in some way from issued stamps, even if the design was identical. A preliminary listing has been made here.

Because the essays in all their various colors have not been examined by the editors, traditional color names have been retained. Some color names have been taken from *Color Standards and Color Nomenclature,* by Robert Ridgway.

Only essays in private hands have been listed. Others exist but are not available to collectors. Some essays were produced after the respective stamps were issued. Year dates are given where information is available.

Essay papers and cards are white, unless described otherwise.

Values for die essays are for essays showing full die sinkage, on intact card backing, where such are known. Measurements are given where such information is available. Cut-down or faulty examples sell for less, often much less. Examples on full-size original card command a premium. Plate essays are valued in the grade of very fine, where such exist. A number of essays are unique or are reported in very limited quantities. Such items are valued in the conditions in which they exist.

The listings are by manufacturer. Basic stamps may appear in two or more places.

This listing is not complete. Other designs, papers and colors exist. The editors would appreciate reports of unlisted items, as well as photos of items listed herein without illustrations.

POSTMASTERS' PROVISIONALS

NON-CONTIGUOUS LISTINGS

Because many listings are grouped by manufacturer, some catalogue numbers are separated.

No. 5-E1 to 5-E2	**follow 11-E16**
No. 11-E17 to 72-E5	**follow 5-E2**
No. 65-E5 to 72-E8	**follow 72-E5**
No. 63-E13 to 113-E2	**follow 72-E8**
No. 112-E2 to 129-E2	**follow 113-E2**
No. 120-E1 to 122-E5	**follow 129-E2**
No. 115-E3a to 129-E6	**follow 122-E5**
No. 115-E11 to 116-E8	**follow 129-E6**
No. 115-E17 to 148-E1	**follow 116-E8**
No. 145-E2 to 179-E3	**follow 148-E1**
No. 156-E2 to 191-E2	**follow 179-E3**
No. 184-E8	**follows 191-E2**
No. 182-E4 to 190-E3	**follow 184-E8**
No. 184-E17 to 293-E11	**follow 190-E3**
No. 285-E10 to 856-E2	**follow 293-E11**

Albany, N.Y.
Gavit & Co.

1Xa-E1

Design size: 23½x25½mm
Die size: 58x48mm

Benjamin Franklin. With crosshatching about 2mm outside border (usually cut off).

1847

1Xa-E1 5c

a. Die on India die sunk on large card, printed through a mat to eliminate cross-hatching

brownish black	*600.*
scarlet	*600.*
red brown	*600.*
blue	*600.*
green	*600.*

b. Die on India; some mounted on small card

bluish black	325.
scarlet	325.
brown	325.
yellow green	325.
gray blue	325.

c. Die on India cut close

black	250.
blue	250.
red brown	250.
scarlet	250.
green	250.
yellow green	250.
brown violet	250.
rose red	250.

d. Die on bond (1858)

bluish black	375.
scarlet	375.
brown	375.
blue	375.
blue green	375.
violet	375.

e. Die on ivory glazed paper (1905)

black	900.
dark brown	900.
scarlet	900.
blue	900.

New York, N.Y.
Rawdon, Wright & Hatch

9X1-E1

Design 22mm wide
Die size: 50x102mm

Vignette of Washington. Two transfers laid down vertically on the die 22mm apart; top one retouched, with frame around it (this is a proof). Values are for combined transfers. Vignette essay exists cut apart from proof, value $200 each.

1845

9X1-E1 5c

a. Die on India (1879)

black	450.
violet black	450.
gray black	450.
scarlet	450.
dull scarlet	450.
orange	450.
brown	450.
dull brown	450.
green	450.
dull green	450.
ultramarine	450.
dull blue	450.
red violet	450.

b. Die on white bond (1879)

gray black	550.
dull scarlet	550.
dull brown	550.
dull green	550.
dull blue	550.

c. Die on white glazed paper, die sunk (1879)

gray black	700.

POSTAGE STAMPS

1847 ISSUE
Rawdon, Wright, Hatch & Edson

The original model for No. 1 exists, engraved vignette of Franklin mounted on frame, part of frame engraved, rest in pencil, ink and a gray wash. Formerly No. 1-E1, now in the National Postal Museum collection.

Engraved vignette only, matted.

1-E2 5c Die on India (1895), brown *2,500.*

1-E3

Engraved frame only, matted from complete die.

1-E3 5c Die on India (1895), brown 2,500.

The 1895 dates are suppositional.

The original model for No. 2 exists, engraved vignette of Washington mounted (replaced) on frame, "POST OFFICE" and "FIVE CENTS" engraved on former No. 1-E1, "U" and "S" at top and "X" in bottom corners in black ink, rest in pencil and a gray wash. Formerly No. 2-E1, now in the National Postal Museum collection.

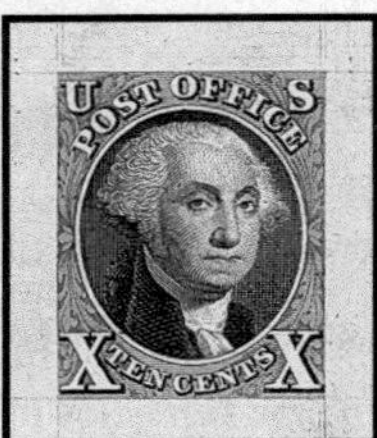
2-E1

Incomplete engraving of entire design, area around vignette incomplete, frame lines and "RWH&E" printer's initials not yet added.

2-E1 10c Die on proof paper, affixed to stiff blue laid paper backing, black —

2-E2

Engraved vignette only.

2-E2 10c Die on India (1895)
black *2,500.*
brownish black *2,500.*
brown *2,500.*

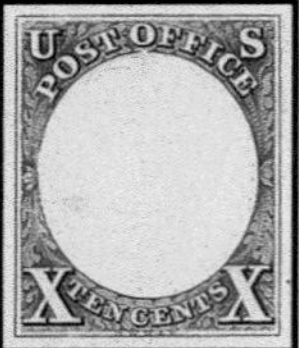
2-E3

Engraved frame only.

2-E3 10c Die on India (1895)
black *4,750.*
brown orange *4,750.*

The 1895 dates are suppositional.

1851 ISSUE

Submitted in Competition for the 1851 Issue Contract
Rawdon, Wright, Hatch & Edson, New York, N.Y.

11-E1

Design size: 18½x23mm
Large 3 in vignette.

11-E1 3c Die on India
black *3,000.*
blue *10,000.*

Submitted in Competition for the 1851 Issue Contract
Henry Benner, Washington, D.C.

11-E2

Design size: 19x24mm
Vignette of Washington.

11-E2 3c
a. Die on India
black *4,500.*
b. Die on proof paper, die sunk on 40x51mm card
black *4,500.*

Submitted in Competition for the 1851 Issue Contract (Nos. 11-E3 and 11-E4)
John E. Gavit & Co., Albany, N.Y.

11-E3

Design size: 19x23mm
Vignette of Franklin. Three states of die. Second state has double line dash above P of POSTAGE, third state has single dash above P and dot in O of POSTAGE.

11-E3 3c
a. Die on India, die sunk on card
warm black *800.*
scarlet *800.*
red brown *800.*
blue green *800.*
b. Die on India, 41x43mm or smaller
black 300.
greenish black 300.
carmine 300.
scarlet 300.
yellow green 300.
brown 300.
blue green 300.
dull blue 300.
dark blue 300.
c. Die on India, cut to shape
warm black 250.
cool black 250.
black 250.
carmine 250.
orange 250.
brown 250.
dark green 250.
yellow green 250.
olive 250.
light blue 250.
dark blue 250.
violet 250.
scarlet 250.
d. Die on bond
cool black 250.
scarlet 250.
orange brown 250.
brown 250.
green 250.
blue 250.
e. Die on ivory glazed paper
black *750.*
dark brown *750.*
scarlet *750.*
blue *750.*
f. Die on thin card, dusky blue, cut to shape *200.*

11-E3g

g. Die on Francis Patent experimental paper with trial cancel
black *1,250.*
dark blue *1,250.*
brown *1,250.*

11-E4

Design size: 19x22mm
Die size: 47x75mm
Vignette of Washington. Two states of die. Second state has small diagonal dash in top of left vertical border below arch.

11-E4 3c
a. Die on India, die sunk on card
black *750.*
scarlet *750.*
brown red *750.*
blue green *750.*
b. Die on India, about 30x40mm or smaller
orange 400.
orange brown 400.
brown 400.
dusky yellow brown 400.
yellow green 400.
blue green 400.
dull blue 400.
red violet 400.
deep red orange 400.
black 400.
c. Die on bond (1858)
black 400.
scarlet 400.
brown 400.
green 400.
blue 400.
d. Die on ivory glazed paper (1858)
black *900.*
dark brown *900.*
scarlet *900.*
blue *900.*
e. Die on proof paper (1858)
cool black *475.*
dull red *475.*
dull brown *475.*
dull blue green *475.*
dull blue *475.*

Bradbury, Wilkinson & Co., England

11-E5

Design size: 20½x23½mm
Vignette of Washington.

11-E5 3c
a. On stiff stamp paper about stamp size
black *1,250.*
violet red *1,250.*
deep carmine *1,250.*
dusky carmine *1,250.*
deep scarlet *1,250.*
orange brown *1,250.*
deep green *1,250.*
blue *1,250.*
ultramarine *1,250.*
brown *1,250.*
b. On card
violet black *1,250.*
dull scarlet *1,250.*
blue *1,250.*
green *1,250.*
brown *1,250.*
c. On stiff bond
brown *1,250.*
blue *1,250.*
violet black *1,250.*

Draper, Welsh & Co.

11-E6

Design size: 18x23mm
Vignette of Washington.

11-E6 3c Surface printed on card, black *750.*

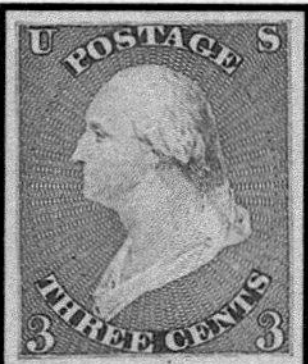
11-E7

Design size: 17½x24mm

Die size: 44x106mm
Engraved vignette of Washington.

11-E7 3c

a. Die on India, about 44x105mm, die sunk on card, in vert. pair with No. 11-E8	
black	*1,500.*
scarlet	*1,500.*
brown red	*1,500.*
green	*1,500.*
b. Die on India, about 40x45mm or smaller	
warm black	*400.*
cool black	*400.*
dark carmine	*400.*
scarlet	*400.*
brown red	*400.*
orange brown	*400.*
brown	*400.*
yellow green	*400.*
blue green	*400.*
blue	*400.*
dull blue	*400.*
brown violet	*400.*
c. Die on India, stamp size	
rose	350.
scarlet	350.
red brown	350.
brown	350.
green	350.
cool black	350.
warm black	350.
yellow green	350.
brown violet	350.
ultramarine blue	350.
d. Die on bond	
black	400.
scarlet	400.
brown	400.
blue green	400.
blue	400.
e. Die on ivory glazed paper	
black	*750.*
dark brown	*750.*
scarlet	*750.*
blue	*750.*

Submitted in Competition for the 1851 Issue Contract

Draper, Welsh & Co., Philadelphia, Pa.

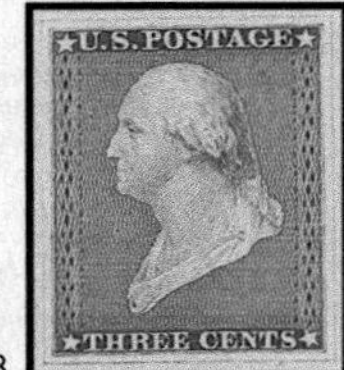

11-E8

Design size: 19½x24mm
Die size: 44x106mm
On same die 30mm below No. 11-E7
Vignette of Washington.

11-E8 3c

a. Die on India, 28x32mm or smaller	
black	*300.*
dark carmine	*300.*
scarlet	*300.*
brown red	*300.*
red brown	*300.*
orange brown	*300.*
brown	*300.*
yellow green	*300.*
green	*300.*
blue green	*300.*
blue	*300.*
b. Die on bond, about 32x40mm	
black	300.
scarlet	300.
brown	300.
green	300.
blue	300.
c. Die on ivory glazed paper	
black	*750.*
dark brown	*750.*
scarlet	*750.*
blue	*750.*

11-E8D

Design size: 18x23mm
Vignette of Washington.
Washington vignette only. Same head as No. 11-E6 through 11-E8, but with more bust. No gridwork in background.

11-E8D 3c Die on proof paper, mounted on card, black *750.*

11-E9

Design size (No. 11-E9a): 18x33mm
Vignette design size (Nos. 11-E9b, 11-E9c): 18x22mm
As No. 11-E8D, gridwork added to background oval.

11-E9 3c

a. Die on India	
black	350.
scarlet	350.
b. Die on India, single line frame	
black	300.
blue	300.
dark carmine	300.
orange red	300.
lilac	300.
brown	300.
scarlet	300.
rose violet	300.
deep yellow green	300.
c. Die on India, imprint of Jocelyn, Draper, Welsh & Co., New York	
black	300.
blue	300.
dark carmine	300.
orange red	300.
lilac	300.
brown	300.
scarlet	300.
rose violet	300.
deep yellow green	300.

Danforth, Bald & Co.

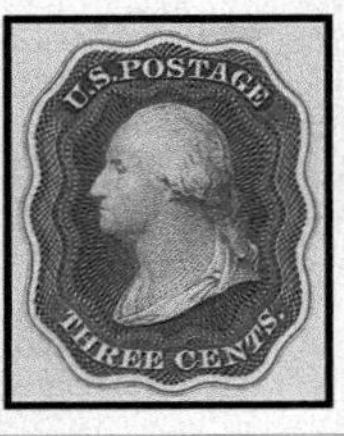

11-E10

Vignette size: 18x22mm
Design size: 20x26mm
Die size: 57x74mm
Vignette of Washington. Double line frame.

11-E10 3c

a. Die on India, die sunk on card	
black	*750.*
scarlet	*750.*
red brown	*750.*
green	*750.*
b. Die on India, off card, about 33x38mm	
black	*200.*
scarlet	*200.*
brown	*200.*
blue	*200.*
green	*200.*
dull violet	*200.*
dull blue	*200.*
red brown	*200.*
rose	*200.*
c. Die on bond, black	*350.*
d. Die on ivory glazed paper	
black	*750.*
dark brown	*750.*
scarlet	*750.*
blue	*750.*

11-E11

Washington vignette only.

11-E11 3c Die on India

black	325.
dull rose	325.
scarlet	325.
orange	325.
brown orange	325.
brown	325.
green	325.
dark blue	325.
dull violet	325.
rose violet	325.

We are *the* Source.

JamesLee.com

America's largest stock of reasonably priced United States Essays and Proofs. See them all on our website!
We are Sellers *and* Buyers! How may we help you?
Over Three Decades Building Collections.

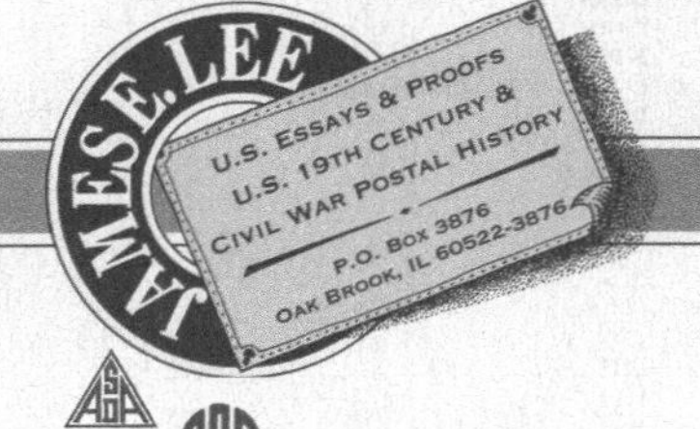

P.O. Box 3876 • Oak Brook, IL 60522-3876
Phone: (847) 910-6048
Email: jim@jameslee.com
Visit us tonight!

Submitted in Competition for the 1851 Issue Contract
Danforth, Bald & Co., Philadelphia, Pa.

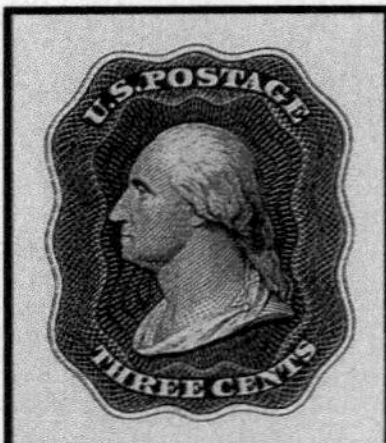

11-E12

Design size: 20x26mm
Die size: 62x66mm
Vignette of Washington. Single line frame. Two states of die. Second state shows scars in lathe lines in front of neck over T, and small dot below design. A third printing has more scars in front of neck.

11-E12 3c
a. Die on India, die sunk on card
black *750.*
scarlet *750.*
brown red *750.*
dusky brown yellow *750.*
brown *750.*
green *750.*
blue *750.*
dull blue *750.*
b. Die on India, about 43x45mm
black *300.*
scarlet *300.*
deep scarlet *300.*
brown *300.*
yellow brown *300.*
green *300.*
yellow green *300.*
blue *300.*
dull blue *300.*
dark blue *300.*
ultramarine blue *300.*
orange *300.*
red *300.*
c. Die on bond
dusky brown yellow *275.*
blue *275.*
d. Die on ivory glazed paper
black *750.*
dark brown *750.*
scarlet *750.*
blue *750.*
e. Plate on thick buff wove
rose 125.
violet brown 125.
orange 125.
dark orange 125.
pink orange 125.
f. Plate on India, dark red orange 150.
g. Plate on ivory wove (head more completely engraved, ruled lines between designs)
black 125.
dark carmine 125.
yellow 125.
blue 125.

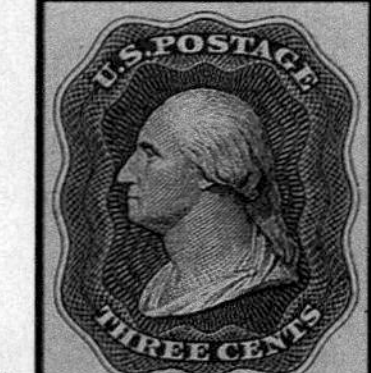

11-E13

Design size: 20x26mm
Die size: 62x66mm
Vignette of Washington. No. 11-E12 reengraved: more dark dots in forehead next to hair, thus line between forehead and hair more distinct.

11-E13 3c
a. Die on India, die sunk on card
black *750.*
scarlet *750.*
brown red *750.*
brown *750.*
green *750.*
b. Die on ivory glazed paper
black *750.*
dark brown *750.*
scarlet *750.*
blue *750.*

Bald, Cousland & Co.

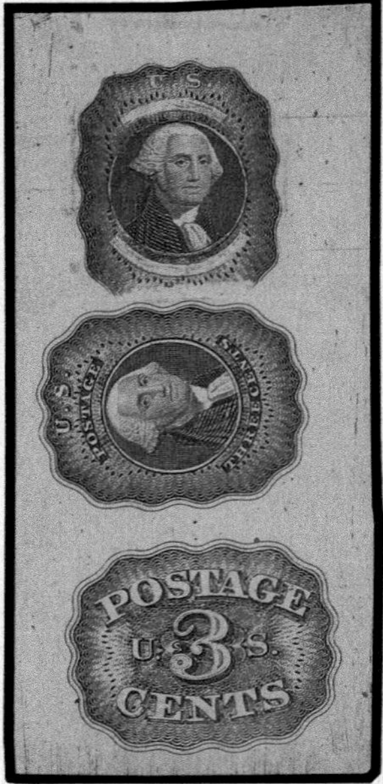

11-E14, 11-E14A, 11-E16

Design size: 22x28mm.
Incomplete design, tablets at top and bottom blank. See No. 11-E14A for listings.

11-E14 3c

Design size: 22x28mm
Die size: 95x43mm
Vignette of Washington. On same die with Nos. 11-E16 and 11-E14. Listings are for the complete triple die essay.

11-E14A 3c
b. Die on India
black *550.*
scarlet *550.*
red brown *550.*
brown *550.*
yellow green *550.*
green *550.*
blue green *550.*
orange brown *550.*
rose pink *550.*
dull blue *550.*
violet *550.*
c. Die on bond
black 350.
scarlet 350.
brown 350.
blue green 350.
blue 350.
d. Die on white glazed paper
black *1,150.*

11-E15

Design size: 28x22½mm
POSTAGE / 3 / CENTS in scalloped frame.

11-E15 3c
a. Die on India, die sunk on card
black *750.*
scarlet *750.*
red brown *750.*
green *750.*
slate *750.*
b. Die on bond, about 40x30mm
black 175.
scarlet 175.
brown 175.
green 175.
blue 175.
slate 275.
c. Die on ivory glazed paper
black *750.*
dark brown *750.*
scarlet *750.*
blue *750.*

11-E16

Design size: 28x22½mm
U.S. at sides of 3.

11-E16 3c
a. Die on India, cut small
black *275.*
light red *275.*
red brown *275.*
brown *275.*
yellow green *275.*
blue green *275.*
green *275.*
blue *275.*
red violet *275.*
b. Die on bond, about 40x30mm
black 175.
scarlet 175.
brown 175.
red brown 175.
green 175.
blue green 175.
blue 175.
violet 175.
slate 175.
c. Die on India, Nos. 11-E14A and 11-E16 with albino 11-E14
black *1,000.*
scarlet *1,000.*
brown *1,000.*
green *1,000.*
blue green *1,000.*
blue *1,000.*
red violet *1,000.*
d. As "c," die on bond
black *750.*
scarlet *750.*
brown *750.*
green *750.*
blue green *750.*
gray blue *750.*
e. As "c," die on ivory glazed paper, 64x78mm, black *1,150.*
f. Die on India, die sunk on card
black *900.*
scarlet *900.*

Toppan, Carpenter, Casilear & Co.

5-E1

Design size: 20½x26mm
Franklin vignette.

5-E1 1c
a. Die on old proof paper, master die shortened to 18½x22½mm, black *1,500.*
b. Die on thick old proof paper, black *1,500.*
c. Pair, Nos. 5-E1b, 11-E23, black *2,000.*

5-E1E

5-E1Ef

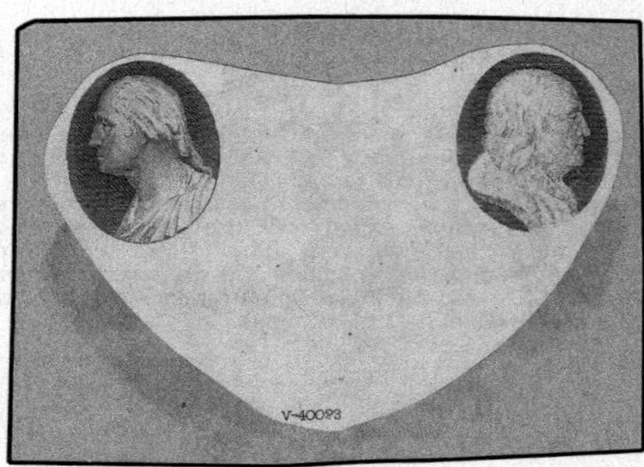

5-E1Eg

Design size: 20x24mm
Similar to No. 5-E1 but with no additional shaded oval border.

5-E1E 1c Die on thin card, black blue —
f. Block of 4 in combination with pair of No. 11-E23, on old proof paper, black *3,500.*
g. Pair, No. 5-E1E in combination with No. 11-E23, on old proof paper, die V-40023, cut to shape to show die number and mounted on 75x54mm card *575.*
h. Pair, No. 5-E1E in combination with No. 11-E23, die on India, die sunk on card, die V-40023 beneath images, black *5,000.*

Nos. 5-E1Eg and 5-E1Eh are essays made by the American Bank Note Co. from the die acquired from Toppan, Carpenter and Company. The die number V-40023 is the new ABNCo. die number. While the essays were produced posthumously, this could prove to be the original die block from which transfers were taken up to be added to bank note designs and later to become the central vignettes for the 1851 postage stamps.

5-E2

Complete design, but with SIX CENTS in value tablet.

5-E2 1c Die on India, black, cut to shape 2,750.

Submitted in Competition for the 1851 Issue Contract (Nos. 11-E17-11-E21)

Toppan, Carpenter, Casilear & Co., Philadelphia, Pa.

11-E17

Design size: 21½x25mm
Die size: 50½x60mm
Vignette of Washington.

11-E17 3c
a. Die on India, die sunk on card, penciled 'By Casilear at lower left, rose carmine 3,000.
b. Die on old ivory paper 2,500.
rose carmine *2,750.*
bluish-black *2,750.*

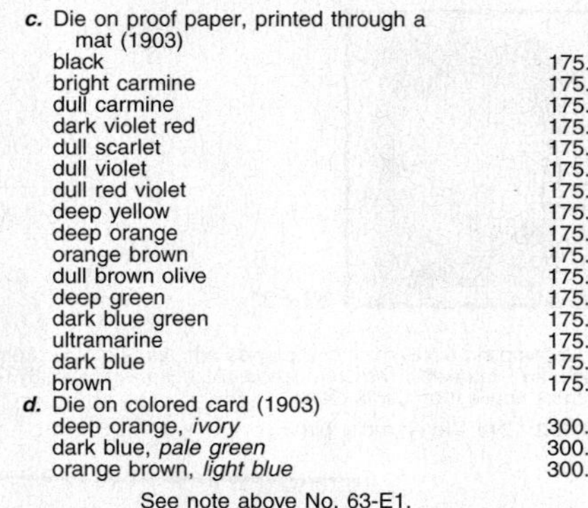

c. Die on proof paper, printed through a mat (1903)

black	175.
bright carmine	175.
dull carmine	175.
dark violet red	175.
dull scarlet	175.
dull violet	175.
dull red violet	175.
deep yellow	175.
deep orange	175.
orange brown	175.
dull brown olive	175.
deep green	175.
dark blue green	175.
ultramarine	175.
dark blue	175.
brown	175.

d. Die on colored card (1903)

deep orange, *ivory*	300.
dark blue, *pale green*	300.
orange brown, *light blue*	300.

See note above No. 63-E1.

No. 11-E17a is also known cut down, and it is worth much less thus.

11-E18

Design size: 20½x22½mm
Washington. Vignette has solid color background. Crack between N and T of CENTS.

11-E18 3c Die on India, card mounted, 24½x25mm
black *2,000.*
carmine *2,000.*

No. 11-E18A

Design size: 20½x22½mm
Washington. Like No. 11-E18 except background of vignette is clearly engraved horizontal and vertical lines. Crack between N and T of CENTS.

11-E18A 3c Die on India, die sunk on 60x50mm card, carmine *7,000.*
b. As No. 11-E18A, cut down to stamp's size, black *2,000.*
c. As No. 11-E18A, on old ivory paper, cut down to stamp size, rose carmine *2,000.*

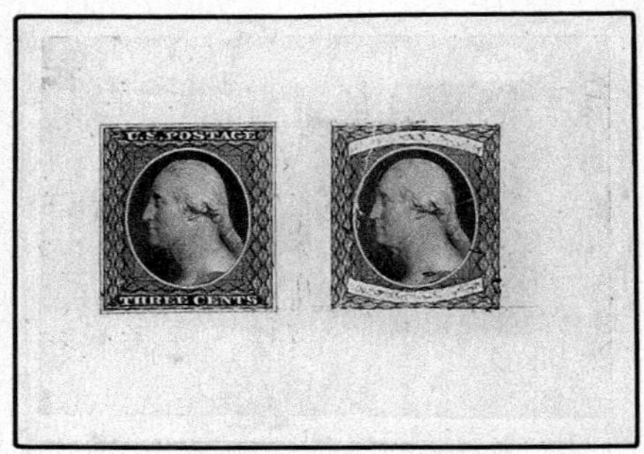

No. 11-E19 On Left, No. 11-E20 On Right

No. 11-E19
Design size: 20½x22½mm
Similar to No. 11-E18, with a slightly modified design, vignette background engraved horiz. and vert. lines. In pair with No. 11-E20.

No. 11-E20
Design size: 20x22½mm
Blank curved top and bottom labels. In pair with 11-E19. Also found in pair with 11-E21.

11-E19 3c Die on India, Nos. 11-E19, 11-E20 mounted on card, black *6,000.*

11-E21

Straight labels. Similar to No. 11-E19 but labels erased and vignette cut out. In pair with No. 11-E20.

11-E21 3c Die on India, Nos. 11-E20, 11-E21 mounted on card, black *4,500.*

11-E22

Die size: 37½x46mm
Similar to issued stamp except lathework impinges on colorless oval.

11-E22 3c Die on India
dusky blue *5,000.*
black *5,000.*
With layout lines *10,000.*

Some students consider No. 11-E22 to be proof strikes of the die used to make the "Roosevelt" and Panama-Pacific small die proofs, as the lathework impinges on the colorless oval of Nos. 11P2 and 11P2a as well.

11-E23

Design size: 18x22mm
Washington vignette only. From master die (21½mm high) with more robe and dark background.

11-E23 3c
a. Master die impression, old proof paper, black *900.*
b. Block of 4, 2mm between ovals, thick old ivory paper, black *3,000.*

11-E24

Washington vignette only, as No. 11-E23, with outer frame added.

11-E24 3c Die on old proof paper, die v 37991, cut to shape to show die number and mounted on 27x37mm card, black *700.*

No. 11-E24 is an essay made by the American Bank Note Co. from a die acquired from Toppan, Carpenter and Company. The die number V 37991 is the new ABNCo. die number.

13-E1

Design as adopted but top label has pencil lettering only, also no lines in leaf ornaments around Xs in top corners.

13-E1 10c Die on India, black *3,000.*

13-E2

Similar to No. 13-E1 but vert. shading around Xs and lines added in leaf ornaments. No lettering in top label.

13-E2 10c Die on India, black *3,000.*

17-E1

Design size: 19x21½mm
Block sinkage size: 57x49mm
Engine engraved frame without labels or interior shadow lines from straight bands and left side rosettes. No small equilateral crosses in central row of diamonds. Original vignette cut out and replaced by engraved vignette of Washington as adopted.

17-E1 12c Die on India, cut close, mounted on block sunk card, 77x57mm, black *10,000.*

17-E2

Similar to adopted design but no small vertical equilateral crosses in center rows of diamond networks at top, sides and bottom.

17-E2 12c Die on India, brown violet, cut close *900.*
17-E3 12c As No. 17-E2, die on wove, brown violet, cut close *750.*

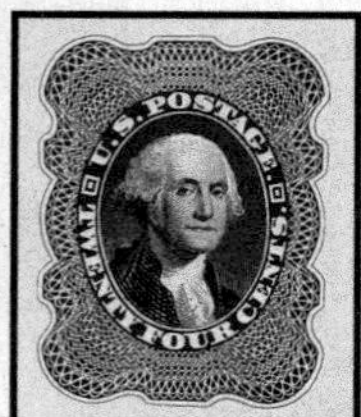

37-E1

Design size: 19½x25½mm
Die size: 46x49mm or larger
Probably not the die used to make the plates. No exterior layout lines. Oval outline recut at bottom of jabot and vignette background etched much darker. Light horizontal lines on stock below chin.

37-E1 24c Die on India, black *2,500.*

37-E2

Incomplete essay for frame only as adopted: no outer frame-line and lathework not retouched. Also known with 37TC1 struck above it on same piece.

37-E2 24c Die on India, black —

38-E1

Incomplete engraving of entire design, lacking text and numerals at top, bottom and sides.

38-E1 30c Die on India, on 37x45mm card, black *7,000.*

38-E2

Design size: 19x24mm
Incomplete engraving of entire design. Scrolls at each side of 30 have only one outer shading line.

38-E2 30c Die on India, black, cut to stamp size, black *1,750.*

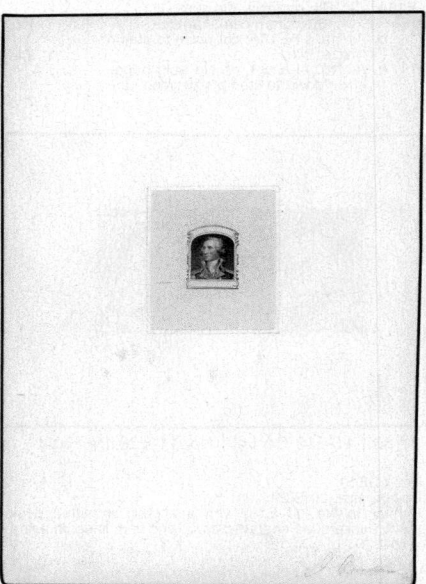

39-E1

Design size: 19x24mm
Incomplete engraving of entire design, lacking "U.S. POSTAGE" at top and "NINETY CENTS" at bottom, incomplete curvature lines in top scroll, signed by engraver on card.

39-E1 90c Die on India (45x52mm), mounted on large card (150x215mm), black —

1861 ISSUE
Toppan, Carpenter & Co.

Examples on 1861 paper and in 1861 colors are rare. Most of the following listed on proof paper, colored card and bond paper are 1903 reprints. Ten sets of reprints on proof paper (and fewer on colored card, bond and pelure papers) supposedly were made for Ernest Schernikow, who bought the original dies about 1903. Similar reprints in similar colors on the same papers also were made of Nos. LO1-E2, 11-E18 and the Philadelphia sanitary fair stamps, plus several master dies of vignettes.

63-E1b

Vignette size: 18½x21½mm
Die size: 49x51mm
Franklin vignette only.

63-E1 1c

a. Die on proof paper (1903)

black	75.
carmine	75.
dark carmine	75.
scarlet	75.
red brown	75.
orange	75.
yellow brown	75.
dark brown	75.
violet brown	75.
light green	75.
green	75.
dark blue	75.
ultramarine	75.
red violet	75.
dark violet	75.
dusky olive green	75.

b. Die on colored card (1903)

orange red, *pale yellow*	*125.*
orange, *pale pink*	*125.*
yellow brown, *buff*	*125.*
dark blue, *pink*	*125.*
dark violet, *pale olive*	*125.*
dull violet, *blue*	*125.*
deep green, *pale blue*	*125.*
violet, *light green*	*125.*

c. Die on green bond (1903)

black	*125.*
dismal red	*125.*
green	*125.*

63-E2b

Franklin vignette with U S POSTAGE at top and ONE CENT at bottom.

63-E2 1c

a. Die on proof paper (1903)

black	100.
carmine	100.
dark carmine	100.
scarlet	100.
red brown	100.
orange	100.
yellow brown	100.
violet brown	100.
gray brown	100.
light green	100.
green	100.
blue	100.
red violet	100.
ultramarine	100.
dusky olive	100.

b. Die on old proof paper, outer line at sides of oval missing (1861), black *1,000.*

c. Die on green bond (1903)

orange	*150.*
orange brown	*150.*
violet	*150.*

d. Die on colored card (1903)

deep green, *pale blue*	*150.*
violet, *light green*	*150.*
dark orange red, *pale dull green*	*150.*
olive, *ivory*	*150.*
brown, *pink*	*150.*
scarlet, *yellow*	*150.*

63-E3

Side ornaments added.

63-E3 1c
a. Die on old proof paper (1861)
black *1,250.*
blue *1,250.*
b. Die on stiff old ivory paper (1861)
black *1,250.*
blue *1,750.*
c. Die on colored card (1903)
black, *ivory* *150.*
brown, *pale pink* *150.*
blue, *blue* *150.*
orange brown, *pale pink* *150.*
gray olive, *ivory* *150.*
gray olive, *buff* *150.*
scarlet, *pale yellow* *150.*
d. Die on proof paper (1903)
black 85.
carmine 85.
dark carmine 85.
scarlet 85.
red brown 85.
orange 85.
yellow brown 85.
violet brown 85.
light green 85.
green 85.
blue 85.
violet 85.
red violet 85.
orange brown 85.
dusky olive 85.
ultramarine 85.
e. Die on green bond (1903)
carmine *150.*
orange *150.*
violet *150.*
f. Die on glazed card, black —

63-E4

With upper and lower right corners incomplete. Serifs of 1s point to right.

63-E4 1c Die on old proof paper (1861), black *2,250.*

63-E4E

As No. 63-E4 but with pencil shading in upper right corner around the "1".

63-E4E 1c Die on old proof paper (1861), black *3,500.*

63-E5

With four corners and numerals in pencil (ornaments differ in each corner).

63-E5 1c Die on old proof paper (1861), blue *2,750.*

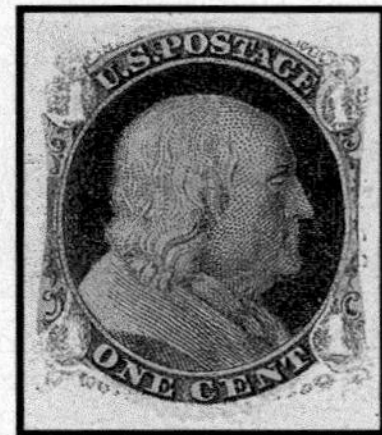

63-E6

As No. 63-E5 but ornaments different.

63-E6 1c Die on old proof paper (1861), blue *3,500.*

63-E7

As Nos. 63-E5 and 63-E6 but ornaments different.

63-E7 1c Die on old proof paper (1861), blue *3,250.*

63-E8

Die proof of No. 5 with lower corners cut out of India paper and resketched in pencil on card beneath.

63-E8 1c Die on India, on card (1861), black *2,000.*

63-E9

Completely engraved design.

63-E9 1c
a. Die on India, cut to shape (1861)
black, on brown toned paper *1,000.*
blue *600.*
b. Die on India, about 58x57mm, die sunk on card (1861)
blue *2,000.*
c. Die on old proof paper, about 48x55mm (1861)
black *2,000.*
d. Die on large old white ivory paper (1861)
black *2,000.*
blue *2,000.*
e. Die on proof paper, printed through mat (1903)
black 100.
carmine 100.
dark carmine 100.
scarlet 100.
orange 100.
orange brown 100.
yellow brown 100.
light green 100.
green 100.
black blue 100.
violet 100.
red violet 100.
violet brown 100.
gray 100.
blue 100.
ultramarine 100.
f. Die on bond (1903)
orange *125.*
dismal blue green *125.*
g. Die on bond, Walls of Troy wmk. (1903)
carmine *200.*
orange red *200.*
orange *200.*
orange brown *200.*
dark green *200.*
light ultramarine *200.*
h. Die on bond, double line of scallops wmk. (1903)
orange red *200.*
dark green *200.*
i. Die on green bond (1903)
dismal carmine *125.*
dismal violet brown *125.*
dull dark green *125.*
j. Die on pinkish pelure (1903)
orange red *300.*
brown red *300.*
brown orange *300.*
dull blue green *300.*
violet *300.*
k. Die on colored card (1903)
black, *pale blue* *225.*
carmine, *pale yellow* *225.*
carmine, *pale pink* *225.*
brown red, *pale pink* *225.*
chestnut, *pale olive* *225.*
dismal olive, *buff* *225.*
ultramarine, *ivory* *225.*
l. Die on stiff card (1903), green *250.*

65-E1

Vignette size: 16½x19mm
Die size: 49x50mm
1851 master die of Washington vignette only.

65-E1 3c
a. Die on proof paper (1903)
black 75.
carmine 75.
dark carmine 75.
scarlet 75.
red brown 75.
orange 75.
brown orange 75.
violet brown 75.
dusky olive 75.
light green 75.
green 75.
dark blue 75.
ultramarine 75.
lilac 75.
red violet 75.
b. Die on green bond (1903)
red *125.*
brown *125.*
blue *125.*
olive *125.*
c. Die on colored card (1903)
carmine, *pale green* *125.*
scarlet, *yellow* *125.*
orange, *ivory* *125.*
olive brown, *blue* *125.*
dark blue, *pink* *125.*
violet, *buff* *125.*
dark green, *pink* *125.*

65-E2

With tessellated frame, bottom label and diamond blocks. Without rosettes, top label and diamond blocks.

65-E2 3c
a. Die on old proof paper (1861)
black *1,000.*
red *1,000.*
b. Die on proof paper, printed through a mat (1903)
black *85.*
carmine *85.*
dark carmine *85.*
scarlet *85.*
orange *85.*
yellow *85.*
yellow brown *85.*
dusky gray *85.*
light green *85.*
green *85.*
black blue *85.*
ultramarine *85.*
lilac *85.*
dark lilac *85.*
red violet *85.*
c. Die on green bond (1903)
black *150.*
dull orange red *150.*
orange *150.*
orange brown *150.*
blue violet *150.*
black blue *150.*
dusky green *150.*

d. Die on dull pale gray blue thin wove (1903)
dull red 300.
orange 300.
yellow brown 300.
dusky green 300.
black blue 300.
e. Die on colored card (1903)
black, *light blue* 150.
orange red, *yellow* 150.
red brown, *ivory* 150.
light green, *pink* 150.
green, *light green* 150.
blue, *buff* 150.
f. Die on India
black —
rose —

65-E3a

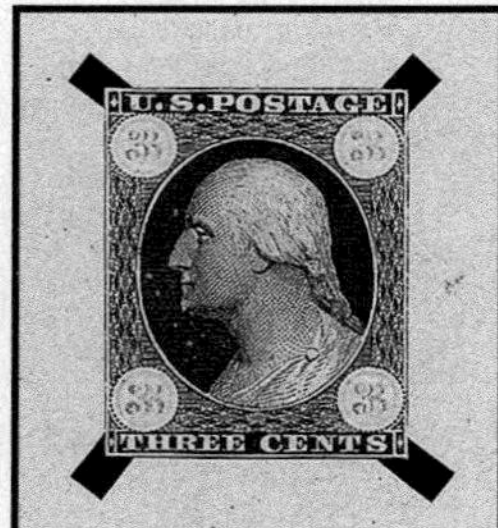
65-E3b

With top label and diamond blocks.

65-E3 3c
a. Die on old proof paper (1861)
brown red 2,500.
black 2,500.
b. Same as No. 65-E3 with numerals in pencil, Die on old proof paper (1861), black 6,000.
c. Die on proof paper, no numerals, printed through a mat (1903)
black 90.
carmine 90.
dark carmine 90.
scarlet 90.
orange 90.
yellow 90.
yellow brown 90.
dusky olive 90.
light green 90.
green 90.
black blue 90.
violet blue 90.
violet brown 90.
lilac 90.
red violet 90.
d. Die on green bond (1903)
dull scarlet 150.
dim red 150.
orange 150.
yellow brown 150.
green 150.
dusky blue 150.
violet 150.
black 150.
e. Die on colored card (1903)
black, *buff* 150.
scarlet, *ivory* 150.
orange, *light yellow* 150.
brown, *light blue* 150.
violet blue, *light pink* 150.
violet, *light green* 150.
f. Die on pink thin wove (1903)
dull yellow 300.
dismal red 300.
yellow brown 300.
dusky blue green 300.
dusky blue 300.

65-E4

Complete die, with numerals in rosette circles.

65-E4 3c
a. Die on India, 75x76mm die sinkage (1861)
black 1,500.
carmine 1,500.
b. Die on old proof paper (1861)
black 1,500.
dark red 1,500.
c. Die on India, cut to shape (1861)
black 1,000.
carmine 1,000.

67-E1a, Die I

67-E1b, Die II

Vignette size: 13½x16mm
Jefferson vignette only. Two dies: die I incomplete, light background in vignette; die II background essentially complete.

67-E1 5c
a. Die I on old proof paper, black (1861) 750.
b. Die II on proof paper (1903)
black 75.
carmine 75.
dark carmine 75.
scarlet 75.
red brown 75.
orange brown 75.
brown 75.
dusky olive 75.
green 75.
dark green 75.
black blue 75.
ultramarine 75.
violet brown 75.
red violet 75.
lilac 75.
c. Die II on colored card (1903)
olive, *buff* 150.
carmine, *pale yellow* 150.
scarlet, *green* 150.
brown, *pink* 150.
black, *ivory* 150.
ultramarine, *pale blue* 150.
d. Die II on green bond (1903)
orange brown 150.
dismal red brown 150.
dark green 150.
violet 150.
black blue 150.
e. Die II on old thin ivory paper (1903)
green 175.
dark carmine 175.
f. Die I on old thin ivory paper (1861), dark blue 1,000.
g. Die I on old proof paper (1861), dusky ultramarine 1,500.
h. Die II on old ivory paper (1861), navy blue 750.

67-E2

Vignette die II framed, with spaces for numerals.

67-E2 5c
a. Die II on proof paper (1903)
black 95.
carmine 95.
dark carmine 95.
scarlet 95.
red brown 95.
orange 95.
yellow brown 95.
dusky olive 95.
violet brown 95.
light green 95.
green 95.
blue 95.
ultramarine 95.
red violet 95.
lilac 95.
b. Die II on colored card (1903)
orange brown, *light yellow* 175.
deep blue, *light pink* 175.
dusky olive, *light buff* 175.
dark green, *pale blue* 175.
red violet, *ivory* 175.
c. Die II on green bond (1903)
orange brown 160.
olive green 160.
violet 160.
blue 160.
ultramarine 160.
d. Die I on old proof paper (1861), black 2,000.

67-E3

67-E3c

With numerals.

67-E3 5c
a. Die I on proof paper, printed through a mat (1903)
black 125.
carmine 125.
dark carmine 125.
scarlet 125.
red brown 125.
yellow brown 125.
dark brown 125.
violet brown 125.
light green 125.
green 125.
dark blue 125.
lilac 125.
ultramarine 125.
red violet 125.
dusky olive 125.
b. Die I on soft laid paper (1861)
black 750.
dark brown 750.
orange brown 750.
c. Die II on old proof paper, pencil designs drawn in corners (1861), black 2,500.
d. Die I on old proof paper, outer lines on corner curves missing (1861), black 500.
e. Die I on colored card (1903)
orange red, *buff* 175.
orange red, *light yellow* 175.
olive green, *pale green* 175.
deep green, *ivory* 175.
dark blue, *light pink* 175.
violet brown, *light blue* 175.
f. Die I on green bond (1903)
black 160.
scarlet 160.
brown 160.
green 160.
g. Die I on yellow pelure (1903)
scarlet 350.
brown red 350.
brown 350.
dark green 350.
violet 350.
blue 350.
h. Die I on bond, Walls of Troy wmk. (1903)
dark orange 250.
blue 250.
carmine 250.
i. Die I on bond, two line scalloped border wmk. (1903)
dark blue green 250.
scarlet 250.

67-E4b

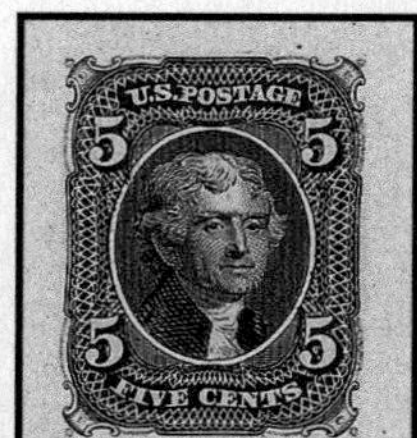
67-E4e

67-E4j

Complete die II design with corner ornaments.

67-E4 5c

a. Die II on India, cut to shape (1861), black *500.*
b. Die II on brown toned paper (1861), cut to shape
black *1,000.*
brown *1,000.*
c. Die II on old proof paper (1861)
orange brown *1,500.*
black *1,500.*
d. Die II on old ivory paper (1861), black *1,500.*
e. Die II on old proof paper, additional frameline drawn on curved corners and small circle drawn in each corner (1861), black *2,500.*
f. Die II on proof paper, printed through a mat (1903)
black 125.
carmine 125.
dark carmine 125.
scarlet 125.
orange 125.
brown 125.
yellow brown 125.
dusky olive 125.
light green 125.
green 125.
blue 125.
black blue 125.
violet brown 125.
red violet 125.
lilac 125.
ultramarine 125.
g. Die II on colored card (1903)
red, *light yellow* *150.*
brown, *buff* *150.*
olive green, *light pink* *150.*
dark violet *150.*
violet brown, *pale green* *150.*
dusky yellow green, *dull pale* *150.*
blue green *150.*
brown, *ivory* *150.*
h. Die II on green bond (1903)
black *125.*
dull dark orange *125.*
violet *125.*
i. Die II on bond, Walls of Troy wmk. (1903)
scarlet *250.*
deep red *250.*
dark green *250.*
j. Die II on bond, two-line scalloped border wmk. (1903)
deep orange *250.*
blue *250.*
k. Die II on greenish pelure (1903)
orange *350.*
olive brown *350.*
dark green *350.*
l. Die II on bluish pelure (1903), red brown *450.*

69-E1

Vignette size: 15x17mm
Washington vignette only. Two dies: die I incomplete, horiz. background lines irregularly spaced, space occurring about every 2mm; die II more engraving on face, horiz. background lines regularly spaced, outer oval border smudged. Die II known only as 1851 master die.

69-E1 12c

a. Die II on old proof paper (1851), black 650.
b. Die I on proof paper (1903)
black 60.
carmine 60.
dark carmine 60.
scarlet 60.
red brown 60.
orange 60.
yellow brown 60.
violet brown 60.
gray brown 60.
light green 60.
green 60.
blue 60.
black blue 60.
red violet 60.
lilac 60.
ultramarine 60.
c. Die I on green bond (1903)
black *150.*
red brown *150.*
brown *150.*
d. Die I on colored card (1903)
dark carmine, *ivory* *150.*
dark carmine, *light blue* *150.*
dark olive, *buff* *150.*
dark green, *light yellow* *150.*
dark blue, *pale green* *150.*
violet brown, *light pink* *150.*

69-E2

Die II with curved labels at top and bottom.

69-E2 12c

a. Die II on proof paper, some printed through a mat (1903)
black 75.
carmine 75.
dark carmine 75.
scarlet 75.
orange 75.
yellow 75.
yellow brown 75.
violet brown 75.
gray brown 75.
light green 75.
green 75.
light blue 75.
black blue 75.
red violet 75.
lilac 75.
ultramarine 75.
b. Die I on old proof paper (1861)
dim red violet *500.*
red violet *500.*
c. Die I on dull light green bond (1903)
black *150.*
dull red *150.*
dim orange *150.*
yellow brown *150.*
dusky green *150.*
dusky blue *150.*
red violet *150.*
d. Die I on pale yellow thin wove (1903)
dim red *200.*
deep orange red *200.*
yellow brown *200.*
dusky blue *200.*
red violet *200.*
e. Die I on colored card (1903)
dull red, *light pink* *150.*
orange red, *buff* *150.*
brown, *light blue* *150.*
dark olive, *light yellow* *150.*
dull dark blue, *ivory* *150.*
violet, *pale green* *150.*

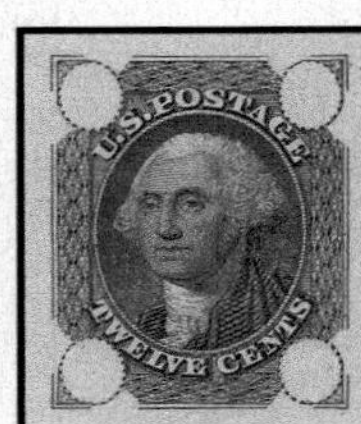
69-E3

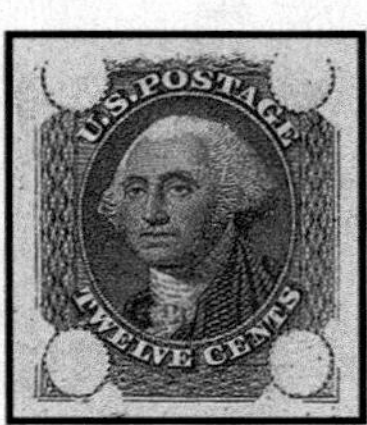
69-E3d

69-E3g

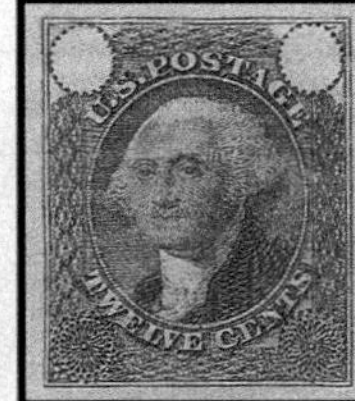
69-E3i

Frame incomplete: all four rosettes blank.

69-E3 12c

a. Die on proof paper (1903)
black 125.
carmine 125.
dark carmine 125.
scarlet 125.
red brown 125.
orange 125.
orange brown 125.
violet brown 125.
light green 125.
green 125.
light blue 125.
black blue 125.
red violet 125.
lilac 125.
ultramarine 125.
b. Die on old proof paper (1861)
black *800.*
olive gray *800.*
c. Die on old ivory, top border and half of rosettes missing (1861), black *800.*
d. Die on stiff old ivory, top border missing (1861), bluish black *800.*
e. Die on colored card, top border missing (1903)
orange brown, *light blue* *175.*
deep green, *light yellow* *175.*
deep blue, *light pink* *175.*
violet, *ivory* *175.*
deep yellow orange, *pale yellow green* *175.*
brown, *buff* *175.*
f. Die on green bond, top border missing (1903)
orange *175.*
green *175.*
violet *175.*
g. Die on old proof paper, 1851 die with border lines complete, upper right rosette blank (1861)
orange *800.*
dark green *800.*
ultramarine *800.*
violet *800.*
h. Die I on old proof paper, vignette background incomplete or worn, stock on neck unfinished (1861) —
i. Die I on old proof paper, as 69-E3h but both upper rosettes blank (1861), ultramarine *1,000.*

69-E3j

69-E3k

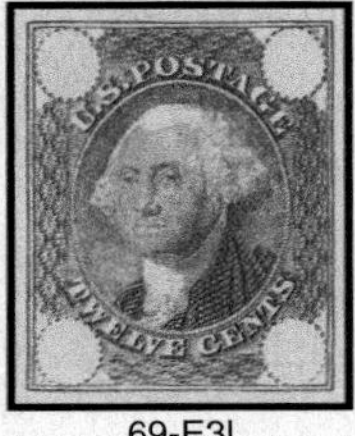
69-E3l

69-E3o

j. Die I on old proof paper, as No. 69-E3h but both upper plus lower left rosettes blank (1861), ultramarine *1,000.*
k. Die I on old proof paper, as No. 69-E3h but both lower plus upper left rosettes blank, corner borders removed around blank rosettes (1861), ultramarine *1,000.*
l. Die I on old proof paper, as No. 69-E3h but all rosettes blank, border lines complete (1861)
dim scarlet *750.*
orange *750.*
green *750.*
ultramarine *750.*
violet *750.*
m. Die I on white wove, as No. 69-E3l (1861), scarlet *750.*
n. Die I on old proof paper, complete design (1861)
orange *1,000.*
dark red *1,000.*
orange red *1,000.*
ultramarine *1,000.*
o. Die I on pale yellow thin wove (1903), dark red *750.*
p. Die I on pink thin wove (1903), blue *750.*
q. Die I on pale pink (1903), blue *750.*

69-E4

69-E4d

69-E4e

Original complete design with numerals in corners.

69-E4 12c
a. Die on India, card mounted (1861)
black *800.*
gray black *800.*
b. Die on India, cut to shape (1861), black *500.*
c. Die on old proof paper (1861), black *500.*
d. Die on old proof paper, corners drawn in pencil (1861), black *2,750.*
e. Die on old proof paper, as No. 69-E3a but numerals sketched in diagonally and vert. (1861), black *3,500.*
f. Die on stiff old ivory paper, as No. 69-E4e but without top border (1861), bluish black *1,500.*
g. Die on thin card, black —

70-E1

Vignette size: 7x16mm
Washington die II vignette only.

70-E1 24c
a. Die II on proof paper (1903)
black 60.
carmine 60.
dark carmine 60.
scarlet 60.
orange 60.
yellow 60.
yellow brown 60.
violet brown 60.
gray olive 60.
light green 60.
green 60.
light blue 60.
black blue 60.
red violet 60.
lilac 60.
b. Die II on green bond (1903)
black *150.*
red brown *150.*
violet *150.*
orange *150.*
c. Die II on colored card (1903)
dull red, *ivory* *150.*
brown red, *buff* *150.*
brown orange, *light pink* *150.*
dark green, *light yellow* *150.*
blue, *pale green* *150.*
violet, *blue* *150.*

70-E2

Washington vignette with oval label. Background complete, eyes retouched.

70-E2 24c
a. Die II on proof paper (1903)
black 60.
carmine 60.
dark carmine 60.
scarlet 60.
orange 60.
yellow 60.
yellow brown 60.
violet brown 60.
light green 60.
green 60.
light blue 60.
black blue 60.
red violet 60.
lilac 60.
gray olive 60.
ultramarine 60.
b. Die I on old proof paper, background lines incomplete (1861)
black *750.*
dim red violet *750.*
c. Die I on colored card (1903)
black, *light pink* *150.*
orange, *buff* *150.*
orange, *light blue* *150.*
dark green, *pale green* *150.*
violet blue, *light yellow* *150.*
violet, *ivory* *150.*
d. Die I on green bond (1903), brown *150.*
e. Die I on dull light blue green bond (1903)
black *150.*
orange red *150.*
orange *150.*
yellow brown *150.*
dusky green *150.*
dull blue *150.*
red violet *150.*
f. Die I on dull pale green blue thin wove (1903)
orange red *300.*
orange *300.*
yellow brown *300.*
dusky green *300.*
dull blue *300.*

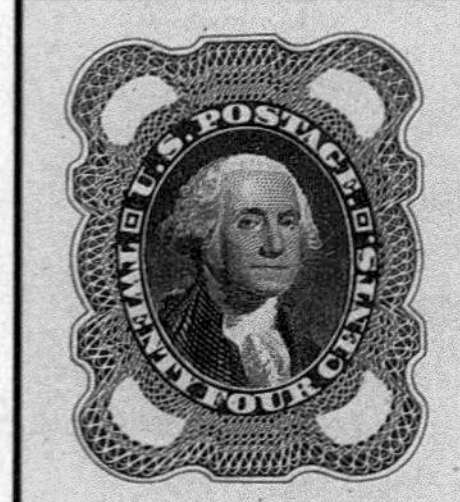

70-E3

With frame. Blank areas in corners for numerals.

70-E3 24c
a. Die on proof paper (1903)
black 100.
carmine 100.
dark carmine 100.
scarlet 100.
orange 100.
yellow brown 100.
orange brown 100.
violet brown 100.
gray olive 100.
light green 100.
green 100.
light blue 100.
black blue 100.
red violet 100.
lilac 100.
ultramarine 100.
b. Die on old proof paper (1861), dusky red violet *1,000.*
c. Die on colored card (1903)
carmine, *light blue* *175.*
blue, *pale green* *175.*
scarlet, *buff* *175.*
yellow brown, *cream* *175.*
dull violet, *pink* *175.*
dusky green, *light yellow* *175.*
gray olive, *ivory* *175.*
d. Die on green bond (1903)
black *175.*
orange brown *175.*
green *175.*

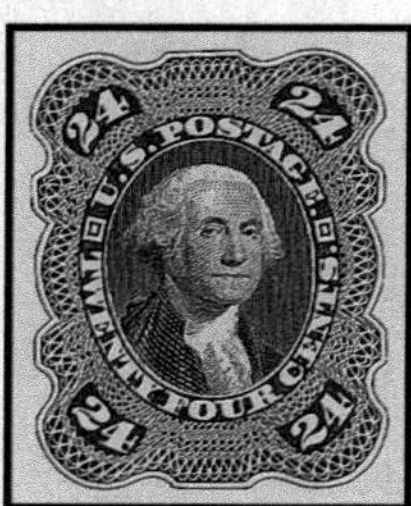

70-E4

Complete design with numerals in corners.

70-E4 24c
a. Die on old proof paper, cut to shape (1861)
lilac *400.*
black *400.*
red violet *400.*
b. Die on India, cut close (1861)
black *400.*
lilac *400.*
brown lilac *400.*
c. Die on India (1861), dark blue *750.*
d. Die on India, mounted on 80x115mm card (1861), lilac *750.*
e. On stiff old ivory paper (1861)
black *1,000.*
lilac *1,000.*
f. Die on proof paper, printed through a mat (1903)
black 125.
carmine 125.
dark carmine 125.
scarlet 125.
red borwn 125.
yellow brown 125.
brown 125.
violet brown 125.
gray olive 125.
light green 125.
green 125.
light blue 125.
black blue 125.
red violet 125.
lilac 125.
ultramarine 125.
g. Die on blue pelure (1903)
dark carmine *300.*
scarlet *300.*
orange *300.*
brown *300.*
dusky green *300.*
h. Die on bond (1903)
black *175.*
scarlet *175.*
orange *175.*
dark green *175.*
blue *175.*
i. Die on green bond (1903)
black *250.*
dark red *250.*
green *250.*
j. Die on bond, Walls of Troy wmk. (1903), dark green *300.*
k. Die on bond, double line of scallops wmk. (1903)
deep orange red *300.*
scarlet *300.*
orange *300.*
light blue *300.*
l. Die on colored card, printed through a mat
dark orange, *ivory* *150.*
dark orange, *light pink* *150.*
brown, *light blue* *150.*
dull dark blue, *pale green* *150.*
violet, *light yellow* *150.*
violet brown, *buff* *150.*

72-E1

Vignette size: 16x17½mm
Washington vignette only.

72-E1 90c
a. Die on proof paper (1903)
black 100.
carmine 100.
dark carmine 100.
scarlet 100.
red brown 100.
orange 100.
orange brown 100.
violet brown 100.
gray olive 100.
light green 100.
green 100.
dark blue 100.
lilac 100.
red violet 100.
yellow brown 100.
ultramarine 100.
b. Die on colored card (1903)
black, *light yellow* *165.*
red brown, *light pink* *165.*
carmine, *buff* *165.*
brown, *pale green* *165.*
dark brown, *light blue* *165.*
ultramarine, *ivory* *165.*
c. Die on dull light blue green bond (1903)
violet brown *165.*
dusky green *165.*
dusky blue *165.*
red violet *165.*

72-E2

Vignette with blank top and bottom labels.

72-E2 90c
a. Die on proof paper (1903)
black 100.
carmine 100.
dark carmine 100.
scarlet 100.
orange 100.
yellow brown 100.
brown 100.
violet brown 100.
gray olive 100.
light green 100.
green 100.

dark blue 100.
red violet 100.
lilac 100.
ultramarine 100.
b. Die on green bond (1903)
dull orange *150.*
dull orange brown *150.*
red violet *150.*
c. Die on colored card (1903)
black, *buff* *185.*
orange red, *light yellow* *185.*
brown, *ivory* *185.*
olive green, *light pink* *185.*
green, *light blue* *185.*
violet brown, *pale green* *185.*

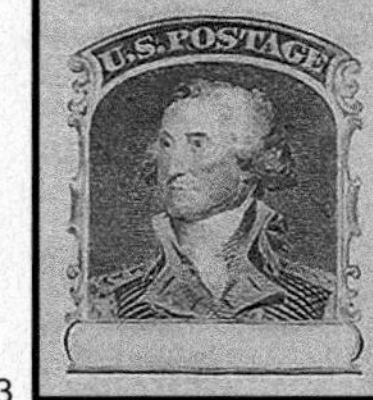
72-E3

U.S. POSTAGE in top label.

72-E3 90c
a. Die on proof paper (1903)
black 125.
carmine 125.
dark carmine 125.
scarlet 125.
yellow 125.
yellow brown 125.
brown 125.
violet brown 125.
gray olive 125.
light green 125.
green 125.
dark blue 125.
lilac 125.
red violet 125.
ultramarine 125.
b. Die on colored card (1903)
orange, *light blue* *185.*
orange red, *light yellow* *185.*
dark blue, *buff* *185.*
violet, *pale green* *185.*
violet brown, *ivory* *185.*
orange brown, *pale pink* *185.*
c. Die on green bond (1903)
black *175.*
brown *175.*
green *175.*

Lower corners of vignette cut out, "NINETY 90 CENTS" in pencil in bottom label.

72-E4 90c Die on India (1861), black *2,000.*

72-E5

Complete design.

72-E5 90c
a. Die on India, cut to shape (1861)
black *350.*
dark blue *350.*
b. Die on India, die sunk on card (1861), blue *2,500.*
c. Die on India, cut close (1861)
black *350.*
blue *350.*
d. Die on proof paper, printed through a mat (1903)
black 175.
carmine 175.
dark carmine 175.
scarlet 175.
orange 175.
yellow brown 175.
brown 175.
violet brown 175.
gray olive 175.
light green 175.
green 175.
dark blue 175.
lilac 175.
red violet 175.
ultramarine 175.
e. Die on colored card (1903)
carmine, *light blue* *250.*
dismal brown, *light pink* *250.*
orange brown, *buff* *250.*
blue, *ivory* *250.*
violet, *pale green* *250.*
green, *pale yellow* *250.*
f. Die on green bond (1903)
dark carmine *225.*
red brown *225.*
green *225.*
g. Die on bond (1903), orange brown *250.*
h. Die on bond, "Bond No. 1" wmk. (1903), orange brown *350.*
i. Die on bond, "Bond No 2" wmk. (1903), orange brown *350.*
j. Die on bond, Walls of Troy wmk. (1903)
carmine *300.*
scarlet *300.*
orange *300.*
dark green *300.*
ultramarine *300.*
k. Die on pink pelure (1903)
brown red *350.*
dull yellow *350.*
very dark green *350.*
dark blue *350.*
dull violet *350.*
l. Die on bond, Double Scallops wmk. (1903), scarlet *300.*

American Bank Note Co.

65-E5

Design size: 19x23 ½mm
Engraved frame with pencil border, center cut out, mounted over 22x27mm engraved vignette of Washington.

65-E5 3c Die on India, black *4,000.*

65-E6

Design size: 19x24 ½mm
Engraved frame with pencil border, center cut out, mounted over engraved ruled background with engraved Washington vignette mounted on it.

65-E6 Three Cents Die on India, on card about 23x27 ½mm, black *2,500.*

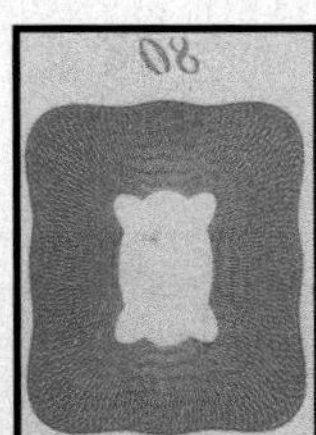
65-E7

Master die No. 80 of frame only.

65-E7 3c Die on India, card mounted
deep orange *2,000.*
dark brown *2,000.*
green *2,000.*
dark blue *2,000.*
black *2,000.*

65-E7A

Design size: 19 ½x24 ½mm
Engraved lathework frame with Bald, Cousland & Co. engraved Washington vignette, blank labels and numeral areas, printed by American Bank Note Co.

65-E7A (3c) Die on India, die sunk on 75x83mm card, black *1,000.*

65-E8

Design size: 19 ½x24 ½mm
Engraved lathework frame with Bald, Cousland & Co. engraved Washington vignette and engraved lettered labels and numerals mounted on it.

65-E8 3c Die on India, on 22x27mm card, black *11,000.*

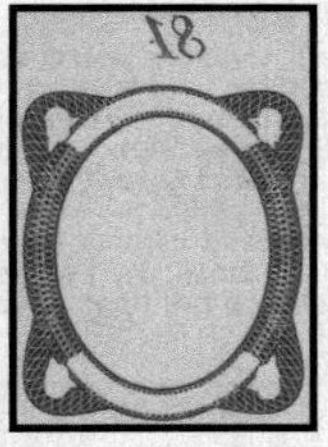
65-E9

Master die No. 81 of frame only.

65-E9 3c Die on India
black *2,750.*
brown yellow *2,750.*
dark green *2,750.*
orange red *2,750.*

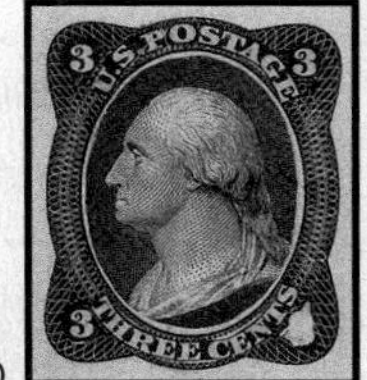
65-E10

Engraved lathework frame with Bald, Cousland & Co. engraved Washington vignette and engraved lettered labels and numerals mounted on it.

65-E10 3c Die on India, on 28x35mm card, black *7,000.*

67-E5

Design size: 21x25mm
Engraved frame used for the 1860 Nova Scotia 5c stamp cut to shape, with engraved lettered labels and Washington vignette No. 209-E7 mounted on it.

67-E5 Five Cents Die on India, on 23x27mm card, black *2,500.*

67-E6

Design size: 19x24
Engraved lathework background with Bald, Cousland & Co. engraved Washington vignette and engraved lettered labels and numerals mounted on it.

67-E6 5c Die on India, mounted on 22x26mm card, black *7,000.*

67-E7

Design size: 19x24mm
Engraved lathework background with Bald, Cousland & Co. engraved Washington vignette and engraved lettered labels and numerals mounted on it.

67-E7 5c Die on India, mounted on 21x26½mm card, black *7,000.*

National Bank Note Co.

The following essays include those formerly listed as Nos. 55-57, 59 and 62 in the Postage section, and the corresponding die and plate essays formerly listed in the Proof section. Former No. 58 is now No. 62B. Former Nos. 60 and 61 are now Nos. 70eTC and 71bTC in the Trial Color Proofs section.

Small die essays from the 1903 Roosevelt albums have "RA" as part of the listing description. Small die essays from the special Panama-Pacific Exposition printings have "PP" as part of the listing description.

63-E10

Frame essay with blank areas for Franklin vignette, labels, numerals, U and S.

63-E10 1c Die on India, black *4,000.*

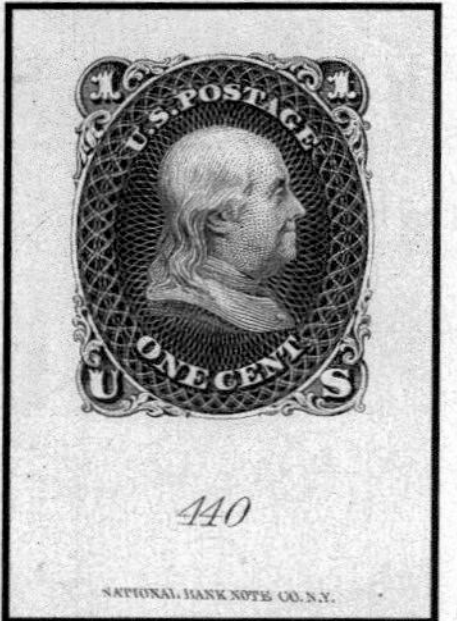

63-E11

Die size: 58x56mm
"Premiere Gravure" die No. 440.

63-E11 1c
- ***a.*** "Premiere Gravure" die essay on India (formerly Nos. 55P1, 55TC1)
  - black *4,000.*
  - indigo *1,500.*
  - ultramarine *2,250.*
- ***b.*** RA "Premiere Gravure" small die essay on white wove, 28x31mm (**formerly No. 55P2**), indigo *325.*
- ***c.*** "Premiere Gravure" plate essay on India (**formerly Nos. 55P3, 55TC3**)
  - indigo *300.*
  - blue —
  - ultramarine *300.*
  - violet ultramarine —
- ***d.*** "Premiere Gravure" plate essay on semitransparent stamp paper (**formerly No. 55TC4**), ultramarine *400.*

63-E11e

- ***e.*** Finished "Premiere Gravure" plate essay on semitransparent stamp paper, perf. 12, gummed (**formerly No. 55**), indigo *50,000.*

No. 63-E11e is valued with perfs cutting slightly into design at top.

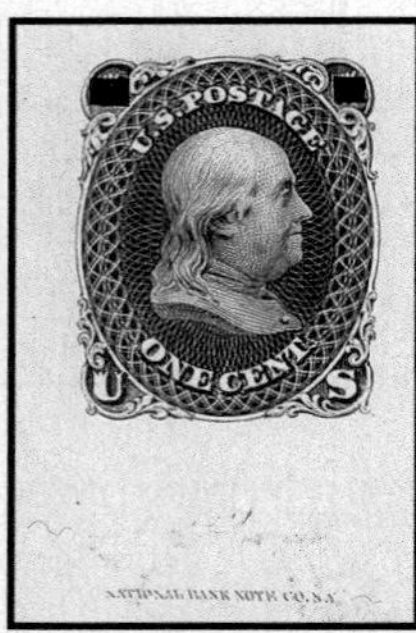

63-E12

Die size: 47x55mm
Apparently complete die except value numerals have been cut out.

63-E12 1c Die on India, die sunk on card, black *1,500.*

65-E11

Die size: 64x76½mm
Incomplete engraving of Washington head only.

65-E11 3c
- ***a.*** Die on India, on card, carmine *750.*
- ***b.*** Die on white glazed paper
  - black *750.*
  - scarlet *750.*
  - brown violet *750.*

65-E12

Die size: 78x55mm
Incomplete engraved design, no scrolls outside framelines, no silhouette under chin, no ornaments on 3s, U and S.

65-E12 3c Die on India, die sunk on card
- black *1,000.*
- blue *1,000.*

65-E13

As No. 65-E12 but ornaments on 3s, U and S. Shows traces of first border design erased. With imprint and No. 441 below design.

65-E13 3c Die on India, card mounted
- scarlet *1,000.*
- brown red *1,000.*
- ultramarine *1,000.*

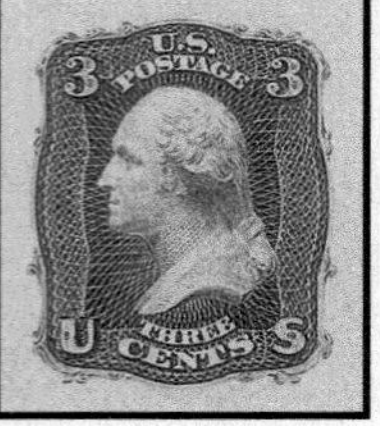

65-E14

Die size: 59x55mm
As No. 65-E13 but with ornaments outside frame.

65-E14 3c Die on India, die sunk on card
- black *750.*
- scarlet *750.*
- pink *1,250.*
- brown orange *750.*
- deep orange red *750.*
- deep red *750.*

65-E15

As No. 65-E14 but top of head silhouetted, lines added or strengthened in hair at top of head, around eye, on chin, in hair behind ear. The three lines on bottom edge of bust extended to back. No imprint or die number on die impression.

65-E15 3c
- ***a.*** Die on India, card mounted, deep orange red *1,000.*
- ***b.*** "Premiere Gravure" die essay on semitransparent stamp paper, 20x25mm-30x37mm
  - deep orange red *750.*
  - deep red orange *750.*
  - dim red *750.*
  - dim deep red *750.*
  - dim orange red *750.*
  - dull pink *750.*
  - dull violet red *750.*
- ***c.*** "Premiere Gravure" die essay on India (**formerly Nos. 56P1, 56TC1**)
  - red *1,350.*
  - black *2,000.*
  - scarlet *2,000.*
  - pink *2,850.*
  - orange red *2,000.*
  - dark orange red *2,000.*
- ***d.*** RA Small die essay on white wove, 28x31mm altered laydown die of complete design but with outer scrolls removed and replaced by ones similar to "Premiere Gravure" design (1903) (**formerly No. 56P2**), dim deep red *325.*

- ***e.*** As "c," PP small die essay on pale cream soft wove, 24x29mm (1915) (**formerly No. 56P2a**), deep red *1,250.*
- ***f.*** "Premiere Gravure" plate No. 2 essay on India (**formerly Nos. 56P3, 56TC3**)
  - red *250.*
  - scarlet *350.*
- ***g.*** "Premiere Gravure" plate essay on semitransparent stamp paper (**formerly Nos. 56aP4, 56TC4**)
  - red, pair with gum *1,750.*
  - black *400.*

65-E15h

- ***h.*** Finished "Premiere Gravure" plate essay on semitransparent stamp paper, perf. 12, gummed (**formerly No. 56**)
  - brown rose *550.*
  - orange red *475.*
  - bright orange red *475.*
  - dark orange red *475.*
  - dim deep red *475.*
  - pink *475.*
  - deep pink *475.*
  - P# block of 8, Impt. (any shade) *20,000.*

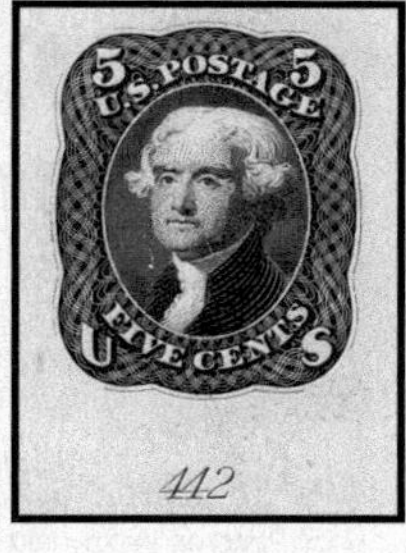
67-E8

Incomplete impression from die No. 442, border lines and corner scrolls missing.

67-E8 5c Die on India, mounted on 34x50mm card, black *1,750.*

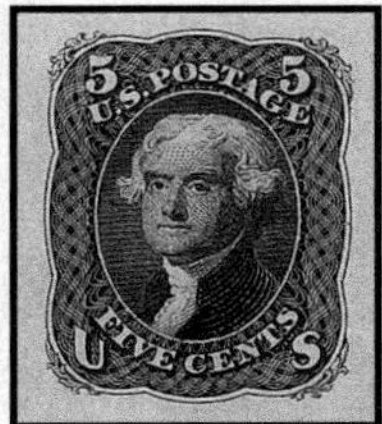
67-E9

Size of die: 58x59mm
"Premiere Gravure" design, with corner scrolls but without leaflets.

67-E9 5c
- ***a.*** "Premiere Gravure" die essay on India, card mounted (formerly No. 57TC1)
  - black *2,500.*
  - scarlet *2,500.*
- ***b.*** RA Small die essay on white wove, 28x31mm, altered laydown die of complete design but with scrolls removed from corners to resemble "Premiere Gravure" (1903) (**formerly No. 57P2), brown** 325.
- ***c.*** As "b," PP die essay on pale cream soft wove, 24x29mm (1915) (**formerly No. 57P2a**), brown *1,750.*
- ***d.*** "Premiere Gravure" plate No. 3 essay on India (**formerly Nos. 57P3, 57TC3**)
  - brown *250.*
  - light brown *300.*
  - dark brown *300.*
  - red brown *300.*

67-E9e

- ***e.*** Finished "Premiere Gravure" plate essay on semitransparent stamp paper, perf. 12, gummed (**formerly No. 57**), brown *30,000.*

68-E1

Design size: 14x17½mm
Die size: 26x31mm
Washington vignette only.

68-E1 10c
- ***a.*** Die on ivory paper, black *1,000.*
- ***b.*** Die on India *1,000.*

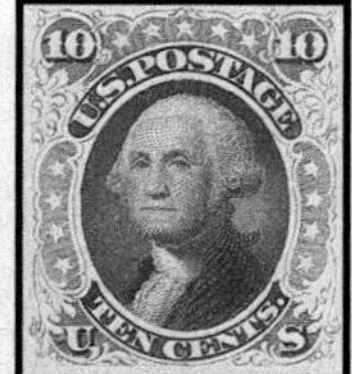
68-E2

Incomplete die No. 443.

68-E2 10c Die on India, 22x26mm, dark green *2,500.*

68-E3

Incomplete die of No. 68P1, thin lines missing on top of frame.

68-E3 10c Die on India
- yellowish green *1,000.*
- dark green *1,000.*

69-E5

Design size: 12½x16mm
Die size: about 62x65mm
Washington vignette only.

69-E5 12c
- ***a.*** Die on India, die sunk on card
  - black *400.*
  - dark red *400.*
  - orange red *400.*
- ***b.*** Die on ivory paper, about 24x28mm
  - black *500.*
  - scarlet *500.*
  - black brown *500.*
  - blue *500.*

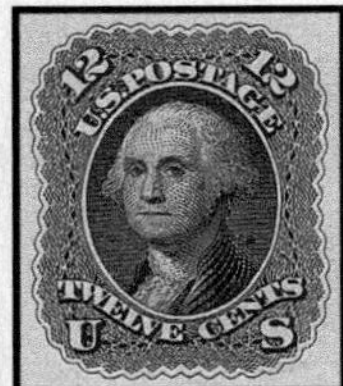
69-E6

Incomplete die No. 444, without corner ornaments.

69-E6 12c
- ***a.*** "Premiere Gravure" die essay on India, mounted on card (**formerly Nos. 59P1, 59TC1**)
  - black *2,500.*
  - scarlet *2,500.*
  - dark green *2,500.*
- ***b.*** RA "Premiere Gravure" small die essay on white wove, 28x31mm (1903) (**formerly No. 59P2**), black *450.*
- ***c.*** PP "Premiere Gravure" small die essay on pale cream soft wove, 24x29mm (1915) (**formerly No. 59P2a**), black *1,750.*
- ***d.*** "Premiere Gravure" plate No. 5 essay on India (**formerly No. 59P3**), black *350.*

69-E6e

- ***e.*** Finished "Premiere Gravure" plate essay on semitransparent stamp paper, perf. 12, gummed (**formerly No. 59**), black *90,000.*

70-E5

Washington vignette in incomplete frame.

70-E5 24c Die on India, black *3,250.*

70-E6

Die size: 56½x56mm
Incomplete die (No. 445): silhouette unfinished, especially scrolls around numerals; shadows over numerals not acid etched.

70-E6 24c Die on India, die sunk on card
- black *900.*
- violet *900.*
- gray violet *900.*
- dark violet *900.*
- scarlet *900.*
- green *900.*
- orange *900.*
- red brown *900.*
- orange brown *900.*
- orange yellow *900.*
- rose red *900.*
- gray *900.*
- steel blue *900.*
- blue *900.*

For finished "Premiere Gravure" trial color plate proof on semitransparent stamp paper, perf 12, gummed (formerly No. 60), see 70TC6 in the Trial Color, Die and Plate Proof section.

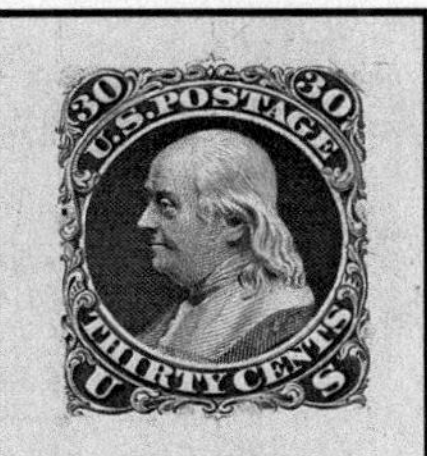
71-E1

Die size: 46x60mm
Incomplete die (No. 446): additional ornaments at top and bottom in pencil, as later engraved.

71-E1 30c Die on India, black *1,750.*

71-E2

"Premiere Gravure" die: left side of frame and silhouette at lower right unfinished.

71-E2 30c
- ***a.*** "Premiere Gravure" die essay on India, die sunk on card (**formerly No. 61TC1**)
  - black *1,750.*
  - green *1,750.*
  - dull gray blue *1,750.*
  - violet brown *1,750.*
  - scarlet *1,750.*
  - dull rose *1,750.*
- ***b.*** "Premiere Gravure" plate essay on India (**formerly No. 61P3**), deep red orange *500.*
- ***c.*** "Premiere Gravure" plate essay on card
  - black (split thin) *500.*
  - blue *750.*
- ***d.*** "Premiere Gravure" plate essay on card, black 12x2mm SPECIMEN overprint, blue *750.*
- ***e.*** "Premiere Gravure" plate essay on semitransparent stamp paper
  - deep red orange *1,250.*

yellow orange *1,250.*
lemon yellow *1,250.*
dark orange yellow *1,250.*
dull orange yellow *1,250.*

For finished "Premiere Gravure" trial color proof on semi-transparent stamp paper, perf 12, gummed (formerly No. 61), see No. 71TC6 in the Trial Color, Die and Plate Proof section.

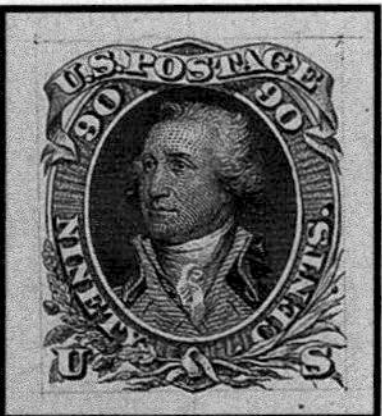

72-E6

Die size: 54x63mm
Incomplete die: without thin lines at bottom of frame and in upper left triangle between label and frame, and without leaves at left of U and right of S.

72-E6 90c Die on India, blue (shades) *1,000.*

72-E7

Similar to 72-E6 but lines added in upper left triangle, leaves added at left of U and at right of S. Exists with and without imprint and Die No. 447 added below design.

72-E7 90c
a. Die on India, die sunk on card, black *1,750.*
b. "Premiere Gravure" die essay on India, thin line under bottom center frame (**formerly Nos. 62P1, 62TC1**)
blue *1,350.*
black *1,750.*
c. RA "Premiere Gravure" small die essay on white wove, 28x31mm (1903) (**formerly No. 62P2**), blue *500.*
d. PP "Premiere Gravure" small die essay on pale cream soft wove, 24x29mm (1915) (**formerly No. 62P2a**), blue *1,750.*
e. "Premiere Gravure" plate essay on India, blue *500.*
f. "Premiere Gravure" plate essay on card, black (split thin) *500.*
g. "Premiere Gravure" plate essay on semi-transparent stamp paper (**formerly Nos. 62aP4, 62TC4**)
blue, pair, gummed *5,500.*
blue green *275.*

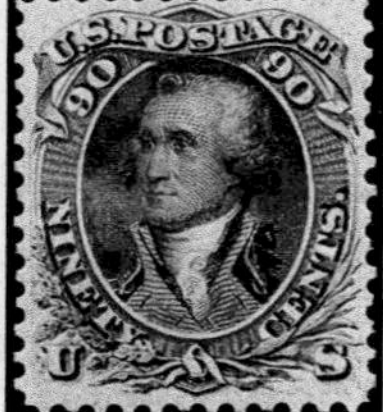

72-E7h

h. Finished "Premiere Gravure" plate essay on semitransparent stamp paper, perf. 12, gummed (**formerly No. 62**), blue *50,000.*

Die size: 54x63mm
Similar to Nos. 72-E6 and 72-E7 but leaf at left of "U" only, no shading around "U" and "S," leaf and some shading missing at bottom right above "S," shading missing in top label, etc., faint ms. "8" at bottom of backing card.

72-E8 90c Die on India, die sunk on 3¼x3½-inch card, dark blue —

63-E13b

63-E13g

Design size: 20x47mm
Die size: 57x95mm
Bowlsby patent coupon at top of 1c stamp design.

63-E13 1c
a. Die on India, die sunk on card
black *1,750.*
red *1,750.*
scarlet *1,750.*
orange *1,750.*
orange brown *1,750.*
brown *1,750.*
yellow brown *1,750.*
blue green *1,750.*
olive green *1,750.*
olive *1,750.*
blue *1,750.*
violet *1,750.*
red violet *1,750.*
gray *1,750.*
gray brown *1,750.*
dull orange yellow *1,750.*
b. Die on white glazed paper
black *1,750.*
dark brown *1,750.*
scarlet *1,750.*
blue *1,750.*
c. Plate on pelure paper, gummed, red *300.*
d. Plate on white paper, red *250.*
e. Plate on white paper, with 13x16mm points-up grill, red *350.*
Split grill *600.*
f. Plate on white paper, perf. all around and between stamp and coupon
red *175.*
blue *175.*
g. Plate on white paper, perf. all around, imperf. between stamp and coupon
red *175.*
blue *175.*
h. Plate on white paper, perf. all around, rouletted between stamp and coupon
red *300.*
blue *300.*
i. Plate on India paper, black 750.

1861-66 Essays
Authors Unknown

73-E2

Design size: 21x26mm

73-E2 2c Pencil and watercolor on thick card, bright green *3,750.*

73-E3

Design size: 21x26mm
Indian vignette. Typographed printings from woodcuts. Plates of three rows of three, one row each of Nos. 73-E3, 73-E4, 73-E5. Listings are of singles.

73-E3 2c
a. Plate on white wove
red *30.*
scarlet *30.*
violet *30.*
black *30.*
blue *30.*
green *30.*
b. Plate on mauve wove
red *50.*
violet *50.*
black *50.*
blue *50.*
green *50.*
c. Plate on yellow wove
red *50.*
violet *50.*
black *50.*
blue *50.*
green *50.*
d. Plate on yellow laid
red *50.*
violet *50.*
black *50.*
blue *50.*
green *50.*
e. Plate on pink laid
red *50.*
violet *50.*
black *50.*
blue *50.*
green *50.*
f. Plate on green laid
red *50.*
violet *50.*
black *50.*
blue *50.*
green *50.*
g. Plate on cream laid
red *50.*
violet *50.*
black *50.*
blue *50.*
green *50.*
h. Plate on pale yellow wove
red *50.*
green *50.*
blue *50.*
i. Plate on yellow-surfaced card, violet *50.*

73-E4

Design size: 23x26½mm
Small head of Liberty in shield. Typographed printings from woodcuts. On plate with Nos. 73-E3 and 73-E5. Listings are of singles.

73-E4 3c
a. Plate on white wove
red *30.*
scarlet *30.*
violet *30.*
black *30.*
blue *30.*
green *30.*
b. Plate on mauve wove, violet *50.*
c. Plate on yellow wove
red *50.*
violet *50.*
black *50.*
blue *50.*
green *50.*
d. Plate on yellow laid
red *50.*
violet *50.*
black *50.*
blue *50.*
green *50.*
e. Plate on pink laid
carmine *50.*
violet *50.*
black *50.*
blue *50.*
green *50.*
f. Plate on green laid
carmine *50.*
green *50.*
dull violet *50.*
blue *50.*
g. Plate on cream laid
red *50.*
violet *50.*
black *50.*
blue *50.*
green *50.*
h. Plate on pale yellow wove
red *50.*
green *50.*
blue *50.*
i. Plate on yellow-surfaced card, violet *50.*
j. Plate on fawn wove, green *50.*

73-E5

Design size: 22½x25½mm

Large head of Liberty. Typographed impressions from woodcut. On plate with Nos. 73-E3 and 73-E4. Listings are of singles.

73-E5 5c
- ***a.*** Plate on white wove
  - red *30.*
  - scarlet *30.*
  - violet *30.*
  - black *30.*
  - blue *30.*
  - green *30.*
- ***b.*** Plate on mauve wove, violet *50.*
- ***c.*** Plate on yellow wove
  - red *50.*
  - violet *50.*
  - black *50.*
  - blue *50.*
  - green *50.*
- ***d.*** Plate on yellow laid
  - red *50.*
  - violet *50.*
  - black *50.*
  - blue *50.*
  - green *50.*
- ***e.*** Plate on pink laid
  - red *50.*
  - black *50.*
  - blue *50.*
  - green *50.*
- ***f.*** Plate on green laid
  - red *50.*
  - violet *50.*
  - black *50.*
  - blue *50.*
  - green *50.*
- ***g.*** Plate on cream laid
  - red *50.*
  - black *50.*
  - blue *50.*
  - green *50.*
- ***h.*** Plate on pale yellow wove
  - red *50.*
  - blue *50.*
  - green *50.*
- ***i.*** Plate on yellow-surfaced card, violet *50.*

73-E6

Size of design: 21x27mm

Indian vignette. Typographed impressions from woodcut.

73-E6 10c
- ***a.*** Die on proof paper
  - black *200.*
  - gray black *200.*
  - carmine *200.*
  - dusky red *200.*
  - brown *200.*
  - green *200.*
  - blue *200.*
  - violet *200.*
- ***b.*** Plate on white paper (pane of 4)
  - red *600.*
  - violet *600.*
  - brown *600.*
  - black *600.*
  - blue *600.*
  - green *600.*
- ***c.*** Plate on soft cream card (pane of 4)
  - black *600.*
  - red *600.*
  - blue *600.*
  - green *600.*
  - red violet *600.*

1864 Decalcomania Essays Re-use Prevention Henry Lowenberg

79-E65P5

79-E66P5

79-E67P5

79-E71P5

79-E72P5

79-E73P5

The following Decalcomania essays, patented in 1864, are plate proofs of the 1861 issue printed on the back of goldbeaters' skin paper and gummed on the side of the impressions. Impressions can be seen on the non-gummed side and show in reverse. The concept was that any attempt to remove the stamp from an envelope would result in the image remaining on the envelope, and the goldbeaters' skin would come off the envelope without an image. All the essays listed below are printed on goldbeaters' skin except where noted, and all are imperforate except one version of the 3c denomination.

Values are for essentially sound examples with a very minimal amount of flaking or creasing.

79-E65P5 3c
- ***a.*** Imperforate
  - rose 50.00
  - blue 150.00
- ***b.*** Perforated, rose 75.00
- ***c.*** Lake on pale blue 300.00

79-E66P5 3c
- ***a.*** Lake 100.00
- ***b.*** Lake on pale green 150.00

79-E67P5 5c
- brown 75.00

79-E68P5 10c
- ***a.*** Green 150.00
- ***b.*** Green on pale rose 250.00

79-E69P5 12c
- black 300.00

79-E70P5 24c
- ***a.*** Lilac 75.00
- ***b.*** Lilac on pale green 250.00

79-E71P5 30c
- ***a.*** Orange 100.00
- ***b.*** Orange on blue-green 250.00

79-E72P5 90c
- dark blue 75.00

79-E73P5 2c
- ***a.*** Black 75.00
- ***b.*** Black on pale rose 250.00

1867 Essays Re-use Prevention Authors Unknown

Unfolded — 79-E1

Folded — 79-E1

Design size (folded): 18x23mm
Design size (unfolded): 18x58mm

Folded and scored four times, horiz. crease at center. Bronze overprint U 2 S, (2 punched out). Lower ⅔ gummed below second fold so top ⅓ could be torn off for canceling.

79-E1 2c On white paper, dull red violet *5,000.*

79-E2

Similar to No. 79-E1 but larger and not folded. Pierced with S-shaped cuts as well as punched out 2.

79-E2 2c
- ***a.*** On white paper, US 7½mm high, bronze, US in dull black *5,000.*
- ***b.*** On white paper, US 10mm high, bronze, US in violet *5,000.*

79-E3

Cuts as on back

U.S. No. 73 as issued but pierced with S-shaped cuts, ovptd. in metallic color.

79-E3 2c Essay on 2c stamp, gold overprint *7,500.*

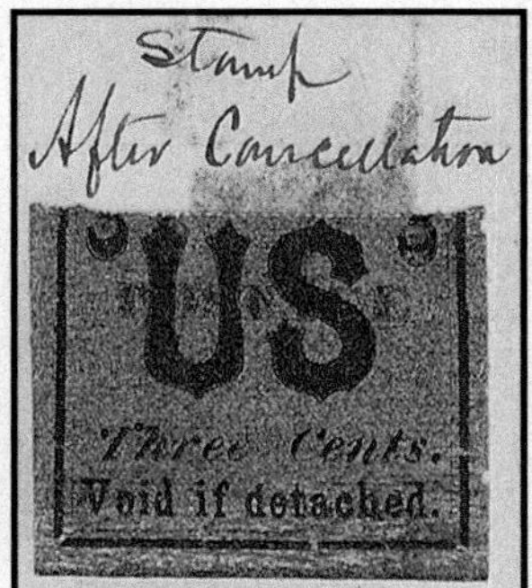

79-E5

Similar to No. 79-E1 but with punched out 3.

79-E4 3c
- ***a.*** On white paper, U 3 S black above, bronze below and on face beneath folds *5,000.*
- ***b.*** On green paper, 3 not punched out, 3 black, POSTAGE blue *5,000.*

79-E4

Similar to No. 79-E4, with "3 U.S. 3 / Three Cents / Void if detached."

79-E5 3c On green paper, black *3,000.*

79-E6

Similar to No. 79-E2 but with punched out 3, gummed.

79-E6 3c
a. On white paper, bronze over violet *3,000.*
b. On white paper, U S black, rest bronze *3,000.*

79-E7

Vignette map of U.S.

79-E7 3c On thick white paper, rouletted, green, gold 3 on map *8,500.*

79-E7A

Similar to 79-E7, without "3" on map.

79-E7A 3c On thick white paper, imperforate block of 9 (unique), black —

1867 Essays
Henry Lowenberg

79-E8

Washington vignette. Printed in reverse on back of transparent paper, reads correctly from front. Plate essays from sheets of 25.

79-E8 3c
a. Plate on onionskin paper, imperf., gummed
brown *10.*
orange brown *10.*
deep orange brown *10.*
orange *10.*
green *10.*
light green *10.*
blue green *10.*
pale green *10.*
red *10.*
light red *10.*
dark red *10.*
violet red *10.*
violet *10.*
light violet *10.*
dull pale violet *10.*
blue *10.*
dark blue *10.*
deep blue *10.*
pale blue *10.*
dull blue *10.*
gold *50.*
gray *7.*
black *7.*
carmine *7.*
b. Plate on onionskin paper, perf. 12, gummed
gray black *25.*
gray *25.*
gray violet *25.*
dull violet *25.*
brown red *25.*
c. Plate on more opaque onionskin paper, imperf.
black *25.*
red violet *25.*
dull violet *25.*
d. Plate on thick transparent paper
gray *25.*
black *25.*

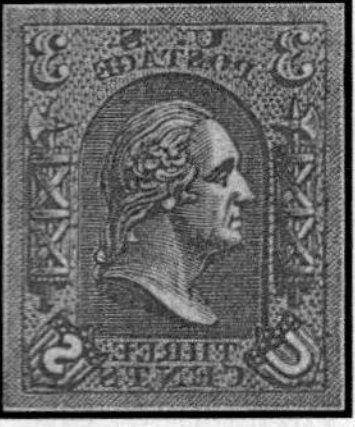
79-E9

Washington vignette. Printed with design reversed on front of various opaque papers, Plate essays are from sheets of 25.

79-E9 3c
a. Plate on white wove, imperf., gummed
blue *10.*
red *10.*
gray *10.*
brown *10.*
orange *10.*
green *10.*
yellow green *10.*
b. Plate on clear white paper, imperf.
orange *10.*
blue *10.*
gray *10.*
dark gray *10.*
c. Plate on thick wove, fugitive ink, perf., gummed
carmine *10.*
violet carmine *10.*
pale dull red *10.*
gray *10.*
pale gray *10.*
pale dull tan *10.*
green *10.*
d. As "c," strip of 3, signed Henry Lowenberg, pale tan *400.*
e. Plate on white chemically treated paper (turns blue if wet), imperf.
carmine *10.*
Prussian blue *10.*
orange *10.*
green *10.*
brown *10.*
black *10.*
f. As "e," perf.
carmine *10.*
scarlet *10.*
orange *10.*
blue *10.*
green *10.*
brown *10.*
g. Plate on India
violet brown *10.*
green *10.*
blue *10.*
dark blue *10.*
h. Plate on India, signed D.H. Craig, red *350.*
i. On white card, 62x72mm, design deeply indented, green *15.*
j. On blue wove, red *15.*
k. On orange laid
black *15.*
gray *15.*
l. On blue laid, scarlet *15.*
m. On white laid, blue *15.*
n. On pink laid, blue *15.*
o. On linen cloth
green *50.*
red *50.*
blue *50.*
p. On glazed white paper, blue *20.*

1867 Essays
John M. Sturgeon

79-E10

Liberty vignette. Curved labels top and bottom. Self-canceling: CANCELLED in colorless sensitive ink, becomes colored when wet. Patented 1867, 1868.

79-E10 10c
a. Die on stiff card, cut close, clearly engraved, not canceled, both labels completely blank, dark carmine *350.*
b. Die on wove, rough impression, CANCELLED diagonally each way, dark carmine *450.*
c. Die on thick white or tinted paper, gummed, rough impression, about 21x26mm, two lines in upper label, one line in lower label
carmine *200.*
dark carmine *200.*
very dark carmine *200.*
green *200.*
dark green *200.*
dull red violet *200.*
d. As "c," on thick pinkish paper, dark green *250.*
g. Single centered in 6-inch wide strip of thick white paper, almost always cut in at top and bottom, dark carmine *400.*
h. Horiz. row of five designs on thick white paper, 10mm apart
dark carmine *1,200.*
dark purple *1,200.*
black *1,200.*
i. Single on blue card, ovptd. seal BRITISH CONSULATE, V.R. in center, black *1,250.*

American Bank Note Co.

79-E11a

Design size: 16x22mm
Vignette of Columbia. Probably submitted by Charles F. Steel.

79-E11 2c and 3c
a. Engraved die on thick yellowish wove, black —

79-E11b

Design size: 18x22mm
Engraving of frame lines, horiz. shading lines and "3" and "2" added to Columbia vignette, black
b. Engraved die on thick yellowish wove, black —
c. Engraved plate on thick yellowish wove, imperf. (usually found in upper left margin blocks)
rose scarlet *300.*
Block of 4 *1,250.*
blue green *300.*
Block of 4 *1,250.*

79-E11d

d. Engraved plate on stamp paper, perf. 12, gummed
black *175.*
rose scarlet *175.*
blue green *175.*
blue *175.*

Author Unknown

79-E12

Design size: 20x26mm

Vignette of Liberty in circle of stars. Vertical color lines outside design to 24x28mm. Curved labels blank. Lithographed.

79-E12 No denomination
- ***a.*** Die on white paper, dull violet *2,750.*
- ***b.*** Die on bluish paper, blue *2,750.*

1867 Grill Essays National Bank Note Co.

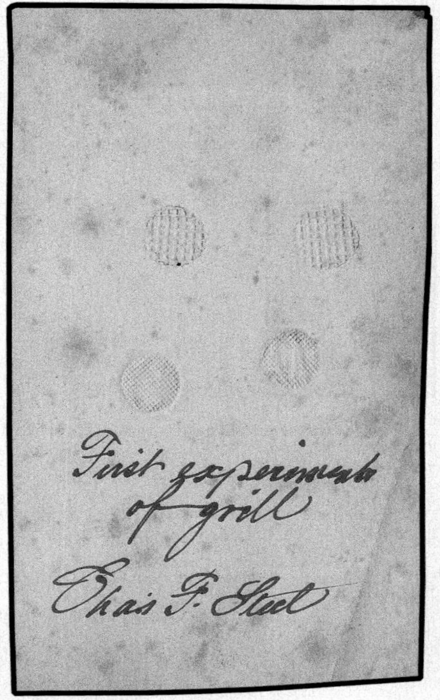

79-E13a

Grill essays patented by Charles F. Steel.

79-E13
- ***a.*** Wove paper, 80x140mm, impressed with four diff. seals, crossed lines and square dots down, circles 11 or 12mm *9,000.*

- ***b.*** Grills in odd shapes on white wove, each about 20x25mm
  - cross *1,500.*
  - star in square *1,500.*
  - horizontal lined oval in square *1,500.*
  - diagonal lined oval in square *1,500.*

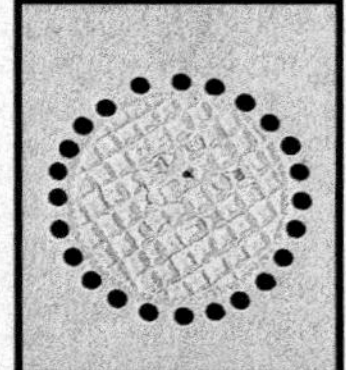

79-E13c

- ***c.*** White wove, gummed, 15mm circle with points down grill, surrounded by 24 perforated holes *1,000.*
- ***d.*** White wove, quadrille batonne watermark, 12mm colored circle with points down grill around 3, roughly grilled colorless 3 below, carmine *1,250.*

79-E13e

- ***e.*** Colorless 12mm grilled circle as on "d," on tan wove, perf. 12 *200.*
- ***f.*** As "e," yellow wove *200.*
- ***g.*** As "e," white wove, block of 6 with ms. "Subject to a half hour pressure after embossing" *3,500.*
- ***h.*** Colorless 15mm points down grilled circle on white wove, perf. 12 *200.*

79-E14a

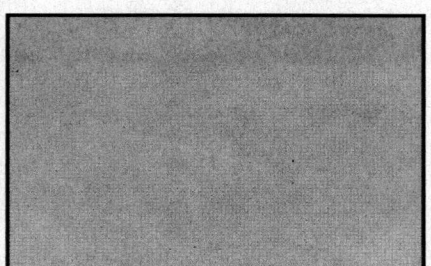

79-E14b

Allover grill.

79-E14
- ***a.*** White wove, about 47x26mm, points down grill, stamped with red 6-digit number 450.
- ***b.*** Wove paper in various colors, about 85x40mm, points up grill as adopted
  - white *200.*
  - pale pink *200.*
  - salmon *200.*
  - light yellow *200.*
  - light gray green *200.*
  - light blue *200.*
  - pale lilac *200.*
  - light gray *200.*

79-E15

Experimental grills on perf. or imperf. stamps or stamp-size pieces of paper.

79-E15
- ***a.*** Allover grill of small squares, points down (points do not break paper as on issued stamp, No. 79)
  - on 3c rose, gummed (No. 65) *250.*
  - on 3c lake, imperf. pair, gummed (No. 66aP4) *250.*
- ***b.*** As "a" but points up, on 3c stamp, perf. 12, gummed
  - black *200.*
  - rose *200.*
- ***c.*** As "a" but points up, imperf pair, gummed
  - 3c rose (**formerly No. 79P4**) *500.*
  - 3c lake (**formerly No. 66aP4**) *500.*

79-E15d

- ***d.*** Allover pinpoint grill (so-called "Music Box" grill), points up, on No. 65 (plates 11, 34, 52) *75.*
- ***e.*** As "d" but points down, on 3c rose (plate 11) *125.*
- ***f.*** 15x16mm grill on stamp size white wove paper, perf. 12, gummed *125.*
- ***g.*** C grill, 13x16mm, points down on stamp size wove paper, perf. 12, gummed
  - white *100.*
  - yellowish *100.*
  - pinkish *100.*
  - blue *100.*
- ***h.*** As "g" but points up, on white wove *100.*
- ***i.*** C grill on 1c stamp (No. 63), points down *5,500.*
- ***j.*** C grill on 3c stamp (No. 65)
  - points up *4,000.*
  - points down *4,000.*

The 3c C grill essay is almost identical to the issued stamp. There are slight differences in the essay grill which match those on No. 79-E15i and Nos. 79-E15k through 79-E15n.

- ***k.*** C grill on 5c stamp (No. 76)
  - points up *4,000.*
  - points down *4,000.*
- ***l.*** C grill on 10c stamp (No. 68)
  - points up *4,000.*
  - points down *4,000.*
- ***m.*** C grill on 12c stamp (No. 69)
  - points up *4,000.*
  - points down *4,000.*
- ***n.*** C grill on 30c stamp (No. 71)
  - points up *4,000.*
  - points down *4,000.*
- ***o.*** E grill, 11x13mm, points up, on stamp size white wove paper, perf. 12, gummed *100.*
- ***p.*** As "o," points down *100.*

1867 "Z" grill Experimental Essays

85C-E1

85C-E1 Sheet of white wove stamp paper, imperf., gummed, with experimental "Z" grill impressions, 11x14mm, points down 175.

85C-E2

85C-E2 Z grill, 11x14mm, points down on stamp size wove paper, perf. 12, partly gummed
- white *200.*
- salmon *200.*
- yellow *200.*
- greenish *200.*
- dull violet *200.*
- pale lilac *200.*

These were made on fully perforated sheet selvage from the 3c and 12c essay panes.

85E-E1 12c Experimental "Z" grill essay, 11x14mm, on heavily horizontally laid paper, gummed, perforated 12
- ***a.*** On thin transparent paper white paper (not laid), blue *250.*
- ***b.*** On salmon paper
  - black *250.*
  - brown *250.*
  - green *250.*
  - blue *250.*
- ***c.*** On deep orange paper
  - black *250.*
  - scarlet *250.*

brown	250.
green	250.
blue	250.
d. On yellow paper	
black	250.
brown	250.
e. On straw paper	
brown	250.
green	250.
f. On green paper	
black	250.
scarlet	250.
brown	250.
green	250.
blue	250.
g. On lilac paper	
black	250.
scarlet	250.
brown	250.
green	250.
blue	250.
h. On pale rose paper	
black	250.
scarlet	250.
brown	250.
green	250.
blue	250.

Continental Bank Note Co.

White wove paper about 6x9 inches with 7x9½mm grills spaced as they would fall on centers of stamps in a sheet.

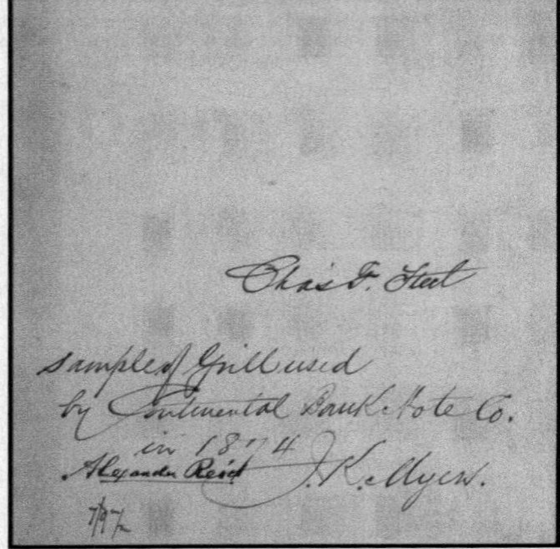

79-E16a

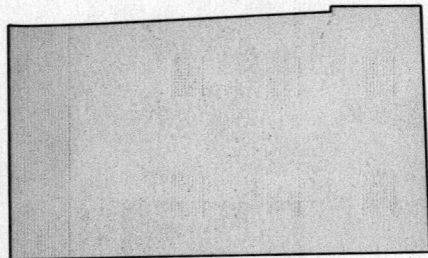

79-E16d

79-E16

a. End roller grill at left, ms. "Chas. F. Steel-Sample of Grill used by Continental Bank Note Co. in 1874. Alexander Reid. J.K. Myers."	*3,000.*
b. Without end roller grill, ms. "Grill of Continental Bank Note Co. Chas. F. Steel."	*3,000.*
c. End roller grill at right, same inscription as "b"	*3,000.*
d. On soft card, six grills	*600.*

Wilbur I. Trafton

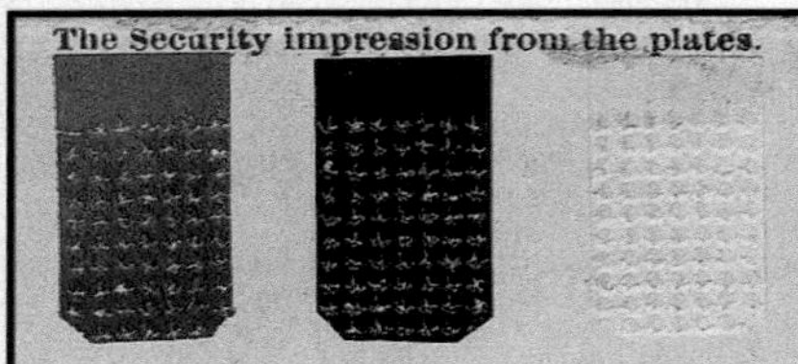

79-E17

Coarse grill in 15mm circle with 7 points up in 11mm, found on 1873 1c, some with 18mm circular cancel, stuck down on printed ad circular along with black, red and albino grill impressions (two each) on paper labeled "The Security Impression from the plates."

79-E17 Entire ad circular with grill examples *750.*

National Bank Note Co.

79-E18

79-E18c

79-E18h

Albino 3 in points down shield-shaped grill in lithographed frame of 3c 1861 stamp.

79-E18 3c

a. Die on thick white paper, gummed	
black	*1,000.*
deep pink	*1,000.*
b. As "a," with Washington, D.C. Feb. 21 pmk.	
black	*1,750.*
deep pink	*1,750.*
c. As "a" but grill with points up, black	*1,000.*
d. As "a," perf. 12, gummed, black	*1,000.*
e. Die on yellow wove, gummed	
black	*1,000.*
red	*1,000.*
f. Die on orange wove	
black	*1,000.*
carmine	*1,000.*
g. Die on yellow laid, black	*1,000.*
h. Numeral handcolored, dull carmine	*1,500.*
i. Frame only, no grill, on grayish wove with pencil "McDonald P.O. Dept. Steel Nature(?)", pale orange brown	*1,500.*

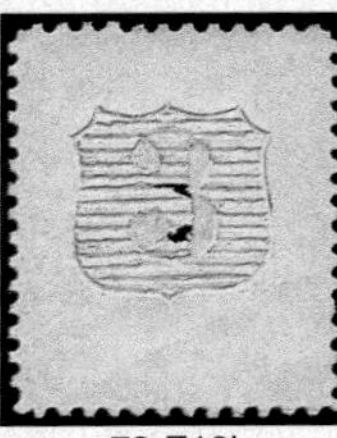

79-E18j

79-E18k

Albino 3 in 13x14mm shield made up of embossed narrow spaced horiz. lines.

j. White wove stamp paper, 22x27mm, perf. 12, gummed 450.

Albino 3 in 13x14mm shield slightly different from No. 79-E18j.

k. As "j," different shield 350.

79-E19a

Illustration reduced.

Typographed impression of frame, lettering and numerals of 3c 1861 stamp with 3 in double lined shield in center. In strip of three about 20mm apart, impression of 3 and shield progressively lighter on impressions two and three.

79-E19 3c

a. Engraved (die No. 1570), green	*3,000.*
b. Typographed in color on white paper	
blue green	*2,750.*
dark red brown	*2,750.*
c. As "b," colored and colorless parts interchanged, on thick paper	
blue green	*2,750.*
dark red brown	*2,750.*

79-E20

Embossed albino shield, uncleared purple ink on rest of die.

79-E20 Shield design, die on card —

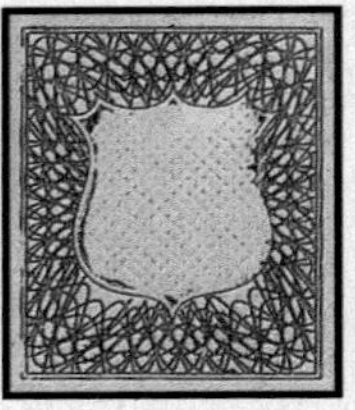

79-E21

Lathework frame with shield shaped vignette cut out, albino 3 in circular grill in center.

79-E21 3c

a. Thick paper, perf. 12	
blue	*500.*
carmine	*500.*
b. At left in strip of 3 with 2 No. 79-E13f, latter black cancels, blue	*3,500.*
c. Lathework frame on thin wove, allover diagonal grill, imperf., gummed, blue	*500.*

79-E22

Lathework frame similar to No. 79-E21 but vignette of 6 horiz. bars with 3 in center printed in glossy ink.

79-E22 3c On pink lilac paper, blue 3,000.

79-E23

Design of 3c 1861 stamp typographed in relief for surface printing. Single impression lightly block sunk 63x62mm in color. Design has 21x26½mm border inside 23x28½mm colorless rectangle.

79-E23 3c

a. Die on 64x75mm ivory paper, black	*400.*
b. Die on India, dull violet-red-red	*325.*
c. Die on 59x54mm stiff white card, color about 40mm wide (not extending to edges)	
light red violet	*325.*
carmine	*325.*
blue	*325.*
d. Washington head only, lines on face around eye, on soft card	
dim blue-green blue	*250.*
dim orange-orange red	*250.*

On 17x21mm plain colored rectangle printed through a mat, surrounded by 55x62mm colorless rectangle, vert. 4½mm wide color bands at sides inside 64x62mm die sinkage.

e. Washington head with dots around eye, on 17x42mm solid color, on 77x45mm stiff white paper, dull violet-red	*250.*
f. India paper on soft white card block sunk 63x62mm, dull violet-red-red with solid color margins	*250.*

Colored India generally cut away outside colorless rectangle 23x28½mm, design heavily embossed through to card beneath.

g. As "f," trimmed to shape	
dark carmine	*350.*
orange	*350.*
blue green	*350.*
red violet	*350.*

h. Complete design on India, sunk on card, trimmed to shape
blue *100.*
dull green blue *100.*
i. Plate typographed on white wove, imperf., gummed
dim red *50.*
dim light orange red *50.*
dim blue green *50.*
dim pale blue *50.*
dim dark blue *50.*
dusky violet red *50.*

Color outside design generally fills rectangle, design impression shows on back.

j. Complete design on glossy sticky paper, deep violet red *150.*
k. As "j," on pelure, perf. 12, gummed, rose *175.*
l. As "k," allover grill, dim red *150.*
m. As "k," 13x16mm grill, gray black *150.*

79-E24 79-E24c

Block sinkage: 65x76mm
Washington head only.

79-E24 3c
a. Lithographed, face dotted, on 65x76mm solid color background
black *750.*
red violet *750.*
olive black *750.*
b. Typographed, background irregular edge, on card, gray black *1,500.*
c. Face lined, on 64x72mm solid color background
black *750.*
scarlet *750.*

79-E25

Plate essays of complete 1861 3c design.

79-E25 3c
a. Plate on hard white transparent wove, dark red *50.*
b. Plate on more opaque white wove, dim red *50.*
c. Plate on Gibson patent starch coated opaque white paper, generally crinkled, lathework design usually poorly printed
orange red *25.*
deep orange red *25.*
pink *25.*
dull yellow *25.*
yellow orange *25.*
dull yellow orange *25.*
brown yellow *25.*
brown *25.*
green *25.*
blue green *25.*
blue *25.*
light blue *25.*
d. Plate on semitransparent white wove
dull pale blue *20.*
green *20.*
dull yellow orange *20.*
e. Plate on pale green paper, clearly printed, dark g-b green *40.*
f. Plate on white wove, 13x16mm points down grill, gummed, dark blue *40.*
g. Plate on lilac gray paper, 13x16mm grill, gummed
dark blue *40.*
dull red *40.*
black *40.*
h. Plate on white paper (ungrilled), perf. 12, gummed
red *25.*
light red *25.*
pale red *25.*
light orange red *25.*
deep yellow orange *25.*
brown *25.*
dark green *25.*
deep blue *25.*
dull g-b blue *25.*
gray black *25.*
i. As "h," ms. A or B in UL corner, red *50.*
j. Plate on white paper, 13x16mm points down grill, perf. 12, gummed
black *25.*
gray black *25.*
pale red *25.*
light red *25.*
orange red *25.*
deep orange yellow *25.*
brown *25.*
dark brown *25.*
green *25.*
blue *25.*
dark blue *25.*
k. As "j," ms. "s No. 6" on back
red *50.*
gray black *50.*
dark blue *50.*
l. As "j," but grill points up
red *40.*
pink *40.*
pale rose *40.*
brown *40.*
orange yellow *40.*
deep red orange *40.*
green *40.*
dull blue *40.*
dull light blue *40.*
m. As "l," pair with blue oval "American Bank Note Co. April 17, '79", pink *150.*
n. Plate on greenish gray chemical paper, 13x16mm grill, perf. 12
black *50.*
green *50.*
dark blue *50.*
orange red *50.*
light yellow gray *50.*
light red gray *50.*
o. As "n," without grill
red *50.*
rose *50.*
p. Plate on pelure, without grill, imperf., gummed, dim red *50.*
q. As "p," perf. 12, dim red *50.*

79-E26c

Illustration Reduced.
Plate impressions of 1861 3c stamp overprinted with various safety network designs. Inks probably fugitive.

79-E26 3c
a. Vert. pair on 58x80mm India, overprint die 54x71mm or more, small ONE repeated in 41 vert. lines per 40mm, rose pink, overprint deep orange yellow *2,000.*
b. As "a," block of 6 inscribed "J. Sangster Pat. 190376, Jan. 6, 1877" *3,500.*
c. 65TC3, "VEINTE" overprint, in miniature sheet of 12, perf. 12, black, overprint orange *7,500.*

Type B

3c 1861 printed in various colors in miniature sheets of 12 with safety ovpts. (Apparently only one sheet printed of each color combination, except two Type D combinations known both perf. and imperf.)

d. Type A
perf. 12, dull violet, overprint gray *425.*
perf. 12, rose red, overprint gray blue *425.*
perf. 12, violet, overprint gray tan *425.*
imperf., pale olive, overprint pale tan *425.*
imperf., green, overprint gray tan *425.*

e. Type B
perf. 12, green, overprint pale tan *425.*
perf. 12, violet, overprint gray tan *425.*
perf. 12, dull red brown, ovpt. pale brown *425.*
perf. 12, dark dull red brown, overprint pale brown *425.*

Type C

Type D

f. Type C
perf. 12, dull violet, overprint gray tan *550.*
perf. 12, dull red, overprint gray blue *550.*
perf. 12, rose red, overprint gray blue *550.*
perf. 12, green, overprint gray tan *550.*
imperf., rose red, overprint pale tan *550.*
imperf., pale rose red, overprint pale tan *550.*
imperf., yellow brown, overprint tan *550.*

g. Type D
perf. 12, dull violet, overprint gray blue *550.*
perf. 12, rose red, overprint gray blue *550.*
perf. 12, light red brown, overprint pale brown *550.*
perf. 12, dark green, overprint dull blue *550.*
imperf., pale olive, overprint tan *550.*
imperf., ultramarine, overprint tan *550.*
imperf., dull violet, overprint gray blue *550.*
imperf., dull violet, overprint pale green *550.*
imperf., dark green, overprint dull blue *550.*

79-E27

79-E27c

Design size: 20½x26½mm
Engraved in relief for surface printing, large 2 vignette, on same die with No. 79-E28, 20mm apart. Also essayed for envelopes on thick papers.

79-E27 2c
a. Untrimmed die, 30x42mm, on paper with "US" monogram, pale rose *850.*
b. Die on stiff glazed paper, 63x50mm, black *600.*
c. Trimmed die on India, on thick soft card, colorless parts in relief
black *450.*
red *450.*
orange *450.*
violet red *450.*
d. Die on 35x40mm white wove, imperf., gummed
blue *450.*
albino *450.*
e. Die on white wove, perf. 12, gummed, smoky violet red *450.*
f. Untrimmed die on white wove, 61x42mm, black *550.*

79-E28

79-E28g

Design size: 21x25½mm

Engraved in relief for surface printing, large 3 in shield vignette, on same die with No. 79-E27, 20mm apart. Also essayed for envelopes on thick papers.

79-E28 3c

a. Untrimmed die on stiff ivory paper, showing color 30x42mm
- black *700.*
- rose *700.*
- orange *700.*
- blue *700.*

b. Untrimmed die on India with No. 79-E27, both embossed, yellow orange *1,000.*

c. Trimmed die heavily struck on India, card mounted, colorless parts in relief
- black *500.*
- red *500.*
- orange *500.*

d. Die on wide laid paper, "US" monogram, perf. 12, gummed
- pale rose *250.*
- dull brown yellow *250.*

e. Die on greenish wove, 10x12mm points down grill, imperf., gummed, dull brown *250.*

f. Die on white paper, perf. 12, gummed
- smoky violet red *250.*
- green *250.*

g. Underprinted design only on thin white wove
- light blue *350.*
- albino *350.*

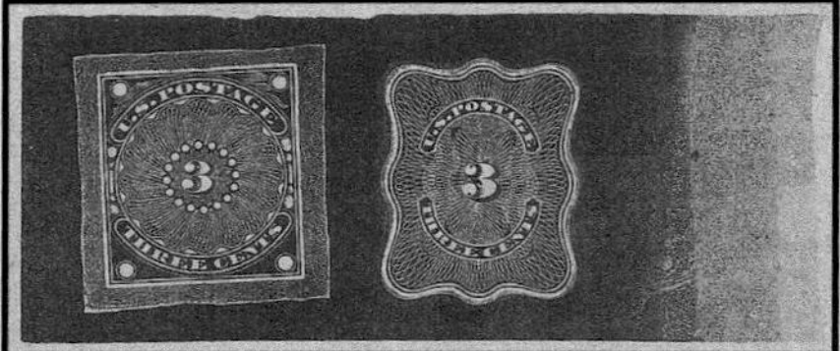
79-E28H

Illustration reduced.

Design size: 68x38mm

Two compound surface-printed designs, "3" within ornate frame.

79-E28H 3c Untrimmed die on wove paper, green *1,250.*

79-E29

1861 1c frame only.

79-E29 1c

a. Die on thin crisp paper, safety design underprint, black on dull olive green *2,750.*

b. Die on pink paper, 18x13mm points down grill, imperf., gummed, red brown *1,750.*

c. Die on pink "laid" paper, red *1,750.*

d. Die on pale pink paper, red brown *1,750.*

e. Die on transparent white paper, red brown *1,750.*

f. Die on thick yellow paper, red brown *1,750.*

g. Die on thin transparent white paper, 11x13mm points down grill, perf. 12, gummed, red brown *1,750.*

h. As "g," imperf. *2,000.*

79-E29i

As No. 79-E29 but with monogram in vignette.

i. Die on transparent white stamp paper, perf. 12, gummed, red brown *11,000.*

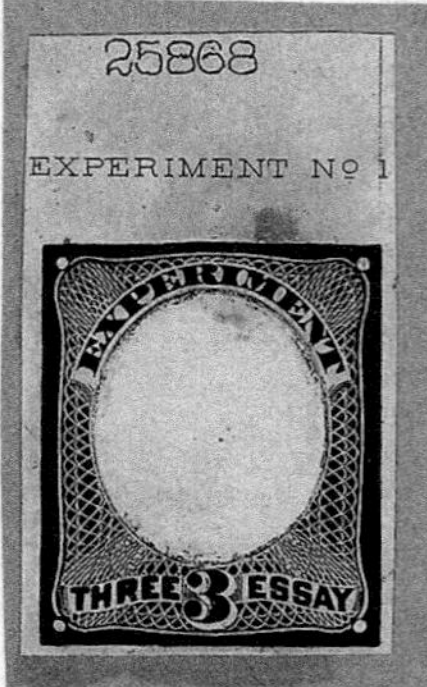

79-E29X

Similar to frame design of No. 79-E32 but with colors reversed, "Experiment" in top label, "THREE 3 ESSAY" in bottom label, blank paste-up in vignette area, "25868" and "EXPERIMENT No. 1" on paper above design. Believed to be a unique American Bank Note Co. essay model.

79-E29X 3c Die on wove, black *1,000.*

79-E30

Design size: 20x26mm

Block size: 64x76½mm

Vignette of Liberty. Typographed.

79-E30 3c

a. Head only on solid color (die size: 67x76mm), on 32x37mm stiff yellowish wove
- black *850.*
- blue green *850.*

b. Vignette only, on 66x100mm card
- black *750.*
- blue green *750.*
- blue *750.*

c. Vignette only, on proof paper
- bright blue *600.*
- blue green *600.*
- black *600.*

d. Complete design, untrimmed block, colorless 22x27 rectangle around design, broad outer edge in color, on stiff yellowish wove
- black *750.*
- blue green *750.*
- violet brown *750.*
- bright violet red *750.*
- red violet *750.*
- buff *750.*

e. As "d," on proof paper
- buff *750.*
- deep blue green *750.*
- red brown *750.*
- carmine *750.*
- black *750.*

f. Die on proof paper, perf. 12, vignette oval perf. 16, carmine *200.*

g. Die on stiff ivory paper about 28x32mm
- black *175.*
- carmine *175.*
- yellow *175.*

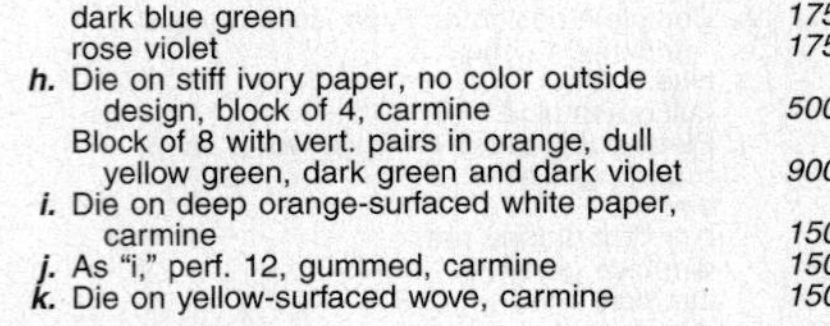
- dark blue green *175.*
- rose violet *175.*

h. Die on stiff ivory paper, no color outside design, block of 4, carmine *500.*

Block of 8 with vert. pairs in orange, dull yellow green, dark green and dark violet *900.*

i. Die on deep orange-surfaced white paper, carmine *150.*

j. As "i," perf. 12, gummed, carmine *150.*

k. Die on yellow-surfaced wove, carmine *150.*

79-E30l

l. Die with outer color removed, on 64x90mm white wove stamp paper with imprint below, imperf., gummed
- carmine *175.*
- scarlet *175.*
- dim orange red *175.*
- orange *175.*
- dull yellow orange *175.*
- pale dull yellow *175.*
- brown *175.*
- lemon *175.*
- yellow green *175.*
- dull olive green *175.*
- dull greenish gray *175.*
- dim blue green *175.*
- dull blue *175.*
- dull red violet *175.*
- pale red violet *175.*

m. As "l," tete-beche pairs, each with imprint
- carmine, orange *350.*
- buff, pale lilac *350.*
- dark orange brown, yellow *350.*
- dull green gray *350.*

79-E30n

n. As "l," perf. 12, vignette oval perf. 16 (also found without paper outside perfs.
- carmine *150.*
- pale rose *150.*
- dim scarlet *150.*
- dull scarlet *150.*
- dim orange red *150.*
- light red brown *150.*
- dark brown *150.*
- orange *150.*
- dull orange *150.*
- dismal orange *150.*
- dull brown orange *150.*
- pale dull yellow *150.*
- dull brown *150.*
- yellow brown *150.*
- dull olive green *150.*
- dim dark yellow orange *150.*
- light yellow green *150.*
- green *150.*
- dim blue green *150.*
- dark blue green *150.*
- dull greenish gray *150.*
- dull yellowish gray *150.*
- dull blue *150.*
- dim red violet *150.*
- dull red violet *150.*
- pale red violet *150.*
- red violet *150.*

79-E30o

o. Plate essay on wove, vertical pair of designs 7mm apart, in two colors shading into each other, imperf.

red brown to dark orange	*150.*
dark orange to brown red	*150.*
brown olive to red brown	*150.*
red brown to yellow green	*150.*
yellow green to dull carmine	*150.*
dull carmine to yellow green	*150.*
blue green to dull carmine	*150.*
brown olive to dull carmine	*150.*
dull carmine to orange	*150.*
orange to deep blue	*150.*
deep blue to orange brown	*150.*
orange brown to dull orange	*150.*
dull carmine to deep blue	*150.*

79-E30p Block

Illustration reduced.

p. As "o," on transparent wove, imperf.

red violet to deep violet	*150.*
deep violet to carmine	*150.*
dull scarlet to gold	*150.*
gold to carmine	*150.*
dark violet to blue green	*150.*
blue green to dark violet red	*150.*
violet to yellow green	*150.*
yellow green to red violet	*150.*

q. As "o," plate on stiff yellowish wove, imperf.

dull carmine to orange	*150.*
orange to deep blue	*150.*
brown olive to brown red	*150.*
brown red to yellow green	*150.*
blue green to dull carmine	*150.*
dull carmine to deep blue	*150.*
deep blue to dark brown	*150.*
dark brown to orange	*150.*

r. As "q," outside edge perf. 12

blue green to dull carmine	*150.*
dull carmine to deep blue	*150.*
deep blue to dark brown	*150.*
dark brown to dull orange	*150.*
dull carmine to dull orange	*150.*
dull orange to deep blue	*150.*
yellow green to dull carmine	*150.*
dull carmine to yellow green	*150.*
brown olive to brown red	*150.*
brown red to yellow green	*150.*

s. As "r," plate in single color, outside edge perf. 12, gummed

carmine	*150.*
dull orange	*150.*
orange brown	*150.*
dark brown	*150.*
brown olive	*150.*
dark blue green	*150.*
violet	*150.*

t. As "s," imperf., gummed

brown	*125.*
brown orange	*125.*
dull blue green	*125.*
deep blue	*125.*
carmine	*125.*

u. As "t," one color directly over another (gives effect of one color), black on scarlet *275.*

v. As "b," heavily stamped on white card, only faint traces of vignette, albino *125.*

w. As "v," printed design at right, very dark blue green *250.*

79-E31a

79-E31b

79-E31c

79-E31d

79-E31e

79-E31f

79-E31g

Same design as No. 79-E30, black green on white wove safety paper, underprinted with different designs in various colors, imperf.

79-E31 3c

a.	Red horiz. diamonds	*1,400.*
b.	Dull yellow green with ONE repeated	*1,400.*
c.	Red with 2 in circular stars	*1,400.*
d.	Red with 2 in ovals	*1,400.*
e.	Red with 3 in diamonds	*1,400.*
f.	Black with 5 in hexagons	*1,400.*
g.	Red with X repeated	*1,400.*

79-E32

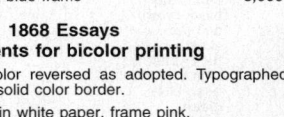

Similar to No. 79-E30f, but perf. vignette removed and frame mounted over 18x23mm Washington vignette.

79-E32 3c Die on 34x40mm white wove, black vignette, blue frame *8,000.*

1868 Essays
Experiments for bicolor printing

1c 1861 design, color reversed as adopted. Typographed frame with 43x60mm solid color border.

79-E33 1c Die on thin white paper, frame pink, vignette dark blue over pink *1,250.*

79-E35a

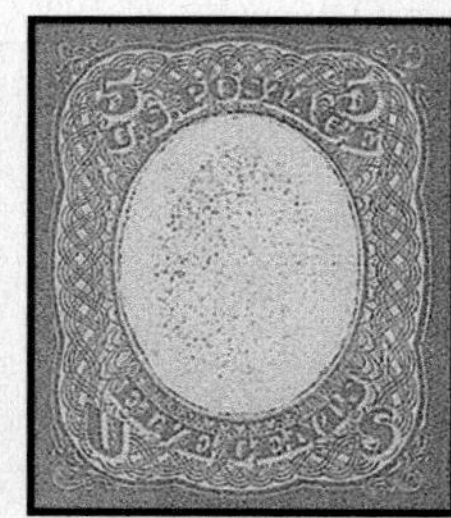

79-E35c

79-E35e

79-E35f

Frame lithographed, colored and colorless parts interchanged, vignette engraved and printed in another color.

Die I: colorless vignette oval (Nos. 79-E35a, 79-E35b)

Die II: vignette with horiz. lines (Nos. 79-E35d through 79-E35f)

79-E35 5c

a. Untrimmed die on thin white paper, 40x60mm (values for cut to stamp size)

frame buff, vignette black	*2,000.*
frame buff, vignette blue	*2,000.*
frame buff, vignette red brown	*2,000.*
frame buff, vignette dark brown	*2,000.*
frame buff, vignette orange	*2,000.*
frame buff, vignette carmine	*2,000.*
frame blue green, vignette dark brown	*2,000.*
frame blue green, vignette red brown	*2,000.*
frame blue green, vignette orange	*2,000.*
frame carmine, vignette blue	*2,000.*
frame carmine, vignette red brown	*2,000.*
frame violet, vignette orange	*2,000.*
frame light red, vignette deep orange red	*2,000.*
frame light red, vignette yellow orange	*2,000.*

b. Die on stiff wove, frame brown, vignette scarlet *2,000.*

c. 45x65mm die impression of lithographed frame only, on ivory paper

black	*2,000.*
blue green	*2,000.*

d. Die on thin white paper

frame violet, vignette carmine	*2,000.*
frame violet, vignette brown	*2,000.*
frame violet, vignette red brown	*2,000.*
frame carmine, vignette black	*2,000.*

e. Vignette only on white glazed paper

black	*2,000.*
blue	*2,000.*
scarlet	*2,000.*
dark brown	*2,000.*

f. As "e," without thin outer frameline, on India

lake	*2,000.*
red	*2,000.*
deep red orange	*2,000.*
scarlet	*2,000.*
deep green	*2,000.*
ultramarine	*2,000.*
black	*2,000.*

79-E36

Die II vignette as No. 79-E35e, with gothic "United States" above.

79-E36 5c

a. Die on white glazed paper
black *450.*

scarlet 450.
dark brown 450.
green 450.
blue 450.

79-E37 79-E37a

Die size: 51x63½
5c 1861 design, color reversed as adopted, vignette mounted on typographed frame.

79-E37 5c
a. Die on white card, frame light blue, vignette black 1,000.
b. Vignette only, die on India, black 350.
c. Vignette only, die on white glazed paper
blue 350.
black 350.
green 350.

100-E1

Design size: 20½x24½mm
Engraved circular Franklin vignette mounted on 43x75mm white card, engraved Washington head mounted thereon; background, silhouette, etc., retouched in black ink. With engraved frame of No. 71-E1 (vignette cut out) mounted over the double vignette.

100-E1 30c Die on India, 30x34mm, black 16,000.

1869 ISSUE
George T. Jones

112-E1a 112-E1b

Design size: 24x30mm
U.S. Grant vignette in frame with blank labels, ovals, etc. Paper overprinted with network of fine colored wavy lines in fugitive inks as on beer stamps.

112-E1 No Denomination
a. Die on India cut to stamp size, 1 color
black 2,250.
blue 2,250.
b. Die on India cut to stamp size, 2 colors (head in black)
blue, light gray overprint 3,250.
red, light gray overprint 3,250.
black, light violet overprint 3,250.
ocher, pale red violet ovpt. 3,250.
carmine, gray overprint 3,250.
blue, yellow overprint 3,250.

113-E1

Design size: 24x30mm
U.S. Treasury Dept. seal in vignette oval.

113-E1 2c
a. Die on India cut to stamp size, 1 color
carmine 2,500.
blue 2,500.
b. Die on India cut to stamp size, 3 colors, black on pale red violet wavy lines and blue green lined vignette 3,750.

Frame as 112-E1 but with Washington vignette and 2c denomination. Another Washington vignette below but in horiz. lined oval frame.

113-E2 2c Die on 1⅝x3½inch India, black 5,000.

National Bank Note Co.

All values originally essayed with numerals smaller than adopted. All designs are same size as issued stamps. Sheets of 150 of 1c-12c, sheets of 50 of 24c-90c. Many colors of plate essays exist from one sheet only, some colors from two sheets and a few from three. Some plate essays exist privately perforated.

112-E2

Die size: 40x65mm
Vignette size: 17mm diameter
Vignette of Franklin.

112-E2 1c Die of vignette only on India
orange 900.
violet brown 900.
black 900.

112-E3

Circle of pearls added to vignette, suggestion for frame and 1 in circle at bottom penciled in.

112-E3 1c Die on India, black 1,500.

112-E4

Complete design as issued but with small value numeral.

112-E4 1c
a. Die on India, die sunk on card
black 1,250.
violet brown 1,250.
dark brown 1,250.
yellow brown 1,250.
scarlet 1,250.
carmine 1,250.
deep violet 1,250.
blue 1,250.
green 1,250.
yellow 1,250.
b. Plate on stamp paper, imperf., gummed
buff 100.
deep orange brown 100.
orange brown 100.
c. Plate on stamp paper, perf. 12, gummed
buff 100.
orange brown 100.
orange 125.
d. As "c," with 9x9mm grill
buff 110.
orange brown 85.
red brown 85.
chocolate 85.
black brown 85.
dull red 85.
violet 110.
dark violet 110.
blue 110.
deep blue 110.
green 110.
yellow 110.
orange 110.
rose red 110.
e. Horiz. pair, one #112-E4c, one #112-E4d 400.

112-E5

Design size: 23x31mm
Die size: 51x55mm
Design as issued but surrounded by fancy frame with flags and shield. Also essayed for envelopes and wrappers on thick paper.

112-E5 1c
a. Die on stamp paper, perf. 12, gummed, gray 3,000.
b. Die on white ivory paper
black 2,000.
black brown 2,000.
scarlet 2,000.
blue 2,000.
c. Die on India
blue 2,000.
blue green 2,000.
d. Die on India, cut to shape
carmine 750.
yellow 750.

113-E3b 113-E3c

Die size: 41x50mm
Design as issued but with small value numeral. Nos. 113-E3a and 113-Eb have incomplete shading around "UNITED STATES."

113-E3 2c
a. Die on India, die sunk on card
black 1,500.
yellow 1,500.
red orange 1,500.
deep scarlet 1,500.
brown 1,500.
green 1,500.
dusky blue 1,500.
deep blue 1,500.
b. Die on India, cut to stamp size
deep orange red 400.
deep orange yellow 400.
blue green 400.
gray black 400.
light blue 400.
rose 400.
c. Complete die on India, die sunk on card
brown 1,500.
rose 1,500.
mauve 1,500.
green 1,500.
dark chocolate 1,500.
red brown 1,500.
d. Plate on stamp paper, perf. 12, gummed
brown 425.
dark brown 425.
yellow 425.
e. As "d," with 9x9mm grill
brown 80.
dark brown 80.
orange brown 80.
dark orange brown 80.
rose 80.
brown rose 80.
copper red 80.
deep copper red 80.
green 80.
deep green 80.
blue green 80.
yellow 80.
orange 80.
dull yellow orange 80.
blue 80.
light violet 80.
violet 80.
dark violet 80.
f. As "e," double grill, orange 300.
g. Horiz. pair, one #113-E3d, one #113-E3e 1,000.

113-E4

Original sketch of postrider, printed "NATIONAL BANK NOTE COMPANY. BUSINESS DEPARTMENT. 1868" at top, pencil instructions at bottom, "Reduce to this length" and "2 copies on one plate. Daguerrotype."

113-E4 2c Drawing on paper, black —

114-E3

Die size: 53x47mm
Design nearly as issued: larger motive above and below "POSTAGE" erased, no shading on numeral shield, top leaves and corner leaves do not touch, no dots in lower corners or scrolls beside bottom of shield, no vert. shading lines in "POSTAGE" label. Small value numeral.

114-E3 3c Die on 30x30mm ivory paper, black *1,500.*

114-E4

Similar to 114-E3, but smaller motive around "POSTAGE," shield shaded.

114-E4 3c
a. Die on India, die sunk on card
black *1,500.*
carmine *1,500.*
scarlet *1,500.*
orange red *1,500.*
yellow orange *1,500.*
dull yellow *1,500.*
red sepia *1,500.*
blue green *1,500.*
blue *1,500.*
dull red *1,500.*
orange brown *1,500.*
b. Die on India, cut to stamp size
black *500.*
rose *500.*
scarlet *500.*
chocolate *500.*
dull dusky orange *500.*
red violet *500.*
blackish slate *500.*

114-E5

Similar to No. 114-E4 but vert. shading lines added to "POSTAGE" frame.

114-E5 3c Die on India
chocolate *1,500.*
dusky yellow orange *1,500.*

114-E6

Completed small numeral die essay: leaves at top and sides touch, dots in lower corners added, vert. shading lines in frame around "POSTAGE," shield shaded darker at bottom, scrolls added to bottom of shield.

114-E6 3c
a. Die on India, card mounted
black *1,750.*
blue *1,750.*
deep orange red *1,750.*
b. Plate on stamp paper, imperf., gummed
ultramarine *125.*
dark ultramarine *125.*
light brown *85.*
red brown *85.*
dark red brown *85.*
pale rose *85.*
rose *85.*
brown rose *85.*
c. Plate on stamp paper, perf. 12, gummed
ultramarine *500.*
dark ultramarine *500.*
d. As "c," with 9x9mm grill
blue *80.*
deep blue *80.*
orange brown *80.*
black brown *80.*
deep black brown *80.*
rose red *80.*
green *80.*
yellow *80.*
orange *80.*
deep orange *80.*
dull violet *80.*
deep violet *80.*
red violet *80.*

114-E7

Same design and color as issued stamp, but with allover essay grill of squares up.

114-E7 3c
a. Imperf., gummed, ultramarine *700.*
b. As "a," 23mm "NATIONAL BANK NOTE CO. N.Y. SEP 27, 1869" circular pmk., ultramarine *1,100.*
c. On thick paper, imperf., gummed, horiz. line defacement, ultramarine *700.*
d. Perf. 12, horiz. line defacement, ultramarine *700.*

115-E1

Die size: 40x60mm
Vignette of Washington. Design as issued 6c stamp but with 5c denomination. Large lettering, large U and S in corners. Also essayed for envelopes on thick paper.

115-E1 6c
a. Die on India, no frameline, solid vignette background, corner spandrels short at centers
black *700.*
carmine *700.*
dismal red brown *700.*
smoky dusky brown *700.*
gray violet *700.*
b. Completed die on India, die sunk on card
black *600.*
carmine *600.*
deep rose *600.*
red violet *600.*
red brown *600.*
deep yellow brown *600.*
black brown *600.*
dull yellow *600.*
orange *600.*
dusky blue *600.*
dusky slate blue *600.*
green *600.*
blue green *600.*
scarlet *600.*
c. Die on proof paper, about 40x65mm
black *600.*
carmine *600.*
scarlet *600.*
red orange *600.*
orange *600.*
dull yellow *600.*
orange brown *600.*
olive brown *600.*
dusky green *600.*
dusky yellow green *600.*
light blue *600.*
deep blue *600.*
red violet *600.*
d. Die on pink bond

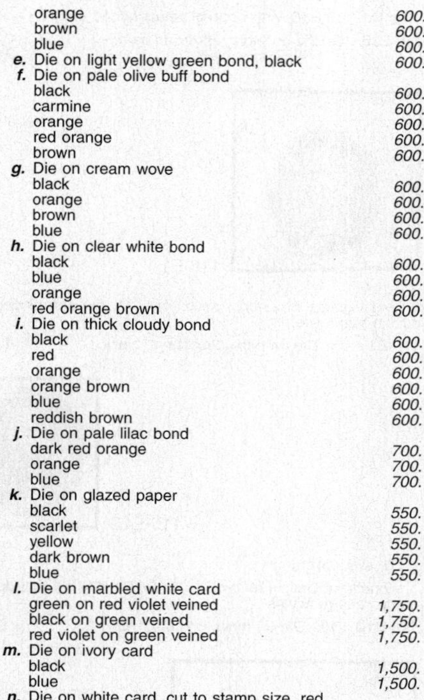

orange *600.*
brown *600.*
blue *600.*
e. Die on light yellow green bond, black *600.*
f. Die on pale olive buff bond
black *600.*
carmine *600.*
orange *600.*
red orange *600.*
brown *600.*
g. Die on cream wove
black *600.*
orange *600.*
brown *600.*
blue *600.*
h. Die on clear white bond
black *600.*
blue *600.*
orange *600.*
red orange brown *600.*
i. Die on thick cloudy bond
black *600.*
red *600.*
orange *600.*
orange brown *600.*
blue *600.*
reddish brown *600.*
j. Die on pale lilac bond
dark red orange *700.*
orange *700.*
blue *700.*
k. Die on glazed paper
black *550.*
scarlet *550.*
yellow *550.*
dark brown *550.*
blue *550.*
l. Die on marbled white card
green on red violet veined *1,750.*
black on green veined *1,750.*
red violet on green veined *1,750.*
m. Die on ivory card
black *1,500.*
blue *1,500.*
n. Die on white card, cut to stamp size, red orange *250.*

115-E2

Die size: 43x63mm
Similar to No. 115-E1 but lettering, U and S smaller.

115-E2 6c
a. Incomplete die on India (incomplete spandrel points, hair on top of head, etc.)
black *750.*
dull red brown *750.*
b. Complete die on India, die sunk on card
black *750.*
blue *750.*
dull dusky violet *750.*
scarlet *750.*
dark orange red *750.*
dim dusky red orange *750.*
dusky green *750.*
dusky green blue green *750.*
dusky blue green *750.*
c. Plate essay on wove, imperf., gummed
deep ultramarine *150.*
orange *150.*
dull red violet *80.*
deep red violet *80.*
red brown *80.*
dull red brown *80.*
buff *80.*
green *80.*
d. Plate essay on wove, perf. 12, gummed
orange *200.*
blue *200.*

115-E3D

Vignette of Washington as used on stamp but with shorter shirt front.

115-E3D 6c Die on India, affixed to card, 35x37mm, black —

115-E3E

As No. 115-E3D, with circle of pearls added around vignette.

115-E3E 6c Die on India, affixed to card, 59x85mm, black 3,000.

116-E1

Oval vignette of Lincoln as on No. 77, but surrounded by double frame line.

116-E1 10c Die on India, 24x24mm, black 1,500.

116-E1D

Die size: 14x18mm

Vignette of Lincoln as on No. 77. As No. 116-E1, but double frame lines removed.

116-E1D 10c Die on India, on card, black 1,150.

116-E1a

Design size:14x14 ½mm

Round vignette of Lincoln as on No. 77, reduced at bottom.

116-E1a Die on India, on card, black 1,700.

116-E1b

Design size: about 19 ½x19 ½mm

Die size: 64x68 ½mm

Head as on No. 77 but less bust, large unshaded collar, no cross shading in triangles between labels and fasces, no shading on diamonds at end of value label.

116-E1b Incomplete die on India, on card, black 6,000.

116-E1c

Small collar, shading on diamonds at end of value label. Also essayed for envelopes on yellow laid paper.

116-E1c Complete die on India, die sunk on card

black 1,100.
brown black 1,100.
gray black 1,100.
carmine 1,100.
scarlet 1,100.
brown red 1,100.
orange 1,100.
deep orange 1,100.
deep red 1,100.
yellow brown 1,100.
yellow 1,100.
green 1,100.
blue green 1,100.
deep blue 1,100.
red violet 1,100.
brown 1,100.

d. Die on proof paper

black 1,000.
carmine 1,000.
bright red 1,000.
orange red 1,000.
orange 1,000.
dark chocolate 1,000.
dusky yellow brown 1,000.
green 1,000.
blue 1,000.
red violet 1,000.

e. Die on ivory paper

black 1,000.
scarlet 1,000.
black brown 1,000.
blue 1,000.

f. Die on clear white thin bond, about 30x35mm

black 1,000.
red orange 1,000.
red brown 1,000.
orange 1,000.
yellow 1,000.
blue 1,000.

g. Die on cloudy cream bond, about 30x35mm

black 1,100.
light red brown 1,100.
red orange 1,100.
blue 1,100.

h. Die on pink bond, about 39x45mm

red orange 1,000.
red brown 1,000.
yellow 1,000.

i. Die on pale greenish gray bond, about 33x37mm

black 1,050.
deep carmine 1,050.
dull scarlet 1,050.
dark brown 1,050.
blue 1,050.

j. Die on marbled white ivory card, about 38x62mm

black on green veined 2,000.
orange red on green veined 2,000.
red orange on green veined 2,000.
dark orange brown on red violet veined 2,000.

k. Plate on stamp paper, imperf., gummed

deep green 150.
blue 125.
ultramarine 125.
dark ultramarine 125.
light ultramarine 125.

l. Plate on stamp paper, perf. 12, gummed

black 1,000.
orange 200.

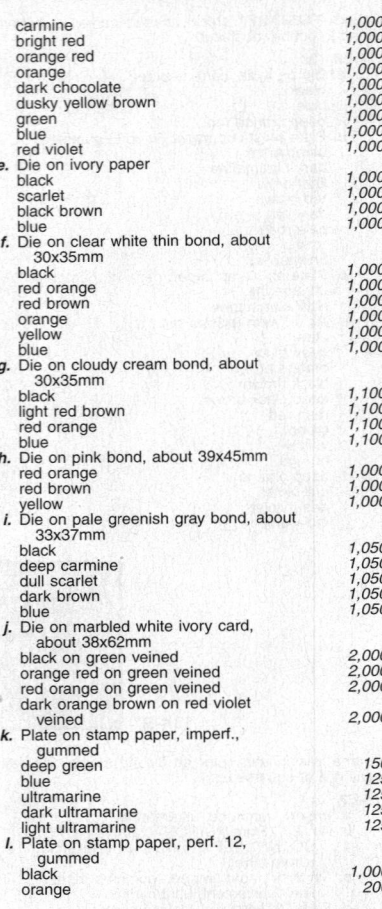

116-E2

Die size: 101x62mm

Vignette of signing the Declaration of Independence as adopted for 24c.

116-E2 10c

a. Die on India, die sunk on card

black 4,250.
carmine 4,250.
dim rose 4,250.
dull scarlet 4,250.
red orange 4,250.
orange yellow 4,250.
red brown 4,250.
orange brown 4,250.
green 4,250.
blue 4,250.
gray 4,250.

b. Die on India, cut to stamp size

black 1,500.
red orange 1,500.
blue green 1,500.
dim rose 1,500.
brown 1,500.
buff 1,500.
dull scarlet 1,500.

Other colors reported to exist.

116-E3

Die size: 63x75mm

Design as adopted for issued stamp, but incomplete shading on bottom ribbon, thin shading lines behind "States," and center of "0" of "10" not filled in.

116-E3 10c Die on India on 61x53mm card, black 2,500.

116-E4

Similar to No. 116-E3 except shading lines added behind "Ten Cents" and center of "0" of "10" filled in.

116-E4 10c Die on India, die sunk on card

black 2,500.
orange 2,500.
blue 2,500.

117-E1

Die size: 47x51 mm

Similar to No. 117 but with smaller value numerals and blunt tip on arrowhead in triangular element to left of "UNITED STATES POSTAGE". Other subtle differences exist.

117-E1 12c

a. Incomplete die on India, on card, black —

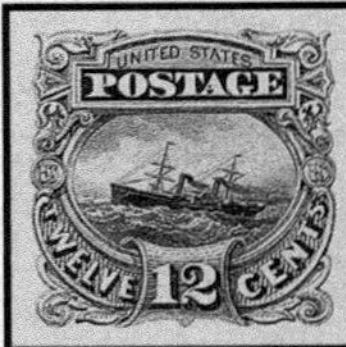

117-E2

Die size: 47x51mm

Design as issued but with smaller value numerals. Sharp tip on arrowhead in triangular element to left of "UNITED STATES POSTAGE". Solid line above dashed line at top of value tablet and curved line added to top-left edge of value tablet. Other subtle differences exist between Nos. 117-E2 and 117-E1.

117-E2 12c

a. Die on card, black 1,600.

b. Vignette die on India, pencil "Adriatic", black 1,600.

c. Complete die on India, die sunk on card

black 1,350.
rose 1,350.
yellow 1,350.
scarlet 1,350.
dark red brown 1,350.
blue green 1,350.
blue 1,350.
dull violet 1,350.
gray black 1,350.
orange brown 1,350.
yellow brown 1,350.
dull orange red 1,350.

d. Die on India, cut to stamp size

black 600.
dusky red orange 600.
deep orange red 600.
dim blue 600.

e. Plate on stamp paper, 9x9mm grill, perf. 12, gummed

green 125.
rose red 125.
pale rose red 125.
yellow brown 125.
red brown 125.
orange 125.
blue 125.
dull violet 125.
dull red violet 125.
yellow orange 125.

117-E2F

Similar to No. 117-E2, but small numeral not printed, large 12 drawn in pencil.

117-E2F 12c Die on India, black 2,750.

117-E3

Typographed small numeral design similar to No. 117-E1, relief engraved for surface printing. Heavier lines, upper label with solid background, letters of "UNITED STATES POSTAGE" colorless. Nos. 117-E3a through 117-E3c from untrimmed die, heavily struck with uncolored areas in relief, color covering borders beyond white line exterior of frame. Untrimmed die size: 58x45mm.

117-E3 12c
- ***a.*** Untrimmed die on card
  - brown red 750.
  - green 750.
  - black 750.
  - red brown 750.
- ***b.*** Untrimmed die on thin pinkish wove
  - gray black 450.
  - dull deep red orange 450.
  - dark red orange 450.
- ***c.*** Untrimmed die on thick white wove
  - carmine 600.
  - green 600.
- ***d.*** Die on white paper, stamp size
  - carmine 400.
  - orange 400.
  - brown 400.
  - lilac 400.
  - green 400.
- ***e.*** Die on thin white wove
  - carmine 400.
  - gray black 400.
  - dull deep red orange 400.
  - deep orange red 400.
- ***g.*** Die on pinkish wove, perf. 12, gummed, red brown 400.
- ***h.*** Die on yellow wove, imperf.
  - gray black 400.
  - carmine 400.
  - red brown 400.
  - dark red violet 400.
- ***i.*** Die on yellow wove, 11x13mm grill, imperf., red brown 400.
- ***j.*** Die on white laid
  - gray 400.
  - gray black 400.
  - brown 400.
  - red brown 400.
- ***k.*** Die on yellow laid
  - red brown 400.
  - brown 400.
  - dull red violet 400.
  - carmine 400.
- ***l.*** Die on salmon laid, red brown 400.
- ***m.*** Die on pinkish laid
  - red brown 400.
  - gray 400.
- ***n.*** Die on pinkish laid, 11x13mm grill, gummed, red brown 400.
- ***o.*** Die on dull red violet laid, gray 400.

117-E4

Vignette size: 15x11mm
Untrimmed die size: 63x32mm
Vignette only, similar to No. 117-E3 but lithographed instead of typographed.

117-E4 12c
- ***a.*** Die on white ivory paper, black 1,000.
- ***b.*** Complete impression from untrimmed stone in solid color about 63x63mm, on white ivory paper, black 750.
- ***c.*** Die on glossy-surfaced thin white wove, trimmed to stamp size
  - carmine 750.
  - rose pink 750.
  - yellow 750.
  - blue green 750.
  - dim red violet 750.
  - pale red violet 750.
  - deep red orange 750.
  - dull dark red orange 750.
  - dull dark yellow orange 750.
  - dark violet red 750.
  - pale gray 750.
- ***d.*** Die on thick white wove
  - yellow 750.
  - violet red 750.
  - deep red violet 750.

118-E1

118-E1a

118-E1 15c Die of vignette only on India, mounted on 62x62mm India, die sunk on card, dark blue 3,500.
- ***a.*** As No. 118-E1, but vignette cut from a plate proof on India, showing framelines on plate, mounted on India, die sunk on card, dark blue —

Type I design but with smaller value numerals.

118-E2 15c Incomplete die (no outer frameline or shading outside frame scrolls) on India, black 4,500.

118-E3

Die size: 62x49mm
Type I design as issued but with smaller value numerals.

118-E3 15c Complete die on India, die sunk on card
- black 5,000.
- scarlet 5,000.
- orange brown 5,000.
- green 5,000.
- dull violet 5,000.
- red brown 5,000.
- blue 5,000.

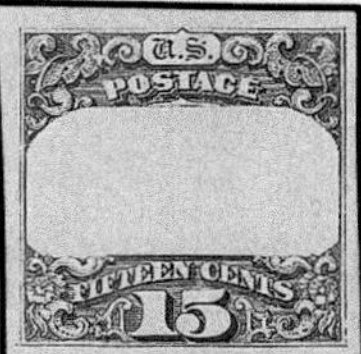
118-E4

Types I and III frame only.

118-E4 15c
- ***a.*** Die on India, red brown 2,750.
- ***b.*** Die on India, with vignette mounted in place, blue frame, yellow vignette 3,750.
- ***c.*** Die on India, with vignette mounted in place, red brown frame, blue vignette 3,500.

118-E5

Type III frame only.

118-E5 15c Die on pink-tinted paper, perforated 3,750.

The type I frame also was used to produce type III stamps, No. 129. On No. 118, the brown fringe lines placed at the sides of the vignette were entered onto the plate one at a time. The lines were not on the die. All positions of the resulting stamp, No. 118, will differ slightly upon close examination.

119-E1a

Type II design with large value numerals as issued.

119-E1 15c
- ***a.*** Type II frame only, die on India
  - black 3,500.
  - red brown 3,500.
- ***b.*** Vignette only, die on India, blue —

119-E1c

- ***c.*** Type II frame with vignette mounted in place, die on India, red brown frame, blue vignette 7,500.
- ***d.*** Type II frame with vignette mounted at right, die on India, red brown frame, blue vignette —

129-E1

Die size: 65x49
Type III design as adopted, except in various single colors, large "15" overprint in diff. color.

129-E1 15c
- ***a.*** Die on India, die sunk on card
  - orange brown, red overprint 3,500.
  - blue green, red overprint 3,500.
  - ultramarine, red overprint 3,500.
  - violet, red overprint 3,500.
  - red brown, red overprint 3,500.
- ***b.*** Die on India, die sunk on card
  - rose red, ultramarine overprint 3,500.
  - dull scarlet, ultramarine overprint 3,500.
  - dark red brown, ultramarine ovpt. 3,500.
- ***c.*** Die on India, die sunk on card
  - scarlet, blue green overprint 3,500.
  - orange brown, blue green overprint 3,500.
  - dark red brown, blue green overprint 3,500.

129-E2

Similar to No. 129-E1 but without the "15" overprint.

129-E2 Die on India, 34x30mm, dark blue 10,000.

120-E1

Die size: 102x63mm
Design nearly as issued, but shading under leaves at top of frame and ribbon over "TWENTY" are unfinished. Small value numerals. Single color.

120-E1 24c Die on India, black 4,000.

120-E2a

120-E2b

Completed small numeral design in single color. No. 120-E2a has 8mm-high bands of shaded colored lines 31mm long overprinted above and below vignette, printed in various single colors with bands in contrasting color.

120-E2 24c
- ***a.*** Die on India
  - black with carmine bands 8,000.
  - black with violet brown bands 8,000.
  - black with brown orange bands 8,000.

orange brown with deep dull violet bands 8,000.
orange brown with blue green bands 8,000.
b. Die on India
black 6,500.
scarlet 6,500.
dark red brown 6,500.
blue 6,500.
violet 6,500.
c. Plate on red salmon tinted paper, black 200.
d. Plate on orange buff tinted paper, black 250.
e. Plate on dull yellowish tinted paper, black 250.
f. Plate on blue tinted paper, black 600.
g. Plate on gray tinted paper, black 500.
h. Plate on India, black 300.
j. Plate on card, imperf., black 350.

120-E3a

120-E3b

120-E3d

No. 120-E3a bicolor design as issued, except vignette printed separately and mounted in place; No. 120-E3b frame only with 3 border lines around vignette space; No. 120-E3c frame only with 2 border lines around vignette space as issued.

120-E3 24c
a. Die on India, card mounted
dull violet frame, green vignette 4,500.
violet frame, red vignette 4,500.
green frame, violet vignette 4,500.
rose frame, green vignette 4,500.
b. Frame die on India, card mounted
black 5,000.
light green 5,000.
dark green 5,000.
c. Frame die on India, block sunk on India, green 5,000.
d. As "b," but frame perforated, and with violet vignette removed and separately die sunk to the right, 108x58mm card 2,000.
e. As "c," but with violet vignette removed from frame and separately die sunk to the right, 88x46mm card. 5,000.

121-E1

Design size: 21½x22mm
Die Size: 71x51mm
Vignette of Surrender of Gen. Burgoyne in ornate frame.

121-E1 30c
a. Die on India, die sunk on card
black 800.
carmine 800.
rose red 800.
light brown red 800.
red brown 800.
brown orange 800.
orange 800.
red orange 800.
yellow green 800.
blue 800.
dull dark violet 800.
yellow brown 800.
scarlet 800.
b. Die on stiff ivory paper
black 650.
c. Die on India, cut to stamp size
dim deep orange red 250.
deep yellow orange 250.
dim deep blue green 250.
dim dusky blue 250.
d. Die on India die sunk on 78x58mm white card
dusky blue 1,000.
e. Die on white card, cut to stamp size
dim orange 500.
f. Die on proof paper, about 70x50mm
black 500.

carmine 500.
scarlet 500.
red orange 500.
green 500.
violet 500.
g. Die on ivory paper, about 64x50mm
black 1,000.
dark brown 1,000.
scarlet 1,000.
blue 1,000.
h. Die on ivory card
black 1,000.
carmine 1,000.
i. Die on clear white bond, about 33x33mm
black 600.
blue 600.
light red brown 600.
orange 600.
j. Die on yellowish cloudy bond, about 34x34mm
black 600.
orange 600.
light red brown 600.
blue 600.
k. Die on smoky yellow greenish bond
black 600.
carmine 600.
orange 600.
l. Die on pink bond, about 40x40mm
blue 600.
dim orange red 600.
orange 600.
m. Die on pale olive buff paper
black 600.
dim orange red 600.
orange 600.
n. Die on thick yellowish wove, dim green blue 600.
o. Die on marbled white ivory card, about 40x60mm
black on green veined 2,500.
black on red violet veined 2,500.
p. Plate essay in black on thin surface-tinted paper
pale gray 275.
salmon red 175.
yellow 175.
orange 275.
orange buff 275.
pink 275.
pale pink 275.
blue 275.
light blue 275.
pale green 275.
brown violet 275.
q. Plate essay in black on India 300.
r. Plate on thick rough pitted card, black 300.

121-E1s

s. Plate on bond, red bands overprinted top and bottom as on No. 120-E2a, dull red violet 350.

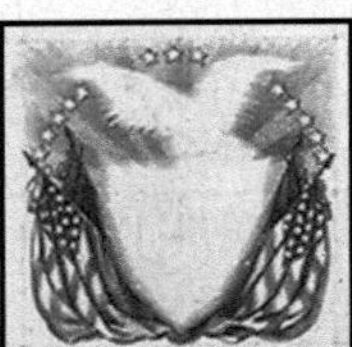

121-E2

Flags, stars and rays only as adopted for issued stamp. Black essay shows traces of vignette also.

121-E2 30c Die on India, mounted on India, block sunk on card
black 7,500.
light ultramarine 6,000.
dark blue 6,000.

121-E3

Eagle, shield and value only as adopted for issued stamp.

121-E3 30c Die on India, card mounted, black 8,500.

122-E1

Die size: 62x69mm
Vignette of Washington in frame similar to that of issued stamp but no shading over U and S in lower corners, small value numerals.

122-E1 90c Die on India, black 3,250.

122-E2

Similar to No. 122-E1 but shading over U and S.

122-E2 90c
a. Die on India, die sunk on card
black 2,500.
carmine 2,500.
scarlet 2,500.
red brown 2,500.
blue green 2,500.
violet 2,500.
b. Plate essay with black vignette on stamp paper, imperf.
dull violet 275.
red brown 275.
orange red 275.
pale orange red 275.
blue 275.

122-E3

Frame as No. 122-E2, vignette oval with narrow-spaced horiz. lines in same color as frame, but no head.

122-E3 90c Plate on medium India paper, imperf.
red brown 225.
blue 225.
dark blue 225.
red violet 225.
dull violet 225.
dark violet 225.
rose red 225.
deep rose red 225.
yellow 225.
orange brown 225.
dark navy blue 225.
blue green 225.
deep blue green 225.
dark blue green 225.
orange 225.

122-E4

122-E4b

Small numeral frame but with black cut down Lincoln vignette on India from No. 77 mounted in place.

122-E4 90c
a. Die on medium India
yellow 3,000.
red brown 3,000.
rose red 3,000.
deep blue green 3,000.
dark navy blue 3,000.
steel blue 3,000.
dull violet 3,000.
b. Plate of Lincoln vignette only, on rough pitted thick gray paper, black 500.
Block of 4 2,250.
c. Die on India, Lincoln vignette as used on No. 77, black 2,500.

122-E5

Similar to No. 122-E1, with Washington vignette but with large numerals as on issued stamp.

122-E5 90c
a. Die on India, die sunk on card
black *5,000.*
carmine *5,000.*
b. Plate of frame only, 2 lines at top, 3 lines at bottom, on India, mounted on block sunk card, rose red *1,250.*
c. As "b," 3 lines at top, 2 lines at bottom
rose red *7,750.*
red brown *1,250.*

Safety paper essays, circa 1868-69, on India paper, underprinted with a stable ink with various engraved safety paper designs in another color.

26 different designs found on 5c (No. 115-E), 10c (No. 116-E), 15c (No. 118-E) and 30c (No. 121-E). The number following the "E" in the listing corresponds to the design numbers identified and illustrated, e.g., No. 115-ESP1 identifies the 5c stamp with safety paper design 1, etc. Stamp color given first.

115-ESP1

Design 1: wavy lines

115-ESP1 5c
carmine on scarlet *3,250.*
orange on scarlet *3,250.*
116-ESP1 10c blue on scarlet *5,000.*
121-ESP1 30c carmine on scarlet *3,500.*

121-ESP2

Design 2: banknote type

115-ESP2 5c
carmine on violet *3,250.*
orange on violet *3,250.*
116-ESP2 10c carmine on violet *5,000.*
121-ESP2 30c
carmine on violet *3,500.*
orange on violet *3,500.*
orange on gray *3,500.*

115-ESP3

Design 3: banknote type

115-ESP3 5c
carmine on orange red *3,250.*
carmine on brown *3,250.*
orange on brown *3,250.*
116-ESP3 10c
carmine on orange red *5,000.*
blue on orange and red *5,000.*
121-ESP3 30c
carmine on orange red *3,500.*
orange on brown *3,500.*

116-ESP4

Design 4: continuous wavy lines

115-ESP4 5c orange on scarlet *3,250.*
116-ESP4 10c
blue on scarlet *5,000.*
carmine on scarlet *5,000.*
121-ESP4 30c black on scarlet *3,500.*

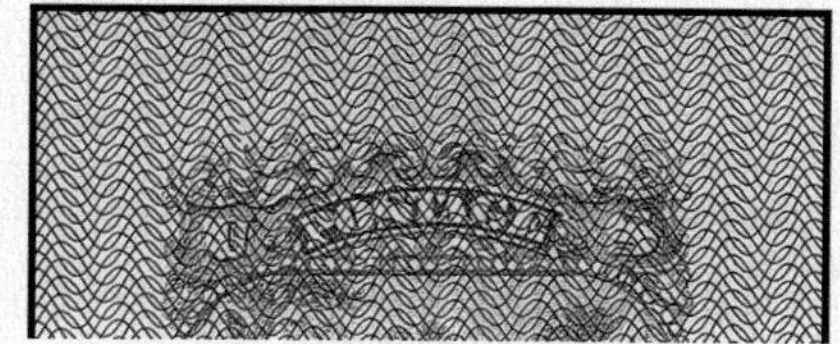

121-ESP5

Design 5: wavy lines

115-ESP5 5c
orange on orange *3,250.*
orange on black *3,250.*
116-ESP5 10c
dark brown on black *5,000.*
orange red on black *5,000.*
carmine on scarlet *5,000.*
121-ESP5 30c
carmine on black *3,500.*
carmine on scarlet *3,500.*

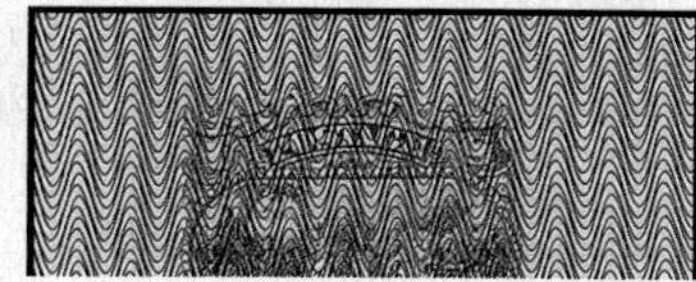

121-ESP6

Design 6: wavy lines

115-ESP6 5c orange on black *3,250.*
116-ESP6 10c blue on black *5,000.*
121-ESP6 30c
carmine on black *3,500.*
orange on black *3,500.*

115-ESP7

Design 7: crossed wavy lines

115-ESP7 5c
carmine on black *3,250.*
orange on black *3,250.*
116-ESP7 10c blue on black *5,000.*
121-ESP7 30c orange on black *3,500.*

116-ESP8

Design 8: wavy lines

115-ESP8 5c carmine on scarlet *3,250.*
116-ESP8 10c
blue on scarlet *5,000.*
carmine on scarlet *5,000.*
orange red on scarlet *5,000.*

118-ESP9

Design 9: wavy lines

118-ESP9 15c
orange brown on orange *3,500.*
blue green on orange *3,500.*
dark blue on orange *3,500.*

118-ESP10

Design 10: continuous whorls

118-ESP10 15c
orange brown on scarlet, horiz. *3,500.*
blue green on scarlet, horiz. *3,500.*
dark blue on scarlet, vert. *3,500.*

118-ESP11

Design 11: banknote type

118-ESP11 15c
orange brown on light scarlet, horiz. *3,500.*
blue green on light scarlet, vert. *3,500.*
dark blue on light scarlet, horiz. *3,500.*

118-ESP12

Design 12: banknote type

118-ESP12 15c
orange brown on deep scarlet *3,500.*
blue green on deep scarlet *3,500.*
dark blue on deep scarlet *3,500.*

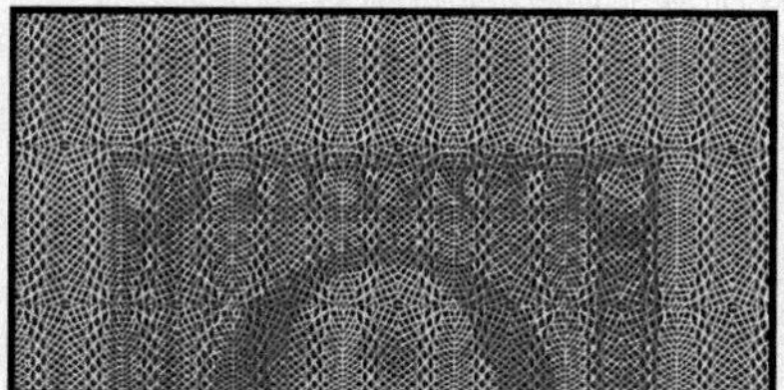

115-ESP13

Design 13: banknote type

115-ESP13 5c orange on brown *3,250.*
116-ESP13 10c
carmine on brown *5,500.*
orange red on brown *5,500.*
blue on brown *5,500.*
121-ESP13 30c carmine on brown *3,500.*

115-ESP14

Design 14: banknote type

115-ESP14 5c
carmine on scarlet 4,000.
black on scarlet 4,000.
116-ESP14 10c
carmine on scarlet 5,500.
orange on scarlet 5,500.
sepia on scarlet 5,500.
blue on scarlet 5,500.
121-ESP14 30c black on scarlet 3,500.

115-ESP15

Design 15: banknote type

115-ESP15 5c carmine on orange brown 3,250.
121-ESP15 30c carmine on deep orange 3,500.

116-ESP16

Design 16: multiple rosettes

115-ESP16 5c orange on scarlet 3,250.
116-ESP16 10c
carmine on scarlet 5,000.
orange red on scarlet 5,000.
sepia on scarlet 5,000.
blue on scarlet 5,000.

115-ESP17

Design 17: multiple oval rosettes

115-ESP17 5c carmine on scarlet 3,250.
121-ESP17 30c
carmine on scarlet 3,500.
orange on scarlet 3,500.

115-ESP18

Design 18: negative stars in diagonal lines

115-ESP18 5c
black on scarlet 3,250.
carmine on scarlet 3,250.
116-ESP18 10c
carmine on scarlet 5,500.
sepia on scarlet 5,500.
121-ESP18 30c carmine on scarlet 3,500.

116-ESP19

Design 19: multiple 6-point stars in lathework

116-ESP19 10c blue on blue green 7,500.
121-ESP19 30c carmine on blue green 3,500.

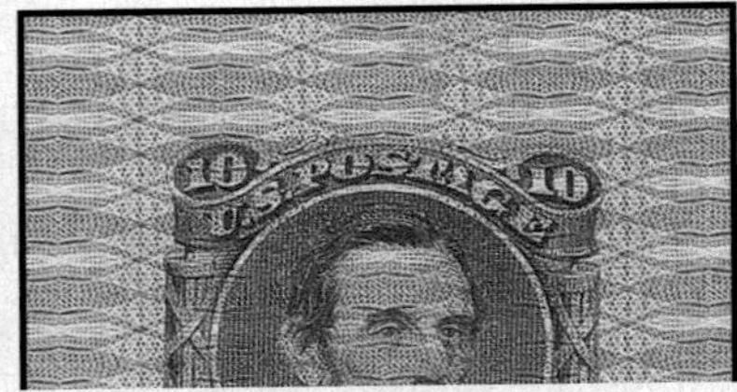
116-ESP20

Design 20: banknote type

116-ESP20 10c
brown on orange 5,500.
blue on orange 5,500.

116-ESP21

Design 21: multiple "ONE"

116-ESP21 10c blue on scarlet 5,500.

115-ESP22

Design 22: multiple "TWO"

115-ESP22 5c orange on scarlet 3,250.
116-ESP22 10c carmine on scarlet 5,500.

115-ESP23

Design 23: multiple "5"s in oval rosettes

115-ESP23 5c black on carmine 3,250.

116-ESP24

Design 24: multiple "TEN 10" with gap between rows of arches

116-ESP24 10c
carmine on scarlet 5,500.
orange red on scarlet 5,500.
brown on scarlet 5,500.
blue on scarlet 5,750.

116-ESP25

Design 25: multiple "TEN 10" with rows of arches touching

115-ESP25 5c
orange on scarlet 3,250.
carmine on scarlet 3,250.
116-ESP25 10c
blue on scarlet 5,500.
carmine on scarlet 5,500.

115-ESP26

Design 26: multiple "50"

115-ESP26 5c
black on black 3,250.
orange on black 3,250.

1870 ISSUE
Continental Banknote Co.
Series 1: Designs derived from concurrent tax paid revenue stamps and essays

145-E1

Vignette of Washington in large ornate "1." Labels and side ornaments not yet engraved.

145-E1 1c engraved die on India, black 1,850.

145-E1C

Continental Bank Note Co. Imprint

Design size: 21x24mm.
Die size: 52x52mm
Vignette of Washington in large ornate "1." Die proofs exist on full size 148x231mm card bearing a handstamped imprint as illustrated. These sell for much more.

145-E1C One Cent
d. Engraved die on India, die sunk on card reduced to about die size
black 1,500.
scarlet 1,500.
green 1,500.
ultramarine 1,500.
blue 1,500.
e. Engraved die essay on India cut close and block sunk on card (about 45x45mm)
scarlet 1,500.

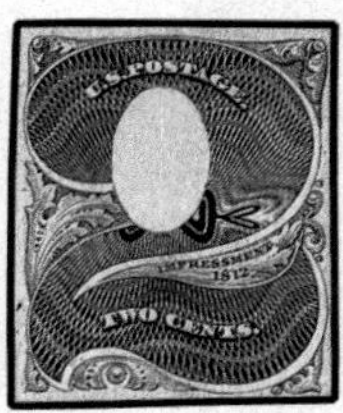

146-E1

Design size: 21x25mm
Die size: 46x45mm
Blank vignette in large ornate "2." Die proofs exist on full size 148x231mm card bearing a handstamped imprint as illustrated with No. 145-E1C.

146-E1 Two cent
a. Engraved die on India, die sunk on card reduced to about die size

black	*1,500.*
scarlet	*1,500.*
green	*1,500.*
ultramarine	*1,500.*
blue	*1,500.*

b. Die essay on India cut close and block sunk on card (about 45x45mm)

scarlet	*1,500.*
green	*1,500.*
blue	*1,500.*

147-E1

Design size: 20x25mm
Die size: 43x48mm
Vignette of Lincoln in large ornate "3" with rounded top. Die proofs exist on full size 148x231mm card bearing a handstamped imprint as illustrated with 145-E1C.

147-E1 Three Cent
a. Engraved die on India, die sunk on card reduced to about die size

black	*2,250.*
scarlet	*2,250.*
green	*2,250.*
blue	*2,250.*

b. Die sunk on proof paper 62x68mm

ultramarine	*2,500.*
black (stamp size)	*1,000.*

c. Engraved die on India, cut close and block sunk on card (about 45x45mm)

scarlet	*1,500.*
green	*1,500.*
blue	*1,500.*

148-E1

Design size: 21½x22½mm
Die size: approx. 51x53mm
Blank vignette in large ornate "6."

148-E1 Six Cent
a. Engraved die on India, die sunk on card reduced to about die size

black	*1,500.*
scarlet	*1,500.*
green	*1,500.*
blue	*1,500.*
ultramarine	*1,500.*

b. Die essay on India cut close and block sunk on card (about 45x45mm)

scarlet	*1,650.*
green	*1,650.*
blue	*1,650.*

Series 2: Variations on a three-cent frame pertaining to a vignette of Columbia

147-E2

Design size: 11½x15½mm
Die size: 47x51mm
Vignette only of Columbia. Continental imprint and die number below design. All known examples have the original die number crossed out by three lines and replaced with V48134 from a reworked die by the American Bank Note Co. Items on Kraft paper are from the archives of the ABNCo.

147-E2
a. Engraved die on India, die sunk on card

black	*1,450.*

b. Die on India reduced and mounted on Kraft paper (from ABNCo. archives)

black	—

Type I: "Flat topped" numeral "3," foliate frame around; 10½x14½ mm oval vignette frame

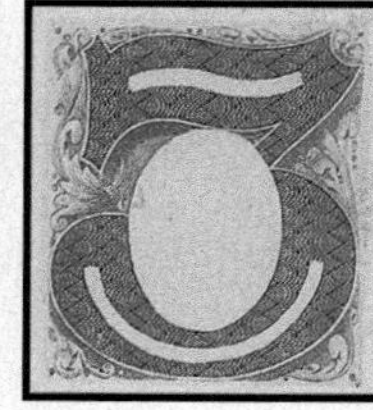

147-E3

Die State 1: blank panels within, no vignette.

147-E3 3c Engraved die on India cut close to design, mounted on India and block sunk on card

black	*2,500.*
green	*2,500.*

147-E3B

No. 147-E2, Columbia vignette in black, cut to shape and mounted in oval.

147-E3B 3c Engraved die on India on card, reduced to approx. 35x41mm

black	*2,750.*
green	*2,750.*

147-E4

Die State 2: As Die State 1 with panels engraved, "THREE CENTS" above, "UNITED STATES POSTAGE" below. Columbia vignette cut to oval shape and pasted in.

147-E4 3c Engraved die on India, die sunk on card

black	*2,250.*
green	*2,000.*

Type II: "Flat topped" numeral; finished panel lettering, 10x14½mm oval vignette frame.

147-E5

Die State 1: numeral only, surrounded by a lined frame 21x25mm without ornamentation.

147-E5 3c Engraved die on India cut close and mounted on card

black	*2,250.*

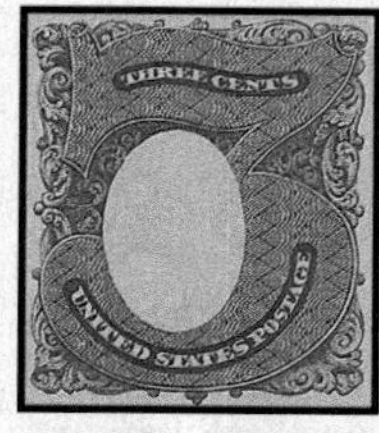

147-E6A

Die State 2: numeral surrounded by scrolled ornamentation, no vignette.

147-E6A 3c Engraved die on India on card, reduced to approx 35x41mm

black	*2,250.*
green	*2,000.*

147-E6B

No. 147-E6A with black Columbia vignette cut to oval and pasted in.

147-E6B 3c Engraved die on India on card, reduced to approx 35x41mm

black	*2,650.*
green	*2,650.*

147-E6C

Die State 3: As Die State 2, but die number "560" added and corrosion marks in vignette frame.

147-E6C 3c Engraved
d. On proof paper reduced to stamp size

black	*1,000.*

e. On India paper reduced to stamp size, on card

green	*2,000.*

f. On India paper, stamp size

green	*750.*

National Banknote Co.

145-E2

Die size: 64x74mm

Engraved vignette of Franklin facing right.

145-E2 1c Die on India, die sunk on card
- black (with pencil lines on bust) *700.*
- dull dark orange *700.*

145-E3

Engraved incomplete Franklin vignette facing right mounted over pencil sketch of frame.

145-E3 1c Die on thin white card, 55x66mm, black *2,850.*

145-E4

Incomplete Franklin vignette mounted on more complete pencil sketch of frame.

145-E4 1c Die on thin white card, orange brown *2,000.*

145-E5

Design size: 20x26mm
Engraved vignette mounted on pencil and watercolor frame design, "U.S. POSTAGE" and "ONE CENT" penciled on card.

145-E5 1c Die on thin white card, 45x51mm, dull dark orange *5,750.*

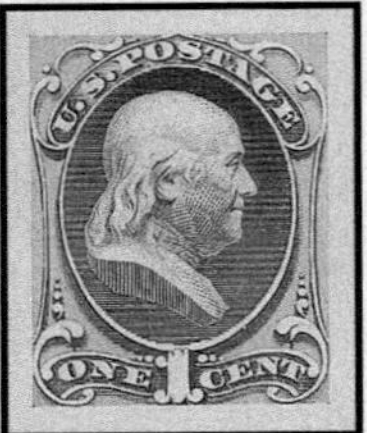

145-E6

Incomplete engraving of entire design; lower edge of bust vert. shading only.

145-E6 1c

a. Die on 64x71mm India, die sunk on card
- ultramarine *475.*
- red *475.*
- orange brown *475.*
- red brown *475.*
- blue green *475.*
- mauve *475.*
- dull lilac *475.*
- black *475.*
- gray *475.*
- carmine *475.*
- carmine rose *475.*
- dull rose *475.*
- dull yellow brown *475.*
- brown violet *475.*
- light green *475.*
- green *475.*
- gray olive *475.*
- yellow *475.*

b. Die on bond, die sunk on card, dark yellow *750.*

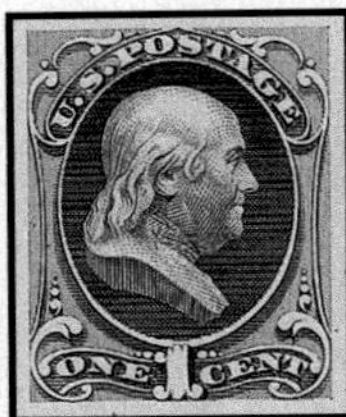

145-E8

Completed die: additional shading lines in background, four horiz. shading lines at top of lower edge of bust.

145-E8 1c

a. Die on India, die sunk on card
- black *475.*
- blue green *475.*
- carmine *475.*
- yellow *475.*
- orange brown *475.*
- orange *475.*
- gray green *475.*
- dull red violet *475.*
- dark blue *475.*

b. Die on ivory glazed paper, 65x72mm
- black *425.*
- black brown *425.*
- scarlet *425.*
- blue *425.*

c. Completed die on thick wove, dismal dusky yellow *425.*

145-E9

Die size: 50½x64mm
Engraved vignette of Franklin facing left, no shading lines at top of bust, etc.

145-E9 1c

a. Die on white glazed paper, black *475.*

b. Die on India, mounted on card stamped "J.I. PEASE.", black *450.*

146-E2

Die size: 62x76mm
Vignette only of Jackson in high stiff collar.

146-E2 2c Die on India, die sunk on card
- black *900.*
- orange brown *900.*

146-E3

Engraved Jackson vignette mounted on watercolor frame.

146-E3 2c Die on thin white card, 46x89mm, black vignette, dark gray frame *5,000.*

146-E4

Engraved Jackson vignette, mounted on watercolor frame (diff. from No. 146-E3).

146-E4 2c Die on thin white card, 46x89mm, black vignette, gray frame *5,000.*

146-E5

Similar to No. 146-E4 but with pencil border around frame.

146-E5 2c Die on thin white card, 45x50mm, dark orange *5,000.*

146-E6

Incomplete die: without shading lines under value ribbon, vert. lines in colorless strips, and broken horiz. lines at top and bottom of frame.

146-E6 2c Die on thin white card, dark orange *2,500.*

146-E7

Die size: 64½x73mm
Completed die of unadopted design.

146-E7 2c

a. Die on India
- carmine *1,000.*
- deep rose *1,000.*
- scarlet *1,000.*
- dim dusky orange orange red *1,000.*
- deep yellow orange *1,000.*
- bone brown *1,000.*
- orange brown *1,000.*
- brown *1,000.*
- canary yellow *1,000.*
- yellow brown *1,000.*
- dark olive green *1,000.*
- green *1,000.*
- dim dusky blue green *1,000.*
- dark blue *1,000.*
- deep ultramarine *1,000.*
- bright blue *1,000.*
- dull violet *1,000.*
- smoky deep red violet red *1,000.*
- gray *1,000.*
- black *1,000.*

b. Die on ivory glazed paper, about 64x77mm
- black *1,000.*
- brown black *1,000.*
- scarlet *1,000.*
- blue *1,000.*

c. Die on thin wove, dark yellow *1,000.*

146-E9

Die size: 62x76mm
Incomplete vignette of Jackson as on issued stamp: incomplete shading in eye and hair in front of ear, right neck tendon on chest not shaded.

146-E9 2c

a. Die on India, on 55x66mm card
- black *750.*
- orange *750.*
- deep yellow orange *750.*

red brown 750.
orange brown 750.
dark blue green 750.
red violet 750.

Also known on 87x143mm card showing full die sinkage, pencil inscribed "2c" above and "Jackson" below sinkage area. Value, *$750.*

The red violet shade also is known cut to shape and mounted on card, presumably as a template for a hand-drawn essay for the frame. Value $1,000.

b. Die on glazed paper, die sinkage 50x63mm, black *1,000.*

146-E10

Completed Jackson vignette.

146-E10 2c Die on glazed paper, black *750.*

146-E11

Engraved vignette with pencil and watercolor frame design, labels blank.

146-E11 2c Die on thin white card, 50x60mm, dim dusky bright blue green vignette, dark green frame *6,250.*

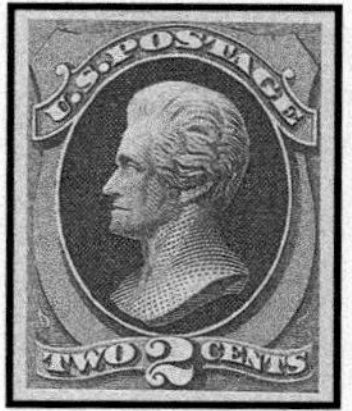

146-E12

Die size: 62x75mm
Incomplete engraving of entire design: no leaves on wide bands at sides below vignette, neck tendon and hair in front of ear changed, top of head incomplete, ear hole too dark. This design essayed for envelopes on thick papers.

146-E12 2c Die on India, die sunk on card

carmine *1,250.*
orange *1,250.*
brown orange *1,250.*
brown *1,250.*
blue *1,250.*
violet *1,250.*
green *1,250.*

147-E7

Incomplete engraved vignette of Lincoln (horiz. line background), mounted on pencil and watercolor frame design.

147-E7 3c Die on thin white card, black vignette, gray black frame *4,000.*

147-E8

Design size: 11x18mm
Incomplete engraving of head only of Washington.

147-E8 3c Die on white glazed paper, black *550.*

147-E9

Die size: 16x20mm
Engraved Washington vignette only as adopted.

147-E9 3c Die on white glazed paper, black *650.*

Nos. 147-E8 and 147-E9 may have been made from completed dies of No. 147 to produce Nos. 184-E9 and 184-E10.

147-E11

Design size: 20x25½mm
Incomplete engraved vignette (horiz. lined background), mounted on pencil and watercolor frame design.

147-E11 3c Die on thin white card, 45x54mm, carmine vignette, dim light red violet red frame *5,000.*

147-E12

Incomplete engraving of entire design: no horizontal lines on nose, parts of hair, chin, collar, forehead unfinished.

147-E12 3c Die on India, die sunk on card

black *575.*
deep red *575.*
carmine *575.*
yellow orange *575.*
brown *575.*
red brown *575.*
dark red brown *575.*
yellow brown *575.*
ultramarine *575.*
dark blue *575.*
dark violet blue *575.*
blue green *575.*
dark red violet *575.*

147-E12A

Similar to No. 147-E12 but two sets of horizontal lines in collar area have been lengthened and strengthened; also 11 scored lines cut across thick ink lines of the shoulder cut of vignette.

147-E12A Die on India, dull grayish red —

147-E13

Issued stamp, No. 147, in trial colors, underprinted network in fugitive ink.

147-E13 3c

a. On thick paper, perf. 12, gummed
gray blue, underprinting gray brown *150.*
gray blue, underprinting olive gray *150.*
green, underprinting olive gray *150.*
dim red, underprinting olive gray *150.*
dull orange, underprinting olive gray *150.*
brown, underprinting olive gray *150.*

b. As "a," faint 6mm-high horiz. bar trial cancel
dim red *450.*
dull orange *450.*

c. As "a," underprinting omitted
gray blue —
dim red —
dull orange —
brown —

d. As "a," imperf, green, underprinting olive gray 325.
Pair *700.*

e. As "d," underprinting omitted 325.
Pair *700.*
P# block of 10 —

Multiples of the No. 147-E13 varieties can be found with fully or partially underprinted stamps in conjunction with underprinting-omitted stamps.

148-E2

Design size: 19½x25½mm
Die size: 63x76mm
Engraved Lincoln vignette only, hair brushed back, horiz. line background.

148-E2 6c Die on India, die sunk on card

black *1,000.*
blue *1,000.*

148-E3

Incomplete engraved Lincoln vignette (horiz. lined background) mounted on pencil and watercolor frame with blank labels. Unique.

148-E3 6c Die on thin white card, 45x52mm, dim blue vignette, dim dark blue frame *14,000.*

148-E4

Incomplete engraving of entire design: horiz. line background in vignette, lines on cheek and hair unfinished, capital "S" and dotted "i" in "Six" and capital "C" in "Cents," plus ornaments in top corners.

148-E4 6c Die on India, on card, about 50x52mm

carmine *700.*
rose *700.*
dull rose *700.*
red violet *700.*
dull violet *700.*
deep ultramarine *700.*
dark black blue *700.*
yellow *700.*
green *700.*
dark green *700.*
dark red brown *700.*
deep yellow brown *700.*
yellow brown *700.*
orange brown *700.*

Incomplete engraving of entire design: horiz. line background in vignette, no shading directly under value label, shadows on "SIX CENTS" and shading on ornaments in upper corners unfinished, capital "S" and dotted "i" in "Six" and capital "C" in "Cents," plus ornaments in top corners.

148-E5 6c Die on India, on card
ultramarine *1,000.*
carmine *1,250.*

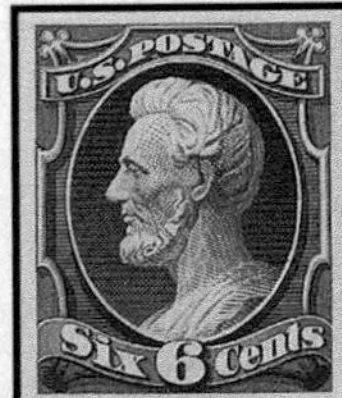
148-E6

Similar to No. 148-E5 but with diagonal lines added to vignette background, capital "S" and dotted "i" in "Six" and capital "C" in "Cents," plus ornaments in top corners. (Essay in orange brown has pencil notations for changes.)

148-E6 6c Die on India, die sunk on card
black *1,000.*
dull carmine *1,000.*
dark rose *1,000.*
yellowish black *1,000.*
brown *1,000.*
gray brown *1,000.*
black brown *1,000.*
yellow *1,000.*
gray olive green *1,000.*
dark green *1,000.*
ultramarine *1,000.*
deep ultramarine *1,000.*
dull ultramarine *1,000.*
violet *1,000.*
dark violet *1,000.*
red violet *1,000.*
orange brown *1,000.*

148-E7

Similar to No. 148-E6 but with dots added to top of hair, capital "S" and dotted "i" in "Six" and capital "C" in "Cents," plus ornaments in top corners.

148-E7 6c Die on India, on card
dark carmine *1,000.*
dull rose *1,000.*
orange *1,000.*
yellow brown *1,000.*
dark brown *1,000.*
black brown *1,000.*
yellow green *1,000.*
blue green *1,000.*
ultramarine *1,000.*
dark red violet *1,000.*

148-E8

Similar to No. 148-E7 but die with lines on cheek softened to dots only, capital "S" and dotted "i" in "Six" and capital "C" in "Cents," plus ornaments in top corners.

148-E8 6c Die on India
yellow green *250.*
brown *250.*
rose *250.*

All known examples are much reduced.

148-E9

Incomplete engraving of entire design, similar to No. 148-E10 but with hair brushed forward as on adopted design but shadow under hair in front of ear is round at bottom, not pointed as on approved design. Shading on cheek behind nostril is dotted instead of lined on completed design, undotted "I" in "SIX" and lower case "c" in "cents," plus no ornaments in top corners. Shading extended at sides.

148-E9 6c Die on India, on card, red violet *1,200.*

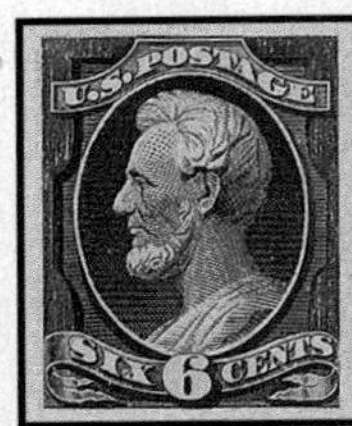
148-E9A

Similar to No. 148-E9, except recessed shadow sections do not continue above "U.S. POSTAGE" label or at sides.

148-E9A 6c Die on India, on card *2,500.*

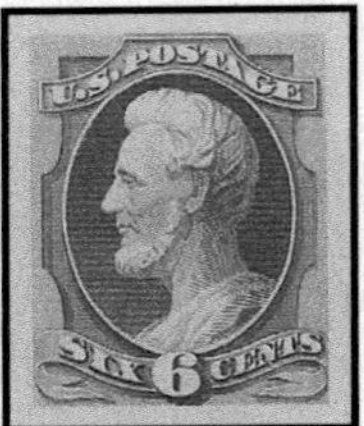
148-E10

Die size: 64x75mm
Frame as adopted, vignette similar to No. 148-E9 but with hair brushed back; lines on cheek. Undotted "I" in "Six" and lower case "c" in "cents," plus no ornaments in top corners. Shading extended at sides.

148-E10 6c
a. Die on India, die sunk on card, deep blue *850.*
b. Die on India, about 30x35mm, carmine *700.*
c. As "a," but no panels above top label, carmine *2,500.*

148-E11

Similar to No. 148-E10a but dots (not lines) on cheek and on lower lip. Shadow under hair in front of ear is rounded at bottom, not pointed as on approved design. Undotted "I" in "Six" and lower case "c" in "cents," plus no ornaments in top corners. Shading extended at sides.

148-E11 6c Die on India, on card
rose pink *700.*
deep rose *700.*
pale rose *700.*
brown rose *700.*
rose carmine *700.*
deep carmine *700.*
brown *700.*
yellow brown *700.*
blue *700.*
red violet *700.*

Die of completed vignette only with hair brushed forward.

148-E12 6c Die on white glazed paper, black *1,500.*

149-E4

Die size: 62x75mm
Vignette of Stanton.

149-E4 7c Die on India, on card, black *1,000.*

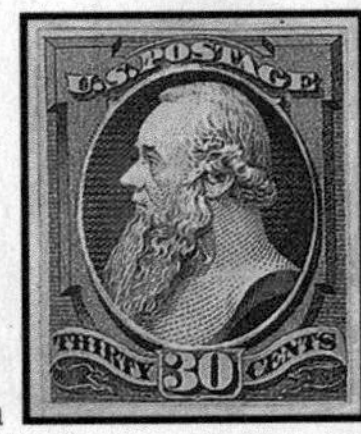
149-E4a

Engraved frame of adopted 30c design but with vignette cut out and mounted over Stanton vignette on India No. 149-E4.

149-E4a Stanton vignette with 30c frame on thin, stiff paper mounted on top, black *500.*

The status of No. 149-E4a has been questioned.

149-E6

Design as issued but shading under ear incomplete.

149-E6 7c Die on India, die sunk on card
black *500.*
dark red *500.*
light red *500.*
gray green *500.*
gray black *500.*
yellow brown *500.*
dark brown *500.*
dull yellow brown *500.*
dull red brown *500.*
blue green *500.*
ultramarine *500.*
dim blue *500.*
lilac *500.*
red orange *500.*
yellow orange *500.*

Similar to No. 149-E6 but with dots added on forehead.

149-E7 7c Die on India, brown *1,250.*

150-E1

Design size: 20x25½mm
Incomplete engraved vignette of Jefferson (horiz. line background) mounted on pencil and watercolor frame design with blank labels.

150-E1 10c Die on thin white card, 45x51mm, black vignette, gray frame *3,000.*

150-E2

Design size: 19½x25½mm
Die size: 62x75mm

Jefferson vignette with incomplete engraving of frame: unfinished shading under "TEN" ribbon, under oval at ends of "U.S. POSTAGE," and under shield over ends of value label ribbons.

150-E2 10c Die on India, on card, deep blue green *2,500.*

Similar to No. 150-E2 but showing horizontal shading lines only.

150-E2A 10c Die on India, die sunk on 152x225mm card

blue green	*750.*
red violet	*750.*

150-E3

Completed engraving of unadopted design.

150-E3 10c

a. Die on India, die sunk on card

carmine	*750.*
rose	*750.*
gray brown rose	*750.*
yellow	*750.*
yellow brown	*750.*
orange	*750.*
orange brown	*750.*
brown	*750.*
chocolate	*750.*
green	*750.*
blue green	*750.*
greenish gray	*750.*
blue	*750.*
dull violet	*750.*
dull red violet	*750.*
dark navy blue	*750.*
ultramarine	*750.*
deep ultramarine	*750.*
dull dusky blue	*750.*
navy blue	*750.*
slate	*750.*

b. Die on bond

dull dusky brown	*500.*
brown gray	*500.*

All known examples of No. 153-E3b are reduced.

150-E4

Three separate designs. Left one dark blue green, similar to No. 150-E3 but shows engraved attempt to remove coat collar to obtain nude neck (some coat still shows under chin). Middle one brown orange (No. 150-E2) with coat collar and top of hair cut out, neck and bust drawn in. Right one black vignette of head finally adopted (No. 150-E7).

150-E4 10c Dies on India, on card *2,500.*

150-E5

Design size: 19½x25½mm

Same frame as No. 150-E2, but Jefferson vignette has hair arranged differently and bust has no clothing.

150-E5 10c

a. Die on India, die sunk on card

black	*600.*
scarlet	*600.*
brown	*600.*
blue	*600.*
green	*600.*

b. Die on ivory glazed paper, 66x75mm

black	*500.*
black brown	*500.*
scarlet	*500.*
blue	*500.*

c. Die on thin wove, dark yellow *500.*

150-E6

Frame of No. 150-E5 with vignette cut out and replaced by black vignette as adopted.

150-E6 10c Die on India

deep orange brown	*1,750.*
black	*1,500.*

150-E7

Die size: 62x76mm

Vignette of Jefferson as adopted.

150-E7 10c Die on India, die sunk on card

dark ultramarine	*700.*
yellow	*700.*
brown	*700.*

151-E1

Design size: 20x25½mm

Engraved vignette of Washington (No. 79-E37b) mounted on incomplete pencil drawing of frame design.

151-E1 12c Die on India, on 38x47½mm card, black vignette, pencil frame *2,500.*

151-E2

Design size: 20x25½mm

Engraved vignette of Washington (No. 79-E37b) mounted on pencil and watercolor frame design with blank labels.

151-E2 12c Die on card, 46x89mm, black vignette, gray frame *3,000.*

151-E3

Design size: 20x25½mm

Engraved vignette of Washington (No. 79-E37b) mounted on pencil and watercolor frame design with ribbons and blank labels.

151-E3 12c Die on card, 46x89mm, black vignette, gray frame *3,000.*

151-E4

Design size: 20x25½mm

Engraved vignette of Washington (No. 79-E37b) mounted on pencil and watercolor frame design with "U, S, 12" and blank labels.

151-E4 12c Die on card, 46x89mm, black vignette, gray frame *3,000.*

151-E5

Design size: 19½x25½mm
Die size: 62x74mm
Vignette of Henry Clay only.

151-E5 12c Die on India, die sunk on card

black	*600.*
deep carmine	*600.*
yellow	*600.*
yellow brown	*600.*
brown orange	*600.*
dark orange brown	*600.*
black brown	*600.*
ultramarine	*600.*
dark blue green	*600.*
red violet	*600.*

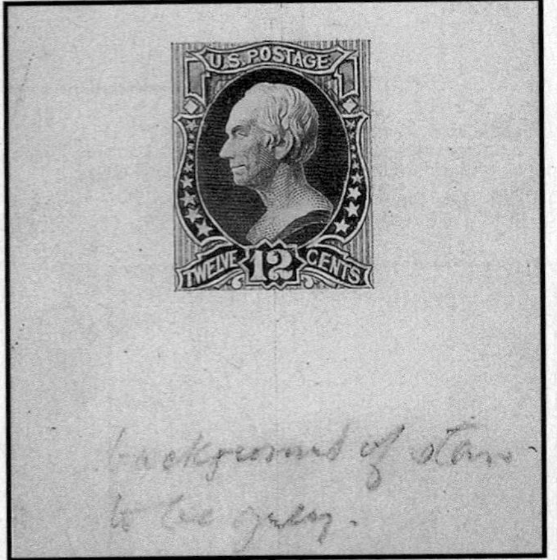

151-E6

Incomplete Clay vignette mounted on watercolor shield-like frame design on gray background, pencil notation "background of stars to be grey."

151-E6 12c Die on card, 53x75mm, blue black vignette, blue frame *4,000.*

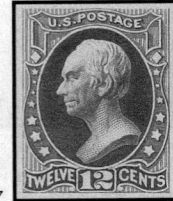

151-E7

Die sinkage size: 63x77mm
Completed die of unadopted design similar to No. 151-E6. This design essayed for envelopes on thick paper.

151-E7 12c

a. Die on India, on card	
deep orange brown	*900.*
green	*900.*
deep ultramarine	*900.*
violet	*900.*
deep red	*900.*
deep orange red	*900.*
orange	*900.*
dusky red	*900.*
b. Die on wove	
carmine	*700.*
orange	*700.*
brown	*700.*
orange brown	*700.*
ultramarine	*700.*
c. Die on card colored yellow, black	*700.*

151-E8

Engraved vignette of Washington mounted on partly complete pencil drawing of frame, pencil notation "new border for clay 12c."

151-E8 12c Die on card, black, pencil frame *2,750.*

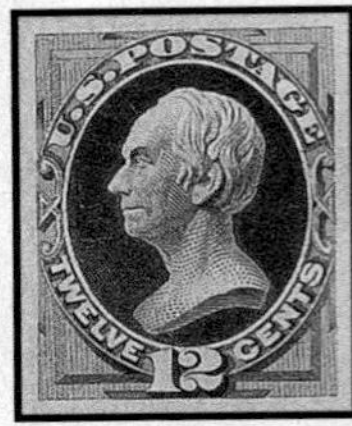

151-E9

Die size: 55x63mm
Incomplete engraving of entire adopted design, without 3 vert. shading lines at left side of lower triangle.

151-E9 12c

a. Die on India, die sunk on card	
black	*650.*
carmine	*650.*
blue green	*650.*
blue	*650.*
light blue	*650.*
orange	*650.*
orange brown	*650.*
dull red	*650.*
brown red	*650.*
b. Die on proof paper, about 38x45mm	
carmine	*650.*
dull carmine	*650.*
orange brown	*650.*
dull red	*650.*
ultramarine	*650.*
c. Die on India, on card, about 30x35mm, dark blue	*650.*

152-E1

Design size: 19½x25mm
Incomplete vignette of Webster with side whiskers bolder than as adopted, mounted on watercolor frame design with 15 and blank labels.

152-E1 15c Die on white card, 40x61mm, dim red vignette, light red violet frame *2,250.*

152-E2

Design size: 19½x25mm
Die size: 63x76mm
Incomplete engraving of vignette only: missing shading under ear and at back of neck.

152-E2 15c Die on India, die sunk on card, black *750.*

152-E3

Vignette similar to No. 152-E2 but with shading under ear, more shading at back of neck.

152-E3 15c Die on India, die sunk on card

black	*700.*
dark orange	*700.*
orange	*700.*
yellow	*700.*
red violet	*700.*
ultramarine	*700.*
brown	*700.*

152-E5

Incomplete engraved design: shading on corner panel bevels incomplete, side whiskers bolder than as adopted. Also essayed for envelopes on thick paper.

152-E5 15c Die on India, die sunk on card, orange brown *750.*

Similar to No. 152-E5 but with pencil marks suggesting shading on corner panels.

152-E6 15c Die on India, orange brown *750.*

152-E7

Similar to No. 152-E5 with engraved shading added to corner panels but white areas incomplete.

152-E7 15c Die on India

orange	*650.*
orange yellow	*650.*
orange brown	*650.*
green	*650.*
red violet	*650.*
rose carmine	*650.*

152-E8

Similar to No. 152-E7 but shading on corner panels complete.

152-E8 15c Die on India, on card, black *1,000.*

153-E1

Design size: 18x23mm
Incomplete engraved vignette of Scott mounted on pencil sketch of partial frame design.

153-E1 24c Die on white card, 33x39mm, dull red violet vignette, pencil frame *1,750.*

153-E2

Design size: 19½x25mm
Complete engraved vignette mounted on pencil and watercolor frame design with "U.S. POSTAGE" in ink.

153-E2 24c Die on white card, 73x110mm, dim blue green *3,250.*

153-E3

Die size: 62x76mm
Incomplete engraved vignette only.

153-E3 24c Die on India, die sunk on card

black	*600.*
yellow	*600.*
yellow brown	*600.*
dark orange brown	*600.*
ultramarine	*600.*
dark ultramarine	*600.*
red violet	*600.*

153-E4

Die size: 62x77mm
Incomplete design as adopted: upper corners not squared outside scrolls, no periods after U and S in stars.

153-E4 24c Die on India, die sunk on card

carmine	*650.*
orange	*650.*
brown orange	*650.*
yellow brown	*650.*
deep brown	*650.*
ultramarine	*650.*
dark red violet	*650.*
green	*650.*

Value off card, cut down, $275.

Previous No. 154-E1 is now No. 149-E4a.

154-E2

Pencil drawing of entire design, labeled "Scott."

154-E2 30c Pencil drawing on white card, 53x92mm *2,400.*

Engraved vignette of Hamilton mounted on pencil drawing of frame.

154-E3 30c Die on card, yellow brown vignette, pencil frame *1,500.*

154-E4

Incomplete engraved vignette of Hamilton.

154-E4 30c Die on India, die sunk on card

yellow brown	*700.*
dark ultramarine blue	*700.*
orange	*700.*

154-E5

Vignette of Hamilton with more engraving on forehead, nose, neck, etc.

154-E5 30c Die on India, die sunk on card

dark red brown	*700.*
dull carmine	*700.*
ultramarine	*700.*

155-E1

Pencil drawing of entire design, labeled "Perry."

155-E1 90c Pencil drawing on white card, 53x92mm *3,000.*

155-E2

Design size: 19½x25mm
Engraved vignette of Perry mounted on pencil and watercolor frame design.

155-E2 90c Die on white card, 73x110mm, dull dark violet vignette, dull red violet frame *3,250.*

155-E3

Die size: 58x79mm
Incomplete engraving of Perry vignette as adopted.

155-E3 90c

a. Die on India, die sunk on card	
black	*1,500.*
deep yellow orange	*600.*
orange brown	*600.*
dark brown	*600.*
dull carmine	*600.*
ultramarine blue	*600.*
dark blue green	*600.*
dark red violet	*600.*
b. Die on white ivory paper, black	*600.*
c. Die on card, carmine	*750.*

155-E4

Similar to No. 155-E3 but more lines in hair above forehead.

155-E4 90c Die on India, on card, black *600.*

155-E5

Incomplete engraving of design as adopted: rope above vignette unfinished. Known in black with pencil drawing of rope beneath on the card; value thus, $3,000. Also essayed for envelopes on thick paper.

155-E5 90c Die on India, die sunk on card

black	*750.*
carmine, off card	*325.*
orange	*750.*
dark orange	*750.*
yellow brown	*750.*
brown	*750.*
deep orange brown	*750.*
deep ultramarine	*750.*
blue green	*750.*
red violet	*750.*

Value off card, cut down, $250.

1873 ISSUE

Continental Bank Note Co.

179-E1

Die size: 20x25mm

Vignette of Taylor by Bureau of Engraving and Printing, in engraved frame.

179-E1 Five Cents, Die on India

black	*4,500.*
blue	*4,500.*

179-E2

Design size: 24x29mm

Vignette of Taylor by Bureau of Engraving and Printing, in ornate wash drawing of frame ("FIVE CENTS" black, on shaded ribbon).

179-E2 5c Die on card, black *4,000.*

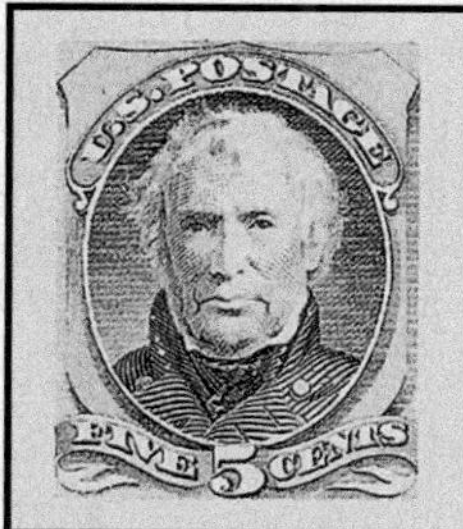

179-E3

Incomplete vignette: hair, coat, background, etc., unfinished.

179-E3 5c Die on India, violet *2,000.*

George W. Bowlsby 1873 essay similar in concept to his No. 63-E13 but without coupon attached. It consisted of an unused 1c stamp (No. 156) with horiz. sewing machine perfs. through center, gummed on upper half only, as described in his Dec. 26, 1865 patent. Stamp was meant to be torn in half by postal clerk as cancellation, to prevent reuse.

156-E1 1c blue *250.*

1876 Experimental Ink and Paper Essays

Plate designs of 1873-75 issues in normal colors, printed on paper tinted with sensitive inks and on heavily laid (horiz.) colored papers (unless otherwise noted).

156-E2 1c Blue on:
carmine *150.*
pale rose *150.*
deep yellow *150.*
pale violet *150.*

158-E1 3c Green on:
pale rose *150.*
deep yellow *150.*
pale violet *150.*

158-E2

158-E2 3c Green on paper covered with pink varnish which vanishes with the color *100.*

158-E3 3c Green on thick white blotting paper which absorbs canceling ink *100.*

161-E1

161-E1 10c Brown on:
pale rose *150.*
deep yellow *150.*
pale violet *150.*

163-E1 15c Yellow orange on:
pale rose *200.*
deep yellow *200.*
pale violet *200.*

165-E1 30c Gray black on:
pale rose *200.*
deep yellow *200.*
pale violet *200.*

166-E1 90c Rose carmine on:
pale rose *200.*
deep yellow *200.*
pale violet *200.*

178-E1

178-E1 2c Vermilion on:
pale rose *150.*
deep yellow *150.*
pale violet *150.*

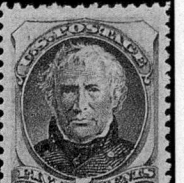

179-E4

179-E4 5c Blue on:
pale rose *300.*
deep yellow *300.*
pale violet *300.*

See No. 147-E13.

1877 Essays
Philadelphia Bank Note Co.

Die essays for this section were all engraved. The frame-only dies for all values of this series were engraved with two values appearing per die, except the 3c (No. 184-E1) which was engraved alone. In each case the listing is under the lower denomination. The Washington vignette associated with each value of the frames is from engraved master die No. 14. (No. 182-E1).

Except as noted, plate essays in this section are all lithographed from a composite stone plate of two panes. The left pane ("plate 1") consists of horiz. rows of four of the 1c, 3c, 7c, 24c and 90c. The right pane ("plate 2") consists of horiz. rows of four 2c, 6c, 12c and 30c. "Printed by Philadelphia Bank Note Co. Patented June 16, 1876" imprint below 2nd and 3rd designs on each row.

See note above No. 63-E1.

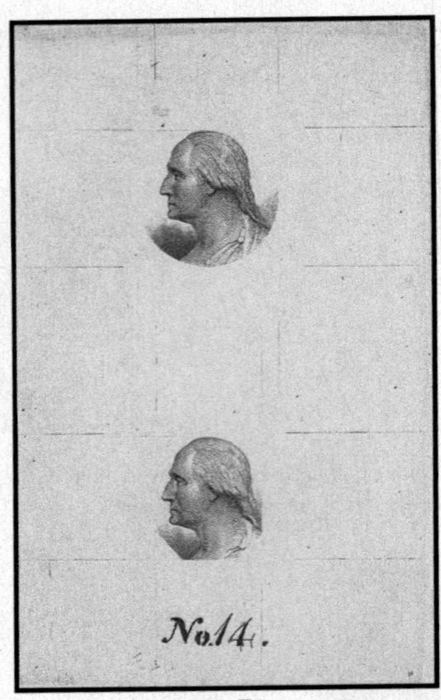

182-E1

Vignette master die "No. 14": two slightly diff. vignettes of Washington, one above the other, bottom one with truncated queue, bust and shading in front of neck.

182-E1
a. Die on old white glazed paper, black *500.*
b. Die on proof paper (1903)
black *100.*
carmine *100.*
dull carmine *100.*
dusky carmine *100.*
yellow *100.*
dull scarlet *100.*
dull orange *100.*
brown orange *100.*
brown *100.*
gray olive *100.*
blue green *100.*
dark green *100.*
black blue *100.*
ultramarine *100.*
violet *100.*
red violet *100.*

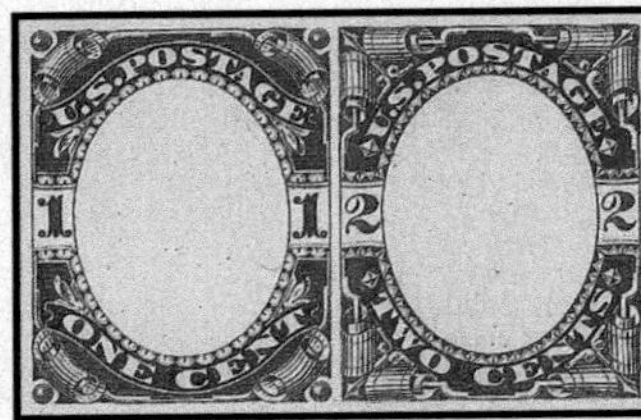
182-E2b

Design size: 20x25mm
Die size: 98x53mm
Frames of 1c and 2c side by side.

182-E2 1c + 2c
a. Die on white pelure
dark carmine *250.*
orange *250.*
brown *250.*
blue green *250.*
blue *250.*
b. Die with vertical line between designs (die size 85x54mm), on India, die sunk on card
dusky red *400.*
deep orange *400.*
orange brown *400.*
dark green *400.*
dark blue *400.*
c. Die on stiff glazed paper, black *400.*
d. Die on proof paper, printed through a mat (1903)
black *100.*
bright carmine *100.*
dull carmine *100.*
dim scarlet *100.*
dark orange *100.*
dull yellow *100.*
dark orange brown *100.*
black olive *100.*
dark blue green *100.*
dark blue *100.*
ultramarine *100.*
dark navy blue *100.*
blue violet *100.*
dull violet *100.*
red violet *100.*
e. Plate sheet of 1c, 2c, 3c, 12c, 24c, 30c, 90c frames only, on card, pale green blue *1,500.*

182-E3b

Complete 1c design, lithographed.

182-E3 1c
a. Plate on stamp paper, imperf., gummed
black *75.*
blue green *75.*
bright ultramarine *75.*
yellow *75.*
b. Plate on stamp paper, perf. 12, gummed
dark red orange *50.*
orange brown *50.*
red brown *50.*
red violet *50.*
violet blue *50.*
ultramarine *50.*
c. Plate 1 "sheet" of 20, complete designs, without imprint, on old glazed paper, imperf., deep brown orange *800.*
d. As "c," with imprint, on old glazed paper, imperf., gummed
black *800.*
dull deep violet red *800.*
ultramarine *800.*
scarlet *800.*
orange *800.*
carmine *800.*
dark carmine *800.*
green *800.*
bluish green *800.*
e. As "d," perf. 12, gummed
dull deep violet red *700.*
ultramarine *700.*
red brown *700.*
violet blue *700.*

Concerning plate 1 sheets of 20, note that composite stone plates also contained the plate 2 sheets of 16 listed as Nos. 183-E2c to 183-E2e. Many such composite sheets remain intact. All separated plate 1 or plate 2 sheets originally were part of a composite sheet.

183-E2b

Complete 2c design, lithographed.

183-E2 2c
a. Plate on stamp paper, imperf.
blue green *60.*
bright ultramarine *60.*
brown *60.*
b. Plate on stamp paper, perf. 12, gummed
bright red orange *35.*
dull red orange *35.*
dark red orange *35.*
red brown *35.*
dark red brown *35.*
dark orange brown *35.*
yellow brown *35.*
dull yellow green *35.*
green *35.*
dull ultramarine *35.*
bright ultramarine *35.*
blue violet *35.*
red violet *35.*
light red violet *35.*
violet red *35.*

c. Plate 2 "sheet" of 16, complete designs, without imprint, on old glazed paper, imperf., deep brown orange *600.*
d. As "c," with imprint, on old glazed paper, imperf., gummed
black *600.*
dull deep violet red *600.*
e. As "d," perf. 12, gummed
dull deep violet red *500.*
deep brown orange *500.*

See note following No. 182-E3e.

184-E1

Design size: 20x25mm
Die size: 54x55mm
Engraved frame of 3c alone on die.

184-E1 3c
a. Die on pelure paper
dark carmine *250.*
dark orange *250.*
orange brown *250.*
bright blue *250.*
green *250.*
dark green *250.*
b. Die on proof paper (1903)
black *100.*
bright carmine *100.*
dull carmine *100.*
dim scarlet *100.*
dark orange *100.*
dull yellow *100.*
dark orange brown *100.*
black olive *100.*
dark rose *100.*
green *100.*
yellow green *100.*
dark blue green *100.*
dark blue *100.*
deep ultramarine *100.*
dark navy blue *100.*
blue violet *100.*
dull violet *100.*
red violet *100.*

184-E2a

184-E2a Variety

Built-up model of engraved frame cut to shape inside and out, mounted atop engraved vignette of the same or different color. Warning: fraudulent models combining engraved and lithographed materials exist.

184-E2 3c
a. Die on proof paper
dark scarlet, cut close *250.*
blue green, cut close *250.*
deep blue, cut close *250.*
deep blue frame, dark scarlet vignette *500.*
blue green frame, dark scarlet vignette *500.*
b. Four examples mounted 2½mm apart on stiff white card, 80x87mm
red *1,000.*
orange brown *1,000.*
green *1,000.*
blue *1,000.*
violet *1,000.*
green frame, light blue vignette *1,000.*

Built-up model as No. 184-E2, vignette as No. 184-E5 with dark background.

184-E3 3c Die on proof paper, scarlet *250.*

184-E4

Complete 3c design, vignette with light background.

184-E4 3c
c. Plate lithographed on stamp paper, imperf.
black *75.*
carmine *75.*
green *75.*
dark green *75.*
bright ultramarine *75.*
orange *75.*

No. 184-E4c exists in two plates of 9 tete-beche, in diff. colors, on same piece of paper. Value, $1,400 sheet of 18.

d. Plate lithographed on stamp paper, perf. 12, gummed
dark red orange *50.*
red brown *50.*
red voilet *50.*
brown orange *50.*
ultramarine *50.*
violet blue *50.*
e. Plate sheet of 9 (3x3), imprint below, on stiff white wove
carmine *300.*
blue green *300.*
f. Plate sheet of 9 (3x3), on glazed thin wove
carmine *300.*
blue green *300.*
blue *300.*
orange *300.*
g. Plate sheet of 9 (3x3), on yellowish wove
carmine *300.*
blue green *300.*
blue *300.*
h. Die of complete design on old stiff glazed paper (die size: 55x66mm), black *350.*
i. Complete die on glazed wove
deep carmine *200.*
scarlet *200.*
ultramarine *200.*
j. Complete die on India, light orange red *200.*
k. Complete die on proof paper (1903)
black *75.*
bright carmine *75.*
dull carmine *75.*
dim scarlet *75.*
dark orange *75.*
dull yellow *75.*
dark orange brown *75.*
black olive *75.*
green *75.*
dark blue green *75.*
deep ultramarine *75.*
dark navy blue *75.*
blue violet *75.*
dull violet *75.*
red violet *75.*
l. Complete die on large colored card (1903)
black, *light green* *150.*
deep scarlet, *ivory* *150.*
red violet, *light blue* *150.*
carmine, *pink* *150.*

184-E5

Design size: 19x24½mm
Die No. 1 size: about 63x94mm Vignette of Washington slightly diff. from rest of series but with quite diff. frame design.

184-E5 3c
a. Die on glazed paper, about 50x75mm, black *350.*
b. Die on proof paper (with and without printing through mats) (1903)
black *100.*
dark carmine *100.*
carmine *100.*
bright carmine *100.*
brown *100.*
red brown *100.*
yellow *100.*
orange *100.*
violet *100.*
red violet *100.*
violet brown *100.*
blue *100.*
steel blue *100.*
light green *100.*
dark green *100.*
dull olive *100.*
c. Die on colored card, 61x93mm (1903)
scarlet, *yellow* *150.*
olive gray, *pale pink* *150.*
dull violet, *buff* *150.*

Plate proofs printed in sheets of 25 (plate size: 140x164mm). A horiz. crack extends through upper 3s from 2mm back of head on position 11 to vignette on position 12.

All plate essay items valued as singles except No. 184-E5d.

d. Engraved plate of 25 on India, mounted on large card, red brown *750.*
e. Plate on proof paper (1903)
black *15.*
blue black *15.*
greenish black *15.*
dull red violet *15.*
dark red violet *15.*
dull violet *15.*
violet brown *15.*
light red brown *15.*
orange brown *15.*
brown carmine *15.*
brown *15.*
dim orange *15.*
yellow *15.*
dull yellow *15.*
carmine *15.*
light carmine *15.*
dark carmine *15.*
dull carmine *15.*
dull scarlet *15.*
dark green *15.*
light green *15.*
dull olive green *15.*
deep ultramarine *15.*
f. Plate on proof paper, perf. 12, lithographed
carmine *100.*
rose lilac *100.*
red orange *100.*
g. Plate on green bond, "Crane & Co. 1887" wmk. (1903)
black *25.*
carmine *25.*
dull carmine *25.*
scarlet *25.*
brown *25.*
brown red *25.*
orange brown *25.*
red violet *25.*
yellow *25.*
orange *25.*
dark green *25.*
light green *25.*
yellow green *25.*
deep ultramarine *25.*
dark navy blue *25.*
h. Plate (printed before plate crack developed) on semiglazed yellowish wove, laid watermark
carmine *30.*
dull red *30.*
bright orange red *30.*
deep orange red *30.*
scarlet *30.*
deep orange *30.*
yellow orange *30.*
orange brown *30.*
orange yellow *30.*
dark yellow green *30.*
dusky blue green *30.*
dull green blue *30.*
violet blue *30.*
red violet *30.*
black *30.*
i. Plate single from sheets of 100 with imprint on yellowish glazed chemically prepared wove, lithographed
black *20.*
brown *20.*
scarlet *20.*
light red *20.*
rose pink *20.*
carmine *20.*
deep carmine *20.*
violet rose *20.*
deep violet rose *20.*
violet red *20.*
red violet *20.*
violet *20.*
blue *20.*
pale blue *20.*
pale dull blue *20.*
yellow *20.*
dull brown yellow *20.*
orange *20.*
red orange *20.*

184-E6

Illustration with card margins reduced.

Similar to No. 184-E1 but engraved vignette of Lincoln on India facing ¾ to right. Each design has vignette attached to frame from behind.

184-E6 3c Four examples mounted on 80x89mm card to resemble block of 4

blue	*3,000.*
green	*3,000.*

Frame of No. 184-E5 with engraved vignette of Lincoln mounted in place.

184-E7 3c Die on card, brown —

There is some doubt whether No. 184-E7 exists as a genuine essay. The editors would like to see authenticated evidence of its existence.

186-E1a

Design size: 20x25mm
Die size: 92x50mm
Frames of 6c and 7c side by side (6c at right).

186-E1 6c + 7c

a. Die on white pelure, orange *375.*

b. Die on proof paper, printed through a mat (1903)

black	*100.*
bright carmine	*100.*
dull carmine	*100.*
dim scarlet	*100.*
dark orange	*100.*
dull yellow	*100.*
dark orange brown	*100.*
black olive	*100.*
green	*100.*
dark blue green	*100.*
dark blue	*100.*
deep ultramarine	*100.*
dark navy blue	*100.*
blue violet	*100.*
dull violet	*100.*
red violet	*100.*

c. Die on white pelure, both 7s reversed on 7c frame, orange *750.*

d. Die on old stiff glazed, black *400.*

186-E2a

Complete 6c design, lithographed.

186-E2 6c

a. Plate on stamp paper, perf. 12, gummed

bright red orange	*35.*
dull red orange	*35.*
dark red orange	*35.*
red brown	*35.*
dark red brown	*35.*
dark orange brown	*35.*
yellow brown	*35.*
dull yellow green	*35.*
green	*35.*
dull ultramarine	*35.*
bright ultramarine	*35.*
blue violet	*35.*
red violet	*35.*
light violet red	*35.*
violet red	*35.*

b. Plate on stamp paper, gummed

ultramarine	*60.*
lilac	*60.*
scarlet	*60.*
orange	*60.*
carmine	*60.*
dark carmine	*60.*
blue green	*60.*

186a-E2b

Complete 7c design, lithographed.

186a-E2 7c

a. Plate on stamp paper, imperf.

black	*75.*
carmine	*75.*
red orange	*75.*
yellow orange	*75.*
green	*75.*
dark green	*75.*
dark blue	*75.*

b. Plate on stamp paper, perf. 12, gummed

red brown	*50.*
dark red orange	*50.*
brown orange	*50.*
red violet	*50.*
ultramarine	*50.*
violet blue	*50.*

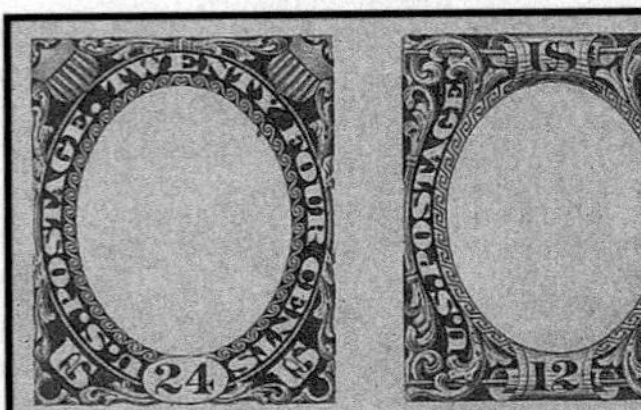

188a-E1b

Design size: 20x25mm
Die size: 78½x64mm
Frames of 12c and 24c side by side (12c on right).

188a-E1 12c + 24c

a. Die on white pelure

deep carmine	*300.*
brown orange	*300.*
orange brown	*300.*
blue green	*300.*
blue	*300.*

b. Die on proof paper, printed through a mat (1903)

black	*100.*
bright carmine	*100.*
dull carmine	*100.*
dim scarlet	*100.*
dark orange	*100.*
dull yellow	*100.*
dark orange brown	*100.*
black olive	*100.*
green	*100.*
dark blue green	*100.*
dark blue	*100.*
deep ultramarine	*100.*
dark navy blue	*100.*
blue violet	*100.*
dull violet	*100.*
red violet	*100.*

c. Die on old stiff glazed, black *400.*

188a-E2a

Complete 12c design, lithographed.

188a-E2 12c

a. Plate on stamp paper, perf. 12, gummed

bright red orange	*35.*
dull red orange	*35.*
dark red orange	*35.*
red brown	*35.*
dark red brown	*35.*
dark orange brown	*35.*
yellow brown	*35.*
dull yellow green	*35.*
green	*35.*
dull ultramarine	*35.*
bright ultramarine	*35.*
blue violet	*35.*
red violet	*35.*
light red violet	*35.*
violet red	*35.*

b. Plate on stamp paper, gummed

ultramarine	*60.*
lilac	*60.*
scarlet	*60.*
orange	*60.*
carmine	*60.*
dark carmine	*60.*
blue green	*60.*

189a-E2a

Complete 24c design, lithographed.

189a-E2 24c

a. Plate on stamp paper, perf. 12, gummed

red brown	*50.*
dark red orange	*50.*
brown orange	*50.*
ultramarine	*50.*
violet blue	*50.*
red violet	*50.*

b. Plate on stamp paper, gummed

ultramarine	*75.*
lilac	*75.*
scarlet	*75.*
orange	*75.*
carmine	*75.*
dark carmine	*75.*
green	*75.*

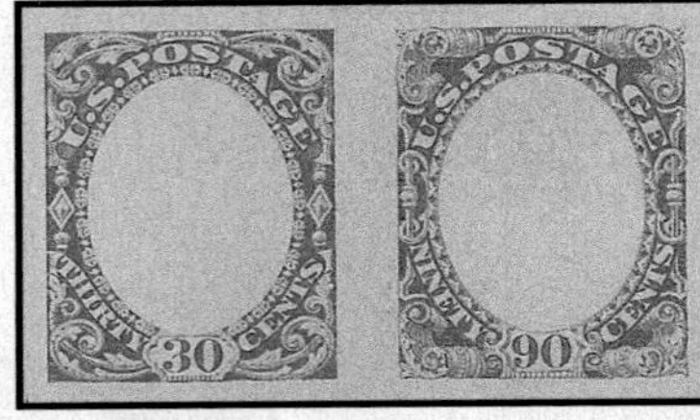

190-E1c

Design size: 20x25mm
Die size: 79x64mm
Frames of 30c and 90c side by side.

190-E1 30c + 90c

a. Die on white pelure

dark carmine	*300.*
dark red orange	*300.*
dark orange brown	*300.*
brown	*300.*
blue green	*300.*
bright blue	*300.*

b. Die on stiff glazed paper, blue black *500.*

c. Die on proof paper, printed through a mat (1903)

black	*100.*
bright carmine	*100.*
dull carmine	*100.*
dim scarlet	*100.*
dark orange	*100.*
dull yellow	*100.*
dark orange brown	*100.*
black olive	*100.*
green	*100.*
dark blue green	*100.*
dark blue	*100.*
deep ultramarine	*100.*
dark navy blue	*100.*
blue violet	*100.*
dull violet	*100.*
red violet	*100.*

190-E2a

Complete 30c design, lithographed.

190-E2 30c
a. Plate on stamp paper, perf. 12, gummed
bright red orange *35.*
dull red orange *35.*
dark red orange *35.*
red brown *35.*
dark red brown *35.*
dark orange brown *35.*
yellow brown *35.*
dull yellow green *35.*
green *35.*
dull ultramarine *35.*
bright ultramarine *35.*
blue violet *35.*
red violet *35.*
light red violet *35.*
violet red *35.*
b. Plate on stamp paper, gummed
ultramarine *60.*
lilac *60.*
scarlet *60.*
orange *60.*
carmine *60.*
dark carmine *60.*
blue green *60.*

191-E2

Complete 90c design, lithographed.

191-E2 90c
a. Plate on stamp paper, perf. 12, gummed
black *50.*
red brown *50.*
dark red orange *50.*
brown orange *50.*
ultramarine *50.*
violet blue *50.*
red violet *50.*
violet red *50.*
dark blue green *50.*
orange brown *50.*
b. Plate on stamp paper, gummed
ultramarine *75.*
lilac *75.*
scarlet *75.*
orange *75.*
carmine *75.*
dark carmine *75.*
green *75.*

1879 Coupon Essay
Azariah B. Harris

184-E8a

Size of coupon design: 25x7½mm
A proposed $300 30-year Postal Revenue Bond with 3.65% interest. Daily coupons 3c each, "Receivable for Postage in all parts of the U.S." after date thereon. Entire bond contained six pages of coupons with 16 rows of four (one for each day of two months); 20% bear month and day, others blank.

184-E8 3c
a. Coupon on bond (dated Jan. or Feb.), imperf., black *350.*
b. Engraved die on old ivory paper (undated), black *1,000.*
c. Single coupon on bond (dated), perf. 12, gummed, blue green *125.*
d. Single coupon on bond (undated), perf. 12, gummed, blue green *50.*

Continental Bank Note Co.

182-E4

Design size: 18x22mm
Die size: 59x67mm

Engraved vignette of Franklin on white background in unadopted frame.

182-E4 1c
a. Die on India, blue *575.*
b. Die on proof paper
black *500.*
dull scarlet *500.*
dull brown *500.*
dull green *500.*
dull blue *500.*
c. Die on ivory glazed paper
black *750.*
black brown *750.*
scarlet *750.*
blue *750.*

All known examples of "b" have reduced margins.

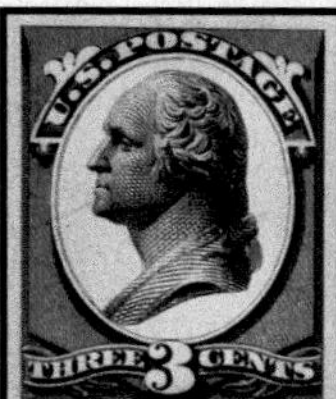

184-E9

Die size: 61½x76½mm
Vignette of Washington on white background in incomplete frame as adopted: no veins in trifoliate ornaments in upper corners.

184-E9 3c Die on India, on card
black *750.*
green *750.*

184-E10

Similar to No. 184-E9 but completed frame with veins in trifoliate ornaments.

184-E10 3c
a. Die on India, die sunk on card, green *750.*
b. Die on proof paper, about 35x40mm
gray black *350.*
dull red *350.*
dull blue *350.*
dull green *350.*
dull brown *350.*
c. Die on ivory glazed paper
black *600.*
black brown *600.*
scarlet *600.*
blue *600.*

Nos. 147-E8 and 147-E9 may have been made from completed dies of No. 147 to produce Nos. 184-E9 and 184-E10.

184-E11

Design size: 17½x21½mm
Die size: 60x75mm
Complete unadopted design with vignette of Liberty on white background.

184-E11 3c
a. Die on India
black *350.*
brown red *350.*
orange *350.*
green *350.*
blue *350.*
scarlet *350.*
b. Die on proof paper
brown *350.*
green *350.*
gray black *350.*
dull red *350.*
dull blue *350.*
c. Die on ivory glazed paper
black *750.*
black brown *750.*
scarlet *750.*
blue *750.*

All known examples of Nos. 184-E11a, 184-E11b have reduced margins.

184-E12

Design size: 19½x24½mm
Die size: 61x71mm
Complete unadopted design with vignette of Washington on white background in frame similar to No. 184-E11 but with numerals of value.

184-E12 3c
a. Die on India, die sunk on card
black *650.*
dull scarlet *650.*
brown *650.*
green *650.*
b. Die on white glazed paper
black *500.*
black brown *500.*
scarlet *500.*
blue *500.*
c. Plate on India (some adhering to original card backing), imperf.
black *100.*
scarlet *100.*
orange red *100.*
green *100.*
d. Plate on white paper, perf. 12, gummed
black *75.*
green *75.*
blue *75.*
brown *75.*
red brown *75.*
orange *75.*
dull scarlet *75.*
orange brown *75.*
e. Plate on Francis Patent bluish chemical paper, perf. 12, gummed
black *150.*
scarlet *150.*
red brown *150.*
brown *150.*
yellow *150.*
green *150.*
gray *150.*
f. Plate on brown chemical paper, perf. 12, gummed
blue *150.*
ultramarine *150.*
g. Hybrid die on India, mounted on India, block sunk on card, green *400.*

184-E13

Design size: 18x22mm
Die size: about 61x62mm
Similar to No. 184-E12 but slightly different frame.

184-E13 3c
a. Die on India, die sunk on card
black *650.*
scarlet *650.*
green *650.*
blue *650.*
black brown *650.*
blue green *650.*
b. Die on ivory glazed paper
black *750.*
black brown *750.*
scarlet *750.*
blue *750.*
c. Plate on India, imperf.
black *100.*
deep scarlet *100.*
green *100.*
dark green *100.*
dark yellow brown *100.*
olive brown *100.*
violet brown *100.*
orange *100.*
d. Plate on stamp paper, perf. 12, gummed
black *75.*
dull scarlet *75.*
blue green *75.*
brown *75.*
red brown *75.*
dull blue *75.*
dark blue *75.*
orange *75.*
yellow *75.*
yellow brown *75.*
gray *75.*

184-E14

Design size: 19x24½mm
Die size: about 67x71mm
Similar to No. 184-E13 but value label with "THREE" above "CENTS."

184-E14 3c
a. Hybrid die on India mounted on India, block sunk on card
brown red 400.
green 400.
b. Die on ivory glazed paper
black 500.
black brown 500.
scarlet 500.
blue 500.
c. Die on proof paper, about 35x35mm
black 300.
dull scarlet 300.
dull brown 300.
dull green 300.
dull blue 300.
brown red 300.
red brown 300.

184-E15

Design size: 20x25½mm
Die size: 60x73mm
Vignette of Indian maiden in headdress, "PORTAGE" error in top label.

184-E15 3c
a. Hybrid die on India, cut close, mounted on India, block sunk on card
black 900.
dark green 900.
b. Die on proof paper, about 28x35mm
black 600.
dull scarlet 500.
dull brown 500.
dull blue 500.
dull green 500.
c. Die on ivory glazed paper
black 750.
black brown 750.
scarlet 750.
blue 750.
d. Die on India, scarlet —

184-E16

Similar to No. 184-E15 but with spelling corrected to "POSTAGE."

184-E16 3c Die on India, cut close, mounted on India, block sunk on card
black 1,250.
blue 1,250.
steel blue 1,250.
carmine 1,250.
scarlet 1,250.
brown 1,250.
dark green 1,250.

190-E3

Die size: 44½x71½mm
Vignette of Hamilton on white background in frame as adopted.

190-E3 30c
a. Die on proof paper, about 35x48mm
gray black 500.
dull red 500.
dull green 500.
dull brown 500.
dull blue 500.
b. Die on ivory glazed paper
black 750.
black brown 750.
scarlet 750.
blue 750.

American Bank Note Co.

184-E17a

184-E17b

Design size: 22x30mm
Silver photo print of engraved vignette of Washington mounted on pencil and ink frame design.

184-E17 3c
a. Die on white card, 38x49mm
light brown vignette, black frame 1,250.
b. Die on white card, 38x50mm
light brown vignette, black frame 1,250.

On No. 184-E17b, the oval frame lines at the sides and the ornaments at top and bottom extend beyond the rectangular frame lines, and the lettering is less complete than on No. 184-E17a.

1881-82 ISSUE
American Bank Note Co.

205-E1

Die size: 59x74mm
Vignette of Garfield in lined oval.

205-E1 5c Die on India, die sunk on card, black 500.

205-E2

Die No. C-47 size: 70x83mm
Vignette of Garfield in beaded oval, in plain border of horiz. lines. Found with and without imprint and die number.

205-E2 5c Die on India, die sunk on card
gray brown 250.
gray black 250.

No. 205-E2 may not be a stamp essay.

205-E3a

205-E3c

Die size: 78x78mm
Vignette of Garfield in beaded oval with cutout at bottom for top of star.

205-E3 5c
a. Die on India, die sunk on card
black 750.
deep red orange 750.
red brown 750.
blue 750.
green 750.
b. Die on ivory glazed paper
black 750.
green 750.
blue 750.
scarlet 750.
red brown 750.
c. Negative impression, solid color outside design, die on India, bright red orange 1,000.

205-E4

Vignette of Garfield as No. 205-E1 in lined oval and finished frame as adopted.

205-E4 5c Die on India, 24x30mm, black 900.

206-E1

Image of unadopted frame, printed on 40x60mm India paper with text and right "1" cut out.

206-E1 1c Black on India 2,500.

206-E1B

Image of frame with "DOS CENTAVOS" in upper label and "ONE CENT" pasted on bottom label, affixed to 57x71mm card with additional pencil sketch at right.

206-E1B 1c Black image affixed to card 2,500.

206-E1C

Design size: 21x26mm
Engraved frame of unadopted design.

206-E1C 1c
 a. Die on white glazed paper, 42x74mm, black *1,000.*
 b. Die on surface-tinted glazed paper, cut close
 green, *buff* *600.*
 black, *orange* *600.*
 brown orange, *blue* *600.*

206-E2

Engraved frame almost identical to No. 206-E1C with small typographed vignette of Peace.

206-E2 1c Die on blue surface-tinted ivory paper, cut close, buff vignette, carmine frame *800.*

206-E3

206-E3c

Vignette of Peace only.

206-E3 1c
 a. Engraved vignette
 black *350.*
 dull red violet *350.*
 b. Typographed vignette *350.*
 c. Die on old proof paper, cut to shape to show AMERICAN BANK NOTE CO. and die number V46742, with die number 340 crossed out by etched lines, mounted on card, black *350.*

Nos. 206-E3a and 206-E3c are essays made by the American Bank Note. Co. from a die acquired from toppan, Carpenter and company. The die number V46742 is the new ABNCo. die number.

206-E4

Engraved frame (No. 206-E1C) with typographed vignette of Lincoln mounted on it. Four diff. colors (dull carmine, dull scarlet, dark brown, green) on cream white ivory paper, 22x27mm each, mounted together on 92x114mm thick white card, ms. "American Bank Note Co. N.Y." at lower right.

206-E4 1c Four designs on cream white ivory on card *2,250.*

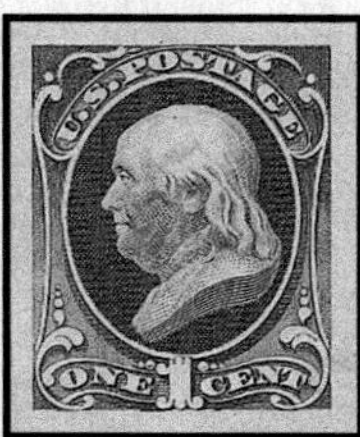
206-E5

Design size: 18x23½mm
Typographed vignette of Lincoln only.

206-E5 1c Die on white ivory paper
 dull carmine *450.*
 dark yellowish brown *450.*
 dull purple *450.*
 dull dark blue *450.*
 orange *450.*

Do not confuse the listed Lincoln vignette, No. 206-E5, with somewhat similar engravings ca. 1894 by Schlecht for currency.

206-E6

Incomplete engraving of complete design as issued: no shading in upper arabesques.

206-E6 1c
 a. Die on India
 gray blue *750.*
 green blue *750.*
 b. Die on India, cut close, on India block sunk on card, deep gray blue *350.*

207-E1

Design size: 20½x25½mm
Die size: 49x54½mm
Engraved unadopted frame design with 3's at sides and large 3 at top.

207-E1 3c
 a. Die on India
 yellow brown *750.*
 dull brown *750.*
 dull blue *750.*
 green *750.*
 b. Die on white glazed paper, 32x38mm
 black *650.*
 dull dark yellow *650.*
 c. Die on surface-tinted ivory paper, cut close
 black, *orange* *500.*
 green, *buff* *500.*
 violet blue, *orange* *500.*

207-E2

Engraved frame as No. 207-E1, with typographed vignette of Peace.

207-E2 3c Die on blue surface-tinted ivory paper, cut close, buff vignette, carmine frame *850.*

207-E3

Engraved frame (No. 207-E1) with typographed vignette of Peace mounted on it. Four diff. color combinations (orange red vignette, dull carmine frame; dull carmine vignette, dull red brown frame; yellow brown vignette and frame; blue green vignette and frame) on cream white ivory paper, 22x27mm each, mounted together on 92x114mm thick white card, ms. "American Bank Note Co. N.Y." at lower right.

207-E3 3c 4 designs on cream white ivory on card *2,500.*

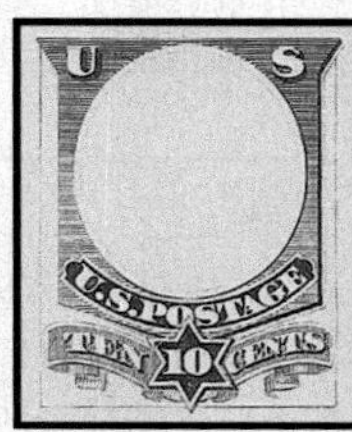

208-E1

Incomplete engraving of design as adopted: unfinished shading on top label and bottom ribbon, four lines between frame sinkage at right and left edges, horiz. line at bottom.

This is a new die engraved by the Bureau of Engraving & Printing for "Roosevelt" proof albums.

208-E1 6c Die on India, on card, black *2,400.*

209-E1

Design size: 20x25mm
Die size: 58x76mm
Engraving of unadopted frame only, no horiz. lines in background.

209-E1 10c Die on thick white card, about 25x33mm
 blue *800.*
 green *800.*

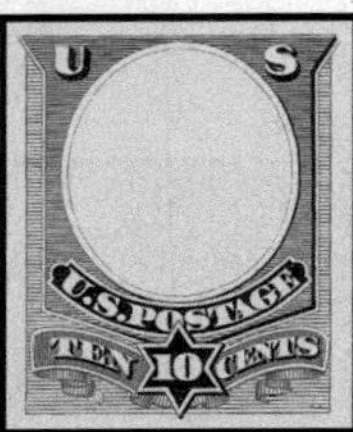

209-E2

Similar to No. 209-E1 but with horiz. lines added to background.

209-E2 10c
a. Die on thick white card
black *700.*
red *700.*
green *700.*
blue *700.*
b. Die on India, on 50x70mm card, black *800.*
c. Die on white glazed paper, black *800.*

209-E3

Engraved frame similar to No. 209-E2 with typographed vignette of Peace.

209-E3 10c
a. Die on blue surface-tinted glazed paper, cut close, buff vignette, carmine frame *650.*
b. Die on orange surface-tinted glazed paper
dull carmine vignette, violet frame *650.*
dull yellow vignette, violet frame *650.*
yellow vignette, green frame *650.*

209-E4

Vignette diameter: 17mm
Engraved Franklin vignette.

209-E4 10c
a. Die on India
black *575.*
dusky carmine *575.*
dull scarlet *575.*
dim orange *575.*
orange brown *575.*
yellow green *575.*
dim blue green *575.*
deep blue *575.*
red brown on blue ground *575.*
dark red violet *575.*
b. Die sunk on glazed paper, approx. 51x69mm
dusky carmine *775.*
dim scarlet *775.*
dim orange *775.*
deep blue *775.*
dim blue green *775.*
dim brown *775.*

209-E5

Design size: 21x26mm
Engraved frame with typographed vignette mounted on it. Four diff. color combinations (dull scarlet vignette, dull carmine frame; dull orange vignette, brown orange frame; yellow brown vignette, dark brown frame; blue green vignette and frame) on cream white ivory paper, 22x27mm each, mounted together on 92x114mm thick white card, ms. "American Bank Note Co. N.Y." at lower right.

209-E5 10c Four designs on cream white ivory on card *2,500.*

209-E6

Vignette diameter: 18mm
Engraved Washington vignette.

209-E6 10c
a. Die on India
black *600.*
dim deep carmine *600.*
dim deep scarlet *600.*
dull orange *600.*
dull brown *600.*
dim blue green *600.*
blue *600.*
dusky red violet *600.*
b. Die sunk on white ivory paper, 55x67mm
dusky carmine *800.*
dull orange *800.*
dull blue green *800.*
scarlet *800.*
dull brown *800.*
red violet *800.*

209-E7

Design size: 21x26mm
Engraved frame with typographed vignette mounted on it. Four diff. color combinations (dull carmine vignette and frame; dull orange vignette, brown orange frame; yellow brown vignette, dark brown frame; blue green vignette and frame) on cream white ivory paper, 22x27mm each, mounted together on 92x114mm thick white card, ms. "American Bank Note Co. N.Y." at lower right.

209-E7 10c
a. Four designs on cream white ivory on card *2,500.*
b. Single composite off card, dull carmine vignette, blue green frame *400.*

Issued stamp, No. 209, in trial color, overprinted network in fugitive ink.

209-E8 10c On thick paper, perf. 12, gummed, sepia, overprint olive gray *150.*

1883 ISSUE
American Bank Note Co.

210-E1

Design size: 20x25½mm
Engraved vignette of Washington (from proof on India of No. 207) with watercolor frame design nearly as adopted but with "TWO" and "CENTS" at an angle, rubber stamp "Feb. 17, 1883" on back.

210-E1 2c Die on white card, 80x90mm, black vignette, gray and white frame *3,000.*

210-E2

Design size: 20x25mm
Engraved vignette of Washington (from proof on India of No. 207) mounted on unadopted watercolor and ink frame design. backstamped "American Bank Note Co. Feb. 27, 1883."

210-E2 2c Die on thick white card, 87x100mm, black and white *3,000.*

210-E3

Design size: 20x25½mm
Engraved vignette of Washington (from proof on India of No. 207) mounted on watercolor frame design as adopted, ms. "2 March 1883 No. 1."

210-E3 2c Die on white card, 80x90mm, black vignette, gray & white frame *6,000.*

210-E4

Design size: 20x25mm
Engraved vignette of Washington on white background mounted on a brush and pen watercolor drawing of unadopted fancy frame design, backstamped "American Bank Note Co. Mar. 2, 1883" and pencil "No. 2."

210-E4 2c Die on white card, 88x101mm, dusky blue green *5,500.*

210-E5

Design size: 20x25mm
Engraved vignette of Washington (from revenue stamp No. RB17) mounted on wash drawing of unadopted ornate frame design, backstamped "American Bank Note Co. Mar. 2, 1883" and pencil "No. 3."

210-E5 2c Die on white card, 88x101mm, blue violet vignette, black frame *2,500.*

211-E1

Design size: 20x25½mm
Engraved vignette of Jackson mounted on unadopted watercolor frame design.

211-E1 4c Die on white card, 70x70mm, blue green vignette and frame *3,500.*

211-E2

Engraved head of Jackson only.

211-E2 4c Die on India, die sunk on card, black *2,500.*

211-E3

Incomplete engraved vignette of Jackson: lower edge of bust incomplete.

211-E3 4c Die on India, die sunk on card
black *2,500.*
green *2,500.*
red brown *2,500.*

Complete engraved vignette of Jackson.

211-E4 4c Die on India, die sunk on card, blue green *2,500.*

Die size: 60x62mm
Complete design as adopted but with pencil sketch of pedestal top under bust.

211-E5 4c Die on India, die sunk on card, gray black *5,750.*

211-E6

Similar to No. 211-E5 but with incomplete shading engraved on pedestal.

211-E6 4c Die on India, die sunk on card, blue green *2,500.*

1887 ISSUE
American Bank Note Co.

212-E1

Die size: 55x63mm
Incomplete engraved vignette of Franklin facing right: horiz. background lines only.

212-E1 1c Die on 32½x35mm card, India mounted, die sunk on card
black *600.*
ultramarine *600.*

212-E2

Die size: 62x62mm
Franklin vignette similar to No. 212-E1 but diagonal lines (in one direction only) added to background.

212-E2 1c Die on India, die sunk on card
black *600.*
ultramarine *600.*

Die size: 55x64mm
Similar to No. 212-E2 but diagonal lines in both directions.

212-E3 1c Die on India, die sunk on card, black *500.*

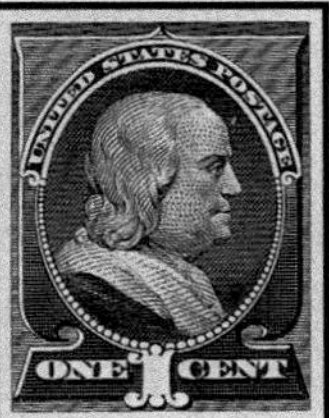

212-E4

Complete design as issued except Franklin facing right.

212-E4 1c
a. Die on India, die sunk on card
black *600.*
ultramarine *600.*
b. Die on ivory glazed paper, about 64x76mm
black *750.*
black brown *750.*
scarlet *750.*
blue *750.*

Die size: 62x62mm
Incomplete vignette of Franklin facing left as adopted.

212-E5 1c Die on India, die sunk on card, ultramarine *450.*

212-E6

Die size: 56x64½mm
Incomplete design as adopted except three lines below value label and taller numeral, shadow on edge of bust and in background below chin too dark.

212-E6 1c Die on India, die sunk on card
ultramarine *750.*
green *750.*

212-E7

Similar to No. 212-E6 but with shadows lightened.

212-E7 1c Die on India, die sunk on card, ultramarine *750.*

1890 ISSUE
American Bank Note Co.

219-E1

Design size: 19x22½mm
Die size: 58x64mm
Engraved die of frame only with blank labels quite similar to adopted design.

219-E1 1c Die on ivory paper, 64x72mm, black *700.*

219-E2

Design size: 19x22mm
Engraved Franklin vignette cut down from 1887 1c stamp (No. 212) mounted on watercolor frame design.

219-E2 1c Die on thick light buff card, ultramarine frame *3,500.*

219-E3

Die size: 62x62mm
Engraved Franklin vignette with lettered label above.

219-E3 1c Die on India, die sunk on card, blue *800.*

219-E4

Engraved die of vignette only with outer line around the oval.

219-E4 1c Die on India, die sunk on card, 71x70mm, ultramarine *800.*

220-E1

Design size: 19x22mm
Engraved Washington vignette from 3c stamp (from proof on India of No. 184) mounted on watercolor frame design.

220-E1 2c Die on thick white card, 62x66mm, light carmine frame *3,750.*

220-E2

Design size: 19x23mm
Engraved Washington vignette cut from 1887 2c stamp (No. 213) mounted on shield-like watercolor frame design.

220-E2 2c Die on thick light buff card, gray frame *3,000.*

220-E3

Design size: 19x23mm

Engraved Washington vignette cut from 1887 2c stamp (No. 213) mounted on watercolor frame design.

220-E3 2c Die on white card, 105x135mm, gray black frame *3,000.*

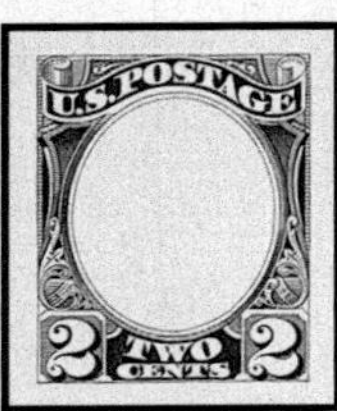

220-E4

Design size: 19x22mm
Die size: 56x63mm
Engraved unadopted frame only.

220-E4 2c Die on white ivory paper, black *1,250.*

220-E5

Die size: 62x62mm
Engraved vignette of Washington in oval line frame.

220-E5 2c Die on India, die sunk on card, dark carmine *800.*

220-E6

Engraved Washington vignette with lettered label above.

220-E6 2c Die on India, dusky carmine *1,250.*

220-E7

Design size: 19x22½mm
Engraved Washington vignette and lettered top label mounted on pencil drawing of frame design adopted, ms. "J.J.M. — engraved background only without figures or words;" backstamped "Nov. 15, 1889 American Bank Note Co."

220-E7 2c Die on 50x55mm white card, mounted on thick white card, 119x122mm, black vignette, pencil frame *3,000.*

220-E8

Design size: 19x22mm
Die size: 56x63mm
Engraved frame only as adopted with numerals, blank curved top label.

220-E8 2c
- ***a.*** Die on ivory paper, 64x71mm, black *900.*
- ***b.*** Die on India, 51x62mm
  - black *700.*
  - brown black *700.*
  - dark brown *700.*
  - dull scarlet *700.*
  - dark blue green *700.*
  - dark blue *700.*
  - red violet *700.*
  - red orange *700.*

220-E9

Incomplete engraving of entire design as adopted: no dots in rectangular spaces between shading lines on cheek under hair in front of ear and on back of neck.

220-E9 2c Die on India, die sunk on card, lake *1,250.*

(Probably by) The Times, Philadelphia

220-E11

Surface-printed essay for proposed business advertising on stamps.

220-E11 2c Die on India, on card, bright green blue —

American Bank Note Co.

221-E1

Engraved 3c frame as adopted with vignette cut out, mounted over photo of James Madison.

221-E1 3c Die on India, cut close, dark green *2,500.*

221-E2

Engraved vignette of Jackson with lettered label above.

221-E2 3c Die on India, die sunk on card, purple *750.*

Design size: 19x22mm
Incomplete engraved design as adopted except Lincoln facing ¾ left: unfinished shading under collar.

222-E1 4c Die on India, die sunk on card, black brown *1,250.*

222-E2

Die No. C-226 size: 62½x62½mm
Completed design with die no. and impt., Lincoln facing ¾ left.

222-E2 4c Die on India, on 25x32mm card, black brown *1,250.*
- ***a.*** Die number and impt. erased, die sunk on card *1,750.*

222-E3

Incomplete engraving as adopted: no wart on face, no lines on shirt.

222-E3 4c Die on India, die sunk on card, black brown *1,500.*

223-E1

Design size: 19x21½mm
Photo of Seward vignette mounted on watercolor frame design.

223-E1 5c Gray and white on light buff paper in upper right corner of short envelope *7,000.*

223-E2

Design size: 19x22mm
Die size: 63x62mm
Incomplete engraved design as adopted except Grant facing ¾ left: hair neatly combed.

223-E2 5c Die on India, die sunk on card
- black *1,750.*
- orange brown *1,750.*

223-E3

Design size: 19x22mm
Die size: 63x62mm
Incomplete engraving of complete bearded left-facing design: eye pupils not solid color, light shading on right side of face, only one diagonal shading line on left coat shoulder.

223-E3 5c Die on India, die sunk on card, chocolate *1,750.*

Similar to No. 223-E3 but more complete. Left beard has no diagonal lines and is light at top center.

223-E4 5c Die on India, die sunk on card, chocolate *1,750.*

223-E5

Third state of die: no horiz. lines on left moustache or under lower lip.

223-E5 5c Die on India, die sunk on card, chocolate *1,750.*

223-E6

Completed left-facing design: shows lines omitted from No. 223-E5, several diagonal shading lines on left shoulder of coat.

223-E6 5c Die on India, die sunk on card
black *700.*
chocolate *700.*

223-E7

Design size: 19x22mm
Die size: 62x62mm
Left-facing design with slightly diff. portrait, hair neatly combed. Horiz. shading lines on left coat shoulder, no wash-etched shadows on coat, beard and tie.

223-E7 5c
a. Die on India, die sunk on card
black *700.*
dark brown *700.*
b. Die on glazed paper, impt. and "ESSAY MARCH 1890"
black *750.*
black brown *750.*
scarlet *750.*
blue *750.*

Design size: 19x22mm
Die similar to No. 223-E7 but diagonal shading lines on left coat shoulder, wash-etched shadows on coat, beard and tie.

223-E8 5c Die on India, on card, brown *700.*

223-E9

Die size: 62x63mm
Engraving of right-facing Grant design diff. than adopted: light oval line around vignette, three diagonal lines on shirtfront under tie. Incomplete engraving: right collar unshaded.

223-E9 5c Die on India, dark orange brown *700.*

223-E10

Similar to No. 223-E9 but engraving completed: right collar shaded.

223-E10 5c
a. Die on India, die sunk on card, dark orange brown *700.*
b. Die on ivory paper, impt. and "ESSAY MARCH 1890"
black *750.*
black brown *750.*
scarlet *750.*
blue *750.*

Ferrotype plate 39x51mm of Grant facing ¾ right, outlines engraved, filled with red.

223-E11 5c Metal plate *650.*

223-E12

Printing from ferrotype plate, No. 223-E11.

223-E12 5c Die on card, 43x56mm, red *1,100.*

226-E1

Design size: 19x22½mm
Incomplete engraved vignette of Webster with curved label above, mounted on pencil drawing of frame design (includes additional pencil drawings of lower part of frame, value lettering), backstamped "D.S. Ronaldson," frame engraver.

226-E1 10c Die on white card, 51x55mm, black *13,500.*

226-E2

Design size: 19x22½mm
Engraving of unadopted frame design.

226-E2 10c Die on white glazed paper, black *1,000.*

226-E3

Design size: 19x22mm
Engraved 10c frame as adopted, vignette cut out and mounted over photo of John Adams.

226-E3 10c Die on India, cut close, dark green *2,500.*

226-E4

Design size: 19x22mm
Engraved 10c frame as adopted, vignette cut out and mounted over photo of William T. Sherman.

226-E4 10c Die on India, cut close, dark green *2,500.*

227-E1

Design size: 19x22½mm
Engraved vignette of Henry Clay with curved label above, mounted on wash drawing of frame design (includes additional enlarged pencil and wash drawing of frame).

227-E1 15c Die on white card, mounted at left on light buff card, 110x123mm (frame drawing at right), black *1,750.*

228-E1

Design size: 17x18½ mm
Die size: 62x61mm
Incomplete engraved vignette of Jefferson with curved lettered label at top: hair shading incomplete.

228-E1 30c Die on India, die sunk on card, black *750.*

228-E2

Design size: 17x18½mm
Similar to No. 228-E1 but more shading on hair, vert. shading lines on chin.

228-E2 30c Die on India, die sunk on card, black *750.*

229-E1

Design size: 17x18½ mm
Die size: 62x62mm
Engraved vignette of Perry with curved lettered label at top.

229-E1 90c Die on India, die sunk on card, red orange *750.*

COLUMBIAN ISSUE

Lyman H. Bagg

230-E1

237-E1

Design sizes: 22x22mm

Left: No. 230-E1 — pencil drawing of Columbus in armor, on paper. "I do not know whether these designs will be of any use to you or not — they are so rough. L.H.B." written at top, "My idea illustrated" at bottom.

Right: No. 237-E1 — pencil drawing of North American continent, on paper.

230-E1 One Cent, Ten Cents, Drawings on 114x72mm white wove, Nos. 230-E1, 237-E1 *6,000.*

American Bank Note Co.

230-E2

230-E3

230-E4

Design size: 33x22mm

Silver print photo vignette of Columbus head mounted on watercolor drawing of unadopted frame design.

230-E2 1c Red violet on stiff white drawing paper *4,500.*

230-E3 1c Blue green on stiff white drawing paper *4,500.*

230-E4 1c Light red on stiff white drawing paper *4,500.*

230-E5

Die size: 57x38mm

Ferrotype metal plate with outline of adopted vignette (reversed) and drawings of Indian man and woman at sides in single line frame 39mm long.

230-E5 1c Metal plate 1,250.

230-E6

Vignette size: 16x15mm

Engraved vignette only as adopted.

230-E6 1c Die on 53x39mm India, on card
- yellow brown *2,000.*
- black *2,000.*

230-E7

Incomplete engraving of vignette, lettering, value numerals and tablet as issued: without palm tree, incomplete shading on and behind Indian and maiden, on Columbus' head, no shading on scrollwork, etc.

230-E7 1c Die on 39x28mm stiff wove, deep blue *2,000.*

230-E8

Incomplete engraving of entire design as issued: maiden's skirt only lightly engraved, chief's torso and shoulder incompletely engraved, incomplete shading in frame design at top, etc.

230-E8 1c Die on India, die sunk on 99x84mm card, deep blue *1,500.*

231-E1

Design size: 34x22mm

Silver print photo of vignette as adopted, mounted on watercolor drawing of unadopted frame design.

231-E1 2c Die on stiff white drawing paper, red violet *8,500.*

Die size: 74x61 ½mm

Incomplete engraving of adopted vignette only.

231-E2 2c Die on India, die sunk on card
- black *1,500.*
- sepia *1,500.*

231-E3

Design size: 35 ½x22mm

Engraved vignette of Columbus asking aid of Isabella as adopted for 5c, mounted on watercolor drawing of frame design similar to that adopted for 2c.

231-E3 2c Die on stiff white drawing paper, dark brown *4,000.*

231-E4

Vignette size: 29x15mm

Die size: 74x61 ½mm

Incomplete engraving of vignette as adopted (probably first state of die): cape on back of central figure incomplete, etc.

231-E4 2c Die on India, die sunk on card, black *2,500.*

231-E5

Incomplete engraving of vignette as adopted (probably second state of die): more shading on top right face, etc.; also pencil sketches for lengthening vignette.

231-E5 2c Die on India, die sunk on card, black *3,250.*

231-E6

Vignette size: 31 ½x15mm

Die size: 74x61 ½mm

Incomplete engraving of vignette, longer than Nos. 231-E4 and 231-E5, later shortened as adopted: Columbus' legs, central figure's cape, etc., are incomplete.

231-E6 2c Die on India, die sunk on card, black *2,500.*

231-E7

Design size: 33x22mm

Die size: 74x61 ½mm

Incomplete engraving of entire design almost as adopted: figures of value narrower, unfinished crosset shadows in lower corners.

Ridgway numbers used for colors of No. 231-E7.

231-E7 2c

a. Die on India, die sunk on card
- 13m/4 smoky dusky o-yellow-orange *1,250.*

b. Die on thin white wove card
- 69o/5 black *800.*
- 1m/0 dusky red *800.*
- 3k/2 dull dark orange-red *800.*
- 5i/0 deep o-orange-red *800.*
- 5j/1 deep v-deep o-orange-red *800.*
- 6i/0 deep m. red-orange *800.*
- 9i/0 deep o-yellow-orange *800.*
- 9m/0 dusky o-red-orange *800.*
- 9m/3 dismal dusky o-red-orange *800.*
- 9m/4 smoky dusky o-red-orange *800.*
- 9n/2 dull v. dusky o-red-orange *800.*
- 10k/0 m. dark orange *800.*
- 11i/0 deep orange *800.*
- 11k/1 dim dark orange *800.*
- 13m/1 dim dusky o-yellow-orange *800.*
- 13m/4 smoky dusky o-yellow-orange *800.*
- 33m/2 dull dusky g-yellow-green *800.*
- 37m/1 dim dusky g-blue-green *800.*
- 43m/2 dull dusky green-blue *800.*
- 49m/0 dusky blue *800.*
- 49m/1 dim dusky blue *800.*
- 55m/2 dull dusky blue-violet *800.*
- 59m/2 dull dusky violet *800.*
- 65m/2 dull dusky r-red-violet *800.*
- 70i/0 deep violet-red-red *800.*

231-E8

Design size: 33x22mm
Incomplete engraving of entire design as adopted: value numerals same as on issued stamp but without thick shading bars at ends of outer frame rectangles, etc.

231-E8 2c Die on India, card mounted, sepia *1,500.*

232-E1

Design size: 33½x22mm
Silver print photo of vignette unadopted for any value (Columbus embarking on voyage of discovery), mounted on watercolor drawing of unadopted frame design.

232-E1 3c Die on stiff white drawing paper, 41x29mm, orange brown *4,000.*

Ferrotype metal plate showing 19x15mm outline of *Santa Maria* (reversed) in 33x15mm vignette frame, outline engraved and filled with red ink.

232-E2 3c Metal plate, 51x30mm *1,250.*

232-E3

Printing from ferrotype plate No. 232-E3.

232-E3 3c Die on stiff white card with rounded corners, 55x42mm, red *1,250.*

232-E4

Vignette size: 30x15mm
Die size: 74x61mm
Incomplete engraving of vignette as adopted: sky composed of horiz. ruled lines, no clouds.

232-E4 3c Die on India, die sunk on card

black	*1,250.*
dark yellow-orange	*1,250.*
sepia	*1,750.*

232-E5

Engraved vignette similar to No. 232-E4 but with "1492 UNITED STATES OF AMERICA 1892" and scrolls around numerals engraved in outline only, pencil outline of frame.

232-E5 3c Die on thick artist's card with beveled edges, 50x38mm, black brown *3,000.*

233-E1

Design size: 33½x22mm
Silver print photo of wash drawing of vignette as adopted, mounted on watercolor drawing of frame design as adopted but titled "COLUMBUS ON VOYAGE OF DISCOVERY. SHIPS AT SEA."

233-E1 4c Die on stiff white drawing paper, 41x29mm, brown red *4,750.*

233-E2

Design size: 33x22mm
Die size: 74x61½mm
Incomplete engraving of complete design as adopted: unfinished crosset shadows in lower corners.

Ridgway numbers used for some colors of No. 233-E2.

233-E2 4c

a. Die on India, die sunk on card

black	*1,250.*
dark yellow orange	*1,250.*

b. Die on thin white wove card, die sunk on card

1m/0 dusky red	*800.*
3i/1 dim deep orange-red	*800.*
3k/2 dull dark orange-red	*800.*
5i/0 deep o-orange-red	*800.*
9i/0 deep o-red-orange	*800.*
9m/1 dim dusky o-red-orange	*800.*
11i/0 deep orange	*800.*
11k/1 dim dark orange	*800.*
11m/2 dull dusky orange	*800.*
13k/1 dim dark o-yellow-orange	*800.*
13m/2 dull dusky o-yellow-orange	*800.*
13k/3 dismal dark o-yellow-orange	*800.*
13k/4 smoky dark o-yellow-orange	*800.*
13m/4 smoky dusky o-yellow-orange	*800.*
15m/2 dull dusky yellow-orange	*800.*
33m/2 dull dusky g-yellow-green	*800.*
35m/5 gloomy dusky green	*800.*
37m/1 dim dusky g-blue-green	*800.*
39m/1 dim dusky blue-green	*800.*
41m/1 dim dusky b-blue-green	*800.*
47m/0 dusky green-blue-blue	*800.*
55m/2 dull dusky blue-violet	*800.*
63m/2 dull dusky red-violet	*800.*
69m/1 dull dusky red-violet-red	*800.*
69k/3 dismal dark red-violet-red	*800.*
71i/0 deep violet-red-red	*800.*
71m/0 dusky violet-red-red	*800.*
71o/5 black	*800.*
ultramarine	*800.*
violet	*800.*
red violet	*800.*
brown violet	*800.*
orange brown	*800.*
dark brown	*800.*

234-E1

Design size: 38½x22mm
Engraved vignette as adopted, mounted on watercolor drawing of frame design similar to but longer than adopted. Vignette also used on No. 231-E3.

234-E1 5c Die on thick artist's card, block sunk as die essay, black brown *8,500.*

234-E2

Design size: 34x22½mm
Die size: 67x63mm
Engraved vignette as adopted, mounted on watercolor drawing of frame design as adopted, pencil "Oct. 5/92," approval monogram of J.D. Macdonough and 7/8x1 1/32 inches. Vignette also used on No. 231-E3.

234-E2 5c Die on thick artist's card, die sunk, black brown & white *4,000.*

234-E3

Vignette size: 29½x15mm
Die size: 74x61½mm
Engraved vignette only as adopted.

234-E3 5c Die on India, die sunk on card, sepia *1,250.*

234-E4

Incomplete engraving of entire design: bench at left has horiz. shading only, incomplete shading in Columbus' face, etc.

234-E4 5c Die on 74x60mm India, on card

sepia	*1,000.*
blue	*1,000.*

235-E1

Ferrotype metal plate with engraved outline design (reversed) of vignette as used on 6c, engraved lines filled with red ink.

235-E1 6c Metal plate, 38x38mm *1,100.*

235-E2

Printing from ferrotype plate No. 235-E1.

235-E2 6c Die on stiff white card with rounded corners, 55x42mm, red *1,250.*

235-E3

Incomplete engraving of frame as adopted: unfinished crosset shadows in lower corners.

235-E3 6c Die on India, black 2,000.

235-E4

Design size: 34x22mm
Die size: 73x60mm
Incomplete engraving of entire design as adopted: neck and shoulder of horse, side figures in niches, crosset shadows in lower corners all unfinished.

235-E4 6c Die on India, die sunk on card, blue violet 1,500.

236-E1

Design size: 33½x22mm
Die size: 73x62mm
Design as adopted but frame incompletely engraved: unfinished crosset shadows in lower corners.

236-E1 8c Die on India, on card, black 2,500.

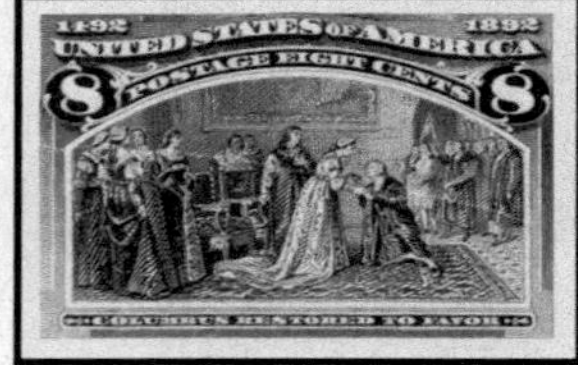

236-E2

Design as adopted but frame incompletely engraved: unfinished crosset shadows in lower corners, incomplete gown at left and faces at right.

236-E2 8c Die on India, on card, black 1,000.

237-E2

Ferrotype metal plate with engraved outline design (reversed) of vignette as used on 10c, engraved lines filled with red ink.

237-E2 10c Metal plate, 43x28mm 1,000.

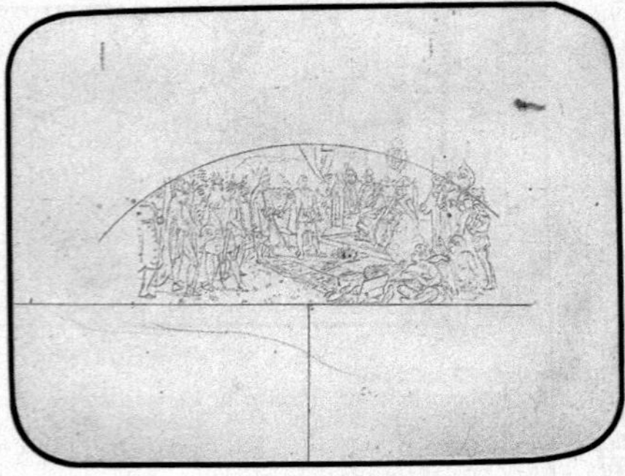

237-E3

Printing from ferrotype plate No. 237-E2.

237-E3 10c Die on stiff white card with rounded corners, 55x42mm, red 1,000.

237-E4

Design size: 33x22mm
Die size: 74x62mm
Incomplete engraving of entire design as adopted: surroundings of Columbus, floor, etc., three figures behind King Ferdinand, crosset shadows in lower corners all unfinished.

237-E4 10c Die on India, card mounted
black brown 1,000.
rose carmine 1,000.

237-E5

Similar to No. 237-E4 but more completely engraved: missing lines on ankle bracelet of Indian, many details in vignette and crosset shadows in lower corners.

237-E5 10c Die on India, die sunk on card
black brown 1,500.
carmine 1,500.

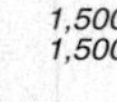

238-E1

Design size: 33½x22mm
Silver print photo of vignette unadopted for any value (Columbus relating incidents of voyage to Ferdinand and Isabella), mounted on watercolor drawing of frame design similar to that adopted.

238-E1 15c Die on stiff white drawing paper, 42x30mm, bright ultramarine 5,000.

238-E2

Vignette size: 30x15mm
Die size: 71x59mm
Incomplete engraving of vignette only as adopted: shading on Columbus' tunic and arms, Isabella's sholder, Ferdinand's robe, seated Indian's robe, robe of kneeling figure in lower left corner, etc., all unfinished.

238-E2 15c Die on India, die sunk on card, black brown 1,500.

238-E3

Complete engraving of vignette adopted.

238-E3 15c Die on India, black brown 1,500.

238-E4

Design size: 33½x22mm
Die size: 73½x62mm
Incomplete engraving of complete design as adopted: shading on Isabella's shoulder, Ferdinand's robe, seated Indian's blanket and crosset shadows in lower corners all unfinished.

238-E4 15c Die on India, on card
black brown 1,500.
blue green 1,500.

239-E1

Design size: 34½x22½mm
Silver print photo of vignette adopted for 15c, mounted on watercolor and ink drawing of unadopted frame design, titled "COLUMBUS PRESENTING NATIVES TO FERDINAND AND ISABELLA."

239-E1 30c Bluish gray on stiff white drawing paper, 42x30mm 5,000.

239-E2

Ferrotype metal plate with engraved outline design (reversed) of vignette as used on 30c, engraved lines filled with red ink.

239-E2 30c Metal plate, 39x29mm 1,000.

239-E3

Printing from ferrotype plate No. 239-E2.

239-E3 30c Die on stiff white card with rounded corners, 55x43mm, red *1,000.*

239-E4

Vignette size: 30x15mm
Die size: 74x62mm
Incomplete engraving of adopted vignette only: table cloth dark at top; horiz. lines on front edge of octagonal footstool, horiz. dots in shadow below windowsill at left, dots on top of head of man standing next to Columbus, etc., all missing.

239-E4 30c Die on India, die sunk on card, black *1,750.*

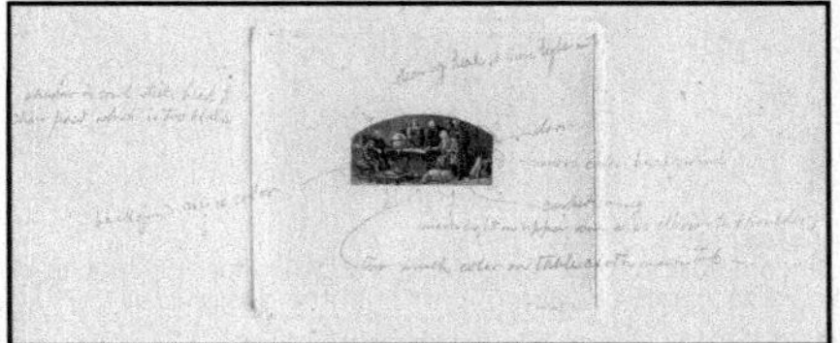

239-E5

Similar to No. 239-E4 but further engraved: has horiz. lines on front of footstool, etc. Eight pencil instructions for finishing vignette engraving written on large card backing, e.g., "Too much color on table cloth near top."

239-E5 30c Die on India, die sunk on 177x117mm card
black *2,000.*
black brown *2,000.*

239-E6

Design size: 33½x22mm
Die size: 74x63mm
Incomplete engraving of entire design as adopted: table cloth dark at top, diagonal dashes in one direction only between horiz. lines at lower left of vignette, etc.

239-E6 30c Die on India, die sunk on card
black *2,000.*
black brown *2,000.*

239-E7

Similar to No. 239-E6 but diagonal dashes in two directions, more dots on head and hand of man seated at near end of table.

239-E7 30c Die on India, die sunk on card
black brown *1,750.*
orange *1,750.*

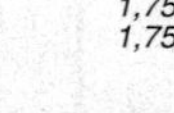

239-E8

Incomplete engraving of entire design: window frame, horiz. shading lines on shoulder of man at right, vert. lines on front of table cloth below Columbus all missing. Lighter shading at top of table cloth as on issued stamp.

239-E8 30c Die on India, on card, orange *2,500.*

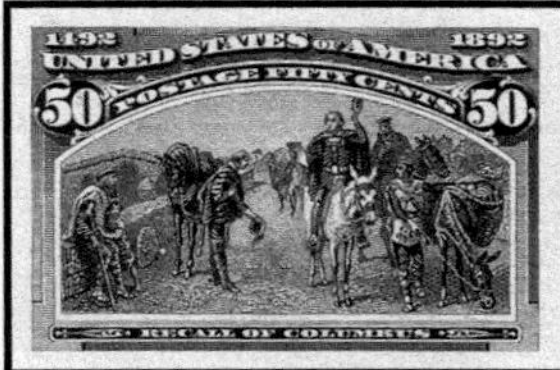

240-E1

Design size: 34x22mm
Die size: Incomplete engraving of entire design as adopted: unfinished shadows between right arm and body of man on donkey, distant object in front of bowing man's head darker than on issued stamp.

240-E1 50c Die on India, on card, slate blue *1,500.*

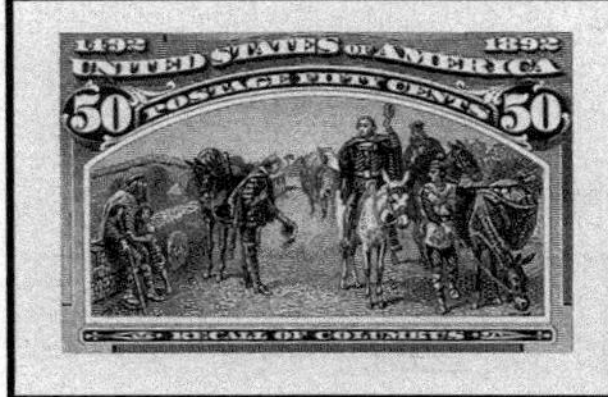

240-E2

Incomplete engraving of entire design: missing dots on donkey's flank and long lines on wrist of bowing man, no etching on two riders or their mounts.

240-E2 50c Die on India, on card, slate blue *1,500.*

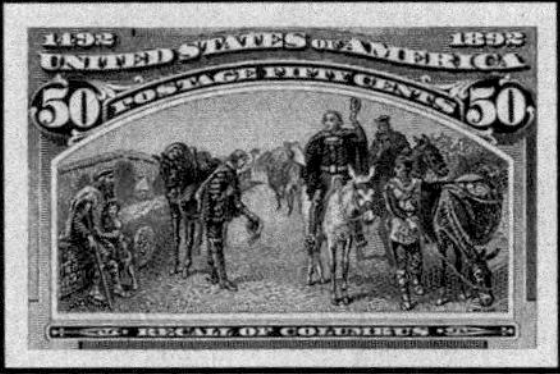

240-E3

Incomplete engraving of entire design: additional engraving on donkey's hindquarters and face of figure to left of Columbus.

240-E3 50c Die on India, on card, slate blue *1,500.*

241-E1

Ferrotype metal plate with engraved outline design (reversed) of vignette as used on $1, engraved lines filled with red ink.

241-E1 $1 Metal plate, 45x29mm *1,000.*

241-E2

Printing from ferrotype plate No. 241-E1.

241-E2 $1 Die on stiff white card with rounded corners, 55½x43mm, red *1,000.*

241-E3

Vignette size: 31x15mm
Die size: 72x59mm
Incomplete engraving of vignette only as adopted (very early state of die): very little shading on Isabella, floor, walls, etc.

241-E3 $1 Die on India, die sunk on card, black brown *2,000.*

241-E4

Incomplete engraving of entire design as adopted: shadow on table cloth, woman in front of table, crosslet shadows at lower corners all unfinished.

241-E4 $1 Die on India, on card, black brown *2,000.*

241-E5

Later state of complete design: horiz. lines in rectangle above Isabella missing.

241-E5 $1 Die on India, die sunk on 86x69mm card, black brown *2,000.*

242-E1

Design size: 33½x22mm
Die size: 75x62mm
Incomplete engraving of entire design as adopted: about 12 horiz. lines missing on back of cape of tall man at right, some

vert. dashes missing on corselet of soldier at right, incomplete foliage over "C" of "COLUMBUS," etc.

242-E1 $2 Die on India, die sunk on card
dull yellow orange *2,000.*
olive brown *2,000.*

243-E1

Ferrotype metal plate with engraved outline design (reversed) of vignette as used on $3, engraved lines filled with red wax.

243-E1 $3 Metal plate, 45x29mm *1,250.*

243-E2

Printing from ferrotype plate No. 243-E1.

243-E2 $3 Die on stiff white card with rounded corners, 55x43mm, red *1,250.*

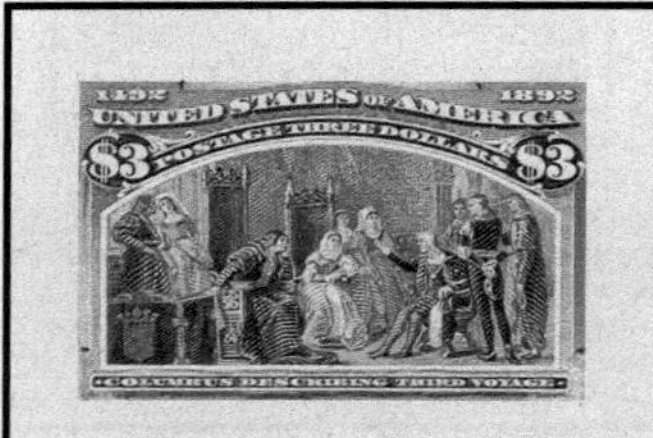

243-E3

Design size: 33½x22mm
Incomplete engraving of entire design as adopted: unshaded crossets in lower corners, shading lines on crossets and frame above title label too light. Pencil marks correct these.

243-E3 $3 Die on India, die sunk on card, dark yellow green *1,500.*

243-E4

Incomplete engraving of entire design as adopted, before etching of shadows on Columbus, Ferdinand, backs of chairs, etc.

243-E4 $3 Die on India, on card, dark red *2,000.*

Ferrotype metal plate with engraved outline design (reversed) of Queen Isabella vignette as used on $4, engraved lines filled with red wax.

244-E1 $4 Metal plate, 33x44mm *1,500.*

244-E2

Printing from ferrotype plate No. 244-E1.

244-E2 $4 Die on stiff white card with rounded corners, 43x55mm, red *1,500.*

244-E3

Vignette diameter: 14mm
Incomplete engraving of Isabella head with background of uniform ruled horiz. lines only, blank circle for Columbus vignette at right adjoining.

244-E3 $4 Die on India, on card, black *3,000.*

Similar to No. 244-E3 but background has diagonal shading also.

244-E4 $4 Die on India, on card, black *3,000.*

244-E5

Design size: about 34x21½mm
Die size: 74½x61½mm
Incomplete engraving of vignettes and lettering only: no diagonal shading lines in background of Columbus vignette.

244-E5 $4 Die on India, die sunk on card
black *3,500.*
dark red *4,000.*

244-E6

Design size: 34x22mm
Same engraving as No. 244-E5 but with wash drawing of frame design as adopted.

244-E6 $4 Die on thick artist's card with beveled edges, 50x39mm, gray black *32,000.*

244-E7

Incomplete engraving of entire design as adopted: shadow at top of vert. bar and lines on leaves at bottom between vignettes unfinished; no circular line bordering vignette at Isabella's right shoulder.

244-E7 $4 Die on India, on card, black brown *2,000.*

244-E8

More complete engraving than No. 244-E7 but still missing circular line at Isabella's shoulder; only light shading on Columbus' collar.

244-E8 $4 Die on India, on card
black brown *2,000.*
dark red —

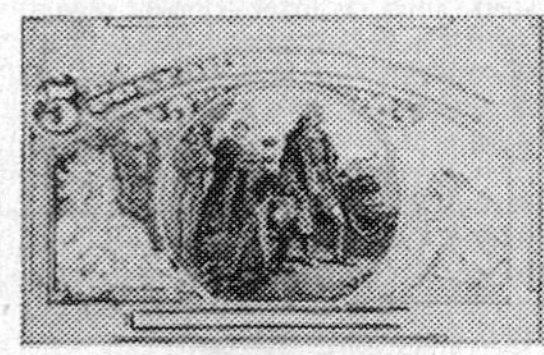

245-E1

Design size: 34½x22½mm
Incomplete engraved vignette as adopted for 1c: missing sky, etc., with pencil drawing of part of frame design.

245-E1 $5 Die on 50x38mm artist's cardboard, on thicker card, 55x43mm, black *4,000.*

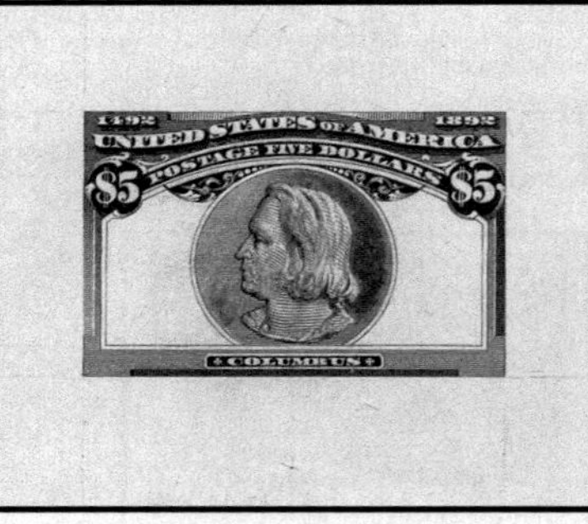

245-E2

Design size: 34x22½mm
Die size: 74½x61½mm
Incomplete engraving of vignette, lettering and frame as adopted (side panels blank): shading unfinished on Columbus' neck, hair and background, and with white and black wash touches.

245-E2 $5 Die on India, die sunk on card, black *3,000.*

245-E3

Similar to No. 245-E2 but further engraved: shading lines on neck, diagonal lines in background, etc.

245-E3 $5 Die on India, on card, 65x54mm, black *3,000.*

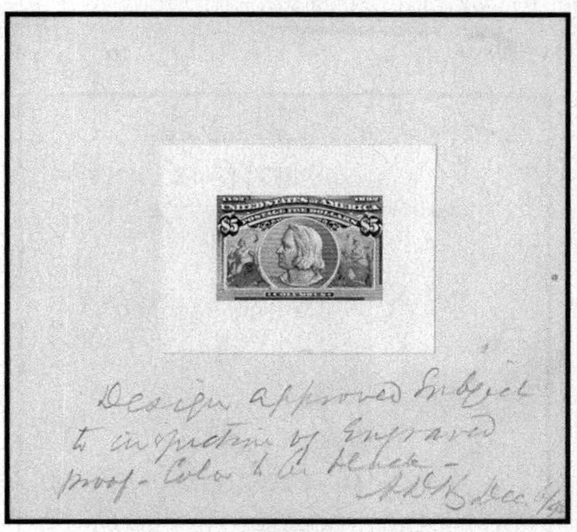

245-E4

Model with photos of female figures mounted each side of vignette, pencil "Design approved subject to inspection of engraved proof, color to be black. A.D.H. Dec. 6 '92" (A.D. Hazen, 3rd asst. PMG).

245-E4 $5 Die on thick white card, on 117x116mm card, black *3,750.*

245-E5

Engraving of No. 245-E3 with retouched photos of side subjects mounted in place.

245-E5 $5 Die on white artist's cardboard, 56½x46mm, die sunk on card, black *2,000.*

245-E6

Design size: 33½x22mm

Incomplete engraving of entire design: one line under "POSTAGE FIVE DOLLARS", no lines outside and no diagonal lines in sky to upper right and upper left of vignette, etc.

245-E6 $5 Die on India, on card, black *2,000.*

245-E7

Similar to No. 245-E2 but with pencil marks to show engraver where to place diagonal shading lines behind head and in front of bust.

245-E7 $5 Die on 65x55mm India, card mounted, black *3,000.*

245-E8

Similar to No. 245-E6 but with pencil marks and white ink suggestions for further engraving.

245-E8 $5 Die on India, die sunk on 83x68mm card, black *2,000.*

245-E9

Similar to No. 245-E6 but further engraved: with diagonal shading above side figures, below numerals and around vignette circle, but still incomplete in arched band above vignette.

245-E9 $5 Die on India, die sunk on 110x83mm card, black *2,000.*

245-E10

Similar to No. 245-E9 but further engraved: with shading lines in arched band above vignette but no shading on pole of liberty cap, object below shield has dotted shading only, spear tip shading incomplete.

245-E10 $5 Die on India, die sunk on 85x70mm card, black *2,000.*

1894 ISSUE
Bureau of Engraving and Printing

The 1c-15c designs of the 1890 issue engraved by the American Bank Note Co. were worked over by the BEP, including the addition of triangles in the upper corners. The 1890 30c was changed to a 50c and the 90c to a $1. Some 1894 essays have American Bank Note Co. imprints below the design.

247-E1

Design size: 18½x22mm

Die size: 61x62mm

Large die engraving of 1890 1c with pencil drawing of UL triangle 3½mm high with straight side next to curved upper label, freehand horiz. ink line at UR.

247-E1 1c Die on India, die sunk on card, black *3,000.*

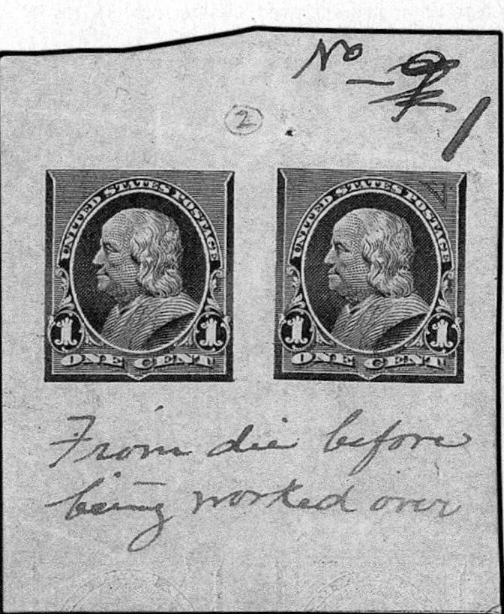

247-E2a

Experimental laydown die with 1890 1c proof 4mm to left of similar design with 15-line high type I triangle in UR corner. Same laydown die also contains two 2c designs 18mm below, 5½mm apart, either uninked or lightly inked in color of 1c (sometimes found separated from 1c designs). No. 247-E2b nearly always found cracked horiz. through designs.

247-E2 1c

a. Die on semiglazed white wove with pencil notations

blue	*1,850.*
ultramarine	*1,850.*

247-E2b

b. Die on white card with pencil notations re color

"1-1 Antwerp, 4 Ultra."	*1,500.*
"2--little lighter--"	*1,500.*
"1 Antwerp blue, 1 Ultra." (not cracked)	*1,750.*
"3 Ul. Blue, 1 Chinese Blue, 2 white"	*1,750.*
"4 Cobalt and Indigo"	*1,500.*
"No 5"	*1,500.*
"No. 6--Antwerp blue"	*1,500.*
"No. 6--with little Antwerp blue"	*1,500.*

247-E3

Die impression of 1890 1c with 15-line high type I triangle in UR corner.

247-E3 1c Die on India, 50x52mm, dusky green *2,500.*

247-E4

Experimental die impression of single 1890 1c with 2c 18mm below, triangles added in ink to upper corners of both designs, ms. "Approved" notations.

247-E4 1c +2c, Die on India, mounted on 57x102mm card, mounted on another card, 144x195mm
green 4,250.
dull violet (without added triangles) 4,000.

247-E5

Large die engraving of 1890 1c with 18-line high triangle in UL corner (inner lines very thick).

247-E5 1c Die on India, die sunk on card, dusky blue green 1,500.

247-E6

Similar to No. 247-E5 but inner line of triangle almost as thin as outer line.

247-E6 1c Die on India, die sunk on card, dusky blue green 1,500.

247-E7

Similar to No. 247-E6 but inner line of triangle same thickness as adopted.

247-E7 1c Die on India, die sunk on card, dusky blue green 1,250.

247-E8

Incomplete engraving of entire design as adopted including triangles: coat collar, scroll under "U," horiz. lines on frame, oval line of vignette, etc., all unfinished; vignette background not re-etched.

247-E8 1c Die on India, die sunk on card
ultramarine 1,000.
blue ("Cobalt 2--Indigo 4") 1,250.
dusky blue green 1,000.

250-E1

Design size: 18½x22mm
Die size: 61x62½mm
Large die engraving of 1890 2c with pencil drawing of UL triangle 2½mm high.

250-E1 2c Die on India, die sunk on card, black 2,300.

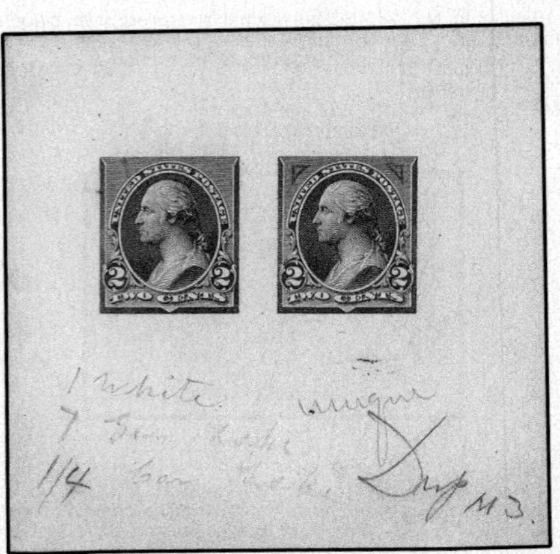

250-E2

Die width: 92mm
Experimental laydown die with 1890 2c proof 5½mm to left of similar design with 14-line high type I triangles in upper corners (found cut apart from No. 247-E2 and used for trial colors as noted thereon in pencil).

250-E2 2c Die on white card
"1 R&D Lake, 1½P. white" 2,000.
"M3 1 white, 7 Gem Lake, ¼ Car. Lake" 2,000.
"2 White, 4 Ger. Lake No. 1, ½ R&D Lake" 2,000.
"Opal Red" 2,000.
"Opal Orange" 2,000.
"Opal Maroon" 2,000.

250-E3

Die size: 61½x62½mm
American Banknote Co. die No. C-224 annealed, with 18-line high type I triangles engraved in upper corners, ms "No. 1" at lower left of card backing.

250-E3 2c Die on India, die sunk on card
medium deep red 1,250.
deep red 1,250.
dusky red 1,250.
dim red 1,250.
medium deep orange-red 1,250.
deep o-orange-red 1,250.
dusky g-blue-green 1,250.
dark medium violet-red-red 1,250.

250-E4

Incomplete engraving of entire design: shadows on frame not etched; lines on foliage, front collar and oval line at vignette bottom not recut; dots instead of lines over corner of eye; only one line on truncated scroll at left of right 2 and no line on similar scroll at right of left 2; shadows of TWO CENTS not etched.

250-E4 2c Die on India, die sunk on card
bright red 1,250.
light red 1,250.
dark red 1,250.
deep orange red 1,250.

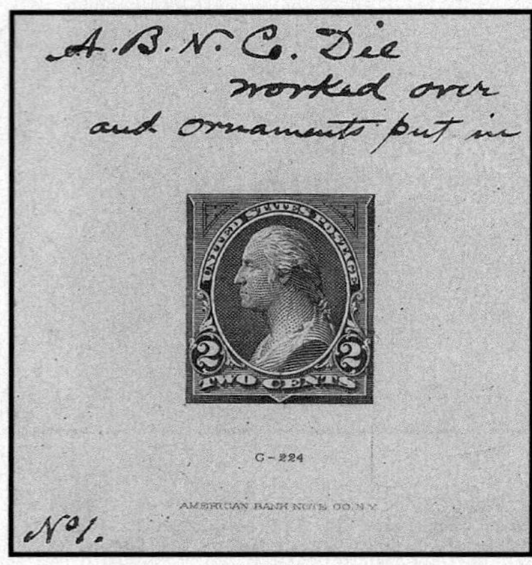

250-E5

Similar to No. 250-E4 but line added to scroll at right of left 2, ms. "A.B.N.Co. Die worked over and ornaments put in" at top, ms. "No. 1" at lower left.

250-E5 2c medium deep red 1,250.

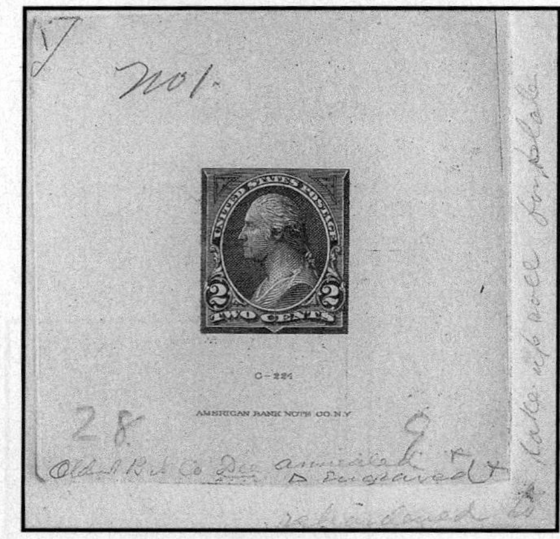

250-E6

Incomplete engraving of entire design: two lines on truncated scroll at left of right 2 (one later removed), scroll at left of right 2 unfinished, profile of nose and forehead darker than on issued stamp, shadows of "TWO CENTS" not etched, short dashes on inside of outer edge of white oval at lower right, veins on scrolls around 2s not recut. Pencil notations incl. "Old A.B.N.Co. annealed & triangles engraved and rehardened to take up roll for plate."

250-E6 2c Die on India, die sunk on card, medium deep red 1,250.

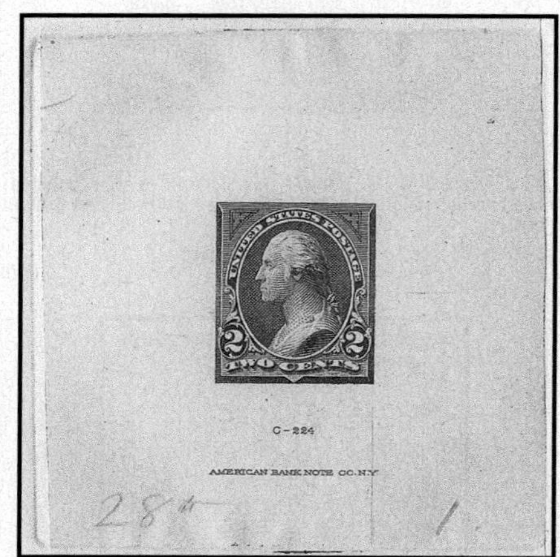

250-E7

Incomplete engraving of entire design: bottom of ear still angular and not yet rounded, dots on lobe not yet gathered into two lines, dot shading under corner of eye not yet gathered into four lines, shadows of "TWO CENTS" have been etched.

250-E7 2c Die on India, die sunk on card, medium deep red *1,000.*

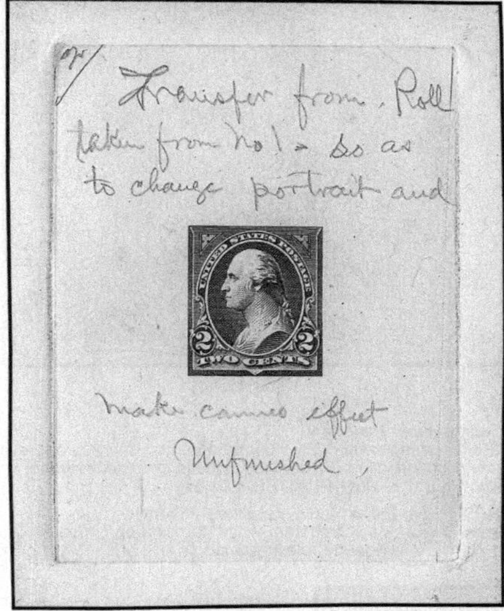

251-E1

Die size: 57x76mm
Incomplete engraving of entire design with type II triangles: top of head not silhouetted. Pencil notation "2/ Transfer from roll taken from No. 1 so as to change portrait and make cameo effect. Unfinished."

251-E1 2c Die on India, die sunk on card
dark violet red *1,000.*
light carmine *1,000.*

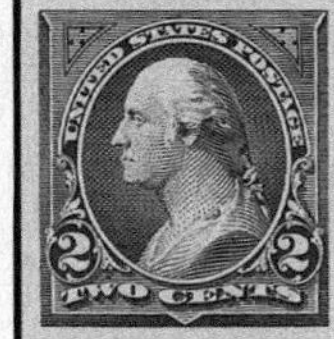

251-E2

Similar to No. 251-E1 but hair in front of ear unfinished, forehead and hair lightened.

251-E2 2c Die on India, die sunk on card, dusky gray *1,250.*

251-E3

Similar to No. 251-E1, made from hardened die, penciled "(Old) No. 2 / Hard" plus suggestions for strengthening design - drawings of nose and eye.

251-E3 2c Die on India, on 55x73mm card, light carmine *1,000.*

252-E1

Die size: 57x81mm
Incomplete engraving of entire design with type III triangles: top of head not silhouetted, unfinished shadow over eye, etc.

252-E1 2c Die on India, die sunk on card, medium deep red *1,000.*

252-E2

Incomplete engraving of entire design with type III triangles: unfinished shadow over eye, etc.

252-E2 2c Die on India, die sunk on card
dusky blue green *2,000.*
dark violet red *1,000.*

252-E3

Design size: 19x22mm
Die size: 56x80½mm
Discarded die, vignette overengraved: too much shading on front hair, cheek, nose, below eye; background too dark; hair in front of ear very prominent.

252-E3 2c Die on India, die sunk on card
light carmine *3,000.*
green, not on card (unique) *3,750.*

253-E1

Die size: 60x63mm
Complete engraved design as adopted but with type II triangles.

253-E1 3c
a. Die on India, die sunk on card
dusky blue green *1,250.*
dark red violet *1,000.*
dusky red violet *1,000.*
b. Die printed directly on card, die sunk on card, violet *1,250.*

254-E1

Design size: about 19x22mm
Die size: 61x63mm
Incomplete engraving of entire design: line under collar wings missing, oval line around vignette not recut; hair, beard, forehead, neck, collar, shirt, etc., all incomplete.

254-E1 4c Die on India, die sunk on card, dark yellow brown *1,500.*

Entire design engraved further than No. 254-E1 but still incomplete: shadows in lettering, etc., not etched, faint lines under collar incomplete, oval around vignette not recut.

254-E2 4c Die on India, die sunk on card, dark yellow brown *1,500.*

254-E3

Entire design engraved further than No. 254-E2 but still incomplete: beard, collar and necktie, etc., unfinished. Some veins recut on foliage under oval label.

254-E3 4c Die on India, die sunk on card, black brown *1,500.*

255-E1

Design size: 19x22mm
Engraved frame of American Bank Note Co. die No. C-227 with triangles, vignette cut out, mounted over engraved vignette of Washington.

255-E1 5c Die on 41x53mm India, on white wove, 48x75mm, black *2,750.*

255-E2

Washington vignette only as on No. 255-E1.

255-E2 5c Die on India, 56-69mm, green *2,000.*

255-E3

Design size: 19x22mm
Engraved frame as adopted with William H. Seward photo mounted on it.

255-E3 5c Die on India, cut close, mounted on 74x84mm white card, black *5,000.*

255-E4

Design size: about 19x22mm
Die size: 62½x75mm
Incomplete engraving of entire design as adopted: no oval border line around vignette.

255-E4 5c Die on India, die sunk on card, orange brown *1,000.*

256-E1

Design size: about 19x22mm
Die size: 62x61½mm
Incomplete engraving of entire design as adopted: white spot on eye and shadows not darkened, diagonal lines missing on beard under mouth, lines on coat unfinished, pencil notations and date "1894" below design.

256-E1 6c Die on India, die sunk on card, dark red 1,250.

256-E2

Entire design engraved further than No. 256-E1 but still incomplete: diagonal lines on beard under mouth incomplete, lines on coat not as dark as on issued stamp.

256-E2 6c Die on India, die sunk on card, dim dusky red 1,000.

257-E1

Design size: about 19x22mm
Die size: 58½x60mm
Incomplete engraving of entire design as adopted: lines on coat not recut darker, vignette background not etched darker.

257-E1 8c Die on India, die sunk on card, dusky red violet 1,000.

258-E1

Design size: about 19x22mm
Die size: 61½x61½mm
Incomplete engraving of entire design as adopted: shading unfinished on cheek, in ear, etc.

258-E1 10c Die on India, die sunk on card, dark brown 1,500.

Entire design engraved further than No. 258-E1 but still incomplete: unfinished shading on cheek under eye.

258-E2 10c Die on India, die sunk on card, red brown 1,500.

260-E1

Die impression of 30c No. 228 with "THIRTY CENTS" crossed out by ink, ms "On roll without the head take out ornament."

260-E1 (50c) Die on India (torn before affixing), on 77x77mm card, black 1,500.

260-E2

Entire design engraved, but without triangles at top corners.

260-E2 50c Die on India, die sunk on 70x115mm card, dark green 2,400.

261-E1

Design size: 19x22mm
Die size: 50x101mm
Large die engraving of 1890 90c with value label and figure circles blank, no triangles.

261-E1 $1 Die on India, die sunk on card, black 2,250.

261-E2

Similar to No. 261-E1 but head further re-engraved and background shadows etched deeper.

261-E2 $1 Die on India, die sunk on card, blue green 2,250.

261-E3

Design size: 19x22mm
Model of engraved Perry vignette mounted on 1890 engraved frame with penciled in triangles, values painted in white and black. Ms. "O.K. July 14/94 TFM" below.

261-E3 $1 Die on India, cut close, mounted on 63x101mm white card, green vignette, black frame 2,000.

261-E4

Similar to No. 261-E3 but with value lettering and circles added, background of circles unfinished, no triangles.

261-E4 $1 Die on India, die sunk on card, dark indigo blue 2,000.

261-E4A

Similar to No. 261-E4 but with engraved triangles added, tiny white space above each numeral.

261-E4A $1 Die on India, die sunk on 67x122mm card, deep blue green 3,500.

261-E5

Incomplete engraving of entire design: hair on top and back of head, whiskers and back of neck, and shading in value circles all unfinished. Triangles are engraved.

261-E5 $1 Die on India, die sunk on card
black 2,000.
orange 2,000.

261-E6

Similar to No. 261-E5 but hair at back of head and whiskers darker, face in front of whiskers darker as on issued stamp. Circular lines extend into colorless vignette oval.

261-E6 $1 Die on India, die sunk on card
black *2,000.*
blue green *2,000.*

261-E7

Design size: 19x21½mm
Die size: 49x100mm
Incomplete engraving of unadopted dollar value design with portrait of Sen. James B. Beck: value label and numerals blank.

261-E7 $1 Die on India, die sunk on card,
black *4,000.*

262-E1

Design size: 19x22mm
Die size: 50x101mm
Incomplete engraving of frame only nearly as adopted: smaller $2's.

262-E1 $2 Die on India, die sunk on card,
blue green *3,000.*

262-E2

Design size: 19x22mm
Die size: 51x112mm
Incomplete engraving of entire design: left value circle blank, right circle engraved $2 outline only, signed by engraver "Lyman F. Ellis."

262-E2 $2 Die on India, die sunk on card,
black *3,000.*

262-E3

Die size: 51x112mm
Incomplete engraving of entire design: vignette shading unfinished, no veins in leaves around value circles.

262-E3 $2 Die on India, die sunk on card,
black *2,500.*

262-E4

Incomplete engraving of entire design: inside of right border line above $2 unfinished, with pencil "line" instruction for border line strengthening, plus penciled "Then O.K./Blue/Lake/Green/Vermilion/Brown/Purple."

262-E4 $2 Die on India, die sunk on
62x128mm card, black *2,500.*

Similar to No. 262-E4 but border line complete.

262-E5 $2 Die on India, die sunk on card,
black *2,500.*

263-E1

263-E1a

Die size: 50x112½mm
Incomplete engraving of entire design: only one line in each scroll at right and left of $5, inner line of right border above $5 unfinished, etc., veins on leaves around right value circle unfinished.

263-E1 $5 Die on India, die sunk on card,
black *3,000.*
a. With photographic portrait of Marshall affixed as vignette with paper hinge *2,500.*

263-E2

Similar to No. 263-E1 but horiz. lines cut into oval line at top and inner oval line above L and R of DOLLARS required retouching as indicated by pencil instructions. Two lines in scrolls around value circles as adopted.

263-E2 $5 Die on India, die sunk on card,
black *3,000.*

The bicolored essays commonly offered as No. 285-293 bicolored proofs can be found under the following listings: Nos. 285-E8, 286-E8, 287-E9, 288-E5, 289-E4, 290-E4, 291-E8, 292-E6, 293-E7. Values are for full-size cards (approximately 8x6 inches).

TRANS-MISSISSIPPI ISSUE

285-E1

Die size: 79x68mm
Incomplete engraving of vignette only: initial state of die, no lines in sky or water.

285-E1 1c Die on India, die sunk on
151x97mm card, black *2,500.*

285-E2

Vignette further engraved: lines in sky and water.

285-E2 1c Die on India, die sunk on card,
black *2,500.*

285-E3

Vignette further engraved: more background lines added.

285-E3 1c Die on India, die sunk on card,
black *2,500.*

285-E4

Vignette further engraved: Indian at right darker, robe shadow etched.

285-E4 1c Die on India, die sunk on card, black *2,500.*

285-E5

Vignette further engraved: rock in water more complete.

285-E5 1c Die on India, die sunk on card, black *2,500.*

285-E6

Design size: 34x22mm
Die size: 73x62mm
Incomplete bicolor engraving of entire design: no second inner line in numerals.

285-E6 1c Die on India, die sunk on card, orange red & black *2,500.*

Die size: 83x68mm
Incomplete engraving of entire design: vignette unfinished and unetched, frame has second inner line in numerals.

285-E7 1c Die on India, die sunk on card, black *3,500.*

285-E8

Die size: 63x51mm
Complete bicolor engraving of entire design.

285-E8 1c Die with black vignette on India, die sunk on card

dark yellow green ("normal" bicolor)	*750.*
dusky green	*2,000.*
dusky blue green	*2,000.*
brown	*2,000.*

285-E9

Die size: 88x70mm
Incomplete engraving of entire design: corn husks and panels in ends of cartouche unfinished, lines under MARQUETTE and MISSISSIPPI not as thick as on completed die.

285-E9 1c Die on India, die sunk on card, dusky green *2,500.*

285-E10

Unfinished frame in red brown missing second inner line in numerals, with black unfinished "Cattle in the Storm" vignette as used on the $1 value, foreground snow at left incomplete.

285-E10 1c Die on India, red brown & black 3,500.

286-E1

Die size: 78x68mm
Incomplete engraving of Mississippi River Bridge vignette (originally intended for 2c but eventually used on $2): initial state of die, very lightly engraved.

286-E1 2c Die on India, die sunk on card, black *3,750.*

286-E2

Vignette further engraved but no lines on bridge beside two trolley cars.

286-E2 2c Die on India, die sunk on card, black *5,000.*

286-E3

Vignette further engraved but foreground between bridge and boat and foretopdeck incomplete, horse truck visible (later removed).

286-E3 2c Die on India, die sunk on card, black *3,000.*

Complete engraving of vignette only.

286-E4 2c Die on India, die sunk on card, black *3,000.*

286-E5

Design size: 137x88½mm
Pencil sketch by R. Ostrander Smith of 2c frame design as adopted except titled "ST. LOUIS BRIDGE."

286-E5 2c Sketch on tracing paper, 178x120mm *1,500.*

286-E6

Design size: 137x89mm
Complete pencil drawing by R.O. Smith of frame design ("P" of "POSTAGE" in ink), titled "ST. LOUIS BRIDGE."

286-E6 2c Drawing on Whatman drawing board, 1889 wmk., 217x163mm *1,500.*

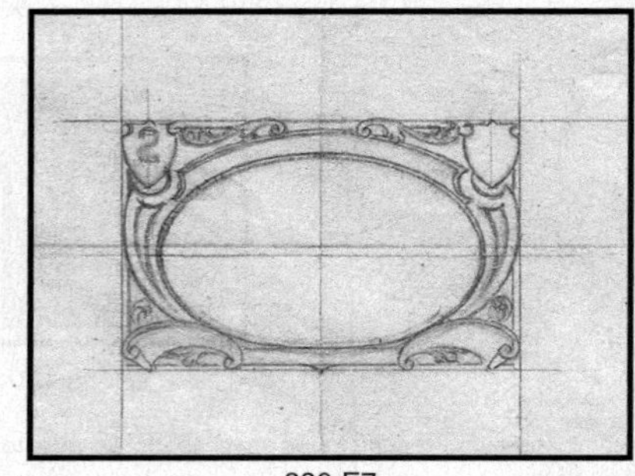

286-E7

Pencil drawing by R.O. Smith, no title.

286-E7 2c Drawing on 72x61mm tracing paper *1,500.*

286-E7A

Ink and wash drawing of frame, stamp size, similar to adopted design.

286-E7A 2c Drawing on hard, thick paper, black *11,000.*

286-E8

Die size: 63x51mm
Complete bicolor engraving of 2c design but with Mississippi River Bridge vignette as used on $2.

Ridgway numbers used for colors of No. 286-E8.

286-E8 2c Die with black vignette on India, die sunk on card

dark red ("normal" bicolor)	*750.*
3k/0 dark orange red	*2,000.*
5k/0 dark o-orange-red	*2,000.*
5m/1 dim dusky o-orange-red	*2,000.*
7i/0 deep red orange	*2,000.*
7m/0 dusky red orange	*2,000.*
9m/0 dusky o-red-orange	*2,000.*
9k/2 dull dark o-red-orange	*2,000.*
13m/3 dismal dusky o-yellow-orange	*2,000.*
35m/1 dim dusky green	*2,000.*
49m/1 dim v. dusky blue	*2,000.*
63m/1 dim dusky red violet	*2,000.*
71-/0 deep violet-red-red	*2,000.*

287-E1

Design size: 28x16.5mm
Die No. 259 size: 77x70mm
Initial state of die, very lightly engraved.

287-E1 4c Die on India, die sunk on card, black *3,000.*

287-E2

Vignette further engraved: sky lines ruled in.

287-E2 4c Die on India, die sunk on card, black *3,000.*

287-E3

Vignette further engraved: more lines added, no right forefoot on bison.

287-E3 4c Die on India, die sunk on card, black *4,500.*

287-E4

Shadow under bison incomplete.

287-E4 4c Die on India, die sunk on card, black *3,750.*

287-E5

Shadow under bison and foreground penciled in.

287-E5 4c Die on India, die sunk on card, black *3,750.*

287-E6

Vignette further engraved: right forefoot added, shadow under bison engraved but not etched.

287-E6 4c Die on India, die sunk on card, black *3,750.*

287-E7

Die size: 83x67mm
Incomplete engraving of entire design: no lines in sky, frame shadow etching unfinished.

287-E7 4c Die on India, die sunk on card
black *3,500.*
deep orange *3,500.*

287-E8

Die size: 63x51mm
Incomplete engraving of entire design: corn husks at lower sides of frame unfinished.

Ridgway numbers used for colors of No. 287-E8.

287-E8 4c Die with black vignette on India, die sunk on card
5k/0 dark o-orange-red *2,000.*
5m/0 dusky o-orange-red *2,000.*
7m/0 dusky red orange *2,000.*
11o/2 dull v. dusky orange *2,000.*
13m/3 dismal dusky o-yellow-orange *2,000.*
35m/1 dim dusky green *2,000.*
39m/1 dim dusky blue green *2,000.*
49o/1 dim v. dusky blue *2,000.*
61k/1 dim dark violet-red violet *2,000.*
63m/1 dim dusky red violet *2,000.*
71m/0 dusky violet-red-red *2,000.*

287-E9

Die size: 62x51mm
Complete bicolor engraving.

287-E9 4c Die with black vignette on India, die sunk on card
red orange ("normal" bicolor) *550.*
deep red orange ("normal" bicolor) *550.*

288-E1

Die size: 75x68mm
Initial state of die, very lightly engraved.

288-E1 5c Die on India, die sunk on card, black *3,500.*

288-E2

Vignette further engraved: lower clouds at right darkened.

288-E2 5c Die on India, die sunk on card, black *5,500.*

288-E3

Vignette further engraved: shading penciled in on figures at right, etc.

288-E3 5c Die on India, die sunk on card, black *3,750.*

288-E4

Vignette further engraved but dots in sky at left of flag unfinished.

288-E4 5c Die on India, die sunk on card, black *3,750.*

288-E5

Design size: 34x22mm
Die size: 63x51mm
Incomplete bicolor engraving of entire design: unfinished crosshatching at left of "FREMONT," lines against bottom label and frame unfinished, no etching on flag.

Ridgway numbers used for colors of No. 288-E5.

288-E5 5c Die with black vignette on India, die sunk on card
49m/1 dim dusky blue ("normal" bicolor) *750.*
49k/1 dim dark blue ("normal" bicolor) *750.*
3k/0 dark orange red *2,000.*
3m/0 dusky orange red *2,000.*
7m/0 dusky red orange *2,000.*
7m/1 dim dusky red orange *2,000.*
9m/0 dusky o-red-orange *2,000.*
11o/2 dull v. dusky orange *2,000.*
37m/1 dim dusky g-blue-green *2,000.*
39m/1 dim dusky blue green *2,000.*
49o/1 dim v. dusky blue *2,000.*
63m/1 dim dusky red violet *2,000.*
71n/0 medium deep violet-red-red *2,000.*
35m/1 dim dusky green *2,000.*

288-E7

Die size: 82x68½mm
Incomplete engraving of entire design: cornhusks, panels at ends of cartouche, mountains, foreground at sides of title label, sky, etc., all unfinished, figures and mountains not etched dark.

288-E7 5c Die on India, die sunk on card, black *3,250.*

Incomplete engraving of vignette: no dots on mountain tops next to right border, unfinished crosshatching at left end of title label.

288-E8 5c Die on India, die sunk on card, black *3,750.*

289-E1

Engraved vignette only of mounted Indian, not used for any value.

289-E1 8c Die on India, on card, black *7,500.*

289-E2

Incomplete engraving of vignette only as adopted: blank area for label wider than completed bicolor vignette, knee of kneeling soldier unfinished, etc.

289-E2 8c Die on India, die sunk on card, black *3,000.*

289-E3

Design size: about 33½x21½mm
Incomplete engraving of frame only: shading of sunken center of cartouche at right of vignette unfinished.

289-E3 8c Die on India, 37x26mm, black *3,000.*

289-E4

Incomplete engraving of entire design: top row of distant shrubbery under "ERICA" missing, crosshatching on distant mountains at left, blades of grass at left end of label, some dots against top label all unfinished.

Ridgway numbers used for colors of No. 289-E4.

289-E4 8c Die with black vignette on India, die sunk on card
dark red ("normal" bicolor) *750.*
dusky red ("normal" bicolor) *750.*
3m/0 dusky orange red *2,750.*
5m/0 dusky o-orange-red *2,750.*
7i/0 deep red orange *2,750.*
7m/0 dusky red orange *2,750.*
9m/0 dusky o-red-orange *2,750.*
11o/2 dull v. dusky orange *2,750.*
35m/1 dim dusky green *2,750.*
39m/1 dim dusky blue-green *2,750.*
49o/1 dim v. dusky blue *2,750.*
63m/1 dim dusky red violet *2,750.*
71-/0 deep violet-red-red *2,750.*

290-E1

Die size: 77x64mm
Incomplete engraving of vignette only: two rows of dots in sky over wagon.

290-E1 10c Die on India, die sunk on card, black *8,500.*

290-E2

Vignette further engraved: three rows of dots in sky over wagon.

290-E2 10c Die on India, die sunk on card, black *3,750.*

290-E3

Vignette further engraved: front of wagon canvas crosshatched.

290-E3 10c Die on India, die sunk on card, black *3,750.*

290-E4

Incomplete bicolor engraving of entire design: cornhusks unfinished, blades of grass to right of girl's feet and some to right of dark horse's feet are missing. Five lines of dots in sky over wagon.

Ridgway numbers used for colors of No. 290-E4.

290-E4 10c Die with black vignette on India, die sunk on card
dull dusky violet blue ("normal" bicolor) *750.*
dusky blue violet ("normal" bicolor) *750.*
1i/0 deep red *2,500.*
3k/0 dark orange red *2,500.*
5k/0 dark o-orange-red *2,500.*
5m/0 dusky o-orange-red *2,500.*
7i/0 deep red orange *2,500.*
9m/0 dusky o-red-orange *2,500.*
11o/2 dull v. dusky orange *2,500.*
35m/1 dim dusky green *2,500.*
39m/1 dim dusky blue green *2,500.*
49o/1 dim v. dusky blue *2,500.*
55m/2 smoky dark v.-blue violet *2,500.*
63m/1 dim dusky red violet *2,500.*
71-/0 deep violet-red-red *2,500.*

290-E6

Incomplete engraving of entire design: cornhusks unfinished, vignette from No. 290-E4 trimmed by engraving to fit frame.

290-E6 10c Die on India, die sunk on card, black brown *3,000.*

Incomplete engraving of entire design: cornhusks and panels at ends of cartouche and both sides and botton of vignette next to border unfinished.

290-E7 10c Die on India, die sunk on card, dull red violet *3,000.*

290-E8

Incomplete engraving of entire design: cornhusks and both sides and bottom of vignette next to border are unfinished, vert. lines on cartouche frame at right of vignette missing.

290-E8 10c Die on India, dull red violet *3,000.*

291-E1

Die size: 76x68mm
Incomplete engraving of vignette only: without sky or mountains.

291-E1 50c Die on India, die sunk on card, black *3,750.*

291-E2

Vignette further engraved: sky ruled in.

291-E2 50c Die on India, die sunk on card, black *3,750.*

291-E3

Vignette further engraved but no shading on distant mountains.

291-E3 50c Die on India, die sunk on card, black *3,750.*

291-E4

Vignette further engraved: light shading on distant mountains.

291-E4 50c Die on India, die sunk on card, black *3,750.*

291-E5

Vignette further engraved: more shading on distant mountains.

291-E5 50c Die on India, die sunk on card, black *3,750.*

291-E6

Vignette further engraved: shadows on miner's hat darker (etched).

291-E6 50c Die on India, die sunk on card, black *3,750.*

291-E7

Vignette further engraved: girth under donkey darkened.

291-E7 50c Die on India, die sunk on card, black *9,000.*

291-E8

Design size: 34x22mm
Die size: 89x71mm
Incomplete bicolor engraving of entire design: shading lines on scroll in LR corner of frame and shrubbery in UL corner of vignette unfinished, sky incomplete.

Ridgway numbers used for colors of No. 291-E8.

291-E8 50c Die with black vignette on India, die sunk on card
dull dusky b-blue-green ("normal" bicolor; die size: 63x51mm) *750.*
dull dusky g-blue-green ("normal" bicolor; die size: 63x51mm) *750.*
1i/0 deep red *2,500.*
3k/0 dark orange red *2,500.*
5m/0 dusky o-orange-red *2,500.*
7m/0 dusky red orange *2,500.*

9i/0 deep o-yellow-orange 2,500.
9m/0 dusky o-red-orange 2,500.
11m/2 dull dusky orange 2,500.
13m/3 dismal dusky o-yellow-orange 2,500.
35m/1 dim dusky green 2,500.
39m/1 dim dusky blue green 2,500.
47n/2 dull v. dusky green-blue blue 2,500.
49o/1 dim v. dusky blue 2,500.
61k/1 dim dark violet-red-violet 2,500.
71m/0 dusky violet-red-red 2,500.

291-E9

Incomplete engraving of entire design: vignette against top frame unfinished.

291-E9 50c Die on India, die sunk on card
black 3,000.
deep red orange 3,000.

291-E10

Incomplete engraving of entire design: engraving on bottom of miner's pan dots only, not lines as on issued stamp.

291-E10 50c Die on wove, dark green 3,000.

292-E1

Incomplete engraving of vignette only: initial state of die, lightly engraved.

292-E1 $1 Die on India, die sunk on card,
black 4,500.

292-E2

Vignette further engraved: light shield-shaped vignette outline (later removed.)

292-E2 $1 Die on India, die sunk on card,
black 4,500.

292-E3

Vignette further engraved: left front hoof of lead bull darker.

292-E3 $1 Die on India, die sunk on card,
black 3,750.

Vignette similar to No. 292-E3 but with penciled modeling in snow and among cattle.

292-E4 $1 Die on India, die sunk on card,
black 3,750.

292-E5

Vignette further engraved: foreground snow at left darkened, shield outline removed.

292-E5 $1 Die on India, die sunk on card,
black 10,000.

292-E6

Incomplete engraving of entire bicolored design: right cornhusk and sky against top of frame unfinished, bull's right forefoot does not touch frame, foreground at right end of label unfinished.

Ridgway numbers used for colors of No. 292-E6, where available.

292-E6 $1 Die with black vignette on India,
die sunk on card
dull violet blue ("normal" bicolor) 750.
dull blue ("normal" bicolor) 750.
dull violet ("normal" bicolor) 3,000.
3k/0 dark orange red 3,000.
5m/0 dusky-o-orange-red 3,000.
7m/0 dusky red orange 3,000.
9m/0 dusky o-red-orange 3,000.
9n/3 dismal v. dusky o-red-orange 3,000.
13n/3 dismal v. dusky o-yellow-orange 3,000.
35m/1 dim dusky green 3,000.
43m/1 dim dusky green blue 3,000.
49m/1 dim dusky blue 3,000.
57k/4 smoky dark violet-blue violet 3,000.
63m/1 dim dusky red violet 3,000.
71-/0 violet-red-red 3,000.
47n/2 dull dusky green blue 3,000.
dark brown 3,000.

292-E7

Incomplete engraving of entire design: left frameline, cornhusks and shading in frame over cornhusks all unfinished.

292-E7 $1 Die on India, die sunk on card,
dusky red orange 3,000.

293-E1

Design size: 34x22mm
Die size: 73x63mm
Vignette of Western mining prospector as used on 50c, but labeled HARVESTING IN THE WEST, frame shows $ same size as numeral 2.

293-E1 $2 Die on India, on card, dusky violet & black 3,500.

293-E2

Die size: 77x66mm
Incomplete engraving of Farming in the West vignette (originally intended for $2 but eventually used on 2c): initial state of die, very lightly engraved.

293-E2 $2 Die on India, die sunk on card,
black 3,000.

293-E3

Vignette further engraved: four horses shaded.

293-E3 $2 Die on India, die sunk on card,
black 3,000.

293-E4

Vignette further engraved: shading added to background figures and horses, pencil shading above and below half horse at left.

293-E4 $2 Die on India, die sunk on card,
black 3,000.

293-E5

Vignette further engraved: foreground and shadows under horse teams darkened, no shading dots above half horse at left, etc.

293-E5 $2 Die on India, die sunk on card,
black 3,000.

293-E6

Vignette further engraved but foreground in front of plow wheel still unfinished.

293-E6 $2 Die on India, die sunk on card,
black 3,000.

293-E7

Die size: 62x51mm
Incomplete engraving of entire bicolor design: only one plowshare shown, label longer, less foreground than on issued stamp.

Ridgway numbers used for colors of No. 293-E7.

293-E7 $2 Die with black vignette on India,
die sunk on card
dusky orange red ("normal" bicolor;
die size: 63x61mm) 750.
dark red orange ("normal" bicolor;
die size: 63x61mm) 750.
1-/0 red 3,000.
3k/0 dark orange red 3,000.
7m/0 dusky red orange 3,000.
35m/1 dim dusky green 3,000.
39m/1 dim dusky blue green 3,000.
45o/1 dim v. dusky blue-green blue 3,000.
45m/2 dull dusky blue-green blue 3,000.
63m/1 dim dusky red violet 3,000.
71i/0 deep violet-red-red 3,000.
47n/2 dull dusky green blue 3,000.

The bicolored essays commonly offered as Nos. 285-293 "bicolored proofs" in "original colors," are Nos. 285-E8, 286-E8, 287-E9, 288-E5, 289-E4, 290-E4, 291-E8, 292-E6 and 293-E7. Value, set of nine $6,550.

293-E8

Die size: 82x68mm

Complete engraving with "HARVESTING IN THE WEST" vignette as adopted but from a die not used for the stamp: horses at left vignette border engraved dark up to border line which is solid complete line at both left and right.

293-E8 $2 Die on India, die sunk on card (marked "Proof from 1st die.")
black *2,500.*
dark orange red *2,500.*

293-E9

Incomplete engraving of entire design as adopted: black wash over engraving on side of bridge and foreground (engraving under wash unfinished).

293-E9 $2 Die on India, die sunk on card, black *3,500.*

293-E10

Complete design, vignette further engraved: engraving completed between title label and steamboat and city next to right frame, near side of bridge and smoke shadow on water lighter than on issued stamp.

293-E10 $2 Die on India, die sunk on card, black *3,500.*

293-E11

Incomplete engraving of entire design: circles in upper corners of vignette next to value ovals, water next to right end of value label, panels at ends of cartouche all unfinished.

293-E11 $2 Die on India, die sunk on card, black *3,500.*

Edward Rosewater

Rosewater, of St. Louis, was asked by the Post Office Dept. in 1897 to submit proposed designs for the Trans-Mississippi Exposition issue. For that reason, they are listed here.

All are drawings on tracing paper, on 91x142mm buff card.

285-E11

Design size: 62x97mm
Wash drawing of cattle.

285-E11 1c dull orange *12,500.*

286-E11

Design size: 57x98mm
Wash drawing of mounted Indian saluting wagon train.

286-E11 2c deep orange red *12,500.*

288-E9

Design size: 61x100mm
Wash drawing of man plowing field.

288-E9 5c dark yellow green *12,500.*

290-E9

Design size: 62x99mm
Wash drawing of train coming around mountain.

290-E9 Ten Cents, dusky blue *12,500.*

292-E9

Design size: 60x98mm
Wash drawing of woman holding light, standing on globe.

292-E9 $1 deep orange yellow *12,500.*

PAN-AMERICAN ISSUE
Bureau of Engraving and Printing

294-E1

Design size: 108x82mm
Preliminary pencil drawing for frame design as adopted.

294-E1 1c Drawing on tracing paper, black *1,500.*

Design size: 114x82½mm
Second state of ink drawing for frame design as adopted.

294-E2 1c Drawing on white card, about 6½x5 inches, black *1,500.*

294-E3

Second state of ink drawing for frame design reduced by Bureau of Engraving and Printing to stamp size.

294-E3 1c Reduced drawing on paper, mounted on 59x38mm black card, black —

294-E4

Similar to No. 294-E2, but design reduced to stamp size and with additional details added to columns and elsewhere, "1" denominations made wider (changed back to narrower on final frame engraving).

294-E4 1c Drawing on paper, mounted on 59x38mm black card, black —

294-E5

Die size: 87x68½mm
Incomplete engraving of vignette only.

294-E5 1c Die on India, die sunk on card, black *1,500.*

295-E1

Design size: 108x82mm
Preliminary pencil drawing of frame similar to that adopted (side ornaments, etc., different); UR corner, etc., unfinished.

295-E1 2c Drawing on tracing paper, black *1,750.*

295-E2

Design size: 114x83mm
Preliminary pencil drawing of frame similar to No. 295-E1 (minor differences) but with UR corner complete.

295-E2 2c Drawing on tracing paper, black *1,750.*

295-E3

Design size: 108x82mm
Preliminary pencil drawing of frame design similar to No. 295-E2 but with minor differences at top, in lettering, etc.

295-E3 2c Drawing on tracing paper, black *1,750.*

295-E4

Design size: 95x70mm
Ink and wash drawing model of frame design as adopted, side torchbearers engraved on India as on U.S. Series of 1901 $10 note.

295-E4 2c Die on white card, about 108x82mm, black *1,750.*

295-E4A

Design size: 88x69mm
Incomplete engraving of vignette only.

295-E4A 2c Die on India, die sunk on card, black *3,500.*

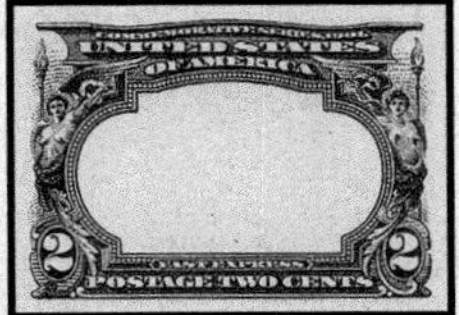
295-E5

Design size: 27x19½mm
Die size: 88x68mm
Complete engraving of frame only as adopted.

295-E5 2c Die on India, die sunk on card, carmine *3,750.*

295-E6

Die size: 88½x69mm
Engraving of entire design with vignette incomplete near frame and on cars.

295-E6 2c Die on India, die sunk on card, carmine & black *4,750.*

296-E1

Preliminary pencil drawing of unadopted frame design.

296-E1 4c Drawing on tracing paper, black *1,750.*

296-E2

Design size: 114x82½mm
Final ink drawing for frame design as adopted.

296-E2 4c Drawing on white card, about 6½x5 inches, black *1,750.*

296-E3

Design size: 27x19mm
Die size: 88x67mm
Incomplete engraving of entire design as adopted: lines missing at base of capitol dome, above driver's head.

296-E3 4c Die on India, die sunk on card, deep red brown & black *1,750.*

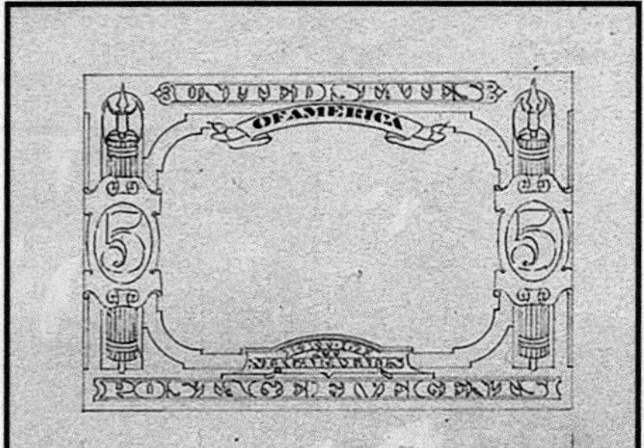

297-E1

Photo reproduction of pencil sketch of unadopted frame design on photosensitive tan paper, reduced to stamp size. Incomplete preliminary pencil drawing of frame design as adopted.

297-E1 5c Photo reproduction on tan paper *1,750.*

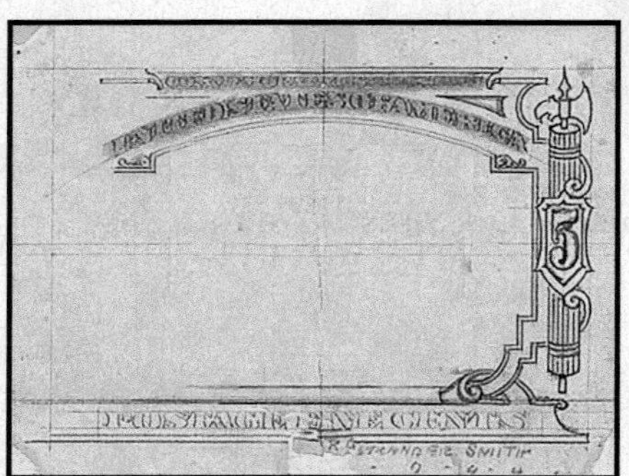

297-E2

Design size: 114x83mm
Incomplete preliminary pencil drawing of frame design as adopted.

297-E2 5c Drawing on tracing paper, black *1,750.*

297-E3

Design size: 114x82½mm
Final ink drawing for frame design as adopted.

297-E3 5c Drawing on white card, about 6½x5 inches, black *1,750.*

297-E4

Photo reproduction of sketch of adopted frame design on photosensitive paper, reduced to stamp size.

297-E4 5c Photo reproduction on tan paper *750.*

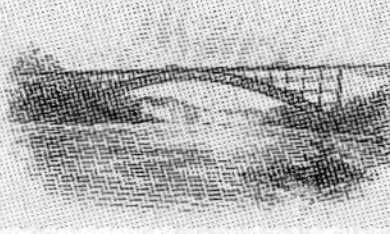

297-E5

Die size: 87x68mm
Incomplete engraving of vignette only.

297-E5 5c Die on India, die sunk on card, black *1,500.*

297-E6

Die size: 87x68mm
As No. 297-E5, but more completely engraved.

297-E6 5c Die on India, die sunk on card, black *1,500.*

297-E7

Design size: 27x19½mm
Die size: 87x68mm
Incomplete engraving of entire design as adopted: shading at bottom of battleaxes and scrolls at ends of title frame unfinished.

297-E7 5c Die on India, die sunk on card, blue & black *1,750.*

298-E1

Design size:108x82mm
Preliminary pencil drawing of unadopted frame design.

298-E1 8c Drawing on tracing paper, black *1,750.*

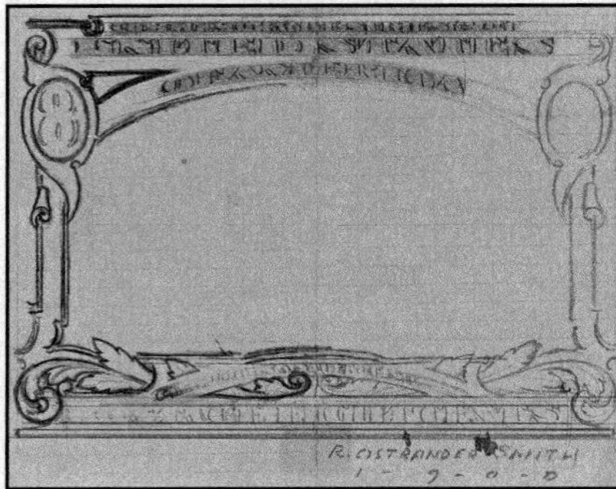

298-E2

Design size: 114x83mm
Incomplete preliminary pencil drawing of unadopted frame design.

298-E2 8c Drawing on tracing paper, black *1,750.*

298-E3

Design size: 114x83mm
Preliminary pencil drawing of unadopted frame design.

298-E3 8c Drawing on tracing paper, black *1,750.*

298-E4

Design size: 114x83mm
Preliminary pencil drawing of frame design as adopted.

298-E4 8c Drawing on tracing paper, black *1,750.*

298-E5

Design size: 114x82½mm
Final ink drawing for frame design as adopted. No. 298-E5 has an example of No. 298 mounted in the vignette area.

298-E5 8c Drawing on white card, about 6½x5 inches, black *1,750.*

298-E6

Design size: 34x26mm
Photo reproduction of sketch of adopted frame design on photosensitive paper, reduced to stamp size.

298-E6 8c Photo reproduction on tan paper *1,750.*

298-E7

Design size: 27x20mm
Die size: 87x69mm
Incomplete engraving of entire design: shading lines of ornaments, scrolls and ribbons at top unfinished, vignette incomplete at right, no etching on building in left foreground.

298-E7 8c Die on India, die sunk on card, bi-colored *1,750.*

299-E1

Design size: 114x83mm
Preliminary pencil drawing of unadopted frame design (small blank oval at center).

299-E1 10c Drawing on tracing paper, black *1,750.*

299-E2

Design size: 114x82½mm
Similar to No. 299-E1 but with outline of eagle and shield in center oval.

299-E2 10c Drawing on tracing paper, black *1,500.*

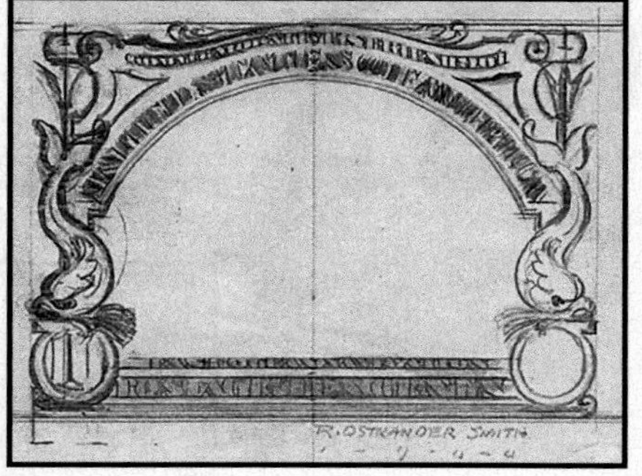

299-E3

Design size: 114x83mm
Preliminary pencil drawing for frame design as adopted.

299-E3 10c Drawing on tracing paper, black *1,750.*

299-E4

Design size: 114x82½mm
Final ink drawing for frame design as adopted.

299-E4 10c Drawing on white card, about 6½x9 inches, black *1,750.*

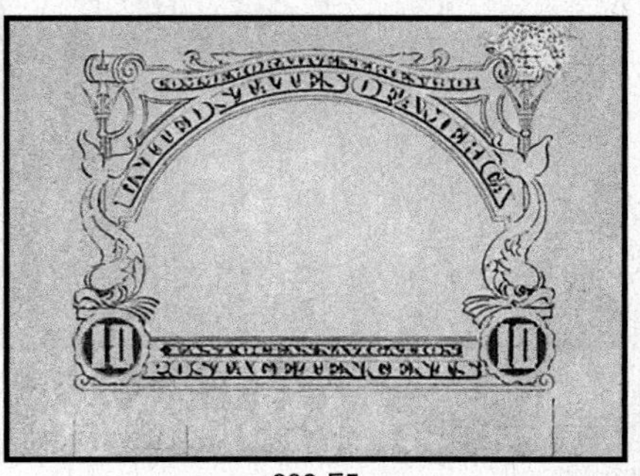
299-E5

Photo reproduction of sketch of adopted frame design on photosensitive paper, reduced to stamp size.

299-E5 10c Photo reproduction on tan paper *750.*

299-E6

Die size: 87x68mm
Incomplete engraving of entire design: frame complete but lines later engraved in the mast, smokestack and sky.

299-E6 10c Die on India, die sunk on card, bi-colored *1,750.*

1902 ISSUE

300-E1

Incomplete engraving of vignette and lower part of frame.

300-E1 1c Die on India, die sunk on card, black *4,000.*

300-E2

Design size: 19x22mm
Die size: 74½x88½mm
Incomplete engraving of entire design: vignette background has horiz. lines only, neckpiece, men at sides, etc., all unfinished.

300-E2 1c Die on India, die sunk on card, black *3,500.*

300-E3

Design size: 136x190mm
Preliminary ink drawing for 5c frame design but later adopted for 1c.

300-E3 1c Drawing on manila paper, blue green, gray blue & black *2,000.*

No. 300-E3 is on the opposite side of the same piece of paper bearing No. 307-E1. Value is for both essays.

300-E4

Design size: 116x135mm
Preliminary pencil and ink drawing for frame design as adopted.

300-E4 1c Drawing on white card, black *3,000.*

301-E1

Design size: 162x188mm
Paper size: 169x214mm
Preliminary pencil drawing of frame design (Raymond Ostrander Smith). Not adopted.

301-E1 2c Drawing on yellowed transparent tracing paper, black *1,500.*

301-E1A

Preliminary pencil and ink drawing of unadopted frame design, on 77x82mm yellowish wove paper, folded vertically and with ink tracing of frame on reverse.

301-E1A 2c Drawing on woven paper, black *2,000.*

301-E1B

Design size: 145x168mm
Preliminary pencil drawing of frame design as adopted.

301-E1B 2c Drawing on tracing paper, black *3,500.*

301-E2

Model with vignette of Houdon bust of Washington, on wash drawing over photo reduced to stamp size for approval by PMG.

301-E2 2c Model mounted on card, black *750.*

301-E3

Design size: 19x22mm
Die size: 75x87½mm
Incomplete engraving of entire design: head unfinished, horiz. background lines only, frame unfinished, lettering either blank or unfinished.

301-E3 2c Die on India, die sunk on card, black *4,000.*

301-E4

Design size: 60x88mm
Preliminary pencil drawing of right numeral 2 design as adopted.

301-E4 2c Drawing on tracing paper, black *500.*

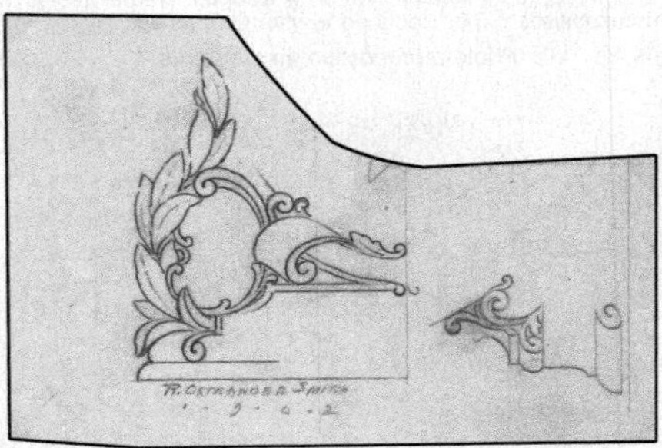

301-E5

Design size: 176x120mm
Preliminary pencil drawing of lower left and upper right design.

301-E5 2c Drawing on tracing paper, black *700.*

301-E6

Design size: 19x22mm
Die size: 74x89mm
Incomplete engraving of entire design: head unfinished, horiz. background lines only, frame almost finished, lettering complete. No. 62057 on back.

301-E6 2c Die on India, die sunk on 153x202mm card, black *3,000.*

302-E1

Design size: 19x22mm
Die size: 74½x88mm
Incomplete engraving of entire design: vignette unfinished, horiz. background lines only, atlantes at sides unfinished. No. 66218 on back.

302-E1 3c Die on India, die sunk on card, black *3,250.*

303-E1

Design size: 19x22mm
Die size: 75x88mm
Incomplete engraving of entire design: vignette unfinished on eyes, hair, beard, etc. No. 58920 on back.

303-E1 4c Die on India, die sunk on card, black *2,500.*

303-E2

Design size: 19x22mm
Incomplete engraving of entire design, shading lines in top of frame unfinished. No. 60085 on back.

303-E2 4c Die on India, die sunk on card, black *2,000.*

303-E3

Photograph of unaccepted design, stamp size, with white wash inside vignette and eagles in corners drawn in pen over portions of photo.

303-E3 4c Retouched photo-sensitive paper, black *900.*

303-E4

Photograph of unaccepted design with additional overlay photo of top portion of frame with eagles similar to those on No. 303-E3.

303-E4 4c Photo-sensitive paper mounted on paper, black *1,100.*

304-E1

Design size: 19x22mm
Die size: 74x87½mm
Rejected die: figure at right poorly draped, blank triangles below "UNITED STATES," no shading in frame around "POSTAGE/FIVE CENTS" except at extreme ends.

304-E1 5c Die on India, die sunk on card, blue *2,300.*

Incomplete engraving of entire design: shading on side figures unfinished.

304-E2 5c Die on India, die sunk on card, blue *1,500.*

304-E3

Design size: 107x110mm
Paper size: 141x128mm
Preliminary pencil and ink drawing of unadopted frame design.

304-E3 5c Drawing on onion skin paper, black *3,000.*

Incomplete engraving of entire design as adopted.

305-E1 6c Die on India, lake *1,250.*

305-E2

Design size: 123x210mm
Preliminary ink drawing for unadopted frame design.

305-E2 6c Drawing on kraft paper, black & blue green *4,500.*

Nos. 305-E2, 306-E3 and 308-E2, are all on same piece of kraft paper, with No. 306-E3 on one side and the other two on the other side. Value is for the entire unit of three essays.

306-E1

Design size: 7x3½ inches
Preliminary pencil drawing of left side of frame design as adopted.

306-E1 8c Drawing on tracing paper, black *2,200.*

306-E2

Die size: 76x89mm
Incomplete engraving of vignette and numerals only: head drapery unfinished, horiz. background lines only.

306-E2 8c Die on India, die sunk on card, black *5,000.*

306-E3

Design size: 165x175mm
Preliminary ink drawing for unadopted frame design.

306-E3 8c Drawing on kraft paper, black, blue & green *4,500.*

See note after No. 305-E2.

307-E1

Design size: 135x174mm
Preliminary ink drawing for unadopted frame design.

307-E1 10c Drawing on kraft paper, gray blue *2,000.*

No. 307-E1 is on the opposite side of the same piece of paper bearing No. 300-E3. Value is for both essays.

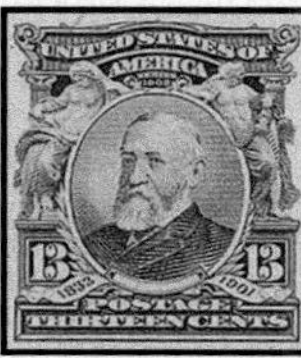

308-E1

Design size: 19x22mm
Die size: 69x85½mm
Incomplete engraving of entire design: hair, beard, right cheek, eyes and right shoulder all unfinished, horiz. background lines only, name panel blank, ribbon shading unfinished, etc. No. 57796 on back.

308-E1 13c Die on India, die sunk on card, black *3,750.*

308-E2

Design size: 177x220mm
Preliminary ink drawing of 3c frame design but later adopted for 13c.

308-E2 13c Drawing on kraft paper, black & blue green 4,500.

See note after No. 305-E2.

Design size: 19x22mm
Die size: 75x78mm
Incomplete engravng with complete portrait and initial lines of frame, blue "66439" handstamp on reverse.

309-E1 15c Die on India, die sunk on 153x204mm card, black 4,000.

310-E1

Design size: 19x22mm
Die size: 74x87 ½mm
Incomplete engraving of entire design: hair and right cheek unfinished, horiz. background lines only, top of frame and eagles unfinished.

310-E1 50c Die on India, die sunk on card, black 4,000.

310-E2

Incomplete engraving of entire design, further engraved than No. 310-E1: oval line outside top label thinner at bottom ends than on issued stamp.

310-E2 50c Die on India, die sunk on card, black 4,000.

312-E1

Design size: 19x22mm
Die size: 76x88mm
Incomplete engraving of entire design: hair, neckpiece, etc., unfinished, horiz. background lines only; top of frame, leaves and numeral surrounds all unfinished.

312-E1 $2 Die on India, die sunk on card, black 4,500.

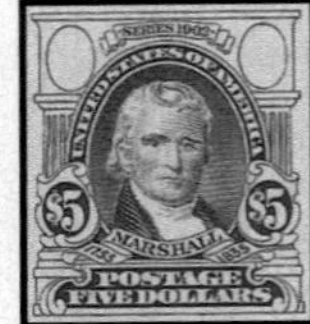

313-E1

Design size: 19x22mm
Die size: 75 ½x87 ½mm
Incomplete engraving of entire design: eyes, cheeks, hair, neckpiece all unfinished, horiz. background lines only, frame engraved in outlines only.

313-E1 $5 Die on India, die sunk on card, dark green 12,000.

319-E1

Design size: 19 ½x22mm
Die size: 75x87 ½mm
Incomplete engraving of entire design from rejected die (central star between UNITED and STATES, four lines above small lettering, bottom of shield curved): name and date ribbon blank.

319-E1 2c Die on India, die sunk on card, carmine 5,250.

319-E2

Incomplete engraving of entire design from rejected die: shading on leaves and vignette completed, lettering added to bottom ribbon and started on label above vignette. Blue pencil note on card backing, "May 1903. This die was abandoned at this stage because of crowded condition of lettering above portrait. G.F.C.S." No. 83909 on back.

319-E2 2c Die on India, die sunk on card, carmine 5,250.

319-E3

Design size: 19 ½x22mm
Die I size: 75 ½x88mm
Incomplete engraving of entire design as adopted (no star between UNITED and STATES, bottom of shield straight): small label above vignëtte is blank.

319-E3 2c Die on India, die sunk on card, black 5,250.

LOUISIANA PURCHASE ISSUE

324-E1

Incomplete engraving of entire design: head, hair, eyes, chin, coat all unfinished, horiz. background lines only, bottom label and upper corner labels blank, frame shading unfinished.

324-E1 2c Die on India, die sunk on card, black 2,500.

325-E1

Incomplete engraving of entire design: head only lightly engraved, horiz. background lines only, laurel leaves unshaded, leaves' background and numeral shields blank.

325-E1 3c Die on India, die sunk on card, black 2,500.

326-E1

Incomplete engraving of entire design: vignette unfinished, horiz. background lines only, much of frame blank or incomplete.

326-E1 5c Die on India, die sunk on card, black blue 2,500.

JAMESTOWN ISSUE

328-E1

Incomplete engraving of entire design: vignette, shading on heads in upper corners, numerals and numeral shields all unfinished.

328-E1 1c Die on pale cream soft wove, 30x24mm, dusky green 1,250.

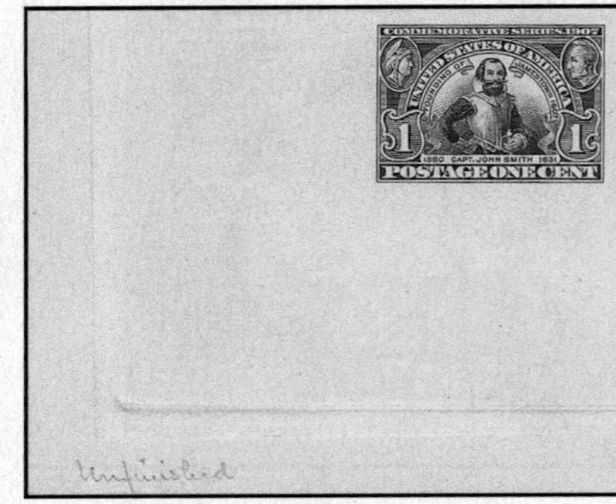

328-E2

Incomplete engraving of entire design: vignette, shading on heads in upper corners, and value tablets unfinished, pencil note "unfinished" at bottom of card.

328-E2 1c Die on India, die sunk on card, 109x94mm, green 2,500.

330-E1

Incomplete engraving of vignette only: collar, hat, corselet, etc., unfinished. No. 245910 on back.

330-E1 5c Die on India, die sunk on card, 123x132mm, black 2,250.

330-E2

Incomplete engraving of entire design: no shading in frame background.

330-E2 5c Die on India, die sunk on card, 109x95mm, blue *6,000.*

330-E3

Incomplete engraving of entire design: shading on corselet and arm of Pocahontas unfinished, horiz. background lines only, shading around date and name ribbon unfinished. No. 247606 on back.

330-E3 5c Die on card, 123x175mm, die sunk, blue *4,250.*

Incomplete engraving of entire design: shading on ribbons unfinished.

330-E4 5c Die on India, die sunk on card, 108x98mm, black *5,000.*

1908 ISSUE

331-E1

Photograph of wash drawing of entire design, head and vignette background retouched with black wash. Ms. "GVLM-Sept. 26th-1908" (PMG) in LR corner of backing card.

331-E1 1c Retouched photo on thick gray cardboard, 83x100mm, black *3,750.*

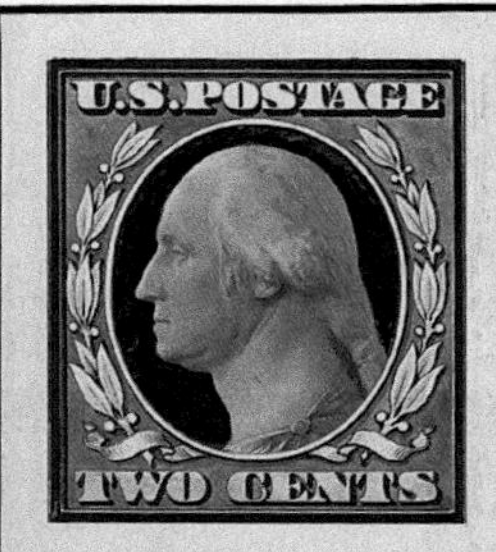

332-E1

Design size: 6⅛x7¼ inches

Wash drawing of frame design with vignette cut out, mounted over retouched glossy black photo of Houdon bust of Washington.

332-E1 Two Cents, Design on drawing paper, black *1,250.*

332-E1A

Design size: 19x22mm

Photograph of wash drawing of entire design, denomination blank, part of design hand-painted in black ink and wash.

332-E1A (2c) Retouched photo on 30x34mm card, black *3,250.*

332-E2

Design size: 19x22mm

Photograph of wash drawing of entire design, almost completely retouched with black ink and wash. Pencil "GVLM" (PMG) at top of backing card.

332-E2 Two Cents, Retouched photo on thick gray cardboard, 81x100mm, black *2,000.*

332-E3

Design size: 19x22mm

Incomplete engraving of entire design: shading on leaves at right unfinished. Pencil "Oct 15 - 1908" at LR of backing card.

332-E3 Two Cents, Die on India, die sunk on card, carmine *1,250.*

333-E1

Design size: 18½x22mm

Engraving of design as adopted except "THREE CENTS" at bottom.

333-E1 Three Cents, Die printed directly on card, deep violet *1,250.*

333-E2

Design size: 19x22mm

Photograph of wash drawing of entire design with "3 CENTS 3" drawn in black and white wash. Ms. "Nov. 24/08. J.E.R." (BEP director) in LR corner of backing card.

333-E2 3c Retouched photo on thick gray cardboard, 80x100mm, black *2,000.*

334-E1

Design size: 18½x22mm

Engraving of design as adopted except "FOUR CENTS" at bottom.

334-E1 Four Cents, Die printed directly on card, orange brown *1,250.*

334-E2

Design size: 19x22mm

Photograph of wash drawing of entire design with "4 CENTS 4" drawn in black and white wash. Ms. "Nov. 24/08. J.E.R." (BEP director) in LR corner of backing card.

334-E2 4c Retouched photo on thick gray cardboard, 80x100mm, black *2,000.*

335-E1

Design size: 18½x22mm

Engraving of design as adopted except "FIVE CENTS" at bottom.

335-E1 Five Cents, Die printed directly on card, blue *1,500.*

335-E2

Design size: 19x22mm

Photograph of wash drawing of entire design with "5 CENTS 5" drawn in black and white wash. Ms. "Nov. 24/08. J.E.R." (BEP director) in LR corner of backing card.

335-E2 5c Retouched photo on thick gray cardboard, 80x100mm, black *2,000.*

336-E1

Design size: 18½x22mm

Incomplete engraving of design with "SIX CENTS" at bottom.

336-E1 Six Cents, Die on India, on card, red orange *1,250.*

336-E2

Design size: 19x22mm

Photograph of wash drawing of entire design with "6 CENTS 6" drawn in black and white wash. Ms. "Nov. 24/08. J.E.R." (BEP director) in LR corner of backing card.

336-E2 6c Retouched photo on thick gray cardboard, 80x100mm, black *2,000.*

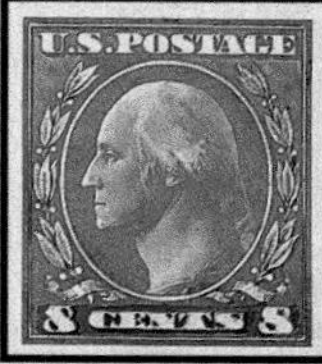

337-E1

Design size: 19x22mm

Photograph of wash drawing of entire design with "8 CENTS 8" drawn in black and white wash. Ms. "Nov. 24/08. J.E.R." (BEP director) in LR corner of backing card.

337-E1 8c Retouched photo on thick gray cardboard, 80x100mm, black *2,000.*

338-E1

Design size: 19x22mm
Photograph of wash drawing of entire design with "10 CENTS 10" drawn in black and white wash. Ms. "Nov. 24/08. J.E.R." (BEP director) in LR corner of backing card.

338-E1 10c Retouched photo on thick gray cardboard, 80x100mm, black *2,000.*

338a-E1

Design size: 18½x22mm
Complete engraving of entire adopted design but a value not issued: "12 CENTS 12" at bottom. Virtually all are stamp size, imperf.

Ridgway numbers used for colors of No. 338a-E1.

338a-E1 12c
a. Die on bluish white wove
41n/1 dim v. dusky b-blue-green *900.*
b. Die on 1f/1 dim pale red wove
c. Die on 7d/1 dim light red orange wove
47m/1 dim dusky g-b. blue *900.*
d. Die on 17b/1 dim bright o-y. yellow wove
1i/0 deep red *900.*
5i/0 deep o-orange-red *900.*
27m/0 dusky green yellow *900.*
37m/0 dusky g-blue-green *900.*
41m/0 dusky b-blue-green *900.*
55m/1 dim dusky blue violet *900.*
59m/1 dim dusky violet *900.*
69m/3 dismal dusky r-violet-red *900.*
e. Die on 19f/0 pale y-orange yellow wove
1i/0 deep red *900.*
15i/1 dim deep yellow orange *900.*
35m/0 dusky green *900.*
43d/1 dim light green blue *900.*
61m/3 dismal dusky v-red-violet *900.*
69o/5 black *900.*
f. Die on 31f/2 dull pale yellow green wove
69o/5 black *900.*
g. Die on 42d/1 dim bright green blue wove
41m/1 dim dusky b-blue-green *900.*
h. Die on 44-/1 dim medium green blue wove
9k/2 dull dark o-r-orange *900.*
i. Die on 45l/1 dim v. dark b-green-blue wove
5i/0 deep o-orange-red *900.*
27m/2 dull dusky green yellow *900.*
j. Die on 69g/0 pale r-v. red wove *900.*
k. Die on dark blue bond, 69o/5 black *900.*

339-E1

Design size: 19x22mm
Photograph of wash drawing of entire design with "13 CENTS 13" drawn in black and white wash. Ms. "Oct. 7-08. J.E.R.-GVLM" (BEP director, PMG) in LL corner of backing card.

339-E1 13c Retouched photo on thick gray cardboard, 80x100mm, black *2,000.*

340-E1

Design size: 19x22mm

Photograph of wash drawing of entire design with "15 CENTS 15" drawn in black and white wash. Ms. "Oct. 7-08. J.E.R.-GVLM" (BEP director, PMG) at bottom of backing card.

340-E1 15c Retouched photo on thick gray cardboard, 80x100mm, black *2,000.*

341-E1

Design size: 19x22mm
Photograph of wash drawing of entire design with "50 CENTS 50" drawn in black and white wash. Ms. "Oct. 7-08. J.E.R.-GVLM" (BEP director, PMG) at bottom of backing card.

341-E1 50c Retouched photo on thick gray cardboard, 80x100mm, black *2,000.*

342-E1

Design size: 19x22mm
Photograph of wash drawing of entire design with "1 DOLLAR 1" drawn in black and white wash. Ms. "Oct. 7-08. J.E.R.-GVLM" (BEP director, PMG) at bottom of backing card.

342-E1 $1 Retouched photo on thick gray cardboard, 80x100mm, black *2,000.*

LINCOLN MEMORIAL ISSUE

Design size: 7x8 inches
Photostat of 1908 2c frame design with wash drawing of ribbons and vignette photo of Lincoln's head.

367-E1 Two Cents, Model of Lincoln design, black *1,500.*

Photo of No. 367-E1 reduced to stamp size, retouched to highlight hair and beard, dates added.

367-E2 Two Cents, Retouched photo, black *1,500.*

367-E3

Design size: 19x22mm
Incomplete engraving of entire design: head, background, name/date ribbon all unfinished.

367-E3 Two Cents, Die on India, die sunk on card, 148x201mm, carmine *3,500.*

ALASKA-YUKON-PACIFIC EXPOSITION ISSUE

370-E1

Design size: 18½x22mm

Wash drawing of frame similar to 1908 2c design with photo of wash drawing of seal on ice cake as vignette. Ms. "#1" at top of backing card.

370-E1 2c Model on card, about 3x4 inches, black *1,500.*

370-E2

Design size: 18½x22mm
Engraved frame similar to 1908 2c but with wash drawing of "1870 1909" in ribbons and "2 CENTS 2" at bottom, vignette cut out, mounted over engraved vignette of Wm. H. Seward from snuff stamp. Ms. "#2" at UL corner of backing card.

370-E2 2c Model on card, about 3x4 inches, black *1,500.*

370-E3

Design size: 27½x20½mm
Photo of seal on ice cake vignette as originally approved, mounted on ink and wash drawing of frame design as approved. Ms. "#3" at UL corner of backing card, engraved Seward vignette pasted on at bottom, "Approved April 3, 1909 FH Hitchcock Postmaster-General" at right.

370-E3 2c Model on glazed card, 93x70mm, black, white and gray *2,250.*

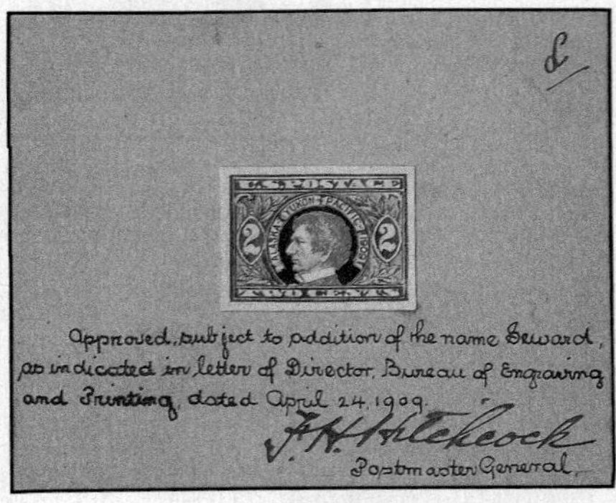

370-E4

Design size: 27½x20mm
Photo of wash drawing of frame and arched ribbon as adopted, vignette cut out, mounted over photo of engraved Seward vignette, background retouched with black wash. Ms. "Approved subject to addition of the name Seward, as indicated in letter of Director, Bureau of Engraving and Printing, dated April 24, 1909. F.H. Hitchcock Postmaster General."

370-E4 2c Model on 93x75mm thick gray card, black *2,250.*

370-E5

Design size: 27x20mm
Retouched photo of wash drawing of adopted frame with seal on ice cake vignette but pencil "WILLIAM H. SEWARD" on white wash ribbon below. Ms. "April 26/09 Approved J.E.R." (BEP director) at LR corner of backing card.

370-E5 2c Retouched photo and pencil on 94x66mm thick gray card, black *2,000.*

Incomplete engraving of entire design: no shading on head or vignette background, no shading lines on ribbons.

370-E6 2c Die on India, die sunk on 8x6 inch card, carmine *2,000.*

370-E7

Design size: 26½x19½mm
Similar to No. 370-E6 but further engraved: face and collar lightly engraved, horiz. background lines only, no shading lines on ribbons.

370-E7 2c Die on wove, 32x26½mm, carmine *2,000.*

372-E1

Wash drawing of adopted vignette design.

372-E1 2c Drawing on artist's cardboard, 11¼x6¾ inches, black *2,000.*

372-E2

Wash drawing of frame design as adopted except "HUDSON-FULTON CENTENARY" at top.

372-E2 2c Drawing on artist's cardboard, 7¾x6¾ inches, black *2,000.*

372-E3

Design size: 33x21½mm
Wash drawing of frame design as adopted with dates "1609-1807" and photo of No. 372-E1 reduced to fit and worked over with wash.

372-E3 2c Model on card, 4x3 inches, black *2,000.*

372-E4

Design size: 33x21½mm
Wash drawing of frame with vignette cut out, mounted over photo of No. 372-E1. Typed/ms. "Approved August 17, 1909 F.H. Hitchcock Postmaster General" and "August 19, 1909 Amend by substituting word 'Celebration' for 'Centenary.' F.H. Hitchcock Postmaster General." Pencil "P.O. 488" in LR corner.

372-E4 2c Model on white card, 129x103mm, black *2,000.*

372-E5

Incomplete engraving of entire design: lettering on flag at masthead of *Clermont* has "N" reversed and no "T."

372-E5 2c Die on wove, 38x27mm, carmine *2,000.*

PANAMA-PACIFIC ISSUE

397-E1

Design size: 27x20mm
Photo of incomplete frame with overlay of circular photo vignette as adopted, with wash drawing of palm trees on each side and "1 CENT 1" in wash. Ms. "Approved July 16, 1912 Frank H. Hitchcock Postmaster General" on backing card.

397-E1 1c Model on card, about 89x77mm, black *1,500.*

Design size: 27x20mm
Photo of incomplete frame with overlay circular photo vignette as adopted, with wash drawing of palm trees on each side and "1 CENT 1" in wash, with "Approved" and signed by the BEP Director J.E. Ralph, but "Opening of Panama Canal 1913" later changed for stamp to "San Francisco 1913."

397-E2 1c Model on thick gray card, 106x86mm, black *1,500.*

398-E1

Design size: about 29½x20mm
Ink and wash drawing of frame design longer than adopted with photo of wash drawing of Golden Gate as eventually used (reduced) on 5c. Backstamp "STAMP DIVISION FEB. 12, 1912 P.O. DEPT" on backing card.

398-E1 2c Model on card, about 4x3 inches, black *1,500.*

398-E2

Design size: 27x20mm
Photo of incomplete frame with photo of wash drawing of vignette as adopted with title "GATUN LOCKS," wash drawing of value numerals. Ms. "Approved Aug. 27, 1912 Frank H. Hitchcock Postmaster General" on backing card.

398-E2 2c Model on thick gray card, 99x72mm, black *1,500.*

Very similar to No. 398-E2 with slightly different wash touch-up and "2"s, with "Approved" and signed by BEP Director J.E. Ralph.

398-E2A 2c Model on thick gray card, 107x86mm, black *1,500.*

398-E3

Completely engraved design as adopted except titled "GATUN LOCKS" in error (design pictures Pedro Miguel locks).

398-E3 2c
- ***a.*** Large die on India, die sunk on card, 202x152mm, carmine *10,000.*
- ***b.*** Small die on India (formerly #398AP2), carmine *6,000.*

398-E4

Design size: 27x20mm
Photo of incomplete engraving (no sky in vignette) with "GATUN LOCKS" in error, ms. "Approved Dec. 17, 1912 Frank Hitchcock Postmaster General" on backing card.

398-E4 2c Model on thick gray card, 97x74mm, black *1,500.*

399-E1

Design size: 27x20mm
Photo of wash drawing of frame design as adopted with photo of wash drawing of adopted vignette mounted in place, with additional hand touch-up done in wash on vignette, ms. "Approved July 16, 1912 Frank H., Hitchcock Postmaster General" on backing card.

399-E1 5c Model on 30x22mm white paper, mounted on card, 97x73mm, black *1,500.*

Very similar to No. 399-E1 with slightly different wash touch-up and no steamship below sun, with "Approved" and signed by BEP Director J.E. Ralph.

399-E2 5c Model on thick gray card, 106x86mm, black *1,500.*

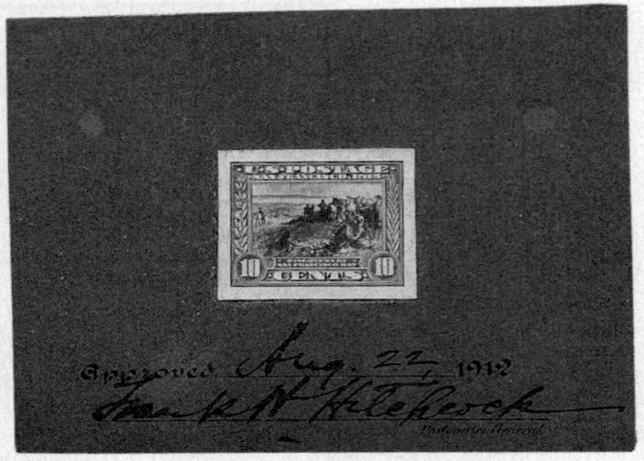

400-E1

Design size: 27x20mm

Photo of wash drawing of frame design as adopted with photo of painting adopted for vignette mounted in place, ms. printed "Approved" and dated and signed " Aug. 22, 1912, Frank H. Hitchcock Postmaster General" on backing card.

400-E1 10c Model on 31x34mm white paper, on thick gray card, 98x73mm, black *1,500.*

Very similar to No. 400-E1 with more extensive touching-up of the vignette and frame, with "Approved" and signed by BEP Director J.E. Ralph.

400-E1A 10c Model on thick gray card, 107x86mm, black *1,500.*

400-E2

Design size: 27x20mm

Photo of wash drawing of frame design as adopted with photo of wash drawing of two galleons at anchor in bay, titled "CABRILLO 1542" mounted in place. Backing card marked "II."

400-E2 10c Model on white paper, on 91x85mm thick gray card, black *1,500.*

400-E3

Design size: 27x20mm

Photo of wash drawing of frame design as adopted with photo of Liberty standing among palm fronds, wash touch-up on vignette and "10" denominations drawn in black and white wash, two battleships in bay. Backing card marked "III."

400-E3 10c Model on white paper, on thick gray card, 90x84mm, black *1,500.*

400-E4

Design size: 27x20mm

Similar to No. 400-E3 but steamships replace battleships. Backing card marked "IV."

400-E4 10c Model on white paper, on thick gray card, 90x83mm, black *1,500.*

400-E5

Design size: 27x20mm

Similar to No. 400-E2 but different hand drawn vignette picturing two galleons under full sail in front of snowclad mountains. Backing card marked "V."

400-E5 10c Model on white paper, on thick gray card, 89x83mm, black *1,500.*

1912 ISSUE

Incomplete engraving of entire design, except value tablet area which is '1 CENT 1' at bottom drawn in wash. Ms. "Approved. July 17, 1911 Frank H. Hitchcock. P.M. Gen." on backing card.

405-E1 1c Model on 3½x3¾-inch card, black *6,000.*

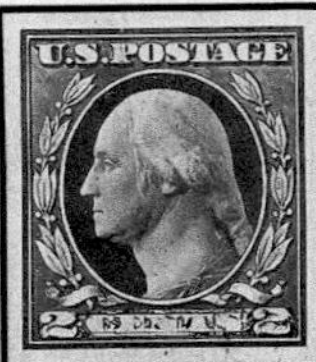

406-E1

Incomplete engraving of entire design, except value tablet area which is '2 CENTS 2' at bottom drawn in wash. Ms. "Approved. July 17, 1911 Frank H. Hitchcock P. M. Gen." on backing card.

406-E1 2c Model on 3⅜x3 11/16-inch card, black —

414-E1

Wash drawing of design as adopted, worked over partial photo with 8 in lower corners drawn in wash. Ms. "Approved. July 17, 1911 Frank H. Hitchcock Postmaster General" on backing card.

414-E1 8c Model on 3½x3¾-inch card, black *2,000.*

414-E2

Vignette of head only without background gridwork, control #490311 on back of card.

414-E2 8c Die on India, die sunk on 152x202mm, olive green *2,250.*

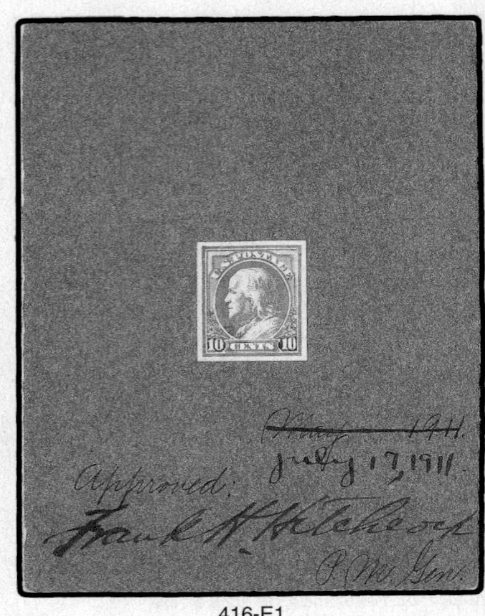

416-E1

Design size: 19x22mm

Photo of wash drawing of generic design with 10 in lower corners drawn in black ink. Ms. "July 17, 1911. (May, 1911 erased) Approved: Frank H. Hitchcock PM Gen" on backing card, backstamped "STAMP DIVISION P.O. DEPT. MAY 15, 1911."

416-E1 10c Model on 87x113mm thick gray card, black *2,000.*

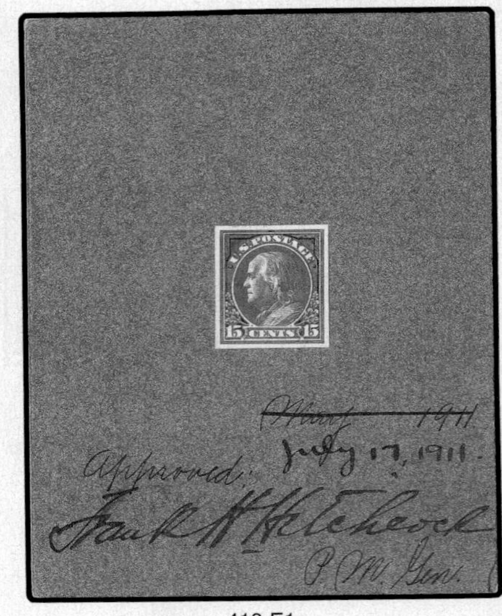

418-E1

Design size: 19x22mm

Photo of wash drawing of generic design with background of frame between oval and outer colorless line in dark gray wash and some colorless retouching, 15 in lower corners drawn in black ink. Ms. "July 17, 1911. (May, 1911 erased) Approved: Frank H. Hitchcock PM Gen" on backing card, backstamped "STAMP DIVISION P.O. DEPT. MAY 15, 1911."

418-E1 15c Model on 87x113mm thick gray card, black *2,000.*

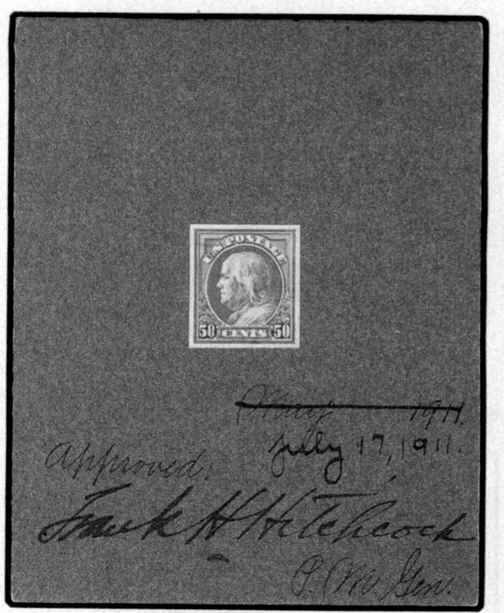

421-E1

Design size: 19x22mm
Photo of wash drawing of generic design with 50 in lower corners drawn in black ink. Ms. "July 17, 1911. (May, 1911 erased) Approved: Frank H. Hitchcock PM Gen" on backing card, backstamped "STAMP DIVISION P.O. DEPT. MAY 15, 1911."

421-E1 50c Model on 77x112mm thick gray card, black *2,000.*

423-E1

Design size: 19x22mm
Photo of wash drawing of generic design with entire value label drawn in black ink. Ms. "July 17, 1911. (May, 1911 erased) Approved: Frank H. Hitchcock PM Gen" on backing card, backstamped "STAMP DIVISION P.O. DEPT. MAY 15, 1911."

423-E1 $1 Model on 87x113mm thick gray card, black *2,000.*

1916 PRECANCEL ESSAYS

499-E1

Design size: 19x22mm
Die size: 90x88mm
"NEW YORK/N.Y." precancel engraved directly onto type I die, printed in one color. Ms. "8/16/22 J.S." in LR corner of backing card on No. 499-E1a. Although dated 1922, records indicate an original proof was pulled in 1916.

499-E1 2c
- ***a.*** Die on India, die sunk on card, lake —
- ***b.*** Die on bond paper, 33x36mm, dark carmine —

1918 ISSUE

Complete engraving of Franklin head only as on $2 and $5 values, no shading around head, control #834424 on back of card.

523-E2 $2 Die on India, die sunk on 151x103mm card, black *1,750.*

523-E3

Design size: 16x18¾mm
Complete engraving of vignette only including shading. Pencil control # "837660 May 1917" on back of India paper, pencil "Schofield" at bottom of backing card (#523-E3a), or control #837662 (1917) on back of card (No. 523-E3b).

523-E3 $2
- ***a.*** Die on 32x33mm India, card mounted, black 1,000.
- ***b.*** Die on wove, die sunk on card, 203x151mm, black 1,000.

PEACE ISSUE

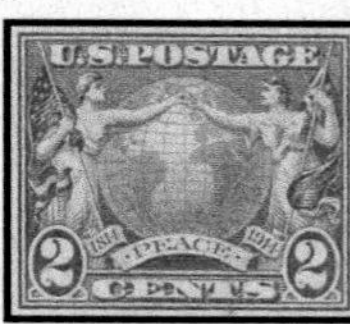
537-E1

Design size: 21½x18½mm
Stamp never issued due to World War I.

537-E1 2c
- ***a.*** Die on India, die sunk on card, deep red 2,250.
- ***b.*** Die on wove, die sunk on card, 201x138mm, signed on card by Harry S. New 4,000.

537-E2

Die size: 22x19mm
Stamp never issued due to World War I.

537-E2 5c
- ***a.*** Die on India, die sunk on card, dim dusky g-b-blue 2,000.
- ***b.*** Die on wove, die sunk on card, 201x138mm, signed on card by Harry S. New 4,000.

SAMUEL F.B. MORSE ISSUE

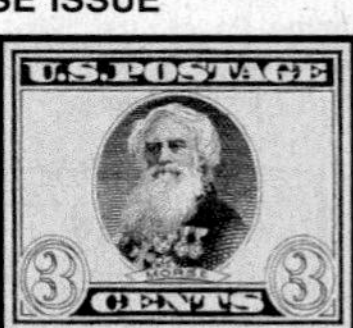
537-E3

Design size: 21½x18½mm
Incomplete engraving of entire design: vignette and lettering finished but blank spaces beside vignette. Backstamped "932944" and "Jan. 1, 1919" or "932945" and "Jan. 7, 1919". Frame design subsequently used for 3c Victory issue, No. 537, though lettering and value numerals made slightly smaller.

537-E3 3c Die on India, die sunk on card, 141x173mm (#932944) or 151x202mm (#932945), black *3,000.*

VICTORY ISSUE

537-E4

Design size: 21½x18½mm
Die size: 85½x75½mm
Incomplete engraving of entire design: no shading in border and some flags unfinished. Backstamped "936356 Jan. 25, 1919."

537-E4 3c Die on India, die sunk on card, black *3,000.*

PILGRIM ISSUE

548-E1

Design size: 26x19mm
Incomplete engraving of entire design: sky blank, sails unshaded.

548-E1 1c Die on India, die sunk on card, 201x151mm, green *1,600.*

Almost complete engraving of entire design as adopted, but no crosshatching behind the "1" denominations.

548-E2 1c Die on India, die sunk on card, 203x151mm, green *1,600.*

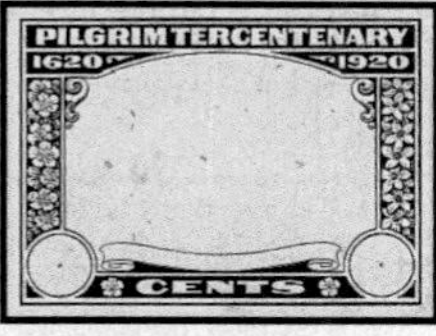
549-E1

Incomplete engraving of frame only: "CENTS" engraved but numeral circles blank (probably an essay for the 2c and 5c).

549-E1 Die on India, die sunk on card
- black *1,600.*
- green *1,600.*

549-E2

Design size: 26x19mm
Incomplete engraving of entire design: vignette unfinished, control #1063097 on back of card.

549-E2 2c Die on India, die sunk on card, 202x151mm, black *1,600.*

549-E3

Incomplete engraving of entire design, virtually complete but no crosshatching behind the numeral "2" denominations.

549-E3 2c
- ***a.*** Die on India, die sunk on card, 202x151mm, control #1063875 on back, black 1,600.
- ***b.*** Die on India, die sunk on card, 202x151mm, control #1064174 or #1064271 on back, carmine rose 1,600.

1922 ISSUE

551-E1

Design size: 19x22mm
Incomplete engraving of entire design as adopted: name label blank, vignette unfinished. Ms. "Approved--Harry S. New" on backing card on olive brown essay; others not signed but with notation of denomination of stamp for color used ("1c" for green, etc.)

551-E1 ½c Die on India, die sunk on 151x202mm card
- olive brown *3,000.*
- green *2,500.*
- carmine *2,500.*
- orange *2,500.*
- rose *2,500.*
- yellow *2,500.*

blue green 2,500.
yellow green 2,500.
carmine rose 2,500.

Incomplete engraving of entire design but further engraved than No. 551-E1: no lines in white oval over ends of title ribbon and ribbon foldunders not etched as darkly as on issued stamp.

551-E2 ½c Die on India, die sunk on 149x201mm card, olive brown 1,500.

555-E2

Complete engraving with cross-hatched lines surrounding bust of Lincoln.

555-E2 3c Die on India, affixed to card, 26x30mm, violet 3,250.

560-E1

Complete engraving with background of cross-hatched lines surrounding slightly larger bust of Grant.

560-E1 8c Die on India, die sunk on 97x111mm card, dark olive green 2,000.

567-E2

Design size: 19x22mm
Engraving of unadopted vignette with unadopted engraved frame cut away.

567-E2 20c Die on India, die sunk on 151x201mm card, cobalt blue 1,750.

568-E2

Design size: 19x15mm
Die size: 88x75mm
Engraving of adopted vignette with engraved frame cut away.

568-E2 25c Die on India, die sunk on 202x151mm card, green 1,750.

Pencil drawings for unadopted frame design, each on thin tissue paper.

555-E1 3c black 1,150.

557-E1

557-E1 5c black 1,150.
557-E2 5c black 1,150.
566-E1 15c black 1,150.
571-E1 $1 black 1,150.

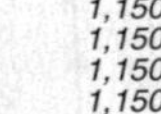

573-E1

Engraving of accepted vignette.

573-E1 $5 Die on India, affixed to card, 73x87mm, blue 3,750.

HUGUENOT-WALLOON TERCENTENARY ISSUE

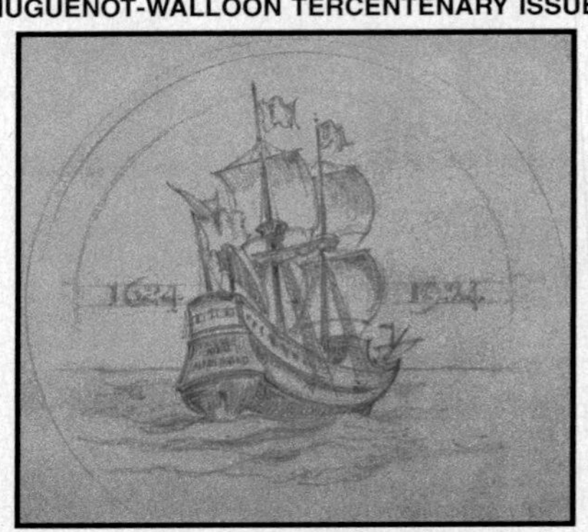

614-E1

Design size: 8½x7¼ inches
Preliminary pencil drawing of *Nieu Nederland* in circular frame. Pencil note: "Reverse--Sailing to America, not away from America--J. B. Stoudt" originally on drawing has been removed.

614-E1 1c black 1,000.

615-E1

Incomplete engraving of entire design, background of vignette incomplete and central figures only roughed in.

615-E1 2c Die on India, 82x69mm, black 4,500.

616-E1

Design size: 5½x3⅛ inches
Wash drawing of design adopted for vignette.

616-E1 5c black 1,500.

617-E1

Almost complete engraving of entire design, lacking strong shading in the foreground of the vignette.

617-E1 1c Die on India, die sunk on card, 126x115mm, green 1,500.

618-E1

Design size: 36x21mm
Incomplete engraving of entire design as adopted: spaces between letters of "BIRTH OF LIBERTY" not solid color.

618-E1 2c Die on India, die sunk on card, black 1,250.

618-E2

Design size: 36x21mm
Incomplete engraving of entire design as adopted: numeral circles blank, many shading lines missing in vignette, no shading around "TWO CENTS," etc.

618-E2 2c Die on India, die sunk on 91x71mm card, black 1,500.

618-E3

Design size: 36x21mm
Engraving of frame only, without vignette or value tablets, control #1317765 on back of card.

618-E3 2c Die on India, die sunk on card, 202x118mm, carmine 1,500.

ERICSSON MEMORIAL ISSUE

Wash drawing of design as adopted, stamp size.

628-E1 5c black 750.

BATTLE OF WHITE PLAINS ISSUE

629-E1

Design size: 8⅜x9 inches
Preliminary ink and watercolor drawing of entire design quite similar to that adopted.

629-E1 2c black & red *750.*

629-E2

Design size: 22x19mm
Card size: 94x66mm
Unfinished engraving of design, vignette, background, foreground, flags and ribbons incomplete, "70010" control number on back.

629-E2 2c Die on India, mounted on card, carmine rose *1,500.*

BURGOYNE CAMPAIGN ISSUE

644-E1

Design size: 22x19mm
Essay size: 25x22mm
Card size: 78x98mm
Photo of wash drawing of unadopted design, on white paper mounted on thick gray card with "Approved" in ink and "May 7, 1927" in pencil subsequently crossed out with "X's."

644-E1 2c black *1,500.*

683-E1

Design size: 13x17 inches
Preliminary ink drawing of design nearly as adopted.

683-E1 2c Drawing on artist's cardboard, black *500.*

American flag and pencil touch-up of outer frame on photo of artist's model with vignette as adopted but entirely different frame.

690-E1 2c black *400.*

702-E1

Engraving of entire design without red cross, engraved cross shows faintly, control #70015 on back of card.

702-E1 2c Die on India, die sunk on 120x142mm card, black *5,000.*

704-E1

Design size: 119x150mm
Preliminary pencil sketch of unadopted ½c design.

704-E1 ½c Drawing on tracing paper, mounted on 195x192mm manila paper, black *1,250.*

718-E1

Design size: 6x7 inches
Watercolor drawing of unadopted design with 2c denomination.

718-E1 2c Drawing on thick artist's card, red *1,250.*

719-E1

Design size: 6x7 inches
Watercolor drawing of entire design similar to that eventually adopted for 5c but with 2c denomination.

719-E1 2c Drawing on thick artist's card, 150x175mm, blue *1,250.*

Engraving of vignette as adopted, within frame, but reversed from final design, without denomination or inscriptions.

742-E1 3c Die on white card, 88x69mm, black *1,750.*

Unadopted engraving of entire design without denomination, portraits as adopted but rest of design different from accepted design, control #70027 on back of card.

786-E1 2c Die on wove, die sunk on card, 202x153mm, carmine *1,500.*

Engravings of Decatur and MacDonough as adopted, widely spaced.

791-E1 2c Die on wove, die sunk on card, 202x153mm, carmine *1,500.*

Engraving of incomplete design without central vignette, control #491747 (1936) on back of card.

791-E2 2c Die on wove, die sunk on card, 198x136mm, carmine *1,500.*

793-E1

Unfinished engravings of three portraits only, control #70031 or 70110 on back.

793-E1 4c Die on wove, die sunk on card, 202x153mm, red brown *2,000.*

PANAMA CANAL ISSUE

856-E1

Design size: 37x21½mm
Essay size: 99x81mm
Card size: 141x117mm
Engraving of unadopted design: "3 CENTS 3" and "25th ANNIVERSARY PANAMA CANAL" changed for final design. "W. O. Marks" at lower right corner, "Engraver's Stock Proof 594256 / Authorized by 'OML'" on reverse.

856-E1 3c Die on India, die sunk on card, deep violet *3,000.*

Unfinished engraving of adopted design, fine horizontal lines in white areas of "FOR DEFENSE" and no dash between "INDUSTRY" and "AGRICULTURE."

899-E1 1c Die on wove, die sunk on card, bright blue green *1,000.*

Engraving of entire design, lacks crosshatching in the shading of background.

899-E2 1c Die on wove, die sunk on card, 140x162mm, green *1,000.*

Engraving of frame as adopted, with "84075" at top and "United States of America" at bottom of die impression, stamped "For Approval" at top of card, signed and dated by four individuals on card.

909-921-E1 5c Die on India, die sunk on card
a. On 227x151mm card, violet *4,000.*
a. On card reduced almost to 89x74mm die size, black *1,500.*

922-E1

Incomplete engraving of entire design, sky unshaded, no smoke from engine, additional background shading missing, blue control number and "MODELING" on reverse of card.

922-E1 3c Die on India, die sunk on card, 200x148mm, violet *2,500.*

As No. 922-E1, with additional background shading added.

922-E2 3c Die on India, die sunk on card, 200x148mm, violet *2,500.*

922-E3

As No. 922-E2, with shading of sky added.

922-E3 3c Die on India, die sunk on card, 200x148mm, violet *2,500.*

922-E4

As No. 922-E3, with additional background and figure shading added.

922-E4 3c Die on India, die sunk on card, 200x148mm, violet *2,500.*

Unadopted design showing steamship under sail, without denomination or background shading, handstamp "Engraver's Stock Proof/Authorized by," initials, "Brooks" (the engraver) in pencil and control #818347A all on back of stamp.

923-E1 3c Die on wove, die sunk on card, 201x152mm, violet *1,500.*

Unfinished engraving of adopted design, lacking smoke from the smokestack and background shading. "Modeling" handstamp and control #818995A on back of card.

923-E2 3c Die on wove, die sunk on card, 201x150mm, violet *1,500.*

Engraved vignette as adopted, "Engraver's Stock Proof/Authorized by," initials, "Brooks" (the engraver) in pencil and control #867263A all on back of stamp.

930-933-E2 Die on wove, die sunk on card, 202x151mm, black *1,500.*

1016-E1

Engraving of adopted design, except "c" cut in design at right where cross should be printed (held in place by tape on back); "Engraver's Stock Proof, Authorized by," initials and blue "103120B" control number on back.

1016-E1 3c Die on wove, die sunk on card, 202x152mm, deep blue *2,500.*

1105-E1

Individual design sizes: 58x33mm; area of 6 designs: 213x87mm

1105-E1 3c Black charcoal on light beige laid artist's paper, irregular 343 x225mm, six hand-drawn designs, note below in blue ink, "First Roughs James Monroe Commemorartive. F. Conley 1957" —

1105-E2

Design size: 43x38mm

1105-E2 3c Pencil drawing of proposed design on tracing paper, irregular 165 x127mm, notes on either side in blue ink, "Trial Layout New Size James Monroe Commemorative." and signed "Frank P. Conley Designer Dec. 1957" —

1105E3

Design size: 32x37mm

1105-E3 3c Pencil drawing of proposed design on tracing paper, irregular 165 x120mm, notes on either side in blue ink, "Trial Layout New Size Jan. 1958 James Monroe stamp" and signed "Frank P. Conley Designer" —

1105-E4

Design size: 41x35mm

1105-E4 3c Black ink drawing of proposed design in format of issued stamp on tracing paper, 207 x133mm, notes on either side in blue ink, "Trial Layout New Size James Monroe stamp" and signed "Frank P. Conley Designer Jan. 1958" —

1128-E1

Design size: 295x178mm

1128-E1 4c Rough sketch in pencil, black pen and blue artist's crayon on tracing paper —

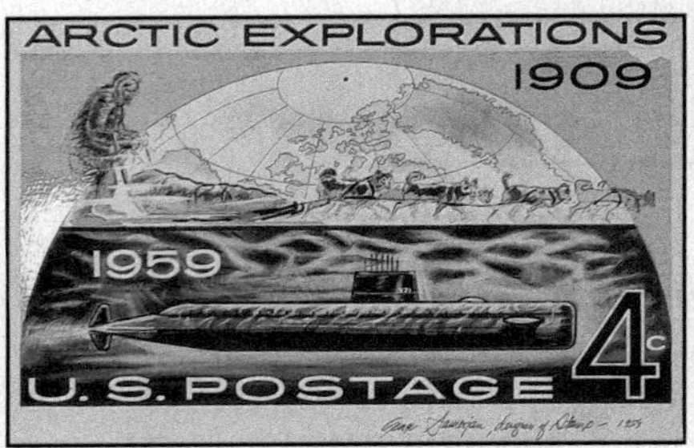

1128-ER2

Design size: 158x95mm

1128-E2 4c Pencil, gray and black watercolor ink, white painted year date, "U.S. Postage," "c" and outline of "4," horizontal background lines on a premade shiny, raised sticker, very close to issued design but with small differences, on white card, signed "George Samerjan, designer of stamp × 1959" beneath in black —

1139-E1

Design size (3): 135x21mm

1139-E1 3c Black charcoal and silver ink rough drawings of three proposed designs on tracing paper, 276 x166mm, no designer notes —

1139-E2

Design size (3): 165x22mm

1139-E2 4c Black and silver ink drawings of three proposed designs on tracing paper, 275x164mm, no designer notes —

E31139

Design size: 35x22mm

1139-E3 4c Dark brown, light brown, dull orange and silver ink handpainted full design on tracing paper, 110 x 92mm, "POSTAGE" on right panel, signed "Frank P. Conley 58" beneath in brown *1,000.*

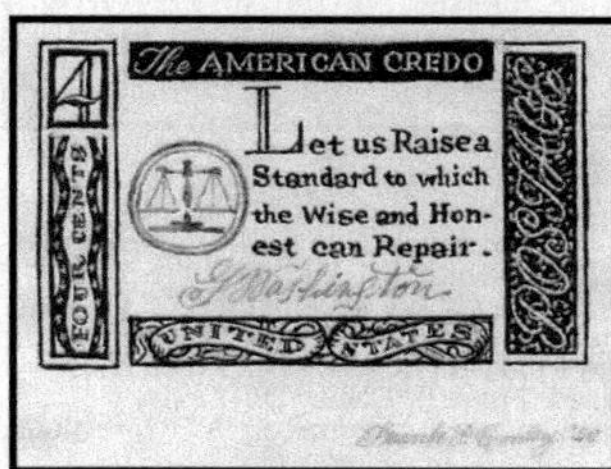

1139-E4

Design size: 35x22mm

1139-E4 4c Dark brown, light brown, dull orange and silver ink handpainted full design on tracing paper, 122 x117mm, "POSTAGE" on right panel, symbol plus other small design differences from #1139-E3, signed "Frank P. Conley '58" beneath in dull orange *1,000.*

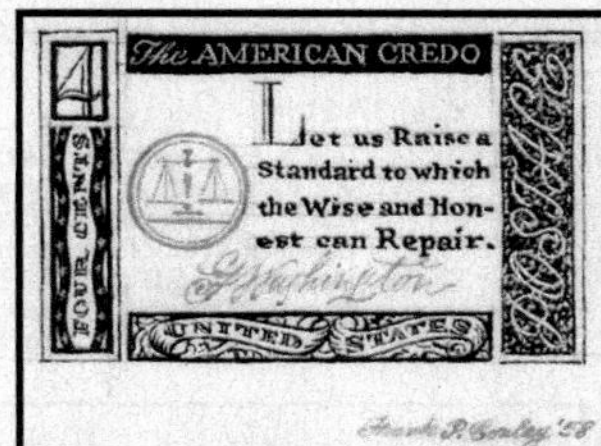

1139-E5

Design size: 35x22mm

1139-E5 4c Dark brown, dull orange and silver ink handpainted full design on tracing paper, 127x216mm, "POSTAGE" on right panel, small design differences from #1139-E3 and 1139-E4, signed "Frank P. Conley '58" beneath in dull orange *1,000.*

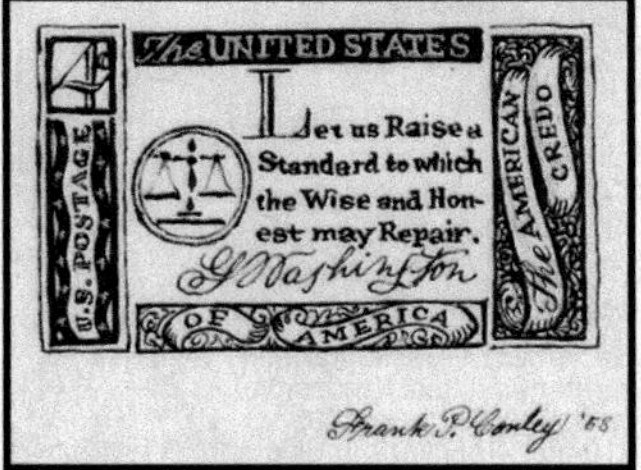

1139-E6

Design size: 35x22mm

1139-E6 4c Brown and silver ink handpainted full design on tracing paper, 274 x152mm, "The AMERICAN CREDO" on right panel, signed "Frank P. Conley '58" beneath in brown *1,000.*

1139-E7

Design size: 35x22mm

1139-E7 4c Dark brown, brown and silver ink handpainted full design on tracing paper, 279 x216mm, "AN AMERICAN CREDO" on right panel, signed "Frank P. Conley '58" beneath in dull orange *1,000.*

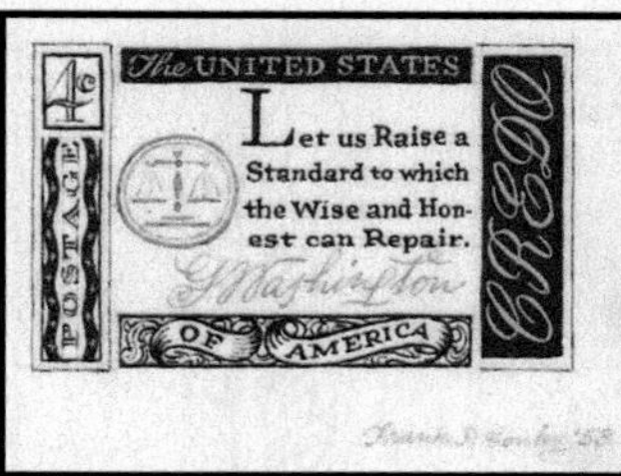

1139-E8

Design size: 35x22mm

1139-E8 4c Dark brown, brown, dull orange and silver ink handpainted full design on tracing paper, 130 x216mm, "CREDO" on right panel, signed "Frank P. Conley '58" beneath in dull orange *1,000.*

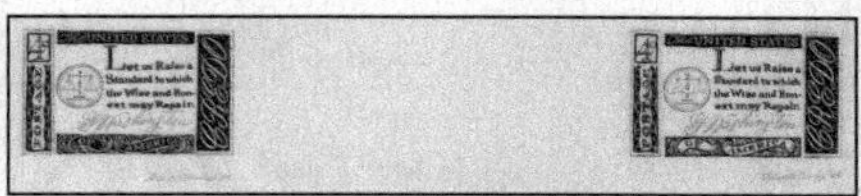
1139-E9

Design size (2): 136x22mm

1139-E9 4c Dark brown, brown, dull orange and silver ink handpainted full designs on tracing paper, 302 x234mm, each with "CREDO" on right panel each with small design differences from #1139-E8, each signed "Frank P. Conley '58" beneath in dull orange —

It is interesting to note that none of the No. 1139 essays contain the text on the center text panel that appears on the issued stamp. Likely, a last-minute change was made.

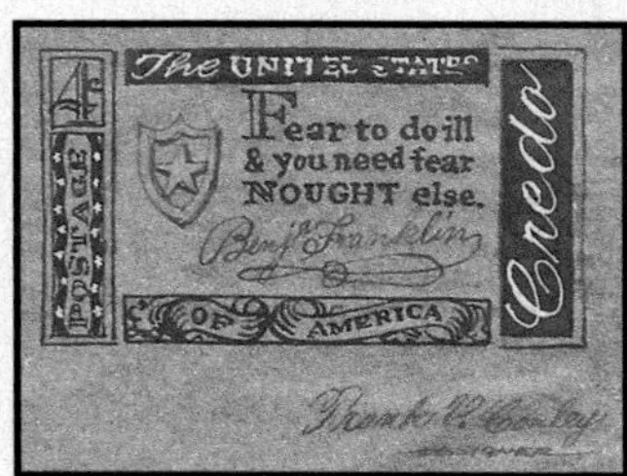

1140-E1

Design size: 32x21mm

1140-E1 4c Red, blue and silver handpainted full design on tracing paper, 129 x 81mm, similar to issued design but with different symbol at left and different Franklin signature, signed "Frank P. Conley designer" beneath in red *1,000.*

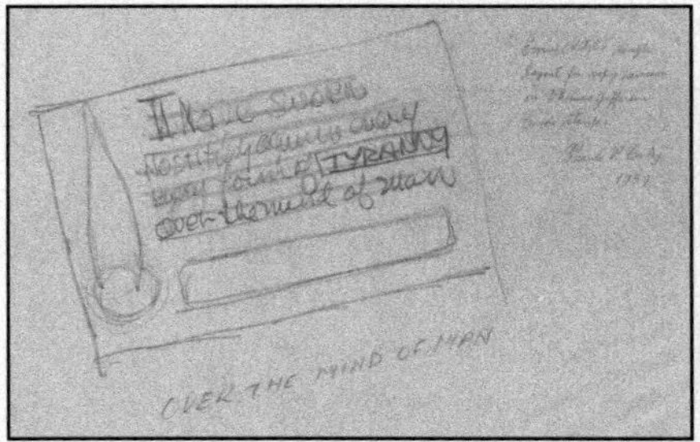

1141-E1

Design size: 125x80mm

1141-E1 4c Rough pencil drawing of proposed design on irregular-sized tracing paper, "Over the mind of man" repeated beneath, "Ervine Metzl's rough layout for copy revision of Thomas Jefferson Credo stamp. Frank P. Conley 1959" at right —

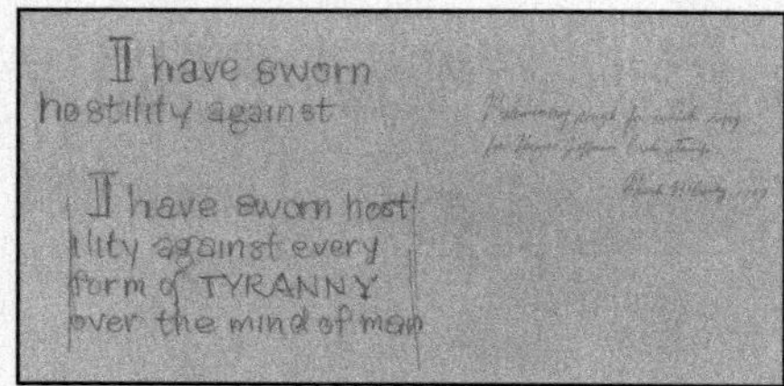

1141-E2

Design size: 90x41mm

1141-E2 4c Rough text only in pencil on irregular-sized tracing paper, part of text repeated above, "Preliminary rough for revised copy for Thomas Jefferson Credo stamp. Frank P. Conley, 1959" at right —

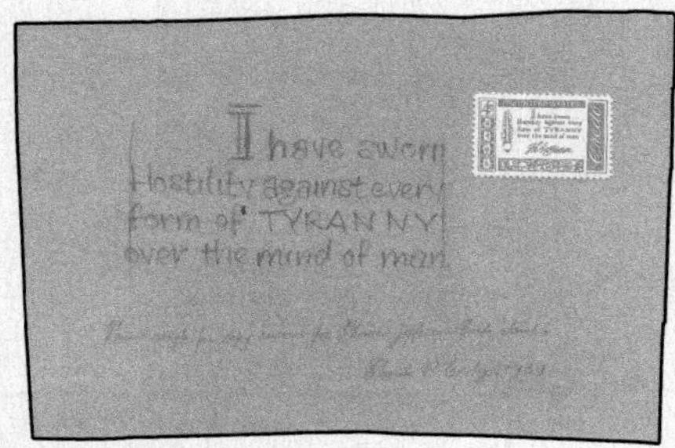

1141-E3

Design size: 98x50mm

1141-E3 4c Rough text only in pencil on tracing paper, 185 x 130mm, "Pencil rough for copy revised for Thomas Jefferson Credo stamp, Frank P. Conley, 1959" beneath —

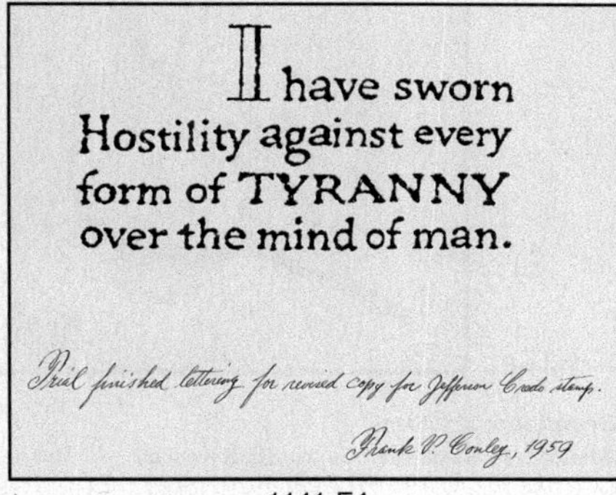

1141-E4

Design size: 69x37mm

1141-E4 4c Black India ink sketch of text only on thin wove paper, 280 x 216mm "Trial finished lettering for revised copy for Jefferson Credo stamp. Frank P. Conley, 1959" beneath —

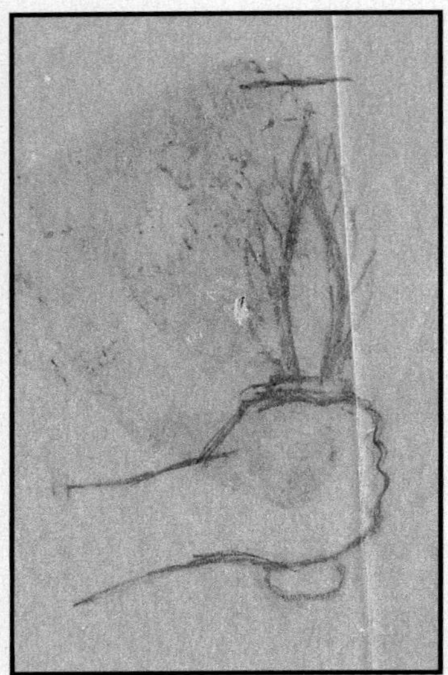

1141-E5

Design size: 33x55mm

1141-E5 4c Pencil sketch of symbol on irregular piece of tracing paper, approximately 220 x110mm, no designer notes —

1141-E6

Design size: 32x55mm

1141-E6 4c Black charcoal sketch of symbol on irregular piece of tracing paper, approximately 200 x120mm, no designer notes —

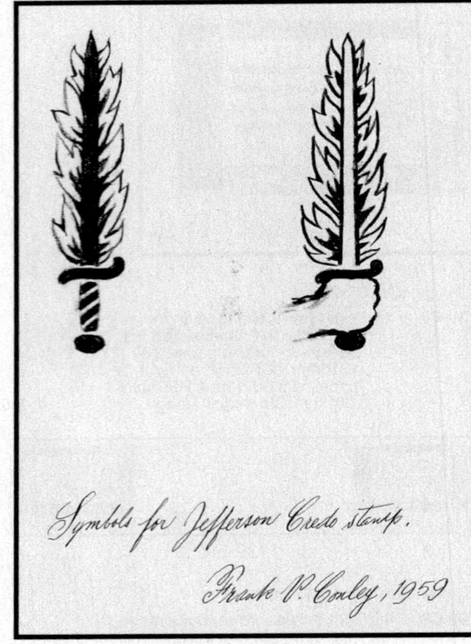

1141-E7

Design size (2): 69x68mm

1141-E7 4c Black charcoal sketches of two symbols on thin wove paper, 280 x216mm, "Symbols for Jefferson Credo stamp, Frank P. Conley, 1959" beneath, in black ink —

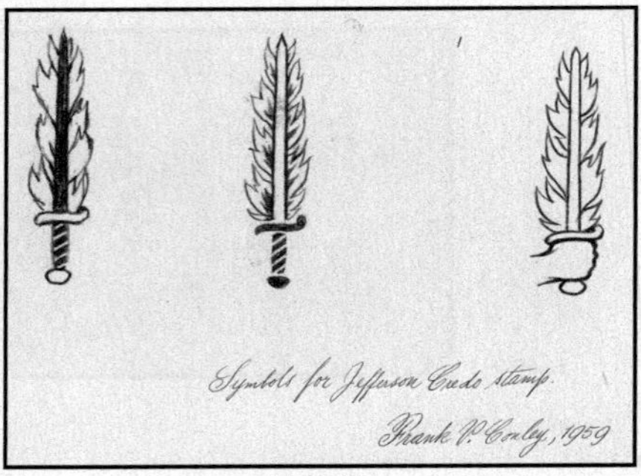

1141-E8

Design size (3): 147x68mm

1141-E8 4c Black charcoal sketches of three symbols on thin wove paper, 280 x216mm, "Symbols for Jefferson Credo stamp. Frank P. Conley, 1959" beneath, in black ink —

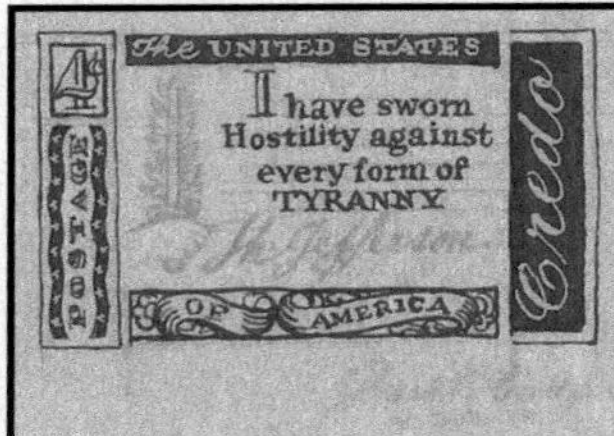

1141-E9

Design size: 37x21mm

1141-E9 4c Dark brown, vermilion and silver handpainted full design on tracing paper, 125 x108mm, signed "Frank P. Conley Designer" beneath in vermilion *1,000.*

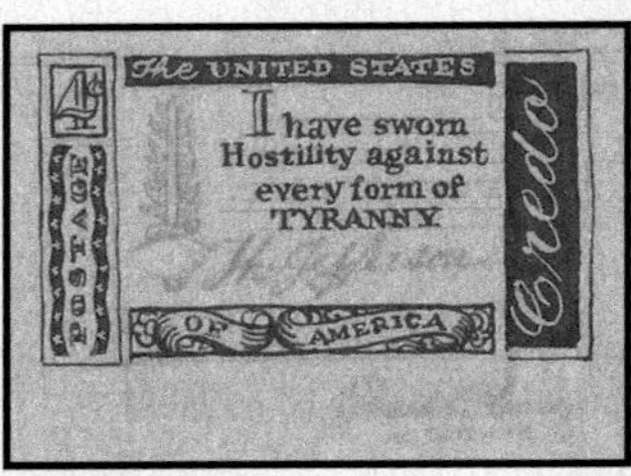

1141-E10

Design size: 37x21mm

1141-E10 4c Dark brown, vermilion and silver handpainted full design on tracing paper, 125 x108mm, different symbol and signature than #1141-E9 or 1141-E11, signed "Frank P. Conley Designer" beneath in vermilion *1,000.*

1141-E11

Design size: 37x21mm

1141-E11 4c Dark brown, vermilion and silver handpainted full design on tracing paper, 125 x108mm, different symbol and signature than #1141-E9 or 1141-E10, signed "Frank P. Conley Designer" beneath in vermilion *1,000.*

1141-E12

Design size (4 together): 156 x121mm

1141-E12 4c Dark brown, vermilion and silver handpainted full designs on thin wove paper, 280 x 216mm, 4 similar but different essays arranged in a square, each with different symbols and signatures (and each different than those on #1141-E9, 1141-E10 and 1141-E11), each signed "Frank P. Conley Designer" beneath in dark brown —

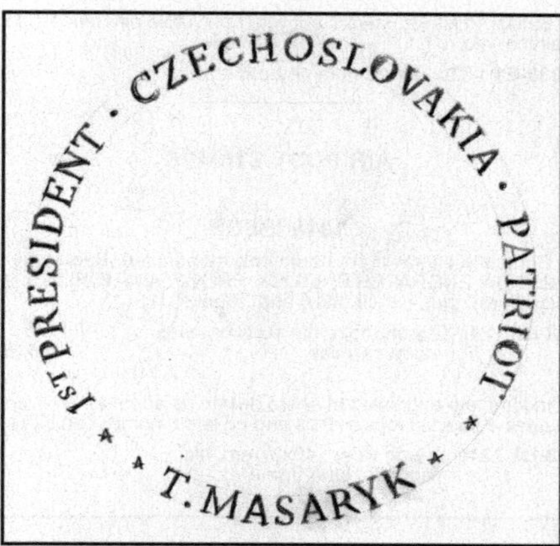

1147-E1

Design size: 157x157mm circle

1147-E1 4c Black charcoal trial design of circular text on medallion on tracing paper, approximately 260 x257mm, double stars before and after name (which does not include middle initial "G"), no dates —

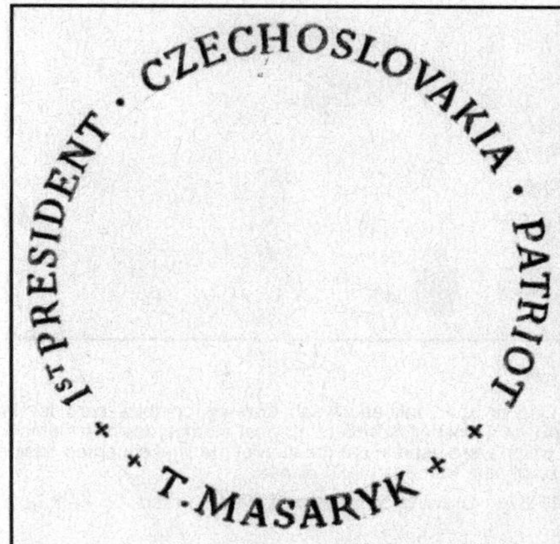

1147-E2

Design size: 159x159mm circle

1147-E2 4c Black charcoal trial design of circular text on medallion on tracing paper, approximately 268 x268mm, double crosses before and after name (which does not include middle initial "G"), no dates —

1147-E3

Design size: 159x159mm circle

1147-E3 4c Black charcoal trial design of circular text on medallion on tracing paper, 255 x255mm, large crosses before and after name, "1850/1937" dates instead of "1918/1935" as on issued stamp —

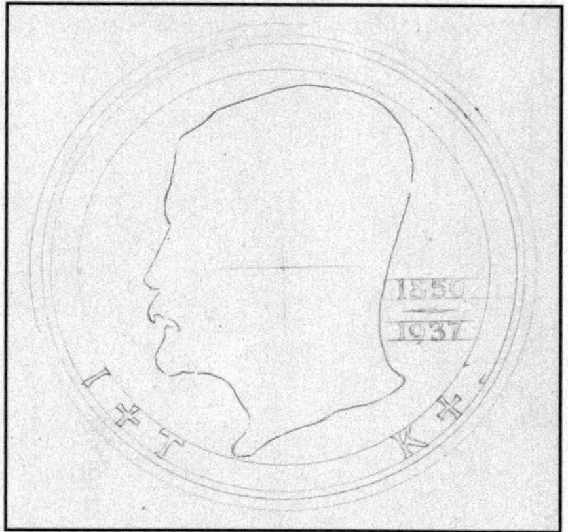

1147-E4

Design size: 173x173mm circle

1147-E4 4c Black pencil design on tracing paper, approximately 250 x290mm with uneven edges, showing circles with outline of Masaryk head, large crosses at bottom before and after name, "1830/1937" dates instead of "1918/1935" as on issued stamp —

1147-E5

Design size: 123x140mm

1147-E5 4c White, tan and black design on 160 x174mm photographic paper with complete design, section showing torch, leaves and ribbons pasted in place, vignette also pasted in place, "1850/1937" dates instead of "1918/1935" as on issued stamp —

Incomplete engraving of vignette, no shading or collar.

2179-E1 20c Die on wove, die sunk on card, red brown *600.*

2179-E2

Similar to No. 2179-E1, but with collar added.

2179-E2 20c Die on wove, die sunk on card, red brown *600.*

Similar to issued stamp, but with substandial differences in shading, etc.

2179-E3 20c Die on India, die sunk on thin card, black *650.*

Image of pine cone portion of stamp, only.

2491-E1 32c Die on India (?), affixed to card, black —

2646a-E1

Design size of each: 54x93mm; "block" size: 116x193mm
Original multicolored art in watercolor and ink.

2646a-E1 25c Four separate designs, each on thin card, mounted in block of 4 format on white card, mounted on blue backing —

2646a-E2

Design size: 126x199mm
Original art in watercolor and ink.

2646a-E2 25c Multicolored art in watercolor and black ink, bird slightly different than #2646a-E1 —

2646a-E3

Design size: 24x38mm
Original art in watercolor and ink.

2646a-E3 25c Multicolored bird slightly different than #2646a-E1 and #2646a-E2, done in stamp size, mounted on white card —

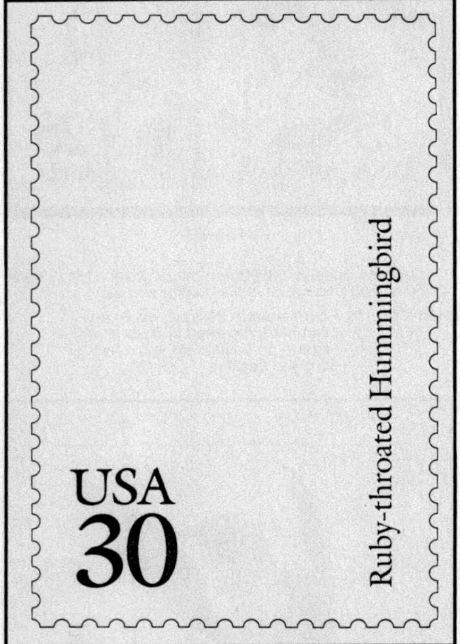

2646a-E4

Design size: 126x198mm
Ink drawing of 30c denomination and text.

2646a-E4 30c Simulated perfs, denomination and text on white card, with measurement notes at left, black —

2646a-E5

Design size: 126x198mm
Ink drawing of final 29c denomination and text.

2646a-E5 29c Simulated perfs, denomination and text on white card, with measurement notes at left, black —

2646a-E6

Design size: 52x129mm; overall size: 65x143mm
Original art in watercolor and black ink.

2646a-E6 25c Multicolored art for proposed booklet cover, later revised, on thin card —

Similar to issued stamp, but with noticeable differences in tie, hairline, etc.

2933-E1 32c Die on gummed paper, brown *1,000.*

AIR POST STAMPS

1918 ISSUE

Complete engraving of frame only as adopted. Backstamped "626646A ENGRAVER'S STOCK PROOF AUTHORIZED BY" (signature), plus pencil "663" and "Weeks" (?).

C3-E1 24c Die on India, die sunk on card, deep carmine *5,000.*

Incomplete engraving of entire design as adopted: unfinished plumes above value numerals and no serial number on biplane.

C3-E2 24c Die on wove, 40x37mm, black vignette, blue frame —

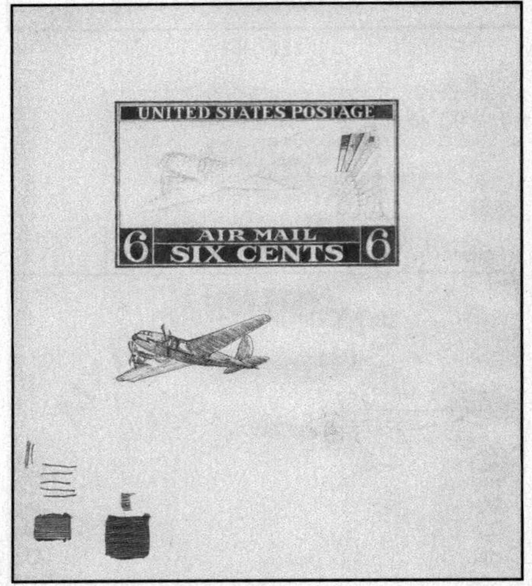

C25-E1

Original pen, ink and wash drawing on thick card for the 1941-44 Transport series of air post stamps, various elements of which were used in the creation of the final accepted design. Size of blue frame is 4⅞x3 inches.

C25-E1 Drawing on thick card, blue and red *3,000.*

Engraving of adopted design except without denomination, "C" punch where denominations go, control #722657A (1942) on back of card.

C25-C31-E2 Die on wove, die sunk on card, 201x150mm, black *5,500.*

SPECIAL DELIVERY STAMPS

1885 ISSUE
American Bank Note Co.

E1-E1

Incomplete engraving of entire design as adopted: ornaments missing at each side of "SPECIAL," line under messenger is in pencil, shading on left side of messenger tablet missing, leaves and vert. background lines unfinished (latter shaded over with pencil).

E1-E1 10c Die on India, dim dusky g-b. green *2,500.*

1888 ISSUE

No. E1P1 with "AT ANY OFFICE" drawn in wash on small piece of thin paper and mounted over "AT A SPECIAL / DELIVERY / OFFICE." Pencil "any post office" and ms. "At once O.K. / J.C.M. 14 Aug. 86" (?) on backing card.

E2-E1 10c Die on India, on card, black *2,500.*

1908 ISSUE
Bureau of Engraving and Printing

E7-E1

Design size: about 8½x7⅛ inches
Preliminary ink and pencil drawing of entire design somewhat similar to that adopted: ("V.S." for U.S. and other minor changes).

E7-E1 10c Drawing on vellum, black —

E7-E2

Design size: about 8½x7⅛ inches
Preliminary ink and pencil drawing of entire design nearly as adopted: ("V.S." for U.S.)

E7-E2 10c Drawing on white drawing paper, black —

E7-E3

Design size: 213½x179mm
Similar to No. E7-E2 but with "U.S."

E7-E3 10c Drawing on white drawing paper, black 750.

E7-E4

Design size: 26x21½mm
Woodblock size: 45x42mm
Woodblock of entire design as adopted with about 5mm colorless border outside design, solid color beyond, engraved on wood by Giraldon of Paris. (One exists with ms. "Wood cut made in Paris by Mr. Whitney Warren — The cuts and the impression therefrom were turned over to the Director of the Bureau of Engraving & Printing, and by him turned over to the Custodian of Dies, Rolls and Plates and given No. 446. They are now held by the Custodian." Another has typewritten "Prints made in Paris, France, from a wood-cut engraving by an unknown engraver from a design made by Mr. Whitney Warren, architect, of New York City." with ms. "Compliments J.E. Ralph" director of B.E.P. and pencil date "9/7/1917.")

Ridgeway numbers used for colors of Nos. E7-E4 and E7-E5.

E7-E4 10c
- ***a.*** Woodcut on 19g/2 yellowish wove
  - 43k/1 dim dark green blue 450.
  - 44m/2 dull dusky m. g-blue 450.
  - 45j/1 dim v. dark b-g-blue 450.
  - 45m/1 dim dusky b-g-blue 450.
- ***b.*** Woodcut on 19f/2 dull faint y-o-yellow wove
  - 43k/1 dim dark g-blue 450.
  - 43m/1 dim dusky g-blue 450.
  - 44k/1 dim dark m. g-blue 450.
  - 44k/2 dull dark m. g-blue 450.
  - 45m/1 dim dusky b-g-blue 450.
  - 45m/2 dull dusky b-g-blue 450.
- ***c.*** Woodcut on 19g/2 dull v. faint y-o-yellow wove
  - 43k/1 dim dark g-blue 450.
  - 43m/1 dim dusky g-blue 450.

E7-E5

Design size: 26x21½mm
Complete engraving of entire design fairly similar to that adopted but with minor differences.

E7-E5 10c
- ***a.*** Die on India, die sunk on card, 37m/0 dusky g-b. green blue 750.
- ***b.*** Die on soft white wove, 30x35mm, 37m/0 dusky g-blue-green 750.

REGISTRATION STAMP

F1-E1

Design size: 19x22½mm
Retouched circular photo of vignette mounted on wash drawing of frame design as adopted. Ms. "Approved July 8/11 — Frank H. Hitchcock — Postmaster General" on backing card.

F1-E1 10c Model on white paper, mounted on thick gray cardboard, 81x92mm, black 1,250.

POSTAGE DUE STAMPS

1879 ISSUE
American Bank Note Co.

J1-E1

Design size: 19½x25½mm
Die size: 54x66½mm
Complete engraving of entire design as adopted except "UNPAID POSTAGE" instead of "POSTAGE DUE" above vignette oval.

J1-E1 1c
- ***a.*** Die on India, die sunk on card
  - orange brown 850.
  - slate gray 850.
  - dark red violet 850.
  - dull yellow 850.
  - light orange 850.
  - red brown 850.
- ***b.*** Die on India, cut small (1-4mm)
  - gray black 300.
  - dull red 300.
  - dull brown 300.
  - dull green 300.
  - dull blue 300.
- ***c.*** Die on India, cut close (0-1mm)
  - orange brown 300.
  - slate gray 300.
  - dark red violet 300.
  - dull yellow 300.
- ***d.*** Die on ivory glazed paper, die sunk
  - black 700.
  - black brown 700.
  - scarlet 700.
  - blue 700.

Design size: 19½x25½mm
Die size: 53½x53½mm
Complete engraving of entire design as adopted except "UNPAID POSTAGE" instead of "POSTAGE DUE" above vignette oval.

J2-E1 2c
- ***a.*** Die on India, die sunk on card
  - dark red violet 850.
  - black 850.
- ***b.*** Die on India, cut small
  - gray black 300.
  - dull red 300.
  - dull brown 300.
  - dull green 300.
  - dull blue 300.
- ***c.*** Die on India, cut close
  - orange brown 300.
  - dark red violet 300.
  - slate gray 400.
- ***d.*** Die on ivory glazed paper, die sunk
  - black 700.
  - black brown 700.
  - scarlet 700.
  - blue 700.

Design size: 19½x25½mm
Die size: 53x53mm
Complete engraving of entire design as adopted except "UNPAID POSTAGE" instead of "POSTAGE DUE" above vignette oval.

J3-E1 3c
- ***a.*** Die on India, die sunk on card, dull yellow 850.
- ***b.*** Die on India, cut small
  - gray black 300.
  - dull red 300.
  - dull brown 300.
  - dull green 300.
  - dull blue 300.
- ***c.*** Die on India, cut close, dull yellow 300.
- ***d.*** Die on ivory glazed paper, die sunk
  - black 700.
  - black brown 700.
  - scarlet 700.
  - blue 700.

Design size: 19½x25½mm
Complete engraving of entire design as adopted except "UNPAID POSTAGE" instead of "POSTAGE DUE" above vignette oval.

J4-E1 5c
- ***a.*** Die on India, die sunk on card, slate gray 850.
- ***b.*** Die on India, cut small
  - gray black 300.
  - dull red 300.
  - dull brown 300.
  - dull green 300.
  - dull blue 300.
- ***c.*** Die on India, cut close
  - orange brown 300.
  - slate gray 300.
  - dark red violet 300.
  - dull yellow 300.
- ***d.*** Die on ivory glazed paper, die sunk
  - black 700.
  - black brown 700.
  - scarlet 700.
  - blue 700.

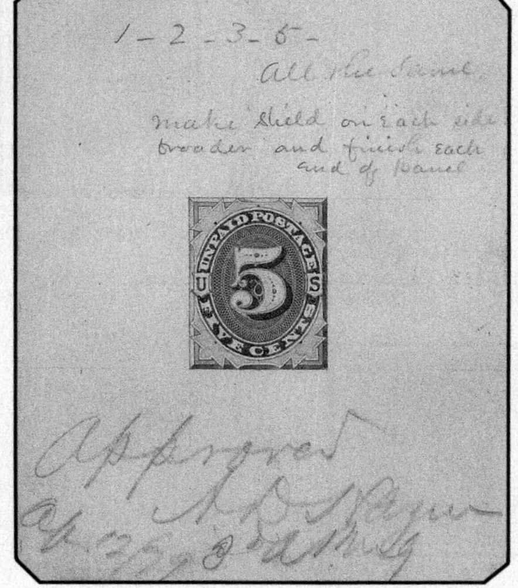

J4-E2

As No. J4-E1 except frame a pencil and wash drawing, vignette engraved numeral and oval lathework numeral cut to shape and pasted over lathework, with design notations.

J4-E2 5c Engraved vignette, frame pencil and wash, on thick card, 70x88mm, brown *4,500.*

1894 ISSUE
Bureau of Engraving and Printing

J31-E1

Design size: 18½x22½mm
Die size: 50x99mm
Incomplete engraving of entire design: no engraved lines on numeral, lathework unfinished on two inclined spots at each side of numeral.

J31-E1 1c Die on India, die sunk on card, deep claret *1,400.*

J31-E2

Design size: 18½x22½mm
Die size: 50x99mm
Incomplete engraving of entire design: engraved lines on numeral but lathework still unfinished on two inclined spots at each side of numeral.

J31-E2 1c Die on India, die sunk on card, claret *1,000.*

J32-E1

Design size: 18½x22½mm
Die size: unknown
Incomplete engraving of entire design: unfinished ornaments by "P" of "POSTAGE" and "E" of "DUE."

J32-E1 2c Die on India, size 26x30mm, deep claret *1,500.*

J33-E1

Incomplete engraving of entire design: blank space for numeral with "3" drawn in pencil.

J33-E1 3c Die on India, die sunk on card, black *1,100.*

J33-E2

Incomplete engraving of entire design: no engraved lines on numeral, bottom lettering in pencil only, no hand retouching of lathework around numeral.

J33-E2 3c Die on India, die sunk on card, black *1,500.*

J33-E3

Incomplete engraving of entire design: no engraved lines on numeral.

J33-E3 3c Die on India, die sunk on card, claret *1,000.*

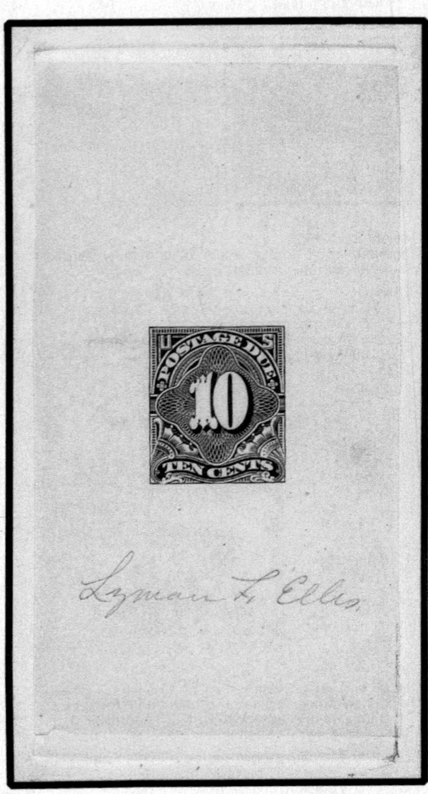

J35-E1

Incomplete engraving of entire design: no engraved lines on numerals, signed by Lyman F. Ellis.

J35-E1 10c Die on India, die sunk on card, black *2,100.*

J36-E1

Incomplete engraving of entire design: no engraved lines on numerals.

J36-E1 30c Die on India, die sunk on card, claret *1,600.*

J37-E1

Incomplete engraving of entire design: 9x9mm blank space for numerals.

J37-E1 50c Die on India, die sunk on card
black *1,600.*
claret *1,600.*

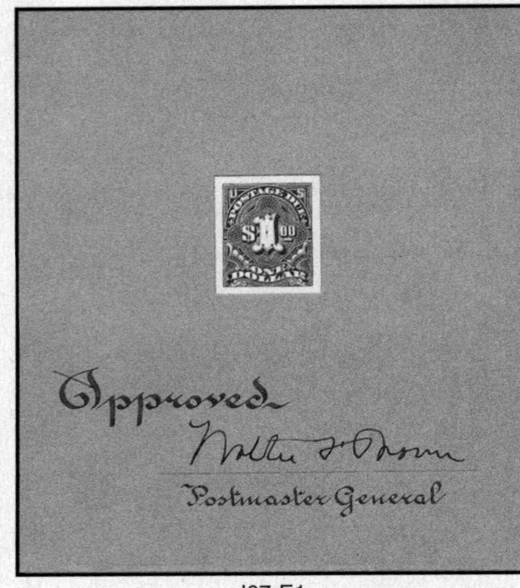

J67-E1

Complete engraving of unissued 1917 denomination with wash drawing in "1" and dollar sign, "Approved / Walter F. Brown (signature) / Postmaster General" below design.

J67A-E1 $1 Die on white card, mounted on gray card, black *21,000.*

OFFICIAL STAMPS

Continental Bank Note Co.
AGRICULTURE

O1-E1

Engraved Franklin vignette with 1 and value label.

O1-E1 1c Die on India, on card (1873), black *2,250.*

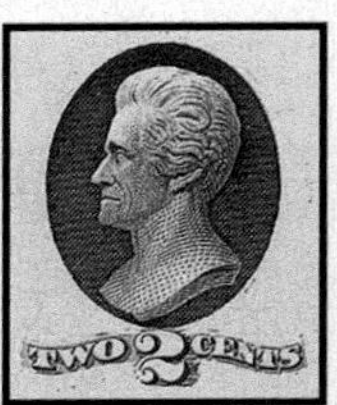

O2-E1

Engraved Jackson vignette with 2 and value label.

O2-E1 2c Die on glazed paper (1873), black *2,250.*

O2-E2

The J37-E2 entry, which sits at the top of the right column, follows:

J37-E2

Incomplete engraving of entire design: numerals engraved but hand engraving to retouch lathework around numerals missing.

J37-E2 50c Die on India, die sunk on card, black *2,300.*

Design size: 20x25mm
Engraved vignette, numeral and value label from 1873 2c (No. O2-E1) mounted on pencil and wash drawing for frame design as adopted for Agriculture set. Pencil signature "J. Claxton" on backing card. Frame differs for each dept.

O2-E2 2c Model on yellowish card, 23x30mm, on 90x118mm white card, black vignette, gray black frame *6,500.*

O3-E1

Washington vignette, 3 and value label.

O3-E1 3c Die on India, card mounted (1873), black *2,250.*

O4-E1

Completed vignette with 6 and value label.

O4-E1 6c Die on India, on card (1873), black *2,400.*

O6-E1

Completed Clay vignette with 12 and value label.

O6-E1 12c Die on white glazed paper (1873), black *2,000.*

O7-E1

Vignette of Webster with 15 below.

O7-E1 15c Die on white glazed paper (1873), black *1,250.*

O9-E1

Completed vignette with 30 below.

O9-E1 30c Die on white glazed paper (1873), black *1,500.*

EXECUTIVE

O12-E1

Design size: 20x25mm
See design note for No. O2-E1.

O12-E1 3c Model on yellowish card, 23x30mm, on 90x118mm white card, black *6,000.*

O12-E2

Design size: 19½x25mm
Die size: 64x76mm
Engraving of complete design of No. O12-E1 with "DEP'T" in top label.

O12-E2 3c
a. Die on India, die sunk on card, green *2,750.*
b. Die on India, cut close
black *2,250.*
green *2,250.*

INTERIOR

O17-E1

Design size: 20x25mm
See design note for No. O2-E1.

O17-E1 3c Model on yellowish card, 23x30mm, on 90x118mm white card, black *9,000.*

JUSTICE

O27-E1

Design size: 20x25mm
See design note for No. O2-E1.

O27-E1 3c Model on yellowish card, 23x30mm, on 90x118mm white card, black *10,000.*

NAVY

O37-E1

Design size: 20x25mm
See design note for No. O2-E1.

O37-E1 3c Model on yellowish card, 23x30mm, on 90x118mm white card, black *4,750.*

O39-E1

Die size: 62x76mm
Completed vignette with 7 and value label.

O39-E1 7c
a. Die on India, on card (1873), black *1,000.*
b. Die on white glazed paper, black *1,000.*

POST OFFICE

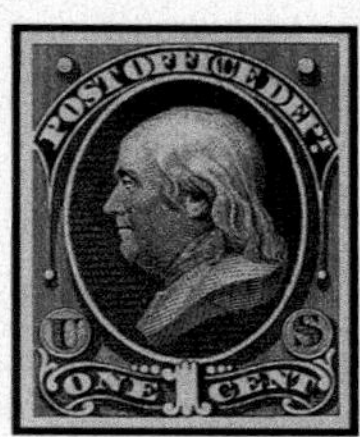

O47-E1

Design size: 19½x25mm
Complete engraving of entire design as adopted except with Franklin vignette instead of large numeral.

O47-E1 1c
a. Die on India, mounted on white ivory card
blue *1,750.*
b. Die on proof paper
gray black *1,250.*
dull scarlet *1,250.*
dull brown *1,250.*
dull green *1,250.*
dull blue *1,250.*
c. Die on ivory glazed paper
brown black *1,750.*
orange red *1,750.*
blue *1,750.*

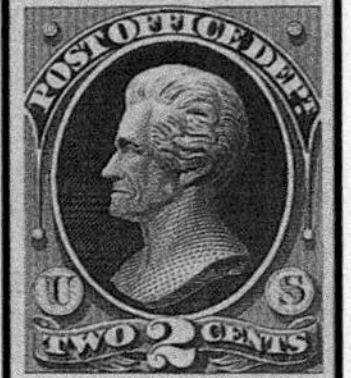

O48-E1

Design size: 19½x25mm

Complete engraving of entire design as adopted except with Jackson vignette instead of large numeral.

O48-E1 2c
- ***a.*** Die on India, mounted on white ivory card
  - orange brown *1,500.*
- ***b.*** Die on proof paper
  - gray black *1,250.*
  - dull scarlet *1,250.*
  - dull brown *1,250.*
  - dull green *1,250.*
  - dull blue *1,250.*
- ***c.*** Die on ivory glazed paper
  - black *1,750.*
  - brown black *1,750.*
  - orange red *1,750.*
  - blue *1,750.*

O49-E1

O49-E2

Design size: 20x25mm
Engraved vignette, numeral and value label from 1873 3c (No. 147-E10) mounted on pencil and wash drawing for frame design not adopted for Post Office set.

O49-E1 3c Model on yellowish card, 23x30mm, on 90x118mm white card, black *5,750.*

O49-E2 3c Model on yellowish card, 23x30mm, on 90x118mm white card, black *5,750.*

O49-E3

Design size: 20x25mm
See design note for No. O2-E1.

O49-E3 3c Model on yellowish card, 23x30mm, on 90x118mm white card, black *5,750.*

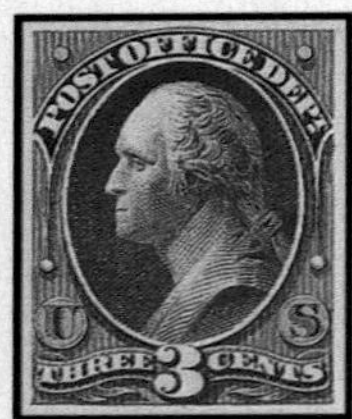
O49-E4

Design size: 19½x25mm
Complete engraving of entire design as adopted except with Washington vignette instead of large numeral.

O49-E4 3c
- ***a.*** Die on India, mounted on white ivory card
  - green *1,500.*
- ***b.*** Die on proof paper
  - gray black *1,250.*
  - dull scarlet *1,250.*
  - dull brown *1,250.*
  - dull green *1,250.*
  - dull blue *1,250.*
- ***c.*** Die on ivory glazed paper
  - brown black *1,750.*
  - orange red *1,750.*
  - blue *1,750.*

O49-E5

1870 1c stamp (No. 145) with vignette cut out, "OFFICIAL 3 STAMP" drawn in pencil on envelope on which stamp is mounted. Blue pencil notations on backing envelope "1st design of official stamp for POD" and "Design by Mr. J. Barber for P O Official."

O49-E5 1c Stamp frame mounted on envelope, ultramarine frame, black vignette *7,500.*

O49-E6

Model of engraved frame from No. O49-E4 with hollow oval engraved lathework band with "OFFICIAL / STAMP" drawn in wash mounted in place, numeral drawn in pencil and wash. Ms. "No. 1" on backing card.

O49-E6 3c Model on stiff white card, 50x75mm, green *7,500.*

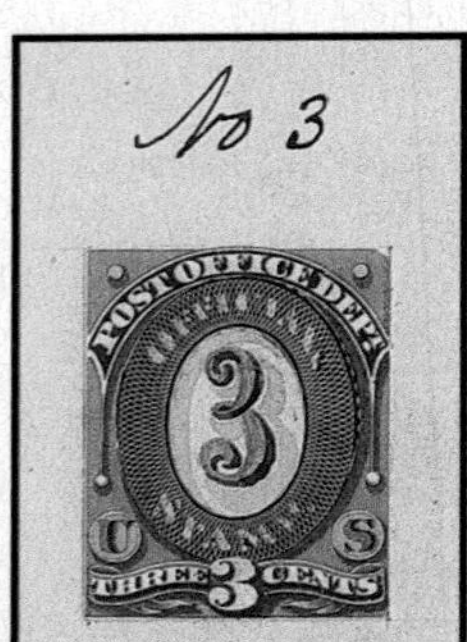

O49-E8

Like No. O49-E6, Ms. "No. 3" on backing card.

O49-E8 3c Model on stiff white card, 50x75mm, green & black *17,500.*

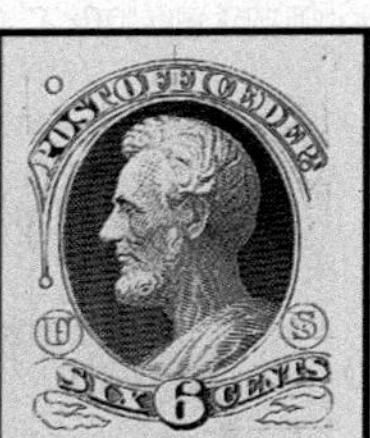
O50-E1

Incomplete engraving of design with Lincoln vignette, without rectangular frame design.

O50-E1 6c Die on white ivory paper, black *4,250.*

O56-E1

Design size: 19½x25mm

Complete engraving of entire design as adopted except with Perry vignette instead of large numeral.

O56-E1 90c
- ***a.*** Die on India, mounted on white ivory card
  - brown *1,500.*
  - blue *1,500.*
  - orange red *1,500.*
- ***b.*** Die on proof paper
  - gray black *1,500.*
  - dull scarlet *1,500.*
  - dull brown *1,500.*
  - dull green *1,500.*
  - dull blue *1,500.*
- ***c.*** Die on ivory glazed paper
  - brown black *1,750.*
  - orange red *1,750.*
  - blue *1,750.*

STATE

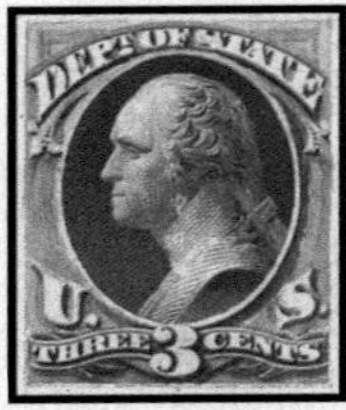
O59-E1

Design size: 20x25mm
Engraved vignette, numeral and value label from 1873 3c (No. 147-E10) mounted on pencil and wash drawing for frame design as adopted for State set. Pencil signature "J. Claxton" on backing card.

O59-E1 3c Model on yellowish card, 23x30mm, on 90x118mm white card, black *4,750.*

O68-E1

Design size: 25½x40mm
Engraved vignette of Seward mounted in watercolor drawing of adopted frame design. Ms. signatures of J. Claxton and Chas. Skinner on backing card.

O68-E1 Two Dollars, Model on 29x43mm grayish white card, mounted on 96x120mm white card, black *7,500.*

O68-E2

Complete engraving of adopted frame only with "TWO DOLLARS." in value label at bottom. With "FIVE DOLLARS." and "TEN DOLLARS." value labels outside design at left and "TWENTY DOLLs." value tablet at right.

O68-E2 Two Dollars, Die on India, black *15,000.*

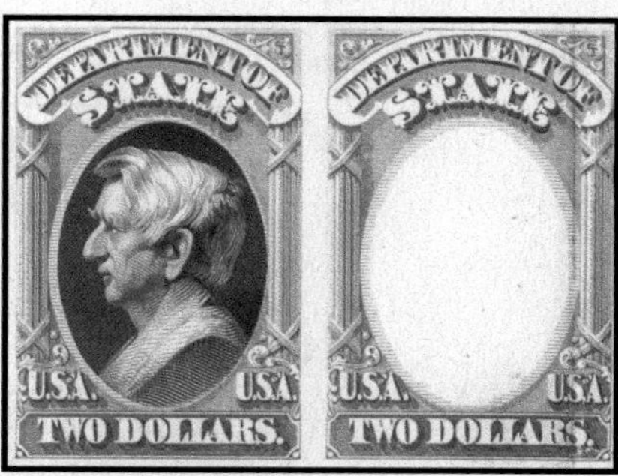

O68-E3

Plate engraved frame only (three examples in a block of four with complete bicolor plate proof of $2 at upper left in block).

O68-E3 Two Dollars, Plate essay on India, green *10,000.*

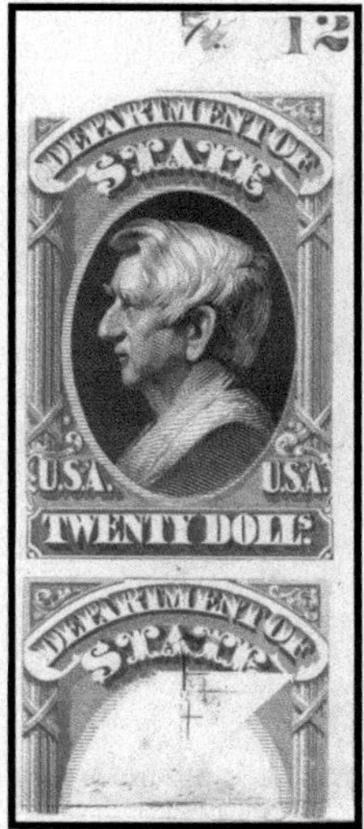

O71-E1

Plate engraving of top half of frame only, paired with $20 plate proof.

O71-E1 Die on India, mounted on card, green *9,000.*

WAR

O85-E1

Design size: 20x25mm

Engraved vignette, numeral and value label from 1873 3c (No. 147-E10) mounted on pencil and wash drawing for frame design as adopted for War set. Pencil signature "J. Claxton" on backing card.

O85-E1 3c Model on yellowish card, 23x30mm, on 90x118mm white card, black *4,750.*

NEWSPAPER AND PERIODICALS

1865 ISSUE
National Bank Note Co.

PR1-E1

Design size: 51x89mm

Typographed design somewhat similar to that adopted but with large Franklin vignette facing left, "PACKAGE" at bottom, other minor differences.

PR1-E1 5c Die on stiff white ivory paper
- deep orange red *2,000.*
- dusky g-b. blue *2,000.*
- bright blue *2,000.*
- *a.* Die on paper with blue ruled lines
  - deep orange red *2,000.*
  - carmine *2,000.*

1875 ISSUE
National Bank Note Co.

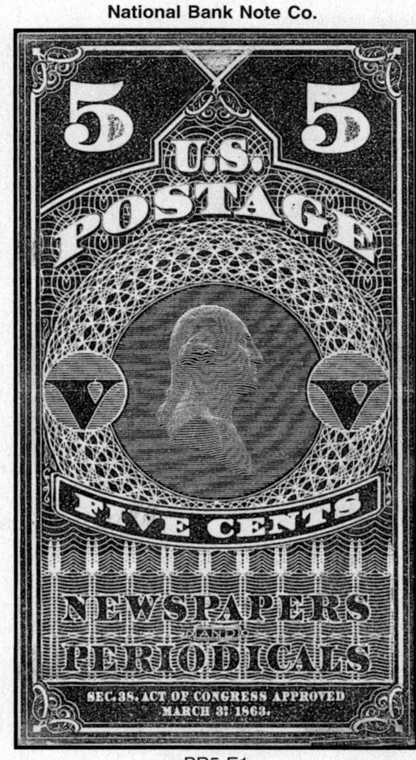

PR5-E1

Design size: 52x96½mm

Typographed design as issued but lacking "National Bank Note Company, New York" imprint at bottom.

PR5-E1 5c Die on wove paper, blue —

1875 ISSUE
Continental Bank Note Co.

PR9-E1

Design size: 19½x25mm

Engraved vignette and numerals (25's) with pencil sketch of unadopted frame design.

PR9-E1 25c Die on India, on card, black *2,750.*

PR9-E2

Design size: 19½x25mm

Complete engraving of unadopted design with "U S" at top and "25 CENTS 25" at bottom.

PR9-E2 25c
- *a.* Die on India, on card
  - black *1,350.*
  - scarlet *1,350.*
  - blue *1,350.*
  - green *1,350.*
- *b.* Die on white ivory paper
  - black *1,350.*
  - black brown *1,350.*
  - scarlet *1,350.*
  - blue *1,350.*

PR9-E3

Engraved unfinished die with final design, blank spaces for numerals and value tablets.

PR9-E3 Blank denomination, die on India, mounted on 27x45mm card, black *1,250.*

PR14-E1

Design size: 25x35mm

Wash drawing of complete design as adopted. Backing card signed by both designers, Chas. Skinner and Jos. Claxton.

PR14-E1 9c Drawing on 26x36mm card, on 56x74mm card, black *900.*

Complete engraving except value tablets blank.

PR16-E1 (12c) Die on India, mounted on 26x40mm card, black *1,700.*

PR23-E1

Design size: 24x35½mm
Wash drawing similar to that adopted, backing card signed by designers Skinner and Claxton, also has pencil "$12" and ms. "Continental Bank Note Co."

PR23-E1 96c Drawing on 88x121mm card, black *900.*

PR27-E1

Design size: 24½x35mm
Incomplete engraving of entire design: unshaded (shading pencilled in) inside left, right and bottom framelines, value label, top of "9." Upper corners unfinished.

PR27-E1 $9 Die on India, die sunk on 76x82mm card, black *1,350.*

PR28-E1

Design size: 24½x35mm
Incomplete engraving of entire design: no shading on dollar signs and numerals. No shading on frame around numerals and around value tablet.

PR28-E1 $12 Die on India, die sunk on 66x80mm card, black *1,350.*

PR28-E2

Incomplete engraving of entire design, shading pencilled in around bottom value tablet and top right and left dollar signs and numerals.

PR28-E2 $12 Die on India, die sunk on card, 75x90mm, black *1,150.*

PR29-E1

Design size: 24x35½mm
Wash drawing similar to that adopted but with "U S" in six-pointed stars instead of at top. Backing card signed by designers Skinner and Claxton, also pencil "31/32" and "8 13/32," pencil "Alter" with lines to stars.

PR29-E1 $24 Drawing on 88x121mm card, black *750.*

PR31-E1

Vignette size: 13½x26mm
Engraved vignette only as adopted.

PR31-E1 $48 Die on India, die sunk on card, black *750.*

PR31-E2

Design size: 24x36mm
Wash drawing similar to that adopted, backing card signed by designers Skinner and Claxton, also has pencil "$48" above each value numeral.

PR31-E2 $48 Drawing on 88x121mm card, black *1,350.*

PR32-E1

Design size: 24½x35½mm
Wash drawing similar to that adopted, backing card signed by designers Skinner and Claxton.

PR32-E1 $60 Drawing on 88x121mm card, black *750.*

1885 ISSUE
American Bank Note Co.

PR81-E1

Design size: 23x25mm
Complete engraving of entire design as adopted for 12c-96c.

PR81-E1 1c
- ***a.*** Die on India, die sunk on card
  - black *1,000.*
- ***b.*** Die on white ivory paper
  - black *600.*
  - black brown *600.*
  - scarlet *600.*
  - blue *600.*

1895 ISSUE
Bureau of Engraving and Printing

PR102-E2

Incomplete engraving of entire design: background at upper ends of value label, shading on side lettering and numerals missing.

PR102-E2 1c Die on India, die sunk on card
- black *900.*
- green *1,250.*

Incomplete engraving of entire design but further engraved than No. PR102-E2: shading on PA is light, no shading on PE of NEWSPAPERS or IO of PERIODICALS and shading on OD is light.

PR102-E3 1c Die on India, die sunk on card, black *900.*

Incomplete engraving of entire design but further engraved than No. PR102-E3: shading on PERIODICALS is finished but not on PAPE.

PR102-E4 1c Die on India, die sunk on card, black *900.*

PR103-E1

Design size: 21½x34½mm
Die size: 56x75½mm
Incomplete engraving of entire design: spaces for numerals and value label blank but with pencil outline of lettering.

PR103-E1 2c Die on India, die sunk on card, black *1,250.*

PR103-E2

Incomplete engraving of entire design but further engraved than No. PR103-E1: shading on leaves at ends of value label unfinished, numerals unshaded, unfinished shading on APE of NEWSPAPERS and RIO of PERIODICALS.

PR103-E2 2c Die on India, black *1,250.*

Incomplete engraving of entire design but further engraved than No. PR103-E2: no shading on PE of NEWSPAPERS, unfinished shading on PA of NEWSPAPERS and RIO of PERIODICALS.

PR103-E3 2c Die on India, die sunk on card, black *1,250.*

PR104-E1

Design size: 21 ½x34 ½mm
Die size: 57x73mm
Incomplete engraving of entire design: spaces for numerals and value label blank but with pencil outline of lettering.

PR104-E1 5c Die on India, die sunk on card, black *1,500.*

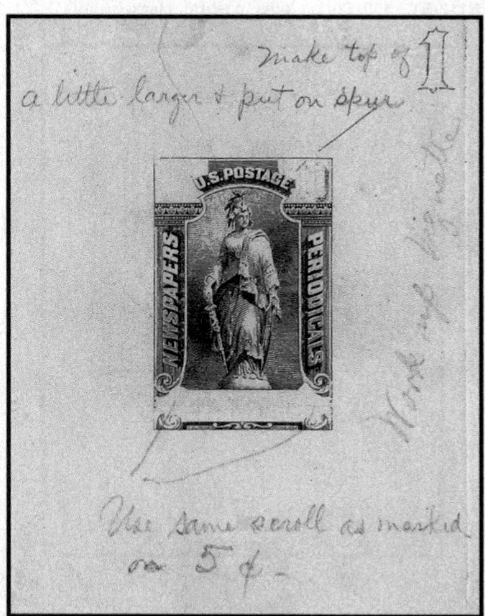

PR105-E1

Design size: 21 ½x34 ½mm
Die size: 56x75mm
Incomplete engraving of entire design: spaces for numerals and value label blank but with pencil outline of lettering.

PR105-E1 10c Die on India, die sunk on card, black *1,600.*

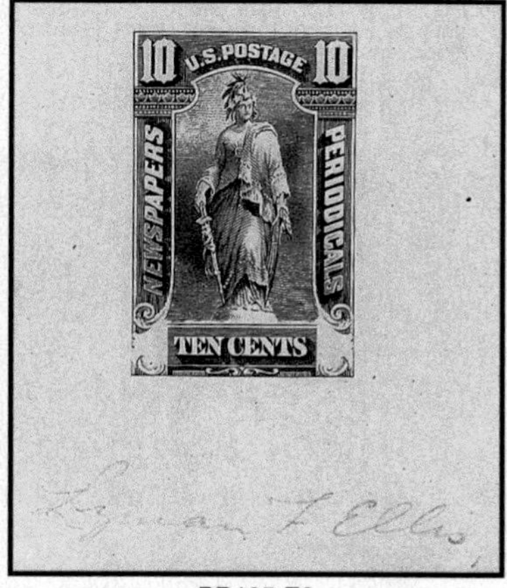

PR105-E2

Incomplete engraving of entire design but further engraved than No. PR105-E1: numerals unfinished, lower corners blank.

PR105-E2 10c Die on India, die sunk on card, black *2,100.*

Incomplete engraving of entire design but further engraved than No. PR105-E2: lower right corner blank.

PR105-E3 10c Die on India, die sunk on card, black *1,250.*

Incomplete engraving of entire design but further engraved than No. PR105-E3: numerals blank, no inner lines.

PR105-E4 10c Die on India, die sunk on card, black *1,250.*

PR105-E5

Design size: 21 ½x34 ½mm
Die size: 56x75mm
Incomplete engraving of entire design (early state of die similar to No. PR105-E1) with "10" pencilled in upper right corner and "TEN CENTS" pencilled in at bottom. Pencil notes on India include "Make top of 1 a little larger and put on spur," "Work up Vignette" and "Use same scrolls as marked on 5c-."

PR105-E5 10c Die on India, die sunk on card, black *2,750.*

PR106-E1

Vignette size: 13x25 ½mm
Die size: 56x72mm
Incomplete engraving of vignette only (transfer of Continental Banknote Co. die for 72c with left side cut off): eagle crest faces front and its right wing is not pointed, shading on left thigh near sword hilt incomplete, bottom of vignette straight instead of curved.

PR106-E1 25c Die on India, die sunk on card
black *3,000.*
deep red *3,000.*

PR106-E2

Design size: about 21x34 ½mm
Die size: 57 ½x75mm
Entire design with frame incompletely engraved: vert. lines around CENTS label missing, no shading on TWENTY FIVE, colorless beads under E and FI of same.

PR106-E2 25c Die on India, die sunk on card
black *3,000.*
deep red *3,000.*

PR106-E3

An impression from No. PR106-E2 with pencil shading on TWENTY FIVE and vert. ink lines in spaces around CENTS label, colorless beads also blacked out in ink. Below engraving are three diff. pencil sketches for shape and shading to be engraved.

PR106-E3 25c Die on India, die sunk on card
black *2,750.*
deep red *2,750.*

PR106-E4

An impression from No. PR106-E2 but with shading suggestions from No. PR106-E3 partly engraved except colorless beads have pencil shading only. Below engraving is pencil sketch for corner of CENTS label.

PR106-E4 25c Die on India, die sunk on card
black *2,650.*
deep red *2,000.*

PR106-E5

Design size: 21½x34½mm
Die size: 55x72mm
Large die proof of PR107 with bottom value label cut out and "TWENTY-FIVE CENTS" pencilled in on backing card.

PR106-E5 25c Die on India, die sunk on card, black *1,500.*

PR107-E1

Incomplete engraving of entire design: eagle's head and much of bottom of stamp's design unfinished, top of frame unfinished, value lettering sketched in pencil.

PR107-E1 50c Die on India, die sunk on card, black *1,950.*

PR107-E3

Incomplete engraving of entire design: top of frame and scrolls below FIFTY CENTS unfinished.

PR107-E3 50c Die on India, die sunk on card, black *1,750.*

PR108-E1

Design size: 24½x37mm
Die size: 75x76mm

Incomplete engraving of entire design: vignette and spaces around numerals incomplete, pencil sketch instructions for engraver at top and side for these spaces.

PR108-E1 $2 Die on India, die sunk on card, black *1,650.*

PR108-E2

Design size: 24½x37mm
Die size: 75x76mm
Incomplete engraving of entire design but further engraved than No. PR108-E1: space for ornaments under POSTAGE blank, numerals unshaded.

PR108-E2 $2 Die on India, die sunk on card, scarlet *1,500.*

Further engraved than No. PR108-E2: scrolls under POSTAGE engraved but unfinished.

PR108-E3 $2 Die on India, die sunk on card, black *1,500.*

Incomplete engraving of design, no frame line under "Postage" and other small differences from final design.

PR110-E1 $10 Die on India, green *1,500.*

PR111-E1

Design size (incomplete): 24½x30mm
Die size: 75x84mm
Incomplete engraving of partial design: spaces for stars and 0s of numerals blank, design missing below bottom of vignette.

PR111-E1 $20 Die on India, die sunk on card, black *1,250.*

PR111-E2

Design size: 24½x35½mm
Incomplete lines below denomination at top, only 7 lines below right "0" of "$20" and 8 lines below left "$20" (issued design has 13 lines in both places), die no. "74" at bottom.

PR111-E2 $20 Die on India, 42x54mm, black *1,850.*

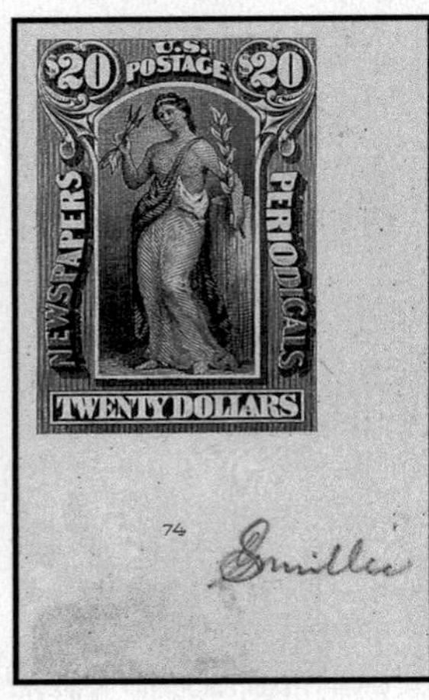

PR111-E3

Design size: 24½x35½mm
Incomplete lines below denomination at top, but with addition of pencil lines of shading to indicate further work needed, die no. "74" at bottom and signed "Smillie" in pencil.

PR111-E3 $20 Die on India, on 71x83mm card, black *1,850.*

PR112-E1

Design size: 24½x35½mm
Die size: 72½x76mm
Incomplete engraving of entire design: upper corners around value numerals unfinished, etc.

PR112-E1 $50 Die on India, on card, black *2,750.*

PR113-E1

Design size: 24½x35½mm
Die size: unknown
Incomplete engraving of entire design: spaces at lower inner corners of value shields blank, shading on numerals and letters at top unfinished.

PR113-E1 $100 Die on India, on card, black *1,850.*

PR113-E2

Design size: 24½x35½mm
Die size: 75x73mm
Further engraved than No. PR113-E1.

PR113-E2 $100 Die on India, die sunk on 80x80mm card, violet *1,750.*

PR113-E3

Further engraved than No. PR113-E2: vignette completed but numerals not shaded, shadows on frame not etched dark.

PR113-E3 $100 Die on India
black *1,750.*
red-violet *1,750.*

Further engraved than No. PR113-E3: numerals shaded, shadows on frame not finally etched, especially above POSTAGE.

PR113-E4 $100 Die on India, black *1,350.*

PARCEL POST STAMPS

Q1-E1

Design size: 35½x23mm
Photo of wash drawing of frame design with numerals, CENT and POST OFFICE CLERK in black ink, vignette in black wash. Ms. "Changed from 15c" and "Approved Nov. 15, 1912 — Frank H. Hitchcock — Postmaster General" on backing card.

Q1-E1 1c Model on thick gray card, 106x91mm, black *5,500.*

Q2-E1

Design size: 35x23½mm
Photo of wash drawing of frame only as adopted. Ms. "Approved Oct. 10, 1912, for border and size of stamps. Engraving to be ⅞ by 1⅜ inches. Frank H. Hitchcock. Postmaster General" on backing card.

Q2-E1 2c Model on thick gray cardboard, 122x110mm, black *3,500.*

Q2-E2

Design size: 35x23mm
Photo of wash drawing of frame design and retouched photo of ship vignette as eventually used for 10c, numerals and STEAMSHIP AND MAIL TENDER in black ink. Ms. "Changed to 10c" and "Approved Oct. 11, 1912. Frank H. Hitchcock. Postmaster General" on backing card.

Q2-E2 2c Model on thick gray cardboard, 110x83mm, black *8,500.*

Q2-E3

Design size: 34x22mm
Photo of wash drawing of entire design with adopted vignette, numerals in white wash and CITY CARRIER in black ink. Ms. "Changed from 5c" and "Approved Nov. 14, 1912. Frank H. Hitchcock. Postmaster General" on backing card.

Q2-E3 2c Model on thick gray cardboard, 111x92mm, black *7,500.*

Design size: 34½x22mm
Engraving of adopted design with blank value tablets and "CITY CARRIER" inscription, mail carrier unfinished.

Q2-E4 2c Die on India, sunk on 118x89mm card, black —

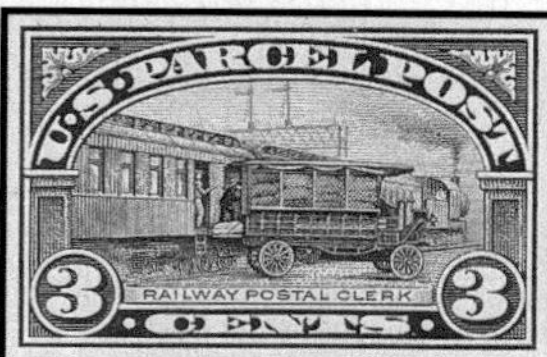

Q3-E1

Design size: 35x23mm
Complete engraving of unadopted design: vignette shows mail truck backing up to railroad mail train with clerk about to handle pouches.

Q3-E1 3c Die on white wove, about 43x31mm, carmine *5,000.*

Q3-E2

Design size: 35x22mm
Photo of wash drawing of entire design with adopted vignette (retouched around door to mail car). Ms. "Approved Feb. 22, 1913. Frank H. Hitchcock. Postmaster General" on backing card.

Q3-E2 3c Model on thick gray cardboard, black *5,000.*

Q3-E3

Design size: 35x22mm
Almost complete engraving of adopted design with subtle differences (most evident in shading on windows), on 100x76mm card, affixed with tape to 125x98mm card, small cutout in design, blue control No. 578444 on back.

Q3-E3 3c Die sunk on card, affixed to card, carmine *4,500.*

Q4-E1

Design size: 33½x22mm
Photo of wash drawing of entire design with adopted vignette, numerals drawn in white and RURAL CARRIER in black ink. Ms. "Changed from 10c" and "Approved Nov. 14, 1912. Frank H. Hitchcock. Postmaster General" on backing card.

Q4-E1 4c Model on thick gray cardboard, 116x92mm, black *5,500.*

Q5-E1

Design size: 35x23mm
Photo of wash drawing of entire design with vignette (retouched) eventually used for 2c, numerals and CITY LETTER CARRIER in black ink and white wash. Ms. "Changed to 2c.--City Carrier" and "Approved Oct. 10, 1912. Frank H. Hitchcock. Postmaster General" on backing card.

Q5-E1 5c Model on thick gray cardboard, 110x84mm, black *5,500.*

Q5-E2

Design size: 33½x21½mm
Photo of wash drawing of entire design with numerals in gray, unadopted vignette with MAIL TRAIN in black ink, first car retouched with wash. Ms. "Approved . . . 1912 / . . . Postmaster General" on backing card.

Q5-E2 5c Model on thick gray cardboard, 104½x92mm, black *2,750.*

Q5-E3

Design size: 33½x22mm

Photo of wash drawing of entire design with numerals in gray, MAIL TRAIN in black ink, first car retouched with wash. Ms. "Approved . . . 1912 / . . . Postmaster General" on backing card.

Q5-E3 5c Model on thick gray cardboard, 104½x92mm, black *5,500.*

Q5-E4

Design size: 33½x22mm
Photo of wash drawing of entire design with numerals in white with black background, MAIL TRAIN and pouch catcher in black ink. Ms. "Approved Nov. 19, 1912 Frank H. Hitchcock Postmaster General" on backing card.

Q5-E4 5c Model on thick gray cardboard, 94x90mm, black *2,250.*

Q5-E5

Design size: 26x16mm
Complete engraving of accepted vignette (smoke from engine reworked from previous essays).

Q5-E5 5c Die on India, die sunk on card, carmine —

Q6-E1

Design size: 35½x23mm
Photo of wash drawing of entire design with vignette (retouched) eventually used for 4c, numerals and RURAL DELIVERY in black ink and white wash. Ms. "Changed to 4c." and "Approved Oct. 10, 1912. Frank H. Hitchcock. Postmaster General" on backing card.

Q6-E1 10c Model on thick gray cardboard, 111x83mm, black *2,500.*

Q6-E2

Design size: 35x23mm
Photo of wash drawing of entire design with adopted vignette, numerals and STEAMSHIP AND MAIL TENDER in black ink and white wash. Ms. "Changed from 2c." and "Approved Nov. 8, 1912. Frank H. Hitchcock. Postmaster General" on backing card.

Q6-E2 10c Model on thick gray cardboard, 116x92mm, black *2,500.*

Q7-E1

Design size: 33½x22mm
Photo of wash drawing of entire design (redrawn in front of autocar and U S MAIL and STATION A) with AUTOMOBILE SERVICE in black ink. Ms. "Approved . . . 1912 / . . . Postmaster General" on backing card.

Q7-E1 15c Model on thick gray cardboard, 115x93mm, black *1,500.*

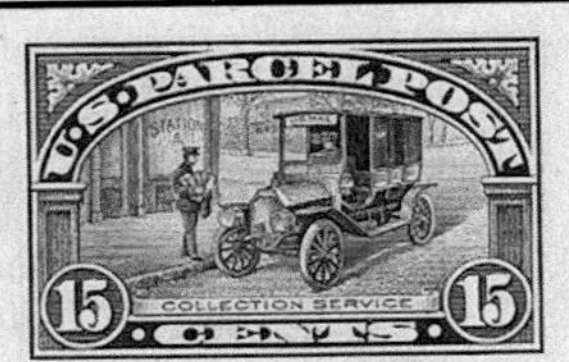

Q7-E2

Design size:
Complete engraving of entire design with unadopted title label "COLLECTION SERVICE" instead of the adopted "AUTOMOBILE SERVICE."

Q7-E2 15c Die on white wove, card mounted, carmine *1,500.*

Q8-E1

Design size: 35x22mm
Incomplete engraved design nearly as adopted: aviator wears football helmet, head tilted far forward and one leg dangling over edge of plane, mail bag "No. 1" at his right while another sack hangs loosely out of plane.

Q8-E1 20c Die on white wove, about 37x24mm, carmine *1,500.*

Q8-E2

Design size: 35x22mm
Photo of incomplete engraved design as adopted. Ms. "Approved Nov. 19, 1912. Frank H. Hitchcock. Postmaster General" on backing card.

Q8-E2 20c Model on thick gray cardboard, 98x95mm, black *2,500.*

Q9-E1

Design size: 34½x22½mm
Photo of wash drawing of entire design with numerals and smoke at right painted in. Ms. "Changed from $1.00." and "Approved Nov. 14, 1912. Frank H. Hitchcock. Postmaster General" on backing card.

Q9-E1 25c Model on thick gray cardboard, 112x92mm, black *2,500.*

Q10-E1

Design size: 35x23mm
Photo of drawing of entire design with vignette eventually used for 25c with roof, smokestacks and smoke drawn in. Typed label "Stamp Division / Feb / 21 / 1912 / P.O. Dept" on back of backing paper.

Q10-E1 50c Model on thick white paper, black *1,500.*

Q10-E2

Design size: 33x21½mm
Photo of wash drawing of frame design with vignette cut out, mounted over photo of wash drawing of unadopted vignette design, retouched with wash on cows, etc., with DAIRYING in black ink. Pencil "Original" and ms. "Approved . . . 1912 / . . . Postmaster General" on backing card.

Q10-E2 50c Model on thick gray cardboard, 98x93mm, black *1,500.*

Q10-E3

Design size: 35x23mm
Complete engraving of entire design with unadopted vignette: silo and barns placed closer to front of design.

Q10-E3 50c Die on white wove, about 43x31mm, carmine *3,000.*

Q10-E4

Design size: 35x22mm
Photo of incomplete engraved design: no vert. lines on frame around corner foliate spandrels or in numeral circles. Ms. "Approved Jan. 8, 1913. Frank H. Hitchcock. Postmaster General" on backing card.

Q10-E4 50c Model on thick gray cardboard, 99x94mm, black *5,500.*

Q11-E1

Design size: 33½x21½mm
Photo of wash drawing of entire design with central horses and thresher retouched. Ms. "Approved Dec. 12, 1912. Frank H. Hitchcock. Postmaster General" on backing card.

Q11-E1 75c Model on thick gray cardboard, 108x89mm, black *5,250.*

Q12-E1

Photo of wash drawing of entire design with vignette much retouched in black ink, numerals, MANUFACTURING and DOLLAR drawn in black ink and white wash. Ms. "Changed to 25c" and "Approved Oct. 22, 1912. Frank H. Hitchcock. Postmaster General" on backing card.

Q12-E1 $1 Model on thick gray cardboard, 114x86mm, black *5,250.*

Q12-E2

Design size: 35x22mm
Photo of wash drawing of complete design with DOLLAR painted in white and black and FRUIT GROWING in black ink, vignette retouched with wash on fruit pickers. Ms. "Approved . . . 1912 . . . Postmaster General" on backing card.

Q12-E2 $1 Model on thick gray cardboard, 105x94mm, black *5,500.*

Q12-E3

Design size: 36x23½mm
Incomplete engraving of entire design: no shading lines in sky. This may be from a rejected die.

Q12-E3 $1 Die on white wove, about 43x31mm, carmine *4,000.*

Q12a-E1

Engraving of entire design as adopted for 1917 offset Documentary Revenues, etc., but with "U.S. PARCEL POST" around value oval.

Q12a-E1	1c Die on card, green	*1,500.*
Q12b-E1	2c Die on card, carmine	*1,500.*
Q12c-E1	3c Die on card, deep violet	*1,500.*
Q12d-E1	4c Die on card, brown	*1,500.*
Q12e-E1	5c Die on card, blue	*1,500.*
Q12f-E1	10c Die on card, orange yellow	*1,500.*
Q12g-E1	15c Die on card, gray	*1,500.*
Q12h-E1	20c Die on wove, carmine rose, affixed to card	*1,500.*

PARCEL POST POSTAGE DUE

Retouched photo of design as adopted, officially dated and approved.

QJQ5-E1a 25c Model, black *1,500.*

CARRIER'S STAMPS

Essays by Toppan, Carpenter, Casilear & Co. in 1851

LO1-E1

Die size: 55x50mm
Unfinished die with outer border in a very incomplete state, pencil "For U.S. Carriers Stamp, Vignette 1851, Toppan, Carpenter Casilier & Co."

1851
LO1-E1 (1c) Die on India, die sunk on 96x76mm card, which is mounted on 101x82mm card, black *9,000.*

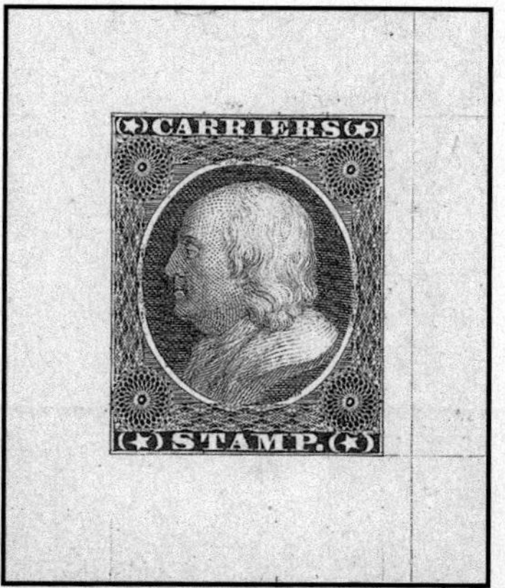
LO1-E1Ab

LO1-E1Ac

LO1-E1Ad

Die size: 57x50mm
Unfinished die with framelines complete at top and bottom, lathework impinging on white oval and rosettes in lower right corner, plus uncleaned horizontal and vertical layout lines.

LO1-E1A (1c)
b. Die on 34x42mm, white bond, black *11,000.*
c. Die on 60x50mm old ivory paper, die sunk, black *11,000.*
d. Die on 62x54mm, pale green bond, red *7,500.*

Essays by Schernikow in 1903 from a new soft steel die made from the original 1851 transfer roll.

LO1-E2

Die size: 50x50mm
Engraving of Franklin vignette only.

1903
LO1-E2 (1c)
a. Die on proof paper

black	*75.*
carmine	*75.*
red	*75.*
light red	*75.*
orange	*75.*
orange brown	*75.*
yellow	*75.*
olive	*75.*
green	*75.*
dark green	*75.*
dark blue	*75.*
violet	*75.*
violet brown	*75.*

b. Die on colored card, about 75x75mm

deep red, *pinkish white*	*175.*
yellow brown, *pale blue*	*175.*
violet brown, *pale green*	*175.*
dark green, *pale pink*	*175.*
dark blue, *pale pink*	*175.*
violet, *pale yellow*	*175.*

c. Die on green bond (die size: 49x50mm)

dull scarlet	*175.*
dull olive	*175.*
dark ultramarine	*175.*

See note above No. 63-E1.

LO1-E3

Design size: 19½x25mm
Die size: 50x50mm
Design as No. LO1-E1, but distinguished by addition of left and right inner frame lines.

1903
LO1-E3 (1c)
a. Die on proof paper

black	*100.*
carmine	*100.*
dark carmine	*100.*
scarlet	*100.*
orange	*100.*
yellow	*100.*
yellow brown	*100.*
olive	*100.*
light green	*100.*
green	*100.*
steel blue	*100.*
violet	*100.*
red violet	*100.*
violet brown	*100.*
ultramarine	*100.*

b. Die on colored card

dull carmine, *pale olive*	*175.*
brown orange, *pink*	*175.*
brown, *pale buff*	*175.*
brown, *pale blue*	*175.*
gray green, *buff*	*175.*
gray green, *yellow*	*175.*
violet, *ivory*	*175.*
dull carmine, *pale blue*	*175.*

c. Die on blue pelure

carmine	*200.*
scarlet	*200.*
orange	*200.*
brown	*200.*
dark green	*200.*

d. Die on green bond

scarlet	*250.*
orange	*250.*
green	*250.*
dull violet	*250.*

e. Die on gummed thick rose paper, cut to stamp size 6,500.

Essays by Clarence Brazer in 1952 using the Schernikow complete die with addition of two diagonal lines in upper right corner.

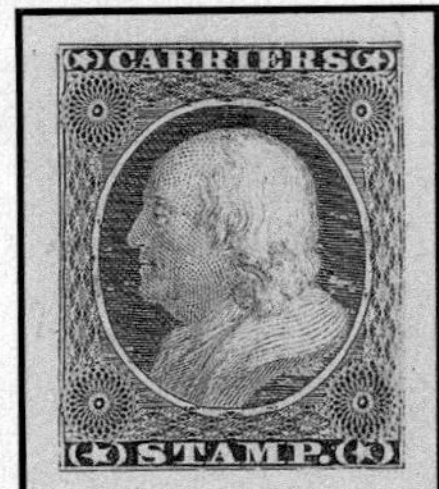

LO1-E4

Die size: 50x50mm

1952

LO1-E4 (1c) Die on approximately 121x125mm glazed card

scarlet	*650.*
brown	*650.*
green	*650.*
red	*650.*

POST OFFICE SEALS

Registry Seals
1872 ISSUE
National Bank Note Co.

OXF1-E1

Design size: 72x40mm
Block size: 100x56½mm

Design cut on a steel block intended for printing by typography from electrotyped clichés. The design is similar to the adopted design except REGISTERED obliterates other words where it touches them. Apparently only one essay block was made and was not itself altered to produce the die with the adopted image from which electrotypes were made for printing. Accordingly, it is likely that a significant proportion of the impressions from the essay die were made subsequent to the pre-production period. Listed in each category are ink colors that have been seen and are known to be from the essay die; others may exist.

The image for OXF1-E1 was pulled from the essay die as if it were a die for intaglio printing. Accordingly, where the image was intended to print in color, this image is clear; and where the image was intended to print clear, this image is colored. Depsite its appearance, it is from the same die as all OXF1 essays.

OXF1-E1

a. Die on card

chocolate	*1,500.*
black	*1,500.*

OXF1-E2

"Colorless borders." The image was pulled from the essay die as if it were for typographic printing, and the ink from the non-image portion of the die was wiped clean before printing. The images printed on card are often, but not always, on India paper impressed on the card. The images on other surfaces do not use India paper and usually do not show the die block impression.

OXF1-E2

a. Die on card

green	*1,000.*
carmine (rose)	*1,000.*
red brown	*1,000.*
orange	*1,000.*
orange brown	*1,000.*
yellow	*1,000.*
blue	*1,000.*
blue (left), green (right)	*1,200.*

b. Die on India

blue	*1,000.*
lavender	*1,000.*

c. Die on bond weight paper

green	*1,000.*
blue	*1,000.*

d. Die on glossy paper or thin card

green	*1,000.*

OXF1-E3

"Colored borders." As No. OXf1-E2 except that the non-image portion of the die was not wiped clean before printing. The colored border area is found both completely and partially colored. Most impressions on card do not use India paper.

OXF1-E3

a. Die on card

green	*1,000.*
rose	*1,000.*
blue	*1,000.*
violet	*1,000.*
brown	*1,000.*

b. Die on India

green	*1,000.*
red	*1,000.*
rose	*1,000.*
orange brown	*1,000.*
yellow	*1,000.*
blue	*1,000.*
violet	*1,000.*

c. Die on bond weight paper

blue	*1,000.*

d. Die on glossy paper or thin card

blue	*1,000.*
brown	*1,000.*

OXF1-E4

As with No. OXF1-E2 except printed on stamp paper, perforated and gummed.

OXF1-E4

a. Die on stamp paper, perf. 12, gummed

blue	*1,000.*
blue (left), green (right)	*1,200.*

Block size: 80x128mm

Engraving of entire design as adopted but in reverse for making typographed block.

OXF1-E5 Die on white wove, chocolate *1,000.*

Post Office Seals
1877 ISSUE

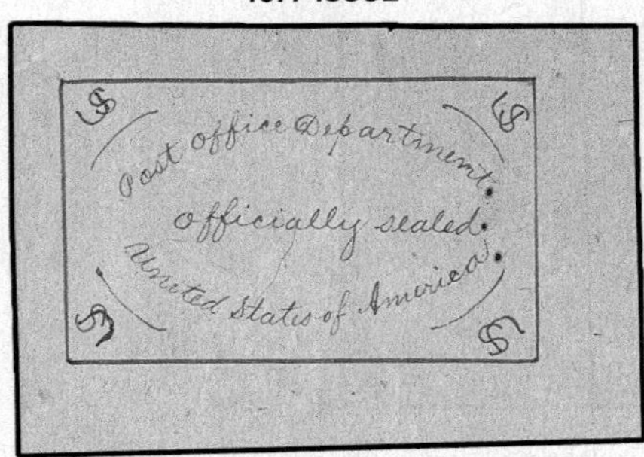

OX1-E1

Preliminary pen and ink concept design on thick light brown paper. Image size: 44x27mm.

OX1-E1 Black *5,500.*

Value based on 2011 auction realization.

OX1-E2

Design size: 44x27mm

Composite model built up from card proofs of intermediate dies; "Post Obitum," the vignette, and the National Bank Note Company imprint cut out and pasted to card. Hand drawn and water-color additions of frame and lettering, Dated Febry 21, 1877 and signed by "Thos. F. Morris" the designer.

OX1-E2 Brown *5,500.*

Value based on 2011 auction realization.

OX1-E3

Design size: 44x27mm

Progressive die essay on India paper on card. Incomplete engraving of entire design with vignette lacking the cap and background, and border lacking the vertical shading lines (probalby unique).

OX1-E3 Brown *1,250.*

OX1-E4

Design size: 44x27mm.

Progressive die essay on India paper. Lacking the vertical shading lines in the border (probably unique).

OX1-E4 Brown *1,000.*

1861 FIRST DESIGN ESSAYS AND TRIAL COLOR PROOFS

For the convenience of collectors and dealers, the Scott editors present here in one location the important 1861 First Design Essays and Trial Color Proofs. The final "stamps" produced with these designs or colors were at one time listed in the Postage section as Nos. 55-57 and 59-62. These so-called "August" issues or "Premiere Gravure" issues, printed on thin and semitransparent stamp paper, gummed and perforated, were not issued as prepared, but were either engraved further to complete the issued designs (1c, 3c, 5c, 12c and 90c) or issued in slightly revised colors (24c and 30c), and they were therefore appropriately moved to the Essay and Trial Color Proof sections of the U.S. Specialized catalogue in 1991.

The 10c denomination of this First Design series, previously No. 58, was pressed into service as an issued stamp, No. 62B, presumably because the demand for this denomination was greater than could be supplied by the plate or plates in use. Former No. 58 and current No. 62B are the same stamp, and it is listed in the Postage section as No. 62B.

The listings here duplicate the listings in the Essay and Trial Color Proof sections rather than replace them. Their listing here is for the convenience of catalogue users only.

Without Dash Below UL Ornament

Die size: 58x56mm
"Premiere Gravure" die No. 440. No dash under the right tip of the ornament at right of the numeral in upper left corner.

63-E11 1c
- *a.* "Premiere Gravure" die essay on India (**formerly Nos. 55P1, 55TC1**)
  - black *4,000.*
  - indigo *1,500.*
  - ultramarine *2,250.*
- *b.* RA "Premiere Gravure" small die essay on white wove, 28x31mm (**formerly No. 55P2**), indigo *325.*
- *c.* "Premiere Gravure" plate essay on India (**formerly Nos. 55P3, 55TC3**)
  - indigo *300.*
  - blue —
  - ultramarine *300.*
  - violet ultramarine —
- *d.* "Premiere Gravure" plate essay on semitransparent stamp paper (**formerly No. 55TC4**), ultramarine *400.*

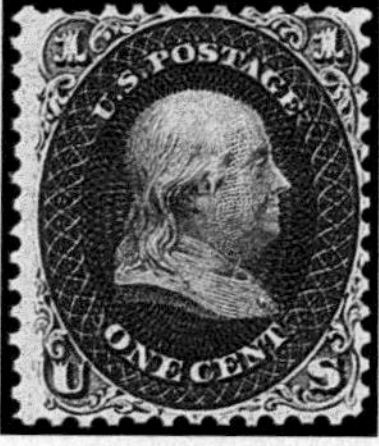
63-E11e

63-E11e 1c **indigo,** finished "Premiere Gravure" plate essay on semitransparent stamp paper, gummed, perf. 12 **(formerly No. 55)** *50,000.*

No. 63-E11e is valued with perfs cutting slightly into design at top.

Without Corner Ornaments

65-E11

Die size: 64x76 ½mm
Incomplete engraving of Washington head only.

65-E11 3c
- *a.* Die on India, on card, carmine *750.*
- *b.* Die on white glazed paper
  - black *750.*
  - scarlet *750.*
  - brown violet *750.*

65-E12

Die size: 78x55mm
Incomplete engraved design, no scrolls outside framelines, no silhouette under chin, no ornaments on 3s, U and S.

65-E12 3c Die on India, die sunk on card
- black *1,000.*
- blue *1,000.*

65-E13

As No. 65-E12 but ornaments on 3s, U and S. Shows traces of first border design erased. With imprint and No. 441 below design.

65-E13 3c Die on India, card mounted
- scarlet *1,000.*
- brown red *1,000.*
- ultramarine *1,000.*

65-E14

Die size: 59x55mm
As No. 65-E13 but with ornaments outside frame.

65-E14 3c Die on India, die sunk on card
- black *750.*
- scarlet *750.*
- pink *1,250.*
- brown orange *750.*
- deep orange red *750.*
- deep red *750.*

"Premiere Gravure" design; no corner ornaments. No imprint or die number on die impression.

65-E15 3c
- *a.* Die on India, card mounted, deep orange red *1,000.*
- *b.* "Premiere Gravure" die essay on semitransparent stamp paper, 20x25mm-30x37mm
  - deep orange red *750.*
  - deep red orange *750.*
  - dim red *750.*
  - dim deep red *750.*
  - dim orange red *750.*
  - dull pink *750.*
  - dull violet red *750.*
- *c.* "Premiere Gravure" die essay on India (**formerly Nos. 56P1, 56TC1**)
  - red *1,350.*
  - black *2,000.*
  - scarlet *2,000.*
  - pink *2,850.*
  - orange red *2,000.*
  - dark orange red *2,000.*
- *d.* RA Small die essay on white wove, 28x31mm altered laydown die of complete design but with outer scrolls removed and replaced by ones similar to "Premiere Gravure" design (1903) (**formerly No. 56P2**), dim deep red *325.*
- *e.* As "c," PP small die essay on pale cream soft wove, 24x29mm (1915) (**formerly No. 56P2a**), deep red *1,250.*
- *f.* "Premiere Gravure" plate No. 2 essay on India (**formerly Nos. 56P3, 56TC3**)
  - red *250.*
  - scarlet *350.*
- *g.* "Premiere Gravure" plate essay on semitransparent stamp paper (**formerly Nos. 56aP4, 56TC4**)
  - red, pair with gum *1,750.*
  - black *400.*

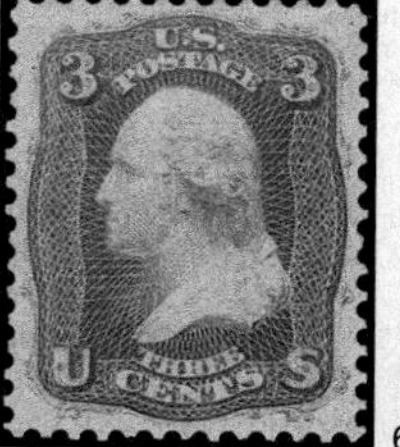
65-E15h

65-E15h 3c **brown rose,** finished "Premiere Gravure" plate essay on semitransparent stamp paper, gummed, perf. 12 **(formerly No. 56)** *550.*
- orange red *475.*
- bright orange red *475.*
- dark orange red *475.*
- dim deep red *475.*
- pink *475.*
- deep pink *475.*
- P# block of 8, Impt. (any shade) *20,000.*

No Leaflets at Corners

67-E8

Incomplete impression from die No. 442, border lines and corner scrolls missing.

67-E8 5c Die on India, mounted on 34x50mm card, black *1,750.*

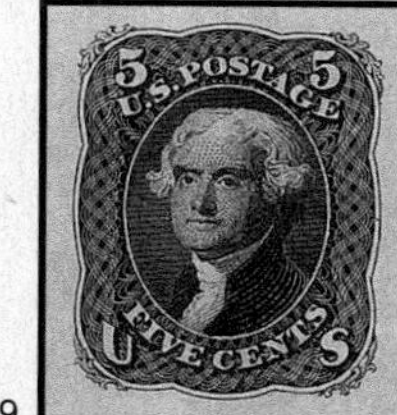
67-E9

Size of die: 58x59mm
"Premiere Gravure" design, with corner scrolls but without leaflets.

67-E9 5c
- *a.* "Premiere Gravure" die essay on India, card mounted (formerly No. 57TC1)
  - black *2,500.*
  - scarlet *2,500.*
- *b.* RA Small die essay on white wove, 28x31mm, altered laydown die of complete design but with scrolls removed from corners to resemble "Premiere Gravure" (1903) (**formerly No. 57P2), brown** 325.
- *c.* As "b," PP die essay on pale cream soft wove, 24x29mm (1915) (**formerly No. 57P2a**), brown *1,750.*

d. "Premiere Gravure" plate No. 3 essay on India (**formerly Nos. 57P3, 57TC3)**

brown	*250.*
light brown	*300.*
dark brown	*300.*
red brown	*300.*

67-E9e

67-E9e 5c **brown,** finished "Premiere Gravure" plate essay on semitransparent stamp paper, gummed, perf. 12 **(formerly No. 57)** *30,000.*

No. 67-E9e is valued with small faults, as all recorded original-gum examples come thus.

One example of No. 67-E9e is known used. It has small faults and a circular datestamp in black.

Without Corner Ornaments

69-E5

Design size: 12½x16mm
Die size: about 62x65mm
Washington vignette only.

69-E5 12c

a. Die on India, die sunk on card

black	*400.*
dark red	*400.*
orange red	*400.*

b. Die on ivory paper, about 24x28mm

black	*500.*
scarlet	*500.*
black brown	*500.*
blue	*500.*

Incomplete die No. 444, without corner ornaments.

69-E6 12c

a. "Premiere Gravure" die essay on India, mounted on card (**formerly Nos. 59P1, 59TC1)**

black	*2,500.*
scarlet	*2,500.*
dark green	*2,500.*

b. RA "Premiere Gravure" small die essay on white wove, 28x31mm (1903) (**formerly No. 59P2**), black *450.*

c. PP "Premiere Gravure" small die essay on pale cream soft wove, 24x29mm (1915) (**formerly No. 59P2a**), black *1,750.*

d. "Premiere Gravure" plate No. 5 essay on India (**formerly No. 59P3**), black *350.*

69-E6e

69-E6e 12c **black,** finished "Premiere Gravure" plate essay on semitransparent stamp paper, gummed, perf. 12 **(formerly No. 59)** *90,000.*

70TC6

No. 70TC6 differs from the issued 1861 24c stamps by its color.

70TC6 24c **dark violet,** finished "Premier Gravure" trial color plate proof on semitransparent stamp paper, gummed, perf. 12 **(formerly No. 60)** *15,000.*

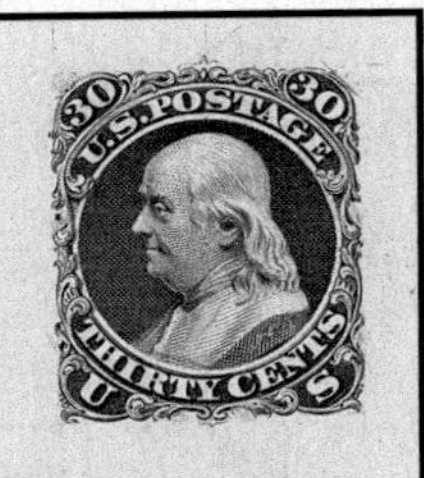

71-E1

Die size: 46x60mm
Incomplete die (No. 446): additional ornaments at top and bottom in pencil, as later engraved.

71-E1 30c Die on India, black *1,750.*

71-E2

"Premiere Gravure" die: left side of frame and silhouette at lower right unfinished.

71-E2 30c

a. "Premiere Gravure" die essay on India, die sunk on card (**formerly No. 61TC1)**

black	*1,750.*
green	*1,750.*
dull gray blue	*1,750.*
violet brown	*1,750.*
scarlet	*1,750.*
dull rose	*1,750.*

b. "Premiere Gravure" plate essay on India (**formerly No. 61P3**), deep red orange *500.*

c. "Premiere Gravure" plate essay on card

black (split thin)	*500.*
blue	*750.*

d. "Premiere Gravure" plate essay on card, black 12x2mm SPECIMEN overprint, blue *750.*

e. "Premiere Gravure" plate essay on semitransparent stamp paper

deep red orange	*1,250.*
yellow orange	*1,250.*
lemon yellow	*1,250.*
dark orange yellow	*1,250.*
dull orange yellow	*1,250.*

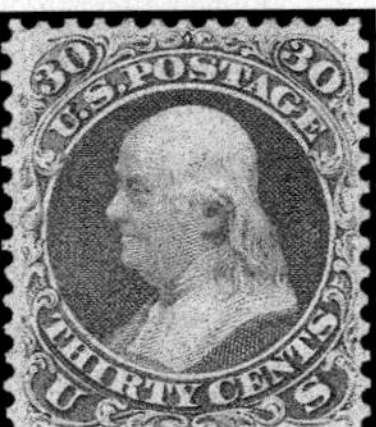

71TC6

No. 71TC6 differs from the issued 1861 30c stamp primarily by its color.

71TC6 30c **red orange,** finished "Premier Gravure" trial color plate proof on semitransparent stamp paper, gummed, perf. 12 **(formerly No. 61)** *40,000.*

No. 71TC6 is valued in the grade of fine.

One example of No. 71TC6 is known used. It has a small repair and is canceled with a quartered cork canel in black.

No Dashes Between the Parallel Angled Lines Above Top Ribbon; No Point of Color at Apex of Lower Angled Line

72-E6

Die size: 54x63mm
Incomplete die: without thin lines at bottom of frame and in upper left triangle between label and frame, and without leaves at left of U and right of S.

72-E6 90c Die on India, blue (shades) *1,000.*

72-E7

Similar to 72-E6 but lines added in upper left triangle, leaves added at left of U and at right of S. Exists with and without imprint and Die No. 447 added below design.

72-E7 90c

a. Die on India, die sunk on card, black *1,750.*

b. "Premiere Gravure" die essay on India, thin line under bottom center frame (**formerly Nos. 62P1, 62TC1)**

blue	*1,350.*
black	*1,750.*

c. RA "Premiere Gravure" small die essay on white wove, 28x31mm (1903) (**formerly No. 62P2**), blue *500.*

d. PP "Premiere Gravure" small die essay on pale cream soft wove, 24x29mm (1915) (**formerly No. 62P2a**), blue *1,750.*

e. "Premiere Gravure" plate essay on India, blue *500.*

f. "Premiere Gravure" plate essay on card, black (split thin) *500.*

g. "Premiere Gravure" plate essay on semitransparent stamp paper (**formerly Nos. 62aP4, 62TC4)**

blue, pair, gummed	*5,500.*
blue green	*275.*

72-E7h

72-E7h 90c **blue,** finished "Premiere Gravure" plate essay on semitransparent stamp paper, gummed, perf. 12 **(formerly No. 62)** *50,000.*

Die size: 54x63mm
Similar to Nos. 72-E6 and 72-E7 but leaf at left of "U" only, no shading around "U" and "S," leaf and some shading missing at bottom right above "S," shading missing in top label, etc., faint ms. "8" at bottom of backing card.

72-E8 90c Die on India, die sunk on 3¼x3½-inch card, dark blue —

2018 Scott Specialty Series Supplement Releases

Start collecting a new country today! Take a look at any of the newly released 2018 Scott Specialty Series and the many different countries that are available. Make sure you don't forget to pick up a classic, durable 3-ring or 2-post binder and slipcase to house your collection.

ASIA

Item#	Country	Retail	AA	Release
275HK18	Hong Kong	$22.99	$19.99	June
618S018	India	$22.99	$19.99	July
510S018	Japan	$45.99	$39.99	July
520S018	People's Republic of China	$22.99	$19.99	July
530S018	Republic of China Taiwan	$22.99	$19.99	July
275SG18	Singapore	$22.99	$19.99	September
622S018	Sri Lanka	$19.99	$16.99	July
540S018	Thailand	$22.99	$19.99	July

NORTH AMERICA

Item#	Country	Retail	AA	Release
170S018	American	$34.99	$29.99	March
240S018	Canada	$25.99	$21.99	May
245S018	Master Canada	$28.99	$24.99	May
430S018	Mexico	$19.99	$16.99	September

EASTERN EUROPE

Item#	Country	Retail	AA	Release
361S018	Baltic States	$19.99	$16.99	August
307S018	Czech Republic & Slovakia	$22.99	$19.99	August
323S018	Hungary	$22.99	$19.99	August
338S018	Poland	$19.99	$16.99	August
360S018	Russia	$34.99	$29.99	September
362UK18	Ukraine	$19.99	$16.99	September

WESTERN EUROPE

Item#	Country	Retail	AA	Release
300S018	Austria	$19.99	$16.99	May
303S018	Belgium	$22.99	$19.99	August
203CY18	Cyprus	$11.99	$9.99	May
345DM18	Denmark	$16.99	$13.99	June
345FI18	Faroe Islands	$11.99	$9.99	June
345FN18	Finland/Aland	$22.99	$19.99	June
310S018	France	$34.99	$29.99	May
626S018	French Southern & Antarctic Territory	$16.99	$13.99	August
315S318	Germany	$16.99	$13.99	May
320S018	Greece	$22.99	$19.99	June
345GR18	Greenland	$16.99	$13.99	June
345IC18	Iceland	$11.99	$9.99	June
201S018	Ireland	$16.99	$13.99	June
325S018	Italy	$22.99	$19.99	September
367S018	Liechtenstein	$11.99	$9.99	June
330S018	Luxembourg	$11.99	$9.99	August
203ML18	Malta	$16.99	$13.99	May
333S018	Monaco & French Andorra	$19.99	$16.99	May
335S018	Netherlands	$40.99	$34.99	August
345NR18	Norway	$11.99	$9.99	June
340S018	Portugal/Azores/Maderia	$22.99	$19.99	September
328S018	San Marino	$11.99	$9.99	July
355S018	Spain & Spanish Andorra	$22.99	$19.99	July
345SW18	Sweden	$16.99	$13.99	September
365S018	Switzerland	$16.99	$13.99	June
375S018	Vatican City	$11.99	$9.99	July

OCEANIA

Item#	Country	Retail	AA	Release
210S018	Australia	$22.99	$19.99	September
211S018	Dependencies of Australia	$22.99	$19.99	September
221S018	Dependencies of New Zealand	$34.99	$29.99	September
625S018	French Polynesia	$11.99	$9.99	August
220S018	New Zealand	$22.99	$19.99	September

UNITED KINGDOM

Item#	Country	Retail	AA	Release
203GB18	Gibraltar	$16.99	$13.99	May
200S018	Great Britain	$22.99	$19.99	May
202GN18	Guernsey & Alderney	$22.99	$19.99	May
202IM18	Isle of Man	$22.99	$19.99	May
202JR18	Jersey	$22.99	$19.99	May
200M018	Great Britain Machins	$9.99	$8.49	July

SOUTH AMERICA

Item#	Country	Retail	AA	Release
642S018	Argentina	$19.99	$16.99	September
644S018	Brazil	$19.99	$16.99	May

CARRIBEAN

Item#	Country	Retail	AA	Release
648S018	Dominican Republic	$16.99	$13.99	September

MIDDLE EAST

Item#	Country	Retail	AA	Release
500S018	Israel Singles	$13.99	$11.89	August
501S018	Israel Tab Singles	$13.99	$11.89	August
505S018	Turkey	$22.99	$19.99	August

SCOTT BINDERS & SLIPCASES

Item#		Retail	AA
ACBR03SET	Large Green 3-Ring, Metal-Hinged, Binder & Slipcase	$79.49	$55.78
ACBR01SET	Small Green 3-Ring, Metal-Hinged, Binder & Slipcase	$79.49	$55.78
ACBS03SET	Large Green Square 2-Post Binder & Slipcase	$92.49	$66.58
ACBUSET	Green Universal Binder & Slipcase (Fit any Scott Album)	$77.49	$53.98

See the Full List of 2018 Scott Supplements at

www.AmosAdvantage.com

or Call 800-572-6885

Outside U.S. & Canada call (937) 498-0800

Ordering Information: *AA prices apply to paid subscribers of Amos Media titles, or for orders placed online. Prices, terms and product availability subject to change. Shipping & Handling: U.S.: Orders total $0-$10.00 charged $3.99 shipping. U.S. Order total $10.01-$79.99 charged $7.99 shipping. U.S. Order total $80.00 or more charged 10% of order total for shipping. Taxes will apply in CA, OH, & IL. Canada: 20% of order total. Minimum charge $19.99 Maximum charge $200.00. Foreign orders are shipped via FedEx Intl. or USPS and billed actual freight.

TRIAL COLOR, DIE AND PLATE PROOFS

PROOFS are known in many styles other than those noted in this section. For the present, however, listings are restricted to die proofs, large and small, and plate proofs on India paper and card, and occasionally on stamp paper or other types of paper. The listing of normal color proofs includes several that differ somewhat from the types and colors of the issued stamps.

Proofs in other than accepted or approved colors exist in a large variety of shades, colors and papers produced at various times by various people for many different reasons. The field is large. Trial Color Proofs are also listed as die proofs, large and small, and plate proofs on a variety of papers. The listings of Trial Color Proofs also include several that are similar to the colors of the issued stamps.

Some Trial Color Proofs are listed out of sequence. Nos. 156TC2-166TC2, the so-called "Goodall" Small Die Proofs in five colors, follow No. 166P4. Nos. O1TC2-O93TC2, another set of "Goodall" Small Die Proofs, follow No. O123P2a. The last set of "Goodall" Small Die Proofs, Nos. PR9TC2-PR32TC2, follow No. PR113P2a. The "Atlanta" set of Plate Proofs in five colors, Nos. 3TC4-LO2TC4, are listed after QE4aP1.

Large Die Proofs are so termed because of the relatively large piece of paper on which they are printed which is about the size of the die block, 40mm by 50mm or larger. The margins of this group of proofs usually are from 15mm to 20mm in width though abnormal examples prevent the acceptance of these measurements as a complete means of identification.

These proofs were prepared in most cases by the original contracting companies and 19th century issues often show the imprint thereof and letters and numbers of identification. They are listed under Large die (P1). The India paper on which these proofs are printed is of an uneven texture and in some respects resembles hand-made paper. These large die proofs were usually mounted on cards though many are found removed from the card. Large Die Proofs autographed by the engraver or officially approved are worth much more, except for those of the 1922-29 period, which are generally approved and signed proofs.

Values for Large Die Proofs are for the full die proofs mounted on cards unless noted otherwise. Full large die proofs measure 5-6" x 7-8". Cut-down Large Die Proofs sell for less. Values for die proofs of the bicolored 1869 issue are for examples which are completely printed. Occasionally the vignette has been cut out and affixed to an impression of the border.

Die Proofs of all United States stamps of later issues exist. Only those known outside of government ownership are listed.

Hybrids are plate proofs of all issues before 1894, and some from 1989-95, which have been cut to shape, mounted and pressed on large cards to resemble large die proofs. These sell for somewhat less than the corresponding large die proofs.

Small Die Proofs are so called because of the small piece of paper on which they are printed. Proofs of stamps issued prior to 1904 are reprints and not in all cases from the same dies as the large die proofs.

Small Die Proofs (Roosevelt Album, Small die (P2)) — These 302 small die proofs are from sets prepared for 85 ("Roosevelt presentation") albums in 1903 by the Bureau of Engraving and Printing but bear no imprint to this effect. The white wove paper on which they are printed is of a fibrous nature. The margins are small, seldom being more than from 3-5mm in width. Values are for proofs affixed to the original gray card backing from the Roosevelt album. Proofs without the card backing sell for less. Small die proofs from the 1903 Roosevelt albums have "RA" as part of the listing description. Small die proofs before 1904 that do not have "RA" as part of the listing description are not from the 1903 Roosevelt albums.

Small Die Proofs (Panama-Pacific Issue, Small die (P2a)) — A special printing of 413 different small die proofs was made in 1915 for the Panama-Pacific Exposition. These have small margins (2½-3mm) and are on soft yellowish wove paper. They are extremely scarce as only 3-5 of each are known and a few exist only in this special printing. 6-10 exist of No. E6 in two slightly different colors. Panama-Pacific small die proofs have "PP" as part of the listing description.

Plate Proofs are, quite obviously, impressions taken from finished plates and differ from the stamps themselves chiefly in their excellence of impression and the paper on which they are printed. Some of the colors vary.

India Paper is a thin, soft, opaque paper which wrinkles when wet. It varies in thickness and shows particles of bamboo.

Card is a plain, clear white card of good quality, which is found in varying thicknesses for different printings. Plate proofs on card were made in five printings in 1879-94. Quantities range from 500 to 3,200 of the card proofs listed between Scott 3P and 245P.

Margin blocks with full imprint and plate number are indicated by the abbreviation "P# blk. of -."

Numbers have been assigned to all proofs consisting of the number of the regular stamp with the suffix letters "TC" to denote Trial Color or "P" to denote Proof.

Some proofs are not identical to the issued stamps. Some of these are now listed in the Essay section. Others have been left in the proof section to keep sets together at this time.

Values are for items in very fine condition. Most "Panama-Pacific" small die proofs are toned. Values are for moderately toned examples. **Plate proof pairs on stamp paper are valued with original gum unless otherwise noted.**

POSTMASTER PROVISIONAL ISSUES

New York

The die proofs are of the No. 9X1 design. All trial color plate proofs and plate proofs in black are from the small sheet of 9. These latter proofs have minutely different design dimensions.

1845

No.	Description	Value
9X1TC2	5c small die on India paper	
b.	**dull dark violet**	300.
c.	**brown violet**	300.
d.	**deep rose violet**	300.
e.	**deep blue**	300.
f.	**dark green**	300.
g.	**orange yellow**	300.
h.	**brown**	300.
9X1TC5	5c plate on bond paper	
a.	**deep blue**	200.
b.	**dk green**	200.
c.	**brown**	200.
d.	**scarlet**	200.

With "Scar" on Neck

No.	Description	Value
9X1TC2	5c small die on India paper	
i.	**dull blue**	175.
j.	**vermilion**	175.

With "Scar" and dot in "P" of "POST"

No.	Description	Value
9X1TC1d	5c large die on thin glazed card	
e.	**deep ultramarine**	450.
f.	**orange vermilion**	450.
g.	**brown black**	450.
9X1TC2	5c small die on India paper	
k.	**dull gray blue**	300.
l.	**deep green**	300.
m.	**dull dark green**	300.
n.	**dark brown red**	300.
o.	**dull dark brown**	300.
p.	**deep blue,** on bond paper	250.
q.	**deep green,** on bond paper	250.
r.	**dull brown red,** on bond paper	250.
s.	**dull dark brown,** on bond paper	250.

Large die trial color proofs with additional impression of the portrait medallion are listed in the Essay section as Nos. 9X1-E1.

No.	Description	Value
9X1P1	5c **black,** large die on India paper	750.
b.	Dot in "P" of "POST" and scar on neck	525.
c.	As "b," on Bond	525.
d.	As "b," on glazed paper	525.
e.	With scar on neck, on Bond	525.
9X1P2	5c **black,** small die on India paper	350.
b.	With scar on neck	300.
c.	Dot in "P" of "POST" and scar on neck	300.
d.	As "b," on Bond	300.
9X1P3	5c **black,** plate on India paper	—
9X1P4	5c As No. 9X1P2c, plate on card	—

The above listed Large Die varieties have an additional impression of the portrait medallion.

No.	Description	Value
9X1P5	5c **black,** plate on bond paper	
a.	Black on white bond	175.
b.	Black on blue bond	150.
	Sheet of 9, either paper	*7,500.*

Providence, R.I.

No.	Description	Value
10X1TC4	5c plate on card	
a.	**gray blue**	250.
b.	**green**	250.
c.	**brown carmine**	250.
d.	**brown**	250.
10X2TC4	10c plate on card	
a.	**gray blue**	450.
b.	**green**	450.
c.	**brown carmine**	450.
d.	**brown**	450.
	Sheet of 12, any color	3,750.
10X1P4	5c **black,** plate on card	300.
10X2P4	10c **black,** plate on card	500.
	Sheet of 12	3,250.

GENERAL ISSUES

1847

No.	Description	Value
1TC1a	5c large die on India paper	
e.	**violet**	1,000.
f.	**dull blue**	1,000.
g.	**blue green**	1,000.
h.	**dull green**	1,000.
i.	**dark green**	1,000.
j.	**orange yellow**	1,000.
k.	**orange vermilion**	1,000.
l.	**scarlet vermilion**	1,000.
m.	**rose lake**	1,000.
n.	**brown red**	1,000.
o.	**black**	1,000.
1TC1b	5c large die on bond paper	
e.	**deep blue**	800.
f.	**dull blue green**	800.
g.	**orange yellow**	800.
h.	**orange vermilion**	800.
i.	**scarlet vermilion**	800.
j.	**black brown**	800.
k.	**black**	800.
1TC1c	5c large die on wove paper	
e.	**deep blue**	800.
f.	**orange yellow**	800.
g.	**deep yellow**	800.
h.	**orange vermilion**	800.
1TC1d	5c large die on thin glazed card	
e.	**deep ultra**	850.
f.	**scarlet vermilion**	850.
g.	**black brown**	850.
h.	**black**	800.
1TC2	5c small die on India paper	
b.	**deep blue**	625.
c.	**blue green**	625.
d.	**dull green,** on bond	600.
e.	**yellow green**	625.
f.	**orange yellow**	625.
g.	**rose lake,** on bond	625.
h.	**dull rose lake,** on bond	625.
i.	**black**	675.
1TC3	5c plate on India paper	
a.	**orange**	600.
b.	**black**	600.
	Double transfer (80R1)	—
	Double transfer (90R1)	—
1P1	5c **red brn,** large die on India paper	800.
a.	White bond paper	800.
b.	Colored bond paper	1,250.
c.	White laid paper	1,000.
d.	Bluish laid paper	800.
e.	Yelsh wove paper	800.
f.	Bluish wove paper	800.
g.	White wove paper	800.
h.	Card	1,000.
i.	Glazed paper	1,000.
1P3	5c **red brn,** plate on India paper	600.
2TC1a	10c large die on India paper	
e.	**violet**	1,000.
f.	**dull blue**	—
g.	**deep blue**	1,000.
h.	**dark green**	1,000.
i.	**orange yellow**	1,000.
j.	**orange vermilion**	1,000.
k.	**golden brown**	1,000.
l.	**light brown**	1,000.
m.	**dark brown**	1,000.

n. **rose lake** 1,000.
o. **yellow green,** on blue pelure paper 1,000.
2TC1b 10c large die on bond paper
e. **deep blue** 800.
f. **blue green** 800.
g. **dull blue green** 800.
h. **dull green** 800.
i. **orange vermilion** 800.
j. **golden brown** 800.
k. **dark brown** 800.
2TC1c 10c large die on wove paper
e. **deep blue** 800.
f. **dull yellow** 800.
g. **orange yellow** 800.
h. **orange vermilion** 800.
2TC1d 10c large die on thin glazed card
e. **deep blue** 850.
f. **scarlet vermilion** 850.
g. **golden brown** 850.
h. **red brown** 675.
i. **dull red** 675.
j. **black brown** 850.
2TC2 10c small die on India paper
b. **deep blue** 675.
c. **dull gray blue,** on bond paper 625.
d. **yellow green** 675.
e. **orange vermilion** 625.
f. **rose lake** 625.
2TC3 10c plate on India paper
a. **orange** 600.
b. **deep brown** 600.

Original trial color die proofs are often cut down and reduced in size; full-size trial color die proofs sell at higher prices. Reprint proofs with cross-hatching are valued as full-size; cut-down examples sell for less.

Nos. 1TC3 and 2TC3 exist with and without "specimen" overprint. Values are for examples without the overprint. Examples with the overprint are equally as scarce but sell for slightly less.

2P1 10c **black,** large die on India paper 800.
a. White bond paper 800.
b. Colored bond paper 1,250.
c. White laid paper 800.
d. Bluish laid paper 800.
e. Yelsh wove paper 800.
f. Bluish wove paper 800.
g. White wove paper 800.
h. Card 1,000.
i. Glazed paper 1,000.
2P3 10c **black,** plate on India paper 900.
Dbl. transfer (31R1) —

Original die proofs are generally found cut to stamp size; full size die proofs sell at higher prices. Reprint proofs with cross-hatching are valued as full size; cut down examples sell for less. Plate proofs overprinted "Specimen" sell for about half the above figures.

Reproductions of 1847 Issue

Actually, official imitations made about 1875 from new dies and plates by order of the Post Office Department.

3TC1a 5c large die on India paper
e. **black** 900.
f. **green** 900.
3TC4 5c plate on card
a. **dull rose lake** 600.
3P1 5c **red brn,** large die on India paper 900.
3P2 5c **red brn,** RA sm die on white wove paper 425.
b. On bond paper 650.
3P2a 5c **red brn,** PP sm die on yelsh wove paper 2,750.
3P3 5c **red brn,** plate on India paper 375.
Block of 4 1,750.
3P4 5c **red brn,** plate on card 250.
Block of 4 1,100.
Plate scratches at UL —
4TC1a 10c large die on India paper
e. **green** 900.
4TC3 10c plate on India paper
a. **green** 750.
4P1 10c **black,** large die on India paper 900.
4P2 10c **black,** RA sm die on white wove paper 425.
b. On bond paper 650.
4P2a 10c **black,** PP sm die on yelsh wove paper 2,750.
4P3 10c **black,** plate on India paper 375.
Block of 4 1,750.
4P4 10c **black,** plate on card 250.
Block of 4 1,100.

1851-60

5TC1a 1c large die on India paper
e. **black** —
5P1 1c **blue,** Type I, large die on India paper *5,000.*
7TC5 1c plate on stamp paper
a. **black** *3,750.*
11TC5 3c plate on stamp paper
a. **black** *3,000.*
11P1 3c **red,** Type I, large die on India paper *5,000.*
11P3 3c **red,** Type I, plate on India paper, brush obliteration 1,000.
Block of 4 5,000.
P# block of 8 *20,000.*
12TC1a 5c large die on India paper
e. **black** *8,500.*
12TC5 5c plate on wove paper
a. **pale brown** 300.
b. **rose brown** 300.
c. **deep red brown** 1,500.
d. **dark olive bister** 300.
e. **olive brown** 300.
f. **olive green** 300.
g. **deep orange** 300.
h. **black** *5,000.*

12P1 5c **brn,** Type I, large die on India paper *7,000.*
12P2a 5c **brn,** Type I, PP sm die on yelsh wove paper *5,000.*
13TC1a 10c large die on India paper
e. **black** *5,000.*
13TC5 10c Plate on wove paper
a. **black** 1,500.
13P1 10c **grn,** Type I, large die on India paper *5,000.*
15TC5 10c plate on wove paper
a. **black** *5,000.*
17P1 12c **black,** large die on India paper *12,500.*
24P3 1c **blue,** Type V (pl. 9), plate on India *1,250.*
Pair *3,000.*
26P3 3c **red,** Type II (pl. 20), plate on India *1,250.*
Pair *3,000.*
30P3 5c **brn,** Type II, plate on India *1,250.*
35P3 10c **grn,** Type V, plate on India *1,250.*
36BP3 12c **blk,** plate III (broken frame lines), plate on India *1,250.*
Block of 4 *5,500.*
36BP5 12c **blk,** plate III (broken frame lines), plate on stamp paper —
Pair —
Block of 4 —
37TC1a 24c large die on India paper
e. **black** *7,000.*
37TC5 24c plate on wove paper
a. **claret brown** 600.
b. **red brown** 600.
c. **orange** 600.
d. **deep yellow** 600.
e. **yellow** 600.
f. **deep blue** 600.
g. **black** —
h. **violet black** 600.
37TC6 24c **red lilac,** on stamp paper, perf 15½, gummed (formerly No. 37b) 1,000.
Block of 4 6,000.
37P1 24c **lilac,** large die on India paper —
37P3 24c **lilac,** plate on India *1,250.*
Pair *3,000.*
37P5 24c **lilac,** plate on stamp paper *1,500.*
Pair *10,000.*
38TC1a 30c large die on India paper
e. **black** *5,000.*
38TC2 30c small die on India paper
b. **black** 1,250.
38TC3 30c plate on India paper
a. **black** 1,400.
Block of 4 9,000.
38TC5 30c plate on wove paper
a. **black** 1,000.
38P1 30c **org,** large die on India paper —
38P2 30c **org,** sm die on white wove paper —
38P3 30c **org,** plate on India *1,250.*
Pair *3,000.*
38P5 30c **org,** plate on stamp paper *1,500.*
Pair *7,750.*

39TC1a 90c large die on India paper
e. **brown orange** *6,000.*
f. **black** *6,000.*
39TC2 90c small die on India paper
b. **black** 1,250.
39TC5 90c plate on wove paper
a. **rose lake** 625.
b. **henna brown** 625.
c. **orange red** 625.
d. **brown orange** 625.
e. **sepia** 625.
f. **dark green** 625.
g. **dark violet brown** 625.
h. **black** 675.

Former Nos. 55-57, 59, 62 are now in the Essay section. Former Nos. 60-61 will be found below as Nos. 70TC3e and 71TC3b, respectively.

39P1 90c **blue,** large die on India paper —
39P2 90c **blue,** sm die on white wove paper —
39P3 90c **blue,** plate on India *1,250.*
Pair *3,000.*
39P5 90c **blue,** plate on stamp paper *4,500.*
Pair *37,500.*

Plate proofs of 24P to 39P are from the original plates. They may be distinguished from the 40P to 47P by the type in the case of the 1c, 3c, 10c and 12c, and by the color in the case of the 5c, 24c, 30c and 90c.

The 3c plate proofs (No. 11) are on proof paper and all known examples have a vertical brush stroke obliteration.

Die proofs of the 30c show full spear point in corners of design.

Reprints of 1857-60 Issue

40TC5 1c plate on wove paper
a. **orange vermilion** 275.
b. **orange** 275.
c. **yellow orange** 275.
d. **orange brown** 275.
e. **dark brown** 275.
f. **dull violet** 275.
g. **violet** 275.
h. **red violet** 275.
i. **gray** 275.
40P1 1c **br blue,** type I, large die on India paper 325.
40P2 1c **br blue,** type I, RA sm die on white wove paper 350.
40P2a 1c **br blue,** type I, PP sm die on yelsh wove paper *2,500.*
40P3 1c **br blue,** type I (new plate), plate on India 90.
Block of 4 550.
40P4 1c **br blue,** type I (new plate), plate on card 50.
Block of 4 220.
40P5 1c **br blue,** type I (new plate), plate on stamp paper 750.

We are *the* Source.

JamesLee.com

America's largest stock of reasonably priced U.S. Die & Plate Proofs. See them all on our website!
We are Sellers *and* Buyers! How may we help you?
Over Three Decades Building Collections.

P.O. Box 3876 • Oak Brook, IL 60522-3876

Phone: (847) 910-6048
Email: jim@jameslee.com

Visit us tonight!

41TC3 3c **red,** plate on India paper —
41P1 3c **scarlet,** type I, large die on India paper 325.
41P2 3c **scarlet,** type I, RA sm die on white wove paper 350.
41P2a 3c **scarlet,** type I, PP sm die on yelsh wove paper *2,500.*
41P3 3c **scarlet,** type I (new plate), plate on India 90.
Block of 4 550.
41P4 3c **scarlet,** type I (new plate), plate on card 75.
Block of 4 330.
41P5 3c **scarlet,** type I (new plate), plate on stamp paper —
42P1 5c **org brn,** type II, large die on India paper 325.
42P2 5c **org brn,** type II, RA sm die on white wove paper 350.
42P3 5c **org brn,** type II (plate II), plate on India
Block of 4 550.
P# blk. of 8 1,450.
42P4 5c **org brn,** type II (plate II), plate on card 50.
Block of 4 220.
P# blk. of 8 —
43P1 10c **grn,** type I, large die on India paper 325.
43P2 10c **grn,** type I, RA sm die on white wove paper 350.
43P2a 10c **grn,** type I, PP sm die on yelsh wove paper *2,500.*
43P3 10c **grn,** type I (new plate), plate on India 90.
Block of 4 550.
43P4 10c **grn,** type I (new plate), plate on card 50.
Block of 4 220.
43P5 10c **grn,** type I (new plate), plate on stamp paper 50.
44P1 12c **greenish blk,** (new die, frame line complete), large die on India paper 325.
44P2 12c **greenish blk,** (new die, frame line complete), RA sm die on white wove paper 350.
44P2a 12c **greenish blk,** (new die, frame line complete), PP sm die on yelsh wove paper *3,500.*
44P3 12c **greenish blk,** (new plate, frame line complete), plate on India 125.
Block of 4 625.
44P4 12c **greenish blk,** (new plate, frame line complete), plate on card 50.
Block of 4 220.
44P5 12c **greenish blk,** (new plate, frame line complete), plate on stamp paper —
45P1 24c **blksh vio,** large die on India paper 325.
45P2 24c **blksh vio,** RA sm die on white wove paper 350.
45P2a 24c **blksh vio,** PP sm die on yelsh wove paper *2,500.*
45P3 24c **blksh vio,** (plate I), plate on India 90.
Block of 4 400.
P# blk. of 8 1,050.
45P4 24c **blksh vio,** (plate I), plate on card 50.
Block of 4 220.
46P1 30c **yel org,** large die on India paper 325.
46P2 30c **yel org,** RA sm die on white wove paper 350.
46P2a 30c **yel org,** PP sm die on yelsh wove paper *2,500.*
46P3 30c **yel org,** (plate I), plate on India 90.
Block of 4 550.
P# blk. of 8 1,450.
46P4 30c **yel org,** (plate I), plate on card 50.
Block of 4 220.
P# blk. of 8 —
47P1 90c **dp blue,** large die on India paper 325.
47P2 90c **dp blue,** RA sm die on white wove paper 350.
47P2a 90c **dp blue,** PP sm die on yelsh wove paper *2,500.*
47P3 90c **dp blue,** (plate I), plate on India 125.
Block of 4 625.
P# blk. of 8 2,000.
47P4 90c **dp blue,** (plate I), plate on card 50.
Block of 4 220.
P# blk. of 8 850.
Nos. 40P4-47P4 (8) 425.00

Nos. 42P2-44P2 were printed from original dies. The 5c shows type I projections at top and bottom. The 12c was printed from a new die and shows complete frame lines.

Nos. 40P1-47P1, large die, exist only as hybrids.

SECOND DESIGNS (Regular Issue)

For "First Designs" see Essay section (former Nos. 55-57, 59, 62), Proofs and Trial Color Proofs (former No. 58) and Trial Color Proofs (former Nos. 60-61).

1861

62BTC1a 10c large die on India paper
e. **black** *2,500.*
62BTC3 10c plate on India paper
a. **green** 300.
b. **light green** 300.
62BP2 10c **dark green,** RA sm die on white wove paper *325.*
62BP3 10c **dark green,** plate on India *375.*
P# blk. of 8 —
63TC1a 1c large die on India paper
e. **black** *2,500.*
63TC2 1c small die on India paper
b. **black** 750.
c. **red** 750.
d. **brown** 750.
e. **green** —
f. **orange** —

63TC5 1c plate on wove paper, imperf.
a. **rose** 40.
b. **deep orange red** 40.
c. **deep red orange** 40.
d. **dark orange** 40.
e. **yellow orange** 40.
f. **orange brown** 40.
g. **dark brown** 40.
h. **yellow green** 40.
i. **green** 40.
j. **blue green** 40.
k. **gray lilac** 40.
l. **gray black** 40.
m. **slate black** 40.
n. **blue** 40.
o. **light blue** 40.
p. **deep blue** 100.
63TC6 1c plate on wove paper, perf.
a. **rose** 50.
b. **deep orange red** 50.
c. **deep red orange** 50.
d. **dark orange** 50.
e. **yellow orange** 50.
f. **orange brown** 50.
g. **dark brown** 50.
h. **yellow green** 50.
i. **green** 50.
j. **blue green** 50.
k. **gray lilac** 50.
l. **gray black** 50.
m. **slate black** 50.
n. **blue** 50.
o. **light blue** 50.
p. **deep blue** 50.

The perforated 1861 1c trial colors are valued with perfs cutting the design on two sides. Well centered examples are extremely scarce and sell for more.

There are many trial color impressions of the issues of 1861 to 1883 made for experimentation with various patent papers, grills, etc. Some are fully perforated, gummed and with grill.

63P1 1c **blue,** large die on India paper 700.
63P2 1c **blue,** RA sm die on white wove paper 225.
63P2a 1c **blue,** PP sm die on yelsh wove paper 2,750.
b. **indigo** 2,750.
63P3 1c **blue,** plate on India 55.
Block of 4 225.
P# blk. of 8 1,500.
63P4 1c **blue,** plate on card 40.
Block of 4 250.
P# blk. of 8 —
64TC6 3c plate on thin stamp paper, perf 12, gummed
a. **carmine pink** —
64P1 3c **pink,** large die on India paper 3,500.
64P2 3c **pink,** RA sm die on white wove paper —
65TC1a 3c large die on India paper
e. **black** 2,500.
f. **black,** on glazed 2,500.
g. **blue green** 2,500.
h. **orange** 2,500.
i. **brown** 2,500.
j. **dark blue** 2,500.
k. **ocher** 2,500.
l. **green** 2,500.
m. **dull red** 2,500.
n. **slate** 2,500.
o. **red brown** 2,500.
p. **deep pink** 2,500.
q. **rose pink** 2,500.
r. **dark rose** 2,500.
65TC6 3c plate on thin stamp paper, perf 12, gummed
a. **dark carmine** —
65P1 3c **rose,** large die on India paper 1,000.
65P2 3c **rose,** RA sm die on white wove paper —
65P2a 3c **rose,** PP sm die on yelsh wove paper 2,750.
65P3 3c **rose,** plate on India 100.
Block of 4 550.
P# blk. of 8 1,500.
a. **dull red** 100.
65P4 3c **rose,** plate on card 150.
65P5 3c **rose,** plate on stamp paper, pair 1,000.
P# blk. of 8 —
67TC1a 5c large die on India paper
e. **black** 2,500.
f. **dark orange** 2,500.
g. **green** 2,500.
h. **ultramarine** 2,500.
i. **gray** 2,500.
j. **rose brown** —
67TC2 5c small die on India paper
b. **black** —
67P1 5c **buff,** large die on India paper *5,000.*
67P2a 5c **buff,** PP sm die on white wove paper *5,000.*
76P1 5c **brown,** large die on India paper 700.
76P2 5c **brown,** RA sm die on white wove paper 225.
76P2a 5c **brown,** PP sm die on yelsh wove paper 2,750.
76P3 5c **brown,** plate on India 45.
Block of 4 225.
P# blk. of 8 1,500.
76P4 5c **brown,** plate on card 30.
Block of 4 140.
P# blk. of 8 —
68TC1a 10c large die on India paper
e. **orange** 2,500.
f. **red brown** 2,500.
g. **dull pink** 2,500.
h. **scarlet** 2,500.
i. **black** 2,500.

j. **ocher** 2,500.
k. **ultramarine** 2,500.
68TC2 10c small die on India paper
b. **black** 550.
68P1 10c **green,** large die on India paper 650.
68P2 10c **green,** RA sm die on white wove paper 225.
68P2a 10c **green,** PP sm die on yelsh wove paper 2,750.
68P3 10c **green,** plate on India 65.
Block of 4 300.
P# blk. of 8 1,500.
68P4 10c **green,** plate on card 30.
Block of 4 140.
P# blk. of 8 —
69TC1a 12c large die on India paper
e. **scarlet vermilion** 2,500.
f. **brown** 2,500.
g. **red brown** 2,500.
h. **green** 2,500.
i. **orange yellow** 2,500.
69TC2 12c small die on India paper
b. **black** 550.
69P1 12c **black,** large die on India paper 700.
69P2 12c **black,** RA sm die on white wove paper 225.
69P2a 12c **black,** PP sm die on yelsh wove paper 2,750.
69P3 12c **black,** plate on India 65.
Block of 4 300.
P# blk. of 8 1,500.
69P4 12c **black,** plate on card 30.
Block of 4 140.
P# blk. of 8 —
70TC1a 24c large die on India paper
e. **scarlet** 2,500.
f. **green** 2,500.
g. **orange** 2,500.
h. **red brown** 2,500.
i. **orange brown** 2,500.
j. **orange yellow** 2,500.
k. **rose red** 2,500.
l. **gray** 2,500.
m. **steel blue** 2,500.
n. **blue** 2,500.
o. **black** 2,500.
p. **violet** 2,500.
70TC2 24c small die on India paper
b. **violet** 375.
70TC2a 24c PP small die on yelsh wove paper
e. **violet** 2,250.
70TC3 24c plate on India paper
a. **violet** 500.
Block of 4 2,250.
70TC5 24c **gray,** on bluish gray stamp paper —
70TC6 24c **dark violet,** semi-transparent stamp paper, perf 12, gummed **(formerly No. 60)** *15,000.*
70P1 24c **red lilac,** large die on India paper —
70P2a 24c **red lilac,** PP sm die on yelsh wove paper 2,750.
70P4 24c **red lilac,** plate on card 500.
78P2 24c **lilac,** RA sm die on white wove paper 225.
78P2a 24c **lilac,** PP sm die on yelsh wove paper 2,750.
78P3 24c **lilac,** plate on India 80.
Block of 4 400.
P# blk. of 8 1,750.
78P4 24c **lilac,** plate on card 75.
Block of 4 375.
P# blk. of 8 —
71TC1a 30c large die on India paper
e. **rose** 2,500.
f. **red orange** 2,500.
71TC2 30c small die on India paper
e. **black** 600.
f. **red orange** 375.
71TC2a 30c PP small die on yelsh wove paper
e. **red orange** 1,250.
71TC6 30c **red orange,** semi-transparent stamp paper, perf 12, gummed **(formerly No. 61)** *45,000.*
71P1 30c **orange,** large die on India paper 500.
71P2 30c **orange,** RA sm die on white wove paper 225.
71P2a 30c **orange,** PP sm die on yelsh wove paper 2,750.
71P3 30c **orange,** plate on India 50.
Block of 4 250.
P# blk. of 8 1,500.
71P4 30c **orange,** plate on card 30.
Block of 4 140.
P# blk. of 8 —
72TC1a 90c large die on India paper
e. **black** 2,500.
f. **ultramarine** 2,500.
g. **bluish gray** 2,500.
h. **violet gray** 2,500.
i. **red brown** 2,500.
j. **orange** 2,500.
k. **yellow orange** 2,500.
l. **scarlet** 2,500.
m. **green** 2,500.
72P1 90c **blue,** large die on India paper 500.
72P2 90c **blue,** RA sm die on white wove paper 225.
72P2a 90c **blue,** PP sm die on yelsh wove paper 2,750.
72P3 90c **blue,** plate on India 50.
Block of 4 250.
P# blk. of 8 1,500.
72P4 90c **blue,** plate on card 30.
Block of 4 140.
P# blk. of 8 —

1861 **Gummed Stamp Paper**

66TC6 3c **lake,** perf. 12 *2,000.*
Pair *4,500.*
Block of 4 *9,250.*
P# strip of 4 *10,000.*
Double transfer *2,250.*
a. Imperf, pair *1,850.*
P# block of 8 —

John N. Luff recorded the plate number for No. 66TC as 34.

74TC6 3c **scarlet,** perf. 12 *7,000.*
Block of 4 *29,000.*
With 4 horiz. black pen strokes *5,500.*
With handstamped cancel *15,000.*
a. Imperf, pair *4,000.*

John N. Luff recorded the plate number for No. 74TC as 19.

1861

66TC2 3c **lake,** RA small die on India paper 250.
66TC2a 3c **lake,** PP small die on yelsh wove paper 1,100.
66TC3 3c **lake,** plate on India paper 150.
Block of 4 850.
P# Block of 8 2,250.
74TC1a 3c **scarlet,** large die on India paper 2,250.
74TC2 3c **scarlet,** RA small die on India paper 375.
74TC2a 3c **scarlet,** small die on yelsh wove paper 1,100.
74TC3 3c **scarlet,** plate on India paper 150.
Block of 4 725.
74TC4 3c **scarlet,** plate on card 150.
Block of 4 725.
P# Block of 8 —

1861-67

73TC1a 2c large die on India paper
e. **dull chalky blue** *8,000.*
f. **green** *8,000.*
g. **dull yellow** *8,000.*
h. **dark orange** *8,000.*
i. **scarlet** *8,000.*
j. **dull rose** *8,000.*
k. **brown** *8,000.*
l. **ultramarine** *8,000.*
73TC3 2c plate on India paper
a. **light blue** 250.
b. **dull chalky blue** 500.
c. **green** 250.
d. **olive green** 250.
e. **blue green** *400.*
f. **vermilion** 250.
g. **scarlet** 250.
h. **dull red** 250.
i. **dull rose** 250.
j. **gray black** 250.
Block of 4 *2,500.*
73P1 2c **black,** die I, large die on India paper 10,000.
a. Die II 2,500.
73P2 2c **black,** die II, RA sm die on white wove paper 1,300.
73P2a 2c **black,** die II, PP sm die on yelsh wove paper 8,750.
73P3 2c **black,** die I, plate on India 150.
Block of 4 750.
P# blk. of 8 2,250.
a. Die II 110.
Block of 4 550.
P# blk. of 8 1,750.
73P4 2c **black,** die I, plate on card, P# block of 8 —
a. Die II 75.
Block of 4 400.
P# blk. of 8 —
77TC1a 15c large die on India paper
e. **deep blue** 2,500.
f. **dark red** 2,500.
g. **orange red** 2,500.
h. **dark orange** 2,500.
i. **yellow orange** 2,500.
j. **dark yellow** 2,500.
k. **sepia** 2,500.
l. **orange brown** 2,500.
m. **red brown** 2,500.
n. **blue green** 2,500.
o. **dusky blue** 2,500.
p. **gray black** 2,500.
77TC3 15c plate on India paper
a. **deep blue** 335.
Block of 4 1,650.
77P1 15c **black,** large die on India paper 1,400.
77P2 15c **black,** RA sm die on white wove paper 500.
77P2a 15c **black,** PP sm die on yelsh wove paper 2,750.
77P3 15c **black,** plate on India 55.
Block of 4 250.
P# blk. of 8 3,000.
77P4 15c **black,** plate on card 45.
Block of 4 200.
P# blk. of 8 —
79P5 3c **rose,** A grill, plate on stamp paper, pair *1,500.*
Block of 4 *4,000.*
P# blk. of 8 *10,000.*
83P5 3c **rose,** C grill, plate on stamp paper, pair *1,750.*
94P5 3c **red,** F grill, plate on stamp paper, pair *1,500.*

The listed plate proofs of the 1c (63P), 5c (76P), 10c (68P) and 12c (69P) are from the 100 subject re-issue plates of 1875. Single proofs of these denominations from the regular issue plates cannot be told apart from the reprints. As the reprint plates had wider spacing between the subjects, multiples can be differentiated. Values are for proofs from the reprint plates. The 2c Die II has a small dot on the left cheek. The 5c has a small notch at the bottom left of the design.

1869

112TC1a 1c large die on India paper
e. **black** 2,500.
112P1 1c **buff,** large die on India paper 750.
112P2 1c **buff,** RA sm die on white wove paper 350.
112P2a 1c **buff,** PP sm die on yelsh wove paper 3,000.
112P3 1c **buff,** plate on India 55.
Block of 4 250.
P# blk. of 10 950.
112P4 1c **buff,** plate on card 65.
Block of 4 300.
113TC1a 2c large die on India paper
e. **black** 2,500.
113P1 2c **brown,** large die on India paper 750.
113P2 2c **brown,** RA sm die on white wove paper 350.
113P2a 2c **brown,** PP sm die on yelsh wove paper 3,500.
113P3 2c **brown,** plate on India 40.
Block of 4 175.
P# blk. of 10 800.
113P4 2c **brown,** plate on card 50.
Block of 4 225.
P# blk. of 10 1,000.
114TC1a 3c large die on India paper
e. **black** 2,500.
114P1 3c **ultra,** large die on India paper 900.
114P2 3c **ultra,** RA sm die on white wove paper 575.
114P2a 3c **ultra,** PP sm die on yelsh wove paper 3,500.
114P3 3c **ultra,** plate on India 45.
Block of 4 190.
P# blk. of 10 1,000.
114P4 3c **ultra,** plate on card 85.
Block of 4 375.
P# blk. of 10 1,250.
115TC1a 6c large die on India paper
e. **deep dull blue** 2,500.
f. **black** 2,500.
115P1 6c **ultra,** large die on India paper 900.
115P2 6c **ultra,** RA sm die on white wove paper 350.
115P2a 6c **ultra,** PP sm die on yelsh wove paper 3,000.
115P3 6c **ultra,** plate on India 45.
Block of 4 190.
P# blk. of 10 1,000.
115P4 6c **ultra,** plate on card 85.
Block of 4 375.
P# blk. of 10 1,250.
116TC1a 10c large die on India paper
e. **black** 2,500.
f. **dull dark violet** 2,500.
g. **deep green** 2,500.
h. **dull dark orange** 2,500.
i. **dull rose** 2,500.
j. **copper red** 2,500.
k. **chocolate** 2,500.
l. **dark Prussian blue** 2,500.
116P1 10c **yellow,** large die on India paper 900.
116P2 10c **yellow,** RA sm die on white wove paper 350.
116P2a 10c **yellow,** PP sm die on yelsh wove paper 3,000.
116P3 10c **yellow,** plate on India 45.
Block of 4 190.
P# blk. of 10 2,000.
116P4 10c **yellow,** plate on card 55.
Block of 4 250.
P# blk. of 10 2,500.
117TC1a 12c large die on India paper
e. **black** 2,500.
117P1 12c **green,** large die on India paper 900.
117P2 12c **green,** RA sm die on white wove paper 350.
117P2a 12c **green,** PP sm die on yelsh wove paper 3,000.
117P3 12c **green,** plate on India 45.
Block of 4 190.
P# blk. of 10 2,250.
117P4 12c **green,** plate on card 55.
Block of 4 265.
P# blk. of 10 2,800.
118TC1a 15c large die on India paper
e. **dull dark violet** 2,500.
f. **deep blue** 2,500.
g. **dull red brown** 2,500.
h. **black** 2,500.
i. **dark blue gray** 2,500.
119P1 15c **brn & bl,** (type II), large die on India paper 550.
119P2 15c **brn & bl,** (type II), RA sm die on white wove paper 450.
119P2a 15c **brn & bl,** (type II), PP sm die on yelsh wove paper 3,000.
119P3 15c **brn & bl,** (type II), plate on India 120.
Block of 4 600.
P# blk. of 8 4,000.
129P1 15c **Reissue,** (type III), large die on India paper 550.
129P2 15c **Reissue,** (type III), RA sm die on white wove paper 450.
129P2a 15c **Reissue,** (type III), PP sm die on yelsh wove paper 3,000.
129P3 15c **Reissue,** (type III), plate on India 350.
Block of 4 1,600.
P# blk. of 8 4,500.
129P4 15c **Reissue,** (type III), plate on card 140.
Block of 4 725.
P# blk. of 8 3,750.
a. Center inverted *(100)* *2,750.*
Block of 4 *15,000.*
P# blk. of 8 *65,000.*
120TC1a 24c large die on India paper
e. **black** 4,500.
120TC3 24c plate on India paper
a. **green & reddish lilac** —
Block of 4 —
P# block of 8 6,000.
120P1 24c **grn & vio,** large die on India paper 550.
120P2 24c **grn & vio,** RA sm die on white wove paper 450.
120P2a 24c **grn & vio,** PP sm die on yelsh wove paper 3,000.
120P3 24c **grn & vio,** plate on India 140.
Block of 4 625.
P# blk. of 8 6,000.
120P4 24c **grn & vio,** plate on card 140.
Block of 4 650.
P# blk. of 8 7,500.
a. Center inverted *(100)* *2,750.*
Block of 4 *15,000.*
P# blk. of 8 *65,000.*
121TC1a 30c large die on India paper
e. **deep blue & deep green** 3,500.
f. **deep brown & blue** 3,500.
g. **golden brown & carmine lake** 3,500.
h. **carmine lake & dull violet** 3,500.
i. **carmine lake & green** 3,500.
j. **carmine lake & brown** 3,500.
k. **carmine lake & black** 3,500.
l. **dull orange red & deep green** 3,500.
m. **deep ocher & golden brown** 3,500.
n. **dull violet & golden brown** 3,500.
o. **black & deep green** 3,500.
121P1 30c **ultra & car,** large die on India paper 1,250.
121P2 30c **ultra & car,** RA sm die on white wove paper 450.
121P2a 30c **ultra & car,** PP sm die on yelsh wove paper 3,000.
121P3 30c **ultra & car,** plate on India 140.
Block of 4 625.
P# blk. of 8 7,500.
121P4 30c **ultra & car,** plate on card 170.
Block of 4 875.
P# blk. of 8 —
a. Flags inverted *(100)* *2,750.*
Block of 4 *15,000.*
P# blk. of 8 *65,000.*
122TC1a 90c large die on India paper
e. **brown & deep green** 3,500.
122TC4 90c Plate on card
a. **green & black** 1,500.
122P1 90c **car & blk,** large die on India paper 550.
122P2 90c **car & blk,** RA sm die on white wove paper 450.
122P2a 90c **car & blk,** PP sm die on yelsh wove paper 5,000.
122P3 90c **car & blk,** plate on India 180.
Block of 4 825.
P# blk. of 8 6,500.
122P4 90c **car & blk,** plate on card 170.
Block of 4 875.
P# blk. of 8 8,250.
a. Center inverted *(100)* *2,750.*
Block of 4 *15,000.*
P# blk. of 8 (unique) *75,000.*
Nos. 112P3-117P3, 119P3-122P3 (10) 855.00
Nos. 112P4-117P4, 120P4-122P4 (9) 875.00

Large die proofs of Nos. 119, 129, 120 and 122 exist only as hybrids.

1880

133P1 1c **dark buff,** large die on India paper 1,000.
133P3 1c **dark buff,** plate on India 100.
Block of 4 450.
P# blk. of 10 1,250.

1870-71 **National Bank Note Co.**

136P5 3c **green,** grill, on stamp paper, pair *1,200.*
P# blk. of 12 *14,000.*
145TC1a 1c large die on India paper
e. **yellow orange** 600.
f. **red brown** 600.
g. **red violet** 600.
h. **black** —
i. **green** 600.
145TC3 1c plate on India paper
a. **black** —
145P1 1c **ultra,** large die on India paper 250.
145P2 1c **ultra,** RA sm die on white wove paper, from new die 175.
145P2a 1c **ultra,** PP sm die on yelsh wove paper 2,500.
145P3 1c **ultra,** plate on India 20.
Block of 4 90.
P# blk. of 12 750.
146TC1a 2c large die on India paper
e. **black** 600.
146P1 2c **red brn,** large die on India paper 250.
146P3 2c **red brn,** plate on India 20.
Block of 4 90.
P# blk. of 12 750.
147TC1a 3c large die on India paper
e. **brown** —
f. **red brown** —
g. **dark red** —
h. **light ultramarine** —
i. **yellow brown** —
j. **dull red violet** —
k. **dull grayish red** —
l. **yellow orange** —
m. **red violet** —
n. **green** —
147TC3 3c plate on India paper
a. **brown** 125.
b. **dark brown** 125.
c. **red brown** 125.
d. **orange brown** 125.
e. **dark red** 125.
f. **light ultramarine** 125.

g. **yellow brown** 125.
h. **dull red violet** 125.
i. **yellow orange** 125.
j. **red violet** 125.
147TC5 3c plate on wove paper
a. **deep red brown** 125.

Former Nos. 147aTC and 147bTC are now listed in the Essay section as No. 147-E13c.

147P1 3c **green,** large die on India paper 300.
147P3 3c **green,** plate on India 20.
Block of 4 90.
P# blk. of 12 750.

The former No. 147Pc4 is now listed in the Essay section as No. 147-E13e.

148TC1a 6c large die on India paper
e. **deep magenta** 600.
f. **ultramarine** 600.
g. **carmine** 600.
h. **maroon** 600.
148P1 6c **carmine,** large die on India paper 1,750.
148P3 6c **carmine,** plate on India 35.
Block of 4 150.
P# blk. of 12 1,400.
149TC1a 7c large die on India paper
e. **black** 550.
149P1 7c **vermilion,** large die on India paper 250.
149P3 7c **vermilion,** plate on India 15.
Block of 4 70.
P# blk. of 12 750.
150TC1a 10c large die on India paper
e. **blue** 550.
f. **dull pale blue** 550.
g. **ultramarine** 550.
h. **blue green** 550.
i. **carmine** 550.
j. **bister** 550.
k. **dull red** 550.
l. **red orange** 550.
m. **yellow brown** 550.
n. **brown orange** 550.
150P1 10c **brown,** large die on India paper 300.
150P3 10c **brown,** plate on India 40.
Block of 4 165.
P# blk. of 12 2,000.
151TC1a 12c large die on India paper
e. **orange** 550.
f. **orange brown** 550.
g. **brown red** 550.
h. **dull red** 550.
i. **carmine** 550.
j. **blue** 550.
k. **light blue** 550.
l. **ultramarine** 550.
m. **green** 550.
151P1 12c **violet,** large die on India paper 250.
151P3 12c **violet,** plate on India 16.
Block of 4 70.
P# blk. of 12 750.
152P1 15c **orange,** large die on India paper 300.
152P3 15c **orange,** plate on India 30.
Block of 4 135.
P# blk. of 12 750.
153TC1a 24c large die on India paper
e. **dark brown** 550.
153P1 24c **purple,** large die on India paper 300.
153P3 24c **purple,** plate on India 30.
Block of 4 135.
P# blk. of 12 750.
154P1 30c **black,** large die on India paper 300.
154P3 30c **black,** plate on India 40.
Block of 4 170.
P# blk. of 12 2,250.
155TC1a 90c large die on India paper
e. **carmine** 550.
f. **ultramarine** 550.
g. **black** 550.
155P1 90c **carmine,** large die on India paper 300.
155P3 90c **carmine,** plate on India 45.
Block of 4 195.
P# blk. of 12 2,500.

Secret Marks on 24, 30 and 90c Dies of the Bank Note Issues

National 24c — Rays of lower star normal.

Continental 24c — Rays of lower star strengthened.

National 30c — Lower line does not join point of shield.

Continental and American 30c — Lower line joins point of shield and bottom line of shield thicker.

National 90c — Rays of star in upper right normal.

Continental and American 90c — Rays of star in upper right strengthened.

1873 Continental Bank Note Co.

156TC1a 1c large die on India paper
e. **scarlet** *1,500.*
156TC3 1c plate on India paper
a. **black** 15.
Block of 4 65.
156TC4 1c plate on card
a. **black** 30.
Block of 4 140.
156P1 1c **ultra,** large die on India paper 450.
156P3 1c **ultra,** plate on India 55.
Block of 4 250.
P# blk. of 14 1,150.
156P4 1c **ultra,** plate on card 300.
157TC1a 2c large die on India paper
e. **black** 850.
f. **dull blue** 850.
g. **rose** 850.
h. **deep rose** 850.
157TC3 2c plate on India paper
a. **black** 15.
Block of 4 65.
157P1 2c **brown,** large die on India paper 350.
157P2 2c **brown,** RA sm die on white wove paper 175.
157P2a 2c **brown,** PP sm die on yelsh wove paper 2,500.
157P3 2c **brown,** plate on India 35.
Block of 4 165.
P# blk. of 14 1,150.
157P4 2c **brown,** plate on card 20.
Block of 4 100.
P# blk. of 14 —
157P5 2c **brown,** plate on stamp paper —
158TC1a 3c large die on India paper
e. **black** 750.
g. **orange red** —
158TC3 3c plate on India paper
a. **black** 12.
Block of 4 55.
158P1 3c **green,** large die on India paper 350.
158P2 3c **green,** RA sm die on white wove paper 175.
158P3 3c **green,** plate on India 55.
Block of 4 220.
P# blk. of 14 1,150.
158P4 3c **green,** plate on card 150.
158P5 3c **green,** plate on stamp paper, pair *150.*
a. On stamp paper, grill, pair *650.*
159TC3 6c plate on India paper
a. **black** 30.
Block of 4 150.
159P1 6c **rose,** large die on India paper 2,000.
159P2 6c **rose,** RA sm die on white wove paper 250.
159P2a 6c **rose,** PP sm die on yelsh wove paper 2,500.
159P3 6c **rose,** plate on India 110.
Block of 4 525.
P# blk. of 12 2,000.
159P4 6c **pink,** plate on card 300.
160TC3 7c plate on India paper
a. **black** 75.
Block of 4 325.
160P1 7c **org vermilion,** large die on India paper 250.
160P2 7c **org vermilion,** RA sm die on white wove paper 175.
160P2a 7c **org vermilion,** PP sm die on yelsh wove paper 2,500.
160P3 7c **org vermilion,** plate on India 35.
Block of 4 165.
P# blk. of 14 1,150.
160P4 7c **org vermilion,** plate on card 20.
Block of 4 100.
P# blk. of 14 —
161P1 10c **brown,** large die on India paper 450.
161P2 10c **brown,** RA sm die on white wove paper 200.
161P3 10c **brown,** plate on India 60.
Block of 4 300.
P# blk. of 14 1,300.
161P4 10c **brown,** plate on card 300.
162P1 12c **blackish vio,** large die on India paper 200.
162P2 12c **blackish vio,** RA sm die on white wove paper 175.
162P2a 12c **blackish vio,** PP sm die on yelsh wove paper 2,500.
162P3 12c **blackish vio,** plate on India 38.
Block of 4 190.
P# blk. of 14 1,150.
162P4 12c **blackish vio,** plate on card 20.
Block of 4 100.
P# blk. of 14 —
162P5 12c **blackish vio,** plate on stamp paper —
163P1 15c **yel org,** large die on India paper 400.
163P2 15c **yel org,** RA sm die on white wove paper 175.
163P2a 15c **yel org,** PP sm die on yelsh wove paper 2,500.
163P3 15c **yel org,** plate on India 65.
Block of 4 250.
P# blk. of 12 1,000.
163P4 15c **yel org,** plate on card 20.
Block of 4 100.
P# blk. of 12 —
164P1 24c **violet,** large die on India paper 400.
164P2 24c **violet,** RA sm die on white wove paper 175.
164P2a 24c **violet,** PP sm die on yelsh wove paper 2,500.
164P3 24c **violet,** plate on India 50.
Block of 4 225.
P# blk. of 12 1,150.
164P4 24c **violet,** plate on card 30.
Block of 4 140.
165P1 30c **gray blk,** large die on India paper 400.
165P2 30c **gray blk,** RA sm die on white wove paper 175.
165P2a 30c **gray blk,** PP sm die on yelsh wove paper 2,500.
165P3 30c **gray blk,** plate on India 40.
Block of 4 200.
P# blk. of 12 1,150.
165P4 30c **gray blk,** plate on card 20.
Block of 4 90.
166P1 90c **rose car,** large die on India paper 400.
166P2 90c **rose car,** RA sm die on white wove paper 175.
166P2a 90c **rose car,** PP sm die on yelsh wove paper 2,500.
166P3 90c **rose car,** plate on India 55.
Block of 4 250.
P# blk. of 12 1,500.
166P4 90c **rose car,** plate on card 40.
Block of 4 190.

Die proofs of the 24c, 30c and 90c show secret marks, as illustrated, but as plates of these denominations were not made from these dies, plate proofs can be identified only by color.

Nos. 159TC2-166TC2 are so-called "Goodall" set of Small Die proofs on India Paper of Official Stamps in five colors

159TC2 6c "Goodall" small die on India paper
b. **black** 600.
c. **deep green** 600.
d. **dull gray blue** 600.
e. **deep brown** 600.
f. **dull red** 600.
160TC2 7c "Goodall" small die on India paper
b. **black** 600.
c. **deep green** 600.
d. **dull gray blue** 600.
e. **deep brown** 600.
f. **dull red** 600.
161TC2 10c "Goodall" small die on India paper
b. **black** 600.
c. **deep green** 600.
d. **dull gray blue** 600.
e. **deep brown** 600.
f. **dull red** 600.
162TC2 12c "Goodall" small die on India paper
b. **black** 600.
c. **deep green** 600.
d. **dull gray blue** 600.
e. **deep brown** 600.
f. **dull red** 600.
163TC2 15c "Goodall" small die on India paper
b. **black** 600.
c. **deep green** 600.
d. **dull gray blue** 600.
e. **deep brown** 600.
f. **dull red** 600.
164TC2 24c "Goodall" small die on India paper
b. **black** 600.
c. **deep green** 600.
d. **dull gray blue** 600.
e. **deep brown** 600.
f. **dull red** 600.
165TC2 30c "Goodall" small die on India paper
b. **black** 600.
c. **deep green** 600.
d. **dull gray blue** 600.
e. **deep brown** 600.
f. **dull red** 600.
166TC2 90c "Goodall" small die on India paper
b. **black** 600.
c. **deep green** 600.
d. **dull gray blue** 600.
e. **deep brown** 600.
f. **dull red** 600.

1875

178P5 2c **vermilion,** plate on stamp paper, pair *600.*
P# blk. of 12 *12,000.*
179TC1a 5c large die on India paper
e. **black** 650.
f. **scarlet** 1,000.

No.	Description	Price
179TC2	5c "Goodall" small die on India paper	
	b. **black**	550.
	c. **deep green**	550.
	d. **deep brown**	550.
	e. **dull red**	550.
	f. **dull gray blue**	550.
179TC3	5c plate on India paper	
	a. **black**	25.
	Block of 4	125.
179TC4	5c Plate on card	
	a. **black**	45.
	Block of 4	200.

1879 American Bank Note Co.

No.	Description	Price
182TC6	1c plate on stamp paper, gummed, perf. 12	
	a. **ultramarine**	300.
	b. **green**	300.
	c. **deep green**	300.
	d. **vermilion**	300.
	e. **brown**	300.
182P1	1c **gray blue,** large die on India paper	525.
182P3	1c **gray blue,** plate on India	60.
	Block of 4	275.
	P# blk. of 12	1,000.
183TC6	2c plate on stamp paper, gummed, perf. 12	
	a. **ultramarine**	300.
	b. **blue**	300.
	c. **green**	300.
183P1	2c **vermilion,** large die on India paper	300.
183P2	2c **vermilion,** RA sm die on white wove paper	190.
183P2a	2c **vermilion,** PP sm die on yelsh wove paper	2,500.
183P3	2c **vermilion,** plate on India	35.
	Block of 4	160.
	P# blk. of 12	600.
183P4	2c **vermilion,** plate on card	25.
	Block of 4	140.
	P# blk. of 12	—
184TC6	3c plate on stamp paper, gummed, perf. 12	
	a. **ultramarine**	300.
	b. **blue**	300.
	c. **vermilion**	300.
	Block of 4	1,100.
	d. **brown**	300.
184P6	3c **green,** plate on stamp paper, pair	*500.*
	P# blk. of 12	—
185TC6	5c plate on stamp paper, gummed, perf. 12	
	a. **ultramarine**	300.
	b. **green**	300.
	c. **vermilion**	300.
185P1	5c **blue,** large die on India paper	450.
185P2	5c **blue,** RA sm die on white wove paper	225.
185P2a	5c **blue,** PP sm die on yelsh wove paper	2,500.
185P3	5c **blue,** plate on India	70.
	Block of 4	325.
	P# blk. of 12	1,300.
185P4	5c **blue,** plate on card	25.
	Block of 4	140.
	P# blk. of 12	—
186TC6	6c plate on stamp paper, gummed, perf. 12	
	a. **ultramarine**	300.
	b. **blue**	300.
	c. **vermilion**	300.
187TC6	10c plate on stamp paper, gummed, perf. 12	
	a. **ultramarine**	300.
	b. **blue**	300.
	c. **vermilion**	300.
	d. **green**	300.
189TC1a	15c large die on India paper	
	e. **orange vermilion**	1,000.
	f. **orange brown**	1,000.
	g. **chestnut brown**	1,000.
	h. **dark brown**	1,000.
	i. **deep green**	1,000.
	j. **black**	1,000.
189TC1d	15c large die on card	
	e. **orange vermilion**	450.
	f. **orange brown**	450.
	g. **chestnut brown**	450.
	h. **dark brown**	450.
	i. **deep green**	450.
	j. **black**	450.
189TC6	15c plate on stamp paper, gummed, perf. 12	
	a. **ultramarine**	300.
	b. **green**	300.
	c. **vermilion**	300.
	d. **brown**	300.
	e. **dull red**	300.
190TC1a	30c large die on India paper	
	e. **black**	1,000.
	f. **orange vermilion**	1,000.
	g. **dark brown**	1,000.
	h. **deep green**	1,000.
	i. **dull red brown**	1,000.
	j. **green**	1,000.
190TC1d	30c large die on card	
	e. **orange vermilion**	450.
	f. **dark brown**	450.
	g. **deep green**	450.
	h. **dull red brown**	450.
	i. **green**	450.
190TC6	30c plate on stamp paper, gummed, perf. 12	
	a. **ultramarine**	300.
	b. **blue**	300.
	c. **green**	300.

See Specimens for No. 189 in deep blue (No. 189S L), No. 209 in green (No. 209S L), No. 210 in pale rose lake (No. 210S L).

No.	Description	Price
190P3	30c **full black,** plate on India	—
	Block of 4	—
190P4	30c **full black,** plate on card	400.
	Block of 4	2,000.
	P# blk. of 12	*7,500.*
191TC1a	90c large die on India paper	
	e. **carmine**	1,000.
	f. **dark brown**	1,000.
	g. **deep dull orange**	1,000.
	h. **indigo**	1,000.
	i. **dull red brown**	1,000.
	j. **black**	1,000.
191TC1d	90c large die on card	
	e. **carmine**	450.
	f. **dark brown**	450.
	g. **deep dull orange**	450.
	h. **indigo**	450.
	i. **dull red brown**	450.
	j. **black**	450.
191P5	90c **car,** plate on stamp paper, pair	*2,250.*
	P# strip of 5	5,000.
193P4	2c **blk brown,** plate on card	400.
	Block of 4	2,000.
	P# blk. of 12	7,500.

1881-82 American Bank Note Co.

No.	Description	Price
205TC1a	5c large die on India paper	
	e. **chestnut brown**	1,000.
	f. **deep dull orange**	1,000.
	g. **pale ultramarine**	1,000.
	h. **deep green**	1,000.
	i. **green**	1,000.
	j. **carmine**	1,000.
	k. **carmine lake**	1,000.
	l. **blue black**	1,000.
205TC1d	5c large die on card	
	e. **chestnut brown**	—
	f. **pale ultramarine**	—
	g. **carmine**	450.
	h. **black** on glazed card	1,000.
205TC3	5c plate on India paper	
	a. **green**	200.
	b. **carmine lake**	225.
205P1	5c **yel brn,** large die on India paper	250.
205P2	5c **yel brn,** RA sm die on white wove paper	200.
205P2a	5c **yel brn,** PP sm die on yelsh wove paper	2,500.
205P3	5c **yel brn,** plate on India	40.
	Block of 4	175.
	P# blk. of 12	1,000.
205P4	5c **yel brn,** plate on card	15.
	Block of 4	100.
	P# blk. of 12	—
	Bottom margin P# block of 30	*2,700.*
206TC1a	1c large die on India paper	
	e. **deep green**	600.
	f. **black**	600.
	g. **ultramarine**	600.
	h. **dark yellow green**	600.
206TC2	1c small die on India paper	
	b. **deep green**	125.
206TC3	1c plate on India paper	
	a. **black**	125.
206P1	1c **blue,** large die on India paper	375.
206P2	1c **blue,** RA sm die on white wove paper	200.
206P2a	1c **blue,** PP sm die on yelsh wove paper	2,500.
206P3	1c **blue,** plate on India	40.
	Block of 4	175.
	P# blk. of 12	1,000.
206P4	1c **blue,** plate on card	20.
	Block of 4	120.
	P# blk. of 12	—
	Bottom margin P# block of 30	*2,700.*
207P1	3c **blue grn,** large die on India paper	375.
207P2	3c **blue grn,** RA sm die on white wove paper	200.
207P2a	3c **blue grn,** PP sm die on yelsh wove paper	2,500.
207P3	3c **blue grn,** plate on India	40.
	Block of 4	175.
	P# blk. of 12	1,000.
207P4	3c **blue grn,** plate on card	20.
	Block of 4	120.
	P# blk. of 12	—
	Bottom margin P# block of 30	*2,700.*
208TC1a	6c large die on India paper	
	e. **deep dull orange**	1,000.
	f. **indigo**	1,250.
	g. **orange vermilion**	1,100.
	h. **dark violet**	1,000.
	i. **chestnut brown**	1,350.
	j. **carmine**	1,250.
208TC1d	6c large die on card	
	e. **deep dull orange**	450.
	f. **orange vermilion**	450.
	g. **dark violet**	450.
	h. **chestnut brown**	450.
208P1	6c **deep rose,** large die on India paper	2,250.
208P2	6c **deep rose,** RA sm die on white wove paper	200.
208P2a	6c **deep rose,** PP sm die on yelsh wove paper	2,500.
	b. **brown red**	2,500.
208P3	6c **deep rose,** plate on India	90.
	Block of 4	425.
	P# blk. of 12	—
	a. **brown red**	100.
208P4	6c **deep rose,** plate on card	60.
	Block of 4	240.
	P# blk. of 12	—
	Bottom margin P# block of 30	*2,700.*
	a. **brown red**	50.
209TC1a	10c large die on India paper	
	e. **carmine**	1,000.
	f. **orange brown**	1,000.
	g. **orange**	1,000.
	h. **deep dull orange**	1,000.
	i. **chestnut brown**	1,000.
	j. **indigo**	1,000.
	k. **pale ultramarine**	1,000.
209TC1d	10c large die on card	
	e. **carmine**	450.
	f. **orange brown**	450.
	g. **deep dull orange**	450.
	h. **chestnut brown**	450.
	i. **indigo**	450.
	j. **pale ultramarine**	450.
	k. **black,** on glazed card	1,000.
209TC4	10c plate on card	
	a. **orange brown**	125.
	b. **green**	125.
209P1	10c **brn,** large die on India paper	800.
209P2	10c **brn,** RA sm die on white wove paper	200.
209P2a	10c **brn,** PP sm die on yelsh wove paper	2,500.
209P3	10c **brn,** plate on India	40.
	Block of 4	170.
	P# blk. of 12	1,000.
209P4	10c **brn,** plate on card	25.
	Block of 4	140.
	P# blk. of 12	—
	Bottom margin P# block of 30	*2,700.*

1883

No.	Description	Price
210TC1a	2c large die on India paper	
	e. **red brown**	1,000.
	f. **deep dull orange**	1,000.
	g. **chestnut brown**	1,000.
	h. **violet rose**	1,000.
	i. **indigo**	1,000.
	j. **black**	1,000.
	k. **pale ultramarine**	1,000.
	l. **olive green**	1,000.
210TC1d	2c large die on card	
	e. **brown red**	450.
	f. **chestnut brown**	450.
	g. **violet rose**	450.
	h. **indigo**	450.
	i. **olive green**	450.
	j. **olive brown**	450.
210TC4	2c plate on card	
	a. **lake**	140.
	b. **rose lake**	140.
	c. **deep carmine**	140.
	d. **deep red**	140.
210P1	2c **red brn,** large die on India paper	400.
210P2	2c **red brn,** RA sm die on white wove paper	200.
210P2a	2c **red brn,** PP sm die on yelsh wove paper	2,500.
210P3	2c **red brn,** plate on India	40.
	Block of 4	180.
	P# blk. of 12	1,000.
210P4	2c **red brn,** plate on card	20.
	Block of 4	110.
	P# blk. of 12	—
	Bottom margin P# block of 30	*2,700.*
210P5	2c **red brn,** plate on stamp paper, pair	—
211TC1a	4c large die on India paper	
	e. **green**	1,000.
	f. **chestnut brown**	1,000.
	g. **orange brown**	1,000.
	h. **pale ultramarine**	1,000.
	i. **dark brown**	1,000.
	j. **black**	1,000.
211TC1d	4c large die on card	
	e. **green**	450.
	f. **chestnut brown**	450.
	g. **orange brown**	450.
	h. **pale ultramarine**	450.
	i. **black**	450.
211P1	4c **grn,** large die on India paper	500.
211P2	4c **grn,** RA sm die on white wove paper	200.
211P2a	4c **grn,** PP sm die on yelsh wove paper	2,500.
211P3	4c **grn,** plate on India	40.
	Block of 4	165.
	P# blk. of 12	1,000.
211P4	4c **grn,** plate on card	25.
	Block of 4	140.
	P# blk. of 12	—
	Bottom margin P# block of 30	*2,700.*
211P5	4c **green,** plate on stamp paper, pair	—

1887-88

No.	Description	Price
212TC1a	1c large die on India paper	
	e. **indigo**	1,000.
	f. **carmine**	1,000.
	g. **green**	1,000.
	h. **deep green**	1,000.
	i. **copper brown**	1,000.
	j. **chestnut brown**	1,000.
212TC1d	1c large die on card	
	e. **green**	450.
	f. **deep green**	450.
	g. **copper brown**	450.
212P1	1c **ultra,** large die on India paper	650.
212P2	1c **ultra,** RA sm die on white wove paper	200.
212P2a	1c **ultra,** PP sm die on yelsh wove paper	2,500.
212P3	1c **ultra,** plate on India	125.
	Block of 4	600.
	P# blk. of 12	2,250.
212P4	1c **ultra,** plate on card	*2,750.*
	Block of 4	—
212P5	1c **ultra,** plate on stamp paper, pair	—

Examples of No. 212P3 mounted on card are frequently offered as No. 212P4.

No.	Description	Price
213P1	2c **grn,** large die on India paper	500.
213P2	2c **grn,** RA sm die on white wove paper	190.
213P2a	2c **grn,** PP sm die on yelsh wove paper	2,500.
213P3	2c **grn,** plate on India	75.
	Block of 4	325.
	P# blk. of 12	1,150.

No.	Description	Value
213P4	2c **grn,** plate on card	50.
	Block of 4	225.
	P# blk. of 12	—
213P5	2c **green,** plate on stamp paper, pair	2,000.
214TC1a	3c large die on India paper	
	e. **green**	1,000.
	f. **dark green**	—
	g. **dark brown**	1,000.
	h. **chestnut brown**	1,000.
	i. **dull red brown**	1,000.
	j. **deep dull orange**	—
214TC1d	3c large die on card	
	e. **green**	450.
	f. **dark green**	—
	g. **dark brown**	450.
	h. **chestnut brown**	450.
	i. **dull red brown**	450.
	j. **deep dull orange**	—
214TC4	3c plate on card	
	a. **dark green**	—
	b. **deep orange brown**	—
	c. **deep dull orange**	—

All of 214TC1s above bear inscription "Worked over by new company, June 29th, 1881."

No.	Description	Value
214P1	3c **vermilion,** large die on India paper	500.
214P2	3c **vermilion,** RA sm die on white wove paper	190.
214P2a	3c **vermilion,** PP sm die on yelsh wove paper	2,500.
214P3	3c **vermilion,** plate on India	75.
	Block of 4	325.
	P# blk. of 12	—
214P4	3c **vermilion,** plate on card	50.
	Block of 4	225.
	P# blk. of 12	—

Nos. 207P1 & 214P1 inscribed: "Worked over by new company, June 29th, 1881."

No.	Description	Value
215P1	4c **car,** large die on India paper	650.
215P2	4c **car,** RA sm die on white wove paper	190.
215P2a	4c **car,** PP sm die on yelsh wove paper	2,500.
215P3	4c **car,** plate on India	95.
	Block of 4	475.
215P4	4c **car,** plate on card	50.
	Block of 4	225.
	P# blk. of 12	—
216P1	5c **indigo,** large die on India paper	650.
216P2	5c **indigo,** RA sm die on white wove paper	190.
216P2a	5c **indigo,** PP sm die on yelsh wove paper	2,500.
216P3	5c **indigo,** plate on India	75.
	Block of 4	325.
216P4	5c **indigo,** plate on card	50.
	Block of 4	225.
	P# blk. of 12	—
216P5	5c **indigo,** plate on stamp paper, pair	*1,400.*
217P1	30c **org brn,** large die on India paper	750.
217P2	30c **org brn,** RA sm die on white wove paper	190.
217P2a	30c **org brn,** PP sm die on yelsh wove paper	2,500.
217P3	30c **org brn,** plate on India	75.
	Block of 4	325.
217P4	30c **org brn,** plate on card	50.
	Block of 4	225.
	P# blk. of 10	—
217P5	30c **org brn,** plate on stamp paper, pair	*1,750.*
218P1	90c **purple,** large die on India paper	1,100.
218P2	90c **purple,** RA sm die on white wove paper	190.
218P2a	90c **purple,** PP sm die on yelsh wove paper	2,500.
218P3	90c **purple,** plate on India	90.
	Block of 4	400.
218P4	90c **purple,** plate on card	50.
	Block of 4	225.
218P5	90c **purple,** plate on stamp paper, pair	—

1890-93

No.	Description	Value
219TC1a	1c large die on India paper	
	e. **green**	400.
	f. **dull violet**	400.
219P1	1c **ultra,** large die on India paper	225.
219P2	1c **ultra,** RA sm die on white wove paper	190.
219P2a	1c **ultra,** PP sm die on yelsh wove paper	2,000.
219P3	1c **ultra,** plate on India	25.
	Block of 4	110.
	P# blk. of 12	500.
219P4	1c **ultra,** plate on card	40.
	Block of 4	180.
	P# blk. of 12	650.
219P5	1c **ultra,** plate on stamp paper, pair	*190.*
219DP1	2c **lake,** large die on India paper	550.
219DP2	2c **lake,** RA sm die on white wove paper	190.
219DP2a	2c **lake,** PP sm die on yelsh wove paper	2,000.
219DP3	2c **lake,** plate on India	80.
	Block of 4	385.
	P# blk. of 12	1,650.
219DP4	2c **lake,** plate on card	165.
	Block of 4	700.
	P# blk. of 12	3,250.
219DP5	2c **lake,** plate on stamp paper, pair	*80.*
	P# blk. of 8	800.
220TC1a	2c large die on India paper	
	e. **dull violet**	400.
	f. **blue green**	400.
	g. **slate black**	400.
220P1	2c **car,** large die on India paper	450.
220P2	2c **car,** RA sm die on white wove paper	190.
220P3	2c **car,** plate on India	300.
	Block of 4	1,250.
	P# blk. of 12	3,850.
220P4	2c **car,** plate on card	200.
	Block of 4	825.
	P# blk. of 12	2,500.
220P5	2c **car,** plate on stamp paper, pair	*125.*
	As No. 220P5, without gum	*60.*
	P# blk. of 12	—
221P1	3c **purple,** large die on India paper	225.
221P2	3c **purple,** RA sm die on white wove paper	190.
221P2a	3c **purple,** PP sm die on yelsh wove paper	2,000.
221P3	3c **purple,** plate on India	35.
	Block of 4	160.
	P# blk. of 12	650.
221P4	3c **purple,** plate on card	25.
	Block of 4	110.
	P# blk. of 12	600.
221P5	3c **purple,** plate on stamp paper, pair	*225.*
222TC1a	4c large die on India paper	
	e. **green**	450.
222TC5	4c plate on wove	
	a. **orange brown**	—
	b. **yellow brown**	—
222P1	4c **dk brn,** large die on India paper	550.
222P2	4c **dk brn,** RA sm die on white wove paper	300.
222P2a	4c **dk brn,** PP sm die on yelsh wove paper	2,000.
222P3	4c **dk brn,** plate on India	35.
	Block of 4	160.
	P# blk. of 12	650.
222P4	4c **dk brn,** plate on card	25.
	Block of 4	110.
	P# blk. of 12	725.
222P5	4c **dk brn,** plate on stamp paper, pair	*210.*
223TC1c	5c Large die on glossy wove paper	
	e. **blue**	400.
	f. **dark brown**	400.
223TC5	5c plate on wove paper	
	a. **bister**	—
	b. **sepia**	—
	c. **black brown**	—
223P1	5c **chocolate,** large die on India paper	225.
223P2	5c **chocolate,** RA sm die on white wove paper	190.
223P2a	5c **chocolate,** PP sm die on yelsh wove paper	2,000.
223P3	5c **chocolate,** plate on India	32.
	Block of 4	135.
	P# blk. of 12	600.
223P4	5c **chocolate,** plate on card	25.
	Block of 4	110.
	P# blk. of 12	625.
223P5	5c **yel brn,** plate on stamp paper, pair	*225.*
224TC1a	6c large die on India paper	
	e. **deep orange red**	400.
224TC5	6c plate on wove paper	
	a. **orange red**	120.
	b. **violet black**	120.
	c. **yellow**	120.
	d. **olive green**	120.
	e. **purple**	120.
	f. **red orange**	120.
	g. **brown**	120.
	h. **red brown**	120.
	i. **orange brown**	120.
	j. **black brown**	120.
	k. **slate green**	120.
	l. **brown olive**	120.
224P1	6c **brn red,** large die on India paper	225.
224P2	6c **brn red,** RA sm die on white wove paper	190.
224P2a	6c **brn red,** PP sm die on yelsh wove paper	2,000.
224P3	6c **brn red,** plate on India	32.
	Block of 4	135.
	P# blk. of 12	600.
224P4	6c **brn red,** plate on card	20.
	Block of 4	85.
	P# blk. of 12	775.
224P5	6c **brn red,** plate on stamp paper, pair	*225.*
225TC1a	8c large die on India paper	
	e. **yellow orange**	—
	f. **green**	—
225TC1d	8c large die on card	
	e. **dark violet red**	400.
	f. **metallic green**	400.
	g. **salmon**	400.
	h. **orange brown**	400.
	i. **light green**	400.
	j. **blue**	400.
	k. **steel blue**	400.
225P1	8c **lilac,** large die on India paper	600.
225P2	8c **lilac,** RA sm die on white wove paper	190.
225P2a	8c **lilac,** PP sm die on yelsh wove paper	2,000.
225P3	8c **lilac,** plate on India	55.
	Block of 4	250.
	P# blk. of 12	1,100.
225P4	8c **lilac,** plate on card	110.
	Block of 4	500.
	P# blk. of 12	2,000.
225P5	8c **lilac,** plate on stamp paper, pair	*1,000.*
226P1	10c **grn,** large die on India paper	225.
226P2	10c **grn,** RA sm die on white wove paper	190.
226P2a	10c **grn,** PP sm die on yelsh wove paper	2,000.
226P3	10c **grn,** plate on India	45.
	Block of 4	200.
	P# blk. of 12	700.
226P4	10c **grn,** plate on card	40.
	Block of 4	180.
	P# blk. of 12	750.
226P5	10c **grn,** plate on stamp paper, pair	*325.*
227P1	15c **indigo,** large die on India paper	300.
227P2	15c **indigo,** RA sm die on white wove paper	190.
227P2a	15c **indigo,** PP sm die on yelsh wove paper	2,000.
227P3	15c **indigo,** plate on India	45.
	Block of 4	190.
	P# blk. of 12	825.
227P4	15c **indigo,** plate on card	40.
	Block of 4	180.
	P# blk. of 12	875.
227P5	15c **indigo,** plate on stamp paper, pair	*625.*
	P# blk. of 12	*5,000.*
228P1	30c **black,** large die on India paper	300.
228P2	30c **black,** RA sm die on white wove paper	190.
228P2a	30c **black,** PP sm die on yelsh wove paper	2,000.
228P3	30c **black,** plate on India	45.
	Block of 4	190.
	P# blk. of 12	825.
228P4	30c **black,** plate on card	45.
	Block of 4	190.
	P# blk. of 12	875.
228P5	30c **black,** plate on stamp paper, pair	*1,000.*
229P1	90c **orange,** large die on India paper	300.
229P2	90c **orange,** RA sm die on white wove paper	190.
229P2a	90c **orange,** PP sm die on yelsh wove paper	2,000.
229P3	90c **orange,** plate on India	60.
	Block of 4	275.
	P# blk. of 12	1,100.
229P4	90c **orange,** plate on card	50.
	Block of 4	225.
	P# blk. of 12	1,150.
229P5	90c **orange,** plate on stamp paper, pair	*1,450.*

Columbian Issue

1893

No.	Description	Value
230P1	1c **blue,** large die on India paper	900.
230P2	1c **blue,** RA sm die on white wove paper	325.
230P2a	1c **blue,** PP sm die on yelsh wove paper	2,000.
230P3	1c **blue,** plate on India	60.
	Block of 4	300.
	P# blk. of 8	800.
230P4	1c **blue,** plate on card	20.
	Block of 4	130.
	P# blk. of 8	425.
231TC1a	2c large die on India paper	
	e. **sepia**	850.
231TC1d	1c large die on card	
	e. **sepia**	850.
	f. **orange brown**	850.
	g. **deep orange**	850.
	h. **light brown**	850.
	i. **blue green**	850.
	j. **bright rose red**	850.
	k. **rose violet**	850.
231P1	2c **violet,** large die on India paper	1,000.
231P2	2c **violet,** RA sm die on white wove paper	350.
231P2a	2c **violet,** PP sm die on yelsh wove paper	2,500.
231P3	2c **violet,** plate on India	350.
	Block of 4	2,000.
	P# blk. of 8	5,000.
231P4	2c **violet,** plate on card	45.
	Block of 4	260.
	P# blk. of 8	750.
	a. "Broken hat" variety, plate on card	130.
231P5	2c **violet,** plate on stamp paper, pair	*2,000.*

Almost all examples of No. 231P5 are faulty. Value is for pair with minimal faults.

No.	Description	Value
232TC1d	3c large die on card	
	e. **sepia**	850.
	f. **blackish green**	850.
	g. **black**	850.
232TC3	3c plate on India paper	
	a. **blackish green**	800.
232P1	3c **green,** large die on India paper	900.
232P2	3c **green,** RA sm die on white wove paper	325.
232P2a	3c **green,** PP sm die on yelsh wove paper	3,000.
232P3	3c **green,** plate on India	95.
	Block of 4	550.
	P# blk. of 8	1,400.
232P4	3c **green,** plate on card	70.
	Block of 4	425.
	P# blk. of 8	1,100.
233TC1d	4c large die on card	
	e. **sepia**	850.
	f. **deep orange**	850.
	g. **light brown**	850.
	h. **blue green**	850.
	i. **rose red**	850.
	j. **rose violet**	850.
233P1	4c **ultra,** large die on India paper	900.
233P2	4c **ultra,** RA sm die on white wove paper	325.
233P2a	4c **ultra,** PP sm die on yelsh wove paper	3,000.
233P3	4c **ultra,** plate on India	95.
	Block of 4	550.
	P# blk. of 8	1,400.
233P4	4c **ultra,** plate on card	70.
	Block of 4	425.
	P# blk. of 8	1,250.
233aP1	4c **blue,** (error) large die on thin card	*2,750.*
234TC1a	5c large die on India paper	
	e. **black**	850.
	f. **dark violet**	850.
	g. **rose violet**	850.
	h. **red violet**	850.
	i. **brown violet**	850.
	j. **deep blue**	850.

k. **deep ultramarine** 850.
l. **black** 850.
m. **green** 850.
n. **deep green** 850.
o. **blue green** —
p. **dark olive green** 850.
q. **deep orange** 850.
r. **orange red** 850.
s. **orange brown** 850.
t. **bright rose red** 850.
u. **claret** 850.
v. **brown rose** 850.
w. **dull rose brown** 850.
x. **sepia** 850.
y. **black brown** —
234TC1d 5c large die on card
e. **dark violet** 850.
f. **rose violet** 850.
g. **blue green** 850.
h. **dark olive green** —
i. **deep orange** —
j. **orange brown** 850.
k. **claret** —
k. **sepia** 850.
m. **black brown** —

The 5c trial color proofs differ from the issued stamp.

234P1 5c **choc,** large die on India paper 900.
234P2 5c **choc,** RA sm die on white wove paper 325.
234P2a 5c **choc,** PP sm die on yelsh wove paper 3,000.
234P3 5c **choc,** plate on India 95.
Block of 4 550.
P# blk. of 8 1,400.
234P4 5c **choc,** plate on card 65.
Block of 4 360.
P# blk. of 8 1,200.
235P1 6c **purple,** large die on India paper 900.
235P2 6c **purple,** RA sm die on white wove paper 325.
235P2a 6c **purple,** PP sm die on yelsh wove paper 3,000.
235P3 6c **purple,** plate on India 95.
Block of 4 550.
P# blk. of 8 1,400.
235P4 6c **purple,** plate on card 70.
Block of 4 425.
P# blk. of 8 1,300.
236P1 8c **magenta,** large die on India paper 900.
236P2 8c **magenta,** RA sm die on white wove paper 325.
236P2a 8c **magenta,** PP sm die on yelsh wove paper 3,000.
236P3 8c **magenta,** plate on India 95.
Block of 4 550.
P# blk. of 8 1,400.
236P4 8c **magenta,** plate on card 150.
Block of 4 925.
P# blk. of 8 2,500.
237TC1a 10c large die on India paper
e. **bright rose red** 1,250.
f. **claret** 1,250.
237P1 10c **blk brn,** large die on India paper 900.
237P2 10c **blk brn,** RA sm die on white wove paper 325.
237P2a 10c **blk brn,** PP sm die on yelsh wove paper 3,000.
237P3 10c **blk brn,** plate on India 95.
Block of 4 550.
P# blk. of 8 1,400.
237P4 10c **blk brn,** plate on card 70.
Block of 4 425.
P# blk. of 8 1,300.
238P1 15c **dk grn,** large die on India paper 900.
238P2 15c **dk grn,** RA sm die on white wove paper 325.
238P2a 15c **dk grn,** PP sm die on yelsh wove paper 3,000.
238P3 15c **dk grn,** plate on India 95.
Block of 4 550.
P# blk. of 8 1,400.
238P4 15c **dk grn,** plate on card 80.
Block of 4 500.
P# blk. of 8 3,000.
239TC1d 30c large die on card
e. **sepia** 1,000.
239TC4 30c plate on card
a. **black** 350.
239P1 30c **org brn,** large die on India paper 900.
239P2 30c **org brn,** RA sm die on white wove paper 325.
239P2a 30c **org brn,** PP sm die on yelsh wove paper 3,000.
239P3 30c **org brn,** plate on India 140.
Block of 4 850.
P# blk. of 8 2,400.
239P4 30c **org brn,** plate on card 100.
Block of 4 600.
P# blk. of 8 2,400.
240TC1d 50c large die on card
e. **sepia** 1,000.
240P1 50c **slate bl,** large die on India paper 900.
240P2 50c **slate bl,** RA sm die on white wove paper 325.
240P2a 50c **slate bl,** PP sm die on yelsh wove paper 3,000.
240P3 50c **slate bl,** plate on India 225.
Block of 4 1,300.
P# blk. of 8 3,250.
240P4 50c **slate bl,** plate on card 120.
Block of 4 725.
P# blk. of 8 2,500.
241P1 $1 **salmon,** large die on India paper 1,150.
241P2 $1 **salmon,** RA sm die on white wove paper 450.
241P2a $1 **salmon,** PP sm die on yelsh wove paper 3,000.
241P3 $1 **salmon,** plate on India 250.
Block of 4 1,600.
P# blk. of 8 3,750.
241P4 $1 **salmon,** plate on card 200.
Block of 4 1,200.
242TC1a $2 large die on India paper
e. **sepia** —
f. **red brown** —
242TC3 $2 plate on India paper
a. **blackish brown** 1,000.
242P1 $2 **brn red,** large die on India paper 1,150.
242P2 $2 **brn red,** RA sm die on white wove paper 450.
242P2a $2 **brn red,** PP sm die on yelsh wove paper 3,000.
242P3 $2 **brn red,** plate on India 290.
Block of 4 1,850.
P# blk. of 8 4,250.
242P4 $2 **brn red,** plate on card 175.
Block of 4 1,050.
P# blk. of 8 3,000.
243P1 $3 **yel grn,** large die on India paper 1,150.
243P2 $3 **yel grn,** RA sm die on white wove paper 450.
243P2a $3 **yel grn,** PP sm die on yelsh wove paper 3,000.
243P3 $3 **yel grn,** plate on India 350.
Block of 4 2,100.
P# blk. of 8 5,000.
243P4 $3 **yel grn,** plate on card 225.
Block of 4 1,300.
P# blk. of 8 3,400.
244P1 $4 **crimson lake,** large die on India paper 1,150.
244P2 $4 **crimson lake,** RA sm die on white wove paper 450.
244P2a $4 **crimson lake,** PP sm die on yelsh wove paper 3,000.
244P3 $4 **crimson lake,** plate on India 450.
Block of 4 2,700.
P# blk. of 8 6,250.
244P4 $4 **crimson lake,** plate on card 275.
Block of 4 1,600.
P# blk. of 8 5,500.
245P1 $5 **black,** large die on India paper 1,150.
245P2 $5 **black,** RA sm die on white wove paper 450.
245P2a $5 **black,** PP sm die on yelsh wove paper 3,000.
245P3 $5 **black,** plate on India 525.
Block of 4 3,100.
P# blk. of 8 7,500.
245P4 $5 **black,** plate on card 375.
Block of 4 2,150.
P# blk. of 8 6,750.
Nos. 230P3-245P3 (16) 3,305.
Nos. 230P4-245P4 (16) 2,110.

This set also exists as Large Die proofs, not die sunk, but printed directly on thin card. Set value $7,000. 1c through 50c, $350 each; $1 through $5, $650 each.

Nos. 234P1, 234P2 differ from issued stamp.

1894 Bureau of Engraving and Printing

246TC1a 1c large die on India paper
e. **dusky blue green** —
f. **dark blue** —
246P1 1c **ultra,** large die on India paper 450.
247P1 1c **blue,** large die on India paper 250.
247P2 1c **blue,** RA sm die on white wove paper 250.
247P2a 1c **blue,** PP sm die on yelsh wove paper 2,000.
247P4 1c **blue,** plate on card 100.
Block of 4 450.
P# blk. of 6 2,250.
248P1 2c **pink,** Type I, large die on India paper —
248P4 2c **pink,** Type I, plate on card 100.
Block of 4 475.
P# blk. of 6 2,500.
250P1 2c **car,** Type I, large die on India paper 250.
250P2 2c **car,** Type I, RA sm die on white wove paper 250.
251P1 2c **car,** Type II, large die on India paper 250.
251P2 2c **car,** Type II, sm die on white wove paper —

The existence of No. 251P2 has been questioned by specialists. The editors would like to see evidence that the item exists.

252P1 2c **car,** Type III, 15-subject die (3x5) on India *6,000.*
Single design 350.
Block of 4 1,500.
253TC1a 3c large die on India paper
e. **light red violet** —
f. **dark red violet** —
253P1 3c **purple,** Triangle I, large die on India paper 750.
253P5 3c **purple,** Triangle I, plate on stamp paper, pair *300.*
Block of 4 *625.*
P# blk. of 6 *7,500.*
253AP1 3c **purple,** Triangle II, large die on India paper 325.
253AP2 3c **purple,** Triangle II, RA sm die on white wove paper 250.
253AP2a 3c **purple,** Triangle II, PP sm die on yelsh wove paper 2,000.
254P1 4c **dk brn,** large die on India paper 600.
254P2 4c **dk brn,** RA sm die on white wove paper 250.
254P2a 4c **dk brn,** PP sm die on yelsh wove paper 2,000.
254P5 4c **dk brn,** plate on stamp paper, pair *275.*
Block of 4 *575.*
P# blk. of 6 *7,500.*
255TC1a 5c large die on India paper
e. **black** 1,250.
255P1 5c **choc,** large die on India paper 250.
255P2 5c **choc,** RA sm die on white wove paper 250.
255P2a 5c **choc,** PP sm die on yelsh wove paper 2,000.
255P5 5c **choc,** plate on stamp paper, pair *300.*
Block of 4 *625.*
P# blk. of 6 *9,500.*
256TC1a 6c large die on India paper
e. **dark brown** 1,000.
256P1 6c **brn,** large die on India paper 250.
256P2 6c **brn,** RA sm die on white wove paper 250.
256P2a 6c **brn,** PP sm die on yelsh wove paper 2,000.
256P4 6c **brn,** plate on card 450.
Block of 4 1,900.
P# blk. of 6 *5,500.*
257TC1a 8c large die on India paper
e. **black** 1,250.
257P1 8c **vio brn,** large die on India paper 250.
257P2 8c **vio brn,** RA sm die on white wove paper 250.
257P2a 8c **vio brn,** PP sm die on yelsh wove paper 2,000.
258TC1a 10c large die on India paper
e. **olive** 1,250.
258P1 10c **grn,** large die on India paper 275.
258P2 10c **grn,** RA sm die on white wove paper 250.
258P2a 10c **grn,** PP sm die on yelsh wove paper 2,000.
258P5 10c **grn,** plate on stamp paper, pair *500.*
Block of 4 *1,100.*
P# blk. of 6 *9,500.*
259TC1a 15c large die on India paper
e. **red violet** 1,250.
f. **dark red orange** 1,250.
259P1 15c **dk bl,** large die on India paper 300.
259P2 15c **dk bl,** RA sm die on white wove paper 250.
259P2a 15c **dk bl,** PP sm die on yelsh wove paper 2,000.
260TC1a 50c large die on India paper
e. **black** 1,500.
260P1 50c **org,** large die on India paper 450.
260P2 50c **org,** RA sm die on white wove paper 210.
260P2a 50c **org,** PP sm die on yelsh wove paper 2,000.
261TC1a $1 large die on India paper
e. **orange** 1,500.
261ATC1a $1 large die on India paper
e. **lake** 1,500.
f. **orange** 1,500.
261AP1 $1 **blk,** large die on India paper 500.
261AP2 $1 **blk,** RA sm die on white wove paper 350.
261AP2a $1 **blk,** PP sm die on yelsh wove paper 2,000.
262TC1a $2 large die on India paper
e. **black** 1,500.
f. **dull violet** 1,500.
g. **violet** 1,500.
h. **turquoise blue** 1,500.
i. **orange brown** 1,500.
j. **olive green** 1,500.
k. **sepia** 1,500.
l. **greenish black** 1,500.
262P1 $2 **dk bl,** large die on India paper 500.
262P2 $2 **dk bl,** RA sm die on white wove paper 350.
262P2a $2 **dk bl,** PP sm die on yelsh wove paper 2,000.
262P4 $2 **dk bl,** plate on card 450.
Block of 4 2,500.
Margin block of 4, arrow *2,750.*
P# blk. of 6 *6,250.*
263TC1a $5 large die on India paper
e. **black** 1,500.
f. **dark yellow** 1,500.
g. **orange brown** 1,500.
h. **olive green** 1,500.
i. **dull violet** 1,500.
j. **sepia** 1,500.
k. **brown red** 1,500.
263P1 $5 **dk grn,** large die on India paper 650.
263P2 $5 **dk grn,** RA sm die on white wove paper 375.
263P2a $5 **dk grn,** PP sm die on yelsh wove paper 2,000.
263P4 $5 **dk grn,** plate on card 450.
Block of 4 2,500.
Margin block of 4, arrow *2,750.*
P# blk. of 6 *6,500.*

1895 Imperf, with gum

264P5 1c **blue,** plate on stamp paper, pair *275.*
Block of 4 *700.*
P# strip of 3 *850.*
P# blk. of 6 *1,150.*
a. Horiz. P# strip of 3, perf horiz., imperf. vert. *19,000.*
267P5 2c **car,** Type III, plate on stamp paper, pair *200.*
Block of 4 *550.*
P# strip of 3 *650.*
P# blk. of 6 *1,100.*
268P5 3c **purple,** plate on stamp paper, pair *250.*
Block of 4 *700.*
P# strip of 3 *950.*
P# blk. of 6 *2,000.*
269P5 4c **dk brn,** plate on stamp paper, pair *250.*
Block of 4 *700.*
P# strip of 3 *1,250.*
P# blk. of 6 *3,250.*
270P5 5c **choc,** plate on stamp paper, pair *250.*
Block of 4 *700.*
P# strip of 3 *950.*
271P5 6c **dull brn,** plate on stamp paper, pair *275.*
Block of 4 *825.*
P# strip of 3 *1,150.*

272P5 8c **vio brn,** plate on stamp paper, pair *400.*
Block of 4 *1,100.*
P# strip of 3 *1,500.*
P# blk. of 6 *3,100.*
273P5 10c **dk grn,** plate on stamp paper, pair *325.*
Block of 4 *900.*
P# strip of 3 *1,250.*
274P5 15c **dk bl,** plate on stamp paper, pair *1,000.*
Block of 4 *2,750.*
P# strip of 3 *3,750.*
275P5 50c **org,** plate on stamp paper, pair *1,100.*
Block of 4 *3,250.*
P# strip of 3 *4,500.*
276P5 $1 **blk,** Type I, plate on stamp paper, pair *1,450.*
Block of 4 *3,750.*
P# strip of 3 *5,250.*
277P5 $2 **brt bl,** plate on stamp paper, pair *3,250.*
Block of 4 *7,500.*
P# strip of 3 *10,500.*
278P5 $5 **dk grn,** plate on stamp paper, pair *3,250.*
Block of 4 *7,500.*
P# strip of 3 *10,500.*

No. 264P5a exists only as a bottom margin P#24 and imprint strip of 3.

1897-1903

279P1 1c **grn,** large die on India paper 700.
279P2 1c **grn,** RA sm die on white wove paper 375.
279P2a 1c **grn,** PP sm die on yelsh wove paper 2,000.
279BdP2a 2c **org red,** Type IV, PP sm die on yelsh wove paper 2,000.
279BfP1 2c **car,** Type IV, large die on India paper 400.
279BfP2a 2c **car,** Type IV, PP sm die on yelsh wove paper 2,000.
280P1 4c **rose brn,** large die on India paper 700.
280P2a 4c **rose brn,** PP sm die on yelsh wove paper 2,000.
281P1 5c **blue,** large die on India paper 700.
281P2 5c **blue,** RA sm die on white wove paper 375.
281P2a 5c **blue,** PP sm die on yelsh wove paper 2,000.
282P1 6c **lake,** large die on India paper 700.
282P2a 6c **lake,** PP sm die on yelsh wove paper 2,000.
283TC1a 10c large die on India paper
e. **orange** 1,250.
f. **sepia** 1,250.
283P1 10c **org brn,** Type II, large die on India paper 800.
283P2 10c **org brn,** Type II, RA sm die on white wove paper 375.
283P2a 10c **org brn,** Type II, PP sm die on yelsh wove paper 2,000.
283aP1 10c **brn,** Type II, large die on India paper 800.
284TC1a 15c large die on India paper
e. **yellowish olive** *1,500.*
f. **red violet** *1,750.*
g. **deep dull green** *1,750.*
284P1 15c **ol grn,** Type II, large die on India paper 800.
284P2 15c **ol grn,** Type II, RA sm die on white wove paper 375.
284P2a 15c **ol grn,** Type II, PP sm die on yelsh wove paper 2,000.

Trans-Mississippi Issue

1898

285TC1a 1c large die on India paper
e. **black** —
285P1 1c **grn,** large die on India paper 850.
285P2 1c **grn,** RA sm die on white wove paper 750.
285P2a 1c **grn,** PP sm die on yelsh wove paper 3,000.
286TC1a 2c large die on India paper
e. **black** —
286TC4 2c plate on card
a. **purple** 2,500.
b. **black** 2,500.
c. **blue** 2,500.
d. **brown** 2,500.
e. **deep carmine rose** 2,500.
286P1 2c **copper red,** large die on India paper 850.
286P2 2c **copper red,** RA sm die on white wove paper 750.
286P2a 2c **copper red,** PP sm die on yelsh wove paper 3,000.
286P4 2c **copper red,** plate on card *10,000.*
287TC1a 4c large die on India paper
e. **black** —
287P1 4c **org,** large die on India paper 850.
287P2 4c **org,** RA sm die on white wove paper 750.
287P2a 4c **org,** PP sm die on yelsh wove paper 3,000.
288TC1a 5c large die on India paper
e. **black** —
f. **orange brown** *2,500.*
288P1 5c **dull bl,** large die on India paper 850.
288P2 5c **dull bl,** RA sm die on white wove paper 750.
288P2a 5c **dull bl,** PP sm die on yelsh wove paper 3,000.
289TC1a 8c large die on India paper
e. **black** —
289P1 8c **vio brn,** large die on India paper 850.
289P2 8c **vio brn,** RA sm die on white wove paper 750.
289P2a 8c **vio brn,** PP sm die on yelsh wove paper 3,000.
290TC1a 10c large die on India paper
e. **black** 1,500.
290TC2 10c small die on India paper
b. **black** 1,250.
290P1 10c **gray vio,** large die on India paper 850.
290P2 10c **gray vio,** RA sm die on white wove paper 750.
290P2a 10c **gray vio,** PP sm die on yelsh wove paper 3,000.
291TC1a 50c large die on India paper
e. **black** 1,500.
291TC2 50c small die on wove paper
b. **black** 2,400.
291P1 50c **sage grn,** large die on India paper 850.
291P2 50c **sage grn,** RA sm die on white wove paper 750.
291P2a 50c **sage grn,** PP sm die on yelsh wove paper 3,000.
292TC1a $1 large die on India paper
e. **black** —
292P1 $1 **blk,** large die on India paper 1,000.
292P2 $1 **blk,** RA sm die on white wove paper 750.
292P2a $1 **blk,** PP sm die on yelsh wove paper 3,000.
293TC1a $2 large die on India paper
e. **black** 5,000.
293P1 $2 **org brn,** large die on India paper 1,000.
293P2 $2 **org brn,** RA sm die on white wove paper 750.
293P2a $2 **org brn,** PP sm die on yelsh wove paper 3,000.
293P4 $2 **org brn,** plate on card 6,000.
Block of 4 *27,500.*
P# blk. of 6 *35,000.*

The bicolored essays commonly offered as Nos. 285-293 bicolored proofs in "original" colors can be found under the following essay listings: Nos. 285-E8, 286-E8, 287-E9, 288-E5, 289-E4, 290-E4, 291-E8, 292-E6, and 293-E7. Value, set of nine $6,550.

Pan-American Issue

1901

294P1 1c **grn & blk,** large die on India paper 575.
294P1a 1c **grn & blk,** large die on wove paper *1,500.*
294P2 1c **grn & blk,** RA sm die on white wove paper 575.
294P2a 1c **grn & blk,** PP sm die on yelsh wove paper 3,000.
295P1 2c **car & blk,** large die on India paper 575.
295P1a 2c **car & blk,** large die on wove paper *1,500.*
295P2 2c **car & blk,** RA sm die on white wove paper 575.
295P2a 2c **car & blk,** PP sm die on yelsh wove paper 3,000.
b. small die proof on yelsh bond *1,250.*
296P1 4c **choc & blk,** large die on India paper 575.
296P1a 4c **choc & blk,** large die on wove paper *1,500.*
296P2 4c **choc & blk,** RA sm die on white wove paper 575.
296P2a 4c **choc & blk,** PP sm die on yelsh wove paper 3,000.
297P1 5c **ultra & blk,** large die on India paper 575.
297P1a 5c **ultra & blk,** large die on wove paper *1,500.*
297P2 5c **ultra & blk,** RA sm die on white wove paper 575.
297P2a 5c **ultra & blk,** PP sm die on yelsh wove paper 3,000.
298TC2 8c small die on wove
b. **violet & black** *2,500.*
298P1 8c **brn vio & blk,** large die on India paper 575.
298P1a 8c **brn vio & blk,** large die on wove paper *1,500.*
298P2 8c **brn vio & blk,** RA sm die on white wove paper 575.
298P2a 8c **brn vio & blk,** PP sm die on yelsh wove paper 3,000.
299P1 10c **yel brn & blk,** large die on India paper 575.
299P1a 10c **yel brn & blk,** large die on wove paper *1,500.*
299P2 10c **yel brn & blk,** RA sm die on white wove paper 575.
299P2a 10c **yel brn & blk,** PP sm die on yelsh wove paper 3,000.

1902-03

300P1 1c **grn,** large die on India paper 1,750.
300P2 1c **grn,** RA sm die on white wove paper 300.
300P2a 1c **grn,** PP sm die on yelsh wove paper 2,500.
301P1 2c **car,** large die on India paper 1,750.
301P2 2c **car,** RA sm die on white wove paper 300.
301P2a 2c **car,** PP sm die on yelsh wove paper 2,500.
302P1 3c **purple,** large die on India paper 1,750.
302P2 3c **purple,** RA sm die on white wove paper 300.
302P2a 3c **purple,** PP sm die on yelsh wove paper 2,500.
303P1 4c **org brn,** large die on India paper 1,750.
303P2 4c **org brn,** RA sm die on white wove paper 300.
303P2a 4c **org brn,** PP sm die on yelsh wove paper 2,500.
304P1 5c **blue,** large die on India paper 1,750.
304P2 5c **blue,** RA sm die on white wove paper 300.
304P2a 5c **blue,** PP sm die on yelsh wove paper 2,500.
305P1 6c **lake,** large die on India paper 1,750.
305P2 6c **lake,** RA sm die on white wove paper 300.
305P2a 6c **lake,** PP sm die on yelsh wove paper 2,500.
306P1 8c **vio blk,** large die on India paper 1,750.
306P2 8c **vio blk,** RA sm die on white wove paper 300.
306P2a 8c **vio blk,** PP sm die on yelsh wove paper 2,500.
307P1 10c **org brn,** large die on India paper 1,750.
307P2 10c **org brn,** RA sm die on white wove paper 300.
307P2a 10c **org brn,** PP sm die on yelsh wove paper 2,500.
308TC1a 13c large die on India paper
e. **gray violet, type I** 1,000.
308P1 13c **dp vio brn,** large die on India paper 1,750.
308P2 13c **dp vio brn,** RA sm die on white wove paper 300.
308P2a 13c **dp vio brn,** PP sm die on yelsh wove paper 2,500.
309P1 15c **ol grn,** large die on India paper 1,750.
309P2 15c **ol grn,** RA sm die on white wove paper 300.
309P2a 15c **ol grn,** PP sm die on yelsh wove paper 2,500.
310P1 50c **org,** large die on India paper 1,750.
310P2 50c **org,** RA sm die on white wove paper 300.
310P2a 50c **org,** PP sm die on yelsh wove paper 2,500.
311P1 $1 **blk,** large die on India paper 1,750.
311P2 $1 **blk,** RA sm die on white wove paper 300.
311P2a $1 **blk,** PP sm die on yelsh wove paper 2,500.
312P1 $2 **blue,** large die on India paper 2,500.
312P2 $2 **blue,** RA sm die on white wove paper 300.
312P2a $2 **blue,** PP sm die on yelsh wove paper 2,500.
313P1 $5 **grn,** large die on India paper 3,000.
313P2 $5 **grn,** RA sm die on white wove paper 375.
313P2a $5 **grn,** PP sm die on yelsh wove paper 2,500.

1903

319TC1a 2c large die on India paper
e. **black,** type I 3,250.
f. **lake,** type I —
319P1 2c **car,** Type I, large die on India paper 1,500.
319FiP1 2c **car,** Type II, large die on India paper 2,750.
319FiP2 2c **car,** Type II, sm die on white wove paper 1,000.
319FiP2a 2c **car,** Type II, PP sm die on yelsh wove paper 3,500.
b. small die proof on yelsh wove paper *1,000.*

Louisiana Purchase Issue

1904

323P1 1c **grn,** large die on India paper 1,400.
323P2 1c **grn,** sm die on white wove paper 750.
323P2a 1c **grn,** PP sm die on yelsh wove paper 3,500.
324P1 2c **car,** large die on India paper 1,400.
324P2 2c **car,** sm die on white wove paper 750.
324P2a 2c **car,** PP sm die on yelsh wove paper 3,500.
325P1 3c **vio,** large die on India paper 1,400.
325P2 3c **vio,** sm die on white wove paper 750.
325P2a 3c **vio,** PP sm die on yelsh wove paper 3,500.
326TC1d 5c large die on thin glazed card
e. **black** 3,500.
326P1 5c **dk bl,** large die on India paper 1,400.
326P2 5c **dk bl,** sm die on white wove paper 750.
326P2a 5c **dk bl,** PP sm die on yelsh wove paper 3,500.
327P1 10c **brn,** large die on India paper 1,400.
327P2 10c **brn,** sm die on white wove paper 750.
327P2a 10c **brn,** PP sm die on yelsh wove paper 3,500.

Jamestown Exposition Issue

1907

328P1 1c **grn,** large die on India paper 1,000.
328P2 1c **grn,** sm die on white wove paper 900.
328P2a 1c **grn,** PP sm die on yelsh wove paper 3,000.
329P1 2c **car,** large die on India paper 1,000.
329P2 2c **car,** sm die on white wove paper 900.
329P2a 2c **car,** PP sm die on yelsh wove paper 3,000.
330TC1a 5c large die on India paper
e. **ultramarine** 1,600.
f. **black** 1,700.
330P1 5c **dk bl,** large die on India paper 1,000.
330P2 5c **dk bl,** sm die on white wove paper 900.
330P2a 5c **dk bl,** PP sm die on yelsh wove paper 3,000.

1908-09

331P1 1c **grn,** large die on India paper 1,250.
331P2 1c **grn,** sm die on white wove paper 725.
331P2a 1c **grn,** PP sm die on yelsh wove paper 2,500.
332TC1a 2c large die on India paper
e. **dull violet** 750.
f. **light ultramarine** 750.
g. **bright ultramarine** 750.
h. **light green** 750.
i. **dark olive green** 750.
j. **golden yellow** 750.
k. **dull orange** 750.
l. **rose carmine** 750.
m. **ultramarine** 750.
n. **black** —
o. **dark blue** —
p. **blue** 850.
q. **lilac brown** 850.
r. **lilac** 850.
s. **blue black** 850.
t. **sage green** 850.
u. **lilac black** 850.
v. **brown** 850.
w. **brown black** 850.
x. **purple** —
y. **orange brown** 850.
z. **ultra,** *orange brown* 750.
aa. **ultra,** *green* 750.
ab. **green,** *pink* 750.
ac. **green,** *rose* 750.
ad. **dark green,** *green* 750.
ae. **green,** *orange brown* 750.
af. **purple,** *orange brown* 750.
ag. **blue,** *yellow* 750.
ah. **green,** *yellow* 750.
ai. **brown,** *orange brown* 750.

aj. **brown**, *yellow* 750.
ak. **green**, *amber yellow* —
332P1 2c **car**, large die on India paper 1,250.
a. **carmine**, large die on amber paper —
b. **carmine**, large die on lt blue paper —
332P2 2c **car**, sm die on white wove paper 725.
332P2a 2c **car**, PP sm die on yelsh wove paper 2,500.
333P1 3c **dp vio**, large die on India paper 1,250.
333P2 3c **dp vio**, sm die on white wove paper 725.
333P2a 3c **dp vio**, PP sm die on yelsh wove paper 2,500.
334P1 4c **brn**, large die on India paper 1,250.
334P2 4c **brn**, sm die on white wove paper 725.
334P2a 4c **brn**, PP sm die on yelsh wove paper 2,500.
335TC1a 5c large die on India paper
e. **green**, *pink* —
335P1 5c **blue**, large die on India paper 1,250.
a. **blue**, large die on salmon paper —
335P2 5c **blue**, sm die on white wove paper 725.
335P2a 5c **blue**, PP sm die on yelsh wove paper 2,500.
336TC1a 6c large die on India paper
e. **brown** —
336P1 6c **red org**, large die on India paper 1,250.
336P2 6c **red org**, sm die on white wove paper 725.
336P2a 6c **red org**, PP sm die on yelsh wove paper 2,500.
337TC1a 8c large die on India paper
e. **green (shades)**, *yellow* —
f. **orange (shades)**, *yellow* —
g. **blue**, *buff* —
h. **blue**, *yellow* —
337P1 8c **ol grn**, large die on India paper 1,250.
a. **olive green**, large die on yellow paper —
337P2 8c **ol grn**, sm die on white wove paper 725.
337P2a 8c **ol grn**, PP sm die on yelsh wove paper 2,500.
338TC1a 10c large die on India paper
e. **carmine**, *pale yellow green* —
f. **brown**, *yellow* —
g. **green**, *pink* —
h. **orange**, *greenish blue* —
i. **brown**, *gray lavender* —
j. **orange**, *orange* —
k. **black**, *pink* —
l. **orange**, *yellow* —
m. **brown** —
n. **carmine** —
o. **blue**, *pink* —
p. **brown**, *pink* —
q. **black** —
338P1 10c **yel**, large die on India paper 1,250.
338P2 10c **yel**, sm die on white wove paper 725.
338P2a 10c **yel**, PP sm die on yelsh wove paper 2,500.
339TC1a 13c large die on India paper
e. **blue**, *yellow* —
f. **sea green**, *deep yellow* —
g. **sea green**, *pale blue* —
h. **deep violet**, *yellow* —
339P1 13c **bl grn**, large die on India paper 1,250.
339P2 13c **bl grn**, sm die on white wove paper 725.
339P2a 13c **bl grn**, PP sm die on yelsh wove paper 2,500.
340TC1a 15c large die on India paper
e. **blue**, *pale lilac* 1,000.
f. **blue**, *greenish blue* 1,000.
g. **blue**, *pink* 1,000.
h. **blue**, *yellow* 1,000.
i. **dark blue**, *buff* 1,000.
j. **orange brown**, *yellow* 1,000.
k. **dark purple**, *yellow* 1,000.
l. **orange**, *yellow* 1,000.
m. **violet**, *yellow* 1,000.
n. **black**, *orange* 1,000.
340P1 15c **pale ultra**, large die on India paper 1,250.
340P2 15c **pale ultra**, sm die on white wove paper 725.
340P2a 15c **pale ultra**, PP sm die on yelsh wove paper 2,500.
341TC1a 50c large die on India paper
e. **lilac**, *light blue* —
f. **dark violet**, *yellow* —
g. **violet**, *yellow* —
h. **orange**, *yellow* —
i. **orange brown**, *yellow* —
341P1 50c **vio**, large die on India paper 1,250.
a. **violet**, large die on pale lilac paper —
b. **violet**, large die on yellow paper —
c. **violet**, large die on greenish paper —
341P2 50c **vio**, sm die on white wove paper 725.
341P2a 50c **vio**, PP sm die on yelsh wove paper 2,500.
342TC1a $1 large die on India paper
e. **brown**, *blue* —
f. **carmine lake** 1,200.
g. **pink** 1,200.
h. **brown**, *blue green* —
i. **violet brown**, *pink* —
j. **violet brown**, *gray* —
342TC2 $1 small die on India paper
b. **carmine lake** 1,100.
c. **pink** 1,100.
342P1 $1 **vio blk**, large die on India paper 1,500.
342P2 $1 **vio blk**, sm die on white wove paper 725.
342P2a $1 **vio blk**, PP sm die on yelsh wove paper 2,500.

Lincoln Memorial Issue

1909

367P1 2c **car**, large die on India paper 1,750.
367P2 2c **car**, sm die on white wove paper 2,000.
367P2a 2c **car**, PP sm die on yelsh wove paper 3,000.

Alaska-Yukon Issue

370P1 2c **car**, large die on India paper 1,100.
370P2 2c **car**, sm die on white wove paper 1,000.
370P2a 2c **car**, PP sm die on yelsh wove paper 3,000.

Hudson-Fulton Issue

372P1 2c **car**, large die on India paper 1,250.
372P2 2c **car**, sm die on white wove paper 1,000.
372P2a 2c **car**, PP sm die on yelsh wove paper 3,000.

Panama-Pacific Issue

1912-13

397P1 1c **grn**, large die on India paper 1,750.
397P2 1c **grn**, sm die on white wove paper 1,500.
397P2a 1c **grn**, PP sm die on yelsh wove paper 3,000.
398P1 2c **car**, large die on India paper 1,750.
398P2 2c **car**, sm die on white wove paper 1,500.
398P2a 2c **car**, PP sm die on yelsh wove paper 3,000.
399P1 5c **blue**, large die on India paper 1,750.
399P2 5c **blue**, sm die on white wove paper 1,500.
399P2a 5c **blue**, PP sm die on yelsh wove paper 3,000.
400TC1a 10c large die on India paper
e. **brown red** 1,750.
400TC2 10c small die on India paper
b. **carmine lake** 1,100.
400P1 10c **org yel**, large die on India paper 1,750.
400P2 10c **org yel**, sm die on white wove paper 1,500.
400P2a 10c **org yel**, PP sm die on yelsh wove paper 3,000.
400AP1 10c **org**, large die on India paper 1,750.
400AP2 10c **org**, sm die on white wove paper 1,500.
400AP2a 10c **org**, PP sm die on yelsh wove paper 3,000.

No. 398P inscribed "Gatun Locks" is listed in the Essay section as No. 398-E3.

1912-19

405P1 1c **grn**, large die on India paper 1,400.
405P2 1c **grn**, sm die on white wove paper 650.
405P2a 1c **grn**, PP sm die on yelsh wove paper 2,500.
406P1 2c **car**, large die on India paper 1,400.
406P1a 2c **car**, large die on white wove paper *2,750.*
406P2 2c **car**, sm die on white wove paper 650.
406P2a 2c **car**, PP sm die on yelsh wove paper 2,500.
407P1 7c **blk**, large die on India paper 1,400.
407P2 7c **blk**, sm die on white wove paper 650.
407P2a 7c **blk**, PP sm die on yelsh wove paper 2,500.
414TC1a 8c large die on India paper
e. **black** 1,750.
414P1 8c **ol grn**, large die on India paper 1,400.
414P2 8c **ol grn**, sm die on white wove paper 650.
414P2a 8c **ol grn**, PP sm die on yelsh wove paper 2,500.
415P1 9c **ol grn**, large die on India paper 1,400.
415P2 9c **ol grn**, sm die on white wove paper 650.
415P2a 9c **ol grn**, PP sm die on yelsh wove paper 2,500.
416P1 10c **org yel**, large die on India paper 1,400.
416P2 10c **org yel**, sm die on white wove paper 650.
416P2a 10c **org yel**, PP sm die on yelsh wove paper 2,500.
434P1 11c **dk grn**, large die on India paper 1,500.
417P1 12c **cl brn**, large die on India paper 1,400.
417P2 12c **cl brn**, sm die on white wove paper 650.
417P2a 12c **cl brn**, PP sm die on yelsh wove paper 2,500.
513TC1a 13c large die on India paper
e. **violet** 650.
f. **lilac** 650.
g. **violet brown** 650.
h. **light ultramarine** 650.
i. **ultramarine** 650.
j. **deep ultramarine** 650.
k. **green** 650.
l. **dark green** 650.
m. **olive green** 650.
n. **orange yellow** 650.
o. **orange** 650.
p. **red orange** 650.
q. **ocher** 650.
r. **salmon red** 650.
s. **brown carmine** 650.
t. **claret brown** 650.
u. **brown** 650.
v. **black brown** 650.
w. **gray** 650.
x. **black** 650.
513P1 13c **apple grn**, large die on India paper 1,500.
418P1 15c **gray**, large die on India paper 1,400.
418P2 15c **gray**, sm die on white wove paper 650.
418P2a 15c **gray**, PP sm die on yelsh wove paper 2,500.
419P1 20c **ultra**, large die on India paper 1,400.
419P2 20c **ultra**, sm die on white wove paper 650.
419P2a 20c **ultra**, PP sm die on yelsh wove paper 2,500.
420P1 30c **org red**, large die on India paper 1,400.
420P2 30c **org red**, sm die on white wove paper 650.
420P2a 30c **org red**, PP sm die on yelsh wove paper 2,500.
421P1 50c **violet**, large die on India paper 1,500.
421P2 50c **violet**, sm die on white wove paper 650.
421P2a 50c **violet**, PP sm die on yelsh wove paper 2,500.
423P1 $1 **vio blk**, large die on India paper 1,400.
423P2 $1 **vio blk**, sm die on white wove paper 650.
423P2a $1 **vio blk**, PP sm die on yelsh wove paper 2,500.

1917-20

502P1 3c **dk vio**, type II, 10-subject die proof (2x5) on India paper, die sunk on card *6,500.*
524TC1a $5 large die on India paper
e. **carmine & black** 1,350.
524P1 $2 **dp grn & blk**, large die on India paper 1,500.
547TC1a $2 large die on India paper
e. **green & black** 1,500.
547P1 $5 **car & blk**, large die on India paper 1,500.

Victory Issue

1919

537P1 3c **violet**, large die on India paper 1,100.
537P2 3c **violet**, sm die on white wove paper 1,500.

Pilgrim Issue

1920

548P1 1c **grn**, large die on India paper 1,250.
548P2 1c **grn**, sm die on white wove paper 1,200.
549P1 2c **car**, large die on India paper 1,250.
549P2 2c **car**, sm die on white wove paper 1,200.
550P1 5c **blue**, large die on India paper 1,250.
550P2 5c **blue**, sm die on white wove paper 1,200.

1922-26

551P1 ½c **ol brn**, large die on India paper 1,500.
551P1a ½c **ol brn**, large die on white wove paper —
551P3 ½c **ol brn**, plate on white wove paper —
551P4 ½c **ol brn**, plate on card —
552TC2 1c small die on thin glazed card
b. **black** —
552P1 1c **dp grn**, large die on India paper 1,000.
552P1a 1c **dp grn**, large die on white wove paper 700.
552P3 1c **dp grn**, plate on white wove paper —
553P1 1½c **yel brn**, large die on India paper 1,000.
553P3 1½c **yel brn**, plate on white wove paper —
554TC2 2c small die on bond paper
b. **black** 1,250.
554P1 2c **car**, large die on India paper 1,000.
554P1a 2c **car**, large die on white wove paper 700.
554P3 2c **car**, plate on white wove paper —
555P1 3c **vio**, large die on India paper 1,250.
555P1a 3c **vio**, large die on white wove paper 1,000.
555P3 3c **vio**, plate on white wove paper —
556P1 4c **yel brn**, large die on India paper 1,200.
556P1a 4c **yel brn**, large die on white wove paper 700.
556P3 4c **yel brn**, plate on white wove paper —
557P1 5c **dk bl**, large die on India paper 1,000.
557P1a 5c **dk bl**, large die on white wove paper 700.
557P3 5c **dk bl**, plate on white wove paper —
558P1 6c **red org**, large die on India paper 1,000.
558P1a 6c **red org**, large die on white wove paper 700.
558P3 6c **red org**, plate on white wove paper —
559P1 7c **blk**, large die on India paper 1,000.
559P1a 7c **blk**, large die on white wove paper 700.
559P3 7c **blk**, plate on white wove paper —
560P1 8c **ol grn**, large die on India paper 1,000.
560P1a 8c **ol grn**, large die on white wove paper 700.
560P3 8c **ol grn**, plate on white wove paper —
561TC1a 9c large die on India paper
e. **red orange** 2,250.
561P1 9c **rose**, large die on India paper 1,000.
561P1a 9c **rose**, large die on white wove paper 700.
561P3 9c **rose**, plate on white wove paper —
562P1 10c **org**, large die on India paper 1,000.
562P1a 10c **org**, large die on white wove paper 700.
562P3 10c **org**, plate on white wove paper —
563TC1a 11c large die on India paper
e. **deep green** 2,250.
563P1 11c **lt bl**, large die on India paper 1,500.
563P1a 11c **lt bl**, large die on white wove paper 700.
563P3 11c **lt bl**, plate on white wove paper —
564P1 12c **brn vio**, large die on India paper 1,000.
564P1a 12c **brn vio**, large die on white wove paper 700.
564P3 12c **brn vio**, plate on white wove paper —
622TC1a 13c large die on India paper
e. **black** 2,250.
622P1 13c **grn**, large die on India paper 1,000.
622P1a 13c **grn**, large die on white wove paper 700.
622P3 13c **grn**, plate on white wove paper —
565TC1a 14c large die on India paper
e. **dark brown** 2,250.
565P1 14c **dk bl**, large die on India paper 1,250.
565P1a 14c **dk bl**, large die on white wove paper 700.
565P3 14c **dk bl**, plate on white wove paper —
566TC1a 15c large die on India paper
e. **black** 2,250.
566P1 15c **grey**, large die on India paper 1,250.
566P1a 15c **grey**, large die on white wove paper 700.
566P3 15c **grey**, plate on white wove paper —
623P1 17c **blk**, large die on India paper 1,000.
623P3 17c **blk**, plate on white wove paper —
567P1 20c **car rose**, large die on India paper 1,000.
567P1a 20c **car rose**, large die on white wove paper 700.
567P3 20c **car rose**, plate on white wove paper —
568P1 25c **dp grn**, large die on India paper 1,000.
568P1a 25c **dp grn**, large die on white wove paper 700.
568P3 25c **dp grn**, plate on white wove paper —
569P1 30c **ol brn**, large die on India paper 1,000.
569P1a 30c **ol brn**, large die on white wove paper 700.
569P3 30c **ol brn**, plate on white wove paper —
570P1 50c **lilac**, large die on India paper 1,250.
570P1a 50c **lilac**, large die on white wove paper 700.
570P3 50c **lilac**, plate on white wove paper —
571P1 $1 **vio brn**, large die on India paper 1,500.
571P1a $1 **vio brn**, large die on white wove paper 700.
571P3 $1 **vio brn**, plate on white wove paper —
572P1 $2 **dp bl**, large die on India paper 2,500.
572P1a $2 **dp bl**, large die on white wove paper 700.
572P2 $2 **dp bl**, small die on India paper —

572P3 $2 **dp bl,** plate on white wove paper —
573P1 $5 **car & dk bl,** large die on India paper 5,000.
573P1b $5 **car & dk bl,** large die on card *1,500.*

Catalogue values for large and small proofs between Nos. 610TC1a and 1193P1 are often based on one-time auction realizations. Because these items range in scarcity from unique to just a few known, actual market prices, when available, may be much higher than the values shown.

Harding Memorial Issue

1923-26

610TC1a 2c large die on India paper
e. **green** *4,000.*
610P1 2c large die on India paper 3,000.
610P1a 2c large die on white wove paper 2,000.
610P2 2c small die on white or yelsh wove paper 1,500.

Huguenot Walloon Issue

614P1 1c large die on India paper 3,000.
614P1a 1c large die on white wove paper 2,000.
614P2 1c small die on white or yelsh wove paper 2,000.
615P1 2c large die on India paper 3,000.
615P1a 2c large die on white wove paper 2,000.
615P2 2c small die on white or yelsh wove paper 2,000.
616P1 5c large die on India paper 3,000.
616P1a 5c large die on white wove paper 2,000.
616P2 5c small die on white or yelsh wove paper 2,000.

Lexington Concord Issue

617P1 1c large die on India paper 3,000.
617P1a 1c large die on white wove paper 2,000.
617P2 1c small die on white or yelsh wove paper 2,000.
618TC1a 2c large die on India paper
e. **black** *3,000.*
618P1 2c large die on India paper 3,000.
618P1a 2c large die on white wove paper 2,000.
618P2 2c small die on white or yelsh wove paper 2,000.
619P1 5c large die on India paper 3,000.
619P1a 5c large die on white wove paper 2,000.
619P2 5c small die on white or yelsh wove paper 2,000.

Norse American Issue

620P1 2c large die on India paper 3,000.
620P1a 2c large die on white wove paper 2,000.
620P2 2c small die on white or yelsh wove paper 2,000.
621P1 5c large die on India paper 3,000.
621P1a 5c large die on white wove paper 2,000.
621P2 5c small die on white or yelsh wove paper 2,000.

Sesquicentennial Exposition Issue

627P1 2c large die on India paper 1,500.
627P1a 2c large die on white wove paper 1,000.
627P2 2c small die on white or yelsh wove paper 1,500.

Ericsson Memorial Issue

628TC1a 5c large die on India paper
e. **dull dusky blue** 1,500.
628TC2 5c small die on India paper
b. **gray blue** 1,000.
628P1 5c large die on India paper 1,500.
628P1a 5c large die on white wove paper 1,000.
628P2 5c small die on white or yelsh wove paper 1,500.

Battle of White Plains Issue

629P1 2c large die on India paper 1,500.
629P1a 2c large die on white wove paper 1,000.
629P2 2c small die on white or yelsh wove paper 1,500.

1927-29

Vermont Sesquicentennial Issue

643P1 2c large die on India paper 1,500.
643P1a 2c large die on white wove paper 1,000.
643P2 2c small die on white or yelsh wove paper 1,500.

Burgoyne Campaign Issue

644P1 2c large die on India paper 1,500.
644P1a 2c large die on white wove paper 1,000.
644P2 2c small die on white or yelsh wove paper 1,500.

Valley Forge Issue

645P1 2c large die on India paper 1,500.
645P1a 2c large die on white wove paper 1,000.
645P2 2c small die on white or yelsh wove paper 1,500.

Aeronautics Conference Issue

649P1 2c large die on India paper 1,500.
649P1a 2c large die on white wove paper 1,000.
649P2 2c small die on white or yelsh wove paper 1,500.
650P1 5c large die on India paper 1,500.
650P1a 5c large die on white wove paper 1,000.
650P2 5c small die on white or yelsh wove paper 1,500.

George Rogers Clark Issue

651P1 2c large die on India paper 1,500.
651P1a 2c large die on white wove paper 1,000.
651P2 2c small die on white or yelsh wove paper 1,500.

Electric Lights Golden Jubilee

654P1 2c large die on India paper 1,500.
654P1a 2c large die on white wove paper 1,000.
654P2 2c small die on white or yelsh wove paper 1,500.

John Sullivan

657P1 2c large die on India paper 1,500.
657P1a 2c large die on white wove paper 1,000.
657P2 2c small die on white or yelsh wove paper 1,500.

Battle of Fallen Timbers Issue

680P1 2c large die on India paper 1,500.
680P1a 2c large die on white wove paper 1,000.
680P2 2c small die on white or yelsh wove paper 1,500.

Ohio River Canalization Issue

681P1 2c large die on India paper 1,500.
681P1a 2c large die on white wove paper 1,000.
681P2 2c small die on white or yelsh wove paper 1,500.

1930-31

Massachusetts Bay Colony Issue

682P1 2c large die on India paper 1,500.
682P1a 2c large die on white wove paper 1,000.
682P2 2c small die on white or yelsh wove paper 1,500.

Carolina Charleston Issue

683P1 2c large die on India paper 1,500.
683P1a 2c large die on white wove paper 1,000.
683P2 2c small die on white or yelsh wove paper 1,500.

Harding & Taft

684P1 1½c **brn,** large die on India paper 1,500.
685P1 4c **brn,** large die on India paper 1,500.

Braddock's Field Issue

688P1 2c large die on India paper 1,500.
688P1a 2c large die on white wove paper 1,000.
688P2 2c small die on white or yelsh wove paper 1,500.

Von Steuben Issue

689P1 2c large die on India paper 1,500.
689P1a 2c large die on white wove paper 1,000.
689P2 2c small die on white or yelsh wove paper 1,500.

Pulaski Issue

690P1 2c large die on India paper 1,500.
690P1a 2c large die on white wove paper 1,000.
690P2 2c small die on white or yelsh wove paper 1,500.

Red Cross Issue

702P1a 2c large die on white wove paper 1,000.
702P2 2c small die on white or yelsh wove paper 1,500.

Yorktown Issue

703P1 2c large die on India paper 1,500.
703P1a 2c large die on white wove paper 1,000.
703P2 2c small die on white or yelsh wove paper 1,500.

Washington Bicentennial

1932

704P1 ½c **ol brn,** large die on India paper 1,000.
704P1a ½c **ol brn,** large die on white wove paper 1,000.
704P2 ½c **ol brn,** sm die on white or yelsh wove paper 1,500.
705P1 1c **grn,** large die on India paper 1,000.
705P1a 1c **grn,** large die on white wove paper 1,000.
705P2 1c **grn,** sm die on white or yelsh wove paper 1,500.
706P1 1½c **brn,** large die on India paper 1,000.
706P1a 1½c **brn,** large die on white wove paper 1,000.
706P2 1½c **brn,** sm die on white or yelsh wove paper 1,500.
707P1 2c **car rose,** large die on India paper 1,000.
707P1a 2c **car rose,** large die on white wove paper 1,000.
707P2 2c **car rose,** sm die on white or yelsh wove paper 1,500.
708P1 3c **dp vio,** large die on India paper 1,000.
708P1a 3c **dp vio,** large die on white wove paper 1,000.
708P2 3c **dp vio,** sm die on white or yelsh wove paper 1,500.
709P1 4c **lt brn,** large die on India paper 1,000.
709P1a 4c **lt brn,** large die on white wove paper 1,000.
709P2 4c **lt brn,** small die on white or yelsh wove paper 1,500.
710P1 5c **blue,** large die on India paper 1,000.
710P1a 5c **blue,** large die on white wove paper 1,000.
710P2 5c **blue,** sm die on white or yelsh wove paper 1,500.
711P1 6c **red org,** large die on India paper 1,000.
711P1a 6c **red org,** large die on white wove paper 1,000.
711P2 6c **red org,** sm die on white or yelsh wove paper 1,500.
711P3 6c **red org,** plate proof on wove paper *2,500.*
712P1 7c **blk,** large die on India paper 1,000.
712P1a 7c **blk,** large die on white wove paper 1,000.
712P2 7c **blk,** sm die on white or yelsh wove paper 1,500.
713P1 8c **ol bis,** large die on India paper 1,000.
713P1a 8c **ol bis,** large die on white wove paper 1,000.
713P2 8c **ol bis,** sm die on white or yelsh wove paper 1,500.
714P1 9c **pale red,** large die on India paper 1,000.
714P1a 9c **pale red,** large die on white wove paper 1,000.
714P2 9c **pale red,** sm die on white or yelsh wove paper 1,500.
715P1 10c **org yel,** large die on India paper 1,000.
715P1a 10c **org yel,** large die on white wove paper 1,000.
715P2 10c **org yel,** sm die on white or yelsh wove paper 1,500.

Winter Olympic Games Issue

716P1 2c large die on India paper 1,000.
716P1a 2c large die on white wove paper 1,000.
716P2 2c small die on white or yelsh wove paper 1,500.

Arbor Day Issue

717P1 2c large die on India paper 1,000.
717P1a 2c large die on white wove paper 1,000.
717P2 2c small die on white or yelsh wove paper 1,500.

Summer Olympic Games Issue

718TC1a 3c large die on India paper
e. **carmine** *7,500.*
718P1 3c large die on India paper *10,000.*
718P1a 3c large die on white wove paper 1,000.
718P2 3c small die on white or yelsh wove paper 1,500.
719P1 5c large die on India paper *15,000.*
719P1a 5c large die on white wove paper 1,000.
719P2 5c small die on white or yelsh wove paper 1,500.

Washington Issue

720TC2 3c small die on bond paper
b. **black** 2,750.
720P1 3c large die on India paper 2,000.

William Penn Issue

724P1 3c large die on India paper 1,000.
724P1a 3c large die on white wove paper 1,000.
724P2 3c small die on white or yelsh wove paper 1,500.

Daniel Webster Issue

725P1 3c large die on India paper 1,000.
725P1a 3c large die on white wove paper 1,000.
725P2 3c small die on white or yelsh wove paper 1,500.

Georgia Bicentennial Issue

1933-34

726P1 3c large die on India paper 1,000.
726P1a 3c large die on white wove paper 1,000.
726P2 3c small die on white or yelsh wove paper 1,500.

Peace of 1783 Issue

727P1 3c large die on India paper 1,000.
727P1a 3c large die on white wove paper 1,000.
727P2 3c small die on white or yelsh wove paper 1,500.

Century of Progress Issue

728P1 1c large die on India paper 1,000.
728P1a 1c large die on white wove paper 1,000.
728P2 1c small die on white or yelsh wove paper 1,500.
729P1 3c large die on India paper 1,000.
729P1a 3c large die on white wove paper 1,000.
729P2 3c small die on white or yelsh wove paper 1,500.

National Recovery Act Issue

732P1a 3c large die on white wove paper 1,000.
732P2 3c small die on white or yelsh wove paper 1,500.

Byrd Antarctic Issue

733P1 3c large die on India paper *1,250.*
733P1a 3c large die on white wove paper 1,000.
733P2 3c small die on white or yelsh wove paper 1,500.

Kosciuszko Issue

734P1 5c large die on India paper *1,250.*
734P1a 5c large die on white wove paper 1,000.
734P2 5c small die on white or yelsh wove paper 1,500.

Maryland Tercentenary Issue

736P1 3c large die on India paper *1,250.*
736P1a 3c large die on white wove paper 1,000.
736P2 3c small die on white or yelsh wove paper 1,500.

Mothers of America Issue

737P1 3c large die on India paper 1,000.
737P1a 3c large die on white wove paper 1,000.
737P2 3c small die on white or yelsh wove paper 1,500.

Wisconsin Tercentenary Issue

739P1a 3c large die on white wove paper 1,000.
739P2 3c small die on white or yelsh wove paper 1,500.

National Parks Year

740P1a 1c large die on white wove paper 1,000.
740P2 1c small die on white or yelsh wove paper 1,500.
741P2 2c small die on white or yelsh wove paper 1,500.
742P1a 3c large die on white wove paper 1,000.
742P2 3c small die on white or yelsh wove paper 1,500.
743P2 4c small die on white or yelsh wove paper 1,500.
744P2 5c small die on white or yelsh wove paper 1,500.
745P2 6c small die on white or yelsh wove paper 1,500.
746P1a 7c large die on white wove paper 1,000.
746P2 7c small die on white or yelsh wove paper 1,500.
747P2 8c small die on white or yelsh wove paper 1,500.
748P1a 9c large die on white wove paper 1,000.
748P2 9c small die on white or yelsh wove paper 1,500.
749P2 10c small die on white or yelsh wove paper 1,500.

Connecticut Tercentennary Issue

1935-37

772TC1d 3c Large die on thin glazed card
e. **black** *1,500.*
772P1 3c large die on India paper *1,500.*
772P2 3c small die on white or yelsh wove paper 1,500.

California Pacific Expo Issue

773TC1d 3c Large die on yellow glazed card
e. **orange red** *1,500.*
773P2 3c small die on white or yelsh wove paper 1,500.

Boulder Dam Issue

774P2 3c small die on white or yelsh wove paper 1,500.

Michigan Centenary Issue

775P2 3c small die on white or yelsh wove paper 1,500.

Texas Centennial Issue

776P2 3c small die on white or yelsh wove paper 1,500.

Rhode Island Tercentenary Issue

777P2 3c small die on white or yelsh wove paper 1,500.

Arkansas Centennial Issue

782P1 3c large die on India paper 1,500.
782P1a 3c large die on white wove paper 1,500.
782P2 3c small die on white or yelsh wove paper 1,500.

Oregon Territory Issue

783P1 3c large die on India paper 1,500.
783P1a 3c large die on white wove paper 1,500.
783P2 3c small die on white or yelsh wove paper 1,500.

Susan B. Anthony Issue

784TC1d 3c large die on glazed card
a. Deep lilac 1,750.
784P2 3c small die on white or yelsh wove paper 1,500.

Army Issue

785TC2 1c small die on bond paper
b. **black** 750.
785P1a 1c large die on white wove paper 1,500.
785P2 1c small die on white or yelsh wove paper 1,500.
786P2 2c small die on white or yelsh wove paper 1,500.
787P1 3c large die on India paper 1,500.
787P1a 3c large die on white wove paper 1,500.
787P2 3c small die on white or yelsh wove paper 1,500.
788TC1a 4c large die on India paper
e. **dark brown** 1,500.
788P2 4c small die on white or yelsh wove paper 1,500.
789TC1a 5c large die on India paper
e. **blue** 1,500.
789P1 5c large die on India paper *1,500.*
789P1a 5c large die on white wove paper 1,500.
789P2 5c small die on white or yelsh wove paper 1,500.

Navy Issue

790P2 1c small die on white or yelsh wove paper 1,500.
791P1 2c large die on India paper 1,500.
791P2 2c small die on white or yelsh wove paper 1,500.
792P2 3c small die on white or yelsh wove paper 1,500.
793TC1a 4c large die on India paper
e. **dark brown** 1,500.
793P2 4c small die on white or yelsh wove paper 1,500.
794P2 5c small die on white or yelsh wove paper 1,500.

Ordinance of 1787 Issue

795P2 3c small die on white or yelsh wove paper 1,500.

Virginia Dare Issue

796P1 5c large die on India paper 1,500.
796P2 5c small die on white or yelsh wove paper 1,500.

Society of Philatelic Americans

797P2 10c small die on white or yelsh wove paper 1,500.

Constitution Sesquicentennial Issue

798TC2 3c small die on bond paper
b. **black** 750.
798P1 3c large die on India paper 1,500.
798P2 3c small die on white or yelsh wove paper 1,500.

Territorial Issues

799TC2 3c small die on bond paper
b. **black** 750.
799P1 3c large die on India paper 1,500.
799P2 3c small die on white or yelsh wove paper 1,500.
800TC2 3c small die on India paper
b. **black** 750.
c. **black,** on bond paper 750.
800P2 3c small die on white or yelsh wove paper 1,500.
801TC1a 3c large die on India paper
e. **black** 1,500.
801TC1b 3c Large die on bond paper
e. **black** 1,500.
801TC2 3c small die on bond paper
b. **black** 750.
801P1 3c large die on India paper 1,500.
801P2 3c small die on white or yelsh wove paper 1,500.
802TC2 3c small die on bond paper
b. **black** 750.
802P1 3c large die on India paper 1,500.
802P2 3c small die on white or yelsh wove paper 1,500.

Presidential Issue

1938

803TC1a ½c large die on India paper
e. **black** *3,000.*
803P1 ½c **dp org,** large die on India paper *2,000.*
803P2 ½c **dp org,** small die on white or yelsh wove paper 3,000.
804P2 1c **grn,** small die on white or yelsh wove paper 3,000.
805P2 1½c **bis brn,** small die on white or yelsh wove paper 3,000.
806P1a 2c **rose car,** large die on white wove paper *1,800.*
806P2 2c **rose car,** small die on white or yelsh wove paper *3,000.*
807P1 3c **dp vio,** large die on glazed card —
807P2 3c **dp vio,** small die on white or yelsh wove paper 3,000.
808P2 4c **red vio,** small die on white or yelsh wove paper 3,000.
809P1 4½c **dk gray,** large die on India paper *1,500.*
809P2 4½c **dk gray,** small die on white or yelsh wove paper 3,000.
810P1 5c **brt bl,** large die on India paper *1,500.*
810P2 5c **brt bl,** small die on white or yelsh wove paper 3,000.
811P2 6c **red org,** small die on white or yelsh wove paper 3,000.
812P1 7c **sepia,** large die on India paper *1,750.*
812P2 7c **sepia,** small die on white or yelsh wove paper 3,000.
813P1a 8c **ol grn,** large die on white wove paper *1,800.*
813P2 8c **ol grn,** small die on white or yelsh wove paper 3,000.
814P1 9c **ol grn,** large die on India paper *1,800.*
814P1a 9c **ol grn,** large die on white wove paper *1,800.*
814P2 9c **ol grn,** small die on white or yelsh wove paper 3,000.
815TC1a 10c large die on India paper
e. **sepia** 1,500.
815P1 10c **brn red,** large die on India paper *2,500.*
815P2 10c **brn red,** small die on white or yelsh wove paper 3,000.
816P2 11c **ultra,** small die on white or yelsh wove paper 3,000.
817P1 12c **brt vio,** large die on India paper *1,500.*
817P2 12c **brt vio,** small die on white or yelsh wove paper 3,000.
818P2 13c **bl grn,** small die on white or yelsh wove paper 3,000.
819P2 14c **blue,** small die on white or yelsh wove paper 3,000.
820P1 15c **bl gray,** large die on India paper *1,800.*
820P1a 15c **bl gray,** large die on white wove paper *1,800.*
820P2 15c **bl gray,** small die on white or yelsh wove paper 3,000.
821P1 16c **blk,** large die on India paper *1,500.*
821P2 16c **blk,** small die on white or yelsh wove paper 3,000.
822P2 17c **rose red,** small die on white or yelsh wove paper 3,000.
823P2 18c **brn car,** small die on white or yelsh wove paper 3,000.
824P1 19c **brt vio,** large die on India paper *1,800.*
824P1a 19c **brt vio,** large die on white wove paper *1,800.*
824P2 19c **brt vio,** small die on white or yelsh wove paper 3,000.
825P1 20c **brt bl grn,** large die on India paper *1,800.*
825P1a 20c **brt bl grn,** large die on white wove paper *1,800.*
825P2 20c **brt bl grn,** small die on white or yelsh wove paper 3,000.
826TC1a 21c large die on India paper
e. **black** *2,000.*
826P2 21c **dull bl,** small die on white or yelsh wove paper 3,000.
827P2 22c **ver,** small die on white or yelsh wove paper 3,000.
828P1 24c **gray blk,** large die on India paper *1,800.*
828P2 24c **gray blk,** small die on white or yelsh wove paper 3,000.
829TC1a 25c large die on India paper
e. **green** *2,000.*
829P2 25c **dp red lilac,** small die on white or yelsh wove paper 3,000.
830P2 30c **dp ultra,** small die on white or yelsh wove paper 3,000.
831P1 50c **lt red vio,** large die on India paper *1,500.*
831P2 50c **lt red vio,** small die on white or yelsh wove paper 3,000.
832P2 $1 **pur & blk,** small die on white or yelsh wove paper 5,000.
833P2 $2 **yel grn & blk,** small die on white or yelsh wove paper 5,000.
834P2 $5 **car & blk,** small die on white or yelsh wove paper 5,000.

Constitution Ratification Issue

1938

835P1 3c large die on India paper 1,500.
835P2 3c small die on white or yelsh wove paper 1,500.

Swedish-Finnish Tercentenary Issue

836TC1a 3c large die on India paper
e. **purple** 1,500.
836P1 3c large die on India paper 1,500.
836P2 3c small die on white or yelsh wove paper 1,500.

Northwest Territory Sesquicentennial

837TC1a 3c large die on India paper
e. **dark purple** 1,500.
837P2 3c small die on white or yelsh wove paper 800.

Iowa Territory Centennial Issue

838P1 3c large die on India paper *1,500.*
838P2 3c small die on white or yelsh wove paper 1,500.

Golden Gate Intl. Exposition Issue

1939

852P1 3c large die on India paper *1,800.*
852P2 3c small die on white or yelsh wove paper 1,500.

New York World's Fair Issue

853P1 3c large die on India paper *1,500.*
853P2 3c small die on white or yelsh wove paper 1,500.

Washington Inauguration Issue

854TC1a 3c large die on India paper
e. **purple** 900.
854P1 3c large die on India paper *1,500.*
854P2 3c small die on white or yelsh wove paper 1,500.

Baseball Centennial Issue

855TC1a 3c large die on India paper
e. **red violet** *2,500.*
855P1 3c large die on India paper *5,000.*
855P1a 3c large die on white wove paper *2,000.*
855P2 3c small die on white or yelsh wove paper 2,500.

Panama Canal Issue

856P1 3c large die on white wove paper 2,250.
856P2 3c small die on white or yelsh wove paper 1,500.

Printing Tercentenary Issue

857P2 3c small die on white or yelsh wove paper 1,500.

Statehood Issue

858P2 3c small die on white or yelsh wove paper 1,500.

Famous Americans Issue

Authors

1940

859P2 1c small die on white or yelsh wove paper 1,500.
860P2 2c small die on white or yelsh wove paper 1,500.
861P2 3c small die on white or yelsh wove paper 1,500.
862TC1a 5c large die on India paper
e. **dull blue** 1,500.
862P1 5c large die on India paper 1,500.
862P2 5c small die on white or yelsh wove paper 1,500.
863P1 10c large die on India paper *2,500.*
863P2 10c small die on white or yelsh wove paper 1,500.

Poets

864P1 1c large die on India paper *1,500.*
864P2 1c small die on white or yelsh wove paper 1,500.
865P2 2c small die on white or yelsh wove paper 1,500.
866TC1a 3c large die on India paper
e. **dark blue violet** 1,500.
866P2 3c small die on white or yelsh wove paper 1,500.
867P1 5c large die on India paper 1,500.
867P2 5c small die on white or yelsh wove paper 1,500.
868P1 10c large die on India paper *1,500.*
868P2 10c small die on white or yelsh wove paper 1,500.

Educators

869P1 1c large die on India paper 1,500.
869P2 1c small die on white or yelsh wove paper 1,500.
870P2 2c small die on white or yelsh wove paper 1,500.
871P2 3c small die on white or yelsh wove paper 1,500.
872P1 5c large die on India paper 1,500.
872P2 5c small die on white or yelsh wove paper 1,500.
873P1 10c large die on India paper 1,500.
873P2 10c small die on white or yelsh wove paper 1,500.

Scientists

874P1 1c large die on India paper *1,500.*
874P2 1c small die on white or yelsh wove paper 1,500.
875P1 2c large die on India paper 1,500.
875P2 2c small die on white or yelsh wove paper 1,500.
876P1 3c large die on India paper 1,500.
876P2 3c small die on white or yelsh wove paper 1,500.
877P2 5c small die on white or yelsh wove paper 1,500.
878P1 10c large die on India paper *1,500.*
878P2 10c small die on white or yelsh wove paper 1,500.

Composers

879P2 1c small die on white or yelsh wove paper 1,500.
880P1 2c large die on India paper 1,500.
880P2 2c small die on white or yelsh wove paper 1,500.
881P2 3c small die on white or yelsh wove paper 1,500.
882P1 5c large die on India paper 1,500.
882P2 5c small die on white or yelsh wove paper 1,500.
883P2 10c small die on white or yelsh wove paper 1,500.

Artists

884P2 1c small die on white or yelsh wove paper 1,500.
885P1 2c large die on wove paper 1,500.
885P2 2c small die on white or yelsh wove paper 1,500.
886P2 3c small die on white or yelsh wove paper 1,500.
887P1 5c large die on India paper 1,500.
887P2 5c small die on white or yelsh wove paper 1,500.
888P1 10c large die on India paper 1,500.
888P2 10c small die on white or yelsh wove paper 1,500.

Inventors

889P2 1c small die on white or yelsh wove paper 1,500.
890P1 2c large die on India paper *1,500.*
890P2 2c small die on white or yelsh wove paper 1,500.
891P1 3c large die on India paper 1,500.
891P2 3c small die on white or yelsh wove paper 1,500.
892P2 5c small die on white or yelsh wove paper 1,500.
893P2 10c small die on white or yelsh wove paper 1,500.

Pony Express Issue

1940
894P1 3c large die on India paper *1,500.*
894P2 3c small die on white or yelsh wove paper 1,500.

Pan American Union Issue

895P2 3c small die on white or yelsh wove paper 1,500.

Idaho Statehood Issue

896P1 3c large die on India paper *1,500.*
896P2 3c small die on white or yelsh wove paper 1,500.

Wyoming Statehood Issue

897TC1a 3c large die on India paper
e. **red violet** 1,500.
897P2 3c small die on white or yelsh wove paper 1,500.

Coronado Expedition Issue

898P1 3c large die on India paper *1,500.*
898P2 3c small die on white or yelsh wove paper 1,500.

National Defense Issue

899P1 1c large die on India paper *1,500.*
899P2 1c small die on white or yelsh wove paper 1,500.
900P1 2c large die on India paper *1,500.*
900P2 2c small die on white or yelsh wove paper 1,500.
901P1 3c large die on India paper *1,500.*
901P2 3c small die on white or yelsh wove paper 1,500.

Thirteenth Amendment Issue

902P1 3c large die on India paper *1,500.*
902P2 3c small die on white or yelsh wove paper 1,500.

Vermont Statehood Issue

1941-44
903P1 3c large die on wove paper 1,750.
903P2 3c small die on white or yelsh wove paper 1,500.

Kentucky Statehood Issue

904P1 3c large die on India paper *1,500.*
904P2 3c small die on white or yelsh wove paper 1,500.

Win the War Issue

905P2 3c small die on white or yelsh wove paper 1,500.

China Resistance Issue

906P2 3c small die on white or yelsh wove paper 1,750.

Allied Nations Issue

907P2 2c small die on white or yelsh wove paper 1,500.

Four Freedoms Issue

908P1 1c large die on India paper *1,500.*
908P2 1c small die on white or yelsh wove paper 1,500.

Overrun Countries Issue

909P2 5c small die on wove paper *600.*
910P2 5c small die on wove paper *600.*
911P2 5c small die on wove paper *600.*
912P2 5c small die on wove paper *600.*
913P2 5c small die on wove paper *600.*
914P2 5c small die on wove paper *600.*
915P2 5c small die on wove paper *600.*
916P2 5c small die on wove paper *600.*
917P2 5c small die on wove paper *600.*
918P2 5c small die on wove paper *600.*
919P2 5c small die on wove paper *600.*
920P2 5c small die on wove paper *600.*
921P2 5c small die on wove paper *600.*

Transcontinental Railroad Issue

922P1 3c large die on India paper *1,500.*
922P2 3c small die on white or yelsh wove paper 1,500.

Steamship Issue

923P1 3c large die on wove paper *1,600.*
923P2 3c small die on white or yelsh wove paper 1,500.

Telegraph Issue

924P1 3c large die on wove paper *1,500.*
924P2 3c small die on white or yelsh wove paper 1,500.

Philippine Issue

925P1 3c large die on India paper *1,500.*
925P2 3c small die on white or yelsh wove paper 1,500.

Motion Picture Issue

926P1 3c large die on India paper *1,500.*
926P2 3c small die on white or yelsh wove paper *1,000.*

Florida Statehood Issue

1945-46
927P1 3c large die on India paper *1,500.*
927P2 3c small die on white or yelsh wove paper 1,500.

United Nations Conference Issue

928P2 5c small die on white or yelsh wove paper 1,500.

Iwo Jima (Marines) Issue

929TC1a 3c large die on India paper
e. **bright purple** *2,300.*
929P2 3c small die on white or yelsh wove paper 1,500.

Franklin D. Roosevelt Issue

930P2 1c small die on white or yelsh wove paper 1,500.
931P1a 2c large die on wove paper *1,750.*
931P2 2c small die on white or yelsh wove paper 1,500.
932P1a 3c large die on wove paper *1,750.*
932P2 3c small die on white or yelsh wove paper 1,500.
933P1a 5c large die on wove paper *1,750.*

Army & Navy Issues

934P1a 3c large die on wove paper *1,500.*
934P2 3c small die on white or yelsh wove paper 1,200.
935P1a 3c large die on wove paper *1,500.*
935P2 3c small die on white or yelsh wove paper 1,500.

Merchant Marine Issue

939P1a 5c large die on wove paper *1,500.*

Tennessee Statehood Issue

941P1a 3c large die on wove paper *1,500.*

Iowa Statehood Issue

942P1a 3c large die on white wove paper *1,500.*

Kearny Expedition Issue

944P1a 3c large die on wove paper *1,500.*

Thomas A. Edison Issue

1947-50
945P1a 3c large die on wove paper *1,500.*

Joseph Pulitzer Issue

946P1a 3c large die on white wove paper *1,500.*

Postage Stamp Centenary Issue

947P1a 3c large die on wove paper 1,500.

Doctors Issue

949P1a 3c large die on wove paper *1,500.*

Utah Issue

950TC1c 3c large die on wove paper
e. **deep brown** *1,500.*

U.S.S. Constitution Issue

951P1a 3c large die on wove paper *1,500.*

Mississippi Territory Issue

955P1a 3c large die on white wove paper 1,500.

Four Chaplains Issue

956P1a 3c large die on wove paper 1,500.

Swedish Pioneers Issue

958P1a 5c large die on wove paper *1,500.*

Progress of Women Issue

959TC1b 3c large die on wove paper
e. **bright violet** *1,750.*
959P1a 3c large die on wove paper *1,500.*

William Allen White Issue

960P1a 3c large die on wove paper *1,500.*

U.S.-Canada Friendship Issue

961TC1b 3c large die on wove paper
e. **brown violet** *1,500.*

Francis Scott Key Issue

962P1a 3c large die on wove paper *1,500.*

Youth Issue

963TC1b 3c large die on white wove paper
e. **violet** *1,500.*

Oregon Statehood Issue

964TC1b 3c large die on wove paper
e. **dull violet** *1,500.*

Harlan Fiske Stone Issue

965P1a 3c large die on wove paper *1,500.*

Clara Barton Issue

967P1a 3c large die on wove paper *2,000.*

Poultry Issue

968TC1b 3c large die on wove paper
e. **red brown** *1,500.*

Volunteer Firemen Issue

971P1a 3c large die on wove paper *1,500.*

Indian Centennial Issue

972P1a 3c large die on wove paper *1,500.*

Rough Riders Issue

973P1a 3c large die on wove paper *1,500.*

Girl Scouts Issue

974P1a 3c large die on white wove paper *1,500.*

Will Rogers Issue

975P1a 3c large die on wove paper *1,750.*

Fort Bliss Centennial Issue

976P1a 3c large die on wove paper *1,500.*

Moina Michael Issue

977P1a 3c large die on white wove paper *1,500.*

Minnesota Territory Issue

981P1a 3c large die on white wove paper *1,500.*

Puerto Rico Election Issue

983P1a 3c large die on wove paper *1,500.*

G.A.R. Issue

985P1a 3c large die on wove paper *1,500.*

American Bankers Assoc. Issue

987TC1b 3c large die on wove paper
e. **dark green** *1,500.*

Samuel Gompers Issue

988P1a 3c large die on wove paper *1,500.*

National Capital Sesquicentennial Issue

989P1a 3c large die on white wove paper *1,500.*
991P1a 3c large die on wove paper *1,500.*
992P1a 3c large die on wove paper *1,500.*

Boy Scouts Issue

995P1a 3c large die on white wove paper *2,000.*

Nevada Centennial Issue

1951-53
999P1a 3c large die on wove paper *1,500.*

Landing of Cadillac Issue

1000P1a 3c large die on wove paper *1,500.*

Colorado Statehood Issue

1001P1a 3c large die on wove paper *1,500.*

American Chemical Society Issue

1002P1a 3c large die on wove paper *1,500.*

Battle of Brooklyn Issue

1003P1a 3c large die on wove paper *1,500.*

Betsy Ross Issue

1004P1a 3c large die on wove paper *1,500.*

4-H Club Issue

1005P1a 3c large die on wove paper *1,500.*

B & O Railroad Issue

1006TC1b 3c large die on wove paper
e. **deep blue** *1,500.*
1006P1a 3c large die on wove paper *1,750.*

A.A.A. Issue

1007P1a 3c large die on wove paper *1,500.*

Grand Coulee Dam Issue

1009P1a 3c large die on wove paper *1,500.*

Lafayette Issue

1010P1a 3c large die on wove paper *1,500.*

Mt. Rushmore Memorial Issue

1011P1a 3c large die on wove paper *1,500.*

Engineering Centennial Issue

1012P1a 3c large die on wove paper 1,500.

Service Women Issue

1013P1a 3c large die on wove paper *1,500.*

Red Cross Issue

1016P1a 3c large die on wove paper *3,000.*

National Guard Issue

1017P1a 3c large die on wove paper *1,500.*

Ohio Statehood Issue

1018P1a 3c large die on wove paper 1,500.

Washington Territory Issue

1019P1a 3c large die on wove paper *1,500.*

Louisana Purchase Issue

1020P1a 3c large die on wove paper *1,500.*

Opening of Japan Centennial Issue

1021P1a 5c large die on wove paper *2,000.*

American Bar Association Issue

1022P1a 3c large die on wove paper *1,500.*

Trucking Industry Issue

1025P1a 3c large die on wove paper *1,500.*

Gen. George S. Patton Issue

1026P1a 3c large die on wove paper 1,500.

Columbia University Issue

1954-98
1029P1a 3c large die on wove paper *1,500.*

Liberty Issue

1030P1a ½c *Franklin,* large die on wove paper *2,500.*
1031P1a 1c *Washington,* large die on wove paper *1,500.*
1032P1a 1½c *Mt. Vernon,* large die on wove paper *1,500.*
1033P1a 2c *Jefferson,* large die on wove paper *1,500.*
1036P1a 4c *Lincoln,* large die on wove paper *1,500.*
1038P1a 5c *Monroe,* large die on wove paper *1,500.*
1039P1a 6c *Roosevelt,* large die on wove paper 1,500.
1044P1a 10c *Independence Hall,* large die on wove paper *1,500.*
1047P1a 20c *Monticello,* large die on wove paper *1,500.*
1049P1a 30c *Lee,* large die on wove paper *2,000.*
1050P1a 40c *Marshall,* large die on wove paper *2,000.*
1051P1a 50c *Anthony,* large die on wove paper *2,000.*
1052P1a $1 *Henry,* large die on wove paper *2,000.*
1053P1a $5 *Hamilton,* large die on wove paper *2,500.*

Nebraska Territory Issue

1060P1a 3c large die on wove paper *1,500.*

George Eastman Issue

1062P1a 3c large die on wove paper *1,500.*

Lewis & Clark Issue

1063P1a 3c large die on wove paper *1,500.*

Pennsylvania Academy of Fine Arts Issue

1064P1a 3c large die on wove paper *1,500.*

Armed Forces Reserve Issue

1067P1a 3c large die on wove paper *1,500.*

New Hampshire Issue

1068P1a 3c large die on wove paper *1,500.*

Soo Locks Issue

1069P1a 3c large die on wove paper *1,500.*

Ft. Ticonderoga Issue

1071P1a 3c large die on wove paper *1,500.*

Benjamin Franklin Issue

1073P1a 3c large die on wove paper *1,500.*

Booker T. Washington Issue

1074P1a 3c large die on wove paper *1,500.*

FIPEX Souvenir Sheet

1076P1a large die on wove paper *1,500.*

Wildlife Conservation Issue

1077P1a 3c large die on wove paper *1,500.*
1078P1a 3c large die on wove paper *1,500.*
1079P1a 3c large die on wove paper *1,500.*

Pure Food & Drug Laws

1080P1a 3c large die on wove paper *1,500.*

Wheatland Issue

1081P1a 3c large die on wove paper *1,500.*

Labor Day Issue

1082P1a 3c large die on wove paper *1,500.*

Nassau Hall Issue

1083P1a 3c large die on wove paper *1,500.*

Children's Issue

1085P1a 3c large die on wove paper *1,500.*

Alexander Hamilton Issue

1086P1a 3c large die on wove paper *1,500.*

Polio Issue

1087P1a 3c large die on wove paper *1,500.*

Coast & Geodetic Survey Issue

1088P1a 3c large die on wove paper 1,500.

Steel Industry Issue

1090P1a 3c large die on wove paper *1,500.*

Oklahoma Statehood Issue

1092P1a 3c large die on wove paper 1,500.

Civil War Centennial Issue

1178P1 4c Ft. Sumter, large die
a. On white wove paper *1,500.*
b. On stiff yellowish bond paper *1,500.*

Project Mercury Issue

1193P1a 4c large die on wove paper *1,500.*

Antarctic Issue

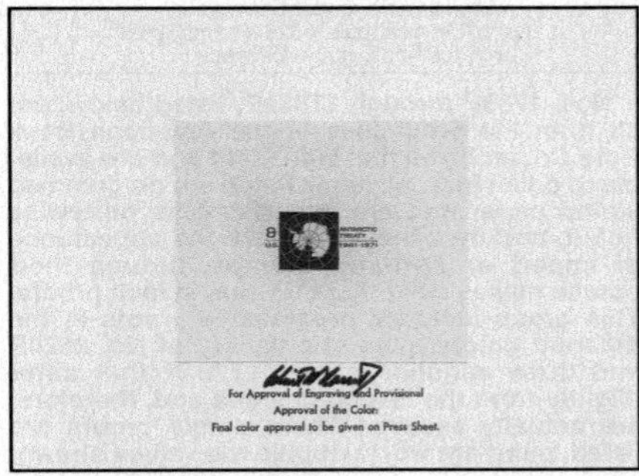

1431P1

1431P1 8c large die on white wove, mounted on card autographed by PMG Winton M. Blount *1,000.*

Olympic Games Issue

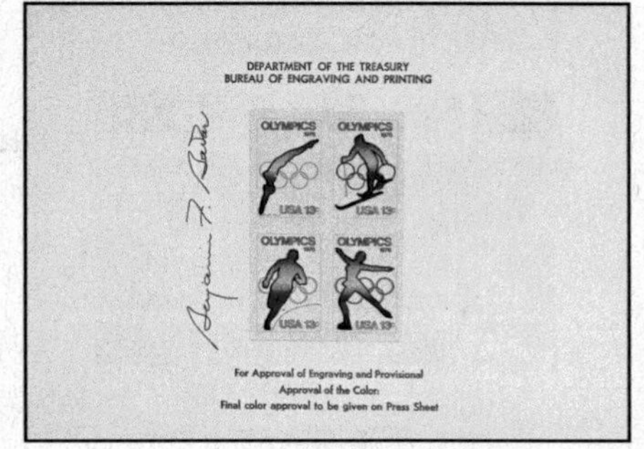

1698aP1

1698aP1 13c large hybrid die proof, mounted on large card imprinted for approval of engraving and color, signed by PMG Benjamin F. Bailar *800.*

Duck Decoy Issue

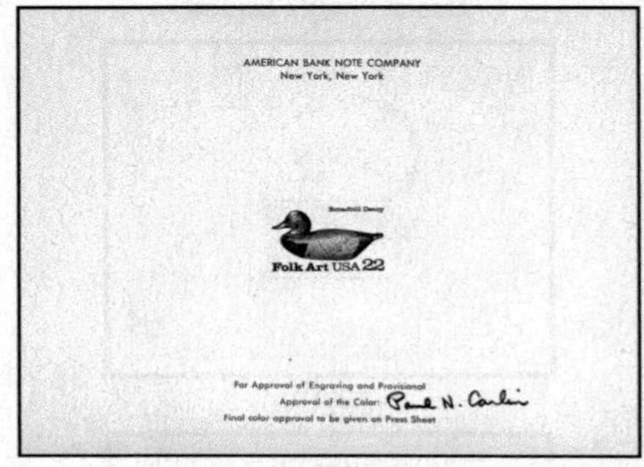

2138P1

2138P1 22c *Broadbill* decoy, large hybrid die proof, mounted on large card imprinted for approval of engraving and color, "Duck Decoys Cylinder Proof," etc. on reverse *240.*

Statue of Liberty, 100th Anniversary

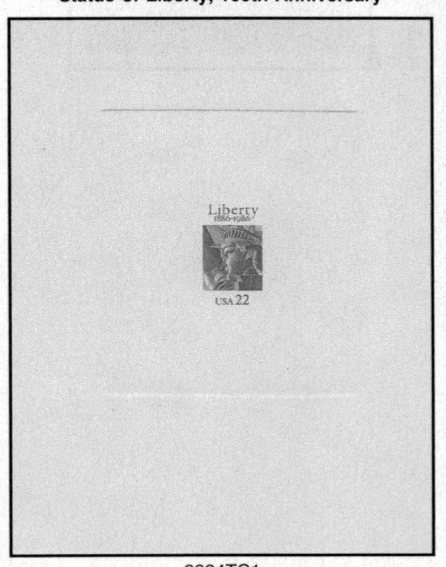

2224TC1

2224TC1e 22c **olive green,** die sunk on card *1,300.*

1988 Winter Olympics, Calgary Issue

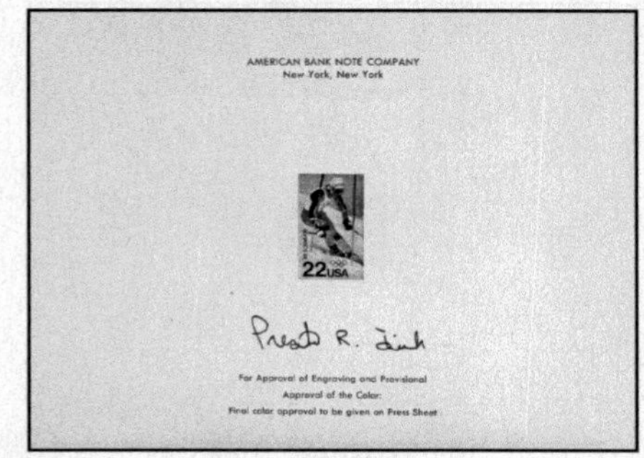

2369P1

2369P1 22c large hybrid die proof, mounted on large card imprinted for approval of engraving and color, "Winter Olympics Stamp From Approved Press Sheet," etc. on reverse *550.*

Moon Landing, 20th Anniversary

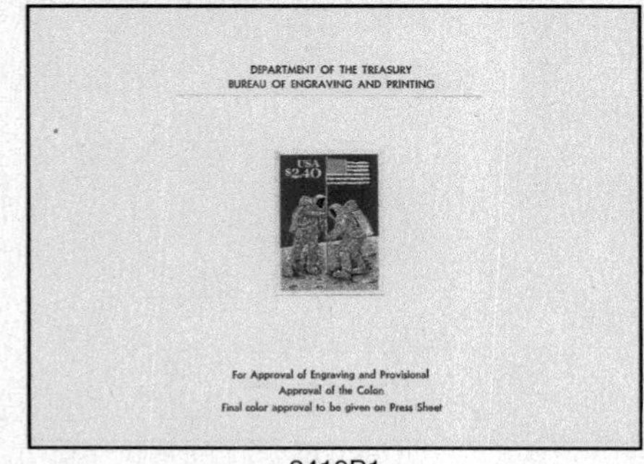

2419P1

2419P1 $2.40 large hybrid die proof, pressed on large card imprinted for approval of engraving and color *2,850.*

Flag and Olympic Rings Issue

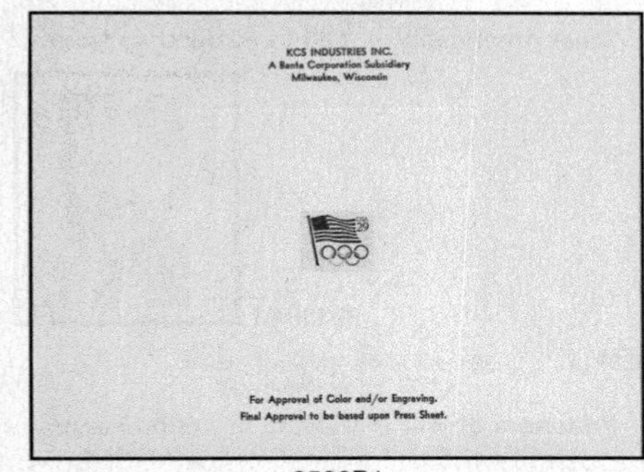

2528P1

2528P1 29c large hybrid die proof, mounted on large card imprinted for approval of engraving and color, "Flag with Olympic Rings Stamp From Approved Press Sheet," etc. on reverse *550.*

Basketball, 100th Anniversary Issue

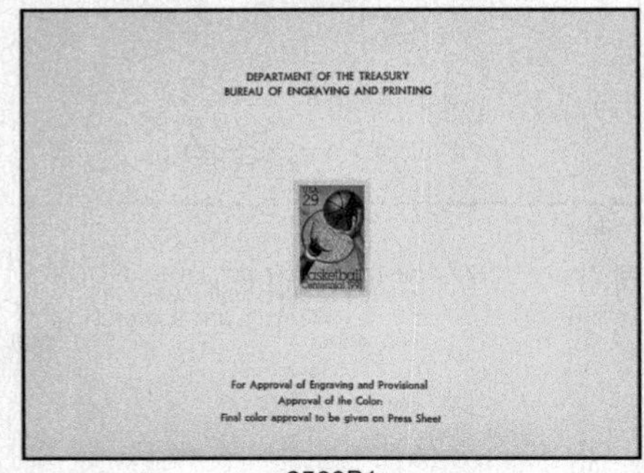

2560P1

2560P1 29c large hybrid die proof, mounted on large card imprinted for approval of engraving and color *950.*

Winter Olympics Issue

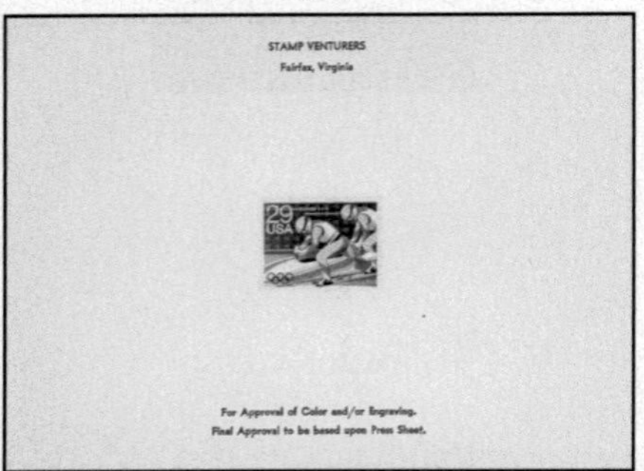

2615P1

2615P1 29c *Bobsledding,* large hybrid die proof, mounted on large card imprinted for approval of engraving and color, "Winter Olympics Stamp from Approved Sheet," etc. on reverse 600.

Summer Olympics Issue

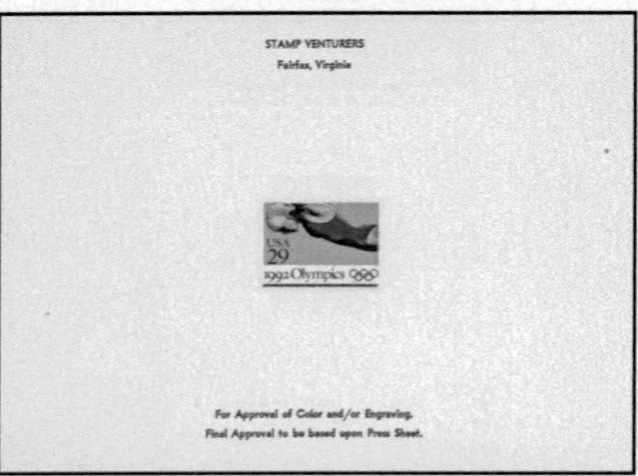

2641P1

2641P1 29c *Swimming,* large hybrid die proof, mounted on large card imprinted for approval of engraving and color, "Summer Olympics Stamp from Approved Sheet," etc. on reverse 500.

Great Americans — Milton S. Hershey Issue

2933P1a

2933P1a 32c large die on wove, dated "7/3/95" at lower right —

Prisoners of War & Missing in Action Issue

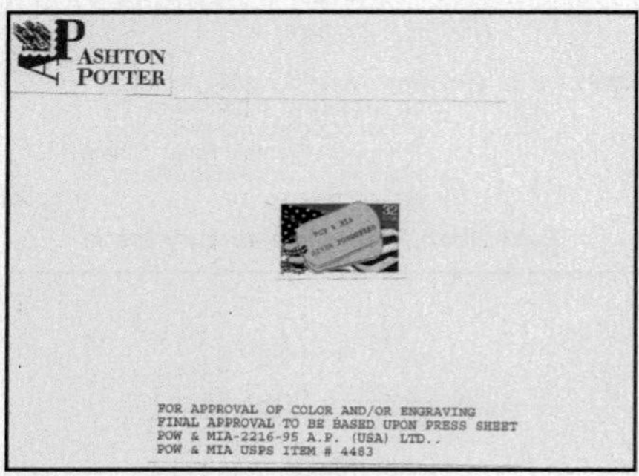

2966P1

2966P1 32c large hybrid die proof, pressed on large card imprinted with Ashton Potter logo and approval information 300.

World War II Issue

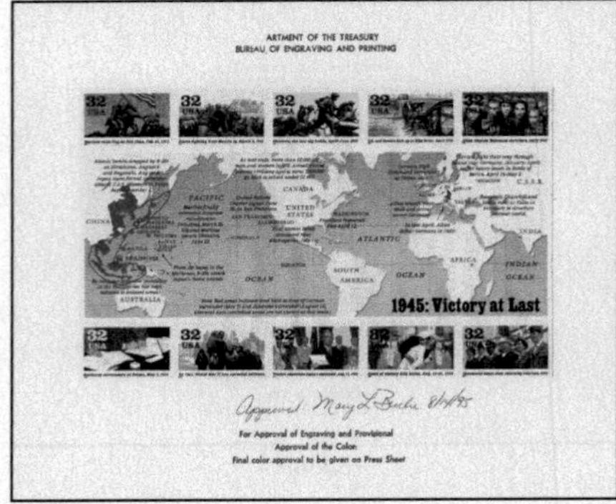

2981P1

2981P1 32c large hybrid die proof, pressed on large card, ms. approved by Mary L. Burke, USPS Production Staff 1,250.

Space Shuttle Issues

3261P

3262P

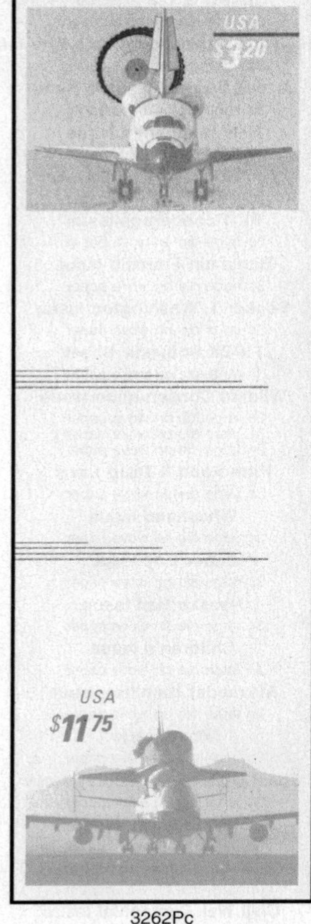

3262Pc

3261P $3.20 **magenta** color only
- ***a.*** On coated paper —
- ***b.*** On uncoated paper —

3262P $11.75 **cyan** color only
- ***a.*** On coated paper —
- ***b.*** On uncoated paper —
- ***c.*** As "a," vertical pair, #3261P and 3262P, with full horiz. gutter between 1,150.
- ***d.*** As "b," vertical pair, #3261P and 3262P, with full horiz. gutter between —

Nos. 1789P through 2788aP, listed below, are all from the proof files of the American Bank Note Co. archives that were sold and are available to collectors. All items listed are on gummed stamp paper and are imperf unless otherwise noted, and they therefore have the appearance of imperf or part-perf stamps, though their source makes clear that they are, in fact, proofs. This group includes progressive proofs in the different colors, plus one variety of No. 2624P and three varieties of No. 2770aP that differ slightly from the issued designs and, therefore, are actually essays. Where single proofs are listed, pairs are worth double the values shown.

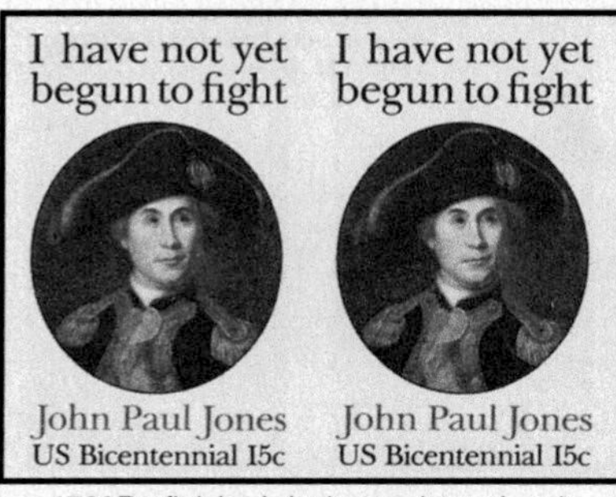

1789Pg finished design as issued, pair

1789Pd blue color only, pair

1979

1789P 15c John Paul Jones
a. Single, red color ("John Paul Jones") only *50.00*
Pair with vert. gutter between —
Pair with horiz. gutter between —
Cross gutter block of four —
b. Single, yellow color only *50.00*
Pair with vert. gutter between —
Pair with horiz. gutter between —
Cross gutter block of four —
c. Single, magenta color only 50.00
Pair with vert. gutter between —
Pair with horiz. gutter between —
Cross gutter block of four —
d. Single, blue color only *50.00*
Pair with vert. gutter between —
Pair with horiz. gutter between —
Cross gutter block of four —
e. Single, black color only *50.00*
Pair with vert. gutter between —
Pair with horiz. gutter between —
Cross gutter block of four —
f. Single, tagging blocks only *50.00*
Pair with vert. gutter between —
Pair with horiz. gutter between —
Cross gutter block of four —
g. Single, finished design as issued *25.00*
Pair *50.00*
Pair with vert. gutter between *700.00*
Pair with horiz. gutter between *600.00*
Cross gutter block of four *3,000.*

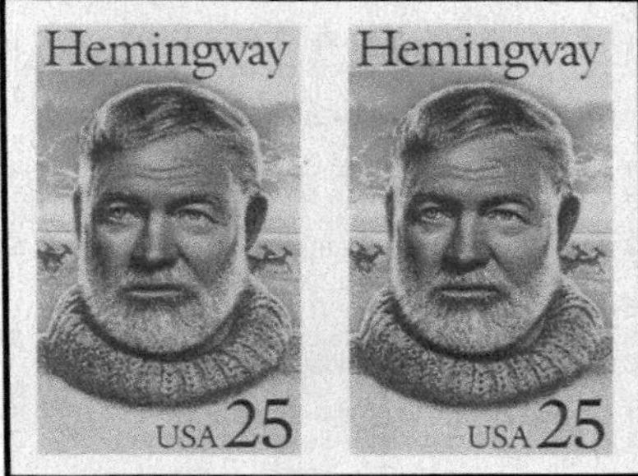

2418P

1989

2418P 25c Ernest Hemingway, pair *2,000.*
Pair with vert. gutter between —
Pair with horiz. gutter between —
Cross gutter block of four —

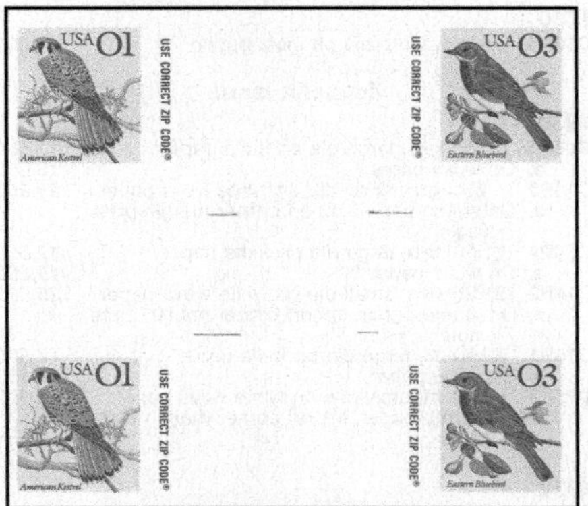

2478Pa cross gutter block

Illustration reduced.

1991

2476P 1c Kestrel, pair *150.*
Pair with vert. gutter between *200.*
Pair with horiz. gutter between *200.*
Cross gutter block of four —
a. Perforated
Pair with vert. gutter between *675.*
Pair with horiz. gutter between *675.*
Cross gutter block of four —

2478P 3c Bluebird, pair *150.*
Pair with vert. gutter between *200.*
Pair with horiz. gutter between *200.*
Cross gutter block of four —
a. Se-tenants, Nos. 2476P and 2478P
Pair, one No. 2476P and one No. 2478P, with vert. gutter between —
Cross gutter block of four, two No. 2476P at left and two No. 2478P at right —
b. Perforated
Pair with vert. gutter between —
Pair with horiz. gutter between —
Cross gutter block of four —
c. Perforated se-tenants
Pair, one No. 2476Pa and one No. 2478Pb, with vert. gutter between —
Cross gutter block of four, two No. 2476Pa at left and two No. 2478Pb at right (unique) —

1990-91

2500aP 25c Olympics, horiz. strip of five *1,500.*
Two strips of five with vert. gutter between —
Two strips of five with horiz. gutter between —
Cross gutter block of four strips of five —

2513P 25c Dwight D. Eisenhower, pair *875.*

2517P (29c) "F" stamp, perforated
Pair with vert. gutter between —
Pair with horiz. gutter between —
Cross gutter block of four (unique) —

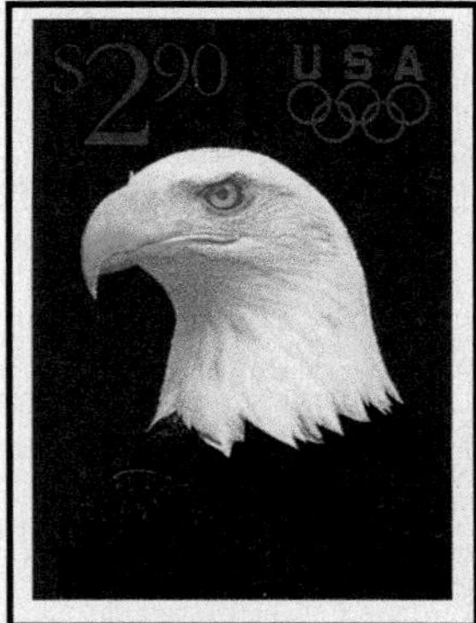

2540Pi with all litho. colors

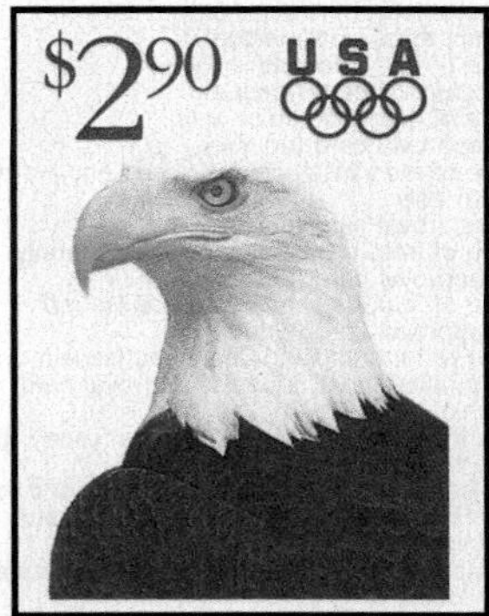

2540Pf magenta, yellow and blue colors only

1991

2540P $2.90 Eagle
a. Single, magenta color only *175.*
Pair with vert. gutter between —
Pair with horiz. gutter between —
Cross gutter block of four —
b. Single, yellow color only *175.*
Pair with vert. gutter between —
Pair with horiz. gutter between —
Cross gutter block of four —
c. Single, blue color only *175.*
Pair with vert. gutter between —
Pair with horiz. gutter between —
Cross gutter block of four —
d. Single, magenta and yellow colors only *175.*
Pair with vert. gutter between —
Pair with horiz. gutter between —
Cross gutter block of four —
e. Single, yellow and blue colors only *175.*
Pair with vert. gutter between —
Pair with horiz. gutter between —
Cross gutter block of four —
f. Single, magenta, yellow and blue colors only *175.*
Pair with vert. gutter between —
Pair with horiz. gutter between —
Cross gutter block of four —
g. Single, black (litho.) color only *175.*
Pair with vert. gutter between —
Pair with horiz. gutter between —
Cross gutter block of four —
h. Single, black (litho.) and yellow colors only *175.*
Pair with vert. gutter between —
Pair with horiz. gutter between —
Cross gutter block of four —
i. Single, all litho. colors but without black engr. *175.*
Pair with vert. gutter between —
Pair with horiz. gutter between —
Cross gutter block of four —
j. Single, finished design as issued *500.*
Pair *1,000.*
Pair with vert. gutter between —
Pair with horiz. gutter between —
Cross gutter block of four —
k. Perforated, all litho. colors but without black engr. —
Pair with vert. gutter between —
Pair with horiz. gutter between —
Cross gutter block of four —
l. Perforated, finished design as issued
Pair with vert. gutter between —
Pair with horiz. gutter between —
Cross gutter block of four —

2605P, with plate numbers

2605P 23c Flag Presorted First Class Coil, vert. pair, uncut between *250.*
Vert. pair, uncut between, with P#A111 —

1992

2624P 1c, 4c and $1 Columbian souvenir sheet *750.*
Pair of sheets —
a. As No. 2624P, but with background of No. 2627P (essay) —

2625P 2c, 3c and $4 Columbian souvenir sheet *750.*
Pair of sheets —

2626P 5c, 30c and 50c Columbian souvenir sheet 750.
Pair of sheets —

2627P 6c, 8c and $3 Columbian souvenir sheet *750.*
Pair of sheets —

2628P 10c, 15c and $2 Columbian souvenir sheet *750.*
Pair of sheets —

2629P $4 Columbian souvenir sheet *750.*
Pair of sheets —

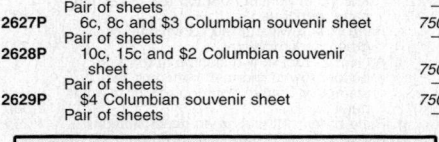

2646aPi finished design as issued

2646aPe brown color only

Illustrations reduced.

2646aP 29c Hummingbirds booklet pane
b. Pane of five, yellow color only *450.*
Two panes of five with vert. gutter between —
Two panes of five with horiz. gutter between —
Cross gutter block of four panes of five —
c. Pane of five, magenta color only *450.*
Two panes of five with vert. gutter between —
Two panes of five with horiz. gutter between —
Cross gutter block of four panes of five —
d. Pane of five, blue color only *450.*
Two panes of five with vert. gutter between —
Two panes of five with horiz. gutter between —
Cross gutter block of four panes of five —
e. Pane of five, brown color (birds) only *450.*
Two panes of five with vert. gutter between —
Two panes of five with horiz. gutter between —
Cross gutter block of four panes of five —
f. Pane of five, brown color ("USA/29") only *450.*
Two panes of five with vert. gutter between —
Two panes of five with horiz. gutter between —
Cross gutter block of four panes of five —
g. Pane of five, green color (frames) only *450.*
Two panes of five with vert. gutter between —
Two panes of five with horiz. gutter between —

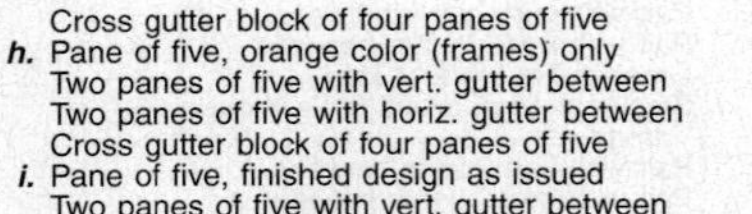

Cross gutter block of four panes of five —
h. Pane of five, orange color (frames) only *450.*
Two panes of five with vert. gutter between —
Two panes of five with horiz. gutter between —
Cross gutter block of four panes of five —
i. Pane of five, finished design as issued *450.*
Two panes of five with vert. gutter between —
Two panes of five with horiz. gutter between —
Cross gutter block of four panes of five —

2718aPd

2718aPe

Illustrations reduced.

2718aP 29c Christmas Toys booklet pane *600.*
Horiz. pair of panes of four *1,500.*
Vert. pair of panes of four *1,500.*
b. As No. 2718aP, pane of four with two stamps at top from bottom row of normal pane and two stamps at bottom from top row of normal pane *1,000.*
c. As No. 2718aP, perforated, pair of panes, uncut horiz. *2,000.*
d. Pane of four with two stamps at top from bottom row of normal pane and two stamps at bottom from top row of normal pane, perforated *1,200.*
e. Pane of four without red "Greetings" or green denominations *1,200.*
f. As No. 2718aPe, two stamps at top from bottom row of "normal" pane and two stamps at bottom from top row of "normal" pane *1,500.*
g. Pane of four without green denominations *1,200.*
h. As No. 2718aPg, two stamps at top from bottom row of "normal" pane and two stamps at bottom from top row of "normal" pane *1,500.*

1993

2737aP 29c American Music booklet pane of eight —
Pair of panes of eight —
c. As No. 2737aP, perforated horiz., uncut vert., pair of panes of eight —
2737bP 29c American Music booklet pane of four *2,000.*
d. As No. 2737bP, perforated horiz., uncut vert., pair of panes of four —
e. Pair of panes, one No. 2737aP + one 2737bP —
f. Pair of panes, one No. 2737aPc + one 2737bPd —

2754Pa

2754Pb

Illustration of No. 2754Pa reduced.

2754P 29c Cherokee Strip Land Run, pair *350.*
Pair with vert. gutter between *400.*
Pair with horiz. gutter between *400.*
Cross gutter block of four *1,500.*
a. Perforated
Pair with vert. gutter between *250.*
Pair with horiz. gutter between *250.*
Cross gutter block of four *750.*
b. As No. 2754P, without purple inscriptions and black denominations, pair —
Pair with vert. gutter between —
Pair with horiz. gutter between —
Cross gutter block of four —
c. Die proof, signed 11/25/92 for color and/or engraving —
2770aP 29c American Musicals booklet pane of four *1,250.*
Pair of panes —
a. Perforated horiz., uncut vert., pair of panes of four —
b. Pane of four, blue color only, with designs slightly different from issued designs (essay) —
c. Pane of four, blue and magenta colors only, with designs slightly different from issued designs (essay) —
d. Pane of four, blue, magenta and yellow colors only, with designs slightly different from issued designs (essay) —
2778aP 29c American Music booklet pane of four
a. Pane of four, yellow color only *300.*
On approval card (unique) —
b. Pane of four, pink color only *300.*
On approval card (unique) —
c. Pane of four, red color only *300.*
On approval card (unique) —
d. Pane of four, blue color only *300.*
On approval card (unique) —
e. Pane of four, black color (frames and wording) only *300.*
On approval card (unique) —
f. Pane of four, black color (Musicians) only *300.*
On approval card (unique) —
g. Pane of four, finished design as issued *1,500.*
On approval card (unique) —
h. Pane of four, finished design as issued, on cromalin paper, taped to approval card (unique) —
i. Booklet cover, finished design as issued, on card stock, pair of covers —
j. Booklet cover, finished design as issued, on cromalin paper, taped to approval card (unique) —
k. Perforated horiz., uncut vert., pair of panes of four *1,500.*

Some of the sets of progressive proofs are in panes that are 2½ to 3½ stamps tall. These sell for somewhat less than the full panes.

About 20 percent of the examples of No. 2778aPk are split into two pieces. From these pieces come horizontal pairs or blocks of booklet stamps imperf vertically.

2788aP

2788aP 29c Classic Books, block of four *400.*
Pair of blocks with vert. gutter between —
Pair of blocks with horiz. gutter between —
Cross gutter block of four blocks —

1995

2587P1b 32c **red brown,** die proof on gummed wove paper, ms "7/17/95" and "#3" below design —

AIR POST

1918

C1P1 6c **org,** large die on India paper *8,500.*
C2P1 16c **grn,** large die on India paper *7,000.*
C3P1 24c **car rose & bl,** large die on India paper *8,500.*

1923

C4P1 8c **dk grn,** large die on India paper *4,750.*
C4P2 8c **dk grn,** small die on white wove paper *5,000.*
C5TC1a 16c large die on India paper
e. **dark green** 5,000.
C5P1 16c **dk bl,** large die on India paper *4,750.*
C5P2 16c **dk bl,** small die on white wove paper *5,000.*
C6P1 24c **car,** large die on India paper *4,750.*
C6P2 24c **car,** small die on white wove paper *5,000.*

1926-27

C7P1 10c **dk bl,** large die on India paper *3,000.*
C8TC1a 15c large die on India paper
e. **orange** 4,750.
C8P1 15c **ol brn,** large die on India paper *3,000.*
C9P1 20c **yel grn,** large die on India paper *3,000.*

Lindbergh Issue

1927

C10P1 10c **dk bl,** large die on India paper *6,000.*
C10P2 10c **dk bl,** small die on white wove paper *7,000.*

1928

C11P1 5c **car & bl,** large die on India paper *11,000.*

1930

C12P1 5c **vio,** large die on India paper *3,000.*

Zeppelin Issue

1930

C13P1 65c **grn,** large die on India paper *17,500.*
a. On wove paper *15,000.*
C13P2 65c **grn,** small die on white wove paper *25,000.*
b. On stamp paper, imperf corner margin plate single —
C14P1 $1.30 **brn,** large die on India paper *17,500.*
a. On wove paper *15,000.*
C14P2 $1.30 **brn,** small die on white wove paper *25,000.*
b. On stamp paper, imperf corner margin plate single —
C15P1 $2.60 **bl,** large die on India paper *17,500.*
a. On wove paper *15,000.*
C15P2 $2.60 **bl,** small die on white wove paper *25,000.*
b. On stamp paper, imperf corner margin plate single —

1932

C17P1 8c **ol bis,** large die on India paper *4,000.*

Century of Progress Issue

1933

C18P1 50c **grn,** large die on India paper *17,500.*
C18P2 50c **grn,** small die on white wove paper *45,000.*

1935-39

C20P2	25c **bl,** small die on white wove paper	*3,250.*
C21P2	20c **grn,** small die on white wove paper	*3,250.*
C22P2	50c **car,** small die on white wove paper	*3,250.*
C23P2	6c **dk bl & car,** small die on white wove paper	*7,000.*
C24P1	30c **dull bl,** large die on India paper	*3,500.*
C24P2	30c **dull bl,** small die on white wove paper	*2,750.*

1941-89

C25P2	6c **car,** small die on white wove paper	*3,000.*
C26P2	8c **ol grn,** small die on white wove paper	*3,000.*
C27P1	10c **vio,** large die on white wove paper	*5,000.*
C27P2	10c **vio,** small die on white wove paper	*3,000.*
C28P2	15c **brn car,** small die on white wove paper	*3,000.*
C29P2	20c **brt grn,** small die on white wove paper	*3,000.*
C30P2	30c **bl,** small die on white wove paper	*3,000.*
C31P2	50c **org,** small die on white wove paper	*3,000.*
C32TC1a	5c large die on India paper	
	***e.* blue**	4,750.
C33P1	5c **car,** large die on white wove paper	*5,500.*
C35TC1a	15c large die on India paper	
	***e.* brown violet**	4,750.
C40P1	6c **car,** large die on white wove paper	*5,000.*
C44P1	25c **rose car,** large die on white wove paper	*5,000.*
C44P2	25c **rose car,** small die on white wove paper	*3,500.*
C45P1	6c **mag,** large die on white wove paper	*6,000.*
C45P2	6c **mag,** small die on white wove paper	*5,000.*
C46P1	80c **brt red vio,** large die on white wove paper	*5,000.*
C46P2	80c **brt red vio,** small die on white wove paper	—
C47P1	6c **car,** large die on white wove paper	*6,000.*
C48P1	4c **brt bl,** large die on white wove paper	—

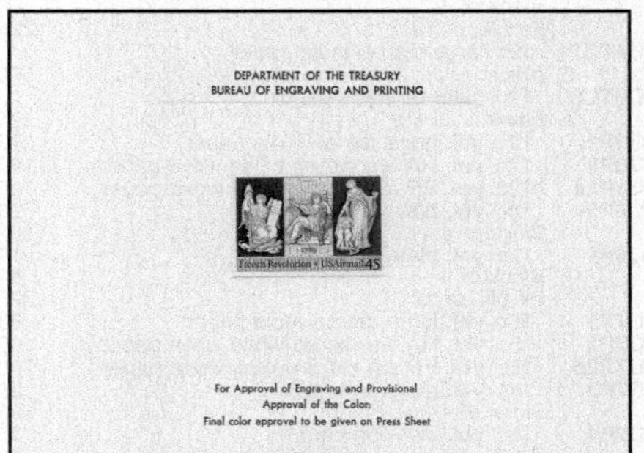

C120P1

C120P1	45c large hybrid die proof, pressed on large card imprinted for approval of engraving and color	1,250.

AIR POST SPECIAL DELIVERY

1934-36

CE1TC1a	16c large die on India paper	
	***e.* black**	4,000.
CE1P2	16c **dk bl,** small die on white wove paper	*4,000.*
CE2P2	16c **red & bl,** small die on white wove paper	*4,000.*

SPECIAL DELIVERY

1885

E1TC1a	10c large die on India paper	
	***e.* black**	3,000.
	***f.* dark brown**	3,000.
E1TC2	10c small die on wove paper	
	***b.* orange yellow**	*2,000.*
E1P1	10c **bl,** large die on India paper	600.
E1P2	10c **bl,** RA sm die on white wove paper	250.
E1P2a	10c **bl,** PP sm die on yelsh wove paper	2,500.
E1P3	10c **bl,** plate on India	35.
	Block of 4	175.
E1P4	10c **bl,** plate on card	30.
	Block of 4	150.
	P# blk. of 8, Impt.	*1,400.*

1888

E2TC1a	10c large die on India paper	
	***e.* black**	3,000.
	***f.* green**	3,000.
E2TC2	10c small die on India paper	
	***b.* olive yellow**	2,000.
E2P1	10c **bl,** large die on India paper	750.
E2P2	10c **bl,** RA sm die on white wove paper	250.
E2P2a	10c **bl,** PP sm die on yelsh wove paper	2,600.
E2P3	10c **bl,** plate on India	35.
	Block of 4	200.
	P# blk. of 8	525.
E2P4	10c **bl,** plate on card	30.
	Block of 4	150.
	P# blk. of 8	—

1893

E3P1	10c **org,** large die on India paper	2,500.
E3P2	10c **org,** RA sm die on white wove paper	300.
E3P2a	10c **org,** PP sm die on yelsh wove paper	4,000.
E3P3	10c **org,** plate on India	75.
	Block of 4	325.
E3P4	10c **org,** plate on card	70.
	Block of 4	310.
	P# blk. of 8, Impt.	1,250.

1894-95

E4P1	10c **bl,** large die on India paper	550.
E4P2	10c **bl,** RA sm die on white wove paper	250.
E4P2a	10c **bl,** PP sm die on yelsh wove paper	3,000.
E4P5	10c **bl,** plate on stamp paper, pair	*6,500.*
E5P5	10c **bl,** plate on stamp paper, pair	*4,500.*
	Block of 4	—
	P# blk. of 6, Impt.	*29,000.*

1902

E6TC1a	10c large die on India paper	
	***e.* orange**	3,750.
	***f.* black**	3,750.
	***g.* rose red**	*3,750.*
E6P1	10c **ultra,** large die on India paper	900.
E6P2	10c **ultra,** RA sm die on white wove paper	250.
E6P2a	10c **ultra,** PP sm die on yelsh wove paper	2,500.

1908

E7TC2	10c small die on India paper	
	***b.* blue**	*3,500.*
	***c.* green**	*3,500.*
E7P1	10c **grn,** large die on India paper	2,750.
E7P2	10c **grn,** sm die on white wove paper	2,000.
E7P2a	10c **grn,** PP sm die on yelsh wove paper	3,000.

1922

E12TC1a	10c large die on India paper	
	***e.* black**	3,250.
E12P1	10c **dp ultra,** large die on India paper	2,000.
E12P1a	10c **dp ultra,** large die on white wove paper	2,250.

1925-54

E13P1	15c **dp org,** large die on India paper	2,000.
E13P2	15c **dp org,** small die on white wove paper	*3,000.*
E14P1	20c **blk,** large die on India paper	2,000.
E14P2	20c **black,** small die on white wove paper	1,500.
E14TC1a	20c large die on India paper	
	***e.* purple**	4,000.
E17P2	13c **bl,** small die on white or yelsh wove paper	*3,000.*
E20P1	20c **dp bl,** large die on India paper	3,000.

REGISTRATION

1911

F1TC1d	10c Large die on glazed card	
	***e.* black**	1,500.
F1P1	10c **ultra,** large die on India paper	10,000.
F1P2	10c **ultra,** sm die on white wove paper	2,000.
F1P2a	10c **ultra,** PP sm die on yelsh wove paper	3,000.

POSTAGE DUE

1879

J1TC1a	1c large die on India paper	
	***e.* black**	500.
	***f.* gray black**	500.
	***g.* ultramarine**	500.
	***h.* blue**	500.
	***i.* blue green**	500.
	***j.* orange**	500.
	***k.* red orange**	500.
	***l.* olive bister**	500.
J1TC2	1c small die on India paper	
	***b.* orange**	100.
J1TC4	1c plate on card	
	***a.* black**	50.
J1P1	1c **brn,** large die on India paper	250.
J1P2	1c **brn,** RA sm die on white wove paper	100.
J1P2a	1c **brn,** PP sm die on yelsh wove paper	750.
J1P3	1c **brn,** plate on India	22.
	Block of 4	105.
	P# blk. of 12	450.
J1P4	1c **brn,** plate on card	15.
	Block of 4	90.
J2TC1a	2c large die on India paper	
	***e.* black**	500.
	***f.* gray black**	500.
	***g.* ultramarine**	500.
	***h.* blue**	500.
	***i.* blue green**	500.
	***j.* orange**	500.
	***k.* red orange**	500.
	***l.* sepia**	500.
J2TC2	2c small die on India paper	
	***b.* orange**	100.
J2P1	2c **brn,** large die on India paper	250.
	***a.* dk brn,** large die on India paper	—
J2P2	2c **brn,** RA sm die on white wove paper	100.
J2P2a	2c **brn,** PP sm die on yelsh wove paper	750.
J2P3	2c **brn,** plate on India	20.
	Block of 4	90.
	P# blk. of 12	425.
J2P4	2c **brn,** plate on card	15.
	Block of 4	90.
J3TC1a	3c large die on India paper	
	***e.* black**	500.
	***f.* ultramarine**	500.
	***g.* blue**	500.
	***h.* blue green**	500.
	***i.* orange**	500.
	***j.* red orange**	500.
	***k.* light brown**	500.
J3TC2	3c small die on India paper	
	***b.* gray black**	100.
	***c.* orange**	500.
J3P1	3c **brn,** large die on India paper	250.
	***a.* dk brn,** large die on India paper	—
J3P2	3c **brn,** RA sm die on white wove paper	100.
	***b.* dk brn,** RA sm die on India paper	—
J3P2a	3c **brn,** PP sm die on yelsh wove paper	750.
J3P3	3c **brn,** plate on India	20.
	Block of 4	90.
	P# blk. of 12	425.
J3P4	3c **brn,** plate on card	15.
	Block of 4	90.
J4TC1a	5c large die on India paper	
	***e.* black**	500.
	***f.* gray black**	500.
	***g.* ultramarine**	500.
	***h.* blue**	500.
	***i.* blue green**	500.
	***j.* orange**	500.
	***k.* red orange**	500.
J4TC2	5c small die on India paper	
	***b.* orange**	500.
J4P1	5c **brn,** large die on India paper	250.
	***a.* dk brn,** large die on India paper	—
J4P2	5c **brn,** RA sm die on white wove paper	100.
J4P2a	5c **brn,** PP sm die on yelsh wove paper	750.
J4P3	5c **brn,** plate on India	20.
	Block of 4	90.
	P# blk. of 12	425.
J4P4	5c **brn,** plate on card	15.
	Block of 4	90.
J5TC1a	10c large die on India paper	
	***e.* black**	500.
	***f.* gray black**	500.
	***g.* blue**	500.
	***h.* olive yellow**	500.
	***i.* blue green**	500.
	***j.* orange**	500.
	***k.* red orange**	500.
	***l.* olive bister**	500.
	***m.* sepia**	500.
	***n.* gray**	500.
J5TC2	10c small die on India paper	
	***b.* orange**	100.
J5P1	10c **brn,** large die on India paper	250.
	***a.* dk brn,** large die on India paper	—
J5P2	10c **brn,** RA sm die on white wove paper	100.
J5P2a	10c **brn,** PP sm die on yelsh wove paper	750.
J5P3	10c **dk brn,** plate on India	32.
	Block of 4	145.
	P# blk. of 12	675.
J5P4	10c **brn,** plate on card	15.
	Block of 4	90.
J6TC1a	30c large die on India paper	
	***e.* black**	500.
	***f.* gray black**	500.
	***g.* blue**	500.
	***h.* blue green**	500.
	***i.* orange**	500.
	***j.* red orange**	500.
	***k.* olive bister**	500.
J6TC2	30c small die on India paper	
	***b.* olive yellow**	100.
	***c.* orange**	100.
	***d.* sepia**	100.
J6P1	30c **brn,** large die on India paper	250.
	***a.* dk brn,** large die on India paper	—
J6P2	30c **brn,** RA sm die on white wove paper	100.
J6P2a	30c **brn,** PP sm die on yelsh wove paper	750.
J6P3	30c **dk brn,** plate on India	32.
	Block of 4	145.
	P# blk. of 12	675.
J6P4	30c **brn,** plate on card	15.
	Block of 4	90.
J7TC1a	50c large die on India paper	
	***e.* black**	500.
	***f.* gray black**	500.
	***g.* blue**	500.
	***i.* blue green**	500.
	***j.* orange**	500.
	***k.* red orange**	500.
	***l.* olive bister**	500.
	***m.* sepia**	500.
	***n.* gray**	500.
J7TC2	50c small die on India paper	
	***b.* blue**	100.
	***c.* olive yellow**	100.
	***d.* orange**	100.
J7P1	50c **brn,** large die on India paper	250.
	***a.* dk brn,** large die on India paper	—
J7P2	50c **brn,** RA sm die on white wove paper	100.
J7P2a	50c **brn,** PP sm die on yelsh wove paper	750.
J7P3	50c **dk brn,** plate on India	32.
	Block of 4	145.
	P# blk. of 12	675.
J7P4	50c **brn,** plate on card	15.
	Block of 4	90.
J1P1-J7P1	1c-50c **brown,** hybrid large die proofs on India paper, cut close and pressed on die sunk card in a "H" pattern	*1,000.*
	Nos. J1P3-J7P3 (7)	178.00
	Nos. J1P4-J7P4 (7)	105.00

1887

J15P2a	1c **red brn,** PP sm die on yelsh wove paper	1,000.
J15P4	1c **red brn,** plate on card	15.
J16P2a	2c **red brn,** PP sm die on yelsh wove paper	1,000.
J16P4	2c **red brn,** plate on card	15.
J17P2a	3c **red brn,** PP sm die on yelsh wove paper	1,000.
J17P4	3c **red brn,** plate on card	20.
J18P2a	5c **red brn,** PP sm die on yelsh wove paper	1,000.
J18P4	5c **red brn,** plate on card	15.
J19P2a	10c **red brn,** PP sm die on yelsh wove paper	1,000.
J19P3	10c **red brn,** plate on India	19.
	Block of 4	90.
	P# blk. of 12	360.

J19P4 10c **red brn,** plate on card 25.
J20P2a 30c **red brn,** PP sm die on yelsh wove paper 1,000.
J20P3 30c **red brn,** plate on India 19.
Block of 4 90.
P# blk. of 12 360.
J20P4 30c **red brn,** plate on card 20.
J21P2a 50c **red brn,** PP sm die on yelsh wove paper 1,000.
J21P3 50c **red brn,** plate on India 45.
Block of 4 210.
P# blk. of 12 900.
J21P4 50c **red brn,** plate on card 25.
Nos. J15P4-J21P4 (7) 135.00

1891-93

J22P1 1c **brt cl,** large die on India paper 140.
J22P2 1c **brt cl,** RA sm die on white wove paper 125.
J22P2a 1c **brt cl,** PP sm die on yelsh wove paper 500.
J22P3 1c **brt cl,** plate on India 12.
Block of 4 65.
J22P4 1c **brt cl,** plate on card 17.
Block of 4 80.
P# blk. of 12 —
J22P5 1c **br cl,** plate on stamp paper, pair *425.*
J23P1 2c **brt cl,** large die on India paper 140.
J23P2 2c **brt cl,** RA sm die on white wove paper 125.
J23P2a 2c **brt cl,** PP sm die on yelsh wove paper 500.
J23P3 2c **brt cl,** plate on India 12.
Block of 4 65.
J23P4 2c **brt cl,** plate on card 17.
Block of 4 80.
P# blk. of 12 —
J23P5 2c **br cl,** plate on stamp paper, pair *425.*
J24P1 3c **brt cl,** large die on India paper 140.
J24P2 3c **brt cl,** RA sm die on white wove paper 125.
J24P2a 3c **brt cl,** PP sm die on yelsh wove paper 500.
J24P3 3c **brt cl,** plate on India 12.
Block of 4 65.
J24P4 3c **brt cl,** plate on card 17.
Block of 4 80.
P# blk. of 12 —
J24P5 3c **br cl,** plate on stamp paper, pair *425.*
J25P1 5c **brt cl,** large die on India paper 140.
J25P2 5c **brt cl,** RA sm die on white wove paper 125.
J25P2a 5c **brt cl,** PP sm die on yelsh wove paper 500.
J25P3 5c **brt cl,** plate on India 12.
Block of 4 65.
J25P4 5c **brt cl,** plate on card 17.
Block of 4 80.
P# blk. of 12 —
J25P5 5c **br cl,** plate on stamp paper, pair *425.*
J26P1 10c **brt cl,** large die on India paper 140.
J26P2 10c **brt cl,** RA sm die on white wove paper 125.
J26P2a 10c **brt cl,** PP sm die on yelsh wove paper 500.
J26P3 10c **brt cl,** plate on India 12.
Block of 4 65.
J26P4 10c **brt cl,** plate on card 17.
Block of 4 80.
P# blk. of 12 —
J26P5 10c **br cl,** plate on stamp paper, pair *425.*
J27P1 30c **brt cl,** large die on India paper 140.
J27P2 30c **brt cl,** RA sm die on white wove paper 125.
J27P2a 30c **brt cl,** PP sm die on yelsh wove paper 500.
J27P3 30c **brt cl,** plate on India 28.
Block of 4 140.
J27P4 30c **brt cl,** plate on card 17.
Block of 4 80.
P# blk. of 12 —
J27P5 30c **br cl,** plate on stamp paper, pair *500.*
J28P1 50c **brt cl,** large die on India paper 140.
J28P2 50c **brt cl,** RA sm die on white wove paper 125.
J28P2a 50c **brt cl,** PP sm die on yelsh wove paper 500.
J28P3 50c **brt cl,** plate on India 19.
Block of 4 90.
J28P4 50c **brt cl,** plate on card 17.
Block of 4 80.
P# blk. of 12 —
J28P5 50c **br cl,** plate on stamp paper, pair *500.*
Nos. J22P3-J28P3 (7) 107.00
Nos. J22P4-J28P4 (7) 119.00

Values for Nos. J22P5-J28P5 are for pairs with original gum and minor faults.

1894

J31P1 1c **cl,** large die on India paper 165.
J31P2 1c **cl,** RA sm die on white wove paper 120.
J31P2a 1c **cl,** PP sm die on yelsh wove paper 500.
J31P5 1c **cl,** plate on stamp paper, pair *225.*
Block of 4 *500.*
J32P1 2c **brt cl,** large die on India paper 165.
J32P2 2c **brt cl,** RA sm die on white wove paper 120.
J32P2a 2c **brt cl,** PP sm die on yelsh wove paper 500.
J32P4 2c **brt cl,** plate on card 200.
Block of 4 900.
P# blk. of 6 3,500.
J33P1 3c **brt cl,** large die on India paper 165.
J33P2 3c **brt cl,** RA sm die on white wove paper 120.
J33P2a 3c **brt cl,** PP sm die on yelsh wove paper 500.
J34P1 5c **brt cl,** large die on India paper 165.
J34P2 5c **brt cl,** RA sm die on white wove paper 120.
J34P2a 5c **brt cl,** PP sm die on yelsh wove paper 500.
J35P1 10c **brt cl,** large die on India paper 165.
J35P2 10c **brt cl,** RA sm die on white wove paper 120.
J35P2a 10c **brt cl,** PP sm die on yelsh wove paper 500.
J36P1 30c **brt cl,** large die on India paper 165.
J36P2 30c **brt cl,** RA sm die on white wove paper 120.
J36P2a 30c **brt cl,** PP sm die on yelsh wove paper 500.
J37P1 50c **brt cl,** large die on India paper 165.
J37P2 50c **brt cl,** RA sm die on white wove paper 120.
J37P2a 50c **brt cl,** PP sm die on yelsh wove paper 500.

1925

J68P1 ½c **dull red,** large die on India paper *5,750.*

1930-31

J69P1 ½c **dp cl,** large die on India paper 450.
J70P1 1c **dp cl,** large die on India paper 450.
J71P1 2c **dp cl,** large die on India paper 450.
J72P1 3c **dp cl,** large die on India paper 450.
J73P1 5c **dp cl,** large die on India paper 450.
J74P1 10c **dp cl,** large die on India paper 450.
J75P1 30c **dp cl,** large die on India paper 450.
J76P1 50c **dp cl,** large die on India paper 450.
J77P1 $1 **dp cl,** large die on India paper 1,750.
J78P1 $5 **dp cl,** large die on India paper 1,750.

PARCEL POST POSTAGE DUE

1912

JQ1P1 1c **dk grn,** large die on India paper 600.
JQ1P2 1c **dk grn,** sm die on white wove paper 500.
JQ1P2a 1c **dk grn,** PP sm die on yelsh wove paper 750.
JQ2P1 2c **dk grn,** large die on India paper 600.
JQ2P2 2c **dk grn,** sm die on white wove paper 500.
JQ2P2a 2c **dk grn,** PP sm die on yelsh wove paper 750.
JQ3P1 5c **dk grn,** large die on India paper 600.
JQ3P2 5c **dk grn,** sm die on white wove paper 500.
JQ3P2a 5c **dk grn,** PP sm die on yelsh wove paper 700.
JQ4P1 10c **dk grn,** large die on India paper 600.
JQ4P2 10c **dk grn,** sm die on white wove paper 500.
JQ4P2a 10c **dk grn,** PP sm die on yelsh wove paper 700.
JQ5P1 25c **dk grn,** large die on India paper 600.
JQ5P2 25c **dk grn,** sm die on white wove paper 500.
JQ5P2a 25c **dk grn,** PP sm die on yelsh wove paper 700.

Specialists have questioned the existence of genuine examples of Nos. JQ1P2, JQ2P2, JQ3P2, JQ4P2 and JQ5P2. The editors would like to see recent authenticated evidence of their existence.

CARRIERS

1851

LO1TC3 1c plate on India paper
a. **deep green** 250.
Block of 4 1,250.
LO1TC5 1c Plate on wove paper
a. **orange** 350.
LO1P1 1c **bl,** *(Franklin)* large die on India paper 800.
LO1P2 1c **bl,** *(Franklin)* RA sm die on white wove paper 300.
LO1P2a 1c **bl,** *(Franklin)* PP sm die on yelsh wove paper 1,500.
LO1P3 1c **bl,** *(Franklin)* plate on India 50.
Block of 4 210.
Cracked plate —
LO1P4 1c **bl,** *(Franklin)* plate on card 30.
Block of 4 125.
Cracked plate —
LO2TC3 plate on India paper
a. **deep green** 250.
Block of 4 1,250.
LO2TC5 plate on wove paper
a. **orange** 350.
LO2P1 1c **bl,** *(Eagle)* large die on India paper 800.
LO2P2 1c **bl,** *(Eagle)* RA sm die on white wove paper 300.
LO2P2a 1c **bl,** *(Eagle)* PP sm die on yelsh wove paper 1,500.
LO2P3 1c **bl,** *(Eagle)* plate on India 50.
Block of 4 210.
Pl # block of 8 675.
LO2P4 1c **bl,** *(Eagle)* plate on card 30.
Block of 4 125.

Nos. LO1P1 and LO2P1 exist only as hybrids.

LOCALS

1844

5L1P1 5c **blk,** large die on India paper *3,500.*

1855

15L18TC3 (1c) plate on India paper
a. **brown** —
b. **blue** —
c. **green** —
d. **reddish brown** —

OFFICIAL
AGRICULTURE

1873

O1TC1a 1c large die on India paper
e. **black** 500.
O1TC3 1c plate on India paper
a. **black** 75.
O1P1 1c **yel,** large die on India paper 80.
O1P2 1c **yel,** RA sm die on white wove paper 100.
O1P2a 1c **yel,** PP sm die on yelsh wove paper 700.
O1P3 1c **yel,** plate on India 20.
Block of 4 100.
O1P4 1c **yel,** plate on card 10.
Block of 4 50.
P# blk. of 12 225.
O2TC1a 2c large die on India paper
e. **black** 500.
O2TC3 2c plate on India paper
a. **black** 75.
O2P1 2c **yel,** large die on India paper 80.
O2P2 2c **yel,** RA sm die on white wove paper 100.
O2P2a 2c **yel,** PP sm die on yelsh wove paper 700.
O2P3 2c **yel,** plate on India 20.
Block of 4 100.
O2P4 2c **yel,** plate on card 10.
Block of 4 50.
P# blk. of 12 225.
O3TC1a 3c large die on India paper
e. **black** 500.
f. **deep green** 500.
O3P1 3c **yel,** large die on India paper 80.
O3P2 3c **yel,** RA sm die on white wove paper 100.
O3P2a 3c **yel,** PP sm die on yelsh wove paper 700.
O3P3 3c **yel,** plate on India 20.
Block of 4 100.
O3P4 3c **yel,** plate on card 10.
Block of 4 50.
P# blk. of 12 225.
O4TC1a 6c large die on India paper
e. **black** 500.
O4TC3 6c plate on India paper
a. **black** 150.
O4P1 6c **yel,** large die on India paper 125.
O4P2 6c **yel,** RA sm die on white wove paper 100.
O4P2a 6c **yel,** PP sm die on yelsh wove paper 700.
O4P3 6c **yel,** plate on India 20.
Block of 4 100.
O4P4 6c **yel,** plate on card 10.
Block of 4 50.
P# blk. of 12 225.
O5TC1a 10c large die on India paper
e. **black** 500.
O5P1 10c **yel,** large die on India paper 80.
O5P2 10c **yel,** RA sm die on white wove paper 100.
O5P2a 10c **yel,** PP sm die on yelsh wove paper 700.
O5P3 10c **yel,** plate on India 20.
Block of 4 100.
O5P4 10c **yel,** plate on card 10.
Block of 4 50.
P# blk. of 12 225.
O6TC1a 12c large die on India paper
e. **black** 500.
O6TC3 12c plate on India paper
a. **black** 75.
O6P1 12c **yel,** large die on India paper 80.
O6P2 12c **yel,** RA sm die on white wove paper 100.
O6P2a 12c **yel,** PP sm die on yelsh wove paper 700.
O6P3 12c **yel,** plate on India 20.
Block of 4 100.
O6P4 12c **yel,** plate on card 10.
Block of 4 50.
P# blk. of 12 225.
O7P1 15c **yel,** large die on India paper 80.
O7P2 15c **yel,** RA sm die on white wove paper 100.
O7P2a 15c **yel,** PP sm die on yelsh wove paper 700.
O7P3 15c **yel,** plate on India 20.
Block of 4 100.
O7P4 15c **yel,** plate on card 10.
Block of 4 50.
P# blk. of 12 225.
O8P1 24c **yel,** large die on India paper 80.
O8P2 24c **yel,** RA sm die on white wove paper 100.
O8P2a 24c **yel,** PP sm die on yelsh wove paper 700.
O8P3 24c **yel,** plate on India 20.
Block of 4 100.
O8P4 24c **yel,** plate on card 10.
Block of 4 50.
P# blk. of 12 225.
O9TC1a 20c large die on India paper
e. **black** 500.
O9P1 30c **yel,** large die on India paper 80.
O9P2 30c **yel,** RA sm die on white wove paper 100.
O9P2a 30c **yel,** PP sm die on yelsh wove paper 700.
O9P3 30c **yel,** plate on India 20.
Block of 4 100.
O9P4 30c **yel,** plate on card 10.
Block of 4 50.
P# blk. of 12 225.
Nos. O1P3-O9P3 (9) 180.00
Nos. O1P4-O9P4 (9) 90.00

EXECUTIVE

O10P1 1c **car,** large die on India paper 100.
O10P2 1c **car,** RA sm die on white wove paper 100.
O10P2a 1c **car,** PP sm die on yelsh wove paper 700.
O10P3 1c **car,** plate on India 20.
Block of 4 100.
O10P4 1c **car,** plate on card 10.
Block of 4 50.
P# blk. of 12 225.
O11TC1a 2c large die on India paper
e. **black** 500.
f. **deep brown** 500.
O11TC3 2c plate on India paper
a. **black** 75.
O11TC4 2c plate on card
a. **brown carmine** 75.
O11P1 2c **car,** large die on India paper 100.
O11P2 2c **car,** RA sm die on white wove paper 100.
O11P2a 2c **car,** PP sm die on yelsh wove paper 700.
O11P3 2c **car,** plate on India 20.
Block of 4 100.
O11P4 2c **car,** plate on card 10.
Block of 4 50.
P# blk. of 12 225.
Foreign entry of 6c Agriculture (pos. 40) —
O12TC1a 3c large die on India paper
e. **black** 500.
f. **deep green** 500.
O12TC3 3c plate on India paper
a. **black** 75.

O12P1 3c **car,** large die on India paper 100.
O12P2 3c **car,** RA sm die on white wove paper 100.
O12P2a 3c **car,** PP sm die on yelsh wove paper 700.
O12P3 3c **car,** plate on India 20.
Block of 4 100.
O12P4 3c **car,** plate on card 10.
Block of 4 50.
P# blk. of 12 225.
O13TC3 6c plate on India paper
a. **black** 90.
O13P1 6c **car,** large die on India paper 100.
O13P2 6c **car,** RA sm die on white wove paper 100.
O13P2a 6c **car,** PP sm die on yelsh wove paper 700.
O13P3 6c **car,** plate on India 20.
Block of 4 125.
O13P4 6c **car,** plate on card 10.
Block of 4 85.
P# blk. of 12 350.
O14TC3 10c plate on India paper
a. **black** 90.
O14P1 10c **car,** large die on India paper 100.
O14P2 10c **car,** RA sm die on white wove paper 100.
O14P2a 10c **car,** PP sm die on yelsh wove paper 700.
O14P3 10c **car,** plate on India 20.
Block of 4 100.
O14P4 10c **car,** plate on card 10.
Block of 4 50.
P# blk. of 12 225.
Nos. O10P3-O14P3 (5) 100.00
Nos. O10P4-O14P4 (5) 50.00

INTERIOR

O15P1 1c **ver,** large die on India paper 80.
O15P2 1c **ver,** RA sm die on white wove paper 100.
O15P2a 1c **ver,** PP sm die on yelsh wove paper 700.
O15P3 1c **ver,** plate on India 20.
Block of 4 100.
O15P4 1c **ver,** plate on card 10.
Block of 4 50.
P# blk. of 12 225.
O16TC1a 2c large die on India paper
e. **black** 500.
f. **deep brown** 500.
O16P1 2c **ver,** large die on India paper 80.
O16P2 2c **ver,** RA sm die on white wove paper 100.
O16P2a 2c **ver,** PP sm die on yelsh wove paper 700.
O16P3 2c **ver,** plate on India 20.
Block of 4 100.
O16P4 2c **ver,** plate on card 10.
Block of 4 50.
P# blk. of 10 200.
O17TC1a 3c large die on India paper
e. **black** 500.
f. **deep green** 500.
O17TC3 3c plate on India paper
a. **black** 90.
O17P1 3c **ver,** large die on India paper 80.
O17P2 3c **ver,** RA sm die on white wove paper 100.
O17P2a 3c **ver,** PP sm die on yelsh wove paper 700.
O17P3 3c **ver,** plate on India 20.
Block of 4 100.
O17P4 3c **ver,** plate on card 10.
Block of 4 50.
P# blk. of 10 225.
O18P1 6c **ver,** large die on India paper 80.
O18P2 6c **ver,** RA sm die on white wove paper 100.
O18P2a 6c **ver,** PP sm die on yelsh wove paper 700.
O18P3 6c **ver,** plate on India 20.
Block of 4 100.
O18P4 6c **ver,** plate on card 10.
Block of 4 50.
P# blk. of 12 250.
O19P1 10c **ver,** large die on India paper 80.
O19P2 10c **ver,** RA sm die on white wove paper 100.
O19P2a 10c **ver,** PP sm die on yelsh wove paper 700.
O19P3 10c **ver,** plate on India 20.
Block of 4 100.
O19P4 10c **ver,** plate on card 10.
Block of 4 50.
P# blk. of 12 225.
O20P1 12c **ver,** large die on India paper 80.
O20P2 12c **ver,** RA sm die on white wove paper 100.
O20P2a 12c **ver,** PP sm die on yelsh wove paper 700.
O20P3 12c **ver,** plate on India 20.
Block of 4 100.
O20P4 12c **ver,** plate on card 10.
Block of 4 50.
P# blk. of 12 225.
O21P1 15c **ver,** large die on India paper 80.
O21P2 15c **ver,** RA sm die on white wove paper 100.
O21P2a 15c **ver,** PP sm die on yelsh wove paper 700.
O21P3 15c **ver,** plate on India 20.
Block of 4 100.
O21P4 15c **ver,** plate on card 10.
Block of 4 50.
P# blk. of 12 225.
O22P1 24c **ver,** large die on India paper 80.
O22P2 24c **ver,** RA sm die on white wove paper 100.
O22P2a 24c **ver,** PP sm die on yelsh wove paper 700.
O22P3 24c **ver,** plate on India 20.
Block of 4 100.
O22P4 24c **ver,** plate on card 10.
Block of 4 50.
P# blk. of 12 225.
O23P1 30c **ver,** large die on India paper 80.
O23P2 30c **ver,** RA sm die on white wove paper 100.
O23P2a 30c **ver,** PP sm die on yelsh wove paper 700.
O23P3 30c **ver,** plate on India 20.
Block of 4 100.
O23P4 30c **ver,** plate on card 10.
Block of 4 50.
P# blk. of 12 225.
O24P1 90c **ver,** large die on India paper 80.
O24P2 90c **ver,** RA sm die on white wove paper 100.
O24P2a 90c **ver,** PP sm die on yelsh wove paper 700.
O24P3 90c **ver,** plate on India 20.
Block of 4 100.
O24P4 90c **ver,** plate on card 10.
Block of 4 50.
P# blk. of 12 225.
Nos. O15P3-O24P3 (10) 200.00
Nos. O15P4-O24P4 (10) 100.00

JUSTICE

O25P1 1c **pur,** large die on India paper 80.
O25P2 1c **pur,** RA sm die on white wove paper 100.
O25P2a 1c **pur,** PP sm die on yelsh wove paper 700.
O25P3 1c **pur,** plate on India 20.
Block of 4 100.
O25P4 1c **pur,** plate on card 10.
Block of 4 50.
P# blk. of 12 225.
O26P1 2c **pur,** large die on India paper 80.
O26P2 2c **pur,** RA sm die on white wove paper 100.
O26P2a 2c **pur,** PP sm die on yelsh wove paper 700.
O26P3 2c **pur,** plate on India 20.
Block of 4 100.
O26P4 2c **pur,** plate on card 10.
Block of 4 50.
P# blk. of 12 225.
O27TC1a 3c large die on India paper
e. **black** 500.
f. **deep green** 500.
O27TC3 3c plate on India paper
a. **black** 90.
b. **bister yellow** 90.
c. **dull orange** 90.
d. **black violet** 90.
O27P1 3c **pur,** large die on India paper 80.
O27P2 3c **pur,** RA sm die on white wove paper 100.
O27P2a 3c **pur,** PP sm die on yelsh wove paper 700.
O27P3 3c **pur,** plate on India 20.
Block of 4 100.
O27P4 3c **pur,** plate on card 10.
Block of 4 50.
P# blk. of 12 225.
Plate Scratches —
O28P1 6c **pur,** large die on India paper 80.
O28P2 6c **pur,** RA sm die on white wove paper 100.
O28P2a 6c **pur,** PP sm die on yelsh wove paper 700.
O28P3 6c **pur,** plate on India 20.
Block of 4 100.
O28P4 6c **pur,** plate on card 10.
Block of 4 50.
P# blk. of 12 225.
O29P1 10c **pur,** large die on India paper 80.
O29P2 10c **pur,** RA sm die on white wove paper 100.
O29P2a 10c **pur,** PP sm die on yelsh wove paper 700.
O29P3 10c **pur,** plate on India 20.
Block of 4 100.
O29P4 10c **pur,** plate on card 10.
Block of 4 50.
P# blk. of 10 225.
O30P1 12c **pur,** large die on India paper 80.
O30P2 12c **pur,** RA sm die on white wove paper 100.
O30P2a 12c **pur,** PP sm die on yelsh wove paper 700.
O30P3 12c **pur,** plate on India 20.
Block of 4 100.
O30P4 12c **pur,** plate on card 10.
Block of 4 50.
P# blk. of 12 225.
O31P1 15c **pur,** large die on India paper 80.
O31P2 15c **pur,** RA sm die on white wove paper 100.
O31P2a 15c **pur,** PP sm die on yelsh wove paper 700.
O31P3 15c **pur,** plate on India 20.
Block of 4 100.
O31P4 15c **pur,** plate on card 10.
Block of 4 50.
P# blk. of 10 225.
O32P1 24c **pur,** large die on India paper 80.
O32P2 24c **pur,** RA sm die on white wove paper 100.
O32P2a 24c **pur,** PP sm die on yelsh wove paper 700.
O32P3 24c **pur,** plate on India 20.
Block of 4 100.
O32P4 24c **pur,** plate on card 10.
Block of 4 50.
P# blk. of 12 225.
Short transfer (pos. 98) —
O33P1 30c **pur,** large die on India paper 80.
O33P2 30c **pur,** RA sm die on white wove paper 100.
O33P2a 30c **pur,** PP sm die on yelsh wove paper 700.
O33P3 30c **pur,** plate on India 20.
Block of 4 100.
O33P4 30c **pur,** plate on card 10.
Block of 4 50.
P# blk. of 12 225.
O34P1 90c **pur,** large die on India paper 80.
O34P2 90c **pur,** RA sm die on white wove paper 100.
O34P2a 90c **pur,** PP sm die on yelsh wove paper 700.
O34P3 90c **pur,** plate on India 20.
Block of 4 100.
O34P4 90c **pur,** plate on card 10.
Block of 4 50.
P# blk. of 12 225.
Nos. O25P3-O34P3 (10) 200.00
Nos. O25P4-O34P4 (10) 100.00

NAVY

O35TC3 1c plate on India paper
a. **black** 90.
O35P1 1c **ultra,** large die on India paper 80.
O35P2 1c **ultra,** RA sm die on white wove paper 100.
O35P2a 1c **ultra,** PP sm die on yelsh wove paper 700.
O35P3 1c **ultra,** plate on India 20.
Block of 4 100.
O35P4 1c **ultra,** plate on card 10.
Block of 4 50.
P# blk. of 12 225.
O36TC1a 2c large die on India paper
e. **black** 500.
f. **deep brown** 500.
O36TC5 2c plate on wove paper, imperf.
a. **deep green** 250.
O36TC6 2c plate on wove paper, perf.
a. **deep green** 250.
b. **black** 250.
O36P1 2c **ultra,** large die on India paper 80.
O36P2 2c **ultra,** RA sm die on white wove paper 100.
O36P2a 2c **ultra,** PP sm die on yelsh wove paper 700.
O36P3 2c **ultra,** plate on India 20.
Block of 4 100.
O36P4 2c **ultra,** plate on card 10.
Block of 4 50.
P# blk. of 12 225.
O37TC1a 3c large die on India paper
e. **black** 500.
f. **deep green** 500.
O37TC3 3c plate on India paper
a. **black** 90.
O37P1 3c **ultra,** large die on India paper 80.
O37P2 3c **ultra,** RA sm die on white wove paper 100.
O37P2a 3c **ultra,** PP sm die on yelsh wove paper 700.
O37P3 3c **ultra,** plate on India 20.
Block of 4 100.
O37P4 3c **ultra,** plate on card 10.
Block of 4 50.
P# blk. of 10 225.
O38P1 6c **ultra,** large die on India paper 80.
O38P2 6c **ultra,** RA sm die on white wove paper 100.
O38P2a 6c **ultra,** PP sm die on yelsh wove paper 700.
O38P3 6c **ultra,** plate on India 20.
Block of 4 100.
O38P4 6c **ultra,** plate on card 15.
Block of 4 75.
P# blk. of 10 350.
O39P1 7c **ultra,** large die on India paper 80.
O39P2 7c **ultra,** RA sm die on white wove paper 100.
O39P2a 7c **ultra,** PP sm die on yelsh wove paper 700.
O39P3 7c **ultra,** plate on India 20.
Block of 4 100.
O39P4 7c **ultra,** plate on card 10.
Block of 4 50.
P# blk. of 10 225.
O40P1 10c **ultra,** large die on India paper 80.
O40P2 10c **ultra,** RA sm die on white wove paper 100.
O40P2a 10c **ultra,** PP sm die on yelsh wove paper 700.
O40P3 10c **ultra,** plate on India 20.
Block of 4 100.
P# blk. of 12 —
O40P4 10c **ultra,** plate on card 10.
Block of 4 50.
P# blk. of 12 225.
O41P1 12c **ultra,** large die on India paper 80.
O41P2 12c **ultra,** RA sm die on white wove paper 100.
O41P2a 12c **ultra,** PP sm die on yelsh wove paper 700.
O41P3 12c **ultra,** plate on India 20.
Block of 4 100.
O41P4 12c **ultra,** plate on card 10.
Block of 4 50.
P# blk. of 12 225.

O42P1	15c **ultra,** large die on India paper	80.
O42P2	15c **ultra,** RA sm die on white wove paper	100.
O42P2a	15c **ultra,** PP sm die on yelsh wove paper	700.
O42P3	15c **ultra,** plate on India	20.
	Block of 4	100.
O42P4	15c **ultra,** plate on card	10.
	Block of 4	50.
	P# blk. of 12	225.
O43P1	24c **ultra,** large die on India paper	80.
O43P2	24c **ultra,** RA sm die on white wove paper	100.
O43P2a	24c **ultra,** PP sm die on yelsh wove paper	700.
O43P3	24c **ultra,** plate on India	20.
	Block of 4	100.
O43P4	24c **ultra,** plate on card	10.
	Block of 4	50.
	P# blk. of 12	225.
O44P1	30c **ultra,** large die on India paper	80.
O44P2	30c **ultra,** RA sm die on white wove paper	100.
O44P2a	30c **ultra,** PP sm die on yelsh wove paper	700.
O44P3	30c **ultra,** plate on India	20.
	Block of 4	100.
O44P4	30c **ultra,** plate on card	10.
	Block of 4	50.
	P# blk. of 12	225.
O45P1	90c **ultra,** large die on India paper	80.
O45P2	90c **ultra,** RA sm die on white wove paper	100.
O45P2a	90c **ultra,** PP sm die on yelsh wove paper	700.
O45P3	90c **ultra,** plate on India	20.
	Block of 4	100.
O45P4	90c **ultra,** plate on card	10.
	Block of 4	50.
	P# blk. of 12	225.
	Short transfer at upper left (106, pos. 1, 5)	—
	Nos. O35P3-O45P3 (11)	220.00
	Nos. O35P4-O45P4 (11)	115.00

POST OFFICE

O47P1	1c **blk,** large die on India paper	80.
O47P2	1c **blk,** RA sm die on white wove paper	100.
O47P2a	1c **blk,** PP sm die on yelsh wove paper	700.
O47P3	1c **blk,** plate on India	20.
	Block of 4	100.
O47P4	1c **blk,** plate on card	10.
	Block of 4	50.
	P# blk. of 10	225.
O48TC1a	2c large die on India paper	
	e. **deep brown**	500.
O48P1	2c **blk,** large die on India paper	80.
O48P2	2c **blk,** RA sm die on white wove paper	100.
O48P2a	2c **blk,** PP sm die on yelsh wove paper	700.
O48P3	2c **blk,** plate on India	20.
	Block of 4	100.
O48P4	2c **blk,** plate on card	10.
	Block of 4	50.
	P# blk. of 14	225.
O49TC1a	3c large die on India paper	
	e. **deep green**	500.
O49P1	3c **blk,** large die on India paper	80.
O49P2	3c **blk,** RA sm die on white wove paper	100.
O49P2a	3c **blk,** PP sm die on yelsh wove paper	700.
O49P3	3c **blk,** plate on India	20.
	Block of 4	100.
O49P4	3c **blk,** plate on card	10.
	Block of 4	50.
	P# blk. of 12	225.
O50TC1a	6c large die on India paper	
	e. **deep brown**	500.
	f. **brown carmine**	500.
O50P1	6c **blk,** large die on India paper	80.
O50P2	6c **blk,** RA sm die on white wove paper	100.
O50P2a	6c **blk,** PP sm die on yelsh wove paper	700.
O50P3	6c **blk,** plate on India	20.
	Block of 4	100.
O50P4	6c **blk,** plate on card	10.
	Block of 4	50.
	P# blk. of 12	225.
O51P1	10c **blk,** large die on India paper	80.
O51P2	10c **blk,** RA sm die on white wove paper	100.
O51P2a	10c **blk,** PP sm die on yelsh wove paper	700.
O51P3	10c **blk,** plate on India	20.
	Block of 4	100.
O51P4	10c **blk,** plate on card	10.
	Block of 4	50.
	P# blk. of 12	225.
O52P1	12c **blk,** large die on India paper	80.
O52P2	12c **blk,** RA sm die on white wove paper	100.
O52P2a	12c **blk,** PP sm die on yelsh wove paper	700.
O52P3	12c **blk,** plate on India	20.
	Block of 4	100.
O52P4	12c **blk,** plate on card	10.
	Block of 4	50.
	P# blk. of 12	225.
O53P1	15c **blk,** large die on India paper	80.
O53P2	15c **blk,** RA sm die on white wove paper	100.
O53P2a	15c **blk,** PP sm die on yelsh wove paper	700.
O53P3	15c **blk,** plate on India	20.
	Block of 4	100.
O53P4	15c **blk,** plate on card	10.
	Block of 4	50.
	P# blk. of 12	225.
O54P1	24c **blk,** large die on India paper	80.
O54P2	24c **blk,** RA sm die on white wove paper	100.
O54P2a	24c **blk,** PP sm die on yelsh wove paper	700.
O54P3	24c **blk,** plate on India	20.
	Block of 4	100.
O54P4	24c **blk,** plate on card	10.
	Block of 4	50.
	P# blk. of 12	225.
O55P1	30c **blk,** large die on India paper	80.
O55P2	30c **blk,** RA sm die on white wove paper	100.
O55P2a	30c **blk,** PP sm die on yelsh wove paper	700.
O55P3	30c **blk,** plate on India	20.
	Block of 4	100.
O55P4	30c **blk,** plate on card	10.
	Block of 4	50.
	P# blk. of 12	225.
O56P1	90c **blk,** large die on India paper	80.
O56P2	90c **blk,** RA sm die on white wove paper	100.
O56P2a	90c **blk,** PP sm die on yelsh wove paper	700.
O56P3	90c **blk,** plate on India	20.
	Block of 4	100.
O56P4	90c **blk,** plate on card	10.
	Block of 4	50.
	P# blk. of 12	225.
	Nos. O47P3-O56P3 (10)	200.00
	Nos. O47P4-O56P4 (10)	100.00

STATE

O57TC1a	1c large die on India paper	
	e. **black**	500.
	f. **light ultramarine**	500.
O57P1	1c **grn,** large die on India paper	80.
O57P2	1c **grn,** RA sm die on white wove paper	100.
O57P2a	1c **grn,** PP sm die on yelsh wove paper	700.
O57P3	1c **grn,** plate on India	20.
	Block of 4	100.
O57P4	1c **grn,** plate on card	10.
	Block of 4	50.
	P# blk. of 12	225.
O58TC1a	2c large die on India paper	
	e. **black**	500.
	f. **deep brown**	500.
O58P1	2c **grn,** large die on India paper	80.
O58P2	2c **grn,** RA sm die on white wove paper	100.
O58P2a	2c **grn,** PP sm die on yelsh wove paper	700.
O58P3	2c **grn,** plate on India	20.
	Block of 4	100.
O58P4	2c **grn,** plate on card	10.
	Block of 4	50.
	P# blk. of 10	225.
O59TC1a	3c large die on India paper	
	e. **black**	500.
O59P1	3c **grn,** large die on India paper	80.
O59P2	3c **grn,** RA sm die on white wove paper	100.
O59P2a	3c **grn,** PP sm die on yelsh wove paper	700.
O59P3	3c **grn,** plate on India	20.
	Block of 4	100.
O59P4	3c **grn,** plate on card	10.
	Block of 4	50.
	P# blk. of 10	225.
O60P1	6c **grn,** large die on India paper	80.
O60P2	6c **grn,** RA sm die on white wove paper	100.
O60P2a	6c **grn,** PP sm die on yelsh wove paper	700.
O60P3	6c **grn,** plate on India	25.
	Block of 4	125.
O60P4	6c **grn,** plate on card	16.
	Block of 4	85.
	P# blk. of 12	375.
O61P1	7c **grn,** large die on India paper	80.
O61P2	7c **grn,** RA sm die on white wove paper	100.
O61P2a	7c **grn,** PP sm die on yelsh wove paper	700.
O61P3	7c **grn,** plate on India	20.
	Block of 4	100.
O61P4	7c **grn,** plate on card	10.
	Block of 4	50.
	P# blk. of 12	225.
O62P1	10c **grn,** large die on India paper	80.
O62P2	10c **grn,** RA sm die on white wove paper	100.
O62P2a	10c **grn,** PP sm die on yelsh wove paper	700.
O62P3	10c **grn,** plate on India	20.
	Block of 4	100.
O62P4	10c **grn,** plate on card	10.
	Block of 4	50.
	P# blk. of 12	225.
O63P1	12c **grn,** large die on India paper	80.
O63P2	12c **grn,** RA sm die on white wove paper	100.
O63P2a	12c **grn,** PP sm die on yelsh wove paper	700.
O63P3	12c **grn,** plate on India	20.
	Block of 4	100.
O63P4	12c **grn,** plate on card	10.
	Block of 4	50.
	P# blk. of 12	225.
O64P1	15c **grn,** large die on India paper	80.
O64P2	15c **grn,** RA sm die on white wove paper	100.
O64P2a	15c **grn,** PP sm die on yelsh wove paper	700.
O64P3	15c **grn,** plate on India	20.
	Block of 4	100.
O64P4	15c **grn,** plate on card	10.
	Block of 4	50.
	P# blk. of 12	225.
O65P1	24c **grn,** large die on India paper	80.
O65P2	24c **grn,** RA sm die on white wove paper	100.
O65P2a	24c **grn,** PP sm die on yelsh wove paper	700.
O65P3	24c **grn,** plate on India	20.
	Block of 4	100.
O65P4	24c **grn,** plate on card	10.
	Block of 4	50.
	P# blk. of 12	225.
O66P1	30c **grn,** large die on India paper	80.
O66P2	30c **grn,** RA sm die on white wove paper	100.
O66P2a	30c **grn,** PP sm die on yelsh wove paper	700.
O66P3	30c **grn,** plate on India	20.
	Block of 4	100.
O66P4	30c **grn,** plate on card	10.
	Block of 4	50.
	P# blk. of 12	225.
O67TC1a	90c large die on India paper	
	e. **black**	500.
O67P1	90c **grn,** large die on India paper	80.
O67P2	90c **grn,** RA sm die on white wove paper	100.
O67P2a	90c **grn,** PP sm die on yelsh wove paper	700.
O67P3	90c **grn,** plate on India	20.
	Block of 4	100.
O67P4	90c **grn,** plate on card	10.
	Block of 4	50.
	P# blk. of 12	225.
O68TC1a	$2 large die on India paper	
	e. **violet & black**	2,500.
	f. **brown red & black**	2,500.
	g. **orange red & slate blue**	2,500.
O68P1	$2 **grn & blk,** large die on India paper	150.
O68P2	$2 **grn & blk,** RA sm die on white wove paper	125.
O68P2a	$2 **grn & blk,** PP sm die on yelsh wove paper	850.
O68P3	$2 **grn & blk,** plate on India	100.
	Block of 4	475.
	Sheet of 10	*4,000.*
O68P4	$2 **grn & blk,** plate on card	35.
	Block of 4	175.
	Sheet of 10	*5,000.*
	a. Invtd. center	*13,500.*
	Half sheet of 5	*70,000.*
O69P1	$5 **grn & blk,** large die on India paper	150.
O69P2	$5 **grn & blk,** RA sm die on white wove paper	125.
O69P2a	$5 **grn & blk,** PP sm die on yelsh wove paper	850.
O69P3	$5 **grn & blk,** plate on India	100.
	Block of 4	475.
	Sheet of 10	*4,000.*
O69P4	$5 **grn & blk,** plate on card	35.
	Block of 4	175.
	Sheet of 10	*5,000.*
	a. Invtd. center	*9,500.*
	Half sheet of 5	*47,500.*
	Sheet of 10	*100,000.*
O70P1	$10 **grn & blk,** large die on India paper	150.
O70P2	$10 **grn & blk,** RA sm die on white wove paper	125.
O70P2a	$10 **grn & blk,** PP sm die on yelsh wove paper	850.
O70P3	$10 **grn & blk,** plate on India	100.
	Block of 4	475.
	Sheet of 10	*4,000.*
O70P4	$10 **grn & blk,** plate on card	35.
	Block of 4	—
	Sheet of 10	*5,000.*
O71P1	$20 **grn & blk,** large die on India paper	150.
O71P2	$20 **grn & blk,** RA sm die on white wove paper	125.
O71P2a	$20 **grn & blk,** PP sm die on yelsh wove paper	900.
O71P3	$20 **grn & blk,** plate on India	100.
	Block of 4	475.
	Sheet of 10	*4,000.*
O71P4	$20 **grn & blk,** plate on card	35.
	Block of 4	175.
	Sheet of 10	*5,000.*
	a. Invtd. center	
	Block of 4	*11,000.*
	Half sheet of 5	*50,000.*
	Nos. O57P3-O71P3 (15)	625.00
	Nos. O57P4-O71P4 (15)	256.00

Nos. O68P1 to O71P1 Large Dies exist as hybrids only.

TREASURY

O72TC1a	1c large die on India paper	
	e. **black**	500.
	f. **light ultramarine**	500.
O72P1	1c **brn,** large die on India paper	80.
O72P2	1c **brn,** RA sm die on white wove paper	100.
O72P2a	1c **brn,** PP sm die on yelsh wove paper	700.
O72P3	1c **brn,** plate on India	20.
	Block of 4	100.

O72P4 1c **brn,** plate on card 10.
Block of 4 50.
P# blk. of 12 225.
O73TC1a 2c large die on India paper
***e.* black** 500.
O73P1 2c **brn,** large die on India paper 80.
O73P2 2c **brn,** RA sm die on white wove paper 100.
O73P2a 2c **brn,** PP sm die on yelsh wove paper 700.
O73P3 2c **brn,** plate on India 20.
Block of 4 100.
O73P4 2c **brn,** plate on card 10.
Block of 4 50.
P# blk. of 12 225.
O74TC1a 3c large die on India paper
***e.* black** 500.
***f.* deep green** 500.
O74P1 3c **brn,** large die on India paper 80.
O74P2 3c **brn,** RA sm die on white wove paper 100.
O74P2a 3c **brn,** PP sm die on yelsh wove paper 700.
O74P3 3c **brn,** plate on India 20.
Block of 4 100.
O74P4 3c **brn,** plate on card 10.
Block of 4 50.
P# blk. of 12 225.
O75TC1a 6c large die on India paper
***e.* black** 500.
O75P1 6c **brn,** large die on India paper 80.
O75P2 6c **brn,** RA sm die on white wove paper 100.
O75P2a 6c **brn,** PP sm die on yelsh wove paper 700.
O75P3 6c **brn,** plate on India 20.
Block of 4 100.
O75P4 6c **brn,** plate on card 15.
Block of 4 75.
P# blk. of 12 375.
O76P1 7c **brn,** large die on India paper 80.
O76P2 7c **brn,** RA sm die on white wove paper 100.
O76P2a 7c **brn,** PP sm die on yelsh wove paper 700.
O76P3 7c **brn,** plate on India 20.
Block of 4 100.
O76P4 7c **brn,** plate on card 10.
Block of 4 50.
P# blk. of 12 225.
O77TC1a 10c large die on India paper
***e.* black** 500.
O77P1 10c **brn,** large die on India paper 80.
O77P2 10c **brn,** RA sm die on white wove paper 100.
O77P2a 10c **brn,** PP sm die on yelsh wove paper 700.
O77P3 10c **brn,** plate on India 20.
Block of 4 100.
O77P4 10c **brn,** plate on card 10.
Block of 4 50.
P# blk. of 12 225.
O78TC1a 12c large die on India paper
***e.* black** 500.
O78P1 12c **brn,** large die on India paper 80.
O78P2 12c **brn,** RA sm die on white wove paper 100.
O78P2a 12c **brn,** PP sm die on yelsh wove paper 700.
O78P3 12c **brn,** plate on India 20.
Block of 4 100.
O78P4 12c **brn,** plate on card 10.
Block of 4 50.
P# blk. of 12 225.
O79TC1a 15c large die on India paper
***e.* black** 500.
O79P1 15c **brn,** large die on India paper 80.
O79P2 15c **brn,** RA sm die on white wove paper 100.
O79P2a 15c **brn,** PP sm die on yelsh wove paper 700.
O79P3 15c **brn,** plate on India 20.
Block of 4 100.
O79P4 15c **brn,** plate on card 10.
Block of 4 50.
P# blk. of 12 275.
O80TC1a 24c large die on India paper
***e.* black** 500.
O80P1 24c **brn,** large die on India paper 80.
O80P2 24c **brn,** RA sm die on white wove paper 100.
O80P2a 24c **brn,** PP sm die on yelsh wove paper 700.
O80P3 24c **brn,** plate on India 20.
Block of 4 100.
O80P4 24c **brn,** plate on card 10.
Block of 4 45.
P# blk. of 12 225.
O81TC1a 30c large die on India paper
***e.* black** 500.
O81P1 30c **brn,** large die on India paper 80.
O81P2 30c **brn,** RA sm die on white wove paper 100.
O81P2a 30c **brn,** PP sm die on yelsh wove paper 700.
O81P3 30c **brn,** plate on India 20.
Block of 4 100.
O81P4 30c **brn,** plate on card 10.
Block of 4 45.
P# blk. of 12 225.
O82TC1a 90c large die on India paper
***e.* black** 500.
O82P1 90c **brn,** large die on India paper 80.
O82P2 90c **brn,** RA sm die on white wove paper 100.
O82P2a 90c **brn,** PP sm die on yelsh wove paper 700.
O82P3 90c **brn,** plate on India 20.
Block of 4 100.
O82P4 90c **brn,** plate on card 10.
Block of 4 50.
P# blk. of 12 225.
Nos. O72P3-O82P3 (11) 220.00
Nos. O72P4-O82P4 (11) 115.00

WAR

O83TC1a 1c large die on India paper
***e.* black** 500.
***f.* light ultramarine** 500.
O83TC3 1c plate on India paper
***a.* black** 80.
O83P1 1c **rose,** large die on India paper 80.
O83P2 1c **rose,** RA sm die on white wove paper 100.
O83P2a 1c **rose,** PP sm die on yelsh wove paper 700.
O83P3 1c **rose,** plate on India 20.
Block of 4 100.
O83P4 1c **rose,** plate on card 10.
Block of 4 50.
P# blk. of 12 225.
O84TC1a 2c large die on India paper
***e.* black** 500.
***f.* deep brown** 500.
O84TC3 2c plate on India paper
***a.* black** 80.
O84TC4 2c plate on card
***a.* black** 75.
O84P1 2c **rose,** large die on India paper 80.
O84P2 2c **rose,** RA sm die on white wove paper 100.
O84P2a 2c **rose,** PP sm die on yelsh wove paper 700.
O84P3 2c **rose,** plate on India 20.
Block of 4 100.
O84P4 2c **rose,** plate on card 10.
Block of 4 50.
O85TC1a 3c large die on India paper
***e.* black** 500.
***f.* deep green** 500.
***g.* chocolate** 675.
O85P1 3c **rose,** large die on India paper 80.
O85P2 3c **rose,** RA sm die on white wove paper 100.
O85P2a 3c **rose,** PP sm die on yelsh wove paper 700.
O85P3 3c **rose,** plate on India 20.
Block of 4 100.
O85P4 3c **rose,** plate on card 10.
Block of 4 50.
Plate flaw at upper left (32R20) —
O86TC3 6c plate on India paper
***a.* black** 80.
O86P1 6c **rose,** large die on India paper 80.
O86P2 6c **rose,** RA sm die on white wove paper 100.
O86P2a 6c **rose,** PP sm die on yelsh wove paper 700.
O86P3 6c **rose,** plate on India 20.
Block of 4 100.
O86P4 6c **rose,** plate on card 10.
Block of 4 50.
P# blk. of 12 225.
O87P1 7c **rose,** large die on India paper 80.
O87P2 7c **rose,** RA sm die on white wove paper 100.
O87P2a 7c **rose,** PP sm die on yelsh wove paper 700.
O87P3 7c **rose,** plate on India 20.
Block of 4 100.
O87P4 7c **rose,** plate on card 10.
Block of 4 50.
P# blk. of 10 225.
O88P1 10c **rose,** large die on India paper 80.
O88P2 10c **rose,** RA sm die on white wove paper 100.
O88P2a 10c **rose,** PP sm die on yelsh wove paper 700.
O88P3 10c **rose,** plate on India 20.
Block of 4 100.
O88P4 10c **rose,** plate on card 10.
Block of 4 50.
P# blk. of 10 225.
O89TC3 12c plate on India paper
***a.* black** 80.
O89P1 12c **rose,** large die on India paper 80.
O89P2 12c **rose,** RA sm die on white wove paper 100.
O89P2a 12c **rose,** PP sm die on yelsh wove paper 700.
O89P3 12c **rose,** plate on India 20.
Block of 4 100.
O89P4 12c **rose,** plate on card 10.
Block of 4 50.
P# blk. of 12 225.
O90P1 15c **rose,** large die on India paper 80.
O90P2 15c **rose,** RA sm die on white wove paper 100.
O90P2a 15c **rose,** PP sm die on yelsh wove paper 700.
O90P3 15c **rose,** plate on India 20.
Block of 4 100.
O90P4 15c **rose,** plate on card 10.
Block of 4 50.
P# blk. of 12 225.
O91P1 24c **rose,** large die on India paper 80.
O91P2 24c **rose,** RA sm die on white wove paper 100.
O91P2a 24c **rose,** PP sm die on yelsh wove paper 700.
O91P3 24c **rose,** plate on India 20.
Block of 4 100.
O91P4 24c **rose,** plate on card 10.
Block of 4 50.
P# blk. of 12 225.
O92P1 30c **rose,** large die on India paper 80.
O92P2 30c **rose,** RA sm die on white wove paper 100.
O92P2a 30c **rose,** PP sm die on yelsh wove paper 700.
O92P3 30c **rose,** plate on India 20.
Block of 4 100.
O92P4 30c **rose,** plate on card 10.
Block of 4 50.
P# blk. of 12 225.
O93P1 90c **rose,** large die on India paper 80.
O93P2 90c **rose,** RA sm die on white wove paper 100.
O93P2a 90c **rose,** PP sm die on yelsh wove paper 700.
O93P3 90c **rose,** plate on India 20.
Block of 4 100.
O93P4 90c **rose,** plate on card 10.
Block of 4 50.
P# blk. of 12 225.
Nos. O83P3-O93P3 (11) 220.00
Nos. O83P4-O93P4 (10) 100.00
Nos. O1P3-O93P3 (92) 1,675.
Nos. O1P4-O93P4 (92) 1,036.

Nos. O83P-O93P exist in a plum shade.

POSTAL SAVINGS MAIL

1911
O124P1 1c **dk vio,** large die on India paper 1,000.
O124P2 1c **dk vio,** sm die on white wove paper 275.
O124P2a 1c **dk vio,** PP sm die on yelsh wove paper 1,000.
O121TC1a 2c large die on India paper
***e.* lake** 500.
O121P1 2c **blk,** large die on India paper 1,000.
O121P2 2c **blk,** sm die on white wove paper 275.
O121P2a 2c **blk,** PP sm die on yelsh wove paper 1,000.
O126TC1c 10c Large die on wove paper
***e.* black** *1,250.*
O126P1 10c **car,** large die on India paper 1,000.
O126P2 10c **car,** sm die on white wove paper 275.
O126P2a 10c **car,** PP sm die on yelsh wove paper 1,000.
O122P1 50c **dk grn,** large die on India paper 1,000.
O122P2 50c **dk grn,** sm die on white wove paper 275.
O122P2a 50c **dk grn,** PP sm die on yelsh wove paper 1,000.
O123P1 $1 **ultra,** large die on India paper 1,000.
O123P2 $1 **ultra,** sm die on white wove paper 275.
O123P2a $1 **ultra,** PP sm die on yelsh wove paper 1,000.

The so-called "Goodall" set of Small Die proofs on India Paper of Official Stamps in five colors
AGRICULTURE

O1TC2 1c "Goodall" small die on India paper
***b.* black** 300.
***c.* deep green** 300.
***d.* dull gray blue** 300.
***e.* deep brown** 300.
***f.* dull red** 300.
O2TC2 2c "Goodall" small die on India paper
***b.* black** 300.
***c.* deep green** 300.
***d.* dull gray blue** 300.
***e.* deep brown** 300.
***f.* dull red** 300.
O3TC2 3c "Goodall" small die on India paper
***b.* black** 300.
***c.* deep green** 300.
***d.* dull gray blue** 300.
***e.* deep brown** 300.
***f.* dull red** 300.
O4TC2 6c "Goodall" small die on India paper
***b.* black** 300.
***c.* deep green** 300.
***d.* dull gray blue** 300.
***e.* deep brown** 300.
***f.* dull red** 300.
O5TC2 10c "Goodall" small die on India paper
***b.* black** 300.
***c.* deep green** 300.
***d.* dull gray blue** 300.
***e.* deep brown** 300.
***f.* dull red** 300.
O6TC2 12c "Goodall" small die on India paper
***b.* black** 300.
***c.* deep green** 300.
***d.* dull gray blue** 300.
***e.* deep brown** 300.
***f.* dull red** 300.
O7TC2 15c "Goodall" small die on India paper
***b.* black** 300.
***c.* deep green** 300.
***d.* dull gray blue** 300.
***e.* deep brown** 300.
***f.* dull red** 300.
O8TC2 24c "Goodall" small die on India paper
***b.* black** 300.
***c.* deep green** 300.
***d.* dull gray blue** 300.
***e.* deep brown** 300.
***f.* dull red** 300.
O9TC2 30c "Goodall" small die on India paper
***b.* black** 300.
***c.* deep green** 300.
***d.* dull gray blue** 300.
***e.* deep brown** 300.

	f. **dull red**	300.

EXECUTIVE

O10TC2	1c “Goodall” small die on India paper	
	b. **black**	300.
	c. **deep green**	300.
	d. **dull gray blue**	300.
	e. **deep brown**	300.
	f. **dull red**	300.
O11TC2	2c “Goodall” small die on India paper	
	b. **black**	300.
	c. **deep green**	300.
	d. **dull gray blue**	300.
	e. **deep brown**	300.
	f. **dull red**	300.
O12TC2	3c “Goodall” small die on India paper	
	b. **black**	300.
	c. **deep green**	300.
	d. **dull gray blue**	300.
	e. **deep brown**	300.
	f. **dull red**	300.
O13TC2	6c “Goodall” small die on India paper	
	b. **black**	300.
	c. **deep green**	300.
	d. **dull gray blue**	300.
	e. **deep brown**	300.
	f. **dull red**	300.
O14TC2	10c “Goodall” small die on India paper	
	b. **black**	300.
	c. **deep green**	300.
	d. **dull gray blue**	300.
	e. **deep brown**	300.
	f. **dull red**	300.

INTERIOR

O15TC2	1c “Goodall” small die on India paper	
	b. **black**	300.
	c. **deep green**	300.
	d. **dull gray blue**	300.
	e. **deep brown**	300.
	f. **dull red**	300.
O16TC2	2c “Goodall” small die on India paper	
	b. **black**	300.
	c. **deep green**	300.
	d. **dull gray blue**	300.
	e. **deep brown**	300.
	f. **dull red**	300.
O17TC2	3c “Goodall” small die on India paper	
	b. **black**	300.
	c. **deep green**	300.
	d. **dull gray blue**	300.
	e. **deep brown**	300.
	f. **dull red**	300.
O18TC2	6c “Goodall” small die on India paper	
	b. **black**	300.
	c. **deep green**	300.
	d. **dull gray blue**	300.
	e. **deep brown**	300.
	f. **dull red**	300.
O19TC2	10c “Goodall” small die on India paper	
	b. **black**	300.
	c. **deep green**	300.
	d. **dull gray blue**	300.
	e. **deep brown**	300.
	f. **dull red**	300.
O20TC2	12c “Goodall” small die on India paper	
	b. **black**	300.
	c. **deep green**	300.
	d. **dull gray blue**	300.
	e. **deep brown**	300.
	f. **dull red**	300.
O21TC2	15c “Goodall” small die on India paper	
	b. **black**	300.
	c. **deep green**	300.
	d. **dull gray blue**	300.
	e. **deep brown**	300.
	f. **dull red**	300.
O22TC2	24c “Goodall” small die on India paper	
	b. **black**	300.
	c. **deep green**	300.
	d. **dull gray blue**	300.
	e. **deep brown**	300.
	f. **dull red**	300.
O23TC2	30c “Goodall” small die on India paper	
	b. **black**	300.
	c. **deep green**	300.
	d. **dull gray blue**	300.
	e. **deep brown**	300.
	f. **dull red**	300.
O24TC2	90c “Goodall” small die on India paper	
	b. **black**	300.
	c. **deep green**	300.
	d. **dull gray blue**	300.
	e. **deep brown**	300.
	f. **dull red**	300.

JUSTICE

O25TC2	1c “Goodall” small die on India paper	
	b. **black**	300.
	c. **deep green**	300.
	d. **dull gray blue**	300.
	e. **deep brown**	300.
	f. **dull red**	300.
O26TC2	2c “Goodall” small die on India paper	
	b. **black**	300.
	c. **deep green**	300.
	d. **dull gray blue**	300.
	e. **deep brown**	300.
	f. **dull red**	300.
O27TC2	3c “Goodall” small die on India paper	
	b. **black**	300.
	c. **deep green**	300.
	d. **dull gray blue**	300.
	e. **deep brown**	300.
	f. **dull red**	300.
O28TC2	6c “Goodall” small die on India paper	
	b. **black**	300.
	c. **deep green**	300.
	d. **dull gray blue**	300.
	e. **deep brown**	300.
	f. **dull red**	300.
O29TC2	10c “Goodall” small die on India paper	
	b. **black**	300.
	c. **deep green**	300.
	d. **dull gray blue**	300.
	e. **deep brown**	300.
	f. **dull red**	300.
O30TC2	12c “Goodall” small die on India paper	
	b. **black**	300.
	c. **deep green**	300.
	d. **dull gray blue**	300.
	e. **deep brown**	300.
	f. **dull red**	300.
O31TC2	15c “Goodall” small die on India paper	
	b. **black**	300.
	c. **deep green**	300.
	d. **dull gray blue**	300.
	e. **deep brown**	300.
	f. **dull red**	300.
O32TC2	24c “Goodall” small die on India paper	
	b. **black**	300.
	c. **deep green**	300.
	d. **dull gray blue**	300.
	e. **deep brown**	300.
	f. **dull red**	300.
O33TC2	30c “Goodall” small die on India paper	
	b. **black**	300.
	c. **deep green**	300.
	d. **dull gray blue**	300.
	e. **deep brown**	300.
	f. **dull red**	300.
O34TC2	90c “Goodall” small die on India paper	
	b. **black**	300.
	c. **deep green**	300.
	d. **dull gray blue**	300.
	e. **deep brown**	300.
	f. **dull red**	300.

NAVY

O35TC2	1c “Goodall” small die on India paper	
	b. **black**	300.
	c. **deep green**	300.
	d. **dull gray blue**	300.
	e. **deep brown**	300.
	f. **dull red**	300.
O36TC2	2c “Goodall” small die on India paper	
	b. **black**	300.
	c. **deep green**	300.
	d. **dull gray blue**	300.
	e. **deep brown**	300.
	f. **dull red**	300.
O37TC2	3c “Goodall” small die on India paper	
	b. **black**	300.
	c. **deep green**	300.
	d. **dull gray blue**	300.
	e. **deep brown**	300.
	f. **dull red**	300.
O38TC2	6c “Goodall” small die on India paper	
	b. **black**	300.
	c. **deep green**	300.
	d. **dull gray blue**	300.
	e. **deep brown**	300.
	f. **dull red**	300.
O39TC2	7c “Goodall” small die on India paper	
	b. **black**	300.
	c. **deep green**	300.
	d. **dull gray blue**	300.
	e. **deep brown**	300.
	f. **dull red**	300.
O40TC2	10c “Goodall” small die on India paper	
	b. **black**	300.
	c. **deep green**	300.
	d. **dull gray blue**	300.
	e. **deep brown**	300.
	f. **dull red**	300.
O41TC2	12c “Goodall” small die on India paper	
	b. **black**	300.
	c. **deep green**	300.
	d. **dull gray blue**	300.
	e. **deep brown**	300.
	f. **dull red**	300.
O42TC2	15c “Goodall” small die on India paper	
	b. **black**	300.
	c. **deep green**	300.
	d. **dull gray blue**	300.
	e. **deep brown**	300.
	f. **dull red**	300.
O43TC2	24c “Goodall” small die on India paper	
	b. **black**	300.
	c. **deep green**	300.
	d. **dull gray blue**	300.
	e. **deep brown**	300.
	f. **dull red**	300.
O44TC2	30c “Goodall” small die on India paper	
	b. **black**	300.
	c. **deep green**	300.
	d. **dull gray blue**	300.
	e. **deep brown**	300.
	f. **dull red**	300.
O45TC2	90c “Goodall” small die on India paper	
	b. **black**	300.
	c. **deep green**	300.
	d. **dull gray blue**	300.
	e. **deep brown**	300.
	f. **dull red**	300.

POST OFFICE

O47TC2	1c “Goodall” small die on India paper	
	b. **black**	300.
	c. **deep green**	300.
	d. **dull gray blue**	300.
	e. **deep brown**	300.
	f. **dull red**	300.
O48TC2	2c “Goodall” small die on India paper	
	b. **black**	300.
	c. **deep green**	300.
	d. **dull gray blue**	300.
	e. **deep brown**	300.
	f. **dull red**	300.
O49TC2	3c “Goodall” small die on India paper	
	b. **black**	300.
	c. **deep green**	300.
	d. **dull gray blue**	300.
	e. **deep brown**	300.
	f. **dull red**	300.
O50TC2	6c “Goodall” small die on India paper	
	b. **black**	300.
	c. **deep green**	300.
	d. **dull gray blue**	300.
	e. **deep brown**	300.
	f. **dull red**	300.
O51TC2	10c “Goodall” small die on India paper	
	b. **black**	300.
	c. **deep green**	300.
	d. **dull gray blue**	300.
	e. **deep brown**	300.
	f. **dull red**	300.
O52TC2	12c “Goodall” small die on India paper	
	b. **black**	300.
	c. **deep green**	300.
	d. **dull gray blue**	300.
	e. **deep brown**	300.
	f. **dull red**	300.
O53TC2	15c “Goodall” small die on India paper	
	b. **black**	300.
	c. **deep green**	300.
	d. **dull gray blue**	300.
	e. **deep brown**	300.
	f. **dull red**	300.
O54TC2	24c “Goodall” small die on India paper	
	b. **black**	300.
	c. **deep green**	300.
	d. **dull gray blue**	300.
	e. **deep brown**	300.
	f. **dull red**	300.
O55TC2	30c “Goodall” small die on India paper	
	b. **black**	300.
	c. **deep green**	300.
	d. **dull gray blue**	300.
	e. **deep brown**	300.
	f. **dull red**	300.
O56TC2	90c “Goodall” small die on India paper	
	b. **black**	300.
	c. **deep green**	300.
	d. **dull gray blue**	300.
	e. **deep brown**	300.
	f. **dull red**	300.

STATE

O57TC2	1c “Goodall” small die on India paper	
	b. **black**	300.
	c. **deep green**	300.
	d. **dull gray blue**	300.
	e. **deep brown**	300.
	f. **dull red**	300.
O58TC2	2c “Goodall” small die on India paper	
	b. **black**	300.
	c. **deep green**	300.
	d. **dull gray blue**	300.
	e. **deep brown**	300.
	f. **dull red**	300.
O59TC2	3c “Goodall” small die on India paper	
	b. **black**	300.
	c. **deep green**	300.
	d. **dull gray blue**	300.
	e. **deep brown**	300.
	f. **dull red**	300.
O60TC2	6c “Goodall” small die on India paper	
	b. **black**	300.
	c. **deep green**	300.
	d. **dull gray blue**	300.
	e. **deep brown**	300.
	f. **dull red**	300.
O61TC2	7c “Goodall” small die on India paper	
	b. **black**	300.
	c. **deep green**	300.
	d. **dull gray blue**	300.
	e. **deep brown**	300.
	f. **dull red**	300.
O62TC2	10c “Goodall” small die on India paper	
	b. **black**	300.
	c. **deep green**	300.
	d. **dull gray blue**	300.
	e. **deep brown**	300.
	f. **dull red**	300.
O63TC2	12c “Goodall” small die on India paper	
	b. **black**	300.
	c. **deep green**	300.
	d. **dull gray blue**	300.
	e. **deep brown**	300.
	f. **dull red**	300.
O63TC2	15c “Goodall” small die on India paper	
	b. **black**	300.
	c. **deep green**	300.
	d. **dull gray blue**	300.
	e. **deep brown**	300.
	f. **dull red**	300.
O64TC2	24c “Goodall” small die on India paper	
	b. **black**	300.
	c. **deep green**	300.
	d. **dull gray blue**	300.
	e. **deep brown**	300.
	f. **dull red**	300.
O65TC2	30c “Goodall” small die on India paper	
	b. **black**	300.
	c. **deep green**	300.
	d. **dull gray blue**	300.
	e. **deep brown**	300.
	f. **dull red**	300.
O66TC2	90c “Goodall” small die on India paper	
	b. **black**	300.
	c. **deep green**	300.
	d. **dull gray blue**	300.
	e. **deep brown**	300.
	f. **dull red**	300.

O68TC2 $2 "Goodall" small die on India paper
b. **scarlet frame, green center** *3,250.*
c. **scarlet frame, black center** *3,250.*
d. **scarlet frame, blue center** *3,250.*
e. **scarlet frame, brown center** *3,250.*
f. **violet frame, black center** *3,250.*
g. **green frame, brown center** *3,250.*
h. **brown frame, green center** *3,250.*
i. **brown frame, black center** *3,250.*
j. **red brown frame, green center** *3,250.*

TREASURY

O72TC2 1c "Goodall" small die on India paper
b. **black** 300.
c. **deep green** 300.
d. **dull gray blue** 300.
e. **deep brown** 300.
f. **dull red** 300.
O73TC2 2c "Goodall" small die on India paper
b. **black** 300.
c. **deep green** 300.
d. **dull gray blue** 300.
e. **deep brown** 300.
f. **dull red** 300.
O74TC2 3c "Goodall" small die on India paper
b. **black** 300.
c. **deep green** 300.
d. **dull gray blue** 300.
e. **deep brown** 300.
f. **dull red** 300.
O75TC2 6c "Goodall" small die on India paper
b. **black** 300.
c. **deep green** 300.
d. **dull gray blue** 300.
e. **deep brown** 300.
f. **dull red** 300.
O76TC2 7c "Goodall" small die on India paper
b. **black** 300.
c. **deep green** 300.
d. **dull gray blue** 300.
e. **deep brown** 300.
f. **dull red** 300.
O77TC2 10c "Goodall" small die on India paper
b. **black** 300.
c. **deep green** 300.
d. **dull gray blue** 300.
e. **deep brown** 300.
f. **dull red** 300.
O78TC2 12c "Goodall" small die on India paper
b. **black** 300.
c. **deep green** 300.
d. **dull gray blue** 300.
e. **deep brown** 300.
f. **dull red** 300.
O79TC2 15c "Goodall" small die on India paper
b. **black** 300.
c. **deep green** 300.
d. **dull gray blue** 300.
e. **deep brown** 300.
f. **dull red** 300.
O80TC2 24c "Goodall" small die on India paper
b. **black** 300.
c. **deep green** 300.
d. **dull gray blue** 300.
e. **deep brown** 300.
f. **dull red** 300.
O81TC2 30c "Goodall" small die on India paper
b. **black** 300.
c. **deep green** 300.
d. **dull gray blue** 300.
e. **deep brown** 300.
f. **dull red** 300.
O82TC2 90c "Goodall" small die on India paper
b. **black** 300.
c. **deep green** 300.
d. **dull gray blue** 300.
e. **deep brown** 300.
f. **dull red** 300.

WAR

O83TC2 1c "Goodall" small die on India paper
b. **black** 300.
c. **deep green** 300.
d. **dull gray blue** 300.
e. **deep brown** 300.
f. **dull red** 300.
O84TC2 2c "Goodall" small die on India paper
b. **black** 300.
c. **deep green** 300.
d. **dull gray blue** 300.
e. **deep brown** 300.
f. **dull red** 300.
O85TC2 3c "Goodall" small die on India paper
b. **black** 300.
c. **deep green** 300.
d. **dull gray blue** 300.
e. **deep brown** 300.
f. **dull red** 300.
O86TC2 6c "Goodall" small die on India paper
b. **black** 300.
c. **deep green** 300.
d. **dull gray blue** 300.
e. **deep brown** 300.
f. **dull red** 300.
O87TC2 7c "Goodall" small die on India paper
b. **black** 300.
c. **deep green** 300.
d. **dull gray blue** 300.
e. **deep brown** 300.
f. **dull red** 300.
O88TC2 10c "Goodall" small die on India paper
b. **black** 300.
c. **deep green** 300.
d. **dull gray blue** 300.
e. **deep brown** 300.
f. **dull red** 300.
O89TC2 12c "Goodall" small die on India paper
b. **black** 300.
c. **deep green** 300.
d. **dull gray blue** 300.
e. **deep brown** 300.
f. **dull red** 300.
O90TC2 15c "Goodall" small die on India paper
b. **black** 300.
c. **deep green** 300.
d. **dull gray blue** 300.
e. **deep brown** 300.
f. **dull red** 300.
O91TC2 24c "Goodall" small die on India paper
b. **black** 300.
c. **deep green** 300.
d. **dull gray blue** 300.
e. **deep brown** 300.
f. **dull red** 300.
O92TC2 30c "Goodall" small die on India paper
b. **black** 300.
c. **deep green** 300.
d. **dull gray blue** 300.
e. **deep brown** 300.
f. **dull red** 300.
O93TC2 90c "Goodall" small die on India paper
b. **black** 300.
c. **deep green** 300.
d. **dull gray blue** 300.
e. **deep brown** 300.
f. **dull red** 300.

POST OFFICE SEALS

1872

OXF1TC1a large die on India paper
e. **ultramarine** *1,000.*
f. **carmine** *1,000.*
g. **brown** *1,000.*
h. **red violet** *1,000.*
OXF1TC2 small die on glossy bond paper
b. **chocolate** *1,000.*
OXF1TC2 small die on card
c. **blue,** colored border *1,000.*
d. **deep blue,** colored border *1,000.*
e. **green,** colored border *1,000.*
f. **chocolate,** colored border *1,000.*
OXF1P1 **grn,** large die on India paper 275.
a. Wove paper *950.*
b. Glazed paper *190.*
OXF1P3 **green,** plate proof on India —
OXF1P4 **grn,** plate on card —

1877

OX1TC1a large die on India paper
e. **blue** 500.
f. **green** 500.
g. **orange** 500.
h. **red orange** 500.
i. **black** 500.
OX1TC5 plate on bond paper, imperf.
a. **green** 500.
OX1TC6 plate on bond paper, perforated & gummed
a. **green** —
OX1P1 **brn,** large die on India paper *1,750.*
OX1P2 **brn,** plate on India paper *125.*
Block of 4 650.

1879

OX2TC1a large die on India paper
e. **black** —
OX2aP1 **brn,** large die on India paper 2,500.
OX2aP3 **brn,** plate on India paper 125.
Block of 4 650.

1888-94

OX5P1 **choc,** large die on India paper *750.*

1901-03

OX11P1 **red brn,** large die on India paper *750.*

No. OX11P is a hybrid proof sunk on card.

1972

OX41P1 Pane of 5, blue line proof —

POSTAL NOTE STAMPS

PN1TC1c 1c large die on white wove paper, imperf.
e. **bister** 12,500.

NEWSPAPER

1865

PR1TC1a 5c large die on India paper
e. **bright red** 600.
f. **deep reddish brown** 3,000.
g. **dark orange** 3,000.
d. **green** 3,000.
PR1P2a 5c **bl,** PP sm die on yelsh wove paper *4,000.*
PR2TC1a 10c large die on India paper
e. **brown** 600.
f. **dull red** 600.
g. **blue** 600.
h. **blue green** 600.
PR2TC5 10c plate on thick cream wove paper
a. **black** 85.
b. **lake** 85.
c. **blue green** 85.
d. **blue** 85.
PR2P1 10c **grn,** large die on India paper 575.
PR2P2 10c **grn,** RA sm die on white wove paper 225.
PR2P2a 10c **grn,** PP sm die on yelsh wove paper *4,000.*
PR2P4 10c **grn,** plate on card 75.
Block of 4 375.
P# blk. of 6 —
PR2P4a 10c **grn,** plate on thin card 85.
Block of 4 425.
PR3TC1a 25c large die on India paper
e. **ocher** 600.
f. **brown** 600.
g. **brick red** 600.
PR3TC1b 25c large die on thin hard paper
e. **carmine** *2,500.*
PR3TC5 25c plate on thick cream wove paper
a. **black** 85.
b. **lake** 85.
c. **blue green** 85.
d. **blue** 85.
PR3P1 25c **org red,** large die on India paper 650.
PR3P2 25c **org red,** RA sm die on white wove paper 225.
PR3P2a 25c **org red,** PP sm die on yelsh wove paper *4,000.*
PR3P4 25c **org red,** plate on card 75.
Block of 4 375.
P# blk. of 6 —
PR3P4a 25c **org red,** plate on thin card 100.
Block of 4 500.
PR4TC1a 5c large die on India paper
e. **blue green,** *greenish* —
PR4TC5 5c plate on thick cream wove paper
a. **black** 85.
b. **lake** 85.
c. **blue green** 85.
d. **blue** 85.
PR4P1 5c **bl,** large die on India paper 575.
PR4P2 5c **bl,** RA sm die on white wove paper 225.
PR4P4 5c **bl,** plate on card 75.
Block of 4 375.
P# blk. of 6 —
PR4P4a 5c **bl,** plate on thin card 85.
Block of 4 425.

1875

PR5P4 5c **dk bl,** plate on card 65.
PR6P4 10c **dp grn,** plate on card 65.
PR7P4 25c **dk car red,** plate on card 65.
PR9TC1a 2c large die on India paper
e. **orange brown** *600.*
f. **black brown** *600.*
g. **blue green** *600.*
PR9TC3 2c plate on India paper
a. **dark carmine** 35.
b. **brown rose** 35.
c. **scarlet** 35.
d. **orange brown** 35.
e. **sepia** 35.
f. **orange yellow** 35.
g. **dull orange** 35.
h. **green** 35.
i. **light ultramarine** 35.
j. **light blue** 35.
k. **dark violet** 35.
l. **violet black** 35.
PR9P1 2c **blk,** large die on India paper 100.
PR9P2 2c **blk,** RA sm die on white wove paper 50.
PR9P2a 2c **blk,** PP sm die on yelsh wove paper 575.
PR9P3 2c **blk,** plate on India paper 15.
Block of 4 65.
P# block of 10 —
PR9P4 2c **blk,** plate on card 12.
Block of 4 55.
P# blk. of 8 —
PR10TC1a 3c large die on India paper
e. **rose lake** *600.*
PR10P1 3c **blk,** large die on India paper 100.
PR10P2 3c **blk,** RA sm die on white wove paper 50.
PR10P2a 3c **blk,** PP sm die on yelsh wove paper 575.
PR10P3 3c **blk,** plate on India paper 15.
Block of 4 65.
Margin block of 8, Impt. and "B" —
PR10P4 3c **blk,** plate on card 12.
Block of 4 55.
P# blk. of 8 —
PR11P1 4c **blk,** large die on India paper 100.
PR11P2 4c **blk,** RA sm die on white wove paper 50.
PR11P2a 4c **blk,** PP sm die on yelsh wove paper 575.
PR11P3 4c **blk,** plate on India paper 15.
Block of 4 65.
PR11P4 4c **blk,** plate on card 12.
Block of 4 55.
PR12P1 6c **blk,** large die on India paper 100.
PR12P2 6c **blk,** RA sm die on white wove paper 50.
PR12P2a 6c **blk,** PP sm die on yelsh wove paper 575.
PR12P3 6c **blk,** plate on India paper 15.
Block of 4 65.
PR12P4 6c **blk,** plate on card 12.
Block of 4 55.
PR13P1 8c **blk,** large die on India paper 100.
PR13P2 8c **blk,** RA sm die on white wove paper 50.
PR13P2a 8c **blk,** PP sm die on yelsh wove paper 575.
PR13P3 8c **blk,** plate on India paper 15.
Block of 4 65.
PR13P4 8c **blk,** plate on card 12.
Block of 4 55.
PR14P1 9c **blk,** large die on India paper 100.
PR14P2 9c **blk,** RA sm die on white wove paper 50.
PR14P2a 9c **blk,** PP sm die on yelsh wove paper 575.
PR14P3 9c **blk,** plate on India paper 15.
Block of 4 65.
PR14P4 9c **blk,** plate on card 12.
Block of 4 55.

PR15P1	10c **blk,** large die on India paper	100.
PR15P2	10c **blk,** RA sm die on white wove paper	50.
PR15P2a	10c **blk,** PP sm die on yelsh wove paper	575.
PR15P3	10c **blk,** plate on India paper	15.
	Block of 4	65.
PR15P4	10c **blk,** plate on card	12.
	Block of 4	55.
PR16TC1a	12c large die on India paper	
e.	**brown rose**	*600.*
f.	**scarlet**	*600.*
g.	**sepia**	*600.*
h.	**green**	*600.*
i.	**light ultramarine**	*600.*
j.	**dark violet**	*600.*
k.	**violet black**	*600.*
l.	**black**	*600.*
PR16TC3	12c plate on India paper	
a.	**dark carmine**	35.
b.	**brown rose**	35.
c.	**scarlet**	35.
d.	**orange brown**	35.
e.	**sepia**	35.
f.	**orange yellow**	35.
g.	**dull orange**	35.
h.	**green**	35.
i.	**light ultramarine**	35.
j.	**light blue**	35.
k.	**dark violet**	35.
l.	**violet black**	35.
m.	**black**	35.
PR16P1	12c **rose,** large die on India paper	100.
PR16P2	12c **rose,** RA sm die on white wove paper	50.
PR16P2a	12c **rose,** PP sm die on yelsh wove paper	575.
PR16P3	12c **rose,** plate on India paper	15.
	Block of 4	65.
PR16P4	12c **rose,** plate on card	12.
	Block of 4	55.
PR17TC1a	24c large die on India paper	
e.	**green**	*600.*
f.	**black**	*600.*
PR17TC3	24c plate on India paper	
a.	**black**	35.
PR17P1	24c **rose,** large die on India paper	100.
PR17P2	24c **rose,** RA sm die on white wove paper	50.
PR17P2a	24c **rose,** PP sm die on yelsh wove paper	575.
PR17P3	24c **rose,** plate on India paper	15.
	Block of 4	65.
PR17P4	24c **rose,** plate on card	12.
	Block of 4	55.
PR18TC1a	36c large die on India paper	
e.	**green**	*600.*
f.	**black**	*600.*
g.	**sepia**	*600.*
PR18TC3	36c plate on India paper	
a.	**black**	35.
PR18P1	36c **rose,** large die on India paper	100.
PR18P2	36c **rose,** RA sm die on white wove paper	50.
PR18P2a	36c **rose,** PP sm die on yelsh wove paper	575.
PR18P3	36c **rose,** plate on India paper	15.
	Block of 4	65.
PR18P4	36c **rose,** plate on card	12.
	Block of 4	55.
PR19TC1a	48c large die on India paper	
e.	**green**	*600.*
f.	**black**	*600.*
g.	**sepia**	*600.*
PR19TC3	48c plate on India paper	
a.	**black**	35.
PR19P1	48c **rose,** large die on India paper	100.
PR19P2	48c **rose,** RA sm die on white wove paper	50.
PR19P2a	48c **rose,** PP sm die on yelsh wove paper	575.
PR19P3	48c **rose,** plate on India paper	15.
	Block of 4	65.
PR19P4	48c **rose,** plate on card	12.
	Block of 4	55.
PR20TC1a	60c large die on India paper	
e.	**black**	*600.*
PR20TC3	60c plate on India paper	
a.	**black**	35.
PR20P1	60c **rose,** large die on India paper	100.
PR20P2	60c **rose,** RA sm die on white wove paper	50.
PR20P2a	60c **rose,** PP sm die on yelsh wove paper	575.
PR20P3	60c **rose,** plate on India paper	15.
	Block of 4	65.
PR20P4	60c **rose,** plate on card	12.
	Block of 4	55.
PR21TC1a	72c large die on India paper	
e.	**black**	*600.*
PR21TC3	72c plate on India paper	
a.	**black**	35.
PR21P1	72c **rose,** large die on India paper	100.
PR21P2	72c **rose,** RA sm die on white wove paper	50.
PR21P2a	72c **rose,** PP sm die on yelsh wove paper	575.
PR21P3	72c **rose,** plate on India paper	15.
	Block of 4	65.
PR21P4	72c **rose,** plate on card	12.
	Block of 4	55.
PR22TC1a	84c large die on India paper	
e.	**black**	*600.*
PR22TC3	84c plate on India paper	
a.	**black**	35.
PR22P1	84c **rose,** large die on India paper	100.
PR22P2	84c **rose,** RA sm die on white wove paper	50.
PR22P2a	84c **rose,** PP sm die on yelsh wove paper	575.
PR22P3	84c **rose,** plate on India paper	15.
	Block of 4	65.
PR22P4	84c **rose,** plate on card	12.
	Block of 4	55.
PR23TC3	96c plate on India paper	
a.	**black**	35.
PR23P1	96c **rose,** large die on India paper	100.
PR23P2	96c **rose,** RA sm die on white wove paper	50.
PR23P2a	96c **rose,** PP sm die on yelsh wove paper	575.
PR23P3	96c **rose,** plate on India paper	15.
	Block of 4	65.
PR23P4	96c **rose,** plate on card	12.
	Block of 4	55.
PR24TC1a	$1.92 large die on India paper	
e.	**orange brown**	*600.*
f.	**green**	*600.*
PR24TC3	$1.92 plate on India paper	
a.	**dark carmine**	35.
b.	**brown rose**	35.
c.	**scarlet**	35.
d.	**orange brown**	35.
e.	**sepia**	35.
f.	**orange yellow**	35.
g.	**dull orange**	35.
h.	**green**	35.
i.	**light ultramarine**	35.
j.	**dark violet**	35.
k.	**violet black**	35.
l.	**black**	35.
PR24P1	$1.92 **dk brn,** large die on India paper	100.
PR24P2	$1.92 **dk brn,** RA sm die on white wove paper	50.
PR24P2a	$1.92 **dk brn,** PP sm die on yelsh wove paper	575.
PR24P3	$1.92 **dk brn,** plate on India paper	18.
	Block of 4	80.
PR24P4	$1.92 **dk brn,** plate on card	15.
	Block of 4	70.
PR25TC1a	$3 large die on India paper	
e.	**dark carmine**	*600.*
f.	**orange yellow**	*600.*
g.	**dull orange**	*600.*
h.	**green**	*600.*
i.	**light ultramarine**	*600.*
j.	**dark violet**	*600.*
k.	**violet black**	*600.*
l.	**black**	*600.*
m.	**brown**	—
PR25TC3	$3 plate on India paper	
a.	**dark carmine**	35.
b.	**brown rose**	35.
c.	**scarlet**	35.
d.	**orange brown**	35.
e.	**sepia**	35.
f.	**orange yellow**	35.
g.	**dull orange**	35.
h.	**green**	35.
i.	**light ultramarine**	35.
j.	**light blue**	35.
k.	**dark violet**	35.
l.	**violet black**	35.
m.	**black**	35.
PR25P1	$3 **ver,** large die on India paper	100.
PR25P2	$3 **ver,** RA sm die on white wove paper	50.
PR25P2a	$3 **ver,** PP sm die on yelsh wove paper	575.
PR25P3	$3 **ver,** plate on India paper	18.
	Block of 4	80.
PR25P4	$3 **ver,** plate on card	15.
	Block of 4	70.
PR26TC1a	$6 large die on India paper	
e.	**dark carmine**	*600.*
f.	**brown rose**	*600.*
g.	**scarlet**	*600.*
h.	**sepia**	*600.*
i.	**orange yellow**	*600.*
j.	**dull orange**	*600.*
k.	**green**	*600.*
l.	**light blue**	*600.*
m.	**dark violet**	*600.*
n.	**violet black**	*600.*
o.	**black**	*600.*
PR26TC3	$6 plate on India paper	
a.	**dark carmine**	35.
b.	**brown rose**	35.
c.	**scarlet**	35.
d.	**orange brown**	35.
e.	**dark brown**	35.
f.	**sepia**	35.
g.	**orange yellow**	35.
h.	**dull orange**	35.
i.	**green**	35.
j.	**light ultramarine**	35.
k.	**light blue**	35.
l.	**dark violet**	35.
m.	**violet black**	35.
n.	**black**	35.
PR26P1	$6 **ultra,** large die on India paper	100.
PR26P2	$6 **ultra,** RA sm die on white wove paper	50.
PR26P2a	$6 **ultra,** PP sm die on yelsh wove paper	575.
PR26P3	$6 **ultra,** plate on India paper	18.
	Block of 4	80.
PR26P4	$6 **ultra,** plate on card	15.
	Block of 4	70.
PR27TC1a	$9 large die on India paper	
e.	**dark carmine**	*600.*
f.	**brown rose**	*600.*
g.	**scarlet**	*600.*
h.	**sepia**	*600.*
i.	**orange yellow**	*600.*
j.	**dull orange**	*600.*
k.	**green**	*600.*
l.	**light ultramarine**	*600.*
m.	**dark violet**	*600.*
n.	**violet black**	*600.*
o.	**black**	*600.*
PR27TC3	$9 plate on India paper	
a.	**dark carmine**	35.
b.	**brown rose**	35.
c.	**scarlet**	35.
d.	**orange brown**	35.
e.	**sepia**	35.
f.	**orange yellow**	35.
g.	**dull orange**	35.
h.	**green**	35.
i.	**light ultramarine**	35.
j.	**light blue**	35.
k.	**dark violet**	35.
l.	**violet black**	35.
m.	**black**	35.
PR27P1	$9 **yel,** large die on India paper	100.
PR27P2	$9 **yel,** RA sm die on white wove paper	50.
PR27P2a	$9 **yel,** PP sm die on yelsh wove paper	575.
PR27P3	$9 **yel,** plate on India paper	18.
	Block of 4	80.
PR27P4	$9 **yel,** plate on card	15.
	Block of 4	70.
PR28TC1a	$12 large die on India paper	
e.	**black**	*600.*
f.	**sepia**	*600.*
g.	**orange brown**	*600.*
PR28P1	$12 **bl grn,** large die on India paper	100.
PR28P2	$12 **bl grn,** RA sm die on white wove paper	50.
PR28P2a	$12 **bl grn,** PP sm die on yelsh wove paper	575.
PR28P3	$12 **bl grn,** plate on India paper	18.
	Block of 4	80.
PR28P4	$12 **bl grn,** plate on card	15.
	Block of 4	70.
PR29TC1a	$24 large die on India paper	
e.	**black**	*600.*
f.	**black brown**	*600.*
g.	**orange brown**	*600.*
h.	**green**	*600.*
PR29TC3	$24 plate on India paper	
a.	**black**	35.
PR29P1	$24 **dk gray vio,** large die on India paper	100.
PR29P2	$24 **dk gray vio,** RA sm die on white wove paper	50.
PR29P2a	$24 **dk gray vio,** PP sm die on yelsh wove paper	575.
PR29P3	$24 **dk gray vio,** plate on India paper	18.
	Block of 4	80.
PR29P4	$24 **dk gray vio,** plate on card	15.
	Block of 4	70.
PR30TC1a	$36 large die on India paper	
e.	**dark carmine**	*600.*
f.	**black**	*600.*
g.	**black brown**	*600.*
h.	**orange brown**	*600.*
i.	**sepia**	*600.*
j.	**violet**	*600.*
k.	**green**	*600.*
PR30TC3	$36 plate on India paper	
a.	**black**	35.
PR30P1	$36 **brn rose,** large die on India paper	100.
PR30P2	$36 **brn rose,** RA sm die on white wove paper	50.
PR30P2a	$36 **brn rose,** PP sm die on yelsh wove paper	575.
PR30P3	$36 **brn rose,** plate on India paper	18.
	Block of 4	90.
PR30P4	$36 **brn rose,** plate on card	15.
	Block of 4	70.
PR31TC1a	$48 large die on India paper	
e.	**violet brown**	*600.*
f.	**black**	*600.*
g.	**sepia**	*600.*
h.	**green**	*600.*
PR31TC3	$48 plate on India paper	
a.	**black**	35.
b.	**violet brown**	35.
PR31P1	$48 **red brn,** large die on India paper	100.
PR31P2	$48 **red brn,** RA sm die on white wove paper	50.
PR31P2a	$48 **red brn,** PP sm die on yelsh wove paper	575.
PR31P3	$48 **red brn,** plate on India paper	23.
	Block of 4	100.
PR31P4	$48 **red brn,** plate on card	15.
	Block of 4	70.
PR32TC1a	$60 large die on India paper	
e.	**dark carmine**	*600.*
f.	**brown rose**	*600.*
g.	**scarlet**	*600.*
h.	**sepia**	*600.*
i.	**orange yellow**	*600.*
j.	**dull orange**	*600.*
k.	**green**	*600.*
l.	**light ultramarine**	*600.*
m.	**orange brown**	*600.*
n.	**violet black**	*600.*
o.	**black**	*600.*
PR32TC3	$60 plate on India paper	
a.	**dark carmine**	35.
b.	**brown rose**	35.
c.	**scarlet**	35.
d.	**sepia**	35.
e.	**orange yellow**	35.
f.	**dull orange**	35.
g.	**green**	35.
h.	**light ultramarine**	35.
i.	**orange brown**	35.

j. **violet black** 35.
k. **black** 35.
PR32P1 $60 **vio,** large die on India paper 100.
PR32P2 $60 **vio,** RA sm die on white wove paper 50.
PR32P2a $60 **vio,** PP sm die on yelsh wove paper 575.
PR32P3 $60 **vio,** plate on India paper 25.
Block of 4 110.
PR32P4 $60 **vio,** plate on card 18.
Block of 4 85.
Nos. PR9P3-PR32P3 (24) 399.00
Nos. PR9P4-PR32P4 (24) 318.00

1879

PR57P1 2c **dp blk,** large die on India paper 100.
PR57P3 2c **dp blk,** plate on India paper 25.
Block of 4 125.
P# block of 10, Impt. —
PR57P4 2c **dp blk,** plate on card 15.
Block of 4 90.
PR58P1 3c **dp blk,** large die on India paper 100.
PR58P3 3c **dp blk,** plate on India paper 25.
Block of 4 125.
PR58P4 3c **dp blk,** plate on card 15.
Block of 4 90.
PR59P1 4c **dp blk,** large die on India paper 100.
PR59P3 4c **dp blk,** plate on India paper 25.
Block of 4 125.
PR59P4 4c **dp blk,** plate on card 15.
Block of 4 90.
PR60P1 6c **dp blk,** large die on India paper 100.
PR60P3 6c **dp blk,** plate on India paper 25.
Block of 4 125.
PR60P4 6c **dp blk,** plate on card 15.
Block of 4 90.
PR61P1 8c **dp blk,** large die on India paper 100.
PR61P3 8c **dp blk,** plate on India paper 25.
Block of 4 125.
PR61P4 8c **dp blk,** plate on card 15.
Block of 4 90.
PR62P1 10c **dp blk,** large die on India paper 100.
PR62P3 10c **dp blk,** plate on India paper 25.
Block of 4 125.
PR62P4 10c **dp blk,** plate on card 15.
Block of 4 90.
PR63P1 12c **red,** large die on India paper 100.
PR63P3 12c **red,** plate on India paper 25.
Block of 4 125.
PR63P4 12c **red,** plate on card 15.
Block of 4 90.
PR64P1 24c **red,** large die on India paper 100.
PR64P3 24c **red,** plate on India paper 25.
Block of 4 125.
PR64P4 24c **red,** plate on card 15.
Block of 4 90.
PR65P1 36c **red,** large die on India paper 100.
PR65P3 36c **red,** plate on India paper 25.
Block of 4 125.
PR65P4 36c **red,** plate on card 15.
Block of 4 90.
PR66P1 48c **red,** large die on India paper 100.
PR66P3 48c **red,** plate on India paper 25.
Block of 4 125.
PR66P4 48c **red,** plate on card 15.
Block of 4 90.
PR67P1 60c **red,** large die on India paper 100.
PR67P3 60c **red,** plate on India paper 25.
Block of 4 125.
PR67P4 60c **red,** plate on card 15.
Block of 4 90.
PR68P1 72c **red,** large die on India paper 100.
PR68P3 72c **red,** plate on India paper 25.
Block of 4 125.
PR68P4 72c **red,** plate on card 15.
Block of 4 90.
PR69P1 84c **red,** large die on India paper 100.
PR69P3 84c **red,** plate on India paper 25.
Block of 4 125.
PR69P4 84c **red,** plate on card 15.
Block of 4 90.
PR70P1 96c **red,** large die on India paper 100.
PR70P3 96c **red,** plate on India paper 25.
Block of 4 125.
PR70P4 96c **red,** plate on card 15.
Block of 4 90.
PR71P1 $1.92 **pale brn,** large die on India paper 100.
PR71P3 $1.92 **pale brn,** plate on India paper 25.
Block of 4 125.
PR71P4 $1.92 **pale brn,** plate on card 15.
Block of 4 90.
PR72P1 $3 **red ver,** large die on India paper 100.
PR72P3 $3 **red ver,** plate on India paper 25.
Block of 4 125.
PR72P4 $3 **red ver,** plate on card 15.
Block of 4 90.
PR73P1 $6 **bl,** large die on India paper 100.
PR73P3 $6 **bl,** plate on India paper 25.
Block of 4 125.
PR73P4 $6 **bl,** plate on card 15.
Block of 4 90.
PR74P1 $9 **org,** large die on India paper 100.
PR74P3 $9 **org,** plate on India paper 25.
Block of 4 125.
PR74P4 $9 **org,** plate on card 15.
Block of 4 90.
PR75P1 $12 **yel grn,** large die on India paper 100.
PR75P3 $12 **yel grn,** plate on India paper 25.
Block of 4 125.
PR75P4 $12 **yel grn,** plate on card 15.
Block of 4 90.
PR76P1 $24 **dk vio,** large die on India paper 100.
PR76P3 $24 **dk vio,** plate on India paper 25.
Block of 4 125.
PR76P4 $24 **dk vio,** plate on card 15.
Block of 4 90.
PR77P1 $36 **Indian red,** large die on India paper 100.
PR77P3 $36 **Indian red,** plate on India paper 25.
Block of 4 125.
PR77P4 $36 **Indian red,** plate on card 15.
Block of 4 90.
PR78P1 $48 **yel brn,** large die on India paper 100.
PR78P3 $48 **yel brn,** plate on India paper 25.
Block of 4 125.
PR78P4 $48 **yel brn,** plate on card 15.
Block of 4 90.
PR79P1 $60 **pur,** large die on India paper 100.
PR79P3 $60 **pur,** plate on India paper 25.
Block of 4 125.
PR79P4 $60 **pur,** plate on card 15.
Block of 4 90.
Nos. PR57P3-PR79P3 (23) 575.00
Nos. PR57P4-PR79P4 (23) 345.00

1885

PR81TC1a 1c large die on India paper
e. **salmon** *600.*
PR81TC3 1c plate on India paper
a. **scarlet** 120.
b. **dark brown** 120.
c. **violet brown** 120.
d. **dull orange** 120.
e. **green** 120.
f. **light blue** 120.
PR81P1 1c **blk,** large die on India paper 100.
PR81P2 1c **blk,** RA sm die on white wove paper 60.
PR81P2a 1c **blk,** PP sm die on yelsh wove paper 600.
PR81P3 1c **blk,** plate on India paper 25.
Block of 4 125.
P# blk. of 8 —
PR81P4 1c **blk,** plate on card 15.
Block of 4 90.
P# blk. of 8 425.
PR82P2a 12c **car,** PP sm die on yelsh wove paper 600.
PR82P3 12c **car,** plate on India paper 25.
Block of 4 125.
PR82P4 12c **car,** plate on card 15.
PR82P5 12c **car,** plate on stamp paper, pair —
PR83P2a 24c **car,** PP sm die on yelsh wove paper 600.
PR83P3 24c **car,** plate on India paper 25.
Block of 4 125.
PR83P4 24c **car,** plate on card 15.
PR83P5 24c **car,** plate on stamp paper, pair —
PR84P2a 36c **car,** PP sm die on yelsh wove paper 600.
PR84P3 36c **car,** plate on India paper 25.
Block of 4 125.
PR84P4 36c **car,** plate on card 15.
PR84P5 36c **car,** plate on stamp paper, pair —
PR85P2a 48c **car,** PP sm die on yelsh wove paper 600.
PR85P3 48c **car,** plate on India paper 25.
Block of 4 125.
PR85P4 48c **car,** plate on card 15.
PR85P5 48c **car,** plate on stamp paper, pair —
PR86P2a 60c **car,** PP sm die on yelsh wove paper 600.
PR86P3 60c **car,** plate on India paper 25.
Block of 4 125.
PR86P4 60c **car,** plate on card 15.
PR86P5 60c **car,** plate on stamp paper, pair —
PR87P2a 72c **car,** PP sm die on yelsh wove paper 600.
PR87P3 72c **car,** plate on India paper 25.
Block of 4 125.
PR87P4 72c **car,** plate on card 15.
PR87P5 72c **car,** plate on stamp paper, pair —
PR88P2a 84c **car,** PP sm die on yelsh wove paper 600.
PR88P3 84c **car,** plate on India paper 25.
Block of 4 125.
PR88P4 84c **car,** plate on card 15.
PR88P5 84c **car,** plate on stamp paper, pair —
PR89P2a 96c **car,** PP sm die on yelsh wove paper 600.
PR89P3 96c **car,** plate on India paper 25.
Block of 4 125.
PR89P4 96c **car,** plate on card 15.
PR89P5 96c **car,** plate on stamp paper, pair —
Nos. PR81P3-PR89P3 (9) 225.00
Nos. PR81P4-PR89P4 (9) 135.00

1895

PR102TC1a 1c large die on India paper
e. **deep scarlet** *600.*
PR102P1 1c **blk,** large die on India paper 125.
PR102P2 1c **blk,** RA sm die on white wove paper 115.
PR102P2a 1c **blk,** PP sm die on yelsh wove paper 600.
PR103P1 2c **blk,** large die on India paper 125.
PR103P2 2c **blk,** RA sm die on white wove paper 115.
PR103P2a 2c **blk,** PP sm die on yelsh wove paper 600.
PR104P1 5c **blk,** large die on India paper 125.
PR104P2 5c **blk,** RA sm die on white wove paper 115.
PR104P2a 5c **blk,** PP sm die on yelsh wove paper 600.
PR105P1 10c **blk,** large die on India paper 125.
PR105P2 10c **blk,** RA sm die on white wove paper 115.
PR105P2a 10c **blk,** PP sm die on yelsh wove paper 600.
PR106TC1a 25c large die on India paper
e. **deep carmine** *600.*
f. **dark carmine** *600.*
PR106P1 25c **car,** large die on India paper 125.
PR106P2 25c **car,** RA sm die on white wove paper 115.
PR106P2a 25c **car,** PP sm die on yelsh wove paper 600.
PR107TC1a 50c large die on India paper
e. **black** *600.*
f. **deep carmine** *600.*
PR107P1 50c **car,** large die on India paper 125.
PR107P2 50c **car,** RA sm die on white wove paper 115.
PR107P2a 50c **car,** PP sm die on yelsh wove paper 600.
PR108TC1a $2 large die on India paper
e. **deep scarlet** *600.*
f. **dark scarlet** *600.*
PR108P1 $2 **scar,** large die on India paper 125.
PR108P2 $2 **scar,** RA sm die on white wove paper 115.
PR108P2a $2 **scar,** PP sm die on yelsh wove paper 600.
PR109TC1a $5 large die on India paper
e. **light ultramarine** *600.*
f. **dark ultramarine** *600.*
PR109P1 $5 **bl,** large die on India paper 125.
PR109P2 $5 **bl,** RA sm die on white wove paper 115.
PR109P2a $5 **bl,** PP sm die on yelsh wove paper 600.
PR110TC1a $10 large die on India paper
e. **black** *600.*
PR110P1 $10 **grn,** large die on India paper 125.
PR110P2 $10 **grn,** RA sm die on white wove paper 115.
PR110P2a $10 **grn,** PP sm die on yelsh wove paper 600.
PR111P1 $20 **slate,** large die on India paper 125.
PR111P2 $20 **slate,** RA sm die on white wove paper 115.
PR111P2a $20 **slate,** PP sm die on yelsh wove paper 600.
PR112TC1a $50 large die on India paper
e. **black** *600.*
f. **deep rose** *600.*
g. **dark rose** *600.*
PR112P1 $50 **car,** large die on India paper 125.
PR112P2 $50 **car,** RA sm die on white wove paper 115.
PR112P2a $50 **car,** PP sm die on yelsh wove paper 600.
PR113TC1a $100 large die on India paper
e. **black** *600.*
PR113P1 $100 **pur,** large die on India paper 125.
PR113P2 $100 **pur,** RA sm die on white wove paper 115.
PR113P2a $100 **pur,** PP sm die on yelsh wove paper 600.

The so-called "Goodall" set of Small Die proofs on India Paper of Newspaper Stamps in five colors

PR9TC2 2c "Goodall" small die on India paper
b. **black** 150.
d. **deep green** 125.
d. **dull gray blue** 125.
e. **deep brown** 125.
f. **dull red** 125.
PR10TC2 3c "Goodall" small die on India paper
b. **black** 150.
c. **deep green** 125.
d. **dull gray blue** 125.
e. **deep brown** 125.
f. **dull red** 125.
PR11TC2 4c "Goodall" small die on India paper
b. **black** 150.
c. **deep green** 125.
d. **dull gray blue** 125.
e. **deep brown** 125.
f. **dull red** 125.
PR12TC2 6c "Goodall" small die on India paper
b. **black** 150.
c. **deep green** 125.
d. **dull gray blue** 125.
e. **deep brown** 125.
f. **dull red** 125.
PR13TC2 8c "Goodall" small die on India paper
b. **black** 150.
c. **deep green** 125.
d. **dull gray blue** 125.
e. **deep brown** 125.
f. **dull red** 125.
PR14TC2 9c "Goodall" small die on India paper
b. **black** 150.
c. **deep green** 125.
d. **dull gray blue** 125.
e. **deep brown** 125.
f. **dull red** 125.
PR15TC2 10c "Goodall" small die on India paper
b. **black** 150.
c. **deep green** 125.
d. **dull gray blue** 125.
e. **deep brown** 125.
f. **dull red** 125.
PR16TC2 12c "Goodall" small die on India paper
b. **black** 150.
c. **deep green** 125.
d. **dull gray blue** 125.
e. **deep brown** 125.
f. **dull red** 125.
PR17TC2 24c "Goodall" small die on India paper
b. **black** 150.
c. **deep green** 125.
d. **dull gray blue** 125.
e. **deep brown** 125.
f. **dull red** 125.
PR18TC2 36c "Goodall" small die on India paper
b. **black** 150.
c. **deep green** 125.

d. **dull gray blue** 125.
e. **deep brown** 125.
f. **dull red** 125.
PR19TC2 48c "Goodall" small die on India paper
b. **black** 150.
c. **deep green** 125.
d. **dull gray blue** 125.
e. **deep brown** 125.
f. **dull red** 125.
PR20TC2 60c "Goodall" small die on India paper
b. **black** 150.
c. **deep green** 125.
d. **dull gray blue** 125.
e. **deep brown** 125.
f. **dull red** 125.
PR21TC2 72c "Goodall" small die on India paper
b. **black** 150.
c. **deep green** 125.
d. **dull gray blue** 125.
e. **deep brown** 125.
f. **dull red** 125.
PR22TC2 84c "Goodall" small die on India paper
b. **black** 150.
c. **deep green** 125.
d. **dull gray blue** 125.
e. **deep brown** 125.
f. **dull red** 125.
PR23TC2 96c "Goodall" small die on India paper
b. **black** 150.
c. **deep green** 125.
d. **dull gray blue** 125.
e. **deep brown** 125.
f. **dull red** 125.
PR24TC2 $1.92 "Goodall" small die on India paper
b. **black** 150.
c. **deep green** 125.
d. **dull gray blue** 125.
e. **deep brown** 125.
f. **dull red** 125.
PR25TC2 $3 "Goodall" small die on India paper
b. **black** 150.
c. **deep green** 125.
d. **dull gray blue** 125.
e. **deep brown** 125.
f. **dull red** 125.
PR26TC2 $6 "Goodall" small die on India paper
b. **black** 150.
c. **deep green** 125.
d. **dull gray blue** 125.
e. **deep brown** 125.
f. **dull red** 125.
PR27TC2 $9 "Goodall" small die on India paper
b. **black** 150.
c. **deep green** 125.
d. **dull gray blue** 125.
e. **deep brown** 125.
f. **dull red** 125.
PR28TC2 $12 "Goodall" small die on India paper
b. **black** 150.
c. **deep green** 125.
d. **dull gray blue** 125.
e. **deep brown** 125.
f. **dull red** 125.
PR29TC2 $24 "Goodall" small die on India paper
b. **black** 150.
c. **deep green** 125.
d. **dull gray blue** 125.
e. **deep brown** 125.
f. **dull red** 125.
PR30TC2 $36 "Goodall" small die on India paper
b. **black** 150.
c. **deep green** 125.
d. **dull gray blue** 125.
e. **deep brown** 125.
f. **dull red** 125.
PR31TC2 $48 "Goodall" small die on India paper
b. **black** 150.
c. **deep green** 125.
d. **dull gray blue** 125.
e. **deep brown** 125.
f. **dull red** 125.
PR32TC2 $60 "Goodall" small die on India paper
b. **black** 150.
c. **deep green** 125.
d. **dull gray blue** 125.
e. **deep brown** 125.
f. **dull red** 125.

PARCEL POST

1912-13
Q1P1 1c **car rose,** large die on India paper 1,400.
Q1P2 1c **car rose,** sm die on India paper 1,200.
Q1P2a 1c **car rose,** PP sm die on yelsh wove paper 2,500.
Q2P1 2c **car rose,** large die on India paper 1,400.
Q2P2 2c **car rose,** sm die on India paper 1,200.
Q2P2a 2c **car rose,** PP sm die on yelsh wove paper 2,500.
Q3P1 3c **car rose,** large die on India paper 1,400.
Q3P2 3c **car rose,** sm die on India paper 1,200.
Q3P2a 3c **car rose,** PP sm die on yelsh wove paper 2,500.
Q4P1 4c **car rose,** large die on India paper 1,400.
Q4P2 4c **car rose,** sm die on India paper 1,200.
Q4P2a 4c **car rose,** PP sm die on yelsh wove paper 2,500.
Q5P1 5c **car rose,** large die on India paper 1,400.
Q5P2 5c **car rose,** sm die on India paper 1,200.
Q5P2a 5c **car rose,** PP sm die on yelsh wove paper 2,500.
Q6P1 10c **car rose,** large die on India paper 1,400.
Q6P2 10c **car rose,** sm die on India paper 1,200.
Q6P2a 10c **car rose,** PP sm die on yelsh wove paper 2,500.
Q7P1 15c **car rose,** large die on India paper 1,400.
Q7P2 15c **car rose,** sm die on India paper 1,200.
Q7P2a 15c **car rose,** PP sm die on yelsh wove paper 2,500.
Q8P1 20c **car rose,** large die on India paper 1,400.
Q8P2 20c **car rose,** sm die on India paper 1,200.
Q8P2a 20c **car rose,** PP sm die on yelsh wove paper 2,500.
Q9P1 25c **car rose,** large die on India paper 1,400.
Q9P2 25c **car rose,** sm die on India paper 1,200.
Q9P2a 25c **car rose,** PP sm die on yelsh wove paper 2,500.
Q10P1 50c **car rose,** large die on India paper 1,400.
Q10P2 50c **car rose,** sm die on India paper 1,200.
Q10P2a 50c **car rose,** PP sm die on yelsh wove paper 2,500.
Q11P1 75c **car rose,** large die on India paper 1,400.
Q11P2 75c **car rose,** sm die on India paper 1,200.
Q11P2a 75c **car rose,** PP sm die on yelsh wove paper 2,500.
Q12P1 $1 **car rose,** large die on India paper 1,400.
Q12P2 $1 **car rose,** sm die on India paper 1,200.
Q12P2a $1 **car rose,** PP sm die on yelsh wove paper 2,500.

SPECIAL HANDLING

1925-28
QE1P1 10c **yel grn,** large die on India paper *2,750.*
QE2P1 15c **yel grn,** large die on India paper *2,750.*
QE3P1 20c **yel grn,** large die on India paper *2,750.*
QE4TC1a 25c large die on India paper
e. **apple green** 2,750.
f. **olive green** 2,750.
g. **light blue green** 2,750.
h. **blue** 2,750.
i. **dark blue** 2,750.
j. **orange yellow** 2,750.
k. **orange** 2,750.
l. **dull rose** 2,750.
m. **carmine lake** 2,750.
n. **carmine rose** 2,750.
o. **brown** 2,750.
p. **gray brown** 2,750.
q. **dark violet brown** 2,750.
r. **gray black** 2,750.
s. **black** 2,750.
QE4P1 25c **dp grn,** large die on India paper *2,750.*
QE4aP1 25c **yel grn,** large die on India paper *3,250.*

THE "ATLANTA" SET OF PLATE PROOFS

A set in five colors on thin card reprinted in 1881 for display at the International Cotton Exhibition in Atlanta, Ga. Blocks exist; they are very rare.

1847 Designs (Reproductions)

3TC4 5c Atlanta plate on card
a. **black** 300.
b. **scarlet** 300.
c. **brown** 300.
d. **green** 300.
e. **blue** 300.
4TC4 10c Atlanta plate on card
a. **black** 300.
b. **scarlet** 300.
c. **brown** 300.
d. **green** 300.
e. **blue** 300.

1851-60 Designs

40TC4 1c Atlanta plate on card
a. **black** 120.
b. **scarlet** 100.
c. **brown** 100.
d. **green** 100.
e. **blue** 100.
41TC4 3c Atlanta plate on card
a. **black** 120.
b. **scarlet** 100.
c. **brown** 100.
d. **green** 100.
e. **blue** 100.
42TC4 5c Atlanta plate on card
a. **black** 120.
b. **scarlet** 100.
c. **brown** 100.
d. **green** 100.
e. **blue** 100.
43TC4 10c Atlanta plate on card
a. **black** 120.
b. **scarlet** 100.
c. **brown** 100.
d. **green** 100.
e. **blue** 100.
44TC4 12c Atlanta plate on card
a. **black** 120.
b. **scarlet** 100.
c. **brown** 100.
d. **green** 100.
e. **blue** 100.
45TC4 24c Atlanta plate on card
a. **black** 120.
b. **scarlet** 100.
c. **brown** 100.
d. **green** 100.
e. **blue** 100.
46TC4 30c Atlanta plate on card
a. **black** 120.
b. **scarlet** 100.
c. **brown** 100.
d. **green** 100.
e. **blue** 100.
47TC4 90c Atlanta plate on card
a. **black** 120.
b. **scarlet** 100.
c. **brown** 100.
d. **green** 100.
e. **blue** 100.

1861-66 Designs

102TC4 1c Atlanta plate on card
a. **black** 100.
b. **scarlet** 90.
c. **brown** 90.
d. **green** 90.
e. **blue** 90.
103TC4 2c Atlanta plate on card
a. **black** 175.
b. **scarlet** 175.
c. **brown** 175.
d. **green** 175.
e. **blue** 175.
104TC4 3c Atlanta plate on card
a. **black** 100.
b. **scarlet** 90.
c. **brown** 90.
d. **green** 90.
e. **blue** 90.
105TC4 5c Atlanta plate on card
a. **black** 100.
b. **scarlet** 90.
c. **brown** 90.
d. **green** 90.
e. **blue** 90.
106TC4 10c Atlanta plate on card
a. **black** 100.
b. **scarlet** 90.
c. **brown** 90.
d. **green** 90.
e. **blue** 90.
107TC4 12c Atlanta plate on card
a. **black** 100.
b. **scarlet** 90.
c. **brown** 90.
d. **green** 90.
e. **blue** 90.
108TC4 15c Atlanta plate on card
a. **black** 100.
b. **scarlet** 90.
c. **brown** 90.
d. **green** 90.
e. **blue** 90.
109TC4 24c Atlanta plate on card
a. **black** 100.
b. **scarlet** 90.
c. **brown** 90.
d. **green** 90.
e. **blue** 90.
110TC4 30c Atlanta plate on card
a. **black** 100.
b. **scarlet** 90.
c. **brown** 90.
d. **green** 90.
e. **blue** 90.
111TC4 90c Atlanta plate on card
a. **black** 100.
b. **scarlet** 90.
c. **brown** 90.
d. **green** 90.
e. **blue** 90.

1869 Designs

123TC4 1c Atlanta plate on card
a. **black** 175.
b. **scarlet** 150.
c. **brown** 150.
d. **green** 150.
e. **blue** 150.
124TC4 2c Atlanta plate on card
a. **black** 175.
b. **scarlet** 150.
c. **brown** 150.
d. **green** 150.
e. **blue** 150.
125TC4 3c Atlanta plate on card
a. **black** 175.
b. **scarlet** 150.
c. **brown** 150.
d. **green** 150.
e. **blue** 150.
126TC4 6c Atlanta plate on card
a. **black** 175.
b. **scarlet** 150.
c. **brown** 150.
d. **green** 150.
e. **blue** 150.
127TC4 10c Atlanta plate on card
a. **black** 175.
b. **scarlet** 150.
c. **brown** 150.
d. **green** 150.
e. **blue** 150.
128TC4 12c Atlanta plate on card
a. **black** 175.
b. **scarlet** 150.
c. **brown** 150.
d. **green** 150.
e. **blue** 150.
129TC4 15c Atlanta plate on card
a. **black frame, scarlet center** 375.
b. **black frame, green center** 375.
c. **scarlet frame, black center** 375.
d. **scarlet frame, blue center** 375.
e. **brown frame, black center** 375.
f. **brown frame, green center** 375.
g. **brown frame, blue center** 375.
h. **green frame, black center** 375.
i. **green frame, blue center** 375.
j. **blue frame, black center** 375.
k. **blue frame, brown center** 375.
l. **blue frame, green center** 375.
130TC4 24c Atlanta plate on card
a. **black frame, scarlet center** 375.
b. **black frame, green center** 375.
c. **black frame, blue center** 375.
d. **scarlet frame, black center** 375.

e. scarlet frame, blue center 375.
f. brown frame, black center 375.
g. brown frame, blue center 375.
h. green frame, black center 375.
i. green frame, brown center 375.
j. green frame, blue center 375.
k. blue frame, brown center 375.
l. blue frame, green center 375.
131TC4 30c Atlanta plate on card
a. black frame, scarlet center 375.
b. black frame, green center 375.
c. black frame, blue center 375.
d. scarlet frame, black center 375.
e. scarlet frame, green center 375.
f. scarlet frame, blue center 375.
g. brown frame, black center 375.
h. brown frame, scarlet center 375.
i. brown frame, blue center 375.
j. green frame, black center 375.
k. green frame, brown center 375.
l. blue frame, scarlet center 375.
m. blue frame, brown center 375.
n. blue frame, green center 375.
132TC4 90c Atlanta plate on card
a. black frame, scarlet center 550.
b. black frame, brown center 550.
c. black frame, green center 550.
d. scarlet frame, blue center 550.
e. brown frame, black center 550.
f. brown frame, blue center 550.
g. green frame, black center *10,000.*
h. green frame, brown center 550.
i. green frame, blue center 550.
j. blue frame, brown center 550.
k. blue frame, green center 550.

1873-75 Designs

156TC4 1c Atlanta plate on card
a. black 55.
b. scarlet 50.
c. brown 50.
d. green 50.
e. blue 50.
157TC4 2c Atlanta plate on card
a. black 55.
b. scarlet 50.
c. brown 50.
d. green 50.
e. blue 50.
158TC4 3c Atlanta plate on card
a. black 60.
b. scarlet 55.
c. brown 55.
d. green 55.
e. blue 55.
159TC4 6c Atlanta plate on card
a. black 65.
b. scarlet 60.
c. brown 60.
d. green 60.
e. blue 60.
160TC4 7c Atlanta plate on card
a. black 55.
b. scarlet 50.
c. brown 50.
d. green 50.
e. blue 50.
161TC4 10c Atlanta plate on card
a. black 55.
b. scarlet 50.
c. brown 50.
d. green 50.
e. blue 50.
162TC4 12c Atlanta plate on card
a. black 55.
b. scarlet 50.
c. brown 50.
d. green 50.
e. blue 50.
163TC4 15c Atlanta plate on card
a. black 55.
b. scarlet 50.
c. brown 50.
d. green 50.
e. blue 50.
164TC4 24c Atlanta plate on card
a. black 55.
b. scarlet 50.
c. brown 50.
d. green 50.
e. blue 50.
165TC4 30c Atlanta plate on card
a. black 60.
b. scarlet 55.
c. brown 55.
d. green 55.
e. blue 55.
166TC4 90c Atlanta plate on card
a. black 55.
b. scarlet 50.
c. brown 50.
d. green 50.
e. blue 50.
179TC4 5c Atlanta plate on card
a. black 80.
b. scarlet 75.
c. brown 75.
d. green 75.
e. blue 75.

POSTAGE DUE

J1TC4 1c Atlanta plate on card
a. black 55.
b. scarlet 50.
c. brown 50.
d. green 50.
e. blue 50.
J2TC4 2c Atlanta plate on card
a. black 55.
b. scarlet 50.
c. brown 50.
d. green 50.
e. blue 50.
J3TC4 3c Atlanta plate on card
a. black 55.
b. scarlet 50.
c. brown 50.
d. green 50.
e. blue 50.
J4TC4 5c Atlanta plate on card
a. black 55.
b. scarlet 50.
c. brown 50.
d. green 50.
e. blue 50.
J5TC4 10c Atlanta plate on card
a. black 55.
b. scarlet 50.
c. brown 50.
d. green 50.
e. blue 50.
J6TC4 30c Atlanta plate on card
a. black 55.
b. scarlet 50.
c. brown 50.
d. green 50.
e. blue 50.
J7TC4 50c Atlanta plate on card
a. black 55.
b. scarlet 50.
c. brown 50.
d. green 50.
e. blue 50.

OFFICIALS

Agriculture

O1TC4 1c Atlanta plate on card
a. black 43.
b. scarlet 37.
c. brown 37.
d. green 37.
e. blue 37.
O2TC4 2c Atlanta plate on card
a. black 43.
b. scarlet 37.
c. brown 37.
d. green 37.
e. blue 37.
O3TC4 3c Atlanta plate on card
a. black 43.
b. scarlet 37.
c. brown 37.
d. green 37.
e. blue 37.
O4TC4 6c Atlanta plate on card
a. black 55.
b. scarlet 50.
c. brown 50.
d. green 50.
e. blue 50.
O5TC4 10c Atlanta plate on card
a. black 43.
b. scarlet 37.
c. brown 37.
d. green 37.
e. blue 37.
O6TC4 12c Atlanta plate on card
a. black 43.
b. scarlet 37.
c. brown 37.
d. green 37.
e. blue 37.
O7TC4 15c Atlanta plate on card
a. black 43.
b. scarlet 37.
c. brown 37.
d. green 37.
e. blue 37.
O8TC4 24c Atlanta plate on card
a. black 43.
b. scarlet 37.
c. brown 37.
d. green 37.
e. blue 37.
O9TC4 30c Atlanta plate on card
a. black 43.
b. scarlet 37.
c. brown 37.
d. green 37.
e. blue 37.

Executive

O10TC4 1c Atlanta plate on card
a. black 43.
b. scarlet 37.
c. brown 37.
d. green 37.
e. blue 37.
O11TC4 2c Atlanta plate on card
a. black 43.
b. scarlet 37.
c. brown 37.
d. green 37.
e. blue 37.
O12TC4 3c Atlanta plate on card
a. black 43.
b. scarlet 37.
c. brown 37.
d. green 37.
e. blue 37.
O13TC4 6c Atlanta plate on card
a. black 43.
b. scarlet 37.
c. brown 37.
d. green 37.
e. blue 37.
O14TC4 10c Atlanta plate on card
a. black 43.
b. scarlet 37.
c. brown 37.
d. green 37.
e. blue 37.

Interior

O15TC4 1c Atlanta plate on card
a. black 43.
b. scarlet 37.
c. brown 37.
d. green 37.
e. blue 37.
O16TC4 2c Atlanta plate on card
a. black 43.
b. scarlet 37.
c. brown 37.
d. green 37.
e. blue 37.
O17TC4 3c Atlanta plate on card
a. black 43.
b. scarlet 37.
c. brown 37.
d. green 37.
e. blue 37.
O18TC4 6c Atlanta plate on card
a. black 55.
b. scarlet 50.
c. brown 50.
d. green 50.
e. blue 50.
O19TC4 10c Atlanta plate on card
a. black 43.
b. scarlet 37.
c. brown 37.
d. green 37.
e. blue 37.
O20TC4 12c Atlanta plate on card
a. black 43.
b. scarlet 37.
c. brown 37.
d. green 37.
e. blue 37.
O21TC4 15c Atlanta plate on card
a. black 43.
b. scarlet 37.
c. brown 37.
d. green 37.
e. blue 37.
O22TC4 24c Atlanta plate on card
a. black 43.
b. scarlet 37.
c. brown 37.
d. green 37.
e. blue 37.
O23TC4 30c Atlanta plate on card
a. black 60.
b. scarlet 55.
c. brown 55.
d. green 55.
e. blue 55.
O24TC4 90c Atlanta plate on card
a. black 43.
b. scarlet 37.
c. brown 37.
d. green 37.
e. blue 37.

Justice

O25TC4 1c Atlanta plate on card
a. black 43.
b. scarlet 37.
c. brown 37.
d. green 37.
e. blue 37.
O26TC4 2c Atlanta plate on card
a. black 43.
b. scarlet 37.
c. brown 37.
d. green 37.
e. blue 37.
O27TC4 3c Atlanta plate on card
a. black 43.
b. scarlet 37.
c. brown 37.
d. green 37.
e. blue 37.
O28TC4 6c Atlanta plate on card
a. black 55.
b. scarlet 50.
c. brown 50.
d. green 50.
e. blue 50.
O29TC4 10c Atlanta plate on card
a. black 43.
b. scarlet 37.
c. brown 37.
d. green 37.
e. blue 37.
O30TC4 12c Atlanta plate on card
a. black 43.
b. scarlet 37.
c. brown 37.
d. green 37.
e. blue 37.
O31TC4 15c Atlanta plate on card
a. black 43.
b. scarlet 37.
c. brown 37.
d. green 37.
e. blue 37.
O32TC4 24c Atlanta plate on card
a. black 43.
b. scarlet 37.
c. brown 37.
d. green 37.
e. blue 37.

O33TC4 30c Atlanta plate on card
a. **black** 60.
b. **scarlet** 55.
c. **brown** 55.
d. **green** 55.
e. **blue** 55.
O34TC4 90c Atlanta plate on card
a. **black** 43.
b. **scarlet** 37.
c. **brown** 37.
d. **green** 37.
e. **blue** 37.

Navy

O35TC4 1c Atlanta plate on card
a. **black** 43.
b. **scarlet** 37.
c. **brown** 37.
d. **green** 37.
e. **blue** 37.
O36TC4 2c Atlanta plate on card
a. **black** 43.
b. **scarlet** 37.
c. **brown** 37.
d. **green** 37.
e. **blue** 37.
O37TC4 3c Atlanta plate on card
a. **black** 43.
b. **scarlet** 37.
c. **brown** 37.
d. **green** 37.
e. **blue** 37.
O38TC4 6c Atlanta plate on card
a. **black** 55.
b. **scarlet** 50.
c. **brown** 50.
d. **green** 50.
e. **blue** 50.
O39TC4 7c Atlanta plate on card
a. **black** 43.
b. **scarlet** 37.
c. **brown** 37.
d. **green** 37.
e. **blue** 37.
O40TC4 10c Atlanta plate on card
a. **black** 43.
b. **scarlet** 37.
c. **brown** 37.
d. **green** 37.
e. **blue** 37.
O41TC4 12c Atlanta plate on card
a. **black** 43.
b. **scarlet** 37.
c. **brown** 37.
d. **green** 37.
e. **blue** 37.
O42TC4 15c Atlanta plate on card
a. **black** 43.
b. **scarlet** 37.
c. **brown** 37.
d. **green** 37.
e. **blue** 37.
O43TC4 24c Atlanta plate on card
a. **black** 43.
b. **scarlet** 37.
c. **brown** 37.
d. **green** 37.
e. **blue** 37.
O44TC4 30c Atlanta plate on card
a. **black** 60.
b. **scarlet** 55.
c. **brown** 55.
d. **green** 55.
e. **blue** 55.
O45TC4 90c Atlanta plate on card
a. **black** 43.
b. **scarlet** 37.
c. **brown** 37.
d. **green** 37.
e. **blue** 37.

Post Office

O48TC4 2c Atlanta plate on card
a. **black** 43.
b. **scarlet** 37.
c. **brown** 37.
d. **green** 37.
e. **blue** 37.
O49TC4 3c Atlanta plate on card
a. **black** 43.
b. **scarlet** 37.
c. **brown** 37.
d. **green** 37.
e. **blue** 37.
O50TC4 6c Atlanta plate on card
a. **black** 43.
b. **scarlet** 37.
c. **brown** 37.
d. **green** 37.
e. **blue** 37.
O51TC4 10c Atlanta plate on card
a. **black** 43.
b. **scarlet** 37.
c. **brown** 37.
d. **green** 37.
e. **blue** 37.
O52TC4 12c Atlanta plate on card
a. **black** 43.
b. **scarlet** 37.
c. **brown** 37.
d. **green** 37.
e. **blue** 37.
O53TC4 15c Atlanta plate on card
a. **black** 43.
b. **scarlet** 37.
c. **brown** 37.
d. **green** 37.
e. **blue** 37.
O54TC4 24c Atlanta plate on card
a. **black** 43.
b. **scarlet** 37.
c. **brown** 37.
d. **green** 37.
e. **blue** 37.
O55TC4 30c Atlanta plate on card
a. **black** 43.
b. **scarlet** 37.
c. **brown** 37.
d. **green** 37.
e. **blue** 37.
O56TC4 90c Atlanta plate on card
a. **black** 43.
b. **scarlet** 37.
c. **brown** 37.
d. **green** 37.
e. **blue** 37.

State

O57TC4 1c Atlanta plate on card
a. **black** 43.
b. **scarlet** 37.
c. **brown** 37.
d. **green** 37.
e. **blue** 37.
O58TC4 2c Atlanta plate on card
a. **black** 43.
b. **scarlet** 37.
c. **brown** 37.
d. **green** 37.
e. **blue** 37.
O59TC4 3c Atlanta plate on card
a. **black** 43.
b. **scarlet** 37.
c. **brown** 37.
d. **green** 37.
e. **blue** 37.
O60TC4 6c Atlanta plate on card
a. **black** 55.
b. **scarlet** 50.
c. **brown** 50.
d. **green** 50.
e. **blue** 50.
O61TC4 7c Atlanta plate on card
a. **black** 43.
b. **scarlet** 37.
c. **brown** 37.
d. **green** 37.
e. **blue** 37.
O62TC4 10c Atlanta plate on card
a. **black** 43.
b. **scarlet** 37.
c. **brown** 37.
d. **green** 37.
e. **blue** 37.
O63TC4 12c Atlanta plate on card
a. **black** 43.
b. **scarlet** 37.
c. **brown** 37.
d. **green** 37.
e. **blue** 37.
O64TC4 15c Atlanta plate on card
a. **black** 43.
b. **scarlet** 37.
c. **brown** 37.
d. **green** 37.
e. **blue** 37.
O65TC4 24c Atlanta plate on card
a. **black** 43.
b. **scarlet** 37.
c. **brown** 37.
d. **green** 37.
e. **blue** 37.
O66TC4 30c Atlanta plate on card
a. **black** 60.
b. **scarlet** 55.
c. **brown** 55.
d. **green** 55.
e. **blue** 55.
O67TC4 90c Atlanta plate on card
a. **black** 43.
b. **scarlet** 37.
c. **brown** 37.
d. **green** 37.
e. **blue** 37.
O68TC4 $2 Atlanta plate on card
a. **scarlet frame, black center** 1,000.
b. **scarlet frame, blue center** 1,000.
c. **brown frame, black center** 1,000.
d. **brown frame, blue center** 1,000.
e. **green frame, brown center** 1,000.
f. **blue frame, brown center** 1,000.
g. **blue frame, green center** 1,000.
O69TC4 $5 Atlanta plate on card
a. **scarlet frame, black center** 1,000.
b. **scarlet frame, blue center** 1,000.
c. **brown frame, black center** 1,000.
d. **brown frame, blue center** 1,000.
e. **green frame, brown center** 1,000.
f. **blue frame, brown center** 1,000.
g. **blue frame, green center** 1,000.
O70TC4 $10 Atlanta plate on card
a. **scarlet frame, black center** 1,000.
b. **scarlet frame, blue center** 1,000.
c. **brown frame, black center** 1,000.
d. **brown frame, blue center** 1,000.
e. **green frame, brown center** 1,000.
f. **blue frame, brown center** 1,000.
g. **blue frame, green center** 1,000.
O71TC4 $20 Atlanta plate on card
a. **scarlet frame, black center** 1,000.
b. **scarlet frame, blue center** 1,000.
c. **brown frame, black center** 1,000.
d. **brown frame, blue center** 1,000.
e. **green frame, brown center** 1,000.
f. **blue frame, brown center** 1,000.
g. **blue frame, green center** 1,000.

Treasury

O72TC4 1c Atlanta plate on card
a. **black** 43.
b. **scarlet** 37.
c. **brown** 37.
d. **green** 37.
e. **blue** 37.
O73TC4 2c Atlanta plate on card
a. **black** 43.
b. **scarlet** 37.
c. **brown** 37.
d. **green** 37.
e. **blue** 37.
O74TC4 3c Atlanta plate on card
a. **black** 43.
b. **scarlet** 37.
c. **brown** 37.
d. **green** 37.
e. **blue** 37.
O75TC4 6c Atlanta plate on card
a. **black** 55.
b. **scarlet** 50.
c. **brown** 50.
d. **green** 50.
e. **blue** 50.
O76TC4 7c Atlanta plate on card
a. **black** 43.
b. **scarlet** 37.
c. **brown** 37.
d. **green** 37.
e. **blue** 37.
O77TC4 10c Atlanta plate on card
a. **black** 43.
b. **scarlet** 37.
c. **brown** 37.
d. **green** 37.
e. **blue** 37.
O78TC4 12c Atlanta plate on card
a. **black** 43.
b. **scarlet** 37.
c. **brown** 37.
d. **green** 37.
e. **blue** 37.
O79TC4 15c Atlanta plate on card
a. **black** 43.
b. **scarlet** 37.
c. **brown** 37.
d. **green** 37.
e. **blue** 37.
O80TC4 24c Atlanta plate on card
a. **black** 43.
b. **scarlet** 37.
c. **brown** 37.
d. **green** 37.
e. **blue** 37.
O81TC4 30c Atlanta plate on card
a. **black** 60.
b. **scarlet** 55.
c. **brown** 55.
d. **green** 55.
e. **blue** 55.
O82TC4 90c Atlanta plate on card
a. **black** 43.
b. **scarlet** 37.
c. **brown** 37.
d. **green** 37.
e. **blue** 37.

War

O83TC4 1c Atlanta plate on card
a. **black** 43.
b. **scarlet** 37.
c. **brown** 37.
d. **green** 37.
e. **blue** 37.
O84TC4 2c Atlanta plate on card
a. **black** 43.
b. **scarlet** 37.
c. **brown** 37.
d. **green** 37.
e. **blue** 37.
O85TC4 3c Atlanta plate on card
a. **black** 43.
b. **scarlet** 37.
c. **brown** 37.
Plate flaw at upper left (32R20) —
d. **green** 37.
e. **blue** 37.
O86TC4 6c Atlanta plate on card
a. **black** 55.
b. **scarlet** 50.
c. **brown** 50.
d. **green** 50.
e. **blue** 50.
O87TC4 7c Atlanta plate on card
a. **black** 43.
b. **scarlet** 37.
c. **brown** 37.
d. **green** 37.
e. **blue** 37.
O88TC4 10c Atlanta plate on card
a. **black** 43.
b. **scarlet** 37.
c. **brown** 37.
d. **green** 37.
e. **blue** 37.
O89TC4 12c Atlanta plate on card
a. **black** 43.
b. **scarlet** 37.
c. **brown** 37.
d. **green** 37.
e. **blue** 37.
O90TC4 15c Atlanta plate on card
a. **black** 43.
b. **scarlet** 37.
c. **brown** 37.

d. **green** 37.
e. **blue** 37.
O91TC4 24c Atlanta plate on card
a. **black** 43.
b. **scarlet** 37.
c. **brown** 37.
d. **green** 37.
e. **blue** 37.
O92TC4 30c Atlanta plate on card
a. **black** 60.
b. **scarlet** 55.
c. **brown** 55.
d. **green** 55.
e. **blue** 55.
O93TC4 90c Atlanta plate on card
a. **black** 43.
b. **scarlet** 37.
c. **brown** 37.
d. **green** 37.
e. **blue** 37.

NEWSPAPERS

PR9TC4 2c Atlanta plate on card
a. **black** 55.
b. **scarlet** 40.
c. **brown** 40.
d. **green** 40.
e. **blue** 40.
PR10TC4 3c Atlanta plate on card
a. **black** 55.
b. **scarlet** 40.
c. **brown** 40.
d. **green** 40.
e. **blue** 40.
PR11TC4 4c Atlanta plate on card
a. **black** 55.
b. **scarlet** 40.
c. **brown** 40.
d. **green** 40.
e. **blue** 40.
PR12TC4 6c Atlanta plate on card
a. **black** 55.
b. **scarlet** 40.
c. **brown** 40.
d. **green** 40.
e. **blue** 40.
PR13TC4 8c Atlanta plate on card
a. **black** 55.
b. **scarlet** 40.
c. **brown** 40.
d. **green** 40.
e. **blue** 40.
PR14TC4 9c Atlanta plate on card
a. **black** 55.
b. **scarlet** 40.
c. **brown** 40.
d. **green** 40.
e. **blue** 40.
PR15TC4 10c Atlanta plate on card
a. **black** 55.
b. **scarlet** 40.
c. **brown** 40.
d. **green** 40.
e. **blue** 40.
PR16TC4 12c Atlanta plate on card
a. **black** 55.
b. **scarlet** 40.
c. **brown** 40.
d. **green** 40.
e. **blue** 40.
PR17TC4 24c Atlanta plate on card
a. **black** 55.
b. **scarlet** 40.
c. **brown** 40.
d. **green** 40.
e. **blue** 40.
PR18TC4 36c Atlanta plate on card
a. **black** 55.
b. **scarlet** 40.
c. **brown** 40.
d. **green** 40.
e. **blue** 40.
PR19TC4 48c Atlanta plate on card
a. **black** 55.
b. **scarlet** 40.
c. **brown** 40.
d. **green** 40.
e. **blue** 40.
PR20TC4 60c Atlanta plate on card
a. **black** 55.
b. **scarlet** 40.
c. **brown** 40.
d. **green** 40.
e. **blue** 40.
PR21TC4 72c Atlanta plate on card
a. **black** 55.
b. **scarlet** 40.
c. **brown** 40.
d. **green** 40.
e. **blue** 40.
PR22TC4 84c Atlanta plate on card
a. **black** 55.
b. **scarlet** 40.
c. **brown** 40.
d. **green** 40.
e. **blue** 40.
PR23TC4 96c Atlanta plate on card
a. **black** 55.
b. **scarlet** 40.
c. **brown** 40.
d. **green** 40.
e. **blue** 40.
PR24TC4 $1.92 Atlanta plate on card
a. **black** 55.
b. **scarlet** 40.
c. **brown** 40.
d. **green** 40.
e. **blue** 40.
PR25TC4 $3 Atlanta plate on card
a. **black** 55.
b. **scarlet** 40.
c. **brown** 40.
d. **green** 40.
e. **blue** 40.
PR26TC4 $6 Atlanta plate on card
a. **black** 55.
b. **scarlet** 40.
c. **brown** 40.
d. **green** 40.
e. **blue** 40.
PR27TC4 $9 Atlanta plate on card
a. **black** 55.
b. **scarlet** 40.
c. **brown** 40.
d. **green** 40.
e. **blue** 40.
PR28TC4 $12 Atlanta plate on card
a. **black** 55.
b. **scarlet** 40.
c. **brown** 40.
d. **green** 40.
e. **blue** 40.
PR29TC4 $24 Atlanta plate on card
a. **black** 55.
b. **scarlet** 40.
c. **brown** 40.
d. **green** 40.
e. **blue** 40.
PR30TC4 $36 Atlanta plate on card
a. **black** 55.
b. **scarlet** 40.
c. **brown** 40.
d. **green** 40.
e. **blue** 40.
PR31TC4 $48 Atlanta plate on card
a. **black** 55.
b. **scarlet** 40.
c. **brown** 40.
d. **green** 40.
e. **blue** 40.
PR32TC4 $60 Atlanta plate on card
a. **black** 55.
b. **scarlet** 40.
c. **brown** 40.
d. **green** 40.
e. **blue** 40.

CARRIERS

LO1TC4 1c Franklin, Atlanta plate on card
a. **black** 120.
b. **scarlet** 110.
c. **brown** 110.
d. **green** 110.
e. **blue** 110.
LO2TC4 1c Eagle, Atlanta plate on card
a. **black** 120.
b. **scarlet** 110.
c. **brown** 110.
d. **green** 110.
e. **blue** 110.

TELEGRAPH

1881 American Rapid Telegraph Co.

1T1TC2 1c small die on India paper
b. **green** 55.
c. **brown** 55.
d. **red** 55.
e. **blue** 55.
f. **bluish green** 55.
1T1P2 1c **blk,** sm die on India paper 80.
1T1P3 1c **blk,** plate on India paper 32.
Pair 68.
1T2P3 3c **org,** plate on India paper 32.
Pair 68.
1T3TC2 5c small die on India paper
b. **green** 55.
c. **black** 55.
d. **red** 55.
e. **blue** 55.
f. **bluish green** 55.
1T3P2 5c **bis brn,** sm die on India paper 80.
1T3P3 5c **bis brn,** plate on India paper 32.
Pair 68.
1T4P1 10c **pur,** large die on India paper *850.*
1T4P3 10c **pur,** plate on India paper 32.
Pair 68.
1T5TC2 15c small die on India paper
b. **red** 55.
c. **black** 55.
d. **brown** 55.
e. **bluish green** 55.
1T5P2 15c **grn,** sm die on India paper 80.
1T5P3 15c **grn,** plate on India paper 32.
Pair 68.
1T6TC2 20c small die on India paper
b. **green** 55.
c. **black** 55.
d. **brown** 55.
e. **blue** 55.
f. **bluish green** 55.
1T6P2 20c **red,** sm die on India paper 80.
1T6P3 20c **red,** plate on India paper 32.
Pair 68.
1T7P2 25c **rose,** sm die on India paper 80.
1T7P3 25c **rose,** plate on India paper 32.
Pair 68.
1T8P3 50c **bl,** plate on India paper 32.
Pair 68.

"Collect"

1T9P3 1c **brn,** plate on India paper 32.
1T10TC2 5c small die on India paper
b. **red** 55.
c. **black** 55.
d. **brown** 55.
e. **green** 55.
f. **bluish green** 55.
1T10P3 5c **bl,** plate on India paper 32.
1T11TC2 15c small die on India paper
b. **red** 55.
c. **black** 55.
d. **brown** 55.
e. **green** 55.
f. **blue** 55.
g. **bluish green** 55.
1T11P3 15c **red brn,** plate on India paper 32.
1T12P1 20c **ol grn,** large die on India paper *850.*
1T12P3 20c **ol grn,** plate on India paper 32.

Office Coupon

1T13P3 1c **brn,** plate on India paper 32.
a. Pair Nos. 1T9P3, 1T13P3 68.
Same, block of 4 145.
1T14TC2 5c small die on India paper
b. **red** 55.
c. **black** 55.
d. **brown** 55.
e. **green** 55.
f. **bluish green** 55.
1T14P3 5c **bl,** plate on India paper 32.
a. Pair Nos. 1T10P3, 1T14P3 68.
Same, block of 4 145.
1T15TC2 15c small die on India paper
b. **red** 55.
c. **black** 55.
d. **brown** 55.
e. **green** 55.
f. **blue** 55.
g. **bluish green** 55.
1T15P3 15c **red brn,** plate on India paper 32.
a. Pair Nos. 1T11P3, 1T15P3 68.
Same, block of 4 145.
1T16P1 20c **ol grn,** large die on India paper *850.*
1T16P3 20c **ol grn,** plate on India paper 32.
a. Pair Nos. 1T12P3, 1T16P3 68.
Same, block of 4 145.

1885 Baltimore & Ohio Telegraph Co.

3T1P3 1c **ver,** plate on India paper 32.
Pair 68.
3T2TC2 5c small die on India paper
b. **dark olive** 65.
3T2P3 5c **bl,** plate on India paper 32.
Pair 68.
3T3P1 10c **red brn,** large die on India paper *900.*
3T3P3 10c **red brn,** plate on India paper 32.
Pair 68.
3T4TC2 25c small die on India paper
b. **dark olive** 65.
3T4P3 25c **org,** plate on India paper 32.
Pair 68.

1886

3T6P3 **blk,** plate on India paper 32.
Pair 68.
3T7P3 1c **grn,** plate on India paper 32.
3T8P3 5c **bl,** plate on India paper 32.
3T9P3 10c **brn,** plate on India paper 32.
3T10P3 25c **org,** plate on India paper 32.

1894-95 Northern New York Telegraph Co.

12T1P4 **green,** plate on card 125.
12T2P4 **red,** plate on card 125.
12T3P4 1c **yellow,** plate on card 40.
12T4P4 10c **blue,** plate on card 40.

1885 Postal Telegraph Co.

15T1TC1a 10c large die on India paper
e. **red** 65.
f. **blue** 65.
g. **black** 65.
15T1TC2 10c small die on India paper
b. **brown red** 65.
15T1TC3 10c plate on India paper
a. **orange** 65.
15T1P2 10c **grn,** sm die on India paper 55.
15T1P3 10c **grn,** plate on India paper 32.
15T2TC1a 15c large die on India paper
e. **red** 65.
f. **blue** 65.
g. **black** 65.
15T2TC2 15c small die on India paper
b. **red** 55.
c. **blue** 55.
15T2TC3 15c plate on India paper
a. **black** 55.
15T2P3 15c **org red,** plate on India paper 32.
15T3TC1a 25c large die on India paper
e. **red** 65.
f. **black** 65.
15T3TC2 25c small die on India paper
b. **brown red** 65.
c. **brown** 55.
15T3TC3 25c plate on India paper
a. **ultramarine** 40.
b. **brown** 40.
15T3P1 25c **bl,** large die on India paper 65.
15T3P3 25c **bl,** plate on India paper 32.
15T4TC1a 50c large die on India paper
e. **red** 65.
f. **blue** 65.
g. **black** 65.
15T4TC2 50c small die on India paper
b. **dull blue** 65.
15T4TC3 50c plate on India paper
a. **black** 40.
15T4P2 50c **brn,** sm die on India paper 65.
15T4P3 50c **brn,** plate on India paper 32.
15T6TC3 plate on India paper
a. **red brown** 40.

Western Union Telegraph Co.

16T1TC3 (1871) plate on India paper
a. **lilac** 20.
Pair 45.
b. **orange** 20.
Pair 45.
c. **black** 20.
Pair 45.
16T1TC4 (1871) plate on card
a. **lilac** 20.
Pair 45.
b. **orange** 20.
Pair 45.
c. **black** 20.
Pair 45.
d. **violet brown** 20.
Pair 45.
e. **light olive** 20.
Pair 45.
f. **brown** 20.
Pair 45.
g. **orange brown** 20.
Pair 45.
h. **blue green** 20.
Pair 45.
16T1P3 (1871) **brn,** plate on India paper 17.
Pair 35.
16T2P3 (1872) **red,** plate on India paper 17.
Pair 35.
16T3P3 (1873) **bl,** plate on India paper 17.
Pair 35.
16T4P3 (1874) **brn,** plate on India paper 17.
Pair 35.
16T5P3 (1875) **dp grn,** plate on India paper 17.
16T6TC3 (1876) plate on India paper
a. **violet blue** 20.
16T6TC4 (1876) plate on card
a. **violet blue** 20.
16T6P3 (1876) **red,** plate on India paper 17.
16T7TC4 (1877) plate on card
a. **orange yellow** 20.
Pair 45.
b. **dark brown** 20.
Pair 45.
c. **black** 20.
Pane of 4 —
16T7P3 (1877) **vio,** plate on India paper —
16T8TC4 (1878) plate on card
a. **dark brown** —
16T8P3 (1878) **gray brn,** plate on India paper 20.
16T9TC4 (1879) plate on card
a. **blue** —
16T9P3 (1879) **bl,** plate on India paper 14.
16T10TC4 (1880) plate on card
a. **violet brown** —
b. **rose** —
16T10P3 (1880) **lil rose,** plate on India paper 16.
16T11P3 (1881) **grn,** plate on India paper 16.
16T12TC3 (1882) plate on India paper
a. **green** —
16T12P3 (1882) **bl,** plate on India paper 20.
16T13P3 (1883) **yel brn,** plate on India paper 16.
16T14P1 (1884) **gray vio,** large die on India paper 250.
16T14P3 (1884) **gray vio,** plate on India paper 20.
16T15P3 (1885) **grn,** plate on India paper 20.
16T16P3 (1886) **brn vio,** plate on India paper 13.
Pair 28.
16T17P3 (1887) **red brn,** plate on India paper 13.
Pair 28.
16T18P3 (1888) **bl,** plate on India paper 13.
Pair 28.
16T19P3 (1889) **ol grn,** plate on India paper 16.
16T22TC4 (1892) plate on card
a. **black** —
16T22P3 (1892) **ver,** plate on India paper 16.
16T30P3 (1900) **red vio,** plate on India paper 28.
16T44TC1a large die on India paper
e. **deep rose** —
f. **carmine lake** —
g. **rose lake** —
h. **deep ultramarine** —
16T44TC1d Large die printed directly on card
e. **dull red** —
f. **orange** —
g. **rose red** —
h. **orange brown** —
i. **ocher** —
j. **dark blue** —
k. **dark ultramarine** —
l. **green** —
m. **brown lake** —
n. **reddish brown** —
o. **sepia** —
p. **sepia,** unsurfaced card —
q. **dull violet** —
r. **slate green** —
s. **slate blue** —
t. **black** —
u. **black,** unsurfaced card —
16T44TC3 Plate on India paper, sheet of 16
a. **deep rose** —
b. **orange** —
c. **dark blue** —
d. **slate green** —
e. **rose lake** —
16T44TC5 Plate on bond paper, sheet of 16
a. **deep rose** —
b. **orange** —
c. **dark blue** —
d. **slate green** —
e. **rose lake** —
f. **sepia** —
16T44P1 (1913) **brn,** large die on India paper —
16T44P2 (1913) **brn,** sm die on India paper —
16T44P3 (1913) **brn,** plate on India paper —
16T99P5 1c **yel grn,** plate on bond 100.
16T100P5 2c **chestnut,** plate on bond 100.
16T101P5 5c **dp bl,** plate on bond 100.
16T102P5 10c **org,** plate on bond 100.
16T103P5 25c **brt car,** plate on bond 100.

REVENUE

1862-68 by Butler & Carpenter, Philadelphia.
1868-75 by Joseph R. Carpenter, Philadelphia.

Several lists of revenue proofs in trial colors have been published, but the accuracy of some of them is questionable. The following listings are limited to items seen by the editors. The list is not complete.

In the following listing the so-called small die proofs on India paper may be, in fact probably are, plate proofs. The editors shall consider them die proofs, however, until they see them in pairs or blocks. Many revenue proofs on India are mounted on card.

First Issue

1862-71

R1P3 1c Express, **red,** plate on India paper 70.
R1P4 1c Express, **red,** plate on card 65.
Block of 4 275.
R2P1 1c Playing Cards, **red,** large die on India paper 600.
R2P3 1c Playing Cards, **red,** plate on India paper 60.
Block of 4 250.
R2P4 1c Playing Cards, **red,** plate on card 65.
Block of 4 275.
R3TC1a 1c **Proprietary,** die on India paper
e. **black** *950.*
R3TC3 1c **Proprietary,** plate on India paper
a. **black** 80.
R3TC4 1c **Proprietary,** plate on card
a. **carmine** 80.
R3TC5 1c **Proprietary,** plate on bond paper
a. **dull red** 125.
b. **orange red** 125.
c. **dull yellow** 125.
d. **violet rose** 125.
e. **deep blue** 125.
f. **red,** *blue* 125.
g. **blue,** perf. & gum 125.
R3TC5 1c **Proprietary,** plate on wove paper
h. **green,** *buff* —
R3P3 1c Proprietary, **red,** plate on India paper 140.
R3P4 1c Proprietary, **red,** plate on card 45.
Block of 4 200.
R4P4 1c Telegraph, **red,** plate on card 28.
Block of 4 125.
R5P2 2c Bank Check, **bl,** sm die on India paper 525.
R5P4 2c Bank Check, **bl,** plate on card 33.
Block of 4 140.
R6P3 2c Bank Check, **org,** plate on India paper 60.
Block of 4 250.
R7TC4 2c **Certificate,** plate on card
a. **ultramarine** 65.
R7P4 2c Certificate, **bl,** plate on card 28.
Block of 4 125.
R8P3 2c Certificate, **org,** plate on India paper 82.
Block of 4 350.
R9P4 2c Express, **bl,** plate on card 28.
Block of 4 125.
R10P1 2c Express, **org,** large die on India paper 600.
R10P3 2c Express, **org,** plate on India paper 60.
Block of 4 250.
R11TC1a 2c **Playing Cards,** die on India paper
e. **black** 500.
R11P4 2c Playing Cards, **bl,** plate on card 38.
Block of 4 160.
R13TC1a 2c **Proprietary,** die on India paper
e. **black** 650.
f. **carmine** 650.
R13TC3 2c **Proprietary,** plate on India paper
a. **black** 75.
R13P2 2c Proprietary, **bl,** sm die on India paper 400.
R13P4 2c Proprietary, **bl,** plate on card 28.
Block of 4 125.
R15TC3 2c **U.S.I.R.,** plate on India paper
a. **black** 110.
R15TC5 2c **U.S.I.R.,** plate on bond paper
a. **violet rose** 110.
b. **light green** 110.
c. **pale blue** 110.
d. **pale rose** 200.
e. **orange,** *blue* —
f. **pale orange,** perf. & gum 110.
R15P3 2c U.S.I.R., **org,** plate on India paper *1,250.*
R16TC5 3c **Foreign Exchange,** plate on bond paper
a. **green,** *blue* 140.
R16TC7 3c **Foreign Exchange,** plate on goldbeater's skin
a. **blue** 110.
R16P1 3c Foreign Exchange, **grn,** large die on India paper 600.
a. R16P1 + R19P1 composite —
R16P3 3c Foreign Exchange, **grn,** plate on India paper 225.
R16P4 3c Foreign Exchange, **grn,** plate on card 38.
Block of 4 160.
R17P1 3c Playing Cards, **grn,** large die on India paper 700.
R17P2 3c Playing Cards, **grn,** sm die on India paper 400.
R17P4 3c Playing Cards, **grn,** plate on card 100.
Block of 4 425.
R18TC1a 3c **Proprietary,** die on India paper
e. **black** 300.
R18P3 3c Proprietary, **grn,** plate on India paper 60.
Block of 4 250.
R18P4 3c Proprietary, **grn,** plate on card 28.
Block of 4 125.
R19P1 3c Telegraph, **grn,** large die on India paper 600.
R19P3 3c Telegraph, **grn,** plate on India paper 225.
R19P4 3c Telegraph, **grn,** plate on card 28.
Block of 4 125.
R20P3 4c Inland Exchange, **brn,** plate on India paper 225.
R20P4 4c Inland Exchange, **brn,** plate on card 28.
Block of 4 125.
R21TC1a 4c **Playing Cards,** die (?) on India paper
e. **black** 300.
R21P2 4c Playing Cards, **vio,** sm die on India paper 400.
R21P4 4c Playing Cards, **vio,** plate on card 95.
Block of 4 400.
R22TC1a 4c **Proprietary,** die on India paper
e. **black** 350.
f. **deep red lilac** 400.
R22TC3 4c **Proprietary,** plate on India paper
a. **black** 110.
R22TC4 4c **Proprietary,** plate on card
a. **red lilac** 110.
R22P1 4c Proprietary, **vio,** large die on India paper 600.
R22P3 4c Proprietary, **vio,** plate on India paper 110.
Block of 4 475.
R22P4 4c Proprietary, **vio,** plate on card 60.
Block of 4 250.
R23P4 5c Agreement, **red,** plate on card 33.
Block of 4 140.
R24TC3 5c **Certificate,** plate on India paper
a. **carmine** 110.
R24P1a 5c R24P1 + R25P1 composite, large die on India paper —
R24P3 5c Certificate, **red,** plate on India paper 95.
Block of 4 400.
R24P4 5c Certificate, **red,** plate on card 110.
R25TC6 5c **Express,** plate on wove paper
a. **pale olive** —
R25P2 5c Express, **red,** sm die on India paper 250.
R25P4 5c Express, **red,** plate on card 33.
Block of 4 145.
R26TC3 5c **Foreign Exchange,** plate on India paper
a. **orange** 110.
R26P4 5c Foreign Exchange, **red,** plate on card 300.
R27P2 5c Inland Exchange, **red,** sm die on India paper 250.
R27P4 5c Inland Exchange, **red,** plate on card 28.
Block of 4 125.
R28TC1a 5c **Playing Cards,** die (?) on India paper
e. **black** 300.
R28P2 5c Playing Cards, **red,** sm die on India paper —
R28P3 5c Playing Cards, **red,** plate on India paper 105.
Block of 4 440.
R28P4 5c Playing Cards, **red,** plate on card 325.
R29TC5 5c **Proprietary,** plate on bond paper
a. **red,** *blue* —
R29P5 5c Proprietary, **red,** plate on blue wove, gummed —
R30TC1a 6c **Inland Exchange,** die on India paper
e. **black** 350.
R30P3 6c Inland Exchange, **org,** plate on India paper 60.
Block of 4 250.
R30P4 6c Inland Exchange, **org,** plate on card 33.
Block of 4 140.
R31TC1a 6c **Proprietary,** die on India paper
e. **black** —
R32TC1a 10c **Bill of Lading,** die on India paper
e. **greenish blue** 350.
f. **dark green,** R32TC1a+R37TC1a composite —
R32P4 10c Bill of Lading, **bl,** plate on card 33.
Block of 4 140.
R33P3 10c Certificate, **bl,** plate on India paper 140.
R33P4 10c Certificate, **bl,** plate on card 33.
Block of 4 140.
R34P4 10c Contract, **bl,** plate on card 33.
Block of 4 140.
R35TC1a 10c **Foreign Exchange,** die (?) on India paper
e. **black** 350.
R35P4 10c Foreign Exchange, **bl,** plate on card 33.
Block of 4 140.
R36P4 10c Inland Exchange, **bl,** plate on card 33.
Block of 4 140.
R37TC1a 10c **Power of Attorney,** die on India paper
e. **greenish blue** 350.
R37P4 10c Power of Attorney, **bl,** plate on card 33.
Block of 4 140.
R38TC1a 10c **Proprietary,** die on India paper
e. **black** 350.
R38P1 10c Proprietary, **bl,** large die on India paper *700.*
R38P3 10c Proprietary, **bl,** plate on India paper 70.
Block of 4 300.
R39P3 15c Foreign Exchange, **brn,** plate on India paper 90.
Block of 4 375.
R39P4 15c Foreign Exchange, **brn,** plate on card 325.
Block of 4 1,600.
R40P3 15c Inland Exchange, **brn,** plate on India paper 120.
R40P4 15c Inland Exchange, **brn,** plate on card 33.
Block of 4 140.
R41P1 20c Foreign Exchange, **red,** large die on India paper 600.
a. R41P1 + R42P1 composite —
R41P3 20c Foreign Exchange, **red,** plate on India paper 90.
Block of 4 375.
R41P4 20c Foreign Exchange, **red,** plate on card 100.
Block of 4 425.
R42P1 20c Inland Exchange, **red,** large die on India paper 600.
R42P2 20c Inland Exchange, **red,** sm die on India paper 250.

R42P3	20c Inland Exchange, **red,** plate on India paper	260.
R42P4	20c Inland Exchange, **red,** plate on card	33.
	Block of 4	140.
R43TC4	25c **Bond,** plate on card	
	***a.* carmine**	90.
R43P4	25c Bond, **red,** plate on card	500.
	Block of 4	2,500.
R44TC5	25c **Certificate,** plate on bond paper	
	***a.* blue**	300.
	***b.* green**	300.
	***c.* orange**	300.
R44P4	25c Certificate, **red,** plate on card	33.
	Block of 4	140.
R45TC1a	25c **Entry of Goods,** hybrid die on India paper	
	***e.* black**	—
R45P4	25c Entry of Goods, **red,** plate on card	550.
R46TC5	25c **Insurance,** plate on bond paper	
	***a.* dull red**	150.
	***b.* vermilion**	170.
	***c.* blue**	170.
	***d.* dark blue**	155.
R46TC7	25c **Insurance,** plate on goldbeater's skin	
	***a.* dull red**	210.
	***b.* vermilion**	210.
	***c.* blue**	215.
	***d.* dark blue**	215.
	***e.* green**	215.
R46P3	25c Insurance, **red,** plate on India paper	60.
	Block of 4	250.
R46P4	25c Insurance, **red,** plate on card	33.
	Block of 4	140.
R47P4	25c Life Insurance, **red,** plate on card	33.
	Block of 4	140.
R48P4	25c Power of Attorney, **red,** plate on card	33.
	Block of 4	140.
R49P4	25c Protest, **red,** plate on card	33.
	Block of 4	140.
R50P4	25c Warehouse Receipt, **red,** plate on card	33.
	Block of 4	140.
R51TC3	30c **Foreign Exchange,** plate on India paper	
	***a.* violet**	130.
	***b.* violet gray**	130.
	***c.* deep red lilac**	155.
	***d.* slate blue**	155.
	***e.* black**	155.
	***f.* red**	155.
R51P3	30c Foreign Exchange, **lil,** plate on India paper	110.
	Block of 4	475.
R51P4	30c Foreign Exchange, **lil,** plate on card	100.
	Block of 4	425.
R52TC3	30c **Inland Exchange,** plate on India paper	
	***a.* deep red lilac**	155.
R52P3	30c Inland Exchange, **lil,** plate on India paper	65.
	Block of 4	275.
R52P4	30c Inland Exchange, **lil,** plate on card	55.
	Block of 4	230.
R53TC1a	40c **Inland Exchange,** hybrid die on India paper	
	***e.* black**	—
R53P3	40c Inland Exchange, **brn,** plate on India paper	150.
R53P4	40c Inland Exchange, **brn,** plate on card	75.
	Block of 4	325.
R54P2	50c Conveyance, **bl,** sm die on India paper	250.
R54P4	50c Conveyance, **bl,** plate on card	33.
	Block of 4	140.
R55TC5	50c **Entry of Goods,** plate on bond paper	
	***a.* orange**	275.
	***b.* green**	275.
	***c.* red**	340.
	***d.* deep blue**	—
R55P3	50c Entry of Goods, **bl,** plate on India paper	65.
	Block of 4	275.
R55P4	50c Entry of Goods, **bl,** plate on card	45.
	Block of 4	190.
R56P3	50c Foreign Exchange, **bl,** plate on India paper	65.
	Block of 4	275.
R56P4	50c Foreign Exchange, **bl,** plate on card	45.
	Block of 4	190.
R57P3	50c Lease, **bl,** plate on India paper	65.
	Block of 4	275.
R57P4	50c Lease, **bl,** plate on card	38.
	Block of 4	160.
R58TC3	50c **Life Insurance,** plate on India paper	
	***a.* ultramarine**	85.
R58P3	50c Life Insurance, **bl,** plate on India paper	65.
	Block of 4	275.
R58P4	50c Life Insurance, **bl,** plate on card	38.
	Block of 4	160.
R59P4	50c Mortgage, **bl,** plate on card	110.
	Block of 4	475.
R60TC1a	50c **Original Process,** die (?) on India paper	
	***e.* black**	280.
R60P3	50c Original Process, **bl,** plate on India paper	65.
	Block of 4	275.
R60P4	50c Original Process, **bl,** plate on card	38.
	Block of 4	160.
R61P4	50c Passage Ticket, **bl,** plate on card	55.
	Block of 4	230.
R62P3	50c Probate of Will, **bl,** plate on India paper	65.
	Block of 4	275.
R62P4	50c Probate of Will, **bl,** plate on card	55.
	Block of 4	230.
R63P4	50c Surety Bond, **bl,** plate on card	55.
	Block of 4	230.
R64TC1a	60c **Inland Exchange,** die (?) on India paper	
	***e.* green**	—
R64P3	60c Inland Exchange, **org,** plate on India paper	55.
R64P4	60c Inland Exchange, **org,** plate on card	38.
	Block of 4	160.
R65TC1a	70c **Foreign Exchange,** die (?) on India paper	
	***e.* orange**	—
	***f.* black**	285.
R65P3	70c Foreign Exchange, **grn,** plate on India paper	120.
R65P4	70c Foreign Exchange, **grn,** plate on card	55.
	Block of 4	230.
R66TC3	$1 **Conveyance,** plate on India paper	
	***a.* carmine**	85.
R66P4	$1 Conveyance, **red,** plate on card	45.
	Block of 4	190.
R67TC3	$1 **Entry of Goods,** plate on India paper	
	***a.* carmine**	60.
R67P1	$1 Entry of Goods, **red,** large die on India paper	525.
R67P4	$1 Entry of Goods, **red,** plate on card	45.
	Block of 4	190.
R68TC3	$1 **Foreign Exchange,** plate on India paper	
	***a.* carmine**	60.
R68P4	$1 Foreign Exchange, **red,** plate on card	33.
	Block of 4	140.
R69TC3	$1 **Inland Exchange,** plate on India paper	
	***a.* carmine**	60.
R69P4	$1 Inland Exchange, **red,** plate on card	55.
	Block of 4	230.
R70TC3	$1 **Lease,** plate on India paper	
	***a.* carmine**	130.
R70P4	$1 Lease, **red,** plate on card	*425.*
R71TC3	$1 **Life Insurance,** plate on India paper	
	***a.* carmine**	75.
R71P4	$1 Life Insurance, **red,** plate on card	33.
	Block of 4	140.
R72TC3	$1 **Manifest,** plate on India paper	
	***a.* carmine**	80.
R72P3	$1 Manifest, **red,** plate on India paper	55.
	Block of 4	—
R72P4	$1 Manifest, **red,** plate on card	33.
	Block of 4	140.
R73TC1a	$1 **Mortgage,** hybrid die on India paper	
	***e.* black**	—
R73TC3	$1 **Mortgage,** plate on India paper	
	***a.* carmine**	85.
R73P4	$1 Mortgage, **red,** plate on card	55.
	Block of 4	230.
R74TC3	$1 **Passage Ticket,** plate on India paper	
	***a.* carmine**	120.
R74P4	$1 Passage Ticket, **red,** plate on card	*425.*
	Block of 4	*1,850.*
R75TC3	$1 **Power of Attorney,** plate on India paper	
	***a.* carmine**	120.
R75P4	$1 Power of Attorney, **red,** plate on card	100.
	Block of 4	425.
R76TC3	$1 **Probate of Will,** plate on India paper	
	***a.* carmine**	60.
R76P4	$1 Probate of Will, **red,** plate on card	33.
	Block of 4	140.
R77P1	$1.30 Foreign Exchange, **org,** large die on India paper	*700.*
R77P3	$1.30 Foreign Exchange, **org,** plate on India paper	140.
	Block of 4	575.
R77P4	$1.30 Foreign Exchange, **org,** plate on card	100.
	Block of 4	425.
R78TC1a	$1.50 **Inland Exchange,** die on India paper	
	***e.* black**	475.
R78P3	$1.50 Inland Exchange, **bl,** plate on India paper	110.
	Block of 4	475.
R78P4	$1.50 Inland Exchange, **bl,** plate on card	45.
	Block of 4	190.
R79P3	$1.60 Foreign Exchange, **grn,** plate on India paper	140.
R79P4	$1.60 Foreign Exchange, **grn,** plate on card	100.
	Block of 4	425.
R80TC3	$1.90 **Foreign Exchange,** plate on India paper	
	***a.* black**	155.
R80P3	$1.90 Foreign Exchange, **vio,** plate on India paper	140.
	Block of 4	575.
R80P4	$1.90 Foreign Exchange, **vio,** plate on card	100.
	Block of 4	425.
R81TC4	$2 **Conveyance,** plate on card	
	***a.* carmine**	85.
R81P3	$2 Conveyance, **red,** plate on India paper	120.
R81P4	$2 Conveyance, **red,** plate on card	33.
	Block of 4	140.
R82TC4	$2 **Mortgage,** plate on card	
	***a.* carmine**	85.
R82P3	$2 Mortgage, **red,** plate on India paper	120.
	Block of 4	—
R82P4	$2 Mortgage, **red,** plate on card	33.
	Block of 4	140.
R83TC1a	$2 **Probate of Will,** hybrid die on India paper	
	***e.* black**	—
R83P4	$2 Probate of Will, **red,** plate on card	110.
	Block of 4	
R84TC1a	$2.50 **Inland Exchange,** die (?) on India paper	
	***e.* black**	120.
R84P3	$2.50 Inland Exchange, **vio,** plate on India paper	250.
R84P4	$2.50 Inland Exchange, **vio,** plate on card	250.
	Block of 4	—
R85TC4	$3 **Charter Party,** plate on thin card	
	***a.* dark green**	—
R85P3	$3 Charter Party, **grn,** plate on India paper	120.
	Block of 4	500.
R85P4	$3 Charter Party, **grn,** plate on card	65.
	Block of 4	275.
R86P1	$3 Manifest, **grn,** large die on India paper	—
R86P2	$3 Manifest, **grn,** sm die on India paper	350.
R86P3	$3 Manifest, **grn,** plate on India paper	180.
R86P4	$3 Manifest, **grn,** plate on card	65.
	Block of 4	275.
R87TC1a	$3.50 **Inland Exchange,** die on India paper	
	***e.* black**	400.
R87P3	$3.50 Inland Exchange, **bl,** plate on India paper	180.
R87P4	$3.50 Inland Exchange, **bl,** plate on card	140.
	Block of 4	575.
R88TC1a	$5 **Charter Party,** hybrid die on India paper	
	***e.* black**	—
R88TC3	$5 **Charter Party,** plate on India paper	
	***a.* carmine**	85.
R88P3	$5 Charter Party, **red,** plate on India paper	70.
	Block of 4	300.
R88P4	$5 Charter Party, **red,** plate on card	55.
	Block of 4	230.
R89TC3	$5 **Conveyance,** plate on India paper	
	***a.* carmine**	90.
R89P3	$5 Conveyance, **red,** plate on India paper	450.
R89P4	$5 Conveyance, **red,** plate on card	55.
	Block of 4	230.
R90P2	$5 Manifest, **red,** sm die on India paper	300.
R90P4	$5 Manifest, **red,** plate on card	55.
	Block of 4	230.
R91TC3	$5 **Mortgage,** plate on India paper	
	***a.* carmine**	90.
R91P3	$5 Mortgage, **red,** plate on India paper	650.
R91P4	$5 Mortgage, **red,** plate on card	55.
	Block of 4	230.
R92P2	$5 Probate of Will, **red,** sm die on India paper	300.
R92P4	$5 Probate of Will, **red,** plate on card	55.
	Block of 4	230.
R93P3	$10 Charter Party, **grn,** plate on India paper	120.
R93P4	$10 Charter Party, **grn,** plate on card	55.
	Block of 4	230.
R94P4	$10 Conveyance, **grn,** plate on card	55.
	Block of 4	230.
R95TC4	$10 **Mortgage,** plate on thin card	
	***a.* yellow green**	—
R95P4	$10 Mortgage, **grn,** plate on card	55.
	Block of 4	230.
R96P1	$10 Probate of Will, **grn,** large die on India paper	*700.*
R96P2	$10 Probate of Will, **grn,** sm die on India paper	300.
R96P4	$10 Probate of Will, **grn,** plate on card	75.
	Block of 4	325.
R97P2	$15 Mortgage, **dk bl,** sm die on India paper	—
R97P3	$15 Mortgage, **dk bl,** plate on India paper	350.
R97P4	$15 Mortgage, **dk bl,** plate on card	180.
	Block of 4	800.
R97eP2	$15 Mortgage, **ultra,** sm die on India paper	—
R97eP4	$15 Mortgage, **ultra,** plate on card	350.
	Block of 4	—
R97fP3	$15 Mortgage, **milky bl,** plate on India paper	290.
R98TC3	$20 **Conveyance,** plate on India paper	
	***a.* red orange**	220.
R98TC4	$20 **Conveyance,** plate on card	
	***a.* red orange**	120.
R98P3	$20 Conveyance, **org,** plate on India paper	220.
	Block of 4	900.
R98P4	$20 Conveyance, **org,** plate on card	100.
	Block of 4	425.
R99TC4	$20 **Probate of Will,** plate on card	
	***a.* red orange**	275.
	***b.* black**	275.
R99P4	$20 Probate of Will, **org,** plate on card	220.
	Block of 4	—
R100P3	$25 Mortgage, **red,** plate on India paper	220.
R100P4	$25 Mortgage, **red,** plate on card	160.
	Block of 4	675.
R101TC1a	$50 **U.S.I.R.,** hybrid die on India paper	
	***e.* black**	—
R101TC5	$50 **U.S.I.R.,** plate on bond paper	
	***a.* orange**	275.
	***b.* deep blue**	275.
R101P3	$50 U.S.I.R., **grn,** plate on India paper	220.
R101P4	$50 U.S.I.R., **grn,** plate on card	230.
	Block of 4	950.
R102TC3	$200 **U.S.I.R.,** plate on India paper	
	***a.* black**	—
	***b.* green & brown red**	2,000.
R102TC4	$200 **U.S.I.R.,** plate on card	
	***a.* black & red**	1,600.
R102TC5	$200 **U.S.I.R.,** plate on bond paper	
	***a.* gray brown & red**	1,600.
R102P3	$200 U.S.I.R., **grn & org red,** plate on India paper	1,400.

Second Issue

1871-72

R104TC5	2c plate on bond paper	
	***a.* pale blue & black**	60.
R105P3	3c **bl & blk,** plate on India paper	20.
	Block of 4	90.

R105P4 3c **bl & blk,** plate on card 15.
Block of 4 65.
P# block of 10 —
R109P3 10c **bl & blk,** plate on India paper 20.
Block of 4 90.
R109P4 10c **bl & blk,** plate on card 15.
Block of 4 65.
P# block of 10 —
R111P3 20c **bl & blk,** plate on India paper 20.
Block of 4 90.
R111P4 20c **bl & blk,** plate on card 15.
Block of 4 65.
P# block of 10 —
R112P3 25c **bl & blk,** plate on India paper 20.
Block of 4 90.
R112P4 25c **bl & blk,** plate on card 15.
Block of 4 65.
P# block of 10 —
R115P3 50c **bl & blk,** plate on India paper 50.
Block of 4 225.
R115P4 50c **bl & blk,** plate on card 15.
Block of 4 65.
P# block of 10 —
R119P3 $1.30 **bl & blk,** plate on India paper 50.
Block of 4 225.
R119P4 $1.30 **bl & blk,** plate on card 38.
Block of 4 160.
P# block of 10 —
R120P3 $1.50 **bl & blk,** plate on India paper 28.
Block of 4 120.
R120P4 $1.50 **bl & blk,** plate on card 22.
Block of 4 100.
Double transfer, design of $1 —
R121P3 $1.60 **bl & blk,** plate on India paper 60.
Block of 4 260.
R121P4 $1.60 **bl & blk,** plate on card 60.
Block of 4 260.
P# block of 10 —
R122P3 $1.90 **bl & blk,** plate on India paper 50.
Block of 4 225.
R122P4 $1.90 **bl & blk,** plate on card 38.
Block of 4 170.
P# block of 10 —
R126P3 $3.50 **bl & blk,** plate on India paper 90.
Block of 4 400.
R126P4 $3.50 **bl & blk,** plate on card 100.
Block of 4 425.
P# block of 8 —
R130P3 $25 **bl & blk,** plate on India paper 150.
Block of 4 650.
R130P4 $25 **bl & blk,** plate on card 110.
Block of 4 500.
P# block of 4 —
R131P3 $50 **bl & blk,** plate on India paper 160.
Block of 4 700.
R131P4 $50 **bl & blk,** plate on card 140.
Block of 4 625.
P# block of 4 —

The "small die proofs" formerly listed under Nos. R103P-R131P are plate proofs from the sheets listed under "Trial Color Proofs."

R132TC1a $200 die on India paper
e. **red, green & black** 2,500.
f. **orange,** master die 2,500.
g. **blue,** master die 2,500.
h. **green,** master die 2,500.
R132P1 $200 **red, bl & blk,** large die on India paper 3,500.
R132P2 $200 **red, bl & blk,** sm die on India paper 2,750.
R132P3 $200 **red, bl & blk,** plate on India paper 2,500.
Red (frame) inverted —
R133TC1a $500 die on India paper
e. **yellow, green & black** *5,000.*
f. **bright green, orange brown & black** *5,000.*
g. **black,** master die *10,000.*
R133TC1b $500 die on bond paper
e. **red, green & black** *5,000.*
f. **light green, light brown & black** *5,000.*
g. **blue, scarlet & black** *5,000.*
R133TC1d $500 die on card
e. **light green, light brown & black** *14,500.*
R133P1 $500 **red, org, grn & blk,** large die on India paper *5,500.*
R133ATC1a $5000 die on India paper
e. **yellow orange, green & black** *20,000.*
f. **olive brown, green & black** *20,000.*
g. **orange red, dark green & black** *20,000.*
h. **orange red, dark blue & black** *20,000.*

The master die is the completed stamp design prior to its division into separate color dies.

Full-size die proofs on full-size card bring substantial premiums above the catalogue values listed for R132TC1a, R133TC1a-R133TC1d, R133ATC1a.

R133AP1 $5000 **red org, dk grn & blk,** large die on India paper *7,500.*

No. R133AP was approved in these colors but never issued. Shade differences of the red orange and dark green colors will be found. It comes both with and without manufacturer's imprints to the left and right of the design. One example exists on bond paper mounted on card with "853½" printed on the lower right card margin.

Due to the unusual manufacturing process of printing these tri-color stamps from single impression plates, proofs with imprints could also be considered to be plate proofs. All are extremely scarce or unique, and are valued in the grade, condition and scarcity in which they exist. For other colors see the trial color proofs listings under No. R133ATC.

Third Issue

1871-72
R134TC4 1c plate on card
a. **brown & black** 60.
R134P4 1c **cl & blk,** plate on card 15.
Block of 4 70.
P# block of 10 —
R135P3 2c **org & blk,** plate on India paper 28.
Block of 4 120.
R135P4 2c **org & blk,** plate on card 15.
Block of 4 70.
P# block of 10 —
R136P3 4c **brn & blk,** plate on India paper 33.
Block of 4 140.
R136P4 4c **brn & blk,** plate on card 15.
Block of 4 70.
P# block of 10 —
R137P3 5c **org & blk,** plate on India paper 33.
Block of 4 140.
R137P4 5c **org & blk,** plate on card 15.
Block of 4 70.
P# block of 10 —
R138P3 6c **org & blk,** plate on India paper 33.
Block of 4 140.
R138P4 6c **org & blk,** plate on card 15.
Block of 4 70.
P# block of 10 —
R139P3 15c **brn & blk,** plate on India paper 33.
Block of 4 140.
R139P4 15c **brn & blk,** plate on card 15.
Block of 4 70.
P# block of 10 —
R140P3 30c **brn & blk,** plate on India paper 38.
Block of 4 160.
R140P4 30c **brn & blk,** plate on card 18.
Block of 4 80.
P# block of 10 —
R141P3 40c **brn & blk,** plate on India paper 38.
Block of 4 160.
R141P4 40c **brn & blk,** plate on card 18.
Block of 4 80.
P# block of 12 —
R142P3 60c **org & blk,** plate on India paper 85.
Block of 4 360.
Foreign entry, design of 70c 225.
R142P4 60c **org & blk,** plate on card 50.
Block of 4 225.
P# block of 10 —
Foreign entry, design of 70c 150.
a. Center inverted *2,250.*
Block of 4 *10,000.*
Foreign entry, design of 70c —
R143P3 70c **grn & blk,** plate on India paper 55.
Block of 4 230.
R143P4 70c **grn & blk,** plate on card 38.
Block of 4 170.
P# block of 10 —
R144P3 $1 **grn & blk,** plate on India paper 50.
Block of 4 210.
R144P4 $1 **grn & blk,** plate on card 38.
Block of 4 170.
P# block of 10 —
R145P3 $2 **ver & blk,** plate on India paper 105.
Block of 4 450.
R145P4 $2 **ver & blk,** plate on card 105.
Block of 4 450.
P# block of 8 —
R146P3 $2.50 **cl & blk,** plate on India paper 65.
Block of 4 260.
R146P4 $2.50 **cl & blk,** plate on card 40.
Block of 4 170.
P# block of 8 —
R147P3 $3 **grn & blk,** plate on India paper 85.
Block of 4 360.
R147P4 $3 **grn & blk,** plate on card 70.
Block of 4 300.
P# block of 8 —
R148P3 $5 **ver & blk,** plate on India paper 85.
Block of 4 360.
R148P4 $5 **ver & blk,** plate on card 55.
Block of 4 240.
P# block of 4 —
R149P3 $10 **grn & blk,** plate on India paper 105.
Block of 4 440.
R149P4 $10 **grn & blk,** plate on card 55.
Block of 4 240.
P# block of 4 —
R150P3 $20 **org & blk,** plate on India paper 150.
Block of 4 650.
R150P4 $20 **org & blk,** plate on card 150.
Block of 4 635.
P# block of 4 —

1875 National Bank Note Co., New York City
R152TC1a 2c Liberty, die on India paper
e. **green** 600.
f. **brown** 600.
g. **black** 600.
R152P1 2c **bl,** (Liberty) large die on India paper 450.
R152P3 2c **bl,** (Liberty) plate on India paper 110.
Block of 4 475.

Documentary

1898
R161TC1a ½c large die on India paper
e. **green** 750.
R163TC1a 1c large die on India paper
e. **green** 750.
f. **black** 750.
R165TC2 1c small die on India paper
b. **green** 650.
R169TC1a 25c large die on India paper
e. **green** 650.
R170TC1a 40c large die on India paper
e. **black** 650.
R172TC1a 80c large die on India paper
e. **green** 1,100.
R173P1 $1 **dk grn,** large die on India paper *600.*
R174TC1a $3 die on India paper
e. **black** 650.
R174P1 $3 **dk brn,** large die on India paper *600.*
R175P1 $5 **org red,** large die on India paper *600.*
R176TC1a $10 die on India paper
e. **green** 650.
R176P1 $10 **blk,** large die on India paper *600.*
R177P1 $30 **red,** large die on India paper *600.*
R178P1 $50 **gray brn,** large die on India paper *600.*

1899
R179TC1a $100 die on India paper
e. **dark green & black** 1,250.
R180P1 $500 **car lake & blk,** large die on India paper *1,650.*
R181TC1a $1000 die on India paper
e. **dark blue & black** 1,250.

1914
R195TC2 ½c small die on wove
b. **black** —
R196TC2 1c small die on wove
b. **blue green** —
R197P2 2c **rose,** sm die on India paper —
R198TC2 3c small die on wove
b. **ultramarine** —
R199TC2 4c small die on wove
b. **brown** —
R200TC2 5c small die on wove
b. **blue** —
R201TC2 10c small die on wove
b. **yellow** —
R202TC2 25c small die on wove
b. **dull violet** —
R203TC2 40c small die on wove
b. **blue green** —
R204TC2 50c small die on wove
b. **red brown** —
R205TC2 80c small die on wove
b. **orange** —

1914-15
R226P1 $500 **bl,** large die on India paper *675.*

1917
R246P1 $30 **dp org,** (without serial No.) large die on India paper *650.*

1940
R298P1 50c **car,** (without ovpt.) large die on India paper *700.*
R305P1 $10 **car,** large die on India paper *825.*
Without overprint —
R306AP1 $50 **car,** large die on India paper *825.*
Without overprint —

1952
R597P1 55c **car,** large die on India paper *675.*

Proprietary

1871-75 Joseph R. Carpenter, Philadelphia
RB1TC5 1c plate on bond paper
a. **blue & black** 70.
b. **scarlet & black** 70.
c. **orange & black** 70.
d. **orange & ultramarine,** on granite bond 60.
RB1P3 1c **grn & blk,** plate on India paper —
RB1P4 1c **grn & blk,** plate on card 12.
Block of 4 52.
P# block of 10 *250.*
RB1P5 1c **grn & blk,** plate on bond 12.
Block of 4 52.
P# block of 10 175.
RB2P3 2c **grn & blk,** plate on India paper 175.
RB2P4 2c **grn & blk,** plate on card 12.
Block of 4 52.
RB2P5 2c **grn & blk,** plate on bond, P# block of 10 175.
RB3TC5 3c Plate on bond paper
a. **blue & black,** with gum 60.
b. **blue & black,** *gray* 60.
RB3TC6 3c plate on wove paper
a. **blue & black** —
RB3P3 3c **grn & blk,** plate on India paper 22.
Block of 4 100.
RB3P4 3c **grn & blk,** plate on card 12.
Block of 4 52.
RB3P5 3c **grn & blk,** plate on bond, P# block of 10 175.
RB4P3 4c **grn & blk,** plate on India paper 22.
Block of 4 100.
RB4P4 4c **grn & blk,** plate on card 12.
Block of 4 52.
RB4P5 4c **grn & blk,** plate on bond, P# block of 10 175.
RB5P3 5c **grn & blk,** plate on India paper 22.
Block of 4 100.
RB5P4 5c **grn & blk,** plate on card 12.
Block of 4 52.
RB5P5 5c **grn & blk,** plate on bond, P# block of 10 175.
RB6P3 6c **grn & blk,** plate on India paper 22.
Block of 4 100.
RB6P4 6c **grn & blk,** plate on card 12.
Block of 4 52.
RB6P5 6c **grn & blk,** plate on bond, P# block of 10 175.
RB7P3 10c **grn & blk,** plate on India paper 22.
Block of 4 100.
RB7P4 10c **grn & blk,** plate on card 12.
Block of 4 52.
RB7P5 10c **grn & blk,** plate on bond, P# block of 10 175.
RB8TC1a 50c Die on India paper
e. **green & brown** 675.
f. **green & purple** 675.

No.	Description	Price
	g. **green & brown red**	675.
	h. **green & violet**	675.
	i. **green & dark carmine**	675.
	j. **ultramarine & red**	675.
RB8P2	50c **grn & blk,** sm die on India paper	1,400.
RB8P4	50c **grn & blk,** plate on card	1,000.
RB9TC1a	$1 die on India paper	
	e. **green & brown**	675.
	f. **green & purple**	675.
	g. **green & violet brown**	675.
	h. **green & brown red**	675.
	i. **green & violet**	675.
	j. **green & dark carmine**	675.
RB9P2	$1 **grn & blk,** sm die on India paper	1,600.
RB9P4	$1 **grn & blk,** plate on card	1,250.
RB10P2	$5 **grn & blk,** sm die on India paper	6,000.
RB10P3	$5 **grn & blk,** plate on India paper	4,500.
RB10P4	$5 **grn & blk,** plate on card	2,750.

1875-83 National Bank Note Co., New York City

No.	Description	Price
RB11TC1a	1c die on India paper	
	e. **brown**	500.
	f. **red brown**	500.
	g. **blue**	500.
	h. **black**	500.
RB11P1	1c **grn,** lg die on India paper	500.
RB11P3	1c **grn,** plate on India paper	65.
	Block of 4	325.
RB11P4	1c **grn,** plate on card	—
RB12TC1a	2c die on India paper	
	e. **green**	500.
	f. **black**	500.
	g. **brown**	500.
	h. **orange brown**	500.
	i. **blue**	500.
RB12P1	2c **brn,** lg die on India paper	500.
RB12P3	2c **brn,** plate on India paper	65.
	Pair	160.
RB12P4	2c **brn,** plate on card	—
RB13TC1a	3c die on India paper	
	e. **brown**	500.
	f. **green**	500.
	g. **blue**	500.
RB13TC3	3c plate on India paper	
	a. **black**	150.
RB13P1	3c **org,** lg die on India paper	500.
RB13P3	3c **org,** plate on India paper	65.
	Pair	160.
RB13P4	3c **org,** plate on card	—
	Pair	—
	Block of 4	—
RB14TC1a	4c die on India paper	
	e. **green**	450.
	f. **black**	450.
	g. **dark brown**	450.
	h. **blue**	450.
RB14TC3	4c plate on India paper	
	a. **black**	150.
RB14P1	4c **red brn,** lg die on India paper	500.
RB14P3	4c **red brn,** plate on India paper	65.
	Pair	160.
RB14P4	4c **red brn,** plate on card	—
	Pair	—
	Block of 4	—
RB15P1	4c **red,** lg die on India paper	500.
RB16TC1a	5c die on India paper	
	e. **green**	450.
	f. **dark slate**	450.
	g. **blue**	450.
RB16P1	5c **blk,** lg die on India paper	500.
RB16P3	5c **blk,** plate on India paper	65.
	Pair	160.
RB16P4	5c **blk,** plate on card	—
	Pair	—
	Block of 4	—
RB17TC1a	6c die on India paper	
	e. **black**	500.
	f. **blue**	500.
	g. **purple**	500.
	h. **dull violet**	500.
	i. **violet**	500.
	j. **violet brown**	500.
	k. **dark brown**	500.
RB17TC3	6c plate on India paper	
	a. **green**	150.
	b. **black**	150.
RB17P1	6c **vio bl,** lg die on India paper	500.
RB17P3	6c **vio bl,** plate on India paper	65.
	Pair	160.
RB18P1	6c **bl,** lg die on India paper	500.
RB18P3	6c **bl,** plate on India paper	175.
	Pair	400.
RB19TC1a	10c die on India paper	
	e. **black**	550.
RB19P1	10c **bl,** lg die on India paper	500.

No. RB19P1 was produced by the Bureau of Engraving and Printing.

SECOND, THIRD AND PROPRIETARY ISSUES

Stamps Nos. R103 to R131, R134 to R150 and RB1 to RB7.

A special composite plate was made and impressions taken in various colors and shades. Although all varieties in all colors must have been made, only those seen by the editors are listed.

CENTERS IN BLACK

1871-75

No.	Description	Price
R103TC3	1c plate on India paper	
	a. **dark purple**	60.
	b. **dull purple**	60.
	d. **brown**	60.
	e. **black brown**	60.
	g. **light blue**	60.
	h. **dark blue**	70.
	i. **ultramarine**	70.
	k. **yellow green**	70.
	n. **green**	65.
	o. **dark green**	65.
	p. **blue green**	65.
	q. **light orange**	65.
	r. **dark orange**	65.
	s. **deep orange**	65.
	t. **scarlet**	65.
	u. **carmine**	65.
	x. **dark brown red**	65.
R103TC7	1c plate on goldbeater's skin	
	a. **dark brown orange**	90.
R104TC3	2c plate on India paper	
	a. **dark purple**	60.
	b. **dull purple**	60.
	d. **brown**	60.
	e. **black brown**	60.
	g. **light blue**	60.
	h. **dark blue**	70.
	i. **ultramarine**	70.
	k. **yellow green**	70.
	l. **dark yellow green**	70.
	n. **green**	65.
	o. **dark green**	65.
	p. **blue green**	65.
	q. **light orange**	65.
	r. **dark orange**	65.
	s. **deep orange**	65.
	t. **scarlet**	65.
	u. **carmine**	65.
	x. **dark brown red**	65.
R104TC7	2c plate on goldbeater's skin	
	a. **dark brown orange**	90.
R105TC3	3c plate on India paper	
	a. **dark purple**	60.
	b. **dull purple**	60.
	d. **brown**	60.
	e. **black brown**	60.
	g. **light blue**	60.
	h. **dark blue**	70.
	i. **ultramarine**	70.
	k. **yellow green**	70.
	n. **green**	65.
	o. **dark green**	65.
	p. **blue green**	65.
	q. **light orange**	65.
	r. **dark orange**	65.
	s. **deep orange**	65.
	t. **scarlet**	65.
	u. **carmine**	65.
	x. **dark brown red**	65.
R105TC7	3c plate on goldbeater's skin	
	a. **dark brown orange**	90.
R106TC3	4c plate on India paper	
	a. **dark purple**	60.
	b. **dull purple**	60.
	d. **brown**	60.
	e. **black brown**	60.
	f. **orange brown**	65.
	g. **light blue**	60.
	h. **dark blue**	70.
	i. **ultramarine**	70.
	k. **yellow green**	70.
	n. **green**	65.
	o. **dark green**	65.
	p. **blue green**	65.
	q. **light orange**	65.
	r. **dark orange**	65.
	s. **deep orange**	65.
	t. **scarlet**	65.
	u. **carmine**	65.
	x. **dark brown red**	65.
R106TC7	4c plate on goldbeater's skin	
	a. **dark brown orange**	90.
R107TC3	5c plate on India paper	
	a. **dark purple**	60.
	b. **dull purple**	60.
	d. **brown**	60.
	e. **black brown**	60.
	f. **orange brown**	65.
	g. **light blue**	60.
	h. **dark blue**	70.
	i. **ultramarine**	70.
	k. **yellow green**	70.
	n. **green**	65.
	o. **dark green**	65.
	p. **blue green**	65.
	q. **light orange**	65.
	r. **dark orange**	65.
	s. **deep orange**	65.
	t. **scarlet**	65.
	u. **carmine**	65.
	v. **dark carmine**	65.
	w. **purplish carmine**	65.
	x. **dark brown red**	65.
R107TC7	5c plate on goldbeater's skin	
	a. **dark brown orange**	90.
R108TC3	6c plate on India paper	
	a. **dark purple**	60.
	b. **dull purple**	60.
	d. **brown**	60.
	e. **black brown**	60.
	f. **orange brown**	65.
	g. **light blue**	60.
	h. **dark blue**	70.
	i. **ultramarine**	70.
	k. **yellow green**	70.
	n. **green**	65.
	o. **dark green**	65.
	p. **blue green**	65.
	q. **light orange**	65.
	r. **dark orange**	65.
	s. **deep orange**	65.
	t. **scarlet**	65.
	u. **carmine**	65.
	v. **dark carmine**	65.
	w. **purplish carmine**	65.
	x. **dark brown red**	65.
R108TC7	6c plate on goldbeater's skin	
	a. **dark brown orange**	90.
R109TC3	10c plate on India paper	
	a. **dark purple**	60.
	b. **dull purple**	60.
	d. **brown**	60.
	e. **black brown**	60.
	g. **light blue**	60.
	h. **dark blue**	70.
	i. **ultramarine**	70.
	k. **yellow green**	70.
	n. **green**	65.
	o. **dark green**	65.
	p. **blue green**	65.
	q. **light orange**	65.
	r. **dark orange**	65.
	s. **deep orange**	65.
	t. **scarlet**	65.
	u. **carmine**	65.
	x. **dark brown red**	65.
R110TC3	15c plate on India paper	
	a. **dark purple**	60.
	b. **dull purple**	60.
	d. **brown**	60.
	e. **black brown**	60.
	f. **orange brown**	65.
	g. **light blue**	60.
	h. **dark blue**	70.
	i. **ultramarine**	70.
	k. **yellow green**	70.
	n. **green**	65.
	o. dark green	65.
	p. **blue green**	65.
	q. **light orange**	65.
	r. **dark orange**	65.
	s. **deep orange**	65.
	t. **scarlet**	65.
	u. **carmine**	65.
	w. **purplish carmine**	65.
	x. **dark brown red**	65.
R111TC3	20c plate on India paper	
	a. **dark purple**	60.
	b. **dull purple**	60.
	d. **brown**	60.
	e. **black brown**	60.
	g. **light blue**	60.
	h. **dark blue**	70.
	i. **ultramarine**	70.
	k. **yellow green**	70.
	n. **green**	65.
	o. **dark green**	65.
	p. **blue green**	65.
	q. **light orange**	65.
	r. **dark orange**	65.
	s. **deep orange**	65.
	t. **scarlet**	65.
	u. **carmine**	65.
	w. **purplish carmine**	65.
	x. **dark brown red**	65.
R111TC7	20c plate on goldbeater's skin	
	a. **dark brown orange**	90.
R112TC3	25c plate on India paper	
	a. **dark purple**	60.
	b. **dull purple**	60.
	d. **brown**	60.
	e. **black brown**	60.
	g. **light blue**	60.
	h. **dark blue**	70.
	i. **ultramarine**	70.
	k. **yellow green**	70.
	l. **dark yellow green**	70.
	n. **green**	65.
	o. **dark green**	65.
	p. **blue green**	65.
	q. **light orange**	65.
	r. **dark orange**	65.
	s. **deep orange**	65.
	t. **scarlet**	65.
	u. **carmine**	65.
	x. **dark brown red**	65.
R112TC7	25c plate on goldbeater's skin	
	a. **dark brown orange**	90.
R113TC3	30c plate on India paper	
	a. **dark purple**	60.
	b. **dull purple**	60.
	d. **brown**	60.
	e. **black brown**	60.
	g. **light blue**	60.
	h. **dark blue**	70.
	i. **ultramarine**	70.
	k. **yellow green**	70.
	n. **green**	65.
	o. **dark green**	65.
	p. **blue green**	65.
	q. **light orange**	65.
	r. **dark orange**	65.
	s. **deep orange**	65.
	t. **scarlet**	65.
	u. **carmine**	65.
	v. **dark carmine**	65.
	w. **purplish carmine**	65.
	x. **dark brown red**	65.
R113TC7	30c plate on goldbeater's skin	
	a. **dark brown orange**	90.
R114TC3	40c plate on India paper	
	a. **dark purple**	60.
	b. **dull purple**	60.
	d. **brown**	60.
	e. **black brown**	60.
	f. **orange brown**	65.
	g. **light blue**	60.
	h. **dark blue**	70.
	i. **ultramarine**	70.
	k. **yellow green**	70.
	n. **green**	65.
	o. **dark green**	65.
	p. **blue green**	65.
	q. **light orange**	65.
	r. **dark orange**	65.

No.	Description	Price
	s. **deep orange**	65.
	t. **scarlet**	65.
	u. **carmine**	65.
	x. **dark brown red**	65.
R115TC3	50c plate on India paper	
	a. **dark purple**	60.
	b. **dull purple**	60.
	d. **brown**	60.
	e. **black brown**	60.
	g. **light blue**	60.
	h. **dark blue**	70.
	i. **ultramarine**	70.
	k. **yellow green**	70.
	n. **green**	65.
	o. **dark green**	65.
	p. **blue green**	65.
	q. **light orange**	65.
	r. **dark orange**	65.
	s. **deep orange**	65.
	t. **scarlet**	65.
	u. **carmine**	65.
	x. **dark brown red**	65.
R116TC3	60c plate on India paper	
	a. **dark purple**	60.
	b. **dull purple**	60.
	d. **brown**	60.
	e. **black brown**	60.
	g. **light blue**	60.
	h. **dark blue**	70.
	i. **ultramarine**	70.
	k. **yellow green**	70.
	n. **green**	65.
	o. **dark green**	65.
	p. **blue green**	65.
	q. **light orange**	65.
	r. **dark orange**	65.
	s. **deep orange**	65.
	t. **scarlet**	65.
	u. **carmine**	65.
	v. **dark carmine**	65.
	x. **dark brown red**	65.
R116TC7	60c plate on goldbeater's skin	
	a. **dark brown orange**	90.
R117TC3	70c plate on India paper	
	a. **dark purple**	60.
	b. **dull purple**	60.
	d. **brown**	60.
	e. **black brown**	60.
	g. **light blue**	60.
	h. **dark blue**	70.
	i. **ultramarine**	70.
	k. **yellow green**	70.
	n. **green**	65.
	o. **dark green**	65.
	p. **blue green**	65.
	q. **light orange**	65.
	r. **dark orange**	65.
	s. **deep orange**	65.
	t. **scarlet**	65.
	u. **carmine**	65.
	x. **dark brown red**	65.
R118TC3	$1 plate on India paper	
	a. **dark purple**	70.
	b. **dull purple**	70.
	d. **brown**	70.
	e. **black brown**	70.
	g. **light blue**	80.
	h. **dark blue**	85.
	i. **ultramarine**	85.
	k. **yellow green**	80.
	n. **green**	75.
	o. **dark green**	75.
	p. **blue green**	75.
	q. **light orange**	75.
	r. **dark orange**	75.
	s. **deep orange**	75.
	t. **scarlet**	80.
	u. **carmine**	80.
	w. **purplish carmine**	80.
	x. **dark brown red**	80.
R118TC7	$1 plate on goldbeater's skin	
	a. **dark brown orange**	90.
R119TC3	$1.30 plate on India paper	
	a. **dark purple**	70.
	b. **dull purple**	70.
	d. **brown**	70.
	e. **black brown**	70.
	g. **light blue**	80.
	h. **dark blue**	85.
	i. **ultramarine**	85.
	k. **yellow green**	80.
	n. **green**	75.
	o. **dark green**	75.
	p. **blue green**	75.
	q. **light orange**	75.
	r. **dark orange**	75.
	s. **deep orange**	75.
	t. **scarlet**	80.
	u. **carmine**	80.
	x. **dark brown red**	80.
R120TC3	$1.50 plate on India paper	
	a. **dark purple**	70.
	b. **dull purple**	70.
	d. **brown**	70.
	e. **black brown**	70.
	g. **light blue**	80.
	h. **dark blue**	85.
	i. **ultramarine**	85.
	k. **yellow green**	80.
	n. **green**	75.
	o. **dark green**	75.
	p. **blue green**	75.
	q. **light orange**	75.
	r. **dark orange**	75.
	s. **deep orange**	75.
	t. **scarlet**	80.
	u. **carmine**	80.
	x. **dark brown red**	80.
R120TC4	$1.50 plate on card	
	a. **bright yellow green**	75.
R121TC3	$1.60 plate on India paper	
	a. **dark purple**	70.
	b. **dull purple**	70.
	d. **brown**	70.
	e. **black brown**	70.
	g. **light blue**	80.
	h. **dark blue**	85.
	i. **ultramarine**	85.
	k. **yellow green**	80.
	n. **green**	75.
	o. **dark green**	75.
	p. **blue green**	75.
	q. **light orange**	75.
	r. **dark orange**	75.
	s. **deep orange**	75.
	t. **scarlet**	80.
	u. **carmine**	80.
	x. **dark brown red**	80.
R122TC3	$1.90 plate on India paper	
	a. **dark purple**	70.
	b. **dull purple**	70.
	d. **brown**	70.
	e. **black brown**	70.
	g. **light blue**	80.
	h. **dark blue**	85.
	i. **ultramarine**	85.
	k. **yellow green**	80.
	n. **green**	75.
	o. **dark green**	75.
	p. **blue green**	75.
	q. **light orange**	75.
	r. **dark orange**	75.
	s. **deep orange**	75.
	t. **scarlet**	80.
	u. **carmine**	80.
	x. **dark brown red**	80.
R122TC4	$1.90 plate on card	
	a. **bright yellow green**	75.
R123TC3	$2 plate on India paper	
	a. **dark purple**	70.
	b. **dull purple**	70.
	d. **brown**	70.
	e. **black brown**	70.
	g. **light blue**	80.
	h. **dark blue**	85.
	i. **ultramarine**	85.
	k. **yellow green**	80.
	n. **green**	75.
	o. **dark green**	75.
	p. **blue green**	75.
	q. **light orange**	75.
	r. **dark orange**	75.
	s. **deep orange**	75.
	t. **scarlet**	80.
	u. **carmine**	80.
	w. **purplish carmine**	80.
	x. **dark brown red**	80.
R123TC4	$2 plate on card	
	a. **bright yellow green**	75.
R123TC7	$2 plate on goldbeater's skin	
	a. **dark brown orange**	90.
R124TC3	$2.50 plate on India paper	
	a. **dark purple**	70.
	b. **dull purple**	70.
	d. **brown**	70.
	e. **black brown**	70.
	g. **light blue**	80.
	h. **dark blue**	85.
	i. **ultramarine**	85.
	k. **yellow green**	80.
	n. **green**	75.
	o. **dark green**	75.
	p. **blue green**	75.
	q. **light orange**	75.
	r. **dark orange**	75.
	s. **deep orange**	75.
	t. **scarlet**	80.
	u. **carmine**	80.
	v. **dark carmine**	80.
	x. **dark brown red**	80.
R125TC3	$3 plate on India paper	
	a. **dark purple**	70.
	b. **dull purple**	70.
	d. **brown**	70.
	e. **black brown**	70.
	g. **light blue**	80.
	h. **dark blue**	85.
	i. **ultramarine**	85.
	k. **yellow green**	80.
	n. **green**	75.
	o. **dark green**	75.
	p. **blue green**	75.
	q. **light orange**	75.
	r. **dark orange**	75.
	s. **deep orange**	75.
	t. **scarlet**	80.
	u. **carmine**	80.
	x. **dark brown red**	80.
R125TC4	$3 plate on card	
	a. **bright yellow green**	75.
R126TC3	$3.50 plate on India paper	
	a. **dark purple**	70.
	b. **dull purple**	70.
	c. **red purple**	75.
	d. **brown**	70.
	e. **black brown**	70.
	g. **light blue**	80.
	h. **dark blue**	85.
	i. **ultramarine**	85.
	k. **yellow green**	80.
	n. **green**	75.
	o. **dark green**	75.
	p. **blue green**	75.
	q. **light orange**	75.
	r. **dark orange**	75.
	s. **deep orange**	75.
	t. **scarlet**	90.
	u. **carmine**	80.
	x. **dark brown red**	80.
R127TC3	$5 plate on India paper	
	a. **dark purple**	70.
	b. **dull purple**	70.
	d. **brown**	70.
	e. **black brown**	70.
	g. **light blue**	80.
	h. **dark blue**	85.
	i. **ultramarine**	85.
	k. **yellow green**	80.
	n. **green**	75.
	o. **dark green**	75.
	p. **blue green**	75.
	q. **light orange**	75.
	r. **dark orange**	75.
	s. **deep orange**	75.
	t. **scarlet**	75.
	u. **carmine**	75.
	w. **purplish carmine**	75.
	x. **dark brown red**	80.
R127TC7	$5 plate on goldbeater's skin	
	a. **dark brown orange**	100.
R128TC	$10 plate on India paper	
	a. **dark purple**	70.
	b. **dull purple**	70.
	d. **brown**	70.
	e. **black brown**	70.
	g. **light blue**	80.
	h. **dark blue**	85.
	i. **ultramarine**	85.
	k. **yellow green**	75.
	n. **green**	75.
	o. **dark green**	75.
	p. **blue green**	75.
	q. **light orange**	75.
	r. **dark orange**	75.
	s. **deep orange**	75.
	t. **scarlet**	75.
	u. **carmine**	80.
	x. **dark brown red**	80.
R128TC4	$10 plate on card	
	a. **bright yellow green**	75.
R129TC3	$20 plate on India paper	
	a. **dark purple**	95.
	b. **dull purple**	95.
	d. **brown**	95.
	e. **black brown**	95.
	g. **light blue**	90.
	h. **dark blue**	90.
	i. **ultramarine**	90.
	k. **yellow green**	85.
	m. **emerald green**	85.
	n. **green**	75.
	o. **dark green**	75.
	p. **blue green**	75.
	q. **light orange**	75.
	r. **dark orange**	85.
	s. **deep orange**	85.
	t. **scarlet**	90.
	u. **carmine**	80.
	v. **dark carmine**	90.
	x. **dark brown red**	80.
R130TC3	$25 plate on India paper	
	a. **dark purple**	100.
	b. **dull purple**	100.
	d. **brown**	100.
	e. **black brown**	100.
	g. **light blue**	90.
	h. **dark blue**	90.
	i. **ultramarine**	90.
	k. **yellow green**	85.
	m. **emerald green**	85.
	n. **green**	75.
	o. **dark green**	75.
	p. **blue green**	75.
	q. **light orange**	75.
	r. **dark orange**	75.
	s. **deep orange**	85.
	t. **scarlet**	90.
	u. **carmine**	80.
	w. **purplish carmine**	90.
	x. **dark brown red**	300.
R130TC7	$5 plate on goldbeater's skin	
	a. **dark brown orange**	100.
R131TC3	$50 plate on India paper	
	a. **dark purple**	95.
	b. **dull purple**	95.
	d. **brown**	95.
	e. **black brown**	95.
	g. **light blue**	90.
	h. **dark blue**	90.
	i. **ultramarine**	90.
	k. **yellow green**	85.
	m. **emerald green**	85.
	n. **green**	75.
	o. **dark green**	75.
	p. **blue green**	75.
	q. **light orange**	75.
	r. **dark orange**	85.
	s. **deep orange**	85.
	t. **scarlet**	90.
	u. **carmine**	80.
	x. **dark brown red**	80.
R131TC4	$50 plate on card	
	a. **bright yellow green**	85.
RB1TC3	1c plate on India paper	
	a. **dark purple**	70.
	b. **dull purple**	70.
	d. **brown**	65.
	e. **black brown**	65.
	g. **light blue**	75.
	h. **dark blue**	75.
	i. **ultramarine**	75.
	k. **yellow green**	70.
	l. **dark yellow green**	70.
	n. **green**	65.
	o. **dark green**	65.
	p. **blue green**	65.

q. light orange 65.
r. dark orange 65.
s. deep orange 65.
t. scarlet 65.
u. carmine 65.
x. dark brown red 65.
RB2TC3 2c plate on India paper
a. dark purple 70.
b. dull purple 70.
d. brown 65.
e. black brown 65.
g. light blue 70.
h. dark blue 70.
i. ultramarine 70.
k. yellow green 70.
n. green 65.
o. dark green 65.
p. blue green 65.
q. light orange 65.
r. dark orange 65.
s. deep orange 65.
t. scarlet 65.
u. carmine 65.
x. dark brown red 65.
RB2TC4 2c plate on card
a. bright yellow green 70.
RB3TC3 3c plate on India paper
a. dark purple 70.
b. dull purple 70.
d. brown 65.
e. black brown 65.
g. light blue 70.
h. dark blue 70.
i. ultramarine 70.
k. yellow green 70.
l. dark yellow green 70.
n. green 65.
o. dark green 65.
p. blue green 65.
q. light orange 65.
r. dark orange 65.
s. deep orange 65.
t. scarlet 65.
u. carmine 65.
x. dark brown red 65.
RB4TC3 4c plate on India paper
a. dark purple 70.
b. dull purple 70.
d. brown 65.
e. black brown 65.
g. light blue 70.
h. dark blue 70.
i. ultramarine 70.
k. yellow green 70.
n. green 65.
o. dark green 65.
p. blue green 65.
q. light orange 65.
r. dark orange 65.
s. deep orange 65.
t. scarlet 65.
u. carmine 65.
x. dark brown red 65.
RB5TC3 5c plate on India paper
a. dark purple 70.
b. dull purple 70.
d. brown 65.
e. black brown 65.
g. light blue 70.
h. dark blue 70.
i. ultramarine 70.
k. yellow green 70.
l. dark yellow green 70.
n. green 65.
o. dark green 65.
p. blue green 65.
q. light orange 65.
r. dark orange 65.
s. deep orange 65.
t. scarlet 65.
u. carmine 65.
x. dark brown red 65.
RB5TC4 5c plate on card
a. bright yellow green 70.
RB6TC3 6c plate on India paper
a. dark purple 70.
b. dull purple 70.
d. brown 65.
e. black brown 65.
g. light blue 70.
h. dark blue 70.
i. ultramarine 70.
k. yellow green 70.
l. dark yellow green 70.
n. green 65.
o. dark green 65.
p. blue green 65.
q. light orange 65.
r. dark orange 65.
s. deep orange 65.
t. scarlet 65.
u. carmine 65.
x. dark brown red 65.
RB7TC3 10c plate on India paper
a. dark purple 70.
b. dull purple 70.
d. brown 65.
e. black brown 65.
g. light blue 70.
h. dark blue 70.
i. ultramarine 70.
k. yellow green 70.
l. dark yellow green 70.
n. green 65.
o. dark green 65.
p. blue green 65.
q. light orange 65.
r. dark orange 65.
s. deep orange 65.
t. scarlet 65.
u. carmine 65.
x. dark brown red 65.

Battleship Type

1898

RB20TC1d ⅛c large die on card
e. light blue *1,000.*
RB20P1 ⅛c yel grn, lg die on India paper *2,000.*
RB21TC1a ¼c large die on India paper
e. dull green 1,300.
RB21P1 ¼c brn, lg die on India paper *2,000.*
RB22TC1a ⅜c large die on India paper
e. dull green 750.
RB22P1 ⅜c dp org, lg die on India paper *2,000.*
RB23P1 ⅝c dp ultra, lg die on India paper *2,000.*
RB24TC1a 1c large die on India paper
e. dull green 750.
RB24P1 1c dk grn, lg die on India paper *2,000.*
RB25P1 1¼c vio, lg die on India paper *2,000.*
RB26TC1a 1⅞c large die on India paper
e. dull green 750.
f. black 750.
RB26P1 1⅞c dull bl, lg die on India paper *2,000.*
RB27TC1a 2c large die on India paper
e. dull green 500.
RB27P1 2c vio brn, lg die on India paper *2,000.*
RB28P1 2½c lake, lg die on India paper *2,000.*
RB29P1 3¾c ol gray, lg die on India paper *2,000.*
RB30P1 4c pur, lg die on India paper *2,000.*
RB31TC1a 5c large die on India paper
e. dull green 500.
RB31P1 5c brn org, lg die on India paper *2,000.*

Stock Transfer

1918-29

RD20TC1a $50 large die on India paper
e. black *2,250.*
f. blue *2,250.*

Wines

1916

RE33P1 3c grn, with "c" punch cancel, lg die on India paper —
RE34P1 4c grn, with "c" punch cancel, lg die on India paper —
RE41P1 20c grn, with "c" punch cancel, lg die on India paper —
RE42TC1a 24c large die on India paper
e. blue —
RE48P1 80c grn, with "c" punch cancel, lg die on India paper —
RE51TC1a $1.60 large die on India paper
e. bister —
RE56P1 $20 grn, lg die on India paper *5,000.*

Playing Cards

1896 **Bureau of Engraving & Printing**

RF1TC1a 2c large die on India paper
e. black, (On hand) *1,500.*
RF2TC1a 2c large die on India paper
e. lake, (Act of) *1,000.*
RF2P1 2c ultra, lg die on India paper 550.
a. blue *1,100.*
RF23P1 10c light blue, large die on India paper *4,500.*

Silver Tax

1941

RG60P1 3c gray, without overprint, with "c" punch cancel, lg die on India paper *1,500.*
RG61P1 4c gray, without overprint, with "c" punch cancel, lg die on India paper *1,500.*
RG66P1 25c gray, without overprint, with "c" punch cancel, lg die on India paper *1,500.*
RG72P1 $3 gray, without overprint, lg die on India paper *1,500.*
RG77P5 $30 gray, plate on stamp paper, imperf., serial #0000 *900.*

Consular Service Fee

1952

RK40P1a $20 violet, large die on wove, on card —

PRIVATE DIE PROPRIETARY

The editors are indebted to Eric Jackson and Philip T. Bansner for the compilation of the following listing of Private Die Proprietary die and plate proofs as well as the corrresponding trial color proofs. The large die proofs range in size and format from die impressions on India die sunk on cards generally up to 6x9 inches, through die impressions on India on or off card in medium to stamp size. Many individual listings are known in more than one size and format. Values reflect the size and format most commonly seen.

Private Die Match Stamps

1864

RO1TC1a 1c large die on India paper
e. black 210.
f. green 360.
RO1P1 1c bl, lg die on India paper 270.
RO2TC1a 1c large die on India paper
e. black 270.
f. green 360.
RO2P1 1c org, lg die on India paper 600.
RO2P3 1c org, plate on India paper 90.
RO3P1 1c bl, lg die on India paper 270.
RO4P1 1c bl, lg die on India paper 600.
RO5TC1a 1c large die on India paper
e. black 330.
f. blue 600.
RO5P1 1c grn, lg die on India paper 600.
RO6TC1a 1c large die on India paper
e. black 360.
f. green 600.
RO6P1 1c bl, lg die on India paper 210.
RO7TC1a 1c large die on India paper
e. black 360.
f. green 360.
g. dull green 600.
RO7P1 1c bl, lg die on India paper 210.
RO9TC1a 1c large die on India paper
e. blue 270.
f. brown 330.
g. dark green 600.
h. green 360.
RO9P1 1c blk, lg die on India paper 210.
RO10TC1a 1c large die on India paper
e. blue 360.
f. green 600.
RO10P1 1c blk, lg die on India paper 220.
RO11TC1a 3c large die on India paper
e. blue 600.
f. green 600.
RO11P1 3c blk, lg die on India paper 300.
RO12TC1a 1c large die on India paper
e. blue 270.
f. green 600.
RO12P1 1c blk, lg die on India paper 270.
RO13TC1a 3c large die on India paper
e. black 600.
f. blue 1,200.
RO13P1 3c grn, lg die on India paper 1,200.
RO14TC1a 1c large die on India paper
e. blue 270.
f. green 600.
RO14P1 1c blk, lg die on India paper 210.
RO15TC1a 1c large die on India paper
e. black 270.
f. blue 270.
RO15P1 1c grn, lg die on India paper 360.
RO16TC1a 1c large die on India paper
e. black 270.
f. green 360.
RO16P1 1c bl, lg die on India paper 270.
RO16P3 1c bl, plate on India paper 60.
RO17TC1a 1c large die on India paper
e. black 270.
f. green 600.
g. green, composite RO17TC+RO19TC 1,500.
RO17P1 1c bl, lg die on India paper 210.
a. 1c+3c bl, RO17P1+RO19TC1e composite 1,200.
b. 1c+3c blk, RO17TC1e+RO19P1 composite 900.
RO19TC1a 3c large die on India paper
e. blue 300.
f. green 125.
RO19P1 3c blk, lg die on India paper 450.
RO20TC1a 1c large die on India paper
e. black 210.
f. green 600.
RO20P1 1c bl, lg die on India paper 210.
RO21TC1a 3c large die on India paper
e. blue 450.
f. green 450.
RO21P1 3c blk, lg die on India paper 300.
RO22TC1a 1c large die on India paper
e. black 360.
RO23TC1a 1c large die on India paper
e. black 270.
f. blue 270.
g. green 600.
RO23P1 1c org, lg die on India paper 270.
RO24TC1a 1c large die on India paper
e. black 270.
f. blue 270.
g. green 600.
RO24P1 1c brn, lg die on India paper 270.
RO25TC1a 12c large die on India paper
e. black 475.
f. blue 900.
g. green 900.
RO26TC1a 1c large die on India paper
e. black 270.
f. blue 270.
g. dark brown 270.
h. green 360.
i. light brown 360.
RO27TC1a 12c large die on India paper
e. black 475.
f. blue 600.
g. green 900.
RO28TC1a 1c large die on India paper
e. black 210.
f. brown 360.
g. green 360.
RO28P1 1c bl, lg die on India paper 360.
RO28P3 1c bl, plate on India paper 90.
RO29TC1a 1c large die on India paper
e. blue 360.
f. green 360.
RO29P1 1c blk, lg die on India paper 210.
RO30TC1a 1c large die on India paper
e. black 210.
f. blue 270.
g. green 360.
h. red 600.
RO30P1 1c grn, lg die on India paper 210.
RO31TC1a 1c large die on India paper
e. blue 360.
f. green 270.
g. red 600.
RO31P1 1c blk, lg die on India paper 210.
RO32TC1a 4c large die on India paper
e. blue 600.
f. brown 600.
g. orange 600.
h. vermilion 600.

RO32P1	4c **blk,** lg die on India paper	360.
RO33P1	4c **grn,** lg die on India paper	270.
RO35TC1a	1c large die on India paper	
	***e.* blue**	360.
	***f.* green**	600.
RO35P1	1c **blk,** lg die on India paper	210.
RO37TC1a	3c large die on India paper	
	***e.* blue**	475.
	***f.* green**	475.
RO37P1	3c **blk,** lg die on India paper	270.
RO38TC1a	1c large die on India paper	
	***e.* blue**	425.
	***f.* dark blue**	600.
	***g.* green**	450.
	***h.* red**	725.
RO38P1	1c **blk,** lg die on India paper	425.
RO39TC1a	1c large die on India paper	
	***e.* black**	360.
RO39P1	1c **grn,** lg die on India paper	600.
RO40P1	1c **bl,** lg die on India paper	210.
RO41TC1a	1c large die on India paper	
	***e.* black**	270.
	***f.* green**	360.
RO41P1	1c **lake,** lg die on India paper	270.
RO42TC1a	1c large die on India paper	
	***e.* black**	360.
	***f.* blue**	360.
	***g.* green**	600.
RO42P1	1c **lake,** lg die on India paper	270.
RO43TC1a	1c large die on India paper	
	***e.* blue**	600.
RO43P1	1c **blk,** lg die on India paper	270.
RO44P1	1c **grn,** lg die on India paper	270.
RO45TC1a	1c large die on India paper	
	***e.* blue**	425.
	***f.* green**	900.
RO45P1	1c **blk,** lg die on India paper	270.
RO46TC1a	1c large die on India paper	
	***e.* blue**	425.
	***f.* dark blue**	600.
	***g.* green**	600.
	***h.* orange**	360.
RO46P1	1c **blk,** lg die on India paper	360.
RO47TC1a	1c large die on India paper	
	***e.* blue**	360.
	***f.* green**	600.
RO47P1	1c **blk,** lg die on India paper	270.
RO47P3	1c **blk,** plate on India paper	90.
RO47P4	1c **blk,** plate on card	75.
RO48P1	1c **blk,** lg die on India paper	600.
RO49TC1a	1c large die on India paper	
	***e.* blue**	270.
	***f.* brown**	600.
	***g.* brown red**	360.
	***h.* dark blue**	600.
	***i.* green**	600.
	***j.* red brown**	600.
RO49P1	1c **blk,** lg die on India paper	210.
RO50P1	1c **blk,** lg die on India paper	450.
RO55TC1a	1c large die on India paper	
	***e.* blue**	450.
RO55P1	1c **blk,** lg die on India paper	300.
RO56TC1a	1c large die on India paper	
	***e.* blue**	900.
	***f.* green**	360.
RO56P1	1c **blk,** lg die on India paper	300.
RO57TC1a	1c large die on India paper	
	***e.* black**	210.
	***f.* blue**	270.
RO57P1	1c **grn,** lg die on India paper	360.
RO58TC1a	1c large die on India paper	
	***e.* black**	360.
	***f.* blue**	270.
	***g.* dark rose**	600.
	***h.* green**	600.
	***i.* rose**	360.
RO58P1	1c **lake,** lg die on India paper	270.
RO58P3	1c **lake,** plate on India paper	75.
RO59TC1a	1c large die on India paper	
	***e.* black**	270.
RO60TC1a	3c large die on India paper	
	***e.* blue**	600.
	***f.* green**	600.
RO60P1	3c **blk,** lg die on India paper	360.
RO61TC1a	1c large die on India paper	
	***e.* black**	210.
	***f.* blue**	360.
RO61P1	1c **grn,** lg die on India paper	360.
RO62TC1a	1c large die on India paper	
	***e.* black**	210.
	***f.* blue**	210.
RO62P1	1c **grn,** lg die on India paper	210.
RO64TC1a	1c large die on India paper	
	***e.* black**	270.
	***f.* blue**	360.
	***g.* green**	360.
RO64P1	1c **lake,** lg die on India paper	270.
RO65TC1a	1c large die on India paper	
	***e.* green**	360.
RO65P1	1c **blk,** lg die on India paper	270.
RO66P1	1c **bl,** lg die on India paper	210.
RO67TC1a	1c large die on India paper	
	***e.* blue**	270.
	***f.* green**	360.
	***g.* red**	600.
	***h.* rose**	600.
RO67P1	1c **blk,** lg die on India paper	210.
RO68TC1a	1c large die on India paper	
	***e.* black**	270.
	***f.* blue**	270.
RO68P1	1c **grn,** lg die on India paper	270.
RO69TC1a	1c large die on India paper	
	***e.* blue**	360.
	***f.* green**	600.
RO69P1	1c **blk,** lg die on India paper	210.
RO71TC1a	1c large die on India paper	
	***e.* black**	300.
	***f.* green**	475.
RO72TC1a	1c large die on India paper	
	***e.* black**	600.
RO72P1	1c **grn,** lg die on India paper	600.
RO73TC1a	1c large die on India paper	
	***e.* blue**	270.
	***f.* green**	360.
	***g.* red**	600.
	***h.* red brown**	270.
RO73P1	1c **blk,** lg die on India paper	210.
RO75P1	1c **car,** lg die on India paper	540.
RO76TC1a	1c large die on India paper	
	***e.* blue**	600.
	***f.* green**	360.
RO76P1	1c **blk,** lg die on India paper	210.
RO77TC1a	1c large die on India paper	
	***e.* black**	270.
	***f.* green**	360.
RO77P1	1c **bl,** lg die on India paper	270.
RO78TC1a	1c large die on India paper	
	***e.* black**	270.
	***f.* dark blue**	600.
	***g.* green**	600.
RO78P1	1c **bl,** lg die on India paper	270.
RO80TC1a	1c large die on India paper	
	***e.* black**	270.
	***f.* green**	600.
RO80P1	1c **bl,** lg die on India paper	600.
RO81TC1a	1c large die on India paper	
	***e.* blue**	210.
	***f.* dark green**	600.
	***g.* green**	270.
	***h.* lake**	600.
	***i.* red**	360.
RO81P1	1c **blk,** lg die on India paper	210.
RO82TC1a	1c large die on India paper	
	***e.* blue**	210.
	***f.* green**	600.
RO82P1	1c **blk,** lg die on India paper	210.
RO83TC1a	1c large die on India paper	
	***e.* black**	210.
	***f.* green**	360.
	***g.* red**	600.
RO83P1	1c **bl,** lg die on India paper	210.
RO84TC1a	1c large die on India paper	
	***e.* blue**	360.
	***f.* green**	600.
RO84P1	1c **blk,** lg die on India paper	210.
RO85TC1a	1c large die on India paper	
	***e.* black**	300.
	***f.* blue**	360.
	***g.* green**	425.
	***h.* orange**	600.
	***i.* vermilion**	600.
RO85P1	1c **brn,** lg die on India paper	360.
RO85P3	1c **brn,** plate on India paper	100.
RO86TC1a	1c large die on India paper	
	***e.* blue**	600.
	***f.* brown**	600.
	***g.* green**	475.
	***h.* orange**	600.
	***i.* red**	600.
RO86P1	1c **blk,** lg die on India paper	300.
RO86P3	1c **blk,** plate on India paper	125.
RO87TC1a	1c large die on India paper	
	***e.* dull rose**	600.
	***f.* orange**	600.
RO87P1	1c **blk,** lg die on India paper	600.
RO87P3	1c **blk,** plate on India paper	50.
RO88TC1a	1c large die on India paper	
	***e.* blue**	360.
	***f.* green**	600.
RO88P1	1c **blk,** lg die on India paper	210.
RO89TC1a	3c large die on India paper	
	***e.* blue**	360.
	***f.* green**	360.
RO89P1	3c **blk,** lg die on India paper	210.
RO90TC1a	6c large die on India paper	
	***e.* blue**	270.
	***f.* brown**	600.
	***g.* green**	600.
	***h.* orange**	600.
RO90P1	6c **blk,** lg die on India paper	210.
RO90P3	6c **blk,** plate on India paper	125.
RO91TC1a	3c large die on India paper	
	***e.* blue**	270.
	***f.* brown**	600.
	***g.* green**	600.
	***h.* orange**	600.
	***i.* red**	600.
RO91P1	3c **blk,** lg die on India paper	270.
RO91P3	3c **blk,** plate on India paper	125.
RO92TC1a	1c large die on India paper	
	***e.* blue**	360.
	***f.* green**	600.
RO92P1	1c **blk,** lg die on India paper	210.
RO94TC1a	3c large die on India paper	
	***e.* blue**	270.
	***f.* brown**	360.
	***g.* green**	270.
	***h.* orange**	360.
	***i.* red**	600.
	***j.* vermilion**	600.
RO94P1	3c **blk,** lg die on India paper	210.
RO94P3	3c **blk,** plate on India paper	175.
RO95TC1a	1c large die on India paper	
	***e.* black**	210.
	***f.* blue**	210.
	***g.* brown**	270.
	***h.* dark blue**	600.
RO95P1	1c **grn,** lg die on India paper	270.
RO96TC1a	1c large die on India paper	
	***e.* black**	210.
	***f.* blue**	270.
RO96P1	1c **grn,** lg die on India paper	360.
RO97TC1a	1c large die on India paper	
	***e.* blue**	360.
RO97P1	1c **blk,** lg die on India paper	210.
RO98P1	1c **grn,** lg die on India paper	270.
RO99TC1a	1c large die on India paper	
	***e.* black**	210.
	***f.* blue**	600.
RO99P1	1c **grn,** lg die on India paper	600.
RO100TC1a	1c large die on India paper	
	***e.* blue**	600.
RO100P1	1c **grn,** lg die on India paper	270.
RO100P3	1c **grn,** plate on India paper	65.
RO101TC1a	3c large die on India paper	
	***e.* black**	210.
	***f.* green**	360.
RO101TC3	3c Plate on India paper	
	***a.* orange**	75.
RO101P3	3c **car,** plate on India paper	75.
RO102TC1a	1c large die on India paper	
	***e.* black**	210.
	***f.* blue**	600.
	***g.* green**	600.
RO102P3	5c **org,** plate on India paper	75.
RO103TC1a	1c large die on India paper	
	***e.* blue**	270.
	***f.* rose**	360.
RO103P1	1c **blk,** lg die on India paper	210.
RO104P1	1c **grn,** lg die on India paper	210.
RO105TC1a	1c large die on India paper	
	***e.* blue**	360.
	***f.* green**	600.
RO105P1	1c **blk,** lg die on India paper	210.
RO105P3	1c **blk,** plate on India paper	100.
RO106TC1a	1c large die on India paper	
	***e.* black**	210.
	***f.* blue**	270.
RO106P1	1c **grn,** lg die on India paper	360.
RO107TC1a	1c large die on India paper	
	***e.* black**	210.
	***f.* green**	360.
RO107P1	1c **bl,** lg die on India paper	270.
RO108P1	1c **red,** lg die on India paper	900.
RO109P1	1c **blk,** lg die on India paper	360.
RO110TC1a	1c large die on India paper	
	***e.* black**	210.
	***f.* blue**	210.
	***g.* orange**	600.
	***h.* red**	270.
RO110P1	1c **grn,** lg die on India paper	210.
RO112TC1a	1c large die on India paper	
	***e.* black**	210.
	***f.* green**	600.
RO112P1	1c **bl,** lg die on India paper	270.
RO112P3	1c **bl,** plate on India paper	100.
RO113TC1a	1c large die on India paper	
	***e.* blue**	360.
	***f.* green**	600.
	***g.* orange**	600.
RO113P1	1c **blk,** lg die on India paper	210.
RO114TC1a	1c large die on India paper	
	***e.* black**	900.
RO114P1	1c **lake,** lg die on India paper	900.
RO115TC1a	1c large die on India paper	
	***e.* black**	210.
	***f.* green**	600.
RO115P1	1c **bl,** lg die on India paper	210.
RO116TC1a	1c large die on India paper	
	***e.* black**	270.
	***f.* green**	360.
RO116P1	1c **bl,** lg die on India paper	210.
RO118TC1a	8c large die on India paper	
	***e.* black**	270.
	***f.* dark blue**	600.
	***g.* green**	600.
RO118P1	8c **bl,** lg die on India paper	600.
RO119TC1a	1c large die on India paper	
	***e.* black**	270.
	***f.* blue**	270.
RO119P1	1c **grn,** lg die on India paper	360.
RO120TC1a	1c large die on India paper	
	***e.* black**	600.
RO120P1	1c+2c **grn,** RO120P1+RS29P1 composite, lg die on India paper	1,500.
RO121TC1a	1c large die on India paper	
	***e.* black**	210.
	***f.* blue**	360.
RO121P1	1c **grn,** lg die on India paper	600.
RO122TC1a	1c large die on India paper	
	***e.* blue**	360.
	***f.* green**	600.
RO122P1	1c **blk,** lg die on India paper	210.
RO123TC1a	1c large die on India paper	
	***e.* blue**	600.
RO123P1	1c **blk,** lg die on India paper	210.
RO124P1	1c **grn,** lg die on India paper	900.
RO125TC1a	1c large die on India paper	
	***e.* black**	270.
RO125P1	1c **bl,** lg die on India paper	360.
RO126P1	1c **blk,** lg die on India paper	210.
RO127TC1a	1c large die on India paper	
	***e.* black**	360.
	***f.* green**	270.
RO127P1	1c **bl,** lg die on India paper	210.
RO128TC1a	1c large die on India paper	
	***e.* black**	270.
	***f.* green**	600.
RO128P1	1c **bl,** lg die on India paper	270.
RO130TC1a	1c large die on India paper	
	***e.* black**	270.
	***f.* green**	360.
RO130P1	1c **bl,** lg die on India paper	600.
RO130P4	1c **bl,** plate on thin card	—
RO131TC1a	1c large die on India paper	
	***e.* black**	210.
	***f.* green**	270.
	***g.* red**	270.
RO131P1	1c **bl,** lg die on India paper	360.
RO132TC1a	1c large die on India paper	
	***e.* black**	270.
	***f.* green**	600.
RO132P1	1c **bl,** lg die on India paper	270.
RO132P3	1c **bl,** plate on India paper	125.

RO133TC1a 1c large die on India paper
e. **blue** 600.
f. **green** 360.
RO133P1 1c **blk,** lg die on India paper 270.
RO134TC1a 1c large die on India paper
e. **black** 360.
f. **green** 360.
RO134TC3 1c plate on India paper
a. **black** 150.
RO134P1 1c **bl,** lg die on India paper 210.
RO134P3 1c **bl,** plate on India paper 75.
RO135TC1a 1c large die on India paper
e. **black** 600.
f. **blue** 360.
g. **green** 360.
h. **rose** 270.
RO135P1 1c **lake,** lg die on India paper 600.
RO136TC1a 1c large die on India paper
e. **black** 270.
f. **green** 360.
RO136P1 1c **bl,** lg die on India paper 210.
RO137TC1a 1c large die on India paper
e. **black** 210.
f. **blue** 210.
g. **green** 600.
RO138TC1a 1c large die on India paper
e. **black** 210.
f. **blue** 600.
RO138P1 1c **grn,** lg die on India paper 210.
RO139TC1a 5c large die on India paper
e. **black** 210.
f. **green** 600.
RO139P1 5c **bl,** lg die on India paper 270.
RO140TC1a 4c large die on India paper
e. **black** 270.
f. **blue** 360.
RO140P1 4c **grn,** lg die on India paper 270.
RO141TC1a 1c large die on India paper
e. **black** 210.
f. **dark blue** 360.
g. **green** 600.
h. **yellow green** 360.
RO141P1 1c **bl,** lg die on India paper 210.
RO142TC1a 1c large die on India paper
e. **black** 210.
f. **blue** 270.
RO142P1 1c **grn,** lg die on India paper 270.
RO143TC1a 3c large die on India paper
e. **black** 210.
f. **blue** 270.
g. **green** 360.
RO143P1 3c **org,** lg die on India paper 270.
RO144TC1a 1c large die on India paper
e. **black** 600.
RO144P1 1c **bl,** lg die on India paper 475.
RO145TC1a 1c large die on India paper
e. **black** 600.
f. **blue** 600.
RO146TC1a 1c large die on India paper
e. **blue** 600.
f. **green** 360.
RO146P1 1c **blk,** lg die on India paper 210.
RO148TC1a 1c large die on India paper
e. **black** 210.
f. **green** 360.
g. **red** 360.
RO148P1 1c **bl,** lg die on India paper 270.
RO148P3 1c **bl,** plate on India paper 100.
RO152TC1a 1c large die on India paper
e. **blue** 360.
f. **green** 360.
RO152P1 1c **blk,** lg die on India paper 210.
RO152P3 1c **blk,** plate on India paper 75.
RO153TC1a 1c large die on India paper
e. **blue** 270.
f. **brown** 360.
g. **green** 270.
h. **orange** 360.
i. **red** 360.
RO153P1 1c **blk,** lg die on India paper 210.
RO153P3 1c **blk,** plate on India paper 75.
RO155TC1a 1c large die on India paper
e. **blue** 270.
f. **green** 600.
RO155P1 1c **blk,** lg die on India paper 210.
RO155P3 1c **blk,** plate on India paper 65.
RO157TC1a 3c large die on India paper
e. **black** 210.
f. **green** 360.
RO157P1 3c **bl,** lg die on India paper 270.
RO157P3 3c **bl,** plate on India paper 80.
RO158TC1a 1c large die on India paper
e. **blue** 360.
f. **green** 600.
RO158P1 1c **blk,** lg die on India paper 210.
RO159TC1a 3c large die on India paper
e. **black** 270.
f. **green** 600.
RO159P1 3c **bl,** lg die on India paper 210.
RO160TC1a 1c large die on India paper
e. **black** 270.
f. **brown** 600.
g. **green** 360.
RO160P1 1c **bl,** lg die on India paper 210.
RO161TC1a 1c large die on India paper
e. **black** 270.
f. **green** 360.
RO161P1 1c **bl,** lg die on India paper 600.
RO163TC1a 1c large die on India paper
e. **blue** 360.
f. **green** 600.
RO163P1 1c **blk,** lg die on India paper 210.
RO164TC1a 1c large die on India paper
e. **black** 600.
RO164P1 1c **lake,** lg die on India paper 600.
RO165TC1a 12c large die on India paper
e. **black** 900.
f. **green** 1,200.
g. **red** 1,200.
RO165P1 12c **bl,** lg die on India paper 900.
RO166TC1a 1c large die on India paper
e. **black** 360.
f. **blue** 270.
g. **green** 600.
h. **red** 210.
RO166P1 1c **ver,** lg die on India paper 270.
RO167TC1a 3c large die on India paper
e. **black** 210.
f. **green** 360.
g. **red** 360.
h. **ultramarine** 360.
RO167P1 3c **bl,** lg die on India paper 210.
RO168TC1a 1c large die on India paper
e. **black** 600.
f. **green** 360.
RO168P1 1c **bl,** lg die on India paper 210.
RO170P1 1c **blk,** lg die on India paper 550.
RO171TC1a 1c large die on India paper
e. **blue** 360.
f. **green** 360.
RO171P1 1c **blk,** lg die on India paper 210.
RO172TC1a 1c large die on India paper
e. **blue** 270.
f. **green** 600.
RO172P1 1c **blk,** lg die on India paper 210.
RO173TC1a 1c large die on India paper
e. **black** 270.
f. **green** 360.
RO173P1 1c **bl,** lg die on India paper 270.
RO173P3 1c **bl,** plate on India paper 75.
RO174TC1a 1c large die on India paper
e. **black** 360.
f. **green** 360.
RO174P1 1c **bl,** lg die on India paper 210.
RO175TC1a 1c large die on India paper
e. **blue** 325.
f. **green** 425.
g. **red** 600.
RO175P1 1c **blk,** lg die on India paper 270.
RO176P1 1c **bl,** lg die on India paper 600.
RO177TC1a 1c large die on India paper
e. **black** 210.
f. **blue** 270.
g. **green** 600.
RO177P1 1c **grn,** lg die on India paper 210.
RO178TC1a 1c large die on India paper
e. **black** 210.
f. **blue** 360.
RO178P1 1c **grn,** lg die on India paper 600.
RO179TC1a 1c large die on India paper
e. **blue** 600.
f. **green** 600.
RO179P1 1c **blk,** lg die on India paper 210.
RO179P3 1c **blk,** plate on India paper 75.
RO179P4 1c **blk,** plate on card 75.
RO180TC1a 1c large die on India paper
e. **blue** 270.
f. **green** 600.
RO180P1 1c **blk,** lg die on India paper 210.
RO180P3 1c **blk,** plate on India paper 80.
RO181TC1a 1c large die on India paper
e. **blue** 600.
f. **green** 360.
RO181P1 1c **blk,** lg die on India paper 210.
RO182TC1a 1c large die on India paper
e. **blue** 360.
f. **green** 360.
RO182P1 1c **blk,** lg die on India paper 210.
RO183TC1a 1c large die on India paper
e. **blue** 775.
f. **green** 775.
RO183P1 1c **blk,** lg die on India paper 600.
RO184TC1a 1c large die on India paper
e. **blue** 270.
f. **brown** 360.
g. **green** 270.
h. **orange** 360.
i. **red** 360.
RO184P1 1c **blk,** lg die on India paper 210.
RO184P3 1c **blk,** plate on India paper 75.
RO185P1 1c+1c **blk,** RO185P1+RO12P1 composite, lg die on India paper 900.
RO186TC1a 1c large die on India paper
e. **black** 210.
RO186P1 1c **bl,** lg die on India paper 270.

Private Die Canned Fruit Stamp

RP1TC1a 1c large die on India paper
e. **black** 475.
RP1P1 1c **grn,** lg die on India paper 475.

Private Die Medicine Stamps

RS1TC1a 1c large die on India paper
e. **blue** 360.
RS1P1 1c **blk,** lg die on India paper 210.
RS1P3 1c **blk,** plate on India paper —
RS4TC1a 1c large die on India paper
e. **green** 600.
RS4P1 1c **blk,** lg die on India paper 270.
RS4P3 1c **blk,** plate on India paper 125.
RS4P4 1c **blk,** plate on card 150.
RS5P1 1c **bl,** lg die on India paper 600.
RS10TC1a 4c large die on India paper
e. **black** 360.
RS10P1 4c **bl,** lg die on India paper 270.
RS10P3 4c **bl,** plate on India paper 125.
RS10P4 4c **bl,** plate on card 150.
RS14TC1a 4c large die on India paper
e. **black** 360.
f. **blue** 360.
RS14P1 4c **grn,** lg die on India paper 600.
RS14P3 4c **grn,** plate on India paper 100.
RS16TC1a 2c large die on India paper
e. **green** 600.
RS16P1 2c **ver,** lg die on India paper 600.
RS18P1 1c **blk,** lg die on India paper 600.
RS18P4 1c **blk,** plate on card 125.
RS19P4 2c **blk,** plate on card 125.
RS20P4 4c **blk,** plate on card 125.
RS21TC1a 1c large die on India paper
e. **blue** 600.
f. **green** 600.
RS21P1 1c **blk,** lg die on India paper 210.
RS21P3 1c **blk,** plate on India paper 125.
RS22TC1a 2c large die on India paper
e. **blue** 600.
f. **green** 600.
RS22P1 2c **blk,** lg die on India paper 270.
RS22P3 2c **blk,** plate on India paper 125.
RS23TC1a 4c large die on India paper
e. **green** 600.
RS23P1 4c **blk,** lg die on India paper 270.
RS23P3 4c **blk,** plate on India paper 125.
RS24TC1a 1c large die on India paper
e. **blue** 600.
f. **green** 600.
RS24P1 1c **blk,** lg die on India paper 210.
RS25TC1a 2c large die on India paper
e. **blue** 600.
f. **green** 600.
RS25P1 2c **blk,** lg die on India paper 210.
RS26TC1a 4c large die on India paper
e. **blue** 600.
f. **green** 600.
RS26P1 4c **blk,** lg die on India paper 210.
RS27TC1a 4c large die on India paper
e. **blue** 270.
f. **green** 600.
RS27P1 4c **blk,** lg die on India paper 210.
RS28TC1a 2c large die on India paper
e. **black** 270.
f. **blue** 270.
RS28P1 2c **grn,** lg die on India paper 210.
RS29TC1a 2c large die on India paper
e. **black,** composite RS29TC+RO30TC 900.
f. **black** 210.
g. **blue** 210.
h. **dark blue** 600.
i. **green** 600.
j. **red** 360.
RS29P1 2c **grn,** lg die on India paper 270.

For composite proof RO120P1 + RS29P1, see No. RO120P1.

RS30TC1a 1c large die on India paper
e. **black** 210.
f. **blue** 600.
g. **green** 600.
h. **red** 600.

For composite proof RO30TC and RS29TC, see No. RS29TC1ae.

RS30P1 1c **lake,** lg die on India paper 360.
RS31TC1a 1c large die on India paper
e. **black** 600.
f. **blue** 270.
g. **red** 600.
RS31P1 1c **grn,** lg die on India paper 210.
RS31P3 1c **grn,** plate on India paper 100.
RS31P4 1c **grn,** plate on card 100.
RS33P1 1c **blk,** lg die on India paper 210.
RS33P3 1c **blk,** plate on India paper 50.
RS33P4 1c **blk,** plate on card 50.
RS34TC1a 1c large die on India paper
e. **blue** 210.
f. **green** 270.
g. **red** 600.
RS34P1 1c **blk,** lg die on India paper 270.
RS35TC1a 1c large die on India paper
e. **blue** 360.
f. **green** 600.
RS35P1 1c **blk,** lg die on India paper 210.
RS36TC1a 1c large die on India paper
e. **black** 600.
f. **dark blue** 600.
g. **green** 600.
h. **ultramarine** 600.
i. **yellow green** 270.
RS36P1 1c **bl,** lg die on India paper 210.
RS37P1 2c **blk,** lg die on India paper 550.
RS38TC1a 2c large die on India paper
e. **blue** 900.
f. **green** 900.
RS38P1 2c **blk,** lg die on India paper 360.
RS39TC1a 1c large die on India paper
e. **blue** 360.
f. **green** 360.
g. **orange** 600.
RS39P1 1c **blk,** lg die on India paper 210.
RS39P3 1c **blk,** plate on India paper 100.
RS39P4 1c **blk,** plate on card 100.
RS40TC1a 2c large die on India paper
e. **black** 270.
f. **blue** 360.
RS40P1 2c **grn,** lg die on India paper 600.
RS40P3 2c **grn,** plate on India paper 100.
RS40P4 2c **grn,** plate on card 100.
RS41TC1a 4c large die on India paper
e. **black** 270.
f. **blue** 600.
g. **green** 600.
RS41P3 4c **brn,** plate on India paper 125.
RS41P4 4c **brn,** plate on card 125.
RS42TC1a 1c large die on India paper
e. **green** 600.
f. **blue** 600.
RS42P1 1c **blk,** lg die on India paper 210.
RS43TC1a 4c large die on India paper
e. **black** 270.
f. **green** 600.
RS43P1 4c **bl,** lg die on India paper 270.
RS44TC1a 1c large die on India paper
e. **green** 900.
RS44P1 1c **blk,** lg die on India paper 725.
RS46TC1a 4c large die on India paper
e. **blue** 270.
f. **green** 360.

Number	Description	Price
RS46P1	4c **blk,** lg die on India paper	210.
RS47TC1a	4c large die on India paper	
	e. **blue**	360.
	f. **brown**	600.
	g. **green**	360.
	h. **orange**	600.
	i. **red**	600.
RS47P1	4c **blk,** lg die on India paper	210.
RS47P3	4c **blk,** plate on India paper	125.
RS49TC1a	4c large die on India paper	
	e. **black**	270.
	f. **blue**	360.
RS49P1	4c **grn,** lg die on India paper	210.
RS50TC1a	1c large die on India paper	
	e. **black**	360.
	f. **blue**	360.
	g. **green**	600.
RS50P1	1c **ver,** lg die on India paper	270.
RS51TC1a	2c large die on India paper	
	e. **blue**	600.
	f. **green**	600.
RS51P1	2c **blk,** lg die on India paper	210.
RS52TC1a	4c large die on India paper	
	e. **blue**	600.
	f. **green**	600.
RS52P1	4c **blk,** lg die on India paper	210.
RS53TC1a	1c large die on India paper	
	e. **blue**	270.
	f. **brown**	360.
	g. **green**	270.
	h. **orange**	360.
	i. **red**	360.
RS53P1	1c **blk,** lg die on India paper	210.
RS53P3	1c **blk,** plate on India paper	125.
RS54TC1a	2c large die on India paper	
	e. **blue**	270.
	f. **brown**	360.
	g. **green**	270.
	h. **orange**	360.
	i. **red**	600.
RS54P1	2c **blk,** lg die on India paper	210.
RS54P3	2c **blk,** plate on India paper	125.
RS55TC1a	4c large die on India paper	
	e. **blue**	270.
	f. **green**	270.
	g. **orange**	270.
	h. **red**	600.
RS55P1	4c **blk,** lg die on India paper	210.
RS55P3	4c **blk,** plate on India paper	125.
RS56TC1a	3c large die on India paper	
	e. **black**	425.
	f. **green**	600.
RS56P1	3c **bl,** lg die on India paper	425.
RS56P3	3c **bl,** plate on India paper	125.
RS57TC1a	6c large die on India paper	
	e. **blue**	270.
	f. **brown**	360.
	g. **green**	270.
	h. **orange**	360.
	i. **red**	360.
RS57P1	6c **blk,** lg die on India paper	210.
RS57P3	6c **blk,** plate on India paper	100.
RS58TC1a	4c large die on India paper	
	e. **blue**	270.
	f. **blue green**	600.
	g. **dark blue**	600.
	h. **green**	270.
	i. **light blue**	600.
	j. **red**	270.
RS58P1	4c **blk,** lg die on India paper	210.
RS59TC1a	1c large die on India paper	
	e. **blue**	360.
	f. **green**	600.
RS59P1	1c **blk,** lg die on India paper	210.
RS60TC1a	1c large die on India paper	
	e. **blue**	600.
RS60P1	1c **blk,** lg die on India paper	210.
RS60P3	1c **blk,** plate on India paper	65.
RS61P1	4c **bl,** lg die on India paper	600.
RS62TC1a	1c large die on India paper	
	e. **brown**	360.
	f. **green**	270.
	g. **orange**	360.
	h. **red**	600.
	i. **vermilion**	600.
RS62P1	1c **blk,** lg die on India paper	270.
RS62P3	1c **blk,** plate on India paper	125.
RS63P1	1c **bl,** lg die on India paper	210.
RS64TC1a	2c large die on India paper	
	e. **blue**	270.
	f. **brown**	360.
	g. **green**	270.
	h. **orange**	360.
	i. **red**	600.
	j. **vermilion**	600.
RS64P1	2c **blk,** lg die on India paper	210.
RS64P3	2c **blk,** plate on India paper	125.
RS65TC1a	4c large die on India paper	
	e. **blue**	600.
	f. **green**	600.
RS65P1	4c **blk,** lg die on India paper	210.
RS66TC1a	1c large die on India paper	
	e. **blue**	360.
	f. **green**	600.
	g. **light green**	600.
	h. **orange**	600.
	i. **rose red**	600.
RS66P1	1c **blk,** lg die on India paper	600.
RS66P4	1c **blk,** plate on card	85.
RS67TC1a	1c large die on India paper	
	e. **green**	600.
RS67P1	1c **blk,** lg die on India paper	210.
RS68P1	2c **blk,** lg die on India paper	210.
RS68P3	2c **blk,** plate on India paper	90.
RS69TC1a	1c large die on India paper	
	e. **blue**	600.
	f. **green**	600.
RS69P1	1c **blk,** lg die on India paper	210.
RS70TC1a	2c large die on India paper	
	e. **blue**	600.
	f. **green**	600.
RS70P1	2c **blk,** lg die on India paper	270.
RS71TC1a	1c large die on India paper	
	e. **blue**	600.
	f. **green**	600.
RS71P1	1c **blk,** lg die on India paper	210.
RS72TC1a	2c large die on India paper	
	e. **blue**	600.
	f. **green**	600.
RS72P1	2c **blk,** lg die on India paper	210.
RS73TC1a	2c large die on India paper	
	e. **black**	600.
	f. **blue**	900.
	g. **red**	1,200.
RS73P1	2c **grn,** lg die on India paper	600.
RS74TC1a	1c large die on India paper	
	e. **blue**	600.
	f. **green**	600.
RS74hTC1a	$100 large die on India paper	
	e. **blue**	600.
	f. **green**	600.
RS74P1	1c **blk,** lg die on India paper	270.
	h. **blk,** $100 instead of $1.00 (error), lg die on India paper	210.
RS75TC1a	1c large die on India paper	
	e. **black**	360.
	f. **green**	600.
RS75P1	1c **bl,** lg die on India paper	210.
RS76TC1a	2c large die on India paper	
	e. **blue**	360.
	f. **green**	360.
RS77P1	2c **blk,** lg die on India paper	270.
RS78P1	2c **dull pur,** lg die on India paper	900.
RS81TC1a	4c large die on India paper	
	e. **black**	270.
	f. **blue**	600.
	g. **green**	600.
RS81P1	4c **brn,** lg die on India paper	270.
RS82P1	2c **blk,** lg die on India paper	210.
RS83TC1a	4c large die on India paper	
	e. **blue**	600.
	f. **green**	600.
RS83P1	4c **blk,** lg die on India paper	270.
RS84TC1a	1c large die on India paper	
	e. **black**	300.
	f. **blue**	425.
	g. **green**	300.
	h. **orange**	775.
	i. **red**	775.
	j. **slate**	775.
RS84P1	1c **lake,** lg die on India paper	600.
RS84P3	1c **lake,** plate on India paper	—
RS84P4	1c **lake,** plate on card	110.
RS85TC1a	4c large die on India paper	
	e. **blue**	330.
	f. **brown**	330.
	g. **green**	360.
	h. **orange**	450.
RS85P1	4c **blk,** lg die on India paper	300.
RS85P3	4c **blk,** plate on India paper	—
RS86TC1a	1c large die on India paper	
	e. **black**	270.
	f. **blue**	270.
RS86P1	1c **grn,** lg die on India paper	210.
RS88TC1a	1c large die on India paper	
	e. **blue**	600.
	f. **green**	600.
RS88P1	1c **blk,** lg die on India paper	270.
RS88P3	1c **blk,** plate on India paper	100.
RS88P4	1c **blk,** plate on card	100.
RS89TC1a	1c large die on India paper	
	e. **green**	360.
RS89P1	1c **blk,** lg die on India paper	600.
RS90P1	1c **bl,** lg die on India paper	270.
RS90P3	1c **bl,** plate on India paper	125.
RS90P4	1c **bl,** plate on card	125.
RS91TC1a	4c large die on India paper	
	e. **blue**	270.
	f. **green**	600.
RS91P1	4c **blk,** lg die on India paper	210.
RS92TC1a	3c large die on India paper	
	e. **blue**	270.
	f. **brown**	360.
	g. **green**	270.
	h. **orange**	360.
	i. **red**	600.
	j. **vermilion**	600.
RS92P1	3c **blk,** lg die on India paper	210.
RS92P3	3c **blk,** plate on India paper	—
RS94TC1a	4c large die on India paper	
	e. **blue**	600.
	f. **green**	600.
RS94P1	4c **blk,** lg die on India paper	210.
RS95TC1a	1c large die on India paper	
	e. **black**	360.
	f. **blue**	270.
RS95TC3	1c plate on India paper	
	a. **dark blue**	90.
RS95P1	1c **grn,** lg die on India paper	270.
RS95P3	1c **grn,** plate on India paper	90.
RS96TC1a	3c large die on India paper	
	e. **blue**	270.
	f. **green**	600.
RS96P1	3c **blk,** lg die on India paper	210.
RS96P3	3c **blk,** plate on India paper	50.
RS97TC1a	1c large die on India paper	
	e. **blue**	360.
	f. **green**	600.
RS97P1	1c **blk,** lg die on India paper	210.
RS98TC1a	1c large die on India paper	
	e. **blue**	270.
	f. **green**	210.
	g. **red**	600.
RS98P1	1c **blk,** lg die on India paper	210.
RS99TC1a	4c large die on India paper	
	e. **blue**	600.
RS99P1	4c **blk,** lg die on India paper	210.
RS100TC1a	6c large die on India paper	
	e. **green**	600.
RS100P1	6c **blk,** lg die on India paper	210.
RS101TC1a	1c large die on India paper	
	e. **blue**	600.
	f. **green**	600.
RS101P1	1c **blk,** lg die on India paper	210.
RS102TC1a	2c large die on India paper	
	e. **black**	210.
	f. **green**	270.
	g. **rose**	270.
RS102P1	2c **bl,** lg die on India paper	210.
RS103TC1a	4c large die on India paper	
	e. **blue**	600.
	f. **green**	600.
RS103P1	4c **blk,** lg die on India paper	210.
RS104P1	3c **blk,** lg die on India paper	900.
RS105P1	3c **brn,** lg die on India paper	725.
RS106TC1a	2c large die on India paper	
	e. **black**	600.
	f. **green**	360.
RS106P1	2c **bl,** lg die on India paper	270.
RS106P3	2c **bl,** plate on India paper	60.
RS107TC1a	3c large die on India paper	
	e. **green,** composite RS107TC+RS109TC	1,500.
	f. **blue**	360.
RS107P1	3c **blk,** lg die on India paper	270.
	a. 3c+6c **blk,** RS107P1+RS109P1 composite, lg die on India paper	1,200.
RS108TC1a	4c large die on India paper	
	e. **blue**	360.
	f. **green**	600.
RS108P1	4c **blk,** lg die on India paper	210.
RS108P3	4c **blk,** plate on India paper	45.
RS109TC1a	6c large die on India paper	
	e. **blue**	360.
RS109P1	6c **blk,** lg die on India paper	270.
RS110TC1a	2c large die on India paper	
	e. **black**	360.
	f. **green**	360.
RS110P1	2c **bl,** lg die on India paper	210.
RS111TC1a	4c large die on India paper	
	e. **blue**	360.
	f. **green**	600.
RS111P1	4c **blk,** lg die on India paper	210.
RS114TC1a	1c large die on India paper	
	e. **green**	360.
RS114P1	1c **blk,** lg die on India paper	270.
	a. 1c+2c **blk,** RS114P1+RS115P1 composite, lg die on India paper	1,200.
RS115P1	2c **bl,** lg die on India paper	270.
RS116TC1a	4c large die on India paper	
	e. **black**	270.
	f. **blue**	360.
	g. **brown**	600.
	h. **green**	600.
	i. **vermilion**	600.
RS116P1	4c **red,** lg die on India paper	270.
RS117TC1a	1c large die on India paper	
	e. **blue**	425.
	f. **green**	900.
RS117P1	1c **blk,** lg die on India paper	300.
RS118TC1a	1c large die on India paper	
	e. **black**	210.
	f. **blue**	270.
	g. **brown red**	360.
	h. **green**	360.
RS118P1	1c **red,** lg die on India paper	360.
RS118P3	1c **red,** plate on India paper	55.
RS118P4	1c **red,** plate on card	50.
RS119P1	1c **blk,** lg die on India paper	270.
RS120TC1a	2c large die on India paper	
	e. **blue**	270.
	f. **brown**	360.
	g. **green**	270.
	h. **orange**	360.
	i. **red**	600.
	j. **vermilion**	600.
RS120P1	2c **blk,** lg die on India paper	210.
RS121TC1a	3c large die on India paper	
	e. **blue**	600.
	f. **green**	600.
RS121P1	3c **blk,** lg die on India paper	270.
RS121P3	3c **blk,** plate on India paper	75.
RS122TC1a	2c large die on India paper	
	e. **blue**	600.
	f. **green**	600.
RS122P1	2c **blk,** lg die on India paper	210.
RS122P3	2c **blk,** plate on India paper	100.
RS123TC1a	4c large die on India paper	
	e. **blue**	270.
	f. **brown**	360.
	g. **green**	270.
	h. **orange**	360.
	i. **red**	600.
	j. **vermilion**	600.
RS123P1	4c **blk,** lg die on India paper	210.
RS123P3	4c **blk,** plate on India paper	125.
RS124TC1a	1c large die on India paper	
	e. **black**	210.
	f. **blue green**	360.
	g. **green**	600.
	h. **orange**	600.
	i. **red**	270.
RS124P1	1c **bl,** lg die on India paper	360.
RS124P3	1c **bl,** plate on India paper	90.
RS124P4	1c **bl,** plate on card	65.
RS126TC1a	1c large die on India paper	
	e. **black**	270.
	f. **blue**	270.
	g. **brown**	360.
	h. **orange**	360.
	i. **red**	600.
	j. **vermilion**	600.
RS126P1	1c **grn,** lg die on India paper	210.
RS127TC1a	4c large die on India paper	
	e. **black**	270.
	f. **blue**	270.

g. brown 270.
h. orange 360.
i. red 600.
j. vermilion 600.
RS127P1 4c grn, lg die on India paper 210.
RS127P3 4c grn, plate on India paper 65.
RS128TC1a 2c large die on India paper
e. black 725.
f. green 475.
g. pale blue 600.
RS128P1 2c bl, lg die on India paper 330.
RS128P3 2c bl, plate on India paper 150.
RS130TC1a 4c large die on India paper
e. black 330.
f. blue 425.
RS130P1 4c grn, lg die on India paper 330.
RS131TC1a 4c large die on India paper
e. blue 270.
f. brown 600.
g. green 360.
h. orange 360.
i. red 600.
j. vermilion 600.
RS131P1 4c blk, lg die on India paper 210.
RS131P3 4c blk, plate on India paper 75.
RS132TC1a 4c large die on India paper
e. blue 600.
f. orange 600.
RS132P4 4c blk, plate on card 75.
RS133TC1a 6c large die on India paper
e. blue 600.
f. green 600.
RS133P1 6c blk, lg die on India paper 210.
RS133P3 6c blk, plate on India paper 125.
RS134TC1a 4c large die on India paper
e. black 360.
f. green 360.
g. red 600.
RS134P1 4c bl, lg die on India paper 270.
RS137P1 4c bl, lg die on India paper 600.
RS138TC1a 1c large die on India paper
e. blue 360.
f. green 600.
g. red 600.
h. yellow green 600.
RS138P1 1c blk, lg die on India paper 210.
RS139TC1a 2c large die on India paper
e. black 270.
f. blue 600.
g. green 600.
h. red 270.
i. rose 600.
RS139TC4 2c plate on card
a. blackish violet 90.
RS141TC1a 4c large die on India paper
e. black 270.
f. blue 360.
RS141P1 4c grn, lg die on India paper 360.
RS141P3 4c grn, plate on India paper 125.
RS142TC1a 1c large die on India paper
e. blue 270.
f. brown 360.
g. green 270.
h. orange 360.
i. red 600.
j. vermilion 600.
RS142P1 1c blk, lg die on India paper 210.
RS143TC1a 4c large die on India paper
e. black 270.
f. blue 270.
RS143P1 4c grn, lg die on India paper 270.
RS144TC1a 1c large die on India paper
e. black 600.
f. green 600.
RS144P1 1c bl, lg die on India paper 210.
RS144P3 1c bl, plate on India paper 100.
RS144P4 1c bl, plate on card 100.
RS145TC1a 2c large die on India paper
e. blue 500.
RS145P1 2c blk, lg die on India paper 175.
RS145P3 2c blk, plate on India paper 100.
RS145P4 2c blk, plate on card 100.
RS146TC1a 4c large die on India paper
e. black 360.
f. blue 360.
RS146P1 4c grn, lg die on India paper 270.
RS146P3 4c grn, plate on India paper 100.
RS146P4 4c grn, plate on card 100.
RS150TC1a 1c large die on India paper
e. black 360.
f. blue 210.
g. carmine 600.
h. green 270.
RS150P1 1c ver, lg die on India paper 270.
RS150P3 1c ver, plate on India paper 100.
RS151TC1a 1c large die on India paper
e. blue 600.
f. carmine 600.
RS151P1 1c blk, lg die on India paper 210.
RS152TC1a 2c large die on India paper
e. black 210.
f. blue 360.
RS152P1 2c grn, lg die on India paper 210.
RS153TC1a 4c large die on India paper
e. blue 900.
f. green 900.
RS153P1 4c blk, lg die on India paper 550.
RS153P3 4c blk, plate on India paper 175.
RS153P4 4c blk, plate on card 150.
RS154TC1a 4c large die on India paper
e. black 600.
RS154P1 4c bl, lg die on India paper 600.
RS155TC1a 2c large die on India paper
e. black 360.
f. blue 270.
g. red 600.
RS155P1 2c grn, lg die on India paper 210.
RS156TC1a 6c large die on India paper
e. blue 270.
f. green 270.
g. red 270.
RS156P1 6c blk, lg die on India paper 210.
RS157TC1a 2c large die on India paper
e. blue 270.
f. green 270.
g. red 600.
h. vermilion 360.
RS157P1 2c blk, lg die on India paper 210.
RS158TC1a 1c large die on India paper
e. black 600.
RS158P1 1c grn, lg die on India paper 600.
RS159TC1a 4c large die on India paper
e. black 450.
RS159P1 4c bl, lg die on India paper 270.
RS160TC1a 6c large die on India paper
e. blue 360.
f. green 600.
RS160P1 6c blk, lg die on India paper 270.
RS161TC1a 4c large die on India paper
e. blue 600.
f. green 900.
RS161P1 4c blk, lg die on India paper 360.
RS161P3 4c blk, plate on India paper 150.
RS162TC1a 1c large die on India paper
e. black 210.
f. green 360.
g. red 600.
RS162P1 1c bl, lg die on India paper 360.
RS163TC1a 4c large die on India paper
e. black 360.
f. green 725.
g. yellow green 725.
RS163P1 4c bl, lg die on India paper 725.
RS164TC1a 1c large die on India paper
e. blue 270.
f. green 600.
RS164P1 1c blk, lg die on India paper 210.
RS165TC1a 4c large die on India paper
e. black 210.
f. blue 270.
RS165P1 4c grn, lg die on India paper 600.
RS166TC1a 1c large die on India paper
e. blue 360.
f. green 600.
RS166P1 1c blk, lg die on India paper 210.
RS169TC1a 4c large die on India paper
e. blue 270.
f. green 600.
g. red 270.
RS169P1 4c blk, lg die on India paper 210.
RS170TC1a 1c large die on India paper
e. blue 360.
f. green 600.
RS170P1 1c blk, lg die on India paper 210.
RS171TC1a 1c large die on India paper
e. black 270.
f. blue 270.
g. brown 360.
h. dull blue 600.
i. green 270.
j. orange 360.
k. red 600.
l. vermilion 600.
RS171P1 1c vio, lg die on India paper 210.
u. pur, lg die on India paper 600.
RS172TC1a 2c large die on India paper
e. blue 270.
f. brown 360.
g. green 270.
h. orange 270.
i. red 600.
j. vermilion 600.
RS172P1 2c blk, lg die on India paper 210.
RS172P3 2c blk, plate on India paper 100.
RS173TC1a 1c large die on India paper
e. black 270.
f. green 270.
g. red 360.
RS173P1 1c bl, lg die on India paper 210.
RS174TC1a 1c large die on India paper
e. black 360.
f. dark blue 600.
g. green 360.
RS174P1 1c bl, lg die on India paper 210.
RS175TC1a 2c large die on India paper
e. black 300.
f. blue 600.
g. green 600.
RS176TC1a 4c large die on India paper
e. blue 450.
f. green 600.
RS176P1 4c blk, lg die on India paper 300.
RS177TC1a 2c large die on India paper
e. blue 900.
f. green 1,200.
RS177P1 2c blk, lg die on India paper 425.
RS178TC1a 6c large die on India paper
e. blue 360.
f. green 600.
RS178P1 1c blk, lg die on India paper 270.
RS179TC1a 2c large die on India paper
e. black 360.
f. blue 450.
RS179P1 2c grn, lg die on India paper 270.
RS180TC1a 3c large die on India paper
e. blue 360.
f. green 360.
RS180P1 3c blk, lg die on India paper 325.
RS180P3 3c blk, plate on India paper 125.
RS181TC1a 4c large die on India paper
e. blue 270.
f. green 600.
RS181P1 4c blk, lg die on India paper 270.
RS182TC1a 4c large die on India paper
e. blue 270.
f. green 270.
g. rose 360.
RS182P1 4c blk, lg die on India paper 210.
RS183TC1a 1c large die on India paper
e. black 600.
f. blue 360.
g. green 600.
h. red 270.
RS183P1 1c ver, lg die on India paper 270.
RS183P3 1c ver, plate on India paper 85.
RS184TC1a 2c large die on India paper
e. blue 360.
f. brown 270.
g. green 270.
h. orange 360.
i. vermilion 360.
RS184P1 2c blk, lg die on India paper 210.
RS184P3 2c blk, plate on India paper 100.
RS185TC1a 1c large die on India paper
e. blue 360.
RS185P1 1c blk, lg die on India paper 210.
RS185P3 1c blk, plate on India paper 100.
RS186TC1a 4c large die on India paper
e. blue 270.
f. green 600.
RS186P1 4c blk, lg die on India paper 210.
RS187TC1a 4c large die on India paper
e. blue 270.
f. brown 360.
g. green 360.
h. orange 600.
i. red 600.
j. vermilion 600.
RS187P1 4c blk, lg die on India paper 210.
RS187P3 4c blk, plate on India paper 100.
RS188TC1a 1c large die on India paper
e. blue 600.
f. green 600.
RS188P1 6c blk, lg die on India paper 360.
RS189TC1a 1c large die on India paper
e. black 210.
f. blue 270.
g. red 270.
RS189P1 1c grn, lg die on India paper 270.
RS190TC1a 2c large die on India paper
e. blue 600.
f. green 600.
RS190P1 2c blk, lg die on India paper 210.
RS191TC1a 4c large die on India paper
e. blue 475.
f. green 475.
RS191P1 4c blk, lg die on India paper 300.
RS192TC1a 6c large die on India paper
e. blue 475.
f. green 475.
g. rose 600.
RS192P1 6c blk, lg die on India paper 300.
RS192P3 6c blk, plate on India paper 125.
RS193TC1a 2c large die on India paper
e. blue 600.
f. green 600.
RS193P1 2c blk, lg die on India paper 210.
RS194TC1a 1c large die on India paper
e. green 210.
RS194P1 1c bl, lg die on India paper 210.
RS195TC1a 2c large die on India paper
e. blue 600.
f. green 600.
RS195P1 2c blk, lg die on India paper 210.
RS196TC1a 1c large die on India paper
e. black 600.
f. green 270.
RS196P1 1c bl, lg die on India paper 210.
RS197TC1a 2c large die on India paper
e. blue 360.
RS197P1 2c blk, lg die on India paper 210.
RS198TC1a 1c large die on India paper
e. green 360.
f. red 600.
RS198P1 1c bl, lg die on India paper 270.
RS199TC1a 2c large die on India paper
e. green 600.
RS199P1 2c bl, lg die on India paper 300.
RS200P1 4c blk, lg die on India paper 210.
RS204TC1a 2c large die on India paper
e. blue 600.
f. green 600.
RS204P1 2c blk, lg die on India paper 210.
RS205TC1a 4c large die on India paper
e. blue 270.
f. green 600.
RS205P1 4c blk, lg die on India paper 210.
RS208TC1a 1c large die on India paper
e. black 270.
f. blue 270.
g. orange 360.
RS208P1 1c grn, lg die on India paper 210.
RS208P3 1c grn, plate on India paper 100.
RS208P4 1c grn, plate on card 95.
RS209TC1a 2c large die on India paper
e. black 600.
f. blue 600.
RS209P1 2c grn, lg die on India paper 270.
RS210TC1a 4c large die on India paper
e. blue 270.
f. green 270.
g. red 270.
RS210P1 4c blk, lg die on India paper 270.
RS212TC1a 1c large die on India paper
e. black 270.
f. blue 360.
g. green 600.
RS212P1 1c grn, lg die on India paper 270.
RS212P3 1c grn, plate on India paper 100.

RS213TC1a 6c large die on India paper
e. **blue** 600.
f. **green** 600.
RS213P1 6c **blk,** lg die on India paper 210.
RS213P3 6c **blk,** plate on India paper 100.
RS213P4 6c **blk,** plate on card 150.
RS214TC1a 4c large die on India paper
e. **blue** 360.
f. **brown** 360.
g. **green** 270.
h. **orange** 360.
i. **red** 600.
j. **vermilion** 600.
RS214P1 4c **blk,** lg die on India paper 210.
RS214P3 4c **blk,** plate on India paper 65.
RS215TC1a 1c large die on India paper
e. **black** 360.
f. **blue** 550.
g. **dark red** 600.
h. **green** 600.
RS215P1 1c **lake,** lg die on India paper 360.
RS216TC1a 1c large die on India paper
e. **blue** 600.
f. **green** 600.
RS216P1 1c **blk,** lg die on India paper 210.
RS216P3 1c **blk,** plate on India paper 75.
RS219P1 4c **bl,** lg die on India paper 360.
RS220TC1a 1c large die on India paper
e. **blue** 360.
RS220P1 1c **blk,** lg die on India paper 210.
RS220P3 1c **blk,** plate on India paper 50.
RS221TC1a 4c large die on India paper
e. **black** 210.
f. **blue** 270.
RS221P1 4c **grn,** lg die on India paper 270.
RS221P3 4c **grn,** plate on India paper 50.
RS222TC1a 8c large die on India paper
e. **green** 600.
RS222P1 8c **blk,** lg die on India paper 210.
RS223TC1a 1c large die on India paper
e. **blue** 360.
f. **brown** 360.
g. **green** 270.
h. **orange** 360.
i. **vermilion** 360.
RS223P1 1c **blk,** lg die on India paper 210.
RS223P3 1c **blk,** plate on India paper —
RS224TC1a 1c large die on India paper
e. **blue** 600.
f. **brown** 360.
g. **green** 270.
h. **orange** 360.
i. **red** 600.
RS224P1 1c **blk,** lg die on India paper 210.
RS224P3 1c **blk,** plate on India paper —
RS225P1 4c **blk,** lg die on India paper 210.
RS226TC1a 1c large die on India paper
e. **black** 425.
RS226P3 1c **bl,** plate on India paper 350.
RS228TC1a 1c large die on India paper
e. **black** 210.
f. **blue** 270.
g. **brown** 600.
h. **green** 270.
i. **orange** 600.
j. **red** 600.
k. **vermilion** 600.
RS228P1 1c **brn,** lg die on India paper 270.
RS228P3 1c **brn,** plate on India paper —
RS229TC1a 2c large die on India paper
e. **black** 270.
f. **blue** 270.
g. **brown** 360.
h. **green** 270.
i. **orange** 270.
j. **red** 360.
k. **vermilion** 600.
RS229P1 1c **choc,** lg die on India paper 210.
RS229P3 1c **choc,** plate on India paper 75.
RS230TC1a 6c large die on India paper
e. **blue** 270.
f. **brown** 360.
g. **green** 270.
h. **orange** 360.
i. **vermilion** 270.
RS230P1 6c **blk,** lg die on India paper 210.
RS230P3 6c **blk,** plate on India paper —
RS231TC1a 6c large die on India paper
e. **black** 1,200.
f. **blue** 1,200.
g. **green** 1,200.
h. **red** 900.
RS231P1 6c **org,** lg die on India paper 900.
RS231P4 6c **org,** plate on card 750.
RS232P1 8c **org,** lg die on India paper 900.
RS236TC1a 4c large die on India paper
e. **blue** 600.
RS236P1 4c **blk,** lg die on India paper 210.
RS239TC1a 2c large die on India paper
e. **black** 270.
f. **blue** 360.
g. **brown** 600.
h. **green** 270.
i. **orange** 360.
j. **vermilion** 600.
RS239P1 2c **ver,** lg die on India paper 270.
RS239P3 2c **ver,** plate on India paper 100.
RS240TC1a 4c large die on India paper
e. **blue** 210.
f. **blue green** 600.
g. **brown** 600.
h. **green** 270.
i. **orange** 270.
j. **red** 600.
k. **vermilion** 270.
RS240P1 4c **blk,** lg die on India paper 210.
RS240P3 4c **blk,** plate on India paper 125.

Proofs of Nos. RS239 and RS240 exist in black on card with the denominations and "USIR" obliterated. These most likely are proofs made in preparation of private die facsimile labels, not proofs of or in preparation of revenue stamps.

RS241TC1a 4c large die on India paper
e. **green** 600.
RS241P1 4c **red,** lg die on India paper 270.
RS242TC1a 1c large die on India paper
e. **blue** 270.
f. **green** 600.
RS242P1 4c **blk,** lg die on India paper 210.
RS242P3 4c **blk,** plate on India paper 80.
RS242P4 4c **blk,** plate on card 75.
RS243TC1a 4c large die on India paper
e. **blue** 600.
f. **green** 600.
RS243P1 4c **blk,** lg die on India paper 210.
RS244TC1a 6c large die on India paper
e. **blue** 600.
f. **green** 600.
RS244P1 6c **blk,** lg die on India paper 210.
RS245TC1a 1c large die on India paper
e. **blue** 600.
RS245P1 1c **blk,** lg die on India paper 300.
RS250TC1a 6c large die on India paper
e. **blue** 600.
f. **green** 600.
RS250P1 6c **blk,** lg die on India paper 210.
RS250P3 6c **blk,** plate on India paper 100.
RS251TC1a 1c large die on India paper
e. **blue** 270.
f. **brown** 270.
g. **green** 270.
RS251P1 1c **blk,** lg die on India paper 210.
RS252TC1a 1c large die on India paper
e. **black** 270.
f. **blue** 270.
g. **brown** 360.
h. **green** 270.
i. **orange** 600.
j. **red** 600.
k. **rose** 270.
RS252P1 1c **ver,** lg die on India paper 210.
RS252P3 1c **ver,** plate on India paper 100.
RS253TC1a 4c large die on India paper
e. **blue** 600.
f. **green** 600.
RS253P1 4c **blk,** lg die on India paper 210.
RS258TC1a 6c large die on India paper
e. **black** 600.
RS258P1 6c **brn,** lg die on India paper 210.
RS259TC1a 1c large die on India paper
e. **blue** 270.
f. **brown** 360.
g. **green** 270.
h. **orange** 360.
i. **red** 600.
j. **vermilion** 600.
RS259P1 1c **blk,** lg die on India paper 210.
RS259P3 1c **blk,** plate on India paper 90.
RS260TC1a 2c large die on India paper
e. **blue** 210.
f. **brown** 360.
g. **green** 270.
h. **orange** 360.
i. **red** 600.
j. **rose** 600.
k. **vermilion** 270.
RS260P1 2c **blk,** lg die on India paper 270.
RS260P3 2c **blk,** plate on India paper 90.
RS261TC1a 4c large die on India paper
e. **blue** 270.
f. **brown** 360.
g. **green** 270.
h. **orange** 360.
i. **red** 600.
j. **vermilion** 600.
RS261P1 4c **blk,** lg die on India paper 210.
RS261P3 4c **blk,** plate on India paper 100.
RS262TC1a 2c large die on India paper
e. **blue** 600.
f. **green** 600.
RS262P1 2c **blk,** lg die on India paper 210.
RS263P1 4c **blk,** lg die on India paper 270.
RS263P3 4c **blk,** plate on India paper 90.
RS264TC1a 4c large die on India paper
e. **blue** 360.
f. **green** 360.
RS264P1 4c **blk,** lg die on India paper 270.
RS264AP1 4c **blk,** lg die on India paper 360.
RS265TC1a 1c large die on India paper
e. **black** 270.
f. **blue** 600.
RS265P1 1c **grn,** lg die on India paper 270.
RS267TC1a 4c large die on India paper
e. **black** 270.
f. **blue** 600.
g. **green** 360.
RS267P1 4c **lake,** lg die on India paper 270.
RS270TC1a 12c large die on India paper
e. **black** 360.
f. **blue** 600.
g. **green** 360.
h. **red** 270.
RS270P1 12c **bl,** lg die on India paper 210.
RS271TC1a 4c large die on India paper
e. **blue** 3,000.
RS271P1 4c **blk,** lg die on India paper 3,000.
RS272TC1a 1c large die on India paper
e. **black** 360.
f. **blue** 360.
RS272P1 1c **grn,** lg die on India paper 270.
RS273TC1a 2c large die on India paper
e. **blue** 600.
RS273P1 2c **blk,** lg die on India paper 210.
RS274TC1a 1c large die on India paper
e. **black** 270.
RS274P1 1c **grn,** lg die on India paper 270.
RS274P3 1c **grn,** plate on India paper 65.
RS274P4 1c **grn,** plate on card 60.
RS275TC1a 2c large die on India paper
e. **black** 270.
f. **blue** 360.
RS276P1 2c **grn,** lg die on India paper 210.
RS278TC1a 2½c large die on India paper
e. **black** *1,200.*
RS280TC1a ¼c large die on India paper
e. **black** *1,200.*
RS300P1 4⅜c **blk,** lg die on India paper *1,200.*
RS302TC1a 2½c large die on India paper
e. **black** *1,200.*
RS303TC1a ⅝c large die on India paper
e. **black** *1,200.*
RS306P1 1¼c **pink,** lg die on India paper *1,200.*

Private Die Perfumery Stamps

RT1P3 2c **bl,** plate on India paper 125.
RT1P4 2c **bl,** plate on card 125.
RT2TC1a 1c large die on India paper
e. **brown** 475.
f. **green** 475.
g. **orange** 360.
h. **red** 600.
RT2P1 1c **blk,** lg die on India paper 270.
RT2P3 1c **blk,** plate on India paper 95.
RT4P1 1c **bl,** lg die on India paper 270.
RT5TC1a 2c large die on India paper
e. **black** 210.
f. **blue** 270.
g. **green** 600.
h. **orange** 600.
RT5TC3 2c plate on India paper
a. **orange** 125.
RT5P3 2c **ver,** plate on India paper 100.
RT6TC1a 1c large die on India paper
e. **blue** 450.
f. **brown** 600.
g. **green** 450.
h. **orange** 600.
i. **red** 600.
RT6P1 1c **blk,** lg die on India paper 300.
RT6P3 1c **blk,** plate on India paper 150.
RT8P1 2c **blk,** lg die on India paper 600.
RT10TC1a 4c large die on India paper
e. **blue** 450.
f. **brown** 600.
g. **green** 475.
h. **orange** 600.
i. **red** 600.
RT10P1 4c **blk,** lg die on India paper 300.
RT10P3 4c **blk,** plate on India paper 150.
RT12TC1a 1c large die on India paper
e. **black** 270.
f. **blue** 270.
g. **green** 600.
RT12TC4 1c plate on card
a. **black** 90.
RT12P1 1c **ver,** lg die on India paper 270.
RT12P3 1c **ver,** plate on India paper —
RT13TC1a 2c large die on India paper
e. **black** 270.
f. **blue** 360.
g. **green** 360.
h. **red** 270.
RT13TC3 2c plate on India paper
a. **black** 75.
RT14TC1a 3c large die on India paper
e. **blue** 1,200.
RT14P1 3c **blk,** lg die on India paper 600.
RT16TC1a 1c large die on India paper
e. **blue** 210.
f. **green** 270.
RT16P1 1c **blk,** lg die on India paper 210.
RT17TC1a 2c large die on India paper
e. **black** 360.
f. **blue** 360.
g. **green** 360.
h. **orange** 600.
RT17P1 2c **brn,** lg die on India paper 210.
RT18TC1a 3c large die on India paper
e. **black** 210.
f. **blue** 210.
g. **green** 600.
h. **orange** 600.
i. **red** 360.
RT18P1 3c **grn,** lg die on India paper 210.
RT19TC1a 1c large die on India paper
e. **black** 600.
RT19P1 1c **ver,** lg die on India paper 270.
RT20TC1a 1c large die on India paper
e. **black** 270.
f. **blue** 360.
g. **green** 210.
RT20P1 1c **grn,** lg die on India paper 270.
RT21TC1a 2c large die on India paper
e. **black** 600.
f. **green** 600.
RT21P1 2c **bl,** lg die on India paper 210.
RT22TC1a 1c large die on India paper
e. **black** 210.
f. **blue** 360.
g. **green** 360.
h. **red brown** 360.
i. **ultramarine** 600.
RT22P1 1c **bl,** lg die on India paper 270.
RT23TC1a 2c large die on India paper
e. **blue** 270.
f. **green** 600.
RT23P1 2c **blk,** lg die on India paper 210.
RT24TC1a 3c large die on India paper
e. **black** 210.
f. **blue** 270.

No.	Description	Value
	g. **green**	360.
	h. **red**	270.
RT25TC1a	4c large die on India paper	
	e. **black**	210.
	f. **blue**	270.
RT25P1	4c **grn,** lg die on India paper	210.
RT26TC1a	1c large die on India paper	
	e. **black**	210.
	f. **blue**	270.
	g. **brown**	360.
	h. **green**	600.
	i. **orange**	360.
	j. **red**	600.
RT26P1	1c **grn,** lg die on India paper	210.
RT27P3	1c **grn,** plate on India paper	100.
RT28TC1a	2c large die on India paper	
	e. **black**	270.
	f. **brown**	360.
	g. **green**	270.
	h. **orange**	360.
	i. **red**	360.
RT28P1	2c **bl,** lg die on India paper	210.
RT30TC1a	3c large die on India paper	
	e. **black**	270.
	f. **blue**	270.
	g. **brown**	360.
	h. **green**	270.
	i. **orange**	360.
	j. **red**	210.
RT30P1	3c **ver,** lg die on India paper	270.
RT32TC1a	4c large die on India paper	
	e. **black**	270.
	f. **blue**	270.
	g. **brown**	600.
	h. **green**	270.
	i. **orange**	270.
	j. **red**	360.
RT32P1	4c **brn,** lg die on India paper	210.

Private Die Playing Card Stamps

No.	Description	Value
RU1P1	5c **blk,** lg die on India paper	*4,000.*
RU2TC1a	2c large die on India paper	
	e. **black**	210.
	f. **blue**	270.
	g. **green**	360.
RU3TC1a	2c large die on India paper	
	e. **blue**	270.
	f. **green**	270.
RU3P1	4c **blk,** lg die on India paper	210.
RU3P3	4c **blk,** plate on India paper	100.
RU4TC1a	5c large die on India paper	
	e. **black**	270.
	f. **green**	360.
RU4P1	5c **bl,** lg die on India paper	210.
RU5TC1a	5c large die on India paper	
	e. **black**	270.
	f. **brown**	360.
	g. **green**	360.
	h. **light brown**	600.
	i. **orange**	600.
	j. **red**	600.
RU5P1	5c **bl,** lg die on India paper	210.
RU6TC1a	10c large die on India paper	
	e. **black**	210.
	f. **green**	360.
RU6P1	10c **bl,** lg die on India paper	600.
RU6P3	10c **bl,** plate on India paper	100.
RU7TC1a	5c large die on India paper	
	e. **blue**	450.
	f. **green**	450.
RU7P1	5c **blk,** lg die on India paper	300.
RU7P3	5c **blk,** plate on India paper	100.
RU7P4	5c **blk,** plate on card	—
RU8TC1a	5c large die on India paper	
	e. **blue**	270.
	f. **green**	270.
	g. **orange**	360.
RU8P1	5c **blk,** lg die on India paper	210.
RU9TC1a	5c large die on India paper	
	e. **blue**	270.
	f. **green**	600.
RU9P1	5c **blk,** lg die on India paper	300.
RU10TC1a	2c large die on India paper	
	e. **black**	240.
	f. **brown**	600.
	g. **green**	600.
RU10P1	2c **bl,** lg die on India paper	210.
RU11TC1a	5c large die on India paper	
	e. **black**	270.
	f. **blue**	270.
	g. **brown**	360.
RU11P1	5c **grn,** lg die on India paper	270.
RU12TC1a	5c large die on India paper	
	e. **blue**	360.
	f. **green**	360.
RU12P1	5c **blk,** lg die on India paper	210.
RU13TC1a	5c large die on India paper	
	e. **green**	210.
RU13P1	5c **bl,** lg die on India paper	360.
RU14TC1a	5c large die on India paper	
	e. **blue**	270.
	f. **brown**	360.
	g. **green**	360.
	h. **light brown**	600.
	i. **orange**	600.
	j. **red**	360.
RU14P1	5c **blk,** lg die on India paper	210.
RU14P3	5c **blk,** plate on India paper	—
RU15TC1a	5c large die on India paper	
	e. **blue**	360.
	f. **green**	360.
RU15P1	5c **blk,** lg die on India paper	400.
RU16P1	5c **blk,** lg die on India paper	600.

Hunting Permit

No.	Year	Denom.	Description	Value
RW1P1	1934	$1	**bl,** lg die on wove paper	—
RW1P2	1934	$1	**bl,** small die on wove paper	*22,500.*
RW2P2	1935	$1	**rose lake,** small die on wove paper	*12,500.*
RW3P1	1936	$1	**brn blk,** lg die on wove paper	*8,500.*
RW3P2	1936	$1	**brn blk,** small die on wove paper	*8,500.*
RW4TC1a		$1	large die on India paper	
			e. **light violet**	*5,500.*
RW4P1	1937	$1	**lt grn,** lg die on wove paper	—
RW4P2	1937	$1	**lt grn,** small die on wove paper	*8,500.*
RW5P1	1938	$1	**lt vio,** lg die on wove paper	—
RW5P2	1938	$1	**lt vio,** small die on wove paper	*8,500.*
RW6P2	1939	$1	**choc,** small die on wove paper	*7,500.*
RW7P2	1940	$1	**sepia,** small die on wove paper	*7,500.*
RW8P1	1941	$1	**brn car,** lg die on wove paper	*7,500.*
RW8P2	1941	$1	**brn car,** small die on wove paper	*7,500.*
RW9P2	1942	$1	**vio brn,** small die on wove paper	*7,500.*
RW10P1	1943	$1	**dp rose,** lg die on wove paper	*7,500.*
RW10P2	1943	$1	**dp rose,** small die on wove paper	*7,500.*
RW11P2	1944	$1	**red org,** small die on wove paper	*7,500.*
RW12TC1a		$1	large die on India paper	
			e. **light violet**	*20,000.*
RW12P1	1945	$1	**blk,** lg die on wove paper	*7,500.*
RW12P2	1945	$1	**blk,** small die on wove paper	*7,500.*
RW13P1	1946	$1	**red brn,** lg die on wove paper	*7,500.*
RW13P2	1946	$1	**red brn,** small die on wove paper	*7,500.*
RW14P1	1947	$1	**blk,** lg die on wove paper	*7,500.*
RW14P2	1947	$1	**blk,** small die on wove paper	*7,500.*
RW15P1	1948	$1	**brt bl,** lg die on wove paper	*9,500.*
RW15P2	1948	$1	**brt bl,** small die on wove paper	*7,500.*
RW16P2	1949	$2	**brt grn,** small die on wove paper	*7,500.*
RW17P2	1950	$2	**vio,** small die on wove paper	*7,500.*
RW18P2	1951	$2	**gray blk,** small die on wove paper	*7,500.*
RW19P1	1952	$2	**dp ultra,** lg die on wove paper	*7,500.*
RW20P2	1953	$2	**dp brn rose,** small die on wove paper	*7,500.*
RW21P2	1954	$2	**blk,** small die on wove paper	*7,500.*
RW22P2	1955	$2	**dk bl,** small die on wove paper	*7,500.*
RW23P1	1956	$2	**blk,** lg die on wove paper	*12,500.*
RW23P2	1956	$2	**blk,** small die on wove paper	*7,500.*
RW24P2	1957	$2	**emerald,** small die on wove paper	*7,500.*
RW25P2	1958	$2	**blk,** small die on wove paper	*7,500.*
RW26P5	1959	$3	**multi,** plate on stamp paper	*3,000.*
RW27P5	1960	$3	**multi,** plate on stamp paper	*3,000.*
RW28P5	1961	$3	**multi,** plate on stamp paper	*3,000.*
RW29P5	1962	$3	**multi,** plate on stamp paper	*3,000.*
RW30P5	1963	$3	**multi,** plate on stamp paper	*3,000.*
RW32P5	1965	$3	**multi,** plate on stamp paper	*3,000.*
RW33P5	1966	$3	**multi,** plate on stamp paper	*3,000.*
RW34P5	1967	$3	**multi,** plate on stamp paper	*3,000.*
RW35P5	1968	$3	**multi,** plate on stamp paper	*3,000.*
RW36P5	1969	$3	**multi,** plate on stamp paper	*3,000.*
RW37P5	1970	$3	**multi,** plate on stamp paper	*3,000.*
RW38P5	1971	$3	**multi,** plate on stamp paper	*3,000.*
RW39P5	1972	$5	**multi,** plate on stamp paper	*3,000.*
RW40P5	1973	$5	**multi,** plate on stamp paper	*3,000.*
RW41P5	1974	$5	**multi,** plate on stamp paper	*3,000.*
RW42P5	1975	$5	**multi,** plate on stamp paper	*3,000.*
RW43P5	1976	$5	**grn & blk,** plate on stamp paper	*3,000.*
RW44P5	1977	$5	**multi,** plate on stamp paper	*3,000.*
RW45P5	1978	$5	**multi,** plate on stamp paper	*3,000.*
RW46P5	1979	$7.50	**multi,** plate on stamp paper	*3,000.*
RW47P5	1980	$7.50	**multi,** plate on stamp paper	*3,000.*
RW48P5	1981	$7.50	**multi,** plate on stamp paper	*3,000.*
RW49P5	1982	$7.50	**multi,** plate on stamp paper	*3,000.*
RW50P5	1983	$7.50	**multi,** plate on stamp paper	*3,000.*

Firearms Transfer

No.	Denom.	Description	Value
RY3P1	$1	**grn,** with "c" punch cancel, lg die on wove paper	*2,000.*

POSTAL SAVINGS

1911

No.	Denom.	Description	Value
PS1P1	10c	**org,** large die on India paper	1,000.
PS1P2a	10c	**org,** PP sm die on yelsh wove paper	750.
PS4P2a	10c	**dp bl,** PP sm die on yelsh wove paper	750.

1940

No.	Denom.	Description	Value
PS7TC1	10c	**black,** large die on India paper, die sunk on 97x110mm card	—
PS7P2	10c	**dp ultra,** sm die on wove paper	1,200.
PS8P2	25c	**dk car rose,** sm die on wove paper	1,200.
PS9TC1	50c	**black,** large die on India paper	—
PS9P2	50c	**dk bl grn,** sm die on wove paper	1,200.
PS10P2	$1	**gray blk,** sm die on wove paper	1,200.

1941

No.	Denom.	Description	Value
PS11P2	10c	**rose red,** sm die on wove paper	1,000.
PS12P2	25c	**bl grn,** sm die on wove paper	1,000.
PS13P2	50c	**ultra,** sm die on wove paper	1,000.
PS14P2	$1	**gray blk,** sm die on wove paper	1,000.
PS15P1	$5	**sepia,** large die on wove paper	*4,000.*
PS15P2	$5	**sepia,** sm die on wove paper	1,000.

WAR SAVINGS STAMP

1942

No.	Denom.	Description	Value
WS7P1	10c	**rose red,** large die on India paper	1,400.

SPECIMEN STAMPS

These are regular stamps overprinted "Specimen." Each number has a suffix letter "S" to denote "specimen." The Scott number is that of the stamp as shown in the regular listings and the second letter "A," etc., indicates the type of overprint. Values are for items of a grade of fine-very fine, with at least part original gum.

Specimen
Type A; 12mm long

Specimen.
Type B; 17mm long

Specimen.
Type C; 32mm long

SPECIMEN.
Type D; Capital Letters 12mm long

Specimen.
Type E; Initial Capital

Specimen.
Type F; 22mm long

SPECIMEN
Type G; 14mm long

SPECIMEN
Type H; 16mm long

Specimen
Type I; 20mm long

Specimen
Type J; 23½mm long

Overprinted in Black

1851-56

7S	A	1c **blue,** type II	*2,500.*
11S	A	3c **dull red,** type I	*6,500.*

1857-60

21S	A	1c **blue,** type III	*1,500.*
24S	A	1c **blue,** type V	*1,000.*
26S	A	3c **dull red,** type III	*1,000.*
30S	A	5c **orange brown,** type II	*1,000.*
30AS	A	5c **brown,** type II	*1,850.*
35S	A	10c **green,** type V	*1,250.*
36BS	A	12c **black**	*3,500.*
37S	A	24c **lilac**	*1,000.*
38S	A	30c **orange**	*1,000.*
26S	F	3c **dull red,** type III	*2,000.*
26S	I	3c **dull red,** type III	*4,000.*

1861

63S	A	1c **blue**	900.
65S	A	3c **rose**	900.
68S	A	10c **dark green**	900.
70S	A	24c **red lilac**	900.
72S	A	90c **blue**	900.
73S	A	2c **black**	*2,250.*
76S	A	5c **brown**	*3,000.*

Type B
Overprint Black, Except As Noted

1861-66

63S	B	1c **blue** *(1300)*	200.
		P# block of 8, Impt.	*1,750.*
		Without period	—
65S	B	3c **rose** *(1500)*	200.
68S	B	10c **dark green** *(1600)*	200.
		P# block of 8, Impt.	—
69S	B	12c **black** (orange) *(1300)*	200.
71S	B	30c **orange** *(1400)*	200.
		P# block of 8, Impt.	*15,000.*
72S	B	90c **blue** *(1394)*	120.
		P# block of 8, Impt.	—
73S	B	2c **black** (vermilion) *(1306)*	350.
		Block of 4	*1,100.*
		Without period	*500.*
		Block of 4, one stamp without period	*1,500.*
76S	B	5c **brown** *(1306)*	200.
		P# block of 8, Impt.	—
77S	B	15c **black** (vermilion) *(1208)*	200.
		Block of 4	*900.*
78S	B	24c **lilac** *(1300)*	250.

1867-68

86S	A	1c **blue**	*1,000.*
85ES	A	12c **black**	*1,000.*
93S	A	2c **black**	*1,100.*
94S	A	3c **rose**	*1,000.*
95S	A	5c **brown**	*5,000.*
97S	A	12c **black**	—
98S	A	15c **black**	*1,000.*
99S	A	24c **gray lilac**	*1,250.*
		Split grill	—
100S	A	30c **orange**	*1,250.*

1869

112S	A	1c **buff**	*1,750.*
113S	A	2c **brown**	*1,750.*
115S	A	6c **ultramarine**	*1,750.*
116S	A	10c **yellow**	*1,750.*
116S	H	10c **yellow**	*2,500.*
117S	A	12c **green**	*2,500.*
119S	A	15c **brown & blue**	*1,750.*
120S	A	24c **green & violet**	*1,750.*
	a.	Without grill	—
121S	A	30c **blue & carmine**	*2,750.*
	a.	Without grill	—
122S	A	90c **carmine & black**	*2,000.*
	a.	Without grill	—
123S	B	1c **buff**	*3,500.*
124S	B	2c **brown**	*3,500.*
125S	B	3c **blue** (blue)	*3,500.*
126S	B	6c **blue** (blue)	*3,500.*
127S	B	10c **yellow** (blue)	—
129S	B	15c **brown & blue** (blue)	*5,250.*

1870-71

145S	A	1c **ultramarine**	*600.*
146S	A	2c **red brown**	*600.*
146S	B	2c **red brown**	*600.*
147S	A	3c **green**	*600.*
148S	A	6c **carmine**	*600.*
149S	A	7c **vermilion**	*600.*
150S	A	10c **brown**	*600.*
151S	A	12c **dull violet**	*600.*
152S	A	15c **bright orange**	*600.*
155S	A	90c **carmine**	*600.*
155S	B	90c **carmine** (blue)	*600.*

1873

158S	B	3c **green** (blue)	*750.*
159S	B	6c **dull pink**	*700.*
160S	B	7c **orange vermilion** (blue)	*700.*
162S	B	12c **blackish violet** (blue)	—
165S	B	30c **greenish black** (blue)	*700.*
166S	B	90c **carmine** (blue)	*750.*

Overprinted in Red

Type D

1879

189S	D	15c **red orange**	80.
190S	D	30c **full black**	80.
191S	D	90c **carmine,** brownish black ovpt.	80.
	a.	Overprint in red	—

1881-82

205S	D	5c **yellow brown**	80.
206S	D	1c **gray blue**	80.
207S	D	3c **blue green**	80.
208S	D	6c **brown red**	80.
209S	D	10c **brown**	80.

1883

210S	D	2c **red brown**	100.
211S	D	4c **blue green**	100.

Handstamped in Dull Purple

Type E

1890-93

219S	E	1c **dull blue**	150.
220S	E	2c **carmine**	150.
221S	E	3c **purple**	150.
222S	E	4c **dark brown**	150.
223S	E	5c **chocolate**	150.
224S	E	6c **dull red**	150.
225S	E	8c **lilac**	150.
226S	E	10c **green**	150.
227S	E	15c **blue**	150.
228S	E	30c **black**	150.
229S	E	90c **orange**	175.

COLUMBIAN ISSUE

Handstamped in Dull Purple

1893

230S	E	1c **deep blue**	400.
		Double overprint	—
231S	E	2c **violet**	400.
232S	E	3c **green**	400.
233S	E	4c **ultramarine**	400.
234S	E	5c **chocolate**	400.
235S	E	6c **purple**	400.
236S	E	8c **magenta**	400.
237S	E	10c **black brown**	400.
238S	E	15c **dark green**	400.
239S	E	30c **orange brown**	400.
240S	E	50c **slate blue**	400.
241S	E	$1 **salmon**	500.
242S	E	$2 **brown red**	500.
243S	E	$3 **yellow green**	550.
244S	E	$4 **crimson lake**	575.
245S	E	$5 **black**	675.

Overprinted in Magenta

Specimen.

Type F

230S	F	1c **deep blue**	550.
232S	F	3c **green**	550.
233S	F	4c **ultramarine**	550.
234S	F	5c **chocolate**	550.
235S	F	6c **purple**	550.
237S	F	10c **black brown**	550.
243S	F	$3 **yellow green**	700.

Overprinted Type H in Black or Red

231S	H	2c **violet** (Bk)	625.
233S	H	4c **ultramarine** (R)	625.
234S	H	5c **chocolate** (R)	625.

Overprinted Type I in Black or Red

231S	I	2c **violet** (R)	625.
232S	I	3c **green** (R)	625.
233S	I	4c **ultramarine** (R)	625.
234S	I	5c **chocolate** (Bk)	625.
235S	I	6c **purple** (R)	625.
236S	I	8c **magenta** (Bk)	625.
237S	I	10c **black brown** (R)	625.
238S	I	15c **dark green** (R)	625.
239S	I	30c **orange brown** (Bk)	625.
240S	I	50c **slate blue** (R)	625.

Handstamped Type E in Purple

1895

264S	E	1c **blue**	90.
267S	E	2c **carmine,** type III	90.
267aS	E	2c **pink,** type III	90.
268S	E	3c **purple**	90.
269S	E	4c **dark brown**	140.

270S	E	5c **chocolate**	90.
271S	E	6c **dull brown**	90.
272S	E	8c **violet brown**	90.
273S	E	10c **dark green**	90.
274S	E	15c **dark blue**	90.
275S	E	50c **orange**	90.
276S	E	$1 **black,** type I	325.
276AS	E	$1 **black,** type II	*2,000.*
277S	E	$2 **dark blue**	300.
278S	E	$5 **dark green**	400.

1897-1903

279S	E	1c **deep green**	90.
279BS	E	2c **light red,** type IV	90.
279BjS	E	2c Booklet pane of 6, **light red,** type IV (Bk)	525.
		Never hinged	750.
		With plate number	1,100.
		Never hinged	1,500.
	a.	As No. 279BjS, inverted overprint on all stamps	*12,500.*
	b.	As No. 279BjS, inverted overprint on one stamp	*12,500.*
	c.	As No. 279BjS, double impression of overprint on bottom two stamps	*12,500.*
280S	E	4c **rose brown**	160.
281S	E	5c **dark blue**	80.
282S	E	6c **lake**	80.
282CS	E	10c **brown,** type I	80.
283S	E	10c **brown,** type II	500.
284S	E	15c **olive green**	80.

Special Printing

In March 1900 one pane of 100 stamps of each of Nos. 279, 279B, 268, 280-282, 272, 282C, 284 and 275-278 were specially handstamped type E "Specimen" in black for displays at the Paris Exposition (1900) and Pan American Exposition (1901). The 2c pane was light red, type IV.

These examples were handstamped by H. G. Mandel and mounted by him in separate displays for the two Expositions. Examples from the panes in addition to those displayed were handstamped "Specimen," but most were destroyed after the Expositions. Examples of all issues that were handstamped are known.

Additional stamps, not from the mounted display panes, do exist with a black "Specimen" handstamp, but it is believed Mandel applied such handstamps to regularly issued stamps from his personal collection. These include Nos. 267, 267a and 279B in pale red.

TRANS-MISSISSIPPI ISSUE

Type F

1898

285S	F	1c **dark yellow green**	850.
289S	F	8c **violet brown**	1,200.

Overprinted in Dull Purple

Type E

285S	E	1c **dark yellow green**	250.
286S	E	2c **copper red**	250.
287S	E	4c **orange**	250.
288S	E	5c **dull blue**	250.
289S	E	8c **violet brown**	250.
290S	E	10c **gray violet**	250.
291S	E	50c **sage green**	550.
292S	E	$1 **black**	800.
293S	E	$2 **orange brown**	950.

PAN-AMERICAN ISSUE

1901

294S	E	1c **green & black**	235.
295S	E	2c **carmine**	235.
296S	E	4c **chocolate & black**	235.
	a.	Center inverted	*11,500.*
297S	E	5c **ultramarine & black**	235.
298S	E	8c **brown violet & black**	235.
299S	E	10c **yellow brown & black**	235.

1902

300S	E	1c **blue green**	150.
301S	E	2c **carmine**	150.
302S	E	3c **bright violet**	150.
303S	E	4c **brown**	150.
304S	E	5c **blue**	150.
305S	E	6c **claret**	150.
306S	E	8c **violet black**	150.
307S	E	10c **pale red brown**	150.
308S	E	13c **purple black**	150.
309S	E	15c **olive green**	150.
310S	E	50c **orange**	150.
311S	E	$1 **black**	300.
312S	E	$2 **dark blue**	400.
313S	E	$5 **dark green**	600.

1903

319S	E	2c **carmine**	110.

LOUISIANA PURCHASE ISSUE

1904

323S	E	1c **green**	350.
324S	E	2c **carmine**	350.
325S	E	3c **violet**	350.
326S	E	5c **dark blue**	350.
327S	E	10c **red brown**	350.

SPECIAL DELIVERY STAMPS

Overprinted in Red **SPECIMEN.**

Type D

1885

E1S	D	10c **blue**	140.

Handstamped in Dull Purple

Type E

1888

E2S	E	10c **blue**	150.

1893

E3S	E	10c **orange**	200.

1894

E4S	E	10c **blue**	300.

1895

E5S	E	10c **blue**	175.

1902

E6S	E	10c **ultramarine**	175.

POSTAGE DUE STAMPS

Overprinted in Red

Type D

1879

J1S	D	1c **brown**	250.00
J2S	D	2c **brown**	250.00
J3S	D	3c **brown**	250.00
J4S	D	5c **brown**	250.00

1884

J15S	D	1c **red brown**	45.00
J16S	D	2c **red brown**	45.00
J17S	D	3c **red brown**	45.00
J18S	D	5c **red brown**	45.00
J19S	D	10c **red brown**	45.00
J20S	D	30c **red brown**	45.00
J21S	D	50c **red brown**	45.00

Specimen.

Handstamped in Dull Purple

Type E

1895

J38S	E	1c **deep claret**	85.00
J39S	E	2c **deep claret**	85.00
J40S	E	3c **deep claret**	85.00
J41S	E	5c **deep claret**	85.00
J42S	E	10c **deep claret**	85.00
J43S	E	30c **deep claret**	85.00
J44S	E	50c **deep claret**	85.00

OFFICIAL STAMPS

Special printings of Official stamps were made in 1875 at the time the other Reprints, Re-issues and Special Printings were printed. The Official stamps reprints received specimen overprints, but philatelists believe they most properly should be considered to be part of the special printings. See Official section after No. O120.

NEWSPAPER STAMPS

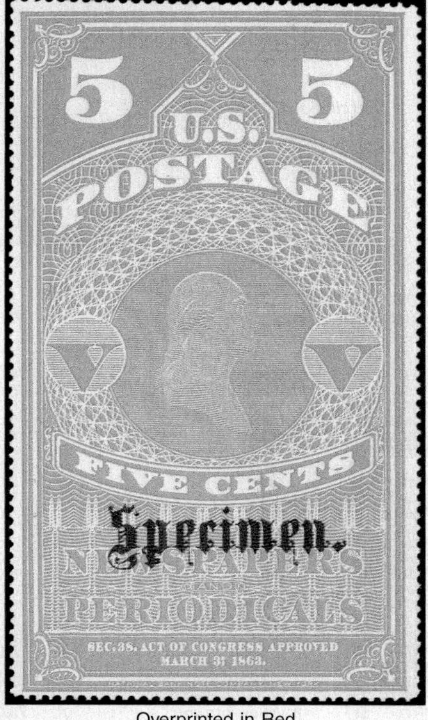

Overprinted in Red

Type C

1865-75

PR2S	C	10c **blue green**	600.00
PR2bS	C	10c **blue green,** pelure paper	*600.00*
PR5S	C	5c **dull blue**	400.00
	a.	Triple overprint	900.00
PR6S	C	10c **dark bluish green**	500.00

Handstamped in Black **Specimen**

Type A

1875

PR9S	A	2c **black**	750.00
PR11S	A	4c **black**	750.00
PR12S	A	6c **black**	750.00
PR16S	A	12c **rose**	750.00

Overprinted in Black, except as noted **Specimen.**

Type B

1875

PR9S	B	2c **black**	125.00
PR10S	B	3c **black**	125.00
PR11S	B	4c **black**	125.00
PR12S	B	6c **black**	125.00
PR13S	B	8c **black**	125.00
PR14S	B	9c **black**	125.00
	a.	Overprint in blue	250.00
PR15S	B	10c **black**	125.00
PR16S	B	12c **rose**	125.00
	a.	Overprint in blue	250.00
PR17S	B	24c **rose**	125.00
	a.	Overprint in blue	250.00
PR18S	B	36c **rose**	125.00
	a.	Overprint in blue	250.00
PR19S	B	48c **rose**	125.00
	a.	Overprint in blue	250.00
PR20S	B	60c **rose**	125.00
	a.	Overprint in blue	250.00
PR21S	B	72c **rose**	125.00
	a.	Overprint in blue	250.00
PR22S	B	84c **rose**	125.00
	a.	Overprint in blue	250.00
PR23S	B	96c **rose**	125.00
	a.	Overprint in blue	250.00

PR24S B $1.92 **dark brown** 125.00
PR25S B $3 **vermilion** 125.00
a. Overprint in blue 250.00
PR26S B $6 **ultramarine** 125.00
a. Overprint in blue 250.00
PR27S B $9 **yellow** 125.00
a. Overprint in blue 250.00
PR28S B $12 **dark green** 125.00
a. Overprint in blue 250.00
PR29S B $24 **dark gray violet** 125.00
a. Overprint in blue 250.00
PR30S B $36 **brown rose** 250.00
PR31S B $48 **red brown** 250.00
PR32S B $60 **violet** 250.00
a. Overprint in blue 250.00

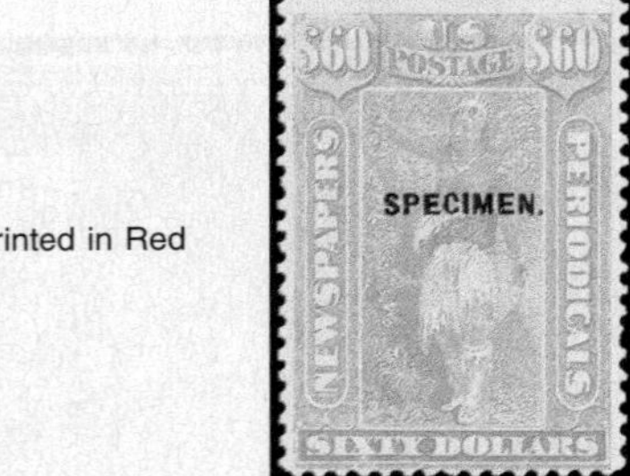

Overprinted in Red

Type D

1875
PR14S D 9c **black** 30.00

1879
PR57S D 2c **black** 75.00
PR58S D 3c **black** 75.00
PR59S D 4c **black** 75.00
PR60S D 6c **black** 75.00
PR61S D 8c **black** 75.00
PR62S D 10c **black** 75.00
a. Double overprint *2,000.*
PR63S D 12c **red** 75.00
PR64S D 24c **red** 75.00
PR65S D 36c **red** 75.00
PR66S D 48c **red** 75.00
PR67S D 60c **red** 75.00
PR68S D 72c **red** 75.00
PR69S D 84c **red** 75.00
PR70S D 96c **red** 75.00
PR71S D $1.92 **pale brown** 75.00
PR72S D $3 **red vermilion** 75.00
PR73S D $6 **blue** 75.00
PR74S D $9 **orange** 75.00
PR75S D $12 **yellow green** 75.00
PR76S D $24 **dark violet** 75.00
PR77S D $36 **Indian red** 75.00
PR78S D $48 **yellow brown** 75.00
PR79S D $60 **purple** 75.00

1885
PR81S D 1c **black** 25.00

Handstamped in Dull Purple

Type E

1879
PR57S E 2c **black** 125.00
PR58S E 3c **black** 125.00
PR59S E 4c **black** 125.00
PR60S E 6c **black** 125.00
PR61S E 8c **black** 125.00
PR62S E 10c **black** 125.00
PR63S E 12c **red** 125.00
PR64S E 24c **red** 125.00
PR65S E 36c **red** 125.00
PR66S E 48c **red** 125.00
PR67S E 60c **red** 125.00
PR68S E 72c **red** 125.00
PR69S E 84c **red** 125.00
PR70S E 96c **red** 125.00
PR71S E $1.92 **pale brown** 125.00
PR72S E $3 **red vermilion** 125.00
PR73S E $6 **blue** 125.00
PR74S E $9 **orange** 125.00
PR75S E $12 **yellow green** 125.00
PR76S E $24 **dark violet** 125.00
PR77S E $36 **Indian red** 125.00
PR78S E $48 **yellow brown** 125.00
PR79S E $60 **purple** 125.00

1885
PR81S E 1c **black** 125.00

1895 **Wmk. 191**
PR114S E 1c **black** 125.00
PR115S E 2c **black** 125.00
PR116S E 5c **black** 125.00
PR117S E 10c **black** 125.00
PR118S E 25c **carmine** 125.00
PR119S E 50c **carmine** 125.00
PR120S E $2 **scarlet** 125.00
PR121S E $5 **dark blue** 125.00
PR122S E $10 **green** 125.00
PR123S E $20 **slate** 125.00
PR124S E $50 **dull rose** 125.00
PR125S E $100 **purple** 125.00

REVENUE STAMPS

SPECIMEN

Type G & A

1862
R5S G 2c Bank Check, **blue** (red) 375.00
R15S A 2c U. S. I. R., **orange** —

SPECIMEN

Type H

R23S H 5c Agreement, **red** 375.00
R34S H 10c Contract, **blue** (red) 375.00
R35eS H 10c Foreign Exchange, **ultra** (red) 375.00
R36S H 10c Inland Exchange, **blue** (red) 375.00
R46S H 25c Insurance, **red** 375.00
R52S H 30c Inland Exchange, **lilac** (red) 375.00
R53S H 40c Inland Exchange, **brown** (red) 375.00
R68S H $1 Foreign Exchange, **red** 375.00

Overprinted in Red

Type I & G

1898
R153S I 1c **green** 475.00

Type G

R163S G 1c **pale blue** 500.00

Overprinted in Red

1875

Type H & G

RB11S H 1c **green** 300.00
RB20S G ⅛c **green** 500.00

Type J

1926-29
RF20S J 10c **blue** 50.00
Joint line pair 250.00
RF23S J 10c **light blue** 100.00
Joint line pair 450.00

PRIVATE DIE MATCH STAMP

Overprinted with Type G in Red

RO133dS G 1c **black**, A. Messinger *500.00*

SAVINGS STAMPS

Overprinted Vertically Reading Down in Red

1911
PS4S 10c **deep blue** 250.00

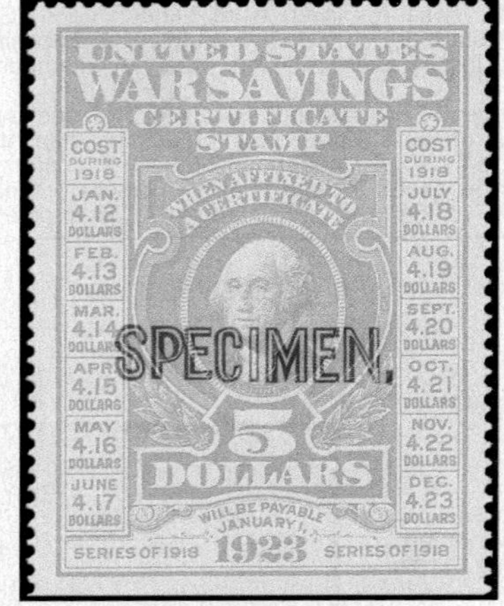

Handstamped in Violet

1917-18
WS1S 25c **deep green** —
WS2S $5 **deep green** —

VARIOUS OVERPRINTS

Overprinted with control numbers in carmine

Type J

1861
63S J A24 1c **pale blue** (overprint 9012) 400.
65S J A25 3c **brown red** (overprint 7890) 400.
Block of 4 *1,750.*
68S J A27 10c **green** (overprint 5678) 400.
69S J A28 12c **gray black** (overprint 4567) 400.
71S J A30 30c **orange** (overprint 2345) 400.
Block of 4 *1,750.*
72S J A31 90c **pale blue** (overprint 1234) 400.
a. Pair, one without overprint —

1863-66
73S J A32 2c **black** (overprint 8901) 400.
Block of 4 *1,750.*
76S J A26 5c **brown** (overprint 6789) 400.
Block of 4 *1,750.*

77S	J	A33	15c **black** (overprint 235)	400.
			Block of 4	*1,750.*
78S	J	A29	24c **gray lilac** (overprint 3456)	400.

Special Printings Overprinted in Red or Blue

Type K

1889

212S	K	A59	1c **ultramarine** (red)	75.00
210S	K	A57	2c **red brown** (blue)	75.00
210S	K	A57	2c **lake** (blue)	75.00
210S	K	A57	2c **rose lake** (blue)	75.00
210S	K	A57	2c **scarlet** (blue)	75.00
214S	K	A46b	3c **vermilion** (blue)	75.00
211S	K	A58	4c **blue green** (red)	75.00
205S	K	A56	5c **gray brown** (red)	75.00
208S	K	A47b	6c **brown red** (blue)	75.00
			P# strip of 7, Impt.	*600.00*
209S	K	A49b	10c **brown** (red)	75.00
			Without overprint	80.00
189S	K	A51a	15c **orange** (blue)	75.00
190S	K	A53	30c **full black** (red)	75.00
191S	K	A54	90c **carmine** (blue)	75.00

Special Printings Overprinted in Red or Blue

Type L

212S	L	A59	1c **ultramarine** (red)	75.00
210S	L	A57	2c **rose lake** (blue)	75.00
			Without overprint	—
214S	L	A46b	3c **purple** (red)	75.00
211S	L	A58	4c **dark brown** (red)	75.00
205S	L	A56	5c **yellow brown** (blue)	75.00
			Without overprint	—
208S	L	A47b	6c **vermilion** (blue)	75.00
209S	L	A49b	10c **green** (red)	75.00
			Without overprint	100.00
189S	L	A51a	15c **blue** (red)	75.00
			Without overprint	100.00
190S	L	A53	30c **full black** (red)	75.00
191S	L	A54	90c **orange** (blue)	75.00

Overprinted with Type K Together with "A" in Black Manuscript

191S	M	A54	90c **carmine** (blue)	140.00
209S	M	A49b	10c **brown** (red)	140.00
211S	M	A58	4c **blue green** (red)	140.00

"SAMPLE A" in Manuscript (red or black)

216S	N	A56	5c **indigo**	160.00

Regular Issues Overprinted in Blue or Red

125 sets were distributed to delegates to the Universal Postal Congress held in Washington, D. C., May 5 to June 15, 1897.

Type O

1897

264S	O	A87	1c **blue**	110.00
267S	O	A88	2c **carmine,** type III	110.00
268S	O	A89	3c **purple**	110.00
269S	O	A90	4c **dark brown**	110.00
270S	O	A91	5c **chestnut**	110.00
271S	O	A92	6c **claret brown**	110.00
272S	O	A93	8c **violet brown**	110.00
273S	O	A94	10c **dark green**	110.00
274S	O	A95	15c **dark blue**	110.00
275S	O	A96	50c **red orange**	110.00
276S	O	A97	$1 **black,** type I	350.00
276AS	O	A97	$1 **black,** type II	300.00
277S	O	A98	$2 **dark blue**	300.00
278S	O	A99	$5 **dark green**	350.00

SPECIAL DELIVERY

E5S	O	SD3	10c **blue** (R)	250.00

POSTAGE DUE

J38S	O	D2	1c **deep claret**	125.00
J39S	O	D2	2c **deep claret**	125.00
J40S	O	D2	3c **deep claret**	125.00
J41S	O	D2	5c **deep claret**	125.00
J42S	O	D2	10c **deep claret**	125.00
J43S	O	D2	30c **deep claret**	125.00
J44S	O	D2	50c **deep claret**	125.00

NEWSPAPERS

PR114S	O	N15	1c **black**	225.00
PR115S	O	N15	2c **black**	225.00
PR116S	O	N15	5c **black**	225.00
PR117S	O	N15	10c **black**	225.00
PR118S	O	N16	25c **carmine**	225.00
PR119S	O	N16	50c **carmine**	225.00
PR120S	O	N17	$2 **scarlet**	225.00
PR121S	O	N18	$5 **dark blue**	225.00
PR122S	O	N19	$10 **green**	225.00
PR123S	O	N20	$20 **slate**	225.00
PR124S	O	N21	$50 **dull rose**	225.00
PR125S	O	N22	$100 **purple**	225.00

ENVELOPES

Overprinted

Type P

U294S	P	1c **blue**	100.00
U296S	P	1c **blue,** *amber*	100.00
U300S	P	1c **blue,** *manila*	100.00
W301S	P	1c **blue,** *manila*	100.00
U304S	P	1c **blue,** *amber manila*	100.00
U311S	P	2c **green,** Die 2	100.00
U312S	P	2c **green,** Die 2, *amber*	100.00
U313S	P	2c **green,** Die 2, *oriental buff*	100.00
U314S	P	2c **green,** Die 2, *blue*	100.00
		a. Double impression of overprint	—
U315S	P	2c **green,** Die 2, *manila*	100.00
W316S	P	2c **green,** Die 2, *manila*	100.00
U317S	P	2c **green,** Die 2, *amber manila*	100.00
U324S	P	4c **carmine**	100.00
U325S	P	4c **carmine,** *amber*	120.00
U330S	P	5c **blue,** Die 1	110.00
U331S	P	5c **blue,** Die 1, *amber*	110.00

Two settings of type P overprint are found.

POSTAL CARDS

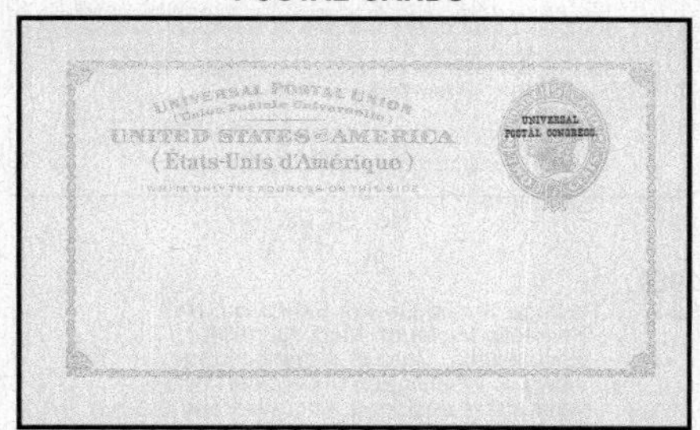

Overprinted Type Q

UX12S	Q	1c **black,** *buff*	600.00
UX13S	Q	2c **blue,** *cream*	600.00

PAID REPLY POSTAL CARDS

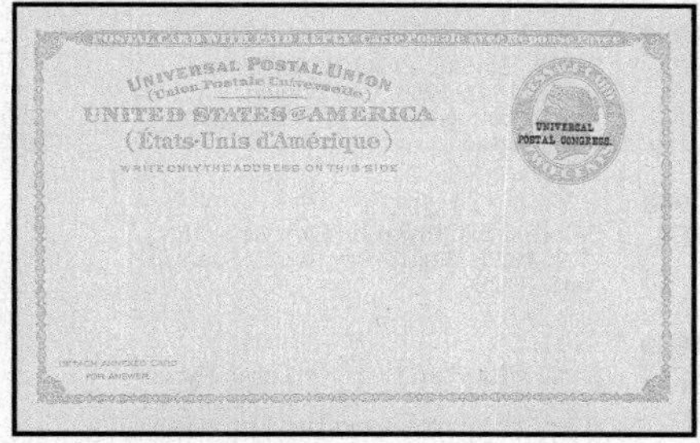

Overprinted Type Q

UY1S	Q	1c **black,** *buff*	600.00
UY2S	Q	2c **blue,** *grayish white*	600.00

As Nos. UY1S-UY2S were made by overprinting unsevered reply cards, values are for unsevered cards.

SOUVENIR CARDS

These cards were issued as souvenirs of the philatelic and numismatic gatherings at which they were distributed by the United States Postal Service (USPS), its predecessor the United States Post Office Department (POD), or the Bureau of Engraving and Printing (BEP). They were not valid for postage. Nos. SC1 and SC3 were produced by members of the trade union now called the International Plate Printers, Die Stampers and Engravers Union. The cards were distributed by the union members.

Listed cards will have a philatelic theme, and most of the cards bear reproductions of United States stamps with the design enlarged, altered by removal of denomination, country name and "Postage" or "Air Mail" or defaced by diagonal bars. The cards are not perforated.

Numismatic cards are listed following the philatelic cards. Cards issued for numismatic shows but showing stamps are listed in the philatelic section.

BEP cards having no obvious philatelic or numismatic theme are not listed.

A forerunner of the souvenir cards is the 1939 Philatelic Truck souvenir sheet which the Post Office Department issued and distributed in various cities visited by the Philatelic Truck. It shows the White House, printed in blue on white paper. A total of 730,040 were printed, 173,220 with gum (first printing, many destroyed) and the rest without gum. Value, with gum, $50; without gum, $8. Some of the first printing was made into coil rolls of 500. A joint line pair and a strip of three (both damaged) are known.

Standard abbreviations:
APS — American Philatelic Society
ASDA — American Stamp Dealers Association

No. SC28

1954

SC1 Postage Stamp Design Exhibition, Natl. Philatelic Museum, Mar. 13, 1954, Philadelphia. Card of 4 monochrome views of Washington. Inscribed: "Souvenir sheet designed, engraved and printed by members, Bureau, Engraving and Printing. Reissued by popular request." *900.00*

1960

SC2 Barcelona, 1st Intl. Philatelic Congress, Mar. 26-Apr. 5, 1960. Vignette, Landing of Columbus from #231. (POD) 200.00

1966

SC3 SIPEX, 6th Intl. Philatelic Exhibition, May 21-30, 1966, Washington. Card of 3 multicolored views of Washington. 50.00
a. Views inverted *725.00*

1968

SC4 EFIMEX, Intl. Philatelic Exhibition, Nov. 1-9, 1968, Mexico City. #292. Spanish text. (POD) 2.25

1969

SC5 SANDIPEX, San Diego Philatelic Exhibition, July 16-20, 1969, San Diego, Cal. Card of 3 multicolored views of Washington. (BEP) 32.50

SC6 ASDA Natl. Postage Stamp Show, Nov. 21-23, 1969, New York. Card of 4 #E4. (BEP) 12.50

1970

SC7 INTERPEX, Mar. 13-15, 1970, New York. Card of 4, #1027, 1035, C35, C38. (BEP) 30.00

SC8 COMPEX, Combined Philatelic Exhibition of Chicagoland, May 29-31, 1970. Card of 4 #C18. (BEP) 7.00

SC9 PHILYMPIA, London Intl. Stamp Exhibition, Sept. 18-26 1970. Card of 3, #548-550. (POD) 1.25

SC10 HAPEX, APS Convention, Nov. 5-8, 1970, Honolulu. Card of 3, #799, C46, C55. (BEP) 6.00

1971

SC11 INTERPEX, Mar. 12-14, 1971, New York. Card of 4 #1193. Background includes #1331-1332, 1371, C76. (BEP) 2.00

SC12 WESTPEX, Western Philatelic Exhibition, Apr. 23-25, 1971, San Francisco. Card of 4, #740, 852, 966, 997. (BEP) 1.50

SC13 NAPEX 71, Natl. Philatelic Exhibition, May 21-23, 1971, Washington. Card of 3, #990, 991, 992. (BEP) 2.00

SC14 TEXANEX 71, Texas Philatelic Association and APS conventions, Aug. 26-29, 1971, San Antonio, Tex. Card of 3, #938, 1043, 1242. (BEP) 2.00

SC15 EXFILIMA 71, 3rd Inter-American Philatelic Exhibition, Nov. 6-14, 1971, Lima, Peru. Card of 3, #1111, 1126, Peru #360. Spanish text. (USPS) 1.00

SC16 ASDA Natl. Postage Stamp Show, Nov. 19-21, 1971, New York. Card of 3, #C13-C15. (BEP) 3.50

SC17 ANPHILEX '71, Anniv. Philatelic Exhibition, Nov. 26-Dec. 1, 1971, New York. Card of 2, #1-2. (BEP) 1.00

1972

SC18 INTERPEX, Mar. 17-19, 1972, New York. Card of 4 #1173. Background includes #976, 1434-1435, C69. (BEP) 1.50

SC19 NOPEX, Apr. 6-9, 1972, New Orleans. Card of 4 #1020. Background includes #323-327. (BEP) 1.50

SC20 BELGICA 72, Brussels Intl. Philatelic Exhibition, June 24-July 9, 1972, Brussels, Belgium. Card of 3, #914, 1026, 1104. Flemish and French text. (USPS) 1.25

SC21 Olympia Philatelie Munchen 72, Aug. 18-Sept. 10, 1972, Munich, Germany. Card of 4, #1460-1462, C85. German text. (USPS) 1.50

SC22 EXFILBRA 72, 4th Inter-American Philatelic Exhibition, Aug. 26-Sept. 2, 1972, Rio de Janeiro, Brazil. Card of 3 #C14, Brazil #C18-C19. Portuguese text. (USPS) 1.00

SC23 Natl. Postal Forum VI, Aug. 28-30, 1972, Washington. Card of 4 #1396. (USPS) 2.00

SC24 SEPAD '72, Oct. 20-22, 1972, Philadelphia. Card of 4 #1044. (BEP) 1.25

SC25 ASDA Natl. Postage Stamp Show, Nov. 17-19, 1972, New York. Card of 4, #883, 863, 868, 888. (BEP) 1.25

SC26 STAMP EXPO, Nov. 24-26, 1972, San Francisco. Card of 4 #C36. (BEP) 1.75

1973

SC27 INTERPEX, Mar. 9-11, 1973, New York. Card of 4 #976. (BEP) 1.50

SC28 IBRA 73 Intl. Philatelic Exhibition, Munich, May 11-20, 1973. #C13. (USPS) 1.00

SC29 COMPEX 73, May 25-27, 1973, Chicago. Card of 4 #245. (BEP) 3.00

SC30 APEX 73, Intl. Airmail Exhibition, Manchester, England, July 4-7, 1973. Card of 3, #C3a, Newfoundland #C4, Honduras #C12. (USPS) 1.00

SC31 POLSKA 73, World Philatelic Exhibition, Poznan, Poland, Aug. 19-Sept. 2, 1973. Card of 3, #1488, Poland #1944-1945. Polish text. (USPS) 1.00

SC32 NAPEX 73, Sept. 14-16, 1973, Washington. Card of 4 #C3. Background includes montage of #C4-C6. (BEP) 2.00

SC33 ASDA Natl. Postage Stamp Show, Nov. 16-18, 1973, New York. Card of 4 #908. Foreground includes #1139-1144. (BEP) 1.00

SC34 STAMP EXPO NORTH, Dec. 7-9, 1973, San Francisco. Card of 4 #C20. (BEP) 2.50

A card of 10, Nos. 1489-1498, was distributed to postal employees. Not available to public. Size: about 14x11 inches.

1974

SC35 Natl. Hobby Industry Trade Show, Feb. 3-6, 1974, Chicago. Card of 4, #1456-1459. Reproductions of silversmith (#1457) and glassmaker (#1456). (USPS) 1.00

SC36 MILCOPEX 1974, Mar. 8-10, 1974, Milwaukee. Card of 4 #C43. (BEP) 1.00

SC37 INTERNABA 1974, June 6, 1974, Basel, Switzerland. Card of 8, #1530-1537. German, French, and Italian text. (USPS) 2.00

SC38 STOCKHOLMIA 74, Intl. Philatelic Exhibition, Sept. 21-29, 1974, Stockholm. Card of 3, #836, Sweden #300, 767. Swedish text. (USPS) 2.00

SC39 EXFILMEX 74, Interamerican Philatelic Exposition, Oct. 26-Nov. 3, 1974, Mexico City. Card of 2, #1157, Mexico #910. Spanish text. (USPS) 2.00

1975

SC40 ESPANA 75, World Stamp Exhibition, Apr. 4-13, Madrid. Card of 3, #233, #1271, Spain #1312. Spanish text. (USPS) 1.00

SC41 NAPEX 75, May 9-11, 1975, Washington. Card of 4 #708. (BEP) 4.00

SC42 ARPHILA 75, June 6-16, 1975, Paris. Card of 3. Designs of #1187, #1207, France #1117. French text. (USPS) 1.75

SC43 Intl. Women's Year, 1975. Card of 3 #872, 878, 959. Reproduction of 1886 dollar bill. (BEP) 15.00

SC44 ASDA Natl. Postage Stamp Show, Nov. 21-23, 1975. Bicentennial series. Card of 4 #1003. (BEP) 10.00

1976

SC45 WERABA 76, 3rd Intl. Space Stamp Exhibition, Apr. 1-4, 1976, Zurich, Switzerland. Card of 2, #1434-1435. (USPS) 2.00

SC46 INTERPHIL 76, 7th Intl. Philatelic Exhibition, May 29-June 6, 1976. Philadelphia. Bicentennial series. Card of 4 #120. (BEP) 6.00

An Interphil '76 card issued by the American Revolution Bicentennial Administration was bound into the Interphil program. It shows an altered #1044 in black brown, the Bicentennial emblem and a view of Independence Hall. Printed by BEP.

SC48 Bicentennial Exposition on Science and Technology, May 30-Sept. 6, 1976, Kennedy Space Center, Fla. #C76. (USPS) 2.50

SC49 STAMP EXPO 76, June 11-13, 1976, Los Angeles. Bicentennial series. Card of 4, #1351, 1352, 1345, 1348. (BEP) 5.00

SC50 Colorado Statehood Centennial, Aug. 1, 1976. Card of 3, #743, 288, 1670. (USPS) 2.50

SC51 HAFNIA 76, Intl. Stamp Exhibition, Copenhagen. Aug. 20-29, 1976. Card of 2, #5, Denmark #2. Danish and English text. (USPS) 2.50

SC52 ITALIA 76, Intl. Philatelic Exhibition, Oct. 14-24, Milan. Card of 3, #1168, Italy #578, 601. Italian text. (USPS) 2.50

SC53 NORDPOSTA 76, North German Stamp Exhibition, Oct. 30-31, Hamburg. Card of 3, #689, Germany #B366, B417. German text. (USPS) 2.50

1977

SC54 MILCOPEX, Milwaukee Philatelic Society, Mar. 4-6, Milwaukee. Card of 2, #733, 1128. (BEP) 1.50

SC55 ROMPEX 77, Rocky Mountain Philatelic Exhibition, May 20-22, Denver. Card of 4 #1001. (BEP) 1.50

SC56 AMPHILEX 77, Intl. Philatelic Exhibition, May 26-June 5, Amsterdam. Card of 3, #1027, Netherlands #41, 294. Dutch text. (USPS) 2.50

SC57 SAN MARINO 77, Intl. PhilatelicExhibition, San Marino, Aug. 28-Sept. 4. Card of 3, #1-2, San Marino #1. Italian text. (USPS) 2.50

SC58 PURIPEX 77, Silver Anniv. Philatelic Exhibit, Sept. 2-5, San Juan, P. R. Card of 4 #801. (BEP) 1.25

SC59 ASDA Natl. Postage Stamp Show, Nov. 15-20, New York. Card of 4 #C45. (BEP) 2.00

1978

SC60 ROCPEX 78, Intl. Philatelic Exhibition, Mar. 20-29, Taipei. Card of 6, #1706-1709, China #1812, 1816. Chinese text. (USPS) 2.50

SC61 NAPOSTA '78 Philatelic Exhibition, May 20-25, Frankfurt. Card of 3, #555, 563, Germany #1216. German text. (USPS) 2.50

SC62 CENJEX 78, Federated Stamp Clubs of New Jersey, 30th annual exhibition, June 23-25, Freehold, NJ. Card of 9, #646, 680, 689, 1086, 1716, 4 #785. (BEP) 2.00

1979

SC63 BRASILIANA 79, Intl. Philatelic Exhibition, Sept. 15-23, Rio de Janeiro. Card of 3, #C91-C92, Brazil #1295. Portuguese text. (USPS) 2.50

SC64 JAPEX 79, Intl. Philatelic Exhibition, Nov. 2-4, Tokyo. Card of 2, #1158, Japan #1024. Japanese text. (USPS) 2.50

1980

SC65 LONDON 1980, Intl. Philatelic Exhibition, May 6-14, London. #329. (USPS) 2.50

SC66 NORWEX 80, Intl. Stamp Exhibition, June 13-22, Oslo. Card of 3, #620-621, Norway #658. Norwegian text. (USPS) 2.50

SC67 NAPEX 80, July 4-6, Washington. Card of 4 #573. (BEP) 8.00

SC68 ASDA Stamp Festival, Sept. 25-28, 1980, New York. Card of 4 #962. (BEP) 9.00

SC69 ESSEN 80, 3rd Intl. Stamp Fair, Nov. 15-19, Essen. Card of 2, #1014, Germany #723. German text. (USPS) 2.50

1981

SC70 STAMP EXPO '81 SOUTH, Mar. 20-22, Anaheim, Calif. Card of 6, #1331-1332, 4 #1287. (BEP) 9.00

SC71 WIPA 1981, Intl. Stamp Exhibition, May 22-31, Vienna. Card of 2, #1252, Austria #789. German text. (USPS) 2.50

SC72 Natl. Stamp Collecting Month, Oct., 1981. Card of 2, #245, 1918. (USPS) 2.50

SC73 PHILATOKYO '81, Intl. Stamp Exhibition, Oct. 9-18. Tokyo. Card of 2, #1531, Japan #800. Japanese text. (USPS) 2.50

SC74 NORDPOSTA 81, North German Stamp Exhibition, Nov. 7-8. Hamburg. Card of 2, #923, Germany #B538. German text. (USPS) 2.50

1982

SC75 MILCOPEX '82, Milwaukee Philatelic Association Exhibition, Mar. 5-7. Card of 4 #1137. (BEP) 9.00

SC76 CANADA 82, Intl. Philatelic Youth Exhibition, May 20-24, Toronto. Card of 2, #116, Canada #15. French and English text. (USPS) 2.50

SC77 PHILEXFRANCE '82, Intl. Philatelic Exhibition, June 11-21, Paris. Card of 2, #1753, France #1480. French text. (USPS) 2.50

SC78 Natl. Stamp Collecting Month, Oct. #C3a. (USPS) 2.50

SC79 ESPAMER '82, Intl. Philatelic Exhibition, Oct. 12-17, San Juan, P.R. Card of 4 #244. English and Spanish text. (BEP) 16.00

SC80 ESPAMER '82, Intl. Philatelic Exhibition, Oct. 12-17, San Juan, P.R. Card of 3, #801, 1437, 2024. Spanish and English text. (USPS) 2.50

1983

SC81 Joint stamp issues, Sweden and US. Mar. 24. Card of 3, #958, 2036, Sweden #1453. Swedish and English text. (USPS) 2.50

SC82 Joint stamp issues, Germany and US. Apr. 29. Card of 2, #2040, Germany #1397. German and English text. (USPS) 2.50

SC83 TEMBAL 83, Intl. Philatelic Exhibition, Mar. 21-29, Basel. Card of 2, #C71, Basel #3L1. German text. (USPS) 2.50

SC84 TEXANEX-TOPEX '83 Exhibition, June 17-19, San Antonio. Card of 5, #1660, 4 #776. (BEP) 12.50

SC85 BRASILIANA 83, Intl. Philatelic Exhibition, July 29-Aug. 7, Rio de Janeiro. Card of 2, #2, Brazil #1. Portuguese text. (USPS) 2.50

SC86 BANGKOK 83, Intl. Philatelic Exhibition, Aug. 4-13, Bangkok. Card of 2, #210, Thailand #1. Thai text. (USPS) 2.50

SC87 Intl. Philatelic Memento, 1983-84. #1387. (USPS) 2.50

SC88 Natl. Stamp Collecting Month, Oct. #293 bicolored. (USPS) 3.50

SC89 Philatelic Show '83, Boston, Oct. 21-23. Card of 2, #718-719. (BEP) 8.50

SC90 ASDA 1983, Natl. Postage Stamp Show, New York, Nov. 17-20. Card of 4 #881. (BEP) 8.50

1984

SC91 ESPANA 84, World Exhibition of Philately. Madrid, Apr. 27-May 6. Card of 4 #241. Enlarged vignette, Landing of Columbus, from #231. English and Spanish text. (BEP) 13.00

SC92 ESPANA 84, Intl. Philatelic Exhibition, Madrid, Apr. 27-May 6. Card of 2, #233, Spain #428. Spanish text. (USPS) 2.50

SC93 Stamp Expo '84 South, Anaheim, CA, Apr. 27-29. Card of 4, #1791-1794. (BEP) 10.00

SC94 COMPEX '84, Rosemont, IL, May 25-27. Card of 4 #728. (BEP) 14.00

SC95 HAMBURG '84, Intl. Exhibition for 19th UPU Congress, Hamburg, June 19-26. Card of 2, #C66, Germany #669. English, French and German text. (USPS) 2.50

SC96 St. Lawrence Seaway, 25th anniv., June 26. Card of 2, #1131, Canada #387. English and French text. (USPS) 2.75

SC97 AUSIPEX '84, Australia's 1st intl. exhibition, Melbourne, Sept. 21-30. Card of 2, #290, Western Australia #1. (USPS) 2.50

SC98 Natl. Stamp Collecting Month, Oct. #2104, tricolored. (USPS) 2.50

SC99 PHILAKOREA '84, Seoul, Oct. 22-31. Card of 2, #741, Korea #994. Korean and English text. (USPS) 2.50

SC100 ASDA 1984, Natl. Postage Stamp Show, New York, Nov. 15-18. Card of 4 #1470. (BEP) 9.00

1985

SC101 Intl. Philatelic Memento, 1985. #2. (USPS) 2.50

SC102 OLYMPHILEX '85. Intl. Philatelic Exhibition, Lausanne. Mar. 18-24. Card of 2, #C106, Switzerland #746. French and English text. (USPS) 2.50

SC103 ISRAPHIL '85. Intl. Philatelic Exhibition, Tel Aviv, May 14-22. Card of 2, #566, Israel #33. Hebrew and English text. (USPS) 2.50

SC104 LONG BEACH '85, Numismatic and Philatelic Exposition, Long Beach, CA, Jan. 31-Feb. 3. Card of 4 #954, plus a Series 1865 $20 Gold Certificate. (BEP) 8.00

SC105 MILCOPEX '85, Milwaukee Philatelic Society annual stamp show, Mar. 1-3. Card of 4 #880. (BEP) 8.00

SC106 NAPEX '85, Natl. Philatelic Exhibition, Arlington, VA, June 7-9. Card of 4 #2014. (BEP) 8.00

SC107 ARGENTINA '85, Intl. Philatelic Exhibition, Buenos Aires, July 5-14. Card of 2, #1737, Argentina #B27. Spanish text. (USPS) 2.50

SC108 MOPHILA '85, Intl. Philatelic Exhibition, Hamburg, Sept. 11-15. Card of 2, #296, Germany #B595. German text. (USPS) 2.50

SC109 ITALIA '85, Intl. Philatelic Exhibition, Rome, Oct. 25-Nov. 3. Card of 2, #1107, Italy #830. Italian text. (USPS) 3.50

1986

SC110 Statue of Liberty Centennial, Natl. Philatelic Memento, 1986. #C87. (USPS) 4.00

SC111 Garfield Perry Stamp Club, Natl. Stamp Show, Cleveland, Mar. 21-23. Card of 4 #306. (BEP) 9.50

SC112 AMERIPEX '86, Intl. Philatelic Exhibition, Chicago, May 22-June 1. Card of 3, #134, 2052, 1474.(BEP) 8.50

SC113 STOCKHOLMIA '86, Intl. Philatelic Exhibition, Stockholm, Aug. 28-Sept. 7. Card of 2, #113, Sweden #253. Swedish text. (USPS) 4.00

SC114 HOUPEX '86, Natl. Stamp Show, Houston. Sept. 5-7. Card of 3, #1035, 1042, 1044A. (BEP) 12.00

SC115 LOBEX '86, Numismatic and Philatelic Exhibition, Long Beach, CA, Oct. 2-5. Long Beach Stamp Club 60th anniv. Card of 4, #291, plus a series 1907 $10 Gold Certificate. (BEP) 15.00

SC116 DCSE '86, Dallas Coin and Stamp Exhibition, Dallas, Dec. 11-14. Card of 4 #550, plus $10,000 Federal Reserve Note. (BEP) 17.50

1987

SC117 CAPEX '87, Intl. Philatelic Exhibition, Toronto, June 13-21. Card of 2, #569, Canada #883. English and French text. (USPS) 5.00

SC118 HAFNIA '87, Intl. Philatelic Exhibition, Copenhagen, Oct. 16-25. Card of 2, #299, Denmark #B52. English and Danish text. (USPS) 5.00

SC119 SESCAL '87, Stamp Exhibition of Southern California, Los Angeles, Oct. 16-18. #798. (BEP) 9.00

SC120 HSNA '87, Hawaii State Numismatic Association Exhibition, Honolulu, Nov. 12-15. #799 and a Series 1923 $5 Silver Certificate. (BEP) 21.00

SC121 MONTE CARLO, Intl. Philatelic Exhibition, Monte Carlo, Nov. 13-17. Card of 3, #2287, 2300, Monaco #1589. French and English text. (USPS) 3.50

1988

SC122 FINLANDIA '88, Intl. Philatelic Exhibition, Helsinki, June 1-12. Card of 2, #836, Finland #768. English and Finnish text. (USPS) 5.00

SC123 STAMPSHOW '88, APS natl. stamp show, Detroit, Aug. 25-28. #835. (BEP) 8.00

SC124 MIDAPHIL '88, Kansas City, Nov. 18-20. #627. (BEP) 9.00

1989

SC125 PHILEXFRANCE '89 intl. philatelic exhibition, Paris, July 7-17. Card of 2, #C120, France #2144. English and French text. (USPS) 6.00

SC126 STAMPSHOW '89, APS natl. stamp show, Anaheim, CA, Aug. 24-27. #565. Various reproductions of the portrait of Chief Hollow Horn Bear from which the stamp was designed. (BEP) 10.00

SC127 WORLD STAMP EXPO '89, Washington, Nov. 17-Dec. 3. Card of 4, #2433a-2433d. Embossed reproductions of Supreme Court, Washington Monument, Capitol and Jefferson Memorial. (USPS) 6.50

1990

SC128 ARIPEX 90, Arizona Philatelic Exhibition, Phoenix, Apr. 20-22. Card of 2, #285 and #285 with black vignette. (BEP) 9.00

SC129 STAMPSHOW '90, APS natl. stamp show, Cincinnati, Aug. 23-26. Card of 2, #286 and essay with frame of #286 in red with vignette of #293 in black. (BEP) 9.00

SC130 STAMP WORLD LONDON 90, London, England, May 3-13. Card of 2, #1, Great Britain #1. (USPS) 7.00

1991

SC131 STAMPSHOW '91, APS natl. stamp show, Philadelphia, Aug. 22-25. Card of 3, #537, Essays #537a-E1, 537b-E1. Embossed figure of "Freedom." (BEP) (card has no year date) 11.00

1992

SC132 World Columbian Stamp Expo, Chicago, May 22-31. Card of 2, #118, 119b. (BEP) 10.00

SC132A OLYMPHILEX '92, Barcelona, Spain, July 30-Aug. 7. Card of 6, #2619, #2637-2641. (USPS) *90.00*

SC133 Savings Bond, produced as gift to BEP employees, available to public. 1954 Savings stamp, Series E War Savings bond. (BEP) 12.00

SC134 STAMPSHOW '92. Oakland, CA (BEP) 11.00

1993

SC135 Combined Federal Campaign, produced as gift to BEP employees, available to public. #1016. Photos of 6 other stamps. (BEP) 12.00

SC136 ASDA stamp show, New York, May 1993. Card of 7 #859, 864, 869, 874, 879, 884, 889 (BEP) 12.00

SC137 Savings Bonds, produced as gift to BEP employees, available to the public Aug. 1993. $200 War Savings Bond, #WS8 (BEP) 15.00

SC138 Omaha Stamp Show, Sept. 1993. Card of 4, #E7, PR2, JQ5, QE4 (BEP) 12.00

SC139 ASDA New York Show, Oct. 1993. Card of 2, #499-E1a and similar with negative New York precancel (BEP) 12.00

1994

SC140 Sandical, San Diego, CA, Feb. 1994. Card of 4 #E4 (BEP) 9.00

SC140A Centennial of U.S. Stamp Production, July 1994, BEP Intaglio Print. Card of 13 Types A87-A99 in black 75.00

SC141 Savings Bonds, produced as a gift to BEP employees, available to the public Aug. 1, 1994. #WS7-WS11. 16.00

SC142 STAMPSHOW '94, APS National Stamp Show Pittsburgh, PA. Card of 3, 1c, 2c and 10c Type D2 11.00

SC143 American Stamp Dealers Association, Nov. 1994, New York, NY. Card of 4, 2c, 12c, $3, $6 Types N4-N5, N7-N8 11.00

1995

SC144 Natl. Exhibition of the Columbus Philatelic Club, Apr. 1995, Columbus, OH. Block of 4 of #261. 11.00

No. 144 was issued folded in half.

SC145 Centennial of U.S. Stamp Production, June 1995, BEP Intaglio Print. Card of 13 of Types A87-A99 in blue 60.00

SC146 Savings Bonds, produced as a gift to BEP employees, available to the public Aug. 1, 1995. Card of 3 #905, 907, 940 14.00

SC147 American Stamp Dealers Association, Nov. 1995, New York, NY. Block of 4, #292 10.50

No. SC147 issued folded in half.

1996

SC148	CAPEX '96, Toronto, Canada, June 1996. Block of 4, #291	11.00
SC149	Olymphilex '96, Atlanta, GA, July-August, 1996, Block of 4, #718	11.00
SC150	Billings Stamp Club, Billings, MT, Oct. 1996, Block of 4, #1130	11.00

1997

SC151	Long Beach Coin & Collectibles Expo, Feb. 1997, Lock Seal revenue stamp	11.00
SC152	PACIFIC 97, May 1997, Process or renovated butter revenue stamp	12.00
SC153	Milcopex, Milwaukee, WI, Sept. 1997, Newspaper Types N15, N16 and N19	12.00

1998

SC154	OKPEX 98, Oklahoma City, OK, May 1998, Block of 4, #922	11.00
SC155	Centennial of Trans-Mississippi Exposition Issue, Sept. 1998, BEP Engraved Print. Card of 9 die impressions in green of designs A100-A108	50.00

1999

SC156	Philadelphia National Stamp Exhibition, Oct. 1999, Card of 4, #RS281, RS284, RS290, RS306	11.00

2003

SC157	Georgia Numismatic Association, Dalton, GA (card of one #C45 in blue gray, without denomination and some inscriptions)	40.00

2005

SC158	ANA Coin, Stamp and Collectibles Show, Las Vegas, Oct. 2005, Card of 7, #999, 1248, RF1, RF11, RF26, 7c essay of #RF11, 5c essay of #RF26	50.00

2006

SC159	ANA World's Fair of Money, Denver, CO, card of #1001 without denomination and some inscriptions, 1908 $10 silver certificate	45.00
SC160	Long Beach Coin, Stamp & Collectible Expo, Long Beach, CA, Sept. 2006, Card of #997 in blue, California state shield, Reverse of Series 1923 $10 United States Note	40.00
SC160A	ANA Coin, Stamp and Collectibles Show, Las Vegas, Oct. 2006, Card of 5, #RF17, RF24, RF27, essay type of RF19, USPO vignette (BEP)	50.00

2007

SC160B	Jamestown 400th Anniv., May 2007, Card of #328-330 in dark blue	45.00
SC161	Whitman Baltimore Coin and Collectibles Convention, Baltimore, MD, Nov. 2007, Card of #962, 1142 in black	30.00

2008

SC162	Florida United Numismatists, Orlando, FL, Jan. 2008, Card of #Q12, 952	30.00
SC163	ANA World's Fair of Money, Baltimore, MD, Aug. 2008, Card of 1⅝ ounce snuff, $19.20 tobacco, 5 Class A cigars stamps	40.00

2009

SC164	ANA National Money Show, Portland, OR, Mar. 2009, Card of #222	40.00
SC165	Whitman Baltimore Coin and Collectibles Convention, Baltimore, MD, Mar. 2009, Card of #77	30.00
SC166	Texas Numismatic Association 51st Texas State Coin and Currency Show, Fort Worth, TX, May 2009, Card of #821	30.00
SC167	American Numismatic Association World's Fair of Money Show, Los Angeles, CA, August 2009, Card of #555	30.00

2010

SC168	ANA National Money Show, Fort Worth, TX, Mar. 2010, Card of #776, 938	40.00
SC169	ANA World's Fair of Money, Boston, MA, Aug. 2010, Card of #951	40.00

Beginning in 2011, the souvenir cards no longer were issued for specific philatelic shows.

2011

SC170	Franklin Commemorative Series - Postmaster, Aug. 2011, Card of #3139a, LO1	40.00

2015

SC171	Centenary of the Opening of the Panama Canal, Card of #399, 400	40.00
SC172	Centenary of the Opening of the Panama Canal, Card of #397, 398	40.00

The numismatic card No. NSC128 also features stamps.

2018

SC173	The Great War 100th Anniversary, Card of #WS4, WS6, $10,000 bond	35.00

NUMISMATIC SOUVENIR CARDS

Included in this section are cards issued by the Bureau of Engraving and Printing showing fractional currency, paper money or parts thereof, for numismatic shows. Not included are press samples sold or given away only at the shows and other special printings. Cards showing both money and stamps are listed in the preceeding section.

Standard abbreviations:

ANA- American Numismatic Association
IPMS- International Paper Money Show
FUN- Florida United Numismatists

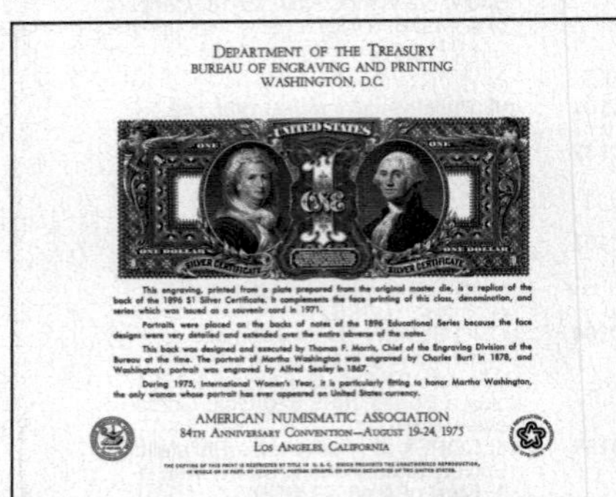

No. NSC8

1969-84

NSC1	ANA	40.00
NSC2	Fresno Numismatic Fair	*150.00*
NSC3	ANA ('70)	40.00
NSC4	ANA ('71)	12.00
NSC5	ANA ('72)	10.00
NSC6	ANA ('73)	14.00
NSC7	ANA ('74)	12.00
NSC8	ANA ('75)	11.00
NSC9	ANA ('76)	11.00
NSC10	ANA ('77)	14.00
NSC11	IPMS ('78)	4.00
NSC12	ANA ('80)	14.00
NSC13	IPMS ('80)	22.00
NSC14	IPMS ('81)	16.00
NSC15	ANA ('81)	14.00
NSC16	IPMS ('82)	13.00
NSC17	ANA ('82)	7.00
NSC18	FUN ('83)	18.00
NSC19	ANA ('83)	12.00
NSC20	FUN ('84)	16.00
NSC21	IPMS ('84)	24.00
NSC22	ANA ('84)	18.00

1985

NSC23	International Coin Club of El Paso	14.00
NSC24	Pacific Northwest Numismatic Assoc.	16.00
NSC25	IPMS	18.00
NSC26	ANA	14.00
NSC27	International Paper Money Convention (IPMC)	16.00

1986

NSC28	FUN	17.00
NSC29	ANA Midwinter	17.00
NSC30	IPMS	12.00
NSC31	ANA	9.00
NSC32	National World Paper Money Convention (NWPMC)	10.00

1987

NSC33	FUN	15.00
NSC34	ANA Midwinter	20.00
NSC35	BEP Fort Worth	16.00
NSC36	IPMS	12.00
NSC37	ANA	12.00
NSC38	Great Eastern Numismatic Association	12.00

1988

NSC39	FUN	10.00
NSC40	ANA Midwinter	17.00
NSC41	IPMS	14.00
NSC42	ANA	20.00
NSC43	Illinois Numismatic Association	14.00

1989

NSC44	FUN	12.00
NSC45	ANA Midwinter	19.00
NSC46	TNA	18.00
NSC47	IPMS	15.00
NSC48	ANA	16.00

1990

NSC49	FUN	14.00
NSC50	ANA Midwinter	14.00
NSC51	Central States Numismatic Society	12.00
NSC52	Dallas Coin and Stamp Exposition	14.00
NSC53	ANA, Seattle, WA	17.00
NSC54	Westex	16.00
NSC55	Hawaii State Numismatic Association (card has no year date)	20.00

1991

NSC56	FUN (card has no year date)	16.00
NSC57	ANA Midwinter, Dallas, Texas (card has no year date)	20.00
NSC58	IPMS (card has no year date)	18.00
NSC59	ANA Convention, Chicago, IL (card has no year date)	20.00

1992

NSC60	FUN	13.00
NSC61	Central States Numismatics Society	20.00
NSC62	IPMS, Memphis, TN	12.00
NSC63	ANA Convention, Orlando, FL	18.00

1993

NSC64	FUN	18.00
NSC65	ANA Convention, Colorado Springs, CO	16.00
NSC66	Texas Numismatic Association Show	16.00
NSC67	Georgia Numismatic Association Show	18.00
NSC68	ANA Convention, Baltimore, MD	16.00
NSC69	IPMS, Memphis, TN	18.00

1994

NSC70	FUN	18.00
NSC71	ANA Convention, New Orleans, LA	22.00
NSC72	European Paper Money Bourse, Netherlands	20.00
NSC73	IPMS, Memphis, TN	20.00
NSC74	ANA Convention, Detroit, MI	16.00

Nos. NSC75-NSC79 were issued folded in half.

1995

NSC75	FUN	20.00
NSC76	New York Intl. Numismatic Convention	16.00
NSC77	IPMS, Memphis, TN	16.00
NSC78	ANA Convention, Anaheim, CA	17.50
NSC79	Long Beach Numismatic/Philatelic Exposition, Long Beach, CA	16.00

1996

NSC80	FUN	18.00
NSC81	Suburban Washington/Baltimore Coin Show	18.00
NSC82	Central States Numismatic Association	25.00
NSC83	ANA Convention, Denver, CO	20.00

1997

NSC84	FUN	22.00
NSC85	Bay State Coin Show	16.00
NSC86	IPMS, Memphis, TN	16.00
NSC87	ANA Convention, New York, NY	22.50

1998

NSC88	FUN	18.00
NSC89	IPMS, Memphis, TN	18.00
NSC90	ANA Convention, Portland, OR	16.00
NSC91	Long Beach Coin & Collectibles Expo, Long Beach, CA	18.00

1999

NSC92	FUN	20.00
NSC93	Bay State Coin Club	22.00
NSC94	IPMS, Memphis, TN	18.00
NSC95	ANA Convention, Rosemont, IL	18.00

2001

NSC96	FUN	18.00
NSC97	IPMS	20.00
NSC98	ANA Convention, Atlanta, GA	20.00
NSC99	Long Beach Coin & Collectibles Expo, Long Beach, CA	18.00

2002

NSC100	FUN	20.00
NSC101	Texas Numismatic Association, Fort Worth	18.00
NSC102	ANA Convention, New York, NY	18.00
NSC103	Long Beach Coin & Collectibles Expo, Long Beach, CA	18.00

2003

NSC104	FUN	35.00

For the 2003 card issued for the Georgia Numismatic Association, Dalton, GA, see No. SC157.

2002

NSC106	ANA Convention, Baltimore, MD	50.00

2003

NSC107	Natl. & World Paper Money Convention, St. Louis, MO	40.00

2004

NSC108	ANA Convention, Portland, OR	60.00
NSC109	ANA Convention, Pittsburgh, PA	35.00

2005

NSC110	FUN	40.00
NSC111	Money Show of the Southwest, Houston, TX	40.00
NSC112	Long Beach Coin & Stamp Expo, Long Beach, CA	45.00
NSC113	ANA National Money Show, Kansas City, MO	35.00
NSC114	ANA World's Fair of Money, San Francisco, CA	35.00

2006

NSC115	ANA National Money Show, Atlanta, GA	45.00

2007

NSC116	ANA National Money Show, Charlotte, NC	35.00
NSC117	ANA World's Fair of Money, Milwaukee, WI	35.00

2008

NSC118	ANA National Money Show, Phoenix, AZ	30.00

2009

NSC119	Central States Numismatic Society, Cincinnati, OH	35.00

2010

NSC120	FUN	35.00

Beginning in 2011, the numismatic souvenir cards no longer were issued for specific numismatic shows.

2011

NSC121	Franklin Commemorative Series - Inventor	40.00
NSC122	Franklin Commemorative Series - Statesman	35.00

2014

NSC123	Defenders of Freedom — Army, dated "2014" at top	40.00
NSC124	Defenders of Freedom — Navy, dated "2014" at top	40.00
NSC125	Defenders of Freedom — Marine Corps, dated "2014" at top	40.00
NSC126	Defenders of Freedom — Air Force, dated "2014" at top	40.00
NSC127	Defenders of Freedom — Coast Guard, dated "2014" at top	40.00

2016

NSC128	Defenders of Freedom — Army, inscribed "Since" and year at top	40.00
NSC129	Defenders of Freedom — Navy, inscribed "Since" and year at top	40.00
NSC130	Defenders of Freedom — Marine Corps, inscribed "Since" and year at top	40.00
NSC131	Defenders of Freedom — Air Force, inscribed "Since" and year at top	40.00
NSC132	Defenders of Freedom — Coast Guard, inscribed "Since" and year at top	40.00

2018

NSC133	The Great War 100th Anniversary, Series 1918 $2 Federal Reserve	35.00
NSC134	The Great War 100th Anniversary, back of Series 1918 $1 Federal Reserve Bank Note	35.00

COMMEMORATIVE PANELS

The U.S. Postal Service began issuing commemorative panels September 20, 1972, with the Wildlife Conservation issue (Scott Nos. 1464-1467). Each panel is devoted to a separate issue. It includes unused examples of the stamp or stamps (usually a block of four), reproduction of steel engravings, and background information on the subject of the issue. Values for panels issued through 1993 are for panels without protective sleeves. Values for panels with protective sleeves are 10% to 25% higher, through 1993. See note preceding No. CP431.

No. CP53

1972

CP1	Wildlife Conservation, #1467a	5.50
CP2	Mail Order, #1468	5.50
CP3	Osteopathic Medicine, #1469	11.00
CP4	Tom Sawyer, #1470	11.00
CP5	Pharmacy, #1473	8.00
CP6	Christmas (angel), #1471	7.50
CP7	Santa Claus, #1472	7.50
CP8	Stamp Collecting, #1474	5.00

1973

CP9	Love, #1475	7.00
CP10	Pamphleteers, #1476	5.00
CP11	George Gershwin, #1484	7.00
CP12	Posting a Broadside, #1477	5.00
CP13	Copernicus, #1488	5.00
CP14	Postal Service Employees, #1489-1498	5.00
CP15	Harry S Truman, #1499	7.00
CP16	Postrider, #1478	7.00
CP17	Boston Tea Party, #1483a	17.50
CP18	Electronics Progress, #1500-1502, C86	7.00
CP19	Robinson Jeffers, #1485	5.00
CP20	Lyndon B. Johnson, #1503	3.00
CP21	Henry O. Tanner, #1486	5.00
CP22	Willa Cather, #1487	5.00
CP23	Drummer, #1479	9.00
CP24	Angus and Longhorn Cattle, #1504	7.00
CP25	Christmas (Madonna), #1507	10.00
CP26	Christmas Tree, needlepoint, #1508	9.00

1974

CP27	Veterans of Foreign Wars, #1525	5.00
CP28	Robert Frost, #1526	5.00
CP29	EXPO '74, #1527	7.00
CP30	Horse Racing, #1528	9.00
CP31	Skylab, #1529	10.00
CP32	Universal Postal Union, #1537a	7.00
CP33	Mineral Heritage, #1541a	9.00
CP34	Kentucky Settlement (Ft. Harrod), #1542	5.00
CP35	First Continental Congress, #1546a	7.00
CP36	Chautauqua, #1505	7.00
CP37	Kansas Wheat, #1506	7.00
CP38	Energy Conservation, #1547	5.00
CP39	Sleepy Hollow Legend, #1548	7.00
CP40	Retarded Children, #1549	5.00
CP41	Christmas (Currier-Ives), #1551	7.00
CP42	Christmas (angel), #1550	7.00

1975

CP43	Benjamin West, #1553	7.00
CP44	Pioneer 10, #1556	10.00
CP45	Collective Bargaining, #1558	5.00
CP46	Contributors to the Cause, #1559-1562	7.00
CP47	Mariner 10, #1557	12.00
CP48	Lexington-Concord Battle, #1563	5.00
CP49	Paul Laurence Dunbar, #1554	7.00
CP50	D. W. Griffith, #1555	9.00
CP51	Battle of Bunker Hill, #1564	7.00
CP52	Military Services (uniforms), #1568a	7.00
CP53	Apollo Soyuz, #1569a	11.00
CP54	World Peace through Law, #1576	5.50
CP55	International Women's Year, #1571	5.50
CP56	Postal Service 200 Years, #1575a	5.00
CP57	Banking and Commerce, #1577a	7.00
CP58	Early Christmas Card, #1580	7.00
CP59	Christmas (Madonna), #1579	7.00

1976

CP60	Spirit of '76, #1631a	9.00
CP61	Interphil '76, #1632	8.50
CP62	State Flags, block of 4 from #1633-1682	16.00
CP63	Telephone Centenary, #1683	7.00
CP64	Commercial Aviation, #1684	8.00
CP65	Chemistry, #1685	9.00
CP66	Benjamin Franklin, #1690	8.00
CP67	Declaration of Independence, #1694a	7.00
CP68	12th Winter Olympics, #1698a	9.00
CP69	Clara Maass, #1699	11.00
CP70	Adolph S. Ochs, #1700	8.00
CP71	Christmas (Currier print), #1702	8.00
CP72	Christmas (Copley Nativity), #1701	10.00

1977

CP73	Washington at Princeton, #1704	10.00
CP74	Sound Recording, #1705	27.50
CP75	Pueblo Art, #1709a	70.00
CP76	Lindbergh Flight, #1710	70.00
CP77	Colorado Statehood, #1711	11.00
CP78	Butterflies, #1715a	14.00
CP79	Lafayette, #1716	11.00
CP80	Skilled Hands for Independence, #1720a	12.00
CP81	Peace Bridge, #1721	12.00
CP82	Battle of Oriskany, #1722	11.00
CP83	Energy Conservation-Development, #1723a	12.00
CP84	Alta California, #1725	12.00
CP85	Articles of Confederation, #1726	18.00
CP86	Talking Pictures, #1727	14.00
CP87	Surrender at Saratoga, #1728	16.00
CP88	Christmas (Washington at Valley Forge), #1729	14.00
CP89	Christmas (rural mailbox), #1730	25.00

1978

CP90	Carl Sandburg, #1731	7.50
CP91	Captain Cook, #1732a	10.00
CP92	Harriet Tubman, #1744	10.00
CP93	American Quilts, #1748a	14.00
CP94	American Dance, #1752a	10.00
CP95	French Alliance, #1753	9.00
CP96	Pap Test, #1754	9.00
CP97	Jimmie Rodgers, #1755	10.00
CP98	Photography, #1758	10.00
CP99	George M. Cohan, #1756	14.00
CP100	Viking Missions, #1759	30.00
CP101	American Owls, #1763a	30.00
CP102	American Trees, #1767a	24.00
CP103	Christmas (Madonna), #1768	12.00
CP104	Christmas (hobby-horse), #1769	12.00

1979

CP105	Robert F. Kennedy, #1770	10.00
CP106	Martin Luther King, Jr., #1771	9.00
CP107	Year of the Child, #1772	7.00
CP108	John Steinbeck, #1773	6.00
CP109	Albert Einstein, #1774	9.00
CP110	Pennsylvania Toleware, #1778a	10.00
CP111	American Architecture, #1782a	9.00
CP112	Endangered Flora, #1786a	9.00
CP113	Seeing Eye Dogs, #1787	7.00
CP114	Special Olympics, #1788	7.00
CP115	John Paul Jones, #1789	8.00
CP116	Olympic Games, #1794a	9.00
CP117	Christmas (Madonna), #1799	9.00
CP118	Christmas (Santa Claus), #1800	9.00
CP119	Will Rogers, #1801	9.00
CP120	Viet Nam Veterans, #1802	9.00
CP121	10c, 31c Olympics, #1790, C97	9.00

1980

CP122	Winter Olympics, #1798a	7.00
CP123	W.C Fields, #1803	12.00
CP124	Benjamin Banneker, #1804	7.00
CP125	Frances Perkins, #1821	5.00
CP126	Emily Bissell, #1823	9.00
CP127	Helen Keller, #1824	5.00
CP128	Veterans Administration, #1825	5.00
CP129	Galvez, #1826	5.00
CP130	Coral Reefs, #1830a	8.00
CP131	Organized Labor, #1831	5.00
CP132	Edith Wharton, #1832	5.00
CP133	Education, #1833	5.00
CP134	Indian Masks, #1837a	12.50
CP135	Architecture, #1841a	7.00
CP136	Christmas Window, #1842	9.00
CP137	Christmas Toys, #1843	9.00

1981

CP138	Dirksen, #1874	6.00
CP139	Young, #1875	8.00
CP140	Flowers, #1879a	9.00
CP141	Red Cross, #1910	7.00
CP142	Savings and Loan, #1911	7.00
CP143	Space Achievements, #1919a	12.00
CP144	Management, #1920	5.00
CP145	Wildlife, #1924a	9.50
CP146	Disabled, #1925	5.00
CP147	Millay, #1926	5.00
CP148	Architecture, #1931a	7.00
CP149	Zaharias, Jones, #1932, 1933	31.50
CP150	Remington, #1934	9.50
CP151	18c, 20c Hoban, #1935, 1936	5.00
CP152	Yorktown, Va. Capes, #1938a	5.00
CP153	Madonna and Child, #1939	7.00
CP154	Teddy Bear, #1940	8.00
CP155	John Hanson, #1941	5.00
CP156	Desert Plants, #1945a	9.50

1982

CP157	FDR, #1950	9.50
CP158	Love, #1951	10.00
CP159	Washington, #1952	11.00
CP160	Birds and Flowers, block of 4 from #1953-2002	31.50
CP161	US-Netherlands, #2003	12.00
CP162	Library of Congress, #2004	10.00
CP163	Knoxville World's Fair, #2009a	9.50
CP164	Horatio Alger, #2010	10.00
CP165	Aging, #2011	10.00
CP166	Barrymores, #2012	11.50
CP167	Dr. Mary Walker, #2013	9.50
CP168	Peace Garden, #2014	10.00
CP169	Libraries, #2015	8.00
CP170	Jackie Robinson, #2016	31.50
CP171	Touro Synagogue, #2017	9.50
CP172	Wolf Trap Farm, #2018	11.25
CP173	Architecture, #2022a	10.00
CP174	Francis of Assisi, #2023	10.00
CP175	Ponce de Leon, #2024	10.00
CP176	Puppy, Kitten, #2025	15.00
CP177	Madonna and Child, #2026	14.00
CP178	Children Playing, #2030a	14.00

1983

CP179	Science, #2031	5.00
CP180	Ballooning, #2035a	7.00
CP181	US-Sweden, #2036	5.00
CP182	CCC, #2037	5.00
CP183	Priestley, #2038	5.00
CP184	Voluntarism, #2039	14.00
CP185	German Immigration, #2040	5.00
CP186	Brooklyn Bridge, #2041	9.00
CP187	TVA, #2042	5.00
CP188	Fitness, #2043	5.00
CP189	Scott Joplin, #2044	5.00
CP190	Medal of Honor, #2045	9.50
CP191	Babe Ruth, #2046	24.00
CP192	Hawthorne, #2047	5.00
CP193	13c Olympics, #2051a	6.50
CP194	28c Olympics, #C104a	6.50
CP195	40c Olympics, #C108a	7.00
CP196	35c Olympics, #C112a	8.00
CP197	Treaty of Paris, #2052	6.00
CP198	Civil Service, #2053	6.00
CP199	Metropolitan Opera, #2054	9.50
CP200	Inventors, #2058a	7.00
CP201	Streetcars, #2062a	9.00
CP202	Madonna and Child, #2063	9.50
CP203	Santa Claus, #2064	9.50
CP204	Martin Luther, #2065	7.00

1984

CP205	Alaska, #2066	5.00
CP206	Winter Olympics, #2070a	6.50
CP207	FDIC, #2071	5.00
CP208	Love, #2072	5.00
CP209	Woodson, #2073	6.25
CP210	Conservation, #2074	5.00
CP211	Credit Union, #2075	5.00
CP212	Orchids, #2079a	7.00
CP213	Hawaii, #2080	7.00
CP214	National Archives, #2081	5.00
CP215	Olympics, #2085a	7.00
CP216	World Expo, #2086	5.00
CP217	Health Research, #2087	5.00
CP218	Fairbanks, #2088	7.00
CP219	Thorpe, #2089	7.00
CP220	McCormack, #2090	7.00
CP221	St. Lawrence Seaway, #2091	7.00
CP222	Waterfowl, #2092	10.00
CP223	Roanoke Voyages, #2093	5.00
CP224	Melville, #2094	6.50
CP225	Horace Moses, #2095	5.00
CP226	Smokey Bear, #2096	22.50
CP227	Roberto Clemente, #2097	30.50
CP228	Dogs, #2101a	9.50
CP229	Crime Prevention, #2102	5.00
CP230	Hispanic Americans, #2103	5.00
CP231	Family Unity, #2104	5.00
CP232	Eleanor Roosevelt, #2105	11.25
CP233	Readers, #2106	4.75
CP234	Madonna and Child, #2107	6.00
CP235	Child's Santa, #2108	6.00
CP236	Vietnam Memorial, #2109	11.25

1985

CP237	Jerome Kern, #2110	7.00
CP238	Bethune, #2137	7.00
CP239	Duck Decoys, #2141a	16.00
CP240	Winter Special Olympics, #2142	5.00
CP241	Love, #2143	5.00
CP242	REA, #2144	5.00
CP243	AMERIPEX '86, #2145	5.00
CP244	Abigail Adams, #2146	5.00
CP245	Bartholdi, #2147	9.50
CP246	Korean Veterans, #2152	9.50
CP247	Social Security, #2153	4.75
CP248	World War I Veterans, #2154	6.00
CP249	Horses, #2158a	13.00
CP250	Education, #2159	4.75
CP251	Youth Year, #2163a	11.50
CP252	Hunger, #2164	4.75
CP253	Madonna and Child, #2165	7.00
CP254	Poinsettias, #2166	7.00

1986

CP255	Arkansas, #2167	4.75
CP256	Stamp Collecting booklet pane, #2201a	7.00
CP257	Love, #2202	9.50
CP258	Sojourner Truth, #2203	9.50
CP259	Texas Republic, #2204	7.00
CP260	Fish booklet pane, #2209a	9.50
CP261	Hospitals, #2210	4.75
CP262	Duke Ellington, #2211	10.00
CP263	Presidents Souvenir Sheet No. 1, #2216	7.00
CP264	Presidents Souvenir Sheet No. 2, #2217	7.00
CP265	Presidents Souvenir Sheet No. 3, #2218	7.00
CP266	Presidents Souvenir Sheet No. 4, #2219	7.00
CP267	Arctic Explorers, #2223a	9.00
CP268	Statue of Liberty, #2224	9.50
CP269	Navajo Art, #2238a	11.00
CP270	T.S. Eliot, #2239	6.50
CP271	Woodcarved Figurines, #2243a	9.50
CP272	Madonna and Child, #2244	7.00
CP273	Village Scene, #2245	7.00

1987

CP274	Michigan, #2246	7.00
CP275	Pan American Games, #2247	4.75
CP276	Love, #2248	7.00
CP277	du Sable, #2249	7.00
CP278	Caruso, #2250	9.50
CP279	Girl Scouts, #2251	11.00
CP280	Special Occasions booklet pane, #2274a	6.50
CP281	United Way, #2275	4.75
CP282	Wildlife, #2286, 2287, 2296, 2297, 2306, 2307, 2316, 2317, 2326, 2327	9.50
CP283	Wildlife, #2288, 2289, 2298, 2299, 2308, 2309, 2318, 2319, 2328, 2329	9.50
CP284	Wildlife, #2290, 2291, 2300, 2301, 2310, 2311, 2320, 2321, 2330, 2331	9.50
CP285	Wildlife, #2292, 2293, 2302, 2303, 2312, 2313, 2322, 2323, 2332, 2333	9.50
CP286	Wildlife, #2294, 2295, 2304, 2305, 2314, 2315, 2324, 2325, 2334, 2335	9.50

1987-90

CP287	Delaware, #2336	9.50
CP288	Pennsylvania, #2337	6.50
CP289	New Jersey, #2338	6.50
CP290	Georgia, #2339	6.50
CP291	Connecticut, #2340	6.50
CP292	Massachusetts, #2341	6.50
CP293	Maryland, #2342	6.50
CP294	South Carolina, #2343	6.50
CP295	New Hampshire, #2344	6.50
CP296	Virginia, #2345	6.50
CP297	New York, #2346	6.50
CP298	North Carolina, #2347	6.50
CP299	Rhode Island, #2348	6.50

1987

CP300	U.S.-Morocco, #2349	5.00
CP301	William Faulkner, #2350	5.00
CP302	Lacemaking, #2354a	9.50
CP303	Drafting of the Constitution booklet pane, #2359a	6.50
CP304	Signing of the Constitution, #2360	7.00
CP305	Certified Public Accounting, #2361	38.00
CP306	Locomotives booklet pane, #2366a	9.00
CP307	Madonna and Child, #2367	6.00
CP308	Christmas Ornaments, #2368	5.00

1988

CP309	Winter Olympics, #2369	6.50
CP310	Australia Bicentennial, #2370	9.50
CP311	James Weldon Johnson, #2371	6.50
CP312	Cats, #2375a	9.50
CP313	Knute Rockne, #2376	13.50
CP314	New Sweden, #C117	6.50
CP315	Francis Ouimet, #2377	20.00
CP316	25c, 45c Love, #2378 and #2379	6.50
CP317	Summer Olympics, #2380	6.50
CP318	Classic Automobiles booklet pane, #2385a	9.50
CP319	Antarctic Explorers, #2389a	7.00
CP320	Carousel Animals, #2393a	9.00
CP321	Special Occasions booklet singles, #2395-2398	7.00
CP322	Madonna and Child, Sleigh, #2399, 2400	7.00

1989

CP323	Montana, #2401	6.50
CP324	A. Philip Randolph, #2402	8.00
CP325	North Dakota, #2403	6.50
CP326	Washington Statehood, #2404	6.50
CP327	Steamboats booklet pane, #2409a	9.50
CP328	World Stamp Expo, #2410	5.00
CP329	Arturo Toscanini, #2411	8.00

1989-90

CP330	House of Representatives, #2412	8.00
CP331	Senate, #2413	8.00
CP332	Executive Branch, #2414	8.00
CP333	Supreme Court, #2415	8.00

1989

CP334	South Dakota, #2416	6.50
CP335	Lou Gehrig, #2417	30.00
CP336	French Revolution, #C120	7.00
CP337	Ernest Hemingway, #2418	11.50
CP338	Letter Carriers, #2420	7.00
CP339	Bill of Rights, #2421	7.00
CP340	Dinosaurs, #2425a	15.00
CP341	Pre-Columbian Artifacts, #2426, C121	7.00
CP342	Madonna, Sleigh with Presents, #2427, 2428	8.00
CP343	Traditional Mail Delivery, #2437a	6.50
CP344	Futuristic Mail Delivery, #C125a	9.50

1990

CP345	Idaho, #2439	6.50
CP346	Love, #2440	6.50
CP347	Ida B. Wells, #2442	10.00
CP348	Wyoming, #2444	6.50
CP349	Classic Films, #2448a	16.00
CP350	Marianne Moore, #2449	5.00
CP351	Lighthouses booklet pane, #2474a	16.00
CP352	Olympians, #2500a	11.50
CP353	Indian Headdresses booklet pane, #2505c	10.00
CP354	Micronesia, Marshall Islands, #2507a	6.50
CP355	Sea Creatures, #2511a	14.00
CP356	Grand Canyon & Tropical Coastline, #2512, C127	8.00
CP357	Eisenhower, #2513	8.00
CP358	Madonna and Child, Christmas Tree, #2514-2515	8.00

1991

CP359	Switzerland, #2532	9.50
CP360	Vermont Statehood, #2533	6.50
CP361	Savings Bonds, #2534	5.50
CP362	Love, #2535-2536	8.00
CP363	William Saroyan, #2538	14.00
CP364	Fishing Flies, #2549a	14.00
CP365	Cole Porter, #2550	7.00
CP366	Antarctic Treaty, C130	6.50
CP367	Operations Desert Shield & Desert Storm, #2551	30.00
CP368	Summer Olympics, #2557a	8.00
CP369	Numismatics, #2558	7.00
CP370	World War II, #2559	11.00
CP371	Basketball, #2560	16.00
CP372	District of Columbia, #2561	7.00
CP373	Comedians, #2566c	12.00
CP374	Jan E. Matzeliger, #2567	8.00
CP375	Space Exploration, #2577a	12.00
CP376	Bering Land Bridge, #C131	7.00
CP377	Madonna and Child, Santa in Chimney, #2578-2579	10.00

1992

CP378	Winter Olympics, #2615a	7.00
CP379	World Columbian Stamp Expo '92, #2616	8.00
CP380	W.E.B. DuBois, #2617	12.00
CP381	Love, #2618	7.00
CP382	Olympic Baseball, #2619	30.00
CP383	Voyages of Columbus, #2623a	8.00
CP384	Columbus, #2624-2625	50.00
CP385	Columbus, #2626, 2629	50.00
CP386	Columbus, #2627-2628	50.00
CP387	New York Stock Exchange, #2630	11.50
CP388	Space Accomplishments, #2634a	11.50
CP389	Alaska Highway, #2635	6.50
CP390	Kentucky Statehood, #2636	6.50
CP391	Summer Olympics, #2641a	8.00
CP392	Hummingbirds, #2646a	11.50
CP393	World War II, #2697	12.00
CP394	Wildflowers, #2647, 2648, 2657, 2658, 2667, 2668, 2677, 2678, 2687, 2688	30.00
CP395	Wildflowers, #2649, 2650, 2659, 2660, 2669, 2670, 2679, 2680, 2689, 2690	30.00
CP396	Wildflowers, #2651, 2652, 2661, 2662, 2671, 2672, 2681, 2682, 2691, 2692	30.00
CP397	Wildflowers, #2653, 2654, 2663, 2664, 2673, 2674, 2683, 2684, 2693, 2694	30.00
CP398	Wildflowers, #2655, 2656, 2665, 2666, 2675, 2676, 2685, 2686, 2695, 2696	30.00
CP399	Dorothy Parker, #2698	6.50
CP400	Dr. Theodore von Karman, #2699	11.25
CP401	Minerals, #2703a	13.00
CP402	Juan Rodriguez Cabrillo, #2704	8.00
CP403	Wild Animals, #2709a	11.25
CP404	Madonna and Child, wheeled toys, #2710, 2714a	11.25
CP405	Chinese New Year, #2720	22.50

1993

CP406	Elvis Presley, #2721	24.00
CP407	Space Fantasy, #2745a	14.00
CP408	Percy Lavon Julian, #2746	12.00
CP409	Oregon Trail, #2747	8.00
CP410	World University Games, #2748	8.00
CP411	Grace Kelly, #2749	22.00
CP412	Oklahoma!, #2722	8.00
CP413	Circus, #2753a	10.00
CP414	Cherokee Strip, #2754	8.00

CP415	Dean Acheson, #2755	11.25
CP416	Sports horses, #2759a	11.50
CP417	Garden flowers, #2764a	9.50
CP418	World War II, #2765	12.00
CP419	Hank Williams, #2723	21.00
CP420	Rock & Roll/Rhythm & Blues, #2737b	22.00
CP421	Joe Louis, #2766	27.50
CP422	Broadway Musicals, #2770a	11.25
CP423	National Postal Museum, #2782a	10.00
CP424	American Sign Language, #2784a	9.00
CP425	Country & Western Music, #2778a	21.00
CP426	Christmas, #2789, 2794a	11.25
CP427	Youth Classics, #2788a	11.25
CP428	Mariana Islands, #2804	9.00
CP429	Columbus' Landing in Puerto Rico, #2805	10.00
CP430	AIDS Awareness, #2806	11.00

Starting with No. CP431, panels are shrink wrapped in plastic with cardboard backing. Shrink wrapping is not suitable for philatelic storage, as the plastic will shrink, bending the panels. Values from 1994 on are for panels without the plastic wrapping.

1994

CP431	Winter Olympics, #2807-2811	14.00
CP432	Edward R. Murrow, #2812	9.50
CP434	Love, #2814	11.25
CP436	Dr. Allison Davis, #2816	11.25
CP437	Chinese New Year, #2817	14.00
CP438	Buffalo Soldiers, #2818	12.00
CP439	Silent Screen Stars, #2828a	14.00
CP440	Garden Flowers, #2829-2833	10.00
CP441	World Cup Soccer, #2837	11.50
CP442	World War II, #2838	12.00
CP443	Norman Rockwell, #2839	18.00
CP444	Moon Landing, #2841	20.00
CP445	Locomotives, #2843-2847	12.00
CP446	George Meany, #2848	6.50
CP447	Popular Singers, #2853a	12.00
CP448	Jazz/Blues Singers, block of 10, 2854-2861	16.00

Block of 10 on No. CP448 may contain different combination of stamps.

CP449	James Thurber, #2862	7.00
CP450	Wonders of the Sea, #2866a	12.00
CP451	Cranes, block of 2 #2868a	12.00
CP453	Christmas Madonna and Child, #2871	7.00
CP454	Christmas stocking, #2872	7.00
CP455	Chinese New Year, #2876	12.00

1995

CP456	Florida Statehood, #2950	10.00
CP457	Earth Day, #2954a	10.00
CP458	Richard M. Nixon, #2955	15.00
CP459	Bessie Coleman, #2956	13.00
CP460	Love, #2957-2958	13.00
CP461	Recreational Sports, #2965a	13.00
CP462	Prisoners of War/Missing in Action, #2966	12.00
CP463	Marilyn Monroe, #2967	24.00
CP464	Texas Statehood, #2968	12.00
CP465	Great Lakes Lighthouses, #2973a	13.00
CP466	United Nations, #2974	10.00
CP467	Carousel Horses, #2979a	15.00
CP468	Woman Suffrage, #2980	9.50
CP469	World War II, #2981	14.00
CP470	Louis Armstrong, #2982	16.00
CP471	Jazz Musicians, #2992a	15.00
CP472	Garden Flowers, #2993-2997	9.00
CP473	Republic of Palau, #2999	9.50
CP474	Naval Academy, #3001	11.00
CP475	Tennessee Williams, #3002	11.50
CP476	Christmas, Madonna and Child, #3003	12.00
CP477	Santa Claus, Children with toys, #3007a	12.00
CP478	James K. Polk, #2587	9.50
CP479	Antique Automobiles, 3023a	16.00

1996

CP480	Utah Statehood, #3024	10.00
CP481	Garden Flowers, #3029a	10.00
CP482	Ernest E. Just, #3058	13.00
CP483	Smithsonian Institution, #3059	9.00
CP484	Chinese New Year, #3060	16.00
CP485	Pioneers of Communication, #3064a	12.00
CP486	Fulbright Scholarships, #3065	9.50
CP487	Summer Olympic Games, #3068, 2 pages	31.50

Beginning with No. CP487, some items contain two pages. One has text and engraved illustrations, the second has the stamp(s).

CP488	Marathon, #3067	12.00
CP489	Georgia O'Keeffe, #3069	9.50
CP490	Tennessee Statehood, #3070	9.50
CP491	Indian Dances, #3076a	15.00
CP492	Prehistoric Animals, #3080a	15.00
CP493	Breast Cancer Awareness, #3081	9.50
CP494	James Dean, #3082	15.00
CP495	Folk Heroes, #3086a	14.00
CP496	Olympic Games, Cent., #3087	11.00
CP497	Iowa Statehood, #3088	9.50
CP498	Rural Free Delivery, #3090	9.50
CP499	Riverboats, #3095a	15.00
CP500	Big Band Leaders, #3099a	14.00
CP501	Songwriters, #3103a	14.00
CP502	F. Scott Fitzgerald, #3104	14.00
CP503	Endangered Species, #3105, 2 pages	24.00
CP504	Computer Technology, #3106	14.00
CP505	Madonna & Child, #3107	13.00
CP506	Family Scenes, #3111a	13.00
CP507	Hanukkah, #3118	12.00
CP507A	Cycling, #3119	30.00

1997

CP508	Chinese New Year, #3120	18.00
CP509	Benjamin O. Davis, Sr., #3121	14.00
CP510	Love Swans, #3123-3124	11.50
CP511	Helping Children Learn, #3125	9.50
CP512	PACIFIC 97 Stagecoach & Ship, #3131a	14.00
CP513	Thornton Wilder, #3134	12.00
CP514	Raoul Wallenberg, #3135	11.25
CP515	Dinosaurs, #3136	22.50
CP516	Bugs Bunny, #3137c	18.00
CP517	PACIFIC 97 Franklin, #3139	38.00
CP518	PACIFIC 97 Washington, #3140	38.00
CP519	Marshall Plan, #3141	11.50
CP520	Classic American Aircraft, #3142, 2 pages	22.50
CP521	Football Coaches, #3146a	18.00
CP522	American Dolls, #3151	40.00
CP523	Humphrey Bogart, #3152	13.00
CP524	"The Stars & Stripes Forever!," #3153	11.25
CP525	Opera Singers, #3157a	12.00
CP526	Composers & Conductors, #3165a	14.00
CP527	Padre Felix Varela, #3166	10.00
CP528	Department of the Air Force, #3167	14.00
CP529	Movie Monsters, #3172a	14.00
CP530	Supersonic Flight, #3173	15.00
CP531	Women in Military Service, #3174	12.00
CP532	Kwanzaa, #3175	10.00
CP533	Madonna & Child, #3176a	14.00
CP534	Holly, #3177a	14.00

1998

CP535	Chinese New Year, #3179	12.00
CP536	Alpine Skiing, #3180	11.25
CP537	Madam C.J. Walker, #3181	12.00

Celebrate the Century

1998-2000

CP537A	1900s, #3182, 2 pages	20.00
CP537B	1910s, #3183, 2 pages	20.00
CP537C	1920s, #3184, 2 pages	18.00
CP537D	1930s, #3185, 2 pages	20.00
CP537E	1940s, #3186, 2 pages	24.00
CP537F	1950s, #3187, 2 pages	17.00
CP537G	1960s, #3188, 2 pages	21.00
CP537H	1970s, #3189, 2 pages	18.00
CP537I	1980s, #3190, 2 pages	17.00
CP537J	1990s, #3191, 2 pages	16.00

1998

CP538	Remember the Maine,inscribed "Key West, Florida" #3192	10.00
	a. Inscribed "Scottsdale, Arizona."	16.00
CP539	Flowering Trees, #3197a	12.00
CP540	Alexander Calder, #3202a	11.50
CP541	Cinco de Mayo, #3203	10.00
CP542	Sylvester & Tweety, #3204c	16.00
CP543	Wisconsin Statehood, #3206	11.25
CP544	Trans-Mississippi, #3209-3210, 2 pages	20.00
CP545	Berlin Airlift, #3211	10.00
CP546	Folk Musicians, #3215a	14.00
CP547	Gospel Singers, #3219a	14.00
CP548	Spanish Settlement, #3220	10.00
CP549	Stephen Vincent Benét, #3221	10.00
CP550	Tropical Birds, #3225a	13.00
CP551	Alfred Hitchcock, #3226	13.00
CP552	Organ & Tissue Donation, #3227	12.00
CP553	Bright Eyes, #3234a	12.00
CP554	Klondike Gold Rush, #3235	10.00
CP555	American Art, #3236	21.00
CP556	American Ballet, #3237	13.00
CP557	Space Discovery, #3242a	14.00
CP558	Giving & Sharing, #3243	10.00
CP559	Madonna & Child, #3244a	14.00
CP560	Wreaths, #3252b	11.25
CP561	Breast Cancer Awareness, #B1	17.00

1999

CP562	Chinese New Year, #3272	12.00
CP563	Malcolm X, #3273	11.25
CP564	Love, #3274a	14.00
CP565	Love, #3275	10.00
CP566	Hospice Care, #3276	10.00
CP567	Irish Immigration, #3286	12.00
CP568	Lunt & Fontanne, #3287	9.50
CP569	Arctic Animals, #3292a	10.00
CP570	Sonoran Desert, #3293, 2 pages	14.00
CP571	Daffy Duck, #3306c	15.00
CP572	Ayn Rand, #3308	18.00
CP573	Cinco de Mayo, #3309	9.50
CP574	John & William Bartram, #3314	10.00
CP575	Prostate Cancer, #3315	10.00
CP576	California Gold Rush, #3316	10.00
CP577	Aquarium Fish, #3320a	10.00
CP578	Extreme Sports, #3324a	10.00
CP579	American Glass, #3328a	10.00
CP580	James Cagney, #3329	10.00
CP581	Honoring Those who Served, #3331	10.00
CP582	Famous Trains, #3337a	13.00
CP583	Frederick Law Olmsted, #3338	10.00
CP584	Hollywood Composers, #3344a	12.00
CP585	Broadway Songwriters, #3350a	12.00
CP586	Insects & Spiders, #3351, 2 pages	18.00
CP587	Hanukkah, #3352	10.00
CP588	NATO, #3354	10.00
CP589	Madonna & Child, #3355	10.00
CP590	Deer, #3359a	10.00
CP591	Kwanzaa, #3368	10.00
CP592	Year 2000, #3369	14.00

2000

CP593	Chinese New Year, #3370	10.00
CP594	Patricia Roberts Harris, #3371	13.00
CP595	Los Angeles Class Submarine, #3372	14.00
CP596	Pacific Coast Rain Forest, #3378, 2 pages	18.00
CP597	Louise Nevelson, #3383a	11.25
CP598	Hubble Space Telescope Images, #3388a	14.00
CP599	American Samoa, #3389	10.00
CP600	Library of Congress, #3390	10.00
CP601	Road Runner & Wile E. Coyote, #3391c	12.00
CP602	Distinguished Soldiers, #3396a	13.00
CP603	Summer Sports, #3397	10.00
CP604	Adoption, #3398	12.00
CP605	Youth Team Sports, #3402a	12.00
CP606	The Stars and Stripes, #3403, 2 pages	21.00
CP607	Legends of Baseball, #3408, 2 pages	24.00
CP608	Stampin' the Future, #3417a	12.00
CP609	California Statehood, #3438	10.00
CP610	Deep Sea Creatures, #3443a	13.00
CP611	Thomas Wolfe, #3444	10.00
CP612	White House, #3445	11.25
CP613	Edward G. Robinson, #3446	8.00

2001

CP614	Non-denominated Love Letters, #3496	12.00
CP615	34c Love, #3497	12.00
CP615A	55c Love, #3499	13.00
CP616	Chinese New Year, #3500	14.00
CP617	Roy Wilkins, #3501	17.00
CP618	Nine-Mile Prairie, #C136	12.00
CP618A	American Illustrators, #3502, 2 pages	22.50
CP619	Diabetes Awareness, #3503	11.25
CP620	Nobel Prize, #3504	14.00
CP621	Pan-American Inverts, #3505, 2 pages	24.00
CP622	Mt. McKinley, #C137	13.00
CP623	Great Plains Prairie, #3506, 2 pages	22.50
CP624	Peanuts Comic Strip, #3507	17.00
CP625	Honoring Veterans, #3508	12.00
CP626	Frida Kahlo, #3509	14.00
CP627	Legendary Playing Fields, #3510-3519	27.50

No. CP627 consists of 2 pages. One has text and engraved illustrations. The other consists of the pane of stamps.

CP628	Leonard Bernstein, #3521	14.00
CP629	Lucille Ball, #3523	14.00
CP630	Amish Quilts, #3527a	14.00
CP631	Carnivorous Plants, #3531a	13.00
CP632	Eid, #3532	10.00
CP633	Enrico Fermi, #3533	11.25
CP634	That's All Folks!, #3535c	14.00
CP635	Madonna & Child, #3536	10.00
CP636	Santas, #3540b	11.25
CP637	James Madison, #3545	12.00
CP638	Thanksgiving, #3546	12.00
CP639	Hanukkah, #3547	10.00
CP640	Kwanzaa, #3548	10.00
CP641	57c Love, #3551	12.00

2002

CP642	Winter Olympics, #3555a	12.00
CP643	Mentoring a Child, #3556	12.00
CP644	Langston Hughes, #3557	12.00
CP645	Happy Birthday, #3558	12.00
CP646	Chinese New Year, #3559	16.00
CP647	U.S. Military Academy Bicentennial, #3560	14.00
CP648	Greetings from America, #3610a	34.00
CP649	Longleaf Pine Forest, #3611	26.00

Nos. CP648 and CP649 each consist of 2 pages. One has text and engraved illustrations. The other contains the pane of stamps.

CP650	Heroes of 2001, #B2	16.00
CP651	Masters of American Photography, #3649	30.00

No. CP651 consists of 2 pages. One has text and engraved illustrations. The other consists of the pane of stamps.

CP652	John James Audubon, #3650	13.50
CP653	Harry Houdini, #3651	13.50
CP654	Andy Warhol, #3652	13.50
CP655	Teddy Bears, #3653-3656	11.00
CP656	37c Love, #3657	10.00
CP657	60c Love, #3658	12.00
CP658	Ogden Nash, #3659	12.00
CP659	Duke Kahanamoku, #3660	17.00
CP660	American Bats, #3664a	17.00
CP661	Women in Journalism, #3668a	14.00
CP662	Irving Berlin, #3669	12.00
CP663	Neuter or Spay, #3671a	12.00
CP664	Hanukkah, #3672	11.25
CP665	Kwanzaa, #3673	11.25
CP666	Eid, #3674	10.00
CP667	Madonna & Child, #3675	12.00
CP668	Christmas Snowmen, #3679a	11.00
CP669	Cary Grant, #3692	13.00
CP670	Hawaiian Missionary Stamps, #3694	26.00

No. CP670 consists of 2 pages. One has text and engraved illustrations. The other contains the pane of stamps.

CP671	Happy Birthday, #3695	10.00
CP672	Greetings from America, #3745a	31.50

No. CP672 consists of 2 pages. One has text and engraved illustrations. The other contains the pane of stamps.

2003

CP673 Thurgood Marshall, #3746 12.00
CP674 Chinese New Year, #3747 13.00
CP675 Zora Neale Hurston, #3748 14.00
CP676 Special Olympics, #3771 13.00
CP677 American Filmmaking: Behind the Scenes, #3772 30.00

No. CP677 consists of 2 pages. One has text and engraved illustrations. The other contains the pane of stamps.

CP678 Ohio Statehood, Bicent., #3773 13.00
CP679 Pelican Island National Wildlife Refuge, #3774 14.00
CP680 Old Glory, #3780b 15.00
CP681 Cesar E. Chavez, #3781 12.00
CP682 Louisiana Purchase, #3782 13.00
CP683 First Flight of Wright Brothers, #3783b 14.00
CP684 Audrey Hepburn, #3786 15.00
CP685 Southeastern Lighthouses, #3791a 14.00
CP686 Arctic Tundra, #3802 26.00
CP687 Korean War Veterans Memorial, #3803 13.00
CP688 Mary Cassatt Paintings, #3807a 13.00
CP689 Early Football Heroes, #3811a 17.00
CP690 Roy Acuff, #3812 13.00
CP691 District of Columbia, #3813 13.00
CP692 Reptiles and Amphibians, #3818a 17.00
CP693 Stop Family Violence, #B3 13.00
CP694 Madonna and Child, #3820 13.00
CP695 Christmas Holiday Music Makers, #3824a 13.00

2004

CP696 Pacific Coral Reef, #3831 26.00

No. CP696 consists of 2 pages. One has text and engraved illustrations. The other contains the pane of stamps.

CP697 Chinese New Year, #3832 13.00
CP698 Love, #3833 13.00
CP699 Paul Robeson, #3834 13.00
CP700 Theodor Seuss Geisel (Dr. Seuss), #3835 17.00
CP701 Love (White Lilacs and Pink Roses), #3836 12.00
CP702 Love (Five Varieties of Pink Roses), #3837 12.00
CP703 U.S. Air Force Academy, #3838 13.00
CP704 Henry Mancini, #3839 13.00
CP705 American Choreographers, #3843a 14.00
CP706 Lewis and Clark, #3854 16.00
CP707 Lewis and Clark booklet pane, #3856b 16.00
CP708 Isamu Noguchi, #3861a 12.00
CP709 National World War II Memorial, #3862 14.00
CP710 Summer Olympics, Athens, Greece, #3863 13.00
CP711 Art of Disney, #3868a 16.00
CP712 USS Constellation, #3869 14.00
CP713 R. Buckminster Fuller, #3870 12.00
CP714 James Baldwin, #3871 11.25
CP715 Martin Johnson Heade, #3872 11.25
CP716 Art of the American Indian, #3873 27.50

No. CP716 consists of 2 pages. One has text and engraved illustrations. The other contains the pane of stamps.

CP717 John Wayne, #3876 17.00
CP718 Sickle Cell Disease, #3877 12.00
CP719 Cloudscapes, #3878 26.00

No. CP719 consists of 2 pages. One has text and engraved illustrations. The other contains the pane of stamps.

CP720 Christmas Madonna, #3879 13.00
CP721 Hanukkah, #3880 10.00
CP722 Kwanzaa, #3881 10.00
CP723 Moss Hart, #3882 11.25
CP724 Christmas Ornaments, #3886a 12.00

2005

CP725 Chinese New Year, #3895 27.50

No. CP725 consists of two pages. One has text and engraved illustrations. The other contains the pane of stamps.

CP726 Marian Anderson, #3896 16.00
CP727 Ronald Reagan, #3897 18.00
CP728 Love, #3898 13.00
CP729 Northeast Deciduous Forest, #3899 26.00

No. CP729 consists of two pages. One has text and engraved illustrations. The other contains the pane of stamps.

CP730 Spring Flowers, #3903a 12.00
CP731 Robert Penn Warren, #3904 10.00
CP732 Yip Harburg, #3905 10.00
CP733 American Scientists, #3909a 11.25
CP734 Modern American Architecture, #3910 26.00

No. CP734 consists of two pages. One has text and engraved illustrations. The other contains the pane of stamps.

CP735 Henry Fonda, #3911 10.00
CP736 Disney Characters, #3915a 20.00
CP737 Advances in Aviation, #3916-3925 29.00

No. CP737 consists of two pages. One has text and illustrations. The other contains the pane of stamps.

CP738 Rio Grande Blankets, #3929a 10.00
CP739 Presidential Libraries, #3930 10.00
CP740 Sporty Cars of the 1950s, #3935b 20.00
CP741 Arthur Ashe, #3936 13.00
CP742 To Form a More Perfect Union, #3937 32.50

No. CP742 consists of two pages. One has text and illustrations. The other contains the pane of stamps.

CP743 Child Health, #3938 10.00
CP744 Let's Dance, #3942a 10.00
CP745 Greta Garbo, #3943 16.00
CP746 Jim Henson and the Muppets, #3944 27.50

No. CP746 consists of two pages. One has text and engraved illustrations. The other contains the pane of stamps.

CP747 Constellations, #3948a 20.00
CP748 Christmas, #3952a 10.00
CP749 Distinguished Marines, #3964a 18.00

2006

CP750 Love, #3976 9.50
CP751 Children's Book Animals, #3994a 20.00

No. CP751 consists of two pages. One has text and illustrations. The other contains the pane of stamps.

CP752 2006 Winter Olympics, #3995 10.00
CP753 Hattie McDaniel, #3996 11.25
CP754 Chinese New Year, #3997 20.00

No. CP754 consists of two pages. One has text and illustrations. The other contains the pane of stamps.

CP755 39c Wedding, #3998 10.00
CP756 63c Wedding, #3999 10.00
CP757 Sugar Ray Robinson, #4020 10.00
CP758 Benjamin Franklin, #4024a 10.00
CP759 Disney Characters, #4028a 10.00
CP760 Love Birds, #4029 10.00
CP761 Katherine Anne Porter, #4030 10.00
CP762 Amber Alert, #4031 10.00
CP763 Wonders of America, #4033-4072 31.50

No. CP763 consists of two pages. One has text and illustrations. The other contains the pane of stamps.

CP764 Samuel de Champlain, #4073 10.00
CP765 Washington 2006 World Philatelic Exhibition, #4075 12.00
CP766 Distinguished American Diplomats, #4076 10.00

No. CP766 consists of two pages. One has text and illustrations. The other contains the pane of stamps.

CP767 Judy Garland, #4077 10.00
CP768 Ronald Reagan, #4078 11.25
CP769 Happy Birthday, #4079 10.00
CP770 Baseball Sluggers, #4083a 11.25
CP771 DC Comics Superheroes, #4084 26.00

No. CP771 consists of two pages. One has text and engraved illustrations. The other contains the pane of stamps.

CP772 Motorcycles, #4088a 12.00
CP773 Quilts of Gee's Bend, Alabama, #4098b 11.25
CP774 Southern Florida Wetland, #4099 26.00

No. CP774 consists of two pages. One has text and engraved illustrations. The other contains the pane of stamps.

CP775 Christmas Madonna, #4100 9.50
CP776 Christmas Snowflakes, #4104a 9.50
CP777 Eid, #4117 9.50
CP778 Hanukkah, #4118 9.50
CP779 Kwanzaa, #4119 9.50
CP780 39c Ella Fitzgerald, #4120 9.50
CP781 39c Oklahoma Statehood, #4121 9.50
CP782 39c Love, #4122 9.50
CP783 84c International Polar Year, #4123 9.50
CP784 39c Henry Wadsworth Longfellow, #4124 9.50
CP785 41c Settlement of Jamestown, #4136 25.00

No. CP785 consists of two pages. One has text and illustrations. The other contains the pane of stamps.

CP786 Star Wars, #4143 25.00

No. CP786 consists of two pages. One has text and engraved illustrations. The other contains the pane of stamps.

CP787 Pacific Lighthouses, #4150a 10.00
CP788 41c Wedding Hearts, #4151 10.00
CP789 58c Wedding Hearts, #4152 10.00
CP790 Pollination, #4156d 13.50
CP791 Marvel Comics Super Heroes, #4159 25.00

No. CP791 consists of two pages. One has text and engraved illustrations. The other contains the pane of stamps.

CP792 Vintage Mahogany Speedboats, #4163a 10.00
CP793 Louis Comfort Tiffany, #4165 10.00
CP794 Disney Characters, #4195a 10.00
CP795 Celebrate, #4196 9.50
CP796 James Stewart, #4197 10.00
CP797 Alpine Tundra, #4198 25.00

No. CP796 consists of two pages. One has text and engraved illustrations. The other contains the pane of stamps.

CP798 Gerald R. Ford, #4199 9.50
CP799 Jury Duty, #4200 9.50
CP800 Mendez v. Westminster School District, #4201 9.50
CP801 Eid, #4202 9.50
CP802 Polar Lights, #4204a 10.00
CP803 Yoda, #4205 10.00
CP804 Christmas Madonna, #4206 10.00
CP805 Christmas Holiday Knits #4210a 10.00
CP806 Hanukkah, #4219 9.50
CP807 Kwanzaa, #4220 9.50

2008

CP808 Chinese New Year, #4221 10.00
CP809 Charles W. Chesnutt, #4222 10.00
CP810 Marjorie Kinnan Rawlings, #4223 10.00
a. With corrected date on panel 10.00
CP811 41c American Scientists, #4227a 10.00
CP812 42c American Journalists, #4252a 10.00
CP813 42c Frank Sinatra, #4265 10.00
CP814 42c Minnesota Statehood, #4266 10.00
CP815 42c Love, #4270 10.00
CP816 42c Wedding Hearts, #4271-4272 10.00
CP817 Charles and Ray Eames, #4333 25.00

No. CP817 consists of two pages. One has text and engraved illustrations. The other contains the pane of stamps.

CP818 Olympic Games, #4334 10.00
CP819 Vintage Black Cinema, #4340a 10.00
CP820 Take Me Out to the Ball Game, #4341 10.00
CP821 Disney Characters - Imagination, #4345a 10.00
CP822 Albert Bierstadt, #4346 10.00
CP823 Latin Jazz, #4349 10.00
CP824 Bette Davis, #4350 10.00
CP825 Great Lakes Dunes, #4352 25.00

No. CP825 consists of two pages. One has text and engraved illustrations. The other contains the pane of stamps.

CP826 Automobiles of the 1950s, #4357a 10.00
CP827 Alzheimer's Disease Awareness, #4358 10.00
CP828 Christmas Madonna, #4359 10.00
CP829 Christmas Nutcrackers, #4363a 10.00

2009

CP830 Alaska Statehood, #4374 10.00
CP831 Chinese New Year, #4375 10.00
CP832 Oregon Statehood, #4376 10.00
CP833 Edgar Allan Poe, #4377 10.00
CP834 44c Abraham Lincoln, #4383a 10.00
CP835 44c Civil Rights Pioneers, #4384 25.00
CP836 44c Bob Hope, #4406 10.00
CP837 44c Anna Julia Cooper, #4408 10.00
CP838 44c Gulf Coast Lighthouses, #4413a 10.00
CP839 44c Early TV Memories, #4414 25.00
CP840 44c Hawaii Statehood, #4415 10.00
CP841 44c Thanksgiving Day Parade, #4420a 10.00
CP842 44c Gary Cooper, #4421 10.00
CP843 44c Supreme Court Justices, #4422 25.00
CP844 44c Kelp Forest, #4423 25.00

2010

CP845 44c Chinese New Year, #4435 10.00
CP846 44c 2010 Winter Olympics, Vancouver, #4436 10.00
CP847 44c Distinguished Sailors, #4443a 10.00
CP848 44c Abstract Expressionists, #4444 25.00
CP849 44c Bill Mauldin, #4445 10.00
CP850 44c Cowboys of the Silver Screen, #4449a 10.00
CP851 44c Animal Rescue, #4460a 10.00
CP852 44c Katharine Hepburn, #4461 10.00
CP853 44c Kate Smith, #4463 10.00
CP854 44c Oscar Micheaux, #4464 10.00
CP855 44c Negro Leagues Baseball, #4466a 10.00
CP856 44c Sunday Funnies, #4471a 10.00
CP857 44c Scouting, #4472 10.00
CP858 44c Winslow Homer, #4473 10.00
CP859 44c Hawaiian Rain Forest, #4474 25.00
CP860 44c Mother Teresa, #4475 10.00
CP861 44c Julia de Burgos, #4476 10.00

2011

CP862 (44c) Chinese New Year, #4492 11.00
CP863 (44c) Kansas Statehood, #4493 11.00
CP864 (44c) Ronald Reagan, #4494 11.00
CP865 (44c) Latin Music Legends, #4501a 11.00
CP866 (44c) Jazz, #4503 11.00
CP867 (44c) Civil War Battles of 1861, #4522-4523 27.00

No. CP867 consists of two pages. One has text and engraved illustrations. The other contains the pane of stamps.

CP868 (44c) Go Green, #4524 27.00

No. CP868 consists of two pages. One has text and engraved illustrations. The other contains the pane of stamps.

CP869 (44c) Helen Hayes, #4525 11.00
CP870 (44c) Gregory Peck, #4526 11.00
CP871 (44c) Mercury Project and Messenger Mission, #4527-4528 11.00
CP872 (44c) Indianapolis 500, #4530 11.00
CP873 (44c) American Scientists, #4544a 11.00
CP874 (44c) Mark Twain, #4545 11.00
CP875 (44c) Pioneers of American Industrial Design, #4546 27.00

No. CP875 consists of two pages. One has text and engraved illustrations. The other contains the pane of stamps.

CP876 (44c) Owney, the Postal Dog, #4547 11.00
CP877 (44c) U.S. Merchant Marine, #4551a 11.00
CP878 (44c) Disney-Pixar Films, Send a Hello, 4557a 11.00
CP879 (44c) Edward Hopper, #4558 11.00
CP880 (44c) Barbara Jordan, #4565 11.00
CP881 (44c) Romare Bearden, 4569a 11.00

2012

CP882 (44c) New Mexico Statehood, #4591 12.00
CP883 (45c) Chinese New Year, #4623 12.00
CP884 (45c) John H. Johnson, #4624 12.00
CP885 (45c) Heart Health, #4625 12.00
CP886 (45c) Arizona Statehood, #4627 12.00
CP887 (45c) Danny Thomas, #4628 12.00
CP888 (45c) Cherry Blossom Centennial, #4652a 12.00
CP889 (45c) William H. Johnson, #4653 12.00
CP890 (45c) Twentieth-Century Poets, #4663a 12.00
CP891 (45c) Civil War Battles of 1862, #4664-4665 27.00

No. CP891 consists of two panes. One has text and engraved illustrations. The other contains the pane of stamps.

CP892 (45c) José Ferrer, #4666 12.00
CP893 (45c) Louisiana Statehood, #4667 12.00

CP894	(45c)	Great Film Directors, #4671a	12.00
CP896	(45c)	Bicycling, #4690a	12.00
CP897	(45c)	Girl Scouts of America, Cent., #4691	12.00
CP898	(45c)	Edith Piaf and Miles Davis, #4693a	12.00
CP895	(45c)	Mail a Smile, #4681a	12.00
CP899	(45c)	Major League Baseball All-Stars, #4697a	12.00
CP900	(45c)	Ted Williams, #4694	12.00
CP901	(45c)	Larry Doby, #4695	12.00
CP902	(45c)	Willie Stargell, #4696	12.00
CP903	(45c)	Joe DiMaggio, #4697	12.00
CP904	(45c)	Innovative Choreographers, #4701a	12.00
CP905	(45c)	Edgar Rice Burroughs, #4702	12.00
CP906	(45c)	USS Constitution, #4703	12.00
CP907	(45c)	O. Henry, #4705	12.00
CP908	(45c)	Earthscapes, #4710	27.00

No. CP908 consists of two panes. One has text and engraved illustrations. The other contains the pane of stamps.

CP909	(45c)	Lady Bird Johnson, #4716	27.00

No. CP909 consists of two panes. One has text and engraved illustrations. The other contains the pane of stamps.

2013

CP910	(45c)	Emancipation Proclamation, #4721	14.00
CP911	(45c)	Chinese New Year, #4726	14.00
CP912	(46c)	Rosa Parks, #4742	14.00
CP913	(46c)	Muscle Cars, #4747a	14.00
CP914	(46c)	Modern Art in America, #4748	29.00

No. CP914 consists of two pages. One has text and engraved illustrations. The other contains the pane of stamps.

CP915	(46c)	La Florida, #4753a	14.00
CP916	(46c)	Lydia Mendoza, #4786	14.00
CP917	(46c)	Civil War Battles of 1863, #4787-4788	14.00

No. CP917 consists of two pages. One has text and engraved illustrations. The other contains the pane of stamps.

CP918	(46c)	Johnny Cash, #4789	14.00
CP919	(46c)	West Virginia Statehood, #4790	14.00
CP920	(46c)	New England Coastal Lighthouses, #4795a	14.00
CP921	(46c)	Building a Nation, #4801	29.00

No. CP921 consists of two pages. One has text and engraved illustrations. The other contains the pane of stamps.

CP922	(46c)	Althea Gibson, #4803	14.00
CP923	(46c)	March on Washington, 50th Anniv., #4804	14.00
CP924	(46c)	Battle of Lake Erie, #4805	14.00
CP925	$2	Inverted Jenny sheet, #4806	29.00

No. CP925 consists of two pages. One has text and engraved illustrations. The other contains the pane of stamps.

CP926	(46c)	Ray Charles, #4807	14.00
CP927	(46c)	Medals of Honor, #4822-4823	29.00

No. CP927 consists of two pages. One has text and engraved illustrations. The other contains the pane of stamps.

CP928	(46c)	Harry Potter, #4825-4844	29.00

No. CP928 consists of two pages. One has text and engraved illustrations. The other contains the pane of stamps.

2014

CP929	(46c)	Chinese New Year, #4846	14.00
CP930	(49c)	Shirley Chisholm, #4856	14.00
CP931	(49c)	Charlton Heston, #4892	14.00
CP932	(49c)	Vintage Circus Posters, #4905a	29.00

No. CP932 consists of two pages. One has text and engraved illustrations. The other contains the pane of stamps.

CP933	(49c)	Harvey Milk, #4906	14.00
CP934	(49c)	Nevada Statehood, #4907	14.00
CP935	(49c)	Medal of Honor — Korean War, #4822a-4823a	29.00

No. CP935 consists of two pages. One has text and engraved illustrations. The other contains the pane of stamps.

CP936	(49c)	Civil War Battles of 1864, #4911a	29.00

No. CP936 consists of two pages. One has text and engraved illustrations. The other contains the pane of stamps.

CP937	(49c)	Farmers Markets, #4915a	14.00
CP938	(49c)	Janis Joplin, #4916	14.00
CP939	(49c)	Bombardment of Fort McHenry, #4921	14.00
CP940	(49c)	Celebrity Chefs, #4926a	14.00
CP941	(49c)	Batman, #4928-4935	29.00

No. CP941 consists of two pages. One has text and engraved illustrations. The other contains the pane of stamps.

CP942	(49c)	Wilt Chamberlain, #4951a	14.00

2015

CP943	(49c)	Battle of New Orleans, #4952	14.00
CP944	(49c)	Chinese New Year, #4957	14.00
CP945	(49c)	Robert Robinson Taylor, #4958	14.00
CP946	(49c)	Martín Ramírez, #4972a	14.00
CP947	(49c)	From Me to You, #4978	14.00
CP948	(49c)	Maya Angelou, #4979	14.00
CP949	(49c)	Civil War Events of 1865, #4981a	29.00

No. CP949 consists of two pages. One has text and engraved illustrations. The other contains the pane of stamps.

CP950	(49c)	Gifts of Friendship, #4983a	14.00
CP951	(49c)	Special Olympics World Games, #4986	14.00
CP952	(49c)	Help Find Missing Children, #4987	14.00
CP953	(49c)	Medal of Honor, #4988a	29.00

No. CP953 consists of two pages. One has text and engraved illustrations. The other contains the pane of stamps.

CP954	(49c)	Coast Guard, #5008	14.00
CP955	(49c)	Elvis Presley, #5009	14.00
CP956	(49c)	World Stamp Show 2016, #5011a	14.00
CP957	(49c)	Ingrid Bergman, #5012	14.00
CP958	(49c)	Paul Newman, #5020	14.00

2016

CP959	(49c)	Richard Allen, #5056	14.00
CP960	(49c)	Chinese New Year, #5057	14.00
CP961	(49c)	Sarah Vaughan, #5059	14.00
CP962	(47c)	Shirley Temple, #5060	14.00
CP963	(47c)	World Stamp Show 2016, #5062-5063	29.00

No. CP963 consists of two pages. One has text and engraved illustrations. The other contains the pane of stamps.

CP964	(47c)	Repeal of the Stamp Act, #5064	29.00

No. CP964 consists of two pages. One has text and engraved illustrations. The other contains the pane of stamps.

CP965	(47c)	Service Cross Medals, #5068a	14.00
CP966	(47c)	Views of Our Planets, #5076a	14.00
CP967	(47c)	Pluto Explored, #5078a	29.00

No. CP967 consists of two pages. One has text and engraved illustrations. The other contains the pane of stamps.

CP968	(47c)	Classics Forever, #5079	29.00

No. CP968 consists of two pages. One has text and engraved illustrations. The other contains the pane of stamps.

CP969	(47c)	National Parks Service, #5080	29.00

No. CP969 consists of two pages. One has text and engraved illustrations. The other contains the pane of stamps.

CP970	(47c)	Indiana Statehood, #5091	14.00
CP971	(47c)	Jaime Escalante, #5100	14.00
CP972	(47c)	Star Trek, #5135a	14.00
CP973	(47c)	Wonder Woman, #5152a	14.00

2017

CP974	(47c)	Chinese New Year, #5154	16.00
CP975	(49c)	Dorothy Height, #5171	16.00
CP976	(49c)	Oscar de la Renta, #5173	32.00

No. CP976 consists of two pages. One has text and engraved illustrations. The other contains the pane of stamps.

CP977	(49c)	Pres. John F. Kennedy, #5175	32.00

No. CP977 consists of two pages. One has text and engraved illustrations. The other contains the pane of stamps.

CP978	(49c)	Nebraska Statehood, #5179	16.00
CP979	(49c)	Mississippi Statehood, #5190	16.00
CP980	(49c)	Henry David Thoreau, #5202	16.00
CP981	(49c)	Sports Balls, #5210a	16.00
CP982	(49c)	Total Eclipse of the Sun, #5211	16.00
CP983	(49c)	Andrew Wyeth, #5212	32.00

No. CP983 consists of two pages. One has text and engraved illustrations. The other contains the pane of stamps.

CP984	(49c)	Disney Villains, #5222a	32.00

No. CP984 consists of two pages. One has text and engraved illustrations. The other contains the pane of stamps.

CP985	(49c)	Sharks, #5227a	16.00
CP986	(49c)	Protect Pollinators, #5232a	16.00
CP987	(49c)	Father Ted Hesburgh, #5241	16.00
CP988	(49c)	National Museum of African American History and Culture, #5251	16.00
CP989	(49c)	History of Ice Hockey, #5253b, and Canada #3039	32.00

No. CP989 consists of two pages. One has text and engraved illustrations. The other contains the pane of stamps.

2018

CP990	(49c)	Chinese New Year, #5254	16.00
CP991	(50c)	Lena Horne, #5259	16.00
CP992	(50c)	Bioluminescent Life, #5273a	32.00

No. CP992 consists of two pages. One has text and engraved illustrations. The other contains the pane of stamps.

CP993	(50c)	Illinois Statehood, #5274	16.00
CP994	(50c)	Mister Rogers, #5275	16.00
CP995	(50c)	STEM Education, #5279a	16.00
CP996	(50c)	U.S. Air Mail Centenary (Blue), #5281	16.00
CP997	(50c)	U.S. Air Mail Centenary (Carmine Lake), #5282	16.00
CP998	(50c)	Sally Ride, #5283	16.00
CP999	(50c)	Flag Act of 1818, Bicent., #5284	16.00
CP1000	(50c)	O Beautiful, #5298	32.00

No. CP1000 consists of two pages. One has text and engraved illustrations. The other contains the pane of stamps.

CP1001	(50c)	Scooby-Doo, #5299	16.00
CP1002	(50c)	World War I, Cent., #5300	16.00
CP1003	(50c)	The Art of Magic, #5305a	16.00
CP1004	(50c)	Dragons, #5310a	16.00
CP1005	(50c)	John Lennon, #5315a	16.00
CP1006	(50c)	First Responders, #5316	16.00
CP1007	(50c)	Hot Wheels Toy Cars, #5321-5330	32.00

No. CP1007 consists of two pages. One has text and engraved illustrations. The other contains the pane of stamps.

Protect Your Collection

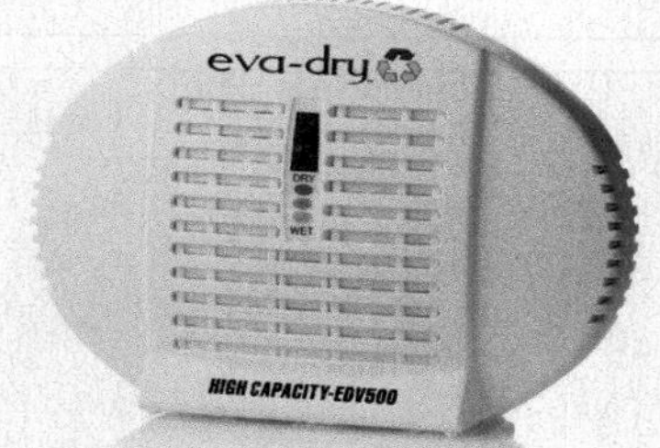

EVA-DRY RENEWABLE DEHUMIDIFIER

The high capacity dehumidifier has been designed to absorb moisture from small enclosed areas. It will help protect valuables from the damaging effects of moisture rot. It is 100% renewable and needs no power to operate. Place the Eva-Dry unit in a closet or any small, enclosed space, and it will start to absorb moisture immediately. For more information, visit AmosAdvantage.com.

- Absorbs 6-8 oz of moisture
- Works in a 500 cubic ft. area
- 100% renewable
- No batteries or cords required
- Lasts up to 10 years
- Spill and mess free

Item#	Retail	AA*
ACC202	$34.95	$31.95

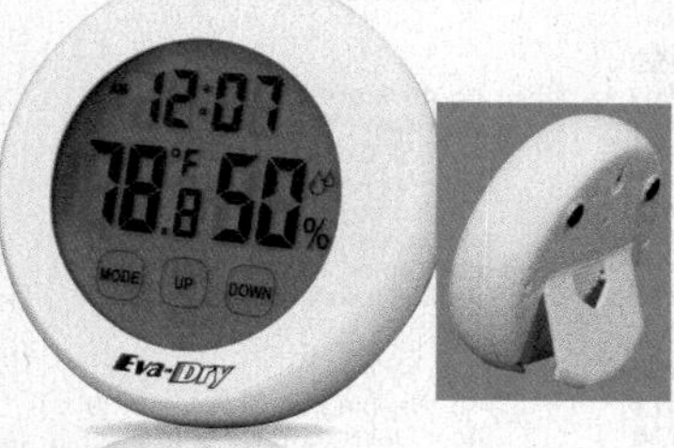

MULTI-FUNCTION HYGROMETER

The Eva-Dry Hygrometer is an affordable and handy way to keep track of the moisture in the environment where your stamps, coins and other collectibles are stored. This multi-use instrument allows for users to keep track of both humidity and temperature with the added bonus of a clock and alarm - all in one unit. The touchscreen display makes using the hygrometer easy while the hanger hole, magnets and built-in stand provide three options for display and use.

• Hygrometer • Thermometer • Clock / Alarm

Item#	Retail	AA*
ACC216	$14.95	$13.95

Visit www.AmosAdvantage.com

Call 1-800-572-6885

Outside U.S. & Canada 937-498-0800

Mail: P.O. Box 4129, Sidney OH 45365

*AA prices apply to paid subscribers of Amos Media titles, or orders placed online. Prices, terms and product availability subject to change. Taxes will apply in CA, OH, & IL. Shipping and handling rates will apply.

SOUVENIR PAGES

These are post office new-issue announcement bulletins, including an illustration of the stamp's design and informative text. They bear an example of the stamp, tied by a first day of issue cancellation. Varieties of bulletin watermarks and text changes, etc., are beyond the scope of this catalogue.

Values for Scott Nos. SP1-SP295 are for folded examples. Values for Official Souvenir Pages (Nos. SP296 on) are for examples that never have been folded.

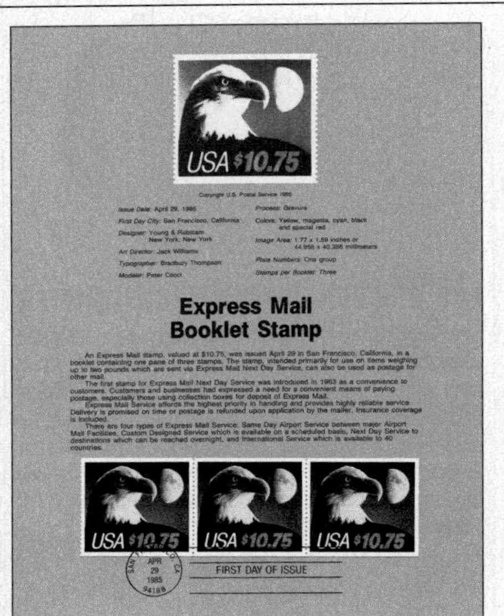

No. SP674a

UNOFFICIAL SOUVENIR PAGES

Liberty Issue

1960-65

No.	Denom.	Description	Value
SP1	1¼c	Palace of Governors, sheet, coil, #1031A, 1054A	50.00
SP2	8c	Pershing, #1214	30.00
SP3	11c	Statue of Liberty, #1044A	27.50
SP4	25c	Revere coil, #1059A	10.00

1959

No.	Denom.	Description	Value
SP5	4c	49 Star Flag, #1132	—
SP6	7c	Hawaii Statehood, #C55	—
SP7	4c	Soil Conservation, #1133	—
SP8	10c	Pan American Games, #C56	—
SP9	4c	Petroleum, #1134	—
SP10	4c	Dental Health, #1135	—
SP11	4c, 8c	Reuter, #1136, 1137	—
SP12	4c	McDowell, #1138	—

1960-61

No.	Denom.	Description	Value
SP13	4c	Washington Credo, #1139	75.00
SP14	4c	Franklin Credo, #1140	75.00
SP15	4c	Jefferson Credo, #1141	75.00
SP16	4c	F.S. Key Credo, #1142	75.00
SP17	4c	Lincoln Credo, #1143	65.00
SP18	4c	P. Henry Credo, #1144	45.00

1961

No.	Denom.	Description	Value
SP19	4c	Boy Scout, #1145	75.00
SP20	4c	Winter Olympics, #1146	75.00
SP21	4c, 8c	Masaryk, #1147, 1148	75.00
SP22	4c	Refugee Year, #1149	45.00
SP23	4c	Water Consevation, #1150	30.00
SP24	4c	SEATO, #1151	30.00
SP25	4c	American Women, #1152	30.00
SP26	10c	Liberty Bell, #C57	—
SP27	15c	Statue of Liberty, #C58	—
SP28	25c	Lincoln, #C59	—
SP29	4c	50 Star Flag, #1153	50.00
SP30	4c	Pony Express, #1154	50.00
SP31	7c	Jet, carmine, #C60	25.00
SP32	7c	Booklet pane of 6, #C60a	37.50
SP33	7c	Jet coil, #C61	17.50
SP34	4c	Handicapped, #1155	50.00
SP35	4c	Forestry Congress, #1156	50.00
SP36	4c	Mexican Independence, #1157	35.00
SP37	4c	U.S., Japan Treaty, #1158	25.00
SP38	4c, 8c	Paderewski, #1159-1160	40.00
SP39	4c	Sen. Taft, #1161	45.00
SP40	4c	Wheels of Freedom, #1162	45.00
SP41	4c	Boys' Clubs, #1163	45.00
SP42	4c	Automated Post Office, #1164	45.00
SP43	4c, 8c	Mannerheim, #1165-1166	45.00
SP44	4c	Camp Fire Girls, #1167	45.00
SP45	4c, 8c	Garibaldi, #1168-1169	45.00
SP46	4c	Sen. George, #1170	45.00
SP47	4c	Carnegie, #1171	45.00
SP48	4c	Dulles, #1172	45.00
SP49	4c	Echo I, #1173	25.00

1961

No.	Denom.	Description	Value
SP50	4c, 8c	Gandhi, #1174-1175	18.00
SP51	4c	Range Conservation, #1176	18.00
SP52	4c	Greeley, #1177	18.00

1961-65

No.	Denom.	Description	Value
SP53	4c	Ft. Sumter, #1178	18.00
SP54	4c	Shiloh, #1179	25.00
SP55	5c	Gettysburg, #1180	8.00
SP56	5c	Wilderness, #1181	8.50
SP57	5c	Appomattox, #1182	8.50

1961

No.	Denom.	Description	Value
SP58	4c	Kansas, #1183	13.50
SP59	13c	Liberty Bell, #C62	18.00
SP60	4c	Sen. Norris, #1184	12.00
SP61	4c	Naval Aviation, #1185	18.00
SP62	4c	Workmen's Compensation, #1186	18.00
SP63	4c	Remington, #1187	11.00
SP64	4c	Sun Yat sen, #1188	18.00
SP65	4c	Basketball, #1189	18.00
SP66	4c	Nursing, #1190	22.50

1962

No.	Denom.	Description	Value
SP67	4c	New Mexico, #1191	11.25
SP68	4c	Arizona, #1192	11.25
SP69	4c	Project Mercury, #1193	9.00
SP70	4c	Malaria, #1194	13.50
SP71	4c	Hughes, #1195	19.00
SP72	4c	Seattle World's Fair, #1196	15.75
SP73	4c	Louisiana, #1197	15.75
SP74	4c	Homestead Act, #1198	15.75
SP75	4c	Girl Scouts, #1199	18.00
SP76	4c	McMahon, #1200	15.75
SP77	4c	Apprenticeship, #1201	15.75
SP78	4c	Rayburn, #1202	15.75
SP79	4c	Hammarskjold, #1203	15.75
SP80	4c	Hammarskjold, yellow inverted, #1204	36.00
SP81	4c	Christmas, #1205	45.00
SP82	4c	Higher Education, #1206	11.00
SP83	8c	Capitol, #C64	13.50
SP83a	8c	Capitol sheet, booklet, coil, #C64, C64b, C65	18.00
SP84	8c	Capitol, tagged, #C64a	34.00
SP85	8c	Capitol booklet single, #C64b	22.50
SP86	8c	Capitol coil, #C65	13.50
SP87	4c	Winslow Homer, #1207	13.50
SP88	5c	Flag, #1208	11.25
SP89	1c	Jackson, #1209	11.25
SP90	5c	Washington, #1213	15.75
SP91	5c	Washington booklet pane of 5 + label, #1213a	27.00
SP92	1c	Jackson coil, #1225	15.75
SP93	5c	Washington coil, #1229	15.75
SP94	15c	Montgomery Blair, #C66	—

1963

No.	Denom.	Description	Value
SP96	5c	Food for Peace, #1231	6.50
SP97	5c	West Virginia, #1232	9.00
SP97A	6c	Eagle, #C67	7.50
SP97B	8c	Amelia Earhart, #C68	18.00
SP98	5c	Emancipation Proclamation, #1233	11.25
SP99	5c	Alliance for Progress, #1234	7.00
SP100	5c	Cordell Hull, #1235	7.00
SP101	5c	Eleanor Roosevelt, #1236	7.00
SP102	5c	Science, #1237	7.00
SP103	5c	City Mail Delivery, #1238	9.00
SP104	5c	Red Cross, #1239	6.25
SP105	5c	Christmas, #1240	8.00
SP106	5c	Audubon, #1241	7.00

1964

No.	Denom.	Description	Value
SP107	5c	Sam Houston, #1242	11.00
SP108	5c	C.M. Russell, #1243	9.00
SP109	5c	N.Y. World's Fair, #1244	8.00
SP110	5c	John Muir, #1245	11.00
SP111	5c	Kennedy (Boston, Mass.) (At least 4 other cities known), #1246	13.50
SP112	5c	New Jersey, #1247	8.00
SP113	5c	Nevada, #1248	8.00
SP114	5c	Register and Vote, #1249	7.00
SP115	5c	Shakespeare, #1250	8.00
SP116	5c	Mayo Brothers, #1251	9.00
SP117	8c	Goddard, #C69	8.00
SP118	5c	Music, #1252	8.00
SP119	5c	Homemakers, #1253	8.00
SP120	5c	Christmas Plants, #1257b	18.00
SP121	5c	Christmas, tagged, #1257c	80.00
SP122	5c	Verrazano Narrows Bridge, #1258	8.00
SP123	5c	Fine Arts, #1259	8.00
SP124	5c	Amateur Radio, #1260	7.00

1965

No.	Denom.	Description	Value
SP125	5c	New Orleans, #1261	7.00
SP126	5c	Sokols, #1262	7.00
SP127	5c	Cancer, #1263	7.00
SP128	5c	Churchill, #1264	7.50
SP129	5c	Magna Carta, #1265	7.00
SP130	5c	I.C.Y., #1266	7.00
SP131	5c	Salvation Army, #1267	7.00
SP132	5c	Dante, #1268	7.00
SP133	5c	Hoover, #1269	7.50
SP134	5c	Fulton, #1270	7.00
SP135	5c	Florida, #1271	7.50
SP136	5c	Traffic Safety, #1272	7.00
SP137	5c	Copley, #1273	7.50
SP138	11c	I.T.U., #1274	7.50
SP139	5c	Stevenson, #1275	7.50
SP140	5c	Christmas, #1276	7.00

Prominent Americans

1965-73

No.	Denom.	Description	Value
SP141	1c	Jefferson, #1278	7.00
SP141a	1c	Jefferson sheet, booklet, coil, #1278, 1278a 1299	6.25
SP142	1c	Jefferson booklet pane of 8, #1278a	7.50
SP143	1¼c	Gallatin, #1279	7.00
SP144	2c	Wright, #1280	5.75
SP145	2c	Wright booklet pane of 5 + label, #1280a	8.50
SP146	3c	Parkman, #1281	7.00
SP147	4c	Lincoln, #1282	5.00
SP148	5c	Washington, #1283	5.00
SP149	5c	Washington, redrawn, #1283B	5.75
SP150	6c	Roosevelt, #1284	5.00
SP151	6c	Roosevelt booklet pane of 8, #1284b	11.50
SP151a	6c	Roosevelt booklet, vert. coil, #1284b, 1298	5.00
SP151b	6c	Roosevelt booklet, horiz. coil, #1284b, 1305	5.00
SP152	8c	Einstein, #1285	9.00
SP153	10c	Jackson, #1286	7.00
SP154	12c	Ford, #1286A	10.00
SP155	13c	Kennedy, #1287	18.00
SP156	15c	Holmes, #1288	9.50
SP157	20c	Marshall, #1289	8.00
SP158	25c	Douglass, #1290	11.00
SP159	30c	Dewey, #1291	27.00
SP160	40c	Paine, #1292	36.00
SP161	50c	Stone, #1293	32.00
SP162	$1	O'Neill, #1294	57.50
SP163	$5	Moore, #1295	135.00
SP164	6c	Roosevelt, vert. coil, #1298	5.00
SP165	1c	Jefferson, coil, #1299	5.75
SP166	4c	Lincoln, coil, #1303	7.00
SP167	5c	Washington, coil, #1304	6.25
SP168	6c	Roosevelt, horiz. coil, #1305	5.75

Nos. 1297, 1305C and 1305E are known on unofficial pages. They are not listed here. For official pages of these issues, see Nos. SP296-SP298.

1966

No.	Denom.	Description	Value
SP169	5c	Migratory Bird Treaty, #1306	9.50
SP170	5c	ASPCA, #1307	7.00
SP171	5c	Indiana, #1308	7.00
SP172	5c	Circus, #1309	8.00
SP173	5c	SIPEX, #1310	6.25
SP174	5c	SIPEX Souvenir Sheet, #1311	6.50
SP175	5c	Bill of Rights, #1312	7.00
SP176	5c	Poland, #1313	7.00
SP177	5c	National Park Service, #1314	7.00
SP178	5c	Marine Corps Reserve, #1315	5.75
SP179	5c	Women's Clubs, #1316	7.00
SP180	5c	Johnny Appleseed, #1317	7.00
SP181	5c	Beautifcation of America, #1318	7.50
SP182	5c	Great River Road, #1319	7.00
SP183	5c	Savings Bonds Servicemen, #1320	7.00
SP184	5c	Christmas, #1321	6.25
SP185	5c	Mary Cassatt, #1322	7.00

1967

No.	Denom.	Description	Value
SP186	8c	Alaska, #C70	9.50
SP187	5c	Grange, #1323	6.25
SP188	20c	Audubon, #C71	9.50
SP189	5c	Canada, #1324	6.25
SP190	5c	Erie Canal, #1325	6.25
SP191	5c	Search for Peace, #1326	7.00
SP192	5c	Thoreau, #1327	6.50
SP193	5c	Nebraska, #1328	6.50
SP194	5c	VOA, #1329	6.50
SP195	5c	Crockett, #1330	7.00
SP196	5c	Space, #1332b	22.50
SP197	5c	Urban Planning, #1333	6.50
SP198	5c	Finland, #1334	7.00
SP199	5c	Eakins, #1335	6.50
SP200	5c	Christmas, #1336	6.25
SP201	5c	Mississippi, #1337	6.25

1968-71

SP202	6c Flags, Giori Press, #1338	5.75
SP203	6c Flag, Huck Press, #1338D	5.00
SP204	8c Flag, #1338F	5.75
SP205	6c Flag coil, #1338A	5.50

1968

SP206	10c 50 star Runway, #C72	8.00
SP207	10c sheet, coil, booklet pane of 8, #C72, C72b, C73	22.50
SP207a	10c sheet, booklet single, coil, #C72, C72b, C73	8.00
SP208	10c 50 star Runway coil, #C73	8.00
SP209	6c Illinois, #1339	5.00
SP210	6c HemisFair, #1340	7.00
SP211	$1 Airlift, #1341	57.50
SP212	6c Youth, #1342	5.00
SP213	10c Air Mail Service, #C74	7.50
SP214	6c Law and Order, #1343	5.00
SP215	6c Register and Vote, #1344	5.00
SP216	6c Historic Flags, #1345-1354	80.00
SP217	6c Disney, #1355	18.00
SP218	6c Marquette, #1356	7.00
SP219	6c Daniel Boone, #1357	7.00
SP220	6c Arkansas River Navigation, #1358	7.00
SP221	6c Leif Erikson, #1359	13.50
SP222	6c Cherokee Strip, #1360	8.00
SP223	6c John Trumbull, #1361	7.00
SP224	6c Waterfowl, #1362	8.00
SP225	6c Christmas, #1363	7.00
SP226	6c Chief Joseph, #1364	8.00
SP227	20c USA, #C75	11.00

1969

SP228	6c Beautification, #1368a	18.00
SP229	6c American Legion, #1369	7.00
SP230	6c Grandma Moses, #1370	6.25
SP231	6c Apollo 8, #1371	13.50
SP232	6c W.C. Handy, #1372	9.00
SP233	6c California, #1373	6.25
SP234	6c Powell, #1374	7.00
SP235	6c Alabama, #1375	7.00
SP236	6c Botanical Congress, #1379a	18.00
SP237	10c Man on the Moon, #C76	12.00
SP238	6c Dartmouth, #1380	7.00
SP239	6c Baseball, #1381	36.00
SP240	6c Football, #1382	13.50
SP241	6c Eisenhower, #1383	7.00
SP242	6c Christmas, #1384	7.00
SP243	6c Hope, #1385	6.25
SP244	45c Special Delivery, #E22	31.50
SP245	6c Harnett, #1386	6.25

1970

SP246	6c Natural History, #1390a	36.00
SP247	6c Maine, #1391	8.00
SP248	6c Wildlife Conservation, #1392	11.00

Regular Issue

1970-71

SP249	6c Eisenhower, #1393	5.00
SP249a	6c sheet, booklet, coil stamps, #1393, 1393a, 1401	7.50
SP249b	6c sheet, coil stamps, #1393, 1401	7.00
SP250	6c Eisenhower booklet pane of 8, #1393a	11.25
SP250a	6c booklet, coil, #1393a, 1401	5.00
SP251	6c Eisenhower booklet pane of 5 + label, #1393b	5.00
SP252	8c Eisenhower, #1394	5.00
SP252a	8c sheet, booklet, coil, #1394-1395, 1402	5.00
SP253	8c Eisenhower booklet pane of 8, #1395a	13.50
SP254	8c Eisenhower booklet pane of 8, #1395b	13.50
SP255	8c U.S.P.S., #1396	9.50
SP256	16c Pyle, #1398	8.00
SP257	6c Eisenhower coil, #1401	6.25
SP258	8c Eisenhower coil, #1402	5.00

1970

SP259	6c Masters, #1405	7.00
SP260	6c Suffrage, #1406	6.25
SP261	6c So. Carolina, #1407	6.25
SP262	6c Stone Mountain, #1408	8.00
SP263	6c Ft. Snelling, #1409	7.00
SP264	6c Anti pollution, #1413a	20.00
SP265	6c Christmas Nativity, #1414	11.50
SP266	6c Christmas Toys, #1418b	9.50
SP267	6c Toys, precanceled, #1418c	40.00
SP268	6c U.N., #1419	8.00
SP269	6c Mayflower, #1420	7.00
SP270	6c DAV, Servicemen, #1422a	25.00

1971

SP271	6c Wool, #1423	8.00
SP272	6c MacArthur, #1424	9.00
SP273	6c Blood Donors, #1425	7.00
SP274	8c Missouri, #1426	7.00
SP275	9c Delta Wing, #C77	8.00
SP276	11c Jet, #C78	8.00
SP276a	11c sheet, booklet, coil, #C78, C78a, C82	11.25
SP277	11c Jet booklet pane, #C78a	16.00
SP278	60c Special Delivery, #E23	22.50
SP279	8c Wildlife, #1430a	13.50
SP280	8c Antarctic Treaty, #1431	11.00
SP281	8c Bicentennial Emblem, #1432	13.50
SP282	17c Statue of Liberty, #C80	13.50
SP283	21c USA, #C81	18.00
SP284	11c Jet coil, #C82	9.00
SP285	8c Sloan, #1433	10.00
SP286	8c Space, #1435b	18.00
SP287	8c Dickenson, #1436	11.25
SP288	8c San Juan, #1437	15.75
SP289	8c Drug Abuse, #1438	9.00
SP290	8c CARE, #1439	9.00
SP291	8c Historic Preservation, #1443a	11.25
SP292	8c Adoration, #1444	9.00
SP293	8c Patridge, #1445	9.00

1972

SP294	8c Lanier, #1446	9.50
SP295	8c Peace Corps, #1447	9.50

OFFICIAL SOUVENIR PAGES

In 1972 the USPS began issuing "official" Souvenir pages by subscription. A few more "unofficials" were produced.

Prominent Americans

1970-78

SP296	3c Parkman, coil, #1297	2.90
SP297	$1 O'Neill, coil, #1305C	11.00
SP298	15c Holmes, coil, #1305E	2.90
SP299	7c Franklin, #1393D	3.60
SP300	14c LaGuardia, #1397	80.00
SP301	18c Blackwell, #1399	2.50
SP302	21c Giannini, #1400	2.90

1972

SP303	2c Cape Hatteras, #1451a	65.00
SP304	6c Wolf Trap Farm, #1452	22.50
SP305	8c Yellowstone, #1453	80.00
SP306	11c City of Refuge, #C84	72.00
SP307	15c Mt. McKinley, #1454	15.75
SP308	8c Family Planning, #1455	650.00

Unofficials exist, value $150.

SP309	8c Colonial Craftsmen, #1459a	10.00
SP310	Olympics, #1460-1462, C85	7.50
	#1460-1462, C85, with #1460 having broken red ring cylinder flaw	*400.00*
SP311	8c PTA, #1463	4.25
SP312	8c Wildlife, #1467a	4.75
SP313	8c Mail Order, #1468	3.00
SP314	8c Osteopathic, #1469	3.75
SP315	8c Tom Sawyer, #1470	5.00
SP316	8c Christmas, #1471-1472	4.25
SP317	8c Pharmacy, #1473	4.75
SP318	8c Stamp Collecting, #1474	3.60

1973

SP319	8c Love, #1475	4.75
SP320	8c Printing, #1476	3.60
SP321	8c Broadside, #1477	3.60
SP322	8c Postrider, #1478	3.60
SP323	8c Drummer, #1479	2.25
SP324	8c Tea Party, #1483a	3.75
SP325	8c Gershwin, #1484	3.75
SP326	8c Jeffers, #1485	3.60
SP327	8c Tanner, #1486	3.75
SP328	8c Cather, #1487	5.25
SP329	8c Copernicus, #1488	4.00
SP330	8c Postal People, #1489-1498	4.00
SP331	8c Truman, #1499	3.60
SP332	Electronics, #1500-1502, C86	7.00
SP333	8c L.B. Johnson, #1503	3.25

1973-74

SP334	8c Cattle, #1504	2.75
SP335	10c Chautauqua, #1505	2.25
SP336	10c Kansas Winter Wheat, #1506	2.00

1973

SP337	8c Christmas, #1507-1508	4.25

Regular Issues

1973-74

SP338	10c Crossed Flags, #1509	2.50
SP339	10c Jefferson Memorial, #1510	2.50
SP340	10c ZIP, #1511	3.60
SP341	6.3c Liberty Bell coil, #1518	2.90
SP341A	13c Winged Envelope, #C79	2.90
SP341B	13c Airmail, coil, #C83	2.90

1974

SP342	18c Statue of Liberty, #C87	5.25
SP343	26c Mt. Rushmore, #C88	3.75
SP344	10c VFW, #1525	2.25
SP345	10c Robert Frost, #1526	3.75
SP346	10c EXPO '74, #1527	4.25
SP347	10c Horse Racing, #1528	4.25
SP348	10c Skylab, #1529	4.00
SP349	10c UPU, #1537a	4.25
SP350	10c Minerals, #1541a	4.25
SP351	10c Ft. Harrod, #1542	2.25
SP352	10c Continental Congress, #1546a	3.75
SP353	10c Energy, #1547	2.25
SP354	10c Sleepy Hollow, #1548	3.75
SP355	10c Retarded Children, #1549	3.00
SP356	10c Christmas, #1550-1552	3.75

1975

SP357	10c Benjamin West, #1553	2.25
SP358	10c Dunbar, #1554	3.60
SP359	10c D.W. Griffith, #1555	3.75
SP360	10c Pioneer, #1556	4.25
SP361	10c Mariner, #1557	4.25
SP362	10c Collective Bargaining, #1558	2.25
SP363	8c Sybil Ludington, #1559	2.25
SP364	10c Salem Poor, #1560	2.90
SP365	10c Haym Salomon, #1561	2.75
SP366	15c Peter Francisco, #1562	2.75
SP367	10c Lexington & Concord, #1563	2.75
SP368	10c Bunker Hill, #1564	2.75
SP369	10c Military Uniforms, #1568a	4.25
SP370	10c Apollo Soyuz, #1570a	5.25
SP371	10c Women's Year, #1571	2.25
SP372	10c Postal Service, #1575	2.90
SP373	10c Peace through Law, #1576	2.25
SP374	10c Banking and Commerce, #1578a	2.75
SP375	10c Christmas, #1579-1580	2.90

Americana Issue

1975-81

SP376	1c, 2c, 3c, 4c Americana, #1581-1585	2.90
SP377	9c Capitol Dome, #1591	2.25
SP378	10c Justice, #1592	2.25
SP379	11c Printing Press, #1593	2.50
SP380	12c Torch sheet, coil, #1594, 1816	2.50
SP381	13c Eagle and Shield, #1596	3.60
SP382	15c Flag sheet, coil, #1597, 1618C	2.25
SP383	16c Statue of Liberty sheet, coil, #1599, 1619	2.50
SP384	24c Old North Church, #1603	2.50
SP385	28c Ft. Nisqually, #1604	2.90
SP386	29c Lighthouse, #1605	3.60
SP387	30c Schoolhouse, #1606	3.25
SP388	50c "Betty" Lamp, #1608	2.90
SP389	$1 Candle Holder, #1610	3.25
SP390	$2 Kerosene Lamp, #1611	4.25
SP391	$5 R. R. Lantern, #1612	8.00
SP392	1c Inkwell, coil, #1811	2.50
SP393	3.1c Guitar, coil, #1613	4.50
SP394	3.5c Violin, coil, #1813	2.25
SP395	7.7c Saxhorns, coil, #1614	2.25
SP396	7.9c Drum, coil, #1615	2.25
SP397	8.4c Piano, coil, #1615C	2.90
SP398	9c Capitol Dome, coil, #1616	2.25
SP398A	10c Justice, coil, #1617	2.25
SP399	13c Liberty Bell, coil, #1618	2.25
SP400	13c 13 star Flag sheet, coil, #1622, 1625	2.25
SP401	9c, 13c Booklet pane, perf. 10, #1623Bc	13.50

1976

SP402	13c Spririt of '76, #1631a	3.60
SP403	25c, 31c Plane and Globes, #C89-C90	2.50
SP404	13c Interphil 76, #1632	2.75
SP405	13c State Flags, #1633-1642	5.75
SP406	13c State Flags, #1643-1652	5.75
SP407	13c State Flags, #1653-1662	5.75
SP408	13c State Flags, #1663-1672	5.75
SP409	13c State Flags, #1673-1682	5.75
SP410	13c Telephone, #1683	2.50
SP411	13c Aviation, #1684	2.50
SP412	13c Chemistry, #1685	2.50
SP413	13c Bicentennial Souvenir Sheet, #1686	7.00
SP414	18c Bicentennial Souvenir Sheet, #1687	7.00
SP415	24c Bicentennial Souvenir Sheet, #1688	7.00
SP416	31c Bicentennial Souvenir Sheet, #1689	7.00
SP417	13c Franklin, #1690	2.00
SP418	13c Declaration of Independence, #1694a	3.25
SP419	13c Olympics, #1698a	3.25
SP420	13c Clara Maass, #1699	4.50
SP421	13c Adolph Ochs, #1700	2.50
SP422	13c Christmas, #1701-1703	2.75

1977

SP423	13c Washington at Princeton, #1704	2.50
SP424	13c Sound Recording, #1705	2.90
SP425	13c Pueblo Pottery, #1709a	4.75
SP426	13c Lindbergh Flight, #1710	2.90
SP427	13c Colorado, #1711	2.00
SP428	13c Butterflies, #1715a	3.60
SP429	13c Lafayette, #1716	2.00
SP430	13c Skilled Hands, #1720a	3.25
SP431	13c Peace Bridge, #1721	2.50
SP432	13c Oriskany, #1722	2.50
SP433	13c Energy, #1724a	2.50
SP434	13c Alta California, #1725	2.50
SP435	13c Articles of Confederation, #1726	3.00
SP436	13c Talking Pictures, #1727	3.00
SP437	13c Saratoga, #1728	2.25
SP438	13c Christmas, #1729-1730	2.25

1978

SP439	13c Sandburg, #1731	2.90
SP440	13c Capt. Cook, #1732, 1733	3.00
SP441	13c Indian Head Penny, #1734	3.00
SP442	15c A Sheet, coil, #1735, 1743	3.75
SP443	15c Roses booklet single, #1737	2.90
SP444	15c Windmills booklet pane of 10, #1742a	7.00
SP445	13c Tubman, #1744	2.90
SP446	13c Quilts, #1748a	3.60
SP447	13c American Dance, #1752a	4.25
SP448	13c French Alliance, #1753	2.50

SP449	13c	Cancer Detection, #1754	3.00
SP450	13c	Jimmie Rodgers, #1755	3.00
SP451	15c	George M. Cohan, #1756	3.00
SP452	13c	CAPEX '78 Souvenir Sheet, #1757	5.00
SP453	15c	Photography, #1758	3.60
SP454	15c	Viking Missions, #1759	4.75
SP455	15c	Owls, #1763a	3.75
SP456	31c	Wright Brothers, #C92a	2.90
SP457	15c	Trees, #1767a	2.90
SP458	15c	Madonna and Child, #1768	2.50
SP459	15c	Hobby Horse, #1769	2.50

1979

SP460	15c	Robert F. Kennedy, #1770	2.90
SP461	15c	Martin Luther King Jr., #1771	3.60
SP462	15c	Year of the Child, #1772	2.25
SP463	15c	John Steinbeck, #1773	4.50
SP464	15c	Einstein, #1774	4.50
SP465	21c	Chanute, #C94a	2.90
SP466	15c	Toleware, #1778a	3.75
SP467	15c	Architecture, #1782a	2.90
SP468	15c	Endangered Flora, #1786a	2.90
SP469	15c	Seeing Eye Dogs, #1787	2.25
SP470	15c	Special Olympics, #1788	2.25
SP471	15c	John Paul Jones, #1789	2.25
SP472	10c	Olympics, #1790	2.50
SP473	15c	Olympics, #1794a	3.60
SP474	31c	Olympics, #C97	3.00

1980

SP475	15c	Winter Olympics, #1798a	3.75

1979

SP476	15c	Madonna and Child, #1799	2.25
SP477	15c	Santa Claus, #1800	2.25
SP478	15c	Will Rogers, #1801	2.90
SP479	15c	Vietnam Veterans, #1802	3.75
SP480	25c	Wiley Post, #C96a	3.00

1980

SP481	15c	W.C. Fields, #1803	3.60
SP482	15c	Benjamin Banneker, #1804	2.90
SP483	15c	Letter Writing Week, #1805-1810	2.90
SP484	18c	B sheet, coil, #1818, 1820	2.25
SP485	18c	B booklet pane of 8, #1819a	2.25
SP486	15c	Frances Perkins, #1821	2.25
SP487	15c	Dolley Madison, #1822	3.00
SP488	15c	Emily Bissell, #1823	3.00
SP489	15c	Helen Keller, #1824	2.25
SP490	15c	Veterans Administration, #1825	2.25
SP491	15c	Galvez, #1826	2.25
SP492	15c	Coral Reefs, #1830a	3.75
SP493	15c	Organized Labor, #1831	2.90
SP494	15c	Edith Wharton, #1832	2.90
SP495	15c	Education, #1833	2.50
SP496	15c	Indian Masks, #1837a	3.60
SP497	15c	Architecture, #1841a	2.90
SP498	40c	Mazzei, #C98	2.75
SP499	15c	Christmas Window, #1842	2.25
SP500	15c	Christmas Toys, #1843	2.90
SP501	28c	Blanche Stuart Scott, #C99	2.75
SP502	35c	Curtiss, #C100	2.75

Great Americans

1980-85

SP503	1c	Dix, #1844	2.50
SP504	2c	Stravinsky, #1845	2.75
SP505	3c	Clay, #1846	2.50
SP506	4c	Schurz, #1847	2.90
SP507	5c	Buck, #1848	2.90
SP508	6c	Lippmann, #1849	2.90
SP509	7c	Baldwin, #1850	2.25
SP510	8c	Knox, #1851	2.25
SP511	9c	Thayer, #1852	2.25
SP512	10c	Russell, #1853	2.25
SP513	11c	Partridge, #1854	2.25
SP514	13c	Crazy Horse, #1855	2.90
SP515	14c	Lewis, #1856	3.75
SP516	17c	Carson, #1857	2.25
SP517	18c	Mason, #1858	2.25
SP518	19c	Sequoyah, #1859	2.25
SP519	20c	Bunche, #1860	3.75
SP520	20c	Gallaudet, #1861	2.25
SP521	20c	Truman, #1862	2.25
SP522	22c	Audubon, #1863	2.90
SP523	30c	Laubach, #1864	2.25
SP524	35c	Drew, #1865	2.25
SP525	37c	Millikan, #1866	2.25
SP526	39c	Clark, #1867	2.25
SP527	40c	Gilbreth, #1868	2.25
SP528	50c	Nimitz, #1869	2.90

1981

SP529	15c	Dirksen, #1874	2.25
SP530	15c	Young, #1875	3.75
SP531	18c	Flowers, #1879a	2.90
SP532	18c	Animals, #1889a	4.50
SP533	18c	Flag sheet, coil, #1890-1891	2.25
SP534	6c, 18c	Booklet pane, #1893a	2.25
SP535	20c	Flag sheet, coil, #1894-1895	2.25
SP536	20c	Flag booklet pane of 6, #1896a	2.25

1982

SP537	20c	Flag booklet pane of 10, #1896b	3.00

Transportation Coils

1981-84

SP538	1c	Omnibus, #1897	2.25
SP539	2c	Locomotive, #1897A	3.00
SP540	3c	Handcar, #1898	2.90
SP541	4c	Stagecoach, #1898A	2.90
SP542	5c	Motorcycle, #1899	4.00
SP543	5.2c	Sleigh, #1900	3.25
SP544	5.9c	Bicycle, #1901	4.50
SP545	7.4c	Baby Buggy, #1902	2.90
SP546	9.3c	Mail Wagon, #1903	2.90
SP547	10.9c	Hansom Cab, #1904	3.00
SP548	11c	Caboose, #1905	2.90
SP549	17c	Electric Auto, #1906	2.25
SP550	18c	Surrey, #1907	3.25
		a. Surrey page with 17c Auto #1906 affixed (error)	—
SP551	20c	Fire Pumper, #1908	3.75

1983

SP552	$9.35	Express Mail single, #1909	67.50
SP552a	$9.35	Express Mail booklet pane of 3, #1909a	125.00

1981

SP553	18c	Red Cross, #1910	2.25
SP554	18c	Savings and Loan, #1911	2.25
SP555	18c	Space Achievements, #1919a	5.00
SP556	18c	Management, #1920	2.25
SP557	18c	Wildlife, #1924a	2.90
SP558	18c	Disabled, #1925	2.25
SP559	18c	Millay, #1926	2.25
SP560	18c	Alcoholism, #1927	2.25
SP561	18c	Architecture, #1931a	3.00
SP562	18c	Zaharias, #1932	13.50
SP563	18c	Jones, #1933	16.50
SP564	18c	Remington, #1934	3.60
SP565	18c, 20c	Hoban, #1935-1936	1.75
SP566	18c	Yorktown, Va. Capes, #1938a	2.90
SP567	20c	Madonna and Child, #1939	2.25
SP568	20c	Teddy Bear, #1940	3.25
SP569	20c	John Hanson, #1941	2.25
SP570	20c	Desert Plants, #1945a	3.00
SP571	20c	C sheet, coil, #1946	2.90
SP572	20c	C Booklet pane of 10, #1948a	2.75

1982

SP573	20c	Bighorn Sheep, #1949a	2.90
SP574	20c	FDR, #1950	2.25
SP575	20c	Love, #1951	2.25
SP576	20c	Washington, #1952	2.90
SP577	20c	Birds and Flowers, #1953-1962	10.00
SP578	20c	Birds and Flowers, #1963-1972	10.00
SP579	20c	Birds and Flowers, #1973-1982	10.00
SP580	20c	Birds and Flowers, #1983-1992	10.00
SP581	20c	Birds and Flowers, #1993-2002	10.00
SP582	20c	US Netherlands, #2003	2.25
SP583	20c	Library of Congress, #2004	2.25
SP584	20c	Consumer Education, #2005	2.90
SP585	20c	Knoxville World's Fair, #2009a	2.25
SP586	20c	Horatio Alger, #2010	2.25
SP587	20c	Aging, #2011	2.25
SP588	20c	Barrymores, #2012	2.90
SP589	20c	Dr. Mary Walker, #2013	2.25
SP590	20c	Peace Garden, #2014	2.25
SP591	20c	Libraries, #2015	2.25
SP592	20c	Jackie Robinson, #2016	12.00
SP593	20c	Touro Synagogue, #2017	2.25
SP594	20c	Wolf Trap Farm, #2018	2.25
SP595	20c	Architecture, #2022a	3.00
SP596	20c	Francis of Assisi, #2023	2.25
SP597	20c	Ponce de Leon, #2024	2.25
SP598	13c	Puppy, Kitten, #2025	2.90
SP599	20c	Madonna and Child, #2026	2.90
SP600	20c	Children Playing, #2030a	3.00

1983

SP601	1c, 4c, 13c	Official Mail, #O127-O129	2.90
SP602	17c	Official Mail, #O130	2.90
SP603	$1	Official Mail, #O132	3.75
SP604	$5	Official Mail, #O133	9.00
SP605	20c	Official Mail coil, #O135	3.00
SP606	20c	Science, #2031	2.25
SP607	20c	Ballooning, #2035a	2.90
SP608	20c	US Sweden, #2036	2.25
SP609	20c	CCC, #2037	2.25
SP610	20c	Priestley, #2038	2.25
SP611	20c	Voluntarism, #2039	2.25
SP612	20c	German Immigration, #2040	2.25
SP613	20c	Brooklyn Bridge, #2041	2.25
SP614	20c	TVA, #2042	2.25
SP615	20c	Fitness, #2043	2.25
SP616	20c	Scott Joplin, #2044	2.25
SP617	20c	Medal of Honor, #2045	4.50
SP618	20c	Babe Ruth, #2046	10.00
SP619	20c	Hawthorne, #2047	2.25
SP620	13c	Olympics, #2051a	2.90
SP621	28c	Olympics, #C104a	2.90
SP622	40c	Olympics, #C108a	2.90
SP623	35c	Olympics, #C112a	2.90
SP624	20c	Treaty of Paris, #2052	2.25
SP625	20c	Civil Service, #2053	2.25
SP626	20c	Metropolitan Opera, #2054	2.75
SP627	20c	Inventors, #2058a	2.75
SP628	20c	Streetcars, #2062a	3.25
SP629	20c	Madonna and Child, #2063	2.25
SP630	20c	Santa Claus, #2064	2.25
SP631	20c	Martin Luther, #2065	3.75

1984-85

SP632	20c	Alaska, #2066	2.25
SP633	20c	Winter Olympics, #2070a	2.90
SP634	20c	FDIC, #2071	2.25
SP635	20c	Love, #2072	2.25
SP636	20c	Woodson, #2073	2.90
SP637	14c, 22c	D sheet, coil, #O138-O139	2.25
SP638	20c	Conservation, #2074	2.25
SP639	20c	Credit Union, #2075	2.25
SP640	20c	Orchids, #2079a	3.75
SP641	20c	Hawaii, #2080	2.75
SP642	20c	National Archives, #2081	2.50
SP643	20c	Olympics, #2085a	2.90
SP644	20c	World Expo, #2086	2.50
SP645	20c	Health Research, #2087	2.50
SP646	20c	Fairbanks, #2088	3.75
SP647	20c	Thorpe, #2089	8.00
SP648	20c	McCormack, #2090	3.75
SP649	20c	St. Lawrence Seaway, #2091	2.25
SP650	20c	Waterfowl, #2092	3.75
SP651	20c	Roanoke Voyages, #2093	2.25
SP652	20c	Melville, #2094	2.50
SP653	20c	Horace Moses, #2095	2.25
SP654	20c	Smokey Bear, #2096	7.50
SP655	20c	Clemente, #2097	11.00
SP656	20c	Dogs, #2101a	3.75
SP657	20c	Crime Prevention, #2102	2.75
SP658	20c	Hispanic Americans, #2103	2.25
SP659	20c	Family Unity, #2104	2.25
SP660	20c	Eleanor Roosevelt, #2105	3.00
SP661	20c	Readers, #2106	2.25
SP662	20c	Madonna and Child, #2107	2.25
SP663	20c	Child's Santa, #2108	2.25
SP664	20c	Vietnam Memorial, #2109	3.75

1985-87

SP665	20c	Jerome Kern, #2110	2.25
SP666	22c	D sheet, coil, #2111-2112	2.25
SP667	22c	D booklet pane of 10, #2113a	2.90
SP668	33c	Verville, #C113	2.25
SP669	39c	Sperry, #C114	2.75
SP670	44c	Transpacific, #C115	2.25
SP671	22c	Flags sheet, coil, #2114-2115	2.25
SP671a	22c	Flag "T" coil, #2115b	2.75
SP672	22c	Flag booklet pane of 5, #2116a	2.25
SP673	22c	Seashells, #2121a	3.75
SP674	$10.75	Express Mail single, #2122	38.00
SP674a	$10.75	Express Mail booklet pane of 3, #2122a	77.50

Transportation Coils

1985-89

SP675	3.4c	School Bus, #2123	2.90
SP676	4.9c	Buckboard, #2124	2.75
SP677	5.5c	Star Route Truck, #2125	2.90
SP678	6c	Tricycle, #2126	2.25
SP679	7.1c	Tractor, #2127	2.50
SP679a	7.1c	Tractor, Zip+4 precancel, #2127b	2.25
SP680	8.3c	Ambulance, #2128	2.25
SP681	8.5c	Tow Truck, #2129	2.25
SP682	10.1c	Oil Wagon, #2130	2.25
SP682a	10.1c	Red precancel, #2130a	2.25
SP683	11c	Stutz Bearcat, #2131	2.75
SP684	12c	Stanley Steamer, #2132	2.90
SP685	12.5c	Pushcart, #2133	2.25
SP686	14c	Iceboat, #2134	2.90
SP687	17c	Dog Sled, #2135	2.25
SP688	25c	Bread Wagon, #2136	2.90

1985

SP689	22c	Bethune, #2137	3.75
SP690	22c	Duck Decoys, #2141a	4.25
SP691	22c	Winter Special Olympics, #2142	2.25
SP692	22c	Love, #2143	2.25
SP693	22c	REA, #2144	2.25
SP694	14c, 22c	Official Mail, #O129A, O136	2.25
SP695	22c	AMERIPEX '86, #2145	2.25
SP696	22c	Abigail Adams, #2146	2.25
SP697	22c	Bartholdi, #2147	2.25
SP698	18c	Washington coil, #2149	2.90
SP699	21.1c	Letters coil, #2150	2.75
SP700	22c	Korean Veterans, #2152	2.90
SP701	22c	Social Security, #2153	2.25
SP702	44c	Serra, #C116	2.25
SP703	22c	World War I Veterans, #2154	3.75
SP704	22c	Horses, #2158a	4.00
SP705	22c	Education, #2159	2.25
SP706	22c	Youth Year, #2163a	4.00
SP707	22c	Hunger, #2164	2.25
SP708	22c	Madonna and Child, #2165	2.25
SP709	22c	Poinsettias, #2166	2.25

1986

SP710	22c	Arkansas, #2167	2.25

Great Americans

1986-94

SP711	1c	Mitchell, #2168	3.75
SP712	2c	Lyon, #2169	2.25
SP713	3c	White, #2170	2.25
SP714	4c	Flanagan, #2171	2.25
SP715	5c	Black, #2172	2.90

SP716	5c Munoz Marin, #2173	2.25
SP717	10c Red Cloud, #2175	3.75
SP718	14c Howe, #2176	2.25
SP719	15c Cody, #2177	2.25
SP720	17c Lockwood, #2178	2.90
SP721	20c Apgar, #2179	3.25
SP722	21c Carlson, #2180	2.25
SP723	23c Cassatt, #2181	2.25
SP724	25c London, #2182	2.25
SP724a	25c London, pane of 10, #2182a	4.00
SP725	28c Sitting Bull, #2183	3.25
SP726	29c Warren, #2184	2.75
SP727	29c Jefferson, #2185	2.25
SP728	35c Chavez, #2186	2.90
SP729	40c Chennault, #2187	2.90
SP730	45c Cushing, #2188	2.25
SP731	52c Humphrey, #2189	2.50
SP732	56c Harvard, #2190	2.50
SP733	65c Arnold, #2191	3.00
SP734	75c Willkie, #2192	3.00
SP735	$1 Revel, #2193	2.75
SP736	$1 Hopkins, #2194	2.75
SP737	$2 Bryan, #2195	4.00
SP739	$5 Harte, #2196	9.00
SP740	25c London, #2197a	2.25

1986

SP741	22c Stamp Collecting, #2201a	3.00
SP742	22c Love, #2202	2.90
SP743	22c Sojourner Truth, #2203	3.75
SP744	22c Texas Republic, #2204	2.25
SP745	22c Fish booklet pane of 5, #2209a	4.25
SP746	22c Hospitals, #2210	2.00
SP747	22c Duke Ellington, #2211	4.25
SP748	22c Presidents Sheet #1, #2216	4.00
SP749	22c Presidents Sheet #2, #2217	4.00
SP750	22c Presidents Sheet #3, #2218	4.00
SP751	22c Presidents Sheet #4, #2219	4.00
SP752	22c Arctic Explorers, #2223a	3.75
SP753	22c Statue of Liberty, #2224	2.75

1987

SP754	2c Locomotive, reengraved, #2226	2.25

1986

SP755	22c Navajo Art, #2238a	3.75
SP756	22c T.S. Eliot, #2239	3.75
SP757	22c Woodcarved Figurines, #2243a	3.75
SP758	22c Madonna and Child, #2244	2.25
SP759	22c Village Scene, #2245	2.25

1987

SP760	22c Michigan, #2246	2.75
SP761	22c Pan American Games, #2247	2.25
SP762	22c Love, #2248	2.25
SP763	22c du Sable, #2249	4.50
SP764	22c Caruso, #2250	2.75
SP765	22c Girl Scouts, #2251	4.25

Transportation Coils

1987-88

SP766	3c Conestoga Wagon, #2252	3.00
SP767	5c, 17.5c Milk Wagon, Racing Car, #2253, 2262	3.00
SP768	5.3c Elevator, #2254	2.50
SP769	7.6c Carreta, #2255	2.50
SP770	8.4c Wheelchair, #2256	2.50
SP771	10c Canal Boat, #2257	2.75
SP772	13c Patrol Wagon, #2258	3.75
SP773	13.2c Coal Car, #2259	3.75
SP774	15c Tugboat, #2260	2.75
SP775	16.7c Popcorn Wagon, #2261	2.75
SP776	20c Cable Car, #2263	2.75
SP777	20.5c Fire Engine, #2264	3.25
SP778	21c Mail Car, #2265	3.25
SP779	24.1c Tandem Bicycle, #2266	2.50

1987

SP780	22c Special Occasions, #2274a	3.00
SP781	22c United Way, #2275	2.25

1987-89

SP782	22c Flag and Fireworks, #2276	2.25
SP783	22c Flag, pair from booklet, #2276a	2.25
SP784	(25c) "E" sheet, coil, #2277, 2279	2.50
SP785	(25c) "E" booklet pane of 10, #2282a	2.90
SP786	25c Flag with Clouds, #2278	2.25
SP787	25c Flag with Clouds booklet pane of 6, #2285c	2.75
SP788	25c Flag over Yosemite coil, block tagging, #2280	2.25
SP788a	25c Flag over Yosemite, prephosphored uncoated paper (mottled tagging), #2280a	2.25
SP789	25c Honeybee coil, #2281	3.25
SP790	25c Pheasant, #2283a	3.75
SP791	25c Owl and Grosbeak, #2285b	2.90
SP792	(25c) "E" Official coil, #O140	2.25
SP793	20c Official coil, #O138B	2.25
SP794	15c, 25c Official coils, #O138A, O141	2.25

1987

SP795	22c Wildlife, #2286-2295	5.00
SP796	22c Wildlife, #2296-2305	5.00
SP797	22c Wildlife, #2306-2315	5.00
SP798	22c Wildlife, #2316-2325	5.00
SP799	22c Wildlife, #2326-2335	5.00

Ratification of the Constitution

1987-90

SP800	22c Delaware, #2336	2.75
SP801	22c Pennsylvania, #2337	2.25
SP802	22c New Jersey, #2338	2.75
SP803	22c Georgia, #2339	2.75
SP804	22c Connecticut, #2340	2.75
SP805	22c Massachusetts, #2341	2.75
SP806	22c Maryland, #2342	2.75
SP807	25c South Carolina, #2343	2.25
SP808	25c New Hampshire, #2344	2.25
SP809	25c Virginia, #2345	2.75
SP810	25c New York, #2346	2.25
SP811	25c North Carolina, #2347	2.75
SP812	25c Rhode Island, #2348	2.25

1987

SP813	22c U.S./Morocco, #2349	2.25
SP814	22c William Faulkner, #2350	4.50
SP815	22c Lacemaking, #2354a	4.75
SP816	22c Constitution, #2359a	2.90
SP817	22c Signing of Constitution, #2360	2.25
SP818	22c Certified Public Accounting, #2361	4.25
SP819	22c Locomotives, #2366a	7.00
SP820	22c Madonna and Child, #2367	2.25
SP821	22c Christmas Ornament, #2368	2.25

1988

SP822	22c Winter Olympics, #2369	2.25
SP823	22c Australia Bicentennial, #2370	2.90
SP824	22c James Weldon Johnson, #2371	2.75
SP825	22c Cats, #2375a	4.50
SP826	22c Knute Rockne, #2376	8.00
SP827	44c New Sweden, #C117	2.25
SP828	45c Samuel P. Langley, #C118	2.25
SP829	25c Francis Ouimet, #2377	10.00
SP830	36c Igor Sikorsky, #C119	2.25
SP831	25c Love, #2378	2.25
SP832	45c Love, #2379	2.25
SP833	25c Summer Olympics, #2380	2.25
SP834	25c Classic Automobiles, #2385a	4.25
SP835	25c Antarctic Explorers, #2389a	2.75
SP836	25c Carousel Animals, #2393a	3.75
SP837	$8.75 Express Mail, #2394	20.00
SP838	25c Special Occasions, #2396a	16.50
SP839	25c Special Occasions, #2398a	16.50
SP840	25c Madonna and Child, #2399	2.25
SP841	25c Village Scene, #2400	2.25

1989

SP842	25c Montana, #2401	2.25
SP843	25c A. Philip Randolph, #2402	2.90
SP844	25c North Dakota, #2403	2.25
SP845	25c Washington Statehood, #2404	2.25
SP846	25c Steamboats, #2409a	4.50
SP847	25c World Stamp Expo, #2410	2.25
SP848	25c Toscanini, #2411	3.75

Branches of Government

1989-90

SP849	25c House of Representatives, #2412	2.25
SP850	25c Senate, #2413	2.25
SP851	25c Executive, #2414	2.25
SP852	25c Supreme Court, #2415	2.25

1989

SP853	25c South Dakota, #2416	2.25
SP854	25c Lou Gehrig, #2417	12.00
SP855	1c Official, litho., #O143	2.25
SP856	45c French Revolution, #C120	3.75
SP857	25c Ernest Hemingway, #2418	4.25
SP858	$2.40 Moon Landing, #2419	14.75
SP859	25c Letter Carriers, #2420	2.25
SP860	25c Bill of Rights, #2421	2.25
SP861	25c Dinosaurs, #2425a	5.00
SP862	25c, 45c Pre-Columbian Artifacts, #2426, C121	2.25
SP863	25c Madonna sheet single, booklet pane of 10, #2427, 2427a	4.75
SP864	25c Sleigh single, booklet pane of 10, #2428, 2429a	4.75
SP865	25c Eagle & Shield, #2431	2.25
SP866	90c World Stamp Expo '89, #2433	10.00
SP867	25c Traditional Mail Delivery, #2437a	3.60
SP868	45c Futuristic Mail Delivery, #C126	3.75
SP869	45c Futuristic Mail Delivery, #C125a	3.75
SP870	25c Traditional Mail Delivery, #2438	4.50

1990

SP871	25c Idaho, #2439	2.25
SP872	25c Love single, booklet pane of 10, #2440, 2441a	3.75
SP873	25c Ida B. Wells, #2442	3.75
SP874	15c Beach Umbrella, #2443a	3.75
SP875	25c Wyoming, #2444	2.90
SP876	25c Classic Films, #2448a	7.00
SP877	25c Marianne Moore, #2449	2.90

Transportation Coils

1990-92

SP879	4c Steam Carriage, #2451	2.25
SP880	5c Circus Wagon, #2452	2.75
SP880A	5c Circus Wagon, #2452B	3.75
SP880B	5c Circus Wagon with cent sign, #2452D	3.60
SP881	5c, 10c Canoe, engr., Tractor Trailer, #2453, 2457	2.50
SP882	5c Canoe, photo., #2454	2.75
SP883	10c Tractor trailer, photo., #2458	3.60
SP891	20c Cog Railway, #2463	2.90
SP892	23c Lunch Wagon, #2464	2.75
SP893	32c Ferry Boat, #2466	2.90
SP895	$1 Seaplane, #2468	4.50

1990-94

SP897	25c Lighthouses, booklet pane of 5, #2474a	7.00
SP898	25c Flag, #2475	2.75

Flora and Fauna Series

SP899	1c, 3c, 30c Kestrel, Bluebird, Cardinal, #2476, 2478, 2480	2.50
SP900	1c Kestrel with cent sign, #2477	2.50
SP901	19c Fawn, #2479	2.50
SP902	45c Pumpkinseed Sunfish, #2481	2.75
SP903	$2 Bobcat, #2482	3.75
SP904	20c Blue jay, #2483	2.50
SP905	29c Wood Ducks booklet panes of 10, #2484a, 2485a	10.00
SP906	29c African Violets bklt. pane of 10, #2486a	3.60
SP907	32c Peach & Pear, #2488b, 2493-2494	3.75
SP908	29c Red Squirrel, #2489	2.75
SP909	29c Red Rose, #2490	2.50
SP910	29c Pine Cone, #2491	2.75
SP911	32c Pink rose, #2492	3.75
SP919	25c Olympians, #2496-2500	4.00
SP920	25c Indian Headdresses, #2505a	4.75
SP921	25c Micronesia, Marshall Islands, #2507a	2.25
SP922	25c Sea Creatures, #2511a	4.75
SP923	25c, 45c Grand Canyon, Tropical Coastline, #2512, C127	2.25
SP924	25c Eisenhower, #2513	2.75
SP925	25c Madonna sheet single, booklet pane of 10, #2514, 2514a	4.25
SP926	25c Christmas Tree sheet single, booklet pane of 10, #2515, 2516a	4.25

1991-95

SP927	(29c) "F" Flower single, coil pair, #2517, 2518	2.25
SP928	(29c) "F" Flower booklet panes of 10, #2519a, 2520a	7.75
SP929	(4c) Make-up Rate, #2521	2.25
SP930	(29c) "F" Flag, #2522	2.75
SP931	(29c) "F" Official coil, #O144	2.25
SP932	29c Mt. Rushmore, #2523	2.75
SP933	29c Mt. Rushmore, photo., #2523A	2.25
SP934	29c Flower single, booklet pane of 10, #2524, 2527a	4.50
SP935	29c Flower coil, #2525	2.25
SP936	29c Flower coil, #2526	2.25
SP937	4c Official, #O146	2.50
SP938	29c Flag, Olympic Rings, #2528a	4.50
SP939	19c Fishing Boat coil, #2529	3.75
SP939A	19c Fishing Boat coil reissue, #2529C	2.90
SP940	19c Ballooning, #2530a	3.75
SP941	29c Flags on Parade, #2531	2.50
SP942	29c Liberty Torch, #2531A	2.50
SP943	50c Switzerland, #2532	2.25
SP944	20c Vermont Statehood, #2533	2.50
SP945	50c Harriet Quimby, #C128	2.75
SP946	29c Savings Bonds, #2534	2.25
SP947	29c, 52c Love, #2535, 2536a, 2537	9.00
SP948	40c William T. Piper, #C129	2.25
SP949	29c William Saroyan, #2538	4.25
SP950	Official 19c, 23c, 29c, #O145, O147-O148	2.50
SP951	$1.00 USPS/Olympic Rings, #2539	3.00
SP952	$2.90 Eagle, #2540	10.00
SP953	$9.95 Eagle, #2541	26.00
SP954	$14 Eagle, #2542	34.00
SP955	$2.90 Futuristic Space Shuttle, #2543	9.00
SP956	$3 Challenger Shuttle, #2544	11.25
SP956A	$10.75 Endeavour Shuttle, #2544A	22.00
SP957	29c Fishing Flies, #2549a	15.75
SP958	29c Cole Porter, #2550	2.75
SP959	50c Antarctic Treaty, #C130	2.75
SP960	29c Desert Shield, Desert Storm, #2551	9.00
SP961	29c 1992 Summer Olympics, #2553-2557	4.75
SP962	29c Numismatics, #2558	3.75
SP963	29c World War II, #2559	9.00
SP964	29c Basketball, #2560	5.00
SP965	29c District of Columbia, #2561	2.25
SP966	29c Comedians, #2566a	5.50
SP967	29c Jan E. Matzeliger, #2567	4.25
SP968	29c Space Exploration, #2577a	9.00
SP969	50c Bering Land Bridge, #C131	2.25

SP970 29c Madonna and Child sheet single, booklet pane of 10, #2578, 2578a 8.00
SP971 29c Santa Claus sheet and booklet singles, #2579, 2580 or 2581, 2582-2585 12.00
SP973 32c James K. Polk, #2587 4.75
SP976 $1 Surrender of Gen. Burgoyne, #2590 3.75
SP978 $5 Washington and Jackson, #2592 11.25
SP980 29c Pledge of Allegiance, #2593a 3.60
SP982 29c Eagle & Shield self-adhesives, #2595-2597 3.00
SP983 29c Eagle self-adhesive, #2598 2.50
SP984 29c Statue of Liberty, #2599 2.50
SP990 (10c) Eagle and Shield coil, #2602 3.75
SP991 (10c) Eagle and Shield coils, #2603-2604 3.75
SP993 23c Stars and Stripes coil, #2605 2.25
SP994 23c USA coil, #2606 2.90
SP994A 23c USA coil, #2607 2.25
SP994B 23c USA coil, #2608 2.50
SP995 29c Flag over White House, #2609 2.50

1992

SP997 29c Winter Olympics, #2611-2615 3.75
SP998 29c World Columbian Stamp Expo '92, #2616 3.00
SP999 29c W.E.B. DuBois, #2617 4.25
SP1000 29c Love, #2618 2.25
SP1001 29c Olympic Baseball, #2619 10.00
SP1002 29c First Voyage of Columbus, #2623a 3.00
SP1003 1c, 4c, $1 First Sighting of Land souvenir sheet, #2624 6.25
SP1004 2c, 3c, $4 Claiming a New World souvenir sheet, #2625 7.50
SP1005 5c, 30c, 50c Seeking Royal Support souvenir sheet, #2626 5.75
SP1006 6c, 8c, $3 Royal Favor Restored souvenir sheet, #2627 7.50
SP1007 10c, 15c, $2 Reporting Discoveries souvenir sheet, #2628 7.50
SP1008 $5 Columbus souvenir sheet, #2629 10.00
SP1009 29c New York Stock Exchange, #2630 2.50
SP1010 29c Space Accomplishments, #2634a 5.25
SP1011 29c Alaska Highway, #2635 2.75
SP1012 29c Kentucky Statehood, #2636 2.50
SP1013 29c Summer Olympics, #2637-2641 3.75
SP1014 29c Hummingbirds, #2646a 7.00
SP1015 29c Wildflowers, #2647-2656 7.00
SP1016 29c Wildflowers, #2657-2666 7.00
SP1017 29c Wildflowers, #2667-2676 7.00
SP1018 29c Wildflowers, #2677-2686 7.00
SP1019 29c Wildflowers, #2687-2696 7.00
SP1020 29c World War II, #2697 5.00
SP1021 29c Dorothy Parker, #2698 2.75
SP1022 29c Dr. Theodore von Karman, #2699 4.25
SP1023 29c Minerals strip of 4, #2703a 4.00
SP1024 29c Juan Rodriguez Cabrillo, #2704 2.75
SP1025 29c Wild Animals, #2709a 5.25
SP1026 29c Madonna and Child sheet single, booklet pane of 10, #2710, 2710a 7.00
SP1027 29c Christmas Toys block of 4, booklet pane of 4 and booklet single, #2714a, 2718a, 2719 4.25
SP1028 29c Chinese New Year, #2720 8.00

1993

SP1029 29c Elvis Presley, #2721 12.00
SP1030 29c Oklahoma!, #2722 2.25
SP1030A 29c Hank Williams sheet stamp, #2723A 4.25
SP1030B 29c Rock & Roll/Rhythm & Blues sheet single, booklet pane of 8, #2737b 22.00

No. SP1030B exists with any one of #2724-2730 affixed along with #2737b.

SP1034 29c Space Fantasy, #2745a 8.00
SP1035 29c Percy Lavon Julian, #2746 3.75
SP1036 29c Oregon Trail, #2747 2.25
SP1037 29c World University Games, #2748 2.25
SP1038 29c Grace Kelly, #2749 7.00
SP1039 29c Circus, #2753a 4.25
SP1040 29c Cherokee Strip, #2754 3.75
SP1041 29c Dean Acheson, #2755 2.25
SP1042 29c Sporting Horses, #2759a 4.75
SP1043 29c Garden Flowers, #2764a 3.75
SP1044 29c World War II, #2765 7.00
SP1045 29c Joe Louis, #2766 11.00
SP1046 29c Broadway Musicals, #2770a 4.25
SP1047 29c National Postal Museum strip of 4, #2782a 3.00
SP1048 29c American Sign Language, #2784a 2.25
SP1049 29c Country & Western Music sheet stamp and booklet pane of 4, #2778a 13.50

No. SP1049 exists with any one of #2771-2774 affixed along with #2778a.

SP1050 10c Official Mail, #O146A 2.50
SP1052 29c Classic Books strip of 4, #2788a 2.90
SP1053 29c Traditional Christmas sheet stamp, booklet pane of 4, #2789, 2790a 4.75
SP1054 29c Contemporary Christmas booklet pane of 10, sheet and self-adhesive single stamps, #2803 11.25

No. SP1054 exists with any one of #2791-2794, 2798a, 2798b, 2799-2802 affixed along with #2803.

SP1055 29c Mariana Islands, #2804 2.25
SP1056 29c Columbus' Landing in Puerto Rico, #2805 2.90
SP1057 29c AIDS Awareness, #2806, 2806b 4.50

1994

SP1058 29c Winter Olympics, #2811a 4.75
SP1059 29c Edward R. Murrow, #2812 3.00
SP1060 29c Love self-adhesive, #2813 3.00
SP1061 29c, 52c Love booklet pane of 10, single sheet stamp, #2814a, 2815 6.25
SP1062 29c Love sheet stamp, #2814C 2.90
SP1063 29c Dr. Allison Davis, #2816 4.50
SP1064 29c Chinese New Year, #2817 3.25
SP1065 29c Buffalo Soldiers, #2818 4.75
SP1066 29c Silent Screen Stars, #2819-2828 5.00
SP1067 29c Garden Flowers, #2833a 5.00
SP1068 29c, 40c, 50c World Cup Soccer, #2834-2836 5.00
SP1069 World Cup Soccer, #2837 5.00
SP1070 29c World War II, #2838 5.75
SP1071 29c, 50c Norman Rockwell stamp, souvenir sheet, #2839-2840 12.00
SP1072 29c, $9.95 Moon Landing, #2841-2842 22.50
SP1073 29c Locomotives, #2847a 7.50
SP1074 29c George Meany, #2848 2.90
SP1075 29c Popular Singers, #2853a 7.00
SP1076 29c Jazz and Blues Singers block of 10, #2854-2861 10.00

Block of 10 on No. SP1076 may contain different combinations of stamps.

SP1077 29c James Thurber, #2862 3.75
SP1078 29c Wonders of the Sea, #2866a 4.50
SP1079 29c Cranes, #2868a 2.90
SP1079A Legends of the West, #2869 20.00
SP1080 29c Traditional Christmas sheet stamp, booklet pane of 10, #2871, 2871b 6.25
SP1081 29c Contemporary Christmas sheet stamp, block of 4 from booklet pane, #2872 4.25
SP1082 29c Contemporary Christmas self-adhesive stamps, #2873-2874 5.00
SP1083 $2 Bureau of Engraving and Printing Souvenir Sheet, #2875 16.00

1995-96

SP1084 29c Chinese New Year, #2876 4.25
SP1085 G make-up rate, G stamps, #2877, 2884, 2890, 2893 3.75
SP1086 G make-up rate, G stamps, #2878, 2880, 2882, 2885, 2888, 2892 3.75
SP1087 G stamps, official G stamp, #2879, 2881, 2883, 2889, O152 3.75
SP1088 G self-adhesive stamps, #2886-2887 7.00
SP1091 32c Flag Over Porch, #2897, 2913, 2915-2916 4.50
SP1096 (5c) Butte coil, #2902 4.00
SP1097 (5c) Mountain coil, #2903, 2904 4.50
SP1099 Butte, Mountain, Juke Box, Auto Tail Fin, Auto, Flag over porch, #2902B, 2904A, 2906, 2910, 2912A, 2915B 4.50
SP1099A Mountain, Juke Box, Flag Over Porch coil and booklet stamps, #2904B, 2912B, 2915D, 2921b 4.50
SP1100 (10c) Auto coil, #2905 4.25
SP1102 Eagle & shield, Flag over porch, #2907, 2920D, 2921 4.25
SP1103 (15c) Auto Tail Fin, #2908-2909 4.25
SP1105 (25c) Juke Box, #2911-2912 2.90
SP1110 32c Flag over Field self-adhesive, #2919 4.25
SP1114 (32c) Non-denominated Love, #2948-2949 2.25
SP1115 32c Florida Statehood, #2950 2.25

Great Americans Series

1995-99

SP1126 32c Milton Hershey, #2933 2.25
SP1127 32c Cal Farley, #2934 2.90
SP1128 32c Henry R. Luce, #2935 5.00
SP1129 32c Lila & DeWitt Wallace, #2936 4.00
SP1131 46c Ruth Benedict, #2938 2.90
SP1133 55c Alice Hamilton, #2940 2.25
SP1134 55c Justin S. Morrill, #2941 5.00
SP1135 77c Mary Breckinridge, #2942 4.50
SP1136 78c Alice Paul, #2943 2.25

1995

SP1141 32c Kids Care, #2954a 2.90
SP1142 32c Richard Nixon, #2955 2.90
SP1143 32c Bessie Coleman, #2956 3.75
SP1144 1-32c Official, #O153-O156 2.50
SP1145 32c, 55c Love (with denominations), #2957-2960 2.90
SP1146 32c Recreational Sports, #2965a 7.00
SP1147 32c Prisoners of War/Missing in Action, #2966 3.00
SP1148 32c Marilyn Monroe, #2967 13.50
SP1149 32c Texas Statehood, #2968 3.60
SP1150 32c Great Lakes Lighthouses, #2973a 8.00
SP1151 32c United Nations, #2974 2.25
SP1152 32c Civil War, #2975 14.00
SP1153 32c Carousel Horses, #2979a 4.75
SP1154 32c Woman Suffrage, #2980 2.25
SP1155 32c World War II, #2981 6.25
SP1156 32c Louis Armstrong, #2982 4.00
SP1157 32c Jazz Musicians, #2992a 7.00
SP1158 32c Garden Flowers, #2997a 5.75
SP1159 60c Eddie Rickenbacker, #2998 3.60
SP1160 32c Republic of Palau, #2999 2.90
SP1161 32c Comic Strip Classics, #3000 14.00
SP1162 32c Naval Academy, #3001 3.60
SP1163 32c Tennessee Williams, #3002 3.60
SP1164 32c Traditional Christmas sheet stamp, booklet pane of 10, #3003, 3003b 5.00
SP1165 32c Contemporary Christmas block of 4, self-adhesive stamps, #3007a, 3010-3011 4.25

No. SP1165 may include different combinations of Nos. 3008-3011.

SP1166 32c Midnight Angel, #3012 3.75
SP1167 32c Children Sledding, #3013 3.75
SP1168 32c Antique Automobiles, #3023a 5.50

1996

SP1169 32c Utah Statehood, #3024 2.90
SP1170 32c Garden Flowers, #3029a 5.25
SP1171 1, 32c Flag Over Porch, Love self-adhesives, Kestrel coil, #2920e, 3030, 3044 12.00

Flora and Fauna Series

1996-99

SP1171A 1c Kestrel, self-adhesive, #3031 5.00
SP1172 2c Woodpecker, #3032 3.00
SP1173 3c Bluebird, #3033 3.00
SP1184 $1 Red Fox, #3036 7.00
SP1185 2c Woodpecker coil, #3045 5.00
SP1187 20c Bluejay self-adhesive coil, booklet stamps, #3048, 3053 4.00
SP1188 32c Yellow Rose, #3049 4.25
SP1189 20c Ring-necked Pheasant, #3050, 3055 5.25
SP1191A 33c Coral Pink Rose, serpentine die cut 10¾x10½, #3052E 5.25
SP1191 33c Coral Pink Rose, #3052 5.25
SP1192 32c Yellow Rose coil, #3054 5.25

1996

SP1197 32c Ernest E. Just, #3058 4.25
SP1198 32c Smithsonian Institution, #3059 2.90
SP1199 32c Chinese New Year, #3060 5.25
SP1200 32c Pioneers of Communication, #3064a 3.75
SP1201 32c Fulbright Scholarships, #3065 2.90
SP1202 50c Jacqueline Cochran, #3066 2.90
SP1203 32c Marathon, #3067 2.90
SP1204 32c Olympic Games, #3068 14.75
SP1205 32c Georgia O'Keeffe, #3069 3.75
SP1206 32c Tennessee Statehood, #3070 2.90
SP1207 32c American Indian Dances, #3076a 3.75
SP1208 32c Prehistoric Animals, #3080a 3.75
SP1209 32c Breast Cancer Awareness, #3081 4.00
SP1210 32c James Dean, #3082 5.25
SP1211 32c Folk Heroes, #3086a 4.50
SP1212 32c Centennial Olympic Games, #3087 4.00
SP1213 32c Iowa Statehood, #3088-3089 4.00
SP1214 32c Rural Free Delivery, #3090 3.00
SP1215 32c Riverboats, #3095b 57.50
SP1216 32c Big Band Leaders, #3099a 5.25
SP1217 32c Songwriters, #3103a 5.25
SP1218 23c F. Scott Fitzgerald, #3104 3.00
SP1219 32c Endangered Species, #3105 16.00
SP1220 32c Computer Technology, #3106 3.00
SP1221 32c Madonna & Child sheet & booklet stamps, #3107, 3112 5.25
SP1222 32c Contemporary Christmas block of 4, self-adhesive stamp, #3111a, 3113 5.25

No. SP1222 may contain Nos. 3114-3116 instead of No. 3113.

SP1223 32c Skaters, #3117 5.25
SP1224 32c Hanukkah, #3118 4.00
SP1225 32c Cycling souvenir sheet, #3119 5.25

1997

SP1226	32c	Chinese New Year, #3120	6.00
SP1227	32c	Benjamin O. Davis, Sr., #3121	5.25
SP1228	32c	Statue of Liberty, #3122	4.50
SP1229	32, 55c	Love Swans, #3123-3124	4.50
SP1230	32c	Helping Children Learn, #3125	4.00
SP1231	32c	Merian Botanical Prints, #3126-3129	4.50
SP1232	32c	PACIFIC 97 Triangles, #3131a	5.25
SP1233	(25c), 32c	Flag Over Porch, Juke Box linerless coils, #3132-3133	4.50
SP1234	32c	Thornton Wilder, #3134	4.00
SP1235	32c	Raoul Wallenberg, #3135	4.00
SP1236	32c	Dinosaurs, #3136	16.00
SP1237	32c	Bugs Bunny, #3137	16.00
SP1238	50c	PACIFIC 97 Franklin, #3139	13.00
SP1239	60c	PACIFIC 97 Washington, #3140	13.00
SP1240	32c	Marshall Plan, #3141	4.50
SP1241	32c	Classic American Aircraft, #3142	16.00
SP1242	32c	Football Coaches, #3146a	13.50
SP1242A	32c	Vince Lombardi, #3147	9.00
SP1242B	32c	Bear Bryant, #3148	9.00
SP1242C	32c	Pop Warner, #3149	9.00
SP1242D	32c	George Halas, #3150	9.00
SP1243	32c	Classic American Dolls, #3151	11.50
SP1244	32c	Humphrey Bogart, #3152	5.25
SP1245	32c	The Stars and Stripes Forever!, #3153	5.25
SP1246	32c	Opera Singers, #3157a	8.50
SP1247	32c	Composers & Conductors, #3165a	10.00
SP1248	32c	Padre Felix Varela, #3155	5.25
SP1249	32c	Department of the Air Force, #3167	9.00
SP1250	32c	Movie Monsters, #3172a	11.00
SP1251	32c	Supersonic Flight, #3173	8.50
SP1252	32c	Women in Military Service, #3174	5.25
SP1253	32c	Kwanzaa, #3175	5.00
SP1254	32c	Madonna and Child, #3176	5.75
SP1255	32c	Holly, #3177	5.75
SP1256	$3	Mars Pathfinder, #3178	15.00

1998

SP1257	32c	Chinese New Year, #3179	5.00
SP1258	32c	Alpine Skiing, #3180	5.00
SP1259	32c	Madam C.J. Walker, #3181	5.00

Celebrate the Century

1998-2000

SP1259A	32c	1900s, #3182	13.50
SP1259B	32c	1910s, #3183	13.50
SP1259C	32c	1920s, #3184	13.50
SP1259D	32c	1930s, #3185	13.50
SP1259E	33c	1940s, #3186	13.50
SP1259F	33c	1950s, #3187	13.50
SP1259G	33c	1960s, #3188	13.50
SP1259H	33c	1970s, #3189	13.50
SP1259I	33c	1980s, #3190	13.50
SP1259J	33c	1990s, #3191	13.50

1998

SP1260	32c	"Remember the Maine," #3192	5.00
SP1261	32c	Flowering Trees, #3197a	7.00
SP1262	32c	Alexander Calder, #3202a	7.00
SP1263	32c	Cinco de Mayo, #3203	5.00
SP1264	32c	Sylvester & Tweety, #3204a	7.00
SP1265	32c	Wisconsin Statehood, #3206	5.00
SP1266	(5c), (25c)	Wetlands, Diner Coils, #3207-3208	5.00
SP1266A	(25c)	Diner coil, #3208A	5.00
SP1267	1c-$2	Trans-Mississippi, #3209	15.75
SP1268	$1	Trans-Mississippi, #3209h	11.00
SP1269	32c	Berlin Airlift, #3211	5.00
SP1270	32c	Folk Musicians, #3215a	7.50
SP1271	32c	Gospel Singers, #3219a	6.25
SP1272	32c	Spanish Settlement, #3220	5.00
SP1273	32c	Stephen Vincent Benét, #3221	5.00
SP1274	32c	Tropical Birds, #3225a	8.00
SP1275	32c	Alfred Hitchcock, #3226	5.50
SP1276	32c	Organ & Tissue Donation, #3227	5.00
SP1277	(10c)	Modern Bicycle, #3229	5.00
SP1278	32c	Bright Eyes, #3234a	7.50
SP1279	32c	Klondike Gold Rush, #3235	5.00
SP1280	32c	American Art, #3236	13.50
SP1281	32c	Ballet, #3237	5.00
SP1282	32c	Space Discovery, #3242a	7.00
SP1283	32c	Giving & Sharing, #3243	5.00
SP1284	32c	Madonna & Child, #3244	5.00
SP1285	32c	Wreaths, #3248a, 3252a	7.00
SP1286	(32+8c)	Breast Cancer Awareness, #B1	5.00
SP1287	(1c), (33c)	Weather Vane, Uncle Sam's Hat, #3257-3258, 3260	5.00
SP1288	22c	Uncle Sam, #3259, 3263	5.00
SP1289	$3.20	Space Shuttle Landing, #3261	15.00
SP1290	$11.75	Piggyback Space Shuttle, #3262	22.50
SP1291	(33c)	Uncle Sam's Hat, #3267-3269	5.75
SP1292	(33c)	Uncle Sam's Hat, #3264, 3266	6.25
SP1293	(5c), (10c)	Wetlands, Eagle & Shield, #3207A, 3270-3271	5.00

1999

SP1294	33c	Chinese New Year, #3272	7.00
SP1295	33c	Malcolm X, #3273	8.50
SP1296	33c	Love, #3274	5.00
SP1297	55c	Love, #3275	5.00
SP1298	33c	Hospice Care, #3276	5.00
SP1299	33c	Flag and City, #3279-3280, 3282	5.00
SP1300	33c	Flag Over Chalkboard, #3283	5.00
SP1301	33c	Irish Immigration, #3286	5.00
SP1302	33c	Lunt & Fontanne, #3287	5.00
SP1303	33c	Arctic Animals, #3292a	7.00
SP1304	33c	Sonoran Desert, #3293	12.00
SP1305	33c	Berries, #3294-3297	6.25
SP1306	33c	Daffy Duck, #3306a	7.00
SP1307	33c	Ayn Rand, #3308	5.00
SP1308	33c	Cinco de Mayo, #3309	5.75
SP1309	33c	Tropical Flowers, #3310-3313	6.25
SP1310	48c	Niagara Falls, #C133	5.75
SP1311	33c	John & William Bartram, #3314	5.00
SP1312	33c	Prostate Cancer, #3315	5.00
SP1313	33c	California Gold Rush, #3316	5.00
SP1314	33c	Aquarium Fish, #3317-3320	6.25
SP1315	33c	Extreme Sports, #3321-3324	6.00
SP1316	33c	American Glass, #3328a	6.25
SP1317	33c	James Cagney, #3329	6.25
SP1318	55c	Billy Mitchell, #3330	6.00
SP1319	40c	Rio Grande, #C134	5.00
SP1320	33c	Honoring Those Who Served, #3331	5.00
SP1321	45c	Universal Postal Union, #3332	5.00
SP1322	33c	Famous Trains, #3337a	7.00
SP1323	33c	Frederick Law Olmsted, #3338	5.75
SP1324	33c	Hollywood Composers, #3344a	12.00
SP1325	33c	Broadway Songwriters, #3350a	12.00
SP1326	33c	Insects & Spiders, #3351	15.00
SP1327	33c	Hanukkah, #3352	5.00
SP1328	22c	Uncle Sam, #3353	5.00
SP1329	33c	Official coil, #O157	5.00
SP1330	33c	NATO, #3354	5.00
SP1331	33c	Madonna & Child, #3355	5.00
SP1332	33c	Christmas Deer, #3359a	6.00
SP1333	33c	Kwanzaa, #3368	5.00
SP1334	33c	Year 2000, #3369	5.00

2000

SP1335	33c	Chinese New Year, #3370	7.00
SP1336	60c	Grand Canyon, #C135	5.00
SP1337	33c	Patricia Roberts Harris, #3371	5.00
SP1338	33c	Berries, dated 2000, #3294a-3296a, 3297c	5.00
SP1339	33c	Los Angeles Class Submarine (sheet stamp), #3372	14.00
SP1340	33c	Pacific Coast Rain Forest, #3378	14.00
SP1341	33c	Louise Nevelson, #3383a	6.50
SP1342	33c	Hubble Space Telescope Images, #3388a	6.50
SP1343	33c	American Samoa, #3389	5.00
SP1344	33c	Library of Congress, #3390	5.00
SP1345	33c	Road Runner & Wile E. Coyote, #3391a	8.00
SP1346	33c	Distinguished Soldiers, 3396a	7.00
SP1347	33c	Summer Sports, #3397	5.00
SP1348	33c	Adoption, #3398	8.00
SP1349	33c	Youth Team Sports, #3402a	5.00
SP1350	33c	The Stars and Stripes, #3403	14.00
SP1351	33c	Legends of Baseball, #3408	18.00
SP1352	33c	Stampin' the Future, #3417a	5.50

Distinguished Americans Series

2000-09

SP1355	10c	Gen. Joseph W. Stilwell, #3420	5.00
SP1357	23c	Wilma Rudolph, #3422, 3436	5.00
SP1361	33c	Claude Pepper, #3426	5.00
SP1362	58c	Margaret Chase Smith, #3427	5.25
SP1362A	59c	James A. Michener, #3427A	5.25
SP1363	63c	Dr. Jonas Salk, #3428	5.25
SP1365	75c	Harriet Beecher Stowe, #3430	5.25
SP1366	76c	Hattie Caraway, #3431	5.00
SP1366A	76c	Edward Trudeau, #3432A	5.25
SP1366B	78c	Mary Lasker, #3432B	5.25
SP1367	83c	Edna Ferber, #3432	5.00
SP1368	87c	Dr. Albert Sabin, #3435	5.25

2000

SP1373	33c	California Statehood, #3438	5.00
SP1374	33c	Deep Sea Creatures, #3443a	6.50
SP1375	33c	Thomas Wolfe, #3444	5.00
SP1376	33c	White House, #3445	5.00
SP1377	33c	Edward G. Robinson, #3446	5.00
SP1378	(10c)	New York Public Library Lion, #3447	5.00
SP1379	(34c)	Flag Over Farm, #3448-3450	5.00
SP1380	(34c)	Statue of Liberty, #3451-3453	5.00
SP1381	(34c)	Flowers, #3454-3457	5.00

2001

SP1382	34c	Statue of Liberty self-adhesive coil, #3466	4.50
SP1382A	21c	American Buffalo, #3467, 3484	4.50
SP1383	21c	American Buffalo, #3468, 3475	4.50
SP1383A	23c	George Washington, #3468A, 3475A	5.00
SP1384	34c	Flag over Farm, #3469	4.50
SP1385	34c	Flag over Farm self-adhesive, #3470	4.50
SP1386	55c	Eagle, #3471	5.00
SP1386A	57c	Eagle, #3471A	4.25
SP1387	$3.50	US Capitol, #3472	11.50
SP1388	$12.25	Washington Monument, #3473	23.25
SP1389	34c	Statue of Liberty, #3476, 3477, 3485	5.25
SP1390	34c	Flowers, #3478-3481	5.25
SP1391	20c	George Washington, #3482	4.50
SP1392	34c	Apple and Orange, #3491, 3492	5.00
SP1393	34c	Flag over Farm self-adhesive booklet, #3495	5.00
SP1394	(34c)	Love, #3496	4.50
SP1395	34c, 55c	Love, #3497, 3499	6.25
SP1396	34c	Chinese New Year, #3500	6.00
SP1397	34c	Roy Wilkins, #3501	7.50
SP1398	34c	American Illustrators, #3502	22.00
SP1399	34c	Official, #O158	4.50
SP1400	70c	Nine-Mile Prairie, #C136	5.00
SP1401	34c	Diabetes Awareness, #3503	5.00
SP1402	34c	Nobel Prize, #3504	5.00
SP1403	1c-80c	Pan-American Inverts, #3505	15.00
SP1404	80c	Mt. McKinley, #C137	6.25
SP1405	34c	Great Plains Prairie, #3506	14.00
SP1406	34c	Peanuts Comic Strip, #3507	10.00
SP1407	34c	Honoring Veterans, #3508	7.00
SP1408	60c	Acadia National Park, #C138	5.00
SP1409	34c	Frida Kahlo, #3509	10.00
SP1410	34c	Legendary Playing Fields, #3510-3519	23.00
SP1411	(10c)	Atlas Statue, #3520	4.50
SP1412	34c	Leonard Bernstein, #3521	5.00
SP1413	(15c)	Woody Wagon, #3522	4.50
SP1414	34c	Lucille Ball, #3523	10.00
SP1415	34c	Amish Quilts, #3524-3527	6.00
SP1416	34c	Carnivorous Plants, #3528-3531	6.00
SP1417	34c	Eid, #3532	4.50
SP1418	34c	Enrico Fermi, #3533	5.00
SP1419	34c	That's All Folks!, #3534a	9.00
SP1420	34c	Christmas Madonna, #3536	4.50
SP1421	34c	Christmas Santas, #3537-3540	5.00
SP1422	34c	James Madison, #3545	4.50
SP1423	34c	Thanksgiving, #3546	4.50
SP1424	34c	Hanukkah, #3547	4.50
SP1425	34c	Kwanzaa, #3548	4.50
SP1426	34c	United We Stand booklet and coil, #3549, 3550	10.00
SP1427	57c	Love, #3551	5.25

2002

SP1428	34c	Winter Olympics, #3552-3555	7.00
SP1429	34c	Mentoring a Child, #3556	4.50
SP1430	34c	Langston Hughes, #3557	7.00
SP1431	34c	Happy Birthday, #3558	4.50
SP1432	34c	Chinese New Year, #3559	5.00
SP1433	34c	US Military Academy, Bicent., #3560	5.00
SP1434	34c	Greetings from America, #3561-3610	27.50
SP1435	34c	Longleaf Pine Forest, #3611	13.50
SP1436	5c	Toleware Coffeepot, #3612	4.50
SP1437	3c	Star, #3613-3615	4.50
SP1438	23c	George Washington, #3616-3618	5.25
SP1439	(37c)	Flag, #3620-3623	6.00
SP1440	(37c)	Toy coils, #3626-3629	7.00

2003

SP1440A	37c	Flag, perf. 11¼, #3629F	4.50

2002

SP1441	37c	Flag, #3630-3631, 3633, 3635	4.50

2003

SP1441A	37c	Flag, self-adhesive booklet stamp, #3637	5.00

2002

SP1442	37c	Toy coils, #3638-3641	5.00

2003

SP1442A	37c	Antique Toys booklet stamps, #3642a, 3643a, 3644a, 3644f	6.00

2002

SP1443	60c	Coverlet Eagle, #3646	4.50
SP1444	$3.85	Jefferson Memorial, #3647	10.00
SP1445	$13.65	Capitol Dome, #3648	23.00
SP1446	(34c+11c)	Heroes of 2001, #B2	13.50
SP1447	37c	Masters of American Photography, #3649	21.50
SP1448	37c	John James Audubon, #3650	5.00
SP1449	37c	Harry Houdini, #3651	5.00
SP1450	37c	Official coil, #O159	4.75
SP1451	37c	Andy Warhol, #3652	5.00
SP1452	37c	Teddy Bears, #3653-3656	5.00
SP1453	37c, 60c	Love, #3657-3658	5.00
SP1454	37c	Ogden Nash, #3659	5.00

SP1455	37c Duke Kahanamoku, #3660	5.75
SP1456	37c American Bats, #3661-3664	7.00
SP1457	37c Women in Journalism, #3665-3668	7.00
SP1458	37c Irving Berlin, #3669	5.00
SP1459	37c Neuter and Spay, #3670-3671	5.00
SP1460	37c Hanukkah, #3672	4.75
SP1461	37c Kwanzaa, #3673	4.75
SP1462	37c Eid #3674	4.75
SP1463	37c Christmas Madonna, #3675	5.00
SP1464	37c Christmas Snowmen, #3676-3679	5.00
SP1465	37c Cary Grant, #3692	7.00
SP1466	(5c) Sea Coast, #3693	5.00
SP1467	37c Hawaiian Missionary Stamps, #3694	11.00
SP1468	37c Happy Birthday, #3695	5.00
SP1469	37c Greetings from America, #3696-3745	31.50

2003

SP1470	37c Thurgood Marshall, #3746	5.25
SP1471	37c Chinese New Year, #3747	5.25
SP1472	37c Zora Neale Hurston, #3748	5.25

American Design Series

2003-14

SP1473	1c Tiffany Lamp, #3749	4.75
SP1473A	1c Tiffany Lamp, litho., #3749A	4.25
SP1475	10c American Clock, #3757	4.75
SP1476	2c Navajo Necklace, #3751-3752, *2005*	4.75
SP1477	2c Navajo Necklace, #3753	4.75
SP1478	3c Silver Coffeepot, #3754	4.75
SP1479	4c Chippendale Chair, #3755	4.75
SP1480	5c Toleware, #3756	4.75
SP1481	2c Navajo Necklace, #3750	4.75
SP1482	1c Tiffany Lamp coil, #3758	5.25
SP1482A	1c Tiffany Lamp coil, litho., #3758A	4.25
SP1482Ab	1c Tiffany Lamp coil, #3758A, dated Apr. 28, 2009	4.25
SP1482C	2c Navajo Necklace coil, #3758B	5.00
SP1483	3c Silver Coffeepot coil, #3759	4.75
SP1484	4c Chippendale Chair coil, #3761	4.75
SP1485	4c Chippendale Chair coil, dated "2013," #3761A	5.00
SP1486	10c American Clock coil, #3762	4.75
SP1487	10c American Clock litho. coil, #3763	4.25
SP1490	$1 Wisdom, #3766	6.25
SP1493	(10c) New York Public Library Lion, perf. 10 vert, #3769	5.25

2004

SP1494	(10c) Atlas Statue, #3770	4.75

2003

SP1495	80c Special Olympics, #3771	5.75
SP1496	37c American Filmmaking: Behind the Scenes, #3772	11.50
SP1497	37c Ohio Statehood, Bicent., #3773	5.25
SP1498	37c Pelican Island National Wildlife Refuge, #3774	5.25
SP1499	(5c) Sea Coast perforated coil, #3775	5.25
SP1500	37c Old Glory, #3776-3780	5.00
SP1501	37c Cesar E. Chavez, #3781	5.25
SP1502	37c Louisiana Purchase, #3782	5.25
SP1503	37c First Flight of Wright Brothers, #3783	5.25
SP1504	37c Purple Heart, #3784	5.25
SP1505	37c Purple Heart, #3784A	5.25
SP1506	37c Audrey Hepburn, #3786	5.75
SP1507	37c Southeastern Lighthouses #3787-3791	6.25
SP1508	(25c) Eagles, two different stamps from #3792-3801	4.50
SP1508A	(25c) Eagles, #3792-3801	7.00
SP1508Ab	(25c) Eagles, dated 2005, #3792a-3801b	7.00
SP1509	37c Arctic Tundra, #3802	11.25
SP1510	37c Korean War Veterans Memorial, #3803	5.25
SP1511	37c Mary Cassatt Paintings, #3804-3807	5.00
SP1512	37c Early Football Heroes, #3808-3811	8.00
SP1513	37c Roy Acuff, #3812	4.75
SP1514	37c District of Columbia, #3813	4.50
SP1515	37c Reptiles And Amphibians, #3814-3818	7.00
SP1516	(37c+8c) Stop Family Violence, #B3	5.00
SP1517	37c Christmas Madonna, #3820	4.50
SP1518	37c Christmas Holiday Music Makers, 2 sets of #3821-3824	5.25
SP1519	37c Snowy Egret coil, #3829	4.50

2004

SP1520	37c Snowy Egret booklet stamp, #3830	4.50
SP1521	37c Pacific Coral Reef, #3831	14.00
SP1522	37c Chinese New Year, #3832	5.00
SP1523	37c Love, #3833	4.50
SP1524	37c Paul Robeson, #3834	4.25
SP1525	37c Theodor Seuss Geisel (Dr. Seuss), #3835	5.00
SP1526	37c Love (White Lilacs and Pink Roses), #3836	4.25
SP1527	60c Love (Five Varieties of Pink Roses), #3837	4.25
SP1528	37c US Air Force Academy, #3838	4.50
SP1529	(5c) Sea Coast coil reprint, serpentine die cut 9½x10, #3785	4.25

A souvenir page containing the original printing of No. 3785 was not prepared as there was no first day cancel applied to that stamp.

SP1530	37c Henry Mancini, #3839	4.50
SP1531	37c American Choreographers, #3840-3843	5.00
SP1532	(25c) Eagles, perforated, #3844-3853	7.00
SP1533	37c Lewis and Clark sheet stamp, #3854 (11 cancels)	9.00
SP1534	37c Lewis and Clark booklet stamps, #3855-3856 (11 cancels)	9.00
SP1535	37c Isamu Noguchi, #3857-3861	5.25
SP1536	37c National World War II Memorial, #3862	4.25
SP1537	37c Summer Olympic Games, Athens, #3863	4.25
SP1538	(5c) Sea Coast coil, perf. 9¾ vert., #3864	4.25
SP1539	37c Disney Characters, #3865-3868	7.00
SP1540	37c USS Constellation, #3869	4.25
SP1541	37c R. Buckminster Fuller, #3870	4.25
SP1542	37c James Baldwin, #3871	4.25
SP1543	37c Martin Johnson Heade, #3872	4.25
SP1544	37c Art of the American Indian, #3873	8.50
SP1547	37c John Wayne, #3876	7.50
SP1548	37c Sickle Cell Disease Awareness, #3877	4.25
SP1549	37c Cloudscapes, #3878	8.50
SP1550	37c Christmas Madonna, #3879	4.75
SP1551	37c Hanukkah, #3880	4.25
SP1552	37c Kwanzaa, #3881	4.25
SP1553	37c Moss Hart, #3882	4.25
SP1554	37c Christmas Santa Claus Ornaments, #3883-3894	7.00

2005

SP1555	37c Chinese New Year double-sided sheet, #3895	16.00

No. SP1555 was sold in a shrink-wrapped package containing the announcement page, a stamp mount, a cardboard backing and one pane of No. 3895 canceled on both sides.

SP1556	37c Marian Anderson, #3896	4.25
SP1557	37c Ronald Reagan, #3897	10.00
SP1558	37c Love, #3898	4.25
SP1559	37c Northeast Deciduous Forest, #3899	12.00
SP1560	37c Spring Flowers, #3900-3903	5.25
SP1561	37c Robert Penn Warren, #3904	4.25
SP1562	37c Yip Harburg, #3905	4.25
SP1563	37c American Scientists, #3906-3909	5.25
SP1564	37c Modern American Architecture, #3910	10.00
SP1565	37c Henry Fonda, #3911	4.25
SP1566	37c Disney Characters, #3912-3915	7.50
SP1567	37c Advances in Aviation, pane of #3916-3925	12.00
SP1568	37c Rio Grande Blankets, #3926-3929	5.25
SP1568A	37c Presidential Libraries, #3930	7.00
SP1569	37c Sporty Cars, #3931-3935	6.00
SP1570	37c Arthur Ashe, #3936	4.50
SP1571	37c To Form a More Perfect Union, #3937	7.00
SP1572	37c Child Health, #3938	4.25
SP1573	37c Let's Dance, #3939-3942	5.00
SP1574	37c Greta Garbo, #3943	5.25
SP1575	37c Jim Henson and the Muppets, #3944	8.00
SP1576	37c Constellations, #3945-3948	5.25
SP1577	37c Christmas, #3949-3960	7.00
SP1578	37c Distinguished Marines, #3961-3964	5.00
SP1579	(37c) Flag and Statue of Liberty, #3965-3967, 3970, 3972, 3974, 3975	7.00

No. SP1579 consists of two sheets.

2006

SP1580	(39c) Love, #3976	4.25
SP1582	39c Flag and Statue of Liberty, #3978, 3981, 3982, 3983, 3985	5.25
SP1583	39c Flag and Statue of Liberty Coil, perf. 10 vert., #3979	5.25
SP1584	39c Flag and Statue of Liberty Coil serpentine die cut 11 vert., #3980	4.25
a.	Like #1584, but dated and canceled 2/8/06, "S" plate number text	4.25
b.	Like #1584a, but with "V" in plate number text	4.25

No. SP1584 is dated and canceled 1/9/06.

SP1585	39c Flag and Statue of Liberty, #3985b	4.25
SP1591	39c Children's Book Animals, #3987-3994	7.00
SP1592	39c Turin Winter Olympics, #3995	4.25
SP1593	39c Hattie McDaniel, #3996	4.25
SP1594	39c Chinese New Year, #3997	8.00
SP1595	63c Bryce Canyon, #C139	4.25
SP1596	75c Great Smoky Mountains National Park, #C140	4.25
SP1597	84c Yosemite National Park, #C141	4.25
SP1598	39c Official, #O160	4.25
SP1599	Weddings, #3998-3999	5.25
SP1600	24c Common Buckey Butterfly, #4000-4002	5.25
SP1601	39c Crops, #4003-4017	9.00
SP1602	$4.05 X-Plane, #4018	8.00
SP1603	$14.40 X-Plane, #4019	20.00
SP1604	39c Sugar Ray Robinson, #4020	4.25
SP1605	39c Benjamin Franklin, #4021-4024	5.25
SP1606	39c Disney Characters, #4025-4028	6.25
SP1607	39c Love, #4029	4.25
SP1608	39c Katherine Anne Porter, #4030	4.25
SP1609	39c Amber Alert, #4031	4.25
SP1610	39c Purple Heart, #4032	4.25
SP1611	39c Wonders of America, #4033-4072	34.00
SP1612	39c Samuel de Champlain, #4073	5.25
SP1613	Samuel de Champlain souvenir sheet, #4074	5.00
SP1614	Washington 2006 World Philatelic Exhibition souvenir sheet, #4075	13.50
SP1615	39c Distinguished American Diplomats souvenir sheet, #4076	5.25
SP1616	39c Judy Garland, #4077	4.25
SP1617	39c Ronald Reagan, #4078	5.00
SP1618	39c Happy Birthday, #4079	4.25
SP1619	39c Baseball Sluggers, #4080-4083	5.75
SP1620	39c DC Comics Superheroes, #4084	12.00
SP1621	39c Motorcycles, #4085-4088	5.25
SP1622	39c Quilts of Gee's Bend, Alabama, #4089-4098	7.00
SP1623	39c Southern Florida Wetland, #4099	9.00
SP1624	$1 Official with solid blue background, #O161	6.25
SP1625	39c Christmas Madonna, #4100	4.25
SP1626	39c Christmas Snowflakes, #4101-4116	7.00
SP1627	39c Eid, #4117	4.25
SP1628	39c Hanukkah, #4118	4.25
SP1629	39c Kwanzaa, #4119	4.25

2007-2012

SP1630	39c Ella Fitzgerald, #4120	4.25
SP1631	39c Oklahoma Statehood, #4121	4.25
SP1632	39c Love, #4122	4.25
SP1633	84c International Polar Year souvenir sheet, #4123	5.75
SP1634	39c Henry Wadsworth Longfellow, #4124	4.25
SP1635	(41c) "Forever" stamps, #4125-4128	5.25
SP1635a	(42c) Forever stamp dated 2008, #4127d	4.25
SP1635b	(42c) Forever stamps dated 2008, #4125b, 4126b	4.25
SP1635c	(42c) Forever stamp dated 2008, #4127f	4.25
SP1635d	(44c) Forever stamp dated 2009, #4127i	4.25
SP1635e	(44c) Forever stamp dated 2009, #4128b	4.25
SP1635f	(44c) Forever stamps dated 2009, #4125f, 4126d	5.25
SP1636	(41c) Non-denominated Flag, #4129-4135	7.00
SP1637	41c Settlement of Jamestown, #4136	4.25
SP1638	26c Florida Panther, #4137, 4139, 4141, 4142	5.25
SP1639	17c Bighorn Sheep, #4138	4.25
SP1640	17c Bighorn Sheep coil, #4140	4.25
SP1641	41c Star Wars, #4143	8.00
SP1642	69c Okefenokee Swamp, #C142	4.25
SP1643	90c Hagatna Bay, Guam, #C143	4.25
SP1644	$4.60 Air Force One, #4144	9.00
SP1645	$16.25 Marine One, #4145	25.00
SP1646	41c Pacific Lighthouses, #4146-4150	6.25
SP1647	41c Official coil, #O162	4.25
SP1648	Love Hearts, #4151-4152	5.25
SP1649	41c Pollination, #4156b, 4156c	7.00
SP1650	(10c) Patriotic Banner, #4157-4158	4.25
SP1651	41c Marvel Comics Superheroes, #4159	13.50
SP1652	41c Vintage Mahogany Speedboats, #4160-4163	6.25
SP1653	41c Purple Heart, #4164	4.25
SP1654	41c Louis Comfort Tiffany, #4165	4.25
SP1655	41c Flowers, #4166-4185	12.00
SP1656	41c Flag, #4186-4191	8.00
SP1657	41c Disney Characters, #4192-4195	7.00
SP1658	41c Celebrate, #4196	4.50
SP1659	41c James Stewart, #4197	4.50
SP1660	41c Alpine Tundra, #4198	9.00
SP1661	41c Gerald R. Ford, #4199	4.25
SP1662	41c Jury Duty, #4200	4.25
SP1663	41c Mendez v. Westminster, #4201	4.25
SP1664	41c Eid, #4202	4.25
SP1665	41c Auroras, #4203-4204	4.25
SP1666	41c Yoda, #4205	5.00
SP1667	41c Christmas Madonna, #4206	4.25
SP1668	41c Christmas Knits, #4209, 4210, 4212, 4215	5.25

No. SP1668 appears to have a representative sampling of Nos. 4207-4218, and other examples may show different stamps from the set.

SP1669	41c Hanukkah, #4219	4.25
SP1670	41c Kwanzaa, #4220	4.25
SP1671	41c Chinese New Year, #4221	4.25
SP1672	41c Charles W. Chesnutt, #4222	4.25
SP1673	41c Marjorie Kinnan Rawlings, #4223	4.25

2008

SP1674	41c American Scientists, #4224-4227	5.25
SP1675	41c Flags, #4230, 4244, 4245, 4247 (lilac sheet)	5.25

No. SP1675 appears to have a representative sampling of Nos. 4228-4231 and Nos. 4244-4247.

SP1676	41c Flags, #4234, 4236, 4237, 4243 (gray sheet)	5.25

No. SP1676 appears to have a representative sampling of Nos. 4232-4243.

SP1677	42c American Journalists, #4248-4252	5.25

SP1678	27c Tropical Fruit, #4253-4262	7.00
SP1679	42c Purple Heart, #4263-4264	4.25
SP1680	42c Frank Sinatra, #4265	4.50
SP1681	72c 13-Mile Woods, New Hampshire, #C144	4.25
SP1682	94c Trunk Bay, St. John, Virgin Islands, #C145	5.00
SP1683	42c Minnesota Statehood, #4266	4.25
SP1684	62c Dragonfly, #4267	5.00
SP1685	$4.80 Mount Rushmore, #4268	10.00
SP1686	$16.50 Hoover Dam, #4269	22.50
SP1687	42c Love, #4270	4.25
SP1688	42c, 59c Wedding Hearts, #4271-4272	5.25
SP1689	42c Flags of Our Nation, #4273-4282	8.50
SP1690	42c Flags of Our Nation, #4283-4292	8.50
SP1691	42c Flags of Our Nation, #4293-4302	8.50
SP1692	44c Flags of Our Nation, #4303-4312	9.00
SP1693	(44c) Flags of Our Nation, #4313-4322	9.00
SP1694	(45c) Flags of Our Nation, #4323-4332	9.00
SP1695	42c Charles and Ray Eames, #4333	12.00
SP1696	42c Summer Olympics, #4334	4.25
SP1697	42c Celebrate, #4335	4.25
SP1698	42c Vintage Black Cinema, #4336-4340	5.25
SP1699	42c Take Me Out to the Ball Game, #4341	4.25
SP1700	42c Disney Characters - Imagination, #4342-4345	7.00
SP1701	42c Albert Bierstadt, #4346	4.25
SP1702	42c Sunflower, #4347	4.25
SP1703	(5c) Sea Coast coil, litho. #4348	4.25
SP1704	42c Latin Jazz, #4349	4.25
SP1705	42c Bette Davis, #4350	4.25
SP1706	42c Eid, #4351	4.25
SP1707	42c Great Lakes Dunes, #4352	9.00
SP1708	42c Automobiles of the 1950s, #4353-4357	5.75
SP1709	42c Alzheimer's Disease Awareness #4358	4.25
SP1710	42c Christmas Madonna, #4359	4.25
SP1711	42c Christmas Nutcrackers, #4362, 4363, 4365, 4368	5.25

No. SP1711 appears to have a representative sampling of Nos. 4360-4371.

SP1712	42c Hanukkah, #4372	4.25
SP1713	42c Kwanzaa, #4373	4.25

2009

SP1714	42c Alaska Statehood, #4374	4.50
SP1715	42c Chinese New Year, #4375	4.50
SP1716	42c Oregon Statehood, #4376	4.50
SP1717	42c Edgar Allan Poe, #4377	4.50
SP1718	$4.95 Redwood Forest, #4378	11.00
SP1719	$17.50 Old Faithful, #4379	25.00
SP1720	42c Abraham Lincoln, #4380-4383	7.00
SP1721	42c Civil Rights Pioneers, #4384	5.25
SP1722	(5c) Patriotic Banner coil, #4385	4.50
SP1723	1c Official, #O163	4.50
SP1724	61c Richard Wright, #4386	6.00
SP1725	28c Polar Bear, Polar Bear coil, #4387, 4389	7.00
SP1726	64c Dolphin #4388	7.00
SP1727	44c Purple Heart #4390	5.00
SP1728	44c Flag, #4391, 4395	5.00
SP1729	44c Flag, #4392-4394	5.00
SP1730	44c Flag, #4396	4.50
SP1731	44c, 61c Wedding Rings, Wedding Cake, #4397-4398	5.75
SP1732	44c The Simpsons, #4399-4403	7.00
SP1733	44c Love, #4404-4405	5.75
SP1734	44c Bob Hope, #4406	5.00
SP1735	44c Celebrate, #4407	5.00
SP1736	44c Anna Julia Cooper, #4408	5.00
SP1737	79c Zion National Park, #C146	7.00
SP1738	98c Grand Teton National Park, #C147	7.00
SP1739	44c Gulf Coast Lighthouses, #4409-4413	7.00
SP1740	44c Early TV Memories, #4414	13.50
SP1741	44c Hawaii Statehood, #4415	5.00
SP1742	44c Eid, #4416	5.00
SP1743	44c Thanksgiving Day Parade, #4417-4420	5.75
SP1744	44c Gary Cooper, #4421	5.00
SP1745	44c Supreme Court Justices, #4422	7.00
SP1746	44c Kelp Forest, #4423	9.00
SP1747	44c Christmas Madonna, #4424	5.00
SP1748	44c Christmas, #4425-4432	7.75
SP1749	44c Hanukkah, #4433	4.50
SP1750	44c Kwanzaa, #4434	4.50

2010

SP1751	44c Chinese New Year, #4435	5.00
SP1752	44c 2010 Winter Olympics, #4436	5.00
SP1753	(44c) Forever stamp, #4437	5.00
SP1754	$4.90 Mackinac Bridge, #4438	11.00
SP1755	$18.30 Bixby Creek Bridge, #4439	27.00
SP1756	44c Distinguished Sailors, #4440-4443	7.00
SP1757	44c Abstract Expressionists, #4444	9.50
SP1758	44c Bill Mauldin, #4445	5.00
SP1759	44c Cowboys of the Silver Screen, #4446-4449	7.00
SP1760	44c Love, #4450	5.00
SP1761	44c Animal Rescue, #4451-4460	9.00
SP1762	44c Katharine Hepburn, #4461	5.00
SP1763	64c Monarch Butterfly, #4462	7.00
SP1764	44c Kate Smith, #4463	5.00
SP1765	44c Oscar Micheaux, #4464	5.00
SP1766	44c Negro Leagues Baseball, #4465-4466	7.00
SP1767	44c Sunday Funnies, #4467-4471	7.00
SP1768	44c Scouting, #4472	5.00
SP1769	44c Winslow Homer, #4473	5.00
SP1770	44c Hawaiian Rain Forest, #4474	9.00
SP1771	44c Mother Teresa, #4475	5.00
SP1772	44c Julia de Burgos, #4476	5.00
SP1773	44c Christmas - Angel with Lute, #4477	5.00
SP1774	44c Christmas - Evergreens, #4478-4485	9.00
SP1775	(44c) Statue of Liberty and Flag coils, #4486, 4488, 4491	7.00

No. SP1775 appears to have a representative sampling of Nos. 4486-4491.

2011

SP1776	(44c) Chinese New Year, #4492	5.00
SP1777	(44c) Kansas Statehood, #4493	5.00
SP1778	(44c) Ronald Reagan, #4494	5.00
SP1779	(5c) Art Deco Bird, #4495	5.00
SP1780	44c Quill and Inkwell, #4496	7.00
SP1781	(44c) Latin Music Legends, #4497-4501	9.00
SP1782	(44c) Celebrate, #4502	5.00
SP1783	(44c) Jazz, #4503	5.00
SP1784	20c George Washington, #4504, 4512	5.00
SP1785	29c Herbs, #4505-4509, 4513-4517	9.00
SP1786	84c Oveta Culp Hobby, #4510	7.00
SP1787	$4.95 New River Gorge Bridge, #4511	9.00
SP1788	(44c) Statue of Liberty Reproduction and Flag ATM booklet stamps, #4518-4519	7.00
SP1789	80c Voyageurs National Park, #C148	7.00
SP1790	(44c) Wedding Roses, #4520	5.00
SP1791	64c Wedding Cake, #4521	7.00
SP1792	(44c) Civil War, #4522-4523	7.00
SP1793	(44c) Go Green, #4524	9.00
SP1794	(44c) Helen Hayes, #4525	5.00
SP1795	(44c) Gregory Peck, #4526	5.00
SP1796	(44c) Mercury Project and Messenger Mission, #4527-4528	7.00
SP1797	(44c) Purple Heart, #4529	5.00
SP1798	(44c) Indianapolis 500, #4530	5.00
SP1799	(44c) Garden of Love, #4531-4540	9.00
SP1800	(44c) American Scientists, #4541-4544	7.00
SP1801	(44c) Mark Twain, #4545	5.00
SP1802	(44c) Pioneers of Industrial Design, #4546	9.00
SP1803	(44c) Owney, the Postal Dog, #4547	5.00
SP1804	(44c) U.S. Merchant Marine, #4548-4551	7.00
SP1805	(44c) Eid, #4552	5.00
SP1806	(44c) Disney-Pixar Films - Send a Hello, #4553-4557	9.00
SP1807	(44c) Edward Hopper, #4558	5.00
SP1808	(44c) Statue of Liberty Reproduction and Flag convertible booklet stamps, #4559, 4560, 4562, 4563	7.00

No. SP1808 appears to have a representative sampling from Nos. 4559-4564.

SP1809	(44c) Barbara Jordan, #4565	5.00
SP1810	(44c+11c) Save Vanishing Species, #B4	5.00
SP1811	(44c) Romare Bearden, #4566-4569	7.00
SP1812	(44c) Christmas - Madonna, #4570	5.00
SP1813	(44c) Christmas - Ornaments, #4571, 4576, 4581, 4582	7.00

No. SP1813 appears to have a representative sampling from Nos. 4571-4582.

SP1814	(44c) Hanukkah, #4583	5.00
SP1815	(44c) Kwanzaa, #4584	5.00

2012

SP1816	(25c) Eagles, #4585-4590	7.00
SP1817	(44c) New Mexico Statehood, #4591	5.00
SP1818	32c Aloha Shirts, #4592-4601	9.00
SP1819	85c Glacier National Park, #C149	7.00
SP1820	65c Wedding Cake, #4602	7.00
SP1821	65c Baltimore Checkerspot Butterfly, #4603	7.00
SP1822	65c Dogs at Work, #4604-4607	9.00
SP1823	85c Birds of Prey, #4608-4612	9.00
SP1824	45c Weather Vanes, #4613-4617	7.00
SP1825	$1.05 Amish Buggy, Lancaster County, Pennsylvania, #C150	7.00
SP1826	(45c) Bonsai, #4618-4622	7.00
SP1827	(45c) Chinese New Year, #4623	5.00
SP1828	(45c) John H. Johnson, #4624	5.00
SP1829	(45c) Heart Health, #4625	5.00
SP1830	(45c) Love, #4626	5.00
SP1831	(45c) Arizona Statehood, #4627	5.00
SP1832	(45c) Danny Thomas, #4628	5.00
SP1833	(45c) Flags, #4632, 4635, 4637, 4638, 4642, 4644, 4645, 4647	9.00

No. SP1833 appears to have a representative sampling from Nos. 4629-4648.

SP1834	$5.15 Sunshine Skyway Bridge, #4649	9.00
SP1835	$18.95 Carmel Mission, #4650	34.00
SP1836	(45c) Cherry Blossom Centennial, #4651-4652	7.00
SP1837	(45c) William H. Johnson, #4653	5.00
SP1838	(45c) Twentieth Century Poets, #4654-4663	9.00
SP1839	(45c) Civil War, #4664-4665	7.00
SP1840	(45c) José Ferrer, #4666	5.00
SP1841	(45c) Louisiana Statehood, #4667	5.00
SP1842	(45c) Great Film Directors, #4668-4671	7.00
SP1843	1c Bobcat, #4672	5.00
SP1844	(45c) Flags (Avery booklet stamps), #4673-4676	7.00
SP1845	(45c) Disney-Pixar Films - Mail a Smile, #4677-4681	9.00
SP1846	32c Aloha Shirts booklet stamps, #4682-4686	9.00
SP1847	(45c) Bicycling, #4687-4690	7.00
SP1848	(45c) Girl Scouts of America, Cent., #4691	5.00
SP1849	(45c) Edith Piaf and Miles Davis, #4692-4693	7.00
SP1850	(45c) Major League Baseball All-Stars, #4694-4697 (dated July 20)	7.00
SP1851	(45c) Ted Williams, #4694 (dated July 21)	5.00
SP1852	(45c) Larry Doby, #4695 (dated July 21)	5.00
SP1853	(45c) Willie Stargell, #4696 (dated July 21)	5.00
SP1854	(45c) Joe DiMaggio, #4697 (dated July 21)	5.00
SP1855	(45c) Innovative Choreographers, #4698-4701	7.00
SP1856	(45c) Edgar Rice Burroughs, #4702	5.00
SP1857	(45c) USS Constitution, #4703	5.00
SP1858	(45c) Purple Heart, #4704	5.00
SP1859	(45c) O. Henry, #4705	5.00
SP1860	(45c) Flags (Ashton-Potter ATM booklet stamps), #4706-4709	7.00
SP1861	(45c) Earthscapes, #4710	13.50
SP1862	(45c) Christmas - Religious, #4711	5.00
SP1863	(45c) Christmas - Santa Over Town, #4712-4715	7.00
SP1864	(45c) Lady Bird Johnson, #4716	7.00
SP1865	$1 Waves of Color, #4717	7.00
SP1866	$2 Waves of Color, #4718	7.00
SP1867	$5 Waves of Color, #4719	11.00
SP1868	$10 Waves of Color, #4720	20.00

2013

SP1869	(45c) Emancipation Proclamation, #4721	5.00
SP1870	46c Kaleidoscope Flowers, #4722-4725	7.00
SP1871	(45c) Chinese New Year, #4726	7.00
SP1872	33c Apples, #4727-4734	9.00
SP1873	66c Wedding Cake, #4735	7.00
SP1874	66c Spicebush Swallowtail Butterfly, #4736	7.00
SP1875	86c Tufted Puffins, #4737	7.00
SP1876	$5.60 Arlington Green Bridge, #4738	9.00
SP1877	$19.95 Grand Central Terminal, #4739	37.50
SP1878	($1.10) Earth, #4740	7.00
SP1879	(46c) Love, #4741	5.00
SP1880	(46c) Rosa Parks, #4742	5.00
SP1881	(46c) Muscle Cars, #4742	7.00
SP1882	(46c) Modern Art in America, #4748	11.00
SP1883	46c Patriotic Star, #4749	5.00
SP1884	(46c) La Florida, #4750-4753	7.00
SP1885	(46c) Vintage Seed Packets, #4754-4763	9.00
SP1886	(46c) Wedding Flowers, #4764	5.00
SP1887	66c Flowers and "Yes I Do," #4765	7.00
SP1888	(46c) Flags For All Seasons, #4769, 4772, 4774, 4775	7.00

No. SP1888 appears to have a representative sampling of Nos. 4766-4777.

SP1889	(46c) Flags For All Seasons booklet stamps, #4778-4785	9.00
SP1890	(46c) Lydia Mendoza, #4786	5.00
SP1891	(46c) Civil War, #4787-4788	7.00
SP1892	(46c) Johnny Cash, #4789	5.00
SP1893	(46c) West Virginia Statehood, #4790	5.00
SP1894	(46c) New England Coastal Lighthouses, #4791-4795	9.00
SP1895	(46c) Flags For All Seasons booklet stamps (Avery Dennison printing), #4796-4799	9.00
SP1896	(46c) Eid, #4800	5.00
SP1897	(46c) Made in America, #4801	36.00

No. SP1897 consists of three pages containing each of the five panes having different margins of No. 4801.

SP1898	1c Bobcat coil, #4802	5.00
SP1899	(46c) Flags For All Seasons booklet stamps (Sennett printing with overall tagging), #4782a-4785a	9.00
SP1900	(46c) Althea Gibson, #4803	5.00
SP1901	(46c) March on Washington, 50th Anniv., #4804	5.00
SP1902	(46c) Battle of Lake Erie, #4805	5.00
SP1903	$2 Inverted Jenny pane, #4806	27.00
SP1904	(46c) Ray Charles, #4807	5.00
SP1905	(10c) Snowflakes, #4808-4812	5.00
SP1906	(46c) Christmas - Holy Family, #4813	5.00
SP1907	($1.10) Christmas - Wreath, #4814	7.00
SP1908	(46c) Christmas - Virgin and Child, #4815	5.00
SP1909	(46c) Christmas - Poinsettias, #4816, 4821	7.00
SP1910	(46c) Christmas - Gingerbread Houses, #4817-4820	9.00
SP1911	(46c) Navy and Army Medals of Honor, #4822-4823	7.00
SP1912	(46c) Hanukkah, #4824	5.00
SP1913	(46c) Harry Potter Characters, #4825-4844	18.00
SP1914	(46c) Kwanzaa, #4845	5.00

2014

SP1915	(46c) Chinese New Year, #4846	5.00
SP1916	(46c) Love, #4847	5.00
SP1917	49c Ferns, #4848-4852	9.00

SP1918	(49c)	Fort McHenry Flag and Fireworks, #4853-4855	7.00
SP1919	(49c)	Shirley Chisholm, #4856	5.00
SP1920	34c	Hummingbird, #4857-4858	7.00
SP1921	70c	Great Spangled Fritillary Butterfly, #4859	7.00
SP1922	21c	Abraham Lincoln, #4860-4861	7.00
SP1923	(49c)	Winter Flowers, #4862-4865	9.00
SP1924	91c	Ralph Ellison, #4866	7.00
SP1925	70c	Wedding Cake, #4867	7.00
SP1926	(49c)	Fort McHenry Flag and Fireworks, #4868-4871	9.50
SP1927	($5.60)	Verrazano-Narrows Bridge, #4872	11.00
SP1928	($19.99)	USS Arizona Memorial, #4873	36.00
SP1929	(49c)	Ferns, #4874-4878	9.00
SP1930	70c	C. Alfred "Chief" Anderson, #4879	7.00
SP1931	(49c)	Jimi Hendrix, #4880	5.00
SP1932	(49c)	Flag For All Seasons booklet stamps, dated "2014," #4782b-4785b	9.00
SP1933	70c	Flowers and "Yes I Do," #4881	7.00
SP1934	(49c)	Songbirds, #4882-4891	11.00
SP1935	(49c)	Charlton Heston, #4892	5.00
SP1936	($1.15)	Global Sea Temperatures Map, #4893	7.00
SP1937	(49c)	Flags, #4894-4897	9.50
SP1938	(49c)	Wedding Flowers, dated "2014," #4764a	5.00
SP1939	(49c)	Circus Posters, #4898-4905	9.00
SP1940		Circus Posters imperforate sheet of 3, #4905c	9.00
SP1941	(49c)	Harvey Milk, #4906	5.00
SP1942	(49c)	Nevada Statehood, #4907	5.00
SP1943	(49c)	Hot Rods, #4908-4909	7.00
SP1944	(49c)	Medal of Honor, dated "2014," #4822a-4823a	7.00
SP1945	(49c)	Civil War, #4910-4911	7.00
SP1946	(49c)	Farmers Markets, #4912-4915	9.00
SP1947	(49c)	Janis Joplin, #4916	5.00
SP1948	(49c)	Christmas - Poinsettia, dated "2014," #4816b	5.00
SP1949	(49c)	Hudson River School Paintings, #4917-4920	9.00
SP1950	(49c)	Fort McHenry, #4921	5.00
SP1951	(49c)	Celebrity Chefs, #4922-4926	9.00
SP1952	($5.75)	Glade Creek Grist Mill, #4927	11.00
SP1953	(49c+11c)	Breast Cancer Research, #B5	5.00
SP1954	(49c)	Batman, #4928-4935	9.00
SP1955	(49c)	Purple Heart, dated "2014," #4704a	5.00
SP1956	($1.15)	Silver Bells Wreath, #4936	7.00
SP1957	(49c)	Winter Fun, #4937-4944	9.00
SP1958	(49c)	Christmas - Magi, #4945	5.00
SP1959	(49c)	Christmas - Rudolph the Red-nosed Reindeer, #4946-4949	9.00
SP1960	(49c)	Wilt Chamberlain, #4950-4951	7.00

2015

SP1961	(49c)	Battle of New Orleans, #4952	5.00
SP1962	$1	Patriotic Waves, #4953	7.00
SP1963	$2	Patriotic Waves, #4954	7.00
SP1964	(49c)	Love, #4955-4956	7.00
SP1965	(49c)	Chinese New Year, #4957	5.00
SP1966	(49c)	Robert Robinson Taylor, #4958	5.00
SP1967	(49c)	Rose and Heart, #4959	5.00
SP1968	70c	Tulip and Heart, #4960	7.00
SP1969	1c	Bobcat, dated "2015," #4672a	5.00
SP1970	(10c)	Flags, #4961-4963	7.00
SP1971	(49c)	Water Lilies, #4964-4967	7.00
SP1972	(49c)	Martín Ramírez, #4968-4972	9.00
SP1973	(49c)	Ferns, lithographed coils, #4973-4977, 4973a-4977a	9.00
SP1974	(49c)	From Me to You, #4978	5.00
SP1975	(49c)	Maya Angelou, #4979	5.00
SP1976	(49c)	Civil War, #4980-4981	7.00
SP1977	(49c)	Gifts of Friendship, #4982-4985	9.00
SP1978	(49c)	Special Olympics World Games, #4986	5.00
SP1979	(49c)	Help Find Missing Children, #4987	5.00
SP1980	(49c)	Medals of Honor, dated "2015," #4822b, 4823b, 4988	7.00
SP1981	(22c)	Emperor Penguins, #4989-4990	7.00
SP1982	(35c)	Coastal Birds, #4991-4998	9.00
SP1983	(71c)	Eastern Tiger Swallowtail Butterfly, #4999	7.00
SP1984	(71c)	Wedding Cake, #5000	7.00
SP1985	(71c)	Flowers and "Yes, I Do," #5001	7.00
SP1986	(71c)	Tulip and Heart, #5002	7.00
SP1987	(93c)	Flannery O'Connor, #5003	7.00
SP1988	(49c)	Summer Harvest, #5004-5007	9.00
SP1989	(49c)	Coast Guard, #5008	5.00
SP1990	(49c)	Elvis Presley, #5009	5.00
SP1991	(49c)	World Stamp Show 2016, #5010-5011	7.00
SP1992	(49c)	Ingrid Bergman, #5012	5.00
SP1993	(25c)	Eagles, #5013-5018	7.00
SP1994	(49c)	Celebrate, #5019	5.00
SP1995	(49c)	Paul Newman, #5020	5.00
SP1996	(49c)	Christmas - A Charlie Brown Christmas, #5021-5030	11.00
SP1997	(49c)	Geometric Snowflakes, #5031-5034	9.00

2016

SP1998	(49c)	Love, #5036	5.00
SP1999	1c	Albemarle Pippin Apples coil, #5037	5.00
SP2000	5c	Pinot Noir Grapes coil, #5038	5.00
SP2001	10c	Red Pears coil, #5039	5.00
SP2002	$6.45	La Cueva del Indio, #5040	11.00
SP2003	$22.95	Columbia River Gorge, #5041	40.50
SP2004	(49c)	Botanical Art, #5042-5051	11.00
SP2005	(49c)	Flag, #5052-5055	9.00
SP2006	(49c)	Richard Allen, #5056	5.50
SP2007	(49c)	Chinese New Year, #5057	5.50
SP2008	($1.20)	Moon, #5058	7.00
SP2009	(49c)	Sarah Vaughan, #5059	5.00
SP2010	(47c)	Shirley Temple, #5060	5.00
SP2011	(5c)	"USA" and Star, #5061	5.00
SP2012	(47c)	World Stamp Show 2016, #5062-5063	7.00
SP2013	(47c)	Repeal of the Stamp Act, #5064	5.00
SP2014	(47c)	Service Cross Medals, #5065-5068	10.00
SP2015	(47c)	Views of Our Planets, #5069-5076	10.00
SP2016	(47c)	Pluto Explored, #5077-5078	7.50
SP2017	(47c)	Classics Forever, #5079a-5079f	10.00
SP2018	(47c)	National Park Service, #5080	16.00
SP2019	(47c)	Colorful Celebrations, #5081-5090	12.00
SP2020	(47c)	Indiana Statehood, #5091	6.00
SP2021	(47c)	Eid, #5092	6.00
SP2022	(47c)	Soda Fountain Favorites, #5093-5097	10.00
SP2023	(25c)	Star Quilts, #5098-5099	6.00
SP2024	(47c)	Jaime Escalante, #5100	6.00
SP2025	(47c)	Pickup Trucks, #5101-5104	10.00
SP2026	(89c)	Henry James, #5105	7.50
SP2027	(47c)	Pets, #5106-5125	20.00
SP2028	(47c)	Songbirds in Snow, #5126-5129	10.00
SP2029	(47c)	Patriotic Spiral, #5130-5131	7.50
SP2030	(47c)	Star Trek, #5132-5135	10.00
SP2031	(68c)	Eastern Tailed-Blue Butterfly, #5136	7.50
SP2032	(47c)	Jack-O'-Lanterns, #5137-5140	10.00
SP2033	(47c)	Kwanzaa, #5141	6.00
SP2034	(47c)	Diwali, #5142	6.00
SP2035	(47c)	Christmas - Madonna and Child, #5143	6.00
SP2036	(47c)	Christmas - Nativity, #5144	6.00
SP2037	(47c)	Christmas - Holiday Windows, #5145-5148	10.00
SP2038	(47c)	Wonder Woman, #5149-5152	10.00
SP2039	(47c)	Hanukkah, #5153	6.00

2017

SP2040	(47c)	Chinese New Year, #5154	6.00
SP2041	(47c)	Love, #5155	6.00
SP2042	$6.65	Lili'uokalani Gardens, #5156	12.50
SP2043	$23.75	Gateway Arch, #5157	47.50
SP2044	(49c)	Flag, #5158, 5160, 5161, 5162	7.50
SP2045	(34c)	Shells, #5163-5170	10.00
SP2046	(49c)	Dorothy Height, #5171	6.00
SP2047	(5c)	"USA" and Star with Blue Frame, #5172	6.00
SP2048	(49c)	Oscar de la Renta, #5173	13.00
SP2049	(21c)	People Wearing Uncle Sam Hats, #5174	6.00
SP2050	(49c)	Pres. John F. Kennedy, #5175	6.00
SP2052	5c	Pinot Noir Grapes, serpentine die cut 11 ¼x11, #5177	6.00
SP2053	10c	Red Pears, serpentine die cut 11 ¼x11, #5178	6.00
SP2054	(49c)	Nebraska Statehood, #5179	6.00
SP2055	(49c)	WPA Posters, #5180-5189	12.00
SP2056	(49c)	Mississippi Statehood, #5190	6.00
SP2057	(70c)	Robert Panara, #5191	7.50
SP2058	(49c)	Delicioso (Latin American Dishes), #5192-5197	10.00
SP2059	($1.15)	Echeveria, #5198	7.50
SP2060	(49c)	Boutonniere, #5199	6.00
SP2061	(70c)	Corsage, #5200	7.50
SP2062	3c	Strawberries coil, #5201	6.00
SP2063	(49c)	Henry David Thoreau, #5202	6.00
SP2064	(49c)	Sports Balls, #5203-5210	10.00
SP2065	(49c)	Total Eclipse of the Sun, #5211	6.00
SP2066	(49c)	Andrew Wyeth Paintings, #5212	13.00
SP2067	(49c)	Disney Villains, #5213-5222	12.00
SP2068	(49c)	Sharks, #5223-5227	10.00
SP2069	(49c)	Protect Pollinators, #5228-5232	10.00
SP2070	(49c)	Flowers from the Garden, #5233-5240	12.00
SP2071	(49c)	Father Ted Hesburgh, #5241-5242	7.50
SP2072	(49c)	The Snowy Day, #5243-5246	10.00
SP2073	(49c)	Christmas Carols, #5247-5250	10.00
SP2074	(49c)	National Museum of African American History and Culture, #5251	6.00
SP2075	(49c)	History of Ice Hockey, #5252-5253	7.50
SP2076	(49c+11c)	Alzheimer's Disease Awareness, #B6	7.50

2018

SP2077	(49c)	Chinese New Year, #5254	6.00
SP2078	(49c)	Love, #5255	6.00
SP2079	2c	Meyer Lemons, #5256	6.00
SP2080	$6.70	Byodo-In Temple, #5257	12.50
SP2081	$24.70	Sleeping Bear Dunes, #5258	47.50
SP2082	(50c)	Lena Horne, #5259	6.00
SP2083	(50c)	Flag, #5260, 5262	7.50
SP2084	(50c)	Bioluminescent Life, #5264-5273	12.00
SP2085	(50c)	Illinois Statehood Bicent., #5274	6.00
SP2086	(50c)	Mister Rogers, #5275	6.00
SP2087	(50c)	Science, Technology Engineering and Mathematics Education, #5276-5279	7.50
SP2088	(50c)	Peace Rose, #5280	6.00
SP2089	(50c)	Blue Air Mail Centenary, #5281	6.00
SP2090	(50c)	Carmine Lake Air Mail Centenary, #5282	6.00
SP2091	(50c)	Sally Ride, #5283	6.00
SP2092	(50c)	Flag Act of 1818, Bicent., #5284	6.00
SP2093	(50c)	Frozen Treats, #5285-5294	6.00
SP2094	$1	Statue of Freedom, #5295	7.50
SP2095	$2	Statue of Freedom, #5296	10.00
SP2096	$5	Statue of Freedom, #5297	11.00
SP2097	(50c)	O Beautiful, #5298	20.00
SP2098	(50c)	Scooby-Doo, #5299	6.00
SP2099	(50c)	World War I, Cent, #5300	6.00
SP2100	(50c)	The Art of Magic, #5301-5305	10.00
SP2101	(50c)	The Art of Magic souvenir sheet, #5306	7.50
SP2102	(50c)	Dragons, #5307-5310	10.00
SP2103	($1.15)	Poinsettia, #5311	7.50
SP2104	(50c)	John Lennon, #5312-5315	10.00
SP2105	(50c)	First Responders, #5316	6.00
SP2106	(50c)	Birds in Winter, #5317-5320	10.00
SP2107	(50c)	Hot Wheels Toy Cars, #5321-5330	11.00
SP2108	(50c)	Christmas - Madonna, #5331	6.00
SP2109	(50c)	Christmas - Santa Claus booklet stamps, #5332-5335	10.00
SP2110	(50c)	Christmas - Santa Claus souvenir sheet, #5336	6.00
SP2111	(50c)	Kwanzaa, #5337	6.00
SP2112	(50c)	Hanukkah, #5338	6.00

2019

SP2113	(50c)	Love, #5339	6.00
SP2114	(50c)	Chinese New Year, #5340	6.00
SP2115	(15c)	People Wearing Uncle Sam's Hat coil stamp, #5341	6.00
SP2117	(70c)	California Dogface Butterfly, #5346	7.50
SP2118	$7.35	Joshua Tree, #5347	15.00
SP2119	$25.50	Bethesda Fountain, #5348	50.00

COMPUTER VENDED POSTAGE

1992

SPCVP1	29c	Postage and Mailing Center (PMC) coil strip of 3, #31	4.25

1994

SPCVP2	29c	Postage and Mailing Center (PMC) horiz. coil strip of 3, #32	4.50

1996

SPCVP3	32c	Postage and Mailing Center (PMC) horiz. strip of 3, #33	5.00

INTERNATIONAL REPLY COUPONS

Coupons produced by the Universal Postal Union for member countries to provide for payment of postage on a return letter from a foreign country. Exchangeable for a stamp representing single-rate ordinary postage (and starting with the use of Type D3, airmail postage) to a foreign country under the terms of contract as printed on the face of the coupon in French and the language of the issuing country and on the reverse in four, five or six other languages.

Postmasters are instructed to apply a postmark indicating date of sale to the left circle on the coupon. When offered for exchange for stamps, the receiving postmaster is instructed to cancel the right circle.

Coupons with no postmark are not valid for exchange. Coupons with two postmarks have been redeemed and normally are kept by the post office making the exchange. **Coupons with one postmark are valued here.** Some coupons with a stamp added to pay an increased rate are listed in footnotes.

The following is a list of all varieties issued by the Universal Postal Union for any or all member countries.

Dates are those when the rate went into effect. The date that any item was put on sale in the United States can be very different.

Type A — Face

Wmk. "25c Union Postale Universelle 25c"

1907-20

A1 Face — Name of country in letters 1½mm high.
Reverse — Printed rules between paragraphs German text contains four lines.

1907-20

A2 Face — Same as A1.
Reverse — Same as A1 but without rules between paragraphs.

1910-20

A3 Face — Same as A1 and A2.
Reverse — Same as A2 except German text has but three lines.

1912-20

A4 Face — Name of country in bold face type; letters 2mm to 2½mm high.
Reverse — Same as A3.

1922-25

A5 Face — French words "le mois d'émission écoulé, deux mois encore."
Reverse — As A3 and A4 but overprinted with new contract in red; last line of red German text has five words.

Wmk. "50c Union Postale Universelle 50c"

1925-26

A6 Face — Same as A5.
Reverse — Four paragraphs of five lines each.

1926-29

A7 Face — French words "il est valable pendant un délai de six mois."
Reverse — As A6 but overprinted with new contract in red; last line of red German text has two words.

Wmk. "40c Union Postale Universelle 40c"

1926-29

A8 Face — Design redrawn. Without lines in hemispheres.
Reverse — Four paragraphs of four lines each.

Type B — Face

1931-35 **Wmk. Double-lined "UPU"**

B1 Face — French words "d'une lettre simple."
Reverse — Four paragraphs of three lines each.

1935-36

B2 Face — French words "d'une lettre ordinaire de port simple."
Reverse — Last line of German text contains two words.

1936-37

B3 Face — Same as B2.
Reverse — Last line of German text contains one word.

1937-40

B4 Face — Same as B2 and B3. "Any Country of the Union."
Reverse — German text is in German Gothic type.

1945

B5 Face — "Any Country of the Universal Postal Union."
Reverse — Each paragraph reads "Universal Postal Union."

Type B5 exists without central printing on face.

1950

B6 Face — Same as B5.
Reverse — Five paragraphs (English, Arabic, Chinese, Spanish, Russian).

1954

B7 Face — Same as B5.
Reverse — Six paragraphs (German, English, Arabic, Chinese, Spanish, Russian.)

Type C — Face

1968 **Wmk. Single-lined "UPU" Multiple**

C1 Face — French words "d'une lettre ordinaire de port simple."
Reverse — Six paragraphs (German, English, Arabic, Chinese, Spanish, Russian).

Foreign coupons, but not U.S., of type C1 are known with large double-lined "UPU" watermark, as on type B coupons.

1971

C2 Face — French words "d'une lettre ordinaire du premier échelon de poids."
Reverse — Six paragraphs (German, English, Arabic, Chinese, Spanish, Russian).

Type D — Face

1975 **Wmk. Single-lined "UPU" Multiple**

D1 Face — French words "d'une lettre ordinaire, expédiée à l'étranger par voie de surface."
Reverse — Six paragraphs (German, English, Arabic, Chinese, Spanish, Russian).

D2 Face — Left box does not have third line of French and dotted circle.
Reverse — Same as D1.

On D1 and D2 the watermark runs horizontally or vertically.

D3 Face — ....aerienne. Left box as D2 with (faculative) added.
Reverse — As D1, all references are to air service.

D4 Face — As D3, "CN 01 / (ancien C22)" replaces "C22."

Type E — Face

Wmk. "UPU" in cross & 8-pointed star horiz. across sheet

2002

E1 Face — Shown
Reverse — Six paragraphs (German, English, Arabic, Chinese, Spanish, Russian), repeating expiration date paragraph in same languages, bar code.

Coupons exist without the validating origination markings. Type E coupons have a bar code on the reverse that identifies the originating country and the date of printing.

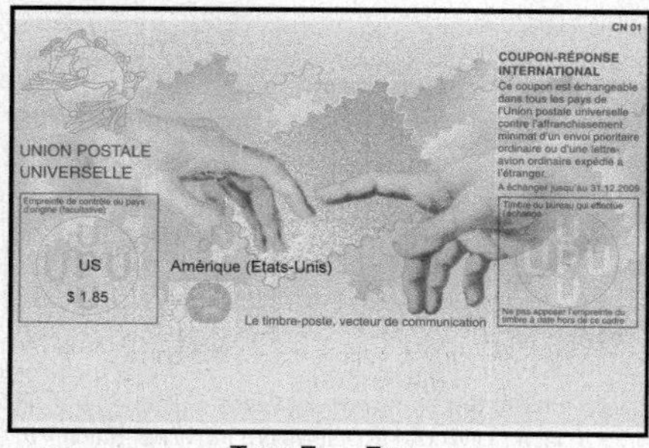

Type F — Face

Wmk. "UPU" in cross & 8-pointed star horiz. across sheet

2006

F1 Face — Shown
Reverse — Six paragraphs (German, English, Arabic, Chinese, Spanish, Russian), repeating expiration date paragraph in same languages, bar code.

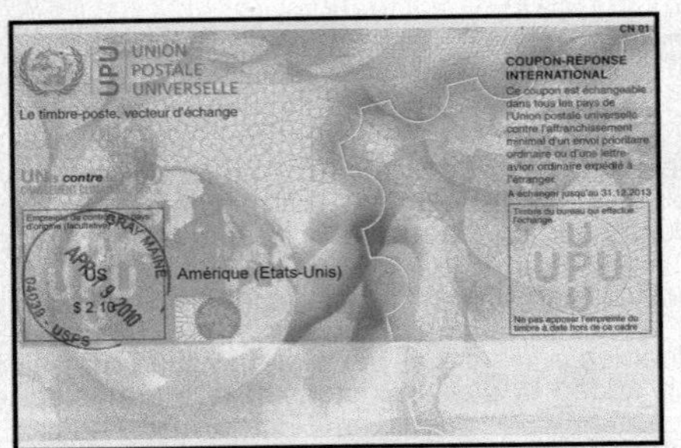

Type G — Face

2009

G1 Face Shown
Reverse Six paragraphs (German, English, Arabic, Chinese, Spanish, Russian), repeating expiration date paragraph in same languages, bar code.

REPLY COUPONS ISSUED FOR THE UNITED STATES

1907, Oct. 1

IRC2 A2 6c **slate green & gray green** 27.50

Rules omitted on reverse.

Earliest documented use: Oct. 10, 1907.

1912

IRC3 A4 6c **slate green & gray green** 32.50

Three line English paragraph on face.

1922, Jan. 1

IRC4 A5 11c **slate green & gray green,** name 81½mm long 25.00

a. Name 88½mm long 25.00

Five line English paragraph on face. Red overprint on reverse.

1925-26

IRC5 A6 11c **slate green & gray green** 22.50

Five line English paragraph on face. No overprint on reverse.

IRC6 A6 9c **slate green & gray green,** *Oct. 1, 1925* 22.50

1926

IRC7 A7 9c **slate green & gray green** 32.50

Four line English paragraph on face. Red overprint on reverse.

IRC8 A8 9c **slate green & gray green** 25.00

Without lines in hemispheres.

1935

IRC9 B2 9c **blue & yellow** 11.00

On reverse, last line of German text contains two words.

1936

IRC10 B3 9c blue and yellow 11.00

On reverse, last line of German text contains one word.

1937

IRC11 B4 9c **blue & yellow** 8.00

On reverse, German text in German Gothic type.

1945

IRC12 B5 9c **blue & yellow,** Italian text on reverse in 4 lines 6.00

a. Italian text on reverse in 3 lines 7.50

On face, "Universal Postal Union" replaces "Union."

1948, Oct. 15

IRC13 B5 11c **blue & yellow** 5.00

1950

IRC14 B6 11c **blue & yellow** 6.00

On reverse, text in English, Arabic, Chinese, Spanish, Russian.

1954, July 1

IRC15 B7 13c **blue & yellow** 6.00

On reverse, text in German, English, Arabic, Chinese, Spanish, Russian.

Varieties: period under "u" of "amount" in English text on reverse, and period under "n" of "amount." Also, country name either 47mm or 50mm long.

No. IRC15 Surcharged in Various Manners

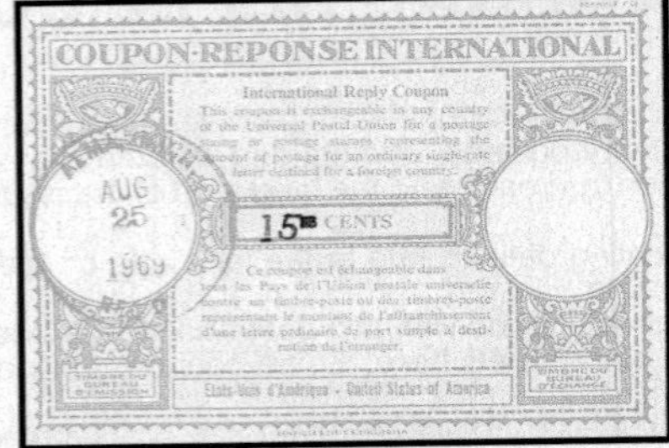

1959, May 2

IRC16 B7 15c on 13c **blue & yellow** 6.00

Individual post offices were instructed to surcharge the 13c coupon, resulting in many types of surcharge in various inks. For example, "REVALUED 15 CENTS," reading vertically; "15," etc.

1959, May 2

IRC17 B7 15c **blue & yellow** 5.00

1964

IRC18 B7 15c **blue & yellow** 5.00

a. Reverse printing 60mm deep instead of 65mm (smaller Arabic characters) 5.00

On face, box at lower left: "Empreinte de contrôle / du Pays d'origine / (date facultative)" replaces "Timbre du / Bureau / d'Emission."

1969

IRC19 C1 15c **blue & yellow** 4.50

1971, July 1

IRC20 C2 22c **blue & yellow** 4.50

No. IRC20 Surcharged in Various Manners

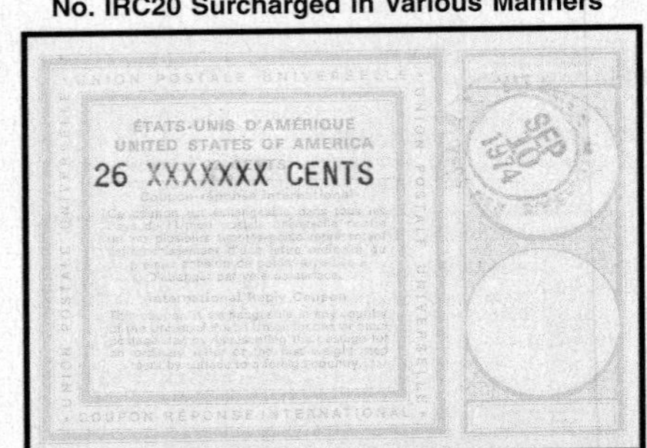

1974, Jan. 5

IRC21 C2 26c on 22c **blue & yellow** 6.50

See note after No. IRC16.

1975, Jan. 2

IRC22 D1 26c **yellow & blue** 4.00

No. IRC22 Surcharged in Various Manners

1976, Jan. 3

IRC23 D1 42c on 26c **yellow & blue** 6.50

See note after No. IRC16. Several post offices are known to have surcharged No. IRC21 (42c on 26c on 22c).

Provisional surcharges on Nos. IRC24-IRC27 were not permitted.

1976, Jan. 3

IRC24 D1 42c **blue & yellow** 4.50

Many foreign countries use non-denominated IRCs. The U.S. has never ordered or used these "generic" items.

1981, July 1

IRC26 D1 65c **blue & yellow** 5.50

1986, Jan. 1

IRC27 D2 80c **blue & yellow** 5.50

1988, Apr. 3

IRC28 D2 95c **blue & yellow** 5.00

IRC29 D3 95c **blue & yellow** 5.00

a. "9.1992" in lower left corner 5.00

Post offices were authorized on July 11, 1995 to revalue remaining stock of 95c IRCs to $1.05 by applying 10c in stamps until new stock (No. 30) arrived. All 95c varieties are known revalued thus.

The date of issue of No. IRC29 is not known. Earliest documented use: Jan. 2, 1992.

No. IRC28 exists with inverted watermark (tops of letters facing right).

1995

IRC30 D4 $1.05 **blue & yellow,** "4.95" in lower left corner 3.75

a. "10.98" in lower left corner 15.00

b. As "a," with "United States of America" in left box 25.00

"1.05" comes 1½mm or 3mm high. 3mm height has numerals more widely spaced.

Earliest documented use: July 12, 1995.

Post offices were authorized on Jan. 7, 2001, to revalue remaining stock of $1.05 IRCs to $1.75 by applying 70c in stamps until new stock arrived. All $1.05 varieties are known revalued thus. Value $7.

2002, Jan. 1

IRC31 E1 $1.75 **multicolored** 3.50

Effective Jan. 8, 2006, the rate increased to $1.85. Post offices were authorized to revalue remaining stock of $1.75 IRCs to $1.85 by applying 10c in stamps.

2006, Aug. 17

IRC32 F1 $1.85 **multicolored** 3.75

Effective May 14, 2007, the rate increased to $2. Post offices were authorized to revalue remaining stock of $1.85 IRCs to $2 by applying 15c in stamps or postal validation imprinter labels.

2009, Aug. 4

IRC33 G1 $2.10 **multicolored** 4.25

The availability of International Reply Coupons ended January 13, 2013, after which they were not supposed to be on sale. They lost their validity December 31, 2013.

POST OFFICE SEALS

Official Seals began to appear in 1872. They do not express any value, having no franking power.

The first seal issued was designed to prevent tampering with registered letters while in transit. It was intended to be affixed over the juncture of the flaps of the large official envelopes in which registered mail letters were enclosed or stamp requisitions were shipped to postmasters and was so used exclusively. Beginning in 1877 (No. OX1 and later), Post Office Seals were used to repair damaged letters, reseal those opened by mistake or by customs inspectors, and to seal letters received by the Post Office unsealed.

Values for unused Post Office Seals are for those without creases. Uncanceled seals without gum will sell for less.

Used Post Office Seals will usually have creases from being applied over the edges of damaged or accidentally opened covers but will have either cancels, precancels or a signature or notation indicating use on the seal. Creased, uncanceled seals without gum are considered used and will sell for less than either an unused or a canceled used seal.

Covers with Post Office Seals are almost always damaged except in cases when the seal was applied to a cover marked "Received Unsealed." The values shown are for covers where the damage is consistent with the application of the seal.

Post Office Seals must be tied or exhibit some auxiliary marking or docketing to qualify for "on cover" values. No. OXF1 must bear a circular date stamp cancel and the cover to which it is affixed must bear the identical cancel to qualify for the "on cover" value.

REGISTRY SEALS

RGS1

National Bank Note Co.

Typographed from copper-faced electrotyped cliches or a plate made from them arranged in a 30-subject format (3x10) cut into two panes of 15 (3x5). Also may have been issued as a pane of 9 (3x3).

1872 Typo. Unwmk. *Perf. 12*

White Wove Paper

OXF1	RGS1	**green**	30.00	7.50
		On cover, Barber signature		40.00
		On cover, Terrell signature		60.00
		Block of 4	*400.00*	
		Upper pane of 15	*1,500.*	
		Lower pane of 15 (unique)	*4,250.*	
	a.	Pelure paper	75.00	40.00
	b.	Imperf., pair	*1,250.*	
	c.	Horizontally laid paper	*500.00*	
	d.	Printed on both sides	*375.00*	
	e.	Printed on both sides, back inverted	*400.00*	
	f.	Double impression	*450.00*	—
	g.	Double impression, one inverted	—	*450.00*

The second impression of Nos. OXF1d and OXF1e are usually faint, and the second impressions on Nos. OXF1f and OXF1g are always faint.

Cancellations

Black	7.50
Blue	+5.00
Red	+15.00
Green	+70.00
Magenta	+50.00
Carrier	+25.00
Panama	—
Shanghai	—

Special Printings

Continental Bank Note Co.

Pane of 30 subjects (5x6)

1875(?) Hard White Wove Paper *Perf. 12*

Without Gum

OXF2	RGS1	**bluish green**	*1,000.*

American Bank Note Co.

Plate of 15 subjects (3x5)

1880(?) Soft Porous Paper *Perf. 12*

Without Gum

OXF3	RGS1	**bluish green**	*1,250.*

POSTAGE STAMP AGENCY SEALS

Used to seal registered pouches containing stamps for distribution to Post Offices.

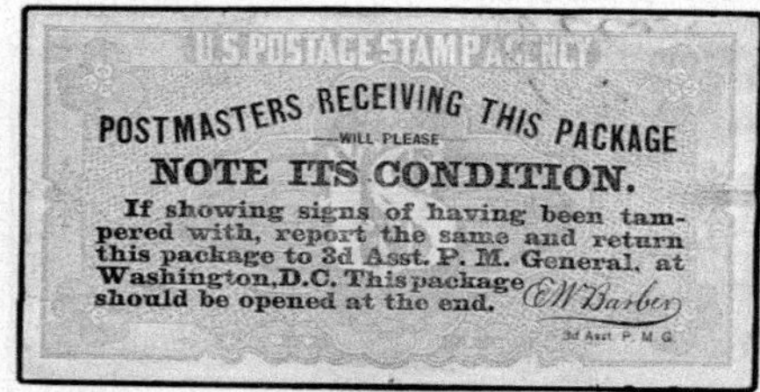

PSA1

Background size: 102x52mm.

Barber Signature

1875-93 Litho. Unwmk. *Die Cut*

OXF4	PSA1	**brown & black**	30.00
		On cover	85.00

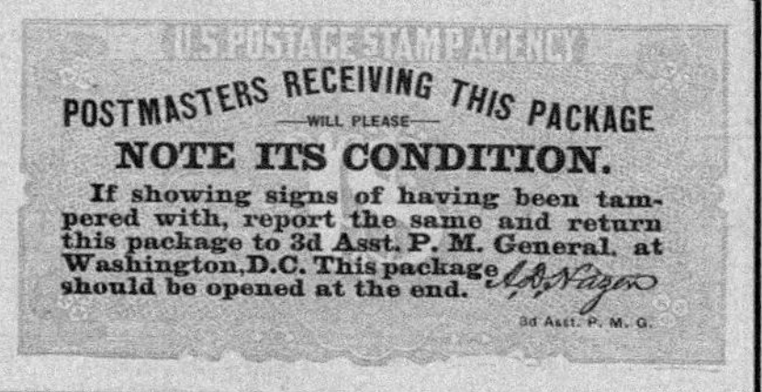

PSA2

Hazen Signature, Text 86mm Wide

OXF5	PSA2	**brown & black,** *1877*	25.00
		On cover	60.00

PSA3

Hazen Signature, Text 87mm Wide

OXF6	PSA3	**pink & red,** *1886*	50.00
		On cover	350.00
	a.	**Salmon & red**	60.00
		On cover	*400.00*

PSA4

Harris Signature

OXF7	PSA4	**pink & red,** *1887*	45.00
		On cover	150.00
	a.	**Salmon & red,**	55.00
		On cover	175.00

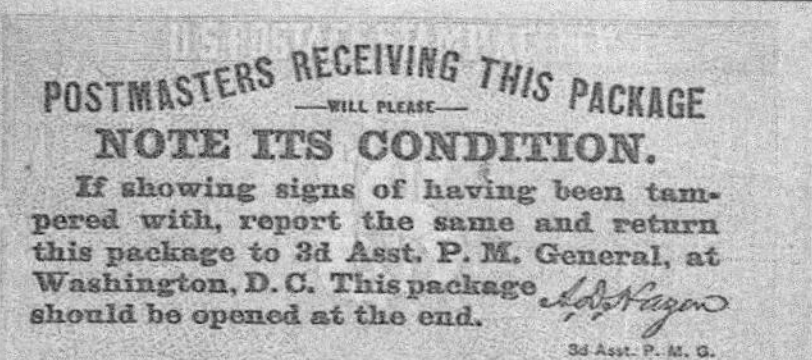

PSA5

Hazen Signature, Text 90½mm Wide

OXF8	PSA5	**pink & red,** *1889*	45.00
		On cover	150.00

PSA6

Craige Signature

OXF9	PSA6	**pink & red,** *1893*	45.00
		On cover	200.00

PSA7

Background size: 120½x67mm.

Craige Signature, "3rd Asst. P.M.G."

1894 Litho. Unwmk. *Die Cut*

OXF10	PSA7	**pink & black**	60.00
		On cover	250.00

PSA8

Craige Signature, "Third Assistant Postmaster General"

OXF11	PSA8	**pink & black**	35.00
		On cover	150.00
	a.	**Deep pink & black**	35.00
		On cover	150.00

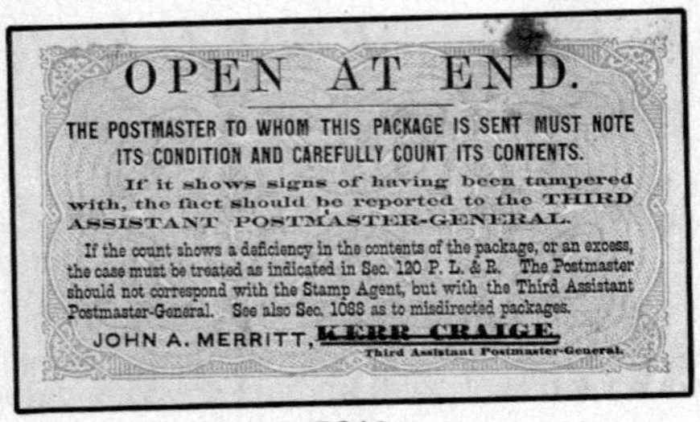

PSA9

"John A. Merritt" in Sans-Serif Capitals at Left. Two Horizontal Lines Obliterating "Kerr Craige."

1897

OXF12 PSA9 **pale pink & black** 100.00
On cover 500.00

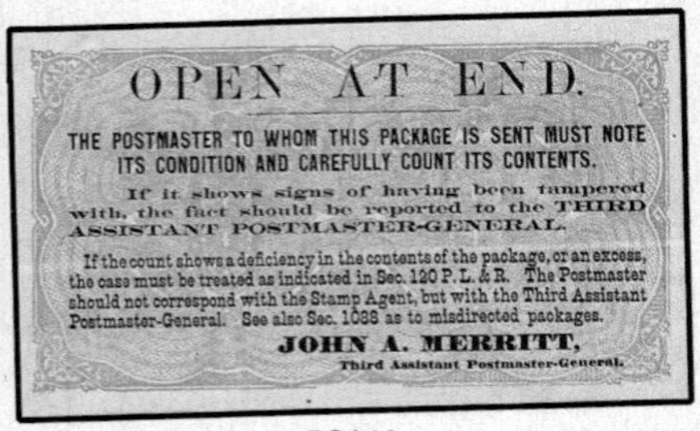

PSA10

Merritt Signature

1897-1914

OXF13 PSA10 **rose & black** 35.00
On cover 130.00

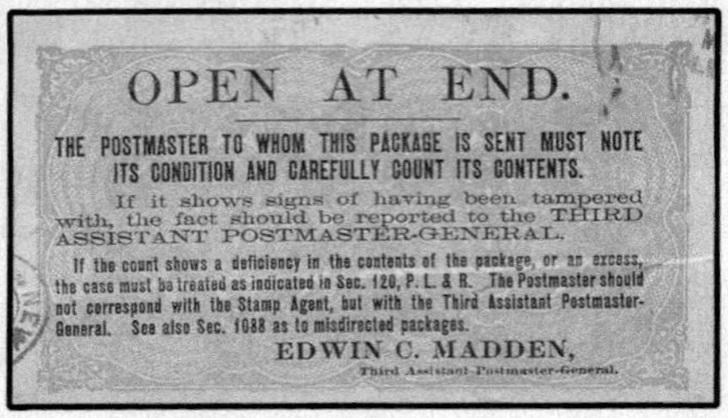

PSA11

Madden Signature

OXF14 PSA11 **rose & black**, *1899* 40.00
On cover 250.00

The first paragraph of text reads: "...MUST NOTE ITS CONDITION AND CAREFULLY COUNT..."

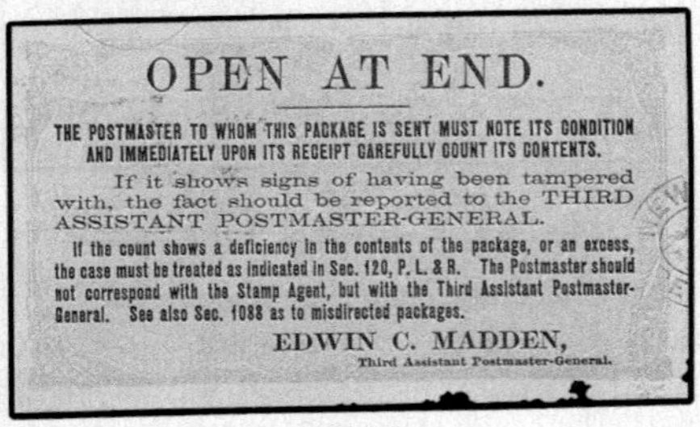

PSA12

OXF14A PSA12 **rose & black**, *1899*
On cover *250.00*

The first paragraph of text reads: "...MUST NOTE ITS CONDITION AND IMMEDIATELY UPON.."

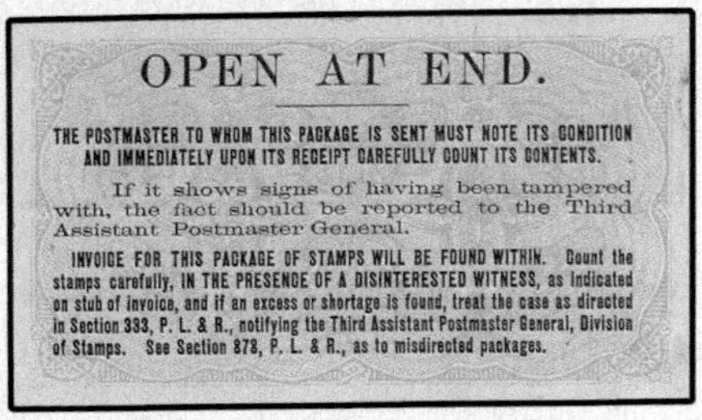

PSA13

"Section 878"

OXF15 PSA13 **rose & black**, *1907* 30.00
On cover 140.00

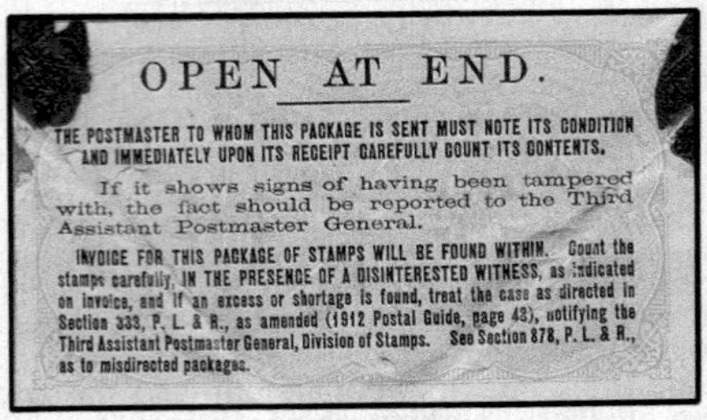

PSA14

OXF15A PSA14 **rose & black**, *1912* —
On cover

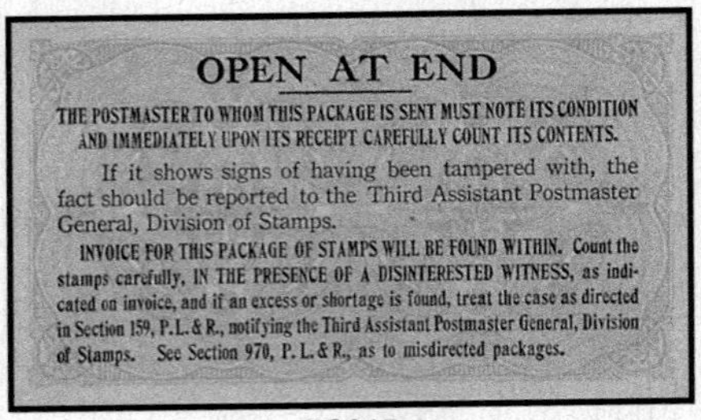

PSA15

"Section 970"

OXF16 PSA15 **rose & black**, *1912* 35.00
On cover 175.00

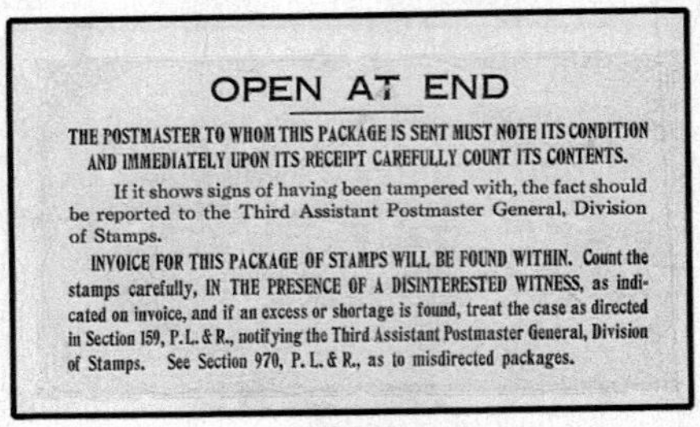

PSA16

OXF17 PSA16 **rose & black**, *1914* 40.00
On cover 175.00

DEAD LETTER OFFICE SEALS

Nos. OXA1-OXA9 were used by general Dead Letter Office personnel. Nos. OXB1-OXB5 appear to have been used only by the Money Division of the Dead Letter Office. Both types were used for forwarding mail and may also have been used to return mail to the sender.

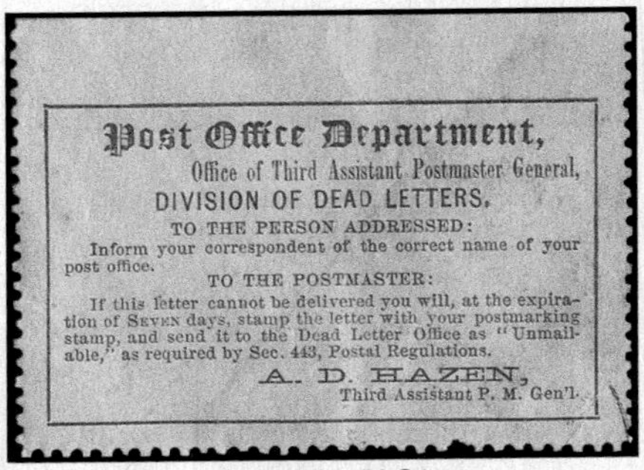

"Hazen" — DLO1

1884 **Litho.** ***Perf. 10½***

OXA1 DLO1 **black** 55.00
On cover 200.00

Perf. 12

OXA1A DLO1 **black** 25.00
On cover 125.00

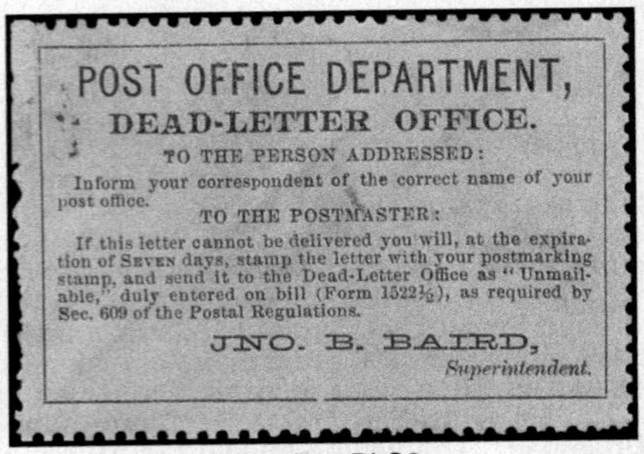

"Baird" — DLO2

1887-88 ***Perf. 10½***

OXA2 DLO2 **black** 55.00
On cover *350.00*

a. Last line of text reads "the Postal Regulations" instead of "Sec. 609 of the Postal Regulations", on cover —

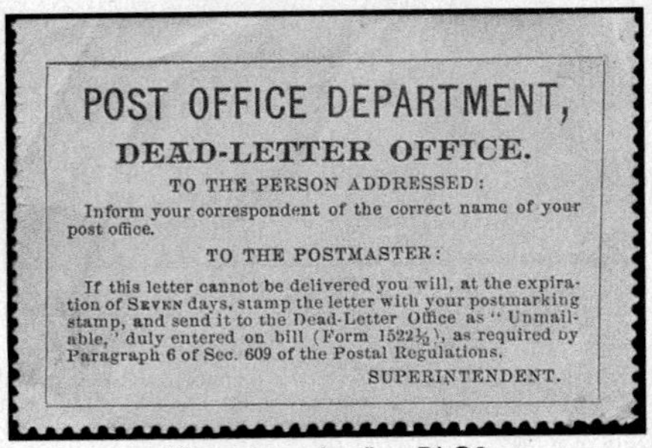

"Superintendent" — DLO3

1891 ***Perf. 10½***

OXA3 DLO3 **black** 35.00
On cover 175.00

Perf. 12

OXA3A DLO3 **black** 30.00
On cover 150.00

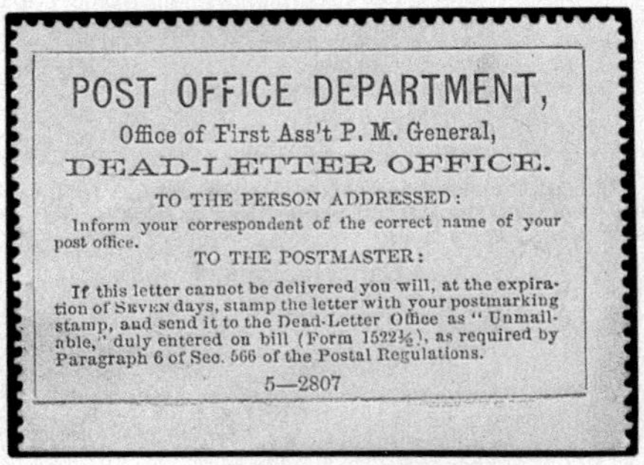

"5-2807" — DLO4

OXA4a

1892 ***Perf. 12***

OXA4 DLO4 **black** 25.00
On cover 125.00

a. With "Sec. 609 of the Postal Regulations" instead of "Sec. 566" —

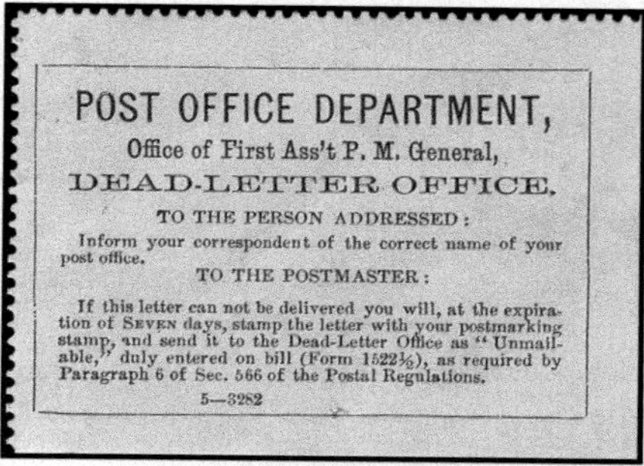
POST OFFICE DEPARTMENT,
Office of First Ass't P. M. General,
DEAD-LETTER OFFICE.
TO THE PERSON ADDRESSED:
Inform your correspondent of the correct name of your post office.
TO THE POSTMASTER:
If this letter can not be delivered you will, at the expiration of SEVEN days, stamp the letter with your postmarking stamp, and send it to the Dead-Letter Office as "Unmailable," duly entered on bill (Form 1522½), as required by Paragraph 6 of Sec. 566 of the Postal Regulations.
5—3282

"5-3282" — DLO5

1895			***Perf. 12***
OXA5	DLO5	**black**	25.00
	On cover		150.00

1898(?)			***Hyphen hole perf. 7***
OXA6	DLO5	**black**	35.00
	On cover		225.00

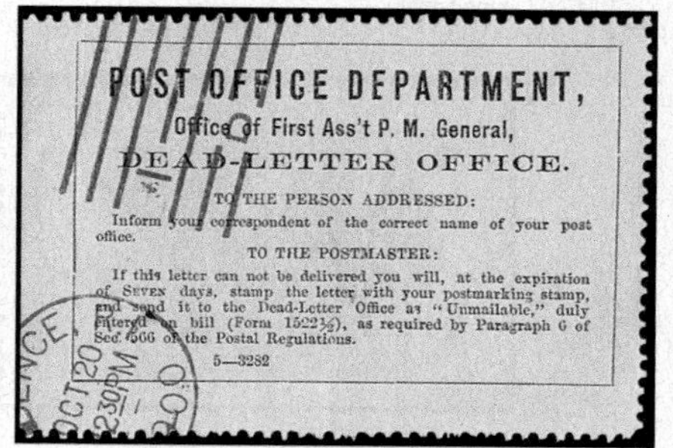
POST OFFICE DEPARTMENT,
Office of First Ass't P. M. General,
DEAD-LETTER OFFICE.
TO THE PERSON ADDRESSED:
Inform your correspondent of the correct name of your post office.
TO THE POSTMASTER:
If this letter can not be delivered you will, at the expiration of SEVEN days, stamp the letter with your postmarking stamp, and send it to the Dead-Letter Office as "Unmailable," duly entered on bill (Form 1522½), as required by Paragraph 6 of Sec. 566 of the Postal Regulations.
5—3282

DLO6

Similar to DLO5 but smaller type used for instructions to the postmasters.

1900			***Perf. 12***
OXA7	DLO6	**black**	45.00
	On cover		250.00

POST OFFICE DEPARTMENT,
Office of First Ass't P. M. General,
DEAD-LETTER OFFICE.
TO THE PERSON ADDRESSED:
Inform your correspondent of the correct name of your post office.
TO THE POSTMASTER:
If this letter can not be delivered you will, at the expiration of SEVEN days, stamp the letter with your postmarking stamp, and send it to the Dead-Letter Office as "Unmailable," duly entered on bill (Form 1522½), as required by Sec. 686 of the Postal Regulations.
5—3282

"5-3282" at Right — DLO7

1902(?) 12			***Perf. 12***
OXA8	DLO7	**black**	25.00
	On cover		125.00

POST OFFICE DEPARTMENT,
Office of First Ass't P. M. General,
DEAD-LETTER OFFICE.
TO THE PERSON ADDRESSED:
Inform your correspondent of the correct name of your post office.
TO THE POSTMASTER:
If this letter can not be delivered you will, at the expiration of SEVEN days, stamp the letter with your postmarking stamp, and send it to the Dead-Letter Office as "Unmailable," duly entered on bill (Form 1522½), as required by Paragraph 6 of Sec. 566 of the Postal Regulations.
5—3282.

"5-3282" at Center — DLO8

1902(?)			***Perf. 12***
OXA9	DLO8	**black**	25.00
	On cover		125.00

DEAD LETTER OFFICE RETURN SEALS

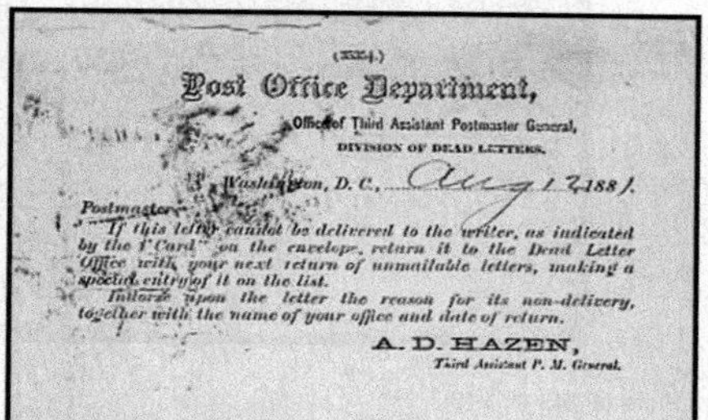
(3354.)
Post Office Department,
Office of Third Assistant Postmaster General,
DIVISION OF DEAD LETTERS.
Washington, D. C., Aug 1 2 188 1
Postmaster:
If this letter cannot be delivered to the writer, as indicated by the "Card" on the envelope, return it to the Dead Letter Office with your next return of unmailable letters, making a special entry of it on the list.
Indorse upon the letter the reason for its non-delivery, together with the name of your office and date of return.
A. D. HAZEN,
Third Assistant P. M. General.

DLO9

Incomplete Year Date ("188 ")

1881-91			***Die Cut***
OXB1	DLO9	**black**	—
	On cover		*1,000.*

(3535.)
Post Office Department,
OFFICE OF THIRD ASSISTANT POSTMASTER GENERAL,
DIVISION OF DEAD LETTERS,
Washington, D. C., May 7, 1883.
If this letter cannot be delivered you will, at the expiration of SEVEN days, stamp the letter with your postmarking stamp, and return it and this circular to the DEAD LETTER OFFICE, with your next RETURN OF UNMAILABLE LETTERS, DULY NUMBERED AND ENTERED ON THE LIST, FORM No. 1522.
A. D. HAZEN,
Third Assistant P. M. General.
To the person addressed: Inform your correspondent of the correct name of your post office.

"1883" — DLO10

Complete Year Date

OXB2	DLO10	**black** (1882)	75.00
	On cover		*400.00*
OXB3	DLO10	**black** (1883)	75.00
	On cover		*400.00*
OXB4	DLO10	**black** (1886)	75.00
	On cover		*400.00*

Post Office Department,
OFFICE OF THIRD ASSISTANT POSTMASTER GENERAL,
DIVISION OF DEAD LETTERS,
Washington, D. C., Nov 16, 188 3
If this letter cannot be delivered you will, at the expiration of SEVEN days, stamp the letter with your postmarking stamp, and return it and this circular to the DEAD LETTER OFFICE, with your next RETURN OF UNMAILABLE LETTERS, DULY NUMBERED AND ENTERED ON THE LIST, FORM No. 1522.
A. D. HAZEN,
Third Assistant P. M. General.
To the person addressed: Inform your correspondent of the correct name of your post office.

DLO11

Incomplete Year Date ("188")

OXB5	DLO11	**black** *1883*	
	On cover		*600.00*

Post Office Department,
DEAD-LETTER OFFICE,
WASHINGTON, D. C., July 20, 188 7
Postmaster:
Upon the delivery of this letter, please obtain the envelope, if agreeable to the party addressed, and return it to the Dead-Letter Office. If the letter cannot be delivered you will, at the expiration of SEVEN days, stamp the letter with your postmarking stamp, and return it and this circular to the DEAD-LETTER OFFICE, ~~with your next RETURN OF UNMAILABLE LETTERS, DULY NUMBERED AND ENTERED ON THE LIST, FORM No. 1522.~~
JNO. B. BAIRD,
Superintendent.

DLO12

Incomplete Year Date ("188")

OXB6	DLO12	**black**	75.00
	On cover		*250.00*

Post Office Department,
DEAD-LETTER OFFICE,
WASHINGTON, D. C., ________, 189
Postmaster:
Upon the delivery of this letter, please obtain the envelope, if agreeable to the party addressed, and return it to the Dead-Letter Office. If the letter can not be delivered, you will, at the expiration of SEVEN days, stamp the letter with your postmarking stamp, and return it and this circular to the DEAD-LETTER OFFICE, with your next RETURN OF UNMAILABLE LETTERS, DULY NUMBERED AND ENTERED ON THE LIST, FORM No. 1522.
5—3194
SUPERINTENDENT.

DLO13

Incomplete Year Date ("189")

OXB7	DLO13	**black** (1891?)	75.00
	On cover		*500.00*
a.	Without form number "5-3194" at LL, on cover		*500.00*

POST OFFICE SEALS

No. OX1 was prepared for use in the Dead Letter Office but was distributed to other offices and used in the same way as later seals. Most on-cover examples are normal Post Office usages from larger East Coast cities. New York and Philadelphia predominate. Very few examples with Dead Letter Office markings are recorded. For that reason, No. OX1 is listed with the other Post Office Seals.

POS1

("Post Obitum" in background.)
National Bank Note Co.
Plate of 50 subjects (5x10)
Silk Paper

1877		**Engr.**		***Perf. 12***
OX1	POS1	**brown**	50.00	27.50
	On cover			*1,000.*
	Block of 4		*400.00*	

Earliest documented use: April 17, 1879.

Cancellations

Used (creased, no gum, or marking without town or date)	27.50
With town marking	+42.50
With town marking and year date	+67.50

POS2

American Bank Note Co.
Plate of 100 subjects (10x10) in two panes of 50 bearing imprint of American Bank Note Co. in the selvage.
(Also plates of 50 (5x10) subjects)

1879 **Engr.** ***Perf. 12***
Thin, crisp, semi-translucent paper, yellowish gum

OX2	POS2	**red brown**	3.00	1.00
	On cover			85.00
	Block of 4		20.00	
	Margin block with imprint		40.00	
a.	**Brown**		10.00	5.00
	On cover			200.00
	Block of 4		70.00	
	Margin block with imprint		100.00	

Seal impression can be clearly seen when viewed from the back.

Panes of 50 (5x10) bearing the imprint of the American Bank Note Co. centered on each side in the top selvage. At least one of the panes used has a reversed "2" to the right of the top imprint.

1879(?)		**Thick, opaque paper**		
OX3	POS2	**yellow brown**	*150.00*	*150.00*

1881(?)
Thin, hard porous paper, clear transparent gum

OX4	POS2	**deep brown**	75.00
	Block of 4		350.00
	Margin block of 4 with imprint (side)		400.00
	Margin block of 6 with imprint (bottom)		550.00
	Margin block of 4 with imprint & reversed "2" (top)		575.00

No. OX4 is the so-called "Special Printing." It was produced from a new plate prepared from the original die. It received little usage, but at least two full panes are known to have existed.

Colors

Beginning with OX5, many Official Seals exhibit a wide variety of shades. Minimal care was exercised in their printing. It is not uncommon for seals within a single pane to vary in shade from dark to very light. No attempt is being made here to list all of the various shades separately.

POS3

Typographed
Without words in lower label.
Outer frame line at top and left is thick and heavy (compare with POS4).
Plate of 72 subjects (8x9)

1888 *Rough perf. 12*

Medium thick, crisp paper

OX5	POS3	**chocolate** (shades)	.75	.75
		On cover		50.00
		Block of 4	5.00	
	a.	Imperf, pair	50.00	
		Pane of 72, imperf	*900.00*	

A perforated pane of 72 exists, but lacks three corner seals.

Imperforates

Imperforates of Nos. OX6, OX7, and OX10 are believed to be printer's waste. No seals were issued imperforate, though some may have been sent to post offices.

Plate of 42 subjects (7x6)

1889 *Rough perf. 12*

Thick to extremely thick paper

OX6	POS3	**chocolate** (shades)	.75	.50
		On cover		40.00
		Block of 4	5.00	
		Pane of 42	—	

1890 *Perf. 12*

OX7	POS3	**bister brown** (shades)	.75	.50
		On cover		40.00
		Block of 4	5.00	
		Pane of 42	—	
	a.	**Rose brown**	4.00	2.50
		On cover		65.00
		Block of 4	22.50	
	b.	**Yellow brown**	2.00	2.00
		On cover		50.00
		Block of 4	10.00	
	c.	Imperf. vertically, pair	50.00	—
	d.	Imperf. horizontally, pair	50.00	—
	e.	Vertical pair, imperf. between	100.00	
	f.	Horizontal pair, imperf. between	100.00	
	g.	Double impression		400.00

Cancellation

Puerto Rico +75.00

Examples of No. OX7 with multiple impressions widely spaced or at angles to each other, are found on normal paper and various documents. These are printer's waste.

1892 *Rouletted 5½*

OX8	POS3	**light brown** (shades)	20.00	15.00
		On cover		*750.00*
		Block of 4	300.00	
		Pane of 42	—	

1895(?) *Hyphen Hole Perf. 7*

OX9	POS3	**gray brown**	7.50	5.00
		On cover		500.00
		Block of 4	200.00	
		Pane of 42	—	

Earliest documented use: Feb. 3, 1897.

1898(?) **Thin soft paper** *Perf. 12*

OX10	POS3	**brown** (shades)	8.00	2.00
		On cover		250.00
		Pane of 42	—	

Cancellation

Cuba —

POS4

Plate of 143 (11x13)

Outer frame line at top and left is thin.
Otherwise similar to POS3.

1900 **Litho.** *Perf. 12*

OX11	POS4	**red brown**	.50	.25
		On cover		30.00
		Block of 4	2.50	
	a.	**Gray brown**	2.00	1.25
		On cover		45.00
		Block of 4	15.00	
	b.	**Dark brown**	2.50	*4.50*
		On cover		85.00
		Block of 4	15.00	
	c.	**Orange brown**	2.50	*2.00*
		On cover		75.00
		Block of 4	11.00	

Most imperfs and part perfs are printers waste. Some genuine perforation errors may have been issued to post offices.

Watermarks

Watermarks cover only a portion of the panes. Many stamps in each pane did not receive any of the watermark. Values for watermarked panes are for examples with at least 50% of the watermark present.

POS4a

Similar to POS3 but smaller.
Design: 38x23mm
Issued in panes of 20 (5x4)

1907 **Typo.** *Perf. 12*

OX12	POS4a	**bright royal blue**	2.00	2.00
		On cover		45.00
		Pane of 20	60.00	
	b.	Wmkd. "Rolleston Mills" in sheet	25.00	25.00
		Block of 4	180.00	

Earliest documented use: June 1, 1907.

OX13	POS4a	**blue** (shades)	.25	.25
		On cover		25.00
		Pane of 20	20.00	
	a.	Wmkd. Seal of U.S. in sheet (2 types)	1.50	1.50
		Pane of 20	50.00	
	b.	Wmkd. "Rolleston Mills" in sheet	1.00	1.00
		Pane of 20	40.00	
	c.	Wmkd. "Birchwood Superfine" in sheet	—	—
		Pane of 20	—	
	d.	Pelure paper	*20.00*	*20.00*
	e.	Toned paper	*25.00*	*25.00*
	f.	Printed on both sides	—	

Numerous varieties such as imperf., part perf., tete beche, and double impressions exist. These seem to be from printer's waste. Some genuine perforation errors may have been issued to post offices.

All recorded examples of No. OX13f show the reverse-side impression inverted in relation to the impression on the face.

1912 *Hyphen Hole 6½*

OX14	POS4a	**blue**	1.75	1.50
		On cover		75.00
		Pane of 20	45.00	
	a.	Wmkd. Seal of U.S. in sheet	10.00	10.00
		Pane of 20	300.00	
	b.	Wmkd. "Rolleston Mills" in sheet	2.50	2.50
		Pane of 20	80.00	

Panes of 10 were made from panes of 20 for use in smaller post offices. Complete booklets with covers exist.

1913 *Perf. 12 x Hyphen Hole 6½*

OX15	POS4a	**blue**	3.50	3.00
		On cover		100.00
		Pane of 20	110.00	
	a.	Hyphen-hole perf 6½ (right) x Perf. 12 (left, top, bottom)	15.00	—
	b.	Wmkd. Seal of U.S. in sheet	4.50	4.00
		Pane of 20	125.00	
	c.	As "a" and "b"	20.00	—

No. OX15a comes from panes that are perfed between the left selvage and the seals.

1913 *Hyphen Hole 6½ x Perf. 12*

OX16	POS4a	**blue**	5.25	5.25
		On cover		400.00
		Pane of 20	250.00	
	a.	Wmkd. Seal of U.S. in sheet	15.00	15.00
		Pane of 20	300.00	
	b.	Wmkd. "Rolleston Mills" in sheet	—	—
		Pane of 20	—	

1916 *Perf. 12*

OX17	POS4a	**black,** *pink*	1.00	1.00
		On cover		100.00
		Pane of 20	75.00	
	a.	Imperf horiz., pane of 20	—	

1917 *Perf. 12*

OX18	POS4a	**black** (shades to gray)	.40	.40
		On cover		27.50
		Pane of 20	40.00	
	b.	Vert. pair, imperf horizontally	25.00	
	c.	Horiz. pair, imperf vertically	20.00	
	d.	Vertical pair, imperf between	60.00	
	e.	Horizontal pair, imperf between	35.00	
	f.	Imperf, pair	50.00	

POS5

Quartermaster General's Office

Issued in panes of 10 (2x5) without selvage.

1919 *Perf. 12*

OX19	POS5	**indigo**	150.	
		Block of 4	*700.*	
		Pane of 10	*1,600.*	

Rouletted 7

OX20	POS5	**indigo**	*4,750.*	*3,250.*

The pane format of No. OX20 is not known. One of the few reported examples is rouletted on four sides.

Nos. OX19-OX20 were used on mail to and from the Procurement Division of the Quartermaster General's Office. After five weeks of use the seals were withdrawn when the Mail and Records Section became a full branch of the Quartermaster General's Office.

POS6

Issued in panes of 20 (5x4) and 16 (4x4).

Panes of 10 were made from panes of 20 for use in smaller post offices. Panes are valued as having the selvage on the left of the pane. Panes without the selvage sell for less. Pairs of imperforate and partially perforated seals are listed with the most common variety having the same paper type and surviving perforation, if any.

Thin, white, crisp paper

The paper used for Nos. OX21-OX27 is thin enough to allow reading text on the envelope.

1919 *Perf. 12 (sometimes rough)*

OX21	POS6	**black** (shades)	.30	.25
		On cover		12.50
		Pane of 20	15.00	
	a.	Imperf, pair	15.00	
		On cover		—
	b.	Vert. pair, imperf horiz.	12.50	
	c.	Horiz. pair, imperf vert.	12.50	
	d.	Vert. pair, imperf btwn.	25.00	
	e.	Horiz. pair, imperf btwn.	25.00	
	f.	Wmkd. eagle and star in sheet (1936?)	2.00	2.00
		Pane of 20	70.00	
	g.	As "f," imperf, pair	35.00	
	h.	As "f," vert. pair, imperf horiz.	27.50	
	i.	As "f," vert. pair, imperf btwn.	40.00	
	j.	As "f," horiz. pair, imperf. vert.	27.50	
	k.	As "f," horiz. pair, imperf. btwn.	40.00	

l. Wmkd. "Certificate Bond," "Made in USA," or McElwain logo in sheet (1936?) 10.00 10.00
Pane of 20 300.00

Earliest documented use: 1920.

1936(?) ***Perf. 12x9***
OX22 POS6 **black** (shades) 7.50 7.50
On cover 85.00
Pane of 20 200.00
a. Vert. pair, imperf. horiz. 50.00
b. Wmkd. eagle and star in sheet 7.50 7.50
Pane of 20 200.00
c. As "b," vert. pair, imperf. horiz. 50.00

Earliest documented use: Oct. 1936 (No. OX22 or OX23.)

1936(?) ***Perf. 12x8½***
OX23 POS6 **black** (shades) 2.50 2.50
On cover 40.00
Pane of 20 75.00
a. Wmkd. eagle and star in sheet 4.00 4.00
Pane of 20 110.00

1927(?) ***Perf. 12½***
OX24 POS6 **gray black,** on cover —

1936(?) ***Perf. 8½***
OX25 POS6 **gray black** —
a. Wmkd. eagle and star in sheet —

1936(?) ***Perf. 12x9½***
OX26 POS6 **gray black,** pane of 20 —

1935(?) ***Perf. 11½***
OX27 POS6 **gray black** *17.50* *17.50*
On cover 50.00

Medium to thick, opaque, egg or cream colored paper

1946(?) ***Perf. 12***
OX28 POS6 **gray black** .40 .40
On cover 25.00
Pane of 20 30.00
a. Vert. pair, imperf btwn. 25.00

1946(?) ***Perf. 12½***
OX29 POS6 **gray black** .50 .50
On cover 27.50
Pane of 20 35.00

1945(?) ***Perf. 12½x9***
OX29A POS6 **gray black** —

1944(?) ***Perf. 12½x8½***
OX30 POS6 **gray black** 1.00 1.00
On cover 32.50
Pane of 20 30.00

1947(?) ***Perf. 8½***
OX31 POS6 **gray black** 1.00 1.00
On cover 32.50
Pane of 20 30.00

1947(?) ***Perf. 8½x12***
OX32 POS6 **gray black** —

1947(?) ***Perf. 8½x8***
OX33 POS6 **gray black,** —
On cover —

1947(?) ***Perf. 8x8½***
OX33A POS6 **gray black** —
On cover —

Thick, gray, very soft paper

1948 ***Perf. 12½ (sometimes rough)***
OX34 POS6 **gray black** 1.00 1.00
On cover 35.00
Pane of 16 45.00

1947 ***Perf. 8½***
OX35 POS6 **gray black** 3.50 3.50
On cover 45.00
Pane of 20 50.00

1948(?) ***Perf. 8½x12½***
OX37 POS6 **gray black** — —

1948 ***Hyphen Hole Perf. 9½***
OX38 POS6 **gray black** 12.50 12.50
On cover 50.00
Pane of 16 250.00
a. Pane of 5, imperf at sides, with tab 125.00

Pane of 5 tab inscribed "16-56146-1 GPO." Pane of 5 also known on cream paper. Seals without the tab generally cannot be distinguished from No. OX39.

1950(?) ***Hyphen Hole Perf. 9½ x Imperf***

Medium thick, cream or white paper
Design width: 37½mm

OX39 POS6 **gray black** .25 .25
On cover 12.50
Pane of 5 with tab 1.25
a. Vert. pair, imperf between 12.50
b. Pane of 5, imperf, with tab 20.00
c. Pane of 5, imperf at top & btwn. rows 2 & 3, 4 & 5 30.00

Pane of 5 tab inscribed, "16-56164-1 GPO."
Earliest documented use: Jan. 23, 1950.

1969(?) ***Hyphen Hole Perf. 9½ x Imperf***

Medium thick, white paper
Design width: 38½mm

OX40 POS6 **gray black** .25 .25
On cover 30.00
Pane of 5 with tab 2.25
a. Vert. pair, imperf. btwn. —
b. Pane of 5, Imperf 35.00
c. Double impression —

Tab inscribed, "c43-16-56164-1 GPO"

Earliest documented use: Feb. 11, 1969.

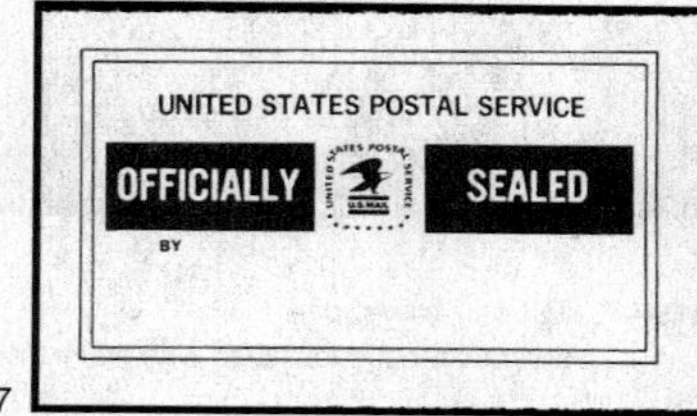

POS7

Design size, Nos. OX41-OX45, 37x21mm.
On Nos. OX41-OX50, tab is inscribed, "LABEL 21, JULY 1971."

1972 **Litho.** ***Rouletted 9½ x Imperf***
OX41 POS7 **black** .25 .25
On cover 12.50
Pane of 5 2.00
a. Imperf, pair 10.00

1972(?) ***Rouletted 6½ x Imperf***
OX42 POS7 **black** .25 .25
On cover 5.00
Pane of 5 2.75

1973(?) **Litho.** ***Hyphen Hole 7 x Imperf***
OX43 POS7 **black** .30 .25
On cover 7.50
Pane of 5 9.00

1976(?) **Litho.** ***Rouletted 8½ x Imperf***
OX44 POS7 **black** .25 .25
On cover 7.50
Pane of 5 2.00

1979(?) **Litho.** ***Perf. 12½ x Imperf***
OX45 POS7 **black** .25 .25
On cover 7.50
Pane of 5 2.25
Small holes .25 .25
On cover 7.50
Pane of 5 2.25

1988(?) **Litho.** ***Die Cut***
Self-Adhesive
OX46 POS7 **black,** 38x21mm, fluorescent paper .25 .25
On cover *7.50*
Pane of 5 3.50
OX47 POS7 **black,** 38x21mm, non-fluorescent paper .25 .25
On cover *7.50*
Pane of 5 3.50
OX48 POS7 **gray** (shades), 37x21mm .25 .25
On cover *7.50*
Pane of 5 3.50
OX49 POS7 **black,** 40x21mm .50 .50
On cover *15.00*
Pane of 5 10.00

On No. OX49, BY is 2x1mm, P of POSTAL is left of P in POSTAL of Emblem. Tab inscribed as No. OX41, but 1's have no bottom serif.

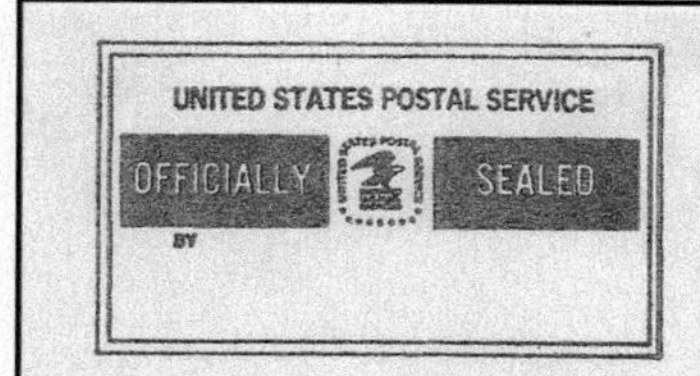

POS7a

Size: 37x21mm
OX50 POS7a **purple** — —
On cover —

Earliest documented use: Dec. 2, 1992.

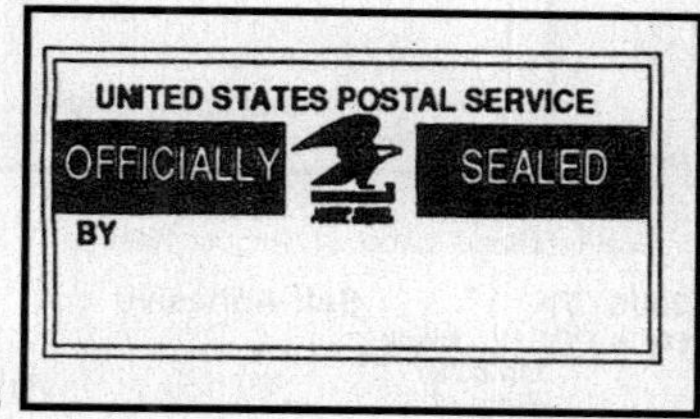

POS8

Tab inscribed "LABEL 21, JAN. 1992."

Size: 44x22mm

1992 **Self-adhesive** ***Die Cut***
OX51 POS8 **black** 1.00 1.00
On cover *25.00*
Pane of 5 10.00

Earliest documented use: Mar. 1992.

Size: 41x21mm

1992? **Self-Adhesive** ***Die Cut***
OX52 POS8 **black** .25 .25
On cover *7.50*
Pane of 5 3.50

No. OX52 exists on both white and brown backing paper. Those on brown backing paper are worth more.

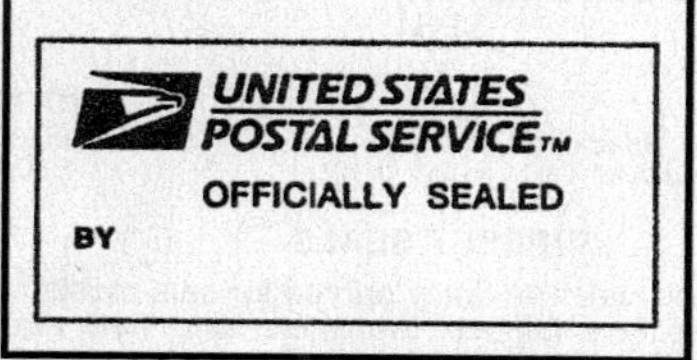

POS9

Tab inscribed "Label 21, April 1994."

1994 **Self-Adhesive** ***Die Cut***
OX53 POS9 **black** .25 .25
On cover *7.50*
Pane of 5 3.50

POS10

Tab inscribed "Label 21, August 1996."

1996 **Self-Adhesive** ***Die Cut***
OX54 POS10 **black** .25 .25
On cover *20.00*
Pane of 5 2.00
a. "OFFICALLY" *.25* .25
On cover 7.50
Pane of 5 *2.00*

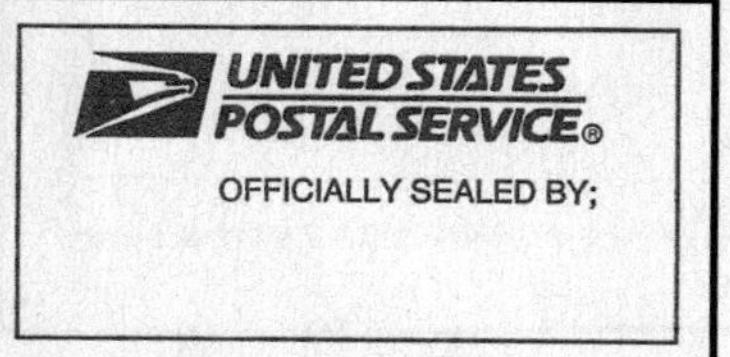

POS11

Tab inscribed "Label 21, August 1996."

1996 **Self-Adhesive** ***Die Cut***
OX55 POS11 **black** .25 .25
On cover 7.50
Pane of 5 3.00

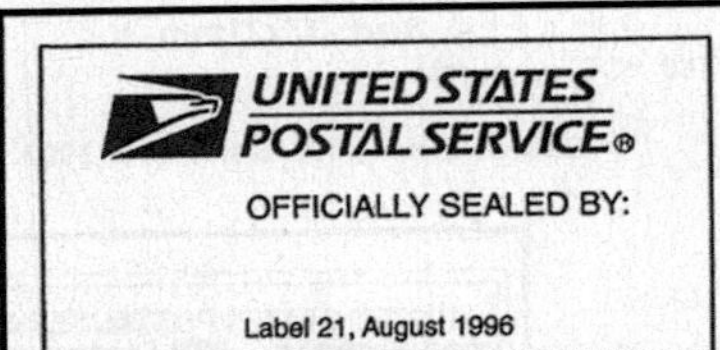

POS12

Seal inscribed “Label 21, August 1996.”

2006 (?) **Self-Adhesive** ***Die Cut***

OX56	POS12	**black**	.25	.25
		On cover		*7.50*
		Pane of 5	3.00	

Although No. OX56 is inscribed “August 1996,” it likely was issued in 2006.

SEA POST SEAL

This seal was used by clerks on North German Lloyd ships on the New York - Bremen route.

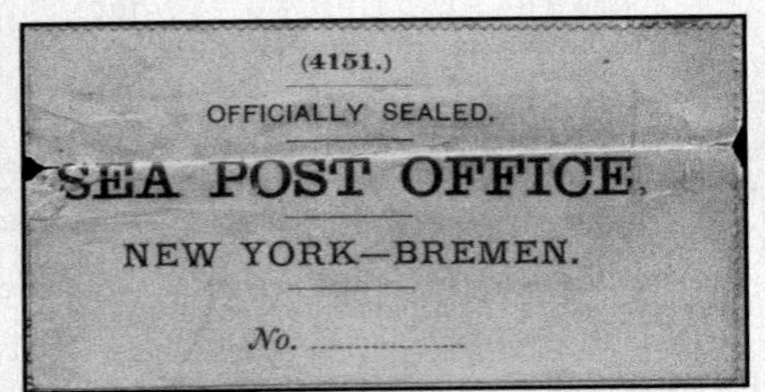

SPS1

1895 (?) ***Perf. 12***

OXSP1	SPS1	**black**	400.00	400.00
		On cover		*1,500.*

TYPESET SEALS

These seals were privately printed for sale mostly to Fourth Class Post Offices. Many are extremely rare. Unquestioned varieties are listed. Many others exist.

All are imperf or die cut except Nos. LOX7-LOX11 and LOX36.

TSS1

LOX1	TSS1	**black**	*350.00*	*350.00*
		On cover		900.00

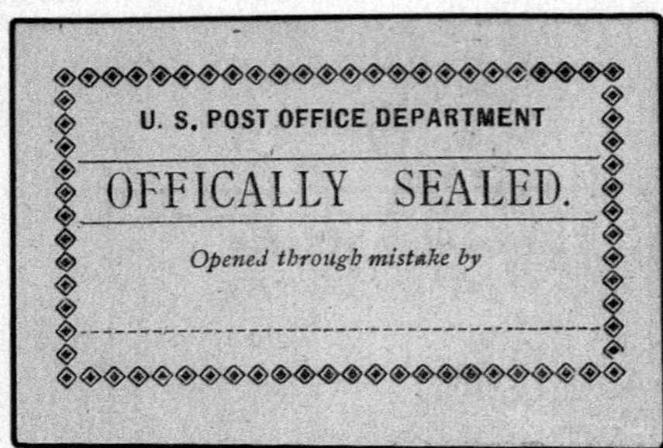

TSS2

LOX2	TSS2	**black,** 15 diamonds vertically in frame	*1,000.*	*1,000.*
	a.	14 diamonds vertically		*450.*
	b.	14 diamonds vertically, no period after “DEPARTMENT”		*450.*
	c.	“OFFICALLY” misspelling, 14 diamonds vertically	*800.*	
		On cover		—

TSS3

LOX3	TSS3	**black**		*1,000.*
		On cover		*1,100.*

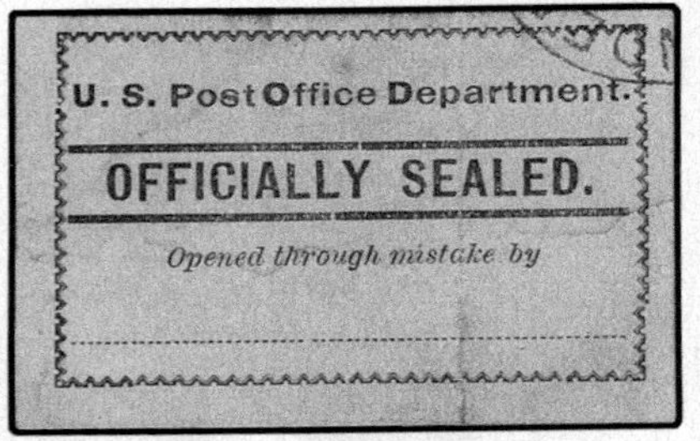

TSS4

LOX4	TSS4	**black,** *pink*		*900.*

No. LOX4 used is valued with minor flaws.

TSS5

LOX5	TSS5	**black**	*400.*	*400.*
LOX5A	TSS5	**black,** *pink*		*1,000.*

TSS6

LOX6	TSS6	**black**		—

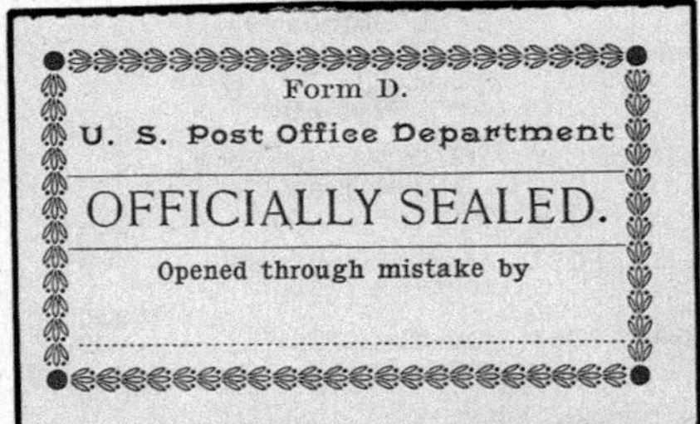

TSS7

Rouletted 9½ horizontally

LOX7	TSS7	**black**	*750.*	*750.*

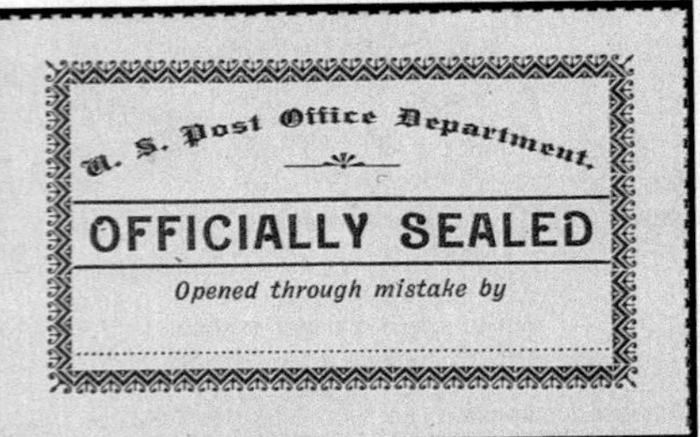

TSS8

Printed and distributed by Morrill Bros., P.O. Supply Printers, Fulton, N.Y., in panes of 4, two tete beche pairs.

Rouletted 11½, 12½, 16½ in black at top & side

LOX8	TSS8	**black,** rouletted 11½	100.00	100.00
		On cover		*750.00*
		On cover with No. OX5		*1,000.*
	a.	**black,** rouletted 12½	100.00	100.00
		On cover		*750.00*
	b.	**black,** rouletted 11½ by 12½	100.00	100.00
		On cover		*750.00*
	c.	**black,** rouletted 12½ by 11½	100.00	100.00
		On cover		*750.00*
		Sheet of 4, 1 each Nos. LOX8, LOX8a-LOX8c	*900.*	
	d.	**black,** rouletted 11½ and 12½ compound by 11½	250.00	150.00
	e.	**black,** rouletted 11½ and 12½ compound by 12½	250.00	150.00
		Sheet of 4, 1 each Nos. LOX8a, LOX8c, LOX8d-LOX8e	*1,250.*	
	f.	**black,** rouletted 16½	300.00	200.00
		On cover		*800.00*
	g.	**black,** rouletted 16½ on 3 sides		300.00

Gauge of rouletting on Nos. LOX8d and LOX8e transitions about one-quarter of way across top edge of seal. A sheet of 4 of No. LOX8f exists and is in the Luff reference collection of the Philatelic Foundation.

TSS9

Solid lines above and below “OFFICIALLY SEALED.”

Rouletted 12½, 16½ in black between

LOX9	TSS9	**black**	*350.00*	*350.00*
		On cover		*1,200.*

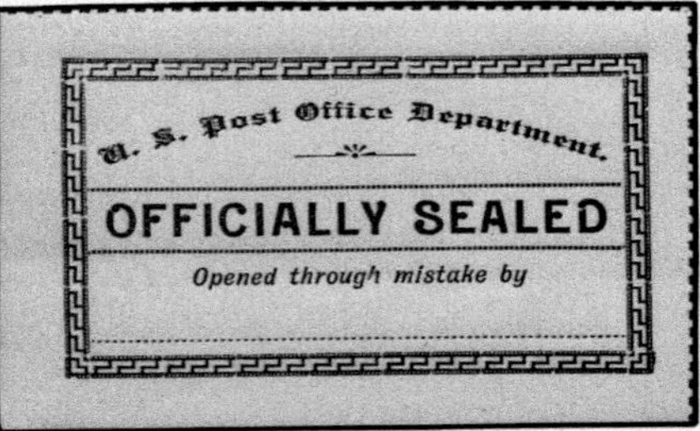

TSS10

Dotted lines above and below “OFFICIALLY SEALED.”

Rouletted 12½ in black

LOX10	TSS10	**black,** *pink*	*300.00*	*450.00*
	a.	Dot after “OFFICIALLY”	*700.00*	

Dyed examples of No. LOX11 are frequently misrepresented as No. LOX10.

Rouletted 11½, 12½ or 16½ in black

LOX11	TSS10	**black,** rouletted 12½ at top and side	2.00	75.00
		On cover		*900.00*
		Sheet of 4	15.00	
	a.	Double impression	*250.00*	
		Sheet of 4	—	
	b.	Double impression, one inverted	*250.00*	
	c.	Dot after “OFFICIALLY”	4.00	100.00
		On cover		*1,500.*
		Sheet of 4, one seal with dot	12.50	
	d.	**black,** rouletted 11½ at top or bottom	200.00	

Sheet of 2, both seals with dot *1,250.*

f. **black,** rouletted 11½ at top and side 100.00

Sheet of 4 *750.00*

g. **black,** rouletted 12½ by 11½ *500.00*

h. **black,** rouletted 16½ at top or bottom 200.00

Sheet of 2, both seals with dot *1,250.*

i. As "h," sheet of 2, tete beche, both seals with dot *1,250.*

j. **black,** rouletted 16½ at top and side 250.00

LOX11E TSS10 **blue,** rouletted 11½ at top or bottom *750.00*

TSS11

Printed and distributed by The Lemoyne Supply Co., Lemoyne, Pa.

LOX12 TSS11 **black** *200.00*

On cover *800.00*

Outer and inner framelines on No. LOX12 have closed mitered corners. Some examples have damaged top corners. Thick lines above and below "OFFICIALLY SEALED."

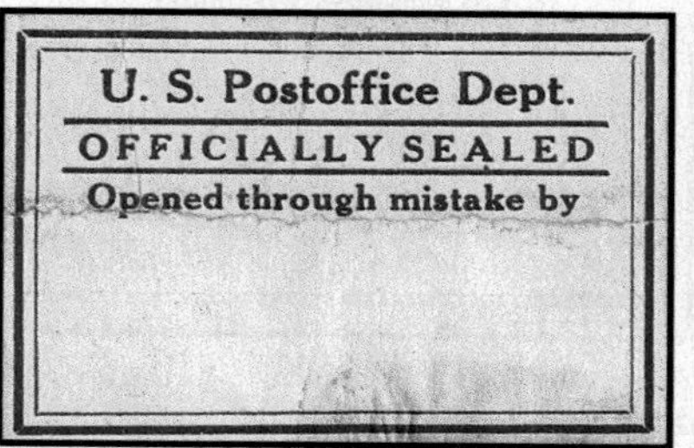

TSS11a

LOX12A TSS11a **blue** *1,250.*

Similar to No. LOX12, but with a different setting of the three lines of type. The frameline corners are mitered but slightly open at the top.

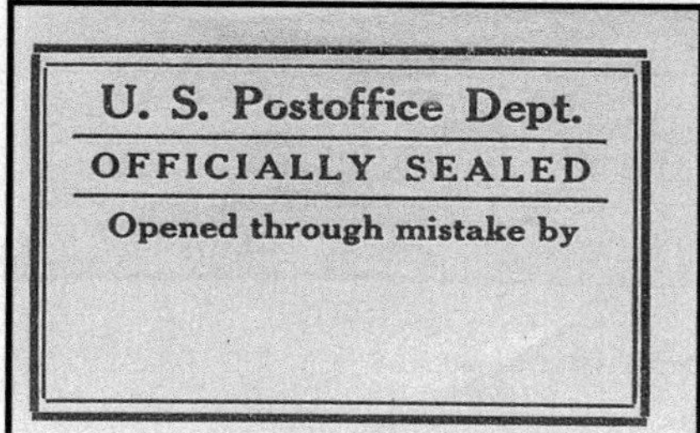

TSS11B

LOX13 TSS11B **blue** *500.00*

LOX13A TSS11B **black** *1,100.*

Outer and inner framelines on Nos. LOX13 and LOX13A have narrow spacing at left and right, and have corner of square-ended rules that are open at the corners. Thin lines above and below "OFFICIALLY SEALED."

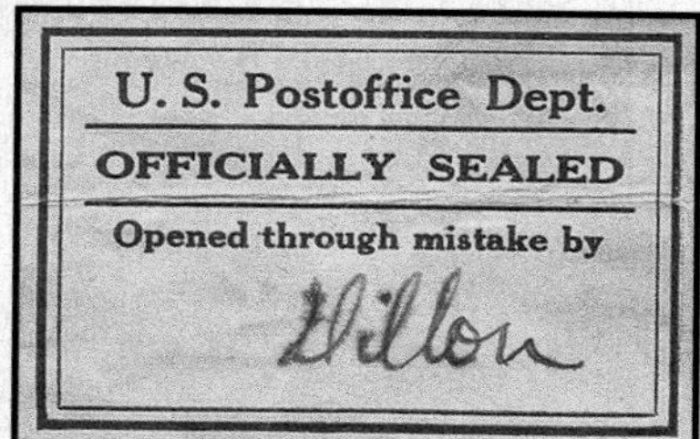

TSS12

LOX14 TSS12 **blue** *1,250.* *1,250.*

Outer and inner framelines on No. LOX14 have wide spacing, and the closed corners are mitered like Nos. LOX12 and LOX12A. "OFFICIALLY SEALED" set in a type face with flatter and wider letters and reduced letter spacing.

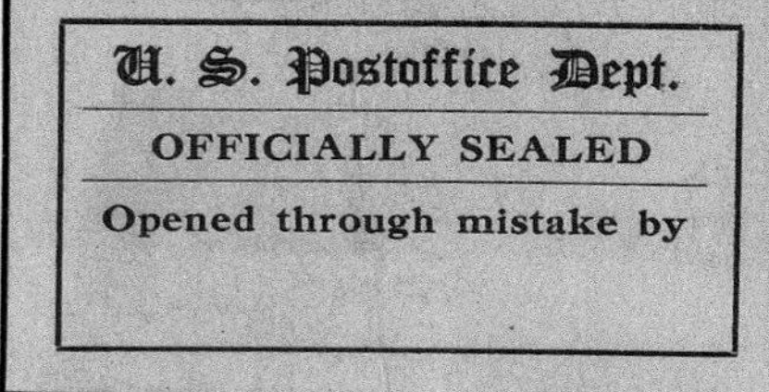

TSS13

LOX15 TSS13 **black** *800.00* *600.00*

On cover *1,250.*

No. LOX15 unused is valued with small faults and crease. See No. LOX29 for a similar design in blue.

TSS14

LOX16 TSS14 **blue** *1,100.* 650.00

No. LOX16 used is valued with usual crease, thin spots and small tear.

TSS15

Period after "Sealed"; 6mm between "Officially" and "Sealed".

LOX17 TSS15 **dark blue** 125.00 *225.00*

On cover *600.00*

a. Printed on both sides *750.00*

LOX18 TSS15 **black** 200.00 —

On cover *750.00*

Two types of No. LOX18: Type I (shown) has first "o" of "Post office" upside-down; Type II corrects the inversion. Both types found with approx. equal frequency.

TSS15A

No period after "Sealed"; 2mm between "Officially" and "Sealed".

LOX18A TSS15A **dark blue** 200.00 400.00

TSS16

LOX19 TSS16 **black** *500.00* *500.00*

TSS16A

LOX19A TSS16a **black** *2,000.*

Type I
TSS17

Type II — Bottom line in heavy type face. Period after "Office." Two different types or settings are known. The illustrated type has a dotted line above "BY" that does not show in the illustration.

LOX20 TSS17 **black,** *light green* (Type I), on cover —

LOX20A TSS17 **black,** *light green* (Type II) *1,500.*

No. LOX20A is valued with major thin at top center. It is unique.

TSS18

LOX21 TSS18 **black** *500.* —

TSS18a

LOX21A TSS18a **black** — *1,000.*
On cover *1,250.*

No. LOX21A unused is valued with crease and small faults.

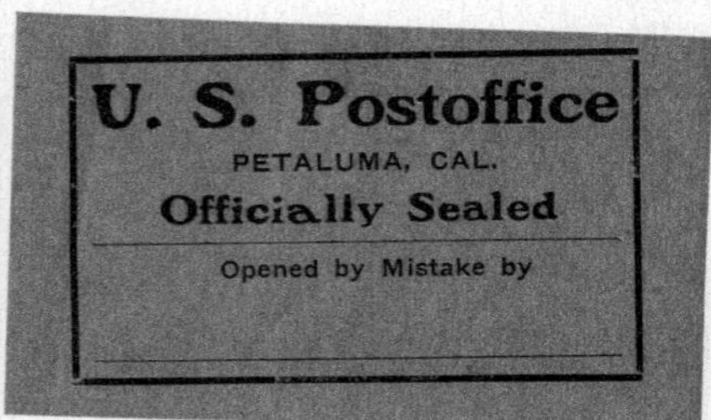

TSS19

LOX22 TSS19 **black,** *blue* *2,150.*

No. LOX22 is unique. It is creased and is valued as such.

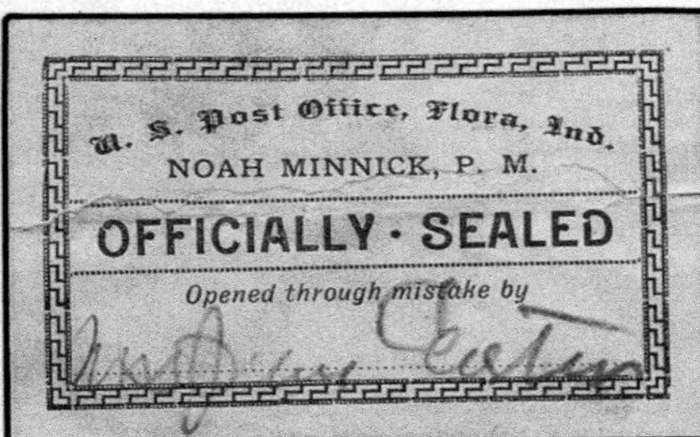

TSS20

LOX23 TSS20 **black** *1,000.*

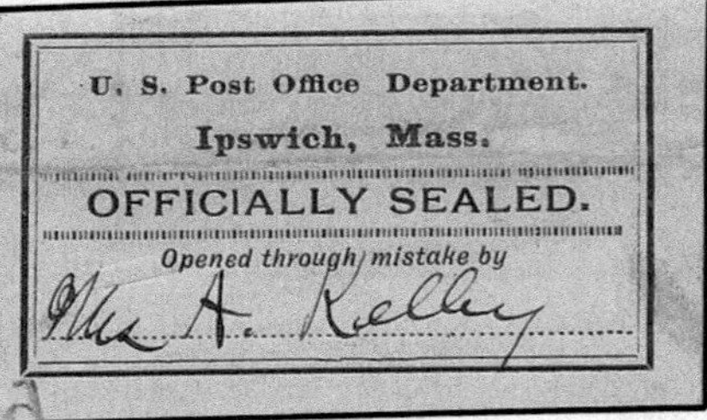

TSS21

LOX24 TSS21 **black,** on cover *2,000.*

TSS22

LOX25 TSS22 **black** *800.*

At least three examples of No. LOX25 exist. All have faults. Value is for the finest example.

TSS23

LOX26 TSS23 **black** *1,400.*

No. LOX26 used is valued with small fault. It is unique.

TSS24

LOX27 TSS24 **black,** *dark brown red* *1,350.*

No. LOX27 is valued with crease and small flaws.

TSS25

LOX28 TSS25 **black** *1,000.*
On cover *2,000.*

The on-cover seal shown was torn in half when the envelope was opened.

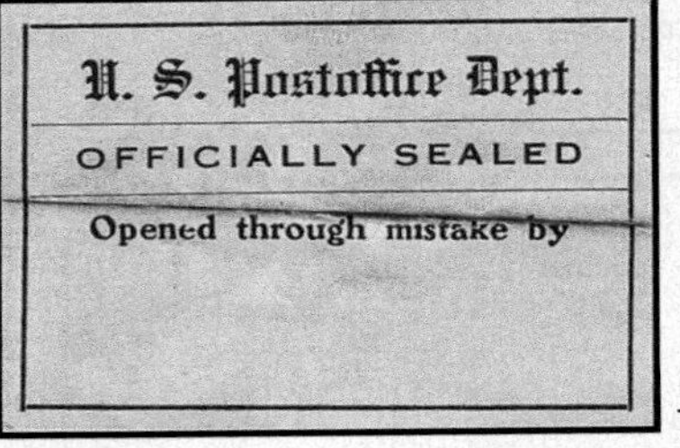

TSS26

LOX29 TSS26 **blue,** on cover *2,000.*

No. LOX29 is unique.

TSS27

LOX30 TSS27 **black,** pair on cover *3,000.*

No. LOX30 is unique. The seals were torn in half when the envelope was opened.

TSS28

LOX31 TSS28 **red,** *cream* *1,500.*

No. LOX31 is unique. It has a thin spot and crease and is valued as such.

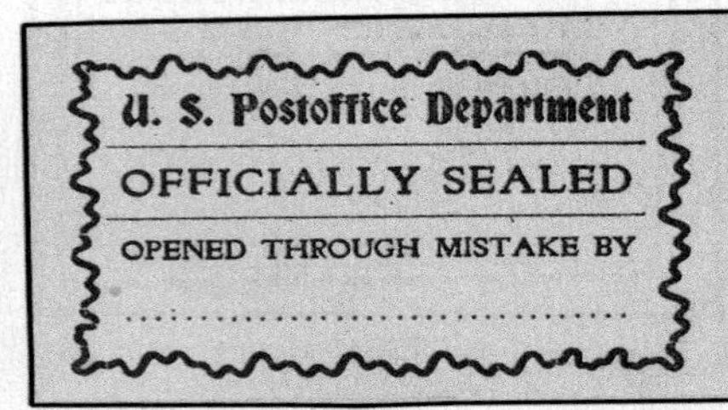

TSS29

LOX32 TSS29 **black** *900.*

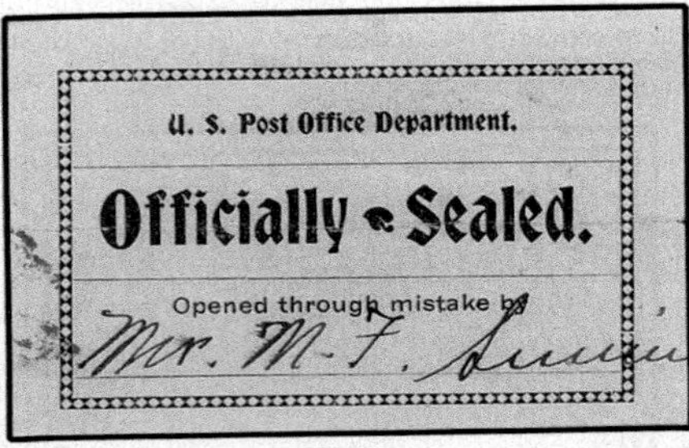

TSS30

LOX33 TSS30 **black** *1,500.*

TSS31

LOX34 TSS31 **red,** *rose* *800.*
On cover *1,100.*

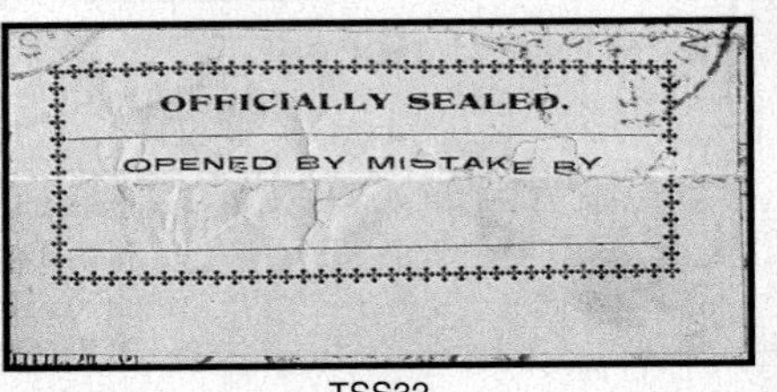

TSS32

LOX35 TSS32 **black,** on cover *1,100.*

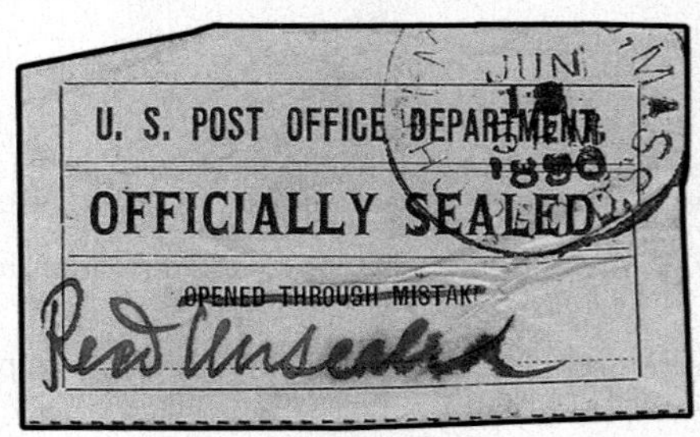

TSS33

Rouletted (at least one side)

LOX36 TSS33 **black** *750.*

TSS34

LOX37 TSS34 **green** *1,500.*

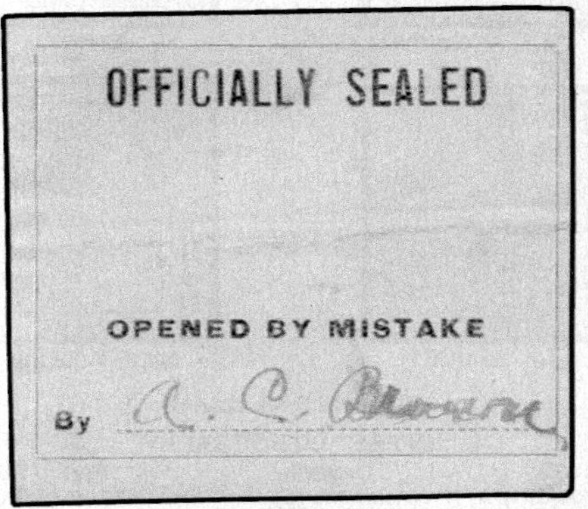

TSS35

LOX38 TSS35 **black,** *tan* *1,000.*

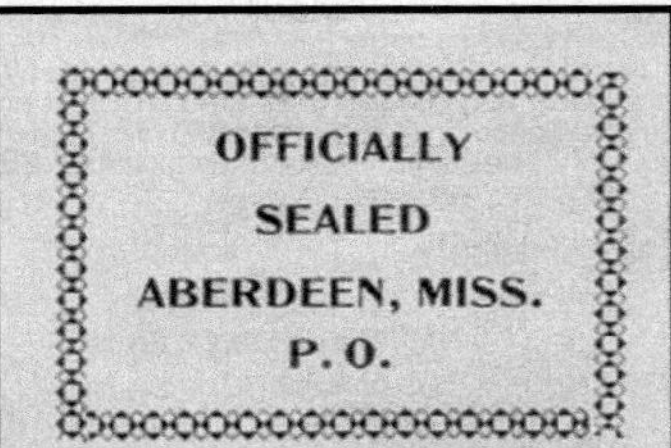

TSS36

LOX39 TSS36 **black,** *tan* *1,250.*

TSS37

LOX40 TSS37 **black,** *tan* *1,200.*

TSS38

LOX41 TSS38 **black** —

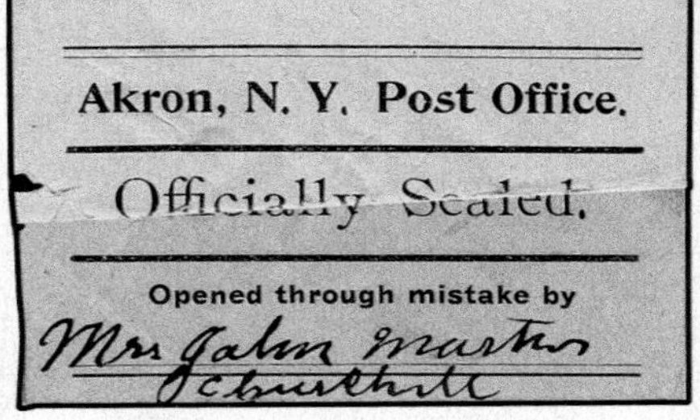

TSS39

LOX42 TSS39 **black,** on cover —

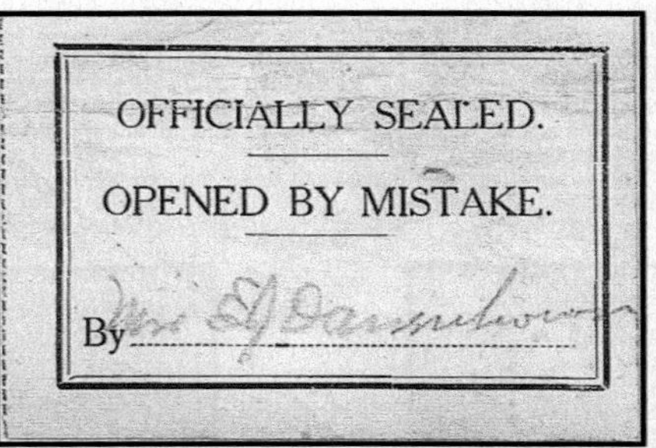

TSS40

LOX43 TSS40 **black** *1,100.*

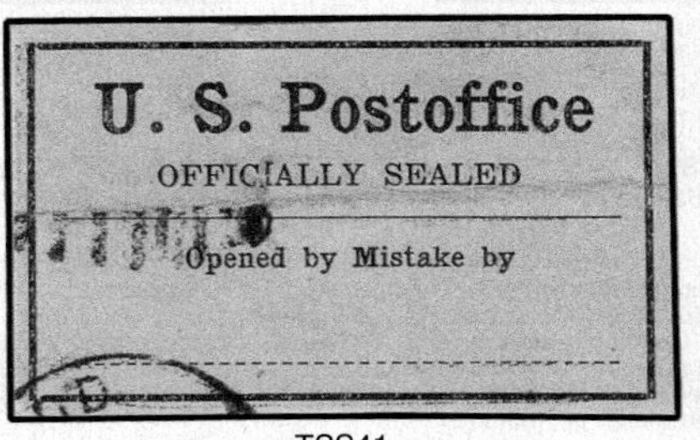

TSS41

LOX44 TSS41 **blue,** *yellow* *1,100.*

TSS42

LOX45 TSS42 **dark blue** *1,000.*

MINT SHEET BINDERS & PAGES

MINT SHEET BINDERS & PAGES

Keep those mint sheets intact in a handsome, 3-ring binder. Just like the cover album, the Mint Sheet album features the "D" ring mechanism on the right hand side of binder so you don't have to worry about damaging your stamps when turning the pages.

Item	Color	Retail	AA*
BINDERS			
MBRD	Red (Burgundy)	$21.99	**$17.99**
MBBL	Blue	$21.99	**$17.99**
MBGY	Gray	$21.99	**$17.99**
MBBK	Black	$21.99	**$17.99**
MINT SHEET PAGE PACKS			
MS1	Black (25 per pack)	$16.99	**$14.99**
SSMP3C	Clear (12 per pack)	$9.95	**$8.95**

BINDER & SHEET PACK COMBOS

Item	Binder Color	Retail	AA*
MBBK3PB	Black (with 25 Black pages)	$33.97	**$29.99**
MBBK3PC	Black (with 24 Clear pages)	$33.97	**$29.99**
MBBL3PB	Blue (with 25 Black pages)	$33.97	**$29.99**
MBBL3PC	Blue (with 24 Clear pages)	$33.97	**$29.99**
MBRD3PB	Burgundy (with 25 Black pages)	$33.97	**$29.99**
MBRD3PC	Burgundy (with 24 Clear pages)	$33.97	**$29.99**
MBGY3PB	Gray (with 25 Black pages)	$33.97	**$29.99**
MBGY3PC	Gray (with 24 Clear pages)	$33.97	**$29.99**

Available from your favorite stamp dealer or direct from:

www.AmosAdvantage.com

1-800-572-6885

Outside U.S. & Canada call (937) 498-0800

P.O. Box 4129, Sidney OH 45365

*AA prices apply to paid subscribers of Amos Media titles, or for orders placed online. Prices, terms and product availability subject to change. Shipping and handling rates apply. Taxes will apply in CA, OH, & IL.

POSTAL COUNTERFEITS

While possession of counterfeit stamps remains contrary to law, U.S. postal counterfeits can now be found in philatelic auctions, exhibits, dealer advertising, and current philatelic literature. Neither the Postal Inspection Service nor the U.S. Secret Service have intervened to confiscate these items.

Before purchasing counterfeits, collectors should obtain a certificate of authenticity (that the item in question is a genuine counterfeit) from a recognized expertizing service.

Values for counterfeits on cover are for contemporaneous usage.

The listings in this section follow standard Scott policy. A comparison of the attributes found in the counterfeit listing with those of the genuine stamp will enable collectors to distinguish the real from the spurious. The description field of each listing contains a letter rarity code keyed to the list below.

Numbers that survive in the hands of collectors:
A = Probably in the low thousands.
B = Probably 500-1500.
C = Probably in the low hundreds.
D = Probably equal to or fewer than 250.
E = Probably equal to or fewer than 100.
F = Probably equal to or fewer than 25.
G = 5 or fewer reported.
H = Unique in philatelic hands.
I = None known in philatelic hands.

Genuine No. 250

No. 250(CF1)

No. 250(CF2)

No. 250(CF3)

Thin coarsely woven white paper

COPPER ELECTROTYPE LITHO PLATE OF 5

1895 *Imperf.*

Size: 19-19.5x22.5-23mm

250(CF1) A88 2c **light rose carmine** *(E)* *225.00*
Full pane of 5 *(G)* 1,500.

Technically, No. 250(CF1) is "unfinished production," not yet perforated as the final product.

No. 250(CF1) has smooth, tending toward brownish gum. Much of the central oval is solid. While No. 250(CF2) is scarce, individual unused examples are not rare. Multiples are very difficult to find.

Genuine examples of No. 250 were printed by recess engraving on smooth white wove paper with smooth, yellowish gum, perf. 12.1. Image size: 19x22mm.

Perf. 11.8

250(CF2) A88 2c **rose carmine** *(C)* *75.00* *150.00*
On cover *(G)* *2,500.*
Strip of 5 *(G)* *800.00*
Block of 4 —

No. 250(CF2) has smooth, tending toward brownish gum. Much of the central oval is solid. Used examples are known on cover. While scarce, individual unused examples are not rare. Multiples are very difficult to find. Each "stamp" in the plate of 5 has minutely different characteristics.

Genuine examples of No. 250 were printed by recess engraving on smooth white wove paper with smooth, yellowish gum, perf. 12.1. Image size: 19x22mm.

Perf. 11.8

250(CF3) A88 2c **light rose carmine** *(C)* *75.00* *150.00*
On official notice from office of third assistant postmaster general to post offices, "stamp" with manuscript or printed "c" *950.00*
On official notice from office of post office inspectors to post offices, "stamp" with punched "c" *950.00*
On cover *(F)* *2,500.*
Strip of 5 *(G)* 750.00

No. 250(CF3) has glossy and whiter gum than Nos. 250(CF1) and 250(CF2).The April 10, 1895, letter used to notify postmasters, describes the color and impression of No.250(CF1) as "the lighter look of more open engraving, but under a magnifying glass, it will be found that this is attributable to the broken lines instead of continuous lines of the genuine steel engraving." Much of the central oval is solid. Used examples are known on cover. While scarce, individual unused examples are not rare. Multiples are very difficult to find. Each "stamp" in the plate of 5 has minutely different characteristics.

Many surviving examples have been marked "C" by postal authorities.

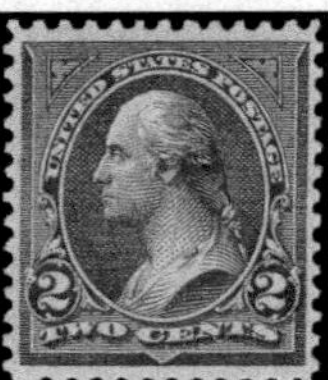
Genuine No. 252

No. 252(CF1)

Thin, see-through white paper

Size: 18.5-19x22mm

1896 **STONE LITHO PLATES** *Perf. 12.1*

252(CF1) A88 2c **pink** *(F)* *1,500.* *1,750.*
Block of 4 —

No. 252(CF1) has good detail, but a flat impression. The width of the oval at the mouth is 13mm. The vast majority of No. 252(CF1) were seized. Very few are known.

Genuine examples of No. 252 were printed by recess engraving on smooth white wove paper with smooth, light yellow gum, perf. 12.1. Image size: 19x22-22.5mm. The width of the oval at the mouth is 13.5mm.

Genuine No. 528

No. 528A(CF1)

Sheets of 10

Size: approximately 18.5-19x21.6mm

ENGRAVING USING A COPPER PLATE

1920 **Unwmk.** *Perf. 11.9*

528A(CF1) A140 2c **carmine** simulating offset Type VI, *(C)* *50.00* *75.00*
Block of 4 *350.00*
Complete cliche of 10 *1,000.*
On cover (Unused) *(G)* *1,000.*
On cover (Used) *(F)* *1,250.*

No. 528A(CF1) appears somewhat brighter than a genuine example and exhibits variable print quality, due to the lack of sufficient lines in the area of the head, especially above the ear. Gum and paper are slightly darker than a genuine example.

Genuine examples of No. 528A were printed by offset lithography and perforated 11. Inking and shading lines are consistently applied across the entire design. Size: 18.5x21.3mm.

Genuine No. 634

No. 634(CF1)

No. 634(CF2)

No. 634(CF3)

Size: 19.5mmx23mm

OFFSET LITHOGRAPHY

1932 **Unwmk.** *Perf. 11.65*

634(CF1) A157 2c **carmine** *(C)* *35.00* *35.00*
On cover (Used) *(F)* *2,000.*
Block of 4 *900.00*

No. 634(CF1) is a fairly crude counterfeit with a heavy, over-inked appearance. It does not have an oversized "S" in "Washington." The gum is a thick yellow brown or whitish. The interior oval is 13.5mm across.

Genuine examples of No. 634 were printed by recess engraving. Inking and shading lines are consistent across the entire design. Perforations gauge 11x10.5. There are horizontal gum breakers. The interior oval is 13.5mm across. Size: 19x22.3mm.

1935 or 1936 *Perf. 14.1*

Thick Paper

Size: 19x22.2mm

634(CF2) A157 2c **carmine** *(C)* *40.00* *40.00*
On cover *(F)* *900.00*
Block of 4 *180.00*
Full pane of 100 (no marginal markings) *2,250.*

1936 **Typo.** *Perf. 11.9*

Thick paper

Size: 18.6-18.8x22.2mm

634(CF3) A157 2c **carmine** *(A)* *20.00* *20.00*
On cover *(F)* *600.00*
Block of 4 *110.00*

All examples of Nos. 634(CF2) and 634(CF3) have an oversize "S" in "Washington." The interior oval is 13.0mm across, and the bust appears visually smaller. Color is flat and image is coarse compared to genuine examples. They appear flat with the inking of uneven quality. Paper and gum are slightly darker than the genuine, and the gum has no gum breakers. Exact quantities are not known, but these are the most often seen U.S. postal counterfeits, both on and off cover, until modern times.

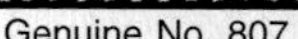
Genuine No. 807

No. 807(CF1)

No. 807(CF2)

1938 Unwmk. *Perf. 11.7*

OFFSET LITHOGRAPHY

Thin, yellowish paper

Size: 19x22.6mm

807(CF1) A279 3c **deep violet** *(C)* 40.00 30.00
On cover *(G)* 300.00
Block of 4 *(G)* 250.00

Imperf

807(CF2) A279 3c **deep violet,** pair *(B)* 80.00 75.00
Block of 4 *(F)* 160.00
Full pane of 100 (no marginal markings) *(G)* 2,500.

Nos. 807(CF1) and 807(CF2) are close to the genuine stamp in color, but the background lines are less distinct, often connected by splotches of ink. There are no horizontal gum breakers. Perforations on No. 807(CF1) range from irregular with small holes to clean and regular. Some examples of 807(CF2) are known with incomplete and inconsistent impressions.

Genuine examples of No. 807 were printed by recess engraving, and have distinct and finely engraved background lines. They are perforated 11x10.5, and have horizontal gum breakers.

Genuine No. 1030

No. 1030(CF1)

1954 Unwmk. *Ragged Perf. 9.9*

SURFACE PRINTED

Soft, low-quality white paper

Size: 19.5x22.25mm

1030(CF1) A477 ½c **light orange**
Pair, on cover *(G)* 4,000.

No. 1030(CF1) appears smaller than a genuine example because there is much more margin around the design. Printing is light and indistinct. For example, the lettering of "U.S. Postage" runs together. On-cover examples contain propaganda items from North Korea that were inserted into the South Korean post with a U.S. return address and forged U.S. cancellation, for delivery in Pusan. No off-cover examples are known. Only two covers are known. See No. 1049(CF1).

Genuine examples of No. 1030 are red orange, are perforated 11x10.5, size: 19x22.5mm. The features of the face are clear and each letter of text is distinct.

Genuine No. 1036

No. 1036(CF1)

1954 Unwmk. *Perf. 12.4*

PHOTOGRAPHIC OFFSET LITHOGRAPHY

Thin shiny paper

Size: 19.75x22mm

1036(CF1) A483 4c **red violet** *(E)* 75.00 50.00
P# block of 4 (P#26401LL) 1,000.
Pane of 100 (with marginal markings including P#26401 at LL) 3,500.

No. 1036(CF1) was produced from photographically prepared plates using coil stamps as the initial model; thus, images of the counterfeit are both shorter and wider than genuine examples. The color is brighter and the design less detailed than the genuine. For example, there is a white space between the shoulders and the background. There is less vertical space between the stamps and more horizontal space. There are no horizontal gum breakers. Perforation holes are very small.

Genuine examples of No. 1036 were printed by recess engraving. The background lines extend all the way to Lincoln's shoulders. Perforations are 11x10.5. Size: 19x22.5mm.

Genuine No. 1044

1954 Unwmk. *Imperf.*

PHOTOGRAPHIC OFFSET LITHOGRAPHY

Slightly yellowish paper

Size: unspecified

1044(CF1) A491 10c **rose lake** *(I)*

No. 1044(CF1) has been reported by the Postal Inspection Service, and one unfinished pane of 100 is in their files.
See *Linn's Stamp News* 10/15/90.

Genuine No. 1049

1954 Unwmk. *Ragged Perf. 9.9*

SURFACE PRINTED

Soft, low-quality white paper

Size: 19.5x22.25mm

1049(CF1) A496 30c **black,** pair on cover with pair of #1030(CF1) *(H)* 9,000.

No. 1049(CF1) appears smaller than genuine examples because there is much more margin around the design. Printing is light and indistinct. For example, the lettering of "U.S. Postage" runs together. The only known cover contains propaganda items from North Korea that was inserted into the South Korean post with a U.S. return address and forged U.S. cancellation for delivery in Pusan. No off-cover examples are known.

Genuine examples of No. 1049 are black, perforated 11x10.5. The features of the face are clear and each letter of text is distinct. Size: 19x22.5mm.

Genuine No. 1052

1954 Unwmk. *Imperf.*

PHOTOGRAPHIC OFFSET LITHOGRAPHY

Slightly yellowish paper

Size: unspecified

1052(CF1) A499 $1 **purple** *(I)*

No. 1052(CF1) has been reported by the Postal Inspection Service, and one unfinished pane of 100 is in their files.
See *Linn's Stamp News* 10/15/90.

Genuine No. 1213

Unknown printing method

1962 Unwmk. *Imperf.*

1213(CF1) A650 5c **dark blue grey**

No. 1213(CF1) is mentioned in the March 1982 issue of *The American Philatelist* as existing, but with no details given. No examples have been seen by the editors.

Genuine No. 1284

No. 1284(CF1)

1966 Unwmk. *Perf. 12.6*

PHOTOGRAPHIC OFFSET LITHOGRAPHY

Size: 22.25x19mm

1284(CF1) A716 6c **grey brown***(G)* 250.00
On cover *(H)* 750.00

No. 1284(CF1) is surface printed, and therefore has parts of the design missing their shading lines and lacking definition. The example on cover is a bottom margin single with thin simulated Electric Eye markings.

Genuine examples of No. 1284 were printed by recess engraving and exhibit a complete design. Perforations gauge 10.5x11. Size: 22.5x18.5mm.

Genuine No. 1287

No. 1287(CF1)

No. 1287(CF1A)

No. 1287(CF3)

1967 Unwmk. *Perf. 11.8*

PHOTOGRAPHIC OFFSET LITHOGRAPHY

Thick white or yellowish paper

Size: 19x22.5mm

Untagged

1287(CF1) A719 13c **red brown** *(B)* 50.00 35.00
Block of 4 225.00
Full pane of 100, no margins 6,000.

Imperf

1287(CF1A) A719 13c **red brown,** pair *(H)* 300.00
On cover, pair *(G)* 500.00

Nos. 1287(CF1) and 1287(CF1A) have a constant variety, a dot over the "c" of "13c." The portrait is closer to red brown than the brown of a genuine example.

No. 1287(CF1) has smooth dull gum without horizontal gum breakers. The portrait is poorly printed, with a wide vertical white line on left cheek. Most examples are poorly centered.

The No. 1287(CF1A pair is unique, without gum, and shows partial plate number 39293 (not a genuine plate number, thought here is a genuine number 29393).

1287(CF2) A719 13c **plum** *(C)* 60.00 *45.00*
On cover *500.00*

Perf. 12.5

1287(CF3) A719 13c **plum** *(C)* 50.00 *35.00*

Nos. 1287(CF2) and 1287(CF3) do not have the "dot over c" variety. They have a darker, more consistent print than No. 1287(CF1), with a thinner white vertical line on left cheek, and very light shading on forehead, upper lip, chin, and around the eyes.

Genuine examples of No. 1287 were printed by recess engraving, with all areas of the face having consistent shading. Color is dark brown. Perforations gauge 11x10.5.

Genuine No. 1288

1968 Unwmk. *Imperf., 12 x imperf., imperf. x 12*
PHOTOGRAPHICALLY PREPARED ALUMINUM OFFSET PLATE
Hard, thin paper with smooth surface

1288(CF1) A720 15c **red**, Type I *(I)*

No. 1288(CF1) has been reported by the Postal Inspection Service, and unfinished panes of 100 are in their files. The counterfeits are reported to be more red than the genuine magenta of No. 1288 and the design is muddy compared to genuine examples. No stamps are fully perforated and some are fully imperf.

See *Linn's Stamp News* 10/18/81.

Genuine examples of No. 1288 were printed by recess engraving, with full and consistent shading throughout the design. Perforations measure 11x10.5.

Genuine No. 1293

1968 Unwmk. *Perf. 11.8*
OFFSET

1293(CF1) A725 50c **rose** *(I)*

No. 1293(CF1) has been reported by the Postal Inspection Service, and unfinished panes of 100 are in their files. Design has less definition and detail than genuine examples.

See *Linn's Stamp News* 2/12/90.

Genuine examples of No. 1293 were printed by recess engraving, so shading is consistent and clear. Perforations gauge 11x10.5.

Geniune No. 1295

No. 1295(CF1)

1966 Offset Unwmk. *Perf. 11.1x10.7*
Medium White Fluorescent Paper, Untagged
Size: 18.7x22.4mm

1295(CF1) A727 $5 black *(H)* 500.00

No. 1295(CF1) lacks the detail and depth of the original. The perforations match well but appear to have been punched vertically. This counterfeit glows blue under both long wave and short wave ultraviolet light. The gum is white, with no gum breakers.

Genuine examples of No. 1295 were printed by recess engraving on untagged paper. There are tagged and untagged versions, the latter glowing green under short wave ultraviolet light. Perforations measure 11.1x10.6 and size is 18.9x22.5mm.

Genuine No. 1393

No. 1393(CF1)

No. 1393(CF2)

1970 Unwmk. *Perf. 10.3*
PHOTOGRAPHIC OFFSET LITHOGRAPHY
Thin white to yellowish paper
Size: 19x22.5mm

1393(CF1) A815 6c **blue black** *(B)* 150.00 *100.00*
On cover *900.00*

Perf. 10.9x10.5

1393(CF2) A815 6c **blue black** *(E)* 150.00 *100.00*
Zip block of 4 350.00
a. **dark slate blue** 200.00 *150.00*
P# block of 4 (P#31920 LR) 900.00

On Nos. 1393(CF1) and 1393(CF2) the shading at the top of the head and in the right ear is partially missing. "Eisenhower" and "USA" are filled in and appear solid. There are no horizontal gum breakers.

Genuine examples of No. 1393 were printed by recess engraving. "Eisenhower" and "USA" can be seen under magnification to be made up of closely spaced engraved diagonal lines. No. 1393 is dark blue grey, has gauge 11x10.5 perforations and has horizontal gum breakers.

Genuine No. 1394

No. 1394(CF1)

No. 1394(CF2)

1971 Unwmk. *Perf. 12.3*
PHOTOGRAPHIC OFFSET LITHOGRAPHY
Thin slightly darker paper
Size: 19.5x20.5mm

1394(CF1) A815a 8c **blk, red & bl grey** *(D)* 50.00 *40.00*

Imperf

1394(CF2) A815a 8c **blk, red & bl grey,** pair *(B)* 60.00 *40.00*
Mail Early block of 6 375.00
Zip block of 4 250.00
P# block of 4 (P# 33063LR) 550.00
Full pane of 100 (with normal marginal markings) 3,500.
Full pane of 100 (with normal marginal markings), horiz. perforations under rows 2, 5 and 8 *(H)* 5,000.

While Nos. 1394(CF1) and 1394(CF2) have higher quality images of Eisenhower than most counterfeits, the printing quality of "Eisenhower" is poor, being light and/or smeared. Black vignette, and blue and red lettering sometimes are misaligned. No. 1394(CF1) has smaller perf holes than genuine examples.

Genuine examples of No. 1394 were printed by recess engraving. Colors are almost always perfectly aligned, and "Eisenhower" and "USA" are clearly and cleanly printed. Perforations gauge 11.

Genuine No. 1474

No. 1474(CF1)

1972 Offset Untagged Unwmk. *Perf. 11.8*
Thin, White Paper
Size: 39x29mm

1474(CF1) A888 8c **multicolored** *(H)*
On cover *750.00*

No. 1474(CF1) has the green a good match with the issued stamp, but the brown in the No. 1 design lacks definition and is a darker brown. Paper is whiter, and the ink glows white under short wave ultraviolet light. Known only on cover together with a genuine 29c stamp to make up the 2003 37c rate. Genuine examples of No. 1474 are lithographed (green) and engraved (brown and black). They are perf. 11.1 and tagged, glowing yellow green under short wave ultraviolet light. Size is 36.5x28mm.

Genuine No. 1509

No. 1509(CF2)

1973 Unwmk. *Perf. 12*
PHOTOGRAPHIC OFFSET LITHOGRAPHY
Untagged

1509(CF1) A928 10c **red & bright blue** 40.00

According to press reports, *Linn's Stamp News* 2/12/90, No. 1509(CF1) shares many of the same characteristics as No. 1509(CF2), but has larger perforation holes and poor reproduction of "United States," which is blotchy with excess ink. Although many were used on mail, the bulk were seized by the Postal Inspection Service. The editors have not seen an example of No. 1509(CF1).

Perf. 12.5
Poor quality medium fluorescent white paper

1509(CF2) A928 10c **red & brt blue** *(D)*

No. 1509(CF2) has small-hole, poorly applied line perforations that were applied from the back. Color is bright blue rather than dark blue, and the stars in the field of stars in the left part of the flag are too large and run into one another or are partially filled by excess ink. Reproduces the vertical joint line characteristic of Huck press printing. Gum is shiny white without horizontal gum breakers.

Genuine examples of No. 1509 were printed by recess engraving. They have well defined stars in the left side flag. They are block tagged and bulls-eye perforated 11x10.5. Gum is shiny yellowish with horizontal gum breakers.

Genuine No. 1510

No. 1510(CF1)

No. 1510(CF4)

1973 Unwmk. *Imperf.*

PHOTOGRAPHIC OFFSET LITHOGRAPHY

Thin white paper, gummed

Size: 19x22.5mm

Untagged

1510(CF1) A924 10c **flat grey blue** *(D)* *75.00*

No. 1510(CF1) is a lower right margin block of 8, with traces of what may be horizotal perf 12 perforations at right. It has the least definition in shading lines present of any of the 1510(CF) counterfeits.

Thick white paper, gummed

1510(CF2) A924 10c **flat grey blue** *(E)* *100.00*

No. 1510(CF2) is missing many of the shading lines in the Jefferson Memorial, especially in the triangular area above the entrance.

Thin white paper, gummed

1510(CF3) A924 10c **deep blue** *(E)* *100.00*

No. 1510(CF3) has a deep blue color and the best defined shading lines of all the No. 1510(CF) imperfs.

Perf. 12.5

Heavy paper

1510(CF4) A924 10c **blue** *(H)* *75.00*

Large dots form background with some appearing in the text and in the right margin on No. 1510(CF4), unlike Nos. 1510(CF1)-1510(CF3). Size: 19.7x22.7mm.

Genuine examples of No. 1510 were printed by recess engraving, and are perforated 11x10.5. They are tagged, and have horizontal gum breakers. They are a darker blue than any 1510(CF).

Genuine No. 1595

No. 1595(CF1)

1975 Unwmk. *Imperf.*

PHOTOGRAPHIC OFFSET LITHOGRAPHY

Off white medium thickness paper

Size: 19x22mm

Untagged

1595(CF1) A998 13c **brown** *(B)* *50.00 45.00*
On cover *400.00*
Block of 4 *225.00*

No. 1595(CF1) reproduces the 13c Liberty Bell design issued in booklet and coil forms only; thus there are straight edges on at least one side of all genuine examples. The counterfeit examples were all produced and sold in strips and sheets that have stamps perforated on all four sides. The bottom of the bell clapper is open, making it look like an "A."

This is the so-called "Boston" counterfeit, printed in sheets of 400, four panes of 100 stamps each.

Genuine No. 1894

1981 Unwmk. *Crude Perf. 9*

PHOTOGRAPHIC OFFSET LITHOGRAPHY

Untagged

1894(CF1) A1281 20c **blk, dk bl & red** *(G)* *100.00*

Imperf

1894(CF2) A1281 20c **blk, dk blue & red** *(I)*

Nos. 1894(CF1) and 1894(CF2) have a gap between the field of stars and the short red stripes. The design has a coarse appearance, especially in the Supreme Court building, and the blue is brighter than that of genuine examples. Nos. 1894(CF1) and 1894(CF2) were written up in the philatelic press, *Linn's Stamp News* 7/4/83, noting that 250,000 perforated examples had been used on mailings, but the editors have not seen an example of either. No. 1894(CF2) exists only in the files of the Postal Inspection Service.

Genuine examples of No. 1894 were printed by recess engraving on white gummed paper with light vertical gum breakers. Authentic stamps do not have a large gap between the field of stars and the short stripes, although freak prints of No. 1894 do exist with this variety. Perforations gauge 11.

Genuine No. 1946

No. 1946(CF1)

1981 Unwmk. *Perf. 12.5*

PHOTOGRAPHIC OFFSET LITHOGRAPHY

Off white thin paper

Size: 20x21.5mm

Untagged

1946(CF1) A1332 (20c) **brown,** Pane of 100 *(H) 2,500.*

Pane of 100 No. 1946(CF1) has marginal markings with the exception of P#; stamps are lined through horizontally. Surface printed on flat-gummed paper with no gloss. Color is flat. Perforations are irregularly spaced.

Genuine examples of No. 1946 were printed by photogravure on white, tagged paper with a light gloss. Perforations gauge 11x10.5. Size: 20x22.75mm.

Genuine No. 2111

1985 Unwmk. *Perf. Unknown*

PHOTOGRAPHIC OFFSET LITHOGRAPHY

Untagged

2111(CF1) A1496 (22c) **gray green** *(I)*

Imperf

2111(CF2) A1496 (22c) **gray green** *(I)*

Discovery of Nos. 2111(CF1) and 2111(CF2) was announced by local law enforcement in Lubbock, Texas, which turned the issues over to the Postal Inspection Service. Images of full panes were subsequently released by the service. They appear to be of better than average quality, but no details are available. See *Linn's Stamp News* 4/23/90.

Genuine examples of No. 2111 were produced by photogravure printing in green, with perfs that gauge 11. Stamps have a yellowish gum, and are tagged. Size: 18x20.5mm.

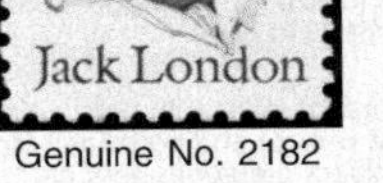

Genuine No. 2182

No. 2182(CF1)

1986 Unwmk. *Crude Perf. 11.25*

PHOTOGRAPHIC OFFSET LITHOGRAPHY

Glossy label-style paper

Untagged

2182(CF1) A1564 25c **blue**
On cover *(G)* *300.00*

Design of No. 2182(CF1) is less detailed and more sketchy than genuine examples of No. 2182 and is composed of a dot pattern, with stripped-in solid lettering. Lighter blue than genuine examples. All examples reported to date are on glossy label-type paper, untagged and on cover.There might have been more than one attempt to counterfeit this stamp.

Genuine examples of No. 2182 were printed by recess engraving on paper with large block tagging. Color is green blue, perforations gauge 11. Size: 18x20.25mm.

Genuine No. 2531

No. 2531(CF1)

1991 UNKOWN PRINTING METHOD Unwmk.

Rouletted 9.5 X 9.25 to simulate perforations

Ungummed white paper with yellowish surface tint

Untagged

2531(CF1) A1883 29c **red, bl & blk** *(B)* *40.00 25.00*
On cover *(F)* *200.00*
Strip of 6 *250.00*

Greenish surfaced paper

2531(CF2) A1883 29c **red, bl & blk** *(B)* *40.00 25.00*
Strip of 6 *250.00*

Nos. 2531(CF1) and 2531(CF2) were printed in six-stamp strips on ungummed paper in Taiwan for use with a paper weight. Some migrated to the U.S. and were sold in 1993. The presence of "29c" violated USPS regulations and encouraged fraudulent use. Top of flag poles and shaded areas of flag are made up of patterns of large dots. There are more areas of shading in the flag than on genuine examples of No. 2531.

A press report in *Stamp Collector* 7/17/93, stated that there was also a domestic counterfeiting operation that produced No. 2531(CF2). Though attempts were made to use them in the mails, the great majority were seized by the Postal Inspection Service. There has been no additional information released that would help identify No. 2531(CF2).

Genuine examples of No. 2531 were printed by photogravure on tagged white paper with no tint on the face of the stamps. The top of the flag pole is made up of fine dots in the shape of a triangle. Perforations gauge 11.

Genuine No. 2938

1995 Unwmk. *Perf. Unknown*

PHOTOGRAPHIC OFFSET LITHOGRAPHY

Untagged

2938(CF1) A2253 46c **carmine** *(I)*

No. 2938(CF1) has been reported by the Postal Inspection Service, which holds unfinished panes in their files. Design has less definition and detail than authentic examples of No. 2938. See *Stamp Collector* 6/22/98.

Genuine examples of No. 2938 were printed by recess engraving on white pre-phosphored paper with embedded tagging. Shading is consistent and clear. Perforations gauge 11. Size: 18.5x21mm.

Genuine No. 3281

No. 3281(CF1)

1999 Unwmk. *Imperf.*

OFFSET LITHOGRAPHY

Heavy slick ungummed paper

Untagged

Coil Stamp Size:18x21mm

3281(CF1) A2540 33c **multicolored,** pair, diagonal black line through "33USA" *(C)* *50.00*

3281(CF2) A2540 33c **multicolored,** pair, without black diagonal line through "33USA" *50.00*

The date and background of No. 3281(CF1) are composed of widely spaced dots with an obvious dot pattern. Image size is the same as the genuine No. 3281. There is no backing paper as there is with genuine self-adhesive stamps. These may have been produced for use in refrigerator magnets sold as an ancillary product by the Postal Service.

Genuine examples of No. 3281 were photogravure-printed, are tagged, die cut 9.8 vertically and have a solid "1999" year date. They are self-adhesive on backing paper.

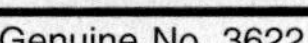
Genuine No. 3622

No. 3622(CF1)

2002 Unwmk. ***Serpentine Die Cut 10 Vert.***

OFFSET LITHOGRAPHY

Thin, shiny paper on thin backing

Self-Adhesive

Untagged

Coil Stamp Size:18x21mm

3622(CF1) A2807 (37c) **multicolored** *(A)* 40.00 30.00
On cover *(D)* 45.00

No. 3622(CF1) is dated "2003" instead of the correct "2002." It has a strong dot pattern that includes black dots in both red and white stripes and in the stars. The red is brighter than in genuine examples and there is a yellowish tint to the white stripes. Sold in rolls of 100 with no plate number. Die cut and image size match genuine examples.

3622(CF2) A2807 (37c) **multicolored** *(A)* 40.00 30.00
On cover *(D)* 45.00

No. 3622(CF2) is similar to No. 3622(CF1), but it is die cut 9.6. It has a bluish tint under longwave and shortwave UV light.

Genuine examples of No. 3622 were photogravure printed on thicker paper and dated "2002." The stripes in the flag are white and there are no black dots in the red and white stripes or the stars.

Genuine No. 3635

No. 3635(CF1)

Serpentine Die Cut 11.3 on 2, 3, or 4 Sides

2002 Unwmk.

OFFSET LITHOGRAPHY

Self-Adhesive

Untagged

Booklet Stamps Size 18.25x21mm

3635(CF1) A2812 37c **multicolored** *(A)* *15.00 30.00*
On cover *(D)* *75.00*
Booklet Pane of 20 *(C)* *350.00*

No. 3635(CF1) lacks microprinting and has shading in the white stripes that has an obvious pattern of dots, giving them a light yellow tint. The paper is slightly darker than genuine examples . All panes seen to date have plate number B5555. Die cut gauge and pattern and image size are similar to genuine examples. Wavy die cuts extend through backing so individual stamps can be separated from the pane with backing intact.

Genuine examples of No. 3635 are yellow-green tagged, have "USPS" microprinted in the top red flag stripe, and are printed by photogravure. The shading in the white stripes looks like the dimpled surface of a paper towel rather than individual dots. Wavy die cuts do not extend through the backing paper.

Genuine No. 3981

No. 3981(CF1)

2006 Unwmk. ***Serpentine Die Cut 9.4 Vert.***

OFFSET LITHOGRAPHY

Untagged

Self-Adhesive

Thin, yellowish slick paper, back and front

Coil Stamps Size 18.5x21mm

3981(CF1) A3040 39c **multicolored** *(B)* *20.00 30.00*

Die Cut 9.5 Vert.

3981(CF2) A3040 39c **multicolored** *(B)* *20.00 30.00*

Nos. 3981(CF1) and 3981(CF2) have "2006" dates composed of dots and the microprinted "USPS" is only a dark patch, not lettering. The dots of the design are indistinct. While untagged, No. 3981(CF1) gives a medium hi-brite bluish violet-white response under shortwave UV, and No. 3981(CF2) exhibits an even higher level of hi-brite response.

Genuine examples of No. 3981 were photogravure printed, die cut 9.4 and have yellow-green tagging. The dots are distinct and there is a distinct microprinted "USPS" in the top red stripe next to the blue field of stars.

Genuine No. 3982

No. 3982(CF1)

2006 Unwmk. ***Serpentine Die Cut 10.5 Vert.***

OFFSET LITHOGRAPHY

Untagged

Self-Adhesive

Thick, slick paper on backing

Coil Stamp Size 19x20.5mm

3982(CF1) A3040 39c **multicolored** *(B)* 20.00 *30.00*

No. 3982(CF1) is slightly smaller than genuine examples, has a solid "2006" date and does not react under UV light. The blue sky is a grid pattern with the white background showing through. The inking pattern is distinct. The die cut matches genuine examples.

3982(CF2) A3040 39c **multicolored** 20.00 *30.00*

No. 3982(CF2) has a design size of 17.4x20mm. It has a fuzzy "2006" year date, and the "39USA" is thinner than on the genuine stamp. It does not react under UV light. It has a crude die cut of 10.5.

3982(CF3) A3040 39c **multicolored** 20.00 *30.00*

No. 3982(CF3) is a very good quality counterfeit. The design is 18x20.8mm, and the die cut is 10.2. It shows bluish under shortwave UV light. Under longwave UV light, the paper is hibrite.

3982(CF4) A3040 39c **multicolored** 20.00 *30.00*

No. 3982(CF4) is similar to No. 3982(CF2). The design is 17.3x19.8mm, and the die cut is a very crude 10.6. It has a greenish tint under shortwave UV light, and is hibrite under longwave UV light.

Genuine examples of No. 3982 were photogravure printed with yellow-green tagging and an image size of 19.5x21.5mm. The "2006" date is composed of dots. The blue sky is solid and the inking pattern is less distinct.

Genuine No. 4125

No. 4125(CF1)

2007 Unwmk. ***Irregular Die Cut***

OFFSET LITHOGRAPHY

Untagged

Self-Adhesive

Glossy surface paper

Booklet Stamps

4125(CF1) A3148 (41c) **multicolored** *(A)* 20.00 *30.00*
Booklet pane of 20, P#V11111 *(D)* *450.00*

No. 4125(CF1) has die cuts that are irregular with no consistent gauge. Transitions at junction of vertical and horizontal die cuts are also irregular and do not bisect the separators as on genuine examples. No. 4125(CF1) is untagged, but gives a bright bluish-violet response to shortwave UV light. All booklets have plate number V11111.

4125(CF2) A3148 (41c) **multicolored** 20.00 *30.00*

No. 4125(CF2) has crude lettering and a large brown "2009" year date. Die cutting is 9.5x9.3. No microprinting. The paper is dead under longwave and shortwave UV light.

4125(CF3) A3148 (41c) **multicolored** — *50.00*

No. 4125(CF3) is imperforate and has no microprinting. It has a crude small reddish brown "2009" year date. The paper has a bluish tint under shortwave UV light, and it shows hibrite under longwave UV light.

Genuine examples of No. 4125 were photogravure printed on matte paper. Die cut is 11.2x10.7. Where horizontal and vertical die cuts meet, they bisect each other. Tagging is yellow-green.

Genuine No. 4133

No. 4133(CF1)

2007 Unwmk. ***Serpentine Die Cut 11 Vert.***

OFFSET LITHOGRAPHY

Untagged

Self-Adhesive

Thin, smooth-backed paper

Coil Stamps

4133(CF1) A3149 (41c) **multicolored** *(A)* *20.00 30.00*

Among the features that distinguish Nos. 4133(CF1)-4133(CF6) from genuine examples are the short lanyard connecting the UL corner of the flag to the halyard and the shading in the flag pole.

On No. 4133(CF1) the laynard is composed of four straight dots. The red stripes of the flag are a grid of red on white. The tan background has a coarse litho dot overlay. The center of the flag pole is unshaded.

4133(CF2) A3149 (41c) **multicolored** *(A)* *20.00 30.00*

On No. 4133(CF2) the laynard is composed of three straight dots. The red stripes of the flag are solid with an overlay of tiny black dots. The yellowish background has a fine litho dot overlay. The flag pole has a vertical row of tiny shading dots in the center of the pole.

4133(CF3) A3149 (41c) **multicolored** *(A)* *20.00 30.00*

On No. 4133(CF3) the laynard is composed of a straight double line of four dots over three dots. The red stripes of the flag are solid with an overlay sprinkling of tiny black dots. The yellowish background has a fine litho dot pattern with large dots interspersed with tiny ones. The flag pole has one unshaded vertical stripe.

4133(CF4) A3149 (41c) **multicolored** *(A)* *20.00 30.00*

On No. 4133(CF4) the laynard is composed of a straight line of four dots. The red stripes of the flag are a coarse grid of red on white. The yellowish background has a coarse dot pattern. The flag pole has a vertical row of tiny shading dots in the center of the pole.

4133(CF5) A3149 (41c) **multicolored** *(A)* *20.00 30.00*

On No. 4133(CF5) the laynard is composed of a straight double line of four dots, with a gap between dots two and three, over three dots. The red stripes of the flag are solid overlaid with a few tiny black dots. The background has a pinkish tint arising from a medium dot pattern that includes a grid of red dots. The flag pole is completely shaded.

4133(CF6) A3149 (41c) **multicolored** *(A)* *20.00 30.00*

On No. 4133(CF6) the laynard is kinked. The red stripes of the flag are solid overlaid with a few tiny black dots. The background has fine dot pattern. The flag pole is completely shaded.

Nos. 4133(CF1)-4133(CF6) were produced on paper that gives a blue-white response under shortwave UV light. The printing of the flag is somewhat embossed into the paper, which shows from the back. Die cutting matches genuine examples. The background is a solid yellow-tan, but overlaid with dots in a pattern that ranges from coarse with large dots to medium to fine with large dots surrounded by tiny ones.

Genuine examples of No. 4133 are tagged yellow-green. The red stripes and tan background are solid. The lanyard is a double line of tiny dots. Shading in the flag pole is uniform both in size of dots and coverage over the pole.

Genuine No. 4187

No. 4187(CF1)

2007 Unwmk. ***Serpentine Die Cut 10.2 Vert.***

OFFSET LITHOGRAPHY

Untagged

Self-Adhesive

Plasticized paper with shiny back

Coil Stamps

4187(CF1) A3184 41c **multicolored** *(A)* *20.00 30.00*

On No. 4187(CF1) the flag laynard is composed of a double row of alternating dots. The right edge of the flag pole is composed of two columns of alternating dots.

4187(CF2) A3187 41c **multicolored** *(A)* *20.00 30.00*

On No. 4187(CF2) the laynard is like No. 4187(CF1). The right side of the flag pole is composed of three columns of alternating dots.

4187(CF3) A3184 41c **multicolored** *(A)* *20.00 30.00*

On No. 4187(CF3) the laynard is composed of a single row of dots. The left edge of the flag pole is composed of three columns of alternating dots.

4187(CF4) A3184 41c **multicolored** *(A)* *20.00 30.00*

On No. 4187(CF4) the laynard is like No. 4187(CF3). The left edge of the flag pole is composed of four rows of alternating dots.

4187(CF5) A3184 41c **multicolored** *(A)* *20.00 30.00*

On No. 4187(CF5) the laynard is composed of a single row of dots linked by an extra dot in the white flag margin to the left of the blue field. The left edge of the flag pole has three rows of alternating dots.

Nos. 4187(CF1)-4187(CF5) have a background of fine dots, and no microprinting. The "41USA" is weakly formed by light blue dots. All give off a blue-white glow under shortwave uv light.

4187(CF6) A3184 41c **multicolored** *(A)* *20.00 30.00*

On No. 4187(CF6) the background is a coarse, more pronounced grid of dots. The red stripes have a distinct grid of blue dots. "41USA" is darker and stronger than on Nos. 4187(CF1)-4187(CF5).

4187(CF7) A3184 41c **multicolored** *(A)* 20.00 *30.00*

No. 4187(CF7) has a lanyard made up of sequential double black dots. The red stripes are solid with a diagonal white-dot pattern. The union is covered with a pattern of red and white dots in the background. The tan background is composed of a coarse dot overlay. The denomination is a light blue. The flag pole is unshaded and is made up of a double column of sequential triple black dots. Die cuts are uneven and approximately 10.3.

4187(CF8) A3184 41c **multicolored** *(A)* 20.00 *30.00*

On No. 4187(CF8), the flag pole, lanyard and color of the denomination and tan background are the same as on No. 4187(CF7), but the red stripes are solid with a diagonal black-dot pattern. The union is covered with a pattern of large red dots in the background. Die cuts are uneven and approximately 10.4.

Genuine examples of No. 4187 are tagged pale green, die cut 11 and have "41USA" printed in solid silver. The background is a solid tan.

Genuine No. 4228

Genuine No. 4229

Genuine No. 4230

Genuine No. 4231

2008 Unwmk. ***Perf. 9.5 Vert.***

OFFSET LITHOGRAPHY

Untagged

Coil Stamps

4228(CF1) A3214 42c **multicolored** *(B)* *30.00 40.00*
4229(CF1) A3215 42c **multicolored** *(B)* *30.00 40.00*
4230(CF1) A3216 42c **multicolored** *(B)* *30.00 40.00*
4231(CF1) A3217 42c **multicolored** *(B)* *30.00 40.00*

Nos. 4228(CF1)-4231(CF1) are known to exist but few specific details are available. The color design size is larger than genuine examples, but the date is not as distinct and the shading dots in the "42" are missing. The perfs match those of genuine examples.

Genuine examples of Nos. 4228-4231 were printed by photogravure.

Genuine No. 4235

No. 4235(CF1)

2008 Unwmk. ***Serpentine Die Cut 9.5 Vert.***

OFFSET LITHOGRAPHY

Untagged

Self-Adhesive

Coil Stamps Size: 17.5x21.25mm

4232(CF1) A3214 42c **multicolored** *(B)* *30.00 40.00*
4233(CF1) A3215 42c **multicolored** *(B)* *30.00 40.00*
4234(CF1) A3216 42c **multicolored** *(B)* *30.00 40.00*
4235(CF1) A3217 42c **multicolored** *(B)* *30.00 40.00*

Nos. 4232(CF1)-4235(CF1) are offset printed. They are taller than genuine examples because of larger top and bottom margins. The shading of the red strips lack the pattern of genuine examples. There is a backdrop of blue and red dots behind the "2008." The date is also closer to the design than on genuine examples.

4235(CF2) A3217 42c **multicolored** *(B)* 30.00 *40.00*

No. 4235(CF2) is similar to No. 4235(CF1), but the year date is lower than either No. 4235(CF1) or the genuine stamp. There are large yellow dots on the design and in the margins.

Genuine examples of Nos. 4232-4325 were printed by lithograph, have a clean, crisp "2008" and darker red stripes than Nos. 4232(CF1)-4235(CF1).

Genuine No. 4390

No. 4390(CF1)

2009 Unwmk. ***Serpentine Die Cut 11¼x10¾***

OFFSET LITHOGRAPHY

Untagged

Self-Adhesive

4390(CF1) A2891 44c **multicolored** 20.00 *30.00*

On No. 4390(CF1), the die cuts are crude and uneven at 11.3x11.3. The microprinting is a blob. Crude lettering that is mostly black but with red, yellow and blue dots. Paper is hibrite under longwave UV light.

Genuine No. 4392

No. 4392(CF1)

2009 Unwmk. ***Serpentine Die Cut 11 Vert.***

OFFSET LITHOGRAPHY

Untagged

Self-Adhesive

Glossy paper

Coil Stamps Size: 18x21mm

4392(CF1) A3342 44c **multicolored** *(A)* *20.00 30.00*

On No. 4392(CF1), the red stripes are a bright red. There is a coarse litho dot pattern in an obvious grid. The stars have a weak grid of multicolored dots.The numerals in the date are composed of dots, and there is no microprinting. Lettering of "USA" is coarsely outlined. While untagged, the paper on Nos. 4392(CF1)-4392(CF4) does respond purplish-white under shortwave uv light.

4392(CF2) A3342 44c **multicolored** *(A)* *20.00 30.00*

The red stripes on No. 4392(CF2) are darker than those on No. 4392(CF1), coming close to matching those on genuine examples. The date is less distinct than on No. 4239(CF1) and appears to be narrower. There is no microprinting. Lettering of "USA" is roughly edged with overlying blue dots.

4392(CF3) A3342 44 **multicolored** *(A)* *20.00 30.00*

The date on No. 4392(CF3) is composed of dots, each of which contains a number of microdots that are visible under 20x magnification, but cannot be resolved by a scanner. The tail of the "9" in the "2009" year date does not extend to the left edge of the digit. There is no microprinting. The lettering of "USA" is coarsely outlined by dots with an overspray of dark blue microdots.

4392(CF4) A3342 44c **multicolored** *(A)* *20.00 30.00*

On No. 4392(CF4) the numerals of the date are surrounded by a heavy spray of dots. The tail of the "9" in the "2009" year date extends to the left edge of the digit. The numerals of the date are composed of microdots, which appear spray painted under 20x magnification. There is no microprinting. Letters of "USA" are sharply edged with an overlay of dark blue microdots.

Genuine examples of No. 4392 were lithographed with microprinted "USPS" in the top red stripe near the blue field, and have yellow-green tagging on prephosphored matte paper. Letters have sharp black outlining. Date and numerals are solid. There is a fine dot pattern in the red stripes. Stars have a regular grid of blue dots.

Genuine No. 4393

No. 4393(CF1)

2009 Unwmk. ***Serpentine Die Cut 9.5 Vert.***

OFFSET LITHOGRAPHY

Untagged

Self-Adhesive

Matte paper

Coil Stamps Size: Variable

4393(CF1) A3342 44c **multicolored** *(A)* *20.00 30.00*

No. 4393(CF1) is 17.7mm wide. The lettering is coarsely outlined and there is no microprinting. There is cyan under the black in the year date and the tail of the "9" in "2009" extends to the edge of the digit.

4393(CF2) A3342 44c **multicolored** *(A)* *20.00 30.00*

No. 4393(CF2) is 17.7mm wide. The lettering is coarsely outlined and there is no microprinting. The crossbar on the "A" of "USA" is tilted to the UR. There is no cyan under the black in the year date and the tail of the "9" in "2009" is short and does not extend to the edge of the digit. There is no distinct dot pattern in the white stripes.

4393(CF3) A3342 44c **multicolored** *(A)* *20.00 30.00*
On cover —

No. 4393(CF3) is 17.7mm wide. The lettering is coarsely outlined and there is no microprinting. The crossbar on the "A" of "USA" is horizontal. There is no cyan under the black in the year date and the tail of the "9" in "2009" is short and does not extend to the edge of the digit. There is no distinct dot pattern in the white stripes.

4393(CF4) A3342 44c **multicolored** *(A)* *20.00 30.00*
On cover —

No. 4393(CF4) is 17.1mm wide. The lettering is coarsely outlined and there is no microprinting. The crossbar on the "A" in "USA" is horizontal. There is no cyan under the black in the year date and the tail of the "9" in "2009" is short and does not extend to the edge of the digit. There is almost no dot pattern in the white stripes.

4393(CF5) A3342 44c **multicolored** *(A)* *20.00 30.00*
On cover —

No. 4393(CF5) is 17.3mm wide. The lettering is coarsely outlined and there is no microprinting. The year date is composed of multicolored dots. There is a distinct dot pattern of shading in the white stripes.

4393(CF6) A3342 44c **multicolored** *(A)* *20.00 30.00*

No. 4393(CF6) is 18mm wide. The lettering is coarsely outlined and there is no microprinting. The year date is composed of multicolored dots. There is a distinct dot pattern of shading in the white stripes.

4393(CF7) A3342 44c **multicolored** *(A)* *20.00 30.00*

No. 4393(CF7) is 18.5mm wide. The lettering is not outlined and there is microprinting. The black year date is distinct and clear. There are black shading dots in the red stripes.

4393(CF8) A3342 44c **multicolored** *(A)* *20.00 30.00*
Strip of 20

No. 4393(CF8) is 18.5mm wide. The lettering is not outlined and there is microprinting. The black year date is distinct and clear. There are black shading lines in the red stripe below the microprinting. There is a black dot that appears just below the microprinted "USPS" on every other stamp in a strip of 20.

4393(CF9) A3342 44c **multicolored** 20.00 *30.00*

On No. 4393(CF9), the design is 18mm wide, and the die cut is 9.4 and crude. The year date is very crude, made up of coarse multicolored dots. There is no microprinting. There is no reaction under shortwave UV light; the paper is hibrite under longwave UV light.

4393(CF10) A3342 44c **multicolored** 20.00 *30.00*

On No. 4393(CF10), the design is 18.2mm wide, and the die cut is 9.5, smooth and even. The year date is crude and made up of coarse multicolored dots. There are large yellow dots across the stamp, including the margins. The white stripes are made up of red, yellow and blue dots, with virtually all of the white stripes covered. There is no microprinting. There is no reaction under shortwave UV light; the paper is hibrite under longwave UV light.

Genuine examples of No. 4393 are photogravure printed with a micorprinted "USPS" at the top of the white stripe at the bottom center. They are tagged yellow-green under shortwave

UV light. They are 18.5mm wide. The lettering is sharply outlined and the date is solid.

Genuine No. 4394

No. 4394(CF1)

2009 Unwmk. *Serpentine Die Cut 8.5 Vert.*

OFFSET LITHOGRAPHY

Untagged

Self-Adhesive

Glossy paper

Coil Stamps Size: 18.5x21.5mm

4394(CF1) A3342 44c **multicolored** *(B)* *30.00 40.00*

No. 4394(CF1) is 24.5mm wide, die cut to die cut, about 1.5mm larger than a genuine example, although the image width is the same. The inscription has coarse outlines. Die cut gauge is similar to genuine, but is not consistent along the stamp edge. Untagged, but under flourescent white light, the blue is not as purple as the genuine. The dot pattern in the white stripes is weak and square where it exists. The date is not as close to the design as on the genuine stamp.

4394(CF2) A3342 44c **multicolored** *(B)* 30.00 *40.00*

On No. 4394(CF2), the die cuts are a crude and uneven 8.3. The stamp and margins are dotted with large yellow dots. The year date is fairly crude. There is no reaction under shortwave UV light, and the paper is hibrite under longwave UV light.

Genuine examples of No. 4394 have an inscription with sharp outline. They are tagged and printed on matte paper. The dots in the white stripes of the flag are in a regular diamond pattern.

Genuine No. 4490

Genuine No. 4491

No. 4490(CF1)

No. 4491(CF1)

2010 Unwmk. *Die Cut 9.5 Vert.*

OFFSET LITHOGRAPHY

Untagged

Self-Adhesive

Glossy paper

Coil Stamps Size: 16x20.7mm

4490(CF1) A3429 (44c) **multicolored** *(B)* *30.00 40.00*

The image on No. 4490(CF1) is smaller than a genuine stamp. The inscription is 20.5mm long. The printing is fuzzy with large litho dots. There is no microprinting, only a dark patch where the microprinting on a genuine stamp is located. The untagged paper gives a strong blue-white response under shortwave uv light.

Image size on genuine examples of No. 4490 is 16.5x21.2mm. The inscription is 21.1mm long. The printing is sharp with small litho dots and a distinct "4EVR" microprinting. Genuine examples have yellow-green tagging on matte paper and are serpentine die cut 8.5 vert.

4491(CF1) A3430 (44c) **multicolored** *(B)* *30.00 40.00*

The image on No. 4491(CF1) is smaller than a genuine stamp. The inscription is 20.5mm long. The printing is fuzzy with large litho dots. There is no microprinting, only a dark patch where the microprinting on a genuine stamp is located. The untagged paper gives a strong blue-white response under shortwave uv light.

Image size on genuine examples of No. 4491 is 16.5x21.2mm. The inscription is 21.1mm long. The printing is sharp with small litho dots and a distinct "4EVR" microprinting. Genuine examples have yellow-green tagging on matte paper and are serpentine die cut 8.5 vert.

Genuine No. 4629

No. 4629(CF1)

2012 Unwmk. *Serpentine Die Cut 8½ Vert.*

OFFSET LITHOGRAPHY

Untagged

Self-Adhesive

4629(CF1) A3537 (45c) **multicolored** — —

No. 4629(CF1) is untagged, and the microprinting is a blob. The letters are made up of lots of multicolored dots. The red stripes are mostly red dots, but on the genuine they are red with a lot of black dots distributed evenly. The stars are made up of tiny red and blue dots. The union is a brighter blue than on genuine stamps.

Genuine No. 4631

No. 4631(CF1)

4631(CF1) A3539 (45c) **multicolored** — —

No. 4631(CF1) has the same characteristics as No. 4629(CF1).

Genuine No. 4632

No. 4632(CF1)

4632(CF1) A3540 (45c) **multicolored** — —

No. 4632(CF1) has the same characteristics as No. 4629(CF1).

Genuine No. 4637

No. 4637(CF1)

No. 4637(CF2)

2014 (?) Unwmk. *Serpentine Die Cut 11 Vert.*

OFFSET LITHOGRAPHY

Untagged

Self-Adhesive Coil Stamp

4637(CF1) A3537 (45c) **multicolored** (A) 25.00 30.00

On cover, single franking 75.00

No. 4637(CF1) is a poor-quality counterfeit. A loose pattern of blue, red and yellow dots makes the background appear grayish. On the genuine stamps, the background is clear. The die-cut peaks are much shorter on the counterfeit than they are on the genuine, and the paper is high-bright, glowing blue under shortwave UV light.The genuine stamps shows the typical yellow-green glow from the prephosphored tagged paper. The red stripes on the flag are thinner than they are on the genuine, and the dot pattern on the flag is quite coarse. There is no microprinted "USPS" on the counterfeit. Rolls of this counterfeit were assembled from strips of eight stamps joined together with tape affixed to the backing paper.

The listing for No. 4637(CF1) on cover is for single-stamp use. Many philatelic covers have been made bearing a genuine No. 4637 and a counterfeit No. 4637(CF1), and such covers will sell for much less. This applies to all Nos. 4637(CF1)-4640(CF1).

2015 (?) Unwmk. *Serpentine Die Cut 11 Vert.*

OFFSET LITHOGRAPHY

Untagged

Self-Adhesive Coil Stamp

4637(CF2) A3537 (45c) **multicolored** (A) — —

On cover, single franking —

No. 4637(CF2) is a high-quality counterfeit. Under shortwave UV light, it does not glow, whereas the genuine stamp shows the typical yellow-green glow from the prephoshored tagged paper. The backing paper of the counterfeit glows blue under shortwave UV light. The red strips on the flag are thinner on the counterfeit than they are on the genuine, and the dot pattern of the flag is slightly coarse compared to the genuine. There is no microprinted "USPS" on the counterfeit.

The listing for No. 4637(CF2) on cover is for single-stamp use. Many philatelic covers have been made bearing a genuine No. 4637 and a counterfeit No. 4637(CF2), and such covers will sell for much less. This applies to all Nos. 4637(CF2)-4640(CF2).

Genuine No. 4638

No. 4638(CF1)

No. 4638(CF2)

4638(CF1) A3538 (45c) **multicolored** (A) 25.00 —

On cover, single franking —

For identifying features of No. 4638(CF1) and cover listing information, see notes under No. 4637(CF1) above.

4638(CF2) A3538 (45c) **multicolored** (A) — —

On cover, single franking —

For identifying features of No. 4638(CF2) and cover listing information, see notes under No. 4637(CF2) above.

Genuine No. 4639

No. 4639(CF1)

No. 4639(CF2)

4639(CF1) A3539 (45c) **multicolored** (A) 25.00 —

On cover, single franking —

For identifying features of No. 4639(CF1) and cover listing information, see notes under No. 4637(CF1) above.

4639(CF2) A3538 (45c) **multicolored** (A) — —

On cover, single franking —

For identifying features of No. 4639(CF2) and cover listing information, see notes under No. 4637(CF2) above.

Genuine No. 4640

No. 4640(CF1)

No. 4640(CF2)

4640(CF1) A3540 (45c) **multicolored** (A) 25.00 —
On cover, single franking —
a. Strip of 4, #4637(CF1)-4640(CF1) 100.00

For identifying features of No. 4640(CF1) and cover listing information, see notes under No. 4637(CF1) above.

4640(CF2) A3540 (45c) **multicolored** (A) — —
On cover, single franking —
a. Strip of 4, #4637(CF2)-4640(CF2) —

For identifying features of No. 4640(CF2) and cover listing information, see notes under No. 4637(CF2) above.

Genuine No. 4770

No. 4770(CF1)

2013 Unwmk. *Serpentine Die Cut 9½*
OFFSET LITHOGRAPHY
Untagged
Self-Adhesive

4770(CF1) A3640 (46c) **multicolored** — —

On No. 4770(CF1), the die cut is 9.4 vertically, generally even but a little crude. No indication of microprinting. The design is smaller than the genuine by about 0.5mm, but it is larger vertically by about 0.5mm. The sky is made up of large multicolored dots, but on the genuine there are only tiny blue dots, evenly distributed. The red stripes include lots of black dots, while on the genuine the stripes are mostly red. The stars are not very clear, and they are filled with fine colored dots. The year date is made up of large multicolored dots.

Genuine No. 4771

No. 4771(CF1)

4771(CF1) A3641 (46c) **multicolored** — —

No. 4771(CF1) has the same characteristics as No. 4770(CF1).

Genuine No. 4772

No. 4772(CF1)

4772(CF1) A3642 (46c) **multicolored** — —

No. 4772(CF1) has the same characteristics as No. 4770(CF1).

Genuine No. 4773

No. 4773(CF1)

4773(CF1) A3643 (46c) **multicolored** — —

No. 4773(CF1) has the same characteristics as No. 4770(CF1).

Genuine No. 4854

No. 4854(CF1)

2014 Unwmk. *Serpentine Die Cut 9¼ Vert.*
OFFSET LITHOGRAPHY
Untagged
Self-Adhesive

4854(CF1) A3716 (49c) **multicolored** — —

On No. 4854(CF1), the colors are washed out, and the black background is covered with tiny red dots. The die cuts are uneven and approximately 9.2. There is a black blur where the "USPS" microprinting should be. The red ink is reactive under shortwave UV light, and the paper is dead under longwave UV light. The white stripes are composed of red and blue dots.

4854(CF2) A3716 (49c) **multicolored** — —

No. 4854(CF2) is untagged, but the red ink reacts under both shortwave UV light and longwave UV light. There is microprinting that is almost readable. Die cutting is uneven at 9.4. "USA" is pinkish red. The year date is partially unreadable. "FOREVER" is made up of many colored dots, and the black background has many red specks. There is very little yellow in the fireworks.

4854(CF3) A3716 (49c) **multicolored** — —

On No. 4854(CF3), the die cuts are very big on both sides (similar to the wavy die cut on the end of rolls). It is untagged, and there is no indication of microprinting. The white stripes, year date and letters are filled with coarse red and blue dots. The blue is almost violet in color.

4854(CF4) A3716 (49c) **multicolored** — —

The die cuts are very big on both sides as on No. 4854(CF3). It is untagged and there is no indication of microprinting. The black background is spotted with tiny red dots. The white stripes are made up of coarse red and blue dots across the left half of the stripes and are limited on the right half. The letters and year date are crude and spotted with coarse red and blue dots. The blue is almost violet in color.

Genuine No. 4868

No. 4868(CF1)

2016 (?) Unwmk. *Serpentine Die Cut 11.2 Vert.*
OFFSET LITHOGRAPHY
Untagged
Self-Adhesive Coil Stamp ("issued" in coil roll of 100)

4868(CF1) A3716 (49c) **multicolored** (A) 10.00 —
On cover, single franking 25.00

No. 4868(CF1) is a fairly convincing counterfeit. It is printed on untagged paper that exhibits a blue glow under shortwave UV light, whereas genuine examples show a yellow-green glow. The counterfeit is serpentine die cut 11.2 vertically, but the genuine stamp is die cut 11 vertically. The microprinted "USPS" in the fireworks above the flagpole is indistinct on the counterfeit but clear on the genuine stamp. The stripes on the flag on the counterfeit are not of uniform thickness, as they are on the genuine stamps, and the first white stripe below the field of stars is complete on the genuine stamp but is missing a portion at left on the counterfeit. The "O" of "FOREVER" is wide on the counterfeit and narrow on the genine. The lithographic dot structure on the counterfeit is large, resulting in a coarseness not seen on the genuine stamp.

The listing for No. 4868(CF1) on cover is for a single-stamp use. Many philatelic covers have been made bearing a genuine No. 4868 and a counterfeit No. 4868(CF1), and such covers will sell for much less.

4868(CF2) A3716 (49c) **multicolored** — —

No. 4868(CF2) is untagged and die cut 10.9. There is no indication of microprinting. There are diagonal lines running from the lower left to the upper right. The lettering is crude. The white stripes are made up of small red and blue dots, and larger yellow dots. The ink and paper have no reaction under either longwave or shortwave UV light.

4868(CF3) A3716 (49c) **multicolored** — —

No. 4868(CF3) is untagged and with smooth and even 11.25 die cuts. The microprinting is blurred. The letters and year date are smooth and white with no dots. The white stripes are made up of coarse red, yellow and blue dots. The red stripes have coarse black dots in them.

4868(CF4) A3716 (49c) **multicolored** — —

No. 4868(CF4) is untagged with uneven 11.25 die cuts. The die cuts are like the teeth on a saw blade. There is a vertical die cut at the top and bottom, but there is also a horizontal die cut near the top. There is no microprinting. The black background is covered with tiny red and blue dots. The edges of the lettering and year date are coarse.

Genuine No. 4955 — A3808

No. 4955(CF1)

No. 4955(CF2)

Genuine No. 4956 — A3809

No. 4956(CF1)

No. 4956(CF2)

2015 (?) Unwmk. *Serpentine Die Cut 11¼*
OFFSET LITHOGRAPHY
Untagged
Self-Adhesive

4955(CF1) A3808 (49c) **red** (A) 3.50 —
On cover, single franking 25.00

No. 4955(CF1) is a fairly convincing counterfeit. It is printed on untagged paper that exhibits a blue glow under shortwave UV light, whereas genuine examples show a yellow-green glow. The counterfeit is die cut 11 ¼, but the genuine stamp is die cut 11. The "2015" at top right of the counterfeit is barely visible, even under magnification. Genuine panes show only serpentine die cutting around the stamps, whereas counterfeits have a striaght-line die cut around the perimeter of the pane and rouletting between each column and row of stamps. The paper of the counterfeit is high-bright and appears shiney when viewed at an angle, whereas the paper of genuine stamps appears dull. On the back liner, the line above the ruled box in the center of genuine panes is much closer to the box in comparison to the line above the box on counterfeit panes. In the last line of text in the ruled box, the word "news" on genuine panes is misspelled "new" on counterfeit panes. The listing for No. 4955(CF1) on cover is for single-stamp use. Many philatelic covers have been made bearing a genuine No. 4955 and a counterfeit No. 4955(CF1), or a pair of Nos. 4955(CF1) and 4956(CF1), and such covers will sell for much less.

The listing for No. 4955(CF1) on cover is for a single-stamp use. Many philatelic covers have been made bearing a genuine

No. 4955 and a counterfeit No. 4955(CF1), and such covers will sell for much less.

4955(CF2) A3809 (49c) **red** (A) — —
On cover, single franking *25.00*

No. 4955(CF2) is a fairly convincing counterfeit. It is untagged, but the surface of the paper is dull like the genuine stamp. The backing text has been corrected.

The listing for No. 4955(CF2) on cover is for a single-stamp use. Many philatelic covers have been made bearing a genuine No. 4955 and a counterfeit No. 4955(CF2), and such covers will sell for much less.

4956(CF1) A3809 (49c) **red & gray** (A) 3.50 —
On cover, single franking —
a. Pair, #4955(CF1)-4956(CF1) 7.50
Pane of 20 75.00

For identifying features of No. 4956(CF1) and cover listing information, see notes under No. 4955(CF1) above.

4956(CF2) A3809 (49c) **red & gray** (A) — —
On cover, single franking *25.00*
a. Pair, #4955(CF2)-4956(CF2) —
Pane of 20 —

For identifying features of No. 4956(CF2) and cover listing information, see note under No. 4955(CF2) above.

Genuine No. 4959 — A3812

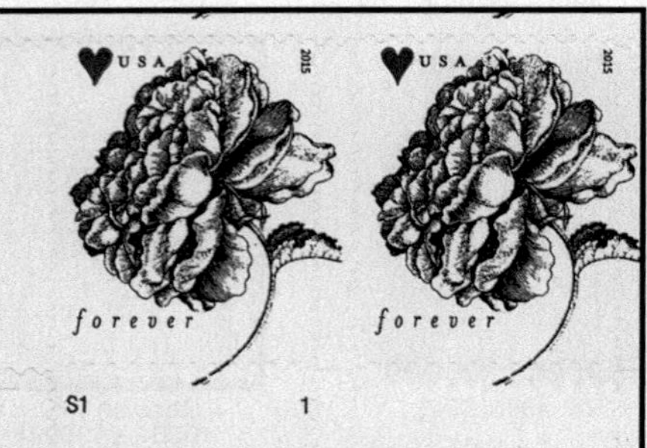

No. 4959(CF1)

No. 4959(CF2)

2015 Unwmk. *Serpentine Die Cut 11¼*

OFFSET LITHOGRAPHY

Untagged

Self-Adhesive

4959(CF1) A3812 (49c) **red & black** 4.00
On cover, single franking *25.00*
Pane of 20 80.00
a. Pane of 20, inverted backing —

No. 4959(CF1) appeared in the marketplace in early 2016. This counterfeit is lithographed, though the ink on the flower "stands up" as on engraved stamps. The overall appearance is slightly fuzzy and darker in color than the genine engraved No. 4959. The die cutting does not match the genuine, and the die cutting in the selvage and between stamps is far from a match with the genuine stamps. The die cut "peaks" are less round than on the genuine, and the counterfeit appears to be on hi-brite paper front and back. When looking at the back of genuine panes, in the last line of the text in the ruled box, the word "news" on genuine stamps in misspelled "new" on counterfeit panes.

The listing for No. 4959(CF1) on cover is for a single-stamp use. Many philatelic covers have been made bearing a genuine No. 4959 and a counterfeit No. 4959(CF1), and such covers will sell for much less.

4959(CF2) A3812 (49c) **red & black** (A) —
On cover, single franking *25.00*
Pane of 20 —

On No. 4959(CF2), the ink does not "stand up" as on genuine stamps and No. 4959(CF1), but the counterfeiter added tiny, raised dots over the surface of the printed flower and its stem, which can be felt by rubbing a fingertip across the stamp. This counterfeit is untagged. On counterfeit panes, there is a slight misalignment of the horizontal and vertical wavy-line die-cutting patterns where the four stamps come together. The printing appears as patterns of dots on counterfeit stamps whereas the genuine engraved stamp appears as a mix of fine lines and dots. The end of the loop of the "5" in the year date points up, whereas the loop points down on the genuine stamp. Panes of the counterfeit have the word "news" misspelled as "new."

The listing for No. 4959CF2) on cover is for a single-stamp use. Many philatelic covers have been made bearing a genuine No. 4959 and a counterfeit No. 4959(CF1), and such covers will sell for much less.

Genuine No. 4991

No. 4991(CF1)

2015 Unwmk. *Serpentine Die Cut 11¼x11*

OFFSET LITHOGRAPHY

Untagged

Self-Adhesive

4991(CF1) A3838(35c) **multicolored** — —

Nos. 4991(CF1)-4994(CF1) are the first counterfeit of a se-tenant issue. Printing quality is good, but the die cutting is not good. Die cutting is uneven, crude and disjointed at 8.25 x8. The microprinting is a gray blob. The font of the "5" of the year date is wrong. On the pane, the plate number is omitted on the bottom left corner. The barcodes are omitted on the back of the pane.

Genuine No. 4992

No. 4992(CF1)

4992(CF1) A3839 (35c) **multicolored** — —

No. 4992(CF1) has the same characteristics as No. 4991(CF1).

Genuine No. 4993

No. 4993(CF1)

4993(CF1) A3840 (35c) **multicolored** — —

No. 4993(CF1) has the same characteristics as No. 4991(CF1).

Genuine No. 4994

No. 4994(CF1)

4994(CF1) A3841 (35c) **multicolored** — —

No. 4994(CF1) has the same characteristics as No. 4991(CF1).

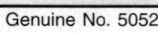

Genuine No. 5052

No. 5052(CF1)

2016 Unwmk. *Serpentine Die Cut 11 Vert.*

OFFSET LITHOGRAPHY

Untagged

Self-Adhesive

5052(CF1) A3887 (49c) **multicolored** — —

No. 5052(CF1) is untagged, and the die cuts are very crude (similar to the wavy die cuts on the ends of rolls). The date is made up of multicolored dots, but is mostly dark blue with red dots. The microprinting is blurred, with the "U" and second "S" being distinguishable. The font of "USA FOREVER" is a little thinner than on the genuine stamp. The image is darker blue overall, and there are lots of extra dots in lines along the top and bottom.

Genuine No. 5053

No. 5053(CF1)

2016 Unwmk. *Serpentine Die Cut 9.5 Vert.*

Self-Adhesive

5053(CF1) A3887 (49c) **multicolored** (A) — —
On cover, single franking *25.00*

No. 5053(CF1) is a convincing counterfeit, but it is not tagged, and the microprinting on the second white stripe is an indistinct blob of ink. On the genuine stamp, "USA" has thick lettering; the same lettering on the counterfeit is noticeably thinner. The "2016" year date is much darker on the counterfeit, and light gray on the genuine stamp. The die cutting on the counterfeit is somewhat uneven.

The listing for No. 5053(CF1) on cover is for a single-stamp use. Many philatelic covers have been made bearing a genuine No. 5053 and a counterfeit No. 5053(CF1), and such covers will sell for much less.

5053(CF2) A3887 (49c) **multicolored** — —

No. 5053(CF2) is untagged, and the die cuts are very crude and are shifted up vertically (very approximately 8.8 x 9.5). The year date is made up of multicolored dots, but it is mostly light green in color. There is no indication of microprinting. The font of "FOREVER" is shorter, thinner and not the same height as "USA."

5053(CF3) A3887 (49c) **multicolored** — —

No. 5053(CF3) is untagged, and the die cutting is approximately 9 to 9.5 and are like a "U" on its side, back and forth. The year date is made up of multicolored dots, but it is mostly light green in color, with red dots. There is no indication of microprinting. The font of "FOREVER" is shorter and thinner than the font of "USA."

5053(CF4) A3887 (49c) **multicolored** — —

No. 5053(CF4) is very similar to No. 5053(CF3), but it is on porous paper. The year date is a solid light green color.

5053(CF5) A3887 (49c) **multicolored** — —

No. 5053(CF5) is untagged and on porous paper. The die cuts are very crude and uneven (very approximately 12). The year date is made up of multicolored dots, but it is mostly gray with red dots. There is no indication of microprinting. The font of "FOREVER" is shorter than the font of "USA."

Genuine No. 5131

No. 5131(CF1)

2016 Unwmk. *Serpentine Die Cut 11.2x10.8*

OFFSET LITHOGRAPHY

Untagged

Self-Adhesive

5131(CF1) A3961 (47c) **multicolored** (A) — —
On cover, single franking —

No. 5131(CF1) is a convincing counterfeit, but it is not tagged, and the microprinted 'USPS' is missing.

The listing for No. 5131(CF1) on cover is for a single-stamp use. Many philatelic covers have been made bearing a genuine No. 5131 and a counterfeit No. 5131(CF1), and such covers will sell for much less.

5131(CF2) A3961 (47c) **multicolored** — —

No. 5131(CF2) is similar to 5131(CF1), but the year date is darker and thicker. Shiny paper. Untagged, and no indication of microprinting. The paper is a brighter white than the genuine stamp, but it is dead under shortwave UV light.

Genuine No. 5142

No. 5142(CF1)

2017 Unwmk. *Serpentine Die Cut 11¼*

OFFSET LITHOGRAPHY

Untagged

Self-Adhesive

5142(CF1) A3972 (47c) **multicolored** (A) 4.00 —
On cover, single franking 25.00
Pane of 20 80.00
Pane of 20 with inverted backing paper —

No. 5142(CF1) is a very convincing counterfeit. The counterfeit is die cut 11¼, whereas the genuine stamp is die cut 11. Die-cut peaks of the counterfeits are shorter and rounder than those of genuine stamps, and on counterfeit panes there is a misalignment of the horizontal and vertical die cutting in some locations where four stamps come together. Counterfeits are untagged and glow blue under shortwave UV light, whereas genuine stamps have block tagging that glows yellow-green. The "2016" year date at right bottom is dark and without a serif at the bottom of the "1" on the counterfeit versus the lighter date with serif on the genuine. The lithographed dot pattern on the counterfeit is much coarser compared to the fine dot pattern of the genuine stamps. Additional differences can be seen on the backing paper in rouletting and serpentine slits, and a vertical pipe missing between "USPS.com/stamps" and "© 2016 USPS" on the counterfeit pane backing.

The listing for No. 5142(CF1) on cover is for single-stamp use. Many philatelic covers have been made bearing a genuine No. 5142 and a counterfeit No. 5142(CF1), and such covers will sell for much less.

Genuine No. 5155

No. 5155(CF1)

2017 Unwmk. *Serpentine Die Cut 11x10¾*

OFFSET LITHOGRAPHY

Untagged

Self-Adhesive

5155(CF1) A3985 (47c) **light blue** (A) 4.00 —
On cover, single franking —
Pane of 20 80.00

No. 5155(CF1) is a very convincing counterfeit. Its color is only slightly lighter than the light blue color of the genuine stamp. The counterfeit is untagged. Die-cut peaks on the counterfeit are more pointed than those on genuine stamps, and the lithographic pattern is coarser. The legible microprinted "USPS" just below the airplane on the genuine stamp appears as an indistinct white spot on the counterfeit.

The listing for No. 5155(CF1) on cover is for a single-stamp use. Many philatelic covers have been made bearing a genuine No. 5155 and a counterfeit No. 5155(CF1), and such covers will sell for much less.

5155(CF2) A3985 (47c) **light blue** — —

Similar to No. 5155(CF1), but the two types can be distinguished by the silhouette of the airplane. On No. 5155(CF1), there are many blue dots in the white area of the plane, but on No. 5155(CF2), there are no dots except on the upper wing. The die cutting is 10.9 x10.8.

Genuine No. 5158

No. 5158(CF1)

2017 Unwmk. *Serpentine Die Cut 11.2 Vert.*

OFFSET LITHOGRAPHY

Untagged

Self-Adhesive

5158(CF1) A3988 (49c) **multicolored** (A) — —
On cover, single franking 25.00

No. 5158(CF1) is a good quality counterfeit, but the printing is darker than on the genuine stamp, it is untagged, and the microprinted "USPS" on the right end of the fourth red stripe is missing. The stamp size of the counterfeit is 23.8mm, more than one full mm wider than the genuine stamp.

5158(CF2) A3988 (49c) **multicolored** — —

No. 5158(CF2) is the first counterfeit coil stamp found with a plate number (#B1111). It is a good quality counterfeit, about the same size as the genuine stamp, but it is untagged and the "USPS" microprinting is not clear, smaller than the genuine at 0.6mm, and is placed on the second white stripe rather than the fourth stripe, which would correspond to the #B1111 plate number. Die cuts are 11, but there is some overlap on the lower half of the stamps. The year date has tiny white dots present. The colors are lighter than the genine stamps, and the dot pattern is very coarse.

5158(CF3) A3988 (49c) **multicolored** — —

No. 5158(CF3) is untagged and has a crude and uneven die cut measuring 10.7. A brighter red was used for this counterfeit compared to the others. The dark blue of the union is a solid color, with the stars having a reddish background made up with a variety of large colored dots. The white along the margins is made up of multicolored dots. The year date is made up of multicolored dots but is predominantly black.

5158(CF4) A3988 (49c) **multicolored** — —

No. 5158(CF4) is very similar to No. 5158(CF3). Untagged and die cut 10.8. Crude perfs, which (like those on No. 5158(CF3) are not complete at the ends. The dark blue and red have vertical lines present. The stars have a red tint and are made up of very light multicolored dots. The margins are white. The year date is made up of tiny multicolored dots but is predominantly gray.

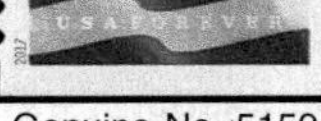
Genuine No. 5159

No. 5159(CF1)

2017 Unwmk. *Serpentine Die Cut 7.8*

OFFSET LITHOGRAPHY

Untagged

Self-Adhesive

5159(CF1) A3988 (49c) **multicolored** (A) — —

No. 5159(CF1) is untagged and has no microprinting. The die cut is 7.8, and the stamps are 23.4mm wide compared to 23mm on the genuine stamps. The die cuts are crude and uneven. The colors are darker than on the genuine stamps. The stars are crude and made up of coarse dots. Found as intact rolls including a wrapper with "1 02" or "4-10" inside a circle.

Genuine No. 5161

No. 5161(CF1)

2018 Unwmk. *Serpentine Die Cut 11.25x10.8*

OFFSET LITHOGRAPHY

Untagged

Self-Adhesive

5161(CF1) A3988 (49c) **multicolored** — —

No. 5161(CF1) is untagged and with blurred microprinting that is slightly smaller than on the genuine stamps. Die cutting is fairly crude and uneven, and cuts do not quite meet. All vertical die cuts are the same pattern, and an easy way to identify this counterfeit with a stamp from the bottom row of the booklet is to examine the fourth die cut from the bottom on the lower right, which is extended. The year date is a solid color, as opposed to black dots on the genuine stamps. Overall, the printing is not as sharp.

Genuine No. 5255

No. 5255(CF1)

2018 Unwmk. *Serpentine Die Cut 11x10.75*

OFFSET LITHOGRAPHY

Untagged

Self-Adhesive

5255(CF1) A4094 (49c) **multicolored** — —

The printing of No. 5255(CF1) is very good, but the genuine stamp has a finer dot pattern. The microprinting is very close, except it is more gray than black, whereas the genuine stamps have microprinting more black than gray, and the genuine stamps have microprinting with a dropped second "S" while the counterfeits do not.

Genuine No. 5260

No. 5260(CF1)

2018 Unwmk. *Serpentine Die Cut 9.6 Vert.*

OFFSET LITHOGRAPHY

Untagged

Self-Adhesive

5260(CF1) A4099 (50c) **multicolored** — —

No. 5260(CF1) is untagged, and the microprinting is a slightly blurred "unas" in lower case letters and inverted. Die cut approximately 9.6, but quite uneven. All of the rolls found were wraped in Ashton-Potter wrappers, held in place by rubber cement. All wrappers have a "2" inside a circle.

5260(CF2) A4099 (50c) **multicolored** — —

No. 5260(CF2) is untagged, and the microprinting on the fourth white stripe is very clear but is in a larger font than the genuine stamps, measuring 1mm wide versus 0.7mm on the genine stamps. All of the wrappers found have a "1" inside a circle. Smooth and even die cut 9.3.

5260(CF3) A4099 (50c) **multicolored** — —

No. 5260(CF3) is untagged, and the microprinting is clear and very close to the genuine. Wrappers found have a "4" inside a circle. Uneven die cut 8.3.

5260(CF4) A4099 (50c) **multicolored** — —

No. 5260(CF4) is similar to No. 5260(CF1). It is untagged, and the microprinting is a blurred "uaas" in lower case letters and inverted. The die cut is 9.6, and there is a straight vertical die cut at the bottom and an uneven die cut at the top.

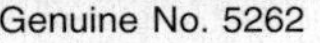
Genuine No. 5262

No. 5262(CF1)

2018 Unwmk. *Serpentine Die Cut 11.25x10.8*

OFFSET LITHOGRAPHY

Untagged

Self-Adhesive

5262(CF1) A4099 (50c) **multicolored** — —

No. 5262(CF1) is similar in characteristics to the booklet counterfeit No. 5161(CF1). It is untagged, the microprinting is fairly convincing, and the die cutting is 11.25 x10.8. All vertical die cuts are the same pattern, and an easy way to identify this counterfeit with a stamp from the bottom row of the booklet is to examine the fourth die cut from the bottom on the lower right, which is extended. The year date is a solid black, as opposed to the black dots on the genuine version. Overall the printing is not as sharp.

5262(CF2) A4099 (50c) **multicolored** — —

No. 5262(CF2) is not of very good quality, is untagged, and the microprinting is slightly larger and is a regular font, not bold as is the genuine. Die cuts are crude and uneven, approximately 11.4 x10.8. The year date is smooth along the edges compared to the genuine.

5262(CF3) A4099 (50c) **multicolored** — —

No. 5262(CF3) is similar to 5262(CF2), but the die cuts are smooth, even and measure 11.2 x10.8.

COUNTERFEIT AIR POST STAMPS

Genuine No. C15

No. C15(CF1)

1930 Unwmk. *Perf. 11.5*

ENGRAVED

Thin white paper

Size: 45x19mm

C15(CF1) AP11 $2.60 **blue** *(F)* *1,500. 1,000.*
a. Large die proof **orange red** *(H)* *2,000.*
b. Large die proof **blue** —

While the objective of this counterfeit was to defraud collectors, the Postal Inspection Service did in fact make an attempt to gather up examples in dealer hands. Few were made, and of these a very small number are known either on philatelic mail or are canceled to order. No. C15(CF1), often called the "Panelli forgery," is a darker blue than genuine examples of No. C15, but the paper is a good match. The counterfeits were printed and perforated individually, so centering and perforating range from credible (10.9) to suspicious (irregular 11.4-12.4x11.4). Examples perforated 11.5 exist. Details for the design are generally unclear, including the numbers on the Zeppelin. The top of the "R" in "GRAF" is very thin, and the lettering in the label in the bottom center of the airship is unreadable.

Perforations on genuine examples of No. C15 gauge 11. The details of engraving are clear and distinct. The bar at the top of the "R" in "GRAF" clearly closes the letter. Gum is of higher quality. Size: 46x18.5mm.

Genuine No. C64

1962 Unwmk. *Perf. Unknown*

PRINTING METHOD UNKNOWN

C64(CF1) AP42 8c **carmine** *(I)*

No. C64(CF1) was mentioned in the March 1982 issue of *The American Philatelist,* but with no details provided. No examples have been seen by the editors.

Genuine No. C79

1973 Unwmk. *Perf. Unknown*

PHOTOGRAPHIC OFFSET LITHOGRAPHY

Untagged

C79(CF1) AP55 13c **carmine** *(I)*

No. C79(CF1) has been reported in the March 1982 issue of *The American Philatelist,* with an illustration of a blurry used example on piece, probably obtained from the U.S. Postal Inspection Service, which holds unfinished panes in their files.

Genuine examples of No. C79 were printed by recess engraving. Perforations gauge 11x10.5.

Genuine No. C126a

No. C126a(CF1)

1989 Unwmk. *Imperf.*

LITHOGRAPHED & ENGRAVED

Yellowish bright flourescent paper

Size: 131x82mm

C126(CF1) AP95-AP98 Souvenir sheet of 4, #a-d *(B)* *200.00*

No. C126(CF1) has a distinct beige tone to the gum. It is cut off center with the entire design lower on the sheet than genuine examples of No. C126. The ink at the right edge of the "45" is poorly wiped so that the blue ink runs irregularly out from the numbers, especially the "5." Under magnification, the images are fuzzy. The text is thinner than on genuine examples, and the paper is thicker.

Genuine examples of No. C126 were produced by lithography with the "US Air Mail 45" engraved. There is little to no bleeding of the blue engraved ink from the "45." Paper is white and the gum is whiter than the counterfeit. There is overall phosphor tagging on the front, although tagging omitted examples have been recorded.

COUNTERFEIT POSTAL CARDS

Genuine No. UX12

1894 UNKNOWN PRINTING METHOD

UX12(CF1) PC7 1c **black,** *buff (G)* — —

No. UX12(CF1) has a poor quality image of Jefferson, but printing of genuine postal cards was so poor that it is difficult to authenticate counterfeits; made even more difficult by the lack of any major flaws in the text. However, there are minor flaws: The bottom of the four-petal ornament near the left end of the upper line is cut off. The similar ornament at the middle of the bottom line has a break in the right side of the upper petal. There is a break in the upper line of the farthest left "hairpin" in the line directly under the "NI" or "UNITED." There are only two examples reported, one mint and one used.

Genuine examples of No. UX12 are only marginally better in paper and printing quality.

Genuine No. UX14

No. UX14(CF1)

No. UX14(CF1) Missing Serifs Flaw Type V

1897 UNKNOWN PRINTING METHOD

UX14(CF1) PC8 1c **black,** *buff (F)* *1,000. 1,750.*

No. UX14(CF1) is poorly printed but not much worse than the average genuine example. The image of Jefferson is dark and muddy. There is one outstanding flaw on all counterfeits: the bottom of the second "T" in "STATES" lacks serifs. Serifs are also often missing on the outside bottom of the "E" next to the "T." The counterfeit can be further subdivided into at least five types as follows:

Type I: Both "T" and "E" affected. Border line weak below "E" of "UNITED." Small downward bend or break in border line of inscription, directly above center of semicircular ornament. There is a short upward extension of the dot at extreme right end of the inscription panel.

Type II: Both "T" and "E" affected. There are small white spots between tops of "ST" in "STATES," and at the upper-left corner of "O" in "OF." The inner edge of the leaf to the left of the mouth is missing.

Type III: Both "T" and "E" affected. Very small clean break in border line over the second "T" in "STATES." Top of "C" in first "Card" is flattened. The vertical stroke of "T" in "Cent" points down over "E" of "AMERICA."

Type IV: Both "T" and "E" affected. The thin line above the inscription is very weak from the beginning of the first "T" to that of the second "T" in "STATES." There is a slight doubling of the thin oval frameline around the portrait at left, opposite Jefferson's mouth.

Type V: Bottom of "T" only, missing serifs.

Counterfeits are sometimes coated on one or both sides to give the impression of a previous private message and/or address being covered. Prior to the discovery of this counterfeit, this was legal and often done to allow for use of postal cards printed with ads or messaging that were excess and had not been used in the post.

Approximately 25 examples of all types are known.

Mint examples of No. UX14(CF1) have no additional printing beyond the ad and address. Used value is for examples cancelled and used in the mail, which are scarce.

Genuine examples of No. UX14 are generally but not always on lighter cards without the missing serifs identifer.

Genuine No. UX100

1983 UNKNOWN PRINTING METHOD

UX100(CF1) PC74 14c **black and white** *(H)* —

No. UX100(CF1) is an altered version of the multicolored No. UX100. The denomination of No. UX100(CF1) has been altered to 14c from the genuine 13c value. According to a press report in *Linn's Stamp News* 3/18/91, multiple examples were produced, but only a single used example is known.

Color Photocopies of Nos. 3750 and 3784

"Not quite" counterfeits:
Items in this category are either officially or privately made stamp look-alikes. While these items fall outside the scope of the listings above due to the almost individual nature of production, it is important to mention their existence and describe the various types that have occurred.

1. Photocopies of stamps—With the increased quality of photocopying, even color reproduction of genuine stamps is not beyond the technology. However, in the experience of the editors, use of photocopies as U.S. postal counterfeits has, until recently, been used mostly to reproduce stamps that are black and white. See the illustration above.
2. Stamps photocopied onto an envelope.
3. Hand-drawn replicas—Must be done item by item, but can be well done.
4. Paste-on replicas from stamp club spoof sheets—for example a 1970 Wilkinsburg Stamp Club sheetlet, a combination of the 6c Apollo 8 stamp and the 6c Botanical Congress block.
5. Paste-on commercial replicas—Usually occurs with a line through the value.
6. Stamp illustrations clipped from dealer or USPS ads, booklet pane covers, etc.
7. Shaved proofs or stamp illustrations on Bureau souvenir cards.
8. Actual stamp designs, but with no value, used as samples in refrigerator magnets sold by the USPS in Walmarts in 1999.
9. Pieces of genuine margins, or dummy stamp images from production sheets used as stamps. One item that has been seen was created using the label from a Pacific 97 sheet.
10. Tagged margin pieces used to facilitate use of non-tagged low-value stamps, and stamp-like images.
11. USPS stationery, including images of genuine stamps folded to resemble postal stationery.
12. Stamp-like images created by companies such as Pitney-Bowes to use in advertising or for use as props in movies.

NONPOSTAL AND REVENUE COUNTERFEITS

The listings of counterfeits in this section are for non-postal and revenue counterfeits that were created to deprive legal authorities (Treasury Department) of lawful monies due them.

The listings follow standard Scott policy. A comparison of the attributes found in the counterfeit listings with those of genuine stamps will enable collectors to distinguish the real from the spurious. The description field of each listing contains a letter rarity code keyed to the list below.

Numbers that survive in the hands of collectors:
E = Probably equal to or fewer than 100
F = Probably equal to or fewer than 25
G = 5 or fewer reported
H = Unique in philatelic hands

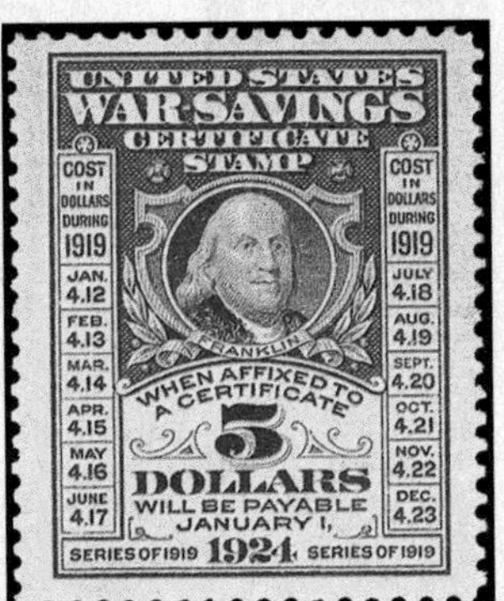

Genuine No. WS4

No. WS4(CF1)

"COUNTERFEIT" handstamp

1919(?) Engr. Unwmk. *Perf. 10.6-10.9 Variable*

WS4(CF1)		$5 **deep blue**, without handstamp (E)	*600.00*
	a.	With handstamp on gum on reverse	*750.00*
	b.	With handstamp on face	*1,000.*

No. WS4(CF1) is a high-quality engraved counterfeit with low-quality perforations, which are variable and somewhat wavering. The paper on the counterfeit is a very light beige, whereas the genuine stamp was printed on white paper and often has an overall blue wash. The counterfeit has flat, white gum. Franklin's head and circular medallion is more finely detailed on the genuine stamp, but overall the counterfeit is very close to the genuine, even in detail. Nos. WS4(CF1) and WS4(CF1b) without gum sell for somewhat less than the values shown, which are for stamps in the grade of very fine and with "original" gum.

Quantities known of the three varieties combined = (E).

Genuine No. R3c

No. R3c(CF1)

1860s Engr. *Perf. 12½*

R3c(CF1)		R1 1c **red** (E)	*900.00*
	a.	Vert. strip of 7 (see footnote)	—

No. R3c(CF1) is a fairly convincing counterfeit, but the foliate ornamentation at top and bottom, and the engraved lines on Washington's coat, are significantly different.

No. R3ca(CF1) actually is a proof impression printed by the Bureau of Engraving and Printing, with a manuscript note on reverse: "Plate engraved by Hart L. Pierce. Impression from cft. plate taken at the Bureau Eng. and Printing."

Genuine No. R86a

No. R86a(CF1)

No. R86c(CF1)

1860s **Engr.** ***Imperf.***

R86a(CF1) R8 $3 **greeen** (G) *7,500.*

No. R86a(CF1) is a fair counterfeit, but there are myriad small differences in all parts of the design.

Perf.

R86c(CF1) R8 $3 **green** (H) —

Genuine No. REA3

No. REA3(CF1)

1860s **Litho.** ***Imperf.***

REA3(CF1) 25c **blue** (H) *6,000.*

REA3(CF1) is a crude lithographed counterfeit of an engraved stamp. In the upper left margin is written, "Counterfeit Rev Stamp. The lithographer was convicted and sentenced to Prison."

Genuine No. REA156

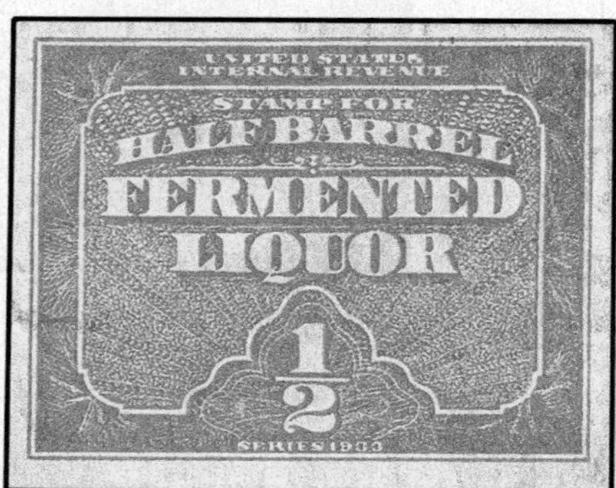

No. REA156(CF1)

1933 **Litho.** ***Imperf.***

REA156(CF1) ½ bbl., **orange,** *light blue* (H) *2,500.*

No. REA156(CF1) is a crude lithographed counterfeit of an engraved stamp. The paper is a much lighter blue than the genuine paper.

Genuine No. RK21

No. RK21(CF1)

1929(?) **Litho.** ***Rough Perfs.***

RK21(CF1) CSF1 10c **orange** (H) *1,750.*

No. RK21(CF1) is a lithographed counterfeit of an engraved stamp. It is canceled by an apparently genuine government handstamp dated Dec. 7, 1920 / Rome Italy.

Genuine No. RO98a

No. RO98a(CF1)

1860s **Litho.** ***Perf. 12¼***

RO98a(CF1) 1c **green** (G) *1,750.*

No. RO98a(CF1) is a crude lithographic counterfeit of an engraved stamp. The most obvious difference, besides the color and uneven perforations, is the background of horizontal lines on No. RO98a(CF1) rather than the lattice-work of diagonal lines on the genuine No. RO98a.

Genuine No. RO112a

No. RO112a(CF1)

1860s **Engr.** ***Perf. 12¼***

RO112a(CF1) 1c **blue** (G) *4,500.*

No. RO112a(CF1) is an engraved counterfeit by Benoni Howard. It differs from the genuine No. RO112a in numerous small details, including the perf. gauge.

TEST STAMPS

Test stamps, also called "dummy stamps," came into being in the late 19th century, and their production continues to the present. These stamps have been printed by both the Bureau of Engraving & Printing and by private companies for use when the Post Office Department, United States Postal Service and other companies wanted to use test stamps rather than accountable paper (i.e., actual stamps that would have to be accounted for).

With the growth of automation and the development of vending equipment in the 20th century, the production and use of test stamps proliferated. A majority are very scarce, as these items generally were not made available to the general public or philatelists.

The test stamps listed here were produced for several purposes:

1. To develop and test production equipment, including printing presses and stamp and booklet manufacturing equipment.
2. To design stamp vending equipment by private companies.
3. To test, adjust and promote stamp affixing equipment by commercial vendors.
4. To test and adjust stamp vending equipment at dispensing sites by the Postal Service and private companies.

The test stamp listings are arranged into two sections, the first being sheet and coil stamps, and the second being booklets. These listings were originally formed by Steven R. Unkrich, in consultation with other leading collectors of test stamps. The listings have since been expanded greatly with the help of the Dummy Stamps Study Group of the United States Stamp Society, headed by Terry Scott. Thanks to Dan Undersander for supplying much of the information in this section's introduction. Those interested in learning more about test (dummy) stamps are invited to join the Dummy Stamps Study Group. Contact Terry Scott at trs@napanet.net.

Blank Design — TE6

Blank Definitive — TE10

Produced by Continental Bank Note Co.

1877-78 Intermediate Paper Unwmk. *Perf. 12*

TD6 TE6 blank *150.00*
Block of 4 *600.00*

Prior to 1877, Continental Bank Note Company used "hard" wove paper. In early 1877, they began using an "intermediate" paper. They switched to a "soft" paper in August 1878 that was used until the company merged with American Bank Note Co. in February 1879. American Bank Note Co. only used "soft" paper.

No. TD6 is the large-size blank sheet stamp (TE6). See Nos. TD10, TD11, TD83, TD84A, TD113, TD114 and TD114A for small-size blank sheet test stamps (TE9).

Automatic Postage Stamp Sticker — TE7

1886 ***Perf. 15¾***

TD7 TE7 **red** —

No. TD7 was produced for Hyde & Company of New York for use in their stamp affixing device.

Burt and Tobey's Stamp Battery — TE8

1890 ***Perf. 12***

TD8 TE8 **light green** *675.00*

Perf. 12¼x12

TD8A TE8 **lavender** —

Nos. TD8 and TD8A have printed simulated perforations in addition to the normal perforations.

The Klein Mfg. Co. — TE9

1890s ***Rouletted 11***

TD9 TE9 **red** —

Blank Sheet Test Stamps

Produced by Bureau of Engraving & Printing

1894 Unwmk. *Perf. 12*

TD10 TE10 blank 75.00
Block of 4 300.00

The BEP produced perf. 12 stamps on unwatermarked paper from July 1894 until switching to double-line watermark 191 paper in April 1895.

Blank Design Type of 1907

Produced by Bureau of Engraving & Printing.

1907 Wmk. 191 *Perf. 12*
Brownish Gum

TD11 TE10 blank 75.00
Block of 4 300.00

On Oct. 26, 1907, the BEP received an order for "500 sheets of postage stamp paper, perforated and gummed, but not printed." These stamps were given to companies that were developing stamp vending machines for the post office.

No. TD11 is known only on paper with reversed forward-stepping watermark. See explanation before listing for No. 264 in the Postage section. For other blank small-size sheet test stamps, see Nos. TD83, TD84, TD84A, TD113, TD114 and TD114A

TE11

TE12

Mailometer Coil — TE12a

1906-09 Unwmk. *Perf. 12*

TD12 TE11 **rose red,** on cover —

Schermack Type III Perforations

TD13 TE12 **red** *450.00*
Pair *900.00*
Pasteup pair —

TD14 TE12a **brown** *150.00*
On cover *525.00*
Pair *350.00*
Guide line pair —
Pasteup pair —
a. Imperf. 100.00
Pair 200.00
b. Pair, No. TD14 + No. TD14a —

Mailometer Type I Perforations

TD14C TE12 **rose red** —
Pair —

A strip of eight No. TD14C is the largest multiple recorded.

TD15 TE12a **brown** *125.00*
Pair *250.00*
Pasteup pair —

Mailometer Type II Perforations

TD15A TE12 **red** —
Pair —
Guide line pair —

TD16 TE12a **brown** —
Pair —
Guide line pair —
Pasteup pair —

Mailometer Type III Perforations

TD17 TE12a **brown** —
Pair —

See Vending and Affixing Machines Perforations section for illustrations of perforation types.

Bureau of Engraving & Printing Test Stamps for Rotary Press Development

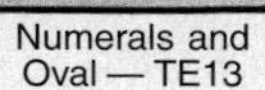

Numerals and Oval — TE13

Numerals and Alexander Hamilton — TE14

Nos. TD18-TD23 were the first test stamps used by the BEP during efforts to develop rotary press printing as a less costly method of stamp production than flat plate printing. Experiments were conducted with intaglio (engraving), letterpress (typography) and offest lithography printing. Engraving was the selected technique. The rotary press was developed under the direction of BEP Director Joseph E. Ralph, but is generally named the Stickney Press after its inventor and patent holder, Benjamin F. Stickney.

1909 Engr. *Imperf.*
Ungummed

TD18 TE13 **red** *2,000.*
Pair *4,000.*
Block of 9 with pencil inscription on back *14,000.*

Inscription on block of 9 reads "first impression printed from an experimental press designed by J. E. Ralph & B. F. Stickney from intaglio roll JER."

1910 Ungummed

TD19 TE14 **red** 125.00
Block of 4 600.00

No. TD19 portrait has facial shading composed of fine lines and dots. Subjects spaced 3½mm horizontally and 2mm vertically.

Typo.
(Letterpress) ***Perf. 12 Vert.***
Ungummed

TD20 TE14 **red** *3,000.*

Perf. 12 Horiz.
Ungummed

TD21 TE14 **red** *1,500.*

Perf. 12
Ungummed

TD22 TE14 **red** —

The portrait on Nos. TD20-TD22 has facial shading composed of fine lines and small squares, open-centered when large.

1910 Offset (Litho.) *Perf. 10¼ Horiz.*

TD23 TE14 **red** 400.00
Pair 800.00
Pair, on cover 1,250.

The portrait of No. TD23 has facial shading composed of dots and short lines providing a coarse appearance.

Pairs invariably have one row of perfs cutting slightly into the stamp design and are valued thus. Stamps in pairs alternate 23mm and 25mm tall.

Nos. TD18-TD22 were made by the BEP; No. TD23 was made by an unknown company. The BEP did not buy an offset press until 1914.

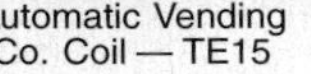

Automatic Vending Co. Coil — TE15

TE15a

1909 ***Imperf.***

TD24 TE15 **red** *275.00*
Pair *550.00*

Block of 4 *1,250.*

U.S. Automatic Vending Co. Type 1 separations

TD24A TE15a **red** *200.00*
Vert. pair *425.00*

Rosback perf 11.75 Vert.

TD24C TE15 **red** *175.00*
Horiz. pair *350.00*
d. Vert. pair, unslit horiz. *350.00*
Block of 4 *1,000.*

Imperf

TD24E TE15 **green** *275.00*
Horiz. pair *550.00*
Vert. pair *650.00*

Simplex Mfg. Co. — TE16

TE16a

1909-10 **Solid Background** ***Imperf.***
TD25 TE16 **red** 250.00

Horizontal Lines in Background

TD26 TE16a **green** 250.00

Simplex Stamp Affixer — TE17

1909-10 ***Imperf.***
TD27 TE17 **red** *500.00*
Vert. pair —

C & R Sales Company, Newark, N.J. — TE17a

Printed by the American Bank Note Co.

1909-11 ***Perf. 12 Horiz.***
TD27A TE17a **red** —
Pair —

C & R Sales Co. was incorporated Oct. 22, 1909 and the company name was changed to Postcraft on Feb. 27, 1911. See No. TD66.

"White Stamp Affixer" Coil — TE17b

1910s ***Perf. 8½ Horiz.***
TD27B TE17b **red** —
Pair —

Test Stamps for Offset Printing

Minerva Facing Right — TE18

Minerva Facing Left (Text Reversed) — TE19

Nos. TD28-TD29 were made to test the Harris offset press at the Bureau of Engraving & Printing. The offset method was not adopted in 1910 but several Harris presses were used to print revenue stamps and the offset postage issues of 1918-20.

1910 **Litho.** ***Imperf.***
Design: 30½x34mm
Ungummed White Wove Paper

TD28 TE18 **red** 650.00
Pair 1,300.
Block of 4 —

Design: 30x33½mm

TD29 TE19 **red** 650.00
Pair 1,300.
Block of 4 —

Nos. TD28 and TD29 were printed from a 192-subject plate to test a Harris press at the Bureau of Engraving and Printing in June 1910. Stamps were printed on watermarked paper, but it appears the watermark only existed in the left and right sheet margins. Stamps almost never show the watermark.

The Minerva stamps are about 50% larger than definitive-size stamps (the design size is about 30x34mm).

The offset method was not adopted in 1910, but several Harris presses were used to print revenue stamps and the offset postage issues of 1918-1920.

"Standard Stamp Affixer" — TE20

1910s ***Perf. 8½ Vert.***
TD30 TE20 **red** —
Pair —

Standard Stamp Affixer Coils

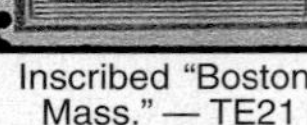

Inscribed "Boston, Mass." — TE21

Inscribed "Everett, Mass." — TE22

Inscribed "Somerville, Mass." — TE23

1910s ***Perf. 10½ Vert.***
TD31 TE21 **green** —
Pair —
TD32 TE21 **red** 20.00
Pair 50.00
TD33 TE22 **green** 20.00
Pair 50.00
TD33A TE22 **red** 20.00
Pair 50.00

Alternating Perf. 8¼ and 8½ Vert.

TD34 TE23 **green** 15.00
Pair 35.00

Perf. 8½ Vert.

TD35 TE23 **light green** 20.00
Pair 50.00

Perf. 10½ Vert.

TD36 TE23 **green** 20.00
Pair 50.00

Alternating Perf. 11 and 10¼ Vert.

TD36A TE23 **red** 20.00
Pair 50.00

Multipost Co. Coil — TE24

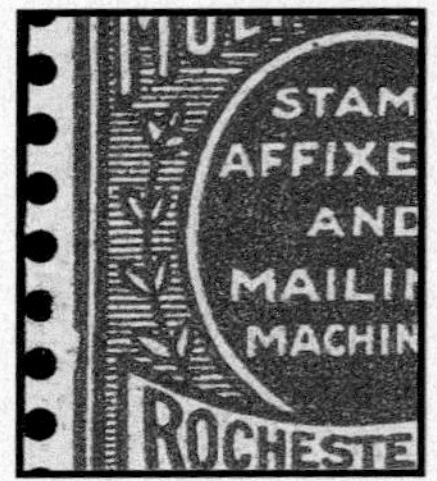
TE24 Detail

TE24a Detail

1910-20 ***Perf. 9¾ Vert.***
TD37 TE24 **red** 5.00
Pair 10.00

Perf. 11½ Vert.

TD37A TE24 **red** —
Pair *150.00*

Perf. 11¾ Vert.

TD37B TE24 **red** —
Pair —

Perf. 10¼ Vert.

TD38 TE24a **red** 20.00
Pair 50.00

No. TD37 has full shading lines, and No. TD38 has shorter shading lines.

No. TD38 exists precanceled Cleveland/Ohio between lines, in violet.

On some rolls of No. TD38, the design of every other stamp is 1mm taller and 1mm wider than on the adjacent stamp. Every other vertical column of perforations has slightly larger diameter perforation holes.

Midland Supply Co. Coil — TE24b

Perf. 10½ Vert.

TD38A TE24b **red** —
Pair —

Extensive Manufacturing Co. Coils — TE25

1911-13 ***Perf. 8½ Horiz.***

TD39 TE25 **red & blue** 20.00
Pair 45.00

Perf. 10¼ Vert.

TD40 TE25 **carmine & black** 35.00
Pair 75.00

Perf. 10¾ Vert.

TD41 TE25 **carmine & black** 35.00
Pair 75.00

Standard Mailing Machine Co. Coils — TE26

1913 ***Perf. 10½ Vert.***

TD42 TE26 **red** 40.00
Pair 80.00
TD43 TE26 **red violet** 40.00
Pair 80.00

Blank Coil Design Type

Blank Coil Design — TE26a

Blank Coil Design — TE26b

1910-27 **Smooth Gum** ***Imperf.***

TD44 TE20 blank —
Pair —

Expertization is recommended for No. TD44.

Perf. 10½ Vert.

TD45 TE26a blank —
Pair —

No. TD45 is 25mm tall while No. TD79 is 23.5mm tall.

Perf. 11 Vert.

TD45A TE26a blank —

Nos. TD45 and TD45A, and possibly TD44, were produced for General Vending Service Company, Baltimore, MD.

Pair —

Schermack Type III Perforations

TD46 TE26a blank —
Pair —
Paste up pair —

Mailometer Type I Perforations

TD47 TE26a blank *100.00*
Pair —
Paste up pair —

Mailometer Type II Perforations

TD48 TE26a blank —
Pair —
Paste up pair —

Mailometer Type III Perforations

TD49 TE26a blank —
Pair —
Paste up pair —

Perf. 11 Vert. Schermack Type I 7-hole Perforations

TD50 TE26a blank —
Pair —

Perf. 10 Vert. Schermack Type I 7-hole Perforations

TD50A TE26a blank —
Pair —

Illustrations of the different private perforation type test stamps are found in the 'Vending & Affixing Machine Perforations' section of this catalogue.

For other blank coil test stamps see Nos. TD75, TD79, TD106 and TD122.

George Washington — TE27

1912 **Without Gum** ***Imperf.***

TD51 TE27 **brown** 100.00
Pair 200.00
Block of 4 450.00

No. TD51 tested a photo-etching process by Bruckmann A. G. of Munich, Germany.

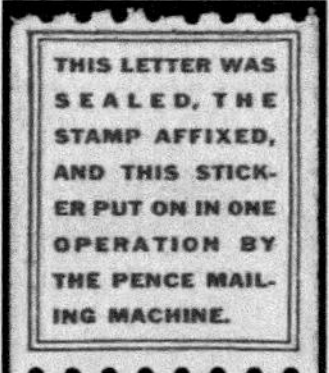
THIS LETTER WAS SEALED, THE STAMP AFFIXED, AND THIS STICKER PUT ON IN ONE OPERATION BY THE PENCE MAILING MACHINE.

Pence Mailing Machine — TE27a

1914 ***Perf 8½ Horiz.***

TD51A TE27a **red** 100.00
Pair —

New Jersey Vending Machine Co. Coil — TE28

1914-16 ***Perf. 10½ Vert.***

TD52 TE28 **red violet** —
Pair —

National Envelope Sealing and Stamp Manufacturing Coils

Brattleboro, VT. — TE29

Boston, Mass. — TE29a

1915 ***Perf. 8½ Horiz.***

TD53 TE29 **red & blue** —
Pair —
TD54 TE29a **red** —
Pair —

U.S. Stamp Distributing and Sales Corporation Coil — TE29b

1919 ***Perf. 11 Horiz.***

TD54A TE29a **red** —
Pair —

Alternating Perf. 8½ and 8¼ Vert.

TD54B TE29b **red** —
Pair —

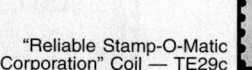

"Reliable Stamp-O-Matic Corporation" Coil — TE29c

1920s ***Perf. 9½ Vert.***

TD54C TE29c **red** —
Pair —

Mailometer Coils — TE30

1922 ***Nine small perforation holes***

TD55 TE30 **red** —
Pair —

Perf. 10¼ Vert. (10 small holes)

TD56 TE30 **violet** —
Pair —
On cover *550.00*

Perf. 12 Vert. (8 small holes)

TD57 TE30 **violet** —
Pair —

Perf. 12 Vert. (9 small holes)

TD57A TE30 **violet** —
Pair —

Perf. 10¼ Vert.

TD58 TE30 **red** —
Pair —
On cover —

TE30a

Perf. 10½ Vert.

TD59 TE30a **red** —
Pair —

TE30b

Perf. 10½ Vert.

TD60 TE30b **red** —
Pair —

TE30c

Perf. 10½ Vert.

TD60A TE30c **red** —
Pair —

Wizard Stamp Affixer Coil — TE31

1912-14 ***Perf. 10¼ Vert.***

TD61 TE31 **red** —
Pair —

Kendall Stamp Affixer — TE32

1917 ***Alternating Perf. 10.6 and 10.4 Vert.***

TD61A TE32 **blue** *300.00*
Pair *650.00*

Wizard Stamp Affixer Coil — TE32a

Wizard Stamp Affixer Coil — TE32b

1920s ***Perf. 10 Vert.***

TD62 TE32a **red & blue** —
Pair —

A large version of design TE32a exists with perforating similar to Schermack Type III. It is 28x41mm and is believed to have been used to test a mechanical mattress label applicator.

TD62A TE32b **red & blue** —
Pair —

On No. TD62A, "MADE IN AMERICA" is outlined in red.

Postage Stamp Machine Co. Coil — TE33

1920s ***Perf. 8½ Vert.***

TD63 TE33 **red** —
Pair —

Natural Method Stamp Affixer — TE33a

1910-30 ***Perf. 11¾ Vert.***

TD63A TE33a **red** —
Pair —

"Security Sealing and Stamping Machine Company" Coil — TE33b

1910-30 ***Perf. 8½ Horiz.***

TD63B TE33b **red** —
Pair —

Licensed Sanitary Postage Coil — TE34

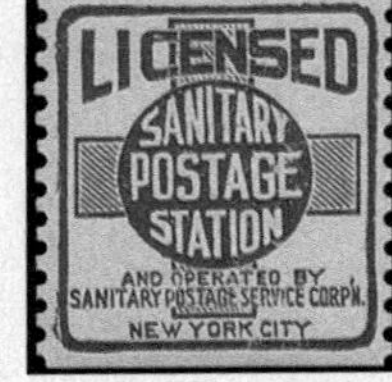

TE34a

1920s ***Perf. 10½ Horiz.***

TD64 TE34 **red** —
Pair —

Perf. 10¾ Vert.

TD65 TE34a **red** 17.50
Pair 35.00

Postcraft Stamp Affixer Coil — TE35

1920s ***Perf. 10 Vert.***

TD66 TE35 **red** —
Pair —

Vidaver Mailing Machine Co. Inc. Coil — TE36

1920s ***Perf. 10½ Vert.***

TD67 TE36 **red** 90.00
Pair 180.00

Agnew Auto Mailing — TE37

1920s ***Perf. 12***

TD68 TE37 **red brown** 45.00
TD68A TE37 **red** —
TD68B TE37 **dark green** —

Molyneux Automatic Mailing Machine Coil — TE38a

1920s ***Perf. 11¾x12***

TD69A TE38a **light blue green** —
TD69B TE38a **orange** —

Stearns-Daniels Co. Coil — TE39

1920s-30s ***Perf. 10¼ Vert.***

TD70 TE39 **green** —
Pair —

RO-TA-RE Stamp Affixer Service Machines Company — TE39a

1910-30 ***Perf. 10¼ Vert.***

TD70A TE39a **blue** —
Pair —

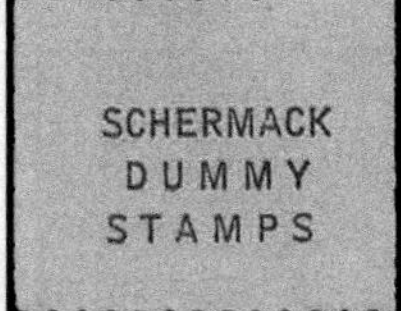

Schermack Dummy Coil — TE41

1920s-30s ***Perf. 10½ Horiz.***

TD72 TE41 **red** —
Pair —

National Postal Meter Co., Inc. Coil — TE42

1920s-30s ***Perf. 9¾ Vert.***

TD73 TE42 **red** —
Pair —

Stampmasters Inc. Coil — TE43

1920s-30s ***Perf. 9¾ Vert.***

TD74 TE43 **violet** 15.00
Pair 30.00

Blank Coil Design Type

Produced by Bureau of Engraving & Printing.

1927-30 ***Perf. 9¾ Vert.***

Horiz. Ribbed Gum

TD75 TE26a blank .60
Pair 1.25

For other blank coil test stamps, see Nos. TD44, TD45, TD45A, TD46, TD47, TD48, TD49, TD50, TD50A, TD79, TD106 and TD122.

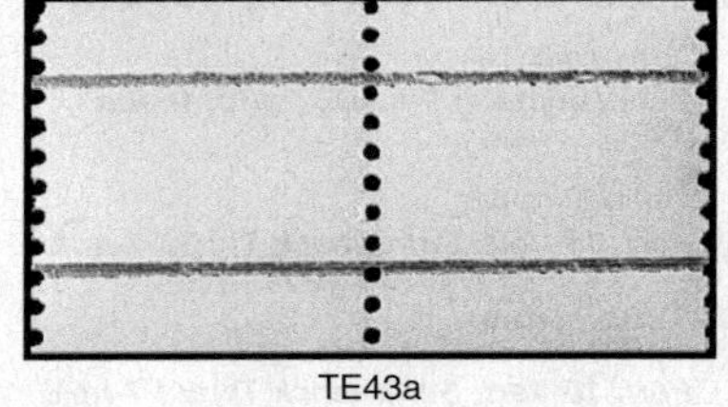

TE43a

With Red Horizontal Lines 13½ mm Apart

TD76 TE43a blank, *1930-40* .60
Pair 1.25
Pair with gap in lines 4.25
Strip of 10 with wide and narrow line gaps 16.00

Gaps appear every six stamps and alternate between wide (3mm) and narrow (2mm) gaps.

Central Machine & Supply Co. Coil — TE44

1930s ***Perf. 9¾ Vert.***
TD77 TE44 **red** —
Pair —

Puritan Mailing Machine Co. Coil — TE45

1930s ***Perf. 8½ Vert.***
TD78 TE45 **red & black** —
Pair —

The Postamper Co. Coil — TE45a

1930s ***Perf. 10½ Vert.***
TD78A TE45a **red** —
Pair —

Peerless Stamp Affixer Coil — TE45b

1930s ***Perf. 10½ Vert.***
TD78B TE45b **red** —
Pair —

Blank Coil Design Type

Zeigle Coil, Blue Paper — TE45c

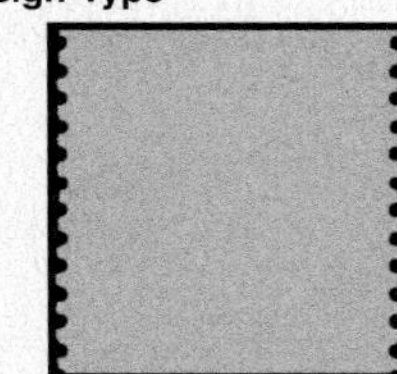
Zeigle Coil, Green Paper — TE45d

Zeigle Coil, Yellow Paper — TE45e

Produced by Electric Vendors (Zeigle), Inc.

1930s ***Perf. 10½ Vert.***

Shiny Smooth Gum

TD79 TE26b blank 14.00
Pair 30.00
TD80 TE45c *blue* 14.00
Pair 30.00
TD81 TE45d *green* 14.00
Pair 30.00
TD82 TE45e *yellow* 14.00
Pair 30.00

Nos. TD79-TD82 are 23.5mm tall. No. TD79 resembles No. TD45, which is 25mm tall.

Blank Design Type

Produced by Bureau of Engraving & Printing.

1920s-1970 ***Perf. 10***

With Gum Breaker Ridges 5½mm Apart

TD83 TE10 blank, *1920s* 25.00
Block of 4 100.00
Vert. pair with horiz. gutter between —

With Gum Breaker Ridges 11mm Apart

Perf. 11¼x10½

TD84 TE10 blank, *1936* 5.00
Block of 4 20.00
Vert. pair with horiz. gutter between 80.00

With Gum Breaker Ridges Alternating Between 5mm and 6.5mm Apart

Perf. 11¼x10½

TD84A TE10 blank, *1956* 10.00
Block of 4 40.00

Genuine examples of No. TD84A are known with blue, green or red defacement markings, and sell for somewhat less thus.

For other small blank sheet test stamps with different gauge perforations, gum breaker spacings, and/or tagging, see Nos. TD10, TD11, TD83, TD84, TD113, TD114 and TD114A.

Blank Commemorative — TE45g

Stamp Size:40x25mm

With Gum Breaker Ridges Alternating Between 5mm and 6.5mm Apart

Brownish Gum

Perf. 11¼x10½

TD85 TE45g blank, *1950s* 50.00
Block of 4 200.00

With Gum Breaker Ridges 11mm Apart

TD85A TE45g blank, *1930s* 50.00
Block of 4 200.00

Produced by American Bank Note Co.

1943 ***Perf. 12***
TD86 TE45g blank —

No. TD86 was produced as a test for the Overrun Countries stamps. No. TD86 exists in a pane of 50 with manuscript markings in the margins.

Multipost Mailing System & Equipment Coil — TE46

1930s-40s ***Perf. 9½ Vert.***
TD87 TE46 **red** —
Pair —

Multipost Co. Walter I. Plant Agent Coil — TE46a

1930s ***Perf. 11¾ Vert.***
TD87A TE46a **red** —
On cover —
Pair —

Multipost Agents The Office Appliance Co. Coil — TE46b

1930s ***Perf. 11¾ Vert.***
TD87B TE46b **red** —
Pair —

Memphis Multipost Coil — TE46c

1930s ***Perf. 10 Vert.***
TD87C TE46c **red** —
Pair —

National Postage Service Coil — TE46d

1930s ***Perf. 9¼ Vert.***
TD87D TE46d **red** —
Pair —

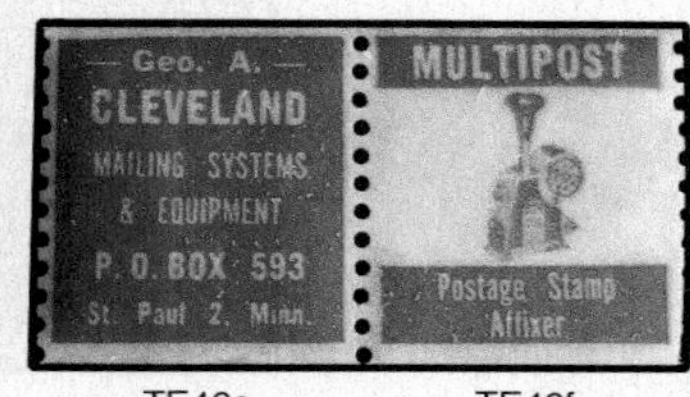

TE46e TE46f

No. TD87E, George A. Cleveland Coil. No. TD87F, Multipost Postage Stamp Affixer Coil.

1930s ***Perf. 10 Vert.***
TD87E TE46e **red** —
TD87F TE46f **red** —
a. Pair, #TD87E-TD87F —

Multipost Mailing Machines Coil — TE46g

1930s ***Perf. 9¾ Vert.***
TD87G TE46g **red** —

Multipost Sales Agency Coil — TE46h

TD87H TE46h **red** —
Pair —

Catalogue values for stamps in this section, from this point to the end, are for Never Hinged items.

Multipost Commercial Controls Coil — TE47

1944-49 *Perf. 9¾ Vert.*

TD88 TE47 **blue** 20.00
Pair 45.00
TD89 TE47 **black** 20.00
Pair 45.00
On cover 75.00
TD90 TE47 **blue black** 20.00
Pair 45.00

Multipost Commercial Controls Multipost Mailmaster Coil — TE48

Multipost Friden Multipost Mailmaster Coil — TE49

1944-49 *Perf. 9¾ Vert.*

TD91 TE48 **violet** 20.00
Pair 50.00
TD92 TE48 **red** 30.00
Pair 50.00
TD93 TE49 **red** 10.00
Pair 22.50

Framed Rectangle — TE50

Printed by Bureau of Engraving & Printing.

1954-56 *Perf. 11.2x10.5*

TD94 TE50 **carmine** 75.00
Block of 4 300.00
P# block of 4, P#141730 or 141731 800.00
a. Imperf. 110.00
Pair 225.00
Block of 4 450.00
P# block of 4, P#141730 or 141731 850.00
Horiz. pair, with vert. gutter with EE dashes between stamps 325.00

No. TD94a and TD97a are often confused with each other. No. TD94a is an imperforate rotary press sheet stamp and thus is slightly narrower and slightly taller (typically 19.0x22.5mm) than No. TD97a, which is an imperforate rotary press coil stamp (typically19.5x22.0mm).

Coil Stamps
Perf. 9¾ Vert.

TD95 TE50 **violet**, large holes 5.00
Pair 10.00
Joint line pair 30.00
On cover with "Parade of Postal Progress" cancel 85.00
Small holes, *1959* 6.00
Pair 15.00
Joint line pair 35.00
a. Imperf., pair 100.00
Joint line pair 300.00

Misperforated examples of No. TD95 are common and sell for less.

TD96 TE50 **red violet,** small holes 2.00
Pair 5.00
Joint line pair 15.00
Large holes 5.00
Pair 12.50
Joint line pair 125.00
On cover with "Parade of Postal Progress" cancel 85.00
a. Imperf., pair *500.00*
Joint line pair *950.00*
Block of 8 with joint line, sheet margin and P#165939 and 165940, unslit horiz. —

See "large hole" and "small hole" illustrations after No. 1053 in Postage section.

TD97 TE50 **carmine** 200.00
Pair 400.00
Joint line pair 600.00
Vert. pair, unslit horiz. —
Block of 10 with joint line and sheet margin, P#164564 or 164565 *2,500.*
a. Imperf., horiz. pair 300.00
Joint line pair 450.00
Block of 10 with joint line and sheet margin, P#164564 or 164565 *2,500.*

All known examples of No. TD97 have been hand cut from perforated coil web sections. All known examples of No. TD97a are cut from imperforate coil web sections. Examples of Nos. TD97 and TD97a are unknown as BEP-produced coils.

See No. TD94a and its footnote.

Kansas Territorial Centennial Experimental TE51

Printed by Eureka Specialty Printing.

1954 *Perf. 12x11¾*

TD98 TE51 **brown, red & yellow** *150.00*
Block of 4 *600.00*

Nebraska Territorial Centennial Experimental — TE52

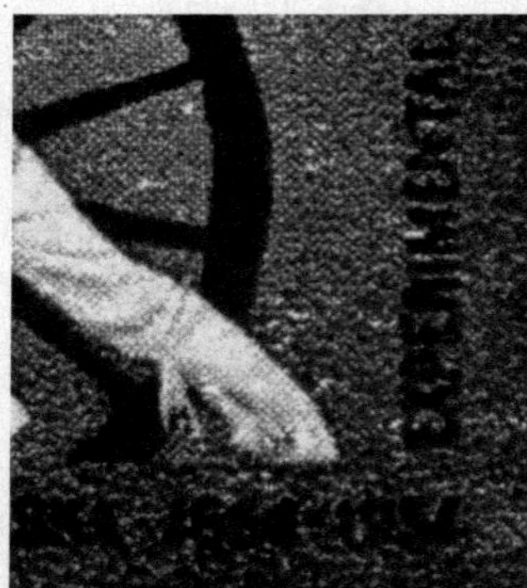
Coarse Impression — TE52 Detail

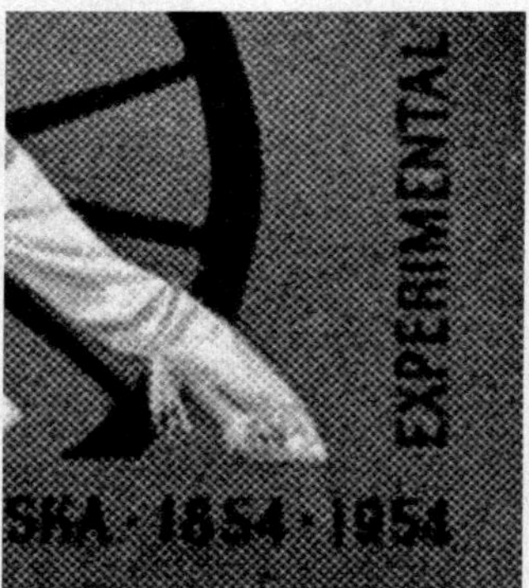

Fine Impression — TE52a Detail

Printed by Eureka Specialty Printing.

1954 **Solid Background** *Imperf.*
Design Size: 37x21mm

TD99 TE52 **brown** *90.00*
Block of 4 *360.00*
a. **brown,** *tan* 150.00
Block of 4 600.00

TD100 TE52 **black** *30.00*
Block of 4 *120.00*
a. **gray** 30.00
Block of 4 120.00
TD101 TE52 **blue** *30.00*
Block of 4 *120.00*
a. **blue,** *tan* *150.00*
Block of 4 600.00

Background of Dots
Ungummed
Imperf

TD101B TE52a **black** 200.00
Block of 4 *800.00*

No. TD101B was printed as a sheet of 50 on ungummed paper. The design is similar to No. TD100, but the background printing is a distinct cross-hatching rather than the usual blurred shading, probably due to two different printing processes being used. Nos. TD99, TD100 and TD101 are only known in blocks of four or fewer; one sheet of 50 of No. TD101B is known.

Eureka Specialty Printing Co. — TE52b

Printed by Eureka Specialty Printing.

1954? *Imperf.*
Design Size: 38x22mm

TD101C TE52b **green** *750.00*
TD101D TE52b **blue** *750.00*
TD101E TE52b **brown** *750.00*
TD101F TE52b **pink** *750.00*

Pitney Bowes Co. — TE53

1958-59 **Tagged** *Imperf.*
Helecon Paper

TD102 TE53 **carmine** —
a. Lumogen paper —
TD103 TE53 **black** —

Helecon paper glows orange red under shortwave UV light. Lumogen paper glows bright yellow-green under shortwave UV light.

Stamp-E-Z Postage Stamp Affixer Coil — TE54

1960s *Imperf.*

TD104 TE54 **red violet** —
Pair —

Perf. 10¼ Vert.

TD104A TE54 **red violet** —
Pair —

Perf. 9¾ Vert.

TD105 TE54 **red** —
Pair —

Blank Coil Design of 1910-27

Produced by Bureau of Engraving & Printing

1960-70s **Overall Tagging** *Perf. 9¾ Vert.*
Dull Gum

TD106 TE26a blank 12.50
Pair 25.00
Joint line pair 100.00

No. TD106 was produced on an inked press. The ink was wiped, but some stamps have wiping marks and black joint lines.

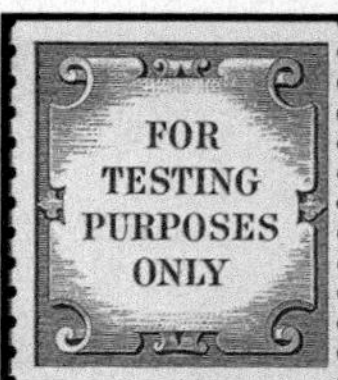

For Testing Purposes Only Coil — TE55

Produced by Bureau of Engraving & Printing.

1962-86 **Engr.** ***Perf. 9¾ Vert.***

Design Size: Approximately 19½mm Wide

TD107 TE55 **black,** untagged, shiny gum 1.00
Pair 2.00
Joint line pair 12.50
a. Tagged, shiny gum 1.00
Pair 2.00
Joint line pair 10.00
b. Tagged, pebble-surfaced gum .50
Pair 1.00
Joint line pair 5.00
c. As "b," imperf. pair 250.00
Joint line pair 750.00
d. Tagged, dull gum .50
Pair 1.00
Joint line pair 5.00
e. Untagged, dull gum 1.00
Pair 2.00
Joint line pair 10.00

No. TD107 is known on hi-brite fluorescent paper.

No. TD107b is known on slightly yellowish paper.

No. TD107b has been found with red, dark red, rose red, blue, blue green, green, orange, violet, brown, black violet, black, gray black, gray and silver defacement lines, which vary in number and thickness and which have been known to have been forged. Some defacement line colors may all be forgeries.

No. TD107e is known on fluorescent and non-fluorescent papers, as well as on papers with diagonal gum striations or wavy, intermittent gum striations.

TD108 TE55 **carmine,** tagged, *1970* 850.00
Pair 1,700.
Joint line pair —

The tagging on Nos. TD108 and TD114 is orange red. All other tagged test stamps except TD102 glow yellow green.

TD109 TE55 **slate green,** untagged, dull gum, *1980* 75.00
Pair 150.00
Joint line pair 400.00
a. Imperf., pair 350.00
Joint line pair 500.00
b. Vert. pair, imperf. horiz. 200.00
P# block of 12 with joint line, imperf or unslit horiz., P# 36111 and 36112 1,500.
c. Tagged, gray paper, shiny gum 160.00
Pair 325.00
Joint line pair —

No. TD109 was sent to Germany in large imperf. and part perforate sheets to test coil production equipment.

TD110 TE55 **orange,** *gray,* tagged, *1975* 1,000.
Pair 2,000.
Joint line pair —

TD111 TE55 **brown,** untagged, *1978* 1.50
Pair 3.00
Joint line pair 30.00

Design Size: Approximately 19mm Wide

TD112 TE55 **black,** untagged, dull gum *1986* .50
Pair 1.00

No. TD107 was printed on the Cottrell press. No. TD112 was printed on the B press.

See Nos. TD121, TD126-TD127, TD133, TD133A, TD136-TD137, and TD140.

"For Testing Purposes Only" Commemorative Size — TE55a

1970 ***Perf. 10½x11¼***

Stamp Size: 25x40mm

Alternating Horizontal Gum Breaker Ridges 4½ and 6½mm Apart

TD112A TE55a **black,** yellow green tagging, shiny pebbled gum —
Block of 4 —

Blank Design Types

Produced by Bureau of Engraving & Printing, with tagging added by Pitney Bowes.

1964-70 ***Perf. 11***

TD113 TE10 blank, yellow green tagging 75.00
Block of 4 300.00

TD114 TE10 blank, orange red tagging 75.00
Block of 4 300.00

Nos. TD113-TD114 was produced as a test for Nos. 1254-1257.

With Gum Breaker Ridges 11mm Apart

Perf. 11¼x10½

TD114A TE10 blank, yellow green tagging *1970* 15.00
Block of 4 60.00
Horiz. pair with vert. gutter between 75.00

For other small blank sheet test stamps with different gauge perforations, gum breaker spacings, and/or tagging, see Nos. TD10, TD83, TD85, TD84A, TD113 and TD114.

Blank Commemorative, Light Brown Paper — TE45h

Perf. 11¼x10½

TD114B TE45h blank, *light brown,* yellow green tagging, *1970* 25.00
Block of 4 100.00
Horiz. pair with vert. gutter between 150.00
Vert. pair with horiz. gutter between 250.00

No. TD114B is a commemorative-size blank stamp on the light brown paper used for the bison stamp No. 1392.

Jefferson Memorial Experimental — TE56

Printed by Bureau of Engraving & Printing.

1966 **Untagged** ***Perf. 11***

Engraved (Multicolor Huck Press)

TD114D TE56 **black & orange** 1,000.
Block of 4 4,000.

No. TD114D was produced as a test for No. 1363, the 1968 Christmas stamp. A similar test stamp (without the three lines of text to the left of the design) was made in 1962 to test the BEP's 3-color sheet-fed Giori press. No examples of that test stamp are currently known in collector hands. All known No. TD114D stamps are without gum.

Flag — TE56a

Produced by Avery Products Corp.

1970s ***Die Cut***

Self-Adhesive

TD115 TE56a **blue,** on roulетted backing paper *300.00*
Block of 4 *1,200.*
a. On imperforate backing paper —

Proclaim Liberty TE57

1970s ***Perf. 12x11.8***

TD116 TE57 **blue, red & green** 75.00

Christmas Test Stamp TE58

Printed by Bureau of Engraving & Printing for Avery Products Corp. to add die cutting.

1973 ***Die Cut***

Self-Adhesive

TD117 TE58 **black,** rouletted backing paper 2.50
Block of 4 with intact matrix 10.00
Pane of 50 150.00
Press sheet of 200 750.00
a. Pair, imperf backing paper —
b. Vert. pair, backing paper rouletted vert. only —

No. TD117 was produced as a test for No. 1552.

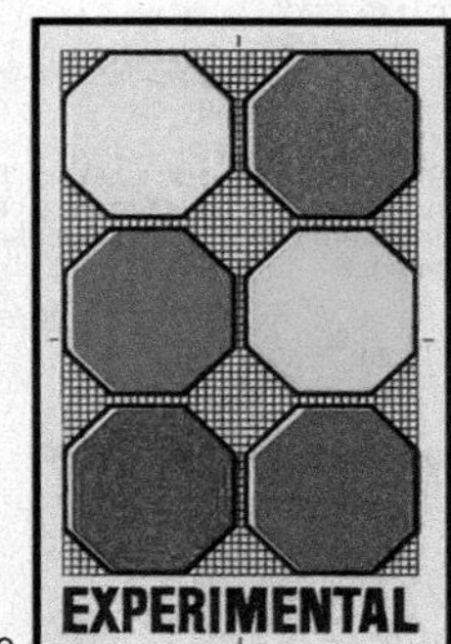

Octagons — TE59

Printed by Bureau of Engraving & Printing.

1979 ***Imperf.***

TD118 TE59 **multicolored** 140.00
Block of 4 600.00
P# block of 4, P#173404 1,200.

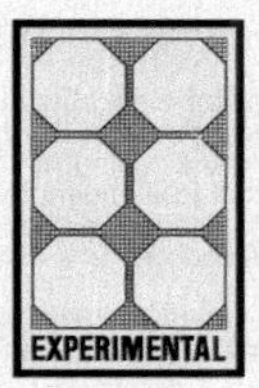

TE59a

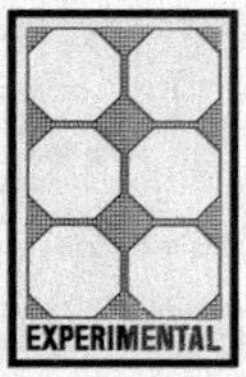

EXPERIMENTAL

TE59b

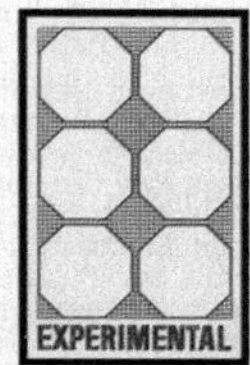

TE59c

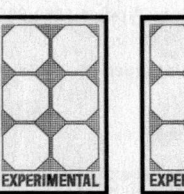

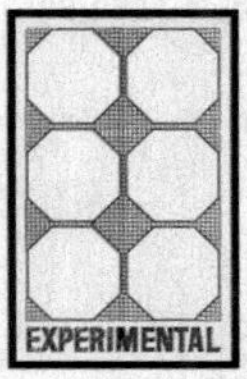

EXPERIMENTAL

TE59d

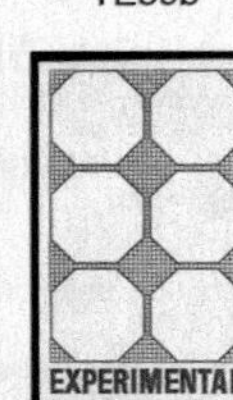

TE59e

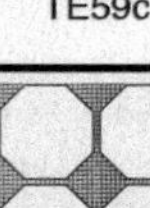

EXPERIMENTAL

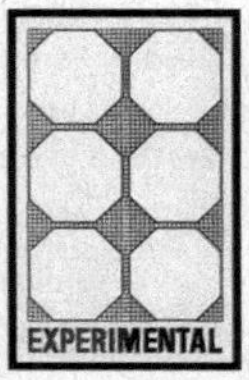

TE59f

Printed by Goebel, GmbH (Germany) from materials supplied by the Bureau of Engraving & Printing.

1979-80 *Imperf.*

TD118A TE59a **black** 200.00
TD118B TE59b **black and blue** 200.00
TD118C TE59c **blue** 200.00
TD118D TE59d **blue and red** 200.00
TD118E TE59e **red** 200.00
TD118F TE59f **red and black** 200.00

A 128-subject web section of Nos. TD118A-TD118F is known to exist. The large botton margin contains a red EE bar under every other column of No. TD118E (TE59e) solid red stamps. These stamps were printed from a 96-subject plate.

Flag and Eagle Over Trees Coil — TE60

Flag and Eagle Over Trees Coil — TE60a

Printed by Stamp Venturers.

1989 *Perf. 10 Vert.*

TD119 TE60 **gray** .25
Pair .50
Strip of 5 with counting number on reverse 50.00

Most examples of Nos. TD119 and TD120 come from coils of 100 stamps. Rolls of 3,000 No. TD119 had a four-digit counting number printed on the reverse of every tenth stamp. Back numbers were used to determine the number of stamps remaining on a roll.

Rouletted

TD120 TE60a **gray** .25
Pair .50

Flag and Eagle Over Trees — TE60b

Printed by Sennett Security Products.

TD120A TE60b **multicolored** 15.00
Pair 35.00

Most examples of No. TD120A have serpentine die cuts that are slightly misplaced into the top of the design. Because the die cutting is shallow, done from the back and hiding in the design, they can appear to be imperforate, but true imperforate examples are unknown. Values shown are for stamps with misplaced die cuts. Examples with correctly placed die cuts command a higher price.

A similar design, in a sheet of 20 commemorative-size multicolor stamps, was distributed as a souvenir at World Stamp Expo 2000.

For Testing Purposes Only Type of 1962-88

Printed by Bureau of Engraving & Printing.

1978 **Photo.** **Untagged** *Imperf.*

TD121 TE55 **black,** shiny gum 75.00
Pair 150.00
Block of 4 400.00
Block of 6 with bottom sheet margin, EE dashes and P#173285 —

No. TD121 was printed on the Andreotti press. A bottom sheet margin block of 18 (9x2) is known with EE dashes, six sets of black color-density bars and P#173285.

Blank Coil Design Type of 1910-27

Produced by Bureau of Engraving & Printing.

1990s **Untagged** *Perf. 9¾ Vert.*

TD122 TE26a blank, coated paper, shiny gum 10.00
Pair 20.00
a. Uncoated paper, shiny gum 10.00
Pair 20.00
b. Coated paper, dull gum 10.00
Pair 20.00
c. Uncoated paper, dull gum —
Pair —

No. TD122 with shiny gum is known on hi-brite fluorescent paper.

Stylized Eagle Coil — TE61

Printed by 3M Corp.

Linerless Self-Adhesive

1992 **Tagged** *Imperf.*

TD123 TE61 **multicolored** 15.00
Pair 30.00
P# strip of 5, #1111 325.00

Stamps have printed simulated perforations only. Vertical pairs (or larger) are known cut from the web.

Rectangle With Thick Lines Coil — TE62

Printed by Bureau of Engraving & Printing.

1996 **Gravure** *Perf. 9¾ Vert.*

TD124 TE62 **blue,** shiny gum 50.00
Pair 100.00
Strip of 5 with one stamp with crudely etched reversed "2" 1,500.
Strip of 5 with one stamp with crudely etched reversed "12" 1,500.

Reversed numbers appear in the center of every 24th stamp.

1994 **Offset**

TD125 TE62 **gray black,** dull gum 125.00
Pair 250.00
a. Shiny gum 125.00
Pair 250.00
Strip of 5, one stamp with etched "VI" 1,250.

Rectangle With Thin Lines, Water-Activated Coil — TE62a

1998(?) *Perf. 9¾ Vert.*

TD125B TE62a **blue,** green tagging, dull gum 200.00
Pair 400.00

The same design was used on self-adhesive coils with serpentine die cut perforations. See No. TD130.

For Testing Purposes Only Type of 1962-88

Printed by Bureau of Engraving & Printing (#TD126), Avery-Dennison (#TD127).

1996 *Die Cut*

Self-Adhesive

TD126 TE55 **black & light blue** .25
Pair .50
P# strip of 5, #1111 5.00

Nos. TD126, TD133 and TD136 appear to be printed on blue paper. Light blue ink was applied in several layers to mask the phosphorescence of the tagged white paper before printing the stamps. A four-digit counting number is on the reverse of the backing paper on every 20th stamp on some rolls. No. TD126 is on backing paper taller than the stamps, with a gap between stamps.

"For Testing Purposes Only" — TE55b

Serpentine Die Cut 11.2 Vert.

TD127 TE55b **black** .25
Pair .50
P# strip of 5, #V1 10.00

No. TD127 has printed simulated perforations in addition to serpentine die cutting. Nos. TD127 and TD137 look similar, but No. TD137 does not have the printed simulated perforations. No. TD127 is on backing paper taller than the stamp.

Polar Bear Ice Skating — TE62b

Printed by Ashton-Potter (USA) Ltd.

1995 **Tagged** ***Serpentine Die Cut 11.5x11.8***

Design Size: 21x35mm

Self-Adhesive

TD127A TE62b **multicolored** 750.00
Block of 4 —
Sheetlet of 20 —

The sheetlet of 20 has vertical and horizontal gutters between the stamps with the matrix removed.

Serpentine Die Cut 11x11.5

Tagged

TD127B TE62b **multicolored** 750.00
Block of 4 —
Sheetlet of 20 —

The sheetlet of 20 has no vertical or horizontal gutters between the stamps.

Avery Dennison — TE62c

Printed by Avery Dennison.

1996 ***Serpentine Die Cut 11x11¼***

Design size: 36x21mm

Self-Adhesive

TD127C TE62c **red** 375.00
Block of 4 with plate position in diagram in selvage *1,750.*
P# block of 4, #V1 *2,250.*

No. TD127C was printed in sheets of 200 stamps as ten 20-stamp panes. It was a test for the Scott Nos. 3091-3095 Riverboats issue. Only one pane of 20 was known in collectors' hands and it was broken into two blocks and twelve singles.

Parrot — TE63

Blank Parrot — TE63a

Parrot — TE63b

Printed by Banknote Corporation of America.

1996 Tagged ***Serpentine Die Cut 11¾x11½***

Design Size: 22x31mm

Self-Adhesive

TD128	TE63	**multicolored**	450.00
		Block of 4	—
TD128A	TE63a	**blank**	40.00
		Block of 4	150.00

Design Size: 25x40mm

Perf. 11½

TD129	TE63b	**multicolored**	—

No. TD128 was printed both in sheets of 50 (10x5) and 20 (54). No. TD128A was produced in panes of 50 (10x5). Both Nos. TD128 and TD128 have die cuts that penetrate the backing paper with horizontal slitting that is approximately 15m long behind each stamp. No. TD128A has horizontal slitting continuous across the backing paper.

No. TD129 was used to test luminescent inks.

Commemorative Size Flower — TE63c

Printed by Dittler Brothers Inc. and American Bank Note Co.

1997 Photo. & Engr. Tagged ***Imperf.***

Self-Adhesive

Design Size: 22x31mm

TD129A	TE63c	**multicolored**	375.00
TD129B	TE63c	**multicolored**	375.00

Nos. TD129A and TD129B were both printed in photogravure and intaglio. No. TD129B has engraved black lines in the flower that do not appear on No. TD129A. See Nos. TDB87-TDB88.

Rectangle With Thin Lines, Self-Adhesive Coil — TE62d

Printed by Bureau of Engraving & Printing.

1998 ***Serpentine Die Cut 9¾ Vert.***

Self-Adhesive

TD130	TE62d	**blue**	125.00
		Pair	250.00
		Strip of 3 with number "3" printed inside one stamp	*1,500.*
		Strip of 5 with number "2" printed inside one stamp	—

No. TD130 is on backing paper taller than the stamp with a gap between the stamps. A four-digit counting number is known on the reverse of the backing paper.

No. TD130 stamps with numbers printed inside one stamp are spaced 21 stamps apart. A four-digit counting number is known on the reverse of the backing paper every 20 stamps.

For water-activated gum with TE62a design, see No. TD125B.

Star Spangled Banner Coil — TE64a

Printing on Liner Paper — TE64b

Printed by Sennett Security Products

1998 Tagged ***Serpentine Die Cut 11¼ Vert.***

Self-Adhesive

TD130A	TE64a	**multicolored**, with stamp image printed on back of liner paper	35.00
		Horizontal pair, with stamp image (TE64b) on liner	75.00
		Vertical pair, with stamp image (TE64b) on liner	75.00
		Block of 4, with stamp image (TE64b) on liner	150.00
		Envelope with 8 #TD130A on back	75.00
		Single #TD130A removed from envelope (no liner paper)	7.50

No. TD130A was printed from 210-subject gravure cylinders with horizontal and vertical spaces between stamps. The black stamp image (TE64b) printed on the back of the liner paper is not aligned with the stamp image. All known examples of No. TD130A attached to liner paper were hand cut from a partially processed coil web section.

Coil rolls of 3,000 stamps, with liner paper taller than the stamps and with a gap between stamps, were used in a USPS recycling test conducted in December 1998. Stamps without liner paper have been removed from the backs of envelopes used in that test and are worth less than stamps on the original liner paper.

See Nos. TD130B and TD130C for self-adhesive Star Spangled Banner coils that do not have spaces between the stamp designs, and No. TD130D for linerless coils.

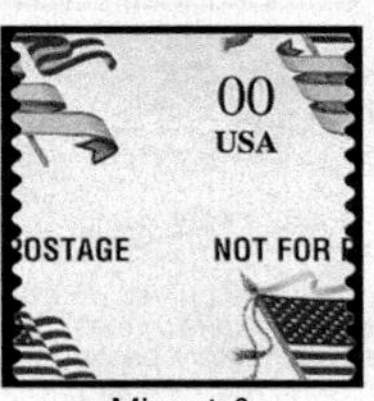

Miscut & Misperforated Coil — TE64c

Imperforate Coil — TE64d

Printed by Sennett Security Products

1998 Tagged ***Serpentine Die Cut 11¼ Vert.***

Self-Adhesive

TD130B	TE64c	**multicolored**	15.00
		Envelope with 8 #TD130B on back	125.00

Imperf.

TD130C	TE64d	**multicolored**, with stamp image (TE64b) printed on back of liner paper	50.00
		Pair	100.00
		Block of 4	225.00
		Block of 4 with web margin showing EE markings	300.00

Nos. TD130B and TD130C were printed from 225-subject gravure cylinders without horizontal and vertical spaces between stamps (intended to be processed into coils of 100). Miscut examples of No. TD130B were created when the die cutting mat intended for No. TD130A (with horizontal and vertical spaces between stamps) was used on the imperforate No. TD130C coil web (without spaces between stamps) to make coils containing 3,000 stamps that could be mechanically applied to the back of envelopes in a USPS test.

The black stamp image (TE64b) printed on the back of No. TD130C is not aligned with the stamp image. All known examples of No. TD130C were hand cut from an imperforate coil web section.

See Nos. TD130A and TD130D for other Star Spangled Banner coils.

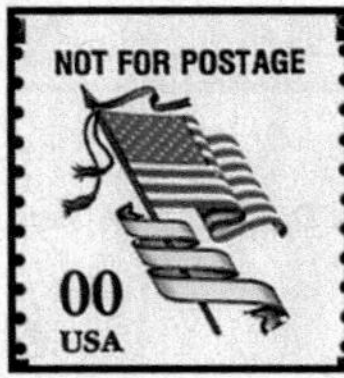

Star Spangled Banner Coil — TE64e

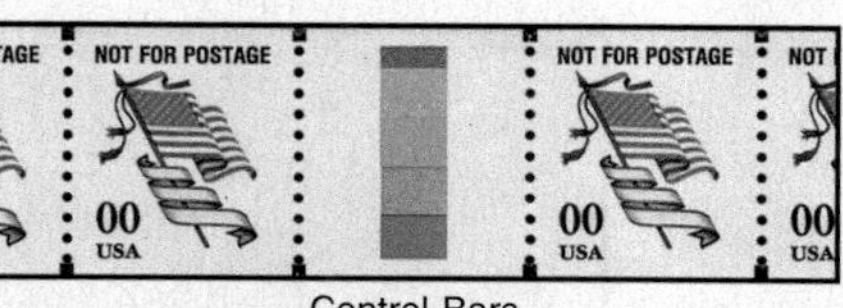

Control Bars

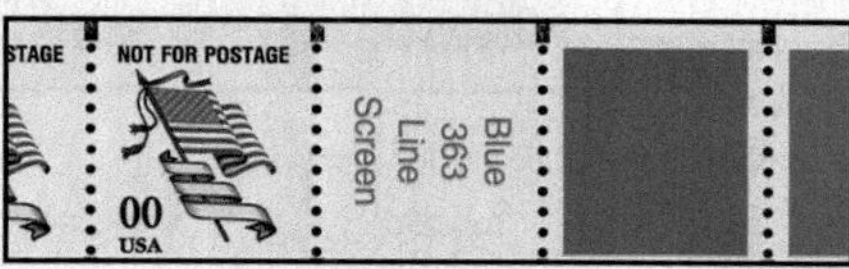

Color Description

Printed by Bureau of Engraving and Printing

1998 Tagged ***Perf. 9¾ Vert.***

Linerless Self-Adhesive

TD130D	TE64e	**multicolored**	30.00
		Pair	60.00
		P# strip of 5, #11111	300.00
		P# strip of 5, #111 1 (missing blue intaglio)	400.00
		Strip of 5, center stamp with multicolor offset color control bars (various combinations exist)	*500.00*
		Strip of 11, center stamp with multicolor offset color control bars, 7 stamps with screen density blocks, 1 stamp with color description	*800.00*

It is possible for the strips of 5 with the center stamp having the offset color control bars to have 15 different color combinations. For the strips of 11 with multicolor offset color control bars, the known colors are magenta, yellow, cyan, blue and black.

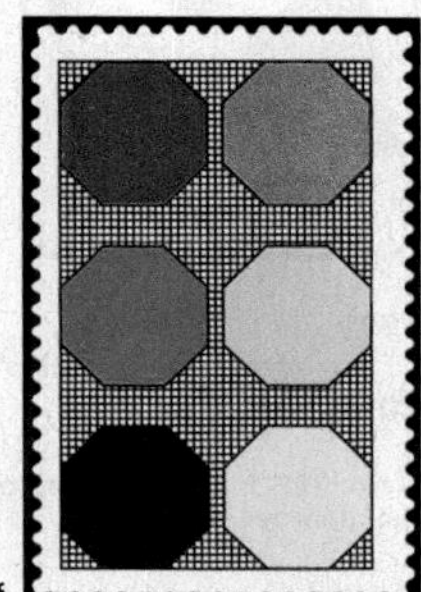
Octagons — TE64f

1998 Tagged ***Serpentine Die Cut 12.6***

Self-Adhesive

TD130E	TE64f	**multicolored**	20.00
		5 #TD130E affixed to envelope back	100.00

All known examples of No. TD130E were affixed to envelope backs for use in USPS mailing tests.

No. TD130E was printed in sheets of 50. Each of the horizontal rows contained stamps with ten different densities in the octagons, ranging from dark colors in the left column of 5 to a very light color in the right column of 5 stamps.

George Clinton — TE64g

1993 Engr. Tagged ***Perf. 11¼x11***

TD130F	TE64g	**blue gray**	150.00
		Block of 4	600.00

No. TD130F was produced by American Bank Note Co. using a die supplied by BEP. No. TD130F has semi-glossy water-activated gum and was printed in panes of 100.

Nos. TDB93 and TDB93A have the same design, but No. TDB93 was produced in 18-stamp self-adhesive convertible booklet panes with serpentine die cutting between the stamps.

Full sheets may have what appears to be unprinted stamps at the right in the margin. Such items are part of the unprinted gutter between panes that have been miscut.

Tropical Fish — TE64h

Printed by Sennett Security Products

1998 **Tagged** ***Imperf.***
Self-Adhesive
Design Size: 36x21½mm

TD130G TE64h **multicolored**		—
	Block of 4	—
	Block of 4, with either top web margin or bottom EE marks	—
	Vertical strip of 6 with 2 each normal, 400- and 500-line screens printing with web margin and EE marks	—

No. TD130G was printed from 84-subject gravure cylinders with three different screen printing intensities on the same sheet. Information printed in the top margin indicates that the top two stamps in the vertical column of 6 stamps were printed with "normal line screens," the middle two were "400 line screens," and the bottom two were "500 line screens." The 500-line screen stamps are noticeably darker than the others. All known examples of No. TD130G were hand cut from an imperforate web section. These test stamps may have been intended to be horizontal coils.

RENA Test Stamp Coil — TE65

1999 ***Die Cut***
Self-Adhesive

TD131 TE65 **blue**		12.50
	Pair	25.00

No. TD131 is on backing paper taller than the stamp with a gap between stamps.

Mailbox Coil — TE66

Printed by Avery Dennison.

2000 ***Imperf.***
Linerless Self-Adhesive

TD132 TE66 **bright magenta**		200.00
	Pair	400.00
a.	Pair with "xxxx" on one stamp	1,500.

Pairs have 1-2mm slit marks between stamps in left and right margins.

For Testing Purposes Only Type of 1962-88

Printed by Bureau of Engraving & Printing.

2000 ***Serpentine Die Cut 9¾ Vert.***
Self-Adhesive

TD133 TE55 **black & light blue**		.50
	Pair	1.00
	P# strip of 5, #1111	4.00

Nos. TD126, TD133 and TD136 appear to be printed on blue paper. Light blue ink was applied in several layers to mask the phosphorescence of the tagged white paper before printing the stamps. A four-digit counting number is on the reverse of the backing paper on every 20th stamp on some rolls. No. TD133 is on backing paper taller than the stamps, with a gap between stamps.

Plate numbers appear every 21 stamps, and a vertical white line can occur at either the far right edge of the numbered stamp or the far left edge of the next stamp to the right. Some unnumbered strips without a plate number also are known with a white line at the far edge of one stamp. The white line is an unprinted gap in the blue.

TD133A TE55 **black**		15.00
	Pair	30.00
	P# strip of 5, #1111	300.00

A four-digit counting number is on the reverse of the backing paper every 20th stamp on some rolls. No. TD133A is on backing paper with no gap between perforation tips.

South Carolina Flag Coil — TE67

Printed by Avery Dennison.

2000 ***Serpentine Die Cut 8½ Vert.***
Self-Adhesive

TD134 TE67 **dark blue**		*450.00*
	Pair	*900.00*
	P# strip of 5, #V1	*2,750.*
TD135 TE67 **light blue**		20.00
	Pair	40.00
	P# strip of 5, #V1	250.00

Plate-number examples of Nos. TD134 and TD135 bear a "2000" year date at lower left.Two rolls of No. TD135 are known with a nine-digit accounting number on the back of the P# stamp, at 35-stamp intervals. The examples known are: 000052763-65 and 000052949-51. This accounting number increases by one digit with each revolution of the stamp-printing sleeve. Value, $300.

For Testing Purposes Only Type of 1962-88

Printed by Bureau of Engraving & Printing (#TD136), Sennett Security Products (#TD137).

For Testing Purposes Only Coil with Vertical Line Between "N" and "L" of "ONLY" — TE55c

1997 ***Serpentine Die Cut 9¾ Vert.***
Self-Adhesive

TD136 TE55c **black & light blue**		.65
	Pair	1.25
	Strip of 5 with white line on left or right margin of center stamp	7.50

Nos. TD126, TD133 and TD136 apear to be printed on blue paper. Light blue ink was applied in several layers to mask the phosphorescence of the tagged white paper before printing the stamps. A four-digit counting number is on the reverse of the backing paper on every 20th stamps on some rolls. No. TD136 is on backing paper taller than the stamps, with a gap between stamps.

For Testing Purposes Only Coil — TE55d

Serpentine Die Cut 11½ Vert.

TD137 TE55d **black**		.50
	Pair	1.00
	P# strip of 5, #S1	4.00

No. TD137 does not have the printed simulation perforations found on No. TD127, and is on backing paper taller than the stamp with a gap between stamps.

SSP Test Void Coil — TE69

Printed by Sennett Security Products.

2005 ***Serpentine Die Cut 10¼ Vert.***
Self-Adhesive

TD138 TE69 **black**		3.75
	Pair	7.50

2000 ***Serpentine Die Cut 11.6 Vert.***
Self-Adhesive

TD138A TE69 **black**		10.00
	Pair	20.00

Nos. TD138 and TD139 have a horizontal and vertical line printed completely around all stamps. The vertical line is not a joint line. Horizontally mis-slit examples show a continuous horizontal line at either the top or bottom of all stamps.

RENA No Postage Test Stamp Coil — TE70

2006 ***Die Cut***
Self-Adhesive

TD139 TE70 **blue**		2.00
	Pair	4.00

No. TD139 is on backing paper taller than the stamp with a gap between stamps.

For Testing Purposes Only Type of 1962-88
Self-Adhesive
Serpentine Die Cut 8.7 Vert.

TD140 TE55 **gray black**		25.00
	Pair	50.00
a.	Vertical pair, backing paper unslit horiz.	*450.00*

The dimensions of the stamp design is slightly larger than other For Testing Purposes Only coils, being 19mm by 22.25mm. No. TD140 is on backing paper taller than the stamp.

TEST BOOKLETS: PANES & COVERS

Test booklets normally are collected as complete booklets, and the major listings are for complete booklets. Very often the booklet panes in different booklets are the same or similar. Booklet panes are presented as lettered minor listings. Where similar booklet panes can be differentiated by gum breaker measurements, size measurements, or other factors, they are given separate minor listings. Single stamps from these booklets are not given minor listings.

This test booklet section is divided into four categories: stapled booklets, folded and glued booklets with water-activated gum, folded and glued booklets with self-adhesive gum, and ATM and Convertible Booklet Test Panes.

All perforation measurements are with tab (staples end) at top of 6-subject booklet panes and with tab (stapled end) on left of 8-subject booklet panes.

STAPLED BOOKLETS

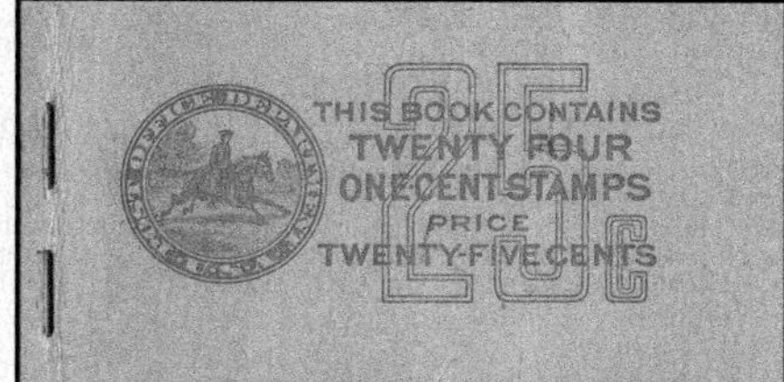

Small Postrider — BC5A

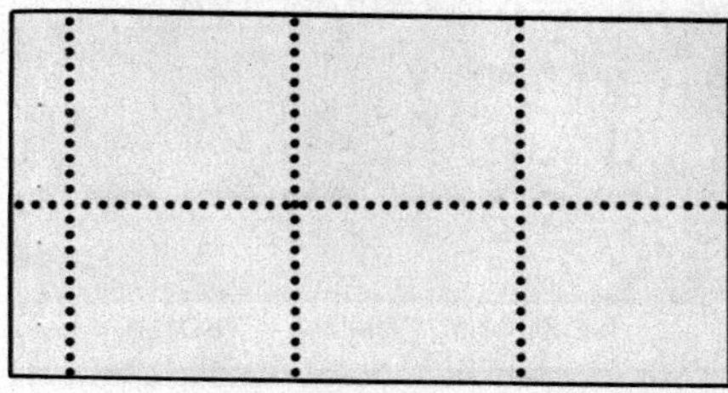

Blank Stamps — TDP1

1927-30 ***Perf. 11¼x10½***

TDB1 BC5A 25c **green,** *green,* 4 #TDB1a —
a. TDP1 pane of 6 —

Horiz. gum breakers are 22mm apart on No. TDB1a. No. TDB1 has 5 waxed glassine interleaves, 1 in front of the first pane and 1 behind each pane.

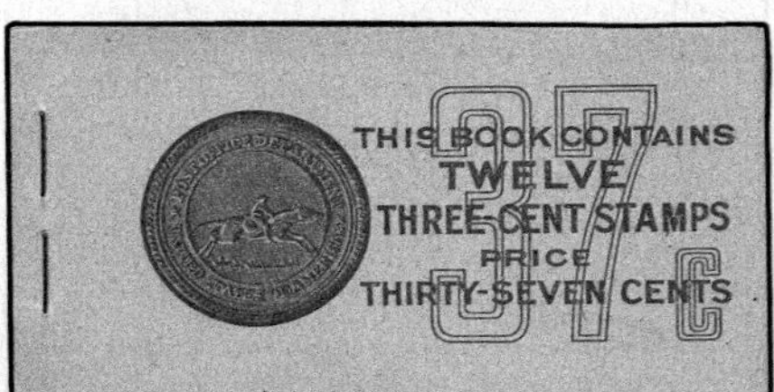

Post Office Seal — BC9A

Blank Stamps—TDP2

1930s

TDB2 BC9A 37c **violet,** *buff,* 2 #TDB2a —
a. TDP1 pane of 6 —
b. Unsevered pair of No. TDB2 booklets containing 2 #TDB2c panes —
c. TDP2 Unsevered pair of TDP1 panes —

No. TDB2b has a double-width cover made up of two unsevered BC9A covers. No. TDB2 has 2 waxed glassine interleaves, 1 behind each pane.

Horiz. gum breakers are 11½mm apart on No. TDB2a.

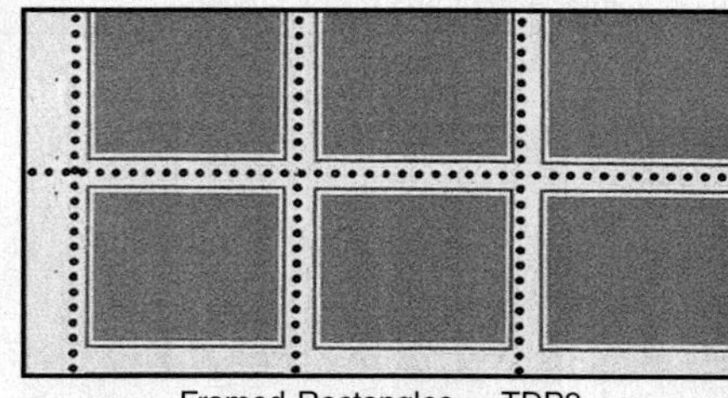

Framed Rectangles — TDP3

1940

TDB3 BC9A 37c **violet,** *buff,* 2 #TDB3a 600.00
a. TDP3 **violet,** pane of 6, hinged 175.00
Never hinged 250.00

Horiz. gum breakers are 11mm apart on No. TDB3a. No. TDB3 has 2 waxed glassine interleaves, 1 behind each pane.

Earliest documented use: Jan. 13, 1941 (single stamp)

Catalogue values for booklet panes in this section, from this point to the end, are for Never Hinged items.

Type of 1940

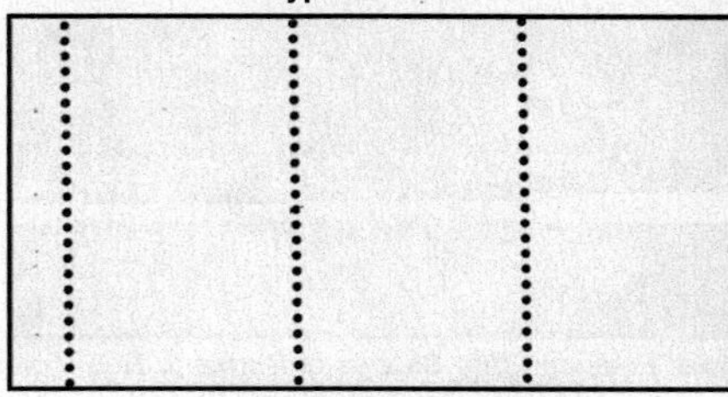

Blank Stamps — TDP4

1940s

TDB4 BC9A 37c **violet,** *buff,* #TDB4a, TDB4b —
a. TDP1 pane of 6 —
b. TDP4 pane of 3, perf. 11¼

Horiz. gum breakers are 6mm apart on Nos. TDB4a and TDB4b. No. TDB4 has 2 waxed glassine interleaves, 1 behind each pane.

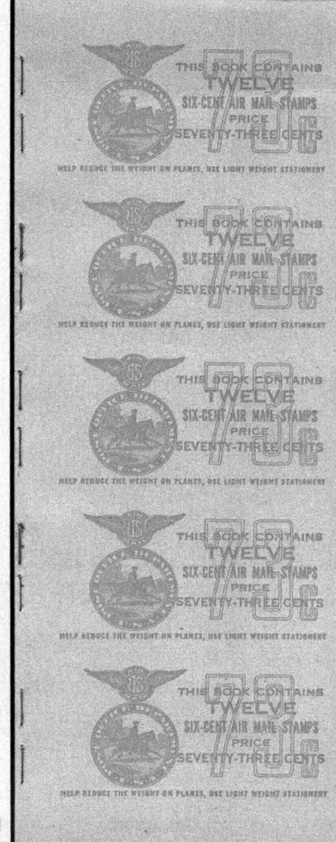

Unsevered Strip of 5 73¢ — BC10

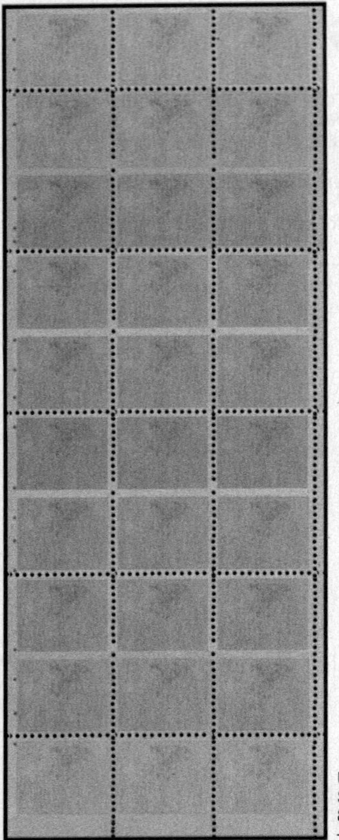

Unsevered Strip of 5 No. 807a Variety — TDP4A

TDP4A Pane of 6

Printed by Bureau of Engraving and Printing

1959 **Untagged** ***Perf. 11¼x10½***

TDB4C BC10 73c **red,** 4 #TDB4Cd #807a variety —
d. TDP4A Pane of 6 —

No. TDB4C booklets were originally discovered in an unsevered strip of five BC10 booklet covers with four strips of five No. 807a under-inked booklet panes within the covers. The No. 807a printer's waste panes are inverted in relation to the booklet covers with the stapling tab at the opposite end of the stapled booklet covers. No. BC10 73¢ red airmail booklet covers, and No. C39a booklet panes, are narrower than the width of the No. 807a panes, and therefore the stamps in the panes would not align with the covers if cut into individual booklets.

No. TDB4Cd horizontal gum breakers are 5½mm apart, and vertical gum breakers alternate 14mm and 8½mm apart. No. TDB4C has four silicone interleaves, one behind each pane. It is unknown if the discovery strip of five connected booklets is still intact and unsevered.

Post Office Seal — BC9H

1959

TDB5 BC9H 97c **blue,** *pink,* 4 #TDB5a 175.00
a. TDP1 pane of 6 —
b. As #TDB5, with silicone interleaves 325.00

Horiz. gum breakers are 5½mm apart, and vert. gum breakers are 21mm apart on No. TDB5a. No. TDB5 has 4 waxed glassine interleaves, and No. TDB5b has 4 silicone interleaves, 1 behind each pane.

U.S. Airmail Wings — BC11C

1959

TDB6 BC11C 85c **blue,** 2 #TDB5a 175.00

Horiz. gum breakers are 5½mm apart on No. TDB6a. Some panes exhibit faint vertical gum breakers, while some panes show no horizontal or vertical gum breakers. No. TDB6 has 2 waxed glassine interleaves, 1 behind each pane.

For Nos. TDB7, TDB8, TDB13, TDB14, TDB15, TDB16, TDB17, TDB18 and TDB19, booklet panes were made from coil stock that had stamp designs rotated 90 degrees from booklet stamps and therefore always appear miscut and misperforated.

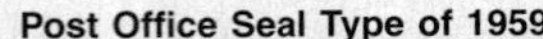

Post Office Seal Type of 1959

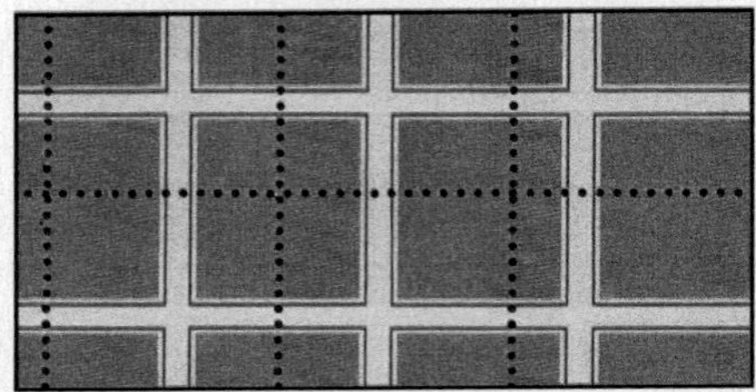

Misperforated and Miscut Framed Rectangles — TDP5

1960-62

TDB7 BC9H 97c **blue,** *pink,* 4 #TDB7a *900.00*
a. TDP5 **red violet,** pane of 6 *200.00*

Horiz. gum breakers are 4½-6½mm apart and vert. gum breakers are 22½mm apart on No. TDB7a. No. TDB7 has 4 glassine interleaves, 1 behind each pane. Some panes show joint lines.

Small Postrider With Shades of Purple to Red Violet "DUMMY" Handstamp — TBC12A

For Testing Purposes Only — TDP6

1962-67 **Untagged**

Shades of Purple to Red Violet 29½x4½mm "DUMMY" Handstamp

TDB8 TBC12A $1 **blue,** 4 #TDB8a 550.00
a. TDP6 **black,** pane of 6 stamps 100.00

Horiz. gum breakers are 5½mm apart and alternating vert. gum breakers are 22½mm and 8½mm apart on No. TDB8a. No. TDB8 has 4 silicone interleaves, 1 behind each pane, and staples at left. No. TDB8 is the only stapled-cover test booklet containing untagged "For Testing Purposes Only" panes. Some panes show joint lines.

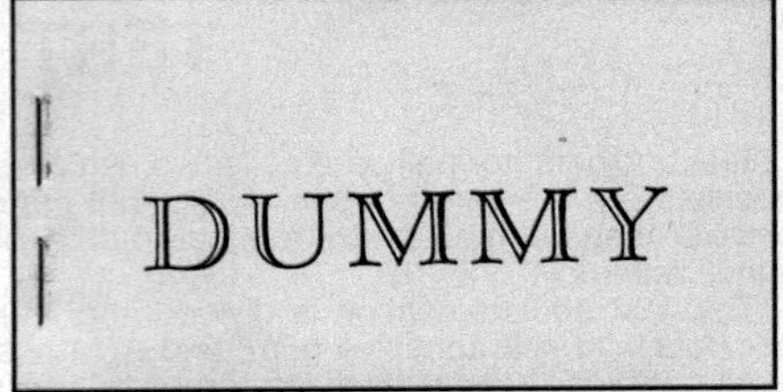

"DUMMY" — TBC12B

1962-67

Black 55x7½mm "DUMMY" Overprint

TDB9 TBC12B **black** 2 #TDB9a 90.00
a. TDP1 pane of 6 4.00

Red 55x7½mm "DUMMY" Overprint

TDB10 TBC12B **red** 2 #TDB9a *1,500.*

Horiz. gum breakers are 11½mm apart, and alternating vert. gum breakers are 14mm and 8½mm apart on No. TDB9a. Nos. TDB9 and TDB10 have 2 glassine interleaves, 1 behind each pane. Two examples of No. TDB10 are recorded. No. TDB9a blank booklet panes are found in Nos. TDB9, TDB10, TDB11 and TDB12.

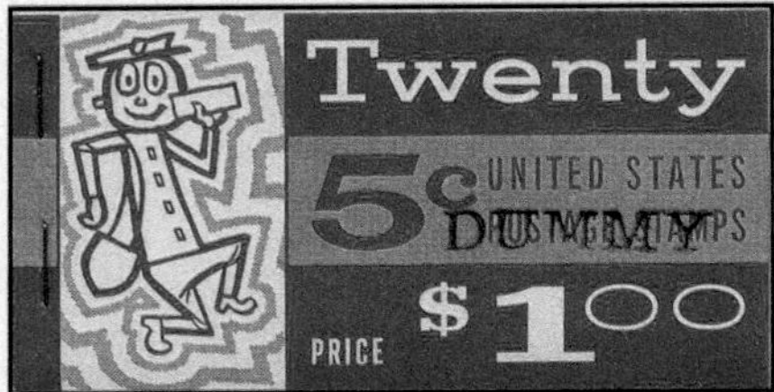

Mr. Zip With "DUMMY" — TBC13A

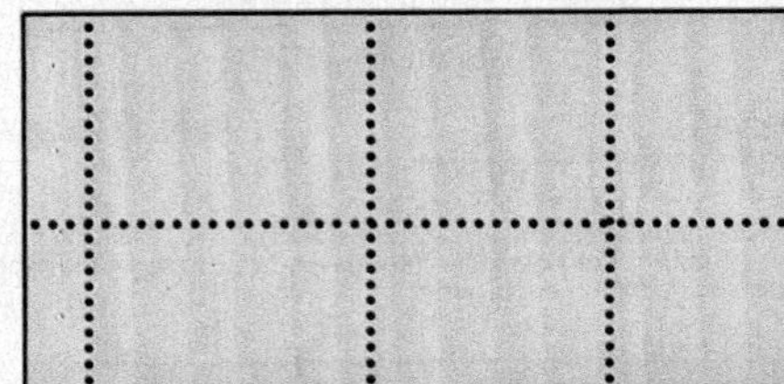

Blank Pane, 3 Sizes of Stamps — TDP1a

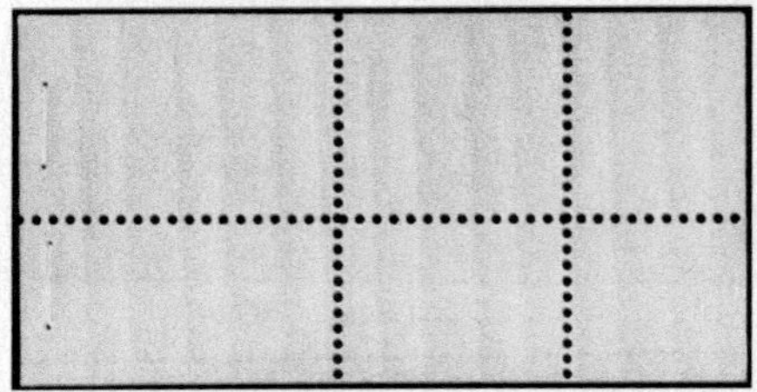

Blank Pane Without Perforated Stapling Tab — TDP1b

1963-66

Shades of Violet to Red Violet 29½x4½mm "DUMMY" Handstamp

TDB11 TBC13A $1 **blue,** 4 #TDB9a 125.00
a. As #TDB11, with 4 #TDB11b 125.00
b. TDP1a pane of 6 25.00
c. As #TDB11, with 4 #TDB11d 225.00
d. TDP1b pane of 6 50.00
e. As No. TDB11, without "DUMMY" handstamp on outside front cover —

Alternating horiz. gum breakers are 4½mm and 6½mm apart, and alternating vert. gum breakers are 14mm and 8½mm apart on Nos. TDB11b and TDB11d.

Mr. Zip with Press-printed "DUMMY" — TBC13B

Red 55x7½mm "DUMMY" Overprint

TDB12 TBC13B $1 **blue,** 4 #TDB9a — 50.00
a. As #TDB12, with different inside front cover — 8.00

No. TDB12 has inside front cover reading "Domestic Postage Rates." No. TDB12a has inside front cover reading "Minute Man — Buy — HOLD US Savings Bonds."

Nos. TDB11-TDB12a have 4 silicone interleaves, 1 behind each pane.

For Nos. TDB13, TDB18, TDB19, TDB20a, TDB21a and TDB21b, the perforation gauge and the gum breaker spacing on the booklet panes are measured with the staple position to the left. The perforation gauge and gum breaker spacing in the small-size booklets (from No. TDB1 to TDB17) are measured with the staple position at the top.

Post Office Seal With Shades of Violet to Red Violet "DUMMY" Handstamp — TBC14A

For Testing Purposes Only — TDP7

1967-68 Tagged *Perf. 11¼x10½*

Shades of Violet to Red Violet 34½x6½mm "DUMMY" Handstamp

TDB13 TBC14A $2 **brown,** 5 #TDB13a — 200.00
a. TDP7 **black,** pane of 8 stamps — 35.00

Horiz. gum breakers are 11mm apart and alternating vert. gum breakers are 14mm and 8½mm apart on No. TDB13a. No. TDB13 has 5 silicone interleaves, 1 behind each pane, and staples at left. Some booklets and panes have felt pen markings along the top and bottom edges placed by the technicians for machine adjustments, and are valued less.

All known No. TDB13 booklet covers are screened at 130 dpi from later 400-subject printings, instead of at 100 dpi from earlier 320-subject printings.

Stamp Silhouette With Purple "DUMMY" Handstamp — TBC15

FTPO Pane Without Perforated Stapling Tab — TDP6a

1960s-72 Tagged *Perf. 11¼x10½*

Purple 34½x6½mm "DUMMY" Handstamp

TDB14 TBC15 $1 **brown,** 4 #TDB14a — 150.00
a. TDP6a **black,** pane of 6 stamps — 35.00

Horiz. gum breakers are 11mm apart and vert. gum breakers are 22mm apart on No. TDB14a. No. TDB14 has 4 silicone interleaves, 1 behind each pane, and staples at left. "Dummy" handstamp is 34½x6½mm. Most booklets have felt pen markings on either the front or back covers and are valued less thus.

No. TDB14a panes do not have a perforated stapling tab. No. TDB14a panes are found in Nos. TDB14, TDB17 and TDB17b booklets.

TBC15A

Inverted FTPO Pane — TDP6b

Shades of Violet 34½x6½mm "DUMMY" Handstamp

Tagged

TDB15 TBC15A $1 **blue,** 4 #TDB15a — 150.00
a. TDP6b **black,** pane of 6 stamps — 35.00
b. No. TDB15 without "DUMMY" handstamp on outside front cover — *600.00*

Horiz. gum breakers are 11mm apart on No. TDB15a. No. TDB15 has 4 silicone interleaves, 1 behind each pane, and staples at left. Some booklets have felt pen markings on either the front or back covers and are valued less.

TBC15B

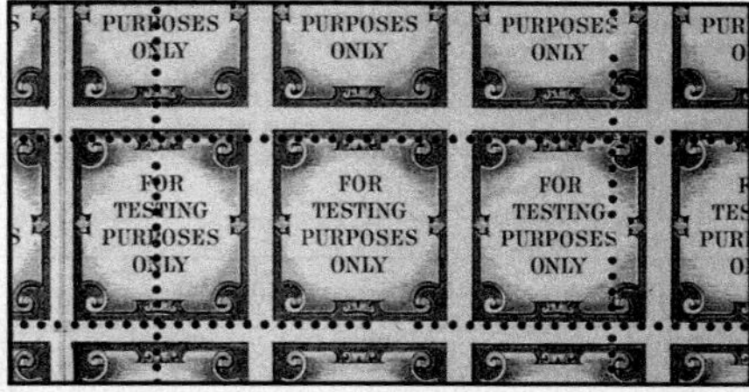

Small FTPO Pane With Perfs. For Large FTPO Pane — TDP6c

Upright FTPO Pane with Stapling at Right, Staples at Left — TDP6d

Shades of Red Violet 29½x4½mm "DUMMY" Handstamp

Tagged

TDB16 TBC15B $1 **claret,** 3 #TDB16a — 400.00
a. TDP6 **black,** pane of 6 stamps — 125.00
b. As #TDB16, with 34½x6½mm "DUMMY" handstamp — 400.00
c. As No. TDB16b, with 3 #TDB16d — *900.00*
d. TDP6c pane of 6 — *300.00*
e. As #TDB16b, with 3 #TDB16f — —
f. TDP6d Pane of 6 — —

Horizontal gum breakers are 11mm apart on Nos. TDB16a and TDB16d. No. TDB16a has perforations made with a 360-subject perforator (used for booklet panes of 6); No. TDB16d has perforations made with a 400-subject perforator (intended for booklet panes of 8). No. TDB16d panes all have two rows of perforations horizontally with one or two rows of perforations vertically on the pane. No. TDB16d is only known in No. TDB16c. Nos. TDB16, TDB16b, TDB16c and TDB16e have three silicone interleaves, one behind each pane, and staples at left.

TBC15C

Shades of Violet to Red Violet 29½x4½mm "DUMMY" Handstamp

Tagged

TDB17 TBC15C $1 **red,** 2 #TDB14a — 300.00
a. As No. TDB17, with 2 No. TDB15a — 300.00
b. As #TDB17, with 34½x6½mm "DUMMY" handstamp — 300.00
c. As #TDB17a, without "DUMMY" handstamp on outside of front cover — *750.00*

Horizontal gum breakers are 11mm apart, and alternating vertical gum breakers are 14 and 8½mm apart on No. TDB17a. Some panes do not show vertical gum breakers. No. TDB17 has 2 silicone interleaves, 1 behind each pane, and staples at left. All known booklets have felt pen markings on either the front or back covers.

Eisenhower With Shades of Red Violet "DUMMY" Handstamp — TBC16

1970-71 Tagged *Perf. 11¼x10½*

Shades of Red Violet 29½x4½mm "DUMMY" Handstamp

TDB18 TBC16 $2 **blue,** 5 #TDB13a — 325.00
a. As #TDB18, with 34½x6½mm "DUMMY" handstamp — 400.00
b. As #TDB18 or TDB18b, without "DUMMY" handstamp on outside of front cover — *800.00*

Horiz. gum breakers are 11mm apart and vert. gum breakers are 22mm apart on No. TDB13a. No. TDB18 has 5 silicone interleaves, 1 behind each pane, and staples at left.

TBC17

Shades of Red Violet to Red 29½x4½mm "DUMMY" Handstamp

TDB19 TBC17 $1.92 **claret,** 3 #TDB13a — 400.00
a. As #TDB19, with shades of red violet to red 34½x6½mm "DUMMY" handstamp — 400.00

No. TDB19 has 3 silicone interleaves, 1 behind each pane, and staples at left.

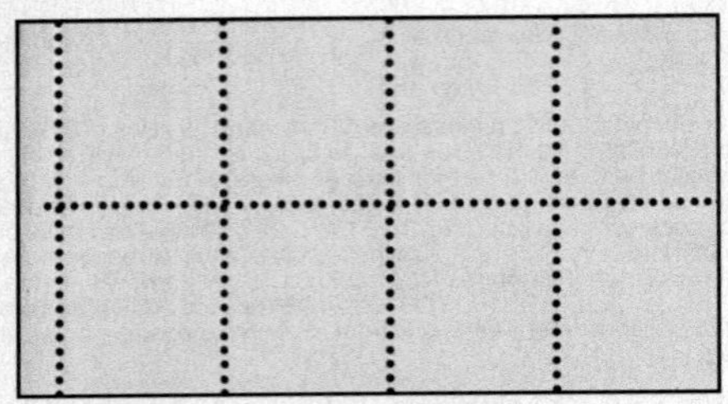
Blank Stamps — TDP8

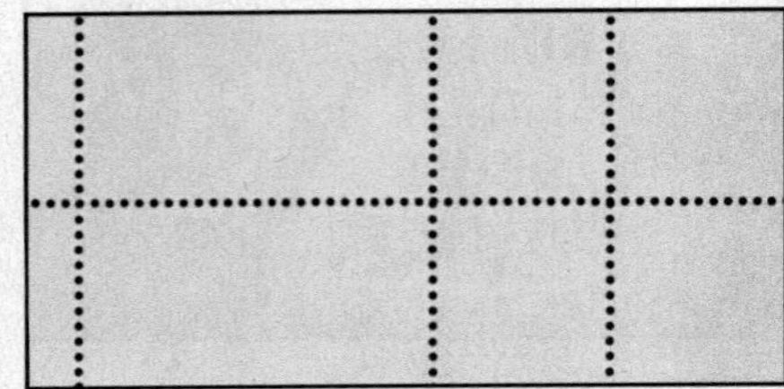
Blank Stamps — TDP9

1970 **Tagged** ***Perf. 11¼x10½***

Shiny Gum with Gum Breaker Ridges 11mm Apart

TDB20a TDP8 pane of 8 stamps, shiny gum, yellow green tagging —
Horiz. pair of 2 blank panes of 8 —
Vert. pair of 2 blank panes of 8 —
Block of 4 blank panes of 8 —

Some stamps are known with a vertical rejection marking.

The No.TDB20a (TDP8 pane) is the same format as the No. 1393a booklet pane.

1972 **Tagged** ***Perf. 10½x11¼***

Dull DAVAC Gum with Gum Breaker Ridges 11mm Apart

Nashua Paper

TDB21a TDP9 pane of 4 stamps + 2 double-width labels dull gum, yellow green tagging —
Horiz. pair of 2 blank panes of 4 stamps + 2 labels —
Vert. pair of 2 blank panes of 4 stamps + 2 labels —
Block of 4 blank panes of 4 stamps + 2 labels —

Some stamps are known with a vertical rejection marking.

The No. TDB21a (TDP9) pane is the same format as the No. 1395c booklet pane.

Dull DAVAC Gum with Gum Breaker Ridges 11mm Apart

Nashua Paper

Perf. 10½x11¼

TDB21b TDP8 pane of 7 stamps + label, dull gum, yellow green tagging —
Horiz. pair of 2 blank panes of 7 stamps + label —
Vert. pair of 2 blank panes of 7 stamps + label —
Block of 4 blank panes of 7 stamps + label —

The No. TDB21b (TDP8) pane is the same format as the No. 1395d booklet pane. No complete booklets containing Nos. TDB20a, TDB21a or TDB21b have been reported.

FOLDED AND GLUED BOOKLETS

Blank Cover TBC20

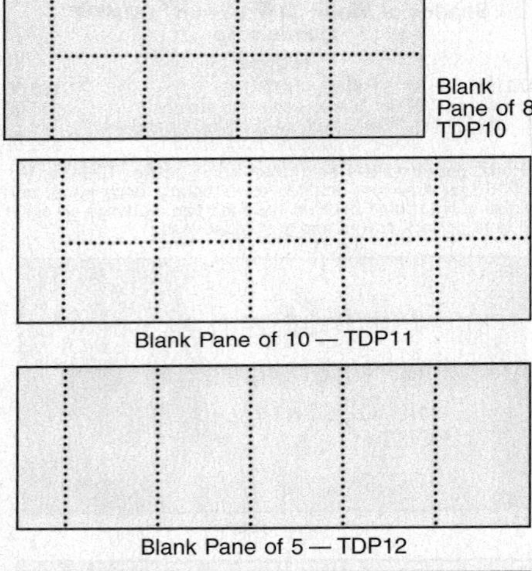
Blank Pane of 8 TDP10

Blank Pane of 10 — TDP11

Blank Pane of 5 — TDP12

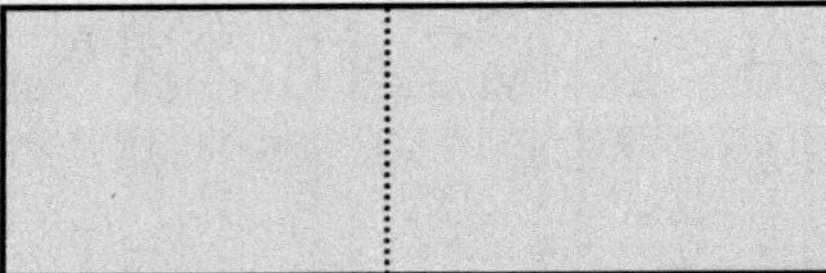
Blank Pane of 2 — TDP12a

Blank Imperf. Pane — TDP12b

Produced by Bureau of Engraving and Printing.

1970s-80s **Untagged** ***Perf. 11x10½***

TDB25 TBC20 blank, #TDB25a 500.00
a. TDP10 pane of 8, dull gum —

Perf. 10x9¾

TDB26 TBC20 blank, 2 #TDB26a 80.00
a. TDP11 pane of 10, shiny gum 35.00

Perf. 10 Horiz.

TDB27 TBC20 blank, #TDB28a 40.00
TDB28 TBC20 blank, 2 #TDB28a 30.00
a. TDP12 pane of 5, dull gum 12.50
b. As #TDB28, with 2 #TDB28c 30.00
c. TDP12 pane of 5, shiny gum 12.50

Produced by KCS Industries

Imperf

TDB29 TBC20 blank, 2 #TDB29a 50.00
a. TDP12b pane of 1, dull gum 22.50

Panes in No. TDB29 lack perforations and are attached to each other and the booklet cover with three glue spots. The booklet cover of No. TDB29 is scored at the pane fold location with approximate gauge 6½.

Perf. 11 Horiz.

TDB30 TBC20 blank, 2 #TDB30a 80.00
a. TDP12a pane of 2, dull gum 35.00
b. As #TDB30, with inverted pane (perfs unaligned with cover fold) —

Panes in No. TDB30 are fastened to each other with 3 glue spots and bottom pane is fastened to booklet cover with a 1mm wide glue line. Covers are known with handstamps "A1" (black), "A2" (orange), "B1" (red), or "B2" (violet) on the front and back cover panels.

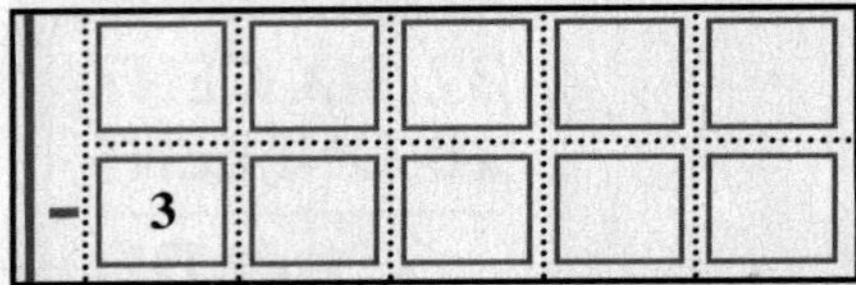

Rectangles and Numeral — TDP13

Made by Goebel, GmbH, Germany, from materials supplied by Bureau of Engraving and Printing

1990s **Untagged** ***Perf. 11x9¾***

TDB30C TBC20 blank, 2 #TDB30Cd *900.00*
d. TDP13 **blue**, pane of 10, shiny gum —

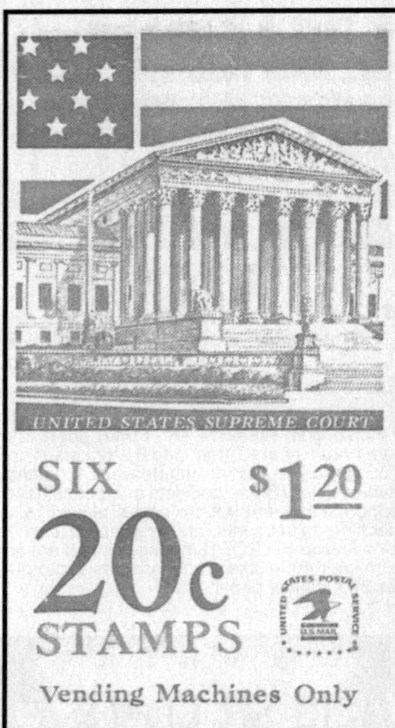

Flag Over Supreme Court BC29

Printed by Bureau of Engraving & Printing.

1985 **Untagged** ***Perf. 10 Horiz.***

TDB31 BC29 $1.20 **red & blue,** #TDB28a *1,500.*

Two examples of No. TDB31 are recorded.

The inside cover printing on No. TDB31 is not the same as the printing used on the issued booklet No. BK139. Instead, it has the inside printing found on the $1.10 Flag over Capital booklet No. BK144.

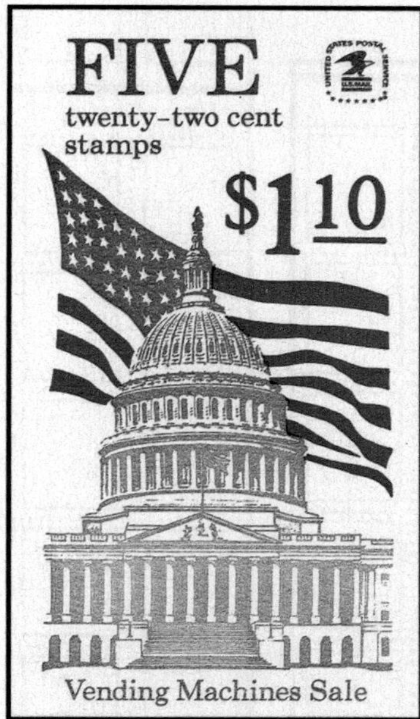

Flag Over Capitol
BC33C

Printed by Bureau of Engraving and Printing.

1985 **Untagged** ***Perf. 10 Horiz.***
TDB32 BC33C $1.10 **red & blue,** #TDB28a 17.50

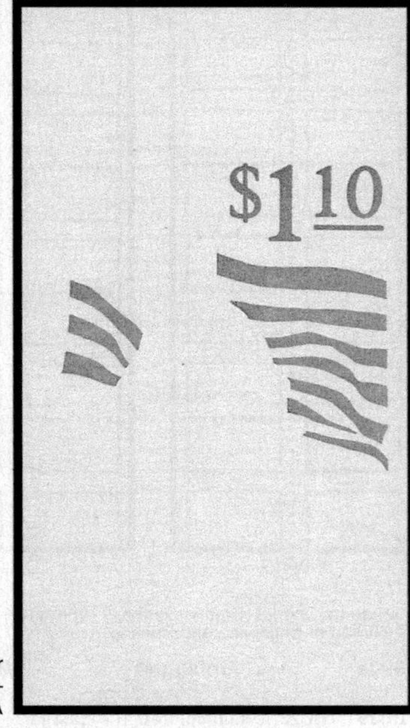

Flag Over Capitol — TBC20A

Printed by Bureau of Engraving and Printing

1985 **Untagged** ***Perf. 10 Horiz.***
TDB32A TBC20A $1.10 **red,** #TDB28a —

Seashells — BC33A

Seashells Without Text — TBC21

Printed by Bureau of Engraving and Printing.

1985 **Untagged** ***Perf. 10x9¾***
TDB33 BC33A $4.40 **multicolored,** 2 #TDB26a *500.00*

Panes are scored at all horizontal perforation rows. Some booklet covers have red felt pen marks on the outside front cover.

TDB34 TBC21 **multicolored,** 2 #TDB26a *500.00*
TDB35 TBC21 **multicolored,** 2 #TDB28a *350.00*

No. TDB35 panes are fastened to the inside of the blank back cover, whereas No. TDB33 and TDB34 booklets have the panes fastened to the inside of the front covers with the Seashell illustrations.

Seven adjacent booklet covers are needed to show the complete design of all 25 seashells for Nos. TDB33-TDB35.

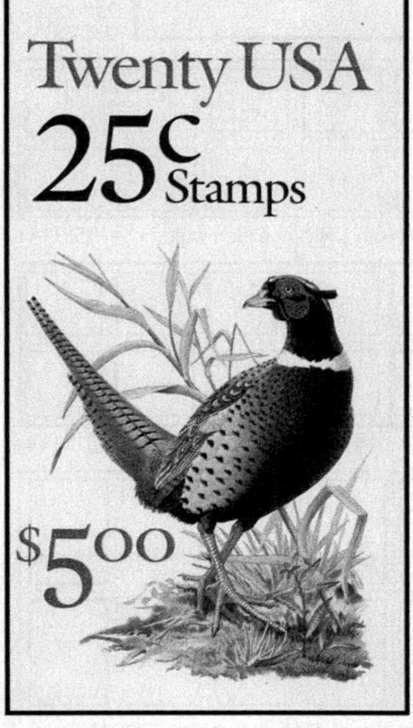

Pheasant — BC41

TDP13a

Printed by American Bank Note Company

1988 **Untagged** ***Perf. 11***
TDB35A BC41 $5 **multicolored,** 2 #TDB35Ab —
b. TDP13a Pane of 4, dull gum —

Jack London — BC43

Printed by Bureau of Engraving and Printing

1988 **Untagged** ***Perf. 11¼***
TDB35C BC43 $5 **multicolored,** 2 #TDB35Cd —
d. TDP11 Pane of 10, dull gum —

No. TDB35C booklets were made by hand using the BEP's proprietary process and were sometimes cut at a slight angle, resulting in a trapezoid-shaped booklet that looked like a "chevron" when opened.

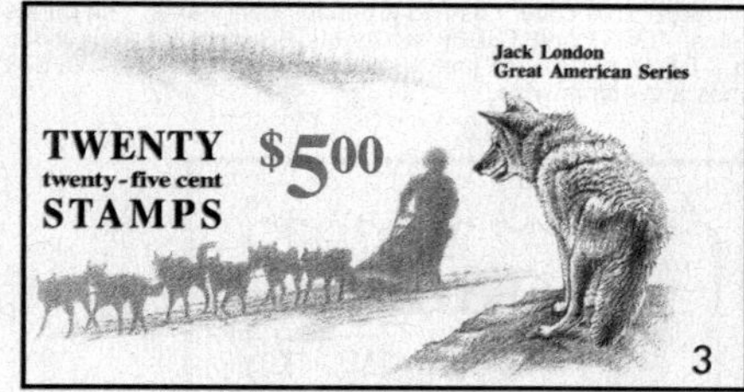

Jack London — TBC22

Made by Goebel, GmbH, Germany, from materials supplied by Bureau of Engraving and Printing.

1988 **Untagged** ***Perf. 11x9¾***
TDB36 TBC22 $5 **multicolored,** 2 #TDB30Cd *350.00*

Panes are scored at all horizontal perforation rows. No. TDB36 booklet covers have a small number (1 to 12) in the lower right corner that match the large number on the booklet panes on the inside (also 1-12). No. TDB36 also exists with mismatched pane and cover numbers. Value, $900.

Some booklet covers have red felt pen marks on the outside front cover. An unpublished quote from George Washington is printed on inside front cover and unissued "American Garden" printed on inside back cover.

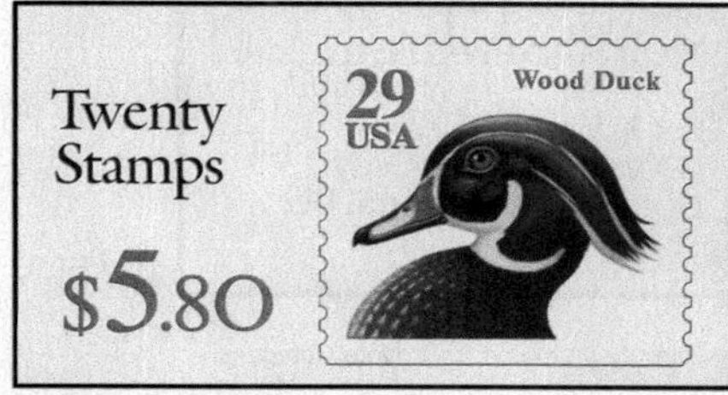

Wood Duck — BC57B

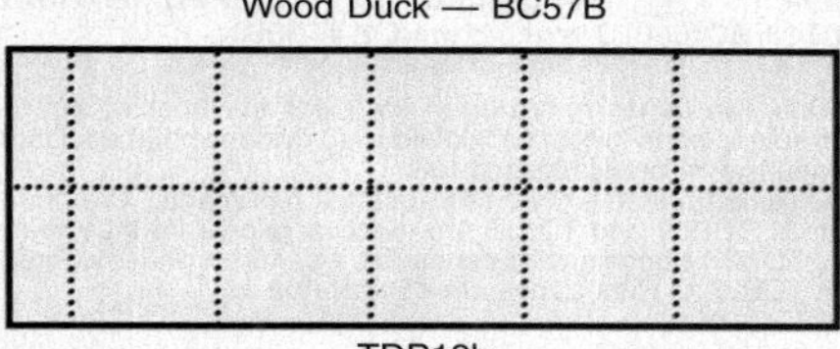
TDP13b

Printed by KCS Industries

1991-92 ***Perf. 11***
TDB36A BC57B $5.80 **multicolored,** 1 #TDB36Ab —
b. TDP13b pane of 10, shiny gum —

Hummingbird — BC80

Printed by American Bank Note Company.

1994 **Untagged** ***Perf. 11 Horiz.***

TDB37 BC80 $5.80 **multicolored,** 4 #TDB37a —
a. TDP12 pane of 5, shiny gum —

Outside front cover has two green felt pen marks. The panes in Nos. TDB37 and TDB38 are identical except for their width. No. TDB37 panes are just 40mm wide, whereas No. TDB38 panes are 45mm wide.

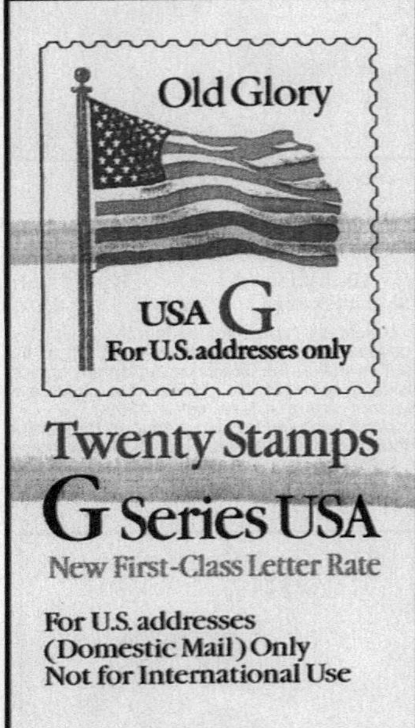

Flag — BC106B

Printed by American Bank Note Company.

1994 **Untagged** ***Perf. 11 Horiz.***

TDB38 BC106B G **multicolored,** 2 #TDB38a —
a. TDP12 pane of 5, shiny gum —

Only two panes remained in the discovery booklet, but the current top pane in that booklet showed evidence that additional pane(s) were once attached to it.

Outside front cover has two aqua felt pen marks. The panes in Nos. TDB37 and TDB38 are identical except for their width. No. TDB37 Hummingbird panes are just 40mm wide, whereas No. TDB38 G Rate panes are 45mm wide.

Flag — BC106C

Printed by KCS Industries

1992-1994 **Tagged** ***Perf. 11***

TDB38B BC106C G **multicolored,** 2 #TDB36Ab 600.00
c. TDP13b pane of 10, shiny gum —

No. TDB38Bc has "© United States Postal Service 1992 / K" on inside of cover above pane tab.

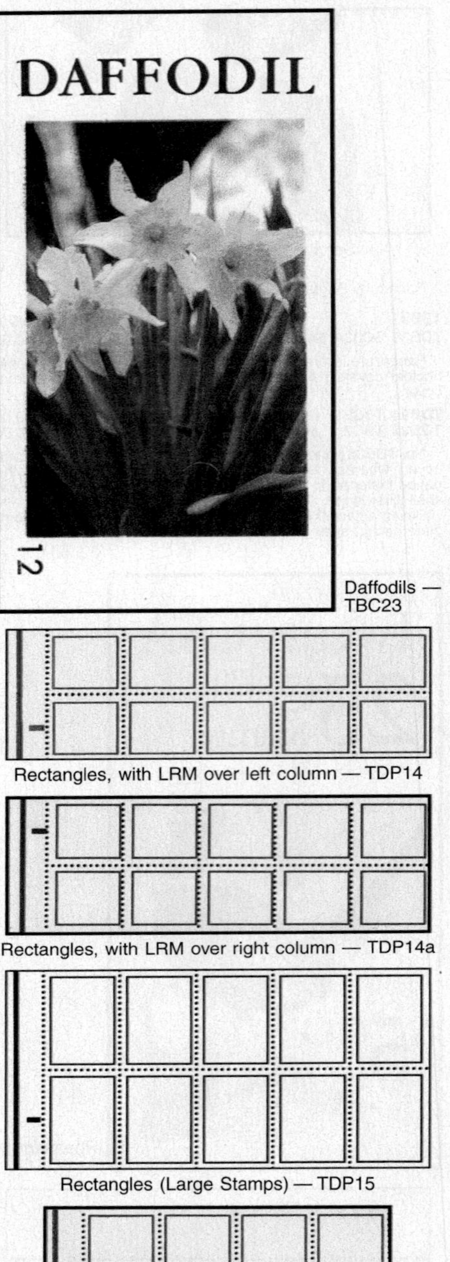

Daffodils — TBC23

Rectangles, with LRM over left column — TDP14

Rectangles, with LRM over right column — TDP14a

Rectangles (Large Stamps) — TDP15

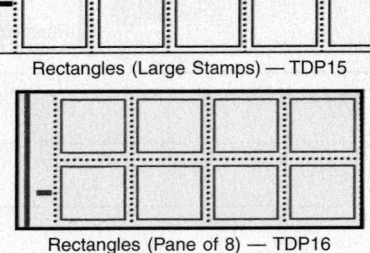

Rectangles (Pane of 8) — TDP16

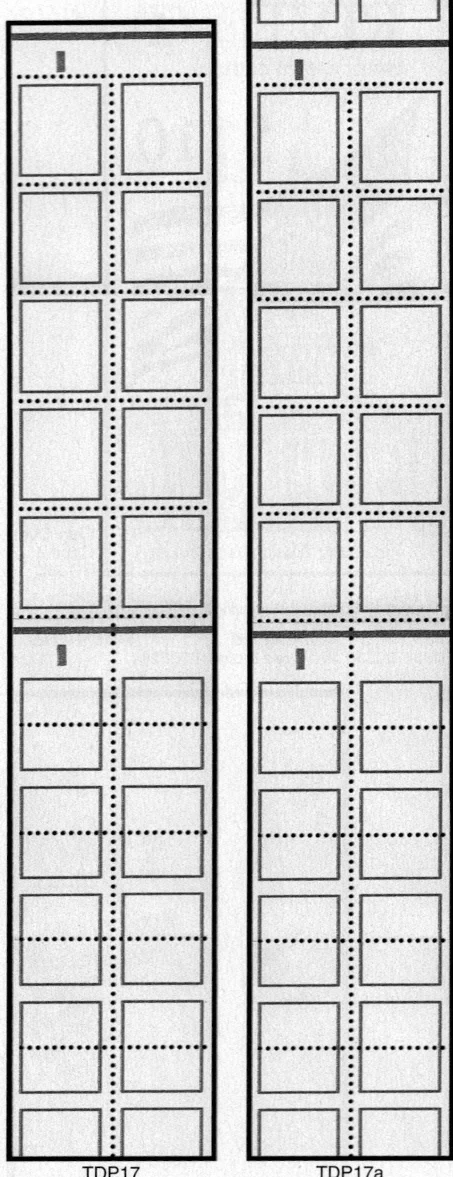

TDP17 TDP17a

Made by Goebel, GmbH, Germany, from materials supplied by Bureau of Engraving and Printing.

1990s **Untagged** ***Perf. 11x9¾***
Shiny Gum

TDB39 TBC23 **multicolored,** 2 #TDB39a 750.00
a. TDP14 **dark blue,** pane of 10, with LRM over the left column 300.00
TDB40 TBC23 **multicolored,** 4 #TDB30Cd —
TDB40B TBC23 **multicolored,** 2 #TDB30Cd —
TDB41 TBC23 **multicolored,** 4 #TDB39a 900.00
a. TDP14 **dark blue,** pane of 10, with LRM over left column —
TDB42 TBC23 **multicolored,** 4 #TDB42a —
a. TDP14a **dark blue,** pane of 10, with LRM over right column —
TDB43 TBC23 **multicolored,** 2 #TDB43a, no printing on inside covers —
a. TDP15 **black,** pane of 10 —
b. As #TDB43, with printing on inside covers 400.00
TDB44 TBC23 **multicolored,** #TDB44a 400.00
a. TDP16 **dark blue,** pane of 8 —
TDB45 TBC23 **multicolored,** #TDB45a, TDB45b 400.00
a. TDP17 **dark blue,** pane of 20, 43x257mm, shiny gum —
b. TDP17a **dark blue,** pane of 20, 43x272mm, shiny gum —

Nos. TDB42 and TDB43 lack printing on inside covers found on Nos. TDB39-TDB41. The numbers on the panes in Nos. TDB40 and TDB40B usually match the numbers on the covers. No. TDB40B also exists with mismatched pane and cover numbers. Value, $900. Numbers on the covers range from 1-12 on Nos. TDB39, TDB40, TDB40B, TDB41, TDB42, and TDB45. Numbers on the covers range from 1-8 on Nos. TDB43 and TDB43b.

No. TDB43b is known with 66.5x84.5mm front covers that show a black EE bar below the Daffodil illustration, and 66.5x81mm front covers that do not show the black EE bar below the Daffodil illustration.

TDP18

TDP19

Tete-beche block found in TDP19

TDP20 TDP21

Made by Goebel, GmbH (Germany) from materials supplied by the Bureau of Engraving and Printing.

Untagged ***Perf. 10x9¾***

TDB46 TBC20 blank, #TDB46a, TDB46b, TDB46c, TDB46d *1,200.*
- ***a.*** TDP18 **black,** pane of 8, 44x100mm, dull gum —
- ***b.*** TDP19 **black,** pane of 10, 44x135mm, dull gum —
- ***c.*** TDP20 **black,** pane of 8, 44x111mm, dull gum —
- ***d.*** TDP21 **black,** pane of 8, 44x111mm, dull gum —

The No. TDB46 booklet panes were printed in gravure by the BEP for use by Goebel GmbH, Germany, to evaluate a new booklet forming machine.

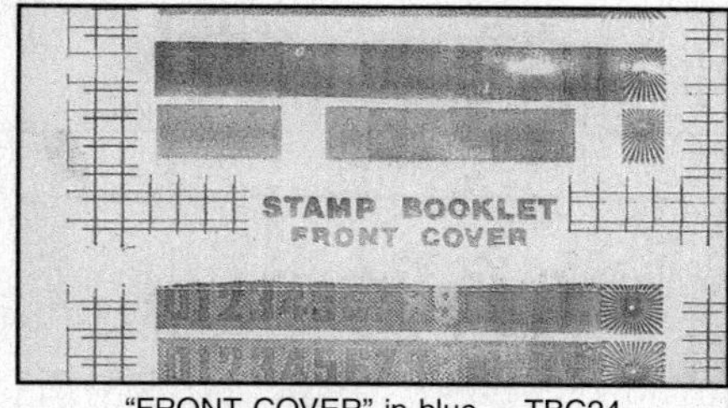

"FRONT COVER" in blue — TBC24

For Testing Purposes Only — TDP22

Overall Tagging ***Perf. 11x10½***

TDB47 TBC24 **red & blue,** #TDB47a *1,200.*
- ***a.*** TDP22 **black,** pane of 8, 44x110mm, dull gum —

No. TDB47a was cut from the web with horizontal perforations between each row of panes. All known panes thus show a partial row of perforations at bottom.

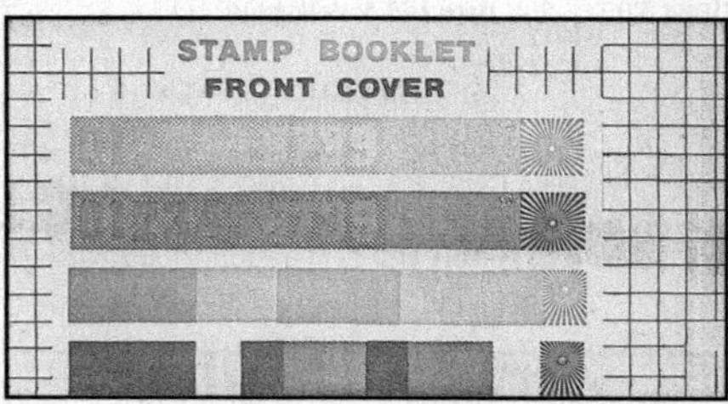

"FRONT COVER" in red — TBC25

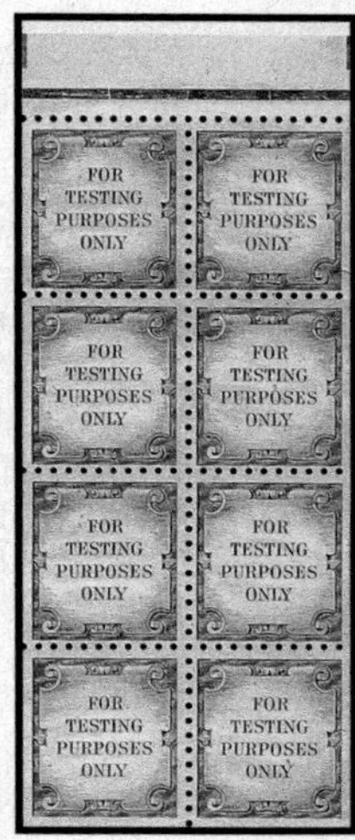

For Testing Purposes Only — TDP23

Overall Tagging ***Perf. 10x9¾***

TDB48 TBC25 **blue & red,** #TDB48a *850.00*
- ***a.*** TDP23 **black,** pane of 8, 44x110mm, dull gum —

SELF-ADHESIVE FOLDED & GLUED BOOKLETS
Blank Cover and Pane Types

1990s ? **Untagged** ***Perf. 11 Horiz.***

TDB60 TBC20 blank, 2 #TDB60a —
- ***a.*** TDP12 blank, pane of 2, self-adhesive, 44x132mm —

Specialists have questioned the existence of No. TDB60. The editors would like to see authenticated evidence of the existence of this booklet.

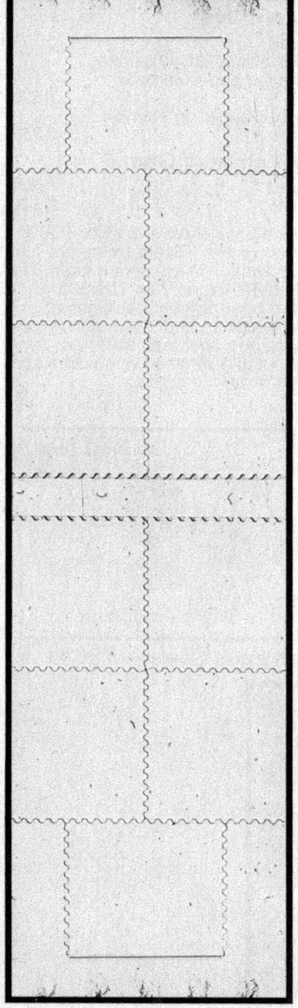

Stamp Layout — TBP61

Blank — TBE39 — TBE39

Serpentine Die Cut 10½x11 on 3 Sides, 10½ on 3 Sides on Stamps at Each End of Pane

1999 **Overall Tagging**

TDB61 TBC20 blank, self-adhesive blank pane of 10, 8 #TDB61a + 2 #TDB61b 150.00
- ***a.*** TBE39 Die cut 10½x11 on 3 sides 10.00
- ***b.*** TBE39 Die cut 10½ on 3 sides 20.00

Stamps in pane have same arrangement as that of the 1999 20c Pheasant booklet, No. BK242A.

All reported No. TDB61 booklets have had the center peel-away strip removed.

ATM and CONVERTIBLE BOOKLET TEST PANES

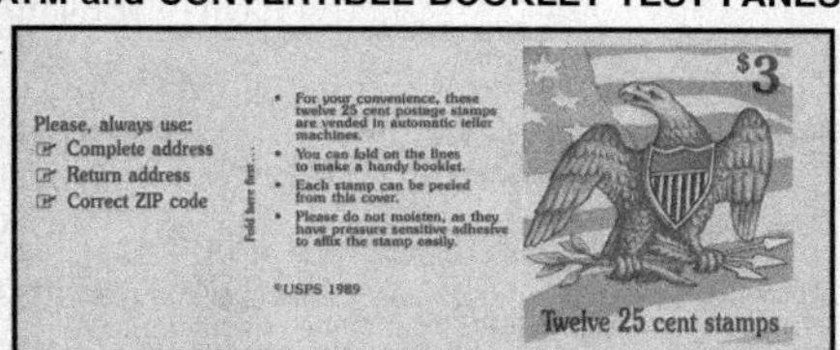

Eagle and Flag Pane Cover — TBC40

Stamp Layout — TBP40

Eagle and Flag — TBE40

Printed by Bureau of Engraving & Printing.

1989 **Tagged** ***Imperf.***

Self-Adhesive

TDB80 TBE40 **multicolored** *125.*

a. TBP40 $3 *red and blue,* (TBC40), pane of 12, slick-surfaced paper on both sides *1,500.*

b. As "a," slick-surfaced paper on stamp side only *2,250.*

Shiny, Water-Activated Gum

TDB81 TBE40 **multicolored** *200.*

a. TBP40 Pane of 12 *2,500.*

The backing paper serves as a booklet cover on No. TDB80a and TDB80b. At least one pane of No. TD80b exists not fully trimmed, with "Paper Corp" handwritten in the right margin. The liner printing is clearly visible on the thinner No. TDB80a when looking at the stamp side of the pane without backlighting.

No. TDB81 does not have a cover, and does not require backing paper since it is printed on paper with water-activated gum. No. TDB81a panes exist not fully trimmed with colored EE registration markings in the left or right margins.

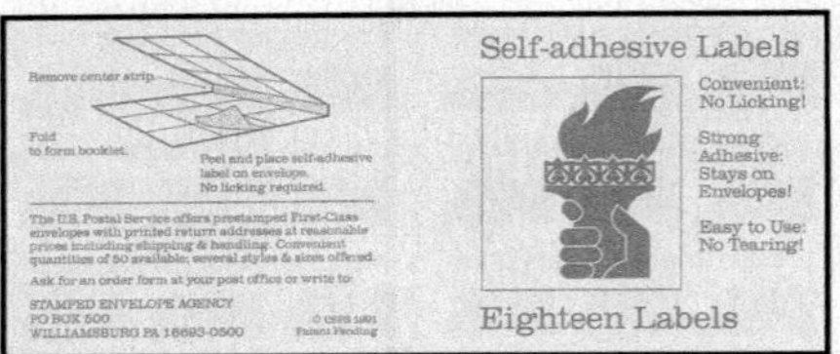

Statue of Liberty Torch Pane Cover — TBC41

Stamp Layout — TBP41

Green Liberty Torch — TBE41

Printed by Avery Dennison.

1990 **Untagged** ***Die Cut***

Self-Adhesive

TDB82 TBE41 **green** .50

a. TBP41 *green* (TBC41), pane of 18 10.00

Individual stamps contain different portions of the "ATM TEST / DEMONSTRATION SHEET" text at the left side.

No. TDB82 is similar in design to No. 2531Ae.

Similar to No. 2475a Overprinted in Black "SPECIMEN / FOR ATM TEST" on Each Stamp

Blank Sheetlet Back — TBC42

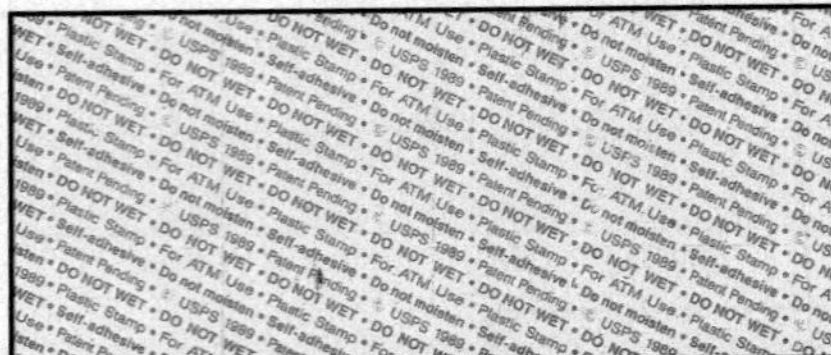

Flag Pane Cover — TBC43

Stamp Layout — TBP42

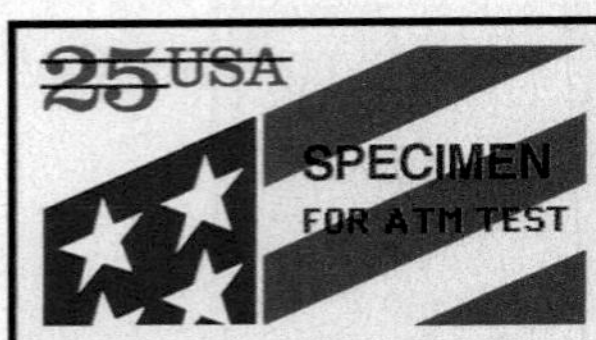

Flag — TBE42

Printed by Avery Dennison.

1990 **Untagged** ***Imperf.***

Printed on Plastic Without Liner Paper

TDB83 TBE42 25c **dark red & dark blue** —

a. TBP42 Pane of 12 with no printing on back (TBC42) —

Die Cut

Printed on Plastic With Self-Adhesive Liner Paper

TDB84 TBE42 25c **dark red & dark blue** —

a. TBP42 Pane of 12 with blue liner writing on back (TBC43) —

A black overprint was applied that reads "SPECIMEN / FOR ATM TEST." The liner writing on the back of No. TDB84a Printed Pane Cover - TBC43 is different than on the issued No. 2475a ATM pane. There are four repeating lines of text that read, "(dot) DO NOT WET (dot / dot) Plastic Stamp (dot) For ATM Use (dot) / (dot) Do not moisten (dot) Self-adhesive (dot) /(dot) (copyright symbol) USPS 1989 (dot) Patent Pending (dot)."

NCR/USPS Flag Sheetlet Back — TBC42A

TDB84B Stamp Layout — TBP42A

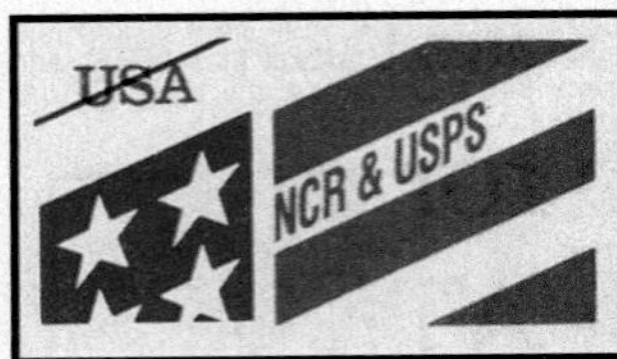

NCR/USPS Flag — TBE42A

Produced by NCR

Without Gum

1990s **Litho.** ***Imperf.***

Untagged

TDB84B TBE42A **red and blue** —

c. TBP42A Pane of 12 with blue printing on back (TBC42A) —

This ATM sheetlet was printed on regular weight plain paper.

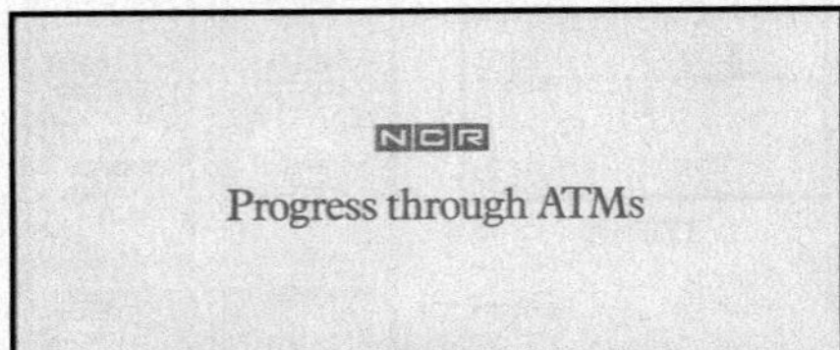

NCR Flag Sheetlet Back — TBC42B

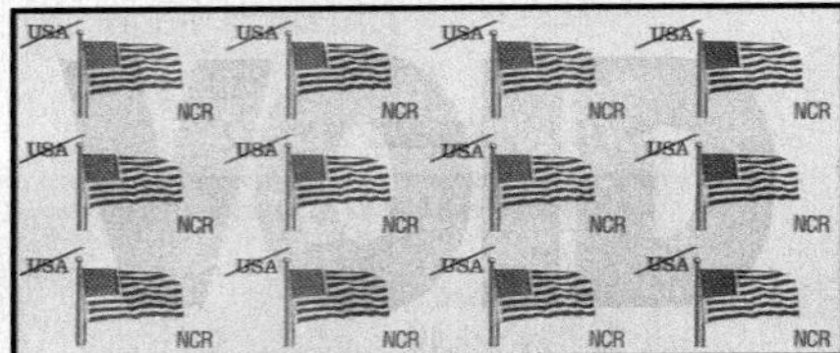

TDB84D Stamp Layout — TBP42B

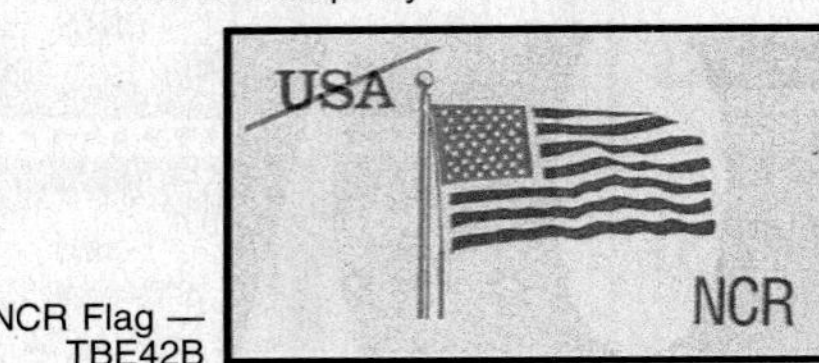

NCR Flag — TBE42B

Produced by NCR

Without Gum

1990s **Litho.** ***Imperf.***

Untagged

TDB84D TBE42B **red and blue** —

e. TBP42B Pane of 12 with red and blue printing on back (TBC42B) —

This ATM sheetlet was printed on regular weight plain paper.

TDB84F Stamp Layout — TBP42C

Red Rose — TBE42C

Without Gum

1990s **Litho.** ***Imperf.***
Untagged

TDB84F TBE42C **red, green and black** —
g. TBP42C Pane of 18 without printing on back (TBC42) —

Stamp Layout — TBP44

Blank — TBE44

Produced by Dittler Brothers.

1992 **Untagged** ***Die Cut***
Self-Adhesive

TDB85 TBE44 **blank** —
a. TBP44 *blank,* pane of 18 *750.00*
b. As "a," without die cuts 300.00

Nos. TDB85a and TDB85b were produced on thick self-adhesive paper similar to No. 2596a postage stamps, and were used for testing Postal Buddy machines. Backing paper of Nos. TDB85a and TDB85b reads "SELF-ADHESIVE DO NOT WET" on the stamp side of the backing paper. The die cuts on the front of No. TDB85 panes and the roulettes on the liner where the center peel strip was supposed to be located are typically misaligned.

Stamp Layout — TBP45

Blank — TBE45

Produced by Bureau of Engraving and Printing.

1996 **Tagged** ***Serpentine Die Cut 10***
Self-Adhesive

TDB86 TBE45 **blank** 30.00
a. TBP45 *blank,* pane of 20 + reorder label (TBC42) 600.00

There is no printing to identify who produced this pane. The "Tic-tac-toe" style of defacement die-cutting in the corner where the reorder label is located on regular panes is only found on Nos. 3112a, 3176a and 3244a convertible booklets produced by the Bureau of Engraving and Printing.

TBC46

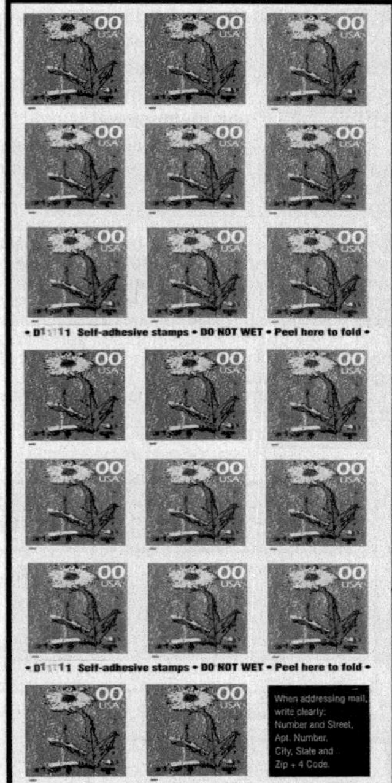

Stamp Layout (Design Size: 18x17mm) TBP46

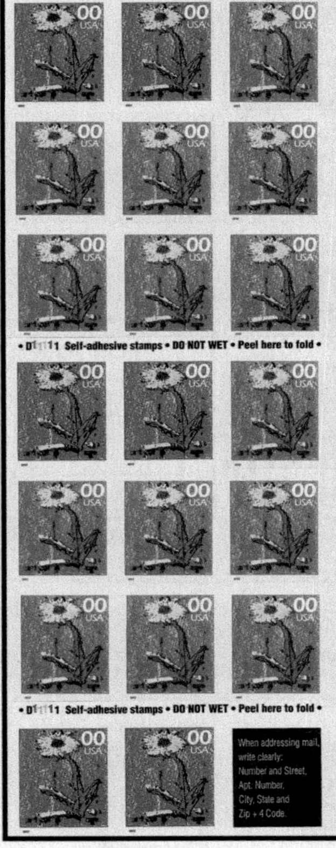

Stamp Layout (Design Size: 18x21mm) TBP47

Flower — TBE46

Flower — TBE47

Printed in a joint venture of Dittler brothers and the American Bank Note Co.

1997 Photo. & Engr. Tagged *Imperf.*
Self-Adhesive

TDB87 TBE46 00c **multicolored** 375.00

Photo.

TDB88 TBE47 00c **multicolored** 250.00

Nos. TBD87 and TDB88 were printed at the same time on the same web. No. TDB87 was printed from one intaglio and five gravure plates, while Nos. TDB88 was printed from just the five gravure plates. Nos. TDB87 and TDB88 were printed in panes of 20 + reorder label, but all known panes have been cut into singles, pairs, strips of 3 or blocks. The backside printing consists of text and emblems related to Dittler Brothers and the American Banknote Company. No. TBC46 back cover image applies to both Nos. TBP46 and TBP47 stamp layout images. Nos. TBP46 and TBP47 stamp layout images and No. TBC46 back cover image were computer generated by reconstructing partial images found on the front and back of individual stamps cut from the panes.

A press sheet containing just the black intaglio printing exists. It has not been cut up.

See Nos. TD129A-TD129B.

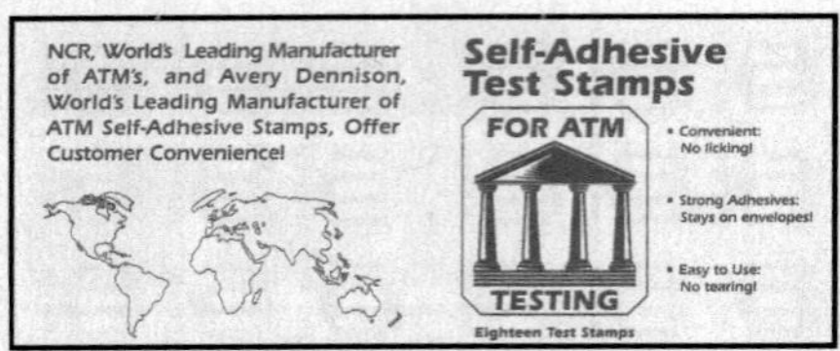

Temple Pane Cover — TBC48

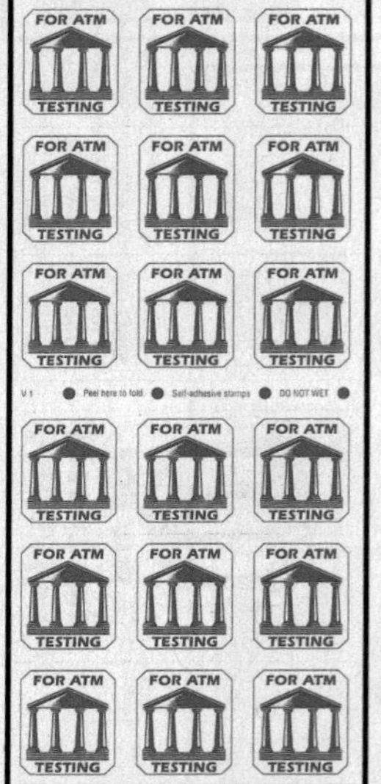

Stamp Layout — TBP48

Temple — TBE48

Printed by Avery Dennison.

1997 Untagged *Die Cut*
Self-Adhesive

TDB89 TBE48 **dark blue** 15.00
a. TBP48 *dark blue* (TBC48), pane of 18 250.00

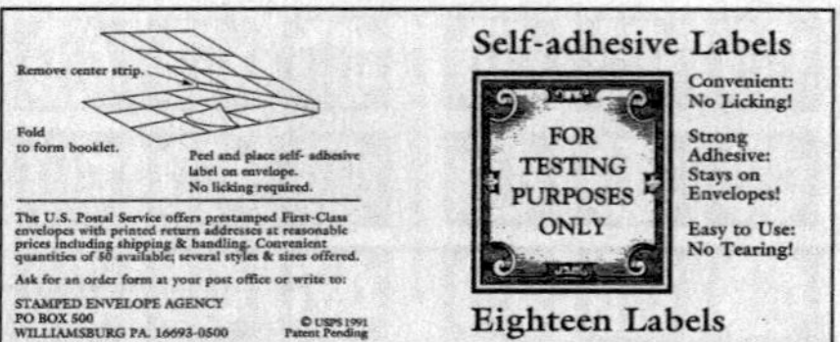

"For Testing Purposes Only" Pane Cover — TBC49

TDB90a, TDB91a, TDB92a
Stamp Layout — TBP49

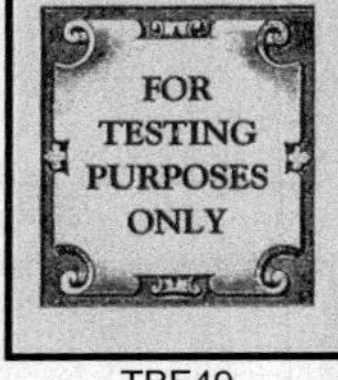

TBE49

TBE50

TBE51

Printed by Avery Dennison.

1997 Untagged *Die Cut*
Self-Adhesive

TDB90 TBE49 **black** 7.00
a. TBP49 *black* (TBC49), pane of 18 130.00

Serpentine Die Cut 7¾

TDB91 TBE50 **black** 1.00
a. TBP49 *black* (TBC49), pane of 18 12.50
TDB92 TBE51 **magenta** 14.00
a. TBP49 *blue* (TBC49), pane of 18 250.00

George Clinton — TBE52

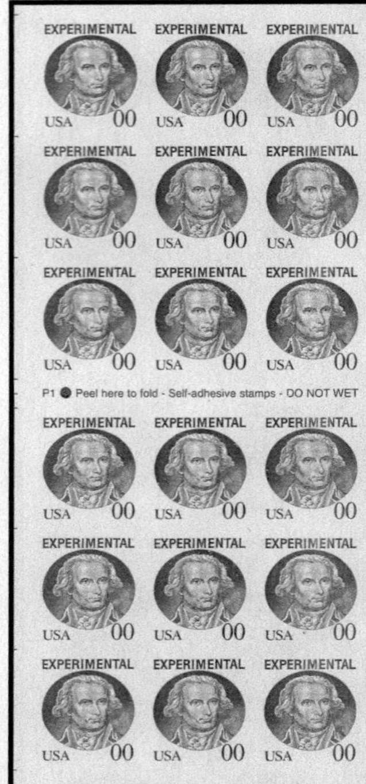

Stamp Layout
TBP52

Printed by Ashton-Potter (USA) Ltd.

Serpentine Die Cut 11¼x11½
1998 Engr. Tagged
Self-Adhesive

TDB93 TBE52 00c **blue gray** 10.00
Envelope with 8 #TDB93 on back —

Imperf.

TDB93A TBE52 00c **blue gray** 15.00
b. TBP52 pane of 18 without printing on back (TBC42) 300.00

No. TDB93 was printed in booklet panes of 18 from a 324-subject plate. Full No. TDB93 booklet panes with serpentine die cuts are unknown in collector hands; all known examples of No. TDB93 were affixed to envelope backs for use in USPS mailing tests.

No. TDB93A is an imperforate convertible booklet pane cut from a press sheet. Each of the 18 panes in the press sheet is separated by a gutter. Various registration marks can be found in some margins and gutters.

See No. TD130F.

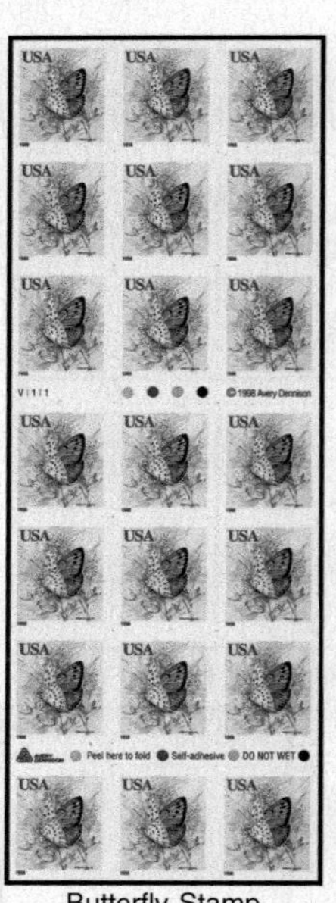

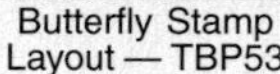

Butterfly Stamp Layout — TBP53

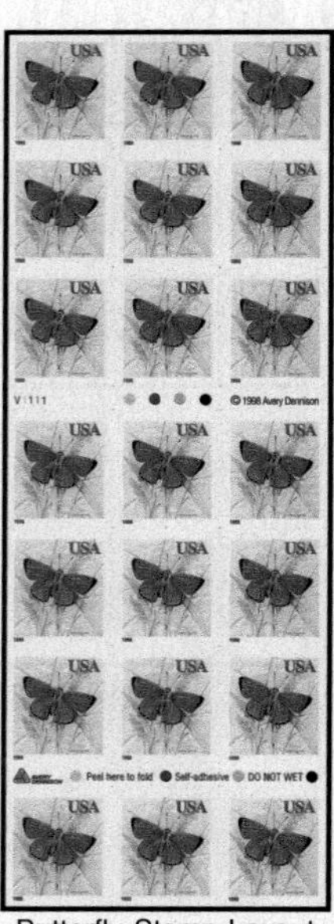

Butterfly Stamp Layout — TBP53a

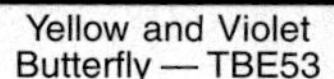

Yellow and Violet Butterfly — TBE53

Orange Butterfly — TBE53a

Printed by Avery Dennison.

1998 Litho. Untagged ***Serpentine Die Cut 11***
Self-Adhesive

TDB94 TBE53 **multicolored** + 1998 date —
TDB95 TBE53a **multicolored** + 1998 date —
a. TBP53-TBP53a *multicolored,* double-sided pane of 42, 21 each #TDB94-TDB95 —

No. TDB95a has a 1998 copyright date in the center peel strip and each stamp has a small black "1998" date under the lower left corner of the design. The center peel strip on each side shows the stamps were copyrighted by Avery Dennison.

Butterfly Stamp Layout — TBP54

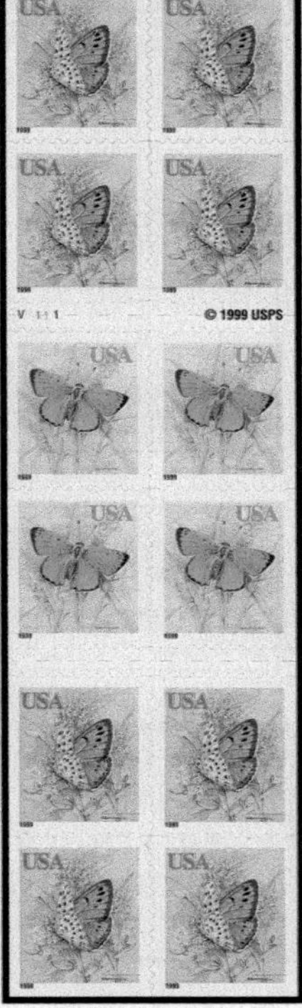

Butterfly Stamp Layout — TBP54a

Printed by Avery Dennison.

1999 Litho. Tagged ***Serpentine Die Cut 11***
Self-Adhesive

TDB96 TBE53 **multicolored** + 1999 date —
TDB97 TBE53a **multicolored** + 1999 date —
a. TBP54-TBP54a *multicolored,* pane of 20, 12 #TDB96, 8 #TDB97 —

No. TDB97a has a 1999 copyright date in the center peel strip and each stamp has a small black 1999 date under the lower left corner of the design. The center peel strip on each side shows these stamps were copyrighted by USPS, rather than Avery Dennison like those on No. TDB95a. The only difference between the TBE53 and TBE53a stamp designs on Nos. TDB95a and TDB97a is the date on the stamps. No. TDB97a is a complete double-sided booklet. Eight stamps plus P# and the booklet cover (TBC54) are printed on one side of the peelable backing paper, and 12 stamps plus P# appear on the other side of the backing paper.

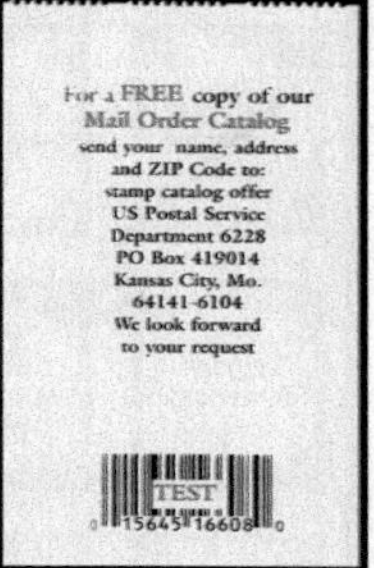

Part of Back Cover — TBC55

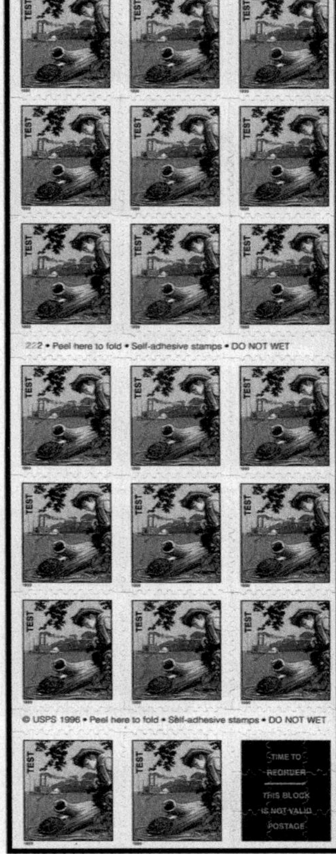

Stamp Layout TBP55

Tom Sawyer — TBE55

Printed by Bureau of Engraving and Printing

1999 Litho. ***Serpentine Die Cut 10***
Self-Adhesive

TDB98 TBE55 **multicolored** —
a. TBP55 *multicolored,* (TBC55) pane of 20 plus reorder label —

The only known example of No. TDB98 has plate #2222, indicating it was printed by the BEP. The "tic-tac-toe" style die cutting on the reorder label was only used on BEP produced convertible booklets. No complete panes are known. The illustration shown is a mockup (the top nine stamps were added to show what a complete pane would look like).

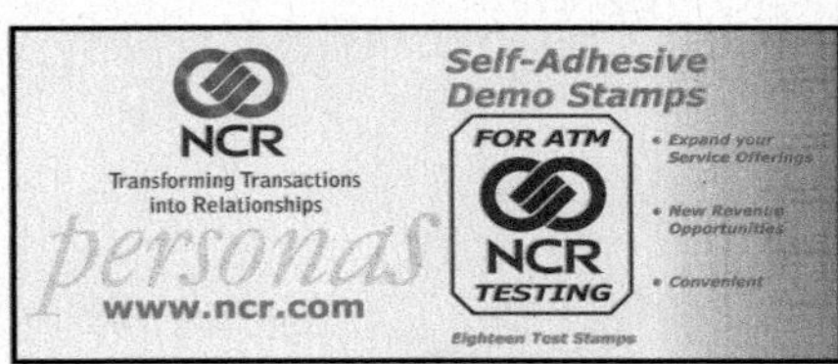

NCR Pane Cover — TBC56

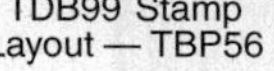

TDB99 Stamp Layout — TBP56

NCR Emblem — TBE56

Printed by Systemedia for NCR.

2000 Litho. Without Gum ***Imperf.***
Untagged

TDB99 TBE56 **black** —
a. TBP56 (TBC56), pane of 18 75.00

This ATM Sheetlet is printed on regular weight plain paper.

Stamp Layout — TBP56A

AutoTell Systems — TBE56A

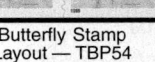

1990s **Without Gum** ***Imperf.***
Untagged

TDB99B TBE56A **black,** *white* —
c. TBP56A pane of 18 with no printing on back (TBC42) —

This ATM sheetlet is printed on regular weight plain white paper.

Stamp Layout — TBP56B

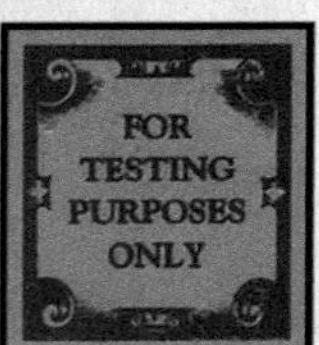

Wincor AutoTell LLC — TBE56B

2000 **Litho.** **Without Gum** ***Imperf.***
Untagged

TDB99D TBE56B **black,** *gray* —
e. TBP56B pane of 18 with no printing on back (TBC42) —

This ATM sheetlet is printed on regular weight plain gray paper made by the Crane Company, using recycled U.S. currency. Some panes show part of the Crane Company watermark that includes the words "OLD MONEY."

Stamp Layout TBP57

"For Test Purposes Only" — TBE57

Printed by Avery Dennison.

2005 **Untagged** ***Serpentine Die Cut 7¾***
Self-Adhesive

TDB100 TBE57 **blue** 7.00
a. TBP57 *black,* (TBC49) pane of 18 110.00

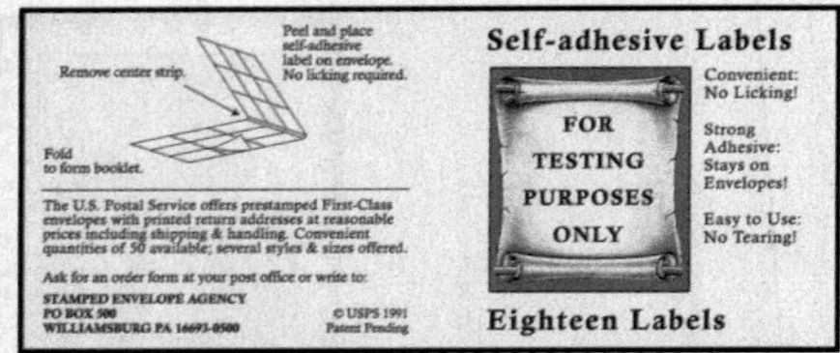

"For Testing Purposes Only" Cover — TBC58

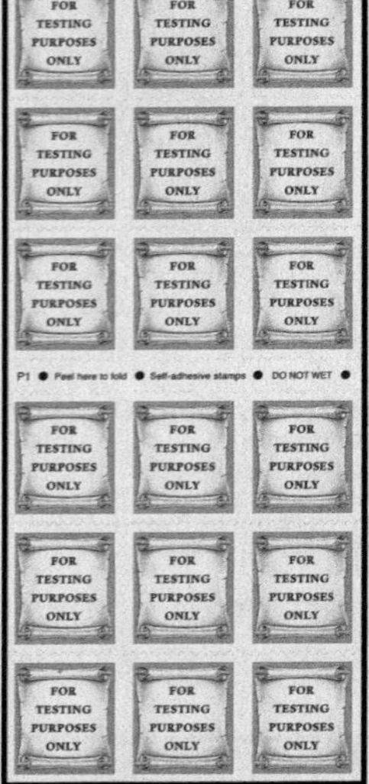

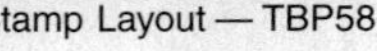

Stamp Layout — TBP58

"For Testing Purposes Only" — TBE58

Printed by Ashton-Potter (USA) Ltd.

2009 ***Serpentine Die Cut 11¼x11***

TDB101 TBE58 **blue** *7.00*
a. TBP58 *black* (TBC58), pane of 18 110.00

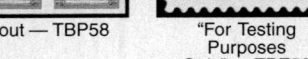

Cover Layout — TBP59

Stamp Layout — TBP59a

Ashton-Potter — TBE59

Printed by Ashton-Potter (USA) Ltd.

2005 **Litho.** ***Serpentine Die Cut 11¼x10¾***
Self-Adhesive

TDB102 TBE59 **multicolored** —
a. TBP59-TBP59a (TBC59), pane of 20 —

No. TDB102 has no plate number in a peel strip. While there is no date printed on the stamps, the panes were likely produced between 2005 and 2007. The peel strips on the side with 8 stamps have 10¾ gauge rouletting, while the peel strips on the side with 12 stamps have no rouletting. The panes were printed on prephosphored paper that was treated to mask the phosphorescence of the yellow green tagging.

TEST STAMP ESSAYS, TRIAL COLOR, AND PLATE PROOFS

TD19P1

Bureau of Engraving & Printing

1910 **Engr.**

TD19P1 **red,** large die on India paper, die sunk on card *2,000.*

No. TD19P1 (199x152mm) has a blue control number "400894" on reverse.

TDP20P1

Bureau of Engraving & Printing

1910 **Typo.**

TD20P1 **black,** large die on thick glazed card *2,000.*

No. TD20P1 (73x83mm) has a control number "420279" and manuscript "first die proof impression of experimental surface die from surface print, JER April 25/10" on reverse.

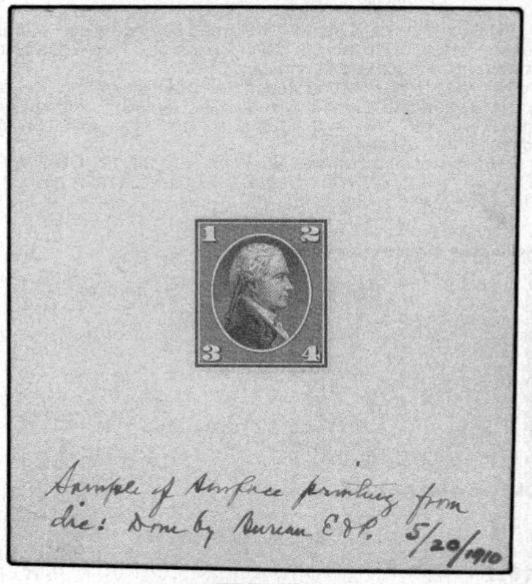

TDP20P2

Bureau of Engraving & Printing

1910 **Typo.**

TD20P2 **red,** large die on thick glazed card *1,500.*

No. TD20P2 (73x83mm) has manuscript inscription in blue ink "Sample of surface printing from die: Done by Bureau E. & P. 5/20/1910" on front below design, with rubber hand-stamp"420270" on reverse. Another TDP@ die pruoof on thick card stock has been cut down to stamp-design size, with control number "42039-" (missing last digit) on reverse, Value, $1,000.

No. TD28TC1ae

Bureau of Engraving & Printing

1910 **Engr.**

TD28TC1a Large die on India, die sunk on card

e.	**blue**	1,000.
f.	**carmine**	1,000.
g.	**dark brown**	1,000.
h.	**dark green**	1,000.
i.	**dark violet brown**	1,000.

TD28TC1d **black,** large die on thick glazed card, die sunk 1,750.

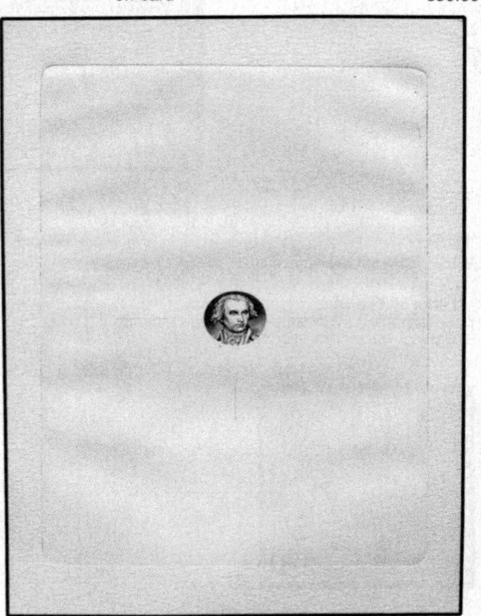

TD130C-E1

Design size: 18x18mm.

Engraved vignette of George Clinton, unfinished design with detail missing on shirt rosette, etc., lines on forehead, shading horizontal.

1993

TD130C-E1 **black,** large die on wove, die sunk on card *850.00*

TD130C-E2

Design size: 18x23mm. Oval size: 18x17mm.

Engraved vignette of George Clinton similar to TD130C-E1, with detail on shirt rosette, hair neatened, no lines on forehead, background shading horizontal.

TD130C-E2 **black,** large die on wove, die sunk on card *850.00*

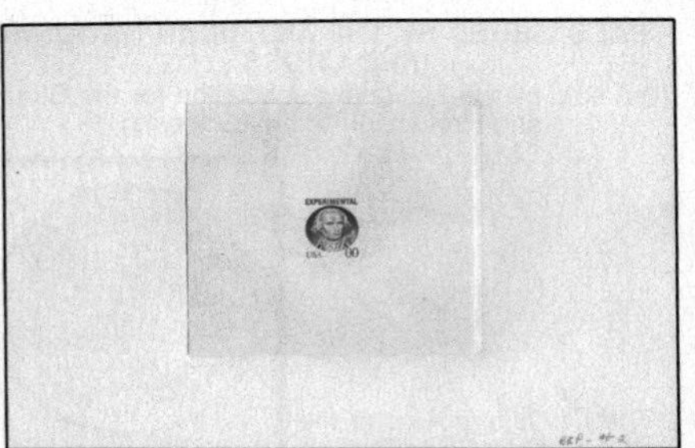

TD130CP1

Design size: 18x23mm. Oval size: 18x16mm.

Engraved complete design as adopted, background at an angle.

TD130CP1 **blue gray,** large die proof, die sunk on card *850.00*

CHRISTMAS SEALS

Issued by the American National Red Cross (1907-1919), the National Tuberculosis Association (1920-1967), the National Tuberculosis and Respiratory Disease Association (1968-1972) and the American Lung Association (1973-).

While the Christmas Seal is not a postage stamp, it has long been associated with the postal service because of its use on letters and packages.

Einar Holboell, an employee of the Danish Post Office, created the Christmas Seal. He believed that seal sales could raise money for charity. The post offices of Denmark, Iceland and Sweden began to sell such seals in the 1904 Christmas season. In the United States, Christmas Seals were first issued in 1907 under the guidance of Emily P. Bissell, following the suggestion of Jacob Riis, social service worker.

Until 1975, all seals (except those of 1907 and 1908 type I) were issued in sheets of 100. The grilled gum (1908) has small square depressions like a waffle. The broken gum (1922), devised to prevent paper curling, consists of depressed lines in the gum, ½mm. apart, forming squares. The vertical and horizontal broken gum (1922, 1923, 1925, 1927-1932) forms diamonds. The perf. 12.00 (1917-1919, 1923, 1925, 1931) has two larger and wider-spaced holes between every 11 smaller holes.

Values are for unused seals with original gum.

Values for covers are for seals that are tied. Values for 1907-24 are for seals tied on post card or postal card; values for 1925-31 are for seals tied either on card or on cover; values for 1932 to present are for seals tied on envelopes. 1907-24 seals on cover and 1932+ seals on card sell for more. Values are for non-philatelic and contemporaneous uses. Philatelic and non-contemporaneous uses are worth considerably less.

SEALS ISSUED BY THE DELAWARE CHAPTER OF THE AMERICAN NATIONAL RED CROSS

CS1 (Type I)

Type II — WX2

Designer — Emily P. Bissell.
Nearly $4,000 worth of seals were sold, $3,000 cleared.

Type I — "Merry Christmas" only.
Type II — "Merry Christmas" and "Happy New Year."

1907 ***Perf. 14***

WX1	CS1 Type I		17.50	
	On cover			*1,000.*
a.	Horiz. pair, imperf. between		*1,000.*	
b.	Horiz. pair, imperf. vert.		*300.00*	
c.	Vert. pair, imperf. between		*650.00*	
WX2	CS1 Type II		15.00	
	On cover			*1,500.*
	On cover, both types I and II			*6,750.*
a.	Vert. pair, imperf. between		*1,000.*	

Types I and II litho. by Theo. Leonhardt & Son, Philadelphia, Pa. The 1st seals were sold Dec. 7, 1907, in Wilmington, Del. Issued in sheets of 228 (19x12). Type II was issued to extend the sale of seals until New Year's Day, 1908. Nos. WX1 and WX2 were sold in only three cities: Wilmington, DE; Philadelphia, PA and Washington D.C. Postmarks from other cities need to be authenticated.

All pairs of No. WX1c also have an imperforate top margin.

Counterfeits of both types exist (perf. 12).

Earliest documented use: No. WX1, Dec. 7, 1907; No. WX2, Dec. 23, 1907.

SEALS ISSUED BY THE AMERICAN NATIONAL RED CROSS

CS2 (Type II)

Designer — Howard Pyle. Sales $135,000.

Type I — frame lines with square corners, small "C" in "Christmas," ear of "8" separate from body of the "8."

Type Ia—frame lines have square corners, small "C" in "Christmas," ear of "8" is joined to the "8."

Type II — frame lines have rounded corners, large "C" in "Christmas," leaves veined.

1908 ***Perf. 14***

WX3	CS2 Type I, perf. 14, smooth gum	35.00	
	On cover		15.00
a.	Perf. 12, smooth gum	45.00	
c.	Perf. 14, grilled gum	100.00	
d.	Perf. 12, grilled gum	50.00	
e.	As #WX3, bklt. pane of 6	500.00	
f.	As "c," bklt. pane of 6	600.00	
g.	As #WX3, bklt. pane of 3	600.00	
	On cover		225.00

Perf. 12

WX3H	CS2 Type Ia, smooth gum	75.00	
	On cover		15.00
i.	Type Ia, grilled gum	60.00	
j.	Type Ia, perf. 14, smooth gum	55.00	
k.	Type Ia, perf. 14, grilled gum	100.00	
WX4	CS2 Type II	30.00	
	On cover		20.00
a.	Booklet pane of 6	190.00	
b.	Booklet pane of 3	125.00	
	On cover		225.00

Type I litho. by Theo. Leonhardt & Son. Sheets of 250 (14x18), with the 1st space in the 9th and 18th rows left blank.

Type II litho. by American Bank Note Co., New York, N.Y. in sheets of 100 (10x10).

Booklet panes have straight edges on 3 sides and perforated on left side where there is a stub, except No. WX4b which is a vert. strip of 3 with stub at top. Panes of 6 were made up in books of 24 and 48 and sold for 25c and 50c, and panes of 3 in books of 9 sold for 10c. The grilled gum has small square depressions like a waffle.

Earliest document use: No. WX3, Nov. 29, 1908; No. WX3g, Dec. 13, 1908; No. WX3H, Nov. 30, 1908; No. WX4, Dec. 2, 1908; No. WX4b, Dec. 2, 1908.

CS3

Designer — Carl Wingate. Sales $250,000.

1909 ***Perf. 12***

WX5	CS3 One type only	1.25	
	On cover		8.00

Litho. by The Strobridge, Cincinnati, Ohio. Seals with a round punched hole of 3½mm are printers' samples.

Earliest document use: Nov. 19, 1909.

CS4

Designer — Frances Thompson. Sales $300,000.

1910 ***Perf. 12***

WX6	CS4 One type only	20.00	
	On cover		8.00
a.	Horiz. pair, imperf. between	—	
b.	Vert. pair, imperf. between	—	

Lithographed by The Strobridge Lithographing Co.
Earliest documented use: Nov. 23, 1910.

SEALS ISSUED BY THE AMERICAN NATIONAL RED CROSS

(But sold by the National Association for the Study and Prevention of Tuberculosis)

"The Old Home Among the Cedars" — CS5 (Type II)

Designer — Anton Rudert under directions of F. D. Millet. Sales $320,000.

Type I — diameter of circle 22mm, solid end in house.
Type II — same circle but thinner, lined end to house.
Type III — diameter of circle 20mm, lined end to house.
Type IV — green windows on house and green berries at bottom.
Type V — design same as types II and III.

1911 ***Perf. 12***

WX7	CS5 Type I	50.00	
	On cover		15.00
WX8	CS5 Type II	120.00	
	On cover		250.00

COIL STAMP

Perf. 8½ Vertically

WX9	CS5 Type III	50.00	
	On cover		*2,000.*

Rouletted 12 in red x 6 colorless

WX9A	CS5 Type IV	*750.00*	
	On cover		*1,500.*

COIL STAMP

WX9B	CS5 Type V	*2,700.*	—
	On cover		

Typo. by Eureka, Scranton, Pa. Type I has name and address of printer and union label in red in top margin. Type II has union label only in green on left margin.

No. WX9B was issued imperforate, but all examples were privately perforated with U.S. Automatic Vending Company type II separations. This is the rarest national seal with only six documented examples.

Earliest documented use: No. WX7, Nov. 24, 1911; No. WX8, Dec. 11, 1911; No. WX9, Dec. 22, 1911; No. WX9A, Dec. 15, 1911; No. WX9B, unknown.

CS6

Designer — John H. Zeh. Sales $402,256.

1912 ***Perf. 12***

WX10	CS6 One type only	11.00	
	On cover		15.00

Lithographed by The Strobridge Lithographing Co.
Earliest documented use: Nov. 26, 1912.

CS7 (Type I)

Designer — C. J. Budd. Sales $449,505.

Type I — with Poinsettia flowers and green circles around red crosses at either side.

Type II — the Poinsettia flowers have been removed, and the bottom left of the upper ribbon with "American Red Cross" has closed curl filled in green.

Type IIa — the Poinsettia flowers have been removed, and the bottom left of the upper ribbon with "American Red Cross" has open curl filled in red.

Type III — the Poinsettia flowers and green circles have been removed.

Type IV — similar to type IIa, with slight differences (the reindeer bodies not filled in, etc.)

1913 ***Perf. 12***

WX11 CS7 Type I *1,400.*
WX12 CS7 Type II 7.50
On cover *1,000.*
WX12A CS7 Type IIa 7.50
On cover *1,500.*
WX13 CS7 Type III 8.50
On cover 15.00

Imperf

WX14 CS7 Type IV *600.00*
On cover *2,000.*

Lithographed by American Bank Note Co.

Only a single sheet of No. WX11 was printed, and it was not sold to the public. Any examples on cover are fakes.

Earliest documented use: No. WX12, Nov. 11, 1913; No. WX12A, Dec. 16, 1913; No. WX13, Nov. 24, 1913; No. WX14; Dec. 24, 1913.

CS8

Designer — Benjamin S. Nash. Sales $555,854.

1914 ***Perf. 12***

WX15 CS8 One type only 10.00
On cover 15.00

Lithographed by The Strobridge Lithographing Co.

Earliest documented use: Nov. 26, 1914.

CS9

Designer — Benjamin S. Nash. Sales $760,000.

1915

WX16 CS9 Perf. 12½ 10.00
On cover 15.00
a. Perf. 12 65.00
On cover 15.00

Lithographed by Andrew B. Graham Co., Washington, D.C.

Earliest documented use: No. WX16, Nov. 22, 1915; No. WX16a, Nov. 22, 1915.

CS10

Designer — T. M. Cleland. Sales $1,040,810.

1916

WX18 CS10 Perf. 12 5.00
On cover 15.00
a. Perf. 12x12½ 6.00
b. Perf. 12½x12 15.00
c. Perf. 12½ 14.00

Lithographed by the Strobridge Lithographing Co.

Earliest documented use: Nov. 27, 1916.

Seals of 1917-21 are on coated paper.

CS11

Designer — T. M. Cleland. Sales $1,815,110.

1917

WX19 CS11 Perf. 12 2.00
On cover 8.00
a. Perf. 12½ 15.00
b. Perf. 12x12 2.00
c. Perf. 12x12½ *20.00*

Typographed by Eureka Specialty Printing Co.

Perf. 12 has two larger and wider-spaced holes between; every eleven smaller holes.

Sheets come with straight edged margins on all four sides also with perforated margins at either right or left. Perforated margins have the union label imprint in green.

Earliest documented use: Oct. 23, 1917.

SEALS ISSUED BY THE AMERICAN NATIONAL RED CROSS

(Distributed by the National Tuberculosis Association)

CS12

Designer — Charles A. Winter.

These seals were given to members and others in lots of 10, the Natl. Tuberculosis Assoc. being subsidized by a gift of $2,500,000 from the American National Red Cross.

To aid the collector in understanding the complex issues Nos. WX21 and WX22, the following abbreviations are used in the listings:

VM — Varying margins: 1918 Type II booklet panes of 10 (2x5) with varying margins, show perfs. or roulettes on one or both sides of the pane. Cut from press sheets with perf. or rouletted vert. gutters. The cut normally was inaccurate, creating a straight edge on one pane and a tiny perf. or rouletted margin on the next pane.
P4S — Perfed on all four sides, from a sheet of 100.
SE3S — Straight edge on three sides of the booklet pane.
SE4S — Straight edge on all four sides of the booklet pane.
PMT — Perforated margin at top.
PMB — Perforated margin at bottom.
PML — Perforated margin at left.
PMR — Perforated margin at right.

Type I — "American Red Cross" 15mm long, heavy circles between date.

Type II — "American Red Cross" 15½mm long, periods between date.

1918

WX21 CS12 Type I, perf. 11½x12, P4S 7.50
On cover 35.00
a. Perf. 12, P4S 10.00
On cover 500.00
b. Perf. 12, booklet pane of 10, P4S 2.00
On cover 500.00
c. Perf. 12x12, booklet pane of 10, SE4S 2.00
d. Perf. 12, booklet pane of 10, SE4S 2.00
e. Perf. 12x12, booklet pane of 10, SE4S 65.00
WX22 CS12 Type II, perf. 12½xRoulette 9½, from booklet pane .60
On cover 40.00
a. Perf. 12½, booklet pane of 10 (2x5), SE3S, PMT 2.00
b. Perf. 12½x12, bklt. pane of 10 (2x5), SE3S, PMT —
d. Roulette 9½xPerf. 12½, bklt. pane of 10 (2x5), SE3S, PMT 50.00
e. Perf. 12½xRoulette 9½, bklt. pane of 10 (2x5), VM, SE at bottom, PMT 25.00
f. Perf. 12½, booklet pane of 10 (2x5), VM, SE at bottom, PMT 25.00
h. Roulette 9½xPerf. 12½, bklt. pane of 10 (2x5), VM, SE at bottom, PMT 25.00
i. Roulette 9½xPerf. 12½ booklet pane of 10 (2x5), VM, roulette 12½ at left, perf. 12½ through the center and at right —
j. Perf. 12½, horiz. booklet pane of 10 (5x2), SE3S, PMR 50.00
k. Perf. 12½, except 2nd & 4th vert. rows perf. 12, horiz. bklt. pane of 10 (5x2), SE left & bottom, cut through perfs at right, PMT —
l. Roulette 9½xPerf. 12½, horiz. booklet pane of 10 (5x2), SE3S, PMR —
m. Perf. 12½, booklet pane of 10 (2x5), SE3S, PML —
n. Perf. 12½, booklet pane of 10 (2x5), SE3S, PMB 35.00

For perf 12, see note following No. WX19.

Type I typographed by Eureka Specialty Printing Co.

Booklet panes of 10 (2x5) normally have straight edges on all four sides. They were cut from the sheets of 100 and can be plated by certain flaws which occur on both. Sheets have union label imprint on top margin in brown.

Type II lithographed by Strobridge Lithographing Co.

Booklet panes are the same but normally have a perforated margin at top and stub attached. These too can be plated by flaws.

The seal with "American Red Cross" 17¼mm long is believed to be an essay.

Earliest documented use: No. WX21, Dec. 13, 1918; No. WX21a-WX21b, Dec. 23, 1918; No. WX22, Dec. 11, 1918.

CS13 (Type I)

Designer — Ernest Hamlin Baker. Sales $3,872,534.

Type I — plume at right side of Santa's cap.

Type II — no plume but a white dot in center of band.

1919

WX24 CS13 Type I, perf. 12 .40
On cover 8.00
a. Perf. 12x12 .60
b. Perf. 12½x12 .50
c. Perf. 12½x12 2.75
WX25 CS13 Type II, perf. 12½ .40
On cover 8.00

For perf 12, see note following No. WX19.

This is the first time the double barred cross, the emblem of the National Tuberculosis Association, appeared in the design of the seals. It is also the last time the red cross emblem of the American National Red Cross was used on seals.

Type I typo. by Eureka, and has union label on margin at left in dark blue. Type II litho. by Strobridge.

Earliest documented use: No. WX24, Dec. 1, 1919; No. WX25, Nov. 28, 1919.

SEALS ISSUED BY THE NATIONAL TUBERCULOSIS ASSOCIATION

CS14

Designer — Ernest Hamlin Baker. Sales $3,667,834.

Type I — size of seal 18x22mm.

Type II — seal 18½x23½mm, letters larger & numerals heavier.

A Great Source for Seals

- 1907-2017 single, pair, block or sheet as required, Slogan Blocks, bklt panes and both types of 1907 .... 152.50
- 1907-16, 1918 U.S. Christmas Seal sheets .... POR
- 1909, 1917, 1919, 1921-26 set of 9 sheets 445.00
- 1927-31, 5 sheets 27.50
- 1932-1981 set of 50 sheets 37.50
- 1930//1977 set of 40 imperforate sheets, 30 are no gum. 168.00
- 1978-87 set of 10 imperforate sheets 40.00
- U.S. Xmas Seal Pricelist, 75 pgs, illustrated 3.00
- 10th Ed. Worldwide Xmas Seal Pricelist, 72 pgs, illustrated 3.00
- All my pricelists on computer CD, with printable albums .... FREE
- Green's Catalog, Section 1, U.S. National Xmas Seals, 2014 Ed. illustrating all regular issue and experiment seals, 200 pages (Computer CD '14 Ed. $8.95) comb bound 24.50

I distribute Green's Catalog and other literature for The Christmas Seal & Charity Stamp Society, as a club project. Visit their site: www.seal-society.org

JOHN DENUNE
234 E. Broadway, Granville, OH 43023
Phone (740) 587-0276
E-mail: john@christmasseals.net
Website: www.christmasseals.net

1920

WX26	CS14 Type I, perf. 12x12½	.50	
	On cover		8.00
a.	Perf. 12	.60	
b.	Perf. 12½x12	35.00	
c.	Perf. 12½	35.00	
WX27	CS14 Type II, perf. 12½	.50	
	On cover		12.00

Type I typo. by Eureka, and has union label imprint and rings on margin at left in dark blue. Type II litho. & offset by Strobridge.

Earliest documented use: No. WX26, Nov. 16, 1920; No. WX27, Dec. 2, 1920.

CS15

Designer — George V. Curtis. Sales $3,520,303.

Type I — dots in the chimney shading and faces are in diagonal lines, dots on chimney are separate except between the 2 top rows of bricks where they are solid.

Type II — dots in the chimney shading and faces are in horiz. lines.

Type III — as Type I except red dots on chimney are mostly joined forming lines, dots between the 2 top rows of bricks are not a solid mass.

1921

WX28	CS15 Type I, perf. 12½	.65	
	On cover		8.00
WX29	CS15 Type II, perf. 12½	.50	
	On cover		8.00
WX29A	CS15 Type III, perf. 12	.50	
	On cover		30.00

Type I typo. by Eureka. Type II offset by Strobridge. Type III typo. by Zeese-Wilkinson Co., Long Island City, N.Y.

Earliest documented use: No. WX28, Nov. 23, 1921; No. WX29, Nov. 27, 1921; No. WX29A, Nov. 23, 1921.

CS16

Designer — T. M. Cleland. Sales $3,857,086.

1922

WX30	CS16 Perf. 12½, broken gum	.80	
	On cover		8.00
a.	Perf. 12, broken gum	3.00	
b.	Perf. 12x12½, broken gum	10.00	
c.	Perf. 12, smooth gum	3.00	
d.	Perf. 12½, vertical broken gum	3.00	

Typographed by Eureka Specialty Printing Co.

The broken gum, which was devised to prevent curling of paper, consists of depressed lines in the gum ½mm apart, forming squares, or vertical broken gum forming diamonds.

Earliest documented use: Nov. 29, 1922.

CS17

Designer — Rudolph Ruzicka. Sales $4,259,660.

1923

WX31	CS17 Perf. 12½, vertical broken gum	.30	
	On cover		8.00
a.	Perf. 12, horizontal broken gum	3.00	
b.	Perf. 12x12, vertical broken gum	3.50	
c.	Perf. 12½x12, vertical broken gum	6.50	
d.	Perf. 12, vertical broken gum	2.00	
e.	Perf. 12x12, vertical broken gum	3.00	

For perf 12, see note following No. WX19.

Typographed by Eureka Specialty Printing Co.

The broken gum on this and issues following printed by Eureka consists of very fine depressed lines forming diamonds.

Earliest documented use: Nov. 16, 1923.

CS18

Designer — George V. Curtis. Sales $4,479,656.

1924

WX32	CS18 One type only	.30	
	On cover		8.00

Offset by Strobridge, E.&D., and U.S.P.& L.

Earliest documented use: Nov. 24, 1924.

CS19 (Type II)

Designer — Robert G. Eberhard. Sales $4,937,786.

Type I — red lines at each side of "1925" do not join red tablet below.

Type II — red lines, as in type I, join red tablet below.

Type III — as type I but shorter rays around flames and "ea" of "Health" smaller.

1925 ***Perf. 12½***

WX35	CS19 Type I, vert. broken gum	.30	
	On cover		15.00
a.	Perf. 12, vertical broken gum	3.50	
b.	Perf. 12x12½ vertical broken gum	.60	
c.	Perf. 12x12½ vert. broken gum	—	
WX36	CS19 Type II	.30	
	On cover		250.00
WX37	CS19 Type III	.75	
	On cover		100.00

For perf 12, see note following No. WX19.

Type I typo. by Eureka. Type II offset by E.&D. Type III litho. by Gugler Lithographing Co., Milwaukee.

Earliest documented use: No. WX35, Nov. 30, 1925; No. WX36, Nov. 30, 1925; No. WX37, Dec. 10, 1925.

CS20

Designer — George V. Curtis. Sales $5,121,872.

1926 ***Perf. 12½***

WX38	CS20 One type only	.25	
	On cover		8.00

Offset by E.&D. and U.S.P.&L.

Printers' marks: E.&D. has a red dot at upper right on seal 91 on some sheets. U.S.P.&L. has a black dot at upper left on seal 56 on some sheets.

Earliest documented use: Nov. 27, 1926.

CS21

Designer — John W. Evans. Sales $5,419,959.

1927

WX39	CS21 Perf. 12, horizontal broken gum	.25	
	On cover		8.00
a.	Smooth gum	1.00	
WX40	CS21 Perf. 12½, no dot	.25	
	On cover		8.00
WX41	CS21 Perf. 12½, one larger red dot in background 1mm above right post of dashboard on sleigh	.25	
	On cover		8.00

"Bonne Sante" added to design and No. WX39a but with body of sleigh myrtle green instead of green were used in Canada.

Offset: Nos. WX39, WX39a by Eureka. No. WX40 by E.&D. No. WX41 by U.S.P.&L.

Printer's marks: Eureka has no mark but can be identified by the perf. 12. E.&D. has red dot to left of knee of 1st reindeer on seal 92. U.S.P.&L. has 2 red dots in white gutter, one at lower left of seal 46 (and sometimes 41) and the other at upper right of seal 55. The perforations often strike out one of these dots.

Earliest documented use: Nos. WX39-WX41, Nov. 18, 1927.

The Gallant Ship "Argosy" — CS22

Designer — John W. Evans. Sales $5,465,738.

Type I — shading on sails broken, dots in flag regular.

Type II — shading on sails broken, dots in flag spotty.

Type III — shading on sails unbroken, dots in flag regular.

1928 ***Perf. 12½***

WX44	CS22 Type I, vertical broken gum	.25	
	On cover		50.00
WX45	CS22 Type II	.25	
	On cover		60.00
WX46	CS22 Type III	.25	
	On cover		60.00

Seals inscribed "Bonne Annee 1929" or the same as type II but green in water, and black lines of ship heavier and deeper color were used in Canada.

Offset: Type I by Eureka, Type II by Strobridge, Type III by E.&D.

Printers' marks: Type I comes with and without a blue dash above seal 10, also with a blue and a black dash. Type II has 2 blue dashes below seal 100. Type III has red dot in crest of 1st wave on seal 92.

Earliest documented use: Nos. WX44, Nov. 20, 1928; No. WX45, Nov. 23, 1928; No. WX46, Dec. 1, 1928.

CS23

Designer — George V. Curtis. Sales $5,546,147.

1929 ***Perf. 12½***

WX49	CS23 Vertical broken gum	.25	
	On cover		20.00
a.	Perf. 12, vertical broken gum	.50	
b.	Perf. 12½x12, vertical broken gum	2.00	
WX50	CS23 Smooth gum	.25	

Seals inscribed "Bonne Sante 1929" or "Christmas Greetings 1929" were used in Canada.

Offset: Nos. WX49-WX49b by Eureka, No. WX50 by E.&D., U.S.P.&L., and R.R. Heywood Co., Inc., New York, N.Y.

Printers' marks: Eureka is without mark but identified by broken gum. E.&D. has a black dot in lower left corner of seal 92. U.S.P.&L. has blue dot above bell on seal 56. Heywood has a blue dot at lower right corner of seal 100.

Earliest documented use: Nos. WX49-WX50, Nov. 29, 1929.

CS24

Designer — Ernest Hamlin Baker, and redrawn by John W. Evans. Sales $5,309,352.

1930 ***Perf. 12½***

WX55	CS24 Vertical broken gum	.25	
	On cover		10.00
a.	Perf. 12, vert. broken gum	.50	
b.	Perf. 12x12, vert. broken gum	.25	
c.	Perf. 12½x12, vertical broken gum	2.50	
d.	Perf. 12, booklet pane of 10, horiz. broken gum	2.50	
WX56	CS24 Smooth gum	.25	

Seals inscribed "Bonne Sante" or "Merry Christmas" on red border of seal were used in Canada.

Offset: Nos. WX55-WX55d by Eureka, No. WX56 by Strobridge, E.&D. and U.S.P.&L.

Printers' marks: Eureka has a dot between the left foot and middle of "M" of "Merry" on seal 1. Strobridge has 2 dashes below "ALL" on seal 100. E.&D. printed on Nashua paper has dot on coat just under elbow on seal 92, and on Gummed Products Co. paper has the dot on seals 91, 92. U.S.P.&L. has a dash which joins tree to top frame line just under "MA" of "Christmas" on seal 55.

The plate for booklet panes was made up from the left half of the regular plate and can be plated by certain flaws which occur on both.

Earliest documented use: No. WX55, Nov. 28, 1930; No. WX56, Nov. 28, 1930.

CS25

Designer — John W. Evans. Sales $4,526,189.

1931 ***Perf. 12½***

WX61 CS25 Horiz. broken gum (see footnote) 3.00
On cover 10.00
WX62 CS25 Horizontal broken gum .25
a. Perf. 12x12½, horiz. broken gum .35
b. Perf. 12x12½, horizontal broken gum 2.50
c. Perf. 12, horizontal broken gum 1.00
g. Perf. 12, vertical broken gum, booklet pane of 10 2.00
h. Perf. 12x12, vertical broken gum, booklet pane of 10 2.00
WX63 CS25 Smooth gum .25

For perf 12, see note following No. WX19.

Offset: Nos. WX61-WX62h by Eureka, No. WX63 by Strobridge. No. WX61 has a green dash across inner green frame line at bottom center on each seal in sheet except those in 1st and last vertical rows and the 2 rows at bottom.

Printers' marks: Eureka has none. Strobridge has the usual 2 dashes under seal 100.

The plate for booklet panes was made up from transfers of 60 seals (12x5). The panes can be plated by minor flaws.

Earliest documented use: Nox. WX61-WX63, Nov. 23, 1931.

CS26

Designer — Edward F. Volkmann. Sales $3,470,637.

1932

WX64 CS26 Perf. 12½x12¾ .25
On cover 10.00
a. Vertical broken gum .50
WX65 CS26 Perf. 12 .25
On cover 10.00
WX66 CS26 Perf. 12½ .25
On cover 10.00
WX67 CS26 Perf. 12½ .25
On cover 10.00

Offset: Nos. WX64 by Eureka, No. WX65 by E.&D., No. WX66 by U.S.P.&L., No. WX67 by Columbian Bank Note Co., Chicago. Nos. WX64, WX67 have a little red spur on bottom inner frame line of each seal, at left corner.

Printers' marks: Eureka has a red dash, in each corner of the sheet, which joins the red border to the red inner frame line. E.&D. has a blue dot in snow at lower left on seal 91. U.S.P.&L. has a blue dot on top of post on seal 56. Columbian Bank Note has small "C" in lower part of girl's coat on seal 82.

Earliest documented use: Nos. WX64-WX67, Nov. 13, 1932.

CS27

Designer — Hans Axel Walleen. Sales $3,429,311.

1933

WX68 CS27 Perf. 12 .25
On cover 45.00
WX69 CS27 Perf. 12½ .25
On cover 45.00

Offset: No. WX68 by Eureka, No. WX69 by Strobridge, U.S.P.&L., and the Columbian Bank Note Co.

Printers' marks; Eureka has rope joining elbow of figure to left on seals 11, 20, 91, 100. Strobridge has the usual 2 dashes under seal 100. U.S.P.&L. has green dot on tail of "s" of "Greetings" on seal 55. Columbian has white "c" on margin, under cross, on seal 93.

Earliest documented use: Nos. WX68-WX69, Oct. 19, 1933.

CS28

Designer — Herman D. Giesen. Sales $3,701,344.

1934

WX72 CS28 Perf. 12½x12¼ .25
On cover 30.00
WX73 CS28 Perf. 12½ (see footnote) .25
On cover 30.00
WX74 CS28 Perf. 12½ (see footnote) .25
On cover 30.00
WX75 CS28 Perf. 12½ (see footnote) .25
On cover 30.00

Offset: No. WX72 by Eureka, No. WX73 by Strobridge, No. WX74 by E.&D. and No. WX75 by U.S.P.&L.

Cutting of blue plate for the under color: Nos. WX72, WX73 (early printing) and WX74 have lettering and date cut slightly larger than ultramarine color. No. WX73 (later printing) has square cutting around letters and date, like top part of letter "T". No. WX75 has cutting around letters and date cut slightly larger.

Printers' marks: Eureka has 5 stars to right of cross on seal 10. Strobridge has 2 blue dashes in lower left corner of seal 91 or in lower right corner of seal 100. E.&D. has a red dot in lower left corner of seal 99. U.S.P.&L. has 5 stars to left of cross on seal 56.

Great Britain issued seals of this design which can be distinguished by the thinner and whiter paper. Sheets have perforated margins on all 4 sides but without any lettering on bottom margin, perf. 12½.

Earliest documented use: Nos. WX72-WX75, Nov. 16, 1934.

CS29

Designer — Ernest Hamlin Baker. Sales $3,946,498.

1935

WX76 CS29 Perf. 12½x12¼ .25
On cover 25.00
WX77 CS29 Perf. 12½ .25
On cover 25.00

Offset: No. WX76 by Eureka, No. WX77 by Strobridge, U.S.P.&L. and Columbian Bank Note Co.

Eureka recut their blue plate and eliminated the faint blue shading around cross, girl's head and at both sides of the upper part of post. U.S.P.& L. eliminated the 2 brown spurs which pointed to the base of cross, in all 4 corners of the sheet.

Printers' marks: Eureka has an extra vertical line of shading on girl's skirt on seal 60. Strobridge has 2 brown dashes in lower right corner of position 100 but sheets from an early printing are without this mark. U.S.P.&L. has a blue dot under post on seal 55. Columbian has a blue "c" under post on seal 99.

The corner seals carry slogans: "Help Fight Tuberculosis," "Protect Your Home from Tuberculosis," "Tuberculosis Is Preventable," "Tuberculosis Is Curable."

Earliest documented use: Nos. WX76-WX77, Nov. 22, 1935.

Printers' marks appear on seal 56 on sheets of 100 unless otherwise noted:

E Eureka Specialty Printing Co.
S Strobridge Lithographing Co. (1930-1958).
S Specialty Printers of America (1975-).
D Edwards & Deutsch Lithographing Co. (E.&D.)
U United States Printing & Lithographing Co. (U.S.P.&L.)
F Fleming-Potter Co., Inc.
W Western Lithograph Co.
B Berlin Lithographing Co. (1956-1969); I. S. Berlin Press (1970-1976); Barton-Cotton (1977-).
R Bradford-Robinson Printing Co.
N Sale-Niagara, Inc.

Seals from 1936 onward are printed by offset.

Seals with tropical gum (dull), starting in 1966, were used in Puerto Rico.

Other printers noted in the listings:

C Cyril Scott (1987-93)
C Connecticut Color (1994-95)
CW Colorform & Webcraft (1995-2000)
M Midland
Mo Moore Response Marketing
V Vertis
WL Wisconsin Label

CS30

Designer — Walter I. Sasse. Sales $4,522,269.

1936 **Pair**

WX80 CS30 Perf. 12½x12 (E) .25
On cover 8.00
WX81 CS30 Perf. 12½ (S,D,U) .25
On cover 8.00

Seals with red background and green cap-band alternate with seals showing green background and red cap-band. The corner seals carry the same slogans as those of 1935.

Two of the three Strobridge printings show vertical green dashes in margin below seal 100, besides "S" on seal 56.

Earliest documented use: Nos. WX80-WX81, Nov. 10, 1936.

CS31

Designer — A. Robert Nelson. Sales $4,985,697.

1937

WX88 CS31 Perf. 12x12½ (E) .25
On cover 8.00
WX89 CS31 Perf. 12½ (S,D,U) .25
On cover 8.00

Positions 23, 28, 73 and 78, carry slogans: "Health for all," "Protect your home," "Preventable" and "Curable."

The "U" printer's mark of U.S.P.&L. appears on seal 55. It is omitted on some sheets.

Earliest documented use: Nos. WX88-WX89, July 20, 1937.

CS32

Designer — Lloyd Coe. Sales $5,239,526.

1938

WX92 CS32 Perf. 12½x12 (E) .25
On cover 8.00
WX93 CS32 Perf. 12½ (S,D,U) .25
On cover 8.00
a. Miniature sheet, imperf. 5.00
On cover 50.00

The corner seals bear portraits of Rene T. H. Laennec, Robert Koch, Edward Livingston Trudeau and Einar Holboll.

No. WX93a contains the 4 corner seals, with the regular seal in the center. It sold for 25 cents.

Earliest documented use: Nos. WX92-WX93, Nov. 18, 1938; No. WX93a, Nov. 24, 1938.

CS33

Designer — Rockwell Kent. Sales $5,593,399.

1939

WX96 CS33 Perf. 12½x12 (E) .25
On cover 8.00
a. Booklet pane of 20, perf. 12 2.00
WX97 CS33 Perf. 12½ (S,D,U) .25
On cover 8.00

The center seals, positions 45, 46, 55, 56, carry slogans: "Health to All," "Protect Your Home." "Tuberculosis Preventable Curable" and "Holiday Greetings."

Printers' marks appear on seal 57.

Earliest documented use: Nos. WX96-WX97, Nov. 18, 1939.

CS34

Designer — Felix L. Martini. Sales $6,305,979.

1940

WX100	CS34	Perf. 12½x12 (E)	.25
		On cover	8.00
WX101	CS34	Perf. 12½x13 (E)	.25
		On cover	8.00
WX103	CS34	Perf. 12½ (S,D,U)	.25
		On cover	8.00

Seals 23, 32 and 34 carry the slogan "Protect Us from Tuberculosis." Each slogan seal shows one of the 3 children.

Earliest documented use: Nos. WX100-WX103, Aug. 12, 1940.

CS35

Designer — Stevan Dohanos. Sales $7,530,496.

1941

WX104	CS35	Perf. 12½x12 (E)	.25
		On cover	8.00
WX105	CS35	Perf. 12½ (S,D,U)	.25
		On cover	8.00

"S" and "U" printers' marks exist on same sheet.

Earliest documented use: Nos. WX104-WX105, Nov. 12, 1941.

CS36

Designer — Dale Nichols. Sales $9,390,117.

1942

WX108	CS36	Perf. 12x12½ (E)	.25
		On cover	8.00
WX109	CS36	Perf. 12½ (S,D,U)	.25
		On cover	8.00

Earliest documented use: Nos. WX108-WX109, Nov. 20, 1942.

CS37

Designer — Andre Dugo. Sales $12,521,494.

Pair

1943

WX112	CS37	Perf. 12½x12 (E)	.25
		On cover	8.00
WX113	CS37	Perf. 12½ (S,D,U)	.25
		On cover	8.00

On alternate seals, the vert. frame colors (blue & red) are transposed as are the horiz. frame colors (buff & black).

Seals where "Joyeux Noel" replaces "Greetings 1943" and "1943" added on curtain or the same as No. WX113 but darker colors were used in Canada.

Earliest documented use: Nos. WX112-WX113, Sept. 29, 1943.

CS38

Designer — Spence Wildey. Sales $14,966,227.

1944

WX118	CS38	Perf. 12½x12 (E)	.25
		On cover	8.00
WX119	CS38	Perf. 12½ (S,D,U)	.25
		On cover	8.00

Seals with "USA" omitted are for Canada.

Earliest documented use: Nos. WX118-WX119, Sept. 28, 1944.

CS39

Designer — Park Phipps. Sales $15,638,755.

1945 **"USA" at Lower Right Corner**

WX124	CS39	Perf. 12½x12 (E)	.25
		On cover	8.00
WX125	CS39	Perf. 12½ (S,D,U)	.25
		On cover	8.00

Seals with "USA" omitted are for Canada.

Earliest documented use: Nos. WX124-WX125, Aug. 6, 1945.

CS40

Designer — Mary Louise Estes and Lloyd Coe. Sales $17,075,608.

1946 **"USA" at Left of Red Cross**

WX130	CS40	Perf. 12½x12 (E)	.25
		On cover	8.00
WX131	CS40	Perf. 12½ (S,D,U)	.25
		On cover	8.00

Seals with "USA" omitted are for Canada and Bermuda.

Printers' marks are on seal 86.

The center seals (45, 46, 55, 56) bear portraits of Jacob Riis, Emily P. Bissell, E. A. Van Valkenburg and Leigh Mitchell Hodges.

Earliest documented use: Nos. WX130-WX131, Oct. 21, 1946.

CS41

Designer — Raymond H. Lufkin. Sales $18,665,523.

1947

WX135	CS41	Perf. 12x12½ (E)	.25
		On cover	8.00
WX136	CS41	Perf. 12½ (S,D,U)	.25
		On cover	8.00

Seals with "USA" omitted are for Canada and Great Britain.

The "U" printer's mark of U.S.P.&L. appears on seal 46.

Earliest documented use: Nos. WX135-WX136, July 25, 1947.

CS42

Designer — Jean Barry Bart. Sales $20,153,834.

1948

WX140	CS42	Perf. 12x12½ (E)	.25
		On cover	8.00
WX141	CS42	Perf. 12½ (S,D,U)	.25
		On cover	8.00

Seals with "USA" omitted are for Canada and Great Britain.

Earliest documented use: Nos. WX140-WX141, Nov. 22, 1948.

CS43

Designer — Herbert Meyers. Sales $20,226,794.

1949

WX145	CS43	Perf. 12x12½ (E)	.25
		On cover	8.00
WX146	CS43	Perf. 12½ (S,D,U)	.25
		On cover	8.00

Seals with "USA" omitted are for Canada & Great Britain.

Earliest documented use: Nos. WX145-WX146, Nov. 19, 1949.

CS44

Designer — Andre Dugo. Sales $20,981,540.

1950

WX150	CS44	Perf. 12½x12 (E)	.25
		On cover	8.00
WX151	CS44	Perf. 12½ (S,D,U,F)	.25
		On cover	8.00

Seals with "USA" omitted are for Canada & Great Britain.

Earliest documented use: Nos. WX150-WX151, Nov. 17, 1950.

CS45

Designer — Robert K. Stephens. Sales $21,717,953.

1951

WX155	CS45	Perf. 12½x12 (E)	.25
		On cover	8.00
WX156	CS45	Perf. 12½ (S,D,U,F)	.25
		On cover	8.00

Seals with "USA" omitted are for Canada.

Earliest documented use: Nos. WX155-WX156, Nov. 12, 1951.

CS46

Designer — Tom Darling. Sales $23,238,148.

1952

WX159 CS46 Perf. 12½x12 (E) .25
On cover 8.00
WX160 CS46 Perf. 12½ (S,D,U,F) .25
On cover 8.00

For Nos. WX159-WX160 overprinted "Ryukyus" in Japanese characters, see Ryukyu Islands Nos. WX1 and WX1a.

Earliest documented use: Nos. WX159-WX160, Nov. 17, 1952.

CS47

Designers — Elmer Jacobs and E. Willis Jones. Sales $23,889,044.

1953

WX164 CS47 Perf. 13 (E) .25
On cover 8.00
WX165 CS47 Perf. 12½ (S,D,U,F) .25
On cover 8.00

Earliest documented use: Nos. WX164-WX165, Oct. 24, 1953.

CS48

Designer — Jorgen Hansen. Sales $24,670,202.

1954 **Block of 4**

WX168 CS48 Perf. 13 (E) .40
On cover, any single 8.00
WX169 CS48 Perf. 12½ (S,U,F,W) .40
On cover, any single 8.00
WX170 CS48 Perf. 11 (D) .50
On cover, any single 8.00

Earliest documented use: Nos. WX168-WX170, Nov. 4, 1954.

CS49

Designer — Jean Simpson. Sales $25,780,365.

1955 **Pair**

WX173 CS49 Perf. 13 (E) .25
On cover, either single 8.00
WX174 CS49 Perf. 12½ (S,U,F,W) .25
On cover, either single 8.00
WX175 CS49 Perf. 11 (D) .25
On cover, either single 8.00

Earliest documented use: Nos. WX173-WX175, Nov. 17, 1955.

CS50

Designer — Heidi Brandt. Sales $26,310,491.

1956 **Block of 4**

WX178 CS50 Perf. 12½x12 (E) 1.00
On cover, any single 8.00
WX179 CS50 Perf. 12½ (E,S,U,F,W) .50
On cover, any single 8.00
WX180 CS50 Perf. 11 (D,B) .40
On cover, any single 8.00
WX183 CS50 "Puerto Rico," perf. 12½ 3.00

Earliest documented use: Nos. WX178-WX180, Nov. 13, 1956.

CS51

Designer — Clinton Bradley. Sales $25,959,998.

1957 **Block of 4**

WX184 CS51 Perf. 13 (E) .40
On cover, any single 8.00
WX185 CS51 Perf. 12½ (S,U,F,W,R) .40
On cover, any single 8.00
WX186 CS51 Perf. 11 (D,B) .50
On cover, any single 8.00
WX187 CS51 Perf. 10½x11 (D) 1.00
On cover, any single 8.00
WX188 CS51 Perf. 10½ (D) 3.00
On cover, any single 8.00
WX190 CS51 "Puerto Rico," perf. 13 3.00

Earliest documented use: Nos. WX184-WX188, Nov. 15, 1957.

CS52

Designer — Alfred Guerra. Sales $25,955,390.

1958 **Pair**

WX191 CS52 Perf. 13 (E) .25
On cover, either single 8.00
WX192 CS52 Perf. 12½ (S,U,F,W,R) .25
On cover, either single 8.00
WX193 CS52 Perf. 10½x11 (B,D) .50
On cover, either single 8.00
WX194 CS52 Perf. 11 (B,D) .35
On cover, either single 8.00
WX196 CS52 "Puerto Rico," perf. 13 1.50

Earliest documented use: Nos. WX191-WX196, Nov. 10, 1958.

CS53

Designer — Katherine Rowe. Sales $26,740,906.

1959 **Pair**

WX197 CS53 Perf. 13 (E) .25
On cover, either single 8.00
WX198 CS53 Perf. 12½ (F,R,W) .25
On cover, either single 8.00
a. Horiz. pair, imperf. btwn. (D) 1.50
On cover 50.00
WX199 CS53 Perf. 10½x11 (B) .50
On cover, either single 8.00
WX200 CS53 Perf. 11 (B,D) .25
On cover, either single 8.00
WX201 CS53 Perf. 10½ (B) 3.50
On cover, either single 8.00
WX203 CS53 "Puerto Rico," perf. 13 1.50

E.&D. omitted every other vertical row of perforation on a number of sheets which were widely distributed as an experiment. No. WX198a (shown above in illustration) is from these sheets.

Earliest documented use: Nos. WX197-WX198, WX199-WX201, Nov. 16, 1959; No. WX198a Dec. 22, 1959.

CS54

Designer — Philip Richard Costigan. Sales $26,259,030.

1960 **Block of 4**

WX204 CS54 Perf. 12½ (E,F,R,W) .35
On cover, any single 8.00
WX205 CS54 Perf. 12½x12 (E) 2.00
On cover, any single 8.00
WX206 CS54 Perf. 11x10½ (B) .35
On cover, any single 8.00
WX207 CS54 Perf. 11 (D) .35
On cover, any single 8.00
a. As #WX207, block of 4, horiz. imperf. between 4.00

Puerto Rico used No. WX204 (E).

Earliest documented use: Nos. WX204-WX207, Nov. 14, 1960.

CS55

Designer — Heidi Brandt. Sales $26,529,517.

1961 **Block of 4**

WX209 CS55 Perf. 12½ (E,F,R,W) .35
On cover, any single 8.00
WX209A CS55 Perf. 12½x12 (E) 2.50
On cover, any single 8.00

WX210 CS55 Perf. 11x10½ (B) .35
On cover, any single 8.00
WX211 CS55 Perf. 11 (D) .35
On cover, any single 8.00

Puerto Rico used No. WX209 (E).
Earliest documented use: Nos. WX209-WX211, Nov. 16, 1961.

CS56

Designer — Paul Dohanos. Sales $27,429,202.

1962 **Block of 4**
WX213 CS56 Perf. 12½ (F,R,W) .35
On cover, any single 8.00
WX214 CS56 Perf. 13 (E) .35
On cover, any single 8.00
WX215 CS56 Perf. 10½x11 (B) .35
On cover, any single 8.00
WX216 CS56 Perf. 11 (D,B) .35
On cover, any single 8.00

Puerto Rico used No. WX214.
Earliest documented use: Nos. WX213-WX216, Nov. 1, 1962.

CS57

Designer — Judith Campbell Piussi. Sales $27,411,806.

1963 **Block of 4**
WX218 CS57 Perf. 12½ (E,F,R,W) .35
On cover, any single 8.00
WX219 CS57 Perf. 11 (B,D) .35
On cover, any single 8.00

Puerto Rico used No. WX218 (E).
Earliest documented use: Nos. WX218-WX219, Nov. 1, 1963.

CS58

Designer — Gaetano di Palma. Sales $28,784,043.

1964 **Block of 4**
WX220 CS58 Perf. 12½ (E,F,R,W) .35
On cover, any single 8.00
WX221 CS58 Perf. 11 (B,D) .35
On cover, any single 8.00

Puerto Rico used No. WX221 (B).
Earliest documented use: Nos. WX220-WX2221, Nov. 9, 1964.

CS59

Designer — Frede Salomonsen. Sales $29,721,878.

1965 **Block of 4**
WX222 CS59 Perf. 12½ (F,W) .35
On cover, any single 8.00
WX223 CS59 Perf. 11 (B,D) .35
On cover, any single 8.00
WX224 CS59 Perf. 13 (E) .35
On cover, any single 8.00

Puerto Rico used No. WX223 (B).
Earliest documented use: Nos. WX222-WX224, Nov. 2, 1965.

CS60

Designer — Heidi Brandt. Sales $30,776,586.

1966 **Block of 8**
WX225 CS60 Perf. 12½ (E,F,W) .65
On cover, any single 8.00
WX226 CS60 Perf. 10½x11 (B) 1.00
On cover, any single 8.00
WX227 CS60 Perf. 11 (D) .65
On cover, any single 8.00

Blocks of four seals with yellow green and white backgrounds alternate in sheet in checkerboard style.
Puerto Rico used No. WX226.
Earliest documented use: Nos. WX225-WX227, Nov. 1, 1966.

Holiday Train — CS61

Designer — L. Gerald Snyder. Sales $31,876,773.
The seals come in 10 designs showing a train filled with Christmas gifts and symbols. The direction of the train is reversed in alternating rows as are the inscriptions "Christmas 1967" and "Greetings 1967." The illustration shows first 2 seals of top row.

1967 **Block of 20 (10x2)**
WX228 CS61 Perf. 13 (E) .65
On cover, any single 8.00
WX229 CS61 Perf. 12½ (F,W) .65
On cover, any single 8.00
WX231 CS61 Perf. 11 (D) .75
On cover, any single 8.00
WX232 CS61 Perf. 11x10½ (B) —
On cover, any single 8.00

Puerto Rico used No. WX229 (F).
Earliest documented use: Nos. WX228-WX232, Nov. 6, 1967.

SEALS ISSUED BY NATIONAL TUBERCULOSIS AND RESPIRATORY DISEASE ASSOCIATION

CS62

Designer — William Eisele. Sales $33,059,107.

1968 **Block of 4**
WX233 CS62 Perf. 13 (E) .50
On cover, any single 8.00
WX234 CS62 Perf. 10½x11 (B) 7.50
On cover, any single 8.00
WX234A CS62 Perf. 10½ (B) 2.00
On cover, any single 8.00
WX235 CS62 Perf. 11 (D) .50
On cover, any single 8.00
WX236 CS62 Perf. 12½ (F,W) .50
On cover, any single 8.00

Pairs of seals with bluish green and yellow backgrounds alternate in sheet in checkerboard style.
Puerto Rico used No. WX236 (F).
Earliest documented use: Nos. WX233-WX236, Oct. 31, 1968.

CS63

Designer — Bernice Kochan. Sales $34,437,591.

1969 **Block of 4**
WX237 CS63 Perf. 13 (E) .35
On cover, any single 8.00
WX238 CS63 Perf. 12½ (F,W) .35
On cover, any single 8.00
WX239 CS63 Perf. 10½x11 (B) .50
On cover, any single 8.00
WX240 CS63 Perf. 11 (B) .50
On cover, any single 8.00

Puerto Rico used No. WX238 (F).
Earliest documented use: Nos. WX237-WX240, Nov. 15, 1969.

CS64

Designer — L. Gerald Snyder. Sales $36,237,977.
Sheets contain 100 different designs, Christmas symbols, toys, decorated windows; inscribed alternately "Christmas 1970" and "Greetings 1970." The illustration shows 6 seals from the center of the sheet.

1970 **Sheet of 100 (10x10)**

WX243 CS64 Perf. 11 (B) 1.25
On cover, any single 8.00
WX244 CS64 Perf. 11x10½ (B) 10.00
On cover, any single 8.00

Puerto Rico used No. WX242 (F).
Earliest documented use: Nos. WX242-WX244, Sept. 24, 1970.

CS65

Designer — James Clarke. Sales $36,120,000.

1971 **Block of 8 (2x4)**
WX245 CS65 Perf. 12½ (E,F) .50
On cover, any single 8.00
WX246 CS65 Perf. 11 (B) .50
On cover, any single 8.00

The 4 illustrated seals each come in a 2nd design arrangement: cross at left, inscriptions transposed, and reversed bugler, candle and tree ornaments. Each sheet of 100 has 6 horiz. rows as shown and 4 rows with 2nd designs.
Puerto Rico used No. WX245 (F).
Eureka printings are found with large "E," small "E" and without "E."
Earliest documented use: Nos. WX245-WX246, Oct. 17, 1971.

CS66

Designer — Linda Layman. Sales $38,000,557.
The seals come in 10 designs showing various holiday scenes with decorated country and city houses, carolers, Christmas trees and snowman. Inscribed alternately "1972 Christmas" and "Greetings 1972." Shown are seals from center of row.

1972 **Strip of 10**
WX247 CS66 Perf. 13 (E) .50
On cover, any single 8.00
WX248 CS66 Perf. 12½ (F) .75
On cover, any single 8.00
WX249 CS66 Perf. 11 (B) .50
On cover, any single 8.00

Seal 100 has designer's name. Puerto Rico used No. WX248.
Earliest documented use: Nos. WX247-WX249, Oct. 31, 1972.

SEALS ISSUED BY AMERICAN LUNG ASSOCIATION

CS67

Designer — Cheri Johnson. Sales $36,902,439.

The seals are in 12 designs representing "The 12 Days of Christmas." Inscribed alternately "Christmas 1973" and "Greetings 1973." Shown is block from center of top 2 rows.

1973 **Block of 12**
WX250 CS67 Perf. 12½ (F), 18x22mm .50
On cover, any single 8.00
a. Size 16½x20½mm (E) .50
On cover, any single 8.00
WX251 CS67 Perf. 11 (B,W) .50
On cover, any single 8.00

Seal 100 has designer's name. Puerto Rico used No. WX250 (F).
Earliest documented use: Nos. WX250-WX251, Nov. 15, 1973.

CS68

Designer — Rubidoux. Sales $37,761,745.

1974 **Block of 4**
WX252 CS68 Perf. 12½ (E,F) .35
On cover, any single 8.00
WX253 CS68 Perf. 11 (B) .35
On cover, any single 8.00

Seal 99 has designer's name. Puerto Rico used No. WX252 (F).
Earliest documented use: Nos. WX252-WX253, Oct. 22, 1974.

CS69

Children's paintings of holiday scenes. Different design for each state or territory. Paintings by elementary school children were selected in a nationwide campaign ending in Jan., 1974.
Sales $34,710,107.

1975 **Sheet of 54 (6x9)**
WX254 CS69 Perf. 12½ (S,F) 1.25
On cover, any single 8.00
WX255 CS69 Perf. 11 (B) 2.50
On cover, any single 8.00

Printers' marks are on seal 28 (New Mexico). Specialty Printers' seals (S) carry union labels: "Scranton 4," "Scranton 7," "E. Stroudsburg."
Puerto Rico used No. WX254 (F).
Earliest documented use: Nos. WX254-WX255, Oct. 19, 1975.

CS70

Continuous village picture covers sheet with Christmas activities and Santa crossing the sky with sleigh and reindeer. No inscription on 34 seals. Others inscribed "Christmas 1976," "Greetings 1976," and (on 9 bottom-row seals) "American Lung Association." Illustration shows seals 11-12, 20-21.
Sales $36,489,207.

1976 **Sheet of 54 (9x6)**
WX256 CS70 Perf. 12½ (F,N) 1.25
On cover, any single 8.00
WX257 CS70 Perf. 11 (B) 2.50
On cover, any single 8.00
WX258 CS70 Perf. 13 (S) 1.25
On cover, any single 8.00

Printers' marks (N, B, S) on seal 32 and (F) on seal 23.
Puerto Rico used No. WX256 (F).
Earliest documented use: Nos. WX256-WX258, Nov. 9, 1976.

CS71

Children's paintings of holiday scenes. Different design for each state or territory.
Sales $37,583,883.

1977 **Sheet of 54 (6x9)**
WX259 CS71 Perf. 12½ (F) 1.25
On cover, any single 8.00
WX260 CS71 Perf. 11 (B) 1.25
On cover, any single 8.00
WX261 CS71 Perf. 13 (S) 1.50
On cover, any single 8.00

Printers' marks on seal 28 (Georgia).
Puerto Rico used No. WX259.
Earliest documented use: Nos. WX259-WX261, Oct. 21, 1977.

CS72

Children's paintings of holiday scenes. Different design for each state or territory.
Sales $37,621,466.

1978 **Sheet of 54 (6x9)**

WX262 CS72 Perf. 12½ (F) 1.25
On cover, any single 8.00
WX263 CS72 Perf. 11 (B) 1.25
On cover, any single 8.00
WX264 CS72 Perf. 13 (S) 1.25
On cover, any single 8.00

Printers' marks on seal 29 (New Hampshire).
Puerto Rico used No. WX262.
Earliest documented use: Nos. WX262-WX264, Oct. 13, 1978.

CS73

1979 **Sheet of 54 (6x9)**

WX265 CS73 Perf. 12½ (F) 1.50
On cover, any single 8.00
WX266 CS73 Perf. 11 (B) 1.25
On cover, any single 8.00
WX267 CS73 Perf. 13 (S) 1.25
On cover, any single 8.00

Printer's marks on seal 22 (Virgin Islands). Puerto Rico used No. WX265.
Earliest documented use: Nos. WX265-WX267, Oct. 9, 1979.

From 1980 on, most Christmas seals exist with a one year earlier date. These are design experiments, which began in 1979, and were used in target markets to help select the following year's Christmas seal. These experiments are not listed.

In 1988, Christmas seals branched out into Easter, or Spring, issues, Hanukkah issues in 1997, and Kwanzaa issues in 2001. These seals are not listed.

Starting in 1983, Spanish-text Christmas seals have been used in Spanish-speaking parts of the United States. These seals are listed.

CS74

1980 **Sheet of 54 (6x9)**

WX268 CS74 Perf. 12½ (F) 1.50
On cover, any single 8.00
WX269 CS74 Perf. 11 (B) 1.50
On cover, any single 8.00
WX270 CS74 Perf. 13 (S) 1.50
On cover, any single 8.00

Earliest documented use: Nos. WX268-WX270, Nov. 13, 1980.

CS75

1981

WX271 CS75 Perf. 12½ (F) .25
On cover 8.00
WX272 CS75 Perf. 11 (B) .25
On cover 8.00
WX273 CS75 Perf. 13 (S) .25
On cover 8.00

Earliest documented use: Nos. WX271-WX273, Oct. 9, 1981.

CS76

1982 **Block of 12 + 2 Gift Tags**

WX274 CS76 Perf. 12½ (F) 1.00
On cover, any single 8.00
a. Spanish text 2.50
WX275 CS76 Perf. 11 (B) 1.50
On cover, any single 8.00
WX276 CS76 Perf. 13 (S) 1.50
On cover, any single 8.00

Earliest documented use: Nos. WX274-WX276, Oct. 5, 1982.

AMERICAN LUNG ASSOCIATION
SEASON'S GREETINGS • 1983

CS77

1983 **Single Seal + Gift Tag**

WX277 CS77 Perf. 12½ (F) .30
On cover, single 8.00
a. Spanish text .50
WX278 CS77 Perf. 11 (B) .35
On cover, single 8.00
WX279 CS77 Perf. 13 (S) .30
On cover, single 8.00

Earliest documented use: Nos. WX277-WX279, Oct. 6, 1983.

CS78

1984 **Block of 12 + 2 Gift Tags**

WX280 CS78 Perf. 11½ (F) 1.00
On cover, any single 8.00
a. Spanish text 1.50
WX281 CS78 Perf. 11 (B) .50
On cover, any single 8.00
WX282 CS78 Perf. 13 (S) .50
On cover, any single 8.00

Earliest documented use: Nos. WX280-WX282, Oct. 24, 1984.

CS79

1985 **Single Seal + Gift Tag**

WX283 CS79 Perf. 11½ (F) 1.00
On cover, single 8.00
a. Spanish text 1.50
WX284 CS79 Perf. 12½, silver foil margins (F) 1.25
On cover, single 8.00
WX285 CS79 Perf. 12½, gold foil margins (F) .50
On cover, single 8.00
WX286 CS79 Perf. 11 (B) .35
On cover, single 8.00
WX287 CS79 Perf. 13 (S) .50
On cover, single 8.00
WX288 CS79 Perf. 12½ (M) .50
On cover, single 8.00

Earliest documented use: Nos. WX283-WX288, Oct. 4, 1985.

CS80

1986 **Block of 4 + 2 Gift Tags**

WX289 CS80 Perf. 12½ (F, M, S) 1.00
On cover, any single 8.00
a. Spanish text 1.50
WX290 CS80 Perf. 12½, silver foil margins (F) 1.25
On cover, any single 8.00
a. From sheet of 42 with no horiz. perfs after rows 1, 4 and 5 (F) 1.25

Earliest documented use: Nos. WX289-WX290, Sept. 18, 1986.

CS81

1987 — Block of 4 + 2 Gift Tags

WX292	CS81	Perf. 11½ (F)	1.00	
		On cover, any single		8.00
	a.	Spanish text	1.50	
WX293	CS81	Perf. 11½, silver foil margins, no horiz. perfs at the folds after rows 1, 4, and 5 (F)	1.50	
		On cover, any single		8.00
WX294	CS81	Perf. 12½ (S)	1.50	
		On cover, any single		8.00
WX295	CS81	Perf. 14½ (C)	5.00	
		On cover, any single		8.00

Earliest documented use: Nos. WX292-WX295, Sept. 21, 1987.

CS82

1988 — Block of 4 + 2 Gift Tags

WX296	CS82	Perf. 11½ (F)	.50	
		On cover, any single		8.00
WX297	CS82	Perf. 11½, silver foil margins, no horiz. perfs at the folds after rows 1, 4, and 5 (F)	1.50	
		On cover, any single		8.00
WX298	CS82	Perf. 12½ (S, C)	1.00	
		On cover, any single		8.00
	a.	Spanish text	1.00	

Earliest documented use: Nos. WX296-WX298, Sept. 29, 1988.

CS83

1989 — Single Seal + Gift Tag

WX299	CS83	Perf. 11½ (F)	.35	
		On cover, single		8.00
	a.	Spanish text	1.00	
WX300	CS83	Perf. 12½, silver foil margins, no horiz. perfs at the folds after rows 1, 4, and 5 (F)	.75	
		On cover, single		8.00
WX301	CS83	Perf. 12½ (S)	.35	
		On cover, single		8.00
WX302	CS83	Self-adhesive, straight die cut over simulated perf. 11½ (printer unknown)	.25	
		On cover, single		8.00

Earliest documented use: Nos. WX299-WX302, Aug. 12, 1989.

CS84

1990 — Single Seal + Gift Tag

WX303	CS84	Perf. 12¼ (F)	.35	
		On cover, single		8.00
	a.	Spanish text, perf. 12½	.75	
WX304	CS84	Perf. 12¼, silver foil margins, no horiz. perfs at the folds after rows 1, 4, and 5 (F)	1.00	
		On cover, single		8.00
WX305	CS84	Perf. 12½ (S)	.75	
		On cover, single		8.00
WX306	CS84	Perf. 10½x10 (C)	.35	
		On cover, single		8.00

Earliest documented use: Nos. WX303-WX306, Oct. 2, 1990.

CS85

1991 — 2 Blocks of 4 + 4 Gift Tags

WX307	CS85	Perf. 10½x11 (F)	1.00	
		On cover, any single		8.00
	a.	Spanish text	2.00	
WX308	CS85	Perf. 12½, silver foil margins (F)	3.50	
		On cover, any single		8.00
WX309	CS85	Perf. 12½, dull silver ink margins (F)	3.50	
		On cover, any single		8.00
WX310	CS85	Perf. 12½ (S)	1.00	
		On cover, any single		8.00
WX311	CS85	Perf. 11 (C)	1.00	
		On cover, any single		8.00

Earliest documented use: Nos. WX307-WX311, Sept. 3, 1991.

CS86

1992 — Single Seal + Gift Tag

WX312	CS86	10½x10 (F)	.35	
		On cover, single		8.00
	a.	Spanish text	.75	
WX313	CS86	Perf. 12½ (S)	.35	
		On cover, single		8.00
WX314	CS86	Perf. 12½, dull silver ink margins (S)	.75	
		On cover, single		8.00
WX315	CS86	Perf. 11 (C)	1.50	
		On cover, single		8.00

Earliest documented use: Nos. WX312-WX315, Aug. 17, 1992.

CS87

1993 — Single Seal + Gift Tag

WX316	CS87	12½ (F)	.25	
		On cover, single		8.00
	a.	Spanish text	.50	
WX317	CS87	Perf. 12½, dull silver ink margins (F)	.75	
		On cover, single		8.00
WX318	CS87	Perf. 12¼ (C)	.25	
		On cover, single		8.00

Earliest documented use: Nos. WX316-WX318, Oct. 9, 1993.

CS88

1994 — Single Seal + Gift Tag

WX319	CS88	12¼, dull silver ink margins (F)	.35	
		On cover, single		8.00
	a.	Spanish text	.35	
WX320	CS88	Self-adhesive, straight die cut, dull silver ink margins, roulette at the folds after rows 2, 5 and 8 (unknown printer)	.50	
		On cover, single		8.00
WX321	CS88	Simulated perf. over roulette, dull silver ink margins (unknown printer)	1.25	
		On cover, single		8.00

Earliest documented use: Nos. WX319-WX321, Oct. 8, 1994.

CS89

1995 **Sheet of 52 + Label**

WX322 CS89 12½, dull silver ink margins (F) 2.25
On cover, any single 8.00

WX323 CS89 12¾x12¼, dull silver ink margins (C) 3.00
On cover, any single 8.00

WX324 CS89 Simulated perf. over roulette, seals 27.75x17.5mm, dull silver ink margins (CW) 3.00
On cover, any single 8.00

WX325 CS89 Simulated perf. over roulette, seals 26x17.5mm, dull silver ink margins (CW) 25.00
On cover, any single 8.00

WX326 CS89 Self-adhesive, straight die cut, dull silver ink margins (unknown printer) 3.00
On cover, any single 8.00
a. Horiz. die cutting omitted (error sheets) 15.00

Earliest documented use: Nos. WX322-WX326, Oct. 3, 1995.

CS90

1996 **Sheet of 53 + Label**

WX327 CS90 Perf. 11½ (F) 1.50
On cover, any single 8.00
a. Spanish text, perf. 12¼ 7.50

WX328 CS90 Perf. 11½, dull silver ink margins (F) 7.50
On cover, any single 8.00

WX329 CS90 Simulated perf. over roulette (CW) 12.50
On cover, any single 8.00

WX330 CS90 Self-adhesive, straight die cut (CW) 7.50
On cover, any single 8.00

Earliest documented use: Nos. WX327-WX330, Oct. 24, 1996.

CS91

1997 **Single Seal + Gift Tag**

WX331 CS91 Perf. 12¼ (F) .35
On cover, single 8.00
a. Spanish text 2.00

WX332 CS91 Simulated perf. over roulette (CW) .35
On cover, single 8.00

WX333 CS91 Self-adhesive, straight die cut with simulated perfs, except roulette in rows 3, 6 and 9 (printer unknown) .35
On cover, single 8.00

WX334 CS91 Self-adhesive, straight die cut (printer unknown) .40
On cover, single 8.00

Earliest documented use: Nos. WX331-WX334, Oct. 30, 1997.

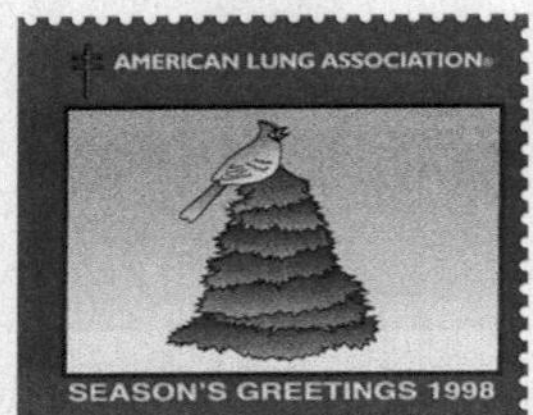

CS92

1998 **Sheet of 36 + 9 Gift Tags**

WX335 CS92 Perf. 12¼ (F) 1.75
On cover, any single 8.00

WX336 CS92 Simulated perf. over roulette (CW) 2.00
On cover, any single 8.00
a. Spanish text 15.00

WX337 CS92 Self-adhesive, serpentine die cut (CW) 1.50
On cover, any single 8.00

WX338 CS92 Self-adhesive, straight die cut, except roulette in rows 3, 6 and 9 (CW) 1.50
On cover, any single 8.00

Earliest documented use: Nos. WX335-WX338, Oct. 26, 1998.

CS93

1999 **Block of 4 + 4 Gift Tags**

WX339 CS93 Self-adhesive, serpentine die cut (F) 1.25
On cover, any single 8.00

WX340 CS93 Simulated perf. over roulette (CW) .75
On cover, any single 8.00
a. Spanish text (CW) 2.25

WX341 CS93 Perf. 9½ (unknown printer) 7.50
On cover, any single 8.00

Earliest documented use: Nos. WX339-WX341, Oct. 26, 1999.

CS94

2000 **Vert. Strip of 4 + 4 Gift Tags**

WX342 CS94 Self-adhesive, serpentine die cut, green tinted gift tags (F) 1.75
On cover, any single 8.00

WX343 CS94 Simulated perf. over roulette (CW) 1.25
On cover, any single 8.00
a. Spanish text (CW) 2.25

WX344 CS94 Self-adhesive, serpentine die cut, gift tags not tinted (CW) .75

Earliest documented use: Nos. WX342-WX344, Oct. 1, 2000.

CS95

2001 **Single Seal + Gift Tag**

WX345 CS95 Self-adhesive, shallow serpentine die cut, high gloss paper, vignette 22x24mm (F) 2.00
On cover, single 8.00

WX346 CS95 Self-adhesive, shallow angular die cut, vignette 22x22mm (WL) 1.00
On cover, single 8.00

WX347 CS95 Re-moist gum, simulated perf. over roulette (V) .35
On cover, single 8.00

WX348 CS95 Self-adhesive, serpentine die cut, satin paper, vignette 22x24mm (V) .30
On cover, single 8.00
a. Spanish text (V) 3.00

Earliest documented use: Nos. WX345-WX348, Oct. 19, 2001.

CS96

2002 **Vert. Strip of 4 + 4 Gift Tags**

WX349 CS96 Self-adhesive, shallow serpentine die cut, vignette 22.5x21mm, with thicker green frame lines (F) 3.50
On cover, any single 8.00

WX350 CS96 Self-adhesive, straight die cut, vignette 22x21mm, with thicker green frame lines (F) 3.50
On cover, any single 8.00

WX351 CS96 Self-adhesive, serpentine die cut, vignette 21.5x21.5mm (Mo) .75
On cover, any single 8.00
a. Spanish text (Mo) —

WX352 CS96 Self-adhesive, serpentine die cut, vignette 22x27mm, silver foil margins (Mo) 1.00
On cover, any single 8.00

WX353 CS96 Self-adhesive, serpentine die cut, vignette 22x26mm, silver foil margins (Mo) 3.00
On cover, any single 8.00

WX354 CS96 Roulette 12½ (Mo) .75
On cover, any single 8.00

Earliest documented use: Nos. WX349-WX354, Nov. 3, 2002.

CS97

2003 **Vert. Strip of 4 + 4 Gift Tags**

WX355 CS97 Roulette 12½ 1.25
On cover, any single 8.00
a. Spanish text 7.50

WX356 CS97 Self-adhesive, serpentine die cut 1.25
On cover, any single 8.00

WX357 CS97 Self-adhesive, serpentine die cut, silver foil margins 2.50
On cover, any single 8.00

Earliest documented use: Nos. WX355-WX357, Oct. 9, 2003.

CS98

2004 **Horiz. Strip of 5**

WX358 CS98 Self-adhesive, serpentine die cut, dark blue margins 1.00

WX359 CS98 Self-adhesive, serpentine die cut, silver foil margins .75
On cover, any single 8.00
a. Spanish text 1.50

WX360 CS98 Self-adhesive, serpentine die cut, silver foil margins, gutter between rows 4 and 5, strip of 5 with gift tag at right 2.50

Earliest documented use: Nos. WX358-WX360, Oct. 9, 2004.

All seals from 2005 through 2013 have silver foil margins.

CS99

2005 **Horiz. Strip of 4 + Gift Tag**

WX361 CS99 Self-adhesive, serpentine die cut 5.00
On cover, any single 8.00
a. Strip of 4 from sheet of 56 or 64, no gift tag .25
b. Spanish text, strip of 4, no gift tag 1.00

Earliest documented use: No. WX361, Oct. 15, 2005.

CS100

2006 **Horiz. Strip of 5 + Gift Tag**

WX362 CS100 Self-adhesive, serpentine die cut 3.00
On cover, any single 8.00
a. Strip of 5 from sheet of 56 or 64, no gift tag .35
b. Spanish text, strip of 5, no gift tag 1.00

Earliest documented use: No. WX362, Sept. 5, 2006.

CS101

2007 **Horiz. Strip of 5 + Gift Tag**

WX363 CS101 Self-adhesive, serpentine die cut, design 17x23.5mm 4.00
On cover, any single 8.00
a. Self-adhesive, serpentine die cut, design 17x24mm, no gift tag .35
On cover, any single 8.00
b. Spanish text, no gift tag 1.00

Earliest documented use: No. WX363, Oct. 2, 2007.

CS102

2008 **Horiz. Strip of 5 + Gift Tag**

WX364 CS102 Self-adhesive, serpentine die cut 4.00
On cover, any single 8.00
a. Strip of 5 from sheet of 56, no gift tag .35

Earliest documented use: No. WX364, Sept. 23, 2008.

CS103

2009 **Horiz. Strip of 4 + 4 Gift Tags**

WX365 CS103 Self-adhesive, serpentine die cut 4.00
On cover, any single 8.00
a. Strip of 4 from sheet of 56, no gift tags .35

Earliest documented use: No. WX365, Aug. 18, 2009.

CS104

2010 **Horiz. Strip of 5 + Gift Tag**

WX366 CS104 Self-adhesive, serpentine die cut 4.00
On cover, any single 8.00
a. Strip of 5 from sheet of 64, no gift tag .50

Earliest documented use: No. WX366, Aug. 18, 2010.

CS105

2011 **Horiz. Strip of 5 + Gift Tag**

WX367 CS105 Self-adhesive, serpentine die cut 4.00
On cover, any single 8.00
a. Strip of 5 from sheet of 56, no gift tag .50

Earliest documented use: No. WX367, Sept. 7, 2011.

CS106

2012 **Horiz. Strip of 7 + Gift Tag**

WX368 CS106 Self-adhesive, serpentine die cut .40
On cover, any single 8.00
a. Strip of 7 from sheet of 56, no gift tag .75

Earliest documented use: No. WX368, Aug. 31, 2012.

CS107

2013 **Horiz. Strip of 7 + Gift Tag**

WX369 CS107 Self-adhesive, serpentine die cut 4.00
On cover, any single 8.00
a. Strip of 7 from sheet of 56, no gift tag .75

Earliest documented use: No. WX369, Sept. 6, 2013.

CS108

2014 **Horiz. Strip of 6**

WX370 CS108 Self-adhesive, serpentine die cut, green margins .75
On cover, any single 8.00

Earliest documented use: No. WX370, Aug. 30, 2014.

CS109

2015 **Horiz. Strip of 7**

WX371 CS109 Self-adhesive, serpentine die cut, silver foil margins, design 20x28mm .75
On cover, any single 8.00
WX372 CS109 Self-adhesive, serpentine die cut, silver foil margins, design 21x20mm 1.25
On cover, any single 8.00

Earliest documented use: Nos. WX371-WX372, Sept. 22, 2015.

CS110

2016 **Horiz. Strip of 7**

WX373 CS110 Self-adhesive, serpentine die cut, white margins, design 21x28mm .40
On cover, any single 8.00
WX374 CS110 Self-adhesive, serpentine die cut, white margins, design 18x25mm 1.25
On cover, any single 8.00

Earliest documented use: Nos. WX373-WX374, Sept. 22, 2016.

CS111

2017 **Horiz. Strip of 7**

WX375 CS111 Self-adhesive, serpentine die cut, white margins, design 21x28mm .40
On cover, any single 8.00
WX376 CS111 Self-adhesive, serpentine die cut, white margins, design 18x25mm 1.25
On cover, any single 8.00

Earliest documented use: Nos. WX375-WX376, Sept. 12, 2017.

CS112

2018 **Horiz. Strip of 7**

WX377 CS112 Self-adhesive, serpentine die cut, red margins, design 21x28mm .75
On cover, any single 8.00

WX378 CS112 Self-adhesive, serpentine die cut, red margins, design 18x25mm 1.25
On cover, any single 8.00

Earliest documented use: Nos. WX377-WX378, Aug. 30, 2018.

SANITARY FAIR

The United States Sanitary Commission was authorized by the Secretary of War on June 9, 1861, and approved by President Lincoln on June 13, 1861. It was a committee of inquiry, advice and aid dealing with the health and general comfort of Union troops, supported by public contributions.

Many Sanitary Fairs were held to raise funds for the Commission, and eight issued stamps. The first took place in 1863 at Chicago, where no stamp was issued. Some Sanitary Fairs advertised on envelopes.

Sanitary Fair stamps occupy a position midway between United States semi-official carrier stamps and the private local posts. Although Sanitary Fair stamps were not valid for U.S. postal service, they were prepared for, sold and used at the fair post offices, usually with the approval and participation of the local postmaster.

The Commission undertook to forward soldiers' unpaid and postage due letters. These letters were handstamped "Forwarded by the U.S. Sanitary Commission."

Details about the Sanitary Fair stamps may be found in the following publications:
American Journal of Philately, Jan. 1889, by J. W. Scott
The Collector's Journal, Aug-Sept. 1909, by C. E. Severn
Scott's Monthly Journal, Jan. 1927 (reprint, Apr. 1973), by Elliott Perry
Stamps, April 24th, 1937, by Harry M. Konwiser
Pat Paragraphs, July, 1939, by Elliott Perry
Covers, Aug. 1952, by George B. Wray
Sanitary Fairs, 1992, by Alvin and Marjorie Kantor
The listings were compiled originally by H. M. Konwiser and Dorsey F. Wheless.

SF1

Albany, New York
Army Relief Bazaar
Setting A: narrow spacing, pane of 12.
Setting B: wider spacing, sheet of 25.

1864, Feb. 22-Mar. 30 **Litho.** ***Imperf.***
Thin White Paper

WV1 SF1 10c **rose** 125.
Used on cover (tied "Albany") 9,500.
Block of 4, setting A 1,200.
Pane of 12, setting A *4,800.*
Block of 4, setting B 500.
Sheet of 25, setting B *3,000.*

WV2 SF1 10c **black** 700.
Block of 5, setting A *4,500.*
Vert. pair, setting B *1,500.*

The No. WV1 tied by Albany cancel on cover is unique. One other cover exists in private hands with the stamp uncanceled and slightly damaged.

Vert. pair is only setting B multiple of No. WV2.

Imitations are typographed in red, blue, black or green on a thin white or ordinary white paper, also on colored papers and are:
(a) Eagle with topknot, printed in sheets of 30 (6x5).
(b) Eagle without shading around it.
(c) Eagle with shading around it, but with a period instead of a circle in "C" of "Cents," and "Ten Cents" is smaller.

SF2

Boston, Mass.
National Sailors' Fair

1864, Nov. 9-22 **Litho.**
Die Cut

WV3 SF2 10c **green** 400.
On 3c envelope #U34 *750.*

Brooklyn, N.Y.
Brooklyn Sanitary Fair
Sheets of 25 (WV4)

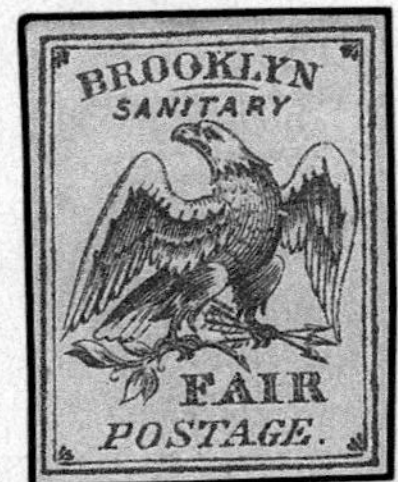

SF3

1864, Feb. 22-Mar. 8 **Litho.** ***Imperf.***

WV4 SF3 (15c) **green** 1,000. *3,600.*
On cover, Fair postmark on envelope *3,000.*
Block of 4 *6,500.*
Block of 6 *10,000.*

WV5 SF3 (25c) **black** *7,000.*
On cover, with 1c local #28L2, Fair postmark on envelope *36,000.*

No. WV4 used is valued canceled by the Fair postmark. Two or more examples also exist with a manuscript cancel. Value with manuscript cancel, $1,100. No. WV5 unused is unique as is the use on cover.

Fakes exist of No. WV4 on pelure paper.

Imitations: *(a)* Typographed and shows "Sanitary" with a heavy cross bar to "T" and second "A" with a long left leg. *(b)* Is a rough typograph print without shading in letters of "Fair."

SF4

SF5

1863, Dec. **Typeset** ***Imperf.***

WV6 SF4 5c **black,** *rosy buff* 800. *200.*
WV7 SF5 10c **green** 1,100.
Tete beche pair *9,000.*

No. WV6 used is believed to be unique. It has a manuscript cancel and is faulty. It is valued thus.

SF6

New York, N.Y.
Metropolitan Fair

1864, Apr. 4-27 **Engr.** ***Imperf.***
Thin White Paper

WV8 SF6 10c **blue** 350.
Sheet of 4 1,750.
WV9 SF6 10c **red** 1,900.
Pair 4,500.
WV10 SF6 10c **black** *28,500.*

Engraved and printed by John E. Gavit of Albany, N.Y. from a steel plate composed of four stamps, 2x2. Can be plated by the positions of scrolls and dots around "Ten Cents."

No. WV10 is unique.

SF7

Philadelphia, Pa.
Great Central Fair

1864, June 7-28 **Engr.** ***Perf. 12***
Printed by Butler & Carpenter, Philadelphia
Sheets of 126 (14x9)

WV11 SF7 10c **blue** 40.00 525.00
On cover tied with Fair postmark *2,250.*
On cover with 3c #65, Fair and Philadelphia postmarks *36,000.*
On cover with two 2c #73, Fair and Philadelphia postmarks *25,000.*
On cover with 3c #65, New York postmark *42,500.*
Block of 4 250.00

WV12 SF7 20c **green** 27.50 500.00
On cover tied with Fair postmark *1,500.*
Block of 4 140.00
Block of 12 475.00
WV13 SF7 30c **black** 35.00 400.00
On cover tied with Fair postmark *8,000.*
Nos. WV11-WV13 on single cover, Fair postmark *10,000.*
On cover with pair of 2c #73, Fair and Philadelphia postmarks *50,000.*
Block of 4 160.00
Block of 6 240.00

Imprint "Engraved by Butler & Carpenter, Philadelphia" on right margin adjoining three stamps.

Used examples of Nos. WV11-WV13 have Fair cancellation.

The No. WV11 covers used with 3c #65 and with 2c #73 are each unique. The New York usage is on a Metropolitan Fair illustrated envelope. The No. WV13 cover with 2c #73 also is unique.

White and amber envelopes were sold by the fair inscribed "Great Central Fair for the Sanitary Commission," showing picture in several colors of wounded soldier, doctors and ambulance marked "U.S. Sanitary Commission." Same design and inscription are known on U.S. envelope No. U46.

A fake June 23, 1864, postmark is known on No. WV11-WV13 stamps and covers.

Imitation of No. WV13 comes typographed in blue or green on thick paper.

SF8

Springfield, Mass.
Soldiers' Fair

1864, Dec. 19-24 **Typo.** ***Imperf.***
WV14 SF8 10c **lilac** 225.00
On unaddressed cover, Fair postmark on envelope 750.00
Horizontal strip of 4 1,000.

Design by Thomas Chubbuck, engraver of the postmaster provisional stamp of Brattleboro, Vt.

One cover exists pencil-addressed to Wm. Ingersoll, Springfield Armory; value slightly more than an unaddressed cover.

A fake postmark is known on No. WV14 covers.

Imitations: (a) Without designer's name in lower right corner, in lilac on laid paper. *(b)* With designer's name, but roughly typographed, in lilac on white wove paper. Originals show 5 buttons on uniform.

SF9

Stamford, Conn.
Soldiers' Fair

1864, July 27-29
WV15 SF9 15c **pale brown** *4,250.* *5,750.*

Originals have tassels at ends of ribbon inscribed "SOLDIERS FAIR." Imitations have leaning "S" in "CENTS" and come in lilac, brown, green, also black on white paper, green on pinkish paper and other colors.

Twelve examples of No. WV15 are recorded.

ESSAY
Great Central Fair, Philadelphia

1864
WV11-E1 Design as issued but value tablets blank, greenish black on glazed paper (unique) —

PROOFS
Metropolitan Fair, New York

1864
WV10P4 10c Plate on card
a. **black** on white card 900.
b. **black** on yellow glazed card —

Great Central Fair, Philadelphia

1864
WV11TC/WV13TC1d 10c and 30c **grnsh blk,** se-tenant, glazed paper, large die —
WV11P4 10c **blue,** plate on card, imperf. 40.00
Block of 4 175.00
WV12TC1a 20c Large die on India paper
e. **vermilion** —
f. **bright blue** —
WV12TC1d 20c Large die on glazed paper
e. **greenish black** —
WV12TC5 20c Plate on wove paper, imperf.
a. **vermilion** 40.00
Block of 4 175.00
b. **orange** 40.00
Block of 4 175.00
c. **brown orange,** opaque wove paper 40.00
Block of 4 175.00
d. **black brown** 40.00
Block of 4 175.00
e. **olive** 40.00
Block of 4 175.00
f. **bright blue** 40.00
Block of 4 175.00
g. **lt. ultramarine** 40.00
Block of 4 175.00
h. **purple** 40.00
Block of 4 175.00
i. **claret** 40.00
Block of 4 175.00
j. **black,** opaque wove paper 40.00
Block of 4 175.00
k. **grey black,** experimental double paper, wove, small x pattern 50.00
Block of 4 225.00
l. **grey black,** experimental double paper, wove, large X pattern 50.00
Block of 4 225.00
m. **grey black,** thin opaque paper 40.00
WV12TC6 20c Plate on wove paper, perf. 12
a. **carmine** 40.00
Block of 4 175.00
b. **vermilion** 40.00
Block of 4 175.00
c. **red brown** 40.00
Block of 4 175.00
d. **bright blue** 40.00
Block of 4 175.00
e. **brown black** 40.00
Block of 4 175.00
f. **black** 40.00
Block of 4 175.00
WV12P4 20c **green,** plate on card, imperf. 40.00
Block of 4 175.00
WV12P5 20c Plate on thick wove paper, imperf.
a. **green** 40.00
Block of 4 175.00
WV12P6 20c Plate on thick wove paper, perf. 12
a. **green** 40.00
Block of 4 175.00
WV13TC1a 30c Large die on India paper
e. **blue** —

Color shades vary widely.

Reprints (1903?) exist of WV11TC-WV13TC, se-tenant vertically, large die on glazed white, pink or yellow card and small die on India paper (mounted se-tenant) in carmine, red carmine, vermilion, orange, brown, yellow brown, olive, yellow green, blue green, gray blue, ultramarine, light violet, violet, claret and gray black.

There also exist large die essay reprints on India paper, green bond paper and glazed cardboard without denomination or with 20c. The 20c value has an added line below the center shield.

WV13P4 30c **black,** plate on card, imperf. 40.00
Block of 4 175.00

ENCASED POSTAGE STAMPS

In early 1862, months after the beginning of the American Civil War, people were conserving resources in anticipation of hard times and shortages ahead. Coins were one of the most hoarded resources, and as a result of this hoarding, coins began to command a premium over paper money. The public was reluctant to spend their coins, fearing the premiums for coins might increase, and a loss might result. Many millions of dollars in gold and silver coins, even copper-nickel cents, disappeared into private hands.

The U.S, Mint began coining copper-nickel cents almost exclusively, but could not meet demand. In response, the public turned to postage stamps to meet small obligations, and shopkeepers were forced to accept stamps as change. Envelopes stating the amount of stamps contained within and cards bearing stamps were sometimes used to keep the stamps from sticking and becoming destroyed, and printers sold advertisements on large numbers of these envelopes. By July 1862, the government had authorized the monetizing of postage stamps and began printing stamp impressions on bank note paper.

On August 12, 1862, John Gault was issued a patent for a "Design for Encasing Government Stamps" to be used as the equivalent of currency. Gault's plans called for a postage stamp to have its corners wrapped around a cardboard circle and show through a thin mica covering. An outer metal frame would hold these items secure, and a heavier brass backing would complete the piece. The brass backing would be suitable for advertising purposes. The resulting piece was about the size of a quarter, but much lighter in weight. The stamps placed in the new encased postage were the 1c, 3c, 5c, 10c, 12c, 24c, 30c and 90c stamps of the 1861 issue. Of course, Gault sold his encased postage at a small markup over the value of the stamp enclosed and the cost of production.

On August 21, 1862, the government issued postage currency in 5c, 10c, 25c and 50c denominations, and fractional currency was issued in 1863. These policies, plus the increased production of brass and copper-nickel coinage in 1863, effectively ended Gault's enterprise. Still, encased postage proved very popular, because it solved the major problems of stamp damage and the necessity of opening stamp envelopes to count the contents. More than 30 companies took advantage of the advertising possibilities and had their ads stamped on the brass backing. Perhaps $50,000 or a little more in encased postage eventually was sold and circulated, not nearly enough by itself to solve the nation's small change crisis. Of the approximately 750,000 pieces sold, only 3,500-7,000 are believed to have survived for collectors.

Values are for very fine examples with mica intact, although signs of circulation and handling are to be expected.

Grading encompasses three areas: 1. Case will show signs of wear or handling and signs of original toning. 2. Mica will be intact with no pieces missing. 3. Stamp will be fresh with no signs of toning or wrinkling.

Examples that came with silvered cases and still have some or all of the original silvering will sell for more than the values shown.

The Eight Stamps of the 1861 Issue Used for Encased Postage

Aerated Bread Co., New York

EP1	1c	*7,000.*
EP1A	5c	*15,000.*

No. EP1A is unique.

Ayer's Cathartic Pills, Lowell, Mass.

Varieties with long and short arrows below legend occur on all denominations.

EP2	1c	550.
EP3	3c	475.
EP4	5c	1,000.
EP5	10c	1,000.
EP6	12c	2,500.
EP7	24c	*3,500.*

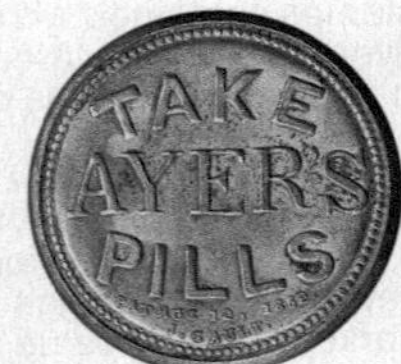

Take Ayer's Pills

EP8	1c	500.
EP9	3c	400.
EP10	5c	1,100.
	a. Ribbed frame	*3,000.*
EP11	10c	1,100.
	a. Ribbed frame	*5,000.*
EP12	12c	2,500.
EP12A	30c	*5,000.*

Nos. EP11a and EP12A each are unique.

Ayer's Sarsaparilla

Three varieties: "AYER'S" small, medium or large.
Example illustrated is the medium variety.

EP13	1c medium "Ayer's"	500.
	a. Small	750.
EP15	3c medium "Ayer's"	400.
	a. Small	650.
	b. Large	450.
	c. Ribbed frame, medium	2,000.
EP16	5c medium "Ayer's"	2,000.
	a. Large	1,500.
EP17	10c medium "Ayer's"	850.
	a. Ribbed frame, medium	2,000.
	b. Small	1,250.
	c. Large	1,400.
EP18	12c medium "Ayer's"	2,250.
	a. Small	2,750.
EP19	24c medium "Ayer's"	1,900.
EP20	30c medium "Ayer's"	*4,500.*

Bailey & Co., Philadelphia

EP21	1c	1,100.
EP22	3c	1,200.
EP23	5c	*2,250.*
EP24	10c	*2,250.*
EP25	12c	*3,000.*

"FANCYGOODS" as one word

"FANCY GOODS" as two words

Joseph L. Bates, Boston

EP26	1c one word	450.
	a. Two words	600.
EP27	3c one word	2,000.
	a. Two words	1,000.
EP28	5c two words	1,250.
	a. One word	1,500.
	b. Ribbed frame, one word	*2,750.*

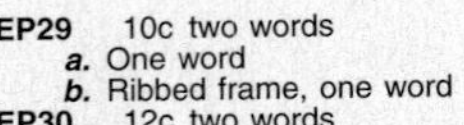

EP29	10c two words	1,750.
	a. One word	1,500.
	b. Ribbed frame, one word	*2,500.*
EP30	12c two words	*3,750.*

Brown's Bronchial Troches

EP31	1c	2,250.
EP32	3c	650.
EP33	5c	450.
EP34	10c	1,000.
EP35	12c	*3,500.*
EP36	24c	*4,000.*
EP37	30c	*4,500.*

F. Buhl & Co., Detroit

EP38	1c	*2,750.*
EP39	3c	*9,000.*
EP40	5c	*2,000.*
EP41	10c	1,750.
EP42	12c	*5,500.*
EP43	24c	*5,500.*

No. EP39 is unique.

Burnett's Cocoaine Kalliston

EP44	1c	750.
EP45	3c	750.
EP46	5c	650.
EP47	10c	700.
EP48	12c	*3,750.*
EP49	24c	*5,000.*
EP50	30c	*4,000.*
EP51	90c	*7,500.*

Burnett's Cooking Extracts

EP52	1c	450.
EP53	3c	500.
EP54	5c	750.
EP55	10c	750.
a.	Ribbed frame	*4,000.*
EP56	12c	*2,000.*
EP57	24c	*5,500.*
EP58	30c	*5,500.*
EP58A	90c	*6,000.*

No. EP58A is unique.

A. M. Claflin, Hopkinton, Mass.

EP59	1c	*11,000.*
EP60	3c	—
EP61	5c	*15,000.*
EP62	10c	*7,500.*
EP63	12c	*16,000.*

No. EP60 is unique.

H. A. Cook, Evansville, Ind.

EP64	5c	*4,000.*
EP65	10c	*3,000.*

Dougan, Hatter, New York

EP66	1c	*2,500.*
EP67	3c	*2,500.*
EP68	5c	*3,750.*
EP69	10c	*3,750.*

Drake's Plantation Bitters

EP70	1c	500.
EP71	3c	500.
EP72	5c	600.
a.	Ribbed frame	*2,500.*
EP73	10c	650.
a.	Ribbed frame	*2,500.*

EP74	12c	*2,000.*
EP75	24c	*3,500.*
EP76	30c	*5,000.*
EP77	90c	*9,500.*

Ellis, McAlpin & Co., Cincinnati

EP78	1c	—
EP79	3c	*2,250.*
EP80	5c	1,250.
EP81	10c	1,100.
EP82	12c	*3,500.*
EP83	24c	*2,750.*

Specialists have questioned the existence of No. EP78. The editors would like to see authenticated evidence of this listing.

G. G. Evans, Philadelphia

EP84	1c	1,750.
EP85	3c	1,750.
EP86	5c	—
EP87	10c	*9,250.*

No. EP87 is believed to be unique.

Gage Bros. & Drake, Tremont House, Chicago

EP88	1c	1,200.
EP89	3c	600.
EP90	5c	750.
EP91	10c	1,100.
a.	Ribbed frame	*4,000.*
EP92	12c	*3,000.*

Only one example of No. EP91a is available to collectors.

J. Gault

EP93	1c	750.
a.	Ribbed frame	*6,500.*
EP95	3c	750.
a.	Ribbed frame	1,400.
EP96	5c	375.
a.	Ribbed frame	575.
EP97	10c	800.
a.	Ribbed frame	750.
EP98	12c	900.
a.	Ribbed frame	*2,500.*
EP99	24c	2,250.
a.	Ribbed frame	*2,750.*
EP100	30c	*2,750.*
a.	Ribbed frame	*4,250.*
EP101	90c	*10,000.*

L. C. Hopkins & Co., Cincinnati

EP102	1c	*2,500.*
EP103	3c	*5,500.*
EP104	5c	*7,500.*
EP105	10c	*6,000.*

Hunt & Nash, Irving House, New York

EP106	1c	*2,000.*
EP107	3c	*2,000.*
a.	Ribbed frame	*3,000.*
EP108	5c	850.
a.	Ribbed frame	900.
EP109	10c	1,300.
a.	Ribbed frame	1,000.
EP110	12c	2,000.
a.	Ribbed frame	*3,000.*
EP111	24c	*3,750.*
a.	Ribbed frame	*4,500.*
EP112	30c	*6,000.*

No. EP112 is unique.

Kirkpatrick & Gault, New York

EP113	1c	500.
EP114	3c	700.
EP115	5c	500.
EP116	10c	600.
EP117	12c	1,400.
EP118	24c	*1,600.*
EP119	30c	*3,750.*
EP120	90c	*10,000.*

Lord & Taylor, New York

EP121	1c	1,250.
EP122	3c	1,500.
EP123	5c	1,100.
EP124	10c	1,250.
EP125	12c	*2,500.*
EP126	24c	*2,750.*
EP127	30c	*3,750.*
EP128	90c	*10,000.*

Mendum's Family Wine Emporium, New York

EP129	1c	1,000.
EP130	3c	1,200.
EP131	5c	1,500.
EP132	10c	*2,750.*
	a. Ribbed frame	*3,000.*
EP133	12c	*3,500.*

B. F. Miles, Peoria

EP134	1c	*25,000.*
EP135	5c	*15,000.*

John W. Norris, Chicago

EP136	1c	*3,000.*
EP137	3c	*3,750.*
EP138	5c	*3,250.*
EP139	10c	*3,000.*

"INSURANCE" Curved

"INSURANCE" Straight

North America Life Insurance Co., N. Y.

EP140	1c Curved	550.
	a. Straight	525.
EP141	3c Straight	800.
	a. Curved	1,750.
EP142	5c Straight	675.
	a. Straight, ribbed frame	1,100.
	b. Curved	*3,000.*
EP143	10c Straight	900.
	a. Straight, ribbed frame	*3,250.*
	b. Curved	1,750.
	c. Curved, ribbed frame	*2,250.*
EP144	12c Straight	*3,000.*
	a. Curved	*4,000.*

No. EP142b is unique. Nos. EP143a and EP144a each may be unique.

Pearce, Tolle & Holton, Cincinnati

EP145	1c	*7,000.*
EP146	3c	*3,000.*
EP147	5c	*3,000.*
EP148	10c	*12,000.*
EP149	12c	*7,000.*
EP150	24c	—

No. EP149 is unique.

The existence of No. EP150 has been questioned by specialists. The editors would like to see authenticated evidence of its existence.

Sands' Ale

EP151	5c	*3,750.*
EP152	10c	*4,500.*
EP153	12c	—
EP154	30c	—

No. EP154 is unique. The case of the known example has been opened. It is possible that the 30c stamp has been substituted for the original stamp and/or the mica has been replaced.

Schapker & Bussing, Evansville, Ind.

EP155	1c	2,500.
EP156	3c	1,250.
EP157	5c	1,600.
EP158	10c	800.
EP159	12c	*5,500.*

John Shillito & Co., Cincinnati

EP160	1c	3,000.
EP161	3c	900.
EP162	5c	600.
EP163	10c	1,000.
EP164	12c	*5,500.*

S. Steinfeld, New York

EP165	1c	*3,250.*
EP166	5c	*7,000.*
EP167	10c	*9,500.*
EP168	12c	*6,000.*

No. EP167 may be unique.

N. G. Taylor & Co., Philadelphia

EP169	1c	*3,250.*
EP170	3c	*3,500.*
EP171	5c	*3,750.*
EP172	10c	*3,750.*
EP173	12c	*4,500.*

No. EP173 is unique.

Weir and Larminie, Montreal

EP174	1c	*4,000.*
EP175	3c	*14,000.*
EP176	5c	—
EP177	10c	*2,500.*

No. EP176 may be unique.

White, the Hatter, New York

EP178	1c	*3,000.*
EP179	3c	*2,750.*
EP180	5c	*5,000.*
EP181	10c	*5,000.*

POSTAGE CURRENCY

Small coins disappeared from circulation in 1861-62 as cash was hoarded. To ease business transactions, merchants issued notes of credit, promises to pay, tokens, store cards, etc. U.S. Treasurer Francis E. Spinner made a substitute for small currency by affixing postage stamps, singly and in multiples, to Treasury paper. He arranged with the Post office to replace worn stamps with new when necessary.

The next step was to print the stamps on Treasury paper. On July 17, 1862, Congress authorized the issue of such "Postage Currency." It remained in use until May 27, 1863. It was not money, but a means of making stamps negotiable.

On Oct. 10, 1863 a second issue was released. These, and the later three issues, did not show stamps and are called Fractional Currency. In 1876 Congress authorized the minting of silver coins to redeem the outstanding fractional currency.

Values quoted are for notes in crisp, new condition, not creased or worn.
Creased or worn notes sell for 25 percent to 75 percent less.
Items valued with a dash are believed to be unique.

Front Engraved and Printed by the National Bank Note Co.
Back Engraved and Printed in Black by the American Bank Note Co.
"A B Co." on Back

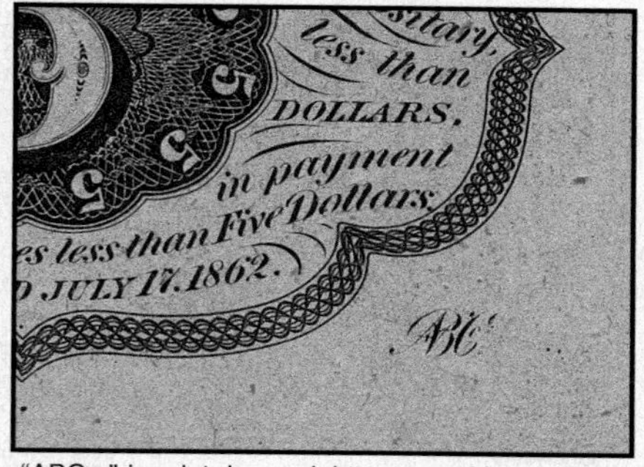

"ABCo." imprint, lower right corner of back (#1-8)

1862, Aug. 21

Perforated Edges-Perf. 12

PC1	5c Bust of Jefferson on 5c stamp, brown	190.00
	a. Inverted back	*950.00*
PC2	10c Bust of Washington on 10c stamp, green	160.00
PC3	25c Five 5c stamps, brown	240.00
PC4	50c Five 10c stamps, green	325.00
	a. Inverted back	*950.00*

Imperforate Edges

PC5	5c Bust of Jefferson on 5c stamp	85.00
	a. Inverted back	*525.00*
PC6	10c Bust of Washington on 10c stamp	85.00
	a. Inverted back	*675.00*
PC7	25c Five 5c stamps	150.00
	a. Inverted back	*600.00*
PC8	50c Five 10c stamps	175.00
	a. Inverted back	*750.00*

No. PC8 exists perforated 14, privately produced.

Front and Back Engraved and Printed by the National Bank Note Co.

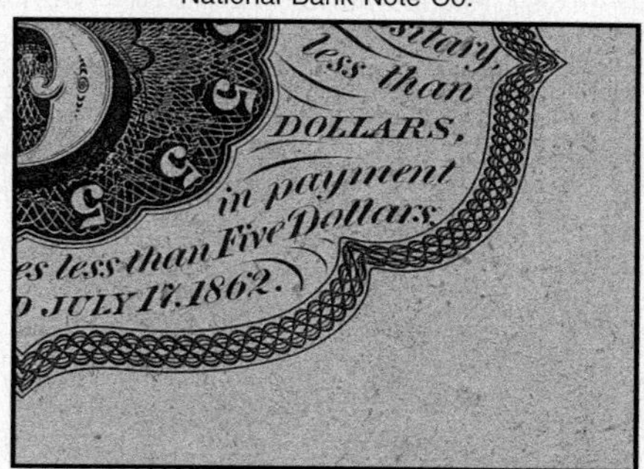

Without "A B Co." on Back

Perforated Edges-Perf. 12

PC9	5c Bust of Jefferson on 5c stamp	230.00
	a. Inverted back	—
PC10	10c Bust of Washington on 10c stamp	250.00
	a. Inverted back	—
PC11	25c Five 5c stamps	340.00
	a. Inverted back	*1,100.*
PC12	50c Five 10c stamps	450.00
	a. Inverted back	—

Imperforate Edges

PC13	5c Bust of Jefferson on 5c stamp	210.00
	a. Inverted back	—
PC14	10c Bust of Washington on 10c stamp	320.00
	a. Inverted back	*1,100.*
PC15	25c Five 5c stamps	425.00
PC16	50c Five 10c stamps	750.00
	a. Inverted back	—

CONFEDERATE STATES OF AMERICA

UNITED STATES STAMPS AND STAMPED ENVELOPES
USED IN THE INDEPENDENT STATES AND IN THE CONFEDERATE STATES

With the secession of South Carolina from the Union on December 20, 1860, a new era began in U.S. history as well as its postal history. Other Southern states quickly followed South Carolina's lead, which in turn led to the formation of the provisional government of the Confederate States of America on February 4, 1861.

President Jefferson Davis' cabinet was completed March 6, 1861, with the acceptance of the position of Postmaster General by John H. Reagan of Texas. The provisional government had already passed regulations that required payment for postage in cash or by the use of the then-current United States stamps and stamped envelopes and that effectively carried over the U.S. 3¢ rate until the new Confederate Post Office Department took over control of the system.

Soon after entering on his duties, Reagan directed the postmasters in the Confederate States and in the newly seceded states to "continue the performance of their duties as such, and render all accounts and pay all moneys (sic) to the order of the Government of the U.S. as they have heretofore done, until the Government of the Confederate States shall be prepared to assume control of its postal affairs."

On May 13, 1861, Postmaster General Reagan issued his proclamation "assuming control and direction of postal service within the limits of the Confederate States of America on and after the first day of June," with new postage rates and regulations. The Federal government suspended operations in the Confederates States (except for western Virginia and the seceding state of Tennessee) by a proclamation issued by Postmaster General Montgomery Blair on May 27, 1861, and June 10 for western and middle Tennessee.

Until the assumption of control by the Confederate Post Office on June 1, 1861, therefore, Southern postmasters continued to use the stamps, stamped envelopes and postal rates of the United States. Stamps soon became scarce in many locations, as the U.S. Post Office was reluctant to re-supply seceded states with additional supplies.

The listings are by Scott number and denomination and, where appropriate, stamps and covers from individual states are indicated. Off-cover stamps are valued in the grade of fine, with the identifying town and date clearly legible. Covers also are valued in the grade of fine, with town and date of use clearly indicated.

TABLE OF SECESSION

	Ordinance of Secession	Admitted to Confederacy	Period for Use of U.S. Stamps: As Independent State	Period for Use of U.S. Stamps: Total to 5/31/1861*
SC	12/20/1860	2/4/1861	46 days	163 days
MS	1/9/1861	2/4/1861	26 days	143 days
FL	1/11/1861	2/4/1861	24 days	142 days
AL	1/11/1861	2/4/1861	24 days	141 days
GA	1/19/1861	2/4/1861	16 days	133 days
LA	1/26/1861	2/4/1861	9 days	126 days
MO	10/31/1861	11/28/1861	—	—
TX	3/2/1861	3/5/1861	3 days	90 days
VA	4/17/1861	5/7/1861	20 days	45 days
AR	5/6/1861	5/18/1861	12 days	26 days
TN	6/8/1861	7/2/1861	24 days	—
NC	5/20/1861	5/27/1861	7 days	12 days

* The use of United States stamps in the seceded States was prohibited after May 31, 1861.

TX — Ordinance of Secession adopted Feb. 1. Popular vote to secede Feb. 23, effective Mar. 2, 1861. Collectors call Texas covers used between Feb. 1 and March 1 inclusive "Transitional Texas Use" covers, and all CSA collectors treat these covers as an integral part of CSA postal history.

Settlers in south Arizona Territory south of the 34th parallel voted to secede 3/16/61 and were accepted into the CSA on Feb. 14, 1862. This was largely symbolic and Confederate forces abanodoned the area in mid-1862.

VA — Ordinance of adopted. Admitted to Confederacy May 7. Scheduled election of May 23 ratified the Ordinance of Secession.

TN — Ordinance passed to "submit to vote of the people a Declaration of Independence, and for other purposes." Adopted May 6. Election took place June 8. General Assembly ratified election June 24.

MO - The Missouri secession vote and admission into the CSA was symbolic, because the Confederacy did not control any part of the state.

KY - Southern sympathizers from a rival government seceded on Nov. 20, 1861. This faction was granted admission to the CSA on Dec. 10, 1861.

Values in the left column are for U.S. stamps and covers bearing U.S. stamps mailed during the dates of Independent Statehood, and values in the right column are for U.S. stamps and covers bearing U.S. stamps mailed during the time after the states were formally admitted to the Confederate States of America.

18	1c Type I, Plate 12	1,000.	1,500.
	On cover	1,500.	1,500.
20	1c Type II, Plate 12	500.	500.
	On cover	1,000.	1,000.
	1c Type II, Plate 11	1,000.	1,000.
	On cover	1,500.	1,500.
21	1c Type III, Plate 12	*5,000.*	*5,000.*
	On cover	7,500.	7,500.
22	1c Type IIIa, Plate 11 or 12	750.	750.
	On cover	1,250.	1,250.
24	1c Type V	150.	150.
	On cover		
	South Carolina	750.	500.
	Mississippi	750.	500.
	Florida	1,250.	750.
	Alabama	750.	500.
	Georgia	750.	500.
	Louisiana	750.	500.
	Texas	1,000.	750.
	Virginia	750.	500.
	Arkansas	—	**
	Tennessee	***	***
	North Carolina	**	**

Uses of U.S. Nos. U19//U24 instead of Nos. 18-24 also are known. Values start at $250 more than the values shown for No. 24 for both Independent State use and for Confederate States of America use.

26	3c Type III	50.	50.
	On cover		
	South Carolina	300.	150.
	Mississippi	325.	175.
	Florida	500.	350.
	Alabama	300.	175.
	Georgia	300.	175.
	Louisiana	300.	175.
	Texas	500.	350.
	Virginia	300.	200.
	Arkansas	*1,250.*	*1,000.*
	Tennessee	***	***
	North Carolina	1,000.	750.

Uses of U.S. Nos. U1//U10 and U26-U27 instead of No. 26 also are known. Values start at the same as the values shown for No. 26 for both Independent State use and for Confederate States of America use. While no examples of No. 26 are known used from either independent or CSA Arkansas, the 3¢ star die envelopes (Nos. U26-U27) are known used during Arkansas' CSA period. Value, $1,250.

29	5c Type I	750.	750.
	On cover	1,250.	1,250.
30A	5c Type II	500.	500.
	On cover	1,000.	1,000.
35	10c Type V	200.	200.
	On cover	1,000.	1,000.
36B	12c Type II, Plate 3	500.	500.
	On cover	1,000.	1,000.
37	24c	1,000.	1,000.
	On cover	*5,000.*	*5,000.*
38	30c	1,000.	1,000.
	On cover	*6,500.*	*5,000.*

** = none known

*** = Tennessee did not formally secede until June 8, 1861, after the C.S.A. Post Office had assumed control over the postal system.

The following Scott numbers were replaced by new varieties in 1857-59. They might exist used in an Independent State or in the C.S.A., but to date none has been found: Nos. 19, 23, 25, 25A, 26A, 27, 28, 28A, 30, 31, 32, 33, 34, 36.

Scott 39, the 90¢ blue of 1860, could have been used from New Orleans, but no such use has been found.

CONFEDERATE STATES OF AMERICA

3¢ 1861 POSTMASTERS' PROVISIONALS

As coinage and United States stamps became scarce in the newly seceded states, postal patrons began having problems buying stamps or paying for letters individually. Even though the U.S. Post Office Department was technically in control of the postal system and southern postmasters were operating under Federal authority, the U.S.P.O. began to cut off supplies to the seceded states.

The U.S. government had made the issuance of postmasters' provisionals illegal many years before, but the southern postmasters had to do what they felt was necessary to allow patrons to pay for postage and make the system work. Therefore, a few postmasters took it upon themselves to issue provisional stamps in the 3¢ rate then in effect. Interestingly, these were stamps and envelopes that the U.S. government did not recognize as legal, but they did do postal duty unchallenged in the Confederate States. Yet the proceeds were to be remitted to the U.S. government in Washington! Six authenticated postmasters' provisionals in the 3¢ rate have been recorded.

Because Tennessee did not join the Confederacy until July 2, 1861, the unissued 3¢ Nashville provisional was produced in a state that was in the process of seceding, while the other provisionals were used in the Confederacy before the assumption of control of the postal service by the Confederate States of America on June 1, 1861.

DARLINGTON C.H., S. C.

E1

Handstamped Envelope

8AXU1 E1 3c black *3,500.*

One example of No. 8AXU1 is recorded, used under a pair of C.S.A. No. 7. To be a provisional, the 3¢ marking must be unused or used under Confederate stamps.

FORT VALLEY, GA.

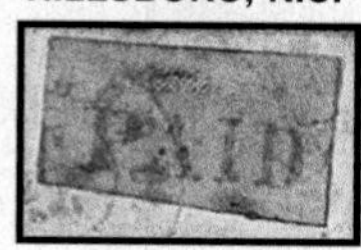

E1

Control

Handstamped Envelope

7AXU1 E1 3c **black** —

HILLSBORO, N.C.

A1

Handstamped Adhesive

1AX1 A1 3c **bluish black,** on cover —

No. 1AX1 is unique. This is the same handstamp as used for No. 39X1. 3c usage is determined from the May 27, 1861 circular date stamp.

Cancellation: black town.

JACKSON, MISS.

E1

Handstamped Envelope

2AXU1 E1 3c **black** *3,500.*

See Nos. 43XU1-43XU4.

MADISON COURT HOUSE, FLA.

A1 "CNETS"

Typeset Adhesive

3AX1 A1 3c **gold** — *20,000.*
On cover *120,000.*
a. "CNETS" *22,500.*

No. 3AX1 on cover and No. 3AX1a are each unique.

Cancellations: black town, oblong paid, ms "Paid in Money," manuscript.

See No. 137XU1.

CONFEDERATE STATES

★ I BUY IT ★ I SELL IT ★

• Help building your collection • Full retail stock online
• Marketing the accumulation of a lifetime or a family inheritance

50 years of philatelic experience specializing in Confederate States.
Researcher, writer and Editor-in-Chief of the 2012 CSA Catalog.

PATRICIA A. KAUFMANN
10194 N. Old State Road, Lincoln, DE 19960
Phone: 302-422-2656 • Fax: 302-424-1990
E-mail: trishkauf@comcast.net

50 YEARS

trishkaufmann.com

Life Member: CSA, APS, APRL, USPCS • Member: ASDA, CCNY, FRPSL

NASHVILLE, TENN.

A1

Typeset Adhesive (5 varieties)

4AX1 A1 3c **carmine** 400.
Horizontal strip of 5 showing all varieties 2,250.

No. 4AX1 was prepared by Postmaster McNish with the U.S. rate, but the stamp was never issued.

Fakes exist of the horizontal strips. Expertization is recommended.

See Nos. 61X2-61XU2.

SELMA, ALA.

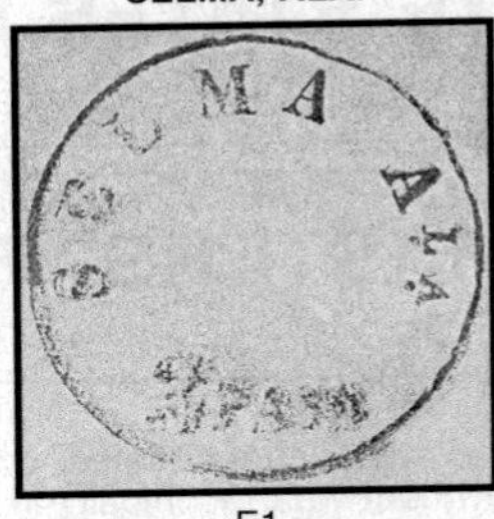

E1

Handstamped Envelope

5AXU1 E1 3c **black** *1,950.*

See Nos. 77XU1-77XU3.

TUSCUMBIA, ALA.

E1

Handstamped Envelope, impression at upper right

6AXU1 E1 3c **dull red,** *buff* *17,500.*

No. 6AXU1 also exists with a 3c 1857 stamp affixed at upper right over the provisional handstamp, tied by black circular "TUSCUMBIA, ALA." town postmark. Value $12,500.

Dangerous forgeries exist of No. 6AXU1.

See Nos. 84XU1-84XU3.

For later additions, listed out of numerical sequence, see:
#*7AXU1*, Fort Valley, Ga.
#*8AXU1*, Darlington, C.H., S.C.

CONFEDERATE POSTMASTERS' PROVISIONALS

These stamps and envelopes were issued by individual postmasters generally during the interim between June 1, 1861, when the use of United States stamps stopped in the Confederacy, and October 16, 1861, when the first Confederate Government stamps were issued. They were occasionally issued at later periods, especially in Texas, when regular issues of government stamps were unavailable.

Canceling stamps of the post offices were often used to produce envelopes, some of which were supplied in advance by private citizens. These envelopes and other stationery therefore may be found in a wide variety of papers, colors, sizes and shapes, including patriotic and semi-official types. It is often difficult to determine whether the impression made by the canceling stamp indicates provisional usage or merely postage paid at the time the letter was deposited in the post office. Occasionally the same mark was used for both purposes.

The press-printed **provisional envelopes are in a different category. They were produced in quantity, using envelopes procured in advance by the postmaster, such as those of Charleston, Lynchburg, Memphis, etc.** *The* **press-printed** *envelopes are listed and valued on all known papers.*

The **handstamped** *provisional envelopes are listed and valued according to type and variety of handstamp, but not according to paper. Many exist on such a variety of papers that they defy accurate, complete listing. The value of a handstamped provisional envelope is determined primarily by the clarity of the markings and its overall condition and attractiveness, rather than the type of paper.*

All handstamped provisional envelopes, when used, should also show the postmark of the town of issue.

Most handstamps are impressed at top right, although they exist from some towns in other positions.

Many illustrations in this section are reduced in size.

Values for envelopes are for entires. Values for stamps of provisional issues are for examples with little or no gum; original gum over a large portion of the stamp will increase the value substantially.

ABERDEEN, MISS.

E1

Handstamped Envelopes

1XU1 E1 5c **black** *7,000.*
a. 10c (ms.) on 5c **black** *9,000.*

No. 1XU1a is unique.

ABINGDON, VA.

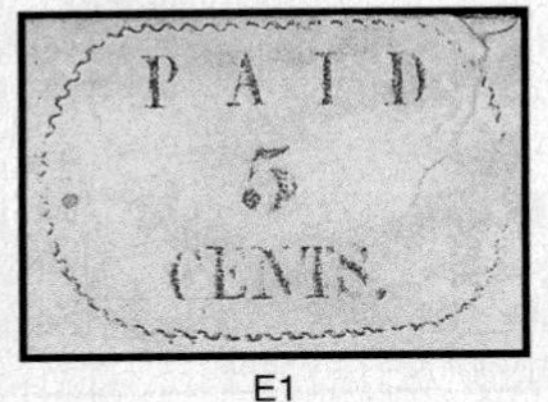

E1

Handstamped Envelopes

2XU1 E1 2c **black** *12,500.*
a. 5c (ms.) on 2c **black** *15,000.*
2XU2 E1 5c **black** 1,750.
On patriotic cover 3,000.
2XU3 E1 10c **black** 2,200. 3,500.

No. 2XU1 is unique. The unused No. 2XU3 is a unique mint example, and the value represents the price realized in a 1997 auction sale. No. 2XU3 used also is unique.

ALBANY, GA.

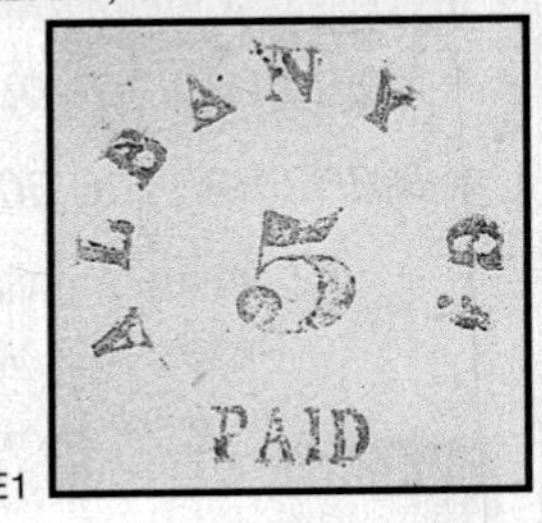

E1

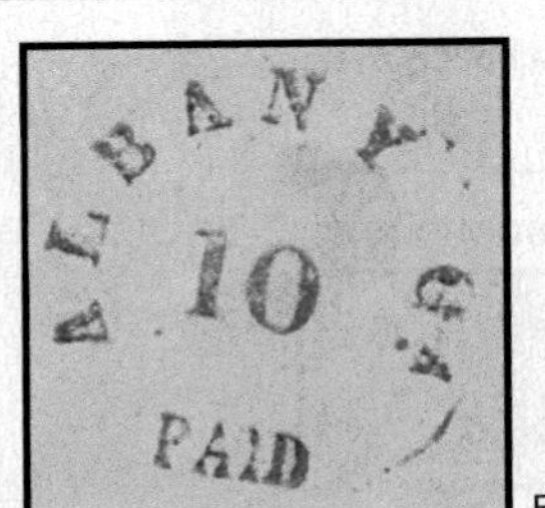

E2

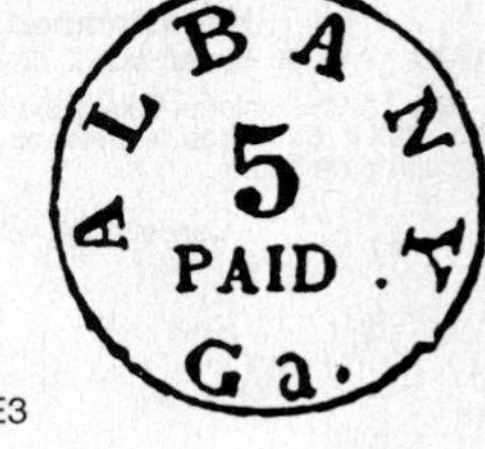

E3

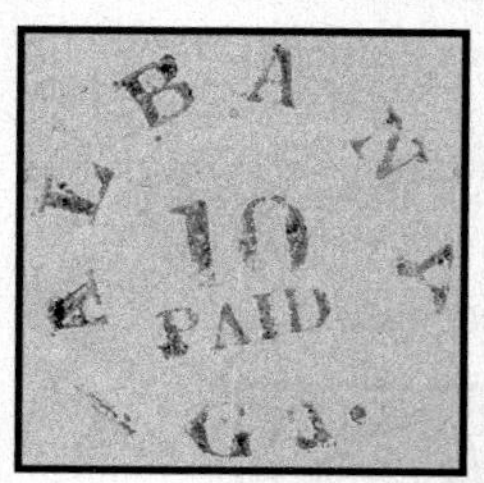

E4

Handstamped Envelopes

3XU1 E1 5c **greenish blue** 1,000.
On patriotic cover —
3XU2 E2 10c **greenish blue** *1,750.*
a. 10c on 5c **greenish blue** *3,500.*
3XU5 E3 5c **greenish blue** —
3XU6 E4 10c **greenish blue** *3,500.*

Only one example each recorded of Nos. 3XU2, 3XU2a and 3XU6. No. 3XU2 is a cover front only and is valued as such. No. 3XU2a is the unique Confederate example of one provisional marking revaluing another.

The existence of No. 3XU5 is in question. The editors would like to see an authenticated example of this marking.

ANDERSON COURT HOUSE, S.C.

E1

E2

E3

Handstamped Envelopes

4XU1 E1 5c **black** 1,000. *2,750.*
4XU2 E2 10c (ms.) **black** *2,750.*
4XU3 E3 (2c) **black,** denomination omitted (circular rate) *2,250.*

ATHENS, GA

A1 (Type I)

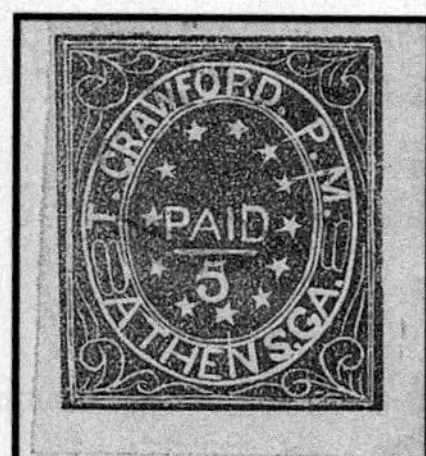

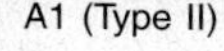
A1 (Type II)

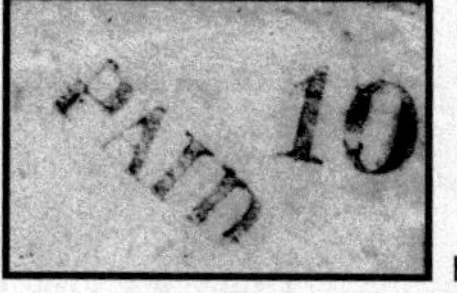

E1

Typographed Adhesives (from woodcuts of two types)

Pairs, both horizontal and vertical, always show one of each type.

5X1 A1 5c **purple** (shades) 1,000. 1,400.
Pair — 3,500.
On cover 2,250.
Pair on cover 7,000.
Strip of 4 on cover (horiz.) *10,000.*
a. Tete beche pair (vertical) *7,500.*
Tete beche pair on cover *20,000.*
5X2 A1 5c **red** 5,750. 5,750.
On cover *17,500.*
Pair on cover —

Cancellations in black: grid, town, "PAID."

The colorless ornaments in the four corners of No. 5X2 were recut making them wider than those in No. 5X1.

Dangerous fakes exist of Nos. 5X1 and 5X2. Certificates of authenticity from recognized committees are strongly recommended.

The existence of a pair on cover of No. 5X2 is in question. The editors would like to see an example of this usage.

Handstamped Envelopes

5XU1 E1 10c **black,** on patriotic cover *2,500.*

The markings on No. 5XU1 are the same as those used on stampless envelopes. On the unique listed example of No. 5XU1, there is a handwritten note on the inside of the flap: 'Andrew had these envelopes stamped & I am obliged to use them or loose the postage.' Two or more similar covers from the same correspondence are known, but without the note under the flap. While these also may be provisional use, it cannot be proven, and these covers are considered handstamp paid covers.

ATLANTA, GA.

E1

E2

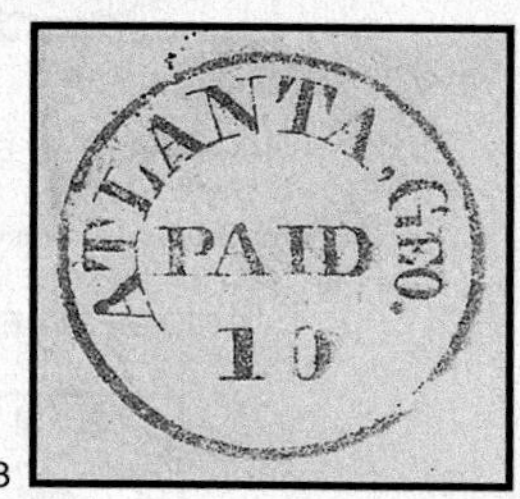

E3

Handstamped Envelopes

6XU1 E1 5c **red** *5,000.*
6XU2 E1 5c **black** 160. 1,000.
On patriotic cover *3,500.*
a. 10c on 5c **black** *2,500.*
On patriotic cover —
6XU3 E2 PAID, black *1,000.*

No. 6UX3 was probably used for drop letters and circulars.

6XU4 E3 2c **black** *3,000.*
6XU5 E3 5c **black** 1,500.
On patriotic cover 3,500.
a. 10c on 5c **black** *2,500.*
6XU6 E3 10c **black** 550.
On patriotic cover —

Only one example recorded of No. 6XU1.

E3

Handstamped Envelopes

6XU8 E3 5c **black** 3,500.
6XU9 E3 10c **black** ("10" upright) 3,250.

Only one example recorded of No. 6XU8.

AUSTIN, MISS.

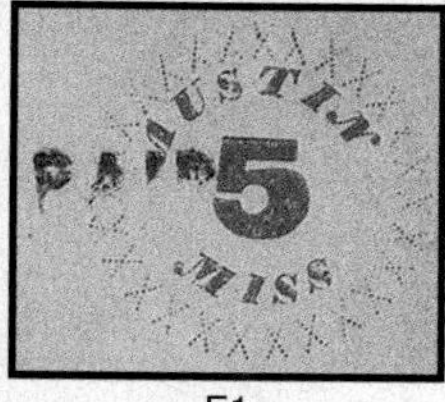

E1

Press-printed Envelope (typeset)

8XU1 E1 5c **red,** *amber* *75,000.*

One example recorded.

Cancellation: black "Paid."

AUSTIN, TEX.

E1a

Handstamped Adhesive

9X1 E1a 10c **black,** *white* or *buff* —
On cover, uncanceled *18,000.*
On cover, tied —

Only one example of No. 9X1 tied on cover is recorded.

Handstamped Envelope

9XU1 E1a 10c **black** 2,500.

Cancellation on Nos. 9X1 and 9XU1: black town.

AUTAUGAVILLE, ALA.

E1

E2

Handstamped Envelopes

10XU1 E1 5c **black** *20,000.*
10XU2 E2 5c **black** *20,000.*

No. 10XU2 is unique.

BALCONY FALLS, VA.

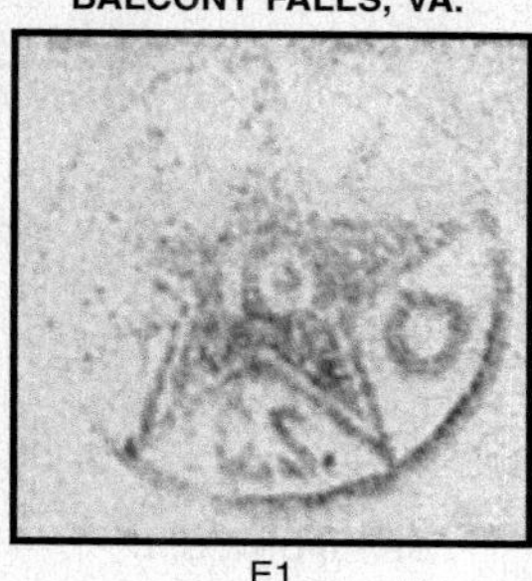
E1

Handstamped Envelope

122XU1 E1 10c **blue** *2,000.*

The use of No. 122XU1 as a provisional marking is in question. The editors would like to see authenticated evidence of its use as a provisional.

BARNWELL COURT HOUSE, S. C.

E1

Handstamped Envelope

123XU1 E1 5c **black** *3,000.*

These are two separate handstamps.

All recorded uses are on addressed covers without postmarks.

BATON ROUGE, LA.

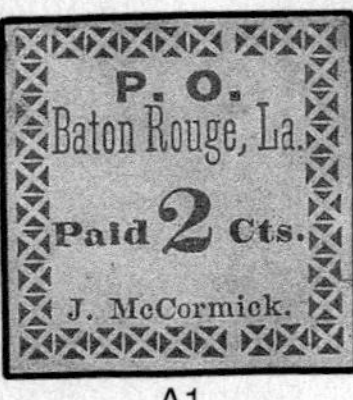

A1

A2

Typeset Adhesives

Ten varieties of each

11X1 A1 2c **green**	*8,250.*	*5,000.*
On cover		*50,000.*
a. "McCcrmick"	*35,000.*	*35,000.*
On cover		*55,000.*
11X2 A2 5c **green & carmine** (Maltese cross border)	1,500.	1,400.
On cover		5,000.
Strip of 3		*7,000.*
Strip of 5		*24,000.*
Canceled in New Orleans, on cover		*15,000.*
a. "McCcrmick"	*10,000.*	*3,500.*
On cover		*15,000.*

Only one example each is recorded of No. 11X1a unused, used and on cover.

The "Canceled in New Orleans" examples entered the mails in New Orleans after having been placed (uncanceled) on riverboats in Baton Rouge. Two such covers are recorded.

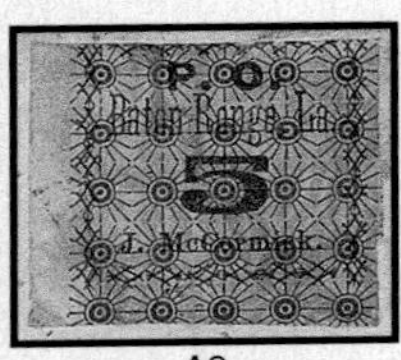

A3

A4

Ten varieties of each

11X3 A3 5c **green & carmine** (crisscross border)	*10,000.*	*4,000.*
On cover		*10,000.*
a. "McCcrmick"		*32,500.*
11X4 A4 10c **blue**		*50,000.*
On cover		*75,000.*

Nos. 11X3a and 11X4 on cover are unique.

Cancellation on Nos. 11X1-11X4: black town.

BEAUFORT, S. C.

E1

Handstamped Envelope

150XU1 E1 5c **black** — *3,500.*

To be the No. 150XU1 provisional, the cover must be unused, used under a Confederate stamp, or used from another town. Two examples are recorded.

BEAUMONT, TEX.

A1

A2

Typeset Adhesives

Several varieties of each

12X1 A1 10c **black,** *yellow*		—
On cover		*55,000.*
12X2 A1 10c **black,** *pink*		*20,000.*

No. 12X1 is smaller than No. 12X2.

On cover		*27,500.*
12X3 A2 10c **black,** *yellow,* on cover		*90,000.*

One example recorded of No. 12X3.

Cancellations: black pen; black town.

BLUFFTON, S. C.

E1

Handstamped Envelope

124XU1 E1 5c **black** *4,750.*

Only one example recorded of No. 124XU1.

BRIDGEVILLE, ALA.

A1

Handstamped Adhesive in black within red pen-ruled squares

13X1 A1 5c **black & red,** pair on cover *20,000.*

Cancellation is black pen.

CAMDEN, S. C.

E1

E2

Handstamped Envelopes

125XU1 E1 5c **black** *2,500.*

125XU2 E2 10c **black** *750.*

No. 125XU2 unused was privately carried and is addressed but has no postal markings. No. 125XU2 is indistinguishable from a handstamp paid cover when used.

CANTON, MISS.

E1

"P" in star is initial of Postmaster William Priestly.

Handstamped Envelopes

14XU1 E1 5c **black** 4,000.

a. 10c (ms.) on 5c **black** 5,000.

CAROLINA CITY, N. C.

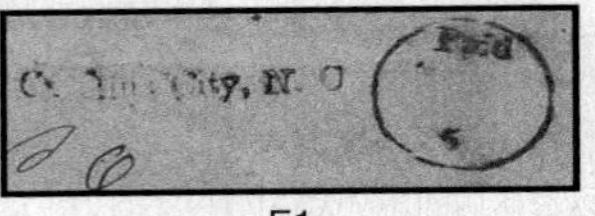

E1

Handstamped Envelope

118XU1 E1 5c **black** *5,000.*

CARTERSVILLE, GA.

E1

Handstamped Envelope

126XU1 E1 (5c) **red** *1,500.*

CHAPEL HILL, N. C.

E1

Handstamped Envelope

15XU1 E1 5c **black** *4,500.*

On patriotic cover 6,000.

CHARLESTON, S. C.

A1

E1

E2

Lithographed Adhesive

16X1 A1 5c **blue** 1,400. 800.
Pair 3,250. 2,200.
On cover *2,250.*
On patriotic cover *11,500.*
Pair, on cover *5,000.*
On cover with No. 112XU1 *22,500.*
Used on cover with C.S.A. 5c #6 to make 10c rate *3,000.*

Values are for stamps showing parts of the outer frame lines on at least 3 sides. The vast majority of this stamp small faults and are valued thus. Completely sound examples are scarce and sell for more.

Cancellation: black town (two types).

Press-printed Envelopes (typographed from woodcut)

16XU1 E1 5c **blue** 1,250. *1,750.*
16XU2 E1 5c **blue,** *amber* 1,250. *2,250.*
16XU3 E1 5c **blue,** *orange* 1,250. *2,250.*
16XU4 E1 5c **blue,** *buff* 1,250. *1,500.*
16XU5 E1 5c **blue,** *blue* 1,250. *2,250.*
16XU6 E2 10c **blue,** *orange* *80,000.*

The No. 16XU6 used entire is unique; value based on 1997 auction sale.
Beware of fakes of the E1 design.

Handstamped Cut Square

16XU7 E2 10c **black** *2,000.*

There is only one example of No. 16XU7. It is a cutout, not an entire. It may not have been mailed from Charleston, and it may not have paid postage.

CHARLOTTE, N. C.

E1

146XU1 E1 5c **blue,** "5" in circle and straight line "PAID" *3,500.*

CHARLOTTESVILLE, VA.

E1

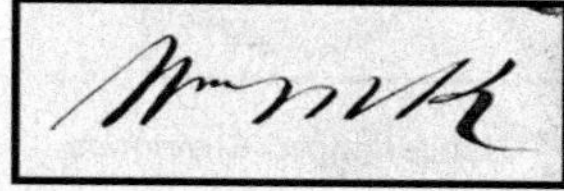
Control

Handstamped Envelopes, Manuscript Initials

127XU1 E1 5c **blue** —
127XU2 E1 10c **blue** —

The control initials appear at the upper right on the front of the envelope.

CHATTANOOGA, TENN.

E1

E2

Handstamped Envelopes

17XU2 E1 5c **black** 1,750.
17XU3 E2 5c on 2c **black** *5,000.*

No. 17XU3 is unique.

CHRISTIANSBURG, VA.

E1

Handstamped Envelopes
Impressed at top right

99XU1 E1 5c **black** *2,250.*
99XU2 E1 5c **blue** *2,000.*
99XU4 E1 5c **green** on U.S. envelope No. U27 *4,500.*
99XU5 E1 10c **blue** *3,500.*

The absence of 5c and 10c handstamped paid markings from this town suggests that Nos. 99XU1-99XU5 were used as both provisional and handstamped paid markings.

COLAPARCHEE, GA.

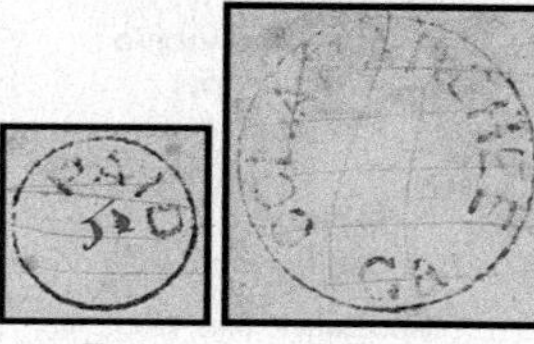
E1 Control

Handstamped Envelope

119XU1 E1 5c **black** *3,500.*

There are only two recorded examples of No. 119XU1, and both are used from Savannah with a general issue stamp. The control appears on the front of the envelope.

COLUMBIA, S. C.

Oval Control

Circular Control

E1

E2

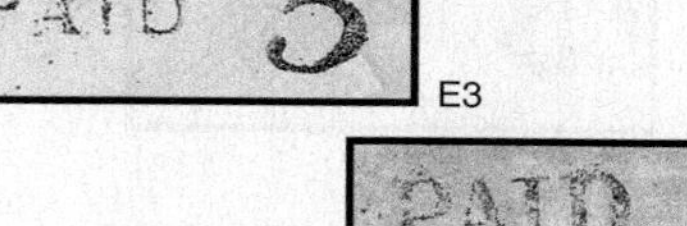

E3

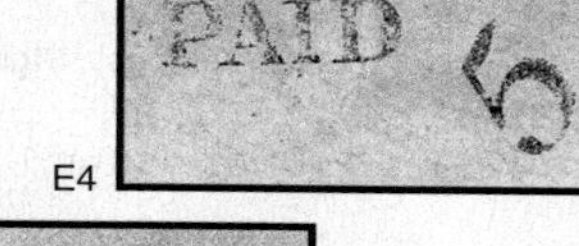

E4

E5

E6

E7

E8

Handstamped Envelopes

18XU1 E1 5c **blue** 550. 900.
Used on cover with C.S.A. 5c #1 or #1c to make 10c rate *3,000.*
Used on cover with C.S.A. 5c #7 to make 10c rate *16,500.*
a. 10c on 5c **blue** *3,500.*
18XU4 E2 5c **blue,** oval control on front *7,500.*
a. Oval control on back *1,250.*
18XU7 E3 5c **blue,** oval control on back 1,000.
18XU8 E4 5c **blue** oval control on back 1,000.
a. Circular control on back 2,000.
18XU9 E4 10c **blue** oval control on back 1,250.
18XU10 E5 10c **blue** oval control on back 1,250.
18XU11 E6 5c **blue** oval control on front *2,500.*
18XU12 E6 10c **blue** oval control on back 1,250.
18XU13 E7 5c **blue** oval control on back 1,000.
a. Circular control on back 1,500.
18XU14 E8 5c **blue** oval control on back 1,000.
a. No control (unused) —

COLUMBIA, TENN.

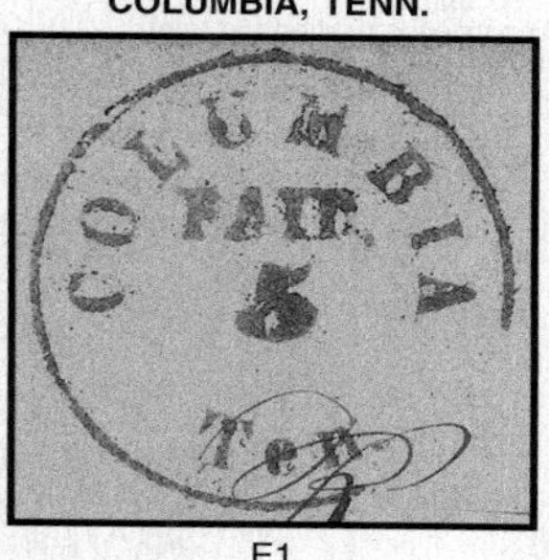

E1

Handstamped Envelope

113XU1 E1 5c **red** *6,000.*

One example recorded.

COLUMBUS, GA.

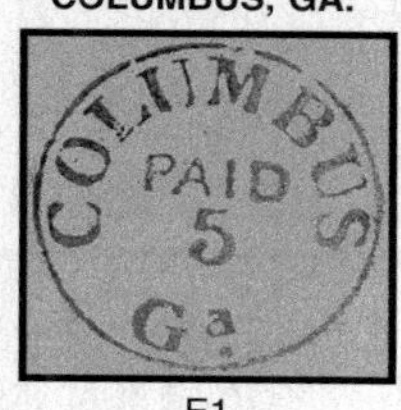

E1

Handstamped Envelopes

19XU1 E1 5c **blue** *900.*
19XU2 E1 10c **red** *3,250.*

COURTLAND, ALA.

E1

Handstamped Envelopes (from woodcut)

103XU1 E1 5c **red** *37,500.*

CUTHBERT, GA

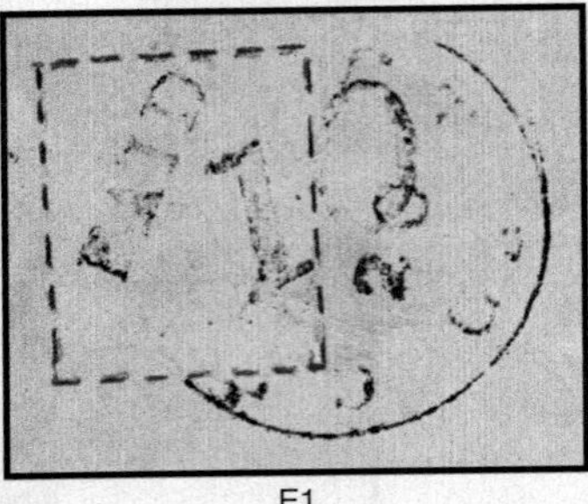
E1

Handstamped Envelope

95XU1 E1 10c **black** *1,000.*

The unique example of No. 95XU1 was used by having a C.S.A. 10c #12c placed over it.

DALTON, GA

E1

Handstamped Envelopes

20XU1 E1 5c **black** *750.*
a. Denomination omitted (5c rate) *875.*
b. 10c (ms.) on 5c **black** *1,500.*
c. 20c (ms.) on 5c **black** —
20XU2 E1 10c **black** *1,250.*

DANVILLE, VA.

A1

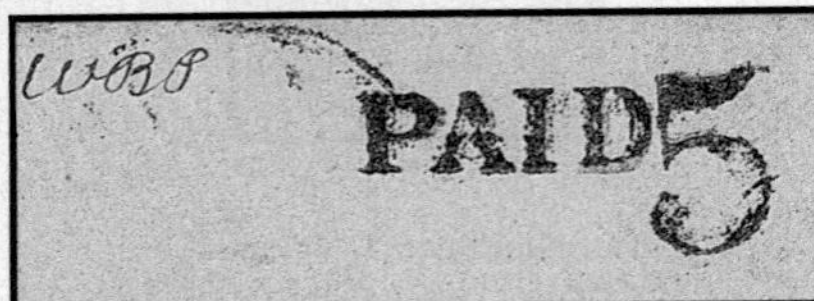

E1

E2

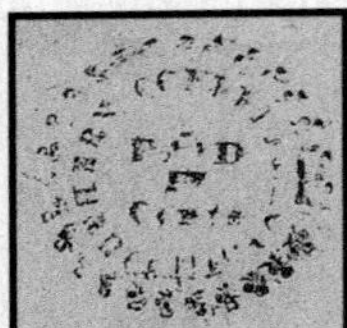

E3

E4

E5

E6

Typeset Adhesive
Wove Paper

21X1 A1 5c **red** *7,500.*
On cover *32,500.*
Cut to shape *6,250.*
On cover, cut to shape *27,500.*

Two varieties known.

Cancellation: blue town.

Laid Paper

21X2 A1 5c **red** *10,000.*

Cancellation: black town.

No. 21X2 is unique.

Press-printed Envelopes (typographed)

Two types: "SOUTHERN" in straight or curved line

Impressed (usually) at top left

21XU1 E1 5c **black** *7,000.*
21XU2 E1 5c **black,** *amber* *7,000.*
21XU3 E1 5c **black,** *dark buff* *7,000.*

The existence of No. 21XU2 is in question. The editors would like to see authenticated evidence of its existence.

Unissued 10c envelopes (type E1, in red) are known. All recorded examples are envelopes that show evidence of added stamps being torn off.

Dangerous forgeries exist of No. 21XU1.

Handstamped Envelopes

21XU3A E2 5c **black** (ms "WBP" initials) *1,000.*
21XU3B E3 5c **black** (ms "WPB" initials) *8,500.*
21XU4 E4 10c **black** *2,500.*
21XU6 E5 10c **black** *2,750.*
21XU7 E6 10c **black** (ms "WBP" initials) —

Types E4 and E5 both exist on one cover.

On No. 21XU3B, the "PAID 5 Cents" handstamp is to the left, and the "PAID" and ms. "5" are toward the right. It is unique.

DEMOPOLIS, ALA.

E1

Handstamped Envelopes, Signature in ms.

22XU1 E1 5c **black** ("Jno. Y. Hall") *3,500.*
22XU2 E1 5c **black** ("J. Y. Hall") *3,500.*
22XU3 E1 5c (ms.) **black** ("J. Y. Hall") *4,000.*

EATONTON, GA.

E1

E2

Handstamped Envelopes

23XU1 E1 5c **black** *3,000.*
a. 10 (ms) on 5c **black** —
23XU2 E2 5c + 5c **black** *5,000.*

EMORY, VA.

A1

Handstamped Adhesives ("PAID" and "5" in circle on selvage of U.S. 1c 1857 issue)
Perf. 15 on three sides

24X1 A1 5c **blue,** on cover, tied *27,500.*

Also known with "5" above "PAID."

Cancellation: blue town.

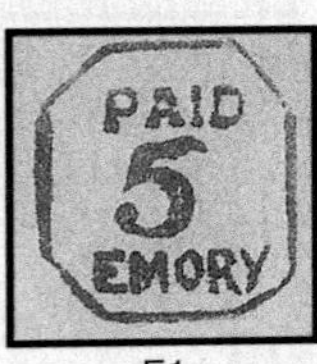

E1

E2

Handstamped Envelopes

24XU1 E1 5c **blue** *4,000.*
24XU2 E2 10c **blue** *5,000.*

One example each recorded of Nos. 24XU1 and 24XU2.

FINCASTLE, VA.

E1

Press-printed Envelope (typeset)

Impressed at top right

104XU1 E1 10c **black** *20,000.*

One example recorded of No. 104XU1.

FORSYTH, GA.

E1

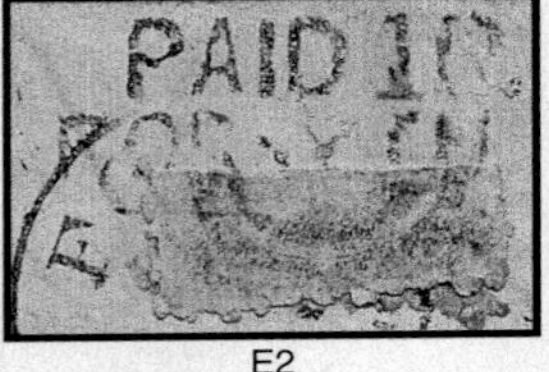
E2

Handstamped Envelope

120XU1 E1 10c **black** *2,000.*
120XU2 E2 10c **black** *1,250.*

Only one example each recorded of Nos. 120XU1 and 120XU2.

The No. 120XU2 cover has a C.S.A. 10c #11 rouletted used over the provisional marking.

FORT VALLEY, GA.

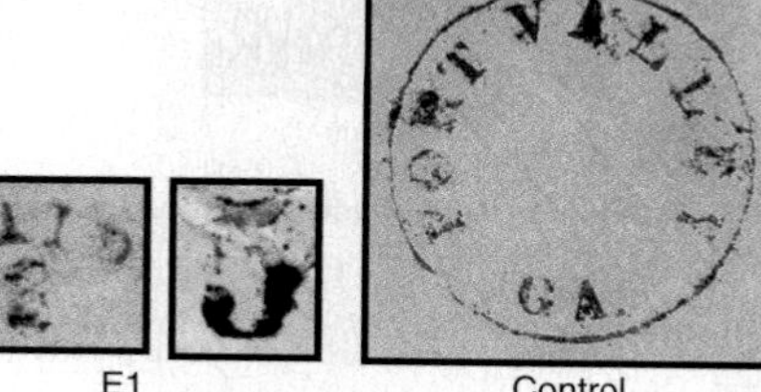

E1 Control

Handstamped Envelope

148XU1 E1 5c on 3c **black** *3,250.*

Black circle control on front of envelope. Unique.

FRANKLIN, N. C.

E1

E2

Press-printed Envelope (typeset) (No. 25XU1) Impressed at top right

25XU1 E1 5c **blue,** *buff* *30,000.*
25XU2 E2 5c **black,** large "5" woodcut in 31mm circular town mark *2,500.*

The one known No. 25XU1 envelope shows black circular Franklin postmark with manuscript date.

FRAZIERSVILLE, S. C.

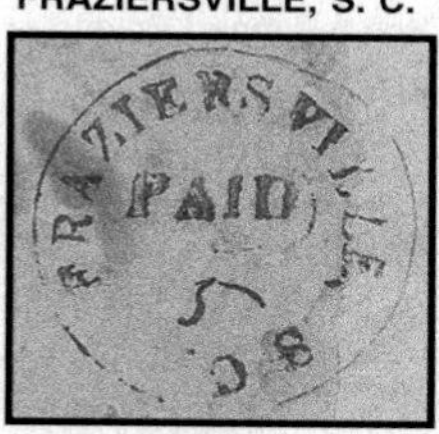

E1

Handstamped Envelope, "5" manuscript

128XU1 E1 5c **black** *5,000.*

Only one example recorded of No. 128XU1.

FREDERICKSBURG, VA.

A1

Sheets of 20, two panes of 10 varieties each

Typeset Adhesives
Thin bluish paper

26X1 A1 5c **blue,** *bluish* 900. 1,250.
Block of 4 4,000.
Sheet of 20 *19,000.*
On cover *5,500.*
Pair on cover *12,000.*
26X2 A1 10c **red (shades),** *bluish* 2,250.
Brown red, *bluish* 1,500.
Block of 4 —

Cancellation: black town.

GAINESVILLE, ALA.

E1 E2 E3

Handstamped Envelopes

27XU1 E1 5c **black** *4,500.*
27XU2 E2 5c **black** *5,000.*
27XU3 E3 10c ("01") **black** *12,000.*

Postmark spells town name "Gainsville."

GALVESTON, TEX.

E1

Handstamped Envelopes

98XU1 E1 5c **black** 500. *1,500.*
98XU2 E1 10c **black** *2,000.*

E2

E3

Handstamped Envelopes

98XU3 E2 10c **black** 550. *2,750.*
98XU4 E2 20c **black** *3,500.*
98XU5 E3 5c **black** *4,500.*

GASTON, N. C.

E1

Handstamped Envelope

129XU1 E1 5c **black** *6,000.*

Only one example recorded of No. 129XU1.

GEORGETOWN, S. C.

E1

Control

E2

Handstamped Envelopes

28XU1 E1 5c **black** *1,000.*
28XU2 E2 5c **black,** separate "5" and straightline "PAID" handstamps, control on reverse — *1,750.*

GOLIAD, TEX.

A1

A2

Typeset Adhesives

29X1 A1 5c **black** *16,500.*
29X2 A1 5c **black,** *gray* *11,500.*
29X3 A1 5c **black,** *rose* *12,000.*
On cover front *47,500.*
29X4 A1 10c **black** — *25,000.*
29X5 A1 10c **black,** *rose* *12,000.*

Type A1 stamps are signed "Clarke-P.M." vertically in black or red.

29X6 A2 5c **black,** *gray* *22,500.*
a. "GOILAD" *12,000.*
Pair, left stamp the error —
29X7 A2 10c **black,** *buff* *12,000.*
On cover *40,000.*
a. "GOILAD" *15,000.*
On cover *30,000.*
29X8 A2 5c **black,** *dark blue,* on cover *18,000.*
29X9 A2 10c **black,** *dark blue* *27,500.*

Cancellations in black: pen, town, "Paid"

GONZALES, TEX.

Colman & Law were booksellers when John B. Law (of the firm) was appointed Postmaster. The firm used a small lithographed label on drugs and on the front or inside of books they sold.

A1

Lithographed Adhesives on colored glazed paper

30X1 A1 (5c) **gold,** *dark blue,* pair on cover, *1861* *15,000.*
30X2 A1 (10c) **gold,** *garnet,* on cover, *1864* *25,000.*
30X3 A1 (10c) **gold,** *black,* on cover, *1865* *50,000.*

Cancellations: black town, black pen. No. 30X1 must bear double-circle town cancel as validating control. The control was applied to the labels in the sheet before their sale as stamps. When used, the stamps bear an additional Gonzales double-circle postmark.

GREENSBORO, ALA.

E1

E2

E3

Handstamped Envelopes

31XU1	E1	5c **black**	*3,000.*
31XU2	E1	10c **black**	*2,750.*
31XU3	E2	10c **black**	*6,000.*
31XU4	E3	10c on 5c **black,** on cover	*3,000.*

GREENSBORO, N. C.

E1

Handstamped Envelope

32XU1 E1 10c **red** 1,250.

GREENVILLE, ALA.

A1

A2

Typeset Adhesives
On pinkish surface-colored glazed paper.

33X1	A1	5c **blue & red**	*28,000.*	
		On cover		*47,500.*
33X2	A2	10c **red & blue,** on cover		*47,500.*

Two used examples each are known of Nos. 33X1-33X2, and all are on covers. Covers bear a postmark but it was not used to cancel the stamps.

The former No. 33X1a has been identified as a fake.

GREENVILLE, TENN.

E1

144XU1 E1 5c **black** *5,000.*

Only one example of No. 144XU1 is recorded.

GREENVILLE COURT HOUSE, S. C.

E1

PAID 10

E2

Control A

Control B

GREENVILLE C.H. JUN 1 S.C

Control C

Handstamped Envelopes (Several types)

34XU1	E1	5c **black**	*2,000.*
34XU2	E2	10c **black**	*2,000.*
a.		20c (ms.) on 10c **black**	*3,000.*

Envelopes must bear one of three different postmark controls on the back. When the control postmark is dated, the date must be the same or prior to the date of the postmark on the front of the envelope.

GREENWOOD DEPOT, VA.

A1

"PAID" Handstamped Adhesive ("PAID" with value and signature in ms.)
Laid Paper

35X1	A1	10c **black,** *gray blue,* uncanceled,		
		on cover	22,500.	
		On cover, tied		—

Six examples recorded of No. 35X1, all on covers. One of these is in the British Library collection. Of the remaining five, only one has the stamp tied to the cover.

Cancellation: black town.

GRIFFIN, GA.

E1

Handstamped Envelopes

102XU1	E1	5c **black**	2,000.
102XU2	E1	10c **black**	*5,000.*

No. 102XU2 is on a large piece of an envelope with July 25 postmark at left. It is unique.

GROVE HILL, ALA.

A1

Handstamped Adhesive (from woodcut)

36X1	A1	5c **black**		—
		On cover, tied	*130,000.*	

Two examples are recorded. One is on cover tied by the postmark. The other is canceled by magenta pen on a cover front.

Cancellations: black town, magenta pen.

HALLETTSVILLE, TEX.

A1

Handstamped Adhesive
Ruled Letter Paper

37X1 A1 10c **black,** *gray blue,* on cover *15,000.*

One example known.

Cancellation: black ms.

HAMBURGH, S. C.

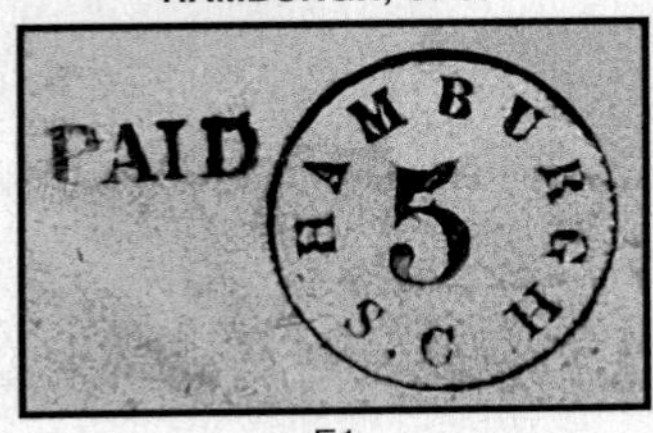
E1

Handstamped Envelope

112XU1	E1	5c **black**	*8,000.*	
		On cover with #16X1 (forwarded)		—

HARRISBURGH (Harrisburg), TEX.

E1

E2

Handstamped Envelope

130XU1	E1	5c **black**	*5,500.*	—
130XU2	E2	10c **black**		

The unused 5c entire is the only example recorded of No. 130XU1

HELENA, TEX.

A1

Typeset Adhesives
Several varieties

38X1 A1 5c **black,** *buff* *22,500. 20,000.*
38X2 A1 10c **black,** *gray* *40,000.*

On 10c "Helena" is in upper and lower case italics.
Used examples are valued with small faults or repairs, as all recorded have faults.

Cancellation: black town.

HILLSBORO, N. C.

A1

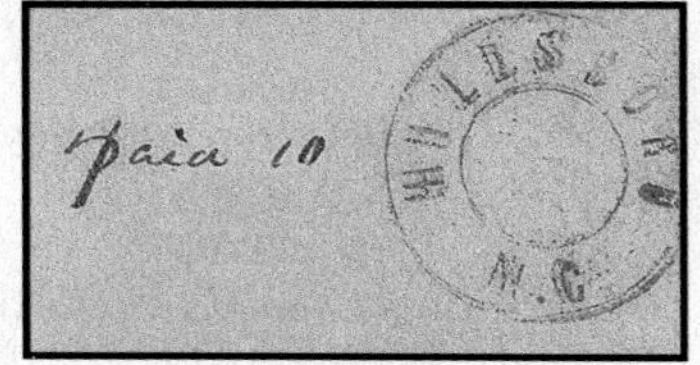

E1

Handstamped Adhesive

39X1 A1 5c **black,** on cover *15,000.*

5c usage is determined by date of June 1, 1861, or later in the dated cancel. No. 39X1 is unique.
See 3c 1861 Postmaster's Provisional No. 1AX1.

Cancellation: black town.

Ms./Handstamped Envelope

39XU1 E1 10c "paid 10" in manuscript with undated blue town cancel as control on face *2,250.*

No. 39XU1 is unique.

HOLLANDALE, TEX.

E1

Handstamped Envelope

132XU1 E1 5c **black** —

HOUSTON, TEX.

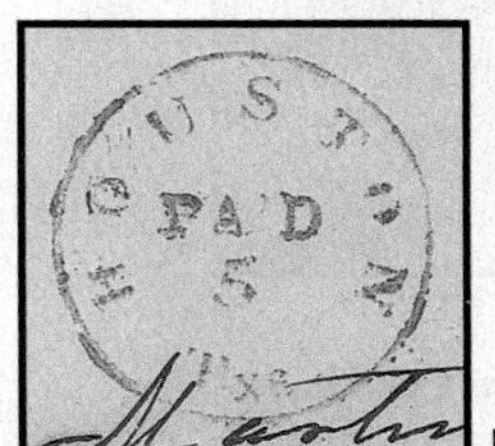

E1

No. 40XU1a

Handstamped Envelopes

40XU1 E1 5c **red** — 800.
On patriotic cover —
a. 10c (ms.) on 5c **red** *11,000.*
40XU2 E1 10c **red** — *2,000.*
40XU3 E1 10c **black** *6,750.*
40XU4 E1 5c +10c **red** *2,500.*
40XU5 E1 10c +10c **red** *2,500.*

Nos. 40XU2-40XU5 show "TEX" instead of "TXS."

HUNTSVILLE, TEX.

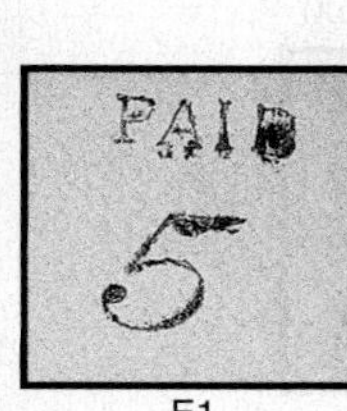

E1

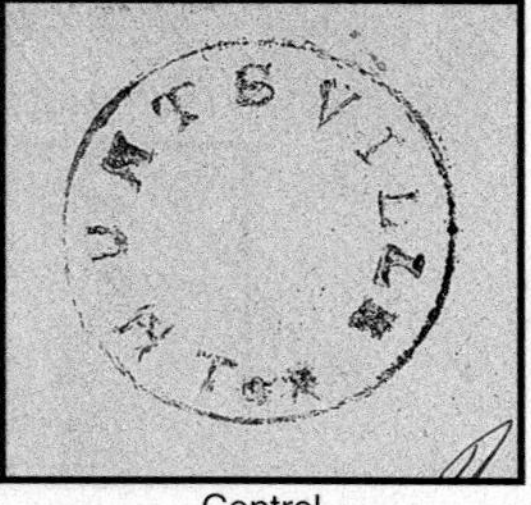

Control

Handstamped Envelope

92XU1 E1 5c **black** *5,000.*

No. 92XU1 exists with "5" outside or within control circle.

INDEPENDENCE, TEX.

A1

A2

Handstamped Adhesives

41X1 A1 10c **black,** *buff,* on cover, uncanceled, cut to shape *20,000.*
41X2 A1 10c **black,** *dull rose,* on cover —

With small "10" and "Pd" in manuscript

41X3 A2 10c **black,** *buff,* on cover, uncanceled, cut to shape *32,500.*
On cover, uncanceled, cut square —

No. 41X1 is unique.
All known examples of Nos. 41X1-41X3 are uncanceled on covers with black "INDEPENDANCE TEX." (sic) postmark.
The existence of No. 41X2 has been questioned by specialists. The editors would like to see authenticated evidence of the existence of this item.

ISABELLA, GA.

E1

Handstamped Envelope, Manuscript "5"

133XU1 E1 5c **black** *5,000.*

Only one example recorded of No. 133XU1.

IUKA, MISS.

E1

Handstamped Envelope

42XU1 E1 5c **black** *1,750.*
On patriotic cover *4,000.*

JACKSON, MISS.

E1

Handstamped Envelopes
Two types of numeral

43XU1 E1 5c **black** 750.
On patriotic cover 3,000.
a. 10c on 5c **black** *2,750.*
b. 5c on 3c **black** *1,500.*
43XU2 E1 10c **black** *2,000.*
a. 5c on 10c **black** *3,750.*
43XU4 E1 10c on 5c **blue** *2,750.*

The 5c also exists on a lettersheet.
See 3c 1861 Postmaster's Provisional No. 2AXU1.

JACKSONVILLE, ALA.

E1

Handstamped Envelope

110XU1 E1 5c **black** — *3,000.*

JACKSONVILLE, FLA.

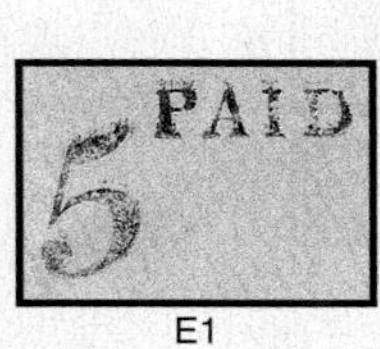

E1

Control

Handstamped Envelope

134XU1 E1 5c **black** *4,000.*

Undated double circle postmark control on reverse. No. 134XU1 is unique.

JETERSVILLE, VA.

A1

Handstamped Adhesive
("5" with ms. "AHA." initials)
Laid Paper

44X1 A1 5c **black,** vertical pair on cover, uncanceled *16,000.*

Initials are those of Postmaster A. H. Atwood.

Cancellation: black town.

JONESBORO, TENN.

E1

Handstamped Envelopes

45XU1 E1 5c **black** *6,000.*
45XU2 E1 5c **dark blue** *5,000.*

KINGSTON, GA.

E1

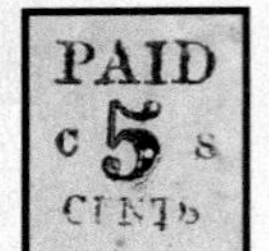

E2

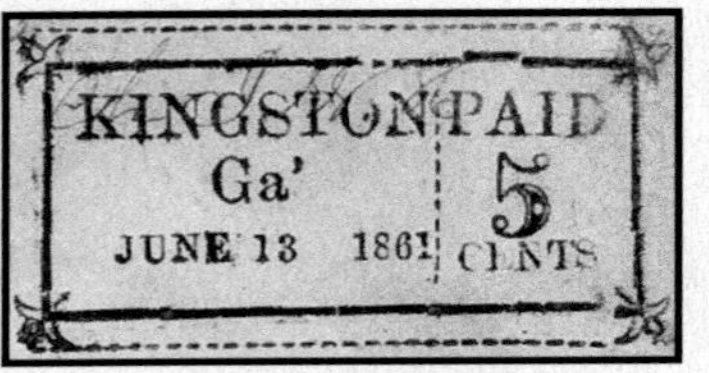

E3

E4

Typeset Envelopes
(design types E1-E2, E4 are handstamps; typeset design E3 probably impressed by hand but possibly press printed)

46XU1 E1 5c **black** 3,000.
46XU2 E2 5c **black** 3,250.
46XU4 E3 5c **black** *12,500.*
46XU5 E4 5c **black** *2,000.*

There is only one recorded example of No. 46XU4.

KNOXVILLE, TENN.

A1

Typographed Adhesives
(stereotype from woodcut)
Grayish Laid Paper

47X1 A1 5c **brick red** *1,750.* 1,400.
Manuscript cancel 650.
Horizontal pair *4,500.* *3,000.*
Vertical pair *4,000.*
Vertical strip of 3 *7,000.*
On cover, tied by handstamp *8,000.*
On cover, manuscript cancel *2,100.*
Pair on cover *7,500.*
47X2 A1 5c **carmine** *2,750.* *2,250.*
Manuscript cancel 1,100.
Vertical strip of 3 —
On cover, tied by handstamp *7,500.*
On cover, manuscript cancel *2,100.*
47X3 A1 10c **green,** on cover *57,750.*

The #47X3 cover is unique. Value is based on 1997 auction sale.

Cancellations in black: town, bars, pen or pencil.

E1

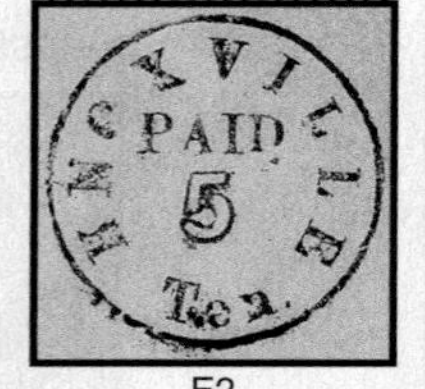

E2

Press-printed Envelopes (typographed)

47XU1 E1 5c **blue** *2,500.*
47XU2 E1 5c **blue,** *orange* *5,000.*
47XU3 E1 10c **red** (cut to shape) *7,500.*
47XU4 E1 10c **red,** *orange* (cut to shape) *7,500.*

Only one example each recorded of Nos. 47XU3 and 47XU4. Dangerous fakes exist of Nos. 47XU1 and 47XU2.

Handstamped Envelopes

47XU5 E2 5c **black** *1,400.*
On patriotic cover *3,750.*
a. 10c on 5c **black** *3,500.*

Type E2 exists with "5" above or below "PAID."

LA GRANGE, TEX.

E1

Handstamped Envelopes

48XU1 E1 5c **black** — 3,250.
48XU2 E1 10c **black** 3,250.

LAKE CITY, FLA.

E1

Control Type A

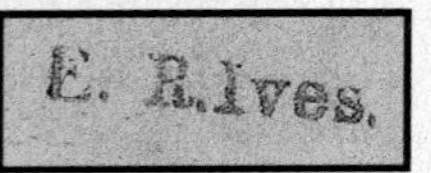

Control Type B

Handstamped Envelope

96XU1 E1 10c **black** *3,500.*

Envelopes have black circle control mark, or printed name of E. R. Ives, postmaster, on back.

LAURENS COURT HOUSE, S. C.

E1

E2

Control

Handstamped Envelopes

116XU1 E1 5c **black** *2,000.*
116XU2 E2 5c **black** *2,000.*

Envelopes have a 25mm undated control mark on reverse. No. 116XU1 is unique.

LENOIR, N. C.

A1

E1

Handstamped Adhesive (from woodcut)
White wove paper with cross-ruled orange lines

49X1 A1 5c **blue & orange** *7,250.* *6,750.*
On cover, pen canceled *15,000.*
On cover, tied by handstamp *22,500.*
a. On paper with narrow-spaced blue vertical lines and no horizontal lines *4,000.*

Cancellations: blue town, blue "Paid" in circle, black pen.

The paper on No. 49X1 has 21-22 vertical orange lines and 3-4 horizontal lines. The paper on No. 49X1a has approximately 53 closely spaced vertical blue lines and no horizontal lines. No. 49X1a is unique, with thins and a repaired tear, and it is valued thus.

Handstamped Envelopes

49XU1 A1 5c **blue** *4,000.*
49XU2 A1 10c (5c+5c) **blue** *25,000.*
49XU3 E1 5c **blue** *4,500.*
49XU4 E1 5c **black** *4,500.*

No. 49XU2 is unique. A variety of No. 49XU3 is recorded with two light strikes of the provisional handstamp, one in blue and one in black.

LEXINGTON, MISS.

E1

Handstamped Envelopes

50XU1 E1 5c **black** *4,500.*
50XU2 E1 10c **black** *6,000.*

Only one example is recorded of No. 50XU2.

LEXINGTON, VA.

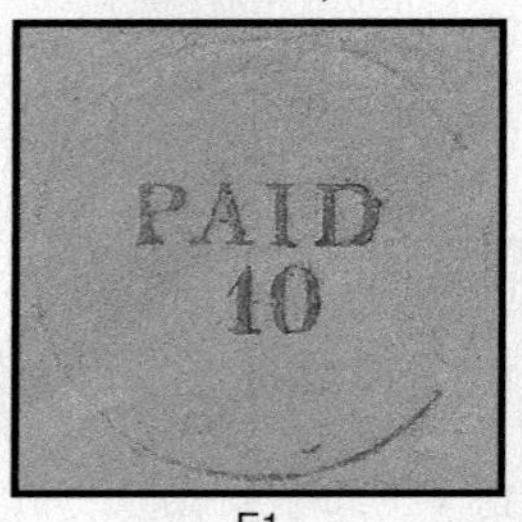

E1

Handstamped Envelopes

135XU1 E1 5c **blue** *350.*
Used with 5c #6 to make 10c rate *500.*
135XU2 E1 10c **blue** *350.*

Nos. 135XU1-135XU2 by themselves are indistinguishable from stampless covers when used.

LIBERTY, VA. (and Salem, Va.)

A1

Typeset Adhesive (probably impressed by hand)
Laid Paper

74X1 A1 5c **black,** on cover, uncanceled, with Liberty postmark *35,000.*
On cover, uncanceled, with Salem postmark *40,000.*

Two known on covers with Liberty, Va. postmark; one cover known with the nearby Salem, Va. office postmark.

LIMESTONE SPRINGS, S. C.

A1

Handstamped Adhesive

121X1 A1 5c **black,** *light blue,* on cover *10,000.*
Two on cover *15,000.*
121X2 A1 5c **black,** *white,* two on cover *32,500.*

Stamps are cut round or rectangular. Covers are not postmarked. The No. 121X2 cover bears the only two recorded examples of this stamp.

LIVINGSTON, ALA.

A1

Lithographed Adhesive

51X1 A1 5c **blue** *15,000.*
On cover *75,000.*
Pair on cover *120,000.*

The pair on cover is unique.

Cancellation: black town.

LYNCHBURG, VA.

A1

E1

Typographed Adhesive
(stereotype from woodcut)

52X1 A1 5c **blue** (shades) *1,800.* *1,500.*
Pair *3,250.*
On cover *6,500.*
Pair on cover *20,000.*

Cancellations: black town, blue town.

Press-printed Envelopes (typographed)

Impressed at top right or left

52XU1 E1 5c **black** *700.00* *4,000.*
52XU2 E1 5c **black,** *amber* *4,000.*
52XU3 E1 5c **black,** *buff* *4,000.*
52XU4 E1 5c **black,** *brown* *4,000.*
On patriotic cover —

MACON, GA.

A1

A2

A3

A4

Typeset Adhesives
Several varieties of type A1, 10 of A2, 5 of A3
Wove Paper

53X1 A1 5c **black,** *light blue green* (shades) 1,250. 1,000.
On cover *6,000.*
Pair on cover *14,000.*
Comma after "OFFICE" 950. 1,100.
Comma after "OFFICE," on cover *7,500.*

Warning: Dangerous forgeries exist of the normal variety and the Comma after "OFFICE" variety. Certificates of authenticity from recognized committees are strongly recommended.

53X3 A2 5c **black,** *yellow* 2,500. 1,250.
On cover *6,000.*
Pair on cover *11,000.*
On patriotic cover, single *7,500.*
Pair on patriotic cover *25,000.*
53X4 A3 5c **black,** *yellow* (shades) 3,000. 2,250.
On cover *7,500.*
Pair on cover *11,000.*
a. Vertical tête bêche pair —
53X5 A4 2c **black,** *gray green* —
On cover *50,000.*

Laid Paper

53X6 A2 5c **black,** *yellow* *6,000.* *6,000.*
On cover *8,000.*
53X7 A3 5c **black,** *yellow* *6,000.*
On cover *9,000.*
53X8 A1 5c **black,** *light blue green* 1,750. *2,250.*
On cover *4,500.*

No. 53X4a is unique.

Cancellations: black town, black "PAID" (2 types).

E1

Handstamped Envelope

Two types: "PAID" over "5," "5" over "PAID"

53XU1 E1 5c **black** 250. 650.
On patriotic cover 1,900.

Values are for "PAID" over "5" variety. "5" over "PAID" is much scarcer.

MADISON, GA.

E1

Handstamped Envelope

136XU1 E1 5c **red** *600.*

No. 136XU1 is indistinguishable from a handstamp paid cover when used.

MADISON COURT HOUSE, FLA.

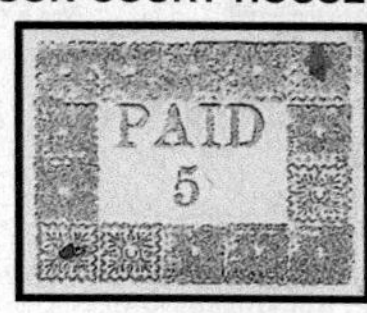

E1

Typeset Envelope

137XU1 E1 5c **black,** *yellow* *35,000.*

No. 137XU1 is unique.
See 3c 1861 Postmaster's Provisional No. 3AX1.

MARIETTA, GA.

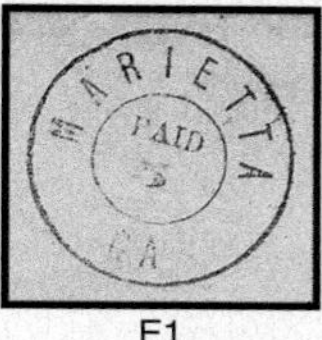

E1

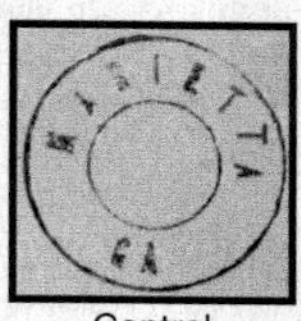

Control

E2

Handstamped Envelopes

54XU1 E1 5c **black** 500.
a. 10c on 5c **black** *1,750.*

With Double Circle Control

54XU3 E1 10c **black**
54XU4 E2 5c **black** *2,000.*

The existence of No. 54XU3 has been questioned by specialists. The editors would like to see authenticated evidence that verifies this listing.

MARION, VA.

A1

Adhesives with Typeset frame and Handstamped numeral in center

55X1 A1 5c **black** *7,500.*
On cover *20,000.*
55X2 A1 10c **black** *16,500.* *10,000.*
On cover *35,000.*
55X3 A1 5c **black,** *bluish,* laid paper — —

The 2c, 3c, 15c and 20c are believed to be bogus items printed later using the original typeset frame.

Cancellations: black town, black "PAID," black manuscript.

MARS BLUFF, S. C.

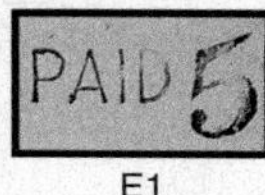

E1

145XU1 E1 5c **black** *2,000.*

The No. 145XU1 marking is a provisional only when unused, used from another town or used under a general issue.

MEMPHIS, TENN.

A1

56X1a Partial Print

A2

Typographed Adhesives
(stereotyped from woodcut)

Plate of 50 (5x10) for the 2c. The stereotypes for the 5c stamps were set in 5 vertical rows of 8, with at least 2 rows set sideways to the right (see Thomas H. Pratt's monograph, "The Postmaster's Provisionals of Memphis").

56X1 A1 2c **blue** (shades) 100. *1,250.*
Block of 4 550.
On cover *12,500.*
Cracked plate (16, 17, 18) 250. *1,350.*
Plate scratch across "GALLA" of "MCGALLAWAY" 200.
a. Partial print 250. —

On No. 56X1a, a breaking off of the plate at the right edge caused incomplete printing (approximately 2/3 of the stamp) on stamps in positions 5, 10, 15, 20 and 50.

56X2 A2 5c **red** (shades) 150. *250.*
Pair *340.* *650.*
Block of 4 *1,000.* —
On cover 2,000.
Pair on cover *4,000.*
Strip of 4 on cover *9,000.*
On patriotic cover *9,000.*
Pair on patriotic cover *12,500.*
a. Tête bêche pair 1,500.
Pair on cover *9,500.*
b. Pair, one sideways 2,500.
c. Pelure paper — —

Cancellation on Nos. 56X1-56X2: black town.

Press-printed Envelopes (typographed)

56XU1 A2 5c **red** (shades) *3,000.*
Used with 5c #56X2 to make 10c rate *6,000.*
56XU2 A2 5c **red,** *amber* *3,000.*
Used with C.S.A. 5c #1 to make 10c rate *8,000.*
Used with #56X2 to make 10c rate *5,500.*
56XU3 A2 5c **red,** *orange* *2,500.*
Used with #56X2 *5,750.*
On patriotic cover —
56XU4 A2 5c **red,** *cream* *5,750.*

Only one example of No. 56XU4 is recorded. It is on a cover on which a C.S.A. No. 11 is affixed over the provisional to pay the postage.

MICANOPY, FLA.

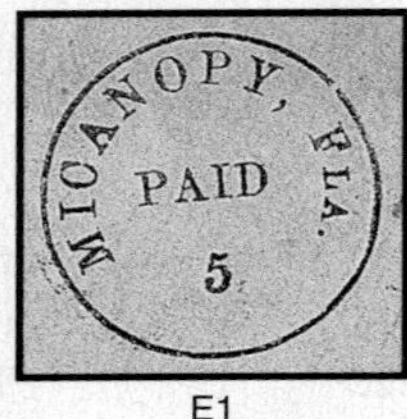

E1

Handstamped Envelope

105XU1 E1 5c **black** *11,500.*
One example recorded.

MILLEDGEVILLE, GA.

E1

E2

E3

Handstamped Envelopes

Two types of No. 57XU5: Type I, tall, thin "1" and "0" of "10"; Type II, short, fat "1" and "0" of "10."

57XU1 E1 5c **black** 500.
a. Wide spacing between "I" and "D" of "PAID" 600.
b. 10c on 5c **black** 1,000.
57XU2 E1 5c **blue** 800.
57XU4 E2 10c **black** 375. 1,200.
a. Wide spacing between "I" and "D" of "PAID" 1,200.
57XU5 E3 10c **black,** type I 450. 800.
a. Type II 1,500.

On No. 57XU4, the "PAID/10" virtually always falls outside the Milledgeville control marking (as in illustration E1).

The existence of No. 57XU2 as a provisional has been questioned by specialists. The editors would like to see authenticated evidence of provisional use of this marking.

MILTON, N. C.

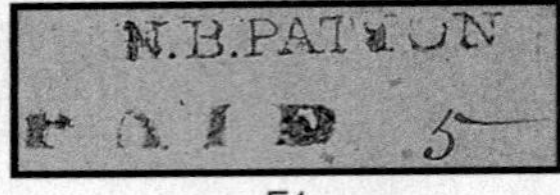

E1

Handstamped Envelope, "5" Manuscript

138XU1 E1 5c **black** *3,750.*

MOBILE, ALA.

A1

Lithographed Adhesives

58X1 A1 2c **black** 2,250. 1,200.
Pair — *2,500.*
On cover *6,000.*
Pair on cover *20,000.*
Three singles on one cover *20,000.*
Five stamps on one cover *24,000.*
58X2 A1 5c **blue** 350. 450.
Pair 900. 1,050.
On cover 2,000.
On cover, canceled in Claiborne, Ala. —
On cover, canceled in Montgomery, Ala. —
Pair on cover 2,750.
Strip of 3 on cover *10,000.*
Strip of 4 on cover *25,000.*
Line through "O" of "Office" (plate scratch) —

Cancellations: black town, express company.

The existence of a strip of 5 of No. 58X2 has been questioned by specialists. The editors would like to see authenticated evidence of the existence of this strip either on or off cover.

MONTGOMERY, ALA.

E1

E1a

Handstamped Envelopes

59XU1 E1 5c **red** *1,100.*
a. 10c on 5c **red** *2,750.*
59XU2 E1 5c **blue** 400. *1,000.*
59XU3 E1a 10c **red** *900.*
59XU4 E1a 10c **blue** *1,250.*
59XU5 E1a 10c **black** 850.

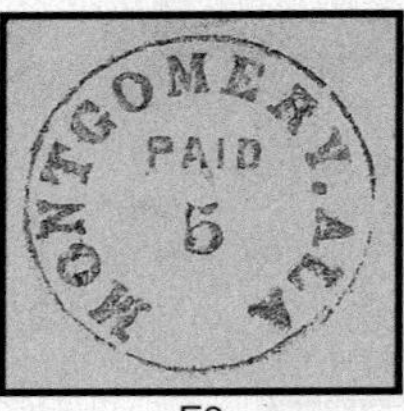

E2

E3

59XU7 E2 2c **red** *2,500.*
59XU7A E2 2c **blue** *3,500.*
59XU8 E2 5c **black** *2,000.*
59XU9 E3 10c **black** *2,000.*
59XU10 E3 10c **red** *1,750.*

The existence of No. 59XU10 is in question. The editors would like to see an authenticated example of this marking.

MOUNT LEBANON, LA.

A1

Woodcut Adhesive (mirror image of design)

60X1 A1 5c **red brown,** on cover *255,000.*

One example known. Value represents sale price at 2009 auction.

Cancellation: black pen.

MOUNT PLEASANT, N. C.

E1

Handstamped Envelope

151XU1 E1 10c **blue** *3,500.*

One example of No. 151XU1 is recorded, posted in January 1866 and covered by a U.S. 3c stamp subsequently removed to reveal the provisional.

NASHVILLE, TENN.

A2

Typographed Adhesives (stereotyped from woodcut)

Gray Blue Ribbed Paper

61X2 A2 5c **carmine** (shades) 1,000. 650.
Pair 2,100.
On cover 3,500.
On patriotic cover *5,000.*
Pair on cover *6,000.*
On cover with U.S. 3c 1857 (express) *25,000.*
a. Vertical tête bêche pair 4,000.
On cover *25,000.*
61X3 A2 5c **brick red** (shades) 900. 700.
Pair 2,000.
On cover 3,500.
On patriotic cover *6,000.*
Pair on cover *7,500.*
On U.S. #U26 (express) *35,000.*
On U.S. #U27 with #26 (express) *25,000.*
a. Vertical tête bêche pair *3,000.*
61X4 A2 5c **gray** (shades) 1,250. 1,500.
On cover *7,500.*
On patriotic cover *12,000.*
Pair on cover *7,500.*
Strip of 5 on cover front *8,750.*
61X5 A2 5c **violet brown** (shades) 1,250. 750.
Block of 4 —
On cover 4,250.
On patriotic cover *35,000.*
Pair on cover *6,000.*
a. Vertical tete beche pair *5,000.* *7,500.*
Pair on cover —
61X6 A2 10c **green** — *7,500.*
On cover *22,500.*
On cover with U.S. 3c 1857 (express) *75,000.*
On U.S. #U26 (express) *90,000.*
On cover with No. 61X2 *27,500.*

Cancellations

Pen Cancel
Blue "Paid"
Blue "Postage Paid"
Blue town
Blue numeral "5"

Blue numeral "10"
Blue express company
Black express company

For the former 61X1, see No. 4AX1 in the 3c 1861 Postmasters' Provisional section.

E1

Handstamped Envelopes

61XU1	E1 5c **blue**		900.
	On patriotic envelope		2,000.
61XU2	E1 10c on 5c **blue**		*2,750.*
	On patriotic cover		*5,500.*

NEW ORLEANS, LA.

A1

A2

Typographed Adhesives (stereotyped from woodcut)

Plate of 40

62X1	A1 2c **blue,** *July 14, 1861*	225.	*800.*
	Pair	650.	*1,650.*
	Block of 4	*6,000.*	
	On cover		*5,000.*
	On patriotic cover		*8,000.*
	Pair on cover		*10,000.*
	Three singles on one cover		*20,000.*
	Three singles + #62X4, on cover		—
	Five singles on one cover		*12,500.*
	Strip of 5 on cover		*30,000.*
a.	Printed on both sides, on cover		*10,500.*
62X2	A1 2c **red** (shades), *Jan. 6, 1862*	190.	*1,000.*
	Pair	475.	
	Block of 4	*1,800.*	
	On cover		*25,000.*
62X3	A2 5c **brown,** *white, June 12, 1861*	300.	200.
	Pair	800.	425.
	Block of 4	2,000.	
	On cover		450.
	On cover from town other than N.O.		*5,000.*
	On patriotic cover		*7,000.*
	Pair on cover		850.
	Strip of 5 on cover		*5,000.*
	On cover with U.S. #26 (Southern Letter Unpaid)		*110,000.*
	On cover with U.S. No. 30A		—
a.	Printed on both sides		*3,750.*
	On cover		*7,500.*
b.	5c **ocher,** *June 18, 1861*	700.	625.
	Pair		1,500.
	On cover		2,750.
	On patriotic cover		*6,000.*
	Pair on cover		3,500.
c.	5c **chocolate brown,** *white*		*1,500.*

The editors would like to see authenticated evidence of the existence of No. 62X3a on cover.

62X4	A2 5c **red brn,** *bluish, Aug. 22, 1861*	325.	200.
	Pair	725.	475.
	Horizontal strip of 6		*3,500.*
	Block of 4		2,200.
	On cover		425.
	On patriotic cover		*10,000.*
	Pair on cover		700.
	Block of 4 on cover		*5,000.*
	Used on cover with C.S.A. 5c #1 to make 10c rate		*27,500.*
a.	Printed on both sides		*3,250.*
	On cover		*9,000.*
62X5	A2 5c **yel brn,** *off-white, Dec. 3, 1861*	160.	*250.*
	Pair	350.	*525.*
	Block of 4	750.	
	On cover		850.
	On patriotic cover		*3,000.*
	Pair on cover		1,200.
	Strip of 5 on cover		—
62X6	A2 5c **red** (shades)	—	*14,000.*
62X7	A2 5c **red** (shades), *bluish*		*15,000.*

Cancellations

Black town (single or double circle New Orleans)
Red town (double circle New Orleans)
Town other than New Orleans
Postmaster's handstamp
Black "Paid"
Express Company
Packet boat, cover "STEAM"

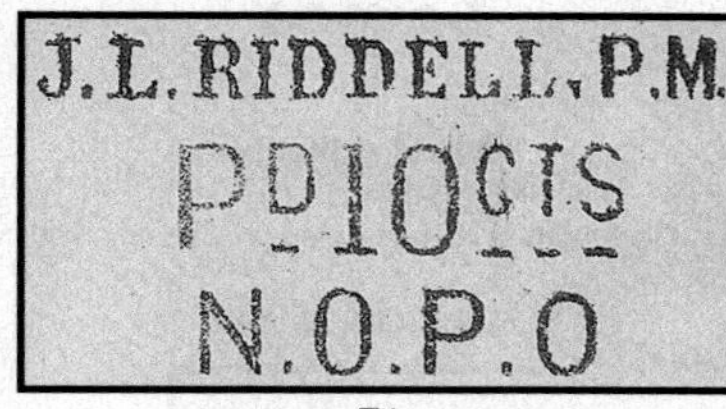

E1

Handstamped Envelopes

62XU1	E1 5c **black**		4,500.
62XU2	E1 10c **black**		*11,500.*

"J. L. RIDDELL, P. M." omitted

62XU3	E1 2c **black**		*9,500.*

Some authorities question the use of No. 62XU3 as a provisional.

NEW SMYRNA, FLA.

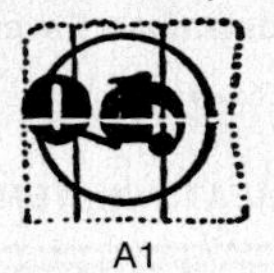
A1

Handstamped Adhesive

On white paper with blue ruled lines

63X1	A1 10c ("O1") on 5c **black**		*50,000.*

One example known. It is uncanceled on a postmarked patriotic cover.

NORFOLK, VA.

E1

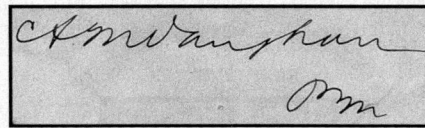

Manuscript Signature

Handstamped Envelopes

Ms Signature on Back

139XU1	E1 5c **blue**	1,000.	*1,750.*
139XU2	E1 10c **blue**		*1,750.*

OAKWAY, S. C.

A1

Handstamped Adhesive (from woodcut)

115X1	A1 5c **black,** on cover		*60,000.*

Two used examples of No. 115X1 are recorded, both on cover. Value represents 2012 auction realization for the cover on which the stamp is tied by manuscript "Paid."

OXFORD, N. C.

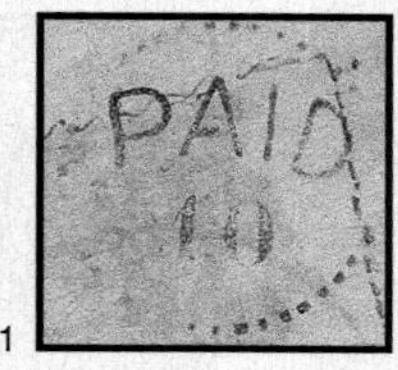

E1

Handstamped Envelope

152XU1	E1 10c **black**		*3,500.*

One example of No. 152XU1 is recorded, covered by a C.S.A. 10¢ No. 12 that paid the postage.

PATTERSON, N. C.

E1

E2

Control

Handstamped Envelopes

149XU1	E1 5c **black**		*750.*
149XU2	E2 10c **black**		*2,500.*

Nos. 149XU1 and 149XU2 must have an undated postmark on the cover as a control.

PENSACOLA, FLA.

E1

Handstamped Envelopes

106XU1	E1 5c **black**		*5,000.*
a.	10c (ms.) on 5c **black**		*5,250.*
	On patriotic cover		*28,000.*

PETERSBURG, VA.

A1

Typeset Adhesive

Ten varieties

Thick white paper

65X1	A1 5c **red** (shades)	*2,250.*	500.
	Pair	*5,000.*	*1,250.*
	Block of 4	*11,000.*	
	On cover		2,250.
	On patriotic cover		—
	Pair on cover		*12,500.*
	Used on cover with C.S.A. 5c #1 to make 10c rate		*57,500.*

Cancellation: blue town.

PITTSYLVANIA COURT HOUSE, VA.

A1

Typeset Adhesives

66X1 A1 5c **dull red,** wove paper *7,500. 9,000.*
Octagonally cut *7,000.*
On cover *40,000.*
On cover, octagonally cut *20,000.*
66X2 A1 5c **dull red,** laid paper *5,500.*
On cover —
Octagonally cut *4,500.*
On cover, octagonally cut *50,000.*

Cancellation: black town.

PLAINS OF DURA, GA.

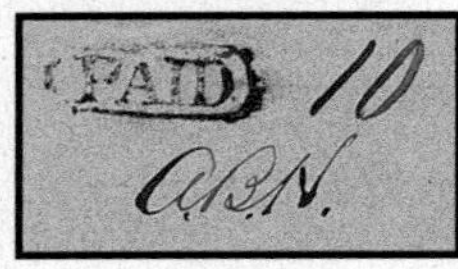
E1

Handstamped Envelopes, Ms. Initials

140XU1 E1 5c **black** —
140XU2 E1 10c **black** *5,000.*

No. 140XU2 is unique.

PLEASANT SHADE, VA.

A1

Typeset Adhesive
Five varieties

67X1 A1 5c **blue** *8,000. 20,000.*
On cover *40,000.*
Pair *13,500.*
Pair on cover *55,000.*
Block of 6 *42,500.*

Cancellation: blue town.

PLUM CREEK, TEX.

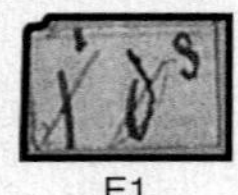
E1

Manuscript Adhesive

141X1 E1 10c **black,** *blue,* on cover —

The stamps have ruled lines with the value "10" in manuscript. Size and shape vary.

PORT GIBSON, MISS.

E1

Manuscript Signature

Handstamped Envelope, Ms Signature

142XU1 E1 5c **black** —

PORT LAVACA, TEX.

A1

Typeset Adhesive

107X1 A1 10c **black,** on cover *25,000.*

One example known. It is uncanceled on a postmarked cover.

RALEIGH, N. C.

E1

Handstamped Envelopes

68XU1 E1 5c **red** 400.
On patriotic cover 5,500.
68XU2 E1 5c **blue** *3,000.*

RHEATOWN, TENN.

A1

Typeset Adhesive
Three varieties

69X1 A1 5c **red** *6,000. 6,500.*
On cover, ms. cancel *20,000.*
On cover, tied by handstamp *37,500.*
Pair *15,000.*

Stamps normally were canceled in manuscript. One cover is known with stamp tied by red town postmark.

Cancellations: red town or black pen.

RICHMOND, TEX.

E1

Handstamped Envelopes or Letter Sheets

70XU1 E1 5c **red** 2,500.
a. 10c on 5c **red** *5,000.*
70XU2 E1 10c **red** 2,000.
a. 15c (ms.) on 10c **red** *5,000.*

RINGGOLD, GA.

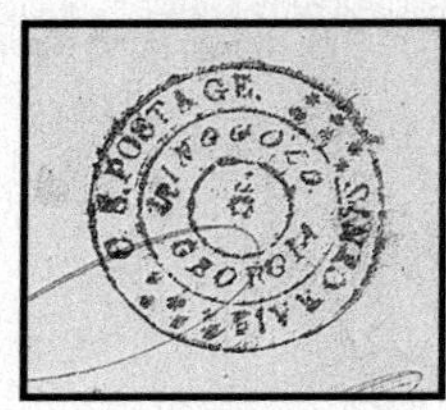
E1

Handstamped Envelope

71XU1 E1 5c **blue black** *8,500.*

RUTHERFORDTON, N. C.

A1

Handstamped Adhesive, Ms. "Paid 5cts"

72X1 A1 5c **black,** cut round, on cover (uncanceled) *60,000.*

No. 72X1 is unique.

SALEM, N. C.

E1

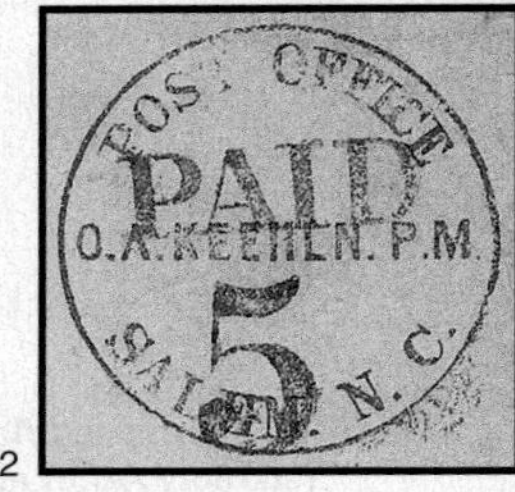

E2

Handstamped Envelopes

73XU1 E1 5c **black** 1,400.
73XU2 E1 10c **black** *3,500.*
73XU3 E2 5c **black** *2,250.*
a. 10c on 5c **black** *2,800.*

Reprints exist on various papers. They either lack the "Paid" and value or have them counterfeited.

Salem, Va.
See No. 74X1 under Liberty, Va.

SALISBURY, N. C.

E1

Press-printed Envelope (typeset)
Impressed at top left

75XU1 E1 5c **black,** *greenish* *15,000.*

One example known. Part of the envelope was torn away (now repaired), leaving part of design missing.

SAN ANTONIO, TEX.

E1

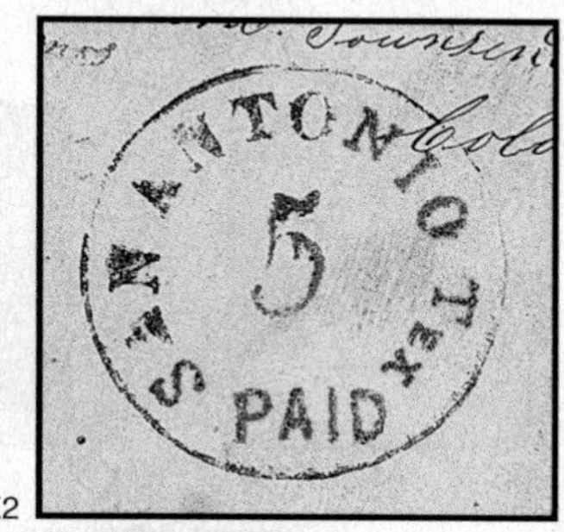
E2

Control

Handstamped Envelopes

76XU1	E1	10c **black**	500.	*2,000.*
76XU1A	E2	5c **black**		*13,000.*
76XU2	E2	10c **black**		*2,500.*

Black circle control mark is on front or back.
One example of No. 76XU1A is recorded.

SAVANNAH, GA.

E1

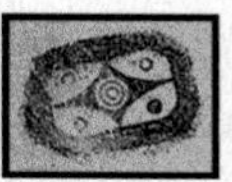
Control

E2

Handstamped Envelopes

101XU1	E1	5c **black**	400.
		On patriotic cover	*8,000.*
a.		10c on 5c **black**	1,500.
101XU2	E2	5c **black**	600.
a.		20c on 5c **black**	*2,000.*
101XU3	E1	10c **black**	750.
101XU4	E2	10c **black**	750.

Envelopes must have octagonal control mark. One example is known of No.101XU2a.

SELMA, ALA.

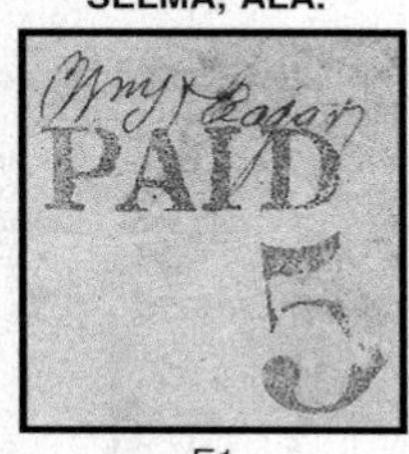
E1

Handstamped Envelopes; Signature in Ms.

77XU1	E1	5c **black**	*1,250.*
a.		10c on 5c **black**	*3,000.*
77XU2	E1	10c **black**	*2,500.*

Signature is that of Postmaster William H. Eagar.
See 3c 1861 Postmaster's Provisional No. 5AX1.

SPARTA, GA.

E1

Handstamped Envelopes

93XU1	E1	5c **red**	—	2,250.
93XU2	E1	10c **red**		*5,000.*

Only one example recorded of No. 93XU2.

SPARTANBURG, S. C.

A1

A2

Handstamped Adhesives
(on ruled or plain wove paper)

78X1	A1	5c **black,** cut to shape	
		Cut square	*27,500.*
		On cover, cut to shape	*20,000.*
		Pair on cover	*30,000.*
		On patriotic cover	*50,000.*
a.		"Paid" instead of denomination, revalued to 5c with "PAID" and "5" in small circle handstamps	—
78X2	A2	5c **black,** *bluish*	*4,000.*
		On cover	*12,500.*
78X3	A2	5c **black,** *brown*	*4,000.*
		On cover	*18,000.*

Among the Nos. 78X1-78X3 stamps, only one sound example of No. 78X1 is recorded cut square (one other stained and defective example is known), and only one No. 78X3 on cover is cut square. All other examples are cut to shape. The only recorded pair of No. 78X1 is on cover. The stamps are cut round, but are still connected. Only one example of No. 78X2 on cover is recorded. Part of the stamp is missing, and the cover is valued thus.

Cancellations: black "PAID," black town.

E1

Control

Handstamped Envelopes

78XU1 E1 10c **black** (control on reverse) *5,000.*

STATESVILLE, N. C.

E1

Handstamped Envelopes

79XU1	E1	5c **black**	*1,500.*
a.		10c on 5c **black**	*3,000.*

Unused examples of No. 79XU1 are reprints.

SUMTER, S. C.

E1

Handstamped Envelopes

80XU1	E1	5c **black**	500.	
a.		10c on 5c **black**		*900.*
80XU2	E1	10c **black**	600.	
a.		2c (ms.) on 10c **black**		*1,100.*

Used examples of Nos. 80XU1-80XU2 are indistinguishable from handstamped "Paid" covers.

TALBOTTON, GA.

E1

Handstamped Envelopes

94XU1	E1	5c **black**	900.
a.		10c on 5c **black**	*2,000.*
94XU2	E1	10c **black**	1,000.

TALLADEGA, ALA.

E1

Handstamped Envelopes

143XU1	E1	5c **black**	*1,500.*	—
143XU2	E1	10c **black**	*1,500.*	—

These same markings were used on handstamped "Paid" covers.

TELLICO PLAINS, TENN.

A1

Typeset Adhesives
Settings of two 5c and one 10c
Laid Paper

81X1	A1	5c **red**	2,500.	—
		On cover		*40,000.*
81X2	A1	10c **red**	4,500.	
a.		Se-tenant pair, Nos. 81X1 and 81X2	*7,500.*	
		Sheet of 3 (5c+5c+10c)	*11,000.*	

Cancellation: black pen.

THOMASVILLE, GA.

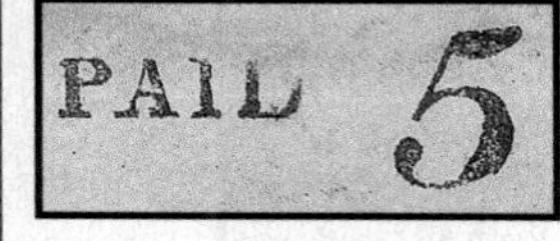
E1

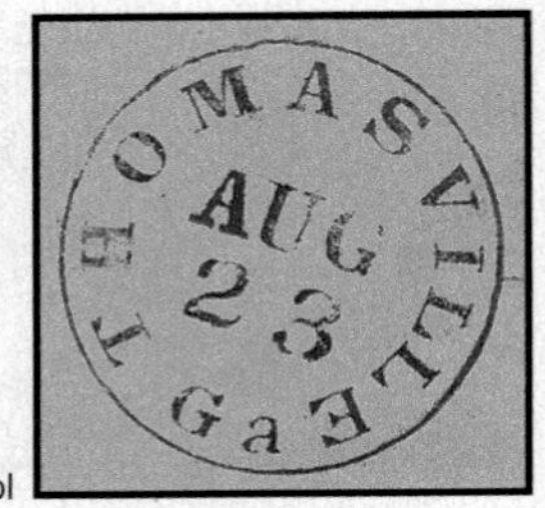

Control

Handstamped Envelopes

82XU1 E1 5c **black** 750.
On patriotic cover *5,000.*

On No. 82XU1, the control is on the reverse of the cover. The dated control is known with five different dates, including June 1, June 13, June 21, and August 23. The patriotic envelope is unique.

E2

82XU2 E2 5c **black** 1,000.

TULLAHOMA, TENN.

E1

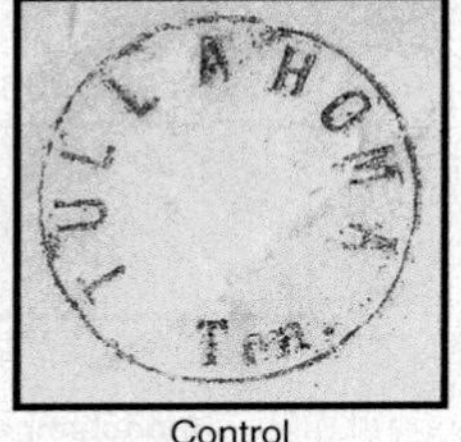

Control

Handstamped Envelope

111XU1 E1 10c **black** *6,000.*

The control appears either on the front or the back of the envelope.

TUSCALOOSA, ALA.

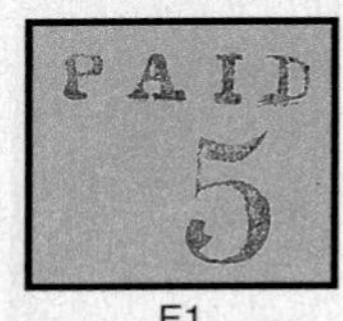

E1

Handstamped Envelopes

83XU1 E1 5c **black** 250.
83XU2 E1 10c **black** 250.

Used examples of Nos. 83XU1-83XU2 are indistinguishable from handstamped "Paid" covers. Some authorities question the use of E1 to produce provisional envelopes.

TUSCUMBIA, ALA.

E1

Handstamped Envelopes

84XU1 E1 5c **black** 4,000.
On patriotic cover 10,000.
84XU2 E1 5c **red** *5,000.*

UNIONTOWN, ALA.

A1

Typeset Adhesives
(settings of 4 (2x2), 4 varieties of each value)
Laid Paper

86X1 A1 2c **dark blue,** *gray blue,* on cover —
86X2 A1 2c **dark blue,** sheet of 4 *40,000.*
86X3 A1 5c **green,** *gray blue* *4,000.* *3,250.*
Pair —
On cover *15,000.*
86X4 A1 5c **green** *4,000.* *3,250.*
On cover *15,000.*
Pair on cover *22,500.*
86X5 A1 10c **red,** *gray blue* —
On cover *40,000.*

Two examples known of No. 86X1, both on cover (drop letters), one uncanceled and one pen canceled.

The only recorded examples of No. 86X2 are in a unique sheet of 4.

The item listed as No. 86X5 used is an uncanceled stamp on a large piece with part of addressee's name in manuscript.

Cancellation on Nos. 86X3-86X5: black town.

UNIONVILLE, S. C.

A1

Handstamped Adhesive
"PAID" and "5" applied separately
Paper with Blue Ruled Lines

87X1 A1 5c **black,** *grayish* —
On cover, uncanceled *17,500.*
On cover, tied —
Pair on patriotic cover *32,500.*

The pair on patriotic cover is the only pair recorded.

Cancellation: black town.

VALDOSTA, GA.

E1

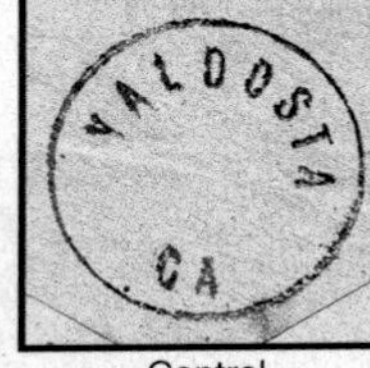

Control

E2

Handstamped Envelopes

100XU1 E1 10c **black** *9,000.*
100XU2 E2 5c +5c **black** —

The black circle control must appear on front of the No. 100XU2 envelope and on the back of the No. 100XU1 envelope.

There is one recorded cover each of Nos. 100XU1-100XU2.

VICTORIA, TEX.

A1

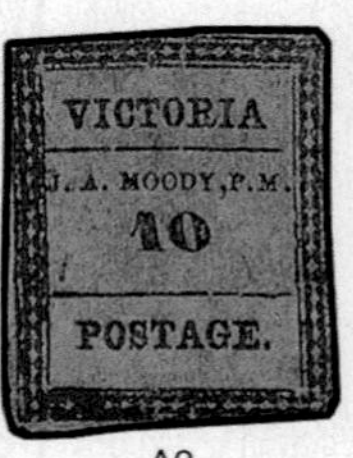

A2

Typeset Adhesives
Surface colored paper

88X1 A1 5c **red brown,** *green* *20,000.*
88X2 A1 10c **red brown,** *green* *22,500.*
On cover *115,000.*
88X3 A2 10c **red brown,** *green,* pelure paper *32,500.* *30,000.*

WALTERBOROUGH, S. C.

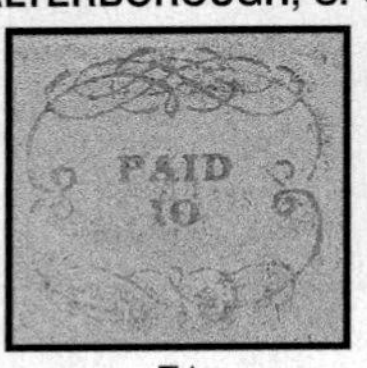

E1

Handstamped Envelopes

108XU1 E1 10c **black,** *buff* —
108XU2 E1 10c **carmine** *4,000.*

The existence of No. 108XU1 is in question. The editors would like to see authenticated evidence of its existence.

WARRENTON, GA.

E1

Handstamped Envelopes

89XU1 E1 5c **black** 2,100.
a. 10c (ms.) on 5c **black** 1,000.

Fakes of the Warrenton provisional marking based on the illustration shown are known on addressed but postally unused covers.

WASHINGTON, GA.

E1

Handstamped Envelope

117XU1 E1 10c **black** *2,000.*

Envelopes must have black circle postmark control on the back. Examples with the undated control on the front are not considered provisional unless a dated postmark is also present.

WEATHERFORD, TEX.

E1

Handstamped Envelopes
(woodcut with "PAID" inserted in type)

109XU1 E1 5c **black** *2,000.*
109XU2 E1 5c +5c **black** *11,000.*

One example is known of No. 109XU2.

WILKESBORO, N. C.

E1

Handstamped Envelope

147XU1 E1 5c **black,** revalued to 10c		—

No. 147XU1 is unique.

WINNSBOROUGH, S. C.

PAID 5

E1

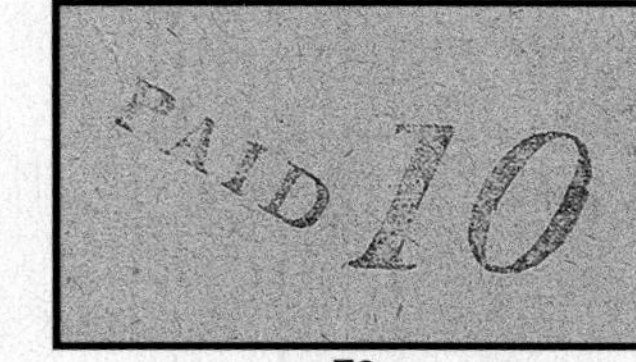

E2

Control

Handstamped Envelopes

97XU1 E1 5c **black**	2,000.
On patriotic cover	*3,750.*
97XU2 E2 10c **black**	*3,000.*

Envelopes must have black circle control on front or back.

WYTHEVILLE, VA.

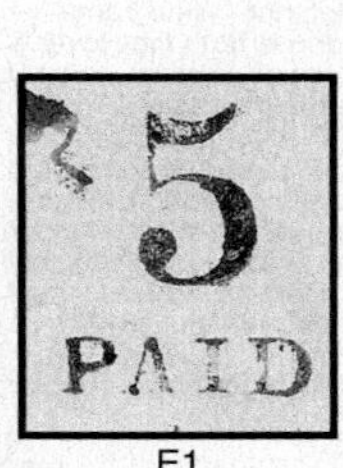

E1

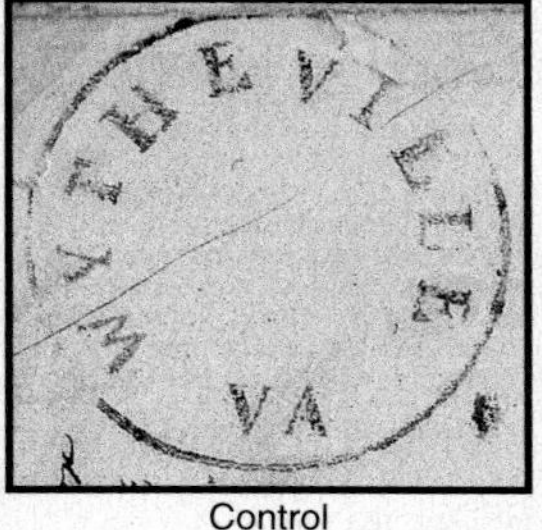

Control

Handstamped Envelope

114XU1 E1 5c **black**	900.

For later additions, listed out of numerical sequence, see:

#74X1, **Liberty, Va.**
#92XU1, **Huntsville, Tex.**
#93XU1, **Sparta, Ga.**
#94XU1, **Talbotton, Ga.**
#95XU1, **Cuthbert, GA**
#96XU1, **Lake City, Fla.**
#97XU1, **Winnsborough, S.C.**
#98XU1, **Galveston, Tex.**
#99XU1, **Christiansburg, Va.**
#100XU1, **Valdosta, Ga.**
#101XU1, **Savannah, Ga.**
#102XU1, **Griffin, Ga.**
#103XU1, **Courtland, Ala.**
#104XU1, **Fincastle, Va.**
#105XU1, **Micanopy, Fla.**
#106XU1, **Pensacola, Fla.**
#107X1, **Port Lavaca, Tex.**
#108XU1, **Walterborough, S.C.**
#109XU1, **Weatherford, Tex.**
#110XU1, **Jacksonville, Ala.**
#111XU1, **Tullahoma, Tenn.**
#112XU1, **Hamburgh, S.C.**
#113XU1, **Columbia, Tenn.**
#114XU1, **Wytheville, Va.**
#115X1, **Oakway, S.C.**
#116XU1, **Laurens Court House, S.C.**
#117XU1, **Washington, Ga.**
#118XU1, **Carolina City, N.C.**
#119XU1, **Colaparchee, Ga.**
#120XU1, **Forsyth, Ga.**
#121XU1, **Limestone Springs, S.C.**
#122XU1, **Balcony Falls, Va.**
#123XU1, **Barnwell Court House, S.C.**
#124XU1, **Bluffton, S.C.**
#125XU1, **Camden, S.C.**
#126XU1, **Cartersville, Ga.**
#127XU1, **Charlottesville, Va.**
#128XU1, **Fraziersville, S.C.**
#129XU1, **Gaston, N.C.**
#130XU1, **Harrisburgh, Tex.**
#132XU1, **Hollandale, Tex.**
#133XU1, **Isabella, Ga.**
#134XU1, **Jacksonville, Fla.**
#135XU1, **Lexington, Va.**
#136XU1, **Madison, Ga.**
#137XU1, **Madison Court House, Fla.**
#138XU1, **Milton, N.C.**
#139XU1, **Norfolk, Va.**
#140XU1, **Plains of Dura, Ga.**
#141X1, **Plum Creek, Tex.**
#142XU1, **Port Gibson, Miss.**
#143XU1, **Talladega, Ala.**
#144XU1, **Greenville, Tenn.**
#145XU1, **Mars Bluff, S.C.**
#146XU1, **Charlotte, N.C.**
#147XU1, **Wilkesboro, N.C.**
#148XU1, **Fort Valley, Ga.**
#149XU1, **Patterson, N.C.**
#150XU1, **Beaufort, S.C.**
#151XU1, **Mount Pleasant, N.C.**
#152XU1, **Oxford, N.C.**

CONFEDERATE STATES OF AMERICA, GENERAL ISSUES

Due to its tendency to damage the paper and the color of the stamps, the gum on most unused Confederate States stamps very often is removed. Values for unused examples of Nos. 1-5 (the lithographed issues), Nos. 6 and 7 (the typographed issues, but not including No. 6 printed by De La Rue and imported), Nos. 8-10 and 13 (the engraved issues), and both the Keatinge & Ball and Archer & Daly printings of Nos. 11 and 12 are for stamps without gum. The De La Rue printed Nos. 6 and 14 are valued both with original gum and without gum. All Confederate States unused and used stamps are valued in the grade of very fine, with fresh color and no faults. Unused stamps that are valued only without gum will sell for about the same prices if they have original gum and are very fine with fresh color, but stamps with original gum will sell for less if they have paper cracks or creases, staining, or other paper problems caused by gum deterioration.

For explanations of various terms used see the notes at the end of the postage listings.

Due to its tendency to damage the paper and color of the stamps, the gum on most (but not all) Confederate States stamps very often is removed. Except for the De La Rue-printed Nos. 6 and 14, which are valued both with original gum and without gum, unused values for all Confederate States stamps are for stamps without gum. Stamps with original gum sell for about the same prices, if the gum has not deteriorated and damaged the paper or stamp color.

Jefferson Davis — A1

All 5c Lithographs were printed by Hoyer & Ludwig, of Richmond, Va.

Stones A or B — First stones used. Earliest dated cancellation October 16, 1861. Plating not completed hence size of sheets unknown. These stones had imprints. Stamps from Stones A or B are nearly all in the olive green shade. Sharp, clear impressions. Distinctive marks are few and minute.

Stone 1 — Earliest dated cancellation October 18, 1861. Plating completed. Sheet consists of four groups of fifty varieties arranged in two panes of one hundred each without imprint. The first small printing was in olive green and later small printings appeared in light and dark green; the typical shade, however, is an intermediate shade of bright green. The impressions are clear though not as sharp as those from Stones A or B. Distinctive marks are discernible.

Stone 2 — Earliest dated cancellation December 2, 1861. Plating completed. Sheet consists of four groups of fifty varieties arranged in two panes of one hundred each without imprint. All shades other than olive green are known from this stone, the most common being a dull green. Poor impressions. Many noticeable distinctive marks.

1861 Litho. Soft Porous Paper *Imperf.*

Stone 2

1	A1 5c **green** (shades)	300.	175.
	bright green	350.	200.
	dull green	275.	175.
	On cover		300.
	Single on cover (overpaid drop letter)		500.
	On wallpaper cover		*1,800.*
	On prisoner's cover		—
	On prisoner's cover with U.S. #65		—
	On prisoner's cover with U.S. #U34		—
	On patriotic cover		2,500.
	Pair	600.	425.
	Pair on cover		500.
	Block of 4	1,750.	1,300.
	Pair with full horiz. gutter between		—
a.	5c **light green**	275.	175.
b.	5c **dark green**	375.	250.

VARIETIES

Spur on upper left scroll (Pos. 21)	425.	275.
Side margin copy showing initials (Pos. 41 or 50)	—	—
Misplaced transfer (clear twin impressions of lower left scrolls — pos. 1 entered over pos. 10)	—	—
Rouletted unofficially	500.	850.
On cover		*1,750.*
Pair on cover		*3,750.*

Cancellations

Blue town	+10.
Red town	+125.
Violet town	+150.
Green town	+175.
Orange town	+225.
Texas town	+35.
Arkansas town	+100.
Florida town	+110.
Kentucky town	+300.
Blue gridiron	+5.
Red gridiron	+50.
Blue concentric	+5.
Star or flowers	+125.
Numeral	+50.
"Paid"	+50.
"Steamboat"	+150.
Express Co.	+350.
Railroad	+300.
Pen Cancel	60.

Stone 1

1	A1 5c **green**	325.	200.
	bright green	350.	200.
	dull green	300.	200.
a.	5c **light green**	300.	200.
b.	5c **dark green**	375.	250.
c.	5c **olive green**	400.	250.
	On cover		300.
	On patriotic cover		2,500.
	Pair	750.	475.
	Pair on cover		600.

	Block of 4	1,650.	1,250.

VARIETIES

Acid flaw	350.	200.
Arrow between panes	600.	325.
Flaw on "at" of "States" (Pos. 38)	325.	225.

Cancellations

Blue town	+10.
Red town	+80.
Green town	+225.
Texas town	+45.
Arkansas town	+90.
Florida town	+110.
Georgia double straightline town	+350.
Kentucky town	+300.
October, 1861, year date	+40.
Blue gridiron	+5.
Red gridiron	+75.
Blue concentric	+5.
Numeral	+50.
"Paid"	+50.
"Steam"	+150.
"Steamboat"	+150.
Express Company	+350.
Railroad	+300.
Pen Cancel	75.

Stones A or B

1c	A1 5c **olive green**	425.	200.
	On cover		400.
	On patriotic cover		*5,000.*
	Pair	900.	450.
	Pair on cover		700.
	Block of 4	2,250.	1,300.

VARIETIES

White curl back of head	450.	275.
Imprint	775.	475.

Cancellations

Blue town	+10.
Red town	+150.
October, 1861, year date	+50.
Blue gridiron	+5.
Blue concentric	+5.
Numeral	+60.
"Paid"	+50.
"Steam"	+150.
Express Co.	+400.
Pen Cancel	90.

JOHN L. KIMBROUGH

CONFEDERATE STATES OF AMERICA

STAMPS & POSTAL HISTORY

CURRENCY

BUYING & SELLING

JOHN L. KIMBROUGH

10140 Wandering Way, Benbrook, Texas 76126

Phone (817) 249-2447

Fax (817) 249-5213

E-mail: JLKCSA@aol.com

www.csastamps.com

CSA • FSDA • TSDA • USPCS

Thomas Jefferson — A2

Hoyer & Ludwig — First stone used. Earliest dated cancellation November 8, 1861. Sheet believed to consist of four groups of fifty varieties each arranged in two panes of one hundred each with imprint at bottom of each pane. Two different imprints are known. Hoyer & Ludwig printings are always in a uniform shade of dark blue. Impressions are clear and distinct, especially so in the early printings. Plating marks are distinct.

J. T. Paterson & Co. — Earliest dated cancellation July 25, 1862. Sheet consists of four groups of fifty varieties each arranged in two panes of one hundred each with imprint at bottom of each pane. Two different imprints are known and at least one pane is known without an imprint. Wide range of shades. Impressions are less clear than those from the Hoyer & Ludwig stone. Paterson stamps show small vertical colored dash below the lowest point of the upper left triangle.

Stone "Y" — Supposedly made by J. T. Paterson & Co., as it shows the distinctive mark of that firm. Plating not completed hence size of sheet unknown. No imprint found. Color is either a light milky blue or a greenish blue. Impressions are very poor and have a blurred appearance. Stone Y stamps invariably show a large flaw at the back of the head as well as small vertical colored dash beneath the upper left triangle.

1861-62 Litho. Soft Porous Paper

Paterson

2	A2 10c **blue**	275.	180.
	On cover		325.
	On wallpaper cover		1,800.
	On patriotic cover		2,250.
	On prisoner's cover with U.S. #65		—
	Pair	650.	425.
	Pair on cover		950.
	Strip of 3 on cover		—
	Block of 4	1,750.	
	Horiz. pair, gutter btwn.	1,500.	
a.	10c **light blue**	300.	200.
b.	10c **dark blue**	700.	300.
c.	10c **indigo**	*5,000.*	*7,500.*
d.	Printed on both sides		*1,750.*

Two examples of No. 2d are recorded. One has a single inverted split impression on the reverse, and the other has a double impression, one inverted, on the reverse.

VARIETIES

Malformed "O" of "POSTAGE" (Pos. 25)	425.	240.
J. T. Paterson & Co. imprint	1,250.	1,250.

Cancellations

Blue town	+10.
Red town	+120.
Green town	+200.
Violet town	—
Texas town	+125.
Arkansas town	+275.
Florida town	+325.
July, 1862, date	+300.
Straight line town	+500.
Blue gridiron	+10.
Red gridiron	+75.
Blue concentric	+10.
Numeral	+80.
"Paid"	+75.
Star or flower	+150.
Railroad	+350.
Express Co.	+300.
Pen Cancel	80.

Hoyer

2b	A2 10c **dark blue**	650.	275.
	On cover		1,000.
	On wallpaper cover		2,000.
	On patriotic cover		3,000.
	On prisoner's cover with U.S. #65		—
	Pair	1,300.	900.
	Pair on cover		1,500.
	Strip of 3 on cover		3,500.
	Block of 4	2,750.	—
d.	Printed on both sides	—	

Specialists have questioned the existence of No. 2bd, the Hoyer & Ludwig printed on both sides. The editors would like to see authenticated evidence of its existence.

VARIETIES

Malformed "T" of "TEN" (Pos. 4)	750.	325.
"G" and "E" of "POSTAGE" joined (Pos. 10)	750.	325.
Circular flaw, upper left star (Pos. 11)	750.	325.
Third spiked ornament at right, white (Pos. 45)	750.	375.
Hoyer & Ludwig imprint	1,000.	850.
Rouletted unofficially		—
On cover		*3,250.*

Cancellations

Blue town	+30.
Red town	+100.
Texas town	+125.
Arkansas town	+275.
Florida town	+325.
Kentucky town	+400.
Nov., 1861, date	+300.
Straight line town	+500.
Blue gridiron	+10.
Red gridiron	+75.
Blue concentric	+10.
Numeral	+75.
"Paid"	+50.
Railroad	+350.
Express Company	+300.
Pen Cancel	95.

Stone Y

2e	A2 10c **light milky blue**	1,250.	325.
	greenish blue	1,400.	375.
	On cover		400.
	On wallpaper cover		1,800.
	On patriotic cover		2,100.
	Pair	3,000.	—
	Block of 4	*10,000.*	2,500.

Cancellations

Blue town	+10.
Red town	+125.
Violet town	+75.
Green town	+300.
Texas town	+125.
Arkansas town	+275.
Florida town	—
Straight line town	+500.
Blue gridiron	+10.
Red gridiron	+75.
Blue concentric	+10.
Numeral	+100.
"Paid"	+100.
Pen Cancel	110.

Andrew Jackson — A3

Sheet consists of four groups of fifty varieties arranged in two panes of 100 each.

One stone only was used. Printed by Hoyer & Ludwig, of Richmond, Va. Issued to prepay drop letter and circular rates. Strips of five used to prepay regular 10c rate, which was changed from 5c on July 1, 1862. Earliest known cancellation, March 21, 1862.

1862 (March?) Soft Porous Paper Litho.

3	A3 2c **green**	1,000.	750.
	light green	1,000.	750.
	dark green	1,000.	800.
	dull yellow green	1,350.	900.
	On cover		*3,500.*
	Pair on cover (double circular rate)		*5,000.*
	Strip of 5 on cover		*13,500.*
	On patriotic cover		—
	Pair	2,100.	—
	Block of 4	6,000.	5,000.
	Block of 5	7,000.	*5,500.*
a.	2c **bright yellow green**	*2,000.*	—
	On cover		*4,000.*
	Pair		—

VARIETIES

Diagonal half used as 1c with unsevered pair, on cover (unique)		*15,000.*
Horiz. pair, vert. gutter between	—	—
Pair, mark between stamps (btwn. Pos. 4 and 5)	2,200.	2,100.
Mark above upper right corner (Pos. 30)	1,050.	850.
Mark above upper left corner (Pos. 31)	1,050.	850.
Acid flaw	1,050.	800.

Cancellations

Blue town	+800.
Red town	+800.
Arkansas town	—
Texas town	+1,250.
Blue gridiron	+250.
"Paid"	—
Express Company	—
Railroad	+3,000.
Pen Cancel	375.

1862 Soft Porous Paper Litho.

Stone 2 — First stone used for printing in blue. Plating is the same as Stone 2 in green. Earliest dated cancellation Feb. 26, 1862. Printings from Stone 2 are found in all shades of blue. Rough, coarse impressions are typical of printings from Stone 2.

Stone 3 — A new stone used for printings in blue only. Earliest dated cancellation April 10, 1862. Sheet consists of four groups of fifty varieties each arranged in two panes of one hundred each without imprint. Impressions are clear and sharp, often having a proof-like appearance, especially in the deep blue printing. Plating marks, while not so large as on Stone 2 are distinct and clearly defined.

Stone 2

4	A1 5c **blue**	225.	125.
	light blue	250.	140.
	Pair	625.	450.

Block of 4 1,300. *2,000.*
Horiz. pair, wide gutter between 1,250. —
Vert. pair, narrow gutter between —
On cover 275.
Single on cover (overpaid drop letter) 400.
Pair on cover 450.
On wallpaper cover 1,250.
On patriotic cover *2,500.*
On prisoner's cover —
On prisoner's cover with U.S. #65 —
a. 5c **dark blue** 275. 175.
b. 5c **light milky blue** 350. 200.

VARIETIES

Spur on upper left scroll (Pos. 21) 250. 150.
Thin hard paper — 150.
Misplaced transfer (faint twin impression of second lower left scroll at left — pos. 2 entered over pos. 10) —

Cancellations

Blue town +20.
Red town +100.
Orange town +400.
Texas town +300.
Arkansas town +325.
Florida town +200.
Straight line town +350.
Blue gridiron +10.
Red gridiron +85.
Star or Flowers +150.
Numeral +85.
Railroad —
"Paid" +50.
"Steamboat" +400.
Express Company —
"Way" +250.
Pen Cancel 65.

Stone 3

4 A1 5c **blue** 750. 250.
a. 5c **dark blue** 800. 275.
b. 5c **light milky blue** 750. 250.
Pair 1,600. 550.
Block of 4 3,750. *2,000.*
On cover 500.
Pair on cover 625.
On patriotic cover *2,750.*
Horiz. pair, wide gutter btwn. —
Vert. pair, narrow gutter between —

Stone 3 stamps can be positively identified by plating only. Color or shade is not a determinant.

VARIETIES

Tops of "C" and "E" of "cents" joined by flaw (Pos. 33) 850. 325.
"Flying bird" above lower left corner ornament (Pos. 19) 850. 325.

Cancellations

Blue town +40.
Red town +100.
Texas town +300.
Arkansas town +325.
Straight line town +325.
Blue gridiron +10.
Star or Flowers +150.
"Paid" +50.
Pen Cancel 90.

1862 (March?) Soft Porous Paper Litho.

Settings of fifty varieties repeated.

Printed by Hoyer & Ludwig, of Richmond, Va. One stone used, being the same as that used for the Hoyer & Ludwig 10c value in blue. Color change occured probably in March, 1862.

There are many shades of this stamp. The carmine is a very dark, bright color and should not be confused with the deeper shade of rose.

Earliest known cancellation, March 10, 1862. The earliest date of usage of the carmine shade is May 1, 1862.

5 A2 10c **rose** (shades) 2,400. 400.
dull rose 2,200. 400.
brown rose 2,650. 800.
deep rose 2,500. 550.
carmine rose 2,650. 850.
On cover 750.
On wallpaper cover *2,000.*
On patriotic cover *3,000.*
On prisoner's cover *5,500.*
On prisoner's cover with U.S. #65 —
Pair 4,900. 1,500.
Strip of 3 — *3,000.*
Block of 4 *12,000.* *4,500.*
a. 10c **carmine** *3,750.* *1,900.*
On cover *5,000.*
On patriotic cover —

VARIETIES

Malformed "T" of "TEN" (Pos. 4) 1,850. 600.
"G" and "E" of "POSTAGE" joined (Pos. 10) 1,850. 600.
Circular flaw, upper left star (Pos. 11) 1,950. 675.
Third spiked ornament at right, white (Pos. 45) 1,950. 675.
Scratched stone (occurring on Pos. 40, 39, 49 and 48, one pane) 1,950. 925.
Imprint 1,750.
Horiz. pair, vert. gutter between —

Cancellations

Blue town +50.
Red town +125.
Green town +350.
Texas town +125.
Arkansas town —
Straight line town +700.
April, 1862, year date —
Blue gridiron +50.
Black concentric +50.
Blue concentric +50.
"Paid" —
Railroad —
Express Company —
Pen Cancel 200.

Jefferson Davis — A4

Plate of 400 in four panes of 100 each. No imprint.

No. 6 represents London printings from De La Rue & Co., a number of sheets being sent over by blockade runners. Fine clear impressions. The gum is light and evenly distributed. Exact date of issue unknown. Earliest known cancellation, April 16, 1862.

Typographed by De La Rue & Co. in London, England

1862 (April) Hard Medium Paper

6 A4 5c **light blue** 18. 28.
No gum 9.
Single on cover used before July 1, 1862 150.
Single on cover (overpaid drop letter) 250.
Single on patriotic cover used before July 1, 1862 2,000.
Single on prisoner's cover used before July 1, 1862 —
On wallpaper cover 1,200.
On patriotic cover 1,200.
On prisoner's cover —
On prisoner's cover with U.S. #65 —
Pair 40. 75.
Pair on cover 100.
Pair on patriotic cover *2,000.*
Block of 4 90. 290.
Block of 4 on cover 900.

Cancellations

Blue town +7.
Red town +55.
Green town +75.
Texas town +65.
Arkansas town +100.
Straight line town +225.
Blue gridiron +2.
Red gridiron +35.
Blue concentric +7.
Express Company +350.
Railroad +250.
"Paid" +50.

1862 (July) Typo. Thin to Thick Paper

Plate of 400 in four panes of 100 each. No imprint.

Locally printed by Archer & Daly of Richmond, Va., from plates made in London, England, by De La Rue & Co. Printed on both imported English and local papers. Earliest known cancellation, July 13, 1862.

No. 7 shows coarser impressions than No. 6, and the color is duller and often blurred. Gum is light or dark and unevenly distributed.

7 A4 5c **blue** (De La Rue thin paper) 22. 22.
Single on cover (overpaid drop letter) 200.
On wallpaper cover 1,200.
On patriotic cover 1,200.
On prisoner's cover —
On prisoner's cover with U.S. #65 *2,500.*
Pair 50. 48.
Pair on cover 95.
Block of 4 110. 350.
Block of 4 on cover 800.
Eight on cover (Trans-Miss. rate) *4,000.*
a. 5c **deep blue** 28. 35.
b. Printed on both sides *2,500.* *1,400.*
Pair *3,000.*
Pair on cover *4,000.*

VARIETIES

White tie (UR30), De La Rue paper 200. 250.
Local paper (thick) 50. 55.
White tie (UR30), local paper (thick) *450.* *450.*
White tie on cover 400.
Vert. plate scratch at right — —
Horiz. pair, vert. gutter between, De La Rue thin paper 200.
Horiz. pair, vert. gutter between, thick local paper *300.*

Cancellations

Blue town +7.
Red town +75.
Brown town +30.
Violet town +110.
Green town +150.
Texas town +90.
Arkansas town +110.
Florida town +140.
Straight line town +250.
Blue gridiron +2.
Red gridiron +60.
Blue concentric +7.
Railroad +250.
Express Company +400.
Design (stars, etc.) +75.
"Paid" +50.

The unissued 10c design A4 was privately printed in various colors for philatelic purposes. (See note below No. 14.)

Counterfeits of the 10c exist.

Andrew Jackson — A5

Sheet of 200 (two panes of 100 each).

One plate. Printed by Archer & Daly of Richmond, Va. Earliest known cancellation. Apr. 21, 1863. Issued to prepay drop letter and circular rates. Strips of five used to prepay regular 10c rate.

1863 (April) Soft Porous Paper Engraved

8 A5 2c **brown red** 75. *350.*
a. 2c **pale red** 90. *450.*
Single on cover, #8 or 8a *1,500.*
On prisoner's cover —
On prisoner's cover with U.S. #65 —
Pair 160. *1,000.*
Pair on cover *3,250.*
On wallpaper cover —
Block of 4 375. —
Block of 5 —
Strip of 5 on cover *4,500.*
Strip of 5 on wallpaper cover —
Strip of 10 on cover —
Double transfer 130. *450.*
Horiz. pair, vert. gutter between 325.

Cancellations

Blue town +35.
Red town +225.
Violet town +300.
Army of Tenn. —
Blue gridiron +35.
Black numeral —
Railroad +325.
Pen cancel 150.

Jefferson Davis "TEN CENTS" — A6

One plate of 200 subjects all of which were probably recut as every example examined to date shows distinct recutting. Plating not completed.

Printed by Archer & Daly of Richmond, Va. First printings in milky blue. First issued in April, 1863. Earliest known cancellation, April 23, 1863.

1863, Apr. Soft Porous Paper Engraved

9 A6 10c **blue** 950. 500.
a. 10c **milky blue** (first printing) 1,050. 550.
b. 10c **gray blue** 1,050. 600.
On cover 1,500.
On wallpaper cover *4,000.*
On patriotic cover *3,500.*
On prisoner's cover —
On prisoner's cover with U.S. #65 —
Pair 2,000. 2,100.
Pair on cover *3,000.*
Block of 4 *5,250.*
Four stamps on one cover (Trans-Mississippi rate) *13,500.*
Curved lines outside the labels at top and bottom are broken in the middle (Pos. 63R) 1,050. 750.
Double transfer 1,100. 950.
Damaged plate 1,200. 1,050.

Cancellations

Blue town +25.
Red town +150.
Green town +600.
Violet town —
Straight line town +500.
April, 1863, year date —
Black gridiron +25.
Blue gridiron +50.
Red gridiron +200.
Railroad +400.
Circle of wedges +1,250.
Pen Cancel 275.

Frame Line "10 CENTS" — A6a

Printed by Archer & Daly of Richmond, Va.

One copper plate of 100 subjects, all but one of which were recut. Earliest known use April 19, 1863.

Stamp design same as Die A (Pos. 11).

Values are for stamps showing parts of lines on at least 3 of 4 sides. Used stamps showing 4 complete lines sell for 400%-500% of the values given. Unused stamps showing 4 complete lines are exceedingly rare (only two recorded), and the sound example is valued at $35,000.

1863, Apr. — Soft Porous Paper — Engraved

		Unused	Used
10	A6a 10c **blue**	5,500.	2,100.
a.	10c **milky blue**	5,500.	2,100.
b.	10c **greenish blue**	6,000.	2,100.
c.	10c **dark blue**	6,000.	2,100.
	On cover		*3,250.*
	On wallpaper cover		*5,000.*
	On patriotic cover		*10,000.*
	On prisoner's cover		*7,250.*
	On prisoner's cover with U.S. #65		—
	Pair	*12,500.*	*6,250.*
	Pair on cover		*7,250.*
	Block of 4	*25,000.*	
	Strip of 4	*25,000.*	
	Strip of 6	—	*21,500.*
	Strip of 7	*47,500.*	
	Double transfer (Pos. 74)	6,250.	2,200.

Cancellations

Blue town	+100.
Red town	+500.
Straight line town	+750.
April, 1863, year date	—
Blue gridiron	+100.
Pen Cancel	1,000.

No Frame Line "10 CENTS" (Die A) — A7

There are many slight differences between A7 (Die A) and A8 (Die B), the most noticeable being the additional line outside the ornaments at the four corners of A8 (Die B).

Stamps were first printed by Archer & Daly, of Richmond, Va. In 1864 the plates were transferred to the firm of Keatinge & Ball in Columbia, S. C., who made further printings from them. Two plates, each with two panes of 100, numbered 1 and 2. First state shows numbers only, later states show various styles of Archer & Daly imprints, and latest show Keatinge & Ball imprints. Archer & Daly stamps show uniformly clear impressions and a good quality of gum evenly distributed (Earliest known cancellation, April 21, 1863); Keatinge & Ball stamps generally show filled in impressions in a deep blue, and the gum is brown and unevenly distributed. (Earliest known cancellation, Oct. 4, 1864). These notes also apply to No. 12.

1863-64 — Thick or Thin Paper — Engraved

		Unused	Used
11	A7 10c **blue**	18.	*20.*
	deep blue, Keatinge & Ball ('64)	17.	*35.*
	On cover		125.
	Single on cover (overpaid drop letter)		200.
	On wallpaper cover		1,200.
	On patriotic cover		1,000.
	On prisoner's cover		750.
	On prisoner's cover with U.S. #65		2,500.
	On cover, dp. blue (K. & B.) ('64)		200.
	On wallpaper cover (K. & B.)		1,250.
	On prisoner's cover (K. & B.) with U.S. #65 ('64)		—
	Pair	40.	*45.*
	Pair on cover		275.
	Block of 4	85.	350.
	Strip of 4 on cover (Trans-Mississippi rate)		*4,000.*
	Margin block of 12, Archer & Daly impt. & P#	450.	
	Margin block of 12, Keatinge & Ball impt. & P#	425.	
a.	10c **milky blue**	55.	60.
b.	10c **dark blue**	25.	30.
c.	10c **greenish blue**	30.	50.
d.	10c **green**	85.	*80.*
e.	Officially perforated 12½ (Archer & Daly printing)	400.	350.
	On cover		*900.*
	On wallpaper cover		—
	Pair	800.	600.
	Pair on cover		*2,750.*
	Block of 4	1,750.	*6,000.*

VARIETIES

Printed on paper with horiz. "textile marks" (lines)	*50.*	*60.*
Horiz. pair, vert. gutter between	125.	
Double transfer	75.	100.
Roulettted unofficially	600.	500.
On cover		800.

Cancellations

Blue town	+5.
Red town	+35.
Orange town	+110.
Brown town	+60.
Green town	+200.
Violet town	+100.
Texas town	+60.
Arkansas town	+125.
Florida town	+200.
Straight line town	+350.
Army of Tenn.	+300.
April, 1863 year date	+75.
"FREE"	+250.
Blue gridiron	+5.
Black concentric circles	+10.
Star	+100.
Crossroads	+150.
"Paid"	+100.
Numeral	+100.
Railroad	+175.
Steamboat	+1,500.

Jefferson Davis (Die B) — A8

Plates bore Nos. 3 and 4, otherwise notes on No. 11 apply.

Earliest known use: Archer & Daly — May 1, 1863; Keatinge & Ball — Sept. 4, 1864.

1863-64 — Thick or Thin Paper — Engraved

		Unused	Used
12	A8 10c **blue**	22.	25.
	deep blue, Keatinge & Ball ('64)	21.	40.
	On cover		135.
	Single on cover (overpaid drop letter)		200.
	On wallpaper cover		1,200.
	On patriotic cover		1,250.
	On prisoner's cover		750.
	On prisoner's cover with U.S. #65		2,500.
	On cover, dp. blue (K. & B.) ('64)		130.
	Pair	48.	55.
	Pair on cover		200.
	Block of 4	110.	300.
	Strip of 4 on cover (Trans-Mississippi rate)		*4,000.*
	Margin block of 12, Archer & Daly impt. & P#	475.	
	Margin block of 12, Keatinge & Ball impt. & P#	425.	
a.	10c **milky blue**	55.	60.
b.	10c **light blue**	21.	22.
c.	10c **greenish blue**	40.	*50.*
d.	10c **dark blue**	24.	25.
e.	10c **green**	150.	140.
f.	Officially perforated 12½ (Archer & Daly printing)	400.	375.
	On cover		*900.*
	Pair	850.	600.
	Pair on cover		—
	Block of 4	2,000.	

VARIETIES

Printed on paper with horiz. "textile marks" (lines)	*50.*	*75.*
Horiz. pair, vert. gutter between	125.	
Double transfer	95.	110.
Roulettted unofficially	—	375.
On cover		850.

Cancellations

Blue town	+5.
Red town	+35.
Brown town	+90.
Green town	+120.
Violet town	+85.
Texas town	+125.
Arkansas town	+150.
Florida town	+200.
Straight line town	+400.
Army of Tenn.	+350.
May, 1863, year date	+60.
Blue gridiron	+5.
Black concentric circles	+10.
Railroad	+175.

George Washington — A9

One plate which consisted of two panes of 100 each. First printings were from plates with imprint in Old English type under each pane, which was later removed. Printed on paper of varying thickness and in many shades of green. This stamp was also used as currency. Earliest known cancellation, June 1, 1863. Forged cancellations exist.

1863 (June?) — Engraved by Archer & Daly

		Unused	Used
13	A9 20c **green**	45.	*400.*
	On cover		*1,250.*
	On wallpaper cover		*2,000.*
	On prisoner's cover		*4,000.*
	On prisoner's cover with U.S. #65		*5,000.*
	Pair	100.	*900.*
	Pair on cover (non-Trans-Mississippi rate)		*4,750.*
	Pair on cover (Trans-Mississippi rate)		*3,000.*
	Block of 4	200.	*3,500.*
	Strip of 4 with imprint	425.	
	Block of 8 with imprint	1,050.	
a.	20c **yellow green**	80.	*450.*
b.	20c **dark green**	65.	*500.*
	Short transfer at right	130.	
c.	20c **bluish green**	100.	—
d.	Diagonal half used as 10c on cover		*1,400.*
	Diagonal half on prisoner's cover		—
	Diagonal half on wallpaper cover		*11,500.*
e.	Horizontal half used as 10c on cover		*2,500.*

VARIETIES

Horizontal pair with gutter between	350.	
Double transfer, 20 doubled (Pos. 24L and 35R)	300.	—
"20" on forehead	*3,000.*	—
Roulettted unofficially		*1,100.*
On cover		*3,750.*

Cancellations

Blue town	+50.
Red town	+200.
Violet town	—
Texas town	+100.
Arkansas town	+400.
Tennessee town	+1,000.
Railroad	—

John C. Calhoun — A10

Typographed by De La Rue & Co., London, England

1862

14	A10 1c **orange**	110.
	No gum	60.
	Pair	225.
	Block of 4	475.
a.	1c **deep orange**	145.
	No gum	85.

No. 14 was never put in use.

Upon orders from the Confederate Government, De La Rue & Co. of London, England, prepared Two Cents and Ten Cents typographed plates by altering the One Cent (No. 14) and the Five Cents (Nos. 6-7) designs previously made by them. Stamps were never officially printed from these plates although privately made prints exist in various colors.

Counterfeits

In 1935 a set of 12 lithographed imitations, later known as the "Springfield facsimiles," appeared in plate form. They are in approximately normal colors on yellowish soft wove paper of modern manufacture.

PROOFS

1861

1P5	5c **green,** plate on wove paper	*1,750.*
2TC5	10c Plate on wove paper (stone Y)	
a.	**black**	*4,500.*
2P5	10c **blue,** plate on wove paper	*1,750.*

1862

6TC1c	5c Die on wove paper	
e.	**dark blue**	1,000.
f.	**black**	1,000.
6TC1d	5c Die on glazed card	
e.	**black**	900.
f.	**pink**	*2,000.*
6TC5	5c Plate on wove paper	
a.	**gray blue**	600.
6P1d	5c **light blue,** die on glazed card	600.
b.	5c **blue** & 1c **orange,** 6P1+14P1 composite die proof on 20x90mm glazed card	*6,500.*
6P5	5c **light blue,** plate on wove paper	150.
	Pair with gutter between	375.
7TC4	5c Plate on thin card	
a.	**carmine**	1,150.
7TC5	5c Plate on wove paper	
a.	**carmine**	1,750.

1863

8TC1c	2c Die on wove paper	
e.	**black**	3,000.
f.	**blue**	3,750.

Nos. 8TC1ab and 8TC1ac have a frame line around the design.

9TC1c	10c Die on wove paper	
	e. **black**	1,500.
11TC1c	10c Die on wove paper	
	e. **black**	—
12P7	10c **deep blue,** plate on thick ribbed paper	750.
13TC1c	20c Die on wove paper	
	e. **red brown**	*4,000.*
13P5a	20c **green,** die on wove paper	*4,000.*

1862

14TC1d	1c Die on glazed card	
	e. **black**	*2,250.*
14TC5	1c Plate on wove paper	
	a. **light yellow brown**	500.
14P1b	1c **orange,** die on glazed card	*2,750.*

SPECIMENS

6s	5c **blue,** "SPECIMEN" diagonal	*7,000.*
14s	1c **orange,** "SPECIMEN" diagonal	*7,000.*
	a. "SPECIMEN" horizontal	—

Nos. 6s and 14s are together on a page originally from the De La Rue archives.

Essay Die Proofs

In working up the final dies, proofs of incomplete designs in various stages were made. Usually dated in typeset lines, they are very rare. Others, of the 10c (No. 12) and the 20c (No. 13) were proofs made as essays from the dies. They are deeply engraved and printed in deep shades of the issued colors, but show only small differences from the stamps as finally issued. All are very rare.

Explanatory Notes

The following notes by Lawrence L. Shenfield explain the various routes, rates and usages of the general issue Confederate stamps.

"Across the Lines" Letters Carried by Private Express Companies

Adams Express Co. and American Letter Express Company Handstamps Used on "Across the Lines" Letters

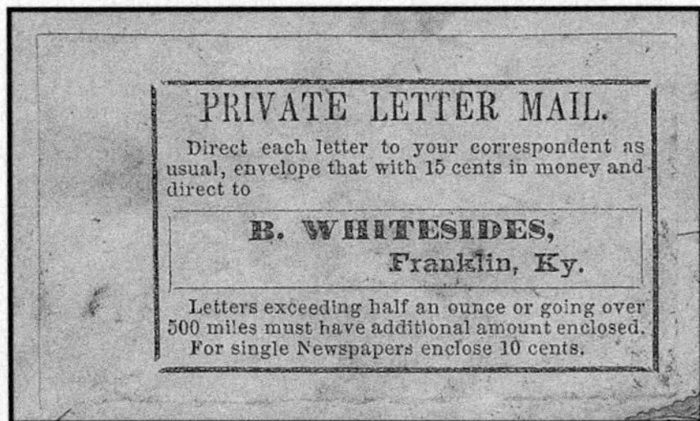
PRIVATE LETTER MAIL.

Direct each letter to your correspondent as usual, envelope that with 15 cents in money and direct to

B. WHITESIDES,
Franklin, Ky.

Letters exceeding half an ounce or going over 500 miles must have additional amount enclosed. For single Newspapers enclose 10 cents.

B. Whitesides Label

About two months after the outbreak of the Civil War, in June, 1861, postal service between North and South and vice versa was carried on largely by Adams Express Company, and the American Letter Express Company. Northern terminus for the traffic was Louisville, Ky.; Southern terminus was Nashville, Tenn. Letters for transmission were delivered to any office of the express company, together with a fee, usually 20c or 25c per ½ ounce to cover carriage. The express company messengers carried letters across the lines and delivered them to their office on the other side, where they were deposited in the Government mail for transmission to addressees, postage paid out of the fee charged. Letters from North to South, always enclosed in 3c U.S. envelopes, usually bear the handstamp of the Louisville office of the express company, and in addition the postmark and "Paid 5" of Nashville, Tenn., indicating its acceptance for delivery at the Nashville Post Office. Letters from South to North sometimes bear the origin postmark of a Southern post office, but more often merely the handstamp of the Louisville express company office applied as the letters cleared through Louisville. The B. Whitesides South to North cover bears a "Private Letter Mail" label. In addition, these covers bear the 3c 1857 U.S. adhesive stamp, cancelled with the postmark and grid of Louisville, Ky., where they went into the Government mail for delivery. Some across-the-lines letters show the handstamp of various express company offices, according to the particular routing the letters followed. On August 26, 1861, the traffic ceased by order of the U.S. Post Office Dept. (Values are for full covers bearing the usual Louisville, Ky., or Nashville, Tenn., handstamps of the express company. Unusual express office markings are rarer and worth more.)

North to South 3c U.S. Envelope, Adams Exp. Co. Louisville, Ky., handstamp	*1,500.*
North to South 3c U.S. Envelope, American Letter Express Co., Ky., handstamp	*2,100.*
South to North 3c 1857, Adams Exp. Co., Louisville, Ky., handstamp	*1,750.*
South to North 3c 1857, American Letter Exp. 250, Nashville, Tenn., handstamp	*2,500.*
South to North 3c 1861, Adams Exp. Co., Louisville, Ky., handstamp	*3,250.*
South to North 3c 1857, B. Whitesides, Franklin, Ky., label	*16,500.*

Blockade-Run Letters from Europe to the Confederate States

Charleston "STEAM-SHIP" in Oval Handstamp

As the Federal Fleet gradually extended its blockade of the Confederate States coastal regions, the South was forced to resort to blockade runners to carry letters to and from outside ports. These letters were all private-ship letters and never bore a foreign stamp if from Europe, nor a Confederate stamp if to Europe. The usual route from Europe was via a West Indies port, Nassau, Bahamas; Hamilton, Bermuda, or Havana, into the Southern ports of Wilmington, N.C. and Charleston, S.C. More rarely such letters came in to Savannah, Mobile and New Orleans. Letters from Europe are the only ones which are surely identified by their markings. They bore either the postmark of Wilmington, N.C., straightline "SHIP" and "12", "22", "32", etc., in manuscript; or the postmark of Charleston, S. C., "STEAMSHIP" in oval, and "12", "22", "32", etc., in manuscript. Very rarely Charleston used a straightline "SHIP" instead of "STEAMSHIP" in oval. All such letters were postage due; the single letter rate of 12c being made up of 2c for the private ship captain plus 10c for the regular single letter Confederate States rate. Over-weight letters were 22c (due), 32c, 42c, etc. A few examples are known on which Confederate General Issue stamps were used, usually as payment for forwarding postage. Covers with such stamps, or with the higher rate markings, 22c, 32, etc., are worth more.

Values are for full covers in fine condition.

Charleston, S.C. "6" handstamp	*2,500.*
Charleston, S.C., postmark, "STEAM—SHIP," and "12" in ms.	*3,000.*
Charleston, S.C., postmark, "SHIP," and "12" in ms.	*3,000.*
Wilmington, N.C., postmark, "SHIP," and "12" in ms.	*3,000.*
Savannah, Ga., postmark "SHIP," and "7" in ms. (*)	*4,000.*
New Orleans, La. postmark, "SHIP" and "10" in ms.	*5,000.*

(* 7c rate: 5c postage before July 1, 1862, plus 2c for ship captain.)

Express Company Mail in the Confederacy

Southern Express Company Handstamps

Shortly after the outbreak of war in 1861, the Adams Express Company divisions operating in the South were forced to suspend operations and turned their Southern lines over to a new company organized under the title Southern Express Company. This express did the bulk of the express business in the Confederacy despite the continued opposition of the Post Office Dept. of the C.S.A. and the ravages of the contending armies upon railroads. Other companies operating in the Confederacy were: South Western Express Co. (New Orleans), Pioneer Express Company, White's Southern Express (only one example known) and some local expresses of limited operation. The first three used handstamps of various designs usually bearing the city name of the office. Postal regulation necessitated the payment of regular Confederate postal rates on letters carried by express companies, express charges being paid in addition. Important letters, particularly money letters, were entrusted to these express companies as well as goods and wares of all kinds. The express rates charged for letters are not known; probably they varied depending upon the difficulty and risk of transmittal. Covers bearing stamps and express company handstamps are very rare.

Prisoner-of-War and Flag-of-Truce Letters

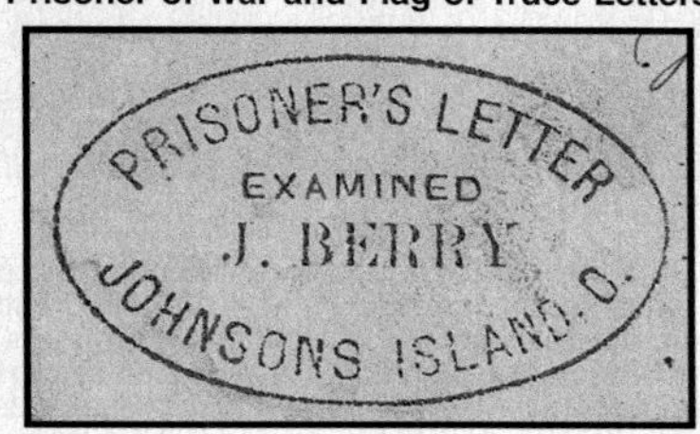

Prison Censor Handstamps

By agreement between the United States and the Confederate States, military prisoners and imprisoned civilians of both sides were permitted to send censored letters to their respective countries. Such letters, if from North to South, usually bore a U.S. 3c 1861 adhesive, postmarked at a city near the prison, to pay the postage to the exchange ground near Old Point Comfort, Va.; and a 10c Confederate stamp, canceled at Richmond, Va. (or "due" handstamp) to pay the Confederate postage to destination. If from South to North, letters usually bore a 10c Confederate stamp canceled at a Southern city (or "paid" handstamp) and a U. S. 3c 1861 adhesive (or "due 3" marking) and the postmark of Old Point Comfort, Va. In addition, prison censor markings, handstamped or manuscript, the name and rank of the soldier, and "Flag of Truce, via Fortress Monroe" in manuscript usually appear on these covers.

Federal prison censor handstamps of various designs are known from these prisons:

Camp Chase, Columbus, O.
David's Island, Pelham, N.Y.
Fort Delaware, Delaware City, Del.
Camp Douglas, Chicago, Ill.
Elmira Prison, Elmira, N.Y.

Johnson's Island, Sandusky, O.
Fort McHenry, Baltimore, Md.
Camp Morton, Indianapolis, Ind.
Fort Oglethorpe, Macon, Ga.
Old Capitol Prison, Washington, D.C.
Point Lookout Prison, Point Lookout, Md.
Fort Pulaski, Savannah, Ga.
Rock Island Prison, Rock Island, Ill.
Ship Island, New Orleans, La.
West's Hospital, Baltimore, Md.
U.S. General Hospital, Gettysburg, Pa.

Several other Federal prisons used manuscript censor markings.

Southern prison censor markings are always in manuscript, and do not identify the prison. The principal Southern prisons were at Richmond and Danville, Va.; Andersonville and Savannah, Ga.; Charleston, Columbia and Florence S.C.; Salisbury, N.C.; Hempstead and Tyler, Tex.

Civilians residing in both the North and the South were also, under exceptional circumstances, permitted to send Flag of Truce letters across the lines. Such covers bore no censor marking nor prison markings, but were always endorsed "via Flag of Truce".

Values will be found under various individual stamps for "on prisoner's cover" and are for the larger prisons. Prisoners' letters from the smaller prisons are much rarer. Only a very small percentage of prisoners' covers bore *both* a U.S. stamp and a Confederate stamp.

The "SOUTHERN LETTER UNPAID" Marking On Northbound Letters of Confederate Origin

By mid-May, 1861, correspondence between the North and South was difficult. In the South, postmasters were resigning and closing their accounts with Washington as the Confederacy prepared to organize its own postal system by June 1. From that date on, town marks and "paid" handstamps (and later postmasters' provisional stamps) were used in all post offices of the seceded states. The three most important Southern cities for clearing mail to the North were Memphis, Nashville and Richmond. The Richmond-Washington route was closed in April; Memphis was closed by June 1st, and mail attempting to cross the lines at these points generally ended up at the dead letter office. However, at Louisville, Kentucky, mail from the South via Nashville continued to arrive in June, July and August. On June 24, 1861, the Post Office Department advised the Louisville post office, "You will forward letters from the South for the Loyal States as unpaid, after removing postage stamps, but foreign letters in which prepayment is compulsory must come to the Dead Letter Office." However, Louisville avoided the task of "removing postage stamps," and instead prepared the "Southern Letter Unpaid" handstamp and special "due 3" markers for use. These markings were applied in the greenish-blue color of the Louisville office to letters of Southern origin that had accumulated, in addition to the usual town mark and grid of Louisville. The letters were delivered in the North as unpaid. Probably Louisville continued to forward such unpaid mail until about July 15. The marking is very rare. Other Southern mail was forwarded from Louisville as late as Aug. 27.

For listings see under U.S. 1857-61 issue, Nos. 26, 35-38. Values shown there are generally for this marking on off-cover stamps. Complete covers bearing stamps showing the full markings are valued from $10,000 upward depending upon the stamps, other postal markings and unusual usages, and condition. Fraudulent covers exist.

Trans-Mississippi Express Mail-the 40c Rate

From the fall of New Orleans on April 24, 1862, the entire reach of the Mississippi River was threatened by the Federal fleets. Late in 1862 the Confederacy experienced difficulty in maintaining regular mail routes trans-Mississippi to the Western states. Private express companies began to carry some mail, but by early 1863 when the Meridian-Jackson-Vicksburg-Shreveport route was seriously menaced, the Post Office Department of the Confederate States was forced to inaugurate an express mail service by contracting with a private company the name of which remains undisclosed. The eastern termini were at Meridian and Brandon, Miss.; the western at Shreveport and Alexandria, La. Letters, usually endorsed "via Meridian (or Brandon)" if going West; "via Shreveport (or Alexandria)" if going East were deposited in any Confederate post office. The rate was 40c per ½ ounce or less. Such Trans-Mississippi Express Mail upon arrival at a terminus was carried by couriers in a devious route across the Mississippi and returned to the regular mails at the nearest terminus on the other side of the river. The precise date of the beginning of the Trans-Mississippi service is not known. The earliest date of use so far seen is November 2, 1863 and the latest use February 9, 1865. These covers can be identified by the written endorsement of the route, but particularly by the rate since many bore no route endorsements.

Strips of four of 10c engraved stamps, pairs of the 20c stamp and various combinations of 10c stamps and the 5c London or Local prints are known; also handstamped Paid 40c marking. No identifying handstamps were used, merely the postmark of the office which received the letter originally. Values for Trans-Mississippi Express covers will be found under various stamps of the General Issues.

A 50c Preferred Mail Express rate, announced in April, 1863, preceded the Trans-Mississippi Express Mail 40c rate. One cover showing this rate is known.

Packet and Steamboat Covers and Markings

Letters carried on Confederate packets operating on coastal routes or up and down the inland waterways were usually handstamped with the name of the packet or marked STEAM or STEAMBOAT. Either United States stamps of the 1857 issue or stamped envelopes of the 1853 or 1860 issues have been found so used, as well as Confederate Postmasters' Provisional and General Issue stamps. Some specially designed pictorial or imprinted packet boat covers also exist. All are scarce and command values from $1,000 upward for handstamped United States envelopes and from $1,500 up for covers bearing Confederate stamps.

The Confederate postal laws did not provide the franking privilege for any mail except official correspondence of the Post Office Department. Such letters could be sent free only when enclosed in officially imprinted envelopes individually signed by the official using them. These envelopes were prepared and issued for Post Office Department use.

The imprints were on United States envelopes of 1853-61 issue, and also on commercial envelopes of various sizes and colors. When officially signed and mailed, they were postmarked, usually at Richmond, Va., with printed or handstamped "FREE". Envelopes are occasionally found unused and unsigned, and more rarely, signed but unused. When such official envelopes were used on other than official Post Office Department business, Confederate stamps were used.

Semi-official envelopes also exist bearing imprints of other government departments, offices, armies, states, etc. Regular postage was required to carry such envelopes through the mails.

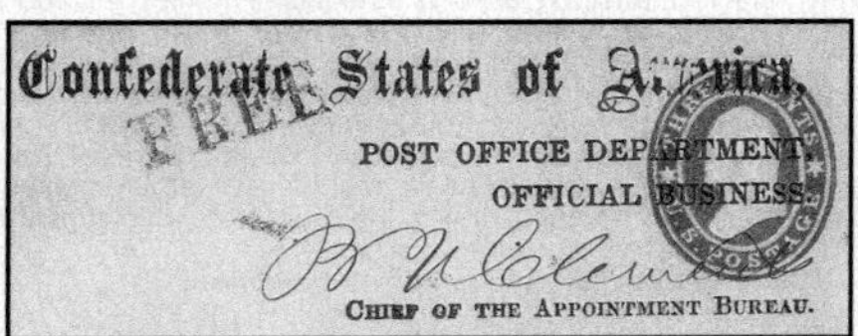

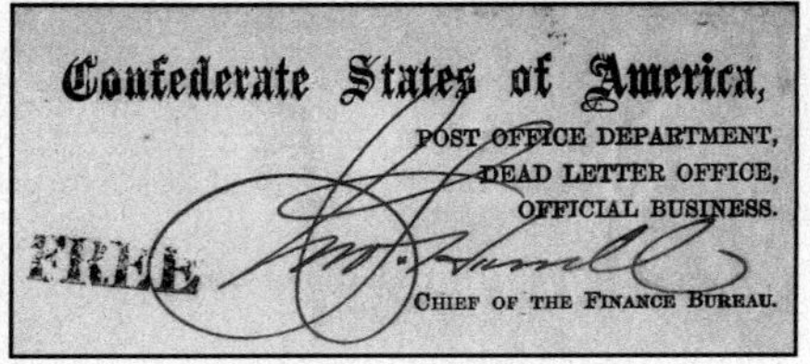

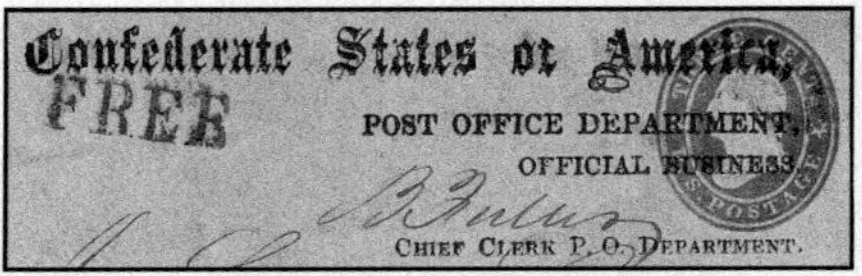

Typical Imprints of Official Envelopes of the Post Office Department. (Many variations of type, style and wording exist.)

Office	Signature
Postmaster General	John H. Reagan
Chief of the Contract Bureau	H. St. Geo. Offutt
Chief of the Appointment Bureau	B. N. Clements
Chief of the Finance Bureau	Jno. L. Harrell
Chief of the Finance Bureau	J. L. Lancaster
Chief of the Finance Bureau	A. Dimitry
Dead Letter Office	A. Dimitry
Dead Letter Office	Jno. L. Harrell
Chief Clerk, P. O. Department	B. Fuller
Chief Clerk	W. D. Miller
Auditor's Office	W. W. Lester
Auditor's Office	B. Baker
Auditor's Office	J. W. Robertson
First Auditor's Office, Treasury Department	J. W. Robertson
First Auditor's Office, Treasury Department	B. Baker
Third Auditor's Office	A. Moise
Third Auditor's Office	I. W. M. Harris
Agency, Post Office Dept. Trans-Miss.	Jas. H. Starr

CANAL ZONE

The Canal Zone, a strip of territory with an area of about 552 square miles following generally the line of the Canal, was under the jurisdiction of the United States, 1904-1979, and under the joint jurisdiction of the United States and Panama, 1979-1999, when the Canal, in its entirety, reverted to Panama.

The Canal organization underwent two distinct and fundamental changes. The construction of the Canal and the general administration of civil affairs were performed by the Isthmian Canal Commission under the provisions of the Spooner Act. This was supplanted in April, 1914, by the Panama Canal Act which established the organization known as The Panama Canal. This was an independent government agency which included both the operation and maintenance of the waterway and civil government in the Canal Zone. Most of the quasi-business enterprises relating to the Canal operation were conducted by the Panama Railroad, an adjunct of The Panama Canal.

A basic change in the mode of operations took effect July 1, 1951, under provisions of Public Law 841 of the 81st Congress. This in effect transferred the Canal operations to the Panama Railroad Co., which had been made a federal government corporation in 1948, and changed its name to the Panama Canal Co. Simultaneously the civil government functions of The Panama Canal, including the postal service, were renamed the Canal Zone Government. The organization therefore consisted of two units — the Panama Canal Co. and Canal Zone Government — headed by an individual who was president of the company and governor of the Canal Zone. His appointment as governor was made by the president of the United States, subject to confirmation by the Senate, and he was ex-officio president of the company.

The Canal Zone Government functioned as an independent government agency, and was under direct supervision of the president of the United States who delegated this authority to the Secretary of the Army.

The Panama Canal is 50 miles long from deep water in the Atlantic to deep water in the Pacific. It runs from northwest to southeast with the Atlantic entrance being 33.5 miles north and 27 miles west of the Pacific entrance. The airline distance between the two entrances is 43 miles. It requires about eight hours for an average ship to transit the Canal. Transportation between the Atlantic and Pacific sides of the Isthmus is available by railway, highway or air.

The Canal Zone Postal Service began operating June 24, 1904, when nine post offices were opened in connection with the construction of the Panama Canal. It ceased Sept. 30, 1979, and the Panama Postal Service took over.

Italicized numbers in parentheses indicate quantity issued.

100 CENTAVOS = 1 PESO
100 CENTESIMOS = 1 BALBOA
100 CENTS = 1 DOLLAR

Catalogue values for unused stamps are for Never Hinged items beginning with No. 118 in the regular postage section and No. C6 in the airpost section.

Map of Panama — A1

Violet to Violet-Blue Handstamp on Panama Nos. 72, 72a-72c, 78, 79.

On the 2c "PANAMA" is normally 13mm long. On the 5c and 10c it measures about 15mm.

On the 2c, "PANAMA" reads up on the upper half of the sheet and down on the lower half. On the 5c and 10c, "PANAMA" reads up at left and down at right on each stamp.

On the 2c only, varieties exist with inverted "V" for "A," accent on "A," inverted "N," etc., in "PANAMA."

1904, June 24 Engr. Unwmk. *Perf. 12*

1 A1 2c **rose**, both "PANAMA" reading up or down *(2600)* 650. 400.
Single on post card *1,650.*
Strip of 3 on cover *1,300.*
Block of 4 3,000. 2,000.
"PANAMA" 15mm long *(260)* 700. 600.
"P NAMA" 700. 600.
a. "CANAL ZONE" inverted *(100)* *1,000.* 850.
Block of 4 *6,000.*
b. "CANAL ZONE" double *4,250.* 2,000.
c. "CANAL ZONE" double, both inverted *20,000.*
d. "PANAMA" reading down and up *(52)* 750. 650.
e. As "d," "CANAL ZONE" invtd. *9,000.* *9,000.*
f. Vert. pair, "PANAMA" reading up on top 2c, down on other *2,100.* *2,100.*
g. As "f," "CANAL ZONE" inverted *20,000.*

2 A1 5c **blue** *(7800)* 300. 190.
On cover 225.
First day cover *7,500.*
Block of 4 1,400. 950.
Left "PANAMA" 2¼mm below bar *(156)* 575. 500.
Colon between right "PANAMA" and bar *(156)* 575. 500.
a. "CANAL ZONE" inverted 775. 600.
On cover *800.*
b. "CANAL ZONE" double 2,250. 1,500.
c. Pair, one without "CANAL ZONE" overprint *5,000.* *5,000.*
d. "CANAL ZONE" overprint diagonal, reading down to right 800. 700.

3 A1 10c **yellow** *(4946)* 400. 210.
On cover 325.
First day cover *5,000.*
Block of 4 1,750. 1,100.
Left "PANAMA" 2¼mm below bar *(100)* 675. 575.
Colon between right "PANAMA" and bar *(100)* 650. 550.
a. "CANAL ZONE" inverted *(200)* 775. 600.
On cover *800.*
b. "CANAL ZONE" double *14,000.*
c. Pair, one without "CANAL ZONE" overprint *6,000.* *5,000.*

Cancellations consist of town and/or bars in magenta or black, or a mixture of both colors.

Nos. 1-3 were withdrawn July 17, 1904.

Forgeries of the "Canal Zone" overprint and cancellations are numerous.

United States Nos. 300, 319, 304, 306 and 307 Overprinted in Black

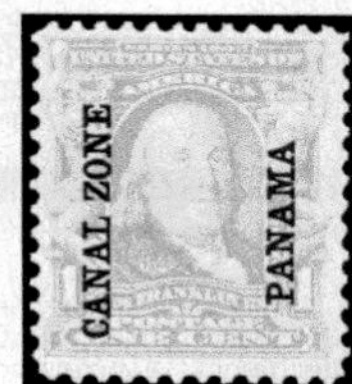

1904, July 18 Wmk. 191

4 A115 1c **blue green** *(43,738)* 35.00 22.50
green 35.00 22.50
On cover 75.00
Block of 4 150.00 140.00
P# strip of 3, Impt. 140.00
P# block of 6, Impt. 900.00

5 A129 2c **carmine** *(68,414)* 25.00 25.00
On cover 75.00
Block of 4 110.00 125.00
P# strip of 3, Impt. 100.00
P# block of 6, Impt. 1,150.
a. 2c **scarlet** 32.50 30.00

6 A119 5c **blue** *(20,858)* 85.00 60.00
On cover 275.00
Block of 4 375.00 325.00
P# strip of 3, Impt. 360.00
P# block of 6, Impt. 1,450.

7 A121 8c **violet black** *(7932)* 130.00 85.00
On cover 500.00
Block of 4 600.00 450.00
P# strip of 3, Impt. 575.00
P# block of 6, Impt. 3,000.

8 A122 10c **pale red brown** *(7856)* 120.00 80.00
On cover 500.00
Block of 4 500.00 475.00
P# strip of 3, Impt. 475.00
P# block of 6, Impt. 2,500.
Nos. 4-8 (5) 395.00 272.50

Nos. 4-8 frequently show minor broken letters.

Cancellations consist of circular town and/or bars in black, blue or magenta.

Beware of fake overprints.

A2

A3

CANAL ZONE Regular Type

CANAL ZONE Antique Type

The Canal Zone overprint on stamps Nos. 9-15 and 18-20 was made with a plate which had six different stages, each with its peculiar faults and errors. Stage 1: Broken CA-L, broken L, A-L spaced, on Nos. 9, 10, 12-15. Stage 2: broken L, Z, N, E, on Nos. 9, 10, 12-14. Stage 3: same as 2 with additional antique ZONE, on Nos. 9, 11-14, 18. Stage 4: same as 3 with additional antique CANAL on Nos. 9, 12, 13. Stage 5: broken E and letters L, Z, N, and words CANAL and ZONE in antique type on Nos. 12-14, 19, 20. Stage 6: same as 5 except for additional antique Z on stamp which had antique L, on No. 12. The Panama overprints can be distinguished by the different shades of the red overprint, the width of the bar, and the word PANAMA. No. 11 has two different Panama overprints; No. 12 has six; No. 13 five; No. 14 two; and Nos. 15, 18-20, one each. In the "8cts" surcharge of Nos. 14 and 15, there are three varieties of the figure "8." The bar is sometimes misplaced so that it appears on the bottom of the stamp instead of the top.

1904-06 Unwmk.

Black Overprint on Stamps of Panama

9 A2 1c **green** *(319,800) Dec. 12, 1904* 2.50 2.00
On cover 12.50
Block of 4 11.00 11.00
Spaced "A L" in "CANAL" *(700)* 110.00 100.00

CANAL ZONE
We Specialize in Canal Zone!
Stamps, Covers,
First Day Covers, First Flight
Covers, Stationery, Books,
Picture Post Cards and
Paper Canal Memorabilia
WE INVITE YOUR
INQUIRIES!
C & H STAMPS
P.O. Box 855
Dewitt, NY 13214-0855
www.CanalZoneStamps.com

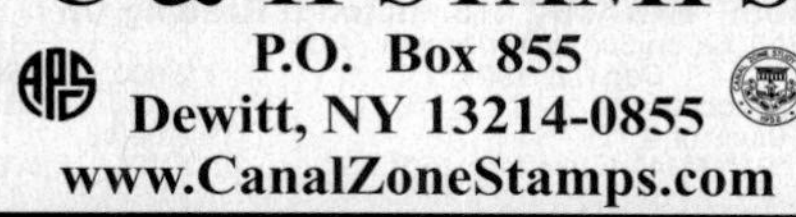

"ON" of "ZONE" dropped 300.00 275.00
On cover 325.00
a. "CANAL" in antique type *(500)* 90.00 90.00
b. "ZONE" in antique type *(1500)* 60.00 60.00
c. Inverted overprint *7,500. 6,000.*
d. Double overprint *2,750. 2,000.*

10 A2 2c **rose** *(367,500) Dec. 12, 1904* 4.00 2.50
On cover 17.50
First day cover *750.00*
Block of 4 19.00 15.00
Spaced "A L" of "CANAL" *(1700)* 85.00 85.00
"ON" of "ZONE" dropped 400.00 400.00
a. Inverted overprint 225.00 275.00
b. "L" of "CANAL" sideways *2,000. 2,250.*

"PANAMA" (15mm long) reading up at left, down at right

Overprint "CANAL ZONE" in Black, "PANAMA" and Bar in Red

11 A3 2c **rose** *(150,000) Dec. 9, 1905* 6.50 4.50
On cover 50.00
Block of 4 30.00 25.00
Inverted "M" in "PANAMA" *(3,000)* 47.50 40.00
"PANAMA" 16mm long *(3000)* 47.50 40.00
a. "ZONE" in antique type *(1500)* 175.00 175.00
b. "PANAMA" overprint inverted, bar at bottom *(200)* 600.00 *675.00*

12 A3 5c **blue** *(400,000) Dec. 12, 1904* 7.50 2.75
On cover 100.00
Block of 4 32.50 20.00
Spaced "A L" in "CANAL" *(300)* 90.00 80.00
"PANAMA" reading up *(2800)* 75.00 70.00
"PANAMA" reading down *(400)* 200.00 180.00
"PANAMA" 16mm long *(1300)* 40.00 37.50
Inverted "M" in "PANAMA" *(1300)* 40.00 37.50
Right "PANAMA" 5mm below bar *(600)* 75.00 70.00
"PANAM" 70.00 65.00
"PAN MA" 75.00 70.00
"ANAMA" 80.00 75.00
a. "CANAL" in antique type *(2750)* 75.00 65.00
b. "ZONE" in antique type *(2950)* 75.00 65.00
c. "CANAL ZONE" double *(200)* 800.00 800.00
d. "PANAMA" double *(120)* 1,100. 1,000.
e. "PANAMA" inverted, bar at bottom 1,000. 1,250.
f. "PANAAM" at right *950.00 850.00*

13 A3 10c **yellow** *(64,900) Dec. 12, 1904* 17.00 12.00
On cover 125.00
Block of 4 100.00 62.50
Spaced "A L" in "CANAL" *(200)* 190.00 180.00
"PANAMA" 16mm long *(400)* 75.00 65.00
"PANAMA" reading down *(200)* 200.00 180.00
Invtd. "M" in "PANAMA" *(400)* 100.00 90.00
Right "PANAMA" 5mm below bar *(398)* 150.00 140.00
Left "PANAMA" touches bar *(400)* 200.00 160.00
a. "CANAL" in antique type *(200)* 180.00 180.00
b. "ZONE" in antique type *(400)* 175.00 160.00
c. "PANAMA" ovpt. double *(80)* 650.00 650.00
d. "PANAMA" overprint in red brown *(5000)* 27.50 22.50
"PANAMA" ovpt. in orange red 32.50 32.50
Nos. 11-13 (3) 31.00 19.25

With Added Surcharge in Red

a

There are three varieties of "8" in the surcharge on Nos. 14-15.

14 A3 8c on 50c **bister brown** *(27,900) Dec. 12, 1904* 25.00 25.00
On cover 200.00
Block of 4 150.00 150.00
Spaced "A L" in "CANAL" *(194)* 160.00 160.00
Right "PANAMA" 5mm below bar *(438)* 200.00 175.00
a. "ZONE" in antique type *(25)* 1,150. 1,150.
b. "CANAL ZONE" inverted *(200)* 450.00 425.00
c. "PANAMA" overprint in rose brown *(6000)* 35.00 35.00
d. As "c," "CANAL" in antique type *(10)* *1,750. 850.00*
e. As "c," "ZONE" in antique type *(10)* *1,750.*
f. As "c," "8 cts" double *(30)* *1,100.*
g. As "c," "8" omitted *4,500.*
h. As "c," "cts 8" —

Nos. 11-14 are overprinted or surcharged on Panama Nos. 77, 77e, 78, 78c, 78d, 78f, 78g, 78h, 79 79c, 79e, 79g and 81 respectively.

On No. 14 with original gum, the gum is almost always disturbed. Unused stamps are valued thus.

Panama No. 74a, 74b Overprinted "CANAL ZONE" in Regular Type in Black and Surcharged Type "a" in Red

Both "PANAMA" (13mm long) Reading Up

15 A3(a) 8c on 50c **bister brown** *(435) Dec. 12, 1904* 2,000. *4,750.*
On cover *10,000.*
Block of 4 *9,000.*
"PANAMA" 15mm long *(50)* 2,400. *5,000.*
"P NAMA" *4,500.*
Spaced "A L" in "CANAL" *(5)* *4,500.*
a. "PANAMA" reading down and up *(10)* *6,000.* —

On No. 15 with original gum, the gum is almost always disturbed. Unused stamps are valued thus.

Map of Panama — A4

Panama Nos. 19 and 21 Surcharged in Black

CANAL ZONE 1 ct. PANAMA PANAMA
a

CANAL ZONE 1 ct. PANAMA PANAMA
b

CANAL ZONE 1 ct. PANAMA PANAMA
c

CANAL ZONE 2 cts. PANAMA PANAMA
d

CANAL ZONE 2 cts. PANAMA PANAMA
e

CANAL ZONE 2 cts. PANAMA PANAMA
f

There were three printings of each denomination, differing principally in the relative position of the various parts of the surcharges. Varieties occur with inverted "V" for the final "A" in "PANAMA," "CA" spaced, "ZO" spaced, "2c" spaced, accents in various positions, and with bars shifted so that two bars appear on top or bottom of the stamp (either with or without the corresponding bar on top or bottom) and sometimes with only one bar at top or bottom.

1906

16 A4 1c on 20c **violet,** type a *(100,000) Mar.* 1.90 1.60
On cover 10.00
Block of 4 8.50 7.50
a. Type b *(100,000) May* 1.90 1.60
On cover 10.00
Block of 4 8.50 7.50
b. Type c *(300,000) Sept.* 1.90 1.50
On cover 10.00
Block of 4 8.50 7.50
Spaced C A 13.00 12.00
c. As No. 16, double surcharge *2,000.*

17 A4 2c on 1p **lake,** type d *(200,000) Mar.* 2.25 2.25
On cover 12.00
Block of 4 12.00 12.00
a. Type e *(200,000) May* 2.25 2.25
On cover 12.00
Block of 4 12.00 12.00
b. Type f *(50,000) Sept.* 20.00 20.00
On cover 75.00
Block of 4 90.00 90.00

Panama Nos. 74, 74a and 74b Overprinted "CANAL ZONE" in Regular Type in Black and Surcharged in Red

b

c

1905-06

Both "PANAMA" Reading Up

18 A3(b) 8c on 50c **bister brown** *(17,500) Nov. 1905* 45.00 45.00
On cover 225.00
Block of 4 200.00 230.00
"PANAMA" 15mm long *(1750)* 90.00 80.00
"P NAMA" 125.00 110.00
a. "ZONE" in antique type *(175)* 200.00 180.00
b. "PANAMA" reading down and up *(350)* 160.00 150.00

19 A3(c) 8c on 50c **bister brown** *(19,000) Apr. 23, 1906* 45.00 37.50
On cover 275.00
Block of 4 200.00 200.00
"PANAMA" 15mm long *(1900)* 85.00 70.00
"P NAMA" 90.00
a. "CANAL" in antique type *(190)* 210.00 180.00
b. "ZONE" in antique type *(190)* 210.00 180.00
c. "8 cts" double *1,100. 1,100.*
d. "PANAMA" reading down and up *(380)* 110.00 90.00

On Nos. 18-19 with original gum, the gum is usually disturbed. Unused stamps are valued thus.

Panama No. 81 Overprinted "CANAL ZONE" in Regular Type in Black and Surcharged in Red Type "c" plus Period

"PANAMA" reading up and down

20 A3(c) 8c on 50c **bister brown** *(19,600) Sept. 1906* 35.00 37.50
On cover 200.00
Block of 4 160.00 170.00
"PANAMA" reading up *(392)* 120.00 110.00
a. "CANAL" antique type *(196)* 200.00 180.00
b. "ZONE" in antique type *(196)* 200.00 180.00
c. "8 cts" omitted *(50)* 800.00 800.00
d. "8 cts" double *1,500.*
e. "cts 8" —

Nos. 14 and 18-20 exist without CANAL ZONE overprint but were not regularly issued and are considered printer's waste. Forgeries of the overprint varieties of Nos. 9-15 and 18-20 are known.

On No. 20 with original gum, the gum is usually disturbed. Unused stamps are valued thus.

Fernández de Córdoba — A5

Vasco Núñez de Balboa — A6

Fernández de Córdoba — A7

Justo Arosemena — A8

Manuel J. Hurtado — A9

José de Obaldía — A10

Engraved by Hamilton Bank Note Co.

Overprinted in Black by Isthmian Canal Commission Press.

1906-07 **Unwmk.** ***Perf. 12***

Overprint Reading Up

21 A5 2c **red & black** *(50,000) Oct. 29, 1906* 25.00 25.00
On cover 55.00
Block of 4 125.00 *175.00*
Narrow spacing between "CANAL" and "ZONE" (6¾mm vs. normal 7¼mm) (pos. 83) — —

a. "CANAL" only 4,000.

Overprint Reading Down

22 A6 1c **green & black** *(2,000,000) Jan. 14, 1907* 2.00 .90
dull green & black 2.00 1.00
On cover 5.00
Block of 4 9.00 7.50
"ANA" for "CANAL" *(1000)* 70.00 70.00
"CAN L" for "CANAL" 80.00 80.00
"ONE" for "ZONE" *(3000)* 80.00 80.00
a. Horiz. pair, imperf. btwn. *(50)* 1,100. 1,100.
b. Vert. pair, imperf. btwn. *(20)* *2,000.* *2,000.*
c. Vert. pair, imperf. horiz. *(20)* *2,250.* *1,750.*
d. Inverted overprint reading up *(100)* 550.00 550.00
e. Double overprint *(300)* 275.00 275.00
f. Double overprint, one inverted 1,750. 1,600.
g. Invtd. center, ovpt. reading up *3,500.* *4,500.*
Pair on cover *18,500.*
Block of 4 *17,000.*
h. Horiz. pair, imperf vert. *5,000.*
23 A7 2c **red & black** *(2,370,000) Nov. 25, 1906* 3.00 1.00
scarlet & black, *1907* 3.00 1.00
On cover 6.00
Block of 4 13.00 8.50
"CAN L" for "CANAL" 45.00
a. Horizontal pair, imperf. between *(20)* 2,000. 2,000.
b. Vertical pair, one without overprint 2,500. 2,500.
c. Double overprint *(100)* 600.00 700.00
d. Double overprint, one diagonal 800.00 800.00
e. Double overprint, one diagonal, in pair with normal 2,500.
f. 2c carmine red & black, *Sept. 9, 1907* 5.00 2.75
g. As "f," inverted center and overprint reading up *14,000.*
On cover *17,500.*
h. As "d," one "ZONE CANAL" *4,000.*
i. "CANAL" double *6,500.*
24 A8 5c **ultramarine & black** *(1,390,000) Dec. 1906* 5.75 2.00
light ultramarine & black 5.75 2.00
blue & black, *Sept. 16, 1907* 5.75 2.00
dark blue & black 5.75 2.25
dull blue & black 5.75 2.25
light blue & black 5.75 2.25
On cover 40.00
Block of 4 25.00 20.00
"CAN L" for "CANAL" 60.00
c. Double overprint *(200)* 500.00 400.00
d. "CANAL" only *(10)* *7,000.*
e. "ZONE CANAL" *5,000.*
25 A9 8c **purple & black** *(170,000) Dec. 1906* 20.00 8.00
On cover 100.00
Block of 4 110.00 55.00
a. Horizontal pair, imperf. between and at left margin *(34)* *1,600.* *4,000.*
26 A10 10c **violet & black** *(250,000) Dec. 1906* 20.00 7.00
On cover 100.00
Block of 4 110.00 50.00
a. Dbl. ovpt., one reading up *(10)* *5,000.*
b. Overprint reading up *5,500.*
Nos. 22-26 (5) 50.75 18.90

The early printings of this series were issued on soft, thick, porous-textured paper. A sizeable proportion of some later printings of Nos. 22, 23 and 24 only appear on hard, thinner, smooth-textured paper.

Normal spacing of the early printings is 7¼mm between the words; later printings, 6¾mm. All were printed on soft, porous-textured paper; Nos. 22-24 also printed on hard, smooth-textured paper.

Nos. 22 and 26 exist imperf. between stamp and sheet margin. Nos. 22-25 occur with "CA" of "CANAL" spaced ½mm further apart on position No. 50 of the setting.

The used pair of No. 25a is unique.

No. 23g is valued in sound condition. Almost all examples are faulty to some degree; value with small faults is approximately $6,000.

Córdoba — A11

Arosemena — A12

Hurtado — A13

José de Obaldía — A14

Engraved by American Bank Note Co.

1909

Overprint Reading Down

27 A11 2c **vermilion & black** *(500,000) May 11, 1909* 12.00 5.00
On cover 15.00
First day cover 750.00
Block of 4 55.00 27.50
a. Horizontal pair, one without overprint *2,500.*
b. Vert. pair, one without ovpt. *3,250.*
28 A12 5c **deep blue & black** *(200,000) May 28, 1909* 40.00 12.50
On cover *225.00*
Block of 4 190.00 60.00
29 A13 8c **violet & black** *(50,000) May 25, 1909* 37.50 14.00
On cover 90.00
Block of 4 190.00 82.50
30 A14 10c **violet & black** *(100,000) Jan. 19, 1909* 40.00 14.00
On cover 85.00
Block of 4 200.00 85.00
a. Horizontal pair, one with "ZONE" omitted *3,000.*
b. Vertical pair, one without overprint *4,000.*
Nos. 27-30 (4) 129.50 45.50

Nos. 27-30 occur with "CA" spaced (position 50).

Do not confuse No. 27 with Nos. 39d or 53a.

On No. 30a, the stamp with "ZONE" omitted is also missing most of "CANAL."

Black Overprint Reading Up

Vasco Núñez de Balboa — A15

Engraved, Printed and Overprinted by American Bank Note Co.

Type I

Type I Overprint: "C" with serifs both top and bottom. "L," "Z" and "E" with slanting serifs.

Compare Type I overprint with Types II to V illustrated before Nos. 38, 46, 52 and 55.

1909-10

31 A15 1c **dark green & black** *(4,000,000) Nov. 8, 1909* 4.25 1.25
On cover 5.00
Block of 4 18.00 6.75
a. Inverted center and overprint reading down *22,500.*
c. Bklt. pane of 6, handmade, perf. margins *500.00*
32 A11 2c **vermilion & black** *(4,000,000) Nov. 8, 1909* 4.50 1.25
On cover 5.00
Block of 4 20.00 6.75
a. Vert. pair, imperf. horiz. 1,000. 1,000.
c. Bklt. pane of 6, handmade, perf. margins *800.00*
d. Double overprint (I) *6,000.*
33 A12 5c **deep blue & black** *(2,000,000) Nov. 8, 1909* 17.00 3.50
On cover 40.00
Block of 4 80.00 20.00
a. Double overprint *(200)* 375.00 375.00
On cover *1,000.*
34 A13 8c **violet & black** *(200,000) Mar. 18, 1910* 11.00 5.00
On cover 75.00
Block of 4 50.00 27.50
a. Vertical pair, one without overprint *(10)* *1,750.*
35 A14 10c **violet & black** *(100,000) Nov. 8, 1909* 47.50 20.00
On cover 100.00
Block of 4 210.00 100.00
Nos. 31-35 (5) 84.25 31.00

Normal spacing between words of overprint on No. 31 is 10mm; on No. 32 it is 8½mm, or less frequently 9¼mm; and on Nos. 33 to 35, 8½mm. Spacing variations are known.

A16

A17

1911, Jan. 14

36 A16 10c on 13c **gray** *(476,700)* 6.00 2.00
On cover 50.00
Block of 4 30.00 15.00
a. "10 cts" inverted 325.00 325.00
b. "10 cts" omitted 300.00

The "10 cts" surcharge was applied by the Isthmian Canal Commission Press after the overprinted stamps were received from the American Bank Note Co.

Many used stamps offered as No. 36b are merely No. 36 from which the surcharge has been chemically removed.

1914, Jan. 6

37 A17 10c **gray** *(200,000)* 47.50 11.00
On cover 85.00
Block of 4 200.00 60.00

Black Overprint Reading Up

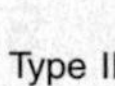

Type II

Type II Overprint: "C" with serif at top only. "L" and "E" with vertical serifs. "O" tilts to left.

1912-16

38 A15 1c **green & black** *(3,000,000) July 1913* 10.00 3.00
On cover 5.50
Block of 4 45.00 20.00
a. Vertical pair, one without overprint 1,750. 1,750.
On cover *2,250.*
b. Booklet pane of 6, imperf. margins *(120,000)* 575.00
c. Booklet pane of 6, handmade, perf. margins *1,000.*
39 A11 2c **vermilion & black** *(7,500,000) Dec. 1912* 8.00 1.10
orange vermilion & black, *1916* 8.00 1.10
On cover 5.00
Block of 4 40.00 6.50
a. Horiz. pair, right stamp without overprint *(20)* *1,250.*
b. Horiz. pair, left stamp without overprint *(10)* *1,500.*
c. Booklet pane of 6, imperf. margins *(194,868)* 550.00
d. Overprint reading down 200.00
e. As "d," inverted center 600.00 *750.00*

Dedicated to the study of stamps & postal history related to the Panama Canal Zone
For information and a complimentary copy of our quarterly publication
The Canal Zone Philatelist
Please write to
Michael D. Drabik, Secretary
P.O. Box 281
Bolton, MA 01740-0281
www.czsg.org

	On cover		*1,000.*
f.	As "e," booklet pane of 6, handmade, perf. margins	*8,000.*	
g.	As "c," handmade, perf. margins	900.00	800.00
h.	As No. 39, "CANAL" only (1)		*2,500.*
40	A12 5c **deep blue & black** *(2,300,000) Dec. 1912*	20.00	2.50
	On cover		35.00
	Block of 4	95.00	12.00
a.	With Cordoba portrait of 2c		*12,500.*
41	A14 10c **violet & black** *(200,000) Feb. 1916*	60.00	7.50
	On cover		80.00
	Block of 4	250.00	37.50
	Nos. 38-41 (4)	98.00	14.10

Normal spacing between words of overprint on the first printing of Nos. 38-40 is 8½mm and on the second printing 9¼mm. The spacing of the single printing of No. 41 and the imperf. margin booklet pane printings of Nos. 38 and 39 is 7¾mm. Minor spacing variations are known.

Map of Panama Canal — A18

Balboa Taking Possession of the Pacific Ocean — A19

Gatun Locks — A20

Culebra Cut — A21

Engraved, Printed and Overprinted by American Bank Note Co.

1915, Mar. 1

Blue Overprint, Type II

42	A18 1c **dark green & black** *(100,000)*	8.75	6.50
	On cover		17.50
	Block of 4	40.00	30.00
	First day cover		200.00
43	A19 2c **carmine & black** *(100,000)*	12.00	4.25
	vermilion & black	12.00	4.25
	On cover		25.00
	First day cover		150.00
	Block of 4	50.00	21.00
44	A20 5c **blue & black** *(100,000)*	10.00	5.75
	On cover		55.00
	Block of 4	45.00	29.00
	First day cover		500.00
45	A21 10c **orange & black** *(50,000)*	19.00	11.00
	On cover		70.00
	Block of 4	80.00	55.00
	First day cover		500.00
	Nos. 42-45 (4)	49.75	27.50

Normal spacing between words of overprint is 9¼mm on all four values except position No. 61 which is 10mm.

Black Overprint Reading Up

Type III

Type III Overprint: Similar to Type I but letters appear thinner, particularly the lower bar of "L," "Z" and "E." Impressions are often light, rough and irregular, and not centered.

Engraved and Printed by American Bank Note Co.
Overprint applied by
Panama Canal Press, Mount Hope, C.Z.

1915-20

46	A15 1c **green & black,** *Dec. 1915*	175.00	125.00
	light green & black, *1920*	250.00	150.00
	Single on postcard		175.00
	Pair on cover		500.00
	Block of 4	775.00	650.00
a.	Overprint reading down *(200)*	375.00	
b.	Double overprint *(385)*	225.00	
c.	"ZONE" double *(2)*	*6,500.*	
d.	Double overprint, one reads "ZONE CANAL" *(13)*	2,000.	
47	A11 2c **orange vermilion & black,** *Aug. 1920*	2,750.	60.00
	On cover		350.00
	Pair on cover		*850.00*
	Block of 4	*11,500.*	500.00
48	A12 5c **deep blue & black,** *Dec. 1915*	425.00	130.00
	On cover		1,000.
	Pair on cover		*2,250.*
	Block of 4	*2,100.*	675.00

Spacing between words of overprint on Nos. 46-48 is 9¼mm; spacing varieties are not known. This should not be confused with a fairly common 9¼mm spacing of the 2c value of type I, nor with an uncommon 9¼mm spacing variety of the 5c of type I.

A22

S. S. "Panama" in Culebra Cut — A23

S. S. "Cristobal" in Gatun Locks — A24

Engraved, Printed and Overprinted by American Bank Note Co.

1917, Jan. 23

Blue Overprint, Type II

49	A22 12c **purple & black** *(314,914)*	17.50	5.25
	On cover		50.00
	First day cover		1,750.
	Block of 4	87.50	27.50
50	A23 15c **bright blue & black**	50.00	17.50
	On cover		135.00
	Block of 4	230.00	95.00
51	A24 24c **yellow brown & black**	35.00	13.00
	On cover		325.00
	Block of 4	180.00	80.00
	Nos. 49-51 (3)	102.50	35.75

Normal spacing between words of overprint is 11¼mm.

Black Overprint Reading Up

Type IV

Type IV Overprint: "C" thick at bottom, "E" with center bar same length as top and bottom bars.

Engraved, Printed and Overprinted by American Bank Note Co.

1918-20

52	A15 1c **green & black** *(2,000,000) Jan. 1918*	32.50	10.00
	On cover		12.50
	Block of 4	150.00	45.00
a.	Overprint reading down	175.00	—
b.	Booklet pane of 6 *(60,000)*	600.00	
c.	Booklet pane of 6, left vertical row of 3 without overprint	*7,500.*	
d.	Booklet pane of 6, right vertical row of 3 with double overprint	*7,500.*	
e.	Horiz. bklt. pair, left stamp without overprint	*3,000.*	
f.	Horiz. bklt. pair, right stamp with double overprint	*3,000.*	
g.	Double overprint, booklet single		3,000.
53	A11 2c **vermilion & black** *(2,000,000) Nov. 1918*	110.00	6.00
	On cover		10.00
	Block of 4	500.00	30.00
a.	Overprint reading down	150.00	150.00
b.	Horiz. pair, right stamp without ovpt. (from misregistered overprints)	2,000.	
c.	Booklet pane of 6 *(34,000)*	1,050.	
d.	Booklet pane of 6, left vertical row of 3 without overprint	*15,000.*	
e.	Horiz. bklt. pair, left stamp without overprint	*3,000.*	
	On cover (unique)		*4,500.*
f.	Horiz. sheet pair, left stamp without overprint (2)	*1,750.*	
54	A12 5c **deep blue & black** *(500,000) Apr. 1920*	150.00	32.50
	On cover		200.00
	Block of 4	825.00	150.00
	Nos. 52-54 (3)	292.50	48.50

Normal spacing between words of overprint on Nos. 52 and 53 is 9¼mm. On No. 54 and the booklet printings of Nos. 52 and 53, the normal spacing is 9mm. Minor spacing varieties are known.

No. 53f is in a block of nine containing two such pairs.

Black Overprint Reading Up

Type V

Type V Overprint: Smaller block type 1¾mm high. "A" with flat top.

1920-21

55	A15 1c **light green & black,** *Apr. 1921*	22.50	3.25
	On cover		8.00
	Block of 4	100.00	16.50
a.	Overprint reading down	300.00	225.00
b.	Horiz. pair, right stamp without ovpt. (10)	*1,750.*	
c.	Horiz. pair, left stamp without ovpt. (21)	1,100.	
d.	"ZONE" only	*4,000.*	—
e.	Booklet pane of 6	*2,250.*	
f.	As No. 55, "CANAL" double (10)	*1,750.*	
g.	Vert. pair, one without overprint (2)	3,000.	
h.	Vert. pair, one "ZONE" only, one without overprint (1)	*4,000.*	
56	A11 2c **orange vermilion & black,** *Sept. 1920*	8.50	1.75
	On cover		7.00
	Block of 4	37.50	8.50
a.	Double overprint *(100)*	500.00	
b.	Double overprint, one reading down *(100)*	600.00	
c.	Horiz. pair, right stamp without overprint (11)	1,400.	
d.	Horiz. pair, left stamp without overprint (20)	1,000.	
e.	Vertical pair, one without overprint	1,500.	
f.	"ZONE" double	900.00	
g.	Booklet pane of 6	900.00	
h.	As No. 56, "CANAL" double	800.00	

57 A12 5c **deep blue & black**, *Apr. 1921* 300.00 45.00
On cover 225.00
Block of 4 1,350. 200.00
a. Horiz. pair, right stamp without overprint *(10)* *2,000.*
b. Horiz. pair, left stamp without overprint *(10)* *2,000.*
Nos. 55-57 (3) 331.00 50.00

Normal spacing between words of overprint on Nos. 55-57 is 9½mm. On booklet printings of Nos. 55 and 56 the normal spacing is 9¼mm.

Drydock at Balboa — A25

U.S.S. "Nereus" in Pedro Miguel Locks — A26

1920, Sept.

Black Overprint Type V

58 A25 50c **orange & black** 250.00 160.00
On cover *1,000.*
Block of 4 1,250. 800.00
59 A26 1b **dark violet & black** *(23,014)* 175.00 50.00
On cover *1,000.*
Block of 4 825.00 300.00

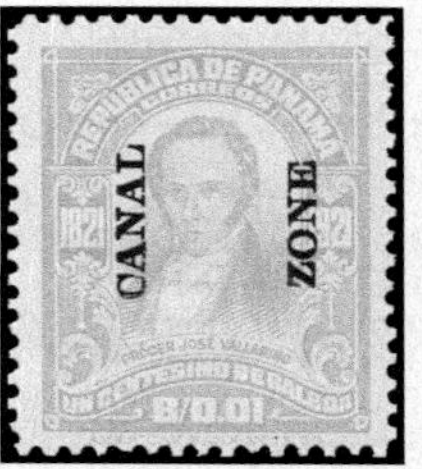

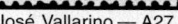

José Vallarino — A27

"Land Gate" — A28

Bolívar's Tribute — A29

Municipal Building in 1821 and 1921 — A30

Statue of Balboa — A31

Tomás Herrera — A32

José de Fábrega — A33

Engraved, Printed and Overprinted by American Bank Note Co.

Type V overprint in black, reading up, on all values except the 5c which is overprinted with larger type in red

1921, Nov. 13

60 A27 1c **green** 3.75 1.50
On cover 6.00
Block of 4 13.00 7.25
a. "CANAL" double *1,900.*
b. Booklet pane of 6 *900.00*
61 A28 2c **carmine** 2.75 1.00
On cover 15.00
Block of 4 12.50 4.50
a. Overprint reading down 200.00 *225.00*
b. Double overprint 900.00
c. Vertical pair, one without overprint *3,500.*
d. "CANAL" double *1,900.*
e. "ZONE" only (1) *4,000.*
f. Booklet pane of 6 *2,000.*
62 A29 5c **blue** (R) 10.00 3.00
On cover 30.00
Block of 4 45.00 18.00
a. Overprint reading down (R) 60.00
63 A30 10c **violet** 18.00 7.50
On cover 60.00
Block of 4 100.00 35.00
a. Overprint, reading down 90.00
64 A31 15c **light blue** 47.50 17.50
On cover 175.00
Block of 4 230.00 95.00
65 A32 24c **black brown** 67.50 22.50
On cover *600.00*
Block of 4 360.00 125.00
66 A33 50c **black** 145.00 85.00
On cover *600.00*
Block of 4 700.00 400.00
Nos. 60-66 (7) 294.50 138.00

Experts question the status of the 5c with a small type V overprint in red or black.

Type III overprint in black, reading up, applied by the Panama Canal Press, Mount Hope, C. Z.

Engraved and printed by the American Bank Note Co.

1924, Jan. 28

67 A27 1c **green** 500. 200.
Single on postcard 350.
Pair on cover 750.
Block of 4 2,250. 900.
a. "ZONE CANAL" reading down 800.
b. "ZONE" only, reading down *1,900.*
c. Se-tenant pair, #67a and 67b *2,750.*

Arms of Panama — A34

1924, Feb.

68 A34 1c **dark green** 10.00 4.50
On cover 12.00
Block of 4 50.00 24.00
69 A34 2c **carmine** 7.00 2.75
carmine rose 7.00 2.75
On cover 15.00
Block of 4 30.00 12.50

The following were prepared for use, but they were not issued.

A34 5c **dark blue** *(600)* 350.
Block of 4 1,750.
A34 10c **dark violet** *(600)* 350.
Block of 4 1,750.
A34 12c **olive green** *(600)* 350.
Block of 4 1,750.
A34 15c **ultramarine** *(600)* 350.
Block of 4 1,750.
A34 24c **yellow brown** *(600)* 350.
Block of 4 1,750.
A34 50c **orange** *(600)* 350.
Block of 4 1,750.
A34 1b **black** *(600)* 350.
Block of 4 1,750.

The 5c to 1b values were prepared for use but never issued due to abrogation of the Taft Agreement which required the Canal Zone to use overprinted Panama stamps. Six hundred of each denomination were not destroyed, as they were forwarded to the Director General of Posts of Panama for transmission to the UPU which then required about 400 sets. Only a small number of sets appear to have reached the public market.

All Panama stamps overprinted "CANAL ZONE" were withdrawn from sale June 30, 1924, and were no longer valid for postage after Aug. 31, 1924.

United States Nos. 551-554, 557, 562, 564-566, 569, 570 and 571 Overprinted in Red (No. 70) or Black (all others)

Type A

Letters "A" with Flat Tops

Printed and Overprinted by the U.S. Bureau of Engraving and Printing.

1924-25 Unwmk. *Perf. 11*

70 A154 ½c **olive brown** *(399,500) Apr. 15, 1925* .25 .70
Never hinged .40
On cover 4.00
On cover, single, with 1c additional on 3rd-class cover 20.00
First day cover 75.00
Block of 4 1.00 3.25
P# block of 6 5.00
71 A155 1c **deep green** *(1,985,000) July 1, 1924* 1.40 1.00
Never hinged 2.50
On cover 4.00
First day cover 75.00
Block of 4 5.75 4.25
P# block of 6 27.50
a. Inverted overprint 500.00 500.00
b. "ZONE" inverted 350.00 325.00
c. "CANAL" only *(20)* 1,150.
d. "ZONE CANAL" *(180)* 400.00
e. Booklet pane of 6 *(43,152)* 80.00 —
f. Se-tenant pair, #71c and 71d *1,750.*
72 A156 1½c **yellow brown** *(180,599) Apr. 15, 1925* 2.00 1.70
brown 2.00 1.70
Never hinged 3.25
On cover 4.00
On cover, single franking, on 3rd-class cover 30.00
First day cover, Nos. 70, 72 80.00
Block of 4 8.75 9.50
P# block of 6 37.50
73 A157 2c **carmine** *(2,975,000) July 1, 1924* 6.75 1.70
Never hinged 10.50
First day cover 80.00
Block of 4 31.00 8.00
P# block of 6 160.00
a. Booklet pane of 6 *(140,000)* 175.00

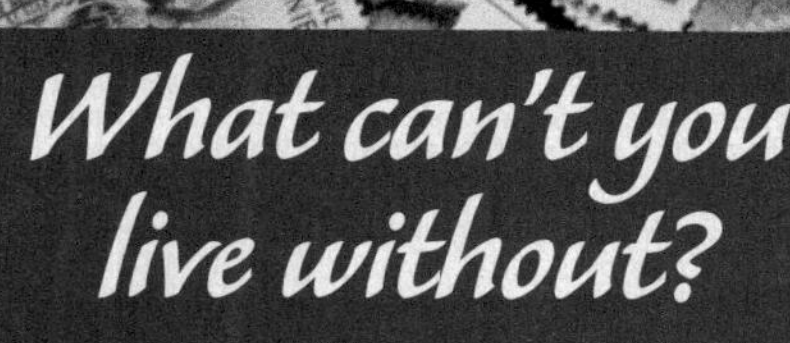
What can't you live without?
POSSESSIONS
From Canal Zone to Puerto Rico plus Spanish era stamps
Request Possessions price list or shop online at:
www.astampdealer4u.com
FRANK BACHENHEIMER
6547 Midnight Pass Rd. #89,
Sarasota, FL 34242
Ph. 941-349-0222

Email: frankb@astampdealer4u.com

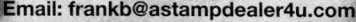

No.	Description	Unused	Used
74	A160 5c **dark blue** *(500,000) July 1, 1924*	16.00	7.00
	Never hinged	25.00	
	On cover		20.00
	Block of 4	67.50	37.50
	P# block of 6	300.00	
75	A165 10c **orange** *(60,000) July 1, 1924*	40.00	20.00
	Never hinged	65.00	
	On cover		45.00
	First day cover		500.00
	Block of 4	190.00	105.00
	P# block of 6	875.00	
76	A167 12c **brown violet** *(80,000) July 1, 1924*	32.50	30.00
	Never hinged	62.50	
	On cover		45.00
	First day cover		750.00
	Block of 4	140.00	130.00
	P# block of 6	475.00	
a.	"ZONE" inverted	*3,750.*	*3,000.*
77	A168 14c **dark blue** *(100,000) June 27, 1925*	27.50	22.50
	Never hinged	45.00	
	On cover		50.00
	First day cover		*500.00*
	Block of 4	120.00	140.00
	P# block of 6	425.00	
78	A169 15c **gray** *(55,000) July 1, 1924*	45.00	37.50
	Never hinged	70.00	
	On cover		52.50
	First day cover		*500.00*
	Block of 4	200.00	190.00
	P# block of 6	825.00	
79	A172 30c **olive brown** *(40,000) July 1, 1924*	32.50	20.00
	Never hinged	52.50	
	On cover		50.00
	Block of 4	140.00	110.00
	P# block of 6	600.00	
	Double transfer (14438 LR79)	600.00	
80	A173 50c **lilac** *(25,000) July 1, 1924*	75.00	45.00
	Never hinged	150.00	
	On cover		*500.00*
	Block of 4	325.00	225.00
	P# block of 6	3,000.	
81	A174 $1 **violet brown** *(10,000) July 1, 1924*	225.00	95.00
	Never hinged	400.00	
	On cover		*1,000.*
	Block of 4	1,000.	500.00
	Margin block of 4, arrow, top or bottom	1,250.	
	P# block of 6	*4,250.*	
	Nos. 70-81 (12)	503.90	282.10

Normal spacing between words of the overprint is 9¼mm. Minor spacing variations are known. The overprint of the early printings used on all values of this series except No. 77 is a sharp, clear impression. The overprint of the late printings, used only on Nos. 70, 71, 73, 76, 77, 78 and 80 is heavy and smudged, with many of the letters, particularly the "A" practically filled.

All examples of Nos. 71b and 76a have a natural straight edge at right.

Booklet panes Nos. 71e, 73a, 84d, 97b, 101a, 106a and 117a were made from 360 subject plates. The handmade booklet panes Nos. 102a, 115c and a provisional lot of 117b were made from Post Office panes from regular 400-subject plates.

United States Nos. 554, 555, 557, 562, 564-567, 569, 570, 571, 623 Overprinted in Red (No. 91) or Black (all others)

Type B

Letters "A" with Sharp Pointed Tops

1925-28 ***Perf. 11***

No.	Description	Unused	Used
84	A157 2c **carmine** *(1,110,000) May 1926*	27.50	8.00
	Never hinged	45.00	
	On cover		11.00
	Block of 4	115.00	37.50
	P# block of 6	375.00	
	P# block of 6 & large 5 point star, side only	*2,000.*	
a.	"CANAL" only *(20)*	*2,250.*	
b.	"ZONE CANAL" *(180)*	425.00	
c.	Horizontal pair, one without overprint	*3,500.*	
d.	Booklet pane of 6 *(82,000)*	175.00	
e.	Se-tenant pair, #84a and 84b	*3,000.*	
85	A158 3c **violet** *(199,200) June 27, 1925*	3.75	3.00
	Never hinged	6.00	
	On cover		6.00
	Block of 4	16.50	12.50
	P# block of 6	165.00	
	"CANAL" in wrong font	*125.00*	*75.00*
	"ZONE" in wrong font	*175.00*	*125.00*
a.	"ZONE ZONE"	550.00	550.00
86	A160 5c **dark blue** *(1,343,147) Jan. 7, 1926*	3.50	2.75
	Never hinged	6.00	
	On cover		20.00
	Block of 4	15.00	12.00
	P# block of 6	165.00	
	Double transfer (15571 UL 86)	—	—
	"CANAL" in wrong font	*175.00*	*75.00*
	"ZONE" in wrong font	*250.00*	*125.00*
a.	"ZONE ZONE" (LR18)	1,000.	
b.	"CANAL" inverted (LR7)	950.00	
c.	Inverted overprint *(80)*	500.00	
d.	Horizontal pair, one without overprint	*3,250.*	
e.	Overprinted "ZONE CANAL" *(90)*	350.00	
f.	"ZONE" only *(10)*	*2,000.*	
g.	Vertical pair, one without overprint, other overprint inverted *(10)*	*2,000.*	
h.	"CANAL" only	*2,000.*	
i.	Se-tenant pair, #86e and 86f	*2,500.*	
87	A165 10c **orange** *(99,510) Aug. 1925*	35.00	12.00
	Never hinged	52.50	
	On cover		40.00
	Block of 4	160.00	72.50
	P# block of 6	500.00	
	"CANAL" in wrong font	*200.00*	*150.00*
	"ZONE" in wrong font	*325.00*	*200.00*
a.	"ZONE ZONE" (LR18)	*3,000.*	
b.	"ZONE" only (1)	*4,000.*	
88	A167 12c **brown violet** *(58,062) Feb. 1926*	20.00	12.50
	Never hinged	34.00	
	On cover		45.00
	Block of 4	100.00	57.50
	P# block of 6	375.00	
	"CANAL" in wrong font	*600.00*	*350.00*
	"ZONE" in wrong font	—	
a.	"ZONE ZONE" (LR18)	*5,000.*	
89	A168 14c **dark blue** *(55,700) Dec. 1928*	27.50	15.00
	Never hinged	45.00	
	On cover		50.00
	Block of 4	125.00	70.00
	P# block of 6	350.00	
90	A169 15c **gray** *(204,138) Nov. 1925*	7.50	4.50
	Never hinged	12.00	
	On cover		15.00
	Block of 4	35.00	21.00
	P# block of 6	200.00	
	P# block of 4, large 5 point star, side only	*3,000.*	
	"CANAL" in wrong font	*250.00*	*175.00*
	"ZONE" in wrong font	*275.00*	*225.00*
a.	"ZONE ZONE" (LR18)	*5,500.*	

It is believed that the four recorded P# blocks of 4 with large 5-point star are the largest known P# multiples from the plate that shows the star.

No.	Description	Unused	Used
91	A187 17c **black** *(199,500) Apr. 5, 1926*	4.50	2.75
	Never hinged	7.50	
	On cover		12.50
	First day cover		*750.00*
	Block of 4	19.00	13.00
	P# block of 6	190.00	
	"Z" of "ZONE" under "A" or "L" of "CANAL"	300.00	
a.	"ZONE" only *(40)*	1,000.	
b.	"CANAL" only *(11)*	1,900.	
c.	"ZONE CANAL" *(450)*	275.00	
d.	Se-tenant pair, #91a and 91c	*1,400.*	
92	A170 20c **carmine rose** *(259,807) Apr. 5, 1926*	7.25	3.25
	Never hinged	12.00	
	On cover		32.50
	First day cover		*750.00*
	Block of 4	32.50	14.00
	P# block of 6	175.00	
a.	"CANAL" inverted (UR48)	*6,500.*	
b.	"ZONE" inverted (LL76)	*4,750.*	
c.	"ZONE CANAL" (LL91)	*4,750.*	

Double transfer (14438 LR79)

No.	Description	Unused	Used
93	A172 30c **olive brown** *(154,700) Dec. 1925*	5.75	3.75
	Never hinged	9.00	
	On cover		60.00
	Block of 4	25.00	19.00
	P# block of 6	250.00	
	Double transfer (14438 LR79)	*550.00*	
	"CANAL" in wrong font	*225.00*	*150.00*
	"ZONE" in wrong font	*275.00*	*200.00*
94	A173 50c **lilac** *(13,533) July 1928*	230.00	165.00
	Never hinged	400.00	
	On cover		*500.00*
	Block of 4	1,100.	750.00
	P# block of 6	2,350.	
	"CANAL" in wrong font	*375.00*	*275.00*
	"ZONE" in wrong font	*425.00*	*350.00*
95	A174 $1 **violet brown** *(20,000) Apr. 1926*	120.00	55.00
	Never hinged	250.00	
	On cover		*1,000.*
	Block of 4	575.00	250.00
	Margin block of 4, arrow, top or bottom	625.00	
	P# block of 6	2,000.	
	"CANAL" in wrong font	*300.00*	*225.00*
	"ZONE" in wrong font	*350.00*	*275.00*
	Nos. 84-95 (12)	492.25	287.50

Nos. 85-88, 90 and 93-95 exist with wrong-font "CANAL" and "ZONE." Positions are: Nos. 85-88 and 90, UL51 (CANAL) and UL82 (ZONE); Nos. 93-95, U51 (CANAL) and U82 (ZONE).

Normal spacing between words of the overprint is 11mm on No. 84; 9mm on Nos. 85-88, 90, first printing of No. 91 and the first, third and fourth printing of No. 92; 7mm on the second printings of Nos. 91-92. Minor spacing varieties exist on Nos. 84-88, 90-92.

Overprint Type B on U.S. Sesquicentennial Stamp No. 627

1926

No.	Description	Unused	Used
96	A188 2c **carmine rose** *(300,000) July 6, 1926*	4.50	3.75
	Never hinged	7.00	
	On cover		8.00
	First day cover		60.00
	Block of 4	20.00	18.00
	P# block of 6	67.50	

On this stamp there is a space of 5mm instead of 9mm between the two words of the overprint.

The authorized date, July 4, fell on a Sunday with the next day also a holiday, so No. 96 was not regularly issued until July 6. But the postmaster sold some stamps and canceled some covers on July 4 for a few favored collectors.

Overprint Type B in Black on U.S. Nos. 583, 584, 591

1926-27 **Rotary Press Printings** ***Perf. 10***

No.	Description	Unused	Used
97	A157 2c **carmine** *(1,290,000) Dec. 1926*	45.00	11.00
	Never hinged	75.00	
	On cover		14.00
	Block of 4	200.00	50.00
	P# block of 4	525.00	
a.	Pair, one without overprint *(10)*	*2,250.*	
b.	Booklet pane of 6 *(58,000)*	500.00	
c.	"CANAL" only *(10)*	*2,000.*	
d.	"ZONE" only	*2,750.*	
98	A158 3c **violet** *(239,600) May 9, 1927*	7.50	4.25
	Never hinged	11.00	
	On cover		12.00
	Block of 4	32.50	19.00
	P# block of 4	120.00	
99	A165 10c **orange** *(128,400) May 9, 1927*	18.00	7.50
	Never hinged	27.50	
	On cover		35.00
	Block of 4	82.50	40.00
	P# block of 4	225.00	
	Nos. 97-99 (3)	70.50	22.75

No. 97d is valued in the grade of fine. Very fine examples are not known.

Overprint Type B in Black on U.S. Nos. 632, 634 (Type I), 635, 637, 642

1927-31 **Rotary Press Printings** ***Perf. 11x10½***

No.	Description	Unused	Used
100	A155 1c **green** *(434,892) June 28, 1927*	1.75	1.40
	Never hinged	2.60	
	On cover		3.00
	Block of 4	7.50	6.75
	P# block of 4	14.50	
a.	Vertical pair, one without overprint *(10)*	*3,250.*	
101	A157 2c **carmine** *(1,628,195) June 28, 1927*	1.75	1.00
	Never hinged	2.50	
	On cover		3.00
	Block of 4	8.00	4.75
	P# block of 4	17.50	
a.	Booklet pane of 6 *(82,108)*	200.00	
102	A158 3c **violet** *(1,250,000) Feb., 1931*	4.25	2.75
	Never hinged	6.25	
	On cover		5.00
	Block of 4	21.00	13.50
	P# block of 4	90.00	
a.	Booklet pane of 6, handmade, perf. margins	*6,500.*	
103	A160 5c **dark blue** *(60,000) Dec. 13, 1927*	25.00	10.00
	Never hinged	45.00	
	On cover		30.00
	Block of 4	110.00	42.50
	P# block of 4	175.00	
104	A165 10c **orange** *(119,800) July, 1930*	17.50	10.00
	Never hinged	26.00	
	On cover		35.00
	Block of 4	77.50	45.00
	P# block of 4	190.00	
	Nos. 100-104 (5)	50.25	25.15

Wet and Dry Printings

Canal Zone stamps printed by both the "wet" and "dry" process are Nos. 105, 108-109, 111-114, 117, 138-140, C21-C24, C26, J25, J27. Starting with Nos. 147 and C27, the Bureau of Engraving and Printing used the "dry" method exclusively. Late dry printings of Nos. 105, 108, 112-114, 117, 138 and 152 also exist with dull gum.

See note on Wet and Dry Printings following U.S. No. 1029.

Maj. Gen. William Crawford Gorgas — A35

Maj. Gen. George Washington Goethals — A36

Gaillard Cut — A37

Maj. Gen. Harry Foote Hodges — A38

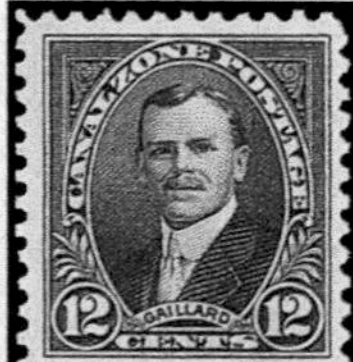

Lt. Col. David Du Bose Gaillard — A39

Maj. Gen. William Luther Sibert — A40

Jackson Smith — A41

Rear Adm. Harry Harwood Rousseau — A42

Col. Sydney Bacon Williamson — A43

Joseph Clay Styles Blackburn — A44

Printed by the U. S. Bureau of Engraving and Printing.
Plates of 400 subjects (except 5c), issued in panes of 100. The 5c was printed from plate of 200 subjects, issued in panes of 50. The 400-subject sheets were originally cut by knife into Post Office panes of 100, but beginning in 1948 they were separated by perforations to eliminate straight edges.

1928-40 Flat Plate Printing Unwmk. *Perf. 11*

105 A35 1c **green** *(22,392,147)* .25 .25
Never hinged .25
P# block of 6 2.50 —
a. Wet printing, yel grn, *Oct. 3, 1928* .25 .25
Never hinged .25
First day cover 17.50
P# block of 6 4.25 —
106 A36 2c **carmine** *(7,191,600) Oct. 1, 1928* .25 .25
Never hinged .30
First day cover 17.50
P# block of 6 3.00 —
a. Booklet pane of 6 *(284,640)* 15.00 *20.00*
Never hinged 22.50

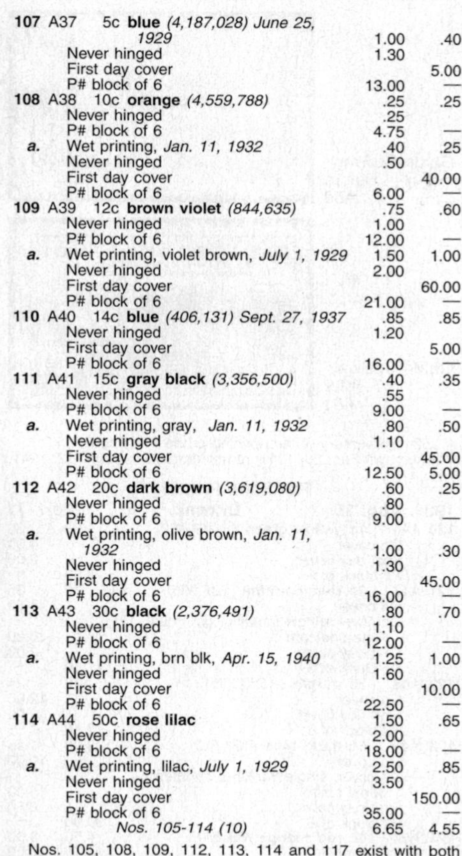
107 A37 5c **blue** *(4,187,028) June 25, 1929* 1.00 .40
Never hinged 1.30
First day cover 5.00
P# block of 6 13.00 —
108 A38 10c **orange** *(4,559,788)* .25 .25
Never hinged .25
P# block of 6 4.75 —
a. Wet printing, *Jan. 11, 1932* .40 .25
Never hinged .50
First day cover 40.00
P# block of 6 6.00 —
109 A39 12c **brown violet** *(844,635)* .75 .60
Never hinged 1.00
P# block of 6 12.00 —
a. Wet printing, violet brown, *July 1, 1929* 1.50 1.00
Never hinged 2.00
First day cover 60.00
P# block of 6 21.00 —
110 A40 14c **blue** *(406,131) Sept. 27, 1937* .85 .85
Never hinged 1.20
First day cover 5.00
P# block of 6 16.00 —
111 A41 15c **gray black** *(3,356,500)* .40 .35
Never hinged .55
P# block of 6 9.00 —
a. Wet printing, gray, *Jan. 11, 1932* .80 .50
Never hinged 1.10
First day cover 45.00
P# block of 6 12.50 5.00
112 A42 20c **dark brown** *(3,619,080)* .60 .25
Never hinged .80
P# block of 6 9.00 —
a. Wet printing, olive brown, *Jan. 11, 1932* 1.00 .30
Never hinged 1.30
First day cover 45.00
P# block of 6 16.00 —
113 A43 30c **black** *(2,376,491)* .80 .70
Never hinged 1.10
P# block of 6 12.00 —
a. Wet printing, brn blk, *Apr. 15, 1940* 1.25 1.00
Never hinged 1.60
First day cover 10.00
P# block of 6 22.50 —
114 A44 50c **rose lilac** 1.50 .65
Never hinged 2.00
P# block of 6 18.00 —
a. Wet printing, lilac, *July 1, 1929* 2.50 .85
Never hinged 3.50
First day cover 150.00
P# block of 6 35.00 —
Nos. 105-114 (10) 6.65 4.55

Nos. 105, 108, 109, 112, 113, 114 and 117 exist with both shiny gum and dull gum.
Coils are listed as Nos. 160-161.

United States Nos. 720 and 695 Overprinted type B

Rotary Press Printing

1933, Jan. 14 *Perf. 11x10½*

115 A226 3c **deep violet** *(3,150,000)* 2.75 .25
Never hinged 4.00
First day cover 12.00
P# block of 4 35.00 —
a. "ZONE" only (1) *4,000.*
b. "CANAL" only *2,600.*
c. Booklet pane of 6, handmade, perf. margins 80.00 —
With plate number *110.00*
d. Vertical pair, one without overprint —
e. Pair without overprint, one with "CANAL ZONE" on reverse, inverted (2) *3,000.*
116 A168 14c **dark blue** *(104,800)* 4.50 3.50
Never hinged 7.00
On cover 60.00
First day cover 20.00
P# block of 4 60.00 —
a. "ZONE CANAL" *(16)* *1,500.*

Maj. Gen. George Washington Goethals — A45

20th anniversary of the opening of the Panama Canal.

1934 Flat Plate Printing Unwmk. *Perf. 11*

117 A45 3c **red violet** .25 .25
Never hinged .30
First day cover 3.00
P# block of 6 1.00 —
a. Booklet pane of 6 *12.50* *32.50*
Never hinged *20.00*

b. As "a," handmade, perf. margins 160.00 —
c. Wet printing, violet, *Aug. 15* .30 .25
P# block of 6 1.90 —

Coil is listed as No. 153.

Catalogue values for unused stamps in this section, from this point to the end, are for Never Hinged items.

United States Nos. 803 and 805 Overprinted in Black

Rotary Press Printing

1939, Sept. 1 Unwmk. *Perf. 11x10½*

118 A275 ½c **red orange** *(1,030,000)* .25 .25
Single franking, with 1c additional on third-class cover 50.00
Single franking, with 1c postal stationery on third-class cover *150.00*
First day cover 1.00
P# block of 4 2.75 —
119 A277 1½c **bister brown** *(935,000)* .25 .25
brown .30 .25
Single franking on third-class cover *50.00*
First day cover 1.00
P# block of 4 2.25 —

Balboa-Before A46

Balboa-After A47

Gaillard Cut-Before A48

Gaillard Cut-After A49

Bas Obispo-Before A50

Bas Obispo-After A51

Gatun Locks-Before A52

Gatun Locks-After A53

Canal Channel-Before A54

Canal Channel-After A55

Gamboa-Before A56

Gamboa-After A57

Pedro Miguel Locks-Before A58

Pedro Miguel Locks-After A59

Gatun Spillway-Before A60

Gatun Spillway-After A61

25th anniversary of the opening of the Panama Canal.
Withdrawn Feb. 28, 1941; remainders burned Apr. 12, 1941.

Flat Plate Printing

1939, Aug. 15 **Unwmk.** ***Perf. 11***

120 A46 1c **yellow green** *(1,019,482)* .60 .30
On cover 4.00
First day cover 2.00
P# block of 6 17.50 —

121 A47 2c **rose carmine** *(227,065)* .70 .35
On cover 7.50
On cover, single franking, on Treaty Rate postcard 40.00
First day cover 2.00
P# block of 6 17.50 —

122 A48 3c **purple** *(2,523,735)* .70 .25
On cover 12.00
First day cover 2.00
P# block of 6 17.50 —

123 A49 5c **dark blue** *(460,213)* 2.00 1.25
On cover 10.00
On cover, single franking, on international cover 15.00
First day cover 2.50
P# block of 6 30.00 —

124 A50 6c **red orange** *(68,290)* 4.50 3.00
On cover 12.00
On cover, single franking, on Steamer/Plane cover to U.S. 25.00
First day cover 6.00
P# block of 6 75.00 —

125 A51 7c **black** *(71,235)* 4.75 3.00
On cover 15.00
First day cover 6.00
P# block of 6 75.00 —

126 A52 8c **green** *(41,576)* 7.00 3.25
On cover 15.00
First day cover 6.00
P# block of 6 85.00 —

127 A53 10c **ultramarine** *(83,571)* 5.50 5.00
On cover 15.00
On cover, single franking, on airmail cover to Costa Rica or Colombia coast 100.00
First day cover 6.00
P# block of 6 85.00 —

128 A54 11c **blue green** *(34,010)* 11.00 8.00
On cover 35.00
First day cover 10.00
P# block of 6 175.00 —

129 A55 12c **brown carmine** *(66,735)* 11.00 7.50
On cover 12.50
First day cover 10.00
P# block of 6 150.00 —

130 A56 14c **dark violet** *(37,365)* 11.00 7.00
On cover 35.00
On cover, single uprating of 1c postal stationery on airmail cover to U.S. 125.00
First day cover 10.00
P# block of 6 175.00 —

131 A57 15c **olive green** *(105,058)* 14.00 5.75
On cover 12.50
First day cover 10.00
P# block of 6 190.00 —

132 A58 18c **rose pink** *(39,255)* 15.00 8.50
On cover 20.00
On cover 20.00
On cover, single franking, on registered cover to Zone or U.S. 40.00
First day cover 10.00
P# block of 6 190.00 —

133 A59 20c **brown** *(100,244)* 17.50 7.00
On cover 35.00
First day cover 10.00
P# block of 6 200.00 —

134 A60 25c **orange** *(34,283)* 27.50 15.00
On cover 175.00
First day cover 20.00
P# block of 6 400.00 —

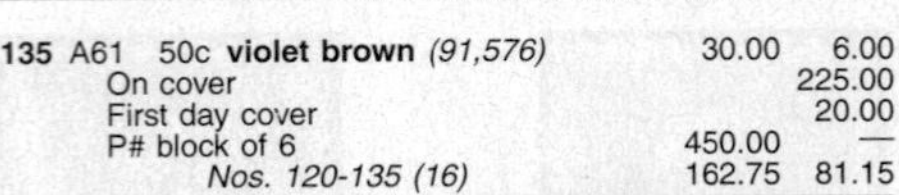

135 A61 50c **violet brown** *(91,576)* 30.00 6.00
On cover 225.00
First day cover 20.00
P# block of 6 450.00 —
Nos. 120-135 (16) 162.75 81.15

Values for Nos. 120-165 on cover and for single franking usages of these issues are for commercial covers dated near the period of availability of the issue in post offices. Philatelically contrived covers are worth less.

Maj. Gen. George W. Davis — A62

Gov. Charles E. Magoon — A63

Theodore Roosevelt — A64

John F. Stevens — A65

John F. Wallace — A66

1946-49 **Unwmk.** ***Perf. 11***
Size: 19x22mm

136 A62 ½c **bright red** *(1,020,000) Aug. 16, 1948* .40 .25
On cover 2.00
On cover, single, with 1c additional on 3rd-class cover 75.00
First day cover 1.25
P# block of 6 3.00 —

137 A63 1½c **chocolate** *(603,600) Aug. 16, 1948* .40 .25
On cover 2.00
On cover, single franking, on 3rd-class cover 100.00
First day cover 1.25
P# block of 6 3.00 —

138 A64 2c **light rose carmine** *(6,951,755)* .25 .25
P# block of 6 .65 —
a. Wet printing, rose carmine, *Oct. 27, 1949* .25 .25
First day cover 1.00
P# block of 6 1.00 —

139 A65 5c **dark blue** .35 .25
P# block of 6 2.50 —
a. Wet printing, deep blue, *Apr. 25, 1946* .60 .25
First day cover 1.00
P# block of 6 4.50 —

140 A66 25c **green** *(1,520,000)* .85 .55
On cover 20.00
P# block of 6 7.00 —
a. Wet printing, yel grn, *Aug. 16, 1948* 3.00 1.00
First day cover 3.50
P# block of 6 24.00 —
Nos. 136-140 (5) 2.25 1.55

See Nos. 155, 162, 164. For overprint, see No. O9.

Map of Biological Area and Coati-mundi A67

25th anniversary of the establishment of the Canal Zone Biological Area on Barro Colorado Island.
Withdrawn Mar. 30, 1951, and remainders destroyed Apr. 10, 1951.

1948, Apr. 17 **Unwmk.** ***Perf. 11***

141 A67 10c **black** *(521,200)*	1.75	1.00
On cover		4.00
On cover, single franking, airmail to Central or S. America		8.00
First day cover		3.00
P# block of 6	15.00	—

"Forty-niners" Arriving at Chagres — A68

Journeying in "Bungo" to Las Cruces — A69

Las Cruces Trail to Panama — A70

Departure for San Francisco — A71

Centenary of the California Gold Rush.
Stocks on hand were processed for destruction on Aug. 11, 1952 and destroyed Aug. 13, 1952.

1949, June 1 **Unwmk.** ***Perf. 11***

142 A68 3c **blue** *(500,000)*	.65	.25
On cover		2.00
On foreign postcard		12.00
First day cover		1.00
P# block of 6	6.50	—
143 A69 6c **violet** *(481,600)*	.65	.30
On cover		2.00
First day cover		1.00
P# block of 6	6.50	—
144 A70 12c **bright blue green** *(230,200)*	1.75	.90
On cover		8.00
First day cover		2.00
P# block of 6	21.00	—
145 A71 18c **deep red lilac** *(240,200)*	2.00	1.50
On cover		8.00
First day cover		3.25
P# block of 6	20.00	—
Nos. 142-145 (4)	5.05	2.95

Workers in Culebra Cut — A72

Contribution of West Indian laborers in the construction of the Panama Canal.
Entire issue sold, none withdrawn and destroyed.

1951, Aug. 15 **Unwmk.** ***Perf. 11***

146 A72 10c **carmine** *(480,000)*	3.50	1.50
On cover		5.00
On cover, single franking, airmail to Central or S. America		12.50
First day cover		3.00
P# block of 6	27.50	—

Centenary of the completion of the Panama Railroad and the first transcontinental railroad trip in the Americas.

Early Railroad Scene — A73

1955, Jan. 28 **Unwmk.** ***Perf. 11***

147 A73 3c **violet** *(994,000)*	1.00	.60
On cover		5.00
First day cover		1.50
P# block of 6	8.00	—

Gorgas Hospital and Ancon Hill — A74

75th anniversary of Gorgas Hospital.

1957, Nov. 17 **Unwmk.** ***Perf. 11***

148 A74 3c **black,** *dull blue green (1,010,000)*	.45	.35
Light blue green paper	.40	.35
On cover		5.00
On postcard or drop-letter rate after Aug. 1, 1958		10.00
First day cover		1.00
P# block of 4	4.25	—

S.S. Ancon — A75

1958, Aug. 30 **Unwmk.** ***Perf. 11***

149 A75 4c **greenish blue** *(1,749,700)*	.40	.30
On cover		4.00
On postcard or drop-letter rate after Jan. 7, 1963		10.00
First day cover		1.00
P# block of 4	3.25	—

Roosevelt Medal and Canal Zone Map — A76

Centenary of the birth of Theodore Roosevelt (1858-1919).

1958, Nov. 15 **Unwmk.** ***Perf. 11***

150 A76 4c **brown** *(1,060,000)*	.60	.30
On cover		4.00
First day cover		1.00
P# block of 4	3.50	—

Boy Scout Badge — A77

50th anniversary of the Boy Scouts of America.

Giori Press Printing

1960, Feb. 8 **Unwmk.** ***Perf. 11***

151 A77 4c **dark blue, red & bister** *(654,933)*	.55	.40
On cover		4.00
First day cover		1.50
P# block of 4	4.50	—

Administration Building, Balboa Heights — A78

1960, Nov. 1 **Unwmk.** ***Perf. 11***

152 A78 4c **rose lilac** *(2,486,725)*	.25	.25
First day cover		1.00
P# block of 4	.90	—

Types of 1934, 1960 and 1946

Coil Stamps

1960-62 **Unwmk.** ***Perf. 10 Vertically***

153 A45 3c **deep violet** *(3,743,959) Nov. 1, 1960*	.25	.25
First day cover		1.00
Pair	.40	.25
Joint line pair	1.10	—
Perf. 10 Horizontally		
154 A78 4c **dull rose lilac** *(2,776,273) Nov. 1, 1960*	.25	.25
First day cover		1.00
Pair	.40	.25
Joint line pair	1.10	—
Perf. 10 Vertically		
155 A65 5c **deep blue** *(3,288,264) Feb. 10, 1962*	.25	.25
First day cover		1.00
Pair	.50	.50
Joint line pair	1.25	—
Nos. 153-155 (3)	.75	.75

Girl Scout Badge and Camp at Gatun Lake — A79

50th anniversary of the Girl Scouts.

Giori Press Printing

1962, Mar. 12 **Unwmk.** ***Perf. 11***

156 A79 4c **blue, dark green & bister** *(640,000)*	.40	.30
On cover		4.00
First day cover *(83,717)*		1.25
P# block of 4	2.75	—

Thatcher Ferry Bridge and Map of Western Hemisphere A80

Opening of the Thatcher Ferry Bridge, spanning the Panama Canal.

Giori Press Printing

1962, Oct. 12 **Unwmk.** ***Perf. 11***

157 A80 4c **black & silver** *(775,000)*	.35	.25
On cover		4.00
First day cover *(65,833)*		1.00
P# block of 4, 2P#	3.75	—
a. Silver (bridge) omitted *(50)*	*8,000.*	
Hinged	*6,000.*	
P# block of 6, black P# only	*55,000.*	

Goethals Memorial, Balboa — A81

Fort San Lorenzo — A82

1968-71 **Giori Press Printing** ***Perf. 11***

158 A81 6c **green & ultra.** *(1,890,000) Mar. 15, 1968*	.30	.30
First day cover		1.00
P# block of 4	2.00	—
159 A82 8c **slate green, blue, dark brown & ocher** *(3,460,000) July 14, 1971*	.35	.25
First day cover		1.00
P# block of 4	2.75	—

Types of 1928, 1932 and 1948
Coil Stamps

1975, Feb. 14 — Unwmk. — *Perf. 10 Vertically*

No.	Description	Unused	Used
160	A35 1c **green** *(1,090,958)*	.25	.25
	First day cover		1.00
	Pair	.40	.30
	Joint line pair	1.00	—
161	A38 10c **orange** *(590,658)*	.70	.40
	First day cover		1.00
	Pair	1.40	.80
	Joint line pair	5.00	—
162	A66 25c **yellow green** *(129,831)*	2.75	2.75
	First day cover		3.00
	Pair	5.50	5.50
	Joint line pair	19.00	—
	Nos. 160-162 (3)	3.70	3.40

Dredge Cascadas A83

1976, Feb. 23 — Giori Press Printing — *Perf. 11*

No.	Description	Unused	Used
163	A83 13c **multicolored** *(3,653,950)*	.35	.25
	On cover		3.00
	First day cover		1.00
	P# block of 4	2.00	—
a.	Booklet pane of 4 *(1,032,400) Apr. 19*	3.00	—

No. 163a exists with and without staple holes in selvage tab.

Stevens Type of 1946

1977 — Rotary Press Printing — *Perf. 11x10½*
Size: 19x22½mm

No.	Description	Unused	Used
164	A65 5c **deep blue** *(1,009,612)*	.60	.85
	P# block of 4	3.50	—
a.	Tagged, dull gum	12.00	15.00
	On cover		150.00
	P# block of 4	125.00	—

No. 164 exists with both shiny gum and dull gum. Stamps with dull gum exist with and without tagging.

No. 164a exists even though there was no equipment in the Canal Zone to detect tagging.

Towing Locomotive, Ship in Lock, by Alwyn Sprague A84

1978, Oct. 25 — *Perf. 11*

No.	Description	Unused	Used
165	A84 15c **dp grn & bl grn** *(2,921,083)*	.35	.25
	On cover		4.00
	First day cover *(81,405)*		1.00
	P# block of 4	2.00	—

AIR POST STAMPS

> Values for Nos. C1-C53 on cover and for single franking usages of these issues are for commercial covers dated near the period of availability of the issue in post offices. Philatelically contrived covers are worth less.

Regular Issue of 1928 Surcharged in Dark Blue

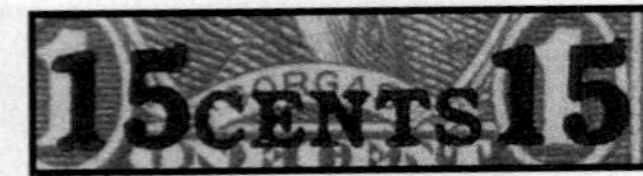

Type I - Flag of "Five" pointing up

Type II - Flag of "5" curved

1929-31 — Flat Plate Printing — Unwmk. — *Perf. 11*

No.	Description	Unused	Used
C1	A35 15c on 1c **green,** type I, *Apr. 1, 1929*	7.50	4.75
	Never hinged	11.50	
	On cover		15.00
	On cover, single franking, to 15c airmail rate countries (Jamaica, Nicaragua, Ecuador or Colombia coast)		60.00
	First day cover		25.00
	Block of 4	32.50	25.00
	P# block of 6	120.00	—
C2	A35 15c on 1c **yellow green,** type II, *Mar. 1931*	60.00	47.50
	Never hinged	120.00	
	On cover		175.00
	Block of 4	300.00	340.00
	P# block of 6	900.00	—
C3	A36 25c on 2c **carmine** *(223,880) Jan. 11, 1929*	3.50	2.00
	Never hinged	5.25	
	On cover		15.00
	First day cover		17.50
	Block of 4	15.00	9.00
	P# block of 6	115.00	—
	Nos. C1-C3 (3)	71.00	54.25

Nos. 114 and 106 Surcharged in Black

1929, Dec. 31

No.	Description	Unused	Used
C4	A44 10c on 50c **lilac** *(116,666)*	8.00	5.75
	Never hinged	12.00	
	On cover		15.00
	On cover, single franking, on airmail cover to Costa Rica or Colombia coast		50.00
	First day cover		25.00
	Block of 4	35.00	25.00
	P# block of 6	120.00	—
C5	A36 20c on 2c **carmine** *(638,395)*	4.50	1.25
	Never hinged	7.50	
	On cover		7.50
	First day cover		20.00
	Block of 4	18.00	6.00
	P# block of 6	110.00	—
a.	Dropped "2" in surcharge *(7,000)*	85.00	60.00

> **Catalogue values for unused stamps in this section, from this point to the end, are for Never Hinged items.**

Gaillard Cut — AP1

Printed by the U. S. Bureau of Engraving and Printing.

Plates of 200 subjects, issued in panes of 50.

1931-49 — Unwmk. — *Perf. 11*

No.	Description	Unused	Used
C6	AP1 4c **red violet** *(525,000) Jan. 3, 1949*	.75	.65
	First day cover		2.00
	P# block of 6	5.25	—
C7	AP1 5c **yellow green** *(9,935,500) Nov. 18, 1931*	.60	.30
	green	.60	.30
	First day cover		10.00
	P# block of 6	4.50	—
C8	AP1 6c **yellow brown** *(9,399,500) Feb. 15, 1946*	.75	.35
	First day cover		2.00
	P# block of 6	5.25	—
C9	AP1 10c **orange** *(5,079,000) Nov. 18, 1931*	1.00	.35
	First day cover		10.00
	P# block of 6	10.00	—
C10	AP1 15c **blue** *(11,072,700) Nov. 18, 1931*	1.25	.30
	pale blue	1.25	.30
	First day cover		15.00
	P# block of 6	11.00	—
C11	AP1 20c **red violet** *(3,184,100) Nov. 18, 1931*	2.00	.25
	deep violet	2.00	.30
	First day cover		35.00
	P# block of 6	20.00	—
C12	AP1 30c **rose lake** *(1,119,500) July 15, 1941*	7.50	1.50
	dull rose	7.50	1.50
	First day cover		22.50
	P# block of 6	60.00	—
C13	AP1 40c **yellow** *(795,600) Nov. 18, 1931*	3.50	1.10
	lemon	3.50	1.10
	First day cover		75.00
	P# block of 6	35.00	—
C14	AP1 $1 **black** *(372,500) Nov. 18, 1931*	10.00	1.60
	First day cover		150.00
	P# block of 6	95.00	—
	Nos. C6-C14 (9)	27.35	6.40

For overprints, see Nos. CO1-CO14.

Douglas Plane over Sosa Hill — AP2

Planes and Map of Central America AP3

Pan American Clipper and Scene near Fort Amador — AP4

Pan American Clipper at Cristobal Harbor — AP5

Pan American Clipper over Gaillard Cut — AP6

Pan American Clipper Landing — AP7

10th anniversary of Air Mail service and the 25th anniversary of the opening of the Panama Canal.

Withdrawn Feb. 28, 1941, remainders burned Apr. 12, 1941.

Flat Plate Printing

1939, July 15 **Unwmk.** ***Perf. 11***

C15 AP2 5c **greenish black** *(86,576)* 3.75 2.25
On cover 7.50
First day cover 5.00
P# block of 6 45.00 —
C16 AP3 10c **dull violet** *(117,644)* 3.50 3.00
On cover 7.50
On cover, single franking, on airmail cover to Costa Rica or Colombia coast 75.00
First day cover 5.00
P# block of 6 47.50 —
C17 AP4 15c **light brown** *(883,742)* 5.00 1.00
On cover 3.00
First day cover 3.00
P# block of 6 57.50 —
C18 AP5 25c **blue** *(82,126)* 17.50 8.00
On cover 15.00
On cover, single franking, to 25c airmail-rate countries (Peru, the Guianas, Haiti, Dominican Republic, etc.) 45.00
First day cover 17.50
P# block of 6 275.00 —
C19 AP6 30c **rose carmine** *(121,382)* 17.50 6.00
On cover 10.00
First day cover 15.00
P# block of 6 200.00 —
C20 AP7 $1 **green** *(40,051)* 45.00 27.50
On cover 200.00
On cover, single franking, on registered airmail cover to Australasia, Asia or Africa 300.00
First day cover 60.00
P# block of 6 525.00 —
Nos. C15-C20 (6) 92.25 47.75

Globe and Wing — AP8

Flat Plate Printing

1951, July 16 **Unwmk.** ***Perf. 11***

C21 AP8 4c **lt red violet** *(1,315,000)* .75 .35
P# block of 6 7.00 —
a. Wet printing, red violet 1.25 .40
1st day card, Balboa Heights 1.50
P# block of 6 10.00 —
C22 AP8 6c **lt brown** *(22,657,625)* .50 .25
P# block of 6 5.00 —
a. Wet printing, brown .95 .35
1st day cover, Balboa Heights 1.00
P# block of 6 7.50 —
C23 AP8 10c **lt red orange** *(1,049,130)* .90 .35
P# block of 6 8.00 —
a. Wet printing, red orange 2.00 .50
1st day cover, Balboa Heights 2.00
P# block of 6 16.00 —
C24 AP8 21c **lt blue** *(1,460,000)* 8.00 4.00
P# block of 6 75.00 —
a. Wet printing, blue 15.00 5.00
1st day cover, Balboa Heights 7.50
P# block of 6 125.00 —
C25 AP8 31c **cerise** *(375,000)* 9.50 3.75
On cover 25.00
On cover, single franking, on airmail cover to Australasia, Asia or Africa 40.00
1st day cover, Balboa Heights 7.50
P# block of 6 80.00 —
a. Horiz. pair, imperf. vert. *(98)* 1,250. —
C26 AP8 80c **lt gray black** *(827,696)* 6.00 1.50
On cover 100.00
P# block of 6 45.00 —
a. Wet printing, gray black 12.50 1.65
1st day cover, Balboa Heights 12.50
1st day cover, Balboa Heights, #C21-C26 20.00
P# block of 6 115.00 —
Nos. C21-C26 (6) 25.65 10.20

See note after No. 114. Total number of first day covers with one or more of Nos. C21-C26, about 12,000.

Flat Plate Printing

1958, Aug. 16 **Unwmk.** ***Perf. 11***

C27 AP8 5c **yellow green** *(899,923)* 1.00 .60
First day cover *(2,176)* 4.50
P# block of 4 6.00 —
C28 AP8 7c **olive** *(9,381,797)* 1.00 .45
First day cover *(2,815)* 4.50
P# block of 4 6.00 —
C29 AP8 15c **brown violet** *(359,923)* 4.50 2.75
First day cover *(2,040)* 6.00
P# block of 4 37.50 —
C30 AP8 25c **orange yellow** *(600,000)* 12.50 2.75
First day cover *(2,115)* 9.00
P# block of 4 125.00 —
C31 AP8 35c **dark blue** *(283,032)* 9.00 2.75
On cover 30.00
On cover, single franking, on airmail cover to Australasia, Asia or Africa 80.00
First day cover *(1,868)* 11.00
P# block of 4 60.00 —
Nos. C27-C31 (5) 28.00 9.30
Nos. C21-C31 (11) 53.65 19.50

See No. C34.

Emblem of US Army Caribbean School — AP9

US Army Caribbean School for Latin America at Fort Gulick.

Giori Press Printing

1961, Nov. 21 **Unwmk.** ***Perf. 11***

C32 AP9 15c **red & blue** *(560,000)* 1.60 .75
On cover 7.50
On cover, single franking, on foreign postcard or letter to Western Hemisphere 10.00
First day cover *(25,949)* 1.75
P# block of 4 9.50 —

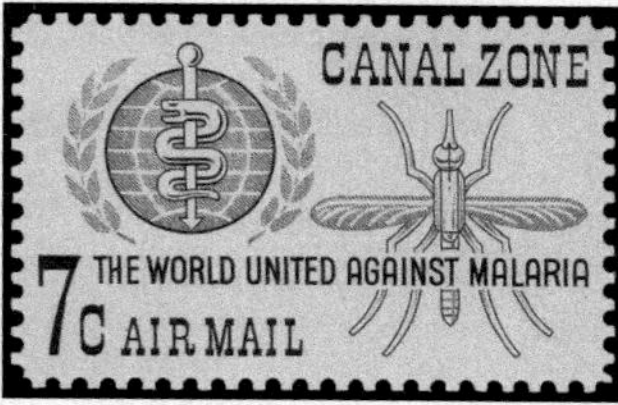

Malaria Eradication Emblem and Mosquito AP10

World Health Organization drive to eradicate malaria.

Giori Press Printing

1962, Sept. 24 **Unwmk.** ***Perf. 11***

C33 AP10 7c **yellow & black** *(862,349)* .50 .40
On cover 5.00
On cover, single franking, airmail to US 10.00
First day cover *(44,433)* 1.00
P# block of 4 3.00 —

Globe-Wing Type of 1951

Rotary Press Printing

1963, Jan. 7 ***Perf. 10½x11***

C34 AP8 8c **carmine** *(5,054,727)* .75 .30
First day cover *(19,128)* 1.00
P# block of 4 4.00 —

Alliance for Progress Emblem AP11

2nd anniv. of the Alliance for Progress, which aims to stimulate economic growth and raise living standards in Latin America.

Giori Press Printing

1963, Aug. 17 **Unwmk.** ***Perf. 11***

C35 AP11 15c **gray, grn & dk ultra** *(405,000)* 1.50 .85
On cover 7.50
On cover, single franking, on foreign postcard or letter to Western Hemisphere 12.50
First day cover *(29,594)* 1.50
P# block of 4 12.50 —

Jet over Canal Zone Views — AP12

50th anniversary of the opening of the Panama Canal.

Designs: 6c, Cristobal. 8c, Gatun Locks. 15c, Madden Dam. 20c, Gaillard Cut. 30c, Miraflores Locks. 80c, Balboa.

Giori Press Printing

1964, Aug. 15 **Unwmk.** ***Perf. 11***

C36 AP12 6c **green & black** *(257,193)* .60 .35
On cover 1.50
1st day cover, Balboa 1.50
P# block of 4 3.75 —
C37 AP12 8c **rose red & black** *(3,924,283)* .60 .35
On cover 1.00
1st day cover, Balboa 1.00
P# block of 4 4.00 —
C38 AP12 15c **blue & black** *(472,666)* 1.25 .75
On cover 7.50
On cover, single franking, on foreign postcard 12.50
1st day cover, Balboa 1.00
P# block of 4 9.25 —
C39 AP12 20c **rose lilac & black** *(399,784)* 1.60 1.00
On cover 15.00
On cover, single franking, to Europe or North Africa 40.00
1st day cover, Balboa 2.00
P# block of 4 10.00 —
C40 AP12 30c **reddish brown & black** *(204,524)* 2.75 2.25
On cover 10.00
On cover, single franking, to Australasia, Asia, or sub-Sahara Africa 50.00
1st day cover, Balboa 3.00
P# block of 4 17.50 —
C41 AP12 80c **olive bister & black** *(186,809)* 4.75 3.00
On cover 75.00
1st day cover, Balboa 4.00
1st day cover, Balboa, #C36-C41 10.00
P# block of 4 26.00 —
Nos. C36-C41 (6) 11.55 7.70

There were 57,822 first day covers with one or more of Nos. C36-C41.

Canal Zone Seal and Jet Plane — AP13

Giori Press Printing

1965, July 15 **Unwmk.** ***Perf. 11***

C42 AP13 6c **green & black** *(548,250)* .50 .30
First day cover, Balboa 2.00
P# block of 4 3.25 —
C43 AP13 8c **rose red & black** *(8,357,700)* .45 .25
First day cover, Balboa 1.00
P# block of 4 3.00 —
C44 AP13 15c **blue & black** *(2,385,000)* .75 .25
On cover, single franking, on foreign postcard or letter to Western Hemisphere 8.00
First day cover, Balboa 1.00
P# block of 4 7.00 —
C45 AP13 20c **lilac & black** *(2,290,699)* .80 .30
On cover, single franking, to Europe or North Africa 15.00
First day cover, Balboa 1.25
P# block of 4 4.25 —
C46 AP13 30c **redsh brn & blk** *(2,332,255)* 1.10 .30
On cover, single franking, to Australasia, Asia or sub-Sahara Africa 25.00
First day cover, Balboa 1.25
P# block of 4 6.00 —
C47 AP13 80c **bister & black** *(1,456,596)* 2.50 .75
On cover 15.00
First day cover, Balboa 2.50
First day cover, Balboa, #C42-C47 7.00
P# block of 4 18.00 —
Nos. C42-C47 (6) 6.10 2.15

No. C46 also exists with dull gum.

There were 35,389 first day covers with one or more of Nos. C42-C47.

1968-76

C48 AP13 10c **dull orange & black** *(10,055,000) Mar. 15, 1968* .35 .25
First day cover, Balboa *(7,779)* 1.00
P# block of 4 3.50 —
a. Booklet pane of 4 *(713,390) Feb. 18, 1970* 4.25 —
First day cover, Balboa *(5,054)* 5.00
C49 AP13 11c **olive & black** *(3,335,000) Sept. 24, 1971* .35 .25
First day cover, Balboa *(10,916)* 1.00
P# block of 4 3.50 —
a. Booklet pane of 4 *(1,277,760) Sept. 24, 1971* 3.50 —
First day cover, Balboa *(2,460)* 5.00
C50 AP13 13c **emerald & black** *(1,865,000) Feb. 11, 1974* .85 .25
First day cover, Balboa *(7,646)* 1.00
P# block of 4 5.00 —
a. Booklet pane of 4 *(619,200) Feb. 11, 1974* 6.00 —
First day cover, Balboa *(3,660)* 5.00
C51 AP13 22c **vio & blk** *(363,720) May 10, 1976* 1.10 *2.00*
On cover, single franking, on foreign postcard 15.00
First day cover, Balboa 2.50
P# block of 4 8.00 —
C52 AP13 25c **pale yellow green & black** *(1,640,441) Mar. 15, 1968* .80 .70
On cover, single franking, to Western Hemisphere 22.50
First day cover, Balboa 1.00
P# block of 4 5.50 —
C53 AP13 35c **salmon & black** *(573,822) May 10, 1976* 1.25 *2.00*
On cover, single franking, to Europe or North Africa 15.00

First day cover, Balboa — 2.50
P# block of 4 — 10.00 —
Nos. C48-C53 (6) — 4.70 *5.45*

No. C50a exists with and without staple holes in selvage tab.
There were 5,047 first day covers with one or more of Nos. C51, C53.

AIR POST OFFICIAL STAMPS

Beginning in March 1915, stamps for use on official mail were identified by a large "P" perforated through each stamp. These were replaced by overprinted issues in 1941. The use of official stamps was discontinued December 31, 1951. During their currency, they were not for sale in mint condition and were sold to the public only when canceled with a parcel post rotary canceler reading "Balboa Heights, Canal Zone" between two wavy lines.

After having been withdrawn from use, mint stamps (except Nos. CO8-CO12 and O3, O8) were made available to the public at face value for three months beginning Jan. 2, 1952. **Values for used examples of Nos. CO1-CO7, CO14, O1-O2, O4-O9, are for canceled-to-order stamps with original gum, postally used stamps being worth more.** Sheet margins were removed to facilitate overprinting and plate numbers are, therefore, unknown.

Air Post Stamps of 1931-41 Overprinted in Black

Two types of overprint

Type I — "PANAMA CANAL" 19-20mm long

1941-42 Unwmk. *Perf. 11*

CO1 AP1 5c **yellow green** *(42,754) Mar. 31, 1941* — 6.50 1.50
green — 6.50 1.50
On cover — 50.00
Block of 4 — 27.50 6.00
CO2 AP1 10c **orange** *(49,723) Mar. 31, 1941* — 8.50 1.75
On cover — 25.00
Block of 4 — 37.50 8.00
CO3 AP1 15c **blue** *(56,898) Mar. 31, 1941* — 11.00 1.75
On cover — 25.00
Block of 4 — 47.50 15.00
CO4 AP1 20c **red violet** *(22,107) Mar. 31, 1941* — 13.00 4.00
deep violet — 13.00 4.00
On cover — 110.00
Block of 4 — 62.50 22.50
CO5 AP1 30c **rose lake** *(22,100) June, 4, 1942* — 17.50 5.00
dull rose — 17.50 4.50
On cover — 40.00
Block of 4 — 80.00 22.50
CO6 AP1 40c **yellow** *(22,875) Mar. 31, 1941* — 17.50 7.50
lemon yellow — 17.50 7.50
On cover — 75.00
Block of 4 — 80.00 37.50
CO7 AP1 $1 **black** *(29,525) Mar. 31, 1941* — 20.00 10.00
On cover — 150.00
Block of 4 — 90.00 45.00
Nos. CO1-CO7 (7) — 94.00 31.50

Overprint varieties occur on Nos. CO1-CO7 and CO14: "O" of "OFFICIAL" over "N" of "PANAMA" (entire third row). "O" of "OFFICIAL" broken at top (position 31). "O" of "OFFICIAL" over second "A" of "PANAMA" (position 45). First "F" of "OFFICIAL" over second "A" of "PANAMA" (position 50).

Type II — "PANAMA CANAL" 17mm long

1941, Sept. 22

CO8 AP1 5c **yellow green** *(2,000)* — — 150.00
On cover — 500.00
Block of 4 — 925.00
CO9 AP1 10c **orange** *(2,000)* — *1,100.* 260.00
On cover — 400.00
Block of 4 — 1,650.
CO10 AP1 20c **red violet** *(2,000)* — — 160.00
On cover — —
Block of 4 — 1,050.
CO11 AP1 30c **rose lake** *(5,000)* — *900.* 60.00
On cover — 125.00
Block of 4 — 325.00
CO12 AP1 40c **yellow** *(2,000)* — — 170.00
On cover — 500.00
Block of 4 — 1,100.
Nos. CO8-CO12 (5) — 800.00

Type I — "PANAMA CANAL" 19-20mm long

1947, Nov.

CO14 AP1 6c **yellow brown** *(33,450)* — 13.00 5.50
On cover — 50.00
Block of 4 — 60.00 25.00
a. Inverted overprint *(50)* — *2,000.*

POSTAGE DUE STAMPS

Prior to 1914, many of the postal issues were handstamped "Postage Due" and used as postage due stamps.

Postage Due Stamps of the United States Nos. J45a, J46a, and J49a Overprinted in Black

1914, Mar. Wmk. 190 *Perf. 12*

J1 D2 1c **rose carmine** *(23,533)* — 85.00 15.00
On cover — 275.00
Block of 4 (2mm spacing) — 425.00 70.
Block of 4 (3mm spacing) — 450.00 80.00
P# block of 6, impt. & star — 1,000. —
J2 D2 2c **rose carmine** *(32,312)* — 250.00 42.50
On cover — 275.00
Block of 4 — 1,250. 200.00
P# block of 6 — 2,000. —
J3 D2 10c **rose carmine** *(92,493)* — 900.00 40.00
On cover — 900.00
Block of 4 (2mm spacing) — 4,000. 170.
Block of 4 (3mm spacing) — 4,000. 170.00
P# block of 6, Impt. & star — *23,000.* —

Many examples of Nos. J1-J3 show one or more letters of the overprint out of alignment, principally the "E."

Two examples exist of the plate block of No. J3. The value reflects the 2009 auction sale of the finer of the two.

San Geronimo Castle Gate, Portobelo (See footnote) — D1

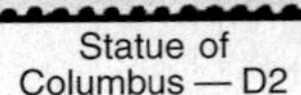

Statue of Columbus — D2

Pedro J. Sosa — D3

1915, Mar. Unwmk. *Perf. 12*

Blue Overprint, Type II, on Postage Due Stamps of Panama

J4 D1 1c **olive brown** *(50,000)* — 11.00 5.00
On cover — 150.00
Block of 4 — 50.00 22.50
J5 D2 2c **olive brown** *(50,000)* — 225.00 17.50
On cover — 425.00
Block of 4 — 975.00 90.00
J6 D3 10c **olive brown** *(200,000)* — 50.00 10.00
On cover — 175.00
Block of 4 — 225.00 45.00
Nos. J4-J6 (3) — 286.00 32.50

Type D1 was intended to show a gate of San Lorenzo Castle, Chagres, and is so labeled. By error the stamp actually shows the main gate of San Geronimo Castle, Portobelo.

Surcharged in Red

1915, Nov. Unwmk. *Perf. 12*

J7 D1 1c on 1c **olive brown** *(60,614)* — 110.00 14.00
On cover — 160.00
Block of 4 — 500.00 65.00
J8 D2 2c on 2c **olive brown** — 22.50 7.50
On cover — 225.00
Block of 4 — 100.00 37.50
J9 D3 10c on 10c **olive brown** *(175,548)* — 22.50 5.00
On cover — 300.00
Block of 4 — 100.00 25.00
Nos. J7-J9 (3) — 155.00 26.50

One of the printings of No. J9 shows wider spacing between "1" and "0." Both spacings occur on the same sheet.

D4

Capitol, Panama — D5

1919, Dec.

Surcharged in Carmine by Panama Canal Press, Mount Hope, C. Z.

"Canal Zone" Type III

J10 D4 2c on 2c **olive brown** — 30.00 11.00
On cover — 350.00
Block of 4 — 130.00 50.00
J11 D5 4c on 4c **olive brown** *(35,695)* — 35.00 12.50
On cover — 400.00
Block of 4 — 160.00 65.00
a. "ZONE" omitted — *9,250.*
b. "4" omitted — *8,500.*

Blue Overprint, Type V, on Postage Due Stamp of Panama

1922

J11C D1 1c **dark olive brown** — — 5.00
d. "CANAL ZONE" reading down — 200.00

United States Postage Due Stamps Nos. J61, J62b and J65b Overprinted

Type A

Letters "A" with Flat Tops

1924, July 1 *Perf. 11*

J12 D2 1c **carmine rose** *(10,000)* — 110.00 27.50
On cover — 100.00
Block of 4 — 475.00 125.00
P# block of 6 — 1,250. —
J13 D2 2c **deep claret** *(25,000)* — 55.00 15.00
On cover — 110.00
Block of 4 — 275.00 65.00
P# block of 6 — 775.00 —
J14 D2 10c **deep claret** *(30,000)* — 250.00 50.00
On cover — 225.00
Block of 4 (2mm spacing) — 1,250. 210.00
Block of 4 (3mm spacing) — 1,250. 210.00
Margin block of 6, imprint, star and P# — *3,500.* —
Nos. J12-J14 (3) — 415.00 92.50

Values for Nos. J12-J29 on cover are for philatelically prepared items. Commercial usages on cover are much more valuable.

United States Nos. 552, 554 and 562 Ovptd. Type A and Additionally Ovptd. at Mount Hope in Red or Blue

1925, Feb. *Perf. 11*

J15 A155 1c **deep green** (R) *(15,000)* — 90.00 15.00
On cover — 110.00
Block of 4 — 400.00 62.50
P# block of 6 — 900.00 —
J16 A157 2c **carmine** (Bl) *(21,335)* — 22.50 7.00
On cover — 67.50
Block of 4 — 100.00 30.00
P# block of 6 — 225.00 —
J17 A165 10c **orange** (R) *(39,819)* — 55.00 11.00
On cover — 90.00
Block of 4 — 260.00 47.50
P# block of 6 — 500.00 —

a. "POSTAGE DUE" double 800.00
b. "E" of "POSTAGE" omitted 750.00
c. As "b," "POSTAGE DUE" double *3,250.*
Nos. J15-J17 (3) 167.50 33.00

Overprinted Type B

Letters "A" with Sharp Pointed Tops

On U.S. Postage Due Stamps Nos. J61, J62, J65, J65a

1925, June 24

J18 D2 1c **carmine rose** *(80,000)* 8.00 2.75
On cover 65.00
Block of 4 35.00 14.00
P# block of 6 90.00 —
"CANAL" in wrong font *125.00 75.00*
"ZONE" in wrong font *175.00 125.00*
a. "ZONE ZONE" (LR18) 1,500.
J19 D2 2c **carmine rose** *(146,430)* 15.00 2.75
On cover 42.50
Block of 4 65.00 14.00
P# block of 6 160.00 —
"CANAL" in wrong font *225.00 175.00*
"ZONE" in wrong font *375.00 225.00*
a. "ZONE ZONE" (LR18) 1,500.
J20 D2 10c **carmine rose** *(153,980)* 150.00 20.00
On cover 300.00
Block of 4, 2mm spacing 650.00 85.00
Block of 4, 3mm spacing 675.00 90.00
P# block of 6, Impt. & Star 1,250. —
"CANAL" in wrong font *175.00 50.00*
"ZONE" in wrong font *200.00 100.00*
a. Vert. pair, one without ovpt. *(10)* *3,000.*
P# block of 6, Impt. & Star *17,500.*
b. 10c **rose red** *250.00* 150.00
On cover —
c. As "b," double overprint *450.00* —
Nos. J18-J20 (3) 173.00 25.50

Nos. J18-J20 exist with wrong font "CANAL" (UL51) and "ZONE" (UL82).

Regular Issue of 1928-29 Surcharged

1929-30

J21 A37 1c on 5c **blue** *(35,990) Mar. 20, 1930* 3.75 1.75
Never hinged 7.50
On cover 75.00
P# block of 6 40.00 —
a. "POSTAGE DUE" missing *(5)* *5,500.*
J22 A37 2c on 5c **blue** *(40,207) Oct. 18, 1930* 6.50 2.50
Never hinged 13.00
On cover 75.00
P# block of 6 70.00 —
J23 A37 5c on 5c **blue** *(35,464) Dec. 1, 1930* 6.50 2.75
Never hinged 13.00
On cover 125.00
P# block of 6 70.00 —
J24 A37 10c on 5c **blue** *(90,504) Dec. 16, 1929* 6.50 2.75
Never hinged 13.00
On cover 75.00
P# block of 6 70.00 —
Nos. J21-J24 (4) 23.25 9.75

On No. J23 the three short horizontal bars in the lower corners of the surcharge are omitted.

Canal Zone Seal — D6

Printed by the U.S. Bureau of Engraving and Printing.

Plates of 400 subjects, issued in panes of 100.

1932-41 **Flat Plate Printing**

J25 D6 1c **claret** *(378,300) Jan. 2, 1932* .25 .25
Never hinged .30
On cover 30.00
P# block of 6 3.00 —
a. Dry printing, red violet .25 .25
Never hinged .35
On cover 32.50
P# block of 6 3.00 —
J26 D6 2c **claret** *(413,800) Jan. 2, 1932* .25 .25
Never hinged .30
On cover 22.50
P# block of 6 3.00 —
J27 D6 5c **claret** *Jan. 2, 1932* .35 .25
Never hinged .50
On cover 25.00
P# block of 6 3.50 —
a. Dry printing, red violet 1.00 .30
Never hinged 1.40
On cover 22.50
P# block of 6 10.00 —
J28 D6 10c **claret** *(400,600) Jan. 2, 1932* 1.75 1.50
Never hinged 2.25
On cover 32.50
P# block of 6 15.00 —
J29 D6 15c **claret** *Apr. 21, 1941* 1.25 1.00
Never hinged 1.60
On cover 37.50
P# block of 6 12.00 —
Nos. J25-J29 (5) 3.85 3.25

See note after No. J14.

OFFICIAL STAMPS

See note at beginning of Air Post Official Stamps

Regular Issues of 1928-34 Overprinted in Black by the Panama Canal Press, Mount Hope, C.Z.

Type 1

Type 2

Type 1 — "PANAMA" 10mm long
Type 2 — "PANAMA" 9mm long

1941, Mar. 31 **Unwmk.** ***Perf. 11***

O1 A35 1c **yellow green,** type 1 *(87,198)* 2.00 .40
Never hinged 3.00
On cover 70.00
O2 A45 3c **deep violet,** type 1 *(34,958)* 3.75 .75
Never hinged 5.75
On cover 90.00
O3 A37 5c **blue,** type 2 *(19,105)* *1,000.* 25.00
On cover *110.00*
O4 A38 10c **orange,** type 1 *(18,776)* 7.50 1.90
Never hinged 11.50
On cover 200.00
O5 A41 15c **gray black,** type 1 *(16,888)* 15.00 2.25
Never hinged 22.00
gray 2.25
On cover 140.00
O6 A42 20c **olive brown,** type 1 *(20,264)* 17.50 2.75
Never hinged 26.00
On cover 100.00
O7 A44 50c **lilac,** type 1 *(19,175)* 42.50 5.50
Never hinged 65.00
rose lilac 5.50
On cover —
O8 A44 50c **rose lilac,** type 1a *(1000)* 550.00

No. O3 exists with "O" directly over "N" of "PANAMA."

No. 139 Overprinted in Black

1947, Feb.

O9 A65 5c **deep blue,** type 1 *(21,639)* 12.50 3.75
Never hinged 20.00
On cover 75.00

POST OFFICE SEALS

POS1

Issued in panes of 8 (2 x 4), without gum, imperforate outer margins.

1907 **Typo.** **Unwmk.** ***Perf. 11½***

OX1 POS1 **blue** 35.00 *50.00*
On cover *1,500.*
Block of 4 150.00
Pane of 8 *750.00*
a. Wmkd. seal of U.S. in sheet 75.00 *125.00*
Block of 4 425.00
Pane of 8 *1,250.*

No. OX1 clichés are spaced 3½mm apart both horizontally and vertically.

1910

OX2 POS1 **ultramarine** 50.00 *65.00*
On cover *1,750.*
Block of 4, cliches ½mm apart horiz. and vert. 225.00
Pane of 8 *1,000.*
Block of 4, cliches 1½mm apart horiz., 4mm vert. 275.00
Pane of 8 *1,100.*
a. Wmkd. "Rolleston Mills" in sheet (½mm spacing) 80.00 *100.00*
Block of 4 350.00
b. Wmkd. U.S. Seal in sheet (1½mm x 4mm spacing) 85.00 *100.00*
Block of 4 350.00
Pane of 8 1,500.

POS2

Printed by the Panama Canal Press, Mount Hope, C.Z.

Issued in panes of 25 (5 x 5), without gum, imperforate outer margins at top, bottom, and left.

Rouletted 6 horizontally in color of seal, vertically without color

1917, Sept. 22

OX3 POS2 **slate violet** (shades) 4.00 4.00
On cover 250.00
Block of 4 17.50
Pane of 25 250.00
a. Wmkd. double lined letters in sheet ("Sylvania") 17.50 *25.00*
Block of 4 85.00
Pane of 25 600.00

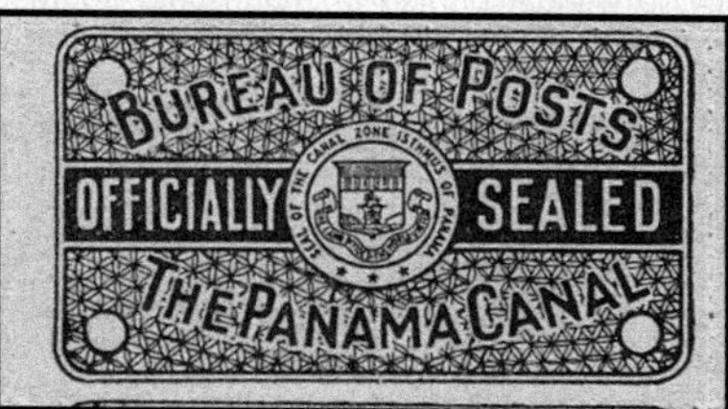

POS3

Issued in panes of 20 (4 x 5), without gum, imperforate outer margins.

1945 ***Rouletted 6, without color***

OX4 POS3 **deep violet blue** (shades) 7.00 *10.00*
On cover 300.00
Block of 4 35.00
Pane of 20 300.00

POS4

Typographed by the Panama Canal Press. Issued in panes of 32 (4 x 8), without gum, imperforate margins except at top of pane.

Size: 46x27mm
Seal Diameter: 13mm

1954, Mar. 8	**Unwmk.**		***Perf. 12½***	
OX5	POS4	**black** *(16,000)*	5.00	5.00
		On cover		200.00
		Block of 4	20.00	
		Pane of 32	200.00	
	a.	Wmkd. Seal of U. S. in sheet	12.50	12.50
		Block of 4	60.00	
		Pane of 32	500.00	
	b.	Double impression	45.00	
	c.	As "a," double impression	75.00	

POS5

Seal Diameter: 11½mm

1961, May 16			***Perf. 12½***	
OX6	POS5	**black** (48,000)	3.00	*5.00*
		On cover		175.00
		Block of 4	12.00	
		Pane of 32	125.00	
	a.	Wmkd. Seal of U.S. in sheet	7.50	7.50
		Block of 4	35.00	
		Pane of 32	300.00	

No. OX6 exists in approximately equal proportions on three types of paper: very thin tissue-like, medium, and heavy opaque.

1974, July 1			***Rouletted 5***	
OX7	POS5	**black**	2.50	*5.00*
		On cover		150.00
		Block of 4	11.00	
		Pane of 32	100.00	

ENVELOPES

Values for cut squares are for examples with fine margins on all sides. Values for unused entires are for those without printed or manuscript address. A "full corner" includes back and side flaps and commands a premium.

Vasco Núñez de Balboa — U1

Fernandez de Córdoba — U2

Envelopes of Panama Lithographed and Overprinted by American Bank Note Co.

1916, Apr. 24			**On White Paper**	
U1	U1	1c **green & black**	14.00	10.00
		Entire	90.00	35.00
	a.	Head and overprint only	—	—
		Entire	*1,750.*	*2,000.*
	b.	Frame only	—	—
		Entire	*1,500.*	*2,500.*
U2	U2	2c **carmine & black**	11.00	4.50
		Entire	85.00	25.00
	a.	2c **red & black**	12.50	4.50
		Entire	85.00	45.00
	b.	Head and overprint only	—	—
		Entire	*750.00*	*1,750.*
	c.	Frame only (red)	—	—
		Entire	*850.00*	*1,750.*
	d.	Frame double (carmine)	—	—
		Entire	*2,250.*	*2,250.*

José Vallarino — U3

"The Land Gate" — U4

1921, Nov. 13			**On White Paper**	
U3	U3	1c **green**	140.00	100.00
		Entire	700.00	375.00
U4	U4	2c **red**	35.00	20.00
		Entire	325.00	125.00

Arms of Panama — U5

Typographed and embossed by American Bank Note Co. with "CANAL ZONE" in color of stamp.

1923, Dec. 15			**On White Paper**	
U5	U5	2c **carmine**	55.00	32.50
		Entire	200.00	125.00

U.S. Nos. U420 and U429 Overprinted in Black by Bureau of Engraving and Printing, Washington, D.C.

1924, July 1				
U6	U92	1c **green** *(50,000)*	3.75	3.00
		Entire	25.00	19.00
		Entire, 1st day cancel		125.00
U7	U93	2c **carmine** *(100,000)*	5.00	3.00
		Entire	35.00	19.00
		Entire, 1st day cancel		125.00

Seal of Canal Zone — U6

Printed by the Panama Canal Press, Mount Hope, C.Z.

1924, Oct.			**On White Paper**	
U8	U6	1c **green** *(205,000)*	2.00	1.00
		Entire	24.00	15.00
U9	U6	2c **carmine** *(1,997,658)*	.75	.40
		Entire	27.50	15.00

Gorgas — U7

Goethals — U8

Typographed and Embossed by International Envelope Corp., Dayton, O.

1932, Apr. 8				
U10	U7	1c **green** *(1,300,000)*	.25	.25
		Entire	3.00	1.10
		Entire, 1st day cancel		35.00
U11	U8	2c **carmine** *(400,250)*	.25	.25
		Entire	3.50	1.75
		Entire, 1st day cancel		35.00

No. U9 Surcharged in Violet by Panama Canal Press, Mount Hope, C.Z. Numerals 3mm high

1932, July 20				
U12	U6	3c on 2c **carmine** *(20,000)*	17.50	6.75
		Entire	225.00	125.00

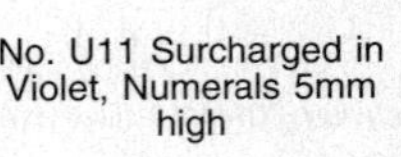
No. U11 Surcharged in Violet, Numerals 5mm high

1932, July 20				
U13	U8	3c on 2c **carmine** *(320,000)*	2.00	1.00
		Entire	25.00	15.00
		Entire, 1st day cancel		75.00

No. U9 Surcharged with Numerals with Serifs and Numerals 4mm high

1934, Jan. 17				
U14	U6	3c on 2c **carmine** *(8,000)*	100.00	60.00
		Entire	425.00	525.00
U15	U8	3c on 2c **carmine** (Numerals 5mm high) *(23,000)*	25.00	15.00
		Entire	250.00	150.00

Typographed and Embossed by International Envelope Corp., Dayton, O.

1934, June 18				
U16	U8	3c **purple** *(2,450,000)*	.25	.25
		Entire	1.20	1.40

1958, Nov. 1				
U17	U8	4c **blue** *(596,725)*	.25	.25
		Entire	1.25	1.25
		Entire, 1st day cancel, Cristobal		2.00

Surcharged at Left of Stamp in Ultra. as No. UX13

1969, Apr. 28				
U18	U8	4c +1c **blue** *(93,850)*	.25	*.25*
		Entire	1.25	*1.60*
		Entire, 1st day cancel		1.50
U19	U8	4c +2c **blue** *(23,125)*	.50	*.65*
		Entire	2.50	*4.00*
		Entire, 1st day cancel		1.50

Ship Passing through Gaillard Cut — U9

Typographed and Embossed by United States Envelope Co., Williamsburg, Pa.

1971, Nov. 17

U20 U9 8c **emerald** *(121,500)* .25 *.30*
Entire .75 .65
Entire, 1st day cancel, Balboa *(9,650)* 1.50

Surcharged at Left of Stamp in Emerald as #UX13

1974, Mar. 2

U21 U9 8c +2c **emerald** .30 *.35*
Entire 1.00 *2.00*
Entire, 1st day cancel 1.25

1976, Feb. 23

U22 U9 13c **violet** *(638,350)* .35 *.40*
Entire .85 .85
Entire, 1st day cancel, Balboa *(9,181)* 1.25

Surcharged at Left of Stamp in Violet as No. UX13

1978, July 5

U23 U9 13c +2c **violet** *(245,041)* .35 *.40*
Entire .85 *2.00*
Entire, 1st day cancel 1.25

AIR POST ENVELOPES

No. U9 Overprinted with Horizontal Blue and Red Bars Across Entire Face. Overprinted by Panama Canal Press, Mount Hope. Boxed inscription in lower left with nine lines of instructions. Additional adhesives required for air post rate.

1928, May 21

UC1 U6 2c **red,** entire *(15,000)* 135.00 65.00
First day cancel 175.00

No. U9 with Similar Overprint of Blue and Red Bars, and "VIA AIR MAIL" in Blue, At Left, no box.

1929

UC2 U6 2c **red,** entire *(60,200)* 65.00 27.50
a. Inscription centered *(10,000) Jan. 11* 325.00 190.00

Earliest known use of No. UC2 is Feb. 6.

DC-4 Skymaster UC1

Typographed and Embossed by International Envelope Corp., Dayton, O.

1949, Jan. 3

UC3 UC1 6c **blue** *(4,400,000)* .25 .25
Entire 4.00 3.50
Entire, 1st day cancel 2.00

1958, Nov. 1

UC4 UC1 7c **carmine** *(1,000,000)* .25 .25
Entire 4.00 3.50
Entire, 1st day cancel 1.50

No. U16 Surcharged at Left of Stamp and Imprinted "VIA AIR MAIL" in Dark Blue

Surcharged by Panama Canal Press, Mount Hope, C.Z.

1963, June 22

UC5 U8 3c + 5c **purple** *(105,000)* 1.00 1.00
Entire 6.00 *10.00*
Entire, 1st day cancel 5.00
a. Double surcharge *1,250.*

Jet Liner and Tail Assembly — UC2

Typographed and Embossed by International Envelope Corp., Dayton, O.

1964, Jan. 6

UC6 UC2 8c **deep carmine** *(600,000)* .35 .35
Entire 2.25 2.50
Entire, 1st day cancel, Balboa *(3,855)* 2.25

No. U17 Surcharged at Left of Stamp as No. UC5 and Imprinted "VIA AIR MAIL" in Vermilion
Surcharged by Canal Zone Press, La Boca, C.Z.

1965, Oct. 15

UC7 U8 4c + 4c **blue** *(100,000)* .50 .40
Entire 4.50 *9.00*
Entire, 1st day cancel 5.00

Jet Liner and Tail Assembly — UC3

Typographed and Embossed by United States Envelope Co., Williamsburg, Pa.

1966, Feb.

UC8 UC3 8c **carmine** *(224,000)* .50 .45
Entire 5.00 5.00

Earliest known use: Feb. 23.

No. UC8 Surcharged at Left of Stamp as No. UX13 in Vermilion
Surcharged by Canal Zone Press, La Boca, C.Z.

1968, Jan. 18

UC9 UC3 8c + 2c **carmine** *(376,000)* .40 .35
Entire 2.75 *5.00*
Entire, 1st day cancel 4.50

No. UC7 with Additional Surcharge at Left of Stamp as No. UX13 and Imprinted "VIA AIR MAIL" in Vermilion
Surcharged by Canal Zone Press, La Boca, C.Z.

1968, Feb. 12

UC10 U8 4c + 4c + 2c **blue** *(224,150)* .60 .50
Entire 2.25 *12.50*
Entire, 1st day cancel 5.00

Type of 1966

Typographed and Engraved by United States Envelope Co., Williamsburg, Pa.

1969, Apr. 1

Luminescent Ink

UC11 UC3 10c **ultramarine** *(448,000)* .60 .40
Entire 4.00 *5.00*
Entire, 1st day cancel, Balboa *(9,583)* 2.00

No. U17 Surcharged at Left of Stamp as Nos. UC5 and UX13, and Imprinted "VIA AIR MAIL" in Vermilion

1971, May 17

UC12 U8 4c + 5c + 2c **blue** *(55,775)* .75 .50
Entire 4.00 *12.50*
Entire, 1st day cancel 5.00

No. UC11 Surcharged in Ultra. at Left of Stamp as No. UX13

1971, May 17

Luminescent Ink

UC13 UC3 10c + 1c **ultramarine** *(152,000)* .45 .40
Entire 4.00 *8.00*
Entire, 1st day cancel 3.50

Type of 1966

Typographed and Engraved by United States Envelope Co., Williamsburg, Pa.

1971, Nov. 17

UC14 UC3 11c **rose red** *(258,000)* .30 .25
Entire 1.25 1.25
Entire, 1st day cancel, Balboa *(3,451)* 1.50
a. 11c **carmine,** stamp tagged, *(395,000)* .30 .25
Entire 1.25 1.25
Entire, 1st day cancel, Balboa *(5,971)* 1.50

The red diamonds around the envelope edges are luminescent on both Nos. UC14 and UC14a. No. UC14 is size 10, No. UC14a size 6¾.

Surcharged at Left of Stamp in Rose Red as No. UX13

1974, Mar. 2

UC15 UC3 11c + 2c **carmine,** tagged *(305,000)* .35 .30
Entire 1.50 *3.00*
Entire, 1st day cancel 1.25
a. 11c + 2c **rose red,** untagged, *(87,000)* .35 .25
Entire 1.75 2.00

No. U21 with Additional Surcharge in Vermilion at Left of Stamp as No. UX13 and Imprinted "VIA AIR MAIL" in Vermilion

1975, May 3

UC16 U9 8c + 2c + 3c **emerald** *(75,000)* .50 .30
Entire 1.25 *3.00*
Entire, 1st day cancel 1.50

REGISTRATION ENVELOPES

RE1

Panama Registration Envelope surcharged by Panama Canal Press, Mount Hope, C.Z.

1918, Oct. 8mm between CANAL & ZONE

UF1 RE1 10c on 5c **black & red,** *cream (10,000),* entire *1,750.* *2,000.*
a. 9¼mm between CANAL & ZONE *(25,000),* entire ('19) *1,300.* *2,000.*

Stamped envelopes inscribed "Diez Centesimos," surcharged with numerals "5" and with solid blocks printed over "Canal Zone," were issued by the Republic of Panama after being rejected by the Canal Zone. Parts of "Canal Zone" are often legible under the surcharge blocks. These envelopes exist without surcharge.

POSTAL CARDS

Values are for Entires

Map of Panama — PC1

Panama Card Lithographed by American Bank Note Co., revalued and surcharged in black by the Isthmian Canal Commission.

1907, Feb. 9

UX1 PC1 1c on 2c **carmine,** "CANAL" 15mm *(50,000)* 40. 25.
a. Double surcharge *1,500.* *2,000.*
b. Double surcharge, one reading down *2,500.*
c. Triple surcharge, one reading down *3,250.*
d. "CANAL" 13mm *(10,000)* 250. 200.
e. As "d," double surcharge *2,400.*

Balboa — PC2

Panama card lithographed by Hamilton Bank Note Co. Overprinted in black by Isthmian Canal Commission.

At least six types of overprint, reading down.

1908, Mar. 3

UX2 PC2 1c **green & black,** "CANAL" 13mm *(295,000)* 190. 80.
- *a.* Double overprint *1,750.* *2,000.*
- *b.* Triple overprint *1,750.* —
- *c.* Period after "ZONE" *(40,000)* 200. 125.
- *d.* "CANAL" 15mm *(30,000)* 200. 125.
- *e.* "ZONE CANAL", reading up *3,500.*
- *f.* Double overprint, one inverted at bottom left *3,000.*

Balboa — PC3

Lithographed by Hamilton Bank Note Co. Overprinted in Black by Panama Canal Press, Mount Hope, C.Z.

1910, Nov. 10

UX3 PC3 1c **green & black** *(40,000)* 190. 70.
- *a.* Double overprint *3,500.*

This card, with overprint reading up, is actually the fourth of seven settings of UX2.

Balboa — PC4

Lithographed and Overprinted by American Bank Note Co.

1913, Mar. 27

UX4 PC4 1c **green & black** *(634,000)* 160. 60.

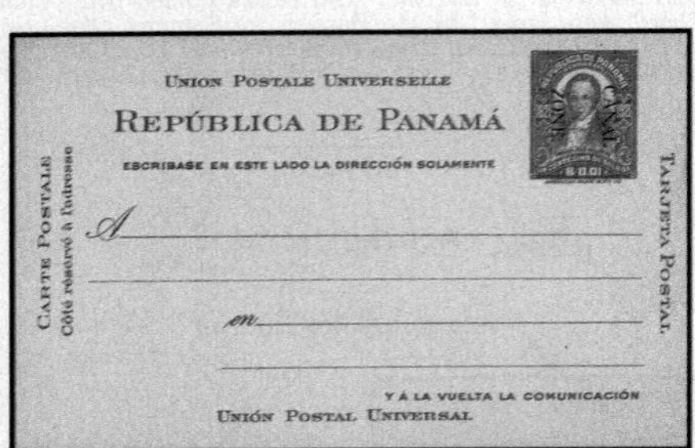

Design of Canal Zone Envelopes Overprinted in black by the American Bank Note Co.

1921, Oct.

UX5 U3 1c **green** 1,000. 450.

Typographed and embossed by American Bank Note Co. with "CANAL ZONE" in color of stamp.

1924, Jan.

UX6 U5 1c **green** 1,050. *1,100.*

U.S. No. UX27 Overprinted by U.S. Gov't. Printing Office at Washington, D.C.

1924, July 1

UX7 PC17 1c **green,** *buff (Jefferson) (50,000)* 80. 35.

Design of Canal Zone Envelope Printed by Panama Canal Press.

1925, Jan.

UX8 U6 1c **green,** *buff (25,000)* 75. 35.
- *a.* Background only *1,800.*

U.S. No. UX27 Overprinted

1925, May

UX9 PC17 1c **green,** *buff (Jefferson) (850,000)* 8.50 5.00

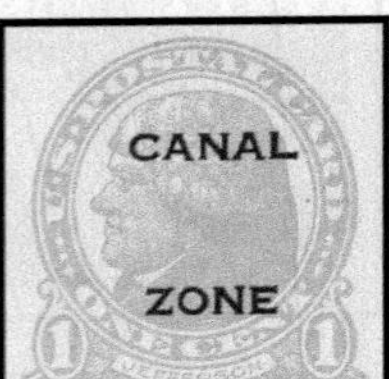

U.S. No. UX27 Overprinted

1935, Oct.

UX10 PC17 1c **green,** *buff (Jefferson) (2,900,000)* 1.80 1.80
- *a.* Double overprint *1,800.*

Used values are for contemporaneous usage without additional postage applied.

Same Overprint on U.S. No. UX38

1952, May 1

UX11 PC22 2c **carmine rose,** *buff (Franklin) (800,000)* 2.00 2.00
1st day cancel, Balboa Heights 3.50

Ship in Lock — PC5

Printed by Bureau of Engraving & Printing, Washington, D.C.

1958, Nov. 1

UX12 PC5 3c **dark blue,** *buff (335,116)* 2.00 *3.00*
First day cancel, Cristobal 1.25

No. UX12 Surcharged at Left of Stamp in Green by Panama Canal Press, Mount Hope, C.Z.

1963, July 27

UX13 PC5 3c + 1c **dark blue,** *buff (78,000)* 4.00 *7.50*
First day cancel 3.50
- *a.* Surcharge inverted at bottom left *750.00*

Ship Passing through Panama Canal — PC6

Printed by Panama Canal Press, Mount Hope, C.Z.

1964, Dec. 1

UX14 PC6 4c **violet blue,** *buff (74,200)* 3.75 *7.50*
1st day cancel, Cristobal *(19,260)* 3.50

Ship in Lock (Towing locomotive at right redrawn) — PC7

Printed by Bureau of Engraving & Printing, Washington, D.C.

1965, Aug. 12

UX15 PC7 4c **emerald** *(95,500)* 1.10 *2.00*
1st day cancel, Cristobal *(20,366)* 1.00

No. UX15 Surcharged at Left of Stamp in Green as No. UX13 by Canal Zone Press, La Boca, C.Z.

1968, Feb. 12

UX16 PC7 4c + 1c **emerald** *(94,775)* 1.10 *4.00*
First day cancel 1.00

Ship-in-Lock Type of 1965

1969, Apr. 1

UX17 PC7 5c **light ultramarine** *(63,000)* 1.00 *2.50*
1st day cancel, Balboa *(11,835)* 1.00

No. UX17 Surcharged at Left of Stamp in Light Ultramarine as No. UX13

1971, May 24

UX18 PC7 5c + 1c **light ultramarine** *(100,500)* .90 *4.00*
First day cancel 1.00

Ship-in-Lock Type of 1965

Printed by Bureau of Engraving & Printing, Washington, D.C.

1974, Feb. 11

UX19 PC7 8c **brown** *(90,895)* 1.00 *2.00*
1st day cancel, Balboa *(10,375)* 1.00

No. UX19 Surcharged at Left of Stamp in Brown as No. UX13

1976, June 1

UX20 PC7 8c + 1c **brown** *(60,249)* .65 *5.00*
First day cancel 1.00

No. UX19 Surcharged at Left of Stamp in Brown as No. UX13

1978, July 5

UX21 PC7 8c + 2c **brown** *(74,847)* 1.00 *5.00*
First day cancel 1.00

AIR POST POSTAL CARDS

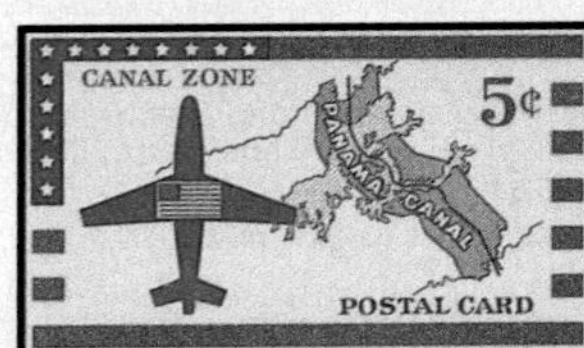

Plane, Flag and Map — APC1

Printed by Bureau of Engraving & Printing, Washington, D.C.

1958, Nov. 1

UXC1 APC1 5c **blue & carmine rose** *(104,957)* 3.00 *7.50*
1st day cancel, Balboa 3.75

No. UXC1 Surcharged at Left of Stamp in Green as No. UX13 by Panama Canal Press, Mount Hope, C.Z.

1963, July 27

UXC2 APC1 5c + 1c **blue & carmine rose** *(48,000)* 8.00 *20.00*
- *a.* Inverted surcharge *1,500.*

First day cancel 5.00

No. UX15 Surcharged at Left of Stamp as No. UX13 and Imprinted "AIR MAIL" in Vermilion

1965, Aug. 18

UXC3 PC7 4c + 2c **emerald** *(41,700)* 3.25 *20.00*
First day cancel 6.00

No. UX15 Surcharged at Left of Stamp as No. UC5 and Imprinted "AIR MAIL" in Vermilion by Canal Zone Press, La Boca, C.Z.

1968, Feb. 12

UXC4 PC7 4c + 4c **emerald** *(60,100)* 2.50 *18.00*
First day cancel 6.00

No. UX17 Surcharged at Left of Stamp as No. UC5 and Imprinted "AIR MAIL" in Vermilion

1971, May 24

UXC5 PC7 5c + 4c **light ultramarine** *(68,000)* .90 *18.00*
First day cancel 6.00

PROOFS

1928-40

106TC1 2c Large die on India paper
a. **black** *1,300.*
113P2 30c **brn blk,** small die on yellowish wove paper 975.

1934

117P1 3c **dp violet,** large die on India paper *(8)* 475.

1939

120P1 1c **yellow green,** large die on India paper *1,300.*
120P2 1c **yel grn,** small die on yellowish wove paper 875.
121P2 2c **rose car,** small die on yellowish wove paper 875.
122P1 3c **purple,** large die on India paper *1,300.*
122P2 3c **purple,** small die on yellowish wove paper 875.
123P1 5c **dk blue,** large die on India paper *1,300.*
123P2 5c **dk blue,** small die on yellowish wove paper 875.
124P2 6c **red org,** small die on yellowish wove paper 875.
125P2 7c **black,** small die on yellowish wove paper 875.
126P1 8c **green,** large die on India paper *1,300.*
126P2 8c **grn,** small die on yellowish wove paper 875.
127P1 10c **ultra,** large die on India paper *1,300.*
127P2 10c **ultra,** small die on yellowish wove paper 875.
128P1 11c **bl grn,** large die on India paper *1,300.*
128P2 11c **bl grn,** small die on yellowish wove paper 875.
129P1 12c **brn car,** large die on India paper *1,300.*
129P2 12c **brn car,** small die on yellowish wove paper 875.
130P2 14c **dk vio,** small die on yellowish wove paper 875.
131P2 15c **ol grn,** small die on yellowish wove paper 875.
132P2 18c **rose pink,** small die on yellowish wove paper 875.
133P1 20c **brown,** large die on India paper *1,300.*
133P2 20c **brn,** small die on yellowish wove paper 875.
134P1 25c **orange,** large die on India paper *1,300.*
134P2 25c **org,** small die on yellowish wove paper 875.
135P1 50c **violet brown,** large die on India paper *1,300.*
135P2 50c **vio brn,** small die on yellowish wove paper 875.

1946-48

136P1 ½c **brt red,** large die on India paper *1,300.*
137P1 1½c **chocolate,** large die on India paper *1,300.*
139P1 5c **dp blue,** large die on India paper *1,300.*
140P1 25c **yellow green,** large die on India paper *1,300.*
141P1 10c **black,** large die on India paper *825.*

1949

142P1 3c **blue,** large die on India paper *1,150.*
143P1 6c **violet,** large die on India paper *1,150.*
144P1 12c **brt bl grn,** large die on India paper *1,150.*
145P1 18c **dp red lilac,** large die on India paper *1,150.*

1951

146P1 10c **carmine,** large die on India paper *1,500.*

1955

147P1 3c **violet,** large die on India paper *1,500.*

Air Post

1931-49

C6P1 4c **red violet,** large die on India paper *1,600.*
C7P1 5c **lt green,** large die on India paper *1,600.*
C8P1 6c **yel brown,** large die on India paper *1,600.*
C13TC1 40c Large die on India paper
a. **orange** *1,600.*

1939

C15P2 5c **grnsh blk,** small die on yellowish wove paper 925.
C15TC1 5c Large die on India paper
a. **scarlet** *1,300.*
C16P1 10c **dull vio,** large die on India paper *1,300.*
C16P2 10c **dull vio,** small die on yellowish wove paper 925.
C17P1 15c **lt brn,** large die on India paper *1,300.*
C17P2 15c **lt brn,** small die on yellowish wove paper 925.
C18P2 25c **blue,** small die on yellowish wove paper 925.
C19P1 30c **rose car,** large die on India paper *1,300.*
C19P2 30c **rose car,** small die on yellowish wove paper 925.
C20P1 $1 **green,** large die on India paper *1,300.*
C20P2 $1 **grn,** small die on yellowish wove paper 925.

1951

C21P1 4c **red vio,** large die on India paper *1,300.*

Only No. 117P1 has more than two examples reported in private collections.

SPECIMENS

Issues of the American Bank Note Co.

Panama stamps overprinted "CANAL ZONE," handstamped SPECIMEN in three fonts and having a 2.5mm round hole punched in the lower right area.

Where a stamp has more than one type of SPECIMEN overprint, the types are listed chronologically by production dates, not alphabetically.

All SPECIMEN handstamps are red unless otherwise indicated. Almost all examples have a pencil notation on reverse giving the 'F' number (ABNCo. order number), sheet position, and sometimes a sheet designation.

Booklet pane specimens from uncut sheets are usually collected in units of two full panes of six with gutter between or in pairs with gutter between. Because most examples are still in a few large multiples and few have been sold publicly, values for these items are not given.

A few assembled Specimen booklets are known with a red handstamped order number on the front cover. Some examples contain panes that are punched and handstamped; other examples have unmarked panes indistinguishable from those of issued booklets if they are removed from their marked covers.

Uncut booklet covers are known, some with a punched "Specimen A. B. N. Co."

Number in parenthesis after denomination and color is quantity known.

SPECIMEN
Type A; 19.8 to 20mm long

SPECIMEN
Type B

Type C; 13.8 to 14.2mm long *SPECIMEN*

Type B subtypes: a, 11.2 to 11.3mm long. b, 13.7 to 13.8mm long. c, 14 to 14.3mm long. d, 15.3mm long.

1909-10 **Portraits Type I**

31S A 1c **dark green & black** *(194)* 25.00
31S C 1c **dark green & black** *(98)* 25.00
32S C 2c **vermilion & black** *(400)* 25.00
33S C 5c **deep blue & black** *(400)* 25.00
34S A 8c **violet & black** *(300)* 25.00
35S A 10c **violet & black** *(100)*

Although known to have existed, the sheet of No. 35S has disappeared. No examples of No. 35S are currently reported in collections.

1911-14 **Maps**

36S C 10c on 13c **gray,** without 10c surcharge *(289)* 35.00
a. Inverted SPECIMEN *(3)* —
b. Double SPECIMEN *(2)* —
37S A 10c **gray** *(299)* 25.00

1912-16 **Portraits Type II**

38S A 1c **green & black** *(100)* 35.00
38S Ba 1c **green & black** *(200)* 25.00
38S Bb 1c **green & black** *(300)* 25.00
38S Bc 1c **green & black** *(300)* 25.00
39S A 2c **vermilion & black,** SPECIMEN in blue *(397)* 25.00
a. Inverted CANAL —
39S A 2c **vermilion & black** *(300)* 25.00
39S Bb 2c **vermilion & black,** SPECIMEN in blue *(300)* 25.00
39S C 2c **vermilion & black** *(300)* 25.00
39S Bc 2c **vermilion & black,** SPECIMEN in blue *(300)* 25.00
39cS Bc 2c **vermilion & black,** SPECIMEN in blue *(74 panes)* —
40S A 5c **deep blue & black** *(400)* 25.00
40S Ba 5c **deep blue & black** *(200)* 25.00
40S C 5c **deep blue & black** *(500)* 25.00
41S Bc 10c **violet & black** *(300)* 25.00

1915-17 **Ninth Series Pictorials**

42S Bb 1c **dark green & black** *(293)* 30.00
43S Bb 2c **carmine & black** *(293)* 30.00
44S Bb 5c **blue & black** *(293)* 30.00
45S Bb 10c **orange & black** *(293)* 30.00
49S Bc 12c **purple & black** *(300)* 30.00
50S Bc 15c **bright blue & black** *(300)* 30.00
51S Bc 24c **yellow brown & black** *(300)* 30.00

1918-20 **Portraits Type IV**

52S Bb 1c **green & black** *(300)* 25.00
52S Bc 1c **green & black** *(300)* 25.00
52bS Bc 1c **green & black** *(48 panes)* —
53S Bc 2c **vermilion & black,** SPECIMEN in blue *(600)* 25.00
a. Double SPECIMEN *(1)* —
53cS Bc 2c **vermilion & black,** *(8 panes)* —
a. 13mm different font SPECIMEN *(2)* —
53cS Bb 2c **vermilion & black,** *(24 panes)* —
53cS Bd 2c **vermilion & black,** *(48 panes)* —
a. Missing SPECIMEN *(2)* —
b. Missing punch hole *(1)* —
54S Bb 5c **blue & black** *(300)* 25.00

1920-21 **Portraits Type V**

55S Bb 1c **light green & black** *(300)* 25.00
55eS Bb 1c **light green & black** *(36 panes)* —
56S Bb 2c **orange vermilion & black** *(400)* 25.00
56S Ba 2c **orange vermilion & black** *(300)* 25.00
56gS Bb 2c **orange vermilion & black** *(48 panes)* —
57S Bb 5c **deep blue & black** *(300)* 25.00
a. Double SPECIMEN *(1)* —

1920 **Ninth Series High Value Pictorials**

58S Bd 50c **orange & black** *(285)* 60.00
59S Bd $1 **dark violet & black** *(273)* 60.00
a. Double SPECIMEN *(1)* —

1921 **Independence Issue**

60S Ba 1c **green** *(300)* 35.00
60bS Ba 1c **green** *(46 panes)* —
61S Ba 2c **carmine** *(300)* 35.00
61fS Ba 2c **carmine** *(47 panes)* —
62S Ba 5c **blue** *(300)* 35.00
63S Ba 10c **violet** *(200)* 35.00
64S Ba 15c **light blue** *(200)* 35.00
65S Ba 24c **black brown** *(200)* 35.00
66S Ba 50c **black** *(200)* 35.00

1924 **Coat of Arms**

68S Ba 1c **dark green** *(300)* 25.00
69S Ba 2c **carmine** *(194)* 25.00

The following unissued stamps have SPECIMEN Type Ba:

A34 1c **dark green** booklet pane *(69 panes)* —
A34 2c **carmine** booklet pane *(71 panes)* —
A34 5c **dark blue** *(300)* 45.00
A34 10c **dark violet** *(300)* 45.00
A34 12c **olive green** *(300)* 45.00
A34 15c **ultramarine** *(300)* 45.00
A34 24c **yellow brown** *(300)* 45.00
A34 50c **orange** *(300)* 45.00
a. Double SPECIMEN *(1)* —
A34 1b **black** *(300)* 45.00
a. Double SPECIMEN *(3)* —

POSTAGE DUES

1915 **Blue Overprints**

J4S A 1c **olive brown** *(300)* 30.00
J5S Bb 2c **olive brown** *(100)* 35.00
J5S A 2c **olive brown** *(200)* 25.00
J6S Ba 10c **olive brown** *(100)* 60.00

1915 **Red Surcharges**

J8S Bc 2c on 2c **olive brown** *(300)* 25.00
J8S Bb 2c on 2c **olive brown** *(300)* 25.00
J9S Bc 10c on 10c **olive brown** *(300)* 30.00

The following unissued stamp with a thin "4" surcharge, unlike the thick "4" found on No. J11, has SPECIMEN Type Bb:

D5 4c on 4c **olive brown** *(300)* 25.00

1922 **Blue Type V Overprint**

J11CS Ba 1c **dark olive brown** *(300)* 25.00

CUBA

After the U.S. battleship "Maine" was destroyed in Havana harbor with a loss of 266 lives in February, 1898, the United States demanded the withdrawal of Spanish troops from Cuba. The Spanish-American War followed. With the peace treaty of Dec. 10, 1898, Spain relinquished Cuba to the United States in trust for its inhabitants. On Jan. 1, 1899, Spanish authority was succeeded by U.S. military rule which lasted until May 20, 1902, when Cuba, as a republic, assumed self-government.

The listings in this catalogue cover the U.S. Administration issue of 1899, the Republic's 1899-1902 issues under U.S. military rule and the Puerto Principe issue of provincial provisionals.

Values for Nos. 176-220 are for stamps in the grade of fine and in sound condition where such exist. Values for Nos. 221-UX2b are for very fine examples.

100 CENTS = 1 DOLLAR

The basic stamps used for overprinting at Puerto Principe are normally poorly centered. Values for Nos. 176-220 are for stamps with fine centering, as typically found. Furthermore, values are for stamps accompanied by certificates issued by competent experts. Convincing fakes and counterfeits are plentiful.

Values for Nos. 221-J4 are for very fine examples.

Puerto Principe Issue

In December, 1898, Puerto Principe, a provincial capital now called Camagüey, ran short of 1c, 2c, 3c, 5c and 10c stamps. The Postmaster ordered Cuban stamps to be surcharged on Dec. 19, 1898.

The surcharging was done to horizontal strips of five stamps, so vertical pairs and blocks do not exist. Five types are found in each setting, and five printings were made. Counterfeits are plentiful.

First Printing

Black Surcharge, 17½mm high

Surcharge measures 17½mm high and is roughly printed in dull black ink.

HABILITADO 2 cents. — Position 1
HABILITADO 2 cents. — Position 2
HABILITADO 2 cents. — Position 3
HABILITADO 2 cents. — Position 4
HABILITADO 2 cents. — Position 5

Position 1 — No serif at right of "t"
Position 2 — Thin numeral except on 1c on 1m No. 176
Position 3 — Broken right foot of "n"
Position 4 — Up-stroke of "t" broken
Position 5 — Broken "DO"

This printing consisted of the following stamps:

176 1c on 1m orange brown, Pos. 1, 2, 3, 4 and 5
178 2c on 2m orange brown, Pos. 1, 3, 4 and 5
179 2c on 2m orange brown, Pos. 2
180 3c on 3m orange brown, Pos. 1, 3, 4 and 5
181 3c on 3m orange brown, Pos. 2
188 5c on 5m orange brown, Pos. 1, 3, 4 and 5
189 5c on 5m orange brown, Pos. 2

Second Printing

Black Surcharge, 17½mm high

This printing was from the same setting as used for the first printing, but the impression is much clearer and the ink quite shiny.

The printing consisted of the following stamps:

179F 3c on 2m orange brown, Pos. 1, 3, 4 and 5
179G 3c on 2m orange brown, Pos. 2
182 5c on 1m orange brown, Pos. 1, 3, 4 and 5
183 5c on 1m orange brown, Pos. 2
184 5c on 2m orange brown, Pos. 1, 3, 4 and 5
185 5c on 2m orange brown, Pos. 2
186 5c on 3m orange brown, Pos. 1, 3, 4 and 5
187 5c on 3m orange brown, Pos. 2
188 5c on 5m orange brown, Pos. 1, 3, 4 and 5
189 5c on 5m orange brown, Pos. 2
190 5c on ½m blue green, Pos. 1, 3, 4 and 5
191 5c on ½m blue green, Pos. 2

Third Printing

Red Surcharge, 20mm high

The same setting as for the first and second was used for the third printing. The 10c denomination first appeared in this printing and position 2 of that value has numerals same as on positions 1, 3, 4 and 5, while position 4 has broken "1" in "10."

The printing consisted of the following stamps:

196 3c on 1c black violet, Pos. 1, 3, 4 and 5
197 3c on 1c black violet, Pos. 2
198 5c on 1c black violet, Pos. 1, 3, 4 and 5
199 5c on 1c black violet, Pos. 2
200 10c on 1c black violet, Pos. 1, 2, 3 and 5
200a 10c on 1c black violet, Pos. 4

Fourth Printing

Black Surcharge, 19½mm high

The same type as before but spaced between so that the surcharge is 2mm taller. Clear impression, shiny ink.

HABILITADO 1 cents. — Position 1
HABILITADO 1 cents. — Position 2
HABILITADO 1 cents. — Position 3
HABILITADO 1 cents. — Position 4
HABILITADO 1 cents. — Position 5

Position 1 — No serif at right of "t"
Position 2 — Broken "1" on No. 177
Position 2 — Thin numerals on 5c stamps
Position 3 — Broken right foot of "n"
Position 4 — Up-stroke of "t" broken
Position 4 — Thin numeral on 3c stamps
Position 5 — Broken "DO"

This printing consisted of the following stamps:

177 1c on 1m orange brn, Pos. 1, 3, 4 and 5
177a 1c on 1m orange brn, Pos. 2
179B 3c on 1m orange brn, Pos. 1, 2, 3 and 5
179D 3c on 1m orange brn, Pos. 4
183B 5c on 1m orange brn, Pos. 1, 3, 4 and 5
189C 5c on 5m orange brn, Pos. 1, 3, 4 and 5
192 5c on ½m blue green, Pos. 1, 3, 4 and 5
193 5c on ½m blue green, Pos. 2

Fifth Printing

Black Surcharge, 19½mm high

HABILITADO 3 cents. — Position 1
HABILITADO 3 cents. — Position 2
HABILITADO 3 eents. — Position 3
HABILITADO 3 cents. — Position 4
HABILITADO 3 cents. — Position 5

Position 1 — Nick in bottom of "e"and lower serif of "s"
Position 2 — Normal surcharge
Position 3 — "eents"
Position 4 — Thin numeral
Position 5 — Nick in upper part of right stroke of "n"

This printing consisted of the following stamps:

201 3c on 1m blue green, Pos. 1, 2 and 5
201b 3c on 1m blue green, Pos. 3
202 3c on 1m blue green, Pos. 4
203 3c on 2m blue green, Pos. 4
203a 3c on 2m blue green, Pos. 3
204 3c on 2m blue green, Pos. 4
205 3c on 3m blue green, Pos. 1, 2 and 5
205b 3c on 3m blue green, Pos. 3
206 3c on 3m blue green, Pos. 4
211 5c on 1m blue green, Pos. 1, 2 and 5
211a 5c on 1m blue green, Pos. 3
212 5c on 1m blue green, Pos. 4
213 5c on 2m blue green, Pos. 1, 2 and 5
213a 5c on 2m blue green, Pos. 3
214 5c on 2m blue green, Pos. 4
215 5c on 3m blue green, Pos. 1, 2 and 5
215a 5c on 3m blue green, Pos. 3
216 5c on 3m blue green, Pos. 4
217 5c on 4m blue green, Pos. 1, 2 and 5
217a 5c on 4m blue green, Pos. 3
218 5c on 4m blue green, Pos. 4
219 5c on 8m blue green, Pos. 1, 2 and 5
219b 5c on 8m blue green, Pos. 3
220 5c on 8m blue green, Pos. 4

Counterfeits exist of all Puerto Principe surcharges. Illustrations have been altered to discourage further counterfeiting.

Regular Issues of Cuba of 1896 and 1898 Surcharged

a

b

Numeral in ( ) after color indicates printing.

Black Surcharge on Nos. 156-158, 160

1898-99

176	(a)	1 cent on 1m **orange brn** (1)	100.00	60.00
177	(b)	1 cents on 1m **org brn** (4)	600.00	115.00
a.		Broken figure "1"	*3,000.*	275.00
b.		Inverted surcharge		*500.00*
d.		Same as "a" inverted		*1,500.*

c

d

178	(c)	2c on 2m **orange brown** (1)	65.00	62.50
a.		Inverted surcharge	500.00	100.00
179	(d)	2c on 2m **orange brown** (1)	82.50	77.50
a.		Inverted surcharge	—	*500.00*

k

l

179B	(k)	3c on 1m **orange brown** (4)	300.	175.
c.		Double surcharge	—	*3,000.*

An unused example is known with "cents" omitted.

179D	(l)	3c on 1m **orange brown** (4)	*1,350.*	*675.00*

e

f

179F (e) 3c on 2m **orange brown** (2) *1,500.*
Value is for example with minor faults.

179G (f) 3c on 2m **orange brown** (2) — *2,000.*
Value is for example with minor faults.

180 (e) 3c on 3m **orange brown** (1) 150. 100.
a. Inverted surcharge 375.
181 (f) 3c on 3m **orange brown** (1) 600. 400.
a. Inverted surcharge *750.*

g

h

i

j

182 (g) 5c on 1m **orange brown** (2) 1,000. 165.
a. Inverted surcharge — *1,000.*
183 (h) 5c on 1m **orange brown** (2) *1,500.* 1,000.
a. Inverted surcharge — *1,500.*
184 (g) 5c on 2m **orange brown** (2) *1,000.* 275.
185 (h) 5c on 2m **orange brown** (2) 1,500. 600.
186 (g) 5c on 3m **orange brown** (2) 1,500. 350.
a. Inverted surcharge 1,200. 700.
187 (h) 5c an 3m **orange brown** (2) — *1,000.*
a. Inverted surcharge — *1,000.*
188 (g) 5c on 5m **orange brown** (1) (2) 145. 230.
a. Inverted surcharge — 750.
b. Double surcharge — —
189 (h) 5c on 5m **orange brown** (1) (2) *3,000.* 425.
a. Inverted surcharge *3,000.* 900.
b. Double surcharge — —
189C (i) 5c on 5m **orange brown** (4) *7,500.*

Values for Nos. 188, 189 are for the first printing.

No. 191

Black Surcharge on No. P25

190 (g) 5c on ½m **blue green** (2) 375. 115.
a. Inverted surcharge 1,000. 210.
b. Pair, one without surcharge 500.
191 (h) 5c on ½m **blue green** (2) 1,000. 275.
a. Inverted surcharge *1,000.*
192 (i) 5c on ½m **blue green** (4) *3,000.* 100.
a. Double surcharge, one diagonal *3,500.* —

Value for No. 190b is for pair with unsurcharged stamp at right. One pair with unsurcharged stamp at left is known.
No. 192a is unique.

193 (j) 5c on ½m **blue green** (4) *900.* 500.

Red Surcharge on No. 161

196 (k) 3c on 1c **black violet** (3) 150. 125.
a. Inverted surcharge 500.
197 (l) 3c on 1c **black violet** (3) 250. 200.
a. Inverted surcharge *1,500.*

198 (i) 5c on 1c **black violet** (3) 92.50 72.50
a. Inverted surcharge 500.
b. Vertical surcharge —
c. Double surcharge *600.* *2,750.*
d. Double inverted surcharge — —

Value for No. 198b is for surcharge reading up. One example is known with surcharge reading down.

199 (j) 5c on 1c **black violet** (3) 150. 115.
a. Inverted surcharge *3,000.*
b. Vertical surcharge — —
c. Double surcharge *3,000.* *3,000.*

m

200 (m) 10c on 1c **black violet** (3) 62.50 *92.50*
a. Broken figure "1" 160.00 *225.00*

Black Surcharge on Nos. P26-P30

201 (k) 3c on 1m **blue green** (5) 350. 350.
a. Inverted surcharge 450.
b. "EENTS" 600. 450.
c. As "b", inverted 850.
202 (l) 3c on 1m **blue green** (5) 1,000. 400.
a. Inverted surcharge 850.
203 (k) 3c on 2m **blue green** (5) 1,650. 400.
a. "EENTS" 1,650. 500.
b. Inverted surcharge 1,500.
c. As "a," inverted *2,750.*
204 (l) 3c on 2m **blue green** (5) *2,750.* *600.*
a. Inverted surcharge *1,500.*
205 (k) 3c on 3m **blue green** (5) 900. 400.
a. Inverted surcharge 750.
b. "EENTS" 1,250. 450.
c. As "b," inverted *2,750.*
206 (l) 3c on 3m **blue green** (5) *1,500.* 550.
a. Inverted surcharge *1,000.*
211 (i) 5c on 1m **blue green** (5) 1,800.
a. "EENTS" — 3,000.
212 (j) 5c on 1m **blue green** (5) — 2,250.
213 (i) 5c on 2m **blue green** (5) 3,000. 1,800.
a. "EENTS" 3,000. 3,000.
214 (j) 5c on 2m **blue green** (5) 3,250. 1,750.
215 (i) 5c on 3m **blue green** (5) 550.
a. "EENTS" 1,000.
216 (j) 5c on 3m **blue green** (5) 3,000. 1,000.
217 (i) 5c on 4m **blue green** (5) *3,000.* 900.
a. "EENTS" *3,000.* 1,500.
b. Inverted surcharge *2,000.*
c. As "a," inverted *3,000.*
218 (j) 5c on 4m **blue green** (5) 3,000. *1,500.*
a. Inverted surcharge *2,000.*
219 (i) 5c on 8m **blue green** (5) *2,500.* 1,250.
a. Inverted surcharge 1,500.
b. "EENTS" 3,000. 2,750.
c. As "b," inverted 2,500.
220 (j) 5c on 8m **blue green** (5) 2,000.
a. Inverted surcharge 2,500.

Puerto Principe pairs, strips and stamps properly canceled on cover are scarce and command high premiums.
Most copies of all but the most common varieties are faulty or have tropical toning. Values are for sound copies where they exist.

United States Stamps Nos. 279, 267, 267b, 279Bf, 279Bh, 268, 281, 282C and 283 Surcharged in Black

1899 **Wmk. 191** ***Perf. 12***

221 A87 1c on 1c **yellow green** 4.50 .40
Never hinged 11.50
On cover 15.00
Block of 4 22.50 4.50
P# strip of 3, Impt. 55.00
P# block of 6, Impt. 290.00
222 A88 2c on 2c **reddish carmine,** type III, *Feb.* 10.00 .75
Never hinged 25.00
On cover 22.50
Block of 4 55.00 8.00
P# strip of 3, Impt. 115.00
P# block of 6, Impt. 650.00
b. 2c on 2c **vermilion,** type III, *Feb.* 10.00 .75
222A A88 2c on 2c **reddish carmine,** type IV, *Feb.* 6.00 .40
Never hinged 15.00
On cover 12.50
Block of 4 30.00 4.50
P# strip of 3, Impt. 65.00
P# block of 6, Impt. 600.00
"CUBA" at bottom *650.00*
"CUPA" (broken letter. pos. 99) 250.00 75.00
c. 2c on 2c **vermilion,** type IV, *Feb.* 6.00 .40
d. As No. 222A, inverted surcharge *5,500.* *4,000.*

223 A88 2½c on 2c **reddish carmine,** type III, *Jan. 2* 6.00 .80
Never hinged 15.00
On cover 20.00
Block of 4 30.00 8.00
P# strip of 3, Impt. 95.00
P# block of 6, Impt. 350.00
b. 2½ on 2c **vermilion,** type III, *Jan. 2* 6.00 .80
223A A88 2½c on 2c **reddish carmine,** type IV, *Jan. 2* 3.50 .50
Never hinged 8.75
On cover 12.50
Block of 4 20.00 4.50
P# strip of 3, Impt. 62.50
P# block of 6, Impt. 250.00
c. 2½c on 2c **vermilion,** type IV, *Jan. 2* 3.50 .50

All 2½c stamps were sold and used as 2 centavo stamps.

224 A89 3c on 3c **purple** 12.00 1.75
Never hinged 30.00
On cover 25.00
Block of 4 57.50 14.00
P# strip of 3, Impt. 110.00
P# block of 6, Impt. 675.00
a. Period between "B" and "A" 40.00 35.00

Two types of surcharge
I — "3" directly over "P"
II — "3" to left over "P"

225 A91 5c on 5c **blue** 12.50 2.00
Never hinged 30.00
On cover 30.00
Block of 4 60.00 15.00
P# strip of 3, Impt. 190.00
P# block of 6, Impt. 800.00
"CUBA" at bottom — —
"CUPA" (broken letter) 80.00 40.00
226 A94 10c on 10c **brown,** type I 25.00 6.00
Never hinged 70.00
On cover 110.00
Block of 4 115.00 45.00
P# strip of 3, Impt. 260.00
P# block of 6, Impt. 1,100.
"CUBA" at bottom 500.00 550.00
b. "CUBA" omitted *7,000.* *4,000.*
226A A94 10c on 10c **brown,** type II *6,000.*
Block of 4 —
Nos. 221-226 (8) 79.50 12.60

No. 226A exists only in the special printing.
The No. 225 "CUPA" variety always has a straight edge at the right.

Special Printing

In March 1900, one pane of 100 each of Nos. 221-225, 226A, J1-J4 and two panes of 50 of No. E1, were specially overprinted for displays at the Paris Exposition (1900) and Pan American Exposition (1901). The 2c pane was light red, type IV. Stamps were handstamped type E "Specimen" in black ink by H. G. Mandel and mounted by him in separate displays for the two Expositions. Additional stamps from each pane were also handstamped "specimen," but most were destroyed after the Expositions. However, because additional stamps that are not Special Printings exist with a black "Specimen" handstamp, expertization by competent authorities is recommended. Nearly all examples remaining bear impression of a dealer's handstamp reading "Special Surcharge" in red ink on the back. Value: Nos. 221-225, each $750; Nos. J1-J4, each $1,500; No. E1, $2,500.

Issues of the Republic under US Military Rule

Statue of Columbus — A20

Royal Palms — A21

Allegory, "Cuba" — A22

Ocean Liner — A23

Cane Field — A24

ORIGINAL RE-ENGRAVED

Re-engraved

The re-engraved stamps issued by the Republic of Cuba in 1905-07 may be distinguished from the Issue of 1899 as follows:

Nos. 227-231 are watermarked U S-C

The re-engraved stamps are unwatermarked.

1c: The ends of the label inscribed "Centavo" are rounded instead of square.

2c: The foliate ornaments, inside the oval disks bearing the numerals of value, have been removed.

5c: Two lines forming a right angle have been added in the upper corners of the label bearing the word "Cuba."

10c: A small ball has been added to each of the square ends of the label bearing the word "Cuba."

Printed by the U.S. Bureau of Engraving and Printing

1899 **Wmk. US-C (191C)** ***Perf. 12***

No.	Description	Unused	Used
227	A20 1c **yellow green**	3.50	.25
	Never hinged	8.75	
	On cover		2.00
	Block of 4	15.00	1.00
	P# block of 10, Impt., type VII	225.00	—
228	A21 2c **carmine**	3.50	.25
	Never hinged	8.75	
	On cover		2.00
	Block of 4	15.00	1.00
	P# block of 10, Impt., type VII	180.00	—
a.	2c **scarlet**	3.50	.25
b.	Booklet pane of 6	*5,500.*	
229	A22 3c **purple**	3.50	.30
	Never hinged	8.75	
	On cover		4.00
	Block of 4	15.00	2.50
	P# block of 10, Impt., type VII	275.00	—
230	A23 5c **blue**	4.50	.30
	Never hinged	11.00	
	On cover		4.00
	Block of 4	21.00	2.50
	P# block of 10, Impt., type VII	450.00	—
231	A24 10c **brown**	11.00	.80
	Never hinged	27.50	
	On cover		6.50
	Block of 4	52.50	5.50
	P# block of 10, Impt., type VII	1,200.	—
	Nos. 227-231 (5)	26.00	1.90

No. 228b was issued by the Republic.

See Nos. 233-237 in Scott Standard Catalogue Vol 2. For surcharge see No. 232.

SPECIAL DELIVERY STAMPS

Issued under Administration of the United States

Special Delivery Stamp of the United States No. E5 Surcharged in Red

1899 **Wmk. 191** ***Perf. 12***

No.	Description	Unused	Used
E1	SD3 10c on 10c **blue**	130.	100.
	Never hinged	300.	
	On cover		450.
	Block of 4	575.	
	Margin block of 4, arrow	650.	
	P# strip of 3, Impt.	1,000.	
	P# block of 6, Impt.	*5,000.*	
a.	No period after "CUBA"	575.	400.
b.	Five dots in curved frame above messenger's head (Pl. 882)	*2,500.*	

Issue of the Republic under US Military Rule

Special Delivery Messenger SD2

Printed by the US Bureau of Engraving and Printing

1899 **Wmk. US-C (191C)**

Inscribed: "Immediata"

No.	Description	Unused	Used
E2	SD2 10c **orange**	52.50	15.00
	Never hinged	120.00	
	On cover		150.00
	Block of 4	250.00	—
	P# strip of 3, Impt., type VII	300.00	
	P# block of 6, Impt., type VII	1,000.	

Re-engraved

In 1902 the Republic of Cuba issued a stamp of design SD2 re-engraved with word correctly spelled "Inmediata." The corrected die was made in 1899 (See No. E3P). It was printed by the U.S. Bureau of Engraving and Printing.

POSTAGE DUE STAMPS

Issued under Administration of the United States

Postage Due Stamps of the United States Nos. J38, J39, J41 and J42 Srchd. in Black Like Nos. 221-226A

1899 **Wmk. 191** ***Perf. 12***

No.	Description	Unused	Used
J1	D2 1c on 1c **deep claret**	45.00	5.25
	Never hinged	110.00	
	Block of 4	210.00	45.00
	P# block of 6, Impt.	*900.00*	
J2	D2 2c on 2c **deep claret**	45.00	5.25
	Never hinged	110.00	
	Block of 4	200.00	30.00
	P# block of 6, Impt.	*900.00*	
a.	Inverted surcharge		*3,750.*
J3	D2 5c on 5c **deep claret**	42.50	5.25
	Never hinged	105.00	
	Block of 4	210.00	45.00
	P# block of 6, Impt.	*900.00*	
	"CUPA" (broken letter)	150.00	140.00
J4	D2 10c on 10c **deep claret**	25.00	2.50
	Never hinged	60.00	
	Block of 4	125.00	27.50
	P# block of 6, Impt.	*800.00*	
	Nos. J1-J4 (4)	157.50	18.25

The No. J3 "CUPA" variety always has a straight edge at right.

ENVELOPES

Values are for Cut Squares

US Envelopes of 1887-99 Surcharged

a

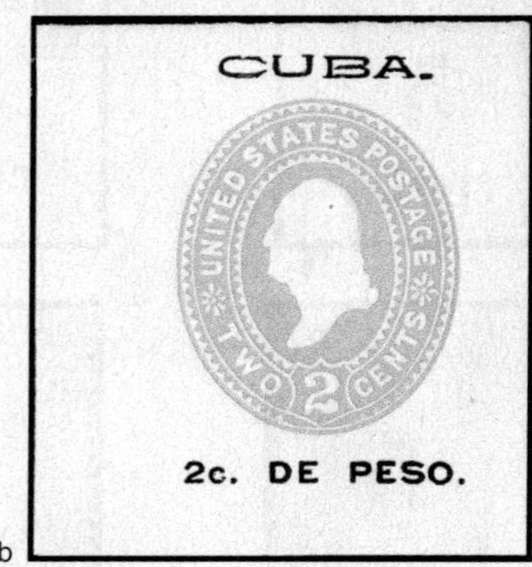

b

1899

No.	Description	Unused	Used
U1	U77 (a) 1c on 1c **green,** *oriental buff* (No. U354)	5.00	3.50
	Entire	12.00	15.00
U2	U77 (a) 1c on 1c **green,** *blue* (No. U355)	2.50	2.50
	Entire	4.00	5:50
a.	Double surcharge, entire	*5,250.*	
U3	U71 (b) 2c on 2c **green** (No. U311)	1.50	1.10
	Entire	3.00	3.50
a.	Double surcharge, entire	*4,500.*	*6,500.*
b.	Inverted surcharge at lower left, entire	—	*4,250.*
U4	U71 (b) 2c on 2c **green,** *amber* (No. U312)	2.75	1.65
	Entire	5.25	6.00
a.	Double surcharge, entire	*5,250.*	
U5	U71 (a) 2c on 2c **green,** *oriental buff* (No. U313)	17.50	8.00
	Entire	47.50	47.50
U6	U79 (a) 2c on 2c **carmine,** *amber* (No. U363)	17.50	17.50
	Entire	47.50	47.50
U7	U79 (a) 2c on 2c **carmine,** *oriental buff* (No. U364)	25.00	25.00
	Entire	100.00	80.00
U8	U79 (a) 2c on 2c **carmine,** *blue* (No. U365)	3.00	2.00
	Entire	7.00	8.00
a.	Double surcharge, entire		*6,750.*
	Nos. U1-U8 (8)	74.75	61.25

In addition to the envelopes listed above, several others are known but were not regularly issued. They are:

1c on 1c green
1c on 1c green, *manila*
2c on 2c carmine
4c on 4c brown
5c on 5c blue

Issue of the Republic under US Military Rule

Columbus — E1

Similar envelopes without watermark on white and amber papers, were issued by the Republic after Military Rule ended in 1902.

1899 Wmk. "US POD '99" in Monogram

U9 E1	1c **green**	.75	.65
	Entire	4.00	4.00
U10 E1	1c **green,** *amber*	1.00	.65
	Entire	4.00	4.00
U11 E1	1c **green,** *oriental buff*	17.50	13.00
	Entire	85.00	42.50
U12 E1	1c **green,** *blue*	25.00	15.00
	Entire	85.00	42.50
U13 E1	2c **carmine**	1.00	.70
	Entire	3.75	3.00
U14 E1	2c **carmine,** *amber*	1.00	.70
	Entire	3.75	3.00
U15 E1	2c **carmine,** *oriental buff*	9.00	7.75
	Entire	35.00	21.00
U16 E1	2c **carmine,** *blue*	25.00	18.00
	Entire	60.00	52.50
U17 E1	5c **blue**	3.25	2.25
	Entire	5.00	2.75
U18 E1	5c **blue,** *amber*	5.50	5.00
	Entire	9.00	6.50
	Nos. U9-U18 (10)	89.00	63.70

WRAPPERS

Issue of the Republic under US Military Rule

1899

W1 E1	1c **green,** *manila*	4.00	10.00
	Entire	11.00	50.00
W2 E1	2c **carmine,** *manila*	12.00	10.00
	Entire	25.00	50.00

POSTAL CARDS

Values are for Entires

U.S. Postal Cards Nos. UX14, UX16 Surcharged

UX1 PC8	1c on 1c **black,** *buff, Jefferson (1,000,000)*	15.00	16.50
a.	No period after "1c"	40.00	75.00
b.	No period after "Peso"	35.00	
c.	Surcharge "2c" (error)	*6,500.*	
UX2 PC3	2c on 2c **black,** *buff, Liberty (583,000)*	15.00	16.50
a.	No period after "Peso"	40.00	75.00
b.	Double surcharge		—

In 1904 the Republic of Cuba revalued remaining stocks of No. UX2 by means of a perforated numeral "1."

PROOFS

1899

227P1	1c **yellow green,** large die on India paper	160.
227P2	1c **yellow green,** RA sm die on white wove paper	160.
227TC1	1c Large die on India paper	
a.	**blue green**	375.
b.	**black**	625.
228P1	2c **carmine,** large die on India paper	160.
228P2	2c **carmine,** RA sm die on white wove paper	160.
228TC1	2c Large die on India paper	
a.	**black**	625.
229P1	3c **purple,** large die on India paper	160.
229P2	3c **purple,** RA sm die on white wove paper	160.
229TC1	3c Large die on India paper	
a.	**black**	375.
230P1	5c **blue,** large die on India paper	160.
230P2	5c **blue,** RA sm die on white wove paper	160.
230TC1	5c Large die on India paper	
a.	**black**	625.
231P1	10c **brown,** large die on India paper	160.
231P2	10c **brown,** RA sm die on white wove paper	160.
231TC1	10c Large die on India paper	
a.	**gray**	625.
b.	**black**	625.

Special Delivery

E2TC1	10c Large die on India paper	
a.	**blue**	3,750.
E3P1	10c **orange** large die on India paper	575.
E3P2	10c **orange** RA sm die on white wove paper	450.

SPECIMEN STAMPS

Handstamped U.S. Type E in Purple or Black

1899

221S	E	1c on 1c **yellow green**	200.
222AS	E	2c on 2c **reddish carmine,** type IV	200.
223AS	E	2½c on 2c **reddish carmine,** type IV	200.
224S	E	3c on 3c **purple**	200.
225S	E	5c on 5c **blue**	200.
226S	E	10c on 10c **brown,** type I	200.
226AS	E	10c on 10c **brown,** type II	*6,000.*

See Special Printing Notice following No. 226A for Special Printings with black "Specimen" handstamps, but note that not all stamps with the black "Specimen" handstamp are Special Printings.

1899

227S	E	1c **yellow green**	225.
228S	E	2c **carmine**	225.
229S	E	3c **purple**	225.
230S	E	5c **blue**	225.
231S	E	10c **brown**	225.

Special Delivery

1899

E1S	E	10c on 10c **blue**	1,500.
a.		Five dots in curved frame above messenger's head	5,250.
E2S	E	10c **orange**	2,100.

Postage Due

1899

J1S	E	1c on 1c **deep claret**	500.
J2S	E	2c on 2c **deep claret**	500.
J3S	E	5c on 5c **deep claret**	500.
J4S	E	10c on 10c **deep claret**	500.

See Special Printing Notice following No. 226A for Special Printings with black "Specimen" handstamps, but note that not all stamps with the black "Specimen" handstamp are Special Printings.

DANISH WEST INDIES AND UNITED STATES VIRGIN ISLANDS

Formerly a Danish colony, these islands were purchased by the United States on March 31, 1917 and have since been known as the U.S. Virgin Islands. They lie east of Puerto Rico, have an area of 132 square miles and had a population of 27,086 in 1911. The capital is Charlotte Amalie (also called St. Thomas). Stamps of Danish West Indies were replaced by those of the United States in 1917. However, for the first six months of U.S. ownership, until September 30, 1917, a postal transition period existed. During this period, either U.S., D.W.I. or mixed frankings could be used. The domestic printed matter or postcard rate was 5 bits or 1 cent, and the foreign printed matter or postcard rate was 10 bits, 2 cents, or 5 bits + 1 cent. The domestic minimum weight letter rate was 10 bits, 2 cents, or 5 bits + 1 cent, while the foreign minimum letter rate was 25 bits, 5 cents, or any combination of U.S. and D.W.I. stamps that together totalled 25 bits or 5 cents.

Letters posted to foreign destinations during the transition period are rare because of World War I. Values for covers listed here are for the period before the transition. Transition-period covers, including those with mixed franking, sell for much more.

100 CENTS = 1 DOLLAR
100 BIT = 1 FRANC (1905)

Wmk. 111 — Small Crown

Wmk. 112 — Crown

Wmk. 113 — Crown

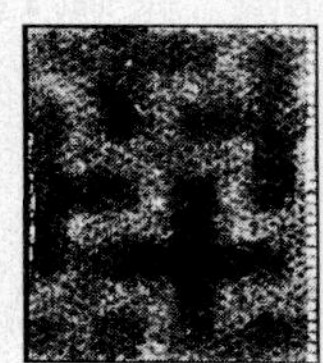
Wmk. 114 — Multiple Crosses

Coat of Arms — A1

1856 Typo. Wmk. 111 *Imperf.*

1 A1	3c **dark carmine,** brown gum	200.	*275.*
	On cover		3,000.
	Block of 4	1,300.	
a.	3c **dark carmine,** yellow gum	225.	*275.*
	On cover		3,000.

Block of 4 2,850.
b. 3c **carmine,** white gum 4,250. —
On cover —

The brown and yellow gums were applied locally.

Reprint: 1981, carmine, back-printed across two stamps ("Reprint by Dansk Post og Telegrafmuseum 1978"), value, pair, $10.

White Paper

1866 Yellow Wavy-line Burelage UR to LL

2 A1 3c **rose** 40. *65.*
On cover 3,000.
Block of 4 200. *350.*
Rouletted 4½ privately 350. 175.
On cover, rouletted 4½ —
Rouletted 9 450. 200.

The value for used blocks is for favor cancel (CTO).

No. 2 reprints, unwatermarked: 1930, carmine, value $100. 1942, rose carmine, back-printed across each row ("Nytryk 1942 G. A. Hagemann Danmark og Dansk Vestindiens Frimaerker Bind 2"), value $50.

1872 ***Perf. 12½***

3 A1 3c **rose** 100. *275.*
On cover *7,500.*
Block of 4 550.

1873 **Without Burelage**

4 A1 4c **dull blue** 250. *475.*
On cover —
Block of 4 1,300.
a. Imperf., pair 775.
b. Horiz. pair, imperf. vert. 575.

The 1930 reprint of No. 4 is ultramarine, unwatermarked and imperf., value $100.

The 1942 4c reprint is blue, unwatermarked, imperf. and has printing on back (see note below No. 2), value $60.

Numeral of Value — A2

D.W.I.
and Scandinavia
• Free Catalog • Stamps
• Postal History • Literature
• Want Lists Filled • Albums
www.JaySmith.com
email:info-x977@JaySmith.com
CALL TOLL FREE
1-800-447-8267
(U.S. and CANADA)
or 336-376-9991
FAX 336-376-6750
Jay Smith
P.O. Box 650-X977
Snow Camp, NC 27349
The Scandinavia Specialist Since 1973

Normal Frame Inverted Frame

The arabesques in the corners have a main stem and a branch. When the frame is in normal position, in the upper left corner the branch leaves the main stem half way between two little leaflets. In the lower right corner the branch starts at the foot of the second leaflet. When the frame is inverted the corner designs are, of course, transposed.

Values for inverted frames, covers and blocks are for the cheapest variety.

White Wove Paper, Printings 1-3 Thin, 4-7 Medium, 8-9 Thick
1c Nine printings
3c Eight printings
4c Two printings
5c Six printings
7c Two printings
10c Seven printings
12c Two printings
14c One printing
50c Two printings

1874-79 **Wmk. 112** ***Perf. 14x13½***

White Wove Paper, Printings 1-3 Thin, 4-7 Medium, 8-9 Thick
1c Nine printings
3c Eight printings
4c Two printings
5c Six printings
7c Two printings
10c Seven printings
12c Two printings
14c One printing
50c Two printings

5 A2 1c **green & brown red** 22.50 *30.00*
On cover 250.00
Block of 4 100.00 *240.00*
a. 1c **green & rose lilac,** thin paper 80.00 *125.00*
b. 1c **green & red violet,** medium paper 45.00 *65.00*
c. 1c **green & claret,** thick paper 20.00 *30.00*
e. As "c," inverted frame 25.00 *32.50*
f. As "a," inverted frame *475.00*

No. 5 exists with a surcharge similar to the surcharge on No. 15, with 10 CENTS value and 1895 date. This stamp is an essay.

6 A2 3c **blue & carmine** 27.50 20.00
On cover 225.00
Block of 4 120.00 —
White "wedge" flaw 52.50 52.50
a. 3c **light blue & rose carmine,** thin paper 65.00 50.00
b. 3c **deep blue & dark carmine,** medium paper 40.00 17.00
c. 3c **greenish blue & lake,** thick paper 32.50 17.00
d. Imperf., pair 375.00 —
e. Inverted frame, thick paper 30.00 20.00
f. As "a," inverted frame *350.00*

7 A2 4c **brown & dull blue** 16.00 *19.00*
On cover 225.00
Block of 4 75.00 —
b. 4c **brown & ultramarine,** thin paper 225.00 *225.00*
c. Diagonal half used as 2c on cover 140.00
d. As "b," inverted frame *900.00* *1,400.*

8 A2 5c **green & gray** 30.00 20.00
On cover 250.00
Block of 4 130.00 —
a. 5c **yellow green & dark gray,** thin paper 55.00 32.50
b. Inverted frame, thick paper 30.00 20.00

9 A2 7c **lilac & orange** 35.00 *95.00*
On cover 1,100.
Block of 4 175.00 —
a. 7c **lilac & yellow** 90.00 *100.00*
b. Inverted frame 65.00 *150.00*

10 A2 10c **blue & brown** 30.00 25.00
On cover 300.00
Block of 4 140.00 —
a. 10c **dark blue & black brown,** thin paper 70.00 40.00
b. Period between "t" & "s" of "cents" 35.00 25.00
c. Inverted frame 27.50 *32.50*

11 A2 12c **red lilac & yellow green** 42.50 *175.00*
On cover 1,750.
Block of 4 230.00 —
a. 12c **lilac & deep green** 160.00 *200.00*

12 A2 14c **lilac & green** 650.00 *1,250.*
On cover —
Block of 4 *4,000.*
a. Inverted frame *2,500.* *3,500.*

13 A2 50c **violet,** thin paper 190.00 *300.00*
On cover 2,500.
Block of 4 1,350.
a. 50c **gray violet,** thick paper 250.00 *375.00*

Issue dates: 1c, 3c, 4c, 14c, Jan. 15, 1874. 7c, July 22, 1874. 5c, 10c, 1876; 12c, 1877; 50c, 1879. Colors of major numbers are generally those of the least expensive of two or more shades, and do not indicate the shade of the first printing.

No. 9 Surcharged in Black

a

1887

14 A2 (a) 1c on 7c **lilac & orange** 100.00 *200.00*
On cover 3,000.
Block of 4 450.00 —
a. 1c on 7c **lilac & yellow** 120.00 *225.00*
b. Double surcharge 250.00 *500.00*
c. Inverted frame 110.00 *350.00*

No. 13 Surcharged in Black

b

1895

15 A2 (b) 10c on 50c **violet,** thin paper 42.50 *67.50*
On cover 275.00
Block of 4 275.00 —

The "b" surcharge also exists on No. 5, with "10" found in two sizes. These are essays.

1896-1901 ***Perf. 13***

16 A2 1c **grn & red vio,** inverted frame ('98) 15.00 *22.50*
On cover 150.00
Block of 4 75.00 —
a. Normal frame 300.00 *450.00*

17 A2 3c **blue & lake,** inverted frame ('98) 12.00 *17.50*
On cover 150.00
Block of 4 55.00 —
White "wedge" flaw 35.00 *45.00*
a. Normal frame 250.00 *425.00*

18 A2 4c **bister & dull blue** ('01) 17.50 11.00
On cover 150.00
Block of 4 77.50 —
a. Diagonal half used as 2c on cover 100.00
b. Inverted frame 60.00 *80.00*
On cover 250.00
c. As "b," diagonal half used as 2c on cover 350.00

19 A2 5c **green & gray,** inverted frame 35.00 35.00
On cover 325.00
Block of 4 160.00 —
a. Normal frame 800.00 *1,200.*

20 A2 10c **blue & brn** ('01) 80.00 *150.00*
On cover 1,150.
Block of 4 475.00 —
a. Inverted frame 1,000. *2,000.*
b. Period between "t" and "s" of "cents" 170.00 160.00
Nos. 16-20 (5) 159.50 *236.00*

Two printings each of Nos. 18-19.

Arms — A5

1900

21 A5 1c **light green** 3.00 3.00
On cover, pair 80.00
On cover, single franking 300.00
Block of 4 12.50 12.50

22 A5 5c **light blue** 17.50 *25.00*
On cover 300.00
Block of 4 80.00 —

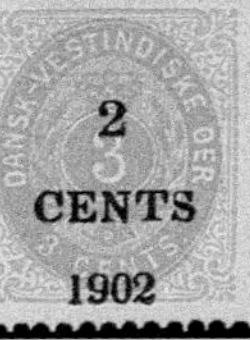

Nos. 6, 17 and 20 Surcharged in Black — c

1902 *Perf. 14x13½*

23 A2 2c on 3c **blue & carmine,** inverted frame 700.00 900.00
On cover 4,000.
Block of 4 3,250.
a. "2" in date with straight tail 750.00 950.00
b. Normal frame —

Perf. 13

24 A2 2c on 3c **blue & lake,** inverted frame 10.00 27.50
On cover 160.00
Block of 4 45.00 —
White "wedge" flaw 55.00 55.00
a. "2" in date with straight tail 12.00 32.50
b. Dated "1901" 750.00 750.00
c. Normal frame 175.00 300.00
d. Dark green surcharge 2,750.
e. As "d" & "a" — —
f. As "d" & "c" —

The overprint on No. 24b exists in two types: with "1901" measuring 2.5 mm or 2.2 mm high.
Only one example of No. 24f can exist.

25 A2 8c on 10c **blue & brown** 25.00 42.50
On cover 225.00
Block of 4 105.00 —
a. "2" with straight tail 30.00 45.00
b. On No. 20b 32.50 45.00
c. Inverted frame 250.00 425.00

Nos. 17 and 20 Surcharged in Black — d

1902 *Perf. 13*

27 A2 2c on 3c **blue & lake,** inverted frame 12.00 32.50
On cover 500.00
Block of 4 52.50 —
White "wedge" flaw 40.00 55.00
a. Normal frame 240.00 425.00
28 A2 8c on 10c **blue & brown** 12.00 12.00
On cover 175.00
Block of 4 52.50 —
a. On No. 20b 18.50 25.00
b. Inverted frame 225.00 400.00
Nos. 23-28 (5) 759.00 1,015.

1903 **Wmk. 113**

29 A5 2c **carmine** 8.00 22.50
On cover 125.00
Block of 4 35.00 —
30 A5 8c **brown** 27.50 35.00
On cover 250.00
Block of 4 115.00 —

King Christian IX — A8

St. Thomas Harbor — A9

1905 **Typo.** *Perf. 13*

31 A8 5b **green** 3.75 3.25
On cover 35.00
Block of 4 17.00 —
32 A8 10b **red** 3.75 3.25
On cover 35.00
Block of 4 16.00 —
33 A8 20b **green & blue** 8.75 8.75
On cover 150.00
Block of 4 40.00 —
34 A8 25b **ultramarine** 8.75 10.50
On cover 85.00
Block of 4 40.00 —
35 A8 40b **red & gray** 8.25 9.50
On cover 225.00
Block of 4 37.50 —
36 A8 50b **yellow & gray** 10.00 10.00
On cover 250.00
Block of 4 42.50 —

Perf. 12

Wmk. Two Crowns (113)

Frame Typographed, Center Engraved

37 A9 1fr **green & blue** 17.50 40.00
On cover 625.00
Block of 4 75.00 —
38 A9 2fr **orange red & brown** 30.00 55.00
On cover 1,100.
Block of 4 150.00 —
39 A9 5fr **yellow & brown** 77.50 275.00
On cover 1,750.
Block of 4 375.00 —
Nos. 31-39 (9) 168.25 415.25

On cover values are for commercial usages, usually parcel address cards. Philatelic covers are valued at approximately 25% of these values.

Nos. 18, 22 and 30 Surcharged in Black

1905 **Wmk. 112** *Perf. 13*

40 A2 5b on 4c **bister & dull blue** 16.00 50.00
On cover 250.00
Block of 4 77.50 —
a. Inverted frame 45.00 90.00
41 A5 5b on 5c **light blue** 10.00 47.50
On cover 250.00
Block of 4 40.00 —

Wmk. 113

42 A5 5b on 8c **brown** 12.50 50.00
On cover 250.00
Block of 4 55.00 —
Nos. 40-42 (3) 38.50 147.50

Favor cancels exist on Nos. 40-42. Value 25% less.

King Frederik VIII — A10

Frame Typographed, Center Engraved

1908 **Wmk. 113** *Perf. 13*

43 A10 5b **green** 1.90 1.90
On cover 22.50
Block of 4 9.50 —
Number block of 6 18.50
44 A10 10b **red** 1.90 1.90
On cover 22.50
Block of 4 9.50 —
Number block of 6 18.50
45 A10 15b **violet & brown** 3.75 4.50
On cover 125.00
Block of 4 19.00 —
Number block of 6 52.50
46 A10 20b **green & blue** 30.00 27.50
On cover 110.00
Block of 4 130.00 —
Number block of 6 375.00
47 A10 25b **blue & dark blue** 1.90 2.50
On cover 35.00
Block of 4 9.00 —
Number block of 6 18.50
48 A10 30b **claret & slate** 50.00 52.50
On cover 350.00
Block of 4 220.00 240.00
Number block of 6 525.00
49 A10 40b **vermilion & gray** 5.75 9.50
On cover 210.00
Block of 4 25.00 —
Number block of 6 55.00
50 A10 50b **yellow & brown** 5.75 14.00
On cover 210.00
Block of 4 25.00 —
Number block of 6 70.00
Nos. 43-50 (8) 100.95 114.30

Printing numbers appear in the selvage, once per pane, in Roman or Arabic numerals.

King Christian X — A11

Frame Typographed, Center Engraved

1915 **Wmk. 114** *Perf. 14x14½*

51 A11 5b **yellow green** 4.00 5.50
On cover 45.00
Block of 4 17.50 —
Number block of 4 40.00
52 A11 10b **red** 4.00 55.00
On cover 110.00
Block of 4 17.50 —
Number block of 4 40.00
53 A11 15b **lilac & red brown** 4.00 55.00
On cover 300.00
Block of 4 17.50 —
Number block of 4 40.00
54 A11 20b **green & blue** 4.00 55.00
On cover 350.00
Block of 4 17.50 —
Number block of 4 40.00
55 A11 25b **blue & dark blue** 4.00 17.50
On cover 110.00
Block of 4 17.50 —
Number block of 4 40.00
56 A11 30b **claret & black** 4.00 100.00
On cover 900.00
Block of 4 17.50 —
Number block of 4 40.00
57 A11 40b **orange & black** 4.00 100.00
On cover 550.00
Block of 4 18.50 —
Number block of 4 40.00
58 A11 50b **yellow & brown** 3.75 100.00
On cover 650.00
Block of 4 17.50 —
Number block of 4 40.00
Nos. 51-58 (8) 31.75 488.00

Forged and favor cancellations exist.
Plate identifications 11-D, 50-D or 50-O are located in the selvage in all four corners of the pane. The 50-D is on all denominations. 11-D, all but the 50b, 50-O, all but 15b, 20b, 25b.

POSTAGE DUE STAMPS

Royal Cipher "Christian Rex" — D1

1902 **Litho.** **Unwmk.** *Perf. 11½*

J1 D1 1c **dark blue** 5.00 17.50
On cover 400.00
Block of 4 25.00
J2 D1 4c **dark blue** 12.50 22.50
On cover 350.00
Block of 4 55.00
J3 D1 6c **dark blue** 22.50 60.00
On cover 450.00
Block of 4 100.00
J4 D1 10c **dark blue** 20.00 65.00
On cover 400.00
Block of 4 95.00
Nos. J1-J4 (4) 60.00 165.00

There are five types of each value. On the 4c they may be distinguished by differences in the figure "4"; on the other values differences are minute.
Used values of Nos. J1-J8 are for canceled stamps. Uncanceled stamps without gum have probably been used. Value 60% of unused. On cover values are for stamps tied by cancellation.
Excellent counterfeits of Nos. J1-J4 exist.

Numeral of value — D2

1905-13 *Perf. 13*

J5 D2 5b **red & gray** 4.50 6.75
On cover 450.00
Block of 4 20.00 —
J6 D2 20b **red & gray** 7.50 14.00
On cover 450.00
Block of 4 32.50 —
J7 D2 30b **red & gray** 6.75 14.00
On cover 450.00
Block of 4 30.00 —
J8 D2 50b **red & gray** 6.00 30.00
On cover 900.00
Block of 4 27.50 —
a. Perf. 14x14½ ('13) 90.00 375.00
Block of 4 400.00 —
b. Perf. 11½ 375.00
Nos. J5-J8 (4) 24.75 64.75

Nos. J5-J8 are known imperforate but were not regularly issued. Excellent counterfeits exist.
See notes following No. J4 for canceled stamps.
No. J8b is valued in the grade of fine.

ENVELOPES

E1

1877-78 **On White Paper**

No.	Type	Description	Unused	Used
U1	E1	2c **light blue** ('78)	5.00	*14.00*
		Entire	20.00	*65.00*
a.		2c **ultramarine**	20.00	*200.00*
		Entire	100.00	*800.00*
U2	E1	3c **orange**	5.00	*12.50*
		Entire	20.00	*65.00*
a.		3c **red orange**	5.50	*12.50*
		Entire	22.50	*65.00*

Three different Crown watermarks are found on entires of No. U1, four on entires of No. U2. Envelope watermarks do not show on cut squares.

POSTAL CARDS

Values are for entire cards.

Italicized numbers in parentheses indicate quantities issued.

Designs of Adhesive Stamps

"BREV-KORT" at top

1877 **Inscription in Three Lines**

No.	Type	Description	Unused	Used
UX1	A2	6c **violet**	40.00	*1,400.*

Used value is for card to foreign destination postmarked before April 1, 1879.

1878-85 **Inscription in Four Lines**

No.	Type	Description	Unused	Used
UX2	A2	2c **light blue** *(8,800)*	22.50	*50.00*
UX3	A2	3c **carmine rose** *(17,700)*	17.50	*35.00*

1888 **Inscription in Five Lines**

No.	Type	Description	Unused	Used
UX4	A2	2c **light blue** *(30,500)*	20.00	*32.50*
UX5	A2	3c **red** *(26,500)*	12.50	*22.50*

Card No. UX5 Locally Surcharged with type "c" but with date "1901"

1901

No.	Type	Description	Unused	Used
UX6	A2	1c on 3c **red** *(2,000)*	50.00	*200.00*

1902

Card No. UX4 Locally Surcharged with type "c," "1902" date

No.	Type	Description	Unused	Used
UX7	A2	1c on 2c **light blue** *(3,000)*	37.50	*160.00*

Card No. UX5 Surcharged similar to type "c" but heavy letters, "1902" date

1902

No.	Type	Description	Unused	Used
UX8	A2	1c on 3c **red** *(7,175)*	12.50	*150.00*

1903

No.	Type	Description	Unused	Used
UX9	A5	1c **light green** *(10,000)*	12.50	*30.00*
UX10	A5	2c **carmine** *(10,000)*	19.00	*70.00*

1905

No.	Type	Description	Unused	Used
UX11	A8	5b **green** *(16,000)*	12.50	*22.50*
UX12	A8	10b **red** *(14,000)*	12.50	*35.00*

1907-08 **Unwmk.**

No.	Type	Description	Unused	Used
UX13	A10	5b **green** ('08) *(30,750)*	9.50	*27.50*
UX14	A10	10b **red** *(19,750)*	12.50	*40.00*

1913 **Wmk. Wood-grain**

No.	Type	Description	Unused	Used
UX15	A10	5b **green** *(10,000)*	90.00	*210.00*
UX16	A10	10b **red** *(10,000)*	100.00	*325.00*

1915-16 **Wmk. Wood-grain**

No.	Type	Description	Unused	Used
UX17	A11	5b **yellow green** *(8,200)*	80.00	*250.00*
UX18	A11	10b **red** ('16) *(2,000)*	100.00	—

PAID REPLY POSTAL CARDS

Designs similar to Nos. UX2 and UX3 with added inscriptions in Danish and French:

Message Card-Four lines at lower left.

Reply Card-Fifth line centered, "Svar. Réponse."

Italicized numbers in parentheses indicate quantities issued.

1883

No.	Type	Description	Unused	Used
UY1	A2	2c +2c **light blue,** unsevered *(2,600)*	25.00	*250.00*
m.		Message card, detached	12.50	*35.00*
r.		Reply card, detached	12.50	*35.00*
UY2	A2	3c +3c **carmine rose,** unsevered	21.00	*150.00*
m.		Message card, detached	12.50	*20.00*
r.		Reply card, detached	12.50	*25.00*

Designs similar to Nos. UX4 and UX5 with added inscription in fifth line, centered in French:

Message Card-"Carte postale avecréponse payée."

Reply Card-"Carte postale-réponse."

1888

No.	Type	Description	Unused	Used
UY3	A2	2c +2c **light blue,** unsevered *(26,000)*	25.00	*125.00*
m.		Message card, detached	10.00	*20.00*
r.		Reply card, detached	10.00	*100.00*
UY4	A2	3c +3c **carmine rose,** unsevered *(5,000)*	22.50	*175.00*
m.		Message card, detached	11.00	*35.00*
r.		Reply card, detached	11.00	*125.00*

No. UY4 Locally Surcharged with type "c" but with date "1901"

1902

No.	Type	Description	Unused	Used
UY5	A2	1c on 3c+1c on 3c **carmine rose,** unsevered *(1,000)*	35.00	*300.00*
m.		Message card, detached	12.50	*50.00*
r.		Reply card, detached	14.00	*75.00*

No. UY4 Surcharged in Copenhagen with type similar to "c" but heavy letters, "1902" date

No.	Type	Description	Unused	Used
UY6	A2	1c on 3c+1c on 3c **carmine rose,** unsevered *(975)*	50.00	*350.00*
m.		Message card, detached	20.00	*60.00*
r.		Reply card, detached	20.00	*75.00*

Designs similar to Nos. UX9 and UX10 with added inscriptions in Danish and English

1903

No.	Type	Description	Unused	Used
UY7	A5	1c +1c **light green,** unsevered *(5,000)*	35.00	*75.00*
m.		Message card, detached	11.00	*20.00*
r.		Reply card, detached	11.00	*25.00*
UY8	A5	2c +2c **carmine,** unsevered *(5,000)*	40.00	*400.00*
m.		Message card, detached	15.00	*50.00*
r.		Reply card, detached	15.00	*75.00*

Designs similar to Nos. UX11 and UX12 with added inscriptions

1905

No.	Type	Description	Unused	Used
UY9	A8	5b +5b **green,** unsevered *(5,000)*	21.00	*75.00*
m.		Message card, detached	10.00	*20.00*
r.		Reply card, detached	10.00	*30.00*
UY10	A8	10b +10b **red,** unsevered *(4,000)*	30.00	*90.00*
m.		Message card	12.50	*25.00*
r.		Reply card, detached	15.00	*35.00*

Designs similar to Nos. UX13, UX14 and UX15 with added inscriptions

1908 **Unwmk.**

No.	Type	Description	Unused	Used
UY11	A10	5b +5b **green,** unsevered *(7,150)*	25.00	*100.00*
m.		Message card, detached	11.00	*30.00*
r.		Reply card, detached	11.00	*35.00*
UY12	A10	10b +10b **red,** unsevered *(6,750)*	25.00	*100.00*
m.		Message card, detached	12.50	*30.00*
r.		Reply card, detached	11.00	*40.00*

1913 **Wmk. Wood-grain**

No.	Type	Description	Unused	Used
UY13	A10	5b +5b **green,** unsevered *(5,000)*	—	
m.		Message card, detached		—
r.		Reply card, detached		—

The 10b + 10b red type A10 with wood-grain watermark was authorized and possibly printed, but no example is known.

REVENUE STAMPS

DANISH WEST INDIES DOCUMENTARY TAX

R1

1907 **Litho.** **Wmk. Crown** ***Perf. 12***

No.	Type	Description	Unused	Used
R1	R1	10b **red & light green**	2.00	*15.00*
		MAK overprint	5.00	
		U.S. usage		*50.00*
a.		Inverted watermark	25.00	*50.00*
R2	R1	50b **green**	15.00	*40.00*
		U.S. usage		*75.00*
a.		Inverted watermark	—	—
R3	R1	1fr **red & gray**	15.00	*40.00*
R4	R1	2fr **black & gray**	2.00	*25.00*
		MAK overprint	3.00	
a.		Inverted watermark	50.00	
R5	R1	3fr **red & blue**	30.00	*50.00*
		U.S. usage		—
R6	R1	5fr **blue**	15.00	*40.00*
		U.S. usage		*150.00*
R7	R1	7fr **red & yellow**	150.00	*200.00*
		U.S. usage		*250.00*
R8	R1	10fr **yellow**	20.00	*75.00*
		U.S. usage		*150.00*
a.		Inverted watermark	—	—
R9	R1	50fr **brown & pink**	300.00	300.00
		U.S. usage		300.00
R10	R1	100fr **black & pink**	400.00	400.00

Nos. R2, R4, R5 and R8 Surcharged

1917 ***Perf. & Printing Methods as Before***

No.	Type	Description	Unused	Used
R11	R1	10b on 50b (No. R2)	*500.00*	*600.00*
		U.S. usage		—
R12	R1	10b on 3fr (No. R5)	*500.00*	
R13	R1	10b on 10fr (No. R8)	*500.00*	
R14	R1	50b on 2fr (No. R4)	*500.00*	
R15	R1	50b on 3fr (No. R5)	*500.00*	
		U.S. usage		*600.00*

UNITED STATES VIRGIN ISLANDS DOCUMENTARY TAX

R2

1919 **Litho.** **Unwmk.** ***Perf. 11***

No.	Type	Description	Unused	Used
R16	R2	10b **red & light green**	50.00	60.00
R17	R2	50b **green**	60.00	40.00
a.		**dark green**	—	40.00
R18	R2	1fr **red & gray**	—	125.00
R19	R2	2fr **black**	—	125.00
a.		**gray black**	—	125.00
R20	R2	3fr **red & blue**	—	150.00
R21	R2	5fr **blue**	—	125.00
R22	R2	7fr **red & yellow**	60.00	*100.00*
R23	R2	10fr **orange**	—	100.00
a.		**dark orange**	—	125.00
R24	R2	50fr **brown & pink**	—	400.00
R25	R2	100fr **black & pink**	—	500.00
a.		**black & red**	—	500.00

1919 ***Perf. 10***

No.	Type	Description	Unused	Used
R27	R2	50b **green**	—	50.00
a.		**dark green**	—	50.00
R28	R2	5fr **blue**	275.00	125.00
R29	R2	10fr **orange**	—	125.00

A 10b red & green, perf. 10, also was produced, but currently no examples have been recorded without surcharges.

No. R16 Surcharged in Black

1921 ***Perf. 11***

No.	Type	Description	Unused	Used
R30	R2	50b on 10b **red & lt grn**	—	*1,500.*

No. R28 With Printed Surcharge in Black

R31	R2	10c on 5fr **blue**	500.00	—

R3

1935 ***Perf. 11***

R32	R3	2c **red & green**	7.50	5.00
a.		2c **red & lt yel green** (thin paper)	12.50	7.50
b.		2c **red & yel green**	12.50	6.00
R33	R3	2c **red & apple green**	25.00	15.00
R34	R3	10c **green**	10.00	10.00
R35	R3	20c **red & gray**	25.00	22.50
R36	R3	20c **red & green**	15.00	10.00
a.		20c **red & yellow green**	15.00	10.00
R37	R3	40c **gray**	15.00	10.00
R38	R3	60c **red & milky blue**	20.00	15.00
a.		60c **red & lt blue**	27.50	15.00
R39	R3	60c **red & dp blue**	15.00	15.00
R40	R3	$1 **blue**	35.00	15.00
R41	R3	$1.40 **red & yellow**	40.00	—
R42	R3	$2 **yellow**	32.50	15.00
R43	R3	$10 **reddish brn & pink**	60.00	*100.00*
R44	R3	$20 **black & pink**	95.00	75.00
R45	R3	$100 **red & green**	—	75.00

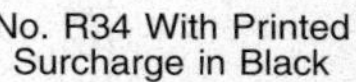

No. R34 With Printed Surcharge in Black

1935 ***Perf. 11***

R47	R3	2c on 10c **green**		*600.00*

1965 **Unwmk.** ***Perf. 12½***

R48	R3	2c **red & yellow green**	4.00	
a.		2c **red & green**	5.00	
R49	R3	10c **green**	15.00	
a.		10c **milky green**	17.50	
R50	R3	20c **red & yellow green**	10.00	
a.		20c **red & green**	10.00	
R51	R3	40c **gray**	10.00	*20.00*
R52	R3	60c **red & light blue**	12.50	
R53	R3	$1 **blue**	15.00	
a.		$1 **milky blue**	15.00	
R54	R3	$2 **yellow**	25.00	*25.00*
R55	R3	$10 **reddish brn & pink**	75.00	
R56	R3	$20 **black & pink**	60.00	
R57	R3	$100 **red & green**	150.00	150.00
R58	R3	$1,000 **green & yellow**		*1,000.*

PLAYING CARDS

Shipments of 10,000 each of Nos. RF1-RF3 were sent to the Virgin Islands on June 17, 1920, Jan. 16, 1926, and Mar. 5, 1934, respectively.

U.S. Playing Card Stamp No. RF3 Surcharged in Carmine

1920 **Engr.** **Wmk. 191R** ***Rouletted 7***

RF1	4c on 2c **blue**	225.00	

U.S. Playing Card Stamp No. RF17 Surcharged in Carmine

1926 ***Rouletted 7***

RF2	4c on (8c) **blue**	75.00	

Same Surcharge on U.S. Type RF4

1934 ***Perf. 11***

RF3	4c on (8c) **light blue**	225.00	125.00

The above stamp with perforation 11 was not issued in the United States without the overprint.

TOBACCO TAX

10b Perf. 10 Revenue Handstamp Surcharged in Black

1933 ***Perf. 10***

RJ1	R2	1b on 10b	100.00	75.00
RJ2	R2	2b on 10b	100.00	100.00
RJ3	R2	3b on 10b	—	75.00
RJ4	R2	5b on 10b	100.00	50.00
RJ5	R2	6b on 10b	110.00	90.00
RJ6	R2	7b on 10b	80.00	*110.00*
RJ7	R2	8b on 10b	—	120.00
RJ8	R2	12b on 10b	100.00	—
RJ9	R2	33b on 10b	150.00	—
RJ10	R2	40b on 10b	175.00	—
RJ11	R2	50b on 10b	140.00	—
RJ12	R2	60b on 10b	200.00	—

See footnote following No. R29 concerning the 10b stamp.

10b Perf. 10 Revenue and Nos. R28-R29 with Typed Surcharges in Black

1933 ***Perf. 10***

RJ13	R2	6b on 10b	125.00	75.00
RJ14	R2	6b on 5fr (No. R28)	85.00	75.00
RJ15	R2	6b on 10fr (No. R29)	125.00	125.00
RJ16	R2	7b on 10fr (No. R29)	175.00	—

No. R16 Handstamp Surcharged in Black

1933 ***Perf. 11***

RJ17	R2	2b on 10b **red & lt grn**	—	125.00

Numeral-only Typed Surcharge on No. R16

1933 ***Perf. 11***

RJ18	R2	6 on 10b **red & lt grn**	85.00	—
RJ19	R2	15 on 10b **red & lt grn**	85.00	—
RJ20	R2	40 on 10b **red & lt grn**	125.00	90.00
RJ21	R2	105 on 10b **red & lt grn**	150.00	—

Typed Surcharge in Black on Nos. R16, R21

1933 ***Perf. 11***

RJ22	R2	6b on 10b **red & lt grn**	125.00	—
RJ23	R2	6b on 5fr **blue**	—	—

Numeral-only Handstamp Surcharge in Black on No. R16

1933 ***Perf. 11***

RJ24	R2	5 on 10b **red & lt grn**	75.00	60.00
RJ25	R2	6 on 10b **red & lt grn**	100.00	100.00
RJ26	R2	7 on 10b **red & lt grn**	50.00	50.00
RJ27	R2	8 on 10b **red & lt grn**	100.00	100.00
RJ28	R2	50 on 10b **red & lt grn**	100.00	75.00

No. RF2 Handstamp Surcharged in Black

1933 ***Rouletted 7***

RJ29	1b on 4c on (8c) **blue**		300.00
RJ30	2b on 4c on (8c) **blue**		300.00
RJ31	3b on 4c on (8c) **blue**		350.00
RJ32	5b on 4c on (8c) **blue**		300.00
RJ33	6b on 4c on (8c) **blue**	275.00	—
RJ34	7b on 4c on (8c) **blue**		350.00
RJ35	8b on 4c on (8c) **blue**		375.00
RJ36	12b on 4c on (8c) **blue**	225.00	—
RJ37	33b on 4c on (8c) **blue**	300.00	200.00
RJ38	40b on 4c on (8c) **blue**	—	—

No. RF2 with Typed Surcharge in Black

RJ39	6b on 4c on (8c) **blue**	250.00	—

ST. CROIX PROVISIONAL TOBACCO TAX

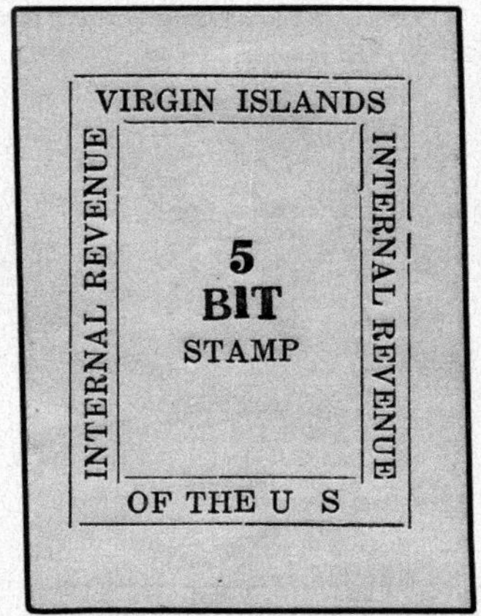

R4

1933-34 **Letterpress** **Without Gum** ***Imperf.***

1RJ1	R4	3b **black**	250.00	—
1RJ2	R4	5b **black**	100.00	—
1RJ3	R4	6b **black**	40.00	—
1RJ4	R4	7b **black**	125.00	125.00

A papermaker's watermark appears on some examples of Nos. 1RJ1-1RJ4.

Handstamp Surcharge in Black on Stamps with No Imprinted Denomination

1RJ5	R4	3b on blank, **black**	250.00	—
1RJ6	R4	7b on blank, **black**	50.00	—
1RJ7	R4	8b on blank, **black**	140.00	—
1RJ8	R4	15b on blank, **black**	160.00	—
1RJ9	R4	40b on blank, **black**		—

Numeral-only Handstamp Surcharge in Black on Nos. 1RJ1-1RJ4

1RJ10 R4 3 on 6b **black** (#1RJ3) —
1RJ11 R4 6 on 3b **black** (#1RJ1) 75.00 —
a. Violet surcharge 200.00 —
1RJ12 R4 6 on 5b **black** (#1RJ2) 250.00 —
1RJ13 R4 6 on 7b **black** (#1RJ4) 100.00 *125.00*
1RJ14 R4 7 on 6b **black** (#1RJ3) 150.00 —
1RJ15 R4 15 on 6b **black** (#1RJ3) 150.00 —

Numeral-only Typed Surcharge in Black on No. 1RJ4

1RJ16 R4 10 on 7b **black** 300.00 —

On No. 1RJ16, typed "XXXX" obliterates the "7" denomination.

CUSTOMS HOUSE INSPECTION FEE

Danish West Indies Postage Due Stamps of 1905-13 Canceled with the "Toldkammer" Canceling Device in Violet or Black

"Toldkammer" Cancel

Litho. ***Perf. 13***

RL1 D2 5b (on #J5) **red & gray** —
RL2 D2 20b (on #J6) **red & gray** *300.00*
RL3 D2 30b (on #J7) **red & gray** *300.00*
RL4 D2 50b (on #J8) **red & gray** *100.00*

GUAM

A former Spanish island possession in the Pacific Ocean, one of the Mariana group, about 1,450 miles east of the Philippines. Captured June 20, 1898, and ceded to the United States by treaty after the Spanish-American War. Stamps overprinted "Guam" were used while the post office was under the jurisdiction of the Navy Department from July 7, 1899, until March 29, 1901, when a Postal Agent was appointed by the Post Office Department and the postal service passed under that Department's control. From this date on Guam was supplied with regular United States postage stamps, although the overprints remained in use for several more years.

Italicized numbers in parentheses indicate quantities issued.

Population 9,000 (est. 1899).

100 CENTS = 1 DOLLAR

United States Nos. 279, 279B, 279Bc, 268, 280a, 281, 282, 272, 282C, 283, 284, 275, 275a, 276 and 276A Overprinted

1899 **Wmk. 191** ***Perf. 12***

Black Overprint

1 A87 1c **deep green** *(25,000)* 20.00 *25.00*
Never hinged 40.00
On cover *200.00*
Block of 4 90.00 *140.00*
P# strip of 3, Impt. 90.00
P# block of 6, Impt. 350.00

A bogus inverted overprint exists.

2 A88 2c **red,** type IV, *Dec. (105,000)* 17.50 *25.00*
light red, type IV 17.50 *25.00*
On cover *200.00*
Never hinged 35.00
Block of 4 85.00 *140.00*
P# strip of 3, Impt. 75.00
P# block of 6, Impt. 300.00 —
a. 2c **rose carmine,** type IV, *Aug. 15* 30.00 30.00
Never hinged 60.00
On cover *225.00*
Block of 4 125.00 *175.00*
P# strip of 3, Impt. 100.00
P# block of 6, Impt. 375.00

3 A89 3c **purple** *(5000)* 140.00 *175.00*
Never hinged 275.00
On cover *400.00*
Block of 4 600.00 *850.00*
P# strip of 3, Impt. 575.00
P# block of 6, Impt. 1,600.

4 A90 4c **lilac brown** *(5000)* 125.00 *175.00*
Never hinged 250.00
On cover *450.00*
Block of 4 550.00 *825.00*
P# strip of 3, Impt. 525.00
P# block of 6, Impt. *1,750.*
Extra frame line at top (Plate 793 R62) —

5 A91 5c **blue** *(20,000)* 32.50 *45.00*
Never hinged 65.00
On cover *200.00*
Block of 4 140.00 *250.00*
P# strip of 3, Impt. 140.00
P# block of 6, Impt. 700.00

6 A92 6c **lake** *(5000)* 125.00 *190.00*
Never hinged 250.00
On cover *450.00*
Block of 4 550.00 *1,000.*
P# strip of 3, Impt. 500.00
P# block of 6, Impt. 1,500.

7 A93 8c **violet brown** *(5000)* 125.00 *160.00*
Never hinged 275.00
On cover *450.00*
Block of 4 575.00 *1,000.*
P# strip of 3, Impt. 575.00
P# block of 6, Impt. 1,250.

8 A94 10c **brown,** type I *(10,000)* 45.00 *55.00*
Never hinged 90.00
On cover *275.00*
Block of 4 200.00 *300.00*
P# strip of 3, Impt. 220.00
P# block of 6, Impt. 1,000.

9 A94 10c **brown,** type II *2,750.* —
Never hinged *5,500.*
Pair —

10 A95 15c **olive green** *(5000)* 150.00 140.00
Never hinged 300.00
On cover *900.00*
Block of 4 650.00 *875.00*
P# strip of 3, Impt. 600.00
P# block of 6, Impt. 2,200.

11 A96 50c **orange** *(4000)* 350.00 *400.00*
Never hinged 700.00
On cover *1,500.*
Block of 4 1,600. *2,000.*
P# strip of 3, Impt. 1,600.
P# block of 6, Impt. 4,500.
a. 50c **red orange** 550.00 —
Never hinged 1,100.

Red Overprint

12 A97 $1 **black,** type I *(3000)* 350.00 *400.00*
Never hinged 700.00
On cover *3,500.*
Block of 4 1,750. *1,750.*
P# strip of 3, Impt. 1,750.
P# block of 6, Impt. *37,500.*

13 A97 $1 **black,** type II *3,750.*
Never hinged —
Block of 4 22,500.
Nos. 1-8,10-12 (11) 1,480. *1,790.*

Counterfeits of the overprint exist.

No. 13 exists only in the special printing.

Special Printing

In March 1900, one pane of 100 stamps of each of Nos. 1-8, 10-12 and two panes of 50 stamps of No. E1 were specially overprinted for displays at the Paris Exposition (1900) and Pan American Exposition (1901). The 2c pane was light red, type IV.

Stamps were handstamped type E "Specimen" in black ink by H. G. Mandel and mounted by him in separate displays for the two Expositions. Additional stamps from each pane were also handstamped "Specimen" but most were destroyed after the Expositions. However, becasue additional stamps that are not Special Printings exist with a black "Specimen" handstamp, expertization by competent authorities is recommended.

J. M. Bartels, a stamp dealer, signed some stamps from these panes "Special Surcharge" in pencil on the gum to authenticate them as coming from the "Mandel" Special Printing panes. In 1904 or later, he handstamped additional surviving examples "Special Surcharge" in red ink on the back as his guarantee. Some of these guaranteed stamps had Mandel's "Specimen" handstamp on the face while others did not. Value (with or without "Specimen" handstamp): Nos. 1-8, 10, each $1,000; Nos. 11, E1, each $1,250; No. 12, $2,000.

SPECIAL DELIVERY STAMP

Special Delivery Stamp of the United States, No. E5 Overprinted diagonally in Red

1899 **Wmk. 191** ***Perf. 12***

E1 SD3 10c **blue** *(5000)* 150. *200.00*
Never hinged 275.
On cover *1,500.*
Block of 4 650.
Margin block of 4, arrow 750.
P# strip of 3, Impt. 900.
P# block of 6, Impt. *4,000.*
a. Dots in curved frame above messenger (Plate 882) 200.
Never hinged 400.
P# block of 6, Impt. (Plate 882) *4,250.*

Counterfeits of the overprint exist.

The special stamps for Guam were replaced by the regular issues of the United States.

GUAM GUARD MAIL

LOCAL POSTAL SERVICE

Inaugurated April 8, 1930, by Commander Willis W. Bradley, Jr., U.S.N., Governor of Guam, for the conveyance of mail between Agaña and the other smaller towns.

Philippines Nos. 290 and 291 Overprinted

1930, Apr. 8 **Unwmk.** ***Perf. 11***

M1 A40 2c **green** *(2,000)* 400. 275.
Never hinged 575.
First day cover 600.
Block of 4 1,700.
P# block of 6 —

M2 A40 4c **carmine** *(3,000)* 225. 150.
Never hinged 325.
First day cover 400.
Block of 4 950.
P# block of 6 —

Counterfeits of overprint exist.

Seal of Guam — A1

Design size: 19x30mm

1930, July 10 **Unwmk.** ***Perf. 12***

Without Gum

M3	A1 1c **red & black** *(1,000)*	120.00	150.00
	On cover		225.00
	Block of 4	525.00	
M4	A1 2c **black & red** *(4,000)*	75.00	95.00
	On cover		250.00
	Block of 4	325.00	
a.	Block of 4 with extra impression of vignette covering the intersection of the block	*10,000.*	

Examples are often found showing parts of watermark "CLEVELAND BOND."

Philippines Nos. 290 and 291 Overprinted in Black

1930, Aug. 21 **Unwmk.** ***Perf. 11***

M5	A40 2c **green** *(20,000)*	2.75	4.50
	Never hinged	4.00	
	On cover		75.00
	Block of 4	12.00	
	P# block of 6	*125.00*	
a.	2c **yellow green**	2.50	4.50
M6	A40 4c **carmine** *(80,000)*	.50	1.75
	Never hinged	1.00	
	On cover		75.00
	Block of 4	2.25	
	P# block of 6	*90.00*	

Same Overprint in Red on Philippines Nos. 290, 291, 292, 293a, and 294

1930, Dec. 29

M7	A40 2c **green** *(50,000)*	.80	2.00
	Never hinged	1.20	
	On cover		50.00
	Block of 4	3.50	
	P# block of 6	*125.00*	
a.	GRAUD (Pos. 63) *(500)*	425.00	
b.	MIAL (Pos. 84) *(500)*	425.00	
M8	A40 4c **carmine** *(50,000)*	.85	1.50
	Never hinged	1.30	
	On cover		50.00
	Block of 4	3.50	
	P# block of 6	*90.00*	
M9	A40 6c **deep violet** *(25,000)*	2.50	4.50
	Never hinged	3.75	
	On cover		60.00
	Block of 4	11.00	
	P# block of 10, Impt.	*250.00*	
M10	A40 8c **orange brown** *(25,000)*	2.50	4.50
	Never hinged	3.75	
	On cover		60.00
	Block of 4	11.00	
	P# block of 10, Impt.	*300.00*	
M11	A40 10c **deep blue** *(25,000)*	2.75	4.50
	Never hinged	4.00	
	On cover		60.00
	Block of 4	11.00	
	P# block of 10, Impt.	*350.00*	

The local postal service was discontinued April 8th, 1931, and replaced by the service of the United States Post Office Department.

ESSAYS

M3-E1

Impression of denomination and inscription only; single impresson in pane of 25.

M3-E1	1c red, on stamp paper with "Cleveland Bond" watermark, perforated vertically	*4,000.*

M3-E2

Design size: 15x25mm
Impression of vignette only.

M3-E2	On smooth, thick, off-white paper	
	black	—
	black on thin book paper	—
	green	—
	reddish brown	—
	blue on cream-colored card	—

SPECIMEN STAMPS

Handstamped U.S. Type E in Purple or Black

1899

1S	E	1c **deep green**	175.00
2aS	E	2c **rose carmine,** type IV	175.00
3S	E	3c **purple**	175.00
4S	E	4c **lilac brown**	175.00
5S	E	5c **blue**	175.00
6S	E	6c **lake**	175.00
7S	E	8c **violet brown**	175.00
8S	E	10c **brown,** type I	175.00
10S	E	15c **olive green**	175.00
11S	E	50c **orange**	350.00
12S	E	$1 **black,** type I	350.00
13S	E	$1 **black,** type II	—

Special Delivery

1899

E1S	E	10c **blue**	500.00
E1aS	E	10c **blue**	—

Values for specimen stamps are for fine-very fine appearing examples with minor faults.

See Special Printing notice after No. 13 for Special Printings with black "Specimen" handstamps, but note that not all stamps with the black "Specimen" handstamp are Special Printings.

HAWAII

Until 1893, Hawaii was an independent kingdom. From 1893-1898 it was a republic. The United States annexed Hawaii in 1898, and it became a Territory on June 14, 1900. Hawaiian stamps remained in use through June 13, 1900, and were replaced by U.S. stamps on June 14. In 1959 Hawaii became the 50th State of the Union. Hawaii consists of about 20 islands in the mid-Pacific, about 2,300 miles southwest of San Francisco. The area is 6,434 square miles and the population was estimated at 150,000 in 1899. Honolulu is the capital.

100 CENTS = 1 DOLLAR

Values of Hawaii stamps vary considerably according to condition. For Nos. 1-4, values are for examples with minor damage that has been skillfully repaired.

A1

A2

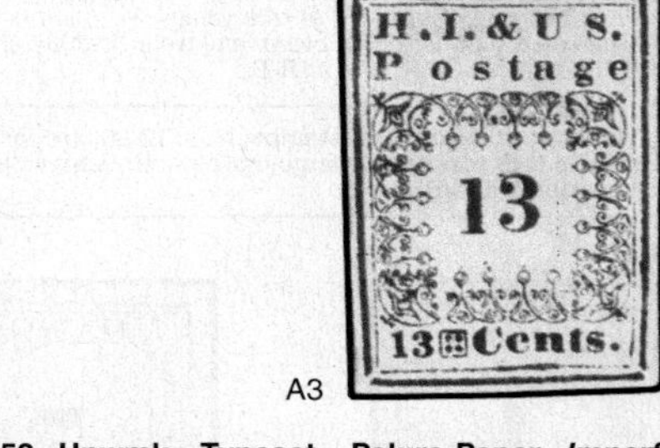

A3

1851-52 **Unwmk.** **Typeset** **Pelure Paper** ***Imperf.***

1	A1 2c **blue**	*625,000.*	*250,000.*
	On cover		*2,250,000.*
2	A1 5c **blue**	*55,000.*	*35,000.*
	On cover		*90,000.*
3	A2 13c **blue**	*37,000.*	*29,000.*
	On cover		*75,000.*
4	A3 13c **blue**	*52,500.*	*35,000.*
	On cover		*80,000.*

Nos. 1-4 are known as the "Missionaries."

Two varieties of each. Nos. 1-4, off cover, are almost invariably damaged.

No. 1 unused and on cover are each unique; the on-cover value is based on a 2013 auction sale.

Values for Nos. 5-82 are for very fine examples. Extremely fine to superb stamps sell at much higher prices, and inferior or poor stamps sell at reduced prices, depending on the condition of the individual example.

King Kamehameha III

A4

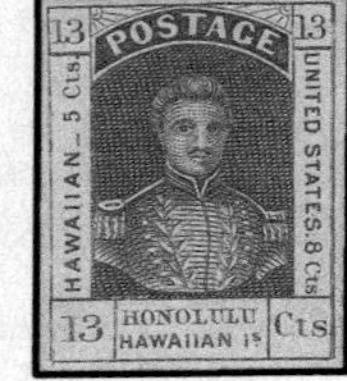

A5

Printed in Sheets of 20 (4x5)

1853 Thick White Wove Paper Engr.

5 A4 5c **blue** 1,900. 1,900.
On cover *5,000.*
On cover with U.S. #17 *12,000.*
Pair *4,000.* *4,750.*
a. Line through "Honolulu" (Pos. 2) *3,000.* *3,000.*
6 A5 13c **dark red** 875. *1,700.*
On cover *22,500.*
On cover with #5 *12,500.*
On cover with U.S. #11 (pair) *22,500.*
On cover with U.S. #17 *32,500.*
On cover with #5 and U.S. #17 *32,500.*
On cover with #8 and U.S. #36b *37,500.*
Pair *2,000.* *4,750.*
Block of 4 *4,000.*
Double transfer —

Black Manuscript Surcharge on Scott 6

1857

7 A6 5c on 13c **dark red** *7,000.* *10,000.*
On cover with pair U.S. #7 and 14 *57,500.*
On cover with pair U.S. #11, 14 *55,000.*
On cover with U.S. #14 *50,000.*
On cover with U.S. #14, 20 *57,500.*
On cover with U.S. #17 *45,000.*

Beware of fake manuscript surcharges. Expertization is strongly recommended.

1857 Thin White Wove Paper

8 A4 5c **blue** 700. *750.*
On cover *2,800.*
On cover with U.S. #11 —
On cover with U.S. #7, 15 *6,000.*
On cover with U.S. #17 *9,000.*
On cover with U.S. #26 —
On cover with U.S. #35 *11,000.*
On cover with U.S. #36 *10,000.*
On cover with U.S. #69 *12,500.*
On cover with U.S. #76 —
Pair 1,650. *2,000.*
Pair on cover *15,000.*
a. Line through "Honolulu" (Pos. 2) *1,350.* *1,350.*
On cover with U.S. #17 *6,500.*
b. Double impression *4,250.* *4,750.*

Hawaiian Islands
Stamp and Coin
In Business since 1973
BUYING & SELLING
Hawaiian Stamps, Covers,
Postal History, Royalty Items,
Autographs, Documents
Whether Common or Rare,
CONTACT US FIRST
For All Your Needs Write or call...
DON MEDCALF, President

WE BUY HAWAIIAN
COINS & MEDALS TOO!

1111 Bishop Street • Honolulu, HI 96813
(808) 531-6251 • info@hawaiianmoney.com

1861 Thin Bluish Wove Paper

9 A4 5c **blue** 400. 400.
On cover *4,500.*
On cover with U.S. #36b *3,250.*
On cover with U.S. #65 *3,000.*
On cover with U.S. #65, 73 *7,750.*
On cover with U.S. #68 *4,250.*
On cover with U.S. #76 *7,000.*
Block of 4 2,000.
a. Line through "Honolulu" (Pos. 2) *950.* *1,000.*
On cover with U.S. #69 *10,000.*

RE-ISSUE

1868 Ordinary White Wove Paper

10 A4 5c **blue** 27.50
Block of 4 130.
a. Line through "Honolulu" (Pos. 2) 80.
In pair with #10 350.
11 A5 13c **dull rose** 325.
Block of 4 1,400.

Remainders of Nos. 10 and 11 were overprinted "SPECIMEN." See Nos. 10S-11Sb.

Nos. 10 and 11 were never placed in use but stamps (both with and without overprint) were sold at face value at the Honolulu post office.

REPRINTS (Official Imitations) 1889

Original

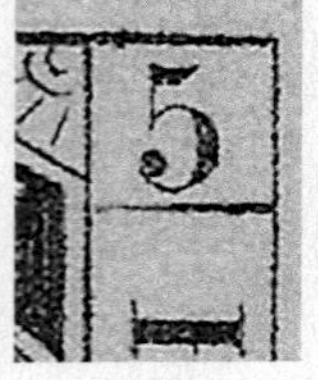

Reprint

Original

Reprint

5c — *Originals have two small dots near the left side of the square in the upper right corner. These dots are missing in the reprints.*

13c — *The bottom of the 3 of 13 in the upper left corner is flattened in the originals and rounded in the reprints. The "t" of "Cts" on the left side is as tall as the "C" in the reprints, but shorter in the originals.*

10R A4 5c **blue** 65.
Block of 4 280.
11R A5 13c **orange red** 300.
Block of 4 1,450.

On August 19, 1892, the remaining supply of reprints was overprinted in black "REPRINT." The reprints (both with and without overprint) were sold at face value.

Quantities sold (including overprints) were 5c-3634 and 13c-1696. See Nos. 10R-S and 11R-S.

Values for the Numeral stamps, Nos. 12-26, are for examples with four reasonably large margins. Unused values are for stamps without gum.

A7

A8

A9

1859-62 Typeset from settings of 10 varieties

12 A7 1c **light blue,** *bluish white* *15,000.* *15,000.*
Pair *37,500.*
a. "1 Ce" omitted *22,500.*
b. "nt" omitted — —

No. 12a is unique.

13 A7 2c **light blue,** *bluish white* *6,250.* *5,000.*
On cover *12,500.*
Block of 4 *27,500.*
a. 2c **dark blue,** *grayish white* *6,750.* *5,000.*
On cover *12,500.*
On cover, both #13 and #13a *40,000.*
b. Comma after "Cents" — *6,750.*
On cover *12,500.*
c. No period after "LETA" — —
14 A7 2c **black,** *greenish blue* ('62) *8,000.* *6,000.*
On cover *10,000.*
a. "2-Cents." —

1859-63

15 A7 1c **black,** *grayish* ('63) 650. *2,750.*
On cover —
Block of 4 3,250.
a. Tête bêche pair *9,000.*
b. "NTER" —
c. Period omitted after "Postage" 850.
d. 1c **black,** *bluish gray* *850.*
Block of 4 —
16 A7 2c **black,** *grayish* 1,000. 850.
On cover *5,000.*
Pair — —
a. "2" at top of rectangle *3,750.* *3,750.*
On cover *13,500.*
b. Printed on both sides — *21,000.*
c. "NTER" *3,250.* *6,500.*
d. 2c **black,** *grayish white* 1,000. 850.
e. Period omitted after "Cents" —
f. Overlapping impressions — —
g. "TAGE" —
17 A7 2c **dark blue,** *bluish* ('63) *12,000.* *8,750.*
Pair *25,000.*
a. "ISL" — —
18 A7 2c **black,** *blue gray* ('63) *3,250.* *6,000.*
On cover *18,000.*
Pair *13,500.*
Thick paper — —

1864-65

19 A7 1c **black** 625. *10,000.*
Pair 1,300.
Block of 4 3,000.
20 A7 2c **black** 775. *1,500.*
On cover *17,500.*
Pair 1,600.
Block of 4 *4,000.*
21 A8 5c **blue,** *blue* ('65) 900. 700.
On cover (pair) *13,000.*
On cover with U.S. #65 —
On cover with U.S. #68 —
On cover with U.S. #76 *8,250.*
Block of 4 *4,500.* —
a. Tête bêche pair *10,500.*
b. 5c **bluish black,** *grayish white* *11,000.* *3,750.*

No. 21b unused is unique. No. 21b used is also unique but defective.

22 A9 5c **blue,** *blue* ('65) 575. *900.*
On cover *13,000.*
On cover with U.S. #76 *9,250.*
On cover with U.S. #63 and 76 —
Block of 4 2,600.
a. Tête bêche pair *18,000.*
b. 5c **blue,** *grayish white* —
c. Overlapping impressions —

1864 Laid Paper

23 A7 1c **black** 300. *2,500.*
On cover with U.S. #76 *12,000.*
Block of 4 1,250.
a. "HA" instead of "HAWAIIAN" *3,500.*
b. Tête bêche pair *6,000.*
c. Tête bêche pair, Nos. 23, 23a *18,000.*
24 A7 2c **black** 350. *1,050.*
Block of 4 1,500.
a. "NTER" *3,250.*
b. "S" of "POSTAGE" omitted *1,500.*
c. Tête bêche pair *7,000.*

A10

1865 **Wove Paper**

25 A10 1c **dark blue**	350.	
Block of 4	1,450.	
a. Double impression	—	
b. With inverted impression of No. 21 on face	*18,500.*	
26 A10 2c **dark blue**	350.	
Block of 4	1,500.	

Nos. 12 to 26 were typeset and were printed in sheets of 50 (5 settings of 10 varieties each). The sheets were cut into panes of 25 (5x5) before distribution to the post offices.

King Kamehameha IV — A11

1861-63 **Litho.** **Horizontally Laid Paper**

27 A11 2c **pale rose**	350.	350.
On cover		*900.*
Pair		—
a. 2c **carmine rose** ('63)	3,000.	2,850.

Vertically Laid Paper

28 A11 2c **pale rose**	325.	325.
On cover		*1,500.*
Block of 4	1,750.	1,650.
a. 2c **carmine rose** ('63)	400.	*450.*
On cover		*2,500.*
Block of 4	1,900.	

RE-ISSUE

1869 **Engr.** **Thin Wove Paper**

29 A11 2c **red**	45.00	—
Block of 4	240.00	

No. 29 was not issued for postal purposes although canceled examples are known. It was sold only at the Honolulu post office, at first without overprint and later with overprint "CANCELLED." See No. 29S.

See note following No. 51.

HAWAII

STAMPS, COVERS, PROOFS, ESSAYS

BUYING & SELLING

Hawaii #78 Specimen Gutter Block of Four
Mint, Never Hinged
12 Cents Blue, 1894, World Class Rarity
Professional Stamp Experts Certificate #01295738

PACIFIC MIDWEST CO.

P.O. Box 730818
SAN JOSE, CA 95173
408-532-7100

EMAIL: GARYUCB@AOL.COM

WE ARE A WORLD CLASS HAWAIIAN DEALER

APS Hawaiian Philatelic Society China Stamp Society

Princess Victoria Kamamalu — A12

King Kamehameha IV — A13

King Kamehameha V — A14

King Kamehameha V — A15

Mataio Kekuanaoa — A16

1864-86 Engr. Wove Paper *Perf. 12*

30	A12 1c **purple** ('86)	11.00	8.00
	Never hinged	25.00	
	On cover		150.00
	Block of 4	55.00	
a.	1c **mauve** ('71)	60.00	20.00
	Never hinged	95.00	
	On cover, pair		550.00
	On cover with #32		*7,000.*
	On cover with U.S. #156		600.00
	Block of 4	300.00	
b.	1c **violet** ('78)	20.00	10.00
	Never hinged	45.00	
	On cover, pair		500.00
	On cover with #35 and #36		*6,000.*
	Block of 4	160.00	200.00
31	A13 2c **rose vermilion**	65.00	12.50
	Never hinged	150.00	
	On cover		200.00
	On cover with #32		*5,000.*
	On cover with U.S. #63 and #65		*11,000.*
	On cover with U.S. #65		*5,000.*
	On cover with U.S. #73		*3,000.*
	On cover with U.S. #76		*1,000.*
	On cover, pair, with pair U.S. #93		*10,000.*
	On cover with #27 and U.S. #76		*15,000.*
	On cover with #32 and #33 and U.S. #148		*8,000.*
	Block of 4	275.00	*400.00*
a.	2c **vermilion** ('86)	55.00	17.50
	Never hinged	130.00	
	On cover		500.00
b.	Half used as 1c on cover with #32		*7,500.*
	As "b," with U.S. #117		*18,000.*
32	A14 5c **blue** ('66)	175.00	30.00
	Never hinged	375.00	
	On cover		250.00
	On cover with any U.S. issues of 1861-68		*5,000.*
	On cover with U.S. #116		*15,000.*
	On cover with U.S. #116 and 69		*25,000.*
	Block of 4	800.00	175.00
33	A15 6c **yellow green** ('71)	45.00	10.00
	Never hinged	100.00	
	On cover		300.00
a.	6c **bluish green** ('78)	35.00	10.00
	Never hinged	85.00	
	On cover		300.00
	On cover with U.S. #179		*1,500.*
	On cover with U.S. #183 + #184		*1,750.*
	On cover with U.S. #185		*1,250.*
	Block of 4	160.00	500.00
b.	As "a," horiz. pair, imperf.	*2,250.*	
34	A16 18c **dull rose** ('71)	100.00	45.00
	Never hinged	220.00	
	On cover		350.00
	On cover with No. 36		—
	On cover with No. 36 and U.S. No. 179		*2,000.*
	On cover with U.S. No. 161		—
	On cover with U.S. No. 163		—
	On cover with U.S. No. 185		*10,000.*
	Block of 4	475.00	—
	Nos. 30-34 (5)	396.00	105.50
	Set, never hinged	860.00	

Half of No. 31 was used with a 5c stamp to make up the 6-cent rate to the United States.

No. 32 has traces of rectangular frame lines surrounding the design. Nos. 39 and 52C have no such frame lines.

King David Kalakaua — A17

Prince William Pitt Leleiohoku — A18

1875

35	A17 2c **brown**	9.00	3.00
	Never hinged	22.00	
	On cover		200.00
	Block of 4	45.00	40.00
36	A18 12c **black**	75.00	32.50
	Never hinged	165.00	
	On cover		400.00
	On cover with U.S. No. 161		—
	On cover with U.S. No. 179b		—
	Block of 4	350.00	—

Princess Likelike — A19

King David Kalakaua — A20

Queen Kapiolani — A21

Statue of King Kamehameha I — A22

King William Lunalilo — A23

Queen Emma Kaleleonalani — A24

1882

37	A19 1c **blue**	11.00	6.00
	Never hinged	27.50	
	On cover		60.00
	Block of 4	55.00	50.00
38	A17 2c **lilac rose**	125.00	47.50
	Never hinged	275.00	
	On cover		150.00
	Block of 4	625.00	
39	A14 5c **ultramarine**	15.00	3.00
	Never hinged	35.00	
	On cover		27.50
	Block of 4	75.00	60.00
a.	Vert. pair, imperf. horiz.	*5,000.*	*6,000.*
40	A20 10c **black**	50.00	25.00
	Never hinged	115.00	
	On cover		160.00
	Block of 4	210.00	140.00
41	A21 15c **red brown**	70.00	27.50
	Never hinged	150.00	
	On cover		200.00
	Block of 4	325.00	200.00
	Nos. 37-41 (5)	271.00	109.00
	Set, never hinged	602.50	

1883-86

42	A19 1c **green**	3.00	2.00
	Never hinged	7.00	
	On cover		25.00
	Block of 4	15.00	14.00
43	A17 2c **rose** ('86)	5.00	1.00
	Never hinged	11.00	
	On cover		25.00
	Block of 4	22.50	12.50
a.	2c **dull red**	65.00	22.50
	Never hinged	140.00	
	Block of 4	310.00	
44	A20 10c **red brown** ('84)	40.00	12.00
	Never hinged	90.00	
	On cover		125.00
	Block of 4	190.00	100.00
45	A20 10c **vermilion**	45.00	14.00
	Never hinged	100.00	
	On cover		125.00
	Block of 4	210.00	85.00
46	A18 12c **red lilac**	90.00	40.00
	Never hinged	225.00	
	On cover		425.00
	Block of 4	435.00	250.00
47	A22 25c **dark violet**	160.00	65.00
	Never hinged	350.00	
	On cover		375.00
	Block of 4	725.00	350.00
48	A23 50c **red**	200.00	95.00
	Never hinged	425.00	
	On cover		525.00
	Block of 4	1,050.	
49	A24 $1 **rose red**	325.00	275.00
	Never hinged	675.00	
	On cover		*8,000.*
	Block of 4	1,500.	
	Maltese cross cancellation		150.00
	Nos. 42-49 (8)	868.00	504.00
	Set, never hinged	1,833.	

Other fiscal cancellations exist on No. 49.

Nos. 48-49 are valued used with postal cancels. Canceled-to-order cancels exist and are worth less.

REPRODUCTION and REPRINT

Yellowish Wove Paper

1886-89 Engr. *Imperf.*

50	A11 2c **orange vermilion**	170.00	
	Never hinged	275.00	
	Block of 4	825.00	
51	A11 2c **carmine** ('89)	35.00	
	Never hinged	50.00	
	Block of 4	160.00	

In 1885, the Postmaster General wished to have on sale complete sets of Hawaii's portrait stamps, but was unable to find either the stone from which Nos. 27 and 28 were printed, or the plate from which No. 29 was printed. He therefore sent an example of No. 29 to the American Bank Note Company, with an order to engrave a new plate like it and print 10,000 stamps therefrom, of which 5000 were overprinted "SPECIMEN" in blue.

The original No. 29 was printed in sheets of fifteen (5x3), but the plate of these "Official Imitations" was made up of fifty stamps (10x5). Later, in 1887, the original die for No. 29 was discovered, and, after retouching, a new plate was made and 37,500 stamps were printed (No. 51). These, like the originals, were printed in sheets of fifteen. They were delivered during 1889 and 1890. In 1892, all remaining unsold in the Post Office were overprinted "Reprint".

No. 29 is red in color, and printed on very thin white wove paper. No. 50 is orange vermilion in color, on medium, white to buff paper. In No. 50 the vertical line on the left side of the portrait touches the horizontal line over the label "Elua Keneta", while in the other two varieties, Nos. 29 and 51, it does not touch the horizontal line by half a millimeter. In No. 51 there are three parallel lines on the left side of the King's nose, while in No. 29 and No. 50 there are no such lines. No. 51 is carmine in color and printed on thick, yellowish to buff, wove paper.

It is claimed that both Nos. 50 and 51 were available for postage, although not made to fill a postal requirement. They exist with favor cancellation. No. 51 also is known postally used. See Nos. 50S-51S.

Queen Liliuokalani — A25

1890-91 *Perf. 12*

52	A25 2c **dull violet** ('91)	15.00	1.50
	Never hinged	25.00	
	On cover		25.00
	Block of 4	70.00	12.00
a.	Vert. pair, imperf. horiz.	*3,750.*	
52C	A14 5c **deep indigo**	125.00	150.00
	Never hinged	280.00	
	On cover		500.00
	Block of 4	600.00	*850.00*

Stamps of 1864-91 Overprinted

Three categories of double overprints:
I. Both overprints heavy.
II. One overprint heavy, one of moderate strength.
III. One overprint heavy, one of light or weak strength.

1893 **Overprinted in Red**

53 A12 1c **violet** 9.00 13.00
Never hinged 20.00
On cover 35.00
Block of 4 42.50 70.00
a. "189" instead of "1893" 600.00 —
b. No period after "GOVT" 275.00 275.00
f. Double overprint (III) 600.00
54 A19 1c **blue** 9.00 15.00
Never hinged 21.00
On cover 40.00
Block of 4 45.00 67.50
b. No period after "GOVT" 140.00 150.00
e. Double overprint (II) 1,500.
f. Double overprint (III) 400.00
55 A19 1c **green** 2.00 3.00
Never hinged 4.00
On cover 25.00
Block of 4 8.00 15.00
d. Double overprint (I) 650.00 650.00
f. Double overprint (III) 250.00 250.00
g. Pair, one without ovpt. 10,000.
56 A17 2c **brown** 12.50 20.00
Never hinged 27.50
On cover 60.00
Block of 4 60.00 120.00
b. No period after "GOVT" 325.00 —
57 A25 2c **dull violet** 2.00 1.50
Never hinged 3.00
On cover 25.00
Block of 4 9.00 6.50
a. "18 3" instead of "1893" 900.00 900.00
d. Double overprint (I) 1,300. 1,000.
f. Double overprint (III) 190.00 190.00
g. Inverted overprint 4,000. 4,750.
58 A14 5c **deep indigo** 15.00 30.00
Never hinged 32.00
On cover 100.00
Block of 4 72.50 140.00
b. No period after "GOVT" 275.00 275.00
f. Double overprint (III) 1,250. 675.00
59 A14 5c **ultramarine** 7.00 3.00
Never hinged 15.00
On cover 40.00
Block of 4 35.00 22.50
d. Double overprint (I) 6,500.
e. Double overprint (II) 3,750. 3,750.
f. Double overprint (III) 600.00
g. Inverted overprint 1,500. 1,500.
60 A15 6c **green** 17.50 25.00
Never hinged 40.00
On cover 140.00
Block of 4 85.00 125.00
d. Double overprint (I) 5,000.
e. Double overprint (II) 1,100.
f. Double overprint (III) 400.00
61 A20 10c **black** 14.00 20.00
Never hinged 30.00
On cover 125.00
Block of 4 65.00 82.50
e. Double overprint (II) 1,000. 900.00
f. Double overprint (III) 225.00
61B A20 10c **red brown** 15,000. 29,000.
Never hinged 25,000.
Block of 4 65,000.
62 A18 12c **black** 14.00 20.00
Never hinged 30.00
On cover 150.00
Block of 4 70.00 110.00
d. Double overprint (I) 1,500.
e. Double overprint (II) 1,100.
f. Double overprint (III) —
63 A18 12c **red lilac** 175.00 250.00
Never hinged 400.00
On cover 550.00
Block of 4 1,000. —
64 A22 25c **dark violet** 35.00 45.00
Never hinged 70.00
On cover 225.00
Block of 4 160.00 200.00
Vert. plate scratch at top 90.00
b. No period after "GOVT" 350.00 350.00
Never hinged 600.00
f. Double overprint (III) 1,250.
Nos. 53-61,62-64 (12) 312.00 445.50
Nos. 53-61, 62-64 never hinged 692.75

Virtually all known examples of No. 61B are cut in at the top.

Overprinted in Black

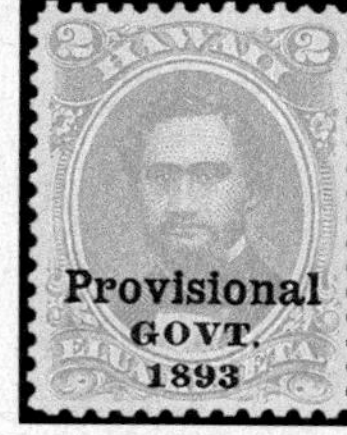

65 A13 2c **vermilion** 85.00 90.00
Never hinged 200.00
On cover 450.00
Block of 4 375.00 500.00
b. No period after "GOVT" 300.00 300.00
66 A17 2c **rose** 2.50 2.50
Never hinged 3.75
On cover 25.00
Block of 4 11.00 11.00
b. No period after "GOVT" 70.00 70.00
d. Double overprint (I) 4,000.
e. Double overprint (II) 2,750.
f. Double overprint (III) 300.00
66C A15 6c **green** 15,000. 29,000.
On cover —
Block of 4 65,000.
67 A20 10c **vermilion** 22.50 30.00
Never hinged 45.00
On cover 125.00
Block of 4 110.00 180.00
f. Double overprint (III) 1,250.
68 A20 10c **red brown** 12.00 13.00
Never hinged 24.00
On cover 100.00
Block of 4 57.50 75.00
f. Double overprint (III) 4,000.
69 A18 12c **red lilac** 350.00 500.00
Never hinged 575.00
On cover 950.00
Block of 4 1,600. 2,400.
70 A21 15c **red brown** 27.50 35.00
Never hinged 55.00
On cover 300.00
Block of 4 120.00 150.00
e. Double overprint (II) 2,000.
71 A16 18c **dull rose** 40.00 40.00
Never hinged 80.00
On cover 225.00
Block of 4 185.00 175.00
a. "18 3" instead of "1893" 525.00 525.00
b. No period after "GOVT" 350.00 350.00
d. Double overprint (I) 650.00
f. Double overprint (III) 275.00 —

WE BUY AND SELL

ALL HAWAII!

OUR EXTENSIVE WEBSITE OF HAWAII ONLY:

www.vogtstamps.com

Stamps. Covers, Postcards, Flight Covers, Documents, Coins, Currency, Paper Ephemera, Autographs, Photographs, Memorabilia, Kahului Railroad. **In short, nearly everything!**

FROM RARITIES TO COMMON GEMS TO NOT

(MANY NOT ON THE MARKET FOR HALF A CENTURY!)

Shows we will be attending with our full Hawaiian stock:

APS, August, Omaha, NE
SESCAL, October, Ontario, CA
Honolulu Stamp and Coin Show,TBA
ORCOEXPO, January 2020, Fullerton, CA
WESTPEX, April 2020

650-344-3401 Phone
650-401-5530 Fax
vogtstamps@aol.com

VOGTSTAMPS-HAWAII

g. Pair, one without ovpt. 3,500.
h. As "b," double overprint (II) 1,750.
72 A23 50c **red** 90.00 *120.00*
Never hinged 180.00
On cover 600.00
Block of 4 400.00 *500.00*
b. No period after "GOVT" *500.00* *500.00*
Never hinged *775.00*
f. Double overprint (III) *1,000.*
73 A24 $1 **rose red** 160.00 *190.00*
Never hinged 325.00
On cover 775.00
Block of 4 700.00 *875.00*
b. No period after "GOVT" *525.00* 500.00
Nos. 65-66,67-73 (9) 789.50 *1,021.*
Nos. 65-66, 67-73 never hinged 1,485.

Coat of Arms — A26

View of Honolulu — A27

Statue of Kamehameha I — A28

Stars and Palms — A29

S. S. "Arawa" — A30

Pres. Sanford Ballard Dole — A31

1894

74 A26 1c **yellow** 2.00 1.50
Never hinged 4.00
On cover 25.00
Block of 4 9.00 9.00
75 A27 2c **brown** 2.00 .60
Never hinged 4.00
On cover 25.00
Block of 4 9.00 7.00
"Flying goose" flaw (48 LR 2) 525.00 475.00
Never hinged 1,100.
Double transfer 5.00 5.00
76 A28 5c **rose lake** 5.00 2.00
Never hinged 11.00
On cover 25.00
Block of 4 25.00 15.00
77 A29 10c **yellow green** 8.00 5.00
Never hinged 18.00
On cover 45.00
Block of 4 35.00 25.00
78 A30 12c **blue** 17.50 *20.00*
Never hinged 37.50
On cover 150.00
Block of 4 65.00 *80.00*
Double transfer 20.00 20.00
79 A31 25c **deep blue** 22.50 17.50
Never hinged 47.50
On cover 100.00
Block of 4 100.00 —
Nos. 74-79 (6) 57.00 *46.60*
Set, never hinged 122.50

Numerous double transfers exist on Nos. 75 and 81.

"CENTS" Added — A32

1899

80 A26 1c **dark green** 2.00 1.50
Never hinged 4.50
On cover 25.00
Block of 4 9.50 7.00
81 A27 2c **rose** 1.50 1.00
Never hinged 3.50
On cover 20.00
Block of 4 6.50 6.00
Double transfer — —
"Flying goose" flaw (48 LR 2) 350.00 350.00
Never hinged 750.00
a. 2c **salmon** 1.50 1.50
Never hinged 3.50
b. Vert. pair, imperf. horiz. *4,250.*
82 A32 5c **blue** 8.00 4.00
Never hinged 20.00
On cover 25.00
Block of 4 40.00 55.00
Nos. 80-82 (3) 11.50 6.50
Set, never hinged 28.00

OFFICIAL STAMPS

Lorrin Andrews Thurston — O1

1896 **Engr.** **Unwmk.** ***Perf. 12***

O1 O1 2c **green** 45.00 20.00
Never hinged 90.00
On cover 400.00
Block of 4 200.00
O2 O1 5c **black brown** 45.00 20.00
Never hinged 90.00
On cover 425.00
Block of 4 200.00
O3 O1 6c **deep ultramarine** 45.00 20.00
Never hinged 90.00
On cover —
Block of 4 200.00
O4 O1 10c **bright rose** 45.00 20.00
Never hinged 90.00
On cover 475.00
Block of 4 200.00
O5 O1 12c **orange** 55.00 22.50
Never hinged 110.00
On cover —
Block of 4 260.00
O6 O1 25c **gray violet** 65.00 22.50
Never hinged 130.00
On cover —
Block of 4 300.00
Nos. O1-O6 (6) 300.00 125.00
Set, never hinged 600.00

Used values for Nos. O1-O6 are for stamps canceled-to-order "FOREIGN OFFICE/HONOLULU H.I." in double circle without date. Values of postally used stamps: Nos. O1-O2, O4, $50 each; No. O3, $125; No. O5, $160; No. O6, $200.

ENVELOPES

Italicized numbers in parentheses indicate quantities issued.

All printed by American Bank Note Co., N.Y.

View of Honolulu Harbor — E1

Envelopes of White Paper, Outside and Inside

1884

U1 E1 1c **light green** *(109,000)* 2.75 3.00
Entire 6.00 *25.00*
a. 1c **green** *(10,000)* 5.00 *15.00*
Entire 15.00 *90.00*
b. 1c **dark green** 10.00 *10.00*
Entire 25.00 *75.00*
c. As No. U1, double impression *5,250.*
U2 E1 2c **carmine** *(386,000 including U2a, U2b)* 2.75 4.00
Entire 5.00 *17.50*
a. 2c **red** 2.75 4.00
Entire 5.00 *17.50*
b. 2c **rose** 2.75 4.00
Entire 5.00 *17.50*
c. 2c **pale pink** *(5,000)* 30.00 30.00
Entire 90.00 *100.00*
U3 E1 4c **red** *(18,000)* 15.00 25.00
Entire 50.00 *150.00*
U4 E1 5c **blue** *(90,775)* 6.50 7.50
Entire 17.50 *30.00*
U5 E1 10c **black** *(3,500 plus)* 25.00 37.50
Entire 100.00 *150.00*

Envelopes White Outside, Blue Inside

U6 E1 2c **rose** 175.00 225.00
Entire 425.00 *6,500.*
U7 E1 4c **red** 175.00 225.00
Entire 425.00 *7,500.*
U8 E1 5c **blue** 225.00 250.00
Entire 575.00 *1,250.*
U9 E1 10c **black** 300.00 450.00
Entire 525.00 —
Nos. U1-U9 (9) 927.00 1,227.

Nos. U1, U2, U4 & U5 Overprinted Locally in Red or Black

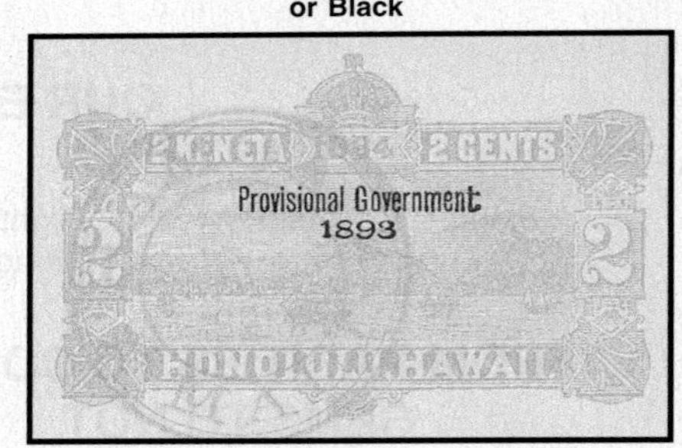

1893

U10 E1 1c **light green** (R) *(16,000)* 6.00 11.00
Entire 12.00 *75.00*
a. Double overprint *2,000.*
Entire *8,000.*
U11 E1 2c **carmine** (Bk) *(37,000)* 3.00 4.00
Entire 6.00 *20.00*
a. Double overprint 600.00
Entire *1,100.* *1,750.*
b. Double overprint, one inverted, entire *1,500.*
c. Double impression *4,750.*

No. U11 is known as an unused entire with a triple overprint, two of the overprints being at the bottom right portion of the envelope. Unique. Value, $9,500.

U12 E1 5c **blue** (R) *(34,891)* 4.50 5.00
Entire 10.00 *15.00*
a. Double overprint 375.00 *400.00*
Entire 700.00 *3,000.*
b. Triple overprint, entire *7,500.*
U13 E1 10c **black** (R) *(17,707 incl. No. U14)* 15.00 20.00
Entire 27.50 *125.00*
a. Double overprint, entire *2,000.* *2,000.*
b. Triple overprint, entire *8,500.*

Envelope No. U9 Overprinted in Red

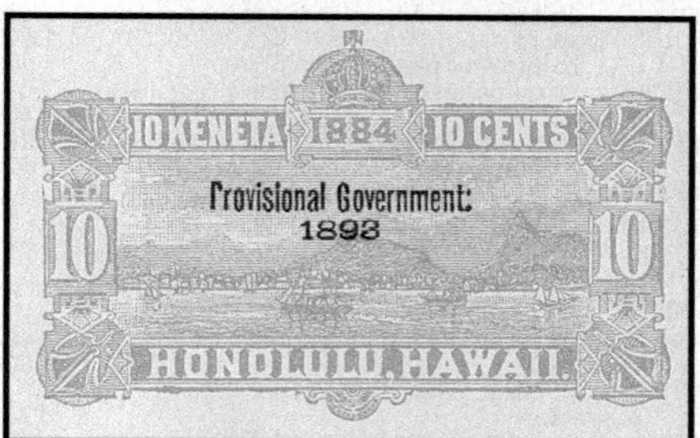

U14 E1 10c **black** (R) 325. *750.00*
Entire 1,100. *13,000.*

SPECIAL DELIVERY ENVELOPE

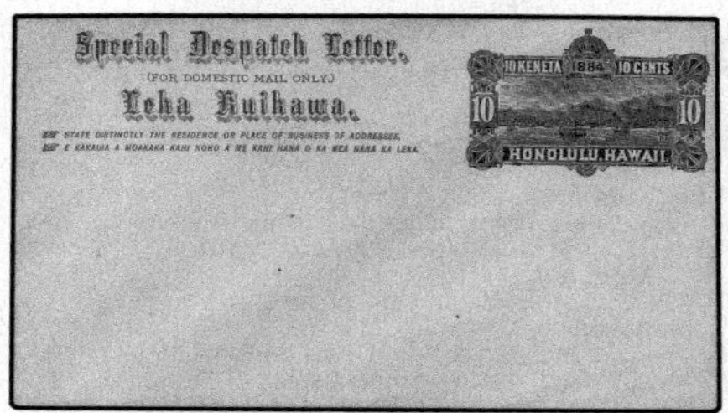

Envelope No. U5 with added inscription "Special Despatch Letter" etc. in red at top left corner
Value is for Entire.

1885

UE1 E1 10c **black** *(2,000)* 175.

Envelope No. UE1 was prepared for use but never issued for postal purposes. Postally used examples exist, but no special delivery service was performed. Favor cancellations exist.

POSTAL CARDS

All printed by American Bank Note Co., N.Y.
Values are for entires.

Queen Liliuokalani — PC1

View of Diamond Head — PC2

Royal Emblems — PC3

1882-92 **Engr.**

UX1 PC1 1c **red,** *buff (125,000)* 30.00 *75.00*
UX2 PC2 2c **black** *(45,000)* 50.00 *90.00*
a. Lithographed ('92) 125.00 200.00
UX3 PC3 3c **blue green** *(21,426)* 67.50 *175.00*

1889 **Litho.**

UX4 PC1 1c **red,** *buff (171,240)* 27.50 *50.00*

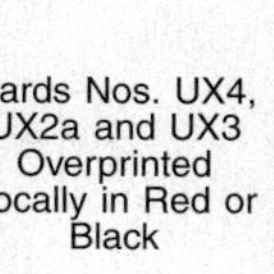

Cards Nos. UX4, UX2a and UX3 Overprinted Locally in Red or Black

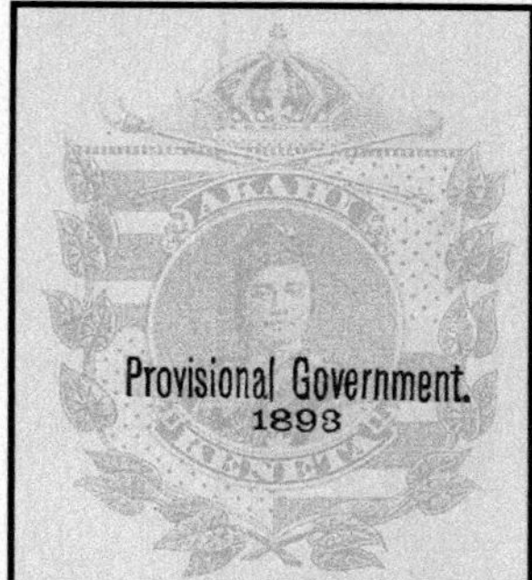

1893

UX5 PC1 1c **red,** *buff* (Bk) *(28,760)* 30.00 *75.00*
a. Double overprint *4,500.* *3,500.*
UX6 PC2 2c **black** (R) *(10,000)* 65.00 *95.00*

No. UX6 is known unused with double overprint, one inverted at lower left of card. Unique. Value, $16,000.

UX7 PC3 3c **blue green** (R) *(8,574)* 80.00 *500.00*
a. Double overprint *18,500.*

No. UX7a is believed to be unique. The second, full-strength overprint is just above the indicium.

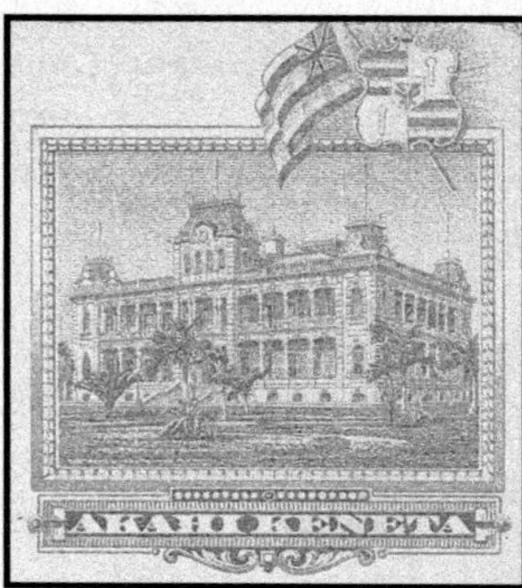

Iolani Palace — PC4

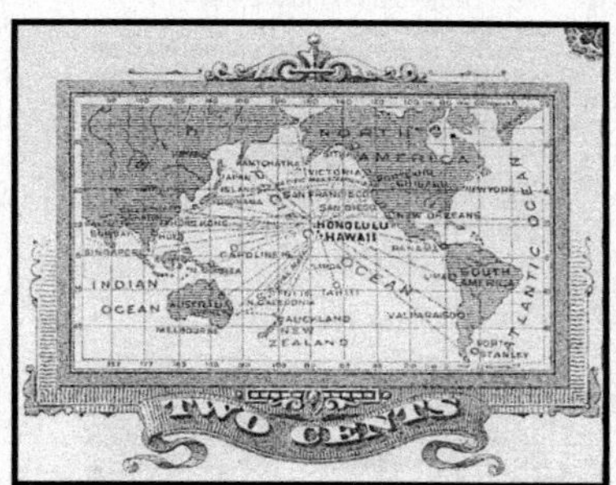

Map of Pacific Ocean, Mercator's Projection — PC5

1894-97 **Litho.**

Border Frame 131½x72½mm

UX8 PC4 1c **red,** *buff (100,000)* 20.00 *40.00*
a. Border frame 132½x74mm ('97) *(200,000)* 20.00 *40.00*
UX9 PC5 2c **green** *(60,000)* 45.00 *80.00*
a. Border frame 132½x74mm ('97) *(190,000)* 45.00 *80.00*

PAID REPLY POSTAL CARDS

Double Cards, Same Designs as Postal Cards With Added Inscriptions

1883 **Litho.**

UY1 PC1 1c +1c **purple,** *buff,* unsevered *(5,000)* 400.00 *450.00*
m. Message card, detached 35.00 *100.00*
r. Reply card, detached 35.00 *100.00*
UY2 PC2 2c +2c **dark blue,** unsevered *(5,000)* 450.00 *500.00*
m. Message card, detached 55.00 *140.00*
r. Reply card, detached 55.00 *140.00*

1889

UY3 PC1 1c +1c **gray violet,** *buff,* unsevered *(5,000)* 450.00 *550.00*
m. Message card, detached 35.00 *110.00*
r. Reply card, detached 35.00 *110.00*
UY4 PC2 2c +2c **sapphire,** unsevered *(5,000)* 450.00 *550.00*
m. Message card, detached 35.00 *90.00*
r. Reply card, detached 35.00 *90.00*

Values for unused unsevered Paid Reply Postal Cards are for cards which have not been folded. Folded cards sell for about 33% of these values.

Detached card used values are for canceled cards with printed messages on the back.

REVENUE STAMPS

R1

R2

R3

R4

R5

R6

Printed by the American Bank Note Co.
Sheets of 70

1877 **Engr.** **Unwmk.** ***Rouletted 8***

R1 R1 25c **green** *(160,000)* 25.00 *20.00*
Never hinged 32.50
R2 R2 50c **yellow orange** *(190,000)* 45.00 20.00
R3 R3 $1 **black** *(580,000)* 45.00 13.00
a. $1 gray 45.00 13.00

Denominations Typo.

R4 R4 $5 **vermilion & violet blue** *(21,000)* 260.00 57.50
R5 R5 $10 **reddish brown & green** *(14,000)* 260.00 65.00
R6 R6 $50 **slate blue & carmine** *(3,500)* *1,050.* *450.00*

No. R6 unused is valued without gum, as all known examples come thus.

Unused values for all revenues except No. R6 are for stamps with original gum. Apparently unused stamps without gum sell for less.

No. R1 Surcharged in Black or Gold

a

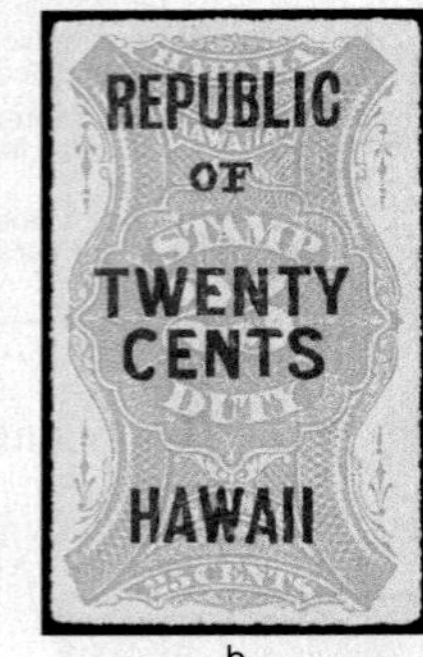

b

1893-94

R7 R1 (a) 20c on 25c **green** 60.00 30.00
Never hinged 80.00
a. Inverted surcharge *1,250.* *900.00*
R8 R1 (b) 20c on 25c **green** (G) 100.00 100.00
Never hinged 175.00
a. Inverted surcharge —
b. Double surcharge — —
c. Double surcharge, one black, one gold — *1,500.*
d. Double surcharge, one gold, one red in different font —
e. Double surcharge, with a single added letter "c" —
f. Double surcharge with two "c" letters added —

On No. R8b, one surcharge is always diagonal. On No. R8c, the black surcharge is 20mm wide, while the normal gold surcharge is 15mm wide.

R7

Sheets of 50

1894 **Litho.** ***Perf. 14***

R9 R7 20c **red** *(10,000)* 375.00 375.00
Never hinged 850.00
a. Imperf. *(25,000)* 575.00 1,200.
Never hinged 1,200.
Pair 1,200.
Never hinged 2,700.

No. R9a is known in an unused pair on paper with "DENNIS" papermaker's watermark.

R10 R7 25c **violet brown** 1,300. 1,000.
Never hinged 2,400.
a. Imperf. 1,900. —
Never hinged 3,800.
Pair 4,250.
Never hinged 7,900.
b. As "a," tete beche pair —

Kamehameha I — R8

Printed by the American Bank Note Co.
Sheets of 100

1897 **Engr.** ***Perf. 12***

R11 R8 $1 **dark blue** *(60,000)* 9.00 9.00
Never hinged 12.50

R9

1901 ***Rouletted 8***

R12 R9 $50 **slate blue & carmine** *(7,000)* 70.00 70.00
Never hinged 120.00

Types of 1877

Printed by the American Bank Note Co.
Sheets of 70

1910-13 **Engr.** ***Perf. 12***

R13 R2 50c **yellow orange** ('13) *(70,000)* 17.50 *30.00*
Never hinged 22.50
R14 R3 $1 **black** ('13) *(35,000)* 22.50 *40.00*
Never hinged 27.50
R15 R4 $5 **vermilion & violet blue** *(14,000)* 45.00 *60.00*
Never hinged 55.00
a. Denomination inverted *10,000.*
R16 R5 $10 **reddish brown & green** *(14,000)* 65.00 *70.00*
Never hinged 75.00

PROOFS

1853

5TC3 5c Plate on wove paper
a. **black** *6,000.*
6TC3 13c Plate on wove paper
a. **black** *6,000.*

1868-89

10TC1a 5c Large die on India paper
e. **orange red** 3,000.
10RTC1a 5c Large die on India paper, on card
e. **orange red** 2,500.
11TC1a 13c Large die on India paper
e. **orange red** 1,000.
11TC3 13c Plate on India paper
a. **orange red** 800.
11RP1 13c **orange red,** large die on India paper *2,500.*
11RP3 13c **orange red,** plate on India paper 800.

1861-63

27TC3 2c Plate on India paper
a. **black** 1,100.

1864-71

30P1 1c **purple,** large die on India paper 900.
30P3 1c **purple,** plate on India paper 400.
Block of 4 1,500.
31P1 2c **rose vermilion,** large die on India paper 900.
31P3 2c **rose vermilion,** plate on India paper 400.
Block of 4 —
31P4 2c **rose vermilion,** plate on card 400.
31TC1a 2c Large die on India paper
e. **green** *2,500.*
32P1 5c **blue,** large die on India paper 900.
32P3 5c **blue,** plate on India paper 400.
32P4 5c **blue,** plate on card 400.
32TC1a 5c Large die on India paper
e. **black** 1,250.
32TC3 5c Plate on India paper
a. **dark red** 400.
b. **orange red** 400.
c. **orange** 400.
d. **red brown** 400.
Block of 4 1,800.
e. **green** 400.
Block of 4 1,800.
f. **dark violet** 400.
Block of 4 1,800.
33P1 6c **green,** large die on India paper 900.
33P3 6c **green,** plate on India paper 400.
Block of 4 1,800.
34P1 18c **dull rose,** large die on India paper 900.
34P3 18c **dull rose,** plate on India paper 400.
Block of 4 1,800.
34P4 18c **dull rose,** plate on card 400.
34TC1a 18c Large die on India paper
e. **orange red** 900.
f. **dark orange** 900.
34TC3 18c Plate on India paper
a. **orange red** 650.

1875

35P1 2c **brown,** large die on India paper 900.
35P3 2c **brown,** plate on India paper 400.
Block of 4 1,800.
35P4 2c **brown,** plate on card 400.
35TC1a 2c Large die on India paper
e. **black** *2,600.*
36P1 12c **black,** large die on India paper 900.
36P3 12c **black,** plate on India paper 400.
36P4 12c **black,** plate on card 400.
36TC1a 12c Large die on India paper
e. **violet blue** 925.

1882

37P3 1c **blue,** plate on India paper 400.
Block of 4 1,800.
37TC1a 1c Large die on India paper
e. **black** *3,750.*
39P1 5c **ultramarine,** large die on India paper 900.
39P3 5c **ultramarine,** plate on India paper 400.
40P1 10c **black,** large die on India paper 900.
40P3 10c **black,** plate on India paper 400.
Block of 4 1,800.
41P3 15c **red brown,** plate on India paper 400.
Block of 4 1,800.
41P4 15c **red brown,** plate on card 400.

1883-86

42P3 1c **green,** plate on India paper 400.
Block of 4 1,800.
42P4 1c **green,** plate on card 400.
43P3 2c **rose,** plate on India paper 400.
Block of 4 1,800.
43P4 2c **rose,** plate on card 400.
47P1 25c **dk violet,** large die on India paper 900.
47P3 25c **dk violet,** plate on India paper 400.
Block of 4 1,800.
47TC1a 25c Large die on India paper
e. **black** *1,000.*
48P1 50c **red,** large die on India paper 1,000.
48P3 50c **red,** plate on India paper 400.
Block of 4 1,800.
48TC1a 50c Large die on India paper
e. **lake** *1,700.*
48TC3 50c Plate on India paper
a. **lake** 500.
49P1 $1 **rose red,** large die on India paper *2,100.*
49P3 $1 **rose red,** plate on India paper 400.
Block of 4 1,800.
49P4 $1 **rose red,** plate on card 500.
49TC1a $1 Large die on India paper
e. **orange red** 1,000.
49TC3 $1 Plate on India paper
a. **black** 400.
b. **orange red** *1,000.*
c. **carmine** *1,000.*
d. **vermilion** *1,000.*
Block of 4 *4,500.*

1886-89

50P1 2c **orange vermilion,** large die on India paper 1,000.
50P3 2c **orange vermilion,** plate on India paper 500.
51P1 2c **carmine,** large die on India paper 1,100.

1890-91

52P1 2c **dull violet,** large die on India paper *4,000.*
52P3 2c **dull violet,** plate on India paper 500.
52P4 2c **dull violet,** plate on card 500.
52CP3 2c **deep indigo,** plate on India paper 500.

1894

74P1 1c **yellow,** large die on India paper 1,000.
74P3 1c **yellow,** plate on India paper 400.
74P4 1c **yellow,** plate on card 400.
75P1 2c **brown,** large die on India paper 1,000.
75P3 2c **brown,** plate on India paper 400.
75TC1a 2c Large die on India paper
e. **dk green** 1,000.
76P1 5c **rose lake,** large die on India paper 1,000.
76P3 5c **rose lake,** plate on India paper 400.
76P4 5c **rose lake,** plate on card 400.
77P1 10c **yellow green,** large die on India paper 1,000.
77P3 10c **yellow green,** plate on India paper 400.
Block of 4 1,800.
77P4 10c **yellow green,** plate on card 400.
77TC1a 2c Large die on India paper
e. **dp blue green** 1,000.
78P1 12c **blue,** large die on India paper 1,000.
78P3 12c **blue,** plate on India paper 400.
78P4 12c **blue,** plate on card 400.
79P1 25c **dp blue,** large die on India paper 1,000.
79P3 25c **dp blue,** plate on India paper 400.
79P4 25c **dp blue,** plate on card 400.

1899

82P3 5c **blue,** plate on India paper 400.
Block of 4 1,800.
82P4 5c **blue,** plate on card 400.

Official

1896

O1P1 2c **green,** large die on India paper 1,000.
O1P3 2c **green,** plate on India paper 500.
O1P4 2c **green,** plate on card 400.
O2P1 5c **blk brown,** large die on India paper 1,000.
O2P3 5c **blk brown,** plate on India paper 500.
O2P4 5c **blk brown,** plate on card 425.
O3P1 6c **dp ultra,** large die on India paper 1,000.
O3P3 6c **dp ultra,** plate on India paper 500.
O3P4 6c **dp ultra,** plate on card 425.
O4P1 10c **brt rose,** large die on India paper 1,000.

O4P3 10c **brt rose,** plate on India paper 500.
Block of 4 —
O4P4 10c **brt rose,** plate on card 425.
O4TC1a 2c Large die on India paper
e. **black** 1,000.
O5P1 12c **orange,** large die on India paper 1,000.
O5P3 12c **orange,** plate on India paper 500.
O5P4 12c **orange,** plate on card 425.
O5TC1a 12c Large die on India paper
e. **black** 1,000.
O6P1 25c **gray violet,** large die on India paper 1,000.
O6P3 25c **gray violet,** plate on India paper 500.
O6P4 25c **gray violet,** plate on card 425.
O6TC1a 25c Large die on India paper
e. **black** 1,000.

Envelopes

Uncleared indicia only

1884

U1P1 1c **green,** large die on India paper *1,000.*
U1TC1a 1c Large die on India paper
e. **black** *750.*
f. **orange** *1,000.*
g. **red** *1,000.*
k. **brown,** on bond paper *1,000.*
U2P1 2c **carmine,** large die on India paper *1,000.*
U2TC1a 2c Large die on India paper
e. **black** *750.*
f. **blue** *1,000.*
g. **orange** *1,000.*
U3P1 4c **red,** large die on India paper *1,000.*
U3TC1a 4c Large die on India paper
e. **black** *750.*
U4P1 5c **blue,** large die on India paper *1,000.*
U4TC1a 5c Large die on India paper
e. **black** *750.*
U5P1 10c **black,** large die on India paper *1,000.*
U5TC1a 10c Large die on India paper
e. **black** *750.*

Postal Cards

Large die proofs are of indicia only, India plate proofs are entire card.

1882-95

UX1P1 1c **red,** large die on India paper *3,500.*
UX1P3 1c **red,** plate on India paper *2,000.*
UX1TC3 1c Plate on India paper
a. **green** *2,000.*
UX2P3 2c **black,** plate on India paper *2,000.*
UX3P1 3c **blue green,** large die on India paper *2,000.*
UX3P3 3c **blue green,** plate on India paper *2,000.*
UX8TC3 1c Plate on India paper
a. **orange** *3,000.*
b. **brown** *3,000.*
UX8TC5 1c Plate on wove paper
a. **orange** *6,000.*

Paid Reply Postal Cards

1889

UY3mTC4 1c **greenish blue,** message card, plate proof on card *9,500.*
UY3rTC4 1c **greenish blue,** reply card, plate proof on card *9,500.*

Revenues

1877-97

R1P3 25c **green,** plate on India paper *600.*
Block of 4 *2,750.*
R1P4 25c **green,** plate on card *600.*
R1TC1a 25c Large die on India paper
e. **blue green** *1,150.*
f. **black** *1,150.*
g. **brown red** *1,150.*
h. **brown** *1,150.*
i. **grayish blue** *1,150.*
R2P3 50c **yellow orange,** plate on India paper *600.*
Block of 4 *2,800.*
R2P4 50c **yellow orange,** plate on card *600.*
R2TC1a 50c Large die on India paper
e. **blue green** *1,150.*
f. **black** *1,150.*
g. **brown red** *1,150.*
h. **brown** *1,150.*
i. **grayish blue** *1,150.*
R3P1 $1 **black,** large die on India paper *1,150.*
R3P3 $1 **black,** plate on India paper *600.*
Block of 4 *2,750.*
R3P4 $1 **black,** plate on card *600.*
R3TC1a $1 Large die on India paper
e. **blue green** *1,150.*
f. **brown red** *1,150.*
g. **brown** *1,150.*
h. **grayish blue** *1,150.*
R4P3 $5 **ver. & violet blue,** plate on India paper *600.*
Block of 4 *2,750.*
R4P4 $5 **ver. & violet blue,** plate on card *400.*
R5P3 $10 **reddish brn & grn,** plate on India paper *600.*
Block of 4 *2,750.*
R5P4 $10 **reddish brn & grn,** plate on card *600.*
R6P3 $50 **slate blue & car,** plate on India paper *600.*
Block of 4 *2,750.*
R6P4 $50 **slate blue & car,** plate on card *800.*
R11P1 $1 **dk blue,** Large die on India paper *1,250.*
R11P3 $1 **dk blue,** plate on India paper *800.*
R11P4 $1 **dk blue,** plate on card *700.*

SPECIMEN STAMPS

Overprinted in Black or Red — Type A

1868

10S A 5c **blue** (R) 25.
Block of 4 130.
a. Line through "Honolulu" (Pos. 2) 110.
11S A 13c **dull rose** 25.
Block of 4 130.

Overprinted in Black — Type B

11S B 13c **dull rose** 275.
Block of 4 1,250.
a. Double overprint, one as #11S A, one as #11S B *4,000.*
b. Period omitted (Pos. 18, 20) 600.

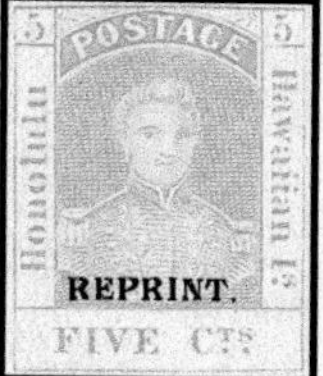

Overprinted in Black — Type C

1889

10RS C 5c **blue** 65.
Block of 4 275.
11RS C 13c **orange red** 240.
Block of 4 1,100.

Overprinted in Black — Type D

1869

29S D 2c **red** 55.
Block of 4 275.

Overprinted in Blue — Type E

1886

50S E 2c **orange vermilion** 65.
Block of 4 300.

Overprinted in Black — Type C

1889

51S C 2c **carmine** 35.
Block of 4 175.

PHILIPPINES

Following the American occupation of the Philippines, May 1, 1898, after Admiral Dewey's fleet entered Manila Bay, an order was issued by the U. S. Postmaster General (No. 201, May 24, 1898) establishing postal facilities with rates similar to the domestic rates.

Military postal stations were established as branch post offices, each such station being placed within the jurisdiction of the nearest regular post office. Supplies were issued to these military stations through the regular post office of which they were branches.

Several post office clerks were sent to the Philippines and the San Francisco post office was made the nearest regular office for the early Philippine mail and the postmarks of the period point out this fact.

U.S. stamps overprinted "PHILIPPINES" were placed on sale in Manila June 30, 1899. Regular U.S. stamps had been in use from early March, and at the Manila post office Spanish stamps were also acceptable.

The first regular post office was established at Cavite on July 30, 1898, as a branch of the San Francisco post office. The first cancellation was a dated handstamp with "PHILIPPINE STATION" and "SAN FRANCISCO, CAL."

On May 1, 1899, the entire Philippine postal service was separated from San Francisco and numerous varieties of postmarks resulted. Many of the early used stamps show postmarks and cancellations of the Military Station, Camp or R.P.O. types, together with "Killers" of the types employed in the U.S. at the time.

The Philippines became a commonwealth of the United States on November 15, 1935, the High Commissioner of the United States taking office on the same day. The official name of the government was "Commonwealth of the Philippines" as provided by Article 17 of the Constitution. Upon the final and complete withdrawal of sovereignty of the United States and the proclamation of Philippine independence on July 4, 1946, the Commonwealth of the Philippines became the "Republic of the Philippines."

Italicized numbers in parentheses indicate quantities issued.

Authority for dates of issue, stamps from 1899 to 1911, and some quantities issued — "The Postal Issues of the Philippines," by F. L. Palmer (New York, 1912). Authority for quantities issued — "NAPP's Numbers, Volume 2," by Joseph M. Napp (2001).

100 CENTS = 1 DOLLAR
100 CENTAVOS = 1 PESO (1906)

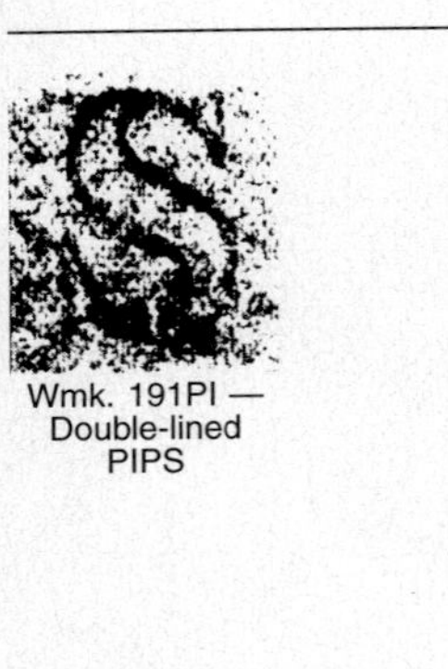
Wmk. 191PI — Double-lined PIPS

Wmk. 190PI — Single-lined PIPS

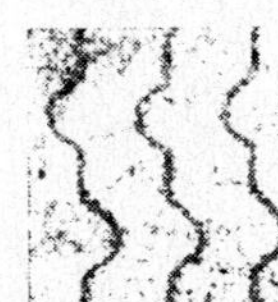
Wmk. 257 — Curved Wavy Lines

Regular Issues of the United States Overprinted in Black

Printed and overprinted by the U.S. Bureau of Engraving and Printing.

1899, June 30 **Unwmk.** ***Perf. 12***

On U.S. Stamp No. 260

212 A96 50c **orange** 300. 225.
Never hinged 775.
On cover —
Block of 4 1,425. —
P# strip of 3, Impt. 1,350.
P# block of 6, Impt. *25,000.*

On U.S. Stamps Nos. 279, 279B, 279Bd, 279Bj, 279Bf, 279Bc, 268, 281, 282C, 283, 284, 275, 275a

Wmk. Double-lined USPS (191)

213 A87 1c **yellow green** *(5,500,000)* 3.50 .60
Never hinged 10.00
On cover 10.00
Block of 4 20.00 5.00
P# strip of 3, Impt. 40.00
P# block of 6, Impt. 225.00
a. Inverted overprint *77,500.*
214 A88 2c **red,** type IV *(6,970,000)* 1.75 .60
light red 1.75 .60
Never hinged 4.25
On cover 10.00
Block of 4 7.00 4.00
P# strip of 3, Impt. 25.00
P# block of 6, Impt. 175.00
a. 2c **orange red,** type IV, *1901* 1.75 .60
pale orange red 1.75 .60
deep orange red, *1903* 1.75 .60
Never hinged 4.25
b. Booklet pane of 6, **red,** type IV *1900* 200.00 *300.00*
orange red, *1901* 250.00 *300.00*
Never hinged 450.00
c. 2c **reddish carmine,** type IV 2.50 1.00
Never hinged 6.00
On cover 12.50
Block of 4 11.00 7.50
P# strip of 3, Impt. 35.00
P# block of 6, Impt. 225.00
d. 2c **rose carmine,** type IV 3.00 1.10
Never hinged 7.25
On cover 15.00
Block of 4 14.00 8.50
P# strip of 3, Impt. 40.00
P# block of 6, Impt. 260.00
e. As "d," double ovpt., one albino 750.00
215 A89 3c **purple** *(673,814)* 9.00 1.25
Never hinged 21.50
On cover 50.00
Block of 4 42.50 13.50
P# strip of 3, Impt. 85.00
P# block of 6, Impt. 550.00
216 A91 5c **blue** *(1,700,000)* 9.00 1.00
Never hinged 21.50
On cover 20.00
Block of 4 42.50 9.00
P# strip of 3, Impt. 85.00
P# block of 6, Impt. 850.00
a. Inverted overprint *6,500.*

No. 216a is valued in the grade of fine.

217 A94 10c **brown,** type I *(500,000)+* 35.00 4.00
Never hinged 80.00
On cover 100.00
Block of 4 160.00 55.00
P# strip of 3, Impt. 175.00
P# block of 6, Impt. 700.00

(+ Quantity includes Nos. 217, 217A)

217A A94 10c **orange brown,** type II *(250,000* 110.00 27.50
Never hinged 275.00
On cover 250.00
Block of 4 525.00 190.00
P# strip of 3, Impt. 800.00
P# block of 6, Impt. *6,000.*

No. 217A was overprinted on U.S. No. 283a, vertical watermark. The watermark on No. 217 is horizontal.

218 A95 15c **olive green** *(200,000)* 40.00 8.00
light olive green 37.50 8.50
Never hinged 95.00
On cover 110.00
Block of 4 175.00 52.50
P# strip of 3, Impt. 200.00
P# block of 6, Impt. 3,000.
219 A96 50c **orange** *(50,000)+* 125.00 37.50
Never hinged 300.00
On cover *400.00*
Block of 4 575.00 *250.00*
P# strip of 3, Impt. 575.00
P# block of 6, Impt. *5,000.*
a. 50c **red orange** 250.00 55.00
Never hinged 600.00
Block of 4 1,700.
Nos. 213-219 (8) 333.25 80.45

(+ Quantity includes Nos. 212, 219, 219a)

Special Printing

In March 1900 one pane of 100 stamps of each of Nos. 213-217, 218, 219 and J1-J5 were specially overprinted for displays at the Paris Exposition (1900) and Pan American Exposition (1901). The 2c pane was light red, type IV.

Stamps were handstampd type E "Specimen" in black ink on the face by H. G. Mandel and mounted by him in separate displays for the two Expositions. Additional stamps from each pane were also handstamped "Specimen" but most were destroyed after the Expositions. However, because additional stamps that are not Special Printings exist with a black "Specimen" handstamp, expertization by competent authorities is recommended.

J. M. Bartels, a stamp dealer, signed some stamps from these panes "Special Surcharge" in pencil on the gum to authenticate them as coming from the "Mandel" Special Printing panes. In 1904 or later, he handstamped additional surviving examples "Special Surcharge" in red ink on the back as his guarantee. Some of these guaranteed stamps had Mandel's "Specimen" handstamp on the face while others did not. Value, each $1,000.

Regular Issue

Same Overprint in Black On U.S. Stamps Nos. 280b, 282 and 272

1901, Aug. 30

220 A90 4c **orange brown** *(404,907)* 35.00 5.00
Never hinged 80.00
On cover 50.00
Block of 4 160.00 50.00
P# strip of 3, Impt. 180.00
P# block of 6, Impt. 750.00
221 A92 6c **lake** *(223,465)* 40.00 7.00
Never hinged 95.00
On cover 65.00
Block of 4 200.00 50.00
P# strip of 3, Impt. 200.00
P# block of 6, Impt. 2,000.
222 A93 8c **violet brown** *(248,000)* 40.00 7.50
Never hinged 95.00
On cover 50.00
Block of 4 200.00 55.00
P# strip of 3, Impt. 200.00
P# block of 6, Impt. 1,000.
Nos. 220-222 (3) 115.00 19.50

Same Overprint in Red On U.S. Stamps Nos. 276, 276A, 277a and 278

223 A97 $1 **black,** type I *(3,000)+* 300.00 200.00
Never hinged 1,000.
On cover *800.00*
Block of 4 1,400.
P# strip of 3, Impt. *1,500.*
P# block of 6, Impt. —

(+ Quantity includes Nos. 223, 223A)

223A A97 $1 **black,** type II 1,500. 750.00
Never hinged 5,000.
On cover —
Block of 4 *8,750.* —
P# strip of 3, Impt., one stamp No. 223 *16,000.*
b. Horiz. pair, Nos. 223 and 223A *3,000.*
224 A98 $2 **dark blue** *(1800)* 350.00 325.00
Never hinged 1,150.
On cover 3,250.
Block of 4 1,600. —
P# strip of 3, Impt. *7,000.*
P# block of 6, Impt. —

225 A99 $5 **dark green** *(782)* 500.00 *900.00*
Never hinged 1,600.
On cover *12,500.*
Block of 4 *3,000.* —
P# strip of 3, Impt. *10,000.*

The existence of a plate block of No. 225 has been questioned by specialists. The editors would like to see evidence of its existence.

Special Printing

Special printings exist of Nos. 227, 221, 223-225, made from defaced plates. These were made for display at the St. Louis Exposition. All but a few copies were destroyed. Most of the existing copies have the handstamp "Special Printing" on the back. Value: Nos. 227, 221, each $775; No. 223, $1,500; No. 224, $2,000; No. 225, $2,500.

Same Overprint in Black On U.S. Stamps Nos. 300 to 310 and Shades

1903-04

226 A115 1c **blue green** *(9,631,172)* 7.00 .40
Never hinged 15.50
On cover 8.25
Block of 4 32.50 4.25
P# strip of 3, Impt. 25.00
P# block of 6, Impt. 300.00
227 A116 2c **carmine** *(850,000)* 9.00 1.10
Never hinged 20.00
On cover 10.00
Block of 4 42.50 6.00
P# strip of 3, Impt. 42.50
P# block of 6, Impt. 400.00
228 A117 3c **bright violet** *(14,500)* 67.50 12.50
Never hinged 150.00
On cover 55.00
Block of 4 275.00 85.00
P# strip of 3, Impt. 275.00
P# block of 6, Impt. 2,000.
229 A118 4c **brown** *(13,000)* 80.00 22.50
Never hinged 175.00
a. 4c **orange brown** 80.00 20.00
Never hinged 175.00
On cover 40.00
Block of 4 350.00 150.00
P# strip of 3, Impt. 325.00
P# block of 6, Impt. 2,500.
230 A119 5c **blue** *(1,211,844)* 17.50 1.00
Never hinged 40.00
On cover 22.50
Block of 4 80.00 7.50
P# strip of 3, Impt. 70.00
P# block of 6, Impt. 1,000.
231 A120 6c **brnsh lake** *(11,500)* 85.00 22.50
Never hinged 190.00
On cover 65.00
Block of 4 350.00 150.00
P# strip of 3, Impt. 350.00
P# block of 6, Impt. 3,000.
232 A121 8c **violet black** *(49,033)* 50.00 15.00
Never hinged 125.00
On cover 300.00
Block of 4 250.00 100.00
P# strip of 3, Impt. 275.00
P# block of 6, Impt. 2,250.
233 A122 10c **pale red brown** *(300,179)* 35.00 2.25
Never hinged 80.00
On cover 27.50
Block of 4 160.00 20.00
P# strip of 3, Impt. 175.00
P# block of 6, Impt. 1,500.
a. 10c **red brown** 35.00 3.00
Never hinged 80.00
On cover 35.00
Block of 4 160.00 32.50
P# strip of 3, Impt. 175.00
P# block of 6, Impt. 1,300.
b. Pair, one without overprint *1,500.*
234 A123 13c **purple black** *(91,341)* 35.00 17.50
Never hinged 80.00
a. 13c **brown violet** 35.00 17.50
Never hinged 80.00
On cover 55.00
Block of 4 150.00 110.00
P# strip of 3, Impt. 175.00
P# block of 6, Impt. 1,850.
235 A124 15c **olive green** *(183,965)* 60.00 15.00
Never hinged 135.00
On cover 100.00
Block of 4 275.00 100.00
P# strip of 3, Impt. 300.00
P# block of 6, Impt. 4,750.
236 A125 50c **orange** *(57,641)* 125.00 35.00
Never hinged 275.00
On cover 300.00
Block of 4 575.00 275.00
P# strip of 3, Impt. 575.00
P# block of 6, Impt. *35,000.*
Nos. 226-236 (11) 571.00 144.75
Set, never hinged 1,285.

Same Overprint in Red On U.S. Stamps Nos. 311, 312 and 313

237 A126 $1 **black** *(5617)* 300.00 200.00
Never hinged 800.00
On cover *1,000.*
Block of 4 1,400. 1,850.
P# strip of 3, Impt. 1,400.
P# block of 6, Impt. *8,500.*
238 A127 $2 **dark blue** *(695)* 550.00 *800.00*
Never hinged 1,500.
Block of 4 *3,000.* —
P# strip of 3, Impt. *3,250.*
P# block of 6, Impt. *37,500.*
239 A128 $5 **dark green** *(746)* 800.00 *2,750.*
Never hinged 2,000.
Block of 4 *3,750.* —
P# strip of 3, Impt. *8,500.*
P# block of 6, Impt. *250,000.*

Same Overprint in Black On U.S. Stamp Nos. 319 and 319c

240 A129 2c **carmine** *(862,245)* 8.00 2.25
Never hinged 17.50
On cover 3.50
Block of 4 35.00 15.00
P# strip of 3, Impt. 45.00
P# block of 6, Impt. 600.00
a. Booklet pane of 6 *1,500.*
b. 2c **scarlet** 8.00 2.75
Never hinged 19.00
On cover 4.00
Block of 4 35.00 17.50
P# strip of 3, Impt. 47.50
P# block of 6, Impt. 650.00
c. As "b," booklet pane of 6 —

Dates of issue:
Sept. 20, 1903, Nos. 226, 227, 236.
Jan. 4, 1904, Nos. 230, 234, 235, 237, 240a.
Nov. 1, 1904, Nos. 228, 229, 231, 232, 233, 238, 239, 240.
Nos. 212 to 240 were withdrawn from sale on Sept. 8, 1906, the remainders being destroyed.

Special Printing

Two sets of special printings exist of the 1903-04 issue. The first consists of Nos. 226, 230, 234, 235, 236, 237 and 240. These were made for display at the St. Louis Exposition. All but a few stamps were destroyed. Most of the existing examples have the handstamp "Special Surcharge" on the back. Value: No. 237, $1,550; others $900.

In 1907 the entire set Nos. 226, 228 to 240, J1 to J7 were specially printed for the Bureau of Insular Affairs on very white paper. They are difficult to distinguish from the ordinary stamps except the Special Delivery stamp which is on U.S. No. E6 (see Philippines No. E2A). Value: No. 237, $1,300; No. 238, $2,600; No. 239, $3,500; J6, $1,600.; J7, $3,250; others, $1,000.

Regular Issue

José Rizal — A40

Printed by the U.S. Bureau of Engraving and Printing.

Plates of 200 subjects in two panes of 100 each.

Booklet panes Nos. 240a, 241b, 242b, 261a, 262b, 276a, 277a, 285a, 286a, 290e, 291b and 292c were made from plates of 180 subjects. No. 214b came from plates of 360 subjects.

Designs: 4c, McKinley. 6c, Ferdinand Magellan. 8c, Miguel Lopez de Legaspi. 10c, Gen. Henry W. Lawton. 12c, Lincoln. 16c, Adm. William T. Sampson. 20c, Washington. 26c, Francisco Carriedo. 30c, Franklin. 1p-10p, Arms of City of Manila.

Wmk. Double-lined PIPS (191PI)

1906, Sept. 8 *Perf. 12*

241 A40 2c **deep green** *(51,000,019)* .40 .25
Never hinged 1.00
P# block of 10, Impt. 40.00
Never hinged 65.00
a. 2c **yellow green** ('10) .60 .25
Never hinged 1.50
Double transfer *40.00*
P# block of 10, Impt. 30.00
Never hinged 50.00
b. Booklet pane of 6 *(720,120)* 750.00 800.00
Never hinged *1,500.*
242 A40 4c **carmine** *(11,000,019)* .50 .25
Never hinged 1.25
P# block of 10, Impt. 35.00
Never hinged 60.00
a. 4c **carmine lake** ('10) 1.00 .25
Never hinged 2.50
P# block of 10, Impt. 40.00
Never hinged 65.00
b. Booklet pane of 6*(300,600)* *650.00* *700.00*
Never hinged *1,250.*
243 A40 6c **violet** *(1,980,019)* 2.50 .25
Never hinged 6.25
P# block of 10, Impt. 75.00
Never hinged 120.00
244 A40 8c **brown** *(770,019)* 4.50 .90
Never hinged 11.00
P# block of 10, Impt. 140.00
Never hinged 225.00
245 A40 10c **blue** *(5,500,019)* 3.50 .30
Never hinged 8.75
P# block of 10, Impt. 85.00
Never hinged 145.00
a. 10c **dark blue** 3.50 .30
Never hinged 8.75
P# block of 10, Impt. 95.00
Never hinged 160.00
246 A40 12c **brown lake** *(670,019)* 9.00 2.50
Never hinged 22.50
P# block of 10, Impt. 300.00
Never hinged 475.00
247 A40 16c **violet black** *(1,300,019)* 6.00 .35
Never hinged 15.00
P# block of 10, Impt. 325.00
Never hinged 475.00
248 A40 20c **orange brown** *(2,100,019)* 7.00 .35
Never hinged 17.50
P# block of 10, Impt. 275.00
Never hinged 450.00
249 A40 26c **violet brown** *(428,000)* 11.00 3.00
Never hinged 27.50
P# block of 10, Impt. 450.00
Never hinged 675.00
250 A40 30c **olive green** *(1,256,019)* 6.50 1.75
Never hinged 16.00
P# block of 10, Impt. 375.00
Never hinged 575.00
251 A40 1p **orange** *(200,019)* 55.00 17.50
Never hinged 130.00
P# block of 10, Impt. 1,350.
Never hinged 2,000.
252 A40 2p **black** *(100,000)* 50.00 1.75
Never hinged 130.00
P# block of 10, Impt. 1,600.
Never hinged 2,500.
253 A40 4p **dark blue** *(10,000)* 160.00 20.00
Never hinged 375.00
P# block of 10, Impt. 2,750.
Never hinged *5,000.*
254 A40 10p **dark green** *(6,019)* 225.00 80.00
Never hinged 575.00
Block of 4 1,100. 400.00
Nos. 241-254 (14) 540.90 129.15
Set, never hinged 1,316.

1909-13 **Change of Colors**

255 A40 12c **red orange** *(300,000)* 11.00 3.00
Never hinged 27.50
P# block of 10, Impt. 425.00
Never hinged 700.00
256 A40 16c **olive green** *(500,000)* 6.00 .75
Never hinged 15.00
P# block of 10, Impt. 250.00
Never hinged 450.00
257 A40 20c **yellow** *(800,000)* 9.00 1.25
Never hinged 22.50
P# block of 10, Impt. 225.00
Never hinged 375.00
258 A40 26c **blue green** *(250,000)* 3.50 1.25
Never hinged 8.75
P# block of 10, Impt. 250.00
Never hinged 425.00
259 A40 30c **ultramarine** *(600,000)* 13.00 3.50
Never hinged 32.50
P# block of 10, Impt. 400.00
Never hinged 625.00
260 A40 1p **pale violet** *(100,000)* 45.00 5.00
Never hinged 110.00
P# block of 10, Impt. 975.00
Never hinged 1,750.
260A A40 2p **violet brown** ('13) *(50,000)* 100.00 12.00
Never hinged 250.00
P# block of 10, Impt. 1,600.
Never hinged *3,500.*
Nos. 255-260A (7) 187.50 26.75
Set, never hinged 466.25

1911 **Wmk. Single-lined PIPS (190PI)** ***Perf. 12***

261 A40 2c **green** *(44,000,000)* .75 .25
Never hinged 1.80
On cover 4.00
P# block of 10, Impt. 25.00
Never hinged 40.00
a. Booklet pane of 6 *(896,160)* *800.00* *900.00*
Never hinged *1,400.*
262 A40 4c **carmine lake** *(6,000,000)* 3.00 .25
Never hinged 6.75
On cover 6.00
P# block of 10, Impt. 50.00
Never hinged 110.00
a. 4c **carmine** — —
P# block of 10, Impt. 150.00
Never hinged 275.00
b. Booklet pane of 6 *(100,020)* *600.00* *700.00*
Never hinged *1,100.*
263 A40 6c **deep violet** *(3,200,000)* 3.00 .25
Never hinged 6.75
P# block of 10, Impt. 90.00
Never hinged 145.00
264 A40 8c **brown** *(1,400,000)* 9.50 .50
Never hinged 21.50
P# block of 10, Impt. 225.00
Never hinged 350.00
265 A40 10c **blue** *(3,700,000)* 4.00 .25
Never hinged 9.00
P# block of 10, Impt. 115.00
Never hinged 180.00
266 A40 12c **orange** *(1,320,000)* 4.00 .45
Never hinged 9.00
P# block of 10, Impt. 235.00
Never hinged 525.00
267 A40 16c **olive green** *(1,000,000)* 4.50 .40
Never hinged 10.00
P# block of 10, Impt. 145.00
Never hinged 225.00
a. 16c **pale olive green** 4.50 .50
Never hinged 10.00
P# block of 10, Impt. 150.00
Never hinged 250.00
268 A40 20c **yellow** *(3,000,000)* 3.50 .25
Never hinged 7.75
P# block of 10, Impt. 140.00
Never hinged 250.00
a. 20c **orange** 4.00 .30
Never hinged 9.00
P# block of 10, Impt. 185.00
Never hinged 300.00
269 A40 26c **blue green** *(249,900)* 6.00 .30
Never hinged 13.50
P# block of 10, Impt. 210.00
Never hinged 375.00

270 A40 30c **ultramarine** *(1,000,000)* 6.00 .50
Never hinged 13.50
P# block of 10, Impt. 175.00
Never hinged 300.00
271 A40 1p **pale violet** *(694,000)* 27.50 .60
Never hinged 62.50
P# block of 10, Impt. 425.00
Never hinged 1,000.
272 A40 2p **violet brown** *(100,000)* 45.00 1.00
Never hinged 100.00
P# block of 10, Impt. 775.00
Never hinged 1,600.
273 A40 4p **deep blue** *(10,000)* 550.00 110.00
Never hinged 1,100.
P# block of 10, Impt. *6,750.*
Never hinged *15,000.*
274 A40 10p **deep green** *(20,000)* 200.00 30.00
Never hinged 400.00
Block of 4 900.00 150.00
Nos. 261-274 (14) 866.75 145.00
Set, never hinged 1,862.

1914
275 A40 30c **gray** *(700,000)* 12.00 .50
Never hinged 27.50
P# block of 10, Impt. 200.00
Never hinged 425.00

1914 ***Perf. 10***
276 A40 2c **green** *(60,000,000)* 3.00 .25
Never hinged 7.00
P# block of 6, no Impt. 25.00
Never hinged 45.00
a. Booklet pane of 6 *(400,080)* *600.00 800.00*
Never hinged *1,250.*
277 A40 4c **carmine** *(2,500,000)* 4.00 .30
Never hinged 9.00
P# block of 6, no Impt. 52.50
Never hinged 90.00
a. Booklet pane of 6 *(56,040)* *600.00*
Never hinged *1,300.*
278 A40 6c **light violet** *(700,000)* 45.00 9.50
Never hinged 100.00
P# block of 10, Impt. 525.00
Never hinged 1,200.
a. 6c **deep violet** 50.00 6.25
Never hinged 110.00
P# block of 10, Impt. 700.00
Never hinged 1,350.
279 A40 8c **brown** *(200,000)* 55.00 10.50
Never hinged 125.00
P# block of 10, Impt. 875.00
Never hinged 2,000.
280 A40 10c **dark blue** *(2,000,000)* 30.00 .25
Never hinged 67.50
P# block of 10, Impt. 375.00
Never hinged 725.00
281 A40 16c **olive green** *(700,000)* 100.00 5.00
Never hinged 225.00
P# block of 10, Impt. *1,200.*
Never hinged *2,500.*
282 A40 20c **orange** *(2,000,000)* 40.00 1.00
Never hinged 85.00
Block of 4 180.00 5.75
283 A40 30c **gray** *(1,300,000)* 60.00 4.50
Never hinged 130.00
P# block of 10, Impt. 1,000.
Never hinged 1,675.
284 A40 1p **pale violet** *(198,000)* 150.00 3.75
Never hinged 350.00
P# block of 10, Impt. *1,800.*
Never hinged *4,000.*
Nos. 276-284 (9) 487.00 35.05
Set, never hinged 1,020.

1918 Wmk. Single-lined PIPS (190PI) ***Perf. 11***
285 A40 2c **green** *(40,000,000)* 21.00 4.25
Never hinged 40.00
P# block of 6, no Impt. 225.00
Never hinged 425.00
a. Booklet pane of 6 *(50,040)* *600.00 800.00*
Never hinged *1,100.*
286 A40 4c **carmine** *(3,000,000)* 26.00 6.00
Never hinged 55.00
P# block of 6, no Impt. 400.00
Never hinged 850.00
a. Booklet pane of 6 *1,350. 2,000.*
287 A40 6c **deep violet** *(1,000,000)* 40.00 6.00
Never hinged 90.00
P# block of 10, Impt. 550.00
Never hinged 1,250.
287A A40 8c **light brown** *(200,000)* 220.00 25.00
Never hinged 400.00
P# block of 10, Impt. *2,750.*
Never hinged *5,000.*
288 A40 10c **dark blue** *(2,000,000)* 60.00 3.00
Never hinged 140.00
P# block of 10, Impt. 650.00
Never hinged 1,400.
289 A40 16c **olive green** *(700,000)* 110.00 10.00
Never hinged 250.00
P# block of 10, Impt. 1,400.
Never hinged *3,200.*
289A A40 20c **orange** *(1,000,000)* 175.00 12.00
Never hinged 400.00
P# block of 10, Impt. 1,950.
Never hinged *4,400.*
289C A40 30c **gray** *(500,000)* 95.00 18.00
Never hinged 215.00
P# block of 10, Impt. 1,500.
Never hinged *3,400.*
289D A40 1p **pale violet** *(200,000)* 100.00 25.00
Never hinged 225.00
P# block of 10, Impt. 1,600.
Never hinged *3,600.*
Nos. 285-289D (9) 847.00 109.25
Set, never hinged 1,815.

1917 Unwmk. ***Perf. 11***
290 A40 2c **yellow green** *(444,746,800)* .25 .25
Never hinged .55
On cover 4.00
P# block of 6, no Impt. 100.00
Never hinged 140.00
a. 2c **dark green** .30 .25
Never hinged .65
green .25 .25
Double transfer — —
P# block of 6, no Impt. 17.50
Never hinged 30.00
b. Vert. pair, imperf. horiz. *2,000.*
c. Horiz. pair, imperf. between *1,500.* —
d. Vertical pair, imperf. btwn. *1,750. 1,000.*
e. Booklet pane of 6 *(3,251,080)* 27.50 *30.00*
Never hinged 60.00
291 A40 4c **carmine** *(50,579,100)* .30 .25
Never hinged .65
On cover 6.00
P# block of 6, no Impt. 15.00
Never hinged 30.00
a. 4c **light rose** .30 .25
Never hinged .65
P# block of 6, no Impt. 15.00
Never hinged 30.00
b. Booklet pane of 6 *(500,820)* 20.00 *22.50*
Never hinged 35.00
292 A40 6c **deep violet** *(8,803,600)* .35 .25
Never hinged .70
P# block of 10, Impt. 22.50
Never hinged 40.00
a. 6c **lilac** .40 .25
Never hinged .80
P# block of 10, Impt. 22.50
Never hinged 40.00
b. 6c **red violet** .40 .25
Never hinged .70
P# block of 10, Impt. 22.50
Never hinged 40.00
c. Booklet pane of 6 *(75)* *550.00 800.00*
Never hinged *900.00*
293 A40 8c **yellow brown** *(6,036,700)* .30 .25
Never hinged .50
P# block of 10, Impt. 25.00
Never hinged 45.00
a. 8c **orange brown** .30 .25
Never hinged .50
P# block of 6, no Impt. 30.00
Never hinged 55.00
294 A40 10c **deep blue** *(15,848,800)* .30 .25
Never hinged .65
P# block of 10, Impt. 19.00
Never hinged 35.00
295 A40 12c **red orange** *(3,396,500)* .35 .25
Never hinged .75
P# block of 10, Impt. 55.00
Never hinged 125.00
296 A40 16c **light olive green** *(3,249,600)* 65.00 .25
Never hinged 130.00
P# block of 10, Impt. 950.00
Never hinged 2,000.
a. 16c **olive bister** 65.00 .50
Never hinged 130.00
P# block of 10, Impt. 1,000.
Never hinged 2,000.
297 A40 20c **orange yellow** *(10,814,600)* .35 .25
Never hinged .75
P# block of 10, Impt. 37.50
Never hinged 85.00
298 A40 26c **green** *(1,595,400)* .50 .45
Never hinged 1.10
P# block of 10, Impt. 47.50
Never hinged 120.00
a. 26c **blue green** .60 .25
Never hinged 1.35
P# block of 10, Impt. 62.50
Never hinged 140.00
299 A40 30c **gray** *(6,031,300)* .55 .25
Never hinged 1.35
P# block of 10, Impt. 52.50
Never hinged 90.00
Dark gray .55 .25
300 A40 1p **pale violet** *(1,173,200)* 40.00 2.00
Never hinged 90.00
P# block of 10, Impt. 375.00
Never hinged 950.00
a. 1p **red lilac** 40.00 2.50
Never hinged 90.00
P# block of 10, Impt. 425.00
Never hinged 1,050.
b. 1p **pale rose lilac** 40.00 1.10
Never hinged 90.00
P# block of 10, Impt. 425.00
Never hinged 1,050.
301 A40 2p **violet brown** *(475,300)* 35.00 1.00
Never hinged 77.50
P# block of 10, Impt. 450.00
Never hinged 1,000.
302 A40 4p **blue** *(541,800)* 32.50 .50
Never hinged 72.50
P# block of 10, Impt. 450.00
Never hinged 1,000.
a. 4p **dark blue** 35.00 .55
Never hinged 77.50
P# block of 10, Impt. 450.00
Never hinged 1,000.
Nos. 290-302 (13) 175.75 6.20
Set, never hinged 377.00

1923-26
303 A40 16c **olive bister** *(Adm. George Dewey) (13,524,300)* 1.00 .25
Never hinged 2.25
P# block of 6, no Impt. 16.50
Never hinged 37.50
a. 16c **olive green** 1.25 .25
Never hinged 2.75
P# block of 6, no Impt. 15.00
Never hinged 35.00
304 A40 10p **deep green** ('26) *(32,400)* 50.00 20.00
Never hinged 110.00
Block of 4 210.00 90.00

Legislative Palace Issue

Issued to commemorate the opening of the Legislative Palace.

Legislative Palace — A42

Printed by the Philippine Bureau of Printing and issued in panes of 50 without plate numbers or imprints.

1926, Dec. 20 Unwmk. ***Perf. 12***
319 A42 2c **green & black** *(502,300)* .50 .25
Never hinged 1.25
First day cover 3.50
Corner margin block of 4 2.50 1.25
Never hinged 5.00
a. Horiz. pair, imperf. between *200.00*
b. Vert. pair, imperf. between *375.00*
320 A42 4c **carmine & black** *(304,150)* .55 .40
Never hinged 1.20
First day cover 3.50
Corner margin block of 4 2.75 1.75
Never hinged 5.50
a. Horiz. pair, imperf. between *275.00*
b. Vert. pair, imperf. between *400.00*
321 A42 16c **olive green & black** *(203,500)* 1.00 .65
Never hinged 2.25
First day cover 10.00
Corner margin block of 4 5.25 3.25
Never hinged 10.75
a. Horiz. pair, imperf. between *250.00*
b. Vert. pair, imperf. between *425.00*
c. Double impression of center *675.00*
322 A42 18c **light brown & black** *(103,700)* 1.10 .50
Never hinged 2.50
First day cover 10.00
Corner margin block of 4 5.25 2.50
Never hinged 10.75
a. Double impression of center *(150)* *850.00*
b. Vertical pair, imperf. between *475.00*
323 A42 20c **orange & black** *(103,200)* 2.00 1.00
Never hinged 4.50
Corner margin block of 4 10.00 6.00
Never hinged 22.50
a. 20c **orange & brown** *(100)* *600.00* —
b. As No. 323, imperf., pair *(50)* *575.00 575.00*
c. As "a," imperf., pair *(100)* *1,750.*
d. Vert. pair, imperf. between *500.00*
324 A42 24c **gray & black** *(103,100)* 1.00 .55
Never hinged 2.25
Corner margin block of 4 5.00 3.00
Never hinged 10.50
a. Vert. pair, imperf. between *500.00*
325 A42 1p **rose lilac & black** *(10,800)* 47.50 50.00
Never hinged 70.00
Corner margin block of 4 225.00 165.00
Never hinged 330.00
a. Vert. pair, imperf. between *500.00*
First day cover, #319-325 400.00
Nos. 319-325 (7) 53.65 53.35
Set, never hinged 83.95

No. 322a is valued in the grade of fine.

Rizal Type of 1906

Coil Stamp

Printed by the U.S. Bureau of Engraving and Printing.

1928 Unwmk. ***Perf. 11 Vertically***
326 A40 2c **green** *(110,000)* 7.50 *12.50*
Never hinged 19.00
On cover 100.00
Pair 17.50 *32.50*
Line pair 55.00 *100.00*
Never hinged 140.00

Types of 1906-1923

1925-31 Unwmk. ***Imperf.***
340 A40 2c **yellow green** ('31) *(99,986)* .50 .50
Never hinged .90
P# block of 6, no Impt. 25.00
Never hinged 37.50
a. 2c **green** ('25) *(51,000)* .80 .75
Never hinged 1.80
P# block of 6, no Impt. 52.50
Never hinged 77.50
341 A40 4c **carmine rose** ('31) *(49,855)* .50 *1.00*
Never hinged 1.00
P# block of 6, no Impt. 27.50
Never hinged 42.50
a. 4c **carmine** ('25) *(25,500)* 1.20 1.00
Never hinged 2.75
P# block of 6, no Impt. 55.00
Never hinged 85.00
342 A40 6c **violet** ('31) *(10,000)* 3.00 3.75
Never hinged 5.00
P# block of 10, Impt. 115.00
Never hinged 160.00

a. 6c **deep violet** ('25) *(5,200)* 12.00 8.00
Never hinged 26.00
P# block of 10, Impt. 300.00
Never hinged 400.00
343 A40 8c **brown** ('31) *(10,000)* 2.00 *5.00*
Never hinged 4.00
P# block of 10, Impt. 125.00
Never hinged 180.00
P# block of 6, no Impt. 120.00
Never hinged 170.00
a. 8c **yellow brown** ('25) *(5,200)* 13.00 8.00
Never hinged 26.00
P# block of 10, Impt. *320.00*
Never hinged 425.00
344 A40 10c **blue** ('31) *(7,000)* 5.00 *7.50*
Never hinged 12.00
P# block of 10, Impt. 375.00
Never hinged 500.00
a. 10c **deep blue** ('25) *(2,200)* 45.00 20.00
Never hinged 100.00
P# block of 10, Impt. *900.00*
Never hinged 1,300.
345 A40 12c **deep orange** ('31) *(7,000)* 8.00 10.00
Never hinged 15.00
P# block of 10, Impt. 500.00
Never hinged 700.00
P# block of 6, no Impt. 475.00
Never hinged 675.00
a. 12c **red orange** ('25) *(2,200)* 60.00 35.00
Never hinged 135.00
P# block of 10, Impt. *1,225.*
Never hinged 1,750.
P# block of 6, no Impt. *1,000.*
346 A40 16c **olive green** *(Dewey)* ('31) *(7,000)* 6.00 7.50
Never hinged 11.00
P# block of 6, no Impt. 375.00
Never hinged 550.00
a. 16c **bister green** ('25) *(2,200)* 42.50 18.00
Never hinged 100.00
P# block of 6, no Impt. *750.00*
Never hinged 1,100.
347 A40 20c **deep yellow orange** ('31) *(7,000)* 5.00 *7.50*
Never hinged 11.00
P# block of 10, Impt. 425.00
Never hinged 600.00
a. 20c **yellow orange** ('25) *(2,200)* 45.00 20.00
Never hinged 100.00
P# block of 10, Impt. *900.00*
Never hinged 1,300.
348 A40 26c **green** ('31) *(7,000)* 6.00 *9.00*
Never hinged 11.00
P# block of 10, Impt. 550.00
Never hinged 775.00
P# block of 6, no Impt. 550.00
Never hinged 775.00
a. 26c **blue green** ('25) *(2,200)* 45.00 25.00
Never hinged 110.00
P# block of 10, Impt. *1,000.*
Never hinged 1,450.
349 A40 30c **light gray** ('31) *(7,000)* 8.00 10.00
Never hinged 16.00
P# block of 10, Impt. 450.00
Never hinged 650.00
a. 30c **gray** ('25) *(2,200)* 45.00 25.00
Never hinged 110.00
P# block of 10, Impt. *950.00*
Never hinged 1,400.
350 A40 1p **light violet** ('31) *(6,395)* 10.00 *15.00*
Never hinged 20.00
P# block of 10, Impt. 875.00
Never hinged 1,250.
a. 1p **violet** ('25) *(2,100)* 200.00 100.00
Never hinged 425.00
P# block of 10, Impt. 3,700.
Never hinged *4,800.*
351 A40 2p **brown violet** ('31) *(3,612)* 30.00 *45.00*
Never hinged 80.00
P# block of 10, Impt. 1,600.
Never hinged 2,200.
a. 2p **violet brown** ('25) *(600)* 400.00 400.00
Never hinged 675.00
P# block of 10, Impt. *5,750.*
Never hinged *8,250.*
352 A40 4p **blue** ('31) *(2,570)* 80.00 90.00
Never hinged 150.00
Block of 4 350.00 —
P# block of 10, Impt. —
a. 4p **deep blue** ('25) *(300)* 2,200. 1,100.
Never hinged 3,500.
Block of 4 *9,000.*
353 A40 10p **green** ('31) *(2,208)* 175.00 *225.00*
Never hinged 300.00
Block of 4 700.00
a. 10p **deep green** ('25) *(200)* 2,750. *2,950.*
Never hinged 4,250.
P# block of 10, Impt., never hinged *45,000.*
Nos. 340-353 (14) 339.00 436.75
Set, never hinged 636.90

Nos. 340a-353a were the original post office issue. These were reprinted twice in 1931 for sale to collectors (Nos. 340-353).

Mount Mayon, Luzon — A43

Post Office, Manila — A44

Pier No. 7, Manila Bay — A45

Vernal Falls, Yosemite Park, California (See Footnote) — A46

Rice Planting — A47

Rice Terraces — A48

Baguio Zigzag — A49

1932, May 3 **Unwmk.** ***Perf. 11***
354 A43 2c **yellow green** *(5,432,000)* .75 .30
Never hinged 1.25
First day cover 2.00
P# block of 6 20.00
Never hinged 25.00
355 A44 4c **rose carmine** *(1,602,800)* .75 .30
Never hinged 1.25
First day cover 2.00
P# block of 6 16.00
Never hinged 20.00
356 A45 12c **orange** *(483,000)* .90 .75
Never hinged 1.30
First day cover 6.50
P# block of 6 32.50
Never hinged 40.00
357 A46 18c **red orange** *(983,400)* 45.00 15.00
Never hinged 72.50
First day cover 16.00
P# block of 6 350.00
Never hinged 550.00
358 A47 20c **yellow** *(441,000)* 1.00 .75
Never hinged 1.60
First day cover 6.50
P# block of 6 32.50
Never hinged 40.00
359 A48 24c **deep violet** *(425,000)* 1.60 1.00
Never hinged 2.75
First day cover 6.50
P# block of 6 35.00
Never hinged 45.00
360 A49 32c **olive brown** *(510,600)* 1.60 1.00
Never hinged 2.75
First day cover 6.50
P# block of 6 27.50
Never hinged 35.00
First day cover, #354-360 50.00
Nos. 354-360 (7) 51.60 19.10
Set, never hinged 83.40

The 18c vignette was intended to show Pagsanjan Falls in Laguna, central Luzon, and is so labeled. Through error the stamp pictures Vernal Falls in Yosemite National Park, California.

For overprints see #C29-C35, C47-C51, C63.

Nos. 302, 302a Surcharged in Orange or Red

1932
368 A40 1p on 4p **blue** (O) *(134,000)* 6.00 1.00
Never hinged 9.75
On cover 1.00
P# block of 10, Impt. 140.00
Never hinged 175.00
a. 1p on 4p **dark blue** (O) 6.00 1.00
Never hinged 9.25
P# block of 10, Impt. 140.00
Never hinged 175.00
369 A40 2p on 4p **dark blue** (R) *(80,000)* 9.00 1.50
Never hinged 15.00
P# block of 10, Impt. 160.00
Never hinged 200.00
a. 2p on 4p **blue** (R) 9.00 1.00
Never hinged 15.00
On cover 2.00
P# block of 10, Impt. 160.00
Never hinged 200.00

Far Eastern Championship

Issued in commemoration of the Tenth Far Eastern Championship Games.

Baseball Players — A50

Tennis Player — A51

Basketball Players — A52

Printed by the Philippine Bureau of Printing.

1934, Apr. 14 **Unwmk.** ***Perf. 11½***
380 A50 2c **yellow brown** *(999,985)* 1.50 .80
brown 1.50 .80
Never hinged 2.25
First day cover 2.00
"T" of "Eastern" malformed 2.00 1.25
381 A51 6c **ultramarine** *(800,000)* .25 .25
pale ultramarine .25 .25
Never hinged .30
First day cover 1.60
a. Vertical pair, imperf. between *700.00*
Never hinged *1,100.*
382 A52 16c **violet brown** *(500,000)* .50 .50
dark violet .50 .50
Never hinged .75
First day cover 2.25
a. Vert. pair, imperf. horiz. *950.00*
Never hinged *1,500.*
Nos. 380-382 (3) 2.25 1.55
Set, never hinged 3.30

José Rizal — A53

Woman and Carabao — A54

La Filipina — A55

Pearl Fishing — A56

Fort Santiago — A57

Salt Spring — A58

Magellan's Landing, 1521 — A59

"Juan de la Cruz" — A60

Rice Terraces — A61

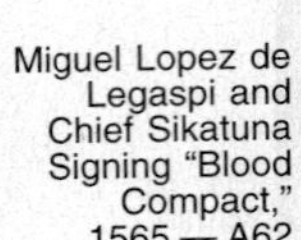

Miguel Lopez de Legaspi and Chief Sikatuna Signing "Blood Compact," 1565 — A62

Barasoain Church, Malolos A63

Battle of Manila Bay, 1898 — A64

Montalban Gorge — A65

George Washington — A66

Printed by U.S. Bureau of Engraving and Printing.

1935, Feb. 15 **Unwmk.** ***Perf. 11***

383 A53 2c **rose** *(62,183,400)*	.25	.25
Never hinged	.25	
First day cover		1.00
P# block of 6	25.00	
Never hinged	35.00	
384 A54 4c **yellow green** *(14,238,193)*	.25	.25
Light yellow green	.25	.25
Never hinged	.25	
First day cover		1.00
P# block of 6	2.00	
Never hinged	2.50	
385 A55 6c **dark brown** *(1,958,928)*	.25	.25
Never hinged	.35	
First day cover		1.00
P# block of 6	12.00	
Never hinged	15.00	
386 A56 8c **violet** *(792,000)*	.25	.25
Never hinged	.35	
First day cover		1.60
P# block of 6	16.00	
Never hinged	20.00	
387 A57 10c **rose carmine** *(341,400)*	.30	.25
Never hinged	.45	
First day cover		1.60
P# block of 6	16.00	
Never hinged	20.00	
388 A58 12c **black** *(319,500)*	.35	.25
Never hinged	.50	
First day cover		1.60
P# block of 6	16.00	
Never hinged	20.00	
389 A59 16c **dark blue** *(2,422,778)*	.35	.25
Never hinged	.55	
First day cover		1.60
P# block of 6	16.00	
Never hinged	20.00	
390 A60 20c **light olive green** *(1,061,400)*	.35	.25
Never hinged	.45	
First day cover		2.25
P# block of 6	20.00	
Never hinged	25.00	
391 A61 26c **indigo** *(212,000)*	.40	.40
Never hinged	.60	
First day cover		3.00
P# block of 6	16.00	
Never hinged	20.00	
392 A62 30c **orange red** *(171,200)*	.40	.40
Never hinged	.60	
First day cover		3.00
P# block of 6	20.00	
Never hinged	25.00	
393 A63 1p **red orange & black** *(80,000)*	2.00	1.25
Never hinged	3.00	
First day cover		8.25
P# block of 4, 2 P#	32.50	
Never hinged	40.00	
394 A64 2p **bister brown & black** *(61,100)*	12.00	2.00
Never hinged	16.00	
First day cover		14.00
P# block of 4, 2 P#	65.00	
Never hinged	75.00	
395 A65 4p **blue & black** *(59,000)*	12.00	4.00
Never hinged	16.00	
First day cover		
P# block of 4, 2 P#	67.50	
Never hinged	85.00	
396 A66 5p **green & black** *(54,000)*	25.00	5.00
Never hinged	50.00	
First day cover		27.50
P# block of 4, 2 P#	110.00	
Never hinged	225.00	
Nos. 383-396 (14)	54.15	15.05
Set, never hinged	74.45	

USED VALUES

Used values in italics are for postally used examples with cancels of the proper function during the correct period of use.

Issues of the Commonwealth

Commonwealth Inauguration Issue

Issued to commemorate the inauguration of the Philippine Commonwealth, Nov. 15, 1935.

"The Temples of Human Progress" — A67

1935, Nov. 15 **Unwmk.** ***Perf. 11***

397 A67 2c **carmine rose** *(1,531,000)*	.25	.25
Never hinged	.35	
First day cover		1.00
P# block of 6	2.40	
Never hinged	3.00	
398 A67 6c **deep violet** *(523,000)*	.25	.25
Never hinged	.35	
First day cover		1.00
P# block of 6	3.20	
Never hinged	4.00	
399 A67 16c **blue** *(313,500)*	.25	.25
Never hinged	.40	
First day cover		1.00
P# block of 6	4.75	
Never hinged	6.00	
400 A67 36c **yellow green** *(261,000)*	.40	.30
Never hinged	.65	
First day cover		1.40
P# block of 6	6.75	
Never hinged	8.50	
401 A67 50c **brown** *(218,500)*	.70	.55
Never hinged	1.00	
First day cover		2.00
P# block of 6	9.50	
Never hinged	12.00	
Nos. 397-401 (5)	1.85	1.60
Set, never hinged	2.75	

Jose Rizal Issue

75th anniversary of the birth of Jose Rizal (1861-1896), national hero of the Filipinos.

Jose Rizal — A68

Printed by the Philippine Bureau of Printing.

1936, June 19 Unwmk. *Perf. 12*
402 A68 2c **yellow brown** *(500,000)* .25 .25
light yellow brown .25 .25
Never hinged .25
First day cover 1.00
403 A68 6c **slate blue** *(300,000)* .25 .25
light slate green .25 .25
Never hinged .25
First day cover 1.00
a. Imperf. vertically, pair *1,000.*
Never hinged *1,500.*
404 A68 36c **red brown** *(200,000)* .50 *.70*
light red brown .50 .70
Never hinged .75
First day cover 2.25
Nos. 402-404 (3) 1.00 1.20
Set, never hinged 1.25

Commonwealth Anniversary Issue

Issued in commemoration of the first anniversary of the Commonwealth.

President Manuel L. Quezon — A69

Printed by U.S. Bureau of Engraving and Printing.

1936, Nov. 15 Unwmk. *Perf. 11*
408 A69 2c **orange brown** *(4,946,816)* .25 .25
Never hinged .30
First day cover 1.00
P# block of 6 6.50
Never hinged 8.00
409 A69 6c **yellow green** *(1,019,900)* .25 .25
Never hinged .30
First day cover 1.00
P# block of 6 6.50
Never hinged 8.00
410 A69 12c **ultramarine** *(527,600)* .25 .25
Never hinged .30
First day cover 1.50
P# block of 6 6.50
Never hinged 8.00
Nos. 408-410 (3) .75 .75
Set, never hinged .90

Stamps of 1935 Overprinted in Black

a

b

1936-37 Unwmk. *Perf. 11*
411 A53(a) 2c **rose,** *Dec. 28, 1936 (84,092,400)* .25 .25
Never hinged .25
First day cover *35.00*
P# block of 6 12.00
Never hinged 15.00
a. Bklt. pane of 6, *Jan. 15 1937 (239,492)* 2.50 2.00
Never hinged 4.00
First day cover *40.00*
b. Hyphen omitted 125.00 100.00
412 A54(b) 4c **yellow green,** *Mar. 29, 1937 (100,000)* .45 *4.00*
Never hinged .70
P# block of 6 35.00
Never hinged 45.00
413 A55(a) 6c **dark brown,** *Oct. 7, 1936 (2,230,394)* .25 .25
Never hinged .25
On cover .25
P# block of 6 5.50
Never hinged 7.00
414 A56(b) 8c **violet,** *Mar. 29, 1937 (627,500)* .25 .25
Never hinged .35
On cover .75
P# block of 6 9.50
Never hinged 12.00
415 A57(b) 10c **rose carmine,** *Dec. 28, 1936 (1,687,550)* .25 .25
Never hinged .25
First day cover 35.00
P# block of 6 4.75
Never hinged 6.00
a. "COMMONWEALT" 20.00 —
Never hinged 30.00
416 A58(b) 12c **black,** *Mar. 29, 1937 (2,118,600)* .25 .25
Never hinged .30
On cover .75
P# block of 6 9.50
Never hinged 12.00
417 A59(b) 16c **dark blue,** *Oct. 7, 1936 (597,300)* .25 .25
Never hinged .40
On cover .75
P# block of 6 12.00
Never hinged 15.00
418 A60(a) 20c **lt olive green,** *Mar. 29, 1937 (100,000)* .90 .40
Never hinged 1.50
On cover .85
P# block of 6 16.00
Never hinged 20.00
419 A61(b) 26c **indigo,** *Mar. 29, 1937 (100,000)* .80 .35
Never hinged 1.40
On cover .85
P# block of 6 20.00
Never hinged 25.00
420 A62(b) 30c **orange red,** *Dec. 28, 1936 (836,252)* .45 .25
Never hinged .75
First day cover *35.00*
P# block of 6 9.50
Never hinged 12.00
421 A63(b) 1p **red org & blk,** *Oct. 7, 1936 (319,250)* .90 .25
Never hinged 1.50
On cover .75
P# block of 4 27.50
Never hinged 35.00
422 A64(b) 2p **bis brn & blk,** *Mar. 29, 1937 (50,000)* 12.50 4.00
Never hinged 21.00
On cover 6.00
P# block of 4 100.00
Never hinged 130.00
423 A65(b) 4p **blue & blk,** *Mar. 29, 1937 (30,000)* 45.00 8.00
Never hinged 72.50
On cover *50.00*
P# block of 4 225.00
Never hinged 375.00
424 A66(b) 5p **green & blk,** *Mar. 29, 1937 (60,500)* 12.50 *25.00*
Never hinged 21.00
On cover *40.00*
P# block of 4 140.00
Never hinged 175.00
Nos. 411-424 (14) 75.00 43.75
Set, never hinged 122.15

Eucharistic Congress Issue

Issued to commemorate the 33rd International Eucharistic Congress held at Manila, Feb. 3-7, 1937.

Map, Symbolical of the Eucharistic Congress Spreading Light of Christianity — A70

FLAT PLATE PRINTING

Plates of 256 subjects in four panes of 64 each.

1937, Feb. 3 Unwmk. *Perf. 11*
425 A70 2c **yellow green** *(4,102,848)* .25 .25
Never hinged .25
First day cover 1.00
P# block of 6 4.00
Never hinged 5.00
426 A70 6c **light brown** *(2,626,240)* .25 .25
Never hinged .25
First day cover 1.00
P# block of 6 4.00
Never hinged 5.00
427 A70 12c **sapphire** *(2,165,440)* .25 .25
Never hinged .25
First day cover 1.00
P# block of 6 4.00
Never hinged 5.00
428 A70 20c **deep orange** *(1,640,640)* .30 .25
Never hinged .50
First day cover 1.00
P# block of 6 5.50
Never hinged 7.00
429 A70 36c **deep violet** *(1,115,840)* .55 .40
Never hinged .80
First day cover 1.40
P# block of 6 8.00
Never hinged 10.00
430 A70 50c **carmine** *(1,115,840)* .70 .35
Never hinged 1.10
First day cover 2.00
P# block of 6 10.00
Never hinged 15.00
Nos. 425-430 (6) 2.30 1.75
Set, never hinged 3.15

Arms of City of Manila — A71

1937, Aug. 27 Unwmk. *Perf. 11*
431 A71 10p **gray** *(70,000)* 5.00 2.00
Never hinged 7.25
P# block of 6 67.50
Never hinged 85.00
432 A71 20p **henna brown** *(90,600)* 4.00 1.40
Never hinged 6.50
First day cover, #431-432 50.00
P# block of 6 65.00
Never hinged 80.00

Stamps of 1935 Overprinted in Black

a

b

1938-40 Unwmk. *Perf. 11*
433 A53(a) 2c **rose,** *1939 (103,549,959)* .25 .25
Never hinged .25
P# block of 6 8.00
Never hinged 10.00
a. Booklet pane of 6 *(157,176)* 3.50 3.50
Never hinged 5.50
b. As "a," lower left-hand stamp overprinted "WEALTH COMMON-" *(24)* *2,000.*
Never hinged *3,250.*
c. Hyphen omitted 100.00 50.00
434 A54(b) 4c **yellow green,** *1940 (72,500)* 3.00 *30.00*
Never hinged 4.75
P# block of 6 35.00
Never hinged 45.00
435 A55(a) 6c **dark brown,** *May 12, 1939 (4,013,440)* .25 .25
Never hinged .40
First day cover *35.00*
P# block of 6 5.50
Never hinged 7.00
a. 6c **golden brown** .25 .25
Never hinged .40
P# block of 6 5.50
Never hinged 7.00
436 A56(b) 8c **violet,** *1939 (1,583,357)* .25 *1.75*
Never hinged .25
P# block of 6 8.00
Never hinged 10.00
a. "COMMONWEALT" (LR 31) 90.00
Never hinged 140.00
437 A57(b) 10c **rose carmine,** *May 12, 1939 (2,695,242)* .25 .25
Never hinged .25
P# block of 6 8.00
Never hinged 10.00
a. "COMMONWEALT" (LR 31) 65.00 —
Never hinged 100.00

438 A58(b) 12c **black,** *1940 (3,765,000)* .25 *1.00*
Never hinged .25
P# block of 6 8.00
Never hinged 10.00
439 A59(b) 16c **dark blue** *(1,415,700)* .25 .25
Never hinged .25
P# block of 6 16.00
Never hinged 20.00
440 A60(a) 20c **light olive green,** *1939 (1,663,799)* .25 .25
Never hinged .25
P# block of 6 12.00
Never hinged 15.00
441 A61(b) 26c **indigo,** *1940 (597,500)* 1.00 *2.50*
Never hinged 1.50
P# block of 6 16.00
Never hinged 20.00
442 A62(b) 30c **orange red,** *May 23, 1939 (643,100)* 3.00 .70
Never hinged 5.00
P# block of 6 22.50
Never hinged 35.00
443 A63(b) 1p **red org & blk,** *Aug. 29, 1938 (1,065,629)* .60 .25
Never hinged 1.00
First day cover *40.00*
P# block of 4 27.50
Never hinged 35.00
444 A64(b) 2p **bister brown & black,** *1939 (98,000)* 10.00 1.00
Never hinged 15.00
P# block of 4 87.50
Never hinged 110.00
445 A65(b) 4p **blue & black,** *1940 (6,500)* 150.00 250.00
Never hinged 325.00
On cover 500.00
P# block of 4 *700.00*
Never hinged *1,500.*
446 A66(b) 5p **green & black,** *1940 (31,500)* 20.00 8.00
Never hinged 35.00
P# block of 4 200.00
Never hinged 250.00
Nos. 433-446 (14) 189.35 *296.45*
Set, never hinged 414.15

Overprint "b" measures 18½x1¾mm.

No. 433b occurs in booklet pane, No. 433a, position 5; all examples are straight-edged, left and bottom.

All bottom plate blocks of Nos. 433-443 have selvage that was shortened by cutting by the Bureau of Engraving and Printint to set up the proper plate size for positioning the small "COMMON-WEALTH" overprint. This selvage reduction cuts through the plate numbers and is the natural format.

First Foreign Trade Week Issue

Nos. 384, 298a and 432 Surcharged in Red, Violet or Black

a

b

c

1939, July 5

449 A54(a) 2c on 4c **yellow green** (R) *(500,000)* .25 .25
Never hinged .35
First day cover 1.40
P# block of 6 13.50
Never hinged 17.00
450 A40(b) 6c on 26c **blue green** (V) *(166,700)* .25 .50
Never hinged .35
First day cover 2.00
Left arrow block of 4 16.00
Never hinged 20.00
a. 6c on 26c **green** 3.00 1.00
Never hinged 5.00
451 A71(c) 50c on 20p **henna brown** (Bk) *(60,000)* 1.25 1.00
Never hinged 2.00
First day cover 5.00
P# block of 6 27.50
Never hinged 35.00
Nos. 449-451 (3) 1.75 1.75
Set, never hinged 2.70

There are no known reports of plate blocks of Nos. 450 or 450a.

Commonwealth 4th Anniversary Issue (#452-460)

Triumphal Arch — A72

Printed by U.S. Bureau of Engraving and Printing.

1939, Nov. 15 **Unwmk.** ***Perf. 11***

452 A72 2c **yellow green** *(1,562,352)* .25 .25
Never hinged .25
First day cover 1.00
P# block of 6 4.00
Never hinged 5.00
453 A72 6c **carmine** *(1,267,717)* .25 .25
Never hinged .25
First day cover 1.00
P# block of 6 5.50
Never hinged 7.00
454 A72 12c **bright blue** *(971,724)* .25 .25
Never hinged .25
First day cover 1.40
P# block of 6 9.50
Never hinged 12.00
Nos. 452-454 (3) .75 .75
Set, never hinged .75

For overprints see Nos. 469, 476.

Malacañan Palace — A73

1939, Nov. 15 **Unwmk.** ***Perf. 11***

455 A73 2c **green** *(1,578,600)* .25 .25
Never hinged .25
First day cover 1.00
P# block of 6 4.00
Never hinged 5.00
456 A73 6c **orange** *(1,252,859)* .25 .25
Never hinged .25
First day cover 1.00
P# block of 6 6.00
Never hinged 7.50
457 A73 12c **carmine** *(935,800)* .25 .25
Never hinged .25
First day cover 1.40
P# block of 6 9.50
Never hinged 12.00
Nos. 455-457 (3) .75 .75
Set, never hinged .75

For overprint, see No. 470.

President Quezon Taking Oath of Office — A74

1940, Feb. 8 **Unwmk.** ***Perf. 11***

458 A74 2c **dark orange** *(1,572,400)* .25 .25
Never hinged .25
First day cover 1.00
P# block of 6 4.00
Never hinged 5.00
459 A74 6c **dark green** *(1,257,900)* .25 .25
Never hinged .25
First day cover 1.00
P# block of 6 6.00
Never hinged 5.00
460 A74 12c **purple** *(980,779)* .25 .25
Never hinged .30
First day cover 1.40
P# block of 6 9.50
Never hinged 12.00
Nos. 458-460 (3) .75 .75
Set, never hinged .80

For overprints, see Nos. 471, 477.

José Rizal — A75

ROTARY PRESS PRINTING

1941, Apr. 14 **Unwmk.** ***Perf. 11x10½***
Size: 19x22½mm

461 A75 2c **apple green** *(59,915,600)* .25 *.50*
Never hinged .25
First day cover 1.00
P# block of 4 2.00
Never hinged 2.50

FLAT PLATE PRINTING

1941, Nov. 14 **Unwmk.** ***Perf. 11***
Size: 18¾x22¼mm

462 A75 2c **pale apple green** 1.00 —
Never hinged 1.25
a. Booklet pane of 6 6.00 —
Never hinged 7.50

No. 461 was issued only in sheets. No. 462 was issued only in booklet panes on Nov. 14, 1941, just before the war, and only a few used stamps and covers exist. All examples have one or two straight edges. Mint booklets reappeared after the war. In August 1942, the booklet pane was reprinted in a darker shade (apple green). However, the apple green panes were available only to U.S. collectors during the war years, so no war-period used stamps from the Philippines exist. Value of apple green booklet pane, never hinged, $6.

For type A75 overprinted, see Nos. 464, O37, O39, N1 and NO1.

Stamps of 1935-41 Handstamped in Violet

1944 **Unwmk.** ***Perf. 11, 11x10½***

463 A53 2c **rose** (On 411), *Dec. 3 (168)* *1,250.* *650.00*
a. Booklet pane of 6 *(28)* *12,500.*
463B A53 2c **rose** (On 433), *Dec. 14 (41)* *2,000.* *1,750.*
464 A75 2c **apple green** (On 461), *Nov. 8 (24,400)* 12.50 10.00
Never hinged 22.50
On cover 20.00
P# block of 4 72.50
Never hinged 110.00
a. Pair, one without ovpt. — —
465 A54 4c **yellow green** (On 384), *Nov. 8 (807)* 47.50 *50.00*
Never hinged 80.00
On cover —
466 A55 6c **dark brown** (On 385), *Dec. 14 (64)* *3,250.* *2,000.*
On cover —
467 A69 6c **yellow green** (On 409), *Dec. 3* 300.00 *150.00*
Never hinged *525.00*
On cover —
468 A55 6c **dark brown** (On 413), *Dec. 28 (206)* *4,750.* *825.00*
On cover —
469 A72 6c **carmine** (On 453), *Nov. 8 (235)* *350.00* *125.00*
On cover —
470 A73 6c **orange** (On 456), *Dec. 14 (141)* *1,750.* *725.00*
On cover —
471 A74 6c **dark green** (On 459), *Nov. 8* *275.00* *225.00*
On cover —
P# block of 6 *1,700.*
472 A56 8c **violet** (On 436), *Nov. 8 (1,643)* 17.50 *30.00*
Never hinged 30.00
On cover —
P# block of 6 250.00
a. Pair, one without ovpt. —
473 A57 10c **carmine rose** (On 415), *Nov. 8 (450)* *350.00* *150.00*
On cover —
474 A57 10c **carmine rose** (On 437), *Nov. 8 (358)* *275.00* *200.00*
Never hinged *475.00*
On cover —
475 A69 12c **ultramarine** (On 410), *Dec. 3* *1,100.* *400.00*
On cover —
476 A72 12c **bright blue** (On 454), *Nov. 8 (36)* *7,000.* *2,500.*
On cover —
477 A74 12c **purple** (On 460), *Nov. 8* *500.00* *275.00*
On cover —

478 A59 16c **dark blue** (On 389), *Dec. 3 (122)*	*3,000.*	—
On cover		—
479 A59 16c **dark blue** (On 417), *Nov. 8 (200)*	*1,500.*	*1,000.*
On cover		—
480 A59 16c **dark blue** (On 439), *Nov. 8 (500)*	*500.00*	*200.00*
On cover		—
P# block of 6	*3,500.*	
481 A60 20c **light olive green** (On 440), *Nov. 8 (1,401)*	140.00	35.00
Never hinged	230.00	
On cover		—
482 A62 30c **orange red** (On 420), *Dec. 3 (248)*	*450.00*	*1,500.*
On cover		—
483 A62 30c **orange red** (On 442), *Dec. 3 (200)*	*800.00*	*375.00*
On cover		—
484 A63 1p **red orange & black** (On 443) *Dec. 3 (21)*	*6,250.*	*4,500.*
On cover		—

Nos. 463-484 are valued in the grade of fine to very fine.

No. 463 comes only from the booklet pane. All examples have one or two straight edges.

Types of 1935-37 Overprinted

a

b

c

1945 Unwmk. *Perf. 11*

485 A53(a) 2c **rose,** *Jan. 19 (65,816,000)*	.25	.25
Never hinged	.25	
First day cover		2.50
P# block of 6	4.00	
Never hinged	5.00	
486 A54(b) 4c **yellow green,** *Jan. 19 (4,986,800)*	.25	.25
Never hinged	.25	
First day cover		2.50
P# block of 6	12.00	
Never hinged	15.00	
487 A55(a) 6c **golden brown,** *Jan. 19 (4,381,440)*	.25	.25
Never hinged	.25	
First day cover		2.50
P# block of 6	4.00	
Never hinged	5.00	
488 A56(b) 8c **violet,** *Jan. 19 (535,000)*	.25	.25
Never hinged	.25	
First day cover		3.00
P# block of 6	5.50	
Never hinged	7.00	
489 A57(b) 10c **rose carmine,** *Jan. 19 (1,060,000)*	.25	.25
Never hinged	.25	
First day cover		3.00
P# block of 6	4.00	
Never hinged	5.00	
490 A58(b) 12c **black,** *Jan. 19 (3,214,200)*	.25	.25
Never hinged	.25	
First day cover		3.50
P# block of 6	4.00	
Never hinged	5.00	
491 A59(b) 16c **dark blue,** *Jan. 19 (1,060,000)*	.25	.25
Never hinged	.30	
First day cover		4.00
P# block of 6	4.00	
Never hinged	5.00	
492 A60(a) 20c **light olive green,** *Jan. 19 (976,800)*	.30	.25
Never hinged	.40	
First day cover		4.25
P# block of 6	9.50	
Never hinged	12.00	
493 A62(b) 30c **orange red,** *May 1 (535,000)*	.50	.35
Never hinged	.75	
First day cover		2.50
P# block of 6	12.50	
Never hinged	16.00	
494 A63(b) 1p **red orange & black,** *Jan. 19 (1,434,400)*	1.10	.25
Never hinged	1.60	
First day cover		6.50
P# block of 4, 2 P#	16.00	
Never hinged	20.00	
495 A71(c) 10p **gray,** *May 1 (22,000)*	55.00	13.50
Never hinged	90.00	
First day cover		20.00
P# block of 6	375.00	
Never hinged	600.00	
496 A71(c) 20p **henna brown,** *May 1 (42,500)*	50.00	15.00
Never hinged	75.00	
First day cover		25.00
P# block of 6	600.00	
Never hinged	750.00	
Nos. 485-496 (12)	108.65	31.10
Set, never hinged	169.55	

José Rizal — A76

ROTARY PRESS PRINTING

1946, May 28 Unwmk. *Perf. 11x10½*

497 A76 2c **sepia** *(53,560,000)*	.25	.25
Never hinged	.25	
P# block of 4	2.00	
Never hinged	2.50	

Later issues, released by the Philippine Republic on July 4, 1946, and thereafter, are listed in Scott's Standard Postage Stamp Catalogue, Vol. 5A.

AIR POST STAMPS

Madrid-Manila Flight Issue

Issued to commemorate the flight of Spanish aviators Gallarza and Loriga from Madrid to Manila.

Regular Issue of 1917-26 Overprinted in Red or Violet

Printed by the Philippine Bureau.

1926, May 13 Unwmk. *Perf. 11*

C1 A40 2c **green** (R) *(9,900)*	20.00	17.50
Never hinged	45.00	
First day cover		26.00
P# block of 6	725.00	
Never hinged	900.00	
C2 A40 4c **carmine** (V) *(8,900)*	30.00	20.00
Never hinged	55.00	
First day cover		26.00
P# block of 6	400.00	
Never hinged	500.00	
a. Inverted overprint *(100)*	*2,600.*	—
C3 A40 6c **lilac** (R) *(5,000)*	75.00	75.00
Never hinged	125.00	
First day cover		40.00
Block of 4	325.00	
C4 A40 8c **orange brown** (V) *(5,000)*	75.00	60.00
Never hinged	125.00	
First day cover		40.00
Block of 4	325.00	
C5 A40 10c **deep blue** (R) *(5,000)*	75.00	60.00
Never hinged	140.00	
First day cover		40.00
Block of 4	325.00	
C6 A40 12c **red orange** (V) *(4,000)*	80.00	65.00
Never hinged	150.00	
First day cover		42.50
Block of 4	350.00	
C7 A40 16c **light olive green** *(Sampson)* (V) *(300)*	*2,800.*	*3,250.*
Block of 4	—	
C8 A40 16c **olive bister** *(Sampson)* (R) *(100)*	*5,000.*	*5,000.*
Block of 4	—	
C9 A40 16c **olive green** *(Dewey)* (V) *(3,600)*	100.00	70.00
Never hinged	160.00	
First day cover		42.50
Block of 4	450.00	
C10 A40 20c **orange yellow** (V) *(4,000)*	100.00	80.00
Never hinged	160.00	
First day cover		42.50
Block of 4	450.00	
C11 A40 26c **blue green** (V) *(3,900)*	100.00	80.00
Never hinged	160.00	
First day cover		45.00
Block of 4	450.00	
C12 A40 30c **gray** (V) *(4,000)*	100.00	80.00
Never hinged	160.00	
First day cover		45.00
Block of 4	450.00	
C13 A40 2p **violet brown** (R) *(900)*	500.00	600.00
Never hinged	1,100.	
On cover		800.00
Block of 4	—	
C14 A40 4p **dark blue** (R) *(700)*	800.00	750.00
Never hinged	1,300.	
On cover		—
Block of 4	—	
C15 A40 10p **deep green** (V) *(500)*	1,000.	1,350.
On cover		—
Block of 4	—	

Same Overprint on No. 269
Wmk. Single-lined PIPS (190)
Perf. 12

C16 A40 26c **blue green** (V) *(100)*	*5,000.*	
Block of 4	—	

Same Overprint on No. 284
Perf. 10

C17 A40 1p **pale violet** (V) *(2,000)*	200.00	225.00
Never hinged	450.00	
On cover		—
First day cover		*225.00*
Block of 4	1,300.	
Bottom margin block of 4, P#	*1,750.*	

Overprintings of Nos. C1-C6, C9-C15 and C17 were made from two plates. Position No. 89 of the first printing shows broken left blade of propeller.

Plate blocks do not exist for Nos, C3-C16 because the Bureau of Engraving & Printing cut off all selvage from these sheets.

London-Orient Flight Issue

Issued Nov. 9, 1928, to celebrate the arrival of a British squadron of hydroplanes.

Regular Issue of 1917-25 Overprinted in Red

1928, Nov. 9 Unwmk. *Perf. 11*

C18 A40 2c **green** *(101,200)*	1.00	1.00
Never hinged	2.00	
First day cover		7.75
P# block of 6	40.00	
Never hinged	50.00	
C19 A40 4c **carmine** *(50,500)*	1.25	1.50
Never hinged	2.00	
First day cover		9.50
P# block of 6	40.00	
Never hinged	50.00	
C20 A40 6c **violet** *(12,600)*	5.00	3.00
Never hinged	10.00	
On cover		4.00
P# block of 6	60.00	
Never hinged	70.00	
C21 A40 8c **orange brown** *(10,000)*	5.00	3.00
Never hinged	10.00	
On cover		5.00
C22 A40 10c **deep blue** *(10,000)*	5.00	3.00
Never hinged	10.00	
On cover		5.00
C23 A40 12c **red orange** *(8,000)*	8.00	4.00
Never hinged	12.00	
On cover		6.00
C24 A40 16c **olive green** (No. 303a) *(12,600)*	8.00	4.00
Never hinged	12.00	
On cover		6.00
C25 A40 20c **orange yellow** *(8,000)*	8.00	4.00
Never hinged	12.00	
On cover		6.00
C26 A40 26c **blue green** *(7,000)*	20.00	8.00
Never hinged	35.00	
On cover		12.00
C27 A40 30c **gray** *(7,000)*	20.00	8.00
Never hinged	35.00	
On cover		12.00

Same Overprint on No. 271
Wmk. Single-lined PIPS (190)
Perf. 12

C28 A40 1p **pale violet** *(6,000)*	55.00	30.00
Never hinged	90.00	
On cover		34.00
Block of 4	800.00	
Never hinged	*1,000.*	
Nos. C18-C28 (11)	136.25	69.50
Set, never hinged	230.00	

Von Gronau Issue

Commemorating the visit of Capt. Wolfgang von Gronau's airplane on its round-the-world flight.

Nos. 354-360 Overprinted

Printed by the Philippine Bureau.

1932, Sept. 27 **Unwmk.** ***Perf. 11***

C29 A43 2c **yellow green** *(100,000)*	.90	.60
Never hinged	1.40	
First day cover		2.00
P# block of 6	12.00	
Never hinged	15.00	
C30 A44 4c **rose carmine** *(80,000)*	.90	.40
Never hinged	1.40	
First day cover		2.00
P# block of 6	16.00	
Never hinged	20.00	
C31 A45 12c **orange** *(55,000)*	1.25	.65
Never hinged	2.00	
On cover		1.00
P# block of 6	12.00	
Never hinged	15.00	
C32 A46 18c **red orange** *(25,305)*	5.00	5.00
Never hinged	8.00	
On cover		7.00
P# block of 6	75.00	
Never hinged	95.00	
C33 A47 20c **yellow** *(30,000)*	3.50	3.50
Never hinged	5.75	
On cover		6.00
P# block of 6	24.00	
Never hinged	30.00	
C34 A48 24c **deep violet** *(30,000)*	3.50	4.00
Never hinged	5.75	
On cover		6.00
P# block of 6	24.00	
Never hinged	30.00	
C35 A49 32c **olive brown** *(30,000)*	3.50	3.00
Never hinged	5.75	
On cover		7.00
First day cover, #C29-C35		35.00
P# block of 6	24.00	
Never hinged	30.00	
Nos. C29-C35 (7)	18.55	17.15
Set, never hinged	31.55	

Rein Issue

Commemorating the flight from Madrid to Manila of the Spanish aviator Fernando Rein y Loring.

Regular Issue of 1917-25 Overprinted in Black

1933, Apr. 11

C36 A40 2c **green** *(95,000)*	.75	.45
Never hinged	1.10	
First day cover		1.60
P# block of 6	120.00	
Never hinged	150.00	
C37 A40 4c **carmine** *(75,000)*	.90	.45
Never hinged	1.40	
First day cover		—
P# block of 6	145.00	
Never hinged	180.00	
C38 A40 6c **deep violet** *(65,000)*	1.10	.80
Never hinged	1.75	
First day cover		3.00
P# block of 10, Impt.	80.00	
Never hinged	100.00	
C39 A40 8c **orange brown** *(35,000)*	3.75	2.00
Never hinged	5.75	
P# block of 10, Impt.	120.00	
Never hinged	150.00	
C40 A40 10c **dark blue** *(35,000)*	3.75	2.25
Never hinged	5.75	
P# block of 10, Impt.	120.00	
Never hinged	150.00	
C41 A40 12c **orange** *(35,000)*	3.75	2.00
Never hinged	5.75	
P# block of 10, Impt.	120.00	
Never hinged	150.00	
C42 A40 16c **olive green** *(Dewey) (35,000)*	3.50	2.00
Never hinged	5.25	
P# block of 6	160.00	
Never hinged	200.00	
C43 A40 20c **yellow** *(35,000)*	3.75	2.00
Never hinged	5.75	
P# block of 10, Impt.	160.00	
Never hinged	200.00	
C44 A40 26c **green** *(35,000)*	3.75	2.75
Never hinged	5.75	
a. 26c **blue green**	4.00	2.00
Never hinged	6.00	
C45 A40 30c **gray** *(30,000)*	4.00	3.00
Never hinged	6.00	
First day cover, #C36-C45		40.00
Nos. C36-C45 (10)	29.00	17.70
Set, never hinged	44.25	

Stamp of 1917 Overprinted

Printed by the Philippine Bureau.

1933, May 26 **Unwmk.** ***Perf. 11***

C46 A40 2c **green** *(500,000)*	.65	.40
Never hinged	1.00	
P# block of 6	12.00	
Never hinged	15.00	

Regular Issue of 1932 Overprinted

C47 A44 4c **rose carmine** *(799,878)*	.30	.25
Never hinged	.45	
P# block of 6	16.00	
Never hinged	20.00	
C48 A45 12c **orange** *(500,000)*	.60	.25
Never hinged	.90	
P# block of 6	20.00	
Never hinged	25.00	
C49 A47 20c **yellow** *(500,000)*	.60	.25
Never hinged	.90	
P# block of 6	20.00	
Never hinged	25.00	
C50 A48 24c **deep violet** *(500,000)*	.65	.25
Never hinged	1.00	
P# block of 6	24.00	
Never hinged	30.00	
C51 A49 32c **olive brown** *(500,000)*	.85	.35
Never hinged	1.40	
First day cover, #C46-C51		35.00
P# block of 6	24.00	
Never hinged	30.00	
Nos. C46-C51 (6)	3.65	1.75
Set, never hinged	5.65	

Transpacific Issue

Issued to commemorate the China Clipper flight from Manila to San Francisco, Dec. 2-5, 1935.

Nos. 387, 392 Overprinted in Gold

1935, Dec. 2 **Unwmk.** ***Perf. 11***

C52 A57 10c **rose carmine** *(500,000)*	.40	.25
Never hinged	.60	
First day cover		2.00
P# block of 6	16.00	
Never hinged	20.00	
C53 A62 30c **orange red** *(300,000)*	.60	.35
Never hinged	.90	
First day cover		3.00
P# block of 6	22.50	
Never hinged	28.00	

Manila-Madrid Flight Issue

Issued to commemorate the Manila-Madrid flight by aviators Antonio Arnaiz and Juan Calvo.

Nos. 291, 295, 298a, 298 Surcharged in Various Colors

Printed by the Philippine Bureau.

1936, Sept. 6

C54 A40 2c on 4c **carmine** (Bl) *(2,000,000)*	.25	.25
Never hinged	.25	
First day cover		1.00
P# block of 6	12.00	
Never hinged	15.00	
C55 A40 6c on 12c **red orange** (V) *(500,000)*	.25	.25
Never hinged	.30	
First day cover		3.00
P# block of 6	20.00	
Never hinged	25.00	
C56 A40 16c on 26c **blue green** (Bk) *(300,000)*	.25	.25
Never hinged	.40	
First day cover		5.00
a. 16c on 26c **green**	2.00	.70
Never hinged	3.00	
Nos. C54-C56 (3)	.75	.75
Set, never hinged	.95	

Air Mail Exhibition Issue

Issued to commemorate the first Air Mail Exhibition, held Feb. 17-19, 1939.

Nos. 298a, 298, 431 Surcharged in Black or Red

Printed by the Philippine Bureau.

1939, Feb. 17

C57 A40 8c on 26c **blue green** (Bk) *(200,000)*	2.00	2.00
Never hinged	4.00	
First day cover		3.50
a. 8c on 26c **green** (Bk)	10.00	4.00
Never hinged	16.00	
C58 A71 1p on 10p **gray** (R) *(30,000)*	8.00	4.00
Never hinged	12.00	
First day cover		8.00
P# block of 6	160.00	
Never hinged	200.00	

Moro Vinta and Clipper — AP1

Printed by the US Bureau of Engraving and Printing.

1941, June 30 **Unwmk.** ***Perf. 11***

C59 AP1 8c **carmine** *(210,000)*	2.00	.60
Never hinged	2.75	
First day cover		2.00
P# block of 6	19.00	
Never hinged	24.00	
C60 AP1 20c **ultramarine** *(25,000)*	3.00	.50
Never hinged	4.00	
First day cover		2.50
P# block of 6	24.00	
Never hinged	30.00	
C61 AP1 60c **blue green** *(50,000)*	3.00	1.00
Never hinged	4.00	
First day cover		3.50
P# block of 6	36.00	
Never hinged	45.00	
C62 AP1 1p **sepia** *(1,110,000)*	.70	.50
Never hinged	1.00	
First day cover		2.25
P# block of 6	12.00	
Never hinged	15.00	
Nos. C59-C62 (4)	8.70	2.60
Set, never hinged	11.75	

For overprint see No. NO7. For surcharges see Nos. N10-N11, N35-N36.

No. C47 Handstamped in Violet

1944, Dec. 3 **Unwmk.** ***Perf. 11***

C63 A44 4c **rose carmine** *(122)*	3,750.	2,750.
On cover		—

SPECIAL DELIVERY STAMPS

U.S. No. E5 Overprinted in Red

a

Printed by U.S. Bureau of Engraving & Printing

Wmk. Double-lined USPS (191)

1901, Oct. 15 *Perf. 12*

E1 SD3 10c **dark blue** *(14,998)* 100. 80.
Never hinged 185.
On cover 350.
Block of 4 500.
P# strip of 3, Impt. 500.
P# block of 6, Impt. *4,000.*
a. Dots in curved frame above messenger (Pl. 882) *175. 160.*
P# block of 6, Impt. (Pl. 882) *6,000.*

Special Delivery Messenger SD2

Wmk. Double-lined PIPS (191PI)

1906, Sept. 8 *Perf. 12*

E2 SD2 20c **deep ultramarine** *(40,019)* 45.00 8.00
Never hinged 90.00
On cover 17.50
P# block of 6, Impt. 2,400.
Never hinged *3,000.*
b. 20c **pale ultramarine** 35.00 8.00
Never hinged 70.00
On cover 17.50
P# block of 6, Impt. 2,600.
Never hinged *3,200.*

See Nos. E3-E6. For overprints see Nos. E7-E10, EO1.

SPECIAL PRINTING

U.S. No. E6 Overprinted in Red

1907 Wmk. Double-lined USPS (191) *Perf. 12*

E2A SD4 10c **ultramarine** *3,250.*
Block of 4 *13,500.*
P# block of 6, Impt. *145,000.*

This stamp was part of the set specially printed for the Bureau of Insular Affairs in 1907. See note following No. 240.
There is only one intact plate block of No. E2A. It is fine and is valued thus.

Wmk. Single-lined PIPS (190PI)

1911, Apr. *Perf. 12*

E3 SD2 20c **deep ultramarine** *(200,000)* 22.00 1.75
Never hinged 42.00
On cover 12.50
P# block of 6 1,600.
Never hinged 2,000.

1916 *Perf. 10*

E4 SD2 20c **deep ultramarine** *(200,000)* 175.00 150.00
Never hinged 275.00
On cover 200.00
P# block of 6 2,000.
Never hinged 2,500.
pale ultramarine —
P# block of 6 *4,400.*
Never hinged *5,500.*

Early in 1919 the supply of Special Delivery stamps in the Manila area was exhausted. A Government decree permitted the use of regular issue postage stamps for payment of the special delivery fee when so noted on the cover. This usage was permitted until the new supply of Special Delivery stamps arrived.

1919 Unwmk. *Perf. 11*

E5 SD2 20c **ultramarine** *(4,195,862)* .60 .25
Never hinged .90
On cover 5.00
P# block of 6 120.00
Never hinged 150.00
a. 20c **pale blue** .75 .25
Never hinged 1.00
On cover 5.25
P# block of 6 160.00
Never hinged 200.00
b. 20c **dull violet** .60 .25
Never hinged .90
On cover 5.00
P# block of 6 160.00
Never hinged 200.00

Type of 1906 Issue

1925-31 Unwmk. *Imperf.*

E6 SD2 20c **dull violet** ('31) *(6,500)* 27.50 *75.00*
Never hinged 40.00
On cover 250.00
P# block of 6 275.00
Never hinged 400.00
a. 20c **violet blue** ('25) *(2,100)* 50.00 —
Never hinged 80.00
On cover —
P# block of 6 525.00
Never hinged 750.00

Type of 1919 Overprinted in Black

1939, Apr. 27 Unwmk. *Perf. 11*

E7 SD2 20c **blue violet** *(1,253,250)* .25 .25
Never hinged .40
First day cover 35.00
P# block of 6 80.00
Never hinged 100.00

Nos. E5b and E7 Handstamped in Violet

1944 Unwmk. *Perf. 11*

E8 SD2 20c **dull violet** (On E5b) *(138)* *1,400. 550.00*
On cover —
Block of 4 *6,000.*
E9 SD2 20c **blue violet** (On E7), *Nov. 8* *(600)* *550.00 250.00*
On cover —
P# block of 6 *4,250.*

Type SD2 Overprinted "VICTORY" As No. 486

1945, May 1 Unwmk. *Perf. 11*

E10 SD2 20c **blue violet** *(578,600)* .70 .55
Never hinged 1.10
First day cover 10.00
P# block of 6 20.00
Never hinged 25.00
a. "IC" close together 3.25 2.75
Never hinged 4.75

Some plate blocks of E10 contain No. E10a. These are very rare.

SPECIAL DELIVERY OFFICIAL STAMP

Type of 1906 Issue Overprinted

1931 Unwmk. *Perf. 11*

EO1 SD2 20c **dull violet** *(46,750)* 3.00 *75.00*
Never hinged 4.50
P# block of 6 150.00
Never hinged 190.00
a. No period after "B" 50.00 *250.00*
Never hinged 75.00
b. Double overprint —

It is strongly recommended that expert opinion be acquired for Nos. EO1 and EO1a used.

POSTAGE DUE STAMPS

U.S. Nos. J38-J44 Overprinted in Black

Printed by the U.S. Bureau of Engraving and Printing.

Wmk. Double-lined USPS (191)

1899, Aug. 16 *Perf. 12*

J1 D2 1c **deep claret** *(340,892)* 7.50 2.50
Never hinged 15.00
On cover 30.00
On cover, used as regular postage 110.00
P# strip of 3, Impt. 125.00
P# block of 6, Impt. *650.00*
J2 D2 2c **deep claret** *(306,983)* 7.50 2.50
Never hinged 15.00
On cover 37.50
P# strip of 3, Impt. 125.00
P# block of 6, Impt. *650.00*
J3 D2 5c **deep claret** *(34,565)* 15.00 2.50
Never hinged 30.00
On cover *70.00*
P# strip of 3, Impt. 200.00
P# block of 6, Impt. *2,000.*
J4 D2 10c **deep claret** *(15,848)* 19.00 5.50
Never hinged 37.50
On cover 100.00
P# strip of 3, Impt. 175.00
P# block of 6, Impt. *1,500.*
J5 D2 50c **deep claret** *(3,216)* 250.00 100.00
Never hinged 425.00
On cover —
P# strip of 3, Impt. 1,100.
P# block of 6, Impt. *18,000.*

No. J1 was used to pay regular postage Sept. 5-19, 1902.

1901, Aug. 31

J6 D2 3c **deep claret** *(14,885)* 17.50 7.00
Never hinged 35.00
On cover 60.00
P# strip of 3, Impt. 175.00
P# block of 6, Impt. *1,250.*
J7 D2 30c **deep claret** *(2,140)* 250.00 110.00
Never hinged 415.00
On cover —
P# strip of 3, Impt. 1,000.
P# block of 6, Impt. *21,500.*
Nos. J1-J7 (7) 566.50 230.00
Set, never hinged 882.50

Post Office Clerk — D3

1928, Aug. 21 Unwmk. *Perf. 11*

J8 D3 4c **brown red** *(948,054)* .25 .25
Never hinged .25
P# block of 6 14.00
Never hinged 17.50

J9 D3 6c **brown red** *(255,490)* .30 .75
Never hinged .45
P# block of 6 14.00
Never hinged 17.50
J10 D3 8c **brown red** *(508,621)* .25 .75
Never hinged .35
P# block of 6 14.00
Never hinged 17.50
J11 D3 10c **brown red** *(254,195)* .30 .75
Never hinged .45
P# block of 6 14.00
Never hinged 17.50
J12 D3 12c **brown red** *(407,457)* .25 .75
Never hinged .35
P# block of 6 14.00
Never hinged 17.50
J13 D3 16c **brown red** *(253,215)* .30 .75
Never hinged .45
P# block of 6 14.00
Never hinged 17.50
J14 D3 20c **brown red** *(259,665)* .30 .75
Never hinged .45
P# block of 6 14.00
Never hinged 17.50
Nos. J8-J14 (7) 1.95 4.75
Set, never hinged 2.75

No. J8 Surcharged in Blue

1937, July 29 **Unwmk.** ***Perf. 11***
J15 D3 3c on 4c **brown red** *(250,000)* .25 .25
Never hinged .35
First day cover 35.00
P# block of 6 18.00
Never hinged 22.50

See note after No. NJ1.

Nos. J8-J14 Handstamped in Violet

1944, Dec. 3 **Unwmk.** ***Perf. 11***
J16 D3 4c **brown red** *(306)* *150.00* —
On cover —
P# block of 6 1,500.
J17 D3 6c **brown red** *(390)* *100.00* —
On cover —
P# block of 6 1,500.
J18 D3 8c **brown red** *(379)* *110.00* *350.00*
On cover —
P# block of 6 1,000.
J19 D3 10c **brown red** *(405)* *100.00* —
On cover —
P# block of 6 1,000.
J20 D3 12c **brown red** *(423)* *100.00* —
On cover —
P# block of 6 1,000.
J21 D3 16c **brown red** *(425)* *100.00* 350.00
On cover —
P# block of 6 1,500.
a. Pair, one without ovpt. —
J22 D3 20c **brown red** *(375)* *110.00* —
On cover —
P# block of 6 1,000.
Nos. J16-J22 (7) *770.00*

OFFICIAL STAMPS

Official Handstamped Overprints

"Officers purchasing stamps for government business may, if they so desire, surcharge them with the letters O.B. either in writing with black ink or by rubber stamps but in such a manner as not to obliterate the stamp that postmasters will be unable to determine whether the stamps have been previously used." C.M. Cotterman, Director of Posts, December 26, 1905.

Beginning January 1, 1906, all branches of the Insular Government used postage stamps to prepay postage instead of franking them as before. Some officials used manuscript, some utilized the typewriting machines but by far the larger number provided themselves with rubber stamps. The majority of these read "O.B." but other forms were: "OFFICIAL BUSINESS" or "OFFICIAL MAIL" in two lines, with variations on many of these.

These "O.B." overprints are known on U.S. 1899-1901 stamps; on 1903-06 stamps in red and blue; on 1906 stamps in red, blue, black, yellow and green.

"O.B." overprints were also made on the centavo and peso stamps of the Philippines, per order of May 25, 1907.

Beginning in 1926 the Bureau of Posts issued press-printed official stamps, but many government offices continued to handstamp ordinary postage stamps "O.B." The press-printed "O.B." overprints are listed below.

During the Japanese occupation period 1942-45, the same system of handstamped official overprints prevailed, but the handstamp usually consisted of "K.P.", initials of the Tagalog words, "Kagamitang Pampamahalaan" (Official Business), and the two Japanese characters used in the printed overprint on Nos. NO1 to NO4.

Legislative Palace Issue of 1926 Overprinted in Red

Printed and overprinted by the Philippine Bureau of Printing.

1926, Dec. 20 **Unwmk.** ***Perf. 12***
O1 A42 2c **green & black** *(90,500)* 3.00 1.00
Never hinged 4.50
On cover 2.00
Block of 4 13.00 5.50
O2 A42 4c **carmine & black** *(90,450)* 3.00 1.25
Never hinged 4.50
On cover 2.00
First day cover 10.00
Block of 4 13.00 5.50
a. Vertical pair, imperf. between 550.00
O3 A42 18c **light brown & black** *(70,000)* 8.00 4.00
Never hinged 12.00
On cover 6.50
Block of 4 36.00 20.00
O4 A42 20c **orange & black** *(70,250)* 7.75 1.75
Never hinged 11.50
On cover 3.00
Block of 4 36.00 8.25
First day cover, #O1-O4 50.00
Nos. O1-O4 (4) 21.75 8.00
Set, never hinged 32.50

Regular Issue of 1917-26 Overprinted

Printed and overprinted by the U.S. Bureau of Engraving and Printing.

1931 **Unwmk.** ***Perf. 11***
O5 A40 2c **green** *(22,940,100)* .40 .25
Never hinged .65
P# block of 6 20.00
Never hinged 25.00
a. No period after "B" 17.50 17.50
Never hinged 27.50
b. No period after "O" 40.00 30.00
O6 A40 4c **carmine** *(5,377,000)* .45 .25
Never hinged .70
P# block of 6 20.00
Never hinged 25.00
a. No period after "B" 40.00 20.00
Never hinged 60.00
O7 A40 6c **deep violet** *(616,500)* .75 .25
Never hinged 1.25
P# block of 10, Impt. 40.00
Never hinged 50.00
O8 A40 8c **yellow brown** *(706,700)* .75 .25
Never hinged 1.25
P# block of 6 32.00
Never hinged 40.00
P# block of 10, Impt. 40.00
Never hinged 50.00
O9 A40 10c **deep blue** *(1,006,800)* 1.20 .25
Never hinged 1.90
P# block of 10, Impt. 32.00
Never hinged 40.00
O10 A40 12c **red orange** *(158,050)* 2.00 .25
Never hinged 3.00
P# block of 6 65.00
Never hinged 80.00
P# block of 10, Impt. 80.00
Never hinged 95.00
a. No period after "B" 80.00 80.00
Never hinged 120.00
O11 A40 16c **light olive green** *(Dewey)* *(824,400)* 1.00 .25
Never hinged 1.50
P# block of 6 24.00
Never hinged 30.00
a. 16c olive bister 2.00 .25
Never hinged 3.00
P# block of 6 20.00
Never hinged 25.00
O12 A40 20c **orange yellow** *(509,050)* 1.25 .25
Never hinged 1.90
P# block of 10, Impt. 75.00
Never hinged 95.00
a. No period after "B" 80.00 80.00
Never hinged 120.00
O13 A40 26c **green** *(68,600)* 2.00 1.00
Never hinged 3.25
P# block of 6 120.00
Never hinged 150.00
a. 26c blue green 2.50 1.50
Never hinged 4.00
P# block of 6 130.00
Never hinged 165.00
O14 A40 30c **gray** *(199,400)* 2.00 .25
Never hinged 3.25
P# block of 10, Impt. 80.00
Never hinged 100.00
Nos. O5-O14 (10) 11.80 3.25
Set, never hinged 18.65

Many collectors prefer to collect the plate blocks of 6 of Nos. O5-O6, O8, O10-O11a and O14 as blocks of 10 so they fit aesthetically with the other plate blocks of 10 with imprints.

Regular Issue of 1935 Overprinted in Black

1935 **Unwmk.** ***Perf. 11***
O15 A53 2c **rose** *(7,927,800)* .25 .25
Never hinged .30
P# block of 6 4.75
Never hinged 6.00
a. No period after "B" 15.00 10.00
Never hinged 22.50
b. No period after "O" — —
O16 A54 4c **yellow green** *(5,079,266)* .25 .25
Never hinged .30
P# block of 6 4.00
Never hinged 5.00
a. No period after "B" 15.00 *40.00*
Never hinged 22.50
O17 A55 6c **dark brown** *(786,896)* .25 .25
Never hinged .40
P# block of 6 8.00
Never hinged 10.00
a. No period after "B" 35.00 35.00
Never hinged 52.50
O18 A56 8c **violet** *(656,200)* .30 .25
Never hinged .45
P# block of 6 9.50
Never hinged 12.00
O19 A57 10c **rose carmine** *(756,100)* .30 .25
Never hinged .45
P# block of 6 8.00
Never hinged 10.00
O20 A58 12c **black** *(104,500)* .75 .25
Never hinged 1.10
P# block of 6 8.00
Never hinged 10.00
O21 A59 16c **dark blue** *(254,800)* .55 .25
Never hinged .85
P# block of 6 8.00
Never hinged 10.00
O22 A60 20c **light olive green** *(203,079)* .60 .25
Never hinged .90
P# block of 6 12.00
Never hinged 15.00
O23 A61 26c **indigo** *(67,750)* .90 .25
Never hinged 1.50
P# block of 6 20.00
Never hinged 25.00
O24 A62 30c **orange red** *(83,500)* .80 .25
Never hinged 1.20
P# block of 6 20.00
Never hinged 25.00
Nos. O15-O24 (10) 4.95 2.50
Set, never hinged 7.40

Nos. 411 and 418 with Additional Overprint in Black

1937-38 **Unwmk.** ***Perf. 11***
O25 A53 2c **rose**, *Apr. 10, 1937* *(11,580,800)* .25 .25
Never hinged .30
First day cover 50.00
P# block of 6 8.00
Never hinged 10.00
a. No period after "B" 25.00 25.00
Never hinged 45.00
b. Period after "B" raised (UL 4) 150.00
O26 A60 20c **light olive green**, *Apr. 26, 1938* *(174,929)* .70 .50
Never hinged 1.10
P# block of 6 20.00
Never hinged 25.00

Regular Issue of 1935 Overprinted In Black

a

b

1938-40	Unwmk.	Perf. 11	
O27 A53(a) 2c **rose** *(23,239,872)*		.25	.25
Never hinged		.30	
P# block of 6		4.75	
Never hinged		6.00	
a. Hyphen omitted		10.00	10.00
Never hinged		15.00	
b. No period after "B"		20.00	*30.00*
Never hinged		30.00	
O28 A54(b) 4c **yellow green** *(85,000)*		.75	1.00
Never hinged		1.10	
P# block of 6		24.00	
Never hinged		30.00	
O29 A55(a) 6c **dark brown** *(393,549)*		.30	.25
Never hinged		.45	
P# block of 6		12.00	
Never hinged		15.00	
O30 A56(b) 8c **violet** *(82,000)*		.75	.85
Never hinged		1.10	
P# block of 6		9.50	
Never hinged		12.00	
O31 A57(b) 10c **rose carmine** *(1,188,735)*		.25	.25
Never hinged		.30	
P# block of 6		16.00	
Never hinged		20.00	
a. No period after "O"		50.00	40.00
Never hinged		75.00	
O32 A58(b) 12c **black** *(340,000)*		.30	.25
Never hinged		.45	
P# block of 6		12.00	
Never hinged		15.00	
O33 A59(b) 16c **dark blue** *(490,000)*		.30	.25
Never hinged		.45	
P# block of 6		16.00	
Never hinged		20.00	
O34 A60(a) 20c **light olive green** ('40) *(162,000)*		.55	.85
Never hinged		.85	
P# block of 6		16.00	
Never hinged		20.00	
O35 A61(b) 26c **indigo** *(77,000)*		1.50	*2.00*
Never hinged		2.25	
P# block of 6		12.00	
Never hinged		15.00	
O36 A62(b) 30c **orange red** *(82,000)*		.75	.85
Never hinged		1.10	
P# block of 6		16.00	
Never hinged		20.00	
Nos. O27-O36 (10)		5.70	6.80
Set, never hinged		8.25	

All bottom plate blocks have the plate numbers cut in half. See note after No. 446.

No. 461 Overprinted in Black — c

ROTARY PRESS PRINTING

1941, Apr. 14	Unwmk.	Perf. 11x10½	
O37 A75(c) 2c **apple green** *(21,087,900)*		.25	*.40*
Never hinged		.30	
First day cover			3.50
P# block of 4		2.00	
Never hinged		2.50	

Nos. O27, O37, O16, O29, O31, O22 and O26 Handstamped in Violet

1944	Unwmk.	Perf. 11, 11x10½	
O38 A53 2c **rose** (On O27) *(128)*		*375.00*	*200.00*
Never hinged		*750.00*	
On cover			—
P# block of 6		*4,000.*	
Never hinged		*5,000.*	
O39 A75 2c **apple green** (On O37) *(13,100)*		15.00	*20.00*
Never hinged		20.00	
On cover			*25.00*
P# block of 4		160.00	
Never hinged		200.00	
O40 A54 4c **yellow green** (On O16) *(2,634)*		45.00	*30.00*
Never hinged		80.00	
On cover			—
P# block of 6		600.00	
Never hinged		750.00	
O40A A55 6c **dark brown** (On O29)		*8,000.*	—
Block of 4		—	
O41 A57 10c **rose carmine** (On O31) *(665)*		*500.00*	
Block of 4		*2,100.*	
a. No period after "O"		*4,000.*	
O42 A60 20c **light olive green** (On O22)		*8,000.*	
O43 A60 20c **light olive green** (On O26)		*1,750.*	
Block of 4		—	

No. 497 Overprinted Type "c" in Black

1946, June 19	Unwmk.	Perf. 11x10½	
O44 A76 2c **sepia** *(10,470,000)*		.25	.25
Never hinged		.25	
P# block of 4		2.00	
Never hinged		2.50	
a. Vertical pair, bottom stamp without ovpt.		—	

POST OFFICE SEALS

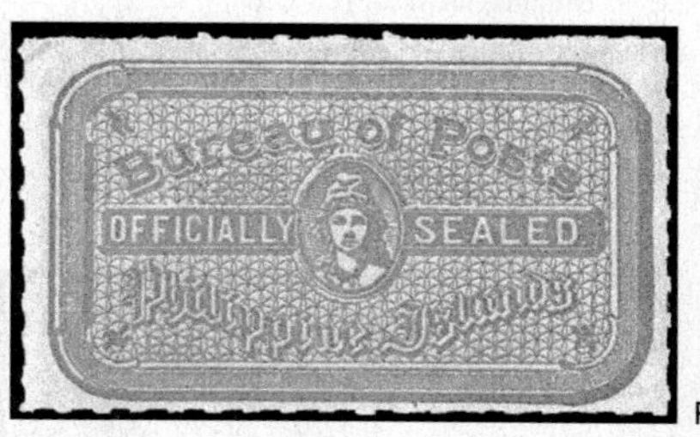

POS1

1906	Litho. Unwmk.	Perf. 12	
OX1 POS1 **light brown**		75.00	75.00
On cover			*1,750.*

Wmk. "PIRS" in Double-lined Capitals

1907		Perf. 12	
OX2 POS1 **light brown**		95.00	95.00
On cover			*2,250.*
	Hyphen-hole Perf. 7		
OX3 POS1 **orange brown**		40.00	*45.00*

1911		Hyphen-hole Perf. 7	
OX4 POS1 **yellow brown**		40.00	*45.00*
On cover			*1,750.*
OX5 POS1 **olive bister**		75.00	75.00
On cover			*1,750.*
a. Unwatermarked		—	
OX6 POS1 **yellow**		75.00	75.00
On cover			*1,750.*

1913	Unwmk.	Hyphen-hole Perf. 7	
OX7 POS1 **lemon yellow**		3.00	*15.00*
On cover			*250.00*
	Perf. 12		
OX8 POS1 **yellow**		150.00	*200.00*
On cover			*2,000.*

Wmk. "USPS" in Single-lined Capitals

Hyphen-hole Perf. 7

OX9 POS1 **yellow**		80.00	50.00
On cover			*1,500.*
a. Rouletted 4½		—	—

1934	Unwmk.	Rouletted	
OX10 POS1 **dark blue**		3.00	*10.00*
On cover			*450.00*

POS2

OX11 POS2 **dark blue**		6.00	*7.50*
On cover			*300.00*

POS3

1938		Hyphen-hole Perf. 7	
OX12 POS3 **dark blue**		3.00	*4.00*
On cover			*175.00*

ENVELOPES

U.S. Envelopes of 1899 Issue Overprinted below stamp in color of the stamp, except where noted

Note: Many envelopes for which there was no obvious need were issued in small quantities. Anyone residing in the Islands could, by depositing with his postmaster the required amount, order any envelopes in quantities of 500, or multiples thereof, provided it was on the schedule of U.S. envelopes.

Such special orders are indicated by a plus sign after the quantity.

1899-1900			
U1 U77 1c **green** (#U352) *(370,000)*		3.00	2.00
Entire		8.75	9.50
U2 U77 1c **green,** *amber* (#U353) *(1,000)*+		18.00	14.00
Entire		40.00	40.00
U3 U77 1c **green,** *amber* (#U353) red overprint *(500)*+		22.50	20.00
Entire		60.00	57.50
U4 U77 1c **green,** *oriental buff* (#U354) *(1,000)*+		14.00	14.00
Entire		30.00	30.00
U5 U77 1c **green,** *oriental buff* (#U354) red overprint *(500)*+		35.00	35.00
Entire		72.50	*72.50*
U6 U77 1c **green,** *blue* (#U355) *(1,000)*+		9.00	9.00
Entire		30.00	30.00
U7 U77 1c **green,** *blue* (#U355) red overprint *(500)*+		20.00	19.00
Entire		72.50	67.50
U8 U79 2c **carmine** (#U362) *(1,180,000)*		1.50	1.50
Entire		4.00	3.00
U9 U79 2c **carmine,** *amber* (#U363) *(21,000)*		5.25	5.00
Entire		15.00	12.50
U10 U79 2c **carmine,** *oriental buff* (#U364) *(10,000)*		5.25	4.75
Entire		17.00	13.50

U11 U79 2c **carmine,** *blue* (#U365) *(10,000)* 4.75 6.25
Entire 12.50 12.00
U12 U81 4c **brown,** *amber* (#U372) *(500)*+ 40.00 35.00
Entire 85.00 *92.50*
a. Double overprint —
Entire *4,000.*
U13 U83 4c **brown** (#U374) *(10,500)* 12.50 9.00
Entire 30.00 *40.00*
U14 U83 4c **brown,** *amber* (#U375) *(500)*+ 55.00 50.00
Entire 175.00 125.00
U15 U84 5c **blue** (#U377) *(20,000)* 6.25 6.00
Entire 13.00 13.00
U16 U84 5c **blue,** *amber* (#U378) *(500)*+ 35.00 35.00
Entire 87.50 *110.00*
Nos. U1-U16 (16) 287.00 265.50

1903 Same Overprint on U.S. Issue of 1903

U17 U85 1c **green** (#U379) *(300,000)* 1.50 1.25
Entire 4.25 4.25
U18 U85 1c **green,** *amber* (#U380) *(1,000)*+ 12.50 12.00
Entire 22.50 *25.00*
U19 U85 1c **green,** *oriental buff* (#U381) *(1,000)*+ 14.50 12.50
Entire 26.00 *24.00*
U20 U85 1c **green,** *blue* (#U382) *(1,500)*+ 12.00 11.00
Entire 26.00 *26.00*
U21 U85 1c **green,** *manila* (#U383) *(500)*+ 20.00 20.00
Entire 45.00 *47.50*
U22 U86 2c **carmine** (#U385) *(150,500)* 5.00 3.50
Entire 7.50 7.00
U23 U86 2c **carmine,** *amber* (#U386) *(500)*+ 17.50 14.00
Entire 35.00 42.50
U24 U86 2c **carmine,** *oriental buff* (#U387) *(500)*+ 17.50 *25.00*
Entire 45.00 —
U25 U86 2c **carmine,** *blue* (#U388) *(500)*+ 17.50 17.50
Entire 40.00
U26 U87 4c **chocolate,** *amber* (#U391) *(500)*+ 55.00 *75.00*
Entire 140.00 *190.00*
a. Double overprint, entire *7,000.*
U27 U88 5c **blue,** *amber* (#U394) *(500)*+ 55.00 —
Entire 125.00 125.00
Nos. U17-U27 (11) 228.00 191.75

Same Overprint on Re-cut U.S. Issue of 1904

1906

U28 U89 2c **carmine** (#U395) 42.50 27.50
Entire 150.00 125.00
U29 U89 2c **carmine,** *Oriental buff* (#U397) 67.50 *110.00*
Entire 225.00 *275.00*

Rizal —E1

E2, McKinley.

1908

U30 E1 2c **green** .50 .25
Entire .85 1.50
U31 E1 2c **green,** *amber* 4.00 2.25
Entire 9.00 8.00
U32 E1 2c **green,** *oriental buff* 5.00 3.00
Entire 9.00 9.00
U33 E1 2c **green,** *blue* 5.00 3.00
Entire 9.00 9.00
U34 E1 2c **green,** *manila (500)* 7.25 —
Entire 15.00 20.00
U35 E2 4c **carmine** .50 .25
Entire 1.40 1.25
U36 E2 4c **carmine,** *amber* 4.00 2.50
Entire 9.00 7.00
U37 E2 4c **carmine,** *oriental buff* 4.25 3.50
Entire 9.00 17.00
U38 E2 4c **carmine,** *blue* 4.00 3.00
Entire 8.50 8.50
U39 E2 4c **carmine,** *manila (500)* 9.00 —
Entire 20.00 30.00
Nos. U30-U39 (10) 43.50 17.75

Rizal — E3

1927, Apr. 5

U40 E3 2c **green** 11.50 9.50
Entire 30.00 25.00
Entire, 1st day cancel *37.50*

"Juan de la Cruz" — E4

1935, June 19

U41 E4 2c **carmine** .35 .25
Entire 1.25 .75
U42 E4 4c **olive green** .50 .30
Entire 1.65 1.10

For surchages see Nos. NU1-NU2.

Nos. U30, U35, U41 and U42 Handstamped in Violet

1944

U42A E1 2c **green** (On U30), entire —
U43 E4 2c **carmine** (On U41) 17.50 14.00
Entire 47.50 *77.00*
U44 E2 4c **carmine,** *McKinley* (On U35) — —
Entire 950.00 *950.00*
U45 E4 4c **olive green** (On U42) 82.50 70.00
Entire 140.00 175.00

WRAPPERS

U.S. Wrappers Overprinted in Color of Stamp

1901

W1 U77 1c **green,** *manila* (No. W357) *(320,000)* 1.50 1.25
Entire 5.00 *10.00*

1905

W2 U85 1c **green,** *manila* (No. W384) 9.00 9.00
Entire 22.50 *25.00*
a. Double overprint, entire *4,500.*
W3 U86 2c **carmine,** *manila* (No. W389) 11.00 10.50
Entire 22.50 *27.50*

Design of Philippine Envelopes

1908

W4 E1 2c **green,** *manila* 2.00 2.00
Entire 11.00 *15.00*

POSTAL CARDS

Values are for Entires.
U.S. Cards Overprinted in Black below Stamp

a

1900, Feb.

UX1 (a) 1c **black** (Jefferson) (UX14) *(100,000)* 17.50 15.00
a. Without period 47.50 75.00
UX2 (a) 2c **black** (Liberty) (UX16) *(20,000)* 40.00 30.00
a. With double "PHILIPPINES" overprint *10,000.* *20,000.*

b

1903, Sept. 15

UX3 (b) 1c **black** (McKinley) (UX18) *1,250.* *1,150.*
UX4 (b) 2c **black** (Liberty) (UX16) *800.* *700.*

c PHILIPPINES.

1903, Nov. 10

UX5 (c) 1c **black** (McKinley) (UX18) 47.50 40.00
UX6 (c) 2c **black** (Liberty) (UX16) 60.00 55.00

d

1906

UX7 (d) 1c **black** (McKinley) (UX18) *275.* *300.*
UX8 (d) 2c **black** (Liberty) (UX16) *1,750.* *1,000.*

Designs same as postage issue of 1906

1907

UX9 A40 2c **black,** *buff* (Rizal) 10.00 8.00
UX10 A40 4c **black,** *buff* (McKinley) 25.00 20.00

Color changes

1911

UX11 A40 2c **blue,** *light blue* (Rizal) 8.00 8.00
a. 2c blue on white 20.00 20.00
UX12 A40 4c **blue,** *light blue* (McKinley) 25.00 25.00

An impression of No. UX11 exists on the back of a U.S. No. UX21.

1915

UX13 A40 2c **green,** *buff* (Rizal) 3.00 2.00
UX14 A40 2c **yellow green,** *amber* 3.50 1.50
UX15 A40 4c **green,** *buff* (McKinley) 20.00 15.00

Design of postage issue of 1935

1935

UX16 A53 2c **red,** *pale buff* (Rizal) 2.50 1.60

No. UX16 Overprinted at left of Stamp **COMMONWEALTH**

1938

UX17 A53 2c **red,** *pale buff* 2.50 1.60

No. UX16 Overprinted **COMMONWEALTH**

UX18 A53 2c **red,** *pale buff* 45.00 45.00

No. UX16 Overprinted **COMMONWEALTH**

UX19 A53 2c **red,** *pale buff* 4.00 4.00

Nos. UX13, UX18 and UX19 Handstamped in Violet

1944

UX20 A40 2c **green,** *buff, Rizal* (On UX13) *225.00 225.00*
UX21 A53 2c **red,** *pale buff* (On UX18) *900.00* —
UX22 A53 2c **red,** *pale buff* (On UX19) *425.00 550.00*

Overprinted in Black at left

1945, Jan. 19

UX23 A76 2c **gray brown,** *pale buff* 1.25 .75
First day cancel 3.25
a. "IC" of "Victory" very close 5.00 3.00

This card was not issued without overprint.

PAID REPLY POSTAL CARDS

U.S. Paid Reply Cards of 1892-93 issues Overprinted with type "a" in blue

1900, Feb.

UY1 2c +2c **blue,** unsevered *(5,000)* 160.00 375.00
m. PM2 Message card, detached 27.50 50.00
r. PR2 Reply card, detached 27.50 50.00
s. As No. UY1, double impression of overprint on message card —

Overprinted type "c" in black

1903

UY2 1c + 1c **black,** *buff,* unsevered *(20,000)* 150.00 375.00
m. PM1 Message card, detached 22.50 25.00
r. PR1 Reply card, detached 22.50 25.00

Overprinted type "c" in black

UY3 2c + 2c **blue,** unsevered *(20,000)* 300.00 *700.00*
m. PM2, Message card, detached 55.00 50.00
r. PR2, Reply card, detached 55.00 50.00

OFFICIAL CARDS

Overprinted at Left of Stamp

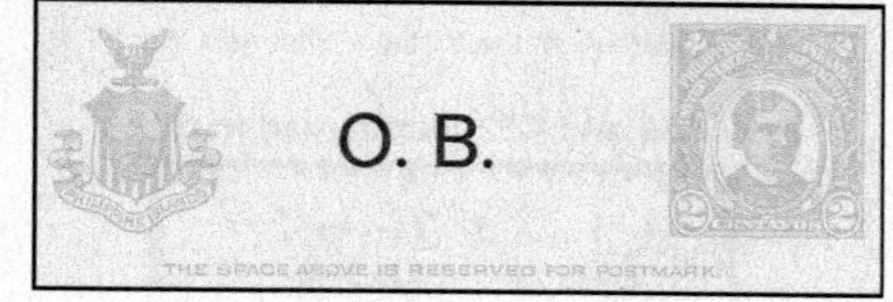

1925 **On postal card No. UX13**

UZ1 A40 2c **green,** *buff* (Rizal) 35.00 35.00

Overprinted at Left of Stamp

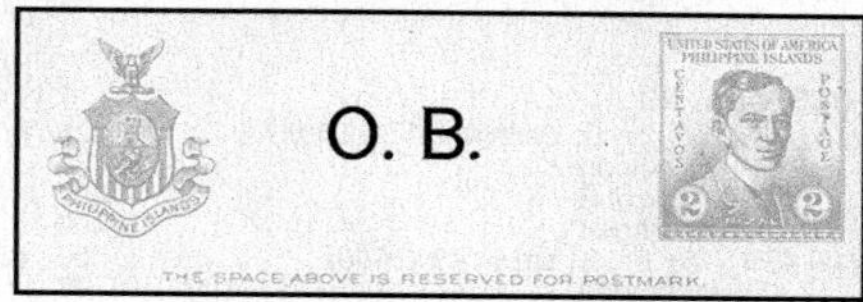

1935 **On postal card No. UX16**

UZ2 A53 2c **red,** *pale buff* 14.00 *17.50*

Overprinted at Left of Stamp

1938 **On postal card No. UX19**

UZ3 A53 2c **red,** *pale buff* 13.00 *17.50*

Overprinted Below Stamp

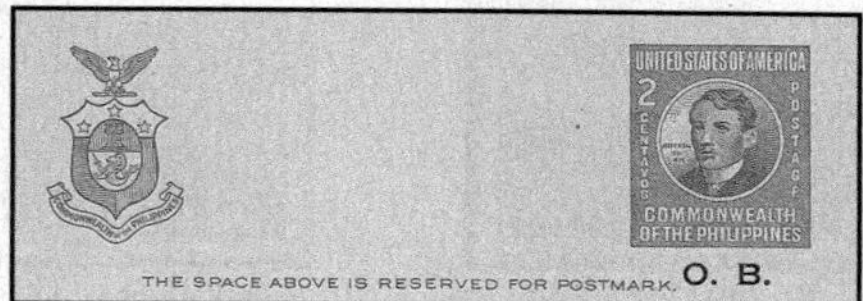

1941 **Design of postage issue of 1941**

UZ4 A75 2c **light green,** *pale buff* 160.00 *200.00*

This card was not issued without overprint.

Postal Card No. UX19 Overprinted at Left of Stamp

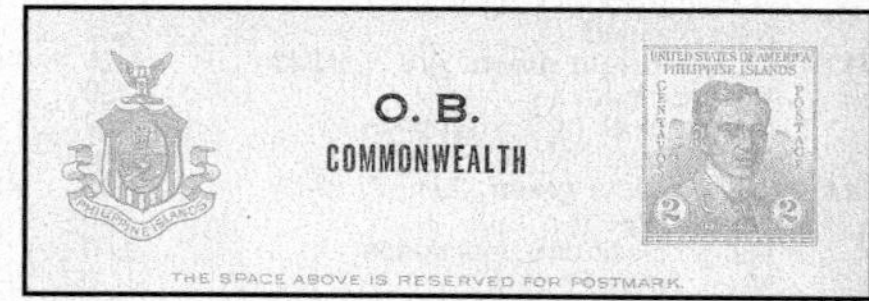

1941

UZ5 A53 2c **red,** *pale buff* 20.00 *25.00*

OCCUPATION STAMPS

Issued Under Japanese Occupation

No. 461 Overprinted in Black

No. 438 Overprinted in Black

No. 439 Overprinted in Black

1942-43 **Unwmk.** ***Perf. 11x10½, 11***

N1 A75 2c **apple green,** *Mar. 4, 1942 (3,000,000)* .25 *1.00*
Never hinged .30
P# block of 4 2.00
Never hinged 2.50
a. Pair, one without overprint —
N2 A58 12c **black,** *Apr. 30, 1943 (310,000)* .25 *2.00*
Never hinged .40
P# block of 6 12.00
Never hinged 15.00
N3 A59 16c **dark blue,** *Mar. 4, 1942 (160,000)* 5.00 3.75
Never hinged 7.50
P# block of 6 37.50
Never hinged 55.00
Nos. N1-N3 (3) 5.50 6.75
Set, never hinged 8.20

Nos. 435a, 435, 442, 443, and 423 Surcharged in Black

a

b

c

d

Type I

Type II

Two types of 50c surcharge
Type I: Center of "A" is a triangle.
Type II: Center of "A" is a pin hole.

1942-43 *Perf. 11*

N4 A55(a) 5(c) on 6c **golden brown** *Sept. 1, 1942 (800,000)* .25 *.75*
Never hinged .35
First day cover, Manila 4.00
P# block of 6 15.00
Never hinged 20.00
a. Top bar shorter and thinner *(200,000)* .25 *1.00*
Never hinged .35
P# block of 6 50.00
Never hinged 60.00
b. 5(c) on 6c **dark brown** .25 *.85*
Never hinged .35
c. As "b," top bar shorter and thinner .25 *1.00*
Never hinged .35
d. Double surcharge, on cover —

N5 A62(b) 16(c) on 30c **orange red**, *Jan. 11, 1943 (210,000)* .25 *.60*
Never hinged .45
First day cover 5.00
P# block of 6 8.00
Never hinged 10.00

N6 A63(c) 50c on 1p **red orange & black**, type II surcharge, *Apr. 30, 1943 (20,000)* .75 *1.25*
Never hinged 1.10
P# block of 4, 2 P# 16.00
Never hinged 20.00
a. Double surcharge *300.00*
b. Type I surcharge 100.00 90.00
Never hinged 125.00
P# block of 4 500.00
Never hinged 600.00

N7 A65(d) 1p on 4p **blue & black**, *Apr. 30, 1943 (19,975)* 100.00 *150.00*
Never hinged 155.00
Inverted "S" in "PESO," position 4 175.00 *225.00*
P# block of 4 525.00
Never hinged 700.00
Nos. N4-N7 (4) 101.25 152.60
Set, never hinged 156.90

On Nos. N4 and N4b, the top bar measures 1½x22½mm. On Nos. N4a and N4c, the top bar measures 1x21mm and the "5" is smaller and thinner.

Bottom plate blocks of Nos. N2 and N3 have selvage reduced through the plate number. See note after No. 446.

The used value for No. N7 is for postal cancellation. Used stamps exist with first day cancellations. They are worth somewhat less.

No. 384 Surcharged in Black

1942, May 18

N8 A54 2(c) on 4c **yellow green** *(100,000)* 4.00 5.00
Never hinged 8.75
First day cover 6.00
P# block of 6 47.50
Never hinged 60.00

Issued to commemorate Japan's capture of Bataan and Corregidor. The American-Filipino forces finally surrendered May 7, 1942. No. N8 exists with "R" for "B" in BATAAN.

No. 384 Surcharged in Black

1942, Dec. 8

N9 A54 5(c) on 4c **yellow green** *(400,000)* .50 *1.00*
Never hinged .75
First day cover 3.00
P# block of 6 20.00
Never hinged 35.00

1st anniversary of the "Greater East Asia War."

Nos. C59 and C62 Surcharged in Black

1943, Jan. 23

N10 AP1 2(c) on 8c **carmine** *(400,000)* .25 *1.00*
Never hinged .35
P# block of 6 20.00
Never hinged 25.00

N11 AP1 5c on 1p **sepia** *(300,000)* .50 *1.50*
Never hinged .75
First day cover, #N10-N11 4.00
P# block of 6 24.00
Never hinged 30.00

1st anniv. of the Philippine Executive Commission.

Nipa Hut — OS1

Rice Planting — OS2

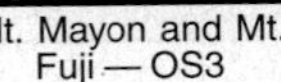

Mt. Mayon and Mt. Fuji — OS3

Moro Vinta — OS4

The "c" currency is indicated by four Japanese characters, "p" currency by two. Nos. N12-N27 were printed in Japan and sheets have marginal inscriptions but no plate numbers.

Engraved; Typographed (2c, 6c, 25c)

1943-44 **Wmk. 257** *Perf. 13*

N12 OS1 1c **deep orange**, *June 7, 1943* .25 .40
Never hinged .30
Margin block of 6, inscription 2.40
Never hinged 3.00

N13 OS2 2c **bright green**, *Apr. 1, 1943* .25 .40
Never hinged .30
Margin block of 6, inscription 2.40
Never hinged 3.00

N14 OS1 4c **slate green**, *June 7, 1943* .25 .40
Never hinged .30
Margin block of 6, inscription 2.40
Never hinged 3.00

N15 OS3 5c **brown**, *Apr. 1, 1943* .25 .40
Never hinged .30
Margin block of 6, inscription 2.40
Never hinged 3.00

N16 OS2 6c **red**, *July 14, 1943* .25 .60
Never hinged .30
Margin block of 6, inscription 2.40
Never hinged 3.00

N17 OS3 10c **blue green**, *July 14, 1943* .25 .40
Never hinged .30
Margin block of 6, inscription 2.40
Never hinged 3.00

N18 OS4 12c **steel blue**, *July 14, 1943* 1.00 1.50
Never hinged 1.50
Margin block of 6, inscription 11.00
Never hinged 14.00

N19 OS4 16c **dark brown**, *July 14, 1943* .25 .40
Never hinged .30
Margin block of 6, inscription 2.40
Never hinged 3.00

N20 OS1 20c **rose violet**, *Aug. 16, 1943* 1.25 1.75
Never hinged 1.90
Margin block of 6, inscription 15.00
Never hinged 19.00

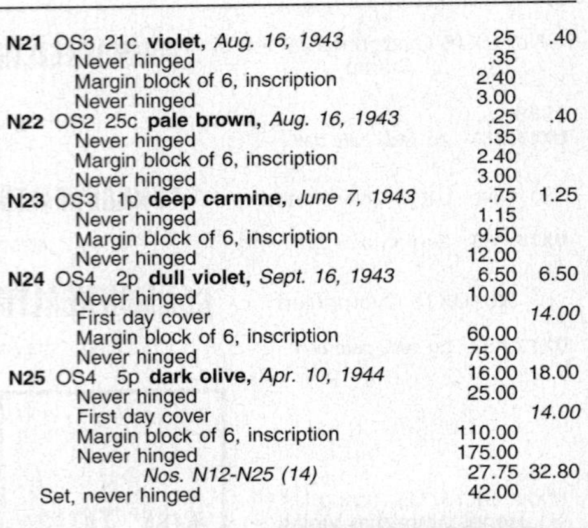

N21 OS3 21c **violet**, *Aug. 16, 1943* .25 .40
Never hinged .35
Margin block of 6, inscription 2.40
Never hinged 3.00

N22 OS2 25c **pale brown**, *Aug. 16, 1943* .25 .40
Never hinged .35
Margin block of 6, inscription 2.40
Never hinged 3.00

N23 OS3 1p **deep carmine**, *June 7, 1943* .75 1.25
Never hinged 1.15
Margin block of 6, inscription 9.50
Never hinged 12.00

N24 OS4 2p **dull violet**, *Sept. 16, 1943* 6.50 6.50
Never hinged 10.00
First day cover *14.00*
Margin block of 6, inscription 60.00
Never hinged 75.00

N25 OS4 5p **dark olive**, *Apr. 10, 1944* 16.00 18.00
Never hinged 25.00
First day cover *14.00*
Margin block of 6, inscription 110.00
Never hinged 175.00
Nos. N12-N25 (14) 27.75 32.80
Set, never hinged 42.00

Map of Manila Bay Showing Bataan and Corregidor — OS5

1943, May 7 **Photo.** **Unwmk.**

N26 OS5 2c **carmine red** .25 *.75*
Never hinged .30
Margin block of 6, inscription 4.00
Never hinged 5.00

N27 OS5 5c **bright green** .25 *1.00*
Never hinged .35
Margin block of 6, inscription 6.50
Never hinged 8.00
Colorless dot after left "5" 4.00 —
First day cover, #N26-N27, Manila 4.00

1st anniversary of the fall of Bataan and Corregidor.

No. 440 Surcharged in Black

1943, June 20 **Engr.** *Perf. 11*

N28 A60 12(c) on 20c **light olive green** *(350,000)* .25 *.75*
Never hinged .35
First day cover 6.00
P# block of 6 11.00
Never hinged 15.00
a. Double surcharge —

350th anniversary of the printing press in the Philippines. "Limbagan" is Tagalog for "printing press."

Rizal Monument, Filipina and Philippine Flag — OS6

1943, Oct. 14 **Photo.** **Unwmk.** *Perf. 12*

N29 OS6 5c **light blue** .25 *.90*
Never hinged .30
a. Imperf. .25 .90

N30 OS6 12c **orange** .25 *.90*
Never hinged .30
a. Imperf. .25 .90

N31 OS6 17c **rose pink** .25 *.90*
Never hinged .30
First day cover, #N29-N31, Manila 3.00
a. Imperf. .25 *.90*
First day cover, #N29a-N31a, Manila 3.00
Nos. N29-N31 (3) .75 *2.70*
Set, never hinged .90

"Independence of the Philippines." Japan granted "independence" Oct. 14, 1943, when the puppet republic was founded.

The imperforate stamps were issued without gum.

Nos. N29-N31 were printed locally and have no plate markings in the selvage.

José Rizal — OS7

Rev. José Burgos — OS8

Apolinario Mabini — OS9

1944, Feb. 17 Litho. Unwmk. *Perf. 12*

N32 OS7 5c **blue** .25 *1.00*
Never hinged .30
a. Imperf. .25 *2.00*
Never hinged .35
N33 OS8 12c **carmine** .25 *1.00*
Never hinged .30
a. Imperf. .25 *2.00*
Never hinged .35
N34 OS9 17c **deep orange** .25 *1.00*
Never hinged .30
First day cover, #N32-N34, Manila 1.00
a. Imperf. .25 *2.00*
Never hinged .35
First day cover, #N32a-N34a, *Apr. 17,* Manila 3.00
Nos. N32-N34 (3) .75 *3.00*
Set, never hinged .90

See No. NB8.

Nos. N32-N34a were printed locally and have no plate markings in the selvage.

Nos. C60 and C61 Surcharged in Black

1944, May 7 Unwmk. *Perf. 11*

N35 AP1 5(c) on 20c **ultramarine** .50 1.00
Never hinged .75
P# block of 6 32.50
Never hinged 40.00
N36 AP1 12(c) on 60c **blue green** *(165,000)* 1.75 1.75
Never hinged 2.50
P# block of 6 42.50
Never hinged 52.50
First day cover, #N35-N36 4.00

2nd anniversary of the fall of Bataan and Corregidor.

José P. Laurel — OS10

1945, Jan. 12 Litho. Unwmk. *Imperf.*
Without Gum

N37 OS10 5c **dull violet brown** .25 *.50*
Never hinged .30
N38 OS10 7c **blue green** .25 *.50*
Never hinged .30
N39 OS10 20c **chalky blue** .25 *.50*
Never hinged .30
First day cover, #N37-N39 3.00
Nos. N37-N39 (3) *.75 1.50*
Set, never hinged .90

Issued belatedly on Jan. 12, 1945, to commemorate the first anniversary of the puppet Philippine Republic, Oct. 14, 1944. "S" stands for "sentimos."

The special cancellation devices prepared for use on Oct. 14, 1944, were employed on "First Day" covers Jan. 12, 1945.

Nos. N37-N39 were printed locally and have no plate markings in the selvage.

OCCUPATION SEMI-POSTAL STAMPS

Woman, Farming and Cannery — OSP1

1942, Nov. 12 Litho. Unwmk. *Perf. 12*

NB1 OSP1 2c + 1c **pale violet** .25 *.60*
Never hinged .30
NB2 OSP1 5c + 1c **brt grn** .25 *1.00*
Never hinged .30
NB3 OSP1 16c + 2c **orange** 25.00 *32.50*
Never hinged 42.00
First day cover, #NB1-NB3 37.50
Nos. NB1-NB3 (3) 25.50 34.10
Set, never hinged 42.60

Issued to promote the campaign to produce and conserve food. The surtax aided the Red Cross.

Nos. NB1-NB3 were printed locally and have no plate markings in the selvage.

Souvenir Sheet

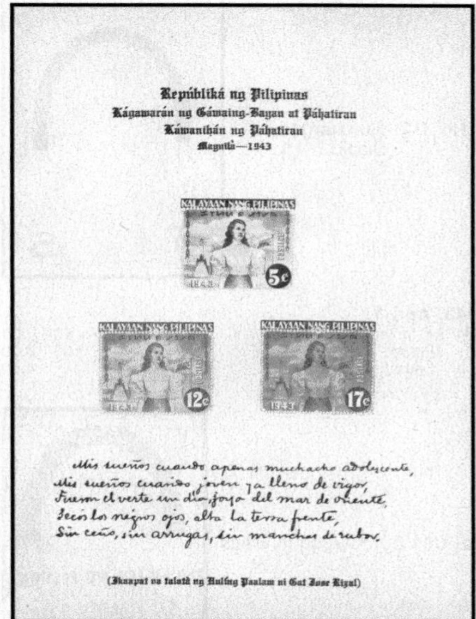

OSP2

Illustration reduced.

1943, Oct. 14 Without Gum *Imperf.*

NB4 OSP2 Sheet of 3 60.00 *17.50*
Sheet with first day cancel and cachet, Manila 17.50
First day cover, Manila —

"Independence of the Philippines."

No. NB4 contains one each of Nos. N29a-N31a. Marginal inscription is from Rizal's "Last Farewell." Sold for 2.50p.

The value of No. NB4 used is for a sheet from a first day cover. Commercially used sheets are extremely scarce and worth much more.

Nos. N18, N20 and N21 Surcharged in Black

1943, Dec. 8 Wmk. 257 *Perf. 13*

NB5 OS4 12c + 21c **steel blue** .25 *1.50*
Never hinged .30
Margin block of 6, inscription 4.00
Never hinged 5.00
NB6 OS1 20c + 36c **rose violet** .25 *1.50*
Never hinged .30
Margin block of 6, inscription 4.00
Never hinged 5.00
NB7 OS3 21c + 40c **violet** .25 *2.00*
Never hinged .30
Margin block of 6, inscription 4.75
Never hinged 6.00
First day cover, #NB5-NB7 2.50
Nos. NB5-NB7 (3) .75 *5.00*
Set, never hinged .90

The surtax was for the benefit of victims of a Luzon flood. "Baha" is Tagalog for "flood."

Souvenir Sheet

OSP3

Illustration reduced.

1944, Feb. 9 Litho. Unwmk. *Imperf.*
Without Gum

NB8 OSP3 Sheet of 3 6.50 3.50
First day cover *4.00*

No. NB8 contains 1 each of Nos. N32a-N34a.

Sheet sold for 1p, surtax going to a fund for the care of heroes' monuments.

The value for No. NB8 used is for a stamp from a first day cover. Commercially used examples are worth much more.

OCCUPATION POSTAGE DUE

No. J15 Overprinted in Blue

1942, Oct. 14 Unwmk. *Perf. 11*

NJ1 D3 3c on 4c **brown red** *(40,000)* 25.00 *35.00*
Never hinged 37.50
First day cover *35.00*
Double bar — —
Right side P# block of 6 200.00
Never hinged 350.00

On examples of No. J15, two lines were drawn in India ink with a ruling pen across "United States of America" by employees of the Short Paid Section of the Manila Post Office to make a provisional 3c postage due stamp which was used from Sept. 1, 1942 (when the letter rate was raised from 2c to 5c) until Oct. 14 when No. NJ1 went on sale. Value on cover, $175.

Bottom plate blocks of 6 of No. NJ1 are much scarcer than the right side plate blocks. Value $325 hinged, $450 nerver hinged.

OCCUPATION OFFICIAL STAMPS

Nos. 461, 413, 435, 435a and 442 Overprinted or Surcharged in Black with Bars and

1943-44 **Unwmk.** ***Perf. 11x10½, 11***

NO1 A75 2c **apple green,** *Apr. 7, 1943 (200,000)* .25 *.75*
Never hinged .30
P# block of 4 6.75
Never hinged 8.50
a. Double overprint *400.00*
Never hinged *600.00*
On cover (double overprint) *1,250.*
NO2 A55 5(c) on 6c **dark brown** (On No. 413), *June 26, 1944 (23,049)* 40.00 *45.00*
Never hinged 55.00
First day cover *125.00*
P# block of 6 290.00
Never hinged 375.00
NO3 A55 5(c) on 6c **golden brown** (On No. 435a), *Apr. 7, 1943 (250,000)* .25 *.90*
Never hinged .35
P# block of 6 14.00
Never hinged 17.50
a. Narrower spacing between bars *(249,951)* .25 *.90*
Never hinged .35
b. 5(c) on 6c dark brown (On No. 435) .25 *.90*
Never hinged .35
c. As "b," narrower spacing between bars .25 *.90*
Never hinged .35
d. Double overprint —
NO4 A62 16(c) on 30c **orange red,** *Apr. 7, 1943 (100,000)* .30 *1.25*
Never hinged .45
P# block of 6 20.00
Never hinged 25.00
a. Wider spacing between bars .30 *1.25*
Never hinged .45
First day cover, Nos. NO1, NO3-NO4 *35.00*
b. Surcharged on No. 420 —
Nos. NO1-NO4 (4) 40.80 47.90
Set, never hinged 56.10

On Nos. NO3 and NO3b the bar deleting "United States of America" is 9¾ to 10mm above the bar deleting "Common." On Nos. NO3a and NO3c, the spacing is 8 to 8½mm.

On No. NO4, the center bar is 19mm long, 3½mm below the top bar and 6mm above the Japanese characters. On No. NO4a, the center bar is 20½mm long, 9mm below the top bar and 1mm above the Japanese characters.

"K.P." stands for Kagamitang Pampamahalaan, "Official Business" in Tagalog.

Nos. 435 and 435a Surcharged in Black

1944, Aug. 28 **Unwmk.** ***Perf. 11***

NO5 A55 (5c) on 6c **golden brown** *(500,000)* .30 *.40*
Never hinged .45
P# block of 6 20.00
Never hinged 25.00
a. 5(c) on 6c **dark brown** .30 *.40*
Never hinged .45
P# block of 6 20.00
Never hinged 25.00

Nos. O34 and C62 Overprinted in Black

a

b

NO6 A60(a) 20c **light olive green** *(200,000)* .40 *.50*
Never hinged .60
P# block of 6 12.00
Never hinged 15.00
NO7 AP1(b) 1p **sepia** *(100,000)* .90 *1.00*
Never hinged 1.45
P# block of 6 20.00
Never hinged 25.00
First day cover, #NO5-NO7 4.00
Nos. NO5-NO7 (3) 1.60 1.90
Set, never hinged 2.05

Bottom plate blocks of Nos. NO3-NO6 have selvage reduced through the plate number. See note after No. 446.

OCCUPATION ENVELOPES

No. U41 Surcharged in Black

1943, Apr. 1

NU1 E4 5c on 2c **carmine** .50 .30
Entire 3.00 3.00
Entire, 1st day cancel 4.00

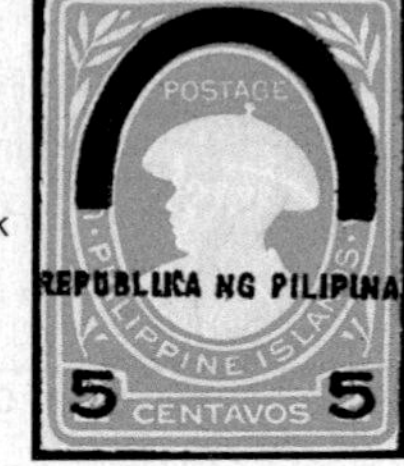

No. U41 Surcharged in Black

1944, Feb. 17

NU2 E4 5c on 2c **carmine** .75 .50
Entire 3.50 *5.00*
Entire, 1st day cancel 7.50
a. Inverted surcharged —
b. Double surcharge —
c. Both 5's missing —

OCCUPATION POSTAL CARDS

Values are for entire cards.
Nos. UX19 and UZ4 Overprinted

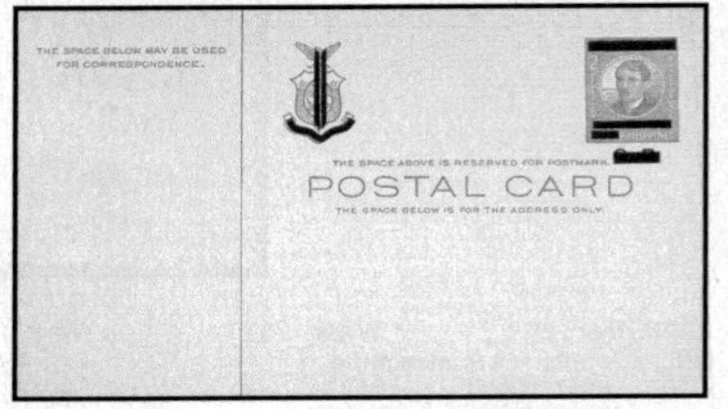

1942

NUX1 A53 2c **red,** *pale buff, Mar. 4, 1942* 15.00 15.00
First day cancel *85.00*
a. Vertical obliteration bars reversed *140.00*
NUX2 A75 2c **light green,** *pale buff, Dec. 12, 1942* 3.00 2.00
First day cancel 6.00

Rice Planting — A77

1943, May 17

NUX3 A77 2c **green** 1.00 *1.00*
First day cancel, Manila 2.00

OCCUPATION OFFICIAL CARDS

Nos. UX19, UX17 and UX18 Overprinted in Black with Bars and

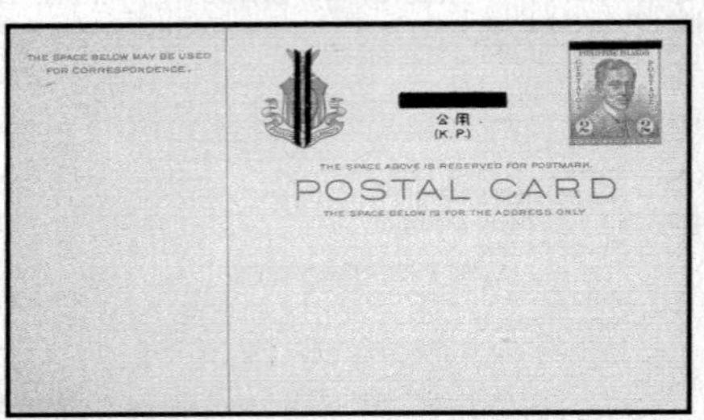

1943, Apr. 7

NUZ1 A53 2c **red,** *pale buff* 5.00 5.00
First day cancel 100.00
a. On No. UX17 — —
b. On No. UX18 *500.00* —

No. NUX3 Overprinted in Black

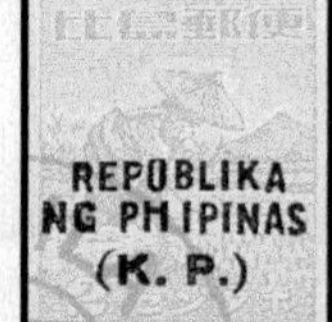

1944, Aug. 28

NUZ2 A77 2c **green** 1.50 *1.00*
First day cancel 2.00
a. Double overprint *700.00*

FILIPINO REVOLUTIONARY GOVERNMENT

Following the defeat of the Spanish fleet by U.S. Commodore Dewey in Manila on May 1, 1898, which essentially ended the Spanish-American War in the Philippines, postal services were disrupted throughout the Philippines. Postal service was reestablished through U.S. Army military stations, beginning in June 1898 near Manila, continuing province by province until culminating at Zamboanga and other cities in the southern areas in late 1899.

Provisional stamps were prepared for use in the central part of the island of Luzon at Malolos in late 1898 under the leadership of General Emilio Aguinaldo, who had proclaimed the Philippine Republic on June 12, 1898. Later, other provisional stamps were prepared by local Filipino insurgents at Iloilo (Panay Island), Bohol, Cebu and Negros, and Spanish period stamps were overprinted and/or surcharged for use by postal officials at Zamboanga and La Union.

The most familiar of these provisionals were the "Aguinaldo" issues of the Filipino Revolutionary Government in central Luzon near Manila. The letters "KKK," the initials of the revolutionary society, "Kataastaasang, Kagalang-galang Katipunan nang Mañga Anak nang Bayan," meaning "Sovereign Worshipful Association of the Sons of the Country," readily identify the Aguinaldo provisionals. Hostilities broke out between the Aguinaldo regime and the occupying American administration in February 1899, and the Filipino-American War continued until the American capture of Aguinaldo on March 23, 1901.

The Aguinaldo regular postage, registration, revenue, newspaper and telegraph stamps were in use in Luzon as early as November 10, 1898, and continued in use through early 1901. Although the postal regulations specified that these stamps be used for their inscribed purpose, they were commonly used interchangeably.

POSTAGE ISSUES

A1

A2

Coat of Arms — A3

1898-99 **Unwmk.** ***Perf. 11½***

Y1 A1 2c **red** 250.00 125.00
On cover *1,500.*
a. Double impression *325.00*
Y2 A2 2c **red** .30 4.00
On cover 350.00
b. Double impression —
d. Horiz. pair, imperf. between —
e. Vert. pair, imperf. between *225.00*
Y3 A3 2c **red** 150.00 *200.00*
On cover *2,000.*

Imperf pairs and pairs, imperf horizontally, have been created from No. Y2e.

REGISTRATION STAMP

RS1

YF1 RS1 8c **green** 5.00 *30.00*
On cover with #Y2 *3,500.*
a. Imperf., pair 400.00
b. Imperf. vertically, pair —

NEWSPAPER STAMP

N1

YP1 N1 1m **black** 2.00 *20.00*
a. Imperf., pair 5.00 *20.00*

PROOFS

1906

241P2 2c **yellow green,** small die on white wove paper 500.
241P2a 2c **yellow green,** PP sm die on yelsh wove paper 750.
242TC1 4c **black,** large die on India paper *1,600.*
242P1 4c **carmine lake,** large die on India paper *1,000.*
242P2 4c **carmine lake,** small die on white wove paper 500.
242P2a 4c **carmine lake,** PP sm die on yelsh wove paper 750.
243P1 6c **violet,** large die on Indian paper *1,000.*
243P2 6c **violet,** small die on white wove paper 500.
243P2a 6c **violet,** PP sm die on yelsh wove paper 750.
244P1 8c **brown,** large die on India paper *1,000.*
244P2 8c **brown,** small die on white wove paper 500.
244P2a 8c **brown,** PP sm die on yelsh wove paper 750.
245P2 10c **dark blue,** small die on white wove paper 500.
245P2a 10c **dark blue,** PP sm die on yelsh wove paper 750.
246P2 12c **brown lake,** small die on white wove paper 500.
246P2a 12c **brown lake,** PP sm die on yelsh wove paper 750.
247P1 16c **violet black,** large die on India paper *1,000.*
247P2 16c **violet black,** small die on white wove paper 500.
247P2a 16c **violet black,** PP sm die on yelsh wove paper 750.
248P2 20c **orange brown,** small die on white wove paper 500.
248P2a 20c **orange brown,** PP sm die on yelsh wove paper 750.
249P2 26c **violet brown,** small die on white wove paper 500.
249P2a 26c **violet brown,** PP sm die on yelsh wove paper 750.
250P1 30c **olive green,** large die on India paper *1,000.*
250P2 30c **olive green,** small die on white wove paper 500.
250P2a 30c **olive green,** PP sm die on yelsh wove paper 750.
251P2 1p **orange,** small die on white wove paper 500.
251P2a 1p **orange,** PP sm die on yelsh wove paper 750.
252P2 2p **black,** small die on white wove paper 500.
252P2a 2p **black,** PP sm die on yelsh wove paper 750.
253P2 4p **dark blue,** small die on white wove paper 500.
253P2a 4p **dark blue,** PP sm die on yelsh wove paper 750.
254P2 10p **dark green,** small die on white wove paper 500.
254P2a 10p **dark green,** PP sm die on yelsh wove paper 750.

1909-13

255P2 12c **red orange,** small die on white wove paper 600.
255P2a 12c **red orange,** PP sm die on yelsh wove paper 625.
256P2 16c **olive green,** small die on white wove paper 600.
256P2a 16c **olive green,** PP sm die on yelsh wove paper 625.
257P2 20c **yellow,** small die on white wove paper 600.
257P2a 20c **yellow,** PP sm die on yelsh wove paper 625.
258P2 26c **blue green,** small die on white wove paper 600.
258P2a 26c **blue green,** PP sm die on yelsh wove paper 625.
259P2 30c **ultramarine,** small die on white wove paper 600.
259P2a 30c **ultramarine,** PP sm die on yelsh wove paper 625.
260P2 1p **pale violet,** small die on white wove paper 600.
260P2a 1p **pale violet,** PP sm die on yelsh wove paper 625.
260AP2 2p **violet brown,** small die on white wove paper 600.
260AP2a 2p **violet brown,** PP sm die on yelsh wove paper 625.
275P2 30c **gray,** small die on white wove paper 600.
275P2a 30c **gray,** PP sm die on yelsh wove paper 625.

1923

303TC1 16c Large die on India paper
a. **olive green** 450.
303P1 16c **olive bister,** large die on India paper 450.

1926

322P4 18c **light brown & black,** plate on glazed card 350.

1932

357TC1 18c Large die on India paper
a. **orange red** 450.
357P1 18c **red orange,** large die on India paper 450.
360TC1 32c Large die on India paper
a. **green** 450.
b. **olive green** 450.

1935

383P1 2c **rose,** large die on India paper 600.
384P1 4c **yellow green,** large die on India paper 600.
385P1 6c **dk brown,** large die on India paper 600.
386P1 8c **violet,** large die on India paper 600.
387P1 10c **rose carmine,** large die on India paper 600.
388P1 12c **black,** large die on India paper 600.
389P1 16c **dk blue,** large die on India paper 600.
390TC1 20c Large die on India paper
a. **black** —
390P1 20c **lt olive green,** large die on India paper 600.
391P1 26c **indigo,** large die on India paper 600.
392P1 30c **orange red,** large die on India paper 600.
393P1 1p **red org & blk,** large die on India paper 600.
394P1 2p **bis brn & blk,** large die on India paper 600.
395P1 4p **blue & blk,** large die on India paper 600.
396P1 5p **grn & blk,** large die on India paper 600.

1936

408TC1 2c Large die on India paper
a. **yellow green** 450.
408P1 2c **orange brown,** large die on India paper 450.

1937

425P2 2c **yellow green,** small die on white wove paper 500.

1939

452P1 2c **yellow green,** large die on India paper *750.*
452P2 2c **yellow green,** small die on white wove paper 500.
453P2 6c **carmine,** small die on white wove paper 500.
454P2 12c **bright blue,** small die on white wove paper 500.
455P1 2c **green,** large die on India paper 750.
455P2 2c **green,** small die on white wove paper 500.
456P2 6c **orange,** small die on white wove paper 500.
457P2 12c **carmine,** small die on white wove paper 500.

1940

458P1 2c **dk orange,** large die on India paper 1,000.
458P2 2c **dk orange,** small die on white wove paper 600.
459P2 6c **dk green,** small die on white wove paper 600.
460P2 12c **purple,** small die on white wove paper 600.

1941

461P2 2c **apple green,** small die on white wove paper 600.

1946

497P1 2c **sepia,** large die on India paper —

AIR POST

1941

C59P2 8c **carmine,** small die on white wove paper 500.
C60P2 20c **ultramarine,** small die on white wove paper 500.
C61P2 60c **blue green,** small die on white wove paper 500.
C62P2 1p **sepia,** small die on white wove paper 500.

SPECIAL DELIVERY

1906

E2TC1 20c **black,** large die on India paper —
E2P1 20c **ultramarine,** large die on wove paper 2,000.
E2TC2 20c Small die on India paper
a. **green** 1,000.
E2P2 20c **ultramarine,** small die on wove paper 1,000.
E2P2a 20c **ultramarine,** PP small die on yelsh wove paper 850.

POSTAGE DUE

1899

J1P2 1c **deep claret,** small die on wove paper 2,750.
J2P2 2c **deep claret,** small die on wove paper 2,750.
J3P2 5c **deep claret,** small die on wove paper 2,750.
J4P2 10c **deep claret,** small die on wove paper 2,750.
J5P2 50c **deep claret,** small die on wove paper 2,750.

1901

J6P2 3c **deep claret,** small die on wove paper 2,750.
J7P2 30c **deep claret,** small die on wove paper 2,750.

SPECIMEN STAMPS

Handstamped US Type E in Purple or Black

1899

213S E 1c **yellow green** 175.00
214dS E 2c **rose carmine,** type IV 175.00
215S E 3c **purple** 175.00
216S E 5c **blue** 175.00
217S E 10c **brown,** type I 175.00
218S E 15c **olive brown** 175.00
219S E 50c **orange** 175.00

See "Special Printings" notice after No. 219 for Special Printings with black "Specimen" handstamp, but note that not all stamps with the black "Specimen" handstamp are Special Printings.

Overprinted US Type R in Black

1917-25

290S R	2c **green**	40.00
291S R	4c **carmine**	40.00
292S R	6c **deep violet**	40.00
293S R	8c **yellow brown**	40.00
294S R	10c **deep blue**	40.00
295S R	12c **red orange**	40.00
297S R	20c **orange yellow**	40.00
298S R	26c **green**	40.00
299S R	30c **gray**	40.00
300S R	1p **pale violet**	40.00
301S R	2p **violet brown**	40.00
302S R	4p **blue**	40.00

1923-26

303S R	16c **olive bister**	40.00
304S R	10p **deep green**	40.00

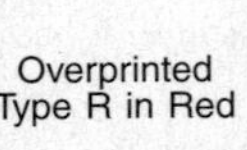
Overprinted Type R in Red

1926

319S R	2c **green & black**	65.00
320S R	4c **carmine & black**	65.00
321S R	16c **olive green & black**	65.00
322S R	18c **light brown & black**	65.00
323S R	20c **orange & black**	65.00
324S R	24c **gray & black**	65.00
325S R	1p **rose lilac & black**	65.00

Overprinted US Type S in Red

1926

319S S	2c **green & black**	65.00
320S S	4c **carmine & black**	65.00
321S S	16c **olive green & black**	65.00
322S S	18c **light brown & black**	65.00
323S S	20c **orange & black**	65.00
324S S	24c **gray & black**	65.00
325S S	1p **rose lilac & black**	65.00

Imperforate examples of this set, on glazed cards with centers in brown, are known with the "Cancelled" overprint. Value, $2,250 for set.

Handstamped "SPECIMEN" in Red Capitals, 13x3mm

1925

340aS S	2c **green**	75.00
341aS S	4c **carmine**	75.00
342aS S	6c **deep violet**	75.00
343aS S	8c **yellow brown**	100.00
344aS S	10c **deep blue**	100.00
345aS S	12c **red orange**	100.00
346aS S	16c **olive bister**	100.00
347aS S	20c **yellow**	100.00
348aS S	26c **blue green**	100.00
349aS S	30c **gray**	100.00
350aS S	1p **violet**	100.00
351aS S	2p **violet brown**	100.00
352aS S	4p **deep blue**	150.00
353aS S	10p **deep green**	250.00

SPECIAL DELIVERY

Overprinted Type R in Black

1919

E5S R	20c **ultramarine**	200.00
E5bS R	20c **dull violet**	—

Handstamped "SPECIMEN" in Red Capitals, 13x3mm

1925

E6aS	20c **violet blue**	300.00

POSTAGE DUE

1899 Overprinted Type E in Black

J1S E	1c **deep claret**	500.00
J2S E	2c **deep claret**	500.00
J3S E	5c **deep claret**	500.00
J4S E	10c **deep claret**	500.00
J5S E	50c **deep claret**	500.00

OFFICIAL

1926 Overprinted Type R in Red

O1S R	2c **green & black**	30.00
O2S R	4c **carmine & black**	30.00
O3S R	18c **light brown & black**	30.00
O4S R	20c **orange & black**	30.00

1926 Overprinted Type S in Red

O1S S	2c **green & black**	30.00
O2S S	4c **carmine & black**	30.00
O3S S	18c **light brown & black**	30.00
O4S S	20c **orange & black**	30.00

PUERTO RICO

(Porto Rico)

United States troops landed at Guanica Bay, Puerto Rico, on July 25, 1898, and mail service between various points in Puerto Rico began soon after under the authority of General Wilson, acting governor of the conquered territory, who authorized a provisional service early in August, 1898. The first Military Postal Station was opened at La Playa de Ponce on August 3, 1898. Control of the island passed formally to the United States on October 18, 1898. Twenty-one military stations operating under the administration of the Military Postal Service were authorized in Puerto Rico after the Spanish-American war. After the overprinted provisional issue of 1900, unoverprinted stamps of the United States replaced those of Puerto Rico.

Name changed to Puerto Rico by Act of Congress, approved May 17, 1932.

Italicized numbers in parentheses indicate quantities issued.

100 CENTS = 1 DOLLAR.

LOCAL ISSUES

Ponce Issue

A11

1898 Unwmk. Handstamped *Imperf.*

200 A11 5c **violet** —

No. 200 is a violet handstamp and control mark used on envelopes. Some examples have no control mark. There are three types of circular markings known, and two control marks. Uses on 2¢ U.S. stamps on cover were strictly as a cancellation, not as local postage. Because genuine usage is extremely difficult to authenticate with certainty, certification by competent authorities is essential.

Coamo Issue

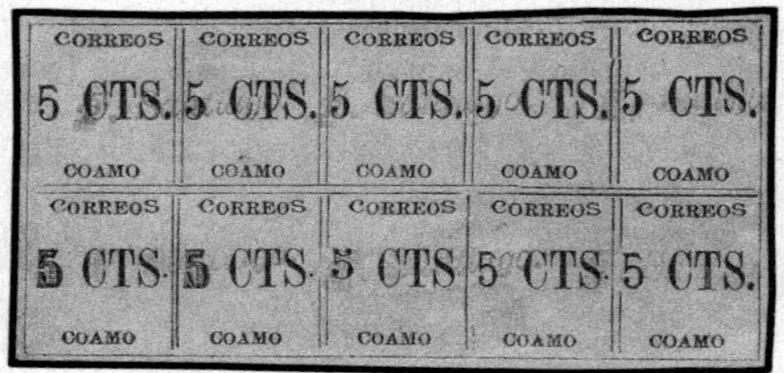

A12 — Setting of 10

Types of "5":
I — Curved flag. Pos. 2, 3, 4, 5.
II — Flag turns down at right. Pos. 1, 9, 10.
III — Fancy outlined "5." Pos. 6, 7.
IV — Flag curls into ball at right. Pos. 8.

Typeset, setting of 10

1898, Aug. Unwmk. *Imperf.*

201 A12 5c **black,** Type I	700.	*1,250.*
Type II	700.	*1,300.*
Type III	775.	*1,400.*
Type IV	850.	*1,550.*
Irregular "block" of 4 showing one of each type	3,750.	
Sheet of 10	10,000.	
On cover		*27,500.*
Pair on cover		—

Blocks not showing all four types and pairs normally sell for 10-20% over the value of the individual stamps.

The stamps bear the control mark "F. Santiago" in violet. About 500 were issued.

Dangerous forgeries exist.

Regular Issue

United States Nos. 279, 279Bf, 281, 272 and 282C Overprinted in Black at 36 degree Angle

1899 Wmk. 191 *Perf. 12*

210 A87 1c **yellow green,** *Mar. 15*	6.00	1.40
Never hinged	13.00	
On cover		50.00
First day cover		—
Block of 4	30.00	10.00
P# strip of 3, Impt.	52.50	
P# block of 6, Impt.	300.00	
a. Overprint at 25 degree angle	8.00	2.25
Never hinged	17.50	
Pair, 36 degree and 25 degree angles	27.50	
"PORTO RICU"	37.50	25.00
211 A88 2c **reddish carmine,** type IV, *Mar. 15*	5.00	1.25
Never hinged	11.00	
On cover		50.00
Block of 4	25.00	10.00
P# strip of 3, Impt.	40.00	
P# block of 6, Impt.	350.00	
"FORTO RICO" (pos. 77)		—
a. Overprint at 25 degree angle, *Mar. 15*	6.50	2.25
Never hinged	14.00	
On cover		50.00
First day cover		—
Block of 4	30.00	17.50
P# strip of 3, Impt.	42.50	
P# block of 6, Impt.	275.00	

No.	Description	Unused	Used
	Pair, 36 degree and 25 degree angles	27.50	
	P# strip of 3, Impt.	100.00	
	P# block of 6, Impt.	700.00	
	"PORTU RICO" (pos. 46)	52.50	20.00
	"PORTO RICU" (pos. 3)	—	
	"PURTO RICO"	—	
	"FURTU RICO"	—	
212	A91 5c **blue**	12.50	2.50
	Never hinged	27.50	
	On cover		50.00
	Block of 4	55.00	27.50
	P# strip of 3, Impt.	70.00	
	P# block of 6, Impt.	350.00	
213	A93 8c **violet brown**	40.00	17.50
	Never hinged	90.00	
	On cover		125.00
	Block of 4	180.00	110.00
	P# strip of 3, Impt.	260.00	
	P# block of 6, Impt.	*5,000.*	
	"FORTO RICO"	95.00	60.00
a.	Overprint at 25 degree angle	45.00	19.00
	Never hinged	100.00	
	Pair, 36 degree and 25 degree angles	110.00	
c.	"PORTO RIC"	150.00	110.00
214	A94 10c **brown,** type I	22.50	6.00
	Never hinged	50.00	
	On cover		120.00
	Block of 4	100.00	45.00
	P# strip of 3, Impt.	150.00	
	P# block of 6, Impt.	1,500.	
	"FORTO RICO"	87.50	70.00
	Nos. 210-214 (5)	86.00	28.65

Misspellings of the overprint on Nos. 210-214 (PORTO RICU, PORTU RICO, FORTO RICO) are actually broken letters.

United States Nos. 279 and 279B Overprinted in Black

1900

No.	Description	Unused	Used
215	A87 1c **yellow green**	7.50	1.40
	Never hinged	17.50	
	On cover		50.00
	Block of 4	32.50	10.00
	P# strip of 3, Impt.	30.00	
	P# block of 6, Impt.	175.00	
216	A88 2c **red,** type IV, *Apr. 2*	5.50	2.00
	Never hinged	12.50	
	On cover		50.00
	Block of 4	25.00	15.00
	P# strip of 3, Impt.	32.50	
	P# block of 6, Impt.	175.00	
b.	Inverted overprint		*12,500.*

Special Printing

In March 1900 one pane of 100 stamps of each of the 1c (No. 215), 2c (No. 216) and 5c, 8c and 10c values, as well as 1c, 2c and 10c postage due stamps were specially overprinted for displays at the Paris Exposition (1900) and Pan American Exposition (1901). These last six items were never regularly issued with the PUERTO RICO overprint and therefore have no Scott catalogue number. The 2c pane was light red, type IV.

Stamps were handstampd type E "Specimen" in black ink by H. G. Mandel and mounted by him in separate displays for the two Expositions. Additional stamps from each pane were also handstamped "Specimen," but most were destroyed after the Expositions. However, because additional stamps that are not Special Printings exist with a black "Specimen" handstamp, expertizaton by competent authorities is reommmended.

J. M. Bartels, a stamp dealer, signed some stamps from these panes "Special Surcharge" in pencil on the gum to authenticate them as coming from the "Mandel" Special Printing panes. In 1904 or later, he handstamped additional surviving examples "Special Surcharge" in red ink on the back as his guarantee. Some of these guaranteed stamps had Mandel's "Specimen" handstamp on the face while others did not. Value, each $2,000.

No Special Printing panes overprinted "Porto Rico" were produced by the government. Stamps do exist with a black type E "Specimen" handstamp, but it is believed that H. G. Mandel applied such handstamps to regularly issued overprinted "Porto Rico" stamps from his personal collection. Examples are known of the 2c type IV, in reddish carmine, 25 degree angle.

AIR POST

In 1938 a series of eight labels, two of which were surcharged, was offered to the public as "Semi-Official Air Post Stamps", the claim being that they had been authorized by the "Puerto Rican postal officials." These labels, printed by the Ever Ready Label Co. of New York, were a private issue of Aerovias Nacionales Puerto Rico, operating a passenger and air express service. Instead of having been authorized by the postal officials, they were at first forbidden but later tolerated by the Post Office Department at Washington.

In 1941 a further set of eight triangular labels was prepared and offered to collectors, and again the Post Office Department officials at Washington objected and forbade their use after September 16, 1941.

These labels represent only the charge for service rendered by a private enterprise for transporting matter outside the mails by plane. Their use did not and does not eliminate the payment of postage on letters carried by air express, which must in every instance be paid by United States postage stamps.

POSTAGE DUE STAMPS

United States Nos. J38, J39 and J42 Overprinted in Black at 36 degree Angle

1899 **Wmk. 191** ***Perf. 12***

No.	Description	Unused	Used
J1	D2 1c **deep claret**	22.50	5.50
	Never hinged	50.00	
	On cover		125.00
	Block of 4	100.00	35.00
	P# strip of 3, Impt.	120.00	
	P# block of 6, Impt.	*625.00*	
a.	Overprint at 25 degree angle	22.50	7.50
	Never hinged	50.00	
	Pair, 36 degree and 25 degree angles	65.00	
	P# strip of 3, Impt.	150.00	
	P# block of 6, Impt.	*750.00*	
J2	D2 2c **deep claret**	20.00	6.00
	Never hinged	45.00	
	On cover		250.00
	Block of 4	80.00	37.50
	P# strip of 3, Impt.	120.00	
	P# block of 6, Impt.	*800.00*	
a.	Overprint at 25 degree angle	20.00	7.00
	Never hinged	45.00	
	Pair, 36 degree and 25 degree angles	60.00	
	P# strip of 3, Impt.	140.00	
	P# block of 6, Impt.	*900.00*	
J3	D2 10c **deep claret**	180.00	55.00
	Never hinged	375.00	
	On cover		—
	Block of 4	800.00	—
a.	Overprint at 25 degree angle	160.00	75.00
	Never hinged	330.00	
	Pair, 36 degree and 25 degree angles	650.00	
	P# strip of 3, Impt., 36 degree and 25 degree angles	*1,250.*	
	P# block of 6, Impt., 36 degree and 25 degree angles	*7,250.*	
	Nos. J1-J3 (3)	222.50	66.50

ENVELOPES

U.S. Envelopes of 1887 Issue Ovptd. in Black

PORTO RICO.

20mm long

Note: Some envelopes for which there was no obvious need were issued in small quantities. Anyone residing in Puerto Rico could, by depositing with his postmaster the required amount, order any envelope in quantities of 500, or multiples thereof, provided it was on the schedule of U.S. envelopes. Such special orders are indicated by a plus sign, i. e., Nos. U15 and U18, and half the quantities of Nos. U16 and U17.

1899-1900

No.	Description	Unused	Used
U1	U71 2c **green** (No. U311) *(3,000)*	16.00	*20.00*
	Entire	40.00	*350.00*
a.	Double overprint, entire	*3,500.*	
U2	U74 5c **blue** (No. U330) *(1,000)*	20.00	20.00
	Entire	55.00	*350.00*
a.	Double overprint, entire		—
b.	Triple overprint, entire		—

U.S. Envelopes of 1899 Overprinted in color of the stamp

PORTO RICO.

21mm long

No.	Description	Unused	Used
U3	U79 2c **carmine** (No. U362) *(100,000)*	3.00	3.00
	Entire	10.00	*12.00*
U4	U84 5c **blue** (No. U377) *(10,000)*	8.00	*9.00*
	Entire	17.50	*32.50*

Overprinted in Black PORTO RICO.

19mm long

No.	Description	Unused	Used
U5	U77 1c **green,** *blue* (No. U355) *(1,000)*		750.
	Entire		1,900.
U6	U79 2c **carmine,** *amber* (No. U363), Die 2 *(500)*	450.	*500.*
	Entire	1,100.	1,100.
U7	U79 2c **carmine,** *oriental buff* (No. U364), Die 2 *(500)*		500.
	Entire		1,100.
U8	U80 2c **carmine,** *oriental buff* (No. U369), Die 3 *(500)*		600.
	Entire		1,300.
U9	U79 2c **carmine,** *blue* (No. U365), Die 2		
	Entire		*4,000.*
U10	U83 4c **brown** (No. U374), Die 3 *(500)*	200.	*500.*
	Entire	500.	*900.*

U.S. Envelopes of 1899 Issue Ovptd.

PUERTO RICO.

23mm long

No.	Description	Unused	Used
U11	U79 2c **carmine** (No. U362) red overprint *(100,000)*	4.00	3.00
	Entire	10.00	*11.00*
U12	U79 2c **carmine,** *oriental buff* (No. U364), Die 2, black overprint *(1,000)*	—	325.00
	Entire	*1,000.*	*1,200.*
U13	U80 2c **carmine,** *oriental buff* (No. U369), Die 3, black overprint *(1,000)*		375.00
	Entire		*1,750.*
U14	U84 5c **blue** (No. U377) blue overprint *(10,000)*	14.00	14.00
	Entire	45.00	*50.00*

Overprinted in Black PUERTO RICO.

No.	Description	Unused	Used
U15	U77 1c **green,** *oriental buff* (No. U354) *(500)+*	20.00	*50.00*
	Entire	75.00	*80.00*
U16	U77 1c **green,** *blue* (No. U355) *(1,000)+*	25.00	*50.00*
	Entire	95.00	*125.00*
U17	U79 2c **carmine,** *oriental buff* (No. U364) *(1,000)+*	20.00	*50.00*
	Entire	95.00	*135.00*
U18	U79 2c **carmine,** *blue* (No. U365) *(500)+*	20.00	*50.00*
	Entire	75.00	*135.00*

There were two settings of the overprint, with minor differences, which are found on Nos. U16 and U17.

WRAPPER

U.S. Wrapper of 1899 Issue Ovptd. in Green

PORTO RICO.

21mm long

No.	Description	Unused	Used
W1	U77 1c **green,** *manila* (No. W357) *(15,000)*	8.00	*35.00*
	Entire	20.00	*110.00*

POSTAL CARDS

Values are for Entires.

Imprinted below stamp PORTO RICO.

1899-1900 **U.S. Postal Card No. UX14**

No.	Description	Unused	Used
UX1	PC8 1c **black,** *buff,* imprint 21mm long	165.	*175.*
b.	Double imprint	*2,250.*	

Imprinted below stamp PORTO RICO.

No.	Description	Unused	Used
UX1A	PC8 1c **black,** *buff,* imprint 20mm long	1,200.	*1,300.*

Imprinted below stamp PORTO RICO.

No.	Description	Unused	Used
UX2	PC8 1c **black,** *buff,* imprint 26mm long	165.	*190.*

Imprinted below stamp PUERTO RICO.

No.	Description	Unused	Used
UX3	PC8 1c **black,** *buff*	150.	*200.*
a.	Double overprint	—	

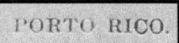

REVENUE STAMPS

U.S. Revenue Stamps Nos. R163, R168-R169, R171 & Type of 1898 Srchd. in Black or Dark Blue

a 

b 

1901 Wmk. 191R *Hyphen-hole Roulette 7*

R1	R15(a)	1c on 1c **pale blue** (Bk)	10.00	8.75
R2	R15(a)	10c on 10c **dark brown**	12.50	10.00
R3	R15(a)	25c on 25c **purple brown**	15.00	11.00
R4	R15(a)	50c on 50c **slate violet**	25.00	16.50
R5	R16(b)	$1 on $1 **pale greenish gray**	62.50	22.50
R6	R16(b)	$3 on $3 **pale greenish gray**	70.00	32.50
R7	R16(b)	$5 on $5 **pale greenish gray**	85.00	37.50
R8	R16(b)	$10 on $10 **pale greenish gray**	120.00	70.00
R9	R16(b)	$50 on $50 **pale greenish gray**	325.00	160.00
		Nos. R1-R9 (9)	725.00	368.75

Lines of 1c surcharge spaced farther apart; total depth of surcharge 15¾mm instead of 11mm.

RECTIFIED SPIRITS

U.S. Wine Stamps of 1933-34 Ovptd. in Red or Carmine

RECTIFIED

SPIRITS

Overprint Lines 14mm Apart, Second Line 25mm Long

1937 Offset Printing Wmk. 191R *Rouletted 7*

RE1	RE5	2c **green**	17.50
RE2	RE5	3c **green**	60.00
RE3	RE5	4c **green**	20.00
RE4	RE5	5c **green**	17.50
RE5	RE5	6c **green**	20.00

Overprint Lines 21½mm Apart, Second Line 23½mm Long

RE6	RE2	50c **green**	30.00
RE7	RE2	60c **green**	27.50

Handstamped overprints are also found on U.S. Wine stamps of 1933-34.

U.S. Wine Stamps of 1933-34 Ovptd. in Black

a 

b 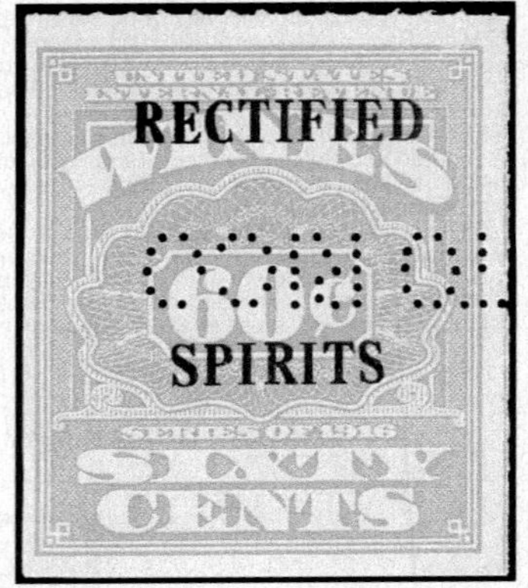

1937 Offset Printing Wmk. 191R *Rouletted 7*

RE8	RE5(a)	1c **green**	22.50
RE9	RE5(a)	2c **green**	12.50
RE10	RE5(a)	3c **green**	60.00
RE11	RE5(a)	5c **green**	12.50
RE12	RE5(a)	6c **green**	15.00
RE12A	RE2(b)	36c **green**	—
RE13	RE2(b)	50c **green**	17.50
RE14	RE2(b)	60c **green**	15.00
RE15	RE2(b)	72c **green**	75.00
RE16	RE2(b)	80c **green**	40.00

U.S. Wine Stamps of 1933-34 Ovptd. in Black

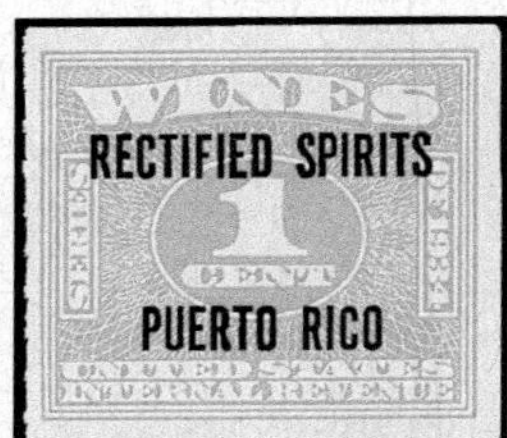

Overprint Lines 9mm Apart

1938 Offset Printing Wmk. 191R *Rouletted 7*

RE17	RE5	½c **green**		2.50
RE18	RE5	1c **green**	42.50	.60
RE19	RE5	2c **green**	42.50	.50
a.		Overprint lines 5.3mm apart		—
RE20	RE5	3c **green**	100.00	3.25
RE21	RE5	4c **green**	—	.65
RE22	RE5	5c **green**	50.00	1.00
RE23	RE5	6c **green**	50.00	1.10
RE24	RE5	10c **green**	100.00	3.50
RE25	RE5	30c **green**		30.00

Overprint Lines 12½mm Apart

RE26	RE2	36c **green**		6.00
RE27	RE2	40c **green**	150.00	5.00
RE28	RE2	50c **green**	140.00	2.50
RE29	RE2	60c **green**	105.00	.45
a.		Inverted overprint		—
RE30	RE2	72c **green**	150.00	4.00
RE31	RE2	80c **green**	150.00	4.00
RE32	RE2	$1 **green**	175.00	7.50

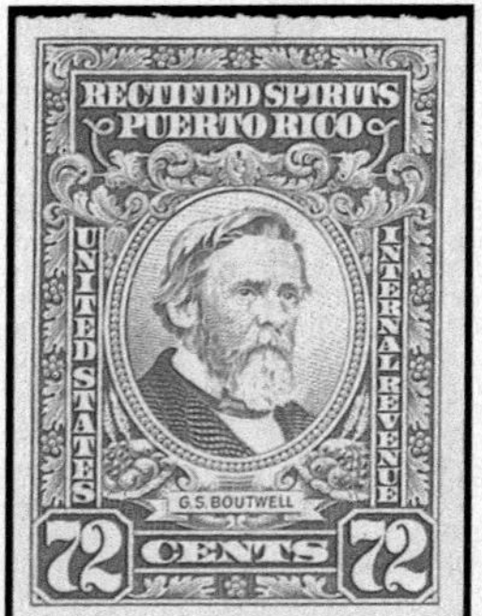

George Sewall Boutwell

Engr. (8c & 58c); Litho.

1942-57 Wmk. 191 *Rouletted 7*

Without Gum

RE33	R1	½c **carmine**	3.50	1.25
RE34	R1	1c **sepia**	8.25	3.50
RE35	R1	2c **bright yellow green**	1.10	.25
RE36	R1	3c **lilac**	70.00	35.00
RE37	R1	4c **olive**	2.25	.50
RE38	R1	5c **orange**	5.00	1.00
RE39	R1	6c **red brown**	4.00	1.25
RE40	R1	8c **bright pink** ('57)	8.25	3.50
RE41	R1	10c **bright purple**	12.50	5.00
RE41A	R1	30c **vermilion**	160.00	
RE42	R1	36c **dull yellow**	250.00	70.00
RE43	R1	40c **deep claret**	20.00	7.00
RE44	R1	50c **green**	11.00	4.00
RE45	R1	58c **red orange**	110.00	7.00
RE46	R1	60c **brown**	1.25	.25
RE47	R1	62c **black**	3.00	.70
RE48	R1	72c **blue**	40.00	1.00
RE49	R1	77½c **olive gray**	11.00	3.50
RE50	R1	80c **brownish black**	14.00	6.00
RE51	R1	$1 **violet**	75.00	25.00
		Nos. RE33-RE51 (20)	810.10	175.70

The 30c is believed not to have been placed in use.

SPECIMEN STAMPS

Handstamped U.S. Type E in Purple or Black

1899

210S	E	1c **yellow green**	200.00
211S	E	2c **reddish carmine,** type IV	200.00
212S	E	5c **blue**	200.00
213S	E	8c **violet brown**	200.00
214S	E	10c **brown**	200.00

Postage Due

1899

J1S	E	1c **deep claret**	500.00
J2S	E	2c **deep claret**	500.00
J3S	E	10c **deep claret**	500.00

See note after No. 216 for Special Printings with black "Specimen" handstamp, but note that not all stamps with the black "Specimen" handstamp are Special Printings.

Revenue

R1S	E	1c on 1c **pale blue**	40.00
R2S	E	10c on 10c **dark brown**	40.00
R3S	E	25c on 25c **purple brown**	40.00
R4S	E	50c on 50c **state violet**	40.00
R5S	E	$1 on $1 **pale greenish gray**	40.00
R6S	E	$3 on $3 **pale greenish gray**	40.00
R7S	E	$5 on $5 **pale greenish gray**	40.00
R8S	E	$10 on $10 **pale greenish gray**	40.00
R9S	E	$50 on $50 **pale greenish gray**	40.00

RYUKYU ISLANDS

rē-'yü-ˌkyü 'ī-ləndz

LOCATION — Chain of 63 islands between Japan and Formosa, separating the East China Sea from the Pacific Ocean.
GOVT. — Semi-autonomous under United States administration.
AREA — 848 sq. mi.
POP. — 945,465 (1970)
CAPITAL — Naha, Okinawa

The Ryukyus were part of Japan until American forces occupied them in 1945. The islands reverted to Japan May 15, 1972.

100 Sen = 1 Yen
100 Cents = 1 Dollar (1958)

In the Provisional Issues and Postal Stationery sections, italicized numbers in parentheses indicate quantity sold.
Values for First Day Covers are for unaddressed, cacheted covers. Values are for official cachets for Scott 1-26, C1-C3 and E1; and for commercial cachets for all others. Early cachets from the Japanese Philatelic Society command substantial premiums.

Catalogue values for unused stamps are for Never Hinged items beginning with Scott 1 in the regular postage section, Scott C1 in the air post section, Scott E1 in the special delivery section, Scott R1 in the revenue section, Scott 91S in the specimen section and Scott RQ1 in the unemployment insurance section.

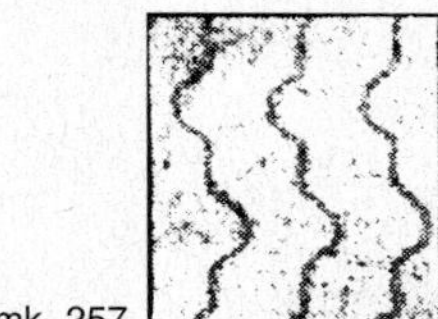

Wmk. 257

Cycad — A1
Lily — A2
Sailing Ship — A3
Farmer — A4

1948-49 Typo. Wmk. 257 *Perf. 13*

Second Printing, July 18, 1949

1	A1 5s **magenta**	2.00	2.00
	Imprint block of 10	30.00	
2	A2 10s **yellow green**	5.00	5.00
	Imprint block of 10	75.00	
3	A1 20s **yellow green**	3.00	3.00
	Imprint block of 10	42.50	
4	A3 30s **vermilion**	1.25	1.25
	Imprint block of 10	18.00	
5	A2 40s **magenta**	1.25	1.25
	Imprint block of 10	18.00	
6	A3 50s **ultramarine**	5.00	*4.00*
	Imprint block of 10	75.00	
7	A4 1y **ultramarine**	5.00	5.00
	Imprint block of 10	75.00	
	Nos. 1-7 (7)	22.50	21.50

First Printing, July 1, 1948

1a	A1 5s **magenta**	3.00	*3.50*
	First day cover		250.00
	Imprint block of 10	45.00	
2a	A2 10s **yellow green**	2.00	*2.00*
	First day cover		250.00
	Imprint block of 10	30.00	
3a	A1 20s **yellow green**	2.00	*2.00*
	First day cover		250.00
	Imprint block of 10	30.00	
4a	A3 30s **vermilion**	4.00	*3.50*
	First day cover		250.00
	Imprint block of 10	45.00	
5a	A2 40s **magenta**	50.00	50.00
	First day cover		250.00
	Imprint block of 10	850.00	
6a	A3 50s **ultramarine**	4.00	4.00
	First day cover		250.00
	Imprint block of 10	55.00	
7a	A4 1y **ultramarine**	400.00	325.00
	First day cover		250.00
	Imprint block of 10	*6,250.*	
	Nos. 1a-7a (7)	465.00	390.00

First printing: thick yellow gum, dull colors, rough perforations, grayish paper. Second printing: white gum, sharp colors, clean-cut and rough perforations, white paper. Third printing (Sept. 28, 1950): 5s to 50s denominations, white gum, clean-cut perforations, cream paper (same values as second printings).

A5

Designs: 50s, Tile rooftop and Shisa. 1y, Ryukyuan girl. 2y, Main hall of Shuri Castle. 3y, Female dragonhead statue. 4y, Two women. 5y, Sea shells.

1950, Jan. 21 Photo. Unwmk. *Perf. 13x13¼*

Off-white Paper

8	A5 50s **dark carmine rose**	.25	.25
	First day cover		20.00
	Imprint block of 6	2.00	
a.	White paper, third printing, *Sept. 6, 1958*	.50	.50
	First day cover		27.50
	Imprint block of 10	6.50	
b.	"White Sky" variety (pos. 76)	3.50	3.50
9	A5 1y **deep blue**	3.25	3.00
	First day cover		20.00
	Imprint block of 6	30.00	
10	A5 2y **rose violet**	9.00	6.00
	First day cover		20.00
	Imprint block of 6	80.00	
11	A5 3y **carmine rose**	22.50	11.00
	First day cover		20.00
	Imprint block of 6	200.00	
12	A5 4y **greenish gray**	11.00	11.00
	First day cover		20.00
	Imprint block of 6	90.00	
13	A5 5y **blue green**	6.50	6.00
	First day cover		20.00
	Imprint block of 6	50.00	
	First day cover, #8-13		200.00
	Nos. 8-13 (6)	52.50	37.25

The original first two printings (No. 8) were printed on off-white paper with yellowish gum and a 5-character imprint in the sheet margin. The first printing is a deep carmine red or dark red, and the second printing a dark carmine rose. The first printing was issued Jan. 21, 1950; the second printing received in Naha Sept. 22, 1950; and the third printing (No. 8a) Sept. 6, 1958. Quantities: first printing: 300,000; second printing: 3,000,000; and third printing: 300,000. The first printing unused is much scarcer than the second printing because most of the first printing was used as postage.

No. 8a has colorless gum and an 8-character imprint in the sheet margin. The color is a deep red.

For No. 8b, a defect in position 76 of the plates used resulted in the sky above the roof being predominantly white in the second printing, whereas in the first printing the 'white sky' is not as pronounced. The master negative and plate were reworked for the third printing, so position 76 in this printing does not have the "white sky" variety.

For surcharges see Nos. 16-17.

Ryukyu University and Female Dragonhead Statue — A6

1951, Feb. 12 *Perf. 13½x13¼*

14	A6 3y **red brown**	45.00	25.00
	First day cover		60.00
	Imprint block of 6	375.00	

Opening of Ryukyu University, Feb. 12.

Ryukyuan Pine Tree — A7

1951, Feb. 19 *Perf. 13¼*

15	A7 3y **dark green**	40.00	22.50
	First day cover		60.00
	Imprint block of 6	360.00	

Reforestation Week, Feb. 18-24.

No. 8 surcharged in Black

16A Type I 16 Type II 16B Type III

There are three types of 10y surcharge:

Type I: narrow-spaced rules, "10" normal spacing, "Kai Tei" characters in 9-point type. First printing, Jan. 1, 1952.

Type II: wide-spaced rules, "10" normal spacing, "Kai Tei" characters in 9-point type. Second printing, June 5, 1952.

Type III: rules and "10" both wide-spaced, "Kai Tei" characters in 8-point type. Third printing, Dec. 8, 1952.

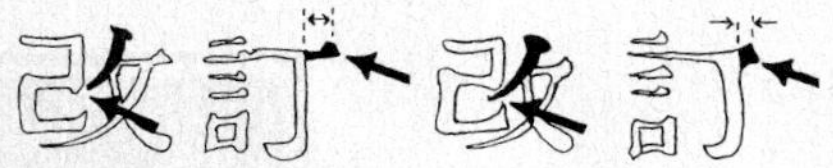

9 Point Kai Tei 8 Point Kai Tei

Both eight and nine point type were used in overprinting Nos. 16-17. In the varieties listed below, the first number indicates the size of the "Kai" character, and the second number is the size of the "Tei" character.

1952 *Perf. 13½x13*

16	A5 10y on 50s **dark carmine rose** (II)	8.00	8.00
	Imprint block of 6	80.00	
	Top imprint block of 4, *Higa Seal* (pos. 8, 9, 18, 19)	70.00	
c.	8/8 point Kai Tei	8.00	8.00
d.	9/8 point Kai Tei	80.00	80.00
e.	9/9-9/8-8/8 se-tenant (horiz. strip of all 3 varieties)	140.00	140.00
	8/8-9/9 horiz. se-tenant pair	30.00	30.00
	9/9-8/8 horiz. se-tenant pair	30.00	30.00
f.	Surcharge transposed	900.00	—
g.	Legend of surcharge only (no obliteration bars)	1,200.	
h.	Wrong font for "0" (pos. 59)	150.00	150.00
i.	Wrong font for "Yen" symbol (pos. 69)	150.00	150.00
j.	Surcharge on "white sky" variety (No. 8b) (pos. 76)	150.00	150.00

On No. 16e, the entire obliteration-bars portion of the surcharge normally under the 10 Yen must be visible at the top of the stamp. Ten examples of No. 16e exist (pos. 91-100) with the full obliteration bars also in the bottom selvage.

Forgeries to defraud the Postal Agency of revenue are known, used only, at the Gusikawa Post Office. Two types. Value, $500 each.

16A A5 10y on 50s **dark carmine rose** (I) 30.00 30.00
Imprint block of 6 280.00
a. 8/8 point Kai Tei 30.00 30.00
8/8-9/9 horiz. se-tenant pair (pos. 23-24) 190.00 240.00
9/9-8/8 horiz. se-tenant pair 110.00 110.00
b. Bottom two bars inverted (pos. 17) 150.00 150.00
c. Wrong font for "0" (pos. 73) 250.00 250.00
d. Surcharge on "white sky" variety (No. 8b) (pos. 76) 250.00 250.00
e. Wide spaced obliterating bars (pos. 72) 150.00 150.00
f. Wide spaced bottom obliterating bars (pos. 86, 95) 80.00 80.00

16B A5 10y on 50s **dark carmine rose** (III) 45.00 35.00
Imprint block of 6 400.00
a. Wrong font for "Yen" symbol (pos. 25, 35, 85) 200.00 200.00
b. Wrong font for "Tei" (pos. 26) 350.00 350.00
c. Asterisk missing (pos. 54) — —
d. "Kai Tei" 1.25mm above asterisk (pos. 54) 350.00 350.00
e. "Kai" omitted (pos. 71) —
f. Narrow spaced "10" (pos. 96) 350.00 350.00
Strip of 3, narrow spaced "10" in center (pos. 95-97) 450.00
g. Surcharge on "white sky" variety (No. 8b) 350.00 350.00
h. Extra wide spaced "10" (pos. 60) 200.00 200.00
i. Asterisk within 2.0mm of "Kai Tei" (pos. 87) 200.00 200.00

The Kai Tei of the third printing measures the same as the 8-point type in the earlier printings but has differing characteristics. The Top curved line of the Kai is shorter and the lower curved line is also much shorter.

No. 10 surcharged 100y in black

17 A5 100y on 2y **rose violet,** Kai Tei characters in 9/9-point type, June 16, 1952 2,000. 1,400.
Hinged 1,600.
Imprint block of 6 17,500.
Top imprint block of 4, *Higa Seal* (pos. 7, 8, 17, 18) 9,500.
a. 8/8 point Kai Tei 2,000. 1,400.
b. 9/8 point Kai Tei 3,250. 3,250.
9/9-9/8-8/8 se-tenant (horiz. strip of all 3 varieties) *9,500. 9,500.*
8/8-9/9 horiz. se-tenant pair *4,750. 4,750.*
9/9-8/8 horiz. se-tenant pair *6,500. 6,500.*
c. Center "0" in wrong font, stamp with 9/9 Kai Tei (pos. 42) 4,000. 4,000.
d. Center "0" in wrong font, stamp with 8/8 Kai Tei (pos. 67, 86) 3,500. 3,500.
e. Center "0" in wrong font, stamp with 9/8 Kai Tei (pos. 53) 5,000. 5,000.
f. Wrong font for last "0" (pos. 59) 5,000. 5,000.
g. Wrong font for "yen" symbol (pos. 69) 5,000. 5,000.
h. "Tei" in wrong font (pos. 9) *4,000. 4,000.*

Varieties of shifted and damaged surcharge characters exist, most notably a damaged ("clipped") Kai.

The "Tei" on No. 17h is the character used on Nos. 16 and 16A.

See note after 16B to differentiate between 8-point and 9-point characters.

Surcharge forgeries are known. Authentication by competant experts is recommended.

Dove, Bean Sprout and Map — A8

1952, Apr. 1 ***Perf. 13¼***
18 A8 3y **deep plum** 80.00 40.00
First day cover 80.00
Imprint block of 10 1,250.

Establishment of the Government of the Ryukyu Islands (GRI), April 1, 1952.

Madanbashi Bridge — A9

Designs: 2y, Main Hall, Shuri Castle. 3y, Shureimon Gate. 6y, Stone Gate, Sogen-ji Temple, Naha. 10y, Benzaiten-do Temple. 30y, Sonohyan Utaki (altar) at Shuri Castle. 50y, Tamaudun (royal mausoleum). Shuri. 100y, Stone Bridge, Hojo Pond, Enkaku Temple.

1952-53 ***Perf. 13x13¼***
19 A9 1y **red,** *Nov. 20, 1952* .30 .30
Imprint block of 10 4.50
20 A9 2y **green,** *Nov. 20, 1952* .40 .40
Imprint block of 10 6.00
21 A9 3y **aquamarine,** *Nov. 20, 1952* .50 .50
First day cover, #19-21 40.00
Imprint block of 10 7.50
22 A9 6y **blue,** *Jan. 20, 1953* 2.00 2.00
First day cover 27.50
Imprint block of 10 34.00
23 A9 10y **crimson rose,** *Jan. 20, 1953* 2.50 1.00
First day cover 47.50
Imprint block of 10 45.00
24 A9 30y **olive green,** *Jan. 20, 1953* 9.00 7.50
First day cover 75.00
Imprint block of 10 160.00
a. 30y **light olive green,** *1958* 50.00
Imprint block of 10 750.00
25 A9 50y **rose violet,** *Jan. 20, 1953* 12.50 9.00
First day cover 125.00
Imprint block of 10 175.00
26 A9 100y **claret,** *Jan. 20, 1953* 15.00 5.00
First day cover 190.00
Imprint block of 10 210.00
First day cover, #22-26 550.00
Nos. 19-26 (8) 42.20 25.70

Reception at Shuri Castle — A10

Perry and American Fleet in Naha Port — A11

1953, May 26 ***Perf. 13x13¼***
27 A10 3y **deep magenta** 12.00 6.50
Imprint block of 6 105.00
28 A11 6y **dull blue** 1.25 1.50
First day cover, #27-28 15.00
Imprint block of 6 10.00

Centenary of the arrival of Commodore Matthew Calbraith Perry at Naha, Okinawa.

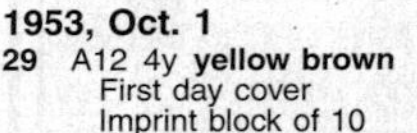

Chofu Ota and Pencil-shaped Matrix — A12

1953, Oct. 1 ***Perf. 13¼x13***
29 A12 4y **yellow brown** 11.00 5.00
First day cover 20.00
Imprint block of 10 140.00

Third Newspaper Week, Oct. 1-7.

Shigo Toma and Pen — A13

1954, Oct. 1
30 A13 4y **blue** 10.00 7.50
First day cover 25.00
Imprint block of 10 135.00

Fourth Newspaper Week, Oct. 1-7.

Ryukyu Pottery — A14

Designs: 4y, Dachibin (sake or water flask). 15y, Tsuikin lacquerware tray. 20y, Kajimayaa pattern on Kijoka-bashofu textile.

1954-55 **Photo.** ***Perf. 13x13¼***
31 A14 4y **brown,** *June 25, 1954* .90 .50
First day cover 10.00
Imprint block of 10 10.00
32 A14 15y **vermilion,** *June 20, 1955* 3.50 3.50
First day cover 12.50
Imprint block of 10 55.00
33 A14 20y **yellow orange,** *June 20, 1955* 2.25 2.25
First day cover 12.50
Imprint block of 10 35.00
First day cover, #32-33 35.00
Nos. 31-33 (3) 6.65 6.25

For surcharges see Nos. C19, C21, C23.

Noguni Shrine and Sweet Potato Plant — A15

1955, Nov. 26 ***Perf. 13¼***
34 A15 4y **blue** 10.00 7.00
First day cover 22.50
Imprint block of 10 125.00

350th anniv. of the introduction of the sweet potato to the Ryukyu Islands.

Stylized Trees — A16

1956, Feb. 18 ***Perf. 13***
35 A16 4y **bluish green** 10.00 6.00
First day cover 20.00
Imprint block of 6 85.00

Arbor Week, Feb. 18-24.

Yanaji (Willow) Dance — A17

8y, Munjuru (Straw Hat) Dance. 14y, Nido Tichiuchi Dance.

1956, May 1 *Perf. 13x13¼*

No.	Type	Description	Unused	Used
36	A17	5y **rose lilac**	1.00	.60
		First day cover		6.50
		Imprint block of 10	15.00	
37	A17	8y **violet blue**	2.00	2.00
		First day cover		6.50
		Imprint block of 10	32.50	
38	A17	14y **reddish brown**	2.50	2.50
		First day cover		6.50
		Imprint block of 10	37.50	
		First day cover, #36-38		35.00
		Nos. 36-38 (3)	5.50	5.10

For surcharges see Nos. C20, C22.

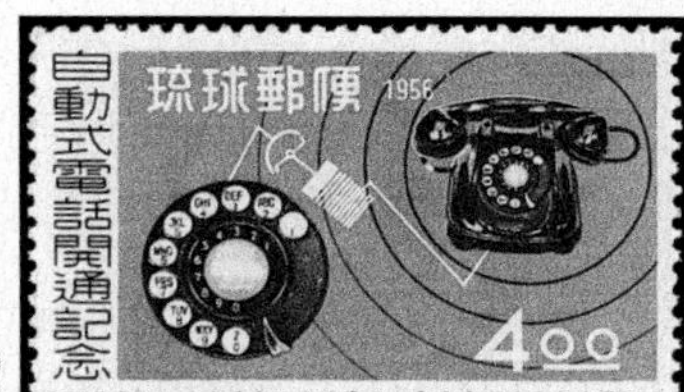

Telephone A18

1956, June 8

No.	Type	Description	Unused	Used
39	A18	4y **violet blue**	12.50	8.00
		First day cover		20.00
		Imprint block of 6	110.00	

Establishment of dial telephone system.

Garland of Pine, Bamboo and Plum — A19

1956, Dec. 1 *Perf. 13¼*

No.	Type	Description	Unused	Used
40	A19	2y **multicolored**	1.60	1.60
		First day cover		3.50
		Imprint block of 10	22.50	

New Year, 1957.

Map of Okinawa and Pencil Rocket — A20

1957, Oct. 1 **Photo.** *Perf. 13*

No.	Type	Description	Unused	Used
41	A20	4y **deep violet blue**	1.00	1.00
		First day cover		6.00
		Imprint block of 10	12.50	

Seventh Newspaper Week, Oct. 1-7.

Phoenix — A21

1957, Dec. 1 *Perf. 13x13¼*

No.	Type	Description	Unused	Used
42	A21	2y **multicolored**	.25	.25
		First day cover		1.50
		Imprint block of 10	3.50	

New Year, 1958.

Ryukyu Stamps — A22

1958, July 1 *Perf. 13½*

No.	Type	Description	Unused	Used
43	A22	4y **multicolored**	.80	.80
		First day cover		1.25
		Imprint block of 4	4.00	

10th anniv. of 1st Ryukyu stamps.

Yen Symbol and Dollar Sign — A23

Perf. 10.3, 10.8, 11.1 & Compound

1958, Sept. 16 **Typo.**

Without Gum

No.	Type	Description	Unused	Used
44	A23	½c **orange**	.80	.80
		Imprint block of 6	7.25	
a.		Imperf., pair	*1,500.*	
b.		Horiz. pair, imperf. between	225.00	
c.		Vert. pair, imperf. between	575.00	
d.		Vert. strip of 4, imperf. between	800.00	
45	A23	1c **yellow green**	1.25	1.25
		Imprint block of 6	10.00	
a.		Horiz. pair, imperf. between	200.00	
b.		Vert. pair, imperf. between	150.00	
c.		Vert. strip of 3, imperf. between	650.00	
d.		Vert. strip of 4, imperf. between	800.00	
e.		Block of 4, imperf. btwn. vert. & horiz.	*10,000.*	
46	A23	2c **dark blue**	2.00	2.00
		Imprint block of 6	16.00	
a.		Horiz. pair, imperf. between	200.00	
b.		Vert. pair, imperf. between	*2,200.*	
c.		Horiz. strip of 3, imperf. between	450.00	
d.		Horiz. strip of 4, imperf. between	700.00	
47	A23	3c **deep carmine**	1.50	1.50
		Imprint block of 6	12.00	
a.		Horiz. pair, imperf. between	200.00	
b.		Vert. pair, imperf. between	150.00	
c.		Vert. strip of 3, imperf. between	400.00	
d.		Vert. strip of 4, imperf. between	750.00	
e.		Block of 4, imperf. btwn. vert. & horiz.	*10,000.*	
48	A23	4c **bright green**	2.00	2.00
		Imprint block of 6	16.00	
a.		Horiz. pair, imperf. between	*400.00*	
b.		Vert. pair, imperf. between	175.00	
49	A23	5c **orange**	4.00	3.75
		Imprint block of 6	32.50	
a.		Horiz. pair, imperf. between	200.00	
b.		Vert. pair, imperf. between	*850.00*	
50	A23	10c **aquamarine**	5.25	4.75
		Imprint block of 6	37.50	
a.		Horiz. pair, imperf. between	200.00	
b.		Vert. pair, imperf. between	150.00	
c.		Vert. strip of 3, imperf. between	750.00	
51	A23	25c **bright violet blue**	7.50	6.00
		Imprint block of 6	57.50	
a.		Gummed paper, perf. 10.3 ('61)	15.00	15.00
		Imprint block of 6	95.00	
b.		Horiz. pair, imperf. between	*2,200.*	
c.		Vert. pair, imperf. between	*5,000.*	
d.		Vert. strip of 3, imperf. between	900.00	
52	A23	50c **gray**	15.00	10.00
		Imprint block of 6	120.00	
a.		Gummed paper, perf. 10.3 ('61)	15.00	15.00
		Imprint block of 6	150.00	
		First day cover, #51a-52a		35.00
b.		Horiz. pair, imperf. between	*1,750.*	
53	A23	$1 **rose lilac**	11.00	5.50
		Imprint block of 6	90.00	
a.		Horiz. pair, imperf. between	450.00	
b.		Vert. pair, imperf. between	*2,250.*	
		Nos. 44-53 (10)	50.30	37.55

Printed locally. Perforation, paper and shade varieties exist. Nos. 51a and 52a are on off-white paper and perf 10.3.

First day covers come with various combinations of stamps: Nos. 44-48, 49-53, 44-53 etc. Values $20 for short set of low values (Nos. 44-48) to $60 for full set on one cover.

Gate of Courtesy — A24

1958, Oct. 15 **Photo.** *Perf. 13x13¼*

No.	Type	Description	Unused	Used
54	A24	3c **multicolored**	1.25	1.25
		First day cover		1.50
		Imprint block of 4	6.25	

Restoration of Shureimon, Gate of Courtesy, on road leading to Shuri City.

Imitations of this stamp were distributed in 1972 to discourage speculation in Ryukyuan stamps. The imitations were printed without gum and have a lengthy message in light blue printed on the back. A second type exists, with printed black perforations and three Japanese characters on the back ("Mozo Hin" — imitation) in black. Value, sheet of 10 $15.

Lion Dance — A25

1958, Dec. 10 *Perf. 13¼x13*

No.	Type	Description	Unused	Used
55	A25	1½c **multicolored**	.30	.30
		First day cover		1.50
		Imprint block of 6	2.00	

New Year, 1959.

Trees and Mountains — A26

1959, Apr. 30 *Perf. 13¼*

No.	Type	Description	Unused	Used
56	A26	3c **blue, yellow green, green & red**	.70	.60
		First day cover		1.00
		Imprint block of 6	5.50	

"Make the Ryukyus Green" movement.

Perforation and Paper Varieties of Ryukyu Islands Scott 44-53

Perforation	Perf.	1/2¢ (No. 44) Paper Type				1¢ (No. 45) Paper Type				2¢ (No. 46) Paper Type				3¢ (No. 47) Paper Type				4¢ (No. 48) Paper Type				5¢ (No. 49) Paper Type				10¢ (No. 50) Paper Type				25¢ (No. 51) Paper Type				50¢ (No. 52) Paper Type				$1 (No. 53) Paper Type			
	ID#	1	2	3	4	1	2	3	4	1	2	3	4	1	2	3	4	1	2	3	4	1	2	3	4	1	2	3	4	1	2	3	4	1	2	3	4	1	2	3	4
11.1 x 11.1	M	*			*	*	*			*			*	*	*		*	*	*			*	*		*	*	*	*		*		*		*				*		*	
11.1 x 10.8	N	*			*	*	*			*			*	*	*		*	*	*		∞	*	?		*	*	*			*		*		*				*		*	
11.1 x 10.3	O	*			*	?	*			*			*	*	*			*				*	*			*				*		*		*				*			
10.8 x 11.1	P	*			*	*	*			*			*	*	*			*	*			*	*		*	*	*			*		*		*				*		*	
10.8 x 10.8	Q	*			*	*	*			*			*	*	*			*	*			*			*	*	*			*	*	*		*				*		*	
10.8 x 10.3	R	*			*	*	*			*			*	?	*			*	*			*				*	*			*				*							
10.3 x 11.1	S	*				*	*			*			*	*	*		*	?	*			*	*		*		*			*								*			
10.3 x 10.8	T	*			*	*	*			*			*	*	*		*		*			*	*			*	*	*										*		*	
10.3 x 10.3	U	*				?	*			*			*	?	*							*	*		*	?	*			\		*		\							

Paper Legend: 1= off-white; 2= white; 3= ivory; 4= thick

Specialists use a shorthand to refer to perf. and paper types: e.g., 50M3 =10¢ stamp, perf. 11.1 x 11.1, ivory paper.

Notes:

* = Verified variety
? = Reported in literature, but unverified variety.
∞ = 48N4 is unknown; however, a single example of 48N exists on a thick white paper unknown used for any other issue.
\ = These particular perf/paper combinations are known only in stamps of the Second (1961) Printing (51a and 52a)

The following are known unused only: 45R1, 45T2, 47O1, 48N4, 53O1.

The following are known used only: 47N4, 47T4, 50M3, 50Q2, 50R2, 50T2, 51P3, 51S1, 53T3.

Chart classifications and data supplied by courtesy of the Ryukyu Philatelic Specialist Society.

Yonaguni Moth — A27

1959, July 23 **Photo.** ***Perf. 13x13¼***

57 A27 3c **multicolored** 1.20 1.00
First day cover 1.50
Imprint block of 6 9.00

Meeting of the Japanese Biological Education Society in Okinawa.

Hibiscus — A28

琉球郵便
Inscribed

Designs: 3c, Fish (Moorish idol). 8c, Sea shell (Phalium bandatum). 13c, Butterfly (Kallinia inachus eucerca), denomination at left, butterfly going up. 17c, Jellyfish (Dactylometra pacifera Goette).

1959, Aug. 10 ***Perf. 12¾x13***

58 A28 ½c **multicolored** .30 .25
Imprint block of 10 3.50
59 A28 3c **multicolored** .75 .40
Imprint block of 10 9.00
60 A28 8c **light ultramarine, black & ocher** 10.00 5.50
Imprint block of 10 180.00
61 A28 13c **light blue, gray & orange** 1.75 1.75
Imprint block of 10 28.50
62 A28 17c **violet blue, red & yellow** 20.00 9.00
Imprint block of 10 330.00
First day cover, #58-62 17.50
Nos. 58-62 (5) 32.80 16.90

Four-character inscription measures 10x2mm on ½c; 12x3mm on 3c, 8c; 8½x2mm on 13c, 17c. See Nos. 76-80.

Toy (Yakaji) — A29

1959, Dec. 1 ***Perf. 13x13¼***

63 A29 1½c **gold & multicolored** .55 .45
First day cover 1.50
Imprint block of 10 8.00

New Year, 1960.

University Badge A30

1960, May 22 **Photo.**

64 A30 3c **multicolored** .95 .75
First day cover 1.25
Imprint block of 6 7.25

10th anniv. opening of Ryukyu University.

Straw Hat Folk Dancer — A31

Designs: 2½c, Nufwabushi. 5c, Hatumabushi. 10c, Hanafu.

1960, Nov. 1 **Photo.** ***Perf. 13¼***

Dark Gray Background

65 A31 1c **yellow, red & violet** 2.00 .80
Imprint block of 10 22.00
66 A31 2½c **crimson, blue & yellow** 3.00 1.00
Imprint block of 10 37.50
67 A31 5c **dark blue, yellow & red** 1.00 .50
Imprint block of 10 11.00
68 A31 10c **dark blue, yellow & red** 1.00 .70
Imprint block of 10 12.00
First day cover, #65-68 5.50
Nos. 65-68 (4) 7.00 3.00

See Nos. 81-87, 220.

Torch and Nago Bay — A32

Runners at Starting Line — A33

1960, Nov. 8 **Litho.** ***Perf. 13x13¼***

72 A32 3c **light blue, green & red** 5.00 3.00
First day cover 3.50
Imprint block of 6 37.50
73 A33 8c **orange & slate green** 1.00 .75
First day cover 1.50
Imprint block of 6 7.50
First day cover, #72-73 5.00

8th Kyushu Inter-Prefectural Athletic Meet, Nago, Northern Okinawa, Nov. 6-7.

Little Egret and Rising Sun — A34

1960, Dec. 1 **Photo.**

74 A34 3c **reddish brown** 5.00 3.50
First day cover 4.00
Imprint block of 6 37.50

National census.

Okinawa Bull Fight — A35

1960, Dec. 10

75 A35 1½c **bister, dark blue & red brown** 1.50 1.50
First day cover 2.00
Imprint block of 6 11.00

New Year, 1961.

Type of 1959 With Japanese Inscription Redrawn

A28a

1960-61 **Photo.**

76 A28a ½c **multicolored,** *Oct. 1961* .60 .45
Imprint block of 10 6.50
77 A28a 3c **multicolored,** *Aug. 23, 1961* 1.00 .35
First day cover 1.50
Imprint block of 10 11.50
78 A28a 8c **light ultramarine, black & ocher,** *July 1, 1960* 1.25 .80
Imprint block of 10 14.50
79 A28a 13c **blue, brown & red,** *July 1, 1960* 1.50 .90
Imprint block of 10 16.00
80 A28a 17c **violet blue, red & yellow,** *July 1, 1960* 12.50 6.00
Imprint block of 10 130.00
First day cover, #78-80 15.00
Nos. 76-80 (5) 16.85 8.50

Size of Japanese inscription on Nos. 78-80 is 10½x1½mm. On No. 79 the denomination is at right, butterfly going down.

Dancer Type of 1960 with "RYUKYUS" Added in English

Designs: 20c, Shudun. 25c, Haodori. 50c, Nubui Kuduchi. $1, Koteibushi.

1961-64 ***Perf. 13¼***

81 A31 1c **multicolored,** *Dec. 5, 1961* .25 .25
First day cover 1.00
Imprint block of 10 2.00
82 A31 2½c **multicolored,** *June 20, 1962* .25 .25
Imprint block of 10 2.25
83 A31 5c **multicolored,** *June 20, 1962* .25 .25
Imprint block of 10 3.00
84 A31 10c **multicolored,** *June 20, 1962* .45 .40
First day cover, #82-84 1.50
Imprint block of 10 5.75
84A A31 20c **multicolored,** *Jan. 20, 1964* 3.00 1.40
First day cover 2.50
Imprint block of 10 35.00
85 A31 25c **multicolored,** *Feb. 1, 1962* 1.00 .90
First day cover 2.00
Imprint block of 10 13.00
86 A31 50c **multicolored,** *Sept. 1, 1961* 2.50 1.40
Imprint block of 10 32.50
87 A31 $1 **multicolored,** *Sept. 1, 1961* 5.50 .25
Imprint block of 10 62.50
First day cover, #86-87 35.00
Nos. 81-87 (8) 13.20 5.10

Pine Tree — A36

1961, May 1 **Litho.**

88 A36 3c **yellow green & red** 1.75 1.25
First day cover 1.50
Imprint block of 6 14.00

"Make the Ryukyus Green" movement.

Naha, Steamer and Sailboat A37

1961, May 20 **Photo.**

89 A37 3c **aquamarine** 2.25 1.50
First day cover 1.75
Imprint block of 6 18.00

40th anniv. of Naha.

White Silver Temple — A38

1961, Oct. 1 Typo. Unwmk. ***Perf. 10¾, 10¾x10¼***

90 A38 3c **red brown** 2.50 2.00
First day cover 2.00
Imprint block of 6 18.00
a. Horiz. pair, imperf. between *1,000.*
b. Vert. pair, imperf. between *700.00*

Merger of townships Takamine, Kanegushiku and Miwa with Itoman.

A 3-cent stamp to commemorate the merger of two cities, Shimoji-cho and Hirara-shi of Miyako Island, was scheduled to be issued on Oct. 30, 1961. However, the merger was called off and the stamp never issued. It features a white chaplet on Kiyako linen on a blue background.

Books and Bird — A39

1961, Nov. 12 **Litho.** ***Perf. 13¼***

91 A39 3c **multicolored** 1.10 .90
First day cover 1.25
Imprint block of 6 10.00

Book Week, 10th anniversary.

Rising Sun and Eagles — A40

1961, Dec. 10 **Photo.**

92 A40 1½c **gold, vermilion & black** 2.00 2.00
First day cover 3.00
Imprint block of 6 16.00

New Year, 1962.

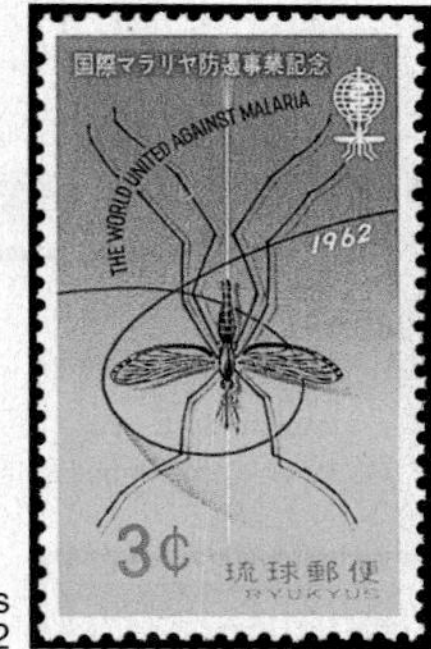

Symbolic Steps, Trees and Government Building — A41

Design: 3c, Government Building.

1962, Apr. 1 ***Perf. 13½***

93 A41 1½c **multicolored** .60 .60
Imprint block of 6 4.75
94 A41 3c **bright green, red & gray** .80 .80
Imprint block of 6 6.50
First day cover, #93-94 2.00

10th anniv. of the Government of the Ryukyu Islands (GRI).

Anopheles Hyrcanus Sinensis — A42

Design: 8c, Malaria eradication emblem and Shurei gate.

1962, Apr. 7 ***Perf. 13¼x13***

95 A42 3c **multicolored** .60 .60
Imprint block of 6 4.50
96 A42 8c **multicolored** .90 .75
Imprint block of 6 7.50
First day cover, #95-96 2.25

World Health Organization drive to eradicate malaria.

Dolls and Toys — A43

1962, May 5 ***Perf. 13x13¼***

97 A43 3c **red, black, blue & buff** 1.10 1.00
First day cover 1.50
Imprint block of 6 9.00

Children's Day, 1962.

Linden or Sea Hibiscus — A44

Flowers: 3c, Deigo tree (Erythrina variegata var. orientealis). 8c, Iju (Schima liukiuensis Nakal). 13c, Touch-me-not (Impatiens balsamina). 17c, Shell flower (Alpinia speciosa).

1962, June 1 **Photo.** ***Perf. 13¼***

98 A44 ½c **multicolored** .35 .25
Imprint block of 10 4.00
99 A44 3c **multicolored** .30 .25
Imprint block of 10 4.50
100 A44 8c **multicolored** .55 .45
Imprint block of 10 6.25
101 A44 13c **multicolored** .75 .60
Imprint block of 10 8.50
102 A44 17c **multicolored** 1.25 .80
Imprint block of 10 14.00
First day cover, #98-102 3.75
Nos. 98-102 (5) 3.20 2.35

See Nos. 107 and 114 for 1½c and 15c flower stamps. For surcharge see No. 190.

Akae (Earthenware)
A45

1962, July 5
103 A45 3c **multicolored** 3.50 2.50
First day cover 2.75
Imprint block of 6 26.00

Philatelic Week, July 5-12.

Japanese Fencing (Kendo)
A46

1962, July 25 ***Perf. 13¼x13***
104 A46 3c **multicolored** 3.50 2.50
First day cover 3.50
Imprint block of 6 26.00

All-Japan Kendo Meeting in Okinawa, July 24-25, 1962.

Rabbit Playing near Water, Bingata Cloth Design — A47

1962, Dec. 10 ***Perf. 13¼***
105 A47 1½c **gold & multicolored** 1.00 .80
First day cover 1.50
Imprint block of 10 12.50

New Year, 1963.

Young Man and Woman, Stone Relief — A48

1963, Jan. 15 **Photo.**
106 A48 3c **gold, black & blue** .90 .80
First day cover 1.50
Imprint block of 6 6.75

Gooseneck Cactus (Epiphyllum strictum) — A49

1963, Apr. 5 ***Perf. 13x13¼***
107 A49 1½c **dark blue green, yellow & pink** .25 .25
First day cover 1.25
Imprint block of 10 1.40

Trees and Wooded Hills — A50

1963, Mar. 25 ***Perf. 13¼***
108 A50 3c **ultramarine, green & red brown** 1.00 .80
First day cover 1.25
Imprint block of 6 7.00

"Make the Ryukyus Green" movement.

Map of Okinawa — A51

1963, Apr. 30
109 A51 3c **multicolored** 1.25 1.00
First day cover 1.50
Imprint block of 6 9.00

Opening of the Round Road on Okinawa.

Hawks over Islands — A52

1963, May 10 **Photo.**
110 A52 3c **multicolored** 1.10 .95
First day cover 1.50
Imprint block of 6 9.00

Bird Day, May 10.

Shioya Bridge — A53

1963, June 5
111 A53 3c **multicolored** 1.10 .95
First day cover 1.40
Imprint block of 6 8.25

Opening of Shioya Bridge over Shioya Bay.

Tsuikin-wan Lacquerware Bowl — A54

1963, July 1 ***Perf. 13¼***
112 A54 3c **multicolored** 2.75 2.50
First day cover 2.75
Imprint block of 6 20.00

Philatelic Week.

Map of Far East and JCI Emblem — A55

1963, Sept. 16 **Photo.**
113 A55 3c **multicolored** .70 .70
First day cover 1.25
Imprint block of 6 6.00

Meeting of the International Junior Chamber of Commerce (JCI), Naha, Okinawa, Sept. 16-19.

Hamaomoto (Crinum asiaticum var. japonica) — A56

1963, Oct. 15 ***Perf. 13x13¼***
114 A56 15c **multicolored** 1.25 .80
First day cover 1.25
Imprint block of 10 17.50

Site of Nakagusuku Castle — A57

1963, Nov. 1 ***Perf. 13¼***
115 A57 3c **multicolored** .60 .60
First day cover 1.25
Imprint block of 6 4.75

Protection of national cultural treasures.

Flame — A58

1963, Dec. 10
116 A58 3c **red, dark blue & yellow** .65 .60
First day cover 1.25
Imprint block of 6 5.00

15th anniv. of the Universal Declaration of Human Rights.

Dragon (Bingata Pattern) — A59

1963, Dec. 10 **Photo.**
117 A59 1½c **multicolored** .55 .50
First day cover 1.50
Imprint block of 10 7.00

New Year, 1964.

Carnation — A60

1964, May 10 ***Perf. 13¼***

118 A60 3c **blue, yellow, black & carmine** .40 .35
First day cover 1.25
Imprint block of 6 3.00

Mothers Day.

Pineapples and Sugar Cane — A61

1964, June 1

119 A61 3c **multicolored** .40 .35
First day cover 1.25
Imprint block of 6 3.00

Agricultural census.

Minsah Obi (Sash Woven of Kapok) — A62

1964, July 1 ***Perf. 13¼***

120 A62 3c **deep blue, rose pink & ocher** .50 .50
First day cover 2.25
Imprint block of 6 4.25
a. 3c **deep blue, deep carmine & ocher** .65 .65
First day cover 2.75
Imprint block of 6 5.00

Philatelic Week.

Girl Scout and Emblem — A63

1964, Aug. 31 **Photo.**

121 A63 3c **multicolored** .40 .35
First day cover 1.25
Imprint block of 6 3.00

10th anniv. of Ryukyuan Girl Scouts.

Shuri Relay Station — A64

Parabolic Antenna and Map — A65

1964, Sept. 1 **Unwmk.**

Black Overprint

122 A64 3c **deep green** .65 .65
Imprint block of 6 5.50
a. Figure "1" inverted 30.00 30.00
b. Overprint inverted *1,500.*
c. Overprint missing *3,500.*
d. Overprint inverted and figure "1" inverted *5,000.*
123 A65 8c **ultramarine** 1.25 1.25
Imprint block of 6 10.00
First day cover, #122-123 4.75
a. Overprint missing *3,500.*

Opening of the Ryukyu Islands-Japan microwave system carrying telephone and telegraph messages. The overprints indicate the system was not actually opened until 1964.

Many of the stamps with overprint errors listed above are damaged. The values listed here are for stamps in very fine condition.

A number of different overprint shifts also exist with the shifts to greater and lesser degrees.

Gate of Courtesy, Olympic Torch and Emblem — A66

1964, Sept. 7 **Photo.** ***Perf. 13¼***

124 A66 3c **ultramarine, yellow & red** .30 .25
First day cover (Sept. 7) 1.25
First day cover (Sept. 6 & 7) 25.00
Imprint block of 6 2.50

Relaying the Olympic torch on Okinawa en route to Tokyo.

Torch arrival was scheduled for Sept. 6. A typhoon delayed arrival until Sept. 7. A small number of covers received both Sept. 6 and 7 cancels.

"Naihanchi," Karate Stance — A67

"Makiwara," Strengthening Hands and Feet — A68

"Kumite," Simulated Combat — A69

1964-65 **Photo.**

125 A67 3c **dull claret, yel & blk,** *Oct. 5, 1964* .50 .45
First day cover 1.25
Imprint block of 6 3.25
126 A68 3c **yel & multi,** *Feb. 5, 1965* .40 .40
First day cover 1.25
Imprint block of 6 3.00
Incomplete vertical stroke in "cent" sign 17.50 17.50
First day cover 25.00
127 A69 3c **gray, red & blk,** *June 5, 1965* .40 .40
First day cover 1.25
Imprint block of 6 3.00
Nos. 125-127 (3) 1.30 1.25

Karate, Ryukyuan self-defense sport.

Miyara Dunchi — A70

1964, Nov. 1

128 A70 3c **multicolored** .30 .25
First day cover 1.25
Imprint block of 6 2.25

Protection of national cultural treasures. Miyara Dunchi was built as a residence by Pei-chin Miyara Touen in 1819.

Snake and Iris (Bingata) — A71

1964, Dec. 10 **Photo.**

129 A71 1½c **multicolored** .30 .25
First day cover 2.00
Imprint block of 10 4.00

New Year, 1965.

Boy Scouts — A72

1965, Feb. 6 ***Perf. 13¼***

130 A72 3c **light blue & multi** .45 .40
First day cover 1.50
Imprint block of 6 4.00

10th anniv. of Ryukyuan Boy Scouts.

Main Stadium, Onoyama A73

1965, July 1 *Perf. 13x13¼*
131 A73 3c **multicolored** .25 .25
First day cover 1.00
Imprint block of 6 2.00

Inauguration of the main stadium of the Onoyama athletic facilities.

Samisen of King Shoko — A74

1965, July 1 **Photo.** *Perf. 13¼*
132 A74 3c **buff & multicolored** .45 .40
First day cover 1.25
Imprint block of 6 3.25

Philatelic Week.

Kin Power Plant — A75

1965, July 1
133 A75 3c **green & multi** .25 .25
First day cover 1.00
Imprint block of 6 2.00

Completion of Kin power plant.

ICY Emblem, Ryukyu Map — A76

1965, Aug. 24 **Photo.**
134 A76 3c **multicolored** .25 .25
First day cover 1.00
Imprint block of 6 1.75

20th anniv. of the UN and International Cooperation Year, 1964-65.

Naha City Hall — A77

1965, Sept. 18
135 A77 3c **blue & multicolored** .35 .25
First day cover 1.00
Imprint block of 6 1.75

Completion of Naha City Hall.

Chinese Box Turtle (Cyclemys flavomarginata) A78

Turtles: No. 137, Hawksbill turtle (Eretochelys imbricata bissa) (denomination at top, country name at bottom). No. 138, Asian terrapin (Geoemyda japonica) (denomination and country name at top).

1965-66 **Photo.** *Perf. 13¼*
136 A78 3c **golden brown & multi,** *Oct. 20, 1965* .30 .30
First day cover 1.00
Imprint block of 6 2.50
137 A78 3c **black, yel & brown,** *Jan. 20, 1966* .30 .30
First day cover 1.00
Imprint block of 6 2.50
138 A78 3c **gray & multicolored,** *Apr. 20, 1966* .30 .30
First day cover 1.00
Imprint block of 6 2.50
Nos. 136-138 (3) .90 .90

Horse (Bingata) — A79

1965, Dec. 10 **Photo.**
139 A79 1½c **multicolored** .25 .25
First day cover 1.50
Imprint block of 10 2.25
a. Gold omitted *2,000. 2,000.*

New Year, 1966.

There are 92 unused and 2 used examples of No. 139a known.

NATURE CONSERVATION ISSUE

Noguchi's Okinawa Woodpecker (Dendrocopus noguchii) — A80

Sika Deer (Cervus nippon var. keramae) — A81

Design: No. 142, Dugong (Dugong dugong).

1966 **Photo.**
140 A80 3c **blue green & multi,** *Feb. 15* .25 .25
First day cover 1.00
Imprint block of 6 1.65
141 A81 3c **blue, red, black, brown & green,** *Mar. 15* .25 .25
First day cover 1.00
Imprint block of 6 1.75
142 A81 3c **blue, yellow green, black & red,** *Apr. 20* .25 .25
First day cover 1.00
Imprint block of 6 1.75
Nos. 140-142 (3) .75 .75

Ryukyu Bungalow Swallow (Hirundo tahitica) — A82

1966, May 10 **Photo.** *Perf. 13¼*
143 A82 3c **sky blue, black & brown** .25 .25
First day cover 1.00
Imprint block of 6 1.10

4th Bird Week, May 10-16.

Lilies and Ruins A83

1966, June 23 *Perf. 13*
144 A83 3c **multicolored** .25 .25
First day cover 1.00
Imprint block of 6 1.00

Memorial Day, end of the Battle of Okinawa, June 23, 1945.

University of the Ryukyus A84

1966, July 1
145 A84 3c **multicolored** .25 .25
First day cover 1.00
Imprint block of 6 1.00

Transfer of the University of the Ryukyus from U.S. authority to the Ryukyu Government.

Chinkin Ukuhan Lacquerware, 18th Century — A85

1966, Aug. 1 *Perf. 13¼*
146 A85 3c **gray & multicolored** .25 .25
First day cover 1.50
Imprint block of 6 1.30

Philatelic Week.

Tile-Roofed House and UNESCO Emblem — A86

1966, Sept. 20 **Photo.**

147 A86 3c **multicolored** .25 .25
First day cover 1.00
Imprint block of 6 1.10

20th anniv. of UNESCO.

Government Museum and Dragon Statue — A87

1966, Oct. 6

148 A87 3c **multicolored** .25 .25
First day cover 1.00
Imprint block of 6 1.00

Completion of the GRI (Government of the Ryukyu Islands) Museum, Shuri.

Tomb of Nakasone-Toyomiya Genga, Ruler of Miyako — A88

1966, Nov. 1 **Photo.**

149 A88 3c **multicolored** .25 .25
First day cover 1.00
Imprint block of 6 1.00

Protection of national cultural treasures.

Ram in Iris Wreath — A89

1966, Dec. 10 **Photo.** ***Perf. 13¼***

150 A89 1½c **dark blue & multicolored** .25 .25
First day cover 1.50
Imprint block of 10 1.10

New Year, 1967.

Clown Fish (Amphiprion frenatus) — A90

Fish: No. 152, Young boxfish (Ostracion cubicus) (white numeral at lower left). No. 153, Forceps fish (Forcipiger longirostris) (pale buff numeral at lower right). No. 154, Spotted triggerfish (Balistoides conspicillum) (orange numeral). No. 155, Saddleback butterflyfish (Chaetodon ephippium) (carmine numeral, lower left).

1966-67

151 A90 3c **orange red & multi,** *Dec. 20, 1966* .25 .25
First day cover 1.00
Imprint block of 6 1.75

152 A90 3c **orange yellow & multi,** *Jan. 10, 1967* .25 .25
First day cover 1.00
Imprint block of 6 1.75

153 A90 3c **multicolored,** *Apr. 10, 1967* .40 .25
First day cover 1.00
Imprint block of 6 2.75

154 A90 3c **multicolored,** *May 25, 1967* .35 .25
First day cover 1.00
Imprint block of 6 2.25

155 A90 3c **multicolored,** *June 10, 1967* .30 .25
First day cover 1.00
Imprint block of 6 1.90
Nos. 151-155 (5) 1.55 1.25

A 3-cent stamp to commemorate Japanese-American-Ryukyuan Joint Arbor Day was scheduled for release on March 16, 1967. However, it was not released. The stamp in light blue and white features American and Japanese flags joined by a shield containing a tree.

Tsuboya Urn — A91

1967, Apr. 20

156 A91 3c **yellow & multicolored** .25 .25
First day cover 1.25
Imprint block of 6 1.65

Philatelic Week.

Episcopal Miter (Mitra mitra) — A92

Seashells: No. 158, Venus comb murex (Murex pecten). No. 159, Chiragra spider (Lambis chiragra). No. 160, Green turban (Turbo marmoratus). No. 161, Bubble conch (Euprotomus bulla).

1967-68 **Photo.** ***Perf. 13¼***

157 A92 3c **light green & multi,** *July 20, 1967* .25 .25
First day cover 1.00
Imprint block of 6 1.25

158 A92 3c **greenish blue & multi,** *Aug. 30, 1968* .25 .25
First day cover 1.00
Imprint block of 6 1.75

159 A92 3c **emerald & multi,** *Jan. 18, 1968* .25 .25
First day cover 1.00
Imprint block of 6 1.65

160 A92 3c **light blue & multi,** *Feb. 20, 1968* .30 .25
First day cover 1.00
Imprint block of 6 1.65

161 A92 3c **bright blue & multi,** *June 5, 1968* .60 .50
First day cover 1.00
Imprint block of 6 4.00
Nos. 157-161 (5) 1.65 1.50

Red-tiled Roofs and ITY Emblem — A93

1967, Sept. 11 **Photo.**

162 A93 3c **multicolored** .25 .25
First day cover 1.00
Imprint block of 6 1.25

International Tourist Year.

Mobile TB Clinic Bus — A94

1967, Oct. 13 **Photo.**

163 A94 3c **lilac & multicolored** .25 .25
First day cover 1.00
Imprint block of 6 1.25

15th anniv. of the Anti-Tuberculosis Society.

Hojo Bridge, Enkaku Temple, 1498 — A95

1967, Nov. 1

164 A95 3c **blue green & multi** .25 .25
First day cover 1.00
Imprint block of 6 1.50

Protection of national cultural treasures.

Monkey (Bingata) — A96

1967, Dec. 11 **Photo.** ***Perf. 13¼***

165 A96 1½c **silver & multi** .25 .25
First day cover 1.50
Imprint block of 10 3.00

New Year, 1968.

TV Tower and Map — A97

1967, Dec. 22

166 A97 3c **multicolored** .25 .25
First day cover 1.00
Imprint block of 6 1.50

Opening of Miyako and Yaeyama television stations.

Dr. Kijin Nakachi and Helper — A98

1968, Mar. 15 **Photo.**

167 A98 3c **multicolored** .30 .25
First day cover 1.00
Imprint block of 6 1.75

120th anniv. of the first vaccination in the Ryukyu Islands, by Dr. Kijin Nakachi.

Pill Box (Inro) — A99

1968, Apr. 18

168 A99 3c **gray & multicolored** .45 .45
First day cover 1.25
Imprint block of 6 3.50

Philatelic Week.

Young Man, Library, Book and Map of Ryukyu Islands — A100

1968, May 13

169 A100 3c **multicolored** .30 .25
First day cover 1.00
Imprint block of 6 1.75

10th International Library Week.

Mailmen's Uniforms and Stamp of 1948 — A101

1968, July 1 **Photo.** ***Perf. 13¼***

170 A101 3c **multicolored** .30 .25
First day cover 1.00
Imprint block of 6 1.75

First Ryukyuan postage stamps, 20th anniv.

Main Gate, Enkaku Temple — A102

1968, July 15 **Photo. & Engr.**

171 A102 3c **multicolored** .30 .25
First day cover 1.00
Imprint block of 6 1.75

Restoration of the main gate Enkaku Temple, built 1492-1495, destroyed during World War II.

Kagiyadefu Old Man's Dance — A103

1968, Sept. 15 **Photo.**

172 A103 3c **gold & multicolored** .30 .25
First day cover 1.00
Imprint block of 6 2.00

Old People's Day.

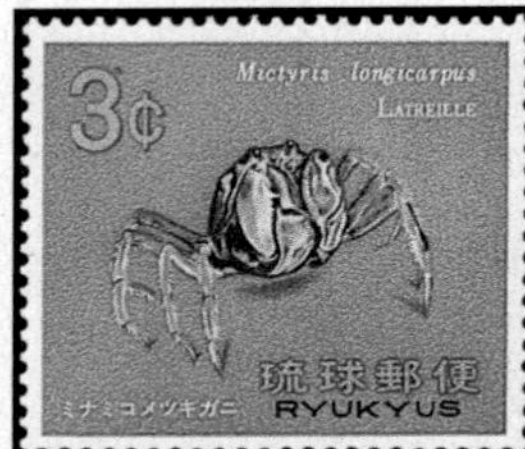

Mictyris Longicarpus — A104

Crabs: No. 174, Uca dubia stimpson. No. 175, Baptozius vinosus. No. 176, Cardisoma carnifex. No. 177, Ocypode ceratophthalma pallas.

1968-69 **Photo.** ***Perf. 13¼***

173 A104 3c **blue, ocher & black,** *Oct. 10, 1968* .30 .25
First day cover 1.25
Imprint block of 6 2.50

174 A104 3c **light blue green & multi,** *Feb. 5, 1969* .35 .30
First day cover 1.25
Imprint block of 6 2.75

175 A104 3c **light green & multi,** *Mar. 5, 1969* .35 .30
First day cover 1.25
Imprint block of 6 2.75

176 A104 3c **light ultra & multi,** *May 15, 1969* .45 .40
First day cover 1.25
Imprint block of 6 3.25

177 A104 3c **light ultra & multi,** *June 2, 1969* .45 .40
First day cover 1.25
Imprint block of 6 3.25

Nos. 173-177 (5) 1.90 1.65

Saraswati Pavilion (Benzaitan-do Temple) — A105

1968, Nov. 1 **Photo.**

178 A105 3c **multicolored** .30 .25
First day cover 1.00
Imprint block of 6 2.00

Restoration of the Sarawati Pavilion (in front of Enkaku Temple), destroyed during World War II.

Tennis Player — A106

1968, Nov. 23 **Photo.**

179 A106 3c **green & multi** .40 .35
First day cover 1.00
Imprint block of 6 3.25

35th All-Japan East-West Men's Soft-ball Tennis Tournament, Naha City, Nov. 23-24.

Cock and Iris (Bingata) — A107

1968, Dec. 10

180 A107 1½c **orange & multi** .25 .25
First day cover 1.50
Imprint block of 10 3.50

New Year, 1969.

Boxer — A108

1969, Jan. 3

181 A108 3c **gray & multi** .40 .30
First day cover 1.00
Imprint block of 6 2.75

20th All-Japan Amateur Boxing Championships held at the University of the Ryukyus, Jan. 3-5.

Ink Slab Screen — A109

1969, Apr. 17 **Photo.** ***Perf. 13¼x13***

182 A109 3c **salmon, indigo & red** .40 .35
First day cover 1.50
Imprint block of 6 2.75

Philatelic Week.

Box Antennas and Map of Radio Link — A110

1969, July 1 **Photo.**

183 A110 3c **multicolored** .30 .25
First day cover 1.00
Imprint block of 6 2.25

Opening of the UHF (radio) circuit system between Okinawa and the outlying Miyako-Yaeyama Islands.

Gate of Courtesy and Emblems — A111

1969, Aug. 1 **Photo.**

184 A111	3c **Prussian blue, gold & vermilion**	.30	.25
	First day cover		1.00
	Imprint block of 6	2.25	

22nd All-Japan Formative Education Study Conf., Naha, Aug. 1-3.

FOLKLORE ISSUE

Tug of War Festival A112

Hari Boat Race A113

Izaiho Ceremony, Kudaka Island A114

Mortar Drum Dance (Ushideiku) A115

Sea God Dance (Ungami) A116

1969-70 **Photo.** ***Perf. 13¼x13***

185 A112	3c **multicolored,** *Aug. 1, 1969*	.30	.25
	First day cover		1.50
	Imprint block of 6	2.25	
186 A113	3c **multicolored,** *Sept. 5, 1969*	.35	.30
	First day cover		1.50
	Imprint block of 6	2.25	
187 A114	3c **multicolored,** *Oct. 3, 1969*	.35	.30
	First day cover		1.50
	Imprint block of 6	2.25	
188 A115	3c **multicolored,** *Jan. 20, 1970*	.50	.45
	First day cover		1.50
	Imprint block of 6	3.50	
189 A116	3c **multicolored,** *Feb. 27, 1970*	.50	.45
	First day cover		1.50
	Imprint block of 6	3.50	
	Nos. 185-189 (5)	2.00	1.75

No. 99 Surcharged

1969, Oct. 15 **Photo.** ***Perf. 13¼***

190 A44	½c on 3c **multicolored**	1.00	1.00
	First day cover		3.00
	Imprint block of 10	13.50	
a.	"1/2c" only surcharge	950.00	

No. 190a are right margin stamps from a pane with a leftward misregistration of the surcharging plate.

Nakamura-ke Farm House, Built 1713-51 — A117

1969, Nov. 1 **Photo.** ***Perf. 13¼x13***

191 A117	3c **multicolored**	.25	.25
	First day cover		1.00
	Imprint block of 6	1.50	

Protection of national cultural treasures.

Statue of Kyuzo Toyama, Maps of Hawaiian and Ryukyu Islands — A118

1969, Dec. 5 **Photo.** ***Perf. 13¼***

192 A118	3c **light ultra & multi**	.50	.50
	First day cover		1.50
	Imprint block of 6	3.75	
a.	Without overprint	*3,000.*	
b.	Wide-spaced bars	*700.00*	*500.00*

70th anniv. of Ryukyu-Hawaii emigration led by Kyuzo Toyama.

The overprint "1969" at lower left and bars across "1970" at upper right was applied before No. 192 was issued.

Dog and Flowers (Bingata) — A119

1969, Dec. 10 ***Perf. 13¼x13***

193 A119	1½c **pink & multicolored**	.25	.25
	First day cover		1.50
	Imprint block of 10	2.75	

New Year, 1970.

Sake Flask Made from Coconut (Yashi-gwa) A120

1970, Apr. 15 **Photo.** ***Perf. 13¼***

194 A120	3c **multicolored**	.25	.25
	First day cover		1.25
	Imprint block of 6	1.75	

Philatelic Week, 1970.

CLASSIC OPERA ISSUE

"The Bell" (Shushin Kaneiri) — A121

Child and Kidnapper (Chunusudu) A122

Robe of Feathers (Mekarushi) A123

Vengeance of Two Young Sons (Nidotichiuchi) A124

The Virgin and the Dragon (Kokonomaki) A125

1970 **Photo.** ***Perf. 13¼***

195 A121	3c **dull blue & multi,** *Apr. 28*	.60	.40
	First day cover		1.75
	Imprint block of 6	4.00	
a.	Souvenir sheet of 4	4.00	4.00
	First day cover		5.00
196 A122	3c **light blue & multi,** *May 29*	.60	.40
	First day cover		1.75
	Imprint block of 6	4.00	
a.	Souvenir sheet of 4	4.00	4.00
	First day cover		5.00
197 A123	3c **bluish green & multi,** *June 30*	.60	.40
	First day cover		1.75
	Imprint block of 6	4.00	
a.	Souvenir sheet of 4	4.00	4.00
	First day cover		5.00
198 A124	3c **dull blue green & multi,** *July 30*	.60	.40
	First day cover		1.75
	Imprint block of 6	4.00	
a.	Souvenir sheet of 4	4.00	4.00
	First day cover		5.00
199 A125	3c **multicolored,** *Aug. 25*	.60	.40
	First day cover		1.75
	Imprint block of 6	4.00	
a.	Souvenir sheet of 4	4.00	4.00
	First day cover		5.00
	Nos. 195-199 (5)	3.00	2.00
	Nos. 195a-199a (5)	20.00	20.00

Underwater Observatory and Tropical Fish — A126

1970, May 22

200 A126 3c **blue green & multi** .30 .25
First day cover 1.25
Imprint block of 6 2.00

Completion of the underwater observatory of Busena-Misaki, Nago.

Noboru Jahana (1865-1908), Politician — A127

Portraits: No. 202, Saion Gushichan Bunjaku (1682-1761), statesman. No. 203, Choho Giwan (1823-1876), regent and poet.

1970-71 **Engr.**

201 A127 3c **rose claret,** *Sept. 25, 1970* .50 .45
First day cover 2.50
Imprint block of 6 3.50
202 A127 3c **dull blue green,** *Dec. 22, 1970* .75 .65
First day cover 2.50
Imprint block of 6 6.00
203 A127 3c **black,** *Jan. 22, 1971* .50 .45
First day cover 2.50
Imprint block of 6 3.50
Nos. 201-203 (3) 1.75 1.55

Map of Okinawa and People — A128

1970, Oct. 1 **Photo.**

204 A128 3c **red & multicolored** .25 .25
First day cover 1.00
Imprint block of 6 1.75

Oct. 1, 1970 census.

Great Cycad of Une — A129

1970, Nov. 2 **Photo.** ***Perf. 13¼***

205 A129 3c **gold & multicolored** .25 .25
First day cover 1.00
Imprint block of 6 1.75

Protection of national treasures.

Japanese Flag, Diet and Map of Ryukyus — A130

1970, Nov. 15 **Photo.**

206 A130 3c **ultramarine & multicolored** .80 .75
First day cover 2.00
Imprint block of 6 6.00

Citizen's participation in national administration to Japanese law of Apr. 24, 1970.

Wild Boar and Cherry Blossoms (Bingata) — A131

1970, Dec. 10 ***Perf. 13¼x13***

207 A131 1½c **multicolored** .25 .25
First day cover 1.50
Imprint block of 10 2.40

New Year, 1971.

Low Hand Loom (Jibata) — A132

Farmer Wearing Palm Bark Raincoat (Shurunnui) and Kuba Leaf Hat (Kubagasa) A133

Fisherman's Wooden Box (Yutui) and Scoop (Umi-fujo) — A134

Designs: No. 209, Woman running a filature (reel). No. 211, Woman hulling rice with cylindrical "Shiri-ushi."

1971 **Photo.** ***Perf. 13¼***

208 A132 3c **light blue & multi,** *Feb. 16* .30 .25
First day cover 1.25
Imprint block of 6 2.00
209 A132 3c **pale green & multi,** *Mar. 16* .30 .25
First day cover 1.25
Imprint block of 6 2.00
210 A133 3c **light blue & multi,** *Apr. 30* .35 .30
First day cover 1.25
Imprint block of 6 2.25
211 A132 3c **yellow & multi,** *May 20* .40 .35
First day cover 1.25
Imprint block of 6 3.00
212 A134 3c **gray & multi,** *June 15* .35 .30
First day cover 1.25
Imprint block of 6 2.25
Nos. 208-212 (5) 1.70 1.45

Water Carrier (Taku) — A135

1971, Apr. 15 **Photo.**

213 A135 3c **blue green & multicolored** .35 .30
First day cover 1.50
Imprint block of 6 2.75

Philatelic Week, 1971.

Old and New Naha, and City Emblem A136

1971, May 20 ***Perf. 13¼x13***

214 A136 3c **ultramarine & multicolored** .25 .25
First day cover 1.00
Imprint block of 6 1.75

50th anniv. of Naha as a municipality.

Ogocho (Caesalpinia pulcherrima) — A137

Design: 2c, Madder (Sandanka).

1971 **Photo.** ***Perf. 13¼***

215 A137 2c **gray & multicolored,** *Sept. 30* .25 .25
First day cover 1.00
Imprint block of 10 3.00
216 A137 3c **gray & multicolored,** *May 10* .25 .25
First day cover 1.00
Imprint block of 10 3.00

GOVERNMENT PARK SERIES

View from Mabuni Hill — A138

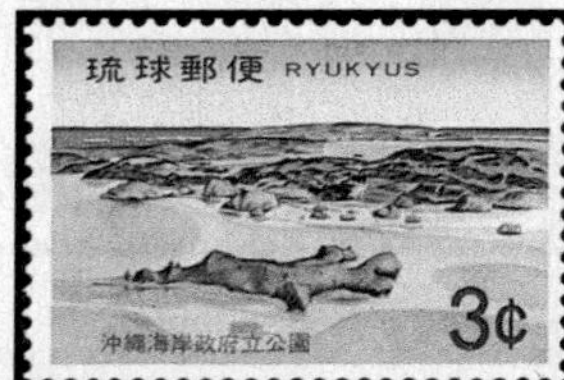

Mt. Arashi from Haneji Sea — A139

Yabuchi Island from Yakena Port — A140

1971-72

217 A138 3c **green & multi,** *July 30, 1971* .25 .25
First day cover 1.25
Imprint block of 6 1.50
218 A139 3c **blue & multi,** *Aug. 30, 1971* .25 .25
First day cover 1.25
Imprint block of 6 1.50
219 A140 4c **multicolored,** *Jan. 20, 1972* .25 .25
First day cover 1.25
Imprint block of 6 1.75
Nos. 217-219 (3) .75 .75

For the 4-cent unissued "stamp" picturing Iriomote Park, originally planned for issue in 1971 but never released, see the note after No. RQ8.

Dancer (Nu-fwa-bushi) — A141

1971, Nov. 1 **Photo.** ***Perf. 13¼***

220 A141 4c **Prussian blue & multicolored** .25 .25
First day cover 1.00
Imprint block of 10 2.50

Deva King (Misshaku Kongo), Torin-ji Temple — A142

1971, Dec. 1

221 A142 4c **deep blue & multicolored** .25 .25
First day cover 1.00
Imprint block of 6 1.50

Protection of national cultural treasures.

Rat and Chrysanthemums — A143

1971, Dec. 10 ***Perf. 13¼x13***

222 A143 2c **brown orange & multi** .25 .25
First day cover 1.50
Imprint block of 10 2.50

New Year, 1972.

Student Nurse — A144

1971, Dec. 24 ***Perf. 13¼***

223 A144 4c **lilac & multicolored** .25 .25
First day cover 1.00
Imprint block of 6 1.50

Nurses' training, 25th anniversary.

A145

A147

Coral Reef — A146

1972 **Photo.**

224 A145 5c **bright blue & multi,** *Apr. 14* .40 .35
First day cover 1.25
Imprint block of 6 2.75
225 A146 5c **gray & multi,** *Mar. 30* .40 .35
First day cover 1.25
Imprint block of 6 2.75
226 A147 5c **ocher & multi,** *Mar. 21* .40 .35
First day cover 1.25
Imprint block of 6 2.75
Nos. 224-226 (3) 1.20 1.05

Dove, U.S. and Japanese Flags — A148

1972, Apr. 17 **Photo.**

227 A148 5c **bright blue & multi** .80 .80
First day cover 1.50
Imprint block of 6 5.50

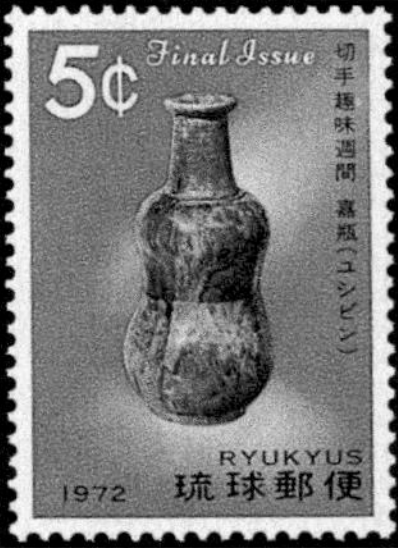

Antique Sake Container (Yushibin) — A149

1972, Apr. 20

228 A149 5c **ultramarine & multicolored** .60 .60
First day cover 1.25
Imprint block of 6 4.50

Ryukyu stamps were replaced by those of Japan after May 15, 1972.

AIR POST STAMPS

Catalogue values for all unused stamps in this section are for Never Hinged items.

Dove and Map of Ryukyus — AP1

1950, Feb. 15 **Photo.** **Unwmk.** ***Perf. 13x13¼***

C1 AP1 8y **bright blue** 110.00 40.00
First day cover 35.00
Imprint block of 6 1,050.
C2 AP1 12y **green** 17.50 17.50
First day cover 35.00
Imprint block of 6 180.00
C3 AP1 16y **rose carmine** 9.00 9.00
First day cover 35.00
Imprint block of 6 80.00
First day cover, #C1-C3 200.00
Nos. C1-C3 (3) 136.50 66.50

Heavenly Maiden AP2

1951-54 ***Perf. 13¼x13***

C4 AP2 13y **blue,** *Oct. 1, 1951* 2.00 2.00
First day cover 60.00
Imprint block of 6, 5-character 300.00
Imprint block of 6, 8-character 30.00
C5 AP2 18y **green,** *Oct. 1, 1951* 3.00 3.00
First day cover 60.00
Imprint block of 6, 5-character 45.00
Imprint block of 6, 8-character 35.00
C6 AP2 30y **cerise,** *Oct. 1, 1951* 4.50 1.50
First day cover 60.00
First day cover, #C4-C6 250.00
Imprint block of 6, 5-character 55.00
Imprint block of 6, 8-character 120.00
C7 AP2 40y **red violet,** *Aug. 16, 1954* 6.50 6.50
First day cover 35.00
Imprint block of 6 72.50
C8 AP2 50y **yellow orange,** *Aug. 16, 1954* 7.50 7.50
First day cover 35.00
Imprint block of 6 82.50
First day cover, #C7-C8 125.00
Nos. C4-C8 (5) 23.50 20.50

Heavenly Maiden Playing Flute — AP3

1957, Aug. 1 **Engr.** ***Perf. 13x13¼***

C9 AP3 15y **blue green** 7.50 4.00
Imprint block of 6 55.00
C10 AP3 20y **rose carmine** 9.00 7.00
Imprint block of 6 67.50
C11 AP3 35y **yellow green** 10.00 8.00
Imprint block of 6 85.00
a. 35y **light yellow green,** *1958* *125.00*
C12 AP3 45y **reddish brown** 14.00 10.00
Imprint block of 6 100.00
C13 AP3 60y **gray** 16.00 12.00
Imprint block of 6 135.00
First day cover, #C9-C13 45.00
Nos. C9-C13 (5) 56.50 41.00

On one printing of No. C10, position 49 shows an added spur on the right side of the second character from the left. Value unused, $175.

Same Surcharged in Brown Red or Light Ultramarine

1959, Dec. 20 **Engr.**

C14 AP3 9c on 15y **blue green** (BrR) 2.50 2.00
Imprint block of 6 20.00
a. Inverted surcharge *800.00*
Imprint block of 6 *5,750.*
b. Pair, one without surcharge —
C15 AP3 14c on 20y **rose carmine** (L.U.) 3.00 3.25
Imprint block of 6 22.50
C16 AP3 19c on 35y **light yellow green** (BrR) 7.00 6.00
Imprint block of 6 52.50
C17 AP3 27c on 45y **reddish brown** (L.U.) 12.50 6.00
Imprint block of 6 110.00

C18 AP3 35c on 60y **gray** (BrR) 11.00 9.00
Imprint block of 6 95.00
First day cover, #C14-C18 35.00
Nos. C14-C18 (5) 36.00 26.25

No. C15 is found with the variety described below No. C13. Value unused, $125.

Nos. 31-33, 36 and 38 Surcharged in Black, Brown, Red, Blue or Green

1960, Aug. 3 **Photo.**

C19 A14 9c on 4y **brown** 2.50 1.00
Imprint block of 10 40.00
a. Surcharge inverted and transposed *12,500.* *12,500.*
b. Inverted surcharge (legend only) *10,000.*
c. Surcharge transposed *800.00*
d. Legend of surcharge only *3,500.*
e. Vert. pair, one without surcharge *11,000.*

Nos. C19c and C19d are from a single sheet of 100 with surcharge shifted downward. Ten examples of No. C19c exist with "9c" also in bottom selvage. No. C19d is from the top row of the sheet.

No. C19e is unique, pos. 100, caused by paper foldover.

C20 A17 14c on 5y **rose lilac** (Br) 3.00 3.00
Imprint block of 10 45.00
C21 A14 19c on 15y **vermilion** (R) 2.50 3.00
Imprint block of 10 37.50
C22 A17 27c on 14y **reddish brown** (Bl) 7.00 2.50
Imprint block of 10 110.00
C23 A14 35c on 20y **yellow orange** (G) 5.00 5.00
Imprint block of 10 72.50
First day cover, #C19-C23 25.00
Nos. C19-C23 (5) 20.00 14.50

Wind God — AP4

Designs: 9c, Heavenly Maiden (as on AP2). 14c, Heavenly Maiden (as on AP3). 27c, Wind God at right. 35c, Heavenly Maiden over treetops.

1961, Sept. 21 ***Perf. 13¼***

C24 AP4 9c **multicolored** .30 .25
Imprint block of 6 2.25
C25 AP4 14c **multicolored** .60 .75
Imprint block of 6 5.00
C26 AP4 19c **multicolored** .70 .85
Imprint block of 6 5.50
C27 AP4 27c **multicolored** 3.00 .60
Imprint block of 6 22.00
C28 AP4 35c **multicolored** 2.00 1.25
Imprint block of 6 16.00
First day cover, #C24-C28 35.00
Nos. C24-C28 (5) 6.60 3.70

AP5

AP6

1963, Aug. 28 ***Perf. 13x13¼***

C29 AP5 5½c **multicolored** .25 .25
First day cover 1.00
Imprint block of 10 3.00
C30 AP6 7c **multicolored** .30 .30
First day cover 1.00
First day cover, #C29-C30 2.50
Imprint block of 10 3.50

SPECIAL DELIVERY STAMP

Catalogue value for the unused stamp in this section is for a Never Hinged item.

Sea Horse and Map of Ryukyus — SD1

1950, Feb. 15 **Unwmk.** **Photo.** ***Perf. 13¼***

E1 SD1 5y **bright blue** 25.00 17.50
First day cover 100.00
Imprint block of 6 300.00

QUANTITIES ISSUED

Regular Postage and Commemorative Stamps

Cat. No.	*Quantity*	*Cat. No.*	*Quantity*
1	90,214	*87*	3,019,000
2	55,901	*88*	298,966
3	94,663	*89*	298,966
4	55,413	*90*	398,901
5	76,387	*91*	398,992
6	117,321	*92*	1,498,970
7	291,403	*93*	598,989
1a	61,000	*94*	398,998
2a-4a	181,000	*95*	398,993
5a	29,936	*96*	298,993
6a	99,300	*97*	398,997
7a	46,000	*98*	9,699,000
8	2,559,000	*99*	10,991,500
8a	300,000	*100*	1,549,000
9	1,198,989	*101*	799,000
10	589,000	*102*	1,299,000
11	479,000	*103*	398,995
12	598,999	*104*	298,892
13	397,855	*105*	1,598,949
14	499,000	*106*	348,989
15	498,960	*107*	10,099,000
16	199,197	*108*	348,865
16A	199,900	*109*	348,937
16B	39,900	*110*	348,962
17	9,800	*111*	348,974
18	299,500	*112*	398,974
19	3,014,427	*113*	398,911
20	3,141,777	*114*	1,199,000
21	2,970,827	*115*	398,948
22	191,917	*116*	398,943
23	1,118,617	*117*	1,698,912
24	276,218	*118*	550,000
24a	ca. 1,300	*119*	549,000
25	231,717	*120*	749,000
26	220,130	*121*	799,000
27	398,993	*122*	389,000
28	386,421	*123*	319,000
29	498,854	*124*	1,999,000
30	298,994	*125-127*	999,000
31	4,768,413	*128*	799,000
32	1,202,297	*129*	1,699,000
33	500,059	*130-131*	799,000
34	298,994	*132*	849,000
35	199,000	*133*	799,000
36	455,896	*134*	1,299,000
37	160,518	*135*	1,099,000
38	198,720	*136*	1,299,000
39	198,199	*137-138*	1,598,000
40	599,000	*139*	3,098,000
41	598,075	*140-142*	1,598,000
42	1,198,179	*143-148*	2,498,000
43	1,625,406	*149*	2,298,000
44	994,880	*150*	3,798,000
45	997,759	*151*	2,298,000
46	996,759	*152-156*	1,998,000
47	2,705,955	*157-158*	1,698,000
48	997,542	*159-160*	1,298,000
49	996,609	*161*	898,000
50	996,928	*162*	1,498,000
51	499,000	*163-164*	1,298,000
52	249,000	*165*	3,998,000
52a	78,415	*166-167*	1,298,000
53	248,700	*168*	998,000
54	1,498,991	*169-179*	898,000
55	2,498,897	*180*	3,198,000
56	1,098,972	*181-189*	898,000
57	998,918	*190*	1,773,050
58	2,699,000	*191*	898,000
59	2,499,000	*192*	864,960
60	199,000	*193*	3,198,000
61	499,000	*194*	898,000
62	199,000	*195-199*	598,000
63	1,498,931	*195a-199a*	124,500
64	798,953	*200-206*	898,000
65-68	999,000	*207*	3,198,000
72	598,912	*208-210*	1,098,000
73	398,990	*211-212*	1,298,000
74	598,936	*213*	1,098,000
75	1,998,992	*214*	1,298,000
76	1,000,000	*215-216*	4,998,000
77	2,000,000	*217*	1,498,000
78	500,000	*218-219*	1,798,000
79-80	400,000	*220*	2,998,000
81	12,599,000	*221*	1,798,000
82	11,979,000	*222*	4,998,000
83	6,850,000	*223*	1,798,000
84	5,099,000	*224-226*	2,498,000
84A	1,699,000	*227*	2,998,000
85	4,749,000	*228*	3,998,000
86	2,099,000		

AIR POST STAMPS

Cat. No.	*Quantity*	*Cat. No.*	*Quantity*
C1-C3	198,000	*C18*	96,650
C4	1,952,348	*C19*	1,033,900
C5	331,360	*C19a*	100
C6	762,530	*C20*	230,000
C7	76,166	*C21*	185,000
C8	122,816	*C22*	191,000
C9	708,319	*C23*	190,000
C10	108,824	*C24*	17,199,000
C11	164,147	*C25*	1,999,000
C12	50,335	*C26*	1,250,000
C13	69,092	*C27*	3,499,000
C14	597,103	*C28*	1,699,000
C15	77,951	*C29*	1,199,000
C16	97,635	*C30*	1,949,000
C17	98,353		

SPECIAL DELIVERY STAMP

Cat. No.	*Quantity*
E1	198,804

Stamps of Japan Overprinted by Postmasters in Four Island Districts

PROVISIONAL ISSUES

Trading Ship — A82

Rice Harvest — A83

Gen. Maresuke Nogi — A84

Admiral Heihachiro Togo — A86

Garambi Lighthouse, Taiwan — A88

Meiji Shrine, Tokyo — A90

Plane and Map of Japan — A92

Kasuga Shrine, Nara — A93

Mount Fuji and Cherry Blossoms — A94

Horyu Temple, Nara — A95

Miyajima Torii, Itsukushima Shrine — A96

Golden Pavilion, Kyoto — A97

Great Budda, Kamakura — A98

Kamatari Fujiwara — A99

War Factory Girl — A144

Hyuga Monument & Mt. Fuji — A146

War Worker & Planes — A147

Palms and Map of "Greater East Asia" — A148

Aviator Saluting & Japanese Flag — A150

Torii of Yasukuni Shrine — A151

Mt. Fuji and Cherry Blossoms — A152

Torii of Miyajima — A153

Garambi Lighthouse, Taiwan — A154

Sun & Cherry Blossoms — A161

Sunrise at Sea & Plane — A162

Coal Miners — A163

Yasukuni Shrine — A164

"Thunderstorm below Fuji," by Hokusai — A167

KUME ISLAND

Values are for unused stamps. Used stamps sell for considerably more, should be expertized and are preferred on cover or document.

A1

Mimeographed
Seal Handstamped in Vermilion

1945, Oct. 1 Without Gum Unwmk. *Imperf.*

				Unused	Used
1X1	A1	7s	**black,** *cream (2,400)*	2,750.	2,500.
			On cover		—
a.			"7" & "SEN" one letter space to left	3,250.	

Printed on legal-size U.S. military mimeograph paper and validated by the official seal of the Kume Island postmaster, Norifume Kikuzato. Valid until May 4, 1946.

Cancellations "20.10.1" (Oct. 1, 1945) or "20.10.6" (Oct. 6, 1945) are by favor. See proofs section for stamps on white watermarked U.S. official bond paper.

AMAMI DISTRICT

Inspection Seal ("Ken," abbreviation for *kensa zumi,* inspected or examined; five types and five colors)

Stamps of Japan 1937-46 Handstamped in Black, Blue, Purple, Vermilion or Red

Typographed, Lithographed, Engraved

1947-48 Wmk. 257 *Perf. 13, Imperf*

				Unused
2X1	A82	½s	**purple,** #257	1,000.
a.			Double seal	—
2X2	A83	1s	**fawn,** #258	—
2X3	A144	1s	**orange brown,** #325	*1,750.*
2X4	A84	2s	**crimson,** #259	600.
a.			2s **vermilion,** #259c	—
b.			Double seal	—
2X5	A84	2s	**rose red,** imperf., #351	2,000.
2X6	A85	3s	**green,** #260	*1,900.*
2X7	A84	3s	**brown,** #329	—
2X8	A161	3s	**rose carmine,** imperf., #352	*1,300.*
a.			Double seal	—
2X9	A146	4s	**emerald,** #330	700.
a.			Double seal	—
2X10	A86	5s	**brown lake,** #331	700.
2X11	A162	5s	**green,** imperf., #353	*1,500.*
2X12	A147	6s	**light ultramarine,** #332	—
2X13	A86	7s	**orange vermilion,** #333	*1,250.*
2X14	A90	8s	**dark purple & pale violet,** #265	*1,500.*
2X15	A148	10s	**crimson & dull rose,** #344	600.
2X16	A152	10s	**red orange,** imperf., #355 *(48)*	*2,500.*
2X17	A93	14s	**rose lake & pale rose,** #268	—
2X18	A150	15s	**dull blue,** #336	600.
2X19	A151	17s	**gray violet,** #337	*1,750.*
2X20	A94	20s	**ultramarine,** #269	*1,750.*
2X21	A152	20s	**blue,** #338	600.
a.			Double seal	—
2X22	A152	20s	**ultramarine,** imperf., #356 *(48)*	*1,750.*
2X23	A95	25s	**dark brown & pale brown,** #270	900.
2X24	A151	27s	**rose brown,** #339	—
2X25	A153	30s	**bluish green,** #340	—
2X26	A153	30s	**bright blue,** imperf., #357	*2,000.*
2X27	A88	40s	**dull violet,** #341	*1,750.*
2X28	A154	40s	**dark violet,** #342	*1,750.*
2X29	A97	50s	**olive & pale olive,** #272	—
2X30	A163	50s	**dark brown,** imperf., #358 *(48)*	*2,000.*
2X31	A164	1y	**deep olive green,** imperf., #359	*2,500.*
2X32	A167	1y	**deep ultramarine,** imperf., #364	—
2X33	A99	5y	**deep gray green,** #274	—
2X34	A99	5y	**deep gray green,** imperf., #360	—

Nos. 2X5, 2X8, 2X11, 2X16, 2X22, 2X26, 2X30, 2X31, 2X32 and 2X34 were issued without gum.

MIYAKO DISTRICT

Personal Seal of Postmaster Jojin Tomiyama

Stamps of Japan 1937-46 Handstamped in Vermilion or Red

Typographed, Lithographed, Engraved

1946-47 Wmk. 257 *Perf. 13*

				Unused	Used
3X1	A144	1s	**orange brown,** #325	125.	
a.			Double seal	—	
3X2	A84	2s	**crimson,** #259	80.	—
a.			2s **vermilion** #259c ('47)	100.	
b.			2s **pink** #259b ('47)	550.	
c.			Horiz. pair, one without seal	*1,200.*	
d.			Double seal	—	
3X3	A84	3s	**brown,** #329	75.	—
3X4	A86	4s	**dark green,** #261	40.	
a.			Double seal	—	
3X5	A86	5s	**brown lake,** #331	550.	—
			On cover with #3X17		—
a.			Double seal	—	
3X6	A88	6s	**orange,** #263	40.	—
a.			Double seal	—	
3X7	A90	8s	**dark purple & pale violet,** #265	40.	—
a.			Double seal	—	
3X8	A148	10s	**crimson & dull rose,** #334	40.	—
			On cover with #3X15		*6,250.*
a.			Double seal	—	
b.			Triple seal	—	
3X9	A152	10s	**red orange,** imperf., #355 ('47) *(1,000)*	100.	
3X10	A92	12s	**indigo,** #267	40.	—
3X11	A93	14s	**rose lake & pale rose,** #268	40.	—
a.			Double seal	—	
3X12	A150	15s	**dull blue,** #336	40.	—
a.			Double seal	—	
b.			Triple seal	—	
3X13	A151	17s	**gray violet,** #337	40.	—
a.			Double seal	—	
3X14	A94	20s	**ultramarine,** #269	—	
3X15	A152	20s	**blue,** #338	40.	—
a.			Double seal	—	
3X16	A152	20s	**ultramarine,** imperf., #356 ('47)	125.	
a.			Double seal	—	
3X17	A95	25s	**dark brown & pale brown,** #270	50.	—
a.			Horiz. pair, one without seal	*300.*	
b.			Double seal	—	
c.			Triple seal	—	
3X18	A153	30s	**bluish green,** #340	40.	—
a.			Double seal	—	
3X19	A88	40s	**dull violet,** #341	250.	—
3X20	A154	40s	**dark violet,** #342	50.	—
a.			Double seal	—	
3X21	A97	50s	**olive & pale olive,** #272	50.	—
a.			Double seal	—	
b.			Triple seal	—	
c.			Quadruple seal	—	
3X22	A163	50s	**dark brown,** #358 ('47) *(750)*	150.	—
a.			Pair, one without seal	*1,200.*	
b.			Double seal	—	
c.			Triple seal	—	
3X23	A98	1y	**brown & pale brown,** #273		*9,000.*
3X24	A167	1y	**deep ultramarine,** #364 ('47) *(500)*	*1,500.*	*600.*

Nos. 3X9, 3X16, 3X22 and 3X24 were issued without gum.

Nos. 3X22 and 3X24 have sewing machine perf.; No. 3X16 exists with that perf. also.

Nos. 3X1-3X2, 3X2a, 3X3-3X5, 3X8 Handstamp Surcharged

1946-47

3X25	A144	1y on 1s **orange brown**	120.	—
3X26	A84	1y on 2s **crimson**	—	
3X27	A84	1y on 3s **brown** ('47)	3,000.	
3X28	A84	2y on 2s **crimson**	130.	—
a.		2y on 2s **vermilion** ('47)	130.	—
b.		Double seal	—	
3X29	A86	4y on 4s **dark green**	100.	—
3X30	A86	5y on 5s **brown lake**	100.	—
3X31	A148	10y on 10s **crimson & dull rose**	100.	—
a.		Double seal	—	

The overwhelming majority of used examples of Miyako District stamps were used on Bulk Mailing Records documents and Letter Content Certification Records documents. Stamps affixed to such documents command a substantial premium above off-document used stamps.

Cancellation: black Miyako cds.

Some time after mid-1964, Tomiyama Jojin, Postmaster of the Miyako District, prepared several "Display Sheets," each containing 29 genuine provisionals used between Feb. 1, 1946, and June 30, 1948. The stamps were from remainder stock. The stamps are canceled "23.6.30," which was backdated to indicate the last day of normal use (June 30, 1948). Six such Display Sheets are recorded at present. Value, $6,000.

OKINAWA DISTRICT

Personal Seal of Postmaster Shiichi Hirata

R1

Japan Nos. 355-356, 358, 364 Overprinted in Black

1947, Nov. 1 Wmk. 257 Litho. *Imperf.*

Without Gum

4X1	A152	10s **red orange** *(13,997)*	1,200.	*1,000.*
		On cover, strip of 3		*9,500.*
		On cover with #4X2		*7,500.*
4X2	A152	20s **ultramarine** *(13,641)*	600.	*1,000.*
a.		Block of 4, one with double seal, one without seal	*3,000.*	
b.		Pair, one without seal	—	
c.		Double seal	—	
4X3	A163	50s **dark brown** *(6,276)*	900.	*700.*
a.		Double seal	—	
4X4	A167	1y **deep ultramarine** *(1,947)*	1,750.	*1,000.*
a.		Double seal	—	

On Revenue Stamp of Japan

4X5	R1	30s **brown** *(14,000)*	*3,500.*	*3,500.*
		On cover		*7,500.*

No. 4X5 is on Japan's current 30s revenue stamp. The Hirata seal validated it for postal use.

Nos. 4X1-4X5 are known with rough sewing machine perforations, full or partial. These are scarce to rare.

YAEYAMA DISTRICT

Personal Seal of Postmaster Kenpuku Miyara

Stamps of Japan 1937-46 Handstamped in Black

Typographed, Engraved, Lithographed

1948 Wmk. 257 *Perf. 13*

5X1	A86	4s **dark green,** #261	1,200.	
5X2	A86	5s **brown lake,** #331	1,200.	
5X3	A86	7s **orange vermilion,** #333	800.	
5X4	A148	10s **crimson & dull rose,** #334	*5,000.*	
5X5	A94	20s **ultramarine,** #269	150.	
		On cover with 2 #5X8		—
a.		Double seal	*600.*	
5X6	A96	30s **peacock blue,** #271	1,000.	
a.		Double seal	—	
5X7	A88	40s **dull violet,** #341	70.	
a.		Double seal	—	
b.		Triple seal	—	
5X8	A97	50s **olive & pale olive,** #272	75.	
a.		Double seal	—	
5X9	A163	50s **dark brown,** imperf., #358 *(250)*	1,350.	
5X10	A99	5y **deep gray green,** #274	2,000.	
a.		Pair, one without seal	—	
b.		Double seal	—	

No. 5X9 was issued without gum.

This handstamp exists double, triple, inverted and in pair, one stamp without overprint.

Provisional postal stationery of the four districts also exists.

LETTER SHEETS

Values are for entires.

Stylized Deigo Blossom — US1

Typographed by Japan Printing Bureau.
Stamp is in upper left corner.

Designer: Shutaro Higa

1948-49

U1	US1	50s **vermilion,** *cream, July 18, 1949 (250,000)*	50.00	60.00
		First day cancel		—
a.		50s **orange red,** *gray, July 1, 1948 (1,000)*	1,500.	—

Banyan Tree — US2

Designer: Ken Yabu

1950, Jan. 21

U2	US2	1y **carmine red,** *cream (250,000)*	40.00	50.00
		First day cancel		—

AIR LETTER SHEETS

DC-4 Skymaster and Shurei Gate — UC1

Designer: Chosho Ashitomi
"PAR AVION" (Bilingual) below Stamp

Litho. & Typo. by Japan Printing Bureau

1952-53

UC1	UC1	12y **light rose,** *pale blue green, Mar. 9, 1953 (76,000)*	20.00	12.50
a.		12y **dull rose,** *pale blue green, Nov. 1, 1952 (50,000)*	30.00	15.00
		First day cancel, No. UC1a		80.00

No. UC1a is on tinted paper with colorless overall inscription "RYUKYU FOREIGN AIRMAIL," repeated in parallel vertical lines, light and indistinct. Dull rose ink of imprinted design and legend "AIR LETTER" appears to bleed. No. UC1 has overall inscription darker and more distinct. Light rose ink of design and legend does not bleed. Model: U.S. No. UC16.

UC2

Litho. & Typo. by Nippon Toppan K.K.
"AEROGRAMME" below Stamp

1955, Sept. 10

UC2	UC2	15y **violet blue & bright red,** *pale yellow green (89,300)*	30.00	15.00
		First day cancel		60.00
a.		15y **violet blue & dull red,** *pale blue green, Oct. 1957 (33,742)*	45.00	25.00

Printing on the envelope stamp is heavier on No. UC2a than on No. UC2.

No. UC2 Surcharged in Red

"13" & "¢" aligned at bot.; 2 thick bars — a

"¢" raised; 2 thick bars — b

"13" & "¢" as in "a"; 4 thin bars — c

"¢" raised; 4 thin bars — d

Printers: Type "a," Nakamura Printing Co., "b" and "d," Okinawa Printing Co., "c," Sun Printing Co.

1958-60

UC3	UC2	13c on 15y type "a," *Sept. 16, 1958 (60,000)*	20.00	18.00
		First day cancel		60.00
a.		Type "b," on No. UC2, *June 1, 1959 (2,000)*	40.00	30.00
b.		Type "b," on No. UC2a *(7,000)*	50.00	30.00
c.		Type "c," on No. UC2, *Sept. 22, 1959 (1,000)*	80.00	80.00
d.		As "c," small wrong font "¢" sign	1,400.	—
e.		Type "c," on No. UC2a *(1,000)*	80.00	80.00
f.		As "e," double surcharge, one on reverse	*3,250.*	
g.		Type "b" and No. 46 on No. UC2a, *Aug. 22, 1960 (1,000)*	550.00	—
h.		Type "d" and Nos. 55, 58 on No. UC2, *Oct. 1, 1960 (1,000)*	450.00	450.00
i.		Type "d" and Nos. 55, 58 on No. UC2a *(2,000)*	300.00	300.00

For Nos. UC3g, UC3h and UC3i, additional stamps have been affixed to make up the 15c rate.

UC3

Lithographed by Japan Printing Bureau

1959, Nov. 10

UC4	UC3	15c **dark blue,** *pale blue (560,000)*	4.00	2.50
		First day cancel		10.00

POSTAL CARDS

Deigo Blossom Type

Values are for entire cards.

Nos. UX1-UX9 are typo., others litho.

Printed by Japan Printing Bureau unless otherwise stated.

Quantities in parentheses; "E" means estimated.

Designer: Shutaro Higa

1948, July 1

UX1 US1 10s **dull red,** *grayish tan (100,000)* 50.00 *60.00*

1949, July 1

UX2 US1 15s **orange red,** *gray (E 175,000)* 40.00 *70.00*
First day cancel —
a. 15s **vermilion,** *tan (E 50,000)* 110.00 *125.00*

Banyan Tree Type

Designer: Ken Yabu

1950, Jan. 21

UX3 US2 50s **carmine red,** *light tan (E 200,000)* 10.00 10.00
First day cancel 60.00
a. Grayish tan card (E 25,000) 25.00 *50.00*

Nos. UX2, UX2a Handstamp Surcharged in Vermilion

19-21x23-25mm — a

22-23x26-27mm — b

20-21x24-24½mm — c

22-23½x25-26mm — d

1951

UX4 US1 (c) 15s + 85s on #UX2 *(E 35,000)* 100. 100.
a. Type "c" on #UX2a *(E 5,000)* 150. 150.
b. Type "a" on #UX2 *(E 39,000)* 75. *100.*
c. Type "a" on #UX2a *1,500.* —
d. Type "b" on #UX2 *1,500.* *1,500.*
e. Type "d" on #UX2 *(E 4,000)* 150. *200.*
f. Type "d" on #UX2a *(E 1,000)* 250. *300.*

Type "a" exists on the 15s cherry blossom postal card of Japan. Value $100.

Crown, Leaf Ornaments

Naha die 21x22mm PC3

Tokyo die 18½x19mm PC4

Designer: Masayoshi Adaniya Koshun Printing Co.

1952

UX5 PC3 1y **vermilion,** *tan, Feb. 8 (400,600)* 50.00 30.00
UX6 PC4 1y **vermilion,** *off-white, Oct. 6 (1,295,000)* 25.00 14.00
a. Tan card, coarse *(50,000)* 30.00 20.00
b. Tan card, smooth *(16,000)* 500.00 150.00

Naminoue Shrine

Naha die 23x25½mm — PC5

Tokyo die 22x24½mm — PC6

Designer: Gensei Agena

1953-57

UX7 PC5 2y **green,** *off-white, Dec. 2, 1953 (1,799,400)* 60.00 20.00
First day cancel 80.00
a. Printed both sides *500.00*
UX8 PC6 2y **green,** *off-white, 1955 (2,799,400)* 15.00 6.00
a. 2y **deep blue green,** *1956 (300,000)* 30.00 16.50
b. 2y **yellow green,** *1957 (2,400,000)* 12.50 3.50
c. As "a," printed on both sides *500.00*
d. As "b," printed on both sides *500.00*

Stylized Pine, Bamboo, Plum Blossoms — PC7

1956 New Year Card

Designer: Koya Oshiro Kotsura and Koshun Printing Companies

1955, Dec. 1

UX9 PC7 2y **red,** *cream* 100.00 45.00
First day cancel 125.00

No. UX9 was printed on rough card (43,400) and smooth-finish card (356,600).

Sun — PC8

1957 New Year Card

Designer: Seikichi Tamanaha Kobundo Printing Co.

1956, Dec. 1

UX10 PC8 2y **brown carmine & yellow,** *off-white (600,000)* 6.00 3.75
First day cancel 10.00

Temple Lion — PC9

1958 New Year Card

Designer: Shin Isagawa Fukuryu Printing Co.

1957, Dec. 1

UX11 PC9 2y **lilac rose,** *off-white (1,000,000)* 1.75 *2.25*
First day cancel 4.00
a. "1" omitted in right date 75.00 75.00
b. Printed on both sides 250.00 *300.00*

Nos. UX8, UX8a and UX8b "Revalued" in Red, Cherry or Pink by Three Naha Printeries

a

b

c

1958-59

UX12 PC6 1½c on 2y **green,** type "a," *Sept. 16 (600,000)* 5.00 5.00
First day cancel 10.00
a. Shrine stamp omitted *750.00* *1,000.*
b. Bar of ½ omitted, top of 2 broken 75.00 *100.00*
c. Type "b," *Nov. (1,000,000)* 10.00 *12.50*
d. Type "c," *1959 (200,000)* 15.00 *22.50*
e. Wrong font "¢," type "c" 30.00 *45.00*
f. "¢" omitted, type "c" *1,500.* 1,500.
g. Double surcharge, type "c" *1,000.* —

Multicolor Yarn Ball — PC10

1959 New Year Card

Designer: Masayoshi Adaniya Kobundo Printing Co.

1958, Dec. 10

UX13 PC10 1½c **black, red, yellow & gray blue,** *off-white (1,514,000)* 1.50 *1.90*
First day cancel 2.00
a. Black omitted —

Toy Pony 19½x23mm — PC11

Designer: Seikichi Tamanaha Kobundo Printing Co.

1959, June 20

UX14 PC11 1½c **dark blue & brown** *(1,140,000)* 1.50 1.25
First day cancel 1.50
a. Dark blue omitted 500.00

Toy Carp and Boy — PC12

1960 New Year Card

Designer: Masayoshi Adaniya

1959, Dec. 1

UX15 PC12 1½c **violet blue, red & black,** *cream (2,000,000)* 1.25 *1.50*

First day cancel 1.75

Toy Pony 21x25mm — PC13

1959, Dec. 30

UX16 PC13 1½c **gray violet & brown,** *cream (3,500,000)* 3.00 .75

First day cancel 2.75

Household Altar — PC14

1961 New Year Card

Designer: Shin Isagawa

1960, Nov. 20

UX17 PC14 1½c **gray, carmine, yellow & black,** *off-white (2,647,591)* 1.50 1.50

First day cancel 1.50

Coral Head — PC15

Summer Greeting Card

Designer: Shinzan Yamada Kidekuni Printing Co.

1961, July 5

UX18 PC15 1½c **ultramarine & cerise,** *off-white (264,900)* 2.25 *3.75*

First day cancel 4.00

Tiger — PC16

1962 New Year Card

Designer: Shin Isagawa

1961, Nov. 15

UX19 PC16 1½c **ocher, black & red,** *off-white (2,891,626)* 1.50 *2.50*

First day cancel 1.65

a.	Red omitted	750.00	—
b.	Red inverted	500.00	—
c.	Red omitted on face, inverted on back	500.00	—
d.	Double impression of red, one inverted	500.00	—
e.	Double impression of ocher & black, red inverted	500.00	—
f.	Double impression of ocher & black, one inverted	500.00	—

Inscribed "RYUKYUS" — PC17

Designer: Seikichi Tamanaha

1961-67

UX20 PC17 1½c **gray violet & brown,** *white ('67) (18,600,000)* 1.00 .50

a.	Off-white card ('66) *(4,000,000)*	1.50	.75
b.	Cream card, *Dec. 23 (12,500,000)*	1.00	.50
	First day cancel		1.35

Ie Island — PC18

Summer Greeting Card

Designer: Shinzan Yamada Sakai Printing Co.

1962, July 10

UX21 PC18 1½c **bright blue, yellow & brown,** *off-white (221,500)* 1.50 *2.50*

First day cancel 3.00

Square notch at left 40.00 *45.00*

New Year Offerings — PC19

1963 New Year Card; Precanceled

Designer: Shin Isagawa Sakai Printing Co.

1962, Nov. 15

UX22 PC19 1½c **olive brown, carmine & black** *(3,000,000)* 1.50 *3.00*

	First day cancel		2.25
a.	Yellow brown background		—
b.	Brown ocher background		—

Ryukyu Temple Dog and Wine Flask Silhouette PC20

International Postal Card

Designer: Shin Isagawa

1963, Feb. 15

UX23 PC20 5c **vermilion, emerald & black,** *pale yellow (150,000)* 1.75 *2.75*

	First day cancel		1.65
a.	Black & emerald omitted	450.00	

Water Strider — PC21

Summer Greeting Card

Designer: Seikichi Tamanaha

1963, June 20

UX24 PC21 1½c **Prussian green & black,** *off-white (250,000)* 4.00 *4.25*

First day cancel 3.50

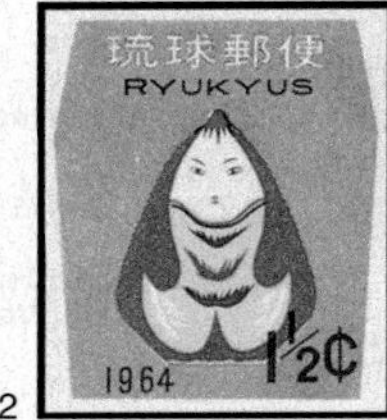

Princess Doll — PC22

1964 New Year Card; Precanceled

Designer: Koya Oshiro

1963, Nov. 15

UX25 PC22 1½c **orange red, yellow & ultra,** *off-white (3,200,000)* 2.00 2.00

First day cancel 2.00

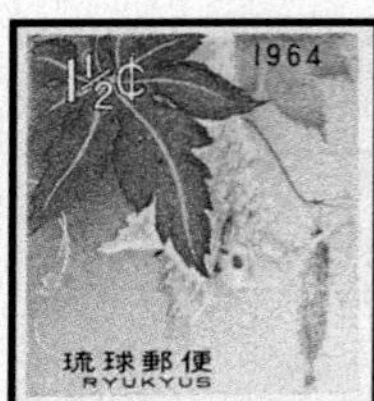

Bitter Melon Vine — PC23

Summer Greeting Card

Designer: Shinzan Yamada

1964, June 20

UX26 PC23 1½c **multicolored,** *off-white (285,410)* 1.40 *2.25*

First day cancel 1.75

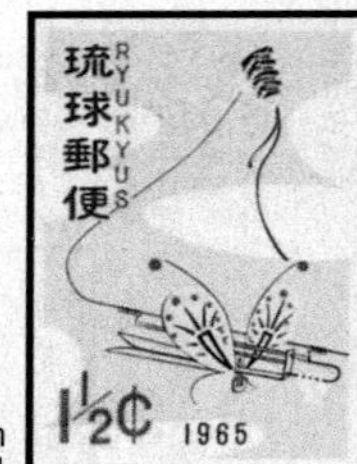

Fighting Kite with Rider — PC24

1965 New Year Card; Precanceled

Designer: Koya Oshiro

1964, Nov. 15

UX27 PC24 1½c **multicolored,** *off-white (4,876,618)* 1.25 *1.75*

First day cancel 2.00

Palm-leaf Fan — PC25

Summer Greeting Card

Designer: Koya Oshiro

1965, June 20
UX28 PC25 1½c **multicolored,** *off-white* *(340,604)* 1.40 *2.50*
First day cancel 1.65

Toy Pony Rider — PC26

1966 New Year Card; Precanceled

Designer: Seikichi Tamanaha

1965, Nov. 15
UX29 PC26 1½c **multicolored,** *off-white* *(5,224,622)* 1.25 *1.75*
First day cancel 1.40
a. Silver (background) omitted 250.00

Fan Palm Dipper — PC27

Summer Greeting Card

Designer: Seikichi Tamanaha

1966, June 20
UX30 PC27 1½c **multicolored,** *off-white* *(339,880)* 1.25 *2.00*
First day cancel 1.40

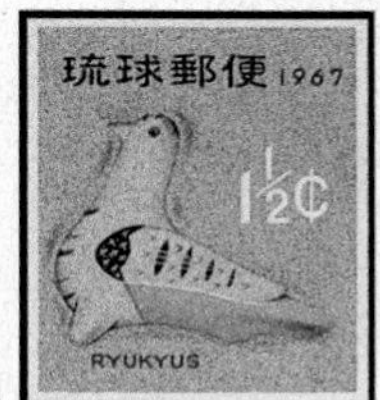

Toy Dove — PC28

1967 New Year Card; Precanceled

Designer: Seikichi Tamanaha

1966, Nov. 15
UX31 PC28 1½c **multicolored,** *off-white* *(5,500,000)* 1.25 *1.75*
First day cancel 1.65
a. Silver (background) omitted *500.00*
b. Gray blue & green omitted *750.00*

Cycad Insect Cage and Praying Mantis — PC29

Summer Greeting Card

Designer: Shin Isagawa

1967, June 20
UX32 PC29 1½c **multicolored,** *off-white* *(350.000)* 1.50 *2.50*
First day cancel 1.75

Paper Doll Royalty — PC30

1968 New Year Card; Precanceled

Designer: Shin Isagawa

1967, Nov. 15
UX33 PC30 1½c **multicolored,** *off-white* *(6,200,000)* 1.10 *1.50*
First day cancel 1.75
a. Gold omitted 500.00

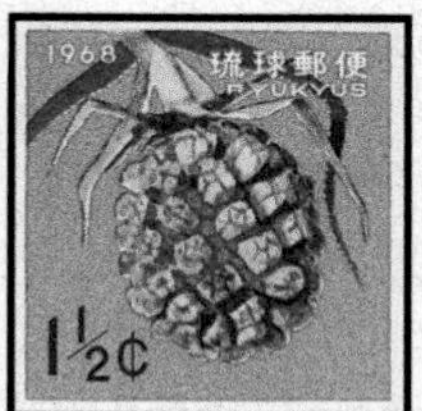

Pandanus Drupe — PC31

Summer Greeting Card

Designer: Seikan Omine

1968, June 20
UX34 PC31 1½c **multicolored,** *off-white* *(350,000)* 1.25 *2.25*
First day cancel 1.75

Toy Lion — PC32

1969 New Year Card; Precanceled

Designer: Teruyoshi Kinjo

1968, Nov. 15
UX35 PC32 1½c **multicolored,** *off-white* *(7,000,000)* 1.10 *1.50*
First day cancel 1.50

Ryukyu Trading Ship — PC33

Summer Greeting Card

Designer: Seikichi Tamanaha

1969, June 20
UX36 PC33 1½c **multicolored,** *(349,800)* 1.25 *2.25*
First day cancel 1.75

Toy Devil Mask — PC34

1970 New Year Card; Precanceled

Designer: Teruyoshi Kinjo

1969, Nov. 15
UX37 PC34 1½c **multicolored** *(97,200,000)* 1.10 *1.50*
First day cancel 1.25

Ripe Litchis — PC35

Summer Greeting Card

Designer: Kensei Miyagi

1970, June 20
UX38 PC35 1½c **multicolored** *(400,000)* 1.40 *2.25*
First day cancel 1.50

Thread-winding Implements for Dance — PC36

1971 New Year Card; Precanceled

Designer: Yoshinori Arakai

1970, Nov. 16
UX39 PC36 1½c **multicolored** *(7,500,000)* 1.10 *1.50*
First day cancel 1.25

Ripe Guavas — PC37

Summer Greeting Card

Designer: Kensei Miyagi

1971, July 10
UX40 PC37 1½c **multicolored** *(400,000)* 1.25 *2.25*
First day cancel 1.25

Pony Type of 1961
Zip Code Boxes in Vermilion

1971, July 10
UX41 PC17 1½c **gray violet & brown** *(3,000,000)* 1.25 *3.50*
First day cancel 2.00

No. UX41 Surcharged below Stamp in Vermilion

改訂2¢

"Revalued 2¢" applied by Nakamura Printing Co.

1971, Sept. 1
UX42 PC17 2c on 1½c **gray violet & brown** *(1,699,569)* 1.10 *2.25*
First day cancel 2.00
a. Inverted surcharge *500.00*
b. Double surcharge *500.00*
c. Surcharge on back *500.00*
e. Surcharge on back, inverted *500.00*

1972 New Year Card; Precanceled

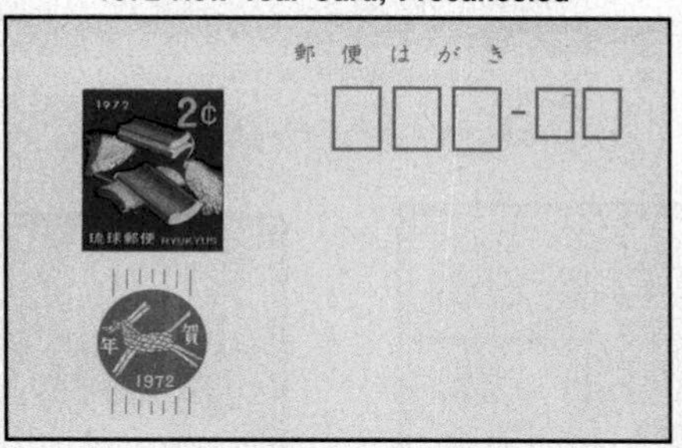

Tasseled Castanets — PC38

Zip Code Boxes in Vermilion

Designer: Yoshinori Arakaki

1971, Nov. 15
UX43 PC38 2c **multicolored** *(8,000,000)* 1.00 *1.50*
First day cancel 1.25

Type of 1961
Zip Code Boxes in Vermilion

1971, Dec. 15
UX44 PC17 2c **gray violet & brown** *(3,500,000)* 1.25 *1.75*
First day cancel 1.65

PAID REPLY POSTAL CARDS

Sold as two attached cards, one for message, one for reply. The major listings are of unsevered cards except Nos. UY4-UY6.

Message

Reply

1948, July 1

UY1 US1 10s + 10s **dull red,** *grayish tan (1,000)* 2,000. —
m. Message card 600. 1,000.
r. Reply card 600. 1,000.

1949, July 18

UY2 US1 15s + 15s **vermilion,** *tan (E 150,000)* 30.00 *40.00*
a. Gray card *(E 75,000)* 75.00 —
First day cancel —
m. Message card 8.00 *16.50*
r. Reply card 8.00 *16.50*

1950, Jan. 21

UY3 US2 50s + 50s **carmine red,** *gray cream (E 130,000)* 25.00 *40.00*
a. Double impression of message card —
b. Light tan card *(E 96,000)* 15.00 —
First day cancel —
m. Message card 3.50 *13.50*
r. Reply card 3.50 *13.50*

No. UY2a Handstamp Surcharged in Vermilion

1951

UY4 US1 1y (15s+85s) message, type "b" *(E 3,000)* 350. 350.
a. Reply, type "b" *(E 3,000)* 350. 350.
b. Message, type "a" *(E 300)* 600. —
c. Reply, type "a" *(E 300)* 600. —
d. Message, type "d" *(E 200)* 500. —
e. Reply, type "d" *(E 200)* 500. —
f. Message, UY2, type "a" *(E 3,000)* 150. *225.*
g. Reply, UY2, type "a" *(E 3,000)* 150. *225.*
h. Message, UY2, type "b" *(E 2,500)* 275. 275.
i. Reply, UY2, type "b" *(E 2,500)* 275. 275.
j. Message, UY2, type "d" *(E 2,800)* 150. *250.*
k. Reply, UY2, type "d" *(E 2,800)* 150. *250.*
l. 1y + 1y unsevered, type "b" *850.*
m. 1y + 1y unsevered, type "a" *1,450.*
n. 1y + 1y unsevered, type "d" *1,200.*
o. 1y + 1y unsevered, UY2, type "a" *360.*
p. 1y + 1y unsevered, UY2, type "b" *650.*
q. 1y + 1y unsevered, UY2, type "d" *360.*
r. 1y + 1y unsevered, UY2, type "c" *3, 500.*
s. Message, UY2, type "c," —
t. Reply, UY2, type "c" —
u. Message, type "c" —
v. Reply, type "c" —
w. As "n," surcharge omitted on reply card —

Types are illustrated above No. UX4.

e

f

g

h

Typographed Surcharge in Vermilion on No. UY2a

UY5 US1 1y (15s+85s) message, type "f" *(E 20,000)* 125. 125.
a. Reply, type "f" *(E 20,000)* 125. 125.
b. Message, type "e" *(E 12,500)* 225. 225.
c. Reply, type "e" *(E 12,500)* 225. 225.
d. Message, type "g" *(E 500)* — —
e. Reply, type "g" *(E 500)* *1,250.* —
f. Message, UY2, type "e" *(E 15,000)* 125. 125.
g. Reply, UY2, type "e" *(E 15,000)* 125. 125.
h. Message, UY2, type "f" *(E 9,000)* 125. 125.
i. Reply, UY2, type "f" *(E 9,000)* 125. 125.
j. Message, UY2, type "g" *(E 500)* *2,000.*
k. Reply, UY2, type "g" *(E 500)* *1,000.* *1,500.*
l. 1y + 1y unsevered, type "e" *1,000.*
m. 1y + 1y unsevered, UY2, type "e" *375.*

Typographed Surcharge Type "h" in Vermilion on No. UY3

UY6 US2 1y (50s+50s) message *(E 35,000)* 125.00 *150.00*
a. Reply *(E 35,000)* 125.00 *150.00*
b. Message, UY3b *(E 10,000)* 125.00 *150.00*
c. Reply, UY3b *(E 10,000)* 125.00 *150.00*

No. UY6 is unknown as a joined card.

Smooth or Coarse Card

1952, Feb. 8

UY7 PC3 1y + 1y **vermilion,** *gray tan (60,000)* 120.00 *140.00*
First day cancel 250.00
m. Message card 25.00 *50.00*
r. Reply card 25.00 *50.00*

1953

UY8 PC4 1y + 1y **vermilion,** *tan (22,900)* 30.00 *40.00*
First day cancel —
a. Off-white card *(13,800)* 40.00 *50.00*
m. Message card 7.50 *19.00*
r. Reply card 7.50 *26.50*

Off-white or Light Cream Card

1953, Dec. 2

UY9 PC5 2y + 2y **green** *(50,000)* 100.00 90.00
First day cancel 150.00
m. Message card 15.00 *25.00*
r. Reply card 15.00 *35.00*

1955, May

UY10 PC6 2y + 2y **green,** *off-white (280,000)* 10.00 —
a. Reply card blank 500.00
m. Message card 3.25 *11.00*
r. Reply card 3.25 *15.00*

No. UY10 Surcharged in Red

1958, Sept. 16

UY11 PC6 1½c on 2y, 1½c on 2y *(95,000)* 8.00 —
First day cancel 22.50
a. Surcharge on reply card only *500.00* —
b. Surcharge on message card only *500.00* —
c. Reply card double surcharge *750.00* —
d. Reply card stamp omitted (surcharge only) *1,000.* —
m. Message card 2.75 *10.00*
r. Reply card 2.75 *16.50*

Surcharge varieties include: "1" omitted; wrong font "2".

Pony Types

1959, June 20

UY12 PC11 1½c + 1½c **dark blue & brown** *(366,000)* 3.50 —
First day cancel 4.00
m. Message card .65 *3.50*
r. Reply card .65 *3.50*

1960, Mar. 10

UY13 PC13 1½c + 1½c **gray violet & brown,** *(150,000)* 7.00 —
First day cancel 5.00
m. Message card 1.50 *5.00*
r. Reply card 1.50 *5.00*

International Type

1963, Feb. 15

UY14 PC20 5c + 5c **vermilion, emerald & black,** *pale yellow (70,000)* 2.50 —
First day cancel 3.00
m. Message card .75 *3.75*
r. Reply card .75 *3.75*

Pony ("RYUKYUS") Type

1963-69

UY15 PC17 1½c + 1½c **gray violet & brown,** *cream, Mar. 15, (800,000)* 2.00 —
First day cancel 2.50
a. Off-white card, *Mar. 13, 1967 (100,000)* 2.25 —
b. White card, *Nov. 22, 1969 (700,000)* 1.75 —
m. Message card detached .40 *4.00*
r. Reply card detached .40 *4.00*

No. UY14 Surcharged below Stamp in Vermilion

1971, Sept. 1

UY16 PC17 2c on 1½c + 2c on 1½c **gray violet & brown** *(80,000)* 2.00 —
First day cancel 2.25
m. Message card .50 *2.50*
r. Reply card .50 *2.50*

Pony ("RYUKYUS") Type
Zip Code Boxes in Vermilion

1971, Nov. 1

UY17 PC17 2c + 2c **gray violet & brown** *(150,000)* 2.00 —
First day cancel 2.50
m. Message card .50 *2.50*
r. Reply card .50 *2.50*

OFFICIAL STAMPS ELECTION POSTAL CARDS

Official election free-mail postal cards were authorized by the United States Civil Administration of the Ryukyus, Ordinance 57, Dec. 18, 1951, as a measure to ensure equal access to voters for each candidate standing in district or general elections in the islands. Under the terms of the ordinance and the local enabling legislation, each candidate, on request, could receive a fixed number of cards per election, which were serviced with no mailing costs to the candidate.

Until the issuance of No. UZE15 in 1960, cards were processed without canceling; beginning with that issue, they were treated as regular postal cards and canceled.

With the exception of pieces bearing emergency handstamp or machine-cancel indicia, the cards were special-order printings (incorporating the election indicium) of designs and types of postal cards concurrently in use as regular postal cards (though at times in different colors).

ELECTION INDICIA

Type I

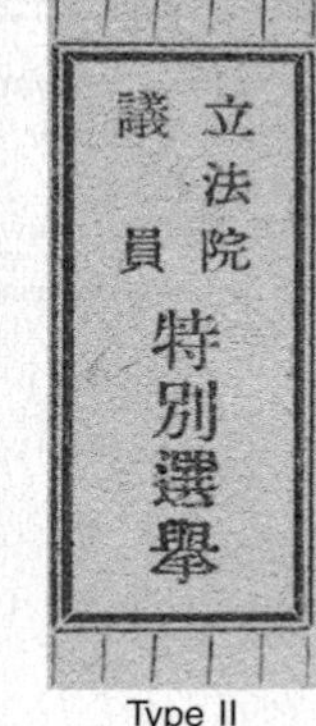

Type II

Type I: Typographed, Size: 18x45mm
Type II: Typographed, Size: 17½x48-49mm

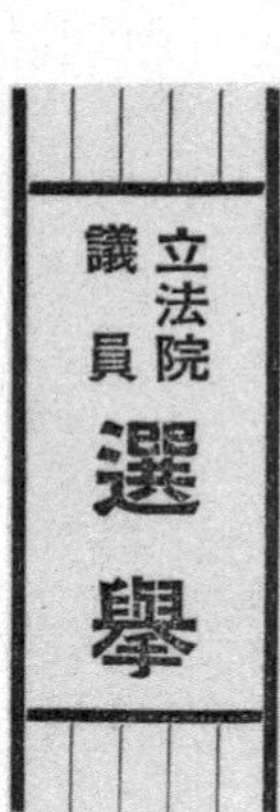

Type III

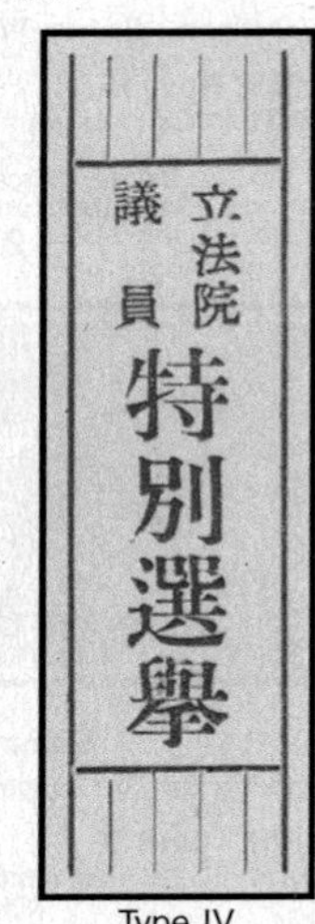

Type IV

Type III: Typographed, Size: 17½x49-51mm
Type IV: Typographed, Size: 16½x62mm

Type IVa

Type V

Type IVa: Like Type IV but with second character from bottom ("SEN") having one stroke at upper left instead of two
Type V: Typographed, Size: 16-17x61-63mm (similar to Type IV, but with different bottom character)

Type VI

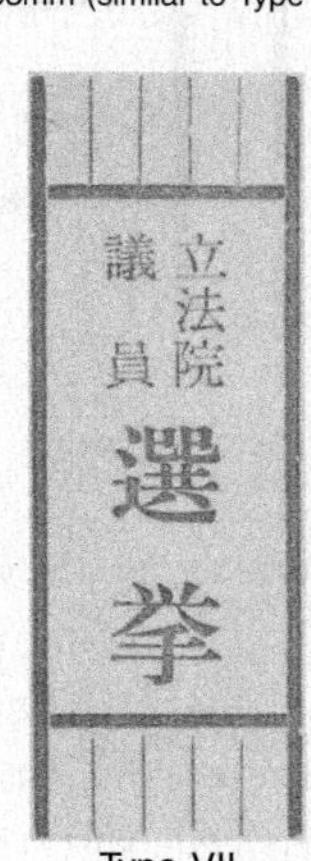

Type VII

Type VI: Typographed, Size: 17½x51-52mm
Type VII: Typographed, Size: 17½x51-52mm (similar to Type VI, but with different bottom character)

Type VIII

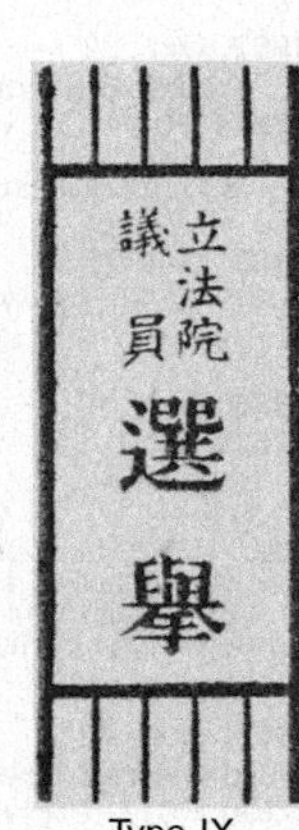

Type IX

Type VIII: Typographed, Size: 17¼-17½x 52mm (similar to Type VII but with second character from bottom ("SEN") having one stroke at upper left instead of two)
Type IX: Handstamped, Size: 17½x51mm

Type X

Type XI

Type X: Typographed, Size: 17½x51-51½mm (similar to Type VIII, but with different appearance of five smaller characters at top)
Type XI: Typographed, Size: 10x31½mm

Type XII

Type XIII

Type XII: Handstamped, Size: 17½-18x49½-51½mm, Thick characters
Type XIII: Handstamped, Size: 17½-18x50¼-51mm, Thin characters

Type XIIIa

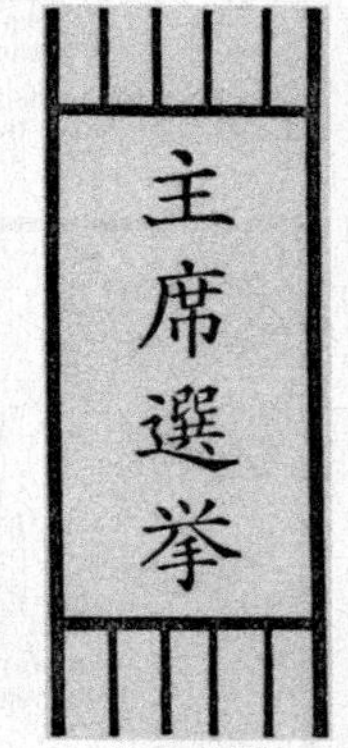

Type XIV

Type XIIIa: Handstamped, Size: 17½-18x50¼x51mm, Thick characters, with shorter lvertical line at lower left.
Type XIV: Typographed, Size: 18x50-50½mm

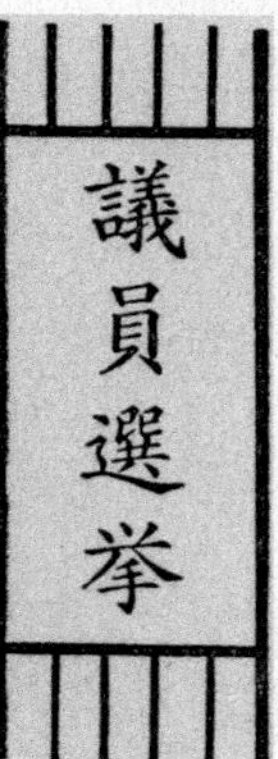

Type XV

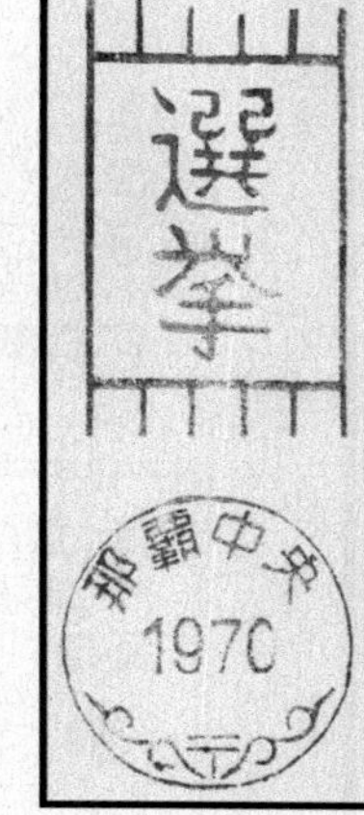

Type XVI

Type XV: Typographed, Size: 18x50-50½mm
Type XVI: Machine cancel, Circle diameter: 20mm, Height of legend box: 23½mm

Type XVIa

Type XVII

Type XVIa: Machine cancel, Circle diameter: 20mm, Height of legend box: 20½-22mm
Type XVII: Typographed, Size: 18½x48½-50mm

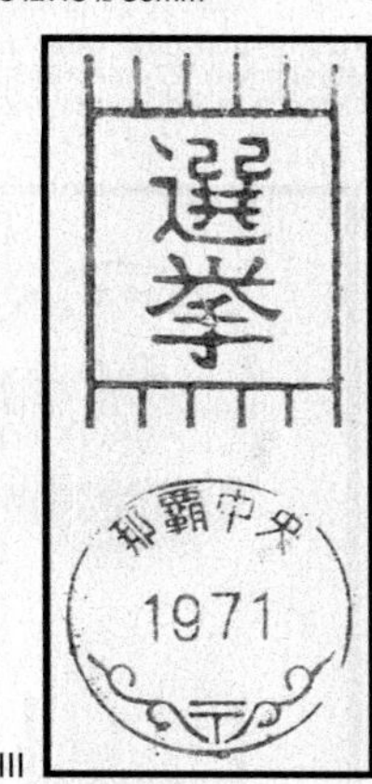

Type XVIII

Type XVIII: Machine cancel, Circle diameter: 20mm, Height of legend box: 20½-22 mm

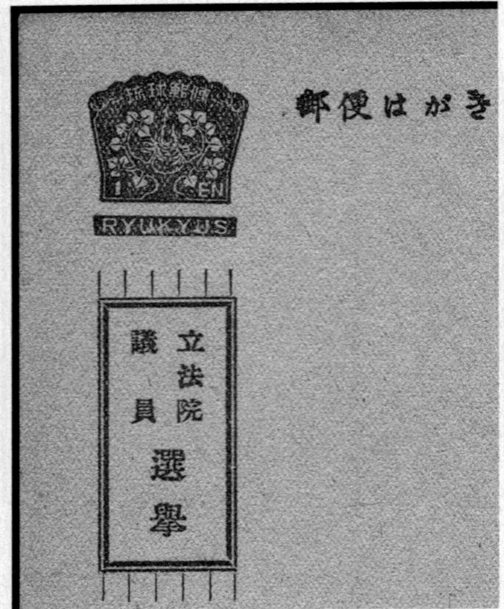

UZE1

1952, Feb. 2 **First General Election**

UZE1 PC3 1y **vermilion,** *tan* coarse (Naha die) + Type I *(345,000)* 300.00 500.00

a. Postmarked (error) —

1952, July 26 **1st District Special Election**

UZE2 PC3 1y **vermilion,** *tan* coarse (Naha die) + Type II *(est. 25,000)* — —

a. 2nd character from bottom in indicium (SEN) inverted — —

Used cards or unused with campaign messages must have reference to the 1st District (Kasari, Amami Gunto) election.

1953, Mar. 3 **4th District Special Election**

UZE3 PC4 1y **vermilion,** *tan* coarse (Tokyo die) + Type II *(est. 10,000)* —

a. Postmarked (error) —

Identifiable only when postmarked (in error, with dates between Mar. 3-Mar.31, 1953) and/or with campaign message in reference to 4th District election (Motobu, Okinawa Gunto).

1953, Mar. 27 **3rd District Special Election**

UZE4 PC4 1y **vermilion,** *tan* coarse (Tokyo die) + Type II *(est. 10,000)* 50.00 —

a. Postmarked (error) —

Identifiable only when postmarked (in error, with dates between Mar. 27-Apr. 1953) and/or with campaign message in reference to 3rd District election (Yagaji, Okinawa Gunto).

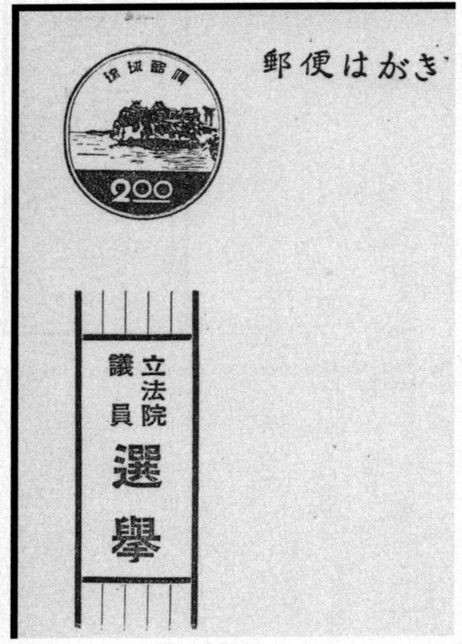

UZE5

1954, Feb. 23 **Second General Election**

UZE5 PC5 2y **rose red,** *off white* (Naha die) + Type III *(70,000)* 45.00 —

a. Postmarked (error) —

1954, Nov. 19 **18th District Special Election**

UZE6 PC6 2y **red,** *off white* (Tokyo die) + Type IV 500.00 —

a. Postmarked (error) —

UZE6A PC6 2y **red,** *off white* (Tokyo die) + Type V 500.00 —

a. Postmarked (error) —

Postal records show receipt of 4,000 total cards of Nos. UZE6 and UZE6A, undefined as to type.

1955, Feb. 15 **20th District Special Election**

UZE7 PC6 2y **dark purple,** *off white* (Tokyo die) + Type IV *(2,000)* 500.00 —

1955, Mar. 8 **23rd District Special Election**

UZE8 PC6 2y **turquoise blue,** *off white* (Tokyo die) + Type V *(2,000)* 500.00 —

a. Postmarked (error) —

1955, June 28 **22nd District Special Election**

UZE9 PC6 2y **dull brown,** *gray cream* (Tokyo die) + Type V *(3,030)* 240.00 —

a. Postmarked (error) —

1956, Feb. 20 **Third General Election**

UZE10 PC6 2y **pale blue green,** *off white* (Tokyo die) + Type VI 75.00 150.00

a. Postmarked (error) —

UZE10A PC6 2y **pale blue green,** *off white* (Tokyo die) + Type VII 75.00 150.00

a. Postmarked (error) —

Postal records show receipt of 65,000 total cards of Nos. UZE10 and UZE10A, undefined as to type.

1956, Oct. 26 **25th District Special Election**

UZE11 PC6 2y **brown red,** *off white* (Tokyo die) + Type IV 300.00 —

UZE11A PC6 2y **brown red,** *off white* (Tokyo die) + Type V 140.00 350.00

Postal records show a total quantity of 3,030 examples of Nos. UZE11 and UZE11A prepared, unidentified as to type, of which 2,000 were issued.

1957, Aug. 5 **18th District Special Election**

UZE12 PC6 2y **lilac,** *off white* (Tokyo die) + Type IVa *(3,030)* 175.00 —

1958, Feb. 25 **Fourth General Election**

UZE13 PC6 2y **deep blue,** *off white* (Tokyo die) + Type VI (bold face print) 130.00 70.00

UZE13A PC6 2y **deep blue,** *off white* (Tokyo die) + Type VI (light face print) 130.00 70.00

UZE13B PC6 2y **deep blue,** *off white* (Tokyo die) + Type VII (bold face print) 130.00 70.00

UZE13C PC6 2y **deep blue,** *off white* (Tokyo die) + Type VII (light face print) 90.00 70.00

Postal records show a total of 140,300 cards of Nos. UZE13-UZE13C prepared in two printings, undefined as to types.

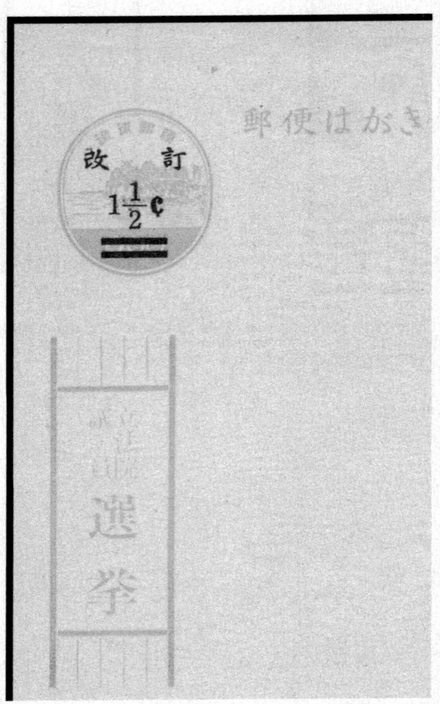

UZE14

1959, July 23 **26th District Special Election**

UZE14 PC6 1½c on 2y **lemon,** *white* (Tokyo die) + Type VIII *(4,100)* 450.00 —

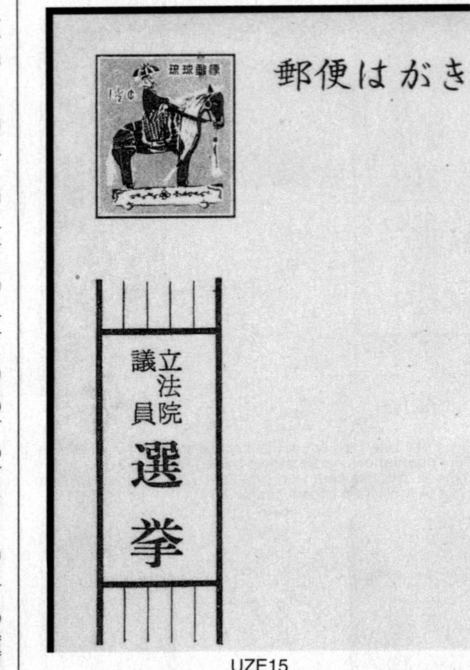

UZE15

1960, Oct. 24 **Fifth General Election**

UZE15 PC11 1½c **indigo & claret brown,** *white* (Naha die) + Type VIII *(150,000)* 50.00 50.00

UZE16 PC13 1½c **violet gray & claret brown,** *cream* (Tokyo die) + Type IX in LL corner *(10,000)* 350.00 *650.00*

1962, Oct. 22 **Sixth General Election**

UZE17 PC17 1½c **violet gray & claret brown,** *cream* + Type VIII 30.00 50.00

b. Election indicium inverted at right side of card —

UZE17A PC17 1½c **violet gray & claret brown,** *cream* + Type X 30.00 50.00

Postal records show a total of 116,000 cards of Nos. UZE17-UZE17A prepared, undefined as to type.

1962, Oct. 22

Sixth General Election Emergency Issue

UZE18 PC17 1½c **violet gray & claret brown,** *cream* + Type IX *(6,000)* 250.00 —

a. Indicium inverted — —

1965, Oct. 25 **Seventh General Election**

UZE19 PC17 1½c **violet gray & claret brown,** *cream* + Type XI *(134,000)* 17.50 90.00

1966, Aug. 1 **3rd District Special Election**

UZE20 PC17 1½c **violet gray & claret brown,** *cream* + Type XI *(est. 3,800)* 500.00

No. UZE20 is a remainder copy of No. UZE19 identifiable only when canceled at the Nakijin Post Office or Nago Central Post Office with verification that the card was delivered to a registered voter of Nakijin between Aug. 1 and Aug. 20, 1966.

1966, Aug. 11

3rd District Special Election Emergency Issue

UZE21 PC17 1½c **violet gray & claret brown,** *cream* + Type XII *(est. 200 for #UZE21 and #UZE22)* 425.00

UZE22 PC17 1½c **violet gray & claret brown,** *cream* + Type XIII 150.00 —

b. Double strike of indicium —

1968, Oct. 21 **First Chief Executive Election**

UZE23 PC17 1½c **violet gray & claret brown,** *white* + Type XIV *(300,000)* 20.00 25.00

1968, Oct. 21 **Eighth General Election**

UZE24 PC17 1½c **violet gray & claret brown,** *white* + Type XV *(142,000)* 20.00 35.00

1970, Oct. 12 **1st District Special Election**

UZE25 PC17 1½c **violet gray & claret brown,** *white* + Type XV *(4,000)* 350.00

No. UZE25 is a remainder card of No. UZE24, identifiable only when canceled at the Higashi, Kunigami, Ogimi or Oku Post Offices between Oct. 12-Oct. 31, 1970.

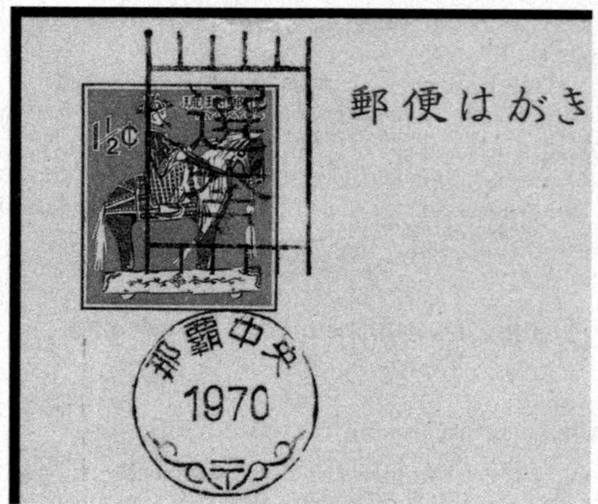

UZE26A

First General Election for Coucilors and Representatives to the Japanese Diet

1970, Oct. 23

UZE26	PC17	1½c	**violet gray & claret brown,** *white* + Type XVI *(300,000)*	250.00	20.00
UZE26A	PC17	1½c	**violet gray & claret brown,** *white* + Type XVIa *(300,000)*	250.00	20.00

Postal records show a total of 171,000 examples of Nos. UZE26-UZE26A prepared, undefined as to type.

Emergency Commercial Card Issue for First General Japanese Diet Election

UZE27	*white or light gray blue* + Type XVI	—	20.00
UZE27A	*white or light gray blue* + Type XVIa	—	20.00

Postal records show a total of 79,000 commercial cards were acquired for official issue as Nos. UZE27-UZE27A after validating. Some of the cards show an imprinted black square, while others show nothing.

1970, Nov. 16 **21st District Special Election**

UZE28	PC17	1½c	**violet gray & claret brown,** *white* + Type XVII *(8,000)*	—	130.00

推薦状

島本「ケン」は言う
「政治は相互の理解と協調と和の中にあり、抵抗や反抗の中にはない。抵抗と反抗はいたずらに憎悪の感情を増し、混乱を招くだけである」と、常に現実を踏へて、前向きに誠実で勇気をもって実践する人、島本「ケン」
島本「ケン」こそは新沖縄建設に必要な人であります。
善意に満ちた、豊かな明るい清らかな新沖縄建設の為に第二十二区から立法院議員に立候補しました
島本「ケン」に絶大なる御支持、御支援を賜ります様お願い申し上げると共に絶対自信をもって「ケン」を推薦致します。

昭和四十五年十一月　日
那覇市古波蔵二四四
島本ケン選挙本部
推薦者

UZE29

1970, Nov. 16 **22nd District Special Election**

UZE29	PC17	1½c	**violet gray & claret brown,** *white* + Type XVII *(2,000)*	—	350.00

No. UZE29 is a remainder card of No. UZE28, identifiable only with the imprinted message shown above of candidate Shimamoto Ken.

UZE30	PC17	1½c	**violet gray & claret brown,** *white* + Type XIII	—	300.00
UZE30A	PC17	1½c	**violet gray & claret brown,** *white* + Type XIIa	—	300.00

Postal records show a total of 2,000 of Nos. UZE30-UZE30A prepared, undefined as to type.

1971, Feb. 15 **7th District Special Election**

UZE31	PC17	1½c	**violet gray & claret brown,** *white* + Type XV *(4,000)*	—	250.00

1971, June 4

Second General Election for Coucilors and Representatives to the Japanese Diet

UZE32	PC17	1½c	**violet gray & claret brown,** *white* + Type XVIII *(25,000)*	—	27.50

Emergency Commercial Card Issue for Second General Japanese Diet Election

UZE33	*white* + Type XVIII, 100x148mm *(25,000)*	—	17.50
b.	Double strike of election indicium, one inverted in LR corner	—	—
c.	Double strike of election indicium, one in lower left corner		—
d.	Election indicium on front and reverse		—
UZE33A	*white* + Type XVIII, 104x150mm *(25,000)*	—	30.00

REVENUE STAMPS

Upon its establishment Apr. 1, 1952, the government of the Ryukyu Islands assumed responsibility for the issuing of and the profit from revenue stamps. The various series served indiscriminately as evidence of payment of the required fees for various legal, realty and general commercial transactions.

1 yen — R1

3

5

10

50

100

500

1000

Designer: Eizo Yonamine

Litho. by Japan Printing Bureau.

1952-54 **Wmk. 257** ***Perf. 13x13½***

R1	R1	1y	**brown**	15.00	10.00
R2	R1	3y	**carmine**	20.00	12.00
R3	R1	5y	**green**	25.00	15.00
R4	R1	10y	**blue**	25.00	20.00
R5	R1	50y	**purple**	30.00	25.00
R6	R1	100y	**yellow brown**	50.00	30.00
R7	R1	500y	**dark green**	350.00	100.00
R8	R1	1,000y	**carmine**	200.00	150.00
			Nos. R1-R8 (8)	715.00	362.00

Issued: #R1-R6, July 15, 1952; #R7-R8, Apr. 16, 1954.

Denomination Vertical

"Cent"

"Dollar"

Litho. by Kobundo Printing Co., Naha

Perf. 10, 10½, 11 and combinations

1958, Sept. 16 **Without Gum** **Unwmk.**

R9	R1	1c	**red brown**	30.00	25.00
a.			Horiz. pair, imperf. between	500.00	
R10	R1	3c	**red**	40.00	35.00
a.			Horiz. pair, imperf. between	500.00	
R11	R1	5c	**green**	50.00	45.00
R12	R1	10c	**blue**	70.00	65.00
a.			Horiz. pair, imperf. between	500.00	
R13	R1	50c	**purple**	135.00	120.00
R14	R1	$1	**sepia**	200.00	175.00
R15	R1	$5	**dark green**	400.00	350.00
R16	R1	$10	**carmine**	450.00	400.00
			Nos. R9-R16 (8)	1,375.	1,215.

R2

R3

R4

Litho. by Japan Printing Bureau.

1959-69 **Wmk. 257** ***Perf. 13x13½***

R17	R2	1c	**brown**	3.00	1.90
R18	R2	3c	**red**	3.00	1.10
R19	R2	5c	**purple**	5.50	3.25
R20	R2	10c	**green**	10.00	6.00
R21	R2	20c	**sepia** ('69)	80.00	55.00
R22	R2	30c	**light olive** ('69)	100.00	65.00
R23	R2	50c	**blue**	40.00	14.00
			Engr.		
R24	R3	$1	**olive**	45.00	12.50
R25	R3	$2	**vermilion** ('69)	250.00	50.00
R26	R3	$3	**purple** ('69)	450.00	60.00
R27	R3	$5	**orange**	120.00	45.00
R28	R3	$10	**dark green**	180.00	60.00
R29	R4	$20	**carmine** ('69)	1,500.	200.00
R30	R4	$30	**blue** ('69)	1,750.	*1,250.*
R31	R4	$50	**black** ('69)	2,000.	*1,750.*
			Nos. R17-R28 (12)	1,287.	373.75

UNEMPLOYMENT INSURANCE

These stamps, when affixed in an official booklet and canceled, certified a one-day contract for a day laborer. They were available to employers at certain post offices on various islands.

Dove — RQ1

Shield — RQ2

Lithographed in Naha

1961, Jan. 10 **Without Gum** **Unwmk.** ***Rouletted***

RQ1	RQ1	2c	**pale red**	800.00	—
RQ2	RQ2	4c	**violet**	60.00	60.00

Redrawn

Lithographed by Japan Printing Bureau

1966, Feb. **Unwmk.** ***Perf. 13x13½***

RQ3	RQ1	2c	**pale red**	—	—
RQ4	RQ2	4c	**violet**	25.00	25.00

Redrawn stamps have bolder numerals and inscriptions, and fewer, stronger lines of shading in background.

Cycad — RQ3

Lithographed by Japan Printing Bureau

1968, Apr. 19 **Wmk. 257** ***Perf. 13x13½***

RQ5	RQ3	8c	**brown**	30.00	30.00

Nos. RQ3-RQ4 Surcharged

1967-72

RQ6	RQ1	8c on 2c **pale red**	60.00	60.00
RQ7	RQ2	8c on 4c **violet** ('72)	30.00	30.00
RQ8	RQ2	12c on 4c **violet** ('71)	25.00	25.00

A 4-cent "stamp" picturing Iriomote Park was originally planned for postage in 1971. Its use was changed, and it became a label that was used on the "Ryukyu Islands Emergency Conversion Confirmation Certificate." Value, $175 unused, $225 on document.

PROVISIONAL ISSUES MIYAKO

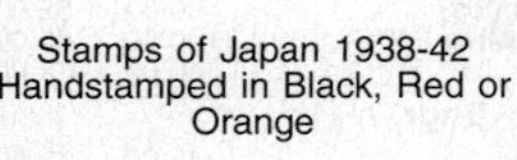

Stamps of Japan 1938-42 Handstamped in Black, Red or Orange

1948 Typo., Litho., Engr. Wmk. 257 *Perf. 13*

3XR1	A84	3s **brown,** #329	60.00	—
a.		Double overprint	—	
3XR2	A86	5s **brown lake,** #331	60.00	—
a.		Horiz. pair, one without revenue overprint	*1,500.*	—
b.		Double overprint	—	
c.		Triple overprint	—	
d.		Quadruple overprint	—	
3XR3	A152	20s **blue,** #338 (R)	40.00	—
a.		Double overprint	—	
b.		Pair, one without overprint	—	
3XR4	A95	25s **dark brown & pale brown,** #270 (R)	40.00	—
a.		Black overprint	600.00	—
b.		Double overprint	—	
c.		Black double overprint	—	
3XR5	A96	30s **peacock blue,** #271 (R)	40.00	—
a.		Double overprint	—	
b.		Triple overprint	—	
3XR6	A154	40s **dark violet,** #342 (R)	40.00	—
a.		Double overprint	—	
3XR7	A97	50s **olive & pale olive,** #272 (R)	120.00	—
a.		Orange overprint	*500.00*	—
b.		Double overprint	—	

Doubled handstamps are known on all values and pairs with one stamp without handstamp exist on the 5s and 20s.

PROVISIONAL ISSUES YAEYAMA

In addition to the continued use of the then-current Japanese revenue stamps in stock from the wartime period, the varying authorities of the Yaeyama Gunto issued three district-specific revenue series, with a total of 28 values. Only those values at present verified by surviving examples are indicated. Numbers are reserved for other values believed to have been issued, but as yet not seen and verified.

No. 5XR2 — R5

No. 5XR3 — R6

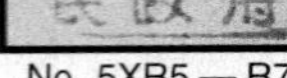

No. 5XR5 — R7

No. 5XR27 — R8

1946 (?) Without Gum *Imperf.*

Value printed, frame handstamped

5XR1	R5	3s **vermilion & black**	—	
5XR2	R5	10s **vermilion & black**	—	—

Validating handstamp below

5XR3	R6	1y **vermilion & black**	—	—

Civil Administration Issues
Value printed, frame handstamped
Cream Paper

1947 (?) Without Gum *Imperf.*

5XR5	R7	10s **vermilion & black**	—	
5XR6	R7	50s **vermilion & black**	—	—

Gunto Government Issues
Value printed, frame handstamped
Cream Paper

1950 (?) Without Gum *Imperf.*

5XR17	R8	10s **vermilion & black**	—	
5XR18	R8	50s **vermilion & black**	—	
a.		50s **vermilion & blue**	—	
5XR20	R8	1.50y **vermilion & black**	—	
5XR22	R8	5y **vermilion & black**	—	
5XR24	R8	20y **vermilion & black**	—	—
5XR27	R8	100y **vermilion & black**	—	

Nos. 5XR17-5XR27 are known with rough perforations, full or partial.

SPECIMEN STAMPS

Regular stamps and postal cards of 1958-65 overprinted with three cursive syllabics *mi-ho-n* ("specimen").

Type A

1961-64 Overprinted in Black

91S	3c **multicolored** *(1,000)*	200.00
118S	3c **multicolored** *(1,100)*	400.00
119S	3c **multicolored** *(1,100)*	350.00

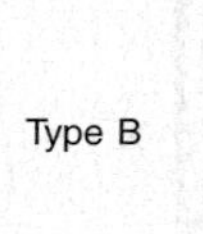

Type B

1964-65 Overprinted in Red or Black

120aS	3c **deep blue, deep carmine & ocher** (R) *(1,500)*	180.00
121S	3c **multicolored** (R) *(1,500)*	160.00
124S	3c **ultra, yel & red** (R) *(5,000)*	30.00
125S	3s **dull claret, yel & black** *(1,500)*	65.00
126S	3c **yellow & multi** *(2,000)*	55.00
127S	3c **gray, red & black** *(2,000)*	55.00
128S	3c **multicolored** *(1,500)*	65.00
129S	1½c **multicolored** (R) *(1,500)*	65.00
130S	3c **light blue & multi** (R) *(1,500)*	180.00
131S	3c **multicolored** (R) *(1,500)*	55.00
132S	3c **buff & multicolored** *(2,000)*	55.00
133S	3c **green & multi** (R) *(2,000)*	45.00
134S	3c **multicolored** *(2,000)*	45.00
135S	3c **blue & multicolored** *(2,000)*	45.00
136S	3c **golden brown & multi** *(2,000)*	45.00
139S	1½c **multicolored** (R) *(2,500)*	45.00

POSTAL CARDS

1964-65

Overprinted Type A or B in Black or Red

UX26S	A	1½c **multicolored** *(1,000)*	450.00
UX27S	B	1½c **multicolored** *(1,000)*	325.00
UX28S	A	1½c **multicolored** *(1,000)*	275.00
UX29S	A	1½c **multicolored** *(1,100)*	225.00

See also Nos. 46TCS and 48TCS following Proofs and Trial Color Proofs.

PROOFS AND TRIAL COLOR PROOFS

1948

1aP2	5s **magenta,** sm die on salmon paper, imperf., without gum	—
2aP2	10s **yellow green,** sm die on salmon paper, imperf., without gum	—
3aP2	20s **yellow green,** sm die on salmon paper, imperf., without gum	—
5aP2	40s **magenta,** sm die on salmon paper, imperf., without gum	—
6aP2	50s **ultramarine,** sm die on salmon paper, imperf., without gum	—
7aP2	1y **ultramarine,** sm die on salmon paper, imperf., without gum	—

Nos. 1aP2-7aP2 are each unique and with stamp-size margins. They may be plate proofs.

Between the printing of Nos. 1a-7a and Nos. 1-7, essay sheets of the series were prepared in Tokyo and overprinted with a swirl-pattern of blue or red dots. These essays sell for about $800 each.

Except for No. 12TC5 4y olive, the proofs and trial color proofs of Nos. 8-13, 18, C1-C3 and E1 are from special plates of 9 subjects.

1950

8TC5	50s plate on soft white paper, imperf., without gum	
a.	**rose**	1,500.
b.	**green**	1,500.
8P5	50s **dark carmine rose,** plate on gummed soft white paper, imperf.	1,250.
9TC5	1y plate on soft white paper, imperf., without gum	
a.	**rose**	1,500.
b.	**green**	1,500.
9P5	1y **deep blue,** plate on gummed soft white paper, imperf.	1,250.
10TC5	2y plate on soft white paper, imperf., without gum	
a.	**rose**	1,500.
b.	**green**	1,500.
10P5	2y **rose violet,** plate on gummed soft white paper, imperf.	1,250.
11TC5	3y plate on soft white paper, imperf., without gum	
a.	**rose**	1,500.
b.	**green**	1,500.
11P5	3y **carmine rose,** plate on gummed soft white paper, imperf.	1,250.
12TC5	4y plate on soft white paper, imperf., without gum	
a.	**rose**	1,500.
b.	**olive**	1,500.
12P5	4y **greenish gray,** plate on gummed soft white paper, imperf.	1,250.
13TC5	5y plate on soft white paper, imperf., without gum	
a.	**rose**	1,500.
b.	**green**	1,500.
13P5	5y **blue green,** plate on gummed soft white paper, imperf.	1,250.

1951 From plates of 50

14P5	3y **red brown,** plate on soft white paper, imperf., without gum	750.

From plates of 80

15P5	3y **dark green,** plate on soft white paper, imperf., without gum	550.

1952 From plates of 18

18TC5	3y plate on whitish paper, imperf, with gum	
a.	**pale salmon**	1,500.
b.	**scarlet**	1,500.
c.	**red orange**	2,000.

Perforated, gummed proof sheets of Nos. 18, 27 and 28 with oversized, untrimmed selvage were printed for display purposes.

The sheets no longer exist. The imprint block of No. 18 exists, plus one single each (with mihon marking) of Nos. 27 and 28.

1958 From plates of 100

46TC5	2c **black,** plate on off white paper, imperf., without gum	700.
48TC5	4c **black,** plate on off white paper, imperf., without gum	700.

AIR POST

1950

C1TC5 8y plate on soft white paper, imperf., without gum
a. **rose** 1,500.
b. **light green** 1,500.
C1P5 8y **bright blue,** plate on gummed soft white paper, imperf. 1,250.
C2TC5 12y plate on soft white paper, imperf., without gum
a. **rose** 1,500.
b. **light green** 1,500.
C2P5 12y **green,** plate on gummed soft white paper, imperf. 1,250.
C3TC5 16y plate on soft white paper, imperf., without gum
a. **rose** 1,500.
C3P5 16y **rose carmine,** plate on gummed soft white paper, imperf. 1,250.

1951 **From plates of 100**

C4P5 13y **blue,** plate on soft white paper, imperf., without gum 850.
C5P5 18y **green,** plate on soft white paper, imperf., without gum 850.
C6P5 30y **cerise,** plate on soft white paper, imperf., without gum 700.

SPECIAL DELIVERY

1950

E1TC5 5y plate on soft white paper, imperf., without gum
a. **rose** 1,500.
b. **green** 1,500.
E1P5 5y **bright blue,** plate on gummed soft white paper, imperf. 1,250.

Official proof folders contain one each of Nos. 8P5-13P5, 12TC5b, C1P5-C3P5 and E1P5. The stamps are securely adhered to the folder. Value, $9,000.

Similar folders exist containing photographs of die proofs in black of the same issues and mockups of Nos. U2, UX3 and UY3.

KUME ISLAND

Plate on U.S. Official Watermarked White Bond Paper

1945 **Imperf., Without Gum**

Seal Handstamped in Vermilion

1X1P5 7s **black** *2,500.*
a. "7" and "SEN" one letter space to left, pos. 8 *3,500.*

SPECIMEN OVERPRINTS ON TRIAL COLOR PROOFS

1961 **Overprinted in Vermillion**

46TCS5 2c **black** *(100)* *750.*
48TCS5 4c **black** *(100)* *750.*

Cursive type used for these two trial color proofs is different from the mihon overprints.

TUBERCULOSIS PREVENTION SEALS

Issued by the Ryukyu Tuberculosis Prevention Association (1952-71) in panes of 100 (Nos. WX1 and WX5) and 20 (Nos. WX2-WX4 and WX6-WX20). The sale of seals provided income beyond government funding for treatment. Seals were sold by the pane for the price of 1 Yen (1952-58) or 1¢ (1959-71) per seal.

Nos. WX1 and WX1a are overprinted U.S. Christmas seals (Nos. WX159-WX160). Nos. WX2-WX20 were printed for the Ryukyu Tuberculosis Prevention Association by the Japan Printing Bureau. Nos. WX2-WX20 bear a year date and the word "GREETINGS." Nos. WX2-WX4 show "RYUKYUS" in kanji, and Nos. WX5-WX20 show "RYUKYUS" in both kanji and English.

Nos. WX1-WX20 were printed on unwatermarked paper. Values are for unused seals with original gum.

Designer — Tom Darling.

1952 **Overprinted in Black** ***Perf. 12½x12***

WX1 CS46 **green, red, yellow & black** *(600,000)* 4.00
Pane of 100 450.00
Imprint single 10.00
Imprint block of 4 25.00
a. Perf 12½ 4.00
Pane of 100 450.00
Imprint single 10.00
Imprint block of 4 25.00

Lithographed by Eureka Specialty Co. (No. WX1) and United States Printing and Lithographing Co. (No. WX1a).

Panes of the 1952 Christmas seals (U.S. Nos. WX159 and WX160) were donated by the National Tuberculosis Association and overprinted "Ryu-Kyu" in kanji by the Koshun Insatsusho in Naha. Printer's marks appear on seal 56 in each pane of 100: "E" for Eureka Specialty Printing Co.; "U" for United States Printing and Lithographing Co. Panes printed by the Strobridge Lithographing Co. ("S"), Edwards & Deutch Lithographing Co. ("D") and the Fleming-Potter Co., Inc. ("F") may also have been overprinted, but these have not been verified.

Imprint appears in selvage below seal 100; imprint of Union Local No. 41 on No. WX1, and imprint of Union Local No. 1 on No. WX1a.

TBS1

Designer — Adaniya Masayoshi.

1953 ***Perf. 13x13¼***

WX2 TBS1 **green, red, & buff** *(780,000)* 2.00
Pane of 20, perf through top and bottom selvage 30.00
Imprint single, type I 5.00
Imprint block of 6 15.00
Pane of 20, perf through top selvage only 30.00
Imprint single, type I 5.00
Imprint block of 6 15.00
a. Imperf *(20,000)* 100.00
Pane of 20 2,250.
Imprint single, type I 150.00
Imprint block of 6 750.00

Imprint appears in selvage below seal 19.

TBS2

Designer — Adaniya Masayoshi.

1954

WX3 TBS2 **light green, red, & black** *(780,000)* 2.00
Pane of 20, perf through top and bottom selvage 30.00
Imprint single, type I 5.00
Imprint block of 6 15.00
Pane of 20, perf through top selvage only 30.00
Imprint single, type I 5.00
Imprint block of 6 15.00
a. Imperf *(20,000)* —
Pane of 20 —
Imprint single, type I —
Imprint block of 6 —

Imprint appears in selvage below seal 19.

TBS3

Designer — Adaniya Masayoshi.

1955

WX4 TBS3 **carmine red, apple green & black** *(1,180,000)* 2.00
Pane of 20, perf through top and bottom selvage 20.00
Imprint single, type I 5.00
Imprint block of 6 10.00
Pane of 20, perf through top selvage only 20.00
Imprint single, type I 5.00
Imprint block of 6 10.00
a. Imperf *(20,000)* 3.00
Pane of 20 50.00
Imprint single, type I 5.00
Imprint block of 6 20.00

Imprint appears in selvage below seal 19.

TBS4

Designer — Adaniya Masayoshi.

1956

WX5 TBS4 **cobalt, carmine red, yellow & black** *(1,460,000)* 2.00
Pane of 100, perf through top and bottom selvage 150.00
Imprint single, type I 5.00
Imprint block of 10 40.00
Control No. strip of 3 15.00
a. Imperf *(40,000)* 5.00
Pane of 100 300.00
Imprint single, type I 20.00
Imprint block of 10 80.00
Control No. strip of 3 50.00

Imprint appears in selvage below seal 98. Five-digit control number appear in right selvage next to seals 20 and 30, or 20, 30 and 40.

Two types of Marginal Imprint on Nos. WX6-WX20

大蔵省印刷局製造	GOVERNMENT PRINTING BUREAU, TOKYO
Type I	Type II

TBS5

Designer — Yamazato Keiichi.

1957

WX6 TBS5 **orange yellow, black, red & light blue** *(1,750,000)* 1.00
Pane of 20, perf through top and bottom selvage 15.00
Imprint single, type I 2.00
Imprint block of 4, type I 4.00
Imprint single, type II 2.00
Imprint block of 4, type II 4.00
a. Imperf *(50,000)* 2.00
Pane of 20 20.00
Imprint single, type I 4.00
Imprint block of 4, type I 10.00
Imprint single, type II 4.00
Imprint block of 4, type II 10.00

Imprint type I appears in selvage below seal 20; imprint type II appears in selvage below seal 17. Legend printed in Japanese in right selvage.

TBS6

Designer — Adaniya Masayoshi.

1958 ***Perf. 13¼x13***

WX7 TBS6 **yellow, blue, carmine red & black** *(1,900,000)* .50
Pane of 20, perf through left and right selvage 8.00
Imprint single, type I 2.00
Imprint block of 4, type I 3.00
Imprint single, type II 2.00
Imprint block of 4, type II 3.00
a. Imperf *(80,000)* 2.00
Pane of 20 20.00
Imprint single, type I 4.00
Imprint block of 4, type I 10.00
Imprint single, type II 4.00
Imprint block of 4, type II 10.00
b. Perf 11 *(20,000)* 10.00
Pane of 20 200.00
Imprint single, type I 25.00

Imprint block of 4, type I 75.00
Imprint single, type II 25.00
Imprint block of 4, type II 75.00

Imprint type I appears in selvage below seal 20; imprint type II appears in selvage below seal 16. Legend printed in Japanese in top selvage. A total of 1,000 imperforate sheets were later perforated (No. WX7b), by order of the Ryukyu Tuberculosis Prevention Association.

TBS7

Designer — Tamanaha Seikichi.

1959 ***Perf. 13x13¼***

WX8 TBS7 **vermilion, mauve, ultramarine & indigo** *(2,100,000)* .50
Pane of 20, perf through top and bottom selvage 8.00
Imprint single, type I 2.00
Imprint block of 4, type I 3.00
Imprint single, type II 2.00
Imprint block of 4, type II 3.00
a. Imperf *(200,000)* 2.00
Pane of 20 20.00
Imprint single, type I 4.00
Imprint block of 4, type I 10.00
Imprint single, type II 4.00
Imprint block of 4, type II 10.00

Imprint type I appears in selvage below seal 20; imprint type II appears in selvage below seal 17. Legend printed in Japanese in right selvage.

TBS8

Designer — Oshiro Kohya.

1960 ***Perf. 13¼x13***

WX9 TBS8 **scarlet, orange, cobalt, bright blue & black** *(2,450,000)* .50
Pane of 20, perf through left and right selvage 8.00
Imprint single, type I 2.00
Imprint block of 4, type I 3.00
Imprint single, type II 2.00
Imprint block of 4, type II 3.00
a. Imperf *(50,000)* 2.00
Pane of 20 20.00
Imprint single, type I 4.00
Imprint block of 4, type I 10.00
Imprint single, type II 4.00
Imprint block of 4, type II 10.00

Imprint type I appears in selvage below seal 20; imprint type II appears in selvage below seal 16. Legend printed in Japanese in top selvage.

TBS9

Designer — Omine Seikan.

1961 ***Perf. 13x13¼***

WX10 TBS9 **multicolored** *(3,450,000)* .30
Pane of 20, perf through top and bottom selvage 6.00
Imprint single, type I .80
Imprint block of 4, type I 2.00
Imprint single, type II .80
Imprint block of 4, type II 2.00
a. Imperf *(50,000)* 1.00
Pane of 20 12.00
Imprint single, type I 3.00
Imprint block of 4, type I 6.00
Imprint single, type II 3.00
Imprint block of 4, type II 6.00

Imprint type I appears in selvage below seal 20; imprint type II appears in selvage below seal 17. Legend printed in Japanese in right selvage.

TBS10

Designer — Kabira Choshin.

1962 ***Perf. 13¼***

WX11 TBS10 **multicolored** *(3,450,000)* .30
Pane of 20, perf through top and bottom selvage 5.00
Imprint single, type I .60
Imprint block of 6, type I 1.50
Imprint single, type II .60
Imprint block of 6, type II 1.50
a. Imperf *(50,000)* .50
Pane of 20 7.00
Imprint single, type I 1.00
Imprint block of 6, type I 2.50
Imprint single, type II 1.00
Imprint block of 6, type II 2.50

Imprint type I appears in selvage below seal 19; imprint type II appears in selvage below seal 17. Legend printed in English in left selvage and in Japanese in right selvage.

TBS11

Designer — Kabira Choshin.

1963 ***Perf. 13x13¼***

WX12 TBS11 **multicolored** *(3,450,000)* .30
Pane of 20, perf through top and bottom selvage 5.00
Imprint single, type I .60
Imprint block of 4, type I 1.50
Imprint single, type II .60
Imprint block of 4, type II 1.50
a. Imperf *(50,000)* .50
Pane of 20 7.00
Imprint single, type I 1.00
Imprint block of 4, type I 2.50
Imprint single, type II 1.00
Imprint block of 4, type II 2.50

Imprint type I appears in selvage below seal 20; imprint type II appears in selvage below seal 17. Legend printed in Japanese in right selvage.

TBS12

Designer — Kabira Choshin.

1964

WX13 TBS12 **multicolored** *(3,650,000)* .30
Pane of 20, perf through top and bottom selvage 5.00
Imprint single, type I .60
Imprint block of 4, type I 1.50
Imprint single, type II .60
Imprint block of 4, type II 1.50
a. Imperf *(50,000)* .50
Pane of 20 7.00
Imprint single, type I 1.00
Imprint block of 4, type I 2.50
Imprint single, type II 1.00
Imprint block of 4, type II 2.50

Imprint type I appears in selvage below seal 20; imprint type II appears in selvage below seal 17. Legend printed in English in left selvage and in Japanese in right selvage.

TBS13

Designer — Oyama Masaru.

1965 ***Perf. 13¼x13***

WX14 TBS13 **dark blue, light green, carmine & pink** *(3,700,000)* .30
Pane of 20, perf through left and right selvage 5.00
Imprint single, type I .60
Imprint block of 4, type I 1.50
Imprint single, type II .60
Imprint block of 4, type II 1.50
a. Imperf *(100,000)* .50
Pane of 20 7.00
Imprint single, type I 1.00
Imprint block of 4, type I 2.50
Imprint single, type II 1.00
Imprint block of 4, type II 2.50

Imprint type I appears in selvage below seal 20; imprint type II appears in selvage below seal 16. Legend printed in English in top selvage and in Japanese in top and bottom selvage.

TBS14

Designer — Kabira Choshin.

1966 ***Perf. 13x13¼***

WX15 TBS14 **dark green, yellow & carmine** *(3,700,000)* .30
Pane of 20, perf through top and bottom selvage 5.00
Imprint single, type I .60
Imprint block of 4, type I 1.50
Imprint single, type II .60
Imprint block of 4, type II 1.50
a. Imperf *(100,000)* .50
Pane of 20 7.00
Imprint single, type I 1.00
Imprint block of 4, type I 2.50
Imprint single, type II 1.00
Imprint block of 4, type II 2.50

Imprint type I appears in selvage below seal 20; imprint type II appears in selvage below seal 17. Legend printed in English in left selvage and in Japanese in right selvage.

TBS15

Designer — Kabira Choshin.

1967

WX16 TBS15 **blue, carmine, yellow & black** *(4,100,000)* .30
Pane of 20, perf through top and bottom selvage 5.00
Imprint single, type I .60
Imprint block of 4, type I 1.50
Imprint single, type II .60
Imprint block of 4, type II 1.50
a. Imperf *(100,000)* .50
Pane of 20 7.00
Imprint single, type I 1.00
Imprint block of 4, type I 2.50
Imprint single, type II 1.00
Imprint block of 4, type II 2.50

Imprint type I appears in selvage below seal 20; imprint type II appears in selvage below seal 17. Legend printed in English in left selvage and in Japanese in right selvage.

TBS16

Designer — Kabira Choshin.

1968

WX17 TBS16 **blue, carmine & black** *(4,400,000)* .30
Pane of 20, perf through top and bottom selvage 5.00
Imprint single, type I .60

	Imprint block of 4, type I	1.50
	Imprint single, type II	.60
	Imprint block of 4, type II	1.50
a.	Imperf *(100,000)*	.50
	Pane of 20	7.00
	Imprint single, type I	1.00
	Imprint block of 4, type I	2.50
	Imprint single, type II	1.00
	Imprint block of 4, type II	2.50

Imprint type I appears in selvage below seal 20; imprint type II appears in selvage below seal 17. Legend printed in English in left selvage and in Japanese in right selvage.

TBS17

Designer — Oshiro Kohya.

1969

WX18	TBS17 **multicolored** *(4,600,000)*	.30
	Pane of 20, perf through top and bottom selvage	5.00
	Imprint single, type I	.60
	Imprint block of 4, type I	1.50
	Imprint single, type II	.60
	Imprint block of 4, type II	1.50
a.	Imperf *(100,000)*	.50
	Pane of 20	7.00
	Imprint single, type I	1.00
	Imprint block of 4, type I	2.50
	Imprint single, type II	1.00
	Imprint block of 4, type II	2.50

Imprint type I appears in selvage below seal 20; imprint type II appears in selvage below seal 17. Legend printed in English in left selvage and in Japanese in right selvage.

TBS18

Designer — Kabira Choshin.

1970

WX19	TBS18 **multicolored** *(4,650,000)*	.30
	Pane of 20, perf through top and bottom selvage	5.00
	Imprint single, type I	.60
	Imprint block of 4, type I	1.50
	Imprint single, type II	.60
	Imprint block of 4, type II	1.50
a.	Imperf *(50,000)*	.50
	Pane of 20	7.00
	Imprint single, type I	1.00
	Imprint block of 4, type I	2.50
	Imprint single, type II	1.00
	Imprint block of 4, type II	2.50

Imprint type I appears in selvage below seal 20; imprint type II appears in selvage below seal 17. Legend printed in English in left selvage and in Japanese in right selvage.

TBS19

Designer — Ashimine Kinsei.

1971

WX20	TBS19 **multicolored** *(4,650,000)*	.30
	Pane of 20, perf through top and bottom selvage	5.00
	Imprint single, type I	.60
	Imprint block of 4, type I	1.50
	Imprint single, type II	.60
	Imprint block of 4, type II	1.50
a.	Imperf *(50,000)*	.50
	Pane of 20	7.00
	Imprint single, type I	1.00
	Imprint block of 4, type I	2.50
	Imprint single, type II	1.00
	Imprint block of 4, type II	2.50

Imprint type I appears in selvage below seal 20; imprint type II appears in selvage below seal 17. Legend printed in English in left selvage and in Japanese in right selvage.

UNITED NATIONS

United Nations stamps are used on UN official mail sent from UN Headquarters in New York City, the UN European Office in Geneva, Switzerland, or from the Donaupark Vienna International Center or Atomic Energy Agency in Vienna, Austria to points throughout the world. They may be used on private correspondence sent through the UN post offices and are valid only at the individual UN post offices.

The UN stamps issued for use in Geneva and Vienna are listed in separate sections. Geneva issues were denominated in centimes and francs and Vienna issues in schillings (now cents and euros) and are valid only in Geneva or Vienna. The UN stamps issued for use in New York, denominated in cents and dollars, are valid only in New York.

Letters bearing Nos. 170-174 provide an exception as they were carried by the Canadian postal system.

See Switzerland Nos. 7O1-7O39 in Volume 6 of the Scott *Standard Postage Stamp Catalogue* for stamps issued by the Swiss Government for official use of the UN European Office and other UN affiliated organizations. See France official stamp listings for stamps issued by the French Government for official use of UNESCO.

+: When following the quantity, this indicates the total printed to date. Unless otherwise noted, these are the initial printing order. Final quantities frequently are not given for definitives and air post stamps. The total printed is shown here.

Blocks of four generally sell for four times the single stamp value.

Values for first day covers are for cacheted and unaddressed covers. Addressed covers sell for much less, and addressed and uncacheted first day covers sell for very little.

For imperforate stamps, see the Proofs section following U.N. Souvenir Cards.

Catalogue values for all unused stamps in this section are for Never Hinged items. Values for used UN stamps are for postally used stamps with contemporaneous cancels. Used stamps soaked off of first day covers sell for less.

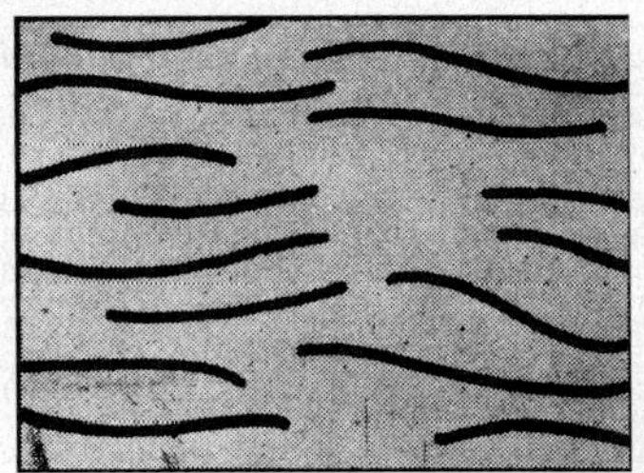

Wmk. 309 — Wavy Lines

Peoples of the World — A1

UN Headquarters Building — A2

"Peace, Justice, Security" — A3

UN Flag — A4

UN International Children's Emergency Fund — A5

World Unity — A6

Printed by Thomas De La Rue & Co., Ltd., London (1c, 3c, 10c, 15c, 20c, 25c), and Joh. Enschedé and Sons, Haarlem, Netherlands (1½c, 2c, 5c, 50c, $1). The 3c, 15c and 25c have frame engraved, center photogravure; other denominations are engraved. Panes of 50. Designed by O. C. Meronti (A1), Leon

Helguera (A2), J. F. Doeve (A3), Ole Hamann (A4), S. L. Hartz (5c) and Hubert Woyty-Wimmer (20c).

Perf. 13x12½, 12½x13

1951 Engr. and Photo. Unwmk.

1	A1 1c **magenta**, *Oct. 24 (8,000,000)*	.25	.25
	First day cover		1.00
	Margin block of 4, UN seal	.25	—
2	A2 1½c **blue green**, *Oct. 24 (7,450,000)*	.25	.25
	First day cover		1.00
	Margin block of 4, UN seal	.25	—
	Precanceled *(361,700)*		*55.00*
3	A3 2c **purple**, *Nov. 16 (8,470,000)*	.25	.25
	First day cover		1.00
	Margin block of 4, UN seal	.25	—
4	A4 3c **magenta & blue**, *Oct. 24 (8,250,000)*	.25	.25
	First day cover		1.00
	Margin block of 4, UN seal	.25	—
5	A5 5c **blue**, *Oct. 24 (6,000,000)*	.25	.25
	First day cover		1.75
	Margin block of 4, UN seal	.40	—
6	A1 10c **chocolate**, *Nov. 16 (2,600,000)*	.25	.25
	First day cover		2.00
	Margin block of 4, UN seal	1.30	—
7	A4 15c **violet & blue**, *Nov. 16 (2,300,000)*	.25	.25
	First day cover		2.00
	Margin block of 4, UN seal	1.30	—
8	A6 20c **dark brown**, *Nov. 16 (2,100,000)*	.30	.25
	First day cover		2.00
	Margin block of 4, UN seal	2.00	—
9	A4 25c **olive gray & blue**, *Oct. 24 (2,100,000)*	.35	.25
	First day cover		2.00
	Margin block of 4, UN seal	2.00	—
10	A2 50c **indigo**, *Nov. 16 (1,785,000)*	3.00	1.50
	First day cover		8.00
	Margin block of 4, UN seal	14.00	—
11	A3 $1 **red**, *Oct. 24 (2,252,500)*	1.25	.90
	First day cover		8.00
	Margin block of 4, UN seal	8.00	—
	Nos. 1-11 (11)	6.65	4.65

First day covers of Nos. 1-11 and C1-C4 total 1,113,216.

The various printings of Nos. 1-11 vary in sheet marginal perforation. Some were perforated through left or right margins, or both; some through all margins.

Sheets of this issue carry a marginal inscription consisting of the UN seal and "First UN/Issue 1951." This inscription appears four times on each sheet. The listing "Margin block of 4, UN seal" or "Inscription block of 4" in this and following issues refers to a corner block.

Sheets of the 1½c, 2c, 50c and $1 have a cut-out of different shape in one margin. The printer trimmed this off entirely on most of the 1½c third printing, and partially on the 1½c fourth printing and $1 fifth and sixth printings.

See UN Offices in Geneva Nos. 4, 14.

Forgeries of the 1½c precancel abound. Examination by a competent authority is necessary.

Veterans' War Memorial Building, San Francisco A7

Issued to mark the 7th anniversary of the signing of the United Nations Charter.

Engraved and printed by the American Bank Note Co., New York. Panes of 50. Designed by Jean Van Noten.

1952, Oct. 24 *Perf. 12*

12	A7 5c **blue** *(1,274,670)*	.50	.35
	First day cover *(160,117)*		1.00
	Inscription block of 4	2.50	—

Globe and Encircled Flame — A8

4th anniversary of the adoption of the Universal Declaration of Human Rights.

Engraved and printed by Thomas De La Rue & Co., Ltd., London. Panes of 50. Designed by Hubert Woyty-Wimmer.

1952, Dec. 10 *Perf. 13½x14*

13	A8 3c **deep green** *(1,554,312)*	.45	.35
	First day cover		2.00
	Inscription block of 4	3.00	—
14	A8 5c **blue** *(1,126,371)*	.55	.40
	First day cover		2.50
	First day cover, #13-14		10.00
	Inscription block of 4	4.00	—

First day covers of Nos. 13 and 14 total 299,309.

Refugee Family — A9

Issued to publicize "Protection for Refugees."

Engraved and printed by Thomas De La Rue & Co., Ltd., London. Panes of 50. Designed by Olav Mathiesen.

1953, Apr. 24 *Perf. 12½x13*

15	A9 3c **dark red brown & rose brown** *(1,299,793)*	.25	.25
	First day cover		2.50
	Inscription block of 4	1.50	—
16	A9 5c **indigo & blue** *(969,224)*	.45	.40
	First day cover		3.75
	First day cover, #15-16		10.00
	Inscription block of 4	3.75	—

First day covers of Nos. 15 and 16 total 234,082.

Envelope, UN Emblem and Map — A10

Issued to honor the Universal Postal Union.

Engraved and printed by Thomas De La Rue & Co., Ltd., London. Panes of 50. Designed by Hubert Woyty-Wimmer.

1953, June 12 *Perf. 13*

17	A10 3c **black brown** *(1,259,689)*	.40	.40
	First day cover		5.00
	Inscription block of 4	2.50	—
18	A10 5c **dark blue** *(907,312)*	1.25	1.00
	First day cover		5.00
	First day cover, #17-18		12.50
	Inscription block of 4	7.50	—

First day covers of Nos. 17 and 18 total 231,627.

Plate number ("1A" or "1B") in color of stamp appears below 47th stamp of sheet.

Gearwheels and UN Emblem — A11

Issued to publicize United Nations activities in the field of technical assistance.

Engraved and printed by Thomas De La Rue & Co. Ltd. London. Panes of 50. Designed by Olav Mathiesen.

1953, Oct. 24 *Perf. 13x12½*

19	A11 3c **dark gray** *(1,184,348)*	.25	.25
	First day cover		2.00
	Inscription block of 4	2.00	—
20	A11 5c **dark green** *(968,182)*	.40	.45
	First day cover		5.00
	First day cover, #19-20		9.00
	Inscription block of 4	5.00	—

First day covers of Nos. 19 and 20 total 229,211.

Hands Reaching Toward Flame — A12

UN PERSONALIZED & EVENT SHEETS

HGPI has one of the largest stocks in the U.S. of these interesting sheets.

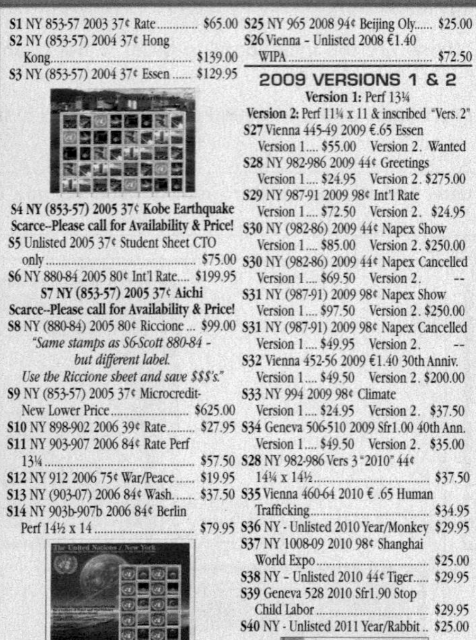

S1 NY 853-57 2003 37¢ Rate $65.00
S2 NY (853-57) 2004 37¢ Hong Kong $139.00
S3 NY (853-57) 2004 37¢ Essen $129.95
S4 NY (853-57) 2005 37¢ Kobe Earthquake Scarce--Please call for Availability & Price!
S5 Unlisted 2005 37¢ Student Sheet CTO only $75.00
S6 NY 880-84 2005 80¢ Int'l Rate $199.95
S7 NY (853-57) 2005 37¢ Aichi Scarce--Please call for Availability & Price!
S8 NY (880-84) 2005 80¢ Riccione ... $99.00
"Same stamps as S6-Scott 880-84 - but different label. Use the Riccione sheet and save $$$'s."
S9 NY (853-57) 2005 37¢ Microcredit-New Lower Price $625.00
S10 NY 898-902 2006 39¢ Rate $27.95
S11 NY 903-907 2006 84¢ Rate Perf 13¼ $57.50
S12 NY 912 2006 75¢ War/Peace $19.95
S13 NY (903-07) 2006 84¢ Wash. $37.50
S14 NY 903b-907b 2006 84¢ Berlin Perf 14½ x 14 .... $79.95
S15 NY 929 2006 84¢ Japan's 50th Ann in the UN $89.00
S16 Vienna {393-97} 2007 € .55 Essen $65.00
S17 NY 934-38 2007 41¢ Rate $24.95
S18 NY 939 2007 90¢ Int'l Rate $29.00
S19 NY 931 2007 84¢ Peaceful Vision $24.95
S20 NY (939) 2007 90¢ Climate Change $42.50
S21 Vienna {404-08} 2007 €.65 World Space Week $59.95
S22 Vienna {422-26} 2008 € .65 Essen $59.95
S23 NY 954-58 2008 42¢ Domestic rate $25.00
S24 NY 959 2008 94¢ Foreign Rate .. $24.95
S25 NY 965 2008 94¢ Beijing Oly $25.00
S26 Vienna - Unlisted 2008 €1.40 WIPA $72.50

2009 VERSIONS 1 & 2
Version 1: Perf 13¼
Version 2: Perf 11¼ x 11 & inscribed "Vers. 2"

S27 Vienna 445-49 2009 €.65 Essen Version 1.... $55.00 Version 2. Wanted
S28 NY 982-986 2009 44¢ Greetings Version 1.... $24.95 Version 2. $275.00
S29 NY 987-91 2009 98¢ Int'l Rate Version 1.... $72.50 Version 2. $24.95
S30 NY (982-86) 2009 44¢ Napex Show Version 1.... $85.00 Version 2. $250.00
S30 NY (982-86) 2009 44¢ Napex Cancelled Version 1.... $69.50 Version 2. --
S31 NY (987-91) 2009 98¢ Napex Show Version 1.... $97.50 Version 2. $250.00
S31 NY (987-91) 2009 98¢ Napex Cancelled Version 1.... $49.95 Version 2. --
S32 Vienna 452-56 2009 €1.40 30th Anniv. Version 1.... $49.50 Version 2. $200.00
S33 NY 994 2009 98¢ Climate Version 1.... $24.95 Version 2. $37.50
S34 Geneva 506-510 2009 Sfr1.00 40th Ann. Version 1.... $49.50 Version 2. $35.00
S28 NY 982-986 Vers 3 "2010" 44¢ 14¼ x 14½ $37.50
S35 Vienna 460-64 2010 € .65 Human Trafficking $34.95
S36 NY - Unlisted 2010 Year/Monkey $29.95
S37 NY 1008-09 2010 98¢ Shanghai World Expo $25.00
S38 NY - Unlisted 2010 44¢ Tiger $29.95
S39 Geneva 528 2010 Sfr1.90 Stop Child Labor $29.95
S40 NY - Unlisted 2011 Year/Rabbit .. $25.00
Working Dogs of the United Nations
S41 NY 1023 2011 98¢ Working Dogs 10 different labels $25.00
S42 Vienna 486-90 2011 € .62 Domestic Rate $32.50
S43 Vienna 491-95 2011 € .70 Vienna Int'l rate $32.50
S44 NY 1037 2012 $1.05 NY Year of the Dragon $25.00
S45 NY 1038 2012 $1.05 Guided Tours $25.00
S46 Vienna 510 2012 € .70 Essen $25.00
S47 NY (1037) 2012 Law of the Sea.. $29.00
S48 NY 1046-47 2012 $1.05 Rio 20/ Tinkerbell $24.95
S49 NY (1037) 2012 $1.05 Manila Declaration $32.50
CHINESE LUNAR CALENDAR
S50 NY 1054 2013 $1.10 Year of the Snake $25.00
S51 NY 1056 2013 $1.10 NY $1.10 Greetings $24.95
S52 NY (1054) 2013 $1.10 40th Ann. of CITES $24.95
S53 NY 1071 2013 $1.10 World Humanitarian Day $25.00
S54 Vienna 538 2013 € .70 Sindelfingen $25.00
S55 (V-538) 2013 € .70 Panama UNCAC $19.95
S56 NY 1079 2014 $1.15 Year of the Horse $25.00
S57 NY 1080 2014 $1.15 Greetings to United Nations NY $25.00
S58 Vienna 543 2014 € .70 35th Anniv $18.95
S59 Geneva 587 2014 Sfr1.30 Greetings from Geneva $25.95
S60 Vienna (510) 2014 € .70 FAO/IAEA 50th Anniv $19.95
S61 NY 1101 2014 $1.15 ASDA $24.95
2015 NY 1102 $1.20 Year of the Ram $25.00
Vienna 557 E8.00 Greetings $22.95
NY 1112 $1.20 Greetings $25.00
Vienna DOHA Crime Prevention ... $19.95
NY 1118 Pope Francis Visit $25.00

COMPLETE UN PRICE LIST AVAILABLE

Strips of 5 & Singles with labels available on our UN Price List.

Gen 606 Sfr1.40 Greetings $26.75
NY 1124 70th Ann. UNESCO $25.00
Vienna 577 70th Anniv UN $25.00
NY (1118) Disability & Devel $25.00
Vienna (577) UNCAC Conference . $19.95
2016 NY 1126 Year of the Monkey ... $25.00
NY 1131 Angry Birds/Green Planet $25.00
Vienna 585 UNIDO Anniv $19.95
NY 1136 65th UNPA $25.00
Vienna 595 Nuclear Test Ban Treaty $19.95
NY 1146 World Post Day $25.00
NY (1126) M.S. Subbulakshmi $25.00
2017 NY 1149 Year of Rooster $25.00
NY 1158 Int'l Happiness Day $25.00
Vien 598 Int'l Happiness Day $25.00
NY 1168 Int'l Day of Yoga $25.00
Vien 610 Traunsee $22.95
2018 NY 1187 Year of the Dog $25.00
Gen 652 Naba - Lugano $30.00
Vien. 662 Rustavelli $22.50
Vien 622 var. UN Headquarters $22.50
NY 1202 Thomas/Global Goals $25.00
NY 1206-07 Diwali $25.00

PERSONALIZED SHEET ERRORS
Visit our Web Store for our latest Selection of Rare Errors including imperfs, Unlisted stamps, missing colors etc.
S6 884b Error VF/NH Sheet Postion 8 + 9 37¢ instead of 80¢–Rare $3,250.00

SATISFACTION GUARANTEED!!!
**Shipping for Personalized Sheets:
Domestic: Please add $6.00 for 1 sheet and $9.50 for sheet orders totaling $150.00 or more. **Foreign shipping including Canada:** Please add $9.50 to Domestic Rates. When ordering ONLY strips or singles, please use our normal terms of sale.

HENRY GITNER PHILATELISTS, INC.
Philately - the quiet excitement!
53 Highland Ave., P.O. Box 3077 • Middletown, NY 10940
1-800-947-8267 (94-STAMP) • 845-343-5151 • Fax 845-343-0068
E-mail: hgitner@hgitner.com • Web: www.hgitner.com

Issued to publicize Human Rights Day.
Engraved and printed by Thomas De La Rue & Co., Ltd., London. Panes of 50. Designed by León Helguera.

1953, Dec. 10 ***Perf. 12½x13***

21 A12 3c **bright blue** *(1,456,928)* .30 .30
First day cover 2.00
Inscription block of 4 1.50 —
22 A12 5c **rose red** *(983,831)* 1.00 1.00
First day cover 4.00
First day cover, #21-22 12.50
Inscription block of 4 5.75 —

First day covers of Nos. 21 and 22 total 265,186.

Ear of Wheat — A13

Issued to honor the Food and Agriculture Organization and printed by Thomas De La Rue & Co., Ltd., London. Panes of 50. Designed by Dirk Van Gelder.

1954, Feb. 11 ***Perf. 12½x13***

23 A13 3c **dark green & yellow** *(1,250,000)* .30 .25
First day cover 2.00
Inscription block of 4 2.25 —
24 A13 8c **indigo & yellow** *(949,718)* .75 .50
First day cover 4.00
First day cover, #23-24 6.00
Inscription block of 4 5.00 —

First day covers of Nos. 23 and 24 total 272,312.

UN Emblem and Anvil Inscribed "ILO" — A14

Design: 8c, inscribed "OIT."
Issued to honor the International Labor Organization.
Engraved and printed by Thomas De La Rue & Co., Ltd., London. Panes of 50. Designed by José Renau.

1954, May 10 ***Perf. 12½x13***

25 A14 3c **brown** *(1,085,651)* .25 .25
First day cover 2.00
Inscription block of 4 1.50 —
26 A14 8c **magenta** *(903,561)* 1.00 .85
First day cover 4.00
First day cover, #25-26 7.50
Inscription block of 4 5.50 —

First day covers of Nos. 25 and 26 total 252,796.

UN European Office, Geneva A15

Issued on the occasion of United Nations Day.
Engraved and printed by Thomas De La Rue & Co., Ltd., London. Panes of 50. Designed by Earl W. Purdy.

1954, Oct. 25 ***Perf. 14***

27 A15 3c **dark blue violet** *(1,000,000)* 1.25 1.00
First day cover 2.00
Inscription block of 4 6.50 —
28 A15 8c **red** *(1,000,000)* .35 .30
First day cover 3.00
First day cover, #27-28 9.00
Inscription block of 4 1.75 —

First day covers of Nos. 27 and 28 total 233,544.

Mother and Child — A16

Issued to publicize Human Rights Day.
Engraved and printed by Thomas De La Rue & Co., Ltd. London. Panes of 50. Designed by Leonard C. Mitchell.

1954, Dec. 10 ***Perf. 14***

29 A16 3c **red orange** *(1,000,000)* 6.00 2.50
First day cover 3.00
Inscription block of 4 35.00 —
30 A16 8c **olive green** *(1,000,000)* 1.00 .35
First day cover 3.75
First day cover, #29-30 12.50
Inscription block of 4 5.00 —

First day covers of Nos. 29 and 30 total 276,333.

Symbol of Flight — A17

Design: 8c, inscribed "OACI."
Issued to honor the International Civil Aviation Organization.
Engraved and printed by Waterlow & Sons, Ltd., London. Panes of 50. Designed by Angel Medina Medina.

1955, Feb. 9 ***Perf. 13½x14***

31 A17 3c **blue** *(1,000,000)* 1.00 .75
First day cover 2.00
Inscription block of 4 6.50 —
32 A17 8c **rose carmine** *(1,000,000)* .60 .50
First day cover 3.00
First day cover, #31-32 9.00
Inscription block of 4 3.25 —

First day covers of Nos. 31 and 32 total 237,131.

UNESCO Emblem A18

Issued to honor the UN Educational, Scientific and Cultural Organization.
Engraved and printed by Waterlow & Sons, Ltd., London. Panes of 50. Designed by George Hamori.

1955, May 11 ***Perf. 13½x14***

33 A18 3c **lilac rose** *(1,000,000)* .35 .30
First day cover 2.00
Inscription block of 4 3.25 —
34 A18 8c **light blue** *(1,000,000)* .30 .30
First day cover 3.00
First day cover, #33-34 7.50
Inscription block of 4 3.00 —

First day covers of Nos. 33 and 34 total 255,326.

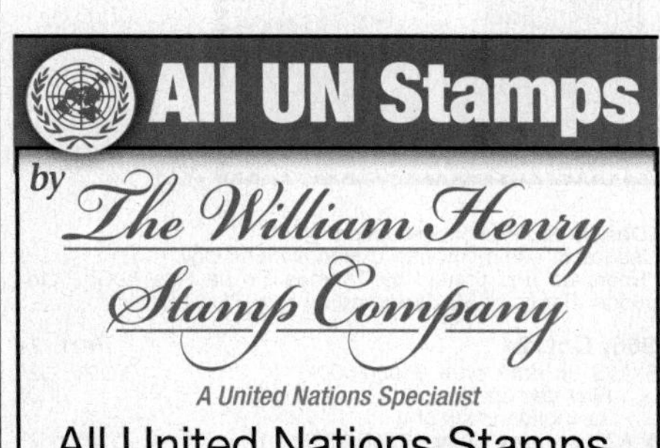

United Nations Charter — A19

Design: 4c, Spanish inscription. 8c, French inscription.
10th anniversary of the United Nations.

Engraved and printed by Waterlow & Sons, Ltd., London. Panes of 50. Designed by Claude Bottiau.

1955, Oct. 24 ***Perf. 13½x14***

35 A19 3c **deep plum** *(1,000,000)* .90 .55
First day cover 3.00
Inscription block of 4 4.25 —
36 A19 4c **dull green** *(1,000,000)* .50 .35
First day cover 3.00
Inscription block of 4 2.75 —
37 A19 8c **bluish black** *(1,000,000)* .35 .25
First day cover 4.00
First day cover, #35-37 11.00
Inscription block of 4 2.50 —
Nos. 35-37 (3) 1.75 1.15

Souvenir Sheet

1955, Oct. 24 **Wmk. 309** ***Imperf.***

38 A19 Sheet of 3 *(250,000)* 50.00 22.50
Hinged 35.00
a. 3c **deep plum** 7.00 3.00
b. 4c **dull green** 7.00 3.00
c. 8c **bluish black** 7.00 3.00
First day cover 18.00
d. As No. 38, corrected plates (see footnote) 55.00 27.50

No. 38 measures 108x83mm and has marginal inscriptions in deep plum.
Two printings were made of the sheet: No. 38 (200,000) and No. 38d (50,000). No. 38 may be distinguished by the broken lines in the background shading on the 8c. It leaves a small white spot below the left leg of the "n" of "Unies." On No. 38d, the broken line was retouched, eliminating the white spot. The 4c was also retouched.
Nos. 38 and 38d used are valued with first day of issue cancels. Postally used examples are worth substantially more.
First day covers of Nos. 35-38 total 455,791.
Examples of No. 38 are known with the 4c and 8c stamps misaligned.

Hand Holding Torch — A20

Issued in honor of Human Rights Day.
Engraved and printed by Waterlow & Sons, Ltd., London. Panes of 50. Designed by Hubert Woyty-Wimmer.

1955, Dec. 9 **Unwmk.** ***Perf. 14x13½***

39 A20 3c **ultramarine** *(1,250,000)* .30 .30
First day cover 1.25
Inscription block of 4 1.80 —
40 A20 8c **green** *(1,000,000)* .40 .30
First day cover 1.25
First day cover, #39-40 2.50
Inscription block of 4 3.00 —

First day covers of Nos. 39 and 40 total 298,038.

All UN Stamps
by The William Henry Stamp Company
A United Nations Specialist
All United Nations Stamps.
All for sale. All the time.
www.AllUNStamps.com
• Mint • Used • Personalized Sheets
• MI4's • FDC's • Sheets • Varieties
• Souvenir Cards • Postal Stationery
• Folders • Year Sets • Collections
SEND FOR FREE U.N. PRICE LIST
P.O. Box 150010 • Kew Gardens, NY 11415-0010
Telephone/Fax: (347) 829-3400
E-Mail: wmhenry@msn.com

Symbols of Telecommunication — A21

Design: 8c, inscribed "UIT."
Issued in honor of the International Telecommunication Union.
Engraved and printed by Thomas De La Rue & Co., Ltd., London. Panes of 50. Designed by Hubert Woyty-Wimmer.

1956, Feb. 17 *Perf. 14*

41 A21 3c **turquoise blue** *(1,000,000)* .25 .25
First day cover 1.25
Inscription block of 4 2.00 —
42 A21 8c **deep carmine** *(1,000,000)* .30 .30
First day cover 1.75
First day cover, #41-42 3.50
Inscription block of 4 3.50 —

Plate number ("1A" or "1B") in color of stamp appears below 47th stamp of sheet.

Globe and Caduceus — A22

Design: 8c, inscribed "OMS."
Issued in honor of the World Health Organization.
Engraved and printed by Thomas De La Rue & Co., Ltd., London. Panes of 50. Designed by Olav Mathiesen.

1956, Apr. 6 *Perf. 14*

43 A22 3c **bright greenish blue** *(1,250,000)* .25 .25
First day cover 1.00
Inscription block of 4 2.00 —
44 A22 8c **golden brown** *(1,000,000)* .25 .25
First day cover 1.50
First day cover, #43-44 10.00
Inscription block of 4 3.00 —

First day covers of Nos. 43 and 44 total 260,853.

General Assembly A23

Design: 8c, French inscription.
Issued to commemorate United Nations Day.
Engraved and printed by Thomas De La Rue & Co., Ltd., London. Panes of 50. Designed by Kurt Plowitz.

1956, Oct. 24 *Perf. 14*

45 A23 3c **dark blue** *(2,000,000)* .25 .25
First day cover 1.00
Inscription block of 4 .75 —
46 A23 8c **gray olive** *(1,500,000)* .25 .25
First day cover 1.00
First day cover, #45-46 5.50
Inscription block of 4 1.30 —

First day covers of Nos. 45 and 46 total 303,560.

Flame and Globe — A24

Issued to publicize Human Rights Day
Engraved and printed by Thomas De La Rue & Co., Ltd., London. Panes of 50. Designed by Rashid-ud Din.

1956, Dec. 10 *Perf. 14*

47 A24 3c **plum** *(5,000,000)* .25 .25
First day cover 1.00
Inscription block of 4 .60 —
48 A24 8c **dark blue** *(4,000,000)* .25 .25
First day cover 1.00
First day cover, #47-48 2.50
Inscription block of 4 1.00 —

First day covers of Nos. 47 and 48 total 416,120.

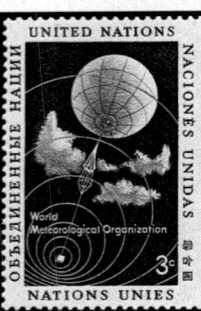

Weather Balloon — A25

Design: 8c, Agency name in French.
Issued to honor the World Meterological Organization.
Engraved and printed by Thomas De La Rue & Co., Ltd., London. Panes of 50. Designed by A. L. Pollock.

1957, Jan. 28 *Perf. 14*

49 A25 3c **violet blue** *(5,000,000)* .25 .25
First day cover 1.00
Inscription block of 4 .50 —
50 A25 8c **dark carmine rose** *(3,448,985)* .25 .25
First day cover 1.00
First day cover, #49-50 1.75
Inscription block of 4 .65 —

First day covers of Nos. 49 and 50 total 376,110.

Badge of UN Emergency Force — A26

Issued in honor of the UN Emergency Force.
Engraved and printed by Thomas De La Rue & Co., Ltd., London. Panes of 50. Designed by Ole Hamann.

1957, Apr. 8 *Perf. 14x12½*

51 A26 3c **light blue** *(4,000,000)* .25 .25
First day cover 1.00
Inscription block of 4 .50 —
52 A26 8c **rose carmine** *(3,000,000)* .25 .25
First day cover 1.00
First day cover, #51-52 1.50
Inscription block of 4 .70 —

First day covers of Nos. 51 and 52 total 461,772.

Nos. 51-52 Re-engraved

1957, Apr.-May *Perf. 14x12½*

53 A26 3c **blue** *(2,736,206)* .25 .25
Inscription block of 4 .75 —
54 A26 8c **rose carmine** *(1,000,000)* .35 .25
Inscription block of 4 2.00 —

On Nos. 53-54 the background within and around the circles is shaded lightly, giving a halo effect. The lettering is more distinct with a line around each letter.

UN Emblem and Globe — A27

Design: 8c, French inscription.
Issued to honor the Security Council.
Engraved and printed by Thomas De La Rue & Co., Ltd., London. Panes of 50. Designed by Rashid-ud Din.

1957, Oct. 24 *Perf. 12½x13*

55 A27 3c **orange brown** *(3,674,968)* .25 .25
First day cover 1.00
Inscription block of 4 .40 —
56 A27 8c **dark blue green** *(2,885,938)* .25 .25
First day cover 1.00
First day cover, #55-56 1.75
Inscription block of 4 .70 —

First day covers of Nos. 55 and 56 total 460,627.

Flaming Torch — A28

Issued in honor of Human Rights Day.
Engraved and printed by Thomas De La Rue & Co., Ltd., London. Panes of 50. Designed by Olav Mathiesen.

1957, Dec. 10 *Perf. 14*

57 A28 3c **red brown** *(3,368,405)* .25 .25
First day cover 1.00
Inscription block of 4 .40 —
58 A28 8c **black** *(2,717,310)* .25 .25
First day cover 1.00
First day cover, #57-58 1.25
Inscription block of 4 .65 —

First day covers of Nos. 57 and 58 total 553,669.

UN Emblem Shedding Light on Atom — A29

Design: 8c, French inscription.
Issued in honor of the International Atomic Energy Agency.
Engraved and printed by the American Bank Note Co., New York. Panes of 50. Designed by Robert Perrot.

1958, Feb. 10 *Perf. 12*

59 A29 3c **olive** *(3,663,305)* .25 .25
First day cover 1.00
Inscription block of 4 .40 —
60 A29 8c **blue** *(3,043,622)* .25 .25
First day cover 1.00
First day cover, #59-60 1.00
Inscription block of 4 .85 —

First day covers of Nos. 59 and 60 total 504,832.

Central Hall, Westminster — A30

Design: 8c, French inscription.
Central Hall, Westminster, London, was the site of the first session of the United Nations General Assembly, 1946.
Engraved and printed by the American Bank Note Co., New York. Panes of 50. Designed by Olav Mathiesen.

1958, Apr. 14 *Perf. 12*

61 A30 3c **violet blue** *(3,353,716)* .25 .25
First day cover 1.00
Inscription block of 4 .40 —
62 A30 8c **rose claret** *(2,836,747)* .25 .25
First day cover 1.00
First day cover, #61-62 1.50
Inscription block of 4 .60 —

First day covers of Nos. 61 and 62 total 449,401.

UN Seal — A31

Engraved and printed by Bradbury, Wilkinson & Co., Ltd., England. Panes of 50. Designed by Herbert M. Sanborn.

1958, Oct. 24 ***Perf. 13½x14***
63 A31 4c **red orange** *(9,000,000)* .25 .25
First day cover 1.00
First day cover of #63 also bearing #64 *85.00*
Inscription block of 4 .50 —

1958, June 2 ***Perf. 13x14***
64 A31 8c **bright blue** *(5,000,000)* .25 .25
First day cover *(219,422)* 1.00
Inscription block of 4 .55 —
Margin block of 4, Bradbury, Wilkinson imprint 3.00 —

Gearwheels — A32

Design: 8c, French inscription.
Issued to honor the Economic and Social Council.
Engraved and printed by the American Bank Note Co., New York. Panes of 50. Designed by Ole Hamann.

1958, Oct. 24 **Unwmk.** ***Perf. 12***
65 A32 4c **dark blue green** *(2,556,784)* .25 .25
First day cover 1.00
Inscription block of 4 .40 —
66 A32 8c **vermilion** *(2,175,117)* .25 .25
First day cover 1.00
First day cover, #65-66 1.00
Inscription block of 4 .70 —

First day covers of Nos. 63, 65 and 66 total 626,236.

Hands Upholding Globe — A33

Issued for Human Rights Day and to commemorate the 10th anniversary of the signing of the Universal Declaration of Human Rights.
Engraved and printed by the American Bank Note Co., New York. Panes of 50. Designed by Leonard C. Mitchell.

1958, Dec. 10 **Unwmk.** ***Perf. 12***
67 A33 4c **yellow green** *(2,644,340)* .25 .25
First day cover 1.00
Inscription block of 4 .40 —
68 A33 8c **red brown** *(2,216,838)* .25 .25
First day cover 1.00
First day cover, #67-68 1.00
Inscription block of 4 .65 —

First day covers of Nos. 67 and 68 total 618,124.

New York City Building, Flushing Meadows A34

Design: 8c, French inscription.

New York City Building at Flushing Meadows, New York, was the site of many General Assembly meetings, 1946-50.
Engraved and printed by Canadian Bank Note Company, Ltd., Ottawa. Panes of 50. Designed by Robert Perrot.

1959, Mar. 30 **Unwmk.** ***Perf. 12***
69 A34 4c **light lilac rose** *(2,035,011)* .25 .25
First day cover 1.00
Inscription block of 4 .40 —
70 A34 8c **aquamarine** *(1,627,281)* .25 .25
First day cover 1.00
First day cover, #69-70 1.25
Inscription block of 4 .60 —

First day covers of Nos. 69 and 70 total 440,955.

A35

Design: UN emblem and symbols of agriculture, industry and trade.
Issued to honor the Economic Commission for Europe.
Engraved and printed by Canadian Bank Note Company, Ltd., Ottawa. Panes of 50. Designed by Ole Hamann.

1959, May 18 **Unwmk.** ***Perf. 12***
71 A35 4c **blue** *(1,743,502)* .25 .25
First day cover 1.00
Inscription block of 4 .60 —
72 A35 8c **red orange** *(1,482,898)* .25 .25
First day cover 1.00
First day cover, #71-72 1.25
Inscription block of 4 .85 —

First day covers of Nos. 71 and 72 total 433,549.

A36

Designs: 4c, Figure Adapted from Rodin's "Age of Bronze." 8c, same, French inscription.
Issued to honor the Trusteeship Council.
Engraved and printed by Canadian Bank Note Co., Ltd., Ottawa. Panes of 50. Designed by León Helguera; lettering by Ole Hamann.

1959, Oct. 23 **Unwmk.** ***Perf. 12***
73 A36 4c **bright red** *(1,929,677)* .25 .25
First day cover 1.00
Inscription block of 4 .60 —
74 A36 8c **dark olive green** *(1,587,647)* .25 .25
First day cover 1.00
First day cover, #73-74 1.25
Inscription block of 4 1.25 —

First day covers of Nos. 73 and 74 total 466,053.

World Refugee Year Emblem — A37

Design: 8c, French inscription.
Issued to publicize World Refugee Year, July 1, 1959-June 30, 1960.
Engraved and printed by Canadian Bank Note Co., Ltd., Ottawa. Panes of 50. Designed by Olav Mathiesen.

1959, Dec. 10 **Unwmk.** ***Perf. 12***
75 A37 4c **olive & red** *(2,168,963)* .25 .25
First day cover 1.00
Inscription block of 4 .50 —
76 A37 8c **olive & bright greenish blue** *(1,843,886)* .25 .25
First day cover 1.00
First day cover, #75-76 1.50
Inscription block of 4 .75 —

First day covers of Nos. 75 and 76 total 502,262.

Chaillot Palace, Paris — A38

Design: 8c, French inscription.
Chaillot Palace in Paris was the site of General Assembly meetings in 1948 and 1951.
Engraved and printed by Thomas De La Rue & Co., Ltd., London. Panes of 50. Designed by Hubert Woyty-Wimmer.

1960, Feb. 29 **Unwmk.** ***Perf. 14***
77 A38 4c **rose lilac & blue** *(2,276,678)* .25 .25
First day cover 1.00
Inscription block of 4 .40 —
78 A38 8c **dull green & brown** *(1,930,869)* .25 .25
First day cover 1.00
First day cover, #77-78 1.75
Inscription block of 4 .70 —

First day covers of Nos. 77 and 78 total 446,815.

Map of Far East and Steel Beam — A39

Design: 8c, French inscription.
Issued to honor the Economic Commission for Asia and the Far East (ECAFE).
Printed by the Government Printing Bureau, Tokyo. Panes of 50. Designed by Hubert Woyty-Wimmer.

1960, Apr. 11 **Photo.** **Unwmk.** ***Perf. 13x13½***
79 A39 4c **deep claret, blue green & dull yellow** *(2,195,945)* .25 .25
First day cover 1.00
Inscription block of 4 .40 —
80 A39 8c **olive green, blue & rose** *(1,897,902)* .25 .25
First day cover 1.00
First day cover, #79-80 1.50
Inscription block of 4 .75 —

First day covers of Nos. 79 and 80 total 415,127.

Tree, FAO and UN Emblems — A40

Design: 8c, French inscription.
Issued to commemorate the Fifth World Forestry Congress, Seattle, Washington, Aug. 29-Sept. 10.
Printed by the Government Printing Bureau, Tokyo. Panes of 50. Designed by Ole Hamann.

1960, Aug. 29 **Photo.** **Unwmk.** ***Perf. 13½***
81 A40 4c **dark blue, green & orange** *(2,188,293)* .25 .25
First day cover 1.00
Inscription block of 4 .40 —
82 A40 8c **yellow green, black & orange** *(1,837,778)* .25 .25
First day cover 1.00
First day cover, #81-82 1.50
Inscription block of 4 .75 —

First day covers of Nos. 81 and 82 total 434,129.

UN Headquarters and Preamble to UN Charter — A41

Design: 8c, French inscription.
Issued to commemorate the 15th anniversary of the United Nations.
Engraved and printed by the British American Bank Note Co., Ltd., Ottawa, Canada. Panes of 50. Designed by Robert Perrot.

1960, Oct. 24 Unwmk. *Perf. 11*

83	A41 4c **blue** *(2,631,593)*	.25	.25
	First day cover		1.00
	Inscription block of 4	.40	—
84	A41 8c **gray** *(2,278,022)*	.25	.25
	First day cover		1.00
	First day cover, #83-84		1.25
	Inscription block of 4	.65	—

Souvenir Sheet

Imperf

85	Sheet of 2 *(1,000,000)*	1.25	1.25
a.	A41 4c **blue**	.55	.55
b.	A41 8c **gray**	.55	.55
	First day cover *(256,699)*		1.00

No. 85 has dark gray marginal inscription. Size: 92x71mm. Broken "I" and "V" flaws occur in "ANNIVERSARY" in marginal inscription. Value $40. Examples are known with the two stamps misaligned.

Block and Tackle — A42

Design: 8c, French inscription.
Issued to honor the International Bank for Reconstruction and Development.
Printed by the Government Printing Bureau, Tokyo. Panes of 50. Designed by Angel Medina Medina.

1960, Dec. 9 Photo. Unwmk. *Perf. 13½x13*

86	A42 4c **multicolored** *(2,286,117)*	.25	.25
	First day cover		1.00
	Inscription block of 4	.40	—
87	A42 8c **multicolored** *(1,882,019)*	.25	.25
	First day cover		1.00
	First day cover, #86-87		1.00
	Inscription block of 4	.60	—

First day covers of Nos. 86 and 87 total 559,708.

Scales of Justice from Raphael's Stanze — A43

Design: 8c, French inscription.
Issued to honor the International Court of Justice.
Printed by the Government Printing Bureau, Tokyo, Japan. Panes of 50. Designed by Kurt Plowitz.

1961, Feb. 13 Photo. Unwmk. *Perf. 13½x13*

88	A43 4c **yellow, orange brown & black** *(2,234,588)*	.25	.25
	First day cover		1.00
	Inscription block of 4	.40	—
89	A43 8c **yellow, green & black** *(2,023,968)*	.25	.25
	First day cover		1.00
	First day cover, #88-89		1.00
	Inscription block of 4	.60	—

First day covers of Nos. 88 and 89 total 447,467.

Seal of International Monetary Fund — A44

Design: 7c, French inscription.
Issued to honor the International Monetary Fund.
Printed by the Government Printing Bureau, Tokyo, Japan. Panes of 50. Designed by Roy E. Carlson and Hordur Karlsson, Iceland.

1961, Apr. 17 Photo. Unwmk. *Perf. 13x13½*

90	A44 4c **bright bluish green** *(2,305,010)*	.25	.25
	First day cover		1.00
	Inscription block of 4	.40	—
91	A44 7c **terra cotta & yellow** *(2,147,201)*	.25	.25
	First day cover		1.00
	First day cover, #90-91		1.00
	Inscription block of 4	.60	—

First day covers of Nos. 90 and 91 total 448,729.

Abstract Group of Flags — A45

Printed by Courvoisier S.A., La Chaux-de-Fonds, Switzerland. Panes of 50. Designed by Herbert M. Sanborn.

1961, June 5 Photo. Unwmk. *Perf. 11½*

92	A45 30c **multicolored** *(3,370,000)*	.45	.30
	First day cover *(182,949)*		1.00
	Inscription block of 4	2.00	—

See UN Offices in Geneva No. 10.

Cogwheel and Map of Latin America — A46

Design: 11c, Spanish inscription.
Issued to honor the Economic Commission for Latin America.
Printed by the Government Printing Bureau, Tokyo. Panes of 50. Designed by Robert Perrot.

1961, Sept. 18 Photo. Unwmk. *Perf. 13½*

93	A46 4c **blue, red & citron** *(2,037,912)*	.25	.25
	First day cover		1.00
	Inscription block of 4	.75	—
94	A46 11c **green, lilac & orange vermilion** *(1,835,097)*	.25	.25
	First day cover		1.00
	First day cover, #93-94		1.00
	Inscription block of 4	1.50	—

First day covers of Nos. 93 and 94 total 435,820.

Africa House, Addis Ababa, and Map — A47

Design: 11c, English inscription.
Issued to honor the Economic Commission for Africa.
Printed by Courvoisier S.A., La Chaux-de-Fonds, Switzerland. Panes of 50. Designed by Robert Perrot.

1961, Oct. 24 Photo. Unwmk. *Perf. 11½*

95	A47 4c **ultramarine, orange, yellow & brown** *(2,044,842)*	.25	.25
	First day cover		1.00
	Inscription block of 4	.30	—
96	A47 11c **emerald, orange, yellow & brown** *(1,790,894)*	.25	.25
	First day cover		1.00
	First day cover, #95-96		1.00
	Inscription block of 4	1.00	—

First day covers of Nos. 95 and 96 total 435,131.

Mother Bird Feeding Young and UNICEF Seal — A48

Designs: 3c, Spanish inscription. 13c, French inscription.
15th anniversary of the United Nations Children's Fund.
Printed by Courvoisier S.A., La Chaux-de-Fonds, Switzerland. Panes of 50. Designed by Minoru Hisano.

1961, Dec. 4 Photo. Unwmk. *Perf. 11½*

97	A48 3c **brown, gold, orange & yellow** *(2,867,456)*	.25	.25
	First day cover		1.00
	Inscription block of 4	.20	—
98	A48 4c **brown, gold, blue & emerald** *(2,735,899)*	.25	.25
	First day cover		1.00
	Inscription block of 4	.30	—
99	A48 13c **deep green, gold, purple & pink** *(1,951,715)*	.25	.25
	First day cover		1.00
	First day cover, #97-99		1.25
	Inscription block of 4	1.00	—
	Nos. 97-99 (3)	.75	.75

First day covers of Nos. 97-99 total 752,979.

Family and Symbolic Buildings A49

Design: 7c, inscribed "Services Collectifs".
Issued to publicize the UN program for housing and urban development, and in connection with the expert committee meeting at UN headquarters, Feb. 7-21.
Printed by Harrison and Sons, Ltd., London, England. Panes of 50. Designed by Olav Mathiesen.

1962, Feb. 28 Photo. Unwmk. *Perf. 14½x14*

Central design multicolored

100	A49 4c **bright blue** *(2,204,190)*	.25	.25
	First day cover		1.00
	Inscription block of 4	.35	—
a.	Black omitted	*200.00*	
b.	Yellow omitted		—
c.	Brown omitted		—
101	A49 7c **orange brown** *(1,845,821)*	.25	.25
	First day cover		1.00
	First day cover, #100-101		1.25
	Inscription block of 4	.65	—
a.	Red omitted		—
b.	Black omitted		—
c.	Gold omitted		—

First day covers of Nos. 100-101 total 466,178.

"The World Against Malaria" — A50

Issued in honor of the World Health Organization and to call attention to the international campaign to eradicate malaria from the world.
Printed by Harrison and Sons, Ltd., London, England. Panes of 50. Designed by Rashid-ud Din.

1962, Mar. 30 Photo. Unwmk. *Perf. 14x14½*
Word frame in gray

102 A50 4c **orange, yellow, brown, green & black** *(2,047,000)* .25 .25
First day cover 1.00
Inscription block of 4 .50 —
103 A50 11c **green, yellow, brown & indigo** *(1,683,766)* .25 .25
First day cover 1.00
First day cover, #102-103 1.25
Inscription block of 4 1.00 —
First day covers of Nos. 102-103 total 522,450.

"Peace" — A51

UN Flag — A52

Hands Combining "UN" and Globe — A53

UN Emblem over Globe — A54

Printed by Harrison & Sons, Ltd. London, England (1c, 3c and 11c), and by Canadian Bank Note Co., Ltd., Ottawa (5c). Panes of 50. Designed by Kurt Plowitz (1c), Ole Hamann (3c), Renato Ferrini (5c) and Olav Mathiesen (11c).

Photo.; Engr. (5c)

1962, May 25 Unwmk. *Perf. 14x14½*

104 A51 1c **vermilion, blue, black & gray** *(5,000,000)* .25 .25
First day cover 1.00
Inscription block of 4 .40 —
105 A52 3c **light green, Prussian blue, yellow & gray** *(5,000,000)* .25 .25
First day cover 1.00
Inscription block of 4 .40 —

Perf. 12

106 A53 5c **dark carmine rose** *(4,000,000)* .25 .25
First day cover 1.00
Inscription block of 4 .75 —

Perf. 12½

107 A54 11c **dark & light blue & gold** *(4,400,000)* .25 .25
First day cover 1.00
First day cover, #104-107 4.50
Inscription block of 4 1.10 —
Nos. 104-107 (4) 1.00 1.00

First day covers of Nos. 104-107 total 738,985.
Size of 5c, No. 106: 36½x23½mm.
See No. 167. See UN Offices in Geneva Nos. 2 and 6.

Flag at Half-mast and UN Headquarters — A55

Issued on the 1st anniversary of the death of Dag Hammarskjold, Secretary General of the United Nations 1953-61, in memory of those who died in the service of the United Nations.
Printed by Courvoisier S. A., La Chaux-de-Fonds, Switzerland. Panes of 50. Designed by Ole Hamann.

1962, Sept. 17 Photo. Unwmk. *Perf. 11½*

108 A55 5c **black, light blue & blue** *(2,195,707)* .25 .25
First day cover 1.00
Inscription block of 4 .75 —
109 A55 15c **black, gray olive & blue** *(1,155,047)* .25 .25
First day cover 1.00
First day cover, #108-109 1.50
Inscription block of 4 1.10 —
First day covers of Nos. 108-109 total 513,963.

World Map Showing Congo — A56

Design: 11c inscribed "Operation des Nations Unies au Congo."
Issued to commemorate the United Nations Operation in the Congo.
Printed by Courvoisier S. A., La Chaux-de-Fonds, Switzerland. Panes of 50. Designed by George Hamori.

1962, Oct. 24 Photo. Unwmk. *Perf. 11½*

110 A56 4c **olive, orange, black & yellow** *(1,477,958)* .25 .25
First day cover 1.00
Inscription block of 4 .75 —
111 A56 11c **blue green, orange, black & yellow** *(1,171,255)* .25 .25
First day cover 1.00
First day cover, #110-111 1.25
Inscription block of 4 1.10 —
First day covers of Nos. 110-111 total 460,675.

Globe in Universe and Palm Frond — A57

Design: 4c, English inscription.
Issued to honor the Committee on Peaceful Uses of Outer Space.
Printed by Bradbury, Wilkinson and Co., Ltd., England. Panes of 50. Designed by Kurt Plowitz.

1962, Dec. 3 Engr. Unwmk. *Perf. 14x13½*

112 A57 4c **violet blue** *(2,263,876)* .25 .25
First day cover 1.00
Inscription block of 4 .35 —
113 A57 11c **rose claret** *(1,681,584)* .25 .25
First day cover 1.00
First day cover, #112-113 1.50
Inscription block of 4 1.10 —
First day covers of Nos. 112-113 total 529,780.

Development Decade Emblem — A58

Design: 11c, French inscription.
UN Development Decade and UN Conference on the Application of Science and Technology for the Benefit of the Less Developed Areas, Geneva, Feb. 4-20.
Printed by Courvoisier S. A., La Chaux-de-Fonds, Switzerland. Panes of 50. Designed by Rashid-ud Din.

1963, Feb. 4 Photo. Unwmk. *Perf. 11½*

114 A58 5c **pale green, maroon, dark blue & Prussian blue** *(1,802,406)* .25 .25
First day cover 1.00
Inscription block of 4 .50 —
115 A58 11c **yellow, maroon, dark blue & Prussian blue** *(1,530,190)* .25 .25
First day cover 1.00
First day cover, #114-115 1.25
Inscription block of 4 .90 —
First day covers of Nos. 114-115 total 460,877.

Stalks of Wheat — A59

Design: 11c, French inscription.
Issued for the "Freedom from Hunger" campaign of the Food and Agriculture Organization.
Printed by Courvoisier S. A., La Chaux-de-Fonds, Switzerland. Panes of 50. Designed by Ole Hamann.

1963, Mar. 22 Photo. Unwmk. *Perf. 11½*

116 A59 5c **vermilion, green & yellow** *(1,666,178)* .25 .25
First day cover 1.00
Inscription block of 4 .50 —
117 A59 11c **vermilion, deep claret & yellow** *(1,563,023)* .25 .25
First day cover 1.00
First day cover, #116-117 1.25
Inscription block of 4 .90 —
First day covers of Nos. 116-117 total 461,868.

Bridge over Map of New Guinea — A60

1st anniversary of the United Nations Temporary Executive Authority (UNTEA) in West New Guinea (West Irian).
Printed by Courvoisier S.A., La Chaux-de-Fonds, Switzerland. Panes of 50. Designed by Henry Bencsath.

1963, Oct. 1 Photo. Unwmk. *Perf. 11½*

118 A60 25c **blue, green & gray** *(1,427,747)* .50 .40
First day cover *(222,280)* 1.00
Inscription block of 4 2.50 —

General Assembly Building, New York — A61

Design: 11c, French inscription.
Since October 1955 all sessions of the General Assembly have been held in the General Assembly Hall, UN Headquarters, NY.
Printed by the Government Printing Bureau, Tokyo. Panes of 50. Designed by Kurt Plowitz.

1963, Nov. 4 Photo. Unwmk. *Perf. 13*

119 A61 5c **violet blue, blue, yellow green & red** *(1,892,539)* .25 .25
First day cover 1.00
Inscription block of 4 .50 —

120 A61 11c **green, yellow green, blue, yellow & red** *(1,435,079)* .25 .25
First day cover 1.00
First day cover, #119-120 1.00
Inscription block of 4 .80 —

First day covers of Nos. 119-120 total 410,306.

Flame — A62

Design: 11c inscribed "15e Anniversaire."
15th anniversary of the signing of the Universal Declaration of Human Rights.
Printed by the Government Printing Bureau, Tokyo. Panes of 50. Designed by Rashid-ud Din.

1963, Dec. 10 Photo. Unwmk. *Perf. 13*

121 A62 5c **green, gold, red & yellow** *(2,208,008)* .25 .25
First day cover 1.00
Inscription block of 4 .60 —

122 A62 11c **carmine, gold, blue & yellow** *(1,501,125)* .25 .25
First day cover 1.00
First day cover, #121-122 1.00
Inscription block of 4 .80 —

First day covers of Nos. 121-122 total 567,907.

Ships at Sea and IMCO Emblem — A63

Design: 11c, inscribed "OMCI."
Issued to honor the Intergovernmental Maritime Consultative Organization.
Printed by Courvoisier S.A., La Chaux-de-Fonds, Switzerland. Panes of 50. Designed by Henry Bencsath; emblem by Olav Mathiesen.

1964, Jan. 13 Photo. Unwmk. *Perf. 11½*

123 A63 5c **blue, olive, ocher & yellow** *(1,805,750)* .25 .25
First day cover 1.00
Inscription block of 4 .60 —

124 A63 11c **dark blue, dark green, emerald & yellow** *(1,583,848)* .25 .25
First day cover 1.00
First day cover, #123-124 1.00
Inscription block of 4 .80 —

First day covers of Nos. 123-124 total 442,696.

World Map, Sinusoidal Projection — A64

Stylized Globe and Weather Vane — A67

Printed by Thomas De La Rue & Co. Ltd., London (2c) and Courvoisier S.A., La Chaux-de-Fonds, Switzerland (7c, 10c and 50c). Panes of 50.
Designed by Ole Hamann (2c), George Hamori (7c, 10c) and Hatim El Mekki (50c).

1964-71 Photo. Unwmk. *Perf. 14*

125 A64 2c **light & dark blue, orange & yellow green** *(3,800,000)* .25 .25
First day cover 1.00
Inscription block of 4 .60 —
a. Perf. 13x13½, *Feb. 24, 1971 (1,500,000)* .25 .25

Perf. 11½

126 A65 7c **dark blue, orange brown & black** *(2,700,000)* .25 .25
First day cover 1.00
Inscription block of 4 .75 —

127 A66 10c **blue green, olive green & black** *(3,200,000)* .25 .25
First day cover 1.00
First day cover, #125-127 4.00
Inscription block of 4 1.00 —

128 A67 50c **multicolored** *(2,520,000)* .55 .45
First day cover *(210,713)* 1.00
Inscription block of 4 3.25 —
Nos. 125-128 (4) 1.30 1.20

Issue dates: 50c, Mar. 6; 2c, 7c, 10c, May 29, 1964.
First day covers of 2c, 7c and 10c total 524,073.
See UN Offices in Geneva Nos. 3 and 12.

Arrows Showing Global Flow of Trade — A68

Design: 5c, English inscription.
Issued to commemorate the UN Conference on Trade and Development, Geneva, Mar. 23-June 15.
Printed by Thomas De La Rue & Co., Ltd., London. Panes of 50. Designed by Herbert M. Sanborn and Ole Hamann.

1964, June 15 Photo. Unwmk. *Perf. 13*

129 A68 5c **black, red & yellow** *(1,791,211)* .25 .25
First day cover 1.00
Inscription block of 4 .50 —

130 A68 11c **black, olive & yellow** *(1,529,526)* .25 .25
First day cover 1.00
First day cover, #129-130 1.25
Inscription block of 4 .80 —

First day covers of Nos. 129-130 total 422,358.

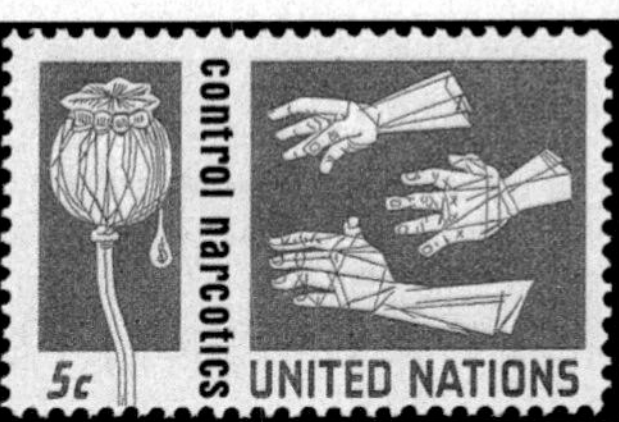

Poppy Capsule and Reaching Hands — A69

Design: 11c, Inscribed "Echec au Stupéfiants."
Issued to honor international efforts and achievements in the control of narcotics.
Printed by the Canadian Bank Note Co., Ottawa. Panes of 50. Designed by Kurt Plowitz.

1964, Sept. 21 Engr. Unwmk. *Perf. 12*

131 A69 5c **rose red & black** *(1,508,999)* .25 .25
First day cover 1.00
Inscription block of 4 .50 —

132 A69 11c **emerald & black** *(1,340,691)* .25 .25
First day cover 1.00
First day cover, #131-132 1.50
Inscription block of 4 1.00 —

First day covers of Nos. 131-132 total 445,274.

Padlocked Atomic Blast — A70

Signing of the nuclear test ban treaty pledging an end to nuclear explosions in the atmosphere, outer space and under water.
Printed by Artia, Prague, Czechoslovakia. Panes of 50. Designed by Ole Hamann.

Litho. and Engr.

1964, Oct. 23 Unwmk. *Perf. 11x11½*

133 A70 5c **dark red & dark brown** *(2,422,789)* .25 .25
First day cover *(298,652)* 1.00
Inscription block of 4 .50 —

Education for Progress — A71

Design: 11c, French inscription.
Issued to publicize the UNESCO world campaign for universal literacy and for free compulsory primary education.
Printed by Courvoisier, S. A., La Chaux-de-Fonds, Switzerland. Panes of 50. Designed by Kurt Plowitz.

1964, Dec. 7 Photo. Unwmk. *Perf. 12½*

134 A71 4c **orange, red, bister, green & blue** *(2,375,181)* .25 .25
First day cover 1.00
Inscription block of 4 .50 —

135 A71 5c **bister, red, dark & light blue** *(2,496,877)* .25 .25
First day cover 1.00
Inscription block of 4 .55 —

136 A71 11c **green, light blue, black & rose** *(1,773,645)* .25 .25
First day cover 1.00
First day cover, #134-136 1.25
Inscription block of 4 1.25 —
Nos. 134-136 (3) .75 .75

First day covers of Nos. 134-136 total 727,875.

Progress Chart of Special Fund, Key and Globe — A72

Design: 11c, French inscription.
Issued to publicize the Special Fund program to speed economic growth and social advancement in low-income countries.
Printed by the Government Printing Bureau, Tokyo. Panes of 50. Designed by Rashid-ud Din, Pakistan.

1965, Jan. 25 Photo. Unwmk. *Perf. 13½x13*

137 A72 5c **dull blue, dark blue, yellow & red** *(1,949,274)* .25 .25
First day cover 1.00
Inscription block of 4 .50 —

138 A72 11c **yellow green, dark blue, yellow & red** *(1,690,908)* .25 .25
First day cover 1.00
First day cover, #137-138 1.00
Inscription block of 4 .75 —
a. Black omitted (UN emblem on key) —

First day covers of Nos. 137-138 total 490,608.

UN Emblem, Stylized Leaves and View of Cyprus — A73

Design: 11c, French inscription.

Issued to honor the United Nations Peace-keeping Force on Cyprus.

Printed by Courvoisier S.A., Switzerland. Panes of 50. Designed by George Hamori, Australia.

1965, Mar. 4 Photo. Unwmk. *Perf. 11½*

No.	Type	Description	Unused	Used
139	A73	5c **orange, olive & black** *(1,887,042)*	.25	.25
		First day cover		1.00
		Inscription block of 4	.50	—
140	A73	11c **yellow green, blue green & black** *(1,691,767)*	.25	.25
		First day cover		1.00
		First day cover, #139-140		1.00
		Inscription block of 4	.75	—

First day covers of Nos. 139-140 total 438,059.

"From Semaphore to Satellite" — A74

Design: 11c, French inscription.

Centenary of the International Telecommunication Union.

Printed by Courvoisier S.A., Switzerland. Panes of 50. Designed by Kurt Plowitz, United States.

1965, May 17 Photo. Unwmk. *Perf. 11½*

No.	Type	Description	Unused	Used
141	A74	5c **aquamarine, orange, blue & purple** *(2,432,407)*	.25	.25
		First day cover		1.00
		Inscription block of 4	.50	—
142	A74	11c **light violet, red orange, bister & bright green** *(1,731,070)*	.25	.25
		First day cover		1.00
		First day cover, #141-142		1.00
		Inscription block of 4	.75	—

First day covers of Nos. 141-142 total 434,393.

ICY Emblem — A75

Design: 15c, French inscription.

20th anniversary of the United Nations and International Cooperation Year.

Printed by Bradbury, Wilkinson and Co., Ltd., England. Panes of 50. Designed by Olav Mathiesen, Denmark.

1965, June 26 Engr. Unwmk. *Perf. 14x13½*

No.	Type	Description	Unused	Used
143	A75	5c **dark blue** *(2,282,452)*	.25	.25
		First day cover		1.00
		Inscription block of 4	.50	—
144	A75	15c **lilac rose** *(1,993,562)*	.25	.25
		First day cover		1.00
		First day cover; #143-144		1.00
		Inscription block of 4	.95	—

Souvenir Sheet

No.	Type	Description	Unused	Used
145	A75	Sheet of two *(1,928,366)*	.35	.35
		First day cover		1.00

No. 145 contains one each of Nos. 143-144 with dark blue and ocher marginal inscription, ocher edging. Size: 92x70mm.

First day covers of Nos. 143-145 total: New York, 748,876; San Francisco, 301,435.

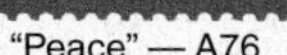
"Peace" — A76

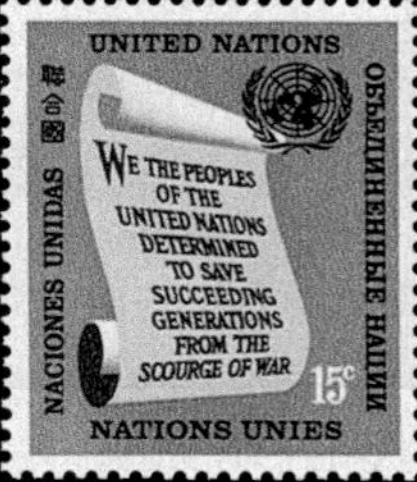

Opening Words, UN Charter — A77

UN Headquarters and Emblem — A78

UN Emblem — A79

UN Emblem Encircled — A80

Printed by Government Printing Bureau, Tokyo (1c); Government Printing Office, Austria (15c, 20c); Government Printing Office (Bundesdruckerei), Berlin (25c), and Courvoisier S.A., Switzerland ($1). Panes of 50.

Designed by Kurt Plowitz US (1c); Olav S. Mathiesen, Denmark (15c); Vergniaud Pierre-Noel, US (20c); Rashid-ud Din, Pakistan (25c), and Ole Hamann, Denmark ($1).

1965-66 Photo. Unwmk. *Perf. 13½x13*

No.	Type	Description	Unused	Used
146	A76	1c **vermilion, blue, black & gray** *(7,000,000)*	.25	.25
		First day cover		1.00
		Inscription block of 4	.40	—

Perf. 14

No.	Type	Description	Unused	Used
147	A77	15c **olive bister, dull yellow, black & deep claret** *(2,500,000)*	.25	.25
		First day cover		1.00
		Inscription block of 4	1.00	—

Perf. 12

No.	Type	Description	Unused	Used
148	A78	20c **dark blue, blue, red & yellow** *(3,000,000)*	.25	.25
		First day cover		1.00
		First day cover, #147-148		1.00
		Inscription block of 4	1.10	—
a.		Yellow omitted		—

Litho. and Embossed

Perf. 14

No.	Type	Description	Unused	Used
149	A79	25c **light & dark blue** *(3,200,000)*	.30	.25
		First day cover		1.00
		First day cover, #146, 149		1.25
		Inscription block of 4	1.40	—
		Inscription block of 6, "Bundesdruckerei Berlin" imprint	20.00	
		First day cover, "Bundesdruckerei," margin block of 6		32.50
a.		25c **light & dark blue,** new dk blue plate/cylinder (see footnote)	.30	.25
		Inscription block of 4	1.40	—
b.		As "a," tagged *('76)*	10.00	10.00
		Inscription block of 4	45.00	—

Photo.

Perf. 11½

No.	Type	Description	Unused	Used
150	A80	$1 **aquamarine & sapphire** *(2,570,000)*	1.60	1.60
		First day cover *(181,510)*		2.00
		Inscription block of 4	7.50	—
		Nos. 146-150 (5)	2.65	2.60

Issued: 1c, No. 149, 9/20/65; No. 149a, 11/5/65; 15c, 20c, 10/25/65; $1, 3/25/66.

First day covers of Nos. 146 and 149 total 443,964. Those of Nos. 147-148 total 457,596.

On No. 149, the dark blue "halo" of the U.N. emblem is large, overlapping the "25c." Marginal inscriptions (U.N. emblem and "1965") are 6mm in diameter, and imprint "Bundesdruckerei Berlin" is present.

On No. 149a, a new dark blue plate/cylinder was used, making the "halo" of the U.N. emblem smaller. Marginal inscriptions are 8mm in diameter and the "Bundesdruckerei" imprint is not present. No. 149b was printed from the new dark blue plate/cylinder.

See UN Offices in Geneva Nos. 5, 9 and 11.

Fields and People — A81

Design: 11c, French inscription.

Issued to emphasize the importance of the world's population growth and its problems and to call attention to population trends and development.

Printed by Government Printing Office, Austria. Panes of 50. Designed by Olav S. Mathiesen, Denmark.

1965, Nov. 29 Photo. Unwmk. *Perf. 12*

No.	Type	Description	Unused	Used
151	A81	4c **multicolored** *(1,966,033)*	.25	.25
		First day cover		1.00
		Inscription block of 4	.40	—
152	A81	5c **multicolored** *(2,298,731)*	.25	.25
		First day cover		1.00
		Inscription block of 4	.40	—
153	A81	11c **multicolored** *(1,557,589)*	.25	.25
		First day cover		1.00
		First day cover, #151-153		1.50
		Inscription block of 4	1.00	—
		Nos. 151-153 (3)	.75	.75

First day covers of Nos. 151-153 total 710,507.

Globe and Flags of UN Members — A82

Design: 15c, French inscription.

Issued to honor the World Federation of United Nations Associations.

Printed by Courvoisier S.A., Switzerland. Panes of 50. Designed by Olav S. Mathiesen, Denmark.

1966, Jan. 31 Photo. Unwmk. *Perf. 11½*

No.	Type	Description	Unused	Used
154	A82	5c **multicolored** *(2,462,215)*	.25	.25
		First day cover		1.00
		Inscription block of 4	.40	—
155	A82	15c **multicolored** *(1,643,661)*	.25	.25
		First day cover		1.00
		First day cover, #154-155		1.25
		Inscription block of 4	1.00	—

First day covers of Nos. 154-155 total 474,154.

WHO Headquarters, Geneva — A83

Design: 11c, French inscription.

Issued to commemorate the opening of the World Health Organization Headquarters, Geneva.

Printed by Courvoisier, S.A., Switzerland. Panes of 50. Designed by Rashid-ud Din.

1966, May 26 Photo. *Perf. 12½x12*

Granite Paper

No.	Type	Description	Unused	Used
156	A83	5c **lt & dk blue, orange, green & bister** *(2,079,893)*	.25	.25
		First day cover		1.00
		Inscription block of 4	.50	—
157	A83	11c **orange, lt & dark blue, green & bister** *(1,879,879)*	.25	.25
		First day cover		1.00
		First day cover, #156-157		1.00
		Inscription block of 4	1.00	—

First day covers of Nos. 156-157 total 466,171.

Coffee — A84

Design: 11c, Spanish inscription.

Issued to commemorate the International Coffee Agreement of 1962.

Printed by the Government Printing Bureau, Tokyo. Panes of 50. Designed by Rashid-ud Din, Pakistan.

1966, Sept. 19 Photo. *Perf. 13½x13*

158 A84 5c **orange, lt blue, green, red & dk brown** *(2,020,308)*	.25	.25
First day cover		1.00
Inscription block of 4	.50	—
159 A84 11c **lt blue, yellow, green, red & dk brown** *(1,888,682)*	.25	.25
First day cover		1.00
First day cover, #158-159		1.00
Inscription block of 4	1.00	—

First day covers of Nos. 158-159 total 435,886.

UN Observer — A85

Issued to honor the Peace Keeping United Nation Observers.

Printed by Courvoisier, S.A. Panes of 50. Designed by Ole S. Hamann.

1966, Oct. 24 Photo. *Perf. 11½*

Granite Paper

160 A85 15c **steel blue, orange, black & green** *(1,889,809)*	.25	.25
First day cover *(255,326)*		1.00
Inscription block of 4	1.10	—

Children of Various Races — A86

Designs: 5c, Children riding in locomotive and tender. 11c, Children in open railroad car playing medical team (French inscription).

20th anniversary of the United Nations Children's Fund (UNICEF).

Printed by Thomas De La Rue & Co., Ltd. Panes of 50. Designed by Kurt Plowitz.

1966, Nov. 28 Litho. *Perf. 13x13½*

161 A86 4c **pink & multi** *(2,334,989)*	.25	.25
First day cover		1.00
Inscription block of 4	.40	—
162 A86 5c **pale green & multi** *(2,746,941)*	.25	.25
First day cover		1.00
Inscription block of 4	.40	—
a. Yellow omitted	—	—
163 A86 11c **light ultramarine & multi** *(2,123,841)*	.25	.25
First day cover		1.00
First day cover, #161-163		1.00
Inscription block of 4	.90	—
b. Dark blue omitted	—	
Nos. 161-163 (3)	.75	.75

First day covers of Nos. 161-163 total 987,271.

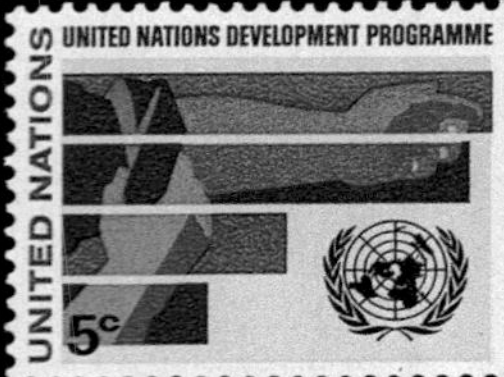

Hand Rolling up Sleeve and Chart Showing Progress — A87

Design: 11c, French inscription.

United Nations Development Program.

Printed by Courvoisier, S.A. Panes of 50. Designed by Olav S. Mathiesen.

1967, Jan. 23 Photo. *Perf. 12½*

164 A87 5c **green, yellow, purple & orange** *(2,204,679)*	.25	.25
First day cover		1.00
Inscription block of 4	.40	—
165 A87 11c **blue, chocolate, light green & orange** *(1,946,159)*	.25	.25
First day cover		1.00
First day cover, #164-165		1.00
Inscription block of 4	1.00	—

First day covers of Nos. 164-165 total 406,011.

Type of 1962 and

UN Headquarters, NY, and World Map — A88

Printed by Courvoisier, S.A. Panes of 50. Designed by Jozsef Vertel, Hungary (1½c); Renato Ferrini, Italy (5c).

1967 Photo. *Perf. 11½*

166 A88 1½c **ultramarine, black, orange & ocher** *(4,000,000)*	.25	.25
First day cover *(199,751)*		1.00
Inscription block of 4	.40	—

Size: 33x23mm

167 A53 5c **red brown, brown & orange yellow** *(5,500,000)*	.25	.25
First day cover *(212,544)*		1.00
Inscription block of 4	.50	—

Issue dates: 1½c, Mar. 17; 5c, Jan. 23.

For 5c of type A88, see UN Offices in Geneva No. 1.

Fireworks — A89

Design: 11c, French inscription.

Issued to honor all nations which gained independence since 1945.

Printed by Harrison & Sons, Ltd. Panes of 50. Designed by Rashid-ud Din.

1967, Mar. 17 Photo. *Perf. 14x14½*

168 A89 5c **dark blue & multi** *(2,445,955)*	.25	.25
First day cover		1.00
Inscription block of 4	.40	—
169 A89 11c **brown lake & multi** *(2,011,004)*	.25	.25
First day cover		1.00
First day cover, #168-169		1.00
Inscription block of 4	.90	—

First day covers of Nos. 168-169 total 390,499.

"Peace" — A90

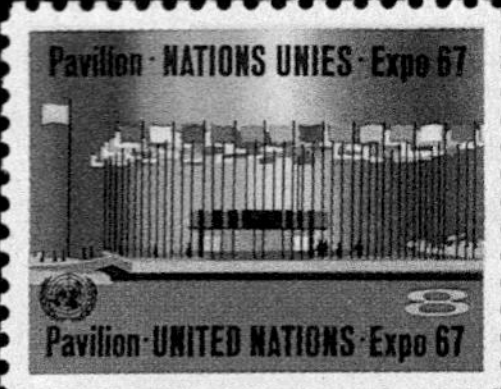

UN Pavilion, EXPO '67 — A91

Designs: 5c, Justice. 10c, Fraternity. 15c, Truth.

EXPO '67, International Exhibition, Montreal, Apr. 28-Oct. 27, 1967.

Under special agreement with the Canadian Government Nos. 170-174 were valid for postage only on mail posted at the UN pavilion during the Fair. The denominations are expressed in Canadian currency.

Printed by British American Bank Note Co., Ltd., Ottawa. The 8c was designed by Olav S. Mathiesen after a photograph by Michael Drummond. The others were adapted by Ole S. Hamann from reliefs by Ernest Cormier on doors of General Assembly Hall, presented to UN by Canada.

1967, Apr. 28 Engr. & Litho. *Perf. 11*

170 A90 4c **red & red brown** *(2,464,813)*	.25	.25
First day cover		1.00
Inscription block of 4	.40	—
171 A90 5c **blue & red brown** *(2,177,073)*	.25	.25
First day cover		1.00
Inscription block of 4	.40	—

Litho.

172 A91 8c **multicolored** *(2,285,440)*	.25	.25
First day cover		1.00
Inscription block of 4	.50	—

Engr. and Litho.

173 A90 10c **green & red brown** *(1,955,352)*	.25	.25
First day cover		1.00
Inscription block of 4	.80	—
174 A90 15c **dark brown & red brown** *(1,899,185)*	.25	.25
First day cover		1.00
First day cover, #170-174		1.00
Inscription block of 4	.85	
Nos. 170-174 (5)	1.25	1.25

First day covers of Nos. 170-174 total 901,625.

Luggage Tags and UN Emblem A92

Issued to publicize International Tourist Year, 1967.

Printed by Government Printing Office, Berlin. Panes of 50. Designed by David Dewhurst.

1967, June 19 Litho. *Perf. 14*

175 A92 5c **reddish brown & multi** *(2,593,782)*	.25	.25
First day cover		1.00
Inscription block of 4	.40	—
176 A92 15c **ultramarine & multi** *(1,940,457)*	.25	.25
First day cover		1.00
First day cover, #175-176		1.00
Inscription block of 4	1.00	—

First day covers of Nos. 175-176 total 382,886.

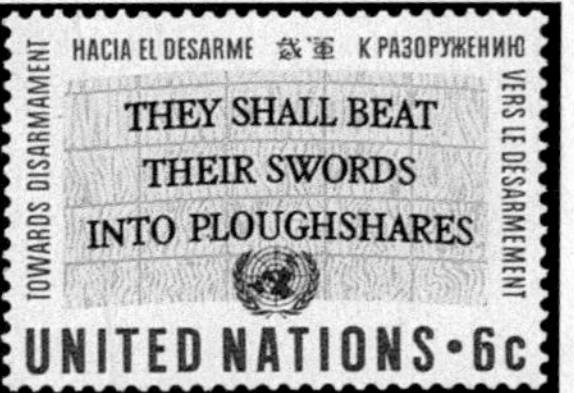

Quotation from Isaiah 2:4 — A93

Design: 13c, French inscription.

Issued to publicize the UN General Assembly's resolutions on general and complete disarmament and for suspension of nuclear and thermonuclear tests.

Printed by Heraclio Fournier S.A., Spain. Panes of 50. Designed by Ole Hamann.

1967, Oct. 24 **Photo.** ***Perf. 14***

177 A93 6c **ultramarine, yellow, gray & brown** *(2,462,277)* .25 .25
First day cover 1.00
Inscription block of 4 .50 —
178 A93 13c **magenta, yellow, gray & brown** *(2,055,541)* .25 .25
First day cover 1.00
First day cover, #177-178 1.00
Inscription block of 4 1.00 —

First day covers of Nos. 177-178 total 403,414.

Art at UN Issue

Miniature Sheet

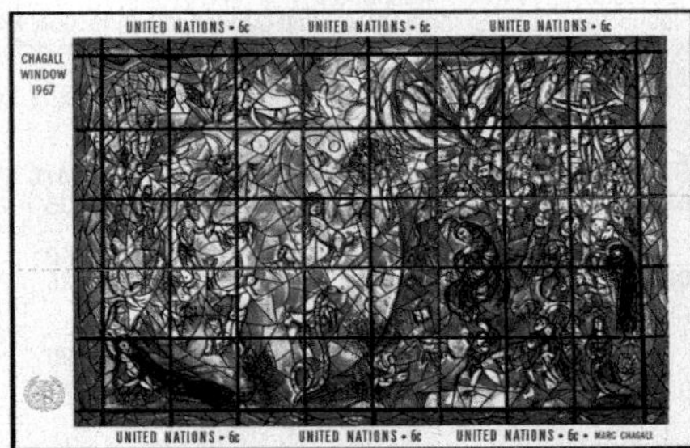

Stained Glass Memorial Window by Marc Chagall, at UN Headquarters — A94

"The Kiss of Peace" by Marc Chagall — A95

Printed by Joh. Enschede and Sons, Netherlands. No. 180 issued in panes of 50. Design adapted by Ole Hamann from photograph by Hans Lippmann.

Sizes: a, 41x46mm. b, 24x46mm. c, 41x33½mm. d, 36x33½mm. e, 29x33½mm. f, 41½x47mm.

1967, Nov. 17 **Litho.** ***Rouletted 9***

179 A94 6c Sheet of 6, #a.-f. *(3,178,656)* .40 .40
First day cover 1.00

Perf. 13x13½

180 A95 6c **multicolored** *(3,438,497)* .25 .25
First day cover 1.00
Inscription block of 4 .50 —

No. 179 contains six 6c stamps, each rouletted on 3 sides, imperf. on fourth side. Size: 124x80mm. On Nos. 179a-179c, "United Nations 6c" appears at top; on Nos. 179d-179f, at bottom. No. 179f includes name "Marc Chagall."

First day covers of Nos. 179-180 total 617,225.

Globe and Major UN Organs — A96

Design: 13c, French inscriptions.

Issued to honor the United Nations Secretariat.

Printed by Courvoisier, S. A., Switzerland. Panes of 50. Designed by Rashid-ud Din.

1968, Jan. 16 **Photo.** ***Perf. 11½***

181 A96 6c **multicolored** *(2,772,965)* .25 .25
First day cover 1.00
Inscription block of 4 .50 —
182 A96 13c **multicolored** *(2,461,992)* .25 .25
First day cover 1.00
First day cover, #181-182 1.00
Inscription block of 4 1.00 —

First day covers of Nos. 181-182 total 411,119.

Art at UN Issue

Statue by Henrik Starcke — A97

The 6c is part of the "Art at the UN" series. The 75c belongs to the regular definitive series. The teakwood Starcke statue, which stands in the Trusteeship Council Chamber, represents mankind's search for freedom and happiness.

Printed by Courvoisier, S.A., Switzerland. Panes of 50.

1968, Mar. 1 **Photo.** ***Perf. 11½***

183 A97 6c **blue & multi** *(2,537,320)* .25 .25
First day cover 1.00
Inscription block of 4 .50 —
184 A97 75c **rose lake & multi** *(2,300,000)* 1.10 .90
First day cover 1.25
First day cover, #183-184 5.00
Inscription block of 4 5.00 —

First day covers of Nos. 183-184 total 413,286.

See UN Offices in Geneva No. 13.

Factories and Chart — A98

Design: 13c, French inscription ("ONUDI," etc.).

Issued to publicize the UN Industrial Development Organization.

Printed by Canadian Bank Note Co., Ltd., Ottawa. Panes of 50. Designed by Ole Hamann.

1968, Apr. 18 **Litho.** ***Perf. 12***

185 A98 6c **greenish blue, lt greenish blue, black & dull claret** *(2,439,656)* .25 .25
First day cover 1.00
Inscription block of 4 .50 —
186 A98 13c **dull red brown, light red brown, black & ultra** *(2,192,453)* .25 .25
First day cover 1.00
First day cover, #185-186 1.00
Inscription block of 4 .80 —

First day covers of Nos. 185-186 total 396,447.

UN Headquarters — A99

Printed by Aspioti Elka-Chrome Mines, Ltd., Athens. Panes of 50. Designed by Olav S. Mathiesen.

1968, May 31 **Litho.** ***Perf. 12x13½***

187 A99 6c **green, blue, black & gray** *(4,000,000)* .25 .25
First day cover *(241,179)* 1.00
Inscription block of 4 .50 —

Radarscope and Globe — A100

Design: 20c, French inscription.

Issued to publicize World Weather Watch, a new weather system directed by the World Meteorological Organization.

Printed by the Government Printing Bureau, Tokyo. Designed by George A. Gundersen and George Fanais, Canada.

1968, Sept. 19 **Photo.** ***Perf. 13x13½***

188 A100 6c **green, black, ocher, red & blue** *(2,245,078)* .25 .25
First day cover 1.00
Inscription block of 4 .50 —
189 A100 20c **lilac, black, ocher, red & blue** *(2,069,966)* .30 .25
First day cover 1.00
First day cover, #188-189 1.00
Inscription block of 4 1.40 —

First day covers of Nos. 188-189 total 620,510.

Human Rights Flame — A101

Design: 13c, French inscription.

Issued for International Human Rights Year, 1968.

Printed by Harrison & Sons, Ltd., England. Designed by Robert Perrot, France.

1968, Nov. 22 **Photo.; Foil Embossed** ***Perf. 12½***

190 A101 6c **bright blue, deep ultra & gold** *(2,394,235)* .25 .25
First day cover 1.00
Inscription block of 4 .50 —
191 A101 13c **rose red, dark red & gold** *(2,284,838)* .25 .25
First day cover 1.00
First day cover, #190-191 1.00
Inscription block of 4 .90 —

First day covers of Nos. 190-191 total 519,012.

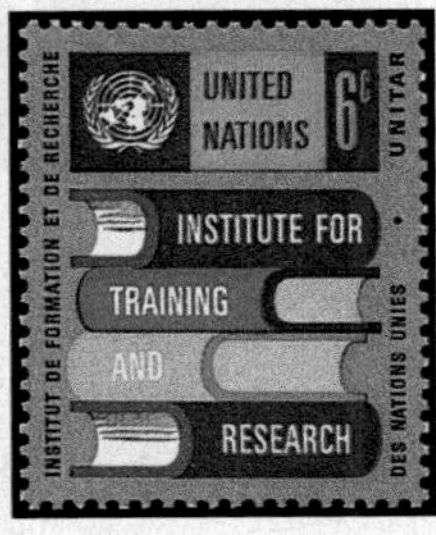

Books and UN Emblem — A102

Design: 13c, French inscription in center, denomination panel at bottom.

United Nations Institute for Training and Research (UNITAR).

Printed by the Government Printing Bureau, Tokyo. Panes of 50. Designed by Olav S. Mathiesen.

1969, Feb. 10 **Litho.** ***Perf. 13½***

192 A102 6c **yellow green & multi** *(2,436,559)* .25 .25
First day cover 1.00
Inscription block of 4 .40 —
193 A102 13c **bluish lilac & multi** *(1,935,151)* .25 .25
First day cover 1.00
First day cover, #192-193 1.00
Inscription block of 4 1.00 —

First day covers of Nos. 192-193 total 439,606.

UN Building, Santiago, Chile A103

Design: 15c, Spanish inscription.

The UN Building in Santiago, Chile, is the seat of the UN Economic Commission for Latin America and of the Latin American Institute for Economic and Social Planning.

Printed by Government Printing Office, Berlin. Panes of 50. Design by Ole Hamann, adapted from a photograph.

1969, Mar. 14 Litho. *Perf. 14*

194 A103 6c **light blue, violet blue & light green** *(2,543,992)* .25 .25
First day cover 1.00
Inscription block of 4 .40 —

195 A103 15c **pink, cream & red brown** *(2,030,733)* .25 .25
First day cover 1.00
First day cover, #194-195 1.00
Inscription block of 4 1.00 —

First day covers of Nos. 194-195 total 398,227.

"UN" and UN Emblem — A104

Printed by Government Printing Bureau, Tokyo. Panes of 50. Designed by Leszek Holdanowicz and Marek Freudenreich, Poland.

1969, Mar. 14 Photo. *Perf. 13½*

196 A104 13c **bright blue, black & gold** *(4,000,000)* .25 .25
First day cover *(177,793)* 1.00
Inscription block of 4 1.00 —

See UN Offices in Geneva No. 7.

UN Emblem and Scales of — A105

Design: 13c, French inscription.

20th anniversary session of the UN International Law Commission.

Printed by Courvoisier S.A., Switzerland. Panes of 50. Designed by Robert Perrot, France.

Granite Paper

1969, Apr. 21 Photo. *Perf. 11½*

197 A105 6c **bright green, ultra & gold** *(2,501,492)* .25 .25
First day cover 1.00
Inscription block of 4 .50 —

198 A105 13c **crimson, lilac & gold** *(1,966,994)* .25 .25
First day cover 1.00
First day cover, #197-198 1.00
Inscription block of 4 .90 —

First day covers of Nos. 197-198 total 439,324.

Allegory of Labor, Emblems of UN and ILO — A106

Design: 20c, French inscription.

Printed by Government Printing Bureau, Tokyo. Panes of 50. Designed by Nejat M. Gur, Turkey.

Issued to publicize "Labor and Development" and to commemorate the 50th anniversary of the International Labor Organization.

1969, June 5 Photo. *Perf. 13*

199 A106 6c **blue, deep blue, yellow & gold** *(2,078,381)* .25 .25
First day cover 1.00
Inscription block of 4 .50 —

200 A106 20c **orange vermilion, magenta, yellow & gold** *(1,751,100)* .25 .25
First day cover 1.00
First day cover, #199-200 1.00
Inscription block of 4 1.40 —

First day covers of Nos. 199-200 total 514,155.

Art at UN Issue

Ostrich, Tunisian Mosaic, 3rd Century — A107

Design: 13c, Pheasant; French inscription.

The mosaic "The Four Seasons and the Genius of the Year" was found at Haidra, Tunisia. It is now at the Delegates' North Lounge, UN Headquarters, New York.

Printed by Heraclio Fournier, S. A., Spain. Panes of 50. Designed by Olav S. Mathiesen.

1969, Nov. 21 Photo. *Perf. 14*

201 A107 6c **blue & multi** *(2,280,702)* .25 .25
First day cover 1.00
Inscription block of 4 .40 —

202 A107 13c **red & multi** *(1,918,554)* .25 .25
First day cover 1.00
First day cover, #201-202 1.00
Inscription block of 4 1.00 —

First day covers of Nos. 201-202 total 612,981.

Art at UN Issue

Peace Bell, Gift of Japanese — A108

Design: 25c, French inscription.

The Peace Bell was a gift of the people of Japan in 1954, cast from donated coins and metals. It is housed in a Japanese cypress structure at UN Headquarters, New York.

Printed by Government Printing Bureau, Tokyo. Panes of 50. Designed by Ole Hamann.

1970, Mar. 13 Photo. *Perf. 13½x13*

203 A108 6c **violet blue & multi** *(2,604,253)* .25 .25
First day cover 1.00
Inscription block of 4 .50 —

204 A108 25c **claret & multi** *(2,090,185)* .30 .25
First day cover 1.00
First day cover, #203-204 1.00
Inscription block of 4 1.50 —

First day covers of Nos. 203-204 total 502,384.

Mekong River, Power Lines and Map of Mekong Delta — A109

Design: 13c, French inscription.

Issued to publicize the Lower Mekong Basin Development project under UN auspices.

Printed by Heraclio Fournier, S.A., Spain. Panes of 50. Designed by Ole Hamann.

1970, Mar. 13 *Perf. 14*

205 A109 6c **dark blue & multi** *(2,207,309)* .25 .25
First day cover 1.00
Inscription block of 4 .40 —

206 A109 13c **deep plum & multi** *(1,889,023)* .25 .25
First day cover 1.00
First day cover, #205-206 1.00
Inscription block of 4 1.00 —

First day covers of Nos. 205-206 total 522,218.

"Fight Cancer" — A110

Design: 13c, French inscription.

Issued to publicize the fight against cancer in connection with the 10th International Cancer Congress of the International Union Against Cancer, Houston, Texas, May 22-29.

Printed by Government Printing Office, Berlin. Panes of 50. Designed by Leonard Mitchell.

1970, May 22 Litho. *Perf. 14*

207 A110 6c **blue & black** *(2,157,742)* .25 .25
First day cover 1.00
Inscription block of 4 .40 —

208 A110 13c **olive & black** *(1,824,714)* .25 .25
First day cover 1.00
First day cover, #207-208 1.00
Inscription block of 4 .90 —

First day covers of Nos. 207-208 total 444,449.

UN Emblem and Olive Branch — A111

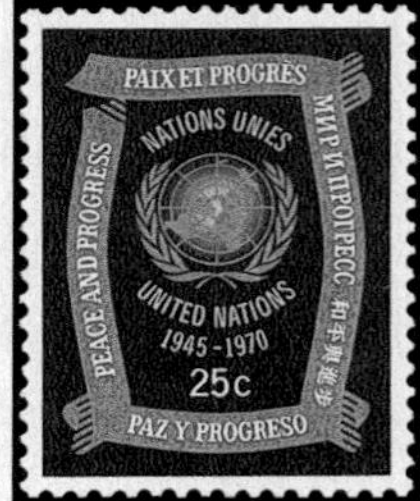

UN Emblem — A112

Design: 13c, French inscription.

25th anniv. of the UN. First day covers were postmarked at UN Headquarters, NY, and at San Francisco.

Printed by Courvoisier, S.A., Switzerland. Designed by Ole Hamann and Olav S. Mathiesen (souvenir sheet).

1970, June 26 Photo. *Perf. 11½*

209 A111 6c **red, gold, dark & light blue** *(2,365,229)* .25 .25
First day cover 1.00
Inscription block of 4 .40 —

210 A111 13c **dark blue, gold, green & red** *(1,861,613)* .25 .25
First day cover 1.00
Inscription block of 4 .90 —

Perf. 12½

211 A112 25c **dark blue, gold & light blue** *(1,844,669)* .35 .25
First day cover 1.00
First day cover, #209-211 1.25
Inscription block of 4 1.50 —
Nos. 209-211 (3) .85 .75

Souvenir Sheet

Imperf

212 Sheet of 3 *(1,923,639)* .80 .80
a. A111 6c **red, gold & multicolored** .25 .25
b. A111 13c **violet blue, gold & multi** .25 .25
c. A112 25c **violet blue, gold & light blue** .30 .30
First day cover 1.00

No. 212 contains 3 imperf. stamps, gold border and violet blue marginal inscription. Size: 94½x78mm.

First day covers of Nos. 209-212 total: New York, 846,389; San Francisco, 471,100.

Scales, Olive Branch and Symbol of Progress — A113

Design: 13c, French inscription.
Issued to publicize "Peace, Justice and Progress" in connection with the 25th anniversary of the United Nations.
Printed by Government Printing Bureau, Tokyo. Panes of 50. Designed by Ole Hamann.

1970, Nov. 20 Photo. *Perf. 13½*

213 A113 6c **gold & multi** *(1,921,441)* .25 .25
First day cover 1.00
Inscription block of 4 .50 —
214 A113 13c **silver & multi** *(1,663,669)* .25 .25
First day cover 1.00
First day cover, #213-214 1.00
Inscription block of 4 1.00 —

First day covers of Nos. 213-214 total 521,419.

Sea Bed, School of Fish and Underwater Research — A114

Issued to publicize peaceful uses of the sea bed.
Printed by Setelipaino, Finland. Panes of 50. Designed by Pentti Rahikainen, Finland.

1971, Jan. 25 Photo. & Engr. *Perf. 13*

215 A114 6c **blue & multi** *(2,354,179)* .25 .25
First day cover *(405,554)* 1.00
Inscription block of 4 .50 —

See UN Offices in Geneva No. 15.

Refugees, Sculpture by Kaare K. Nygaard — A115

International support for refugees.
Printed by Joh. Enschede and Sons, Netherlands. Panes of 50. Designed by Dr. Kaare K. Nygaard and Martin J. Weber.

1971, Mar. 2 Litho. *Perf. 13x12½*

216 A115 6c **brown, ocher & black** *(2,247,232)* .25 .25
First day cover 1.00
Inscription block of 4 .40 —
217 A115 13c **ultramarine, greenish blue & black** *(1,890,048)* .25 .25
First day cover 1.00
First day cover, #216-217 1.00
Inscription block of 4 1.00 —

First day covers of Nos. 216-217 total 564,785.
See UN Offices in Geneva No. 16.

Wheat and Globe — A116

Publicizing the UN World Food Program.
Printed by Heraclio Fournier, S.A., Spain. Panes of 50. Designed by Olav S. Mathiesen.

1971, Apr. 13 Photo. *Perf. 14*

218 A116 13c **red & multicolored** *(1,968,542)* .25 .25
First day cover *(409,404)* 1.00
Inscription block of 4 1.00 —

See UN Offices in Geneva No. 17.

UPU Headquarters, Bern — A117

Opening of new Universal Postal Union Headquarters, Bern.
Printed by Courvoisier, S.A. Panes of 50. Designed by Olav S. Mathiesen.

1971, May 28 Photo. *Perf. 11½*

219 A117 20c **brown orange & multi** *(1,857,841)* .30 .25
First day cover *(375,119)* 1.00
Inscription block of 4 1.30 —

See UN Offices in Geneva No. 18.

A118

"Eliminate Racial Discrimination" A119

International Year Against Racial Discrimination.
Printed by Government Printing Bureau, Tokyo. Panes of 50. Designers: Daniel Gonzague (8c); Ole Hamann (13c).

1971, Sept. 21 Photo. *Perf. 13½*

220 A118 8c **yellow green & multi** *(2,324,349)* .25 .25
First day cover 1.00
Inscription block of 4 .40 —
221 A119 13c **blue & multi** *(1,852,093)* .25 .25
First day cover 1.00
First day cover, #220-221 1.00
Inscription block of 4 1.00 —

First day covers of Nos. 220-221 total 461,103.
See UN Offices in Geneva Nos. 19-20.

UN Headquarters, New York — A120

UN Emblem and Symbolic Flags — A121

No. 222 printed by Heraclio Fournier, S.A., Spain. No. 223 printed by Government Printing Bureau, Tokyo. Panes of 50. Designers: O. S. Mathiesen (8c); Robert Perrot (60c).

1971, Oct. 22 Photo. *Perf. 13½*

222 A120 8c **violet blue & multi** *(5,600,000)* .25 .25
First day cover 1.00
Inscription block of 4 .60 —

Perf. 13

223 A121 60c **ultra & multi** *(3,500,000)+* .80 .80
First day cover 1.25
First day cover, #222-223 2.50
Inscription block of 4 3.75 —

First day covers of Nos. 222-223 total 336,013.

Maia, by Pablo Picasso — A122

To publicize the UN International School.
Printed by Courvoisier, S.A. Panes of 50. Designed by Ole Hamann.

1971, Nov. 19 Photo. *Perf. 11½*

224 A122 8c **olive & multi** *(2,668,214)* .25 .25
First day cover 1.00
Inscription block of 4 .50 —
225 A122 21c **ultra & multi** *(2,040,754)* .25 .25
First day cover 1.00
First day cover, #224-225 1.50
Inscription block of 4 1.50 —

First day covers of Nos. 224-225 total 579,594.
See UN Offices in Geneva No. 21.

Letter Changing Hands A123

Printed by Bundesdruckerei, Berlin. Panes of 50. Designed by Olav S. Mathiesen.

1972, Jan. 5 Litho. *Perf. 14*

226 A123 95c **carmine & multi** *(2,000,000)* 1.30 1.10
First day cover *(188,193)* 1.25
Inscription block of 4 5.75 —

"No More Nuclear Weapons" A124

To promote non-proliferation of nuclear weapons.
Printed by Heraclio Fournier, S. A., Spain. Panes of 50. Designed by Arne Johnson, Norway.

1972, Feb. 14 Photo. *Perf. 13½x14*

227 A124 8c **dull rose, black, blue & gray** *(2,311,515)* .25 .25
First day cover *(268,789)* 1.00
Inscription block of 4 .60 —

See UN Offices in Geneva No. 23.

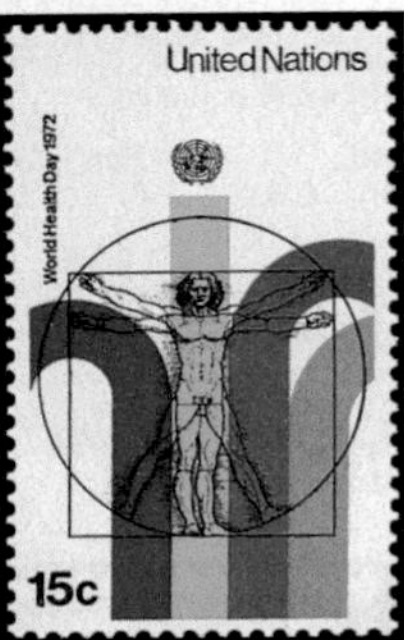

Proportions of Man, by Leonardo da Vinci — A125

World Health Day, Apr. 7.
Printed by Setelipaino, Finland. Panes of 50. Designed by George Hamori.

1972, Apr. 7 Litho. & Engr. *Perf. 13x13½*

228 A125 15c **black & multi** *(1,788,962)* .25 .25
First day cover *(322,724)* 1.00
Inscription block of 4 1.00 —

See UN Offices in Geneva No. 24.

"Human Environment" — A126

UN Conf. on Human Environment, Stockholm, June 5-16, 1972.
Printed by Joh. Enschede and Sons, Netherlands. Panes of 50. Designed by Robert Perrot.

1972, June 5 Litho. & Embossed *Perf. 12½x14*

229 A126 8c **red, buff, green & blue** *(2,124,604)* .25 .25
First day cover 1.00
Inscription block of 4 .50 —
230 A126 15c **blue green, buff, green & blue** *(1,589,943)* .25 .25
First day cover 1.00
First day cover, #229-230 1.00
Inscription block of 4 1.10 —

First day covers of Nos. 229-230 total 437,222.
See UN Offices in Geneva Nos. 25-26.

"Europe" and UN Emblem — A127

Economic Commission for Europe, 25th anniversary.
Printed by Government Printing Bureau, Tokyo. Panes of 50. Designed by Angel Medina Medina.

1972, Sept. 11 Litho. *Perf. 13x13½*

231 A127 21c **yellow brown & multi** *(1,748,675)* .30 .30
First day cover *(271,128)* 1.00
Inscription block of 4 1.50 —

See UN Offices in Geneva No. 27.

Art at UN Issue

The Five Continents by José Maria Sert — A128

Design shows part of ceiling mural of the Council Hall, Palais des Nations, Geneva. It depicts the five continents joining in space.
Printed by Courvoisier, S. A. Panes of 50. Designed by Ole Hamann.

1972, Nov. 17 Photo. *Perf. 12x12½*

232 A128 8c **gold, brown & golden brown** *(2,573,478)* .25 .25
First day cover 1.00
Inscription block of 4 .50 —
233 A128 15c **gold, blue green & brown** *(1,768,432)* .25 .25
First day cover 1.00
First day cover, #232-233 1.00
Inscription block of 4 1.10 —

First day covers of Nos. 232-233 total 589,817.
See UN Offices in Geneva Nos. 28-29.

Olive Branch and Broken Sword — A129

Disarmament Decade, 1970-79.
Printed by Ajans-Turk, Turkey. Panes of 50. Designed by Kurt Plowitz.

1973, Mar. 9 Litho. *Perf. 13½x13*

234 A129 8c **blue & multi** *(2,272,716)* .25 .25
First day cover 1.00
Inscription block of 4 .50 —
235 A129 15c **lilac rose & multi** *(1,643,712)* .25 .25
First day cover 1.00
First day cover, #234-235 1.00
Inscription block of 4 1.40 —

First day covers of Nos. 234-235 total 548,336.
See UN Offices in Geneva Nos. 30-31.

Poppy Capsule and Skull — A130

Fight against drug abuse.
Printed by Heraclio Fournier, S.A., Spain. Panes of 50. Designed by George Hamori.

1973, Apr. 13 Photo. *Perf. 13½*

236 A130 8c **deep orange & multi** *(1,846,780)* .25 .25
First day cover 1.00
Inscription block of 4 .50 —
237 A130 15c **pink & multi** *(1,466,806)* .25 .25
First day cover 1.00
First day cover, #236-237 1.00
Inscription block of 4 1.40 —

First day covers of Nos. 236-237 total 394,468.
See UN Offices in Geneva No. 32.

Honeycomb A131

5th anniversary of the United Nations Volunteer Program.
Printed by Heraclio Fournier, S.A., Spain. Panes of 50. Designed by Courvoisier, S.A.

1973, May 25 Photo. *Perf. 14*

238 A131 8c **olive bister & multi** *(1,868,176)* .25 .25
First day cover 1.00
Inscription block of 4 .50 —
239 A131 21c **gray blue & multi** *(1,530,114)* .30 .30
First day cover 1.00
First day cover, #238-239 1.00
Inscription block of 4 1.50 —

First day covers of Nos. 238-239 total 396,517.
See UN Offices in Geneva No. 33.

Map of Africa with Namibia — A132

To publicize Namibia (South-West Africa) for which the UN General Assembly ended the mandate of South Africa and established the UN Council for Namibia to administer the territory until independence.
Printed by Heraclio Fournier, S.A., Spain. Panes of 50. Designed by George Hamori.

1973, Oct. 1 Photo. *Perf. 14*

240 A132 8c **emerald & multi** *(1,775,260)* .25 .25
First day cover 1.00
Inscription block of 4 .60 —
241 A132 15c **bright rose & multi** *(1,687,782)* .25 .25
First day cover 1.00
First day cover, #240-241 1.00
Inscription block of 4 1.40 —

First day covers of Nos. 240-241 total 385,292.
See UN Offices in Geneva No. 34.

UN Emblem and Human Rights Flame — A133

25th anniversary of the adoption and proclamation of the Universal Declaration of Human Rights.
Printed by Government Printing Bureau, Tokyo. Panes of 50. Designed by Alfred Guerra.

1973, Nov. 16 Photo. *Perf. 13½*

242 A133 8c **deep carmine & multi** *(2,026,245)* .25 .25
First day cover 1.00
Inscription block of 4 .60 —
243 A133 21c **blue green & multi** *(1,558,201)* .25 .25
First day cover 1.00
First day cover, #242-243 1.00
Inscription block of 4 1.40 —

First day covers of Nos. 242-243 total 398,511.
See UN Offices in Geneva Nos. 35-36.

ILO Headquarters, Geneva — A134

New Headquarters of International Labor Organization.
Printed by Heraclio Fournier, S.A., Spain. Panes of 50. Designed by Henry Bencsath.

1974, Jan. 11 **Photo.** ***Perf. 14***
244 A134 10c **ultra & multi** *(1,734,423)* .25 .25
First day cover 1.00
Inscription block of 4 .75 —
245 A134 21c **blue green & multi** *(1,264,447)* .30 .25
First day cover 1.00
First day cover, #244-245 1.00
Inscription block of 4 1.50 —

First day covers of Nos. 244-245 total 282,284.
See UN Offices in Geneva Nos. 37-38.

UPU Emblem and Post Horn Encircling Globe — A135

Centenary of Universal Postal Union.
Printed by Ashton-Potter Ltd., Canada. Panes of 50. Designed by Arne Johnson.

1974, Mar. 22 **Litho.** ***Perf. 12½***
246 A135 10c **gold & multi** *(2,104,919)* .25 .25
First day cover *(342,774)* 1.00
Inscription block of 4 1.00 —

See UN Offices in Geneva Nos. 39-40.

Art at UN Issue

Peace Mural, by Candido Portinari — A136

The mural, a gift of Brazil, is in the Delegates' Lobby, General Assembly Building.
Printed by Heraclio Fournier, S.A., Spain. Panes of 50. Design adapted by Ole Hamann.

1974, May 6 **Photo.** ***Perf. 14***
247 A136 10c **gold & multi** *(1,769,342)* .25 .25
First day cover 1.00
Inscription block of 4 .75 —
248 A136 18c **ultra & multi** *(1,477,500)* .35 .30
First day cover 1.00
First day cover, #247-248 1.00
Inscription block of 4 1.40 —

First day covers of Nos. 247-248 total 271,440.
See UN Offices in Geneva Nos. 41-42.

Dove and UN Emblem — A137

UN Headquarters — A138

Globe, UN Emblem, Flags — A139

Printed by Heraclio Fournier, S.A., Spain. Panes of 50.
Designed by Nejut M. Gur (2c); Olav S. Mathiesen (10c); Henry Bencsath (18c).

1974, June 10 **Photo.** ***Perf. 14***
249 A137 2c **dark & light blue** *(6,900,000)* .25 .25
First day cover 1.00
Inscription block of 4 .25 —
250 A138 10c **multicolored** *(4,000,000)* .25 .25
First day cover 1.00
Inscription block of 4 .60 —
251 A139 18c **multicolored** *(2,300,000)* .25 .25
First day cover 1.00
First day cover, #249-251 1.00
Inscription block of 4 1.40 —
Nos. 249-251 (3) .75 .75

First day covers of Nos. 249-251 total 307,402.
+ Printing orders to Feb. 1990.

Children of the World — A140

World Population Year
Printed by Heraclio Fournier, S.A., Spain. Panes of 50. Designed by Henry Bencsath.

1974, Oct. 18 **Photo.** ***Perf. 14***
252 A140 10c **light blue & multi** *(1,762,595)* .25 .25
First day cover 1.00
Inscription block of 4 1.00 —
253 A140 18c **lilac & multi** *(1,321,574)* .35 .25
First day cover 1.00
First day cover, #252-253 1.00
Inscription block of 4 1.50 —

First day covers of Nos. 253-254 total 354,306.
See UN Offices in Geneva Nos. 43-44.

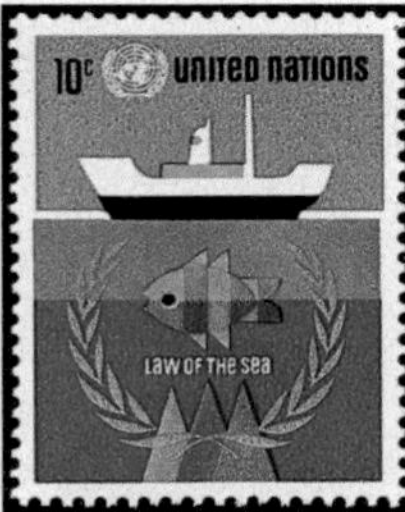

Law of the Sea — A141

Declaration of UN General Assembly that the sea bed is common heritage of mankind, reserved for peaceful purposes.
Printed by Heraclio Fournier, S.A., Spain. Panes of 50. Designed by Asher Kalderon.

1974, Nov. 22 **Photo.** ***Perf. 14***
254 A141 10c **green & multi** *(1,621,328)* .25 .25
First day cover 1.00
Inscription block of 4 .75 —
255 A141 26c **orange red & multi** *(1,293,084)* .35 .30
First day cover 1.00
First day cover, #254-255 1.00
Inscription block of 4 1.60 —

First day covers of Nos. 254-255 total 280,686.
See UN Offices in Geneva No. 45.

Satellite and Globe — A142

Peaceful uses (meteorology, industry, fishing, communications) of outer space.
Printed by Setelipaino, Finland. Panes of 50. Designed by Henry Bencsath.

1975, Mar. 14 **Litho.** ***Perf. 13***
256 A142 10c **multicolored** *(1,681,115)* .25 .25
First day cover 1.00
Inscription block of 4 .75 —
257 A142 26c **multicolored** *(1,463,130)* .35 .30
First day cover 1.00
First day cover, #256-257 1.00
Inscription block of 4 1.50 —

First day covers of Nos. 256-257 total 330,316.
See UN Offices in Geneva Nos. 46-47.

Equality Between Men and Women — A143

International Women's Year
Printed by Questa Colour Security Printers, Ltd., England. Panes of 50. Designed by Asher Kalderon and Esther Kurti.

1975, May 9 **Litho.** ***Perf. 15***
258 A143 10c **multicolored** *(1,402,542)* .25 .25
First day cover 1.00
Inscription block of 4 .75 —
259 A143 18c **multicolored** *(1,182,321)* .35 .30
First day cover 1.00
First day cover, #258-259 1.00
Inscription block of 4 1.50 —

First day covers of Nos. 258-259 total 285,466.
See UN Offices in Geneva Nos. 48-49.

UN Flag and "XXX" — A144

30th anniversary of the United Nations.
Printed by Ashton-Potter, Ltd., Canada. Nos. 260-261 panes of 50. Stamps designed by Asher Calderon, sheets by Olav S. Mathiesen.

1975, June 26 **Litho.** ***Perf. 13***
260 A144 10c **olive bister & multi** *(1,904,545)* .25 .25
First day cover 1.00
Inscription block of 4 .75 —
261 A144 26c **purple & multi** *(1,547,766)* .40 .35
First day cover 1.00
First day cover, #260-261 1.00
Inscription block of 4 1.90 —

Souvenir Sheet

Imperf

262 Sheet of 2 *(1,196,578)* .60 .50
a. A144 10c **olive bister & multicolored** .25 .25
b. A144 26c **purple & multicolored** .35 .25
First day cover 1.00

No. 262 has blue and bister margin with inscription and UN emblem.
First day covers of Nos. 260-262 total: New York 477,912; San Francisco, 237,159.
See Offices in Geneva Nos. 50-52.

Hand Reaching up over Map of Africa and Namibia — A145

"Namibia-United Nations direct responsibility." See note after No. 241.
Printed by Heraclio Fournier S.A., Spain. Panes of 50. Designed by Henry Bencsath.

1975, Sept. 22 **Photo.** ***Perf. 13½***
263 A145 10c **multicolored** *(1,354,374)* .25 .25
First day cover 1.00
Inscription block of 4 .75 —
264 A145 18c **multicolored** *(1,243,157)* .30 .30
First day cover 1.00
First day cover, #263-264 1.00
Inscription block of 4 1.50 —

First day covers of Nos. 263-264 total 281,631.
See UN Offices in Geneva Nos. 53-54.

Wild Rose Growing from Barbed Wire — A146

United Nations Peace-keeping Operations
Printed by Setelipaino, Finland. Panes of 50. Designed by Mrs. Eeva Oivo.

1975, Nov. 21 **Engr.** ***Perf. 12½***
265 A146 13c **ultramarine** *(1,628,039)* .25 .25
First day cover 1.00
Inscription block of 4 1.00 —
266 A146 26c **rose carmine** *(1,195,580)* .40 .40
First day cover 1.00
First day cover, #265-266 1.00
Inscription block of 4 1.90 —

First day covers of Nos. 265-266 total 303,711.
See UN Offices in Geneva Nos. 55-56.

Symbolic Flags Forming Dove — A147

UN Emblem — A149

People of All Races A148

United Nations Flag — A150

Dove and Rainbow — A151

Printed by Ashton-Potter, Ltd., Canada (3c, 4c, 30c, 50c), and Questa Colour Security Printers, Ltd., England (9c). Panes of 50.
Designed by Waldemar Andrzesewski (3c); Arne Johnson (4c); George Hamori (9c, 30c); Arthur Congdon (50c).

1976 **Litho.** ***Perf. 13x13½, 13½x13***
267 A147 3c **multicolored** *(4,000,000)* .25 .25
First day cover 1.00
Inscription block of 4 .40 —
268 A148 4c **multicolored** *(4,000,000)* .25 .25
First day cover 1.00
Inscription block of 4 .50 —

Photo.
Perf. 14

269 A149 9c **multicolored** *(3,270,000)+* .25 .25
First day cover 1.00
Inscription block of 4 .70 —

Litho.
Perf. 13x13½

270 A150 30c **blue, emerald & black** *(2,500,000)* .35 .35
First day cover 2.00
Inscription block of 4 1.90 —
271 A151 50c **yellow green & multi** *(2,000,000)* .65 .65
First day cover 1.00
First day cover, #267-268, 270-271 1.50
Inscription block of 4 3.50 —
Nos. 267-271 (5) 1.75 1.75

Issue dates: 3c, 4c, 30c, 50c, Jan. 6; 9c, Nov. 19.
First day covers of Nos. 267-268, 270-271 total 355,165; of Nos. 269 and 280 total 366,556.
See UN Offices in Vienna No. 8.

Interlocking Bands and UN Emblem — A152

World Federation of United Nations Associations.
Printed by Heraclio Fournier, S.A., Spain. Panes of 50. Designed by George Hamori.

1976, Mar. 12 **Photo.** ***Perf. 14***
272 A152 13c **blue, green & black** *(1,331,556)* .25 .25
First day cover 1.00
Inscription block of 4 .80 —
273 A152 26c **green & multi** *(1,050,145)* .35 .30
First day cover 1.00
First day cover, #272-273 1.00
Inscription block of 4 1.60 —

First day covers of Nos. 272-273 total 300,775.
See UN Offices in Geneva No. 57.

Cargo, Globe and Graph — A153

UN Conference on Trade and Development (UNCTAD), Nairobi, Kenya, May 1976.
Printed by Courvoisier, S.A. Panes of 50. Designed by Henry Bencsath.

1976, Apr. 23 **Photo.** ***Perf. 11½***
274 A153 13c **deep magenta & multi** *(1,317,900)* .25 .25
First day cover 1.00
Inscription block of 4 .80 —
275 A153 31c **dull blue & multi** *(1,216,959)* .40 .30
First day cover 1.00
First day cover, #274-275 1.00
Inscription block of 4 1.90 —

First day covers of Nos. 274-275 total 234,657.
See UN Offices in Geneva No. 58.

Houses Around Globe — A154

Habitat, UN Conference on Human Settlements, Vancouver, Canada, May 31-June 11.
Printed by Heraclio Fournier, S.A., Spain. Panes of 50. Designed by Eliezer Weishoff.

1976, May 28 **Photo.** ***Perf. 14***
276 A154 13c **red brown & multi** *(1,346,589)* .25 .25
First day cover 1.00
Inscription block of 4 .75 —
277 A154 25c **green & multi** *(1,057,924)* .40 .30
First day cover 1.00
First day cover, #276-277 1.00
Inscription block of 4 1.75 —

First day covers of Nos. 276-277 total 232,754.
See UN Offices in Geneva Nos. 59-60.

Magnifying Glass, Sheet of Stamps, UN Emblem — A155

United Nations Postal Administration, 25th anniversary.
Printed by Courvoisier, S.A. Designed by Henry Bencsath.

1976, Oct. 8 **Photo.** ***Perf. 11½***
278 A155 13c **blue & multi** *(1,996,309)* .25 .25
First day cover 1.00
Inscription block of 4 .90 —
279 A155 31c **green & multi** *(1,767,465)* 1.40 1.40
First day cover 1.50
First day cover, #278-279 2.00
Inscription block of 4 6.25 —
Panes of 20, #278-279 26.00 —

First day covers of Nos. 278-279 total 366,784.
Upper margin blocks are inscribed "XXV ANNIVERSARY"; lower margin blocks "UNITED NATIONS POSTAL ADMINISTRATION."
See UN Offices in Geneva Nos. 61-62.

Grain — A156

World Food Council.
Printed by Questa Colour Security Printers, Ltd., England. Panes of 50. Designed by Eliezer Weishoff.

1976, Nov. 19 **Litho.** ***Perf. 14½***
280 A156 13c **multicolored** *(1,515,573)* .25 .25
First day cover 1.00
Inscription block of 4 1.10 —

See UN Offices in Geneva No. 63.

WIPO Headquarters, Geneva — A157

World Intellectual Property Organization (WIPO).
Printed by Heraclio Fournier, S. A., Spain. Panes of 50. Designed by Eliezer Weishoff.

1977, Mar. 11 **Photo.** ***Perf. 14***
281 A157 13c **citron & multi** *(1,330,272)* .25 .25
First day cover 1.00
Inscription block of 4 .75 —
282 A157 31c **bright green & multi** *(1,115,406)* .45 .35
First day cover 1.00
First day cover, #281-282 1.00
Inscription block of 4 2.00 —

First day covers of Nos. 281-282 total 364,184.
See UN Offices in Geneva No. 64.

Drops of Water Falling into Funnel — A158

UN Water Conference, Mar del Plata, Argentina, Mar. 14-25.
Printed by Government Printing Bureau, Tokyo. Panes of 50.
Designed by Elio Tomei.

1977, Apr. 22 Photo. *Perf. 13½x13*

283 A158 13c **yellow & multi** *(1,317,536)* .25 .25
First day cover 1.00
Inscription block of 4 .75 —
284 A158 25c **salmon & multi** *(1,077,424)* .40 .35
First day cover 1.00
First day cover, #283-284 1.00
Inscription block of 4 2.00 —

First day covers of Nos. 283-284 total 321,585.
See UN Offices in Geneva Nos. 65-66.

Burning Fuse Severed — A159

UN Security Council.
Printed by Heraclio Fournier, S.A., Spain. Panes of 50.
Designed by Witold Janowski and Marek Freudenreich.

1977, May 27 Photo. *Perf. 14*

285 A159 13c **purple & multi** *(1,321,527)* .25 .25
First day cover 1.00
Inscription block of 4 .75 —
286 A159 31c **dark blue & multi** *(1,137,195)* .45 .30
First day cover 1.00
First day cover, #285-286 1.00
Inscription block of 4 2.00 —

First day covers of Nos. 285-286 total 309,610.
See UN Offices in Geneva Nos. 67-68.

"Combat Racism" — A160

Fight against racial discrimination.
Printed by Setelipaino, Finland. Panes of 50. Designed by Bruno K. Wiese.

1977, Sept. 19 Litho. *Perf. 13½x13*

287 A160 13c **black & yellow** *(1,195,739)* .25 .25
First day cover 1.00
Inscription block of 4 .75 —
288 A160 25c **black & vermilion** *(1,074,639)* .40 .30
First day cover 1.00
First day cover, #287-288 1.00
Inscription block of 4 1.75 —

First day covers of Nos. 287-288 total 356,193.
See UN Offices in Geneva Nos. 60-70.

Atom, Grain, Fruit and Factory — A161

Peaceful uses of atomic energy.
Printed by Heraclio Fournier, S.A., Spain. Panes of 50.
Designed by Henry Bencsath.

1977, Nov. 18 Photo. *Perf. 14*

289 A161 13c **yellow bister & multi** *(1,316,473)* .25 .25
First day cover 1.00
Inscription block of 4 .75 —
290 A161 18c **dull green & multi** *(1,072,246)* .30 .25
First day cover 1.00
First day cover, #289-290 1.00
Inscription block of 4 1.40 —

First day covers of Nos. 289-290 total 325,348.
See UN Offices in Geneva Nos. 71-72.

Opening Words of UN Charter — A162

"Live Together in Peace" — A163

People of the World — A164

Printed by Questa Colour Security Printers, United Kingdom. Panes of 50. Designed by Salahattin Kanidinc (1c); Elio Tomei (25c); Paula Schmidt ($1).

1978, Jan. 27 Litho. *Perf. 14½*

291 A162 1c **gold, brown & red** *(4,800,000)+* .25 .25
First day cover 1.00
Inscription block of 4 .20 —
292 A163 25c **multicolored** *(3,000,000)+* .35 .30
First day cover 1.00
Inscription block of 4 1.40 —
293 A164 $1 **multicolored** *(3,400,000)+* 1.25 1.25
First day cover 1.00
First day cover, #291-293 1.75
Inscription block of 4 5.25 —
Nos. 291-293 (3) 1.85 1.80

+ Printing orders to Sept. 1989.
First day covers of Nos. 291-293 total 264,782.
See UN Offices in Geneva No. 73.

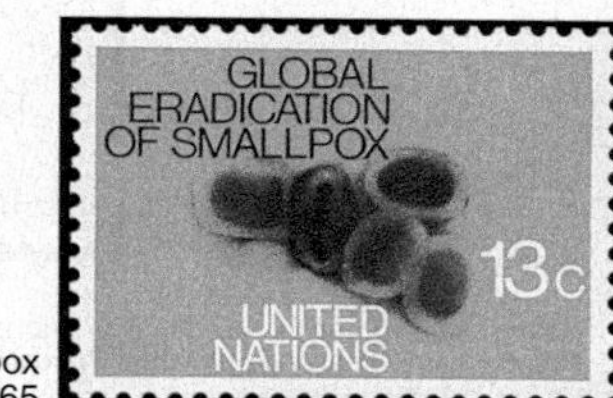

Smallpox Virus — A165

Global eradication of smallpox.
Printed by Courvoisier, S.A. Panes of 50. Designed by Herbert Auchli.

1978, Mar. 31 Photo. *Perf. 12x11½*

294 A165 13c **rose & black** *(1,188,239)* .25 .25
First day cover 1.00
Inscription block of 4 .75 —
295 A165 31c **blue & black** *(1,058,688)* .40 .40
First day cover 1.00
First day cover, #294-295 1.25
Inscription block of 4 1.75 —

First day covers of Nos. 294-295 total 306,626.
See UN Offices in Geneva Nos. 74-75.

Open Handcuff — A166

Liberation, justice and cooperation for Namibia.
Printed by Government Printing Office, Austria. Panes of 50.
Designed by Cafiro Tomei.

1978, May 5 Photo. *Perf. 12*

296 A166 13c **multicolored** *(1,203,079)* .25 .25
First day cover 1.00
Inscription block of 4 .75 —
297 A166 18c **multicolored** *(1,066,738)* .30 .25
First day cover 1.00
First day cover, #296-297 1.00
Inscription block of 4 1.40 —

First day covers of Nos. 296-297 total 324,471.
See UN Offices in Geneva No. 76.

Multicolored Bands and Clouds — A167

International Civil Aviation Organization for "Safety in the Air."
Printed by Heraclio Fournier, S.A., Spain. Panes of 50.
Designed by Cemalettin Mutver.

1978, June 12 Photo. *Perf. 14*

298 A167 13c **multicolored** *(1,295,617)* .25 .25
First day cover 1.00
Inscription block of 4 .75 —
299 A167 25c **multicolored** *(1,101,256)* .35 .30
First day cover 1.00
First day cover, #298-299 1.00
Inscription block of 4 1.50 —

First day covers of Nos. 298-299 total 329,995.
See UN Offices in Geneva Nos. 77-78.

General Assembly — A168

Printed by Government Printing Bureau, Tokyo. Panes of 50.
Designed by Jozsef Vertel.

1978, Sept. 15 Photo. *Perf. 13½*

300 A168 13c **multicolored** *(1,093,005)* .25 .25
First day cover 1.00
Inscription block of 4 .75 —
301 A168 18c **multicolored** *(1,065,934)* .35 .30
First day cover 1.00
First day cover, #300-301 1.00
Inscription block of 4 1.50 —

First day covers of Nos. 300-301 total 283,220.
See UN Offices in Geneva Nos. 79-80.

Hemispheres as Cogwheels
A169

Technical Cooperation Among Developing Countries Conference, Buenos Aires, Argentina, Sept. 1978.

Printed by Heraclio Fournier, S.A., Spain. Panes of 50. Designed by Simon Keter and David Pesach.

1978, Nov. 17 **Photo.** ***Perf. 14***

302 A169 13c **multicolored** *(1,251,272)* .25 .25
First day cover 1.00
Inscription block of 4 1.00 —
303 A169 31c **multicolored** *(1,185,213)* .50 .40
First day cover 1.00
First day cover, #302-303 1.25
Inscription block of 4 2.25 —

First day covers of Nos. 302-303 total 272,556.
See UN Offices in Geneva No. 81.

Hand Holding Olive Branch — A170

Various Races Tree — A171

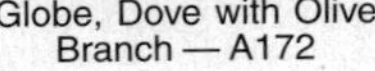

Globe, Dove with Olive Branch — A172

Birds and Globe — A173

Printed by Heraclio Fournier, S.A., Spain. Panes of 50. Designed by Raymon Müller (5c); Alrun Fricke (14c); Eliezer Weishoff (15c); Young Sun Hahn (20c).

1979, Jan. 19 **Photo.** ***Perf. 14***

304 A170 5c **multicolored** *(3,000,000)* .25 .25
First day cover 1.00
Inscription block of 4 .40 —
305 A171 14c **multicolored** *(3,000,000)+* .25 .25
First day cover 1.00
Inscription block of 4 .80 —
306 A172 15c **multicolored** *(3,000,000)+* .25 .25
First day cover 1.00
Inscription block of 4 1.25 —
307 A173 20c **multicolored** *(3,400,000)+* .30 .25
First day cover 1.00
First day cover, #304-307 2.25
Inscription block of 4 1.40 —
Nos. 304-307 (4) 1.05 1.00

First day covers of Nos. 304-307 total 295,927.
\+ Printing orders to June 1990.

UNDRO Against Fire and Water — A174

Office of the UN Disaster Relief Coordinator (UNDRO).
Printed by Heraclio Fournier, S.A., Spain. Panes of 50. Designed by Gidon Sagi.

1979, Mar. 9 **Photo.** ***Perf. 14***

308 A174 15c **multicolored** *(1,448,600)* .25 .25
First day cover 1.00
Inscription block of 4 .85 —
309 A174 20c **multicolored** *(1,126,295)* .35 .30
First day cover 1.00
First day cover, #308-309 1.25
Inscription block of 4 1.50 —

First day covers of Nos. 308-309 total 266,694.
See UN Offices in Geneva Nos. 82-83.

Child and IYC Emblem — A175

International Year of the Child.
Printed by Heraclio Fournier, S.A., Spain. Panes of 20 (5x4). Designed by Helena Matuszewska (15c) and Krystyna Tarkowska-Gruszecka (31c).

1979, May 4 **Photo.** ***Perf. 14***

310 A175 15c **multicolored** *(2,290,329)* .25 .25
First day cover 1.00
Inscription block of 4 1.00 —
311 A175 31c **multicolored** *(2,192,136)* .35 .35
First day cover 1.00
First day cover, #310-311 2.25
Inscription block of 4 1.50 —
Panes of 20, #310-311 12.00

First day covers of Nos. 310-311 total 380,022.
See UN Offices in Geneva Nos. 84-85.

Map of Namibia, Olive Branch — A176

For a free and independent Namibia.
Printed by Ashton-Potter Ltd., Canada. Panes of 50. Designed by Eliezer Weishoff.

1979, Oct. 5 **Litho.** ***Perf. 13½***

312 A176 15c **multicolored** *(1,470,231)* .25 .25
First day cover 1.00
Inscription block of 4 .75 —
313 A176 31c **multicolored** *(1,355,323)* .30 .35
First day cover 1.00
First day cover, #312-313 1.25
Inscription block of 4 1.50 —

First day covers of Nos. 312-313 total 250,371.
See UN Offices in Geneva No. 86.

Scales and Sword of Justice — A177

International Court of Justice, The Hague, Netherlands.
Printed by Setelipaino, Finland. Panes of 50. Designed by Henning Simon.

1979, Nov. 9 **Litho.** ***Perf. 13x13½***

314 A177 15c **multicolored** *(1,244,972)* .25 .25
First day cover 1.00
Inscription block of 4 .75 —
315 A177 20c **multicolored** *(1,084,483)* .30 .35
First day cover 1.00
First day cover, #314-315 1.25
Inscription block of 4 1.50 —

First day covers of Nos. 314-315 total 322,901.
See UN Offices in Geneva Nos. 87-88.

Graph of Economic Trends — A178

Key — A179

New International Economic Order.
Printed by Questa Colour Security Printers, United Kingdom. Panes of 50. Designed by Cemalettin Mutver (15c), George Hamori (31c)

1980, Jan. 11 **Litho.** ***Perf. 15x14½***

316 A178 15c **multicolored** *(1,163,801)* .25 .25
First day cover 1.00
Inscription block of 4 .85 —
317 A179 31c **multicolored** *(1,103,560)* .45 .35
First day cover 1.00
First day cover, #316-317 1.00
Inscription block of 4 2.00 —

First day covers of Nos. 316-317 total 211,945.
See UN Offices in Geneva No. 89; Vienna No. 7.

Women's Year Emblem — A180

United Nations Decade for Women.
Printed by Questa Colour Security Printers, United Kingdom. Panes of 50. Designed by Susanne Rottenfusser.

1980, Mar. 7 **Litho.** ***Perf. 14½x15***

318 A180 15c **multicolored** *(1,409,350)* .25 .25
First day cover 1.00
Inscription block of 4 .75 —
319 A180 20c **multicolored** *(1,182,016)* .30 .25
First day cover 1.00
First day cover, #318-319 1.00
Inscription block of 4 1.50 —

First day covers of Nos. 318-319 total 289,314.
See UN Offices in Geneva Nos. 90-91; Vienna Nos. 9-10.

UN Emblem and "UN" on Helmet — A181

Arrows and UN Emblem — A182

United Nations Peace-keeping Operations.
Printed by Joh. Enschede en Zonen, Netherlands. Panes of 50. Designed by Bruno K. Wiese (15c), James Gardiner (31c)

1980, May 16 **Litho.** ***Perf. 14x13***

320 A181 15c **blue & black** *(1,245,521)* .25 .25
First day cover 1.00
Inscription block of 4 .90 —
321 A182 31c **multicolored** *(1,191,009)* .40 .40
First day cover 1.00
First day cover, #320-321 1.00
Inscription block of 4 2.10 —

First day covers of Nos. 320-321 total 208,442.
See UN Offices in Geneva No. 92; Vienna No. 11.

"35" and Flags — A183

Globe and Laurel — A184

35th Anniversary of the United Nations.
Printed by Ashton-Potter Ltd, Canada. Nos. 322-323, panes of 50. Designed by Cemalettin Matver (15c), Mian Mohammad Saeed (31c).

1980, June 26 **Litho.** ***Perf. 13x13½***

322 A183 15c **multicolored** *(1,554,514)* .25 .25
First day cover 1.00
Inscription block of 4 .85 —
323 A184 31c **multicolored** *(1,389,606)* .40 .35
First day cover 1.00
First day cover, #322-323 1.00
Inscription block of 4 1.90 —

Souvenir Sheet

Imperf

324 Sheet of 2 *(1,215,505)* .65 .65
a. A183 15c **multicolored** .25 .25
b. A184 31c **multicolored** .40 .40
First day cover 1.00

First day covers of Nos. 322-324 total: New York, 369,345; San Francisco, 203,701.
See UN Offices in Geneva Nos. 93-95; Vienna Nos. 12-14.

Flag of Turkey — A185

Printed by Courvoisier, S.A., Switzerland. Panes of 16. Designed by Ole Hamann.
Each pane contains 4 blocks of 4 (Nos. 325-328, 329-332, 333-336, 337-340). A se-tenant block of 4 designs centers each pane.

1980, Sept. 26 **Litho.** ***Perf. 12***
Granite Paper

325 A185 15c shown *(3,490,725)* .25 .25
326 A185 15c Luxembourg *(3,490,725)* .25 .25
327 A185 15c Fiji *(3,490,725)* .25 .25
328 A185 15c Viet Nam *(3,490,725)* .25 .25
a. Se-tenant block of 4, #325-328 1.10 1.10
329 A185 15c Guinea *(3,442,633)* .25 .25
330 A185 15c Surinam *(3,442,633)* .25 .25
331 A185 15c Bangladesh *(3,442,633)* .25 .25
332 A185 15c Mali *(3,442,633)* .25 .25
a. Se-tenant block of 4, #329-332 1.10 1.10
333 A185 15c Yugoslavia *(3,416,292)* .25 .25
334 A185 15c France *(3,416,292)* .25 .25
335 A185 15c Venezuela *(3,416,292)* .25 .25
336 A185 15c El Salvador *(3,416,292)* .25 .25
a. Se-tenant block of 4, #333-336 1.10 1.10
337 A185 15c Madagascar *(3,442,497)* .25 .25
338 A185 15c Cameroon *(3,442,497)* .25 .25
339 A185 15c Rwanda *(3,442,497)* .25 .25
340 A185 15c Hungary *(3,442,497)* .25 .25
a. Se-tenant block of 4, #337-340 1.10 1.10
First day covers of Nos. 325-340, each .35
Set of 4 diff. panes of 16 7.00
Nos. 325-340 (16) 4.00 4.00

First day covers of Nos. 325-340 total 6,145,595.
See Nos. 350-365, 374-389, 399-414, 425-440, 450-465, 477-492, 499-514, 528-543, 554-569, 690-697, 719-726, 744-751, 795-802, 921-924, 1063-1066, 1083-1086, 1150-1157, 1179-1186.

Symbolic Flowers — A186

Symbols of Progress — A187

Printed by Ashton-Potter Ltd., Canada. Panes of 50. Designed by Eliezer Weishoff (15c), Dietman Kowall (20c).

1980, Nov. 21 **Litho.** ***Perf. 13½x13***

341 A186 15c **multicolored** *(1,192,165)* .25 .25
First day cover 1.00
Inscription block of 4 1.00 —
342 A187 20c **multicolored** *(1,011,382)* .40 .35
First day cover 1.00
First day cover, #341-342 1.00
Inscription block of 4 1.75 —

First day covers of Nos. 341-342 total 232,149.
See UN Offices in Geneva, Nos. 96-97; Vienna Nos. 15-16.

Inalienable Rights of the Palestinian People — A188

Printed by Courvoisier S.A., Switzerland. Panes of 50. Designed by David Dewhurst.

1981, Jan. 30 **Photo.** ***Perf. 12x11½***

343 A188 15c **multicolored** *(993,489)* .30 .25
First day cover *(127,187)* 1.00
Inscription block of 4 1.25 —

See UN Offices in Geneva No. 98; Vienna No. 17.

Interlocking Puzzle Pieces — A189

Stylized Person — A190

International Year of the Disabled.
Printed by Heraclio Fournier S.A., Spain. Panes of 50. Designed by Sophia Van Heeswijk (20c) and G.P. Van der Hyde (35c).

1981, Mar. 6 **Photo.** ***Perf. 14***

344 A189 20c **multicolored** *(1,218,371)* .25 .25
First day cover 1.00
Inscription block of 4 1.10 —
345 A190 35c **black & orange** *(1,107,298)* .40 .45
First day cover 1.00
First day cover, #344-345 1.25
Inscription block of 4 2.00 —

First day covers of Nos. 344-345 total 204,891.
See UN Offices in Geneva Nos. 99-100; Vienna Nos. 18-19.

Art at UN Issue

Desislava and Sebastocrator Kaloyan, Bulgarian Mural, 1259, Boyana Church, Sofia — A191

Printed by Courvoisier. Panes of 50. Designed by Ole Hamann.

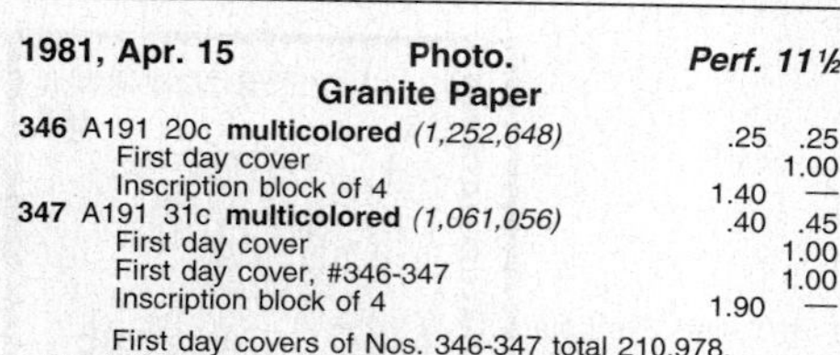

1981, Apr. 15 **Photo.** ***Perf. 11½***
Granite Paper

346 A191 20c **multicolored** *(1,252,648)* .25 .25
First day cover 1.00
Inscription block of 4 1.40 —
347 A191 31c **multicolored** *(1,061,056)* .40 .45
First day cover 1.00
First day cover, #346-347 1.00
Inscription block of 4 1.90 —

First day covers of Nos. 346-347 total 210,978.
See UN Offices in Geneva No. 101; Vienna No. 20.

Solar Energy — A192

Conference Emblem — A193

Conference on New and Renewable Sources of Energy, Nairobi, Aug. 10-21.
Printed by Setelipaino, Finland. Panes of 50. Designed by Ulrike Dreyer (20c); Robert Perrot (40c).

1981, May 29 **Litho.** ***Perf. 13***

348 A192 20c **multicolored** *(1,132,877)* .25 .25
First day cover 1.00
Inscription block of 4 1.00 —
349 A193 40c **multicolored** *(1,158,319)* .50 .50
First day cover 1.00
First day cover, #348-349 1.25
Inscription block of 4 2.25 —

First day covers of Nos. 348-349 total 240,205.
See UN Offices in Geneva No. 102; Vienna No. 21.

Flag Type of 1980

Printed by Courvoisier, S.A., Switzerland. Panes of 16. Designed by Ole Hamann.
Each pane contains 4 blocks of 4 (Nos. 350-353, 354-357, 358-361, 362-365). A se-tenant block of 4 designs centers each pane.

1981, Sept. 25 **Granite Paper** **Litho.**

350 A185 20c Djibouti *(2,342,224)* .25 .25
351 A185 20c Sri Lanka *(2,342,224)* .25 .25
352 A185 20c Bolivia *(2,342,224)* .25 .25
353 A185 20c Equatorial Guinea *(2,342,224)* .25 .25
a. Se-tenant block of 4, #350-353 1.50 1.50
354 A185 20c Malta *(2,360,297)* .25 .25
355 A185 20c Czechoslovakia *(2,360,297)* .25 .25
356 A185 20c Thailand *(2,360,297)* .25 .25
357 A185 20c Trinidad & Tobago *(2,360,297)* .25 .25
a. Se-tenant block of 4, #354-357 1.50 1.50
358 A185 20c Ukrainian SSR *(2,344,755)* .25 .25
359 A185 20c Kuwait *(2,344,755)* .25 .25
360 A185 20c Sudan *(2,344,755)* .25 .25
361 A185 20c Egypt *(2,344,755)* .25 .25
a. Se-tenant block of 4, #358-361 1.50 1.50
362 A185 20c US *(2,450,537)* .25 .25
363 A185 20c Singapore *(2,450,537)* .25 .25
364 A185 20c Panama *(2,450,537)* .25 .25
365 A185 20c Costa Rica *(2,450,537)* .25 .25
a. Se-tenant block of 4, #362-365 1.50 1.50
First day covers, #350-365, each .40
Set of 4 diff. panes of 16 10.00
Nos. 350-365 (16) 4.00 4.00

First day covers of Nos. 350-365 total 3,961,237.

Seedling and Tree Cross-section A194

"10" and Symbols of Progress — A195

United Nations Volunteers Program, 10th anniv.
Printed by Walsall Security Printers, Ltd., United Kingdom. Pane of 50. Designed by Gabriele Nussgen (18c), Angel Medina Medina (28c).

1981, Nov. 13 **Litho.**

366 A194 18c **multicolored** *(1,246,833)* .25 .25
First day cover 1.00
Inscription block of 4 1.25 —
367 A195 28c **multicolored** *(1,282,868)* .55 .55
First day cover 1.00
First day cover, #366-367 1.00
Inscription block of 4 2.50 —

First day covers of Nos. 366-367 total 221,106.
See UN Offices in Geneva Nos. 103-104; Vienna Nos. 22-23.

A196

A197

A198

Respect for Human Rights (17c), Independence of Colonial Countries and People (28c), Second Disarmament Decade (40c).
Printed by Courvoisier, S.A., Switzerland. Panes of 50. Designed by Rolf Christianson (17c); George Hamori (28c); Marek Kwiatkowski (40c).

1982, Jan. 22 ***Perf. 11½x12***

368 A196 17c **multicolored** *(3,000,000)+* .25 .25
First day cover 1.00
Inscription block of 4 1.10 —
369 A197 28c **multicolored** *(3,000,000)+* .45 .40
First day cover 1.00
Inscription block of 4 2.00 —
370 A198 40c **multicolored** *(3,000,000)* .75 .70
First day cover 1.00
First day cover, #368-370 1.25
Inscription block of 4 3.25 —
Nos. 368-370 (3) 1.45 1.35

First day covers of Nos. 368-370 total 243,073.

Sun and Hand Holding Seedling — A199

Sun, Plant Land and Water — A200

10th Anniversary of United Nations Environment Program.

Printed by Joh. Enschede En Zonen, Netherlands. Panes of 50. Designed by Philine Hartert (20c); Peer-Ulrich Bremer (40c).

1982, Mar. 19 **Litho.** ***Perf. 13½x13***

371 A199 20c **multicolored** *(1,017,117)* .25 .25
First day cover 1.00
Inscription block of 4 1.10 —
372 A200 40c **multicolored** *(884,798)* .65 .65
First day cover 1.00
First day cover, #371-372 1.25
Inscription block of 4 3.00 —

First day covers of Nos. 371-372 total 288,721.
See UN Offices in Geneva Nos. 107-108; Vienna Nos. 25-26.

UN Emblem and Olive Branch in Outer Space — A201

Exploration and Peaceful Uses of Outer Space.
Printed By Enschede. Panes of 50. Designed by Wiktor C. Nerwinski.

1982, June 11 **Litho.** ***Perf. 13x13½***

373 A201 20c **multicolored** *(1,083,426)* .45 .45
First day cover *(156,965)* 1.00
Inscription block of 4 2.00 —

See UN Offices in Geneva Nos. 109-110; Vienna No. 27.

Flag Type of 1980

Printed by Courvoisier. Panes of 16. Designed by Ole Hamann.
Issued in 4 panes of 16. Each pane contains 4 blocks of four (Nos. 374-377, 378-381, 383-385, 386-389). A se-tenant block of 4 designs centers each pane.

1982, Sept. 24 **Litho.** ***Perf. 12***
Granite Paper

374 A185 20c Austria *(2,314,006)* .25 .25
375 A185 20c Malaysia *(2,314,006)* .25 .25
376 A185 20c Seychelles *(2,314,006)* .25 .25
377 A185 20c Ireland *(2,314,006)* .25 .25
a. Se-tenant block of 4, #374-377 1.50 1.50
378 A185 20c Mozambique *(2,300,958)* .25 .25
379 A185 20c Albania *(2,300,958)* .25 .25
380 A185 20c Dominica *(2,300,958)* .25 .25
381 A185 20c Solomon Islnads *(2,300,958)* .25 .25
a. Se-tenant block of 4, #378-381 1.50 1.50
382 A185 20c Philippines *(2,288,589)* .25 .25
383 A185 20c Swaziland *(2,288,589)* .25 .25
384 A185 20c Nicaragua *(2,288,589)* .25 .25
385 A185 20c Burma *(2,288,589)* .25 .25
a. Se-tenant block of 4, #382-385 1.50 1.50
386 A185 20c Cape Verde *(2,285,848)* .25 .25
387 A185 20c Guyana *(2,285,848)* .25 .25
388 A185 20c Belgium *(2,285,848)* .25 .25
389 A185 20c Nigeria *(2,285,848)* .25 .25
a. Se-tenant block of 4, #386-389 1.50 1.50
First day cover, #374-389, each .40
Set of 4 diff. panes of 16 9.00
Nos. 374-389 (16) 4.00 4.00

First day covers of Nos. 374-389 total 3,202,744.

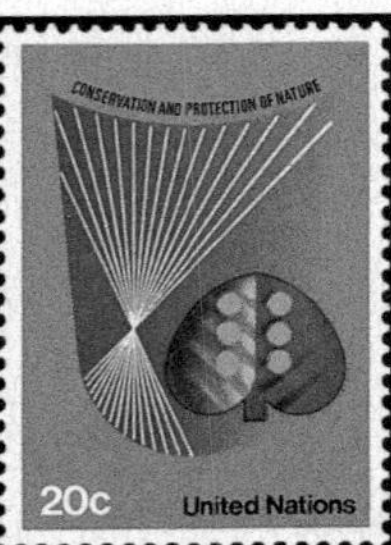

Conservation and Protection of Nature — A202

Printed by Fournier. Panes of 50. Designed by Hamori.

1982, Nov. 19 **Photo.** ***Perf. 14***

390 A202 20c Leaf *(1,110,027)* .30 .30
First day cover 1.00
margin block of 4, inscription 1.60 —
391 A202 28c Butterfly *(848,772)* .55 .50
First day cover 1.00
First day cover, #390-391 1.00
Inscription block of 4 2.25 —

First day covers of Nos. 390-391 total 214,148.
See UN Offices in Geneva Nos. 111-112; Vienna Nos. 28-29.

A203

A204

World Communications Year
Printed by Walsall. Panes of 50. Designed by Hanns Lohrer (A203) and Lorena Berengo (A204).

1983, Jan. 28 **Litho.** ***Perf. 13***

392 A203 20c **multicolored** *(1,282,079)* .25 .25
First day cover 1.00
Inscription block of 4 1.00 —
393 A204 40c **multicolored** *(931,903)* .65 .65
First day cover 1.00
First day cover, #392-393 1.00
Inscription block of 4 3.25 —

First day covers of Nos. 392-393 total 183,499.
See UN Offices in Geneva No. 113; Vienna No. 30.

A205

A206

Safety at Sea.
Printed by Questa. Panes of 50. Designed by Jean-Marie Lenfant (A205), Ari Ron (A206).

1983, Mar. 18 **Litho.** ***Perf. 14½***

394 A205 20c **multicolored** *(1,252,456)* .25 .25
First day cover 1.00
Inscription block of 4 1.25 —
395 A206 37c **multicolored** *(939,910)* .60 .55
First day cover 1.00
First day cover, #394-395 1.00
Inscription block of 4 2.50 —

First day covers of Nos. 394-395 total 199,962.
See UN Offices in Geneva Nos. 114-115; Vienna Nos. 31-32.

World Food Program — A207

Printed by Government Printers Bureau, Japan. Designed by Marek Kwiatkowski.

1983, Apr. 22 **Engr.** ***Perf. 13½***

396 A207 20c **rose lake** *(1,238,997)* .35 .35
First day cover *(180,704)* 1.00
Inscription block of 4 1.50 —

See UN Offices in Geneva No. 116; Vienna Nos. 33-34.

A208

A209

UN Conference on Trade and Development.

Printed by Carl Uberreuter Druck and Verlag M. Salzer, Austria. Panes of 50. Designed by Dietmar Braklow (A208), Gabriel Genz (A209).

1983, June 6 Litho. *Perf. 14*

397 A208 20c **multicolored** *(1,060,053)* .25 .35
First day cover 1.00
Inscription block of 4 1.25 —
398 A209 28c **multicolored** *(948,981)* .70 .65
First day cover 1.25
First day cover, #397-398 1.40
Inscription block of 4 2.75 —

First day covers of Nos. 397-398 total 200,131.
See UN Offices in Geneva Nos. 117-118; Vienna Nos. 35-36.

Flag Type of 1980

Printed by Courvoisier. Panes of 16. Designed by Ole Hamann.

Issued in 4 panes of 16. Each pane contains 4 blocks of four (Nos. 399-402, 403-406, 407-410, 411-414). A se-tenant block of 4 designs centers each pane.

1983, Sept. 23 Photo. *Perf. 12*
Granite Paper

399 A185 20c Great Britain *(2,490,599)* .25 .25
400 A185 20c Barbados *(2,490,599)* .25 .25
401 A185 20c Nepal *(2,490,599)* .25 .25
402 A185 20c Israel *(2,490,599)* .25 .25
a. Se-tenant block of 4, #399-402 1.50 1.50
403 A185 20c Malawi *(2,483,010)* .25 .25
404 A185 20c Byelorussian SSR *(2,483,010)* .25 .25
405 A185 20c Jamaica *(2,483,010)* .25 .25
406 A185 20c Kenya *(2,483,010)* .25 .25
a. Se-tenant block of 4, #403-406 1.50 1.80
407 A185 20c People's Republic of China *(2,474,140)* .25 .25
408 A185 20c Peru *(2,474,140)* .25 .25
409 A185 20c Bulgaria *(2,474,140)* .25 .25
410 A185 20c Canada *(2,474,140)* .25 .25
a. Se-tenant block of 4, #407-410 1.50 1.80
411 A185 20c Somalia *(2,482,070)* .25 .25
412 A185 20c Senegal *(2,482,070)* .25 .25
413 A185 20c Brazil *(2,482,070)* .25 .25
414 A185 20c Sweden *(2,482,070)* .25 .25
a. Se-tenant block of 4, #411-414 1.50 1.80
First day cover, #399-414, each .40
Set of 4 diff. panes of 16 10.00
Nos. 399-414 (16) 4.00 4.00

First day covers of Nos. 399-414 total 2,214,134.

Window Right — A210

Peace Treaty with Nature — A211

35th Anniversary of the Universal Declaration of Human Rights.

Printed by Government Printing Office, Austria. Panes of 16 (4x4). Designed by Friedensreich Hundertwasser, Austria.

1983, Dec. 9 Photo. & Engr. *Perf. 13½*

415 A210 20c **multicolored** *(1,591,102)* .30 .25
First day cover 1.00
Inscription block of 4 1.25 —
416 A211 40c **multicolored** *(1,566,789)* .70 .65
First day cover 1.25
First day cover, #415-416 1.40
Inscription block of 4 3.00 —
Panes of 16, #415-416 16.00

First day covers of Nos. 415-416 total 176,269.
See UN Offices in Geneva Nos. 119-120; Vienna Nos. 37-38.

International Conference on Population — A212

Printed by Bundesdruckerei, Federal Republic of Germany. Panes of 50. Designed by Marina Langer-Rosa and Helmut Langer, Federal Republic of Germany.

1984, Feb. 3 Litho. *Perf. 14*

417 A212 20c **multicolored** *(905,320)* .25 .25
First day cover 1.00
Inscription block of 4 1.40 —
418 A212 40c **multicolored** *(717,084)* .65 .65
First day cover 1.00
First day cover, #417-418 1.00
Inscription block of 4 2.50 —

First day covers of Nos. 417-418 total 118,068.
See UN Offices in Geneva No. 121; Vienna No. 39.

Tractor Plowing A213

Rice Paddy A214

World Food Day, Oct. 16

Printed by Walsall Security Printers, Ltd., United Kingdom. Panes of 50. Designed by Adth Vanooijen, Netherlands.

1984, Mar. 15 Litho. *Perf. 14½*

419 A213 20c **multicolored** *(853,641)* .30 .30
First day cover 1.00
Inscription block of 4 1.50 —
420 A214 40c **multicolored** *(727,165)* .60 .60
First day cover 1.00
First day cover, #419-420 1.40
Inscription block of 4 2.50 —

First day covers of Nos. 419-420 total 116,009.
See UN Offices in Geneva Nos. 122-123; Vienna Nos. 40-41.

Grand Canyon — A215

Ancient City of Polonnaruwa, Sri Lanka — A216

World Heritage

Printed by Harrison and Sons, United Kingdom. Panes of 50. Designs adapted by Rocco J. Callari, U.S., and Thomas Lee, China.

1984, Apr. 18 Litho. *Perf. 14*

421 A215 20c **multicolored** *(814,316)* .25 .25
First day cover 1.00
Inscription block of 4 1.00 —
422 A216 50c **multicolored** *(579,136)* .75 .75
First day cover 1.00
First day cover, #421-422 1.10
Inscription block of 4 3.50 —

First day covers of Nos. 421-422 total 112,036.
See Nos. 601-602, UN Offices in Geneva Nos. 124-125, 211-212; Vienna Nos. 42-43, 125-126.

A217

A218

Future for Refugees

Printed by Courvoisier. Panes of 50. Designed by Hans Erni, Switzerland.

1984, May 29 Photo. *Perf. 11½*

423 A217 20c **multicolored** *(956,743)* .30 .30
First day cover 1.00
Inscription block of 4 1.25 —
424 A218 50c **multicolored** *(729,036)* .90 .90
First day cover 1.00
First day cover, #423-424 1.25
Inscription block of 4 4.00 —

First day covers of Nos. 423-424 total 115,789.
See UN Offices in Geneva Nos. 126-127; Vienna Nos. 44-45.

Flag Type of 1980

Printed by Courvoisier. Panes of 16. Designed by Ole Hamann.

Issued in 4 panes of 16. Each pane contains 4 blocks of four (Nos. 425-428, 429-432, 433-436, 437-440). A se-tenant block of 4 designs centers each pane.

1984, Sept. 21 Photo. *Perf. 12*
Granite Paper

425 A185 20c Burundi *(1,941,471)* .25 .25
426 A185 20c Pakistan *(1,941,471)* .25 .25
427 A185 20c Benin *(1,941,471)* .25 .25
428 A185 20c Italy *(1,941,471)* .25 .25
a. Se-tenant block of 4, #425-428 1.80 1.80
429 A185 20c Tanzania *(1,969,051)* .25 .25
430 A185 20c United Arab Emirates *(1,969,051)* .25 .25
431 A185 20c Ecuador *(1,969,051)* .25 .25
432 A185 20c Bahamas *(1,969,051)* .25 .25
a. Se-tenant block of 4, #429-432 1.80 1.80
433 A185 20c Poland *(2,001,091)* .25 .25
434 A185 20c Papua New Guinea *(2,001,091)* .25 .25
435 A185 20c Uruguay *(2,001,091)* .25 .25
436 A185 20c Chile *(2,001,091)* .25 .25
a. Se-tenant block of 4, #433-436 1.80 1.80
437 A185 20c Paraguay *(1,969,875)* .25 .25
438 A185 20c Bhutan *(1,969,875)* .25 .25
439 A185 20c Central African Republic *(1,969,875)* .25 .25

440 A185 20c Australia *(1,969,875)* .25 .25
a. Se-tenant block of 4, #437-440 1.80 1.80
First day cover, #425-440, each .50
Set of 4 diff. panes of 16 15.00
Nos. 425-440 (16) 4.00 4.00

First day covers of Nos. 425-440 total 1,914,972.

International Youth Year — A219

Printed by Waddingtons Ltd., United Kingdom. Panes of 50. Designed by Ramon Mueller, Federal Republic of Germany.

1984, Nov. 15 Litho. *Perf. 13½*
441 A219 20c **multicolored** *(884,962)* .35 .35
First day cover 1.00
Inscription block of 4 1.25 —
442 A219 35c **multicolored** *(740,023)* .85 .85
First day cover 1.00
First day cover, #441-442 1.25
Inscription block of 4 4.25 —

First day covers of Nos. 441-442 total 125,315.
See UN Offices in Geneva No. 128; Vienna Nos. 46-47.

ILO Turin Center — A220

Printed by the Government Printing Bureau, Japan. Panes of 50. Engraved by Mamoru Iwakuni and Hiroshi Ozaki, Japan.

1985, Feb. 1 Engr. *Perf. 13½*
443 A220 23c **blue** *(612,942)* .45 .45
First day cover *(76,541)* 1.00
Inscription block of 4 2.00 —

See UN Offices in Geneva Nos. 129-130; Vienna No. 48.

UN University A221

Printed by Helio Courvoiser, Switzerland. Panes of 50. Designed by Moshe Pereg, Israel, and Hinedi Geluda, Brazil.

50c, Farmer plowing, discussion group.

1985, Mar. 15 Photo. *Perf. 11½*
444 A221 50c multi *(625,043)* .95 .95
First day cover *(77,271)* 1.25
Inscription block of 4 4.25 —

See UN Offices in Geneva Nos. 131-132; Vienna No. 49.

Peoples of the World United — A222

Painting UN Emblem — A223

Printed by Carl Ueberreuter Druck and Verlag M. Salzer, Austria. Panes of 50. Designed by Fritz Henry Oerter, Federal Republic of Germany (22c), and Rimondi Rino, Italy ($3).

1985, May 10 Litho. *Perf. 14*
445 A222 22c **multicolored** *(2,000,000)+* .30 .30
First day cover 1.00
Inscription block of 4 1.25 —
446 A223 $3 **multicolored** *(2,000,000)+* 3.75 1.50
First day cover 3.50
First day cover, #445-446 5.75
Inscription block of 4 16.50 —

First day covers of Nos. 445-446 total 88,613.
See UN Offices in Geneva Nos. 133-134; Vienna Nos. 50-51.

The Corner, 1947 — A224

Alvaro Raking Hay, 1953 — A225

UN 40th anniversary. Oil paintings (details) by American artist Andrew Wyeth (b. 1917). Printed by Helio Courvoisier, Switzerland. Nos. 447-448 panes of 50. Designed by Rocco J. Callari, U.S., and Thomas Lee, China (#449).

1985, June 26 Photo. *Perf. 12 x 11½*
447 A224 22c **multicolored** *(944,960)* .35 .35
First day cover 1.00
Inscription block of 4 1.25 —
448 A225 45c **multicolored** *(680,079)* 1.00 1.00
First day cover 1.00
First day cover, #447-448 1.50
Inscription block of 4 4.00 —

Souvenir Sheet

Imperf

449 Sheet of 2 *(506,004)* 1.10 1.30
a. A224 22c **multicolored** .40 .50
b. A225 45c **multicolored** .70 .80
First day cover 1.00

First day covers of Nos. 447-449 total; New York, 210,189; San Francisco, 92,804.
See UN Offices in Geneva Nos. 135-137; Vienna Nos. 52-54.

Flag Type of 1980

Printed by Helio Courvoisier, Switzerland. Designed by Ole Hamann.
Issued in panes of 16; each contains 4 blocks of four (Nos. 450-453, 454-457, 458-461, 462-465). A se-tenant block of 4 designs is at the center of each pane.

1985, Sept. 20 Photo. *Perf. 12*
Granite Paper
450 A185 22c Grenada *(1,270,755)* .30 .30
451 A185 22c Federal Republic of Germany *(1,270,755)* .30 .30
452 A185 22c Saudi Arabia *(1,270,755)* .30 .30
453 A185 22c Mexico *(1,270,755)* .30 .30
a. Se-tenant block of 4, #450-453 2.75 3.00
454 A185 22c Uganda *(1,216,878)* .30 .30
455 A185 22c St. Thomas & Prince *(1,216,878)* .30 .30
456 A185 22c USSR *(1,216,878)* .30 .30
457 A185 22c India *(1,216,878)* .30 .30
a. Se-tenant block of 4, #454-457 2.75 3.00
458 A185 22c Liberia *(1,213,231)* .30 .30
459 A185 22c Mauritius *(1,213,231)* .30 .30
460 A185 22c Chad *(1,213,231)* .30 .30
461 A185 22c Dominican Republic *(1,213,231)* .30 .30
a. Se-tenant block of 4, #458-461 2.75 3.00
462 A185 22c Sultanate of Oman *(1,215,533)* .30 .30
463 A185 22c Ghana *(1,215,533)* .30 .30
464 A185 22c Sierra Leone *(1,215,533)* .30 .30
465 A185 22c Finland *(1,215,533)* .30 .30
a. Se-tenant block of 4, #462-465 2.75 3.00
First day covers, #460-465, each .50
Set of 4 diff. panes of 16 16.00
Nos. 450-465 (16) 4.80 4.80

First day covers of Nos. 450-465 total 1,774,193.

UNICEF Child Survival Campaign — A226

Printed by the Government Printing Bureau, Japan. Panes of 50. Designed by Mel Harris, United Kingdom (#466) and Dipok Deyi, India (#467).

1985, Nov. 22 Photo. & Engr. *Perf. 13½*
466 A226 22c Asian Toddler *(823,724)* .30 .30
First day cover 1.00
Inscription block of 4 1.40 —
467 A226 33c Breastfeeding *(632,753)* .65 .65
First day cover 1.00
First day cover, #466-467 1.75
Inscription block of 4 2.75 —

First day covers of Nos. 466-467 total 206,923.
See UN Offices in Geneva Nos. 138-139; Vienna Nos. 55-56.

Africa in Crisis — A227

Printed by Helio Courvoisier, Switzerland. Pane of 50. Designed by Wosene Kosrof, Ethiopia.

1986, Jan. 31 Photo. *Perf. 11½x12*
468 A227 22c **multicolored** *(708,169)* .40 .40
First day cover *(80,588)* 1.25
Inscription block of 4 1.90 —

Campaign against hunger. See UN Offices in Geneva No. 140; Vienna No. 57.

Water Resources A228

Printed by the Government Printing Bureau, Japan. Pane of 40, 2 blocks of 4 horizontal by 5 blocks of 4 vertical. Designed by Thomas Lee, China.

1986, Mar. 14 Photo. *Perf. 13½*
469 A228 22c Dam *(525,839)* .60 .60
470 A228 22c Irrigation *(525,839)* .60 .60
471 A228 22c Hygiene *(525,839)* .60 .60
472 A228 22c Well *(525,839)* .60 .60
a. Block of 4, #469-472 2.75 2.75
First day cover, #472a 4.50
First day cover, #469-472, each 1.50
Inscription block of 4, #469-472 3.25 —
Pane of 40, #469-472 35.00

UN Development Program. No. 472a has continuous design.
First day covers of Nos. 469-472 total 199,347.
See UN Offices in Geneva Nos. 141-144; Vienna Nos. 58-61.

Human Rights Stamp of 1954 — A229

Stamp collecting: 44c, Engraver. Printed by the Swedish Post Office, Sweden. Panes of 50. Designed by Czeslaw Slania and Ingalill Axelsson, Sweden.

1986, May 22 **Engr.** ***Perf. 12½***

473 A229 22c **dark violet & bright blue** *(825,782)* .25 .25
First day cover 1.00
Inscription block of 4 1.40 —
474 A229 44c **brown & emerald green** *(738,552)* .75 .75
First day cover 1.00
First day cover, #473-474 1.25
Inscription block of 4 2.75 —

First day covers of Nos. 473-474 total: New York, 121,143; Chicago, 89,557.
See UN Offices in Geneva Nos. 146-147; Vienna Nos. 62-63.

Bird's Nest in Tree — A230

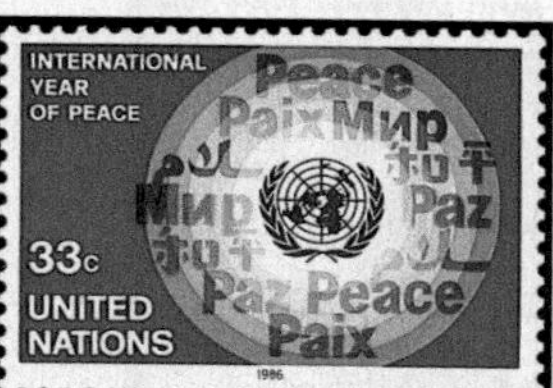

Peace in Seven Languages A231

Printed by the Government Printing Bureau, Japan. Panes of 50. Designed by Akira Iriguchi, Japan (#475), and Henryk Chylinski, Poland (#476).

1986, June 20 **Photo. & Embossed** ***Perf. 13½***

475 A230 22c **multicolored** *(836,160)* .50 .50
First day cover 1.00
Inscription block of 4 2.25 —
476 A231 33c **multicolored** *(663,882)* 1.25 1.25
First day cover 2.00
First day cover, #475-476 4.50
Inscription block of 4 6.00 —

International Peace Year.
First day covers of Nos. 475-476 total 149,976.
See UN Offices in Geneva Nos. 148-149; Vienna Nos. 64-65.

Flag Type of 1980

Printed by Helio Courvoisier, Switzerland. Designed by Ole Hamann. Issued in panes of 16; each contains 4 blocks of four (Nos. 477-480, 481-484, 485-488, 489-492). A se-tenant block of 4 designs centers each pane.

1986, Sept. 19 **Photo.** ***Perf. 12***
Granite Paper

477 A185 22c New Zealand *(1,150,584)* .30 .30
478 A185 22c Lao PDR *(1,150,584)* .30 .30
479 A185 22c Burkina Faso *(1,150,584)* .30 .30
480 A185 22c Gambia *(1,150,584)* .30 .30
a. Se-tenant block of 4, #477-480 2.75 3.00
481 A185 22c Maldives *(1,154,870)* .30 .30
482 A185 22c Ethiopia *(1,154,870)* .30 .30
483 A185 22c Jordan *(1,154,870)* .30 .30
484 A185 22c Zambia *(1,154,870)* .30 .30
a. Se-tenant block of 4, #481-484 2.75 3.00
485 A185 22c Iceland *(1,152,740)* .30 .30
486 A185 22c Antigua & Barbuda *(1,152,740)* .30 .30
487 A185 22c Angola *(1,152,740)* .30 .30
488 A185 22c Botswana *(1,152,740)* .30 .30
a. Se-tenant block of 4, #485-488 2.75 3.00
489 A185 22c Romania *(1,150,412)* .30 .30
490 A185 22c Togo *(1,150,412)* .30 .30
491 A185 22c Mauritania *(1,150,412)* .30 .30
492 A185 22c Colombia *(1,150,412)* .30 .30
a. Se-tenant block of 4, #489-492 2.75 3.00
First day covers, #477-492, each .50
Set of 4 diff. panes of 16 16.00
Nos. 477-492 (16) 4.80 4.80

First day covers of Nos. 477-492 total 1,442,284.

Souvenir Sheet

World Federation of UN Associations, 40th anniv. — A232

Printed by Johann Enschede and Sons, Netherlands. Designed by Rocco J. Callari, U.S.
Designs: 22c, Mother Earth, by Edna Hibel, U.S. 33c, Watercolor by Salvador Dali (b. 1904), Spain. 39c, New Dawn, by Dong Kingman, U.S. 44c, Watercolor by Chaim Gross, U.S.

1986, Nov. 14 **Litho.** ***Perf. 13x13½***

493 A232 Sheet of 4 *(433,888)* 2.50 2.50
a. 22c **multicolored** .30 .40
b. 33c **multicolored** .40 .40
c. 39c **multicolored** .60 .50
d. 44c **multicolored** .90 .75
First day cover *(106,194)* 2.00

No. 493 has inscribed margin picturing UN and WFUNA emblems.
See UN Offices in Geneva No. 150; Vienna No. 66.

Trygve Halvdan Lie (1896-1968), first Secretary-General — A233

Printed by the Government Printing Office, Austria. Panes of 50. Designed by Rocco J. Callari, U.S., from a portrait by Harald Dal, Norway.

1987, Jan. 30 **Photo. & Engr.** ***Perf. 13½***

494 A233 22c **multicolored** *(596,440)* .75 .75
First day cover *(84,819)* 1.25
Inscription block of 4 3.25 —

See Offices in Geneva No. 151; Vienna No. 67.

International Year of Shelter for the Homeless A234

Printed by Johann Enschede and Sons, Netherlands. Panes of 50. Designed by Wladyslaw Brykczynski, Poland.
Designs: 22c, Surveying and blueprinting. 44c, Cutting lumber.

1987, Mar. 13 **Litho.** ***Perf. 13½x12½***

495 A234 22c **multicolored** *(620,627)* .35 .35
First day cover 1.25
Inscription block of 4 1.60 —
496 A234 44c **multicolored** *(538,096)* .90 .90
First day cover 1.75
First day cover, #495-496 2.50
Inscription block of 4 4.25 —

First day covers of Nos. 495-496 total 94,090.
See Offices in Geneva Nos. 154-155; Vienna Nos. 68-69.

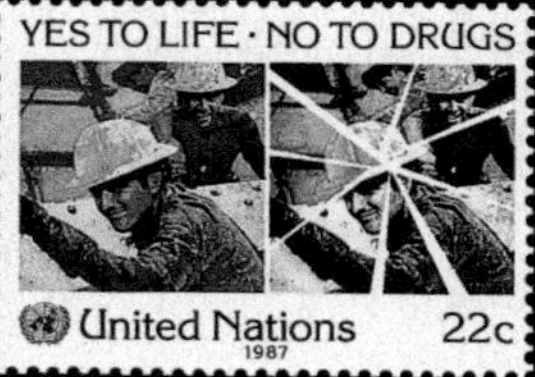

Fight Drug Abuse — A235

Printed by the House of Questa, United Kingdom. Panes of 50. Designed by Susan Borgen and Noel Werrett, U.S.

Designs: 22c, Construction. 33c, Education.

1987, June 12 **Litho.** ***Perf. 14½x15***

497 A235 22c **multicolored** *(674,563)* .45 .45
First day cover 1.00
Inscription block of 4 2.25 —
498 A235 33c **multicolored** *(643,153)* .90 .90
First day cover 1.00
First day cover, #497-498 1.75
Inscription block of 4 4.50 —

First day covers of Nos. 497-498 total 106,941.
See Offices in Geneva Nos. 156-157; Vienna Nos. 70-71.

Flag Type of 1980

Printed by Courvoisier. Designed by Ole Hamann.
Issued in panes of 16; each contains 4 block of four (Nos. 499-502, 503-506, 507-510, 511-514). A se-tenant block of 4 designs centers each pane.

1987, Sept. 18 **Photo.** ***Perf. 12***
Granite Paper

499 A185 22c Comoros *(1,235,828)* .30 .35
500 A185 22c Yemen PDR *(1,235,828)* .30 .35
501 A185 22c Mongolia *(1,235,828)* .30 .35
502 A185 22c Vanuatu *(1,235,828)* .30 .35
a. Se-tenant block of 4, #499-502 3.25 3.25
503 A185 22c Japan *(1,244,534)* .30 .35
504 A185 22c Gabon *(1,244,534)* .30 .35
505 A185 22c Zimbabwe *(1,244,534)* .30 .35
506 A185 22c Iraq *(1,244,534)* .30 .35
a. Se-tenant block of 4, #503-506 3.25 3.25
507 A185 22c Argentina *(1,238,065)* .30 .35
508 A185 22c Congo *(1,238,065)* .30 .35
509 A185 22c Niger *(1,238,065)* .30 .35
510 A185 22c St. Lucia *(1,238,065)* .30 .35
a. Se-tenant block of 4, #507-510 3.25 3.25
511 A185 22c Bahrain *(1,239,323)* .30 .35
512 A185 22c Haiti *(1,239,323)* .30 .35
513 A185 22c Afghanistan *(1,239,323)* .30 .35
514 A185 22c Greece *(1,239,323)* .30 .35
a. Se-tenant block of 4, #511-514 3.25 3.25
First day covers, #499-514, each 1.00
Set of 4 diff. panes of 16 17.50
Nos. 499-514 (16) 4.80 5.60

United Nations Day — A236

Printed by The House of Questa, United Kingdom. Panes of 12. Designed by Elisabeth von Janota-Bzowski (#515) and Fritz Henry Oerter (#516), Federal Republic of Germany.
Designs: Multinational people in various occupations.

1987, Oct. 23 **Litho.** ***Perf. 14½x15***

515 A236 22c **multicolored** *(1,119,286)* .35 .35
First day cover 1.00
Inscription block of 4 1.75 —
516 A236 39c **multicolored** *(1,065,468)* .55 .55
First day cover 1.25
First day cover, #515-516 1.60
Inscription block of 4 2.25 —
Panes of 12, #515-516 12.00

See Offices in Geneva Nos. 158-159; Vienna Nos. 74-75.

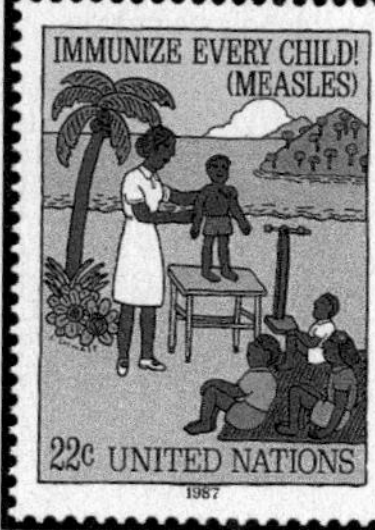

Immunize Every Child — A237

Printed by The House of Questa, United Kingdom. Panes of 50. Designed by Seymour Chwast, U.S.
Designs: 22c, Measles. 44c, Tetanus.

1987, Nov. 20 **Litho.** ***Perf. 15x14½***

517 A237 22c **multicolored** *(660,495)* .75 .75
First day cover 1.50
Inscription block of 4 2.75 —
518 A237 44c **multicolored** *(606,049)* 1.50 1.50
First day cover 1.50
First day cover, #517-518 2.00
Inscription block of 4 7.50 —

See Offices in Geneva Nos. 160-161; Vienna Nos. 76-77.

Intl. Fund for Agricultural Development (IFAD)
A238

Printed by CPE Australia Ltd., Australia. Panes of 50. Designed by Santiago Arolas, Switzerland.
Designs: 22c, Fishing. 33c, Farming.

1988, Jan. 29 **Litho.** ***Perf. 13½***

519 A238 22c **multicolored** *(392,649)* .35 .35
First day cover 1.00
Inscription block of 4 1.50 —
520 A238 33c **multicolored** *(475,185)* .75 .75
First day cover 1.25
First day cover, #519-520 2.50
Inscription block of 4 3.50 —

See Offices in Geneva Nos. 162-163; Vienna Nos. 78-79.

A239

Printed by Heraclio Fournier, S.A., Spain. Panes of 50. Designed by David Ben-Hador, Israel.

1988, Jan. 29 **Photo.** ***Perf. 13½x14***

521 A239 3c **multicolored** *(3,000,000)+* .25 .25
First day cover 1.00
Inscription block of 4 .75 —

Survival of the Forests — A240

Printed by The House of Questa, United Kingdom. Panes of six se-tenant pairs. Designed by Braldt Bralds, the Netherlands.
Tropical rain forest: 25c, Treetops. 44c, Ground vegetation and tree trunks. Printed se-tenant in a continuous design.

1988, Mar. 18 **Litho.** ***Perf. 14x15***

522 A240 25c **multicolored** *(647,360)* .75 .75
First day cover 2.00
523 A240 44c **multicolored** *(647,360)* 1.00 1.00
First day cover 4.50
a. Pair, #522-523 2.00 *3.00*
First day cover, #523a 6.50
Inscription block of 4 6.00
Pane of 12, #522-523 14.00

See Offices in Geneva Nos. 165-166; Vienna Nos. 80-81.

Intl. Volunteer Day — A241

Printed by Johann Enschede and Sons, the Netherlands. Panes of 50. Designed by James E. Tennison, U.S.
Designs: 25c, Edurahon. 50c, Vocational training, horiz.

1988, May 6 **Litho.** ***Perf. 13x14, 14x13***

524 A241 25c **multicolored** *(688,444)* .45 .45
First day cover 1.00
Inscription block of 4 2.00 —
525 A241 50c **multicolored** *(447,784)* .95 .95
First day cover 1.50
First day cover, #524-525 1.75
Inscription block of 4 4.25 —

See Offices in Geneva Nos. 167-168; Vienna Nos. 82-83.

Health in Sports — A242

Printed by the Government Printing Bureau, Japan. Panes of 50. Paintings by LeRoy Neiman, American sports artist.
Designs: 25c, Cycling, vert. 35c, Marathon.

1988, June 17 **Litho.** ***Perf. 13½x13, 13x13½***

526 A242 25c **multicolored** *(658,991)* .45 .45
First day cover 1.75
Inscription block of 4 2.25 —
527 A242 38c **multicolored** *(420,421)* 1.00 1.00
First day cover 2.00
First day cover, #526-527 3.50
Inscription block of 4 6.00 —

See Offices in Geneva Nos. 169-170; Vienna Nos. 84-85.

Flag Type of 1980

Printed by Helio Courvoisier, Switzerland. Designed by Ole Hamann, Denmark. Issued in panes of 16; each contains 4 blocks of four (Nos. 528-531, 532-535, 536-539 and 540-543). A se-tenant block of 4 centers each pane.

1988, Sept. 15 **Photo.** ***Perf. 12***
Granite Paper

528 A185 25c Spain *(1,029,443)* .45 .45
529 A185 25c St. Vincent & Grenadines *(1,029,443)* .45 .45
530 A185 25c Ivory Coast *(1,029,443)* .45 .45
531 A185 25c Lebanon *(1,029,443)* .45 .45
a. Se-tenant block of 4, #528-531 3.00 3.00
532 A185 25c Yemen (Arab Republic) *(1,010,774)* .45 .45
533 A185 25c Cuba *(1,010,774)* .45 .45
534 A185 25c Denmark *(1,010,774)* .45 .45
535 A185 25c Libya *(1,010,774)* .45 .45
a. Se-tenant block of 4, #532-535 3.00 3.00
536 A185 25c Qatar *(1,016,941)* .45 .45
537 A185 25c Zaire *(1,016,941)* .45 .45
538 A185 25c Norway *(1,016,941)* .45 .45
539 A185 25c German Democratic Republic *(1,016,941)* .45 .45
a. Se-tenant block of 4, #536-539 3.00 3.00
540 A185 25c Iran *(1,009,234)* .45 .45
541 A185 25c Tunisia *(1,009,234)* .45 .45
542 A185 25c Samoa *(1,009,234)* .45 .45
543 A185 25c Belize *(1,009,234)* .45 .45
a. Se-tenant block of 4, #540-543 3.00 3.00
First day covers, #528-543, each 1.00
Set of 4 diff. panes of 16 21.00
Nos. 528-543 (16) 7.20 7.20

See note after No. 340.

Universal Declaration of Human Rights, 40th. Anniv. — A243

Printed by Helio Couvoisier, Switzerland. Panes of 50. Designed by Rocco J. Callari, U.S.

1988, Dec. 9 **Photo. & Engr.** ***Perf. 11x11½***

544 A243 25c **multicolored** *(893,706)* .45 .45
First day cover 1.75
Inscription block of 4 2.25 —

Souvenir Sheet

545 A243 $1 **multicolored** *(411,863)* 1.00 1.00
First day cover 1.75

No. 545 has multicolored decorative margin inscribed with the preamble to the human rights declaration in English.
See Offices in Geneva Nos. 171-172; Vienna Nos. 86-87.

World Bank — A244

Printed by Johann Enschede and Sons, the Netherlands. Panes of 50. Designed by Saturnino Lumboy, Philippines.

1989, Jan. 27 **Litho.** ***Perf. 13x14***

546 A244 25c Energy and nature *(612,114)* .60 .60
First day cover 1.25
Inscription block of 4 2.50 —
547 A244 45c Agriculture *(528,184)* 1.10 1.10
First day cover 1.50
First day cover, #546-547 1.75
Inscription block of 4 5.50 —

First day covers of Nos. 546-547 total 103,087 (NYC), 56,501 (Washington).
See Offices in Geneva Nos. 173-174; Vienna Nos. 88-89.

A245

UN Peace-Keeping Force, awarded 1988 Nobel Peace Prize.
Printed by CPE Australia, Ltd., Australia. Panes of 50. Designed by Tom Bland, Australia.

1989, Mar. 17 **Litho.** ***Perf. 14x13½***

548 A245 25c **multicolored** *(808,842)* .45 .45
First day cover *(52,115)* 1.25
Inscription block of 4 2.00 —

See Offices in Geneva No. 175; Vienna No. 90.

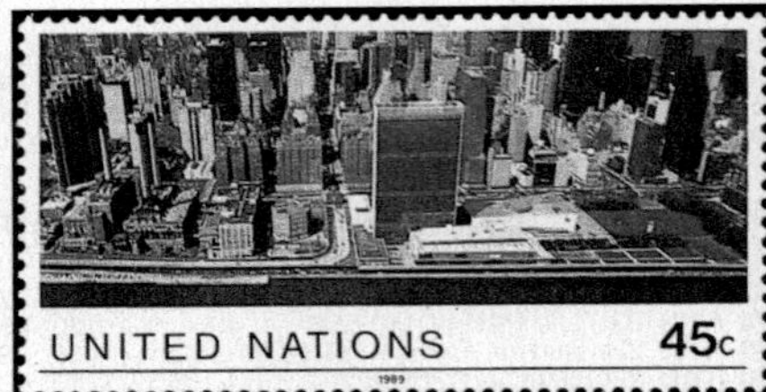

Aerial Photograph of New York Headquarters — A246

Printed by Johann Enschede and Sons, the Netherlands. Panes of 25. Designed by Rocco J. Callari, United States, from a photograph by Simon Nathan.

1989, Mar. 17 **Litho.** ***Perf. 14½x14***

549 A246 45c **multicolored** *(2,000,000)+* .65 .65
First day cover *(41,610)* 1.50
Inscription block of 4 2.75 —

World Weather Watch, 25th Anniv. (in 1988) — A247

Printed by Johann Enschede and Sons, the Netherlands. Panes of 50.

Satellite photographs: 25c, Storm system off the U.S. east coast. 36c, Typhoon Abby in the north-west Pacific.

1989, Apr. 21 Litho. *Perf. 13x14*

550 A247 25c **multicolored** *(849,819)* .50 .50
First day cover 1.25
Inscription block of 4 2.25 —
551 A247 36c **multicolored** *(826,547)* 1.10 1.10
First day cover 1.75
First day cover, #550-551 2.00
Inscription block of 4 6.50 —

First day covers of Nos. 550-551 total 92,013.

See Offices in Geneva Nos. 176-177; Vienna Nos. 91-92.

Offices in Vienna, 10th Anniv.
A248 A249

Printed by the Government Printing Office, Austria. Panes of 25. Designed by Paul Flora (25c) and Rudolf Hausner (90c), Austria.

Photo. & Engr., Photo. (90c)

1989, Aug. 23 *Perf. 14*

552 A248 25c **multicolored** *(580,663)* 1.25 1.25
First day cover 2.25
Inscription block of 4 5.00 —
553 A249 90c **multicolored** *(505,776)* 2.50 2.50
First day cover 3.00
First day cover, #552-553 5.00
Inscription block of 4 7.00 —
Panes of 25, #552-553 70.00

First day covers of Nos. 552-553 total 89,068.

See Offices in Geneva Nos. 178-179; Vienna Nos. 93-94.

Flag Type of 1980

Printed by Helio Courvoisier, Switzerland. Designed by Ole Hamann, Denmark. Issued in panes of 16; each contains 4 blocks of 4 (Nos. 554-557, 558-561, 562-565, 566-569). A se-tenant block of 4 designs centers each pane.

1989, Sept. 22 Photo. *Perf. 12*
Granite Paper

554 A185 25c Indonesia *(959,076)* .55 .55
555 A185 25c Lesotho *(959,076)* .55 .55
556 A185 25c Guatemala *(959,076)* .55 .55
557 A185 25c Netherlands *(959,076)* .55 .55
a. Se-tenant block of 4, #554-557 3.25 3.25
558 A185 25c South Africa *(960,502)* .55 .55
559 A185 25c Portugal *(960,502)* .55 .55
560 A185 25c Morocco *(960,502)* .55 .55
561 A185 25c Syrian Arab Republic *(960,502)* .55 .55
a. Se-tenant block of 4, #558-561 3.25 3.25
562 A185 25c Honduras *(959,814)* .55 .55
563 A185 25c Kampuchea *(959,814)* .55 .55
564 A185 25c Guinea-Bissau *(959,814)* .55 .55
565 A185 25c Cyprus *(959,814)* .55 .55
a. Se-tenant block of 4, #562-565 3.25 3.25
566 A185 25c Algeria *(959,805)* .55 .55
567 A185 25c Brunei *(959,805)* .55 .55
568 A185 25c St. Kitts and Nevis *(959,805)* .55 .55
569 A185 25c United Nations *(959,805)* .55 .55
a. Se-tenant block of 4, #566-569 3.25 3.25
First day covers, #554-569, each 1.25
Set of 4 diff. panes of 16 30.00
Nos. 554-569 (16) 8.80 8.80

First day covers of Nos. 554-569 total 794,934.

Declaration of Human Rights, 40th Anniv. (in 1988) — A250

Printed by Johann Enschede and Sons, the Netherlands. Panes of 12+12 se-tenant labels containing Articles 1 (25c) or 2 (45c) inscribed in English, French or German. Designed by Rocco J. Callari and Robert Stein, US.

Paintings: 25c, The Table of Universal Brotherhood, by Jose Clemente Orozco. 45c, Study for Composition II, by Vassily Kandinsky.

1989, Nov. 17 Litho. *Perf. 13½*

570 A250 25c **multicolored** *(1,934,135)* .35 .35
First day cover 1.00
Inscription block of 3 + 3 labels 1.10 —
571 A250 45c **multicolored** *(1,922,171)* .80 .80
First day cover 1.50
First day cover, #570-571 1.50
Inscription block of 3 + 3 labels 2.50 —
Panes of 12, #570-571 12.00

First day covers of Nos. 570-571 total 146,489 (NYC), 46,774 (Washington).

See Nos. 582-583, 599-600, 616-617, 627-628; Offices in Geneva Nos. 180-181, 193-194, 209-210, 224-225, 234-235; Vienna Nos. 95-96, 108-109, 123-124, 139-140, 150-151.

Intl. Trade Center — A251

Printed by House of Questa, United Kingdom. Panes of 50. Designed by Richard Bernstein, US.

1990, Feb. 2 Litho. *Perf. 14½x15*

572 A251 25c **multicolored** *(429,081)* 1.00 1.00
First day cover *(52,614)* 1.00
Inscription block of 4 4.00 —

See Offices in Geneva No. 182; Vienna No. 97.

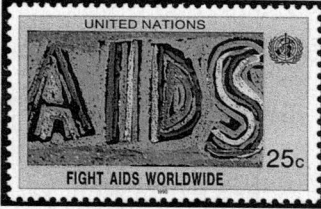

Fight AIDS Worldwide A252

Printed by Johann Enschede and Sons, the Netherlands. Panes of 50. Designed by Jacek Tofil, Poland (25c) and Fritz Henry Oerter, Federal Republic of Germany (40c).

Design: 40c, Shadow over crowd.

1990, Mar. 16 Litho. *Perf. 13½x12½*

573 A252 25c **multicolored** *(492,078)* .35 .35
First day cover 1.00
Inscription block of 4 1.50 —
574 A252 40c **multicolored** *(394,149)* 1.15 1.15
First day cover 1.25
First day cover, #573-574 3.50
Inscription block of 4 5.00 —

First day covers of Nos. 573-574 total 95,854.

See Offices in Geneva Nos. 184-185, Vienna Nos. 99-100.

Medicinal Plants — A253

Printed by Helio Courvoisier, Switzerland. Panes of 50. Designed by Rocco J. Callari & Robert Stein, US from illustrations from "Curtis's Botanical Magazine".

25c, Catharanthus roseus. 90c, Panax quinquefolium.

1990, May 4 Photo. Granite Paper *Perf. 11½*

575 A253 25c multi *(796,792)* .45 .45
First day cover 1.00
Inscription block of 4 1.75 —
576 A253 90c multi *(605,617)* 1.40 1.40
First day cover 1.25
First day cover, #575-576 2.50
Inscription block of 4 5.50 —

First day covers of Nos. 575-576 total 100,548.

See Offices in Geneva Nos. 186-187, Vienna Nos. 101-102.

United Nations, 45th Anniv. A254

Printed by Johann Enschede and Sons, the Netherlands. Panes of 50. Designed by Kris Geysen, Belgium (25c), Nejat M. Gur, Turkey (45c), Robert Stein, US (No. 579).

Design: 45c, "45," emblem.

1990, June 26 Litho. *Perf. 14½x13*

577 A254 25c **multicolored** *(581,718)* .50 .50
First day cover 1.00
Inscription block of 4 2.25 —
578 A254 45c **multicolored** *(582,769)* 1.90 1.90
First day cover 1.00
First day cover, #577-578 2.00
Inscription block of 4 8.00 —

Souvenir Sheet

579 Sheet of 2, #577-578 *(315,946)* 3.50 3.50
First day cover 3.50

First day covers of Nos. 577-579 total 129,011.

See Offices in Geneva Nos. 188-190; Vienna Nos. 103-105.

Crime Prevention — A255

Printed by Heraclio Fournier, S.A. Spain. Panes of 50. Designed by Josef Ryzec, Czechoslovakia.

1990, Sept. 13 Photo. *Perf. 14*

580 A255 25c Crimes of youth *(533,089)* .65 .65
First day cover 1.00
Inscription block of 4 3.00 —
581 A255 36c Organized crime *(427,215)* 1.25 1.25
First day cover 1.75
First day cover, #580-581 2.50
Inscription block of 4 5.75 —

First day covers of Nos. 580-581 total 68,660.

See Offices in Geneva Nos. 191-192; Vienna Nos. 106-107.

Human Rights Type of 1989

Printed by Johann Enschede and Sons, the Netherlands. Panes of 12+12 se-tenant labels containing Articles 7 (25c) or 8 (45c) inscribed in English, French or German. Designed by Rocco J. Callari and Robert Stein, US.

Artwork: 25c, Fragment from the sarcophagus of Plotinus, c. 270 A.D. 45c, Combined Chambers of the High Court of Appeal by Charles Paul Renouard.

1990, Nov. 16 Litho. *Perf. 13½*

582 A250 25c **black, gray & tan** *(1,492,950)* .35 .35
First day cover 1.00
Inscription block of 3 + 3 labels 1.10 —
583 A250 45c **black & brown** *(1,490,934)* .65 .65
First day cover 1.00
First day cover, #582-583 1.50
Inscription block of 3 + 3 labels 2.75 —
Panes of 12, #582-583 14.00

First day covers of Nos. 582-583 total 108,560.

See Offices in Geneva Nos. 193-194; Vienna Nos. 108-109.

Economic Commission for Europe — A256

Printed by Heraclio Fournier, S.A., Spain. Panes of 40. Designed by Carlos Ochagavia, Argentina.

1991, Mar. 15 **Litho.** ***Perf. 14***

584 A256 30c Two storks *(590,102)* .85 .85
585 A256 30c Woodpecker, ibex *(590,102)* .85 .85
586 A256 30c Capercaille, plover *(590,102)* .85 .85
587 A256 30c Falcon, marmot *(590,102)* .85 .85
a. Block of 4, #584-587 3.40 3.40
First day cover, #587a 4.00
First day cover, #584-587, any single 4.50
Inscription block of 4, #587a 5.00 —
Pane of 40, #584-587 35.00

First day covers of Nos. 584-587 total 53,502.
See Offices in Geneva Nos. 195-198; Vienna Nos. 110-113.

Namibian Independence A257

Printed by Heraclio Fournier, S.A., Spain. Designed by Rocco J. Callari, US, from photographs by John Isaac, India.

1991, May 10 **Litho.** ***Perf. 14***

588 A257 30c Dunes, Namib Desert *(360,825)* .50 .50
First day cover 1.00
Inscription block of 4 2.25 —
589 A257 50c Savanna *(415,648)* 1.10 1.00
First day cover 1.25
First day cover, #588-589 2.50
Inscription block of 4 4.75 —

First day covers of Nos. 588-589 total 114,258.
See Offices in Geneva Nos. 199-200; Vienna Nos. 114-115.

A258

The Golden Rule by Norman Rockwell — A259

UN Headquarters, New York — A260

Printed by Johann Enschede and Sons, the Netherlands (30c), Helio Courvoisier, S.A., Switzerland (50c), and by Government Printing Bureau, Japan ($2). Panes of 50. Designed by Rocco J. Callari (30c), Norman Rockwell, US (50c), Rocco J. Callari and Robert Stein, US ($2).

1991 **Litho.** ***Perf. 13½***

590 A258 30c **multi,** *Sept. 11, (2,000,000)+* .60 .60
First day cover 1.00
Inscription block of 4 2.50 —

Photo.

Perf. 12x11½

591 A259 50c **multi,** *Sept. 11, (2,000,000)+* 1.00 1.00
First day cover 1.00
Inscription block of 4 5.00

Engr.

592 A260 $2 **dark blue,** *May 10, (2,000,000)+* 2.75 2.75
First day cover 2.75
Inscription block of 4 11.00 —

First day covers of Nos. 590-591 total 66,016, No. 592, 36,022.
See Offices in Geneva Nos. 199-200; Vienna Nos. 114-115.

Rights of the Child — A261

Printed by The House of Questa, United Kingdom. Panes of 50. Designed by Nicole Delia Legnani, US (30c) and Alissa Duffy, US (70c).

1991, June 14 **Litho.** ***Perf. 14½***

593 A251 30c Children, globe *(440,151)* 1.00 1.00
First day cover 1.00
Inscription block of 4 4.50 —
594 A261 70c House, rainbow *(447,803)* 2.00 2.00
First day cover 1.50
First day cover, #593-594 2.00
Inscription block of 4 9.00 —

First day covers of Nos. 593-594 total 96,324.
See Offices in Geneva Nos. 203-204; Vienna Nos. 117-118.

Banning of Chemical Weapons A262

Printed by Heraclio Fournier, S.A., Spain. Panes of 50. Designed by Oscar Asboth, Austria (30c), Michael Granger, France (90c).
Design: 90c, Hand holding back chemical drums.

1991, Sept. 11 **Litho.** ***Perf. 13½***

595 A262 30c **multicolored** *(367,548)* .75 .75
First day cover 1.25
Inscription block of 4 3.75 —
596 A262 90c **multicolored** *(346,161)* 2.25 2.25
First day cover 1.50
First day cover, #595-596 2.50
Inscription block of 4 11.00 —

First day covers of Nos. 595-596 total 91,552.
See Offices in Geneva Nos. 205-206; Vienna Nos. 119-120.

UN Postal Administration, 40th Anniv. — A263

Printed by The House of Questa, United Kingdom. Panes of 25. Designed by Rocco J. Callari, US.

1991, Oct. 24 **Litho.** ***Perf. 14x15***

597 A263 30c No. 1 *(442,548)* .65 .65
First day cover 1.00
Inscription block of 4 2.75 —
598 A263 40c No. 3 *(419,127)* .85 .85
First day cover 1.00
First day cover, #597-598 1.50
Inscription block of 4 4.00 —
Panes of 25, #597-598 45.00

First day covers of Nos. 597-598 total 81,177 (New York), 58,501 (State College, PA).
See Offices in Geneva Nos. 207-208; Vienna Nos. 121-122.

Human Rights Type of 1989

Printed by Johann Enschede and Sons, the Netherlands. Panes of 12+12 se-tenant labels containing Articles 13 (30c) or 14 (50c) inscribed in English, French or German. Designed by Robert Stein, US.
Artwork: 30c, The Last of England, by Ford Madox Brown. 40c, The Emigration to the East, by Tito Salas.

1991, Nov. 20 **Litho.** ***Perf. 13½***

599 A250 30c **multicolored** *(1,261,198)* .35 .35
First day cover 1.00
Inscription block of 3 + 3 labels 1.75 —
600 A250 50c **multicolored** *(1,255,077)* .80 1.00
First day cover 1.00
First day cover, #599-600 2.25
Inscription block of 3 + 3 labels 3.50 —
Panes of 12, #599-600 14.00

First day covers of Nos. 599-600 total 136,605.
See Offices in Geneva Nos. 209-210; Vienna Nos. 123-124.

World Heritage Type of 1984

Printed by Cartor S.A., France. Panes of 50. Designed by Robert Stein, U.S.
Designs: 30c, Uluru Natl. Park, Australia. 50c, The Great Wall of China.

1992, Jan. 24 **Litho.** ***Perf. 13***

Size: 35x28mm

601 A215 30c **multicolored** *(337,717)* .55 .55
First day cover 1.00
Inscription block of 4 2.50 —
602 A215 50c **multicolored** *(358,000)* .90 .90
First day cover 1.25
First day cover, #601-602 1.75
Inscription block of 4 4.25 —

First day covers of Nos. 601-602 total 62,733.
See Offices in Geneva Nos. 211-212; Vienna Nos. 125-126.

Clean Oceans — A264

Printed by The House of Questa, United Kingdom. Panes of 12. Designed by Braldt Bralds, Netherlands.

1992, Mar. 13 **Litho.** ***Perf. 14***

603 A264 29c Ocean surface *(983,126)* .45 .50
604 A264 29c Ocean bottom *(983,126)* .45 .50
a. Pair, #603-604 .90 1.10
First day cover, #604a 2.00
First day cover, #603-604, any single 1.00
Inscription block of 4, #603-604 3.25 —
Pane of 12, #603-604 9.00

First day covers of Nos. 603-604 total 75,511.
See Offices in Geneva Nos. 214-215, Vienna Nos. 127-128.

Earth Summit — A265

Printed by Helio Courvoisier S.A., Switzerland. Panes of 40. Designed by Peter Max, US.
Designs: No. 605, Globe at LR. No. 606, Globe at LL. No. 607, Globe at UR. No. 608, Globe at UL.

1992, May 22 **Photo.** ***Perf. 11½***

605 A265 29c **multicolored** *(806,268)* .65 .65
606 A265 29c **multicolored** *(806,268)* .65 .65
607 A265 29c **multicolored** *(806,268)* .65 .65
608 A265 29c **multicolored** *(806,268)* .65 .65
a. Block of 4, #605-608 4.00 3.50
First day cover, #608a 3.50
First day cover, #605-608, each 7.50
Inscription block of 4, #608a 5.00 —
Pane of 40, #605-608 27.50

First day covers of Nos. 605-608a total 110,577.
See Offices in Geneva Nos. 216-219, Vienna Nos. 129-132.

Mission to Planet Earth — A266

Printed by Helio Courvoisier, S.A., Switzerland. Designed by Attilla Hejja, US.

Designs: No. 609, Satellites over city, sailboats, fishing boat. No. 610, Satellite over coast, passenger liner, dolphins, whale, volcano.

1992, Sept. 4 **Photo.** ***Rouletted 8***
Granite Paper

609 A266 29c **multicolored** *(643,647)* 1.50 1.50
610 A266 29c **multicolored** *(643,647)* 1.50 1.50
a. Pair, #609-610 3.00 3.00
First day cover, #610a 5.00
First day cover, #609-610, each 11.00
Inscription block of 4 9.00 —
Pane of 10, #609-610 21.00

First day covers of Nos. 609-610a total 69,343.
See Offices in Geneva Nos. 220-221, Vienna Nos. 133-134.

Science and Technology for Development A267

Printed by Unicover Corp., US. Designed by Saul Mandel, US.

Design: 50c, Animal, man drinking.

1992, Oct. 2 **Litho.** ***Perf. 14***

611 A267 29c **multicolored** *(453,365)* .40 .40
First day cover 1.00
Inscription block of 4 1.75 —
612 A267 50c **multicolored** *(377,377)* .70 .70
First day cover 1.00
First day cover, #611-612 4.25
Inscription block of 4 3.25

First day covers of Nos. 611-612 total 69,195.
See Offices in Geneva Nos. 222-223, Vienna Nos. 135-136.

UN University Building, Tokyo A268

UN Headquarters, New York — A269

Printed by Cartor SA, France (4c, 40c), Walsall Security Printers, Ltd., UK (29c). Designed by Banks and Miles, UK (4c, 40c), Robert Stein, US (29c).

Design: 40c, UN University Building, Tokyo, diff.

1992, Oct. 2 **Litho.** ***Perf. 14, 13½x13 (29c)***

613 A268 4c **multicolored** *(1,500,000)+* .25 .25
First day cover 1.00
Inscription block of 4 .70 —
614 A269 29c **multicolored** *(1,750,000)+* .50 .50
First day cover 1.00
Inscription block of 4 2.25 —
615 A268 40c **multicolored** *(1,500,000)+* .65 .65
First day cover 1.00
First day cover, #613-615 2.00
Inscription block of 4 3.75 —
Nos. 613-615 (3) 1.40 1.40

First day covers of Nos. 613-615 total 62,697.

Human Rights Type of 1989

Printed by Johann Enschede and Sons, the Netherlands. Panes of 12+12 se-tenant labels containing Articles 19 (29c) and 20 (50c) inscribed in English, French or German. Designed by Robert Stein, US.

Artwork: 29c, Lady Writing a Letter with her Maid, by Vermeer. 50c, The Meeting, by Ester Almqvist.

1992, Nov. 20 **Litho.** ***Perf. 13½***

616 A250 29c **multicolored,** *(1,184,531)* .40 .40
First day cover 1.50
Inscription block of 3 + 3 labels 1.75 —
617 A250 50c **multicolored,** *(1,107,044)* .60 .60
First day cover 1.50
First day cover, #616-617 2.25
Inscription block of 3 + 3 labels 2.75 —
Panes of 12, #616-617 14.00

First day covers of Nos. 616-617 total 104,470.
See Offices in Geneva Nos. 224-225; Vienna Nos. 139-140.

Aging With Dignity — A270

Printed by Cartor SA, France. Designed by C.M. Dudash, US.

Designs: 29c, Elderly couple, family. 52c, Old man, physician, woman holding fruit basket.

1993, Feb. 5 **Litho.** ***Perf. 13***

618 A270 29c **multicolored** *(336,933)* .45 .45
First day cover 1.00
Inscription block of 4 2.25 —
619 A270 52c **multicolored** *(308,080)* 1.00 1.00
First day cover 1.00
First day cover, #618-619 1.25
Inscription block of 4 4.75 —

First day covers of Nos. 618-619 total 52,932.
See Offices in Geneva Nos. 226-227; Vienna Nos. 141-142.

Endangered Species A271

Printed by Johann Enschede and Sons, the Netherlands. Designed by Rocco J. Callari and Norman Adams, US.

Designs: No. 620, Hairy-nosed wombat. No. 621, Whooping crane. No. 622, Giant clam. No. 623, Giant sable antelope.

1993, Mar. 2 **Litho.** ***Perf. 13x12½***

620 A271 29c **multicolored** *(1,200,000)+* .45 .45
621 A271 29c **multicolored** *(1,200,000)+* .45 .45
622 A271 29c **multicolored** *(1,200,000)+* .45 .45
623 A271 29c **multicolored** *(1,200,000)+* .45 .45
a. Block of 4, #620-623 2.00 2.00
First day cover, #623a 3.75
First day cover, #620-623, each 2.00
Inscription block of 4, #623a 2.50 —
Pane of 16, #620-623 9.00

First day covers of Nos. 620-623a total 64,794.
See Nos. 639-642, 657-660, 674-677, 700-703, 730-733, 757-760, 773-776, 789-792, 818-821, 842-845, 858-861, 876-879; 908-911, 925-928, 949-952, 975-978, 999-1002, 1031-1034, 1042-1045, 1074-1077; Offices in Geneva Nos. 228-231, 246-249, 264-267, 280-283, 298-301, 318-321, 336-339, 352-355, 367-370, 386-389, 407-410, 418-421, 436-439, 453-456, 465-468, 480-483, 496-499, 513-516, 540-543, 549-552, 572-575; Vienna Nos. 143-146, 162-165, 180-183, 196-199, 214-217, 235-238, 253-256, 269-272, 284-287, 308-311, 329-332, 342-345, 360-363, 376-379, 388-391, 417-420, 438-441, 465-468, 501-504, 511-514, 534-537.

Healthy Environment A272

Printed by Leigh-Mardon Pty. Limited, Australia. Designed by Milton Glaser, US.

Designs: 29c, Personal. 50c, Family.

1993, May 7 **Litho.** ***Perf. 15x14½***

624 A272 29c Man *(430,463)* .50 .50
First day cover 1.00
Inscription block of 4 2.25 —
625 A272 50c Family *(326,692)* .90 .90
First day cover 1.00
First day cover, #624-625 2.00
Inscription block of 4 3.75 —

WHO, 45th anniv. First day covers of Nos. 624-625 total 55,139.
See Offices in Geneva Nos. 232-233; Vienna Nos. 147-148.

A273

Printed by House of Questa, Ltd., United Kingdom. Designed by Salahattin Kanidinc, US.

1993, May 7 **Litho.** ***Perf. 15x14***

626 A273 5c **multicolored** *(1,500,000)+* .25 .25
First day cover *(23,452)* 1.00
Inscription block of 4 .65 —

Human Rights Type of 1989

Printed by Johann Enschede and Sons, the Netherlands. Panes of 12 + 12 se-tenant labels containing Articles 25 (29c) and 26 (35c) inscribed in English, French or German. Designed by Robert Stein, US.

Artwork: 29c, Shucking Corn, by Thomas Hart Benton. 35c, The Library, by Jacob Lawrence.

1993, June 11 **Litho.** ***Perf. 13½***

627 A250 29c **multicolored** *(1,049,134)* .40 .40
First day cover 1.00
Inscription block of 3 + 3 labels 1.75 —
628 A250 35c **multicolored** *(1,045,346)* .45 .45
First day cover 1.00
First day cover, #627-628 1.25
Inscription block of 3 + 3 labels 2.50 —
Panes of 12, #627-628 16.00

First day covers of Nos. 627-628 total 77,719.
See Offices in Geneva Nos. 234-235; Vienna Nos. 150-151.

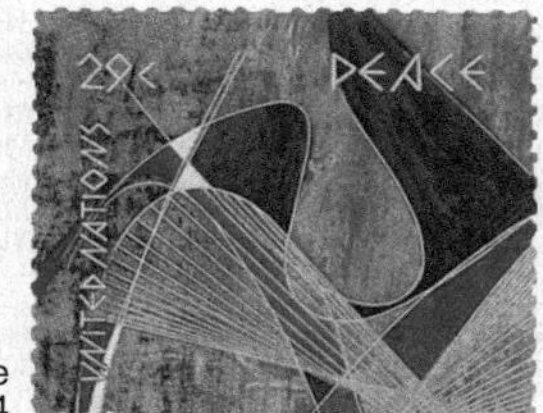

Intl. Peace Day — A274

Printed by the PTT, Switzerland. Designed by Hans Erni, Switzerland.

Denomination at: #629, UL. #630, UR. #631, LL. #632, LR.

1993, Sept. 21 **Litho. & Engr.** ***Rouletted 12½***

629 A274 29c **blue & multi** *(298,367)* 1.00 1.00
630 A274 29c **blue & multi** *(298,367)* 1.00 1.00
631 A274 29c **blue & multi** *(298,367)* 1.00 1.00
632 A274 29c **blue & multi** *(298,367)* 1.00 1.00
a. Block of 4, #629-632 6.00 6.00
First day cover, #629-632, each 5.00
First day cover, #632a 6.00
Inscription block of 4, #632a 7.50 —
Pane of 40, #629-632 65.00

First day covers of Nos. 629-632a total 41,743.
See Offices in Geneva Nos. 236-239; Vienna Nos. 152-155.

Environment-Climate — A275

Printed by House of Questa, Ltd., United Kingdom. Designed by Braldt Bralds, Netherlands.

Designs: No. 633, Chameleon. No. 634, Palm trees, top of funnel cloud. No. 635, Bottom of funnel cloud, deer, antelope. No. 636, Bird of paradise.

1993, Oct. 29 **Litho.** ***Perf. 14½***

633 A275 29c **multicolored** *(383,434)* .90 .90
634 A275 29c **multicolored** *(383,434)* .90 .90
635 A275 29c **multicolored** *(383,434)* .90 .90
636 A275 29c **multicolored** *(383,434)* .90 .90
a. Strip of 4, #633-636 4.75 4.75
First day cover, #636a 2.75
First day cover, #633-636, each 3.75
Inscription block, 2 #636a 10.00 —
Pane of 24, #633-636 30.00

First day covers of Nos. 633-636a total 38,182.
See Offices in Geneva Nos. 240-243; Vienna Nos. 156-159.

Intl. Year of the Family — A276

Printed by Cartor S.A., France. Designed by Rocco J. Callari, US.

Designs: 29c, Mother holding child, two children, woman. 45c, People tending crops.

1994, Feb. 4 **Litho.** ***Perf. 13.1***

637 A276 29c **green & multi** *(590,000)+* .70 .70
First day cover 1.00
Inscription block of 4 3.25 —
638 A276 45c **blue & multi** *(540,000)+* .90 .90
First day cover 1.00
First day cover, #637-638 1.25
Inscription block of 4 4.00 —

First day covers of Nos. 637-638 total 47,982. See Offices in Geneva Nos. 244-245; Vienna Nos. 160-161.

Endangered Species Type of 1993

Printed by Johann Enschede and Sons, the Netherlands. Designed by Rocco J. Callari, US (frame), and Kerrie Maddeford, Australia (stamps).

Designs: No. 639, Chimpanzee. No. 640, St. Lucia Amazon. No. 641, American crocodile. No. 642, Dama gazelle.

1994, Mar. 18 **Litho.** ***Perf. 12.7***

639 A271 29c **multicolored** *(1,200,000)+* .45 .45
640 A271 29c **multicolored** *(1,200,000)+* .45 .45
641 A271 29c **multicolored** *(1,200,000)+* .45 .45
642 A271 29c **multicolored** *(1,200,000)+* .45 .45
a. Block of 4, #639-642 2.00 2.00
First day cover, #642a 3.50
First day cover, #639-642, each 1.50
Inscription block of 4, #642a 2.50 —
Pane of 16, #639-642 8.50

First day covers of Nos. 639-642 total 79,599. See Offices in Geneva Nos. 246-249; Vienna Nos. 162-165.

Protection for Refugees — A277

Printed by Leigh-Mardon Pty. Limited, Australia. Designed by Francoise Peyroux, France.

1994, Apr. 29 **Litho.** ***Perf. 14.3x14.8***

643 A277 50c **multicolored** *(600,000)+* .90 .90
First day cover *(33,558)* 1.25
Inscription block of 4 4.50 —

See Offices in Geneva No. 250; Vienna No. 166.

Dove of Peace — A278

Sleeping Child, by Stanislaw Wyspianski — A279

Mourning Owl, by Vanessa Isitt — A280

Printed by Cartor S.A., France, and Norges Banks Seddeltrykkeri, Norway (#646).

1994, Apr. 29 **Litho.** ***Perf. 12.9***

644 A278 10c **multicolored** *(1,000,000)+* .25 .25
First day cover 1.00
Inscription block of 4 .75 —
645 A279 19c **multicolored** *(1,000,000)+* .30 .30
First day cover 1.25
Inscription block of 4 1.50 —

Engr.

Perf. 13.1

646 A280 $1 **red brown** *(1,000,000)+* 1.50 1.50
First day cover 3.00
Inscription block of 4 7.00 —
Nos. 644-646 (3) 2.05 2.05

First day covers of Nos. 644-646 total 48,946.

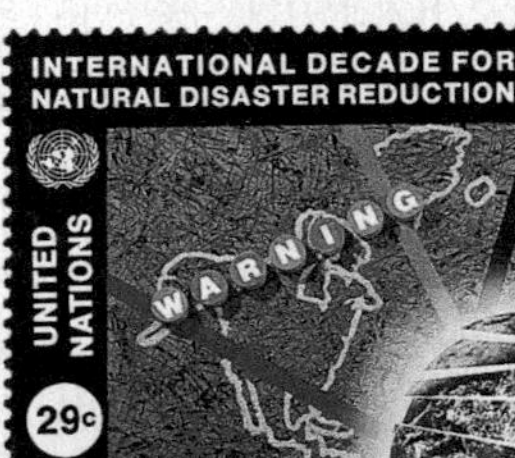

Intl. Decade for Natural Disaster Reduction — A281

Printed by The House of Questa, UK. Designed by Kenji Koga, Japan.

Earth seen from space, outline map of: #647, North America. #648, Eurasia. #649, South America, #650, Australia and South Asia.

1994, May 27 **Litho.** ***Perf. 13.9x14.2***

647 A281 29c **multicolored** *(630,000)+* 1.75 1.75
648 A281 29c **multicolored** *(630,000)+* 1.75 1.75
649 A281 29c **multicolored** *(630,000)+* 1.75 1.75
650 A281 29c **multicolored** *(630,000)+* 1.75 1.75
a. Block of 4, #647-650 7.50 7.50
First day cover, #650a 7.50
First day cover, #647-650, each 6.00
Inscription block of 4, #650a 8.00 —
Pane of 40, #647-650 75.00

First day covers of Nos. 647-650 total 37,135. See Offices in Geneva Nos. 251-254; Vienna Nos. 170-173.

Population and Development A282

Printed by Johann Enschede and Sons, the Netherlands. Designed by Jerry Smath, US.

Designs: 29c, Children playing. 52c, Family with house, car, other possessions.

1994, Sept. 1 **Litho.** ***Perf. 13.2x13.6***

651 A282 29c **multicolored** *(590,000)+* .40 .40
First day cover 1.00
Inscription block of 4 2.00 —
652 A282 52c **multicolored** *(540,000)+* .80 .80
First day cover 1.00
First day cover, #651-652 2.25
Inscription block of 4 3.75 —

First day covers of Nos. 651-652 total 45,256.
See Offices in Geneva Nos. 258-259; Vienna Nos. 174-175.

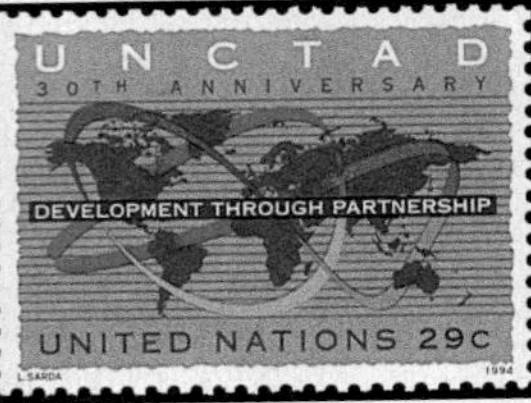

UNCTAD, 30th Anniv. — A283

Printed by Johann Enschede and Sons, the Netherlands. Designed by Luis Sarda, Spain.

1994, Oct. 28

653 A283 29c **multicolored** *(590,000)+* .40 .40
First day cover 1.00
Inscription block of 4 1.75 —
654 A283 50c **multi, diff.** *(540,000)+* .80 .80
First day cover 1.00
First day cover, #653-654 1.50
Inscription block of 4 3.00

First day covers of Nos. 653-654 total 42,763. See Offices in Geneva Nos. 260-261; Vienna Nos. 176-177.

UN, 50th Anniv. — A284

Printed by Swiss Postal Service. Designed by Rocco J. Callari, US.

1995, Jan. 1 **Litho. & Engr.** ***Perf. 13.4***

655 A284 32c **multicolored** *(938,644)* .90 .90
First day cover *(39,817)* 1.25
Inscription block of 4 4.00 —

See Offices in Geneva No. 262; Vienna No. 178.

Social Summit, Copenhagen — A285

Printed by Austrian Government Printing Office.
Designed by Friedensreich Hundertwasser.

1995, Feb. 3 **Photo. & Engr.** ***Perf. 13.6x13.9***

656 A285 50c **multicolored** *(495,388)* 1.00 1.00
First day cover *(31,797)* 2.00
Inscription block of 4 4.00 —

See Offices in Geneva No. 263; Vienna No. 179.

Endangered Species Type of 1993

Printed by Johann Enschede and Sons, the Netherlands. Designed by Chris Calle, US.

Designs: No. 657, Giant armadillo. No. 658, American bald eagle. No. 659, Fijian/Tongan banded iguana. No. 660, Giant panda.

1995, Mar. 24 **Litho.** ***Perf. 13x12½***

657 A271 32c **multicolored** *(756,000)+* .40 .40
658 A271 32c **multicolored** *(756,000)+* .40 .40
659 A271 32c **multicolored** *(756,000)+* .40 .40
660 A271 32c **multicolored** *(756,000)+* .40 .40
a. Block of 4, 657-660 2.25 2.25
First day cover, #660a 5.00
First day cover, #657-660, each 1.75
Inscription block of 4, #660a 2.50 —
Pane of 16, #657-660 9.00

First day covers of Nos. 657-660 total 67,311. See Offices in Geneva Nos. 264-267; Vienna Nos. 180-183.

Intl. Youth Year, 10th Anniv. — A286

Printed by The House of Questa (UK). Designed by Gottfried Kumpf, Austria.
Designs: 32c, Seated child. 55c, Children cycling.

1995, May 26 Litho. *Perf. 14.4x14.7*

661 A286 32c **multicolored** *(358,695)* .55 .55
First day cover 1.00
Inscription block of 4 2.50 —
662 A286 55c **multicolored** *(288,424)* .95 .95
First day cover 1.00
First day cover, #661-662 1.50
Inscription block of 4 4.25 —

First day covers of Nos. 661-662 total 42,846. See Offices in Geneva Nos. 268-269; Vienna Nos. 184-185.

UN, 50th Anniv. — A287

Printed by Johann Enschede Security Printing, the Netherlands. Designed by Paul and Chris Calle, US.
Designs: 32c, Hand with pen signing UN Charter, flags. 50c, Veterans' War Memorial, Opera House, San Francisco.

1995, June 26 Engr. *Perf. 13.3x13.6*

663 A287 32c **black** *(501,961)* .55 .55
First day cover 1.00
Inscription block of 4 2.25 —
664 A287 50c **maroon** *(419,932)* 1.00 1.00
First day cover 1.00
First day cover, #663-664 1.50
Inscription block of 4 4.25 —

Souvenir Sheet

Litho. & Engr.

Imperf

665 Sheet of 2, #663-664 *(347,963)+* 3.00 3.00
a. A287 32c **black** 1.25 1.25
b. A287 50c **maroon** 1.50 1.50
First day cover 2.75

First day covers of Nos. 663-665 total: New York, 69,263; San Francisco, 53,354.
No. 665 exists with gold China 1996 overprint. Value $20.
See Offices in Geneva Nos. 270-272; Vienna Nos. 186-188.

4th World Conference on Women, Beijing — A288

Printed by Postage Stamp Printing House, MPT, People's Republic of China. Designed by Ting Shao Kuang, People's Republic of China.
Designs: 32c, Mother and child. 40c, Seated woman, cranes flying above.

1995, Sept. 5 Photo. *Perf. 12*

666 A288 32c **multicolored** *(561,847)* .50 .50
First day cover 1.25
Inscription block of 4 2.25 —

Size: 28x50mm

667 A288 40c **multicolored** *(499,850)* .85 .85
First day cover 1.25
First day cover, #666-667 2.50
Inscription block of 4 3.75 —

First day covers of Nos. 666-667 total 103,963. See Offices in Geneva Nos. 273-274; Vienna Nos. 189-190.

UN Headquarters A289

Designed by John B. De Santis, Jr. US.

1995, Sept. 5 Litho. *Perf. 15*

668 A289 20c **multicolored** .35 .35
First day cover *(18,326)* 1.50
Inscription block of 4 2.00 —

Miniature Sheet

United Nations, 50th Anniv. — A290

Designed by Ben Verkaaik, Netherlands.
Printed by House of Questa, UK.
Designs: #669a-669 l, Various people in continuous design (2 blocks of six stamps with gutter between).

1995, Oct. 24 Litho. *Perf. 14*

669 A290 Sheet of 12 *(214,639 sheets)* 5.00 5.00
First day cover 12.00
a.-l. 32c any single .40 .40
First day cover, #669a-669l, each 7.00
670 Souvenir booklet *(85,256 booklets)* 5.50
a. A290 32c Booklet pane of 3, vert. strip of 3 from UL of sheet 1.35 1.35
b. A290 32c Booklet pane of 3, vert. strip of 3 from UR of sheet 1.35 1.35
c. A290 32c Booklet pane of 3, vert. strip of 3 from LL of sheet 1.35 1.35
d. A290 32c Booklet pane of 3, vert. strip of 3 from LR of sheet 1.35 1.35
First day covers, #670a-670d, set booklet tab singles 100.00

First day covers of Nos. 669-670 total 47,632. See Offices in Geneva Nos. 275-276; Vienna Nos. 191-192.

WFUNA, 50th Anniv. — A291

Designed by Rudolf Mirer, Switzerland.
Printed by Johann Enschede and Sons, the Netherlands.

1996, Feb. 2 Litho. *Perf. 13x13½*

671 A291 32c **multicolored** *(580,000)+* .50 .50
First day cover 1.00
Inscription block of 4 2.25 —

See Offices in Geneva No. 277; Vienna No. 193.

Mural, by Fernand Leger — A292

Designed by Fernand Leger, France.
Printed by House of Questa, UK.

1996, Feb. 2 Litho. *Perf. 14½x15*

672 A292 32c **multicolored** *(780,000)+* .45 .45
First day cover 1.25
Inscription block of 4 2.00 —
673 A292 60c **multi, diff.** *(680,000)+* .95 .95
First day cover 1.75
First day cover, #672-673 2.25
Inscription block of 4 4.00 —

Endangered Species Type of 1993

Printed by Johann Enschede and Sons, the Netherlands. Designed by Diane Bruyninckx, Belgium.

Designs: No. 674, Masdevallia veitchiana. No. 675, Saguaro cactus. No. 676, West Australian pitcher plant. No. 677, Encephalartos horridus.

1996, Mar. 14 Litho. *Perf. 12½*

674 A271 32c **multicolored** *(640,000)+* .45 .45
675 A271 32c **multicolored** *(640,000)+* .45 .45
676 A271 32c **multicolored** *(640,000)+* .45 .45
677 A271 32c **multicolored** *(640,000)+* .45 .45
a. Block of 4, #674-677 2.25 2.25
First day cover, #677a 5.00
First day cover, #674-677, each 1.75
Inscription block of 4, #677a 2.75 —
Pane of 16, #674-677 10.00

See Offices in Geneva Nos. 280-283; Vienna Nos. 196-199.

City Summit (Habitat II) — A293

Printed by Johann Enschede and Sons, the Netherlands. Designed by Teresa Fasolino, US.

Designs: No. 678, Deer. No. 679, Man, child, dog sitting on hill, overlooking town. No. 680, People walking in park, city skyline. No. 681, Tropical park, Polynesian woman, boy. No. 682, Polynesian village, orchids, bird.

1996, June 3 Litho. *Perf. 14x13½*

678 A293 32c **multicolored** *(475,000)+* .80 .80
679 A293 32c **multicolored** *(475,000)+* .80 .80
680 A293 32c **multicolored** *(475,000)+* .80 .80
681 A293 32c **multicolored** *(475,000)+* .80 .80
682 A293 32c **multicolored** *(475,000)+* .80 .80
a. Strip of 5, #678-682 7.00 7.00
First day cover, #682a 6.00
First day cover, #678-682, each 7.00
Inscription block of 10, 2 #682a 14.50
Sheet of 25 35.00

See Offices in Geneva Nos. 284-288; Vienna Nos. 200-204.

Sport and the Environment — A294

Printed by The House of Questa, UK. Designed by LeRoy Neiman, US.

Designs: 32c, Men's basketball. 50c, Women's volleyball, horiz.

1996, July 19 Litho. *Perf. 14x14½, 14½x14*

683 A294 32c **multicolored** *(680,000)+*	.65	.65
First day cover		1.25
Inscription block of 4	3.00	—
684 A294 50c **multicolored** *(680,000)+*	1.40	1.40
First day cover		1.50
First day cover, #683-684		1.75
Inscription block of 4	6.25	—

Souvenir Sheet

685 A294 Sheet of 2, #683-684 *(370,000)+*	2.50	2.50
First day cover		2.50

See Offices in Geneva Nos. 289-291; Vienna Nos. 205-207.
1996 Summer Olympic Games, Atlanta, GA.

Plea for Peace — A295

Printed by House of Questa, UK.
Designed by: 32c, Peng Yue, China. 60c, Cao Chenyu, China.

Designs: 32c, Doves. 60c, Stylized dove.

1996, Sept. 17 Litho. *Perf. 14½x15*

686 A295 32c **multicolored** *(580,000)+*	.50	.50
First day cover		1.00
Inscription block of 4	2.25	—
687 A295 60c **multicolored** *(580,000)+*	.90	.90
First day cover		1.00
First day cover, #686-687		1.75
Inscription block of 4	4.25	—

See Offices in Geneva Nos. 292-293; Vienna Nos. 208-209.

UNICEF, 50th Anniv. — A296

Printed by The House of Questa, UK. Designed by The Walt Disney Co.

Fairy Tales: 32c, Yeh-Shen, China. 60c, The Ugly Duckling, by Hans Christian Andersen.

1996, Nov. 20 Litho. *Perf. 14½x15*

688 A296 32c **multicolored** *(1,000,000)+*	.45	.45
First day cover		1.00
Pane of 8 + label	4.00	
689 A296 60c **multicolored** *(1,000,000)+*	1.10	1.10
First day cover		1.00
First day cover, #688-689		2.00
Pane of 8 + label	12.00	

See Offices in Geneva Nos. 294-295; Vienna Nos. 210-211.

Flag Type of 1980

Printed by Helio Courvoisier, S.A., Switzerland. Designed by Oliver Corwin,US, and Robert Stein, UN. Each pane contains 4 blocks of 4 (Nos. 690-693, 694-697). A se-tenant block of 4 designs centers each pane.

1997, Feb. 12 Photo. *Perf. 12*

Granite Paper

690 A185 32c Tajikistan *(940,000)+*	.75	1.00
691 A185 32c Georgia *(940,000)+*	.75	1.00
692 A185 32c Armenia *(940,000)+*	.75	1.00
693 A185 32c Namibia *(940,000)+*	.75	1.00
a. Block of 4, #690-693	9.00	13.00
694 A185 32c Liechtenstein *(940,000)+*	.75	1.00
695 A185 32c Republic of Korea *(940,000)+*	.75	1.00
696 A185 32c Kazakhstan *(940,000)+*	.75	1.00
697 A185 32c Latvia *(940,000)+*	.75	1.00
a. Block of 4, #694-697	9.00	13.00
First day cover, #690-697, each		3.00
Set of 2 panes of 16	34.00	

First day covers of Nos. 690-697 total 136,114.

Cherry Blossoms, UN Headquarters — A297

Peace Rose — A298

Printed by The House of Questa, Ltd., UK.

1997, Feb. 12 Litho. *Perf. 14½*

698 A297 8c **multicolored** *(700,000)+*	.25	.25
First day cover		1.00
Inscription block of 4	.70	—
699 A298 55c **multicolored** *(700,000)+*	.90	.90
First day cover		1.25
First day cover, #698-699		2.50
Inscription block of 4	3.75	—

First day covers of Nos. 698-699 total 34,794.

Endangered Species Type of 1993

Printed by Johann Enschedé and Sons, the Netherlands. Designed by Rocco J. Callari, US.
Designs: No. 700, African elephant. No. 701, Major Mitchell's cockatoo. No. 702, Black-footed ferret. No. 703, Cougar.

1997, Mar. 13 Litho. *Perf. 12½*

700 A271 32c **multicolored** *(532,000)+*	.40	.40
701 A271 32c **multicolored** *(532,000)+*	.40	.40
702 A271 32c **multicolored** *(532,000)+*	.40	.40
703 A271 32c **multicolored** *(532,000)+*	.40	.40
a. Block of 4, #700-703	2.25	2.25
First day cover, #703a		3.00
First day cover, #700-703, each		2.50
Inscription block of 4, #703a	2.50	
Pane of 16	9.00	

First day covers of Nos. 700-703 total 66,863.
See Offices in Geneva Nos. 298-301; Vienna Nos. 214-217.

Earth Summit, 5th Anniv. — A299

Printed by Helio Courvoisier SA, Switzerland. Designed by Peter Max, US.
Designs: No. 704, Sailboat. No. 705, Three sailboats. No. 706, Two people watching sailboat, sun. No. 707, Person, sailboat.
$1, Combined design similar to Nos. 704-707.

1997, May 30 Photo. *Perf. 11.5*

Granite Paper

704 A299 32c **multicolored** *(328,566)*	.90	.90
705 A299 32c **multicolored** *(328,566)*	.90	.90
706 A299 32c **multicolored** *(328,566)*	.90	.90
707 A299 32c **multicolored** *(328,566)*	.90	.90
a. Block of 4, #704-707	5.00	5.00
First day cover, #707a		3.00
First day cover, #704-707, each		6.00
Inscription block of 4, #707a	6.00	

Souvenir Sheet

708 A299 $1 **multicolored** *(181,667)*	3.25	3.25
First day cover		2.75
a. Ovptd. in sheet margin *(154,435)*	*17.50*	*17.50*
First day cover, #708a		16.50

First day covers of Nos. 704-708 total: New York, 52,528; San Francisco, 49,197.
See Offices in Geneva Nos. 302-306; Vienna Nos. 218-222.
No. 708 contains one 60x43mm stamp. Overprint in sheet margin of No. 708a reads "PACIFIC 97 / World Philatelic Exhibition / San Francisco, California / 29 May - 8 June 1997".

Transportation — A300

Printed by The House of Questa, UK. Panes of 20. Designed by Michael Cockcroft, UK.

Ships: No. 709, Clipper ship. No. 710, Paddle steamer. No. 711, Ocean liner. No. 712, Hovercraft. No. 713, Hydrofoil.

1997, Aug. 29 Litho. *Perf. 14x14½*

709 A300 32c **multicolored** *(303,767)*	.65	.65
710 A300 32c **multicolored** *(303,767)*	.65	.65
711 A300 32c **multicolored** *(303,767)*	.65	.65
712 A300 32c **multicolored** *(303,767)*	.65	.65
713 A300 32c **multicolored** *(303,767)*	.65	.65
a. Strip of 5, #709-713	4.25	4.25
First day cover, #713a		4.00
First day cover, #709-713, each		5.75
Inscription block of 10, 2#713a	10.00	
Sheet of 20	20.00	

First day covers of Nos. 709-713 total 29,287.
See Offices in Geneva Nos. 307-311; Vienna Nos. 223-227.
No. 713a has continuous design.

Philately — A301

Printed by Joh. Enschedé and Sons, the Netherlands. Panes of 20. Designed by Robert Stein, US.
Designs: 32c, No. 473. 50c, No. 474.

1997, Oct. 14 Litho. *Perf. 13½x14*

714 A301 32c **multicolored** *(363,237)*	.60	.60
First day cover		1.25
Inscription block of 4	3.00	—
715 A301 50c **multicolored** *(294,967)*	1.50	1.50
First day cover		1.50
First day cover, #714-715		4.00
Inscription block of 4	6.75	—

First day covers of Nos. 714-715 total 43,684.
See Offices in Geneva Nos. 312-313; Vienna Nos. 228-229.

World Heritage Convention, 25th Anniv. — A302

Printed by Government Printing Office, Austria. Panes of 20. Designed by Robert Stein, US, based on photographs by Guo Youmin, People's Republic of China.
Terracotta warriors of Xian: 32c, Single warrior. 60c, Massed warriors. No. 718a, like #716. No. 718b, like #717. No. 718c, like Geneva #314. No. 718d, like Geneva #315. No. 718e, like Vienna #230. No. 718f, like Vienna #231.

1997, Nov. 19 Litho. *Perf. 13½*

716 A302 32c **multicolored** *(549,095)*	.75	.75
First day cover		1.25
Inscription block of 4	3.25	—
717 A302 60c **multicolored** *(505,265)*	1.25	1.25
First day cover		1.75
First day cover, #716-717		3.50
Inscription block of 4	5.25	—
718 Souvenir booklet *(304,406 booklets)*	8.50	
a.-f. A302 8c any single	.35	.35
g. Booklet pane of 4 #718a	1.40	1.40

h.	Booklet pane of 4 #718b	1.40	1.40
i.	Booklet pane of 4 #718c	1.40	1.40
j.	Booklet pane of 4 #718d	1.40	1.40
k.	Booklet pane of 4 #718e	1.40	1.40
l.	Booklet pane of 4 #718f	1.40	1.40

First day covers of Nos. 716-718 total 33,386.

See Offices in Geneva Nos. 314-316; Vienna Nos. 230-232.

Flag Type of 1980

Printed by Helio Courvoisier, S.A., Switzerland. Designed by Oliver Corwin, and Robert Stein, US. Each pane contains 4 blocks of 4 (Nos. 719-722, 723-726). A se-tenant block of 4 designs centers each pane.

No. 719, Micronesia. No. 720, Slovakia. No. 721, Democratic People's Republic of Korea. No. 722, Azerbaijan. No. 723, Uzbekistan. No. 724, Monaco. No. 725, Czech Republic. No. 726, Estonia.

1998, Feb. 13 Photo. *Perf. 12*
Granite Paper

719	A185 32c multi *(718,000)+*	.80	.80
720	A185 32c multi *(718,000)+*	.80	.80
721	A185 32c multi *(718,000)+*	.80	.80
722	A185 32c multi *(718,000)+*	.80	.80
a.	Block of 4, #719-722	12.50	12.50
723	A185 32c multi *(718,000)+*	.80	.80
724	A185 32c multi *(718,000)+*	.80	.80
725	A185 32c multi *(718,000)+*	.80	.80
726	A185 32c multi *(718,000)+*	.80	.80
a.	Block of 4, #723-726	12.50	12.50
	First day cover, #719-726, each		2.50
	Set of 2 panes of 16	40.00	
	Nos. 719-726 (8)	6.40	6.40

A303

A304

A305

Printed by The House of Questa, UK. Designed by Zhang Le Lu, China (1c), Robert Stein, US (2c), Gregory Halili, Philippines (21c). Panes of 20.

1998, Feb. 13 Litho. *Perf. 14½x15, 15x14½*

727	A303 1c **multicolored** *(1,000,000)+*	.25	.25
	First day cover		1.00
	Inscription block of 4	.20	—
728	A304 2c **multicolored** *(1,000,000)+*	.25	.25
	First day cover		1.00
	Inscription block of 4	.20	—
729	A305 21c **multicolored** *(1,000,000)+*	.40	.40
	First day cover		1.25
	First day cover, #727-729		4.00
	Inscription block of 4	1.75	—
	Nos. 727-729 (3)	.90	.90

Endangered Species Type of 1993

Printed by Johann Enschedé and Sons, the Netherlands. Designed by Rocco J. Callari, US and Pat Medearis-Altman, New Zealand.

Designs: No. 730, Lesser galago. No. 731, Hawaiian goose. No. 732, Golden birdwing. No. 733, Sun bear.

1998, Mar. 13 Litho. *Perf. 12½*

730	A271 32c **multicolored** *(502,000)+*	.45	.45
731	A271 32c **multicolored** *(502,000)+*	.45	.45
732	A271 32c **multicolored** *(502,000)+*	.45	.45
733	A271 32c **multicolored** *(502,000)+*	.45	.45
a.	Block of 4, #730-733	2.25	2.25
	First day cover, #733a		4.00
	First day cover, #730-733, each		3.50
	Inscription block of 4, #733a	2.50	—
	Pane of 16	10.00	

See Offices in Geneva Nos. 318-321; Vienna Nos. 235-238.

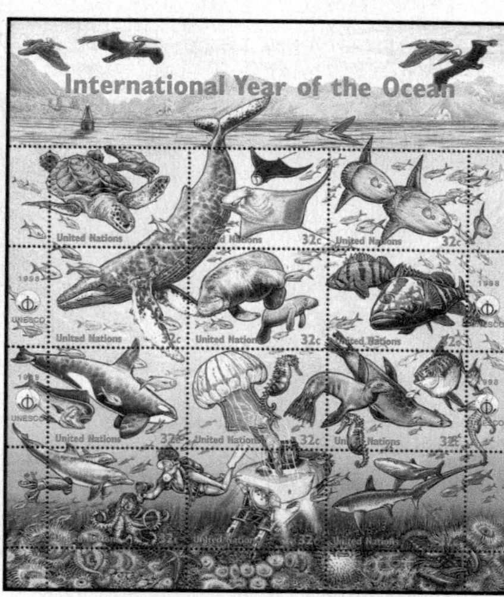

Intl. Year of the Ocean — A306

Printed by Johann Enschedé and Sons, the Netherlands. Designed by Larry Taugher, US.

1998, May 20 Litho. *Perf. 13x13½*

734	A306 Sheet of 12 *(280,000)+*	12.50	12.50
	First day cover		9.00
a.-l.	32c any single	1.00	1.00
	First day cover, #734a-734l, each		3.50

See Offices in Geneva No. 322; Vienna No. 239.

Rain Forests A307

Printed by Government Printing Bureau, Japan. Designed by Rick Garcia, US.

1998, June 19 Litho. *Perf. 13x13½*

735	A307 32c Jaguar *(570,000)+*	.50	.50
	First day cover		2.50
	Inscription block of 4	2.25	—

Souvenir Sheet

736	A307 $2 like #735 *(280,000)+*	3.00	3.00
	First day cover		3.00

See Offices in Geneva Nos. 323-324; Vienna Nos. 240-241.

U.N. Peacekeeping Forces, 50th Anniv. — A308

Printed by Helio Courvoisier, S.A. (Switzerland). Designed by Andrew Davidson, UK.

Designs: 33c, Commander with binoculars. 40c, Two soldiers on vehicle.

1998, Sept. 15 Photo. *Perf. 12*

737	A308 33c **multicolored** *(485,000)+*	.50	.50
	First day cover		1.50
	Inscription block of 4	2.25	—
738	A308 40c **multicolored** *(445,000)+*	.75	.75
	First day cover		1.50
	First day cover, #737-738		2.00
	Inscription block of 4	3.75	—

See Offices in Geneva Nos. 325-326; Vienna Nos. 242-243.

Universal Declaration of Human Rights, 50th Anniv. — A309

Printed by Cartor Security Printing (France). Designed by Jean-Michel Folon, France.

Stylized people: 32c, Carrying flag. 55c, Carrying pens.

1998, Oct. 27 Litho. & Photo. *Perf. 13*

739	A309 32c **multicolored** *(485,000)+*	.45	.45
	First day cover		1.50
	Inscription block of 4	2.25	—
740	A309 55c **multicolored** *(445,000)+*	.90	.90
	First day cover		1.50
	First day cover, #739-740		7.00
	Inscription block of 4	4.00	—

See Offices in Geneva Nos. 327-328; Vienna Nos. 244-245.

Schönbrunn Palace, Vienna — A310

Printed by the House of Questa, UK. Panes of 20. Designed by Robert Stein, US.

Designs: 33c, #743f, The Gloriette. 60c, #743b, Wall painting on fabric (detail), by Johann Wenzl Bergl, vert. No. 743a, Blue porcelain vase, vert. No. 743c, Porcelain stove, vert. No. 743d, Palace. No. 743e, Great Palm House (conservatory).

1998, Dec. 4 Litho. *Perf. 14*

741	A310 33c **multicolored** *(485,000)+*	.55	.55
	First day cover		1.25
	Inscription block of 4	2.00	—
742	A310 60c **multicolored** *(445,000)+*	1.25	1.00
	First day cover		1.50
	First day cover, #741-742		2.50
	Inscription block of 4	4.50	—

Souvenir Booklet

743	Booklet *(110,000)+*	19.50	
a.-c.	A310 11c any single	.35	.35
d.-f.	A310 15c any single	1.40	1.40
g.	Booklet pane of 4 #743d	5.50	5.50
h.	Booklet pane of 3 #743a	1.00	1.00
i.	Booklet pane of 3 #743b	1.00	1.00
j.	Booklet pane of 3 #743c	1.00	1.00
k.	Booklet pane of 4 #743e	5.50	5.50
l.	Booklet pane of 4 #743f	5.50	5.50

See Offices in Geneva Nos. 329-331; Vienna Nos. 246-248.

Flag Type of 1980

Printed by Helio Courvoisier S.A., Switzerland. Designed by Oliver Corwin, Robert Stein and Blake Tarpley, US. Each pane contains 4 blocks of 4 (Nos. 744-747, 748-751). A se-tenant block of 4 designs centers each pane.

1999, Feb. 5 Photo. *Perf. 12*

744	A185 33c Lithuania *(524,000)+*	.75	.75
745	A185 33c San Marino *(524,000)+*	.75	.75
746	A185 33c Turkmenistan *(524,000)+*	.75	.75
747	A185 33c Marshall Islands *(524,000)+*	.75	.75
a.	Block of 4, #744-747	8.00	8.00
748	A185 33c Moldova *(524,000)+*	.75	.75
749	A185 33c Kyrgyzstan *(524,000)+*	.75	.75
750	A185 33c Bosnia & Herzegovina *(524,000)+*	.75	.75
751	A185 33c Eritrea *(524,000)+*	.75	.75
a.	Block of 4, #748-751	8.00	8.00
	First day cover, #744-751, each		2.75
	Set of 2 panes of 16	35.00	
	Nos. 744-751 (8)	6.00	6.00

First day covers of Nos. 744-751 total 102,040.

Flags and Globe — A311

Roses — A312

Designed by Blake Tarpley (#752), Rorie Katz, (#753), US.
Printed by Johann Enschedé and Sons, the Netherlands (#752), Helio Courvoisier SA, Switzerland (#753).

1999, Feb. 5 **Litho.** ***Perf. 14x13½***

752 A311 33c **multicolored** *(960,000)+* .50 .50
First day cover 1.00
Inscription block of 4 2.25 —

Photo.
Granite Paper
Perf. 11½x12

753 A312 $5 **multicolored** *(420,000)+* 7.50 7.50
First day cover 5.50
First day cover, #752-753 6.50
Inscription block of 4 25.00 —

First day covers of Nos. 752-753 total 32,142.

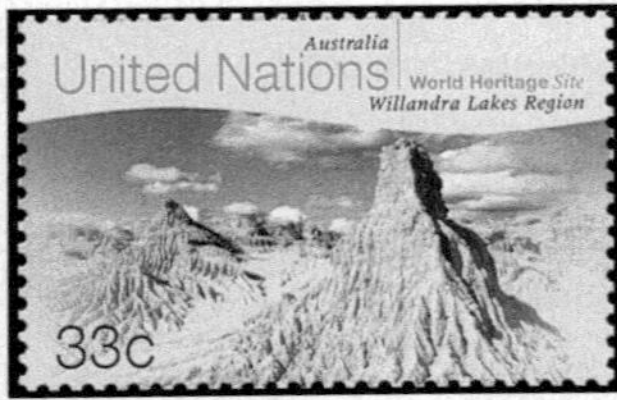

World Heritage Sites, Australia A313

Printed by House of Questa, UK. Panes of 20. Designed by Passmore Design, Australia.
Designs: 33c, #756f, Willandra Lakes region. 60c, #756b, Wet tropics of Queensland. No. 756a, Tasmanian wilderness. No. 756c, Great Barrier Reef. No. 756d, Uluru-Kata Tjuta Natl. Park. No. 756e, Kakadu Natl. Park.

1999, Mar. 19 **Litho.** ***Perf. 13***

754 A313 33c **multicolored** *(480,000)+* .60 .60
First day cover 2.00
Inscription block of 4 3.00 —
755 A313 60c **multicolored** *(440,000)+* 1.25 1.25
First day cover 2.00
First day cover, #754-755 3.00
Inscription block of 4 6.00 —

Souvenir Booklet

756 Booklet *(97,000)+* 35.00
a.-c. A313 5c any single .70 .70
d.-f. A313 15c any single 1.50 1.50
g. Booklet pane of 4, #756a 2.80 2.80
h. Booklet pane of 4, #756d 6.00 6.00
i. Booklet pane of 4, #756b 2.80 2.80
j. Booklet pane of 4, #756e 6.00 6.00
k. Booklet pane of 4, #756c 2.80 2.80
l. Booklet pane of 4, #756f 6.00 6.00

First day covers of Nos. 754-756 total 42,385.
See Offices in Geneva Nos. 333-335; Vienna Nos. 250-252.

Endangered Species Type of 1993

Printed by Johann Enschedé and Sons, the Netherlands. Designed by Jimmy Wang, China.
Designs: No. 757, Tiger. No. 758, Secretary bird. No. 759, Green tree python. No. 760, Long-tailed chinchilla.

1999, Apr. 22 **Litho.** ***Perf. 12½***

757 A271 33c **multicolored** *(494,000)+* .60 .60
758 A271 33c **multicolored** *(494,000)+* .60 .60
759 A271 33c **multicolored** *(494,000)+* .60 .60
760 A271 33c **multicolored** *(494,000)+* .60 .60
a. Block of 4, #757-760 2.40 2.40
First day cover, #760a 3.50
First day cover, #757-760, each 2.25
Inscription block of 4, #760a 2.75 —
Pane of 16 10.00

First day covers of Nos. 757-760 total 49,656.
See Offices in Geneva Nos. 336-339; Vienna Nos. 253-256.

UNISPACE III, Vienna — A314

Printed by Helio Courvoisier SA, Switzerland. Designed by Attila Hejja, US.
Designs: No. 761, Probe on planet's surface. No. 762, Planetary rover. No. 763, Composite of Nos. 761-762.

1999, July 7 **Photo.** ***Rouletted 8***

761 A314 33c **multicolored** *(1,000,000)+* .50 .50
762 A314 33c **multicolored** *(1,000,000)+* .50 .50
a. Pair, #761-762 1.75 1.75
First day cover, #762a 2.00
First day cover, #761-762, each 8.00
Inscription block of 4 4.00 —
Pane of 10, #761-762 10.00 —

Souvenir Sheet
Perf. 14½

763 A314 $2 **multicolored** *(530,000)+* 4.00 4.00
First day cover 3.00
a. Ovptd. in sheet margin 18.00 18.00
First day cover 8.00

No. 763a was issued 7/7/00 and is overprinted in violet blue "WORLD STAMP EXPO 2000 / ANAHEIM, CALIFORNIA / U.S.A./ 7-16 JULY 2000."
First day covers of Nos. 761-763 total 48,190.
See Offices in Geneva Nos. 340-342; Vienna Nos. 257-259.

UPU, 125th Anniv. — A315

Printed by Helio Courvoisier S.A., Switzerland. Panes of 24. Designed by Mark Hess, US.

Various people, 19th century methods of mail transportation, denomination at: No. 764, UL. No. 765, UR. No. 766, LL. No. 767, LR.

1999, Aug. 23 **Photo.** ***Perf. 11¾***

764 A315 33c **multicolored** *(378,000)+* .45 .45
765 A315 33c **multicolored** *(378,000)+* .45 .45
766 A315 33c **multicolored** *(378,000)+* .45 .45
767 A315 33c **multicolored** *(378,000)+* .45 .45
a. Block of 4, #764-767 2.50 2.50
Inscription block of 4 3.00 —
First day cover, #767a 2.00
First day covers, #764-767, set of 4 individual covers 25.00
Sheet of 20 17.00

First day covers of Nos. 764-767 total 25,294.
See Offices in Geneva Nos. 343-346; Vienna Nos. 260-263.

In Memoriam — A316

Printed by Walsall Security Printers, Ltd., United Kingdom. Panes of 20. Designed by Robert Stein, US.

Designs: 33c, $1, UN Headquarters. Size of $1 stamp: 34x63mm.

1999, Sept. 21 **Litho.** ***Perf. 14½x14***

768 A316 33c **multicolored** *(550,000)+* .80 .80
Inscription block of 4 4.00 —
First day cover 1.25

Souvenir Sheet
Perf. 14

769 A316 $1 **multicolored** *(235,000)+* 2.00 2.00
First day cover 1.75

First day covers of Nos. 768-769 total 42,130.
See Offices in Geneva Nos. 347-348, Vienna Nos. 264-265.

Education, Keystone to the 21st Century — A317

Printed by Government Printing Office, Austria. Panes of 20. Designed by Romero Britto, Brazil.

1999, Nov. 18 **Litho.** ***Perf. 13½x13¾***

770 A317 33c Two readers *(450,000)+* .50 .50
First day cover 1.25
Inscription block of 4 2.25 —
771 A317 60c Heart *(430,000)+* 1.00 1.00
First day cover 1.75
First day cover, #770-771 2.50
Inscription block of 4 4.50 —

First day covers of Nos. 770-771 total 34,679.
See Offices in Geneva Nos. 349-350, Vienna Nos. 266-267.

International Year of Thanksgiving — A318

Printed by Cartor Security Printing, France. Panes of 20. Designed by Rorie Katz, US.

2000, Jan. 1 **Litho.** ***Perf. 13¼x13½***

772 A318 33c **multicolored** *(550,000)+* .75 .75
First day cover 1.25
Inscription block of 4 3.25 —

On No. 772 parts of the design were applied by a thermographic process producing a shiny, raised effect. See Offices in Geneva No. 351, Vienna No. 268.

Endangered Species Type of 1993

Printed by Johann Enschedé and Sons, the Netherlands. Designed by Suzanne Duranceau, Canada.
Designs: No. 773, Brown bear. No. 774, Black-bellied bustard. No. 775, Chinese crocodile lizard. No. 776, Pygmy chimpanzee.

2000, Apr. 6 **Litho.** ***Perf. 12¾x12½***

773 A271 33c **multicolored** *(490,000)+* .50 .50
774 A271 33c **multicolored** *(490,000)+* .50 .50
775 A271 33c **multicolored** *(490,000)+* .50 .50
776 A271 33c **multicolored** *(490,000)+* .50 .50
a. Block of 4, #773-776 2.50 2.50
First day cover, #776a 2.75
First day cover, #773-776, each 1.50
Inscription block of 4, #776a 2.75 —
Pane of 16 10.00

See Offices in Geneva Nos. 352-355; Vienna Nos. 269-272.

Our World 2000 — A319

Printed by Cartor Security Printing, France. Panes of 20. Designed by Robert Stein, US.

Winning artwork in Millennium painting competition: 33c, Crawling Toward the Millennium, by Sam Yeates, US. 60c, Crossing, by Masakazu Takahata, Japan, vert.

2000, May 30 Litho. *Perf. 13x13½, 13½x13*

777 A319 33c **multicolored** *(400,000)+* .60 .60
First day cover 1.00
Inscription block of 4 2.50 —
778 A319 60c **multicolored** *(360,000)+* 1.00 1.00
First day cover 1.00
First day cover, #777-778 2.00
Inscription block of 4 4.50 —

See Offices in Geneva No. 356-357, Vienna No. 273-274.

UN, 55th Anniv. — A320

Printed by Cartor Security Printing, France. Panes of 20. Designed by Rorie Katz, US.

Designs: 33c, Workmen removing decorative discs in General Assembly Hall, 1956. 55c, UN Building in 1951.

2000, July 7 Litho. *Perf. 13¼x13*

779 A320 33c **multicolored** *(400,000)+* .55 .55
First day cover 1.00
Inscription block of 4 2.50 —
780 A320 55c **multicolored** *(360,000)+* .95 .95
First day cover 1.00
First day cover, #779-780 2.00
Inscription block of 4 4.25 —

Souvenir Sheet

781 A320 Sheet of 2, #779-780 *(277,000)+* 3.00 3.00
First day cover 2.50

See Offices in Geneva No. 358-360, Vienna No. 275-277.

International Flag of Peace — A321

Printed by House of Questa, UK. Panes of 20. Designed by Mateja Prunk, Slovenia.

2000, Sept. 15 Litho. *Perf. 14½x14*

782 A321 33c **multicolored** *(400,000)+* .65 .65
First day cover 1.25
Inscription block of 4 2.60 —

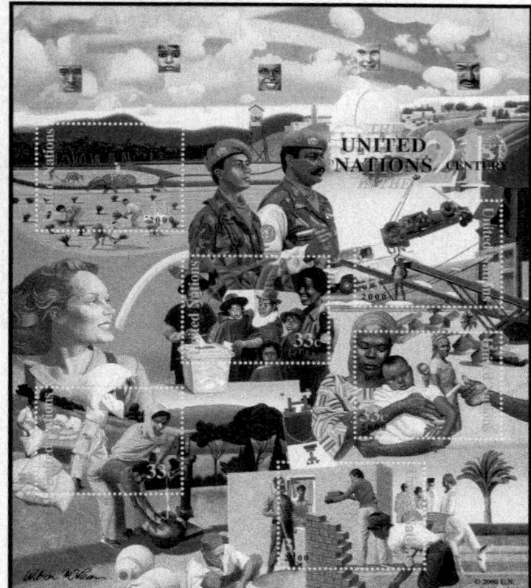

The UN in the 21st Century — A322

Printed by Government Printing Office, Austria. Designed by Wilson McLean, UK.

No. 783: a, Farmers, animals in rice paddy. b, Vehicle chassis being lifted. c, People voting. d, Baby receiving inoculation. e, Woman, man at pump. f, Mason, construction workers.

2000, Sept. 15 Litho. *Perf. 14*

783 A322 Sheet of 6 *(274,000)+* 7.50 7.50
First day cover 7.50
a.-f. 33c any single 1.25 1.25
First day covers, each 6.00

See Offices in Geneva No. 361; Vienna No. 278.

World Heritage Sites, Spain — A323

Printed by House of Questa, UK. Panes of 20. Designed by Robert Stein, US.

Designs: Nos. 784, 786a, Alhambra, Generalife and Albayzin, Granada. Nos. 785, 786d, Amphitheater of Mérida. #786b, Walled Town of Cuenca. #786c, Aqueduct of Segovia. #786e, Toledo. #786f, Güell Park, Barcelona.

2000, Oct. 6 Litho. *Perf. 14¾x14½*

784 A323 33c **multicolored** *(400,000)+* .55 .55
First day cover 1.25
Inscription block of 4 2.60 —
785 A323 60c **multicolored** *(360,000)+* 1.10 1.10
First day cover 1.25
First day cover, #784-785 2.00
Inscription block of 4 5.00 —

Souvenir Booklet

786 Booklet *(63,000)+* 15.00
a.-c. A323 5c any single .45 .45
d.-f. A323 15c any single .80 .80
g. Booklet pane of 4, #786a 1.80 1.80
h. Booklet pane of 4, #786d 3.20 3.20
i. Booklet pane of 4, #786b 1.80 1.80
j. Booklet pane of 4, #786e 3.20 3.20
k. Booklet pane of 4, #786c 1.80 1.80
l. Booklet pane of 4, #786f 3.20 3.20

See Offices in Geneva Nos. 362-364, Vienna Nos. 279-281.

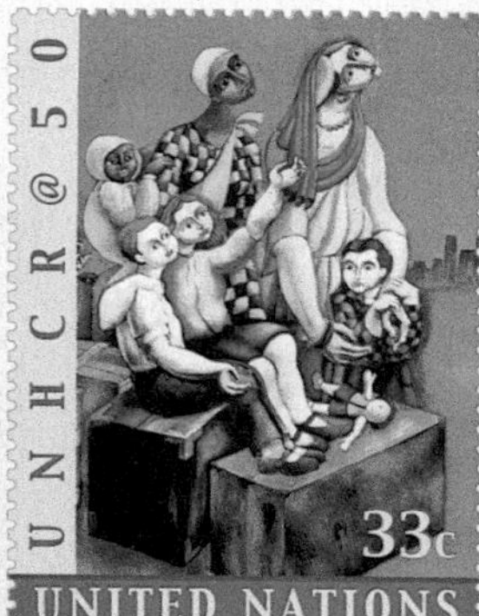

Respect for Refugees — A324

Printed by Johann Enschedé and Sons, the Netherlands. Panes of 20. Designed by Yuri Gevorgian, Armenia.

2000, Nov. 9 Litho. *Perf. 13¼x12¾*

787 A324 33c **multicolored** *(540,000)+* .75 .75
First day cover 1.50
Inscription block of 4 3.25 —

Souvenir Sheet

788 A324 $1 **multicolored** *(225,000)+* 2.00 2.00
First day cover 2.00

See Offices in Geneva Nos. 365-366, Vienna Nos. 282-283.

Endangered Species Type of 1993

Printed by Johann Enschedé and Sons, the Netherlands. Designed by Grace DeVito, US.

Designs: No. 789, Common spotted cuscus. No. 790, Resplendent quetzal. No. 791, Gila monster. No. 792, Guereza.

2001, Feb. 1 Litho. *Perf. 12¾x12½*

789 A271 34c **multicolored** *(430,000)+* .60 .60
790 A271 34c **multicolored** *(430,000)+* .60 .60
791 A271 34c **multicolored** *(430,000)+* .60 .60
792 A271 34c **multicolored** *(430,000)+* .60 .60
a. Block of 4, #789-792 2.40 2.40
First day cover, #792a 3.50
First day cover, #789-792 each 1.25
Inscription block of 4, #792a 2.75 —
Pane of 16 10.00

See Offices in Geneva Nos. 367-370; Vienna Nos. 284-287.

Intl. Volunteers Year — A325

Printed by Johann Enschedé and Sons, the Netherlands. Panes of 20. Designed by Rorie Katz and Robert Stein, US.

Paintings by: 34c, Jose Zaragoza, Brazil. 80c, John Terry, Australia.

2001, Mar. 29 Litho. *Perf. 13¼*

793 A325 34c **multicolored** *(390,000)+* .65 .65
First day cover 1.25
Inscription block of 4 2.60
794 A325 80c **multicolored** *(360,000)+* 1.60 1.60
First day cover 1.75
First day cover, #793-794 2.50
Inscription block of 4 6.50

See Offices in Geneva Nos. 371-372; Vienna Nos. 288-289.

Flag Type of 1980

Printed by Helio Courvoisier, Switzerland. Designed by Ole Hamann. Issued in panes of 16; each contains 4 blocks of 4 (Nos. 795-798, 799-802). A se-tenant block of 4 designs centers each pane.

No. 795, Slovenia. No. 796, Palau. No. 797, Tonga. No. 798, Croatia. No. 799, Former Yugoslav Republic of Macedonia. No. 800, Kiribati. No. 801, Andorra. No. 802, Nauru.

2001, May 25 Photo. *Perf. 12*

Granite Paper

795 A185 34c multi *(460,000)+* 1.25 1.25
796 A185 34c multi *(460,000)+* 1.25 1.25
797 A185 34c multi *(460,000)+* 1.25 1.25
798 A185 34c multi *(460,000)+* 1.25 1.25
a. Block of 4, #795-798 15.00 15.00
799 A185 34c multi *(460,000)+* 1.25 1.25
800 A185 34c multi *(460,000)+* 1.25 1.25
801 A185 34c multi *(460,000)+* 1.25 1.25

802 A185 34c multi *(460,000)+* 1.25 1.25
a. Block of 4, #799-802 15.00 15.00
First day cover, #795-802, each 1.25
Set of 2 panes of 16 40.00
Nos. 795-802 (8) 10.00 10.00

Sunflower — A326

Rose — A327

Printed by Johann Enschedé and Sons, the Netherlands. Panes of 20. Designed by Rorie Katz, US.

2001, May 25 Litho. *Perf. 13¼x13¾*

803 A326 7c **multicolored** *(550,000)+* .25 .25
First day cover 1.00
Margin block of 4, inscription .50 —
804 A327 34c **multicolored** *(650,000)+* .60 .60
First day cover 1.00
First day cover, #803-804 1.40
Margin block of 4, inscription 3.00 —

World Heritage Sites, Japan — A328

Printed by Johann Enschedé and Sons, the Netherlands. Panes of 20. Designed by Rorie Katz, US.

Designs: 34c, #807a, Kyoto. 70c, #807d, Shirakawa-Go and Gokayama. #807b, Nara. #807c, Himeji-Jo. #807e, Itsukushima Shinto Shrine. #807f, Nikko.

2001, Aug. 1 Litho. *Perf. 12¾x13¼*

805 A328 34c **multicolored** *(380,000)+* .60 .60
First day cover 1.25
Inscription block of 4 2.50 —
806 A328 70c **multicolored** *(360,000)+* 1.25 1.25
First day cover 1.25
First day cover, #805-806 2.00
Inscription block of 4 5.50 —

Souvenir Booklet

807 Booklet *(51,000)+* 14.00
a.-c. A328 5c any single .40 .40
d.-f. A328 20c any single .75 .75
g. Booklet pane of 4, #807a 1.60 1.60
h. Booklet pane of 4, #807d 3.00 3.00
i. Booklet pane of 4, #807b 1.60 1.60
j. Booklet pane of 4, #807e 3.00 3.00
k. Booklet pane of 4, #807c 1.60 1.60
l. Booklet pane of 4, #807f 3.00 3.00

See Offices in Geneva Nos. 373-375, Vienna Nos. 290-292.

Dag Hammarskjöld (1905-61), UN Secretary General — A329

Printed by Banknote Corporation of America, US. Panes of 20. Designed by Robert Stein, US.

2001, Sept. 18 Engr. *Perf. 11x11¼*

808 A329 80c **blue** *(530,000)+* 1.50 1.50
First day cover 2.00
Inscription block of 4 6.00 —

See Offices in Geneva No. 376, Vienna No. 293.

A330

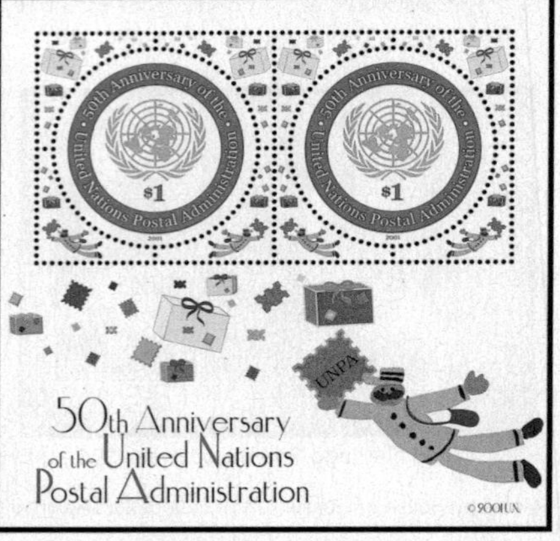

UN Postal Administration, 50th Anniv. — A331

Printed by Johann Enschedé and Sons, the Netherlands. Panes of 20. Designed by Rorie Katz, US.

2001, Oct. 18 Litho. *Perf. 13½*

809 A330 34c Stamps, streamers *(350,000)+* .55 .55
First day cover 1.00
Inscription block of 4 2.75 —
810 A330 80c Stamps, gifts *(310,000)+* 1.50 1.50
First day cover 1.25
First day cover, #809-810 2.00
Inscription block of 4 6.50 —

Souvenir Sheet

811 A331 Sheet of 2 #811a *(180,000)+* 8.00 8.00
a. $1 **blue & light blue,** 38mm diameter 4.00 4.00
First day cover 10.00

See Offices in Geneva Nos. 377-379, Vienna Nos. 294-296.

Climate Change — A332

Printed by Walsall Security Printers Limited, UK. Panes of 24. Designed by Robert Giusti, US.

Designs: No. 812, Canada geese, greenhouses, butterfly, thistle. No. 813, Canada geese, iceberg, penguins, tomato plant. No. 814, Palm tree, solar collector. No. 815, Hand planting ginkgo cutting.

2001, Nov. 16 Litho. *Perf. 13¼*

812 A332 34c **multicolored** *(70,500)+* 1.00 1.00
813 A332 34c **multicolored** *(70,500)+* 1.00 1.00
814 A332 34c **multicolored** *(70,500)+* 1.00 1.00
815 A332 34c **multicolored** *(70,500)+* 1.00 1.00
a. Horiz. strip, #812-815 4.00 4.00
Inscription block of 8 8.00 —
First day cover, #815a 2.75
First day cover, #812-815, each 9.00
Pane of 24 24.00 —

See Offices in Geneva Nos. 380-383, Vienna Nos. 297-300.

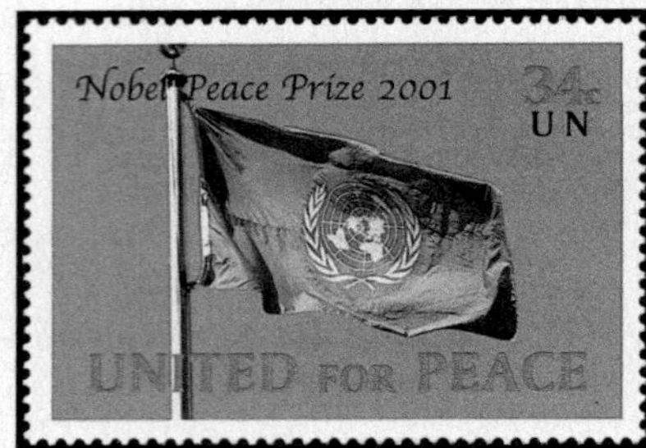

Awarding of Nobel Peace Prize to Secretary General Kofi Annan and UN — A333

Printed by Cartor S. A., France. Panes of 12. Designed by Robert Stein, US.

2001, Dec. 10 Litho. *Perf. 13¼*

816 A333 34c **multicolored** *(840,000)+* .70 .70
Inscription block of 4 3.50 —
First day cover 1.00
Pane of 12 11.50 —

See Offices in Geneva Nos. 384, Vienna Nos. 301.

Children and Stamps — A334

Printed by Government Printing Office, Austria. Panes of 20. Designed by Jerry Smath, US.

2002, Mar. 1 Litho. *Perf. 13¾*

817 A334 80c **multicolored** *(420,000)+* 1.40 1.40
First day cover 1.50
Inscription block of 4 6.00 —

Endangered Species Type of 1993

Printed by Johann Enschedé and Sons, the Netherlands. Designed by Teresa Fasolino, US.

Designs: No. 818, Hoffmann's two-toed sloth. No. 819, Bighorn sheep. No. 820, Cheetah. No. 821, San Esteban Island chuckwalla.

2002, Apr. 4 Litho. *Perf. 12¾x12½*

818 A271 34c **multicolored** *(414,000)+* .80 .80
819 A271 34c **multicolored** *(414,000)+* .80 .80
820 A271 34c **multicolored** *(414,000)+* .80 .80
821 A271 34c **multicolored** *(414,000)+* .80 .80
a. Block of 4, #818-821 3.25 3.25
First day cover, #821a 3.50
First day cover, #818-821 each 1.50
Inscription block of 4, #821a 3.50 —
Pane of 16 13.50 —

See Offices in Geneva Nos. 386-389; Vienna 308-311.

Independence of East Timor — A335

Printed by The House of Questa, UK. Designed by Karen Kelleher, US. Panes of 20

Designs: 34c, Wooden ritual mask. 57c, Decorative door panel.

2002, May 20 **Litho.** ***Perf. 14x14½***

822 A335 34c **multicolored** *(355,000)+* .70 .70
First day cover 1.25
Inscription block of 4 3.00 —
823 A335 57c **multicolored** *(325,000)+* 1.20 1.20
First day cover 1.50
First day cover, #822-823 2.50
Inscription block of 4 5.00 —

See Offices in Geneva Nos. 390-391; Vienna Nos. 312-313.

Intl. Year of Mountains A336

Printed by Cartor Security Printing, France. Designed by Robert Stein and Rorie Katz, US.

Designs: No. 824, Khan Tengri, Kyrgyzstan. No. 825, Mt. Kilimanjaro, Tanzania. No. 826, Mt. Foraker, US. No. 827, Paine Grande, Chile.

2002, May 24 **Litho.** ***Perf. 13x13¼***

824 A336 34c **multicolored** *(1,362,000)+* .75 .75
First day cover 3.00
825 A336 34c **multicolored** *(1,362,000)+* .75 .75
First day cover 3.00
826 A336 80c **multicolored** *(1,362,000)+* 1.25 1.50
First day cover 5.00
First day cover, #824, 826 3.25
827 A336 80c **multicolored** *(1,362,000)+* 1.25 1.50
a. Vert. strip or block of four, #824-827 6.00 8.00
First day cover 5.00
First day cover, #825, 827 3.25
First day cover, #823-827 3.00
Pane of 12, 3 each #824-827 20.00 —

See Offices in Geneva Nos. 392-395; Vienna Nos. 314-317.

World Summit on Sustainable Development, Johannesburg A337

Printed by The House of Questa, UK. Designed by Peter Max, US.

Designs: No. 828, Sun, Earth, planets, stars. No. 829, Three women. No. 830, Sailboat. No. 831, Three faceless people.

2002, June 27 **Litho.** ***Perf. 14½x14***

828 A337 37c **multicolored** *(1,350,000)+* .75 .75
First day cover 1.25
829 A337 37c **multicolored** *(1,350,000)+* .75 .75
First day cover 1.25
830 A337 60c **multicolored** *(1,350,000)+* 1.25 1.25
First day cover 2.00
First day cover, #828, 830 2.25
831 A337 60c **multicolored** *(1,350,000)+* 1.25 1.25
a. Vert. strip or block of four, #828-831 6.00 6.00
First day cover 2.00
First day cover, #829, 831 2.25
First day cover, #828-831 4.50
Pane of 12, 3 each #828-831 20.00 —

See Offices in Geneva Nos. 396-399; Vienna Nos. 318-321.

World Heritage Sites, Italy — A338

Printed by Cartor Security Printing, France. Panes of 20. Designed by Rorie Katz, US.

Designs: 37c, #834d, Florence. 70c, #834a, Amalfi Coast. #834b, Aeolian Islands. #834c, Rome. #834e, Pisa. #834f, Pompeii.

2002, Aug. 30 **Litho.** ***Perf. 13½x13¼***

832 A338 37c **multicolored** *(365,000)+* .70 .70
First day cover 1.25
Inscription block of 4 3.00 —
833 A338 70c **multicolored** *(345,000)+* 1.40 1.40
First day cover 2.40
First day cover, #832-833 3.00
Inscription block of 4 6.00 —

Souvenir Booklet

834 Booklet *(52,000)+* 16.00
a.-c. A338 5c any single .40 .40
d.-f. A338 15c any single .90 .90
g. Booklet pane of 4, #834d 3.60 3.60
h. Booklet pane of 4, #834a 1.60 1.60
i. Booklet pane of 4, #834e 3.60 3.60
j. Booklet pane of 4, #834b 1.60 1.60
k. Booklet pane of 4, #834f 3.60 3.60
l. Booklet pane of 4, #834c 1.60 1.60

See Offices in Geneva Nos. 400-402, Vienna Nos. 322-324.
See Italy Nos. 2506-2507.

AIDS Awareness — A339

Printed by Walsall Security Printers Limited, UK. Panes of 20. Designed by Rorie Katz, US.

2002, Oct. 24 **Litho.** ***Perf. 13½***

835 A339 70c **multicolored** *(365,000)+* 1.50 1.50
Inscription block of 4 6.50
First day cover, #835 2.00
Pane of 20 30.00

See No. B1, Offices in Geneva Nos. 403, B1, Vienna Nos. 325, B1.

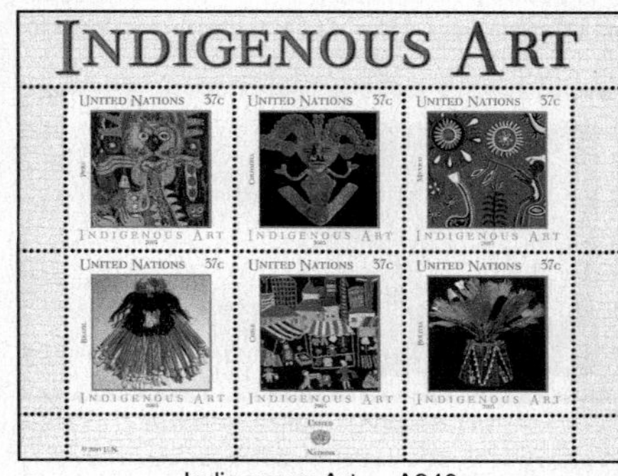

Indigenous Art — A340

Printed by House of Questa, UK.
Designed by Rorie Katz and Robert Stein, US.

No. 836: a, Detail of Paracas textile, Peru. b, Sinu culture anthropo-zoomorphic pendant, Colombia. c, Hicholi Indian embroidery, Mexico. d, Rigpaktsa back ornament, Brazil. e, Wool crafts, Chile. f, Huari feathered woven hat, Bolivia.

2003, Jan. 31 **Litho.** ***Perf. 14¼***

836 A340 Sheet of 6 *(165,000)+* 8.50 8.50
First day cover 7.50
a.-f. 37c Any single 1.40 1.40

See Offices in Geneva No. 405; Vienna No. 326.

Clasped Hands — A341

UN Emblem — A342

UN Headquarters A343

Printed by House of Questa, UK (23c, 37c); Walsall Security Printers Ltd., UK (70c). Designed by Rorie Katz, US (23c, 37c), Robert Stein and Rorie Katz (70c). Panes of 20.

2003, Mar. 28 **Litho.** ***Perf. 14¼***

837 A341 23c **multicolored** *(870,000)+* .40 .40
First day cover 1.00
Inscription block of 4 1.75 —

Litho. with Foil Application

838 A342 37c **gold & multicolored** *(870,000)+* .60 .60
First day cover 1.00
Inscription block of 4 2.75 —

Litho. with Hologram

Perf. 13¼x12¾

839 A343 70c **multicolored** *(910,000)+* 1.40 1.40
First day cover 1.75
First day cover, #837-839 3.00
Inscription block of 4 5.75 —

Powered Flight, Cent. — A344

Printed by Government Printing Office, Austria. Designed by Robert Stein, US. Panes of 16 (eight pairs).

2003, Mar. 28 **Litho.** ***Perf. 13½x13¾***

840 23c **multicolored** *(175,000)+* 1.25 1.25
841 70c **multicolored** *(175,000)+* 2.75 2.75
a. A344 Tete beche pair, #840-841 4.00 4.00
First day cover, #841a 2.75
Inscription block of 4 8.00

Endangered Species Type of 1993

Printed by Johann Enschedé and Sons, the Netherlands. Designed by Joseph Hautman, US.

Designs: No. 842, Great hornbill. No. 843, Scarlet ibis. No. 844, Knob-billed goose. No. 845, White-faced whistling duck.

2003, Apr. 3 **Litho.** ***Perf. 12¾x12½***

842 A271 37c **multicolored** *(364,000)+* .80 .80
843 A271 37c **multicolored** *(364,000)+* .80 .80
844 A271 37c **multicolored** *(364,000)+* .80 .80
845 A271 37c **multicolored** *(364,000)+* .80 .80
a. Block of 4, #842-845 3.25 3.25
First day cover, #845a 3.00
First day cover, #842-845 each 1.00
Inscription block of 4, #845a 3.75 —
Pane of 16 13.50 —

See Offices in Geneva Nos. 407-410; Vienna 329-332.

Intl. Year of Freshwater A345

Printed by De La Rue Global Services, United Kingdom. Panes of 20. Designed by Rick Garcia, US.

2003, June 20 **Litho.** ***Perf. 14¼x14½***

846 A345 23c Wildlife, garbage *(211,000)+* 1.50 1.50
847 A345 37c Trees, canoe *(211,000)+* 2.00 2.00
a. Horiz. pair, #846-847 7.50 7.50
First day cover, #847a 3.00
Inscription block of 4 15.00 —

See Offices in Geneva, Nos. 411-412; Vienna Nos. 333-334.

Ralph Bunche (1903-71), Diplomat — A346

Printed by Johann Enschedé and Sons, the Netherlands. Panes of 20. Designed by Rorie Katz, US.

Litho. With Foil Application

2003, Aug. 7 ***Perf. 13½x14***

848 A346 37c **blue & multicolored** *(405,000)+* .80 .80
First day cover 1.75
Inscription block of 4 3.50 —
Pane of 20 16.50 —

See Offices in Geneva No. 413; Vienna No. 336.

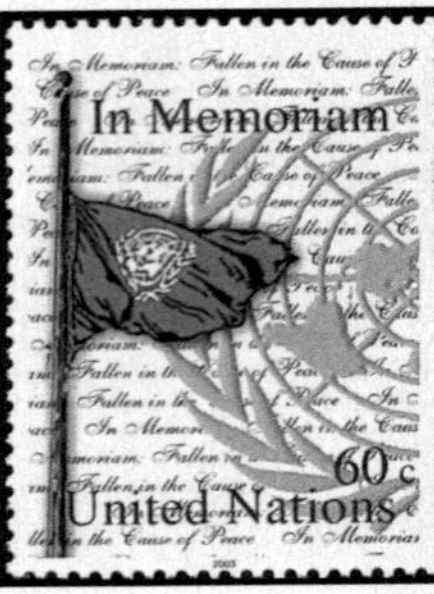

In Memoriam of Victims of Aug. 19 Bombing of UN Complex in Baghdad, Iraq — A347

Printed by Cartor Security Printing, France. Panes of 20. Designed by Jenny J. Karia and Robert Stein, US.

2003, Oct. 24 **Litho.** ***Perf. 13¼x13***

849 A347 60c **multicolored** *(850,000)+* 1.25 1.25
First day cover 2.00
Inscription block of 4 5.00 —
Pane of 20 25.00 —

See Offices in Geneva No. 414, Vienna No. 337.

World Heritage Sites, United States A348

Printed by De La Rue Global Services, United Kingdom. Panes of 20. Designed by Rorie Katz, US.

Designs: 37c, #852a, Yosemite National Park. 60c, #852d, Hawaii Volcanoes National Park. #852b, Great Smoky Mountains National Park. #852c, Olympic National Park. #852e, Everglades National Park. #852f, Yellowstone National Park.

2003, Oct. 24 **Litho.** ***Perf. 14½x14¼***

850 A348 37c **multicolored** *(303,000)+* .90 .90
First day cover 1.25
Inscription block of 4 3.75 —
851 A348 60c **multicolored** *(193,000)+* 1.50 1.50
First day cover 2.10
First day cover, #850-851 3.00
Inscription block of 4 6.50 —

Souvenir Booklet

852 Booklet *(38,500)+* 14.00
a.-c. A348 10c any single .35 .35
d.-f. A348 20c any single .70 .70
g. Booklet pane of 4 #852a 1.40 1.40
h. Booklet pane of 4 #852d 2.80 2.80
i. Booklet pane of 4 #852b 1.40 1.40
j. Booklet pane of 4 #852e 2.80 2.80
k. Booklet pane of 4 #852c 1.40 1.40
l. Booklet pane of 4 #852f 2.80 2.80

See Offices in Geneva Nos. 415-417, Vienna Nos. 338-340.

UN Security Council — A349

UN Emblem — A350

UN General Assembly — A351

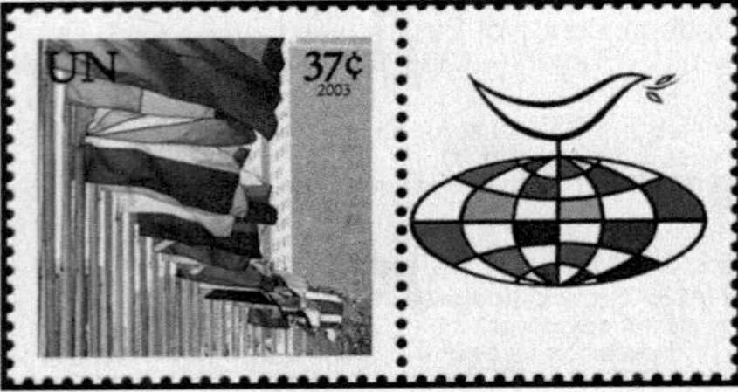

Flags — A352

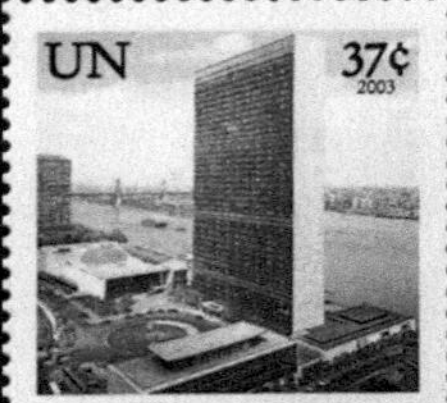

UN Headquarters — A353

2003, Nov. 26 **Litho.** ***Perf. 13¼***

853 A349 37c **multicolored** + label 12.50 12.50
854 A350 37c **multicolored** + label 12.50 12.50
855 A351 37c **multicolored** + label 12.50 12.50
856 A352 37c **multicolored** + label 12.50 12.50
857 A353 37c **multicolored** + label 12.50 12.50
a. Vert. strip of 5, #853-857, + 5 labels 65.00 65.00
Sheet, 4 #857a 260.00 —
First day cover, #857a —
First day cover, #853-857, each 15.00

The full sheet sold for $14.95 with or without personalized labels. The personalization of labels was available only at UN Headquarters, and not through mail order.

One thousand full sheets with sheet margins inscribed "Hong Kong Stamp Expo" were sold only at that venue. Value $135. Also exists with sheet margins inscribed "Essen." Value $125.

A sheet containing two strips of five stamps similar to Nos. 853-857 but dated "2005" and ten labels sold for $4.95. These sheets were only available canceled. Value $100. An imperforate error of this sheet is known.

Endangered Species Type of 1993

Printed by Johann Enschedé and Sons, the Netherlands. Designed by Yuan Lee, U.S.

Designs: No. 858, American black bear. No. 859, Musk deer. No. 860, Golden snub-nosed monkey. No. 861, Wild yak.

2004, Jan. 29 **Litho.** ***Perf. 12¾x12½***

858 A271 37c **multicolored** *(316,000)+* .90 .90
859 A271 37c **multicolored** *(316,000)+* .90 .90
860 A271 37c **multicolored** *(316,000)+* .90 .90
861 A271 37c **multicolored** *(316,000)+* .90 .90
a. Block of 4, #858-861 3.60 3.60
First day cover, #861a 4.00
First day cover, #858-861, each 1.50
Inscription block of 4, #861a 3.75 —
Pane of 16 15.00 —

See Offices in Geneva Nos. 418-421; Vienna Nos. 342-345.

Indigenous Art Type of 2003

Printed by Johann Enschedé and Sons, the Netherlands. Designed by Rorie Katz and Robert Stein, US.

No. 862: a, Viking wood carving depicting Saga of Sigurd Favnesbane, Norway. b, Stele, Italy. c, Detail of matador's suit, Spain. d, Amphora, Greece. e, Bronze figurine of bull, Czech Republic. f, Detail of lacquer box illustration depicting scene from "On the Seashore," by Alexander Pushkin, Russia.

2004, Mar. 4 **Litho.** ***Perf. 13¼***

862 A340 Sheet of 6 *(134,000)+* 6.00 6.00
First day cover 8.50
a.-f. 37c Any single 1.00 1.00
First day cover, a.-f., each 3.00

See Offices in Geneva No. 422; Vienna No. 346.

Road Safety — A354

Printed by Cartor Security Printing. Panes of 20. Designed by Michel Granger, France.

Road map art with: 37c, Automobile with road signs, city skyline. 70c, Automobile, hand, vert.

2004, Apr. 7 Litho. *Perf. 13x13¼, 13¼x13*

863 A354 37c **multicolored** *(266,000)+*		.85	.85
First day cover			1.25
Inscription block of 4		3.50	—
864 A354 70c **multicolored** *(196,000)+*		1.40	1.40
First day cover			2.50
First day cover, #863-864			3.75
Inscription block of 4		6.50	—

See Offices in Geneva Nos. 423-424, Vienna Nos. 347-348.

Japanese Peace Bell, 50th Anniv. — A355

Printed by Imprimerie des Timbres-Poste, France. Panes of 20. Designed by Martin Mörck, Norway.

2004, June 3 Litho. & Engr. *Perf. 13¼x13*

865 A355 80c **multicolored** *(376,000)+*	1.25	1.25
First day cover		2.25
Inscription block of 4	5.50	—
Pane of 20	27.50	

See Offices in Geneva No. 425; Vienna No. 349.

World Heritage Sites, Greece — A356

Printed by Johann Enschedé and Sons, the Netherlands. Panes of 20. Designed by Rorie Katz, US.

Designs: No. 866, Acropolis, Athens. Nos. 867, 868e, Delos. No. 868a, Delphi. No. 868b, Pythagoreion and Heraion of Samos. No. 868c, Olympia. No. 868d, Mycenae and Tiryns.

2004, Aug. 12 Litho. *Perf. 14x13¼*

866 A356 37c **multicolored** *(275,000)+*	.70	.70
First day cover		1.25
Inscription block of 4	2.75	—
a. Booklet pane of 4	3.00	—
867 A356 60c **multicolored** *(195,000)+*	1.10	1.10
First day cover		2.10
First day cover, #866-867		2.75
Inscription block of 4	4.75	—

Souvenir Booklet

868 Booklet, #866a, 868f-868j *(31,000)+*	15.00	
a.-d. A356 23c any single	.55	.55
e. A356 37c multi	.90	.90
f. Booklet pane of 4 #868a	2.20	2.20
g. Booklet pane of 4 #868b	2.20	2.20
h. Booklet pane of 4 #868c	2.20	2.20
i. Booklet pane of 4 #868d	2.20	2.20
j. Booklet pane of 4 #868e	3.60	3.60

See Offices in Geneva Nos. 426-428, Vienna Nos. 350-352. No. 868 sold for $7.20.

My Dream for Peace — A357

Printed by Government Printing Office, Austria. Panes of 20.

Winning designs of Lions Club International children's global peace poster contest by: 37c, Sittichok Pariyaket, Thailand. 80c, Bayan Fais Abu Bial, Israel.

2004, Sept. 21 Litho. *Perf. 14*

869 A357 37c **multicolored** *(276,000)+*	.60	.60
First day cover		1.25
Inscription block of 4	2.75	—
Pane of 20	12.00	—
870 A357 80c **multicolored** *(206,000)+*	1.40	1.40
First day cover		2.25
First day cover, #869-870		3.00
Inscription block of 4	6.00	—
Pane of 20	28.00	—

See Offices in Geneva Nos. 429-430, Vienna Nos. 353-354.

A358

Human Rights — A359

Printed by Banknote Corportation of America, US. Designed by Yuri Gervorgian, Armenia.

2004, Oct. 14 Litho. *Perf. 11¼*

871 A358 37c **multicolored** *(464,000)+*	.75	.75
First day cover		1.25
Pane of 8	6.00	—
872 A359 70c **multicolored** *(464,000)+*	1.40	1.40
First day cover		2.40
First day cover, #871-872		3.00
Pane of 8	11.50	—

See Offices in Geneva Nos. 431-432, Vienna Nos. 355-356.

Disarmament A360

Printed by Government Printing Office, Austria. Designed by Michel Granger, France.

2004, Oct. 15 Litho. *Perf. 13¾*

873 A360 37c **multicolored** *(270,000)+*	.80	.80
First day cover		2.00
Inscription block of 4	3.25	—
Pane of 20	16.50	—

The U.N. Postal Administration announced that it would begin offering canceled-to-order stamps at the same price as mint stamps, effective Feb. 4, 2005. It has been reliably reported that this did not happen.

United Nations, 60th Anniv. — A361

Printed by Banknote Corporation of America, US. Designed by Czeslaw Slania, Sweden.

2005, Feb. 4 Litho. & Engr. *Perf. 11x11¼*

874 A361 80c **multicolored** *(395,000)+*	1.50	1.50
First day cover		2.50
Inscription block of 4	6.25	—
Pane of 20	30.00	

Souvenir Sheet

Litho.

Imperf

875 A361 $1 **multicolored** *(135,000)+*	17.50	17.50
First day cover		12.00

See Offices in Geneva Nos. 434-435; Vienna Nos. 357-358.

Endangered Species Type of 1993

Printed by Johann Enschedé and Sons, the Netherlands. Designed by Boris Zlotsky, US.

Designs: No. 876, Blue orchid. No. 877, Swan orchid. No. 878, Christmas orchid. No. 879, Aerangis modesta.

2005, Mar. 3 Litho. *Perf. 12¾x12½*

876 A271 37c **multicolored** *(248,000)+*	1.10	1.10
877 A271 37c **multicolored** *(248,000)+*	1.10	1.10
878 A271 37c **multicolored** *(248,000)+*	1.10	1.10
879 A271 37c **multicolored** *(248,000)+*	1.10	1.10
a. Block of 4, #876-879	4.50	4.50
First day cover, #879a		3.75
First day cover, #876-879, each		1.50
Inscription block of 4, #879a	4.75	—
Pane of 16	18.00	

See Offices in Geneva Nos. 436-439; Vienna Nos. 360-363.

Non-Violence, Sculpture by Carl Fredrik Reuterswärd, New York — A362

Armillary Sphere, Sculpture by Paul Manship, Geneva — A363

Terra Cotta Warriors, Vienna — A364

Single Form, Sculpture by Barbara Hepworth, New York — A365

Sphere Within a Sphere, Sculpture by Arnaldo Pomodoro, New York — A366

2005, Mar. 3 **Litho.** ***Perf. 13¼***

No.	Type	Description	Unused	Used
880	A362	80c **multicolored** + label	*50.00*	*50.00*
881	A363	80c **multicolored** + label	*50.00*	*50.00*
882	A364	80c **multicolored** + label	*50.00*	*50.00*
883	A365	80c **multicolored** + label	*50.00*	*50.00*
884	A366	80c **multicolored** + label	*50.00*	*50.00*
a.		Vert. strip of 5, #880-884, + 5 labels	*250.00*	*250.00*
		Sheet, 2 #884a	*500.00*	—
		First day cover, #884a		—
		First day cover, #880-884, each		15.00
b.		Sheet of 10, both #884 37c (error)	*3,250.*	
c.		Vert. strip of 5, #884 37c (error)	*1,450.*	

The full sheet sold for $14.95 with or without personalized labels. The personalization of labels was available only at UN Headquarters, and not through mail order.

The full sheet exists with sheet margins and labels commemorating the Riccione 2005 Philatelic Exhibition. This sheet went on sale 8/20/05 and was also sold for $14.95. Value $175.

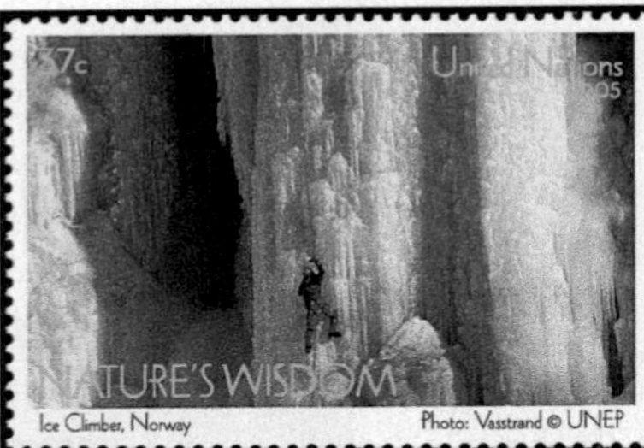

Nature's Wisdom — A367

Printed by Cartor Security Printing, France. Panes of 20. Designed by Robert Stein, US.

Designs: 37c, Ice climber, Norway. 80c, Egret, Japan.

2005, Apr. 21 **Litho.** ***Perf. 13½x13¼***

No.	Type	Description	Unused	Used
885	A367	37c **multicolored** *(280,000)+*	.65	.65
		First day cover		1.40
		Inscription block of 4	2.75	—
		Pane of 20	13.00	—
886	A367	80c **multicolored** *(200,000)+*	1.50	1.50
		First day cover		3.00
		First day cover, #885-886		3.50
		Inscription block of 4	6.00	—
		Pane of 20	30.00	—

See Offices in Geneva Nos. 440-441, Vienna Nos. 364-365.

Intl. Year of Sport — A368

Printed by Cartor Security Printing, France. Designed by Roland Hirter, Switzerland.

2005, June 3 **Litho.** ***Perf. 13x13¼***

No.	Type	Description	Unused	Used
887	A368	37c Sailing *(255,000)+*	.65	.65
		First day cover		1.25
		Inscription block of 4	2.75	—
		Pane of 20	13.00	—
888	A368	70c Running *(185,000)+*	1.25	1.25
		First day cover		2.50
		First day cover, #887-888		3.50
		Inscription block of 4	5.25	—
		Pane of 20	25.00	—

See Offices in Geneva Nos. 442-443; Vienna Nos. 366-367.

World Heritage Sites, Egypt — A369

Printed by Johann Enschedé and Sons, the Netherlands. Panes of 20. Designed by Rorie Katz, US.

Designs: Nos. 889, 891a, Memphis and its Necropolis. Nos. 890, 891d, Ancient Thebes. No. 891b, Philae. No. 891c, Abu Mena. No. 891e, Islamic Cairo. No. 891f, St. Catherine area.

2005, Aug. 4 **Litho.** ***Perf. 14x13¼***

No.	Type	Description	Unused	Used
889	A369	37c **multicolored** *(275,000)+*	.60	.60
		First day cover		1.40
		Inscription block of 4	2.75	—
890	A369	80c **multicolored** *(195,000)+*	1.40	1.40
		First day cover		3.00
		First day cover, #889-890		3.50
		Inscription block of 4	6.00	—

Souvenir Booklet

No.	Description	Unused	Used
891	Booklet, #891g-891l *(29,000)+*	15.00	
a.-c.	A369 23c any single	.50	.50
d.-f.	A369 37c any single	.75	.75
g.	Booklet pane of 4 #891a	2.00	2.00
h.	Booklet pane of 4 #891b	2.00	2.00
i.	Booklet pane of 4 #891c	2.00	2.00
j.	Booklet pane of 4 #891d	3.00	3.00
k.	Booklet pane of 4 #891e	3.00	3.00
l.	Booklet pane of 4 #891f	3.00	3.00

See Offices in Geneva Nos. 444-446, Vienna Nos. 368-370.

My Dream for Peace Type of 2004

Printed by Government Printing Office, Austria. Panes of 20. Winning designs of Lions Club International children's global peace poster contest by: 37c, Vittoria Sansebastiano, Italy. 80c, Jordan Harris, US.

2005, Sept. 21 **Litho.** ***Perf. 14***

No.	Type	Description	Unused	Used
892	A357	37c **multicolored** *(270,000)+*	.60	.60
		First day cover		1.40
		Inscription block of 4	2.75	—
		Pane of 20	12.00	—
893	A357	80c **multicolored** *(200,000)+*	1.40	1.40
		First day cover		3.00
		First day cover, #892-893		3.50
		Inscription block of 4	5.75	—
		Pane of 20	28.00	—

See Offices in Geneva Nos. 447-448, Vienna Nos. 371-372.

Food for Life A370

Printed by Government Printing Office, Austria. Designed by Andrew Davidson, United Kingdom.

Designs: 37c, Oats, children and adults. 80c, Wheat, mothers breastfeeding babies.

2005, Oct. 20 **Litho.** ***Perf. 13¾***

No.	Type	Description	Unused	Used
894	A370	37c **multicolored** *(245,000)+*	.60	.60
		First day cover		1.25
		Inscription block of 4	2.75	—
		Pane of 20	12.00	—
895	A370	80c **multicolored** *(185,000)+*	1.40	1.40
		First day cover		2.75
		First day cover, #894-895		3.25
		Inscription block of 4	5.75	—
		Pane of 20	28.00	—

See Offices in Geneva Nos. 449-450; Vienna Nos. 373-374.

Stylized Flags in Heart and Hands — A371

Printed by Cartor Security Printing, France. Panes of 20. Designed by Eliezer Weishoff, Israel.

2006, Feb. 3 **Litho.** ***Perf. 13x13¼***

No.	Type	Description	Unused	Used
896	A371	25c **multicolored** *(670,000)+*	.75	.75
		First day cover		1.75
		Inscription block of 4	2.75	—
		Pane of 20	13.50	—

Indigenous Art Type of 2003

Printed by Johann Enschedé and Sons, the Netherlands. Designed by Robert Stein, US.

No. 897 — Musical instruments: a, Drum, Ivory Coast. b, Drum, Tunisia. c, Stringed instruments, Morocco. d, Drums, Sudan. e, Instruments, Cameroun. f, Harp, Congo.

2006, Feb. 3 **Litho.** ***Perf. 13¼***

No.	Type	Description	Unused	Used
897	A340	Sheet of 6 *(88,000)+*	10.00	10.00
		First day cover		6.50
a.-f.		37c Any single	1.50	1.50

See Offices in Geneva No. 452; Vienna No. 375.

UN Symbols Type of 2003

2006, Mar. 6 **Litho.** ***Perf. 13¼***

No.	Type	Description	Unused	Used
898	A349	39c **multicolored** + label	5.00	5.00
899	A350	39c **multicolored** + label	5.00	5.00
900	A351	39c **multicolored** + label	5.00	5.00
901	A352	39c **multicolored** + label	5.00	5.00
902	A353	39c **multicolored** + label	5.00	5.00
a.		Vert. strip of 5, #898-902, + 5 labels	25.00	25.00
		Sheet, 4 #902a	100.00	—

The full sheet sold for $14.95 with or without personalized labels. The personalization of labels was available only at UN Headquarters, and not through mail order.

Sculpture Type of 2005

2006, Mar. 6 **Litho.** ***Perf. 13¼***

No.	Type	Description	Unused	Used
903	A362	84c **multicolored** + label	12.00	12.00
a.		Perf. 14½x14 + label	16.00	16.00

904 A363 84c **multicolored** + label 12.00 12.00
a. Perf. 14½x14 + label 16.00 16.00
905 A364 84c **multicolored** + label 12.00 12.00
a. Perf. 14½x14 + label 16.00 16.00
906 A365 84c **multicolored** + label 12.00 12.00
a. Perf. 14½x14 + label 16.00 16.00
907 A366 84c **multicolored** + label 12.00 12.00
a. Perf. 14½x14 + label 16.00 16.00
b. Vert. strip of 5, #903-907, + 5 labels *60.00 60.00*
Sheet, 2 #907b *120.00 120.00*
c. Vert. strip of 5, #903a-907a, + 5 labels *80.00 80.00*
Sheet, 2 #907c *160.00 160.00*

The full sheet sold for $14.95 with or without personalized labels. The personalization of labels was available only at UN Headquarters, and not through mail order.

Nos. 903a-907a issued 9/21/06. Nos. 903a-907a were from sheet for 2006 Berlin Stamp Show. The year "2006" is slightly smaller on Nos. 903a-907a than on Nos. 903-907.

Full sheets with different margins were sold at the Washington 2006 World Philatelic Exhibition, where the labels could be personalized. These are worth slightly more than the generic No. 907b sheet.

Endangered Species Type of 1993

Printed by Johann Enschedé and Sons, the Netherlands. Designed by John D. Dawson, US.

Designs: No. 908, Golden mantella. No. 909, Panther chameleon. No. 910, Peruvian rainbow boa. No. 911, Dyeing poison frog.

2006, Mar. 16 **Litho.** ***Perf. 12¾x12½***
908 A271 39c **multicolored** *(212,000)+* .90 .90
909 A271 39c **multicolored** *(212,000)+* .90 .90
910 A271 39c **multicolored** *(212,000)+* .90 .90
911 A271 39c **multicolored** *(212,000)+* .90 .90
a. Block of 4, #908-911 3.60 3.60
First day cover, #911a 4.50
First day cover, #908-911, each 1.75
Inscription block of 4, #911a 3.75 —
Pane of 16 14.50 —

See Offices in Geneva Nos. 453-456; Vienna Nos. 376-379.

Dove Between War and Peace — A372

Designed by Armando Milani, Italy.

2006, Apr. 10 **Litho.** ***Perf. 13¼***
912 A372 75c **multicolored** + label 5.50 5.00
First day cover 10.00
Sheet of 10 + 10 labels 55.00 —

The full sheet sold for $14.95 with or without personalized labels. The personalization of labels was available only at UN Headquarters, and not through mail order.

Intl. Day of Families A373

Printed by Johann Enschedé and Sons, the Netherlands. Designed by Shelly Bartek, US.

Designs: 39c, Family harvesting grapes. 84c, Children playing with toy sailboats.

2006, May 27 **Litho.** ***Perf. 14x13½***
913 A373 39c **multicolored** *(226,000)+* .70 .70
First day cover 1.25
Inscription block of 4 3.00 —
Pane of 20 14.00 —
914 A373 84c **multicolored** *(186,000)+* 1.50 1.50
First day cover 2.75
First day cover, #913-914 3.25
Inscription block of 4 6.25 —
Pane of 20 30.00 —

See Offices in Geneva Nos. 457-458; Vienna Nos. 380-381.

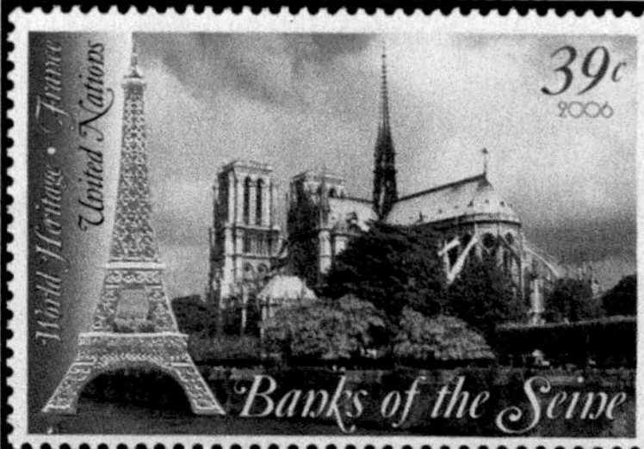

World Heritage Sites, France — A374

Printed by Cartor Security Printing, France. Panes of 20. Designed by Robert Stein, US.

Eiffel Tower and: Nos. 915, 917a, Banks of the Seine. Nos. 916, 917d, Roman Aqueduct. No. 917b, Provins. No. 917c, Carcasonne. No. 917e, Mont Saint-Michel. No. 917f, Chateau de Chambord.

Litho. & Embossed with Foil Application

2006, June 17 ***Perf. 13½x13¼***
915 A374 39c **multicolored** *(260,000)+* .75 .75
First day cover 2.25
Inscription block of 4 3.25 —
916 A374 84c **multicolored** *(180,000)+* 1.75 1.75
First day cover 4.25
First day cover, #889-890 3.50
Inscription block of 4 7.50 —

Souvenir Booklet

917 Booklet, #917g-917l *(28,000)+* 16.00
a.-c. A374 24c any single .50 .50
d.-f. A374 39c any single .80 .80
g. Booklet pane of 4 #917a 2.00 2.00
h. Booklet pane of 4 #917b 2.00 2.00
i. Booklet pane of 4 #917c 2.00 2.00
j. Booklet pane of 4 #917d 3.25 3.25
k. Booklet pane of 4 #917e 3.25 3.25
l. Booklet pane of 4 #917f 3.25 3.25

See Offices in Geneva Nos. 459-461, Vienna Nos. 382-384.

My Dream for Peace Type of 2004

Printed by Cartor Security Printing, France. Panes of 20.

Winning designs of Lions Club International children's global peace poster contest by: 39c, Cheuk Tat Li, Hong Kong. 84c, Kosshapan Paitoon, Thailand.

2006, Sept. 21 **Litho.** ***Perf. 13½x13***
918 A357 39c **multicolored** *(246,000)+* .80 .80
First day cover 1.25
Inscription block of 4 3.25 —
Pane of 20 16.00 —
919 A357 84c **multicolored** *(186,000)+* 1.75 1.75
First day cover 2.75
First day cover, #918-919 3.00
Inscription block of 4 7.00 —
Pane of 20 35.00 —

See Offices in Geneva Nos. 462-463; Vienna Nos. 385-386.

Flags and Coins — A375

Printed by Cartor Security Printing, France. Designed by Rorie Katz, US.

No. 920 — Flag of: a, People's Republic of China, 1 yuan coin. b, Australia, 1 dollar coin. c, Ghana, 50 cedi coin. d, Israel, 10 agorot coin. e, Russia, 1 ruble coin. f, Mexico, 10 peso coin. g, Japan, 10 yen coin. h, Cambodia, 200 riel coin.

2006, Oct. 5 **Litho.** ***Perf. 13¼x13***
920 Sheet of 8 8.00 8.00
a.-h. A375 39c Any single 1.00 1.00
First day cover 10.00

A column of rouletting in the middle of the sheet separates it into two parts. See Nos. 930, 953, 998, 1022, 1039, 1078, 1103; Offices in Geneva Nos. 464, 469, 484, 512, 532, 546, 576, 594; Vienna Nos. 387, 392, 421, 459, 483, 507, 539, 558.

Flag Type of 1980

Printed by Government Printing Office, Austria. Designed by Rorie Katz, US. Issued in panes of 16; each pane contains 4 blocks of 4. A se-tenant block of 4 designs centers each pane.

2007, Feb. 2 **Litho.** ***Perf. 14***
921 A185 39c Tuvalu *(275,000)+* 1.10 1.10
922 A185 39c Switzerland *(275,000)+* 1.10 1.10
923 A185 39c Timor-Leste *(275,000)+* 1.10 1.10
924 A185 39c Montenegro *(275,000)+* 1.10 1.10
a. Block of 4, #921-924 12.50 12.50
First day cover, #921-924, each 1.50
Pane of 16 24.00
Nos. 921-924 (4) 4.40 4.40

Endangered Species Type of 1993

Printed by Johann Enschedé and Sons, the Netherlands. Designed by John Rowe, US.

Designs: No. 925, Drill. No. 926, Common squirrel monkey. No. 927, Ring-tailed lemur. No. 928, Collared mangabey.

2007, Mar. 15 **Litho.** ***Perf. 12¾x12½***
925 A271 39c **multicolored** *(212,000)+* .85 .85
926 A271 39c **multicolored** *(212,000)+* .85 .85
927 A271 39c **multicolored** *(212,000)+* .85 *.85*
928 A271 39c **multicolored** *(212,000)+* .85 .85
a. Block of 4, #925-928 3.50 3.50
First day cover, #928a 3.50
First day cover, #925-928, each 1.75
Inscription block of 4, #928a 4.00 —
Pane of 16 14.00 —

See Offices in Geneva Nos. 465-468; Vienna Nos. 388-391.

UN Emblem — A376

Designed by Robert Stein.

2007, Feb. 5 **Litho.** ***Perf. 14½x14***
929 A376 84c **dark blue** + label *17.50 17.50*
First day cover, strip of 5 + 5 labels *55.00*
Sheet of 10 + 10 labels *175.00* —

The full sheet sold for $14.95. The sheet has two each of five different labels that could not be personalized. The sheet was distributed to members of the Japanese mission on Sept. 21, 2006, but it was not sold to the public until 2007. The sheet's availability to the public was not announced through press releases or on the UNPA website prior to the day of issue or afterward. It was sent to standing order customers in May 2007.

Compare with Type A377.

Flags and Coins Type of 2006

Printed by Cartor Security Printing, France. Designed by Rorie Katz, US.

No. 930 — Flag of: a, Brazil, 50 centavo coin. b, Thailand, 1 baht coin. c, Viet Nam, 5,000 dong coin. d, Ecuador, 10 centavo coin. e, India, 5 rupee coin. f, South Africa, 5 cent coin. g, Barbados, 25 cent coin. h, Republic of Korea, 500 won coin.

2007, May 3 **Litho.** ***Perf. 13¼x13***
930 Sheet of 8 *(125,000)+* 9.00 9.00
a.-h. A375 39c Any single 1.10 1.10
First day cover 12.50

A column of rouletting in the middle of the sheet separates it into two parts. See Offices in Geneva No. 469; Vienna No. 392.

UN Emblem — A377

2007, June 1 **Litho.** ***Perf. 13¼***
931 A377 84c **blue** + label *4.50 4.50*
First day cover, strip of 5 + 5 labels —
Sheet of 10 + 10 labels *45.00* —

The full sheet sold for $14.95. The sheet has two each of five different labels that could not be personalized.

Compare with Type A376.

Peaceful Visions — A378

Printed by Lowe-Martin Company, Canada. Designed by Slavka Kolesar, Canada. Panes of 20.
Designs: 39c, "Nest." 84c, "Sisters Weave the Olive Branch."

2007, June 1 Litho. *Perf. 13x12½*

932	A378 39c **multicolored** *(264,000)+*	.90	.90
	First day cover		1.50
	Inscription block of 4	3.60	—
	Pane of 20	18.00	—
933	A378 84c **multicolored** *(214,000)+*	1.80	1.80
	First day cover		3.25
	First day cover, #932-933		3.75
	Inscription block of 4	7.25	—
	Pane of 20	36.00	—

See Offices in Geneva Nos. 470-471; Vienna Nos. 398-399.

UN Symbols Type of 2003

2007, May 14 Litho. *Perf. 13¼*

934	A349 41c **multicolored** + label	3.25	3.25
935	A350 41c **multicolored** + label	3.25	3.25
936	A351 41c **multicolored** + label	3.25	3.25
937	A352 41c **multicolored** + label	3.25	3.25
938	A353 41c **multicolored** + label	3.25	3.25
a.	Vert. strip of 5, #934-938, + 5 labels	17.00	17.00
	First day cover, #938a		—
	Sheet, 4 #938a	67.50	—

The full sheet sold for $14.95 with or without personalized labels. The personalization of labels was available only at UN Headquarters, and not through mail order.

UN Flag — A379

2007, May 14 Litho. *Perf. 13¼*

939	A379 90c **blue** + label	*6.00*	*6.00*
	First day cover		65.00
	Sheet of 10 + 10 labels	*60.00*	—

The full sheet sold for $14.95. The sheet has two each of five different labels that could not be personalized.
A second printing of No. 939 has the "U" and "N" more closely spaced, and it has different labels and different pane borders. Value about the same.

Helmet of UN Peacekeeper — A380

Printed by Lowe-Martin Group, Canada. Panes of 20.

2007, Aug. 9 Litho. *Perf. 12½x13¼*

940	A380 90c **multicolored** *(550,000)+*	1.90	1.90
	First day cover		3.00
	Inscription block of 4	7.60	—
	Pane of 20	38.00	—

World Heritage Sites, South America — A381

Printed by Lowe-Martin Group, Canada. Panes of 20. Designed by Rorie Katz, US.
Designs: No. 941, Galapagos Islands, Ecuador. Nos. 942, 943a, Rapa Nui, Chile. No. 943b, Cueva de las Manos, Argentina. No. 943c, Machu Picchu, Peru. No. 943d, Tiwanaku, Bolivia. No. 943e, Iguaçu National Park, Brazil.

2007, Aug. 9 Litho. *Perf. 13¼x13*

941	A381 41c **multicolored** *(254,000)+*	.85	.85
	First day cover		1.50
	Inscription block of 4	3.40	—
a.	Booklet pane of 4	3.40	—
942	A381 90c **multicolored** *(254,000)+*	1.90	1.90
	First day cover		3.25
	First day cover, #941-942		3.75
	Inscription block of 4	7.60	—

Souvenir Booklet

943	Booklet, #941a, 943f-943j *(26,500)+*	17.00	
a.-c.	A381 26c Any single	.60	.60
d.-e.	A381 41c Either single	1.00	1.00
f.	Booklet pane of 4 #943a	2.40	2.40
g.	Booklet pane of 4 #943b	2.40	2.40
h.	Booklet pane of 4 #943c	2.40	2.40
i.	Booklet pane of 4 #943d	4.00	4.00
j.	Booklet pane of 4 #943e	4.00	4.00

See Offices in Geneva Nos. 472-474, Vienna Nos. 400-402. No. 943 sold for $8.50.

Humanitarian Mail — A382

Printed by Lowe-Martin Group, Canada. Panes of 10.

2007, Sept. 6 Litho. *Perf. 12½x13¼*

944	A382 90c **multicolored** *(288,000)+*	1.90	1.90
	First day cover		3.50
	Inscription block of 4	7.75	—
	Pane of 10	19.00	—

See Offices in Geneva No. 475, Vienna No. 403, Switzerland No. 9O21.

Space for Humanity A383

Printed by Johann Enschedé and Sons, the Netherlands. Panes of 6. Designed by Donato Giancola, US.
Designs: 41c, Space Shuttle. 90c, Astronauts spacewalking. $1, International Space Station.

2007, Oct. 25 Litho. *Perf. 13½x14*

945	A383 41c **multicolored** *(264,000)+*	.85	.85
	First day cover		1.50
	Inscription block of 4	3.40	—
	Sheet of 6	5.10	—
946	A383 90c **multicolored** *(264,000)+*	1.90	1.90
	First day cover		3.25
	First day cover, #945-946		4.00
	Inscription block of 4	7.60	—
	Sheet of 6	11.40	—

Souvenir Sheet

947	A383 $1 **multicolored** *(110,000)+*	2.50	2.50
	First day cover		4.00
a.	With World Space Week emblem in margin *(110,000)+*	3.00	3.00
	First day cover		4.00

See Offices in Geneva Nos. 476-478, Vienna Nos. 409-411.

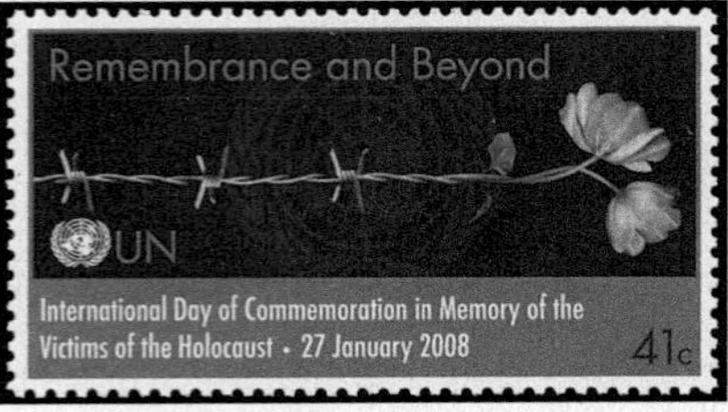

Intl. Holocaust Remembrance Day — A384

Printed by Lowe-Martin Company, Canada. Panes of 9. Designed by Matías Delfino, Argentina.

2008, Jan. 27 Litho. *Perf. 13*

948	A384 41c **multicolored** *(495,000)+*	.85	.85
	First day cover		1.90
	Sheet of 9	7.75	—

See Offices in Geneva No. 479, Vienna No. 412, Israel No. 1715.

Endangered Species Type of 1993

Printed by Johann Enschedé and Sons, the Netherlands. Designed by Suzanne Duranceau, Canada.
Designs: No. 949, South African fur seal. No. 950, Orange cup coral. No. 951, Longsnout seahorse. No. 952, Gray whale.

2008, Mar. 6 Litho. *Perf. 12¾x12½*

949	A271 41c **multicolored** *(164,000)+*	1.00	1.00
950	A271 41c **multicolored** *(164,000)+*	1.00	1.00
941	A271 41c **multicolored** *(164,000)+*	1.00	1.00
952	A271 41c **multicolored** *(164,000)+*	1.00	1.00
a.	Block of 4, #949-952	4.00	4.00
	First day cover, #952a		4.50
	First day cover, #949-952, each		1.75
	Inscription block of 4, #952a	4.25	—
	Pane of 16	16.00	—

See Offices in Geneva Nos. 480-483; Vienna Nos. 417-420.

Flags and Coins Type of 2006

Printed by Cartor Security Printing, France. Designed by Rorie Katz, US.
No. 953 — Flag of: a, United Kingdom, 2 pound coin. b, Singapore, 5 dollar coin. c, Colombia, 500 peso coin. d, Sri Lanka, 10 rupee coin. e, Philippines, 1 peso coin. f, Indonesia, 500 rupiah coin. g, United Arab Emirates, 1 dirham coin. h, Libya, 50 dinar coin.

2008, May 8 Litho. *Perf. 13¼x13*

953	Sheet of 8 *(100,000)+*	7.00	7.00
a.-h.	A375 41c Any single	.85	.85
	First day cover		9.25

A column of rouletting in the middle of the sheet separates it into two parts. See Offices in Geneva No. 484; Vienna No. 421.

Sculpture and Flags — A385

UN Flag — A386

UN General Assembly — A387

Flags — A388

UN Headquarters — A389

Designed by Rorie Katz, US.

2008, May 12 Litho. *Perf. 13¼*

954	A385 42c **multicolored** + label	*3.50*	*3.50*
955	A386 42c **multicolored** + label	*3.50*	*3.50*
956	A387 42c **multicolored** + label	*3.50*	*3.50*
957	A388 42c **multicolored** + label	*3.50*	*3.50*
958	A389 42c **multicolored** + label	*3.50*	*3.50*
a.	Vert. strip of 5, #954-958, + 5 labels	*17.50*	*17.50*
	First day cover, #958a		—
	Sheet, 4 #958a	*70.00*	—

The full sheet sold for $14.95 with or without personalized labels. The personalization of labels was available only at UN Headquarters, and not through mail order.

UN Emblem — A390

Designed by Rorie Katz, US.

2008, May 12 Litho. *Perf. 13¼*

959	A390 94c **blue** + label	*4.50*	*4.50*
	First day cover		—
	Sheet of 10 + 10 labels	*45.00*	—

The full sheet sold for $14.95 with or without labels that could be personalized. There are five non-personalized labels. The personalization of labels was available only at UN Headquarters, and not through mail order.

Wheelchair Accessibility Symbol — A391

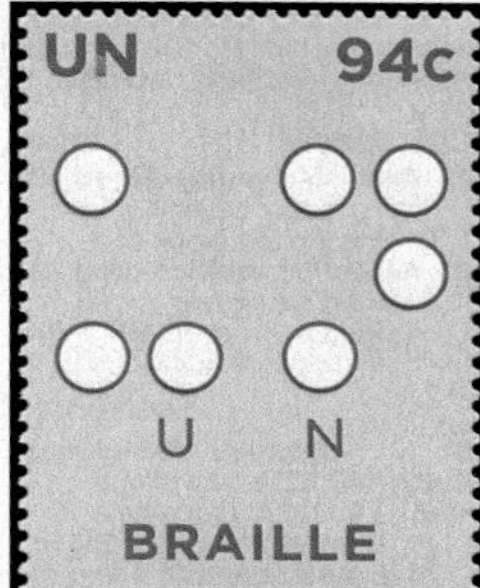

"UN" in Braille — A392

Printed by Johann Enschedé and Sons, the Netherlands. Panes of 20. Designed by Rorie Katz, US.

2008, June 6 Litho. & Embossed *Perf. 14x13¼*

960	A391 42c **blue & yellow** *(224,000)+*	.85	.85
	First day cover		1.60
	Inscription block of 4	3.40	—
	Sheet of 20	17.00	—
961	A392 94c **yellow & blue** *(174,000)+*	1.90	1.90
	First day cover		3.50
	First day cover, #960-961		4.00
	Inscription block of 4	7.60	—
	Sheet of 20	38.00	—

Convention on the Rights of Persons with Disabilities. See Offices in Geneva Nos. 485-486, Vienna Nos. 427-428.

Sport for Peace — A393

Printed by Johann Enschedé and Sons, the Netherlands. Panes of 9 (#962-963). Designed by Romero Britto, Brazil.
Designs: 42c, $1.25, Sprinter. 94c, Hurdler.

2008, Aug. 8 Litho. *Perf. 14½*

962	A393 42c **multicolored** *(389,700)+*	.85	.85
	First day cover		1.60
	Inscription block of 4	3.40	—
	Pane of 9	7.75	—
963	A393 94c **multicolored** *(389,700)+*	1.90	1.90
	First day cover		3.50
	First day cover, #962-963		4.00
	Inscription block of 4	7.60	—
	Pane of 9	17.50	—

Souvenir Sheet

Perf. 12¾x13¼

964	A393 $1.25 **multicolored** *(150,000)+*	6.00	6.00
	First day cover		5.00

2008 Summer Olympics, Beijing. See Offices in Geneva Nos. 487-489, Vienna Nos. 429-431.

Sport for Peace — A394

2008, Aug. 8 Litho. *Perf. 13¼*

965	A394 94c **multicolored** + label	*3.75*	*3.75*
	First day cover		12.50
	Pane of 10 + 10 labels	*37.50*	—

2008 Summer Olympics, Beijing. The full pane sold for $14.95 with or without personalized labels. There are two non-personalized labels. The personalization of labels was available only at UN Headquarters, and not through mail order.

No. 965 is often collected as a single stamp with the two different labels attached; value thus $6.50.

"We Can End Poverty" — A395

Printed by Sweden Post, Sweden. Panes of 20.
Winning designs in children's art contest by: 42c, Grace Tsang, Hong Kong. 94c, Bryan Jevoncia, Indonesia, vert.

2008, Sept. 18 Litho. *Perf. 12¾x12½*

966	A395 42c **multicolored** *(225,000)+*	.85	.85
	First day cover		1.25
	Inscription block of 4	3.40	—
	Sheet of 20	17.00	—

Perf. 12½x12¾

967	A395 94c **multicolored** *(165,000)+*	1.90	1.90
	First day cover		3.25
	First day cover, #966-967		4.00
	Inscription block of 4	7.60	—
	Sheet of 20	38.00	—

See Offices in Geneva Nos. 490-491, Vienna Nos. 432-433.

Climate Change Types of Geneva and Vienna and

A396

Climate Change — A397

Printed by Lowe-Martin Group, Canada. Panes of 4. Designed by Rorie Katz, US.

No. 968 — Parched ground and snail shell with quarter of Earth in: a, LR. b, LL. c, UR. d, UL.

No. 969 — Coral reef with quarter of Earth in: a, LR. b, LL. c, UR. d, UL.

No. 970: a, Like #969a. b, Like #969b. c, Like #969c. d, Like #969d. e, Like Geneva #493a. f, Like Geneva #493b. g, Like Geneva #493c. h, Like Geneva #493d. i, Like Vienna #434a. j, Like Vienna #434b. k, Like Vienna #434c. l, Like Vienna #434d. m, Like Geneva #492a. n, Like Geneva #492b. o, Like Geneva #492c. p, Like Geneva #492d. q, Like Vienna #435a. r, Like Vienna #435b. s, Like Vienna #435c. t, Like Vienna #435d.

All stamps have blue panels inscribed "Climate Change."

2008, Oct. 23 Litho. *Perf. 13¼x13*

968	Sheet of 4 *(100,000)+*	4.75	4.75
a.-d.	A396 42c Any single	1.10	1.10
	First day cover		4.50
e.	Booklet pane of 4, #968a-968d	6.00	6.00
969	Sheet of 4 *(100,000)+*	10.00	10.00
a.-d.	A397 94c Any single	2.50	2.50
	First day cover		9.75
	First day cover, #968-969		14.00

Souvenir Booklet

970	Booklet, #968e, 970u-970y *(22,500)+*	20.00	
a.-d.	A397 27c Any single	.75	.75
e.-h.	G77 27c Any single	.75	.75
i.-l.	V72 27c Any single	.75	.75
m.-p.	G76 42c Any single	1.00	1.00
q.-t.	V73 42c Any single	1.00	1.00
u.	Booklet pane of 4, #970a-970d	3.00	3.00
v.	Booklet pane of 4, #970e-970h	3.00	3.00
w.	Booklet pane of 4, #970i-970l	3.00	3.00
x.	Booklet pane of 4, #970m-970p	4.00	4.00
y.	Booklet pane of 4, #970q-970t	4.00	4.00

No. 970 sold for $9. See Offices in Geneva Nos. 492-494, Vienna Nos. 434-436.

Paintings of Flowers by Jaime Arredondo — A398

Printed by Lowe-Martin Company, Inc., Canada. Panes of 20.
Designs: 1c, Cielo rosado. 9c, Rosa de sangre. 10c, Espíritu de mujer.

2009, Feb. 6 **Litho.** ***Perf. 13¼***

971 A398 1c **multicolored** *(570,000)+* .30 .30
First day cover 1.90
Inscription block of 4 1.50 —
Sheet of 20 3.00 —
972 A398 9c **multicolored** *(570,000)+* .30 .30
First day cover 1.90
Inscription block of 4 1.50 —
Sheet of 20 3.00 —
973 A398 10c **multicolored** *(570,000)+* .30 .30
First day cover 1.90
First day cover, #971-973 3.75
Inscription block of 4 1.50 —
Sheet of 20 3.00 —
Nos. 971-973 (3) .90 .90

U Thant (1909-74), Secretary General — A399

Printed by Johann Enschedé and Sons, the Netherlands. Panes of 20.

Litho. With Foil Application

2009, Feb. 6 ***Perf. 14x13½***

974 A399 94c **purple & multicolored** *(255,000)+* 2.00 2.00
First day cover 3.00
Inscription block of 4 8.00 —
Sheet of 20 40.00 —

See Offices in Geneva No. 495, Vienna No. 437.

Endangered Species Type of 1993

Printed by Johann Enschedé and Sons, the Netherlands. Designed by Roger Kent, United Kingdom.
Designs: No. 975, Emperor dragonfly. No. 976, Southern wood ant. No. 977, Rosalia longicorn. No. 978, Apollo butterfly.

2009, Apr. 16 **Litho.** ***Perf. 12¾x12½***

975 A271 42c **multicolored** *(156,000)+* 1.25 1.25
976 A271 42c **multicolored** *(156,000)+* 1.25 1.25
977 A271 42c **multicolored** *(156,000)+* 1.25 1.25
978 A271 42c **multicolored** *(156,000)+* 1.25 1.25
a. Block of 4, #975-978 5.00 5.00
First day cover, #978a 5.00
First day cover, #975-978, each 1.50
Inscription block of 4, #978a 5.00 —
Pane of 16 20.00 —
b. Pane of 16, imperf. *5,000.*

See Offices in Geneva Nos. 496-499; Vienna Nos. 438-441.

World Heritage Sites, Germany — A400

Printed by Johann Enschedé and Sons, the Netherlands. Panes of 20. Designed by Grit Fiedler, Germany.
Designs: Nos. 979, 981a, Town Hall and Roland on the Marketplace, Bremen. Nos. 980, 981d, Aachen Cathedral. No. 981b, Wartburg Castle. No. 981c, Palaces and Parks of Potsdam and Berlin. No. 981e, Luther Memorials in Eisleben and Wittenberg. No. 981f, Monastic Island of Reichenau.

2009, May 7 **Litho.** ***Perf. 14x13½***

979 A400 44c **multicolored** *(220,000)+* .90 .90
First day cover 1.25
Inscription block of 4 3.60 —
980 A400 98c **multicolored** *(220,000)+* 2.00 2.00
First day cover 3.00
First day cover, #979-980 4.00
Inscription block of 4 8.00 —

Souvenir Booklet

981 Booklet, #981g-981l *(21,000)+* 20.00
a.-c. A400 27c any single .60 .60
d.-f. A400 42c any single 1.00 1.00
g. Booklet pane of 4 #981a 2.40 2.40
h. Booklet pane of 4 #981b 2.40 2.40
i. Booklet pane of 4 #981c 2.40 2.40
j. Booklet pane of 4 #981d 4.00 4.00
k. Booklet pane of 4 #981e 4.00 4.00
l. Booklet pane of 4 #981f 4.00 4.00

See Offices in Geneva Nos. 500-502, Vienna Nos. 442-444.

UN Flag — A401

Let Us Beat Swords Into Plowshares, Sculpture by Evgeny Vuchetich — A402

Single Form, Sculpture by Barbara Hepworth — A403

Window Cleaner — A404

UN Headquarters — A405

2009, June 5 **Litho.** ***Perf. 13¼***

982 A401 44c **multicolored** + label *2.00 2.00*
a. Perf. 11¼x11 + label *10.00 10.00*
b. Perf. 14¼x14½ + label *1.80 1.80*
983 A402 44c **multicolored** + label *2.00 2.00*
a. Perf. 11¼x11 + label *10.00 10.00*
b. Perf. 14¼x14½ + label *1.80 1.80*
984 A403 44c **multicolored** + label *2.00 2.00*
a. Perf. 11¼x11 + label *10.00 10.00*
b. Perf. 14¼x14½ + label *1.80 1.80*
985 A404 44c **multicolored** + label *2.00 2.00*
a. Perf. 11¼x11 + label *10.00 10.00*
b. Perf. 14¼x14½ + label *1.80 1.80*
986 A405 44c **multicolored** + label *2.00 2.00*
a. Perf. 11¼x11 + label *10.00 10.00*
b. Perf. 14¼x14½ + label *1.80 1.80*
c. Vert. strip of 5, #982-986, + 5 labels *10.00 10.00*
Sheet, 4 #986c *40.00 —*
d. Vert. strip of 5, #982a-986a, + 5 labels *50.00 50.00*
Sheet, 4 #986d *200.00 —*
e. Vert. strip of 5, #982b-986b, + 5 labels *9.00 7.50*
Sheet, 4 #986e *37.50 —*

The full sheets sold for $14.95 with or without personalized labels. The personalization of labels was available only at UN Headquarters, and not through mail order. The sheet of No. 986d has "ver. 2" in the lower right selvage. The sheet of No. 986e has "Ver. 3" in the lower right selvage.

Flags and UN Headquarters — A406

Single Form, Sculpture by Barbara Hepworth — A407

UN Flag — A408

Sphere Within a Sphere, Sculpture by Arnaldo Pomodoro — A409

UN Headquarters and Chrysler Building — A410

2009, June 5 Litho. *Perf. 13¼*

987 A406 98c **multicolored** + label	*4.00*	*4.00*
a. Perf. 11¼x11 + label	*9.00*	*9.00*
b. Perf. 14¼x14½ + label	*3.50*	*3.50*
988 A407 98c **multicolored** + label	*4.00*	*4.00*
a. Perf. 11¼x11 + label	*9.00*	*9.00*
b. Perf. 14¼x14½ + label	*3.50*	*3.50*
989 A408 98c **multicolored** + label	*4.00*	*4.00*
a. Perf. 11¼x11 + label	*9.00*	*9.00*
b. Perf. 14¼x14½ + label	*3.50*	*3.50*
990 A409 98c **multicolored** + label	*4.00*	*4.00*
a. Perf. 11¼x11 + label	*9.00*	*9.00*
b. Perf. 14¼x14½ + label	*3.50*	*3.50*
991 A410 98c **multicolored** + label	*4.00*	*4.00*
a. Perf. 11¼x11 + label	*9.00*	*9.00*
b. Perf. 14¼x14½ + label	*3.50*	*3.50*
c. Vert. strip of 5, #987-991, + 5 labels	*20.00*	*20.00*
Sheet, 2 #991c	*40.00*	—
d. Vert. strip of 5, #987a-991a, + 5 labels	*45.00*	*45.00*
Sheet, 2 #991d	*90.00*	—
e. Vert. strip of 5, #987b-991b, + 5 labels	*17.50*	*17.50*
Sheet, 2 #991e	*35.00*	—

The full sheets sold for $14.95 with or without personalized labels. The personalization of labels was available only at UN Headquarters, and not through mail order. The sheet of No. 991d has "ver. 2" in the lower right selvage. The sheet of No. 991e has "VER. 3" in the lower right selvage.

Economic and Social Council — A411

Printed by Sweden Post, Sweden. Panes of 20. Designed by Rorie Katz, US.

Designs: 44c, Water and sanitation. 98c, Traditional medicines.

2009, Aug. 6 Litho. *Perf. 12¾x12½*

992 A411 44c **multicolored** *(220,000)+*	2.00	.90
First day cover		1.60
Inscription block of 4	6.00	—
Sheet of 20	30.00	—
993 A411 98c **multicolored** *(170,000)+*	5.00	2.00
First day cover		3.50
First day cover, #992-993		4.25
Inscription block of 4	16.00	—
Sheet of 20	80.00	—

See Offices in Geneva Nos. 503-504, Vienna Nos. 450-451.

UN Emblem — A412

2009, Sept. 22 Litho. *Perf. 13¼*

994 A412 98c **multicolored** + label	*5.50*	*5.50*
Sheet of 10 + 10 labels	*55.00*	—
a. Perf. 11¼x11 + label	*5.00*	*5.00*
Sheet of 10 + 10 labels	*50.00*	—

The full sheets sold for $14.95 with or without personalized labels. There are five different non-personalized labels. The personalization of labels was available only at UN Headquarters, and not through mail order. The sheet of No. 994a has "ver. 2" in the lower right selvage.

Miniature Sheet

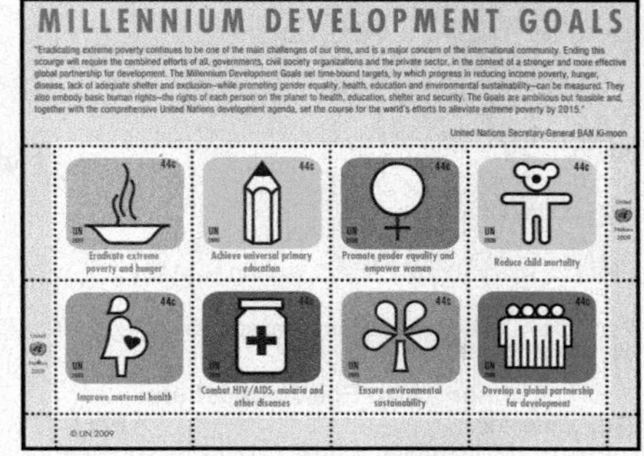

Millennium Development Goals — A413

Printed by Lowe Martin Group, Canada.
Designed by Rorie Katz, US.

No. 995: a, Bowl of hot food. b, Pencil. c, Female symbol. d, Teddy bear. e, Pregnant woman, heart. f, Medicine bottle. g, Stylized tree. h, Conjoined people.

2009, Sept. 25 Litho. *Perf. 13¼*

995 A413 Sheet of 8 *(60,000)+*	10.00	10.00
First day cover		9.75
a.-h. 44c Any single	1.20	1.20

See Offies in Geneva No. 505; Vienna No. 457.

Mohandas K. Gandhi — A414

Printed by Lowe-Martin Group, Canada. Designed by Dr. Ferdie Pacheco, US. Panes of 20.

2009, Oct. 2 Litho. *Perf. 13¼*

996 A414 $1 **multicolored** *(570,000)+*	2.25	2.25
First day cover		3.00
Inscription block of 4	10.00	—
Pane of 20	45.00	—

Miniature Sheet

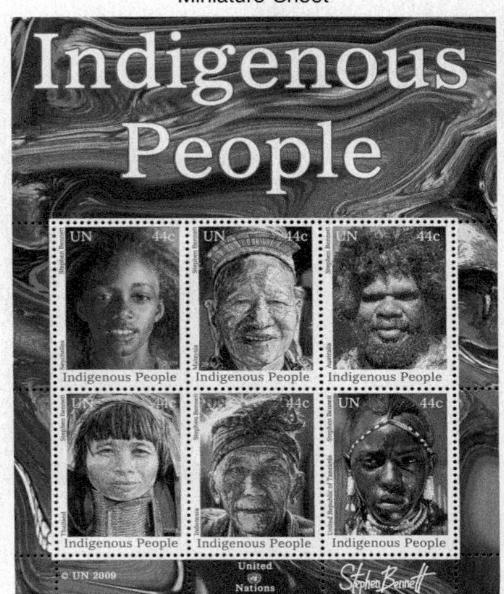

Indigenous People — A415

Printed by Lowe-Martin Group, Canada. Designed by Stephen Bennett, US.

No. 997 — Portraits of person from: a, Seychelles. b, Malaysia. c, Australia. d, Thailand. e, Indonesia. f, Tanzania.

2009, Oct. 8 Litho. *Perf. 12½*

997 A415 Sheet of 6 *(65,000)+*	7.00	7.00
a.-f. 44c Any single	1.15	1.15
First day cover		10.00

See Offices in Geneva No. 511, Vienna No. 458.

Flags and Coins Type of 2006

Printed by Cartor Security Printing, France. Designed by Rorie Katz, US.

No. 998 — Flag of: a, Bahamas, 10 cent coin. b, Jamaica, 20 dollar coin. c, Honduras, 50 centavo coin. d, Kuwait, 100 fils coin. e, Panama, 1 cuarto de Balboa coin. f, Guatemala, 50 centavo coin. g, St. Lucia, 1 cent coin. h, Yemen, 20 rial coin.

2010, Feb. 5 Litho. *Perf. 13¼x13*

998 Sheet of 8 *(66,000)+*	9.75	9.75
a.-h. A375 44c Any single	1.20	1.20
First day cover		10.00

A column of rouletting in the middle of the sheet separates it into two parts. See Offices in Geneva No. 512; Vienna No. 459.

Endangered Species Type of 1993

Printed by Johann Enschedé and Sons, the Netherlands. Designed by Rosie Sanders, United Kingdom.

Designs: No. 999, Monkey puzzle tree. No. 1000, Quiver tree. No. 1001, Bristlecone pine tree. No. 1002, Scarlet ball cactus.

2010, Apr. 15 Litho. *Perf. 12¾x12½*

999 A271 44c **multicolored** *(140,000)+*	1.25	1.25
1000 A271 44c **multicolored** *(140,000)+*	1.25	1.25
1001 A271 44c **multicolored** *(140,000)+*	1.25	1.25
1002 A271 44c **multicolored** *(150,000)+*	1.25	1.25
a. Block of 4, #999-1002	5.00	5.00
First day cover, #1002a		5.00
First day cover, #999-1002, each		2.00
Inscription block of 4, #1002a	5.25	—
Pane of 16	20.00	—

See Offices in Geneva Nos. 513-516; Vienna Nos. 465-468.

The stamp pictured above was printed in limited quantities and sold for far more than face value. The label attached to the stamp could not be personalized. Value for stamp and label, $3. A similar stamp dated "2011" with a different label attached exists.

One Planet, One Ocean Types of Geneva and Vienna and

A416

One Planet, One Ocean — A417

Printed by Johann Enschedé and Sons, the Netherlands. Designed by Robert Wyland, US.

No. 1003: a, Turtle at top, eel at left, fish at LR. b, Fish at LL, turtle's flipper at bottom. c, Fish at left, yellow sponge at LR, Lobster at right. d, Lobster at left, turtle at right.

No. 1004: a, Octopus at left, fish at LR. b, Fish at left and right, turtle's head at bottom. c, Lobster at left. fish at LL and LR. d, Fish at LL and LR, turtle's body at UR.

No. 1005: a, Like #1003a. b, Like #1003b, c, Like #1003c, d, Like #1003d. e, Like Vienna #471a. f, Like Vienna #471b. g, Like Vienna #471c, h, Like Vienna #471d. i, Like Geneva #519a. j, Like Geneva #519b, k, Like Geneva #519c. l, Like Geneva #519d. m, Like #1004a. n, Like #1004b. o, Like #1004c, p, Like #1004d. q, Like Vienna #472a. r, Like Vienna #472b. s, Like Vienna #472c. t, Like Vienna #472d. u, Like Geneva #520a. v, Like Geneva #520b. w, Like Geneva #520c. x, Like Geneva #520d.

2010, May 6 **Litho.** ***Perf. 14x13¼***

1003 A416 Sheet of 4 *(65,000)+* 3.60 3.60
a.-d. 44c Any single .90 .90
1004 A417 Sheet of 4 *(65,000)+* 8.00 8.00
a.-d. 98c Any single 2.00 2.00
First day cover, #1003-1004 16.50

Souvenir Booklet

Perf. 13¼x13

1005 Booklet, #1005y-1005z, 1005aa-1005ad *(21,000)+* 18.00
a.-d. A416 28c any single .60 .60
e.-h. V91 28c any single .60 .60
i.-l. G85 28c any single .60 .60
m.-p. A417 44c any single .90 .90
q.-t. V92 44c any single .90 .90
u.-x. G86 44c any single .90 .90
y. Booklet pane of 4 #1005a-1005d 2.40 2.40
z. Booklet pane of 4 #1005e-1005h 2.40 2.40
aa. Booklet pane of 4 #1005i-1005l 2.40 2.40
ab. Booklet pane of 4 #1005m-1005p 3.60 3.60
ac. Booklet pane of 4 #1005q-1005t 3.60 3.60
ad. Booklet pane of 4 #1005u-1005x 3.60 3.60

Intl. Oceanographic Commission, 50th anniv. See Offices in Geneva Nos. 519-521, Vienna Nos. 471-473.

People of Different Cultures — A418

People of Different Cultures as New York Buildings — A419

Printed by Lowe-Martin Group, Canada. Designed by Christopher Corr, United Kingdom.

2010, June 4 **Litho.** ***Perf. 13***

1006 A418 3c **multicolored** *(400,000)+* .25 .25
First day cover 2.00
Inscription block of 4 .25 —
Pane of 20 1.25 —
1007 A419 4c **multicolored** *(400,000)+* .25 .25
First day cover 2.00
First day cover, #1006-1007 2.00
Inscription block of 4 .35 —
Pane of 20 1.60 —

UN Headquarters and New York Skyline — A420

Shanghai Skyline — A421

2010, June 4 **Litho.** ***Perf. 13¼***

1008 A420 98c **multicolored** 3.00 3.00
1009 A421 98c **multicolored** 3.00 3.00
a. Horiz. pair, #1008-1009 6.00 6.00
Pane, 5 #1009a 30.00 —

Expo 2010, Shanghai. Nos. 1008-1009 were sold only in full panes for $14.95.

United Nations, 65th Anniv. — A422

Printed by Lowe-Martin Group, Canada. Designed by Rorie Katz, United States.

Litho. With Foil Application

2010, June 28 ***Perf. 13¼***

1010 A422 98c **light blue & gold** *(150,000)+* 2.25 2.25
First day cover 3.25
Inscription block of 4 9.00 —
Pane of 15 32.50 —

Souvenir Sheet

1011 Sheet of 2 #1011a *(36,000)+* 5.00 5.00
a. A422 98c **dark blue & gold** 2.50 2.50
First day cover 7.50

See Offices in Geneva No. 522, Vienna No. 474.

A423

A424

A425

A426

United Nations Sea Transport — A427

Printed by UAB Garsu Pasaulis, Lithuania. Designed by Simon Williams, United Kingdom.

2010, Sept. 2 **Litho.** ***Perf. 13¼x13***

1012 A423 44c **multicolored** *(128,000)+* .90 .90
1013 A424 44c **multicolored** *(128,000)+* .90 .90
1014 A425 44c **multicolored** *(128,000)+* .90 .90
1015 A426 44c **multicolored** *(128,000)+* .90 .90
1016 A427 44c **multicolored** *(128,000)+* .90 .90
a. Horiz. strip of 5, #1012-1016 4.50 4.50
First day cover, #1016a 6.00
First day cover, #1012-1016, each 4.50
Inscription block of 10 9.00 —
Pane of 20 18.00 —

See Offices in Geneva Nos. 523-527, Vienna Nos. 475-479.

Intl. Year of Biodiversity — A428

Printed by Lowe-Martin Group, Canada. Panes of 20. Designed by Deborah Halperin, US.

Drawings from Art Forms from Nature, by Ernst Heinrich: 15c, Hummingbird. $1.50, Liverwort.

2010, Oct. 18 **Litho.** ***Perf. 13***

1017 A428 15c **multicolored** *(400,000)+* .30 .30
First day cover 1.25
Inscription block of 4 1.20 —
Pane of 20 6.00 —
1018 A428 $1.50 **multicolored** *(400,000)+* 3.00 3.00
First day cover 5.75
First day cover, #1017-1018 4.75
Inscription block of 4 12.00 —
Pane of 20 60.00 —

See Offices in Geneva Nos. 517-518; Vienna Nos. 469-470.

Miniature Sheet

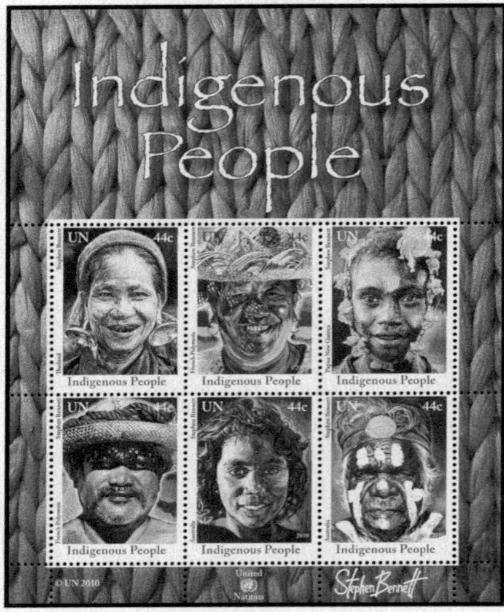

Indigenous People — A429

Printed by Lowe-Martin Group, Canada. Designed by Stephen Bennett, US.

No. 1019 — Portraits of person from: a, Thailand. b, French Polynesia (woman, denomination in black). c, Papua New Guinea. d, French Polynesia (man, denomination in white). e, Australia (child). f, Australia (old man with headband).

2010, Oct. 21 **Litho.** ***Perf. 13***

1019 A429 Sheet of 6 *(55,000)+* 6.00 6.00
a.-f. 44c Any single 1.00 1.00
First day cover 8.00

See Offices in Geneva No. 529; Vienna No. 480.

United Nations Headquarters, New York — A430

Printed by Cartor Security Printing, France. Panes of 20. Designed by Scott Solberg, US.

United Nations Headquarters: 11c, Aerial view. $5, Ground-level view.

2011, Feb. 4 **Litho.** ***Perf. 13***

1020 A430 11c **multicolored** *(400,000)+* .25 .25
First day cover 1.25
Inscription block of 4 1.00 —
Pane of 20 5.00 —
1021 A430 $5 **multicolored** *(400,000)+* 9.00 9.00
First day cover 13.50
First day cover, #1020-1021 12.50
Inscription block of 4 37.50 —
Pane of 20 200.00 —

See Offices in Geneva Nos. 530-531; Vienna Nos. 481-482.

Flags and Coins Type of 2006

Printed by Cartor Security Printing, France. Designed by Rorie Katz, US.

No. 1022 — Flag of: a, Mauritius, 1 rupee coin. b, Guyana, 10 dollar coin. c, Timor, 5 cent coin. d, Iceland, 100 krónur coin. e, Chile, 1 peso coin. f, Norway, 20 kroner coin. g, Fiji, 50 cent coin. h, Comoro Islands, 100 franc coin.

2011, Mar. 3 **Litho.** ***Perf. 13¼x13***

1022 Sheet of 8 *(60,000)+* 8.75 8.75
a.-h. A375 44c Any single 1.10 1.10
First day cover 9.75

A column of rouletting in the middle of the sheet separates it into two parts. See Offices in Geneva No. 532; Vienna No. 483.

UN Emblem — A431

2011, Apr. 7 **Litho.** ***Perf. 14¾***

1023 A431 98c **blue** + label *4.00 4.00*
Sheet of 10 + 10 labels *32.00* —

The full sheets sold for $14.95. There are 10 different non-personalized labels.

Human Space Flight, 50th Anniv. — A432

Printed by Lowe-Martin Group, Canada. Designed by Peter Bollinger, US.

No. 1024: Various parts of outer space scene.

No. 1025, vert.: a, Cosmonaut and rocket. b, Astronaut on ladder of Lunar Module.

2011, Apr. 12 **Litho.** ***Perf. 13x13¼***

1024 A432 Sheet of 16 *(52,000)+* 16.00 16.00
First day cover 17.50

a.-p. 44c any single 1.00 1.00

Souvenir Sheet

1025 A432 Sheet of 2 15.00 15.00
First day cover 4.25
a. 44c **multicolored** 4.50 4.50
b. 98c **multicolored** 11.50 11.50

See Offices in Geneva Nos. 533-534; Vienna Nos. 484-485. No. 1024 contains two 40x48mm stamps that were printed as part of a larger sheet of six stamps, Vienna No. 485c, which was broken up into its component two-stamp souvenir sheets, and also sold as one unit. Value $90, complete unit.

UNESCO World Heritage Sites in Nordic Countries — A433

Printed by Johann Enschedé and Sons, the Netherlands. Panes of 20. Designed by Rorie Katz, US.

Designs: 44c, Surtsey Volcanic Island, Iceland. 98c, Drottningholm Castle, Sweden.

2011, May 5 **Litho.** ***Perf. 14x13½***

1026 A433 44c **multicolored** *(190,000)+* .90 .90
First day cover 1.60
Inscription block of 4 3.60 —
Pane of 20 18.00 —
1027 A433 98c **multicolored** *(190,000)+* 2.00 2.00
First day cover 3.50
First day cover, #1025-1026 4.25
Inscription block of 4 8.00 —
Pane of 20 40.00 —

See Offices in Geneva Nos. 535-536; Vienna Nos. 496-497.

AIDS Ribbon — A434

Printed by Lowe-Martin Group, Canada. Panes of 4. Designed by Rorie Katz, US.

2011, June 3 **Litho.** ***Die Cut***

Self-Adhesive

1028 A434 44c **red & blue** *(200,000)+* 1.75 1.75
Pane of 4 7.00
First day cover, pane of 4 5.25

See Offices in Geneva No. 537; Vienna No. 498.

Economic and Social Council (ECOSOC) — A435

Printed by Cartor Security Printing, France. Panes of 20. Designed by Rorie Katz, US.

Education: 44c, Child and teacher. 98c, Child writing on blackboard.

2011, July 1 **Litho.** ***Perf. 14¼***

1029 A435 44c **multicolored** *(180,000)+* 1.50 1.50
First day cover 1.60
Inscription block of 4 6.00 —
Pane of 20 30.00 —

1030 A435 98c **multicolored** *(180,000)+* 3.50 3.50
First day cover 3.50
First day cover, #1029-1030 5.00
Inscription block of 4 14.00 —
Pane of 20 70.00 —

See Offices in Geneva Nos. 538-539; Vienna Nos. 499-500.

Endangered Species Type of 1993

Printed by Johann Enschedé and Sons, the Netherlands. Designed by Wendy Wray, U.S.

Designs: No. 1031, Bali starling. No. 1032, California condor. No. 1033, Japanese crane. No. 1034, Black-fronted piping-guan.

2011, Sept. 7 **Litho.** ***Perf. 12¾x12½***

1031 A271 44c **multicolored** *(116,000)+* 1.10 1.10
1032 A271 44c **multicolored** *(116,000)+* 1.10 1.10
1033 A271 44c **multicolored** *(116,000)+* 1.10 1.10
1034 A271 44c **multicolored** *(116,000)+* 1.10 1.10
a. Block of 4, #1031-1034 4.40 4.40
First day cover, #1034a 5.00
First day cover, #1031-1034, each 2.00
Inscription block of 4, #1034a 4.50 —
Pane of 16 22.50 —

See Offices in Geneva Nos. 540-543; Vienna Nos. 501-504.

Intl. Year of Forests — A436

Printed by Lowe-Martin Group, Canada. Panes of 8. Designed by Sergio Baradat, U.S.

Designs: 44c, Tree with wildlife, man with mask. 98c, Tree roots.

Litho. With Foil Application

2011, Oct. 13 ***Perf. 12½***

1035 44c **multicolored** *(92,000)+* 1.25 1.25
1036 98c **multicolored** *(92,000)+* 2.50 2.50
a. A436 Vert. pair, #1035-1036 3.75 3.75
First day cover, #1036a 4.25
Pane of 8 15.00 —

See Offices in Geneva Nos. 544-545; Vienna Nos. 505-506.

UN Emblem — A437

2012, Jan. 23 **Litho.** ***Perf. 14¾***

1037 A437 $1.05 **blue** + label *2.75 2.75*
Sheet of 10 + 10 labels *27.50* —

The full sheet sold for $14.95. The generic label exists as shown, and with dragon in yellow against red background. Labels could be personalized. The personalization of labels was available only at UN Headquarters, and not through mail order.

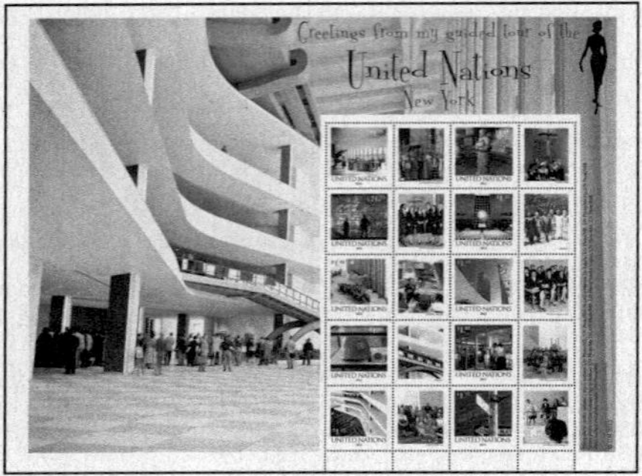

A438

No. 1038: a, Desk in lobby. b, Sculpture of Jesus holding lamb. c, Stained-glass window. d, Meeting room. e, Guided tour. f, Flags in front of United Nations buildings. g, United Nations Peacekeepers helmet in showcase. h, Gift shop. i, View of curved floors above lobby. j, Street signs.

2012, Jan. 23 **Litho.** ***Perf. 14¾***
1038 A438 Sheet of 10 *30.00 30.00*
a.-j. $1.05 Any single + label *3.00 3.00*

The full sheet sold for $14.95. The generic labels are shown. Labels could be personalized. The personalization of labels was available only at UN Headquarters, and not through mail order.

Flags and Coins Type of 2006

Printed by Cartor Security Printing, France. Designed by Rorie Katz, US.

No. 1039 — Flag of: a, Nepal, 1 rupee coin. b, Bahrain, 100 fils coin. c, Paraguay, 1000 guarani coin. d, Ethiopia, 25 cent coin. e, Peru, 1 sol coin. f, Solomon Islands, 20 cent coin. g, Dominican Republic, 1 peso coin. h, Canada, 1 dollar coin.

2012, Feb. 3 **Litho.** ***Perf. 13¼x13***
1039 Sheet of 8 *(43,000)+* 7.25 7.25
a.-h. A375 45c Any single .90 .90
First day cover 10.00

A column of rouletting in the middle of the sheet separates it into two parts. See Offices in Geneva No. 546; Vienna No. 507.

A439

Autism Awareness — A440

Printed by Joh. Enschedé Stamps Security Printers, Netherlands. Panes of 20.

Drawings by autistic people: No. 1040, An Abstract Garden II, by Trent Altman, U.S. No. 1041, Crazy Love, by Hannah Kandel, U.S.

2012, Apr. 2 **Litho.** ***Perf. 14x13½***
1040 A439 $1.05 **multicolored** *(100,000)+* 2.10 2.10
1041 A440 $1.05 **multicolored** *(100,000)+* 2.10 2.10
a. Pair, #1040-1041 4.20 4.20
First day cover, #1040-1041 5.75
Inscription block of 4 8.50 —
Pane of 20 42.00 —

See Offices in Geneva Nos. 547-548; Vienna Nos. 508-509.

Endangered Species Type of 1993

Printed by Johann Enschedé and Sons, the Netherlands. Designed by Diana Marques, Portugal.

Designs: No. 1042, Giant panda. No. 1043, Short-horned chameleon. No. 1044, Oncilla. No. 1045, Cotton-headed tamarin.

2012, Apr. 19 **Litho.** ***Perf. 12¾x12½***
1042 A271 45c **multicolored** *(108,000)+* 1.10 1.10
1043 A271 45c **multicolored** *(108,000)+* 1.10 1.10
1044 A271 45c **multicolored** *(108,000)+* 1.10 1.10
1045 A271 45c **multicolored** *(108,000)+* 1.10 1.10
a. Block of 4, #1042-1045 4.40 4.40
First day cover, #1045a 5.00
First day cover, #1042-1045, each 2.00
Inscription block of 4, #1045a 4.50 —
Pane of 16 22.50 —

See Offices in Geneva Nos. 549-552; Vienna Nos. 511-514.

Tinker Bell — A441

Tinker Bell — A442

2012, June 1 **Litho.** ***Perf. 14¾***
1046 A441 $1.05 **multicolored** + label *3.00 3.00*
1047 A442 $1.05 **multicolored** + label *3.00 3.00*
a. Vert. pair, #1046-1047, + 2 labels *6.00 6.00*
Sheet of 10, 5 each #1046-1047, + 10 labels *30.00 30.00*

The full sheet sold for $14.95. The generic labels are shown. Labels could be personalized. The personalization of labels was available only at UN Headquarters, and not through mail order.

Rio + 20 Conference on Sustainable Development, Rio de Janeiro — A443

Printed by Lowe-Martin Group, Canada. Panes of 20. Designed by Gail Armstrong, United Kingdom.

2012, June 1 **Litho.** ***Perf. 13x13¼***
1048 A443 $1.05 **multicolored** *(146,000)+* 2.10 2.10
First day cover 3.50
Inscription block of 4 8.40 —
Pane of 20 42.50 —

See Offices in Geneva No. 553; Vienna No. 515.

Sport for Peace — A444

Printed by Cartor Security Printing, France. Panes of 9. Designed by Daniel Stolle, Finland.

2012 Paralympics events: 45c, Goalball. $1.05, Sitting volleyball.

Litho. With Foil Application

2012, Aug. 17 ***Perf. 14½***
1049 A444 45c **multicolored** *(121,500)+* .90 .90
First day cover 1.60
Inscription block of 4 3.60 —
Pane of 9 8.25 —
1050 A444 $1.05 **multicolored** *(121,500)+* 2.10 2.10
First day cover 3.75
First day cover, #1049-1050 4.25
Inscription block of 4 8.40 —
Pane of 9 19.00 —
a. Souvenir sheet of 1 *(34,000)+* 3.50 3.50
First day cover 3.25

See Offices in Geneva Nos. 554-555; Vienna Nos. 516-517.

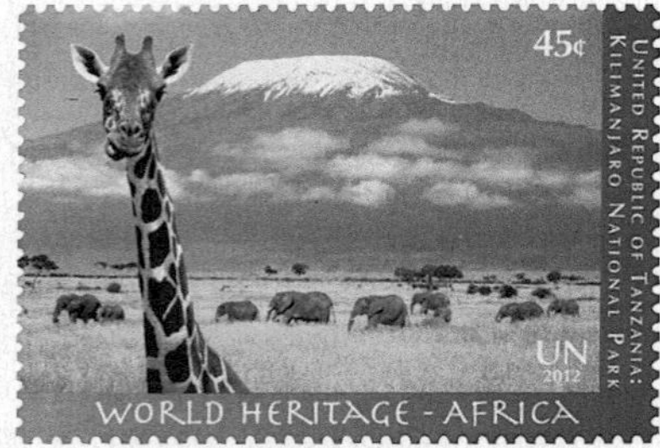

UNESCO World Heritage Sites in Africa — A445

Printed by Lowe-Martin Group, Canada. Panes of 20. Designed by Rorie Katz, US.

Designs: 45c, Kilamanjaro National Park, Tanzania. $1.05, Old Towns of Djenné, Mali.

2012, Sept. 5 **Litho.** ***Perf. 13¼***
1051 A445 45c **multicolored** *(150,000)+* .90 .90
First day cover 1.60
Inscription block of 4 3.60 —
Pane of 20 18.00 —
1052 A445 $1.05 **multicolored** *(150,000)+* 2.10 2.10
First day cover 3.75
First day cover, #1051-1052 4.25
Inscription block of 4 8.50 —
Pane of 20 42.50 —

See Offices in Geneva Nos. 556-557; Vienna Nos. 518-519.

Miniature Sheet

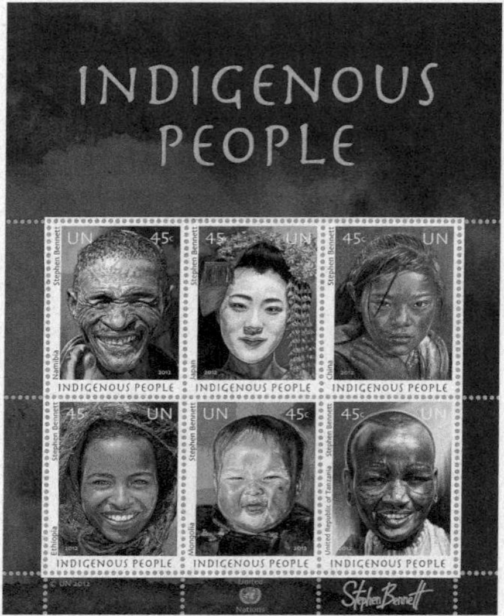

Indigenous People — A446

Printed by Lowe-Martin Group, Canada. Designed by Stephen Bennett, US.

No. 1053 — Portrait of person from: a, Namibia. b, Japan. c, China. d, Ethiopia. e, Mongolia. f, Tanzania.

2012, Oct. 11 **Litho.** ***Perf. 13¼x13***
1053 A446 Sheet of 6 *(43,000)+* 5.50 5.50
a.-f. 45c Any single .90 .90
First day cover 8.00

See Offices in Geneva No. 558; Vienna No. 520.

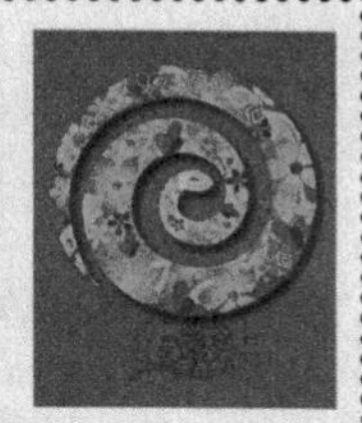

UN Emblem — A447

2013, Jan. 28 Litho. *Perf. 14¾*

1054 A447 $1.10 **multicolored** + label *4.00 4.00*
Sheet of 10 + 10 labels *40.00* —

The full sheet sold for $14.95. The generic label exists as shown, and with snake against red background. Labels could be personalized. The personalization of labels was available only at UN Headquarters, and not through mail order.

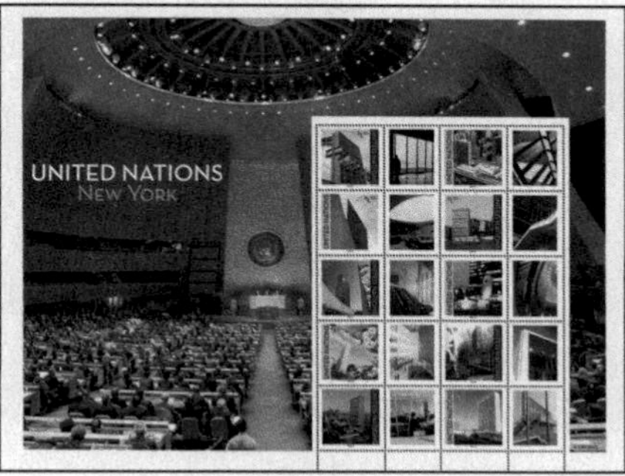

A448

No. 1055: a, Flags in front of Secretariat Building, brown panel at right. b, Aerial view of headquarters and East River, yellow orange panel at left. c, Secretariat Building and wall of General Assembly building, yellow orange panel at left. d, Headquarters and East River, brown panel at right. e, General Asembly and Secretariat Buildings, flags at right, brown panel at right. f, Sculpture and fountain at night, yellow orange panel at left. g, Secretariat Building and cherry blossoms, yellow orange panel at left. h, Secretariat Building, trees without leaves, flags at left, brown panel at right. i, Aerial view of headquarters at night, brown panel at right. j, Headquarters, yellow panel at left.

2013, Jan. 28 Litho. *Perf. 14¾*

1055 A448 Sheet of 10 *30.00 30.00*
a.-j. $1.10 Any single + label *3.00 3.00*

The full sheet sold for $14.95. The generic labels are shown. Labels could be personalized. The personalization of labels was available only at UN Headquarters, and not through mail order.

World Radio Day — A449

Printed by Lowe-Martin Group, Canada. Panes of 20. Designed by Rorie Katz, US.

Designs: 46c, Radio antenna. $1.10, Audrey Hepburn at microphone.

2013, Feb. 13 Litho. *Perf. 13¼x13*

1056 A449 46c **multicolored** *(135,200)+* .95 .95
First day cover 1.60
Inscription block of 4 3.80 —
Pane of 20 19.00 —
1057 A449 $1.10 **multicolored** *(135,200)+* 2.25 2.25
First day cover 3.75
First day cover, #1056-1057 4.50
Inscription block of 4 9.00 —
Pane of 20 45.00 —

See Offices in Geneva Nos. 559-560; Vienna Nos. 521-522.

Circle of People A450

United Nations Headquarters — A451

Printed by Johann Enschedé and Sons, the Netherlands. Panes of 20. Designed by Sergio Baradat, US.

2013, Mar. 5 Litho. *Perf. 14x13½*

1058 A450 $1.10 **multicolored** *(200,000)+* 2.25 2.25
First day cover 3.00
Inscription block of 4 9.00 —
Pane of 20 45.00 —

Perf. 13½x14

1059 A451 $3 **multicolored** *(200,000)+* 6.00 6.00
First day cover 8.00
First day cover, #1058-1059 10.00
Inscription block of 4 24.00 —
Pane of 20 120.00 —

See Offices in Geneva Nos. 561-562; Vienna Nos. 523-524.

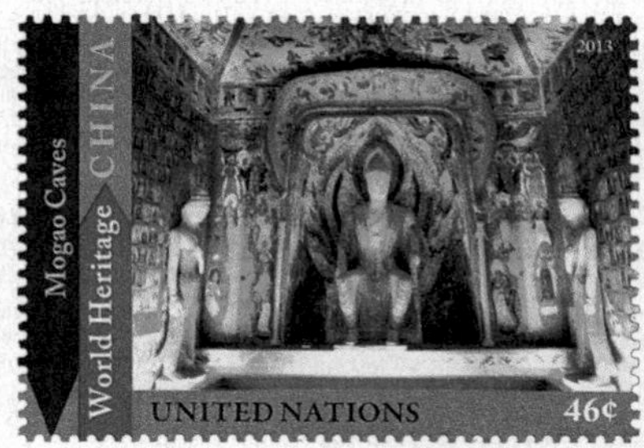

World Heritage Sites, China — A452

Printed by Johann Enschedé and Sons, the Netherlands. Panes of 20. Designed by Sergio Baradat, U.S.

Designs: Nos. 1060, 1062a, Mogao Caves. Nos. 1061, 1062d, Imperial Palace, Beijing. No. 1062b, Potala Palace, Lhasa. No. 1062c, Great Wall of China. No. 1062e, Mount Huangshan. No. 1062f, Mausoleum of the First Qing Emperor.

2013, Apr. 11 Litho. *Perf. 14x13½*

1060 A452 46c **multicolored** *(150,000)+* .95 .95
First day cover 1.60
Inscription block of 4 3.80 —
Pane of 20 19.00 —
1061 A452 $1.10 **multicolored** *(150,000)+* 2.25 2.25
First day cover 3.75
First day cover, #1060-1061 4.50
Inscription block of 4 9.00 —
Pane of 20 45.00 —

Souvenir Booklet

1062 Booklet, #1062g-1062l *(18,000)+* 20.00
a.-c. A452 33c any single .70 .70
d.-f. A452 46c any single .95 .95
g. Booklet pane of 4 #1062a 2.80 —
h. Booklet pane of 4 #1062b 2.80 —
i. Booklet pane of 4 #1062c 2.80 —
j. Booklet pane of 4 #1062d 3.80 —
k. Booklet pane of 4 #1062e 3.80 —
l. Booklet pane of 4 #1062f 3.80 —

See Offices in Geneva Nos. 563-565, Vienna Nos. 525-527.

Flag Type of 1980

Printed by Lowe Martin Group, Canada. Designed by Rorie Katz, US. Issued in panes of 16; each pane contains 4 blocks of 4. A se-tenant block of 4 designs centers each pane.

2013, May 2 Litho. *Perf. 13*

1063 A185 $1.10 Myanmar *(144,000)+* 2.25 2.25
1064 A185 $1.10 Russian Federation *(144,000)+* 2.25 2.25
1065 A185 $1.10 South Sudani *(144,000)+* 2.25 2.25
1066 A185 $1.10 Cape Verde *(144,000)+* 2.25 2.25
a. Block of 4, #1063-1066 9.00 9.00
First day cover, #1063-1066, each 3.50
Pane of 16 36.00
Nos. 1063-1066 (4) 9.00 9.00

World Oceans Day — A453

Printed by Lowe-Martin Group, Canada. Designed by Rorie Katz, US.

No. 1067 — Fish from *One Fish, Two Fish, Red Fish, Blue Fish*, by Dr. Seuss: a, Green fish, red fish, sign. b, Red fish facing right. c, Green fish facing left, sign. d, Yellow fish, sign. e, Blue fish. f, Red fish facing left, sign. g, Red fish facing right, water droplets, tail of yellow and red fish, sign. h, Yellow and red fish, green fish, side of blue fish. i, Head of blue fish, sign post. j, Sign and wave. k, Sign, red fish, side and tail of blue fish, wave. l, Side of blue fish, green fish, wave.

2013, May 31 Litho. *Perf. 13*

1067 A453 Sheet of 12 *(47,000)+* 11.50 11.50
First day cover 14.50
a.-l. 46c any single .95 .95

See Offices in Geneva No. 566; Vienna No. 528.

Nebulae — A454

Printed by UAB Garsu Pasaulis, Lithuania. Panes of 8. Designed by Sergio Baradat, U.S.

Designs: No. 1068, V838 Mon. No. 1069, WR 25, Tr16-244. 46c, 30 Doradus.

2013, Aug. 9 Litho. *Perf. 13¼*

1068 A454 $1.10 **multicolored** *(116,000)+* 2.25 2.25
1069 A454 $1.10 **multicolored** *(116,000)+* 2.25 2.25
a. Pair, #1068-1069 4.50 4.50
First day cover, #1069a 6.00
Inscription block of 4 9.00 —
Pane of 8 18.00 —

Souvenir Sheet

1070 A454 46c **multicolored** *(29,000)+* 2.50 2.50
First day cover 2.00

No. 1070 contains one 44x44mm stamp. See Offices in Geneva Nos. 567-569; Vienna Nos. 529-531.

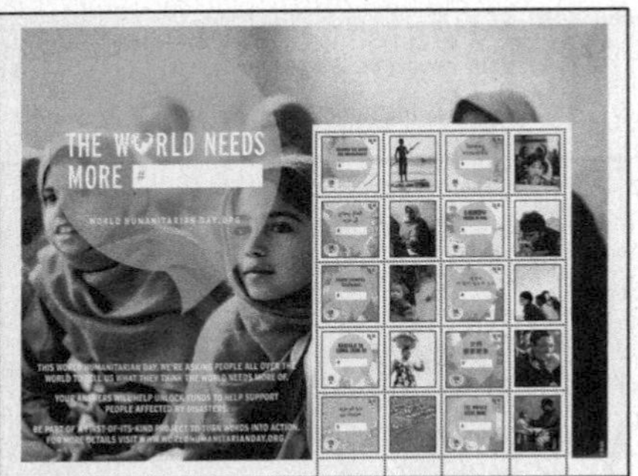

World Humanitarian Day — A455

No. 1071 — "The World Needs More" in speech balloon in: a, Somali (Uduunku. . .). b, Thai. c, Arabic (people in background). d, Portuguese (O Mundo. . .). e, Russian. f, Korean. g, Swahili (Mahitaji. . .). h, Chinese. i, Urdu (aerial view of village in background). j, English.

2013, Aug. 19 **Litho.** ***Perf. 14¾***

1071 A455 Sheet of 10 *30.00 30.00*
a.-j. $1.10 Any single + label *3.00 3.00*

The full sheet sold for $14.95. The generic labels are shown. Labels could be personalized. The personalization of labels was available only at UN Headquarters, and not through mail order.

Works of Disabled Artists — A456

Printed by UAB Garsu Pasaulis, Lithuania. Panes of 20. Designed by Rorie Katz, U.S.

Designs: 46c, Self-portrait II by Chuck Close, U.S. $1.10, Tears and Laughter, by Josephine King, United Kingdom.

2013, Sept. 20 **Litho.** ***Perf. 13¼x13***

1072 A456 46c **multicolored** *(148,000)+* .95 .95
First day cover 1.60
Inscription block of 4 3.80 —
Pane of 20 19.00 —
1073 A456 $1.10 **multicolored** *(148,000)+* 2.25 2.25
First day cover 3.75
First day cover, #1072-1073 4.50
Inscription block of 4 9.00 —
Pane of 20 45.00 —

See Offices in Geneva Nos. 570-571; Vienna Nos. 532-533.

Endangered Species Type of 1993

Printed by Johann Enschedé and Sons, the Netherlands. Designed by Fernando J. S. Correia, Portugal.

Designs: No. 1074, Asian tapir. No. 1075, Mongoose lemur. No. 1076, Flat-headed cat. No. 1077, Aye-aye.

2013, Oct. 10 **Litho.** ***Perf. 12¾x12½***

1074 A271 $1.10 **multicolored** *(108,000)+* 2.50 2.50
1075 A271 $1.10 **multicolored** *(108,000)+* 2.50 2.50
1076 A271 $1.10 **multicolored** *(108,000)+* 2.50 2.50
1077 A271 $1.10 **multicolored** *(108,000)+* 2.50 2.50
a. Block of 4, #1074-1077 10.00 10.00
First day cover, #1077a 11.00
First day cover, #1074-1077, each 3.50
Inscription block of 4, #1077a 10.00 —
Pane of 16 40.00 —

See Offices in Geneva Nos. 572-575; Vienna Nos. 534-537.

Flags and Coins Type of 2006

Printed by Cartor Security Printing, France. Designed by Rorie Katz, US.

No. 1078 — Flag of: a, Montenegro, 20 cent coin. b, Grenada, 5 cent coin. c, United States, 25 cent coin. d, Gabon, 100 franc coin. e, Palau, 1 cent coin. f, Niger, 100 franc coin. g, Saint Kitts and Nevis, 5 cent coin. h, Venezuela, 1 bolivar coin.

2013, Nov. 6 **Litho.** ***Perf. 13¼x13***

1078 Sheet of 8 *(41,000)+* 7.75 7.75
a.-h. A375 46c Any single .95 .95
First day cover 10.50

A column of rouletting in the middle of the sheet separates it into two parts. See Offices in Geneva No. 576; Vienna No. 539.

UN Emblem — A457

2014, Jan. 28 **Litho.** ***Perf. 14¾***

1079 A457 $1.15 **multicolored** + label *3.00 3.00*
Sheet of 10 + 10 labels *30.00 —*

The full sheet sold for $14.95. The generic label exists as shown, with horse on orange background. Labels could be personalized. The personalization of labels was available only at UN Headquarters, and not through mail order. See Nos. 1149, 1187, 1209.

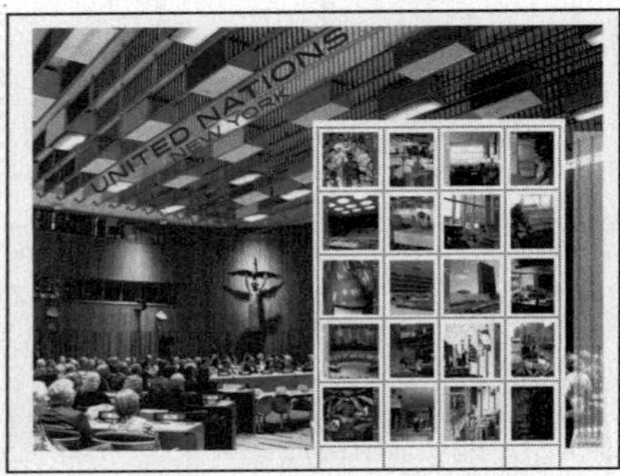

A458

No. 1080: a, The Golden Rule, mosaic by Norman Rockwell, dark green panel at right. b, Renovated Delegate's Lounge, yellow green panel at left. c, Renovated ECOSOC Chamber, red brown panel at left. d, Dag Hammarskjold Library, dark blue panel at right. e, Helmet of United Nations Peacekeeper and United Nations Flag, dark blue panel at right. f, United Nations Headquarters, dark green panel at left. g, Renovated Security Council Chamber, yellow green panel at left. h, Flags of member nations, red brown panel at right. i, Mankind's Struggle for Lasting Peace, by José Vela-Zanetti, dark blue panel at right. j, Relational Painting No. 90, by Fritz Glarner, yellow green panel at left.

2014, Jan. 28 **Litho.** ***Perf. 14¾***

1080 A458 Sheet of 10 *30.00 30.00*
a.-j. $1.15 Any single + label *3.00 3.00*

The full sheet sold for $14.95. The generic labels are shown. Labels could be personalized. The personalization of labels was available only at UN Headquarters, and not through mail order.

International Day of Happiness — A459

Printed by Lowe-Martin Group, Canada. Panes of 20. Designed by Rorie Katz, U.S.

Designs: 47c, Woman smiling, photograph by Mario Castello, "Happy." $1.15, People kissing on beach, photograph by Henryk T. Kaiser, "Feliz."

2014, Mar. 17 **Litho.** ***Perf. 13¼x13***

1081 A459 47c **multicolored** *(130,000)+* .95 .95
First day cover 1.60
Inscription block of 4 3.80 —
Pane of 20 19.00 —
1082 A459 $1.15 **multicolored** *(130,000)+* 2.40 2.40
First day cover 4.00
First day cover, #1081-1082 4.75
Inscription block of 4 9.60 —
Pane of 20 48.00 —

See Offices in Geneva Nos. 577-578; Vienna Nos. 540-541.

Flag Type of 1980

Printed by Lowe Martin Group, Canada. Designed by Rorie

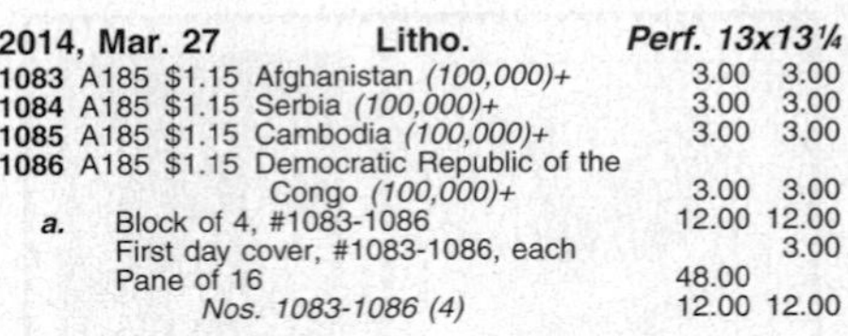

2014, Mar. 27 **Litho.** ***Perf. 13x13¼***

1083 A185 $1.15 Afghanistan *(100,000)+* 3.00 3.00
1084 A185 $1.15 Serbia *(100,000)+* 3.00 3.00
1085 A185 $1.15 Cambodia *(100,000)+* 3.00 3.00
1086 A185 $1.15 Democratic Republic of the Congo *(100,000)+* 3.00 3.00
a. Block of 4, #1083-1086 12.00 12.00
First day cover, #1083-1086, each 3.00
Pane of 16 48.00
Nos. 1083-1086 (4) 12.00 12.00

Miniature Sheet

International Year of Jazz — A460

Printed by Cartor Security Printing, France. Designed by Sergio Baradat, U.S.

No. 1087: a, Trumpeter with cap and mute in trumpet. b, Silhouette of trumpeter in tan. c, Saxophone. d, Trumpet. e, Silhouette of trumpeter in lilac. f, Saxophonist wearing hat. g, Man with hat holding trombone. h, Green saxophone. i, Saxophonist without hat. j, Trombone. k, Trumpeter wearing hat. l, Microphone.

2014, Apr. 30 **Litho.** ***Perf. 13x13¼***

1087 A460 Sheet of 12 *(45,000)+* 12.00 12.00
First day cover 15.00
a.-l. 49c Any single 1.00 1.00

See Offices in Geneva No. 579; Vienna No. 542.

A461

A462

Printed by Lowe-Martin Group, Canada. Panes of 20. Designed by Sergio Baradat, U.S.

2014, June 6 **Litho.** ***Perf. 13¼x13***

1088 A461 33c **multicolored** *(140,000)+* .70 .70
First day cover 1.00
Inscription block of 4 2.80 —
Pane of 20 14.00 —

1089 A462	$2 **multicolored** *(140,000)+*	4.00	4.00
	First day cover		6.00
	First day cover, #1088-1089		6.25
	Inscription block of 4	16.00	—
	Pane of 20	80.00	—

See Offices in Geneva Nos. 580-581; Vienna Nos. 544-545.

Taj Mahal and Tourists — A463

Taj Mahal and Pink Sky — A464

Taj Mahal and Sun A465

Taj Mahal and Reflecting Pool — A466

Taj Mahal and Camel A467

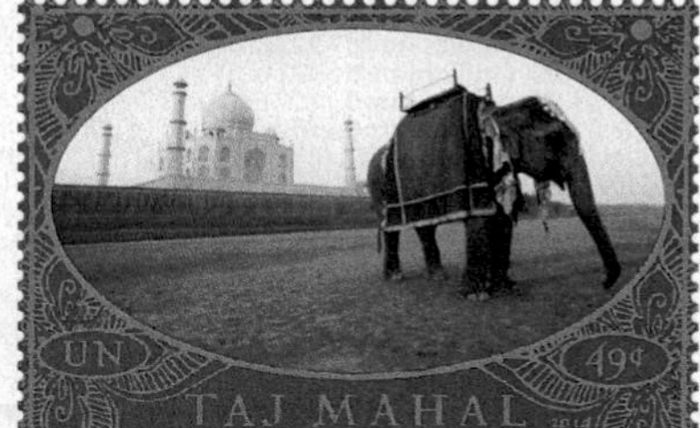

Taj Mahal and Elephant — A468

Printed by Lowe-Martin Group, Canada. Panes of 20. Designed by Rorie Katz, U.S.

2014, July 16 **Engr.** ***Perf. 13¼x13***

1090 A463	49c **multicolored** *(130,000)+*	1.00	1.00
	First day cover		1.75
	Inscription block of 4	4.00	—
	Pane of 20	20.00	—
1091 A464	$1.15 **multicolored** *(130,000)+*	2.40	2.40
	First day cover		4.00
	First day cover, #1090-1091		4.75
	Inscription block of 4	9.60	—
	Pane of 20	48.00	—

Souvenir Booklet

1092	Booklet, #1092g-1092l *(14,000)+*	20.50	
a.	A463 34c multi	.70	.70
b.	A465 34c multi	.70	.70
c.	A466 34c multi	.70	.70
d.	A464 49c multi	1.00	1.00
e.	A467 49c multi	1.00	1.00
f.	A468 49c multi	1.00	1.00
g.	Booklet pane of 4 #1092a	2.80	—
h.	Booklet pane of 4 #1092b	2.80	—
i.	Booklet pane of 4 #1092c	2.80	—
j.	Booklet pane of 4 #1092d	4.00	—
k.	Booklet pane of 4 #1092e	4.00	—
l.	Booklet pane of 4 #1092f	4.00	—

See Offices in Geneva Nos. 582-584, Vienna Nos. 546-548.

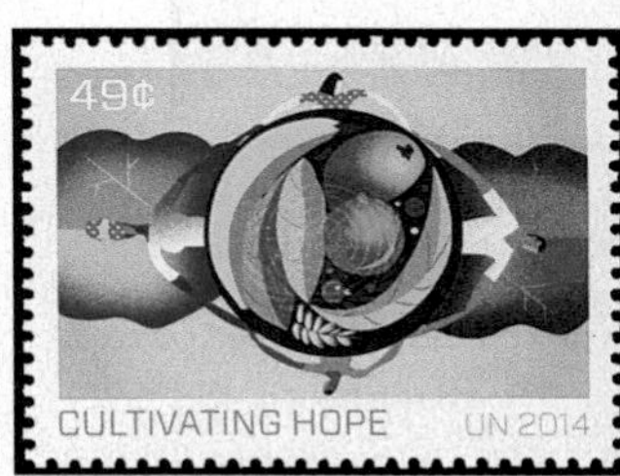

International Year of Family Farming A469

Printed by Lowe-Martin Group, Canada. Panes of 20. Designed by Sergio Baradat, U.S.

Designs: 49c, People and fruits. $1.15, People fishing.

2014, Aug. 21 **Litho.** ***Perf. 13x13¼***

1093 A469	49c **multicolored** *(120,000)+*	1.00	1.00
	First day cover		1.75
	Inscription block of 4	4.00	—
	Pane of 20	20.00	—
1094 A469	$1.15 **multicolored** *(120,000)+*	2.40	2.40
	First day cover		4.00
	First day cover, #1093-1094		4.75
	Inscription block of 4	9.60	—
	Pane of 20	48.00	—

See Offices in Geneva Nos. 585-586; Vienna Nos. 549-550.

Global Education First Initiative A470

Printed by Lowe-Martin Group, Canada. Panes of 20. Designed by Oamul Lu, People's Republic of China.

Designs: $1.15, Teacher and students in forest. $1.50, Chemistry teacher and student.

2014, Sept. 18 **Litho.** ***Perf. 13x13¼***

1095 A470	$1.15 **multicolored** *(130,000)+*	2.40	2.40
	First day cover		3.50
	Inscription block of 4	9.75	—
	Pane of 20	48.00	—

Souvenir Sheet

Perf. 12½

1096 A470	$1.50 **multicolored** *(35,000)+*	5.00	5.00
	First day cover		5.00

No. 1096 contains one 32x32mm stamp. See Offices in Geneva Nos. 588-589; Vienna Nos. 551-552.

Endangered Species A471

Printed by Johann Enschedé and Sons, the Netherlands. Designed by Amadeo Bachar, U.S.

Maps and: No. 1097, Denise's pygmy seahorses. No. 1098, Whale shark. No. 1099, Scalloped hammerhead shark. No. 1100, Asian arowana.

2014, Oct. 23 **Litho.** ***Perf. 12¾x12½***

1097 A471	$1.15 **multicolored** *(100,000)+*	2.40	2.40
1098 A471	$1.15 **multicolored** *(100,000)+*	2.40	2.40
1099 A471	$1.15 **multicolored** *(100,000)+*	2.40	2.40
1100 A471	$1.15 **multicolored** *(100,000)+*	2.40	2.40
a.	Block of 4, #1097-1100	9.75	9.75
	First day cover, #1100a		11.00
	First day cover, #1097-1100, each		3.50
	Inscription block of 4, #1100a	9.75	—
	Pane of 16	39.00	—

See Offices in Geneva Nos. 590-593; Vienna Nos. 553-556.

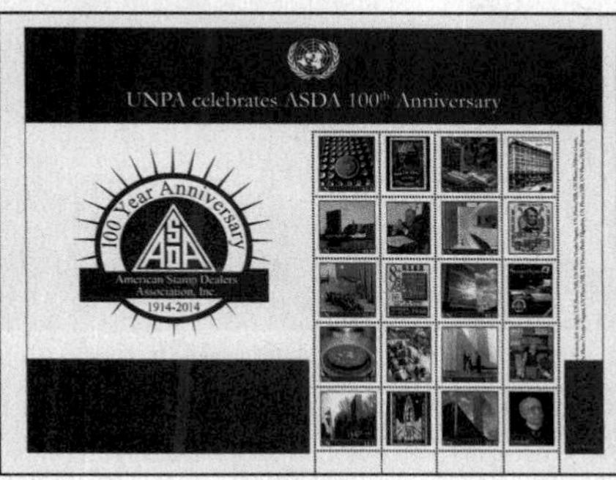

A472

No. 1101: a, United Nations emblem in gray, bottom panel in blue. b, Aerial view of United Nations Headquarters, bottom panel in red, year date at left. c, View of United Nations Headquarters from across East River, bottom panel in red, year date at right. d, Interior balconies, bottom panel in blue. e, Crowd in lobby, bottom panel in blue. f, Sun reflecting off United Nations Building, street lights, bottom panel in red. g, United Nations emblem in brown, bottom panel in red. h, Woman and two men near General Assembly Building, bottom panel in blue. i, United Nations Building, flags, trees without leaves, bottom panel in blue. j, General Assembly and United Nations Buildings, bottom panel in red.

2014, Oct. 23 **Litho.** ***Perf. 14¾***

1101 A472	Sheet of 10	*30.00*	*30.00*
a.-j.	$1.15 Any single + label	*3.00*	*3.00*

The full sheet sold for $14.95. The generic labels are shown. Labels could be personalized. The personalization of labels was available only at UN Headquarters, and not through mail order.

UN Emblem — A473

Designed by Rorie Katz, U.S.

2015, Jan. 23 **Litho.** ***Perf. 14¾***

1102 A473	$1.15 **multicolored** + label	*3.00*	*3.00*
	Sheet of 10 + 10 labels	*30.00*	—

The full sheet sold for $14.95. The generic label exists as shown, with ram on deep bister background. Labels could be personalized. The personalization of labels was available only at UN Headquarters, and not through mail order.

Flags and Coins Type of 2006

Printed by Cartor Security Printing, France. Designed by Rorie Katz, U.S.

No. 1103 — Flag of: a, Kiribati, 10 cent coin. b, Tonga, 2 seniti coin. c, Costa Rica, 10 centimos coin. d, Bhutan, 25 chetrum coin. e, Zimbabwe, 5 dollar coin. f, Angola, 1 kwanza coin. g, Congo Democratic Republic, 1 franc coin. h, Liberia, 25 cent coin.

2015, Feb. 6 Litho. ***Perf. 13¼x13***

1103 Sheet of 8 *(38,000)+* 8.00 8.00
a.-h. A375 49c Any single 1.00 1.00
First day cover 11.00

A column of rouletting in the middle of the sheet separates it into two parts. See Offices in Geneva No. 594; Vienna No. 558.

Miniature Sheets

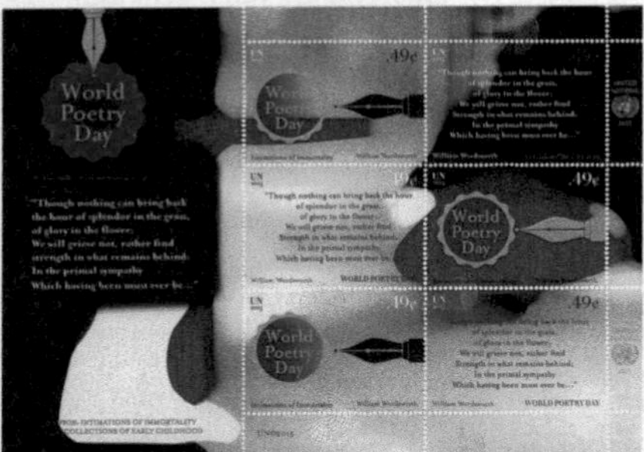

A474

World Poetry Day — A475

Printed by Cartor Security Printing. France. Designed by Sergio Baradat, U.S.

No. 1104: a, Black pen, denomination in red brown. b, William Wordsworth quotation in cream, denomination in red. c, Wordsworth quotation in red brown, denomination in white. d, Gold pen, denomination in white. e, Black pen, denomination in white. f, Wordsworth quotation in black, denomination in red brown.

No. 1105: a, Gold pen, denomination in white, tree top and rose in background. b, José Martí quotation, denomination in lilac, tree tops in background. c, Martí quotation, denomination in white, tree top and rose in background. d, Gold pen, denomination in lilac, tree trunks and tree top in background. e, Gold pen, denomination in lilac, tree trunks and rose in background. f, Martí quotation, denomination in lilac, tree trunks in background.

2015, Mar. 20 Litho. ***Perf. 14½x14¼***

1104 A474 Sheet of 6 *(35,000)+* 6.00 6.00
a.-f. 49c Any single 1.00 1.00
1105 A475 Sheet of 6 *(35,000)+* 14.50 14.50
a.-f. $1.20 Any single 2.40 2.40
First day cover, #1104-1105 26.00

See Offices in Geneva Nos. 595-596; Vienna Nos. 559-560.

Endangered Species — A476

Printed by Johann Enschedé and Sons, the Netherlands. Designed by John Keulemans and William Hart, United Kingdom.

Designs: No. 1106, King bird-of-paradise. No. 1107, Blue bird-of-paradise. No. 1108, Princess Stephanie's bird-of-paradise. No. 1109, Carola's parotia.

2015, Apr. 16 Litho. ***Perf. 12½x12¾***

1106 A476 $1.20 **multicolored** *(92,000)+* 2.40 2.40
1107 A476 $1.20 **multicolored** *(92,000)+* 2.40 2.40
1108 A476 $1.20 **multicolored** *(100,000)+* 2.40 2.40
1109 A476 $1.20 **multicolored** *(100,000)+* 2.40 2.40
a. Block of 4, #1106-1109 9.75 9.75
First day cover, #1109a 11.50
First day cover, #11106-1109, each 3.75
Inscription block of 4, #1109a 9.75 —
Pane of 16 39.00 —
Nos. 1106-1109 (4) 9.60 9.60

See Offices in Geneva Nos. 597-600; Vienna Nos. 561-564.

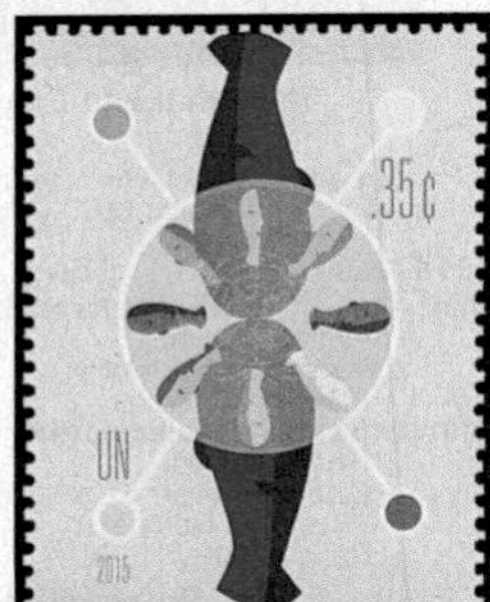

A477

A478

Printed by Lowe-Martin Group, Canada. Panes of 20. Designed by Sergio Baradat, U.S.

2015, May 7 Litho. ***Perf. 13¼x13***

1110 A477 35c **multicolored** *(130,000)+* .70 .70
First day cover 1.60
Inscription block of 4 2.80 —
Pane of 20 14.00 —
1111 A478 40c **multicolored** *(130,000)+* .80 .80
First day cover 1.90
First day cover, #1110-1111 2.60
Inscription block of 4 3.60 —
Pane of 20 16.00 —

See Offices in Vienna Nos. 565-566.

Miniature Sheet

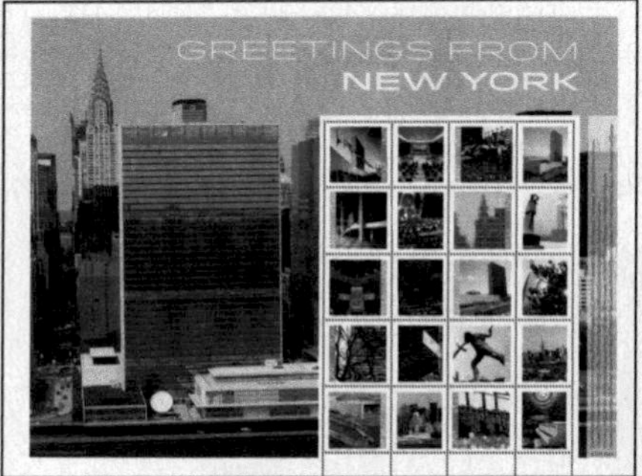

A479

No. 1112: a, United Nations Headquarters and flags, panel at right. b, Flags, panel at left. c, Stairway and pillars, panel at left. d, Reflection of buildings in windows, panel at right. e, Circular meeting room, panel at right. f, United Nations Headquarters, panel at left. g, Trees and United Nations Building, panel at left. h, Let Us Beat Swords Into Plowshares statue, panel at right. i, General Assembly Building, flags and street, panel at right. j, Arrival sculpture, panel at left.

2015, May 7 Litho. ***Perf. 14¾***

1112 A479 Sheet of 10 *30.00 30.00*
a.-j. $1.20 Any single + label *3.00 3.00*

The full sheet sold for $14.95. The generic labels are shown. Labels could be personalized. The personalization of labels was available only at UN Headquarters, and not through mail order.

World Heritage Sites, Southeast Asia — A480

Printed by Johann Enschedé and Sons, the Netherlands. Panes of 20. Designed by Sergio Baradat, U.S.

Designs: Nos. 1113, 1115a, Luang Prabang, Laos. Nos. 1114, 1115d, Borobodur Temple, Indonesia. No. 1115b, Angkor Wat, Cambodia. No. 1115c, Ayutthaya, Thailand. No. 1115e, Cordillera, Philippines. No. 1115f, Hué Monuments, Viet Nam.

2015, June 5 Litho. ***Perf. 14x13½***

1113 A480 49c **multicolored** *(130,000)+* 1.00 1.00
First day cover 1.60
Inscription block of 4 4.00 —
Pane of 20 20.00 —
1114 A480 $1.20 **multicolored** *(130,000)+* 2.40 2.40
First day cover 4.00
First day cover, #1113-1114 4.75
Inscription block of 4 9.60 —
Pane of 20 48.00 —

Souvenir Booklet

1115 Booklet, #1115g-1115l *(13,000)+* 20.50
a.-c. A480 35c any single .70 .70
d.-f. A480 49c any single 1.00 1.00
g. Booklet pane of 4 #1115a 2.80 —
h. Booklet pane of 4 #1115b 2.80 —
i. Booklet pane of 4 #1115c 2.80 —
j. Booklet pane of 4 #1115d 4.00 —
k. Booklet pane of 4 #1115e 4.00 —
l. Booklet pane of 4 #1115f 4.00 —

See Offices in Geneva Nos. 601-603, Vienna Nos. 567-569.

End Violence Against Children — A481

Printed by Cartor Security Printing, France. Panes of 20. Designed by Chris Sharp, U.S.

Designs: 49c, Armed violence reduction. $1.20, Sexual violence against children.

2015, Aug. 20 Litho. ***Perf. 14½x14¼***

1116 A481 49c **multicolored** *(120,000)+* 1.00 1.00
First day cover 1.60
Inscription block of 4 4.00 —
Pane of 20 20.00 —
1117 A481 $1.20 **multicolored** *(120,000)+* 2.40 2.40
First day cover 4.00
First day cover, #1116-1117 4.75
Inscription block of 4 9.60 —
Pane of 20 48.00 —

See Offices in Geneva Nos. 604-605; Vienna Nos. 570-571.

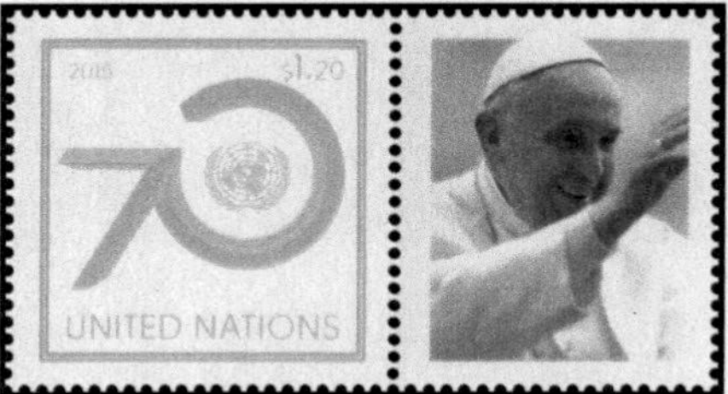

United Nations, 70th Anniv. — A482

Designed by Sergio Baradat, U.S.

2015, Sept. 25 Litho. ***Perf. 14¾***

1118 A482 $1.20 **multicolored** + label *3.00 3.00*
Sheet of 10 + 10 labels *30.00* —

The full sheet sold for $14.95. The generic label exists as shown, depicting Pope Francis. Labels could be personalized. The personalization of labels was available only at UN Headquarters, and not through mail order. On. Sept. 27, No. 1118

was issued in a sheet of 10 + 10 labels depicting Chinese characters.
See Vienna No. 577.

General Assembly Hall A483

Visitors Lobby A484

Security Council A485

Woodrow Wilson Reading Room of Dag Hammarskjöld Library — A486

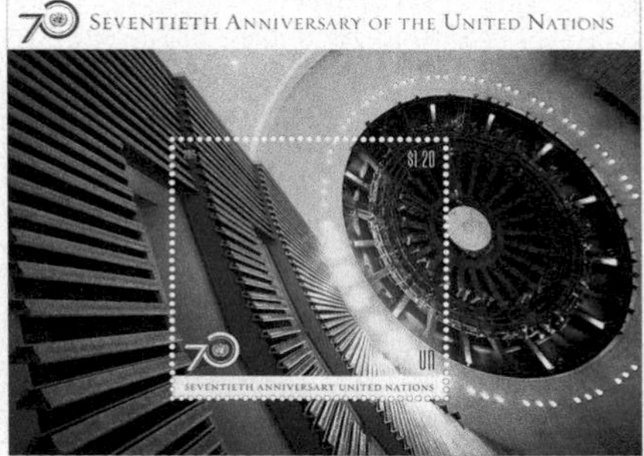

General Assembly Hall — A487

Printed by Cartor Security Printing, France. Panes of 6. Designed by Rorie Katz, U.S.

2015, Oct. 25 Litho. *Perf. 13¾*

1119	A483	49c **multicolored** *(105,000)+*	1.00	1.00
1120	A484	49c **multicolored** *(105,000)+*	1.00	1.00
a.		Pair, #1119-1120	2.00	2.00
		First day cover, #1119-1120		2.75
		Inscription block of 4	4.00	—
		Pane of 6	6.00	—
1121	A485	$1.20 **multicolored** *(105,000)+*	2.40	2.40
1122	A486	$1.20 **multicolored** *(105,000)+*	2.40	2.40
a.		Pair, #1121-1122	4.80	4.80
		First day cover, #1119-1120		6.75
		Inscription block of 4	9.60	—
		Pane of 6	14.50	—
		Nos. 1119-1122 (4)	6.80	6.80

Souvenir Sheet

Perf. 13½

1123	A487	$1.20 **multicolored** *(35,000)+*	4.00	4.00
		First day cover		3.75

United Nations, 70th anniv. See Offices in Geneva Nos. 607-611; Vienna Nos. 572-576.

United Nations Educational, Scientific and Cultural Organization (UNESCO), 70th Anniv. — A488

2015, Nov. 5 Litho. *Perf. 14¾*

1124	A488	$1.20 **multicolored** + label	*3.50*	*3.50*
		Sheet of 10 + 10 labels	*35.00*	—

The full sheet sold for $14.95. Ten different generic labels, one of which is shown, are on the sheet. Labels could be personalized. The personalization of labels was available only at UN Headquarters, and not through mail order.

21st United Nations Climate Change Conference, Paris — A489

Printed by La Poste, France. Panes of 30. Designed by Rorie Katz, U.S.

2015, Nov. 24 Litho. *Perf. 13¼*

1125	A489	$1.20 **multicolored** *(120,000)+*	2.40	2.40
		First day cover		3.75
		Inscription block of 4	9.60	—
		Pane of 30	72.00	—

Values are for stamps with surrounding selvage. See Offices in Geneva No. 612; Vienna No. 578.

UN Emblem — A490

2016, Jan. 8 Litho. *Perf. 14¾*

1126	A490	$1.20 **multicolored** + label	*3.00*	*3.00*
		Sheet of 10 + 10 labels	*30.00*	—

The full sheet sold for $14.95. The generic label, with monkey on red background, is shown. A sheet of 10 No. 1126 + 10 labels depicting M. S. Subbulaskshmi was issued on Oct. 2, 2016. Labels could be personalized. The personalization of labels was available only at UN Headquarters, and not through mail order.

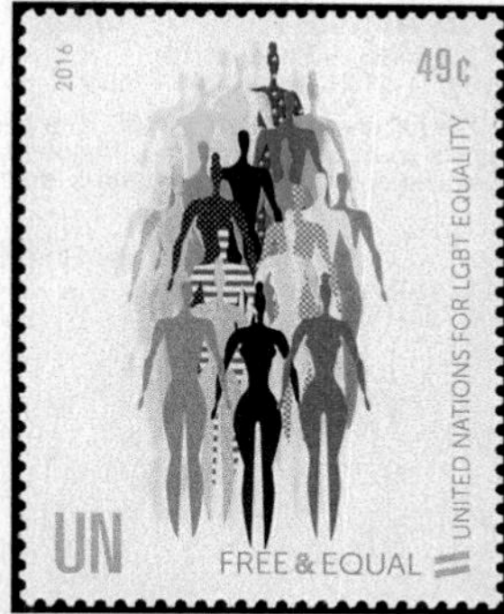

Free and Equal — A491

Printed by Cartor Security Printing, France. Panes of 20. Designed by Sergio Baradat, U.S.
Designs: 49c, Group of stylized people. $1.20, Woman with butterfly wings.

2016, Feb. 5 Litho. *Perf. 13½x13¼*

1127	A491	49c **multicolored** *(120,000)+*	1.00	1.00
		First day cover		1.60
		Inscription block of 4	4.00	—
		Pane of 20	20.00	—
1128	A491	$1.20 **multicolored** *(120,000)+*	2.40	2.40
		First day cover		4.00
		First day cover, #1127-1128		4.75
		Inscription block of 4	9.60	—
		Pane of 20	48.00	—

See Offices in Geneva Nos. 613-614; Vienna Nos. 579-580.

HeForShe Movement — A492

Printed by Lowe-Martin Group, Canada. Panes of 20. Designed by Mirko Ilic, U.S.
Designs: 49c, Man, green background. $1.20, Woman, yellow background.

2016, Mar. 8 Litho. *Perf. 12½x13*

1129	A492	49c **multicolored** *(120,000)+*	1.00	1.00
		First day cover		1.60
		Inscription block of 4	4.00	—
		Pane of 20	20.00	—
1130	A492	$1.20 **multicolored** *(120,000)+*	2.40	2.40
		First day cover		4.00
		First day cover, #1129-1130		4.75
		Inscription block of 4	9.60	—
		Pane of 20	48.00	—

See Offices in Geneva Nos. 615-616; Vienna Nos. 581-582.

Miniature Sheet

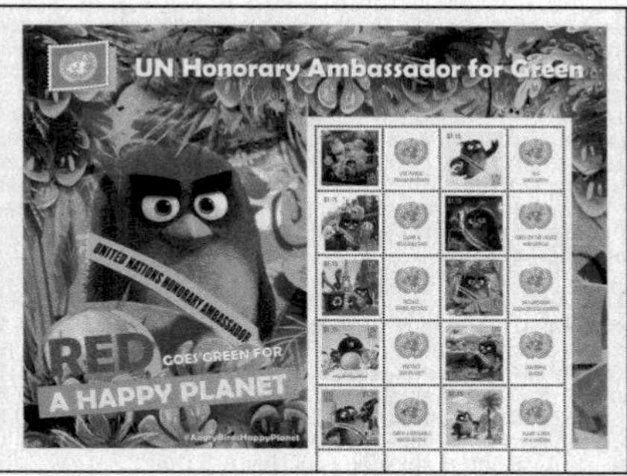

Angry Birds — A493

No. 1131: a, Red, the Pigs, double-decker bus. b, Red with wing extended. c, Red and five Hatchlings. d, Red, New York City skyscrapers. e, Red, Eiffel Tower, recycling container. f, Red in jungle. g, Earth, Hatchlings, Chuck, Red, Bomb, Stella and Matilda. h, Red turning faucet, Pigs in tub. i, Red drinking from squirt bottle, Lower Manhattan skyline. j, Red with shovel, Pyramids.

2016, Apr. 22 **Litho.** ***Perf. 14¾***

1131	A493	Sheet of 10	*30.00*	*30.00*
a.-j.		$1.15 Any single + label	*3.00*	*3.00*

The full sheet sold for $14.95. The generic labels are shown. Labels could be personalized. The personalization of labels was available only at UN Headquarters, and not through mail order.

Miniature Sheets

A494

International Dance Day — A495

Printed by Cartor Security Printing. France. Designed by Sergio Baradat, U.S.

No. 1132 — Illustration of Chinese dancers by Marcos Chin: a, Woman with arm extended upward. b, Two women, denomination in magenta. c, Woman facing left with arm extended outward. d, Two women, denomination in white. e, Woman with closed eyes. f, Woman with closed eyes with two pale yellow lines touching flower.

No. 1133 — Illustration of Thai dancers by Chin: a, Back of dancer's head, hand of another dancer. b, Dancer wearing mask, leg and arm of other dancers. c, Dancer with costume with blue shoulders, dancer with arm extended. d, Dancer with arm extended, leg and arm of other dancers. e, Two dancers with green and yellow costumes. f, Dancer with hand and arm from other dancers.

2016, Apr. 29 **Litho.** ***Perf. 13¼x13***

1132	A494	Sheet of 6 *(32,500)+*	5.75	5.75
a.-f.		47c Any single	.95	.95
1133	A495	Sheet of 6 *(32,500)+*	14.50	14.50
a.-f.		$1.15 Any single	2.40	2.40
		First day cover, #1132-1133		26.00
g.		As #1133, with "Thailand 2018 / World Stamp Exhibition / 28 Nov. - 3 Dec." overprinted in sheet margin	14.50	14.50

Issued: No. 1133g, 11/28/18. See Offices in Geneva Nos. 617-618; Vienna Nos. 583-584.

International Day of United Nations Peacekeepers — A496

Printed by Lowe-Martin Group, Canada. Panes of 20. Designed by Sergio Baradat, U.S.

Designs: 47c, Peacekeeper saluting. $1.15, Man disabling landmine.

Litho. With Foil Application

2016, May 29 ***Perf. 13¼x13***

1134	A496	47c **multicolored** *(150,000)+*	.95	.95
		First day cover		1.60
		Inscription block of 4	3.80	—
		Pane of 20	19.00	—
1135	A496	$1.15 **multicolored** *(150,000)+*	2.40	2.40
		First day cover		4.00
		First day cover, #1134-1135		4.50
		Inscription block of 4	9.60	—
		Pane of 20	48.00	—

See Offices in Geneva Nos. 619-620; Vienna Nos. 586-587.

Miniature Sheet

United Nations Postal Administration, 65th Anniv. — A497

No. 1136 — Old United Nations stamps: a, New York #1. b, New York #127. c, Vienna #86. d, New York #415. e, New York #301. f, New York #548. g, New York #474. h, Vienna #100. i, New York #476. j, Vienna #122.

2016, May 30 **Litho.** ***Perf. 14¾***

1136	A497	Sheet of 10	*30.00*	*30.00*
a.-j.		$1.15 Any single + label	*3.00*	*3.00*

The full sheet sold for $14.95. The generic labels are shown. Labels could be personalized. The personalization of labels was available only at UN Headquarters, and not through mail order.

Sport for Peace — A498

Printed by Cartor Security Printing, France. Panes of 6. Designed by Sergio Baradat and Linsey Thoeng, U.S.

Olympic rings and: No. 1137, Shot put, high jump. No. 1138, Runner, javelin. No. 1139, Dove facing left. No. 1140, Dove facing right.

2016, July 22 **Litho.** ***Perf. 14¼***

1137	A498	47c **multicolored** *(84,000)+*	.95	.95
1138	A498	47c **multicolored** *(84,000)+*	.95	.95
a.		Pair, #1137-1138	1.90	1.90
		First day cover, #1137-1138		2.60
		Inscription block of 4	3.80	—
		Pane of 6	5.75	—
1139	A498	$1.15 **multicolored** *(84,000)+*	2.40	2.40
1140	A498	$1.15 **multicolored** *(84,000)+*	2.40	2.40
		Inscription block of 4	9.60	—
		Pane of 6	14.50	—
		Nos. 1137-1140 (4)	6.70	6.70

See Offices in Geneva Nos. 621-624; Vienna Nos. 588-591.

Souvenir Sheet

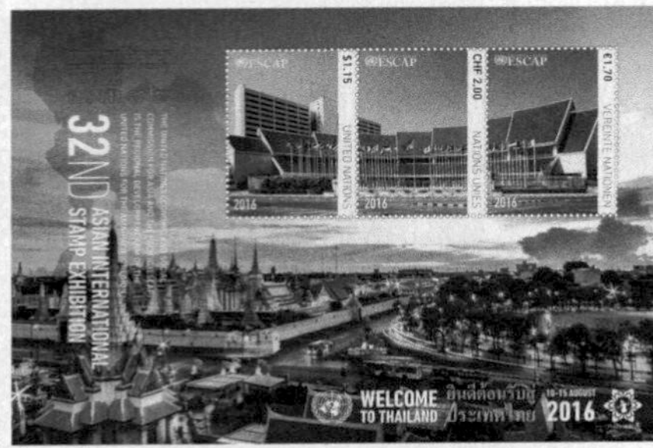

United Nations Economic and Social Commission for Asia and the Pacific Building, Bangkok — A499

Printed by Beijing Postage Stamp Printing House, People's Republic of China.

No. 1141: a, Left third of building, b, Center third of building, c, Right third of building.

2016, Aug. 10 **Litho.** ***Perf. 13¼x13***

1141	A499	Sheet of 3	24.00	24.00
a.		$1.15 multi	5.00	5.00
b.		2fr multi	9.50	9.50
c.		€1.70 multi	8.50	8.50

32nd Asian International Stamp Exhibition. No. 1141 sold for $6.

World Heritage Sites, Czech Republic — A500

Printed by Cartor Security Printing, France. Panes of 20. Designed by Sergio Baradat, U.S.

Designs: Nos. 1142, 1144a, Historic Center of Prague. Nos. 1143, 1144d, Holy Trinity Column, Olomouc. No. 1144b, Gardens and Castle at Kromeríz. No. 1144c, Historic Town Center of Kutná Hora. No. 1144e, Lednice-Valtice Cultural Landscape. No. 1144f, Historic Center of Cesky Krumlov.

2016, Sept. 8 **Litho.** ***Perf. 14¼***

1142	A500	47c **multicolored** *(110,000)+*	.95	.95
		First day cover		1.60
		Inscription block of 4	3.80	—
		Pane of 20	19.00	—
1143	A500	$1.15 **multicolored** *(110,000)+*	2.40	2.40
		First day cover		4.00
		First day cover, #1142-1143		4.50
		Inscription block of 4	9.60	—
		Pane of 20	48.00	—

Souvenir Booklet

1144		Booklet, #1144g-1144l	20.00	
a.-c.	A500	34c any single	.70	.70
d.-f.	A500	47c any single	.95	.95
g.		Booklet pane of 4 #1144a	2.80	—
h.		Booklet pane of 4 #1144b	2.80	—
i.		Booklet pane of 4 #1144c	2.80	—
j.		Booklet pane of 4 #1144d	3.80	—
k.		Booklet pane of 4 #1144e	3.80	—
l.		Booklet pane of 4 #1144f	3.80	—

See Offices in Geneva Nos. 625-627; Vienna Nos. 592-594, Czech Republic Nos. 3683-3684.

Miniature Sheet

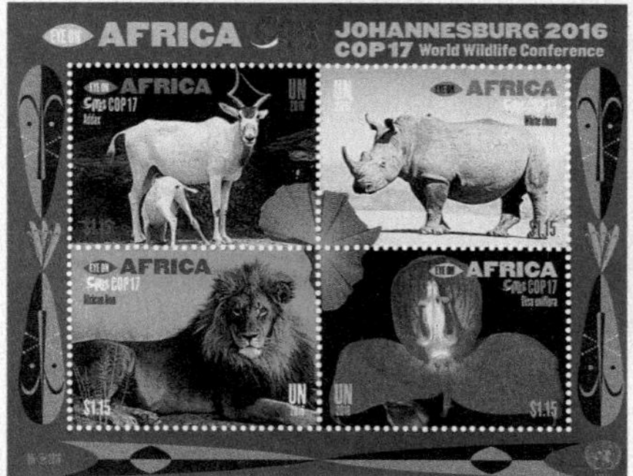

World Wildlife Conference, Johannesburg — A501

Printed by Cartor Security Printing, France. Designed by Sergio Baradat, U.S.

No. 1145 — Part of map of Africa and: a, Addax. b, White rhinoceros. c, African lion. d, Disa uniflora.

2016, Sept. 24 Litho. *Perf. 13x13½*

1145	A501	Sheet of 4 *(30,000)+*	9.75	9.75
a.-d.		$1.15 Any single	2.40	2.40
		First day cover		11.00

See Offices in Geneva No. 628; Vienna No. 596.

Miniature Sheet

World Post Day — A502

No. 1146 — Mail box from: a, Japan. b, Spain. c, Germany. d, Brazil. e, China. f, Denmark. g, India. h, Austria. i, England. j, United States.

2016, Oct. 6 Litho. *Perf. 14¾*

1146	A502	Sheet of 10	*30.00*	*30.00*
a.-j.		$1.15 Any single + label	*3.00*	*3.00*

The full sheet sold for $14.95. The generic labels are shown. Labels could be personalized. The personalization of labels was available only at UN Headquarters, and not through mail order.

Sustainable Development Goals — A503

Printed by Lowe-Martin, Canada. Designed by Lindsey Thoeng, U.S.

No. 1147 — Inscription: a, 1 No poverty. b, 2 Zero hunger. c, 3 Good health and well-being. d, 4 Quality education. e, 5 Gender equality. f, 6 Clean water and sanitation. g, 7 Affordable and clean energy. h, 8 Decent work and economic growth. i, 9 Industry, innovation and infrastructure. j, 10 Reduced inequalities. k, 11 Sustainable cities and communities. l, 12 Responsible consumption and production. m, 13 Climate action. n, 14 Life below water. o, 15 Life on land. p, 16 Peace, justice and strong institutions. q, 17 Partnerships for the goals.

2016, Oct. 24 Litho. *Perf. 13¼*

1147	A503	Sheet of 17 + label *(28,000)+*	17.00	17.00
a.-q.		47c Any single	1.00	1.00
		First day cover		21.00

See Offices in Geneva No. 629; Vienna No. 597.

Souvenir Sheet

Monkey King From Chinese Novel *Journey to the West* — A504

No. 1148 — Various depictions of Monkey King with inscriptions in: a, English. b, French. c, German.

Litho. With Foil Application

2016, Dec. 2 *Perf. 12*

1148	A504	Sheet of 3	20.00	20.00
a.		$1.15 multi	4.00	4.00
b.		2fr multi	7.00	7.00
c.		€1.70 multi	6.75	6.75

33rd Asian International Stamp Exhibition, Nanning, People's Republic of China. No. 1148 sold for $6.

United Nations Emblem Type of 2014 Dated "2017" in Purple

2017, Jan. 13 Litho. *Perf. 14¾*

1149	A457	$1.15 **multicolored** + label	*3.00*	*3.00*
		Sheet of 10 + 10 labels	*30.00*	—

The full sheet sold for $14.95. The generic label exists as shown, with rooster on red background. Labels could be personalized. The personalization of labels was available only at UN Headquarters, and not through mail order.

Flag Type of 1980

Printed by Lowe Martin Company, Inc., Canada. Designed by Sergio Baradat, U.S. Issued in panes of 16; each pane contains 4 blocks of 4. A se-tenant block of 4 designs centers each pane.

2017, Feb. 3 Litho. *Perf. 13x13¼*

1150	A185	$1.15 Albania *(88,000)+*	2.40	2.40
1151	A185	$1.15 Benin *(88,000)+*	2.40	2.40
1152	A185	$1.15 Bulgaria *(88,000)+*	2.40	2.40
1153	A185	$1.15 Comoros *(88,000)+*	2.40	2.40
a.		Block of 4, #1150-1153	9.75	9.75
1154	A185	$1.15 Congo Republic *(88,000)+*	2.40	2.40
1155	A185	$1.15 Ethiopia *(88,000)+*	2.40	2.40
1156	A185	$1.15 Georgia *(88,000)+*	2.40	2.40
1157	A185	$1.15 Iraq *(88,000)+*	2.40	2.40
a.		Block of 4, #1154-1157	9.75	9.75
		First day cover, #1150-1157, each		4.00
		Set of 2 different panes of 16	96.00	
		Nos. 1150-1157 (8)	19.20	19.20

Miniature Sheet

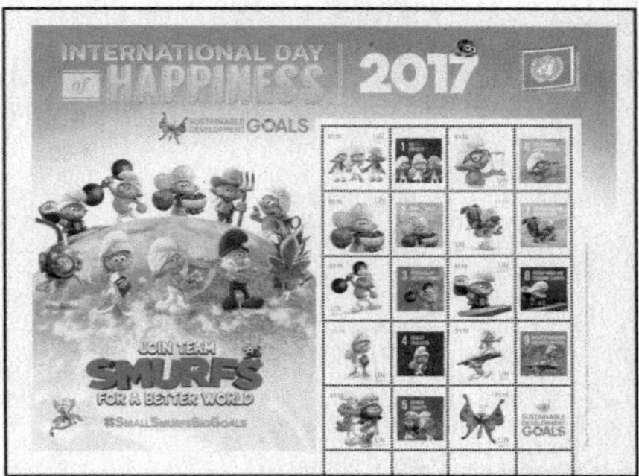

A505

No. 1158: a, Three Smurfs. b, Smurf holding glass of water. c, Smurf holding fruit. d, Smurf with backpack with solar panels. e, Smurf lifting dumbbell. f, Smurf carrying mallet. g, Smurf holding book. h, Two Smurfs with ladder. i, Male and female Smurfs. j, Butterfly.

2017, Mar. 20 Litho. *Perf. 14¾*

1158	A505	Sheet of 10	*30.00*	*30.00*
a.-j.		$1.15 Any single + label	*3.00*	*3.00*

The full sheet sold for $14.95. The generic labels are shown. Labels could be personalized. The personalization of labels was available only at UN Headquarters, and not through mail order.

Miniature Sheets

A506

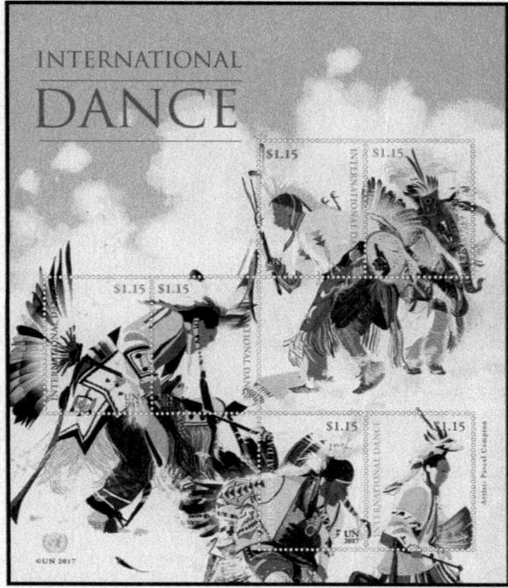

International Dance — A507

Printed by Cartor Security Printing. France. Designed by Sergio Baradat, U.S.

No. 1159 — Illustration of Polynesian dancers by Pascal Campion: a, Woman with arms raised, denomination at LR. b, Woman with arms raised, denomination at UL. c, Two women wearing head coverings, red necklace, denomination at UR. d, One woman wearing head covering and red necklace, denomination at UR. e, Woman with feathered headdress, green necklace, hair of another woman at right, denomination at UR. f, Woman wearing feathered headdress and green necklace, denomination at UR.

No. 1160 — Illustration of Native American tribal dancers by Campion: a, Dancer facing right, denomination in blue at UL. b, Dancer, denomination in orange at UL. c, Back of dancer, denomination in gray lilac at UR. d, Dancer looking downward, denomination in gray lilac at UL. e, Dancer with headband over eyebrows, denomination in orange red at UR, "International Dance" in white. f, Dancer, denomination in orange red at UR, "International Dance" in light blue.

2017, Mar. 23 Litho. *Perf. 13¼x13*

1159	A506	Sheet of 6 *(22,000)+*	6.00	6.00
a.-f.		49c Any single	1.00	1.00
1160	A507	Sheet of 6 *(22,000)+*	14.50	14.50
a.-f.		$1.15 Any single	2.40	2.40
		First day cover, #1159-1160		27.00

See Offices in Geneva Nos. 630-631; Vienna Nos. 599-600.

Souvenir Sheet

Australian Animals — A508

No. 1161: a, Koalas. b, Kangaroos. c, Emu.

Litho. With Foil Application

2017, Mar. 30 ***Perf. 13¼x13***

1161 A508 Sheet of 3		12.00	12.00
a.	$1.15 multi	4.00	4.00
b.	2fr multi	4.00	4.00
c.	€1.70 multi	3.75	3.75

2017 FIAP International Stamp Exhibition, Melbourne, Australia. No. 1161 sold for $6.

Endangered Species — A509

Printed by Johann Enschedé and Sons, the Netherlands. Designed by Rorie Katz, U.S.

Designs: No. 1162, Masobe gecko. No. 1163, Thresher shark. No. 1164, Clarion angelfish. No. 1165, Blaine's fishhook cactus.

2017, May 11 **Litho.** ***Perf. 12¾x12½***

1162 A509 $1.15 **multicolored** *(64,000)+*		2.40	2.40
1163 A509 $1.15 **multicolored** *(64,000)+*		2.40	2.40
1164 A509 $1.15 **multicolored** *(64,000)+*		2.40	2.40
1165 A509 $1.15 **multicolored** *(64,000)+*		2.40	2.40
a.	Block of 4, #1162-1165	9.75	9.75
	First day cover, #1165a		12.00
	First day cover, #1162-1165, each		4.25
	Inscription block of 4, #1165a	9.75	—
	Pane of 16	39.00	—
	Nos. 1162-1165 (4)	9.60	9.60

See Offices in Geneva Nos. 632-635; Vienna Nos. 601-604.

World Environment Day — A510

Printed by Lowe-Martin Group, Canada. Panes of 20. Designed by Sergio Baradat, U.S.

Designs: 49c, Hopewell Rocks, New Brunswick, Canada. $1.15, Polar bear, Baffin Island, Nunavut, Canada.

2017, June 5 **Litho.** ***Perf. 13¼***

1166 A510 49c **multicolored** *(110,000)+*		1.00	1.00
	First day cover		2.10
	Inscription block of 4	4.00	—
	Pane of 20	20.00	—
1167 A510 $1.15 **multicolored** *(110,000)+*		2.40	2.40
	First day cover		5.00
	First day cover, #1166-1167		5.50
	Inscription block of 4	9.60	—
	Pane of 20	48.00	—

See Offices in Geneva Nos. 636-637; Vienna Nos. 605-606.

Miniature Sheet

International Day of Yoga — A511

No. 1168: a, Orange woman on stomach holding her legs. b, Dark blue man siting with legs raised. c, Blue woman with arms extended. d, Beige man sitting with legs crossed and arms raised. e, Purple man with arms extended leaning backward to touch toes. f, Light blue woman bent backward with feet and hands on ground. g, Blue violet woman bent backward to touch raised leg. h, Red woman on one knee. i, Pale blue woman with arms extended touching raised leg. j, Orange man bent over with hands on ground.

2017, June 21 **Litho.** ***Perf. 14¾***

1168 A511 Sheet of 10		*30.00*	*30.00*
a.-j.	$1.15 Any single + label	*3.00*	*3.00*

The full sheet sold for $14.95. The generic labels are shown. Labels could be personalized. The personalization of labels was available only at UN Headquarters, and not through mail order.

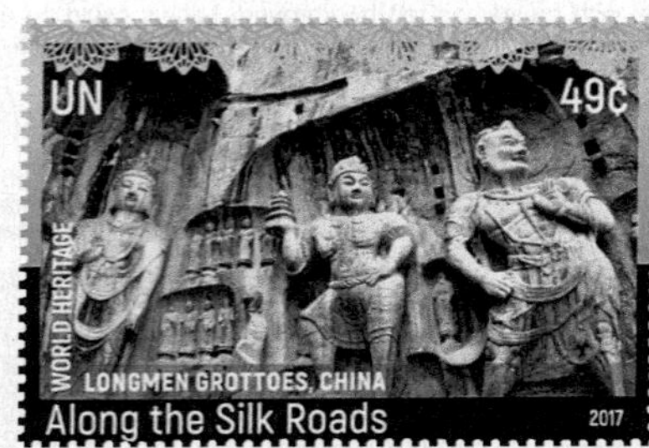

World Heritage Sites Along the Silk Roads — A512

Printed by Cartor Security Printing, France. Panes of 20. Designed by Sergio Baradat, U.S.

Designs: Nos. 1169, 1171a, Longmen Grottoes, People's Republic of China. Nos. 1170, 1171d, Sulaiman-Too Sacred Mountain, Kyrgyzstan. No. 1171b, Historic Center of Bukhara, Uzbekistan. No. 1171c, Tabriz Historic Bazaar Complex, Iran. No. 1171e, Kunya-Urgench, Turkmenistan. No. 1171f, Safranbolu, Turkey.

2017, Aug. 3 **Litho.** ***Perf. 14¼***

1169 A512 49c **multicolored** *(110,000)+*		1.00	1.00
	First day cover		2.10
	Inscription block of 4	4.00	—
	Pane of 20	20.00	—
1170 A512 $1.15 **multicolored** *(110,000)+*		2.40	2.40
	First day cover		5.00
	First day cover, #1169-1170		5.50
	Inscription block of 4	9.60	—
	Pane of 20	48.00	—

Souvenir Booklet

1171	Booklet, #1171g-1171l *(8,500)+*	22.50	
a.-c.	A512 34c any single	.75	.75
d.-f.	A512 49c any single	1.10	1.10
g.	Booklet pane of 4 #1171a	3.00	—
h.	Booklet pane of 4 #1171b	3.00	—
i.	Booklet pane of 4 #1171c	3.00	—
j.	Booklet pane of 4 #1171d	4.50	—
k.	Booklet pane of 4 #1171e	4.50	—
l.	Booklet pane of 4 #1171f	4.50	—

Complete booklet sold for $11. See Offices in Geneva Nos. 638-640; Vienna Nos. 607-609.

Doves A513

Moths A514

Doves — A515

Printed by Johann Enschedé and Sons, the Netherlands. Panes of 20. Designed by Stranger and Stranger, U.S.

2017, Sept. 21 **Litho.** ***Perf. 14x14¼***

1172 A513 49c **multicolored** *(110,000)+*		1.00	1.00
	First day cover		1.90
	Inscription block of 4	4.00	—
	Pane of 20	20.00	—
1173 A514 $1.15 **multicolored** *(110,000)+*		2.40	2.40
	First day cover		4.50
	First day cover, #1172-1173		5.00
	Inscription block of 4	9.60	—
	Pane of 20	48.00	—

Souvenir Sheet

Perf. 14¼x13¾

1174 A515 $1.15 **multicolored** *(27,000)+*		2.40	2.40
	First day cover		4.00

International Day of Peace. See Offices in Geneva Nos. 641-643; Vienna Nos. 611-613.

World Food Day — A516

Printed by Royal Johann Enschedé. Panes of 20. Designed by Helen Dardik, Canada.

Designs: 49c, Vegetables. $1.15, Bowls of food, jar of oil.

2017, Oct. 16 **Litho.** ***Perf. 13¼x14***

1175 A516 49c **multicolored** *(110,000)+*		1.00	1.00
	First day cover		2.10
	Inscription block of 4	4.00	—
	Pane of 20	20.00	—
1176 A516 $1.15 **multicolored** *(110,000)+*		2.40	2.40
	First day cover		5.00
	First day cover, #1175-1176		5.50
	Inscription block of 4	9.60	—
	Pane of 20	48.00	—

See Offices in Geneva Nos. 644-645; Vienna Nos. 614-615.

Souvenir Sheet

Universal Declaration of Human Rights — A517

Printed by Johann Enschedé Stamps Security Printers, B.V., the Netherlands. Designed by Rorie Katz, U.S. No. 1177 — Text of Universal Declaration of Human Rights in: a, English. b, French. c, German.

Litho. With Foil Application

2017, Oct. 27 ***Perf. 14x13¼***

1177 A517 Sheet of 3 *(30,000)+* 12.00 12.00
a. $1.15 multi 4.00 4.00
b. 2fr multi 4.00 4.00
c. €1.70 multi 4.00 4.00

United Nations Expo 2017, Bellefonte, Pennsylvania. No. 1177 sold for $6.

Souvenir Sheet

Landmarks in Paris — A518

Printed by Johann Enschedé Stamps Security Printers, B.V., the Netherlands. Designed by Sergio Baradat, U.S. No. 1178: a, Fame of Louis XVI, statue by Antoine Coysevox. b, Fontaines de la Concorde. c, Gargolye on Notre Dame Cathedral.

2017, Nov. 9 **Litho.** ***Perf. 13¼x14***

1178 A518 Sheet of 3 *(20,000)+* 12.00 12.00
a. $1.15 multi 4.00 4.00
b. 2fr multi 4.00 4.00
c. €1.70 multi 4.00 4.00

Autumn Philatelic Show, Paris. No. 1178 sold for $6.

Flag Type of 1980

Printed by Lowe Martin Group, Canada. Designed by Rorie Katz, U.S. Issued in panes of 16; each pane contains 4 blocks of 4. A se-tenant block of 4 designs centers each pane.

2018, Jan. 12 **Litho.** ***Perf. 13x13¼***

1179 A185 $1.15 Lesotho *(88,000)+* 2.40 2.40
1180 A185 $1.15 Libya *(88,000)+* 2.40 2.40
1181 A185 $1.15 Mozambique *(88,000)+* 2.40 2.40
1182 A185 $1.15 Romania *(88,000)+* 2.40 2.40
a. Block of 4, #1179-1182 9.75 9.75
1183 A185 $1.15 Rwanda *(88,000)+* 2.40 2.40
1184 A185 $1.15 Seychelles *(88,000)+* 2.40 2.40
1185 A185 $1.15 South Africa *(88,000)+* 2.40 2.40
1186 A185 $1.15 Ukraine *(88,000)+* 2.40 2.40
a. Block of 4, #1183-1186 9.75 9.75
First day cover, #1179-1186, each 4.25
Set of 2 different panes of 16 78.00
Nos. 1179-1186 (8) 19.20 19.20

United Nations Emblem Type of 2014 Dated "2018" in Purple

2018, Feb. 2 **Litho.** ***Perf. 14¾***

1187 A457 $1.15 **multicolored** + label *3.00 3.00*
Sheet of 10 + 10 labels *30.00* —

The full sheet sold for $14.95. The generic label depicts a dog. Labels could be personalized. The personalization of labels was available only at UN Headquarters, and not through mail order.

Endangered Species A519

Printed by Johann Enschedé Stamps Security Printers, the Netherlands. Designed by Rorie Katz, U.S.

Designs: No. 1188, Red-crested turaco. No. 1189, Andean hairy armadillo. No. 1190, Lurestan newt. No. 1191, Goldenseal.

2018, Mar. 2 **Litho.** ***Perf. 12¾x12½***

1188 A519 $1.15 **multicolored** *(64,000)+* 2.40 2.40
1189 A519 $1.15 **multicolored** *(64,000)+* 2.40 2.40
1190 A519 $1.15 **multicolored** *(64,000)+* 2.40 2.40
1191 A519 $1.15 **multicolored** *(64,000)+* 2.40 2.40
a. Block of 4, #1188-1191 9.75 9.75
First day cover, #1191a 12.00
First day cover, #1188-1191, each 4.25
Inscription block of 4, #1191a 9.75 —
Pane of 16 39.00 —
Nos. 1188-1191 (4) 9.60 9.60

See Offices in Geneva Nos. 646-649; Vienna Nos. 616-619.

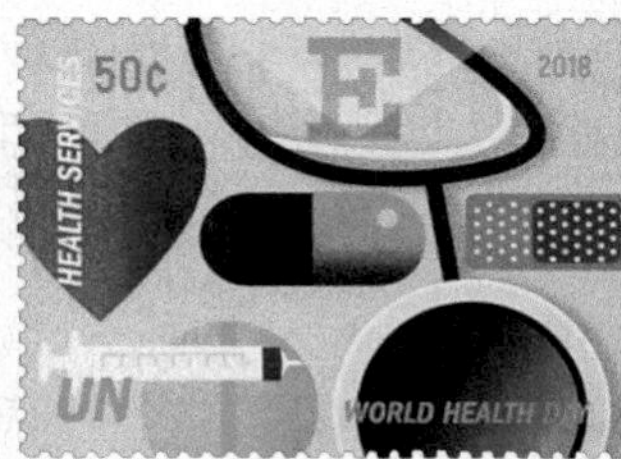

World Health Day — A520

Printed by Lowe-Martin Group, Canada. Panes of 20. Designed by Sergio Baradat, U.S.

Designs: 50c, Heart, pill, bandage, letter from eye chart, syringe and stethoscope. $1.15, Head with gears, heart, clock, stylized people, circle with arrows.

2018, Apr. 6 **Litho.** ***Perf. 13x13¼***

1192 A520 50c **multicolored** *(110,000)+* 1.00 1.00
First day cover 2.10
Inscription block of 4 4.00 —
Pane of 20 20.00 —
1193 A520 $1.15 **multicolored** *(110,000)+* 2.40 2.40
First day cover 5.00
First day cover, #1192-1193 5.50
Inscription block of 4 9.60 —
Pane of 20 48.00 —

See Offices in Geneva Nos. 650-651; Vienna Nos. 620-621.

Universal Declaration of Human Rights, 70th Anniv. — A521

Printed by Lowe-Martin Group, Canada. Panes of 20. Designed by Rorie Katz, U.S.

2018, May 3 **Litho.** ***Perf. 13¼***

1194 A521 $2.50 **multicolored** *(100,000)+* 5.00 5.00
First day cover 7.25
Inscription block of 4 20.00 —
Pane of 20 100.00 —

United Nations Headquarters A522

Printed by Lowe-Martin Group, Canada. Panes of 20. Designed by Rorie Katz, U.S.

2018, May 29 **Litho.** ***Perf. 13¼***

1195 A522 65c **multicolored** *(270,000)+* 1.40 1.40
First day cover 2.75
Inscription block of 4 5.75 —
Pane of 20 28.00 —

UNISPACE + 50 Conferences — A523

Printed by Johann Enschedé Stamps BV, Netherlands. Panes of 20. Designed by Sergio Baradat, U.S. Designs: 50c, Milky Way Galaxy. No. 1197, International Space Station and Space Shuttle Endeavour.

No. 1198, Astronaut Scott Kelly during spacewalk.

2018, June 20 **Litho.** ***Perf. 14x14¼***

1196 A523 50c **multicolored** *(90,000)+* 1.00 1.00
First day cover 2.10
Inscription block of 4 4.00 —
Pane of 20 20.00 —
1197 A523 $1.15 **multicolored** *(90,000)+* 2.40 2.40
First day cover 5.00
First day cover, #1196-1197 5.50
Inscription block of 4 9.60 —
Pane of 20 48.00 —

Souvenir Sheet

Perf. 13¾

1198 A523 $1.15 **multicolored** *(24,000)+* 2.40 2.40
First day cover 4.25

No. 1198 contains one 45x45mm stamp. See Offices in Geneva Nos. 653-655; Vienna Nos. 623-625.

World Heritage Sites in the United Kingdom — A524

Printed by Cartor Security Printing, France. Panes of 20. Designed by Rorie Katz, U.S.

Designs: Nos. 1199, 1201a, Giant's Causeway. Nos. 1200, 1201d, Palace of Westminster. No. 1201b, Stonehenge. No. 1201c, Conwy Castle. No. 1201e, Edinburgh. No. 1201f, Maritime Greenwich.

2018, Aug. 15 **Litho.** ***Perf. 14¼***

1199 A524 50c **multicolored** *(104,000)+* 1.00 1.00
First day cover 2.10
Inscription block of 4 4.00 —
Pane of 20 20.00 —
1200 A524 $1.15 **multicolored** *(104,000)+* 2.40 2.40
First day cover 5.00
First day cover, #1199-1200 5.50
Inscription block of 4 9.60 —

	Pane of 20	48.00	—

Souvenir Booklet

1201	Booklet, #1201g-1201l *(7,500)+*	22.50	
a.-c.	A524 35c any single	.75	.75
d.-f.	A524 50c any single	1.10	1.10
g.	Booklet pane of 4 #1201a	3.00	—
h.	Booklet pane of 4 #1201b	3.00	—
i.	Booklet pane of 4 #1201c	3.00	—
j.	Booklet pane of 4 #1201d	4.50	—
k.	Booklet pane of 4 #1201e	4.50	—
l.	Booklet pane of 4 #1201f	4.50	—

Complete booklet sold for $11. See Offices in Geneva Nos. 657-659; Vienna Nos. 626-628.

Miniature Sheet

Thomas the Tank Engine — A525

No. 1202: a, Thomas and four people. b, Reg lifting bicycle. c, Thomas, conductor holding potted plant. d, Ashima and Thomas. e, Thomas and Nia. f, Passenger car, children and tuba. g, Thomas and giraffe. h, Monkeys on Thomas. i, Water splashing on grimy Thomas. j, Nia, Thomas and ring of colors.

2018, Sept. 12 **Litho.** ***Perf. 14¾***

1202	A525 Sheet of 10	*30.00*	*30.00*
a.-j.	$1.15 Any single + label	*3.00*	*3.00*

The full sheet sold for $14.95. The generic labels are shown. Labels could be personalized. The personalization of labels was available only at UN Headquarters, and not through mail order.

Souvenir Sheet

Characters From Cantonese Opera *Hua Mulan* — A526

Printed by Cartor Security Printing, France. Designed by Ye Luying, China. No. 1203: a, Baozhen. b, Guanyu. c, Mulan.

2018, Sept. 21 **Litho.** ***Perf. 13¼x13***

1203	A526 Sheet of 3 *(18,000)+*	13.00	13.00
a.	$1.15 multi	4.25	4.25
b.	2fr multi	4.25	4.25
c.	€1.80 multi	4.25	4.25

Macao 2018 Asian International Stamp Exhibition. The vignettes are laser cut. No. 1203 sold for $6.30.

Miniature Sheet

International Music Day — A527

Printed by Johann Enschedé Stamps BV, the Netherlands. Designed by Sergio Baradat, U.S.

No. 1204: a, Trombone. b, Flute and clarinet. c, Cornet. d, Tuba, bell at right. e, Tuba, bell at left, red in background. f, French horn, red in background. g, Trumpet, bell at UR. h, Baritone horn. i, Saxophone. j, French horn, blue in background. k, Trumpet, bell at LR. l, Tuba, bell at left, blue in background.

2018, Oct. 1 **Litho.** ***Perf. 14x13¼***

1204	A527 Sheet of 12 *(18,000)+*	12.00	12.00
	First day cover		16.00
a.-l.	50c Any single	1.00	1.00

See Offices in Geneva No. 660; Vienna No. 629.

Non-Violence, Sculpture by Carl Fredrik Reuterswärd — A528

Printed by Johann Enschedé Stamps BV, the Netherlands. Panes of 50. Designed by Martin Mörck, Norway.

2018, Oct. 2 **Litho.** ***Perf. 13¼x14***

1205	A528 1c **multicolored** *(600,000)+*	.25	.25
	First day cover		3.00
	Inscription block of 4	.25	—

See Offices in Vienna Nos. 630-631.

Diwali Candles — A529

Diwali Candles — A530

2018, Oct. 19 **Litho.** ***Perf. 14¾***

1206	A529 $1.15 **multicolored** + label	*3.00*	*3.00*
1207	A530 $1.15 **multicolored** + label	*3.00*	*3.00*
a.	Vert. pair, #1206-1207, + 2 labels	*6.00*	*6.00*
	Sheet of 10, 5 each #1206-1207, + 10 labels	*30.00*	*30.00*

The full sheet sold for $14.95. The generic labels are shown. Labels could be personalized. The personalization of labels was available only at UN Headquarters, and not through mail order.

Souvenir Sheet

Arena di Verona — A531

Printed by La Poste, France. Designed by Chris Thornock, U.S.

No. 1208: a, Left side of Arena. b, Central portion of Arena with four upper-tier arches. c, Right side of Arena.

2018, Nov. 23 **Litho.** ***Perf. 13¼x13***

1208	A531 Sheet of 3 *(18,000)+*	13.00	13.00
a.	$1.15 multi	4.25	4.25
b.	2fr multi	4.25	4.25
c.	€1.80 multi	4.25	4.25

Veronafil 2018 Stamp Exhibition, Verona, Italy. No. 1208 sold for $6.30.

United Nations Emblem Type of 2014 Dated "2019" in Purple

2019, Jan. 11 **Litho.** ***Perf. 14¾***

1209	A457 $1.15 **multicolored** + label	*3.00*	*3.00*
	Sheet of 10 + 10 labels	*30.00*	—

The full sheet sold for $14.95. The generic label depicts a pig. Labels could be personalized. The personalization of labels was available only at UN Headquarters, and not through mail order.

Miniature Sheet

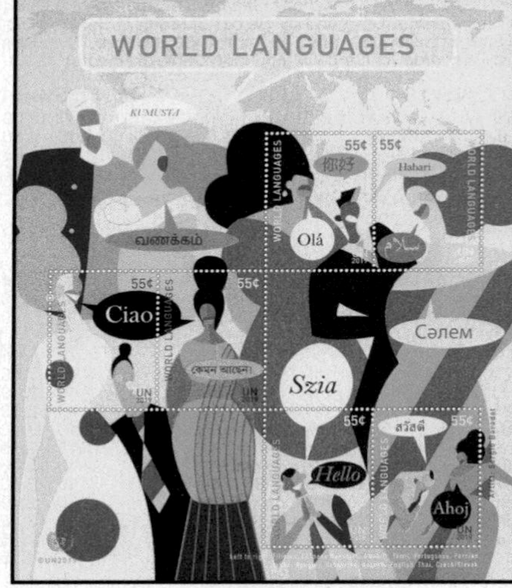

World Languages — A532

Printed by Cartor Security Printing. France. Designed by Sergio Baradat, U.S.

No. 1210 — Word bubbles with word for "Hello" in: a, Chinese and Portuguese (Olá). b, Swahili (Habari) and Persian. c, Italian (Ciao). d, Bengali. e, English. f, Thai and Czech or Slovak (Ahoj).

2019, Feb. 21 **Litho.** ***Perf. 13¼x13***

1210	A532 Sheet of 6 *(22,000)+*	6.75	6.75
a.-f.	55c Any single	1.10	1.10
	First day cover, #1210		11.00

See Offices in Geneva No. 661; Vienna No. 632.

Stop Sexual Exploitation and Abuse — A533

Printed by Lowe-Martin Group, Canada. Panes of 20. Designed by Chris Gash, U.S.

2019, Mar.15 Litho. *Perf. 13¼x13*

1211 A533 85c **multicolored** *(140,000)+*	1.75	1.75
First day cover		3.75
Inscription block of 4	7.00	—
Pane of 20	35.00	—

Endangered Species A534

Printed by Johann Enschedé Stamps Security Printers, the Netherlands. Designed by Rongliang Wang, People's Republic of China.

Designs: No. 1212, Hawksbill turtle. No. 1213, Queen conch. No. 1214, Mushroom coral. No. 1215, Humpback whale.

2019, Apr. 26 Litho. *Perf. 12¾x12½*

1212 A534 $1.15 **multicolored** *(60,000)+*	2.40	2.40
1213 A534 $1.15 **multicolored** *(60,000)+*	2.40	2.40
1214 A534 $1.15 **multicolored** *(60,000)+*	2.40	2.40
1215 A534 $1.15 **multicolored** *(60,000)+*	2.40	2.40
a. Block of 4, #1212-1215	9.75	9.75
First day cover, #1215a		12.00
First day cover, #1212-1215, each		4.50
Inscription block of 4, #1215a	9.75	—
Pane of 16	39.00	—

See Offices in Geneva Nos. 663-666; Vienna Nos. 634-637.

2019 END-OF-YEAR ISSUES

The UNPA has announced that the following items will be issued in late 2019. Dates and denominations are tentative.

World Bee Day, *May 20,* $3 souvenir sheet; Geneva 2.60fr souvenir sheet; Vienna €2.70 souvenir sheet.

Kofi Annan, *May 31,* $1.30 stamp.

Panda Twin Global Animal Goodwill Ambassadors, *June 11,* souvenir sheet with China 2019 World Stamp Exhibition emblem in sheet margin containing $1.15 stamp, 2fr Geneva stamp, and €1.80 Vienna stamp; and *July 31,* souvenir sheet with Singpex 2019 emblem in sheet margin containing same stamps.

International Labor Organization, Cent., *June 280,* strip of five 55c stamps; Geneva strip of five 1fr stamps; Vienna strip of five 80c stamps, souvenir card.

Vienna International Center and United Nations Postal Administration Vienna, 40th Anniv., *Aug. 23,* strip of five different Vienna 90c stamps + 5 labels in sheet of 10 stamps + 10 labels.

Vienna International Center, 40th Anniv., *Aug. 24,* Vienna 90c stamped envelope.

Climate Change, *Sept. 6,* 55c, $1.15 stamps, $1.15 souvenir sheet; Geneva 1fr, 1.50fr stamps, 2fr souvenir sheet; Vienna 80c, 90c stamps, €1.80 souvenir sheet.

Mahatma Gandhi, 150th Anniv. of Birth, *Oct. 2,* $2.75 stamp.

United Nations Postal Administration Geneva, 50th Anniv., *Oct. 4,* sheet of ten Geneva 1.50fr stamps + 10 labels.

World Heritage, Cuba, *Oct. 24,* 55c, $1.15 stamps, prestige booklet; Geneva 1fr, 1.50fr stamps, prestige booklet; Vienna 90c, €1.80 stamps; prestige booklet.

Hello Kitty and Global Goals, sheet of ten $1.15 stamps + 10 labels.

Listings as of 11AM, Aug. 14, 2019.

SEMI-POSTAL STAMPS

Souvenir Sheet

AIDS Awareness — SP1

Printed by Walsall Security Printers Limited, UK. Designed by Rorie Katz, US.

2002, Oct. 24 Litho. *Perf. 14½*

B1 SP1 37c + 6c **multicolored** *(175,000)+*	3.50	3.50
First day cover, #B1		3.50

See Offices in Geneva No. B1, Vienna No. B1.

AIR POST STAMPS

Plane and Gull — AP1

Swallows and UN Emblem AP2

Engraved and printed by Thomas De La Rue & Co., Ltd., London. Panes of 50. Designed by Ole Hamann (AP1) and Olav Mathiesen (AP2).

1951, Dec. 14 Unwmk. *Perf. 14*

C1 AP1 6c **henna brown** *(2,500,000)*	.25	.25
First day cover		2.00
Inscription block of 4	.25	—
C2 AP1 10c **bright blue green** *(2,750,000)*	.30	.30
First day cover		2.00
Inscription block of 4	1.10	—
C3 AP2 15c **deep ultramarine** *(3,250,000)*	.40	.40
First day cover		3.00
Inscription block of 4	1.60	—
a. 15c **Prussian blue**	65.00	
C4 AP2 25c **gray black** *(2,250,000)*	.85	.85
First day cover		7.50
First day cover, #C1-C4		30.00
Inscription block of 4	4.75	—
Nos. C1-C4 (4)	1.80	1.80

First day covers of Nos. 1-11 and C1-C4 total 1,113,216.

Early printings of Nos. C1-C4 have wide, imperforate sheet margins on three sides. Later printings were perforated through all margins.

Airplane Wing and Globe — AP3

Engraved and printed by Thomas De La Rue & Co., Ltd., London. Panes of 50. Designed by W. W. Wind.

1957, May 27 *Perf. 12½x14*

C5 AP3 4c **maroon** *(5,000,000)*	.25	.25
First day cover *(282,933)*		1.00
Inscription block of 4	.30	—

For 5c see No. C6.

Type of 1957 and

UN Flag and Plane — AP4

Engraved and printed by Waterlow & Sons, Ltd., London. Panes of 50. Designed by W. W. Wind (5c) and Olav Mathiesen (7c).

1959, Feb. 9 Unwmk. *Perf. 12½x13½*

C6 AP3 5c **rose red** *(4,000,000)*	.25	.25
First day cover		1.00
Inscription block of 4	.50	—
Perf. 13½x14		
C7 AP4 7c **ultramarine** *(4,000,000)*	.25	.25
First day cover		1.00
First day cover, #C6-C7		17.50
Inscription block of 4	.75	—

First day covers of Nos. C6 and C7 total 413,556.

Outer Space — AP5

UN Emblem — AP6

Bird of Laurel Leaves — AP7

Printed by Courvoisier S.A., La Chaux-de-Fonds, Switzerland. Panes of 50. Designed by Claude Bottiau (6c), George Hamori (8c) and Kurt Plowitz (13c).

1963, June 17 Photo. Unwmk. *Perf. 11½*

C8 AP5 6c **black, blue & yellow green** *(4,000,000)*	.25	.25
First day cover		1.00
Inscription block of 4	.45	—

C9 AP6 8c **yellow, olive green & red** *(4,000,000)* .25 .25
First day cover 1.00
Inscription block of 4 .60 —

Perf. 12½x12

C10 AP7 13c **ultra, aquamarine, gray & carmine** *(2,700,000)* .25 .25
First day cover 1.00
First day cover, #C8-C10 8.50
Inscription block of 4 .90 —

First day covers of Nos. C8-C10 total 535,824.

"Flight Across the Globe" — AP8

Jet Plane and Envelope — AP9

Printed by the Austrian Government Printing Office, Vienna, Austria. Panes of 50. Designed by Ole Hamann (15c) and George Hamori (25c).

Perf. 11½x12, 12x11½

1964, May 1 **Photo.** **Unwmk.**

C11 AP8 15c **violet, buff, gray & pale green** *(3,000,000)* .30 .30
First day cover 1.00
Inscription block of 4 1.40 —
a. Gray omitted *225.00*

C12 AP9 25c **yellow, orange, gray, blue & red** *(2,000,000)* .50 .50
First day cover 1.00
First day cover, #C11-C12 8.00
Inscription block of 4 2.50 —
Nos. C8-C12 (5) 1.55 1.55

First day covers of Nos. C11-C12 total 353,696.
For 75c in type AP8, see UN Offices in Geneva No. 8.

Jet Plane and UN Emblem — AP10

Printed by Setelipaino, Finland. Panes of 50. Designed by Ole Hamann.

1968, Apr. 18 **Litho.** ***Perf. 13***

C13 AP10 20c **multicolored** *(3,000,000)* .35 .35
First day cover *(225,378)* 1.00
Inscription block of 4 1.60 —

Wings, Envelopes and UN Emblem — AP11

Printed by Setelipaino, Finland. Panes of 50. Designed by Olav S. Mathiesen.

1969, Apr. 21 **Litho.** ***Perf. 13***

C14 AP11 10c **orange vermilion, orange, yellow & black** *(4,000,000)* .25 .25
First day cover *(132,686)* 1.00
Inscription block of 4 .75 —

UN Emblem and Stylized Wing — AP12

Birds in Flight — AP13

Clouds AP14

"UN" and Plane — AP15

Printed by Government Printing Bureau, Japan (9c); Heraclio Fournier, S. A., Spain (11c, 17c); Setelipaino, Finland (21c). Panes of 50. Designed by Lyell L. Dolan (9c), Arne Johnson (11c), British American Bank Note Co. (17c) and Asher Kalderon (21c).

1972, May 1 **Litho. & Engr.** ***Perf. 13x13½***

C15 AP12 9c **light blue, dark red & violet blue** *(3,000,000)+* .25 .25
First day cover 1.00
Inscription block of 4 .50 —

Photo.

Perf. 14x13½

C16 AP13 11c **blue & multicolored** *(3,000,000)+* .25 .25
First day cover 1.00
Inscription block of 4 .75 —

Perf. 13½x14

C17 AP14 17c **yellow, red & orange** *(3,000,000)+* .25 .25
First day cover 1.00
Inscription block of 4 1.10 —

Perf. 13

C18 AP15 21c **silver & multi** *(3,500,000)* .25 .25
First day cover 1.00
First day cover, #C15-C18 3.50
Inscription block of 4 1.25 —
Nos. C15-C18 (4) 1.00 1.00

First day covers of Nos. C15-C18 total 553,535.

Globe and Jet — AP16

Pathways Radiating from UN Emblem AP17

Bird in Flight, UN Headquarters AP18

Printed by Setelipaino, Finland. Panes of 50. Designed by George Hamori (13c), Shamir Bros. (18c) and Olav S. Mathiesen (26c).

1974, Sept. 16 **Litho.** ***Perf. 13, 12½x13 (18c)***

C19 AP16 13c **multicolored** *(2,500,000)+* .25 .25
First day cover 1.00
Inscription block of 4 .80 —

C20 AP17 18c **gray olive & multicolored** *(2,000,000)* .25 .25
First day cover 1.00
Inscription block of 4 1.10 —

C21 AP18 26c **blue & multi** *(2,000,000)* .35 .35
First day cover 1.25
First day cover, #C19-C21 2.50
Inscription block of 4 1.60 —
Nos. C19-C21 (3) .85 .85

First day covers of Nos. C19-C21 total 309,610.

Winged Airmail Letter — AP19

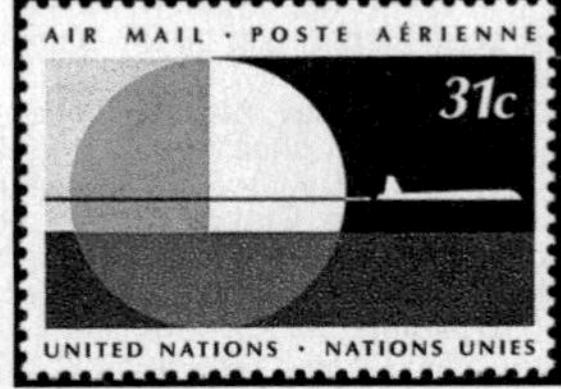

Symbolic Globe and Plane — AP20

Printed by Heraclio Fournier, S.A. Panes of 50. Designed by Eliezer Weishoff (25c) and Alan L. Pollock (31c).

1977, June 27 **Photo.** ***Perf. 14***

C22 AP19 25c **greenish blue & multi** *(2,000,000)+* .35 .35
First day cover 1.25
Inscription block of 4 1.60 —

C23 AP20 31c **magenta** *(2,000,000)* .45 .45
First day cover 1.25
First day cover, #C22-C23 1.50
Inscription block of 4 1.90 —

First day covers of Nos. C22-C23 total 209,060.

ENVELOPES

Used values for all postal stationery are for non-philatelic contemporaneous usages.

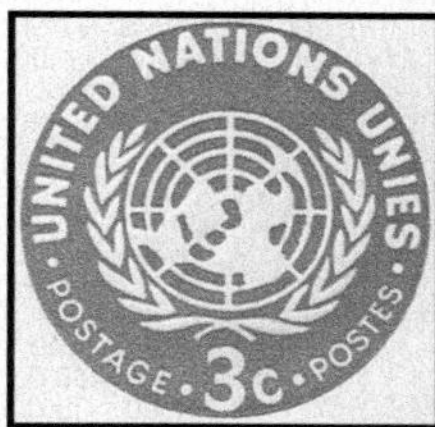

Emblem of United Nations — U1

Printed by the International Envelope Corp., Dayton, Ohio. Die engraved by the American Bank Note Co., New York.

1953, Sept. 15 **Embossed**
U1 U1 3c **blue,** entire *(555,000)* .25 .25
Entire, first day cancel *(102,278)* .50

Printed by International Envelope Corp., Dayton, Ohio.

1958, Sept. 22 **Embossed**
U2 U1 4c **ultramarine,** entire *(1,000,000)* .25 .25
Entire, first day cancel *(213,621)* .50

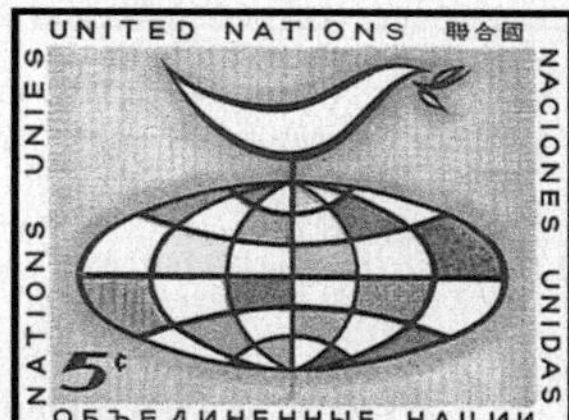

Stylized Globe and Weather Vane — U2

Printed by United States Envelope Co., Springfield, Mass. Designed by Hatim El Mekki.

1963, Apr. 26 **Litho.**
U3 U2 5c **multicolored,** entire *(1,115,888)* .25 .25
Entire, first day cancel *(165,188)* .75

Printed by Setelipaino, Finland.

1969, Jan. 8 **Litho.**
U4 U2 6c **black, blue, magenta & dull yellow,** entire *(850,000)* .25 .25
Entire, first day cancel *(152,593)* .75

Headquarters Type of Regular Issue, 1968

Printed by Eureka Co., a division of Litton Industries.

1973, Jan. 12 **Litho.**
U5 A99 8c **sepia, blue & olive,** entire *(700,000)* .45 .50
Entire, first day cancel *(145,510)* .75

Headquarters Type of Regular Issue, 1974

Printed by United States Envelope Co., Springfield, Mass.

1975, Jan. 10 **Litho.**
U6 A138 10c **blue, olive bister & multi,** entire *(547,500)* .40 .40
Entire, first day cancel *(122,000)* .90

Bouquet of Ribbons — U3

Printed by Carl Ueberreuter Druck and Verlag M. Salzer, Austria. Designed by George Hamori, Australia.

1985, May 10 **Litho.**
U7 U3 22c **multicolored,** entire *(250,000)* 3.25 1.75
Entire, first day cancel *(28,600)* 1.00

New York Headquarters U4

Printed by Mercury Walch, Australia. Designed by Rocco J. Callari, United States.

1989, Mar. 17 **Litho.**
U8 U4 25c **multicolored,** entire *(350,000)* 2.00 2.00
Entire, first day cancel *(28,567)* 3.00

For surcharge see No. U9A.

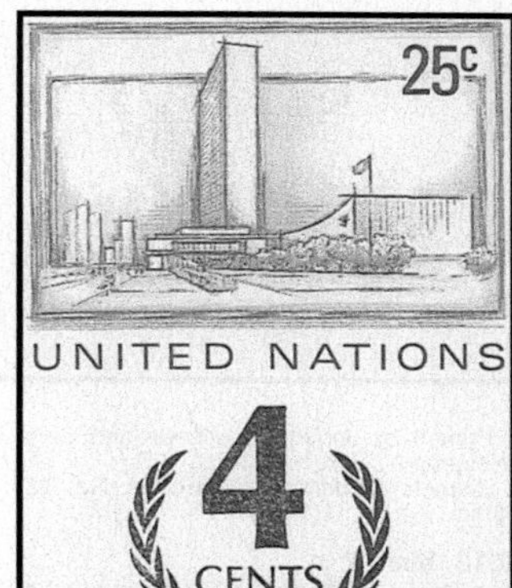

No. U8 Surcharged

1991, Apr. 15 **Litho.**
U9 U4 25c +4c **multicolored,** entire *(50,000)+* 3.00 *6.00*
Entire, first day cover 5.00

No. U8 Surcharged

1995 **Litho.**
U9A U4 25c +7c **multicolored,** entire 2.50 *6.00*
Entire, first day cover 6.00

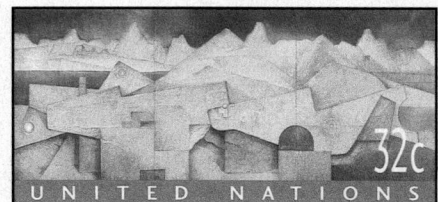

Cripticandina, by Alfredo La Placa — U5

Illustration reduced.
Design sizes: No. U10, 79x38mm. No. U11, 89x44mm.

1997, Feb. 12 **Litho.**
U10 U5 32c **multicolored,** #6¾, entire *(65,000)+* 2.00 2.00
Entire, first day cancel 5.50
U11 U5 32c **multicolored,** #10, entire *(80,000)+* 2.00 2.00
Entire, first day cancel 3.50

Nos. U10-U11 Surcharged

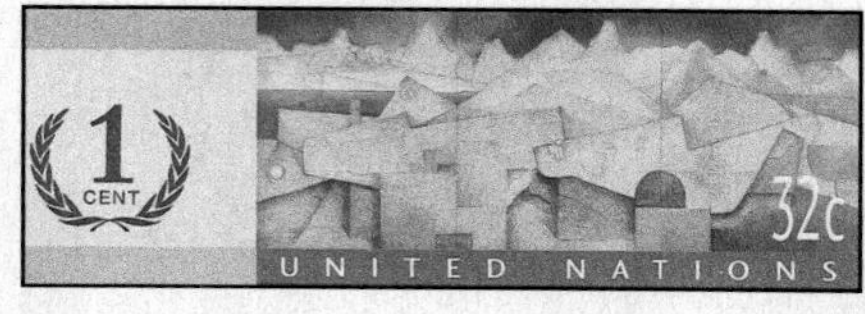

1999, Jan. 10 **Litho.**
U12 U5 32c +1c **multicolored,** on #U10, entire 2.00 2.00
First day cancel, entire 2.50
U13 U5 32c +1c **multicolored,** on #U11, entire 2.25 2.25
First day cancel, entire 2.50

New York Headquarters — U6

Design sizes: No. U14, 34x34mm. No. U15, 36x36mm.

2001, May 25 **Litho.**
U14 U6 34c **multicolored,** #6¾, entire 1.00 .90
Entire, first day cancel 1.10
U15 U6 34c **multicolored,** #10, entire 1.00 .90
Entire, first day cancel 1.10

Nos. U14-U15 Surcharged

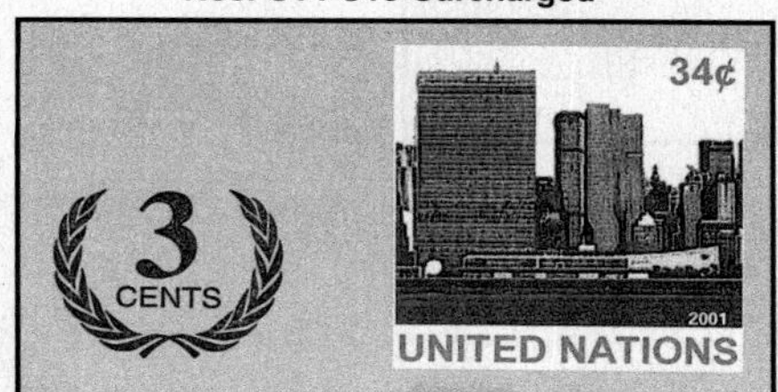

2002, June 30 **Litho.**
U16 U6 34c +3c **multicolored,** entire (#U14) 2.00 *3.00*
Entire, first day cancel 2.00
U17 U6 34c +3c **multicolored,** entire (#U15) 2.00 *3.00*
Entire, first day cancel 2.00

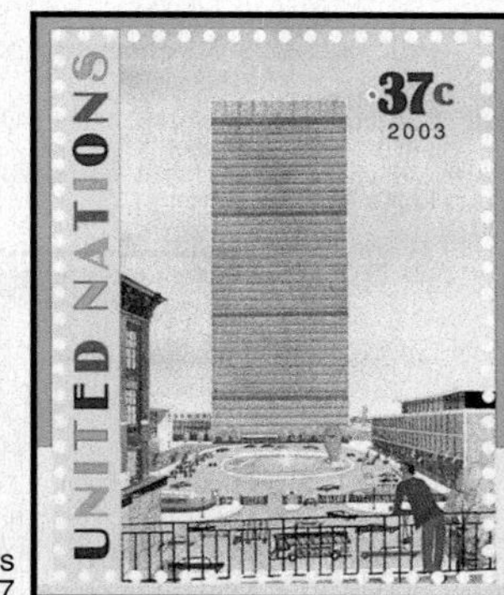

UN Headquarters U7

Printed by Australia Post Spintpak, Australia.
Design sizes: No. U18, 37x47mm. No. U19, 40x52mm.

2003, Mar. 28 **Litho.**
U18 U7 37c **multicolored,** #6¾, entire *(62,000)+* 1.25 .50
Entire, first day cancel 1.50
U19 U7 37c **multicolored,** #10, entire *(72,000)+* 1.25 .50
Entire, first day cancel 1.50

Nos. U18-U19 Surcharged

2006, Jan. 8 **Litho.**
U20 U7 37c +2c **multicolored,** entire (#U18) 1.75 *2.50*
Entire, first day cancel 1.50
U21 U7 37c +2c **multicolored,** entire (#U19) 1.50 *2.50*
Entire, first day cancel 2.00

Nos. U18-U19 Surcharged Like No. U20

2007, May 14 **Litho.**
U22 U7 37c +4c **multicolored,** entire (#U18) 1.75 *2.50*
Entire, first day cancel 2.75
U23 U7 37c +4c **multicolored,** entire (#U19) 1.75 *2.50*
Entire, first day cancel 6.00

United Nations Emblem — U8

Printed by Lowe-Martin Group, Canada. Designed by Robert Stein, US.
Design sizes: No. U24, 22x28mm. No. U25, 29x38mm.

2007, Aug. 9 **Litho.**
U24 U8 41c **multicolored,** #6¾, entire *(35,000)+* 1.75 1.50
Entire, first day cancel 2.50
U25 U8 41c **multicolored,** #10, entire *(35,000)+* 1.50 1.10
Entire, first day cancel 2.50

Nos. U24-U25 Surcharged Like No. U20

2008, May 12 **Litho.**
U26 U8 41c +1c **multicolored,** entire (#U24) 2.50 *3.00*
Entire, first day cancel 3.00
U27 U8 41c +1c **multicolored,** entire (#U25) 2.50 *3.00*
Entire, first day cancel 3.00

Nos. U24-U25 Surcharged Like No. U20

2009, June 5 **Litho.**
U28 U8 41c +3c **multicolored,** entire (#U24) 3.00 *4.00*
Entire, first day cancel 4.00
U29 U8 41c +3c **multicolored,** entire (#U25) 3.00 *4.00*
Entire, first day cancel 4.00

UN Headquarters and Cherry Blossoms — U9

Printed by Johann Enschedé and Sons, the Netherlands. Designed by Rorie Katz, United States.
Design size: No. U30, 32x28mm. No. U31, 42x32mm.

2010, June 4 **Litho.**
U30 U9 44c **multicolored,** #6¾, entire *(24,000)+* 2.50 2.00
Entire, first day cancel 4.00
U31 U9 44c **multicolored,** #10, entire *(25,000)+* 2.50 2.00
Entire, first day cancel 4.00

Nos. U30-U31 Surcharged

2012, Jan. 23 **Litho.**
U32 U9 44c+1c **multicolored,** entire (#U30) 3.00 *4.00*
Entire, first day cancel 4.00
U33 U9 44c+1c **multicolored,** entire (#U31) 3.50 *4.00*
Entire, first day cancel 5.00

Circle and Dots U10

Printed by Johann Enschedé and Sons, the Netherlands. Designed by Sergio Baradat, U.S.
Diameter of denomination circle: No. U34, 16mm. No. U35, 18mm.

2013, Mar. 5 **Litho.**
U34 U10 46c **orange,** #6¾, entire *(17,000)+* 2.50 1.25
Entire, first day cancel *4.75*
U35 U10 46c **orange,** #10, entire *(18,000)+* 3.00 1.50
Entire, first day cancel *4.75*

Nos. U34-U35 Surcharged Like No. U20

2014, June 6 **Litho.**
U36 U10 46c+3c **multicolored,** entire (#U34) 1.25 1.25
Entire, first day cancel 1.25
U37 U10 46c+3c **multicolored,** entire (#U35) 1.25 1.25
Entire, first day cancel 1.25

United Nations Headquarters, Emblem and *Single Form* Sculpture, by Barbara Hepworth — U11

Printed by Lowe-Martin Group, Canada. Designed by Sergio Baradat, U.S.
Design sizes: No. U38, 25x34mm. No. U39, 32x45mm.

2017, Apr. 13 **Litho.**
U38 U11 49c **multicolored,** #6¾, entire *(20,000)+* 1.50 1.50
Entire, first day cancel 2.50
U39 U11 49c **multicolored,** #10, entire *(23,000)+* 1.50 1.50
Entire, first day cancel 2.50

Nos. U38-U39 Surcharged Like No. U12

2018, May 25 **Litho.**
U40 U11 49c+1c **multicolored,** entire (#U38) 1.60 1.60
Entire, first day cancel 1.60
U41 U11 49c+1c **multicolored,** entire (#U39) 1.60 1.60
Entire, first day cancel 1.60

Nos. U38-U39 Surcharged Like No. U20

2019, Feb. 1 **Litho.**
U42 U11 49c+6c **multicolored,** entire (#U38) 1.75 1.75
Entire, first day cancel 1.75
U43 U11 49c+6c **multicolored,** entire (#U39) 1.75 1.75
Entire, first day cancel 1.75

AIR POST ENVELOPES AND AIR LETTER SHEETS

Used values for all postal stationery are for non-philatelic contemporaneous usages.

Letter Sheet
Type of Air Post Stamp of 1951
Inscribed "Air Letter" at Left

Printed by Dennison & Sons, Long Island City, NY.

1952, Aug. 29 **Litho.**
UC1 AP2 10c **blue,** *bluish,* entire *(187,000)* 17.50 17.50
Entire, 1st day cancel *(57,274)* 4.00

Designed by C. Mutver.

Letter Sheet
Inscribed "Air Letter" and "Aerogramme" at Left

1954, Sept. 14 **Litho.**
UC2 AP2 10c **royal blue,** *bluish,* entire, *(207,000)* 9.50 5.00
Entire, 1st day cancel *400.00*
a. No white border, *1958 (148,800)* 7.00 *8.00*

No. UC2 was printed with a narrow white border (½ to 1mm wide) surrounding the stamp. On No. UC2a, this border has been partly or entirely eliminated.

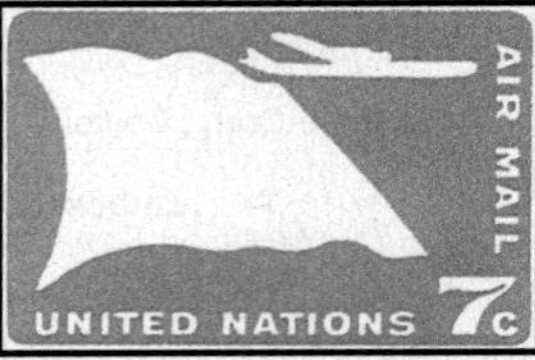

UN Flag and Plane — UC1

(UN Emblem Embossed)

Printed by International Envelope Corp., Dayton, O.
Die engraved by American Bank Note Co., New York.

1959, Sept. 21 **Embossed**
UC3 UC1 7c **blue,** entire *(550,000)* .90 *1.25*
Entire, 1st day cancel *(172,107)* .90

Letter Sheet
Type of Air Post Stamp of 1959

Printed by Thomas De La Rue & Co., Ltd., London.

1960, Jan. 18 **Litho.**
UC4 AP4 10c **ultramarine,** *bluish,* entire *(405,000)* .65 .65
Entire, 1st day cancel *(122,425)* .45

Printed on protective tinted paper containing colorless inscription "United Nations" in the five official languages of the UN.

Letter Sheet
Type of Air Post Stamp of 1951
Inscribed "Correo Aereo" instead of "Poste Aerienne"

Printed by Thomas De La Rue & Co., Ltd., London.

1961, June 26 **Litho.**
UC5 AP1 11c **ultramarine,** *bluish,* entire *(550,000)* .50 .50
Entire, 1st day cancel *(128,557)* .50
a. 11c **dark blue,** *green* entire, *July 16, 1965 (419,000)* 1.25 —

Printed on protective tinted paper containing colorless inscription "United Nations" in the five official languages of the UN.

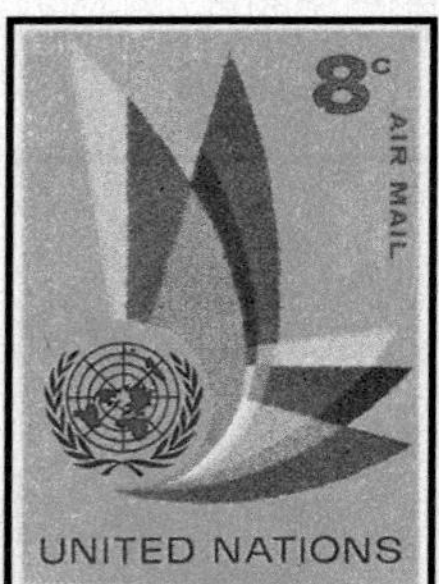

UN Emblem — UC2

Printed by United States Envelope Co., Springfield, Mass. Designed by George Hamori.

1963, Apr. 26 **Litho.**
UC6 UC2 8c **multicolored,** entire *(880,000)* .30 .30
Entire, 1st day cancel *(165,208)* 1.00

Letter Sheet

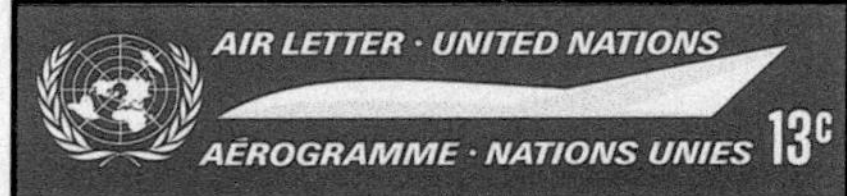

UN Emblem and Stylized Plane — UC3

Printed by Setelipaino, Finland. Designed by Robert Perrot.

1968, May 31 **Litho.**
UC7 UC3 13c **violet blue & light blue,** entire *(750,000)* .30 .30
Entire, 1st day cancel *(106,700)* .50

Type of 1963

Printed by Setelipaino, Finland.

1969, Jan. 8 **Litho.**
UC8 UC2 10c **pink, Prussian blue, orange & sepia,** entire *(750,000)* .35 .35
Entire, 1st day cancel *(153,472)* .40

Letter Sheet

UN Emblem, "UN," Globe and Plane — UC4

Printed by Joh. Enschede and Sons. Designed by Edmondo Calivis, Egypt. Sheet surface printed in greenish blue.

1972, Oct. 16 **Litho.**
UC9 UC4 15c **violet blue & greenish blue,** entire *(500,000)* .60 .60
Entire, 1st day cancel *(85,500)* .80

Bird Type of Air Post Stamp, 1972

Printed by Eureka Co., a division of Litton Industries.

1973, Jan. 12 **Litho.**
UC10 AP13 11c **blue & multicolored,** entire *(700,000)* .40 .40
Entire, 1st day cancel *(134,500)* .80

Globe and Jet Air Post Type of 1974

Printed by United States Envelope Co., Springfield, Mass.

1975, Jan. 10 **Litho.**
UC11 AP16 13c **blue & multicolored,** entire *(555,539)* .60 .60
Entire, 1st day cancel *(122,000)* .80

Letter Sheet
Headquarters Type of Regular Issue, 1971

Printed by Joh. Enschede and Sons, Netherlands.

1975, Jan. 10 **Photo.**
UC12 A120 18c **blue & multicolored,** entire *(400,000)* .60 .60
Entire, 1st day cancel *(70,500)* .80

Letter Sheet

"UN" Emblem and Birds UC5

Printed by Joh. Enschede and Sons. Designed by Angel Medina Medina.

1977, June 27 **Litho.**
UC13 UC5 22c **multicolored,** entire *(400,000)* .65 .60
Entire, 1st day cancel *(70,000)* .80

Letter Sheet

Paper Airplane UC6

Printed by Joh. Enschede and Sons. Designed by Margaret-Ann Champion.

1982, Apr. 28 **Litho.**
UC14 UC6 30c **black,** *pale green,* entire *(400,000)* 1.50 1.50
Entire, 1st day cancel *(61,400)* 1.25

Letter Sheet No. UC14 Surcharged

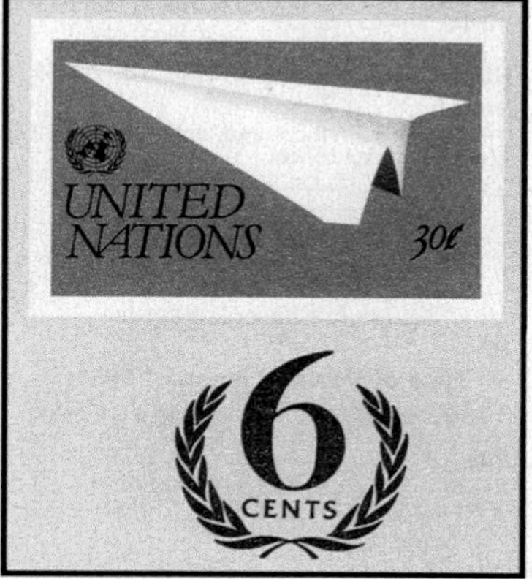

1987, July 7 **Litho.**
UC15 UC6 30c + 6c **black,** *green,* entire *(43,000)* *52.50 50.00*
Entire, 1st day cancel 45.00

New York Headquarters UC7

Printed by Mercury Walch, Australia. Designed by Thomas Lee, China.

1989, Mar. 17 **Litho.**
UC16 UC7 39c **multicolored,** entire *(350,000)* 3.00 3.00
Entire, 1st day cancel *(14,798)* 5.00

No. UC16 Surcharged

1991, Feb. 12 **Litho.**
UC17 UC7 39c + 6c **multicolored,** entire *(35,563)* 18.50 27.50
Entire, first day cancel 7.50

UC8

Designed by Robert Stein. Printed by Mercury-Walch, Australia.

1992, Sept. 4 **Litho.**
UC18 UC8 45c **multicolored,** entire, *(185,000)+* 2.75 3.00
First day cancel 10.00

Letter Sheet No. UC18 Surcharged

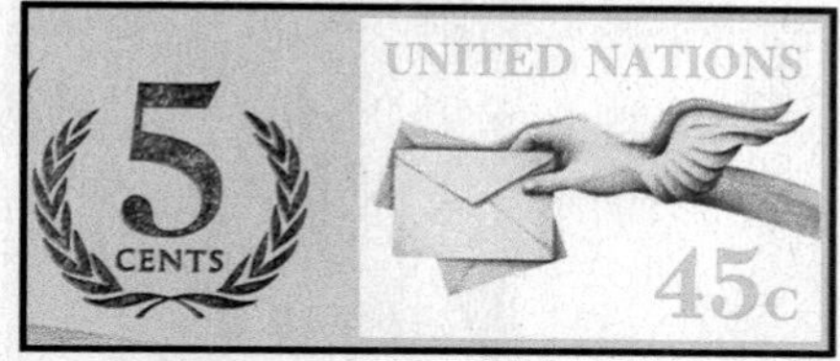

1995, July 9 **Litho.**
UC19 UC8 45c +5c **multicolored,** entire 4.50 7.50
First day cover 9.00

Cherry Blossoms — UC9

1997, Mar. 13 **Litho.**
UC20 UC9 50c **multicolored,** entire *(115,000)+* 3.50 2.00
Entire, first day cancel 5.00

No. UC20 Surcharged

1999, Aug. 23 **Litho.**
UC21 UC9 50c +10c **multicolored,** entire 2.25 *4.00*
Entire, first day cancel 3.00

No. UC20 Surcharged

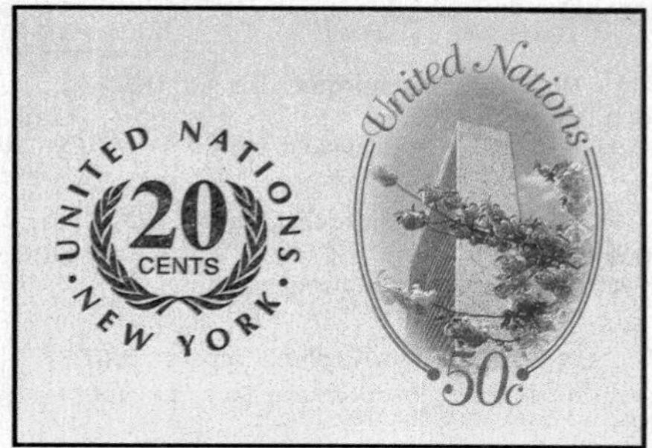

2001, Jan. 9 **Litho.**
UC22 UC9 50c +20c **multicolored,** entire 2.00 *4.00*
Entire, first day cancel 3.50

Cherry Blossoms at New York Headquarters UC10

2001, May 25 **Litho.**
UC23 UC10 70c **multicolored,** entire 2.00 1.75
Entire, first day cancel 8.00

No. UC23 Surcharged

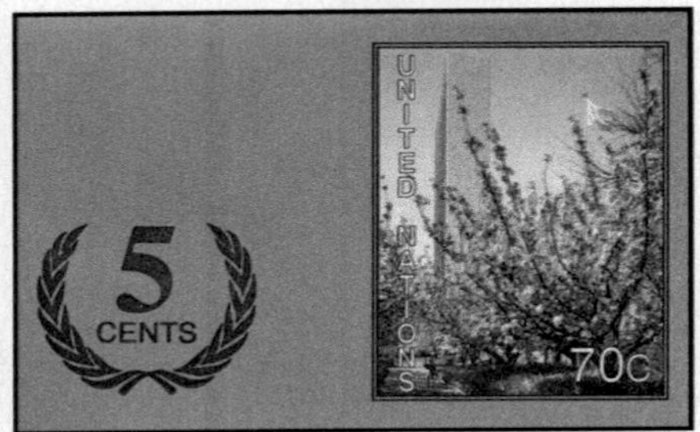

2006, Jan. 8 **Litho.**
UC24 UC10 70c +5c **multicolored,** entire 2.50 3.00
Entire, first day cancel 3.00

No. UC23 Surcharged Like No. UC24

2007, May 14 **Litho.**
UC25 UC10 70c +20c **multicolored,** entire 3.25 *4.00*
Entire, first day cancel 3.50

United Nations Emblem and Airplane UC11

Printed by Sprintpak, Australia. Designed by Robert Stein, US.

2007, Aug. 9 **Litho.**
UC26 UC11 90c **multicolored,** entire *(40,000)+* 2.75 2.75
Entire, first day cancel 3.25

No. UC26 Surcharged Like No. UC24

2008, May 12 **Litho.**
UC27 UC11 90c +4c **multicolored,** entire 2.25 *4.00*
Entire, first day cancel 3.00

No. UC26 Surcharged Like No. UC24

2009, June 5 **Litho.**
UC28 UC11 90c +8c **multicolored,** entire 2.25 *4.00*
Entire, first day cancel 3.50

UN Emblem and Airplane Type of 2007

Printed by Johann Enschedé and Sons, the Netherlands. Designed by Rorie Katz, United States.

2010, June 4 **Litho.**
UC29 UC11 98c **multicolored,** entire *(25,000)+* 3.00 2.25
Entire, first day cancel 4.00

No. UC29 Surcharged Like No. UC24

2012, Jan. 23 **Litho.**
UC30 UC11 98c+7c **multicolored,** entire 2.40 *4.00*
Entire, first day cancel 2.75

Surcharge on No. UC30 is below the indicium.

Circle and Dots Envelope Type of 2013

Printed by Johann Enschedé and Sons, the Netherlands. Designed by Sergio Baradat, U.S.

2013, Mar. 5 **Litho.**
UC31 U10 $1.10 **orange,** entire *(17,000)+* 2.40 2.40
Entire, first day cancel 2.40

No. UC31 Surcharged Like No. UC24

2014, June 6 **Litho.**
UC32 U10 $1.10+5c **multicolored,** entire 2.50 2.50
Entire, first day cancel 2.50

POSTAL CARDS

Values are for entire cards.

Type of Postage Issue of 1951

Printed by Dennison & Sons, Long Island City, N.Y.

1952, July 18 **Litho.**
UX1 A2 2c **blue,** *buff (899,415)* .25 .25
First day cancel *(116,023)* .45

Printed by British American Bank Note Co., Ltd., Ottawa, Canada.

1958, Sept. 22 **Litho.**
UX2 A2 3c **gray olive,** *buff (575,000)* .25 .25
First day cancel *(145,557)* .45

World Map, Sinusoidal Projection — PC1

Printed by Eureka Specialty Printing Co., Scranton, Pa.

1963, Apr. 26 **Litho.**
UX3 PC1 4c **light blue, violet blue, orange & bright citron** *(784,000)* .25 .25
First day cancel *(112,280)* .45
a. Bright citron omitted —

UN Emblem and Post Horn — PC2

Printed by Canadian Bank Note Co., Ltd., Ottawa. Designed by John Mason.

1969, Jan. 8 **Litho.**
UX4 PC2 5c **blue & black** *(500,000)* .25 .25
First day cancel *(95,975)* .45

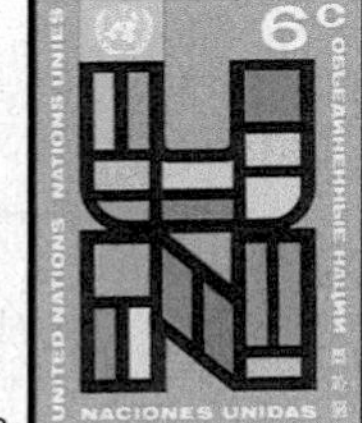

"UN" — PC3

Printed by Government Printing Bureau, Tokyo. Designed by Asher Kalderon.

1973, Jan. 12 **Litho.**
UX5 PC3 6c **gray & multicolored** *(500,000)* .25 .25
First day cancel *(84,500)* .50

Type of 1973

Printed by Setelipaino, Finland.

1975, Jan. 10 **Litho.**
UX6 PC3 8c **light green & multi** *(450,000)* .60 .60
First day cancel *(72,500)* .45

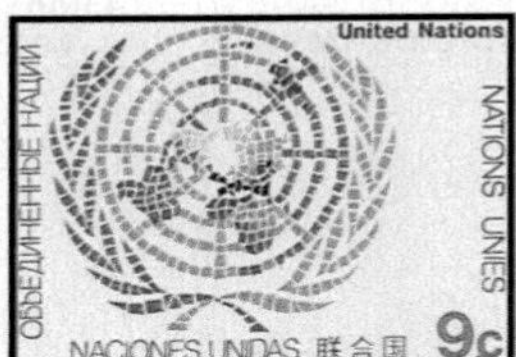

UN Emblem — PC4

Printed by Setelipaino, Finland. Designed by George Hamori.

1977, June 27 **Litho.**
UX7 PC4 9c **multicolored** *(350,000)* .60 .60
First day cancel *(70,000)* .45

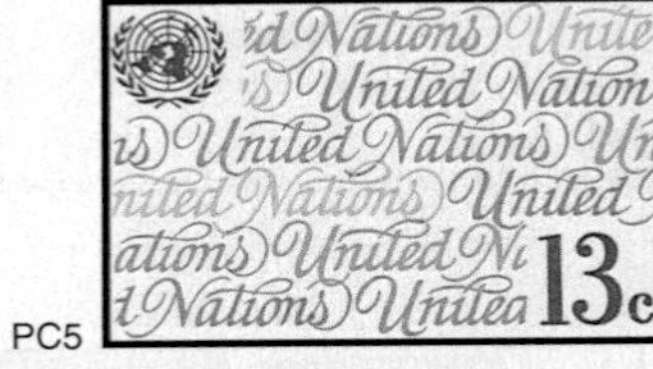

PC5

Printed by Courvoisier. Designed by Salahattin Kanidinc.

1982, Apr. 28 **Photo.**
UX8 PC5 13c **multicolored** *(350,000)* .60 .60
First day cancel *(59,200)* .50

Views of New York Headquarters PC6

Designs: No. UX9, Spring at U.N. Headquarters, vert. No. UX10, Cherry Blossoms, U.N. Gardens, vert. No. UXC11, Row of Flags of member states. No. UX12, U.N. General Assembly. No. UX13, River view, U.N. Headquarters. No. UX14, U.N. Headquarters, vert. No. UX15, Row of flags of member states, vert. No. UX16, Night view, U.N. Headquarters, vert. No. UX17, U.N. Security Council. No. UX18, U.N. Gardens.

Printed by Johann Enschede and Sons, the Netherlands. Designed by Thomas Lee, China, from photographs.

1989, Mar. 17 **Litho.**
UX9 PC6 15c **multicolored** *(120,000)+* .65 1.00
First day cancel 2.00
UX10 PC6 15c **multicolored** *(120,000)+* .65 1.00
First day cancel 2.00
UX11 PC6 15c **multicolored** *(120,000)+* .65 1.00
First day cancel 2.00
UX12 PC6 15c **multicolored** *(120,000)+* .65 1.00
First day cancel 2.00
UX13 PC6 15c **multicolored** *(120,000)+* .65 1.00
First day cancel 2.00
UX14 PC6 36c **multicolored** *(120,000)+* .85 1.50
First day cancel 2.00
UX15 PC6 36c **multicolored** *(120,000)+* .85 1.50
First day cancel 2.00
UX16 PC6 36c **multicolored** *(120,000)+* .85 1.50
First day cancel 2.00
UX17 PC6 36c **multicolored** *(120,000)+* .85 1.50
First day cancel 2.00
UX18 PC6 36c **multicolored** *(120,000)+* .85 1.50
First day cancel 2.00
Nos. UX9-UX18 (10) 7.50 12.50

Nos. UX9-UX13 and UX14-UX18 sold only in sets. Nos. UX9-UX13 sold for $2 and Nos. UX14-UX18 sold for $3.
First day cancels of Nos. UX9-UX18 total 125,526.

New York Headquarters Type of 1991

Printed by Mercury-Walch, Australia.

1992, Sept. 4 **Litho.**
UX19 A260 40c **blue** *(150,000)+* 3.50 4.00
First day cancel *(9,603)* 10.00

Secretariat Building, Roses — PC7

UN Complex — PC8

Printed by Mercury-Walsh, Australia.

1998, May 20 **Litho.**

UX20 PC7 21c **multicolored** *(150,000)+* 1.25 1.25
First day cancel 1.50

UX21 PC8 50c **multicolored** *(150,000)+* 2.00 2.00
First day cancel 2.25

Illustrations of the buildings and other scenes are shown on the back of each card.

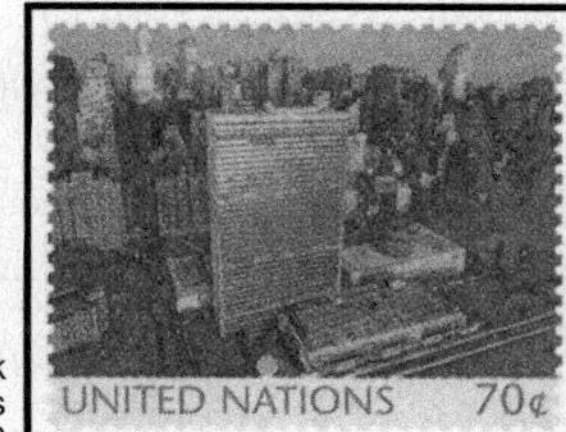

New York Headquarters PC9

2001, May 25 **Litho.**

UX22 PC9 70c **multicolored** 1.75 1.75
Entire, first day cancel 1.75

No. UX20 Surcharged

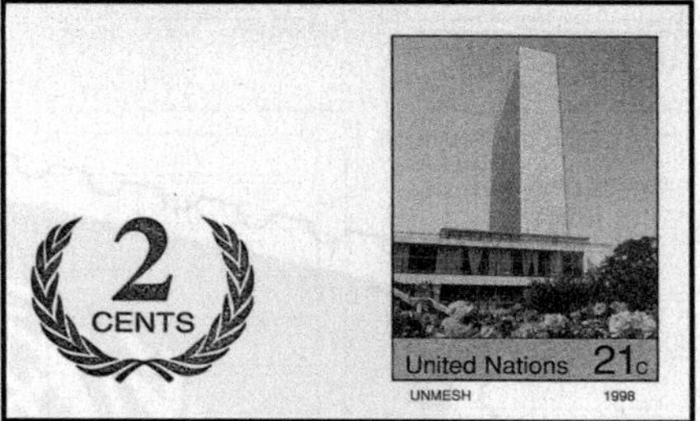

2002, June 30 **Litho.**

UX23 PC7 21c +2c **multicolored** 1.10 *2.00*
First day cancel 7.50

PC10

PC11

PC12

PC13

PC14

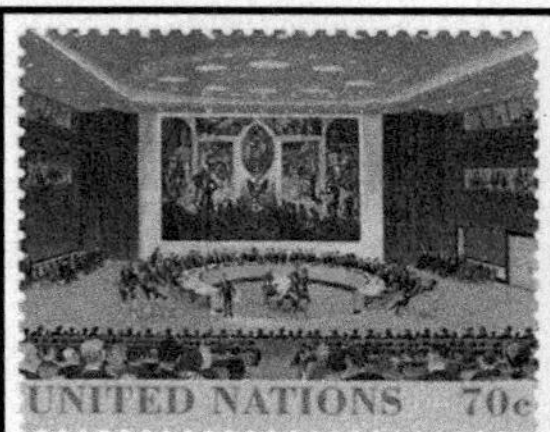

PC15

PC16

PC18

PC17

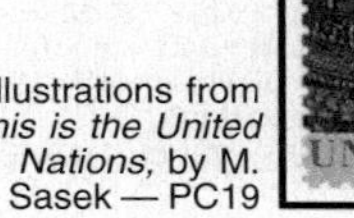

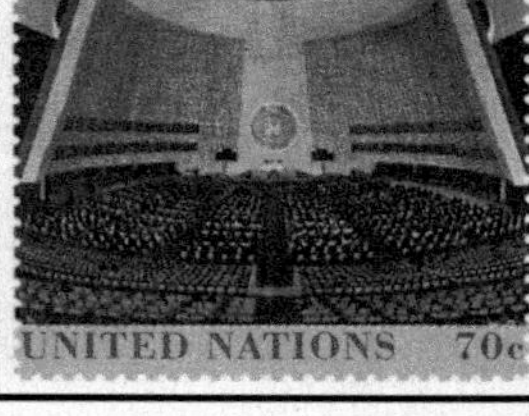

Illustrations from *This is the United Nations,* by M. Sasek — PC19

Printed by Banknote Corporation of America, US.

2003, Mar. 28 **Litho.**

UX24 PC10 23c **multicolored** *(61,500)+* .75 .75
Entire, first day cancel .75

UX25 PC11 23c **multicolored** *(61,500)+* .75 .75
Entire, first day cancel .75

UX26 PC12 23c **multicolored** *(61,500)+* .75 .75
Entire, first day cancel .75

UX27 PC13 23c **multicolored** *(61,500)+* .75 .75
Entire, first day cancel .75

UX28 PC14 23c **multicolored** *(61,500)+* .75 .75
Entire, first day cancel .75

UX29 PC15 70c **multicolored** *(86,500)+* 1.40 1.40
Entire, first day cancel 1.25

UX30 PC16 70c **multicolored** *(86,500)+* 1.40 1.40
Entire, first day cancel 1.25

UX31 PC17 70c **multicolored** *(86,500)+* 1.40 1.40
Entire, first day cancel 1.25

UX32 PC18 70c **multicolored** *(86,500)+* 1.40 1.40
Entire, first day cancel 1.25

UX33 PC19 70c **multicolored** *(86,500)+* 1.40 1.40
Entire, first day cancel 1.25

Nos. UX24-UX33 (10) 10.75 10.75

Nos. UX24-UX28 and UX29-UX33 were sold only in shrink-wrapped sets.

AIR POST POSTAL CARDS

Values are for entire cards.

Type of Air Post Stamp of 1957

Printed by British American Bank Note Co., Ltd., Ottawa.

1957, May 27 **Litho.**

UXC1 AP3 4c **maroon,** *buff (631,000)* .25 .30
First day cancel *(260,005)* .50

No. UXC1 Srchd. in Maroon at Left of Stamp

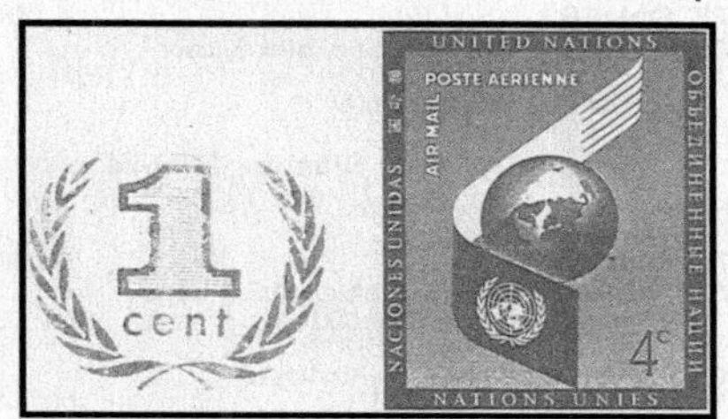

1959, June 5 **Litho.**

UXC2 AP3 4c + 1c **maroon,** buff (1,119,000) .30 .50
Cancel first day of public use, June 8 300.00
a. Double Surcharge —
b. Inverted Surcharge —
c. Double surcharge, one inverted *200.00*

This surcharge also exists on a No. U1 envelope. Status uncertain.

Type of Air Post Stamp, 1957

Printed by Eureka Specialty Printing Co., Scranton, Pa.

1959, Sept. 21 **Litho.**

UXC3 AP3 5c **crimson,** *buff (500,000)* .65 .65
First day cancel *(119,479)* .45

Outer Space — APC1

Printed by Eureka Specialty Printing Co., Scranton, Pa.

1963, Apr. 26 **Litho.**

UXC4 APC1 6c **black & blue** *(350,000)* .55 .60
First day cancel *(109,236)* .40

APC2

Printed by Eureka-Carlisle Co., Scranton, Pa. Designed by Olav S. Mathiesen.

1966, June 9 **Litho.**

UXC5 APC2 11c **dark red, rose, yellow & brown** *(764,500)* .30 .30
First day cancel *(162,588)* .40

1968, May 31 **Litho.**

UXC6 APC2 13c **dark green, bright green & yellow** *(829,000)* .40 .40
First day cancel *(106,500)* .45

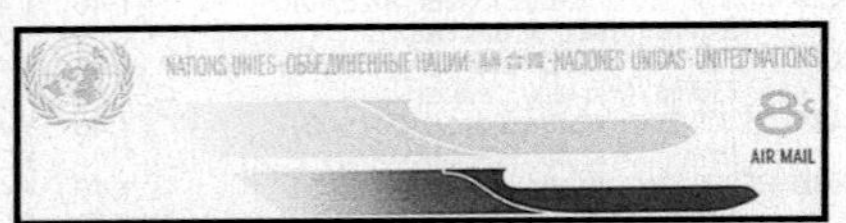

UN Emblem and Stylized Planes — APC3

Printed by Canadian Bank Note Co., Ltd., Ottawa. Designed by Lawrence Kurtz.

1969, Jan. 8 **Litho.**

UXC7 APC3 8c **gray, dull yellow, lt blue, indigo & red** *(500,000)* .65 .65
First day cancel *(94,037)* .40

Type of Air Post Stamp of 1972

Printed by Government Printing Bureau, Tokyo. Designed by L. L. Dolan.

1972, Oct. 16 **Litho.**

UXC8 AP12 9c **orange, red, gray & green** *(500,000)* .45 .45
First day cancel *(85,600)* .50

Type of 1969

Printed by Government Printing Bureau, Tokyo

1972, Oct. 16 **Litho.**

UXC9 APC3 15c **lilac, light blue, pink & carmine** *(500,000)* .50 .50
First day cancel *(84,800)* .45

Types of Air Post Stamps, 1972-74

Printed by Setelipaino, Finland.

1975, Jan. 10 **Litho.**

UXC10 AP14 11c **greenish blue, blue & dark blue** *(250,000)* .50 .50
First day cancel *(70,500)* .45

UXC11 AP17 18c **gray & multicolored** *(250,000)* .50 .50
First day cancel *(70,500)* .45

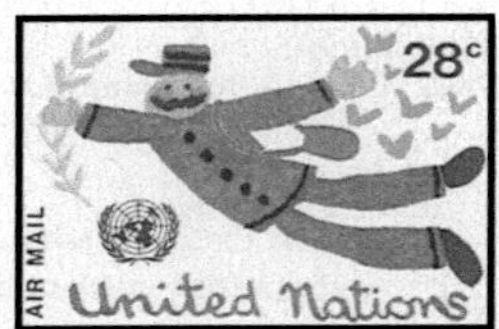

Flying Mailman — APC4

Printed by Courvoisier. Designed by Arieh Glaser.

1982, Apr. 28 **Photo.**

UXC12 APC4 28c **multicolored** *(350,000)* .45 .50
First day cancel *(58,700)* 1.40

VARIO STOCK SHEETS

Vario stock sheets offer unparalleled quality and versatility.

They're a convenient and easy way to store and organize stamps. Vario stock sheets are carefully manufactured to be free of harmful plasticized PVC, and softeners. Vario stock will fit all standard 3-ring binders and are available in a variety of sizes.

NOTE: Black sheets have pockets on both sides. Clear sheets have pockets on one side only. "S" in item number denotes black page. "C" in item number denotes clear page.

Sold in packages of 5. Retail $5.75 **AA* $4.89**

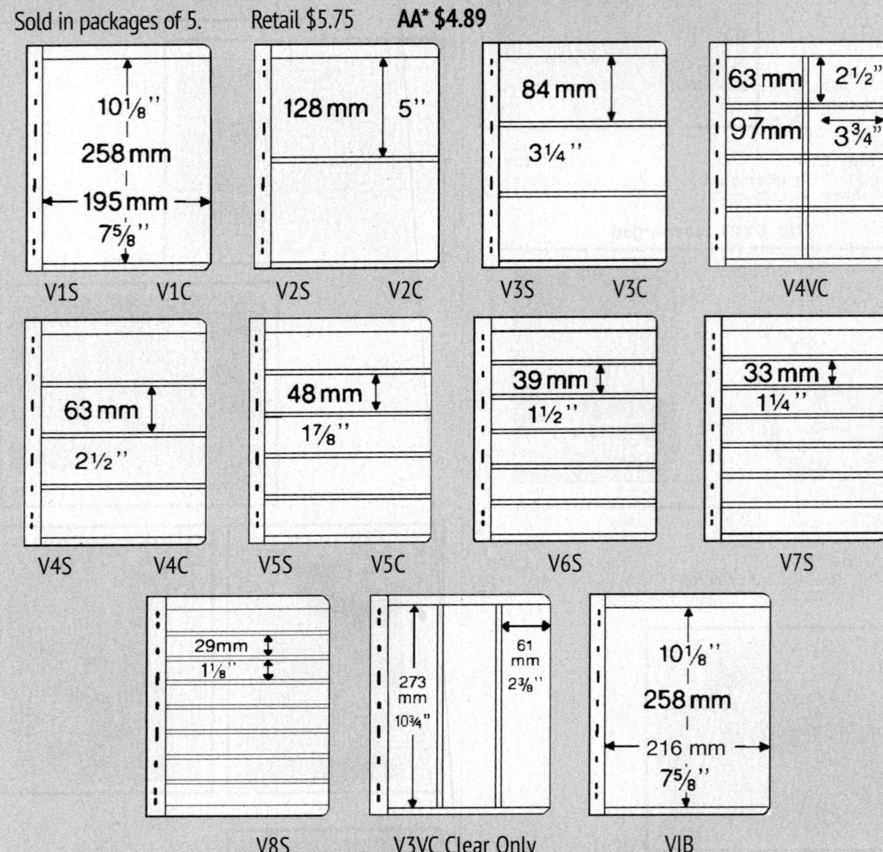

THREE-RING BINDERS

We have the binders for you! Take a look at our handsome matching binder & slipcase sets. These great sets are available in blue or black. If you prefer a heavy duty binder, check out our metal-hinged, thick panel binder. What are you waiting for?

Item	Description	Retail	AA*
SSBSBL	Blue 3-Ring Binder and Slipcase	$21.99	**$17.99**
SSBSBK	Black 3-Ring Binder and Slipcase	$21.99	**$17.99**
SSBMBK	Black Metal Hinged 3-Ring Binder	$24.99	**$19.99**

1-800-572-6885 • Outside U.S. & Canada (937) 498-0800

Visit us at: www.AmosAdvantage.com

Shipping & Handling: United States: Order total $0-$10.00 charged $3.99 shipping. United States - Order total $10.01-$79.99 charged $7.99 shipping. United States - Order total $80.00 or more charged 10% of order total for shipping. Maximum Freight Charge $45.00. Canada: 20% of order total. Minimum charge $19.99 Maximum charge $200.00. Foreign orders are shipped via FedEx Intl. or USPS and billed actual freight. **Ordering Information:** *AA prices apply to paid subscribers of Amos Media titles, or orders placed online. Prices, terms and product availability subject to change. Shipping and handling rates will apply.

Mail Orders To: Amos Media Co., P.O. Box 4129, Sidney OH 45365

OFFICES IN GENEVA, SWITZERLAND

For use only on mail posted at the Palais des Nations (UN European Office), Geneva. Inscribed in French unless otherwise stated.

100 Centimes = 1 Franc

Catalogue values for all unused stamps in this country are for Never Hinged items.

Types of United Nations Issues 1961-69 and

United Nations European Office, Geneva — G1

Printed by Setelipaino, Finland (5c, 70c, 80c, 90c, 2fr, 10fr), Courvoisier, S.A., Switzerland (10c, 20c, 30c, 50c, 60c, 3fr). Government Printing Office, Austria (75c) and Government Printing Office, Federal Republic of Germany (1fr).
Panes of 50. 30c designed by Ole Hamann, others as before.

Designs: 5c, UN Headquarters, New York, and world map. 10c, UN flag. 20c, Three men united before globe. 50c, Opening words of UN Charter. 60c, UN emblem over globe. 70c, "un" and UN emblem. 75c, "Flight Across Globe." 80c, UN Headquarters and emblem. 90c, Abstract group of flags. 1fr, UN emblem. 2fr, Stylized globe and weather vane. 3fr, Statue by Henrik Starcke. 10fr, "Peace, Justice, Security."
The 20c, 80c and 90c are inscribed in French. The 75c and 10fr carry French inscription at top, English at bottom.

1969-70 Photo. Unwmk.
Perf. 13 (5c, 70c, 90c); 12½x12 (10c);

1 A88 5c **purple & multi,** *Oct. 4, 1969 (3,300,000)* .25 .30
First day cover 1.00
Inscription block of 4 .40 —
a. Green omitted —
2 A52 10c **salmon & multi,** *Oct. 4, 1969 (4,300,000)+* .25 .30
First day cover 1.00
Inscription block of 4 .40 —

Perf. 11½ (20c-60c, 3fr)

3 A66 20c **black & multi,** *Oct. 4, 1969 (4,500.000)* .25 .30
First day cover 1.00
Inscription block of 4 .50 —
4 G1 30c **dark blue & multi,** *Oct. 4, 1969 (3,000,000)* .25 .30
First day cover 1.00
Inscription block of 4 .60 —
5 A77 50c **ultra & multi,** *Oct. 4, 1969 (3,300,000)* .25 .30
First day cover 1.25
Inscription block of 4 .80 —
6 A54 60c **dark brown, salmon & gold,** *Apr. 17, 1970 (3,300,000)+* .25 .30
First day cover 1.00
Inscription block of 4 1.25 —
7 A104 70c **red, black & gold,** *Sept. 22, 1970 (3,300,000)+* .30 .35
First day cover 1.00
Inscription block of 4 1.50 —

Perf. 11½x12 (75c)

8 AP8 75c **carmine rose & multi,** *Oct. 4, 1969 (3,300,000)+* .35 .40
First day cover 1.00
Inscription block of 4 1.75 —

Perf. 13½x14 (80c)

9 A78 80c **blue green, red & yellow,** *Sept. 22, 1970 (3,300,000)* .35 .40
First day cover 1.00
Inscription block of 4 1.75 —
10 A45 90c **blue & multi,** *Sept. 22, 1970 (3,300,000)* .40 .45
First day cover 1.00
Inscription block of 4 1.75 —

Litho. & Embossed
Perf. 14 (1fr)

11 A79 1fr **light & dark green,** *Oct. 4, 1969 (3,000,000)* .40 .45
First day cover 1.00
Inscription block of 4 2.00 —

Photo.
Perf. 12x11½ (2fr)

12 A67 2fr **blue & multi,** *Sept. 22, 1970 (3,000,000)+* .75 .85
First day cover 2.00
Inscription block of 4 3.50 —
13 A97 3fr **olive & multi,** *Oct. 4, 1969 (3,000,000)+* 1.00 1.10
First day cover 2.25
Inscription block of 4 5.00 —

Engr.
Perf. 12 (10fr)

14 A3 10fr **dark blue,** *Apr. 17, 1970 (2,250,000)+* 3.50 3.75
First day cover 8.50
Inscription block of 4 16.00 —
Nos. 1-14 (14) 8.55 9.55

+ Printing orders to June 1984.
First day covers of Nos. 1-5, 8, 11, 13 total 607,578; of Nos. 6 and 14, 148,055; of Nos. 7, 9-10 and 12, 226,000.

Sea Bed Type of UN

1971, Jan. 25 Photo. & Engr. *Perf. 13*
15 A114 30c **green & multi** *(1,935,871)* .25 .30
First day cover *(152,590)* 1.00
Inscription block of 4 .65 —

Refugee Type of UN

1971, Mar. 12 Litho. *Perf. 13x12½*
16 A115 50c **deep carmine, deep orange & black** *(1,820,114)* .25 .30
First day cover *(148,220)* 1.00
Inscription block of 4 1.05 —

World Food Program Type of UN

1971, Apr. 13 Photo. *Perf. 14*
17 A116 50c **dark violet & multi** *(1,824,170)* .25 .30
First day cover *(151,580)* 1.00
Inscription block of 4 1.05 —

UPU Headquarters Type of UN

1971, May 28 Photo. *Perf. 11½*
18 A117 75c **green & multi** *(1,821,878)* .35 .40
First day cover *(140,679)* 1.00
Inscription block of 4 1.00 —

Eliminate Racial Discrimination Types of UN

Designed by Daniel Gonzague (30c) and Ole Hamann (50c).

1971, Sept. 21 Photo. *Perf. 13½*
19 A118 30c **blue & multi** *(1,838,474)* .25 .30
First day cover 1.00
Inscription block of 4 1.00 —
20 A119 50c **yellow green & multi** *(1,804,126)* .25 .30
First day cover 1.00
First day cover, #19-20 1.25
Inscription block of 4 1.10 —

First day covers of Nos. 19-20 total 308,420.

Picasso Type of UN

1971, Nov. 19 Photo. *Perf. 11½*
21 A122 1.10fr **multicolored** *(1,467,993)* .75 .80
First day cover *(195,215)* 1.25
Inscription block of 4 3.00 —

Palais des Nations, Geneva — G2

Printed by Courvoisier, S. A. Panes of 50. Designed by Ole Hamann.

1972, Jan. 5 Photo. *Perf. 11½*
22 G2 40c **olive, blue, salmon & dark green** *(3,500,000)+* .25 .30
First day cover *(152,300)* 1.00
Inscription block of 4 1.05 —

+ Initial printing order.

Nuclear Weapons Type of UN

1972, Feb. 14 Photo. *Perf. 13½x14*
23 A124 40c **yellow, green, black, rose & gray** *(1,567,305)* .25 .30
First day cover *(151,350)* 1.00
Inscription block of 4 1.25 —

World Health Day Type of UN

1972, Apr. 7 Litho. & Engr. *Perf. 13x13½*
24 A125 80c **black & multi** *(1,543,368)* .45 .50
First day cover *(192,600)* 1.00
Inscription block of 4 2.00 —

Human Environment Type of UN
Lithographed & Embossed

1972, June 5 *Perf. 12½x14*
25 A126 40c **olive, lemon, green & blue** *(1,594,089)* .25 .30
First day cover 1.00
Inscription block of 4 1.00 —
26 A126 80c **ultra, pink, green & blue** *(1,568,009)* .45 .50
First day cover 1.40
First day cover, #25-26 1.75
Inscription block of 4 1.80 —

First day covers of Nos. 25-26 total 296,700.

Economic Commission for Europe Type of UN

1972, Sept. 11 Litho. *Perf. 13x13½*
27 A127 1.10fr **red & multi** *(1,604,082)* 1.00 1.10
First day cover *(149,630)* 1.75
Inscription block of 4 4.25 —

Art at UN (Sert) Type of UN

1972, Nov. 17 Photo. *Perf. 12x12½*
28 A128 40c **gold, red & brown** *(1,932,428)* .30 .35
First day cover 1.00
Inscription block of 4 1.25 —
29 A128 80c **gold, brown & olive** *(1,759,600)* .60 .65
First day cover 1.25
First day cover, #28-29 1.75
Inscription block of 4 2.50 —

First day covers of Nos. 28-29 total 295,470.

Disarmament Decade Type of UN

1973, Mar. 9 Litho. *Perf. 13½x13*
30 A129 60c **violet & multi** *(1,586,845)* .40 .45
First day cover 1.00
Inscription block of 4 1.60 —
31 A129 1.10fr **olive & multi** *(1,408,169)* .85 .90
First day cover 1.40
First day cover, #30-31 1.75
Inscription block of 4 3.50 —

First day covers of Nos. 30-31 total 260,680.

Drug Abuse Type of UN

1973, Apr. 13 Photo. *Perf. 13½*
32 A130 60c **blue & multi** *(1,481,432)* .45 .50
First day cover *(144,760)* 1.00
Inscription block of 4 1.90 —

Volunteers Type of UN

1973, May 25 Photo. *Perf. 14*
33 A131 80c **gray green & multi** *(1,443,519)* .35 .40
First day cover *(143,430)* 1.10
Inscription block of 4 1.50 —

Namibia Type of UN

1973, Oct. 1 Photo. *Perf. 13½*
34 A132 60c **red & multi** *(1,673,898)* .35 .40
First day cover *(148,077)* 1.00
Inscription block of 4 1.50 —

Human Rights Type of UN

1973, Nov. 16 Photo. *Perf. 13½*
35 A133 40c **ultramarine & multi** *(1,480,791)* .30 .35
First day cover 1.00
Inscription block of 4 1.25 —
36 A133 80c **olive & multi** *(1,343,349)* .50 .55
First day cover 1.25
First day cover, #35-36 1.75
Inscription block of 4 2.10 —

First day covers of Nos. 35-36 total 438,260.

ILO Headquarters Type of UN

1974, Jan. 11 Photo. *Perf. 14*
37 A134 60c **violet & multi** *(1,212,703)* .45 .50
First day cover 1.00
Inscription block of 4 1.90 —
38 A134 80c **brown & multi** *(1,229,851)* .65 .70
First day cover 1.10
First day cover, #37-38 1.25
Inscription block of 4 2.75 —

First day covers of Nos. 37-38 total 240,660.

Centenary of UPU Type of UN

1974, Mar. 22 Litho. *Perf. 12½*
39 A135 30c **gold & multi** *(1,567,517)* .25 .30
First day cover 1.00
Inscription block of 4 1.25 —

40 A135 60c **gold & multi** *(1,430,839)* .60 .65
First day cover 1.25
First day cover, #39-40 1.50
Inscription block of 4 2.50 —

First day covers of Nos. 39-40 total 231,840.

Art at UN (Portinari) Type of UN

1974, May 6 Photo. *Perf. 14*

41 A136 60c **dark red & multi** *(1,202,357)* .40 .45
First day cover 1.00
Inscription block of 4 1.75 —
42 A136 1fr **green & multi** *(1,230,045)* .70 .75
First day cover 1.20
First day cover, #41-42 1.50
Inscription block of 4 3.00 —

First day covers of Nos. 41-42 total 249,130.

World Population Year Type of UN

1974, Oct. 18 Photo. *Perf. 14*

43 A140 60c **bright green & multi** *(1,292,954)* .50 .55
First day cover 1.00
Inscription block of 4 2.25 —
44 A140 80c **brown & multi** *(1,221,288)* .70 .75
First day cover 1.00
First day cover, #43-44 1.25
Inscription block of 4 3.25 —

First day covers of Nos. 43-44 total 189,597.

Law of the Sea Type of UN

1974, Nov. 22 Photo. *Perf. 14*

45 A141 1.30fr **blue & multicolored** *(1,266,270)* 1.00 1.10
First day cover *(181,000)* 1.25
Inscription block of 4 4.00 —

Outer Space Type of UN

1975, Mar. 14 Litho. *Perf. 13*

46 A142 60c **multicolored** *(1,339,704)* .50 .55
First day cover 1.00
Inscription block of 4 2.00 —
47 A142 90c **multicolored** *(1,383,888)* .75 .80
First day cover 1.00
First day cover, #46-47 1.50
Inscription block of 4 3.25 —

First day covers of Nos. 46-47 total 250,400.

International Women's Year Type of UN

1975, May 9 Litho. *Perf. 15*

48 A143 60c **multicolored** *(1,176,080)* .40 .45
First day cover 1.00
Inscription block of 4 1.90 —
49 A143 90c **multicolored** *(1,167,863)* .70 .75
First day cover 1.00
First day cover, #48-49 1.50
Inscription block of 4 3.25 —

First day covers of Nos. 48-49 total 250,660.

30th Anniversary Type of UN

1975, June 26 Litho. *Perf. 13*

50 A144 60c **green & multi** *(1,442,075)* .40 .45
First day cover 1.00
Inscription block of 4 2.00 —
51 A144 90c **violet & multi** *(1,612,411)* .70 .75
First day cover 1.00
First day cover, #50-51 1.25
Inscription block of 4 3.25 —

Souvenir Sheet

Imperf

52 Sheet of 2 *(1,210,148)* 1.00 1.10
a. A144 60c **green & multicolored** .30 .35
b. A144 90c **violet & multicolored** .60 .65
First day cover 1.25

No. 52 has blue and bister margin with inscription and UN emblem. Size: 92x70mm.
First day covers of Nos. 50-52 total 402,500.

Namibia Type of UN

1975, Sept. 22 Photo. *Perf. 13½*

53 A145 50c **multicolored** *(1,261,019)* .30 .35
First day cover 1.00
Inscription block of 4 1.25 —
54 A145 1.30fr **multicolored** *(1,241,990)* .85 .90
First day cover 1.10
First day cover, #53-54 1.25
Inscription block of 4 4.00 —

First day covers of Nos. 53-54 total 226,260.

Peace-keeping Operations Type of UN

1975, Nov. 21 Engr. *Perf. 12½*

55 A146 60c **greenish blue** *(1,249,305)* .35 .40
First day cover 1.00
Inscription block of 4 1.50 —
56 A146 70c **bright violet** *(1,249,935)* .65 .65
First day cover 1.00
First day cover, #55-56 1.25
Inscription block of 4 2.75 —

First day covers of Nos. 55-56 total 229,245.

WFUNA Type of UN

1976, Mar. 12 Photo. *Perf. 14*

57 A152 90c **multicolored** *(1,186,563)* .90 .95
First day cover 1.00
Inscription block of 4 4.00 —

First day covers of No. 57 total 121,645.

UNCTAD Type of UN

1976, Apr. 23 Photo. *Perf. 11½*

58 A153 1.10fr **sepia & multi** *(1,167,284)* .90 .95
First day cover *(107,030)* 1.25
Inscription block of 4 4.00 —

Habitat Type of UN

1976, May 28 Photo. *Perf. 14*

59 A154 40c **dull blue & multi** *(1,258,986)* .25 .30
First day cover 1.00
Inscription block of 4 1.00 —
60 A154 1.50fr **violet & multi** *(1,110,507)* .75 .80
First day cover 1.25
First day cover, #59-60 1.60
Inscription block of 4 3.50 —

First day covers of Nos. 59-60 total 242,530.

UN Emblem, Post Horn and Rainbow — G3

UN Postal Administration, 25th anniversary.
Printed by Courvoisier, S.A. Panes of 20 (5x4). Designed by Hector Viola.

1976, Oct. 8 Photo. *Perf. 11½*

61 G3 80c **tan & multicolored** *(1,794,009)* .50 .55
First day cover 2.00
Inscription block of 4 2.50 —
62 A3 1.10fr **light green & multi** *(1,751,178)* 1.60 1.75
First day cover 2.00
Inscription block of 4 8.00 —
First day cover, #61-62 3.00
Panes of 20, #61-62 37.50

Upper margin blocks are inscribed "XXVe ANNIVERSAIRE"; lower margin blocks "ADMINISTRATION POSTALE DES NATIONS UNIES."
First day covers of Nos. 61-62 total 152,450.

World Food Council Type of UN

1976, Nov. 19 Litho. *Perf. 14½*

63 A156 70c **multicolored** *(1,507,630)* .50 .55
First day cover *(170,540)* 1.00
Inscription block of 4 2.25 —

WIPO Type of UN

1977, Mar. 11 Photo. *Perf. 14*

64 A157 80c **red & multi** *(1,232,664)* .60 .65
First day cover *(212,470)* 1.00
Inscription block of 4 2.75 —

Drop of Water and Globe — G4

UN Water Conference, Mar del Plata, Argentina, Mar. 14-25.
Printed by Government Printing Bureau, Tokyo. Panes of 50. Designed by Eliezer Weishoff.

1977, Apr. 22 Photo. *Perf. 13½x13*

65 G4 80c **ultramarine & multi** *(1,146,650)* .50 .55
First day cover 1.00
Inscription block of 4 2.25 —
66 G4 1.10fr **dark carmine & multi** *(1,138,236)* .80 .85
First day cover 1.25
First day cover, #65-66 1.75
Inscription block of 4 3.50 —

First day covers of Nos. 65-66 total 289,836.

Hands Protecting UN Emblem — G5

UN Security Council.
Printed by Heraclio Fournier, S.A., Spain. Panes of 50. Designed by George Hamori.

1977, May 27 Photo. *Perf. 11*

67 G5 80c **blue & multi** *(1,096,030)* .50 .55
First day cover 1.00
Inscription block of 4 2.25 —
68 G5 1.10fr **emerald & multi** *(1,075,925)* .80 .85
First day cover 1.25
First day cover, #67-68 1.75
Inscription block of 4 3.50 —

First day covers of Nos. 67-68 total 305,349.

Colors of Five Races Spun into One Firm Rope — G6

Fight against racial discrimination.
Printed by Setelipaino, Finland. Panes of 50. Designed by M. A. Munnawar.

1977, Sept. 19 Litho. *Perf. 13½x13*

69 G6 40c **multicolored** *(1,218,834)* .25 .30
First day cover 1.00
Inscription block of 4 1.10 —
70 G6 1.10fr **multicolored** *(1,138,250)* .65 .70
First day cover 1.25
First day cover, #69-70 1.75
Inscription block of 4 2.75 —

First day covers of Nos. 69-70 total 308,722.

Atomic Energy Turning Partly into Olive Branch — G7

Peaceful uses of atomic energy.
Printed by Heraclio Fournier, S.A., Spain. Panes of 50. Designed by Witold Janowski and Marek Freudenreich.

1977, Nov. 18 Photo. *Perf. 14*

71 G7 80c **dark carmine & multi** *(1,147,787)* .55 .60
First day cover 1.00
Inscription block of 4 2.50 —
72 G7 1.10fr **Prussian blue & multi** *(1,121,209)* .75 .80
First day cover 1.20
First day cover, #71-72 1.50
Inscription block of 4 3.50 —

First day covers of Nos. 71-72 total 298,075.

"Tree" of Doves — G8

Printed by Questa Colour Security Printers, United Kingdom. Panes of 50. Designed by M. Hioki.

1978, Jan. 27 Litho. *Perf. 14½*

73 G8 35c **multicolored** *(3,000,000)*+ .25 .30
First day cover *(259,735)* 1.00
Inscription block of 4 .75 —

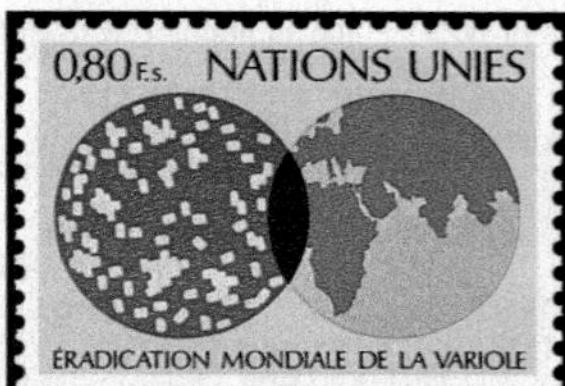

Globes with Smallpox Distribution — G9

Global eradication of smallpox.
Printed by Courvoisier, S.A. Panes of 50. Designed by Eliezer Weishoff.

1978, Mar. 31 **Photo.** ***Perf. 12x11½***

74 G9 80c **yellow & multi** *(1,116,044)*	.60	.65
First day cover		1.00
Inscription block of 4	2.50	—
75 G9 1.10fr **light green & multi** *(1,109,946)*	.90	.95
First day cover		1.25
First day cover, #74-75		2.00
Inscription block of 4	3.75	—

First day covers of Nos. 74-75 total 254,700.

Namibia Type of UN

1978, May 5 **Photo.** ***Perf. 12***

76 A166 80c **multicolored** *(1,183,208)*	.85	.90
First day cover *(316,610)*		1.00
Inscription block of 4	3.50	—

Jets and Flight Patterns — G10

International Civil Aviation Organization for "Safety in the Air."
Printed by Heraclio Fournier, S.A., Spain. Panes of 50. Designed by Tomas Savrda.

1978, June 12 **Photo.** ***Perf. 14***

77 G10 70c **multicolored** *(1,275,106)*	.40	.45
First day cover		1.00
Inscription block of 4	1.75	—
78 G10 80c **multicolored** *(1,144,339)*	.70	.75
First day cover		1.00
First day cover, #77-78		1.60
Inscription block of 4	3.00	—

First day covers of Nos. 77-78 total 255,700.

General Assembly, Flags and Globe — G11

Printed by Government Printing Bureau, Tokyo. Panes of 50. Designed by Henry Bencsath.

1978, Sept. 15 **Photo.** ***Perf. 13½***

79 G11 70c **multicolored** *(1,204,441)*	.45	.50
First day cover		1.00
Inscription block of 4	2.25	—
80 G11 1.10fr **multicolored** *(1,183,889)*	.85	.90
First day cover		1.25
First day cover, #79-80		1.75
Inscription block of 4	3.75	—

First day covers of Nos. 79-80 total 245,600.

Technical Cooperation Type of UN

1978, Nov. 17 **Photo.** ***Perf. 14***

81 A169 80c **multicolored** *(1,173,220)*	.70	.75
First day cover *(264,700)*		1.00
Inscription block of 4	3.25	—

Seismograph Recording Earthquake — G12

Office of the UN Disaster Relief Coordinator (UNDRO).
Printed by Heraclio Fournier, S.A., Spain. Panes of 50. Designed by Michael Klutmann.

1979, Mar. 9 **Photo.** ***Perf. 14***

82 G12 80c **multicolored** *(1,183,155)*	.50	.55
First day cover		1.00
Inscription block of 4	2.00	—
83 G12 1.50fr **multicolored** *(1,168,121)*	.80	.85
First day cover		1.40
First day cover, #82-83		1.90
Inscription block of 4	3.50	—

First day covers of Nos. 82-83 total 162,070.

Children and Rainbow — G13

International Year of the Child.
Printed by Heraclio Fournier, S.A., Spain. Panes of 20 (5x4). Designed by Arieh Glaser.

1979, May 4 **Photo.** ***Perf. 14***

84 G13 80c **multicolored** *(2,251,623)*	.35	.40
First day cover		1.25
Inscription block of 4	1.60	—
85 G13 1.10fr **multicolored** *(2,220,463)*	.65	.70
First day cover		1.75
Inscription block of 4	2.75	—
First day cover, #84-85		1.25
Panes of 20, #84-85	20.00	

First day covers of Nos. 84-85 total 176,120.

Namibia Type of UN

1979, Oct. 5 **Litho.** ***Perf. 13½***

86 A176 1.10fr **multicolored** *(1,229,830)*	.60	.65
First day cover *(134,160)*		1.25
Inscription block of 4	2.25	—

Women's Year Emblem — G15

United Nations Decade for Women.
Printed by Questa Colour Security Printers, United Kingdom. Panes of 50. Designed by M.A. Munnawar.

1980, Mar. 7 **Litho.** ***Perf. 14½x15***

90 G15 40c **multicolored** *(1,265,221)*	.30	.35
First day cover		1.00
Inscription block of 4	1.40	—
91 G15 70c **multicolored** *(1,240,375)*	.70	.75
First day cover		1.10
First day cover, #90-91		1.25
Inscription block of 4	3.50	—

First day covers of Nos. 90-91 total 204,350.

Peace-keeping Operations Type of UN

1980, May 16 **Litho.** ***Perf. 14x13***

92 A181 1.10fr **blue & green** *(1,335,391)*	.85	.90
First day cover *(184,700)*		1.00
Inscription block of 4	3.50	—

35th Anniversary Type of UN and Dove and "35" — G16

35th Anniversary of the United Nations.
Printed by Ashton-Potter Ltd., Canada. Panes of 50. Designed by Gidon Sagi (40c), Cemalattin Mutver (70c).

1980, June 26 **Litho.** ***Perf. 13x13½***

93 G16 40c **blue green & black** *(1,462,005)*	.35	.35
First day cover		1.00
Inscription block of 4	1.40	—
94 A183 70c **multicolored** *(1,444,639)*	.65	.70
First day cover		1.00
First day cover, #93-94		1.50
Inscription block of 4	3.00	—

Souvenir Sheet

Imperf

95	Sheet of 2 *(1,235,200)*	1.10	1.20
a.	G16 40c **blue green & black**	.30	.35
b.	A183 70c **multicolored**	.80	.85
	First day cover		1.00

First day covers of Nos. 93-95 total 379,800.

International Court of Justice, Scales — G14

International Court of Justice, The Hague, Netherlands.
Printed by Setelipaino, Finland. Panes of 50. Designed by Kyohei Maeno.

1979, Nov. 9 **Litho.** ***Perf. 13x13½***

87 G14 80c **multicolored** *(1,123,193)*	.40	.45
First day cover		1.00
Inscription block of 4	1.75	—
88 G14 1.10fr **multicolored** *(1,063,067)*	.60	.65
First day cover		1.25
First day cover, #87-88		1.75
Inscription block of 4	2.75	—

First day covers of Nos. 87-88 total 158,170.

New Economic Order Type of UN

1980, Jan. 11 **Litho.** ***Perf. 15x14½***

89 A179 80c **multicolored** *(1,315,918)*	.85	.90
First day cover *(176,250)*		1.00
Inscription block of 4	3.50	—

ECOSOC Type of UN and

Family Climbing Line Graph — G17

Printed by Ashton-Potter Ltd., Canada. Panes of 50. Designed by Eliezer Weishoff (40c), A. Medina Medina (70c).

1980, Nov. 21 **Litho.** ***Perf. 13½x13***

96 A186 40c **multicolored** *(986,435)*	.30	.35
First day cover		1.00
Inscription block of 4	1.25	—
97 G17 70c **multicolored** *(1,016,462)*	.60	.65
First day cover		1.00
First day cover #96-97		1.50
Inscription block of 4	2.50	—

Economic and Social Council.
First day covers of Nos. 96-97 total 210,460.

Palestinian Rights

Printed by Courvoisier S.A., Switzerland. Panes of 50.
Designed by David Dewhurst.

1981, Jan. 30 Photo. *Perf. 12x11½*
98 A188 80c **multicolored** *(1,031,737)* .55 .60
First day cover *(117,480)* 1.00
Inscription block of 4 2.75 —

International Year of the Disabled.

Printed by Heraclio Fournier S.A., Spain. Panes of 50.
Designed by G.P. Van der Hyde (40c) and Sophia van Heeswijk (1.50fr).

1981, Mar. 6 Photo. *Perf. 14*
99 A190 40c **black & blue** *(1,057,909)* .25 .30
First day cover 1.00
Inscription block of 4 1.00 —
100 V4 1.50fr **black & red** *(994,748)* 1.00 1.10
First day cover 1.25
First day cover, #99-100 1.75
Inscription block of 4 4.00 —

First day covers of Nos. 99-100 total 202,853.

Art Type of UN

1981, Apr. 15 Photo. *Perf. 11½*
Granite Paper
101 A191 80c **multicolored** *(1,128,782)* .80 .85
First day cover *(121,383)* 1.00
Inscription block of 4 3.75 —

Energy Type of 1981

1981, May 29 Litho. *Perf. 13*
102 A192 1.10fr **multicolored** *(1,096,806)* .75 .80
First day cover *(113,700)* 1.25
Inscription block of 4 3.50 —

Volunteers Program Type and

Symbols of Science, Agriculture and Industry — G18

Printed by Walsall Security Printers, Ltd., United Kingdom. Panes of 50.
Designed by Gabriele Nussgen (40c), Bernd Mirbach (70c).

1981, Nov. 13 Litho.
103 A194 40c **multicolored** *(1,032,700)* .45 .50
First day cover 1.00
Inscription block of 4 2.25 —
104 G18 70c **multicolored** *(1,123,672)* .90 .95
First day cover 1.00
First day cover, #103-104 1.50
Inscription block of 4 4.25 —

First day covers of Nos. 103-104 total 190,667.

Fight against Apartheid — G19

Flower of Flags — G20

Printed by Courvoisier, S.A., Switzerland. Panes of 50.
Designed by Tomas Savrda (30c); Dietmar Kowall (1fr).

1982, Jan. 22 *Perf. 11½x12*
105 G19 30c **multicolored** *(3,000,000)+* .25 .30
First day cover 1.00
Inscription block of 4 1.10 —
106 G20 1fr **multicolored** *(3,000,000)+* .80 .85
First day cover 1.00
First day cover, #105-106 1.25
Inscription block of 4 3.25 —

First day covers of Nos. 105-106 total 199,347.

Human Environment Type of UN and

Sun and Leaves — G21

10th Anniversary of United Nations Environment Program.
Printed by Joh. Enschede en Zonen, Netherlands. Panes of 50. Designed by Sybille Brunner (40c); Philine Hartert (1.20fr).

1982, Mar. 19 Litho. *Perf. 13½x13*
107 G21 40c **multicolored** *(948,743)* .30 .35
First day cover 1.00
Inscription block of 4 1.50 —
108 A199 1.20fr **multicolored** *(901,096)* 1.10 1.40
First day cover 1.10
First day cover, #107-108 1.40
Inscription block of 4 5.25 —

First day covers of Nos. 107-108 total 190,155.

Outer Space Type of UN and

Satellite, Applications of Space Technology G22

Exploration and Peaceful Uses of Outer Space.
Printed by Enschede. Panes of 50. Designed by Wiktor C. Nerwinski (80c) and George Hamori (1fr).

1982, June 11 Litho. *Perf. 13x13½*
109 A201 80c **multicolored** *(964,593)* .60 .65
First day cover 1.00
Inscription block of 4 3.00 —
110 G22 1fr **multicolored** *(898,367)* .80 .85
First day cover 1.25
First day cover, #109-110 1.50
Inscription block of 4 3.75 —

First day covers of Nos. 109-110 total 205,815.

Conservation & Protection of Nature

1982, Nov. 19 Photo. *Perf. 14*
111 A202 40c Bird *(928,143)* .45 .50
First day cover 1.00
Inscription block of 4 2.10 —
112 A202 1.50fr Reptile *(847,173)* 1.10 1.20
First day cover 1.25
First day cover, #111-112 1.75
Inscription block of 4 5.25 —

First day covers of Nos. 111-112 total 198,504.

World Communications Year

1983, Jan. 28 Litho. *Perf. 13*
113 A204 1.20fr **multicolored** *(894,025)* 1.25 1.40
First day cover *(131,075)* 1.25
Inscription block of 4 5.25 —

Safety at Sea Type of UN and

G23

Designed by Valentin Wurnitsch (A22).

1983, Mar. 18 Litho. *Perf. 14½*
114 A205 40c **multicolored** *(892,365)* .40 .45
First day cover 1.00
Inscription block of 4 1.75 —
115 G23 80c **multicolored** *(882,720)* .80 .85
First day cover 1.00
First day cover, #114-115 1.50
Inscription block of 4 3.50 —

First day covers of Nos. 114-115 total 219,592.

World Food Program

1983, Apr. 22 Engr. *Perf. 13½*
116 A207 1.50fr **blue** *(876,591)* 1.25 1.40
First day cover 1.25
Inscription block of 4 5.25 —

Trade Type of UN and

G24

Designed by Wladyslaw Brykczynski (A23).

1983, June 6 Litho. *Perf. 14*
117 A208 80c **multicolored** *(902,495)* .50 .55
First day cover 1.00
Inscription block of 4 2.50 —
118 G24 1.10fr **multicolored** *(921,424)* .90 .95
First day cover 1.00
First day cover, #117-118 1.40
Inscription block of 4 4.00 —

First day covers of Nos. 117-118 total 146,507.

Homo Humus Humanitas — G25

Right to Create — G26

35th Anniversary of the Universal Declaration of Human Rights.
Printed by Government Printing Office, Austria. Designed by Friedensreich Hundertwasser, Austria. Panes of 16 (4x4).

1983, Dec. 9 Photo. & Engr. *Perf. 13½*
119 G25 40c **multicolored** *(1,770,921)* .45 .50
First day cover 1.00
Inscription block of 4 2.00 —
120 G26 1.20fr **multicolored** *(1,746,735)* .95 1.00
First day cover 1.10
Inscription block of 4 4.25 —
First day cover, #119-120 1.40
Panes of 16, #119-120 22.50

First day covers of Nos. 119-120 total 315,052.

International Conference on Population Type

1984, Feb. 3 Litho. *Perf. 14*
121 A212 1.20fr **multicolored** *(776,879)* .90 .95
First day cover *(105,377)* 1.00
Inscription block of 4 4.00 —

Fishing G27

Women Farm Workers, Africa — G28

World Food Day, Oct. 16
Printed by Walsall Security Printers, Ltd., United Kingdom. Panes of 50. Designed by Adth Vanooijen, Netherlands.

1984, Mar. 15 Litho. *Perf. 14½*

122 G27 50c **multicolored** *(744,506)*	.30	.35
First day cover		1.00
Inscription block of 4	1.60	—
123 G28 80c **multicolored** *(784,047)*	.60	.65
First day cover		1.25
First day cover, #122-123		1.75
Inscription block of 4	2.75	—

First day covers of Nos. 122-123 total 155,234.

Valletta, Malta — G29

Los Glaciares National Park, Argentina — G30

World Heritage
Printed by Harrison and Sons, United Kingdom. Panes of 50. Designs adapted by Rocco J. Callari, US, and Thomas Lee, China.

1984, Apr. 18 Litho. *Perf. 14*

124 G29 50c **multicolored** *(763,627)*	.60	.65
First day cover		1.00
Inscription block of 4	2.50	—
125 G30 70c **multicolored** *(784,489)*	.85	.90
First day cover		1.25
First day cover, #124-125		1.75
Inscription block of 4	4.50	—

First day covers of Nos. 124-125 total 164,498.

G31

G32

Future for Refugees
Printed by Courvoisier. Panes of 50. Designed by Hans Erni, Switzerland.

1984, May 29 Photo. *Perf. 11½*

126 G31 35c **multicolored** *(880,762)*	.30	.35
First day cover		1.00
Inscription block of 4	1.50	—
127 G32 1.50fr **multicolored** *(829,895)*	1.10	1.20
First day cover		1.25
First day cover, #126-127		1.75
Inscription block of 4	5.00	—

First day covers of Nos. 126-127 total 170,306.

International Youth Year — G33

Printed by Waddingtons Ltd., United Kingdom. Panes of 50. Designed by Eliezer Weishoff, Israel.

1984, Nov. 15 Litho. *Perf. 13½*

128 G33 1.20fr **multicolored** *(755,622)*	1.25	1.40
First day cover *(96,680)*		1.00
Inscription block of 4	5.50	—

ILO Type of UN and

ILO Turin Center — G34

Printed by the Government Printing Bureau, Japan. Panes of 50. Engraved by Mamoru Iwakuni and Hiroshi Ozaki, Japan (No. 129) and adapted from photographs by Rocco J. Callari, US, and Thomas Lee, China (No. 130).

1985, Feb. 1 Engr. *Perf. 13½*

129 A220 80c **dull red** *(654,431)*	.70	.75
First day cover		1.00
Inscription block of 4	3.00	—
130 G34 1.20fr U Thant Pavilion *(609,493)*	1.10	1.20
First day cover		1.50
First day cover, #129-130		2.25
Inscription block of 4	4.75	—

First day covers of Nos. 129-130 total 118,467.

UN University Type

50c, Pastoral scene, advanced communications.

1985, Mar. 15 Photo. *Perf. 11½*

131 A221 50c multi *(625,087)*	.60	.65
First day cover		1.00
Inscription block of 4	2.75	—
132 A221 80c like No. 131 *(712,674)*	1.00	1.10
First day cover		1.25
First day cover, #131-132		1.75
Inscription block of 4	4.50	—

First day covers of Nos. 131-132 total 93,324.

Flying Postman — G35

Interlocked Peace Doves — G36

Printed by Carl Ueberreuter Druck and Verlag M. Salzer, Austria. Panes of 50. Designed by Arieh Glaser, Israel (No. 133), and Carol Sliwka, Poland (No. 134).

1985, May 10 Litho. *Perf. 14*

133 G35 20c **multicolored** *(2,000,000)+*	.25	.30
First day cover		1.00
Inscription block of 4	1.25	—
134 G36 1.20fr **multicolored** *(2,000,000)+*	1.25	1.40
First day cover		1.50
First day cover, #133-134		2.00
Inscription block of 4	6.00	—

First day covers of Nos. 133-134 total 103,165.

40th Anniversary Type

Designed by Rocco J. Callari, U.S., and Thomas Lee, China (No. 137).

1985, June 26 Photo. *Perf. 12 x 11½*

135 A224 50c **multicolored** *(764,924)*	.60	.65
First day cover		1.00
Inscription block of 4	2.50	—
136 A225 70c **multicolored** *(779,074)*	.90	.95
First day cover		1.25
First day cover, #135-136		2.00
Inscription block of 4	4.00	—

Souvenir Sheet

Imperf

137 Sheet of 2 *(498,041)*	2.25	2.40
a. A224 50c **multicolored**	.85	.90
b. A225 70c **multicolored**	1.10	1.20
First day cover		1.25

First day covers of Nos. 135-137 total 252,418.

UNICEF Child Survival Campaign Type

Printed by the Government Printing Bureau, Japan. Panes of 50. Designed by Mel Harris, United Kingdom (No. 138) and Adth Vanooijen, Netherlands (No. 139).

1985, Nov. 22 Photo. & Engr. *Perf. 13½*

138 A226 50c Three girls *(657,409)*	.40	.45
First day cover		1.00
Inscription block of 4	2.00	—
139 A226 1.20fr Infant drinking *(593,568)*	1.10	1.20
First day cover		1.25
First day cover, #138-139		1.75
Inscription block of 4	4.50	—

First day covers of Nos. 138-139 total 217,696.

Africa in Crisis Type

Printed by Helio Courvoisier, Switzerland. Panes of 50. Designed by Alemayehou Gabremedhiu, Ethiopia.

1986, Jan. 31 Photo. *Perf. 11½x12*

140 A227 1.40fr Mother, hungry children *(590,576)*	1.25	1.40
First day cover *(80,159)*		2.00
Inscription block of 4	5.25	—

UN Development Program Type

Forestry. Printed by the Government Printing Bureau, Japan. Pane of 40, 2 blocks of 4 horizontal and 5 blocks of 4 vertical. Designed by Thomas Lee, China.

1986, Mar. 14 Photo. *Perf. 13½*

141 A228 35c Erosion control *(547,567)*	1.60	1.75
142 A228 35c Logging *(547,567)*	1.60	1.75
143 A228 35c Lumber transport *(547,567)*	1.60	1.75
144 A228 35c Nursery *(547,567)*	1.60	1.75
a. Block of 4, #141-144	6.50	7.50
First day cover, #144a		8.50
First day cover, #141-144, each		2.50
Inscription block of 4, #144a	7.50	—
Pane of 40, #141-144	70.00	

No. 144a has a continuous design.
First day covers of Nos. 141-144 total 200,212.

Dove and Sun — G37

Printed by Questa Color Security Printers, Ltd., United Kingdom. Panes of 50. Designed by Ramon Alcantara Rodriguez, Mexico.

1986, Mar. 14 Litho. *Perf. 15x14½*

145 G37 5c **multicolored** *(2,000,000)+* .25 .30
First day cover *(58,908)* 1.00
Inscription block of 4 .60 —

Stamp Collecting Type

Designs: 50c, UN Human Rights stamp. 80c, UN stamps. Printed by the Swedish Post Office, Sweden. Panes of 50. Designed by Czeslaw Slania and Ingalill Axelsson, Sweden.

1986, May 22 Engr. *Perf. 12½*

146 A229 50c **dark green & henna brown** *(722,015)* .60 .65
First day cover 1.50
Inscription block of 4 2.50 —
147 A229 80c **dark green & yellow orange** *(750,945)* .90 .95
First day cover 1.50
First day cover, #146-147 1.75
Inscription block of 4 3.75 —

First day covers of Nos. 146-147 total 137,653.

Flags and Globe as Dove — G38

Peace in French — G39

International Peace Year. Printed by the Government Printing Bureau, Japan. Panes of 50. Designed by Renato Ferrini, Italy (No. 148), and Salahattin Kanidinc, US (No. 149).

1986, June 20 Photo. & Embossed *Perf. 13½*

148 G38 45c **multicolored** *(620,978)* .60 .65
First day cover 1.00
Inscription block of 4 2.75 —
149 G39 1.40fr **multicolored** *(559,658)* 1.25 1.40
First day cover 1.60
First day cover, #148-149 3.00
Inscription block of 4 5.50 —

First day covers of Nos. 148-149 total 123,542.

WFUNA Anniversary Type
Souvenir Sheet

Printed by Johann Enschede and Sons, Netherlands. Designed by Rocco J. Callari, US.

Designs: 35c, Abstract by Benigno Gomez, Honduras. 45c, Abstract by Alexander Calder (1898-1976), US. 50c, Abstract by Joan Miro (b. 1893), Spain. 70c, Sextet with Dove, by Ole Hamann, Denmark.

1986, Nov. 14 Litho. *Perf. 13x13½*

150 Sheet of 4 *(478,833)* 3.75 4.00
a. A232 35c **multicolored** .50 .55
b. A232 45c **multicolored** .70 .75
c. A232 50c **multicolored** .90 1.00
d. A232 70c **multicolored** 1.25 1.40
First day cover *(58,452)* 2.00

No. 150 has inscribed margin picturing UN and WFUNA emblems.

Trygve Lie Type

1987, Jan. 30 Photo. & Engr. *Perf. 13½*

151 A233 1.40fr **multicolored** *(516,605)* 1.10 1.20
First day cover *(76,152)* 1.50
Inscription block of 4 5.50 —

Sheaf of Colored Bands, by Georges Mathieu — G40

Armillary Sphere, Palais des Nations — G41

Printed by Helio Courvoisier, Switzerland (No. 152), and the Government Printing Bureau, Japan (No. 153). Panes of 50. Designed by Georges Mathieu (No. 152) and Rocco J. Callari (No. 153), US.

Photo., Photo. & Engr. (#153)

1987, Jan. 30 *Perf. 11½x12, 13½*

152 G40 90c **multicolored** *(1,600,000)+* .65 .70
First day cover 1.00
Inscription block of 4 3.00 —
153 G41 1.40fr **multicolored** *(1,600,000)+* 1.25 1.40
First day cover 1.00
First day cover, #152-153 2.00
Inscription block of 4 5.00 —

First day covers of Nos. 152-153 total 85,737.

Shelter for the Homeless Type

Designs: 50c, Cement-making and brick-making. 90c, Interior construction and decorating.

1987, Mar. 13 Litho. *Perf. 13½x12½*

154 A234 50c **multicolored** *(564,445)* .50 .55
First day cover 1.00
Inscription block of 4 2.50 —
155 A234 90c **multicolored** *(526,646)* 1.00 1.10
First day cover 1.10
First day cover, #154-155 2.00
Inscription block of 4 4.25 —

First day covers of Nos. 154-155 total 100,366.

Fight Drug Abuse Type

Designs: 80c, Mother and child. 1.20fr, Workers in rice paddy.

1987, June 12 Litho. *Perf. 14½x15*

156 A235 80c **multicolored** *(634,776)* .50 .55
First day cover 1.25
Inscription block of 4 3.00 —
157 A235 1.20fr **multicolored** *(609,475)* 1.00 1.10
First day cover 1.75
First day cover, #156-157 2.50
Inscription block of 4 4.75 —

First day covers of Nos. 156-157 total 95,247.

UN Day Type

Designed by Elisabeth von Janota-Bzowski (35c) and Fritz Oerter (50c).

Designs: Multinational people in various occupations.

1987, Oct. 23 Litho. *Perf. 14½x15*

158 A236 35c **multicolored** *(1,114,756)* .55 .60
First day cover 1.60
Inscription block of 4 2.50 —
159 A236 50c **multicolored** *(1,117,464)* .80 .85
First day cover 1.90
Inscription block of 4 3.50 —
First day cover, #158-159 2.50
Panes of 12, #158-159 15.00

Immunize Every Child Type

Designs: 90c, Whooping cough. 1.70fr, Tuberculosis.

1987, Nov. 20 Litho. *Perf. 15x14½*

160 A237 90c **multicolored** *(634,614)* 1.50 1.65
First day cover 1.00
Inscription block of 4 6.25 —
161 A237 1.70fr **multicolored** *(607,725)* 2.75 3.00
First day cover 1.25
First day cover, #160-161 2.50
Inscription block of 4 11.50 —

IFAD Type

Designs: 35c, Flocks, dairy products. 1.40fr, Fruit.

1988, Jan. 29 Litho. *Perf. 13½*

162 A238 35c **multicolored** *(524,817)* .35 .40
First day cover 1.00
Inscription block of 4 1.90 —
163 A238 1.40fr **multicolored** *(499,103)* 1.40 1.50
First day cover 1.50
First day cover, #162-163 2.00
Inscription block of 4 7.00 —

For A Better World — G42

Printed by Heraclio Fournier, S.A., Spain. Panes of 50. Designed by Bjorn Wiinblad, Denmark.

1988, Jan. 29 Photo. *Perf. 14*

164 G42 50c **multicolored** *(1,600,000)+* .80 .85
First day cover 2.00
Inscription block of 4 3.75 —

Survival of the Forests Type

Pine forest: 50c, Treetops, mountains. 1.10fr, Lake, tree trunks. Printed se-tenant in a continuous design.

1988, Mar. 18 Litho. *Perf. 14x15*

165 A240 50c **multicolored** *(728,569)* 1.25 1.40
First day cover 4.00
166 A240 1.10fr **multicolored** *(728,569)* 3.50 3.75
First day cover 6.00
a. Pair, #165-166 5.50 6.00
First day cover, #166a 10.00
Inscription block of 4, 2 #166a 12.50 —
Pane of 12, #165-166 30.00

Intl. Volunteer Day Type

Designed by Christopher Magadini, US.

Designs: 80c, Agriculture, vert. 90c, Veterinary medicine, horiz.

1988, May 6 Litho. *Perf. 13x14, 14x13*

167 A241 80c **multicolored** *(612,166)* .80 .85
First day cover 1.50
Inscription block of 4 4.00 —
168 A241 90c **multicolored** *(467,334)* 1.00 1.10
First day cover 1.75
First day cover, #167-168 3.50
Inscription block of 4 4.25 —

Health in Sports Type

Paintings by LeRoy Neiman, American sports artist: 50c, Soccer, vert. 1.40fr, Swimming.

1988, June 17 Litho. *Perf. 13½x13, 13x13½*

169 A242 50c **multicolored** *(541,421)* .40 .45
First day cover 1.25
Inscription block of 4 3.00 —
170 A242 1.40fr **multicolored** *(475,445)* 1.40 1.50
First day cover 2.40
First day cover, #169-170 3.00
Inscription block of 4 10.00 —

Universal Declaration of Human Rights 40th Anniv. Type

1988, Dec. 9 Photo. & Engr. *Perf. 12*

171 A243 90c **multicolored** *(745,508)* .70 .75
First day cover 2.50
Inscription block of 4 3.25 —

Souvenir Sheet

172 A243 2fr **multicolored** *(517,453)* 2.75 3.00
First day cover 4.00

World Bank Type

80c, Telecommunications. 1.40fr, Industry.

1989, Jan. 27 Litho. *Perf. 13x14*

173 A244 80c multi *(524,056)* 1.00 1.10
First day cover 1.50
Inscription block of 4 4.50 —
174 A244 1.40fr multi *(488,058)* 2.00 2.20
First day cover 2.40
First day cover, #173-174 3.50
Inscription block of 4 9.00 —

First day covers of Nos. 173-174 total 111,004.

Peace-Keeping Force Type

1989, Mar. 17 *Perf. 14x13½*

175 A245 90c **multicolored** *(684,566)* 1.25 1.40
First day cover *(52,463)* 1.00
Inscription block of 4 6.75 —

World Weather Watch Type

Satellite photographs: 90c, Europe under the influence of Arctic air. 1.10fr, Surface temperatures of sea, ice and land surrounding the Kattegat between Denmark and Sweden.

1989, Apr. 21 Litho. *Perf. 13x14*

176 A247 90c **multicolored** *(864,409)* 1.25 1.40
First day cover 1.50
Inscription block of 4 5.50 —
177 A247 1.10fr **multicolored** *(853,556)* 2.00 2.20
First day cover 1.90
First day cover, #176-177 3.00
Inscription block of 4 9.00 —

First day covers of Nos. 176-177 total 83,343.

Offices in Vienna, 10th Anniv.
G43 G44

Printed by Government Printing Office, Austria. Panes of 25. Designed by Anton Lehmden (50c) and Arik Brauer (2fr), Austria.

Photo., Photo. & Engr. (2fr)

1989, Aug. 23 *Perf. 14*

178 G43 50c **multicolored** *(605,382)* .75 1.10
First day cover 1.25
Inscription block of 4 3.50 —
179 G44 2fr **multicolored** *(538,140)* 2.50 3.75
First day cover 2.75
Inscription block of 4 10.50 —
First day cover, #178-179 3.25
Panes of 25, #178-179 80.00

First day covers of Nos. 178-179 total 83,304.

Human Rights Type of 1989

Printed by Johann Enschede and Sons, the Netherlands. Panes of 12+12 se-tenant labels containing Articles 3 (35c) or 4 (80c) inscribed in English, French or German. Designed by Rocco J. Callari and Robert Stein, US.

Artwork: 35c, Young Mother Sewing, by Mary Cassatt. 80c, The Unknown Slave, sculpture by Albert Mangones.

1989, Nov. 17 Litho. *Perf. 13½*

180 A250 35c **multicolored** *(1,923,818)* .35 .40
First day cover 1.25
Inscription block of 3 + 3 labels 1.60 —
181 A250 80c **multicolored** *(1,917,953)* 1.00 1.10
First day cover 3.00
Inscription block of 3 + 3 labels 4.50 —
First day cover, #180-181 4.50
Panes of 12, #180-181 17.50

First day covers of Nos. 180-181 total 134,469.

See Nos. 193-194, 209-210, 234-235.

Intl. Trade Center Type

1990, Feb. 2 Litho. *Perf. 14½x15*

182 A251 1.50fr **multicolored** *(409,561)* 2.25 2.50
First day cover *(61,098)* 3.50
Inscription block of 4 11.00 —

G45

Printed by Heraclio Fournier, S.A., Spain. Designed by Guy Breniaux, France and Elizabeth White, US.

1990, Feb. 2 Photo. *Perf. 14x13½*

183 G45 5fr **multicolored** *(1,600,000)*+ 4.75 5.25
First day cover *(54,462)* 7.00
Inscription block of 4 21.00 —

G46

Fight AIDS Worldwide — G46a

Fight AIDS Type

Designed by Jacek Tofil, Poland (50c) and Lee Keun Moon, Korea (80c).

Designs: 50c, "SIDA." 80c, Proportional drawing of man like the illustration by Leonardo da Vinci.

1990, Mar. 16 Litho. *Perf. 13½x12½*

184 G46 50c **multicolored** *(480,625)* 1.00 1.10
First day cover 1.25
Inscription block of 4 5.00 —
185 G46a 80c **multicolored** *(602,721)* 1.75 1.90
First day cover 1.50
First day cover, #184-185 2.00
Inscription block of 4 7.75 —

First day covers of Nos. 184-185 total 108,364.

Medicinal Plants Type

1990, May 4 Photo. Granite Paper *Perf. 11½*

186 A253 90c Plumeria rubra *(625,522)* 1.00 1.10
First day cover 1.40
Inscription block of 4 5.00 —
187 A253 1.40fr Cinchona officinalis *(648,619)* 2.00 2.20
First day cover 2.25
First day cover, #186-187 3.50
Inscription block of 4 9.50 —

First day covers of Nos. 186-187 total 114,062.

UN 45th Anniv. Type

Designed by Fritz Henry Oerter and Ruth Schmidthammer, Federal Republic of Germany (90c), Michiel Mertens, Belgium (1.10fr), Robert Stein, US (No. 190).

"45," emblem and: 90c, Symbols of clean environment, transportation and industry. 1.10fr, Dove in silhouette.

1990, June 26 Litho. *Perf. 14½x13*

188 A254 90c **multicolored** *(557,253)* 1.10 1.20
First day cover 1.40
Inscription block of 4 5.25 —
189 A254 1.10fr **multicolored** *(519,635)* 2.25 2.50
First day cover 2.00
First day cover, #188-189 3.00
Inscription block of 4 9.50 —

Souvenir Sheet

190 Sheet of 2, #188-189 *(401,027)* 6.00 6.50
First day cover 4.50

First day covers of Nos. 188-190 total 148,975.

Crime Prevention Type

1990, Sept. 13 Photo. *Perf. 14*

191 A255 50c Official corruption *(494,876)* 1.25 1.40
First day cover 1.40
Inscription block of 4 5.50 —
192 A255 2fr Environmental crime *(417,033)* 3.00 3.25
First day cover 3.25
First day cover, #191-192 4.50
Inscription block of 4 15.00 —

First day covers of Nos. 191-192 total 76,605.

Human Rights Type of 1989

Panes of 12+12 se-tenant labels containing Articles 9 (35c) or 10 (90c) inscribed in French, German or English.

Artwork: 35c, The Prison Courtyard by Vincent Van Gogh. 90c, Katho's Son Redeems the Evil Doer From Execution by Albrecht Durer.

1990, Nov. 16 Litho. *Perf. 13½*

193 A250 35c **multicolored** *(1,578,828)* .45 .50
First day cover 2.75
Inscription block of 3 + 3 labels 1.75 —
194 A250 90c **black & brown** *(1,540,200)* 1.25 1.40
First day cover 6.00
Inscription block of 3 + 3 labels 4.50 —
First day cover, #193-194 2.50
Panes of 12, #193-194 20.00

First day covers of Nos. 193-194 total 100,282.

Panes of 12+12 se-tenant labels containing Articles 9 (35c) or 10 (90c) inscribed in French, German or English.

Economic Commission for Europe Type

1991, Mar. 15 Litho. *Perf. 14*

195 A256 90c Owl, gull *(643,143)*+ 1.40 1.60
First day cover 3.00
196 A256 90c Bittern, otter *(643,143)*+ 1.40 1.60
First day cover 3.00
197 A256 90c Swan, lizard *(643,143)*+ 1.40 1.60
First day cover 3.00
198 A256 90c Great crested grebe *(643,143)*+ 1.40 1.60
First day cover 3.00
a. Block of 4, #195-198 5.60 6.50
First day cover, #198a 5.50
Inscription block of 4, #198a 7.00 —
Pane of 40, #195-198 52.50

First day covers of Nos. 195-198a total 75,759.

Namibian Independence Type

1991, May 10 Litho. *Perf. 14*

199 A257 70c Mountains *(328,014)* 1.00 1.10
First day cover 1.60
Inscription block of 4 4.25 —
200 A257 90c Baobab tree *(395,362)* 2.00 2.20
First day cover 2.25
First day cover, #199-200 5.00
Inscription block of 4 9.00 —

First day covers of Nos. 199-200 total 94,201.

Ballots Filling Ballot Box — G47

UN Emblem — G48

Printed by House of Questa, United Kingdom. Designed by Ran Banda Mawilmada, Sri Lanka (80c), Maurice Gouju, France (1.50fr).

1991, May 10 Litho. *Perf. 15x14½*

201 G47 80c **multicolored** *(1,600,000)*+ .75 .80
First day cover 1.75
Inscription block of 4 3.25 —
202 G48 1.50fr **multicolored** *(1,600,000)*+ 2.00 2.20
First day cover 3.25
First day cover, #201-202 3.75
Inscription block of 4 9.00 —

First day covers of Nos. 201-202 total 77,590.

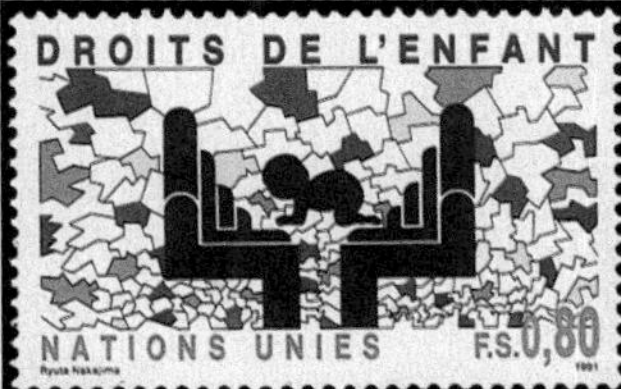

G49

Rights of the Child — G50

Printed by The House of Questa. Panes of 50. Designed by Ryuta Nakajima, Japan (80c) and David Popper, Switzerland (1.10fr).

1991, June 14 Litho. *Perf. 14½*

203 G49 80c Hands holding infant *(469,962)* 1.00 1.10
First day cover 1.75
Inscription block of 4 5.00 —
204 G50 1.10fr Children, flowers *(494,382)* 2.00 2.20
First day cover 2.25
First day cover, #203-204 3.25
Inscription block of 4 9.50 —

First day covers of Nos. 203-204 total 97,732.

G51

Banning of Chemical Weapons
G52

Printed by Heraclio Fournier S.A. Panes of 50. Designed by Oscar Asboth, Austria (80c), Michel Granger, France (1.40fr).

1991, Sept. 11 Litho. *Perf. 13½*
205 G51 80c **multicolored** *(345,658)* 2.00 2.20
First day cover 1.75
Inscription block of 4 8.50
206 G52 1.40fr **multicolored** *(366,076)* 3.00 3.25
First day cover 2.50
First day cover, #205-206 3.50
Inscription block of 4 13.50 —

First day covers of Nos. 205-206 total 91,887.

UN Postal Administration, 40th Anniv. Type

1991, Oct. 24 *Perf. 14x15*
207 A263 50c UN NY No. 7 *(506,839)* .80 .85
First day cover 1.25
Inscription block of 4 3.75 —
208 A263 1.60fr UN NY No. 10 *(580,493)* 2.20 2.40
First day cover 3.00
Inscription block of 4 9.75 —
First day cover, #207-208 3.25
Panes of 25, #207-208 75.00

First day covers of Nos. 207-208 total 88,784.

Human Rights Type of 1989

Panes of 12+12 se-tenant labels containing Articles 15 (50c) or 16 (90c) inscribed in French, German or English.
Artwork: 50c, Early Morning in Rio...1925, by Paul Klee. 90c, Marriage of Giovanni (?) Arnolfini and Giovanna Cenami (?), by Jan Van Eyck.

1991, Nov. 20 Litho. *Perf. 13½*
209 A250 50c **multicolored** *(1,295,172)* .75 .80
First day cover 3.25
Inscription block of 3 + 3 labels 2.40 —
210 A250 90c **multicolored** *(1,324,091)* 1.25 1.40
First day cover 6.75
Inscription block of 3 + 3 labels 3.80 —
First day cover, #209-210 2.00
Panes of 12, #209-210 25.00

First day covers of Nos. 209-210 total 139,904.

World Heritage Type of 1984

Designs: 50c, Sagarmatha Natl. Park, Nepal. 1.10fr, Stonehenge, United Kingdom.

1992, Jan. 24 Litho. *Perf. 13*
Size: 35x28mm
211 G29 50c **multicolored** *(468,647)* .80 .85
First day cover 1.25
Inscription block of 4 3.75 —
212 G29 1.10fr **multicolored** *(369,345)* 1.90 2.10
First day cover 2.25
First day cover, #211-212 3.00
Inscription block of 4 8.00 —

First day covers of Nos. 211-212 total 77,034.

G53

Printed by The House of Questa. Panes of 50. Designed by Nestor Jose Martin, Argentina.

1992, Jan. 24 Litho. *Perf. 15x14½*
213 G53 3fr **multicolored** *(1,600,000)+* 3.00 3.25
First day cover *(36,135)* 4.00
Inscription block of 4 12.00 —

Clean Oceans Type

1992, Mar. 13 Litho. *Perf. 14*
214 A264 80c Ocean surface, diff. *(850,699)* .90 .95
215 A264 80c Ocean bottom, diff. *(850,699)* .90 .95
a. Pair, #214-215 1.80 *2.10*
First day cover, #215a 2.75
First day cover, #214-215, each 1.75
Inscription block of 4, 2 #215a 5.00 —
Pane of 12, #214-215 11.00

First day covers of Nos. 214-215a total 90,725.

Earth Summit Type

Designs: No. 216, Rainbow. No. 217, Two clouds shaped as faces. No. 218, Two sailboats. No. 219, Woman with parasol, boat, flowers.

1992, May 22 Photo. *Perf. 11½*
216 A265 75c **multicolored** *(826,543)* 1.50 1.60
217 A265 75c **multicolored** *(826,543)* 1.50 1.60
218 A265 75c **multicolored** *(826,543)* 1.50 1.60
219 A265 75c **multicolored** *(826,543)* 1.50 1.60
a. Block of 4, #216-219 6.00 6.50
First day cover, #219a 4.00
First day cover, #216-219, each 6.00
Inscription block of 4, #216-219 6.50 —
Pane of 40, #216-219 60.00

First day covers of Nos. 216-219a total 74,629.

Mission to Planet Earth Type

Designs: No. 220, Space station. No. 221, Probes near Jupiter.

1992, Sept. 4 Photo. *Rouletted 8*
Granite Paper
220 A266 1.10fr **multicolored** *(668,241)* 2.40 2.60
221 A266 1.10fr **multicolored** *(668,241)* 2.40 2.60
a. Pair, #220-221 5.00 5.25
First day cover, #221a 5.00
First day cover, #220-221, each 10.00
Inscription block of 4, 2 #220-221 11.00 —
Pane of 10, #220-221 25.00

First day covers of Nos. 220-221 total 76,060.

Science and Technology Type of 1992

Designs: 90c, Doctor, nurse. 1.60fr, Graduate seated before computer.

1992, Oct. 2 Litho. *Perf. 14*
222 A267 90c **multicolored** *(438,943)* 1.25 1.40
First day cover 1.60
Inscription block of 4 5.00 —
223 A267 1.60fr **multicolored** *(400,701)* 3.00 3.25
First day cover 2.50
First day cover, #222-223 3.25
Inscription block of 4 12.00 —

First day covers of Nos. 222-223 total 75,882.

Human Rights Type of 1989

Panes of 12+12 se-tenant labels containing Articles 21 (50c) and 22 (90c) inscribed in French, German or English.
Artwork: 50c, The Oath of the Tennis Court, by Jacques Louis David. 90c, Rocking Chair I, by Henry Moore.

1992, Nov. 20 Litho. *Perf. 13½*
224 A250 50c **multicolored,** *(1,201,788)* .75 .80
First day cover 7.00
Inscription block of 3 + 3 labels 2.75 —
225 A250 90c **multicolored,** *(1,179,294)* 1.25 1.40
First day cover 7.00
Inscription block of 3 + 3 labels 4.25 —
First day cover, #224-225 1.75
Panes of 12, #224-225 24.00

First day covers of Nos. 224-225 total 104,491.

Aging With Dignity Type

Designs: 50c, Older man coaching soccer. 1.60fr, Older man working at computer terminal.

1993, Feb. 5 Litho. *Perf. 13*
226 A270 50c **multicolored** *(483,452)* .50 .55
First day cover 1.00
Inscription block of 4 2.75 —
227 A270 1.60fr **multicolored** *(331,008)* 1.50 1.65
First day cover 2.75
First day cover, #226-227 3.00
Inscription block of 4 7.50 —

First day covers of Nos. 226-227 total 61,361.

Endangered Species Type

Designed by Rocco J. Callari, US, and Betina Ogden, Australia.
Designs: No. 228, Pongidae (gorilla). No. 229, Falco peregrinus (peregrine falcon). No. 230, Trichechus inunguis (Amazonian manatee). No. 231, Panthera uncia (snow leopard).

1993, Mar. 2 Litho. *Perf. 13x12½*
228 A271 80c **multicolored** *(1,200,000)+* 1.10 1.20
229 A271 80c **multicolored** *(1,200,000)+* 1.10 1.20
230 A271 80c **multicolored** *(1,200,000)+* 1.10 1.20
231 A271 80c **multicolored** *(1,200,000)+* 1.10 1.20
a. Block of 4, #228-231 4.50 4.80
First day cover, #231a 5.00
First day cover, #228-231, each 2.00
Inscription block of 4, #228-231 4.50 —
Pane of 16, #228-231 19.00

First day covers of Nos. 228-231a total 75,363.

Healthy Environment Type

1993, May 7 Litho. *Perf. 15x14½*
232 A272 60c **Neighborhood** *(456,304)* .75 .80
First day cover 1.25
Inscription block of 4 3.50 —
233 A272 1fr **Urban skyscrapers** *(392,015)* 1.75 1.90
First day cover 2.00
First day cover, #232-233 3.25
Inscription block of 4 7.50 —

First day covers of Nos. 232-233 total 59,790.

Human Rights Type of 1989

Printed in panes of 12 + 12 se-tenant labels containing Article 27 (50c) and 28 (90c) inscribed in French, German or English.
Artwork: 50c, Three Musicians, by Pablo Picasso. 90c, Voice of Space, by Rene Magritte.

1993, June 11 Litho. *Perf. 13½*
234 A250 50c **multicolored** *(1,166,286)* .75 .80
First day cover 3.50
Inscription block of 3 + 3 labels 2.50 —
235 A250 90c **multicolored** *(1,122,348)* 1.75 1.90
First day cover 4.50
Inscription block of 3 + 3 labels 5.50 —
First day cover, #234-235 2.00
Panes of 12, #234-235 25.00

First day covers of Nos. 234-235 total 83,432.

Intl. Peace Day Type

Denomination at: No. 236, UL. No. 237, UR. No. 238, LL. No. 239, LR.

1993, Sept. 21 Litho. & Engr. *Rouletted 12½*
236 A274 60c **purple & multi** *(357,760)* 2.00 2.20
237 A274 60c **purple & multi** *(357,760)* 2.00 2.20
238 A274 60c **purple & multi** *(357,760)* 2.00 2.20
239 A274 60c **purple & multi** *(357,760)* 2.00 2.20
a. Block of 4, #236-239 8.00 9.00
First day cover, #239a 5.50
First day cover, #236-239, each 5.00
Inscription block of 4, #239a 9.50 —
Pane of 40, #236-239 75.00

First day covers of Nos. 236-239a total 47,207.

Environment-Climate Type

1993, Oct. 29 Litho. *Perf. 14½*
240 A275 1.10fr Polar bears *(391,593)* 2.40 2.40
241 A275 1.10fr Whale sounding *(391,593)* 2.40 2.40
242 A275 1.10fr Elephant seal *(391,593)* 2.40 2.40
243 A275 1.10fr Penguins *(391,593)* 2.40 2.40
a. Strip of 4, #240-243 9.75 10.75
First day cover, #243a 7.25
First day cover, #240-243, each 6.00
Inscription block of 8, 2 #243a 22.50 —
Pane of 24, #240-243 52.50

First day covers of Nos. 240-243a total 41,819.

Intl. Year of the Family Type of 1993

Designs: 80c, Parents teaching child to walk. 1fr, Two women and child picking plants.

1994, Feb. 4 Litho. *Perf. 13.1*
244 A276 80c **rose violet & multi** *(535,000)+* 1.00 1.10
First day cover 1.75
Inscription block of 4 4.75 —
245 A276 1fr **brown & multi** *(535,000)+* 1.40 1.50
First day cover 2.00
First day cover, #244-245 3.25
Inscription block of 4 6.25 —

First day covers of Nos. 244-245 total 50,080.

Endangered Species Type of 1993

Designed by Rocco J. Callari (frame) and Leon Parson, US (stamps).
Designs: No. 246, Mexican prairie dog. No. 247, Jabiru. No. 248, Blue whale. No. 249, Golden lion tamarin.

1994, Mar. 18 Litho. *Perf. 12.7*
246 A271 80c **multicolored** *(1,200,000)+* 1.10 1.20
247 A271 80c **multicolored** *(1,200,000)+* 1.10 1.20
248 A271 80c **multicolored** *(1,200,000)+* 1.10 1.20
249 A271 80c **multicolored** *(1,200,000)+* 1.10 1.20
a. Block of 4, #246-249 4.50 5.00
First day cover, #249a 5.50
First day cover, #246-249, each 1.75
Inscription block of 4, #246-249 4.75 —
Pane of 16, #246-249 20.00

First day covers of Nos. 246-249a total 82,043.

Protection for Refugees Type of 1994

Design: 1.20fr, Hand lifting figure over chasm.

1994, Apr. 29 Litho. *Perf. 14.3x14.8*
250 A277 1.20fr **multicolored** *(550,000)+* 2.25 2.40
First day cover *(33,805)* 2.50
Inscription block of 4 10.00 —

Intl. Decade for Natural Disaster Reduction Type of 1994

Earth seen from space, outline map of: No. 251, North America. No. 252, Eurasia. No. 253, South America. No. 254, Australia and South Pacific region.

1994, May 27 Litho. *Perf. 13.9x14.2*

251 A281 60c **multicolored** *(570,000)+* 1.75 1.90
252 A281 60c **multicolored** *(570,000)+* 1.75 1.90
253 A281 60c **multicolored** *(570,000)+* 1.75 1.90
254 A281 60c **multicolored** *(570,000)+* 1.75 1.90
a. Block of 4, #251-254 7.00 7.75
First day cover, #254a 7.00
First day cover, #251-254, each 5.00
Inscription block of 4, #254a 9.50 —
Pane of 40, #251-254 75.00

First day covers of Nos. 251-254a total 37,595.

Palais des Nations, Geneva — G54

Creation of the World, by Oili Maki — G55

Printed by House of Questa, United Kingdom. Designed by Rocco J. Callari, US.

1994, Sept. 1 Litho. *Perf. 14.3x14.6*

255 G54 60c **multicolored** *(1,075,000)+* .75 .80
First day cover 1.10
Inscription block of 4 3.25 —
256 G55 80c **multicolored** *(1,075,000)+* 1.00 1.10
First day cover 1.50
Inscription block of 4 4.25 —
257 G54 1.80fr **multi,** diff. *(1,075,000)+* 2.25 2.50
First day cover 2.75
Inscription block of 4 9.50 —
First day cover, #255-257 4.50
Nos. 255-257 (3) 4.00 4.40

First day covers of Nos. 255-257 total 51,637.

Population and Development Type of 1994

Designs: 60c, People shopping at open-air market. 80c, People on vacation crossing bridge.

1994, Sept. 1 Litho. *Perf. 13.2x13.6*

258 A282 60c **multicolored** *(535,000)+* 1.00 1.10
First day cover 1.25
Inscription block of 4 4.50 —
259 A282 80c **multicolored** *(535,000)+* 1.25 1.40
First day cover 1.75
Inscription block of 4 6.50 —
First day cover, #258-259 3.00

First day covers of Nos. 258-259 total 50,443.

UNCTAD Type of 1994

1994, Oct. 28

260 A283 80c **multi,** diff. *(535,000)+* 1.10 1.20
First day cover 1.75
Inscription block of 4 5.00 —
261 A283 1fr **multi,** diff. *(535,000)+* 1.50 1.65
First day cover 2.00
Inscription block of 4 6.75 —
First day cover, #260-261 3.50
a. Grayish green omitted —
Inscription block of 4 —

First day covers of Nos. 260-261 total 48,122.

UN 50th Anniv. Type of 1995

1995, Jan. 1 Litho. & Engr. *Perf. 13.4*

262 A284 80c **multicolored** *(823,827)* 1.10 1.20
First day cover *(38,988)* 3.00
Inscription block of 4 5.00 —

Social Summit Type of 1995

1995, Feb. 3 Photo. & Engr. *Perf. 13.6x13.9*

263 A285 1fr **multi,** diff. *(452,116)* 1.25 1.40
First day cover *(35,246)* 2.00
Inscription block of 4 6.00 —

Endangered Species Type of 1993

Designed by Sibylle Erni, Switzerland.

Designs: No. 264, Crowned lemur, Lemur coronatus. No. 265, Giant Scops owl, Otus gurneyi. No. 266, Zetek's frog, Atelopus varius zeteki. No. 267, Wood bison, Bison bison athabascae.

1995, Mar. 24 Litho. *Perf. 13x12½*

264 A271 80c **multicolored** *(730,000)+* 1.10 1.20
265 A271 80c **multicolored** *(730,000)+* 1.10 1.20
266 A271 80c **multicolored** *(730,000)+* 1.10 1.20
267 A271 80c **multicolored** *(730,000)+* 1.10 1.20
a. Block of 4, 264-267 4.50 5.00
First day cover, #267a 4.50
First day cover, #264-267, each 1.60
Inscription block of 4, #267a 5.25 —
Pane of 16, #264-267 18.50

First day covers of Nos. 264-267a total 71,907.

Intl. Youth Year Type of 1995

Designs: 80c, Farmer on tractor, fields at harvest time. 1fr, Couple standing by fields at night.

1995, May 26 Litho. *Perf. 14.4x14.7*

268 A286 80c **multicolored** *(294,987)* 1.25 1.40
First day cover 1.75
Inscription block of 4 5.50 —
269 A286 1fr **multicolored** *(264,823)* 2.00 2.20
First day cover 2.00
First day cover, #268-269 4.00
Inscription block of 4 9.00 —

First day covers of Nos. 268-269 total 45,665.

UN, 50th Anniv. Type of 1995

Designs: 60c, Like No. 663. 1.80fr, Like No. 664.

1995, June 26 Engr. *Perf. 13.3x13.6*

270 A287 60c **maroon** *(352,336)* .80 .85
First day cover .90
Inscription block of 4 3.75 —
271 A287 1.80fr **green** *(377,391)* 3.00 3.25
First day cover 3.00
First day cover, #270-271 4.00
Inscription block of 4 13.00 —

Souvenir Sheet
Litho. & Engr.
Imperf

272 Sheet of 2, #270-271 *(251,272)* 4.25 4.50
a. A287 60c **maroon** 1.00 1.10
b. A287 1.80fr **green** 3.25 3.40
First day cover 8.00

First day covers of Nos. 270-272 total 72,666.

Conference on Women Type of 1995

Designs: 60c, Black woman, cranes flying above. 1fr, Women, dove.

1995, Sept. 5 Photo. *Perf. 12*

273 A288 60c **multicolored** *(342,336)* 1.00 1.10
First day cover 1.25
Inscription block of 4 4.50 —

Size: 28x50mm

274 A288 1fr **multicolored** *(345,489)* 2.00 2.20
First day cover 2.25
First day cover, #273-274 3.25
Inscription block of 4 9.00 —

First day covers of Nos. 273-274 total 57,542.

UN People, 50th Anniv. Type of 1995

1995, Oct. 24 Litho. *Perf. 14*

275 Sheet of 12 *(216,832 sheets)* 14.00 15.00
First day cover 20.00
a.-l. A290 30c each 1.20 1.20
First day cover, #275a-275l, each 7.00
276 Souvenir booklet, *(74,151 booklets)* 15.00
a. A290 30c Booklet pane of 3, vert. strip of 3 from UL of sheet 3.75 3.75
b. A290 30c Booklet pane of 3, vert. strip of 3 from UR of sheet 3.75 3.75
c. A290 30c Booklet pane of 3, vert. strip of 3 from LL of sheet 3.75 3.75
d. A290 30c Booklet pane of 3, vert. strip of 3 from LR of sheet 3.75 3.75

First day covers of Nos. 275-276d total 53,245.

WFUNA, 50th Anniv. Type

Design: 80c, Fishing boat, fish in net.

1996, Feb. 2 Litho. *Perf. 13x13½*

277 A291 80c **multicolored** *(550,000)+* 1.25 1.40
First day cover 2.00
Inscription block of 4 6.50 —

The Galloping Horse Treading on a Flying Swallow, Chinese Bronzework, Eastern Han Dynasty (25-220 A.D.) — G56

Palais des Nations, Geneva — G57

Printed by House of Questa, UK.

1996, Feb. 2 Litho. *Perf. 14½x15*

278 G56 40c **multicolored** *(1,125,000)+* .50 .55
First day cover 1.25
Inscription block of 4 2.50 —
279 G57 70c **multicolored** *(1,125,000+)* .90 .95
First day cover 1.50
First day cover, #278-279 3.50
Inscription block of 4 4.00 —

Endangered Species Type of 1993

Designs: No. 280, Paphiopedilum delenatii. No. 281, Pachypodium baronii. No. 282, Sternbergia lutea. No. 283, Darlingtonia californica.

1996, Mar. 14 Litho. *Perf. 12½*

280 A271 80c **multicolored** *(680,000)+* 1.00 1.10
281 A271 80c **multicolored** *(680,000)+* 1.00 1.10
282 A271 80c **multicolored** *(680,000)+* 1.00 1.10
283 A271 80c **multicolored** *(680,000)+* 1.00 1.10
a. Block of 4, #280-283 4.00 4.50
First day cover, #280-283, each 2.00
First day cover, #283a 4.50
Inscription block of 4, #283a 4.25 —
Pane of 16, #280-283 16.00

City Summit Type of 1996

Designs: No. 284, Asian family. No. 285, Oriental garden. No. 286, Fruit, vegetable vendor, mosque. No. 287, Boys playing ball. No. 288, Couple reading newspaper.

1996, June 3 Litho. *Perf. 14x13½*

284 A293 70c **multicolored** *(420,000)+* 1.50 1.65
285 A293 70c **multicolored** *(420,000)+* 1.50 1.65
286 A293 70c **multicolored** *(420,000)+* 1.50 1.65
287 A293 70c **multicolored** *(420,000)+* 1.50 1.65
288 A293 70c **multicolored** *(420,000)+* 1.50 1.65
a. Strip of 5, #284-288 7.50 8.25
First day cover, #288a 11.00
First day cover, #284-288, each 5.00
Inscription block of 10, 2 #288a 20.00

Sport and the Environment Type

Designs: 70c, Cycling, vert. 1.10fr, Sprinters.

1996, July 19 Litho. *Perf. 14x14½, 14½x14*

289 A294 70c **multicolored** *(625,000)+* 1.00 1.10
First day cover 1.50
Inscription block of 4 4.75 —
290 A294 1.10fr **multicolored** *(625,000)+* 1.50 1.65
First day cover 2.25
First day cover, #289-290 4.50
Inscription block of 4 7.50 —

Souvenir Sheet

291 A294 Sheet of 2, #289-290 *(345,000)+* 3.00 3.25
First day cover 12.00

Plea for Peace Type

Designed by: 90c, Chen Yu, China. 1.10fr, Zhou Jing, China.

Designs: 90c, Tree filled with birds, vert. 1.10fr, Bouquet of flowers in rocket tail vase, vert.

1996, Sept. 17 Litho. *Perf. 15x14½*

292 A295 90c **multicolored** *(550,000)+* 1.25 1.40
First day cover 1.50
Inscription block of 4 5.50 —
293 A295 1.10fr **multicolored** *(550,000)+* 1.50 1.65
First day cover 2.25
First day cover, #292-293 3.75
Inscription block of 4 7.50 —

UNICEF Type

Fairy Tales: 70c, The Sun and the Moon, South America. 1.80fr, Ananse, Africa.

1996, Nov. 20 Litho. *Perf. 14½x15*

294 A296 70c **multicolored** *(1,000,000)+* .80 .85
First day cover 1.50
Pane of 8 + label 6.50
295 A296 1.80fr **multicolored** *(1,000,000)+* 2.00 2.20
First day cover 3.00
First day cover, #294-295 4.00
Pane of 8 + label 17.50

UN Flag — G58

Palais des Nations Under Construction by Massimo Campigli — G59

Printed by The House of Questa, Ltd., UK.

1997, Feb. 12 Litho. *Perf. 14½*

296 G58 10c **multicolored** *(600,000)+* .25 .30
First day cover 1.25
Inscription block of 4 .55 —
297 G59 1.10fr **multicolored** *(700,000)+* 1.25 1.40
First day cover 2.25
First day cover, #296-297 3.50
Inscription block of 4 5.00 —

First day covers of Nos. 296-297 total 41,186.

Endangered Species Type of 1993

Designs: No. 298, Ursus maritimus (polar bear). No. 299, Goura cristata (blue-crowned pigeon). No. 300, Amblyrhynchus cristatus (marine iguana). No. 301, Lama guanicoe (guanaco).

1997, Mar. 13 Litho. *Perf. 12½*

298 A271 80c **multicolored** *(620,000)+* .90 .95
299 A271 80c **multicolored** *(620,000)+* .90 .95
300 A271 80c **multicolored** *(620,000)+* .90 .95
301 A271 80c **multicolored** *(620,000)+* .90 .95
a. Block of 4, #298-301 3.60 3.90
First day cover, #301a 5.00
First day cover, #298-301, each 2.50
Inscription block of 4, #301a 4.00
Pane of 16 17.50

First day covers of Nos. 298-301 total 71,905.

Earth Summit Anniv. Type

Designs: No. 302, Person flying over mountain. No. 303, Mountain, person's face. No. 304, Person standing on mountain, sailboats. No. 305, Person, mountain, trees.
1.10fr, Combined design similar to Nos. 302-305.

1997, May 30 Photo. *Perf. 11½*

Granite Paper

302 A299 45c **multicolored** *(227,187)* 1.00 1.10
303 A299 45c **multicolored** *(227,187)* 1.00 1.10
304 A299 45c **multicolored** *(227,187)* 1.00 1.10
305 A299 45c **multicolored** *(227,187)* 1.00 1.10
a. Block of 4, #302-305 4.00 4.50
First day cover, #305a 8.00
First day cover, #302-305, each 6.00
Inscription block of 4, #305a 6.25

Souvenir Sheet

306 A299 1.10fr **multicolored** *(176,386)* 4.00 4.25
First day cover 5.00

First day covers of Nos. 302-306 total 55,389.

Transportation Type of 1997

Air transportation: No. 307, Zeppelin, Fokker tri-motor. No. 308, Boeing 314 Clipper, Lockheed Constellation. No. 309, DeHavilland Comet. No. 310, Boeing 747, Illyushin jet. No. 311, Concorde.

1997, Aug. 29 Litho. *Perf. 14x14½*

307 A300 70c **multicolored** *(271,575)* 1.00 1.10
308 A300 70c **multicolored** *(271,575)* 1.00 1.10
309 A300 70c **multicolored** *(271,575)* 1.00 1.10
310 A300 70c **multicolored** *(271,575)* 1.00 1.10
311 A300 70c **multicolored** *(271,575)* 1.00 1.10
a. Strip of 5, #307-311 5.00 5.50
First day cover, #311a 7.00
First day cover, #307-311, each 4.75
Margin block of 10, 2#311a 12.50

No. 311a has continuous design.
First day covers of Nos. 307-311 total 33,303.

Philately Type

Designs: 70c, No. 146. 1.10fr, No. 147.

1997, Oct. 14 Litho. *Perf. 13½x14*

312 A301 70c **multicolored** *(254,406)* .80 .85
First day cover 1.75
Inscription block of 4 3.25 —
313 A301 1.10fr **multicolored** *(303,125)* 1.50 1.65
First day cover 2.25
First day cover, #312-313 6.00
Inscription block of 4 6.25 —

First day covers of Nos. 312-313 total 47,528.

World Heritage Convention Type

Terracotta warriors of Xian: 45c, Single warrior. 70c, Massed warriors. No. 316a, like NY No. 716. No. 316b, like NY No. 717. No. 316c, like Geneva No. 314. No. 316d, like Geneva No. 315. No. 316e, like Vienna No. 230. No. 316f, like Vienna No. 231.

1997, Nov. 19 Litho. *Perf. 13½*

314 A302 45c **multicolored** *(409,820)* 1.25 1.40
First day cover 1.40
Inscription block of 4 5.50 —
315 A302 70c **multicolored** *(414,059)* 2.25 2.50
First day cover 1.50
First day cover, #314-315 4.00
Inscription block of 4 9.50 —
316 Souvenir booklet *(275,114 booklets)* 12.00
a.-f. A302 10c any single .45 .50
g. Booklet pane of 4 #316a 2.00 2.00
h. Booklet pane of 4 #316b 2.00 2.00
i. Booklet pane of 4 #316c 2.00 2.00
j. Booklet pane of 4 #316d 2.00 2.00
k. Booklet pane of 4 #316e 2.00 2.00
l. Booklet pane of 4 #316f 2.00 2.00

First day covers of Nos. 314-316 total 40,366.

Palais des Nations, Geneva — G60

Printed by The House of Questa, UK. Designed by UN (2fr).

1998, Feb. 13 Litho. *Perf. 14½x15*

317 G60 2fr **multicolored** *(550,000)+* 1.50 1.65
First day cover 6.00
Inscription block of 4 6.00 —

Endangered Species Type of 1993

Designed by Rocco J. Callari, US and Suzanne Duranceau, Canada.

Designs: No. 318, Macaca thibetana (short-tailed Tibetan macaque). No. 319, Phoenicopterus ruber (Caribbean flamingo). No. 320, Ornithoptera alexandrae (Queen Alexandra's birdwing). No. 321, Dama mesopotamica (Persian fallow deer).

1998, Mar. 13 Litho. *Perf. 12½*

318 A271 80c **multicolored** *(560,000)+* 1.00 1.10
319 A271 80c **multicolored** *(560,000)+* 1.00 1.10
320 A271 80c **multicolored** *(560,000)+* 1.00 1.10
321 A271 80c **multicolored** *(560,000)+* 1.00 1.10
a. Block of 4, #318-321 4.00 4.50
First day cover, #321a 6.00
First day cover, #318-321, each 5.00
Inscription block of 4, #321a 4.25 —
Pane of 16 16.00

Intl. Year of the Ocean — G61

Designed by Jon Ellis, US.

1998, May 20 Litho. *Perf. 13x13½*

322 G61 Pane of 12 *(270,000)+* 11.00 12.00
First day cover 10.00
a.-l. 45c any single .90 1.00
First day cover, #322a-322l, each 3.00

Rain Forests Type

1998, June 19 *Perf. 13x13½*

323 A307 70c Orangutans *(430,000)+* .90 1.00
First day cover 5.00
Inscription block of 4 4.00 —

Souvenir Sheet

324 A307 3fr like #323 *(250,000)+* 4.00 7.50
First day cover 7.00

Peacekeeping Type

Designs: 70c, Soldier with two children. 90c, Two soldiers, children.

1998, Sept. 15 Photo. *Perf. 12*

325 A308 70c **multicolored** *(400,000)+* .85 .90
First day cover 1.50
Inscription block of 4 3.50 —
326 A308 90c **multicolored** *(390,000)+* 1.40 1.50
First day cover 4.00
First day cover, #325-326 5.00
Inscription block of 4 6.00 —

Declaration of Human Rights Type of 1998

Designs: 90c, Stylized birds. 1.80fr, Stylized birds flying from hand.

1998, Oct. 27 Litho. & Photo. *Perf. 13*

327 A309 90c **multicolored** *(400,000)+* .95 1.05
First day cover 2.00
Inscription block of 4 4.00 —
328 A309 1.80fr **multicolored** *(390,000)+* 2.00 2.20
First day cover 3.50
First day cover, #327-328 5.00
Inscription block of 4 8.00 —

Schönbrunn Palace Type

Designs: 70c, No. 331b, Great Palm House. 1.10fr, No. 331d, Blue porcelain vase, vert. No. 331a, Palace. No. 331c, The Gloriette (archway). No. 331e, Wall painting on fabric (detail), by Johann Wenzl Bergl, vert. No. 331f, Porcelain stove, vert.

1998, Dec. 4 Litho. *Perf. 14*

329 A310 70c **multicolored** *(375,000)+* .90 1.00
First day cover 1.50
Inscription block of 4 3.75 —
330 A310 1.10fr **multicolored** *(375,000)+* 1.20 1.30
First day cover 2.25
First day cover, #329-330 5.00
Inscription block of 4 5.25 —

Souvenir Booklet

331 Booklet *(100,000)+* 21.50
a.-c. A310 10c any single .55 .55
d.-f. A310 30c any single 1.65 1.65
g. Booklet pane of 4 #331a 2.20 2.20
h. Booklet pane of 3 #331d 5.00 5.00
i. Booklet pane of 3 #331e 5.00 5.00
j. Booklet pane of 3 #331f 5.00 5.00
k. Booklet pane of 4 #331b 2.20 2.20
l. Booklet pane of 4 #331c 2.20 2.20

Palais Wilson, Geneva — G62

Designed and printed by Helio Courvoisier, SA, Switzerland.

1999, Feb. 5 Photo. *Perf. 11½*

Granite Paper

332 G62 1.70fr **brown red** *(600,000)+* 1.75 1.90
First day cover *(25,568)* 3.50
Inscription block of 4 8.50 —

World Heritage, Australia Type

Designs: 90c, No. 335e, Kakadu Natl. Park. 1.10fr, No. 335c, Great Barrier Reef. No. 335a, Tasmanian Wilderness. No. 335b, Wet tropics of Queensland. No. 335d, Uluru-Kata Tjuta Natl. Park. No. 335f, Willandra Lakes region.

1999, Mar. 19 Litho. *Perf. 13*

333 A313 90c **multicolored** *(420,000)+* 1.25 1.40
First day cover 2.00
Inscription block of 4 5.75 —
334 A313 1.10fr **multicolored** *(420,000)+* 1.50 1.65
First day cover 2.25
First day cover, #333-334 4.50
Inscription block of 4 8.00 —

Souvenir Booklet

335 Booklet *(90,000)+* 16.50
a.-c. A313 10c any single .45 .50
d.-f. A313 20c any single .90 1.00
g. Booklet pane of 4, #335a 1.80 2.00
h. Booklet pane of 4, #335d 3.60 4.00
i. Booklet pane of 4, #335b 1.80 2.00
j. Booklet pane of 4, #335e 3.60 4.00
k. Booklet pane of 4, #335c 1.80 2.00
l. Booklet pane of 4, #335f 3.60 4.00

First day covers of Nos. 333-335 total 44,622.

Endangered Species Type of 1993

Designed by Tim Barrall, US.

Designs: No. 336, Equus hemionus (Asiatic wild ass). No. 337, Anodorhynchus hyacinthinus (hyacinth macaw). No. 338,

Epicrates subflavus (Jamaican boa). No. 339, Dendrolagus bennettianus (Bennetts' tree kangaroo).

1999, Apr. 22 Litho. *Perf. 12½*
336 A271 90c **multicolored** *(488,000)+* 1.00 1.10
337 A271 90c **multicolored** *(488,000)+* 1.00 1.10
338 A271 90c **multicolored** *(488,000)+* 1.00 1.10
339 A271 90c **multicolored** *(488,000)+* 1.00 1.10
a. Block of 4, #336-339 4.00 4.50
First day cover, #339a 5.75
First day cover, #336-339, each 2.00
Inscription block of 4, #339a 4.50 —
Pane of 16 16.00

First day covers of Nos. 336-339 total 52,856.

UNISPACE III Type

Designs: No. 340, Farm, satellite dish. No. 341, City, satellite in orbit. No. 342, Composite of Nos. 340-341.

1999, July 7 Photo. *Rouletted 8*
340 A314 45c **multicolored** *(925,000)+* .90 1.00
341 A314 45c **multicolored** *(925,000)+* .90 1.00
a. Pair, #340-341 2.00 2.20
First day cover, #341a 2.25
First day cover, #340-341, each 14.00
Inscription block of 4 5.00 —
Pane of 10, #340-341 9.50 —

Souvenir Sheet

Perf. 14½
342 A314 2fr **multicolored** *(275,000)+* 4.50 5.00
First day cover 6.00
a. Ovptd. in sheet margin 9.50 10.50
First day cover 19.00

No. 342a is ovptd. in violet blue "PHILEXFRANCE 99 / LE MONDIAL DU TIMBRE / PARIS / 2 AU 11 JUILLET 1999.
First day covers of Nos. 340-342 total 63,412.

UPU Type

Various people, early 20th century methods of mail transportation, denomination at: No. 343, UL. No. 344, UR. No. 345, LL. No. 346, LR.

1999, Aug. 23 Photo. *Perf. 11¾*
343 A315 70c **multicolored** *(336,000)+* .90 1.00
344 A315 70c **multicolored** *(336,000)+* .90 1.00
345 A315 70c **multicolored** *(336,000)+* .90 1.00
346 A315 70c **multicolored** *(336,000)+* .90 1.00
a. Block of 4, #343-346 3.60 4.00
First day cover, #346a 3.50
First day cover, #343-346, each 1.50
Inscription block of 4, #346a 3.75 —

First day covers of Nos. 343-346 total 27,041.

In Memoriam Type

Designs: 1.10fr, 2fr, Armillary sphere, Palais de Nations. Size of 2fr stamp: 34x63mm.

1999, Sept. 21 Litho. *Perf. 14½x14*
347 A316 1.10fr **multicolored** *(400,000)+* 1.25 1.40
First day cover 3.00
Inscription block of 4 5.50 —

Souvenir Sheet

Perf. 14
348 A316 2fr **multicolored** *(225,000)+* 3.00 3.25
First day cover 3.50

First day covers of Nos. 347-348 total 46,527.

Education Type

90c, Rainbow over globe. 1.80fr, Fish, tree, globe, book.

1999, Nov. 18 Litho. *Perf. 13½x13¾*
349 A317 90c Rainbow over globe *(350,000)+* .75 .80
First day cover 1.75
Inscription block of 4 3.25 —
350 A317 1.80fr Fish, tree, globe, book *(370,000)+* 1.75 1.90
First day cover 3.50
First day cover, #349-350 4.50
Inscription block of 4 7.25 —

First day covers of Nos. 349-350 total 37,925.

Intl. Year Of Thanksgiving Type

2000, Jan 1 Litho. *Perf. 13¼x13½*
351 A318 90c **multicolored** *(450,000)+* 1.00 1.10
First day cover 3.00
Inscription block of 4 4.50 —

On No. 351 portions of the design were applied by a thermographic process producing a shiny, raised effect.

Endangered Species Type of 1993

Designed by Robert Hynes, US.
Designs: No. 352, Hippopotamus amphibius (hippopotamus). No. 353, Coscoroba coscoroba (Coscoroba swan). No. 354, Varanus prasinus (emerald monitor). No. 355, Enhydra lutris (sea otter).

2000, Apr. 6 Litho. *Perf. 12¾x12½*
352 A271 90c **multicolored** *(488,000)+* 1.25 1.40
353 A271 90c **multicolored** *(488,000)+* 1.25 1.40
354 A271 90c **multicolored** *(488,000)+* 1.25 1.40
355 A271 90c **multicolored** *(488,000)+* 1.25 1.40
a. Block of 4, #352-355 5.00 5.75
First day cover, #355a 5.00
First day cover, #352-355, each 1.90
Inscription block of 4, #355a 5.25 —
Pane of 16 20.00

Our World 2000 Type

Winning artwork in Millennium painting competition: 90c, The Embrace, by Rita Adaimy, Lebanon. 1.10fr, Living Single, by Richard Kimanthi, Kenya, vert.

2000, May 30 Litho. *Perf. 13x13½, 13½x13*
356 A319 90c **multicolored** *(330,000)+* 1.00 1.10
First day cover 1.75
Inscription block of 4 4.00 —
357 A319 1.10fr **multicolored** *(330,000)+* 1.25 1.40
First day cover 2.25
First day cover, #356-357 3.50
Inscription block of 4 5.00 —

55th Anniversary Type

Designs: 90c, Trygve Lie, Harry S Truman, workers at cornerstone dedication ceremony, 1949. 1.40fr, Window cleaner on Secretariat Building, General Assembly Hall under construction, 1951.

2000, July 7 Litho. *Perf. 13¼x13*
358 A320 90c **multicolored** *(370,000)+* 1.00 1.10
First day cover 1.75
Inscription block of 4 4.00 —
359 A320 1.40fr **multicolored** *(370,000)+* 1.50 1.65
First day cover 2.60
First day cover, #358-359 3.75
Inscription block of 4 6.00 —

Souvenir Sheet

360 A320 Sheet of 2, #358-359 *(235,000)+* 3.50 3.75
First day cover 3.25

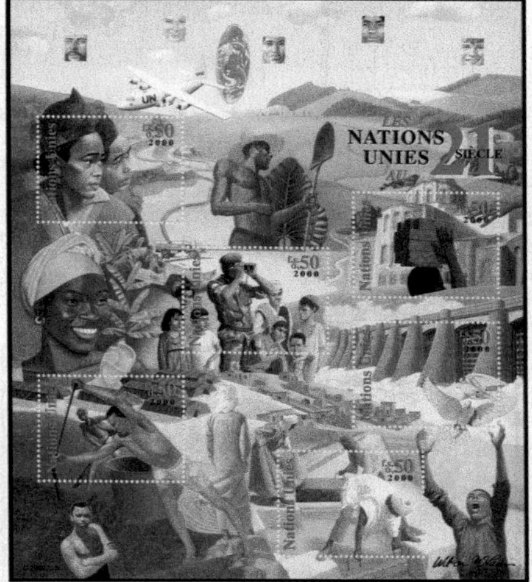

The UN in the 21st Century — G63

Printed by Government Printing Office, Austria. Designed by Wilson McLean, UK.

No. 361: a, Two people, terraced rice paddy. b, Man carrying bricks on head. c, UN Peacekeeper with binoculars. d, Dam, doves. e, Men with shovels. f, People working on irrigation system.

2000, Sept. 15 Litho. *Perf. 14*
361 G63 Pane of 6 *(266,000)+* 9.00 10.00
First day cover 7.50
a.-f. 50c any single 1.50 1.65
First day covers, each 5.00

World Heritage, Spain Type

Designs: Nos. 362, 364b, Walled Town of Cuenca. Nos. 363, 364e, Toledo. No. 364a, Alhambra, Generalife and Albayzin, Granada. No. 364c, Aqueduct of Segovia. No. 364d, Amphitheater of Mérida. No. 364f, Güell Park, Barcelona.

2000, Oct. 6 Litho. *Perf. 14¾x14½*
362 A323 1fr **multicolored** *(340,000)+* 1.40 1.50
First day cover 1.90
Inscription block of 4 5.75 —
363 A323 1.20fr **multicolored** *(340,000)+* 1.60 1.75
First day cover 2.25
First day cover, #362-363 3.50
Inscription block of 4 6.50 —

Souvenir Booklet

364 Booklet *(64,000)+* 11.00
a.-c. A323 10c any single .30 .35
d.-f. A323 20c any single .60 .65
g. Booklet pane of 4, #364a 1.20 1.40
h. Booklet pane of 4, #364d 2.40 2.60
i. Booklet pane of 4, #364b 1.20 1.40
j. Booklet pane of 4, #364e 2.40 2.60
k. Booklet pane of 4, #364c 1.20 1.40
l. Booklet pane of 4, #364f 2.40 2.60

Respect for Refugees Type

Designs: 80c, 1.80fr, Refugee with cane, four other refugees.

2000, Nov. 9 Litho. *Perf. 13¼x12¾*
365 A324 80c **multicolored** *(400,000)+* 1.25 1.40
First day cover 1.75
Inscription block of 4 4.50 —

Souvenir Sheet

366 A324 1.80fr **multicolored** *(215,000)+* 2.50 2.75
First day cover 3.00

Endangered Species Type of 1993

Printed by Johann Enschedé and Sons, the Netherlands. Designed by Higgins Bond, US.
Designs: No. 367, Felis lynx canadensis (North American lynx). No. 368, Pavo muticus (green peafowl). No. 369, Geochelone elephantopus (Galapagos giant tortoise). No. 370, Lepilemur spp. (sportive lemur).

2001, Feb. 1 Litho. *Perf. 12¾x12½*
367 A271 90c **multicolored** *(448,000)+* 1.25 1.40
368 A271 90c **multicolored** *(448,000)+* 1.25 1.40
369 A271 90c **multicolored** *(448,000)+* 1.25 1.40
370 A271 90c **multicolored** *(448,000)+* 1.25 1.40
a. Block of 4, #367-370 5.00 5.75
First day cover, #370a 5.50
First day cover, #367-370 each 1.90
Inscription block of 4, #370a 5.25 —
Pane of 16 20.00

Intl. Volunteers Year — G64

Printed by Johann Enschedé and Sons, the Netherlands. Panes of 20. Designed by Rorie Katz and Robert Stein, US.
Paintings by: 90c, Ernest Pignon-Ernest, France. 1.30fr, Paul Siché, France.

2001, Mar. 29 Litho. *Perf. 13¼*
371 G64 90c **multicolored** *(350,000)+* 1.10 1.20
First day cover 1.75
Inscription block of 4 4.50
372 G64 1.30fr **multicolored** *(340,000)+* 1.60 1.75
First day cover 2.40
First day cover, #371-372 3.50
Inscription block of 4 6.50

World Heritage, Japan Type

Designs: 1.10fr, No. 375b, Nara. 1.30fr, No. 375e, Itsukushima Shinto Shrine. No. 375a, Kyoto. No. 375c, Himeji-Jo. No. 375d, Shirakawa-Go and Gokayama. No. 375f, Nikko.

2001, Aug. 1 Litho. *Perf. 12¾x13¼*
373 A328 1.10fr **multicolored** *(350,000)+* 1.30 1.40
First day cover 2.00
Inscription block of 4 5.75 —
374 A328 1.30fr **multicolored** *(350,000)+* 1.50 1.65
First day cover 2.40
First day cover, #373-374 3.75
Inscription block of 4 6.50 —

Souvenir Booklet

375 Booklet *(52,000)+* 15.00
a.-c. A328 10c any single .50 .55
d.-f. A328 30c any single .75 .80
g. Booklet pane of 4, #375a 2.00 2.20
h. Booklet pane of 4, #375d 3.00 3.20
i. Booklet pane of 4, #375b 2.00 2.20
j. Booklet pane of 4, #375e 3.00 3.20
k. Booklet pane of 4, #375c 2.00 2.20
l. Booklet pane of 4, #375f 3.00 3.20

Dag Hammarskjöld Type

2001, Sept. 18 Engr. *Perf. 11x11¼*
376 A329 2fr **carmine lake** *(380,000)+* 2.50 2.75
First day cover 3.25
Inscription block of 4 10.00 —

UN Postal Administration, 50th Anniv. Types

2001, Oct. 18 Litho. *Perf. 13½*
377 A330 90c Stamps, globe *(310,000)+* 1.00 1.10
First day cover 1.60
Inscription block of 4 4.25 —
378 A330 1.30fr Stamps, horns *(310,000)+* 1.75 1.90
First day cover 2.40
First day cover, #377-378 3.50
Inscription block of 4 8.00 —

Souvenir Sheet

379 A331 Sheet of 2 *(175,000)+* 12.50 13.50
a. 1.30fr **red & light blue,** 38mm diameter 5.00 5.50
b. 1.80fr **red & light blue,** 38mm diameter 7.50 8.00
First day cover 8.00

Climate Change Type

Designs: No. 380, Lizard, flowers, shoreline. No. 381, Windmills, construction workers. No. 382, Non-polluting factory. No. 383, Solar oven, city, village, picnickers.

2001, Nov. 16 **Litho.** ***Perf. 13¼***

380 A332 90c **multicolored** *(73,500)+* 1.10 1.20
381 A332 90c **multicolored** *(73,500)+* 1.10 1.20
382 A332 90c **multicolored** *(73,500)+* 1.10 1.20
383 A332 90c **multicolored** *(73,500)+* 1.10 1.20
a. Horiz. strip, #380-383 4.50 5.00
Inscription block of 8 9.00 —
First day cover, #383a 5.25
First day covers, #380-383, each 6.00
Pane of 24 26.00 —

Nobel Peace Prize Type

2001, Dec. 10 **Litho.** ***Perf. 13¼***

384 A333 90c **multicolored** *(840,000)+* 1.10 1.20
Inscription block of 4 4.50 —
First day cover 1.75
Pane of 12 13.50 —

Palais des Nations — G65

Printed by Government Printing Office, Austria. Panes of 20. Designed by Robert Stein, US.

2002, Mar. 1 **Litho.** ***Perf. 13¾***

385 G65 1.30fr **multicolored** *(630,000)+* 1.40 1.50
First day cover 2.25
Inscription block of 4 5.75 —

Endangered Species Type of 1993

Printed by Johann Enschedé and Sons, the Netherlands. Designed by Lori Anzalone, US.

Designs: No. 386, Cacajao calvus (white uakari). No. 387, Mellivora capensis (honey badger). No. 388, Otocolobus manul (manul). No. 389, Varanus exantematicus (Bosc's monitor).

2002, Apr. 4 **Litho.** ***Perf. 12¾x12½***

386 A271 90c **multicolored** *(420,000)+* 1.50 1.65
387 A271 90c **multicolored** *(420,000)+* 1.50 1.65
388 A271 90c **multicolored** *(420,000)+* 1.50 1.65
389 A271 90c **multicolored** *(420,000)+* 1.50 1.65
a. Block of 4, #386-389 6.00 6.75
First day cover, #389a 5.50
First day cover, #386-389 each 1.90
Inscription block of 4, #389a 6.25 —
Pane of 16 24.00 —

Independence of East Timor Type

Designs: 90c, Wooden statue of male figure. 1.30fr, Carved wooden container.

2002, May 20 **Litho.** ***Perf. 14x14½***

390 A335 90c **multicolored** *(305,000)+* 1.25 1.40
First day cover 1.90
Inscription block of 4 5.00 —
391 A335 1.30fr **multicolored** *(295,000)+* 1.75 1.90
First day cover 2.60
First day cover, #390-391 3.75
Inscription block of 4 7.00 —

Intl. Year of Mountains Type

Designs: No. 392, Weisshorn, Switzerland. No. 393, Mt. Fuji, Japan. No. 394, Vinson Massif, Antarctica. No. 395, Mt. Kamet, India.

2002, May 24 **Litho.** ***Perf. 13x13¼***

392 A336 70c **multicolored** *(1,230,000)+* 1.00 1.10
First day cover 1.40
393 A336 70c **multicolored** *(1,230,000)+* 1.00 1.10
First day cover 1.40
394 A336 1.20fr **multicolored** *(1,230,000)+* 1.75 1.90
First day cover 2.40
First day cover, #392, 394 3.25
395 A336 1.20fr **multicolored** *(1,230,000)+* 1.75 1.90
a. Vert. strip or block of four, #392-395 7.50 8.50
First day cover 2.40
First day cover, #392, 395 3.25
First day cover, #392-395 6.00
Pane of 12, 3 each #392-395 22.50 —

World Summit on Sustainable Development (Peter Max) Type

Designs: No. 396, Sun, birds, flowers, heart. No. 397, Three faceless people, diff. No. 398, Three women, diff. No. 399, Sailboat, mountain.

2002, June 27 **Litho.** ***Perf. 14½x14***

396 A337 90c **multicolored** *(1,215,000)+* 1.25 1.40
First day cover 1.90
397 A337 90c **multicolored** *(1,215,000)+* 1.25 1.40
First day cover 1.90
398 A337 1.80fr **multicolored** *(1,215,000)+* 2.50 2.75
First day cover 3.50
First day cover, #396, 398 4.00
399 A337 1.80fr **multicolored** *(1,215,000)+* 2.50 2.75
a. Vert. strip or block of four, #396-399 9.00 10.00
First day cover 3.50
First day cover, #397, 399 4.00
First day cover, #396-399 8.00
Pane of 12, 3 each #396-399 22.50 —

World Heritage, Italy Type

Designs: 90c, No. 402e, Pisa. 1.30fr, No. 402b, Aeolian Islands. No. 402a, Amalfi Coast. No. 402c, Rome. No. 402d, Florence. No. 402f, Pompeii.

2002, Aug. 30 **Litho.** ***Perf. 13½x13¼***

400 A338 90c **multicolored** *(355,000)+* 1.25 1.40
First day cover 1.90
Inscription block of 4 5.00 —
401 A338 1.30fr **multicolored** *(355,000)+* 2.00 2.20
First day cover 2.75
First day cover, #400-401 4.00
Inscription block of 4 8.25 —

Souvenir Booklet

402 Booklet *(51,000)+* 29.00
a.-c. A338 10c any single .60 .80
d.-f. A338 20c any single 1.75 2.00
g. Booklet pane of 4, #402d 7.00 8.00
h. Booklet pane of 4, #402a 2.40 2.75
i. Booklet pane of 4, #402e 7.00 8.00
j. Booklet pane of 4, #402b 2.40 2.75
k. Booklet pane of 4, #402f 7.00 8.00
l. Booklet pane of 4, #402c 2.40 2.75

AIDS Awareness Type

2002, Oct. 24 **Litho.** ***Perf. 13½***

403 A339 1.30fr **multicolored** *(305,000)+* 2.00 2.20
Inscription block of 4 7.75 —
First day cover, #403 2.60
Pane of 20 40.00 —

Entry of Switzerland into United Nations — G66

Printed by House of Questa, UK. Panes of 20. Designed by Thierry Clauson, Switzerland.

2002, Oct. 24 **Litho.** ***Perf. 14½x14¾***

404 G66 3fr **multicolored** *(580,000)+* 3.50 3.75
Inscription block of 4 14.00 —
First day cover, #404 5.00
Pane of 20 70.00 —

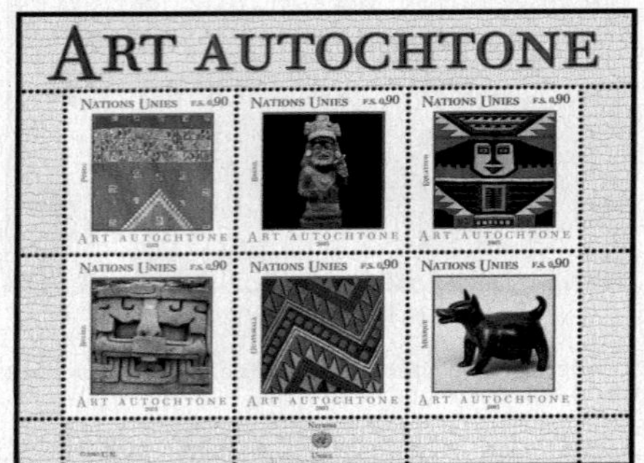

Indigenous Art — G67

Printed by House of Questa, UK.
Designed by Rorie Katz and Robert Stein, US.

No. 405: a, Detail of Inca poncho, Peru. b, Bahia culture seated figure, Brazil. c, Blanket, Ecuador. d, Mayan stone sculpture, Belize. e, Embroidered fabric, Guatemala. f, Colima terra-cotta dog sculpture, Mexico.

2003, Jan. 31 **Litho.** ***Perf. 14¼***

405 G67 Pane of 6 *(168,000)+* 7.50 8.50
First day cover 9.75
a.-f. 90c Any single 1.25 1.35
First day cover, a.-f., each 2.50

New Inter-Parliamentary Union Headquarters, Geneva — G68

Printed by House of Questa, UK. Panes of 20. Designed by Cyril Wursten, Switzerland.

2003, Feb. 20 **Litho.** ***Perf. 14½x14***

406 G68 90c **multicolored** *(480,000)+* 1.75 1.75
Inscription block of 4 7.25 —
First day cover 2.00
Pane of 20 25.00 —

Endangered Species Type of 1993

Printed by Johann Enschedé and Sons, the Netherlands. Designed by James Hautman, US.

Designs: No. 407, Branta ruficollis (red-breasted goose). No. 408, Geronticus calvus (bald ibis). No. 409, Dendrocygna bicolor (fulvous whistling duck). No. 410, Ramphastos vitellinus (channel-billed toucan).

2003, Apr. 3 **Litho.** ***Perf. 12¾x12½***

407 A271 90c **multicolored** *(368,000)+* 1.25 1.25
408 A271 90c **multicolored** *(368,000)+* 1.25 1.25
409 A271 90c **multicolored** *(368,000)+* 1.25 1.25
410 A271 90c **multicolored** *(368,000)+* 1.25 1.25
a. Block of 4, #407-410 5.00 5.00
First day cover, #410a 6.25
First day cover, #407-410 each 2.10
Inscription block of 4, #410a 5.60 —
Pane of 16 22.50 —

International Year of Freshwater Type of 2003

2003, June 20 **Litho.** ***Perf. 14¼x14½***

411 A345 70c Waterfall *(255,000)+* 1.25 1.25
412 A345 1.30fr People, mountain *(255,000)+* 2.25 2.25
a. Horiz. pair, #411-412 5.00 5.00
First day cover, #412a 3.75
Inscription block of 4 10.50 —

Ralph Bunche Type
Litho. With Foil Application

2003, Aug. 7 ***Perf. 13½x14***

413 A346 1.80fr **brown red & multicolored** *(300,000)+* 2.75 2.75
First day cover 3.50
Inscription block of 4 12.50
Pane of 20 55.00

In Memoriam Type of 2003

2003, Oct. 24 **Litho.** ***Perf. 13¼x13***

414 A347 85c **multicolored** *(700,000)+* 1.50 1.50
First day cover 2.10
Inscription block of 4 6.00 —
Pane of 20 30.00 —

World Heritage Sites, United States Type

Designs: 90c, No. 417b, Great Smoky Mountains National Park. 1.30fr, No. 417f, Yellowstone National Park. No. 417a, Yosemite National Park. No. 417c, Olympic National Park. No. 417d, Hawaii Volcanoes National Park. No. 417e, Everglades National Park.

2003, Oct. 24 **Litho.** ***Perf. 14½x14¼***

415 A348 90c **multicolored** *(205,000)+* 1.50 1.50
First day cover 2.10
Inscription block of 4 6.25 —
416 A348 1.30fr **multicolored** *(205,000)+* 2.25 2.25
First day cover 3.25
First day cover, #415-416 4.50
Inscription block of 4 9.25 —

Souvenir Booklet

417 Booklet *(39,000)+* 12.00
a.-c. A348 10c any single .30 .30
d.-f. A348 30c any single .65 .65
g. Booklet pane of 4 #417a 1.20 1.20
h. Booklet pane of 4 #417d 2.60 2.60
i. Booklet pane of 4 #417b 1.20 1.20
j. Booklet pane of 4 #417e 2.60 2.60
k. Booklet pane of 4 #417c 1.20 1.20
l. Booklet pane of 4 #417f 2.60 2.60

Endangered Species Type of 1993

Printed by Johann Enschedé and Sons, the Netherlands. Designed by Yuan Lee, US.

Designs: No. 418, Ursus thibetanus (Asiatic black bear). No. 419, Hippocamelus antisensis (Northern Andean deer). No. 420, Macaca silenus (Lion-tailed macaque). No. 421, Bos gaurus (Gaur).

2004, Jan. 29 **Litho.** ***Perf. 12¾x12½***

418 A271 1fr **multicolored** *(300,000)+* 1.60 1.60
419 A271 1fr **multicolored** *(300,000)+* 1.60 1.60
420 A271 1fr **multicolored** *(300,000)+* 1.60 1.60
421 A271 1fr **multicolored** *(300,000)+* 1.60 1.60
a. Block of 4, #418-421 6.50 6.50
First day cover, #421a 7.50
First day cover, #418-421, each 2.50
Inscription block of 4, #421a 7.50 —
Pane of 16 27.50 —

Indigenous Art Type of 2003

Printed by Johann Enschedé and Sons, the Netherlands.
Designed by Rorie Katz and Robert Stein, US.

No. 422: a, Decoration for cows, Switzerland. b, Stone Age terra cotta sculpture of seated woman, Romania. c, Butter stamps, France. d, Detail of herald's tabard, United Kingdom. e, Woodcut print of medieval Cologne, Germany. f, Mesolithic era terra cotta sculpture of mother and child, Serbia and Montenegro.

2004, Mar. 4 **Litho.** ***Perf. 13¼***

422 G67 Sheet of 6 *(102,000)+* 7.50 7.50
First day cover 12.00
a.-f. 1fr Any single 1.25 1.25

Road Safety Type

Road map art with: 85c, Man on hand. 1fr, Person, seat belt, vert.

2004, Apr. 7 Litho. *Perf. 13x13¼, 13¼x13*

423 A354 85c **multicolored** *(185,000)+* 1.40 1.40
First day cover 2.10
Inscription block of 4 6.00 —
424 A354 1fr **multicolored** *(185,000)+* 1.75 1.75
First day cover 2.50
First day cover, #423-424 4.00
Inscription block of 4 7.25 —

See France No. 3011.

Japanese Peace Bell, 50th Anniv. Type

2004, June 3 Litho. & Engr. *Perf. 13¼x13*

425 A355 1.30fr **multicolored** *(230,000)+* 2.00 2.00
First day cover 3.00
Inscription block of 4 8.50 —
Pane of 20 45.00

World Heritage Sites, Greece Type

Designs: 1fr, No. 428b, Delphi. 1.30fr, No. 428e, Pythagoreion and Heraion of Samos. No. 428a, Acropolis, Athens. No. 428c, Olympia. No. 428d, Delos. No. 428f, Mycenae and Tiryns.

2004, Aug. 12 Litho. *Perf. 14x13¼*

426 A356 1fr **multicolored** *(180,000)+* 1.50 1.50
First day cover 2.25
Inscription block of 4 6.50 —
427 A356 1.30fr **multicolored** *(180,000)+* 2.00 2.00
First day cover 3.00
First day cover, #426-427 4.50
Inscription block of 4 8.50 —

Souvenir Booklet

428 Booklet *(33,000)+* 13.50
a.-c. A356 20c any single .30 .30
d.-f. A356 50c any single .80 .80
g. Booklet pane of 4 #428a 1.25 1.25
h. Booklet pane of 4 #428b 1.25 1.25
i. Booklet pane of 4 #428c 1.25 1.25
j. Booklet pane of 4 #428d 3.25 3.25
k. Booklet pane of 4 #428e 3.25 3.25
l. Booklet pane of 4 #428f 3.25 3.25

My Dream for Peace Type

Winning designs of Lions Club International children's global peace poster contest by: 85c, Anggun Sita Rustinya, Indonesia. 1.20fr, Amanda Nunez, Belize.

2004, Sept. 21 Litho. *Perf. 14*

429 A357 85c **multicolored** *(195,000)+* 1.40 1.40
First day cover 1.90
Inscription block of 4 5.75
Pane of 20 28.00
430 A357 1.20fr **multicolored** *(195,000)+* 2.00 2.00
First day cover 2.75
First day cover, #429-430 4.00
Inscription block of 4 8.25
Pane of 20 40.00

G69

Human Rights — G70

Printed by Banknote Corporation of America, US. Designed by Yuri Gervorgian, Armenia. Panes of 8.

2004, Oct. 14 Litho. *Perf. 11¼*

431 G69 85c **multicolored** *(408,000)+* 1.25 1.25
First day cover 2.10
Pane of 8 10.00 —
432 G70 1.30fr **multicolored** *(408,000)+* 2.25 2.25
First day cover 3.25
First day cover, #431-432 4.50
Pane of 8 18.00 —

Sports — G71

Printed by Cartor Security Printing, France. Designed by Roland Hirter, Switzerland. Panes of 20.

2004, Nov. 23 Litho. *Perf. 13x13½*

433 G71 180c **multicolored** *(216,000)+* 3.25 3.25
First day cover 4.00
Inscription block of 4 13.00 —
Pane of 20 65.00 —

See Switzerland No. 1196.

United Nations, 60th Anniv. Type of 2005

Printed by Banknote Corporation of America, US. Designed by Czeslaw Slania, Sweden.

2005, Feb. 4 Litho. & Engr. *Perf. 11x11¼*

434 A361 1.30fr **multicolored** *(270,000)+* 2.50 2.50
First day cover 3.50
Inscription block of 4 10.00 —
Pane of 20 50.00 —

Souvenir Sheet

Litho.

Imperf

435 A361 3fr **multicolored** *(125,000)+* 7.50 7.50
First day cover 6.75

Endangered Species Type of 1993

Printed by Johann Enschedé and Sons, the Netherlands. Designed by Boris Zlotsky, US.

Designs: No. 436, Laelia milleri. No. 437, Psygmorchis pusilla. No. 438, Dendrobium cruentum. No. 439, Orchis purpurea.

2005, Mar. 3 Litho. *Perf. 12¾x12½*

436 A271 1fr **multicolored** *(248,000)+* 2.00 2.00
437 A271 1fr **multicolored** *(248,000)+* 2.00 2.00
438 A271 1fr **multicolored** *(248,000)+* 2.00 2.00
439 A271 1fr **multicolored** *(248,000)+* 2.00 2.00
a. Block of 4, #436-439 8.00 8.00
First day cover, #439a 8.75
First day cover, #436-439, each 3.00
Inscription block of 4, #439a 8.75 —
Pane of 16 32.50

Nature's Wisdom — G72

Printed by Cartor Security Printing, France. Panes of 20. Designed by Robert Stein, US.

Designs: 1fr, Children collecting water, India. 80c, Ruby brittle star, Bahamas.

2005, Apr. 21 Litho. *Perf. 13½x13¼*

440 G72 1fr **multicolored** *(180,000)+* 1.75 1.75
First day cover 2.75
Inscription block of 4 7.25 —
Pane of 20 35.00 —
441 G72 1.30fr **multicolored** *(180,000)+* 2.00 2.00
First day cover 3.75
First day cover, #440-441 5.50
Inscription block of 4 9.25 —
Pane of 20 40.00 —

Intl. Year of Sport Type

Printed by Cartor Security Printing, France. Designed by Roland Hirter, Switzerland.

2005, June 3 Litho. *Perf. 13x13¼*

442 A368 1fr Wheelchair racing *(185,000)+* 1.75 1.75
First day cover 2.75
Inscription block of 4 7.75 —
Pane of 20 35.00 —
443 A368 1.30fr Cycling *(185,000)+* 2.25 2.25
First day cover 3.75
First day cover, #442-443 5.50
Inscription block of 4 9.25 —
Pane of 20 45.00 —

World Heritage Sites, Egypt Type

Printed by Johann Enschedé and Sons, the Netherlands. Panes of 20. Designed by Rorie Katz, US.

Designs: Nos. 444, 446b, Philae. Nos. 445, 446e, Islamic Cairo. No. 446a, Memphis and its Necropolis. No. 446c, Abu Mena. No. 446d, Ancient Thebes. No. 446f, St. Catherine area.

2005, Aug. 4 Litho. *Perf. 14x13¼*

444 A369 1fr **multicolored** *(180,000)+* 2.00 2.00
First day cover 2.75
Inscription block of 4 8.00 —
445 A369 1.30fr **multicolored** *(180,000)+* 2.50 2.50
First day cover 3.75
First day cover, #444-445 5.50
Inscription block of 4 10.00 —

Souvenir Booklet

446 Booklet, #446g-446l *(31,000)+* 16.50
a.-c. A369 20c any single .40 .40
d.-f. A369 50c any single .90 .90
g. Booklet pane of 4 #446a 1.60 1.60
h. Booklet pane of 4 #446b 1.60 1.60
i. Booklet pane of 4 #446c 1.60 1.60
j. Booklet pane of 4 #446d 3.75 3.75
k. Booklet pane of 4 #446e 3.75 3.75
l. Booklet pane of 4 #446f 3.75 3.75

My Dream for Peace Type

Winning designs of Lions Club International children's global peace poster contest by: 1fr, Marisa Harun, Indonesia. 1.30fr, Carlos Javier Parramón Teixidó, Spain.

2005, Sept. 21 Litho. *Perf. 14*

447 A357 1fr **multicolored** *(175,000)+* 1.75 1.75
First day cover 2.60
Inscription block of 4 7.25
Pane of 20 35.00
448 A357 1.30fr **multicolored** *(175,000)+* 2.00 2.00
First day cover 3.50
First day cover, #447-448 5.00
Inscription block of 4 8.25
Pane of 20 40.00

Food for Life Type

Printed by Government Printing Office, Austria. Designed by Andrew Davidson, United Kingdom.

Designs: 1fr, Rye, airplane dropping parcels, camel caravan. 1.30fr, Sorghum, people carrying grain sacks, trucks.

2005, Oct. 20 Litho. *Perf. 13¾*

449 A370 1fr **multicolored** *(170,000)+* 1.90 1.90
First day cover 2.60
Inscription block of 4 7.75 —
Pane of 20 38.00 —
450 A370 1.30fr **multicolored** *(170,000)+* 2.40 2.40
First day cover 3.50
First day cover, #449-450 5.00
Inscription block of 4 9.75 —
Pane of 20 48.00 —

Armillary Sphere, Palais des Nations — G73

Printed by Cartor Security Printing, France. Panes of 20. Designed by Rorie Katz, United States.

Litho. with Hologram

2006, Feb. 3 *Perf. 13¼x13½*

451 G73 1.30fr **multicolored** *(280,000)+* 2.25 2.25
First day cover 3.25
Inscription block of 4 9.00 —
Pane of 20 45.00 —

Indigenous Art Type of 2003

Printed by Johann Enschedé and Sons, the Netherlands. Designed by Robert Stein, US.

No. 452 — Musical instruments: a, Bell, Benin. b, Drum, Swaziland. c, Sanza, Congo. d, Stringed instruments, Cape Verde. e, Caixixi, Ghana. f, Bells, Central Africa.

2006, Feb. 3 **Litho.** ***Perf. 13¼***
452 G67 Pane of 6 *(91,000)+* 12.00 12.00
First day cover 14.00
a.-f. 1.20fr Any single 2.00 2.00

Endangered Species Type of 1993

Printed by Johann Enschedé and Sons, the Netherlands. Designed by John D. Dawson, US.

Designs: No. 453, Dyscophus antongilii. No. 454, Chamaeleo dilepsis. No. 455, Corallus caninus. No. 456, Phyllobates vittatus.

2006, Mar. 16 **Litho.** ***Perf. 12¾x12½***
453 A271 1fr **multicolored** *(228,000)+* 1.75 1.75
454 A271 1fr **multicolored** *(228,000)+* 1.75 1.75
455 A271 1fr **multicolored** *(228,000)+* 1.75 1.75
456 A271 1fr **multicolored** *(228,000)+* 1.75 1.75
a. Block of 4, #453-456 7.00 7.00
First day cover, #456a 7.75
First day cover, #453-456, each 2.60
Inscription block of 4, #456a 7.00 —
Pane of 16 28.00

Intl. Day of Families Type

Printed by Johann Enschedé and Sons, the Netherlands. Designed by Shelly Bartek, US.
Designs: 1fr, Family reading together. 1.30fr, Family on motorcycle.

2006, May 27 **Litho.** ***Perf. 14x13½***
457 A373 1fr **multicolored** *(150,000)+* 1.25 1.25
First day cover 2.50
Inscription block of 4 5.00 —
Pane of 20 25.00 —
458 A373 1.30fr **multicolored** *(150,000)+* 1.75 1.75
First day cover 3.25
First day cover, #457-458 5.00
Inscription block of 4 7.00 —
Pane of 20 35.00 —

World Heritage Sites, France Type

Printed by Cartor Security Printing, France. Panes of 20. Designed by Robert Stein, US.
Eiffel Tower and: Nos. 459, 461b, Provins. Nos. 460, 461e, Mont Saint-Michel. No. 461a, Banks of the Seine. No. 461c, Carcasonne. No. 461d, Roman Aqueduct. No. 446f, Chateau de Chambord.

Litho. & Embossed with Foil Application

2006, June 17 ***Perf. 13½x13¼***
459 A374 1fr **multicolored** *(280,000)+* 1.75 1.75
First day cover 2.50
Inscription block of 4 7.00 —
460 A374 1.30fr **multicolored** *(280,000)+* 2.25 2.25
First day cover 3.25
First day cover, #444-445 5.00
Inscription block of 4 9.00 —

Souvenir Booklet

461 Booklet, #461g-461l *(29,000)+* 15.00
a.-c. A374 20c any single .35 .35
d.-f. A374 50c any single .85 .85
g. Booklet pane of 4 #461a 1.40 1.40
h. Booklet pane of 4 #461b 1.40 1.40
i. Booklet pane of 4 #461c 1.40 1.40
j. Booklet pane of 4 #461d 3.50 3.50
k. Booklet pane of 4 #461e 3.50 3.50
l. Booklet pane of 4 #461f 3.50 3.50

See France Nos. 3219-3220.

My Dream for Peace Type of 2004

Printed by Cartor Security Printing, France. Panes of 20.
Winning designs of Lions Club International children's global peace poster contest by: 85c, Ariam Boaglio, Italy. 1.20fr, Sierra Spicer, US.

2006, Sept. 21 **Litho.** ***Perf. 13½x13***
462 A357 85c **multicolored** *(160,000)+* 1.60 1.60
First day cover 2.40
Inscription block of 4 6.40 —
Pane of 20 32.00 —
463 A357 1.20fr **multicolored** *(160,000)+* 2.25 2.25
First day cover 3.25
First day cover, #462-463 4.75
Inscription block of 4 9.00 —
Pane of 20 45.00 —

Flags and Coins Type

Printed by Cartor Security Printing, France. Designed by Rorie Katz, US.
No. 464 — Flag of: a, Uganda, 500 shilling coin. b, Luxembourg, 1 euro coin. c, Cape Verde, 20 escudo coin. d, Belgium, 1 euro coin. e, Italy, 1 euro coin. f, New Zealand, 1 dollar coin. g, Switzerland, 2 franc coin. h, Lebanon, 500 pound coin.

2006, Oct. 5 **Litho.** ***Perf. 13¼x13***
464 Pane of 8 15.00 15.00
a.-h. A375 85c Any single 1.50 1.50
First day cover 14.50
First day cover, #464a-464h, each 5.00

A column of rouletting in the middle of the pane separates it into two parts.

Endangered Species Type of 1993

Printed by Johann Enschedé and Sons, the Netherlands. Designed by John Rowe, US.
Designs: No. 465, Theropithecus gelada. No. 466, Cercopithecus neglectus. No. 467, Varecia variegata. No. 468, Hylobates moloch.

2007, Mar. 15 **Litho.** ***Perf. 12¾x12½***
465 A271 1fr **multicolored** *(208,000)+* 1.75 1.75
466 A271 1fr **multicolored** *(208,000)+* 1.75 1.75
467 A271 1fr **multicolored** *(208,000)+* 1.75 1.75
468 A271 1fr **multicolored** *(208,000)+* 1.75 1.75
a. Block of 4, #465-468 7.00 7.00
First day cover, #468a 8.25
First day cover, #465-468, each 2.75
Inscription block of 4, #468a 7.00 —
Pane of 16 28.00 —

Flags and Coins Type of 2006

Printed by Cartor Security Printing, France. Designed by Rorie Katz, US.
No. 469 — Flag of: a, Burkina Faso, 500 franc coin. b, France, 50 cent coin. c, Moldova, 50 bani coin. d, Papua New Guinea, 1 kina coin. e, Bolivia, 1 boliviano coin. f, Myanmar, 100 kyat coin. g, Mali, 500 franc coin. h, Tunisia, 5 dinar coin.

2007, May 3 **Litho.** ***Perf. 13¼x13***
469 Sheet of 8 *(125,000)+* 12.50 12.50
a.-h. A375 85c Any single 1.50 1.50
First day cover 14.50
First day cover, #469a-469h, each 2.50

A column of rouletting in the middle of the sheet separates it into two parts.

Peaceful Visions Type of 2007

Printed by Lowe-Martin Company, Canada. Designed by Slavka Kolesar, Canada. Panes of 20.
Designs: 1.20fr, "Harvest for All." 1.80fr, "This Dream Has Wings."

2007, June 1 **Litho.** ***Perf. 13x12½***
470 A378 1.20fr **multicolored** *(156,000)+* 2.25 2.25
First day cover 3.00
Inscription block of 4 9.00 —
Pane of 20 45.00 —
471 A378 1.80fr **multicolored** *(156,000)+* 3.25 3.25
First day cover 4.50
First day cover, #470-471 6.50
Inscription block of 4 13.00 —
Pane of 20 65.00 —

World Heritage Sites, South America Type

Printed by Lowe-Martin Group, Canada. Panes of 20. Designed by Rorie Katz, US.
Designs: Nos. 472, 474a, Tiwanaku, Bolivia. Nos. 473, 474f, Machu Picchu, Peru. No. 474b, Iguaçu National Park, Brazil. No. 474c, Galapagos Islands, Ecuador. No. 474d, Rapa Nui, Chile. No. 474e, Cueva de las Manos, Argentina.

2007, Aug. 9 **Litho.** ***Perf. 13¼x13***
472 A381 1fr **multicolored** *(150,000)+* 1.90 1.90
First day cover 2.50
Inscription block of 4 7.60 —
473 A381 1.80fr **multicolored** *(150,000)+* 3.25 3.25
First day cover 4.50
First day cover, #472-473 6.00
Inscription block of 4 13.00 —

Souvenir Booklet

474 Booklet, #474g-474l *(27,000)+* 16.00
a.-c. A381 20c Any single .40 .40
d.-f. A381 50c Any single .90 .90
g. Booklet pane of 4 #474a 1.60 1.60
h. Booklet pane of 4 #474b 1.60 1.60
i. Booklet pane of 4 #474c 1.60 1.60
j. Booklet pane of 4 #474d 3.60 3.60
k. Booklet pane of 4 #474e 3.60 3.60
l. Booklet pane of 4 #474f 3.60 3.60

Humanitarian Mail Type

Printed by Lowe-Martin Group, Canada. Panes of 10.

2007, Sept. 6 **Litho.** ***Perf. 12½x13¼***
475 A382 1.80fr **multicolored** *(320,000)+* 3.00 3.00
First day cover 4.25
Inscription block of 4 12.00 —
Pane of 10 30.00 —

Space for Humanity Type

Printed by Johann Enschedé and Sons, the Netherlands. Panes of 6. Designed by Donato Giancola, US.
Designs: 1fr, Astronaut spacewalking. 1.80fr, International Space Station, space probe, Jupiter.
3fr, Astronauts spacewalking.

2007, Oct. 25 **Litho.** ***Perf. 13½x14***
476 A383 1fr **multicolored** *(252,000)+* 1.90 1.90
First day cover 2.50
Inscription block of 4 7.60 —
Pane of 6 11.40 —
477 A383 1.80fr **multicolored** *(252,000)+* 3.25 3.25
First day cover 4.50
First day cover, #476-477 6.00
Inscription block of 4 13.00 —
Pane of 6 19.50 —

Souvenir Sheet

478 A383 3fr **multicolored** *(110,000)+* 7.50 7.50
First day cover 6.50

Intl. Holocaust Remembrance Day Type

Printed by Lowe-Martin Company, Canada. Panes of 9. Designed by Matías Delfino, Argentina.

2008, Jan. 27 **Litho.** ***Perf. 13***
479 A384 85c **multicolored** *(495,000)+* 3.00 3.00
First day cover 2.75
Pane of 9 27.00 —

Endangered Species Type of 1993

Printed by Johann Enschedé and Sons, the Netherlands. Designed by Suzanne Duranceau, Canada.
Designs: No. 480, Odobenus rosmarus. No. 481, Platygyra daedalea. No. 482, Hippocampus bargibanti. No. 483, Delphinapterus leucas.

2008, Mar. 6 **Litho.** ***Perf. 12¾x12½***
480 A271 1fr **multicolored** *(172,000)+* 2.00 2.00
481 A271 1fr **multicolored** *(172,000)+* 2.00 2.00
482 A271 1fr **multicolored** *(172,000)+* 2.00 2.00
483 A271 1fr **multicolored** *(172,000)+* 2.00 2.00
a. Block of 4, #480-483 8.00 8.00
First day cover, #483a 9.00
First day cover, #480-483, each 3.00
Inscription block of 4, #483a 8.00 —
Pane of 16 32.00 —

Flags and Coins Type of 2006

Printed by Cartor Security Printing, France. Designed by Rorie Katz, US.
No. 484 — Flag of: a, Madagascar, 1 ariary coin. b, Rwanda, 50 franc coin. c, Benin, 10 franc coin. d, Iran, 500 rial coin. e, Namibia, 5 dollar coin. f, Maldives, 1 rufiyaa coin. g, Albania, 10 lek coin. h, Turkey, 1 lira coin.

2008, May 8 **Litho.** ***Perf. 13¼x13***
484 Sheet of 8 *(100,000)+* 15.00 15.00
a.-h. A375 85c Any single 1.75 1.75
First day cover 17.00
First day cover, #484a-484h 3.50

A column of rouletting in the middle of the sheet separates it into two parts.

Handshake — G74

Sign Language — G75

Printed by Johann Enschedé and Sons, the Netherlands. Panes of 20. Designed by Rorie Katz, US.

2008, June 6 **Litho. & Embossed** ***Perf. 14x13¼***
485 G74 1fr **orange & red** *(142,000)+* 2.25 2.25
First day cover 3.00
Inscription block of 4 9.00 —
Sheet of 20 45.00 —
486 G75 1.80fr **red & orange** *(142,000)+* 4.00 4.00
First day cover 5.25
First day cover, #485-486 7.25
Inscription block of 4 16.00 —
Sheet of 20 80.00 —

Convention on the Rights of Persons with Disabilities.

Sport for Peace Type of 2008

Printed by Johann Enschedé and Sons, the Netherlands. Panes of 9 (Nos. 487-488). Designed by Romero Britto, Brazil.
Designs: 1fr, 3fr, Gymnast. 1.80fr, Tennis player.

2008, Aug. 8 **Litho.** ***Perf. 14½***
487 A393 1fr **multicolored** *(330,030)+* 2.25 2.25
First day cover 3.00
Inscription block of 4 9.00 —
Pane of 9 21.00 —
488 A393 1.80fr **multicolored** *(330,030)+* 4.00 4.00
First day cover 5.00
First day cover, #487-488 7.00
Inscription block of 4 16.00 —
Pane of 9 36.00 —

Souvenir Sheet

Perf. 12¾x13¼

489 A393 3fr **multicolored** *(160,000)+* 9.00 9.00
First day cover 7.50

2008 Summer Olympics, Beijing.

"We Can End Poverty" Type of 2008

Printed by Sweden Post, Sweden. Panes of 20.
Winning designs in children's art contest by: 1fr, Ranajoy Banerjee, India, vert. 1.80fr, Elizabeth Elaine Chun Nig Au, Hong Kong, vert.

2008, Sept. 18 Litho. *Perf. 12½x12¾*
490 A395 1fr **multicolored** *(130,000)+* 2.25 2.25
First day cover 3.00
Inscription block of 4 9.00 —
Sheet of 20 45.00 —
491 A395 1.80fr **multicolored** *(130,000)+* 3.75 3.75
First day cover 5.00
First day cover, #490-491 7.00
Inscription block of 4 15.00 —
Sheet of 20 75.00 —

Climate Change Types of New York and Vienna and

G76

Climate Change — G77

Printed by Lowe-Martin Group, Canada. Panes of 4. Designed by Rorie Katz, US.
No. 492 — Polar bear with quarter of Earth in: a, LR. b, LL. c, UR. d, UL.
No. 493 — Ship and sea ice with quarter of Earth in: a, LR. b, LL. c, UR. d, UL.
No. 494: a, Like New York #969a. b, Like New York #969b. c, Like New York #969c. d, Like New York #969d. e, Like Geneva #493a. f, Like Geneva #493b. g, Like Geneva #493c. h, Like Geneva #493d. i, Like Vienna #434a. j, Like Vienna #434b. k, Like Vienna #434c. l, Like Vienna #434d. m, Like New York #968a. n, Like New York #968b, o, Like New York #968c, p, Like New York #968d. q, Like Geneva #492a. r, Like Geneva #492b. s, Like Geneva #492c. t, Like Geneva #492d. u, Like Vienna #435a. v, Like Vienna #435b. w, Like Vienna #435c. x, Like Vienna #435d.
All stamps have red panels inscribed "Changement de climat."

2008, Oct. 23 Litho. *Perf. 13¼x13*
492 Sheet of 4 *(100,000)+* 10.50 10.50
a.-d. G76 1.20fr Any single 2.60 2.60
First day cover 11.00
493 Sheet of 4 *(100,000)+* 15.50 15.50
a.-d. G77 1.80fr Any single 3.75 3.75
First day cover 16.50
First day cover, #492-493 27.50

Souvenir Booklet

494 Booklet, #494y-494ad *(22,000)+* 25.00
a.-d. A397 35c Any single .75 .75
e.-h. G77 35c Any single .75 .75
i.-l. V72 35c Any single .75 .75
m.-p. A396 50c Any single 1.00 1.00
q.-t. G76 50c Any single 1.00 1.00
u.-x. V73 50c Any single 1.00 1.00
y. Booklet pane of 4, #494a-494d 3.00 3.00
z. Booklet pane of 4, #494e-494h 3.00 3.00
aa. Booklet pane of 4, #494i-494l 3.00 3.00
ab. Booklet pane of 4, #494m-494p 4.25 4.25
ac. Booklet pane of 4, #494q-494t 4.25 4.25
ad. Booklet pane of 4, #494u-494x 4.25 4.25

U Thant Type of 2009

Printed by Johann Enschedé and Sons, the Netherlands. Panes of 20.

Litho. With Foil Application

2009, Feb. 6 *Perf. 14x13½*
495 A399 1.30fr **red & multi** *(150,000)+* 3.25 3.25
First day cover 3.50
Inscription block of 4 13.00 —
Sheet of 20 65.00 —

Endangered Species Type of 1993

Printed by Johann Enschedé and Sons, the Netherlands. Designed by Roger Kent, United Kingdom.
Designs: No. 496, Maculinea arion. No. 497, Dolomedes plantarius. No. 498, Cerambyx cerdo. No. 499, Coenagrion mercuriale.

2009, Apr. 16 Litho. *Perf. 12¾x12½*
496 A271 1fr **multicolored** *(144,000)+* 1.90 1.90
497 A271 1fr **multicolored** *(144,000)+* 1.90 1.90
498 A271 1fr **multicolored** *(144,000)+* 1.90 1.90
499 A271 1fr **multicolored** *(144,000)+* 1.90 1.90
a. Block of 4, #496-499 7.75 7.75
First day cover, #499a 8.50
First day cover, #496-499, each 2.75
Inscription block of 4, #499a 7.75 —
Pane of 16 31.00 —
b. Pane of 16, imperf. *5,000.*

World Heritage Sites, Germany Type of 2009

Printed by Johann Enschedé and Sons, the Netherlands. Panes of 20. Designed by Grit Fiedler, Germany.
Designs: Nos. 500, 502b, Wartburg Castle. Nos. 501, 502f, Monastic Island of Reichenau. No. 502a, Town Hall and Roland on the Marketplace, Bremen. No. 502c, Palaces and Parks of Potsdam and Berlin. No. 502d, Aachen Cathedral. No. 502e, Luther Memorials in Eisleben and Wittenberg.

2009, May 7 Litho. *Perf. 14x13½*
500 A400 1fr **multicolored** *(155,000)+* 2.25 2.25
First day cover 2.75
Inscription block of 4 9.00 —
501 A400 1.30fr **multicolored** *(155,000)+* 2.75 2.75
First day cover 3.50
First day cover, #500-501 5.50
Inscription block of 4 11.00 —

Souvenir Booklet

502 Booklet, #502g-502l *(22,000)+* 18.00
a.-c. A400 30c any single .55 .55
d.-f. A400 50c any single .90 .90
g. Booklet pane of 4 #502a 2.25 2.25
h. Booklet pane of 4 #502b 2.25 2.25
i. Booklet pane of 4 #502c 2.25 2.25
j. Booklet pane of 4 #502d 3.75 3.75
k. Booklet pane of 4 #502e 3.75 3.75
l. Booklet pane of 4 #502f 3.75 3.75

Economic and Social Council (ECOSOC) Type of 2009

Printed by Sweden Post, Sweden. Panes of 20. Designed by Rorie Katz, US.
Designs: 85c, Improving maternal health. 1.80fr, Access to essential medicines.

2009, Aug. 6 Litho. *Perf. 12¾x12½*
503 A411 85c **multicolored** *(130,000)+* 2.00 2.00
First day cover 2.40
Inscription block of 4 8.00 —
Sheet of 20 40.00 —
504 A411 1.80fr **multicolored** *(130,000)+* 4.00 4.00
First day cover 5.00
First day cover, #503-504 6.50
Inscription block of 4 16.00 —
Sheet of 20 80.00 —

Millennium Development Goals Type of 2009

Miniature Sheet

Printed by Lowe Martin Group, Canada.
Designed by Rorie Katz, US.

No. 505: a, Bowl of hot food. b, Pencil. c, Female symbol. d, Teddy bear. e, Pregnant woman, heart. f, Medicine bottle. g, Stylized tree. h, Conjoined people.

2009, Sept. 25 Litho. *Perf. 13¼*
505 A413 Sheet of 8 *(65,000)+* 18.00 18.00
First day cover 20.00
a.-h. 1.10fr Any single 2.25 2.25

Palais des Nations — G78

Palais des Nations — G79

Flags of United Nations and Switzerland — G80

Meeting Room — G81

Armillary Sphere — G82

2009, Oct. 2 Litho. *Perf. 13¼*
506 G78 1fr **multicolored** + label *6.00 6.00*
a. Perf. 11¼x11 + label *5.00 5.00*
507 G79 1fr **multicolored** + label *6.00 6.00*
a. Perf. 11¼x11 + label *5.00 5.00*
508 G80 1fr **multicolored** + label *6.00 6.00*
a. Perf. 11¼x11 + label *5.00 5.00*
509 G81 1fr **multicolored** + label *6.00 6.00*
a. Perf. 11¼x11 + label *5.00 5.00*
510 G82 1fr **multicolored** + label *6.00 6.00*
a. Perf. 11¼x11 + label *5.00 5.00*
b. Vert. strip of 5, #506-510, + 5 labels *30.00 30.00*
Sheet, 2 #510b *60.00* —
c. Vert. strip of 5, #506a-510a, + 5 labels *25.00 25.00*
Sheet, 2 #510c *50.00* —

United Nations Postal Administration in Geneva, 40th anniv. The full sheets sold for €19.90 or $14.95. Labels could not be personalized. The sheet of No. 510c has "VER. 2" in the lower right selvage.

Miniature Sheet

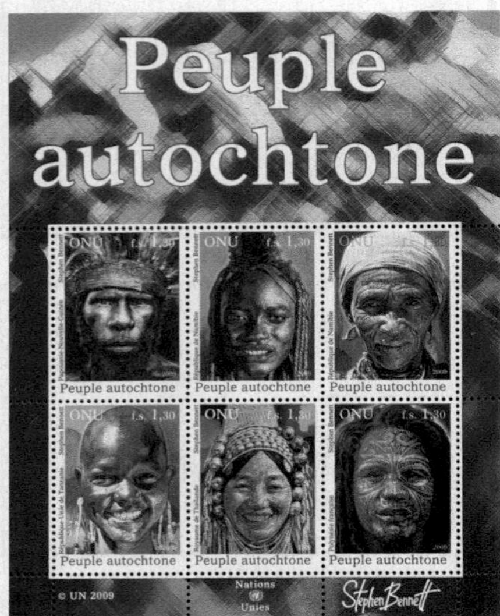

Indigenous People — G83

Printed by Lowe-Martin Group, Canada. Designed by Stephen Bennett, US.

No. 511 — Portraits of person from: a, Papua New Guinea. b, Namibia (young woman). c, Namibia (old man). d, Tanzania. e, Thailand. f, French Polynesia.

2009, Oct. 8 Litho. *Perf. 12½*

511	G83	Sheet of 6 *(70,000)+*	16.00	16.00
a.-f.		1.30fr Any single	2.60	2.60
		First day cover		18.00

Flags and Coins Type of 2006

Printed by Cartor Security Printing, France. Designed by Rorie Katz, US.

No. 512 — Flag of: a, Equatorial Guinea, 100 franc coin. b, Laos, 20 kip coin. c, Seychelles, 5 rupee coin. d, Mauritania, 1 ougiya coin. e, Argentina, 1 peso coin. f, Morocco, 1 dirham coin. g, Sudan, 20 piaster coin. h, Brunei, 50 cent coin.

2010, Feb. 5 Litho. *Perf. 13¼x13*

512		Sheet of 8 *(68,000)+*	15.00	15.00
a.-h.	A375	85c Any single	1.75	1.75
		First day cover		17.00

A column of rouletting in the middle of the sheet separates it into two parts.

Endangered Species Type of 1993

Printed by Johann Enschedé and Sons, the Netherlands. Designed by Rosie Sanders, United Kingdom.

Designs: No. 513, Fouquieria columnaris. No. 514, Aloe arborescens. No. 515, Galanthus krasnovii. No. 516, Dracaena draco.

2010, Apr. 15 Litho. *Perf. 12¾x12½*

513	A271	1fr **multicolored** *(132,000)+*	2.25	2.25
514	A271	1fr **multicolored** *(132,000)+*	2.25	2.25
515	A271	1fr **multicolored** *(132,000)+*	2.25	2.25
516	A271	1fr **multicolored** *(132,000)+*	2.25	2.25
a.		Block of 4, #513-516	9.00	9.00
		First day cover, #516a		10.00
		First day cover, #513-516, each		3.25
		Inscription block of 4, #516a	9.00	—
		Pane of 16	36.00	—

Intl. Year of Biodiversity — G84

Printed by Lowe-Martin Group, Canada. Panes of 20. Designed by Deborah Halperin, US.

Drawings from Art Forms from Nature, by Ernst Heinrich: 1.60fr, Arachnid. 1.90fr, Starfish.

2010, Apr. 15 Litho. *Perf. 13*

517	G84	1.60fr **multicolored** *(400,000)+*	3.75	3.75
		First day cover		4.50
		Inscription block of 4	15.00	—
		Sheet of 20	75.00	—
518	G84	1.90fr **multicolored** *(400,000)+*	4.25	4.25
		First day cover		5.25
		First day cover, #517-518		8.75
		Inscription block of 4	17.00	—
		Sheet of 20	85.00	—

One Planet, One Ocean Types of New York and Vienna and

G85

One Planet, One Ocean — G86

Printed by Johann Enschedé and Sons, the Netherlands. Designed by Robert Wyland, US.

No. 519: a, Turtles at left and top, fish at bottom. b, Hammerhead shark. c, Fish at left and center, corals. d, Fish at left, coral.

No. 520: a, Dolphins. b, Shark, head of fish at right, small fish in background. c, Ray and fish. d, Fish at bottom, coral and sponges.

No. 521: a, Like New York #1003a. b, Like New York #1003b, c, Like New York #1003c, d, Like New York #1003d. e, Like Vienna #471a. f, Like Vienna #471b. g, Like Vienna #471c, h, Like Vienna #471d. i, Like #519a. j, Like #519b, k, Like #519c. l, Like #519d. m, Like New York #1004a. n, Like New York #1004b. o, Like New York #1004c, p, Like New York #1004d. q, Like Vienna #472a. r, Like Vienna #472b. s, Like Vienna #472c. t, Like Vienna #472d. u, Like #520a. v, Like #520b. w, Like #520c. x, Like #520d.

2010, May 6 Litho. *Perf. 14x13¼*

519	G85	Sheet of 4 *(65,000)+*	8.00	8.00
a.-d.		85c Any single	2.00	2.00
520	G86	Sheet of 4 *(65,000)+*	10.00	10.00
a.-d.		1fr Any single	2.50	2.50
		First day cover, #519-520		20.50

Souvenir Booklet
Perf. 13¼x13

521		Booklet, #521y-521z, 521aa-521ad *(22,000)+*	22.00	
a.-d.	A416	30c any single	.70	.70
e.-h.	V91	30c any single	.70	.70
i.-l.	G85	30c any single	.70	.70
m.-p.	A417	50c any single	1.10	1.10
q.-t.	V92	50c any single	1.10	1.10
u.-x.	G86	50c any single	1.10	1.10
y.		Booklet pane of 4 #521a-521d	2.80	2.80
z.		Booklet pane of 4 #521e-521h	2.80	2.80
aa.		Booklet pane of 4 #521i-521l	2.80	2.80
ab.		Booklet pane of 4 #521m-521p	4.40	4.40
ac.		Booklet pane of 4 #521q-521t	4.40	4.40
ad.		Booklet pane of 4 #521u-521x	4.40	4.40

Intl. Oceanographic Commission, 50th anniv.

United Nations, 65th Anniv. Type of 2010

Printed by Lowe-Martin Group, Canada. Designed by Rorie Katz, United States.

Litho. With Foil Application

2010, June 28 *Perf. 13¼*

522	A422	1.90fr **red & gold** *(135,000)+*	4.00	4.00
		First day cover		5.00
		Inscription block of 4	16.00	—
		Pane of 15	60.00	—
a.		Souvenir sheet of 2 *(40,500)+*	8.00	8.00
		First day cover, #522a		8.75

G87

G88

G89

G90

United Nations Land Transport — G91

Printed by UAB Garsu Pasaulis, Lithuania. Designed by Simon Williams, United Kingdom.

2010, Sept. 2 Litho. *Perf. 13¼x13*

523	G87	1fr **multicolored** *(120,000)+*	1.80	1.80
524	G88	1fr **multicolored** *(120,000)+*	1.80	1.80
525	G89	1fr **multicolored** *(120,000)+*	1.80	1.80
526	G90	1fr **multicolored** *(120,000)+*	1.80	1.80
527	G91	1fr **multicolored** *(120,000)+*	1.80	1.80
a.		Horiz. strip of 5, #523-527	9.00	9.00
		First day cover, #527a		11.50
		First day cover, #523-527, each		3.25
		Inscription block of 10	21.00	—
		Pane of 20	42.00	—

Miniature Sheet

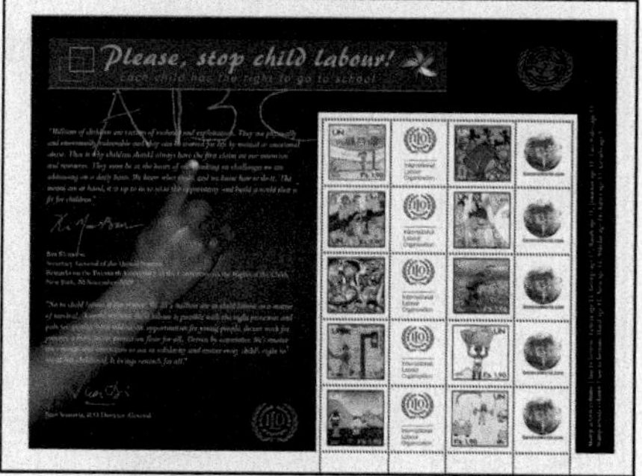

Campaign Against Child Labor — G92

No. 528: a, Child, buildings, road, burning can. b, Child with full basket on back, children playing in background. c, Child working, children on school bus. d, Child with mining helmet, three other children. e, Child near tubs, children working, child being beaten. f, Child with hoe. g, Marionette, traffic light. h, Child carrying basket on head. i, Children on rock field near hills. j, Child holding bags in road.

2010, Sept. 2 Litho. *Perf. 14¾*
528 G92 Sheet of 10 + 10 labels 32.50 32.50
a.-j. 1.90fr Any single + label 3.25 3.25

No. 528 sold for $14.95, 15fr and €11.46, each of which was far lower than the level at which 19fr, the total face value of the stamps on the sheet, was worth on the day of issue. Labels could not be personalized.

Miniature Sheet

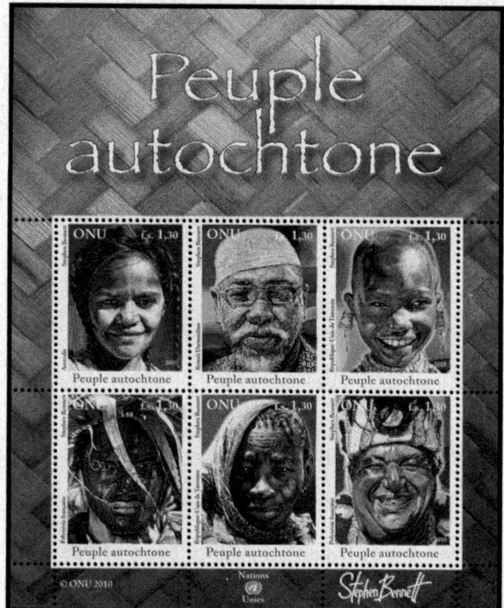

Indigenous People — G93

Printed by Lowe-Martin Group, Canada. Designed by Stephen Bennett, US.
No. 529 — Portraits of person from: a, Australia. b, Brunei. c, Tanzania (girl with bald head). d, French Polynesia (man with headdress of leaves). e, Tanzania (man with headdress). f, French Polynesia (man with white headdress).

2010, Oct. 21 Litho. *Perf. 13*
529 G93 Pane of 6 *(55,000)+* 14.50 14.50
a.-f. 1.30fr Any single 2.40 2.40
First day cover 18.50

United Nations Headquarters, Geneva — G94

Printed by Cartor Security Printing, France. Panes of 20. Designed by Scott Solberg, US.
United Nations Headquarters, Geneva: 10c, Aerial view. 50c, Ground-level view.

2011, Feb. 4 Litho. *Perf. 13*
530 G94 10c **multicolored** *(400,000)+* .35 .35
First day cover 1.25
Inscription block of 4 1.40 —
Pane of 20 7.00 —
531 G94 50c **multicolored** *(400,000)+* 1.25 1.25
First day cover 2.75
First day cover, #530-531 2.25
Inscription block of 4 5.00 —
Pane of 20 25.00 —

Flags and Coins Type of 2006

Printed by Cartor Security Printing, France. Designed by Rorie Katz, US.
No. 532 — Flag of: a, Mongolia, 500 tugrik coin. b, Senegal, 500 franc coin. c, Egypt, 100 piaster coin. d, Congo, 100 franc coin. e, Nicaragua, 1 Córdoba coin. f, Central African Republic, 100 franc coin. g, Algeria, 5 dinar coin. h, Ukraine, 5 hryvnia coin.

2011, Mar. 3 Litho. *Perf. 13¼x13*
532 Sheet of 8 *(60,000)+* 15.00 15.00
a.-h. A375 85c Any single 1.75 1.75
First day cover 17.00

A column of rouletting in the middle of the sheet separates it into two parts.

Human Space Flight, 50th Anniv. — G95

Printed by Lowe-Martin Group, Canada. Designed by Peter Bollinger, US.
No. 533: Various parts of outer space scene.
No. 534, vert.: a, International Space Station. b, International Space Station, diff.

2011, Apr. 12 Litho. *Perf. 13x13¼*
533 G95 Sheet of 16 *(55,000)+* 18.00 18.00
First day cover 20.00
a.-p. 50c any single 1.10 1.10

Souvenir Sheet

534 G95 Sheet of 2 15.00 15.00
First day cover 5.00
a. 85c **multicolored** 6.50 6.50
b. 1fr **multicolored** 8.50 8.50

No. 534 contains two 40x48mm stamps that were printed as part of a larger sheet of six stamps, Vienna No. 485c, which was broken up into its component two-stamp souvenir sheets, and also sold as one unit. Value, $90, complete unit.

UNESCO World Heritage Sites in Nordic Countries Type of 2011

Printed by Johann Enschedé and Sons, the Netherlands. Panes of 20. Designed by Rorie Katz, US.
Designs: 85c, Kronborg Castle, Denmark. 1fr, Suomenlinna Fortress, Finland.

2011, May 5 Litho. *Perf. 14x13½*
535 A433 85c **multicolored** *(140,000)+* 1.90 1.90
First day cover 2.75
Inscription block of 4 7.60 —
Pane of 20 30.00 —
536 A433 1fr **multicolored** *(140,000)+* 2.25 2.25
First day cover 3.25
First day cover, #535-536 5.00
Inscription block of 4 9.00 —
Pane of 20 45.00 —

AIDS Ribbon Type of 2011

Printed by Lowe-Martin Group, Canada. Panes of 4. Designed by Rorie Katz, US.

2011, June 3 Litho. *Die Cut*
Self-Adhesive
537 A434 1.30fr **red & orange** *(220,000)+* 5.00 5.00
Pane of 4 20.00
First day cover, pane of 4 14.50

ECOSOC Type of 2011

Printed by Cartor Security Printing, France. Panes of 20. Designed by Rorie Katz, US.
Education: 1fr, Girls taking notes. 1.30fr, Girls at computers.

2011, July 1 Litho. *Perf. 14¼*
538 A435 1fr **multicolored** *(130,000)+* 3.00 3.00
First day cover 3.50
Inscription block of 4 12.00 —
Pane of 20 60.00 —
539 A435 1.30fr **multicolored** *(130,000)+* 4.00 4.00
First day cover 4.50
First day cover, #538-539 7.00
Inscription block of 4 16.00 —
Pane of 20 80.00 —

Endangered Species Type of 1993

Printed by Johann Enschedé and Sons, the Netherlands. Designed by Wendy Wray, U.S.
Designs: No. 540, Strigops habroptilus (Kakapo). No. 541, Lophophorus impejanus (Himalayan monal). No. 542, Ciconia nigra (Black stork). No. 543, Pithecophaga jeffreyi (Philippine eagle).

2011, Sept. 7 Litho. *Perf. 12¾x12½*
540 A271 1fr **multicolored** *(112,000)+* 2.60 2.60
541 A271 1fr **multicolored** *(112,000)+* 2.60 2.60
542 A271 1fr **multicolored** *(112,000)+* 2.60 2.60
543 A271 1fr **multicolored** *(112,000)+* 2.60 2.60
a. Block of 4, #540-543 10.40 10.40
First day cover, #543a 11.50
First day cover, #540-543, each 3.75
Inscription block of 4, #543a 10.40 —
Pane of 16 42.00 —

Intl. Year of Forests Type of 2011

Printed by Lowe-Martin Group, Canada. Panes of 8. Designed by Sergio Baradat, U.S.
Designs: 85c, Birds and butterflies, tree tops. 1.40fr, Fish and coral.

Litho. With Foil Application
2011, Oct. 13 *Perf. 12½*
544 85c **multicolored** *(88,000)+* 2.25 2.25
545 1.40fr **multicolored** *(88,000)+* 3.75 3.75
a. A436 Vert. pair, #544-545 6.00 6.00
First day cover, #545a 6.75
Pane of 8 24.00 —

Flags and Coins Type of 2006

Printed by Cartor Security Printing, France. Designed by Rorie Katz, US.
No. 546 — Flag of: a, Saudi Arabia, 100 halala coin. b, Georgia, 2 lari coin. c, Democratic People's Republic of Korea, 50 won coin. d, Lesotho, 50 lisente coin. e, Serbia, 5 dinar coin. f, Djibouti, 20 franc coin. g, Belize, 1 dollar coin. h, Liechtenstein, 20 centime coin.

2012, Feb. 3 Litho. *Perf. 13¼x13*
546 Sheet of 8 *(48,000)+* 16.50 16.50
a.-h. A375 85c Any single 2.00 2.00
First day cover 18.50

A column of rouletting in the middle of the sheet separates it into two parts.

G96

Autism Awareness — G97

Printed by Joh. Enschedé Stamps Security Printers, Netherlands. Panes of 20.
Drawings by autistic people: No. 547, Victory, by J.A. Tan, Canada. No. 548, Untitled drawing, by Michael Augello, U.S.

2012, Apr. 2 Litho. *Perf. 14x13½*
547 G96 1.40fr **multicolored** *(85,000)+* 3.50 3.50
548 G97 1.40fr **multicolored** *(85,000)+* 3.50 3.50
a. Pair, #547-548 7.00 7.00
First day cover, #547, 548 7.75
Inscription block of 4 14.00 —
Pane of 20 70.00 —

Endangered Species Type of 1993

Printed by Johann Enschedé and Sons, the Netherlands. Designed by Diana Marques, Portugal.
Designs: No. 549, Panthera tigris altaica. No. 550, Psitacella picta. No. 551, Iguana iguana. No. 552, Propithecus tattersalli.

2012, Apr. 19 Litho. *Perf. 12¾x12½*
549 A271 1fr **multicolored** *(102,000)+* 2.40 2.40
550 A271 1fr **multicolored** *(102,000)+* 2.40 2.40
551 A271 1fr **multicolored** *(102,000)+* 2.40 2.40
552 A271 1fr **multicolored** *(102,000)+* 2.40 2.40
a. Block of 4, #549-552 9.75 9.75
First day cover, #552a 10.50
First day cover, #549-552, each 3.50
Inscription block of 4, #552a 9.75 —
Pane of 16 39.00 —

Rio + 20 Type of 2012

Printed by Lowe-Martin Group, Canada. Panes of 20. Designed by Shailesh Khandeparkar, India.

2012, June 1 Litho. *Perf. 13x13¼*
553 A443 1.40fr **multicolored** *(116,000)+* 4.00 4.00
First day cover 4.50
Inscription block of 4 16.00 —
Pane of 20 80.00 —

Sport for Peace Type of 2012

Printed by Cartor Security Printing, France. Panes of 9. Designed by Daniel Stolle, Finland.
2012 Paralympics events: 1fr, Track. 1.40fr, Archery.

Litho. With Foil Application

2012, Aug. 17 *Perf. 14½*
554 A444 1fr **multicolored** *(126,000)+* 2.40 2.40
First day cover 3.25
Inscription block of 4 9.60 —
Pane of 9 22.00 —
555 A444 1.40fr **multicolored** *(126,000)+* 3.50 3.50
First day cover 4.50
First day cover, #554-555 7.75
Inscription block of 4 14.00 —
Pane of 9 31.50 —
a. Souvenir sheet of 1 *(37,000)+* 3.50 3.50
First day cover 4.50

UNESCO World Heritage Sites in Africa Type of 2012

Printed by Lowe-Martin Group, Canada. Panes of 20. Designed by Rorie Katz, US.
Designs: 85c, Virunga National Park, Congo Democratic Republic. 1fr, Amphitheater of El Jem, Tunisia.

2012, Sept. 5 Litho. *Perf. 13¼*
556 A445 85c **multicolored** *(120,000)+* 2.00 2.00
First day cover 3.00
Inscription block of 4 8.00 —
Pane of 20 40.00 —
557 A445 1fr **multicolored** *(120,000)+* 2.40 2.40
First day cover 3.25
First day cover, #556-557 5.25
Inscription block of 4 9.75 —
Pane of 20 48.00 —

Miniature Sheet

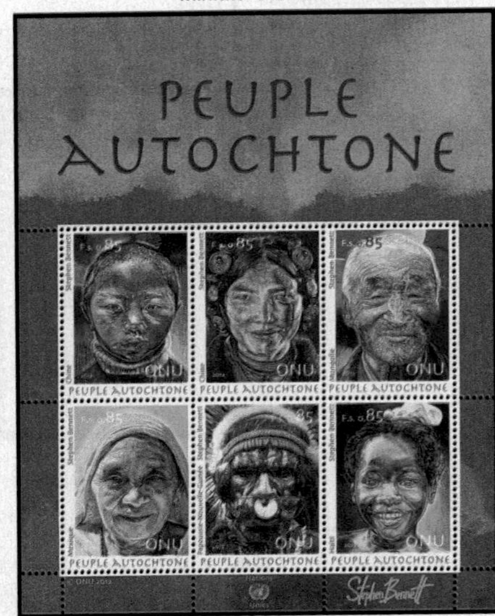

Indigenous People — G98

Printed by Lowe-Martin Group, Canada. Designed by Stephen Bennett, US.
No. 558 — Portrait of person from: a, China. b, Tibet, China. c, Mongolia. d, Mexico. e, Papua New Guinea. f, Haiti.

2012, Oct. 11 Litho. *Perf. 13¼x13*
558 G98 Sheet of 6 *(39,000)+* 13.50 13.50
a.-f. 85c Any single 2.25 2.25
First day cover 14.00

World Radio Day Type of 2013

Printed by Lowe-Martin Group, Canada. Panes of 20. Designed by Rorie Katz, US.
Designs: 1.40fr, Reporter with microphone and tape recorder. 1.90fr, Engineers in studio.

2013, Feb. 13 Litho. *Perf. 13¼x13*
559 A448 1.40fr **multicolored** *(105,700)+* 3.50 3.50
First day cover 4.25
Inscription block of 4 14.00 —
Pane of 20 70.00 —
560 A448 1.90fr **multicolored** *(105,700)+* 4.50 4.50
First day cover 5.75
First day cover, #559-560 9.00
Inscription block of 4 18.00 —
Pane of 20 90.00 —

Person on Leaf — G99

Dove and People — G100

Printed by Johann Enschedé and Sons, the Netherlands. Panes of 20. Designed by Sergio Baradat, US.

2013, Mar. 5 Litho. *Perf. 14x13½*
561 G99 1fr **multicolored** *(200,000)+* 2.40 2.40
First day cover 3.25
Inscription block of 4 9.60 —
Pane of 20 48.00 —

Perf. 13½x14
562 G100 1.40fr **multicolored** *(200,000)+* 3.50 3.50
First day cover 4.50
First day cover, #561-562 6.75
Inscription block of 4 14.00 —
Pane of 20 70.00 —

World Heritage Sites, China, Type of 2013

Printed by Johann Enschedé and Sons, the Netherlands. Panes of 20. Designed by Sergio Baradat, U.S.
Designs: Nos. 563, 565b, Potala Palace, Lhasa. Nos. 564, 565e, Mount Huangshan. No. 565a, Mogao Caves. No. 565c, Great Wall of China. No. 565d, Imperial Palace, Beijing. No. 565f, Mausoleum of the First Qing Emperor.

2013, Apr. 11 Litho. *Perf. 14x13½*
563 A452 1.40fr **multicolored** *(128,600)+* 3.50 3.50
First day cover 4.25
Inscription block of 4 14.00 —
Pane of 20 70.00 —
564 A452 1.90fr **multicolored** *(128,600)+* 4.50 4.50
First day cover 5.75
First day cover, #563-564 8.75
Inscription block of 4 18.00 —
Pane of 20 90.00 —

Souvenir Booklet

565 Booklet, #565g-565l *(20,000)+* 24.00
a.-c. A452 30c any single .75 .75
d.-f. A452 50c any single 1.25 1.25
g. Booklet pane of 4 #565a 3.00 —
h. Booklet pane of 4 #565b 3.00 —
i. Booklet pane of 4 #565c 3.00 —
j. Booklet pane of 4 #565d 5.00 —
k. Booklet pane of 4 #565e 5.00 —
l. Booklet pane of 4 #565f 5.00 —

World Oceans Day — G101

Printed by Lowe-Martin Group, Canada. Designed by Rorie Katz, US.
No. 566 — Fish from *One Fish, Two Fish, Red Fish, Blue Fish,* by Dr. Seuss: a, Three red fish facing right. b, Green fish, tail of yellow fish. c, Three red fish facing right, part of tail of red fish. d, Two entire green fish facing left, tail of bottom fish ends above "n" in "océan." e, Red fish with eye open facing left. f, Tail of red fish, yellow and red fish facing left. g, Red fish facing right, water droplets. h, Yellow and red fish facing right. i, Two green fish facing left, tail of bottom fish ends to right of "océan." j, Red fish and wave. k, Two green fish, red fish, wave. l, Yellow fish in car, wave.

2013, May 31 Litho. *Perf. 13*
566 G101 Sheet of 12 *(48,000)+* 20.00 20.00
First day cover 26.50
a.-l. 85c any single 1.60 1.60

Nebulae Type of 2013

Printed by UAB Garsu Pasaulis, Lithuania. Panes of 8. Designed by Sergio Baradat, U.S.
Designs: No. 567, NGC 2346. No. 568, Sh 2-106. 1fr, Messier 16.

2013, Aug. 9 Litho. *Perf. 13¼*
567 A454 1.40fr **multicolored** *(112,000)+* 3.50 3.50
568 A454 1.40fr **multicolored** *(112,000)+* 3.50 3.50
a. Pair, #567-568 7.00 7.00
First day cover, #568a 7.75
Inscription block of 4 14.00 —
Pane of 8 28.00 —

Souvenir Sheet

569 A454 1fr **multicolored** *(31,000)+* 2.40 2.40
First day cover 3.50

No. 569 contains one 44x44mm stamp.

Works of Disabled Artists Type of 2013

Printed by UAB Garsu Pasaulis, Lithuania. Panes of 20. Designed by Rorie Katz, U.S.
Designs: 1.40fr, See the Girl with the Red Dress On, by Sargy Mann, United Kingdom. 1.90fr, Performers in China Disabled People's Performing Art Troupe, People's Republic of China.

2013, Sept. 20 Litho. *Perf. 13¼x13*
570 A456 1.40fr **multicolored** *(118,200)+* 3.50 3.50
First day cover 4.25
Inscription block of 4 14.00 —
Pane of 20 70.00 —
571 A456 1.90fr **multicolored** *(118,200)+* 4.50 4.50
First day cover 5.75
First day cover, #570-571 9.00
Inscription block of 4 18.00 —
Pane of 20 90.00 —

Endangered Species Type of 1993

Printed by Johann Enschedé and Sons, the Netherlands. Designed by Sara Menon, Italy.
Designs: No. 572, Smutsia temminckii. No. 573, Perodicticus potto. No. 574, Tarsius syrichta. No. 575, Pteropus livingstonii.

2013, Oct. 10 Litho. *Perf. 12¾x12½*
572 A271 1.40fr **multicolored** *(96,000)+* 3.25 3.25
573 A271 1.40fr **multicolored** *(96,000)+* 3.25 3.25
574 A271 1.40fr **multicolored** *(96,000)+* 3.25 3.25
575 A271 1.40fr **multicolored** *(96,000)+* 3.25 3.25
a. Block of 4, #572-575 13.00 13.00
First day cover, #575a 14.00
First day cover, #572-575, each 4.25
Inscription block of 4, #575a 13.00 —
Pane of 16 52.00 —

Flags and Coins Type of 2006

Printed by Cartor Security Printing, France. Designed by Rorie Katz, US.

No. 576 — Flag of: a, Ivory Coast, 100 franc coin. b, Marshall Islands, 10 cent coin. c, Andorra, 20 cent coin. d, Guinea-Bissau, 100 franc coin. e, Kenya, 20 shilling coin. f, Antigua and Barbuda, 5 cent coin. g, Tajikistan, 50 diram coin. h, Micronesia, 5 cent coin.

2013, Nov. 6 Litho. *Perf. 13¼x13*

576	Sheet of 8 *(40,000)+*	26.00	26.00
a.-h.	A375 1.40fr Any single	3.25	3.25
	First day cover		28.00

A column of rouletting in the middle of the sheet separates it into two parts.

International Day of Happiness Type of 2014

Printed by Lowe-Martin Group, Canada. Panes of 20. Designed by Rorie Katz, U.S.

Designs: 1fr, A Sweet Dog's Muzzle, photograph by Jaymi Heimbuch, "Heureux." 1.40fr, Two women making heart with hands, photograph by Glow Images, Chinese characters for "Happy."

2014, Mar. 17 Litho. *Perf. 13¼x13*

577	A459 1fr **multicolored** *(90,000)+*	2.50	2.50
	First day cover		3.25
	Inscription block of 4	10.00	—
	Pane of 20	50.00	—
578	A459 1.40fr **multicolored** *(90,000)+*	3.50	3.50
	First day cover		4.50
	First day cover, #577-578		7.00
	Inscription block of 4	14.00	—
	Pane of 20	70.00	—

Miniature Sheet

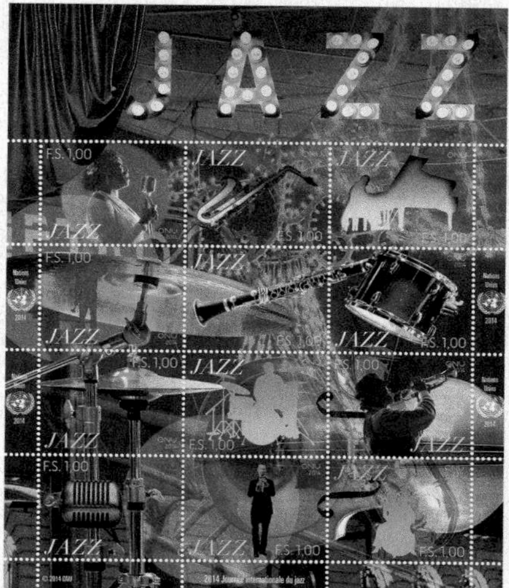

International Year of Jazz — G102

Printed by Cartor Security Printing, France. Designed by Sergio Baradat, U.S.

No. 579: a, Woman behind microphone. b, Saxophone. c, Silhouette of pianist at grand piano. d, Cymbal and silhouette of man holding trumpet. e, Cymbal and clarinet. f, Clarinet and drum. g, Hi-hat. h, Silhouette of drummer and drum set. i, Trumpeter with hat. j, Microphone and cymbal stands. k, Clarinetist. l, Bass player.

2014, Apr. 30 Litho. *Perf. 13x13¼*

579	G102 Sheet of 12 *(45,000)+*	29.50	29.50
	First day cover		31.00
a.-l.	1fr Any single	2.40	2.40

G103

G104

Printed by Lowe-Martin Group, Canada. Panes of 20. Designed by Sergio Baradat, U.S.

2014, June 6 Litho. *Perf. 13¼x13*

580	G103 2.20fr **multicolored** *(106,000)+*	5.50	5.50
	First day cover		6.25
	Inscription block of 4	22.00	—
	Pane of 20	110.00	—
581	G104 2.60fr **multicolored** *(106,000)+*	6.50	6.50
	First day cover		7.50
	First day cover, #580-581		13.00
	Inscription block of 4	26.00	—
	Pane of 20	130.00	—

Taj Mahal Types of 2014

Printed by Lowe-Martin Group, Canada. Panes of 20. Designed by Rorie Katz, U.S.

2014, July 16 Engr. *Perf. 13¼x13*

582	A465 1.40fr **multicolored** *(110,000)+*	3.50	3.50
	First day cover		4.25
	Inscription block of 4	14.00	—
	Pane of 20	70.00	—
583	A467 1.90fr **multicolored** *(110,000)+*	4.75	4.75
	First day cover		5.75
	First day cover, #582-583		9.25
	Inscription block of 4	19.00	—
	Pane of 20	95.00	—

Souvenir Booklet

584	Booklet, #584g-584l *(14,000)+*	24.00	
a.	A463 30c multi	.75	.75
b.	A465 30c multi	.75	.75
c.	A466 50c multi	1.25	1.25
d.	A464 50c multi	1.25	1.25
e.	A467 30c multi	.75	.75
f.	A468 50c multi	1.25	1.25
g.	Booklet pane of 4 #584a	3.00	—
h.	Booklet pane of 4 #584b	3.00	—
i.	Booklet pane of 4 #584c	3.00	—
j.	Booklet pane of 4 #584d	5.00	—
k.	Booklet pane of 4 #584e	5.00	—
l.	Booklet pane of 4 #584f	5.00	—

International Year of Family Farming G105

Printed by Lowe-Martin Group, Canada. Panes of 20. Designed by Sergio Baradat, U.S.

Designs: 1.30fr, African villagers harvesting produce. 1.60fr, Farming family, farm and animals.

2014, Aug. 21 Litho. *Perf. 13x13¼*

585	G105 1.30fr **multicolored** *(90,000)+*	3.25	3.25
	First day cover		4.00
	Inscription block of 4	13.00	—
	Pane of 20	65.00	—
586	G105 1.60fr **multicolored** *(90,000)+*	4.00	4.00
	First day cover		5.00
	First day cover, #585-586		8.25
	Inscription block of 4	16.00	—
	Pane of 20	80.00	—

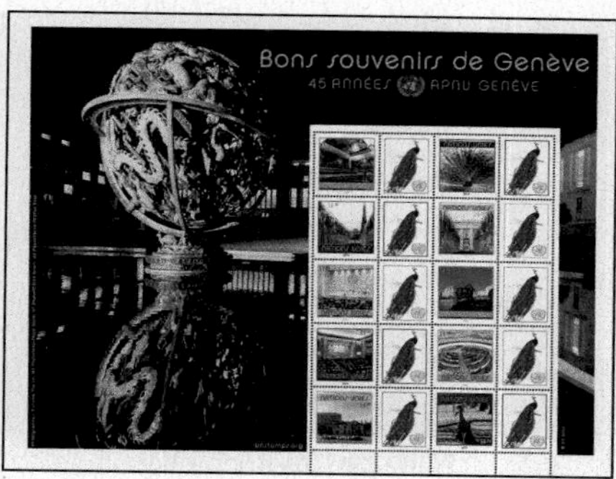

G106

No. 587: a, Room with painted ceiling. b, Peacock with spread tail. c, Rows of flags, brown panel at bottom. d, Rows of flags near Palais des Nations, tan panel at top. e, Meeting hall with United nations emblem on rear wall. f, Armillary sphere and Palais des Nations. g, Meeting hall with movie screen on rear wall. h, Circular meeting hall. i, Farm animals on grass near buildings. j, Peacock with tail down.

2014, Sept. 12 Litho. *Perf. 14¾*

587	G106 Sheet of 10	*35.00*	*35.00*
a.-j.	1.30fr Any single + label	*3.50*	*3.50*

The full sheet sold for 14.95fr. The generic labels are shown. Labels could be personalized.

Global Education First Initiative Type of 2014

Printed by Lowe-Martin Group, Canada. Panes of 20. Designed by Oamul Lu, People's Republic of China.

Designs: No. 588, Students in art museum. No. 589, Student in library.

2014, Sept. 18 Litho. *Perf. 13x13¼*

588	A470 1.90fr **multicolored** *(100,000)+*	4.75	4.75
	First day cover		5.75
	Inscription block of 4	19.00	—
	Pane of 20	95.00	—

Souvenir Sheet

Perf. 12½

589	A470 1.90fr **multicolored** *(34,000)+*	4.75	4.75
	First day cover		6.25

No. 589 contains one 32x32mm stamp.

Endangered Species Type of 2014

Printed by Johann Enschedé and Sons, the Netherlands. Designed by Amadeo Bachar, U.S.

Maps and: No. 590, Arapaima gigas. No. 591, Cetorhinus maximus. No. 592, Pristis pristis. No. 593, Acipenser baerii.

2014, Oct. 23 Litho. *Perf. 12¾x12½*

590	A471 1.40fr **multicolored** *(88,000)+*	3.50	3.50
591	A471 1.40fr **multicolored** *(88,000)+*	3.50	3.50
592	A471 1.40fr **multicolored** *(88,000)+*	3.50	3.50
593	A471 1.40fr **multicolored** *(88,000)+*	3.50	3.50
a.	Block of 4, #590-593	14.00	14.00
	First day cover, #593a		15.00
	First day cover, #590-593, each		4.50
	Inscription block of 4, #593a	14.00	—
	Pane of 16	56.00	—

Flags and Coins Type of 2006

Printed by Cartor Security Printing, France. Designed by Rorie Katz, U.S.

No. 594 — Flag of: a, Vanuatu, 10 vatu coin. b, Nauru, 1 dollar coin. c, Eritrea, 100 cent coin. d, El Salvador, 1 colon coin. e, Mozambique, 50 centavo coin. f, Burundi, 1 franc coin. g, Turkmenistan, 10 tenge coin. h, Guinea, 1 franc coin.

2015, Feb. 6 Litho. *Perf. 13¼x13*

594	Sheet of 8 *(40,000)+*	16.50	16.50
a.-h.	A375 90c Any single	2.00	2.00
	First day cover		18.50

A column of rouletting in the middle of the sheet separates it into two parts.

Miniature Sheets

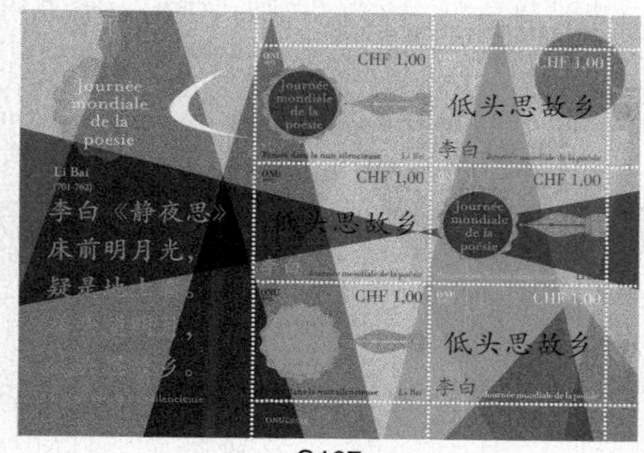

G107

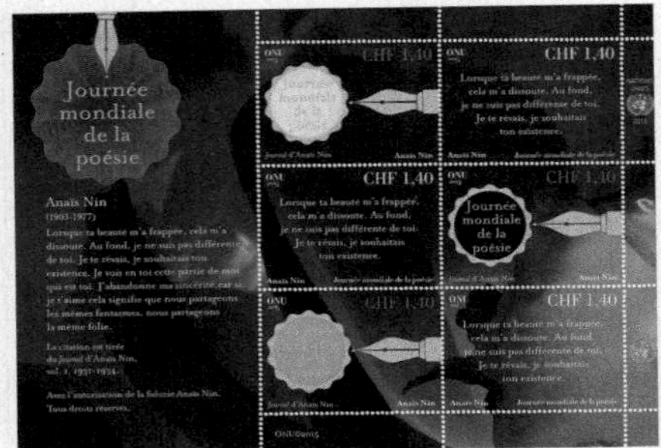

World Poetry Day — G108

Printed by Cartor Security Printing. France. Designed by Sergio Baradat, U.S.

No. 595: a, Pen and gray circle. b, Li Bai quotation in Chinese, denomination in light blue green. c, Li Bai quotation in Chinese, denomination in red. d, Pen and red circle. e, Pen and orange circle. f, Li Bai quotation in Chinese, denomination in white.

No. 596: a, Pen and light green circle. b, Anais Nin quotation, denomination and "Journée mondiale de poésie" in light blue. c, As "b," with "Journée mondiale de poésie" in white, dark blue area below and to left of date. d, Pen and black circle. e, Pen and lilac circle. f, As "c," with dark blue area below and to right of date.

2015, Mar. 20 **Litho.** ***Perf. 14½x14¼***

595	G107	Sheet of 6 *(37,000)+*	14.00	14.00
a.-f.		1fr Any single	2.25	2.25
596	G108	Sheet of 6 *(37,000)+*	19.50	19.50
a.-f.		1.40fr Any single	3.25	3.25
		First day cover, #595-596		37.00

Endangered Species Type of 2015

Printed by Johann Enschedé and Sons, the Netherlands. Designed by John Keulemans and William Hart, United Kingdom.

Designs: No. 597, Diphyllodes respublica. No. 598, Ptiloris paradiseus. No. 599, Semioptera wallacii. No. 600, Paradisaea decora.

2015, Apr. 16 **Litho.** ***Perf. 12½x12¾***

597	A476	1.40fr **multicolored** *(80,000)+*	3.25	3.25
598	A476	1.40fr **multicolored** *(80,000)+*	3.25	3.25
599	A476	1.40fr **multicolored** *(80,000)+*	3.25	3.25
600	A476	1.40fr **multicolored** *(80,000)+*	3.25	3.25
a.		Block of 4, #597-600	13.00	13.00
		First day cover, #600a		14.00
		First day cover, #597-600, each		4.25
		Inscription block of 4, #600a	13.00	—
		Pane of 16	52.00	—
		Nos. 597-600 (4)	13.00	13.00

World Heritage Sites, Southeast Asia, Type of 2015

Printed by Johann Enschedé and Sons, the Netherlands. Panes of 20. Designed by Sergio Baradat, U.S.

Designs: Nos. 601, 603b, Angkor Wat, Cambodia. Nos. 602, 603e, Cordillera, Philippines. No. 603a, Luang Prabang, Laos. No. 603c, Ayutthaya, Thailand. No. 565d, Borobudur Temple, Indonesia. No. 603f, Hué Monuments, Viet Nam.

2015, June 5 **Litho.** ***Perf. 14x13½***

601	A480	1.40fr **multicolored** *(110,000)+*	3.25	3.25
		First day cover		4.00
		Inscription block of 4	13.00	—
		Pane of 20	65.00	—
602	A480	1.90fr **multicolored** *(110,000)+*	4.50	4.50
		First day cover		5.50
		First day cover, #601-602		8.75
		Inscription block of 4	18.00	—
		Pane of 20	90.00	—

Souvenir Booklet

603		Booklet, #603g-603l *(13,000)+*	23.50	
a.-c.	A480	30c any single	.70	.70
d.-f.	A480	50c any single	1.25	1.25
g.		Booklet pane of 4 #603a	2.80	—
h.		Booklet pane of 4 #603b	2.80	—
i.		Booklet pane of 4 #603c	2.80	—
j.		Booklet pane of 4 #603d	5.00	—
k.		Booklet pane of 4 #603e	5.00	—
l.		Booklet pane of 4 #603f	5.00	—

End Violence Against Children Type of 2015

Printed by Cartor Security Printing, France. Panes of 20. Designed by Chris Sharp, U.S.

Designs: 1fr, Child marriage. 1.40fr, Child trafficking.

2015, Aug. 20 **Litho.** ***Perf. 14½x14¼***

604	A481	1fr **multicolored** *(90,000)+*	2.40	2.40
		First day cover		3.25
		Inscription block of 4	9.60	—
		Pane of 20	48.00	—
605	A481	1.40fr **multicolored** *(90,000)+*	3.25	3.25
		First day cover		4.50
		First day cover, #605-606		6.50
		Inscription block of 4	13.00	—
		Pane of 20	65.00	—

Miniature Sheet

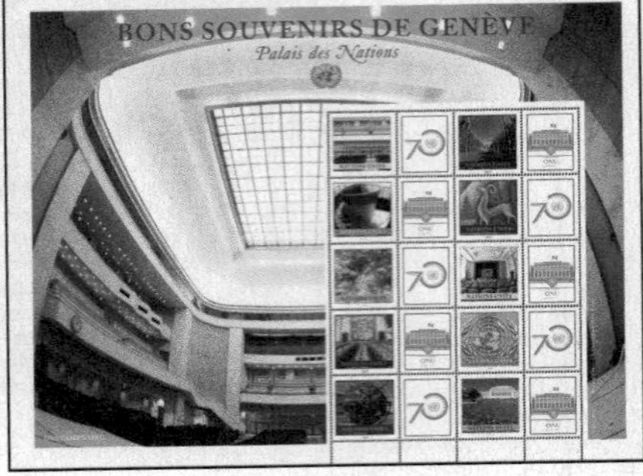

G109

No. 606: a, Balcony above auditorium seats. b, Flags. c, Spiral staircase. d, Stylized horned mammal. e, Painting of trees. f, Auditorium seats facing stage with dais. g, Side view of auditorium seats, painting on wall. h, United Nations emblem. i, Armillary Sphere. j, Palais des Nations and flowers.

2015, Sept. 3 **Litho.** ***Perf. 14¾***

606	G109	Sheet of 10 + 10 labels	*35.00*	*35.00*
a.-j.		1.40fr Any single + label	*3.50*	*3.50*

The full sheet sold for $18.39 or 14.95fr. The generic labels are shown. Labels could be personalized. The personalization of labels was available only at UN Headquarters, and not through mail order.

Visitors Lobby G110

ECOSOC Chamber G111

Façade of Secretariat G112

Chairs in ECOSOC Chamber G113

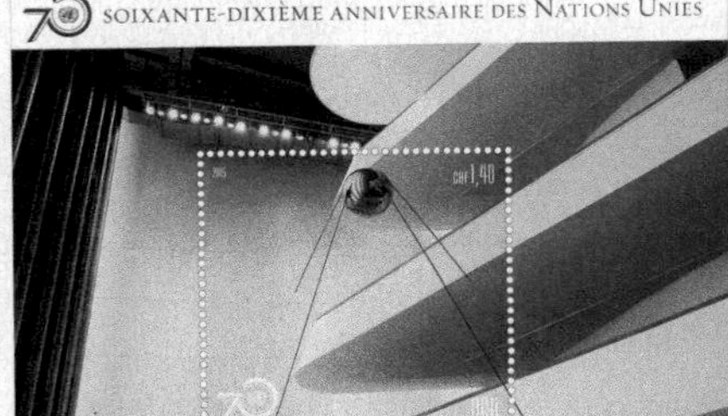

Visitors Lobby — G114

Printed by Cartor Security Printing, France. Panes of 6. Designed by Rorie Katz, U.S.

2015, Oct. 25 **Litho.** ***Perf. 13¾***

607	G110	1fr **multicolored** *(96,000)+*	2.40	2.40
608	G111	1fr **multicolored** *(96,000)+*	2.40	2.40
a.		Pair, #607-608	4.80	4.80
		First day cover, #607-608		5.25
		Inscription block of 4	9.60	—
		Pane of 6	14.50	—
609	G112	1.90fr **multicolored** *(96,000)+*	4.50	4.50
610	G113	1.90fr **multicolored** *(96,000)+*	4.50	4.50
a.		Pair, #609-610	9.00	9.00
		First day cover, #609-610		10.00
		Inscription block of 4	18.00	—
		Pane of 6	27.00	—
		Nos. 607-610 (4)	13.80	13.80

Souvenir Sheet

Perf. 13½

611	G114	1.40fr **multicolored** *(37,000)+*	4.50	4.50
		First day cover		4.25

United Nations, 70th anniv.

21st United Nations Climate Change Conference, Paris — G115

Printed by La Poste, France. Panes of 30. Designed by Rorie Katz, U.S.

2015, Nov. 24 **Litho.** ***Perf. 13¼***

612	G115	1.40fr **multicolored** *(84,000)+*	3.25	3.25
		First day cover		4.25
		Inscription block of 4	13.00	—
		Pane of 30	97.50	—

Values are for stamps with surrounding selvage.

Free and Equal Type of 2016

Printed by Cartor Security Printing, France. Panes of 20. Designed by Sergio Baradat, U.S.

Designs: 1fr, Lesbians. 1.50fr, Gay family.

2016, Feb. 5 **Litho.** ***Perf. 13½x13¼***

613	A491	1fr **multicolored** *(90,000)+*	2.25	2.25
		First day cover		3.00
		Inscription block of 4	9.00	—
		Pane of 20	45.00	—

614 A491 1.50fr **multicolored** *(90,000)+*	3.50	3.50
First day cover		4.50
First day cover, #613-614		6.50
Inscription block of 4	14.00	—
Pane of 20	70.00	—

HeForShe Type of 2016

Printed by Lowe-Martin Group, Canada. Panes of 20. Designed by Mirko Ilic, U.S.

Designs: 1fr, Man, blue background. 2fr, Woman, mauve background.

2016, Mar. 8 Litho. *Perf. 12½x13*

615 A492 1fr **multicolored** *(90,000)+*	2.25	2.25
First day cover		3.00
Inscription block of 4	9.00	—
Pane of 20	45.00	—
616 A492 2fr **multicolored** *(90,000)+*	4.50	4.50
First day cover		5.75
First day cover, #615-616		7.75
Inscription block of 4	18.00	—
Pane of 20	90.00	—

Miniature Sheets

G116

International Dance Day — G117

Printed by Cartor Security Printing. France. Designed by Sergio Baradat, U.S.

No. 617 — Illustration of Swedish dancers by Karin Römark: a, Two male dancers. b, Male dancer on one knee with female dancer. c, Male dancer with yellow cap and female dancer. d, Male dancer with red cap and vest with female dancer. e, Three dancers, with woman with red skirt at LR. f, Three dancers, with woman with blue skirt at LR.

No. 618 — Illustration of African dancers by Rönmark: a, Four dancers with sticks. b, Three dancers with sticks. c, Dancers without sticks. d, Dancer with blue and white mask. e, Two masked dancers with sticks. f, Masked dancer with two sticks.

2016, Apr. 29 Litho. *Perf. 13¼x13*

617 G116 Sheet of 6 *(30,000)+*	13.50	13.50
a.-f. 1fr Any single	2.25	2.25
618 G117 Sheet of 6 *(30,000)+*	20.00	20.00
a.-f. 1.50fr Any single	3.25	3.25
First day cover, #617-618		37.50

International Day of United Nations Peacekeepers Type of 2016

Printed by Lowe-Martin Group, Canada. Panes of 20. Designed by Sergio Baradat, U.S.

Designs: 1fr, Helmeted peacekeepers. 1.50fr, Peacekeeper with African women.

Litho. With Foil Application

2016, May 29 *Perf. 13¼x13*

619 A496 1fr **multicolored** *(120,000)+*	2.25	2.25
First day cover		3.00
Inscription block of 4	9.00	—
Pane of 20	45.00	—
620 A496 1.50fr **multicolored** *(120,000)+*	3.50	3.50
First day cover		4.50
First day cover, #619-620		6.50
Inscription block of 4	14.00	—
Pane of 20	70.00	—

Sport for Peace Type of 2016

Printed by Cartor Security Printing, France. Panes of 6. Designed by Sergio Baradat and Linsey Thoeng, U.S.

Olympic rings and: No. 621, Rowers, denomination at UR. No. 622, Rowers, denomination at UL. No. 623, Rhythmic gymnast facing forward, eyes open. No. 624, Rhythmic gymnast facing left, eyes closed.

2016, July 22 Litho. *Perf. 14¼*

621 A498 1fr **multicolored** *(90,000)+*	2.25	2.25
622 A498 1fr **multicolored** *(90,000)+*	2.25	2.25
a. Pair, #621-622	4.50	4.50
First day cover, #621-622		5.25
Inscription block of 4	9.00	—
Pane of 6	13.50	—
623 A498 2fr **multicolored** *(90,000)+*	4.50	4.50
624 A498 2fr **multicolored** *(90,000)+*	4.50	4.50
a. Pair, #623-624	9.00	9.00
First day cover, #623-624		10.50
Inscription block of 4	18.00	—
Pane of 6	27.00	—
Nos. 621-624 (4)	13.50	13.50

Souvenir sheets of three bearing three stamps, one from each office are listed under United Nations, Offices in New York as Nos. 1141, 1161, 1177-1178, 1203, and 1208.

World Heritage Sites, Czech Republic Type of 2016

Printed by Cartor Security Printing, France. Panes of 20. Designed by Sergio Baradat, U.S.

Designs: Nos. 625, 627b, Gardens and Castle at Kromeríz. Nos. 626, 627e, Lednice-Valtice Cultural Landscape. No. 627a, Historic Center of Prague. No. 627c, Historic Town Center of Kutná Hora. No. 627d, Holy Trinity Column, Olomouc. No. 627f, Historic Center of Cesky Krumlov.

2016, Sept. 8 Litho. *Perf. 14¼*

625 A500 1fr **multicolored** *(90,000)+*	2.25	2.25
First day cover		3.00
Inscription block of 4	9.00	—
Pane of 20	45.00	—
626 A500 1.50fr **multicolored** *(90,000)+*	3.50	3.50
First day cover		4.50
First day cover, #625-626		6.75
Inscription block of 4	14.00	—
Pane of 20	70.00	—

Souvenir Booklet

627 Booklet, #627g-627l	22.00	
a.-c. A500 30c any single	.65	.65
d.-f. A500 50c any single	1.10	1.10
g. Booklet pane of 4 #627a	2.75	—
h. Booklet pane of 4 #627b	2.75	—
i. Booklet pane of 4 #627c	2.75	—
j. Booklet pane of 4 #627d	4.50	—
k. Booklet pane of 4 #627e	4.50	—
l. Booklet pane of 4 #627f	4.50	—

Miniature Sheet

World Wildlife Conference, Johannesburg — G118

Printed by Cartor Security Printing, France. Designed by Sergio Baradat, U.S.

No. 628 — Part of map of Africa and: a, Grue royale (gray-crowned crane). b, Mantella madagascariensis. c, Gorille des montagnes (mountain gorilla). d, Avonia quinaria.

2016, Sept. 24 Litho. *Perf. 13x13½*

628 G118 Sheet of 4 *(30,000)+*	18.00	18.00
a.-d. 2fr Any single	4.50	4.50
First day cover		19.00

Sustainable Development Goals Type of 2016

Printed by Lowe-Martin, Canada. Designed by Lindsey Thoeng, U.S.

No. 629 — Inscription: a, 1 Pas de pauvreté. b, 2 Faim "zéro." c, 3 Bonne santé et bien-être. d, 4 Éducation de qualité. e, 5 Égalité entre les sexes. f, 6 Eau propre et assainissement. g, 7 Énergie propre et d'un coût abordable. h, 8 Travail décent et croissance éconnomique. i, 9 Industrie, innovation et infrastructure. j, 10 Inégalités réduites. k, 11 Villes et communautés durables. l, 12 Consommation et production responsables. m, 13 Mesures relatives à la lutte contre les changements climatiques. n, 14 Vie aquatique. o, 15 Vie terrestre. p, 16 Paix, justice et institutions efficaces. q, 17 Partneriats pour la réalisation des objectifs.

2016, Oct. 24 Litho. *Perf. 13¼*

629 Sheet of 17 + label *(28,000)+*	39.00	39.00
a.-q. A503 1fr Any single	2.25	2.25
First day cover		42.00

Miniature Sheets

G119

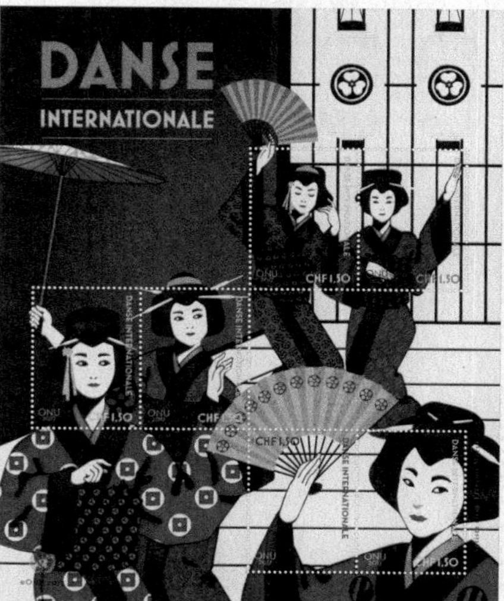

International Dance — G120

Printed by Cartor Security Printing. France. Designed by Sergio Baradat, U.S.

No. 630 — Illustration of Quadrille dancers by Jean François Martin: a, Female dancer wearing red mask facing right, striped pole. b, Male dancer wearing brown mask, harlequin costume, facing right. c, Masked male dancer with red mask facing right. d, Female dancer with brown mask facing left. e, Woman holding black mask facing right. f, Man wearing tan mask facing left.

No. 631 — Illustration of Japanese fan dancers by Martin: a, Dancer holding fan and other hand near her hair. b, Dancer with arm upraised at UR. c, Head of dancer, hand of dancer holding umbrella. d, Dancer, part of fan at LR, e, Dancer's hand holding fan. f, Face of dancer, no hands visible.

2017, Mar. 23 Litho. *Perf. 13¼x13*

630 G119 Sheet of 6 *(22,000)+*	13.00	13.00
a.-f. 1fr Any single	2.10	2.10
631 G120 Sheet of 6 *(22,000)+*	19.50	19.50
a.-f. 1.50fr Any single	3.25	3.25
First day cover, #630-631		37.50

Endangered Species Type of 2017

Printed by Johann Enschedé and Sons, the Netherlands. Designed by Rorie Katz, U.S.

Designs: No. 632, Rhampholeon spp. No. 633, Mobula spp. No. 634, Adansonia grandidieri. No. 635, Scaphiophryne marmorata.

2017, May 11 Litho. *Perf. 12¾x12½*

632 A509 1.50fr **multicolored** *(68,000)+* 3.25 3.25
633 A509 1.50fr **multicolored** *(68,000)+* 3.25 3.25
634 A509 1.50fr **multicolored** *(68,000)+* 3.25 3.25
635 A509 1.50fr **multicolored** *(68,000)+* 3.25 3.25
a. Block of 4, #632-635 13.00 13.00
First day cover, #635a 15.00
First day cover, #632-635, each 5.00
Inscription block of 4, #635a 13.00 —
Pane of 16 52.00 —
Nos. 632-635 (4) 13.00 13.00

World Environment Day Type of 2017

Printed by Lowe-Martin Group, Canada. Panes of 20. Designed by Sergio Baradat, U.S.

Designs: 1fr, Snowy owl, Quebec, Canada. 2fr, Red maple and aspen trees, Canada.

2017, June 5 Litho. *Perf. 13¼*

636 A510 1fr **multicolored** *(80,000)+* 2.25 2.25
First day cover 3.25
Inscription block of 4 9.00 —
Pane of 20 45.00 —
637 A510 2fr **multicolored** *(80,000)+* 4.50 4.50
First day cover 6.50
First day cover, #636-637 8.25
Inscription block of 4 18.00 —
Pane of 20 90.00 —

World Heritage Sites Along the Silk Roads Type of 2017

Printed by Cartor Security Printing, France. Panes of 20. Designed by Sergio Baradat, U.S.

Designs: Nos. 638, 640b, Historic Center of Bukhara, Uzbekistan. Nos. 639, 640e, Kunya-Urgench, Turkmenistan. No. 640a, Longmen Grottoes, People's Republic of China. No. 640c, Tabriz Historic Bazaar Complex, Iran. No. 640d, Sulaiman-Too Sacred Mountain, Kyrgyzstan. No. 640f, Safranbolu, Turkey.

2017, Aug. 3 Litho. *Perf. 14¼*

638 A512 1fr **multicolored** *(80,000)+* 2.40 2.40
First day cover 3.75
Inscription block of 4 9.60 —
Pane of 20 48.00 —
639 A512 1.50fr **multicolored** *(80,000)+* 3.50 3.50
First day cover 5.50
First day cover, #638-639 7.50
Inscription block of 4 14.00 —
Pane of 20 70.00 —

Souvenir Booklet

640 Booklet, #640g-640l *(8,500)+* 26.50
a.-c. A512 30c any single .80 .80
d.-f. A512 50c any single 1.40 1.40
g. Booklet pane of 4 #640a 3.20 —
h. Booklet pane of 4 #640b 3.20 —
i. Booklet pane of 4 #640c 3.20 —
j. Booklet pane of 4 #640d 5.60 —
k. Booklet pane of 4 #640e 5.60 —
l. Booklet pane of 4 #640f 5.60 —

Hare, Fox, and Dove — G121

Heads and Flowers — G122

Heads and Flowers — G123

Printed by Johann Enschedé and Sons, the Netherlands. Panes of 20. Designed by Stranger & Stranger, U.S.

2017, Sept. 21 Litho. *Perf. 14¼x14*

641 G121 1fr **multicolored** *(80,000)+* 2.40 2.40
First day cover 3.50
Inscription block of 4 9.60 —
Pane of 20 48.00 —
642 G122 2fr **multicolored** *(80,000)+* 4.75 4.75
First day cover 7.00
First day cover, #641-642 8.75
Inscription block of 4 19.00 —
Pane of 20 95.00 —

Souvenir Sheet
Perf. 14¼x13¾

643 G123 2fr **multicolored** *(25,000)+* 4.75 4.75
First day cover 6.25

International Day of Peace.

World Food Day Type of 2017

Printed by Royal Johann Enschedé. Panes of 20. Designed by Helen Dardik, Canada.

Designs: 1fr, Milk, yogurt and cheeses. 1.50fr, Fruits.

2017, Oct. 16 Litho. *Perf. 13¼x14*

644 A516 1fr **multicolored** *(80,000)+* 2.40 2.40
First day cover 3.75
Inscription block of 4 9.60 —
Pane of 20 48.00 —
645 A516 1.50fr **multicolored** *(80,000)+* 3.50 3.50
First day cover 5.50
First day cover, #644-645 7.50
Inscription block of 4 14.00 —
Pane of 20 70.00 —

Endangered Species Type of 2018

Printed by Johann Enschedé Stamps Security Printers, the Netherlands. Designed by Rorie Katz, U.S.

Designs: No. 646, Saiga tatarica. No. 647, Uncarina grandidieri. No. 648, Polymita picta. No. 649, Carcharhinus falciformis.

2018, Mar. 2 Litho. *Perf. 12¾x12½*

646 A519 1.50fr **multicolored** *(68,000)+* 3.50 3.50
647 A519 1.50fr **multicolored** *(68,000)+* 3.50 3.50
648 A519 1.50fr **multicolored** *(68,000)+* 3.50 3.50
649 A519 1.50fr **multicolored** *(68,000)+* 3.50 3.50
a. Block of 4, #646-649 14.00 14.00
First day cover, #649a 15.50
First day cover, #646-649, each 5.00
Inscription block of 4, #649a 14.00 —
Pane of 16 56.00 —
Nos. 646-649 (4) 14.00 14.00

World Health Day Type of 2018

Printed by Lowe-Martin Group, Canada. Panes of 20. Designed by Sergio Baradat, U.S.

Designs: 1fr, Microbes and microscope. 2fr, Child, apple, pencil, triangle, numbers, glass of milk.

2018, Apr. 6 Litho. *Perf. 13x13¼*

650 A520 1fr **multicolored** *(80,000)+* 2.25 2.25
First day cover 3.50
Inscription block of 4 9.00 —
Pane of 20 45.00 —
651 A520 2fr **multicolored** *(80,000)+* 4.50 4.50
First day cover 6.75
First day cover, #650-651 8.50
Inscription block of 4 18.00 —
Pane of 20 90.00 —

Miniature Sheet

G124

No. 652: a, Cathedral of St. Lawrence belltower and buildings on hillside. b, Bank with curved glass facade. c, Table and chairs along footpath in city. d, Villa Saroli (yellow building). e, People near door of Santa Maria degli Angioli Church. f, Lugano Arts and Cultural Center (building with four large windows). g, Storefronts along hill on Via Cattedrale. h, Gates of Villa Ciani. i, Arches along Via della Posta. j, William Tell Monument.

2018, May 17 Litho. *Perf. 14¾*

652 G124 Sheet of 10 + 10 labels *38.50 38.50*
a.-j. 1.50fr Any single + label *3.75 3.75*

The full sheet sold for $19.06 or 16.95fr. The generic labels are shown. Labels could be personalized. The personalization of labels was available only at UN Headquarters, and not through mail order.

UNISPACE + 50 Conferences Type of 2018

Printed by Johann Enschedé Stamps BV, Netherlands. Panes of 20. Designed by Sergio Baradat, U.S. Designs: 1fr, View of Earth from space. 1.50fr, Launch of Tiangong 1.

2fr, Widefield Infrared Survey Explorer photograph of Comet 65P/Gunn.

2018, June 20 Litho. *Perf. 14x14¼*

653 A523 1fr **multicolored** *(70,000)+* 2.25 2.25
First day cover 3.75
Inscription block of 4 9.00 —
Pane of 20 45.00 —
654 A523 1.50fr **multicolored** *(70,000)+* 3.50 3.50
First day cover 5.50
First day cover, #653-654 7.25
Inscription block of 4 14.00 —
Pane of 20 70.00 —

Souvenir Sheet
Perf. 13¾

655 A523 2fr **multicolored** *(22,000)+* 4.50 4.50
First day cover 6.25

No. 655 contains one 45x45mm stamp.

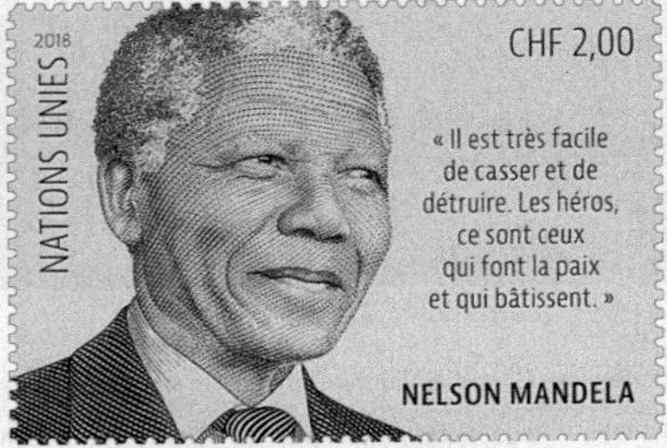

Nelson Mandela (1918-2013), President of South Africa — G125

Printed by Lowe-Martin Group, Canada. Panes of 20. Designed by Martin Morck, Norway.

2018, July 18 Litho. *Perf. 13¼*

656 G125 2fr **buff & black** *(260,000)+* 4.50 4.50
First day cover 6.25
Inscription block of 4 18.00 —
Pane of 20 90.00 —

World Heritage Sites in the United Kingdom Type of 2016

Printed by Cartor Security Printing, France. Panes of 20. Designed by Rorie Katz, U.S.

Designs: Nos. 657, 659b, Stonehenge. Nos. 658, 659e, Edinburgh. No. 659a, Giant's Causeway. No. 659c, Conwy Castle.

No. 659d, Palace of Westminster. No. 659f, Maritime Greenwich.

2018, Aug. 15 **Litho.** ***Perf. 14¼***

657 A524 1fr **multicolored** *(74,000)+* 2.25 2.25
First day cover 3.50
Inscription block of 4 9.00 —
Pane of 20 45.00 —
658 A524 1.50fr **multicolored** *(74,000)+* 3.50 3.50
First day cover 5.50
First day cover, #657-658 7.25
Inscription block of 4 14.00 —
Pane of 20 70.00 —

Souvenir Booklet

659 Booklet, #659g-659l *(7,000)+* 23.50
a.-c. A524 30c any single .75 .75
d.-f. A524 50c any single 1.10 1.10
g. Booklet pane of 4 #659a 3.00 —
h. Booklet pane of 4 #659b 3.00 —
i. Booklet pane of 4 #659c 3.00 —
j. Booklet pane of 4 #659d 4.75 —
k. Booklet pane of 4 #659e 4.75 —
l. Booklet pane of 4 #659f 4.75 —

Miniature Sheet

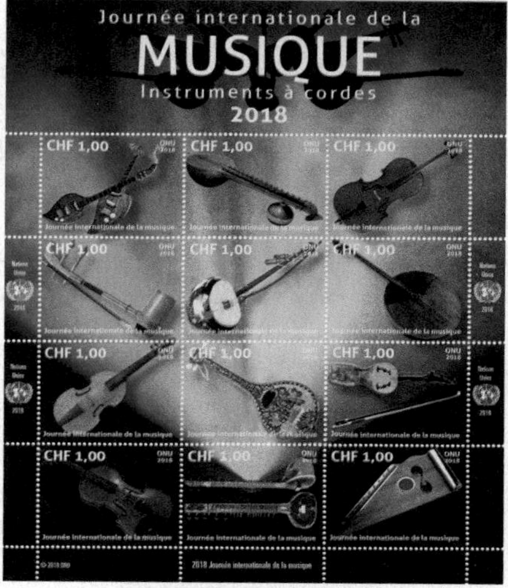

International Music Day — G126

Printed by Johann Enschedé Stamps BV, the Netherlands. Designed by Sergio Baradat, U.S.

No. 660: a, Electric guitars with carved necks. b, Veena. c, Cello. d, Erhu. e, Ektara. f, Domra. g, Viola da gamba. h, Bazouki. i, Stringed instrument with bow. j, Violin with chin rest. k, Sitars. l, Zither.

2018, Oct. 1 **Litho.** ***Perf. 14x13¼***

660 G126 Sheet of 12 *(19,000)+* 27.00 27.00
First day cover 29.00
a.-l. 1fr Any single 2.25 2.25

Miniature Sheet

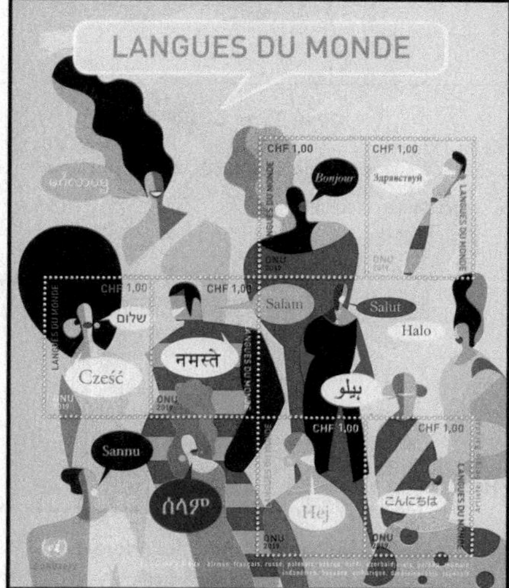

World Languages — G127

Printed by Cartor Security Printing. France. Designed by Sergio Baradat, U.S.

No. 661 — Word bubbles with word for "Hello" in: a, French (Bonjour). b, Russian ("Langues du Monde" in lilac). c, Hebrew and Polish (Czesc), d, Hindi ("Langues du Monde" in white). e, Danish or Swedish (Hej). f, Japanese ("Langues du Monde" in dark gray).

2019, Feb. 21 **Litho.** ***Perf. 13¼x13***

661 G127 Sheet of 6 *(22,000)+* 13.50 13.50
a.-f. 1fr Any single 2.25 2.25
First day cover, #661 17.00

Gender Equality — G128

Printed by Lowe-Martin Group, Canada. Panes of 20. Designed by Chris Gash, U.S.

2019, Mar.15 **Litho.** ***Perf. 13¼x13***

662 G128 1.50fr **multicolored** *(170,000)+* 3.50 3.50
First day cover 5.25
Inscription block of 4 14.00 —
Pane of 20 70.00 —

Endangered Species Type of 2019

Printed by Johann Enschedé Stamps Security Printers, the Netherlands. Designed by Rongliang Wang, People's Republic of China.

Designs: No. 663, Hippocampus kuda. No. 664, Dugong dugon. No. 665, Stylophora pistillata. No. 666, Lamna nasus.

2019, Apr. 26 **Litho.** ***Perf. 12¾x12½***

663 A534 1.50fr **multicolored** *(56,000)+* 3.25 3.25
664 A534 1.50fr **multicolored** *(56,000)+* 3.25 3.25
665 A534 1.50fr **multicolored** *(56,000)+* 3.25 3.25
666 A534 1.50fr **multicolored** *(56,000)+* 3.25 3.25
a. Block of 4, #663-666 13.50 13.50
First day cover, #666a 15.50
First day cover, #663-666, each 5.25
Inscription block of 4, #666a 13.50 —
Pane of 16 54.00 —
Nos. 663-666 (4) 13.00 13.00

2019 END-OF-YEAR ISSUES

See end of New York postage listings.

SEMI-POSTAL STAMP

AIDS Awareness Semi-postal Type
Souvenir Sheet

2002, Oct. 24 **Litho.** ***Perf. 14½***

B1 SP1 90c + 30c **multicolored** *(171,000)+* 4.00 4.00
First day cover, #B1 5.00

AIR LETTER SHEET

Used values for all postal stationery are for non-philatelic contemporaneous usages.

UN Type of 1968

Printed by Setelipaino, Finland. Designed by Robert Perrot.

1969, Oct. 4 **Litho.**

UC1 UC3 65c **ultra & light blue,** entire *(350,000)* .50 *1.50*
Entire, first day cancel *(52,000)* .75

POSTAL CARDS

UN Type of 1969 and Type of Air Post Postal Card, 1966

Printed by Courvoisier, S.A., Switzerland. Designed by John Mason (20c) and Olav S. Mathiesen (30c).

Wmk. Post Horn, Swiss Cross, "S" or "Z"

1969, Oct. 4 **Litho.**

UX1 PC2 20c **olive green & black,** *buff (415,000)* .25 .30
First day cancel *(51,500)* .50
UX2 APC2 30c **violet blue, blue, light & dark green,** *buff (275,000)* .25 .30
First day cancel *(49,000)* .50

No. UX2, although of design APC2, is not inscribed "Poste Aerienne" or "Air Mail."

UN Emblem — GPC1

UN Emblem and Ribbons — GPC2

Printed by Setelipaino, Finland. Designed by Veronique Crombez (40c) and Lieve Baeten (70c).

1977, June 27 **Litho.**

UX3 GPC1 40c **multicolored** *(500,000)* .30 .30
First day cancel *(65,000)* .55
UX4 GPC2 70c **multicolored** *(300,000)* .40 .40
First day cancel *(65,000)* .50

A second printing of No. UX3 was made in 1984. It was released after the Swiss postal card rate had been increased to 50c so instructions were issued that all cards must have a 10c stamp affixed before being sold. A few were sold in NY without the added stamp. The card stock differs from the original printing.

Emblem of the United Nations — GPC3

Peace Dove — GPC4

Printed by Johann Enschede en Zonen, Netherlands. Designed by George Hamori, Australia (50c) and Ryszard Dudzicki, Poland (70c).

1985, May 10 **Litho.**

UX5 GPC3 50c **multicolored** *(300,000)* 1.00 3.50
First day cancel *(34,700)* 1.00
UX6 GPC4 70c **multicolored** *(300,000)* 3.25 3.25
First day cancel *(34,700)* 2.00

No. UX6 Surcharged in Lake

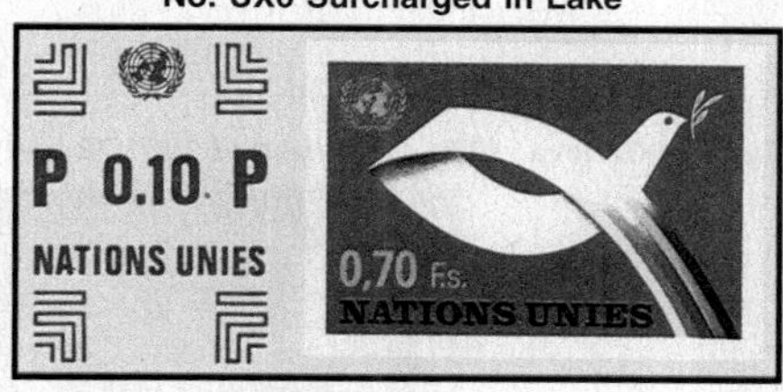

1986, Jan. 2 **Litho.**

UX7 GPC4 70c + 10c **multi** *(90,500)* 2.50 2.50
First day cancel *(8,000 est.)* 10.00

Type of 1990

Printed by Mercury-Walch, Australia.

1992, Sept. 4 **Litho.**

UX8 G45 90c **multicolored** *(150,000)+* 1.75 1.75
First day cancel *(12,385)* 5.00

No. UX5 Surcharged in Lake like No. UX7

1993, May 7 **Litho.**

UX9 GPC3 50c +10c **multicolored** *(47,000)+* 1.50 1.50
First day cancel 15.00

Palais des Nations — GPC5

Printed by Leigh Mardon Pty. Limited, Australia.

1993, May 7 **Litho.**

UX10 GPC5 80c **multicolored** *(200,000)+* 3.00 3.00
First day cancel 4.50

#UX5, UX10 Surcharged in Carmine like #UX7

1996, Mar. 22 **Litho.**

UX11 GPC3 50c +20c **multi** 3.00 3.00
First day cancel 4.00
UX12 GPC5 80c +30c **multi** 3.00 3.00
First day cancel 4.00

Assembly Hall — GPC6

Palais des Nations — GPC7

Printed by Mercury-Walsh, Australia.

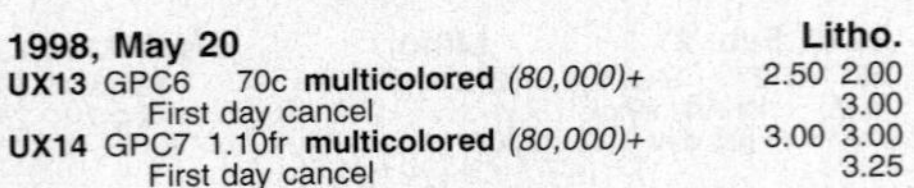

1998, May 20 **Litho.**

UX13 GPC6 70c **multicolored** *(80,000)+* 2.50 2.00
First day cancel 3.00
UX14 GPC7 1.10fr **multicolored** *(80,000)+* 3.00 3.00
First day cancel 3.25

Illustrations of the buildings are shown on the back of each card.

Type of 2002

Printed by Johann Enschedé and Sons, the Netherlands.

2002, Mar. 1 **Litho.**

UX15 G65 1.30fr **multicolored** *(68,000)+* 1.75 1.75
First day cancel 2.00

Nos. UX8, UX13 and UX14 Surcharged Like No. UX7, But With Serifed Numerals

2004, Sept. 21 **Litho.**

UX16 GPC6 70c +15c **multicolored** 2.00 2.00
First day cancel 2.50
UX17 G45 90c +10c **multicolored** 2.25 2.25
First day cancel 2.75
UX18 GPC7 1.10fr +10c **multicolored** 2.50 2.50
First day cancel 3.00

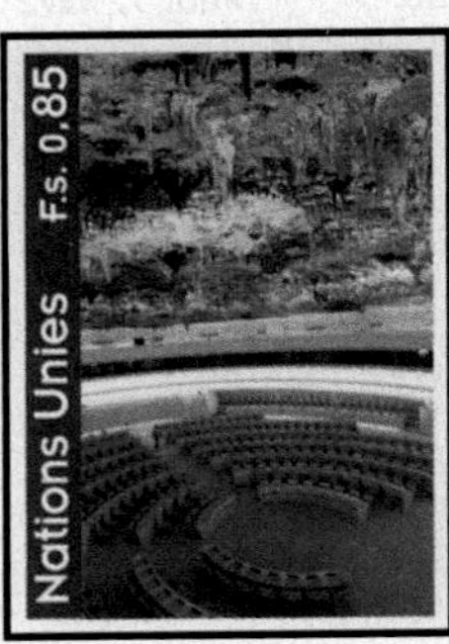

Ceiling Sculpture, Human Rights and Alliance of Civilization Chamber — GPC8

The Broken Chair Memorial GPC9

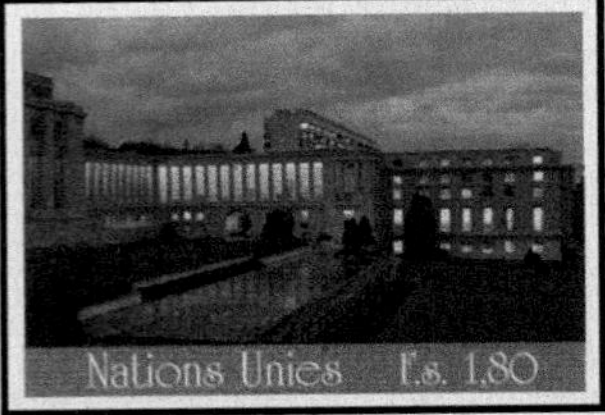

League of Nations Building GPC10

2009, May 7 **Litho.**

UX19 GPC8 85c **multicolored** 2.25 2.25
First day cancel 3.00
UX20 GPC9 1fr **multicolored** 2.50 2.50
First day cancel 4.00
UX21 GPC10 1.80fr **multicolored** 4.25 4.25
First day cancel 6.00

No. UX21 Surcharged Like No. UX7, But With Serifed Numerals

2010 **Litho.**

UX22 GPC10 1.80fr +10c **multicolored** 4.00 4.00
First day cancel 6.00

No. UX15 Surcharged Like No. UX16

2016, July 20 **Litho.**

UX23 G65 1.30fr +20c **multicolored** 4.50 4.50
First day cancel 6.50

OFFICES IN VIENNA, AUSTRIA

For use only on mail posted at the Vienna International Center for the UN and the International Atomic Energy Agency.

100 Groschen = 1 Schilling
100 Cents = 1 Euro (2002)

Type of Geneva, 1978, UN Types of 1961-72 and

Donaupark, Vienna — V1

Aerial View — V2

Printed by Helio Courvoisier S.A., Switzerland. Panes of 50. Designed by Henryk Chylinski (4s); Jozsef Vertel (6s).

1979, Aug. 24 **Photo.** ***Perf. 11½***
Granite Paper

1 G8 50g **multicolored** *(3,500,000)+* .25 .30
First day cover 1.00
Inscription block of 4 .40 —
2 A52 1s **multicolored** *(3,800,000)+* .25 .30
First day cover 1.00
Inscription block of 4 .50 —
3 V1 4s **multicolored** *(3,500,000)+* .25 .30
First day cover 1.00
Inscription block of 4 1.10 —
4 AP13 5s **multicolored** *(3,500,000)+* .30 .35
First day cover 1.00
Inscription block of 4 1.40 —
5 V2 6s **multicolored** *(4,500,000)+* .35 .35
First day cover 1.25
Inscription block of 4 1.75 —
6 A45 10s **multicolored** *(3,500,000)+* .60 .70
First day cover 2.00
Inscription block of 4 3.25 —
Nos. 1-6 (6) 2.00 2.30

\+ Printing orders to Mar. 1993.
No. 4 is not inscribed "Air Mail," No. 6 has no frame.
First day covers of Nos. 1-6 total 1,026,575.

New Economic Order Type of UN

1980, Jan. 11 **Litho.** ***Perf. 15x14½***

7 A178 4s **multicolored** *(1,418,418)* .60 .70
First day cover 1.25
Inscription block of 4 *6.00* —

Value for margin inscription block is for one from bottom of sheet. One from top is about twice the value shown.

Dove Type of UN

1980, Jan. 11 **Litho.** ***Perf. 14x13½***

8 A147 2.50s **multicolored** *(3,500,000)+* .25 .30
First day cover 1.00
Inscription block of 4 1.25 —

First day covers of Nos. 7-8 total 336,229.

Women's Year Emblem on World Map — V3

United Nations Decade for Women

Printed by Questa Colour Security Printers, United Kingdom. Panes of 50. Designed by Gunnar Janssen.

1980, Mar. 7 **Litho.** ***Perf. 14½x15***

9 V3 4s **light green & dark green** *(1,569,080)* .40 .45
First day cover 1.00
Inscription block of 4 1.75 —

10 V3 6s **bister brown** *(1,556,016)* .75 .85
First day cover 1.25
First day cover, #9-10 1.50
Inscription block of 4 3.25 —

First day covers of Nos. 9-10 total 443,893.

Peace-keeping Operations Type of UN

1980, May 16 Litho. *Perf. 14x13*

11 A182 6s **multicolored** *(1,719,852)* .40 .45
First day cover *(323,923)* 1.00
Inscription block of 4 2.00 —

35th Anniversary Types of Geneva and UN

1980, June 26 Litho. *Perf. 13x13½*

12 G16 4s **carmine rose & black** *(1,626,582)* .35 .40
First day cover 1.00
Inscription block of 4 1.60 —
13 A184 6s **multicolored** *(1,625,400)* .60 .65
First day cover 1.25
Inscription block of 4 2.75 —

Souvenir Sheet
Imperf

14 Sheet of 2 *(1,675,191)* .90 1.00
a. G16 4s carmine rose & black .25 .30
b. A184 6s multicolored .65 .30
First day cover 1.00

First day covers of Nos. 12-14 total 657,402.

ECOSOC Types of UN and Geneva

Printed by Ashton-Potter Ltd., Canada. Panes of 50. Designed by Dietman Kowall (4s), Angel Medina Medina (6s).

1980, Nov. 21 Litho. *Perf. 13½x13*

15 A187 4s **multicolored** *(1,811,218)* .30 .35
First day cover 1.00
Inscription block of 4 1.50 —
16 G17 6s **multicolored** *(1,258,420)* .60 .30
First day cover 1.00
First day cover #15-16 1.25
Inscription block of 4 2.50 —

Economic and Social Council (ECOSOC).
First day covers of Nos. 15-16 total 224,631.

Palestinian Rights Type of UN

Printed by Courvoisier S.A., Switzerland. Panes of 50. Designed by David Dewhurst.

1981, Jan. 30 Photo. *Perf. 12x11½*

17 A188 4s **multicolored** *(1,673,310)* .45 .50
First day cover *(208,812)* 1.00
Inscription block of 4 2.00 —

Disabled Type of UN and

Interlocking Stitches — V4

International Year of the Disabled.
Printed by Heraclio Fournier S.A., Spain. Panes of 50. Designed by Sophia van Heeswijk.

1981, Mar. 6 Photo. *Perf. 14*

18 A189 4s **multicolored** *(1,508,719)* .40 .45
First day cover 1.00
Inscription block of 4 1.75 —
19 V4 6s **black & orange** *(1,569,385)* .60 .70
First day cover 1.00
First day cover, #18-19 1.25
Inscription block of 4 2.75 —

First day covers of Nos. 18-19 total 290,603.

Art Type of UN

1981, Apr. 15 Photo. *Perf. 11½*
Granite Paper

20 A191 6s **multicolored** *(1,643,527)* .75 .85
First day cover *(196,916)* 1.00
Inscription block of 4 3.25 —

Energy Type of UN

1981, May 29 Litho. *Perf. 13*

21 A193 7.50s **multicolored** *(1,611,130)* .70 .80
First day cover *(216,197)* 1.00
Inscription block of 4 3.00 —

Volunteers Program Types

1981, Nov. 13 Litho.

22 A195 5s **multicolored** *(1,582,780)* .40 .45
First day cover 1.00
Inscription block of 4 2.25 —

23 G18 7s **multicolored** *(1,516,139)* .90 1.00
First day cover 1.00
First day cover, #22-23 1.00
Inscription block of 4 4.25 —

First day covers of Nos. 22-23 total 282,414.

"For a Better World" — V5

Printed by Courvoisier, S.A., Switzerland. Sheets of 50. Designed by Eliezer Weishoff.

1982, Jan. 22 *Perf. 11½x12*

24 V5 3s **multicolored** *(3,300,000)+* .35 .40
First day cover *(203,872)* 1.00
Inscription block of 4 1.75

Human Environment Types of UN and Geneva

10th Anniversary of United Nations Environment Program. Printed by Joh. Enschede en Zonen, Netherlands. Panes of 50. Designed by Peer-Ulrich Bremer (5s); Sybille Brunner (7s).

1982, Mar. 19 Litho. *Perf. 13½x13*

25 A200 5s **multicolored** *(1,312,765)* .40 .45
First day cover 1.00
Inscription block of 4 1.90 —
26 G21 7s **multicolored** *(1,357,513)* .80 .90
First day cover 1.00
First day cover, #25-26 1.25
Inscription block of 4 3.75 —

First day covers of Nos. 25-26 total 248,576.

Outer Space Type of Geneva

Exploration and Peaceful Uses of Outer Space. Printed by Enschede. Panes of 50. Designed by George Hamori.

1982, June 11 Litho. *Perf. 13x13½*

27 G22 5s **multicolored** *(1,339,038)* .60 .70
First day cover *(150,845)* 1.75
Inscription block of 4 3.00 —

Conservation & Protection of Nature Type

1982, Nov. 16 Photo. *Perf. 14*

28 A202 5s Fish *(1,202,694)* .50 .60
First day cover 1.00
Inscription block of 4 2.50 —
29 A202 7s Animal *(1,194,403)* .70 .80
First day cover 1.00
First day cover, #28-29 1.40
Inscription block of 4 3.00 —

First day covers of Nos. 28-29 total 243,548.

World Communications Year Type

1983, Jan. 28 Litho. *Perf. 13*

30 A203 4s **multicolored** *(1,517,443)* .40 .45
First day cover *(150,541)* 1.40
Inscription block of 4 2.10 —

Safety at Sea Types of Geneva and UN

1983, Mar. 18 Litho. *Perf. 14½*

31 G23 4s **multicolored** *(1,506,052)* .40 .45
First day cover 1.00
Inscription block of 4 2.00 —
32 A206 6s **multicolored** *(1,527,990)* .65 .75
First day cover 1.00
First day cover, #31-32 2.25
Inscription block of 4 2.75 —

First day covers of Nos. 31-32 total 219,118.

World Food Program Type

1983, Apr. 22 Engr. *Perf. 13½*

33 A207 5s **green** *(1,419,237)* .45 .50
First day cover 1.00
Inscription block of 4 2.25 —
34 A207 7s **brown** *(1,454,227)* .70 .80
First day cover 1.00
First day cover, #33-34 1.25
Inscription block of 4 2.75 —

First day covers of Nos. 33-34 total 212,267.

UN Conference on Trade and Development Types of Geneva and UN

1983, June 6 Litho. *Perf. 14*

35 G24 4s **multicolored** *(1,544,973)* .30 .35
First day cover 1.00
Inscription block of 4 1.90 —

36 A209 8.50s **multicolored** *(1,423,172)* .75 .85
First day cover 1.00
First day cover, #35-36 1.25
Inscription block of 4 3.25 —

First day covers of Nos. 35-36 total 184,023.

The Second Skin — V6

Right to Think — V7

35th Anniversary of the Universal Declaration of Human Rights

Printed by Government Printing Office, Austria. Designed by Friedensreich Hundertwasser, Austria. Panes of 16 (4x4).

1983, Dec. 9 Photo. & Engr. *Perf. 13½*

37 V6 5s **multicolored** *(2,163,419)* .40 .45
First day cover 1.25
Inscription block of 4 2.00
38 V7 7s **multicolored** *(2,163,542)* .65 .75
First day cover 1.25
First day cover, #37-38 2.25
Inscription block of 4 3.00
Panes of 16, #37-38 17.50

First day covers of Nos. 37-38 total 246,440.

International Conference on Population Type

Printed by Bundesdruckerei, Federal Republic of Germany. Panes of 50. Designed by Marina Langer-Rosa and Helmut Langer, Federal Republic of Germany.

1984, Feb. 3 Litho. *Perf. 14*

39 A212 7s **multicolored** *(1,135,791)* .65 .75
First day cover *(80,570)* 1.50
Inscription block of 4 2.75 —

Field Irrigation V8

Harvesting Machines V9

World Food Day, Oct. 16

Printed by Walsall Security Printers, Ltd., United Kingdom. Panes of 50. Designed by Adth Vanooijen, Netherlands.

1984, Mar. 15 Litho. *Perf. 14½*

40 V8 4.50s **multicolored** *(994,106)* .40 .45
First day cover 1.00
Inscription block of 4 2.00 —

41 V9 6s **multicolored** *(1,027,115)* .65 .75
First day cover 1.00
First day cover #40-41 2.25
Inscription block of 4 2.50 —

First day covers of Nos. 40-41 total 194,546.

Serengeti Park, Tanzania — V10

Ancient City of Shiban, People's Democratic Rep. of Yemen — V11

World Heritage

Printed by Harrison and Sons, United Kingdom. Panes of 50. Designs adapted by Rocco J. Callari, US, and Thomas Lee, China.

1984, Mar. 15 **Litho.** ***Perf. 14***

42 V10 3.50s **multicolored** *(957,518)* .25 .30
First day cover 1.25
Inscription block of 4 1.25 —
43 V11 15s **multicolored** *(928,794)* 1.25 1.40
First day cover 1.75
First day cover, #42-43 2.50
Inscription block of 4 5.75 —

First day covers of Nos. 42-43 total 193,845.

V12

V13

Future for Refugees

Designed by Hans Erni, Switzerland.
Printed by Courvoisier. Panes of 50.

1984, May 29 **Photo.** ***Perf. 11½***

44 V12 4.50s **multicolored** *(1,086,393)* .45 .50
First day cover 1.25
Inscription block of 4 2.25 —
45 V13 8.50s **multicolored** *(1,109,865)* 1.25 1.40
First day cover 1.75
First day cover, #44-45 2.25
Inscription block of 4 5.75 —

First day covers of Nos. 44-45 total 185,349.

International Youth Year — V14

Printed by Waddingtons Ltd., United Kingdom. Panes of 50. Designed by Ruel A. Mayo, Phillipines.

1984, Nov. 15 **Litho.** ***Perf. 13½***

46 V14 3.50s **multicolored** *(1,178,833)* .45 .50
First day cover 1.25
Inscription block of 4 2.10 —
47 V14 6.50s **multicolored** *(1,109,337)* .70 .80
First day cover 1.50
First day cover, #46-47 2.25
Inscription block of 4 3.25 —

First day covers of Nos. 46-47 total 165,762.

ILO Type of Geneva

Printed by the Government Printing Bureau, Japan. Panes of 50. Adapted from photographs by Rocco J. Callari, US, and Thomas Lee, China.

1985, Feb. 1 **Engr.** ***Perf. 13½***

48 G34 7.50s U Thant Pavilion *(948,317)* .75 .85
First day cover *(115,916)* 1.75
Inscription block of 4 3.50 —

UN University Type

Printed by Helio Courvoisier, Switzerland. Panes of 50. Designed by Moshe Pereg, Israel, and Hinedi Geluda, Brazil.

1985, Mar. 15 **Photo.** ***Perf. 11½***

49 A221 8.50s Rural scene, lab researcher *(863,673)* .75 .85
First day cover *(108,479)* 1.75
Inscription block of 4 3.75 —

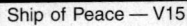

Ship of Peace — V15

Shelter under UN Umbrella — V16

Printed by Carl Ueberreuter Druck and Verlag M. Salzer, Austria. Panes of 50. Designed by Ran Banda Mawilmada, Sri Lanka (4.50s), and Sophia van Heeswijk, Federal Republic of Germany (15s).

1985, May 10 **Litho.** ***Perf. 14***

50 V15 4.50s **multicolored** *(2,000,000)+* .30 .35
First day cover .75
Inscription block of 4 1.50 —
51 V16 15s **multicolored** *(2,000,000)+* 2.00 2.25
First day cover 2.75
First day cover, #50-51 3.50
Inscription block of 4 9.50 —

First day covers of Nos. 50-51 total 142,687.

40th Anniversary Type

Designed by Rocco J. Callari, U.S., and Thomas Lee, China (No. 54).

1985, June 26 **Photo.** ***Perf. 12 x 11½***

52 A224 6.50s **multicolored** *(984,820)* .90 1.00
First day cover 1.25
Inscription block of 4 4.25 —
53 A225 8.50s **multicolored** *(914,347)* 1.40 1.60
First day cover 1.75
First day cover, #52-53 2.50
Inscription block of 4 6.25 —

Souvenir Sheet

Imperf

54 Sheet of 2 *(676,648)* 2.50 2.75
a. A224 6.50s **multi** 1.00 1.10
b. A225 8.50s **multi** 1.40 1.50
First day cover 2.50

First day covers of Nos. 52-54 total 317,652.

UNICEF Child Survival Campaign Type

Printed by the Government Printing Bureau, Japan. Panes of 50. Designed by Mel Harris, United Kingdom (No. 55) and Vreni Wyss-Fischer, Switzerland (No. 56).

4s, Spoonfeeding children. 6s, Mother hugging infant.

1985, Nov. 22 **Photo. & Engr.** ***Perf. 13½***

55 A226 4s multi *(889,918)* .75 .85
First day cover 1.50
Inscription block of 4 3.50 —
56 A226 6s multi *(852,958)* 1.40 1.60
First day cover 1.50
First day cover, #55-56 2.50
Inscription block of 4 6.00 —

First day covers of Nos. 55-56 total 239,532.

Africa in Crisis Type

Printed by Helio Courvoisier, Switzerland. Panes of 50. Designed by Tesfaye Tessema, Ethiopia.

1986, Jan. 31 **Photo.** ***Perf. 11½x12***

57 A227 8s **multicolored** *(809,854)* .80 .90
First day cover *(99,996)* 2.75
Inscription block of 4 3.50 —

UN Development Program Type

Printed by the Government Printing Bureau, Japan. Panes of 40, 2 blocks of 4 horizontal and 5 blocks of 4 vertical. Designed by Thomas Lee, China.

Agriculture: No. 58, Developing crop strains. No. 59, Animal husbandry. No. 60, Technical instruction. No. 61, Nutrition education.

1986, Mar. 14 **Photo.** ***Perf. 13½***

58 A228 4.50s multi *(730,691)* 1.40 1.60
59 A228 4.50s multi *(730,691)* 1.40 1.60
60 A228 4.50s multi *(730,691)* 1.40 1.60
61 A228 4.50s multi *(730,691)* 1.40 1.60
a. Block of 4, #58-61 6.25 7.00
First day cover, #61a 6.75
First day cover, #58-61, each 2.00
Inscription block of 4, #58-61 7.00 —
Pane of 40, #58-61 60.00

No. 61a has a continuous design.

First day covers of Nos. 58-61 total 227,664.

Stamp Collecting Type

Designs: 3.50s, UN stamps. 6.50s, Engraver. Printed by the Swedish Post Office, Sweden. Panes of 50. Designed by Czeslaw Slania and Ingalill Axelsson, Sweden.

1986, May 22 **Engr.** ***Perf. 12½***

62 A229 3.50s **dk ultra & dk brown** *(874,119)* .40 .45
First day cover 1.50
Inscription block of 4 2.25 —
63 A229 6.50s **int blue & brt rose** *(877,284)* .90 1.00
First day cover 1.50
First day cover, #62-63 2.25
Inscription block of 4 4.50 —

First day covers of Nos. 62-63 total 150,836.

Olive Branch, Rainbow, Earth — V17

International Peace Year. Printed by the Government Printing Bureau, Japan. Panes of 50. Designed by Milo Schor, Israel (No. 64), and Mohammad Sardar, Pakistan (No. 65).

Photogravure & Embossed

1986, June 20 ***Perf. 13½***

64 V17 5s shown *(914,699)* .75 .85
First day cover 1.50
Inscription block of 4 3.75 —
65 V17 6s Doves, UN emblem *(818,386)* 1.00 1.10
First day cover 1.50
First day cover, #64-65 2.50
Inscription block of 4 4.50 —

First day covers of Nos. 64-65 total 169,551.

WFUNA Anniversary Type

Souvenir Sheet

Printed by Johann Enschede and Sons, Netherlands. Designed by Rocco J. Callari, US.

Designs: 4s, White stallion by Elisabeth von Janota-Bzowski, Germany. 5s, Surrealistic landscape by Ernst Fuchs, Austria. 6s, Geometric abstract by Victor Vasarely (b. 1908), France. 7s, Mythological abstract by Wolfgang Hutter (b. 1928), Austria.

1986, Nov. 14 **Litho.** ***Perf. 13x13½***

66 Sheet of 4 *(668,264)* 4.00 4.25
a. A232 4s **multicolored** .75 .80
b. A232 5s **multicolored** .85 .90

c. A232 6s **multicolored** 1.00 1.10
d. A232 7s **multicolored** 1.25 1.40
First day cover *(121,852)* 4.00

No. 66 has inscribed margin picturing UN and WFUNA emblems.

Trygve Lie Type

Photogravure & Engraved

1987, Jan. 30 ***Perf. 13½***
67 A233 8s **multicolored** *(778,010)* .70 .80
First day cover *(94,112)* 2.50
Inscription block of 4 3.50 —

Shelter for the Homeless Type

Designs: 4s, Family and homes. 9.50s, Family entering home.

1987, Mar. 13 **Litho.** ***Perf. 13½x12½***
68 A234 4s **multicolored** *(704,922)* .50 .55
First day cover 1.25
Inscription block of 4 2.40 —
69 A234 9.50s **multicolored** *(671,200)* 1.10 1.25
First day cover 1.75
First day cover, #68-69 2.75
Inscription block of 4 4.75 —

First day covers of Nos. 68-69 total 117,941.

Fight Drug Abuse Type

Designs: 5s, Soccer players. 8s, Family.

1987, June 12 **Litho.** ***Perf. 14½x15***
70 A235 5s **multicolored** *(869,875)* .40 .45
First day cover 1.40
Inscription block of 4 2.40 —
71 A235 8s **multicolored** *(797,889)* .90 1.00
First day cover 1.75
First day cover, #70-71 2.75
Inscription block of 4 4.00 —

First day covers of Nos. 70-71 total 117,964.

Donaupark, Vienna — V18

Peace Embracing the Earth — V19

Printed by The House of Questa, United Kingdom. Panes of 50. Designed by Henry Bencsath, US (2s), and Eliezer Weishoff, Israel (17s).

1987, June 12 **Litho.** ***Perf. 14½x15***
72 V18 2s **multicolored** *(2,000,000)+* .30 .35
First day cover 1.25
Inscription block of 4 1.40 —
73 V19 17s **multicolored** *(2,000,000)+* 1.60 1.75
First day cover 2.50
First day cover, #72-73 3.50
Inscription block of 4 7.00 —

First day covers of Nos. 72-73 total 111,153.

UN Day Type

Designed by Elisabeth von Janota-Bzowski (5s) and Fritz Henry Oerter (6s), Federal Republic of Germany.
Designs: Multinational people in various occupations.

1987, Oct. 23 **Litho.** ***Perf. 14½x15***
74 A236 5s **multicolored** *(1,575,731)* .75 .85
First day cover 1.40
Inscription block of 4 3.75 —
75 A236 6s **multicolored** *(1,540,523)* .90 1.00
First day cover 1.75
First day cover, #74-75 2.75
Inscription block of 4 4.25 —
Panes of 12, #74-75 22.00

Immunize Every Child Type

Designs: 4s, Poliomyelitis. 9.50s, Diphtheria.

1987, Nov. 20 **Litho.** ***Perf. 15x14½***
76 A237 4s **multicolored** *(793,716)* .75 .85
First day cover 1.00
Inscription block of 4 4.00 —
77 A237 9.50s **multicolored** *(769,288)* 2.00 2.25
First day cover 1.90
First day cover, #76-77 2.75
Inscription block of 4 8.25 —

IFAD Type

Designs: 4s, Grains. 6s, Vegetables.

1988, Jan. 29 **Litho.** ***Perf. 13½***
78 A238 4s **multicolored** *(697,307)* .40 .45
First day cover 1.25
Inscription block of 4 2.75 —
79 A238 6s **multicolored** *(701,521)* .90 1.00
First day cover 1.75
First day cover, #78-79 2.75
Inscription block of 4 4.25 —

Survival of the Forests Type

Deciduous forest in fall: 4s, Treetops, hills and dales. 5s, Tree trunks. Printed se-tenant in a continuous design.

1988, Mar. 18 **Litho.** ***Perf. 14x15***
80 A240 4s **multicolored** *(990,607)* 2.25 2.40
First day cover 4.50
81 A240 5s **multicolored** *(990,607)* 3.00 3.25
First day cover 5.50
a. Pair, #80-81 5.25 5.75
First day cover, #81a 9.00
Inscription block of 4, #80-81 12.00 —
Pane of 12, #80-81 30.00

Intl. Volunteer Day Type

Designed by George Fernandez, U.S.
Designs: 6s, Medical care, vert. 7.50s, Construction.

1988, May 6 **Litho.** ***Perf. 13x14, 14x13***
82 A241 6s **multicolored** *(701,167)* .75 .85
First day cover 1.40
Inscription block of 4 4.00 —
83 A241 7.50s **multicolored** *(638,240)* 1.00 1.10
First day cover 1.60
First day cover, #82-83 3.00
Inscription block of 4 5.75 —

Health in Sports Type

Paintings by LeRoy Neiman, American Sports artist: 6s, Skiing, vert. 8s, Tennis.

1988, June 17 **Litho.** ***Perf. 13½x13, 13x13½***
84 A242 6s **multicolored** *(668,902)* .90 1.00
First day cover 1.40
Inscription block of 4 5.00 —
85 A242 8s **multicolored** *(647,915)* 1.40 1.60
First day cover 2.00
First day cover #84-85 4.00
Inscription block of 4 8.50 —

Universal Declaration of Human Rights 40th Anniv. Type

1988, Dec. 9 **Photo. & Engr.** ***Perf. 11½***
86 A243 5s **multicolored** *(1,080,041)* .50 .55
First day cover 2.50
Inscription block of 4 3.00 —

Souvenir Sheet

87 A243 11s **multicolored** *(688,994)* 1.25 1.40
First day cover 4.75

No. 87 has multicolored decorative margin inscribed with preamble to the human rights declaration in German.

World Bank Type

1989, Jan. 27 **Litho.** ***Perf. 13x14***
88 A244 5.50s Transportation *(682,124)* 1.10 1.25
First day cover 1.40
Inscription block of 4 5.25 —
89 A244 8s Health care, education *(628,649)* 1.75 1.90
First day cover 2.00
First day cover, #88-89 3.00
Inscription block of 4 8.25 —

First day covers of Nos. 88-89 total 135,964.

Peace-Keeping Force Type

1989, Mar. 17 ***Perf. 14x13½***
90 A245 6s **multicolored** *(912,731)* .85 .95
First day cover *(81,837)* 2.00
Inscription block of 4 4.00 —

World Weather Watch Type

Satellite photograph and radar image: 4s, Helical cloud formation over Italy, the eastern Alps, and parts of Yugoslavia. 9.50s, Rainfall in Tokyo, Japan.

1989, Apr. 21 **Litho.** ***Perf. 13x14***
91 A247 4s **multicolored** *(948,680)* 1.00 1.10
First day cover 1.40
Inscription block of 4 4.50 —
92 A247 9.50s **multicolored** *(880,138)* 2.10 2.25
First day cover 2.00
First day cover, #91-92 4.00
Inscription block of 4 10.50 —

First day covers of Nos. 91-92 total 116,846.

Offices in Vienna, 10th Anniv.
V20 V21

Printed by the Government Printing Office, Austria. Panes of 25. Designed by Gottfried Kumpf (5s) and Andre Heller (7.50s), Austria.

Photo. & Engr., Photo. (7.50s)

1989, Aug. 23 ***Perf. 14***
93 V20 5s **multicolored** *(958,339)* 1.25 1.50
First day cover 1.25
Inscription block of 4 8.50 —
94 V21 7.50s **multicolored** *(785,517)* 1.25 1.50
First day cover 3.00
First day cover, #93-94 4.00
Inscription block of 4 8.50 —
Panes of 25, #93-94 *70.00*

First day covers of Nos. 93-94 total 210,746.

Human Rights Type of 1989

Panes of 12+12 se-tenant labels containing Articles 5 (4s) or 6 (6s) inscribed in German, English or French.
Paintings: 4s, The Prisoners, by Kathe Kollwitz. 6s, Justice, by Raphael.

1989, Nov. 17 **Litho.** ***Perf. 13½***
95 A250 4s **multicolored** *(2,267,450)* .50 .55
First day cover 2.50
Inscription block of 3 + 3 labels 1.75 —
96 A250 6s **multicolored** *(2,264,876)* .75 .85
First day cover 3.50
First day cover, #95-96 3.00
Inscription block of 3 + 3 labels 2.50 —
Panes of 12, #95-96 15.00

First day covers of Nos. 95-96 total 183,199.
See Nos. 108-109, 123-124, 150-151.

Intl. Trade Center Type

1990, Feb. 2 **Litho.** ***Perf. 14½x15***
97 A251 12s **multicolored** *(559,556)* 1.25 1.40
First day cover *(77,928)* 4.00
Inscription block of 4 5.50 —

Painting by Kurt Regschek V22

Printed by the National Postage Stamps and Fiduciary Printing Works, France. Designed by Robert J. Stein, US.

1990, Feb. 2 **Litho.** ***Perf. 13x13½***
98 V22 1.50s **multicolored** *(1,000,000)+* .30 .35
First day cover *(64,622)* 2.50
Inscription block of 4 1.40 —

Fight AIDS Type — V23

Designed by Jacek Tofil, Poland (5s), Orlando Pelaez, Colombia (11s).
Designs: 5s, "SIDA." 11s, Stylized figures, ink blot.

1990, Mar. 16 **Litho.** ***Perf. 13½x12½***
99 V23 5s **multicolored** *(623,155)* 1.00 1.10
First day cover 1.50
Inscription block of 4 6.00 —
100 V23 11s **multicolored** *(588,742)* 2.25 2.40
First day cover 2.50
First day cover, #99-100 4.75
Inscription block of 4 11.50 —

First day covers of Nos. 99-100 total 123,657.

Medicinal Plants Type

1990, May 4 Photo. Granite Paper ***Perf. 11½***

101 A253 4.50s Bixa orellana *(709,840)* 1.25 1.40
First day cover 1.50
Inscription block of 4 5.50 —
102 A253 9.50s Momordica charantia *(732,883)* 2.50 2.75
First day cover 2.50
First day cover, #101-102 4.75
Inscription block of 4 10.50 —

First day covers of Nos. 101-102 total 117,545.

UN 45th Anniv. Type

Designed by Talib Nauman, Pakistan (7s), Marleen Bosmans (9s), Robert Stein, US (No. 105).
Designs: 7s, 9s, "45" and emblem.

1990, June 26 Litho. ***Perf. 14½x13***

103 A254 7s **multicolored** *(604,878)* 1.40 1.60
First day cover 1.75
Inscription block of 4 6.00 —
104 A254 9s **multicolored, diff.** *(550,902)* 2.40 2.75
First day cover 2.25
First day cover, #103-104 4.00
Inscription block of 4 10.50 —

Souvenir Sheet

105 Sheet of 2, #103-104 *(423,370)* 5.00 5.50
First day cover 3.50

First day covers of Nos. 103-105 total 181,174.

Crime Prevention Type

1990, Sept. 13 Photo. ***Perf. 14***

106 A255 6s Domestic violence *(661,810)* 1.00 1.10
First day cover 1.50
Inscription block of 4 5.50 —
107 A255 8s Crimes against cultural heritage *(607,940)* 2.25 2.50
First day cover 2.25
First day cover, #106-107 3.00
Inscription block of 4 11.00 —

First day covers of Nos. 106-107 total 112,193.

Human Rights Type of 1989

Panes of 12+12 se-tenant labels containing Articles 11 (4.50s) or 12 (7s) inscribed in German, English or French.
Paintings: 4.50s, Before the Judge, by Sandor Bihari. 7s, Young Man Greeted by a Woman Writing a Poem, by Suzuki Harunobu.

1990, Nov. 16 Litho. ***Perf. 13½***

108 A250 4.50s **multicolored** *(1,684,833)* .30 .35
First day cover 2.50
Inscription block of 3 + 3 labels 1.25 —
109 A250 7s **multicolored** *(1,541,022)* .90 1.00
First day cover 3.50
First day cover, #108-109 2.50
Inscription block of 3 + 3 labels 4.25 —
Panes of 12, #108-109 20.00

First day covers of Nos. 108-109 total 168,831.

Economic Commission for Europe Type

1991, Mar. 15 Litho. ***Perf. 14***

110 A256 5s Weasel, hoopoe *(727,436)* 1.40 1.60
111 A256 5s Warbler, swans *(727,436)* 1.40 1.60
112 A256 5s Badgers, squirrel *(727,436)* 1.40 1.60
113 A256 5s Fish *(727,436)* 1.40 1.60
a. Block of 4, #110-113 5.60 6.50
First day cover, No. 113a 5.00
First day cover, Nos. 110-113, each 3.25
Inscription block of 4, #110-113 6.50 —
Pane of 40, #110-113 57.50

First day covers of Nos. 110-113 total 81,624.

Namibian Independence Type

1991, May 10 Litho. ***Perf. 14***

114 A257 6s Mountains, clouds *(531,789)* 1.00 1.25
First day cover 2.50
Inscription block of 4 4.25 —
115 A257 9.50s Dune, Namib Desert *(503,735)* 2.25 2.50
First day cover 3.75
First day cover, #114-115 4.50
Inscription block of 4 9.50 —

First day covers of Nos. 114-115 total 111,184.

V24

Printed by House of Questa, United Kingdom. Designed by Marina Langer-Rosa, Germany.

1991, May 10 Litho. ***Perf. 15x14½***

116 V24 20s **multicolored** *(1,750,000)+* 1.75 2.00
First day cover *(60,843)* 4.00
Inscription block of 4 7.50 —

V25

Rights of the Child — V26

Printed by The House of Questa. Panes of 50. Designed by Anna Harmer, Austria (7s) and Emiko Takegawa, Japan (9s).

1991, June 14 Litho. ***Perf. 14½***

117 V25 7s Stick drawings *(645,145)* 1.00 1.25
First day cover 1.75
Inscription block of 4 4.25 —
118 V26 9s Child, clock, fruit *(568,214)* 1.50 1.75
First day cover 2.25
First day cover, #117-118 3.50
Inscription block of 4 6.50 —

First day covers of Nos. 117-118 total 120,619.

V27

Banning of Chemical Weapons V28

Printed by Heraclio Fournier, S.A. Panes of 50. Designed by Oscar Asboth, Austria (5s), Michel Granger, France (10s).

1991, Sept. 11 Litho. ***Perf. 13½***

119 V27 5s **multicolored** *(469,454)* .75 .90
First day cover 1.40
Inscription block of 4 3.50 —
120 V28 10s **multicolored** *(525,704)* 1.75 2.00
First day cover 2.50
First day cover, #119-120 3.00
Inscription block of 4 7.50 —

First day covers of Nos. 119-120 total 116,862.

UN Postal Administration, 40th Anniv. Type

1991, Oct. 24 Litho. ***Perf. 14x15***

121 A263 5s UN NY No. 8 *(564,450)* .75 .90
First day cover 1.40
Inscription block of 4 4.00 —
122 A263 8s UN NY No. 5 *(609,830)* 1.50 1.75
First day cover 2.10
First day cover, #121-122 3.25
Inscription block of 4 7.00 —
Panes of 25, #121-122 57.50

First day covers of Nos. 121-122 total 107,802.

Human Rights Type of 1989

Panes of 12+12 se-tenant labels containing Articles 17 (4.50s) or 18 (7s) inscribed in German, English or French.
Artwork: 4.50s, Pre-columbian Mexican pottery. 7s, Windows, by Robert Delaunay.

1991, Nov. 20 Litho. ***Perf. 13½***

123 A250 4.50s **black & brown** *(1,717,097)* .50 .55
First day cover 2.75
Inscription block of 3 + 3 labels 3.00 —
124 A250 7s **multicolored** *(1,717,738)* .80 .90
First day cover 5.00
First day cover, #123-124 1.75
Inscription block of 3 + 3 labels 5.00 —
Panes of 12+12 labels, #123-124 25.00 25.00

First day covers of Nos. 123-124 total 204,854.

World Heritage Type of 1984

Designs: 5s, Iguacu Natl. Park, Brazil. 9s, Abu Simbel, Egypt.

1992, Jan. 24 Litho. ***Perf. 13***
Size: 35x28mm

125 V10 5s **multicolored** *(586,738)* .75 .90
First day cancel 1.50
Inscription block of 4 3.50 —
126 V10 9s **multicolored** *(476,965)* 1.60 1.80
First day cancel 2.75
First day cancel, #125-126 4.00
Inscription block of 4 6.75 —

First day covers of Nos. 125-126 total 93,016.

Clean Oceans Type

1992, Mar. 13 Litho. ***Perf. 14***

127 A264 7s Ocean surface, diff. *(1,121,870)* 1.00 1.10
128 A264 7s Ocean bottom, diff. *(1,121,870)* 1.00 1.10
a. Pair, #127-128 2.25 2.50
First day cover, #128a 3.25
First day cover, #127-128, any single 2.00
Inscription block of 4, 2 each #127-128 5.00 —
Pane of 12, #127-128 14.00

First day covers of Nos. 127-128 total 128,478.

Earth Summit Type

1992, May 22 Photo. ***Perf. 11½***

129 A265 5.50s Man in space *(784,197)* 1.30 1.50
130 A265 5.50s Sun *(784,197)* 1.30 1.50
131 A265 5.50s Man fishing *(784,197)* 1.30 1.50
132 A265 5.50s Sailboat *(784,197)* 1.30 1.50
a. Block of 4, #129-132 5.50 6.00
First day cover, #132a 6.50
First day cover, #129-132, any single 4.00
Inscription block of 4, #129-132 7.00 —
Pane of 40, #129-132 60.00

First day covers of Nos. 129-132a total 82,920.

Mission to Planet Earth Type

Designs: No. 133, Satellite, person's mouth. No. 134, Satellite, person's ear.

1992, Sept. 4 Photo. ***Rouletted 8***
Granite Paper

133 A266 10s **multicolored** *(881,716)* 3.00 3.25
134 A266 10s **multicolored** *(881,716)* 3.00 3.25
a. Pair, #133-134 6.00 6.50
First day cover, #134a 5.00
First day cover, #133-134, any single 10.00
Inscription block of 4, #133-134 15.00 —
Pane of 10, #133-134 35.00

First day covers of Nos. 133-134 total 99,459.

Science and Technology Type of 1992

Designs: 5.50s, Woman emerging from computer screen. 7s, Green thumb growing flowers.

1992, Oct. 2 Litho. ***Perf. 14***

135 A267 5.50s **multicolored** *(482,830)* .75 .85
First day cover 1.75
Inscription block of 4 3.75 —
136 A267 7s **multicolored** *(500,517)* 1.40 1.60
First day cover 2.00
First day cover, #135-136 4.00
Inscription block of 4 6.75 —

First day covers of Nos. 135-136 total 98,091.

V29

Intl. Center, Vienna — V30

Printed by Walsall Security Printers, Ltd., UK. Designed by Gundi Groh, Austria (5.50s), Rocco J. Callari, US (7s).

1992, Oct. 2 **Litho.** ***Perf. 13x13½***
137 V29 5.50s **multicolored** *(2,100,000)+* .90 1.00
First day cover 1.25
Inscription block of 4 4.25 —

Perf. 13½x13

138 V30 7s **multicolored** *(2,100,000)+* 1.25 1.40
First day cover 2.00
First day cover, #137-138 3.50
Inscription block of 4 6.00 —

First day covers of Nos. 137-138 total 151,788.

Human Rights Type of 1989

Panes of 12+12 se-tenant labels containing Articles 23 (6s) and 24 (10s) inscribed in German, English or French.

Artwork: 6s, Les Constructeurs, by Fernand Leger. 10s, Sunday Afternoon on the Island of Le Grande Jatte, by Georges Seurat.

1992, Nov. 20 **Litho.** ***Perf. 13½***
139 A250 6s **multicolored,** *(1,536,516)* .75 .85
First day cover 5.00
Inscription block of 3 + 3 labels 3.00 —
140 A250 10s **multicolored,** *(1,527,861)* 1.25 1.40
First day cover 11.00
Inscription block of 3 + 3 labels 5.50 —
First day cover, #139-140 2.00
Panes of 12, #139-140 30.00 30.00

Aging With Dignity Type

Designs: 5.50s, Elderly couple, family working in garden. 7s, Older woman teaching.

1993, Feb. 5 **Litho.** ***Perf. 13***
141 A270 5.50s **multicolored** *(428,886)* .75 .85
First day cover 1.60
Inscription block of 4 4.50 —
142 A270 7s **multicolored** *(459,471)* 1.40 1.60
First day cover 2.00
First day cover, #141-142 3.00
Inscription block of 4 7.50 —

First day covers of Nos. 141-142 total 87,052.

Endangered Species Type

Designed by Rocco J. Callari and Steve Brennan, US.

Designs: No. 143, Equus grevyi (Grevy's zebra). No. 144, Spheniscus humboldti (Humboldt's penguins). No. 145, Varanus griseus (desert monitor). No. 146, Canis lupus (gray wolf).

1993, Mar. 2 **Litho.** ***Perf. 13x12½***
143 A271 7s **multicolored** *(1,200,000)+* .90 1.00
144 A271 7s **multicolored** *(1,200,000)+* .90 1.00
145 A271 7s **multicolored** *(1,200,000)+* .90 1.00
146 A271 7s **multicolored** *(1,200,000)+* .90 1.00
a. Block of 4, #143-146 3.60 4.00
First day cover, #146a 5.25
First day cover, #143-146, any single 1.75
Inscription block of 4, #146a 4.00 —
Pane of 16, #143-146 15.00

First day covers of Nos. 143-146a total 106,211.

Healthy Environment Type

1993, May 7 **Litho.** ***Perf. 15x14½***
147 A272 6s **Wave in ocean** *(517,433)* 1.25 1.40
First day cover 1.50
Inscription block of 4 5.25 —
148 A272 10s **Globe** *(453,123)* 2.00 2.25
First day cover 2.25
First day cover, #147-148 3.50
Inscription block of 4 8.75 —

First day covers of Nos. 147-148 total 79,773.

V31

Designed by Marek Kwiatkowski, Poland. Printed by Helio Courvoisier S.A., Switzerland.

1993, May 7 **Photo.** ***Perf. 11½***
Granite Paper
149 V31 13s **multicolored** *(1,500,000)+* 2.00 2.25
First day cover 1.25
Inscription block of 4 8.50 —

Human Rights Type of 1989

Printed in sheets of 12 + 12 se-tenant labels containing Article 29 (5s) and 30 (6s) inscribed in German, English or French.

Artwork: 5s, Lower Austrian Peasants' Wedding, by Ferdinand G. Waldmuller. 6s, Outback, by Sally Morgan.

1993, June 11 **Litho.** ***Perf. 13½***
150 A250 5s **multicolored** *(1,532,531)* .80 .90
First day cover 2.50
Inscription block of 3 + 3 labels 3.25 —
151 A250 6s **multicolored** *(1,542,716)* 1.00 1.10
First day cover 3.50
First day cover, #150-151 1.50
Inscription block of 3 + 3 labels 4.25 —
Panes of 12, #150-151 22.00 25.00

First day covers of Nos. 150-151 total 128,687.

Intl. Peace Day Type

Denomination at: No. 152, UL. No. 153, UR. No. 154, LL. No. 155, LR.

1993, Sept. 21 **Litho. & Engr.** ***Rouletted 12½***
152 A274 5.50s **green & multi** *(445,699)* 1.80 2.00
153 A274 5.50s **green & multi** *(445,699)* 1.80 2.00
154 A274 5.50s **green & multi** *(445,699)* 1.80 2.00
155 A274 5.50s **green & multi** *(445,699)* 1.80 2.00
a. Block of 4, #152-155 7.25 8.25
First day cover, #155a 4.00
First day cover, #152-155, any single 2.25
Inscription block of 4, #155a 8.75 —
Pane of 40, #152-155 80.00

First day covers of Nos. 152-155a total 67,075.

Environment-Climate Type

Designs: No. 156, Monkeys. No. 157, Bluebird, industrial pollution, volcano. No. 158, Volcano, nuclear power plant, tree stumps. No. 159, Cactus, tree stumps, owl.

1993, Oct. 29 **Litho.** ***Perf. 14½***
156 A275 7s **multicolored** *(484,517)* 2.50 2.75
157 A275 7s **multicolored** *(484,517)* 2.50 2.75
158 A275 7s **multicolored** *(484,517)* 2.50 2.75
159 A275 7s **multicolored** *(484,517)* 2.50 2.75
a. Strip of 4, #156-159 10.00 11.00
First day cover, #159a 9.50
First day cover, #156-159, any single 4.00
Inscription block of 8, 2 #159a 22.50 —
Pane of 24, #156-159 60.00

First day covers of Nos. 156-159a total 61,946.

Intl. Year of the Family Type of 1993

Designs: 5.50s, Adults, children holding hands. 8s, Two adults, child planting crops.

1994, Feb. 4 **Litho.** ***Perf. 13.1***
160 A276 5.50s **blue green & multi** *(650,000)+* 1.00 1.10
First day cover 1.60
Inscription block of 4 4.25 —
161 A276 8s **red & multi** *(650,000)+* 1.25 1.40
First day cover 2.25
First day cover, #160-161 3.00
Inscription block of 4 5.50 —

First day covers of Nos. 160-161 total 78,532.

Endangered Species Type of 1993

Designed by Rocco J. Callari, US (frame), and Paul Margocsy, Australia (stamps).

Designs: No. 162, Ocelot. No. 163, White-breasted silver-eye. No. 164, Mediterranean monk seal. No. 165, Asian elephant.

1994, Mar. 18 **Litho.** ***Perf. 12.7***
162 A271 7s **multicolored** *(1,200,000)+* 1.00 1.10
163 A271 7s **multicolored** *(1,200,000)+* 1.00 1.10
164 A271 7s **multicolored** *(1,200,000)+* 1.00 1.10
165 A271 7s **multicolored** *(1,200,000)+* 1.00 1.10
a. Block of 4, #162-165 4.00 4.40
First day cover, #165a 6.00
First day cover, #162-165, each 2.25
Inscription block of 4, #165a 4.50 —
Pane of 16, #162-165 16.50

First day covers of Nos. 162-165a total 104,478.

Protection for Refugees Type

Design: 12s, Protective hands surround group of refugees.

1994, Apr. 29 **Litho.** ***Perf. 14.3x14.8***
166 A277 12s **multicolored** *(650,000)+* 1.50 1.75
First day cover *(49,519)* 3.00
Inscription block of 4 8.00 —

V32

V33

V34

Designed by Masatoshi Hioki, Japan (No. 167), Ramon Alcantara Rodriguez, Mexico (No. 168), Eliezer Weishoff, Israel (No. 169).

Printed by Cartor, S.A., France.

1994, Apr. 29 **Litho.** ***Perf. 12.9***
167 V32 50g **multicolored** *(1,450,000)+* .25 .30
First day cover 1.25
Inscription block of 4 .40 —
168 V33 4s **multicolored** *(1,150,000)+* .40 .45
First day cover 1.25
Inscription block of 4 2.75 —
169 V34 30s **multicolored** *(560,000)+* 4.00 4.50
First day cover 5.00
Inscription block of 4 20.00 —
Nos. 167-169 (3) 4.65 5.25

First day covers of Nos. 167-169 total 74,558.

Intl. Decade for Natural Disaster Reduction Type

Earth seen from space, outline map of: No. 170, North America. No. 171, Eurasia. No. 172, South America. No. 173, Australia and South Asia.

1994, May 27 **Litho.** ***Perf. 13.9x14.2***
170 A281 6s **multicolored** *(690,000)+* 1.75 1.90
171 A281 6s **multicolored** *(690,000)+* 1.75 1.90
172 A281 6s **multicolored** *(690,000)+* 1.75 1.90
173 A281 6s **multicolored** *(690,000)+* 1.75 1.90
a. Block of 4, #170-173 7.00 7.75
First day cover, #173a 6.00
First day cover, #170-173, each 3.25
Inscription block of 4, #173a 8.50 —
Pane of 40, #170-173 82.50

First day covers of Nos. 170-173a total 52,502.

Population and Development Type

Designs: 5.50s, Women teaching, running machine tool, coming home to family. 7s, Family on tropical island.

1994, Sept. 1 **Litho.** ***Perf. 13.2x13.6***
174 A282 5.50s **multicolored** *(650,000)+* .90 1.00
First day cover 2.00
Inscription block of 4 3.75 —
175 A282 7s **multicolored** *(650,000)+* 1.50 1.75
First day cover 2.00
First day cover, #174-175 5.00
Inscription block of 4 6.50 —

First day covers of Nos. 174-175 total 67,423.

UNCTAD Type

1994, Oct. 28
176 A283 6s **multi, diff.** *(650,000)+* .90 1.00
First day cover 1.25
Inscription block of 4 4.25 —
177 A283 7s **multi, diff.** *(650,000)+* 1.50 1.75
First day cover 1.75
First day cover, #176-177 3.00
Inscription block of 4 7.00 —

First day covers of Nos. 176-177 total 67,064.

UN 50th Anniv. Type

1995, Jan. 1 **Litho. & Engr.** ***Perf. 13.4***
178 A284 7s **multicolored** *(742,052)* 1.25 1.40
First day cover *(118,537)* 2.00
Inscription block of 4 5.50 —

Social Summit Type

1995, Feb. 3 **Photo. & Engr.** ***Perf. 13.6x13.9***
179 A285 14s **multi, diff.** *(595,554)* 2.00 2.25
First day cover *(51,244)* 3.50
Inscription block of 4 9.00 —

Endangered Species Type of 1993

Designed by Salvatore Catalano, US.

Designs: No. 180, Black rhinoceros, Diceros bicornis. No. 181, Golden conure, Aratinga guarouba. No. 182, Douc langur, Pygathrix nemaeus. No. 183, Arabian oryx, Oryx leucoryx.

1995, Mar. 24 **Litho.** ***Perf. 13x12½***
180 A271 7s **multicolored** *(938,000)+* 1.00 1.10
181 A271 7s **multicolored** *(938,000)+* 1.00 1.10
182 A271 7s **multicolored** *(938,000)+* 1.00 1.10
183 A271 7s **multicolored** *(938,000)+* 1.00 1.10
a. Block of 4, 180-183 4.00 4.50
First day cover, #183a 4.50

First day cover, #180-183, each 2.00
Inscription block of 4, #183a 5.00 —
Pane of 16, #180-183 17.50

First day covers of Nos. 180-183a total 95,401.

Intl. Youth Year Type

Designs: 6s, Village in winter. 7s, Teepees.

1995, May 26 **Litho.** ***Perf. 14.4x14.7***
184 A286 6s **multicolored** *(437,462)* .80 .90
First day cover 1.50
Inscription block of 4 3.25 —
185 A286 7s **multicolored** *(409,449)* 1.00 1.10
First day cover 2.50
First day cover, #184-185 4.25
Inscription block of 4 4.25 —

First day covers of Nos. 184-185 total 60,979.

UN, 50th Anniv. Type

Designs: 7s, Like No. 663. 10s, Like No. 664.

1995, June 26 **Engr.** ***Perf. 13.3x13.6***
186 A287 7s **green** *(433,922)* 1.20 1.30
First day cover 2.00
Inscription block of 4 5.00 —
187 A287 10s **black** *(471,198)* 1.75 1.90
First day cover 1.75
First day cover, #186-187 4.00
Inscription block of 4 8.00 —

Souvenir Sheet
Litho. & Engr.
Imperf

188 Sheet of 2, #186-187 *(367,773)* 2.75 3.10
a. A287 7s **green** 1.10 1.25
b. A287 10s **black** 1.60 1.80
First day cover 6.50

First day covers of Nos. 186-188b total 171,765.

Conference on Women Type

Designs: 5.50s, Women amid tropical plants. 6s, Woman reading, swans on lake.

1995, Sept. 5 **Photo.** ***Perf. 12***
189 A288 5.50s **multicolored** *(549,951)* .80 .90
First day cover 1.50
Inscription block of 4 3.50 —

Size: 28x50mm

190 A288 6s **multicolored** *(556,569)* 1.20 1.30
First day cover 1.50
First day cover, #189-190 3.50
Inscription block of 4 5.25 —

First day covers of Nos. 189-190 total 71,976.

UN People, 50th Anniv. Type

1995, Oct. 24 **Litho.** ***Perf. 14***
191 Sheet of 12 *(280,528 sheets)* 9.00 10.00
First day cover 16.00
a.-l. A290 3s any single .75 .85
First day cover, #191a-191 l, each 1.25
192 Souvenir booklet, *(95,449 booklets)* 9.00
a. A290 3s Booklet pane of 3, vert. strip of 3 from UL of sheet 2.25 2.75
b. A290 3s Booklet pane of 3, vert. strip of 3 from UR of sheet 2.25 2.75
c. A290 3s Booklet pane of 3, vert. strip of 3 from LL of sheet 2.25 2.75
d. A290 3s Booklet pane of 3, vert. strip of 3 from LR of sheet 2.25 2.75

First day covers of Nos. 191-192d total 107,436.

WFUNA, 50th Anniv. Type

Design: 7s, Harlequin holding dove.

1996, Feb. 2 **Litho.** ***Perf. 13x13½***
193 A291 7s **multicolored** *(655,000)+* 1.00 1.10
First day cover 2.00
Inscription block of 4 4.50 —

UN Flag — V35

Abstract, by Karl Korab — V36

Printed by House of Questa, UK.

1996, Feb. 2 **Litho.** ***Perf. 15x14½***
194 V35 1s **multicolored** *(1,180,000)+* .25 .30

195 V36 10s **multicolored** *(880,000)+* 1.60 1.75
First day cover 2.75
First day cover, #194-195 4.50
Inscription block of 4 7.00 —

Endangered Species Type of 1993

Designs: No. 196, Cypripedium calceolus. No. 197, Aztekium ritteri. No. 198, Euphorbia cremersii. No. 199, Dracula bella.

1996, Mar. 14 **Litho.** ***Perf. 12½***
196 A271 7s **multicolored** *(846,000)+* .75 .85
197 A271 7s **multicolored** *(846,000)+* .75 .85
198 A271 7s **multicolored** *(846,000)+* .75 .85
199 A271 7s **multicolored** *(846,000)+* .75 .85
a. Block of 4, #196-199 3.00 3.40
First day cover, #199a 4.50
First day cover, #196-199, each 2.00
Inscription block of 4, #199a 4.00 —
Pane of 16, #196-199 13.00

City Summit Type

Designs: No. 200, Arab family selling fruits, vegetables. No. 201, Women beside stream, camels. No. 202, Woman carrying bundle on head, city skyline. No. 203, Woman threshing grain, yoke of oxen in field. No. 204, Native village, elephant.

1996, June 3 **Litho.** ***Perf. 14x13½***
200 A293 6s **multicolored** *(500,000)+* 1.50 1.75
201 A293 6s **multicolored** *(500,000)+* 1.50 1.75
202 A293 6s **multicolored** *(500,000)+* 1.50 1.75
203 A293 6s **multicolored** *(500,000)+* 1.50 1.75
204 A293 6s **multicolored** *(500,000)+* 1.50 1.75
a. Strip of 5, #200-204 7.50 9.00
First day cover, #204a 11.50
First day cover, #200-204, each 4.50
Inscription block of 10, 2 #204a 16.00

Sport and the Environment Type

6s, Men's parallel bars (gymnastics), vert. 7s, Hurdles.

1996, July 19 **Litho.** ***Perf. 14x14½, 14½x14***
205 A294 6s **multicolored** *(730,000)+* .80 .90
First day cover 2.75
Inscription block of 4 3.75 —
206 A294 7s **multicolored** *(730,000)+* .90 1.00
First day cover 3.00
First day cover, #205-206 6.00
Inscription block of 4 4.25 —

Souvenir Sheet

207 A294 Sheet of 2, #205-206 *(500,000)+* 1.75 1.90
First day cover 10.00

Plea for Peace Type

Designed by: 7s, Du Keqing, China. 10s, Xu Kangdeng, China.

Designs: 7s, Dove and butterflies. 10s, Stylized dove, diff.

1996, Sept. 17 **Litho.** ***Perf. 14½x15***
208 A295 7s **multicolored** *(655,000)+* .80 .90
First day cover 1.50
Inscription block of 4 3.75 —
209 A295 10s **multicolored** *(655,000)+* 1.20 1.40
First day cover 2.50
First day cover, #208-209 5.00
Inscription block of 4 5.75 —

UNICEF Type

Fairy Tales: 5.50s, Hansel and Gretel, by the Brothers Grimm. 8s, How Maui Stole Fire from the Gods, South Pacific.

1996, Nov. 20 **Litho.** ***Perf. 14½x15***
210 A296 5.50s **multicolored** *(1,160,000)+* .90 1.00
First day cover 1.25
Pane of 8 + label 8.00
211 A296 8s **multicolored** *(1,160,000)+* 1.40 1.60
First day cover 2.00
First day cover, #210-211 4.00
Pane of 8 + label 12.00

V37

V38

Printed by The House of Questa, Ltd., UK.
Phoenixes Flying Down (Detail), by Sagenji Yoshida.

1997, Feb. 12 **Litho.** ***Perf. 14½***
212 V37 5s **multicolored** *(750,000)+* .80 .90
First day cover 1.25
Inscription block of 4 3.40 —

213 V38 6s **multicolored** *(1,050,000)+* .90 1.00
First day cover 1.50
First day cover, #212-213 4.00
Inscription block of 4 4.00 —

First day covers of Nos. 212-213 total 156,021.

Endangered Species Type of 1993

Designs: No. 214, Macaca sylvanus (Barbary macaque). No. 215, Anthropoides paradisea (blue crane). No. 216, Equus przewalskii (Przewalski horse). No. 217, Myrmecophaga tridactyla (giant anteater).

1997, Mar. 13 **Litho.** ***Perf. 12½***
214 A271 7s **multicolored** *(710,000)+* .75 .85
215 A271 7s **multicolored** *(710,000)+* .75 .85
216 A271 7s **multicolored** *(710,000)+* .75 .85
217 A271 7s **multicolored** *(710,000)+* .75 .85
a. Block of 4, #214-217 3.00 3.40
First day cover, #217a 6.00
First day cover, #214-217, each 3.75
Inscription block of 4, #217a 4.50
Pane of 16 13.50

First day covers of Nos. 214-217 total 86,406.

Earth Summit Anniv. Type

Designs: No. 218, Person running. No. 219, Hills, stream, trees. No. 220, Tree with orange leaves. No. 221, Tree with pink leaves.

11s, Combined design similar to Nos. 218-221.

1997, May 30 **Photo.** ***Perf. 11.5***
Granite Paper
218 A299 3.50s **multicolored** *(282,016)* 1.50 1.75
219 A299 3.50s **multicolored** *(282,016)* 1.50 1.75
220 A299 3.50s **multicolored** *(282,016)* 1.50 1.75
221 A299 3.50s **multicolored** *(282,016)* 1.50 1.75
a. Block of 4, #218-221 6.00 7.00
First day cover, #221a 10.00
First day cover, #218-221, each 4.75
Inscription block of 4, #221a 7.00

Souvenir Sheet

222 A299 11s **multicolored** *(221,434)* 2.40 2.60
First day cover 12.00

First day covers of Nos. 218-222 total 62,390.

Transportation Type

Ground transportation: No. 223, 1829 Rocket, 1901 Darraque. No. 224, Steam engine from Vladikawska Railway, trolley. No. 225, Double-decker bus. No. 226, 1950s diesel locomotive, semi-trailer. No. 227, High-speed train, electric car.

1997, Aug. 29 **Litho.** ***Perf. 14x14½***
223 A300 7s **multicolored** *(356,097)* 1.25 1.40
224 A300 7s **multicolored** *(356,097)* 1.25 1.40
225 A300 7s **multicolored** *(356,097)* 1.25 1.40
226 A300 7s **multicolored** *(356,097)* 1.25 1.40
227 A300 7s **multicolored** *(356,097)* 1.25 1.40
a. Strip of 5, #223-227 6.25 7.00
First day cover, #227a 16.00
First day cover, #223-227, each 4.75
Inscription block of 10, 2#227a 13.50

No. 227a has continuous design.
First day covers of Nos. 223-227 total 44,877.

Philately Type

Designs: 6.50s, No. 62. 7s, No. 63.

1997, Oct. 14 **Litho.** ***Perf. 13½x14***
228 A301 6.50s **multicolored** *(379,767)* .80 .90
First day cover 2.50
Inscription block of 4 4.00 —
229 A301 7s **multicolored** *(378,107)* .90 1.00
First day cover 3.50
First day cover, #228-229 6.00
Inscription block of 4 4.50 —

First day covers of Nos. 228-229 total 57,651.

World Heritage Convention Type

Terracotta warriors of Xian: 3s, Single warrior. 6s, Massed warriors. No. 232a, like No. 716. No. 232b, like No. 717. No. 232c, like Geneva No. 314. No. 232d, like Geneva No. 315. No. 232e, like Vienna No. 230. No. 232f, like Vienna No. 231.

1997, Nov. 19 **Litho.** ***Perf. 13½***
230 A302 3s **multicolored** *(528,352)* 1.00 1.10
First day cover 1.50
Inscription block of 4 4.25 —
231 A302 6s **multicolored** *(530,947)* 2.00 2.25
First day cover 2.75
First day cover, #230-231 5.00
Inscription block of 4 9.00 —
232 Souvenir booklet *(298,055 booklets)* 12.00
a.-f. A302 1s any single .50 .55
g. Booklet pane of 4 #232a 2.00 2.25
h. Booklet pane of 4 #232b 2.00 2.25
i. Booklet pane of 4 #232c 2.00 2.25
j. Booklet pane of 4 #232d 2.00 2.25
k. Booklet pane of 4 #232e 2.00 2.25
l. Booklet pane of 4 #232f 2.00 2.25

First day covers of Nos. 230-232 total 71,708.

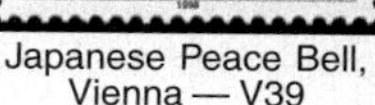

Japanese Peace Bell, Vienna — V39

Vienna Subway, Vienna Intl. Center — V40

Printed by The House of Questa, UK. Panes of 20.
Designed by Heinz Pfeifer, Austria (6.50s), Pigneter, Austria (9s).

1998, Feb. 13 Litho. *Perf. 15x14½*
233 V39 6.50s **multicolored** *(670,000)+* .80 .90
First day cover 3.25
Inscription block of 4 3.50 —
234 V40 9s **multicolored** *(770,000)+* 1.00 1.10
First day cover 4.50
First day cover, #233-234 3.00
Inscription block of 4 4.25 —

Endangered Species Type of 1993

Designed by Rocco J. Callari, US and Robert Hynes, US.
Designs: No. 235, Chelonia mydas (green turtle). No. 236, Speotyto cunicularia (burrowing owl). No. 237, Trogonoptera brookiana (Rajah Brooke's birdwing). No. 238, Ailurus fulgens (lesser panda).

1998, Mar. 13 Litho. *Perf. 12½*
235 A271 7s **multicolored** *(620,000)+* .75 .85
236 A271 7s **multicolored** *(620,000)+* .75 .85
237 A271 7s **multicolored** *(620,000)+* .75 .85
238 A271 7s **multicolored** *(620,000)+* .75 .85
a. Block of 4, #235-238 3.00 3.40
First day cover, #238a 5.00
First day cover, #235-238, each 2.50
Inscription block of 4, #238a 3.50 —
Pane of 16 12.50

Intl. Year of the Ocean — V41

Designed by Yuan Lee, China.

1998, May 20 Litho. *Perf. 13x13½*
239 V41 Sheet of 12 *(345,000)+* 9.50 10.75
a.-l. 3.50s any single .80 .90
First day cover, 3239 17.00
First day cover, #239a-239l, each 3.00

Rain Forests Type

1998, June 19 *Perf. 13x13½*
240 A307 6.50s Ocelot *(590,000)+* .90 1.00
First day cover 4.00
Inscription block of 4 4.75 —

Souvenir Sheet

241 A307 22s like #240 *(340,000)+* 3.00 3.25
First day cover 5.25

Peacekeeping Type of 1998

Designs: 4s, Soldier passing out relief supplies. 7.50s, UN supervised voting.

1998, Sept. 15 Photo. *Perf. 12*
242 A308 4s multicolored *(555,000)+* .50 .60
First day cover 1.25
Inscription block of 4 2.00 —
243 A308 7.50s multicolored *(545,000)+* 1.00 1.10
First day cover 1.75
First day cover, #242-243 4.00
Inscription block of 4 4.25 —

Declaration of Human Rights Type

Designs: 4.50s, Stylized person. 7s, Gears.

1998, Oct. 27 Litho. & Photo. *Perf. 13*
244 A309 4.50s multicolored *(555,000)+* .80 .90
First day cover 1.50
Inscription block of 4 3.25 —
245 A309 7s multicolored *(545,000)+* 1.25 1.40
First day cover 2.75
First day cover, #244-245 4.00
Inscription block of 4 5.00 —

Schönbrunn Palace Type

Designs: 3.50s, No. 248d, Palace. 7s, No. 248c, Porcelain stove, vert. No. 248a, Blue porcelain vase, vert. No. 248b, Wall painting on fabric (detail), by Johann Wenzl Bergl, vert. No. 248e, Great Palm House (conservatory). No. 248f, The Gloriette (archway).

1998, Dec. 4 Litho. *Perf. 14*
246 A310 3.50s **multicolored** *(615,000)+* .60 .70
First day cover 2.00
Inscription block of 4 2.50 —
247 A310 7s **multicolored** *(615,000)+* 1.10 1.25
First day cover 2.75
First day cover, #246-247 4.00
Inscription block of 4 4.50 —

Souvenir Booklet

248 Booklet *(158,000)+* 20.00
a.-c. A310 1s any single .60 .70
d.-f. A310 2s any single 1.20 1.30
g. Booklet pane of 4 #248d 4.80 5.25
h. Booklet pane of 3 #248a 1.80 2.00
i. Booklet pane of 3 #248b 1.80 2.00
j. Booklet pane of 3 #248c 1.80 2.00
k. Booklet pane of 4 #248e 4.80 5.25
l. Booklet pane of 4 #248f 4.80 5.25

Volcanic Landscape — V42

Designed by Peter Pongratz, Austria. Printed by Johann Enschedé and Sons, the Netherlands.

1999, Feb. 5 Litho. *Perf. 13x13½*
249 V42 8s **multicolored** *(660,000)+* 1.25 1.40
First day cover *(33,022)* 4.00
Inscription block of 4 7.50 —

World Heritage, Australia Type

Designs: 4.50s, No. 252d, Uluru-Kata Tjuta Natl. Park. 6.50s, No. 252a, Tasmanian Wilderness. No. 252b, Wet tropics of Queensland. No. 252c, Great Barrier Reef. No. 252e, Kakadu Natl. Park. No. 252f, Willandra Lakes region.

1999, Mar. 19 Litho. *Perf. 13*
250 A313 4.50s **multicolored** *(540,000)+* .75 .85
First day cover 1.25
Inscription block of 4 3.00 —
251 A313 6.50s **multicolored** *(540,000)+* 1.10 1.25
First day cover 1.50
First day cover, #250-251 4.50
Inscription block of 4 4.50 —

Souvenir Booklet

252 Booklet *(116,000)+* 12.00
a.-c. A313 1s any single .35 .40
d.-f. A313 2s any single .65 .70
g. Booklet pane of 4, #252a 1.40 1.60
h. Booklet pane of 4, #252d 2.60 2.80
i. Booklet pane of 4, #252b 1.40 1.60
j. Booklet pane of 4, #252e 2.60 2.80
k. Booklet pane of 4, #252c 1.40 1.60
l. Booklet pane of 4, #252f 2.60 2.80

First day covers of Nos. 250-252 total 65,123.

Endangered Species Type of 1993

Designed by Jeffrey Terreson, US.
Designs: No. 253, Pongo pygmaeus (oran-utan). No. 254, Pelecanus crispus (Dalmatian pelican). No. 255, Eunectes notaeus (yellow anaconda). No. 256, Caracal.

1999, Apr. 22 Litho. *Perf. 12½*
253 A271 7s **multicolored** *(552,000)+* .75 .85
254 A271 7s **multicolored** *(552,000)+* .75 .85
255 A271 7s **multicolored** *(552,000)+* .75 .85
256 A271 7s **multicolored** *(552,000)+* .75 .85
a. Block of 4, #253-256 3.00 3.40
First day cover, #256a 6.00
First day cover, #253-256, each 2.25
Inscription block of 4, #256a 3.75 —
Pane of 16 12.50

First day covers of Nos. 253-256 total 66,733.

UNISPACE III Type

Designs: No. 257, Satellite over ships. No. 258, Satellite up close. No. 259, Composite of Nos. 257-258.

1999, July 7 Photo. *Rouletted 8*
257 A314 3.50s **multicolored** *(1,200,000)+* .75 .85
258 A314 3.50s **multicolored** *(1,200,000)+* .75 .85
a. Pair, #257-258 1.60 1.70
First day cover, #258a 3.00
First day cover, #257-258, each 2.50
Inscription block of 4 6.50 —
Pane of 10, #257-258 9.00 —

Souvenir Sheet

Perf. 14½
259 A314 13s **multicolored** *(350,000)+* 4.50 5.00
First day cover 5.00

First day covers of Nos. 257-259 total 72,143.

UPU Type

Various people, late 20th century methods of mail transportation, denomination at: No. 260, UL. No. 261, UR. No. 262, LL. No. 263, LR.

1999, Aug. 23 Photo. *Perf. 11¾*
260 A315 6.50s **multicolored** *(417,000)+* 1.00 1.10
261 A315 6.50s **multicolored** *(417,000)+* 1.00 1.10
262 A315 6.50s **multicolored** *(417,000)+* 1.00 1.10
263 A315 6.50s **multicolored** *(417,000)+* 1.00 1.10
a. Block of 4, #260-263 4.00 4.50
First day cover, #263a 4.50
First day cover, #260-263, each 2.00
Inscription block of 4 4.50 —

First day covers of Nos. 260-263 total 38,453.

In Memoriam Type

Designs: 6.50s, 14s, Donaupark. Size of 14s stamp: 34x63mm.

1999, Sept. 21 Litho. *Perf. 14½x14*
264 A316 6.50s **multicolored** *(530,000)+* .90 1.00
First day cover 3.00
Inscription block of 4 4.50 —

Souvenir Sheet

Perf. 14
265 A316 14s **multicolored** *(338,000)+* 3.00 3.25
First day cover 4.00

First day covers of Nos. 264-265 total 61,089.

Education Type

1999, Nov. 18 Litho. *Perf. 13½x13¾*
266 A317 7s Boy, girl, book *(490,000)+* .75 .85
First day cover 1.60
Inscription block of 4 3.25 —
267 A317 13s Group reading *(490,000)+* 1.75 1.90
First day cover 3.00
First day cover, #266-267 4.00
Inscription block of 4 6.50 —

First day covers of Nos. 266-267 total 48,590.

Intl. Year of Thanksgiving Type

2000, Jan. 1 Litho. *Perf. 13¼x13½*
268 A318 7s **multicolored** *(510,000)+* .80 .90
First day cover 3.00
Inscription block of 4 4.75 —

On No. 268 parts of the design were applied by a thermographic process producing a shiny, raised effect.

Endangered Species Type of 1993

Designed by Lori Anzalone, US.
Designs: No. 269, Panthera pardus (leopard). No. 270, Platalea leucorodia (white spoonbill). No. 271, Hippocamelus bisulcus (huemal). No. 272, Orcinus orca (killer whale).

2000, Apr. 6 Litho. *Perf. 12¾x12½*
269 A271 7s **multicolored** *(548,000)+* 1.10 1.25
270 A271 7s **multicolored** *(548,000)+* 1.10 1.25
271 A271 7s **multicolored** *(548,000)+* 1.10 1.25
272 A271 7s **multicolored** *(548,000)+* 1.10 1.25
a. Block of 4, #269-272 4.50 5.00
First day cover, #272a 6.00
First day cover, #269-272, each 2.00
Inscription block of 4, #272a 4.75 —
Pane of 16 18.00

Our World 2000 Type

Winning artwork in Millennium painting competition: 7s, Tomorrow's Dream, by Voltaire Perez, Philippines. 8s, Remembrance, by Dimitris Nalbandis, Greece, vert.

2000, May 30 Litho. *Perf. 13x13½, 13½x13*
273 A319 7s **multicolored** *(430,000)+* .60 .70
First day cover 1.75
Inscription block of 4 2.75 —
274 A319 8s **multicolored** *(430,000)+* .75 .85
First day cover 2.00
First day cover, #273-274 3.00
Inscription block of 4 3.25 —

55th Anniversary Type

Designs: 7s, Secretariat Building, unfinished dome of General Assembly Hall, 1951. 9s, Trygve Lie and Headquraters Advisory Committee at topping-out ceremony, 1949.

2000, July 7 **Litho.** ***Perf. 13¼x13***

275 A320 7s **multicolored** *(440,000)+* .90 1.00
First day cover 1.75
Inscription block of 4 4.50 —
276 A320 9s **multicolored** *(440,000)+* 1.25 1.40
First day cover 2.25
First day cover, #275-276 3.00
Inscription block of 4 6.00 —

Souvenir Sheet

277 A320 Sheet of 2, #275-276 *(300,000)+* 2.75 3.25
First day cover 3.25

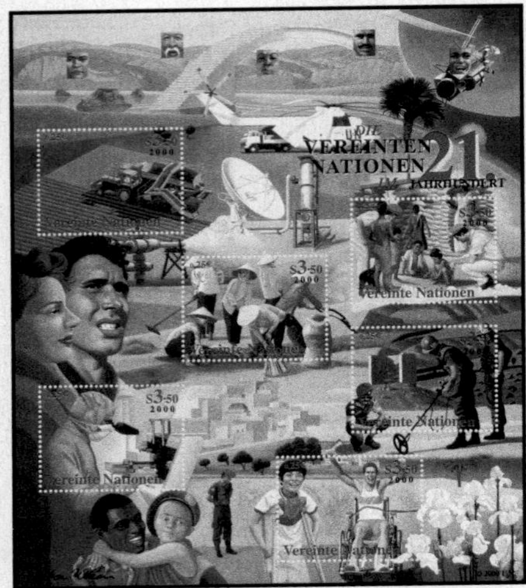

The UN in the 21st Century — V43

Printed by Government Printing Office, Austria. Designed by Wilson McLean, UK.

No. 278: a, Farm machinery. b, UN Peacekeepers and children. c, Oriental farm workers. d, Peacekeepers searching for mines. e, Medical research. f, Handicapped people.

2000, Sept. 15 **Litho.** ***Perf. 14***

278 V43 Sheet of 6 *(330,000)+* 7.50 8.50
First day cover 5.00
a.-f. 3.50s any single 1.25 1.40
First day cover, #278a-278f, each 4.00

World Heritage, Spain Type

Designs: Nos. 279, 281c, Aqueduct of Segovia. Nos. 280, 281f, Güell Park, Barcelona. No. 281a, Alhambra, Generalife and Albayzín, Granada. No. 281b, Walled Town of Cuenca. No. 281d, Amphitheater of Mérida. No. 281e, Toledo.

2000, Oct. 6 **Litho.** ***Perf. 14¾x14½***

279 A323 4.50s **multicolored** *(430,000)+* .80 .90
First day cover 1.25
Inscription block of 4 3.00 —
280 A323 6.50s **multicolored** *(430,000)+* 1.20 1.40
First day cover 1.75
First day cover, #279-280 2.40
Inscription block of 4 4.00 —

Souvenir Booklet

281 Booklet *(92,000)+* 9.00
a.-c. A323 1s any single .25 .30
d.-f. A323 2s any single .50 .55
g. Booklet pane of 4, #281a 1.00 1.10
h. Booklet pane of 4, #281d 2.00 2.25
i. Booklet pane of 4, #281b 1.00 1.10
j. Booklet pane of 4, #281e 2.00 2.25
k. Booklet pane of 4, #281c 1.00 1.10
l. Booklet pane of 4, #281f 2.00 2.25

Respect for Refugees Type

Designs: 7s, 25s, Refugee with hat, three other refugees.

2000, Nov. 9 **Litho.** ***Perf. 13¼x12¾***

282 A324 7s **multicolored** *(530,000)+* 1.10 1.25
First day cover 1.75
Inscription block of 4 4.50 —

Souvenir Sheet

283 A324 25s **multicolored** *(273,000)+* 3.75 4.25
First day cover 4.50

Endangered Species Type of 1993

Printed by Johann Enschedé and Sons, the Netherlands. Designed by Betina Ogden, Australia.

Designs: No. 284, Tremarctos ornatus (spectacled bear). No. 285, Anas laysanensis (Laysan duck). No. 286, Proteles cristatus (aardwolf). No. 287, Trachypithecus cristatus (silvered leaf monkey).

2001, Feb. 1 **Litho.** ***Perf. 12¾x12½***

284 A271 7s **multicolored** *(540,000)+* 1.10 1.25
285 A271 7s **multicolored** *(540,000)+* 1.10 1.25
286 A271 7s **multicolored** *(540,000)+* 1.10 1.25
287 A271 7s **multicolored** *(540,000)+* 1.10 1.25
a. Block of 4, #284-287 4.50 5.00
First day cover, #287a 5.00
First day cover, #284-287 each 1.75
Inscription block of 4, #287a 4.25 —
Pane of 16 16.00

Intl. Volunteers Year — V44

Printed by Johann Enschedé and Sons, the Netherlands. Panes of 20. Designed by Rorie Katz and Robert Stein, US.

Paintings by: 10s, Nguyen Thanh Chuong, Viet Nam. 12s, Ikko Tanaka, Japan.

2001, Mar. 29 **Litho.** ***Perf. 13¼***

288 V44 10s **multicolored** *(440,000)+* 1.40 1.60
First day cover 2.00
Inscription block of 4 5.75
289 V44 12s **multicolored** *(430,000)+* 1.75 1.90
First day cover 2.40
First day cover, #288-289 3.75
Inscription block of 4 7.00

World Heritage, Japan Type

Designs: 7s, No. 290c, Himeji-Jo. 15s, No. 291f, Nikko. No. 292a, Kyoto. No. 292b, Nara. No. 292d, Shirakawa-Go and Gokayama. No. 292e, Itsukushima Shinto Shrine.

2001, Aug. 1 **Litho.** ***Perf. 12¾x13¼***

290 A328 7s **multicolored** *(440,000)+* 1.00 1.10
First day cover 1.40
Inscription block of 4 4.00 —
291 A328 15s **multicolored** *(440,000)+* 2.10 2.25
First day cover 3.00
First day cover, #290-291 3.75
Inscription block of 4 8.50 —

Souvenir Booklet

292 Booklet *(78,000)+* 11.50
a.-c. A328 1s any single .30 .35
d.-f. A328 2s any single .60 .70
g. Booklet pane of 4, #292a 1.20 1.40
h. Booklet pane of 4, #292d 2.40 2.75
i. Booklet pane of 4, #292b 1.20 1.40
j. Booklet pane of 4, #292e 2.40 2.75
k. Booklet pane of 4, #292c 1.20 1.40
l. Booklet pane of 4, #292f 2.40 2.75

Dag Hammarskjöld Type

2001, Sept. 18 **Engr.** ***Perf. 11x11¼***

293 A329 7s **green** *(480,000)+* 1.00 1.10
First day cover 2.00
Inscription block of 4 4.25 —

UN Postal Administration, 50th Anniv. Types

2001, Oct. 18 **Litho.** ***Perf. 13½***

294 A330 7s Stamps, balloons *(380,000)+* 1.00 1.10
First day cover 1.60
Inscription block of 4 4.00 —
295 A330 8s Stamps, cake *(380,000)+* 1.10 1.25
First day cover 1.75
First day cover, #294-295 2.75
Inscription block of 4 4.50 —

Souvenir Sheet

296 A331 Sheet of 2 *(225,000)+* 7.50 8.00
a. 7s **green & light blue,** 38mm diameter 2.50 2.75
b. 21s **green & light blue,** 38mm diameter 5.00 5.50
First day cover 7.00

Climate Change Type

Designs: No. 297, Solar panels, automobile at pump. No. 298, Blimp, bicyclists, horse and rider. No. 299, Balloon, sailboat, lighthouse, train. No. 300, Bird, train, traffic signs.

2001, Nov. 16 **Litho.** ***Perf. 13¼***

297 A332 7s **multicolored** *(87,000)+* 1.00 1.10
298 A332 7s **multicolored** *(87,000)+* 1.00 1.10
299 A332 7s **multicolored** *(87,000)+* 1.00 1.10
300 A332 7s **multicolored** *(87,000)+* 1.00 1.10
a. Horiz. strip, #297-300 5.00 5.50
Inscription block of 8 8.25 —
First day cover, #300a 4.50
First day cover, #297-300 each 6.00
Pane of 24 30.00 —

Nobel Peace Prize Type

2001, Dec. 10 **Litho.** ***Perf. 13¼***

301 A333 7s **multicolored** *(1,260,000)+* 1.00 .55
Inscription block of 4 5.00 —
First day cover 1.60
Pane of 12 14.00 —

100 Cents = 1 Euro (€)

Austrian Tourist Attractions V45

Printed by House of Questa, UK. Panes of 20. Designed by Rorie Katz, US.

Designs: 7c, Semmering Railway. 51c, Pferdschwemme, Salzburg. 58c, Aggstein an der Donau Ruins. 73c, Hallstatt. 87c, Melk Abbey. €2.03, Kapitelschwemme, Salzburg.

2002, Mar. 1 **Litho.** ***Perf. 14½x14***

302 V45 7c **multicolored** *(860,000)+* .25 .30
First day cover 1.25
Inscription block of 4 .75 —
303 V45 51c **multicolored** *(960,000)+* .90 1.25
First day cover 1.40
Inscription block of 4 4.00 —
304 V45 58c **multicolored** *(860,000)+* 1.00 1.10
First day cover 1.60
Inscription block of 4 4.25 —
305 V45 73c **multicolored** *(760,000)+* 1.25 1.40
First day cover 2.00
Inscription block of 4 5.50 —
306 V45 87c **multicolored** *(760,000)+* 1.75 2.00
First day cover 2.40
Inscription block of 4 7.25 —
307 V45 €2.03 **multicolored** *(710,000)+* 3.50 3.75
First day cover 5.50
First day cover, #288-289 10.50
Inscription block of 4 15.00 —
Nos. 302-307 (6) 8.65 9.80

Endangered Species Type of 1993

Printed by Johann Enschedé and Sons, the Netherlands. Designed by Tim Barrall, US.

Designs: No. 308, Hylobates syndactylus (siamang). No. 309, Spheniscus demersus (jackass penguin). No. 310, Prionodon linsang (banded linsang). No. 311, Bufo retiformis (Sonoran green toad).

2002, Apr. 4 **Litho.** ***Perf. 12¾x12½***

308 A271 51c **multicolored** *(500,000)+* 1.25 1.25
309 A271 51c **multicolored** *(500,000)+* 1.25 1.25
310 A271 51c **multicolored** *(500,000)+* 1.25 1.25
311 A271 51c **multicolored** *(500,000)+* 1.25 1.25
a. Block of 4, #308-311 5.00 5.00
First day cover, #311a 4.75
First day cover, #308-311 each 1.75
Inscription block of 4, #311a 5.25 —
Pane of 16 18.00 —

Independence of East Timor Type

Designs: 51c, Deer horn container with carved wooden stopper. €1.09, Carved wooden tai weaving loom.

2002, May 20 **Litho.** ***Perf. 14x14½***

312 A335 51c **multicolored** *(384,000)+* 1.00 1.00
First day cover 1.50
Inscription block of 4 4.50 —
313 A335 €1.09 **multicolored** *(374,000)+* 2.25 2.25
First day cover 3.25
First day cover, #312-313 4.00
Inscription block of 4 9.50 —

Intl. Year of Mountains Type

Designs: No. 314, Mt. Cook, New Zealand. No. 315, Mt. Robson, Canada. No. 316, Mt. Rakaposhi, Pakistan. No. 317, Mt. Everest (Sagarmatha), Nepal.

2002, May 24 **Litho.** ***Perf. 13x13¼***

314 A336 22c **multicolored** *(1,335,000)+* .40 .40
First day cover 1.25
315 A336 22c **multicolored** *(1,335,000)+* .40 .40
First day cover 1.25
316 A336 51c **multicolored** *(1,335,000)+* 1.00 1.00
First day cover 1.50
First day cover, #314, 316 2.25
317 A336 51c **multicolored** *(1,335,000)+* 1.00 1.00
a. Vert. strip or block of four, #314-317 10.00 10.00
First day cover 1.50
First day cover, #315, 317 2.25
First day cover, #314-317 3.75
Pane of 12, 3 each #314-317 10.00 —

World Summit on Sustainable Development (Peter Max) Type

Designs: No. 318, Rainbow. No. 319, Three women, diff. No. 320, Three faceless people. No. 321, Birds, wave.

2002, June 27 **Litho.** ***Perf. 14½x14***

318 A337 51c **multicolored** *(1,305,000)+* 1.00 1.00
First day cover 1.50
319 A337 51c **multicolored** *(1,305,000)+* 1.00 1.00
First day cover 1.50
320 A337 58c **multicolored** *(1,305,000)+* 1.25 1.25
First day cover 1.60
First day cover, #318, 320 2.50
321 A337 58c **multicolored** *(1,305,000)+* 1.25 1.25
a. Vert. strip or block of four, #318-321 8.50 8.50
First day cover 1.60

First day cover, #319, 321 2.50
First day cover, #318-321 3.75
Pane of 12, 3 each #318-321 13.50 —

World Heritage, Italy Type

Designs: 51c, No. 324f, Pompeii. 58c, No. 324c, Rome. No. 324a, Amalfi Coast. No. 324b, Aeolian Islands. No. 324d, Florence. No. 324e, Pisa.

2002, Aug. 30 Litho. *Perf. 13½x13¼*
322 A338 51c **multicolored** *(400,000)+* 1.10 1.10
First day cover 1.75
Inscription block of 4 4.50 —
323 A338 58c **multicolored** *(400,000)+* 1.25 1.25
First day cover 2.00
First day cover, #322-323 3.00
Inscription block of 4 5.00 —

Souvenir Booklet

324 Booklet *(71,000)+* 15.00
a.-c. A338 7c any single .40 .40
d.-f. A338 15c any single .85 .85
g. Booklet pane of 4, #324d 3.40 3.40
h. Booklet pane of 4, #324a 1.60 1.60
i. Booklet pane of 4, #324e 3.40 3.40
j. Booklet pane of 4, #324b 1.60 1.60
k. Booklet pane of 4, #324f 3.40 3.40
l. Booklet pane of 4, #324c 1.60 1.60

AIDS Awareness Type

2002, Oct. 24 Litho. *Perf. 13½*
325 A339 €1.53 **multicolored** *(370,000)+* 2.50 2.75
Inscription block of 4 13.00
First day cover, #325 4.00
Pane of 20 65.00

Indigenous Art — V46

Printed by House of Questa, UK.
Designed by Rorie Katz and Robert Stein, US.

No. 326: a, Mola, Panama. b, Mochican llama-shaped spouted vessel, Peru. c, Tarabuco woven cloth, Bolivia. d, Masks, Cuba. e, Aztec priest's feather headdress, Mexico. f, Bird-shaped staff head, Colombia.

2003, Jan. 31 Litho. *Perf. 14¼*
326 V46 Sheet of 6 *(212,000)+* 7.50 7.50
First day cover 8.25
a.-f. 51c Any single 1.25 1.25
First day cover, a.-f., each 3.00

Austrian Tourist Attractions Type of 2002

Printed by House of Questa, UK. Designed by Rorie Katz, US. Panes of 20.
Designs: 25c, Kunsthistorisches Museum, Vienna. €1, Belvedere Palace, Vienna.

2003, Mar. 28 Litho. *Perf. 14½x14*
327 V45 25c **multicolored** *(650,000)+* .55 .55
First day cover 1.25
Inscription block of 4 2.25 —
328 V45 €1 **multicolored** *(650,000)+* 2.25 2.25
First day cover 3.25
First day cover, #327-328 3.50
Inscription block of 4 9.00 —

Endangered Species Type of 1993

Printed by Johann Enschedé and Sons, the Netherlands. Designed by Robert Hautman, US.
Designs: No. 329, Anas formosa (Baikal teal). No. 330, Bostrychia hagedash (Hadada ibis). No. 331, Ramphastos toco (toco toucan). No. 332, Alopochen aegyptiacus (Egyptian goose).

2003, Apr. 3 Litho. *Perf. 12¾x12½*
329 A271 51c **multicolored** *(432,000)+* 1.25 1.25
330 A271 51c **multicolored** *(432,000)+* 1.25 1.25
331 A271 51c **multicolored** *(432,000)+* 1.25 1.25
332 A271 51c **multicolored** *(432,000)+* 1.25 1.25
a. Block of 4, #329-332 5.00 5.00
First day cover, #332a 5.25
First day cover, #329-332 each 1.90
Inscription block of 4, #332a 5.50 —
Pane of 16 20.00 —

International Year of Freshwater Type of 2003

2003, June 20 Litho. *Perf. 14¼x14½*
333 A345 55c Bridge, bird *(316,000)+* 3.00 3.00
334 A345 75c Horse, empty river *(316,000)+* 5.00 5.00
a. Horiz. pair, #333-334 8.00 8.00
First day cover, #334a 3.75
Inscription block of 4 15.00 —

Austrian Tourist Attractions Type of 2002

Printed by Johann Enschedé and Sons, the Netherlands. Panes of 20. Designed by Rorie Katz, US.
Design: 4c, Schloss Eggenberg, Graz.

2003, Aug. 7 Litho. *Perf. 14x13¼*
335 V45 4c **multicolored** *(650,000)+* .45 .45
First day cover 1.25
Inscription block of 4 1.80
Pane of 20 9.00

Ralph Bunche Type

Litho. With Foil Application

2003, Aug. 7 *Perf. 13½x14*
336 A346 €2.10 **olive green & multicolored** *(384,000)+* 3.50 3.50
First day cover 5.50
Inscription block of 4 15.00
Pane of 20 70.00

In Memoriam Type of 2003

2003, Oct. 24 Litho. *Perf. 13¼x13*
337 A347 €2.10 **multicolored** *(670,000)+* 5.00 5.00
First day cover 6.25
Inscription block of 4 22.00 —
Pane of 20 110.00 —

World Heritage Sites, United States Type

Designs: 55c, No. 340c, Olympic National Park. 75c, No. 340e, Everglades National Park. No. 340a, Yosemite National Park. No. 340b, Great Smoky Mountains National Park. No. 340d, Hawaii Volcanoes National Park. No. 340f, Yellowstone National Park.

2003, Oct. 24 Litho. *Perf. 14½x14¼*
338 A348 55c **multicolored** *(275,000)+* 1.50 .75
First day cover 2.10
Inscription block of 4 6.00 —
339 A348 75c **multicolored** *(275,000)+* 2.00 1.00
First day cover 2.75
First day cover, #338-339 4.25
Inscription block of 4 8.00 —

Souvenir Booklet

340 Booklet *(57,500)+* 14.50
a.-c. A348 15c any single .55 .55
d.-f. A348 20c any single .65 .65
g. Booklet pane of 4 #340a 2.10 2.10
h. Booklet pane of 4 #340d 2.60 2.60
i. Booklet pane of 4 #340b 2.10 2.10
j. Booklet pane of 4 #340e 2.60 2.60
k. Booklet pane of 4 #340c 2.10 2.10
l. Booklet pane of 4 #340f 2.60 2.60

Austrian Tourist Attractions Type of 2002

Printed by Imprimerie de Timbres-Poste, France.
Design: 55c, Schloss Schönbrunn, Vienna.

2004, Jan. 29 Litho. *Perf. 13x13¼*
341 V45 55c **multicolored** *(740,000)+* 1.50 1.50
First day cover 2.10
Inscription block of 4 6.00 —
Pane of 20 30.00 —

Endangered Species Type of 1993

Printed by Johann Enschedé and Sons, the Netherlands. Designed by Yuan Lee, U.S.
Designs: No. 342, Melursus ursinus (Sloth bear). No. 343, Cervus eldi (Eld's deer). No. 344, Cercocebus torquatus (Cherry-crowned mangabey). No. 345, Bubalus arnee (Wild water buffalo).

2004, Jan. 29 Litho. *Perf. 12¾x12½*
342 A271 55c **multicolored** *(376,000)+* 1.50 1.50
343 A271 55c **multicolored** *(376,000)+* 1.50 1.50
344 A271 55c **multicolored** *(376,000)+* 1.50 1.50
345 A271 55c **multicolored** *(376,000)+* 1.50 1.50
a. Block of 4, #342-345 6.00 6.00
First day cover, #345a 6.50
First day cover, #342-345, each 2.25
Inscription block of 4, #345a 7.00 —
Pane of 16 25.00 —

Indigenous Art Type of 2003

Printed by Johann Enschedé and Sons, the Netherlands.
Designed by Rorie Katz and Robert Stein, US.

No. 346: a, Illuminated illustration from the Book of Kells, Ireland. b, Easter eggs, Ukraine. c, Venus of Willendorf, Paleolithic age limestone statue, Austria. d, Flatatunga panel, Iceland. e, Neolithic era idol, Hungary. f, Illuminated illustration from medical treatise, Portugal.

2004, Mar. 4 Litho. *Perf. 13¼*
346 V46 Sheet of 6 *(133,000)+* 12.00 12.00
First day cover 10.50
a.-f. 55c Any single 2.00 2.00
First day cover, a.-f., each 2.75

Road Safety Type

Road map art with: 55c, Automobile, alcohol bottles. 75c, Road, clouds in traffic light colors, vert.

2004, Apr. 7 Litho. *Perf. 13x13¼, 13¼x13*
347 A354 55c **multicolored** *(225,000)+* 1.25 1.25
First day cover 2.10
Inscription block of 4 6.00 —
348 A354 75c **multicolored** *(225,000)+* 1.75 1.75
First day cover 2.75
First day cover, #338-339 4.25
Inscription block of 4 8.00 —

Japanese Peace Bell, 50th Anniv. Type

2004, June 3 Litho. & Engr. *Perf. 13¼x13*
349 A355 €2.10 **multicolored** *(280,000)+* 4.50 4.50
First day cover 6.25
Inscription block of 4 22.00 —
Pane of 20 110.00

World Heritage Sites, Greece Type

Designs: 55c, No. 352f, Mycenae and Tiryns. 75c, No. 352e, Olympia. No. 352a, Acropolis, Athens. No. 352b, Delos. No. 352c, Delphi. No. 352d, Pythagoreion and Heraion of Samos.

2004, Aug. 12 Litho. *Perf. 14x13¼*
350 A356 55c **multicolored** *(250,000)+* 1.75 1.75
First day cover 1.90
Inscription block of 4 7.25 —
351 A356 75c **multicolored** *(250,000)+* 2.25 2.25
First day cover 2.75
First day cover, #350-351 4.00
Inscription block of 4 9.25 —

Souvenir Booklet

352 Booklet *(49,000)+* 16.00
a.-d. A356 25c any single .60 .60
e.-f. A356 30c either single .70 .70
g. Booklet pane of 4 #352a 2.40 2.40
h. Booklet pane of 4 #352b 2.40 2.40
i. Booklet pane of 4 #352c 2.40 2.40
j. Booklet pane of 4 #352d 2.40 2.40
k. Booklet pane of 4 #352e 2.80 2.80
l. Booklet pane of 4 #352f 2.80 2.80

My Dream for Peace Type

Winning designs of Lions Club International children's global peace poster contest by: 55c, Henry Ulfe Renteria, Peru. €1, Michelle Fortaliza, Philippines.

2004, Sept. 21 Litho. *Perf. 14*
353 A357 55c **multicolored** *(235,000)+* 1.40 1.40
First day cover 1.90
Inscription block of 4 5.75
Pane of 20 28.00
354 A357 €1 **multicolored** *(235,000)+* 2.50 2.50
First day cover 3.50
First day cover, #353-354 4.50
Inscription block of 4 10.00
Pane of 20 50.00

V47

Human Rights — V48

Printed by Banknote Corporation of America, US. Designed by Yuri Gervorgian, Armenia. Panes of 8.

2004, Oct. 14 Litho. *Perf. 11¼*
355 V47 55c **multicolored** *(480,000)+* 1.00 1.00
First day cover 2.00
Pane of 8 12.00 —

356 V48 €1.25 **multicolored** *(480,000)+* 3.00 3.00
First day cover 4.50
First day cover, #355-356 5.75
Pane of 8 28.00 —

United Nations, 60th Anniv. Type of 2005

Printed by Banknote Corporation of America, US. Designed by Czeslaw Slania, Sweden.

2005, Feb. 4 **Litho. & Engr.** ***Perf. 11x11¼***
357 A361 55c **multicolored** *(310,000)+* 2.50 2.50
First day cover 2.60
Inscription block of 4 10.50 —
Pane of 20 50.00 —

Souvenir Sheet
Litho.
Imperf

358 A361 €2.10 **multicolored** *(165,000)+* 6.50 6.50
First day cover 6.25

International Center, Vienna — V49

Printed by Cartor Security Printing, France.

Litho. with Hologram

2005, Feb. 4 ***Perf. 13½x13¼***
359 V49 75c **multicolored** *(360,000)+* 2.25 2.25
First day cover 3.25
Inscription block of 4 9.00 —
Pane of 20 45.00 —

Endangered Species Type of 1993

Designs: No. 360, Ansellia africana. No. 361, Phragmipedium kovachii. No. 362, Cymbidium ensifolium. No. 363, Renanthera imschootiana.

2005, Mar. 3 **Litho.** ***Perf. 12¾x12½***
360 A271 55c multicolored 1.40 1.40
361 A271 55c multicolored 1.40 1.40
362 A271 55c multicolored 1.40 1.40
363 A271 55c multicolored 1.40 1.40
a. Block of 4, #360-363 6.00 6.00
First day cover, #363a 7.00
First day cover, #360-363, each 2.25
Inscription block of 4, #363a 6.25 —
Pane of 16 24.00 —

Nature's Wisdom — V50

Printed by Cartor Security Printing, France. Panes of 20. Designed by Robert Stein, US.
Designs: 55c, Desert landscape, China. 80c, Cheetah family, Africa.

2005, Apr. 21 **Litho.** ***Perf. 13½x13¼***
364 V50 55c **multicolored** *(230,000)+* 1.60 1.60
First day cover 2.40
Inscription block of 4 6.50 —
Pane of 20 32.50 —
365 V50 75c **multicolored** *(230,000)+* 2.25 2.25
First day cover 3.50
First day cover, #364-365 4.75
Inscription block of 4 9.00 —
Pane of 20 45.00 —

Intl. Year of Sport Type

Printed by Cartor Security Printing, France. Designed by Roland Hirter, Switzerland.

2005, June 3 **Litho.** ***Perf. 13x13¼***
366 A368 55c Equestrian *(245,000)+* 1.60 1.60

367 A368 €1.10 Soccer *(245,000)+* 3.25 3.25
First day cover 4.50
First day cover, #366-367 6.00
Inscription block of 4 13.00 —
Pane of 20 65.00 —

World Heritage Sites, Egypt Type

Printed by Johann Enschedé and Sons, the Netherlands. Panes of 20. Designed by Rorie Katz, US.
Designs: Nos. 368, 370c, Abu Mena. Nos. 369, 370f, St. Catherine area. No. 370a, Memphis and its Necropolis. No. 370b, Philae. No. 370d, Ancient Thebes. No. 370e, Islamic Cairo.

2005, Aug. 4 **Litho.** ***Perf. 14x13¼***
368 A369 55c **multicolored** *(250,000)+* 1.60 1.60
First day cover 2.40
Inscription block of 4 6.50 —
369 A369 75c **multicolored** *(250,000)+* 2.25 2.25
First day cover 3.25
First day cover, #368-369 4.75
Inscription block of 4 9.00 —

Souvenir Booklet

370 Booklet, #370g-370l *(45,000)+* 19.50
a.-c. A369 25c any single .75 .75
d.-f. A369 30c any single .85 .85
g. Booklet pane of 4 #370a 3.00 3.00
h. Booklet pane of 4 #370b 3.00 3.00
i. Booklet pane of 4 #370c 3.00 3.00
j. Booklet pane of 4 #370d 3.50 3.50
k. Booklet pane of 4 #370e 3.50 3.50
l. Booklet pane of 4 #370f 3.50 3.50

No. 370 sold for €6.80.

My Dream for Peace Type

Winning designs of Lions Club International children's global peace poster contest by: 55c, Lee Min Gi, Republic of Korea. €1, Natalie Chan, US.

2004, Sept. 21 **Litho.** ***Perf. 14***
371 A357 55c **multicolored** *(225,000)+* 1.60 1.60
First day cover 2.25
Inscription block of 4 6.50
Pane of 20 32.00
372 A357 €1 **multicolored** *(225,000)+* 2.75 2.75
First day cover 4.00
First day cover, #371-372 5.25
Inscription block of 4 11.00
Pane of 20 55.00

Food for Life Type

Printed by Government Printing Office, Austria. Designed by Andrew Davidson, United Kingdom.
Designs: 55c, Corn, people with food bowls, teacher and students. €1.25, Rice, helicopter dropping food, elephant caravan.

2005, Oct. 20 **Litho.** ***Perf. 13¾***
373 A370 55c **multicolored** *(210,000)+* 1.60 1.60
First day cover 2.10
Inscription block of 4 6.50 —
Pane of 20 32.00 —
374 A370 €1.25 **multicolored** *(210,000)+* 3.50 3.50
First day cover 4.75
First day cover, #373-374 6.00
Inscription block of 4 14.00 —
Pane of 20 70.00 —

Indigenous Art Type of 2003

Printed by Johann Enschedé and Sons, the Netherlands. Designed by Robert Stein, US.

No. 375 — Musical instruments: a, Drum, Guinea. b, Whistle, Congo. c, Horn, Botswana. d, Drums, Burundi. e, Harp, Gabon. f, Bell, Nigeria.

2006, Feb. 3 **Litho.** ***Perf. 13¼***
375 V46 Sheet of 6 *(117,000)+* 12.00 12.00
First day cover 8.00
a.-f. 55c Any single 2.00 2.00
First day cover, #375a-375f, each 4.50

Endangered Species Type of 1993

Printed by Johann Enschedé and Sons, the Netherlands. Designed by John D. Dawson, US.

Designs: No. 376, Dendrobates pumilio. No. 377, Furcifer lateralis. No. 378, Corallus hortulanus. No. 379, Dendrobates leucomelas.

2006, Mar. 16 **Litho.** ***Perf. 12¾x12½***
376 A271 55c **multicolored** *(260,000)+* 1.50 1.50
377 A271 55c **multicolored** *(260,000)+* 1.50 1.50
378 A271 55c **multicolored** *(260,000)+* 1.50 1.50
379 A271 55c **multicolored** *(260,000)+* 1.50 1.50
a. Block of 4, #376-379 6.00 6.00
First day cover, #379a 6.75
First day cover, #376-379, each 2.40
Inscription block of 4, #379a 6.00 —
Pane of 16 24.00

Intl. Day of Families Type

Printed by Johann Enschedé and Sons, the Netherlands. Designed by Shelly Bartek, US.
Designs: 55c, Family at water pump. €1.25, Family preparing food.

2006, May 27 **Litho.** ***Perf. 14x13½***
380 A373 55c **multicolored** *(190,000)+* 1.25 1.25
First day cover 2.00
Inscription block of 4 5.00 —
Pane of 20 25.00 —
381 A373 €1.25 **multicolored** *(190,000)+* 2.50 2.50
First day cover 4.50
First day cover, #380-381 5.75
Inscription block of 4 10.00 —
Pane of 20 50.00 —

World Heritage Sites, France Type

Printed by Cartor Security Printing, France. Panes of 20. Designed by Robert Stein, US.
Eiffel Tower and: Nos. 382, 384c, Carcasonne. Nos. 383, 384f, Chateau de Chambord. No. 384a, Banks of the Seine. No. 384b, Provins. No. 384d, Roman Aqueduct. No. 384e, Mont Saint-Michel.

Litho. & Embossed with Foil Application

2006, June 17 ***Perf. 13½x13¼***
382 A374 55c **multicolored** *(220,000)+* 1.50 1.50
First day cover 2.25
Inscription block of 4 6.00 —
383 A374 75c **multicolored** *(220,000)+* 2.00 2.00
First day cover 3.00
First day cover, #368-369 4.50
Inscription block of 4 8.00 —

Souvenir Booklet

384 Booklet, #384g-384l *(41,000)+* 18.00
a.-c. A374 25c any single .65 .65
d.-f. A374 30c any single .80 .80
g. Booklet pane of 4 #384a 2.60 2.60
h. Booklet pane of 4 #384b 2.60 2.60
i. Booklet pane of 4 #384c 2.60 2.60
j. Booklet pane of 4 #384d 3.25 3.25
k. Booklet pane of 4 #384e 3.25 3.25
l. Booklet pane of 4 #384f 3.25 3.25

No. 384 sold for €6.80.

My Dream for Peace Type of 2004

Printed by Cartor Security Printing, France. Panes of 20.
Winning designs of Lions Club International children's global peace poster contest by: 55c, Klara Thein, Germany. €1, Laurensia Levina, Indonesia.

2006, Sept. 21 **Litho.** ***Perf. 13½x13***
385 A357 55c **multicolored** *(200,000)+* 1.60 1.60
First day cover 2.25
Inscription block of 4 6.40 —
Pane of 20 32.00 —
386 A357 €1 **multicolored** *(200,000)+* 3.00 3.00
First day cover 4.00
First day cover, #385-386 5.50
Inscription block of 4 12.00 —
Pane of 20 60.00 —

Flags and Coins Type

Printed by Cartor Security Printing, France. Designed by Rorie Katz, US.
No. 387 — Flag of: a, Gambia, 1 dalasi coin. b, Pakistan, 1 rupee coin. c, Afghanistan, 2 afghani coin. d, Austria, 1 euro coin. e, Germany, 50 cent coin. f, Haiti, 50 centimes coin. g, Denmark, 20 krone coin. h, Netherlands, 1 euro coin.

2006, Oct. 5 **Litho.** ***Perf. 13¼x13***
387 Sheet of 8 14.00 14.00
a.-h. A375 55c Any single 1.75 1.75
First day cover 14.50
First day cover, #387a-387h, each 5.00

A column of rouletting in the middle of the sheet separates it into two parts.

Endangered Species Type of 1993

Printed by Johann Enschedé and Sons, the Netherlands. Designed by John Rowe, US.
Designs: No. 388, Chlorocebus aethiops. No. 389, Nasalis larvatus. No. 390, Papio hamadryas. No. 391, Erythrocebus patas.

2007, Mar. 15 **Litho.** ***Perf. 12¾x12½***
388 A271 55c **multicolored** *(256,000)+* 1.60 1.60
389 A271 55c **multicolored** *(256,000)+* 1.60 1.60
390 A271 55c **multicolored** *(256,000)+* 1.60 1.60
391 A271 55c **multicolored** *(256,000)+* 1.60 1.60
a. Block of 4, #388-391 6.40 6.40
First day cover, #391a 7.50
First day cover, #388-391, each 2.60
Inscription block of 4, #391a 6.40 —
Pane of 16 26.00 —

Flags and Coins Type of 2006

Printed by Cartor Security Printing, France. Designed by Rorie Katz, US.
No. 392 — Flag of: a, Trinidad and Tobago, 50 cent coin. b, Sierra Leone, 10 cent coin. c, Hungary, 100 forint coin. d, San Marino, 2 euro coin. e, Croatia, 1 kuna coin. f, Spain, 1 euro coin. g, Kazakhstan, 100 tenge coin. h, Ireland, 5 cent coin.

2007, May 3 **Litho.** ***Perf. 13¼x13***
392 Sheet of 8 *(155,000)+* 13.00 13.00
a.-h. A375 55c Any single 1.60 1.60
First day cover 15.00
First day cover, #392a-392h, each 5.00

A column of rouletting in the middle of the sheet separates it into two parts.

Five 55c stamps depicting views of the Vienna International Center and the United Nations flag were released May 3, 2007. The editors have reason to believe that these stamps were not sold at the UN Post Office in Vienna. Value, strip of 5 with labels $45, sheet of 10 $90.

Peaceful Visions Type of 2007

Printed by Lowe-Martin Company, Canada. Designed by Slavka Kolesar. Panes of 20.
Designs: 55c, "The Sowers." €1.25, "We All Thrive Under the Same Sky."

2007, June 1 Litho. *Perf. 13x12½*
398 A378 55c **multicolored** *(200,000)+* 1.60 1.60
First day cover 2.25
Inscription block of 4 6.40 —
Pane of 20 32.00 —
399 A378 €1.25 **multicolored** *(200,000)+* 3.75 3.75
First day cover 5.00
First day cover, #398-399 6.25
Inscription block of 4 15.00 —
Pane of 20 75.00 —

World Heritage Sites, South America Type

Printed by Lowe-Martin Group, Canada. Panes of 20. Designed by Rorie Katz, US.
Designs: Nos. 400, 402e, Iguaçu National Park, Brazil. Nos. 401, 402b, Cueva de las Manos, Argentina. No. 402a, Rapa Nui, Chile. No. 402c, Machu Picchu, Peru. No. 402d, Tiwanaku, Bolivia. No. 474f, Galapagos Islands, Ecuador.

2007, Aug. 9 Litho. *Perf. 13¼x13*
400 A381 55c **multicolored** *(210,000)+* 2.00 2.00
First day cover 2.50
Inscription block of 4 8.00 —
401 A381 75c **multicolored** *(210,000)+* 2.75 2.75
First day cover 3.50
First day cover, #400-401 5.00
Inscription block of 4 11.00 —

Souvenir Booklet

402 Booklet, #402g-402l *(37,000)+* 20.00
a.-c. A381 25c Any single .75 .75
d.-f. A381 30c Any single .90 .90
g. Booklet pane of 4 #402a 3.00 3.00
h. Booklet pane of 4 #402b 3.00 3.00
i. Booklet pane of 4 #402c 3.00 3.00
j. Booklet pane of 4 #402d 3.60 3.60
k. Booklet pane of 4 #402e 3.60 3.60
l. Booklet pane of 4 #402f 3.60 3.60

Humanitarian Mail Type

Printed by Lowe-Martin Group, Canada. Panes of 10.

2007, Sept. 6 Litho. *Perf. 12½x13¼*
403 A382 75c **multicolored** *(310,000)+* 2.25 2.25
First day cover 3.25
Inscription block of 4 9.00 —
Pane of 10 22.50 —

Five 65c stamps depicting the International Space Station, astronauts and planets were released Oct. 1, 2007. The editors have reason to believe that these stamps were not sold at the UN Post Office in Vienna. Value, strip of 5 with labels $60, sheet of 10 $100.

Space for Humanity Type

Printed by Johann Enschedé and Sons, the Netherlands. Panes of 6. Designed by Donato Giancola, US.
Designs: 65c, Space stations. €1.15, Space Station. €2.10, Space probe, Jupiter.

2007, Oct. 25 Litho. *Perf. 13½x14*
409 A383 65c **multicolored** *(306,000)+* 2.00 2.00
First day cover 2.60
Inscription block of 4 8.00 —
Pane of 6 12.00 —
410 A383 €1.15 **multicolored** *(306,000)+* 3.50 3.50
First day cover 4.75
First day cover, #409-410 6.25
Inscription block of 4 14.00 —
Pane of 6 21.00 —

Souvenir Sheet

411 A383 €2.10 **multicolored** *(130,000)+* 8.00 8.00
First day cover 7.25

Intl. Holocaust Remembrance Day Type

Printed by Lowe-Martin Company, Canada. Panes of 9. Designed by Matías Delfino, Argentina.

2008, Jan. 27 Litho. *Perf. 13*
412 A384 65c **multicolored** *(540,000)+* 3.00 3.00
First day cover 3.25
Pane of 9 27.00 —

Johann Strauss Memorial, Vienna — V61

Pallas Athene Fountain, Vienna — V62

Pegasus Fountain, Salzburg V63

Statue, Belvedere Palace Gardens, Vienna — V64

Printed by Johann Enschedé and Sons, the Netherlands. Panes of 20. Designed by Rorie Katz, US.

2008, Jan. 28 Litho. *Perf. 13½x14*
413 V61 10c **black** *(320,000)+* .35 .35
First day cover .50
Inscription block of 4 1.40 —
Pane of 20 7.00 —

Perf. 14x13½

414 V62 15c **black** *(320,000)+* .50 .50
First day cover .75
Inscription block of 4 2.00 —
Pane of 20 10.00 —
415 V63 65c **black** *(320,000)+* 2.25 2.25
First day cover 3.25
Inscription block of 4 9.00 —
Pane of 20 45.00 —
416 V64 €1.40 **black** *(320,000)+* 4.75 4.75
First day cover 7.00
Inscription block of 4 19.00 —
Pane of 20 95.00 —
Nos. 413-416 (4) 7.85 7.85

Endangered Species Type of 1993

Printed by Johann Enschedé and Sons, the Netherlands. Designed by Suzanne Duranceau, Canada.
Designs: No. 4170, Mirounga angustirostris. No. 418, Millepora alcicornis. No. 419, Hippocampus histrix. No. 420, Physeter catodon.

2008, Mar. 6 Litho. *Perf. 12¾x12½*
417 A271 65c **multicolored** *(212,000)+* 2.50 2.50
418 A271 65c **multicolored** *(212,000)+* 2.50 2.50
419 A271 65c **multicolored** *(212,000)+* 2.50 2.50
420 A271 65c **multicolored** *(212,000)+* 2.50 2.50
a. Block of 4, #417-420 10.00 10.00
First day cover, #420a 9.50
First day cover, #417-420, each 3.25
Inscription block of 4, #420a 10.50 —
Pane of 16 40.00 —

Flags and Coins Type of 2006

Printed by Cartor Security Printing, France. Designed by Rorie Katz, US.
No. 421 — Flag of: a, Poland, 5 zloty coin. b, Latvia, 1 lat coin. c, Portugal, 1 euro coin. d, Armenia, 500 dram coin. e, Sweden, 1 krona coin. f, Cyprus, 1 euro coin. g, Slovakia, 1 koruna coin. h, Qatar, 50 dirham coin.

2008, May 8 Litho. *Perf. 13¼x13*
421 Sheet of 8 *(120,000)+* 18.00 18.00
a.-h. A375 65c Any single 2.25 2.25
First day cover 20.00

A column of rouletting in the middle of the sheet separates it into two parts.

Five 65c stamps depicting the Vienna International Center and its artwork were released May 12, 2008. The editors have reason to believe that these stamps were not sold at the UN Post Office in Vienna. Value, strip of 5 with labels $30, sheet of 10 $60.

Graduate — V70

Stylized Person, Heart, Brain, Hands — V71

Printed by Johann Enschedé and Sons, the Netherlands. Panes of 20. Designed by Rorie Katz, US.

2008, June 6 Litho. & Embossed *Perf. 14x13¼*
427 V70 55c **green & violet** *(186,000)+* 2.00 2.00
First day cover 2.50
Inscription block of 4 8.00 —
Sheet of 20 40.00 —
428 V71 €1.40 **violet & green** *(186,000)+* 5.00 5.00
First day cover 6.50
First day cover, #427-428 7.75
Inscription block of 4 20.00 —
Sheet of 20 100.00 —

Convention on the Rights of Persons with Disabilities.

Sport for Peace Type of 2008

Printed by Johann Enschedé and Sons, the Netherlands. Panes of 9 (Nos. 429-430). Designed by Romero Britto, Brazil.
Designs: 65c, Man on rings. €1.30, €2.10, Swimmer.

2008, Aug. 8 Litho. *Perf. 14½*
429 A393 65c **multicolored** *(435,600)+* 2.25 2.25
First day cover 3.00
Inscription block of 4 9.00 —
Pane of 9 21.00 —
430 A393 €1.30 **multicolored** *(435,600)+* 4.50 4.50
First day cover 6.00
First day cover, #429-430 7.75
Inscription block of 4 18.00 —
Pane of 9 41.00 —

Souvenir Sheet

Perf. 12¾x13¼

431 A393 €2.10 **multicolored** *(200,000)+* 9.00 9.00
First day cover 8.00
a. Overprinted in sheet margin 10.00 10.00
First day cover 8.00

2008 Summer Olympics, Beijing. No. 431a is overprinted in black "Peking 2008" and medals with UN emblem.

"We Can End Poverty" Type of 2008

Printed by Sweden Post, Sweden. Panes of 20.
Winning designs in children's art contest: 65c, By Mariam Marukian, Armenia. 75c, By Rufaro Duri, Zimbabwe, vert.

2008, Sept. 18 Litho. *Perf. 12¾x12½*
432 A395 65c **multicolored** *(160,000)+* 2.25 2.25
First day cover 3.25
Inscription block of 4 9.00 —

Sheet of 20 45.00 —

Perf. 12½x12¾

433 A395 75c **multicolored** *(160,000)+* 2.60 2.60
First day cover 3.75
First day cover, #432-433 5.75
Inscription block of 4 10.50 —
Sheet of 20 52.00 —

Five €1.40 stamps depicting views of the Vienna International Center and its artwork were released Sept. 18, 2008. The editors have reason to believe that these stamps were not sold at the UN Post Office in Vienna. Value, strip of 5 with labels $40, sheet of 10 $80.

Climate Change Types of New York and Geneva and

V72

Climate Change — V73

Printed by Lowe-Martin Group, Canada. Panes of 4. Designed by Rorie Katz, US.

No. 434 — Smokestacks with quarter of Earth in: a, LR. b, LL. c, UR. d, UL.

No. 435 — Cut trees with quarter of Earth in: a, LR. b, LL. c, UR. d, UL.

No. 436: a, Like New York #969a. b, Like New York #969b. c, Like New York #969c. d, Like New York #969d. e, Like Geneva #493a. f, Like Geneva #493b. g, Like Geneva #493c. h, Like Geneva #493d. i, Like Vienna #434a. j, Like Vienna #434b. k, Like Vienna #434c. l, Like Vienna #434d. m, Like New York #968a. n, Like New York #968b, o, Like New York #968c, p, Like New York #968d. q, Like Geneva #492a. r, Like Geneva#492b. s, Like Geneva #492c. t, Like Geneva #492d. u, Like Vienna #435a. v, Like Vienna #435b. w, Like Vienna #435c. x, Like Vienna #435d.

All stamps have green panels inscribed "Klimawandel."

2008, Oct. 23 Litho. *Perf. 13¼x13*

434 Sheet of 4 *(120,000)+* 9.00 9.00
a.-d. V72 65c Any single 2.25 2.25
First day cover 9.75
435 Sheet of 4 *(120,000)+* 16.00 16.00
a.-d. V73 €1.15 Any single 4.00 4.00
First day cover 17.00
First day cover, #434-435 27.00

Souvenir Booklet

436 Booklet, #436y-436ad *(31,000)+* 27.00
a.-d. A397 30c Any single 1.00 1.00
e.-h. G77 30c Any single 1.00 1.00
i.-l. V72 30c Any single 1.00 1.00
m.-p. A396 35c Any single 1.10 1.10
q.-t. G76 35c Any single 1.10 1.10
u.-x. V73 35c Any single 1.10 1.10
y. Booklet pane of 4, #436a-436d 4.25 4.25
z. Booklet pane of 4, #436e-436h 4.25 4.25
aa. Booklet pane of 4, #436i-436l 4.25 4.25
ab. Booklet pane of 4, #436m-436p 4.75 4.75
ac. Booklet pane of 4, #436q-436t 4.75 4.75
ad. Booklet pane of 4, #436u-436x 4.75 4.75

U Thant Type of 2009

Printed by Johann Enschedé and Sons, the Netherlands. Panes of 20.

Litho. With Foil Application

2009, Feb. 6 *Perf. 14x13½*

437 A399 €1.15 **green & multicolored** *(180,000)+* 4.50 4.50
First day cover 4.25
Inscription block of 4 18.00 —
Sheet of 20 90.00 —

Endangered Species Type of 1993

Printed by Johann Enschedé and Sons, the Netherlands. Designed by Roger Kent, United Kingdom.

Designs: No. 438, Trogonoptera brookiana. No. 439, Pandinus imperator. No. 440, Carabus intricatus. No. 441, Brachypelma smithi.

2009, Apr. 16 Litho. *Perf. 12¾x12½*

438 A271 65c **multicolored** *(184,000)+* 2.00 2.00
439 A271 65c **multicolored** *(184,000)+* 2.00 2.00
440 A271 65c **multicolored** *(184,000)+* 2.00 2.00
441 A271 65c **multicolored** *(184,000)+* 2.00 2.00
a. Block of 4, #438-441 8.00 8.00
First day cover, #441a 8.50
First day cover, #438-441, each 2.75
Inscription block of 4, #441a 8.00 —
Pane of 16 32.00 —

World Heritage Sites, Germany Type of 2009

Printed by Johann Enschedé and Sons, the Netherlands. Panes of 20. Designed by Grit Fiedler, Germany.

Designs: Nos. 442, 444c, Palaces and Parks of Potsdam and Berlin. Nos. 443, 444e, Luther Memorials in Eisleben and Wittenberg. No. 444a, Town Hall and Roland on the Marketplace, Bremen. No. 444b, Wartburg Castle. No. 444d, Aachen Cathedral. No. 444f, Monastic Island of Reichenau.

2009, May 7 Litho. *Perf. 14x13½*

442 A400 65c **multicolored** *(190,000)+* 1.90 1.90
First day cover 2.50
Inscription block of 4 7.75 —
443 A400 €1.40 **multicolored** *(320,000)+* 4.00 4.00
First day cover 5.25
First day cover, #500-501 6.75
Inscription block of 4 16.00 —

Souvenir Booklet

444 Booklet, #444g-444l *(32,000)+* 20.00
a.-c. A400 30c any single .75 .75
d.-f. A400 35c any single .90 .90
g. Booklet pane of 4 #444a 3.00 3.00
h. Booklet pane of 4 #444b 3.00 3.00
i. Booklet pane of 4 #444c 3.00 3.00
j. Booklet pane of 4 #444d 3.60 3.60
k. Booklet pane of 4 #444e 3.60 3.60
l. Booklet pane of 4 #444f 3.60 3.60

Memorial Plaza, Vienna International Center — V74

The First Swallows, Sculpture by Juozas Mikenas — V75

Conference Building, Vienna International Center — V76

Butterfly Tree, by Rudolf Hausner — V77

Flags in Memorial Plaza — V78

2009, May 7 Litho. *Perf. 13¼*

445 V74 65c **multicolored** + label *5.00 5.00*
a. Perf. 11¼x11 *10.00 10.00*
446 V75 65c **multicolored** + label *5.00 5.00*
a. Perf. 11¼x11 *10.00 10.00*
447 V76 65c **multicolored** + label *5.00 5.00*
a. Perf. 11¼x11 *10.00 10.00*
448 V77 65c **multicolored** + label *5.00 5.00*
a. Perf. 11¼x11 *10.00 10.00*
449 V78 65c **multicolored** + label *5.00 5.00*
a. Perf. 11¼x11 *10.00 10.00*
b. Vert. strip of 5, #445-449, + 5 labels *25.00 25.00*
Sheet, 2 #449b *50.00* —
c. Vert. strip of 5, #445a-449a, + 5 labels *50.00 50.00*
Sheet, 2 #449c *100.00* —

The full sheets sold for €11.69 or $14.95. Labels could not be personalized. The sheet of No. 449c has "ver. 2" in the lower right selvage.

Economic and Social Council (ECOSOC) Type of 2009

Printed by Sweden Post, Sweden. Panes of 20. Designed by Rorie Katz, US.

Designs: 55c, Combat HIV/AIDS, malaria and other diseases. 65c, Reduce child mortality.

2009, Aug. 6 Litho. *Perf. 12¾x12½*

450 A411 55c **multicolored** *(160,000)+* 2.25 2.25
First day cover 2.60
Inscription block of 4 9.00 —
Sheet of 20 45.00 —
451 A411 65c **multicolored** *(160,000)+* 3.50 3.50
First day cover 3.00
First day cover, #450-4513 4.75
Inscription block of 4 14.00 —
Sheet of 20 70.00 —

V79

V80

V81

V82

Vienna International Center, 30th Anniv. — V83

2009, Aug. 24	**Litho.**	***Perf. 13¼***	
452 V79 €1.40 **multicolored** + label		*6.00*	*6.00*
a. Perf. 11¼x11		*20.00*	*20.00*
453 V80 €1.40 **multicolored** + label		*6.00*	*6.00*
a. Perf. 11¼x11		*20.00*	*20.00*
454 V81 €1.40 **multicolored** + label		*6.00*	*6.00*
a. Perf. 11¼x11		*20.00*	*20.00*
455 V82 €1.40 **multicolored** + label		*6.00*	*6.00*
a. Perf. 11¼x11		*20.00*	*20.00*
456 V83 €1.40 **multicolored** + label		*6.00*	*6.00*
a. Perf. 11¼x11		*20.00*	*20.00*
b. Vert. strip of 5, #452-456, + 5 labels		*30.00*	*30.00*
Sheet, 2 #456b		*60.00*	—
c. Vert. strip of 5, #452a-456a, + 5 labels		*100.00*	*100.00*
Sheet, 2 #456c		*200.00*	—

The full sheets sold for €19.90 or $27.75. Labels could not be personalized. The sheet of No. 456c has "ver. 2" in the lower right selvage.

Millennium Development Goals Type of 2009

Miniature Sheet

Printed by Lowe Martin Group, Canada. Designed by Rorie Katz, US.

No. 457: a, Bowl of hot food. b, Pencil. c, Female symbol. d, Teddy bear. e, Pregnant woman, heart. f, Medicine bottle. g, Stylized tree. h, Conjoined people.

2009, Sept. 25	**Litho.**	***Perf. 13¼***	
457 A413 Sheet of 8 *(75,000)+*		16.00	16.00
First day cover			18.00
a.-h. 65c Any single		2.00	2.00

Miniature Sheet

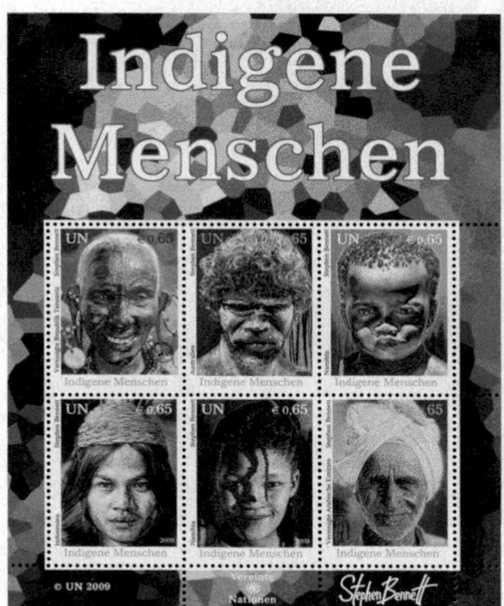

Indigenous People — V84

Printed by Lowe-Martin Group, Canada. Designed by Stephen Bennett, US.

No. 458 — Portraits of person from: a, Tanzania. b, Australia. c, Namibia (small child). d, Indonesia. e, Namibia (young girl). f, Untied Arab Emirates.

2009, Oct. 8	**Litho.**	***Perf. 12½***	
458 V84 Sheet of 6 *(80,000)+*		12.00	12.00
a.-f. 65c Any single		2.00	2.00
First day cover			14.00

Flags and Coins Type of 2006

Printed by Cartor Security Printing, France. Designed by Rorie Katz, US.

No. 459 — Flag of: a, Romania, 1 ban coin. b, Slovenia, 5 cent coin. c, Azerbaijan, 10 giapik coin. d, Bangladesh, 5 taka coin. e, Belarus, 1 ruble coin. f, Malta, 1 euro coin. g, Swaziland, 1 lilangeni coin. h, Jordan, 10 piaster coin.

2010, Feb. 5	**Litho.**	***Perf. 13¼x13***	
459 Sheet of 8 *(88,000)+*		16.00	16.00
a.-h. A375 65c Any single		2.00	2.00
First day cover			19.50

A column of rouletting in the middle of the sheet separates it into two parts.

People Pulling Rope — V85

Person With Hands Over Eyes — V86

Woman Touching Her Shoulder — V87

Man With Wheelbarrow — V88

Blue Heart — V89

Designed by Rorie Katz, US.

2010, Feb. 5	**Litho.**	***Perf. 11¼x11***	
460 V85 65c **multicolored** + label		*4.50*	*4.50*
461 V86 65c **multicolored** + label		*4.50*	*4.50*
462 V87 65c **multicolored** + label		*4.50*	*4.50*
463 V88 65c **multicolored** + label		*4.50*	*4.50*
464 V89 65c **multicolored** + label		*4.50*	*4.50*
a. Vert. strip of 5, #460-464, + 5 labels		*22.50*	*22.50*
Sheet, 2 #464a		*45.00*	—

The full sheet sold for $14.95 or €19.90. The labels could not be personalized.

Endangered Species Type of 1993

Printed by Johann Enschedé and Sons, the Netherlands. Designed by Rosie Sanders, United Kingdom.

Designs: No. 465, Mammillaria zeilmanniana. No. 466, Hoodia gordonii. No. 467, Welwitschia mirabilis. No. 468, Euphorbia milii.

2010, Apr. 15	**Litho.**	***Perf. 12¾x12½***	
465 A271 65c **multicolored** *(148,000)+*		2.25	2.25
466 A271 65c **multicolored** *(148,000)+*		2.25	2.25
467 A271 65c **multicolored** *(148,000)+*		2.25	2.25
468 A271 65c **multicolored** *(148,000)+*		2.25	2.25
a. Block of 4, #465-468		9.00	9.00
First day cover, #468a			9.75
First day cover, #465-468, each			3.25
Inscription block of 4, #468a		9.00	—
Pane of 16		36.00	—

Intl. Year of Biodiversity — V90

Printed by Lowe-Martin Group, Canada. Panes of 20. Designed by Deborah Halperin, US.

Drawings from Art Forms from Nature, by Ernst Heinrich: 5c, Colonial algae. 20c, Boxfish.

2010, Apr. 15	**Litho.**	***Perf. 13***	
469 V90 5c **multicolored** *(400,000)+*		.25	.25
First day cover			1.90
Inscription block of 4		.80	—
Sheet of 20		4.00	—
470 V90 20c **multicolored** *(400,000)+*		.70	.70
First day cover			2.25
First day cover, #469-470			1.90
Inscription block of 4		2.80	—
Sheet of 20		14.00	—

One Planet, One Ocean Types of New York and Geneva and

V91

One Planet, One Ocean — V92

Printed by Johann Enschedé and Sons, the Netherlands. Designed by Robert Wyland, US.

No. 471: a, Dolphin at left, fish at right. b, Fish at top, shark in center. c, Dolphin at left, fish at right and bottom. d, Fish at left, top and right.

No. 472: a, Dolphins. b, Shark and fish at center, ray at bottom. c, Fish at left, turtle at bottom. d, Fish and coral.

No. 473: a, Like New York #1003a. b, Like New York #1003b, c, Like New York #1003c, d, Like New York #1003d. e, Like #471a. f, Like #471b. g, Like #471c, h, Like #471d. i, Like Geneva # 519a. j, Like Geneva #519b, k, Like Geneva # 519c. l, Like Geneva #519d. m, Like New York #1004a. n, Like New York #1004b. o, Like New York #1004c, p, Like New York #1004d. q, Like #472a. r, Like #472b. s, Like #472c. t, Like #472d. u, Like Geneva #520a. v, Like Geneva #520b. w, Like Geneva #520c. x, Like Geneva #520d.

2010, May 6	**Litho.**	***Perf. 14x13¼***	
471 V91 Sheet of 4 *(75,000)+*		7.75	7.75
a.-d. 55c Any single		1.90	1.90
472 V92 Sheet of 4 *(75,000)+*		9.00	9.00
a.-d. 65c Any single		2.25	2.25
First day cover, #471-472			20.00

Souvenir Booklet

Perf. 13¼x13

473	Booklet, #473y-473z, 473aa-473ad *(32,000)+*	27.00	
a.-d.	A416 30c any single	1.00	1.00
e.-h.	V91 30c any single	1.00	1.00
i.-l.	G85 30c any single	1.00	1.00
m.-p.	A417 35c any single	1.25	1.25
q.-t.	V92 35c any single	1.25	1.25
u.-x.	G86 35c any single	1.25	1.25
y.	Booklet pane of 4 #473a-473d	4.00	4.00
z.	Booklet pane of 4 #473e-473h	4.00	4.00
aa.	Booklet pane of 4 #473i-473l	4.00	4.00
ab.	Booklet pane of 4 #473m-473p	5.00	5.00
ac.	Booklet pane of 4 #473q-473t	5.00	5.00
ad.	Booklet pane of 4 #473u-473x	5.00	5.00

Intl. Oceanographic Commission, 50th anniv.

United Nations, 65th Anniv. Type of 2010

Printed by Lowe-Martin Group, Canada. Designed by Rorie Katz, United States.

Litho. With Foil Application

2010, June 28 *Perf. 13¼*

474	A422 75c **green & gold** *(150,000)+*	3.00	3.00
	First day cover		3.25
	Inscription block of 4	12.50	—
	Pane of 15	45.00	—
a.	Souvenir sheet of 2 *(50,500)+*	6.00	6.00
	First day cover, #474a		6.50

V93

V94

V95

V96

United Nations Air Transport — V97

Printed by UAB Garsu Pasaulis, Lithuania. Designed by Simon Williams, United Kingdom.

2010, Sept. 2 **Litho.** *Perf. 13¼x13*

475	V93 65c **multicolored** *(132,000)+*	1.90	1.90
476	V94 65c **multicolored** *(132,000)+*	1.90	1.90
477	V95 65c **multicolored** *(132,000)+*	1.90	1.90
478	V96 65c **multicolored** *(132,000)+*	1.90	1.90
479	V97 65c **multicolored** *(132,000)+*	1.90	1.90
a.	Horiz. strip of 5, #475-479	9.50	9.50
	First day cover, #479a		10.50
	First day cover, #475-479, each		3.25
	Inscription block of 10	19.00	—
	Pane of 20	38.00	—

Miniature Sheet

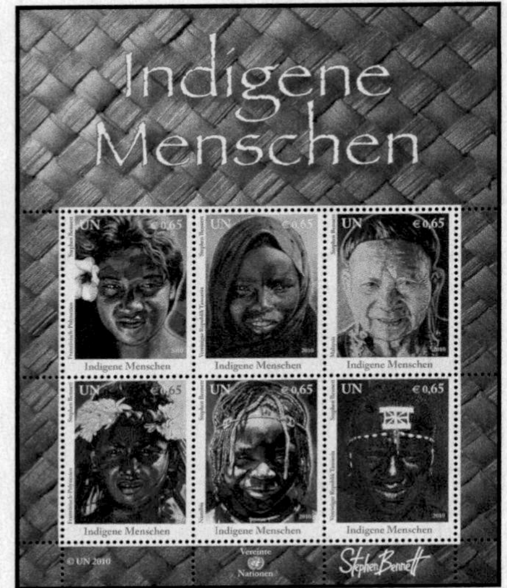

Indigenous People — V98

Printed by Lowe-Martin Group, Canada. Designed by Stephen Bennett, US.

No. 480 — Portraits of person from: a, French Polynesia (denomination in white). b, Tanzania (child with cloth head covering). c, Malaysia. d, French Polynesia (denomination in white and green). e, Namibia. f, Tanzania (man with band around forehead).

2010, Oct. 21 **Litho.** *Perf. 13*

480	V98 Pane of 6 *(65,000)+*	11.50	11.50
a.-f.	65c Any single	1.90	1.90
	First day cover		13.50

United Nations Headquarters, Vienna — V99

Printed by Cartor Security Printing, France. Panes of 20. Designed by Scott Solberg, US.

United Nations Headquarters, Geneva: €1.25, Aerial view. €2.85, Ground-level view.

2011, Feb. 4 **Litho.** *Perf. 13*

481	V99 €1.25 **multicolored** *(400,000)+*	3.75	3.75
	First day cover		4.25
	Inscription block of 4	15.00	—
	Pane of 20	75.00	—
482	V99 €2.85 **multicolored** *(400,000)+*	8.25	8.25
	First day cover		9.50
	First day cover, #481-482		13.00
	Inscription block of 4	33.00	—
	Pane of 20	165.00	—

Flags and Coins Type of 2006

Printed by Cartor Security Printing, France. Designed by Rorie Katz, US.

No. 483 — Flag of: a, Lithuania, 2 lita coin. b, Greece, 1 euro coin. c, Kyrgyzstan, 50 tyiyn coin. d, Oman, 100 baisa coin. e, Estonia, 2 euro coin. f, Czech Republic, 5 koruna coin. g, Uzbekistan, 100 som coin. h, Monaco, 1 euro coin.

2011, Mar. 3 **Litho.** *Perf. 13¼x13*

483	Sheet of 8 *(70,000)+*	15.00	15.00
a.-h.	A375 65c Any single	1.75	1.75
	First day cover		17.00

A column of rouletting in the middle of the sheet separates it into two parts.

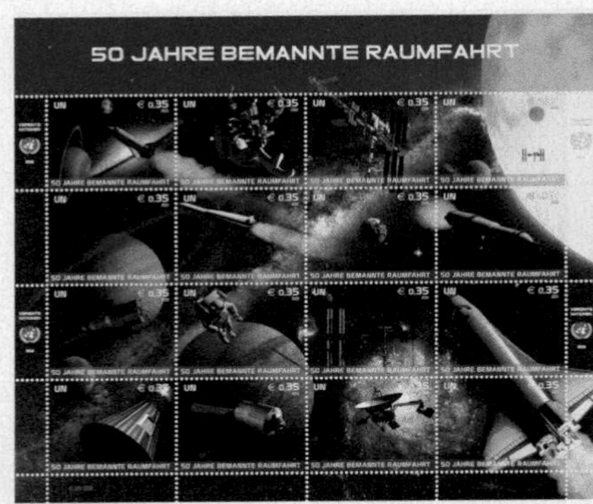

Human Space Flight, 50th Anniv. — V100

Printed by Lowe-Martin Group, Canada. Designed by Peter Bollinger, US.

No. 484: Various parts of outer space scene.

No. 485, vert.: a, Space Shuttle. b, Space Station.

2011, Apr. 12 **Litho.** *Perf. 13x13¼*

484	V100 Sheet of 16 *(65,000)+*	16.50	16.50
	First day cover		18.50
a.-p.	35c any single	1.00	1.00

Souvenir Sheet

485	V100 Sheet of 2	12.00	12.00
	First day cover		4.50
a.	55c **multicolored**	5.50	5.50
b.	65c **multicolored**	6.50	6.50
c.	Souvenir sheet of 6, New York #1025a-1025b, Geneva #534a-b, Vienna #485a-485b *(68,000)+*	42.50	42.50
	First day cover, #485c		13.00

No. 485 contains two 40x48mm stamps that were printed as part of a larger sheet of six stamps, No. 485c, which was broken up into its component two-stamp souvenir sheets, and also sold as one unit. Value $90, complete unit.

Vienna International Center and Flagpoles — V101

Fish-eye View of Vienna International Center and Flagpole — V102

Vienna International Center and Train — V103

Aerial View of Vienna International Center — V104

Vienna International Center and Water — V105

Detail From La Pioggia, Stadt Unter de Regen, by Friedensreich Hundertwasser — V106

Hand in Hand, by Hans Dietrich — V107

The Scholars Pavilion — V108

Detail From Grupo Expectante, by Alfredo Sosabravo — V109

Yes to Life, No to Drugs, by Sami Burhan — V110

2011, May 1	**Litho.**	***Perf. 14¾***	
486	V101 62c **multicolored** + label	*2.50*	*2.50*
487	V102 62c **multicolored** + label	*2.50*	*2.50*
488	V103 62c **multicolored** + label	*2.50*	*2.50*
489	V104 62c **multicolored** + label	*2.50*	*2.50*
490	V105 62c **multicolored** + label	*2.50*	*2.50*
a.	Vert. strip of 5, #486-490, + 5 labels	*15.00*	*15.00*
	Sheet, 4 #490a	*60.00*	—
491	V106 70c **multicolored** + label	*3.00*	*3.00*
492	V107 70c **multicolored** + label	*3.00*	*3.00*
493	V108 70c **multicolored** + label	*3.00*	*3.00*
494	V109 70c **multicolored** + label	*3.00*	*3.00*
495	V110 70c **multicolored** + label	*3.00*	*3.00*
a.	Vert. strip of 5, #491-495, + 5 labels	*17.50*	*17.50*
	Sheet, 2 #495a	*35.00*	—
	Nos. 486-495 (10)	*25.50*	*25.50*

The full sheet of Nos. 486-490 sold for $21.45 or €12.40. The full sheet of Nos. 491-495 sold for $14.26 or €9.90. The labels could be personalized.

UNESCO World Heritage Sites in Nordic Countries Type of 2011

Printed by Johann Enschedé and Sons, the Netherlands. Panes of 20. Designed by Rorie Katz, US.

Designs: 62c, Urnes Stave Church, Norway. 70c, Struve Geodetic Arc, Norway, Finland and Sweden.

2011, May 5	**Litho.**	***Perf. 14x13½***	
496	A433 62c **multicolored** *(160,000)+*	1.90	1.90
	First day cover		2.75
	Inscription block of 4	7.60	—
	Pane of 20	30.00	—
497	A433 70c **multicolored** *(160,000)+*	2.10	2.10
	First day cover		3.00
	First day cover, #496-497		4.75
	Inscription block of 4	8.40	—
	Pane of 20	42.00	—

AIDS Ribbon Type of 2011

Printed by Lowe-Martin Group, Canada. Panes of 4. Designed by Rorie Katz, US.

2011, June 3	**Litho.** **Self-Adhesive**	***Die Cut***	
498	A434 70c **red & green** *(260,000)+*	2.40	2.40
	Pane of 4	9.75	
	First day cover, pane of 4		10.50

ECOSOC Type of 2011

Printed by Cartor Security Printing, France. Panes of 20. Designed by Rorie Katz, US.

Education: 62c, Children with musical instruments. 70c, Woman teaching reading to old man.

2011, July 1	**Litho.**	***Perf. 14¼***	
499	A435 62c **multicolored** *(150,000)+*	3.00	3.00
	First day cover		3.00
	Inscription block of 4	12.00	—
	Pane of 20	60.00	—
500	A435 70c **multicolored** *(150,000)+*	4.00	4.00
	First day cover		3.50
	First day cover, #499-500		5.50
	Inscription block of 4	16.00	—
	Pane of 20	80.00	—

Endangered Species Type of 1993

Printed by Johann Enschedé and Sons, the Netherlands. Designed by Wendy Wray, U.S.

Designs: No. 501, Cyanoramphus novaezelandiae (Red-fronted parakeet). No. 502, Haliaeetus albicilla (White-tailed eagle). No. 503, Probosciger aterrimus (Black palm cockatoo). No. 504, Caloenas nicobarica (Nicobar pigeon).

2011, Sept. 7	**Litho.**	***Perf. 12¾x12½***	
501	A271 70c **multicolored** *(132,000)+*	2.50	2.50
502	A271 70c **multicolored** *(132,000)+*	2.50	2.50
503	A271 70c **multicolored** *(132,000)+*	2.50	2.50
504	A271 70c **multicolored** *(132,000)+*	2.50	2.50
a.	Block of 4, #501-504	10.00	10.00
	First day cover, #504a		9.75
	First day cover, #501-504, each		3.25
	Inscription block of 4, #504a	10.00	—
	Pane of 16	40.00	—

Intl. Year of Forests Type of 2011

Printed by Lowe-Martin Group, Canada. Panes of 8. Designed by Sergio Baradat, U.S.

Designs: 62c, Tree top, crosses, circles and ovals. 70c, Stylized people and trees.

Litho. With Foil Application

2011, Oct. 13		***Perf. 12½***	
505	62c **multicolored** *(100,000)+*	2.00	2.00
506	70c **multicolored** *(100,000)+*	2.25	2.25
a.	A436 Vert. pair, #505-506	4.25	4.25
	First day cover, #506a		5.25
	Pane of 8	17.00	—

Flags and Coins Type of 2006

Printed by Cartor Security Printing, France. Designed by Rorie Katz, US.

No. 507 — Flag of: a, Cameroun, 100 franc coin. b, Samoa, 2 tala coin. c, Surinam, 5 cent coin. d, Macedonia, 50 denar coin. e, Bulgaria, 50 stotinka coin. f, Tanzania, 100 shilling coin. g, Finland, 1 euro coin. h, Cuba, 1 peso coin.

2012, Feb. 3	**Litho.**	***Perf. 13¼x13***	
507	Sheet of 8 *(56,000)+*	16.50	16.50
a.-h.	A375 70c Any single	2.00	2.00
	First day cover		18.50

A column of rouletting in the middle of the sheet separates it into two parts.

V111

Autism Awareness — V112

Printed by Johann Enschedé Stamps Security Printers, Netherlands. Panes of 20.

Drawings by autistic people: No. 508, The Path, by Ryan Smoluk, Canada. No. 509, Untitled drawing, by Colm Isherwood, Ireland.

2012, Apr. 2	**Litho.**	***Perf. 14x13½***	
508	V111 70c **multicolored** *(90,000)+*	2.25	2.25
509	V112 70c **multicolored** *(90,000)+*	2.25	2.25
a.	Pair, #508-509	4.50	4.50
	First day cover, #508, 509		5.25
	Inscription block of 4	9.00	—
	Pane of 20	45.00	—

UN Emblem — V113

2012, Apr. 12 **Litho.** ***Perf. 14½***
510 V113 70c **purple, black** + label 3.50 3.50
Sheet of 10 + 10 labels 35.00 35.00

The full sheet sold for $14.52 or €9.90. The labels could be personalized.

Endangered Species Type of 1993

Printed by Johann Enschedé and Sons, the Netherlands. Designed by Diana Marques, Portugal.

Designs: No. 511, Panthera uncia. No. 512, Polyplectron schleiermacheri. No. 513, Tyto novaehollandiae. No. 514, Ambystoma mexicanum.

2012, Apr. 19 **Litho.** ***Perf. 12¾x12½***
511 A271 70c **multicolored** *(121,600)+* 2.25 2.25
512 A271 70c **multicolored** *(121,600)+* 2.25 2.25
513 A271 70c **multicolored** *(121,600)+* 2.25 2.25
514 A271 70c **multicolored** *(121,600)+* 2.25 2.25
a. Block of 4, #511-514 9.00 9.00
First day cover, #514a 9.25
First day cover, #511-514, each 3.00
Inscription block of 4, #514a 9.00 —
Pane of 16 36.00 —

Rio + 20 Type of 2012

Printed by Lowe-Martin Group, Canada. Panes of 20. Designed by Fei, People's Republic of China.

2012, June 1 **Litho.** ***Perf. 13x13¼***
515 A443 70c **multicolored** *(136,000)+* 2.10 2.10
First day cover 3.25
Inscription block of 4 8.40 —
Pane of 20 42.00 —

Sport for Peace Type of 2012

Printed by Cartor Security Printing, France. Panes of 9. Designed by Daniel Stolle, Finland.

2012 Paralympics events: 62c, Wheelchair basketball. 70c, Paralympic table tennis.

Litho. With Foil Application

2012, Aug. 17 ***Perf. 14½***
516 A444 62c **multicolored** *(153,000)+* 1.90 1.90
First day cover 2.75
Inscription block of 4 7.60 —
Pane of 9 17.50 —
517 A444 70c **multicolored** *(153,000)+* 2.10 2.10
First day cover 3.25
First day cover, #516-517 5.00
Inscription block of 4 8.40 —
Pane of 9 42.00 —
a. Souvenir sheet of 1 *(43,000)+* 2.10 2.10
First day cover 3.25

UNESCO World Heritage Sites in Africa Type of 2012

Printed by Lowe-Martin Group, Canada. Panes of 20. Designed by Rorie Katz, US.

Designs: 62c, Kenya Lake System, Kenya. 70c, Medina of Marrakesh, Morocco.

2012, Sept. 5 **Litho.** ***Perf. 13¼***
518 A445 62c **multicolored** *(140,000)+* 1.75 1.75
First day cover 2.60
Inscription block of 4 7.00 —
Pane of 20 35.00 —
519 A445 70c **multicolored** *(140,000)+* 2.00 2.00
First day cover 3.00
First day cover, #518-519 4.75
Inscription block of 4 8.00 —
Pane of 20 40.00 —

Miniature Sheet

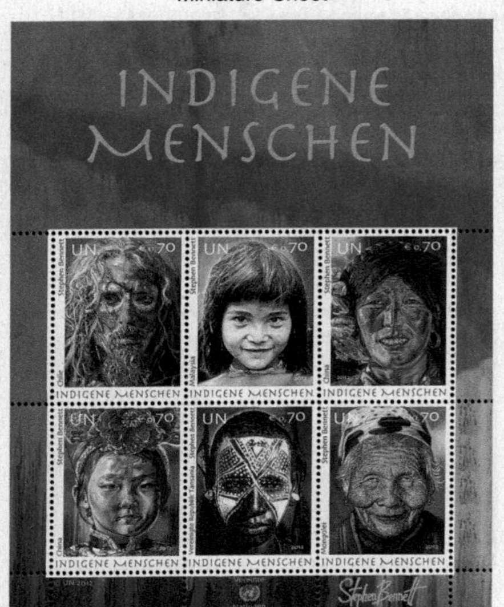

Indigenous People — V114

Printed by Lowe-Martin Group, Canada. Designed by Stephen Bennett, US.

No. 520 — Portrait of person from: a, Chile. b, Malaysia. c, China (woman with black hair). d, China (woman with flower in hair). e, Tanzania. f, Mongolia.

2012, Oct. 11 **Litho.** ***Perf. 13¼x13***
520 V114 Sheet of 6 *(49,000)+* 11.50 11.50
a.-f. 70c Any single 1.90 1.90
First day cover 13.50

World Radio Day Type of 2013

Printed by Lowe-Martin Group, Canada. Panes of 20. Designed by Rorie Katz, US.

Designs: 70c, Microphone and scripts. €1.70, Boy with radio.

2013, Feb. 13 **Litho.** ***Perf. 13¼x13***
521 A448 70c **multicolored** *(126,700)+* 2.00 2.00
First day cover 2.60
Inscription block of 4 8.00 —
Pane of 20 40.00 —
522 A448 €1.70 **multicolored** *(126,700)+* 5.00 5.00
First day cover 6.25
First day cover, #521-522 8.00
Inscription block of 4 20.00 —
Pane of 20 100.00 —

People in Handprint V115

People in Heart — V116

Printed by Johann Enschedé and Sons, the Netherlands. Panes of 20. Designed by Sergio Baradat, US.

2013, Mar. 5 **Litho.** ***Perf. 14x13½***
523 V115 62c **multicolored** *(200,000)+* 1.90 1.90
First day cover 2.25
Inscription block of 4 7.60 —
Pane of 20 38.00 —

Perf. 13½x14

524 V116 €2.20 **multicolored** *(200,000)+* 6.50 6.50
First day cover 7.75
First day cover, #523-524 9.00
Inscription block of 4 26.00 —
Pane of 20 130.00 —

World Heritage Sites, China, Type of 2013

Printed by Johann Enschedé and Sons, the Netherlands. Panes of 20. Designed by Sergio Baradat, U.S.

Designs: Nos. 525, 527c, Great Wall of China. Nos. 526, 527f, Mausoleum of the First Qing Emperor. No. 527a, Mogao Caves. No. 527b, Potala Palace, Lhasa. No. 527d, Imperial Palace, Beijing. No. 527e, Mount Huangshan.

2013, Apr. 11 **Litho.** ***Perf. 14x13½***
525 A452 70c **multicolored** *(150,000)+* 2.00 2.00
First day cover 2.60
Inscription block of 4 8.00 —
Pane of 20 40.00 —
526 A452 €1.70 **multicolored** *(150,000)+* 5.00 5.00
First day cover 6.25
First day cover, #525-526 8.00
Inscription block of 4 20.00 —
Pane of 20 100.00 —

Souvenir Booklet

527 Booklet, #527g-527l *(27,000)+* 25.00
a.-c. A452 30c any single .85 .85
d.-f. A452 40c any single 1.10 1.10
g. Booklet pane of 4 #527a 3.50 —
h. Booklet pane of 4 #527b 3.50 —
i. Booklet pane of 4 #527c 3.50 —
j. Booklet pane of 4 #527d 4.75 —
k. Booklet pane of 4 #527e 4.75 —
l. Booklet pane of 4 #527f 4.75 —

World Oceans Day — V117

Printed by Lowe-Martin Group, Canada. Designed by Rorie Katz, US.

No. 528 — Fish from *One Fish, Two Fish, Red Fish, Blue Fish,* by Dr. Seuss: a, Green fish facing left, wave. b, Red fish facing right. c, Three green fish on plate. d, Red fish, back half of red fish, wave. e, Red fish facing left, front half of red fish facing right. f, Two red fish facing left. g, Two green fish facing right, wave. h, Red fish facing right, head of blue fish wearing hat. i, Yellow fish with green star, wave. j, Yellow fish, back of blue fish, wave. k, Two red fish, body of blue fish. l, Tail of yellow fish, two green fish facing left, wave.

2013, May 31 **Litho.** ***Perf. 13***
528 V117 Sheet of 12 *(53,000)+* 24.00 24.00
First day cover 26.00
a.-l. 70c any single 2.00 2.00

Nebulae Type of 2013

Printed by UAB Garsu Pasaulis, Lithuania. Panes of 8. Designed by Sergio Baradat, U.S.

Designs: No. 529, NGC 7293. No. 530, NGC 1850. 62c, Eagle Nebula.

2013, Aug. 9 **Litho.** ***Perf. 13¼***
529 A454 €1.70 **multicolored** *(136,000)+* 5.00 5.00
530 A454 €1.70 **multicolored** *(136,000)+* 5.00 5.00
a. Pair, #529-530 10.00 10.00
First day cover, #5308a 11.00
Inscription block of 4 20.00 —
Pane of 8 40.00 —

Souvenir Sheet

531 A454 62c **multicolored** *(37,000)+* 1.90 1.90
First day cover 2.75

No. 531 contains one 44x44mm stamp.

Works of Disabled Artists Type of 2013

Printed by UAB Garsu Pasaulis, Lithuania. Panes of 20. Designed by Rorie Katz, U.S.

Designs: 70c, Electro Man, by Pete Eckert, U.S. €1.70, Dive Bomb, by Matt Sesow, U.S.

2013, Sept. 20 **Litho.** ***Perf. 13¼x13***
532 A456 70c **multicolored** *(129,500)+* 2.00 2.00
First day cover 2.60
Inscription block of 4 8.00 —
Pane of 20 40.00 —
533 A456 €1.70 **multicolored** *(129,500)+* 5.00 5.00
First day cover 6.25
First day cover, #532-533 8.00
Inscription block of 4 20.00 —
Pane of 20 100.00 —

Endangered Species Type of 1993

Printed by Johann Enschedé and Sons, the Netherlands. Designed by Emily S. Damstra, Canada.

Designs: No. 534, Hemigalus derbyanus. No. 535, Bubo ascalaphus. No. 536, Nycticebus coucang. No. 537, Zaglossus spp.

2013, Oct. 10 **Litho.** ***Perf. 12¾x12½***
534 A271 70c **multicolored** *(120,000)+* 2.00 2.00
535 A271 70c **multicolored** *(120,000)+* 2.00 2.00
536 A271 70c **multicolored** *(120,000)+* 2.00 2.00
537 A271 70c **multicolored** *(120,000)+* 2.00 2.00
a. Block of 4, #534-537 8.00 8.00
First day cover, #537a 9.00
First day cover, #534-537, each 3.00
Inscription block of 4, #537a 8.00 —
Pane of 16 32.00 —

UN Emblem — V118

2013, Oct. 24 Litho. *Perf. 14½*

538	V118 70c **gray blue & blue** + label	*4.00*	*4.00*
	Sheet of 10 + 10 labels	*30.00*	—

The full sheet sold for $14.20 or €9.90. The labels could be personalized.

Flags and Coins Type of 2006

Printed by Cartor Security Printing, France. Designed by Rorie Katz, US.

No. 539 — Flag of: a, Malaysia, 50 sen coin. b, Nigeria, 1 naira coin. c, Zambia, 20 ngwee coin. d, Togo, 100 franc coin. e, Dominica, 5 cent coin. f, Chad, 100 franc coin. g, St. Vincent and the Grenadines, 5 cent coin. h, Syria, 25 pound coin.

2013, Nov. 6 Litho. *Perf. 13¼x13*

539	Sheet of 8 *(48,000)+*	16.00	16.00
a.-h.	A375 70c Any single	2.00	2.00
	First day cover		18.00

A column of rouletting in the middle of the sheet separates it into two parts.

International Day of Happiness Type of 2014

Printed by Lowe-Martin Group, Canada. Panes of 20. Designed by Rorie Katz, U.S.

Designs: 90c, Happy Asian Boy at the Park, photograph by Alan Levenson, Russian word for "Happy." €1.70, Barbary Macacque with Baby, photograph by Gerhard Schulz, Arabic word for "Happy."

2014, Mar. 17 Litho. *Perf. 13¼x13*

540	A459 90c **multicolored** *(100,000)+*	2.75	2.75
	First day cover		3.50
	Inscription block of 4	11.00	—
	Pane of 20	55.00	—
541	A459 €1.70 **multicolored** *(100,000)+*	5.25	5.25
	First day cover		6.50
	First day cover, #540-541		8.75
	Inscription block of 4	21.00	—
	Pane of 20	105.00	—

Miniature Sheet

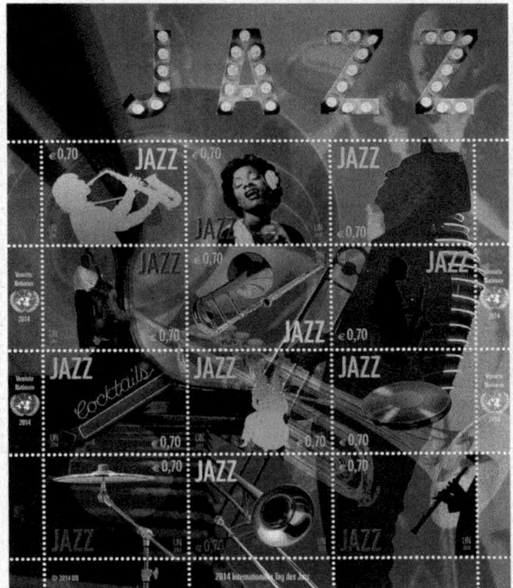

International Year of Jazz — V119

Printed by Cartor Security Printing, France. Designed by Sergio Baradat, U.S.

No. 542: a, Silhouette of saxophonist in blue. b, Woman singing. c, Silhouette of man in red, neon lights. d, Bass player. e, Trombone in gold. f, Silhouette of saxophonist in black, silhouette of man holding trombone. g, "Cocktails" neon sign . h, Silhouette of bass player in orange. i, Stack of record albums. j, Cymbal. k, Trombone in silver. l, Silhouette of clarinetist in black.

2014, Apr. 30 Litho. *Perf. 13x13¼*

542	V119 Sheet of 12 *(50,000)+*	24.00	24.00
	First day cover		27.00
a.-l.	70c Any single	2.00	2.00

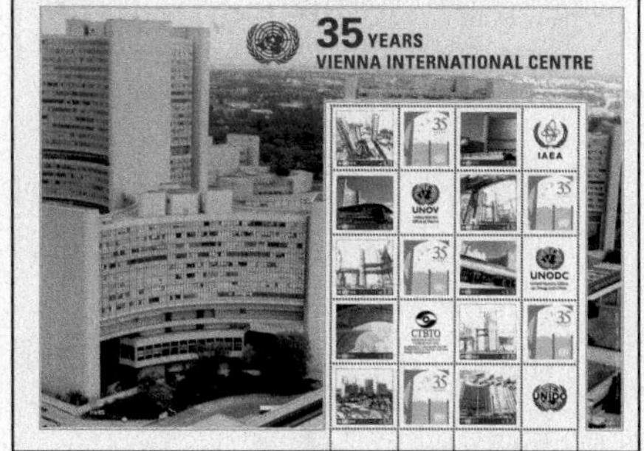

Vienna International Center, 35th Anniv. — V120

Designed by Eduardo Sinoy, U.S.

No. 543: a, Vienna International Center under construction (towers and shadows), red panel. b, Vienna International Center, street light at left, green panel. c, Vienna International Center, curved building at left, green panel. d, Vienna International Center under construction (arch in foreground, cranes at right), red panel. e, Vienna International Center under construction (cranes at left, center and right), red panel. f, Doorway to Vienna International Center, green panel. g, View of curved buildings of Vienna International Center looking up from ground, green panel. h, Vienna International Center under construction (two cranes on central tower), red panel. i, Completed Vienna International Center, red panel. j, Flags in front of Vienna International Center.

2014, May 8 Litho. *Perf. 14¾*

543	V120 Sheet of 10 + 10 labels	*30.00*	*30.00*
a.-j.	70c Any single + label	*3.00*	*3.00*

The full sheet sold for $14.80 or €9.90. The generic labels are shown. Labels could be personalized.

V121

V122

Printed by Lowe-Martin Group, Canada. Panes of 20. Designed by Sergio Baradat, U.S.

2014, June 6 Litho. *Perf. 13¼x13*

544	V121 70c **multicolored** *(116,000)+*	2.10	2.10
	First day cover		2.75
	Inscription block of 4	8.40	—
	Pane of 20	42.00	—
545	V122 €1.70 **multicolored** *(116,000)+*	5.25	5.25
	First day cover		6.50
	First day cover, #544-545		8.25
	Inscription block of 4	21.00	—
	Pane of 20	105.00	—

Taj Mahal Types of 2014

Printed by Lowe-Martin Group, Canada. Panes of 20. Designed by Rorie Katz, U.S.

2014, July 16 Engr. *Perf. 13¼x13*

546	A466 90c **multicolored** *(120,000)+*	2.75	2.75
	First day cover		3.50
	Inscription block of 4	11.00	—
	Pane of 20	55.00	—
547	A468 €1.70 **multicolored** *(120,000)+*	5.25	5.25
	First day cover		6.50
	First day cover, #546-547		8.75
	Inscription block of 4	21.00	—
	Pane of 20	105.00	—

Souvenir Booklet

548	Booklet, #548g-548l *(18,000)+*	25.00	
a.	A463 30c multi	.85	.85
b.	A465 30c multi	.85	.85
c.	A466 30c multi	.85	.85
d.	A464 40c multi	1.20	1.20
e.	A467 40c multi	1.20	1.20
f.	A468 40c multi	1.20	1.20
g.	Booklet pane of 4 #548a	3.40	—
h.	Booklet pane of 4 #548b	3.40	—
i.	Booklet pane of 4 #548c	3.40	—
j.	Booklet pane of 4 #548d	4.80	—
k.	Booklet pane of 4 #548e	4.80	—
l.	Booklet pane of 4 #548f	4.80	—

International Year of Family Farming V123

Printed by Lowe-Martin Group, Canada. Panes of 20. Designed by Sergio Baradat, U.S.

Designs: 62c, Indian farmers collecting harvested straw and grain. €1.70, Asian farmers, bull, terraced fields.

2014, Aug. 21 Litho. *Perf. 13x13¼*

549	V123 62c **multicolored** *(100,000)+*	1.90	1.90
	First day cover		2.40
	Inscription block of 4	7.60	—
	Pane of 20	38.00	—
550	V123 €1.70 **multicolored** *(100,000)+*	5.25	5.25
	First day cover		6.50
	First day cover, #549-550		8.00
	Inscription block of 4	21.00	—
	Pane of 20	105.00	—

Global Education First Initiative Type of 2014

Printed by Lowe-Martin Group, Canada. Panes of 20. Designed by Oamul Lu, People's Republic of China.

Designs: €1.70, Children boarding school bus. €2, Tree growing from book held by students.

2014, Sept. 18 Litho. *Perf. 13x13¼*

551	A470 €1.70 **multicolored** *(110,000)+*	5.25	5.25
	First day cover		6.25
	Inscription block of 4	21.00	—
	Pane of 20	105.00	—

Souvenir Sheet

Perf. 12½

552	A470 €2 **multicolored** *(42,000)+*	6.00	6.00
	First day cover		6.25

No. 552 contains one 32x32mm stamp.

Endangered Species Type of 2014

Printed by Johann Enschedé and Sons, the Netherlands. Designed by Amadeo Bachar, U.S.

Maps and: No. 553, Cheilinus undulatus. No. 554, Carcharodon carcharias. No. 555, Manta birostris. No. 556, Polyodon spathula.

2014, Oct. 23 Litho. *Perf. 12¾x12½*

553	A471 70c **multicolored** *(108,000)+*	2.10	2.10
554	A471 70c **multicolored** *(108,000)+*	2.10	2.10
555	A471 70c **multicolored** *(108,000)+*	2.10	2.10
556	A471 70c **multicolored** *(108,000)+*	2.10	2.10
a.	Block of 4, #553-556	8.50	8.50
	First day cover, #556a		9.50
	First day cover, #553-556, each		3.00
	Inscription block of 4, #556a	8.50	—
	Pane of 16	34.00	—

Miniature Sheet

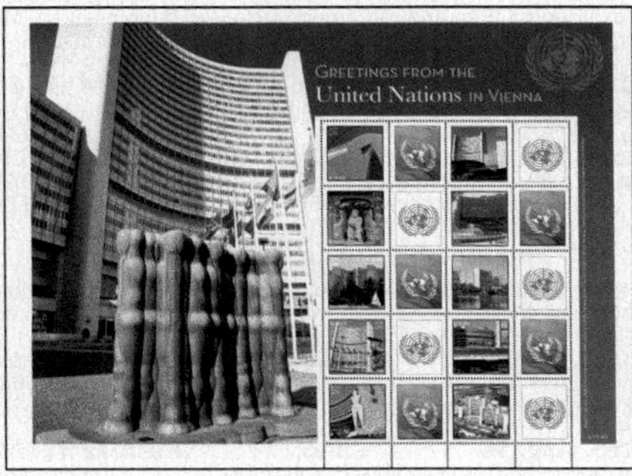

V124

Designed by Rorie Katz, U.S.

No. 557: a, Flag on pole as seen from base of pole. b, Vienna International Center, structure in shadow at bottom. c, Persian Scholars Pavilion. d, Vienna International Center and fountain.

e, Sailboat and Vienna International Center. f, Rowboat on water near Vienna International Center. g, Vienna International Center, flags and sculpture. h, Entrance to Vienna International Center. i, Woman Free sculpture near Vienna International Center. j, Aerial view of Vienna International Center.

2015, Jan. 23 Litho. *Perf. 14¾*

557 V124 Sheet of 10 *30.00 30.00*
a.-j. 80c Any single + label *3.00 3.00*

The full sheet sold for $15 or €10.90. The generic labels are shown. Labels could be personalized.

Flags and Coins Type of 2006

Printed by Cartor Security Printing, France. Designed by Rorie Katz, U.S.

No. 558 — Flag of: a, Tuvalu, 10 cent coin. b, Malawi, 1 kwacha coin. c, Iraq, 50 dinar coin. d, St. Thomas and Prince Islands, 250 dobra coin. e, Botswana, 10 thebe coin. f, Uruguay, 5 peso coin. g, Bosnia and Herzegovina, 20 pfennig coin. h, Somalia, 25 shilling coin.

2015, Feb. 6 Litho. *Perf. 13¼x13*

558 Sheet of 8 *(45,000)+* 18.00 18.00
a.-h. A375 80c Any single 2.25 2.25
First day cover 20.00

A column of rouletting in the middle of the sheet separates it into two parts.

Miniature Sheets

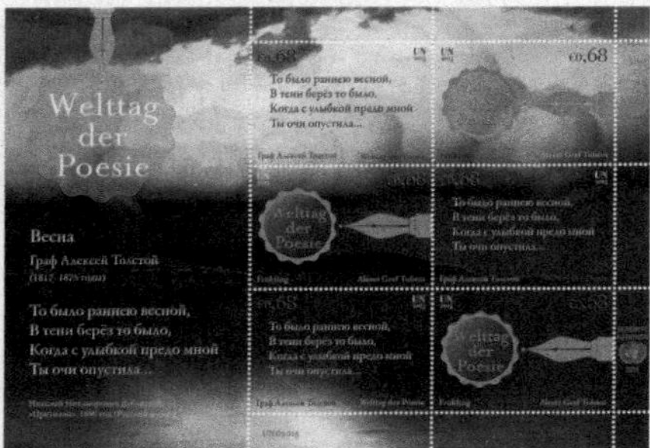

V125

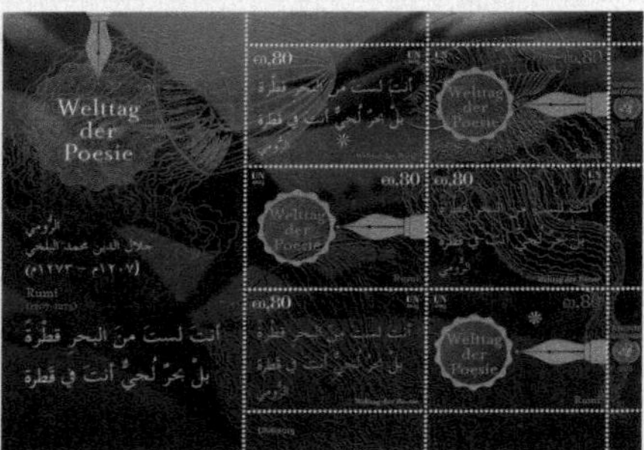

World Poetry Day — V126

Printed by Cartor Security Printing. France. Designed by Sergio Baradat, U.S.

No. 559: a, Aleksey Tolstoy quotation in Russian in red brown, date in purple, "Welttag der Poesie" in red. b, Pen and circle, date in black, "Frühling" in purple. c, Pen and circle, date and "Frühling" in white, clouds above land in background. d, Tolstoy quotation in Russian in white, date in white, "Welttag der Poesie" in red. e, Tolstoy quotation in white, date and "Welttag der Poesie" in white. f, As "c," brown background.

No. 560: a, Rumi quotation in Arabic in light blue. b, Pen and red brown circle, denomination in red, purple jellyfish in background. c, Pen and red brown circle, denomination in white. d, Rumi quotation in orange, purple jellyfish tentacles in background. e, Rumi quotation in orange, red jellyfish tentacles in background. f, Pen and red brown circle, red denomination, red and purple jellyfish tentacles in background.

2015, Mar. 20 Litho. *Perf. 14½x14¼*

559 V125 Sheet of 6 *(42,000)+* 11.50 11.50
a.-f. 68c Any single 1.90 1.90
560 V126 Sheet of 6 *(42,000)+* 13.50 13.50
a.-f. 80c Any single 2.25 2.25
First day cover, #559-560 28.50

Endangered Species Type of 2015

Printed by Johann Enschedé and Sons, the Netherlands. Designed by John Keulemans and William Hart, United Kingdom.

Designs: No. 561, Pteridophora alberti. No. 562, Astrapia splendidissima. No. 563, Paradisaea apoda. No. 564, Lophorina superba.

2015, Apr. 16 Litho. *Perf. 12½x12¾*

561 A476 80c **multicolored** *(100,000)+* 2.00 2.00
562 A476 80c **multicolored** *(100,000)+* 2.00 2.00
563 A476 80c **multicolored** *(100,000)+* 2.00 2.00
564 A476 80c **multicolored** *(100,000)+* 2.00 2.00
a. Block of 4, #561-564 8.00 8.00
First day cover, #564a 9.00
First day cover, #561-564, each 3.00
Inscription block of 4, #564a 8.00 —
Pane of 16 32.00 —
Nos. 561-564 (4) 8.00 8.00

V127

V128

Printed by Lowe-Martin Group, Canada. Panes of 20. Designed by Sergio Baradat, U.S.

2015, May 7 Litho. *Perf. 13¼x13*

565 V127 68c **multicolored** *(110,000)+* 1.75 1.75
First day cover 2.50
Inscription block of 4 7.00 —
Pane of 20 35.00 —
566 V128 80c **multicolored** *(110,000)+* 2.00 2.00
First day cover 3.00
First day cover, #565-566 4.75
Inscription block of 4 8.00 —
Pane of 20 40.00 —

World Heritage Sites, Southeast Asia Type of 2015

Printed by Johann Enschedé and Sons, the Netherlands. Panes of 20. Designed by Sergio Baradat, U.S.

Designs: Nos. 567, 569c, Ayutthaya, Thailand. Nos. 568, 569f, Hué Monuments, Viet Nam. No. 569a, Luang Prabang, Laos. No. 569b, Angkor Wat, Cambodia. No. 569d, Borobudur Temple, Indonesia. No. 569e, Cordillera, Philippines.

2015, June 5 Litho. *Perf. 14x13½*

567 A480 80c **multicolored** *(120,000)+* 2.00 2.00
First day cover 2.60
Inscription block of 4 8.00 —
Pane of 20 40.00 —
568 A480 €1.70 **multicolored** *(120,000)+* 4.25 4.25
First day cover 5.50
First day cover, #567-568 7.25
Inscription block of 4 17.00 —
Pane of 20 85.00 —

Souvenir Booklet

569 Booklet, #569g-569l *(17,000)+* 21.00
a.-c. A480 30c any single .75 .75
d.-f. A480 40c any single 1.00 1.00
g. Booklet pane of 4 #569a 3.00 —
h. Booklet pane of 4 #569b 3.00 —
i. Booklet pane of 4 #569c 3.00 —
j. Booklet pane of 4 #569d 4.00 —
k. Booklet pane of 4 #569e 4.00 —
l. Booklet pane of 4 #569f 4.00 —

End Violence Against Children Type of 2015

Printed by Cartor Security Printing, France. Panes of 20. Designed by Chris Sharp, U.S.

Designs: 68c, Gender-based violence. 80c, Child labor.

2015, Aug. 20 Litho. *Perf. 14½x14¼*

570 A481 68c **multicolored** *(100,000)+* 1.75 1.75
First day cover 2.50
Inscription block of 4 7.00 —
Pane of 20 35.00 —
571 A481 80c **multicolored** *(100,000)+* 2.00 2.00
First day cover 3.00
First day cover, #570-571 4.75
Inscription block of 4 8.00 —
Pane of 20 40.00 —

ECOSOC Chamber V129

Trusteeship Council V130

Visitors Lobby V131

General Assembly Hall V132

Trusteeship Council — V133

Printed by Cartor Security Printing, France. Panes of 6. Designed by Rorie Katz, U.S.

2015, Oct. 25 Litho. *Perf. 13¾*

572	V129	80c **multicolored** *(111,000)+*	2.00	2.00
573	V130	80c **multicolored** *(111,000)+*	2.00	2.00
a.		Pair, #572-573	4.00	4.00
		First day cover, #572-573		4.75
		Inscription block of 4	8.00	—
		Pane of 6	12.00	—
574	V131	€1.70 **multicolored** *(111,000)+*	4.25	4.25
575	V132	€1.70 **multicolored** *(111,000)+*	4.25	4.25
a.		Pair, #574-575	8.50	8.50
		First day cover, #574-575		9.75
		Inscription block of 4	17.00	—
		Pane of 6	25.50	—
		Nos. 572-575 (4)	12.50	12.50

Souvenir Sheet

Perf. 13½

576	V133	€1.70 **multicolored** *(42,000)+*	4.25	4.25
		First day cover		5.25

United Nations, 70th anniv.

United Nations, 70th Anniv. Type of 2015

Designed by Sergio Baradat, U.S.

2015, Nov. 5 Litho. *Perf. 14¾*

577	A482	80c **multicolored** + label	*4.00*	*4.00*
		Sheet of 10 + 10 labels	*40.00*	—

The full sheet sold for $13.45 or €10.90. The sheet contains ten different generic labels. Labels could be personalized. The personalization of labels was available only at UN Headquarters, and not through mail order.

21st United Nations Climate Change Conference, Paris — V134

Printed by La Poste, France. Panes of 30. Designed by Rorie Katz, U.S.

2015, Nov. 24 Litho. *Perf. 13¼*

578	V134	80c **multicolored** *(90,000)+*	3.00	3.00
		First day cover		3.50
		Inscription block of 4	12.00	—
		Pane of 30	60.00	—

Values are for stamps with surrounding selvage.

Free and Equal Type of 2016

Printed by Cartor Security Printing, France. Panes of 20. Designed by Sergio Baradat, U.S.

Designs: 68c, Person coming out of closet. 80c, Gay men.

2016, Feb. 5 Litho. *Perf. 13½x13¼*

579	A491	68c **multicolored** *(100,000)+*	1.75	1.75
		First day cover		2.50
		Inscription block of 4	7.00	—
		Pane of 20	35.00	—
580	A491	80c **multicolored** *(100,000)+*	2.00	2.00
		First day cover		3.00
		First day cover, #579-580		4.50
		Inscription block of 4	8.00	—
		Pane of 20	40.00	—

HeForShe Type of 2016

Printed by Lowe-Martin Group, Canada. Panes of 20. Designed by Mirko Ilic, U.S.

Designs: 1fr, Man, red background. 2fr, Woman, orange brown background.

2016, Mar. 8 Litho. *Perf. 12½x13*

581	A492	68c **multicolored** *(100,000)+*	1.75	1.75
		First day cover		2.25
		Inscription block of 4	7.00	—
		Pane of 20	35.00	—
582	A492	80c **multicolored** *(100,000)+*	2.00	2.00
		First day cover		2.75
		First day cover, #581-582		4.25
		Inscription block of 4	8.00	—
		Pane of 20	40.00	—

Miniature Sheets

V135

International Dance Day — V136

Printed by Cartor Security Printing. France. Designed by Sergio Baradat, U.S.

No. 583 — Illustration of Spanish dancers by Allison Seiffer: a, Female dancer with fan. b, Male dancer with crossed arms. c, Red dress of dancer. d, Female dancer with male guitarist. e, Feet of dancer in ochre and green dress. f, Feet of male and female dancers, rose on floor.

No. 584 — Illustration of Middle Eastern dancers by Seiffer: a, Head of female dancer, "Welttanztag" in red, denomination in yellow. b, Head of female dancer, "Welttanztag" and denomination in red. c, Torso of dancer. d, Dancer, "Welttanztag" in black, denomination in yellow. e, Feet of dancer, "Welttanztag" in black. f, Feet of dancer and drum, "Welttanztag" in yellow.

2016, Apr. 29 Litho. *Perf. 13¼x13*

583	V135	Sheet of 6 *(35,000)+*	10.00	10.00
a.-f.		68c Any single	1.60	1.60
584	V136	Sheet of 6 *(35,000)+*	12.00	12.00
a.-f.		80c Any single	2.00	2.00
		First day cover, #583-584		25.50

United Nations Industrial Development Organization, 50th Anniv. — V137

2016, May 12 Litho. *Perf. 14¾*

585	V137	80c **multicolored** + label	*2.60*	*2.60*
		Sheet of 10 + 10 labels	*26.50*	—

The full sheet sold for $13.12 and €10.90. One of the ten different generic labels is shown. Labels could be personalized. The personalization of labels was available only at UN Headquarters, and not through mail order.

International Day of United Nations Peacekeepers Type of 2016

Printed by Lowe-Martin Group, Canada. Panes of 20. Designed by Sergio Baradat, U.S.

Designs: 68c, Peacekeepers and African children. 80c, Peacekeepers in tank, Africans.

Litho. With Foil Application

2016, May 29 *Perf. 13¼x13*

586	A496	68c **multicolored** *(130,000)+*	1.75	1.75
		First day cover		2.50
		Inscription block of 4	7.00	—
		Pane of 20	35.00	—
587	A496	80c **multicolored** *(130,000)+*	2.00	2.00
		First day cover		3.00
		First day cover, #586-587		4.50
		Inscription block of 4	8.00	—
		Pane of 20	40.00	—

Sport for Peace Type of 2016

Printed by Cartor Security Printing, France. Panes of 6. Designed by Sergio Baradat and Linsey Thoeng, U.S.

Olympic rings and: No. 588, Weight lifting, denomination at LR. No. 589, Weight lifting, denomination at LL. No. 590, Fencing, denonomiation at UR. No. 591, Fencing, denonomiation at UL.

2016, July 22 Litho. *Perf. 14¼*

588	A498	68c **multicolored** *(105,000)+*	1.75	1.75
589	A498	68c **multicolored** *(105,000)+*	1.75	1.75
a.		Pair, #588-589	3.50	3.50
		First day cover, #588-589		4.00
		Inscription block of 4	7.00	—
		Pane of 6	10.50	—
590	A498	€1.70 **multicolored** *(105,000)+*	4.25	4.25
591	A498	€1.70 **multicolored** *(105,000)+*	4.25	4.25
a.		Pair, #590-591	8.50	8.50
		First day cover, #590-591		9.75
		Inscription block of 4	17.00	—
		Pane of 6	25.50	—
		Nos. 588-591 (4)	12.00	12.00

Souvenir sheets of three bearing three stamps, one from each office are listed under United Nations, Offices in New York as Nos. 1141, 1161, 1177-1178, 1203, and 1208.

World Heritage Sites, Czech Republic Type of 2016

Printed by Cartor Security Printing, France. Panes of 20. Designed by Sergio Baradat, U.S.

Designs: Nos. 592, 594c, Historic Town Center of Kutná Hora. Nos. 593, 594f, Historic Center of Cesky Krumlov. No. 594a, Historic Center of Prague. No. 594b, Gardens and Castle at Kroměríz. No. 594d, Holy Trinity Column, Olomouc. Nos. 594e, Lednice-Valtice Cultural Landscape.

2016, Sept. 8 Litho. *Perf. 14¼*

592	A500	68c **multicolored** *(100,000)+*	1.75	1.75
		First day cover		2.25
		Inscription block of 4	7.00	—
		Pane of 20	35.00	—
593	A500	€1.70 **multicolored** *(100,000)+*	4.25	4.25
		First day cover		5.50
		First day cover, #592-593		6.75
		Inscription block of 4	17.00	—
		Pane of 20	85.00	—

Souvenir Booklet

594		Booklet, #594g-594l	20.50	
a.-c.	A500	30c any single	.65	.65
d.-f.	A500	40c any single	1.00	1.00
g.		Booklet pane of 4 #594a	2.75	—
h.		Booklet pane of 4 #594b	2.75	—
i.		Booklet pane of 4 #594c	2.75	—
j.		Booklet pane of 4 #594d	4.00	—
k.		Booklet pane of 4 #594e	4.00	—
l.		Booklet pane of 4 #594f	4.00	—

Comprehensive Nuclear Test-Ban Treaty Organization, 20th Anniv. — V138

2016, Sept. 23 Litho. *Perf. 14¾*

595	V138	80c **multicolored** + label	*4.00*	*4.00*
		Sheet of 10 + 10 labels	*40.00*	—

The full sheet sold for $13.27 and €10.90. One of the ten different generic labels is shown. Labels could be personalized. The personalization of labels was available only at UN Headquarters, and not through mail order.

Miniature Sheet

World Wildlife Conference, Johannesburg — V139

Printed by Cartor Security Printing, France. Designed by Sergio Baradat, U.S.

No. 596 — Part of map of Africa and: a, Nilkrokodil (Nile crocodile). b, Kapgeier (Cape vulture). c, Steppenschuppentier (Cape pangolin). d, Mystacidium capense.

2016, Sept. 24 — Litho. — *Perf. 13x13½*

596 V139 Sheet of 4 *(35,000)+* 17.00 17.00
a.-d. €1.70 Any single 4.25 4.25
First day cover 17.50

Sustainable Development Goals Type of 2016

Printed by Lowe-Martin, Canada. Designed by Lindsey Thoeng, U.S.

No. 597 — Inscription: a, 1 Keine armut. b, 2 Kein hunger. c, 3 Gesundheit und wohlergehen. d, 4 Hochwertige bildung. e, 5 Geschlechter-gleighheit. f, 6 Sauberes wasser und sanitär-einrichtungen. g, 7 Bezahlbare und saubere energie. h, 8 Menschenwürdige arbeit und wirtschafts-wachstum. i, 9 Industrie, innovation und infrastruktur. j, 10 Weniger ungleichheiten. k, 11 Nachhaltige städte und gemeinden. l, 12 Nachhaltige/r konsum und produktion. m, 13 Massnahmen zum klimaschutz. n, 14 Leben unter wasser. o, 15 Leben an land. p, 16 Frieden, gerechtigkeit und starke institutionen. q, 17 Partnerschaften zur erreichung der ziele.

2016, Oct. 24 — Litho. — *Perf. 13¼*

597 Sheet of 17 + label *(30,000)+* 28.50 28.50
a.-q. A503 68c Any single 1.60 1.60
First day cover 32.00

Miniature Sheet

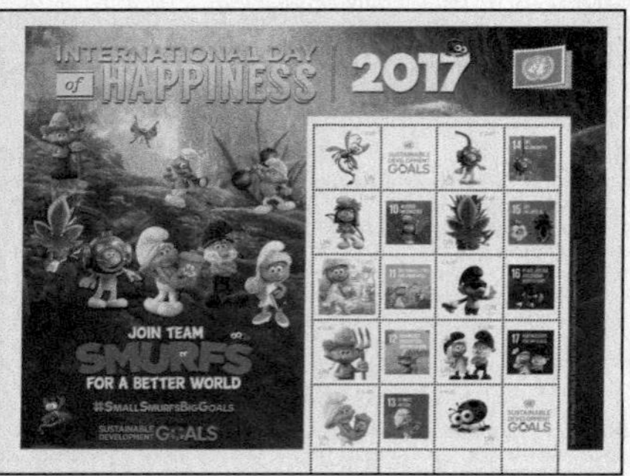

V140

No. 598: a, Insect. b, Smurf wearing diving helmet. c, Smurf holding archery bow. d, Flower with eyes. e, Smurf in park. f, Smurf with police hat, whistle and baton. g, Smurf holding pitchfork. h, Two Smurfs wearing red caps. i, Smurf holding garbage can. j, Ladybug.

2017, Mar. 20 — Litho. — *Perf. 14¾*

598 V140 Sheet of 10 + 10 labels *30.00 30.00*
a.-j. 80c Any single + label *3.00 3.00*

The full sheet sold for $14.95. The generic labels are shown. Labels could be personalized.

Miniature Sheets

V141

International Dance — V142

Printed by Cartor Security Printing. France. Designed by Sergio Baradat, U.S.

No. 599 — Illustration of Samba dancers by Victo Ngai: a, Lion's head. b, Black and tan female dancers. c, Dancers holding drums. d, Black female dancer. e, White female dancer. f, Brown female dancer.

No. 600 — Illustration of Ballet dancers by Ngai: a, Blue dancer with hand bent downward. b, Blue dancer with arm raised above head. c, Blue dancer with arms extended to side. d, Dancer with black dress. e, Head of dancer, tip of dress at bottom. f, Head of dancer facing right.

2017, Mar. 23 — Litho. — *Perf. 13¼x13*

599 V141 Sheet of 6 *(28,000)+* 9.75 9.75
a.-f. 68c Any single 1.60 1.60
599g As #599, with Brasilia 2017 World Stamp Exhibition emblem overprinted in sheet margin 10.50 10.50
600 V142 Sheet of 6 *(28,000)+* 11.50 11.50
a.-f. 80c Any single 1.90 1.90
First day cover, #599-600 25.50

Issued: No. 599g, 10/24.

Endangered Species Type of 2017

Printed by Johann Enschedé and Sons, the Netherlands. Designed by Rorie Katz, U.S.

Designs: No. 601, Capra caucasica. No. 602, Nautilidae spp. No. 603, Siphonochilus aethiopicus. No. 604, Lygodactylus williamsi.

2017, May 11 — Litho. — *Perf. 12¾x12½*

601 A509 80c **multicolored** *(76,000)+* 1.90 1.90
602 A509 80c **multicolored** *(76,000)+* 1.90 1.90
603 A509 80c **multicolored** *(76,000)+* 1.90 1.90
604 A509 80c **multicolored** *(76,000)+* 1.90 1.90
a. Block of 4, #601-604 7.75 7.75
First day cover, #604a 9.25
First day cover, #601-604, each 3.50
Inscription block of 4, #604a 7.75 —
Pane of 16 31.00 —
Nos. 601-604 (4) 7.60 7.60

World Environment Day Type of 2017

Printed by Lowe-Martin Group, Canada. Panes of 20. Designed by Sergio Baradat, U.S.

Designs: 68c, Supreme Court, Ottawa, Ontario, Canada. €1.70, Moraine Lake, Canada.

2017, June 5 — Litho. — *Perf. 13¼*

605 A510 68c **multicolored** *(90,000)+* 1.60 1.60
First day cover 2.60
Inscription block of 4 6.40 —
Pane of 20 32.00 —
606 A510 €1.70 **multicolored** *90,000)+* 4.00 4.00
First day cover 6.50
First day cover, #605-606 7.25
Inscription block of 4 16.00 —
Pane of 20 80.00 —

World Heritage Sites Along the Silk Roads Type of 2017

Printed by Cartor Security Printing, France. Panes of 20. Designed by Sergio Baradat, U.S.

Designs: Nos. 607, 609c, Tabriz Historic Bazaar Complex, Iran. Nos. 608, 609f, Safranbolu, Turkey. No. 609a, Longmen Grottoes, People's Republic of China. No. 609b, Historic Center of Bukhara, Uzbekistan. No. 609d, Sulaiman-Too Sacred Mountain, Kyrgyzstan. No. 609e, Kunya-Urgench, Turkmenistan.

2017, Aug. 3 — Litho. — *Perf. 14¼*

607 A512 80c **multicolored** *(90,000)+* 2.00 2.00
First day cover 3.25
Inscription block of 4 8.00 —
Pane of 20 40.00 —
608 A512 €1.70 **multicolored** *(90,000)+* 4.25 4.25
First day cover 6.75
First day cover, #607-608 8.00
Inscription block of 4 17.00 —
Pane of 20 85.00 —

Souvenir Booklet

609 Booklet, #609g-609l *(10,500)+* 23.50
a.-c. A512 30c any single .85 .85
d.-f. A512 40c any single 1.10 1.10
g. Booklet pane of 4 #609a 3.40 —
h. Booklet pane of 4 #609b 3.40 —
i. Booklet pane of 4 #609c 3.40 —
j. Booklet pane of 4 #609d 4.40 —
k. Booklet pane of 4 #609e 4.40 —
l. Booklet pane of 4 #609f 4.40 —

Miniature Sheet

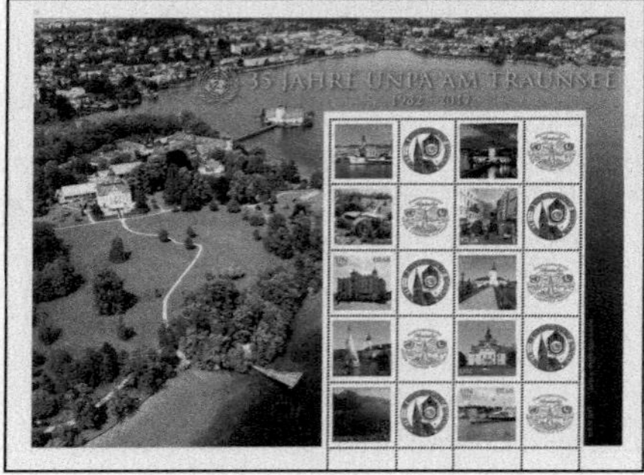

V143

No. 610: a, Traunsee with ships and lakeshore buildings. b, Ort Castle and bridge at dusk. c, Aerial view of Cumberland Castle. d, Street in Gmunden, Austria. e, Gmunden City Hall. f, Ort Castle and bridge. g, Sailboat near Ort Castle. h, Villa Toscana. i, Aerial view of Traunsee. j, Ships on Traunsee.

2017, Aug. 24 — Litho. — *Perf. 14¾*

610 V143 Sheet of 10 + 10 labels *27.50 27.50*
a.-j. 68c Any single + label *2.75 2.75*

United Nations Postal Administration on the Traunsee, 35th anniv. The full sheet sold for $13.64. The generic labels are shown. Labels could be personalized.

Hands and Flower V144

Handshake and Flowers — V145

Handshake and Flowers — V146

Printed by Johann Enschedé and Sons, the Netherlands. Panes of 20. Designed by Stranger and Stranger, U.S.

2017, Sept. 21 **Litho.** ***Perf. 14x14¼***

611 V144 68c **multicolored** *(90,000)+* 1.75 1.75
First day cover 2.75
Inscription block of 4 7.00 —
Pane of 20 35.00 —
612 V145 €1.70 **multicolored** *(90,000)+* 4.25 4.25
First day cover 6.75
First day cover, #611-612 7.75
Inscription block of 4 17.00 —
Pane of 20 85.00 —

Souvenir Sheet

Perf. 14¼x13¾

613 V146 €1.70 **multicolored** *(33,000)+* 4.25 4.25
First day cover 6.00

International Day of Peace.

World Food Day Type of 2017

Printed by Royal Johann Enschedé. Panes of 20. Designed by Helen Dardik, Canada.

Designs: 68c, Breads and grains. 80c, Steak, fish, chicken drumstick, shrimp, egg, beans, lemon slice.

2017, Oct. 16 **Litho.** ***Perf. 13¼x14***

614 A516 68c **multicolored** *(90,000)+* 1.75 1.75
First day cover 3.25
Inscription block of 4 7.00 —
Pane of 20 35.00 —
615 A516 80c **multicolored** *(90,000)+* 2.00 2.00
First day cover 4.00
First day cover, #614-615 5.50
Inscription block of 4 8.00 —
Pane of 20 40.00 —

Endangered Species Type of 2018

Printed by Johann Enschedé Stamps Security Printers, the Netherlands. Designed by Rorie Katz, U.S.

Designs: No. 616, Hoodia pilifera. No. 617, Mantella madagascariensis. No. 618, Pangshua sylhetensis. No. 619, Hippocampus zebra.

2018, Mar. 2 **Litho.** ***Perf. 12¾x12½***

616 A519 80c **multicolored** *(76,000)+* 2.00 2.00
617 A519 80c **multicolored** *(76,000)+* 2.00 2.00
618 A519 80c **multicolored** *(76,000)+* 2.00 2.00
619 A519 80c **multicolored** *(76,000)+* 2.00 2.00
a. Block of 4, #616-619 8.00 8.00
First day cover, #619a 10.50
First day cover, #616-619, each 3.75
Inscription block of 4, #619a 8.00 —
Pane of 16 32.00 —
Nos. 616-619 (4) 8.00 8.00

World Health Day Type of 2018

Printed by Lowe-Martin Group, Canada. Panes of 20. Designed by Sergio Baradat, U.S.

Designs: 68c, Medical worker, people, globe, caduceus. €1.70, Coins entering piggy bank with white cross.

2018, Apr. 6 **Litho.** ***Perf. 13x13¼***

620 A520 68c **multicolored** *(90,000)+* 1.90 1.90
First day cover 2.75
Inscription block of 4 7.60 —
Pane of 20 38.00 —
621 A520 €1.70 **multicolored** *(90,000)+* 4.50 4.50
First day cover 7.00
First day cover, #620-621 8.00
Inscription block of 4 18.00 —
Pane of 20 90.00 —

United Nations Emblem — V147

2018 **Litho.** ***Perf. 14¾***

622 V147 80c **multicolored** + label *2.75 2.75*
Sheet of 10 + 10 labels *29.00* —
a. Less distinct year date and frame, lighter blue emblem *2.75 2.75*
Sheet of 10 #622a + 10 labels *29.00* —

Issued: No. 622, 5/26; No. 622a, 7/30. The full sheet sold for $14.32 and €10.90. One of the ten different generic labels is shown. Labels could be personalized. The personalization of labels was available only at UN Headquarters, and not through mail order.

UNISPACE + 50 Conferences Type of 2018

Printed by Johann Enschedé Stamps BV, Netherlands. Panes of 20. Designed by Sergio Baradat, U.S. Designs: 68c, Great Red Spot of Jupiter. 80c, Aurora Australis from International Space Station.

€1.70, View of river delta from Copernicus Sentinel satellite.

2018, June 20 **Litho.** ***Perf. 14x14¼***

623 A523 68c **multicolored** *(80,000)+* 1.90 1.90
First day cover 3.50
Inscription block of 4 7.60 —
Pane of 20 45.00 —
624 A523 80c **multicolored** *(80,000)+* 2.25 2.25
First day cover 4.00
First day cover, #623-624 5.75
Inscription block of 4 9.00 —
Pane of 20 45.00 —

Souvenir Sheet

Perf. 13¾

625 A523 €1.70 **multicolored** *(27,000)+* 4.50 4.50
First day cover 6.25

No. 625 contains one 45x45mm stamp.

World Heritage Sites In the United Kingdom Type of 2018

Printed by Cartor Security Printing, France. Panes of 20. Designed by Rorie Katz, U.S.

Designs: Nos. 626, 628c, Conwy Castle. Nos. 627, 628f, Maritime Greenwich. No. 628a, Giant's Causeway. No. 628b, Stonehenge. No. 628d, Palace of Westminster. No. 628e, Edinburgh.

2018, Aug. 15 **Litho.** ***Perf. 14¼***

626 A524 90c **multicolored** *(80,000)+* 2.40 2.40
First day cover 3.25
Inscription block of 4 9.60 —
Pane of 20 48.00 —
627 A524 €1.80 **multicolored** *(90,000)+* 4.75 4.75
First day cover 6.75
First day cover, #626-627 8.00
Inscription block of 4 19.00 —
Pane of 20 95.00 —

Souvenir Booklet

628 Booklet, #628g-628l *(9,000)+* 25.50
a.-c. A524 35c any single 1.00 1.00
d.-f. A524 40c any single 1.10 1.10
g. Booklet pane of 4 #628a 4.00 —
h. Booklet pane of 4 #628b 4.00 —
i. Booklet pane of 4 #628c 4.00 —
j. Booklet pane of 4 #628d 4.50 —
k. Booklet pane of 4 #628e 4.50 —
l. Booklet pane of 4 #628f 4.50 —

Miniature Sheet

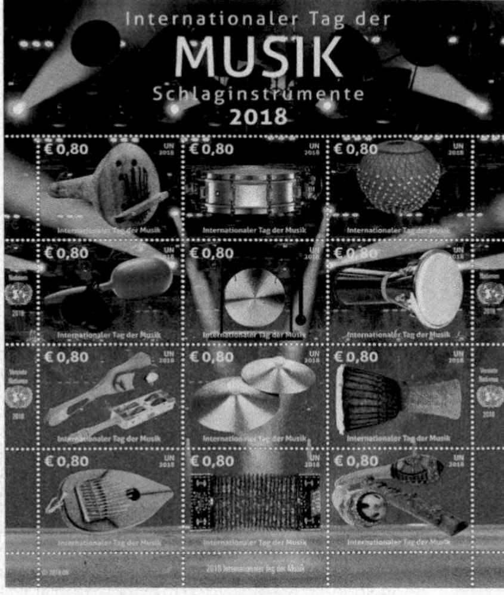

International Music Day — V148

Printed by Johann Enschedé Stamps BV, the Netherlands. Designed by Sergio Baradat, U.S.

No. 629: a, Kalimba with three holes. b, Snare drum. c, Shekere. d, Castanets. e, Gong. f, Hourglass drum. g, Castanet with handles and tambourine stick. h, Cymbals. i, Djembe drum. j, Kalimba with one hole. k, Button accordion. l, Maracas and decorated stick.

2018, Oct. 1 **Litho.** ***Perf. 14x13¼***

629 V148 Sheet of 12 *(24,000)+* 24.50 24.50
First day cover 27.00
a.-l. 80c Any single 2.00 2.00

V149

Non-Violence, Sculpture by Carl Fredrik Reuterswärd — V150

Printed by Johann Enschedé Stamps BV, the Netherlands. Panes of 20. Designed by Martin Mörck, Norway.

2018, Oct. 2 **Litho.** ***Perf. 14x14¼***

630 V149 90c **multicolored** *(300,000)+* 2.40 2.40
First day cover 3.25
Inscription block of 4 9.60 —
Pane of 20 48.00 —
631 V150 €2.30 **multicolored** *(200,000)+* 6.00 6.00
First day cover 8.25
First day cover, #630-631 10.00
Inscription block of 4 24.00 —
Pane of 20 120.00 —

Miniature Sheet

World Languages — V151

Printed by Cartor Security Printing. France. Designed by Sergio Baradat, U.S.

No. 632 — Word bubbles with word for "Hello" in: a, Serbian or Croatian ("Sprachen der Welt" and denomination in red). b, Arabic ("Sprachen der Welt" and denomination in white). c, Korean ("Sprachen der Welt" in white, denomination in black), d, Dutch or German or Norwegian (Hallo). e, Greek and Turkish (Merhaba). f, Spanish (Hola).

2019, Feb. 21 **Litho.** ***Perf. 13¼x13***

632 V151 Sheet of 6 *(28,000)+* 12.50 12.50
a.-f. 80c Any single 2.00 2.00
First day cover, #632 15.50

Migration — V152

Printed by Lowe-Martin Group, Canada. Panes of 20. Designed by Chris Gash, U.S.

2019, Mar.15 **Litho.** ***Perf. 13¼x13***

633 V152 €1.80 **multicolored** *(170,000)+* 4.75 4.75
First day cover 6.50
Inscription block of 4 19.00 —
Pane of 20 95.00 —

Endangered Species Type of 2019

Printed by Johann Enschedé Stamps Security Printers, the Netherlands. Designed by Rongliang Wang, People's Republic of China.

Designs: No. 634, Anguilla anguilla. No. 635, Dermochelys coriacea. No. 636, Acropora spp. No. 637, Huso huso.

2019, Apr. 26 **Litho.** ***Perf. 12¾x12½***

634 A534 90c **multicolored** *(60,000)+* 2.25 2.25
635 A534 90c **multicolored** *(60,000)+* 2.25 2.25
636 A534 90c **multicolored** *(60,000)+* 2.25 2.25
637 A534 90c **multicolored** *(60,000)+* 2.25 2.25
a. Block of 4, #634-637 9.25 9.25
First day cover, #637a 11.00
First day cover, #634-637, each 4.25
Inscription block of 4, #637a 9.25 —
Pane of 16 37.00 —
Nos. 634-637 (4) 9.00 9.00

2019 END-OF-YEAR ISSUES

See end of New York postage listings.

SEMI-POSTAL STAMP

AIDS Awareness Semi-postal Type

Souvenir Sheet

2002, Oct. 24 **Litho.** ***Perf. 14½***

B1 SP1 51c + 25c **multicolored** *(220,000)+* 3.50 3.50
First day cover, #B1 3.50

ENVELOPES

Used values for all postal stationery are for non-philatelic contemporaneous usages.

Donaupark, Vienna — VU1

Printed by Mercury-Walch Pty. Ltd. (Australia). Designed by Hannes Margreiter (Austria).

Design: 7s, Landscape. Design at lower left shows Vienna landmarks (6s), river scene (7s).

1995, Feb. 3 **Litho.**

U1 VU1 6s **multicolored,** entire *(128,000)+* 2.00 2.00
First day cancel *(14,132)* 2.75
U2 VU1 7s **multicolored,** entire *(128,000)+* 2.00 2.00
First day cancel *(9,684)* 3.50

VU2

Printed by Mercury-Walch Pty. Ltd. (Australia).

1998, Mar. 13 **Litho.**

U3 VU2 13s **multicolored,** entire *(87,000)+* 3.50 3.00
Entire, first day cancel 3.50

VU3

Vienna International Center — VU4

Printed by Australia Post Sprintpak (Australia). Designed by Robert Stein (US).

2002, June 27 **Litho.**

U4 VU3 51c **multicolored,** entire *(93,000)+* 2.00 2.00
Entire, first day cancel 2.00
U5 VU4 €1.09 **multicolored,** entire *(88,000)+* 2.60 2.60
Entire, first day cancel 3.25

Nos. U4-U5 Surcharged

2003, June 2 **Litho.**

U6 VU3 51c +4c **multicolored,** entire 4.00 *6.00*
Entire, first day cancel 3.75
U7 VU4 €1.09 +16c **multicolored,** entire 5.25 *8.00*
Entire, first day cancel 4.75

UN Flag — VU5

Dove With Olive Branch — VU6

Printed by Government Printing Office, Austria. Designed by Rorie Katz, US.

2004, June 3 **Litho.**

U8 VU5 55c **multicolored,** entire *(53,000)+* 2.25 1.75
Entire, first day cancel 2.50
U9 VU6 €1.25 **multicolored,** entire *(48,000)+* 4.00 2.75
Entire, first day cancel 4.00

Nos. U8-U9 Surcharged Like No. U6

2007, Sept. 3 **Litho.**

U10 VU5 55c +10c **multicolored,** entire 3.25 *4.00*
Entire, first day cancel 3.75
U11 VU6 €1.25 +15c **multicolored,** entire 5.00 *6.00*
Entire, first day cancel 5.00

Vienna International Center — VU7

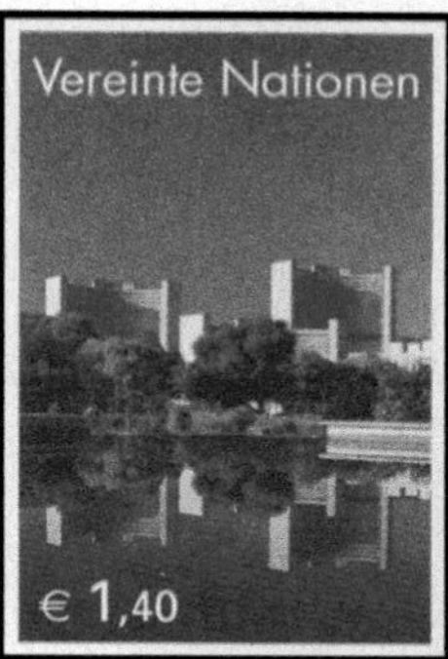

Vienna International Center — VU8

Designed by Rorie Katz, US.

2009, May 7 **Litho.**
U12 VU7 65c **multicolored,** entire 3.25 3.25
Entire, first day cancel 3.00
U13 VU8 €1.40 **multicolored,** entire 5.00 5.00
Entire, first day cancel 5.00

Nos. U12-U13 Surcharged Like No. U6

2011, May 5 **Litho.**
U14 VU7 65c +5c **multicolored,** entire 3.50 *4.00*
Entire, first day cancel 4.50
U15 VU8 €1.40 +30c **multicolored,** entire 6.50 *8.00*
Entire, first day cancel 7.50

Surcharges on Nos. U14-U15 are vertical, reading up.

United Nations Emblem — VU9

Printed by Lowe-Martin Group, Canada. Designed by Sergio Baradat, U.S.

2015, May 7 **Litho.**
U16 VU9 68c **dull orange,** entire *(9,000)+* 3.00 3.00
Entire, first day cancel 3.00
U17 VU9 80c **yellow green,** entire *(9,000)+* 3.25 3.25
Entire, first day cancel 3.25
U18 VU9 €1.70 **lilac,** entire *(9,000)+* 5.50 5.50
Entire, first day cancel 5.50
Nos. U16-U18 (3) 11.75 11.75

Vienna International Center — VU10

Printed by Goessler, Austria. Designed by Adolf Tuma, Austria.

2016, July 20 **Litho.**
U19 VU10 68c **multicolored** *(8,000)+* 3.50 3.50
First day cancel 4.50

AIR LETTER SHEETS

VLS1

Printed by Joh. Enschede and Sons. Designed by Ingrid Ousland.

1982, Apr. 28 **Litho.**
UC1 VLS1 9s **multi,** *light green,* entire *(650,000)* 1.50 1.50
First day cancel *(120,650)* 1.50

No. UC1 Surcharged in Lake

1986, Feb. 3 **Litho.**
UC2 VLS1 9s +2s **multi,** *light green,* entire *(131,190)* 45.00 *75.00*
First day cancel *(18,500)* 10.00

Birds in Flight, UN Emblem VLS2

Printed by Mercury-Walch, Australia. Designed by Mieczyslaw Wasiliewski, Poland.

1987, Jan. 30 **Litho.**
UC3 VLS2 11s **bright blue,** entire *(414,000)* 2.00 2.00
First day cancel *(48,348)* 4.00

No. UC3 Surcharged

1992, Jan. 1 **Litho.**
UC4 VLS2 11s +1s **bright blue,** entire *(80,000)* 45.00 *75.00*
First day cancel 30.00

Donaupark, Vienna — VLS3

Designed by Rocco J. Callari. Printed by Mercury-Walch, Australia.

1992, Sept. 4 **Litho.**
UC5 VLS3 12s **multicolored,** entire *(200,000)+* 6.50 6.50
First day cancel *(16,261)* 27.50

POSTAL CARDS

Olive Branch — VPC1

Bird Carrying Olive Branch — VPC2

Printed by Courvoisier. Designed by Rolf Christianson (3s), M.A. Munnawar (5s).

1982, Apr. 28 **Photo.**
UX1 VPC1 3s **multicolored,** *cream (500,000)* .80 .90
First day cancel *(93,010)* 1.65
UX2 VPC2 5s **multicolored** *(500,000)* .75 1.00
First day cancel *(89,502)* 1.65

Emblem of the United Nations — VPC3

Printed by Johann Enschede en Zonen, Netherlands. Designed by George Hamori, Australia.

1985, May 10 **Litho.**
UX3 VPC3 4s **multicolored** *(350,000)* 1.50 3.50
First day cancel *(53,450)* 3.00

No. UX2 Surcharged

1992, Jan. 1 **Photo.**
UX4 VPC2 5s +1s **multicolored** *(71,700)* 25.00 *30.00*
First day cancel 25.00

Type of 1990

Printed by Mercury-Walch, Australia.

1992, Sept. 4 **Litho.**
UX5 V22 6s **multicolored** *(445,000)+* 1.75 2.75
First day cancel *(16,359)* 10.00

See No. UX9.

Type of 1985

Printed by Leigh Mardon Pty. Limited, Australia.

1993, May 7 **Litho.**
UX6 A222 5s **multicolored** *(450,000)* 19.00 19.00
First day cancel 10.00

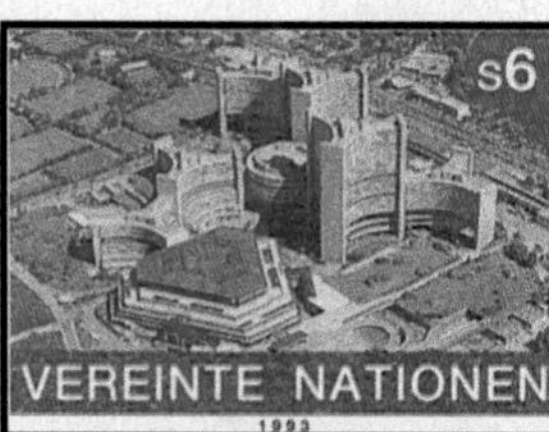

Donaupark, Vienna — VPC4

Printed by Leigh Mardon Pty. Limited, Australia.

1993, May 7 **Litho.**
UX7 VPC4 6s **multicolored** *(450,000)+* 4.00 4.00
First day cancel 6.00

See No. UX10.

No. UX6 with design of Vienna No.1 Added

1994, Jan. 1 **Litho.**
UX8 A222+G8 5s +50g **multi** *(350,000)+* 2.50 *5.00*
First day cancel 4.00

No. UX5 with design of Vienna #167 Added

1997, July 1 **Litho.**
UX9 V22+V32 6s +50g **multi** 2.50 *3.00*
First day cancel 3.50

No. UX7 with design of Vienna #194 Added

UX10 VPC4+V35 6s +1s **multi** 3.00 *4.00*
First day cancel 4.00

VPC5

Designed by Günter Leidenfrost.

1998, May 20 **Litho.**
UX11 VPC5 6.50s **multicolored** *(137,000)+* 1.50 1.50
First day cancel 2.00

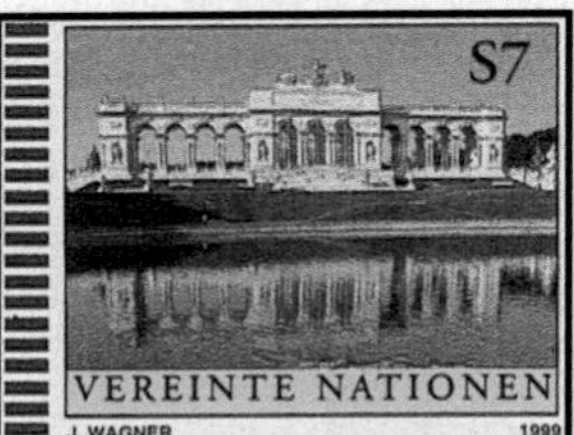

The Gloriette — VPC6

1999, Feb. 5 **Litho.**
UX12 VPC6 7s **multicolored** *(136,000)+* 2.00 2.00
First day cancel 2.50

Type of 1983

2000, June 2 **Litho.**
UX13 V7 7s **multicolored** 2.25 2.25
First day cancel 2.25

Clock Tower, Graz, Austria — VPC7

Printed by Johann Enschedé and Sons, the Netherlands. Designed by Robert Stein, US.

2002, Mar. 1 **Litho.**
UX14 VPC7 51c **multicolored** *(83,000)+* 1.50 1.50
First day cancel 1.50

No. UX14 Surcharged

2003, June 2 **Litho.**
UX15 VPC7 51c +4c **multicolored** 2.75 *4.00*
First day cancel 2.75

Vienna International Center — VPC8

Printed by Government Printing Office, Austria. Designed by Rorie Katz, US.

2004, June 3 **Litho.**
UX16 VPC8 55c **multicolored** *(63,000)+* 2.60 1.25
First day cancel 3.00

No. UX16 Surcharged Like No. UX15

2007, Sept. 3 **Litho.**
UX17 VPC8 55c +10c **multicolored,** entire 3.75 *5.00*
Entire, first day cancel 4.00

Vienna International Center — VPC9

2009, May 7 **Litho.**
UX18 VPC9 65c **multicolored** 3.50 3.50
First day cancel 3.50

Vienna International Center and Flagpoles — VPC10

Designs: 70c, Fish-eye view of Vienna International Center and flagpole. €1.70, Vienna International Center at night.

2011, May 5 **Litho.**
UX19 VPC10 62c **multicolored** 3.75 3.75
First day cancel 3.75
UX20 VPC10 70c **multicolored** 4.25 4.25
First day cancel 4.50
UX21 VPC10 €1.70 **multicolored** 8.00 8.00
First day cancel 8.00
Nos. UX19-UX21 (3) 13.25 13.25

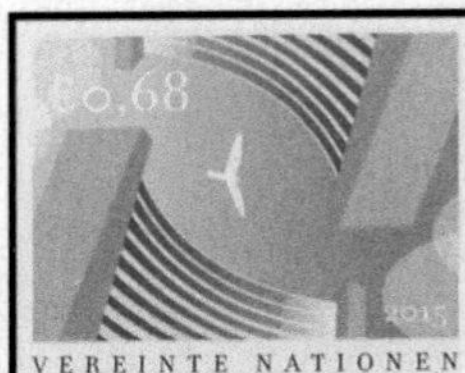

Dove and Vienna International Center — VPC11

Vienna International Center — VPC12

Woman Free, Sculpture by Edwina Sandys — VPC13

Printed by Lowe-Martin Group, Canada. Designed by Sergio Baradat, U.S.

2015, May 7 **Litho.**
UX22 VPC11 68c **multicolored** *(11,000)+* 3.00 3.00
First day cancel 3.00
UX23 VPC12 80c **multicolored** *(11,000)+* 3.25 3.25
First day cancel 3.25
UX24 VPC13 €1.70 **multicolored** *(11,000)+* 5.50 5.50
First day cancel 5.50
Nos. UX22-UX24 (3) 11.75 11.75

Nos. UX22, UX24 Surcharged With Vertical Surcharge Similar to No. UX15

2018, Aug. 23 **Litho.**
UX25 VPC11 68c+22c **multicolored,** entire (#UX22) 3.75 *3.75*
Entire, first day cancel 3.75
UX26 VPC13 €1.70+10c **multicolored,** entire (#UX24) 6.25 *6.25*
Entire, first day cancel 6.25

U.N. SOUVENIR CARDS

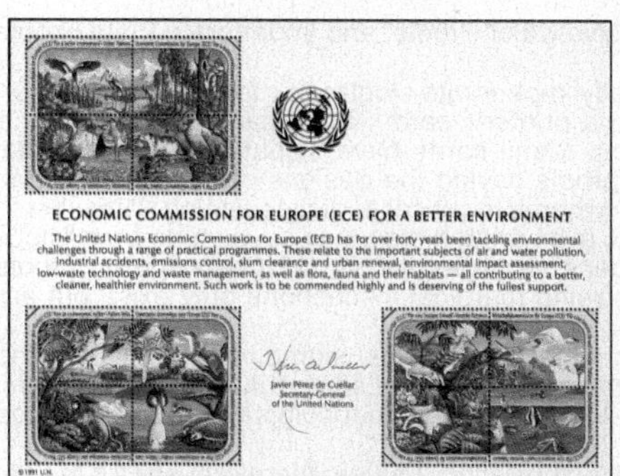

No. 39

These cards were issued by the United Nations Postal Administration and were not valid for postage.

Each card bears reproductions of UN stamps and a statement by the Secretary-General in English.

Values are for mint cards without cancels.

No.	Description	Value
SC1	World Health Day, Apr. 7, 1972. Card of 5: #43, 102, 156, 207, 228.	.65

A second printing shows several minor differences.

No.	Description	Value
SC2	Art on UN Stamps, Nov. 17, 1972. Card of 11: #170, 171, 173, 174, 180, 183, 201, 202, 203, 224, 232. #201, 202 form a simulated setenant pair	.45
SC3	Disarmament Decade, Mar. 9, 1973. Card of 5: #133, 147, 177, 227, 234	.50
SC4	Declaration of Human Rights, 25th Anniversary, Nov. 16, 1973. Card of 10: #13, 22, 29, 39, 47, 58, 68, 121, 190, 242	.75
SC5	UPU centenary, Mar. 22, 1974. Card of 7: #17, 18, 219, 246; Geneva 18, 39, 40.	.75
SC6	World Population Year, Oct. 18, 1974. Card of 7: #151, 152, 153, 252, 253; Geneva 43, 44.	2.50
SC7	Peaceful Uses of Outer Space, Mar. 14, 1975. Card of 6: #112, 113, 256, 257; Geneva 46, 47.	2.00
SC8	UN Peace Keeping Operations, Nov. 21, 1975. Card of 9: #52, 111, 118, 139, 160, 265, 266; Geneva 55, 56.	2.00
SC9	World Federation of United Nations Associations, Mar. 12, 1976. Card of 5: #154, 155, 272, 273; Geneva 57.	2.00
SC10	World Food Council, Nov. 19, 1976. Card of 6: #116, 117, 218, 280; Geneva 17, 63.	2.50
SC11	World Intellectual Property Organization (WIPO), Mar. 11, 1977. Card of 15: #17, 23, 25, 31, 33, 41, 43, 49, 59, 86, 90, 123, 281, 282; Geneva 64.	2.50
SC12	Combat Racism, Sept. 19, 1977. Card of 8: #220, 221, 287, 288; Geneva 19, 20, 69, 70.	2.50
SC13	Namibia, May 5, 1978. Card of 10: #240, 241, 263, 264, 296, 297; Geneva 34, 53, 54, 76.	1.00
SC14	Intl. Civil Aviation Organization, June 12, 1978. Card of 6: #31, 32, 298, 299; Geneva 77, 78.	2.50
SC15	Intl. Year of the Child, May 4, 1979. Card of 9: #5, 97, 161, 162, 163, 310, 311; Geneva 84, 85.	.75
SC16	Intl. Court of Justice, Nov. 9, 1979. Card of 6: #88, 89, 314, 315; Geneva 87, 88.	.75
SC17	UN Decade for Women, Mar. 7, 1980. Card of 4: #258, 318; Geneva 90; Vienna 9.	7.50
SC18	Economic and Social Council, Nov. 7, 1980. Card of 8; #65, 66, 341, 342; Geneva 96, 97; Vienna 15, 16.	.75
SC19	Intl. Year of Disabled Persons, Mar. 6, 1981. Card of 6; #344, 345; Geneva 99, 100; Vienna 18, 19.	.65
SC20	New and Renewable Sources of Energy, May 29, 1981. Card of 4; #348, 349; Geneva 102; Vienna 21.	1.00
SC21	Human Environment, Mar. 19, 1982. Card of 5: #230, 371; Geneva 26, 107; Vienna 25	.75
SC22	Exploration and Peaceful Uses of Outer Space, June 11, 1982. Card of 7: #112, 256, 373; Geneva 46, 109, 110; Vienna 27.	1.40
SC23	Safety at Sea, Mar. 18, 1983. Card of 8: #123, 124, 394, 395; Geneva 114, 115; Vienna 31, 32.	1.10
SC24	Trade and Development, June 6, 1983. Card of 11: #129, 130, 274, 275, 397, 398; Geneva 58, 117, 118; Vienna 31, 32.	1.50
SC25	Intl. Conference on Population, Feb. 3, 1984. Card of 10: #151, 153, 252, 253, 417, 418; Geneva 43, 44, 121; Vienna 39.	2.00
SC26	Intl. Youth Year, Nov. 15, 1984. Card of 5: #441, 442; Geneva 128; Vienna 46, 47.	3.00
SC27	ILO Turin Center, Feb. 1, 1985. Card of 8: #25, 200, 244, 443; Geneva 37, 129, 130; Vienna 48.	2.75
SC28	Child Survival Campaign, Nov. 22, 1985. Card of 6: #466, 467; Geneva 138, 139; Vienna 55, 56.	3.00
SC29	Stamp Collecting, May 22, 1986. Card of 5: #278, 473; Geneva 61, 147; Vienna 63.	*8.25*

No. 29 with stitch marks has been removed from the Ameripex program. Value is one-half that of unstitched card.

No.	Description	Value
SC30	Intl. Peace Year, June 20, 1986. Card of 6: #475, 476; Geneva 148, 149; Vienna 64, 65.	4.00
SC31	Shelter for the Homeless, Mar. 13, 1987. Card of 6: #495, 496; Geneva 154, 155; Vienna 68, 69.	2.50
SC32	Immunize Every Child, Nov. 20, 1987. Card of 13: #44, 103, 157, 208, 294, 517, 518; Vienna 76, 77.	3.00
SC33	Intl. Volunteer Day, May 6, 1988. Card of 10; #239, 367, 524, 525; Geneva 103, 167, 168; Vienna 23, 82, 83.	4.00
SC34	Health in Sports, June 17, 1988. Card of 6; #526, 527; Geneva 169, 170; Vienna 84, 85.	5.00
SC35	World Bank, Jan. 27, 1989. Card of 8; #86-87, 546-547; Geneva 173-174; Vienna 88-89.	5.00
SC36	World Weather Watch, Apr. 21, 1989. Card of 10; #49-50, 188-189, 550-551; Geneva 176-177; Vienna 91-92.	5.00
SC37	Fight AIDS Worldwide, Mar. 16, 1990. Card of 6, #573-574; Geneva 184-185; Vienna 99-100	6.50
SC38	Crime Prevention, Sept. 13, 1990. Card of 6; #580-581; Geneva 191-192; Vienna 106-107.	6.00
SC39	Economic Commission for Europe, Mar. 15, 1991. Card of 12; #584-587; Geneva 195-198; Vienna 110-113.	6.00
SC40	Rights of the Child, June 14, 1991. Card of 6; #593-594; Geneva 203-204; Vienna 117-118.	7.00
SC41	Mission to Planet Earth, Sept. 4, 1992, Card of 6, #609-610; Geneva 220-221; Vienna 133-134	14.00
SC42	Science and Technology for Development, Oct. 2, 1992, Card of 6, #611-612; Geneva 222-223; Vienna 135-136	15.00
SC43	Healthy Environment, May 7, 1993, Card of 6, #624-625; Geneva #232-233; Vienna #147-148	14.00
SC44	Peace, Sept. 21, 1993, Card of 12, #629-632; Geneva #236-239; Vienna #152-155	16.00

No. 44 exists overprinted in gold with Hong Kong '94 emblem.

No.	Description	Value
SC45	Intl. Year of the Family, Feb. 4, 1994, Card of 6, #637-638; Geneva #244-245; Vienna #160-161	13.50
SC46	Population & Development, 1994, Card of 9, #151, 651-652; Geneva #43, 258-259; Vienna #39, 174-175	12.50
SC47	World Summit for Social Development, 1995, Card of 3, #656; Geneva #263; Vienna #179	10.50
SC48	Intl. Youth Year, 1995, Card of 9, #441, 661-662; Geneva #128, 268-269; Vienna #46, 184-185	14.00
SC49	WFUNA, 1996, Card of 3, #671; Geneva #277; Vienna #193	12.00
SC50	UNICEF, 1996, Card of 6, #688-689; Geneva #294-295; Vienna #210-211	9.00
SC51	Philately, 1997, Card of 6, #714-715; Geneva #312-313; Vienna #228-229	12.50
SC52	Peacekeeping, #737-738; Geneva #325-326; Vienna #242-243	9.00
SC53	Universal Declaration of Human Rights, #739-740; Geneva #327-328; Vienna #244-245	9.00
SC54	UPU, #767a; Geneva #346a; Vienna #263a	5.00
SC55	Respect for Refugees, #787; Geneva #365; Vienna #282	6.00
SC56	Intl. Volunteers Year, #793-794; Geneva #371-372; Vienna #288-289	4.00
SC57	Johannesburg Summit on Sustainable Development, #828-831; Geneva #396-399; Vienna #318-321	5.00
SC58	International Year of Freshwater, #846-8471; Geneva #411-412; Vienna #333-334	5.00
SC59	Japanese Peace Bell, 50th Anniv., #865; Geneva #425; Vienna #349	6.50
SC60	Nature's Wisdom, #885-886; Geneva #440-441; Vienna #364-365	5.00
SC61	Intl. Day of Families, #913-914, Geneva #457-458, Vienna #380-381	5.00
SC62	As #SC61, with Washington 2006 World Philatelic Exhibition emblem and text	*22.50*

No. SC62 was only sold canceled.

No.	Description	Value
SC63	Peaceful Visions, #932, Geneva #470-471, Vienna #398-399	6.50

A "souvenir card" depicting no stamps was released in 2008 with the "We Can End Poverty" set. It sold for $1.75. Value, $5.

2009

No.	Description	Value
SC64	Economic and Social Council (ECOSOC), #992-993, Geneva #503-504, Vienna #450-451	7.50

2010

No.	Description	Value
SC65	International Year of Biodiversity, #1017-1018, Geneva #517-518, Vienna #469-470	12.00

2011

No.	Description	Value
SC66	AIDS Ribbon, #1028, Geneva #537, Vienna #498	5.50

2012

No.	Description	Value
SC67	Rio + 20, #1048, Geneva #553, Vienna #515	7.50

2013

No.	Description	Value
SC68	Works of Disabled Artists, #1072-1073, Geneva #570-571, Vienna #532-533	6.50

A "souvenir card" depicting no stamps was released in 2014 with the "International Year of Jazz" set. It sold for $1.75. Value, $5.

2016

No.	Description	Value
SC69	Free and Equal, #1127-1128, Geneva #613-614, Vienna #579-580	4.25

A "souvenir card" depicting no stamps was issued in 2017 with the "World Environment Day" set. It sold for $2. Value, $4.

U.N. PROOFS

Proofs of United Nations stamps are known in four basic types: Die Proofs, Trial Color Proofs, Progressive Color Proofs, and Imperforate Plate Proofs on gummed stamp paper.

Die Proofs (PD suffix) for United Nations stamps show the design of the issued stamp. They are usually imperforate singles printed on stamp paper, that are either affixed to a backing paper that is a component of a printer's card, or affixed directly to a printer's card. These cards usually have a handstamp denoting the status of the proof (approved, approved with corrections, not approved, etc.). Many cards have signatures of UN Postal Administration officials. Cards with an "approved" handstamp and/or signature do not always contain proofs having the designs of the actual stamp produced for sale. As most proof cards have a handstamp, the listings mention specific handstamps only when it is critical to distinguishing items. Items not affixed to cards that are indistinguishable from imperforate singles of the issued stamps are not listed, even though they may have come from "stock sheet style" proof cards that have approval handstamps. Items affixed to art boards available to the general public are not considered to be proofs unless they are identified, usually by handstamps, that they are proofs. Die proofs of sheet layouts showing marginal inscriptions only exist, but are beyond the scope of these listings.

Trial Color Proofs (TC suffix) show the design of the stamp, but with one or more colors differing from that of the actual stamp. Items will be listed as trial color proofs when they differ significantly from the issued color. As evidenced by printer's identification numbers on some trial color proof cards, shades of individual items may differ slightly, but two similar yet discrete shades may fall under one color description. Trial colors can sometimes be found on cards with die proofs.

Progressive Color Proofs (PP suffix) are a set of color proofs containing the number of items stated in the listing. Values, therefore, are for the set of singles (unless otherwise mentioned in the description), not a single progressive color proof from that set. Numbers in parentheses represent the total number of complete sets that were created. Partial sets are not listed if complete sets are known.

Imperforate Plate Proofs (PI suffix) are usually found on gummed stamp paper. Any exceptions are noted in the listing description. Numbers in parentheses represent the total number of imperforate proof stamps created. Many items have inked fingerprints on the reverse as a security device. Values are for pairs unless otherwise stated. Many gutter pairs will have creases. Some gutter pairs will have marginal inscriptions. These are worth more.

Organization of listings Listings have all of the New York, Geneva and Vienna stamps and souvenir cards for any set all together. The first part of an item's catalogue number is the same catalogue number as shown in the listings for stamps and postal stationery. The prefix "G" is before the catalogue number for items from Geneva; prefix "V" for items from Vienna. Items with prefix "SC" are souvenir cards, and catalogue numbers without prefix are from New York. The suffix describing the type of proof follows the catalogue number. Die proofs (suffix PD) are the first proof category in the listings, and will be followed by the other categories in the same order as listed above. Each proof category will list New York items first, followed by Geneva items, Vienna items, and then souvenir cards.

Often cards of proofs will contain all of the items in an issued set. The catalogue numbers for cards that contain New York, Geneva and Vienna proofs are organized by the highest New York catalogue number of the various die proof items in the set. If there are no New York items in the card, then the numbering will be organized by the highest Geneva or Vienna catalogue number in the card of die proofs. Cards that contain both die proofs and trial color proofs are catalogued under the die proofs.

Numbers in parentheses represent the total number of items created. The number of items coming in part or in total from printer's archives are approximations. Listings for single proofs affixed to cards do not usually mention that they are affixed to a card. Cards containing more than one proof will have a minor letter following the PD suffix, and the listing will detail the component parts, as some cards may in the future be broken down by owners into individual proof items. Cutting up cards, however, may destroy their value, as listings are often based on the presence of the handstamp. Removing proofs from the card will lower their value, as it may then be impossible to distinguish them from imperforate singles.

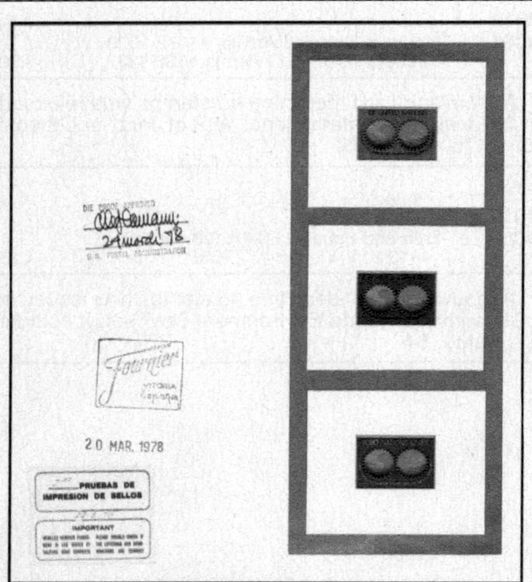

No. 303PDa — A Typical Die Proof Card

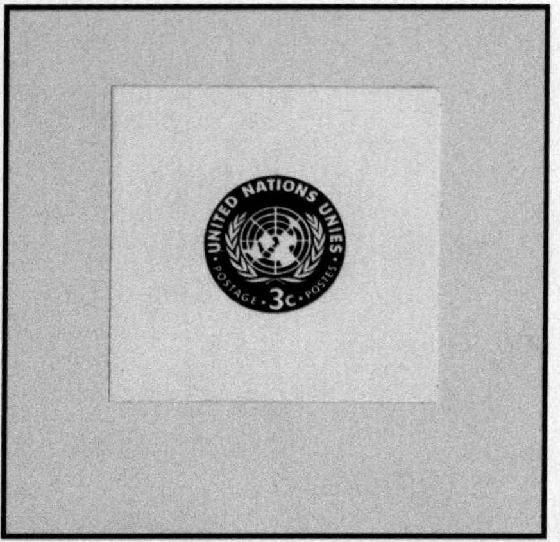

No. U1TC in Black — A Typical Trial Color Proof

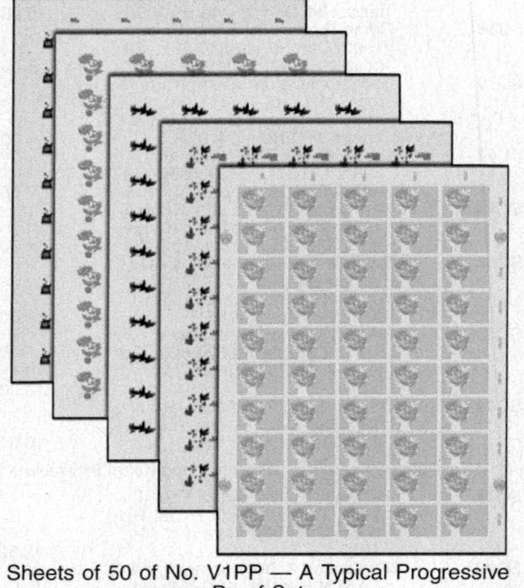

Sheets of 50 of No. V1PP — A Typical Progressive Proof Set

No. 1PI — A Typical Pair of Imperforate Plate Proofs

New York #1-11
Definitives

1951

1PD	(1)	600.
2PD	(3)	500.
3PD	(3)	450.
3PDa	Card, #3PD, 3TC blue violet (1)	575.
4PD	(1)	600.
5PD	(1)	575.
5PDa	Card, #5PD, 5TC dark blue violet	1,150.
6PD	(1)	600.
6PDa	Card, #1PD, 6PD (3)	3,100.
7PD	(1)	600.
8PD	(4)	300.
9PD	(1)	600.
9PDa	Card, #4PD, 7PD, 9PD, essays of #7, 9 (1)	1,850.
9PDb	Card, #9PD, 9TC green (1)	825.
10PD	(1)	500.
11PD	(4)	475.
2TC	indigo (1)	—
3TC	red violet (2)	
3TC	dark red (2)	350.
3TC	red orange (1)	450.
3TC	carmine (3)	—
3TC	orange red (3)	—
3TCa	Card, #3TC carmine, #3TC orange red (1)	700.
5TC	orange red (1)	750.
5TC	brown (1)	750.
5TC	bright blue (1)	—
5TC	light blue (1)	—
5TC	dark blue (1)	—
5TC	black (1)	—
5TC	red orange (1)	—
5TCa	Card, #5TC black, 5TC brown (1)	925.
10TC	black (1)	—
10TC	dark green (1)	—
10TCa	Card, #10TC blue green , #10TC yellow green (1)	—
11TC	dark red, 2 impressions side by side (1)	—
11TC	purple, 2 impressions side by side (1)	—
11TCa	dark blue (2 impressions side by side below two impressions of #5TC (1)	—
1PI	Pair (25)	1,000.
2PI	Pair (5)	—
5PI	Pair (42)	350.
	Vert. pair with horiz. gutter (8)	—
6PI	Pair (25)	375.
8PI	Pair (50)	500.
11PI	Pair (3)	800.

Imperforate printer's waste has impression of No. 6 with stamps of other countries.

New York #12
Signing of UN Charter, 7th Anniv.

1952

12PD	(3)	—
12TC	dark blue (2)	—
12TC	black (2)	—
12TC	green (2)	—
12TC	light blue (1)	—

New York #13-14
Universal Declaration of Human Rights, 4th Anniv.

1952

13PDa	Card, #13PD and two #13TC in slightly different shades (1)	975.
14PDa	Card, #14PD and two #14TC in slightly different shades (1)	975.
14PDb	Card, #13PD, 14PD (1)	—

New York #15-16
Protection for Refugees

1953

15PD	(1)	450.
16PD	(1)	450.
16PDa	Card, #15PD, 16PD (3)	775.
16PDb	Card, #15PD, 16PD, 16TC indigo (1)	875.
16PDc	Card, #16PDb and card, #15PD, 15TC, 16PD (some staining) (1)	575.
15PI	Pair (80)	400.
	Vert. pair with horiz. gutter (20)	—
16PI	Pair (80)	400.
	Vert. pair with horiz. gutter (20)	—

New York #17-18
Universal Postal Union

1953

17PDa	Card, #17PD, 17TC red brown, 17TC ultramarine, 17TC blue	2,000.
17PDb	Card, #17PD, 17TC violet brown (1)	—
18PDa	Card, #18PD, 18TC bright blue (1)	—
18PDb	Card, #17PDa, 18PDa (1)	—
17PI	Pair (82)	200.
	Horiz. pair with vert. gutter (8)	—
18PI	Pair (84)	200.
	Horiz. pair with vert. gutter (6)	—

Approximately half of PI items are stained and glued on cardboard. Imperforate printer's waste has No. 17 with No. 18 and impressions of other items on the reverse.

New York #19-20
Technical Assistance

1953

20PDa	Card, #19PD-20PD, #19TC-20TC in slightly different shades (2)	1,250.

New York #21-22
Human Rights Day

1953

22PDa	Card, #23PD-24PD, two #23TC, two #24TC in slightly different shades (2)	1,600.
21PI	Pair (40)	350.
	Vert. pair with horiz. gutter (10)	—
22PI	Pair (40)	350.
	Vert. pair with horiz. gutter (10)	—

New York #23-24
Food and Agricultural Organization

1954

24PDa	Card, #23PD-24PD, two #23TC-24TC in slightly different colors (2)	1,600.
23PI	Pair (40)	225.
	Vert. pair with horiz. gutter (10)	—
24PI	Pair (40)	225.
	Vert. pair with horiz. gutter (120)	—

New York #25-26
International Labor Organization

1954

25PDa	Card, #25PD, two #25TC in slightly different shades, three #26TC in purple shades (2)	2,400.
26PDa	Card, #25PD-26PD, #26TC in slightly different shade (2)	—
25PI	Pair (40)	350.
	Vert. pair with horiz. gutter (10)	—
26PI	Pair (40)	350.
	Vert. pair with horiz. gutter (10)	—

New York #27-28
United Nations Day

1954

27PI	Pair (40)	300.
	Horiz. pair with vert. gutter (10)	—
28PI	Pair (40)	300.
	Horiz. pair with vert. gutter (10)	—

New York #29-30
Human Rights Day

1954

29PD	(5)	350.
30PD	(5)	350.
29PI	Pair (40)	350.
	Vert. pair with horiz. gutter (10)	—
30PI	Pair (40)	—
	Vert. pair with horiz. gutter (10)	—

New York #31-32
International Civil Aviation Organization

1955

31PDa	Card, #31PD, two #31TC in different blue shades (3)	—
32PDa	Card, #32PD, three #32TC in different red shades (3)	1,400.
32PDb	Card, #31PD-32PD, #31TC-#32TC in different shades, three essays of #31-32 (1)	1,650.
31TC	black (1)	—
32TC	black (1)	—
31PI	Pair (171)	225.
	Horiz. pair with vert. gutter (26)	—
32PI	Pair (130)	225.
	Horiz. pair with vert. gutter (20)	—

No. 31PI exists with and without punch holes.

New York #33-34
UN Educational, Scientific and Cultural Organization

1955

33PD	(1)	—
33PDa	Card, #33PD, two #33TC in different shades (3)	700.
34PD	(1)	—
34PDa	Card, #34PD, two #34TC in different shades (3)	700.
33TC	black (1)	—
34TC	black (1)	—
33PI	Pair (128)	—
	Horiz. pair with vert. gutter (16)	—
34PI	Pair (90)	—
	Horiz. pair with vert. gutter (10)	—

No. 33PI exists with and without punch holes.

New York #35-38
UN, 10th Anniv.

1955

35PDa	Card, #35PD, two #35TC in different shades (2)	2,400.
35PDb	Card, #35PD, #35TC in lighter shade (1)	—
36PDa	Card, #36PD, two #36TC in different shades (3)	—
37PDa	Card, #37PD, two #37TC in different shades (3)	—
38PD	Sheet of #38 with security punches (2)	1,950.
38bPD	Watermarked sheet of nine #38b and nine #38c with security punches (1)	4,250.
38cPD	Watermarked sheet of nine #38c with security punches (1)	5,000.
35TC	carmine (1)	—
35TC	black (1)	—
36TC	black (1)	—
37TC	black (1)	—
38PP	4 items (9 souvenir sheets)	—
38PP	Retouch, 2 items (9 souvenir sheets)	—
35PI	Pair (130)	325.
	Horiz. pair with vert. gutter (20)	—
36PI	Pair (130)	325.
	Horiz. pair with vert. gutter (20)	—
37PI	Pair (180)	325.
	Horiz. pair with vert. gutter (30)	—
38PI	Pairs of souvenir sheets (16)	3,000.
	Single with sheet margin (4)	850.
38PI	Retouch Pairs of souvenir sheets (4)	—
	Retouch, single with sheet margin (1)	—

No. 37PI exists with and without punch holes.

New York #39-40
Human Rights Day

1955

39PDa	Card, #39PD, two #39TC in different shades (2)	850.
40PDa	Card, #40PD, two #40TC in different shades (2)	850.
39TC	black (1)	—
40TC	black (1)	—
40TCa	Card, #39TC in aquamarine, #40TC in dark green and two essays (1)	1,250.
39PI	Pair (180)	425.
	Vert. pair with horiz. gutter (20)	—
40PI	Pair (130)	425.
	Vert. pair with horiz. gutter (20)	—

No. 39PI exists with and without punch holes.

New York #41-42
International Telecommunication Union

1956

41PD	(2)	300.
42PD	(2)	300.
41PI	Pair (40)	350.
	Horiz. pair with vert. gutter (10)	—
42PI	Pair (40)	350.
	Horiz. pair with vert. gutter (10)	—

New York #43-44
World Health Organization

1956

43PD	(2)	225.
44PD	(2)	225.
43PI	Pair (40)	250.
	Vert. pair with horiz. gutter (10)	—
44PI	Pair (40)	250.
	Vert. pair with horiz. gutter (10)	—

Nos. 43PI-44PI have "Colour approved" handstamped in margin.

New York #45-46
General Assembly

1956

45PD	(7)	275.
46PD	(7)	275.
45PI	Pair (40)	350.
	Horiz. pair with vert. gutter (10)	—
46PI	Pair (40)	350.
	Horiz. pair with vert. gutter (10)	—

New York #47-48
Human Rights Day

1956

47PD	(2)	375.
48PD	(2)	375.
47TC	red (3)	400.
47TC	carmine (3)	—
48TC	blue (6)	400.
47PI	Pair (40)	300.
	Horiz. pair with vert. gutter (10)	—
48PI	Pair (40)	300.
	Horiz. pair with vert. gutter (10)	—

New York #49-50
World Meteorological Organization

1957

49PD	(2)	275.
50PD	(2)	275.
49TC	blue (3)	250.
50TC	carmine rose (3)	250.
49PI	Pair (40)	—
	Vert. pair with horiz. gutter (10)	—
50PI	Pair (40)	—
	Vert. pair with horiz. gutter (10)	—

Nos. 49PI-50PI have "Colour approved" handstamped in margin.

New York #51-52
UN Emergency Force

1957

51PD	(7)	275.
52PD	(7)	275.
51PI	Pair (40)	—
	Horiz. pair with vert. gutter (10)	—
52PI	Pair (40)	—
	Horiz. pair with vert. gutter (10)	—

New York #55-56
Security Council

1957

55PD	(6)	275.
56PD	(11)	275.
55TC	golden brown (6)	—
55TC	brown (5)	—
55PI	Pair (40)	—
	Vert. pair with horiz. gutter (10)	—
56PI	Pair (40)	—
	Vert. pair with horiz. gutter (10)	—

New York #57-58
Human Rights Day

1957

57PD	(12)	275.
58PD	(9)	275.
57TC	light red brown (1)	300.
58TC	dark blue (3)	—
58TC	gray green (6)	300.
57PI	Pair (50)	—
58PI	Pair (50)	—

Nos. 57TC-58TC have handstamps with "Approved" crossed out.

New York #59-60
International Atomic Energy Agency

1958

59PD	(12)	250.
60PD	(13)	250.
59TC	emerald (7)	—
59TC	black (7)	350.
60TC	black (8)	350.
59PI	With security punch (358 pairs)	—
	Cross gutter block, with security punch (4)	—
	Horiz. pair with vert. gutter, with security punch (52)	—
	Vert. pair with horiz. gutter, with security punch (32)	—
60PI	Pair with security punch (358)	—
	Cross gutter block, with security punch (4)	—
	Horiz. pair with vert. gutter, with security punch (52)	—
	Vert. pair with horiz. gutter, with security punch (32)	—

New York #61-62
Central Hall, Site of First General Assembly Meeting

1958

61PD	(8)	275.
62PD	(8)	275.
61TC	black (3)	275.
62TC	black (3)	275.
61PI	With security punch (358 pairs)	—
	Cross gutter block, with security punch (4)	—
	Horiz. pair with vert. gutter, with security punch (32)	—
	Vert. pair with horiz. gutter, with security punch (52)	—
62PI	Pair with security punch (358)	—
	Cross gutter block, with security punch (4)	—
	Horiz. pair with vert. gutter, with security punch (32)	—
	Vert. pair with horiz. gutter, with security punch (52)	—

New York #63-64
UN Emblem

1958

63PD	(21)	250.
64PD	(7)	250.
64PDa	Card, #64PD, #64TC Prussian blue, #64TC ultramarine (2)	975.
63TC	brown orange (3)	300.
64TC	light blue (1)	300.
64TC	ultramarine (1)	500.
63PI	Pair (80)	—
	Vert. pair with horiz. gutter (20)	—
64PI	Pair (80)	—
	Vert. pair with horiz. gutter (20)	—

No. 63TC is affixed to cards inscribed "D."

New York #65-66
Economic and Social Council

1958

65PD	(8)	250.
66PD	(7)	250.
65TC	black (2)	325.
65TC	orange brown (1)	—
65TC	green (1)	—
65TC	red orange (1)	—
66TC	black (2)	325.
65PI	Pair with security punch (358)	—
	Cross gutter block, with security punch (4)	—
	Horiz. pair with vert. gutter, with security punch (32)	—
	Vert. pair with horiz. gutter, with security punch (52)	—
66PI	Pair with security punch (358)	—
	Cross gutter block, with security punch (4)	—
	Horiz. pair with vert. gutter, with security punch (32)	—
	Vert. pair with horiz. gutter, with security punch (52)	—

New York #67-68
Human Rights Day

1958

67PD	(5)	300.
68PD	(5)	300.
67TC	black (2)	425.
68TC	black (1)	425.
67PI	Pair (358)	—
	Cross gutter block, with security punch and "SPECIMEN" ovpt. (4)	—
	Horiz. pair with vert. gutter, with security punch and "SPECIMEN" ovpt. (52)	—
	Vert. pair with horiz. gutter, with security punch and "SPECIMEN" ovpt. (32)	—
68PI	Pair (358)	—
	Cross gutter block, with security punch and "SPECIMEN" ovpt. (4)	—
	Horiz. pair with vert. gutter, with security punch and "SPECIMEN" ovpt. (52)	—
	Vert. pair with horiz. gutter, with security punch and "SPECIMEN" ovpt. (32)	—

Essays of Nos. 67 and 68 without denominations exist in issued colors and black.

New York #69-70
New York City Building, Flushing Meadows

1959

69PD	(7)	300.
70PD	(7)	300.
69PI	Pair (216)	—
	Cross gutter block (3)	—
	Horiz. pair with vert. gutter (54)	—
	Vert. pair with horiz. gutter (24)	—
70PI	Pair (216)	—
	Cross gutter block (3)	—
	Horiz. pair with vert. gutter (54)	—
	Vert. pair with horiz. gutter (24)	—

New York #71-72
Economic Commission for Europe

1959

71PD	(7)	275.
72PD	(7)	275.
71PI	Pair (216)	—
	Cross gutter block (3)	—
	Horiz. pair with vert. gutter (24)	—
	Vert. pair with horiz. gutter (54)	—
72PI	Pair (216)	—
	Cross gutter block (3)	—
	Horiz. pair with vert. gutter (24)	—
	Vert. pair with horiz. gutter (54)	—

New York #73-74
Trusteeship Council

1959

73PD	(5)	300.
74PD	(5)	300.
73TC	orange red (2)	—
73PI	Pair (216)	—
	Cross gutter block (3)	—
	Horiz. pair with vert. gutter (24)	—
	Vert. pair with horiz. gutter (54)	—
74PI	Pair (216)	—
	Cross gutter block (3)	—
	Horiz. pair with vert. gutter (24)	—
	Vert. pair with horiz. gutter (54)	—

No. 73TC has handstamps with words "Color and" crossed out.

New York #75-76
World Refugee Year

1959

75PD	(6)	300.
76PD	(5)	300.
75TC	purple & red (3)	—
76TC	olive & Prussian blue (2)	—
76TC	purple & green (3)	—
75PI	Pair (216)	—
	Cross gutter block (3)	—
	Horiz. pair with vert. gutter (54)	—
	Vert. pair with horiz. gutter (24)	—
76PI	Pair (216)	—
	Cross gutter block (3)	—
	Horiz. pair with vert. gutter (54)	—
	Vert. pair with horiz. gutter (24)	—

New York #77-78
Chaillot Palace

1960

77PD	(4)	250.
78PD	(4)	250.
78TC	brown & blue green(1)	325.
78TC	blue & red (1)	325.
78TCa	Card, #78TC brown & blue green, #78TC blue &red (1)	—
77PI	Pair (25)	—
78PI	Pair (25)	—

New York #79-80
Economic Commission for Asia and the Far East

1960

79PD	(1)	—
80PDa	Card, #79PD, #80PD (1)	—
80PDb	Card, two #79PD, two #80PD (1)	1,250.
79PI	Pair (50)	—
80PI	Pair (50)	—

New York #81-82
World Forestry Congress

1960

81PD	(2)	425.
82PDa	Card, #81PD-82PD (3)	350.
81PI	Pair (100)	—
82PI	Pair (100)	—

New York #83-85
UN, 15th Anniv.

1960

83PD	(5)	325.
84PD	(6)	325.
85PD	(2)	700.
83TC	black (1)	—
83TC	bright blue (2)	—
83PI	Pair (144)	—
	Cross gutter block (2)	—
	Horiz. pair with vert. gutter (36)	—
	Vert. pair with horiz. gutter (16)	—
84PI	Pair (119)	—
	Cross gutter block (2)	—
	Horiz. pair with vert. gutter (36)	—
	Vert. pair with horiz. gutter (16)	—
85PI	Pair (16)	—
	Cross gutter block (2)	—
	Horiz. pair with vert. gutter (8)	—
	Vert. pair with horiz. gutter (8)	—

An essay in blue has diagonal lines in background rather than cross-hatching.

New York #86-87
International Bank for Reconstruction and Development

1960

87PDa	Card, 2 #86PD, 2 #87PD (2)	1,150.
87PDb	Card, #86PD-87PD with simulated perforations (1)	—
86PI	Pair (100)	—
87PI	Pair (100)	—

New York #88-89
International Court of Justice

1961

89PDa	Card, #88PD-89PD affixed, dated 10/31/61 (2)	450.
89PDb	Card, 2 #88PD, 2 #89PD, disapproved (2)	—
88PI	Pair (100)	—
89PI	Pair (100)	—

New York #90-91
International Monetary Fund

1961

91PDa	Card with 2 #90PD, 2 #91PD in slightly different shades (1)	1,300.
90PI	Pair (100)	—
91PI	Pair (50)	—

New York #92
Abstract Flags

1961

92PI	Pair (80)	—
	Horiz. pair with vert. gutter (20)	—

New York #93-94
Economic Commission for Latin America

1961

93PDa	Card, 2 #93PD, 2 essays of #94 (2)	—
94PDa	Card, 2 #94PD (1)	400.

Essays of No. 94 lack serifs in "1's."

New York #95-96
Economic Commission for Africa

1961

96PDa	Card with #95PD-96PD affixed (8)	500.
95PP	4 items (100)	—
96PP	8 items (100)	—
95PI	Pair (100)	—
96PI	Pair (100)	—

New York #97-99
UN Children's Fund (UNICEF)

1961

99PDa	Card, #97PD-99PD, with approval handstamp (3)	1,050.
99PDb	Card, #97PD-99PD, no approval handstamp (5)	600.
97PP	4 items (80)	—
	Vert. pair with horiz. gutter (10)	—
98PP	4 items (80)	—
	Vert. pair with horiz. gutter (10)	—
99PP	4 items (80)	—
	Vert. pair with horiz. gutter (10)	—
97PI	Pair (80)	—
	Vert. pair with horiz. gutter (20)	—
98PI	Pair (80)	—
	Vert. pair with horiz. gutter (20)	—
99PI	Pair (80)	—
	Vert. pair with horiz. gutter (20)	—

New York #100-101
Housing and Urban Development Program

1962

100PD	With approval handstamp (3)	200.
101PD	With approval handstamp (3)	200.
100PI	Pair with oval "Harrison's Photogravure Specimen" handstamp (25)	350.
101PI	Pair with oval "Harrison's Photogravure Specimen" handstamp (25)	350.

Three essays each of Nos. 100 and 101 have larger numerals than issued stamps are are on cards marked "disapproved."

New York #102-103
Malaria Eradication Campaign

1962

102PD	(5)	400.
103PD	(5)	400.

New York #104-107
Definitives

1962

104PD	(5)	400.
105PD	(7)	425.
106PD	With approval handstamp & signature (2)	400.
107PD	(3)	500.
104PI	Pair with oval "Harrison's Photogravure Specimen" handstamp (25)	250.
105PI	Pair with oval "Harrison's Photogravure Specimen" handstamp (25)	250.
107PI	Pair with oval "Harrison's Photogravure Specimen" handstamp (25)	250.
	Same, without handstamp (25)	400.

Three essays of No. 106 have indistinct line between "U" and "N," and are on cards marked "disapproved."

New York #108-109
Death of Dag Hammarskjold, 1st Anniv.

1962

108PDa	Card, #108PD, essay of #109 (1)	—
109PDa	Card, #109PD, essay of #108 (1)	—
109PDb	Card, #108PD-#109PD (2)	600.

108PI Pair (80) —
Vert. pair with horiz. gutter (20) —
109PI Pair (80) —
Vert. pair with horiz. gutter (20) —

Essays of Nos 108-109 lack denomination.

New York #110-111
UN Operation in the Congo

1962

111PDa Card, 3 #110PD, 3 #111PD (1) 1,150.
111PDb Card, #111PD, essay of #110 (2) 550.
110PP 4 items (80) —
Horiz. pair with vert. gutter (10) —
111PP 4 items (80) —
Horiz. pair with vert. gutter (10) —
110PI Pair (80) —
Horiz. pair with vert. gutter (20) —
111PI Pair (80) —
Horiz. pair with vert. gutter (20) —

Essays of No. 110 have 5c denomination.

New York #112-113
Committee on Peaceful Uses of Outer Space

1962

112PD (2) —
113PD (1) —
113PDa Card, #112PD-113PD (3) 500.

Essays similar to Nos. 112PD-113PD have text in white panel below palm frond.

New York #114-115
UN Development Decade

1963

115PDa Card, #114PD, 2 #115PD (one in slightly different shade) with approval handstamp (3) 875.
115PDb Card, #114PD-115PD (3) 400.
114PP 4 items (80) —
Vert. pair with horiz. gutter (10) —
115PP 4 items (80) —
Vert. pair with horiz. gutter (10) —
114PI Pair (80) —
Vert. pair with horiz. gutter (20) —
115PI Pair (80) —
Vert. pair with horiz. gutter (20) —

New York #116-117
Freedom from Hunger Campaign

1963

116PD (1) —
117PD (1) —
117PDa Card, #116PD-117PD (5) 500.
116PP 3 items (80) —
Horiz. pair with vert. gutter (10) —
117PP 3 items (80) —
Horiz. pair with vert. gutter (10) —
116PI Pair (80) —
Horiz. pair with vert. gutter (20) —
117PI Pair (80) —
Horiz. pair with vert. gutter (20) —

Essays similar to Nos. 116PD-117PD have taller numerals and lettering.

New York #118
UN Temporary Executive Authority in West New Guinea

1963

118PD With approval handstamp (2) 400.
118PDa Card, #118PD (approved), #118TC (not approved) (3) 500.
118TCa Card, 2 #118TC (disapproved or with instructions to printer) (3) 500.
118PP 3 items (100) —
Horiz. pair with vert. gutter (10) —
118PI Pair (100) —
Horiz. pair with vert. gutter (20) —

No. 118TC has right side of map in a lighter shade of green.

New York #119-120
General Assembly Building, New York

1963

120PDa Card, #119PD-120PD (2) 400.

New York #121-122
Universal Declaration of Human Rights, 15th Anniv.

1963

121PD (2) 250.
122PD (2) 250.
121PI Pair (100) —
122PI Pair (100) —

Essays similar to Nos. 121PD-122PD have top line of frame text flush left rather than centered, and are on a disapproved card.

New York #123-124
Intergovernmental Maritime Consultative Organization

1964

124PDa Card, #123PD-124PD (3) 550.
123PP 4 items (80) —
Horiz. pair with vert. gutter (10) —
124PP 4 items (80) —
Horiz. pair with vert. gutter (10) —
123PI Pair (80) —
Horiz. pair with vert. gutter (20) —
124PI Pair (80) —
Horiz. pair with vert. gutter (20) —

New York #125-128
Definitives

1964

125PD (3) 275.
125PDa Card, #125 perforated with approval handstamp (1) —
126PD (3) 240.
127PDa Card, #126PD-127PD with approval handstamp (3) 550.
127PDb Card, #127PD (approved), #127PD (not approved, in slightly different shade, #126PD (disapproved in slightly different shade (3) 925.
128PD (3) 240.
125PP 3 items (100) —
126PI 3 items (80) —
Vert. pair with horiz. gutter (10) —
127PP 4 items (80) —
Horiz. pair with vert. gutter (10) —
128PP 4 items (80) —
Horiz. pair with vert. gutter (10) —
125PI Pair (65) —
Horiz. pair with vert. gutter (10) —
126PI Pair (80) —
Vert. pair with horiz. gutter (20) —
127PI Pair (80) —
Horiz. pair with vert. gutter (20) —
128PI Pair (80) —
Horiz. pair with vert. gutter (20) —

Essays similar to No. 125PD have larger numerals and blue text.

New York #129-130
UN Conference on Trade and Development

1964

129PD (6) 250.
130PD (6) 250.
129PI Pair (25) —
130PI Pair (25) —

New York #131-132
Narcotics Control

1964

131PD (2) 250.
132PD (2) 250.
132PDa Card, #131PD-132PD (3) 600.

New York #133
Nuclear Test Ban Treaty

1964

133TC dark red & black, perforated, litho. & engr. (1) 300.
133TC lilac, perforated, engr. (20) —
133TCa Card, 2 #133TC dark red & dark brown, litho. & vignette essay, litho. (1) —
133TCb Card, #133TC dark red & black, engr. & 5 vignette essays, engr. (1) —
133TCc Card, 11 #133TC in red, claret, brown rose, brown, dark brown, dull blue, blue, blue violet, gray, dark gray, black, engr. (1) —

New York #134-136
Education for Progress Campaign

1964

135PD (1) —
136PDa Card, #134PD-136PD, with approval stamp (3) —
136PDb Card, #134PD-136PD, without approval stamp (2) 300.
136PDc Card, #134PD, #136PD, without approval stamp (1) 450.
134PP 4 items (80) —
Horiz. pair with vert. gutter (10) —
135PP 4 items (80) —
Horiz. pair with vert. gutter (10) —
136PP 4 items (80) —
Horiz. pair with vert. gutter (10) —
134PI Pair (80) —
Horiz. pair with vert. gutter (20) —
135PI Pair (80) —
Horiz. pair with vert. gutter (20) —
136PI Pair (80) —
Horiz. pair with vert. gutter (20) —

New York #137-138
Special Fund Program

1965

137PD (2) 225.
138PD (2) 225.
138PDa Card, #137PD-138PD, with approval stamp (1) 500.
138PDb Card, #137PD-138PD, without approval stamp (1) —

New York #139-140
UN Peace-Keeping Force in Cyprus

1965

140PDa Card #139PD-140PD, with approval stamp (5) 500.
140PP 3 items (80) —
Vert. pair with horiz. gutter (10) —
139PI Pair (40) —
Vert. pair with horiz. gutter (10) —
140PI Pair (40) —
Vert. pair with horiz. gutter (10) —

Smaller-size essays (30x38mm) of Nos. 139-140 are in three cards with approval stamps.

New York #141-142
International Telecommunication Union

1965

142PDa Card, #141PD-142PD, with approval stamp (3) 500.
142PDb Card, #141PD-142PD, no approval stamp (3) 450.
142PDc Card, #141PD-142PD, #141TC dated "8.2.65" (3) 925.
141PP 4 items (80) —
Horiz. pair with vert. gutter (10) —
142PP 4 items (80) —
Horiz. pair with vert. gutter (10) —
141PI Pair (80) —
Horiz. pair with vert. gutter (20) —
142PI Pair (80) —
Horiz. pair with vert. gutter (20) —

No. 141TC has orange yellow lines instead of orange lines.

New York #143-145
UN, 20th Anniv. and International Cooperation Year

1965

143PD (3) 275.
143PDa Card, #143PD, 144TC orange red (3) 825.
144PD (3) 275.
144PDa Card, #143PD-144PD, with approval stamp (7) 500.
145PD Imperforate sheet with manuscript printer's instructions (4) —
Issued souvenir sheet, perforated (on printer's card) (1) 110.
145PDa #143PD, #144PD affixed to #145 souvenir sheet margin (5) 600.

New York #146-150
Definitives

1965-66

146PD (7) 200.
148PDa Block of 12 perforated stamps with approval handstamp in margin (2) 140.
148PDb Card, #147-148 perforated, with approval handstamp (3) 500.
149PD Perforated, with approval handstamp (2) 250.
149PDa Card, #149PD (2nd printing), #149PD, first printing, perforated, with approval handstamp (2) 600.
150PD (3) 240.
149TC Prussian blue & dark blue, perforated (1) —
150PP 3 items (80), affixed on cards —
Horiz. pair with vert. gutter (10) —
150PI Pair (161) 375.
Horiz. pair with vert. gutter (19) —

Two cards without approval handstamp have perforated essays of both Nos. 147 and 148. The essay of No. 147 has larger numerals and the essay of No. 148 has bright yellow text at bottom. No. 150PI has had extra glue applied.

New York #151-153
Population Trends and Development

1965

152PDa Card, #151PD-152PD, 153TC, perforated, with approval handstamp (2) 825.

No. 153TC has "Nations Unies" in black instead of gray.

New York #154-155
World Federation of United Nations Associations

1966

155PDa Card, #154-155PD with approval handstamp (3) 500.
154PP 4 items (80) —
Vert. pair with horiz. gutter (10) —
155PP 4 items (80) —
Vert. pair with horiz. gutter (10) —
154PI Pair (80) —
Vert. pair with horiz. gutter (20) —
155PI Pair (80) —
Vert. pair with horiz. gutter (20) —

New York #156-157
World Health Organization

1966

157TCa Card, #156TC-157TC, with approval handstamp (3) 500.
156PP 4 items (50) —
157PP 4 items (80) —
Horiz. pair with vert. gutter (10) —

156PI Pair (65) —
Horiz. pair with vert. gutter (10) —
157PI Pair (80) —
Horiz. pair with vert. gutter (20) —

Nos. 156TC and 157TC have side and front of building the same shade of blue.

New York #158-159
International Coffee Agreement of 1962

1966
159PDa Card, #158PD-159PD (3) 625.

New York #160
UN Observers

1964
160PD (2) on cards dated "3.2.1966" 125.
160PP 4 items (50) —
160PI Pair (65) —
Vert. pair with horiz. gutter (10) —

Two essays of No. 160 with white text lines larger and closer together are on cards dated "17.1.1966."

New York #161-163
UNICEF, 20th Anniv.

1966
161PD (3) 250.
162PD (3) 250.
163PD (3) 250.
161PI Pair (72) —
Cross gutter block (1) —
Horiz. pair with vert. gutter (18) —
Vert. pair with horiz. gutter (8) —
162PI Pair (72) —
Cross gutter block (1) —
Horiz. pair with vert. gutter (18) —
Vert. pair with horiz. gutter (8) —
163PI Pair (72) —
Cross gutter block (1) —
Horiz. pair with vert. gutter (18) —
Vert. pair with horiz. gutter (8) —

New York #164-165
UN Development Program

1967
165PDa Card, # 164PD-165PD, dated "6.9. 1966" (3) 725.
165PDb Card, #165PD, 2 #164PD, with approval handstamp, dated "4.10.66" (6) 925.
164PI Pair (40) —
Horiz. pair with vert. gutter (10) —
165PI Pair (40) —
Horiz. pair with vert. gutter (10) —

New York #166-167
Definitives

1967
166PD (6) 225.
166PDa Card, 2 #166PD (3) 575.
167PD (3) 200.
167TC With brown line separating "UN" in vignette, on card dated "27.4.1966" (3) 250.
166PP 4 items (80) —
Vert. pair with horiz. gutter (10) —
167PP 3 items (80) —
Horiz. pair with vert. gutter (10) —
166PI Pair (80) —
Vert. pair with horiz. gutter (20) —
167PI Pair (80) —
Horiz. pair with vert. gutter (20) —

New York #168-169
Independence

1967
168PD (2) 250.
169PD (3) 250.

New York #170-174
EXPO '67

1967
170PD (1) 300.
171PD (1) 300.
172PD (3) 300.
173PD (1) 300.
174PD (3) 300.
170PP 2 items (144) —
Cross gutter block (1) —
Horiz. pair with vert. gutter (8) —
Vert. pair with horiz. gutter (18) —
171PP 2 items (144) —
Cross gutter block (1) —
Horiz. pair with vert. gutter (8) —
Vert. pair with horiz. gutter (18) —
172PP 3 items (144) —
Cross gutter block (1) —
Horiz. pair with vert. gutter (18) —
Vert. pair with horiz. gutter (8) —
173PP 2 items (144) —
Cross gutter block (1) —
Horiz. pair with vert. gutter (8) —
Vert. pair with horiz. gutter (18) —
174PP 2 items (144) —
Cross gutter block (1) —
Horiz. pair with vert. gutter (8) —
Vert. pair with horiz. gutter (18) —
170PI Pair (72) —
Cross gutter block (1) —
Horiz. pair with vert. gutter (8) —
Vert. pair with horiz. gutter (18) —
171PI Pair (72) —
Cross gutter block (1) —
Horiz. pair with vert. gutter (8) —
Vert. pair with horiz. gutter (18) —
172PI Pair (72) —
Cross gutter block (1) —
Horiz. pair with vert. gutter (18) —
Vert. pair with horiz. gutter (8) —
173PI Pair (72) —
Cross gutter block (1) —
Horiz. pair with vert. gutter (8) —
Vert. pair with horiz. gutter (18) —
174PI Pair (72) —
Cross gutter block (1) —
Horiz. pair with vert. gutter (8) —
Vert. pair with horiz. gutter (18) —

New York #175-176
International Tourist Year

1967
176PDa #175-176, perforated, affixed to printer's card (2) 600.

New York #177-178
Towards Disarmament

1967
177PD (3) —
178PD (3) 200.
178TC Wall text in copper, gold lines in wall (1) 110.
178TC Wall text in copper, blue gray lines in wall (3) 110.
178TC Wall text in brown, silver lines in wall (1) 110.
178TC Wall text in brown, blue gray lines in wall (3) 110.

New York #179-180
Chagall Stained Glass Windows

1967
179PP 8 items (29) —
180PP 8 items (29) —
179PI Pair on card stock (24) 1,050.
180PI Pair on card stock (135) 650.
Horiz. pair with vert. gutter, on card stock (15) —
180PI Pair on stamp paper (75) 525.

Essays of Nos. 179-180 in 5c denomination exist.

New York #181-182
UN Secretariat

1968
181PD (1) 110.
182PD (1) 110.
182PDa Card, #181PD-182PD (1) —
181PP 5 items (160) —
Horiz. pair with vert. gutter (20) —
182PP 5 items (160) —
Horiz. pair with vert. gutter (20) —
181PI Pair (80) —
Horiz. pair with vert. gutter (20) —
182PI Pair (80) —
Horiz. pair with vert. gutter (20) —

New York #183-184
Art at the UN

1968
183PD (1) 250.
184PD (1) 250.
184PDa Card, #183PD-184PD, dated "5.12.67" (2) —
184TCa Card, #183TC-184TC, dated "10.XI.67" (3) 725.
183PP 5 items (80) —
Vert. pair with horiz. gutter (10) —
184PP 5 items (80) —
Vert. pair with horiz. gutter (10) —
183PI Pair (65) —
Vert. pair with horiz. gutter (10) —
184PI Pair (80) —
Vert. pair with horiz. gutter (20) —

No. 183TC has a bright blue frame; No. 184TC a birght red frame.

New York #185-186
UN Industrial Development Orgainzation

1968
185PD (4) 325.
186PD (3) 500.
186TC brown frame, deep blue "ONUDI" (2) —
185PP 4 items, affixed to cards (3) —
186PP 4 items, affixed to cards (3) —
185PI Pair with security punch (25) 250.
186PI Pair with security punch (25) 250.

New York #187
UN Headquarters

1964
187TC light gray roof in foreground, numbered 34 or 38, dated July 7, 1967 (2) 140.
187TC With wide curved white line under window of General Assembly building, numbered 397 or 404, dated 11.8.1967 (2) 125.
187TC With halo around UN emblem, dated Feb. 12, 1968 (2) 240.
187PP 11 items, on card with staple holes (3) —
187PI Pair with "Specimen" overprint (80) 250.
Vert. pair with horiz. gutter, with "Specimen" overprint (20) —
187PI Pair without "Specimen" overprint (80) 375.
Vert. pair with horiz. gutter, without "Specimen" overprint (20) —

New York #188-189
World Weather Watch

1968
189PDa Card, #188PD-189PD (1) 500.
188PP 5 items (100) —
189PP 5 items (100)

New York #190-191
International Human Rights Year

1968
190PD (6) 210.
191PD (6) 210.
190PP 4 items (100) —
191PP 4 items (100) —
190PI Pair (50) —
191PI Pair (50) —

New York #192-193
UN Institute for Training and Research

1969
193PDa Card, #192PD-193PD (2) 425.
192PP 6 items (50) —
193PP 6 items (100) —
192PI Pair (15) 425.
193PI Pair (15) 425.

New York #194-195
Economic Commission for Latin America

1969
195PDa #194-195, perforated, affixed to printer's card (4) 425.

New York #196
"UN" and Emblem

1969
196PD With approval handstamp (2) 250.
196TC Card, #196PD, 196TC dark blue background (2) —
196PP 3 items (100) —

New York #197-198
UN International Law Commission

1969
198PDa Card, #197PD-198PD (9) 650.
197PP 4 items (80) —
Horiz. pair with vert. gutter (10) —
198PP 4 items (80) —
Horiz. pair with vert. gutter (10) —
197PI (40 pairs) —
Horiz. pair with vert. gutter (10) —
198PI (40 pairs) —
Horiz. pair with vert. gutter (10) —

New York #199-200
Labor and Development

1969
199PD With approval handstamp (1) —
200PD (1) —
200PDa Card, #199PD-200PD, with approval handstamp (1) 425.
199TC Men in dark blue, perforated (3) —
200TC Rose pink background, perforated (3) —
200PP 4 items (91) —

Geneva #1-14
Definitives

1969-70
G1PD (2) 200.
G3PD (1) —
G3PDa Card, 2 #G3PD, with approval handstamp (2) —
G4PD (2) —
G5PD (3) 325.
G7PD (1) 250.
G8PD Perforated, on card with approval handstamp (2) 275.
G8PDa Perforated layout sheet proof with 4 #G8PD affixed (1) —
G8PDb Partial perforated layout sheet proof with 2 #G8PD affixed (1) —
G9PD (1) 275.
G10PD (1) 200.
G11PD (1) —
G12PD (1) 225.
G13PD (4) 240.
G14PD (3) 225.
G1TC Black panel behind "UN" (1) —
G6TCa Card, #G6PD, #G6TC pewter emblem, dated "7.10.69" (3) —
G6TCb Card, #G6TC silver emblem, 2 #G6PD dated "17.9.69" (3) —

G6TCc Card, #G6PD, #G6TC orange denomination, dated "27.8.69" (3) —
G12TC gray background, on card marked "Rejected" (2) 325.
G1PP 3 items, perforated (100) —
G2PP 5 items (160) —
Horiz. pair with vert. gutter (20) —
G3PP 5 items (160) —
Horiz. pair with vert. gutter (20) —
G4PP 5 items (151) —
Horiz. pair with vert. gutter (20) —
G5PP 4 items (160) —
Vert. pair with horiz. gutter (20) —
G6PP 3 items (160) —
Horiz. pair with vert. gutter (20) —
G7PP 4 items (100) —
G8PP 8 items (150) —
G9PP 6 items (100) —
G10PP 8 items (100) —
G12PP 6 items (100) —
G13PP 5 items (160) —
Vert. pair with horiz. gutter (20) —
G2PI Pair (80) —
Horiz. pair with vert. gutter (20) —
G3PI Pair (80) —
Horiz. pair with vert. gutter (20) —
G4PI Pair (73) —
Horiz. pair with vert. gutter (20) —
G5PI Pair (80) —
Vert. pair with horiz. gutter (20) —
G6PI Pair (80) —
Horiz. pair with vert. gutter (20) —
G7PI Pair (50) —
G8PI Pair (75) —
G9PI Pair (50) —
G10PI Pair (50) —
G13PI Pair (80) —
Vert. pair with horiz. gutter (20) —

Four essays of No. G2 exist, having "0" below "F" jutting out to left. Two essays of No. G10 with small "F.S." are on rejected cards.

New York #201-202
Mosaic Art at the UN

1969
201PD (3) 210.
202PD (3) 210.
202PDa Card, #201PD-202PD (2) —
201PP 8 items (100) —
202PP 8 items (100) —
201PI Pair (50) —
202PI Pair (50) —

New York #203-204
Peace Bell

1970
204PDa Card, 2 each #203PD-204PD (2) 1,300.
203PP 5 items (100) —
204PP 5 items (100) —

About half of Nos. 203PP and 204PP have faults.

New York #205-206
Lower Mekong Basin Development Project

1970
205PD (2) 250.
206PD (2) 250.
205PP 10 items (100) —
206PP 10 items (100) —
205PI Pair (50) —
206PI Pair (50) —

New York #207-208
Fight Cancer

1970
207PD Perforated, non-glossy paper, on piece of printer's card (1) —
208PD Perforated, non-glossy paper, on piece of printer's card (1) —
208PDa Card, #207PD-208PD, perforated, non-glossy paper (1) —
208PDb Card, 2 #207PD-208PD, perforated, non-glossy paper, with approval handstamp (1) 1,050.
208PDc #207-208, perforated, glossy paper, on printer's card (2) —
207PP 2 items (50) —
208PP 2 items (50) —
207PI Pair (50) —
208PI Pair (50) —

New York #209-212
UN, 25th Anniv.

1970
209PD (2) —
210PD (2) —
211PD On card (3) —
211PDa Card, #209PD-211PD (2) 750.
212PD (1) 275.
212PDa Card, #209PD-212PD (1) —
209PP 4 items (180) —
Horiz. pair with vert. gutter (10) —
210PP 5 items (180) —
Horiz. pair with vert. gutter (10) —
211PP 3 items (180) —
Vert. pair with horiz. gutter (10) —
212PP 5 items (22) —
209PI Pair (80) —
Horiz. pair with vert. gutter (20) —
210PI Pair (80) —
Horiz. pair with vert. gutter (20) —
211PI Pair (80) —
Vert. pair with horiz. gutter (20) —
212PI Pair (12) —

New York #213-214
Peace, Justice and Progress

1970
214PDa Card, #213PD-214PD (3) 600.
214PDb Card, 2 each #213PD-214PD (2) 1,300.
213PP 4 items (50) —
214PP 4 items (50) —

New York #215, Geneva #15
Peaceful Uses of the Sea Bed

1971
215PD (2) 200.
G15PD (1) —
215PP 6 items (100) —
G15PP 6 items (100) —
215PI Pair (50) —
G15PI Pair (50) —

New York #216-217, Geneva #16
International Support for Refugees

1971
217PDa Card, #216PD-217PD, #G16PD (2) 775.
216PP 4 items (80) —
Horiz. pair with vert. gutter (10) —
217PP 4 items (80) —
Horiz. pair with vert. gutter (10) —
G16PP 4 items (160) —
Horiz. pair with vert. gutter (20) —
216PI Pair (80) —
Horiz. pair with vert. gutter (20) —
217PI Pair (80) —
Horiz. pair with vert. gutter (20) —
G16PI Pair (80) —
Horiz. pair with vert. gutter (20) —

New York #218, Geneva #17
World Food Program

1971
218PD (4) 225.
G17PD (4) 225.
G17TC (1) 375.
218PP 6 items (100) —
G17PP 6 items (100) —
218PI Pair (50) —
G17PI Pair (50) —

New York #219, Geneva #18
Universal Postal Union

1971
219PDa Card, #219PD, #G18PD (3) 550.
219PP 5 items (130) —
Horiz. pair with vert. gutter (10) —
G18PP 5 items (150) —
219PI Pair (80) —
Horiz. pair with vert. gutter (20) —
G18PI Pair (80) —
Horiz. pair with vert. gutter (20) —

New York #220-221, Geneva #19-20
International Year Against Racial Discrimination

1971
221PDa Card, #220PD-221PD, #G19PD-G20PD and 4 similar items with slightly different colors (1) 2,400.
221PDb Card with affixed plastic sheet with #220PD-221PD, #G19PD-G20PD affixed (1) 600.
221PDc Cut-up card, #220PD-221PD, G19PD-G20PD (1) —
220PP 5 items (100) —
221PP 5 items (75) —
G19PP 5 items (100) —
G20PP 5 items (100) —

New York #222-223
UN Headquarters, New York

1971
222PD (4) 275.
223PD (2) 275.
222PP 8 items (91) —
223PP 5 items (92) —
222PI Pair (175) —

Two sheets of 50 of No. 222PI are "approved."

New York #224-225, Geneva #21
UN International School

1971
225PDa Card, #224PD-225PD, G21PD, with approval stamp (2) 750.
225PDb Card or sheet, #224PD-225PD, 1fr essay of #G21 (3) 925.
224PP 5 items (180) —
Vert. pair with horiz. gutter (10) —
225PP 5 items (100) —
Vert. pair with horiz. gutter (10) —
G21PP 5 items (180) —
Vert. pair with horiz. gutter (10) —
224PI Pair (80) —
Vert. pair with horiz. gutter (20) —
225PI Pair (80) —
Vert. pair with horiz. gutter (20) —
G21PI Pair (80) —
Vert. pair with horiz. gutter (20) —

New York #226, Geneva #22
Definitives

1972
226PD Perforated on printer's card (3) 225.
G22PD (5) 225.
226PP 4 items (100) —
G22PP 4 items (180) —
Horiz. pair with vert. gutter (10) —
226PI Pair (50) —
G22PI Pair (80) —
Horiz. pair with vert. gutter (20) —

New York #227, Geneva #23
Non-proliferation of Nuclear Weapons

1972
227PD (2) 200.
G23PD (2) 225.
227PP 6 items (100) —
G23PP 6 items (100) —
227PI Pair (50) —
G23PI Pair (50) —

Two essays each of Nos. 227 and G23 lacking strong gray billowing in center of cloud exist on cards dated "22.Set.1971."

New York #228, Geneva #24, Souvenir Card #1
World Health Day

1972
228PDa Card, #228PD, #G24PD with approval handstamp (1) 500.
G24PD (1) —
SC1PD Card with stamps with simulated perforations and cancels (2) 600.
228PP 8 items (80) —
Vert. pair with horiz. gutter (10) —
G24PP 8 items (160) —
Vert. pair with horiz. gutter (20) —
G24PI Pair (180) —
Vert. pair with horiz. gutter (20) —

New York #229-230, Geneva #25-26
UN Conference on Human Environment

1972
229PD (1) —
230PDa Card, #229PD-230PD, #G25PD-G26PD (3) 450.
230PDb Card, #230PD, #G25PD-G26PD (1) —
229PP 6 items (288) —
Cross gutter block (2) —
Horiz. pair with vert. gutter (16) —
Vert. pair with horiz. gutter (36) —
230PP 6 items (288) —
Cross gutter block (2) —
Horiz. pair with vert. gutter (16) —
Vert. pair with horiz. gutter (36) —
G25PP 6 items (288) —
Cross gutter block (2) —
Horiz. pair with vert. gutter (16) —
Vert. pair with horiz. gutter (36) —
G26PP 6 items (288) —
Cross gutter block (2) —
Horiz. pair with vert. gutter (16) —
Vert. pair with horiz. gutter (36) —
229PI Pair (144) —
Cross gutter block (2) —
Horiz. pair with vert. gutter (16) —
Vert. pair with horiz. gutter (36) —
230PI Pair (144) —
Cross gutter block (2) —
Horiz. pair with vert. gutter (16) —
Vert. pair with horiz. gutter (36) —
G25PI Pair (144) —
Cross gutter block (2) —
Horiz. pair with vert. gutter (16) —
Vert. pair with horiz. gutter (36) —
G26PI Pair (144) —
Cross gutter block (2) —
Horiz. pair with vert. gutter (16) —
Vert. pair with horiz. gutter (36) —

New York #231, Geneva #27
Economic Commission for Europe

1972
231PDa Card, #231PD, #G27PD (4) 550.
231PP 8 items (100) —
G27PP 8 items (50) —

New York #232-233, Geneva #28-29, Souvenir Card #2
Art at the UN

1972
232PDa Card, #232PD, #233TC text in dull blue green, #G28PD-G29PD (1) 975.
G28PD (1) —
G29PDa Card, #G28PD-G29PD, #233TC text in dull blue green (1) —
G29PDb Card, #G29PD, #233TC text in dull blue green (1) —
SC2PD (25) —
SC2PDa Defaced card, with corrections marked in blue (8) —
SC2TC Untrimmed card, signature in light blue(3) 160.
G28PP 3 items (50) —
G29PP 3 items (50) —
232PI Pair (80) —
Vert. pair with horiz. gutter (20) —
233PI Pair (80) —
Vert. pair with horiz. gutter (20) —

G28PI	Pair (80)	—
	Vert. pair with horiz. gutter (20)	—
G29PI	Pair (80)	—
	Vert. pair with horiz. gutter (20)	—

New York #234-235, Geneva #30-31, Souvenir Card #3
Disarmament Decade

1973

235PDa	Card, #234PD-235PD, #G30PD-G31PD, with approval handstamp (1)	825.
SC3PD	With printer's stamp or approval handstamp (9)	110.
234PP	8 items (130)	—
	Horiz. pair with vert. gutter (20)	—
235PP	8 items (100)	—
G30PP	8 items (130)	—
	Horiz. pair with vert. gutter (20)	—
G31PP	8 items (100)	—
234PI	Pair (230)	—
	Horiz. pair with vert. gutter (20)	—
235PI	Pair (230)	—
	Horiz. pair with vert. gutter (20)	—
G30PI	Pair (205)	—
	Horiz. pair with vert. gutter (20)	—
G31PI	Pair (230)	—
	Horiz. pair with vert. gutter (20)	—

Two examples of #SC3PD are cut in half.

New York #236-237, Geneva #32
Fight Against Drug Abuse

1973

236PD	(1)	—
237PDa	Card, #236PD-237PD, #G32PD with approval handstamp (4)	725.
237PDb	Card, #237PD, #G32PD with approval handstamp (1)	—
237PDc	Card, #237PD, #G32PD, 9c essay of #236 (6)	—
236PP	8 items (75)	—
237PP	8 items (100)	—
G32PP	8 items (50)	—
236PI	Pair (50)	—
237PI	Pair (50)	—
G32PI	Pair (50)	—

New York #238-239, Geneva #33
UN Volunteer Program

1973

239PDa	Card, #238PD-239PD, #G33PD (9)	600.
238PP	8 items (80)	—
239PP	8 items (100)	—
G33PP	8 items (50)	—
238PI	Pair (50)	—
239PI	Pair (50)	—
G33PI	Pair (25)	—

New York #240-241, Geneva #34
Namibia

1973

241PDa	Card, #240PD-241PD, #G34PD (1)	—
241PDb	Card, #240PD-241PD, #G34PD, essays of #240-241, #G34 with Africa outlined in gold (3)	1,400.
240PP	8 items (100)	—
241PP	8 items (100)	—
G34PP	8 items (50)	—
240PI	Pair (50)	—
241PI	Pair (50)	—
G34PI	Pair (50)	—

Two cards containing only the essays exist.

New York #242-243, Geneva #35-36, Souvenir Card #4
Universal Declaration of Human Rights, 25th Anniv.

1973

242PD	(9)	275.
243PDa	Card, #242PD-243PD, #G35PD-G36PD (6)	1,300.
243PDb	Card, #242PD-243PD (9)	725.
243PDc	Card, #243PD, #G35PD-G36PD (1)	—
SC4PD	With approval handstamp (3)	—
242PP	5 items (100)	—
243PP	5 items (100)	—
G35PP	5 items (100)	—
G36PP	5 items (50)	—
SC4PP	2 items (1)	—
SC4PI	untrimmed card (1)	—

No. SC4PP may not be a complete set of progressive proofs.

New York #244-245, Geneva #37-38
New International Labor Organization Headquarters

1974

245PDa	Card, #245PD, #G37PD-G38PD, 8c essay of #244 (4)	1,200.
244PP	8 items (75)	—
245PP	8 items (75)	—
G37PP	8 items (50)	—
G38PP	8 items (50)	—
244PI	Pair (50)	—
245PI	Pair (50)	—
G37PI	Pair (50)	—
G38PI	Pair (50)	—

New York #246, Geneva #39-40, Souvenir Card #5
Universal Postal Union, Cent.

1974

246PD	(1)	—
246PDa	Card, #246PD, #G39PD-G40PD (7)	925.
G40PDa	Card, #G39PD-G40PD (1)	—
SC5PD	Affixed to card (5)	400.
SC5PDa	Card with printer instructions in ink (1)	—
SC5PDb	Progressive proof sheet with printer instructions in ink (1)	400.
246PP	6 items (100)	—
G39PP	5 items (50)	—
G40PP	5 items (50)	—
246PI	Pair (25)	—
G39PI	Pair (25)	—
G40PI	Pair (25)	—

New York #247-248, Geneva #41-42
Art at the UN

1974

247PDa	Card, #247PD, #G41PD-G42PD, 15c essay of #248 (5)	1,250.
248PDa	Card, #247PD-248PD, #G41PD-G42PD (3)	925.
247PP	8 items (100)	—
248PP	8 items (100)	—
G41PP	8 items (50)	—
G42PP	8 items (50)	—
247PI	Pair (50)	—
248PI	Pair (50)	—
G41PI	Pair (50)	—
G42PI	Pair (50)	—

New York #249-251
Definitives

1974

249PD	Affixed on perforated blank (1)	—
250PD	Affixed on perforated blank (1)	—
250PDa	Taped to card (1)	—
250PDb	Card, #250PD, 251TC with darker brown background, essay of #249 with flat top "S," with "21.DIC.1973" date and approval stamp (2)	—
251PD	Affixed on perforated blank (1)	125.
251PDa	Card, #249PD, #251PD, with "17.ENE.1974" date and approval stamp (3)	500.
251TCa	Darker brown background, on cards dated "21.DIC.1973" (3)	—
250PP	10 items (50)	—
251PP	8 items (35)	—
249PI	Pair (200)	—
250PI	Pair (50)	—
251PI	Pair (100)	—

New York #252-253, Geneva #43-44, Souvenir Card #6
World Population Year

1974

252PDa	Card, #252PD, #G44PD, 21c essay of #253, 40c essay of #G43 in se-tenant strip (5)	725.
253PDa	Card, #252PD-253PD, G44PD, 40c essay of #G43 in se-tenant strip (4)	800.
SC6PD	With approval handstamp (10)	—
252PP	10 items (50)	—
253PP	10 items (50)	—
G43PP	10 items (50)	—
G44PP	10 items (50)	—
252PI	Pair (50)	—
253PI	Pair (50)	—
G43PI	Pair (50)	—
G44PI	Pair (50)	—

All examples of No. SC6PD show the 40c essay.

New York #254-255, Geneva #45
Law of the Sea

1974

255PDa	Card, #254PD-255PD, #G45TC with blue green sky (3)	800.
254PP	10 items (50)	—
255PP	10 items (50)	—
G45PP	10 items (50)	—
254PI	Pair (50)	—
255PI	Pair (50)	—
G45PI	Pair (50)	—

New York #256-257, Geneva #46-47, Souvenir Card #7
Peaceful Uses of Outer Space

1975

256PDa	Card, #256PD, #G46PD-G47PD (1)	—
257PD	Cut from #256PDa (1)	—
257PDa	Card, #256PD-257PD, G46PD-G47PD (3)	825.
SC7PD	with approval handstamp (4)	—
256PP	8 items (150)	—
257PP	8 items (150)	—
G46PP	8 items (50)	—
G47PP	8 items (50)	—
256PI	Pair (100)	—
257PI	Pair (100)	—
G46PI	Pair (50)	—
G47PI	Pair (50)	—

New York #258-259, Geneva #48-49
International Women's Year

1975

258PD	On card dated "16 Oct. 1974" (4)	250.
259PD	(4)	250.
G48PD	On card dated "16 Oct. 1974" (4)	325.
G49PD	(4)	325.
258TC	bright blue background (on cards dated "17 Sep. 1974") (4)	—
G48TC	red brown background (on cards dated "17 Sep. 1974") (4)	—
258PP	6 items (50)	—
259PP	6 items (50)	—
G48PP	6 items (50)	—
G49PP	6 items (50)	—
258PI	Pair (50)	—
259PI	Pair (50)	—
G48PI	Pair (50)	—
G49PI	Pair (50)	—

Six essays of the 18c stamp with "Nations Unies" inscription, and six essays of the 90c stamp with "United Nations" inscription exist.

New York #260-262, Geneva #50-52
UN, 30th Anniv.

1975

261PDa	Card, #260PD-261PD, #G51PD, #G50TC in olive green, se-tenant (4)	1,200.
262PD	(5)	500.
G52PD	(1)	—
G52TC	With #G52aTC olive green (5)	700.
260PP	6 items (50)	—
261PP	6 items (50)	—
262PP	10 items (6)	—
G50PP	6 items (50)	—
G51PP	6 items (50)	—
G52PP	10 items (6)	—
260PI	Pair (50)	—
261PI	Pair (50)	—
262PI	Pair of souvenir sheets (26)	—
G50PI	Pair (50)	—
G51PI	Pair (50)	—
G52PI	Pair of souvenir sheets (26)	—

New York #263-264, Geneva #53-54
Namibia

1975

264PDa	Card, #263PD-264PD, #G53PD-G54PD (9)	975.
263PP	8 items (50)	—
264PP	8 items (50)	—
G53PP	8 items (50)	—
G54PP	7 items (50)	—
263PI	Pair (50)	—
264PI	Pair (50)	—
G53PI	Pair (50)	—
G54PI	Pair (50)	—

New York #265-266, Geneva #55-56, Souvenir Card #8
UN Peacekeeping Operations

1975

266PDa	Card, #265PD-266PD, #G55PD-G56PD (3)	1,300.
266PDb	Card, #266PD, #G55PD-G56PD, 10c essay of #265 (5)	1,200.
SC8PD	With approval handstamp (5)	—
265PI	Pair (25)	—
266PI	Pair (25)	—
G55PI	Pair (25)	—
G56PI	Pair (25)	—

New York #267-271
Definitives

1976

267PD	(4)	225.
268PD	(3)	350.
269PD	(5)	110.
270PD	(8)	225.
271PD	(4)	200.
271TC	Dark green background (not approved cards dated "30 June 1975" (5)	—
267PP	10 items (25)	—
268PP	8 items (50)	—
269PP	3 items (50)	—
270PP	6 items (50)	—
271PP	10 items (25)	—
267PI	Pair (50)	—
268PI	Pair (50)	—
269PI	Pair (50)	—
270PI	Pair (50)	—
271PI	Pair (50)	—

New York #272-273, Geneva #57, Souvenir Card #9
World Federation of United Nations Associations

1976

273PDa	Card, #272PD-273PD, #G57PD (4)	825.
SC9PD	With approval handstamp dated "18 Sep 1975" (4)	—
SC9TC	With light blue denominations on 1966 stamp (not approved) (5)	—
272PP	6 items (50)	—
273PP	6 items (50)	—
G57PP	6 items (50)	—
272PI	Pair (50)	—
273PI	Pair (50)	—
G57PI	Pair (50)	—

New York #274-275, Geneva #58
UN Conference on Trade and Development

1976

G58PDa	Card, #G58PD, non-denominated essays of #274-275 (5)	725.
274PP	5 items (130)	—
	Vert. pair with horiz. gutter (10)	—
275PP	5 items (130)	—
	Vert. pair with horiz. gutter (10)	—
G58PP	5 items (150)	—
274PI	Pair (80)	—
	Vert. pair with horiz. gutter (20)	—
275PI	Pair (80)	—
	Vert. pair with horiz. gutter (20)	—
G58PI	Pair (80)	—
	Vert. pair with horiz. gutter (20)	—

New York #276-277, Geneva #59-60
UN Conference on Human Settlements

1976

277PDa	Card, #276PD-277PD, #G59PD-G60PD (4)	1,100.
276PP	12 items (50)	—
277PP	12 items (50)	—
G59PP	12 items (50)	—
G60PP	12 items (50)	—
276PI	Pair (50)	—
277PI	Pair (50)	—
G59PI	Pair (50)	—
G60PI	Pair (50)	—

New York #278-279, Geneva #61-62
UN Postal Administration, 25th Anniv.

1976

279PDa	Card, #278PD-279PD, #G61PD-G62PD (5)	700.
278PP	5 items (64)	—
	Horiz. pair with vert. gutter (4)	—
	Vert. pair with horiz. gutter (4)	—
279PP	5 items (64)	—
	Horiz. pair with vert. gutter (4)	—
	Vert. pair with horiz. gutter (4)	—
G61PP	5 items (72)	—
	Horiz. pair with vert. gutter (4)	—
G62PP	5 items (63)	—
	Horiz. pair with vert. gutter (4)	—
	Vert. pair with horiz. gutter (4)	—

New York #280, Geneva #63, Souvenir Card #10
World Food Council

1976

280PD	(5)	200.
G63PD	(5)	200.
SC10PD	With approval handstamp (12)	—
280PP	2 items (50)	—
G63PP	2 items (50)	—
280PI	Pair (50)	—
G63PI	Pair (50)	—

New York #281-282, Geneva #64, Souvenir Card #11
World Intellectual Property Organization

1977

282PDa	Card, #281PD-282PD, #G64PD (4)	650.
SC11PD	With approval handstamp (4)	—
281PP	8 items (50)	—
282PP	8 items (50)	—
G64PP	8 items (50)	—
281PI	Pair (50)	—
282PI	Pair (50)	—
G64PI	Pair (50)	—

New York #283-284, Geneva #65-66
UN Water Conference

1977

283PD	Cut out from #284PDb (1)	—
284PDa	Card, #283PD-284PD, #G65PD-G66PD (2)	925.
284PDb	Card, #284PD, #G65PD-G66PD (1)	—
284PDc	Card, #284PD, #G66PD (1)	—
283PP	6 items (50)	—
284PP	6 items (50)	—
G65PP	5 items (50)	—
G66PP	5 items (50)	—
283PI	Pair (50)	—
284PI	Pair (50)	—
G65PI	Pair (50)	—
G66PI	Pair (50)	—

New York #285-286, Geneva #67-68
UN Security Council

1977

286PDa	Card, #285PD-286PD, essays of #G67-G68 with small top Chinese character (4)	975.
G68PDa	Card, #G67PD-G68PD (large Chinese character) (4)	450.
286PP	8 items (50)	—
G67PP	8 items (50)	—
G68PP	8 items (50)	—
285PI	Pair (50)	—
286PI	Pair (50)	—
G67PI	Pair (50)	—
G68PI	Pair (50)	—

A card with the two essays only (a cutout of No. 286PDa) with "not approved" handstamp exists.

New York #287-288, Geneva #69-70, Souvenir Card #12
Combat Racism

1977

288PDa	Card, #287PD-288PD (4)	425.
G70PDa	Card, #G69PD-G70PD (4)	500.
SC12PD	With approval handstamp and specimen perfin (5)	—
287PP	3 items (50)	—
288PP	3 items (50)	—
G69PP	6 items (150)	—
G70PP	6 items (150)	—
287PI	Pair (175)	—
288PI	Pair (175)	—
G69PI	Pair (225)	—
G70PI	Pair (225)	—

New York #289-290, Geneva #71-72
Peaceful Uses of Atomic Energy

1977

290PDa	Card, #289PD-290PD, #G71PD-G72PD (4)	1,100.
290PDb	Card, #289PD-290PD, #G71PD, essay of #G72 with capital "F" in "Fins" (5)	975.
289PP	8 items (50)	—
290PP	8 items (50)	—
G71PP	6 items (50)	—
G72PP	6 items (50)	—
289PI	Pair (50)	—
290PI	Pair (50)	—
G71PI	Pair (50)	—
G72PI	Pair (50)	—

New York #291-293, Geneva #73
Definitives

1978

291PD	(4)	200.
292PD	(5)	225.
293PD	(4)	200.
G73PD	With approval handstamp (4)	225.
G73TC	Tree in deep brown (with "not approved" handstamp (6)	175.
G73PP	6 items (50)	—
291PI	Pair (50)	—
292PI	Pair (50)	—
293PI	Pair (75)	—
G73PI	Pair (50)	—

Six essays of No. 293 having "C" in Naciones not even with "A" exist on card with "not approved" handstamp.

New York #294-295, Geneva #74-75
Global Eradication of Smallpox

1978

295PDa	Card, #294PD-295PD, #G74PD-G75PD (5)	1,000.
294PP	2 items (50)	—
295PP	2 items (50)	—
G74PP	4 items (50)	—
G75PP	4 items (50)	—
294PI	Pair (50)	—
295PI	Pair (50)	—
G74PI	Pair (50)	—
G75PI	Pair (50)	—

New York #296-297, Geneva #76, Souvenir Card #13
Liberation, Justice and Cooperation for Namibia

1978

296PD	On perforated sheet layout (2)	—
297PD	On perforated sheet layout (1)	—
297PDa	Card, #296-297, #G76, perforated (4)	725.
297PDb	Card, #296-297 perforated, essay of #G76 ("F." and "S." same size, not approved) (5)	725.
G76PD	On perforated sheet layout (9)	—
SC13PD	With approval handstamp (5)	110.
296PP	6 items (50)	—
297PP	6 items (50)	—
G76PP	6 items (50)	—
296PI	Pair (50)	—
297PI	Pair (50)	—
G76PI	Pair (50)	—

The essay of No. G76 exists on a not approved perforated sheet layout.

New York #298-299, Geneva #77-78, Souvenir Card #14
Safety in the Air

1978

298PDa	Card, #298PD, #G77PD-G78PD (1)	—
299PD	Cut out from #298PDa (1)	—
299PDa	Card, #298PD-299PD, #G77PD-G78PD (3)	875.
SC14PD	With approval handstamp (4)	—
298PP	10 items (50)	—
299PP	10 items (50)	—
G77PP	6 items (50)	—
G78PP	6 items (50)	—
298PI	Pair (50)	—
299PI	Pair (50)	—
G77PI	Pair (50)	—
G78PI	Pair (50)	—

New York #300-301, Geneva #79-80
UN General Assembly

1978

301PDa	Card, #300PD-301PD, #G79PD-G80PD (4)	975.
300PP	4 items (50)	—
301PP	5 items (50)	—
G79PP	6 items (50)	—
G80PP	6 items (50)	—
300PI	Pair (25)	—
301PI	Pair (25)	—
G79PI	Pair (25)	—
G80PI	Pair (25)	—

New York #302-303, Geneva #81
Technical Cooperation Conference

1978

303PDa	Card, #302PD-303PD, #G81PD (3)	975.
302PP	10 items (50)	—
303PP	10 items (50)	—
G81PP	8 items (50)	—
302PI	Pair (50)	—
303PI	Pair (50)	—
G81PI	Pair (50)	—

Five not approved cards have essays of the set showing black behind closer cogwheels and text close to bottom frame. Value $725.

New York #304-307
Definitives

1979

304PD	(1)	—
304PDa	Card, #304PD-307PD (9)	—
304PDb	Card, #304PD, essays of #305, 306, 307 with inked-in corrections for printer (2)	875.
307PDa	Card, #305PD-307PD (3)	725.
304PP	8 items (50)	—
305PP	8 items (50)	—
306PP	6 items (50)	—
307PP	4 items (50)	—
304PI	Pair (50)	—
305PI	Pair (50)	—
306PI	Pair (75)	—
307PI	Pair (75)	—

Three cut-up not approved cards exist containing the three essays with inked-in corrections.

Nos. 306PI and 307PI include 25 pairs of reprints.

New York #308-309, Geneva #82-83
UN Disaster Relief Coordinator

1979

309PDa	Card, #308PD-309PD (4)	425.
G83PDa	Card, #G82PD-G83PD (1)	—
G83PDb	Card, #G82PD-G83PD, essays of #308-309 with inked-in corrections for printer (3)	875.
308PP	9 items (50)	—
309PP	9 items (50)	—
G82PP	4 items (50)	—
G83PP	4 items (50)	—
308PI	Pair (50)	—
309PI	Pair (50)	—
G82PI	Pair (50)	—
G83PI	Pair (50)	—

Two not approved cards contain the essays with inked-in corrections for printer.

New York #310-311, Geneva #84-85, Souvenir Card #15
International Year of the Child

1979

310PDa	Card, #310PD, essays of #G84-G85 (with IYC emblem above bottom of children's feet) (1)	—
311PD	Cut out from #310PDa (1)	—
311PDa	Card, #310PD-311PD, essays #G84-G85 (2)	1,350.
G85PDa	Card, #G84PD-G85PD (4)	625.
SC15PD	With manuscript approval (4)	—
310PP	9 items (20)	—
311PP	9 items (20)	—
G84PP	8 items (20)	—
G85PP	10 items (20)	—
310PI	Pair (40)	140.
311PI	Pair (40)	140.
G84PI	Pair (20)	140.
G85PI	Pair (20)	140.

One cut up not approved card contains the two essays. Five essays of No. SC15 marked "not approved" show the stamp essays.

Vienna #1-6
Definitives

1979

V6PDa	Card, #V1PD-V6PD (5)	2,000.
V1PP	5 items (50)	—
V2PP	5 items (150)	—
V3PP	5 items (50)	—
V4PP	5 items (50)	—
V5PP	5 items (50)	—
V6PP	5 items (50)	—
V1PI	Pair (50)	—
V2PI	Pair (150)	—
V3PI	Pair (50)	—

V4PI	Pair (50)	—
V5PI	Pair (50)	—
V6PI	Pair (50)	—

New York #312-313, Geneva #86
Namibia

1979

313PDa	Card, #312PD-313PD, #G86PD (4)	825.
312PP	8 items (50)	—
313PP	8 items (50)	—
G86PP	8 items (50)	—
312PI	Pair (50)	—
313PI	Pair (50)	—
G86PI	Pair (50)	—

One card of No. 313PDa is badly damaged.

New York #314-315, Geneva #87-88, Souvenir Card #16
International Court of Justice

1979

315PDa	Card, #314PD-315PD, #G87PD-G88PD 2 each (4)	1,650.
SC16PD	With "not approved" handstamp and "Specimen" perfin (5)	—
314PP	4 items (50)	—
315PP	4 items (50)	—
G87PP	6 items (50)	—
G88PP	7 items (50)	—
314PI	Pair (50)	—
315PI	Pair (50)	—
G87PI	Pair (50)	—
G88PI	Pair (50)	—

New York #316-317, Geneva #89, Vienna #7
New International Economic Order

1980

316PD	(11)	225.
317PD	(5)	200.
G89PD	With approval handstamp (5)	175.
V7PD	(5)	225.
316PP	4 items (50)	—
317PP	4 items (50)	—
G89PP	4 items (50)	—
V7PP	5 items (50)	—
316PI	Pair (50)	—
317PI	Pair (50)	—
G89PI	Pair (50)	—
V7PI	Pair (50)	—

Five cards of No. 316PD are marked "not approved" but there are no discernable differences between it and approved proofs. Six "not approved" cards have essays of No. G89 with text "Nouvel International Economique Ordre." Six "not approved" cards have essays of No. V7 with the same text.

Vienna #8
Definitive

1980

V8PD	(4)	200.
V8PP	11 items, perforated (250)	—
V8PI	Pair (25)	—

New York #318-319, Geneva #90-91, Vienna #9-10, Souvenir Card #17
Decade for Women

1980

318PD	(13)	225.
319PD	(11)	200.
G90PD	(13)	225.
G91PD	(5)	225.
V9PD	(5)	175.
V10PD	(5)	200.
SC17PD	With approval handstamp (5)	175.
318PP	4 items (50)	—
319PP	4 items (50)	—
G90PP	4 items (50)	—
G91PP	4 items (50)	—
V9PP	3 items (50)	—
V10PP	2 items (50)	—
318PI	Pair (50)	—
319PI	Pair (50)	—
G90PI	Pair (50)	—
G91PI	Pair (50)	—
V9PI	Pair (50)	—
V10PI	Pair (50)	—

New York #320-321, Geneva #92, Vienna #11
UN Peace-keeping Operations

1980

321PDa	Card, #320PD-321PD, #V11PD, essay of #G92 with "de" on top line (3)	975.
G92PD	(4)	240.
320PP	2 items (50)	—
321PP	8 items (50)	—
G92PP	4 items (50)	—
V11PP	12 items (50)	—
320PI	Pair (50)	—
321PI	Pair (50)	—
G92PI	Pair (50)	—
V11PI	Pair (50)	—

New York #322-324, Geneva #93-95, Vienna #12-14
UN, 35th Anniv.

1980

324PDa	Card, #324PD, #G95D, #V14PD (4)	1,050.
324PDb	Card, #322PD-324PD, #G93PD-G94PD, #V12PD-V14PD, essay of #G95 with incomplete marginal inscription (3)	1,050.
322PP	8 items (50)	—
323PP	8 items (50)	—
G93PP	6 items (300)	—
G94PP	13 items (650)	—
V12PP	3 items (50)	—
V13PP	8 items (50)	—
322PI	Pair (100)	—
323PI	Pair (100)	—
G93PI	Pair (100)	—
G94PI	Pair (100)	—
V12PI	Pair (175)	—
V13PI	Pair (100)	—

New York #325-340
Flags

1980

325PD	Cut from #340PDa (1)	—
332PD	Cut from #340PDa (1)	—
340PDa	Card, #325PD-340PD (4)	3,500.
340PDb	Card, #326PD-331PD, #333PD-340PD (1)	—
325-340PP	Set of 20 sheets (1)	—
325-340PI	Set of 4 sheets (2)	—

On Nos. 325-340PP, there are five progressive proof sheets per issued sheet.

New York #341-342, Geneva #96-97, Vienna #15-16, Souvenir Card #18
Economic and Social Council

1980

342PDa	Sheet, #341PD-342PD, #G96PD-G97PD, #V15PD-V16PD (4)	110.
G96PD	(4)	—
G97PD	(4)	—
V15PD	(4)	—
V16PD	(4)	—
SC18PD	(4)	—
341PP	6 items (50)	—
342PP	6 items (50)	—
G96PP	6 items (50)	—
G97PP	6 items (50)	—
V15PP	6 items (50)	—
V16PP	6 items (50)	—
341PI	Pair (50)	—
342PI	Pair (50)	—
G96PI	Pair (50)	—
G97PI	Pair (50)	—
V15PI	Pair (50)	—
V16PI	Pair (50)	—

An essay of No. SC18 with curved cancel on 4s stamp has "not approved" handstamp.

New York #343, Geneva #98, Vienna #17
Inalienable Rights of the Palestinian People

1981

343TCa	Card, #343TC blue, #G98PD, #V17PD (1)	625.
G98PD	(5)	—
V17PD	(5)	—
343PP	4 items (50)	—
G98PP	5 items (50)	—
V17PP	4 items (50)	—
343PI	Pair (50)	—
G98PI	Pair (50)	—
V17PI	Pair (50)	—

New York #344-345, Geneva #99-100, Vienna #18-19, Souvenir Card #19
Intl. Year of the Disabled

1980

344PD	Cut out from #G100PDa (1)	—
344PDa	Card, #344PD, #G99PD-G100PD, #V18PD-V19PD, 31c essay of #345 (4)	1,450.
344PDb	Card, #344PD, #G100PD, #V18PD-V19PD (4)	—
G100PDa	Card, #G100PD, #V18PD-V19PD (1)	—
SC19PD	With "not approved" handstamp (9)	110.
344PP	6 items (50)	—
345PP	2 items (50)	—
G99PP	2 items (50)	—
G100PP	2 items (50)	—
V18PP	6 items (50)	—
V19PP	2 items (50)	—
344PI	Pair (50)	—
345PI	Pair (50)	—
G99PI	Pair (50)	—
G100PI	Pair (50)	—
V18PI	Pair (50)	—
V19PI	Pair (50)	—

All die proof cards are stamped "not approved." One example of No. SC19PD has "35c" covering "31c."

New York #346-347, Geneva #101, Vienna #20
Art at the UN

1981

347PDa	Card, #346PD-347PD, #G101PD, #V20PD (1)	1,050.
347PDb	Card, #347PD, #G101PD, #V20PD, 15c essay of #346 (not approved) (6)	—
346PP	5 items (50)	—
347PP	5 items (50)	—
G101PP	5 items (50)	—
V20PP	5 items (50)	—
346PI	Pair (50)	—
347PI	Pair (50)	—
G101PI	Pair (50)	—
V20PI	Pair (50)	—

New York #348-349, Geneva #102, Vienna #21, Souvenir Card #20
Conference on New and Renewable Sources of Energy

1981

348PDa	Card, #348PD, #G102PD, #V21PD, 31c essay of #349 (3)	925.
SC20PD	With approval and specimen handstamps (4)	—
348PP	6 items (50)	—
349PP	4 items (50)	—
G102PP	6 items (50)	—
V21PP	4 items (50)	—
348PI	Pair (50)	—
349PI	Pair (50)	—
G102PI	Pair (50)	—
V21PI	Pair (50)	—

All examples of No. SC20PD have the 31c essay.

New York #350-365
Flags

1981

357PDa	Card, #350PD-357PD (5)	—
365PDa	Card, #358PD-365PD (5)	2,300.
350-365PP	Set of 19 sheets (1)	—
350-365PI	Set of 4 sheets (2)	4,600.

On Nos. 350-365PP, there are four progressive sheets for the issued sheet containing Nos. 354-357, and five progressive proof sheets per issued sheet for the issued sheets containing Nos. 350-353, 358-361 and 362-365. Two sets of imperforate sheets of Nos. 350-353 and two sets of imperforate sheets of Nos. 354-357 exist with 15c denominations are essays.

New York #366-367, Geneva #103-104, Vienna #22-23
Volunteers Program, 10th Anniv.

1981

367PDa	Card, #367PD, #G103PD-G104PD, #V22PD-V23PD, 20c essay of #366 (3)	1,450.
G103TC	white background (1)	—
V22TC	white background (1)	—
V23TC	white background (1)	—
366PI	Pair (50)	—
367PI	Pair (50)	—
G103PI	Pair (50)	—
G104PI	Pair (50)	—
V22PI	Pair (50)	—
V23PI	Pair (50)	—

New York #368-370, Geneva #105-106, Vienna #24
Definitives

1982

370PDa	Card, #368PD-370PD, #G106PD, #V24PD, essay of #G105 with no "l'" before "apartheid" (5)	1,450.
368PP	5 items (50)	—
369PP	5 items (50)	—
370PP	5 items (50)	—
G105PP	4 items (50)	—
G106PP	5 items (50)	—
V24PP	5 items (50)	—
368PI	Pair (50)	—
369PI	Pair (50)	—
370PI	Pair (50)	—
G105PI	Pair (50)	—
C106PI	Pair (50)	—
V24PI	Pair (50)	—

One example of No. 370PDa has all stamps canceled and #G105 altered.

New York #371-372, Geneva #107-108, Vienna #25-26, Souvenir Card #21
Environment Program, 10th Anniv.

1982

372PDa	Card, #371PD-372PD, #G107PD, #V25PD-V26PD, 1.30fr essay of #G108 (5)	1,600.
372PDb	Card, #372PD, #G107PD-G108PD, #V25PD-V26PD, 18c essay of #371 (4)	1,450.
SC21PD	(5)	—
371PP	8 items (50)	—
372PP	7 items (50)	—
G107PP	12 items (50)	—
G108PP	8 items (50)	—
V25PP	7 items (50)	—
V26PP	11 items (50)	—
371PI	Pair (50)	—
372PI	Pair (50)	—

G107PI	Pair (50)	—
G108PI	Pair (50)	—
V25PI	Pair (50)	—
V26PI	Pair (50)	—

One example of No. 372PDb has had some stamps defaced. Five essays of No. SC21PD show the 18c essay, with one altered to change 18c to 20c.

New York #373, Geneva #109-110, Vienna #27, Souvenir Card #22

Exploration and Peaceful Uses of Outer Space

1982

373PDa	Card, #373PD, #G109PD-G110PD, #V27PD (4)	925.
G109PD	(4)	—
G110PD	(4)	—
V27PD	(4)	—
SC22PD	(4)	—
373PP	6 items (50)	—
G109PP	6 items (50)	—
G110PP	14 items (50)	—
V27PP	14 items (50)	—
373PI	Pair (50)	—
G109PI	Pair (50)	—
G110PI	Pair (50)	—
V27PI	Pair (50)	—

New York #374-389

Flags

1982

381PDa	Card, #374PD-381PD (5)	2,000.
389PDa	Card, #382PD-389PD (4)	2,000.
374-389PP	Set of 20 sheets (1)	—
374-389PI	Set of 4 sheets (2)	5,250.

On Nos. 374-389PP, there are five progressive proof sheets per issued sheet.

New York #390-391, Geneva #111-112, Vienna #28-29

Conservation and Protection of Nature

1982

390PDa	Card, #390PD, #G111PD, #V29PD, essays of #G112 and #V28 (1)	—
391PD	(1)	—
391PDa	Card, #390PD-391PD, #G111PD, #V29PD, essays of #G112 and #V28 (3)	1,400.
G112PD	(3)	250.
V29PD	(3)	200.
390PP	10 items (50)	—
391PP	10 items (50)	—
G111PP	10 items (50)	—
G112PP	10 items (50)	—
V28PP	10 items (50)	—
V29PP	10 items (50)	—
390PI	Pair (50)	—
391PI	Pair (50)	—
G111PI	Pair (50)	—
G112PI	Pair (50)	—
V28PI	Pair (50)	—
V29PI	Pair (50)	—

Essays of No. G112 have snake with lighter stripes. Essays of No. V28 have umlaut missing one dot.

New York #392-393, Geneva #113, Vienna #30

World Communications Year

1983

392PD	(5)	225.
393PD	(4)	200.
G113PD	(4)	200.
V30PD	(5)	200.
392TC	Dark blue and green colors switched (4)	300.
V30TC	Dark blue and green colors switched (3)	325.
392PP	10 items (50)	—
393PP	15 items (50)	—
G113PP	15 items (50)	—
V30PP	10 items (50)	—
392PI	Pair (50)	—
393PI	Pair (50)	—
G113PI	Pair (50)	—
V30PI	Pair (50)	—

New York #394-395, Geneva #114-115, Vienna #31-32, Souvenir Card #23

Safety at Sea

1983

395PDa	Card, #394PD-395PD, #G114PD-G115PD, #V31PD-V32PD, #394TC-395TC, #G114TC (1)	—
395PDb	Card, #394PD-395PD, #G114PD (4)	750.
G115PDa	Card, #G115PD, #V31PD-V32PD, #394TC-395TC,#G114TC(10)	—
SC23PD	(5)	—
SC23TC	(6)	—
394PP	10 items (50)	—
395PP	8 items (50)	—
G114PP	11 items (50)	—
G115PP	5 items (50)	—
V31PP	5 items (50)	—
V32PP	8 items (50)	—
394PI	Pair (50)	—
395PI	Pair (50)	—
G114PI	Pair (50)	—
G115PI	Pair (50)	—
V31PI	Pair (50)	—
V32PI	Pair (50)	—

Nos. 394TC and G114TC have orange buoy lights instead of red, and No. 395TC has red violet line in ship instead of orange. These appear on No. SC23TC.

New York #396, Geneva #116, Vienna #33-34

World Food Program

1983

396PD	(3)	225.
G116PD	(3)	225.
V33PD	(3)	200.
V34PD	(3)	225.
396PI	Pair (25)	—
G116PI	Pair (25)	—
V33PI	Pair (25)	—
V34PI	Pair (25)	—

New York #397-398, Geneva #117-118, Vienna #35-36, Souvenir Card #24

UN Conference on Trade and Development

1983

398PDa	Card, #397PD-398PD, #G117PD-G118PD, #V35PD-V36PD, approval handstamp (4)	—
398PDb	Card, #397PD-398PD, #G117PD, #V36PD, essays of #G118 and #V35, (not approved, undated) (5)	1,300.
398PDc	As #398PDb, with red dot essays (not approved, dated) (5)	—
SC24PD	With approval handstamp (4)	—
SC24TC	With "not approved" handstamp (5)	—
397PP	5 items (50)	—
398PP	7 items (50)	—
G117PP	5 items (50)	—
G118PP	6 items (50)	—
V35PP	6 items (50)	—
V36PP	7 items (50)	—
397PI	Pair (50)	—
398PI	Pair (50)	—
G117PI	Pair (50)	—
G118PI	Pair (50)	—
V35PI	Pair (50)	—
V36PI	Pair (50)	—

Essays of Nos. G118 and V35 have blue rectangle instead of blue and yellow triangles on bottom row of flags, along with other differences. No. 398PDb has essays showing flag with green dot in 3rd row; No. 398PDc has red dot on this flag. No. SC24TC has Nos. G118 and V35 with lighter box bottom.

New York #399-414

Flags

1983

403PD	With approval handstamp (1)	240.
406PDa	Card, #399PD-402PD, 404PD-406PD, #403 essay (5)	1,600.
414PDa	Card, #407PD, 409PD-414PD, #408 essay (5)	2,100.
399-414PP	Set of 20 sheets (1)	—
399-414PI	Set of 4 sheets (2)	5,000.

The essay of No. 403 has fewer sun rays than on the issued stamp. The essay of No. 408 has incomplete ring above crest and thinner garlands at left and right. Nos. 413PD-414PD are marked "not approved" on No. 414PDa, but there is no appreciable difference between these and the issued stamps. On Nos. 399-414PP, there are five progressive proof sheets per issued sheet.

New York #415-416, Geneva #119-120, Vienna #37-38

Universal Declaration of Human Rights, 35th Anniv.

1983

415PD	mounted on presentation folder, perforated	450.
416PD	mounted on presentation folder, perforated	450.
G120PDa	Card, #G119PD-G120PD (10)	500.
V37PD	mounted on presentation folder, perforated	325.
V38PD	mounted on presentation folder, perforated	400.
415PP	7 items, with "Muster" overprint (32)	—
415PPa	6 items, without "Muster" overprint (24)	—
	Horiz. pair with vert. gutter, without "Muster" overprint (4)	—
416PP	7 items, with "Muster" overprint (24)	—
	Horiz. pair with vert. gutter, with "Muster" overprint (16)	—
416PPa	6 items, without "Muster" overprint (24)	—
	Horiz. pair with vert. gutter, without "Muster" overprint (4)	—
G119PP	7 items, with "Muster" overprint (24)	—
	Horiz. pair with vert. gutter, with "Muster" overprint (16)	—
G119PPa	6 items, without "Muster" overprint (24)	—
	Horiz. pair with vert. gutter, without "Muster" overprint (4)	—
G120PP	7 items, with "Muster" overprint (24)	—
	Horiz. pair with vert. gutter, with "Muster" overprint (16)	—
G120PPa	6 items, without "Muster" overprint (24)	—
	Horiz. pair with vert. gutter, without "Muster" overprint (4)	—
V37PP	7 items, with "Muster" overprint (24)	—
	Horiz. pair with vert. gutter, with "Muster" overprint (16)	—
V37PPa	6 items, without "Muster" overprint (24)	—
	Horiz. pair with vert. gutter, without "Muster" overprint (4)	—
V38PP	7 items, with "Muster" overprint (24)	—
	Horiz. pair with vert. gutter, with "Muster" overprint (16)	—
V38PPa	6 items, without "Muster" overprint (24)	—
	Horiz. pair with vert. gutter, without "Muster" overprint (4)	—
415PI	Pair (64)	—
	Horiz. pair with vert. gutter (16)	—
416PI	Pair (64)	—
	Horiz. pair with vert. gutter (16)	—
G119PI	Pair (64)	—
	Horiz. pair with vert. gutter (16)	—
G120PI	Pair (64)	—
	Horiz. pair with vert. gutter (16)	—
V37PI	Pair (64)	—
	Horiz. pair with vert. gutter (16)	—
V38PI	Pair (64)	—
	Horiz. pair with vert. gutter (16)	—

On Nos. 415PP-416PP, G119PP-G120PP, V37PP-V38PP, one of the items with "Muster" overprint is a finished imperforate.

New York #417-418, Geneva #121, Vienna #39, Souvenir Card #25

Intl. Conference on Population

1984

417PD	(4)	240.
418PD	(4)	250.
G121PD	(4)	250.
V39PD	(4)	250.
SC25PD	With "not approved" handstamp (9)	—
417PP	8 items (50)	—
418PP	7 items (50)	—
G121PP	8 items (50)	—
V39PP	8 items (50)	—
417PI	Pair (50)	—
418PI	Pair (50)	—
G121PI	Pair (50)	—
V39PI	Pair (50)	—

No. 418PP does not include the blue progressive proof found in No. 417PP.

New York #419-420, Geneva #122-123, Vienna #40-41

World Food Day

1984

419PD	(5)	—
420PDa	Card, #419PD-420PD, #G122PD-G123PD, #V40PD-V41PD with "not approved" handstamp (8)	1,500.
419PP	6 items (50)	—
420PP	6 items (50)	—
G122PP	6 items (50)	—
G123PP	6 items (50)	—
V40PP	6 items (50)	—
V41PP	6 items (50)	—
419PI	Pair (50)	—
420PI	Pair (50)	—
G122PI	Pair (50)	—
G123PI	Pair (50)	—
V40PI	Pair (50)	—
V41PI	Pair (50)	—

There is no appreciable difference between approved and not approved examples of No. 419PD.

New York #421-422, Geneva #124-125, Vienna #42-43

World Heritage Sites

1984

422PDa	Card, #421PD-422PD, with approval handstamp (4)	875.
G125PDa	Card, #G124PD-G125PD, with approval handstamp (4)	625.
V43PDa	Card, #V42PD-V43PD, with approval handstamp (4)	625.
V43TCa	Card, #V42PD (darker sky), V43PD prussian blue sky, "not approved" handstamp (8)	875.
421PP	6 items (80)	—
	Horiz. pair with vert. gutter (10)	—
422PP	6 items (80)	—
	Horiz. pair with vert. gutter (10)	—
G124PP	6 items (80)	—
	Horiz. pair with vert. gutter (10)	—
G125PP	6 items (80)	—
	Horiz. pair with vert. gutter (10)	—
V42PP	6 items (80)	—
	Horiz. pair with vert. gutter (10)	—
V43PP	6 items (80)	—
	Horiz. pair with vert. gutter (10)	—
421PI	Pair (80)	—
	Horiz. pair with vert. gutter (20)	—
422PI	Pair (80)	—
	Horiz. pair with vert. gutter (20)	—
G124PI	Pair (80)	—
	Horiz. pair with vert. gutter (20)	—
G125PI	Pair (80)	—
	Horiz. pair with vert. gutter (20)	—

V42PI	Pair (80)	—
	Horiz. pair with vert. gutter (20)	—
V43PI	Pair (80)	—
	Horiz. pair with vert. gutter (20)	—

Four cards like No. 422PDa with "not approved" handstamp contain essays with slightly different vignettes having taller sky area that is brighter blue and with less distinct designs. Four cards like No. G125PDa contain essays lacking "F.S." before denominations.

New York #423-424, Geneva #126-127, Vienna #44-45
Future for Refugees

1984

424PDa	Card, #423PD-424PD, #G126PD-G127PD, #V44PD-V45PD (2)	—
424PDb	Card, #423PD, #G127PD, 2 each #424PD, #G126PD, #V44PD-V45PD (3)	—
424PDc	Card, #423PD-424PD, #G126PD-G127PD, #V44PD-V45PD, #423TC-424TC, #G126TC-G127TC, V44TC-V45TC (5)	2,750.
424TCa	Card, #423TC-424TC, #G126TC-G127TC, #V44TC-V45TC (1)	—
423PP	2 items (50)	—
G126PP	2 items (50)	—
G127PP	2 items (50)	—
V44PP	2 items (50)	—
V45PP	2 items (50)	—
423PI	Pair (50)	—
424PI	Pair (25)	—
G126PI	Pair (50)	—
G127PI	Pair (50)	—
V44PI	Pair (50)	—
V45PI	Pair (50)	—

Trial color items have backgrounds in buff.

New York #425-440
Flags

1984

432PDa	Card, #429PD-432PD (1)	925.
432PDb	Card, 2 each #429PD-432PD (2)	—
436PDa	Card, #425PD, 427PD, 433PD-436PD, essays of #426, 428 (5)	1,850.
440PDa	Card, #437PD-440PD (1)	925.
440PDb	Card, 2 each #437PD-440PD (2)	—
425-440PP	Set of 21 sheets (1)	—
425-440PI	Set of 4 sheets (2)	4,250.

Essays of Nos. 426 and 428 have country name in smaller type. On Nos. 425-440PP, there are six progressive proof sheets for the issued sheet containing Nos. 429-432, and five progressive proof sheets for the issued sheets containing Nos. 425-428, 433-436 and 437-440.

New York #441-442, Geneva #128, Vienna #46-47, Souvenir Card #26
Intl. Youth Year

1984

441PD	With approval handstamp (4)	350.
442PD	With approval handstamp (3)	240.
G128PD	With approval handstamp (4)	300.
V46PD	(4)	250.
V47PD	(4)	300.
SC26PD	With approval handstamp (4)	—
G128TC	Greenish black strand in center (not approved) (5)	325.
SC26TC	With #G128TC "not approved" handstamp (5)	—
441PP	7 items (50)	—
442PP	9 items (50)	—
G128PP	9 items (50)	—
V46PP	7 items (50)	—
V47PP	7 items (50)	—
441PI	Pair (50)	—
442PI	Pair (50)	—
G128PI	Pair (50)	—
V46PI	Pair (50)	—
V47PI	Pair (50)	—

Five "not approved" essays of No. 441 and four of No. 442 have "N" in "Nations" not touching white frame at bottom. A card with a cutout version of the approved No. 442, but with a "not approved" handstamp, and a card with a cutout essay of No. 442 with an "approved" handstamp exist, probably in error.

New York #443, Geneva #129-130, Vienna #48, Souvenir Card #27
Intl. Labor Organization

1985

443PD	Card, imperforate sheet of 50 stamps (1)	—
443PDa	Card, #443PD (single), #G129PD (single) (4)	500.
G130PDa	Card, #G130PD (single), #V48PD (single) (4)	550.
V48PD	Card, imperforate sheet of 50 stamps (4)	—
SC27PD	With approval handstamp (4)	—
443PI	Pair (50)	—
G129PI	Pair (50)	—
G130PI	Pair (50)	—
V48PI	Pair (50)	—

Essays of No. SC27 exist which have the 1954 stamp with a buff background.

New York #444, Geneva #131-132, Vienna #49
UN University

1985

444PDa	Card, #444PD, #G131PD-G132PD, #V49PD, with approval handstamp (5)	1,150.
G132TC	Bright colors in background ("not approved" handstamp) (6)	400.
444PP	6 items (50)	—
G131PP	6 items (50)	—
G132PP	6 items (50)	—
V49PP	6 items (50)	—
444PI	Pair (50)	—
G131PI	Pair (50)	—
G132PI	Pair (50)	—
V49PI	Pair (50)	—

New York #445-446, Geneva #133-134, Vienna #50-51
Definitives

1985

445PDa	Card, #445PD, #G133PD-G134PD, #V50PD-V51PD, #446TC ("not approved handstamp") (4)	1,600.
446PDa	Card, #445PD-446PD, #G134PD (4)	775.
445PP	4 items (50)	—
446PP	5 items (50)	—
G133PP	7 items (50)	—
G134PP	3 items (50)	—
V50PP	5 items (50)	—
V51PP	5 items (50)	—
V50PI	Pair (50)	—
V51PI	Pair (50)	—

No. 446TC has a lighter blue emblem. Other items in No. 445PDa were declared "not approved," but do not have any appreciable difference from approved items.

New York #447-449, Geneva #135-137, Vienna #52-54
UN, 40th Anniv.

1985

447PDa	Card, 4 each #447PD, #G135PD, #V52PD (1)	—
448PDa	Card, 4 each #448PD, #G136PD, #V53PD (1)	—
449PDa	Card, #447PD-449PD, #G135PD-G137PD, #V52PD-V54PD (1)	1,850.
449PDb	Card, #449PD, #G137PD, #V54PD (4)	—
447PP	5 items (50)	—
448PP	5 items (50)	—
449PP	6 items (36)	—
G135PP	5 items (50)	—
G136PP	5 items (50)	—
G137PP	6 items (36)	—
V52PP	5 items (50)	—
V53PP	5 items (50)	—
V54PP	6 items (36)	—
447PI	Pair (50)	—
448PI	Pair (50)	—
449PI	Pair of souvenir sheets (27)	—
G135PI	Pair (50)	—
G136PI	Pair (50)	—
G137PI	Pair of souvenir sheets (27)	—
V52PI	Pair (50)	—
V53PI	Pair (50)	—
V54PI	Pair of souvenir sheets (27)	—

New York #450-465
Flags

1985

465PDa	Card, #450PD-455PD, 457PD-465PD, essay of #456 (5)	2,900.
450-465PP	Set of 24 sheets (1)	—
450-465PI	Set of 4 sheets (2)	4,000.

Essay of Nos. 456 has thin-lined star. On Nos. 425-440PP, there are six progressive proof sheets per issued sheet.

New York #466-467, Geneva #138-139, Vienna #55-56, Souvenir Card #28
UNICEF Child Survival Campaign

1985

466PD	(4)	300.
466PDa	Card, with cut-up pane of 50 (1)	—
467PD	(4)	—
467PDa	Card, with cut-up pane of 50 (1)	—
G138PD	(4)	300.
G138PDa	Card, with cut-up pane of 50 (1)	—
G139PD	(4)	225.
G139PDa	Card, with cut-up pane of 50 (1)	—
V55PD	(4)	300.
V55PDa	Card, with cut-up pane of 50 (1)	—
V56PD	(4)	250.
V56PDa	Card, with cut-up pane of 50 (1)	—
SC28PD	(4)	—
466PP	5 items (50)	—
467PP	5 items (50)	—
G138PP	5 items (50)	—
G139PP	5 items (50)	—
V55PP	5 items (50)	—
V56PP	5 items (50)	—
466PI	Pair (50)	—
467PI	Pair (50)	—
G138PI	Pair (50)	—
G139PI	Pair (50)	—
V55PI	Pair (50)	—
V56PI	Pair (50)	—

New York #468, Geneva #140, Vienna #57
Africa in Crisis

1986

468PDa	Card, #468PD, #G140PD, essay of #V57 (4)	—
468PP	5 items (50)	—
G140PP	4 items (50)	—
V57PP	4 items (50)	—
468PI	Pair (50)	—
G140PI	Pair (50)	—
V57PI	Pair (50)	—

One example of No. 468PDa has essay of No. V57 corrected to show small loop of "8" at top as in the issued stamp.

New York #472a, Geneva #144a, Vienna #61a
UN Development Program

1986

472aPD	(4)	825.
472aPDa	Card, pane of 10 blocks (2)	—
G144aPD	(4)	825.
G144aPDa	Card, pane of 10 blocks (2)	—
V61aPD	(4)	825.
V61aPDa	Card, pane of 10 blocks (2)	—
472aPP	6 items (10 blocks)	—
G144aPP	6 items (10 blocks)	—
V61aPP	6 items (10 blocks)	—
472aPI	Pair (20)	—
G144aPI	Pair (20)	—
V61aPI	Pair (20)	—

Geneva #145
Definitive

1986

G145PD	(5)	—
G145PP	5 items (50)	—
G145PI	Pair (50)	—

New York #473-474, Geneva #146-147, Vienna #62-63, Souvenir Card #29
Philately

1986

473PDa	Partial pane of 39 with approval handstamp on reverse (1)	—
473PDb	Full pane of 50 with approval handstamp on reverse (3)	—
474PDa	Imperforate pane of 50 with approval handstamp on reverse (4)	—
G146PDa	Imperforate pane of 50 with approval handstamp on reverse (4)	—
G147PDa	Partial pane of 41 with approval handstamp on reverse (1)	—
G147PDb	Full pane of 50 with approval handstamp on reverse (3)	—
V62PDa	Imperforate pane of 50 with approval handstamp on reverse (4)	—
V63PDa	Partial pane of 41 with approval handstamp on reverse (1)	—
V63PDb	Full pane of 50 with approval handstamp on reverse (4)	—
SC29PD	(3)	—
473TC	greenish black (5)	725.
474TC	purple (1)	725.
474TC	blue (1)	725.
474TC	red brown (1)	725.
474TC	olive brown (1)	725.
474TC	dark green (1)	725.
G146TC	purple (1)	725.
G146TC	blue (1)	725.
G146TC	reddish purple (1)	725.
G146TC	greenish black (1)	725.
G146TC	dark olive brown (1)	725.
G147TC	dark blue (5)	775.
V62TC	purple (1)	725.
V62TC	blue (1)	725.
V62TC	red brown (1)	725.
V62TC	greenish black (1)	725.
V62TC	dark olive brown (1)	725.
V63TC	greenish black (5)	775.

New York #475-476, Geneva #148-149, Vienna #64-65, Souvenir Card #30
International Peace Year

1986

475PD	(4)	300.
475PDa	Card, imperforate pane of 50 (1)	—
476PD	(4)	250.
476PDa	Card, imperforate pane of 50 (1)	—
G148PD	(4)	450.
G148PDa	Card, imperforate pane of 50 (1)	—
G149PD	(4)	250.
V64PD	(1)	300.
V65PD	(4)	—
V65PDa	Card, imperforate pane of 50 (1)	—
SC30PD	(4)	—
475PP	4 items (50)	—
476PP	4 items (50)	—
G148PP	4 items (50)	—
G149PP	4 items (50)	—
V64PP	4 items (50)	—
V65PP	3 items (50)	—
475PI	Pair (50)	—
476PI	Pair (50)	—
G148PI	Pair (50)	—
G149PI	Pair (50)	—
V64PI	Pair (50)	—
V65PI	Pair (50)	—

Essays of No. V64 with 7s denominations exist in three cards with singles and one card with an imperforate pane of 50.

New York #477-492
Flags

1986

492PDa	Card, #477PD-492PD (5)	3,250.
477-492PP	Set of 24 sheets (1)	—
477-492PI	Set of 4 sheets (2)	4,000.

On Nos. 477-492PP, there are six progressive proof sheets per issued sheet.

New York #493, Geneva #150, Vienna #66
World Federation of UN Associations, 40th Anniv.

1986

493PD	(3)	525.
493PDa	Imperforate souvenir sheet with cancel lines added (1)	—
G150PD	(3)	300.
G150PDa	Imperforate souvenir sheet with cancel lines added (1)	—
V66PD	(3)	400.
V66PDa	Imperforate souvenir sheet with cancel lines added (1)	—
493PP	8 items (16)	—
G150PP	11 items (16)	—
V66PP	6 items (16)	—
493PI	souvenir sheets (32)	—
G150PI	souvenir sheets (32)	—
V66PI	souvenir sheets (32)	—

New York #494, Geneva #151, Vienna #67
Trygve Lie

1987

494PD	On imperforate sheet layout (1)	—
494PDa	Card, #494PD, #G151PD, V67PD (4)	725.
G151PD	On imperforate sheet layout (1)	—
V67PD	On imperforate sheet layout (1)	—
494PP	10 items (50)	—
G151PP	10 items (50)	—
V67PP	10 items (50)	—
494PI	Pair (50)	—
G151PI	Pair (100)	—
V67PI	Pair (50)	—

Geneva #152-153
Definitives

1987

G152PD	(1)	375.
G153PD	(4)	—
G153TCa	Card, 2 #G153TC dark blue panel (5)	—
G153TCb	Card, imperforate pane of 50 #G153TC dark blue panel (2)	525.
G152PP	6 items (50)	—
G153PP	5 items (50)	—
G152PI	Pair (50)	—
G153PI	Pair (50)	—

Six essays of No. G152 with design 33mm high exist on cards marked "approved text only."

New York #495-496, Geneva #154-155, Vienna #68-69, Souvenir Card #31
International Year of Shelter for the Homeless

1987

496PDa	Card, #495PD-496PD, #G154PD-G155PD, #V68PD-V69PD (4)	1,350.
SC31PD	(3)	—
495PP	6 items (80)	—
	Horiz. pair with vert. gutter (10)	—
496PP	6 items (80)	—
	Horiz. pair with vert. gutter (10)	—
G154PP	6 items (80)	—
	Horiz. pair with vert. gutter (10)	—
G155PP	6 items (80)	—
	Horiz. pair with vert. gutter (10)	—
V68PP	6 items (80)	—
	Horiz. pair with vert. gutter (10)	—
V69PP	6 items (80)	—
	Horiz. pair with vert. gutter (10)	—
495PI	Pair (80)	—
	Horiz. pair with vert. gutter (20)	—
496PI	Pair (80)	—
	Horiz. pair with vert. gutter (20)	—
G154PI	Pair (80)	—
	Horiz. pair with vert. gutter (20)	—
G155PI	Pair (80)	—
	Horiz. pair with vert. gutter (20)	—
V68PI	Pair (80)	—
	Horiz. pair with vert. gutter (20)	—
V69PI	Pair (80)	—
	Horiz. pair with vert. gutter (20)	—

New York #497-498, Geneva #156-157, Vienna #70-71
Fight Drug Abuse

1987

498PDa	Card, #497PD-498PD, #G156PD-G157PD, #V70PD-V71PD with approval handstamp (5)	1,450.
497PP	8 items (50)	—
498PP	8 items (50)	—
G156PP	8 items (50)	—
G157PP	8 items (50)	—
V70PP	8 items (50)	—
V71PP	8 items (50)	—
497PI	Pair (100)	—
498PI	Pair (100)	—
G156PI	Pair (100)	—
G157PI	Pair (100)	—
V70PI	Pair (100)	—
V71PI	Pair (100)	—

Six "not approved" cards contain essays of the six stamps, each lacking the white line separating the halves of the vignette.

Vienna #72-73
Definitives

1987

V73PDa	Card, #V72PD-V73PD (5)	575.
V72PP	8 items (50)	—
V73PP	7 items (50)	—
V72PI	Pair (100)	—
V73PI	Pair (100)	—

New York #499-514
Flags

1987

511PDa	Card, #500PD, 501PD, 503PD, 507PD, 509PD, 511PD (1)	—
514PDa	Card, #499PD-514PD (5)	3,750.
514PDb	Card, #499PD, 500PD, 502PD, 504PD-506PD, 508PD, 510PD, 512PD-514PD (1)	—
499-514PP	Set of 24 sheets (1)	—
499-502PI	Sheet (2)	—
503-506PI	Sheet (2)	—

On Nos. 499-514PP, there are six progressive proof sheets per issued sheet.

New York #515-516, Geneva #158-159, Vienna #74-75
United Nations Day

1987

515PDa	Card, #515PD, #V74PD, essay of #G158 (1)	—
516PDa	Card, #516PD, #G159PD, #V75PD (1)	—
516PDb	Card, #515PD-516PD, #G159PD, #V74PD-V75PD, essay of #G158 (4)	1,250.
515PP	8 items (36)	—
	Cross gutter block (3)	—
	Horiz. pair with vert. gutter (6)	—
	Vert. pair with horiz. gutter (18)	—
516PP	8 items (36)	—
	Cross gutter block (3)	—
	Horiz. pair with vert. gutter (6)	—
	Vert. pair with horiz. gutter (18)	—
G158PP	8 items (36)	—
	Cross gutter block (3)	—
	Horiz. pair with vert. gutter (6)	—
	Vert. pair with horiz. gutter (18)	—
G159PP	8 items (36)	—
	Cross gutter block (3)	—
	Horiz. pair with vert. gutter (6)	—
	Vert. pair with horiz. gutter (18)	—
V74PP	8 items (36)	—
	Cross gutter block (3)	—
	Horiz. pair with vert. gutter (6)	—
	Vert. pair with horiz. gutter (18)	—
V75PP	8 items (36)	—
	Cross gutter block (3)	—
	Horiz. pair with vert. gutter (6)	—
	Vert. pair with horiz. gutter (18)	—
515PI	Pair (12)	—
516PI	Pair (12)	—
G158PI	Pair (28)	—
	Cross gutter block (3)	—
	Horiz. pair with vert. gutter (6)	—
	Vert. pair with horiz. gutter (18)	—
G159PI	Pair (28)	—
	Cross gutter block (3)	—
	Horiz. pair with vert. gutter (6)	—
	Vert. pair with horiz. gutter (18)	—
V74PI	Pair (28)	—
	Cross gutter block (3)	—
	Horiz. pair with vert. gutter (6)	—
	Vert. pair with horiz. gutter (18)	—
V75PI	Pair (28)	—
	Cross gutter block (3)	—
	Horiz. pair with vert. gutter (6)	—
	Vert. pair with horiz. gutter (18)	—

Essay of No. G158 lacks accent in "Journée."

New York #517-518, Geneva #160-161, Vienna #76-77, Souvenir Card #32
Immunize Every Child

1987

518PDa	Card, #517PD-518PD, #G161PD, #V76PD-V77PD, 35c essay of #G160 (11)	1,500.
SC32PD	(11)	—
517PP	11 items (50)	—
518PP	11 items (50)	—
G160PP	11 items (50)	—
G161PP	12 items (50)	—
V76PP	12 items (50)	—
V77PP	9 items (50)	—
5178PI	Pair (50)	—
518PI	Pair (50)	—
G160PI	Pair (75)	—
G161PI	Pair (75)	—
V76PI	Pair (75)	—
V77PI	Pair (75)	—

All examples of No. SC32PD have the essay of No. G160. There is no appreciable difference between approved and not approved examples of Nos. 518PDa or SC32PD.

New York #519-520, Geneva #162-163, Vienna #78-79
International Fund for Agricultural Development

1988

520PDa	Card, #519PD-520PD, #G162PD-G163PD, #V78PD-V79PD (4)	1,550.
519PP	8 items (50)	—
520PP	8 items (50)	—
G162PP	9 items (50)	—
G163PP	9 items (50)	—
V78PP	9 items (50)	—
V79PP	9 items (50)	—
519PI	Pair (50)	—
520PI	Pair (50)	—
G162PI	Pair (50)	—
G163PI	Pair (50)	—
V78PI	Pair (50)	—
V79PI	Pair (50)	—

New York #521, Geneva #164
Definitives

1988

521PD	(4)	575.
G164PD	(6)	300.
521PP	6 items (50)	—
G164PP	11 items (50)	—
521PI	Pair (50)	—
G164PI	Pair (50)	—

New York #523a, Geneva #166a, Vienna #81a
Survival of the Forests

1988

523aPDa	Card, imperforate pane of 6 pairs with approval handstamp (6)	2,750.
523aPDb	Card, perforated pane of 6 pairs with approval handstamp (1)	—
G166aPDa	Card, imperforate pane of 6 pairs with approval handstamp (7)	2,400.
V81aPDa	Card, imperforate pane of 6 pairs with approval handstamp (7)	2,400.
523aPP	8 items (6 pairs)	—
G166aPP	8 items (6 pairs)	—
V81aPP	8 items (6 pairs)	—
523aPI	Pair (12)	—
G166aPI	Pair (24)	—
V81aPI	Pair (24)	—

Panes on Nos. 523aPDa, 523aPDb, G166aPDa, V81aPDa are not affixed to cards but are between stamp mounts.

New York #524-525, Geneva #167-168, Vienna #82-83, Souvenir Card #33
Intl. Volunteer Day

1988

524PDa	Card, #524PD, #G167PD-G168PD, #V82PD-V83PD with approval handstamp (4)	1,400.
525PDa	Card, #525PD, #G168PD, #V83PD, essays of #524, #G167, #V82 with "not approved" handstamp (4)	875.
SC33PD	(4)	—
SC33TC	light blue signature (4)	—
524PP	6 items (40)	—
525PP	6 items (40)	—
525PPa	Horiz. se-tenant pair with vert. gutter, #524PP-525PP (10)	—
G167PP	6 items (40)	—
G168PP	6 items (40)	—
G168PPa	Horiz. se-tenant pair with vert. gutter, #G167PP-G168PP (10)	—
V82PP	6 items (40)	—
V83PP	6 items (40)	—
V83PPa	Horiz. se-tenant pair with vert. gutter, #V82PP-V83PP (10)	—
524PI	Pair (70)	—
525PI	Pair (70)	—
G167PI	Pair (70)	—
G168PI	Pair (70)	—
V82PI	Pair (70)	—
V83PI	Pair (70)	—

Essays have incomplete dates at bottom.

New York #526-527, Geneva #169-170, Vienna #84-85, Souvenir Card #34
Health in Sports

1988

526PD	With approval handstamp(2)	250.
526PDa	Card, #526PD, #527TC (1)	—
526PDb	Card, imperforate pane of 50 #526PD (1)	—
527PD	(6)	150.
527PDa	Card, 2 #527PD (1)	—
527PDb	Card, imperforate pane of 50 #527PD (2)	—
G169PD	(6)	350.
G169PDa	Card, 2 #G169PD (1)	—
G169PDb	Card, imperforate pane of 50 #G169PD (2)	—
G170PD	With approval handstamp (2)	350.
G170PDa	Card, #G170PD, #G170TC (1)	—
G170PDb	Card, imperforate pane of 50 #G170PD (1)	—
V84PD	With approval handstamp (2)	450.
V84PDa	Card, #V84PD, #V84TC (1)	—
V84PDb	Card, imperforate pane of 50 #V84PD (1)	—
V85PD	(6)	450.

V85PDa	Card, 2 #V85PD (1)	—
V85PDb	Card, imperforate pane of 50 #V85PD (2)	—
SC34PD	With approval handstamp (5)	—
526TC	Card, darker brown in LL part of vignette (not approved) (4)	325.
526TCa	Card, imperforate pane of 50 #526TC (1)	—
G170TC	Card, black "F.S." (not approved) (4)	—
G170TCa	Card, imperforate pane of 50 #G170TC (1)	—
V84TC	Card, red splotches in UL of vignette (not approved) (4)	325.
V84TCa	Card, imperforate pane of 50 #V84TC (109)	—
SC34TC	With #526TC (not approved) (4)	—
526PP	4 items (50)	—
527PP	4 items (50)	—
G169PP	4 items (50)	—
G170PP	4 items (50)	—
V84PP	5 items (50)	—
V85PP	4 items (50)	—
526PI	Pair (50)	—
527PI	Pair (50)	—
G169PI	Pair (50)	—
G170PI	Pair (45)	—
V84PI	Pair (50)	—
V85PI	Pair (50)	—

There is no appreciable difference between approved and not approved examples of Nos. 527PD, G169PD and V85PD.

New York #528-543
Flags

1988

543PDa	Card, #540PD, 543PD (2)	425.
543PDb	Card, #540PD, 543PD, 22c essays of #528-539, 541-542 (2)	—
528-543PP	Set of 24 sheets (1)	—
528-543PI	Set of 4 sheets (2)	3,000.

Nine cards each containing 22c essays of Nos. 528-543 exist. Value $2,900 each. On Nos. 528-543PP, there are six progressive proof sheets per issued sheet.

New York #544-545, Geneva #171-172, Vienna #86-87
Universal Declaration of Human Rights, 40th Anniv.

1988

545PDa	Card, #544PD-545PD, #G171PD-G172PD, #V86PD-V87PD (5)	2,900.
G172PDa	Card, #172PD, 90c essay of #G172 (6)	775.
544PP	6 items (50)	—
545PP	6 items (1)	—
G171PP	6 items (50)	—
G172PP	6 items (1)	—
V86PP	6 items (50)	—
V87PP	6 items (1)	—
544PI	Pair (50)	—
545PI	souvenir sheets (2)	650.
G171PI	Pair (50)	—
G172PI	souvenir sheets (2)	975.
V86PI	Pair (50)	625.
V87PI	souvenir sheets (2)	—

New York #546-547, Geneva #173-174, Vienna #88-89, Souvenir Card #35
World Bank

1989

547PDa	Card, #546PD-547PD, #G173PD-G174PD, #V88PD-V89PD with approval handstamp (4)	1,250.
547PDb	Card, #547PD in slightly lighter colors, #V88PD, #G173TC, essays of #546, #G174, #V89 (5)	1,150.
SC35PD	With "29 Aug. 1988" handstamp on back (4)	—
546PP	6 items (40)	—
547PP	6 items (40)	—
547PPa	Vert. se-tenant pair with horiz. gutter, #546PP-547PP (10)	—
G173PP	6 items (40)	—
G174PP	6 items (40)	—
G174PPa	Vert. se-tenant pair with horiz. gutter, #G173PP-G174PP (10)	—
V88PP	6 items (40)	—
V89PP	6 items (40)	—
V89PPa	Vert. se-tenant pair with horiz. gutter, #V88PP-V89PP (10)	—
546PI	Pair (40)	—
547PI	Pair (40)	—
G173PI	Pair (70)	—
G174PI	Pair (70)	—
G174PIa	Vert. se-tenant pair with horiz. gutter, #G173PI-G174PI (10)	—
V88PI	Pair (50)	—
V89PI	Pair (50)	—

No. G173TC has lighter orange background. Essays of Nos. 546, G174, and V89 have incomplete years at bottom.

New York #548, Geneva #175, Vienna #90
UN Peace-keeping Force

1989

548PD	Imperforate pane of 50 with "not approved" handstamp (1)	—
548PDa	Card, #548PD, #G175PD, #V90PD (5)	—
G175PD	Imperforate pane of 50 with "not approved" handstamp (1)	—
V90PD	Imperforate pane of 50 with "not approved" handstamp (1)	—
548PP	6 items (90)	—
	Horiz. pair with vert. gutter (5)	—
G175PP	6 items (90)	—
	Horiz. pair with vert. gutter (5)	—
V90PP	6 items (90)	—
	Horiz. pair with vert. gutter (5)	—
548PI	Pair (70)	—
G175PI	Pair (138)	—
	Horiz. pair with vert. gutter (10)	—
V90PI	Pair (138)	—
	Horiz. pair with vert. gutter (10)	—

There is no appreciable difference between approved and not approved examples of No. 548PDa.

New York #549
Definitive

1989

549PD	(9)	—
549PP	6 items (64)	—
	Cross gutter block (1)	—
	Horiz. pair with vert. gutter (8)	—
	Vert. pair with horiz. gutter (8)	—
549PI	Pair (24)	—

There is no appreciable difference between approved and not approved examples of No. 549PD.

New York #550-551, Geneva #176-177, Vienna #91-92, Souvenir Card #36
World Weather Watch

1989

551PDa	Card, #550PD-551PD, #G176PD-G177PD, #V91PD-V92PD (9)	—
SC36PD	(4)	—
550PP	6 items (40)	—
551PP	6 items (40)	—
551PPa	Vert. se-tenant pair with horiz. gutter, #550PP-551PP (10)	—
G176PP	6 items (40)	—
G177PP	6 items (40)	—
G177PPa	Vert. se-tenant pair with horiz. gutter, #G176PP-G177PP (10)	—
V91PP	6 items (40)	—
V92PP	6 items (40)	—
V92PPa	Vert. se-tenant pair with horiz. gutter, #V91PP-V92PP (10)	—
550PI	(50 pairs)	—
551PI	(50 pairs)	—
G176PI	(70 pairs)	—
G177PI	(70 pairs)	—
G177PIa	Vert. se-tenant pair with horiz. gutter, #G176PI-G177PI (10)	—
V91PI	(50 pairs)	—
V92PI	(50 pairs)	—

There is no appreciable difference between approved and not approved examples of No. 551PDa.

New York #552-553, Geneva #178-179, Vienna #93-94
Offices in Vienna, 10th Anniv.

1989

552PD	With approval handstamp (4)	—
553PD	(4)	—
G178PD	(4)	—
G179PDa	Card, #G179PD, #G179TC orange background, #G179TC dull green background (4)	—
V93PD	(4)	—
V94PD	(9)	—
552PP	10 items (25)	—
553PP	12 items (25)	—
G178PP	10 items (25)	—
G179PP	10 items (25)	—
V93PP	10 items (25)	—
V94PP	10 items (25)	—
552PI	(24 pairs)	—
553PI	(24 pairs)	—
G178PI	(24 pairs)	—
G179PI	(24 pairs)	—
V93PI	(24 pairs)	—
V94PI	(24 pairs)	—

Five not approved essays of #552 have clearly defined cross-hatching in background. There is no appreciable difference between approved and not approved examples of No. V94PD. One item from No. G179PP and V93PP is blank as it is from progressive proof sheet showing only black sheet margins.

New York #554-569
Flags

1989

568PDa	Card, #558PD-561PD, 563PD, 564PD, 566PD-568PD (6)	—
569PDa	Card, #554PD-569PD (5)	—
554-569PP	Set of 24 sheets (1)	—
554-569PI	Set of 4 sheets (2)	—

On Nos. 554-569PP, there are six progressive proof sheets per issued sheet.

New York #570-571, Geneva #180-181, Vienna #95-96
Human Rights

1989

570PD	Strip of 3 + 3 labels (4)	—
571PD	Strip of 3 + 3 labels (4)	—
571PDa	Card, #570PD-571PD, #G180PD-G181PD, #V95PD-V96PD (5)	—
G180PD	3 singles or strip of 3 + 3 labels (4)	—
G181PD	Strip of 3 + 3 labels (4)	—
V95PD	Strip of 3 + 3 labels (4)	—
V96PD	3 singles or strip of 3 + 3 labels (4)	—
570PP	6 items (20)	—
	Cross gutter block (1)	—
	Horiz. pair with vert. gutter (2)	—
	Vert. pair with horiz. gutter (10)	—
571PP	6 items (20)	—
	Cross gutter block (1)	—
	Horiz. pair with vert. gutter (2)	—
	Vert. pair with horiz. gutter (10)	—
G180PP	6 items (20)	—
	Cross gutter block (1)	—
	Horiz. pair with vert. gutter (2)	—
	Vert. pair with horiz. gutter (10)	—
G181PP	6 items (20)	—
	Cross gutter block (1)	—
	Horiz. pair with vert. gutter (2)	—
	Vert. pair with horiz. gutter (10)	—
V95PP	6 items (48)	—
	Cross gutter block (1)	—
	Horiz. pair with vert. gutter (2)	—
	Vert. pair with horiz. gutter (10)	—
V96PP	6 items (48)	—
	Cross gutter block (1)	—
	Horiz. pair with vert. gutter (2)	—
	Vert. pair with horiz. gutter (10)	—
570PI	(12 pairs)	—
	Cross gutter block (1)	—
	Horiz. pair with vert. gutter (2)	—
	Vert. pair with horiz. gutter (10)	—
571PI	(12 pairs)	—
	Cross gutter block (1)	—
	Horiz. pair with vert. gutter (2)	—
	Vert. pair with horiz. gutter (10)	—
G180PI	(20 pairs)	—
	Cross gutter block (1)	—
	Horiz. pair with vert. gutter (2)	—
	Vert. pair with horiz. gutter (10)	—
G181PI	(20 pairs)	—
	Cross gutter block (1)	—
	Horiz. pair with vert. gutter (2)	—
	Vert. pair with horiz. gutter (10)	—
V95PI	(20 pairs)	—
	Cross gutter block (1)	—
	Horiz. pair with vert. gutter (2)	—
	Vert. pair with horiz. gutter (10)	—
V96PI	(20 pairs)	—
	Cross gutter block (1)	—
	Horiz. pair with vert. gutter (2)	—
	Vert. pair with horiz. gutter (10)	—

New York #572, Geneva #182, Vienna #97
International Trade Center

1990

572PDa	Card, #572PD, #G182PD, #V97PD with approval handstamp (5)	—
572TCa	Card, #572TC blue green ship, #G182TC red orange ship, #V97TC light pink building, with "not approved" handstamp (6)	—
572PP	9 items (50)	—
G182PP	7 items (50)	—
V97PP	8 items (50)	—
572PI	(50 pairs)	—
G182PI	(75 pairs)	—
V97PI	(50 pairs)	—

Geneva #183, Vienna #98
Definitives

1990

G183PD	(6)	—
V98PD	Proof on large sheet with approval or "not approved" handstamp, and set of 7 progressive proofs on large sheets (9)	—
G183PP	9 items (1)	—
V98PP	7 items (50)	—
G183PI	(50 pairs)	—
V98PI	(50 pairs)	—

The not approved proofs of No. V98PD are slightly lighter in color than the approved proofs.

New York #573-574, Geneva #184-185, Vienna #99-100, Souvenir Card #37
Fight AIDS Worldwide

1990

573PDa	Card, #573PD, #G184PD, #V99PD (4)	—
574PDa	Card, #574PD, #G185PD, #573TC white background, #G184TC white background, #V99TC white background, 10s essay of #V100 (4)	—
SC37PD	(4)	—
573PP	7 items (50)	—
574PP	6 items (50)	—
G184PP	7 items (50)	—
G185PP	7 items (50)	—
V99PP	7 items (50)	—
V100PP	6 items (50)	—
573PI	(50 pairs)	—
574PI	(50 pairs)	—
G184PI	(75 pairs)	—
G185PI	(75 pairs)	—
V99PI	(75 pairs)	—
V100PI	(75 pairs)	—

New York #575-576, Geneva #186-187, Vienna #101-102
Medicinal Plants

1990
576PDa Card, #575PD-576PD, #G186PD-G187PD, #V101PD-V102PD (4) —
G187PD (4) —
G186PP 6 items (50) —
G187PP 6 items (50) —
V101PP 6 items (50) —
V102PP 6 items (50) —
575PI (50 pairs) —
576PI (50 pairs) —
G186PI (50 pairs) —
G187PI (50 pairs) —
V101PI (50 pairs) —
V102PI (50 pairs) —

New York #577-579, Geneva #188-190, Vienna #103-105
United Nations, 45th Anniv.

1990
578PDa Card, #577PD-578PD, #G188PD-G189PD, 6s essay of #V103, 8s essay of #V104 (4) —
579PDa Card, #579PD, #G190PD, #V105PD (4) —
577PP 8 items (320) —
Horiz. pair with vert. gutter (40) —
578PP 8 items (320) —
Horiz. pair with vert. gutter (40) —
579PP 8 items (100) —
G188PP 10 items (160) —
Horiz. pair with vert. gutter (20) —
G189PP 8 items (320) —
Horiz. pair with vert. gutter (40) —
G190PP 9 items (100) —
V103PP 8 items (320) —
Horiz. pair with vert. gutter (40) —
V104PP 8 items (320) —
Horiz. pair with vert. gutter (40) —
V105PP 8 items (100) —
577PI (80 pairs) —
Horiz. pair with vert. gutter (10) —
578PI (80 pairs) —
Horiz. pair with vert. gutter (10) —
579PI (100 souvenir sheets) —
G188PI (260 pairs) —
Horiz. pair with vert. gutter (40) —
G189PI (260 pairs) —
Horiz. pair with vert. gutter (40) —
G190PI (100 souvenir sheets) —
V103PI (260 pairs) —
Horiz. pair with vert. gutter (40) —
V104PI (260 pairs) —
Horiz. pair with vert. gutter (40) —
V105PI (100 souvenir sheets) —

New York #580-581, Geneva #191-192, Vienna #106-107, Souvenir Card #38
Crime Prevention

1990
581PDa Card, #580PD-581PD, #G191PD-G192PD, #V106PD-V107PD, #SC38PD (5) —
580PP 8 items (50) —
581PP 8 items (50) —
G191PP 8 items (50) —
G192PP 8 items (50) —
V106PP 8 items (100) —
V107PP 8 items (100) —
580PI (50 pairs) —
581PI (50 pairs) —
G191PI (75 pairs) —
G192PI (75 pairs) —
V106PI (75 pairs) —
V107PI (75 pairs) —

New York #582-583, Geneva #193-194, Vienna #108-109,
Human Rights

1990
582PDa Strip of 3 + 3 labels (9) —
583PDa Strip of 3 + 3 labels with approval handstamp (4) —
G193PDa Strip of 3 + 3 labels (9) —
G194PDa Strip of 3 + 3 labels (9) —
V108PDa Strip of 3 + 3 labels (9) —
V109PDa Strip of 3 + 3 labels (9) —
583TCa Strip of 3 + 3 labels (chocolate panels) with "not approved" handstamp (5) —
582PP 6 items (20) —
Cross gutter block (1) —
Horiz. pair with vert. gutter (2) —
Vert. pair with horiz. gutter (10) —
583PP 6 items (20) —
Cross gutter block (1) —
Horiz. pair with vert. gutter (2) —
Vert. pair with horiz. gutter (10) —
G193PP 6 items (20) —
Cross gutter block (1) —
Horiz. pair with vert. gutter (2) —
Vert. pair with horiz. gutter (10) —
G194PP 8 items (20) —
Cross gutter block (1) —
Horiz. pair with vert. gutter (2) —
Vert. pair with horiz. gutter (10) —
V108PP 6 items (20) —
Cross gutter block (1) —
Horiz. pair with vert. gutter (2) —
Vert. pair with horiz. gutter (10) —
V109PP 6 items (20) —
Cross gutter block (1) —
Horiz. pair with vert. gutter (2) —
Vert. pair with horiz. gutter (10) —
582PI (20 pairs) —
Cross gutter block (1) —
Horiz. pair with vert. gutter (2) —
Vert. pair with horiz. gutter (10) —
583PI (20 pairs) —
Cross gutter block (1) —
Horiz. pair with vert. gutter (2) —
Vert. pair with horiz. gutter (10) —
G193PI (20 pairs) —
Cross gutter block (1) —
Horiz. pair with vert. gutter (2) —
Vert. pair with horiz. gutter (10) —
G194PI (20 pairs) —
Cross gutter block (1) —
Horiz. pair with vert. gutter (2) —
Vert. pair with horiz. gutter (10) —
V108PI (20 pairs) —
Cross gutter block (1) —
Horiz. pair with vert. gutter (2) —
Vert. pair with horiz. gutter (10) —
V109PI (20 pairs) —
Cross gutter block (1) —
Horiz. pair with vert. gutter (2) —
Vert. pair with horiz. gutter (10) —

There is no appreciable difference between approved and not approved examples of Nos. 582PD, G193PD, G194PD, V108PD and V109PD.

New York #587a, Geneva #198a, Vienna #113a, Souvenir Card #39
Economic Council for Europe

1991
587aPDa Card, #587aPD, #G198aPD, #V113aPD with printed perforations (2) —
587aPDb Card, #587aPDa, SC39PD (1) —
SC39PD (1) —
587aPP 13 items (20 blocks) —
G198aPP 13 items (20 blocks) —
V113aPP 13 items (20 blocks) —
587aPI (40 blocks) —
G198aPI (40 blocks) —
V113aPI (40 blocks) —

Second sets of blocks of Nos. 587aPP and G198aPP with 10 items, and No. V113aPP with 11 items (some items differing from the 13 item set) exist.

New York #588-589, Geneva #199-200, Vienna #114-115
Namibian Independence

1991
588PDa Card, #588PD, #G199PD-G200PD, #V114PD-V115PD, 36c essay of #589 (8) —
589PDa Card, #588PD-589PD, #G199PD-G200PD, #V114PD-V115PD (1) —
588PP 7 items (50) —
589PP 7 items (50) —
G199PP 8 items (50) —
G200PP 8 items (50) —
V114PP 6 items (50) —
V115PP 6 items (50) —
588PI (100 pairs) —
589PI (100 pairs) —
G199PI (75 pairs) —
G200PI (75 pairs) —
V114PI (75 pairs) —
V115PI (75 pairs) —

New York #590-592, Geneva #201-202, Vienna #116
Definitives

1991
590PD With approval handstamp (4) —
592PD (4) —
592PDa Card, imperforate pane of 50 (1) —
G201PD (5) —
G202PDa Card, #G201PD-G202PD, #G213PD, #V116PD (4) —
590TC deep blue background (not approved) (5) —
592TC black (1) —
590PP 8 items (80) —
Horiz. pair with vert. gutter (10) —
591PP 4 items (150) —
G201PP 8 items (50) —
G202PP 7 items (50) —
V116PP 7 items (50) —
590PI (90 pairs) —
Horiz. pair with vert. gutter (10) —
591PI (175 pairs) —
592PI (50 pairs) —
G201PI (75 pairs) —
G202PI (100 pairs) —
V116PI (75 pairs) —

An essay of No. 592 with emblem in solid color exists.

New York #593-594, Geneva #203-204, Vienna #117-118, Souvenir Card #40
Rights of the Child

1991
593PDa Card, #593PD, #G203PD-G204PD, #V117PD-V118PD, 90c essay of #594 (6) —
594PDa Card, #593PD-594PD, #G203PD-G204PD, #V117PD-V118PD (4) —
594PDb Card, #593PD-594PD (4) —
SC40PD (4) —
593PP 9 items (50) —
594PP 9 items (50) —
G203PP 8 items (50) —
G204PP 7 items (50) —
V117PP 7 items (50) —
V118PP 7 items (50) —
SC40PP 15 items (1) —
593PI (75 pairs) —
594PI (75 pairs) —
G203PI (75 pairs) —
G204PI (75 pairs) —
V117PI (75 pairs) —
V118PI (75 pairs) —

No. SC40PP may not be a complete set of progressive proofs. Five essays of No. SC40PD with the 90c essay of No. 594 exist; one is attached to No. 593PDa.

New York #595-596, Geneva #205-206, Vienna #119-120,
Banning of Chemical Weapons

1991
596PDa Card, #595PD-596PD, #G205PD-G206PD, #V119PD-V120PD with approval handstamp (5) —
596PDb Card, #596PD, #G206PD, #V120PD, essays of #595, #G205, #V119 (each with gray panels taller than numerals) with "not approved" handstamp (4) —
595PP 9 items (50) —
596PP 9 items (50) —
G205PP 9 items (100) —
G206PP 9 items (100) —
V119PP 8 items (50) —
V120PP 8 items (50) —
595PI (125 pairs) —
596PI (125 pairs) —
G205PI (125 pairs) —
G206PI (125 pairs) —
V119PI (125 pairs) —
V120PI (125 pairs) —

Second sets of six items of Nos. 595PP-596PP, G205PP-G206PP, and V119PP-V120PP exist. Some items differ from those found in the listed sets.

New York #597-598, Geneva #207-208, Vienna #121-122
UN Postal Administration, 40th Anniv.

1991
598PDa Card, #597PD-598PD, #G207PD-G208PD, #V121PD-V122PD (4) —
597TCa Card, #597TC, #G207TC-G208TCD, #V121TC-V122TC (each with white background), 36c essay of #598 (6) —
597PP 2 items (64) —
Cross gutter block (1) —
Horiz. pair with vert. gutter (8) —
Vert. pair with horiz. gutter (8) —
598PP 2 items (64) —
Cross gutter block (1) —
Horiz. pair with vert. gutter (8) —
Vert. pair with horiz. gutter (8) —
G207PP 2 items (64) —
Cross gutter block (1) —
Horiz. pair with vert. gutter (8) —
Vert. pair with horiz. gutter (8) —
G208PP 2 items (64) —
Cross gutter block (1) —
Horiz. pair with vert. gutter (8) —
Vert. pair with horiz. gutter (8) —
V121PP 2 items (64) —
Cross gutter block (1) —
Horiz. pair with vert. gutter (8) —
Vert. pair with horiz. gutter (8) —
V122PP 2 items (64) —
Cross gutter block (1) —
Horiz. pair with vert. gutter (8) —
Vert. pair with horiz. gutter (8) —
597PI (120 pairs) —
Cross gutter block (3) —
Horiz. pair with vert. gutter (24) —
Vert. pair with horiz. gutter (24) —
598PI (120 pairs) —
Cross gutter block (3) —
Horiz. pair with vert. gutter (24) —
Vert. pair with horiz. gutter (24) —
G207PI (120 pairs) —
Cross gutter block (3) —
Horiz. pair with vert. gutter (24) —
Vert. pair with horiz. gutter (24) —
G208PI (120 pairs) —
Cross gutter block (3) —
Horiz. pair with vert. gutter (24) —
Vert. pair with horiz. gutter (24) —
V121PI (120 pairs) —
Cross gutter block (3) —
Horiz. pair with vert. gutter (24) —
Vert. pair with horiz. gutter (24) —
V122PI (120 pairs) —
Cross gutter block (3) —
Horiz. pair with vert. gutter (24) —
Vert. pair with horiz. gutter (24) —

Four cross gutter blocks, 32 horizontal pairs with vertical gutters and 32 vertical pairs with horizontal gutters can be cut from four perforated sheets of Nos. 597PI-598PI, G207PI-G208PI, V119PI-V120PI. No. 598PI is difficult to distinguish from one item from No. 598PP.

New York #599-600, Geneva #209-210, Vienna #123-124, Human Rights

1991

599PDa Strip of 3 + 3 labels with approval handstamp (4) —
600PDa Strip of 3 + 3 labels with approval handstamp (4) —
G209PDa Strip of 3 + 3 labels with approval handstamp (4) —
G210PDa Strip of 3 + 3 labels with approval handstamp (4) —
V123PDa Strip of 3 + 3 labels with approval handstamp (4) —
V124PDa Strip of 3 + 3 labels with approval handstamp (4) —
599TC Strip of 3 (dark gray background) + 3 labels with "not approved" handstamp (5) —
600TC Strip of 3 (dark green background) + 3 labels with "not approved" handstamp (5) —
G209TC Strip of 3 (light brown in painting) + 3 labels with "not approved" handstamp (5) —
G210TC Strip of 3 (dark green background) + 3 labels with "not approved" handstamp (5) —
V124TC Strip of 3 (black background) + 3 labels with "not approved" handstamp (5) —
599PP 6 items (20) —
Cross gutter block (1) —
Horiz. pair with vert. gutter (2) —
Vert. pair with horiz. gutter (10) —
600PP 6 items (20) —
Cross gutter block (1) —
Horiz. pair with vert. gutter (2) —
Vert. pair with horiz. gutter (10) —
G209PP 6 items (20) —
Cross gutter block (1) —
Horiz. pair with vert. gutter (2) —
Vert. pair with horiz. gutter (10) —
G210PP 6 items (20) —
Cross gutter block (1) —
Horiz. pair with vert. gutter (2) —
Vert. pair with horiz. gutter (10) —
V123PP 6 items (20) —
Cross gutter block (1) —
Horiz. pair with vert. gutter (2) —
Vert. pair with horiz. gutter (10) —
V124PP 6 items (20) —
Cross gutter block (1) —
Horiz. pair with vert. gutter (2) —
Vert. pair with horiz. gutter (10) —
599PI (56 pairs) —
Cross gutter block (1) —
Horiz. pair with vert. gutter (2) —
Vert. pair with horiz. gutter (10) —
600PI (56 pairs) —
Cross gutter block (1) —
Horiz. pair with vert. gutter (2) —
Vert. pair with horiz. gutter (10) —
G209PI (56 pairs) —
Cross gutter block (1) —
Horiz. pair with vert. gutter (2) —
Vert. pair with horiz. gutter (10) —
G210PI (56 pairs) —
Cross gutter block (1) —
Horiz. pair with vert. gutter (2) —
Vert. pair with horiz. gutter (10) —
V123PI (56 pairs) —
Cross gutter block (1) —
Horiz. pair with vert. gutter (2) —
Vert. pair with horiz. gutter (10) —
V124PI (56 pairs) —
Cross gutter block (1) —
Horiz. pair with vert. gutter (2) —
Vert. pair with horiz. gutter (10) —

New York #601-602, Geneva #211-212, Vienna #125-126, World Heritage

1992

602PDa Card, #601PD-602PD (5) —
G212PDa Card, #G211PD-G212PD (5) —
V126PDa Card, #V125PD-V126PD (5) —
601PP 6 items (50) —
602PP 6 items (50) —
G211PP 6 items (50) —
G212PP 6 items (50) —
V125PP 6 items (50) —
V126PP 6 items (50) —
601PI (50 pairs) —
602PI (50 pairs) —
G211PI (50 pairs) —
G212PI (50 pairs) —
V125PI (50 pairs) —
V126PI (50 pairs) —

Geneva #213 Definitive

1992

G213PP 6 items (50) —
G213PI (75 pairs) —

See No. G202PDa.

New York #604a, Geneva #215a, Vienna #128a Clean Oceans

1992

604aPDa Card, imperforate pane of 6 #604aPD (2) —
604aPDb Card, as "a," with one pair removed (1) —
G215aPDa Card, imperforate pane of 6 #G215aPD (2) —
G215aPDb (Card, as "a," with one pair removed (1) —
V128aPDa Card, imperforate pane of 6 #V128aPD (2) —
V128aPDb Card, as "a," with one pair removed (1) —
604aPP 8 items, vert. pair of pairs with narrow horiz. gutter (20) —
Cross gutter block (1) —
Horiz. pair of pairs with vert. gutter (4) —
Vert. pair of pairs with wide horiz. gutter (10) —
G215aPP 8 items, vert. pair of pairs with narrow horiz. gutter (20) —
Cross gutter block (1) —
Horiz. pair of pairs with vert. gutter (4) —
Vert. pair of pairs with wide horiz. gutter (10) —
V128aPP 8 items, vert. pair of pairs with narrow horiz. gutter (20) —
Cross gutter block (1) —
Horiz. pair of pairs with vert. gutter (4) —
Vert. pair of pairs with wide horiz. gutter (10) —
604aPI Vert. pair of pairs with narrow horiz. gutter (20) —
Cross gutter block (1) —
Horiz. pair of pairs with vert. gutter (4) —
Vert. pair of pairs with wide horiz. gutter (10) —
G215aPI Vert. pair of pairs with narrow horiz. gutter (20) —
Cross gutter block (1) —
Horiz. pair of pairs with vert. gutter (4) —
Vert. pair of pairs with wide horiz. gutter (10) —
V128aPI Vert. pair of pairs with narrow horiz. gutter (20) —
Cross gutter block (1) —
Horiz. pair of pairs with vert. gutter (4) —
Vert. pair of pairs with wide horiz. gutter (10) —

New York #608a, Geneva #219a, Vienna #132a Earth Summit

1992

608aPDa Card, #608aPD, #G219aPD, #V132aPD (5) —
608aPP 4 items (10) —
G219aPP 4 items (10) —
V132aPP 4 items (10) —
608aPI (20 blocks) —
G219aPI (20 blocks) —
V132aPI (20 blocks) —

New York #609-610, Geneva #220-221, Vienna #133-134 Mission to Planet Earth

1992

610PDa Card, #610aPD, G221aPD, #V134aPD (3) —
SC41PD (3) —
610aPP 6 items (5) —
G221aPP 6 items (5) —
V134aPP 6 items (5) —
610aPI (10 pairs) —
G221aPI (10 pairs) —
V134aPI (10 pairs) —

One item in No. G221aPP is a blank from a sheet showing marginal inscriptions only.

New York #611-612, Geneva #222-223, Vienna #135-136, Souvenir Card #42 Science and Technology for Development

1992

611PDa Card, 2 #611PD, 2 #V136PD (4) —
612PDa Card, #611PD-612PD, #G222PD-G223PD, #V135PD-V136PD (4) —
SC42PD (18) —
611PP 6 items (50) —
612PP 6 items (50) —
G222PP 6 items (50) —
G223PP 6 items (50) —
V135PP 6 items (50) —
V136PP 6 items (50) —
611PI (100 pairs) —
612PI (100 pairs) —
G222PI (100 pairs) —
G223PI (100 pairs) —
V135PI (100 pairs) —
V136PI (100 pairs) —

There is no appreciable difference between approved and not approved die proofs.

New York #613-615, Vienna #137-138 Definitives

1992

614PDa Card, #614PD, #V137PD-V138PD (4) —
615PDa Card, #613PD, #615PD (3) —
613PP 6 items (50) —
614PP 6 items (50) —
615PP 6 items (50) —
V137PP 6 items (50) —
V138PP 6 items (50) —
613PI (50 pairs) —
614PI (269 pairs) —
Cross gutter block (2) —
Horiz. pair with vert. gutter (36) —
Vert. pair with horiz. gutter (16) —
615PI (50 pairs) —
V137PI (269 pairs) —
Cross gutter block (2) —
Horiz. pair with vert. gutter (16) —
Vert. pair with horiz. gutter (36) —
V138PI (269 pairs) —
Cross gutter block (2) —
Horiz. pair with vert. gutter (36) —
Vert. pair with horiz. gutter (16) —

Three "not approved" cards containing essays of Nos. 613 and 615 lacking year date and designer inscriptions exist.

New York #616-617, Geneva #224-225, Vienna #139-140 Human Rights

1992

616PDa Strip of 3 + 3 labels (4) —
617PDa Strip of 3 + 3 labels (4) —
G224PDa Strip of 3 + 3 labels (4) —
G225PDa Strip of 3 + 3 labels (4) —
V139PDa Strip of 3 + 3 labels (4) —
V140PDa Strip of 3 + 3 labels (4) —
G225TCa Strip of 3 (dark brown background under chair) + 3 labels (not approved) (5) —
616PP 6 items (20) —
Cross gutter block (1) —
Horiz. pair with vert. gutter (2) —
Vert. pair with horiz. gutter (10) —
617PP 6 items (20) —
Cross gutter block (1) —
Horiz. pair with vert. gutter (2) —
Vert. pair with horiz. gutter (10) —
G224PP 6 items (20) —
Cross gutter block (1) —
Horiz. pair with vert. gutter (2) —
Vert. pair with horiz. gutter (10) —
G225PP 6 items (20) —
Cross gutter block (1) —
Horiz. pair with vert. gutter (2) —
Vert. pair with horiz. gutter (10) —
V139PP 6 items (20) —
Cross gutter block (1) —
Horiz. pair with vert. gutter (2) —
Vert. pair with horiz. gutter (10) —
V140PP 6 items (20) —
Cross gutter block (1) —
Horiz. pair with vert. gutter (2) —
Vert. pair with horiz. gutter (10) —
616PI (32 pairs) —
Cross gutter block (4) —
Horiz. pair with vert. gutter (8) —
Vert. pair with horiz. gutter (40) —
617PI (32 pairs) —
Cross gutter block (4) —
Horiz. pair with vert. gutter (8) —
Vert. pair with horiz. gutter (40) —
G224PI (32 pairs) —
Cross gutter block (4) —
Horiz. pair with vert. gutter (8) —
Vert. pair with horiz. gutter (40) —
G225PI (32 pairs) —
Cross gutter block (4) —
Horiz. pair with vert. gutter (8) —
Vert. pair with horiz. gutter (40) —
V139PI (32 pairs) —
Cross gutter block (4) —
Horiz. pair with vert. gutter (8) —
Vert. pair with vert. gutter (40) —
V140PI (32 pairs) —
Cross gutter block (4) —
Horiz. pair with vert. gutter (8) —
Vert. pair with horiz. gutter (40) —

Five "not approved" cards contain 4.50s essays of No. V139, and five "not approved" cards contain 9.50s essays of No. V140.

New York #618-619, Geneva #226-227, Vienna #141-142 Aging With Dignity

1993

618PDa Card, #618PD, #G226PD-G227PD, #V141PD-V142PD, #619TC yellow flowers (not approved) (5) —
619PDa Card, #618PD-619PD, #V141PD-V142PD, #G226TC pink denomination, #G227TC yellow denomination, with approval handstamp (4) —
619TCb Card, #618TC-619TC, #G226TC-G227TC, #V141TC-V142TC, each with white denominations (5) —
618PP 7 items (50) —
619PP 7 items (50) —
G226PP 7 items (50) —
G227PP 7 items (50) —
V141PP 7 items (50) —

V142PP 7 items (50) —
618PI (50 pairs) —
619PI (50 pairs) —
G226PI (50 pairs) —
G227PI (50 pairs) —
V141PI (50 pairs) —
V142PI (50 pairs) —

New York #623a, Geneva #231a, Vienna #146a Endangered Species

1993
623aPDa Card, imperforate pane of 4 blocks of #623aPD (3) —
G231aPDa Card, imperforate pane of 4 blocks of #G231aPD (4) —
V146aPDa Card, imperforate pane of 4 blocks of #V146aPD (3) —
G231aTCa Card, imperforate pane of 4 blocks of #G231aTC black (1) —
G231aPP 6 items (4 blocks) —
Cross gutter block (1) —
Horiz. pair with vert. gutter (2) —
Vert. pair with horiz. gutter (4) —
V146aPP 6 items (4 blocks) —
Cross gutter block (1) —
Horiz. pair with vert. gutter (2) —
Vert. pair with horiz. gutter (4) —
623aPI (20 blocks) —
Cross gutter block (8) —
Horiz. pair with vert. gutter (8) —
Vert. pair with horiz. gutter (16) —
G231aPI (44 blocks) —
Cross gutter block (10) —
Horiz. pair with vert. gutter (10) —
Vert. pair with horiz. gutter (20) —
V146aPI (20 blocks) —
Cross gutter block (8) —
Horiz. pair with vert. gutter (8) —
Vert. pair with horiz. gutter (16) —

New York #624-625, Geneva #232-233, Vienna #147-148, Souvenir Card #43 Healthy Environment

1993
625PDa Card, #624PD-625PD, #V147PD-V148PD, 90c essay of #G232, 1.10fr essay of #G233 (4) —
SC43PD (4) —
624PP 6 items (50) —
625PP 6 items (50) —
G232PP 6 items (50) —
G233PP 6 items (50) —
V147PP 6 items (50) —
V148PP 6 items (50) —
624PI (50 pairs) —
625PI (50 pairs) —
G232PI (50 pairs) —
G233PI (50 pairs) —
V147PI (50 pairs) —
V148PI (50 pairs) —

New York #626, Vienna #149 Definitives

1993
626PD (5) —
V149PD (5) —
626PP 8 items (144) —
Cross gutter block (1) —
Horiz. pair with vert. gutter (18) —
Vert. pair with horiz. gutter (8) —
V149PP 5 items (50) —
626PI (194 pairs) —
Cross gutter block (2) —
Horiz. pair with vert. gutter (36) —
Vert. pair with horiz. gutter (16) —
V149PI (50 pairs) —

New York #627-628, Geneva #234-235, Vienna #150-151 Human Rights

1993
627PDa Strip of 3 + 3 labels (4) —
628PDa Strip of 3 + 3 labels (4) —
G234PDa Strip of 3 + 3 labels (4) —
G235PDa Strip of 3 + 3 labels (4) —
V150PDa Strip of 3 + 3 labels (3) —
V151PDa Strip of 3 + 3 labels (4) —
627PP 6 items (20) —
Cross gutter block (1) —
Horiz. pair with vert. gutter (2) —
Vert. pair with horiz. gutter (10) —
628PP 6 items (20) —
Cross gutter block (1) —
Horiz. pair with vert. gutter (2) —
Vert. pair with horiz. gutter (10) —
G234PP 6 items (20) —
Cross gutter block (1) —
Horiz. pair with vert. gutter (2) —
Vert. pair with horiz. gutter (10) —
G235PP 6 items (20) —
Cross gutter block (1) —
Horiz. pair with vert. gutter (2) —
Vert. pair with horiz. gutter (10) —
627PI (20 pairs) —
Cross gutter block (1) —
Horiz. pair with vert. gutter (2) —
Vert. pair with horiz. gutter (10) —
628PI (20 pairs) —
Cross gutter block (1) —
Horiz. pair with vert. gutter (2) —
Vert. pair with horiz. gutter (10) —
G234PI (20 pairs) —
Cross gutter block (1) —
Horiz. pair with vert. gutter (2) —
Vert. pair with horiz. gutter (10) —
G235PI (20 pairs) —
Cross gutter block (1) —
Horiz. pair with vert. gutter (2) —
Vert. pair with horiz. gutter (10) —
V150PI (6 pairs) —
V151PI (6 pairs) —

New York #632a, Geneva #239a, Vienna #155a, Souvenir Card #44 International Peace Day

1993
632aPD (4) —
G239aPD (4) —
V155aPD (4) —
SC44PD (4) —
632aPP 7 items (10 blocks) —
G239aPP 7 items (10 blocks) —
V155aPP 7 items (10 blocks) —
632aPI (40 blocks) —
G239aPI (40 blocks) —
V155aPI (40 blocks) —

New York #636a, Geneva #243a, Vienna #159a Environment & Climate

1993
636aPDa Card, #636aPD, #V159aPD (4) —
G243aPD (4) —
636aPP 8 items (6 strips) —
Horiz. pair of strips with vert. gutter (6) —
G243aPP 8 items (6 strips) —
Horiz. pair of strips with vert. gutter (6) —
V155aPP 8 items (6 strips) —
Horiz. pair of strips with vert. gutter (6) —
636aPI (18 strips) —
Horiz. pair of strips with vert. gutter (18) —
G243aPI (18 strips) —
Horiz. pair of strips with vert. gutter (18) —
V159aPI (18 strips) —
Horiz. pair of strips with vert. gutter (18) —

New York #637-638, Geneva #244-245, Vienna #160-161, Souvenir Card #45 International Year of the Family

1994
638PDa Card, #637PD-638PD, #G244PD-G245PD, #V160PD-V161PD (4) —
SC45PD (4) —
637PP 11 items (50) —
638PP 11 items (50) —
G244PP 10 items (50) —
G245PP 10 items (50) —
V160PP 11 items (50) —
V161PP 11 items (50) —
637PI (100 pairs) —
638PI (100 pairs) —
G244PI (100 pairs) —
G245PI (100 pairs) —
V160PI (100 pairs) —
V161PI (100 pairs) —

New York #642a, Geneva #249a, Vienna #165a Endangered Species

1994
642aPDa Card, imperforate pane of 4 #642aPD (9) —
G249aPDa Card, imperforate pane of 4 #G249aPD (4) —
V165aPDa Card, imperforate pane of 4 #V165aPD (4) —
642aPP 6 items (4 blocks) —
Cross gutter block (2) —
Horiz. pair with vert. gutter (2) —
Vert. pair with horiz. gutter (4) —
G249aPP 6 items (4 blocks) —
Cross gutter block (2) —
Horiz. pair with vert. gutter (2) —
Vert. pair with horiz. gutter (4) —
V165aPP 6 items (4 blocks) —
Cross gutter block (2) —
Horiz. pair with vert. gutter (2) —
Vert. pair with horiz. gutter (4) —
642aPI (16 blocks) —
Cross gutter block (8) —
Horiz. pair with vert. gutter (8) —
Vert. pair with horiz. gutter (16) —
G249aPI (16 blocks) —
Cross gutter block (8) —
Horiz. pair with vert. gutter (8) —
Vert. pair with horiz. gutter (16) —
V165aPI (16 blocks) —
Cross gutter block (8) —
Horiz. pair with vert. gutter (8) —
Vert. pair with horiz. gutter (16) —

There is no appreciable difference between appoved and not approved examples of No. 642aPD. Five cards with imperforate panes of 40c essays of No. G249a and five cards with imperforate panes of 5s essays of No. V165a exist.

New York #643, Geneva #250, Vienna #166 Protection for Refugees

1994
643PDa Card, #643PD, #G250PD, #V166PD (4) —
643PP 8 items (50) —
G250PP 8 items (50) —
V166PP 6 items (50) —
643PI (69 pairs) —
Horiz. pair with vert. gutter (8) —
G250PI (69 pairs) —
Horiz. pair with vert. gutter (8) —
V166PI (69 pairs) —
Horiz. pair with vert. gutter (8) —

New York #644-646, Vienna #167-169 Definitives

1994
645PDa Card, #644PD-645PD, #V167PD-V169PD (5) —
646PD (1) —
644PP 6 items (50) —
645PP 6 items (50) —
V167PP 12 items (50) —
V168PP 11 items (50) —
V169PP 11 items (50) —
644PI (100 pairs) —
645PI (100 pairs) —
646PI (50 pairs) —
V167PI (100 pairs) —
V168PI (100 pairs) —
V169PI (100 pairs) —

There is no appreciable difference between approved and not approved examples of No. 645PDa.

New York #650a, Geneva #254a, Vienna #173a International Decade for Natural Disaster Reduction

1994
650aPDa Card, #650aPD, #G254aPD, #V173aPD (5) —
650aPP 6 items (16 blocks) —
Cross gutter block (1) —
Horiz. pair with vert. gutter (8) —
Vert. pair with horiz. gutter (2) —
G254aPP 6 items (16 blocks) —
Cross gutter block (1) —
Horiz. pair with vert. gutter (8) —
Vert. pair with horiz. gutter (2) —
V173aPP 6 items (16 blocks) —
Cross gutter block (1) —
Horiz. pair with vert. gutter (8) —
Vert. pair with horiz. gutter (2) —
650aPI (48 blocks) —
Cross gutter block (3) —
Horiz. pair with vert. gutter (24) —
Vert. pair with horiz. gutter (6) —
G254aPI (48 blocks) —
Cross gutter block (3) —
Horiz. pair with vert. gutter (24) —
Vert. pair with horiz. gutter (6) —
V173aPI (48 blocks) —
Cross gutter block (3) —
Horiz. pair with vert. gutter (24) —
Vert. pair with horiz. gutter (6) —

Geneva #255-257 Definitives

1994
G257PDa Card, #G255PD-G257PD (5) —
G255PP 10 items (144) —
Cross gutter block (1) —
Horiz. pair with vert. gutter (18) —
Vert. pair with horiz. gutter (8) —
G256PP 10 items (144) —
Cross gutter block (1) —
Horiz. pair with vert. gutter (18) —
Vert. pair with horiz. gutter (8) —
G257PP 11 items (144) —
Cross gutter block (1) —
Horiz. pair with vert. gutter (18) —
Vert. pair with horiz. gutter (8) —
G255PI (288 pairs) —
Cross gutter block (4) —
Horiz. pair with vert. gutter (72) —
Vert. pair with horiz. gutter (32) —
G256PI (288 pairs) —
Cross gutter block (4) —
Horiz. pair with vert. gutter (72) —
Vert. pair with horiz. gutter (32) —
G257PI (288 pairs) —
Cross gutter block (4) —
Horiz. pair with vert. gutter (72) —
Vert. pair with horiz. gutter (32) —

New York #651-652, Geneva #258-259, Vienna #174-175, Souvenir Card #46 Population and Development

1994
652PDa Card, #651PD-652PD, #G258PD-G259PD, #V174PD-V175PD (4) —
SC46PD (4) —
G258PP 6 items (40) —
G259PP 6 items (40) —
G259PPa Horiz. se-tenant pair with vert. gutter, #G258PP-G259PP (10) —
V174PP 6 items (40) —
V175PP 6 items (40) —
V175PPa Horiz. se-tenant pair with vert. gutter, #V174PP-V175PP (10) —
651PI (50 pairs) —
652PI (50 pairs) —
G258PI (70 pairs) —
G259PI (70 pairs) —
G259PIa Horiz. se-tenant pair with vert. gutter, #G258PI-G259PI (10) —
V174PI (70 pairs) —

V175PI (70 pairs) —
V175PIa Horiz. se-tenant pair with vert. gutter, #V174PI-V175PI (10) —

New York #653-654, Geneva #260-261, Vienna #176-177
UNCTAD, 30th Anniv.

1994
653PP 15 items (40) —
654PP 15 items (40) —
654PPa Horiz. se-tenant pair with vert. gutter, #653PP-654PP (10) —
G260PP 16 items (40) —
G261PP 16 items (40) —
G261PPa Horiz. se-tenant pair with vert. gutter, #G260PP-G261PP (10) —
V176PP 14 items (40) —
V177PP 14 items (40) —
V177PPa Horiz. se-tenant pair with vert. gutter, #V176PP-V177PP (10) —
653PI (60 pairs) —
654PI (60 pairs) —
654PIa Horiz. se-tenant pair with vert. gutter, #653PI-654PI (30) —
G260PI (60 pairs) —
G261PI (60 pairs) —
G261PIa Horiz. se-tenant pair with vert. gutter, #G260PI-G261PI (30) —
V176PI (60 pairs) —
V177PI (60 pairs) —
V177PIa Horiz. se-tenant pair with vert. gutter, #V176PI-V177PI (30) —

Two items from No. G260PP and one from No. V176PP are blank due to color arrangement on progressive proof sheet.

New York # 655, Geneva #262, Vienna #178
United Nations, 50th Anniv.

1995
655PD (3) —
G262PD (3) —
V178PD (3) —
655PP 8 items (50) —
G262PP 8 items (50) —
V178PP 8 items (50) —
655PI (100 pairs) —
G262PI (200 pairs) —
V178PI (200 pairs) —

New York #656, Geneva #263, Vienna #179, Souvenir Card #47
World Summit for Social Development, Copenhagen

1995
656PDa Card, #656PD, #G263PD, #V179PD (3) —
SC47PD Card, 4 #SC47PD (1) —
656PP 12 items (25) —
G263PP 8 items (25) —
V179PP 8 items (25) —
656PI (24 pairs) —
G263PI (24 pairs) —
V179PI (24 pairs) —

New York #660a, Geneva #267a, Vienna #183a
Endangered Species

1995
660aPDa Card, imperforate pane of 4 blocks, #660aPD (5) —
660aPDb Card, broken imperforate pane of 4 blocks, #660aPD (1) —
660aPDc Card, 2 imperforate panes of 4 blocks, #660aPD (1) —
G267aPDa Card, imperforate pane of 4 blocks, #G267aPD (6) —
G267aPDb Card, 2 imperforate panes of 4 blocks, #G267aPD (1) —
V183aPDa Card, imperforate pane of 4 blocks, #V183aPD with "14. Okt. 1994" handstamp (approved) (3) —
V183aTCa Card, imperforate pane of 4 blocks, #V183aTC (violet blue sky on #181TC), not approved (3) —
V183aTCb Card, 2 imperforate pane of 4 blocks, #V183aTC, not approved (1) —
660aPP 6 items (9 blocks) —
Cross gutter block (3) —
Horiz. pair with vert. gutter (4) —
Vert. pair with horiz. gutter (7) —
G267aPP 6 items (12 blocks) —
Cross gutter block (3) —
Horiz. pair with vert. gutter (4) —
Vert. pair with horiz. gutter (6) —
V183aPP 6 items (12 blocks) —
Cross gutter block (3) —
Horiz. pair with vert. gutter (4) —
Vert. pair with horiz. gutter (7) —
660aPI (11 blocks) —
Cross gutter block (3) —
Horiz. pair with vert. gutter (4) —
Vert. pair with horiz. gutter (7) —
G267aPI (16 blocks) —
Cross gutter block (3) —
Horiz. pair with vert. gutter (4) —
Vert. pair with horiz. gutter (6) —
V183aPI (11 blocks) —
Cross gutter block (3) —
Horiz. pair with vert. gutter (4) —
Vert. pair with horiz. gutter (7) —

Three cross gutter blocks, four horizontal pairs with vertical gutters, seven vertical pairs with horizontal gutters and nine blocks with untrimmed margins can be cut from perforated sheets of Nos. V180PI-V183PI.

New York #661-662, Geneva #268-269, Vienna #184-185, Souvenir Card #48
International Youth Year

1995
662PDa Card, #661PD-662PD, #G268PD-G269PD, #V184PD-V185PD (6) —
SC48PD (6) —
661PP 5 items (160) —
Cross gutter block (5) —
Horiz. pair with vert. gutter (25) —
Vert. pair with horiz. gutter (44) —
662PP 8 items (160) —
Cross gutter block (5) —
Horiz. pair with vert. gutter (25) —
Vert. pair with horiz. gutter (44) —
G268PP 6 items (208) —
Cross gutter block (5) —
Horiz. pair with vert. gutter (25) —
Vert. pair with horiz. gutter (44) —
G269PP 5 items (208) —
Cross gutter block (5) —
Horiz. pair with vert. gutter (25) —
Vert. pair with horiz. gutter (44) —
V184PP 7 items (101) —
Cross gutter block (2) —
Horiz. pair with vert. gutter (11) —
Vert. pair with horiz. gutter (12) —
V185PP 6 items (197) —
Cross gutter block (5) —
Horiz. pair with vert. gutter (25) —
Vert. pair with horiz. gutter (44) —
661PI (128 pairs) —
Cross gutter block (5) —
Horiz. pair with vert. gutter (25) —
Vert. pair with horiz. gutter (44) —
662PI (128 pairs) —
Cross gutter block (5) —
Horiz. pair with vert. gutter (25) —
Vert. pair with horiz. gutter (44) —
G268PI (128 pairs) —
Cross gutter block (5) —
Horiz. pair with vert. gutter (25) —
Vert. pair with horiz. gutter (44) —
G269PI (128 pairs) —
Cross gutter block (5) —
Horiz. pair with vert. gutter (25) —
Vert. pair with horiz. gutter (44) —
V184PI (128 pairs) —
Cross gutter block (5) —
Horiz. pair with vert. gutter (25) —
Vert. pair with horiz. gutter (44) —
V185PI (128 pairs) —
Cross gutter block (5) —
Horiz. pair with vert. gutter (25) —
Vert. pair with horiz. gutter (44) —

New York #663-665, Geneva #270-272, Vienna #186-188
United Nations, 50th Anniv.

1995
664PDa Card, # 664PD, #663TC maroon, #663TC dark blue, #663TC green, #664TC dark blue, #664TC green (3) —
663PI (80 pairs) —
664PI (80 pairs) —
664PIa Horiz. se-tenant pair with vert. gutter, #663PI-664PI (40) —
665PI (8 pairs of souvenir sheets) —
G270PI (80 pairs) —
G271PI (80 pairs) —
G271PIa Horiz. se-tenant pair with vert. gutter, #G270PI-G271PI (40) —
G272PI (8 pairs of souvenir sheets) —
V186PI (80 pairs) —
V187PI (80 pairs) —
V187PIa Horiz. se-tenant pair with vert. gutter, #V186PI-V187PI (40) —
V188PI (8 pairs of souvenir sheets) —

Three cards with non-engraved essays of No. 665 in red violet exist.

New York #666-667, Geneva #273-274, Vienna #189-190
Fourth World Conference on Women

1995
666PP 10 items, perforated (275) —
667PP 10 items, perforated (250) —
G273PP 10 items, perforated (100) —
G274PP 10 items, perforated (250) —
V189PP 9 items, perforated (275) —
V190PP 9 items, perforated (275) —
666PI (144 pairs) —
667PI (144 pairs) —
G273PI (108 pairs) —
G274PI (144 pairs) —
V189PI (132 pairs) —
V190PI (144 pairs) —

On No. V189PP and V190PP, 125 sets have a red and multicolored item while the remaining 150 sets have a blue and multicolored item.

New York #668
UN Headquarters

1995
668PD (5) —
668PP 6 items (162) —
Horiz. pair with vert. gutter (9) —
Vert. pair with horiz. gutter (5) —
668PI (85 pairs) —
Horiz. pair with vert. gutter (9) —
Vert. pair with horiz. gutter (5) —

New York #669-670, Geneva #275-276, Vienna #191-192
United Nations, 50th Anniversary

1995
669PD (4) —
G275PD (4) —
V191PD (4) —
669PP 6 items (6) —
G275PP 8 items (6) —
V191PP 7 items (6) —
669PI (2 full panes) —
669PIa (3 pairs of full panes) —
670PI (3 booklets) —
G275PI (2 full panes) —
G275PIa (3 pairs of full panes) —
G276PI (3 booklets) —
V191PI (2 full panes) —
V191PIa (4 pairs of full panes) —
V192PI (3 booklets) —

New York #671, Geneva #277, Vienna #193, Souvenir Card #49
World Federation of United Nations Associations, 50th Anniv.

1996
671PDa Card, #671PD, #G277PD, #V193PD (3) —
SC49PD (4) —
671PP 6 items (150) —
Horiz. pair with vert. gutter (25) —
G277PP 6 items (150) —
Horiz. pair with vert. gutter (25) —
V193PP 6 items (305) —
Cross gutter block (5) —
Horiz. pair with vert. gutter (40) —
Vert. pair with horiz. gutter (30) —
671PI (155 pairs) —
Horiz. pair with vert. gutter (55) —
G277PI (155 pairs) —
Horiz. pair with vert. gutter (55) —
V193PI (264 pairs) —
Cross gutter block (11) —
Horiz. pair with vert. gutter (88) —
Vert. pair with horiz. gutter (63) —

New York #672-673, Geneva #278-279, Vienna #194-195
Definitives

1996
673PDa Card, #672PD-673PD, #G278PD-G279PD, #V194PD-V195PD with approval handstamp (4) —
673PDb Card, #673PD, #672TC gray in vignette, #G278TC-G279TC tan background in panel, essays of #V194PD-V195PD (larger frames) (not approved) (4) —
673PDc #673PDa and 673PDb stapled together (1) —
672PP 8 items (144) —
Cross gutter block (1) —
Horiz. pair with vert. gutter (18) —
Vert. pair with horiz. gutter (8) —
673PP 8 items (144) —
Cross gutter block (1) —
Horiz. pair with vert. gutter (18) —
Vert. pair with horiz. gutter (8) —
G278PP 8 items (144) —
Cross gutter block (1) —
Horiz. pair with vert. gutter (18) —
Vert. pair with horiz. gutter (8) —
G279PP 8 items (144) —
Cross gutter block (1) —
Horiz. pair with vert. gutter (18) —
Vert. pair with horiz. gutter (8) —
V194PP 8 items (144) —
Cross gutter block (1) —
Horiz. pair with vert. gutter (18) —
Vert. pair with horiz. gutter (8) —
V195PP 8 items (144) —
Cross gutter block (1) —
Horiz. pair with vert. gutter (18) —
Vert. pair with horiz. gutter (8) —
672PI (216 pairs) —
Cross gutter block (3) —
Horiz. pair with vert. gutter (54) —
Vert. pair with horiz. gutter (16) —
673PI (144 pairs) —
Cross gutter block (3) —
Horiz. pair with vert. gutter (54) —
Vert. pair with horiz. gutter (16) —
G278PI (216 pairs) —
Cross gutter block (3) —
Horiz. pair with vert. gutter (54) —
Vert. pair with horiz. gutter (24) —
G279PI (216 pairs) —
Cross gutter block (3) —
Horiz. pair with vert. gutter (54) —
Vert. pair with horiz. gutter (24) —

V194PI (216 pairs) —
Cross gutter block (3) —
Horiz. pair with vert. gutter (24) —
Vert. pair with horiz. gutter (36) —
V195PI (216 pairs) —
Cross gutter block (3) —
Horiz. pair with vert. gutter (24) —
Vert. pair with horiz. gutter (36) —

New York #677a, Geneva #283a, Vienna #199a
Endangered Species

1996
677aPDa Card, imperforate pane of 4 blocks, #677aPD (3) —
677aPDb Card, broken imperforate pane of 4 blocks, #677aPD (1) —
G283aPDa Card, imperforate pane of 4 blocks, #G283aPD (3) —
G283aPDb Card, broken imperforate pane of 4 blocks, #G283aPD (1) —
V199aPDa Card, imperforate pane of 4 blocks, #V199aPD (3) —
V199aPDb Card, broken imperforate pane of 4 blocks, #V199aPD (1) —
677aPP 6 items (14 blocks) —
Cross gutter block (5) —
Horiz. pair with vert. gutter (6) —
Vert. pair with horiz. gutter (11) —
G283aPP 6 items (14 blocks) —
Cross gutter block (5) —
Horiz. pair with vert. gutter (6) —
Vert. pair with horiz. gutter (11) —
V199aPP 6 items (14 blocks) —
Cross gutter block (5) —
Horiz. pair with vert. gutter (6) —
Vert. pair with horiz. gutter (11) —
677aPI (25 blocks) —
Cross gutter block (11) —
Horiz. pair with vert. gutter (12) —
Vert. pair with horiz. gutter (23) —
G283aPI (25 blocks) —
Cross gutter block (11) —
Horiz. pair with vert. gutter (12) —
Vert. pair with horiz. gutter (23) —
V199aPI (25 blocks) —
Cross gutter block (11) —
Horiz. pair with vert. gutter (12) —
Vert. pair with horiz. gutter (23) —

New York #682a, Geneva #288a, Vienna #204a
City Summit

1996
682aPDa Card, imperforate pane of 5 strips, #682aPD (4) —
G288aPDa Card, imperforate pane of 5 strips, #G288aPD (4) —
V204aPDa Card, imperforate pane of 5 strips, #V204aPD (4) —
682aPP 10 items (15 horiz. pairs of strips with vert. gutter) —
G288aPP 10 items (24 horiz. pairs of strips with vert. gutter) —
Cross gutter block of strips (3) —
V204aPP 10 items (15 horiz. pairs of strips with vert. gutter) —
682aPI (35 horiz. pairs of strips with vert. gutter) —
G288aPI (56 horiz. pairs of strips with vert. gutter) —
Cross gutter block of strips (7) —
V204aPI (35 horiz. pairs of strips with vert. gutter) —

New York #683-685, Geneva #289-291, Vienna #205-207
Sport and the Environment

1996
684PDa Card, #683PD-684PD (10) —
685PD (10) —
G290PDa Card, #G289PD-G290PD (10) —
G291PD (10) —
V206PDa Card, #V205PD-V206PD (10) —
V207PD (10) —
683PP 8 items (88) —
Cross gutter block (2) —
Horiz. pair with vert. gutter (16) —
Vert. pair with horiz. gutter (11) —
684PP 8 items (88) —
Cross gutter block (2) —
Horiz. pair with vert. gutter (11) —
Vert. pair with horiz. gutter (16) —
685PP 12 items (25 souvenir sheets) —
G289PP 8 items (88) —
Cross gutter block (2) —
Horiz. pair with vert. gutter (16) —
Vert. pair with horiz. gutter (11) —
G290PP 8 items (88) —
Cross gutter block (2) —
Horiz. pair with vert. gutter (11) —
Vert. pair with horiz. gutter (16) —
G291PP 10 items (25 souvenir sheets) —
V205PP 8 items (88) —
Cross gutter block (2) —
Horiz. pair with vert. gutter (16) —
Vert. pair with horiz. gutter (11) —
V206PP 8 items (88) —
Cross gutter block (2) —
Horiz. pair with vert. gutter (11) —
Vert. pair with horiz. gutter (16) —
V207PP 11 items (25 souvenir sheets) —
683PI (44 pairs) —
Cross gutter block (2) —
Horiz. pair with vert. gutter (16) —
Vert. pair with horiz. gutter (11) —
684PI (44 pairs) —
Cross gutter block (2) —
Horiz. pair with vert. gutter (11) —
Vert. pair with horiz. gutter (16) —
685PI (75 souvenir sheets) —
G289PI (88 pairs) —
Cross gutter block (4) —
Horiz. pair with vert. gutter (32) —
Vert. pair with horiz. gutter (22) —
G290PI (88 pairs) —
Cross gutter block (4) —
Horiz. pair with vert. gutter (22) —
Vert. pair with horiz. gutter (32) —
G291PI (75 souvenir sheets) —
V205PI (132 pairs) —
Cross gutter block (6) —
Horiz. pair with vert. gutter (48) —
Vert. pair with horiz. gutter (33) —
V206PI (132 pairs) —
Cross gutter block (6) —
Horiz. pair with vert. gutter (33) —
Vert. pair with horiz. gutter (48) —
V207PI (75 souvenir sheets) —

New York #686-687, Geneva #292-293, Vienna #208-209
Plea for Peace

1996
687PDa Card, #686PD-687PD, #G292PD-G293PD, #V208PD-V209PD (4) —
686PP 10 items (112) —
Cross gutter block (3) —
Horiz. pair with vert. gutter (14) —
Vert. pair with horiz. gutter (24) —
687PP 10 items (112) —
Cross gutter block (3) —
Horiz. pair with vert. gutter (14) —
Vert. pair with horiz. gutter (24) —
G292PP 10 items (112) —
Cross gutter block (3) —
Horiz. pair with vert. gutter (24) —
Vert. pair with horiz. gutter (14) —
G293PP 10 items (112) —
Cross gutter block (2) —
Horiz. pair with vert. gutter (24) —
Vert. pair with horiz. gutter (14) —
V208PP 10 items (112) —
Cross gutter block (3) —
Horiz. pair with vert. gutter (14) —
Vert. pair with horiz. gutter (24) —
V209PP 10 items (112) —
Cross gutter block (3) —
Horiz. pair with vert. gutter (14) —
Vert. pair with horiz. gutter (24) —
686PI (104 pairs) —
Cross gutter block (3) —
Horiz. pair with vert. gutter (14) —
Vert. pair with horiz. gutter (24) —
687PI (104 pairs) —
Cross gutter block (3) —
Horiz. pair with vert. gutter (14) —
Vert. pair with horiz. gutter (24) —
G292PI (80 pairs) —
Cross gutter block (3) —
Horiz. pair with vert. gutter (24) —
Vert. pair with horiz. gutter (14) —
G293PI (80 pairs) —
Cross gutter block (3) —
Horiz. pair with vert. gutter (24) —
Vert. pair with horiz. gutter (14) —
V208PI (80 pairs) —
Cross gutter block (3) —
Horiz. pair with vert. gutter (14) —
Vert. pair with horiz. gutter (24) —
V209PI (80 pairs) —
Cross gutter block (3) —
Horiz. pair with vert. gutter (14) —
Vert. pair with horiz. gutter (24) —

New York #688-689, Geneva #294-295, Vienna #210-211, Souvenir Card #50
UNICEF, 50th Anniv.

1996
689PDa Imperforate pane, #689PD (4) —
G294PDa Imperforate pane, #G294PD (4) —
G295PDa Imperforate pane, #G295PD (6) —
V210PDa Imperforate pane, #V210PD (on photographic paper) (2) —
V211PDa Imperforate pane, #V211PD (4) —
SC50PD (1) —
688PP 10 items (18) —
Cross gutter block (6) —
Horiz. pair with vert. gutter (12) —
Vert. pair with horiz. gutter (15) —
689PP 11 items (18) —
Cross gutter block (6) —
Horiz. pair with vert. gutter (12) —
Vert. pair with horiz. gutter (15) —
G294PP 9 items (18) —
Cross gutter block (6) —
Horiz. pair with vert. gutter (12) —
Vert. pair with horiz. gutter (15) —
G295PP 9 items (18) —
Cross gutter block (6) —
Horiz. pair with vert. gutter (12) —
Vert. pair with horiz. gutter (15) —
V210PP 9 items (18) —
Cross gutter block (6) —
Horiz. pair with vert. gutter (18) —
Vert. pair with horiz. gutter (14) —
V211PP 9 items (18) —
Cross gutter block (6) —
Horiz. pair with vert. gutter (18) —
Vert. pair with horiz. gutter (14) —
688PI (12 pairs) —
Cross gutter block (18) —
Horiz. pair with vert. gutter (36) —
Vert. pair with horiz. gutter (45) —
689PI (12 pairs) —
Cross gutter block (18) —
Horiz. pair with vert. gutter (36) —
Vert. pair with horiz. gutter (45) —
G294PI (12 pairs) —
Cross gutter block (18) —
Horiz. pair with vert. gutter (36) —
Vert. pair with horiz. gutter (45) —
G295PI (12 pairs) —
Cross gutter block (18) —
Horiz. pair with vert. gutter (36) —
Vert. pair with horiz. gutter (45) —
V210PI (12 pairs) —
Cross gutter block (18) —
Horiz. pair with vert. gutter (36) —
Vert. pair with horiz. gutter (45) —
V211PI (12 pairs) —
Cross gutter block (18) —
Horiz. pair with vert. gutter (36) —
Vert. pair with horiz. gutter (45) —

Two of the No. G295PDa items are on photographic paper. Four cards with imperforate panes of 32c Hansel & Gretel essays exist. Four cards with imperforate panes of 5.50s Yeh-Shen essays exist. Four essays of No. SC50 showing these two essay items exist.

New York #690-697
Flags

1997
690-697PP Set of 20 sheets (1) —
690-697PI Set of 2 sheets (3) —

On Nos. 690-697PP, there are ten progressive proof sheets per issued sheet.

New York #698-699, Geneva #296-297, Vienna #212-213
Definitives

1997
698PDa Card, #698PD, #G296PD-G297PD, #V212PD-V213PD (1) —
699PDa Card, #698PD-699PD, #G296PD-G297PD, #V212PD-V213PD (4) —
698PP 8 items (84) —
Cross gutter block (3) —
Horiz. pair with vert. gutter (18) —
Vert. pair with horiz. gutter (14) —
699PP 8 items (84) —
Cross gutter block (3) —
Horiz. pair with vert. gutter (14) —
Vert. pair with horiz. gutter (18) —
G296PP 8 items (84) —
Cross gutter block (3) —
Horiz. pair with vert. gutter (14) —
Vert. pair with horiz. gutter (18) —
G297PP 8 items (84) —
Cross gutter block (3) —
Horiz. pair with vert. gutter (14) —
Vert. pair with horiz. gutter (18) —
V212PP 10 items (84) —
Cross gutter block (3) —
Horiz. pair with vert. gutter (18) —
Vert. pair with horiz. gutter (14) —
V213PP 10 items (84) —
Cross gutter block (3) —
Horiz. pair with vert. gutter (18) —
Vert. pair with horiz. gutter (14) —
698PI (60 pairs) —
Cross gutter block (3) —
Horiz. pair with vert. gutter (18) —
Vert. pair with horiz. gutter (14) —
699PI (60 pairs) —
Cross gutter block (3) —
Horiz. pair with vert. gutter (14) —
Vert. pair with horiz. gutter (18) —
G296PI (60 pairs) —
Cross gutter block (3) —
Horiz. pair with vert. gutter (14) —
Vert. pair with horiz. gutter (18) —
G297PI (60 pairs) —
Cross gutter block (3) —
Horiz. pair with vert. gutter (14) —
Vert. pair with horiz. gutter (18) —
V212PI (60 pairs) —
Cross gutter block (3) —
Horiz. pair with vert. gutter (18) —
Vert. pair with horiz. gutter (14) —
V213PI (60 pairs) —
Cross gutter block (3) —
Horiz. pair with vert. gutter (18) —
Vert. pair with horiz. gutter (14) —

New York #703a, Geneva #301a, Vienna #217a
Endangered Species

1997
703aPDa Card, imperforate pane of 4 blocks #703aPD, imperforate pane of 4 blocks #G301aPD (4) —
V217aPDa Card, imperforate pane of 4 blocks #V217aPD (4) —
703aPP 6 items (4 blocks) —
Cross gutter block (2) —
Horiz. pair with vert. gutter (2) —
Vert. pair with horiz. gutter (4) —
G301aPP 6 items (4 blocks) —
Cross gutter block (2) —
Horiz. pair with vert. gutter (2) —
Vert. pair with horiz. gutter (4) —

V217aPP 6 items (4 blocks) —
Cross gutter block (2) —
Horiz. pair with vert. gutter (2) —
Vert. pair with horiz. gutter (4) —
703aPI (12 blocks) —
Cross gutter block (6) —
Horiz. pair with vert. gutter (6) —
Vert. pair with horiz. gutter (12) —
G301aPI (12 blocks) —
Cross gutter block (6) —
Horiz. pair with vert. gutter (6) —
Vert. pair with horiz. gutter (12) —
V217aPI (12 blocks) —
Cross gutter block (6) —
Horiz. pair with vert. gutter (6) —
Vert. pair with horiz. gutter (12) —

New York #707a, 708, Geneva #305a, 306, Vienna #221a, 222
Earth Summit

1997
707aPP 6 items (6 blocks) —
708PP 6 items (1 souvenir sheet) —
708aPP 6 items (1 souvenir sheet) —
G305aPP 6 items (6 blocks) —
V221aPP 6 items (6 blocks) —
707aPI (15 blocks) —
708PI (6 souvenir sheets) —
708aPI (6 souvenir sheets) —
G305aPI (15 blocks) —
G306PI (6 souvenir sheets) —
V221aPI (15 blocks) —
V222PI (6 souvenir sheets) —

New York #713a, Geneva #311a, Vienna #227a
Transportation

1997
713aPDa Imperforate pane, #713aPD (9) —
G311aPDa Imperforate pane, #G311aPD (9) —
V227aPDa Imperforate pane, #V227aPD (9) —
713aPP 9 items (6 strips) —
Cross gutter block of strips (1) —
Horiz. pair of strips with vert. gutter (6) —
Vert. pair of strips with horiz. gutter (1) —
G311aPP 10 items (6 strips) —
Cross gutter block of strips (1) —
Horiz. pair of strips with vert. gutter (6) —
Vert. pair of strips with horiz. gutter (1) —
V227aPP 9 items (6 strips) —
Cross gutter block of strips (1) —
Horiz. pair of strips with vert. gutter (6) —
Vert. pair of strips with horiz. gutter (1) —
713aPI (14 strips) —
Cross gutter block of strips (1) —
Horiz. pair of strips with vert. gutter (6) —
Vert. pair of strips with horiz. gutter (1) —
G311aPI (14 strips) —
Cross gutter block of strips (1) —
Horiz. pair of strips with vert. gutter (6) —
Vert. pair of strips with horiz. gutter (1) —
V227aPI (14 strips) —
Cross gutter block of strips (1) —
Horiz. pair of strips with vert. gutter (6) —
Vert. pair of strips with horiz. gutter (1) —

New York #714-715, Geneva #312-313, Vienna #228-229, Souvenir Card #51
Philately

1997
715TCa Card, #714TC-715TC, #G312TC-G313TC, #V228TC-V229TC, all with white denominations (4) —
715TCb Card, #714TC-715TC, #G312TC-G313TC, #V228TC-V229TC, all with light blue green backgrounds (1) —
SC51PD (4) —
714PP 11 items (33) —
Horiz. pair with vert. gutter (6) —
715PP 11 items (33) —
Horiz. pair with vert. gutter (6) —
715PPa Cross gutter block, 2 each #714PP-715PP (2) —
715PPb Vert. pair with horiz. gutter, #714PP-715PP (11) —
G312PP 11 items (33) —
Horiz. pair with vert. gutter (6) —
G313PP 11 items (33) —
Horiz. pair with vert. gutter (6) —
G313PPa Cross gutter block, 2 each #G312PP-G313PP (2) —
G313PPb Vert. pair with horiz. gutter, #G312PP-G313PP (11) —
V228PP 10 items (33) —
Horiz. pair with vert. gutter (6) —
V229PP 10 items (33) —
Horiz. pair with vert. gutter (6) —
V229PPa Cross gutter block, 2 each #V228PP-V229PP (2) —
V229PPb Vert. pair with horiz. gutter, #V228PP-V229PP (11) —
714PI (48 pairs) —
Horiz. pair with vert. gutter (18) —
715PI (48 pairs) —
Horiz. pair with vert. gutter (18) —
715PIa Cross gutter block, 2 each #714PI-715PI (6) —
715PIb Vert. pair with horiz. gutter, #714PI-715PI (33) —
G312PI (48 pairs) —
Horiz. pair with vert. gutter (18) —
G313PI (48 pairs) —
Horiz. pair with vert. gutter (18) —
G313PIa Cross gutter block, 2 each #G312PI-G313PI (6) —
G313PIb Vert. pair with horiz. gutter, #G312PI-G313PI (33) —
V228PI (48 pairs) —
Horiz. pair with vert. gutter (18) —
V229PI (48 pairs) —
Horiz. pair with vert. gutter (18) —
V229PIa Cross gutter block, 2 each #V228PI-V229PI (6) —
V229PIb Vert. pair with horiz. gutter, #V228PI-V229PI (33) —

On Nos. 714PP-715PP, G312PP-G313PP and V228PP-V229PP some progressive proof items are blank due to color arrangements on sheets.

New York #716-717, Geneva #314-315, Vienna #230-231
World Heritage

1997
717PDa Stapled set of 6 layout sheets with #716PD-717PD, #G314PD-G315PD, #V230PD-V231PD affixed (3) —
716PP 10 items (20) —
717PP 10 items (20) —
G314PP 10 items (20) —
G315PP 10 items (20) —
V230PP 10 items (20) —
V231PP 10 items (20) —
716PI (30 pairs) —
717PI (30 pairs) —
G314PI (30 pairs) —
G315PI (30 pairs) —
V230PI (30 pairs) —
V231PI (30 pairs) —

New York #719-726
Flags

1998
719-726PP Set of 20 sheets (1) —
719-726PI Set of 2 sheets (3) —

On Nos. 719-726PP, there are ten progressive proof sheets per issued sheet.

New York #727-729, Geneva #317, Vienna #233-234
Definitives

1998
727PDa Card, #727PD, #G317TC black (1) —
729PDa Card, #727PD-729PD, #G317PD, #V233PD-V234PD (4) —
727PP 10 items (84) —
Cross gutter block (3) —
Horiz. pair with vert. gutter (14) —
Vert. pair with horiz. gutter (18) —
728PP 8 items (84) —
Cross gutter block (3) —
Horiz. pair with vert. gutter (14) —
Vert. pair with horiz. gutter (18) —
729PP 9 items (84) —
Cross gutter block (3) —
Horiz. pair with vert. gutter (18) —
Vert. pair with horiz. gutter (14) —
G317PP 10 items (84) —
Cross gutter block (3) —
Horiz. pair with vert. gutter (14) —
Vert. pair with horiz. gutter (18) —
V233PP 8 items (84) —
Cross gutter block (3) —
Horiz. pair with vert. gutter (18) —
Vert. pair with horiz. gutter (14) —
V234PP 10 items (84) —
Cross gutter block (3) —
Horiz. pair with vert. gutter (18) —
Vert. pair with horiz. gutter (14) —
727PI (60 pairs) —
Cross gutter block (3) —
Horiz. pair with vert. gutter (14) —
Vert. pair with horiz. gutter (18) —
728PI (60 pairs) —
Cross gutter block (3) —
Horiz. pair with vert. gutter (14) —
Vert. pair with horiz. gutter (18) —
729PI (60 pairs) —
Cross gutter block (3) —
Horiz. pair with vert. gutter (18) —
Vert. pair with horiz. gutter (14) —
G317PI (60 pairs) —
Cross gutter block (3) —
Horiz. pair with vert. gutter (14) —
Vert. pair with horiz. gutter (18) —
V233PI (60 pairs) —
Cross gutter block (3) —
Horiz. pair with vert. gutter (18) —
Vert. pair with horiz. gutter (14) —
V234PI (60 pairs) —
Cross gutter block (3) —
Horiz. pair with vert. gutter (18) —
Vert. pair with horiz. gutter (14) —

New York #733a, Geneva #321a, Vienna #238a
Endangered Species

1998
733PDa Card, imperforate pane of 4 blocks, #733aPD (1) —
733PDb Card, broken imperforate pane of 4 blocks, #733aPD (1) —
G321PDa Card, imperforate pane of 4 blocks, #G321aPD (1) —
G321PDb Card, broken imperforate pane of 4 blocks, #G321aPD (1) —
V238PDa Card, imperforate pane of 4 blocks, #V238aPD (1) —
V238PDb Card, broken imperforate pane of 4 blocks, #V238aPD (1) —
733aPP 6 items (4 blocks) —
Cross gutter block (2) —
Horiz. pair with vert. gutter (2) —
Vert. pair with horiz. gutter (4) —
G321aPP 4 items (4 blocks) —
Cross gutter block (2) —
Horiz. pair with vert. gutter (2) —
Vert. pair with horiz. gutter (4) —
V238aPP 6 items (4 blocks) —
Cross gutter block (2) —
Horiz. pair with vert. gutter (2) —
Vert. pair with horiz. gutter (4) —
733aPI (12 blocks) —
Cross gutter block (2) —
Horiz. pair with vert. gutter (2) —
Vert. pair with horiz. gutter (4) —
G321aPI (12 blocks) —
Cross gutter block (2) —
Horiz. pair with vert. gutter (2) —
Vert. pair with horiz. gutter (4) —
V238aPI (12 blocks) —
Cross gutter block (2) —
Horiz. pair with vert. gutter (2) —
Vert. pair with horiz. gutter (4) —

No. G321aPP is not a complete set, as there are no black only and cyan only items.

New York #734, Geneva #322, Vienna #239
International Year of the Ocean

1998
734PD (not approved) (4) —
G322PD (4) —
V239PD (4) —
734PP 6 items (6 panes) —
G322PP 6 items (6 panes) —
V239PP 6 items (6 panes) —
734PI (18 panes) —
G322PI (18 panes) —
V239PI (18 panes) —

New York #735-736, Geneva #323-324, Vienna #240-241
Rain Forests

1998
735PDa Card, imperforate pane of 20 #735PD (8) —
736PDa Card, #736PD, #G324PD, #V241PD (8) —
G323PDa Card, imperforate pane of 20 #G323PD (8) —
V240PDa Card, imperforate pane of 20 #V240PD (8) —
735PP 6 items (see note) —
G323PP 6 items (see note) —
V240PP 6 items (see note) —
735PI (see note) —
G323PI (see note) —
V240PI (see note) —

There are two types of Nos. 735PP and V240PP, one with cats lacking spots on the red item, the other with the cat with spots on the magenta item. There are 20 of each type.

There are two types of No. G323PP, one with orangutan with small dots in eyes on the cyan item, the other with large dots in eyes.

Similarly, there are two types of Nos. 735PI, G323PI and V240PI, one with a lighter background, the other with a bolder background. There are 20 pairs of each type.

New York #737-738, Geneva #325-326, Vienna #242-243, Souvenir Card #52
UN Peacekeeping Forces, 50th Anniv.

1998
737TC Dark blue panel (on Cromalin paper) (5) —
738TC Dark blue panel (on Cromalin paper) (5) —
G325TC Dark blue panel (on Cromalin paper) (5) —
G326TC Dark blue panel (on Cromalin paper) (5) —
V242TC Dark blue panel (on Cromalin paper) (5) —
V243TC Dark blue panel (on Cromalin paper) (5) —
SC52PD (4) —
737PP 10 items (20) —
738PP 10 items (20) —
G325PP 10 items (20) —
G326PP 10 items (20) —
V242PP 10 items (20) —
V243PP 10 items (20) —
737PI (20 pairs) —
738PI (20 pairs) —
G325PI (20 pairs) —

G326PI	(20 pairs)	—
V242PI	(20 pairs)	—
V243PI	(20 pairs)	—

New York #739-740, Geneva #327-328, Vienna #244-245, Souvenir Card #53

Universal Declaration of Human Rights, 50th Anniv.

1998

740PDa	Card, #739PD-740PD, #G327PD-G328PD, #V244PD-V245PD (4)	—
SC53PD	(4)	—
739PP	8 items (64)	—
	Cross gutter block (2)	—
	Horiz. pair with vert. gutter (8)	—
	Vert. pair with horiz. gutter (16)	—
740PP	8 items (64)	—
	Cross gutter block (2)	—
	Horiz. pair with vert. gutter (8)	—
	Vert. pair with horiz. gutter (16)	—
G327PP	8 items (64)	—
	Cross gutter block (2)	—
	Horiz. pair with vert. gutter (8)	—
	Vert. pair with horiz. gutter (16)	—
G328PP	8 items (64)	—
	Cross gutter block (2)	—
	Horiz. pair with vert. gutter (8)	—
	Vert. pair with horiz. gutter (16)	—
V244PP	8 items (64)	—
	Cross gutter block (2)	—
	Horiz. pair with vert. gutter (8)	—
	Vert. pair with horiz. gutter (16)	—
V245PP	8 items (64)	—
	Cross gutter block (2)	—
	Horiz. pair with vert. gutter (8)	—
	Vert. pair with horiz. gutter (16)	—
739PI	(52 pairs)	—
	Cross gutter block (2)	—
	Horiz. pair with vert. gutter (8)	—
	Vert. pair with horiz. gutter (16)	—
740PI	(52 pairs)	—
	Cross gutter block (2)	—
	Horiz. pair with vert. gutter (8)	—
	Vert. pair with horiz. gutter (16)	—
G327PI	(52 pairs)	—
	Cross gutter block (2)	—
	Horiz. pair with vert. gutter (8)	—
	Vert. pair with horiz. gutter (16)	—
G328PI	(52 pairs)	—
	Cross gutter block (2)	—
	Horiz. pair with vert. gutter (8)	—
	Vert. pair with horiz. gutter (16)	—
V244PI	(52 pairs)	—
	Cross gutter block (2)	—
	Horiz. pair with vert. gutter (8)	—
	Vert. pair with horiz. gutter (16)	—
V245PI	(52 pairs)	—
	Cross gutter block (2)	—
	Horiz. pair with vert. gutter (8)	—
	Vert. pair with horiz. gutter (16)	—

New York #741-743, Geneva #329-331, Vienna #246-248

Schönbrunn Palace

1998

742PDa	Card, blocks of 4, #741PD-742PD (3)	—
742PDb	Card, cut apart blocks of 4, #741PD-742PD (1)	—
G330PDa	Card, blocks of 4, #G329PD-G330PD (3)	—
G330PDb	Card, cut apart blocks of 4, #G329PD-G330PD (1)	—
V247PDa	Card, blocks of 4, #V246PD-V247PD (3)	—
V247PDb	Card, cut apart blocks of 4, #V246PD-V247PD (1)	—
742TCa	Card, block of 4 #742TC dark blue denomination (on photographic paper) (1)	—
743TCa	Card, strips of 3, #743aTC-743cTC bright red violet denomination (on photographic paper) (1)	—
743TCb	Card, blocks of 4, #743dTC-743fTC bright red violet denomination (on photographic paper) (1)	—
743TCc	Entire booklet (black & white, on photographic paper) (1)	—
G330TCa	Card, blocks of 4, #G329TC-G330TC bright red violet denominations (on photographic paper) (1)	—
G331TCa	Card, blocks of 4, #G331aTC-G331cTC bright red violet denomination (on photographic paper) (1)	—
G331TCb	Card, strips of 3, #G331dTC-G331fTC bright red violet denomination (on photographic paper) (1)	—
G331TCc	Entire booklet (black & white, on photographic paper) (1)	—
V247TCa	Card, block of 4 #V247TC bright green denomination (on photographic paper) (1)	—
V248TCa	Card, strips of 3, #V248aTC-V248cTC bright red violet denomination (on photographic paper) (1)	—
V248TCb	Card, blocks of 4, #V248dTC-V248fTC bright red violet denomination (on photographic paper) (1)	—
V248TCc	Entire booklet (black & white, on photographic paper) (1)	—
741PP	10 items (24)	—
	Vert. pair with horiz. gutter (3)	—
742PP	10 items (24)	—
	Horiz. pair with vert. gutter (3)	—
742PPa	Cross gutter block, 2 #741PP-742PP (1)	—
742PPb	Vert. pair with horiz. gutter, #741PP-742PP (8)	—
G329PP	10 items (24)	—
	Vert. pair with horiz. gutter (3)	—
G330PP	10 items (24)	—
	Horiz. pair with vert. gutter (3)	—
G330PPa	Cross gutter block, 2 #G329PP-G330PP (1)	—
G330PPb	Vert. pair with horiz. gutter, #G329PP-G330PP (8)	—
V246PP	10 items (24)	—
	Vert. pair with horiz. gutter (3)	—
V247PP	10 items (24)	—
	Horiz. pair with vert. gutter (3)	—
V247PPa	Cross gutter block, 2 #V246PP-V247PP (1)	—
V247PPb	Vert. pair with horiz. gutter, #V246PP-V247PP (8)	—
741PI	(32 pairs)	—
	Vert. pair with horiz. gutter (3)	—
742PI	(32 pairs)	—
	Horiz. pair with vert. gutter (3)	—
742PIa	Cross gutter block, 2 #741PI-742PI (1)	—
742PIb	Vert. pair with horiz. gutter, #741PI-742PI (8)	—
G329PI	(32 pairs)	—
	Vert. pair with horiz. gutter (3)	—
G330PI	(32 pairs)	—
	Horiz. pair with vert. gutter (3)	—
G330PIa	Cross gutter block, 2 #G329PI-G330PI (1)	—
G330PIb	Vert. pair with horiz. gutter, #G329PI-G330PI (8)	—
V246PI	(32 pairs)	—
	Vert. pair with horiz. gutter (3)	—
V247PI	(32 pairs)	—
	Horiz. pair with vert. gutter (3)	—
V247PIa	Cross gutter block, 2 #V246PI-V247PI (1)	—
V247PIb	Vert. pair with horiz. gutter, #V246PI-V247PI (8)	—

Five cards with blocks of four essays with gold frames over vignette exist for each of the New York, Geneva and Vienna pairings.

New York #744-751

Flags

1999

744-751PP	Set of 20 sheets (1)	—
744-751PI	Set of 2 sheets (4)	—

On Nos. 744-751PP, there are ten progressive proof sheets per issued sheet.

New York #752-753, Geneva #332, Vienna #249

Definitives

1999

752PDa	Card, #752PD, #V249PD (3)	—
752PDb	Card, #752PD, #V249PD, #753TC lacking gray in pink frame boxes (1)	—
753PDa	Card, block of 4, #753PD (2)	—
753TC	Lacking gray in pink frame boxes (3)	—
G332TC	red (4)	—
G332TC	brown (4)	—
752PP	9 items (48)	—
	Cross gutter block (1)	—
	Horiz. pair with vert. gutter (6)	—
	Vert. pair with horiz. gutter (8)	—
753PP	10 items (20)	—
V249PP	9 items (48)	—
	Cross gutter block (1)	—
	Horiz. pair with vert. gutter (6)	—
	Vert. pair with horiz. gutter (8)	—
752PI	(24 pairs)	—
	Cross gutter block (3)	—
	Horiz. pair with vert. gutter (18)	—
	Vert. pair with horiz. gutter (24)	—
753PI	(20 pairs)	—
G332PI	(20 pairs)	—
V249PI	(72 pairs)	—
	Cross gutter block (3)	—
	Horiz. pair with vert. gutter (18)	—
	Vert. pair with horiz. gutter (24)	—

New York #754-756, Geneva #333-335, Vienna #250-252

World Heritage

1999

755PDa	Card, pairs of #754PD-755PD, #G333PD-G334PD, #V250PD-V251PD (1)	—
756PDa	Card, pairs of #756aPD-756fPD (1)	—
756PDb	Sheet, pairs of #754PD-755PD, #756aPD-756fPD, #G333PD-G334PD, #G335aPD-G335fPD, #V250PD-V251PD, #V252aPD-V252fPD (2)	—
756PDc	Cut-up section of #756PDb with pairs of stamps issued in sheets (2)	—
756PDd	Cut-up section of #756PDb with pairs of stamps issued in booklets (2)	—
754TC	Black and white image on layout sheet of photographic paper (2)	—
755TC	Black and white image on layout sheet of photographic paper (2)	—
G333TC	Black and white image on layout sheet of photographic paper (2)	—
G334TC	Black and white image on layout sheet of photographic paper (2)	—
V250TCa	Black and white image on layout sheet of photographic paper (2)	—
V250TCb	2 pairs of black and white images on layout sheet of photographic paper, affixed to card (1)	—
V251TCa	Black and white image on layout sheet of photographic paper (2)	—
V251TCb	2 pairs of black and white images on layout sheet of photographic paper, affixed to card (1)	—
754PP	6 items (32)	—
	Horiz. pair with vert. gutter (8)	—
755PP	6 items (32)	—
	Horiz. pair with vert. gutter (8)	—
755PPa	Cross gutter block, 2 #754PP-755PP (2)	—
755PPb	Vert. pair with horiz. gutter, #754PP-755PP (8)	—
G333PP	6 items (32)	—
	Horiz. pair with vert. gutter (8)	—
G334PP	6 items (32)	—
	Horiz. pair with vert. gutter (8)	—
G334PPa	Cross gutter block, 2 #G333PP-G334PP (2)	—
G334PPb	Vert. pair with horiz. gutter, #G333PP-G334PP (8)	—
V250PP	6 items (32)	—
	Horiz. pair with vert. gutter (8)	—
V251PP	6 items (32)	—
	Horiz. pair with vert. gutter (8)	—
V251PPa	Cross gutter block, 2 #V250PP-V251PP (2)	—
V251PPb	Vert. pair with horiz. gutter, #V250PP-V251PP (8)	—
754PI	(52 pairs)	—
	Horiz. pair with vert. gutter (16)	—
755PI	(52 pairs)	—
	Horiz. pair with vert. gutter (16)	—
755PIa	Cross gutter block, 2 #754PI-755PI (4)	—
755PIb	Vert. pair with horiz. gutter, #754PI-755PI (16)	—
G333PI	(36 pairs)	—
	Horiz. pair with vert. gutter (8)	—
G334PI	(36 pairs)	—
	Horiz. pair with vert. gutter (8)	—
G334PIa	Cross gutter block, 2 #G333PI-G334PI (2)	—
G334PIb	Vert. pair with horiz. gutter, #G333PI-G334PI (8)	—
V250PI	(36 pairs)	—
	Horiz. pair with vert. gutter (8)	—
V251PI	(36 pairs)	—
	Horiz. pair with vert. gutter (8)	—
V251PIa	Cross gutter block, 2 #V250PI-V251PI (2)	—
V251PIb	Vert. pair with horiz. gutter, #V250PI-V251PI (8)	—

New York #760a, Geneva #339a, Vienna #256a

Endangered Species

1999

760aPDa	Card, imperf pane of 4 blocks, #760aPD (2)	—
760aPDb	Card, 2 each #757PD-760PD (1)	—
G339aPDa	Card, 2 each #G336PD-G339PD (on Cromalin paper), broken pane of 80c essays of #G336-G339 (1)	—
V256aPDa	Card, imperf pane of 4 blocks, #V256aPD (3)	—
V256aPDb	Card, 2 each #V253PD-V256PD (1)	—
760aPP	6 items (4 blocks)	—
	Cross gutter block (2)	—
	Horiz. pair with vert. gutter (2)	—
	Vert. pair with horiz. gutter (4)	—
G339aPP	6 items (4 blocks)	—
	Cross gutter block (2)	—
	Horiz. pair with vert. gutter (2)	—
	Vert. pair with horiz. gutter (4)	—
V256aPP	6 items (4 blocks)	—
	Cross gutter block (2)	—
	Horiz. pair with vert. gutter (2)	—
	Vert. pair with horiz. gutter (4)	—
760aPI	(12 blocks)	—
	Cross gutter block (2)	—
	Horiz. pair with vert. gutter (2)	—
	Vert. pair with horiz. gutter (4)	—
G339aPI	(12 blocks)	—
	Cross gutter block (2)	—
	Horiz. pair with vert. gutter (2)	—
	Vert. pair with horiz. gutter (4)	—
V256aPI	(12 blocks)	—
	Cross gutter block (2)	—
	Horiz. pair with vert. gutter (2)	—
	Vert. pair with horiz. gutter (4)	—

Three cards exist containing imperforate panes of four blocks of the 80c essays.

New York #762a, 763, Geneva #341a, 342, Vienna #258a, 259
UNISPACE III

1999

762aPDa Card, imperforate pane of 5 pairs, #762aPD (3) —
763PD With printed perforations on overlay (3) —
763aPD With printed perforations on overlay (2) —
G341aPDa Card, imperforate pane of 5 pairs, #G341aPD (4) —
G342PD With printed perforations on overlay (2) —
G342aPD With printed perforations on overlay (2) —
V258aPDa Card, imperforate pane of 5 pairs, #V258aPD (4) —
V259PD With printed perforations on overlay (2) —
762PP 8 items (5 pairs) —
762aPP 8 items (1 souvenir sheet) —
763PP 9 items (1 pair) —
763aPP 10 items (1 souvenir sheet) —
762aPI (10 pairs) —
763PI (3 souvenir sheets) —
763aPI (4 souvenir sheets) —
G341aPI (10 pairs) —
G342PI (3 souvenir sheets) —
V258aPI (10 pairs) —
V259PI (3 souvenir sheets) —

New York #767a, Geneva #346a, Vienna #263a, Souvenir Card #54
Universal Postal Union, 125th Anniv.

1999

767aPDa Card, #767aPD, #G346aPD, #V263aPD with approval handstamp (4) —
767aTCa Card, #767aTC, #G346aTCD, #V263aTC (dark blue denominations, not approved (4) —
SC54PD (4) —
767aPP 8 items (6 blocks) —
G346aPP 8 items (6 blocks) —
V263aPP 8 items (6 blocks) —
767aPI (12 blocks) —
G346aPI (12 blocks) —
V263aPI (12 blocks) —

New York #768-769, Geneva #347-348, Vienna #264-265
In Memoriam

1999

769PDa Card, #768PD-769PD (4) —
G348PDa Card, #G347PD-G348PD (4) —
V265PDa Card, #V264PD-V265PD (4) —
768PP 10 items (66) —
Cross gutter block (2) —
Horiz. pair with vert. gutter (12) —
Vert. pair with horiz. gutter (11) —
769PP 10 items (24 souvenir sheets) —
G347PP 10 items (66) —
Cross gutter block (2) —
Horiz. pair with vert. gutter (12) —
Vert. pair with horiz. gutter (11) —
G348PP 10 items (24 souvenir sheets) —
V264PP 10 items (66) —
Cross gutter block (2) —
Horiz. pair with vert. gutter (12) —
Vert. pair with horiz. gutter (11) —
V265PP 10 items (24 souvenir sheets) —
768PI (52 pairs) —
Cross gutter block (2) —
Horiz. pair with vert. gutter (12) —
Vert. pair with horiz. gutter (11) —
769PI (24 souvenir sheets) —
G347PI (52 pairs) —
Cross gutter block (2) —
Horiz. pair with vert. gutter (12) —
Vert. pair with horiz. gutter (11) —
G348PI (24 souvenir sheets) —
V264PI (52 pairs) —
Cross gutter block (2) —
Horiz. pair with vert. gutter (12) —
Vert. pair with horiz. gutter (11) —
V265PI (24 souvenir sheets) —

New York #770-771, Geneva #349-350, Vienna #266-267
Education

1999

771PDa Card, #770PD-771PD, #G349PD-G350PD, #V266PD-V267PD with approval handstamp (4) —
771PDb Card, #770PD, #G350PD, #V266PD-V267PD, #771TC red denomination, #G349TC red violet denomination with "approved with corrections" handstamp (4) —
770PP 9 items (20) —
771PP 8 items (20) —
G349PP 7 items (20) —
G350PP 7 items (20) —
V266PP 7 items (20) —
V267PP 8 items (20) —
770PI (20 pairs) —
771PI (20 pairs) —
G349PI (30 pairs) —
G350PI (30 pairs) —
V266PI (30 pairs) —
V267PI (30 pairs) —

New York #772, Geneva #351, Vienna #268
International Year of Thanksgiving

2000

772PDa Card, #772PD, #G351PD, #V268PD (4) —
772TCa Card, #772TC, #G351TC, #V268TC, all with black background (4) —
772PP 12 items (32) —
Horiz. pair with vert. gutter (4) —
G351PP 12 items (32) —
Horiz. pair with vert. gutter (4) —
V268PP 12 items (32) —
Horiz. pair with vert. gutter (4) —
772PI (36 pairs) —
Horiz. pair with vert. gutter (4) —
G351PI (36 pairs) —
Horiz. pair with vert. gutter (4) —
V268PI (36 pairs) —
Horiz. pair with vert. gutter (4) —

New York #776a, Geneva #355a, Vienna #272a
Endangered Species

2000

776aPDa Card, imperforate pane of 4 blocks, #776aPD (3) —
776aPDb Card, 3 each #773PD-776PD (1) —
G355aPDa Card, imperforate pane of 4 blocks, #G355aPD, imperforate pane of 4 blocks, #V272aPD (3) —
G355aPDb Card, 3 each #G352PD-G355PD, #V269PD-V272PD (1) —
776aPP 6 items (4 blocks) —
Cross gutter block (2) —
Horiz. pair with vert. gutter (2) —
Vert. pair with horiz. gutter (4) —
G355aPP 6 items (4 blocks) —
Cross gutter block (2) —
Horiz. pair with vert. gutter (2) —
Vert. pair with horiz. gutter (4) —
V272aPP 6 items (4 blocks) —
Cross gutter block (2) —
Horiz. pair with vert. gutter (2) —
Vert. pair with horiz. gutter (4) —
776aPI (12 blocks) —
Cross gutter block (2) —
Horiz. pair with vert. gutter (2) —
Vert. pair with horiz. gutter (4) —
G355aPI (12 blocks) —
Cross gutter block (2) —
Horiz. pair with vert. gutter (2) —
Vert. pair with horiz. gutter (4) —
V272aPI (12 blocks) —
Cross gutter block (2) —
Horiz. pair with vert. gutter (2) —
Vert. pair with horiz. gutter (4) —

New York #777-778, Geneva #356-357, Vienna #273-274
Our World 2000

2000

778PDa Card, #777PD-778PD, #G356PD-G357PD, #V273PD-V274PD (4) —
778PDb Card, #777PD-778PD, #G356PD-G357PD, #V274PD, #V273TC black denomination, with "not approved" handstamp (2) —
777PP 8 items (64) —
Cross gutter block (2) —
Horiz. pair with vert. gutter (16) —
Vert. pair with horiz. gutter (8) —
778PP 8 items (64) —
Cross gutter block (2) —
Horiz. pair with vert. gutter (8) —
Vert. pair with horiz. gutter (16) —
G356PP 8 items (64) —
Cross gutter block (2) —
Horiz. pair with vert. gutter (8) —
Vert. pair with horiz. gutter (16) —
G357PP 8 items (64) —
Cross gutter block (2) —
Horiz. pair with vert. gutter (16) —
Vert. pair with horiz. gutter (8) —
V273PP 8 items (64) —
Cross gutter block (2) —
Horiz. pair with vert. gutter (16) —
Vert. pair with horiz. gutter (8) —
V274PP 8 items (64) —
Cross gutter block (2) —
Horiz. pair with vert. gutter (8) —
Vert. pair with horiz. gutter (16) —
777PI (52 pairs) —
Cross gutter block (2) —
Horiz. pair with vert. gutter (16) —
Vert. pair with horiz. gutter (8) —
778PI (52 pairs) —
Cross gutter block (2) —
Horiz. pair with vert. gutter (8) —
Vert. pair with horiz. gutter (16) —
G356PI (52 pairs) —
Cross gutter block (2) —
Horiz. pair with vert. gutter (16) —
Vert. pair with horiz. gutter (8) —
G357PI (52 pairs) —
Cross gutter block (2) —
Horiz. pair with vert. gutter (8) —
Vert. pair with horiz. gutter (16) —
V273PI (52 pairs) —
Cross gutter block (2) —
Horiz. pair with vert. gutter (16) —
Vert. pair with horiz. gutter (8) —
V274PI (52 pairs) —
Cross gutter block (2) —
Horiz. pair with vert. gutter (8) —
Vert. pair with horiz. gutter (16) —

New York #779-781, Geneva #358-360, Vienna #275-277
United Nations, 55th Anniv.

2000

780TCa Card, #779TC-780TC, #G358TC-G359TC, #V275TC-V276TC (all with white denominations with colored outlines (4) —
781TCa Card, #781TC, #G360TC, #V277TC (all with white denominations with colored outlines (4) —
781TCb Card, #779TC-781TC ultramarine & silver (2) —
781TCc Card, #779TC-781TC blue & silver (2) —
781TCd Card, #781TC, #G360TC silver backgrounds, white denominations with colored outlines (5) —
G359TCa Card, #G358TC-G359TC brown red & silver (2) —
G360TCa Card, #G358TC-G360TC carmine & silver (2) —
G360TCb Card, #G358TC-G360TC cerise & silver (2) —
V277TCa Card, #V275TC-V277TC green & silver (2) —
V277TCb Card, #V275TC-V277TC dark green & silver (2) —
V277TCc Silver background, white denominations with green outlines (5) —
779PP 7 items (128) —
Cross gutter block (4) —
Horiz. pair with vert. gutter (16) —
Vert. pair with horiz. gutter (32) —
780PP 7 items (128) —
Cross gutter block (4) —
Horiz. pair with vert. gutter (16) —
Vert. pair with horiz. gutter (32) —
781PP 6 items (60 souvenir sheets) —
G358PP 9 items (128) —
Cross gutter block (4) —
Horiz. pair with vert. gutter (16) —
Vert. pair with horiz. gutter (32) —
G359PP 9 items (128) —
Cross gutter block (4) —
Horiz. pair with vert. gutter (16) —
Vert. pair with horiz. gutter (32) —
G360PP 9 items (60 souvenir sheets) —
V275PP 10 items (128) —
Cross gutter block (4) —
Horiz. pair with vert. gutter (16) —
Vert. pair with horiz. gutter (32) —
V276PP 10 items (128) —
Cross gutter block (4) —
Horiz. pair with vert. gutter (16) —
Vert. pair with horiz. gutter (32) —
V277PP 10 items (60 souvenir sheets) —
779PI (84 pairs) —
Cross gutter block (4) —
Horiz. pair with vert. gutter (16) —
Vert. pair with horiz. gutter (32) —
780PI (84 pairs) —
Cross gutter block (4) —
Horiz. pair with vert. gutter (16) —
Vert. pair with horiz. gutter (32) —
781PI (60 souvenir sheets) —
G358PI (84 pairs) —
Cross gutter block (4) —
Horiz. pair with vert. gutter (16) —
Vert. pair with horiz. gutter (32) —
G359PI (84 pairs) —
Cross gutter block (4) —
Horiz. pair with vert. gutter (16) —
Vert. pair with horiz. gutter (32) —
V275PI (84 pairs) —
Cross gutter block (4) —
Horiz. pair with vert. gutter (16) —
Vert. pair with horiz. gutter (32) —
V276PI (84 pairs) —
Cross gutter block (4) —
Horiz. pair with vert. gutter (16) —
Vert. pair with horiz. gutter (32) —
781PI (60 souvenir sheets) —

One item in Nos. G358PP and G359PP is blank, coming from sheet with marginal inscriptions only.

New York #782
International Flag of Peace

2000

782PD With approval handstamp (4) —
782TC Black and white photocopy of layout of pane of 20, with approval handstamp and signature (1) —
782PP 9 items (96) —
Cross gutter block (2) —
Horiz. pair with vert. gutter (16) —
Vert. pair with horiz. gutter (8) —
782PI (96 pairs) —
Cross gutter block (6) —
Horiz. pair with vert. gutter (48) —
Vert. pair with horiz. gutter (24) —

An essay with "age 12" after artist's name exists in five cards and a black and white layout of the pane of 20 on photographic paper.

New York #783, Geneva #361, Vienna #278
UN in the 21st Century

2000

783PDa Card, #783PD, #G361PD, #V278PD with approval handstamp (4) —

783TCa Card, #783TC, #G361TC, #V278TC all with washed-out colors, with "not approved" handstamp (5) —
783PP 8 items (1) —
G361PP 8 items (1) —
V278PP 8 items (1) —
783PI (2 sheets) —
G361PI (2 sheets) —
V278PI (2 sheets) —

New York #784-786, Geneva #362-364, Vienna #279-281
World Heritage

2000
785PDa Card, #784PD-785PD, #G362PD-G364PD, #V279PD-V280PD (4) —
784TC Black and white image of pane of 20 on layout sheet on photographic paper (1) —
785TC Black and white image of pane of 20 on layout sheet on photographic paper (1) —
G362TC Black and white image of pane of 20 on layout sheet on photographic paper (1) —
G363TC Black and white image of pane of 20 on layout sheet on photographic paper (1) —
V279TC Black and white image of pane of 20 on layout sheet on photographic paper (1) —
V280TC Black and white image of pane of 20 on layout sheet on photographic paper (1) —
784PP 9 items (24) —
Vert. pair with horiz. gutter (3) —
785PP 9 items (24) —
Vert. pair with horiz. gutter (3) —
785PPa Cross gutter block, 2 #784PP-785PP (1) —
785PPb Horiz. pair with vert. gutter, #784PP-785PP (8) —
786iPPa 9 items, Strip of #786gPP-786iPP, with vert. gutters between (4) —
G362PP 9 items (24) —
Vert. pair with horiz. gutter (3) —
G363PP 9 items (24) —
Vert. pair with horiz. gutter (3) —
G363PPa Cross gutter block, 2 #G362PP-G363PP (1) —
G363PPb Horiz. pair with vert. gutter, #G362PP-G363PP (8) —
V279PP 7 items (24) —
Vert. pair with horiz. gutter (3) —
V280PP 7 items (24) —
Vert. pair with horiz. gutter (3) —
V280PPa Cross gutter block, 2 #V279PP-V280PP (1) —
V280PPb Horiz. pair with vert. gutter, #V279PP-V280PP (8) —
784PI (32 pairs) —
Vert. pair with horiz. gutter (3) —
785PI (32 pairs) —
Vert. pair with horiz. gutter (3) —
785PIa Cross gutter block, 2 #784PI-785PI (1) —
785PIb Horiz. pair with vert. gutter, #784PI-785PI (8) —
786gPI (5 booklet panes) —
786hPI (5 booklet panes) —
786iPI (5 booklet panes) —
786iPIa Strip of #786gPI-786iPI, with vert. gutters between (4) —
786jPI (5 booklet panes) —
786kPI (5 booklet panes) —
786lPI (5 booklet panes) —
G362PI (32 pairs) —
Vert. pair with horiz. gutter (3) —
G363PI (32 pairs) —
Vert. pair with horiz. gutter (3) —
G363PIa Cross gutter block, 2 #G362PI-G363PI (1) —
G363PIb Horiz. pair with vert. gutter, #G362PI-G363PI (8) —
G364gPI (5 booklet panes) —
G364hPI (5 booklet panes) —
G364iPI (5 booklet panes) —
G364jPI (5 booklet panes) —
G364kPI (5 booklet panes) —
G364lPI (5 booklet panes) —
V279PI (82 pairs) —
Vert. pair with horiz. gutter (3) —
V280PI (32 pairs) —
Vert. pair with horiz. gutter (3) —
V280PIa Cross gutter block, 2 #V279PI-V280PI (1) —
V280PIb Horiz. pair with vert. gutter, #V279PI-V280PI (8) —
V281gPI (5 booklet panes) —
V281hPI (5 booklet panes) —
V281iPI (5 booklet panes) —
V281jPI (5 booklet panes) —
V281kPI (5 booklet panes) —
V281lPI (5 booklet panes) —

Some pairs of No. V279PI are defaced with blue marker.

New York #787-788, Geneva #365-366, Vienna #282-283, Souvenir Card #55
Respect for Refugees

2000
787PDa Card, #787PD, #G365PD, #V282PD (4) —
788PDa Card, #788PD, #G366PD, #V283PD (4) —
SC55PD (4) —
787PP 6 items (32) —
Horiz. pair with vert. gutter (4) —
788PP 6 items (20 souvenir sheets) —
G365PP 6 items (32) —
Cross gutter block (1) —
Horiz. pair with vert. gutter (6) —
Vert. pair with horiz. gutter (8) —
G366PP 6 items (20 souvenir sheets) —
V282PP 6 items (32) —
Horiz. pair with vert. gutter (4) —
V283PP 6 items (20 souvenir sheets) —
787PI (36 pairs) —
Horiz. pair with vert. gutter (4) —
788PI (20 souvenir sheets) —
G365PI (44 pairs) —
Cross gutter block (1) —
Horiz. pair with vert. gutter (6) —
Vert. pair with horiz. gutter (8) —
G366PI (20 souvenir sheets) —
V282PI (36 pairs) —
Horiz. pair with vert. gutter (4) —
V283PI (20 souvenir sheets) —

AIR POST STAMPS
New York #C1-C4
Plane and Gull, Swallows and UN Emblem

1951
C1PD (1) —
C2PD (1) —
C3PD (1) —
C4PD (1) —
C1PI (25 pairs) —
C2PI (25 pairs) —
C3PI (25 pairs) —
C4PI (25 pairs) —

New York #C5
Airplane Wing and Globe

1957
C5PD (4) —
C5TC brown (not approved) (5) —
C5TC indigo (5) —
C5PI (40 pairs) —
Vert. pair with horiz. gutter (10) —

New York #C6-C7
Airplane Wing and Globe; UN Flag and Plane

1959
C6PD (1) —
C6PDa Card, #C6PD, 2 #C6TC in slightly different shades (2) —
C6PDb Card, 2 #C6PD, 2 #C7TC Prussian blue (1) —
C7PD (1) —
C7PDa Card, #C7PD, #C7TC Prussian blue, #C7TC dark blue (2) —
C6TC black (1) —
C7TC black (1) —
C6PI (115 pairs) —
Vert. pair with horiz. gutter (10) —
C7PI (90 pairs) —
Horiz. pair with vert. gutter (10) —

New York #C8-C10
Definitives

1963
C10PDa Card, #C8PD-C10PD (3) —
C10PDb Card, #C8PD, #C10PD, 3 #C9PD (3) —
C8PP 3 items (80) —
Horiz. pair with vert. gutter (10) —
C9PP 4 items (80) —
Vert. pair with horiz. gutter (10) —
C10PP 4 items (80) —
Horiz. pair with vert. gutter (10) —
C8PI (80 pairs) —
Horiz. pair with vert. gutter (20) —
C9PI (80 pairs) —
Vert. pair with horiz. gutter (20) —
C10PI (80 pairs) —
Horiz. pair with vert. gutter (20) —

New York #C11-C12
Definitives

1964
C11PDa Card, #C11PD, #C12TC peach and brown background (disapproved) (2) —
C12PD (2) —
C12PDa Card, #C11PD-C12PD (4) —
C11PI (25 pairs) —
C12PI (25 pairs) —

New York #C13
Jet and UN Emblem

1968
C13PD (3) —
C13PDa Card, #C13PD, 2 #C13TC with slightly different shades (2) —
C13PP 9 items, perforated, mounted on card (1) —

New York #C14
Wings, Envelopes and UN Emblem

1969
C14PD (4) —
C14PP 6 items, perforated (50) —

New York #C15-C18
Definitives

1972
C15PD (2) —
C16PD With approval handstamp (2) —
C17PD (2) —
C18PD (2) —
C16TC dark blue emblem (dated 16. Oct. 1971) (2) —
C15PP 4 items (100) —
C16PP 10 items (100) —
C17PP 4 items (100) —
C18PP 10 items (160) —
Horiz. pair with vert. gutter (20) —
C16PI (50 pairs) —
C17PI (50 pairs) —

New York #C19-C21
Definitives

1974
C19PD (3) —
C20PD (3) —
C21PD (3) —
C19PP 8 items (50) —
C21PP 5 items (50) —
C19PI (50 pairs) —
C20PI (50 pairs) —
C21PI (50 pairs) —

Five cards with essays of No. C21 with incorrect Russian inscription exist.

New York #C22-C23
Definitives

1977
C22PD With approval handstamp (4) —
C22TC Gray wings and envelope, with "not approved" handstamp (2) —
C23PD (1) —
C23PDa Card, #C23PD, #C22TC gray wings and envelope (3) —
C22PP 6 items (50) —
C22PI (50 pairs) —
C23PI (50 pairs) —

ENVELOPES
New York #U1
UN Emblem

1952
U1PD (1) —
U1TC black (1) —

New York #U2
UN Emblem

1958
U2PD with manuscript approval (2) —
U2TC black, on card, with manuscript approval (1) —

New York #U3
Stylized Globe and Weather Vane

1963
U3PD (2) —
U3PI Indicia only on small piece of paper (1) —

See No. UC6PI.

New York #U5
UN Headquarters

1973
U5PD (41) —
U5PP 6 items (5) —
U5PI Unfolded and uncut (2) —

New York #U6
UN Headquarters

1975
U6PD With approval handstamp (5) —
U6PDa Die cut and unfolded, without approval handstamp (4) —

New York #U7
Bouquet of Ribbons

1985
U7PD Indicia only, in folder (9) —

Vienna #U1-U2
Donaupark

1995
VU1PD On Cromalin paper (approved) (6) —
VU1PDa On AGFA paper (not approved) (5) —
VU2PD On Cromalin paper (approved) (6) —
VU2PDa On AGFA paper (not approved) (5) —

New York #U10-U11
Cripticandina

1997
U10PD On Cromalin paper (4) —
U11PD On Cromalin paper (4) —

Vienna #U3
Landscape

1998

VU3PD On Cromalin paper (4) —

AIR POST ENVELOPES & AIR LETTER SHEETS

New York #UC1 Swallows and UN Emblem

1952

UC1PI (32) —
UC1PIa On white paper (22) —

New York #UC3
UN Flag and Plane Envelope

1959

UC3PD (1) —

New York #UC4
UN Flag and Plane Letter Sheet

1960

UC4PD (1) —

Two "not approved" essays exist with diagonal lines rather than bars around envelope.

New York #UC5 Plane and Gull

1961

UC5PD With approval handstamp (1) —
UC5aPD With approval handstamp (3) —

New York #UC6
UN Emblem

1963

UC6PDa Sheet, #UC6PD, #U3PD, with approval handstamp (2) —
UC6PI (1) —
UC6PIa Sheet, #UC6PD (2 sizes), #U3PD (2 sizes) (6) —
UC6PIb As #UC6PIa with one #U3PI removed (1) —

New York #UC7
UN Emblem and Stylized Plane

1968

UC7PD With specimen perfin and approval handstamp (7) —

New York #UC8
UN Emblem

1969

UC8PD With specimen perfin at left (4) —

Geneva #UC1
UN Emblem and Stylized Plane

1969

GUC1PD With specimen perfin and approval handstamp (1) —
GUC1TC light blue (2) —
GUC1TC ultramarine (3) —

New York #UC9
UN Emblem, "UN," Globe and Plane

1972

UC9PD With approval handstamp (2) —

New York #UC10
Birds in Flight

1973

UC10PDa Small envelope, die cut and folded, with approval handstamp (1) —
UC10PDb Large envelope, partially folded, with approval handstamp (2) —
UC10PPa Uncut and unfolded, large and small envelopes (6 items) —

Three sets of essays exist with blue UN inscriptions close.

New York #UC11
Globe and Jet

1975

UC11PD With approval handstamp (5) —
UC11PDa Die cut and unfolded, without approval handstamp (1) —

New York #UC12
UN Headquarters

1975

UC12PD With approval handstamp (1) —

New York #UC13
UN Emblem and Birds

1977

UC13PD With approval handstamp (2) —

Five "not approved" essays have design flaw at end of orange line.

New York #UC14, Vienna #UC1
Paper Airplane, Dove

1982

UC14PD With approval handstamp (3) —
UC14PDa On thin card stock (1) —
VUC1PD With approval handstamp (3) —
VUC1PDa On thin card stock (1) —

Vienna #UC3
Birds in Flight and UN Emblem

1987

VUC3PD On plastic, with approval handstamp (4) —

New York #UC16
UN Headquarters

1989

UC16PD With approval handstamp (approved) (3) —
UC16PDa With approval handstamp (not approved) (10) —

Vienna #UC5
Donaupark

1992

VUC5PD On Cromalin paper (3) —

New York #UC19
Winged Hand With Envelopes Surcharge

1995

UC19PD On Cromalin paper (1) —

New York #UC20
Cherry Blossoms

1997

UC20PD (5) —

POSTAL CARDS

New York #UX1
UN Headquarters

1952

UX1TC olive brown, on white paper (1) —
UX1PI (4 pairs) —

New York #UX2
UN Headquarters

1958

UX2PD With approval handstamp (2) —

New York #UX3
World Map

1963

UX3PD (2) —

New York #UX4
UN Emblem and Post Horn

1969

UX4PD With approval handstamp on reverse (1) —

Geneva #UX1-UX2
UN Emblem and Post Horn, Stylized Space View

1969

GUX1PD With approval handstamp (3) —
GUX1PI (53 pairs) —
GUX2PI (52 pairs) —

New York #UX5
"UN"

1973

UX5PD (1) —

Five "not approved" essays similar to #UX5 exist. Ten 7c essays exist, three with approval handstamp, the others lacking any handstamp.

New York #UX6
"UN"

1975

UX6PD With specimen perfin and approval handstamp (4) —

Five "not approved" essays have incorrect Russian inscription.

New York #UX7, Geneva #UX3-UX4
UN Emblem, UN Emblem in Rectangles, UN Emblem and Ribbons

1977

UX7PD With specimen perfin at left (4) —
GUX3PD With specimen perfin (5) —
GUX4PD With specimen perfin at left (4) —

New York #UX8, Vienna #UX1-UX2
"United Nations," Olive Branch, Bird Carrying Olive Branch

1982

UX8PD (2) —
VUX1PD With approval handstamp on reverse (4) —
VUX2PD With approval handstamp on reverse (16) —

Geneva #UX5-UX6, Vienna #UX3
Peace Dove, UN Emblem

1985

GUX5PD (3) —
GUX6PD With approval handstamp on reverse (3) —
VUX3PD (3) —

One example of No. GUX5PD has inked lines at left of card. One example of No. GUX6PD has inked lines around address lines.

New York #UX9-UX18
Views of UN Headquarters

1989

UX9PD Message side (4) —
UX9PDa Picture side (4) —
UX10PD Message side (4) —
UX10PDa Picture side (4) —
UX11PD Message side (4) —
UX11PDa Picture side (4) —
UX12PD Message side (4) —
UX12PDa Picture side (4) —
UX13PD Message side (4) —
UX13PDa Picture side (4) —
UX14PD Message side (4) —
UX14PDa Picture side (4) —
UX15PD Message side (4) —
UX15PDa Picture side (4) —
UX16PD Message side (4) —
UX16PDa Picture side (4) —
UX17PD Message side (4) —
UX17PDa Picture side (4) —
UX18PD Message side (4) —
UX18PDa Picture side (4) —

New York #UX19, Geneva #UX8, Vienna #UX5
UN Headquarters, Palais des Nations, Regschek Painting

1992

UX19PD On Cromalin paper (4) —
GUX8PD On Cromalin paper (4) —
VUX5PD On Cromalin paper (4) —
VUX5PDa Sheet, #GUX8PD, #VUX5PD on Cromalin paper (1) —
UX19TC ultramarine (1) —

Geneva #UX10, Vienna #UX6-UX7
Palais des Nations, Peoples of the World United, Donaupark

1993

GUX10PD On Cromalin paper (4) —
VUX6PD On Cromalin paper (4) —
VUX7PD On Cromalin paper (4) —

Vienna #UX12
The Gloriette

1999

VUX12TCa Light blue text (4) —

AIR POST POSTAL CARDS

New York #UXC1
UN Flag and Plane

1957

UXC1PD With printer and approval handstamps (6) —
UXC1PI (30 pairs) —

New York #UXC3
Airplane Wing and Globe

1959

UXC3PD With approval handstamp (3) —

Six essays of No. UXC3 lacking outlined letters on "Airmail" and "Poste Aerienne" exist.

New York #UXC4
Outer Space

1963

UXC4PD (2) —

New York #UXC6
Outer Space

1968

UXC6PD With "Canceled" perfin (2) —
UXC6PDa Strip of 3 cards with 2 "Canceled" perfins (2) —

New York #UXC7
UN Emblem and Stylized Planes

1969

UXC7PD (1) —
UXC7TC black (2) —

New York #UXC8
UN Emblem and Stylized Wing

1972

UXC8PDa	Folder with mounted #UXC8PD with approval handstamp, and #UXC8 (2)	—

New York #UXC9
UN Emblem and Stylized Planes

1972

UXC9PD	Folder with mounted #UXC9, with approval handstamp (2)	—

New York #UXC10-UXC11
Clouds; Pathways

1975

UXC10PD	With specimen perfin and approval handstamp (4)	—
UXC11PD	With specimen perfin and approval handstamp (4)	—
UXC10TC	With manuscript "Lighter as on sample," and approval handstamp (not approved) (5)	—

New York #UXC12
Flying Mailman

1982

UXC12PD	With approval handstamp on reverse (5)	—

U.N. TEMPORARY EXECUTIVE AUTHORITY, WEST NEW GUINEA

Located in the western half of New Guinea, southwest Pacific Ocean, the former Netherlands New Guinea became a territory under the administration of the United Nations Temporary Executive Authority on Oct. 1, 1962. The size was 151,789 sq. mi. and the population was estimated at 730,000 in 1958. The capital was Hollandia.

The territory came under Indonesian administration on May 1, 1963. For stamps issued by Indonesia see listings following Indonesia in Volume 3.

100 Cents = 1 Gulden

Catalogue values for all unused stamps in this country are for Never Hinged items.

First Printing (Hollandia)

Netherlands New Guinea Stamps of 1950-60 Overprinted

Overprint size: 17x3½mm. Top of "N" is slightly lower than the "U," and the base of the "T" is straight, or nearly so.

Photo.; Litho. (#4, 6, 8)

1962, Oct. 1 Unwmk. *Perf. 12½x12, 12½x13½*

1	A4	1c	**vermilion & yellow**, *Oct. 1*	.25	.25
2	A1	2c	**deep orange**, *Oct. 1*	.25	.25
3	A4	5c	**chocolate & yellow**, *Oct. 1*	.25	.25
4	A5	7c	**org red, bl & brn vio**, *Nov. 1*	.25	*.35*
5	A4	10c	**aqua & red brown**, *Oct. 1*	.25	*.35*
6	A5	12c	**green, bl & brn vio**, *Nov. 1*	.25	*.35*
7	A4	15c	**deep yel & red brn**, *Nov. 1*	.45	.45
8	A5	17c	**brown violet & blue**, *Oct. 1*	.55	*.70*
9	A4	20c	**lt bl grn & red brn**, *Nov. 1*	.60	*.75*
10	A6	25c	**red**, *Oct. 1*	.40	*.55*
11	A6	30c	**deep blue**, *Oct. 1*	.75	.75
12	A6	40c	**deep orange**, *Oct. 1*	.75	.75
13	A6	45c	**dark olive**, *Nov. 1*	1.25	*1.50*
14	A6	55c	**slate blue**, *Nov. 1*	*29.00*	2.25
15	A6	80c	**dull gray violet**, *Nov. 1*	6.00	6.00
16	A6	85c	**dark violet brown**, *Nov. 1*	3.00	3.00
17	A6	1g	**plum**, *Oct. 1*	9.25	3.00

Engr.

18	A3	2g	**reddish brown**, *Oct. 1*	12.50	30.00
19	A3	5g	**green**, *Oct. 1*	9.00	8.00
			Nos. 1-19 (19)	75.00	59.50

Overprinted locally and sold in West New Guinea. Stamps of the second printing were used to complete sets sold to collectors.

Second Printing (Haarlen, Netherlands)

Overprint size: 17x3½mm. Top of the "N" is slightly higher than the "U," and the base of the "T" is concave.

Photo.; Litho. (#4a, 6a, 8a)

1962 Unwmk. *Perf. 12½x12, 12½x13½*

1a	A4	1c	**vermilion & yellow**	.25	.25
2a	A1	2c	**deep orange**	.25	.25
3a	A4	5c	**chocolate & yellow**	.25	.25
4a	A5	7c	**org red, bl & brn vio**	.25	.25
5a	A4	10c	**aqua & red brown**	.25	.25
6a	A5	12c	**green, bl & brn vio**	.25	.25
7a	A4	15c	**deep yel & red brn**	.50	.25
8a	A5	17c	**brown violet & blue**	.60	.40
9a	A4	20c	**lt blue grn & red brn**	.60	.40
10a	A6	25c	**red**	.35	.35
11a	A6	30c	**deep blue**	.90	.40
12a	A6	40c	**deep orange**	.90	.40
13a	A6	45c	**dark olive**	1.75	.75
14a	A6	55c	**slate blue**	5.00	1.00
15a	A6	80c	**dull gray violet**	7.00	*9.00*
16a	A6	85c	**dark violet brown**	3.75	*4.75*
17a	A6	1g	**plum**	4.25	2.00

Engr.

18a	A3	2g	**reddish brown**	16.00	*27.50*
19a	A3	5g	**green**	8.00	6.50
			Nos. 1a-19a (19)	51.10	55.20

Overprinted in the Netherlands and sold by the UN in New York.

Third Printing

Overprint 14mm long.

Photo.; Litho. (#4b, 6b, 8b)

1963, Mar. Photo. Unwmk. *Perf. 12½x12*

1b	A4	1c	**vermilion & yellow**	*5.00*	*3.00*
3b	A4	5c	**chocolate & yellow**	*6.00*	*4.00*
4b	A5	7c	**org red, bl & brn vio**	*20.00*	*20.00*
5b	A4	10c	**aqua & red brown**	*6.00*	*4.00*
6b	A5	12c	**green, bl & brn vio**	*35.00*	*35.00*
7b	A4	15c	**deep yel & red brn**	*130.00*	*130.00*
8b	A5	17c	**brown violet & blue**	*15.00*	*12.00*
9b	A4	20c	**lt blue grn & red brn**	*7.50*	*5.00*
			Nos. 1b-9b (8)	*224.50*	*213.00*

The third printing was applied in West New Guinea and it is doubtful whether it was regularly issued. Used values are for canceled to order stamps.

Fourth Printing

Overprint 19mm long.

Photogravure

1963, Mar. Unwmk. *Perf. 12½x12*

1c	A4	1c	**vermilion & yellow**	*50.00*	*50.00*
5c	A4	10c	**aqua & red brown**	*150.00*	*150.00*

The fourth printing was applied in West New Guinea and it is doubtful whether it was regularly issued. Used values are for canceled to order stamps.

U.N. TRANSITIONAL AUTHORITY IN EAST TIMOR

A30

2000, Apr. 29 **Litho.** ***Perf. 12x11¾***

350	A30 Dom. red & multi	*35.00*	*102.50*
351	A30 Int. blue & multi	*47.50*	*112.50*
	First day cover, #350, 351		*80.00*

No. 350 sold for 10c and No. 351 sold for 50c on day of issue.

U.N. INTERIM ADMINISTRATION, KOSOVO

These stamps were issued by the United Nations Interim Administration Mission in Kosovo and the Post & Telecommunications of Kosovo. Service was local for the first two months, with international use starting in mid-May 2000.

Starting with No. 6, stamps were not made available to collectors through the United Nations Postal Administration.

100 pfennigs = 1 mark
100 cents = €1 (2002)

Catalogue values for all unused stamps in this country are for Never Hinged items.

Stamps Issued for Kosovo by the United Nations Interim Administration

Peace in Kosovo — A1

Printed by La Poste, France. Panes of 40. Designed by Shyqri Nimani, Kosovo.

Designs: 20pf, Mosaic depicting Orpheus, c. 5th-6th cent., Podujeve. 30pf, Dardinian idol, Museum of Kosovo. 50pf, Silver coin of Damastion from 4th cent. B.C. 1m, Statue of Mother Teresa, Prizren. 2m, Map of Kosovo.

Perf. 13½x13, 13½x13¼ (30pf)

2000, Mar. 14 **Litho.** **Unwmk.**

1	A1 20pf **multicolored**	.65	.65
	First day cover		1.50
2	A1 30pf **multicolored**	1.25	1.25
	First day cover		1.50
3	A1 50pf **multicolored**	1.60	1.60
	First day cover		2.25
4	A1 1m **multicolored**	2.00	1.80
	First day cover		4.50
5	A1 2m **multicolored**	3.75	3.50
	First day cover		9.00
	First day cover, #1-5		12.00
	Nos. 1-5 (5)	9.25	8.80

Nos. 1-5 were demonetized July 1, 2002.

Peace in Kosovo — A2

Designs: 20pf, Bird. 30pf, Street musician. 50pf, Butterfly and pear. 1m, Children and stars. 2m, Globe and handprints.

2001, Nov. 12 **Litho.** ***Perf. 14***

6	A2 20pf **multicolored**	1.00	1.00
7	A2 30pf **multicolored**	1.25	1.25
8	A2 50pf **multicolored**	2.00	2.00
9	A2 1m **multicolored**	4.00	4.00
10	A2 2m **multicolored**	7.50	7.50
	First day cover, #6-10		22.00
	Nos. 6-10 (5)	15.75	15.75

100 Cents = 1 Euro (€)

Peace in Kosovo Type of 2001 With Denominations in Euros Only

2002, May 2 **Litho.** ***Perf. 14***

11	A2 10c Like #6	.75	.75
12	A2 15c Like #7	1.00	1.00
13	A2 26c Like #8	1.50	1.50
14	A2 51c Like #9	4.50	4.50
15	A2 €1.02 Like #10	8.00	8.00
	First day cover, #11-15		20.00
	Nos. 11-15 (5)	15.75	15.75

Christmas — A3

Designs: 50c, Candles and garland. €1, Stylized men.

2003, Dec. 20 **Litho.** ***Perf. 14***

16	A3 50c **multicolored** *(30,000)*	*7.50*	*7.50*
17	A3 €1 **multicolored** *(30,000)*	*14.50*	*14.50*
	First day cover, #16-17		*20.00*

Return of Refugees — A4

Five Years of Peace — A5

2004, June 29 **Litho.** ***Perf. 13¼x13***

18	A4 €1 **multicolored** *(40,000)*	*7.00*	*7.00*
19	A5 €2 **multicolored** *(40,000)*	*16.00*	*16.00*
	First day cover, #18-19		*25.00*

Musical Instruments — A6

2004, Aug. 31 **Litho.** ***Perf. 13¼x13***

20	A6 20c Flute *(30,000)*	*5.00*	*5.00*
21	A6 30c Ocarina *(30,000)*	*10.00*	*10.00*
	First day cover, #20-21		*12.00*

Aprons — A7

Vests — A8

Designs: 20c, Apron from Prizren. 30c, Apron from Rugova. 50c, Three vests. €1, Two vests.

2004, Oct. 28 **Litho.** ***Perf. 13x13¼***

22 A7 20c **multicolored** *(30,000)* *5.50 5.50*
23 A7 30c **multicolored** *(30,000)* *8.50 8.50*
24 A8 50c **multicolored** *(30,000)* *12.00 12.00*
25 A8 €1 **multicolored** *(30,000)* *26.00 26.00*
First day cover, #22-25 *30.00*
Nos. 22-25 (4) *52.00 52.00*

Mirusha Waterfall — A9

2004, Nov. 26 **Litho.** ***Perf. 13x13¼***

26 A9 €2 **multicolored** *(40,000)* *7.50 7.50*
First day cover *7.50*

House — A10

2004, Dec. 14 **Litho.** ***Perf. 13x13¼***

27 A10 50c **multicolored** *(40,000)* *4.50 4.50*
First day cover *8.00*

Flowers — A11

2005, June 29 **Litho.** ***Perf. 13½***

28 A11 15c Peony *(50,000)* *2.25 2.25*
29 A11 20c Poppies *(50,000)* *3.25 3.25*
30 A11 30c Gentian *(50,000)* *5.00 5.00*
First day cover, #28-30 *17.00*
Nos. 28-30 (3) *10.50 10.50*

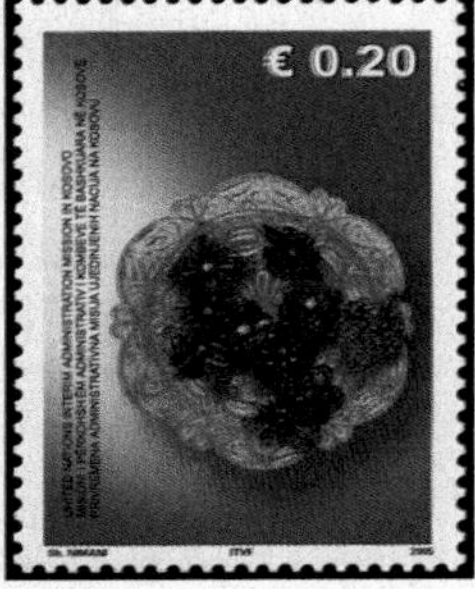

A12

Handicrafts — A13

2005, July 20 ***Perf. 13¼x13***

31 A12 20c shown *(40,000)* *2.50 2.50*
32 A12 30c Cradle *(40,000)* *3.00 3.00*
33 A13 50c shown *(40,000)* *3.25 3.25*
34 A12 €1 Necklace *(40,000)* *4.25 4.25*
First day cover, #31-34 *17.00*
Nos. 31-34 (4) *13.00 13.00*

Village — A14

Town — A15

City — A16

2005, Sept. 15 ***Perf. 13x13½***

35 A14 20c **multicolored** *(50,000)* *2.00 2.00*
36 A15 50c **multicolored** *(110,000)* *3.00 3.00*
37 A16 €1 **multicolored** *(110,000)* *6.00 6.00*
First day cover, #35-37 *17.00*
Nos. 35-37 (3) *11.00 11.00*

Archaeological Artifacts — A17

2005, Nov. 2 ***Perf. 13½x13***

38 A17 20c shown *(25,000)* *1.25 1.25*
39 A17 30c Statue *(25,000)* *1.75 1.75*
40 A17 50c Sculpture *(25,000)* *2.50 2.50*
41 A17 €1 Helmet *(25,000)* *7.50 7.50*
First day cover, #38-41 *17.00*
Nos. 38-41 (4) *13.00 13.00*

Minerals A18

2005, Dec. 10 ***Perf. 13x13½***

42 A18 €2 **multicolored** *(45,000)* *10.00 10.00*
First day cover *10.00*

A19

Europa — A20

2006, July 20 ***Perf. 13¼x13***

43 A19 50c **multicolored** *(60,000)* *2.25 2.25*
44 A20 €1 **multicolored** *(60,000)* *4.25 4.25*
First day cover, #43-44 *10.00*

Exists Imperf. Value set: 2 pairs $75.

Fauna A21

2006, May 23 **Litho.** ***Perf. 13***

45 A21 15c Wolf *(190,000)* *1.00 1.00*
46 A21 20c Cow *(190,000)* *1.25 1.25*
47 A21 30c Pigeon *(190,000)* *1.40 1.40*
48 A21 50c Swan *(190,000)* *1.60 1.60*
49 A21 €1 Dog *(190,000)* *2.75 2.75*
a. Souvenir sheet, #45-49, + label *(15,000)* *8.75 8.75*
First day cover, #45-49 *22.00*
First day cover, #49a *15.00*
Nos. 45-49 (5) *8.00 8.00*

Nos. 45-49 were printed by CPU. Stamps with "Leoprint" imprint are from No. 63a.

No. 49a exists in two shades of green selvage.

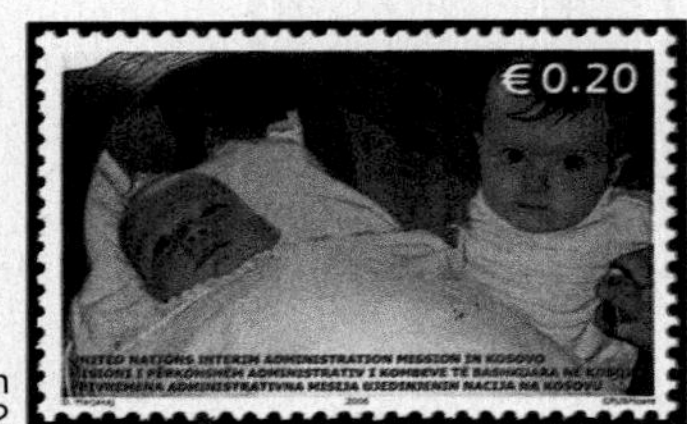

Children A22

Designs: 20c, Children in cradle. 30c, Children reading. 50c, Girls dancing. €1, Child in water.

2006, June 30 **Litho.** ***Perf. 13***

50 A22 20c **multicolored** *(40,000)* *1.00 1.00*
51 A22 30c **multicolored** *(40,000)* *1.25 1.25*
52 A22 50c **multicolored** *(40,000)* *1.75 1.75*
53 A22 €1 **multicolored** *(40,000)* *3.50 3.50*
a. Souvenir sheet, #50-53 *(12,500)* *7.75 7.75*
First day cover, #50-53 *20.00*
First day cover, #53a *22.00*
Nos. 50-53 (4) *7.50 7.50*

Nos. 50-53 were printed by CPU & Moare. No. 53a was printed by two printers: 7,500 inscribed "CPU&Moare," and 5,000 inscribed "Leoprint."

No. 53a exists imperforate. Value $75.

A23

A24

A25

Tourist Attractions A26

2006, Sept. 1 **Litho.** ***Perf. 13***

54 A23 20c **multicolored** *(40,000)* *1.00 1.00*
55 A24 30c **multicolored** *(40,000)* *1.25 1.25*
56 A25 50c **multicolored** *(40,000)* *1.75 1.75*
57 A26 €1 **multicolored** *(40,000)* *3.25 3.25*
a. Souvenir sheet, #54-57 *(12,500)* *9.50 9.50*
First day cover, #54-57 *20.00*
First day cover, #57a *22.00*
Nos. 54-57 (4) *7.25 7.25*

Nos. 54-57 were printed by CPU & Moare. No. 57a was printed by two printers: 7,500 inscribed "CPU&Moare," and 5,000 inscribed "Leoprint."

Intl. Peace Day — A27

2006, Sept. 21 **Litho.** ***Perf. 13***

58 A27 €2 **multicolored** *(40,000)* *7.00 7.00*
Min. sheet of 4 *55.00*
First day cover *12.50*
First day cover, min. sheet of 4 *30.00*

No. 58 was printed by CPU.

Ancient Coins — A28

Various coins.

2006, Nov. 1 **Litho.** ***Perf. 13***

59 A28 20c **multicolored** *(30,000)* *1.00 1.00*
60 A28 30c **multicolored** *(30,000)* *1.50 1.50*
61 A28 50c **multicolored** *(30,000)* *1.75 1.75*
62 A28 €1 **multicolored** *(30,000)* *3.25 3.25*
a. Souvenir sheet, #59-62 *(15,000)* *9.50 9.50*
First day cover, #59-62 *20.00*
First day cover, #62a *22.00*
Nos. 59-62 (4) *7.50 7.50*

Nos. 59-62 were printed by CPU. Stamps with "Leoprint" imprint are from No. 63a.

Sculpture — A29

2006, Dec. 1 **Litho.** ***Perf. 13***

63 A29 €2 **multicolored** *(45,000)* *8.00 8.00*
a. Miniature sheet, #45-57, 59-63, + 2 labels *(5,000)* *80.00 80.00*
First day cover *10.00*
First day cover, #63a *90.00*

Issue dates: No. 63, Dec. 1. No. 63a, Dec. 15.

No. 63 is inscribed "CPU&Moare." No. 63a stamps are inscribed "CPU" or "CPU&Moare" throughout the sheet as they were inscribed when originally printed. Leoprint also printed No. 63a. Those stamps are inscribed "Leoprint."

Convention on the Rights of Persons With Disabilities — A30

Emblems of handicaps and: 20c, Children and butterfly. 50c, Handicapped women. 70c, Map of Kosovo. €1, Stylized flower.

2007, Apr. 23 **Litho.** ***Perf. 14x14¼***

64 A30 20c **multicolored** *(15,000)* *1.25 1.25*
65 A30 50c **multicolored** *(15,000)* *2.50 2.50*
66 A30 70c **multicolored** *(15,000)* *3.00 3.00*
67 A30 €1 **multicolored** *(15,000)* *3.75 3.75*
a. Souvenir sheet, #64-67 *(20,000)* *12.50 12.50*
First day cover, #64-67 *12.50*
First day cover, #67a *12.50*
Nos. 64-67 (4) *10.50 10.50*

Color shades vary widely. Printer's waste of this issue exists in the marketplace, including partial prints, missing design elements, and missing colors.

Two varieties of No. 67a, exist differing in text surrounding the stamps. It has not been established if both varieties were officially issued.

Scouting, Cent. — A31

Europa — A32

2007, May 12 **Litho.** ***Perf. 13¼***

68 A31 70c **multicolored** *(35,000)* *4.25 4.25*
69 A32 €1 **multicolored** *(35,000)* *6.25 6.25*
a. Souvenir sheet, #68-69 *(15,000)* *90.00 90.00*
First day cover, #68-69 *12.50*
First day cover, #69a *45.00*

Nos. 68-69 exist imperf. Value, $40 each pair.

No. 69a exists with perforations inverted (leaving the stamps imperforate). Value, $250.

A33

A34

A35

International Children's Day — A36

2007, June 1 **Litho.** ***Perf. 13¼***

70 A33 20c **multicolored** *(38,000)* *1.25 1.25*
71 A34 30c **multicolored** *(38,000)* *1.50 1.50*
72 A35 70c **multicolored** *(38,000)* *2.50 2.50*
73 A36 €1 **multicolored** *(38,000)* *4.00 4.00*
First day cover, #70-73 *15.00*
Nos. 70-73 (4) *9.25 9.25*

Nos. 70-73 exist imperf. Value, set $45

Native Costumes — A37

Designs: 20c, Serbian woman. 30c, Prizren Region woman. 50c, Sword dancer. 70c, Drenica Region woman. €1, Shepherd, Rugova.

2007, July 6 **Litho.** ***Perf. 13½x13¼***

74 A37 20c **multicolored** *(35,000)*	*1.25*	*1.25*
75 A37 30c **multicolored** *(35,000)*	*1.75*	*1.75*
76 A37 50c **multicolored** *(35,000)*	*2.00*	*2.00*
77 A37 70c **multicolored** *(35,000)*	*2.50*	*2.50*
78 A37 €1 **multicolored** *(35,000)*	*3.25*	*3.25*
a. Souvenir sheet, #74-78, + label *(15,000)*	*12.50*	*12.50*
First day cover, #74-78		*17.50*
First day cover, #78a		*17.50*
Nos. 74-78 (5)	*10.75*	*10.75*

Masks — A38

Various masks.

2007, Sept. 11 **Litho.** ***Perf. 13½x13¼***

79 A38 15c **multicolored** *(38,000)*	*.75*	*.75*
80 A38 30c **multicolored** *(38,000)*	*1.00*	*1.00*
81 A38 50c **multicolored** *(38,000)*	*2.00*	*2.00*
82 A38 €1 **multicolored** *(38,000)*	*3.00*	*3.00*
First day cover, #79-82		*15.00*
Nos. 79-82 (4)	*6.75*	*6.75*

Sports — A39

Designs: 20c, Soccer ball, basketball, two people standing, person in wheelchair. 50c, Wrestlers. €1, Symbols of 24 sports.

2007, Oct. 2 **Litho.** ***Perf. 13¼x13½***

83 A39 20c **multicolored** *(38,000)*	*1.00*	*1.00*
84 A39 50c **multicolored** *(38,000)*	*2.25*	*2.25*
85 A39 €1 **multicolored** *(38,000)*	*4.00*	*4.00*
First day cover, #83-85		*15.00*
Nos. 83-85 (3)	*7.25*	*7.25*

Nos. 83-85 exist imperf. Value, set $65.

Architecture — A40

Designs: 30c, Stone bridge, Vushtrri. 50c, Hamam, Prizren. 70c, Tower. €1, Tower, diff.

2007, Nov. 6 **Litho.** ***Perf. 13¼***

86 A40 30c **multicolored** *(38,000)*	*1.50*	*1.50*
87 A40 50c **multicolored** *(38,000)*	*2.00*	*2.00*
88 A40 70c **multicolored** *(38,000)*	*2.50*	*2.50*
89 A40 €1 **multicolored** *(38,000)*	*3.50*	*3.50*
First day cover, #86-89		*17.50*
Nos. 86-89 (4)	*9.50*	*9.50*

Nos. 86-89 exist imperf. Value, set $85.

Locomotives A41

Designs: €1, Diesel locomotive. €2, Steam locomotive

2007, Dec. 7 **Litho.** ***Perf. 13¼***

90 A41 €1 **multicolored** *(50,000)*	*4.00*	*4.00*
91 A41 €2 **multicolored** *(50,000)*	*8.00*	*8.00*
First day cover, #90-91		*22.50*

Nos. 90-91 exist imperf. Value, set $125.

Skanderbeg (1405-68), Albanian National Hero — A42

2008, Jan. 17 **Litho.** ***Perf. 13¼***

92 A42 €2 **multicolored** *(140,000)*	*7.50*	*7.50*
First day cover		*10.00*

No. 92 exists imperf. Value, $35.

Kosovo declared its independence from Serbia on Feb. 17, 2008, ending the United Nations Interim Administration. Stamps issued after Feb. 17, 2008, by the Republic of Kosovo will be listed under Kosovo in the *Scott Standard Postage Stamp Catalogue*.

INTRODUCING THE SCOTT RAIL TRANSPORTATION ALBUM

PART 1 • 1869-2017

- 1st Full Color Scott Stamp Album!
- Covers North, Central & South America
- Includes Train, Locomotive, Subway & Railed Themed Stamps
- Displays Single Stamps with Scott Numbers
- 50+ Acid-Free Heavy White Paper Stock
- Includes a Small Green, Metal Hinged, 3-ring Specialty Binder

Item#	Retail	AA
440NCSALB	$111.98	$69.99

For More Information Visit www.AmosAdvantage.com/Rail or call 1-800-572-6885

INDEX TO ADVERTISERS – 2020 U.S. SPECIALI[ZED]

DEALERS...TAKE ADVANTAGE OF AMOS HOBBY'S ADVERTISING OPPORTUNITIES!

SCOTT GIVES YOU THE AMERICAN MARKET...AND AN EVER INCREASING WORLD MARKET!
Present Your Buying or Selling Messages, in Your Specialty Area, to Serious Collectors by placing Your Advertisements in Scott Products!

2021 SCOTT CATALOGUES

Call now to reserve ad space and to receive advertising information. If you're interested in specific positions...call or write as soon as possible.

LINN'S STAMP NEWS

Whether you're buying or selling, our readership of active mail-order collectors offers you a perfect opportunity for increased sales and contacts.

SCOTT U.S. POCKET CAT.

Now a full-color reference, this popular annual catalogue can bring you many new customers. Thousands are sold each year to active and beginning collectors.

For Information Call 1-800-895-9881, FAX 1-800-340-9501
Visit our web site: www.scottonline.com
or write SCOTT, P.O. Box 4129, Sidney, OH 45365-4129 USA

3 1333 04889 2804

2020 UNITED STATES SPECIALIZED DEALER DIRECTORY YELLOW PAGE LISTINGS

Appraisals

DR. ROBERT FRIEDMAN & SONS STAMP & COIN BUYING CENTER
2029 W. 75th St.
Woodridge, IL 60517
PH: 800-588-8100
FAX: 630-985-1588
stampcollections@drbobstamps.com
www.drbobfriedmanstamps.com

Argentina

GUILLERMO JALIL
Maipu 466,local 4
1006 Buenos Aires
Argentina
guillermo@jalilstamps.com
philatino@philatino.com
www.philatino.com
www.jalilstamps.com

Auctions

DUTCH COUNTRY AUCTIONS
The Stamp Center
4115 Concord Pike
Wilmington, DE 19803
PH: 302-478-8740
FAX: 302-478-8779
auctions@dutchcountryauctions.com
www.dutchcountryauctions.com

British Commonwealth

COLLECTORS EXCHANGE ORLANDO STAMP SHOP
1814A Edgewater Drive
Orlando, FL 32804
PH: 407-620-0908
PH: 407-947-8603
FAX: 407-730-2131
jlatter@cfl.rr.com
www.BritishStampsAmerica.com
www.OrlandoStampShop.com

British Commonwealth

ARON R. HALBERSTAM PHILATELISTS, LTD.
PO Box 150168
Van Brunt Station
Brooklyn, NY 11215-0168
PH: 718-788-3978
arh@arhstamps.com
www.arhstamps.com

Buying

DR. ROBERT FRIEDMAN & SONS STAMP & COIN BUYING CENTER
2029 W. 75th St.
Woodridge, IL 60517
PH: 800-588-8100
FAX: 630-985-1588
stampcollections@drbobstamps.com
www.drbobfriedmanstamps.com

Canada

CANADA STAMP FINDER
PO Box 92591
Brampton, ON L6W 4R1
PH: 514-238-5751
Toll Free in North America:
877-412-3106
FAX: 323-315-2635
canadastampfinder@gmail.com
www.canadastampfinder.com

Collections

DR. ROBERT FRIEDMAN & SONS STAMP & COIN BUYING CENTER
2029 W. 75th St.
Woodridge, IL 60517
PH: 800-588-8100
FAX: 630-985-1588
stampcollections@drbobstamps.com
www.drbobfriedmanstamps.com

Ducks

MICHAEL JAFFE
PO Box 61484
Vancouver, WA 98666
PH: 360-695-6161
PH: 800-782-6770
FAX: 360-695-1616
mjaffe@brookmanstamps.com
www.brookmanstamps.com

MILLER'S STAMP COMPANY
P.O. Box 1011
Niantic, CT 06357
www.millerstamps.com
PH: 860-908-6200

Netherlands

HENRY GITNER PHILATELISTS, INC.
PO Box 3077-S
Middletown, NY 10940
PH: 845-343-5151
PH: 800-947-8267
FAX: 845-343-0068
hgitner@hgitner.com
www.hgitner.com

New Issues

DAVIDSON'S STAMP SERVICE
Personalized Service since 1970
PO Box 36355
Indianapolis, IN 46236-0355
PH: 317-826-2620
ed-davidson@earthlink.net
www.newstampissues.com

Stamp Stores

California

BROSIUS STAMP, COIN & SUPPLIES
2105 Main St.
Santa Monica, CA 90405
PH: 310-396-7480
brosius.stamp.coin@hotmail.com

Connecticut

MILLER'S STAMP COMPANY
P.O. Box 1011
Niantic, CT 06357
www.millerstamps.com
PH: 860-908-6200

Delaware

DUTCH COUNTRY AUCTIONS
The Stamp Center
4115 Concord Pike
Wilmington, DE 19803
PH: 302-478-8740
FAX: 302-478-8779
auctions@dutchcountryauctions.com
www.dutchcountryauctions.com

Florida

DR. ROBERT FRIEDMAN & SONS STAMP & COIN BUYING CENTER
PH: 800-588-8100
FAX: 630-985-1588
stampcollections@drbobstamps.com
www.drbobfriedmanstamps.com

Stamp Stores

Illinois

DR. ROBERT FRIEDMAN & SONS STAMP & COIN BUYING CENTER
2029 W. 75th St.
Woodridge, IL 60517
PH: 800-588-8100
FAX: 630-985-1588
stampcollections@drbobstamps.com
www.drbobfriedmanstamps.com

Indiana

KNIGHT STAMP & COIN CO.
237 Main St.
Hobart, IN 46342
PH: 219-942-4341
PH: 800-634-2646
knight@knightcoin.com
www.knightcoin.com

Missouri

DAVID SEMSROTT STAMPS
11239 Manchester Rd.
St. Louis Kirkwood, MO 63122
PH: 314-984-8361
fixodine@sbcglobal.net
www.DavidSemsrott.com

New Jersey

BERGEN STAMPS & COLLECTIBLES
306 Queen Anne Rd.
Teaneck, NJ 07666
PH: 201-836-8987
bergenstamps@gmail.com

TRENTON STAMP & COIN CO
Thomas DeLuca
Store: Forest Glen Plaza
1804 Highway 33
Hamilton Square, NJ 08690
Mail: PO Box 8574
Trenton, NJ 08650
PH: 609-584-8100
FAX: 609-587-8664
TOMD4TSC@aol.com

New York

CHAMPION STAMP CO., INC.
432 West 54th St.
New York, NY 10019
PH: 212-489-8130
FAX: 212-581-8130
championstamp@aol.com
www.championstamp.com

Stamp Stores

New York

CK STAMPS
42-14 Union St. # 2A
Flushing, NY 11355
PH: 917-667-6641
ckstampsllc@yahoo.com

Ohio

HILLTOP STAMP SERVICE
Richard A. Peterson
PO Box 626
Wooster, OH 44691
PH: 330-262-8907 (0)
PH: 330-201-1377 (H)
hilltopstamps@sssnet.com
www.hilltopstamps.com

Supplies

BROOKLYN GALLERY COIN & STAMP, INC.
8725 4th Ave.
Brooklyn, NY 11209
PH: 718-745-5701
FAX: 718-745-2775
info@brooklyngallery.com
www.brooklyngallery.com

Topicals - Columbus

MR. COLUMBUS
PO Box 1492
Fennville, MI 49408
PH: 269-543-4755
David@MrColumbus1492.com
www.MrColumbus1492.com

United Nations

BRUCE M. MOYER
Box 12031
Charlotte, NC 28220
PH: 908-237-6967
moyer@unstamps.com
www.unstamps.com

WILLIAM HENRY STAMP CO.
PO Box 150010
Kew Gardens, NY 11415
PH/FAX: 347-829-3400
wmhenry@msn.com
www.allunstamps.com

Worldwide

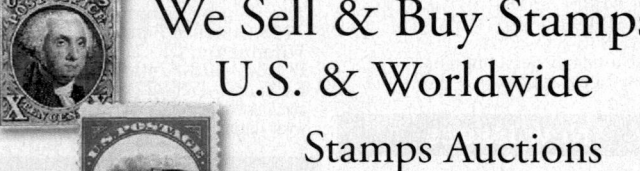

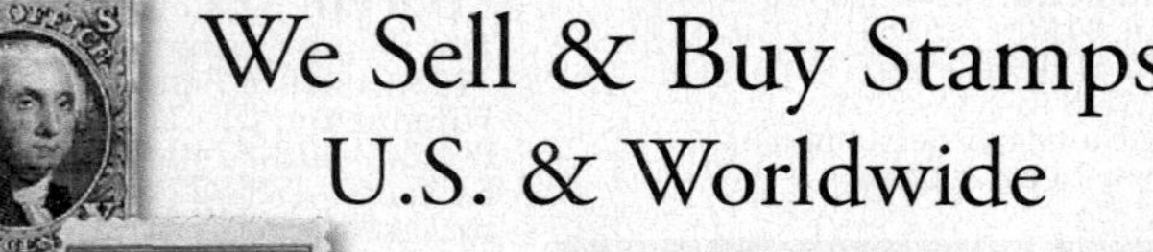
We Sell & Buy Stamps
U.S. & Worldwide
Stamps Auctions
from $0.01 on eBay

CK Stamps LLC • 917-667-6641
42-14 Union St. #2A; Flushing, NY 11355
ckstampsllc@yahoo.com
www.CKstamps.com

APS #216955

United States

ACS STAMP COMPANY
2914 W 135th Ave
Broomfield, Colorado 80020
303-841-8666
www.ACSStamp.com

BROOKMAN STAMP CO.
PO Box 90
Vancouver, WA 98666
PH: 360-695-1391
PH: 800-545-4871
FAX: 360-695-1616
info@brookmanstamps.com
www.brookmanstamps.com

MILLER'S STAMP COMPANY
P.O. Box 1011
Niantic, CT 06357
www.millerstamps.com
PH: 860-908-6200

U.S. - Classics

MILLER'S STAMP COMPANY
P.O. Box 1011
Niantic, CT 06357
www.millerstamps.com
PH: 860-908-6200

U.S. Classics/Moderns

BARDO STAMPS
PO Box 7437
Buffalo Grove, IL 60089
PH: 847-634-2676
jfb7437@aol.com
www.bardostamps.com

U.S.-Collections Wanted

DUTCH COUNTRY AUCTIONS
The Stamp Center
4115 Concord Pike
Wilmington, DE 19803
PH: 302-478-8740
FAX: 302-478-8779
auctions@dutchcountryauctions.com
www.dutchcountryauctions.com

DR. ROBERT FRIEDMAN & SONS STAMP & COIN BUYING CENTER
2029 W. 75th St.
Woodridge, IL 60517
PH: 800-588-8100
FAX: 630-985-1588
stampcollections@drbobstamps.com
www.drbobfriedmanstamps.com

MILLER'S STAMP COMPANY
P.O. Box 1011
Niantic, CT 06357
www.millerstamps.com
PH: 860-908-6200

U.S. - Rare Stamps

MILLER'S STAMP COMPANY
P.O. Box 1011
Niantic, CT 06357
www.millerstamps.com
PH: 860-908-6200

Wanted - Worldwide Collections

DUTCH COUNTRY AUCTIONS
The Stamp Center
4115 Concord Pike
Wilmington, DE 19803
PH: 302-478-8740
FAX: 302-478-8779
auctions@dutchcountryauctions.com
www.dutchcountryauctions.com

Wanted - U.S. Collections

BROOKMAN STAMP CO.
PO Box 90
Vancouver, WA 98666
PH: 360-695-1391
PH: 800-545-4871
FAX: 360-695-1616
info@brookmanstamps.com
www.brookmanstamps.com

Websites

ACS STAMP COMPANY
2914 W 135th Ave
Broomfield, Colorado 80020
303-841-8666
www.ACSStamp.com

MILLER'S STAMP COMPANY
P.O. Box 1011
Niantic, CT 06357
www.millerstamps.com
PH: 860-908-6200

Worldwide-Collections

DR. ROBERT FRIEDMAN & SONS STAMP & COIN BUYING CENTER
2029 W. 75th St.
Woodridge, IL 60517
PH: 800-588-8100
FAX: 630-985-1588
stampcollections@drbobstamps.com
www.drbobfriedmanstamps.com

Eastern Auctions Ltd.

Would like to showcase your collection.

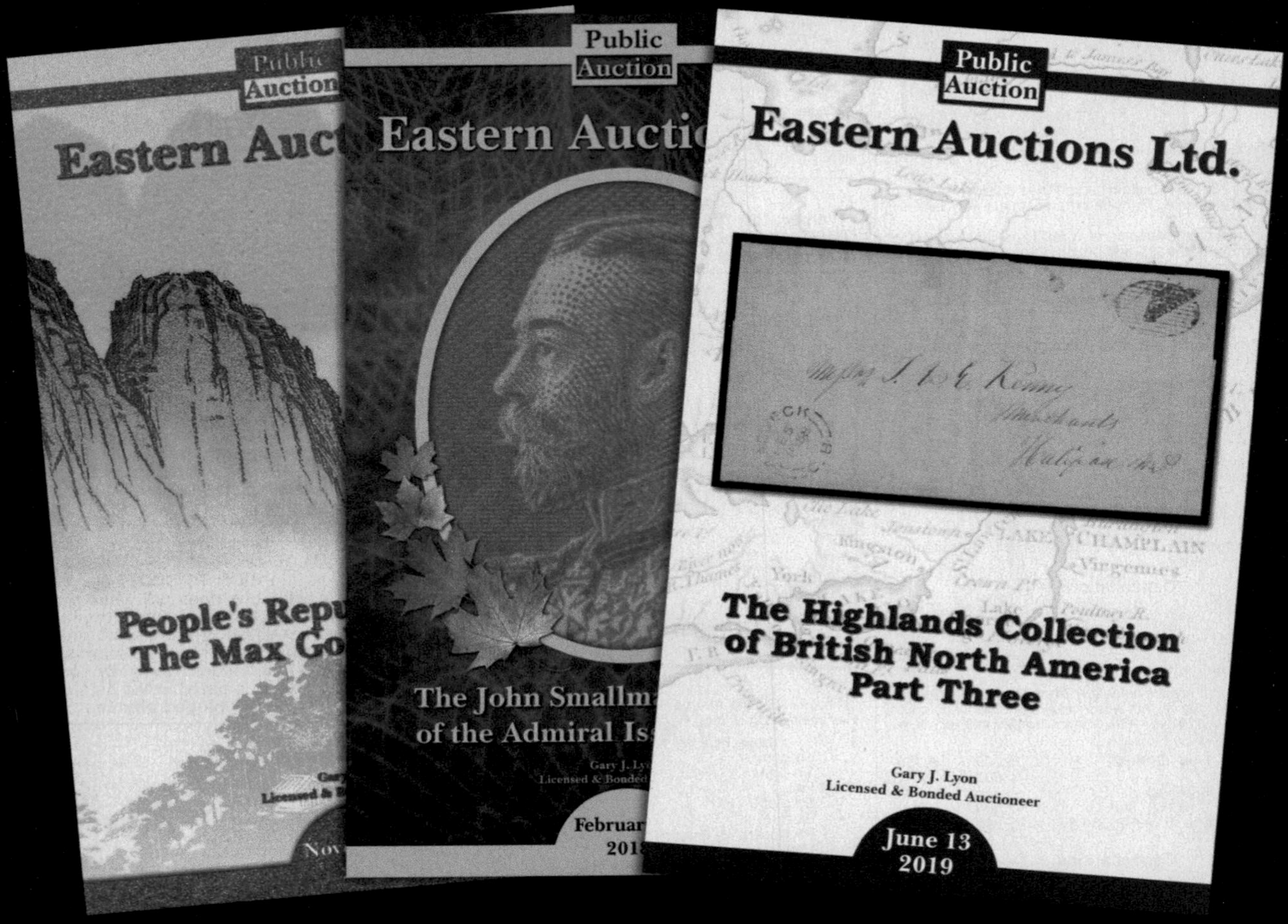

Public Auction
Eastern Auctions Ltd.
The Highlands Collection of British North America Part Three
Gary J. Lyon
Licensed & Bonded Auctioneer
June 13 2019

Canada's most trusted auction house

Since 1980 we have steadily built a reputation for outstanding realizations. Numerous record prices have been achieved for superior quality stamps. Take advantage of our friendly and professional service. Your collection will be described by our expert lotters and lavishly illustrated in our deluxe catalogue. Commission rates are very competitive and prompt payment is always guaranteed.

Contact us today for further details.

Eastern Auctions Ltd.

P.O. Box 250 - Bathurst - New Brunswick - E2A 3Z2 - Canada
Tel: 1(506) 548-8986 - Fax: 1(506) 546-6627
Email: easternauctions@nb.aibn.com - Website: www.easternauctions.com

Type IIIa

Type III — The top and bottom curved lines outside the labels are broken in the middle. The side ornaments are substantially complete.

The most desirable examples of type III are those showing the widest breaks in the top and bottom framelines.

A special example is 99R2. All other stamps come from plate 4 and almost all show the breaks in the lines less clearly defined. Some of these breaks, especially of the bottom line, are very small.

Type IIIa — Similar to III with the outer line broken at top or, rarely, at bottom but not both. The side ornaments are substantially complete.

No.	Description	Unused	Used
8	A8 1c **blue**, type III (Plate 4) see below for 99R2	25,000.	1,600.
	No gum	*7,500.*	
	On cover		1,800.
	Pair	*55,000.*	3,500.
	Pair, types III, IIIa	*35,000.*	*3,000.*
	Pair, types III, II	—	—
	Strip of 3		*8,500.*
	Block of 4, types II, III	—	
	Block of 4, types III, IIIa	—	—

Earliest documented use: July 7, 1857 (on off-cover stamp); May 1, 1857 (on cover).

Cancellations

Blue	+75.
Red	+200.
Red Carrier	+250.
Black Carrier	+250.
Pen Cancel	800.

Values for type III are for at least a 2mm break in each outer line. Examples of type III with wider breaks in outer lines command higher prices; those with smaller breaks sell for much less.

No.	Description	Unused	Used
(8)	A8 1c **blue**, type III (99R2)	*35,000.*	*5,750.*
	No gum	*10,000.*	
	Pair, types III (99R2), II	—	*10,500.*
	Pair, types III (99R2), IIIa	*42,500.*	—
	Block of 4, type III (99R2), 3 type II	*45,000.*	
	On cover (99R2)		*15,000.*

Cancellations

Blue	+150.00
Green	—
"Paid"	—
Red Carrier	+500.00

No.	Description	Unused	Used
8A	A8 1c **blue**, type IIIa (Plate 1E) *July 1, 1851*	6,000.	800.
	No gum	2,250.	
	On cover		875.
	Pair	*12,500.*	2,300.
	Double transfer, one inverted (81L1E)	*6,500.*	1,100.
	Plate 1E (100R), break in lower line	—	—
	Plate 2 (100R), break in lower line	—	—
	Plate 4, *April, 1857*	*6,250.*	1,200.
	No gum	2,350.	
	On cover		1,350.
	Pair	*13,500.*	2,500.
	Block of 4	—	*9,500.*

Earliest documented uses: July 3, 1851 (Plate 1E); Apr. 4, 1857 (Plate 4).

Cancellations

Blue	+50.00
Red	+125.00
"Paid"	+90.00
Black Carrier	+175.00
Red Carrier	+175.00
Pen Cancel	375.00

Values are for stamps with at least a 2mm break in the top outer line. Examples with a wider break or a break in the lower line command higher prices, those with a smaller break sell for less.

PETER MOSIONDZ, JR.

Serving Collectors Since 1968

Quality Pre-1940 U.S. Stamps
Accurately Graded
Properly Attributed

Free Price List or Visit
www.mosiondz.com

26 Cameron Circle
Laurel Springs, NJ 08021
856-627-6865
earlyusstamps@comcast.net

"Paid" Cancellations

Values for "Paid" cancellations are for those OTHER than the common Boston type. See Postal Markings in the Introduction for illustrations.

A9

Type IV. Similar to type II, but with the curved lines outside the labels recut at top or bottom or both.

No.	Description	Unused	Used
9	A9 1c **blue**, type IV, *1852*	725.00	90.00
	No gum	240.00	
	On cover		110.00
	Pair	1,650.	190.00
	Strip of 3	2,600.	300.00
	Block of 4	3,500.	*1,750.*
	P# block of 8, Impt. (Plate 1)	—	
	Double transfer	850.00	95.00
	Triple transfer, one inverted (71L, 81L and 91L Plate 1L)	900.00	145.00
	Cracked plate	900.00	145.00
	On cover		—
	Bottom frameline broken (30L, 50L, 67R, 89R, 90R, 99R Plate 1L), late printings	—	240.00
	Perf. 12½, unofficial		*10,000.*
	Strip of 3		—
a.	Printed on both sides, reverse inverted		*50,000.*
b.	Diagonal half used as ½c on cover		*60,000.*

No. 9a is unique.

The No. 9b cover, a printed-matter circular mailed in 1853, is unique. The circular likely should have been sent at the 1c rate for printed matter in effect at the time. However, both the sending (New Haven, Conn.) and receiving (Hartford, Conn.) post offices treated it as fully prepaid with ½c postage applied. Value is based on 2013 auction realization.

See note concerning unofficial perfs following listings for No. 11.

VARIETIES OF RECUTTING

Stamps of this type were printed from Plate 1 after it had been reentered and recut in 1852. All but one stamp (4R, see No. 7 for listings) were recut and all varieties of recutting are listed below:

Variety	Unused	Used
Recut once at top and once at bottom, (113 on plate)	750.00	90.00
Recut once at top, (40 on plate)	775.00	95.00
Recut once at top and twice at bottom, (21 on plate)	800.00	100.00
Recut twice at bottom, (11 on plate)	825.00	115.00
Recut once at bottom, (8 on plate)	850.00	120.00
Recut once at bottom and twice at top, (4 on plate)	900.00	130.00
Recut twice at bottom and twice at top, (2 on plate)	950.00	230.00

Earliest documented use: June 5, 1852.

Cancellations

Blue	+5.00
Red	+40.00
Ultramarine	+150.00
Brown	+100.00
Green	+400.00
Violet	+350.00
1853 year date	+250.00
1855 year date	+10.00
1856 year date	+7.50
1857 year date	+10.00
"Paid"	+10.00
"U. S. PAID"	+50.00
"Way"	+50.00
"Free"	+75.00
Railroad	+75.00
"Steam"	+60.00
Numeral	+10.00
"Steamboat"	+90.00
"Steamship"	+60.00
Red Carrier	+15.00
Black Carrier	+25.00
U. S. Express Mail	+60.00
Express Company	—
Packet boat	+500.00
Printed precancel "PAID"	+2,500.
Printed precancel "paid"	+2,500.
Pen Cancel	45.00

These 1c stamps were often cut apart carelessly, destroying part or all of the top and bottom lines. When this was done, it is difficult to determine whether a stamp is type II, III, IIIa or IV without identifying the position. Such mutilated examples sell for much less.

PLEASE NOTE:

Stamps are valued in the grade of very fine unless otherwise indicated.

Values for early and valuable stamps are for examples with certificates of authenticity from acknowledged expert committees, or examples sold with the buyer having the right of certification. This applies to examples with original gum as well as examples without gum. Beware of stamps offered "as is," as the gum on some unused stamps offered with "original gum" may be fraudulent, and stamps offered as unused without gum may in some cases be altered or faintly canceled used stamps.

VALUES FOR NEVER-HINGED STAMPS PRIOR TO SCOTT No. 182

This catalogue does not value pre-1879 stamps in never-hinged condition. Premiums for never-hinged condition in the classic era invariably are even larger than those premiums listed for the 1879 and later issues. Generally speaking, the earlier the stamp is listed in the catalogue, the larger will be the never-hinged premium.

Washington — A10

All of the 3c stamps of the 1851 and 1857 issues were recut at least to the extent of the outer frame lines, sometimes the inner lines at the sides (type II stamps), and often other lines in triangles, diamond blocks, label blocks and/or top/bottom frame lines. Some of the most prominent varieties are listed below each major listing (others are described in "The 3c Stamp of U.S. 1851-57 Issue," by Carroll Chase).

Type I

THREE CENTS. Issued July 1, 1851 (Plate 1E).

Type I — There is an outer frame line on all four sides. The outer frame lines at the sides are always recut.

No.	Description	Unused	Used
10	A10 3c **orange brown**, type I (Plates 1E, 1i)	4,000.	185.00
	No gum	1,500.	
	deep orange brown	4,250.	215.00

Quality Classic U.S. Stamps and Postal History

Simply Stated

We Build ...

We Buy...

We Sell... Great Collections

STANLEY M. PILLER & ASSOCIATES

Established 1968

Office: 800 S. Broadway, Suite 201 • Walnut Creek, CA 94596

Mailing Address: P.O. Box 559 • Alamo, CA 94507

Phone: 925-938-8290 • Fax: 925-938-8812

Email: stmpdlr@aol.com • Web: www.smpiller.com

APS

No gum	1,650.	
On cover, orange brown		260.00
On cover (3c circular rate - 1000-1500 miles)		1,000.
Pair	9,000.	550.00
Pair on cover (double rate)		650.00
Pair on cover (6c West Coast rate)		800.00
Strip of 3	*15,000.*	1,200.
Block of 4	*23,500.*	—
Pair, types I, II	*12,000.*	*825.00*
Double transfer		215.00
Gash on shoulder		215.00
On part India paper		*1,000.*

VARIETIES OF RECUTTING

1 line recut in upper left triangle	4,250.	205.00
1 line recut in upper left triangle, 2 lines recut at top of upper right diamond block (27R1E)		500.00

Earliest documented uses: July 1, 1851 (Plate 1E) (FDC); July 12, 1851 (Plate 1i).

Cancellations

Blue	+10.00
Red	+20.00
Orange red	+25.00
Brown	+40.00
Ultramarine	+100.00
Green	+235.00
Violet	+250.00
1851 year date	*+1,500.*
1852 year date	+750.00
"Paid"	+5.00
"Way"	+40.00
"Way" with numeral	+150.00
"Free"	+50.00
Numeral	+15.00
Railroad	+50.00
U. S. Express Mail	+20.00
"Steam"	+35.00
"Steamship"	+60.00
"Steamboat"	+70.00
Packet Boat	+300.00
Black Carrier (circular)	+400.00
Blue Carrier (circular)	+600.00
Blue Carrier (New Orleans "snowshovel")	+400.00
Green Carrier (New Orleans "snowshovel")	+500.00
Canadian	—
Territorial	+200.00
Pen Cancel	65.00

Type II

Type II — As type I, but with the inner lines at the sides added by recutting on the plate.

10A A10 3c **orange brown,** type II (Plates 1E, 1i, 2E, 5E, 0)	3,250.	145.00
No gum	1,250.	
deep orange brown	3,500.	185.00
No gum	1,300.	
copper brown (Plate 2E only)	*4,250.*	900.00
No gum	*1,600.*	
On cover, orange brown		190.00
On cover, copper brown		*1,100.*
On cover (3c circular rate - 1000-1500 miles)		1,000.
Pair	7,500.	500.00
Pair on cover (double rate)		550.00
Pair on cover (6c West Coast rate)		675.00
Strip of 3	*10,500.*	1,200.
Block of 4	*15,000.*	—
Double transfer		165.00
Triple transfer		425.00
Gash on shoulder		155.00
Dot in lower right diamond block (69L5E)		325.00
On part-India paper		*1,250.*
b. Printed on both sides		*55,000.*

Only one example of No. 10Ab is recorded.

VARIETIES OF RECUTTING

All of these stamps also were recut at least to the extent of the outer frame lines at the sides and the inner lines at the sides (the basic type II criteria).

Left inner line only recut		200.00
Right inner line only recut		160.00
1 line recut in upper left triangle		160.00
2 lines recut in upper left triangle		160.00
3 lines recut in upper left triangle		180.00
5 lines recut in upper left triangle (47L0)		*1,500.*
1 line recut in lower left triangle		160.00
1 line recut in lower right triangle		160.00
2 lines recut in lower right triangle (57L0)		*1,500.*
2 lines recut in upper left triangle and 1 line recut in lower right triangle		220.00
1 line recut in upper right triangle		170.00
1 line recut in both upper left and upper right triangles (68, 70L0)	4,250.	260.00
Upper part of top label and diamond block recut	4,000.	150.00
Top label and right diamond block joined		180.00
Top label and left diamond block joined at top (6R2E, 100R2E)		300.00
Lower label and right diamond block joined		210.00
1 line recut at bottom of lower left diamond block (34R2E)		1,500.
Vertical line ties upper left corner of upper left diamond block to top frame line (45R2E)		1,000.

Earliest documented uses: July 1, 1851 (Plate 1E) (FDC); July 12, 1851 (Plate 1i); July 23, 1851 (Plate 2E); July 19, 1851 (Plate 5E); Sept. 6, 1851 (Plate 0).

Cancellations

Blue	+5.00
Red	+15.00
Orange red	+20.00
Orange	—
Brown	+40.00
Ultramarine	+100.00
Green	+225.00
Violet	+250.00
1851 year date	*+1,000.*
1852 year date	+750.00
"Paid"	+5.00
"Way"	+40.00
"Way" with numeral	+150.00
"Free"	+100.00
Numeral	+15.00
Railroad	+50.00
U. S. Express Mail	+20.00
"Steam"	+35.00
"Steamship"	+60.00
"Steamboat"	+70.00
Packet Boat	+300.00
Black Carrier (circular)	+400.00
Blue Carrier (circular)	+600.00
Blue Carrier (New Orleans "snowshovel")	+400.00
Green Carrier (New Orleans "snowshovel")	+500.00
Canadian	—
Territorial	+200.00
Pen Cancel	65.00

11 A10 3c **dull red** (1855), type I (Plates 4, 6, 7, 8)	250.00	15.00
orange red (1855)	250.00	15.00
rose red (1855)	250.00	15.00
No gum	100.00	
brownish carmine (1856)	275.00	18.00
No gum	110.00	
claret (1857)	325.00	22.50
No gum	120.00	
deep claret (1857)	350.00	27.50
No gum	125.00	
plum (1857)	—	*2,000.*
No gum	—	
pinkish		*5,500.*
On cover, dull red		17.50
On cover, orange red		19.00
On cover, brownish carmine		24.00
On cover, claret		27.50
On cover, plum		*3,500.*
On propaganda cover, dull red		400.00
Pair	650.00	62.50
Pair on cover (double rate)		70.00
Pair on cover (6c West Coast rate)		—
Pair, types I, II	—	
Strip of 3	1,100.	140.00
Block of 4	2,100.	1,000.
P# block of 8, Impt.	*7,500.*	
Double transfer	300.00	18.00
Gash on shoulder	300.00	17.00
Worn plate	275.00	13.00
Perf. 12½, unofficial		*5,000.*
On cover		*8,000.*

The unofficial perf varieties listed under Nos. 7, 11 and 11A represent the first perforated stamps in the U. S. made using a true perforating machine. Known as the "Chicago perfs," both the perf. 11 and perf. 12½ stamps were made by Dr. Elijah W. Hadley, using a machine of his construction. None of the perf 11 stamps are believed to have been used.

VARIETIES OF RECUTTING

All of these stamps were recut at least to the extent of three outer frame lines (including both sides) and often other lines in triangles, diamond blocks, label blocks and/or top/bottom frame lines. Some of the most prominent varieties are listed below.

Lines on bust and bottom of medallion circle recut (47R6)	*1,400.*	600.00
Top label and right diamond block joined	300.00	16.00
Top label and right diamond block joined at top and bottom (68R4)	325.00	17.50
Lower label and right diamond block joined	325.00	17.50
Extra line at right	325.00	17.50

Earliest documented uses: Mar. 28, 1855 (Plate 4); Feb. 18, 1856 (Plate 6); Feb. 9, 1856 (Plate 7); Apr. 14, 1856 (Plate 8).

Cancellations

Blue	+4.00
Red	+10.00
Orange red	+5.00
Orange	+250.00
Brown	+75.00
Magenta	+50.00
Ultramarine	+40.00
Green	+125.00
Violet	+250.00
Purple	+250.00
Olive	+200.00
Yellow	+7,500.
1855 year date	+50.00
1856 year date	+12.50
1857 year date	+12.50
1858 year date	+1.00
1859 year date	+25.00
"Paid"	+1.50
"Way"	+10.00
"Free"	+25.00
Numeral, "3" or "5"	+25.00
Numeral, number greater than "5"	—
Railroad	+20.00
Supplemental Mail Type A	*+2,500.*
"Steam"	+25.00
"Ship"	+25.00
"New York Ship"	+35.00
"Steamboat"	+45.00
"Steamship"	+45.00
Packet boat	+120.00
Express Company	+120.00
Black Carrier	+60.00
Red Carrier (New York)	+100.00
Blue Carrier (New Orleans)	+300.00
Green Carrier (New Orleans)	+500.00
Canada	—
Territorial	+200.00
Pen Cancel	7.50

11A A10 3c **dull red** (1853-54-55), type II (Plates 1L, 2L, 3, 5L)	250.00	15.00
orange red (1855)	250.00	15.00
rose red (1854-55)	250.00	15.00
No gum	85.00	
brownish carmine (1851-52)	280.00	20.00
No gum	95.00	
claret (1852)	300.00	22.50
No gum	115.00	
experimental orange brown (1851-52, Plate 1L))	—	300.00
plum (1857)		*2,200.*
pinkish		*6,000.*
On cover, dull red		17.50
On cover, orange red		19.00
On cover, brownish carmine		26.00
On cover, claret		27.50
On cover, experimental orange brown (Plate 1L)		700.00
On cover, plum		*3,500.*
On propaganda cover, dull red		400.00
On cover (3c circular rate - 1000-1500 miles)		850.00
Pair	550.00	62.50
Pair on cover (double rate)		70.00
Pair on cover (6c West Coast rate)		100.00
Strip of 3	1,050.	140.00
Block of 4	2,000.	1,000.
P# block of 8, Impt.	*4,500.*	
Double transfer in "Three Cents"	275.00	18.00
Double transfer line through "Three Cents" and rosettes double (92L1L)	400.00	70.00
Double transfer, "Gents" instead of "Cents" (66R2L)	400.00	55.00
Triple transfer (92L2L)	400.00	55.00
Gash on shoulder	275.00	17.00
Dot in lower right diamond block (69L5L)	350.00	45.00
Major cracked plate (84L, 94L, 9R, Plate 5L)	*775.00*	160.00
Intermediate cracked plate (80L, 96L, 71R, Plate 5L)	*500.00*	80.00
Minor cracked plate (8L, 27L, 31L, 44L, 45L, 51L, 55L, 65L, 71L, 72L, 74L, 78L, 79L, 7R, Plate 5L)	*375.00*	60.00
Worn plate	250.00	13.00
Perf. about 11, unofficial	*6,500.*	
Block of 4	*27,500.*	
Perf. 12½, unofficial		*5,000.*
On cover		*8,000.*
Pair on cover		—
c. Vertical half used as 1c on cover		*5,000.*
Strip of 4 No. 11Ac used as 6c on cover		*15,000.*
d. Diagonal half used as 1c on cover		*5,000.*
e. Double impression		*30,000.*

The unofficial perf varieties listed represent the first perforated stamps in the U. S. made using a true perforating machine. Known as the "Chicago perfs," both were made by Dr. Elijah W. Hadley, using a machine of his construction. None of the perf 11 stamps are believed to have been used.

The strip of 4 No. 11Ac on cover is the only recorded multiple of a bisected stamp in United States philately.

Schuyler J. Rumsey Philatelic Auctions

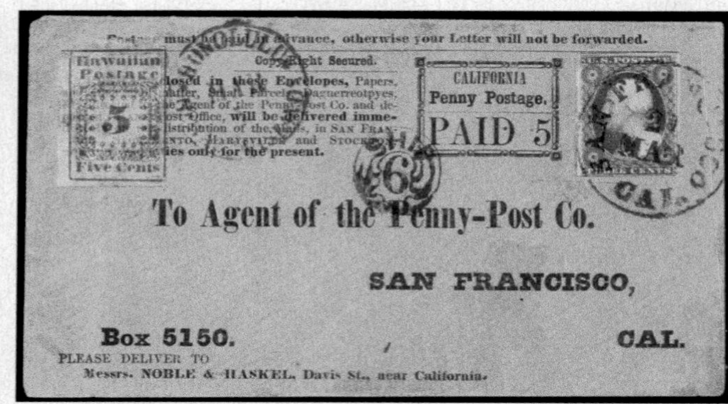

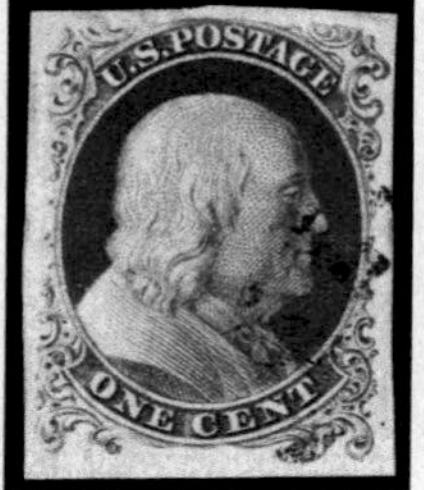

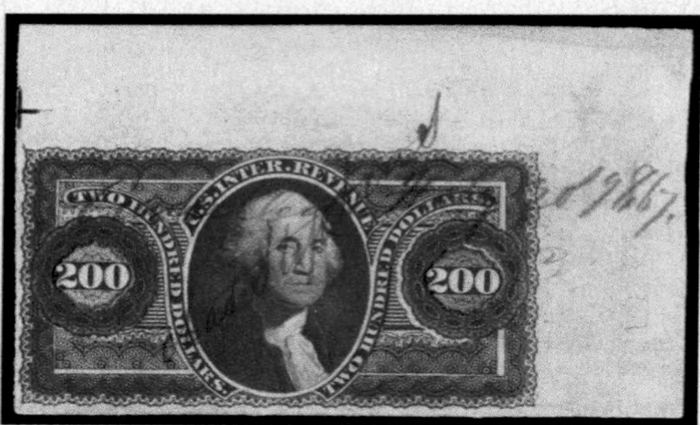

When choosing an auction house, you should also consider the things they don't sell.

Knowledge. Experience. Integrity. Things that cannot be bought, bartered or sold. Yet they're responsible for realizing the highest prices for your stamps. At Rumsey Auctions, we've built our reputation on these qualities as much as on the impressive financial results we achieve for our clients. Please call or email us and let us show you how much we can do for you.

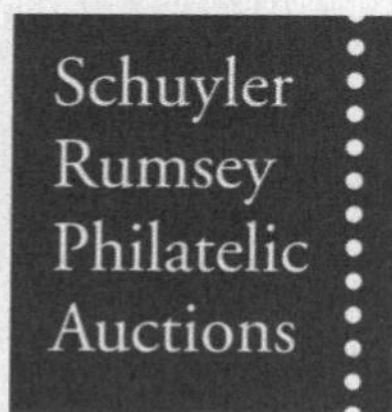

415 781 5127 | srumsey@rumseyauctions.com | visit us at www.rumseyauctions.com

VARIETIES OF RECUTTING

All of these stamps also were recut at least to the extent of the outer lines at the sides and the inner frame lines at the sides (the basic type II criteria).

Right inner line only recut	300.00	17.50
1 line recut in upper left triangle	300.00	16.00
2 lines recut in upper left triangle	300.00	16.00
3 lines recut in upper left triangle	325.00	16.00
5 lines recut in upper left triangle (95L1L)	650.00	200.00
1 line recut in lower left triangle	325.00	16.00
1 line recut in lower right triangle	300.00	16.00
1 line recut in upper right triangle	425.00	18.00
1 line recut in UL, LL and LR triangles (49L1L, 95R3)	475.00	32.50
2 lines recut in UL triangle, 1 line recut in LL triangle (9L1L)	475.00	32.50
Recut button on shoulder (10R2L)	600.00	175.00
Upper part of top label and diamond block recut	275.00	16.00
Top label and right diamond block joined	300.00	16.00
Top label and left diamond block joined	325.00	17.50
Lower label and right diamond block joined	325.00	17.50
1 extra vertical line outside of left frame line (29L, 39L, 49L, 59L, 69L, 79L, Plate 3)	300.00	17.50
2 extra vertical lines outside of left frame line (89L, 99L, Plate 3)	375.00	32.50
1 extra vertical line outside of right frame line (58L, 68L, 78L, 88L, 98L, Plate 3)	425.00	20.00
No inner line and frame line close to design at right (9L, 19L, Plate 3)	375.00	32.50
No inner line and frame line close to design at left (70, 80, 90, 100L, Plate 3)	325.00	19.00

Earliest documented uses: Oct. 6, 1851 (Plate 1L); Jan. 7, 1852 (Plate 2L); Jan. 15, 1852 (Plate 3); July 13, 1855 (Plate 5L).

Cancellations

Blue	+1.00
Red	+7.50
Orange red	+25.00
Orange	+250.00
Brown	+75.00
Magenta	+50.00
Ultramarine	+40.00
Green	+175.00
Violet	+250.00
Purple	+250.00
Olive	+200.00
Yellow	*+7,500.*
Yellow, on cover	*15,000.*
1852 year date	*+300.00*
1852 year date, on cover	1,000.
1853 year date	+100.00
1854 year date	—
1855 year date	+50.00
1856 year date	+12.50
"Paid"	+1.50
"Way"	+10.00
"Way" with numeral	+60.00
"Free"	+25.00
Numeral	+7.50
Railroad	+20.00
U. S. Express Mail	+5.00
Supplemental Mail Type A	*+2,500.*
"Steam"	+15.00
"Ship"	+20.00
"New York Ship"	+35.00
"Steamboat"	+45.00
"Steamship"	+45.00
Packet boat	+120.00
Express Company	+120.00
Black Carrier	+60.00
Red Carrier (New York)	+50.00
Blue Carrier (New Orleans)	+200.00
Green Carrier (New Orleans)	+350.00
Canada	—
Territorial	+100.00
Pen Cancel	7.50

Thomas Jefferson — A11

FIVE CENTS

Type I — Projections on all four sides.

12	A11 5c **red brown,** type I, *1856*	*30,000.*	700.
	dark red brown	*30,000.*	700.
	No gum	*11,000.*	
	On domestic cover		1,150.
	Single on cover to France		1,600.
	Strip of 3 on cover to France		5,750.
	Pair	*67,500.*	1,600.
	Strip of 3	*100,000.*	3,750.
	Block of 4	*300,000.*	*45,000.*
	Double transfer (40R1)		*1,000.*
	Defective transfer (23R1)		*1,200.*

Earliest documented use: Mar. 24, 1856.

Cancellations

Red	+175.
Magenta	+200.
Blue	+150.
Brown	+100.
Green	+1,000.
1856 year date	+25.
1857 year date	+25.
1858 year date	—
"Paid"	+200.
"Steamship"	+200.
U.S. Express Mail	+200.
Express Company	+400.
"Steamboat"	+350.
Railroad	+400.
Numeral	+1,000.
Pen Cancel	350.

Washington — A12

TEN CENTS

Type I — The "shells" at the lower corners are practically complete. The outer line below the label is very nearly complete. The outer lines are broken above the middle of the top label and the "X" in each upper corner. Beware of type V perforated (No. 35) trimmed to resemble type I imperforate (No. 13). Note that the pearls on No. 35 normally will be missing from each end of the lower label.

Types I, II, III and IV have complete ornaments at the sides of the stamps, and three pearls at each outer edge of the bottom panel.

Type I comes only from the bottom row of both panes of Plate 1.

13	A12 10c **green,** type I, *1855*	*19,000.*	800.
	dark green	*19,000.*	800.
	yellowish green	*19,000.*	800.
	No gum	*8,500.*	
	On domestic cover		900.
	Pair	*42,500.*	1,800.
	Strip of 3		2,900.
	Vert. pair, types III, I	*26,000.*	1,450.
	Vert. pair, types IV, I (86, 96L1)		*10,000.*
	Vertical strip of 3, types II, III, I		4,250.
	Block of 4, types III, I	*55,000.*	*10,500.*
	Block of 4, types III, IV, I		*16,000.*
	Double transfer (100R1)	*20,000.*	875.
	"Curl" in left "X" (99R1)	*20,000.*	875.

Earliest documented use: July 11, 1855.

Cancellations

Blue	+50.
Red	+100.
Magenta	+200.
Orange	—
1855 year date	+25.
1856 year date	+25.
1857 year date	+25.
"Paid"	+50.
"Steamship"	+150.
Railroad	+175.
Territorial	+400.
Numeral	+50.
U.S. Express Mail	—
Pen Cancel	400.

A13

Type II — The design is complete at the top. The outer line at the bottom is broken in the middle. The shells are partly cut away, as shown.

14	A13 10c **green,** type II, *1855*	5,000.	140.
	dark green	5,000.	140.
	yellowish green	5,000.	140.
	No gum	1,800.	
	On domestic cover		190.
	Pair	11,000.	300.
	Strip of 3	17,000.	600.
	Block of 4	*25,000.*	*4,000.*
	Pair, types II, III	11,000.	310.
	Pair, types II, IV	*42,500.*	*2,000.*
	Vertical strip of 3, types II, III, IV		*2,400.*
	Block of 4, types II, III	—	*3,500.*
	Block of 4, types II, IV		—
	Block of 4, types II, III, IV		*10,000.*
	Double transfer (31L, 51L, and 20R, Plate 1)	5,500.	220.
	"Curl" opposite "X" (10R1)	5,500.	240.

Earliest documented use: May 12, 1855.

Cancellations

Blue	+15.
Red	+25.
Brown	+75.
Ultramarine	+100.
Magenta	+150.
Green	+200.
Violet	+150.
1855 year date	+100.
1856 year date	+50.
1857 year date	+10.
1858 year date	+10.
"Paid"	+25.
"Way"	+75.
"Free"	+75.
Railroad	+75.
Steamship	+75.
Steamboat	+100.
Numeral	+50.
Territorial	+150.
Express Company	+200.
U. S. Express Mail	+75.
Pen Cancel	60.

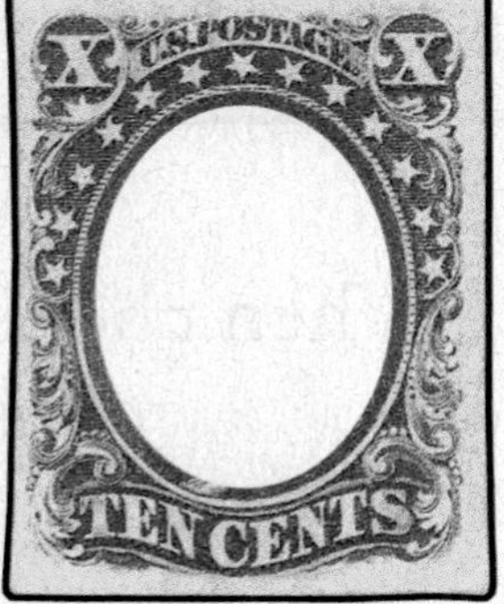

A14

Type III — The outer lines are broken above the top label and the "X" numerals. The outer line at the bottom and the shells are partly cut away, as shown, similar to type II.

15	A14 10c **green,** type III, *1855*	5,000.	140.
	dark green	5,000.	140.
	yellowish green	5,000.	140.
	No gum	1,800.	
	On domestic cover		190.
	Pair	11,000.	300.
	Strip of 3	17,000.	600.
	Pair, types III, IV	*40,000.*	*2,000.*
	Double transfer at top and at bottom		—
	"Curl" on forehead (85L1)	5,500.	240.
	"Curl" to right of left "X" (87R1)	5,500.	240.

Earliest documented use: May 19, 1855.

Cancellations

Blue	+15.
Red	+25.
Orange red	+35.
Magenta	+100.
Violet	+150.

We are quite clearly one of the TOP STAMP BUYERS IN AMERICA Because we are fair, open, and *FAST*.

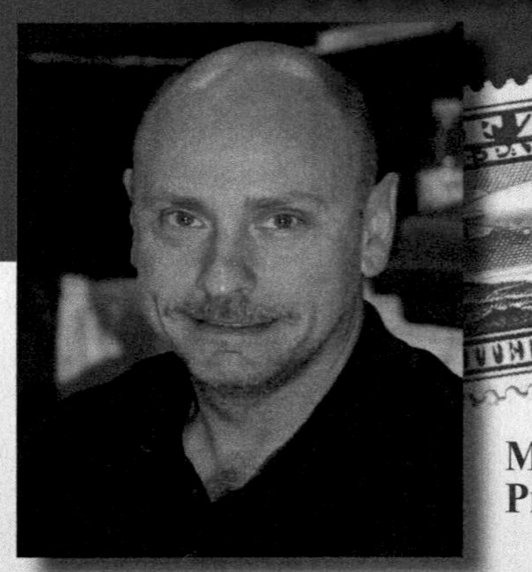

Mark Eastzer
President

"I won't waste a minute of your time. You won't find a more aggressive buyer of United States specialized material anywhere in America. So... why take a chance? Before you take someone else's offer, please do call me toll free today. It's worth a phone call right now."

GET OUR OFFER!

Call Toll Free: 800-470-7708

Wait a minute. Selling U.S. FULL SHEETS?

We're the #1 buyer...and a huge buyer of all kinds of full sheets.

We will come to you with a SOLID, REALISTIC AND ATTRACTIVE OFFER. THE REASON: we hate to lose OUT TO ANYONE ELSE! Count on us for an offer that'll make you smile! Want proof? **Call us now!** It just might be the best phone call you've made in a long, long time!

Philately's History

Club Pin

Millions of Pins Spread the Good Word

When the Ivory Stamp Club of the Air was founded in the 1930s, it was not too long after stamp collector President Franklin Roosevelt was elected by the voters. The Ivory Soap people who ran the nationally-broadcast program thought that, like the election campaign, a special imitation gold cloisonne pin might prove effective in spreading the Word. It was of very high quality and free. Millions of kids wore it proudly and for years thereafter! Mark Eastzer

Now BUYING PSE Graded Stamps! Please Call with offer!

We're not just buying. Please send us your want list or needs.

MARKEST Stamp Co.

Box 176 • Lynbrook, NY 11563
Phone:1-800-470-7708
Fax: (516) 599-1180
Email: markest@optonline.net

www.markest.com

Do You Collect Coins? DON'T FORGET! We are major COIN & CURRENCY BUYERS! Call Us Today!

Brown +75.
Orange +100.
Green +300.
1855 year date —
1856 year date +50.
1857 year date +10.
1858 year date +10.
"Paid" +25.
Steamship +75.
U. S. Express Mail +75.
"MAIL ROUTE" +1,500.
Express Company +200.
Packet boat —
"too late" +500.
Canada (on cover) +1000.
Territorial +150.
Railroad +75.
Numeral +50.
Pen Cancel 60.

A15

Type IV — The outer lines have been recut at top or bottom or both.

16 A15 10c **green,** type IV, *1855* *37,500.* 1,600.
dark green *37,500.* 1,600.
yellowish green *37,500.* 1,600.
No gum *15,000.*
On domestic cover 1,900.
Pair — 4,250.
Block of 4 (54-55, 64-65L) —

VARIETIES OF RECUTTING

Eight stamps on Plate 1 were recut. All are listed below.

Outer line recut at top (65L, 74L, 86L, and 3R, Plate 1) *37,500.* 1,600.
Outer line recut at bottom (54L, 55L, 76L, Plate 1) *39,000.* 1,700.
Outer line recut at top and bottom (64L1) *45,000.* 2,150.

Positions 65L1 and 86L1 have both "X" ovals recut at top, as well as the outer line.

Earliest documented use: June 4, 1855.

Cancellations

Blue +90.
Red +185.
Brown +250.
1857 year date —
1859 year date —
"Paid" +150.
Steamship +300.
Territorial +500.
Express Company +800.
Numeral +150.
Pen Cancel 800.

Types I, II, III and IV occur on the same sheet, so it is possible to obtain pairs and blocks showing combinations of types. For listings of type combinations in pairs and blocks, see Nos. 13-15.

Washington — A16

17 A16 12c **gray black,** *July 1, 1851* 6,250. 250.
No gum 2,100.
black 7,500. 325.
No gum 2,500.
Single, on cover 1,500.
Single on cover with No. 11 to France 1,100.
Pair *17,500.* 575.
Pair, on cover to England 750.
Block of 4 *45,000.* *5,500.*
Double transfer 6,500. 275.
Triple transfer (5R1 & 49R1) 6,750. 425.
Not recut in lower right corner 6,500. 300.
Recut in lower left corner (43L, 53L, 63L, 73L and 100L, Plate 1) 6,500. 375.
Cracked plate (32R1) —
On part-India paper *7,000.* *1,200.*
On very thin paper *1,750.*
No gum *4,500.*
a. Diagonal half used as 6c on cover *2,500.*
Diagonal half used as 6c on "Via Nicaragua" cover *5,000.*
b. Vertical half used as 6c on cover *8,500.*
c. Printed on both sides *40,000.*

Earliest documented use: Aug. 4, 1851.

Cancellations

Red +30.
Orange red +55.
Blue +15.
Brown +60.
Magenta +75.
Orange +150.
Green +600.
"Paid" +25.
"Way" +75.
Steamship +100.
Steamboat +125.
Supplementary Mail Type A +125.
Railroad +100.
"Honolulu" in red (on cover) +400.
U. S. Express Mail +125.
Pen Cancel 125.

Please Note:
Stamps are valued in the grade of very fine unless otherwise indicated.
Values for early and valuable stamps are for examples with certificates of authenticity from acknowledged expert committees, or examples sold with the buyer having the right of certification. This applies to examples with original gum as well as examples without gum. Beware of stamps offered "as is," as the gum on some unused stamps offered with "original gum" may be fraudulent, and stamps offered as unused without gum may in some cases be altered or faintly canceled used stamps.

Values for 1857-61 issues are for examples that clearly show all the illustrated type characteristics. Stamps that have weakly defined or missing type characteristics sell for less.

Nos. 18-39 have small or very small margins. The values take into account the margin size. See footnotes for more specific information on selected issues.

SAME DESIGNS AS 1851-57 ISSUES
Printed by Toppan, Carpenter & Co.

1857-61 ***Perf. 15½***

18 A5 1c **blue,** type I (Plate 12), *1861* 2,100. 450.
No gum 800.
On cover 600.
On patriotic cover 1,400.
Pair 4,500. 1,000.
Strip of 3 7,000. 2,000.
Block of 4 *14,000.*
Short ornaments at either top or bottom —
Pair, types I, II 3,500. 850.
Pair, types I, IIIa 4,700. 1,050.
Block of 4, types I, II *8,750.* 5,000.
Block of 4, types I, II, IIIa *10,500.* 6,250.
Double transfer 2,600. 500.
Cracked plate (91R12) 700.

Plate 12 consists of types I & II. A few positions are type IIIa. Late printings of position 46L12 are type III.

Earliest documented use: Jan. 25, 1861.

Cancellations

Blue +20.
Red +70.
Violet +150.
Steamboat +100.
"Paid" +25.
"Free" +750.
Black Carrier +85.
Red Carrier +95.
Numeral —
Pen Cancel 250.

19 A6 1c **blue,** type Ia (Plate 4) *42,500.* *9,000.*
No gum *20,000.*
On cover *9,500.*
Pair *95,000.* *20,000.*
Strip of 3 *140,000.* *32,500.*
Vertical pair, types Ia, III *65,000.* *12,500.*
Vertical pair, types Ia, IIIa *50,000.* *10,500.*
Pair, types Ia, Ic — —
Strip of 3, types Ia, Ia, Ic (94-96R4 or 96-98R4) —
Block of 4, types Ia, Ic, and IIIa *100,000.*
Block of 4, pair type Ia and types III or IIIa — —
"Curl on shoulder" (97L4) *45,000.* *10,000.*

No. 19 is valued in the grade of fine.

Examples of this stamp exist with perforations not touching the design at any point. Such examples command very high prices.

Type Ia comes only from the bottom row of both panes of Plate 4. Two strips of three, types Ia, Ia, Ic ("F" relief) are recorded.

Earliest documented use: Sept. 9, 1857. No. 19 is known on a folded circular with Aug. 1 postmark, but the year of use has not been certified.

Cancellations

Red Carrier +200.
Blue —
Green +1,750.
Pen Cancel 4,000.

19b A6 1c **blue,** type Ic ("E" relief, less distinct examples) *4,250.* *2,500.*
No gum *1,750.*
On cover *3,500.*
Horizontal pair (81-82R4) —
Pair, types Ic, III — —
Pair, types Ic, IIIa —
blue, type Ic ("F" relief, best examples, 91, 96R4) *20,000.* *7,250.*
No gum *9,000.*
On cover *8,750.*

Type Ic — Same as Ia, but bottom right plume and ball ornament incomplete. Bottom left plume complete or nearly complete. Best examples are from bottom row, "F" relief, positions 91 and 96R4. Less distinct examples are "E" reliefs from 5th and 9th rows, positions 47L, 49L, 83L, 49R, 81R, 82R, and 89R, Plate 4, and early impressions of 41R4. Several combination type multiples can be found in the unused complete left pane of 100 from Plate 4.

Examples of the "F" relief type Ic stamps exist with perforations not touching the design at any point. Such examples command a substantial premium.

Cancellations

Pen ("E" relief) *1,000.*
Blue ("F" relief) —
Red ("F" relief) —
Pen ("F" relief) *3,000.*

20 A7 1c **blue,** type II (Plate 2) 850. 260.
No gum 375.
On cover 325.
Pair 1,800. 625.
Strip of 3 3,000. 1,000.
Block of 4 *6,000.* 2,500.
Double transfer (Plate 2) 900. 300.
Double transfer (89R2) *2,250.* *1,500.*
Major cracked plate (2L, 13L, 23L, Plate 2) 3,400. 1,400.
Intermediate cracked plate (12L2) 2,400. 1,200.
Minor cracked plate (33L2) 2,400. 800.
Reconstruction of the major plate crack (5 stamps: 2L2, 12L2, 13L2, 23L2, 33L2) *5,000.*
Plate 1L (4R1L only, double transfer), *July 1857* 1,000.
Pair, types II (4R1L), IV *2,500.*
Plate 4 3,500. *1,250.*
On cover *1,500.*
Pair 7,500. *2,750.*
Vertical pair, types II, III — —
Strip of 3 — —
Double transfer (10R4) 3,750. *1,800.*
"Curl in hair" (3R, 4R4) — *1,350.*
Plate 11 1,700. 750.
On cover 1,000.
On patriotic cover —
Pair 3,600. 1,650.
Strip of 3 —
Double transfer — —
Plate 12 1,050. 300.
On cover 350.
On patriotic cover 700.
Pair 2,200. 650.
Strip of 3 3,500. 1,050.
Block of 4 *6,000.* *2,500.*
Double transfer — —

Earliest documented uses: July 26, 1857 (Plate 2), July 26, 1857 (Plate 4), Jan. 12, 1861 (Plate 11), Jan. 21, 1861 (Plate 12).

No. 20, plate 2, is also known on two folded circulars dated July 24 and July 25, respectively, but no postal year date or docketing verifies the actual day of mailing.

Cancellations

Blue +15.
Red +35.
Green +200.
1857 year date +10.
1858 year date +5.
1861 year date +5.
"FREE" —
1863 year date +200.
"Paid" +15.
Railroad +60.
"Way" +75.
Steamboat +75.
STEAM SHIP —
Red Carrier +40.
Black Carrier +50.
Pen Cancel 135.

21 A8 1c **blue,** type III (Plate 4), see below for 99R2 *17,500.* 1,600.
No gum *6,000.*
On cover 2,000.
Pair *40,000.* 3,750.
Strip of 3 6,250.
Block of 4 —
Pair, types III, IIIa *22,500.* 2,500.
Vert. strip of 3, types II, IIIa, III *3,000.*
On cover 6,000.
Block of 4, types III, IIIa —
Plate 12 (46L12) *9,000.* *6,000.*
a. Horiz. pair, imperf between *20,000.*

Earliest documented use: Sept. 18, 1857.

Cancellations

Blue +50.
Red +90.
Green +750.
1858 year date +35.
"Paid" +60.

	Black Carrier		+175.
	Red Carrier		+200.
	Pen Cancel		1,000.

Values for type III are for at least a 2mm break in each outer line. Examples of type III with wider breaks in outer lines command higher prices; those with smaller breaks sell for less.

No. 21a is unique and is contained in a strip of three. Value reflects auction sale in 1999.

(21)	A8 1c **blue,** type III (99R2)	—	*8,000.*
	On cover		*12,500.*
	Pair, types III (99R2), II		—
	Pair, types III (99R2), IIIa		—
	Strip of 3, types III (99R2), II, IIIa		—
	Block of 9, one type III (99R2), others type II	*115,000.*	

Two unused examples of No. 21, position 99R2, are recorded; one is in a block of 9. Only three covers are recorded bearing No. 21 (99R2).

Earliest documented use: Oct. 27, 1857.

22	A8 1c **blue,** type IIIa (Plate 4)	2,200.	475.
	No gum	825.	
	On cover		525.
	Pair	4,850.	1,050.
	Vertical pair, types IIIa, II	—	*1,850.*
	Strip of 3	7,250.	1,700.
	Block of 4	*13,000.*	*5,500.*
	Block of 4, types IIIa, II	—	—
	Double transfer	2,400.	525.
	Plate 2 (100R)	—	—
	Plate 11 and Plate 12	2,400.	500.
	On cover		550.
	On patriotic cover		1,000.
	Pair	*5,400.*	1,100.
	Vert. pair, types IIIa, II (Plate 11)	*4,750.*	1,500.
	Strip of 3	*8,500.*	1,750.
	Strip of 3, types IIIa, II, I (46-48L12)		—
	Block of 4	*13,000.*	
	Block of 4, types IIIa, II (Plate 11)	*12,500.*	*4,250.*
	Double transfer	2,500.	525.
	Triple transfer (Plate 11)	*3,250.*	*1,900.*
	Bottom line broken (46L12)	—	*1,900.*

Beware of pairs of No. 22 with faint blind perforations between that sometimes are offered as pairs imperf. between.

Earliest documented uses: July 26, 1857 (Plate 4), Dec. 1860 (day unknown) (dated cancel on off-cover stamp) (Plate 11), Dec. 31, 1860, (on cover) (Plate 11), Jan. 25, 1861 (Plate 12).

Cancellations

	Blue		+20.
	Red		+75.
	Green		+350.
	1857 year date		—
	1858 year date		—
	1861 year date		—
	1863 year date		—
	"Paid"		+50.
	"Steamboat"		—
	Red Carrier		+50.
	Black Carrier		+85.
	Blue Carrier		+120.
	Pen Cancel		250.
23	A9 1c **blue,** type IV	*10,000.*	700.
	No gum	4,250.	
	On cover		1,100.
	Pair	*22,500.*	2,000.
	Strip of 3	*35,000.*	2,750.
	Block of 4		*25,000.*
	Double transfer	*11,000.*	950.
	Triple transfer, one inverted (71L1L, 81L1L and 91L1L)	*17,500.*	2,500.
	On cover		—
	Cracked plate	*10,500.*	*1,000.*
	Bottom line broken (89R1L)	—	*1,900.*

No. 23 is valued in the grade of fine with perforations touching or cutting slightly on one two sides.

Three or four used blocks of No. 23 are presently known. Value of used block of four is based on 1998 auction sale of the well-centered block of 5 sold at auction in 1998. Other blocks are poorly centered and will sell for much less.

VARIETIES OF RECUTTING

Recut once at top and once at bottom, (113 on plate)	10,000.	900.
Recut once at top, (40 on plate)	10,250.	950.
Recut once at top and twice at bottom, (21 on plate)	10,500.	950.
Recut twice at bottom, (11 on plate)	10,250.	975.
Recut once at bottom, (8 on plate)	10,500.	1,000.
Recut twice at top and once at bottom, (4 on plate)	11,000.	1,025.
Recut twice at top and twice at bottom, (2 on plate)	11,500.	1,025.

One example of the "recut twice at top and once at bottom" variety is pos. 71L1L, valued separately under the main listing.

Earliest documented use: July 25, 1857.

Cancellations

Blue	+25.
Red	+100.
1857 year date	+50.
"Paid"	+25.
Red Carrier	+125.
Black Carrier	+150.
Railroad	+150.
"Way"	+120.
"Steamboat"	+135.
"Steam"	+100.
Pen Cancel	425.

Franklin — A20

Type V — Similar to type III of 1851-57 but with side ornaments partly cut away. About one-half of all positions have side scratches. Wide breaks in top and bottom framelines.

Type Va — Stamps from Plate 5 with almost complete ornaments at right side and no side scratches. Many, but not all, stamps from Plate 5 are Type Va, the remainder being Type V.

24	A20 1c **blue,** type V (Plates 5, 7, 8, 9, 10) *1857*	140.00	37.50
	No gum	60.00	
	On cover		45.00
	On patriotic cover		300.00
	Pair	300.00	82.50
	Strip of 3	475.00	140.00
	Block of 4	800.00	425.00
	P# strip of 4, Impt.	1,400.	
	P# block of 8, Impt.	4,500.	—
	Double transfer at top (8R and 10R, Plate 8)	200.00	82.50
	Double transfer at bottom (52R9)	260.00	90.00
	Curl on shoulder, (57R, 58R, 59R, 97R, 98R, 99R, Plate 7)	200.00	65.00
	Long curl in hair and curl over "C" of "Cent" (52, 92R8)	290.00	120.00
	With "Earring" below ear (10L9)	575.00	90.00
	Curl over "C" of "Cent" (92R8)	210.00	65.00
	Curl over "E" of "Cent" (41R and 81R8)	230.00	77.50
	Curl in hair, 23L7; 39, 69L8; 34, 74R9	200.00	55.00
	Horizontal dash in hair (24L7)	310.00	80.00
	Horizontal dash in hair (36L8)	310.00	80.00
	Plate 5, type V	*1,250.*	120.00
	On cover		140.00
	No gum	*400.00*	
	Pair	*2,750.*	*260.00*
	Strip of 3	—	*500.00*
	Pair, types V, Va	*1,500.*	*675.00*
	Curl on shoulder (48L5)	—	300.00
	Curl in "O" of "ONE" (62L5)	—	300.00
	Plate 5, type Va	1,000.	300.00
	No gum	400.00	
	On cover (Type Va)		400.00
	Pair (Type Va)	—	—
	Strip of 3 (Type Va)	—	—
	Block of 4 (Type Va)	—	—
b.	Laid paper		*7,500.*

Earliest documented uses: Dec. 2, 1857 (Plate 5); Dec. 31, 1857 (Plate 7); Nov. 17, 1857 (Plate 8); Aug. 2, 1859 (Plate 9); May 5, 1860 (Plate 10).

Cancellations

	Blue		+2.50
	Red		+15.00
	Green		+250.00
	Brown		+150.00
	Magenta		+150.00
	Ultramarine		+100.00
	1857 year date		+70.00
	1858 year date		+2.50
	1859 year date		+2.50
	1860 year date		+2.50
	1861 year date		+2.50
	1862 year date		—
	1863 year date		+250.00
	Printed Precancel "CUMBERLAND, ME." (on cover)		*25,000.*
	"Paid"		+5.00
	"Free"		+25.00
	Railroad		+50.00
	Numeral		+12.50
	Express Company		+90.00
	Steamboat		+55.00
	"Steam"		+30.00
	Steamship		+40.00
	Packet boat		—
	Supp. Mail Type A, B, or C		+55.00
	"Way"		+30.00
	Red Carrier		+20.00
	Black Carrier		+12.50
	Blue Carrier		+50.00
	"Old Stamps-Not Recognized"		+1,500.
	Territorial		+80.00
	Pen Cancel		17.50
25	A10 3c **rose,** type I (Plates 4, 6, 7, 8)	2,750.	180.00
	rose red	2,750.	180.00
	dull red	2,750.	180.00
	No gum	950.	
	On cover		190.00
	brownish carmine		225.00
	On cover		375.00
	claret	3,000.	190.00
	No gum	1,050.	
	On patriotic cover		525.00
	Pair	*6,000.*	400.00

STEVE MALACK STAMPS

Buying & Selling Quality United States

We are one of the fastest growing stamp companies in the United States with an ever-changing inventory and top-of-the-line customer satisfaction. Call or write with your collecting interests, and we will send you a price list that suits your needs... We are sure that YOU will be another satisfied customer.

COMPUTERIZED WANT LIST SERVICE
Send us your want list, and we will take it from there!! QUALITY-PRICE-SERVICE-INTEGRITY

NO INTERNET ACCESS?
Then call or write for your FREE PRICE LIST!! Please specify: XF/SUPERB Mint or Used, Plate Blocks, GRADED STAMPS, U.S. Regular Mint & Used!!

Check Out Our Website: www.MALACK.com

Over 15,000 U.S. stamps, all with color photos! • Over 2,500 PSE Graded Stamps

P.O. Box #5628 • Endicott, NY 13763 • 607-862-9441 (Phone/FAX) • E-mail: Steve@Malack.com

Strip of 3	*9,500.*	575.00
Block of 4	*15,000.*	7,000.
Double transfer	3,000.	210.00
Worn plate	2,750.	175.00
Major cracked plate (47R, 48R, Plate 7)	*4,750.*	750.00
Gash on shoulder	3,000.	195.00
b. Vert. pair, imperf. horizontally		*25,000.*

No. 25 is valued in the grade of fine with perforations touching or cutting slightly on one or two sides.

All type I perforated stamps were printed from 4 of the plates used to print the imperf. stamps, so many varieties exist both imperf. and perf.

VARIETIES OF RECUTTING

Lines on bust and bottom of medallion circle recut (47R6)	—	1,750.
Top label and right diamond block joined	—	600.00
Top label and right diamond block joined at top and bottom (68R4)	—	1,250.
Lower label and right diamond block joined	—	600.00
Extra line at right	—	750.00

All varieties of recutting listed under No. 11 are found on No. 25.

Earliest documented use: May 9, 1857 (Plate 4); April 30, 1857 (Plate 6); Feb. 28, 1857 (Plate 7); April 15, 1857 (Plate 8).

Cancellations

Blue	+7.50
Red	+20.00
Orange red	+40.00
Orange	+175.00
Brown	+100.00
Ultramarine	+125.00
Green	+250.00
1857 year date	+10.00
1858 year date	+10.00
1859 year date	+10.00
"Paid"	+5.00
"Way"	+20.00
Numeral	+10.00
Railroad	+25.00
"Steam"	+20.00
Steamship	+35.00
Steamboat	+45.00
Packet Boat	+50.00
Supplementary Mail Type A	+40.00
U. S. Express Mail	+7.50
Express Company	+65.00
Black Carrier	+30.00
"Old Stamps-Not Recognized"	+1,000.
Territorial	+50.00
Printed precancel "Cumberland, Me." (on cover)	—
Pen Cancel	65.00

25A A10 3c **rose,** type II, (Plates 2L, 3, 5L)	9,000.	850.
rose red	9,000.	850.
dull red	9,000.	850.
No gum	4,000.	
On cover		950.
claret	9,250.	1,000.
No gum	4,250.	
Pair	*19,500.*	2,000.
Strip of 3	*32,500.*	3,100.
Block of 4	—	—
Double transfer "Gents" instead of "Cents" (66R2L)	—	2,000.
Triple transfer	—	1,650.
Dot in lower right diamond block (69L5L)	—	*1,000.*
Major cracked plate (84L, 94L, 9R, Plate 5L)	*10,000.*	1,500.
Intermediate cracked plate (80L, 96L, 71R, Plate 5L)	*10,000.*	1,100.
Minor cracked plate (8L, 27L, 31L, 44L, 45L, 51L, 55L, 65L, 71L and 72L, 74L, 78L, 79L, 7R, Plate 5L)	*9,250.*	950.
Gash on shoulder	9,250.	950.
Worn plate	9,000.	850.

No. 25A is valued in the grade of fine with perforations touching or cutting slightly on one two sides.

The used block of four, a right margin block showing the center line, is believed to be unique.

All type II perforated stamps were printed from 3 of the plates used to print the imperf. stamps, so most varieties exist both imperf. and perf. See "Varieties of Recutting" under No. 11A — All these varieties also exist on No. 25A except the "5 lines recut in upper left triangle" variety. Nos. 25A printed from plates 2L and 5L are much scarcer than stamps printed from plate 3.

VARIETIES OF RECUTTING

Recut inner line only at right		1,050.
1 extra vertical line outside of left frame line (29L, 39L, 49L, 59L, 69L, 79L, Plate 3)	—	1,100.
2 extra vertical lines outside of left frame line (89L, 99L, Plate 3)	—	1,200.
1 extra vertical line outside of right frame line (58L, 68L, 78L, 88L, 98L, Plate 3)	—	1,200.
No inner line and frame line close to design at right (9L, 19L, Plate 3)	—	1,150.
No inner line and frame line close to design at left (70L, 80L, 90L, 100L, Plate 3)	—	1,100.
Lower label and lower right diamond block joined at top (25L5L)		*2,300.*
Recut button (10R2L)		1,900.

Earliest documented use: July 16, 1857 (Plate 2L); July 16, 1857 (Plate 3); April 15, 1857 (Plate 5L).

Cancellations

Blue	+50.00
Red	+100.00
Orange red	+150.00
Orange	+300.00
Brown	+150.00
Ultramarine	+200.00
Green	+500.00
1857 year date	+20.00
1858 year date	+20.00
1859 year date	+20.00
"Paid"	+20.00
"Way"	+50.00
Numeral	+50.00
Railroad	+70.00
"Steam"	+40.00
Steamship	+50.00
Steamboat	+90.00
Packet Boat	+80.00
Supplementary Mail Type A	+80.00
Express Company	+120.00
Black Carrier	+50.00
Green Carrier (New Orleans "snow shovel")	—
Territorial	+100.00
Pen Cancel	450.00

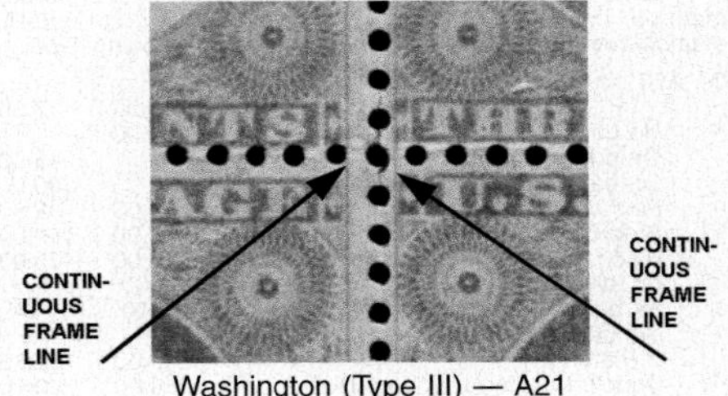

Washington (Type III) — A21

Type III — There are no outer frame lines at top and bottom. The side frame lines were recut so as to be continuous from the top to the bottom of the plate. Stamps from the top or bottom rows show the ends of the side frame lines and may be mistaken for Type IV.

Beware of type III stamps with frame lines that stop at the top of the design (from top row of plate) or bottom of the design (from bottom row of plate). These are often mistakenly offered as No. 26A.

26 A21 3c **dull red,** type III (Plates 9, 12-28)	65.00	10.00
red	65.00	10.00
rose	65.00	10.00
No gum	27.50	
brownish carmine	140.00	21.00
No gum	47.50	
claret	160.00	26.00
No gum	55.00	
orange brown	—	550.00
plum		*5,000.*
On cover, dull red		11.00
On cover, brownish carmine		40.00
On cover, orange brown		*700.00*
On patriotic cover		150.00
On Confederate patriotic cover		2,000.
On Pony express cover		—
Pair	150.00	22.50
Strip of 3	220.00	42.50
Block of 4	450.00	175.00
P# block of 8, Impt.	4,250.	
Double transfer	100.00	21.00
Double transfer, rosettes double and line through "Postage" and "Three Cents" (87R15)	—	*2,500.*
Left frame line double	100.00	21.00
Right frame line double	100.00	21.00
Cracked plate (71L18)	*1,000.*	*400.00*
Cracked plate (62L, 72L, Plate 18)	*750.00*	*250.00*
Damaged transfer above lower left rosette	75.00	12.00
Same, retouched	95.00	13.00
Same, retouched with 2 vertical lines	130.00	14.00
Same, both damaged areas retouched	310.00	100.00
Pair, both damaged areas retouched (8, 9R20)	500.00	175.00
"Quadruple" plate flaw (18L28)	—	*2,000.*
1 line recut in upper left triangle	200.00	75.00
5 lines recut in upper left triangle (52L25)		500.00
Inner line recut at left		*500.00*
Inner line recut at right	—	*1,000.*
Worn plate	65.00	10.00
b. Horiz. pair, imperf. vertically	*14,000.*	
On cover		—
c. Vert. pair, imperf. horizontally		*16,000.*
d. Horizontal pair, imperf. between		—
e. Double impression		*15,000.*
On cover		—

Frame line double varieties are separate and distinct for virtually the entire length of the stamp. Examples with partly split lines are worth considerably less.

Earliest documented use: Sept. 14, 1857.

Cancellations

Blue	+1.00
Red	+3.00
Orange red	+10.00
Orange	+150.00
Brown	+100.00
Ultramarine	+120.00
Violet	+100.00
Green	+150.00
1857 year date	+3.00
1858-1861 year date	+1.00
Printed Circular Precancel "Cumberland, Me." (on cover)	—
"Paid"	+1.00
"Paid All"	+15.00
"Free"	+20.00
"Collect"	+40.00
Numeral, "3" or "5"	+2.50
Numeral, number greater than "5"	—
"Steam"	+12.50
Steamer	—
Steamboat	+22.50
Steamship	+22.50
"Way"	+12.50
Railroad	+15.00
U. S. Express Mail	+20.00
Express Company	+65.00
Packet boat	+65.00
Supp. Mail Type A, B or C	+500.00
Black Carrier	+30.00
Red Carrier	+25.00
"Southn. Letter Unpaid"	+750.00
Territorial	+20.00
"Old Stamps-Not Recognized"	+500.00
On cover	*12,500.*
Pen Cancel	4.00

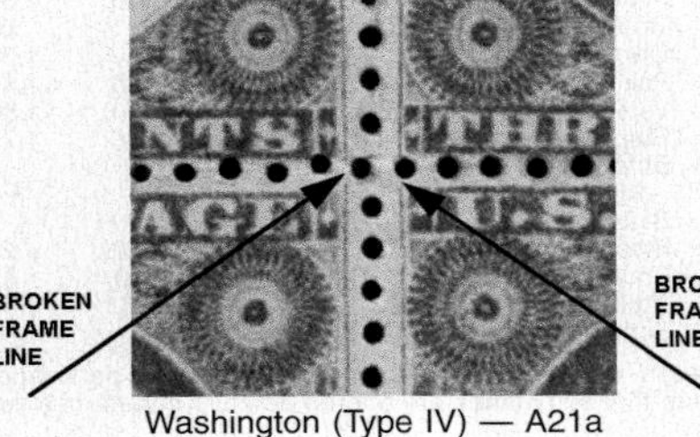

Washington (Type IV) — A21a

Type IV — As type III, but the side frame lines extend only to the top and bottom of the stamp design. All Type IV stamps are from plates 10 and 11 (each of which exists in three states), and these plates produced only Type IV. The side frame lines were recut individually for each stamp, thus being broken between the stamps vertically.

Beware of type III stamps with frame lines that stop at the top of the design (from top row of plate) or bottom of the design (from bottom row of plate). These are often mistakenly offered as No. 26A.

26A A21a 3c **dull red,** type IV (Plates 10-11)	600.00	150.00
brownish carmine	600.00	150.00
rose	600.00	150.00
No gum	260.00	
claret	650.00	170.00
No gum	275.00	
orange red	—	*190.00*
On cover		200.00
On patriotic cover		450.00
Pair	1,250.	325.00
Strip of 3	2,000.	600.00
Block of 4	*4,750.*	*2,500.*
P# block of 8, Impt.	*16,000.*	
Double transfer	675.00	225.00
Double transfer, line through rosettes (61R10i, 61R10L, 98R10i, 98R10L)	—	925.00
Double transfer of rosettes and lower part of stamp (91R11L)	—	270.00
Triple transfer	—	475.00
Damaged transfer above lower left rosette	650.00	175.00
Same, retouched	625.00	170.00
Same, both damaged areas retouched (10R11)		325.00
Inner line recut at right	—	325.00
Inner line recut at left (79L10)	—	525.00
Left frame line double (70, 80, 90, 100R11)	—	225.00
Worn plate	600.00	140.00
f. Horiz. strip of 3, imperf. vert., on cover		*14,500.*

No. 26Af is unique.

Earliest documented use: July 11, 1857.

Cancellations

Blue	+10.00
Red	+20.00
Orange red	+30.00
Orange	+150.00
Brown	+100.00
Ultramarine	+100.00
Violet	+150.00
Green	+175.00
1857 year date	+2.50
1858 or 1859 year date	+1.50
"Paid"	+2.50
"Paid All"	+15.00
"Free"	+20.00
"Collect"	+40.00
Numeral	+2.50
"Steam"	+15.00
Steamer	—
Steamboat	+25.00
Steamship	+25.00
"Way"	+15.00

Railroad		+17.50
U. S. Express Mail		+17.50
Express Company		+65.00
Packet boat		+65.00
Black Carrier		+30.00
Red Carrier		+20.00
Territorial		+30.00
Pen Cancel		40.00
27 A11 5c **brick red,** type I, *1858*	*80,000.*	1,450.
No gum	*20,000.*	
On cover		1,800.
On patriotic cover		4,750.
Pair	*175,000.*	3,500.
Strip of 3		*6,000.*
Block of 4	*475,000.*	*40,000.*
Defective transfer (23R1)	—	—

The unused block of 4 is unique. Value reflects 2019 auction sale price.

Earliest documented use: Oct. 6, 1858.

Cancellations

Blue	+225.
Red	+250.
Ultramarine	+500.
1859 year date	+50.
1860 year date	+50.
"Paid"	+50.
Supplementary Mail Type A	+150.
"Steamship"	+150.
N.Y. Ocean Mail	+1,000.
Pen Cancel	850.

28 A11 5c **red brown,** type I	*60,000.*	1,100.
pale red brown	*60,000.*	1,100.
No gum	15,000.	
On cover		1,300.
Pair	*125,000.*	2,400.
Strip of 3		4,000.
Block of 4	*90,000.*	*8,000.*
Defective transfer (23R1)		—
b. **Bright red brown**	70,000.	2,250.
No gum	20,000.	

The value of the block of 4 of No. 28 is based on the 2009 auction sale of the finest original-gum block, which grades Average-Fine.

Earliest documented use: Aug. 23, 1857 (No. 28).

Cancellations

Blue	+75.
Ultramarine	+200.
Red	+125.
1857 year date	+20.
1858 year date	+15.
"Paid"	+35.
Railroad	+75.
"Short Paid"	—
Pen Cancel	525.

28A A11 5c **Indian red,** type I, *1858*	*160,000.*	3,500.
No gum	*40,000.*	
On cover		5,000.
Pair		*7,500.*
Strip of 3		*13,000.*
Block of 4		—

There are only five recorded examples of No. 28A with any amount of original gum. Value is for a fine stamp, the highest recorded grade (two thus).

Earliest documented use: Mar. 31, 1858.

Cancellations

Red	+250.
Blue	+350.
1858 year date	+50.
1859 year date	+25.
Pen Cancel	1,650.

29 A11 5c **brown,** type I, *1859*	5,500.	350.
pale brown	5,500.	350.
deep brown	5,500.	350.
yellowish brown	5,500.	350.
No gum	1,750.	
On cover		500.
Pair	*12,000.*	750.
Strip of 3	*19,000.*	1,200.
Block of 4	*90,000.*	*5,000.*
Defective transfer (23R1)	—	—

Earliest documented use: Mar. 21, 1859.

Cancellations

Blue	+25.
Ultramarine	+175.
Red	+75.
Brown	+100.
Magenta	+150.
Green	+550.
1859 year date	+10.
1860 year date	+10.
"Paid"	+15.
"Steam"	+75.
Steamship	+100.
Numeral	+80.
Pen Cancel	160.

Jefferson — A22

FIVE CENTS.
Type II — The projections at top and bottom are partly cut away. Several minor types could be made according to the extent of cutting of the projections.

30 A22 5c **orange brown,** Type II, *1861*	1,200.	*1,300.*
deep orange brown	1,200.	*1,300.*
No gum	500.	
On cover		*2,250.*
On patriotic cover		—
Pair	2,700.	*3,250.*
Strip of 3	4,250.	—
Block of 4	*7,000.*	—

Earliest documented use: May 8, 1861.

Cancellations

Blue	+30.
Red	+75.
Green	+1,000.
"Paid"	+75.
Steamship	+110.
Supplementary Mail Type A	+150.
Railroad	—
Pen Cancel	650.

30A A22 5c **brown,** type II, *1860*	2,200.	280.
dark brown	2,200.	280.
yellowish brown	2,200.	280.
No gum	825.	
On cover		325.
On patriotic cover		—
Pair	4,750.	575.
Strip of 3	*7,500.*	950.
Block of 4	*25,000.*	*3,250.*
Cracked plate	—	
b. Printed on both sides		*35,000.*

Earliest documented use: May 4, 1860.

Cancellations

Blue	+50.
Red	+75.
Magenta	+100.
Brown	+100.
Green	+400.
"Paid"	+20.
Supplementary Mail Type A	+50.
"Steamship"	+50.
"Steam"	+50.
Express Company	+300.
Railroad	—
Packet boat	—
Pen Cancel	140.

31 A12 10c **green,** type I	*35,000.*	1,100.
dark green	*35,000.*	1,100.
bluish green	*35,000.*	1,100.
yellowish green	*35,000.*	1,100.
No gum	*11,500.*	
On domestic cover		1,300.
On patriotic cover		3,500.
Pair	*75,000.*	2,400.
Vertical pair, types III, I	*45,000.*	1,500.
Vertical pair, types IV, I (86, 96 L 1)		—
Strip of 3		—
Vertical strip of 3, types II, III, I		—
Block of 4, types III, I	*80,000.*	—
Block of 4, types III, IV, I		*9,500.*
Vertical block of 6, 2 each types II, III, I	*100,000.*	
Double transfer (100R1)	*37,500.*	1,250.
"Curl" in left "X" (99R1)	*37,500.*	1,250.

Type I comes only from the bottom row of both panes of Plate 1.

Earliest documented use: Aug. 25, 1857.

Cancellations

Blue	+50.
Red	+100.
Green	+650.
Supplementary Mail Type A	—
"Steamship"	+100.
Canadian	—
Pen Cancel	600.

Act of February 27, 1861. Ten cent rate of postage to be prepaid on letters conveyed in the mail from any point in the United States east of the Rocky Mountains to any State or Territory on the Pacific Coast and vice versa, for each half-ounce.

32 A13 10c **green,** type II	5,750.	190.
dark green	5,750.	190.
bluish green	5,750.	190.
yellowish green	5,750.	190.
No gum	2,000.	
On domestic cover		230.
On pony express cover		8,500.
Pair	*12,000.*	400.
Strip of 3	—	600.
Block of 4	*30,000.*	*4,500.*
Pair, types II, III	*12,000.*	450.
Pair, types II, IV	*60,000.*	2,500.
Vertical strip of 3, types II, III, IV		—
On cover		—
Block of 4, types II, III	*30,000.*	*3,500.*
Block of 4, types II, IV		—
Block of 4, types II, III, IV	*95,000.*	*18,000.*
Double transfer (31L, 51L and 20R, Plate 1)	6,250.	235.
"Curl opposite left X" (10R1)		260.

Earliest documented use: July 27, 1857 (dated cancel on off-cover stamp), Aug. 8, 1857 (on cover).

Cancellations

Blue	+15.
Red	+35.
Orange "PAID"	—
Brown	+125.
Green	+300.
"Paid"	+20.
1857 year date	+10.
Supplementary Mail Type A	—
Steamship	+50.
Packet boat	—
Railroad	—
Express Company	—
Pen Cancel	90.

33 A14 10c **green,** type III	5,750.	180.
dark green	5,750.	180.
bluish green	5,750.	180.
yellowish green	5,750.	180.
No gum	2,000.	
On domestic cover		225.
Pair	*12,000.*	400.
Strip of 3	—	600.
Pair, types III, IV		2,500.
"Curl" on forehead (85L1)	—	250.
"Curl in left X" (87R1)		250.

Earliest documented use: Aug. 8, 1857.

Cancellations

Blue	+15.
Red	+35.
Brown	+125.
Ultramarine	+150.
1857 year date	+10.
"Paid"	+20.
"Steam"	+45.
Steamboat	—
Steamship	+50.
Numeral	+20.
Packet boat	—
Pen Cancel	90.

34 A15 10c **green,** type IV	*50,000.*	2,100.
dark green	*50,000.*	2,100.
bluish green	*50,000.*	2,100.
yellowish green	*50,000.*	2,100.
No gum	*20,000.*	
On domestic cover		2,500.
Pair		*5,500.*
Block of 4 (54-55, 64-65L)		—

VARIETIES OF RECUTTING

Eight stamps on Plate I were recut. All are listed below.

Outer line recut at top (65L, 74L, 86L and 3R, Plate I)	*50,000.*	2,100.
Outer line recut at bottom (54L, 55L, 76L, Plate 1)	*52,500.*	2,250.
Outer line recut at top and bottom (64L1)	*55,000.*	2,600.

Earliest documented use: Oct. 5, 1857.

Cancellations

Blue	+100.
Red	+175.
Steamship	+200.
Packet boat	—
Pen Cancel	1,100.

Types I, II, III and IV occur on the same sheet, so it is possible to obtain pairs and blocks showing combinations of types. For listings of type combinations in pairs and blocks, see Nos. 31-33.

Example I Example II

Washington (Two typical examples) — A23

Type V — The side ornaments are slightly cut away. Usually only one pearl remains at each end of the lower label, but some examples show two or three pearls at the right side. At the bottom the outer line is complete and the shells nearly so. The outer lines at top are complete except over the right "X."

35 A23 10c **green,** type V, (Plate 2), *1859*	210.00	55.00
dark green	210.00	55.00
yellowish green	210.00	55.00
No gum	95.00	
On domestic cover		67.50
On patriotic cover		625.00

On pony express cover		—
On cover to Canada		120.00
Pair	450.00	120.00
Block of 4	1,100.	600.00
P# block of 8, Impt.	*17,500.*	
Double transfer at bottom (47R2)	275.00	80.00
Small "Curl" on forehead (37, 78L2)	250.00	67.50
Curl in "e" of "cents" (93L2)	300.00	80.00
Curl in "t" of "cents" (73R2)	300.00	80.00
Cracked plate		—

Earliest documented use: Apr. 29, 1859.

Cancellations

Red	+7.50
Orange red	+12.50
Orange	+150.00
Brown	+100.00
Blue	+5.00
Magenta	+100.00
Green	+225.00
1859 year date	+5.00
"Paid"	+5.00
"Paid All"	—
"Free"	+75.00
Red carrier	—
Railroad	+40.00
Steamship	+35.00
"Steam"	+30.00
Numerals	+15.00
Supp. Mail Type A or C	+60.00
Express Company	+135.00
"Southn Letter Unpaid"	—
Territorial	—
Pen Cancel	25.00

TWELVE CENTS. Printed from two plates.

Plate 1 (No. 36) — Outer frame lines were recut on the plate and are complete. Very narrow spacing of stamps on the plate.

No. 36, Outer frame lines recut on plate

36	A16 12c **black** (Plate 1)	1,700.	300.
	gray black	1,700.	300.
	No gum	500.	
	Single on cover		700.
	Single on cover with No. 26 to France		475.
	Pair on cover to England		850.
	Pair on patriotic cover		—
	Pair	4,000.	700.
	Block of 4	*10,000.*	2,750.
	Not recut in lower right corner	2,000.	350.
	Recut in lower left corner (43, 53, 63, 73, 100L)	2,000.	350.
	Double transfer	2,000.	350.
	Triple transfer	2,200.	—
a.	Diagonal half used as 6c on cover		*17,500.*
c.	Horizontal pair, imperf. between		*12,500.*

Earliest documented use: July 30, 1857.

Cancellations

Blue	+10.
Red	+20.
Brown	+75.
Magenta	+75.
Green	—
1857 year date	+100.
"Paid"	+10.
Supplementary Mail Type A	+60.
Express Company	—
Railroad	+60.
Numeral	+20.
"Southn Letter Unpaid"	—
Pen Cancel	150.

Typical No. 36B, outer frame lines not recut

Plate 3 (No. 36B) — Weak outer frame lines from the die were not recut and are noticeably uneven or broken, sometimes partly missing. Somewhat wider spacing of stamps on the plate.

36B	A16 12c **black** (Plate 3)	700.	250.
	intense black	700.	250.
	No gum	325.	
	Single on cover		1,150.
	Single on cover with No. 26 to France		450.
	Pair on cover to England		800.
	Pair	1,500.	600.
	Block of 4	5,000.	3,250.
	Double frame line at right	750.	275.
	Double frame line at left	750.	275.
	Vertical line through rosette (95R3)	875.	325.

Earliest documented use: June 1, 1860. (The previously listed Dec. 3, 1859, cover requires expertization in order to be considered.)

Cancellations

Blue	+20.
Red	+40.
Brown	+85.
Magenta	+60.
Green	+275.
1860 year date	+100.
1861 year date	+50.
"Paid"	+12.
Supplementary Mail Type A	+300.
Express Company	—
Railroad	+65.
Numeral	+25.
"Southn Letter Unpaid"	—
Pen Cancel	125.

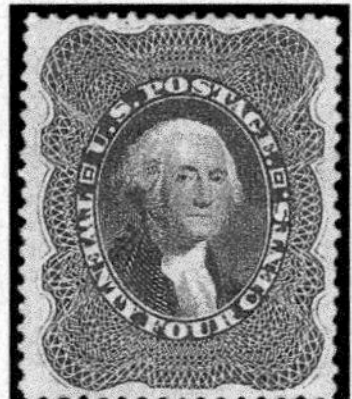

Washington — A17

Franklin — A18

37	A17 24c **gray lilac**, *1860*	1,450.	375.
a.	24c **gray**	1,450.	375.
	No gum	500.	
	On cover to England		1,000.
	On patriotic cover		*4,000.*
	Pair	3,150.	800.
	Block of 4	*10,000.*	*6,500.*
	P# block of 12, Impt.	*40,000.*	

The technical configuration of a No. 37 plate block is eight stamps. The unique plate block currently is contained in the listed block of twelve stamps.

Earliest documented use: July 7, 1860.

Cancellations

Blue	+20.
Red	+65.
Magenta	+110.
Violet	+175.
Green	+525.
1860 year date	+15.
"Paid"	+25.
"Paid All"	+50.
"Free"	+150.
Supplementary Mail Type A	+150.
Railroad	+150.
Packet Boat	+200.
Red Carrier	—
Numeral	+40.
"Southn Letter Unpaid"	—
Mexico	—
Pen Cancel	200.

See Trial Color Proofs for the 24c red lilac.

38	A18 30c **orange**, *1860*	1,900.	425.
	yellow orange	1,900.	425.
	reddish orange	1,900.	425.
	No gum	700.	
	On cover to Germany or France		*1,350.*
	On patriotic cover		*7,500.*
	Pair	*4,250.*	950.
	Block of 4	*14,000.*	*6,750.*
	Double transfer (89L1 and 99L1)	2,150.	500.
	Recut at bottom (52L1)	2,400.	550.
	Cracked plate	—	—
	Curl above "U" of "U.S." (64R1)	—	—

Earliest documented use: Aug. 8, 1860.

Cancellations

Blue	+30.
Red	+50.
Magenta	+90.
Violet	+250.
Green	+1,100.
1860 year date	+30.
"Paid"	+35.
"Free"	—
Black town	+30.
Supplementary Mail Type A	+125.
Steamship	—
N.Y. Ocean Mail	+100.
Express Company	—
Pen Cancel	210.

Washington — A19

39	A19 90c **blue**, *1860*	3,000.	*11,000.*
	deep blue	3,000.	*11,000.*
	No gum	1,300.	
	On cover		*225,000.*
	Pair	*6,250.*	—
	Block of 4	*75,000.*	*45,000.*
	Double transfer at bottom	3,250.	—
	Double transfer at top	3,250.	—
	Short transfer at bottom right and left (13L1 and 68R1)	3,250.	

The used block of 4 is believed to be unique and has perfs trimmed off at left and bottom clear of design. Value is based on 1993 auction sale.

Earliest documented use: Sept. 11, 1860.

Cancellations

Red	10,000.
Black	+200.
Blue	+400.
Red town	+1,200.
Black town	+1,000.
1861 year date	+1,000.
Boston "Paid"	+750.
Red Carrier	—
N.Y. Ocean Mail	+1,000.
Pen Cancel	3,250.

Genuine cancellations on the 90c are very scarce.

All used examples of No. 39 must be accompanied by certificates of authenticity issued by recognized expertizing committees.

See Die and Plate Proofs for imperfs. on stamp paper.

REPRINTS OF 1857-60 ISSUE

These were not valid for postal use, though one example each of Nos. 43 and 45 are known with contemporaneous cancels.

Produced by the Continental Bank Note Co.

White paper, without gum.

The 1, 3, 10 and 12c were printed from new plates of 100 subjects each differing from those used for the regular issue.

1875 ***Perf. 12***

40	A5 1c **bright blue** *(3846)*	*575.*	
	Pair	*1,200.*	
	Block of 4	*3,250.*	
	Cracked plate, pos. 91	*700.*	
	Double transfer, pos. 94	*700.*	
41	A10 3c **scarlet** *(479)*	*2,750.*	
42	A22 5c **orange brown** *(878)*	*1,150.*	
	Pair	*2,750.*	
	Vertical margin strip of 4, Impt. & P#	*11,500.*	
43	A12 10c **blue green** *(516)*	*2,500.*	13,000.
	Pair	*6,000.*	
44	A16 12c **greenish black** *(489)*	*2,750.*	
	Pair	*7,000.*	
45	A17 24c **blackish violet** *(479)*	*3,000.*	10,000.
46	A18 30c **yellow orange** *(480)*	*3,000.*	
47	A19 90c **deep blue** *(454)*	*3,500.*	

Nos. 41-46 are valued in the grade of fine.

Nos. 40-47 exist imperforate. Very infrequent sales preclude establishing a value at this time. One set of imperforate pairs is recorded and it sold for $110,000 in a 2009 auction. An imperforate horizontal strip of 3 of No. 44 also is recorded.

Numbers in parentheses are quantities sold.

Produced by the National Bank Note Co.

Franklin

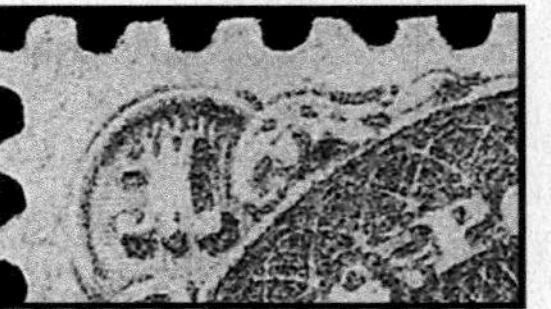

A24

Washington

A25

Jefferson

A26

Washington — A27

A27

A27a

Washington

A28

Washington — A29

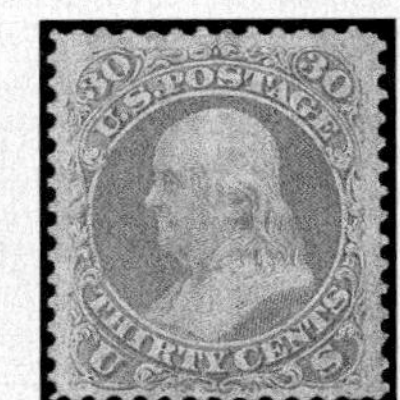

Franklin — A30

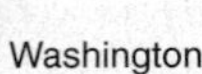

Washington

A31

1c — There is a dash under the tip of the ornament at right of the numeral in upper left corner.

3c — Ornaments at corners end in a small ball.

5c — There is a leaflet in the foliated ornaments at each corner.

10c (A27) — A heavy curved line has been cut below the stars and an outer line added to the ornaments above them.

WANTED TO BUY

STAMPS, COINS AND BANKNOTES

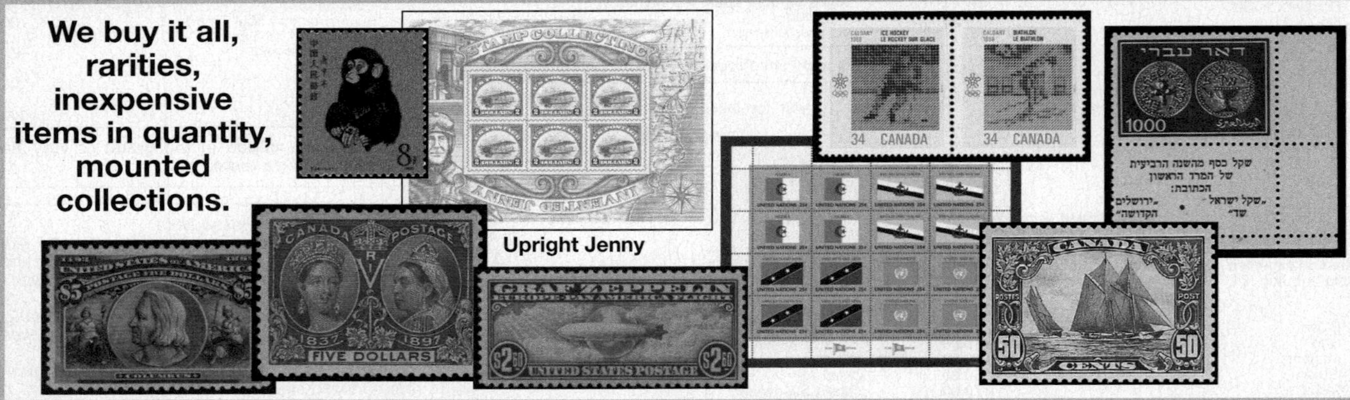

We are leading buyers and suppliers of U.S., Canada, Israel and world wide. We buy it all!!! We travel for valuable lots. Send #10 SASE or by email for Israel, Iran, Russia, Germany, Vatican, U.N. and U.S. Buy & Sell Lists.

IDEAL

STAMP COMPANY, INC.

Sam Malamud

ifsda

172 Empire Boulevard, Third Floor
Brooklyn, NY 11225
PH: 1-212-629-7979 • FAX: 1-212-629-3350
Email: info@idealny.com
Cell: 917-991-8383

Trusted for over 50 Years - Established in 1960

12c — There are corner ornaments consisting of ovals and scrolls.

90c — Parallel lines form an angle above the ribbon with "U. S. Postage"; between these lines there is a row of dashes and a point of color at the apex of the lower line.

Patriotic Covers covering a wide range of historical interest were used during the Civil War period, in the North as well as the South, and are collected by manufacturer and topic as well as generally, both used and unused. There are believed to be 12,500 or more Northern varieties and 300 or more Southern varieties.

During the war, these stamps were used as small change until Postage Currency was issued.

The Act of Congress of March 3, 1863, effective July 1, 1863, created a rate of three cents for each half ounce, first class domestic mail. This Act was the first law which established uniform rate of postage regardless of the distance. This rate remained in effect until Oct. 1, 1883.

Plates of 200 subjects in two panes of 100 each.

The following items, formerly listed here as Nos. 55-62, are considered to be essays or trial color proofs. They will be found in a separate listing between the Essay section and the Proof section of this catalog. Previous No. 58 has been combined with No. 62B.

Formerly	Currently	Formerly	Currently
55	63-E11e	59	69-E6e
56	65-E15h	60	70TC6
57	67-E9e	61	71TC6
58	62B	62	72-E7h

The paper of Nos. 62B-72 is thicker and more opaque than the essays and trial color proofs, except Nos. 62B, 70c, and 70d.

1861 ***Perf. 12***

No.	Description	Unused	Used
62B	A27a 10c **dark green**	*8,500.*	1,600.
	dark yellow green	*8,250.*	1,600.
	No gum	*3,600.*	
	On cover		2,100.
	On patriotic cover		3,000.
	Pair	*18,000.*	3,750.
	Block of 4	*37,500.*	*13,500.*
	Foreign entry 94R4	*9,500.*	—
	Block of 4, one stamp 94R4	*40,000.*	

The foreign entry is of the 90c 1861.

Earliest documented use: Sept. 17, 1861.

Cancellations

Red	+110.
Blue	+70.
"Paid"	+60.
Steamship	+100.
Express Company	+200.
Supplementary Mail Type A	+125.

1861-62 ***Perf. 12***

No.	Description	Unused	Used
63	A24 1c **blue,** *Aug. 17, 1861*	275.00	45.00
	pale blue	275.00	45.00
	bright blue	275.00	45.00
	No gum	100.00	
	On cover (single)		52.50
	On prisoner's letter		—
	On patriotic cover		225.00
	Pair	600.00	95.00
	Block of 4	1,600.	500.00
	P# block of 8, Impt.	*6,500.*	
	Double transfer	—	57.50
	Dot in "U"	300.00	50.00
a.	1c **ultramarine**	*2,500.*	*1,900.*
	No gum	*1,000.*	
	dark ultramarine	*5,000.*	*2,000.*
	No gum	*2,250.*	
b.	1c **dark blue**	800.00	*875.00*
	No gum	300.00	
c.	Laid paper, horiz. or vert.	*8,500.*	*4,500.*
	Block of four		*27,500.*
d.	Vertical pair, imperf. horiz.		—
e.	Printed on both sides, reverse inverted	—	*35,000.*

The editors would like to see authenticated evidence of the existence of No. 63d.

Earliest documented use: Aug. 17, 1861 (dated cancel on off-cover stamp); Aug. 21, 1861 (on cover).

Cancellations

Blue	+5.00
Red	+15.00
Magenta	+50.00
Green	+250.00
Violet	+70.00
1861 year date	+7.50
1865 year date	+2.00
1866 year date	+2.00
"Free"	+40.00
"Paid"	+2.50
"Paid All"	+15.00
Supp. Mail Type A or B	+30.00
Steamship	+35.00
Steam	+40.00
Express Company	+175.00
Red Carrier	+20.00
Black Carrier	+25.00
Railroad	+40.00
Numeral	+20.00
"Steamboat"	+50.00
Printed Precancel "CUMBERLAND, ME."	—

No.	Description	Unused	Used
64	A25 3c **pink,** *Aug. 17, 1861*	*14,000.*	600.00
	No gum	*5,000.*	
	On cover		775.00
	On patriotic cover		1,400.
	Pair	*30,000.*	*1,750.*
	Block of 4	*65,000.*	—

Earliest documented use: Aug. 17, 1861 (FDC).

Cancellations

Blue	+50.00
Red	+150.00
Green	+500.00
1861 date	—
"Paid"	+25.00
"Free"	+175.00
"Ship"	+85.00
Supplementary Mail Type B	+150.00
Railroad	+125.00
Steamboat	+175.00

No.	Description	Unused	Used
a.	3c **pigeon blood pink**	*50,000.*	*4,500.*
	No gum	*15,000.*	
	On cover		*5,000.*
	On patriotic cover		*7,500.*

Earliest documented use: Aug. 21, 1861.

No.	Description	Unused	Used
b.	3c **rose pink,** *Aug. 17, 1861*	600.00	150.00
	No gum	250.00	
	On cover		180.00
	On patriotic cover		250.00
	Pair	1,350.	325.00
	Block of 4	3,250.	850.00

Earliest documented use: Aug. 17, 1861 (FDC).

Cancellations

Blue	+15.00
Red	+30.00
Orange red	+40.00
Green	+180.00
Orange	—
"Paid"	+10.00
"Free"	+75.00
Supplementary Mail Type C	—
Numeral "15" (on No. 64b)	—
"Ship"	+30.00
Railroad	+60.00
Steamboat	+90.00

No.	Description	Unused	Used
65	A25 3c **rose**	125.00	3.00
	bright rose	125.00	3.00
	dull red	125.00	3.00
	rose red	125.00	3.00
	No gum	50.00	
	On cover		3.50
	On patriotic cover		90.00
	On prisoner's letter		150.00
	On pony express cover		—
	Pair	270.00	6.75
	Block of 4	700.00	42.50
	P# block of 8, Impt.	4,750.	
	Double transfer	160.00	6.00
	Cracked plate	—	—
	brown red	*275.00*	5.50
	No gum	100.00	
	pale brown red	*210.00*	5.50
	No gum	70.00	
	dull brown red	*250.00*	5.50
	No gum	90.00	
	Block of 4	*1,250.*	
	deep pinkish rose	*290.00*	30.00
	On cover		—
b.	Laid paper, horiz. or vert.	—	*1,100.*
d.	Vertical pair, imperf. horiz.	*12,500.*	*1,500.*
	No gum	*5,000.*	
e.	Printed on both sides, reverse inverted	*40,000.*	*8,000.*
	Pair	*82,500.*	
	Printed on both sides, reverse not inverted		7,000.
f.	Double impression		*12,500.*

See Die and Plate Proofs for imperfs. on stamp paper.

Earliest documented use: Aug. 19, 1861.

Cancellations

Blue	+1.00
Ultramarine	+2.75
Brown	+50.00
Red	+3.00
Orange red	+3.50
Violet	+75.00
Magenta	+8.00
Green	+100.00
Olive	+100.00
Orange	+150.00
Yellow	*+3,500.*
1861 year date	+2.00
1867 or 1868 year date	+1.00
"Paid"	+.35
"Paid All"	+7.50
"Mails Suspended"	—
Railroad	+12.50
"Way"	+20.00
"Free"	+20.00
"Collect"	+35.00
"Ship"	+15.00
"U. S. Ship"	+35.00
"Steam"	+12.00
Steamship	+15.00
Steamboat	+20.00
"Ship Letter"	+35.00
Red Carrier	+15.00
Blue Carrier	+25.00
Black Carrier	+20.00
Supplementary Mail Type A, B or C	+15.00
Numeral, "3" or "5"	+3.00
Numeral, number greater than "5"	—
Express Company	+90.00
Army Field Post	+60.00
Packet Boat	+40.00
"Registered"	+30.00
"Postage Due"	+25.00
"Advertised"	+15.00
"U.STATES"	+300.00
Territorial	+25.00
St. Thomas	—
China	—

The 3c lake can be found under No. 66TC6 in the Trial Color, Die and Plate Proofs section.

No.	Description	Unused	Used
67	A26 5c **buff**	*27,500.*	750.
	No gum	*10,500.*	
	On cover		1,000.
	On patriotic cover		*3,750.*
	Pair	*60,000.*	1,900.
	Block of 4	*25,000.*	*13,000.*
a.	5c **brown yellow**	*30,000.*	1,100.
	No gum	*11,500.*	
b.	5c **olive yellow**	—	4,750.

The unused block of 4 is unique but very faulty. Value is based on 2019 auction sale.

Earliest documented uses: Aug. 19, 1861 (No. 67); Aug. 21, 1861 (No. 67a); Sept. 18, 1861 (on off-cover No. 67b).

Cancellations

Red	+60.00
Blue	+30.00
Magenta	+250.00
Green	+900.00
1861 year date	+10.00
"Paid"	+25.00
Supplementary Mail Type A	+100.00
Express Company	+250.00
Numeral	+50.00
"Steamship"	+100.00

Values of Nos. 67, 67a, 67b reflect the normal small margins.

No.	Description	Unused	Used
68	A27 10c **green**	950.	55.00
	yellow green	900.	55.00
	No gum	375.	
	On cover		75.00
	On patriotic cover		375.00
	On cover to Canada		100.00
	Pair	2,100.	115.00
	Block of 4	*5,500.*	650.00
	P# block of 8, Impt.	*20,000.*	
	Double transfer	1,150.	60.00
	deep yellow green on thin paper	1,250.	62.50
a.	10c **dark green**	1,350.	85.00
	blue green	1,350.	85.00
	No gum	500.	
b.	Vertical pair, imperf. horiz.		*30,000.*

Earliest documented use: Aug. 20, 1861.

Cancellations

Blue	+5.00
Red	+10.00
Purple	+50.00
Magenta	+50.00
Brown	+50.00
Green	+250.00
1865 year date	+3.50
"Paid"	+2.50
"Collect"	+32.50
"Short Paid"	+50.00
"P.D." in circle	+30.00
"Free"	+50.00
Numeral	+7.50
Red Carrier	+65.00
Railroad	+20.00
Steamship	+15.00
"Steamboat"	+35.00
Supplementary Mail Type A	+30.00
Red Supp. Mail Type D	+1,000.
Express Company	+70.00
China	—
Japan	+200.00
St. Thomas	—
"U. States"	+300.00

Stamps are valued in the grade of very fine unless otherwise indicated.

Please Note:

Values for early and valuable stamps are for examples with certificates of authenticity from acknowledged expert committees, or examples sold with the buyer having the right of certification.

This applies to unused examples with original gum as well as examples without gum. It also applies to used stamps.

Beware of stamps offered "as is," as the gum on some unused stamps offered with "original gum" may be fraudulent, and stamps offered as unused without gum may in some cases be altered or faintly canceled used stamps.

No.	Description	Unused	Used
69	A28 12c **black**	1,700.	95.00
	gray black	1,700.	105.00
	No gum	675.	
	intense black	1,800.	110.00
	No gum	700.	
	On domestic cover		135.00
	On patriotic cover		850.00
	On cover to France or Germany with #65		160.00
	Pair	3,750.	230.00
	Block of 4	*10,000.*	1,100.
	Double transfer of top frame line	1,800.	125.00

Double transfer of bottom frame line 1,800. 125.00
Double transfer of top and bottom frame lines 1,900. 130.00

Earliest documented use: Aug. 30, 1861.

Cancellations

Blue +15.00
Ultramarine —
Red +40.00
Purple +110.00
Magenta +100.00
Green +550.00
1861 year date +5.00
"Paid" +5.00
"Registered" +35.00
Supp. Mail Type A, B or C +45.00
Express Company +175.00
Railroad +50.00
Numeral +15.00

70 A29 24c **red lilac** 3,000. 300.00
No gum 1,150.
On cover 350.00
On patriotic cover *3,000.*
Pair 6,500. 625.00
Block of 4 *15,000.* *3,000.*
Scratch under "A" of "Postage" —
a. 24c **brown lilac** 3,250. 325.00
No gum 1,250.
Block of 4 *17,000.* *3,500.*
b. 24c **steel blue** ('61) *16,500.* 850.00
No gum *6,250.*
On cover 1,300.
Block of 4 *75,000.*
c. 24c **violet,** thin paper, *Aug. 20, 1861* *35,000.* 2,250.
No gum *13,500.*
d. 24c **pale gray violet,** thin paper *25,000.* 3,250.
No gum *6,000.*

There are numerous shades of the 24c stamp in this and the following issue.

Color changelings, especially of No. 78, are frequently offered as No. 70b. Obtaining a certificate from an acknowledged expert committee is strongly advised.

Nos. 70c and 70d are on a thinner, harder and more transparent paper than Nos. 70, 70a, 70b or the latter Nos. 78, 78a, 78b and 78c. No. 70eTC (formerly No. 60, see Trial Color Proofs section) is distinguished by its distinctive dark color.

Earliest documented uses: Jan. 7, 1862 (No. 70); Feb. 5, 1862 (No. 70a); Sept. 21, 1861 (No. 70b); Aug. 20, 1861 (No. 70c); Sept. 10, 1861 (No. 70d).

Cancellations, No. 70

Blue +25.00
Red +40.00
Magenta +200.00
Brown +125.00
Green +400.00
1865 year date +5.00
"Paid" +15.00
Supp. Mail Types A or B +75.00
Express Company +350.00

71 A30 30c **orange** 2,600. 210.
deep orange 2,600. 250.
No gum 950.
On cover to France or Germany 380.
On patriotic cover *3,500.*
Pair 5,750. 460.
Block of 4 *17,000.* *2,500.*
P# strip of 4, Impt. —
a. Printed on both sides —

Values for No. 71 are for examples with small margins, especially at sides. Large-margined examples sell for much more.

Earliest documented use: Aug. 20, 1861.

Cancellations

Blue +15.00
Magenta +100.00
Brown +100.00
Red +35.00
Green —
"Paid" +20.00
"Paid All" +50.00
"Registered" —
Railroad —
Packet Boat —
"Steamship" +75.00
Supplementary Mail Type A +75.00
Red Supp. Mail Type D —
Express Company +350.00
Japan —

72 A31 90c **blue** 3,000. 600.
dull blue 3,000. 600.
No gum 1,200.
On cover *25,000.*
Pair *6,500.* 1,300.
Block of 4 *32,500.* *5,000.*
P# strip of 4, Impt. *50,000.*
a. 90c **pale blue** 3,000. 650.
No gum 1,200.
b. 90c **dark blue** 3,750. 950.
No gum 1,500.

The unique plate number and imprint strip of 4 of No. 72 has no gum and is valued thus.

Earliest documented use: Nov. 27, 1861.

Cancellations

Blue +60.
Red +125.
Green +1,000.
1865 year date +35.
"Paid" +25.
"Registered" +75.
Express Company +500.
Supplementary Mail Type A +100.

Nos. 68a, 69, 71 and 72 exist as imperforate sheet-margin singles with pen cancel. They were not regularly issued.

The 90c was distributed to several post offices in the last two weeks of August, 1861.

Owing to the Civil War, stamps and stamped envelopes in current use or available for postage in 1860, were demonetized by various post office orders, beginning in August, 1861, and extending to early January, 1862.

P. O. Department Bulletin.

"A reasonable time after hostilities began in 1861 was given for the return to the Department of all these (1851-56) stamps in the hands of postmasters, and as early as 1863 the Department issued an order declining to longer redeem them."

The Act of Congress, approved March 3, 1863, abolished carriers' fees and established a prepaid rate of two cents for drop letters, making necessary the 2-cent Jackson (No. 73).

Free City Delivery was authorized by the Act of Congress of March 3, 1863, effective in 49 cities with 449 carriers, beginning July 1, 1863.

Produced by the National Bank Note Co.
DESIGNS AS 1861 ISSUE

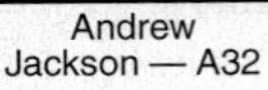

Andrew Jackson — A32

Abraham Lincoln — A33

1861-66 ***Perf. 12***

73 A32 2c **black,** *1863* 325.00 55.00
gray black 325.00 55.00
intense black 325.00 60.00
No gum 140.00
On cover 75.00
On prisoner's letter —
On patriotic cover *2,000.*
Pair 700.00 120.00
Block of 4 *2,750.* *2,000.*
P# strip of 4, Impt. *4,500.*
P# block of 8, Impt. *15,000.*
Double transfer 375.00 60.00
Major double transfer of top left corner and "Postage" ("Atherton shift") *12,500.*
Major double transfer of right side, pos. 81, right pane ("Preston shift") *5,000.* *4,000.*
Major double transfer of frame in all corners plus hair and chin ("Metzger shift") —
Triple transfer —
Short transfer 350.00 60.00
Cracked plate — —
a. Diagonal half used as 1c as part of 3c rate on cover 1,500.
Diagonal half used as 1c as part of 2c drop rate on cover —
b. Diagonal half used alone as 1c on cover *3,000.*
c. Horiz. half used as 1c as part of 3c rate on cover *3,500.*
d. Vert. half used as 1c as part of 3c rate on cover 2,000.
e. Vert. half used alone as 1c on cover *4,000.*
f. Printed on both sides, reverse not inverted *27,500.*
Printed on both sides, reverse inverted *6,500.* *20,000.*
g. Laid paper — *11,500.*

No. 73f unused is unique. It has perfs cut off on two sides and is valued thus.

Earliest documented use: July 1, 1863 (dated cancel on off-cover stamp); July 6, 1863 (on cover).

Cancellations

Blue +15.00
Brown +75.00
Red +50.00
Orange red +70.00
Magenta +200.00
Ultramarine +150.00
Orange +200.00
Green +600.00
1863 year date +5.00
Printed Precancel "Jefferson, Ohio" —
"PAID ALL" +40.00
"Paid" +10.00
Numeral +15.00
"Way" +150.00
Railroad +300.00
"Steam" +40.00
Steamship +100.00
"Steamboat" +65.00
"Ship Letter" +150.00
Black Carrier +20.00
Blue Carrier +35.00
Supp. Mail Type A or B +100.00
Express Company +300.00
"Short Paid" +250.00
Territorial +100.00
"Forwarded by U.S. Consul . . . Japan" +2,000.
China —

The 3c scarlet, design A25, can be found under No. 74TC6 in the Trial Color, Die and Plate Proofs section.

75 A26 5c **red brown** 5,750. 425.
dark red brown 5,750. 425.
No gum 2,100.
On cover 700.
On patriotic cover *4,000.*
Pair *12,000.* 1,100.
Block of 4 *62,500.* *7,500.*
Double transfer *6,000.* 475.

Values for No. 75 reflect the normal small margins.

Earliest documented use: Jan. 2, 1862.

Cancellations

Blue +30.
Red +60.
Magenta +90.
Green +1,000.
"Paid" +25.
Supplementary Mail Type A +50.
Express Company +300.

76 A26 5c **brown,** *1863* 1,400. 120.
pale brown 1,400. 120.
dark brown 1,400. 135.
No gum 550.
On cover 180.
On patriotic cover 2,000.
Pair 3,000. 275.
Block of 4 *8,250.* *1,200.*
P# strip of 4, Impt. *15,000.*
Double transfer of top frame line 1,450. 140.
Double transfer of bottom frame line 1,450. 140.
Double transfer of top and bottom frame lines 1,550. 160.
a. 5c **black brown** 2,250. 400.
No gum 850.
Block of 4 *9,000.* *2,100.*
b. Laid paper —

Values of Nos. 76, 76a reflect the normal small margins. The plate no. strip of 4 with imprint of No. 76 is unique.

Earliest documented use: Feb. 3, 1863.

Cancellations

Blue +15.00
Ultramarine +150.
Magenta +75.00
Red +45.00
Brown +150.00
Green +750.00
1865 year date +10.00
"Paid" +15.00
"Short Paid" +75.00
Supp. Mail Type A or F +55.00
Express Company +175.00
"Steamship" +65.00
Packet boat —
"Forwarded by U.S. Consul . . . Japan" —

77 A33 15c **black,** *April 1866* 5,000. 175.
full black 5,000. 175.
No gum 1,900.
On cover to France or Germany 225.
Pair 10,000. 375.
Block of 4 *32,500.* *1,500.*
P# block of 8, Impt. —
Double transfer 5,000. 240.
Cracked plate — 240.

Earliest documented use: April 21, 1866.

Cancellations

Blue +15.
Indigo +25.
Purple +90.
Lavender (Philadelphia) +135.
Violet +90.
Magenta +100.
Red +50.
Brown +125.
Green +500.
Ultramarine +100.
"Paid" +20.
"Short Paid" +85.
"Insufficiently Paid" or "Insufficiently Prepaid" +130.
"Ship" +50.
Steamship +50.
Supplementary Mail Type A +90.
French anchor in lozenge +75.

78 A29 24c **lilac,** *1862* 2,750. 400.
No gum 950.
dark lilac 2,750. 425.
No gum 950.
On cover 425.
Pair 6,000. 825.
Block of 4 *18,000.* *2,750.*
Scratch under "A" of "Postage" — —
a. 24c **grayish lilac** 2,750. 425.
No gum 950.
b. 24c **gray** 2,750. 450.
No gum 950.

c. 24c **blackish violet**	95,000.	17,500.
No gum	30,000.	
On cover		25,000.

Only three examples are recorded of No. 78c unused with original gum. No. 78c unused with and without gum are valued in the grade of fine-very fine.

d. Printed on both sides, reverse inverted		22,500.
On cover		35,000.

No. 78d off cover and on cover are each unique.

Earliest documented uses: Oct. 23, 1862 (No. 78a); Oct. 29, 1862 (No. 78b); May 1, 1863 (No. 78c).

Cancellations

Blue	+20.00
Red	+40.00
Magenta	+90.00
Green	+600.00
"Paid"	+15.00
Numeral	+20.00
Supplementary Mail Type A	+50.00
"Free"	+100.00

Nos. 73, 76-78 exist as imperforate sheet-margin singles, all with pen cancel except No. 76 which is uncanceled. They were not regularly issued.

SAME DESIGNS AS 1861-66 ISSUES

Printed by the National Bank Note Co.

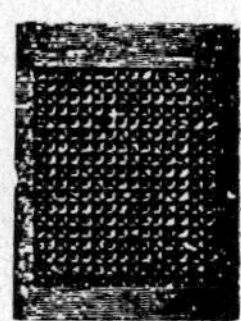

Grill

Embossed with grills of various sizes. Some authorities believe that more than one size of grill probably existed on one of the grill rolls.

A peculiarity of the United States issues from 1867 to 1870 is the grill or embossing. The object was to break the fiber of the paper so that the ink of the canceling stamp would soak in and make washing for a second using impossible. The exact date at which grilled stamps came into use is unsettled. Luff's "Postage Stamps of the United States" places the date as probably August 8, 1867.

Horizontal measurements are given first.

GRILL WITH POINTS UP

Grills A and C were made by a roller covered with ridges shaped like an inverted V. Pressing the ridges into the stamp paper forced the paper into the pyramidal pits between the ridges, causing irregular breaks in the paper. Grill B was made by a roller with raised bosses.

A. GRILL COVERING THE ENTIRE STAMP

1867 ***Perf. 12***

79 A25 3c **rose**	8,500.	1,300.
No gum	2,750.	
On cover		1,800.
Pair	18,000.	3,250.
Block of 4	55,000.	
b. Printed on both sides		—

Earliest documented use: Aug. 13, 1867.

Cancellations

Blue	+125.
Ultramarine	+325.
Railroad	—

Values for No. 79 are for fine-very fine examples with minor perf. faults. Examples with complete or virtually complete perforations sell for much more.

An essay (#79-E15) which is often mistaken for No. 79 shows the points of the grill as small squares faintly impressed in the paper but not cutting through it. On the issued stamp the grill generally breaks through the paper. Examples without defects are rare.

See Die and Plate Proofs for imperf. on stamp paper.

80 A26 5c **brown**	400,000.	
a. 5c **dark brown**	400,000.	
81 A30 30c **orange**	225,000.	

Four examples of Nos. 80 and 80a (two of each shade), and eight examples of No. 81 (one in the New York Public Library Miller collection and not available to collectors) are known. All are more or less faulty and/or off center. Values are for off-center examples with small perforation faults.

B. GRILL ABOUT 18x15mm (22x18 POINTS)

82 A25 3c **rose**	900,000.	

The four known examples of No. 82 are valued in the grade of fine.

Earliest documented use: Feb. 1?, 1869 (dated cancel on off-cover stamp).

C. GRILL ABOUT 13x16mm (16 TO 17 BY 18 TO 21 POINTS)

The grilled area on each of four C grills in the sheet may total about 18x15mm when a normal C grill adjoins a fainter grill extending to the right or left edge of the stamp. This is caused by a partial erasure on the grill roller when it was changed to produce C grills instead of the all-over A grill. Do not mistake these for the B grill. Unused exists and is very rare, value unused $7,500; value used $2,750; on cover $4,500.

83 A25 3c **rose**	5,500.	1,100.
No gum	2,000.	
On cover		1,250.
Pair	12,000.	3,250.
Block of 4	30,000.	—
Double grill	6,750.	2,000.
Grill with points down	6,250.	1,400.

Earliest documented use: Nov. 16, 1867.

Cancellation

Blue	+100.

See Die and Plate Proofs for imperf. on stamp paper.
The 1c, 3c, 5c, 10c, 12c, 30c of 1861 are known with experimental C grills. They are listed in the Essays section. The 3c differs slightly from No. 83.

GRILL WITH POINTS DOWN

The grills were produced by rollers with the surface covered, or partly covered, by pyramidal bosses. On the D, E and F grills the tips of the pyramids are vertical ridges. On the Z grill the ridges are horizontal.

D. GRILL ABOUT 12x14mm (15 BY 18 TO 19 POINTS)

84 A32 2c **black**	16,000.	4,750.
No gum	6,500.	
On cover		5,250.
Pair	35,000.	10,000.
Block of 4	100,000.	—
Double transfer	—	—
Split grill		5,000.

No. 84 is valued in the grade of fine.

Earliest documented use: Feb. 15, 1868.

Cancellations

Red	+400.
Blue	+750.
"Paid All"	+100.

85 A25 3c **rose**	8,000.	1,100.
No gum	2,400.	
On cover		1,250.
Pair	17,000.	2,500.
Block of 4	45,000.	—
Double grill	—	
Split grill		1,200.

Earliest documented use: Feb. 1, 1868 (on cover front); Feb. 2, 1868 (on full cover).

Cancellations

Blue	+50.
Green	+450.
"Paid"	+50.

Z. GRILL ABOUT 11x14mm (14 TO 15 BY 17 OR 18 POINTS)

(1c, 10c, 15c 17 rows; 2c, 3c, 12c 18 rows)

85A A24 1c **blue**		3,000,000.

Two examples of No. 85A are currently recorded. One is contained in the New York Public Library collection, which is on long-term loan to the Smithsonian National Postal Museum.

85B A32 2c **black**	17,500.	1,100.
No gum	6,750.	
On cover		1,300.
Pair	32,500.	2,600.
Block of 4	75,000.	10,000.
Double transfer	19,000.	1,200.
Major double transfer ("Preston shift")		—
Double grill		—
Split grill		—

Earliest documented use: Jan. 17, 1868 (on piece); Jan. 20, 1868 (on cover).

Cancellations

Blue	+250.
Red	+350.
Black Carrier	+75.
"Paid All"	+75.

85C A25 3c **rose**	25,000.	3,250.
No gum	9,000.	
On cover		3,750.
Pair		—
Block of 4	120,000.	
Double grill	27,000.	

Earliest documented use: Jan. 29, 1868.

Cancellations

Green	+600.
Blue	+100.
Red	+250.
"Paid"	+50.

85D A27 10c **green**		750,000.

Six examples of No. 85D are known. One is contained in the New York Public Library collection. Value is for a well-centered example with small faults.

85E A28 12c **intense black**	25,000.	2,400.
black	25,000.	2,400.
No gum	8,500.	
On cover		2,900.
Strip of 3		—
Block of 4	77,500.	—
Double transfer of top frame line		2,500.

Earliest documented use: Feb. 12, 1868.

The unused block of four of No. 85E is unique, and it has fine centering and a small fault. Value is based on 2019 auction sale.

85F A33 15c **black**		2,000,000.

Two examples of No. 85F are documented, one in the grade of very good, the other extremely fine. Value is for the extremely fine example.

E. GRILL ABOUT 11x13mm (14 BY 16 TO 18 POINTS)

86 A24 1c **blue**	3,000.	425.
No gum	1,100.	
a. 1c **dull blue**	3,000.	400.
No gum	1,100.	
On cover		550.
Pair	6,500.	900.
Block of 4	20,000.	3,500.
Double grill	—	550.
Split grill	3,250.	550.
Very thin paper		—

Earliest documented use: Mar. 9, 1868.

Cancellations

Blue	+25.
Red	+80.
Green	+450.
"Paid"	+25.
Steamboat	+90.
Red Carrier	+110.

87 A32 2c **black**	1,700.	190.
gray black	1,700.	190.
No gum	650.	
intense black	1,800.	220.
No gum	700.	
On cover		275.
Pair	3,750.	400.
Block of 4	8,750.	6,250.
P# strip of 4, Impt.	9,750.	
Double grill	—	—
Double grill, one split	—	
Triple grill		—
Split grill	2,000.	210.
Grill with points up	—	
Double transfer	1,850.	210.
Major double transfer ("Preston shift")		—
a. Diagonal half used as 1c on cover		2,000.
b. Vertical half used as 1c on cover		2,000.
c. Horizontal half used as 1c on cover		2,000.

Earliest documented use: Feb. 27, 1868.

Cancellations

Blue	+10.00
Purple	+100.00
Brown	+40.00
Red	+65.00
Magenta	+200.00
Green	+1,000.
"Paid"	+10.00
Steamship	+60.00
Black Carrier	+35.00
"Paid All"	+20.00
"Short Paid"	+65.00
Japan	—

88 A25 3c **rose**	950.	30.00
pale rose	950.	30.00
rose red	950.	30.00
No gum	350.	
On cover		35.00
Pair	2,000.	65.00
Block of 4	6,000.	350.00
P# block of 8, Impt.	13,000.	
Double grill	—	—
Double grill, one split	—	—
Triple grill	—	—
Split grill	1,050.	35.00
Very thin paper	1,000.	35.00
a. 3c **lake red**	1,250.	75.00
No gum	475.	
b. Two diagonal halves from different stamps used as 3c stamp (fraudulent use), one half having grill with points up, on cover		—

Earliest documented use: Feb. 12, 1868.

Cancellations

Blue	+5.00
Red	+10.00
Ultramarine	+40.00
Green	+110.00
"Paid"	+5.00
"Way"	+30.00
Numeral, "3" or "5"	+5.00
Numeral, number greater than "5"	—
Steamboat	+35.00
Railroad	+25.00
Express Company	+80.00

89 A27 10c **green**	5,000.	325.
dark green	5,000.	325.
blue green	5,000.	325.
No gum	2,000.	
On cover		425.
Pair	10,000.	700.
Block of 4	24,000.	3,500.
Double grill	6,500.	500.
Split grill	5,250.	350.
Double transfer	—	350.
Very thin paper	5,250.	350.

Earliest documented use: Feb. 21, 1868.

Cancellations

Blue	+30.
Red	+75.
"Paid"	+15.
Steamship	+50.

Certification and Grading Excellence Since 1987

Founded by noted U.S. Classics Expert, J. Randall Shoemaker, PSAG commits to providing unparalleled certification and grading of all United States, Canada and Canadian Province stamps.

- Finest US and Canadian Experts, 25 years Expertizing Experience
- Competitively Priced Graded & Ungraded certificates at the same price
- GRADING singles, pairs, blocks, plate blocks, booklet panes and souvenir sheets for US & BNA
- Comprehensive References • Best Turnaround Time in the Trade
- Consistent Standardized Third Party Grading

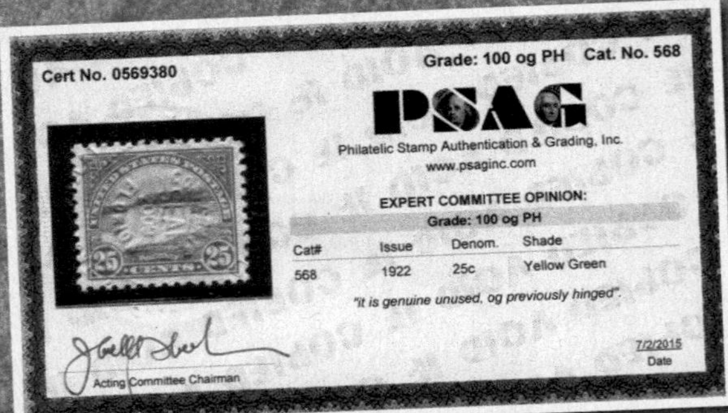

SMALL SIZE

LARGE SIZE

FEE SCHEDULE (All United States, Canada & Provinces, Canal Zone & Hawaii)

SERVICE	FEE	ITEMS THAT CAN BE SUBMITTED	MINIMUM QUANTITY	MAX SCOTT VALUE	MAX FEE	APPROX TURNAROUND
ECONOMY	$20	1932 to date (US#643 to date, C19 to date, RW35 to date, E14 to date) No ERRORS, FREAKS & ODDITIES	5	$100	$20	30 Business Days
REGULAR	5.0% Scott Value (Min $35)	1847 to 1931 (US# 1-642, C1-18, RW 1-34, E1-E13, J1-J78, Revenues, etc)	1	No Max Value	$500	30 Business Days
SPECIALIZED	5.0% Scott Value (Min $45)	1847 to date (Private Vending Coils, Postal Stationary, Postmaster Provisionals, Special Printings, Covers, Locals/Carriers	1	No Max Value	$500	Varies
EXPRESS	Add $20 to Each Item		1	No Max Value	$20	20 Business Days

Additional Services Include: REMOVE Grade from Previous PSAG Certificate ($15), ADD Grade to Previous PSAG Certificate ($15), Duplicate Certificate at time of submission ($5), Duplicate Certificate at later date ($10), Reconsideration (no charge if opinion changes, $25), Plating Charge for Original Plating ($30), Confirmation of Plating ($10)

*If the FINAL OPINION indicates a lesser fee than as submitted, PSAG will reduce the final fee for that item. Conversely, if the FINAL OPINION indicates a Higher Fee for that item, PSAG will raise the final fee. If Scott Catalog does not list a value, PSAG will estimate a reasonable market value to assign a fee for that item.

**PSAG reserves the right to refuse any submission.

www.psaginc.com

Philatelic Stamp Authentication and Grading

P.O. Box 41-0880 Melbourne, FL 32941-0880
Phone: 305.345.9864 • E-Mail: info@psaginc.com

No.	Description	Unused	Used
	French anchor in lozenge		—
	Japan		+225.
90	A28 12c **black**	4,750.	375.
	gray black	4,750.	375.
	intense black	4,750.	375.
	No gum	1,900.	
	On cover		525.
	Pair	*10,000.*	800.
	Block of 4	*35,000.*	*2,850.*
	Double transfer of top frame line	5,000.	400.
	Double transfer of bottom frame line	5,000.	450.
	Double transfer of top and bottom frame lines	5,250.	450.
	Double grill	5,500.	700.
	Split grill	5,000.	400.

Earliest documented use: Mar. 3, 1868.

Cancellations

Cancellation	Value
Blue	+25.
Red	+75.
Purple	+150.
Green	+400.
Railroad	+100.
"Paid"	+30.

No.	Description	Unused	Used
91	A33 15c **black**	12,500.	600.
	gray black	12,500.	600.
	No gum	4,500.	
	On cover		700.
	Pair	*26,000.*	1,300.
	Block of 4	*65,000.*	*12,500.*
	Double grill	—	950.
	Split grill	—	675.

Earliest documented use: May 2, 1868.

Cancellations

Cancellation	Value
Blue	+30.
Magenta	+150.
Red	+125.
"Paid"	+30.
Supplementary Mail Type A	+150.

F. GRILL ABOUT 9x13mm (12 BY 16 TO 18 POINTS)

No.	Description	Unused	Used
92	A24 1c **blue**	2,800.	425.
	dark blue	2,800.	425.
	No gum	925.	
a.	1c **pale blue**	2,300.	375.
	No gum	700.	
	On cover		475.
	Pair	6,000.	900.
	Block of 4	*16,000.*	3,250.
	Double transfer	3,000.	475.
	Double grill	—	800.
	Split grill	3,000.	500.
	Double grill, one split		—
	Very thin paper	3,000.	750.

Earliest documented use: Aug. 11, 1868.

Cancellations

Cancellation	Value
Blue	+20.00
Red	+50.00
Green	+450.00
"Paid"	+10.00
Red Carrier	+60.00
"Paid All"	+15.00

No.	Description	Unused	Used
93	A32 2c **black**	450.	55.00
	gray black	450.	55.00
	No gum	155.	
	On cover		70.00
	Pair	950.	120.00
	Block of 4	2,600.	525.00
	P# strip of 4, Impt.	*6,500.*	
	P# block of 8, Impt.	—	
	Double transfer	500.	62.50
	Double grill	—	170.00
	Split grill	500.	60.00
	Double grill, one split		—
	Double grill, one quadruple split	*1,100.*	—
	Very thin paper	550.	60.00
a.	Vertical half used as 1c as part of 3c rate on cover		*1,250.*
b.	Diagonal half used as 1c as part of 3c rate on cover		*1,250.*
c.	Horizontal half used alone as 1c on cover		*2,500.*
d.	Diagonal half used alone as 1c on cover		*2,500.*

Earliest documented use: Mar. 27, 1868.

Cancellations

Cancellation	Value
Blue	+8.00
Red	+20.00
Green	+250.00
"Paid"	+5.00
"Paid All"	+15.00
Black Carrier	+20.00
Red Carrier	+30.00
Japan	+350.00

No.	Description	Unused	Used
94	A25 3c **red**	350.	10.00
	rose red	350.	10.00
a.	3c **rose**	350.	10.00
	No gum	150.	
	On cover		11.00
	Pair	750.	21.00
	Block of 4	*3,000.*	175.00
	P# block of 8, Impt.	*9,500.*	
	Double transfer	400.	25.00
	Double grill		—
	Double grill, one normal, one partial with points up		—
	Triple grill	—	300.00
	End roller grill		450.00
	Split grill	375.	15.00
	Quadruple split grill	650.	175.00
	Double grill, one quadruple split		—
	Grill with points up		—
	On cover		7,500.
	Very thin paper	375.	10.50
c.	Vertical pair, imperf. horiz.	*15,000.*	
	Block of 4	*40,000.*	
d.	Printed on both sides	*9,000.*	*42,500.*

Seven examples of No. 94d are recorded. Six are in the top row of an unused top margin imprint block of 18 (6x3).

Earliest documented use: Mar. 21, 1868.

Cancellations

Cancellation	Value
Blue	+.25
Ultramarine	+30.00
Red	+15.00
Violet	+70.00
Green	+70.00
Numeral, "3" or "5"	+3.00
Numeral, number greater than "5"	—
"Paid"	+2.25
"Paid All"	+12.50
"Free"	+20.00
Railroad	+30.00
Steamboat	+40.00
Packet boat	+80.00
Express Company	+50.00

See Die and Plate Proofs for imperf. on stamp paper.

No.	Description	Unused	Used
95	A26 5c **brown**	3,250.	850.
	No gum	1,200.	
	dark brown	3,500.	950.
	No gum	1,300.	
	On cover		900.
	Pair	6,750.	1,800.
	Block of 4	*17,000.*	*9,000.*
	Double transfer of top frame line	—	—
	Double transfer of bottom frame line	—	
	Double grill	—	—
	Split grill	4,000.	900.
	Very thin paper	3,750.	900.
a.	5c **black brown**	4,500.	2,300.
	No gum	1,750.	

Earliest documented use: Aug. 19, 1868.

Cancellations

Cancellation	Value
Blue	+25.
Magenta	+90.
Violet	+90.
Red	+80.
Green	+500.
"Paid"	+25.
"Free"	+250.
"Steamship"	+150.

Values of Nos. 95, 95a reflect the normal small margins.

No.	Description	Unused	Used
96	A27 10c **yellow green**	2,500.	240.
	green	2,750.	240.
	blue green	2,500.	240.
	dark green	2,500.	320.
	No gum	825.	
	On cover		285.
	Pair	5,250.	520.
	Block of 4	*26,000.*	*3,500.*
	P# strip of 4, Impt.	*50,000.*	
	Double transfer	—	—
	Double grill	—	380.
	Split grill	2,750.	270.
	Quadruple split grill		675.
	Very thin paper	2,750.	260.

Earliest documented use: May 28, 1868.

Cancellations

Cancellation	Value
Blue	+10.00
Red	+35.00
Magenta	+40.00
Green	+300.00
"Paid"	+10.00
"Free"	+50.00
Supplementary Mail Type A	—
Steamship	+75.00
Japan	+200.00
China	—

No.	Description	Unused	Used
97	A28 12c **black**	2,800.	250.
	gray black	2,800.	250.
	No gum	1,000.	
	On cover		300.
	Pair	6,000.	525.
	Block of 4	*40,000.*	*2,500.*
	P# strip of 4, Impt.	*50,000.*	
	Double transfer of top frame line	3,250.	280.
	Double transfer of bottom frame line	3,250.	280.
	Double transfer of top and bottom frame lines	—	300.
	Double grill	—	475.
	Triple grill		—
	Split grill	3,250.	280.
	End roller grill		—
	Very thin paper	3,250.	325.

Earliest documented use: May 27, 1868.

Cancellations

Cancellation	Value
Blue	+10.00
Red	+50.00
Magenta	+50.00
Brown	+50.00
Green	+250.00
Purple	+150.00
"Paid"	+20.00
"Insufficiently Prepaid"	+100.00
"Paid All"	+25.00
Supplementary Mail Type A	+50.00

No.	Description	Unused	Used
98	A33 15c **black**	4,250.	275.
	gray black	4,250.	275.
	No gum	1,600.	
	On cover		300.
	Pair	*9,000.*	600.
	Block of 4	*35,000.*	*6,000.*
	P# block of 8, Impt.	*165,000.*	
	Double transfer of upper right corner	—	500.
	Double grill	4,750.	425.
	Split grill	4,500.	300.
	Quadruple split grill	5,000.	575.
	Very thin paper	4,750.	475.

Earliest documented use: May 4, 1868.

The plate block of No. 98 is unique; value reflects sale price in 2019 auction.

Cancellations

Cancellation	Value
Blue	+20.00
Magenta	+75.00
Red	+100.00
Orange red	+40.00
Green	+300.00
Orange	+190.00
Purple	+100.00
Lavender (Philadelphia)	+160.00
"Paid"	+20.00
"Insufficiently Prepaid"	+135.00
"Insufficiently Paid"	+135.00
Japan	+300.00
Supplementary Mail Type A	+90.00
French anchor in lozenge	+75.00

No.	Description	Unused	Used
99	A29 24c **gray lilac**	8,500.	1,500.
	gray	8,500.	1,500.
	No gum	3,250.	
	On cover		2,500.
	Pair	*18,000.*	3,250.
	Block of 4	*45,000.*	*10,500.*
	P# block of 8, Impt.	*155,000.*	
	Double grill	9,500.	2,300.
	Split grill	8,750.	1,600.
	Scratch under "A" of "Postage"	—	

Earliest documented use: Jan. 5, 1869.

The plate block of No. 99 is unique; value reflects sale price in 2019 auction.

Cancellations

Cancellation	Value
Blue	+100.
Red	+200.
"Paid"	+50.

No.	Description	Unused	Used
100	A30 30c **orange**	9,000.	950.
	deep orange	9,000.	950.
	No gum	3,300.	
	On cover		1,800.
	Pair	*19,000.*	1,900.
	Block of 4	*45,000.*	*10,000.*
	Double grill	11,500.	1,650.
	Split grill	9,250.	1,050.
	Double grill, one split		—
	Double grill, one quadruple split		—
	Triple grill, two split		—

Values for No. 100 are for examples with small margins, especially at sides. Large-margined examples sell for much more.

Earliest documented use: Nov. 10, 1868.

Cancellations

Cancellation	Value
Blue	+50.
Red	+120.
Magenta	+150.
Green	+500.
"Paid"	+50.
Steamship	+1,250.
Supplementary Mail Type A	+100.
French anchor in lozenge	—
Japan	+400.

No.	Description	Unused	Used
101	A31 90c **blue**	14,500.	2,250.
	dark blue	14,500.	2,250.
	No gum	5,500.	
	On cover		*100,000.*
	Pair	*31,500.*	4,750.
	Block of 4	*75,000.*	*25,000.*
	Double grill	*19,000.*	
	Split grill	15,000.	2,400.

Two usages on cover are recorded (one being a cover front). Value is for use on full cover to Peru.

Some authorities believe that more than one size of grill probably existed on one of the grill rolls.

Earliest documented use: May 8, 1869.

Cancellations

Cancellation	Value
Blue	+150.
Red	+300.
Japan	+600.
"Paid"	+50.

RE-ISSUE OF 1861-66 ISSUES

Produced by the National Bank Note Co.

Without grill, hard white paper, with white crackly gum.

The 1, 2, 5, 10 and 12c were printed from new plates of 100 subjects each.

1875 ***Perf. 12***

No.	Description	Unused	Used
102	A24 1c **blue** *(3195)*	*750.*	*1,600.*
	No gum	*300.*	
	On cover		—
	Block of 4	*7,000.*	—
103	A32 2c **black** *(979)*	*3,500.*	*11,000.*
	No gum	*1,600.*	
	Block of 4	*65,000.*	
104	A25 3c **brown red** *(465)*	*3,750.*	*14,000.*
	No gum	*1,700.*	
	Block of 4	*90,000.*	
105	A26 5c **brown** *(672)*	*2,500.*	*6,500.*
	No gum	*1,150.*	
	Block of 4	*90,000.*	

106	A27 10c **green** *(451)*	2,900.	125,000.
	No gum	1,400.	
	Block of 4	90,000.	
107	A28 12c **black** *(389)*	3,500.	13,000.
	No gum	1,600.	
	Block of 4	115,000.	
108	A33 15c **black** *(397)*	4,500.	32,500.
	No gum	2,100.	
	Block of 4	90,000.	
109	A29 24c **deep violet** *(346)*	6,000.	18,000.
	No gum	2,750.	
	Block of 4	115,000.	
110	A30 30c **brownish orange** *(346)*	5,750.	18,000.
	No gum	2,800.	
	Pair	15,500.	
	Block of 4	115,000.	
111	A31 90c **blue** *(317)*	7,000.	225,000.
	No gum	3,500.	

Earliest documented uses: No. 102, July 25, 1881; No. 104, July ?, 1883 (dated cancel on off-cover stamp); No. 111, Nov. 30, 1888 (dated cancel on off-cover stamp). Any 2c with the "star-on-cheek" variety that is not grilled is a No. 103. Some examples of the "F" grill, No. 93, also show the "star-on-cheek" variety.

These stamps can be distinguished from the 1861-66 issue by the brighter colors, the sharper proof-like impressions and the paper which is very white instead of yellowish. The gum is almost always somewhat yellowed with age, and unused stamps with original gum are valued with such gum.

Numbers in parentheses are quantities sold.

While it was legal to use Nos. 102-111 as postage, their actual use is generally rare and is mostly confined to dealers using them on registered mail. Examination by recognized expert authorities is recommended.

Five examples are recorded of No. 111 used, one of which has a non-contemporaneous cancel. Value is for centered and sound example (two are known thus).

PLEASE NOTE:

Stamps are valued in the grade of very fine unless otherwise indicated.

Values for early and valuable stamps are for examples with certificates of authenticity from acknowledged expert committees, or examples sold with the buyer having the right of certification. This applies to examples with original gum as well as examples without gum. Beware of stamps offered "as is," as the gum on some unused stamps offered with "original gum" may be fraudulent, and unused stamps offered without may in some cases be altered or faintly canceled used stamps.

VALUES FOR NEVER-HINGED STAMPS PRIOR TO SCOTT No. 182

This catalogue does not value pre-1879 stamps in never-hinged condition. Premiums for never-hinged condition in the classic era invariably are even larger than those premiums listed for the 1879 and later issues. Generally speaking, the earlier the stamp is listed in the catalogue, the larger will be the never-hinged premium.

Produced by the National Bank Note Co.

Plates for the 1c, 2c, 3c, 6c, 10c and 12c consisted of 300 subjects in two panes of 150 each. For the 15c, 24c, 30c and 90c plates of 100 subjects each.

NOTE: Stamps of the 1869 issue without grill cannot be guaranteed except when unused and with the original gum or traces of the original gum.

Franklin — A34

Post Horse and Rider — A35

G. Grill measuring 9½x9mm
(12 by 11 to 11½ points)

1869 Hard Wove Paper *Perf. 12*

112	A34 1c **buff**	575.	130.
	brown orange	575.	130.
	dark brown orange	625.	175.
	No gum	210.	
	On cover, single		260.
	Pair	1,200.	275.
	Block of 4	*5,500.*	*2,250.*
	Margin block of 4, arrow	*5,750.*	
	Margin block of 4, P#	*6,250.*	
	Double transfer	—	—
	Double grill	1,350.	300.
	Split grill	725.	180.
	Double grill, one split		—
	Double grill, one quadruple split		—
b.	Without grill, original gum	*32,500.*	

Earliest documented use: Apr. 1, 1869.

Cancellations

Blue	+25.
Ultramarine	+600.
Magenta	+150.
Purple	+175.
Red	+100.
Green	+700.
"Paid"	+50.
Numeral	+100.
Steamship	+135.
Black town	+30.
Blue town	+30.
Red town	+90.
Black Carrier	+80.
Blue Carrier	+100.
Japan	+1,000.
China (Shanghai fancy star), on cover	*+11,000.*

113	A35 2c **brown**	500.	80.
	pale brown	500.	80.
	dark brown	525.	90.
	yellow brown	500.	80.
	No gum	190.	
	On cover, single		140.
	Pair	1,100.	170.
	Block of 4	3,750.	1,350.
	Margin block of 4, arrow	3,850.	
	P# block of 10, Impt.	*55,000.*	
	Double grill	—	310.
	Split grill	650.	125.
	Quadruple split grill	—	
	End roller grill	925.	
	Double transfer		110.
b.	Without grill, original gum	*14,000.*	
c.	Half used as 1c on cover, diagonal, vertical or horizontal		*6,000.*
d.	Printed on both sides		*62,500.*

Earliest documented use: Mar. 20, 1869.

Cancellations

Blue	+50.
Red	+75.
Orange red	+90.
Orange	+250.
Magenta	+80.
Purple	+100.
Ultramarine	+150.
Green	+500.
Brown	+150.
"FREE"	—
"Paid"	+15.
"Paid All"	+25.
Steamship	+75.
Black town	+10.
Blue town	+30.
Japan	+400.
Blue Carrier	+90.
Black Carrier	+80.
China	—
Printed Precancellation "Jefferson, Ohio"	+6,500.

Locomotive — A36

Washington — A37

114	A36 3c **ultramarine**	225.	16.00
	pale ultramarine	225.	16.00
	dark ultramarine	250.	19.00
	No gum	90.	
	blue	625.	100.00
	No gum	225.	
	On cover		24.00
	Pair	525.	35.00
	Block of 4	1,250.	450.00
	Margin block of 4, arrow	1,450.	
	P# block of 10, Impt.	*7,500.*	
	Double transfer	300.	35.00
	Double grill	525.00	95.00
	Triple grill	—	—
	Sextuple grill	—	*7,000.*
	Split grill	275.	30.00
	Quadruple split grill	550.	130.00
	Double grill, one split		—
	Double grill, one quadruple split		—
	End roller grill	—	—
	Grill with points up		—
	Gray paper	—	100.00
	On cover		750.00
	Without grill		—
	Cracked plate	—	160.00
a.	Without grill, original gum	*13,000.*	*18,000.*
	Without grill, gray paper		3,750.
b.	Vert. one-third used as 1c on cover		—
c.	Vert. two-thirds used as 2c on cover		*10,000.*
d.	Double impression		*15,000.*
e.	Printed on both sides, reverse inverted		*55,000.*

The grill-with-points-up variety is found on a unique margin "pair" of stamps where the paper was folded over prior to perforating and grilling. The stamps have drastic freak perfs.

Two examples used are recorded for No. 114a on normal paper and two used examples on gray paper. On normal paper, there exist a used single with original gum and black pen cancel (2015 Philatelic Foundation certificate), and a single on cover that was lifted to check for grill and replaced (2011 Philatelic Foundation certificate). No. 114a used on gray paper exists as a strip of three on piece (1978 Philatelic Foundation certificate), and as a single on advertising cover, lifted and hinged back in place (2015 Philatelic Foundation certificate).

Nos. 114d and 114e each are unique. No. 114d has a preprinting paper fold. The existence of a genuine example of No. 114d has been questioned by specialists. The editors would like to see evidence of its existence with an updated certificate.

Earliest documented use: Mar. 27, 1869.

Cancellations

Blue	+5.
Ultramarine	+25.
Magenta	+35.
Purple	+75.
Violet	+65.
Red	+15.
Orange red	+20.
Brown	+200.
Green	+300.
Orange	—
Yellow	—
Black town	+3.
Blue town	+7.
Red town	+30.
Numeral	+15.
"Paid"	+20.
"Paid All"	+15.
"Steamboat"	—
"Lake Champlain S.B." (steamboat), on cover	—
"Steamship"	+50.
Ship	+35.
"U. S. Ship"	+450.
Railroad	+30.
Packet Boat	+100.
Blue Carrier	+40.
Black Carrier	+30.
Express Company	+250.
"Way"	—
"Free"	+150.
Alaska	—
French anchor in lozenge	—
Japan	+600.

The authenticity of the yellow cancel has been questioned by some specialists. The editors would like to see an expertizing certificate for this stamp and cancel.

115	A37 6c **ultramarine**	2,500.	200.
	pale ultramarine	2,500.	
	No gum	1,000.	
	On cover		475.
	Pair	5,250.	475.
	Block of 4	*16,500.*	*9,000.*
	Margin block of 4, arrow	*17,500.*	
	Double grill	—	550.
	Split grill	3,000.	280.
	Quadruple split grill	—	750.
	Double transfer		250.
b.	Vertical half used as 3c on cover		*50,000.*

Earliest documented use: Apr. 26, 1869.

No. 115b is unique.

Cancellations

Blue	+25.
Brown	+125.
Magenta	+50.
Purple	+85.
Red	+75.
Green	+1,000.
"Paid"	+15.
"Paid All"	+25.
Black town	+30.
"Short Paid"	+75.
"Insufficiently Paid"	+75.
Steamship	+45.
Railroad	+50.
Japan	+1,500.

Shield and Eagle — A38

S.S. "Adriatic" — A39

116	A38 10c **yellow**	1,850.	110.
	yellowish orange	1,850.	110.
	No gum	725.	
	On cover		375.
	Pair	4,000.	270.
	Block of 4	*14,000.*	*8,000.*
	Margin block of 4, arrow	*14,500.*	
	Double grill	—	350.
	Split grill	2,100.	150.
	End roller grill	—	—

Earliest documented use: Apr. 1, 1869.

Cancellations

Blue	+35.
Magenta	+80.
Purple	+250.
Violet	—
Red	+40.
Ultramarine	+300.
Green	+5,000.
Black town	+20.

Numeral	—
Steamship	+35.
Railroad	+45.
"Paid"	+15.
"Paid All"	+30.
"Insufficiently Paid"	+50.
Supplementary Mail Type A	+150.
Express Company	—
Alaska	+5,000.
St. Thomas	—
Hawaii	—
Japan	+200.
China, Shanghai circle of wedges	—

117 A39 12c **green**	1,850.	130.
yellowish green	1,850.	130.
bluish green	2,100.	175.
No gum	725.	
On cover		450.
Pair	4,000.	310.
Block of 4	*14,000.*	*1,800.*
Margin block of 4, arrow	*14,500.*	
Double grill	—	400.
Split grill	2,150.	170.
Double grill, one quadruple split		—
End roller grill		575.

Earliest documented use: Apr. 1, 1869.

Cancellations

Blue	+125.
Magenta	+125.
Purple	+250.
Brown	+300.
Red	+150.
Green	+3,500.
Numeral	+125.
"Paid"	+25.
"Paid All"	+40.
"Too Late"	+100.
"Insufficiently Paid"	+125.
Black town	+35.
Red town	+250.
Japan	+950.

Landing of Columbus — A40

No. 118 has horizontal shading lines at the left and right sides of the vignette.

118 A40 15c **brown & blue,** type I, Picture unframed	9,000.	800.
dark brown & blue	9,000.	800.
No gum	3,250.	
On cover		1,800.
Pair	*20,000.*	1,800.
Block of 4	*60,000.*	*30,000.*
Double grill	*15,000.*	1,050.
Split grill	10,500.	900.
a. Without grill, original gum	*11,500.*	

Earliest documented use: Mar. 31, 1869 (dated cancel on off-cover stamp); Apr. 2, 1869 (on cover).

Cancellations

Blue	+75.
Red	+135.
Magenta	+250.
Brown	+150.
"Paid"	+50.
"Paid All"	+100.
"Insufficiently Paid"	+150.
Black town	+50.
Blue town	+150.
Steamship	+100.

A40a

No. 119 has diagonal shading lines at the left and right sides of the vignette.

119 A40a 15c **brown & blue,** type II, Picture framed	2,750.	190.
dark brown & blue	2,750.	190.
No gum	975.	
On cover		800.
Pair	6,000.	425.
Block of 4	*16,500.*	*9,000.*
P# block of 8, Impt.	*45,000.*	
Double transfer	—	—
Double grill	4,750.	475.
Split grill	3,000.	300.
b. Center inverted	*1,000,000.*	*22,500.*
No gum	*700,000.*	
c. Center double, one inverted		*80,000.*

Earliest documented use: Apr. 5, 1869.

Cancellations

Blue	+60.
Ultramarine	—
Purple	+150.
Magenta	+135.
Red	+150.
Brown	+200.
Green	+1,500.
Numeral	+75.
"Paid"	+25.
"Paid All"	+35.
Black town	+30.
Blue town	+75.
Red town	+200.
"Steamship"	+75.
Supp. Mail Type A or F	+40.
Japan	+500.

Most examples of No. 119b are faulty. Values are for fine centered examples with only minimal faults. Three examples of No. 119b unused are recorded; only one has original gum.

Three examples of No. 119c are recorded. Value is for the finer of the two sound examples.

The Declaration of Independence — A41

120 A41 24c **green & violet**	7,500.	600.
bluish green & violet	7,500.	600.
No gum	2,600.	
On cover, domestic usage		*12,500.*
On cover, foreign usage		*35,000.*
Pair	*21,000.*	1,300.
Block of 4	*52,500.*	*20,000.*
Double grill	—	2,000.
Split grill	8,000.	750.
a. Without grill, original gum	*14,000.*	
b. Center inverted	*750,000.*	*37,500.*
On cover		*130,000.*
Pair		*110,000.*
Block of 4		*750,000.*

Earliest documented use: Apr. 7, 1869 (No. 120); Mar. 1874 (No. 120b).

Cancellations

Blue	+300.
Red	+500.
Black town	+100.
Red town	+400.
"Paid All"	+150.
"Steamship"	+250.
Supp. Mail Type A	+200.
China	+750.

Most examples of No. 120b are faulty. Values are for fine centered examples with only minimal faults. No. 120b unused is valued without gum, as all of the three examples available to collectors are without gum.

Shield, Eagle and Flags — A42

Lincoln — A43

121 A42 30c **ultramarine & carmine**	4,000.	375.
ultramarine & dark carmine	4,000.	400.
No gum	1,450.	
On cover, domestic usage		*17,500.*
On cover, foreign usage		*35,000.*
Pair	*9,500.*	850.
Block of 4	*40,000.*	*3,750.*
Double grill	—	1,400.
Split grill	5,000.	500.
Double grill, one split		—
Double paper (without grill), original gum	*7,000.*	
Block of 4	—	
a. Without grill, original gum	*10,000.*	
Block of 4	*45,000.*	
P# block of 8, Impt.	*100,000.*	
b. Flags inverted	*750,000.*	*90,000.*
No gum	*300,000.*	

Seven examples of No. 121b unused are recorded. Only one has part of its original gum.

Earliest documented use: May 22, 1869.

Cancellations

Blue	+250.
Red	+250.
Brown	+600.
Purple	+1,000.
Green	+7,500.
"Paid"	+50.
"Paid All"	+250.
Black town	+100.
Steamship	+85.
"Steam"	+70.
Supp. Mail Type A	+75.
French anchor in lozenge	+400.
Japan	+800.
China, Shanghai circle of wedges	—

122 A43 90c **carmine & black**	11,000.	1,800.
carmine rose & black	11,000.	1,800.
No gum	3,750.	
On cover		*430,000.*
Pair	*28,000.*	*8,000.*
Block of 4	*75,000.*	*55,000.*
Block of 6	*140,000.*	
Split grill	—	—
a. Without grill, original gum	*22,500.*	

Cancellations

Blue	+1,100.
Red	+1,000.
Orange red	+750.
Brown	+2,000.
Purple	+3,000.
Ultramarine	+1,750.
Black town	+1,500.
Red town	+1,750.
Magenta town	+2,500.
"Paid"	—
"Paid All"	—
N.Y. steamship	+1,000.

Nos. 112, 114, 117, 118, 120b, 121, 122 exist as imperf. singles. They were not regularly issued.

No. 122 on cover is unique. Value reflects 2009 auction sale price. The block of six (two recorded) is the largest multiple known of No. 122.

CANCELLATIONS

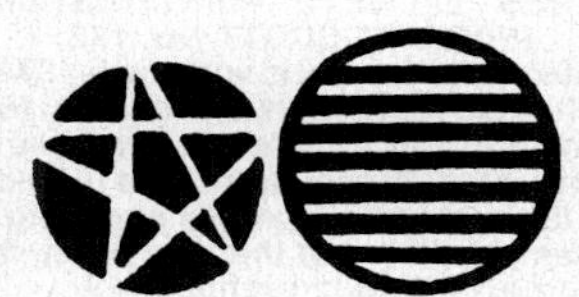

The common type of cancellation on the 1869 issue is the block or cork similar to illustrations above. Japanese cancellations seen on this issue (not illustrated) resulted from the sale of U.S. stamps in Japanese cities where post offices were maintained for mail going from Japan to the United States.

RE-ISSUE OF 1869 ISSUE

Produced by the National Bank Note Co.

Without grill, hard white paper, with white crackly gum.

The gum is almost always somewhat yellowed with age, and unused stamps with original gum are valued with such gum.

A new plate of 150 subjects was made for the 1c. The plate for the frame of the 15c was made using the same die as that used to make the type I frame for No. 118. For No. 118, the lines on each side of the vignette area were entered onto the plate itself, one position at a time. Upon close examination, each stamp position will be found to exhibit minute differences in these horizontal fringe lines.

1875 ***Perf. 12***

123 A34 1c **buff** *(10,000)*	525.	425.
No gum	220.	
Block of 4	*5,500.*	
On cover		*3,000.*
124 A35 2c **brown** *(4755)*	600.	750.
No gum	250.	
Block of 4	*7,000.*	
On cover		*12,500.*
125 A36 3c **blue** *(1406)*	*5,000.*	*27,500.*
No gum	2,500.	
On cover		—

Cancellation

Supplementary Mail Type F	—

Very few authenticated sound used examples of No. 125 are recorded. The used value is for an attractive fine to very fine example with minimal faults. Examples of No. 114 with faint or pressed-out grill are frequently offered as No. 125. Expertization by competent authorities is required.

126 A37 6c **blue** *(2226)*	1,80.	*3,000.*
No gum	800.	
Block of 4	*40,000.*	
On cover		—

		Unused	Used
127 A38 10c **yellow** *(1947)*		1,600.	1,800.
	No gum	700.	
	Block of 4	*22,500.*	
	On cover		*22,500.*
128 A39 12c **green** *(1584)*		2,000.	*3,000.*
	No gum	900.	
	Block of 4	*45,000.*	
	On cover		—
129 A40 15c **brown & blue,** Type III, *(1981)*		1,300.	1,000.
	No gum	625.	
	Pair		*6,000.*
	Block of 4	*42,500.*	
	On cover		*22,500.*
a.	Imperf. horizontally, single	*14,000.*	*30,000.*
	No gum	*5,000.*	

Two used examples of No. 129a are recorded. Both have faults and are valued thus.

130 A41 24c **green & violet** *(2091)*		2,000.	1,600.
	No gum	900.	
	Pair		*10,000.*
	On cover		*27,500.*
131 A42 30c **ultra & carmine** *(1535)*		2,250.	2,750.
	No gum	1,000.	
	Pair		*28,000.*
132 A43 90c **carmine & black** *(1356)*		3,750.	*6,000.*
	No gum	1,500.	
	Pair		*32,500.*
	Block of 4	*35,000.*	
	P# block of 10, Impt.	*325,000.*	

Numbers in parentheses are quantities sold.

While use of Nos. 123-133 for postage was legal, such use is scarce. Expertization is recommended.

Earliest documented uses:
No. 123, Dec. 9, 1877;
No. 124, Mar. 20, 1880;
No. 127, Nov. 11, 1880;
No. 128, Mar. 20, 1880.
No. 129, Mar. 20, 1880;
No. 130, Mar. 27, 1880.

RE-ISSUE OF 1869 ISSUE

Produced by the American Bank Note Co.

Without grill, soft porous paper.

1880-82

133 A34 1c **buff,** issued with gum (5,000)		325.	*550.*
	No gum	140.	
	Block of 4, with gum	1,650.	
	Margin block of 10, Impt. & P#	*22,500.*	
	On cover		1,900.
a.	1c **brown orange,** issued without gum, *1881-82* (18,252)	325.	
	Block of 4, without gum	1,500.	
	Margin block of 10, Impt. & P#, without gum	*24,000.*	

Earliest documented use: Oct. 5, 1880 (No. 133).

Beware of No. 133 unused without gum offered as No. 133a. Certification is recommended for No. 133a.

PRODUCED BY THE NATIONAL BANK NOTE COMPANY

Plates of 200 subjects in two panes of 100 each.

Franklin

A44

Jackson

A45

Washington

A46

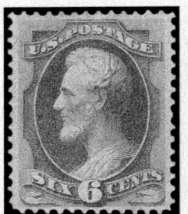

Lincoln

A47

Edwin M. Stanton

A48

Jefferson

A49

Henry Clay

A50

Daniel Webster

A51

General Winfield Scott — A52

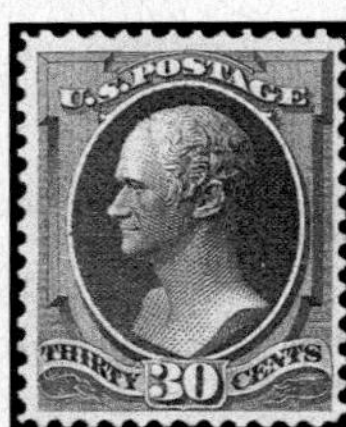
Alexander Hamilton — A53

Commodore Oliver Hazard Perry — A54

H. GRILL ABOUT 10x12mm (11 TO 13 BY 14 TO 16 POINTS)

The "H" grills can be separated into early state and late state, based on the shape of the tip of the grill. Early-state grills show a point or very small vertical line at the tip of the pyramid, while late-state grills show the pyramid tips truncated and flat.

Early-state "H" grills tend to be on vertical-mesh wove paper, while later printings and all late-state grills were printed on horizontal-mesh wove paper, resulting in stamp designs being approximately ¼mm shorter than the designs printed on vertical-mesh wove paper. The late-stage "H" grills virtually all seem to have been used only after Jan. 1873.

Poor printing quality often resulted in grills that show only a few grill points or a very few rows of points. This is especially true of the "H" grills. When there are not enough grill points to clearly identify whether the grill is an "H" or an "I," it must be assumed it is the lower-valued "H" grill variety. Authentication is advised for these stamps with high catalogue values.

Killer cancellation of the oval grid type with letters or numeral centers was first used in 1876 Bank Note issues. By order of the Postmaster-General (July 23, 1860) it was prohibited to use the town mark as a canceling instrument, and a joined town-and-killer duplex cancellation was developed.

Numeral cancellations-see "Postal Markings-Examples."

White Wove Paper, Thin to Medium Thick.

1870-71 ***Perf. 12***

134 A44 1c **ultramarine,** *Apr. 1870*		2,000.	200.00
	pale ultramarine	2,000.	200.00
	dark ultramarine	2,000.	200.00
	No gum	700.	
	On cover		240.00
	Pair	*4,250.*	450.00
	Block of 4	*12,000.*	1,250.
	Double transfer	2,250.	225.00
	Double grill	—	340.00
	Split grill	2,500.	225.00
	Quadruple split grill	—	525.00
	End roller grill		675.00
b.	Pair, one without grill	—	

Earliest documented use: Apr. 9, 1870.

Cancellations

Blue	+25.00
Red	+50.00
Green	+150.00
"Paid"	+10.00
"Paid All"	+20.00
"Steamship"	+45.00

135 A45 2c **red brown,** *Apr. 1870*		1,000.	75.00
	pale red brown	1,000.	75.00
	dark red brown	1,000.	75.00
	No gum	360.	
	On cover		100.00
	Pair	2,100.	160.00
	Block of 4	5,500.	500.00
	Double grill	1,400.	145.00
	Split grill	1,050.	90.00
	Quadruple split grill	*2,250.*	240.00
	End roller grill	*1,750.*	*400.00*

Grill with points up 500.00
b. Diagonal half used as 1c on cover —
c. Vertical half used as 1c on cover —
d. Pair, one without grill —
Strip of 6, five without grill —

Earliest documented use: July 14, 1870.

Cancellations

Blue +10.00
Red +20.00
Brown +15.00
Green +100.00
"Paid" +5.00
"Paid All" +10.00
Numeral +5.00
China —

136 A46 3c **green,** *Mar. 1870* 575. 32.50
pale green 575. 32.50
yellow green 575. 32.50
deep green 575. 32.50
No gum 190.
On cover 37.50
Pair 1,200. 67.50
Block of 4 3,000. 240.00
P# block of 10, Impt. *52,500.*
Double transfer — 37.50
Double grill 950. 90.00
Split grill 625. 37.50
Quadruple split grill — 150.00
End roller grill 275.00
Cracked plate — 100.00
b. Printed on both sides —

Earliest documented use: Mar. 24, 1870.

Cancellations

Blue +5.00
Purple +10.00
Magenta +10.00
Red +10.00
Orange red +10.00
Orange +25.00
Brown +2.50
Green +60.00
"Paid" +2.50
Railroad +10.00
"Steamship" +20.00
"Paid All" +15.00
Numeral +4.00
"Free" +25.00

See Die and Plate Proofs for imperf. on stamp paper.

137 A47 6c **carmine,** *Apr. 1870* 5,000. 400.
pale carmine 5,000. 400.
carmine rose 5,000. 400.
No gum 1,750.
On cover 500.
Pair *10,000.* 850.
Block of 4 *27,500.*
Double grill — 750.
Split grill *5,250.* 475.
Quadruple split grill — 1,000.
End roller grill *6,500.* *825.*
b. Pair, one without grill —
Strip of 4 + single, one in strip without grill, on cover —

Earliest documented use: Apr. 11, 1870.

Cancellations

Blue +50.
Red +75.
"Paid" +35.

138 A48 7c **vermilion,** *1871* 4,250. 500.
deep vermilion 4,250. 500.
No gum 1,550.
On cover 700.
Pair 9,000. 1,050.
Block of 4 *24,000.*
Double grill 775.
Split grill 4,500. 525.
Quadruple split grill 925.
End roller grill *950.*
b. Pair, one without grill —
Strip of 3, two without grill —

Earliest documented use: Feb. 12, 1871.

Cancellations

Blue +25.00
Purple +35.00
Red +50.00
Green +250.00
"Paid" +25.00

The 7c stamps, Nos. 138 and 149, were issued for a 7c rate of July 1, 1870, to Prussia, German States and Austria, including Hungary, via Hamburg (on the Hamburg-American Line steamers), or Bremen (on North German Lloyd ships), but issue was delayed by the Franco-Prussian War.

The rate for this service was reduced to 6c in 1871.

For several months there was no 7c rate, but late in 1871 the Prussian closed mail rate via England was reduced to 7c which revived an important use for the 7c stamps.

The rate to Denmark direct via Baltic Lloyd ships, or via Bremen and Hamburg as above, was 7c from Jan. 1, 1872.

139 A49 10c **brown,** *Apr. 1870* 7,500. 800.
yellow brown 7,500. 800.
dark brown 7,500. 800.
No gum 2,700.
On cover 1,000.
Pair *15,500.* 1,650.
Block of 4 *37,500.* —
Double grill — 1,350.
Split grill 7,750. 825.
End roller grill *1,650.*
b. Pair, one without grill, one with split grill, on cover —

Earliest documented use: May 6, 1870.

Cancellations

Blue +50.
Red +100.
"Steamship" +50.
Supplementary Mail Type A —
"Honolulu Paid All" —

140 A50 12c **dull violet,** *Apr. 1870* 32,500. 3,500.
No gum *17,500.*
On cover *6,500.*
Pair *65,000.* *7,750.*
Strip of 3 *15,000.*
Strip of 4 *20,000.*
Block of 4 *190,000.*
Double grill —
Split grill — 4,000.
End roller grill *7,250.*

Earliest documented use: June 17, 1870.

Cancellations

Blue +125.
Red +300.
"Paid all" —

141 A51 15c **orange,** *Apr. 1870* 7,500. 1,500.
bright orange 7,500. 1,500.
deep orange 7,500. 1,500.
No gum 2,500.
On cover 2,250.
Pair 16,000. 3,250.
Block of 4 *45,000.* —
Double grill *4,500.*
Double grill, one split —
Split grill 7,750. 1,600.
Quadruple split grill —

Earliest documented use: June 2, 1870.

Cancellations

Blue +50.
Purple +100.
Red +150.
Green +400.
"PAID" —

142 A52 24c **purple** — 6,500.
On cover —
Pair, double grill —
Split grill —
End roller grill —
Grill with points up —

Earliest documented use: July 11, 1872.

Cancellations

Red +750.
Blue +4,000.
Purple +2,500.

The pair of No. 142 is the unique multiple of this stamp.

143 A53 30c **black,** *Apr. 1870* 20,000. 3,750.
full black 20,000. 3,750.
No gum 7,500.
On cover 4,750.
Pair *42,500.* 8,000.
Block of 4 *100,000.* —
Double grill —
End roller grill *5,250.*

Earliest documented use: Aug. 18, 1870.

Cancellations

Blue +75.
Red +125.

144 A54 90c **carmine,** *Apr. 12, 1870* 25,000. 2,250.
dark carmine 25,000. 2,250.
No gum 10,000.
On cover —
Pair *55,000.* 5,000.
Block of 4 *125,000.* *13,500.*
Double grill —
Split grill 2,500.

Cancellations

Blue +80.
Red +140.

I. GRILL ABOUT 8½x10mm (10 TO 11 BY 10 TO 13 POINTS)

The "I" grills can be separated into early state and late state, based on the shape of the tip of the grill. Early state grills show small tips of the pyramid, while late state grills show the pyramid tips truncated and flat.

Early state "I" grills tend to be on vertical-mesh wove paper, while later printings and all late-state grills were printed on horizontal-mesh wove paper, resulting in stamp designs being approximately ¼mm shorter than the designs printed on vertical-mesh wove paper. The late-stage "I" grills all seem to have been used only after Jan. 1873.

Values are for stamps with grills that are clearly identifiable. Poor printing quality often resulted in grills that show only a few grill points or a very few rows of points. When there are not enough grill points to clearly identify whether the grill is an "H" or an "I," it must be assumed it is the lower-valued "H" grill variety. Authentication is advised for these stamps with high catalogue values.

134A A44 1c **ultramarine,** *1870* *2,750.* *375.00*
pale ultramarine —
No gum *800.00*
Pair *9,000.*
Block of 4 *30,000.*
On cover —
Split grill — *400.00*

Cancellations

Blue +150.00
Green +150.00
"Paid" +20.00

135A A45 2c **red brown,** *1870* *2,000.* *325.00*
On cover —
Split grill —
Quadruple split grill —

Earliest documented use: July 21, 1870.

136A A46 3c **green,** *1870* *850.00* *100.00*
On cover —
Pair — —
Block of 4 — —
Double grill —
Split grill *1,100.* —
Quadruple split grill — —
a. Pair, one without grill — —
On cover —

Earliest documented use: June 27, 1870.

Cancellations

Blue —
Red —
Green —
"Paid All" —

137A A47 6c **carmine,** *1870* *7,000.* *950.00*
Strip of 3 —

Cancellations

Blue town —

138A A48 7c **vermilion,** *1871* *6,500.* *850.00*
No gum *2,200.*
Split grill —
Double grill, both split —
Quadruple split grill —

Cancellations

Blue +200.00
Red +150.00

139A A49 10c **brown,** *1870* *17,500.* *8,500.*
Pair, on cover 12,000.
Split grill —

There are two unused examples of No. 139A recorded. One is fine and the other is very fine plus. The catalogue value is for the latter. The pair on cover is the only example of No. 139A on cover. One stamp in the pair is defective, and the cover is valued thus.

Earliest documented use: Mar. 8, 1871.

Cancellation

Red +100.00

140A A50 12c **dull violet,** *1870* *30,000.*

Two examples are recorded of No. 140A unused, and it is valued in the grade of fine.

141A A51 15c **orange,** *1870* *16,500.* *7,500.*
On cover —
Block of 4 —

Three singles and a block of 4 are recorded of No. 141A unused. Value for unused single is for a fine example. The unique unused block has original gum and faults.

Earliest documented use: June 15, 1870.

Cancellations

Red +100.00
N. YORK STEAMSHIP —

143A A53 30c **black,** *1870* *75,000.*

Only one recorded example of No. 143A, which is valued in the grade of fine-very fine.

144A A54 90c **carmine,** *1870* — *15,000.*

The unused No. 144A has a vertically split grill and is unique.

PRODUCED BY THE NATIONAL BANK NOTE COMPANY.

White Wove Paper, Thin to Medium Thick.
Issued (except 3c, 6c and 7c) in April, 1870.
Without Grill.

1870-71 ***Perf. 12***

145 A44 1c **ultramarine** 650. 20.00
pale ultramarine 650. 20.00
dark ultramarine 650. 20.00
gray blue 650. 20.00
No gum 240.
On cover 22.50
Pair 1,350. 42.50
Block of 4 3,500. 100.00
P# block of 12, Impt. *9,000.*
Double transfer — 25.00
Worn plate 650. 20.00

Only one plate block of No. 145 is known in private hands. It is of average condition and is without gum. Value is based on 2019 auction sale.

Earliest documented use: May 7, 1870.

Cancellations

Blue +1.50
Ultramarine +2.50
Magenta +2.00
Purple +2.00
Brown +2.00
Red +5.00
Green +55.00
"Paid" +3.00
"Paid All" +15.00
"Steamship" +25.00
Railroad +20.00
Numeral +2.00

146	A45 2c **red brown**	325.	17.50
	pale red brown	325.	17.50
	dark red brown	325.	17.50
	No gum	135.	
	orange brown	350.	20.00
	No gum	140.	
	On cover		20.00
	Pair	675.	37.50
	Block of 4	1,800.	125.00
	P# block of 10, Impt.	*13,000.*	
	Double transfer	—	20.00
a.	Diagonal half used as 1c on cover		*700.00*
b.	Vertical half used as 1c on cover		*800.00*
c.	Horiz. half used as 1c on cover		*800.00*
d.	Double impression	*9,000.*	

The No. 146 plate block is unique. Value is based on 2019 auction sale. No. 146d is also unique. It has VG-Fine centering and faults and is valued thus.

Earliest documented use: May 7, 1870.

Cancellations

Blue	+1.00
Purple	+1.25
Red	+3.00
Green	+55.00
Brown	+1.25
"Paid"	+2.00
"Paid All"	+10.00
Numeral	+2.00
"Steamship"	+22.50
Black Carrier	+12.50
Japan	—
China	—
Curacao	—

Major Plate Crack At Bottom

147	A46 3c **green**	200.	1.80
	pale green	200.	1.80
	dark green	200.	1.80
	No gum	80.	
	yellow green	225.	1.90
	No gum	90.	
	On cover		2.30
	Pair	425.	3.75
	Block of 4	1,200.	24.00
	P# block of 10, Impt.	*6,000.*	
	Double transfer	—	11.00
	Short transfer at bottom	225.	20.00
	Cracked plate	—	55.00
	Major plate crack at bottom (91L, plate ?)		*400.00*
	On cover		*800.00*
	Worn plate	220.	1.80
a.	Printed on both sides, reverse inverted		*17,500.*
b.	Double impression		*30,000.*
	On cover		—

Nos. 147a and 147b are valued in the grade of fine.

See Die and Plate Proofs for imperf. on stamp paper.

Earliest documented use: Mar. 1, 1870.

Cancellations

Blue	+.25
Purple	+.50
Magenta	+.50
Brown	+1.50
Red	+2.50
Ultramarine	+2.00
Green	+55.00
Orange	+750.00
"Paid"	+2.00
"Paid All"	+10.00
"Free"	+15.00
Numeral	+2.00
Railroad	+10.00
Express Company	—
"Steamboat"	+20.00
"Steamship"	+17.50
Ship	+15.00
Japan	+75.00

148	A47 6c **carmine**	900.	22.50
	dark carmine	900.	22.50
	rose	900.	22.50
	No gum	290.	
	On cover		27.50
	Pair	1,900.	55.00
	Block of 4	4,750.	325.00
	Double transfer		32.50
	brown carmine	1,050.	65.00
	No gum	340.	
	violet carmine	1,200.	190.00
	No gum	400.	
a.	Vertical half used as 3c on cover		*6,500.*
b.	Double impression, on cover		*20,000.*
c.	Double paper	—	*100.00*

No. 148b is unique.

Earliest documented use: Mar. 28, 1870.

Cancellations

Blue	+1.50
Purple	+3.00
Violet	+4.00
Ultramarine	+5.00
Brown	+2.00
Red	+5.00
Claret	+10.00
Orange red	+7.00
Orange	+20.00
Green	+150.00
"Paid"	+3.00
"Steamship"	+25.00
"Paid All"	+15.00
Numeral	—
Supp. Mail Type A or D	+35.00
China	+90.00
Japan	+150.00

149	A48 7c **vermilion,** *Mar. 1871*	900.	90.00
	deep vermilion	900.	90.00
	No gum	290.	
	On cover		150.00
	Pair	1,900.	200.00
	Block of 4	5,500.	*775.00*
	Cracked plate		160.00

Earliest documented use: May 11, 1871.

Cancellations

Blue	+2.50
Purple	+7.50
Ultramarine	+12.50
Red	+10.00
Green	+450.00
Japan	+150.00

150	A49 10c **brown**	2,000.	35.00
	dark brown	2,000.	35.00
	yellow brown	2,000.	35.00
	No gum	800.	
	On cover		47.50
	Pair	4,250.	72.50
	Block of 4	10,000.	*275.00*
	P# block of 10, Impt.	—	
	Double transfer	—	85.00

Earliest documented use: May 14, 1870 (stamp on piece); May 19, 1870 (on cover).

Cancellations

Blue	+1.00
Purple	+2.00
Magenta	+2.00
Ultramarine	+4.00
Red	+4.00
Orange red	+5.00
Orange	+10.00
Green	+120.00
Brown	+3.00
"Paid All"	+20.00
"Steamship"	+20.00
Supp. Mail Type A or D	+25.00
Japan	+120.00
China	—
St. Thomas	—

151	A50 12c **dull violet**	2,850.	200.00
	violet	2,850.	200.00
	dark violet	2,850.	200.00
	No gum	1,050.	
	On cover		450.00
	Pair	6,000.	425.00
	Block of 4	*14,000.*	*2,250.*

Earliest documented use: July 9, 1870.

Cancellations

Blue	+25.00
Ultramarine	+1,000.
Magenta	+10.00
Red	+15.00
Orange	—
Green	+150.00
"Paid All"	+25.00
"Steamship"	+50.00
Supp. Mail Type A or D	+40.00
Japan	—

152	A51 15c **bright orange**	3,500.	210.00
	deep orange	3,500.	210.00
	No gum	1,300.	
	On cover		350.00
	Pair	7,500.	450.00
	Block of 4	*17,500.*	*1,850.*
a.	Double impression		*9,000.*

No. 152a is unique. It has fine centering and faults and is valued thus.

Earliest documented use: June 24, 1870.

Cancellations

Blue	+7.50
Magenta	+7.50
Ultramarine	+10.00
Red	+15.00
Purple	+250.00
"Paid"	+12.50
"Steamship"	+40.00
Supp. Mail Type A or F	+30.00
China	—

153	A52 24c **purple**	1,700.	210.00
	bright purple	1,700.	210.00
	No gum	600.	
	On cover		*1,500.*
	Pair	3,600.	450.00
	Block of 4	*13,000.*	*3,500.*
a.	Double paper	—	—

Earliest documented use: Nov. 18, 1870.

Cancellations

Red	+15.00
Blue	+5.00
Purple	+7.50
China	—
"Paid"	+25.00
Town	+15.00
"Steamship"	—
Supp. Mail Type A, D or F	+30.00

154	A53 30c **black**	7,000.	275.00
	full black	7,000.	300.00
	No gum	2,600.	
	On cover		875.00
	Pair	*15,000.*	575.00
	Block of 4	*37,500.*	

Earliest documented use: July 9, 1870.

Cancellations

Blue	+5.00
Brown	+50.00
Magenta	+15.00
Red	+50.00
"Steamship"	+55.00
Supplementary Mail Type A	+40.00

155	A54 90c **carmine**	5,000.	325.00
	dark carmine	5,000.	325.00
	No gum	1,800.	
	On cover		—
	Pair	*10,500.*	675.00
	Block of 4	*25,000.*	2,250.
	P# strip of 5, Impt.	*35,000.*	

Earliest documented use: Sept. 1, 1872.

Cancellations

Blue	+10.00
Purple	+15.00
Magenta	+15.00
Green	+275.00
Red	+50.00
Town	+20.00
Supp. Mail Type A or F	+40.00
Japan	—

Alan E. Cohen

Dealer in High Grade Stamps

Visit our website today.

www.alanecohen.com

P. O. Box 929
New York, NY 10025
212-280-7865

e-mail: alanecohen@mindspring.com

PLEASE NOTE:

Stamps are valued in the grade of very fine unless otherwise indicated.

Values for early and valuable stamps are for examples with certificates of authenticity from acknowledged expert committees, or examples sold with the buyer having the right of certification. This applies to examples with original gum as well as examples without gum. Beware of stamps offered "as is," as the gum on some unused stamps offered with "original gum" may be fraudulent, and stamps offered as unused without gum may in some cases be altered or faintly canceled used stamps.

VALUES FOR NEVER-HINGED STAMPS PRIOR TO SCOTT No. 182

This catalogue does not value pre-1879 stamps in never-hinged condition. Premiums for never-hinged condition in the classic era invariably are even larger than those premiums listed for the 1879 and later issues. Generally speaking, the earlier the stamp is listed in the catalogue, the larger will be the never-hinged premium.

PRINTED BY THE CONTINENTAL BANK NOTE COMPANY

Plates of 200 subjects in two panes of 100 each.

Designs of the 1870-71 Issue with secret marks on the values from 1c to 15c, as described and illustrated:

The object of secret marks was to provide a simple and positive proof that these stamps were produced by the Continental Bank Note Company and not by their predecessors.

Almost all of the stamps of the Continental Bank Note Co. printing including the Department stamps and some of the Newspaper stamps may be found upon a paper that shows more or less the characteristics of a ribbed paper. The ribbing may be oriented either vertically or horizontally, with horizontal ribbing being far more common than vertical ribbing. Values are for the most common varieties.

Franklin — A44a

1c. In the pearl at the left of the numeral "1" there is a small crescent.

Jackson — A45a

2c. Under the scroll at the left of "U. S." there is a small diagonal line. This mark seldom shows clearly. The stamp, No. 157, can be distinguished by its color.

Washington — A46a

3c. The under part of the upper tail of the left ribbon is heavily shaded.

Lincoln — A47a

6c. The first four vertical lines of the shading in the lower part of the left ribbon have been strengthened.

Stanton — A48a

7c. Two small semi-circles are drawn around the ends of the lines that outline the ball in the lower right hand corner.

Jefferson — A49a

10c. There is a small semi-circle in the scroll at the right end of the upper label.

Clay — A50a

12c. The balls of the figure "2" are crescent shaped.

Webster — A51a

15c. In the lower part of the triangle in the upper left corner two lines have been made heavier forming a "V." This mark can be found on some of the Continental and American (1879) printings, but not all stamps show it.

Secret marks were added to the dies of the 24c, 30c and 90c but new plates were not made from them. The various printings of the 30c and 90c can be distinguished only by the shades and paper.

Experimental J. Grill about 7x9½mm exists on all values except 24c and 90c. Grill was composed of truncated pyramids and was so strongly impressed that some points often broke through the paper.

White Wove Paper, Thin to Thick Without Grill

1873, July (?) *Perf. 12*

		Unused	Used
156	A44a 1c **ultramarine**	200.	5.75
	pale ultramarine	200.	5.75
	gray blue	200.	5.75
	blue	200.	5.75
	No gum	90.	
	dark ultramarine	225.	5.75
	No gum	95.	
	On cover		7.25
	Pair	425.	12.00
	Block of 4	1,000.	47.50
	P# block of 12, Impt.	*7,000.*	
	P# block of 14, Impt.	*9,500.*	
	Double transfer	275.	10.00
	Ribbed paper	325.	25.00
	Paper with silk fibers	—	35.00
	Cracked plate		—
	Paper cut with "cogwheel" punch	*425.*	
a.	Double paper	*2,000.*	*500.00*
e.	With grill	*2,000.*	
f.	Imperf., pair	—	*1,500.*

The No. 156 plate block is unique. Value is 1998 auction sale.

No. 156f may not have been regularly issued.

Earliest documented use: Aug. 22, 1873.

Cancellations

Blue	+.25
Purple	+.35
Magenta	+.35
Ultramarine	+1.00
Red	+3.50
Orange red	+4.00
Orange	+5.00
Brown	+20.00
Green	+60.00
"Paid All"	+7.00
"Paid"	+1.00
Railroad	+12.00
"Free"	+12.00
Black carrier	+15.00
Numeral	+2.50
Alaska	—
Japan	—
Printed "G." Precancel (Glastonbury, Conn.)	+200.00
Printed Star Precancel (Glen Allen, Va.)	+100.00

		Unused	Used
157	A45a 2c **brown**	325.	22.50
	dark brown	325.	22.50
	dark reddish brown	325.	22.50
	yellowish brown	325.	22.50
	No gum	125.	
	With secret mark	350.	25.00
	No gum	140.	
	On cover		27.50
	Pair	675.	47.50
	Block of 4	1,650.	180.00
	P# block of 12, Impt.	*12,000.*	
	P# block of 14, Impt.	*13,000.*	
	Ribbed paper	475.	55.00
	Double transfer	—	27.50
	Cracked plate		—
a.	Double paper	*1,500.*	200.00
	On cover		*2,500.*
c.	With grill	*1,850.*	*750.00*
d.	Double impression		*16,500.*
e.	Vertical half used as 1c on cover		*1,000.*

No. 157d is unique.

Earliest documented use: July 12, 1873.

Cancellations

Blue	+.75
Magenta	+1.00
Purple	+1.00
Red	+5.00
Orange red	+5.50
Orange	+7.50
Green	+100.00
"Paid"	+2.50
"Insufficiently Paid"	—
"Paid All"	+13.50
"P. D." in circle	+15.00
Town	+2.00
Numeral	+1.50
Black Carrier	+8.50
"Steamship"	+15.00
Supplementary Mail Type F	+5.00
China	—
Japan	+100.00
Printed Star Precancellation (Glen Allen, Va.)	—

		Unused	Used
158	A46a 3c **green**	110.	1.00
	bluish green	110.	1.00
	yellow green	110.	1.00
	dark yellow green	110.	1.00
	dark green	110.	1.00
	No gum	40.	
	olive green, ribbed paper	*375.*	15.00
	No gum	*140.*	
	On cover		1.20
	Pair	230.	2.10
	Block of 4	550.	14.50
	P# strip of 5, Impt.	700.	
	P# strip of 6, Impt.	825.	
	P# block of 10, Impt.	2,600.	
	P# block of 12, Impt.	*3,750.*	
	P# block of 14, Impt.	*5,000.*	
	Paper cut with "cogwheel" punch	290.	*400.*
	On cover		—
	Ribbed paper	290.	10.00
	Paper with silk fibers	—	10.00
	Cracked plate	—	32.50
	Double transfer	—	6.00
	Short transfer at bottom		15.00
a.	Double paper	600.	100.00
	P# strip of 6, Impt.	*4,250.*	
e.	With grill	*550.*	
	End roller grill	*1,250.*	*425.*
h.	Horizontal pair, imperf. vert.		—
i.	Horizontal pair, imperf. between		*1,300.*
j.	Double impression		*7,000.*
k.	Printed on both sides		*20,000.*

Nos. 158j and 158k are valued in the grade of fine.

See Die and Plate Proofs for imperfs. on stamp paper, with and without grill.

Earliest documented use: July 17, 1873.

Cancellations

Blue	+.10
Magenta	+.20
Purple	+.20
Ultramarine	+1.25
Red	+2.50
Orange red	+2.75
Orange	+3.50
Green	+25.00
Town	+.05
"Paid"	+2.50
"Paid All"	+20.00
"Free"	+15.00
Numeral	+1.00
China	—
Railroad	+7.00
"R. P. O."	+1.50
"P. D." in circle	—
"Steamboat"	—
"Steamship"	—
Supplementary Mail Type D	+11.00
Supplementary Mail Type F	+8.50
Express Company	—
Black Carrier	+8.00
Red Carrier	+25.00
Japan	+65.00
Alaska	—

		Unused	Used
159	A47a 6c **dull pink**	375.	18.00
	brown rose	450.	18.00
	No gum	120.	
	On cover		27.50
	Pair	800.	37.50
	Block of 4	2,250.	*130.00*
	P# block of 12, Impt. (dull pink)	*15,000.*	
	P# block of 12, Impt. (brown rose)	*16,500.*	
	Ribbed paper	—	60.00
	Paper with colored fibers	—	70.00
a.	Diagonal half used as 3c on cover		*7,250.*
b.	With grill	*1,800.*	
	End roller grill	*2,400.*	
c.	Double paper	—	*900.00*

Earliest documented use: June 8, 1873.

No. 159a is unique.

No. 159b is valued in the grade of fine.

Cancellations

Blue	+1.00
Indigo	+2.50
Magenta	+1.50
Purple	+1.50

Violet		+3.00
Ultramarine		+2.50
Red		+7.50
Orange red		+9.00
Green		+100.00
Numeral		+1.50
"Paid"		+10.00
"Paid All"		+15.00
Supp. Mail Type D, E or F		+35.00
Japan		+100.00
China		+125.00
Railroad		+6.00
"R. P. O."		+3.00

160	A48a 7c **orange vermilion**	1,000.	85.00
	vermilion	1,000.	85.00
	No gum	350.	
	On cover		160.00
	Pair	2,300.	180.00
	Block of 4	6,000.	
	P# block of 12, Impt.	*18,500.*	
	Double transfer of "7 cents" (1R22)	—	200.00
	Double transfer in lower left corner	—	150.00
	Ribbed paper	—	140.00
	Paper with silk fibers	1,900.	200.00
a.	With grill	*3,500.*	
b.	Double paper		—

The plate block of 12 is in fine condition. It is unique.

Earliest documented use: Sept. 10, 1873.

Cancellations

Blue	+4.00
Red	+10.00
Purple	+10.00
Brown	+5.00
"Paid"	+15.00

161	A49a 10c **brown**	800.	25.00
	dark brown	800.	25.00
	yellow brown	800.	25.00
	No gum	250.	
	On cover		40.00
	Pair	1,800.	52.50
	Block of 4	4,750.	*200.00*
	P# block of 10, Impt.	*18,500.*	
	P# block of 12, Impt.	*21,500.*	
	Ribbed paper	—	90.00
	Paper with silk fibers	1,400.	100.00
	Double transfer	—	52.50
a.	Double paper	*3,500.*	*900.00*
c.	With grill	*3,750.*	
d.	Horizontal pair, imperf. between		*15,000.*

Earliest documented use: Aug. 2, 1873.

No. 161d is unique. It has a small fault and is valued thus.

Cancellations

Blue	+1.50
Ultramarine	—
Purple	+2.00
Red	+6.00
Orange red	+7.00
Orange	+10.00
Magenta	+2.00
Brown	+20.00
Green	+100.00
"Paid"	+4.00
"P. D." in circle	+20.00
"Steamship"	+15.00
Supplementary Mail Type E	+7.00
Supplementary Mail Type F	+2.50
Japan	+100.00
China	—
Alaska	—

162	A50a 12c **blackish violet**	2,200.	135.00
	No gum	725.	
	On cover		325.00
	Pair	4,750.	280.00
	Block of 4	*12,000.*	*1,000.*
	Ribbed paper	—	350.00
a.	With grill	*5,500.*	

Earliest documented use: Jan. 3, 1874.

Cancellations

Blue	+2.50
Ultramarine	+15.00
Brown	+5.00
Red	+15.00
Magenta	+200.00
Purple	+500.00
Supplementary Mail Type D	+15.00
Japan	+200.00

163	A51a 15c **yellow orange**	1,900.	150.00
	pale orange	1,900.	150.00
	reddish orange	1,900.	150.00
	No gum	650.	
	On cover		340.00
	Pair	4,000.	325.00
	Block of 4	*11,000.*	*1,150.*
	P# strip of 5, Impt.	*15,000.*	
	Paper with silk fibers	3,000.	250.00
	Vertical ribbed paper	3,000.	250.00
a.	With grill	*5,750.*	
b.	Double paper		*1,250.*

Earliest documented use: July 22, 1873.

Cancellations

Blue	+5.00
Purple	+10.00
Red	+20.00
Green	+350.00
Brown	—
Supplementary Mail Type E	—
Supplementary Mail Type F	+10.00
"Steamship"	—
Numeral	+7.50
Puerto Rico	—
China	—

164	A52 24c **purple**		*357,500.*

The Philatelic Foundation has certified as genuine a 24c on vertically ribbed paper, and that is the unique stamp listed as No. 164. Specialists believe that only Continental used ribbed paper. It is not known for sure whether or not Continental also printed the 24c value on regular paper; if it did, specialists currently are not able to distinguish these from No. 153. The catalogue value represents a 2004 auction sale price realized.

165	A53 30c **gray black**	3,750.	135.
	greenish black	3,750.	135.
	No gum	1,200.	
	On cover		*700.*
	Pair	8,000.	280.
	Block of 4	*19,000.*	*1,200.*
	P# strip of 5, Impt.	15,000.	
	Double transfer	—	155.
	Ribbed paper	4,500.	145.
	Paper with silk fibers	—	—
a.	Double paper		
c.	With grill	*22,500.*	

Earliest documented use: Oct. 14, 1874.

Cancellations

Purple	+10.00
Blue	+5.00
Red	+25.00
Brown	+30.00
Magenta	+10.00
"Steamship"	—
Supplementary Mail Type E	+10.00
Supplementary Mail Type F	+5.00
Japan	+200.00

166	A54 90c **rose carmine**	2,100.	275.00
	pale rose carmine	2,100.	275.00
	No gum	700.	
	On cover		*7,500.*
	Pair	*4,500.*	575.00
	Block of 4	*12,500.*	*2,500.*
	P# strip of 5, Impt.	*13,000.*	

Earliest documented use: June 25, 1875.

Cancellations

Blue	+10.
Purple	+40.
Red	+40.
Supplementary Mail Type F	+30.

SPECIAL PRINTING OF 1873 ISSUE

Produced by the Continental Bank Note Co.

1875 ***Perf. 12***

Hard, white wove paper, without gum

167	A44a 1c **ultramarine**	*14,000.*	
168	A45a 2c **dark brown**	*6,000.*	
169	A46a 3c **blue green**	*21,500.*	—
	On cover		—
170	A47a 6c **dull rose**	*18,000.*	
171	A48a 7c **reddish vermilion**	*4,000.*	
172	A49a 10c **pale brown**	*17,000.*	
173	A50a 12c **dark violet**	*5,500.*	
	Horizontal pair	—	
174	A51a 15c **bright orange**	*15,500.*	
175	A52 24c **dull purple**	*3,400.*	*22,500.*
	Horizontal pair	—	
176	A53 30c **greenish black**	*12,000.*	
177	A54 90c **violet carmine**	*18,000.*	

Although perforated, these stamps were usually cut apart with scissors. As a result, the perforations are often much mutilated and the design is frequently damaged.

These can be distinguished from the 1873 issue by the shades; also by the paper, which is very white instead of yellowish.

These and the subsequent issues listed under the heading of "Special Printings" are special printings of stamps then in current use which, together with the reprints and re-issues, were made for sale to collectors. They were available for postage except for the Officials, Newspaper and Periodical, and demonetized issues.

Only No. 169 is documented on cover (unique; postmarked Mar. 5, 1876).

Only three examples of No. 175 used have been certified. They all have small faults and are valued thus.

While use of Nos. 167-177 for postage was legal, actual use was almost non-existent. Expertization strongly recommended.

PRINTED BY THE CONTINENTAL BANK NOTE COMPANY

REGULAR ISSUE

Yellowish Wove Paper

1875 ***Perf. 12***

178	A45a 2c **vermilion,** *June 1875*	325.	15.00
	No gum	100.	
	On cover		17.50
	Pair	675.	32.50
	Block of 4	1,650.	130.00
	P# strip of 6, Impt.	*3,000.*	
	P# block of 12, Impt.	—	
	P# block of 14, Impt.	*7,250.*	
	Double transfer		—
	Ribbed paper	—	—
	Paper with silk fibers	400.	30.00
a.	Double paper	—	—
b.	Half used as 1c on cover		*750.00*
c.	With grill	*1,250.*	*2,750.*

See Die and Plate Proofs for imperf. on stamp paper.

The previously listed EDU has been found to be erroneous. The editors welcome new verified early dates in 1875.

Cancellations

Blue	+.50
Purple	+.75
Magenta	+.75
Red	+6.00
"Paid"	+8.00
"Steamship"	—
Supplementary Mail Type F	+5.50
Black Carrier	+15.00
Railroad	+12.50

Zachary Taylor — A55

179	A55 5c **blue,** *June 1875*	700.	25.00
	dark blue	700.	25.00
	bright blue	700.	25.00
	light blue	700.	25.00
	No gum	225.	
	greenish blue	725.	30.00
	No gum	240.	
	On cover		40.00
	Pair	1,500.	52.50
	Block of 4	3,750.	375.00
	Cracked plate	—	*170.00*
	Double transfer	—	37.50
	Ribbed paper		—
	Paper with silk fibers	—	50.00
a.	Double paper	*950.*	
c.	With grill	*9,500.*	
	End roller grill	—	

Earliest documented use: July 10, 1875.

Cancellations

Blue	+1.00
Ultramarine	+3.00
Purple	+2.00
Magenta	+2.00
Red	+10.00
Green	+70.00
Numeral	+5.00
Railroad	+17.50
"Steamship"	+12.50
Ship	+12.50
Supplementary Mail Type E	+5.00
Supplementary Mail Type F	+2.00
China	—
Japan	+125.00
Peru	—

The five cent rate to foreign countries in the Universal Postal Union began on July 1, 1875. No. 179 was issued for that purpose.

SPECIAL PRINTING OF 1875 ISSUE

Produced by the Continental Bank Note Co.

Hard, White Wove Paper, without gum

1875

180	A45a 2c **carmine vermilion**	*70,000.*	
181	A55 5c **bright blue**	*450,000.*	

Unlike Nos. 167-177, Nos. 180-181 were seldom cut apart with scissors.

Numbers sold: No. 180, 917; No. 181, 317. However, fewer than 25 No. 180 and fewer than 10 No. 181 have been expertized and are available to collectors.

IMPORTANT INFORMATION
REGARDING VALUES FOR
NEVER-HINGED STAMPS

Collectors should be aware that the values given for never-hinged stamps from No. 182 on are for stamps in the grade of very fine, just as the values for all stamps in the catalogue are for very fine stamps unless indicated otherwise. The never-hinged premium as a percentage of value will be larger for stamps in extremely fine or superb grades, and the premium will be smaller for fine-very fine, fine or poor examples. This is particularly true of the issues of the late-19th and early-20th centuries.

VALUES FOR NEVER-HINGED STAMPS
PRIOR TO SCOTT 182

This catalogue does not value pre-1879 stamps in never-hinged condition. Premiums for never-hinged condition in the classic era invariably are even larger than those premiums listed for the 1879 and later issues. Generally speaking, the earlier the stamp is listed in the catalogue, the larger will be the never-hinged premium.

NEVER-HINGED PLATE BLOCKS

Values given for never-hinged plate blocks are for blocks in which all stamps have original gum that has never been hinged and has no disturbances, and all selvage, whether gummed or ungummed, has never been hinged.

For values of the most popular U.S. stamps in various conditions, including never hinged from No. 182 on, and in the grades of very good, fine, fine to very fine, very fine, very fine to extremely fine, extremely fine, extremely fine to superb, and superb, see the *Scott Stamp Values U.S. Specialized by Grade*, updated and issued each year as part of this U.S. specialized catalogue. This section is located after Postage and before Semi-Postal Stamps.

PRINTED BY THE AMERICAN BANK NOTE COMPANY

The Continental Bank Note Co. was consolidated with the American Bank Note Co. on February 4, 1879. The American Bank Note Company used many plates of the Continental Bank Note Company to print the ordinary postage, Departmental and Newspaper stamps. Therefore, stamps bearing the Continental Company's imprint were not always its product.

The A. B. N. Co. also used the 30c and 90c plates of the N. B. N. Co. Some of No. 190 and all of No. 217 were from A. B. N. Co. plate 405.

Early printings of No. 188 were from Continental plates 302 and 303 which contained the normal secret mark of 1873. After those plates were re-entered by the A. B. N. Co. in 1880, pairs or multiple pieces contained combinations of normal, hairline or missing marks. The pairs or other multiples usually found contain at least one hairline mark which tended to disappear as the plate wore.

A. B. N. Co. plates 377 and 378 were made in 1881 from the National transfer roll of 1870. No. 187 from these plates has no secret mark.

Identification by Paper Type:

Collectors traditionally have identified American Bank Note Co. issues by the soft, porous paper on which they were printed. However, the Continental Bank Note Co. used some intermediate papers as early as 1877 and a soft paper from August 1878 through early 1879, before the consolidation of the companies. When the consolidation occurred in the late afternoon of Feb. 4, 1879, American Bank Note Co. took over the presses, plates, paper, ink, and the employees of Continental. Undoubtedly they also acquired panes of finished stamps and sheets of printed stamps that had not yet been gummed and/or perforated. Since the soft paper that was in use at the time of the consolidation and after is approximately the same texture and thickness as the soft paper that American Bank Note Co. began using regularly in June or July of 1879, all undated soft paper stamps have traditionally been classified as American Bank Note Co. printings.

However, if a stamp bears a dated cancellation or is on a dated cover from Feb. 4, 1879 or earlier, collectors (especially specialist collectors) must consider the stamp to be a Continental Bank Note printing. Undated stamps off cover, and stamps and covers dated Feb. 5 or later, traditionally have been considered to be American Bank Note Co. printings since that company held the contract to print U.S. postage stamps beginning on that date. The most dedicated and serious specialist students sometimes attempt to determine the stamp printer of the issues on soft, porous paper in an absolute manner (by scientifically testing the paper and/or comparing printing records).

Earliest documented uses for American Bank Note Co. issues are given for stamps on the soft, porous paper that has been traditionally associated with that company. But, for reasons given above, sometimes that date will precede the Feb. 4, 1879 consolidation date.

SAME AS 1870-75 ISSUES
Soft Porous Paper

1879 ***Perf. 12***

182 A44a 1c **dark ultramarine**	200.	6.00
blue	200.	6.00
gray blue	200.	6.00
Never hinged	675.	
No gum	80.	
On cover		6.50
Pair	425.	12.50
Block of 4	1,200.	67.50
P# block of 12, Impt.	*7,000.*	
P# block of 10, Impt.	4,250.	
Double transfer	—	12.50

Earliest documented use: Jan. 3, 1879.

Cancellations

Blue	+.20
Magenta	+.30
Purple	+.30
Red	+7.00
Printed Star Precancellation (Glen Allen, Va.)	+125.00
Green	+35.00
"Paid"	+4.00
Supplementary Mail Type F	+10.00
Railroad	+12.50
Printed "G." Precancellation (Glastonbury, Conn.)	+100.00

183 A45a 2c **vermilion**	100.	5.00
orange vermilion	100.	5.00
Never hinged	370.	
No gum	40.	
On cover		5.50
Pair	210.	11.00
Block of 4	550.	55.00
P# block of 10, Impt.	*4,000.*	
P# block of 12, Impt.	*4,500.*	
Double transfer	—	—
a. Double impression	—	*5,500.*
b. Half used as 1c on cover		*750.00*

No. 183a is valued in the grade of fine.

Earliest documented use: Aug. 19, 1878.

Cancellations

Blue	+.25
Purple	+.40
Magenta	+.40
Red	+6.00
Green	+175.00
"Paid"	+5.00
"Paid All"	—
"Ship"	—
Numeral	+4.00
Railroad	+15.00
Supplementary Mail Type F	+8.00
China	—
Printed Star Precancellation in black (Glen Allen, Va.)	+350.00
Printed Star Precancellation in red (Glen Allen, Va.)	+1,750.

184 A46a 3c **green**	90.	1.00
light green	90.	1.00
dark green	90.	1.00
Never hinged	325.	
No gum	35.	
On cover		1.10
Pair	190.	2.10
Block of 4	450.	12.50
P# block of 10, Impt.	1,300.	
Never hinged	*3,000.*	
P# block of 12, Impt.	1,525.	
P# block of 14, Impt.	1,900.	
Double transfer	—	—
Short transfer	—	7.00
b. Double impression		*5,000.*

No. 184b is valued in the grade of fine.

See Die and Plate Proofs for imperf. on stamp paper.

Earliest documented use: July 2, 1878.

Cancellations

Blue	+.10
Magenta	+.15
Purple	+.15
Violet	+.15
Brown	+1.00
Red	+7.50
Green	+25.00
"Paid"	+3.00
"Free"	+15.00
Numeral	+2.00
Railroad	+12.50
"Steamboat"	—
Supplementary Mail Type F	+8.00
Printed Star Precancel (Glen Allen, Va.)	—
China	+60.00
Alaska	—

185 A55 5c **blue**	500.	16.00
light blue	500.	16.00
bright blue	500.	16.00
dark blue	500.	16.00
Never hinged	*1,600.*	
No gum	155.	
On cover		27.50
Pair	1,050.	35.00
Block of 4	2,500.	190.00
P# block of 10, Impt.	*17,500.*	
Double transfer		—
Short transfer at top		—

Earliest documented use: Jan. 16, 1879.

Cancellations

Blue	+.25
Purple	+1.00
Magenta	+1.00
Ultramarine	+3.50
Red	+7.50
Railroad	+20.00
Numeral	+2.00
Supplementary Mail Type F	+1.50
"Steamship"	+35.00
China	+60.00
Peru	—
Panama	—

186 A47a 6c **pink**	900.	22.50
dull pink	900.	22.50
brown rose	900.	22.50
Never hinged	*3,100.*	
No gum	275.	
On cover		27.50
Pair	2,000.	50.00
Block of 4	4,000.	*475.00*

Earliest documented use: April 18, 1879.

Cancellations

Blue	+.50
Ultramarine	+3.50
Purple	+1.00
Magenta	+1.00
Red	+12.00
Supplementary Mail Type F	+8.00
Railroad	+20.00
Numeral	+4.00
China	+100.00

187 A49 10c **brown,** without secret mark	3,000.	40.00
yellow brown	3,000.	40.00
Never hinged	*10,000.*	
No gum	1,000.	
On cover		57.50
Pair	6,250.	85.00
Block of 4	*14,000.*	—
Double transfer	—	57.50
a. Double paper	*10,000.*	—

Earliest documented use: Sept. 5, 1879.

Cancellations

Blue	+.50
Magenta	+1.50
Red	+10.00
"Paid"	+3.50
Supplementary Mail Type F	+3.00
China	+70.00

188 A49a 10c **brown,** with secret mark	1,800.	30.00
yellow brown	1,800.	30.00
Never hinged	*6,000.*	
No gum	650.	
black brown	2,100.	60.00
Never hinged	*6,500.*	
No gum	750.	
On cover		45.00
Pair	3,750.	62.50
Block of 4	*9,500.*	325.00
Pair, one stamp No. 187	*9,000.*	725.00
Double transfer		47.50
Cracked plate	—	—

Earliest documented use: Oct. 5, 1878.

Cancellations

Blue	+.50
Ultramarine	+3.00
Purple	+2.00
Magenta	+2.00
Red	+10.00
Green	+70.00
"Paid"	+7.50
Supplementary Mail Type F	+5.00
Numeral	+3.00
Printed Star Precancel (Glen Allen, Va.)	—

189 A51a 15c **red orange**	180.	27.50
orange	180.	27.50
yellow orange	180.	27.50
Never hinged	600.	
No gum	70.	
On cover		82.50
Pair	375.	60.00
Block of 4	1,100.	250.00
P# block of 12, Impt.	*5,000.*	
Never hinged	*8,500.*	
Double transfer		—

Earliest documented use: Jan. 20, 1879.

Cancellations

Blue	+1.50
Purple	+3.00
Magenta	+3.00
Ultramarine	+5.00
Red	+12.00
"Steamship"	+22.50
Supplementary Mail Type E	—
Supplementary Mail Type F	+5.00
Japan	+120.00
China	—

190 A53 30c **full black**	850.	90.00
greenish black	850.	90.00
Never hinged	*2,800.*	
No gum	300.	
On cover		450.00

Pair 1,800. 200.00
Block of 4 4,250. 575.00
P# block of 10, Impt. *17,000.*

Earliest documented use: April 5, 1881.

Cancellations

Blue +1.50
Purple +3.00
Magenta +3.00
Red +20.00
Supplementary Mail Type F +6.00
"Steamship" +35.00
Tahiti —
Samoa —

191 A54 90c **carmine** 2,000. 350.00
rose 2,000. 350.00
carmine rose 2,000. 350.00
Never hinged *7,000.*
No gum 650.
On cover *5,000.*
Pair 4,500. 725.00
Block of 4 *12,000.* 2,000.
P# strip of 5, Impt. *12,500.*
a. Double paper —

See Die and Plate Proofs for imperf. on stamp paper.

Earliest documented use: May 27, 1882 (dated cancel on off-cover stamp), June 24, 1882 (on cover).

Cancellations

Blue +15.00
Purple +20.00
Red +45.00
Supplementary Mail Type F +20.00

SPECIAL PRINTING OF 1879 ISSUE

Produced by the American Bank Note Co.

1880 ***Perf. 12***

Soft porous paper, without gum

192 A44a 1c **dark ultramarine** *57,500.*
193 A45a 2c **black brown** *16,000.*
194 A46a 3c **blue green** *120,000.*
195 A47a 6c **dull rose** *67,500.*
196 A48a 7c **scarlet vermilion** *6,750.*
197 A49a 10c **deep brown** *34,500.*
Double transfer —
198 A50a 12c **blackish purple** *9,500.*
199 A51a 15c **orange** *29,000.*
200 A52 24c **dark violet** *9,000.*
201 A53 30c **greenish black** *20,000.*
202 A54 90c **dull carmine** *29,000.*
203 A45a 2c **scarlet vermilion** *100,000.*
204 A55 5c **deep blue** *240,000.*

Nos. 192 and 194 are valued in the grade of fine.

No. 197 was printed from Continental plate 302 (or 303) after plate was re-entered. Therefore, the stamp may show normal, hairline or missing secret mark.

The Post Office Department did not keep separate records of the 1875 and 1880 Special Printings of the 1873 and 1879 issues, but the total quantity sold of both is recorded. Census research indicates that numbers sold of the two sets were approximately equal.

Unlike the 1875 hard-paper Special Printings (Nos. 167-177), the 1880 soft-paper Special Printings were never cut apart with scissors.

While use of Nos. 192-204 for postage was legal, no used examples are recorded. Expertization by competent authorities would be required to establish use.

Numbers Sold of 1875 and 1880 Special Printings.

1c ultramarine & dark ultramarine *(388)*
2c dark brown & black brown *(416)*
2c carmine vermilion & scarlet vermilion *(917)*
3c blue green *(267)*
5c bright blue & deep blue *(317)*
6c dull rose *(185)*
7c reddish vermilion & scarlet vermilion *(473)*
10c pale brown & deep brown *(180)*
12c dark violet & blackish purple *(282)*
15c bright orange & orange *(169)*
24c dull purple & dark violet *(286)*
30c greenish black *(179)*
90c violet carmine & dull carmine *(170)*

REGULAR ISSUE

Printed by the American Bank Note Co.

James A. Garfield — A56

1882

205 A56 5c **yellow brown** 240. 15.00
brown 240. 15.00
gray brown 240. 15.00
Never hinged 775.
No gum 90.
On cover 27.50
Pair 500. 32.50
Block of 4 1,150. 135.00
P# strip of 5, Impt. 1,750.
P# block of 10, Impt., no gum *5,750.*
P# block of 12, Impt. *9,750.*

Earliest documented use: Feb. 18, 1882.

Cancellations

Blue +.75
Purple +1.00
Magenta +1.00
Red +7.00
"Ship" —
Numeral +2.00
Supplementary Mail Type F +2.50
Red Express Co. —
China +125.00
Japan +125.00
Samoa +150.00
Puerto Rico —

SPECIAL PRINTING

Printed by the American Bank Note Co.

1882 ***Perf. 12***

Soft porous paper, without gum

205C A56 5c **gray brown** *50,000.*

Although Post Office records indicate that 2,463 examples of the 5c Garfield Special Printing were sold, almost all of these stamps appear to have been from supplies of the regular issue No. 205. The actual Special Printings, No. 205C, came from a small supply sent to the Third Assistant Post Master General before the regular issue was available. Only 22 examples have been certified as genuine Special Printings.

While use of No. 205C for postage was legal, no used examples are recorded.

DESIGNS OF 1873 RE-ENGRAVED

Franklin — A44b

1c — The vertical lines in the upper part of the stamp have been so deepened that the background often appears to be solid. Lines of shading have been added to the upper arabesques.

1881-82

206 A44b 1c **gray blue,** *Aug. 1881* 70.00 1.00
ultramarine 70.00 1.25
dull blue 70.00 1.00
slate blue 70.00 1.25
Never hinged 225.00
No gum 25.00
On cover 1.75
Pair 160.00 2.60
Block of 4 375.00 17.50
P# strip of 5, Impt. 500.00
P# strip of 6, Impt. 575.00
P# block of 10, Impt. *1,800.*
Never hinged *2,750.*
P# block of 12, Impt. *2,000.*
Never hinged *3,000.*
Double transfer 105.00 6.00
Punched with 8 small holes in a circle *200.00*
P# block of 10, Impt. (8-hole punch) *2,750.*
a. Double impression —

No. 206a is a partial double impression, with "ONE 1 CENT," etc. at bottom doubled.

Earliest documented use: Oct. 11, 1881.

Cancellations

Purple +.10
Magenta +.10
Blue +.20
Red +3.00
Orange red +3.50
Orange +5.00
Green +50.00
"Paid" +4.75
"Paid All" +12.00
Numeral +3.50
Supplementary Mail Type F +5.00
Railroad +10.00
Printed Star Precancel (Glen Allen, Va.) +80.00
China —

Washington — A46b

3c. The shading at the sides of the central oval appears only about one-half the previous width. A short horizontal dash has been cut about 1mm below the "TS" of "CENTS."

207 A46b 3c **blue green,** *July 16, 1881* 80.00 .80
green 80.00 .80
yellow green 80.00 .80
Never hinged 2.50
No gum 27.50
On cover .95
Pair 170.00 1.70
Block of 4 375.00 30.00
P# strip of 5, Impt. 525.00
P# block of 10, Impt. *1,750.*
Never hinged *2,750.*
Double transfer — 12.00
Cracked plate —
Punched with 8 small holes in a circle *220.00*
P# block of 10, Impt. (8-hole punch) *3,000.*
c. Double impression *5,000.*
On cover *5,500.*

Earliest documented use: Aug. 7, 1881.

Cancellations

Purple +.10
Magenta +.10
Blue +.25
Brown +1.50
Red +2.50
"Paid" +3.00
"Paid All" —
Numeral +2.50
"Ship" —
Railroad +5.00
Supplementary Mail Type F +8.00
Printed Star Precancellation (Glen Allen, Va.) —

Lincoln — A47b

6c. On the original stamps four vertical lines can be counted from the edge of the panel to the outside of the stamp. On the re-engraved stamps there are but three lines in the same place.

208 A47b 6c **rose** 800. 100.00
dull rose 800. 100.00
Never hinged 2,500.
No gum 240.
On cover (rose) 130.00
Pair (rose) 1,700. 210.00
Block of 4 (rose) 4,000. 900.00
P# block of 10, Impt. *11,500.*
Double transfer 850. 140.00
a. 6c **deep brown red** 550. 170.00
Never hinged 1,750.
No gum 150.
pale brown red 475. 120.00
Never hinged 1,400.
No gum 130.
On cover (deep brown red) *400.00*
Pair (deep brown red) 1,200. 360.00
Block of 4 (deep brown red) 2,900. 1,250.
P# strip of 5, Impt. 3,650.
P# strip of 6, Impt. *4,500.*
P# block of 10, Impt. *9,500.*
P# block of 12, Impt. —

Earliest documented use: June 1, 1882.

Cancellations

Magenta +3.00
Purple +5.00
Blue +5.00
Red +15.00
Supplementary Mail Type F +10.00

Jefferson — A49b

10c. On the original stamps there are five vertical lines between the left side of the oval and the edge of the shield. There are only four lines on the re-engraved stamps. In the lower part of the latter, also, the horizontal lines of the background have been strengthened.

209 A49b 10c **brown,** *Apr. 1882* 160. 6.00
yellow brown 160. 6.00
orange brown 160. 6.00
Never hinged 475.
No gum 65.
dark brown 175. 10.00
purple brown 200. 20.00
olive brown 200. 20.00
Never hinged 525.
No gum 55.
On cover 11.00
Pair 350. 12.50
Block of 4 875. 40.00
P# strip of 5, Impt. 1,175.
P# strip of 6, Impt. 1,375.
P# block of 10, Impt. *3,750.*
P# block of 12, Impt. *4,500.*
Never hinged *8,750.*
b. 10c **black brown** 3,000. 375.00
Never hinged 6,000.
No gum 950.
On cover *550.00*
Pair — 775.00
Block of 4 — —
c. Double impression —

Specimen stamps (usually overprinted "Sample") without overprint exist in a brown shade that differs from No. 209. The unoverprinted brown specimen is cheaper than No. 209. Expertization is recommended.

Earliest documented use: May 4, 1882.

Cancellations

Purple	+.50
Magenta	+.50
Blue	+1.00
Red	+4.00
Green	+35.00
Numeral	+2.00
"Paid"	+2.50
Supplementary Mail Type F	+3.00
Express Company	—
Japan	+75.00
China	—
Samoa	—

Printed by the American Bank Note Company.

Washington — A57

Jackson — A58

Nos. 210-211 were issued to meet the reduced first class rate of 2 cents for each half ounce, and the double rate, which Congress approved Mar. 3, 1883, effective Oct. 1, 1883.

1883, Oct. 1 ***Perf. 12***

210 A57 2c **red brown**	45.	.75
dark red brown	45.	.75
orange brown	45.	.75
Never hinged	135.	
No gum	17.	
On cover		.85
Pair	95.	1.60
Block of 4	230.	12.50
P# strip of 5, Impt.	275.	
P# strip of 6, Impt.	340.	
P# block of 10, Impt.	*1,050.*	
P# block of 12, Impt.	*1,300.*	
Double transfer	50.	2.25

See Die and Plate Proofs for imperf. on stamp paper.

Earliest documented use: Oct. 1, 1883 (FDC).

Cancellations

Purple	+.10
Magenta	+.10
Blue	+.20
Violet	+.30
Brown	+.30
Red	+3.50
Green	+25.00
Numeral	+2.50
"Paid"	+3.00
Railroad	+5.00
Express Company	—
Supplementary Mail Type F	+5.00
"Ship"	—
"Steamboat"	—
China	—

211 A58 4c **blue green**	225.	25.00
deep blue green	225.	25.00
Never hinged	800.	
No gum	80.	
On cover		50.00
Pair	475.	52.50
Block of 4	1,075.	130.00
P# strip of 5, Impt.	1,700.	
P# strip of 6, Impt.	2,000.	
P# block of 10, Impt.	*6,500.*	
P# block of 12, Impt.	*7,500.*	
Never hinged	*8,250.*	
Double transfer	—	—
Cracked plate	—	

See Die and Plate Proofs for imperf. on stamp paper.

Earliest documented use: Oct. 1, 1883 (FDC).

Cancellations

Purple	+1.00
Magenta	+1.00
Green	+50.00
Blue	+1.00
Numeral	+2.00
Supplementary Mail Type F	+5.00

SPECIAL PRINTING

Printed by the American Bank Note Company.

1883-85 **Soft porous paper** ***Perf. 12***

211B A57 2c **pale red brown,** with gum ('85)	375.	—
Never hinged	900.	
No gum	130.	
Block of 4	1,650.	
c. Horizontal pair, imperf. between	*2,000.*	
Never hinged	*3,000.*	
Top margin strip of 6, "Steamer-American Bank Note Co." imprint	*35,000.*	

Earliest documented use: May 23, 1885 (dated cancel on off-cover stamp).

No. 211B is from a special trial printing by a new steam-powered American Bank Note Company press. Approximately 1,000 of these stamps (in sheets of 200 with an imperf gutter between the panes of 100) were delivered as samples to the Third Assistant Postmaster General and subsequently made their way to the public market.

While use of No. 211B for postage was legal, actual usage was rare. Expertization is strongly recommended for suspected used examples.

211D A58 4c **deep blue green,** without gum *47,500.*

Postal records indicate that 26 examples of No. 211D were sold. Records also indicate an 1883 delivery and sales of 55 examples of the 2c red brown stamp, but there is no clear evidence that these can be differentiated from no gum examples of No. 210. No used examples of No. 211D are recorded.

REGULAR ISSUE

Printed by the American Bank Note Company.

Franklin — A59

1887 ***Perf. 12***

212 A59 1c **ultramarine,** *June*	90.00	2.50
bright ultramarine	90.00	2.50
Never hinged	290.00	
No gum	35.00	
On cover		3.25
Pair	190.00	5.25
Block of 4	425.00	37.50
P# strip of 5, Impt.	575.00	
P# strip of 6, Impt.	675.00	
P# block of 10, Impt.	*1,500.*	
Never hinged	*3,250.*	
P# block of 12, Impt.	*1,850.*	
Double transfer		—

See Die and Plate Proofs for imperf. on stamp paper.

Earliest documented use: July 15, 1887. The previously listed July 7, 1887, cover has not been adequately documented. The editors would like to see authenticated evidence of its existence.

Cancellations

Purple	+.10
Magenta	+.10
Blue	+.10
Red	+5.50
Numeral	+2.00
Railroad	+10.00
Supplementary Mail Type F	+5.00
China	—

213 A57 2c **green,** *Sept. 10*	40.00	.60
bright green	40.00	.60
dark green	40.00	.60
Never hinged	120.00	
No gum	15.00	
On cover		.75
Pair	85.00	1.30
Block of 4	190.00	10.50
P# strip of 5, Impt.	275.00	
P# strip of 6, Impt.	340.00	
P# block of 10, Impt.	*1,250.*	
Never hinged	*2,250.*	
P# block of 12, Impt.	*1,500.*	
Double transfer	—	3.25
b. Printed on both sides		—

See Die and Plate Proofs for imperf. on stamp paper.

Earliest documented use: Sept. 20, 1887 (dated cancel on off-cover stamp); Sept. 21, 1887 (on cover).

Cancellations

Purple	+.10
Magenta	+.10
Blue	+.90
Red	+5.00
Green	+25.00
"Paid"	+5.00
Railroad	+12.00
Numeral	+2.00
"Steam"	—
"Steamboat"	—
Supplementary Mail Type F	+7.50
China	—
Japan	—

214 A46b 3c **vermilion,** *Sept.*	60.00	50.00
Never hinged	180.00	
No gum	25.00	
On cover (single)		90.00
Pair	130.00	110.00
Block of 4	300.00	*350.00*
P# strip of 5, Impt.	400.00	
P# strip of 6, Impt.	475.00	
P# block of 10, Impt.	*1,300.*	
Never hinged	*2,750.*	
P# block of 12, Impt.	*1,500.*	

Earliest documented use: Sept. 23, 1887.

Cancellations

Purple	+5.00
Magenta	+5.00
Green	+150.00
Blue	+10.00
Supplementary Mail Type F	+15.00
Railroad	+30.00

Printed by the American Bank Note Company.

SAME AS 1870-83 ISSUES

1888 ***Perf. 12***

215 A58 4c **carmine,** *Nov.*	180.	25.00
rose carmine	180.	25.00
pale rose	180.	25.00
Never hinged	525.	
No gum	60.	
On cover		47.50
Pair	375.	52.50
Block of 4	850.	175.00
P# strip of 5, Impt.	1,350.	
Never hinged	*3,500.*	
P# strip of 6, Impt.	1,600.	
P# block of 10, Impt.	*4,500.*	
Never hinged	*6,500.*	
P# block of 12, Impt.	*5,300.*	

Earliest documented use: Dec. 26, 1888.

The earliest documented use of No. 215 has been questioned by specialists, even though the cover currently has a certificate of genuineness. The owner of this cover should contact the Scott editor for resubmission information.

Cancellations

Blue	+1.00
Red	+5.00
Purple	+2.00
Magenta	+2.00
Supplementary Mail Type F	+5.00

216 A56 5c **indigo,** *Feb.*	200.	17.50
deep blue	200.	17.50
Never hinged	625.	
No gum	75.	
On cover		35.00
Pair	425.	37.50
Block of 4	950.	140.00
P# strip of 5, Impt.	1,250.	
P# strip of 6, Impt.	1,750.	
P# block of 10, Impt.	*8,000.*	
P# block of 12, Impt.	*8,750.*	

Earliest documented use: Mar. 15, 1888.

Cancellations

Purple	+1.00
Magenta	+1.00
Blue	+1.00
Supplementary Mail Type F	+3.00
China	+85.00
Japan	+85.00
Puerto Rico	+75.00
Samoa	—

217 A53 30c **orange brown,** *Jan.*	250.	90.00
deep orange brown	250.	90.00
Never hinged	900.	
No gum	80.	
On cover		*1,400.*
Pair	575.	210.00
Block of 4	1,400.	650.00
P# strip of 5, Impt.	*2,200.*	
P# block of 10, Impt.	*8,500.*	
P# block of 12, Impt.	—	

Earliest documented use: April 16, 1888.

Cancellations

Blue	+5.00
Magenta	+10.00
Supplementary Mail Type F	+10.00
"Paid All"	+25.00
"Paid"	+15.00

218 A54 90c **purple,** *Feb.*	800.	225.00
bright purple	800.	225.00
Never hinged	2,500.	
No gum	250.	
On cover		*10,000.*
Pair	1,800.	500.
Block of 4	*4,750.*	1,400.
P# strip of 5, Impt.	*5,750.*	
P# block of 10, Impt.	*22,500.*	
P# block of 12, Impt.	—	

Earliest documented use: June 26, 1888 (dated cancel on off-cover stamp); Oct. 29, 1888 (on cover).

Cancellations

Blue	+80.00
Purple	+100.00
Supplementary Mail Type F	+25.00

See Die and Plate Proofs for imperfs. on stamp paper.

Printed by the American Bank Note Company.

Plates for the 1c were of 400 subjects in four panes of 100 each. Plates for the 2c were first of 400 subjects in four panes of 100 each, and later of 200 subjects in two panes of 100 each. All other values were from plates of 200 subjects in two panes of 100 each. Plates of 400 of the 1c and 2c show imprints in the side margins.

We'll buy your U.S. and Foreign stamp collections now and pay a price that just might amaze you.

Dr. Bob Friedman has been the nation's largest buyer and seller of United States and Foreign stamp collections for over 40 years.

We are a family owned and operated business and take great pride in our reputation for honesty and integrity. You can count on us to professionally examine all of the valuable philatelic material you have for sale and make you an attractive Full Market offer – whether a small valuable collection or a huge accumulation.

We generally have five million dollars available for immediate purchases. Our relationships are personal and confidential between you and Dr. Bob Friedman and over 95% of our offers for collections through the years have been accepted.

HERE ARE SOME SERIOUS FACTORS TO CONSIDER:

- **We will always offer to buy all of your valuable stamp collection.**
- **Dr. Bob Friedman can immediately travel to you for your valuable stamp collection.** No heavy lifting, no headaches, no need to pack and ship, and immediate on-the-spot payment.
- **Need an immediate response?** You may wish to ship your collection to us by UPS for an immediate offer and an overnight check. We can pay all shipping charges of collections sent to us. We can also provide all shipping and packing materials at your request.

Coin and Currency Collections wanted. Highest prices paid.

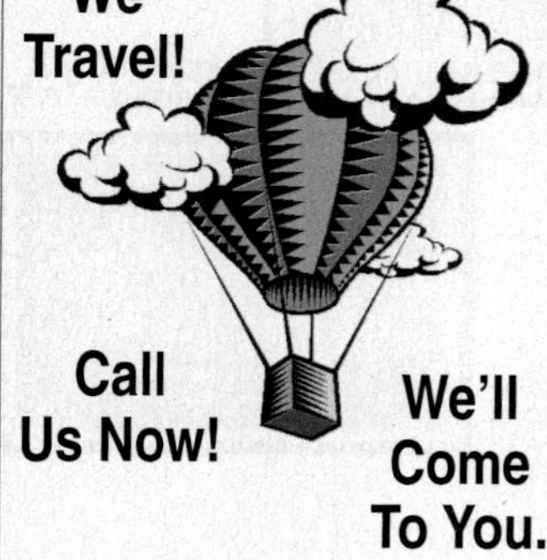

Call Toll Free & Ask For Dr. Bob:

1-800-588-8100

Dr. Robert Friedman

STAMPS

Dr. Robert Friedman Stamp Company
Dept. SC • 2029 West 75th Street • Woodridge IL 60517
Toll Free: (800) 588-8100 • Fax: (815) 725-4134
Visit our website: www.drbobfriedmanstamps.com
E-Mail: stampcollections@drbobstamps.com

Franklin — A60

Washington — A61

Jackson — A62

Lincoln — A63

Ulysses S. Grant — A64

Garfield — A65

William T. Sherman — A66

Daniel Webster — A67

Henry Clay — A68

Jefferson — A69

Perry — A70

1890-93 ***Perf. 12***

219 A60 1c **dull blue,** *Feb. 22, 1890* 20.00 .75
deep blue 20.00 .75
ultramarine 20.00 .75
Never hinged 65.00
On cover .80
Block of 4 85.00 5.25
P# strip of 5, Impt. & letter 125.00
P# strip of 6, Impt. & letter 150.00
P# strip of 7, Impt. & letter 175.00
P# block of 10, Impt. & letter 775.00
P# block of 12, Impt. & letter 1,075.
P# block of 14, Impt. & letter 1,450.
Never hinged *5,000.*
Double transfer — —

Earliest documented use: Feb 27, 1890.

Cancellations

Samoa —
China —

219D A61 2c **lake,** *Feb. 22, 1890* 160.00 5.50
Never hinged 500.00
On cover 7.50
Block of 4 675.00 47.50
P# strip of 5, Impt. 950.00
P# block of 10, Impt. 3,500.
Never hinged *6,500.*
Double transfer — —

Earliest documented use: Feb. 22, 1890 (FDC).

Cancellation

Supplementary Mail Type F +3.00

220 A61 2c **carmine,** *1890* 20.00 .70
dark carmine 20.00 .70
carmine rose 20.00 .70
rose 20.00 .70
Never hinged 60.00
On cover .75
Block of 4 85.00 3.00
P# strip of 5, Impt. & letter 125.00
P# strip of 6, Impt. & letter 150.00
Never hinged 290.00
P# strip of 7, Impt. & letter 175.00
P# block of 10, Impt. & letter 575.00
P# block of 12, Impt. & letter 900.00
Never hinged *1,350.*
P# block of 14, Impt. & letter 1,050.
Never hinged —
Double transfer — 3.25

a. Cap on left "2" (Plates 235-236, 246-247-248) 150.00 12.50
Never hinged 425.00
Block of 4 675.00 *150.00*
P# block of 10, Impt. *12,000.*
Never hinged *25,000.*
Pair, Nos. 220, 220a — —
Never hinged —

c. Cap on both "2's" (Plates 245, 246) 650.00 35.00
Never hinged 1,800.
Pair, Nos. 220a, 220c — —
Never hinged —

The No. 220 with "cap on right 2" variety is due to imperfect inking, not a plate defect.

Earliest documented uses: Feb. 18, 1890 (No. 220); Sept. 9, 1892 (No. 220a); July 7, 1892 (No. 220c).

Cancellations

Blue +.05
Purple +.05
Supp. Mail Types F or G +3.00
China +20.00

221 A62 3c **purple,** *Feb. 22, 1890* 55.00 9.00
bright purple 55.00 9.00
dark purple 55.00 9.00
Never hinged 175.00
On cover 17.50
Block of 4 250.00 55.00
P# strip of 5, Impt. 375.00
P# block of 10, Impt. 2,750.
Never hinged *4,000.*

Earliest documented use: Feb. 28, 1890.

Cancellation

Samoa —

222 A63 4c **dark brown,** *June 2, 1890* 80.00 4.75
blackish brown 80.00 4.75
Never hinged 240.00
On cover 10.00
Block of 4 400.00 35.00
P# strip of 5, Impt. 500.00
P# block of 10, Impt. 3,500.
Never hinged *9,000.*
Double transfer 95.00 25.00

Earliest documented use: July 16, 1890.

Cancellation

China +50.00

223 A64 5c **chocolate,** *June 2, 1890* 60.00 4.75
yellow brown 60.00 4.75
Never hinged 185.00
On cover 12.50
Block of 4 260.00 27.50
P# strip of 5, Impt. 350.00
P# block of 10, Impt. 2,800.
Never hinged 6,250.
Double transfer 85.00 5.25

Earliest documented use: June 14, 1890.

Cancellations

China +35.00
Samoa —
Supp. Mail Types F or G +7.50

224 A65 6c **brown red,** *Feb. 22, 1890* 50.00 25.00
dark brown red 50.00 25.00
Never hinged 160.00
On cover 40.00
Block of 4 250.00 130.00
P# strip of 5, Impt. 350.00
P# block of 10, Impt. 2,750.
Never hinged *4,500.*

Earliest documented use: May 8, 1890.

Cancellation

Supplementary Mail Type F +3.00

225 A66 8c **lilac,** *Mar. 21, 1893* 45.00 17.00
grayish lilac 45.00 17.00
magenta 45.00 17.00
Never hinged 135.00
On cover 32.50
Block of 4 200.00 100.00
P# strip of 5, Impt. 275.00
P# block of 10, Impt. 1,900.
Never hinged 3,250.

The 8c was issued because the registry fee was reduced from 10 to 8 cents effective Jan. 1, 1893.

Earliest documented use: May 4, 1893.

226 A67 10c **green,** *Feb. 22, 1890* 160.00 5.00
bluish green 160.00 5.00
dark green 160.00 5.00
Never hinged 475.00
On cover 10.00
Block of 4 700.00 42.50
P# strip of 5, Impt. 925.00
P# block of 10, Impt. 3,750.
Never hinged *6,000.*
Double transfer — —

Earliest documented use: Mar. 5, 1890.

Cancellations

Samoa —
Supp. Mail Type F or G +2.50

227 A68 15c **indigo,** *Feb. 22, 1890* 180.00 25.00
deep indigo 180.00 25.00
Never hinged 550.00
On cover 60.00
Block of 4 800.00 135.00
P# strip of 5, Impt. 1,250.
P# block of 10, Impt. *8,500.*
Never hinged *15,000.*
Double transfer — —
Triple transfer —

Earliest documented use: May 16, 1890.

Cancellation

Supplementary Mail Type F +3.00

228 A69 30c **black,** *Feb. 22, 1890* 280.00 30.00
gray black 280.00 30.00
full black 280.00 30.00
Never hinged 850.00
On cover *600.00*
Block of 4 1,300. 200.00
P# strip of 5, Impt. 1,800.
P# block of 10, Impt. *22,500.*
Never hinged —
Double transfer — —

Earliest documented use: April 14, 1890.

Cancellation

Supplementary Mail Type F +5.00

229 A70 90c **orange,** *Feb. 22, 1890* 450.00 130.00
yellow orange 450.00 130.00
red orange 450.00 130.00
Never hinged 1,350.
On cover —
Block of 4 2,000. 750.00
P# strip of 5, Impt. 2,750.
P# block of 10, Impt. *27,500.*
Never hinged *42,500.*
Short transfer at bottom — —
Nos. 219-229 (12) 1,560. 257.45

Earliest documented use: May 16, 1890 (dated cancel on off-cover stamp); Feb. 7, 1892 (on cover).

Cancellation

Supp. Mail Type F or G +10.00

VALUES FOR VERY FINE STAMPS
Please note: Stamps are valued in the grade of Very Fine unless otherwise indicated.

COLUMBIAN EXPOSITION ISSUE

World's Columbian Exposition, Chicago, Ill., May 1 - Oct. 30, 1893, celebrating the 400th anniv. of the discovery of America by Christopher Columbus.

See Nos. 2624-2629 for souvenir sheets containing stamps of designs A71-A86 but with "1992" at upper right.

Columbus in Sight of Land — A71

Landing of Columbus — A72

"Santa Maria," Flagship of Columbus — A73

YES! WE'RE THE #1 BUYERS.
BUT IF YOU'RE BUYING <u>SEE</u> OUR WEBSITE!

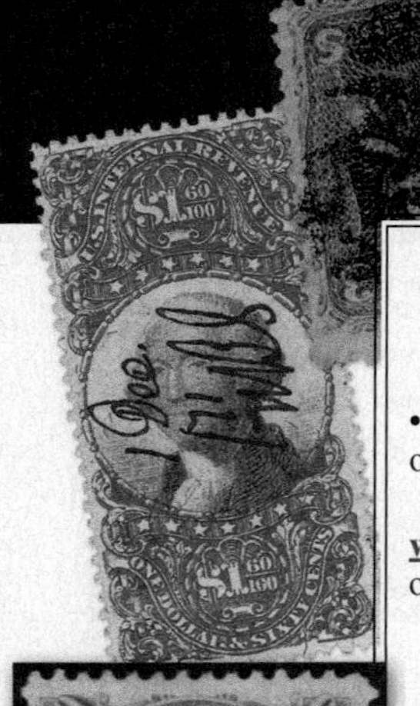

Entering our 40th year, our Guiding Philosophy remains:

"Whether Buying or Selling U.S. or Foreign stamps and collections, we want you to enjoy dealing with us as much as we enjoy dealing with you."

• **BUYING?** Our HUGE inventory of U.S. stamps is unmatched! And our coverage of the rest of the world also is formidable!

We make it easy for you! You can browse our vast inventory at:
www.GaryPosnerInc.com (where you will also find on the right of our home page a link to our PSE Graded stamps on the Collectors Corner site, as well as our major show schedule).

On eBay at www.ebay.com/str/garyposner with Best Offer options.
On HipStamp at https://www.hipstamp.com/store/garyposnerinc

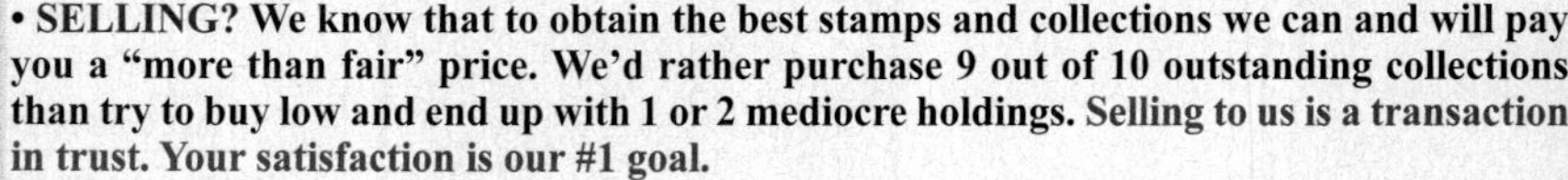

• SELLING? We know that to obtain the best stamps and collections we can and will pay you a "more than fair" price. We'd rather purchase 9 out of 10 outstanding collections than try to buy low and end up with 1 or 2 mediocre holdings. Selling to us is a transaction in trust. Your satisfaction is our #1 goal.

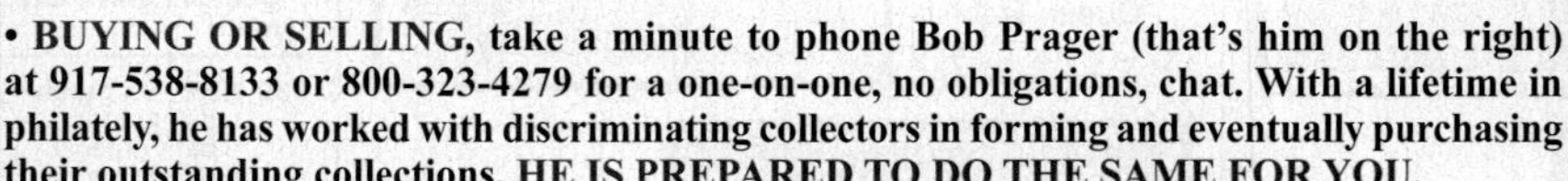

• BUYING OR SELLING, take a minute to phone Bob Prager (that's him on the right) at 917-538-8133 or 800-323-4279 for a one-on-one, no obligations, chat. With a lifetime in philately, he has worked with discriminating collectors in forming and eventually purchasing their outstanding collections. HE IS PREPARED TO DO THE SAME FOR YOU.

Our Reputation: It's a fact: more than half of our fine clients have come to us because of other clients. Our **outstanding national and international reputation** is so valuable—***and cherished by us***—that we protect it by making absolutely certain that the needs and wishes of the people we serve are honored every minute of every transaction—**BUYING and SELLING both United States and Foreign Material.**

Ask around. Check our references (we'll be pleased to show them to you). You'll see how our longstanding firm commitment to every individual we serve every day <u>is our reputation</u>—***and our most important asset***.

Call Toll Free • 800-323-4279

"There are many very good reasons why the greatest of **U.S. & Foreign stamps** have consistently passed through our hands. We carefully serve the very personal interests of every individual client. You can feel free to come to us because you can **ALWAYS** trust us to be confidential, expert, fair, and prompt."

Bob Prager

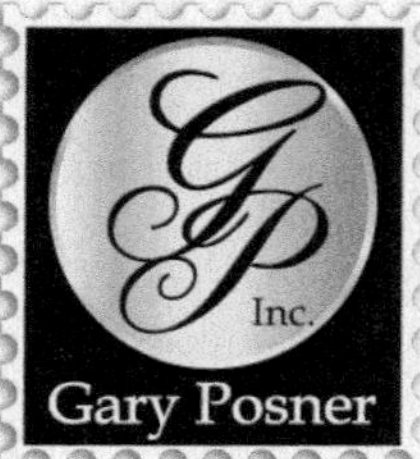

GARY POSNER,

Over 39 years in business • Phone: 800-323-4279 • Fax: 516-599-2145
265 Sunrise Highway • Suite 1-308 • Rockville Centre, NY 11570
Local Ph: 516-599-5969 • Cell 917-538-8133
Email: garyposnerinc@aol.com

www.GaryPosnerInc.com

We Also
BUY GOLD!

Fleet of Columbus — A74

Columbus Soliciting Aid from Queen Isabella — A75

Columbus Welcomed at Barcelona — A76

Columbus Restored to Favor — A77

Columbus Presenting Natives — A78

Columbus Announcing His Discovery — A79

Columbus at La Rábida — A80

Recall of Columbus — A81

Queen Isabella Pledging Her Jewels — A82

Columbus in Chains — A83

Columbus Describing His Third Voyage — A84

Queen Isabella and Columbus — A85

Columbus — A86

P AMERICAN BANK NOTE COMPANY. No. 67

Type of imprint and plate number

Exposition Station Handstamp Postmark

Printed by the American Bank Note Company.
Plates of 200 subjects in two panes of 100 each (1c, 2c).
Plates of 100 subjects in two panes of 50 each (2c-$5).
Issued (except 8c) Jan. 1 (a Sunday) and Jan. 2 (Monday), 1893. Jan. 1 and Jan. 2 first day covers are documented for the 1c, 2c, 3c, 4c, 5c and 10c. Jan. 2-only first day covers exist for the 6c and $2. See the First Day Cover section for values.

1893 *Perf. 12*

230 A71 1c **deep blue**	14.00	.40
blue	14.00	.40
pale blue	14.00	.40
Never hinged	32.50	
On cover		.90
Pair on cover, Expo. station machine canc.		100.00
Pair on cover, Expo. station duplex handstamp canc.		175.00
Block of 4	60.00	7.00
P# strip of 3, Impt.	60.00	
P# strip of 4, Impt. & letter	95.00	
P# block of 6, Impt.	450.00	
Never hinged	625.00	
P# block of 8, Impt. & letter	700.00	
Never hinged	1,000.	
Double transfer	19.00	.75
Cracked plate	80.00	

Earliest documented use: Jan. 1, 1893 (FDC).

Cancellations

China	—
Philippines	—

"Broken hat" variety

231 A72 2c **brown violet**	12.50	.30
deep brown violet	12.50	.30
gray violet	12.50	.30
Never hinged	31.00	
On cover		.35
On cover or card, Expo. station machine cancel		55.00
On cover or card, Expo. station duplex handstamp cancel		110.00
Block of 4	55.00	4.50
P# strip of 3, Impt.	55.00	
P# strip of 4, Impt. & letter	90.00	
Never hinged	225.00	
P# block of 6, Impt.	550.00	
Never hinged	750.00	
P# block of 8, Impt. & letter	800.00	
Never hinged	1,100.	
Double transfer	17.50	.35
Triple transfer	50.00	—
Quadruple transfer	80.00	
Broken hat on third figure to left of Columbus	55.00	3.50
Never hinged	160.00	
Broken frame line	16.00	.45
Recut frame lines	16.00	—
Cracked plate	65.00	—

There are a number of different versions of the broken hat variety, some of which may be progressive.
Earliest documented use: Jan. 1, 1893 (FDC).

Cancellations

China	—
Supplementary Mail Type G	+3.50

See Die and Plate Proofs for the 2c, imperf. on stamp paper.

232 A73 3c **green**	35.00	15.00
dull green	35.00	15.00
dark green	35.00	15.00
Never hinged	97.50	
On cover		30.00
On cover, Expo. station machine canc.		225.00
On cover, Expo. station duplex handstamp cancel		325.00
Block of 4	150.00	130.00
P# strip of 3, Impt.	150.00	
Never hinged	290.00	
P# strip of 4, Impt. & letter	230.00	
Never hinged	475.00	
P# block of 6, Impt.	700.00	
Never hinged	1,250.	
P# block of 8, Impt. & letter	1,175.	
Never hinged	2,000.	
Double transfer	52.50	—

Earliest documented use: Jan. 1, 1893 (FDC).

Cancellations

China	—
Supp. Mail Type F or G	+7.50

233 A74 4c **ultramarine**	50.00	8.00
dull ultramarine	50.00	8.00
deep ultramarine	50.00	8.00
Never hinged	140.00	
On cover		22.50
On cover, Expo. station machine canc.		275.00
On cover, Expo. station duplex handstamp cancel		400.00
Block of 4	225.00	67.50
P# strip of 3, Impt.	225.00	
P# strip of 4, Impt. & letter	360.00	—
P# block of 6, Impt.	950.00	
Never hinged	1,600.	
P# block of 8, Impt. & letter	1,700.	
Never hinged	3,000.	
Double transfer	85.00	—
a. 4c **blue** (error)	*17,500.*	*16,500.*
Never hinged	*32,500.*	
Block of 4	*90,000.*	—
Never hinged	*150,000.*	
P# strip of 4, Impt., letter	*150,000.*	

No. 233a exists in two shades. No. 233a used is valued with small faults, as almost all examples come thus.

Earliest documented use: Jan. 1, 1893 (FDC).

Cancellation

Supplementary Mail Type G	+3.00

234 A75 5c **chocolate**	50.00	8.50
pale brown	50.00	8.50
yellow brown	50.00	8.50
dark chocolate	50.00	8.50
Never hinged	140.00	
On cover		22.50
On cover, Expo. station machine canc.		275.00
On cover, Expo. station duplex handstamp cancel		400.00
Block of 4	225.00	75.00
P# strip of 3, Impt.	225.00	
P# strip of 4, Impt. & letter	375.00	

P# block of 6, Impt. 1,200.
Never hinged 2,100.
P# block of 8, Impt. & letter 2,500.
Never hinged 4,250.
Double transfer 105.00 —

Earliest documented use: Jan. 1, 1893 (FDC).

Cancellations

China —
Philippines —
Supplementary Mail Type F +3.00

235 A76 6c **purple** 50.00 22.50
dull purple 50.00 22.50
Never hinged 140.00
a. 6c **red violet** 50.00 22.50
Never hinged 140.00
On cover 45.00
On cover, Expo. station machine canc. 300.00
On cover, Expo. station duplex handstamp cancel 450.00
Block of 4 225.00 150.00
P# strip of 3, Impt. 225.00
P# strip of 4, Impt. & letter 360.00
P# block of 6, Impt. 1,150.
Never hinged 2,000.
P# block of 8, Impt. & letter 1,800.
Never hinged 3,100.
Double transfer 70.00 30.00

Earliest documented use: Jan. 2, 1893 (FDC).

Cancellations

China —
Supplementary Mail Type F +5.00

236 A77 8c **magenta,** *Mar. 1893* 47.50 10.00
light magenta 47.50 10.00
dark magenta 47.50 10.00
Never hinged 140.00
On cover 20.00
On cover, Expo. station machine canc. 300.00
On cover, Expo. station duplex handstamp cancel 475.00
Block of 4 225.00 85.00
P# strip of 3, Impt. 210.00
P# strip of 4, Impt. & letter 340.00
P# block of 6, Impt. 1,025.
Never hinged 1,650.
P# block of 8, Impt. & letter 1,550.
Never hinged 2,600.
Double transfer 57.50 —

Earliest documented use: Mar. 18, 1893.

Cancellations

China —
Supplementary Mail Type F +4.50

237 A78 10c **black brown** 90.00 8.00
dark brown 90.00 8.00
gray black 90.00 8.00
Never hinged 250.00
On cover 27.50
On cover, Expo. station machine canc. 400.00
On cover, Expo. station duplex handstamp cancel 550.00
Block of 4 400.00 80.00
P# strip of 3, Impt. 400.00
P# strip of 4, Impt. & letter 600.00
Never hinged 1,350.
P# block of 6, Impt. 3,000.
Never hinged *4,500.*
P# block of 8, Impt. & letter 4,500.
Never hinged *8,000.*
Double transfer 115.00 12.50
Triple transfer —

Earliest documented use: Jan. 1, 1893 (FDC).

Cancellations

Philippines —
Supp. Mail Types F or G +4.00

238 A79 15c **dark green** 200.00 72.50
green 200.00 72.50
dull green 200.00 72.50
Never hinged 600.00
On cover 210.00
On cover, Expo. station machine canc. 700.00
On cover, Expo. station duplex handstamp cancel *1,000.*
Block of 4 850. 600.00
P# strip of 3, Impt. 825.
P# strip of 4, Impt. & letter 1,350.
P# block of 6, Impt. *3,500.*
Never hinged *6,000.*
P# block of 8, Impt. & letter *5,500.*
Never hinged *12,000.*
Double transfer — —

Earliest documented use: Jan. 26, 1893.

Cancellations

China +75.00
Supp. Mail Type F or G +10.00

239 A80 30c **orange brown** 225.00 90.00
bright orange brown 225.00 90.00
Never hinged 675.00
On cover 375.00
On cover, Expo. station machine canc. *1,250.*
On cover, Expo. station duplex handstamp cancel *1,750.*
Block of 4 1,075. 850.00
P# strip of 3, Impt. 1,000.
P# strip of 4, Impt. & letter 1,450. —
P# block of 6, Impt. *7,500.*
Never hinged *12,500.*
P# block of 8, Impt. & letter *10,500.*
Never hinged *17,000.*

Earliest documented use: Jan. 10, 1893 (dated cancel on off-cover stamp); Feb. 8, 1893 (cover).

Cancellation

Supp. Mail Types F or G +25.00

240 A81 50c **slate blue** 425. 175.
dull slate blue 425. 175.
Never hinged 1,250.
No gum 190.
On cover 600.
On cover, Expo. station machine canc. *1,750.*
On cover, Expo. station duplex handstamp cancel 2,250.
Block of 4 1,750. 2,000.
P# strip of 3, Impt. 1,750.
P# strip of 4, Impt. & letter *3,250.* —
Never hinged 6,750.
P# block of 6, Impt. *10,500.*
Never hinged *18,000.*
P# block of 8, Impt. & letter *22,500.*
Never hinged *36,000.*
Double transfer — —
Triple transfer — —

Earliest documented use: Feb. 8, 1893.

Cancellation

Supp. Mail Types F or G +30.00

241 A82 $1 **salmon** 1,000. 525.
dark salmon 1,000. 525.
Never hinged 3,400.
No gum 500.
On cover *1,800.*
On cover, Expo. station machine canc. *3,500.*
On cover, Expo. station duplex handstamp cancel 4,500.
Block of 4 4,500. *5,000.*
P# strip of 3, Impt. 4,750.
P# strip of 4, Impt. & letter 8,250.
P# block of 6, Impt. *45,000.*
P# block of 8, Impt. & letter *75,000.*
Never hinged *130,000.*
Double transfer — —

Earliest documented use: Jan. 11, 1893 (dated cancel on off-cover stamp); Jan. 21, 1893 (on cover).

Cancellation

Supp. Mail Types F or G +50.

242 A83 $2 **brown red** 1,050. 525.
deep brown red 1,050. 525.
Never hinged 3,500.
No gum 500.
On cover *1,900.*

Send For Our New Current Quarterly U.S. Color CATALOG

Over 1,000 Graded Stamps!!
150 Pages
U.S. Stamps from 1847-1938
Over 3,000 STAMPS!!
A listing of over 2,000 F-VF and VF Mint & Used Stamps also included.

Send $3.00 Catalog Sent Priority Mail.
Sorry, no catalogs sent overseas but please see our online catalogue at: www.centurystamps.com.
Limit one catalog per request.

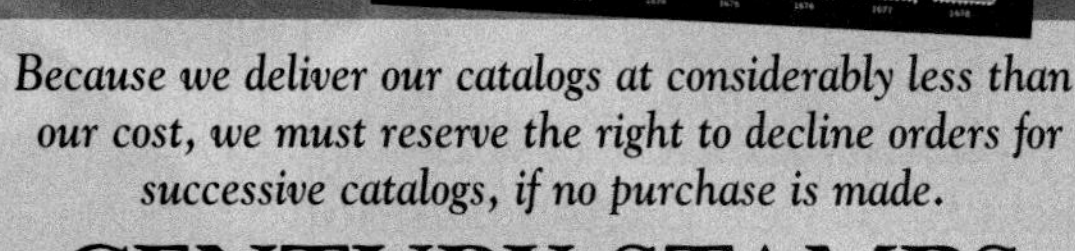

Because we deliver our catalogs at considerably less than our cost, we must reserve the right to decline orders for successive catalogs, if no purchase is made.

CENTURY STAMPS
42 Years of Quality & Service
P.O. Box 69, Dept. S, Huntington Sta., NY 11746
Phone: 631-385-4647 Fax: 631-385-4699
See our online catalogue at: www.century-stamps.com
email: centurystamps@hotmail.com

On cover, Expo. station machine canc.		*3,500.*
On cover, Expo. station duplex handstamp cancel		*4,500.*
Block of 4	4,600.	*5,500.*
P# strip of 3, Impt.	5,250.	
P# strip of 4, Impt. & letter	8,500.	
P# block of 6, Impt.	*150,000.*	
P# block of 8, Impt. & letter	*225,000.*	

Earliest documented use: Jan. 2, 1893 (FDC).

Cancellations

Supplementary Mail Type G	+50.

The No. 242 plate block of 8 is believed to be unique.

243 A84 $3 **yellow green**	1,350.	750.
pale yellow green	1,350.	750.
Never hinged	4,250.	
No gum	675.	
a. $3 **olive green**	1,350.	750.
Never hinged	4,250.	
No gum	675.	
On cover		*2,500.*
On cover, Expo. station machine canc.		*5,000.*
On cover, Expo. station duplex handstamp cancel		*7,000.*
Block of 4	*8,250.*	*10,000.*
P# strip of 3, Impt.	*7,500.*	
P# strip of 4, Impt. & letter	*13,500.*	
P# block of 6, Impt.	*200,000.*	

Earliest documented use: Mar. 24, 1893.

244 A85 $4 **crimson lake**	2,000.	950.
Never hinged	7,000.	
No gum	1,000.	
a. $4 **rose carmine**	2,000.	950.
pale aniline rose	2,000.	1,000.
Never hinged	7,000.	
No gum	1,000.	
On cover		*4,000.*
On cover, Expo. station machine canc.		*6,500.*
On cover, Expo. station duplex handstamp cancel		*9,000.*
Block of 4	*10,000.*	*15,000.*
P# strip of 3, Impt.	*11,500.*	
P# strip of 4, Impt. & letter	*40,000.*	
P# block of 6, Impt.	*500,000.*	
P# block of 8, Impt. & letter	—	

The No. 244 plate block of 8 is unique; it has full original gum with light hinge marks.

Earliest documented use: Mar. 24, 1893.

Cracked Plate

245 A86 $5 **black**	2,300.	1,150.
grayish black	2,300.	1,150.
Never hinged	9,500.	
No gum	1,150.	
On cover		*4,750.*
On cover, Expo. station machine canc.		*15,000.*
On cover, Expo. station duplex handstamp cancel		*17,500.*
Block of 4	*11,500.*	*15,000.*

WALTER KASELL STAMPS

Quality United States Stamps
Classics, U.S. Possessions & Plate Blocks
175 Richdale Ave., Cambridge, MA 02140
(617) 694-9360
Email: wbkasell@yahoo.com

P# strip of 3, Impt.	*13,500.*	
P# strip of 4, Impt. & letter	*55,000.*	
Never hinged	*150,000.*	
P# block of 6, Impt.	*290,000.*	
Never hinged	—	
P# block of 8, Impt. & letter	*325,000.*	
Cracked plate		—

Earliest documented use: Jan. 6, 1893.

The No. 245 plate block of 8 is unique; it has traces of original gum.

See Nos. 2624-2629 for souvenir sheets containing stamps of designs A71-A86 but with "1992" at upper right.

Nos. 230-245 exist imperforate; not issued. See Die and Plate proofs for the 2c.

Never-Hinged Stamps

See note before No. 182 regarding premiums for never-hinged stamps.

BUREAU ISSUES

In the following listings of postal issues mostly printed by the Bureau of Engraving and Printing at Washington, D.C., the editors acknowledge with thanks the use of material prepared by the Catalogue Listing Committee of the Bureau Issues Association.

The Bureau-printed stamps until 1965 were engraved except the Offset Issues of 1918-19 (Nos. 525-536). Engraving and lithography were combined for the first time for the Homemakers 5c (No. 1253). The Bureau used photogravure first in 1971 on the Missouri 8c (No. 1426).

Stamps in this section that were not printed by the Bureau begin with Nos. 909-921 and are so noted.

"*On cover*" listings carry through No. 701. Beyond this point a few covers of special significance are listed. Many Bureau Issue stamps are undoubtedly scarce properly used on cover. Most higher denominations exist almost exclusively on pieces of package wrapping and usually in combination with other values. Collector interest in covers is generally limited to fancy cancellations, attractive corner cards, uses abroad and other special usages.

Plate number blocks are valued unused. Although many exist used, and are scarcer in that condition, they tend to sell for less than the value of the unused examples because they are less sought after.

IMPRINTS AND PLATE NUMBERS

In listing the Bureau of Engraving & Printing Imprints, the editors have followed the classification of types adopted by the Bureau Issues Association. Types I, II, IV, V and VIII occur on postage issues and are illustrated below. Types III, VI and VII occur only on Special Delivery plates, so are illustrated with the listings of those stamps; other types are illustrated with the listings of the issues on which they occur.

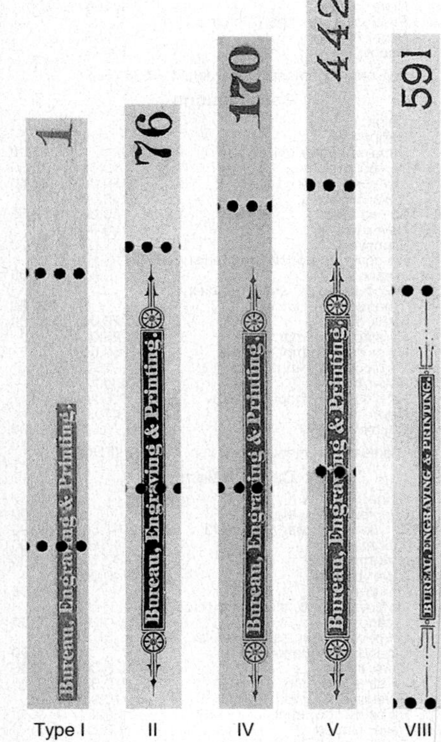

Type I II IV V VIII

In listing Imprint blocks and strips, the editors have designated for each stamp the various types known to exist. If, however, the Catalogue listing sufficiently describes the Imprint, no type number is given. Thus a listing reading: "P# block of 6, Impt. (Imprint) & A" in the 1912-14 series would not be followed by a type number as the description is self-explanatory. Values are for the most common types.

PLATE POSITIONS

At the suggestion of the Catalogue Listing Committee of the Bureau Issues Association (now the United States Stamp Society), all plate positions of these issues are indicated by giving the plate number first, next the pane position, and finally the stamp position. For example: 20234 L.L. 58.

Franklin — A87

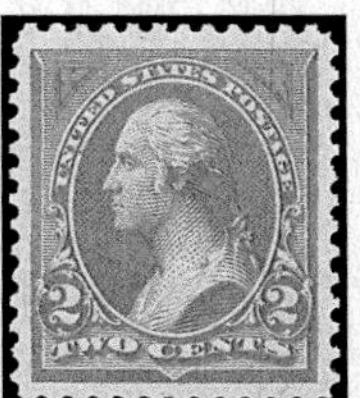

Washington — A88

Jackson — A89

Lincoln — A90

Grant — A91

Garfield — A92

Sherman — A93

Webster — A94

Clay — A95

Jefferson — A96

Perry — A97

James Madison — A98

John Marshall — A99

Designed by Thomas F. Morris.

REGULAR ISSUE

Plates for the issue of 1894 were of two sizes: 400 subjects for all 1c, 2c and 10c denominations; 200 subjects for all 6c, 8c, 15c, 50c, $1.00, $2.00 and $5.00, and both 400 and 200 subjects for the 3c, 4c and 5c denominations; all issued in panes of 100 each.

1894 **Unwmk.** ***Perf. 12***

246	A87 1c **ultramarine,** *Oct. 1894*	30.00	7.00
	bright ultramarine	30.00	7.00
	dark ultramarine	30.00	7.00
	Never hinged	90.00	
	On cover		22.50
	Block of 4	130.00	45.00
	P# strip of 3, Impt., T I	135.00	
	Never hinged	300.00	
	P# block of 6, Impt., T I	500.00	
	Never hinged	1,000.	
	Double transfer	37.50	8.00

Earliest documented use: Oct. 17, 1894.

Cancellation

	China		—
247	A87 1c **blue**	60.00	4.00
	bright blue	60.00	4.00
	dark blue	60.00	4.00
	Never hinged	175.00	
	On cover		18.50
	Block of 4	260.00	27.50
	P# strip of 3, Impt., T I or II	275.00	
	Never hinged	575.00	
	P# block of 6, Impt., T I or II	850.00	
	Never hinged	1,750.	
	Double transfer	—	5.00

Earliest documented use: Nov. 5, 1894.

Triangle A (Type I)

TWO CENTS

Type I (Triangle A). The horizontal lines of the ground work run across the triangle and are of the same thickness within it as without.

Triangle B (Type II)

Type II (Triangle B). The horizontal lines cross the triangle but are thinner within it than without. Other minor design differences exist, but the change to Triangle B is a sufficient determinant.

Triangle C (Types III and IV)

Type III (Triangle C). The horizontal lines do not cross the double lines of the triangle. The lines within the triangle are thin, as in Type II. The rest of the design is the same as Type II, except that most of the designs had the dot in the "S" of "CENTS" removed. Stamps with this dot present are listed; some specialists refer to them as "Type IIIa" varieties.

Type IV (Triangle C). See No. 279B and its varieties. Type IV is from a new die with many major and minor design variations including, (1) re-cutting and lengthening of hairline, (2) shaded toga button, (3) strengthening of lines on sleeve, (4) additional dots on ear, (5) "T" of "TWO" straight at right, (6) background lines extend into white oval opposite "U" of "UNITED." Many other differences exist.

For further information concerning type IV, see also George Brett's article in the Sept. 1993 issue of the "The United States Specialist" and the 23-part article by Kenneth Diehl in the Dec. 1994 through Aug. 1997 issues of the "The United States Specialist."

248	A88 2c **pink,** type I, *Oct. 1894*	30.00	9.00
	pale pink	30.00	9.00
	Never hinged	90.00	
	On cover		16.00
	Block of 4	130.00	47.50
	P# strip of 3, Impt., T I or II	125.00	
	Never hinged	300.00	
	P# block of 6, Impt., T I or II	325.00	
	Never hinged	750.00	
	Double transfer	—	—
a.	Vert. pair, imperf horiz.	*5,500.*	

Earliest documented use: Oct. 16, 1894.

249	A88 2c **carmine lake,** type I, *Oct. 1894*	150.00	7.00
	dark carmine lake	150.00	7.00
	Never hinged	450.00	
	On cover		12.50
	Block of 4	650.00	45.00
	P# strip of 3, Impt., T I or II	650.00	
	Never hinged	1,400.	
	P# block of 6, Impt., T I or II	2,750.	
	Never hinged	5,750.	
	Double transfer	—	8.00
a.	Double impression		—
250	A88 2c **carmine,** type I, *Oct. 1894*	29.00	3.00
	dark carmine	30.00	5.00
	Never hinged	85.00	
	On cover		4.00
	Block of 4	125.00	20.00
	P# strip of 3, Impt., T I or II	120.00	
	Never hinged	290.00	
	P# block of 6, Impt., T I or II	375.00	
	Never hinged	800.00	
a.	2c **rose,** type I, *Oct. 1894*	36.00	6.00
	Never hinged	105.00	
	On cover		7.25
	Block of 4	155.00	27.50
	P# strip of 3, Impt., T I or II	155.00	
	Never hinged	360.00	
	P# block of 6, Impt., T I or II	475.00	
	Never hinged	1,000.	
b.	2c **scarlet,** type I, *Jan. 1895*	26.00	3.00
	Never hinged	80.00	
	On cover		6.00
	Block of 4	110.00	32.50
	P# strip of 3, Impt., T I or II	105.00	
	Never hinged	250.00	
	P# block of 6, Impt., T I or II	350.00	
	Never hinged	750.00	
	Double transfer	—	5.50
d.	Horizontal pair, imperf. between	*2,000.*	

Earliest documented uses: Oct. 11, 1894 (No. 250), Oct. 13, 1894 (No. 250a), Jan. 17, 1895 (No. 250b).

Counterfeits exist of No. 250. See the Postal Counterfeits section of this catalog.

251	A88 2c **carmine,** type II, *Feb. 1895*	400.00	14.00
	dark carmine	400.00	14.00
	Never hinged	1,200.	
	On cover		22.50
	Block of 4	1,700.	105.00
	P# strip of 3, Impt., T II	1,600.	
	Never hinged	4,500.	
	P# block of 6, Impt., T II	4,000.	
	Never hinged	8,000.	
a.	2c **scarlet,** type II, *Feb. 1895*	375.00	13.00
	Never hinged	1,125.	
	On cover		21.00
	Block of 4	1,600.	100.00
	P# strip of 3, Impt., T II	1,500.	
	Never hinged	4,250.	
	P# block of 6, Impt., T II	3,500.	
	Never hinged	7,500.	

Earliest documented uses: Feb. 12, 1895 (No. 251, dated cancel on off-cover stamp); Feb. 16, 1895 (No. 251, on cover); Feb. 19, 1895 (No. 251a).

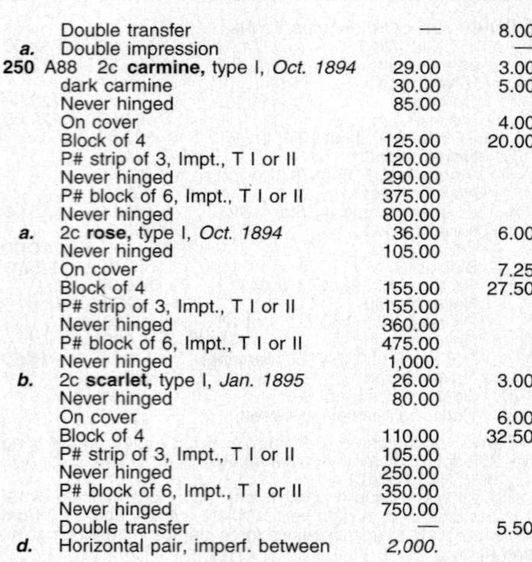

Visit our website today.

www.alanecohen.com

P. O. Box 929
New York, NY 10025
212-280-7865

e-mail: alanecohen@mindspring.com

252 A88 2c **carmine,** type III, *Mar. 1895* 135.00 13.00
pale carmine 135.00 13.00
Never hinged 400.00
On cover 22.50
Block of 4 600.00 120.00
P# strip of 3, Impt., T II or IV 600.00
Never hinged 1,400.
P# block of 6, Impt., T II or IV 2,100.
Never hinged 4,500.
a. 2c **scarlet,** type III, *Mar. 1895* 120.00 15.00
Never hinged 360.00
On cover 20.00
Block of 4 500.00 115.00
P# strip of 3, Impt., T II or IV 500.00
Never hinged 1,200.
P# block of 6, Impt., T II or IV 1,850.
Never hinged 4,000.
Dot in "S" of "CENTS" (carmine) 140.00 16.50
Never hinged 400.00
b. Horiz. pair, imperf. vert. *5,000.*
c. Horiz. pair, imperf. between *5,500.*

Earliest documented uses: Apr. 2, 1895 (dated cancel tying No. 252 dot in "S" variety on piece); Apr. 5, 1895 (No. 252); Apr. 17, 1895 (No. 252a).

No. 252b is unique and exists only as a horizontal top plate-number strip of 3. A right vertical plate-number strip of 3 from the same plate exists containing three stamps imperforate at left and right.

Counterfeits exist of No. 252. See the Postal Counterfeits section of this catalog.

253 A89 3c **purple,** *Sept. 1894* 120.00 12.00
dark purple 120.00 12.00
Never hinged 360.00
On cover 27.50
Block of 4 500.00 85.00
Margin block of 4, arrow, R or L 525.00
P# strip of 3, Impt., T I or II 475.00
Never hinged 1,200.
P# block of 6, Impt., T I or II 1,500.
Never hinged 3,250.

Earliest documented use: Oct. 20, 1894 (dated cancel on off-cover stamp); Nov. 15, 1894 (on cover).

See Die and Plate Proofs for imperf. on stamp paper.

254 A90 4c **dark brown,** *Sept. 1894* 200.00 11.00
brown 200.00 11.00
Never hinged 600.00
On cover 22.50
Block of 4 850.00 60.00
Margin block of 4, arrow, R or L 875.00
P# strip of 3, Impt., T I or II 800.00
Never hinged 1,950.
P# block of 6, Impt., T I or II 2,300.
Never hinged 5,000.

Earliest documented use: Oct. 16, 1894 (dated cancel on off-cover stamp); Nov. 2, 1894 (on cover).

See Die and Plate Proofs for imperf. on stamp paper.

Cancellation

Supplementary Mail Type F +2.00

255 A91 5c **chocolate,** *Sept. 1894* 120.00 9.00
deep chocolate 120.00 9.00
yellow brown 120.00 9.00
Never hinged 360.00
On cover 22.50
Block of 4 500.00 52.50
Margin block of 4, arrow, R or L 525.00
P# strip of 3, Impt., T I, II or IV 500.00
Never hinged 1,200.
P# block of 6, Impt., T I, II or IV 1,500.
Never hinged 3,000.
Double transfer 150.00 10.00
Worn plate, diagonal lines missing in oval background 140.00 10.00
c. Vert. pair, imperf. horiz. *3,500.*
P# block of 6, Impt., T IV *15,000.*

The plate block of No. 255c is in a unique block of 9 stamps. Beware of a No. 255Pb plate block that is known to have been reperforated to resemble No. 255c.

Earliest documented use: Oct. 23, 1894.

See Die and Plate Proofs for imperf. on stamp paper.

Cancellations

Supplementary Mail Type G +2.00
China —

256 A92 6c **dull brown,** *July 1894* 160.00 27.50
Never hinged 475.00
On cover 50.00
Block of 4 700.00 185.00
Margin block of 4, arrow, R or L 725.00
P# strip of 3, Impt., T I 675.00
Never hinged 1,650.
P# block of 6, Impt., T I 3,250. —
Never hinged *6,500.*
a. Vert. pair, imperf. horiz. *3,000.*
P# block of 6, Impt., T I *30,000.*

Earliest documented use: Aug. 11, 1894.

257 A93 8c **violet brown,** *Mar. 1895* 160.00 20.00
bright violet brown 160.00 20.00
Never hinged 475.00
On cover 50.00
Block of 4 700.00 130.00
Margin block of 4, arrow, R or L 725.00
P# strip of 3, Impt., T I 675.00
Never hinged 1,600.
P# block of 6, Impt., T I 2,500.
Never hinged *5,500.*

Earliest documented use: May 8, 1895.

258 A94 10c **dark green,** *Sept. 1894* 275.00 20.00
green 275.00 20.00
dull green 275.00 20.00
Never hinged 850.00
On cover 37.50
Block of 4 1,150. 100.00
P# strip of 3, Impt., T I 1,250.
Never hinged 2,700.
P# block of 6, Impt., T I 3,250.
Never hinged *6,750.*
Double transfer 325.00 22.50

Earliest documented use: Oct. 2, 1894.

See Die and Plate Proofs for imperf. on stamp paper.

Cancellations

China —
Supp. Mail Types F, G +2.00

259 A95 15c **dark blue,** *Oct. 1894* 275.00 65.00
indigo 275.00 65.00
Never hinged 850.00
On cover 125.00
Block of 4 1,150. 425.00
Margin block of 4, arrow, R or L 1,200.
P# strip of 3, Impt., T I 1,250.
Never hinged 2,750.
P# block of 6, Impt., T I 4,750.
Never hinged *9,500.*

Earliest documented use: Dec. 6, 1894.

Cancellation

China —

260 A96 50c **orange,** *Nov. 1894* 475. 140.
deep orange 475. 140.
Never hinged 1,425.
On cover 950.
Block of 4 2,250. 1,100.
Margin block of 4, arrow, R or L 2,350.
P# strip of 3, Impt., T I 2,300.
Never hinged *4,750.*
P# block of 6, Impt., T I 20,000.
Never hinged *32,500.*

Earliest documented use: Dec. 12, 1894 (dated cancel on off-cover stamp); Jan. 15, 1895 (on cover).

Cancellations

Supp. Mail Type F or G —
China —

Type I

Type II

ONE DOLLAR

Type I. The circles enclosing "$1" are broken where they meet the curved line below "One Dollar."

Type II. The circles are complete.

The fifteen left columns of impressions from the plate of 200 subjects are Type I, the other five columns being Type II.

261 A97 $1 **black,** type I, *Nov. 1894* 1,000. 350.
grayish black 1,000. 350.
Never hinged 3,150.
No gum 400.
On cover *2,750.*
Block of 4 4,500. *2,100.*
Margin block of 4, arrow, L 4,750.
P# strip of 3, Impt., T V 4,250.
P# block of 6, Impt., T V *20,000.*

Earliest documented use: Jan. 18, 1895.

261A A97 $1 **black,** type II, *Nov. 1894* 2,100. 800.
Never hinged 6,500.
No gum 850.
On cover *4,500.*
Block of 4 *9,000.* *5,000.*
Margin block of 4, arrow, R *9,500.*
Horizontal pair, types I and II *4,000.* *1,400.*
Block of 4, two each of types I and II *9,500.* —
P# strip of 3, Impt., T V, one stamp No. 261 10,000.
P# block of 6, Impt., T V, two stamps No. 261 *75,000.*

Earliest documented use: Mar. 22, 1895. A Mar. 11, 1895, cover has been reported. The editors would like to see evidence of certification of this date.

262 A98 $2 **bright blue,** *Dec. 1894* 2,750. 1,200.
Never hinged 8,750.
No gum 1,100.
dark blue 2,900. 1,250.
Never hinged 9,250.
On cover *5,000.*
Block of 4 *12,500.* *9,500.*
Margin block of 4, arrow, R or L *13,000.*
P# strip of 3, Impt., T V *13,500.*
P# block of 6, Impt., T V *45,000.*

The only recorded plate block of 6 of No. 262 has average centering and is valued as such.

Earliest documented use: July 6, 1895 (dated cancel on off-cover stamp); July 15, 1895 (on cover).

263 A99 $5 **dark green,** *Dec. 1894* 4,000. 2,600.
Never hinged 14,000.
No gum 2,100.
On cover —
Block of 4 *20,000.* *16,000.*
Margin block of 4, arrow, R or L *21,000.*
P# strip of 3, Impt., T V *25,000.*

Earliest documented use: July 6, 1896 (dated cancel on off-cover stamp).

Top plate block positions on the unwatermarked dollar-denomination stamps, Nos. 261, 261A, 262 and 263, do not exist. The Bureau of Engraving and Printing trimmed the top selvage before issuing the panes. Therefore, only bottom position plate blocks exist for these stamps.

REGULAR ISSUE

Designed by Thomas F. Morris.

(Actual size of letter)

repeated in rows, thus

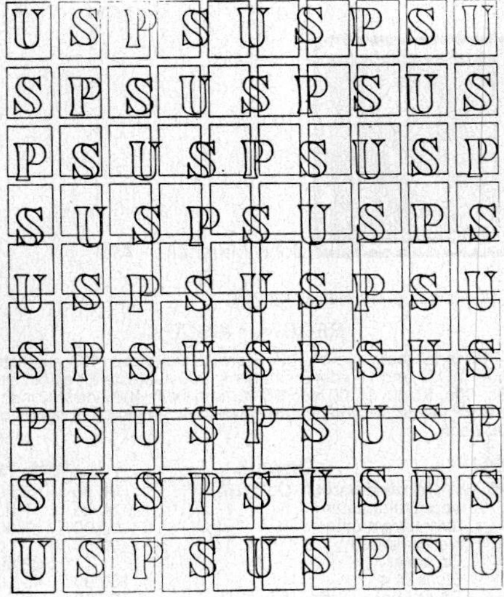

Watermarks are viewed from the back of the stamp.

Note that the letters "USPS" in watermark 191 occur in a pattern called "backward stepping." That is, each row of letters begins one letter to the left of the row above. A second variety of this watermark was discovered in 2009. In this "forward-stepping" watermark, each row of letters begins one letter to the right of the row above.

All watermarked Bureau issues printed before Jan. 1903 were on paper with the backward-stepping watermark. After 1902, stamps printed in fiscal years 1902-03, 1903-04, 1906-07 and 1909-10 have backward-stepping watermarks, while stamps printed in fiscal years 1904-05, 1905-06, 1907-08 and 1908-09 have forward-stepping watermarks.

Some issues are found only on paper with the forward-stepping watermark. These include Nos. 357-366, 367-369 and TD10.

Twelve stamps have been confirmed on which both types of watermark appear. They are Nos. 300, 301, 319, 331a, 332a, 343, 344, E6 and J39-J42. Many more are expected to exist thus and should be reported to the editors.

It is expected that exceptions to the general rules will be found occasionally, and the editors welcome new reports by collectors and dealers.

HORIZONTAL WATERMARK ORIENTATIONS

USPS — Normal; Reversed; Inverted; Inverted Reversed

VERTICAL WATERMARK ORIENTATIONS

Normal; Reversed; Inverted; Inverted Reversed

This catalog does not list the different watermark orientations shown above for individual stamps. What research has been done indicates many stamp issues show most or all of the orientations, and most orientations do not appear to be very much scarcer than the others.

Watermark 191

The letters stand for "United States Postage Stamp."

Plates for the 1895 issue were of two sizes:

400 subjects for all 1c, 2c and 10c denominations; 200 subjects for all 3c, 4c, 5c, 6c, 8c, 15c, 50c, $1, $2 and $5; all issued in panes of 100 each.

Printings from the 400 subject plates show the watermark reading horizontally, on the 200 subject printings the watermark reads vertically.

Same as 1894 Issue

Wmk. 191 Horizontally or Vertically

1895 ***Perf. 12***

No.	Description	Unused	Used
264	A87 1c **blue,** *Apr. 1895*	6.00	.60
	dark blue	6.00	.60
	pale blue	6.00	.60
	Never hinged	17.50	
	On cover		1.25
	Block of 4	26.00	5.00
	P# strip of 3, Impt., T I, II, IV or V	26.00	
	Never hinged	65.00	
	P# block of 6, Impt., T I, II, IV or V	240.00	
	Never hinged	450.00	
	Double transfer	—	1.10

Earliest documented use: May 16, 1895.

The bottom margin plate-number strip of 3, imperforate vertically, formerly No. 264a, is now listed in the Proofs section as No. 264P5a.

Cancellations

China		—
Philippines		—
Samoa		—

No.	Description	Unused	Used
265	A88 2c **carmine,** type I, *May 1895*	35.00	3.50
	deep carmine	35.00	3.50
	Never hinged	105.00	
	On cover		5.50
	Block of 4	150.00	18.00
	P# strip of 3, Impt., T II	130.00	
	Never hinged	325.00	
	P# block of 6, Impt., T II	450.00	
	Never hinged	900.00	
	Double transfer	50.00	7.25

Earliest documented use: May 2, 1895.

No.	Description	Unused	Used
266	A88 2c **carmine,** type II, *May 1895*	40.00	5.50
	Never hinged	120.00	
	On cover		8.50
	Block of 4	240.00	40.00
	Horizontal pair, types II and III	220.00	17.50
	Never hinged	600.00	
	P# strip of 3, Impt., T II or IV	150.00	
	Never hinged	375.00	
	P# block of 6, Impt., T II or IV	525.00	
	Never hinged	1,100.	

Earliest documented use: May 27, 1895.

No.	Description	Unused	Used
267	A88 2c **carmine,** type III, *May 1895*	5.50	.50
	deep carmine	5.50	.50
	reddish carmine	5.50	.50
	Never hinged	16.00	
	On cover		.65
	Block of 4	24.00	3.50
	P# strip of 3, Impt., T II, IV or V	22.50	
	Never hinged	57.50	
	P# block of 6, Impt., T II, IV or V	190.00	
	Never hinged	325.00	
	Dot in "S" of "CENTS"	7.50	.60
	Never hinged	22.50	
	Double transfer	16.50	1.30
a.	2c **pink,** type III, *Nov. 1897*	20.00	5.00
	Never hinged	60.00	
	bright pink	25.00	7.50
	Never hinged	75.00	
	On cover		6.00
	Block of 4	90.00	32.50
	P# strip of 3, Impt., T II, IV or V	75.00	
	Never hinged	200.00	
	P# block of 6, Impt., T II, IV or V	425.00	
	Never hinged	825.00	
	Dot in "S" of "CENTS"	35.00	5.50
	Never hinged	110.00	
b.	2c **vermilion,** type III, *early 1899*	*50.00*	15.00
c.	2c **rose carmine,** type III, *Mar. 1899*	—	—

No. 267-267c type III plate numbers run through plate #503. No. 279B type IV plate numbers start at #505.

Earliest documented uses:
No. 267, May 23, 1895;
No. 267 with dot in "S", July 15, 1895;
No. 267a, Dec. 8, 1897;
No. 267a with dot in "S", Mar. 18, 1898.

Cancellations

Green		—
China		—
Hawaii		—
Philippines		—
Samoa		—

The three left vertical rows of impressions from plate 170 are Type II, the balance being Type III.

No.	Description	Unused	Used
268	A89 3c **purple,** *Oct. 1895*	37.50	2.25
	dark purple	37.50	2.25
	Never hinged	115.00	
	On cover		8.00
	Block of 4	160.00	21.00
	Margin block of 4, arrow, R or L	175.00	
	P# strip of 3, Impt., T II or V	150.00	
	Never hinged	400.00	
	P# block of 6, Impt., T II or IV	725.00	
	Never hinged	1,300.	
	Double transfer	45.00	4.75

Earliest documented use: Dec. 1, 1895.

Cancellations

Guam		—
China		—
Philippines		—

No.	Description	Unused	Used
269	A90 4c **dark brown,** *June, 1895*	42.50	3.50
	dark yellow brown	42.50	3.50
	Never hinged	125.00	
	On cover		8.00
	Block of 4	180.00	35.00
	Margin block of 4, arrow, R or L	200.00	
	P# strip of 3, Impt., T I, II, IV or V	180.00	
	Never hinged	450.00	
	P# block of 6, Impt., T I, II, IV or V	775.00	
	Never hinged	1,600.	
	Double transfer	50.00	5.50

Earliest documented use: June 24, 1895.

Cancellations

Philippines		—
China		—
Samoa		—

No.	Description	Unused	Used
270	A91 5c **chocolate,** *June, 1895*	35.00	3.50
	deep brown	35.00	3.50
	chestnut	35.00	3.50
	Never hinged	105.00	
	On cover		8.00
	Block of 4	150.00	30.00
	Margin block of 4, arrow, R or L	160.00	
	P# strip of 3, Impt., T I, II, IV or V	145.00	
	Never hinged	375.00	
	P# block of 6, Impt., T I, II, IV or V	675.00	
	Never hinged	1,300.	
	Double transfer	42.50	5.00
	Worn plate, diagonal lines missing in oval background	37.50	3.75

Earliest documented use: Sept. 12, 1895.

Cancellations

China		—
Supplementary Mail G		+2.50

No.	Description	Unused	Used
271	A92 6c **dull brown,** *Aug. 1895*	110.00	8.50
	claret brown	110.00	8.50
	Never hinged	325.00	
	On cover		27.50
	Block of 4	525.00	70.00
	Margin block of 4, arrow, R or L	550.00	
	P# strip of 3, Impt., T I, IV or V	475.00	
	Never hinged	1,200.	
	P# block of 6, Impt., T I, IV or V	2,900.	
	Never hinged	5,500.	
	Very thin paper	130.00	9.50
a.	Wmkd. USIR	*15,000.*	*8,500.*
	Pair	—	—

Earliest documented use: Sept. 14, 1895.

Cancellation

Philippines		—

No. 271a unused is valued in the grade of fine.

Nos. 271a, 272a must have an identifiable portion of the letters "I" or "R." Single stamps from the same sheets, but showing the "U" or "S" are considered to be Nos. 271 and 272.

No.	Description	Unused	Used
272	A93 8c **violet brown,** *July 1895*	70.00	2.75
	dark violet brown	70.00	2.75
	Never hinged	210.00	
	On cover		14.00
	Block of 4	300.00	17.50
	Margin block of 4, arrow, R or L	310.00	
	P# strip of 3, Impt., T I, IV or V	300.00	
	Never hinged	750.00	
	P# block of 6, Impt., T I, IV or V	975.00	
	Never hinged	2,100.	
	Double transfer	85.00	4.25
a.	Wmkd. USIR	*6,000.*	950.00
	Block of 4		*5,500.*
	P# strip of 3 Impt., T I	*18,000.*	

Earliest documented use: Sept. 11, 1895.

Cancellations

China		—
Guam		—
Philippines		—
Puerto Rico, 1898		—
Samoa		—
Supplementary Mail Type G		+2.50

No.	Description	Unused	Used
273	A94 10c **dark green,** *June 1895*	95.00	2.25
	green	95.00	2.25
	Never hinged	280.00	
	On cover		15.00
	Block of 4	400.00	21.00
	P# strip of 3, Impt., T I or IV	410.00	
	Never hinged	1,000.	
	P# block of 6, Impt., T I or IV	1,750.	
	Never hinged	3,500.	
	Double transfer	120.00	4.75

Earliest documented use: July 25, 1895.

Cancellations

Green		—
China		—
Cuba		—
Philippines		—
Supp. Mail Types F, G		+2.00

No.	Description	Unused	Used
274	A95 15c **dark blue,** *Sept. 1895*	200.00	17.50
	indigo	200.00	17.50
	Never hinged	600.00	
	On cover		55.00
	Block of 4	875.00	105.00
	Margin block of 4, arrow, R or L	900.00	
	P# strip of 3, Impt., T I or IV	825.00	
	Never hinged	2,200.	
	P# block of 6, Impt., T I or IV	4,500.	
	Never hinged	*10,000.*	

Earliest documented use: May 5, 1896.

Cancellations

China		—
Philippines		—
Supplementary Mail Type G		+3.00

No.	Description	Unused	Used
275	A96 50c **orange,** *Nov. 1895*	240.	40.00
	Never hinged	725.	
	On cover		400.00
	Block of 4	1,075.	225.00
	Margin block of 4, arrow, R or L	1,125.	
	P# strip of 3, Impt., T I	1,000.	
	P# block of 6, Impt., T I	*7,500.*	
	Never hinged	*17,500.*	
a.	50c **red orange**	325.	47.50
	Never hinged	975.	
	On cover		425.00
	Block of 4	1,500.	275.00
	Margin block of 4, arrow, R or L	1,550.	
	P# strip of 3, Impt., T I	1,500.	
	P# block of 6, Impt., T I	*7,000.*	

Earliest documented use: May 5, 1896.

Cancellations

China		—
Philippines		—
Supp. Mail Types F, G		+5.

No.	Description	Unused	Used
276	A97 $1 **black,** type I, *Aug. 1895*	600.	95.
	greenish black	600.	95.
	Never hinged	1,800.	
	No gum	250.	
	On cover		*2,250.*
	Block of 4	2,600.	750.
	Margin block of 4, arrow, L	2,700.	
	P# strip of 3, Impt., T V	*3,000.*	
	Never hinged	*6,000.*	
	P# block of 6, Impt., T V	*40,000.*	

Earliest documented use: April 9, 1897.

Cancellation

Philippines		—

No.	Description	Unused	Used
276A	A97 $1 **black,** type II, *Aug. 1895*	1,250.	200.
	greenish black	1,250.	200.
	Never hinged	3,750.	
	No gum	500.	
	On cover		*3,750.*
	Block of 4	5,500.	1,500.
	Margin block of 4, arrow, R	5,750.	
	Horizontal pair, types I and II	*2,250.*	*2,600.*
	Block of 4, two each of types I and II	*6,000.*	*6,500.*
	P# strip of 3, Impt., T V, one stamp No. 276	*5,000.*	
	P# block of 6, Impt., T V, two stamps No. 276	*125,000.*	

Earliest documented use: Apr. 6, 1896.

Cancellations

China		—
Philippines		—

The fifteen left columns of impressions from the plate of 200 subjects are Type I, the other five columns being Type II.

No.	Description	Unused	Used
277	A98 $2 **bright blue**	900.	400.
	Never hinged	2,900.	
	No gum	375.	
a.	$2 **dark blue**	900.	400.
	Never hinged	2,900.	
	No gum	375.	

	On cover		*3,500.*
	Block of 4	*4,000.*	*3,000.*
	Margin block of 4, arrow, R or L	*4,250.*	
	P# strip of 3, Impt., T V	*4,500.*	*2,000.*
	P# block of 6, Impt., T V	*90,000.*	

Earliest documented use: July 18, 1895.

Cancellation

	Supplementary Mail Type G		—
278	A99 $5 **dark green,** *Aug. 1895*	2,000.	600.
	Never hinged	6,250.	
	No gum	800.	
	On cover		*10,000.*
	Block of 4	*9,000.*	*4,000.*
	Margin block of 4, arrow, R or L	*9,500.*	
	P# strip of 3, Impt., T V	*9,750.*	
	P# block of 6, Impt., T V	*200,000.*	

The plate block of 6 of No. 278 is unique.

Earliest documented use: Nov. 3, 1896.

See Die and Plate Proofs for imperf. or horiz. pair, imperf. vert. (1c) on stamp paper.

REGULAR ISSUE

Designed by Thomas F. Morris.

Plates for the sheet stamps for the 1897-1903 issue were of two sizes:

400 subjects for the 1c and 2c denominations; 200 subjects for all 4c, 5c, 6c and 15c denominations; and both 400 and 200 for the 10c denomination; all issued in panes of 100 each.

Printings from the 400 subject plates show the watermark reading horizontally. On the 200 subject plate printings the watermark reads vertically.

Plates for booklet panes for the 1897-1903 issue were of two sizes: 360 subjects and 180 subjects. Printings from the 360-subject plates show the watermark reading horizontally, while printings from the 180-subject plates show the watermark reading vertically.

In January, 1898, the color of the 1-cent stamp was changed to green and in March, 1898, that of the 5-cents to dark blue in order to conform to the colors assigned these values by the Universal Postal Union. These changes necessitated changing the colors of the 10c and 15c denominations in order to avoid confusion.

Wmk. 191 Horizontally or Vertically

1897-1903 ***Perf. 12***

279	A87 1c **deep green,** horizontal watermark, *Jan. 1898*	9.00	.50
	green	9.00	.50
	yellow green	9.00	.50
	dark yellow green	9.00	.50
	Never hinged	25.00	
	On cover		.60
	Block of 4	37.50	5.00
	P# strip of 3, Impt., T V	37.50	—
	Never hinged	85.00	
	P# block of 6, Impt., T V	185.00	
	Never hinged	350.00	
	Double transfer	12.00	1.10
a.	1c **deep green, vertical** watermark (error), *May 1902*	*50.00*	*7.50*
	Never hinged	*150.00*	
	On cover		*22.50*
	Block of 4	*200.00*	
	P# strip of 3, Impt., T V	*350.00*	
	Never hinged	*700.00*	

Earliest documented use: Jan. 31, 1898

Cancellations

	China		—
	Guam		—
	Puerto Rico, 1898		—
	Philippines		—
279B	A88 2c **red,** type IV *May 1899*	9.00	.40
	light red, *May 1899*	9.00	.40
	Never hinged	25.00	
	deep red, *Sept. 1901*	13.50	1.25
	Never hinged	32.50	
	On cover		.50
	Block of 4	37.50	3.00
	P# strip of 3, Impt., T V	37.50	
	Never hinged	85.00	
	P# block of 6, Impt., T V	200.00	
	Never hinged	360.00	
	P# strip of 4, Impt., T V (plate 802, UR position)	*250.00*	
	P# block of 8, Impt., T V (plate 802, UR position)	*750.00*	
	Double transfer	18.00	.75
	Triple transfer	—	
	Triangle at upper right without shading	22.50	6.00
c.	2c **rose carmine,** type IV, *Mar. 1899*	275.00	220.00
	bright carmine rose, *Mar. 1899*	275.00	220.00
	Never hinged	850.00	
	pinkish rose carmine	—	
	Never hinged	—	
	Block of 4	1,200.	—
	P# strip of 3, Impt., T V	1,150.	
	Never hinged	2,750.	
	P# block of 6, Impt., T V	4,000.	

No. 279Bc in the pinkish rose carmine shade is essentially the same shade as the rose carmine stamp, but the ink contains a pink pigment from an aniline ink that causes fluorescence under ultraviolet light.

d.	2c **orange red,** type IV, horizontal watermark, *June 1900*	11.50	2.00
	pale orange red	11.50	2.00
	dark orange red, *Sept. 1902*	11.50	2.00
	deep orange red, *Jan. 1903*	11.50	2.00
	Never hinged	32.50	
	On cover		2.50
	Block of 4	50.00	12.50
	P# strip of 3, Impt., T V	42.50	
	Never hinged	115.00	
	P# block of 6, Impt., T V	220.00	
	Never hinged	400.00	
e.	2c **orange red,** type IV, **vertical** watermark (error), *May 1902*	*55.00*	*12.50*
	Never hinged	*170.00*	
	On cover		*22.50*
	Block of 4	*250.00*	
	P# strip of 3, Impt., T V	*325.00*	
	Never hinged	*800.00*	
	P# block of 6, Impt., T V, never hinged	*2,850.*	
f.	2c **carmine,** type IV, *Nov. 1897*	10.00	2.00
	reddish carmine, *Dec. 1898*	10.00	2.00
	Never hinged	27.50	
	On cover		2.25
	Block of 4	42.50	12.50
	P# strip of 3, Impt., T V	40.00	
	Never hinged	95.00	
	P# block of 6, Impt., T V	220.00	
	Never hinged	385.00	
g.	2c **pink,** type IV, *Nov. 1897*	55.00	7.50
	Never hinged	165.00	
	bright pink	65.00	15.00
	Never hinged	200.00	
	On cover		8.00
	Block of 4	250.00	40.00
	P# strip of 3, Impt., T V	190.00	
	Never hinged	550.00	
	P# block of 6, Impt., T V	625.00	
	Never hinged	1,250.	
h.	2c **vermilion,** type IV, *Jan. 1899*	12.50	3.00
	pale vermilion	12.50	3.00
	Never hinged	35.00	
	On cover		5.00
	Block of 4	47.50	20.00
	P# strip of 3, Impt., T V	45.00	
	Never hinged	120.00	
	P# block of 6, Impt., T V	235.00	
	Never hinged	425.00	
i.	2c **brown orange,** type IV, *Jan. 1899*	*400.00*	*100.00*
	Never hinged	*950.00*	
	P# strip of 3, Impt., T V	*1,500.*	
j.	Booklet pane of 6, **red,** type IV, horizontal watermark, *Apr. 18, 1900*	500.00	*3,000.*
	light red	500.00	*3,000.*
	orange red, *1901*	500.00	*3,000.*
	Never hinged	1,000.	
k.	Booklet pane of 6, **red,** type IV, vertical watermark ('02)	500.00	—
	Never hinged	1,000.	
	orange red	750.00	—
	Never hinged	1,500.	
l.	As No. 279B, all color missing (FO)	*500.00*	

No. 279Bl must be collected se-tenant with a partially printed stamp.

Earliest documented uses:
No. 279B, July 6, 1899;
No. 279Bc, Mar 30, 1899;
No. 279Bc in bright rose carmine, July 16, 1899;
No. 279Bd, June 8, 1900;
No. 279Bf, Nov. 18, 1897;
No. 279Bg, Dec. 1, 1897;
No. 279Bh, Feb. 27, 1899;
No. 279Bj booklet single (red), May 4, 1900;
No. 279Bj booklet single (orange red), May 7, 1902.

Cancellations

	Puerto Rico, 1898		—
	Philippines, 1898		—
	Guam, 1899 or 1900		—
	Supplementary Mail Type G		+4.00
	Cuba, 1898		—
	China		+35.00
	Samoa		+20.00
280	A90 4c **rose brown,** *Oct. 1898*	30.00	3.25
	Never hinged	80.00	
a.	4c **lilac brown**	30.00	3.25
	brownish claret	30.00	4.00
	Never hinged	80.00	
b.	4c **orange brown**	30.00	3.00
	Never hinged	80.00	
	On cover		7.50
	Block of 4	130.00	25.00
	Margin block of 4, arrow, R or L	140.00	
	P# strip of 3, Impt., T V	110.00	
	Never hinged	300.00	
	P# block of 6, Impt., T V	700.00	
	Never hinged	1,250.	
	Double transfer	35.00	5.00
	Extra frame line at top (Plate 793 R 62)	55.00	9.50

Earliest documented use: Nov. 13, 1898.

Cancellations

	Supplementary Mail Type G		+3.00
	China		+35.00
	Philippines		+20.00
	Samoa		—
281	A91 5c **dark blue,** *Mar. 1898*	32.50	2.25
	blue	32.50	2.25
	bright blue	32.50	2.25
	Never hinged	100.00	
	On cover		10.00
	Block of 4	140.00	14.00
	Margin block of 4, arrow, R or L	150.00	
	P# strip of 3, Impt., T V	135.00	
	Never hinged	340.00	
	P# block of 6, Impt., T V	650.00	
	Never hinged	1,250.	
	Double transfer	42.50	4.50
	Worn plate (diagonal lines missing in oval background)	37.50	2.75

Earliest documented use: Mar. 19, 1898.

Cancellations

	Puerto Rico, 1898		—
	Supplementary Mail Type G		+4.00
	China		—
	Cuba		—
	Guam		—
	Philippines		—
	Samoa		—
282	A92 6c **lake,** *Dec. 1898*	45.00	6.50
	claret	45.00	6.50
	Never hinged	140.00	
	On cover		17.50
	Block of 4	190.00	50.00
	Margin block of 4, arrow, R or L	200.00	
	P# strip of 3, Impt., T V	190.00	
	Never hinged	475.00	
	P# block of 6, Impt., T V	900.00	
	Never hinged	1,650.	
	Double transfer	55.00	9.00
a.	6c **purple lake**	75.00	20.00
	Never hinged	225.00	
	Block of 4	350.00	110.00
	Margin block of 4, arrow	375.00	
	P# strip of 3, Impt., T V	325.00	
	Never hinged	800.00	
	P# block of 6, Impt., T V	1,300.	
	Never hinged	2,300.	

Earliest documented use: Mar. 13, 1899.

Cancellations

	Supplementary Mail Type G		+4.00
	China		—
	Philippines		—

Type I. The tips of the foliate ornaments do not impinge on the white curved line below "ten cents."

282C	A94 10c **brown,** type I, *Nov. 1898*	175.00	6.50
	dark brown	175.00	6.50
	Never hinged	525.00	
	On cover		18.00
	Block of 4	750.00	57.50
	P# strip of 3, Impt., T IV or V	725.00	
	Never hinged	1,750.	
	P# block of 6, Impt., T IV or V	2,600.	
	Never hinged	*4,500.*	
	Double transfer	220.00	11.00

Earliest documented use: Dec. 10, 1898.

Cancellation

	Supplementary Mail Type G		+2.50

Type II. The tips of the ornaments break the curved line below the "e" of "ten" and the "t" of "cents."

283	A94 10c **orange brown,** type II, horizontal watermark	150.00	6.00
	brown	150.00	6.00
	yellow brown	150.00	6.00
	Never hinged	450.00	
	On cover		17.50
	Block of 4	650.00	50.00
	P# strip of 3, Impt., T V	550.00	
	Never hinged	1,500.	
	P# block of 6, Impt., T V	1,900.	
	Never hinged	3,750.	
	Double transfer		—
	Pair, type I and type II	*15,000.*	*6,000.*
a.	10c **orange brown,** type II, vertical watermark, *early 1900*	*250.00*	*15.00*
	Never hinged	*775.00*	
	On cover		*35.00*
	Block of 4	*1,050.*	
	Margin block of 4, arrow, R or L	1,100.	—
	P# strip of 3, Impt., T V	*1,100.*	
	Never hinged	*2,750.*	
	P# block of 6, Impt., T V	*3,000.*	
	Never hinged	*5,500.*	

Earliest documented use: Mar. 13, 1899.

Cancellations

	Supplementary Mail Type G		+2.50
	China		—
	Puerto Rico		—

On the 400 subject plate 932, all are Type I except the following: UL 20; UR 11, 12, 13; LL 61, 71, 86, these 7 being Type II.

284	A95 15c **olive green,** *Nov. 1898*	150.00	13.00
	dark olive green	150.00	13.00
	Never hinged	475.00	
	On cover		32.50
	Block of 4	650.00	90.00
	Margin block of 4, arrow, R or L	700.00	

P# strip of 3, Impt., T IV 600.00
Never hinged 1,575.
P# block of 6, Impt., T IV 2,250.
Never hinged 4,250.

Earliest documented use: Mar. 3, 1899.

Cancellations

Supp. Mail Type F or G +2.50
China —
Samoa —

Nos. 279-284 (8) 600.50 38.40

For "I.R." overprints, see Nos. R153-R155A.

VALUES FOR VERY FINE STAMPS
Please note: Stamps are valued in the grade of Very Fine unless otherwise indicated.

TRANS-MISSISSIPPI EXPOSITION ISSUE

Omaha, Nebr., June 1 - Nov. 1, 1898.

Jacques Marquette on the Mississippi A100

Farming in the West — A101

Indian Hunting Buffalo — A102

John Charles Frémont on the Rocky Mountains A103

Troops Guarding Wagon Train — A104

Hardships of Emigration A105

Western Mining Prospector A106

Western Cattle in Storm — A107

Mississippi River Bridge, St. Louis — A108

Exposition Station Handstamp Postmark

Designed by Raymond Ostrander Smith.

Plates of 100 (10x10) subjects, divided vertically into 2 panes of 50.

See Nos. 3209-3210 for bi-colored reproductions of Nos. 285-293.

1898, June 17 **Wmk. 191** ***Perf. 12***

285 A100 1c **dark yellow green** 27.50 7.00
yellow green 27.50 7.00
green 27.50 7.00
Never hinged 82.50
On cover 10.00
On card, Expo. station canc. 200.00
Pair, on cover, Expo. station canc. 300.00
Block of 4 120.00 47.50
Margin block of 4, arrow, R or L 130.00 —
P# pair, Impt., T VIII 65.00
Never hinged 175.00
P# strip of 3, Impt., T VIII 115.00
Never hinged 275.00
P# block of 4, Impt., T VIII 275.00
Never hinged 440.00
P# block of 6, Impt., T VIII 500.00
Never hinged 800.00
Double transfer 37.50 8.00

Earliest documented use: June 17, 1898 (FDC).

Cancellations

Supp. Mail Type F or G +1.50
China —
Philippines —
Puerto Rico, 1898 —

286 A101 2c **copper red** 25.00 2.75
brown red 25.00 2.75
light brown red 25.00 2.75
Never hinged 72.50
On cover 3.75
On cover, Expo. station canc. 175.00
Block of 4 110.00 16.00
Margin block of 4, arrow, R or L 120.00 —
P# pair, Impt., T VIII 60.00
Never hinged 160.00
P# strip of 3, Impt., T VIII 105.00
Never hinged 250.00
P# block of 4, Impt., T VIII 260.00
Never hinged 430.00
P# block of 6, Impt., T VIII 500.00
Never hinged 800.00
Double transfer 35.00 4.00
Worn plate 27.50 3.25

Earliest documented use: June 17, 1898 (FDC).

Cancellations

China —
Hawaii —
Puerto Rico, 1898 —
Philippines —

287 A102 4c **orange** 110.00 25.00
deep orange 110.00 25.00
Never hinged 330.00
On cover 60.00
On cover, Expo. station canc. 750.00
Block of 4 475.00 190.00
Margin block of 4, arrow, R or L 460.00 —
P# pair, Impt., T VIII 275.00
Never hinged 725.00
P# strip of 3, Impt., T VIII 425.00
Never hinged 1,050.
P# block of 4, Impt., T VIII 850.00
Never hinged 1,550.
P# block of 6, Impt., T VIII 1,750.
Never hinged 3,250.

Earliest documented use: June 17, 1898 (FDC).

Cancellations

Supp. Mail Type F or G +5.00
China —
Philippines —

288 A103 5c **dull blue** 100.00 25.00
bright blue 100.00 25.00
Never hinged 300.00
On cover 50.00
On cover, Expo. station canc. 500.00
Block of 4 430.00 160.00
Margin block of 4, arrow, R or L 450.00 —
P# pair, Impt., T VIII 260.00 —
Never hinged 675.00
P# strip of 3, Impt., T VIII 400.00
Never hinged 950.00
P# block of 4, Impt., T VIII 800.00
Never hinged 1,600.
P# block of 6, Impt., T VIII 1,600.
Never hinged 3,250.

Earliest documented use: June 17, 1898 (FDC).

Cancellations

Supp. Mail Type F or G +5.00
China —
Philippines —
Puerto Rico, 1898 —

289 A104 8c **violet brown** 140.00 47.50
dark violet brown 140.00 47.50
Never hinged 430.00
On cover 120.00
On cover, Expo. station canc. 1,000.
Block of 4 600.00 300.00
Margin block of 4, arrow, R or L 625.00 —
P# pair, Impt., T VIII 350.00
P# strip of 3, Impt., T VIII 625.00
P# block of 4, Impt., T VIII 1,950.
Never hinged 3,400.
P# block of 6, Impt., T VIII 3,250.
Never hinged 5,500.
a. Vert. pair, imperf. horiz. *27,500.*
P# block of 4, Impt., T VIII *160,000.*

Earliest documented use: June 17, 1898 (FDC).

Cancellations

Philippines —
Samoa —

290 A105 10c **gray violet** 140.00 35.00
blackish violet 140.00 35.00
Never hinged 425.00
On cover 90.00
On cover, Expo. station canc. 750.00
Block of 4 600.00 210.00
Margin block of 4, arrow, R or L 625.00 —
P# pair, Impt., T VIII 375.00
Never hinged 1,025.
P# strip of 3, Impt., T VIII 550.00
Never hinged 1,500.
P# block of 4, Impt., T VIII 2,100.
Never hinged 3,600.
P# block of 6, Impt., T VIII 3,500.
Never hinged 6,000.

Earliest documented use: June 17, 1898 (FDC).

Cancellations

Supplementary Mail Type G +5.00
China —
Philippines —

291 A106 50c **sage green** 600.00 175.00
dark sage green 600.00 175.00
Never hinged 1,800.
On cover 1,750.
Block of 4 2,750. 1,250.
Margin block of 4, arrow, R or L 3,000. —
P# pair, Impt., T VIII 1,800.
Never hinged 4,350.
P# strip of 3, Impt., T VIII *2,750.*
Never hinged *6,900.*
P# block of 4, Impt., T VIII *17,500.*
Never hinged *27,500.*
P# block of 6, Impt., T VIII *30,000.*
Never hinged *70,000.*

Earliest documented use: June 17, 1898 (FDC).

Cancellations

Supp. Mail Type F or G +25.
Cuba —
Philippines —

292 A107 $1 **black** 1,500. 700.
Never hinged 3,750.
No gum 850.
On cover *4,500.*
Block of 4 *7,000.* *4,000.*
Margin block of 4, arrow, R or L *7,250.*
P# pair, Impt., T VIII *4,000.*
Never hinged *8,750.*
P# strip of 3, Impt., T VIII *6,500.*
Never hinged *15,000.*
P# block of 4, Impt., T VIII *35,000.*
Never hinged *52,500.*
P# block of 6, Impt., T VIII *65,000.*
Never hinged *100,000.*

Earliest documented use: June 17, 1898 (FDC).

Cancellation

Philippines —

293 A108 $2 **orange brown** 1,900. 1,050.
dark orange brown 1,900. 1,050.
Never hinged 5,750.
No gum 950.
On cover *12,500.*
Block of 4 *8,000.* *6,000.*

Margin block of 4, arrow, R or L	*8,250.*	
P# pair, Impt., T VIII	*9,000.*	
Never hinged	*16,500.*	
P# strip of 3, Impt., T VIII	*15,000.*	
P# block of 4, Impt., T VIII	*100,000.*	
Never hinged	—	
P# block of 6, Impt., T VIII	*175,000.*	
Nos. 285-293 (9)	4,543.	2,067.

Earliest documented use: June 24, 1898.

Never-Hinged Stamps

See note before No. 182 regarding premiums for never-hinged stamps.

PAN-AMERICAN EXPOSITION ISSUE

Buffalo, N.Y., May 1 - Nov. 1, 1901.
On sale May 1-Oct. 31, 1901.

Fast Lake Navigation (Steamship "City of Alpena") — A109

Empire State Express — A110

Electric Automobile in Washington — A111

Bridge at Niagara Falls — A112

Canal Locks at Sault Ste. Marie — A113

Fast Ocean Navigation (Steamship "St. Paul") — A114

Exposition Station Duplex Handstamp Cancellation

Exposition Station Machine Cancellation

Designed by Raymond Ostrander Smith.

Plates of 200 subjects in two panes of 100 each.

1901, May 1 Wmk. 191 *Perf. 12*

294 A109 1c **green & black**	16.00	3.00
dark blue green & black	16.00	3.00
Never hinged	40.00	
On cover		4.50
On Expo. cover or card, Expo. station machine canc.		50.00
On Expo. cover or card, Expo. station duplex handstamp canc.		170.00
Block of 4	67.50	25.00
Margin block of 4, top arrow & markers	70.00	
Margin block of 4, bottom arrow & markers & black P#	72.50	
P# strip of 3, Impt., T V	75.00	
Never hinged	150.00	
P# block of 6, Impt., T V	300.00	
Never hinged	475.00	
P# strip of 5, bottom Impt. T V, two P#, arrow & markers	110.00	
Never hinged	250.00	
Margin block of 10, bottom Impt., T V, two P#, arrow & markers	700.00	
Never hinged	1,100.	
Double transfer	25.00	5.25
a. Center inverted	*12,500.*	*25,000.*
Never hinged	*22,500.*	
On cover		—
Block of 4	*75,000.*	
P# strip of 4, Impt.	*167,500.*	

Earliest documented uses: May 1, 1901 (No. 294 FDC); Aug. 2, 1901 (No. 294a). The No. 294a cover sold at auction in 1999 for $121,000. Two other uses on cover are recorded.

295 A110 2c **carmine & black**	15.00	1.00
carmine & gray black	15.00	1.00
dark carmine & black	15.00	1.00
rose carmine & black	15.00	1.00
scarlet & black	15.00	1.00
Never hinged	37.50	
On cover		1.50
On Expo. cover or card, Expo. sta. machine cancel		60.00
On Expo. cover or card, Expo. sta. duplex handstamp canc.		200.00
Block of 4	62.50	8.00
Margin block of 4, top arrow & markers	65.00	
P# block of 4, bottom arrow & markers and black P#	67.50	
P# strip of 3, Impt., T V	62.50	
Never hinged	135.00	
P# block of 6, Impt., T V	300.00	
Never hinged	475.00	
P# strip of 5, bottom Impt., T V, two P#, arrow & markers	125.00	
Never hinged	240.00	
P# block of 10, bottom Impt., T V, two P#, arrow & markers	600.00	
Never hinged	1,000.	
Double transfer	24.00	2.25
a. Center inverted	*50,000.*	*55,000.*
Block of 4	*900,000.*	

Almost all unused examples of No. 295a have partial or disturbed gum. Values are for examples with full original gum that is slightly disturbed. Value for No. 295a used is for a well-centered example with faults, as there are no known fault-free examples.

Earliest documented use: May 1, 1901 (No. 295 FDC); Feb. 26, (1902?) (No. 295a, dated cancel on off-cover stamp). The dated No. 295a stamp is the only used example showing a date of any kind. Sold at auction in 2007 for $83,375.

The block of 4 of No. 295a is unique. Value reflects sale price at 2009 auction.

296 A111 4c **deep red brown & black**	70.00	18.00
chocolate & black	70.00	18.00
Never hinged	170.00	
On cover		42.50
On cover, Expo. station machine cancel		350.00
On cover, Expo. station duplex handstamp canc.		*750.00*
Block of 4	300.00	140.00
Margin block of 4, top arrow & markers	320.00	
P# block of 4, bottom arrow & markers & black P#	340.00	
P# strip of 3, Impt., T V	300.00	
Never hinged	650.00	
P# block of 6, Impt., T V	2,000.	
Never hinged	*3,250.*	
P# strip of 5, bottom Impt., T V, two P#, arrow & markers	550.00	
Never hinged	1,125.	
P# block of 10, bottom Impt., T V, two P#, arrow & markers	*4,000.*	
Never hinged	*5,750.*	
a. Center inverted	*85,000.*	—
Block of 4	*400,000.*	
P# strip of 4, Impt.	*450,000.*	

No. 296a was a Special Printing and not regularly issued. Almost all unused examples of No. 296a have partial or disturbed gum. Values are for examples with full orginal gum that is slightly disturbed.

See No. 296a-S, "Specimen" Stamps.

Earliest documented use: May 1, 1901 (FDC).

297 A112 5c **ultramarine & black**	75.00	17.00
dark ultramarine & black	75.00	17.00
Never hinged	180.00	
On cover		45.00
On cover, Expo. station machine cancel		350.00
On cover, Expo. station duplex handstamp canc.		*750.00*
Block of 4	325.00	130.00
Margin block of 4, top arrow & markers	350.00	
P# block of 4, bottom arrow & markers & black P#	375.00	
P# strip of 3, Impt., T V	310.00	
Never hinged	625.00	
P# block of 6, Impt., T V	2,100.	
Never hinged	*3,600.*	
P# strip of 5, bottom Impt., T V, two P#, arrow & markers	625.00	
Never hinged	1,250.	
P# block of 10, bottom Impt., T V, two P#, arrow & markers	*4,250.*	
Never hinged	*6,000.*	

Earliest documented use: May 1, 1901 (FDC).

298 A113 8c **brown violet & black**	90.00	50.00
purplish brown & black	90.00	50.00
Never hinged	230.00	
On cover		110.00
On cover, Expo. station machine cancel		*750.00*
On cover, Expo. station duplex handstamp canc.		*1,250.*
Block of 4	400.00	425.00
Margin block of 4, top arrow & markers	425.00	
P# block of 4, bottom arrow & markers & black P#	475.00	
P# strip of 3, Impt., T V	400.00	
Never hinged	850.00	
P# block of 6, Impt., T V	*3,800.*	
Never hinged	*6,000.*	
P# strip of 5, bottom Impt., T V, two P#, arrow & markers	800.00	
Never hinged	1,600.	
P# block of 10, bottom Impt., T V, two P#, arrow & markers	*6,500.*	
Never hinged	*9,000.*	

Earliest documented use: May 1, 1901 (FDC).

299 A114 10c **yellow brown & black**	115.00	30.00
dark yellow brown & black	115.00	32.50
Never hinged	300.00	
On cover		125.00
On cover, Expo. station machine cancel		*1,000.*
On cover, Expo. station duplex handstamp canc.		*1,500.*
Block of 4	525.00	250.00
Margin block of 4, top arrow & markers	550.00	
P# block of 4, bottom arrow & markers & black P#	625.00	
P# strip of 3, Impt., T V	525.00	
Never hinged	1,100.	
P# block of 6, Impt., T V	6,500.	
Never hinged	*8,500.*	
P# strip of 5, bottom Impt., T V, two P#, arrow & markers	1,075.	
Never hinged	2,150.	
P# block of 10, bottom Impt., T V, two P#, arrow & markers	*9,500.*	
Never hinged	*13,000.*	
Nos. 294-299 (6)	381.00	119.00
Nos. 294-299, never hinged	957.50	

Earliest documented use: May 1, 1901 (FDC).

VALUES FOR VERY FINE STAMPS

Please note: Stamps are valued in the grade of Very Fine unless otherwise indicated.

Franklin — A115

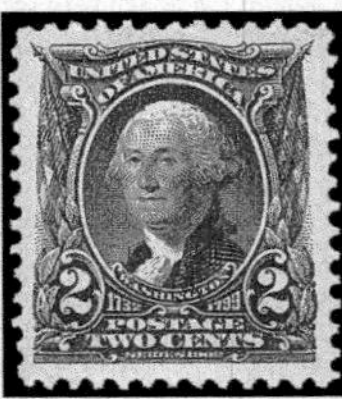

Washington — A116

Jackson — A117

Grant — A118

Lincoln — A119

Garfield — A120

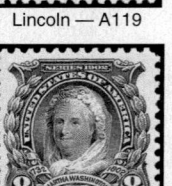

Martha Washington — A121

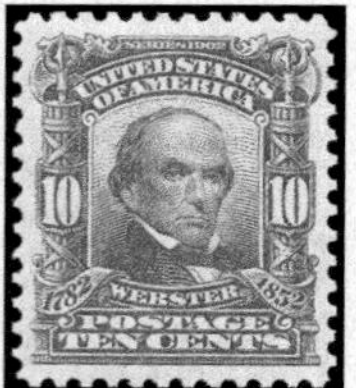

Daniel Webster — A122

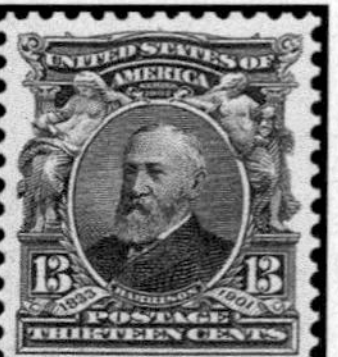

Benjamin Harrison — A123

Henry Clay — A124

Jefferson — A125

David G. Farragut — A126

Madison — A127

Marshall — A128

REGULAR ISSUE

Designed by Raymond Ostrander Smith and/or Clair Aubrey Huston.

Plates of 400 subjects in four panes of 100 each for all values from 1c to 15c inclusive. Certain plates of 1c, 2c type A129, 3c and 5c show a round marker in margin opposite the horizontal guide line at right or left.

Plates of 200 subjects in two panes of 100 each for 15c, 50c, $1, $2 and $5.

Many stamps of this issue are known with blurred printing due to having been printed on dry paper.

1902-03 **Wmk. 191** ***Perf. 12***

300 A115	1c **blue green,** *Feb. 1903*	12.00	.25
	green	12.00	.25
	deep green	12.00	.25
	gray green	12.00	.25
	yellow green	12.00	.25
	Never hinged	30.00	
	On cover		.75
	Block of 4	52.50	3.50
	P# strip of 3, Impt., T V	50.00	
	Never hinged	100.00	
	P# block of 6, Impt., T V	225.00	
	Never hinged	350.00	
	Double transfer	17.50	1.00
	Worn plate	13.00	.35
	Cracked plate	14.00	.30
b.	Booklet pane of 6, *Mar. 6, 1907*	600.00	*11,500.*
	Never hinged	1,150.	
	Wmk. horiz.	*2,000.*	

Earliest documented uses: Feb. 3, 1903 (No. 300); Mar. 22, 1907 (No. 300b single).

301 A116	2c **carmine,** *Jan. 22, 1903*	15.00	.50
	bright carmine	15.00	.50
	deep carmine	15.00	.50
	carmine rose	15.00	.50
	Never hinged	37.50	
	On cover		1.00
	Block of 4	62.50	5.50
	P# strip of 3, Impt., T V	60.00	
	Never hinged	120.00	
	P# block of 6, Impt., T V	275.00	
	Never hinged	425.00	
	Double transfer	27.00	1.40
	Cracked plate	—	1.40
c.	Booklet pane of 6, *Jan. 24, 1903*	500.00	*6,000.*
	Never hinged	950.00	

Earliest documented use: Jan. 26, 1903 (No. 301); Mar. 28, 1903 (No. 301c single); Apr. 4, 1903 (No. 301c pane).

Four unused single imperforate sheet margin examples of No. 301 are recorded. These are considered printer's waste, but they are sought by specialists. Value, $5,000.

302 A117	3c **bright violet,** *Feb. 1903*	55.00	3.75
	violet	55.00	3.75
	deep violet	55.00	3.75
	Never hinged	140.00	
	On cover		11.00
	Block of 4	230.00	32.50
	P# strip of 3, Impt., T V	215.00	
	Never hinged	425.00	
	P# block of 6, Impt., T V	750.00	
	Never hinged	1,300.	
	Double transfer	77.50	4.50
	Cracked plate	—	—

Earliest documented use: Mar. 14, 1903.

303 A118	4c **brown,** *Feb. 1903*	55.00	2.25
	dark brown	60.00	2.25
	yellow brown	55.00	2.25
	orange brown	55.00	2.25
	red brown	55.00	2.25
	Never hinged	140.00	
	On cover		12.00
	Block of 4	230.00	25.00
	P# strip of 3, Impt., T V	220.00	
	Never hinged	450.00	
	P# block of 6, Impt., T V	825.00	
	Never hinged	1,500.	
	Double transfer	72.50	2.50

Earliest documented use: Mar. 10, 1903.

304 A119	5c **blue,** *Jan. 1903*	60.00	2.00
	pale blue	60.00	2.00
	bright blue	60.00	2.00
	dark blue	65.00	2.00
	Never hinged	150.00	
	On cover		6.00
	Block of 4	250.00	12.50
	P# strip of 3, Impt., T V	240.00	
	Never hinged	500.00	
	P# block of 6, Impt., T V	775.00	—
	Never hinged	1,350.	
	Double transfer	82.50	3.50
	Cracked plate	75.00	5.00

Earliest documented use: Feb. 9, 1903.

305 A120	6c **claret,** *Feb. 1903*	60.00	5.50
	deep claret	60.00	5.50
	brownish lake	65.00	5.50
	dull brownish lake	65.00	5.50
	Never hinged	150.00	
	On cover		16.00
	Block of 4	260.00	50.00
	P# strip of 3, Impt., T V	260.00	
	Never hinged	575.00	
	P# block of 6, Impt., T V	850.00	
	Never hinged	1,500.	
	Double transfer	65.00	6.25

Earliest documented use: April 14, 1903.

306 A121	8c **violet black,** *Dec. 1902*	45.00	3.25
	black	45.00	3.25
	slate black	45.00	3.25
	gray lilac	45.00	3.25
	Never hinged	110.00	
	lavender	65.00	4.00
	Never hinged	160.00	
	On cover		8.00
	Block of 4	190.00	30.00
	P# strip of 3, Impt., T V	175.00	
	Never hinged	360.00	
	P# block of 6, Impt., T V	700.00	
	Never hinged	1,150.	
	Double transfer	50.00	4.50

Earliest documented use: Dec. 27, 1902.

307 A122	10c **pale red brown,** *Feb. 1903*	60.00	3.00
	red brown	60.00	3.00
	dark red brown	75.00	3.00
	Never hinged	150.00	
	On cover		9.50
	Block of 4	260.00	19.00
	P# strip of 3, Impt., T V	250.00	
	Never hinged	525.00	
	P# block of 6, Impt., T V	1,000.	
	Never hinged	1,800.	
	Double transfer	70.00	11.00

Earliest documented use: Mar. 7, 1903.

308 A123	13c **purple black,** *Nov. 1902*	40.00	10.00
	brown violet	40.00	10.00
	Never hinged	100.00	
	On cover		37.50
	Block of 4	175.00	100.00
	P# strip of 3, Impt., T V	165.00	
	Never hinged	350.00	
	P# block of 6, Impt., T V	675.00	
	Never hinged	1,150.	

Earliest documented use: Nov. 18, 1902.

309 A124	15c **olive green,** *May 27, 1903*	185.00	12.50
	dark olive green	185.00	12.50
	Never hinged	475.00	
	On cover		75.00
	Block of 4	775.00	100.00
	Margin block of 4, arrow	800.00	
	P# strip of 3, Impt., T V	750.00	
	Never hinged	1,650.	
	P# block of 6, Impt., T V	3,250.	
	Never hinged	5,500.	
	Double transfer	210.00	16.00

Earliest documented use: July 1903 (on registry tag); Sept. 11, 1903 (on cover).

310 A125	50c **orange,** *Mar. 23, 1903*	400.	35.00
	deep orange	400.	35.00
	Never hinged	1,150.	
	On cover		700.00
	Block of 4	1,800.	250.00
	Margin block of 4, arrow	1,900.	
	P# strip of 3, Impt., T V	1,700.	
	Never hinged	4,250.	
	P# block of 6, Impt., T V	*7,250.*	

Earliest documented use: Oct. 6, 1903 (on cover front).

311 A126	$1 **black,** *June 5, 1903*	600.00	90.00
	grayish black	600.00	90.00
	Never hinged	1,800.	
	No gum	240.00	
	On cover		1,500.
	Block of 4	2,750.	600.00
	Margin block of 4, arrow	3,000.	
	P# strip of 3, Impt., T V	3,000.	
	P# block of 6, Impt., T V	*27,500.*	

Earliest documented use: Sept. 30, 1903.

312 A127	$2 **dark blue,** *June 5, 1903*	800.00	190.00
	blue	800.00	190.00
	Never hinged	2,475.	
	No gum	325.00	
	On cover		2,500.
	Block of 4	3,500.	1,900.
	Margin block of 4, arrow	3,750.	
	P# strip of 3, Impt., T V	4,100.	
	P# block of 6, Impt., T V	*35,000.*	

Earliest documented use: Feb. 17, 1904.

Alan E. Cohen

Dealer in
High Grade Stamps

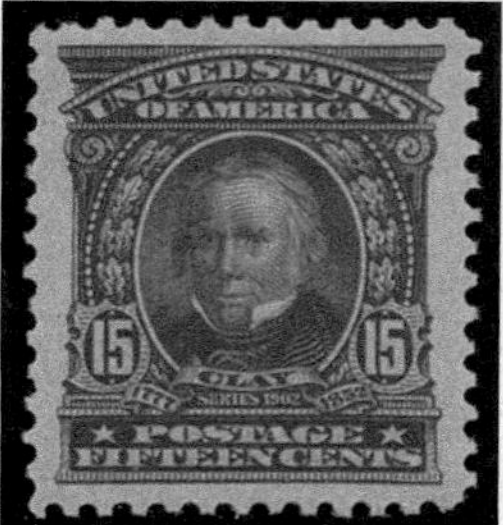

Visit our website today.

www.alanecohen.com

P. O. Box 929
New York, NY 10025
212-280-7865

e-mail: alanecohen@mindspring.com

313 A128 $5 **dark green,** *June 5, 1903* 2,000. 675.00
Never hinged *6,250.*
No gum 750.00
On cover *5,000.*
Block of 4 *11,000.* *6,000.*
Margin block of 4, arrow *11,500.*
P# strip of 3, Impt., T V *9,750.*
P# block of 6, Impt., T V *170,000.*

Earliest documented use: Feb. 17, 1904.

Nos. 300-313 (14) 4,387. 1,033.

For listings of designs A127 and A128 with Perf. 10 see Nos. 479 and 480.

Earliest documented use dates for imperforates are for the imperforate sheet stamps, not for imperforate stamps with vending and affixing machine perforations or for flat plate imperforate coil stamps. EDU dates for VAMP and flat plate imperf coil stamps are shown in their respective sections later in the catalogue.

1906-08 ***Imperf.***

314 A115 1c **blue green,** *Oct. 2, 1906* 14.00 17.50
green 14.00 17.50
deep green 14.00 17.50
Never hinged 30.00
On cover 32.50
Pair 30.00 40.00
Never hinged 60.00
Block of 4 62.50 *95.00*
Never hinged 130.00
Corner margin block of 4 70.00 *100.00*
Margin block of 4, arrow 72.50 *105.00*
Margin block of 4, arrow & round marker 170.00 150.00
Center line block 130.00 130.00
Never hinged 250.00
P# block of 6, Impt. 200.00 —
Never hinged 325.00
Double transfer 28.00 22.50

Earliest documented use: Dec. 20, 1906.

For imperforate coil varieties of No. 314, see the Imperforate Flat Plate Coil Stamps section in this catalogue.

314A A118 4c **brown,** *May 12, 1908* *100,000.* *50,000.*
Never hinged *230,000.*
On cover *140,000.*
Pair *250,000.*
Strip of 3 *300,000.*
Guide line pair *375,000.*

This stamp was issued imperforate but all examples were privately perforated with large oblong perforations at the sides (Schermack type III).

Two guide line pairs of No. 314A are recorded, one fine-very fine and the other extremely fine. The extremely fine example sold for $460,000 in a 2009 auction.

Beware of examples of No. 303 with trimmed perforations and fake private perfs. added.

Used and on-cover values are for contemporaneous usage.

Earliest documented use: May 27, 1908.

315 A119 5c **blue,** *Mar. 30, 1908* 300. *1,250.*
Never hinged 575.
On cover, pair *70,000.*
Pair 625. *11,500.*
Never hinged 1,250.
Block of 4 1,250. *27,500.*
Never hinged 2,500.
Corner margin block of 4 1,300.
Margin block of 4, arrow 1,800.
Margin block of 4, arrow & round marker 2,500.
Never hinged *3,750.*
Center line block *9,000.*
Never hinged *12,500.*
P# block of 6, Impt. 3,000. —
Never hinged 4,750.

Earliest documented use: Sept. 15, 1908 (pair on piece).

Beware of examples of No. 304 with perforations removed.

Used examples of No. 315 must have contemporaneous cancels and certificate of authenticity issued by a recognized expertizing committee. Single examples of No. 315 on cover must be accompanied by a certificate of authenticity.

COIL STAMPS

Warning! Imperforate stamps are known fraudulently perforated to resemble coil stamps and part-perforate varieties. Fully perforated stamps and booklet stamps also are known with perforations fraudulently trimmed off to resemble coil stamps.

1908 ***Perf. 12 Horizontally***

316 A115 1c **blue green,** *Feb. 18* *160,000.*
Pair *375,000.*
Guide line pair *500,000.*

See No. 314V in the Imperforate Flat Plate Coil Stamps section of this catalogue for the imperforate counterpart to this perforated coil stamp.

317 A119 5c **blue,** *Feb. 24* *6,000.* —
Never hinged *12,000.*
Pair *15,000.*
Never hinged *45,000.*
Guide line pair *70,000.*
Never hinged *160,000.*

Earliest documented use: Sept. 18, 1908.

Perf. 12 Vertically

318 A115 1c **blue green,** *July 31* *4,250.*
Never hinged *9,500.*
Pair *11,000.*
Guide line pair *35,000.*
Double transfer —

See No. 314H in the Imperforate Flat Plate Coil Stamps section of this catalogue for the imperforate counterpart to this perforated coil stamp.

No. 316 is valued in the grade of fine to very fine. There are no very fine examples recorded.

The No. 317 mint, never hinged guide line pair is valued in the grade of fine-very fine.

The No. 318 mint never hinged single is valued in the grade of fine.

Coil stamps for use in vending and affixing machines are perforated on two sides only, either horizontally or vertically. They were first issued in 1908, using perf. 12. This was changed to 8½ in 1910, and to 10 in 1914.

Imperforate sheets of certain denominations were sold to the vending machine companies which applied a variety of private perforations and separations (see Vending and Affixing Machine Perforations section of this catalogue).

Several values of the 1902 and later issues are found on an apparently coarse-ribbed paper. This is caused by worn blankets on the printing presses and is not a true paper variety.

All examples of Nos. 316-318 must be accompanied by certificates of authenticity issued by recognized expertizing committees.

Washington — A129

Plate of 400 subjects in four panes of 100 each.

Type I

Type II

Designed by Clair Aubrey Huston.

The two large arrows in the illustrations highlight the two major differences of the type II stamps: closing of the thin left border line next to the laurel leaf, and strengthening of the inner frame line at the lower left corner. The small arrows point out three minor differences that are not always easily discernible: strengthening of shading lines under the ribbon just above the "T" of "TWO," a shorter shading line to the left of the "P" in "POSTAGE," and shortening of a shading line in the left side ribbon.

Type I

1903 **Wmk. 191** ***Perf. 12***

319 A129 2c **carmine,** *Nov. 12* 6.00 .25
bright carmine 6.00 .25
red 6.00 .25
Never hinged 15.00
On cover .30
Block of 4 25.00 2.50
P# strip of 3, Impt., T V 24.00
Never hinged 55.00
P# block of 6, Impt., T V 180.00
Never hinged 310.00
Double transfer 12.50 2.00

a. 2c **lake** —
b. 2c **carmine rose** 15.00 .40
Never hinged 45.00
On cover .60
Block of 4 65.00 9.00
P# strip of 3, Impt., T V 60.00
Never hinged 175.00
P# block of 6, Impt., T V 375.00
Never hinged 650.00
c. 2c **scarlet** 10.00 .30
Never hinged 25.00
On cover .40
Block of 4 42.50 6.00
P# strip of 3, Impt., T V 40.00
Never hinged 85.00
P# block of 6, Impt., T V 250.00
Never hinged 375.00
d. Vert. pair, imperf. horiz., No. 319 *7,500.*
Never hinged *17,500.*
e. Vert. pair, imperf. between —
r. Vert. pair, rouletted between *4,000.*

During the use of No. 319, the postmaster of San Francisco discovered in his stock panes that had the perforations missing between the top two rows of stamps. To facilitate their separation, the imperf rows were rouletted, and the stamps were sold over the counter. These vertical pairs with regular perfs all around and rouletted between are No. 319r. No 319e is from a different source. One example has been authenticated, and collectors are warned that other pairs exist with faint blind perfs or indentations from the perforating machine.

g. Booklet pane of 6, **carmine** 125.00 *450.00*
Never hinged 240.00
Wmk. horizontal *3,000.*
Never hinged *5,000.*
n. Booklet pane of 6, **carmine rose** 275.00 *700.00*
Never hinged 500.00
p. Booklet pane of 6, **scarlet** 185.00 *625.00*
Never hinged 350.00

Earliest documented uses:
No. 319, Nov. 18, 1903;
No. 319b, Nov. 3, 1903;
No. 319c, Dec. 16, 1903;
No. 319g single, Dec. 7, 1903;
No. 319p single, Apr. 12, 1904.

"Gash on Face" Variety, Type II

The gash may appear as double lines due to different plate wiping techniques.

Type II

1908 **Wmk. 191** ***Perf. 12***

319F A129 2c **lake** 10.00 .30
carmine lake 10.00 .30
Never hinged 25.00
On cover .75
Block of 4 42.50 5.50
P# strip of 3, Impt., T V 45.00
Never hinged 95.00
P# block of 6, Impt., T V 325.00
Never hinged 475.00
"Gash on face" plate flaw (carmine lake, 4671 LL 16) —

i. 2c **carmine** 65.00 *50.00*
red 65.00 *50.00*
Never hinged 150.00
Block of 4 275.00
P# strip of 3, Impt., T V *250.00*
Never hinged *500.00*
P# block of 6, Impt., T V, never hinged *2,500.*
On cover *150.00*
j. 2c **carmine rose** 100.00 1.75
Never hinged 225.00
Block of 4 450.00 20.00
P# strip of 3, Impt., T V 525.00
P# block of 6, Impt., T V *1,400.*
k. 2c **scarlet** 70.00 2.00
Never hinged 160.00
Block of 4 300.00 15.00
P# strip of 3, Impt., T V 350.00
P# block of 6, Impt., T V *1,100.*
h. Booklet pane of 6, **carmine** 900.00 —
Never hinged 1,500.
l. Booklet pane of 6, **scarlet** —
q. Booklet pane of 6, **lake** 300.00 *800.00*
Never hinged 575.00

Earliest documented uses:
No. 319F, Sept. 25, 1908;
No. 319Fi, June 5, 1908;

No. 319Fj, June 30, 1908;
No. 319Fk, June 11, 1908;
No. 319Fh single, June 8, 1908.

Type I

1906 **Wmk. 191** ***Imperf.***

320 A129 2c **carmine,** *Oct. 2* 15.00 *19.00*
Never hinged 32.50
On cover 25.00
Pair 32.50 *42.50*
Never hinged 70.00
Block of 4 65.00 *87.50*
Corner margin block of 4 67.50 *110.00*
Margin block of 4, arrow 70.00 *120.00*
Margin block of 4, arrow & round marker —
Center line block 145.00 *225.00*
Never hinged 240.00
P# block of 6, Impt., T V, carmine 200.00 —
Never hinged 325.00
Double transfer 24.00 21.50

Earliest documented use: Oct. 16, 1906.

b. 2c **scarlet** 17.50 15.00
Never hinged 37.50
On cover 22.50
Pair 37.50
Never hinged 80.00
Block of 4 72.50
Corner margin block of 4 75.00
Margin block of 4, arrow 77.50 —
Center line block 200.00 —
Never hinged 320.00
P# block of 6, Impt., T V 225.00
Never hinged 350.00
c. 2c **carmine rose** 75.00 42.50
Never hinged 150.00

For imperforate coil varieties of No. 320, see the Imperforate Flat Plate Coil Stamps section in this catalogue.

Type II

1908 **Wmk. 191** ***Imperf.***

320A A129 2c **lake** 45.00 50.00
carmine lake 45.00 50.00
Never hinged 100.00
On cover *100.00*
Pair 100.00 *120.00*
Never hinged 225.00
Block of 4 200.00 *275.00*
Corner margin block of 4 205.00
Margin block of 4, arrow 210.00
Center line block 425.00 —
Never hinged 700.00
P# block of 6, Impt., T V 725.00 —
Never hinged 1,150.
"Gash on face" plate flaw (see No. 319F) —
d. 2c **carmine** *135.00* —
Never hinged *200.00*
On cover *2,500.*
Pair *290.00*
Never hinged *525.00*
Guide line pair *500.00* *6,000.*

No. 320Ad was issued imperforate, but all examples were privately perforated with large oblong perforations at the sides (Schermack type III).

COIL STAMPS

1908 ***Perf. 12 Horizontally***

321 A129 2c **carmine,** type I, pair, *Feb. 18* *600,000.*
On cover, single *310,000.*
Guide line pair —

See No. 320V in the Imperforate Flat Plate Coil Stamps section of this catalogue for the imperforate counterpart to this perforated coil stamp.

Four authenticated unused pairs of No. 321 are known and available to collectors. A fifth, unauthenticated pair is in the New York Public Library Miller collection, which is on long-term loan to the Smithsonian National Postal Museum. The value for an unused pair is for a fine-very fine example. Two fine pairs are recorded and one very fine pair.

There are no authenticated unused or off-cover used single stamps recorded. Two on-cover singles are known, both used from Indianapolis in 1908.

The Dec. 20, 1908, legal-size cover has not been seen in decades; the Oct. 2, 1908, cover sold in 2018 and is the cover valued.

Numerous counterfeits exist.

Earliest documented use: Oct. 2, 1908.

Perf. 12 Vertically

322 A129 2c **carmine,** type II, *July 31* *7,000.* —
Never hinged *15,000.*
Pair *17,500.*
Guide line pair *35,000.*
Double transfer —

See No. 320H in the Imperforate Flat Plate Coil Stamps section of this catalogue for the imperforate counterpart to this perforated coil stamp.

This Government Coil Stamp should not be confused with those of the International Vending Machine Co., which are perforated 12½.

All examples of Nos. 321-322 must be accompanied by certificates of authenticity issued by recognized expertizing committees.

VALUES FOR VERY FINE STAMPS
Please note: Stamps are valued in the grade of Very Fine unless otherwise indicated.

LOUISIANA PURCHASE EXPOSITION ISSUE

St. Louis, Mo., Apr. 30 - Dec. 1, 1904

Robert R. Livingston — A130

Thomas Jefferson — A131

James Monroe — A132

William McKinley — A133

Map of Louisiana Purchase — A134

Designed by Clair Aubrey Huston.

Plates of 100 (10x10) subjects, divided vertically into 2 panes of 50.

Exposition Station Machine Cancellation

1904, Apr. 30 **Wmk. 191** ***Perf. 12***

323 A130 1c **green** 22.50 4.75
dark green 22.50 4.75
Never hinged 60.00
On cover 7.00
On Expo. card, Expo. station machine canc. 40.00
On Expo. card, Expo. station duplex handstamp canc. 100.00
Block of 4 100.00 35.00
Margin block of 4, arrow, R or L 110.00 —
P# pair, Impt., T V 70.00
Never hinged 160.00
P# strip of 3, Impt., T V 95.00
Never hinged 210.00
P# block of 4, Impt., T V 190.00
Never hinged 325.00
P# block of 6, Impt., T V 400.00
Never hinged 600.00
Diagonal line through left "1" (2138 L 2) 45.00 12.50
Double transfer —

Earliest documented use: Apr. 30, 1904 (FDC).

324 A131 2c **carmine** 22.50 2.00
bright carmine 22.50 2.00
orange carmine — —
Never hinged 60.00
On cover 3.00
On Expo. cover, Expo. station machine canc. 60.00

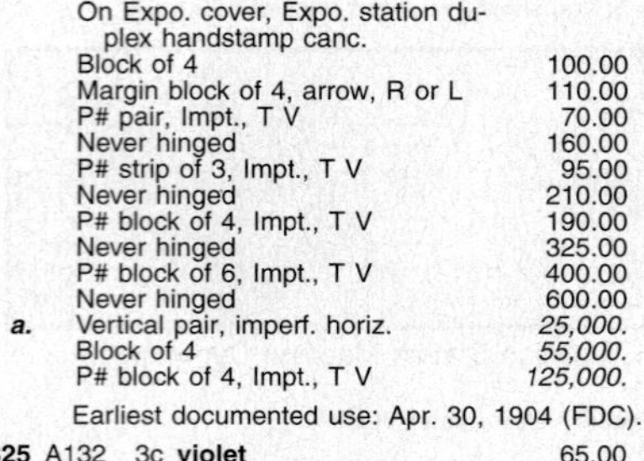

On Expo. cover, Expo. station duplex handstamp canc. 150.00
Block of 4 100.00 17.50
Margin block of 4, arrow, R or L 110.00 —
P# pair, Impt., T V 70.00
Never hinged 160.00
P# strip of 3, Impt., T V 95.00
Never hinged 210.00
P# block of 4, Impt., T V 190.00
Never hinged 325.00
P# block of 6, Impt., T V 400.00
Never hinged 600.00
a. Vertical pair, imperf. horiz. *25,000.*
Block of 4 *55,000.*
P# block of 4, Impt., T V *125,000.*

Earliest documented use: Apr. 30, 1904 (FDC).

325 A132 3c **violet** 65.00 27.50
Never hinged 170.00
On cover 65.00
On cover, Expo. station machine canc. 200.00
On cover, Expo. station duplex handstamp canc. *400.00*
Block of 4 280.00 225.00
Margin block of 4, arrow, R or L 300.00 —
P# pair, Impt., T V 180.00
Never hinged 400.00
P# strip of 3, Impt., T V 280.00
Never hinged 625.00
P# block of 4, Impt., T V 575.00
Never hinged 1,050.
P# block of 6, Impt., T V 950.00
Never hinged 1,750.
Double transfer —

Earliest documented use: Apr. 30, 1904 (FDC).

326 A133 5c **dark blue** 70.00 22.50
Never hinged 180.00
On cover 50.00
On cover, Expo. station machine canc. 400.00
On cover, Expo. station duplex handstamp canc. *500.00*
Block of 4 300.00 200.00
Margin block of 4, arrow, R or L 325.00 —
P# pair, Impt., T V 190.00
Never hinged 425.00
P# strip of 3, Impt., T V 300.00
Never hinged 675.00
P# block of 4, Impt., T V 625.00
Never hinged 1,150.
P# block of 6, Impt., T V 1,000.
Never hinged 1,850.

Earliest documented use: Apr. 30, 1904 (FDC).

327 A134 10c **red brown** 125.00 27.50
dark red brown 125.00 27.50
Never hinged 300.00
On cover 125.00
On cover, Expo. station machine canc. 450.00
On cover, Expo. station duplex handstamp canc. *750.00*
Block of 4 525.00 225.00
Margin block of 4, arrow, R or L 575.00 —
P# pair, Impt., T V 325.00
Never hinged 800.00
P# strip of 3, Impt., T V 600.00
Never hinged 1,400.
P# block of 4, Impt., T V 1,250.
Never hinged 2,150.
P# block of 6, Impt., T V 2,250.
Never hinged 4,000.

Earliest documented use: Apr. 30, 1904 (FDC).

Nos. 323-327 (5) 305.00 84.25
Nos. 323-327, never hinged 770.00

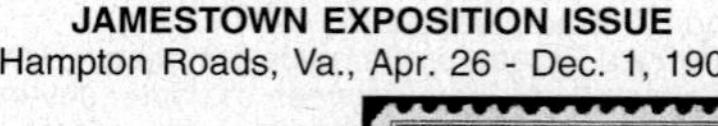

JAMESTOWN EXPOSITION ISSUE

Hampton Roads, Va., Apr. 26 - Dec. 1, 1907

Captain John Smith — A135

Founding of Jamestown — A136

Pocahontas — A137

Plates of 200 subjects in two panes of 100 each.

Exposition Station Machine Cancellation

Designed by Clair Aubrey Huston.

1907 Wmk. 191 *Perf. 12*

328	A135 1c **green,** *Apr. 26*	27.50	4.50
	dark green	27.50	4.50
	Never hinged	70.00	
	On cover		8.00
	On Expo. card, Expo. station machine canc.		25.00
	On Expo. card, Expo. station duplex handstamp canc.		125.00
	Block of 4	115.00	50.00
	Margin block of 4, arrow	120.00	—
	P# strip of 3, Impt., T V	112.50	
	Never hinged	260.00	
	P# block of 6, Impt., T V	550.00	
	Never hinged	825.00	
	Double transfer	35.00	5.50

Earliest documented use: Apr. 26, 1907 (FDC).

329	A136 2c **carmine,** *Apr. 26*	30.00	4.00
	bright carmine	30.00	4.00
	Never hinged	80.00	
	On cover		6.00
	On Expo. cover, Expo. station machine canc.		100.00
	On Expo. cover, Expo. station duplex handstamp canc.		150.00
	Block of 4	130.00	35.00
	Margin block of 4, arrow	140.00	—
	P# strip of 3, Impt., T V	125.00	
	Never hinged	300.00	
	P# block of 6, Impt., T V	625.00	
	Never hinged	900.00	
	Double transfer	40.00	5.50
a.	2c **carmine lake**	—	

Earliest documented use: Apr. 26, 1907 (FDC).

330	A137 5c **blue**	140.00	30.00
	deep blue	140.00	30.00
	Never hinged	350.00	
	On cover		80.00
	On cover, Expo. station machine canc.		350.00
	On cover, Expo. station duplex handstamp canc.		*500.00*
	Block of 4	600.00	225.00
	Margin block of 4, arrow	625.00	—
	P# strip of 3, Impt., T V	550.00	
	Never hinged	1,300.	
	P# block of 6, Impt., T V	3,000.	
	Never hinged	5,750.	
	Double transfer	160.00	35.00

Earliest documented use: May 8, 1907.

Nos. 328-330 (3)	197.50	38.50
Nos. 328-330, never hinged	500.00	

REGULAR ISSUE

Plates of 400 subjects in four panes of 100 each for all values 1c to 15c inclusive.

Plates of 200 subjects in two panes of 100 each for 50c and $1 denominations.

In 1909 the Bureau prepared certain plates with horizontal spacings of 3mm between the outer seven vertical stamp rows and 2mm between the others. This was done to try to counteract the effect of unequal shrinkage of the paper. *However, some unequal shrinkage still did occur and intermediate spacings are frequently found.* The listings of 2mm and 3mm spacings are for exact measurements. Intermediate spacings sell for approximately the same as the cheaper of the two listed spacings.

All such plates were marked with an open star added to the imprint and exist on the 1c, 2c, 3c, 4c, and 5c denominations only. A small solid star was added to the imprint and plate number for 1c plate No. 4980, 2c plate No. 4988 and for the 2c Lincoln. All other plates for this issue are spaced 2mm throughout.

There are several types of some of the 2c and 3c stamps of this and succeeding issues. These types are described under the dates at which they first appeared. Illustrations of Types I-VII of the 2c (A140) and Types I-IV of the 3c (A140) are reproduced by permission of H. L. Lindquist.

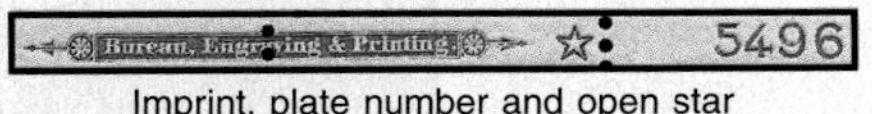
Imprint, plate number and open star

Imprint, plate number and small solid star

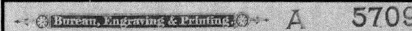

Imprint, plate number and "A"

(Illustrations reduced in size)

"A" and number only

Number only

The above illustrations are several of the styles used on plates of issues from 1908 to date.

The previously listed "China Clay Paper" stamps, formerly Scott 331b-332b and 333a-340a, have been removed from the catalogue. Research has shown that the "experimental paper" explanation for the existence of these stamps was incorrect. The only paper experiment during this time period was the 35 percent rag stock paper (Blue Paper, Scott 357-366, 369) of 1909. The stamps previously known as "China Clay Paper" stamps were, in fact, normal stamps printed on paper that was defective to varying degrees. These interesting varieties, which have nothing to do with China clay, can appear to be thin, thick, translucent, opaque, somewhat dark or very dark, but they are not the kind of items that the Scott catalogue or other catalogues normally list. This is not to say that these various paper varieties are of no value or are not of great interest to specialists of the stamps from this period. It is only to say that these various types and degrees of paper varieties are subjects which are beyond the scope of stamp catalogues. Specialist collectors will no doubt continue to study and treasure these varieties.

Franklin — A138

Washington — A139

1908-09 Wmk. 191 *Perf. 12*

331	A138 1c **green,** *Dec. 1908*	6.25	.40
	bright green	6.25	.40
	dark green	6.25	.40
	yellow green	6.25	.40
	Never hinged	16.00	
	On cover		.55
	Block of 4 (2mm spacing)	27.50	2.50
	Block of 4 (3mm spacing)	30.00	3.00
	P# block of 6, Impt., T V	100.00	
	Never hinged	175.00	
	P# block of 6, Impt. & star	95.00	
	Never hinged	160.00	
	P# block of 6, Impt. & small solid star (plate 4980)	*1,500.*	
	Never hinged	*2,250.*	
	Double transfer	100.00	100.00
	Cracked plate	—	—
a.	Booklet pane of 6, *Dec. 1908*	150.00	*700.00*
	Never hinged	300.00	

No. 331 exists in horizontal pair, imperforate between, a variety resulting from booklet experiments. Not regularly issued. Value in the grade of fine, $3,750.

No. 331a used is valued with a contemporaneous cancel. A certificate of authenticity is advised.

Earliest documented uses: Dec. 1, 1908 (No. 331); Dec. 2, 1908 (No. 331a single) (FDC).

332	A139 2c **carmine,** *Nov. 1908*	5.75	.35
	light carmine	5.75	.35
	dark carmine	5.75	.35
	Never hinged	14.00	
	On cover		.40
	Block of 4 (2mm spacing)	25.00	2.00
	Block of 4 (3mm spacing)	27.50	2.50
	P# block of 6, Impt., T V	90.00	
	Never hinged	150.00	
	P# block of 6, Impt. & star	85.00	
	Never hinged	140.00	
	P# block of 6, Impt. & small solid star (plate 4988)	*1,750.*	
	Never hinged	*2,750.*	
	Double transfer	12.00	—
	Foreign entry, design of 1c (plate 5299)	*2,250.*	*2,750.*
	On cover		*8,000.*
	Rosette crack	—	
	Cracked plate	—	—
a.	Booklet pane of 6	135.00	*500.00*
	Never hinged	240.00	
b.	2c **lake**	*4,250.*	

No. 332a used is valued with a contemporaneous cancel. A certificate of authenticity is advised.

No. 332 with foreign entry, used, is valued in the grade of fine and with a contemporaneous cancel.

No. 332b is valued in the grade of fine.

Earliest documented uses: Dec. 2, 1908 (No. 332), Nov. 16, 1908 (No. 332a single) (FDC).

Washington — A140

TYPE I

THREE CENTS

Type I. The top line of the toga rope is weak and the rope shading lines are thin. The 5th line from the left is missing. The line between the lips is thin. (For descriptions of 3c types II, III and IV, see notes and illustrations preceding Nos. 484, 529-530.)

Used on both flat plate and rotary press printings.

333	A140 3c **deep violet,** type I, *Dec. 1908*	27.50	3.00
	violet	27.50	3.00
	light violet	27.50	3.00
	Never hinged	70.00	
	On cover		8.50
	Block of 4 (2mm spacing)	120.00	26.50
	Block of 4 (3mm spacing)	125.00	29.00
	P# block of 6, Impt., T V	375.00	
	Never hinged	600.00	
	P# block of 6, Impt. & star	400.00	
	Never hinged	650.00	
	Double transfer	35.00	5.75

Earliest documented use: Jan. 12, 1909.

334	A140 4c **orange brown,** *Dec. 1908*	35.00	1.50
	brown	35.00	1.50
	light brown	35.00	1.50
	dark brown	35.00	1.50
	Never hinged	87.50	
	On cover		7.00
	Block of 4 (2mm spacing)	150.00	12.50
	Block of 4 (3mm spacing)	160.00	14.00
	P# block of 6, Impt., T V	450.00	
	Never hinged	725.00	
	P# block of 6, Impt. & star	450.00	
	Never hinged	725.00	
	Double transfer	52.50	—

Earliest documented use: Jan. 12, 1909.

335	A140 5c **blue,** *Dec. 1908*	45.00	2.25
	bright blue	45.00	2.25
	dark blue	45.00	2.25
	Never hinged	110.00	
	On cover		8.50
	Block of 4 (2mm spacing)	190.00	20.00
	Block of 4 (3mm spacing)	200.00	17.50
	P# block of 6, Impt., T V	525.00	
	Never hinged	1,000.	
	P# block of 6, Impt. & star	550.00	
	Never hinged	1,050.	
	Double transfer	55.00	—

Earliest documented use: Jan. 10, 1909.

336	A140 6c **red orange,** *Jan. 1909*	60.00	6.00
	pale red orange	60.00	6.00
	orange	60.00	6.00
	Never hinged	140.00	
	On cover		22.50
	Block of 4	260.00	50.00
	P# block of 6, Impt., T V	750.00	
	Never hinged	1,500.	

Earliest documented use: Jan. 6, 1909.

337	A140 8c **olive green,** *Dec. 1908*	45.00	2.75
	deep olive green	45.00	2.75
	Never hinged	105.00	
	On cover		18.00
	Block of 4	190.00	22.50
	P# block of 6, Impt., T V	525.00	
	Never hinged	875.00	
	Double transfer	57.50	—

Earliest documented use: Jan. 8, 1909.

338	A140 10c **yellow,** *Jan. 1909*	67.50	1.80
	Never hinged	160.00	
	On cover		10.00
	Block of 4	280.00	15.00
	P# block of 6, Impt., T V	800.00	
	Never hinged	1,500.	
	Double transfer	—	—
	Very thin paper	—	

Earliest documented use: Jan. 18, 1909.

339	A140 13c **blue green,** *Jan. 1909*	37.50	17.50
	deep blue green	37.50	17.50
	Never hinged	90.00	

On cover 110.00
Block of 4 160.00 175.00
P# block of 6, Impt., T V 500.00
Never hinged 875.00
Line through "TAG" of "POSTAGE" (4948 LR 96) 70.00 —

Earliest documented use: Mar. 5, 1909.

340 A140 15c **pale ultramarine,** *Jan. 1909* 65.00 6.00
ultramarine 65.00 6.00
Never hinged 150.00
On cover 125.00
Block of 4 270.00 65.00
P# block of 6, Impt., T V 650.00
Never hinged 1,250.

Earliest documented use: Mar. 12, 1909.

341 A140 50c **violet,** *Jan. 13, 1909* 275.00 20.00
dull violet 275.00 20.00
Never hinged 650.00
On cover *5,000.*
Block of 4 1,200. 150.00
Margin block of 4, arrow, right or left 1,250.
P# block of 6, Impt., T V *6,000.* —
Never hinged *13,500.*

Earliest documented use: Oct. 21, 1909 (on registered cover front); June 2, 1916 (on complete cover).

342 A140 $1 **violet brown,** *Jan. 29, 1909* 450.00 90.00
light violet brown 450.00 90.00
Never hinged 1,050.
On cover *6,000.*
Block of 4 2,000. 700.00
Margin block of 4, arrow, right or left 2,150. 725.00
P# block of 6, Impt., T V *20,000.*
Never hinged *32,500.*
Double transfer — —

Earliest documented use: July 3, 1909 (on parcel tag with two No. 334); July 26, 1909 (on cover).

Nos. 331-342 (12) 1,120. 151.55

For listings of other perforated sheet stamps of A138, A139 and A140 see:
Nos. 357-366 Bluish paper
Nos. 374-382, 405-407 Single line wmk. Perf. 12
Nos. 423A-423C Single line wmk. Perf 12x10
Nos. 423D-423E Single line wmk. Perf 10x12
Nos. 424-430 Single line wmk. Perf. 10
Nos. 461 Single line wmk. Perf. 11
Nos. 462-469 unwmk. Perf. 10
Nos. 498-507 unwmk. Perf. 11
Nos. 519 Double line wmk. Perf. 11
Nos. 525-530 and 536 Offset printing
Nos. 538-546 Rotary press printing

Plate Blocks

Scott values for plate blocks printed from flat plates are for very fine side and bottom positions. Top position plate blocks with full wide selvage sell for more.

Earliest documented use dates for imperforates are for the imperforate sheet stamps, not for imperforate stamps with vending and affixing machine perforations or for flat plate imperforate coil stamps. EDU dates for VAMP and flat plate imperf coil stamps are shown in their respective sections later in the catalogue.

Imperf

343 A138 1c **green,** *Dec. 1908* 4.50 *5.00*
dark green 4.50 *5.00*
yellowish green 4.50 *5.00*
Never hinged 9.00
On cover 12.00
Pair 9.50 *11.00*
Never hinged 20.00
Block of 4 (2mm or 3mm spacing) 21.00 25.00
Corner margin block of 4, 2mm or 3mm 22.50 27.50
Margin block of 4, arrow, 2mm or 3mm 24.00 *27.50*
Center line block 32.50 *40.00*
Never hinged 60.00
P# block of 6, Impt., T V 50.00 —
Never hinged 80.00
P# block of 6, Impt. & star 62.50 —
Never hinged 97.50
P# block of 6, Impt. & small solid star (plate 4980) *675.00*
Never hinged *1,050.*
Double transfer 11.00 8.00

Earliest documented use: Jan. 4, 1909.

344 A139 2c **carmine,** *Dec. 1908* 4.50 2.75
light carmine 4.50 2.75
dark carmine 4.50 2.75
Never hinged 9.00
On cover 8.00
Pair 9.50 7.00
Never hinged 20.00
Block of 4 (2mm or 3mm spacing) 20.00 16.00
Corner margin block of 4, 2mm or 3mm 22.50 22.50
Margin block of 4, arrow, 2mm or 3mm 24.00 22.50
Center line block 37.50 *40.00*
Never hinged 67.50
P# block of 6, Impt., T V 77.50 —
Never hinged 120.00
P# block of 6, Impt. & star 70.00 —
Never hinged 110.00
Double transfer 11.50 3.50
Foreign entry, design of 1c (plate 5299) — —

Earliest documented use: Dec. 7, 1908.

The existence of the foreign entry on the imperforate sheet stamp No. 344 has been questioned by specialists. The editors would like to see evidence of the existence of the item, either unused or used.

345 A140 3c **deep violet,** type I, *1909* 9.00 *20.00*
violet 9.00 *20.00*
Never hinged 19.00
On cover 65.00
Pair 19.00 *50.00*
Never hinged 40.00
Block of 4 40.00 *110.00*
Corner margin block of 4 42.50 *115.00*
Margin block of 4, arrow 42.50 *115.00*
Center line block 75.00 *140.00*
Never hinged 135.00
P# block of 6, Impt., T V 155.00 —
Never hinged 240.00
Double transfer 21.00 —

Earliest documented use: Feb. 13, 1909.

346 A140 4c **orange brown,** *Feb. 25, 1909* 12.50 *20.00*
brown 12.50 *20.00*
Never hinged 25.00
On cover 100.00
Pair 27.50 *60.00*
Never hinged 55.00
Block of 4 (2 or 3mm spacing) 57.50 *130.00*
Corner margin block of 4 (2 or 3mm spacing) 62.50 *135.00*
Margin block of 4, arrow, (2 or 3mm spacing) 67.50 *135.00*
Center line block 125.00 *220.00*
Never hinged 225.00
P# block of 6, Impt., T V 175.00 —
Never hinged 275.00
P# block of 6, Impt. & star 210.00 —
Never hinged 325.00
Double transfer 32.50 —

Earliest documented use: Mar. 13, 1909.

347 A140 5c **blue,** *Feb. 25, 1909* 25.00 *32.50*
dark blue 25.00 *32.50*
Never hinged 50.00
On cover 140.00
Pair 55.00 *100.00*
Never hinged 110.00
Block of 4 110.00 *220.00*
Corner margin block of 4 115.00 *235.00*
Margin block of 4, arrow 125.00 *245.00*
Center line block 220.00 *325.00*
Never hinged 400.00
P# block of 6, Impt., T V 275.00 —
Never hinged 500.00
Cracked plate —

Earliest documented use: Mar. 4, 1909.

Nos. 343-347 (5) 55.50 *80.25*
Nos. 343-347, never hinged 129.00

For listings of other imperforate stamps of designs A138, A139 and A140 see Nos. 383, 384, 408, 409 and 459 Single line wmk.
Nos. 481-485 unwmk.
Nos. 531-535 Offset printing

The values for used coil singles, pairs and line pairs are for examples with contemporaneous cancels that can be authenticated by expertizing committees. Used coils with cancels most commonly from the 1950s exist, and these and stamps with other non-contemporaneous cancels sell for less than the values shown.

COIL STAMPS

1908-10 ***Perf. 12 Horizontally***

348 A138 1c **green,** *Dec. 29, 1908* 40.00 *55.00*
dark green 40.00 *55.00*
Never hinged 80.00
On cover 90.00
Pair 100.00 *160.00*
Never hinged 225.00
Guide line pair 300.00 *800.00*
Never hinged 650.00

Earliest documented use: Jan. 25, 1909.

349 A139 2c **carmine,** *Jan. 1909* 100.00 *150.00*
dark carmine 100.00 *150.00*
Never hinged 225.00
On cover 180.00
Pair 260.00 *400.00*
Never hinged 600.00
Guide line pair 550.00 *1,300.*
Never hinged 1,350.
Foreign entry, design of 1c (plate 5299) — *3,000.*

Earliest documented use: May 14, 1909.

350 A140 4c **orange brown,** *Aug. 15, 1910* 140.00 *240.00*
Never hinged 325.00
On cover 375.00
Pair 375.00 *750.00*
Never hinged 900.00
Guide line pair 1,175. *4,000.*
Never hinged 2,600.

Earliest documented use: Mar. 22, 1912.

351 A140 5c **blue,** *Jan. 1909* 140.00 *300.00*
dark blue 140.00 *300.00*
Never hinged 325.00
On cover 625.00
Pair 400.00 *825.00*
Never hinged 850.00
Guide line pair 1,075. *3,000.*
Never hinged 2,350.
Nos. 348-351 (4) 420.00 745.00

Earliest documented use: Sept. 21, 1909.

See Nos. 343V-347V in the Imperforate Flat Plate Coil Stamps section of this catalogue for the imperforate counterparts to these perforated coil stamps.

1909 ***Perf. 12 Vertically***

352 A138 1c **green,** *Jan. 1909* 100.00 *225.00*
dark green 100.00 *225.00*
Never hinged 230.00
On cover 350.00
Pair (2mm spacing) 260.00 *650.00*
Never hinged 570.00
Pair (3mm spacing) 250.00 *625.00*
Never hinged 550.00
Guide line pair 825.00 *1,650.*
Never hinged 1,800.
Double transfer —

353 A139 2c **carmine,** *Jan. 12, 1909* 90.00 *220.00*
dark carmine 90.00 *220.00*
Never hinged 200.00
On cover 375.00
Pair (2mm spacing) 240.00 *600.00*
Never hinged 525.00
Pair (3mm spacing) 225.00 *575.00*
Never hinged 500.00
Guide line pair 750.00 *2,500.*
Never hinged 1,750.

Earliest documented use: June 14, 1909.

354 A140 4c **orange brown,** *Feb. 23, 1909* 200.00 *275.00*
Never hinged 425.00
On cover 450.00
Pair (2mm spacing) 500.00 *825.00*
Never hinged 1,100.
Pair (3mm spacing) 475.00 *825.00*
Never hinged 1,050.
Guide line pair 1,400. *2,000.*
Never hinged 3,000.

Earliest documented use: June 9, 1909.

355 A140 5c **blue,** *Feb. 23, 1909* 210.00 *300.00*
Never hinged 450.00
On cover 475.00
Pair 525.00 *875.00*

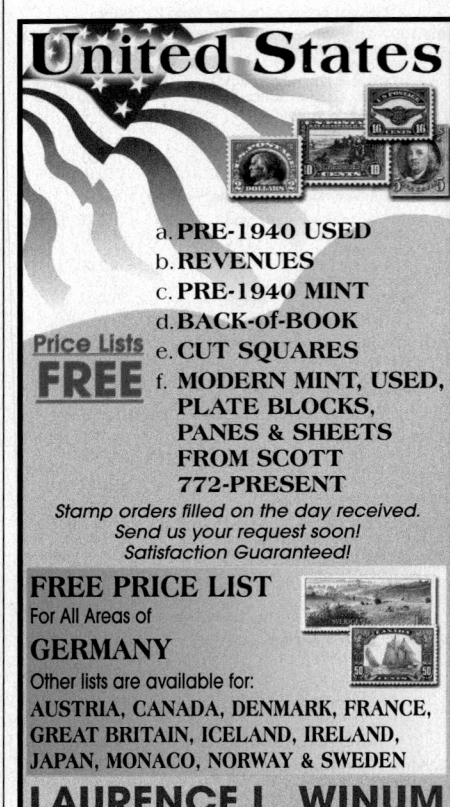

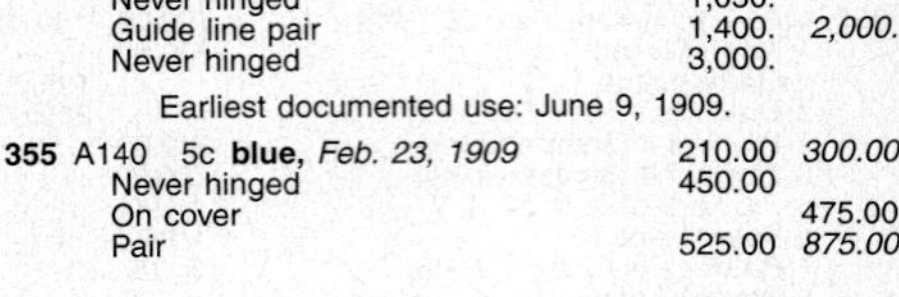

United States
a. PRE-1940 USED
b. REVENUES
c. PRE-1940 MINT
d. BACK-of-BOOK
e. CUT SQUARES
f. MODERN MINT, USED, PLATE BLOCKS, PANES & SHEETS FROM SCOTT 772-PRESENT
Price Lists FREE
Stamp orders filled on the day received.
Send us your request soon!
Satisfaction Guaranteed!
FREE PRICE LIST
For All Areas of
GERMANY
Other lists are available for:
AUSTRIA, CANADA, DENMARK, FRANCE, GREAT BRITAIN, ICELAND, IRELAND, JAPAN, MONACO, NORWAY & SWEDEN
LAURENCE L. WINUM
P.O. Box 247, Dept. S, Walden, NY 12586
APS 51900 • ARA 1970 • Est. 1964
1-800-914-8090
Email: winum@frontiernet.net

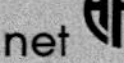

Never hinged 1,100.
Guide line pair 1,500. 4,000.
Never hinged 3,250.

Earliest documented use: Oct. 25, 1909.

See Nos. 343H-347H in the Imperforate Flat Plate Coil Stamps section of this catalogue for the imperforate counterparts to these perforated coil stamps.

These Government Coil Stamps, Nos. 352-355, should not be confused with those of the International Vending Machine Co., which are perf. 12½-13.

356 A140 10c **yellow,** *Jan. 7, 1909* 3,250. 6,000.
Never hinged 8,000.
On cover 10,000.
Pair 7,000. 15,000.
Never hinged 17,500.
Guide line pair 16,000. 29,000.
Never hinged 45,000.

Earliest documented uses: Mar. 9, 1909 (dated cancel on off-cover stamp); July 6, 1909 (on cover).

The used guide line pair of No. 356 is unique. Value reflects price realized at auction in 2002.

For listings of other coil stamps of designs A138 A139 and A140 see:
Nos. 385-396, 410-413, 441-459, single line watermark.
Nos. 486-496, unwatermarked.

Beware of stamps offered as No. 356 which may be examples of No. 338 with perfs. trimmed at top and/or bottom. Beware also of plentiful fakes in the marketplace of Nos. 348-355, made by fraudulently perforating imperforate stamps or by fraudulently trimming perforations off fully perforated stamps. Authentication of all these coils is advised.

BLUISH PAPER

This was made with 35 percent rag stock instead of all wood pulp. The "bluish" color (actually grayish blue) goes through the paper showing clearly on the back as well as on the face.

1909 ***Perf. 12***

357 A138 1c **green,** *Feb. 16, 1909* 90.00 160.00
Never hinged 190.00
On postcard 185.00
On cover 260.00
Block of 4 (2mm spacing) 380.00 1,000.
Block of 4 (3mm spacing) 750.00
P# block of 6, Impt., T V 1,100.
Never hinged 1,850.
P# block of 6, Impt. & star 3,100.
Never hinged 5,200.

Earliest documented use: Feb. 21, 1909.

358 A139 2c **carmine,** *Feb. 16, 1909* 80.00 150.00
Never hinged 170.00
On cover 200.00
Block of 4 (2mm spacing) 350.00 1,000.
Block of 4 (3mm spacing) 450.00
P# block of 6, Impt., T V 1,000.
Never hinged 1,800.
P# block of 6, Impt. & star 1,650.
Never hinged 2,750.
Double transfer 750.00

Earliest documented use: Feb. 23, 1909.

359 A140 3c **deep violet,** type I 1,800. 12,500.
Never hinged 4,000.
On cover —
Block of 4 7,750.
P# block of 6, Impt., T V 25,000.
Never hinged 35,000.

Earliest documented use: Dec. 27, 1910.

360 A140 4c **orange brown** 27,500.
Never hinged 80,000.
Block of 4 125,000.
P# strip of 3, Impt., T V 165,000.

The No. 360 plate number strip of three is unique.

361 A140 5c **blue** 5,750. 20,000.
Never hinged 14,500.
On cover 27,500.
Block of 4 25,000. —
P# block of 6, Impt., T V 140,000.

Only two examples of No. 361 used off cover (three additional on cover) are recorded. Value used is for the better of the two examples, which is well-centered but has two reattached perforations.

The No. 361 plate block is unique.

Earliest documented use: May 18, 1910.

362 A140 6c **red orange** 1,250. 12,500.
Never hinged 3,000.
On cover 22,500.
Block of 4 5,250.
P# block of 6, Impt., T V 17,500.
Never hinged 30,000.

Earliest documented use: Sept. 14, 1911.

363 A140 8c **olive green** 30,000.
Never hinged 85,000.
Block of 4 135,000.
P# strip of 3, Impt., T V 125,000.

The No. 363 plate number strip of three is unique.

364 A140 10c **yellow** 1,600. 10,000.
Never hinged 4,000.
On cover —
Block of 4 7,000.
P# block of 6, Impt., T V 40,000.

Earliest documented use: Feb. 3, 1910.

365 A140 13c **blue green** 2,600. 4,000.
Never hinged 6,000.
On cover —
Block of 4 11,500. 17,500.
P# strip of 3, Impt. T V 10,000.
P# block of 6, Impt., T V 52,500. —
Never hinged 90,000.

366 A140 15c **pale ultramarine** 1,250. 15,000.
Never hinged 3,000.
On cover —
Block of 4 6,000.
P# block of 6, Impt., T V 16,000.
Never hinged 30,000.

Earliest documented use: Jan. 15, 1911.

Nos. 360 and 363 were not regularly issued.

Used examples of Nos. 357-366 must bear contemporaneous cancels, and Nos. 359-366 used must be accompanied by certificates of authenticity issued by recognized expertizing committees.

IMPORTANT INFORMATION
REGARDING VALUES FOR
NEVER-HINGED STAMPS

Collectors should be aware that the values given for never-hinged stamps from No. 182 on are for stamps in the grade of very fine, just as the values for all stamps in the catalogue are for very fine stamps unless indicated otherwise. The never-hinged premium as a percentage of value will be larger for stamps in extremely fine or superb grades, and the premium will be smaller for fine-very fine, fine or poor examples. This is particularly true of the issues of the late-19th and early-20th centuries.

VALUES FOR NEVER-HINGED STAMPS
PRIOR TO SCOTT 182

This catalogue does not value pre-1879 stamps in never-hinged condition. Premiums for never-hinged condition in the classic era invariably are even larger than those premiums listed for the 1879 and later issues. Generally speaking, the earlier the stamp is listed in the catalogue, the larger will be the never-hinged premium.

NEVER-HINGED PLATE BLOCKS

Values given for never-hinged plate blocks are for blocks in which all stamps have original gum that has never been hinged and has no disturbances, and all selvage, whether gummed or ungummed, has never been hinged.

For values of the most popular U.S. stamps in various conditions, including never hinged from No. 182 on, and in the grades of very good, fine, fine to very fine, very fine, very fine to extremely fine, extremely fine, extremely fine to superb, and superb, see the *Scott Stamp Values U.S. Specialized by Grade*, updated and issued each year as part of this U.S. specialized catalogue. This section is located after Postage and before Semi-Postal Stamps.

LINCOLN CENTENARY OF BIRTH ISSUE

Lincoln — A141

Designed by Clair Aubrey Huston.

Plates of 400 subjects in four panes of 100 each

1909 **Wmk. 191** ***Perf. 12***

367 A141 2c **carmine,** *Feb. 12* 4.50 1.75
bright carmine 4.50 1.75
Never hinged 9.50
On cover 4.00
Block of 4 (2mm spacing) 19.00 15.00
Block of 4 (3mm spacing) 19.00 15.00
P# block of 6, Impt. & small solid star 200.00
Never hinged 275.00
Double transfer 7.50 2.75

Earliest documented use: Feb. 12, 1909 (FDC).

Imperf

368 A141 2c **carmine,** *Feb. 12* 12.50 19.00
Never hinged 24.00
On cover 37.50
Pair 27.50 45.00
Never hinged 57.50
Block of 4 (2mm or 3mm spacing) 55.00 90.00
Corner margin block of 4 60.00 90.00
Margin block of 4, arrow 62.50 95.00
Center line block 140.00 125.00
Never hinged 250.00
P# block of 6, Impt. & small solid star 200.00 —
Never hinged 390.00
Double transfer 35.00 27.50

Earliest documented use: Feb. 12, 1909 (FDC).

See Nos. 368V and 368H in the Imperforate Flat Plate Coil Stamps section of this catalogue for imperforate coil stamps of this design.

BLUISH PAPER

Perf. 12

369 A141 2c **carmine,** *Feb.* 150.00 225.00
Never hinged 300.00
On cover 375.00
Block of 4 (2mm or 3mm spacing) 650.00 1,250.
P# block of 6, Impt. & small solid star 2,750.
Never hinged 4,000.
Double transfer 225.00 —

Earliest documented use: Feb. 27, 1909 (dated cancel on off-cover stamp); Mar. 27, 1909 (on cover).

Used examples of No. 369 must bear contemporaneous cancels. Expertizing is recommended.

ALASKA-YUKON-PACIFIC EXPOSITION ISSUE

Seattle, Wash., June 1 - Oct. 16, 1909

William H. Seward — A142

Designed by Clair Aubrey Huston.

Plates of 280 subjects in four panes of 70 each

1909 **Wmk. 191** ***Perf. 12***

370 A142 2c **carmine,** *June 1* 6.75 2.00
bright carmine 6.75 2.00
Never hinged 15.00
On cover 5.00
On Expo. card or cover, Expo. station machine canc. 65.00
On Expo. card or cover, Expo. station duplex handstamp canc. 250.00
Block of 4 29.00 18.00
P# block of 6, Impt., T V 200.00
Never hinged 320.00
Double transfer (5249 UL 8) 10.00 4.75
a. Imperf. (error), P#5209 block of 6 —

Earliest documented use: June 1, 1909 (FDC).

No. 370a comes from error panes found in perforated stock. Plate 5209 was used only to print the perforated Alaska-Yukon-Pacific Exposition issue. No 370a can only be collected as a plate-number stamp or multiple. Without an attached plate number 5209, the stamps from this pane cannot be differentiated from No. 371.

Imperf

371 A142 2c **carmine,** *June* 14.00 21.00
Never hinged 30.00
On cover 40.00
On cover, Expo. station machine canc. 450.00
Pair 30.00 47.50
Never hinged 65.00
Block of 4 67.50 120.00
Corner margin block of 4 72.50 —
Margin block of 4, arrow 75.00 130.00
Center line block 160.00 175.00
Never hinged 275.00
P# block of 6, Impt., T V 225.00 —
Never hinged 350.00
Double transfer 27.50 27.50

Earliest documented use: June 7, 1909.

HUDSON-FULTON CELEBRATION ISSUE

Tercentenary of the discovery of the Hudson River and the centenary of Robert Fulton's steamship, the "Clermont."

Henry Hudson's "Half Moon" and Fulton's Steamship "Clermont" A143

Designed by Clair Aubrey Huston.

Plates of 240 subjects in four panes of 60 each

1909, Sept. 25 **Wmk. 191** ***Perf. 12***

372 A143 2c **carmine** 10.00 4.75
Never hinged 21.00
On cover 8.50
Block of 4 42.50 30.00
P# block of 6, Impt., T V 280.00
Never hinged 425.00
Double transfer (5393 and 5394) 20.00 5.00

Earliest documented use: Sept. 25, 1909 (FDC).

Imperf

373 A143 2c **carmine**		20.00	27.50
	Never hinged	40.00	
	On cover		40.00
	Pair	42.50	60.00
	Never hinged	87.50	
	Block of 4	90.00	130.00
	Corner margin block of 4	95.00	—
	Margin block of 4, arrow	100.00	135.00
	Center line block	210.00	160.00
	Never hinged	360.00	
	P# block of 6, Impt., T V	240.00	—
	Never hinged	375.00	
	Double transfer (5393 and 5394)	55.00	32.50

Earliest documented use: Sept. 25, 1909 (FDC).

Earliest documented use dates for imperforates are for the imperforate sheet stamps, not for imperforate stamps with vending and affixing machine perforations or for flat plate imperforate coil stamps. EDU dates for VAMP and flat plate imperf coil stamps are shown in their respective sections later in the catalogue.

REGULAR ISSUE
DESIGNS OF 1908-09 ISSUES

In this issue the Bureau used three groups of plates:

(1) The old standard plates with uniform 2mm spacing throughout (6c, 8c, 10c and 15c values);

(2) Those having an open star in the margin and showing spacings of 2mm and 3mm between stamps (for all values 1c to 10c); and

(3) A third set of plates with uniform spacing of approximately 2¾mm between all stamps. These plates have imprints showing

a. "Bureau of Engraving & Printing," "A" and number.

b. "A" and number only.

c. Number only.

(See above No. 331)

These were used for the 1c, 2c, 3c, 4c and 5c values.

On or about Oct. 1, 1910 the Bureau began using paper watermarked with single-lined letters:

(Actual size of letter)

repeated in rows, this way:

Watermark 190

Plates of 400 subjects in four panes of 100 each

1910-11 **Wmk. 190** ***Perf. 12***

374 A138 1c **green,** *Nov. 23, 1910*		6.00	.25
	light green	6.00	.25
	dark green	6.00	.25
	Never hinged	14.00	
	On cover		.30
	Block of 4 (2mm spacing)	26.00	3.25
	Block of 4 (3mm spacing)	28.00	3.00
	P# block of 6, Impt., & star	100.00	
	Never hinged	160.00	
	P# block of 6, Impt. & "A"	125.00	—
	Never hinged	175.00	
	Double transfer	13.00	—
	Cracked plate	—	—
	Pane of 60	*2,250.*	—
a.	Booklet pane of 6, *Oct. 7, 1910*	225.00	*400.00*
	Never hinged	375.00	
b.	Double impression		*300.00*

Earliest documented uses: Dec. 31, 1910 (No. 374); Feb. 28, 1911 (No. 374a single).

Panes of 60 of No. 374 were regularly issued in Washington, D.C. during Sept. and Oct., 1912. They were made from the six outer vertical rows of imperforate "Star Plate" sheets that had been rejected for use in vending machines on account of the 3mm spacing.

These panes have sheet margins on two adjoining sides and are imperforate along the other two sides. Upper and lower right panes show plate number, star and imprint on both margins; upper and lower left panes show plate number, star and imprint on side margins, but only the imprint on top or bottom margins.

375 A139 2c **carmine,** *Nov. 23, 1910*		6.00	.25
	bright carmine	6.00	.25
	dark carmine	6.00	.25
	Never hinged	14.00	
	On cover		.30
	Block of 4 (2mm spacing)	26.00	2.00
	Block of 4 (3mm spacing)	25.00	1.75
	P# block of 6, Impt. & star	125.00	
	Never hinged	185.00	
	P# block of 6, Impt. & "A"	135.00	
	Never hinged	200.00	
	Cracked plate	—	—
	Double transfer	12.00	—
	Foreign entry, design of 1c (plate 5299)	—	*1,450.*
a.	Booklet pane of 6, *Nov. 30, 1910*	125.00	*300.00*
	Never hinged	200.00	
b.	2c **lake**	*800.00*	—
	Never hinged	*1,750.*	
c.	As "b," booklet pane of 6	*10,000.*	
d.	Double impression	*750.00*	—
	Never hinged	*1,500.*	

Earliest documented uses: Dec. 3, 1910 (No. 375); April 27, 1911 (No. 375a single).

376 A140 3c **deep violet,** type I, *Jan. 16, 1911*		18.00	2.00
	violet	18.00	2.00
	Never hinged	40.00	
	lilac	22.50	2.25
	Never hinged	50.00	
	On cover		8.00
	Block of 4 (2mm spacing)	77.50	15.00
	Block of 4 (3mm spacing)	80.00	14.00
	P# block of 6, Impt. & star	300.00	
	Never hinged	450.00	
	P# block of 6	325.00	
	Never hinged	475.00	

Earliest documented use: June 9, 1911.

377 A140 4c **brown,** *Dec. 1910*		27.50	1.00
	dark brown	27.50	1.00
	orange brown	27.50	1.00
	Never hinged	65.00	
	On cover		7.50
	Block of 4 (2mm spacing)	125.00	6.50
	Block of 4 (3mm spacing)	120.00	6.00
	P# block of 6, Impt. & star	325.00	
	Never hinged	450.00	
	P# block of 6	350.00	
	Never hinged	550.00	
	Double transfer	—	—

Earliest documented use: Dec. 23, 1910.

378 A140 5c **blue,** *Jan. 25, 1911*		27.50	.75
	light blue	27.50	.75
	dark blue	27.50	.75
	bright blue	27.50	.75
	Never hinged	65.00	
	On cover		5.25
	Block of 4 (2mm spacing)	125.00	6.00
	Block of 4 (3mm spacing)	120.00	5.00
	P# block of 6, Impt., T V	350.00	
	Never hinged	550.00	
	P# block of 6, Impt. & star	350.00	
	Never hinged	550.00	
	P# block of 6, "A"	400.00	
	Never hinged	625.00	
	P# block of 6	400.00	
	Never hinged	625.00	
	Double transfer	—	—

Earliest documented use: Feb. 14, 1911.

379 A140 6c **red orange,** *Jan. 1911*		37.50	1.25
	light red orange	37.50	1.25
	Never hinged	85.00	
	On cover		13.00
	Block of 4 (2mm spacing)	160.00	13.50
	Block of 4 (3mm spacing)	155.00	12.00
	P# block of 6, Impt., T V	500.00	
	Never hinged	800.00	
	P# block of 6, Impt. & star	440.00	
	Never hinged	700.00	

Earliest documented use: Jan. 12, 1911.

380 A140 8c **olive green,** *Feb. 8, 1911*		90.00	15.00
	dark olive green	90.00	15.00
	Never hinged	200.00	
	On cover		45.00
	Block of 4 (2mm spacing)	400.00	100.00
	Block of 4 (3mm spacing)	400.00	95.00
	P# block of 6, Impt., T V	1,100.	
	Never hinged	1,900.	
	P# block of 6, Impt., & star	*1,300.*	
	Never hinged	*2,200.*	

Earliest documented use: May 27, 1911.

381 A140 10c **yellow,** *Jan. 1911*		85.00	6.00
	Never hinged	200.00	
	On cover		22.50
	Block of 4 (2mm spacing)	360.00	50.00
	Block of 4 (3mm spacing)	360.00	47.50
	P# block of 6, Impt., T V	1,150.	
	Never hinged	2,000.	
	P# block of 6, Impt. & star	1,250.	
	Never hinged	2,250.	

Earliest documented use: Jan. 21, 1911.

382 A140 15c **pale ultramarine,** *Mar. 1, 1911*		225.00	20.00
	Never hinged	500.00	
	On cover		100.00
	Block of 4	950.00	125.00
	P# block of 6, Impt., T V	2,500.	
	Never hinged	4,500.	

Earliest documented use: April 25, 1911.

Nos. 374-382 (9)	522.50	46.50

Earliest documented use dates for imperforates are for the imperforate sheet stamps, not for imperforate stamps with vending and affixing machine perforations or for flat plate imperforate coil stamps. EDU dates for VAMP and flat plate imperf coil stamps are shown in their respective sections later in the catalogue.

1910, Dec. ***Imperf.***

383 A138 1c **green**		2.50	*2.75*
	dark green	2.50	*2.75*
	yellowish green	2.50	*2.75*
	bright green	2.50	*2.75*
	Never hinged	5.00	
	On cover		6.00
	Pair	5.25	*6.00*
	Never hinged	11.00	
	Block of 4 (2mm or 3mm spacing)	12.50	*20.00*
	Corner margin block of 4	13.50	
	Margin block of 4, arrow	14.00	*22.50*
	Center line block	27.50	25.00
	Never hinged	47.50	
	P# block of 6, Impt., & star	50.00	—
	Never hinged	80.00	
	P# block of 6, Impt. & "A"	85.00	—
	Never hinged	130.00	
	Double transfer	6.75	—

Earliest documented use: Jan. 28, 1911.

Rosette plate crack on head

384 A139 2c **carmine**		4.00	2.75
	light carmine	4.00	2.75
	Never hinged	8.00	
	dark carmine	55.00	14.00
	On cover		4.00
	Horizontal pair	11.00	8.25
	Never hinged	22.00	
	Vertical pair	9.00	6.75
	Never hinged	18.00	
	Block of 4 (2mm or 3mm spacing)	25.00	17.50
	Corner margin block of 4	27.50	21.50
	Margin block of 4, arrow	29.00	22.50
	Center line block	52.50	*55.00*

WALTER KASELL STAMPS

Quality United States Stamps
Classics, U.S. Possessions & Plate Blocks
175 Richdale Ave., Cambridge, MA 02140
(617) 694-9360
Email: wbkasell@yahoo.com

Never hinged	85.00	
P# block of 6, Impt. & star	130.00	—
Never hinged	200.00	
P# block of 6, Impt. & "A"	170.00	—
Never hinged	260.00	
Double transfer	8.00	—
Rosette plate crack on head	*150.00*	—

Earliest documented use: Dec. 8, 1910.

The values for used coil singles, pairs and line pairs are for examples with contemporaneous cancels that can be authenticated by expertizing committees. Used coils with cancels most commonly from the 1950s exist, and these and stamps with other non-contemporaneous cancels sell for less than the values shown.

COIL STAMPS

1910, Nov. 1 ***Perf. 12 Horizontally***

385 A138 1c **green**	45.00	*50.00*
dark green	45.00	*50.00*
Never hinged	100.00	
On cover		90.00
Pair	110.00	*250.00*
Never hinged	240.00	
Guide line pair	450.00	*850.00*
Never hinged	1,000.	
386 A139 2c **carmine**	120.00	90.00
light carmine	120.00	90.00
Never hinged	260.00	
On cover		175.00
Pair	275.00	*375.00*
Never hinged	600.00	
Guide line pair	1,600.	*2,500.*
Never hinged	3,500.	

Earliest documented use: Dec. 9, 1910.

See Nos. 383V-384V in the Imperforate Flat Plate Coil Stamps section of this catalogue for the imperforate counterparts to these perforated coil stamps.

1910-11 ***Perf. 12 Vertically***

387 A138 1c **green,** *Nov. 1, 1910*	190.00	140.00
Never hinged	400.00	
On cover		250.00
Pair (2mm spacing)	450.00	*450.00*
Never hinged	1,000.	
Pair (3mm spacing)	475.00	*425.00*
Never hinged	1,050.	
Guide line pair	1,250.	*2,500.*
Never hinged	2,500.	

Earliest documented use: Nov. 5, 1910.

388 A139 2c **carmine,** *Nov. 1, 1910*	1,400.	*2,250.*
Never hinged	3,250.	
On cover		*3,000.*
Pair (2mm spacing)	3,500.	*7,500.*
Never hinged	7,500.	
Pair (3mm spacing)	3,750.	*8,000.*
Never hinged	7,750.	
Guide line pair	*9,000.*	*50,000.*
Never hinged	*24,000.*	

The used guide line pair of No. 388 is unique. It is the center pair in a strip of four, is fine-very fine and is valued thus.

Stamps offered as No. 388 frequently are privately perforated examples of No. 384, or examples of No. 375 with top and/or bottom perfs trimmed.

Earliest documented use: Jan. 4, 1911.

See Nos. 383H-384H in the Imperforate Flat Plate Coil Stamps section of this catalogue for the imperforate counterparts to these perforated coil stamps.

389 A140 3c **deep vio.,** type I, *Jan. 24, 1911*	*110,000.*	*10,000.*
Never hinged	*240,000.*	
On cover		*27,500.*
Pair	*240,000.*	*42,500.*

No. 389 is valued in the grade of fine.

Only a small supply of this coil was used at Orangeburg, N.Y. The used pair listed is part of a strip of 3 (three such strips exist). Each strip is in average grade or condition, and the pairs are valued thus. No other used multiples are recorded. There is only one mint, never-hinged example recorded.

Stamps offered as No. 389 sometimes are examples of No. 376 with top and/or bottom perfs trimmed. Expertization by competent authorities is recommended.

Earliest documented use: Mar. 8, 1911.

Beware of plentiful fakes in the marketplace of Nos. 385-389, made by fraudulently perforating the 1c and 2c imperforate stamps or by fraudulently trimming perforations off fully perforated stamps.

1910 ***Perf. 8½ Horizontally***

390 A138 1c **green,** *Dec. 12, 1910*	4.50	*14.00*
dark green	4.50	*14.00*
Never hinged	10.00	
On cover		17.50
Pair	10.50	*45.00*
Never hinged	22.00	
Guide line pair	35.00	*125.00*
Never hinged	72.50	
Double transfer	—	—

Earliest documented use: Oct. 5, 1911.

391 A139 2c **carmine,** *Dec. 23, 1910*	42.50	*50.00*
light carmine	42.50	*50.00*
Never hinged	90.00	
On cover		70.00
Pair	110.00	170.00
Never hinged	240.00	
Guide line pair	260.00	*1,500.*
Never hinged	575.00	

Earliest documented use: May 3, 1911.

See Nos. 383V-384V in the Imperforate Flat Plate Coil Stamps section of this catalogue for the imperforate counterparts to these perforated coil stamps.

1910-13 ***Perf. 8½ Vertically***

392 A138 1c **green,** *Dec. 12, 1910*	27.50	*50.00*
dark green	27.50	*50.00*
Never hinged	65.00	
On cover		75.00
Pair	67.50	*145.00*
Never hinged	145.00	
Guide line pair	190.00	*500.00*
Never hinged	400.00	
Double transfer	—	—

Earliest documented use: Dec. 16, 1910.

393 A139 2c **carmine,** *Dec. 16, 1910*	45.00	*55.00*
dark carmine	45.00	55.00
Never hinged	105.00	
On cover		90.00
Pair	120.00	140.00
Never hinged	260.00	
Guide line pair	300.00	*450.00*
Never hinged	650.00	

Earliest documented use: Dec. 27, 1910.

See Nos. 383H-384H in the Imperforate Flat Plate Coil Stamps section of this catalogue for the imperforate counterparts to these perforated coil stamps.

394 A140 3c **deep violet,** type I, *Sept. 1911*	60.00	65.00
violet	60.00	65.00
red violet	60.00	65.00
Never hinged	135.00	
On cover		125.00
Pair (2mm spacing)	150.00	*220.00*
Never hinged	350.00	
Pair (3mm spacing)	145.00	*200.00*
Never hinged	325.00	
Guide line pair	425.00	*650.00*
Never hinged	925.00	

Earliest documented use: Sept. 18, 1911.

395 A140 4c **brown,** *Apr. 15, 1912*	60.00	*65.00*
dark brown	60.00	*65.00*
Never hinged	135.00	
On cover		125.00
Pair (2mm spacing)	150.00	190.00
Never hinged	350.00	
Pair (3mm spacing)	140.00	190.00
Never hinged	325.00	
Guide line pair	475.00	*650.00*
Never hinged	1,100.	

Earliest documented use: June 21, 1912.

396 A140 5c **blue,** *Mar. 1913*	60.00	*65.00*
dark blue	60.00	*65.00*
Never hinged	135.00	
On cover		120.00
Pair	160.00	190.00
Never hinged	375.00	
Guide line pair	425.00	*825.00*
Never hinged	975.00	

Earliest documented use: April 5, 1913.

Beware of plentiful fakes in the marketplace of Nos. 390-393, made by fraudulently perforating imperforate stamps.

PANAMA-PACIFIC EXPOSITION ISSUE

San Francisco, Cal., Feb. 20 - Dec. 4, 1915

Vasco Nunez de Balboa — A144

Pedro Miguel Locks, Panama Canal — A145

Golden Gate — A146

Discovery of San Francisco Bay — A147

Exposition Station Cancellation.

Designed by Clair Aubrey Huston.

Plates of 280 subjects in four panes of 70 each.

1913 **Wmk. 190** ***Perf. 12***

397 A144 1c **green,** *Jan. 1, 1913*	15.00	2.00
deep green	15.00	2.00
yellowish green	15.00	2.00
Never hinged	35.00	
On cover		3.50
On Expo. card, Expo. station 1915 machine cancel		*30.00*
Pair on cover, Expo. station 1915 duplex handstamp cancel		*150.00*
Block of 4	65.00	14.00
P# block of 6	300.00	
Never hinged	450.00	
Double transfer	20.00	3.25

Earliest documented use: Jan. 1, 1913 (FDC).

398 A145 2c **carmine,** *Jan. 1913*	16.00	1.00
deep carmine	16.00	1.00
Never hinged	35.00	
On cover		1.75
On cover, Expo. station 1915 machine cancel		75.00
On cover, Expo. station 1915 duplex handstamp cancel		*250.00*
Block of 4	67.50	10.00
P# block of 6	400.00	
Never hinged	625.00	
Double transfer	35.00	3.50
a. 2c **carmine lake**	*1,500.*	
Never hinged	*2,500.*	
b. 2c **lake**	*5,250.*	3,000.
Never hinged	*8,500.*	

Earliest documented use: Jan. 17, 1913.

399 A146 5c **blue,** *Jan. 1, 1913*	65.00	10.00
dark blue	65.00	10.00
Never hinged	150.00	
On cover		27.50
On cover, Expo. station 1915 machine cancel		300.00
Block of 4	280.00	70.00
P# block of 6	1,900.	
Never hinged	3,200.	

Earliest documented use: Jan. 1, 1913 (FDC).

400 A147 10c **orange yellow,** *Jan. 1, 1913*	110.00	20.00
Never hinged	250.00	
On cover		57.50
On cover, Expo. station 1915 machine cancel		500.00
Block of 4	475.00	150.00
P# block of 6	2,250.	
Never hinged	3,750.	

Earliest documented use: Jan. 1, 1913 (FDC).

400A A147 10c **orange,** *Aug. 1913*	175.00	22.50
Never hinged	390.00	
On cover		75.00
On cover, Expo. station 1915 machine cancel		550.00
Block of 4	725.00	120.00
P# block of 6	*10,000.*	
Never hinged	*18,000.*	

Earliest documented use: Nov. 12, 1913.

Nos. 397-400A (5)	381.00	55.50
Nos. 397-400A, never hinged	830.00	

1914-15 ***Perf. 10***

401 A144 1c **green,** *Dec. 1914*	25.00	7.00
dark green	25.00	7.00
Never hinged	60.00	
On cover		16.00
On Expo. card, Expo. station 1915 machine cancel		75.00

Block of 4	110.00	47.50
P# block of 6	400.00	
Never hinged	650.00	

Earliest documented use: Dec. 21, 1914.

402 A145 2c **carmine,** *Jan. 1915*	65.00	3.00
deep carmine	65.00	3.00
red	65.00	3.00
Never hinged	160.00	
On cover		6.50
On cover, Expo. station 1915 machine cancel		150.00
On cover, Expo. station 1915 duplex handstamp cancel		450.00
Block of 4	280.00	20.00
P# block of 6	1,200.	
Never hinged	3,000.	

Earliest documented use: Jan. 13, 1915.

403 A146 5c **blue,** *Feb. 1915*	150.00	17.50
dark blue	150.00	17.50
Never hinged	375.00	
On cover		55.00
On cover, Expo. station 1915 machine cancel		450.00
Block of 4	650.00	125.00
P# block of 6	3,800.	
Never hinged	6,500.	

Earliest documented use: Feb. 6, 1915.

404 A147 10c **orange,** *July 1915*	650.00	70.00
Never hinged	1,600.	
On cover		175.00
On cover, Expo. station 1915 machine cancel		600.00
Block of 4	*3,000.*	500.00
P# block of 6	*10,000.*	
Never hinged	20,000.	

Earliest documented use: Aug. 27, 1915.

Nos. 401-404 (4)	890.00	97.50
Nos. 401-404, never hinged	2,195.	

VALUES FOR VERY FINE STAMPS

Please note: Stamps are valued in the grade of Very Fine unless otherwise indicated.

REGULAR ISSUE

Washington — A140

The plates for this and later issues were the so-called "A" plates with uniform spacing of 2¾mm between stamps.

Plates of 400 subjects in four panes of 100 each for all values 1c to 50c inclusive.

Plates of 200 subjects in two panes of 100 each for $1 and some of the 50c (No. 422) denomination.

1912-14 **Wmk. 190** ***Perf. 12***

405 A140 1c **green,** *Feb. 1912*	6.50	.25
light green	6.50	.25
dark green	6.50	.25
yellowish green	6.50	.25
Never hinged	15.00	
On cover		.30
Block of 4	28.00	2.50
P# block of 6, Impt. & "A"	125.00	
Never hinged	200.00	
P# block of 6, "A"	115.00	
Never hinged	185.00	
P# block of 6	110.00	
Never hinged	170.00	
Cracked plate	14.50	—
Double transfer	8.50	—
a. Vert. pair, imperf. horiz.	*2,000.*	—
b. Booklet pane of 6, *1912*	65.00	*75.00*
Never hinged	110.00	
c. Double impression		*5,500.*

Earliest documented uses: Feb. 2, 1912 (No. 405); Jan. 16, 1912 (No. 405b single).

TYPE I

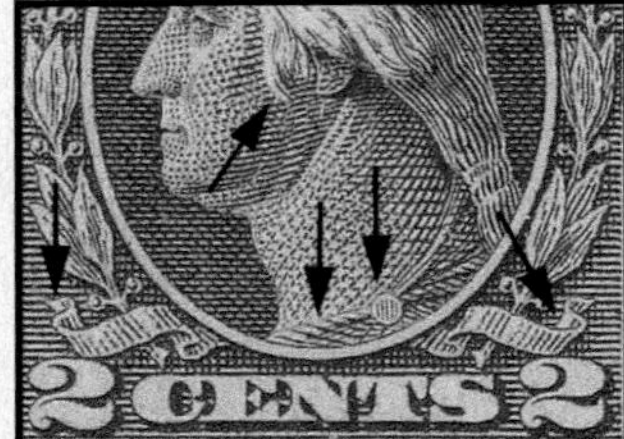

TWO CENTS

Type I. There is one shading line in the first curve of the ribbon above the left "2" and one in the second curve of the ribbon above the right "2."

The button of the toga has only a faint outline.

The top line of the toga rope, from the button to the front of the throat, is also very faint.

The shading lines of the face terminate in front of the ear with little or no joining, to form a lock of hair.

Used on both flat plate and rotary press printings.

406 A140 2c **carmine,** type I, *Feb. 1912*	6.50	.25
bright carmine	6.50	.25
Never hinged	15.00	
dark carmine	7.00	.25
Never hinged	16.00	
On cover		.30
Block of 4	28.00	2.50
P# block of 6, Impt. & "A"	150.00	
Never hinged	240.00	
P# block of 6, "A"	140.00	
Never hinged	230.00	
P# block of 6	125.00	
Never hinged	200.00	
P# single, Electrolytic, (Pl. 6023)	*2,500.*	
Never hinged	*4,000.*	
Double transfer	9.00	—
a. Booklet pane of 6, *Feb. 8, 1912*	65.00	*90.00*
Never hinged	110.00	
b. Double impression	*1,250.*	—
c. 2c **lake,** type I	*2,000.*	*6,000.*
Never hinged	*3,750.*	

Earliest documented uses: Feb. 15, 1912 (No. 406); May 2, 1912 (No. 406a single).

407 A140 7c **black,** *Apr. 1914*	70.00	14.00
grayish black	70.00	14.00
intense black	70.00	14.00
Never hinged	150.00	
On cover		75.00
Block of 4	310.00	100.00
P# block of 6	1,200.	
Never hinged	2,000.	

Earliest documented use: May 1, 1914.

Earliest documented use dates for imperforates are for the imperforate sheet stamps, not for imperforate stamps with vending and affixing machine perforations or for flat plate imperforate coil stamps. EDU dates for VAMP and flat plate imperf coil stamps are shown in their respective sections later in the catalogue.

Plate Blocks

Scott values for plate blocks printed from flat plates are for very fine side and bottom positions. Top position plate blocks with full wide selvage sell for more.

1912 ***Imperf.***

408 A140 1c **green,** *Mar. 1912*	1.00	1.00
yellowish green	1.00	1.00
dark green	1.00	1.00
Never hinged	2.00	
On cover		1.75
Pair	2.10	2.10
Never hinged	4.20	
Block of 4	4.20	4.20
Corner margin block of 4	4.30	4.30
Margin block of 4, arrow	4.40	4.40
Center line block	10.00	10.00
Never hinged	17.50	
P# block of 6, Impt. & "A," T, B or L	45.00	—
Never hinged	75.00	
P# block of 6, Impt. & "A," at right	*550.00*	—
Never hinged	*850.00*	
P# block of 6, "A"	26.00	—
Never hinged	45.00	
P# block of 6	18.00	—
Never hinged	29.00	
Double transfer	2.40	2.40
Cracked plate	—	—

Earliest documented use: April 26, 1912.

409 A140 2c **carmine,** type I, *Feb. 1912*	1.20	1.20
deep carmine	1.20	1.20
scarlet	1.20	1.20
Never hinged	2.40	
On cover		2.00
Pair	2.50	2.50
Never hinged	5.00	
Block of 4	5.00	5.00
Corner margin block of 4	5.25	
Margin block of 4, arrow	5.50	5.50
Center line block	11.00	11.00
Never hinged	19.00	
P# block of 6, Impt. & "A"	47.50	—
Never hinged	80.00	
P# block of 6, "A"	45.00	—
Never hinged	75.00	
P# block of 6	35.00	—
Never hinged	57.50	
Cracked plate (Plates 7580, 7582)	14.00	—

Earliest documented use: Apr. 15, 1912.

In late 1914, the Post Office at Kansas City, Missouri, had on hand a stock of imperforate sheets of 400 of stamps Nos. 408 and 409, formerly sold for use in vending machines, but not then in demand. In order to make them salable, they were rouletted with ordinary tracing wheels and were sold over the counter with official approval of the Post Office Department given January 5, 1915.

These stamps were sold until the supply was exhausted. Except for one full sheet of 400 of each value, all were cut into panes of 100 before being rouletted and sold. They are known as "Kansas City Roulettes". Value, authenticated blocks of 4, 1c *$100*, 2c *$200*. No. 408 is known as a block of four imperforate between vertically. Approximately 20 uses on cover are recorded. Most unused examples have authentication initials on reverse (MOC, ERW, WW, WDW, WCM).

Earliest documented uses of "Kansas City Roulettes": Oct. 22, 1914 (No. 408); Nov. 25, 1914 (No. 409).

COIL STAMPS

1912 ***Perf. 8½ Horizontally***

410 A140 1c **green,** *Mar. 1912*	6.00	*12.50*
dark green	6.00	*12.50*
Never hinged	13.00	
On cover		17.50
Pair	15.00	*42.50*
Never hinged	32.50	
Guide line pair	30.00	*100.00*
Never hinged	65.00	
Double transfer	—	—

Earliest documented use: Apr. 17, 1912.

411 A140 2c **carmine,** type I, *Mar. 1912*	10.00	*17.50*
deep carmine	10.00	*17.50*
Never hinged	22.50	
On cover		22.50
Pair	25.00	*55.00*
Never hinged	55.00	
Guide line pair	55.00	*175.00*
Never hinged	125.00	
Double transfer	12.50	—

Earliest documented use: June 5, 1912.

See Nos. 408V-409V in the Imperforate Flat Plate Coil Stamps section of this catalogue for the imperforate counterparts to these perforated coil stamps.

Perf. 8½ Vertically

412 A140 1c **green,** *Mar. 18, 1912*	25.00	*40.00*
deep green	25.00	40.00
Never hinged	55.00	
On cover		50.00
Pair	60.00	120.00
Never hinged	130.00	
Guide line pair	120.00	*250.00*
Never hinged	260.00	

Earliest documented use: May 21, 1912.

413 A140 2c **carmine,** type I, *Mar. 1912*	60.00	50.00
dark carmine	60.00	50.00
Never hinged	130.00	
On cover		60.00
Pair	125.00	100.00
Never hinged	260.00	
Guide line pair	275.00	*325.00*
Never hinged	575.00	
Double transfer	70.00	—
Nos. 410-413 (4)	101.00	120.00

Earliest documented use: April 16, 1912.

See Nos. 408H-409H in the Imperforate Flat Plate Coil Stamps section of this catalogue for the imperforate counterparts to these perforated coil stamps.

Alan E. Cohen

Dealer in High Grade Stamps

Visit our website today.

www.alanecohen.com

P. O. Box 929
New York, NY 10025
212-280-7865

e-mail: alanecohen@mindspring.com

Beware of plentiful fakes in the marketplace of Nos. 410-413, made by fraudulently perforating imperforate stamps.

Franklin — A148

1912-14 **Wmk. 190** ***Perf. 12***

No.	Description	Unused	Used
414	A148 8c **pale olive green,** *Feb. 1912*	37.50	2.00
	olive green	37.50	2.00
	Never hinged	90.00	
	On cover		15.00
	Block of 4	160.00	15.00
	P# block of 6, Impt. & "A"	475.00	
	Never hinged	800.00	

Earliest documented use: May 23, 1912.

No.	Description	Unused	Used
415	A148 9c **salmon red,** *Apr. 1914*	47.50	14.00
	rose red	47.50	14.00
	Never hinged	110.00	
	On cover		50.00
	Block of 4	200.00	125.00
	P# block of 6	650.00	
	Never hinged	1,100.	

Earliest documented use: May 1, 1914.

No.	Description	Unused	Used
416	A148 10c **orange yellow,** *Jan. 1912*	37.50	.80
	yellow	37.50	.80
	Never hinged	90.00	
	On cover		2.75
	Block of 4	160.00	5.25
	P# block of 6, Impt. & "A"	500.00	
	Never hinged	825.00	
	P# block of 6, "A"	550.00	
	Never hinged	900.00	
	Double transfer	—	—
a.	10c **brown yellow**	*1,250.*	
	Never hinged	*2,750.*	

Earliest documented use: Feb. 12, 1912.

No.	Description	Unused	Used
417	A148 12c **claret brown,** *Apr. 1914*	37.50	5.00
	deep claret brown	37.50	5.00
	Never hinged	90.00	
	On cover		25.00
	Block of 4	170.00	37.50
	P# block of 6	625.00	
	Never hinged	1,050.	
	Double transfer	50.00	—
	Triple transfer	70.00	—

Earliest documented use: May 5, 1914.

No.	Description	Unused	Used
418	A148 15c **gray,** *Feb. 1912*	77.50	4.00
	dark gray	77.50	4.00
	Never hinged	175.00	
	On cover		17.50
	Block of 4	325.00	35.00
	P# block of 6, Impt. & "A"	675.00	
	Never hinged	1,400.	
	P# block of 6, "A"	850.00	
	Never hinged	1,550.	
	P# block of 6	1,000.	
	Never hinged	1,700.	
	Double transfer	—	—

Earliest documented use: Apr. 26, 1912.

No.	Description	Unused	Used
419	A148 20c **ultramarine,** *Apr. 1914*	175.00	17.50
	dark ultramarine	175.00	17.50
	Never hinged	375.00	
	On cover		*150.00*
	Block of 4	750.00	130.00
	P# block of 6	2,000.	
	Never hinged	3,500.	

Earliest documented use: May 1, 1914.

No.	Description	Unused	Used
420	A148 30c **orange red,** *Apr. 1914*	105.00	17.50
	dark orange red	105.00	17.50
	Never hinged	230.00	
	On cover		*250.00*
	Block of 4	440.00	130.00
	P# block of 6	1,450.	
	Never hinged	2,400.	

Earliest documented use: May 1, 1914.

No.	Description	Unused	Used
421	A148 50c **violet,** *1914*	325.00	27.50
	bright violet	325.00	27.50
	Never hinged	725.00	
	On cover		*2,000.*
	Block of 4	1,400.	200.00
	P# block of 6	*10,000.*	
	Never hinged	*16,000.*	

Earliest documented use: May 1, 1914.

No. 421 almost always has an offset of the frame lines on the back under the gum. No. 422 does not have this offset.

1912, Feb. 12 **Wmk. 191**

No.	Description	Unused	Used
422	A148 50c **violet**	210.00	25.00
	Never hinged	475.00	
	On cover		*2,000.*
	Block of 4	900.00	160.00
	Margin block of 4, arrow, R or L	950.00	
	P# block of 6, Impt. & "A"	*4,750.*	
	Never hinged	*7,500.*	

Earliest documented use: Oct. 31, 1914.

No.	Description	Unused	Used
423	A148 $1 **violet brown**	450.00	80.00
	Never hinged	950.00	
	On cover		*7,000.*
	Block of 4	1,900.	1,000.
	Margin block of 4, arrow, R or L	2,000.	
	P# block of 6, Impt. & "A"	*13,500.*	
	Never hinged	*70,000.*	
	Double transfer (5782 L 66)	575.00	—

Earliest documented use: July 15, 1915.

During the United States occupation of Vera Cruz, Mexico, from April to November, 1914, letters sent from there show Provisional Postmarks.

For other listings of perforated sheet stamps of design A148, see:

Nos. 431-440 — Single line wmk. Perf. 10
Nos. 460 — Double line wmk. Perf. 10
Nos. 470-478 — Unwmkd. Perf. 10
Nos. 508-518 — Unwmkd. Perf. 11

1914 Compound Perforations

As the Bureau of Engraving and Printing made the changeover to perf 10 from perf 12, in the normal course of their stamp production they perforated limited quantities of 1c, 2c and 5c stamps with the old 12-gauge perforations in one direction and the new 10-gauge perforations in the other direction. These were not production errors. These compound-perforation stamps previously were listed as Nos. 424a, 424b, 425c, 425d and 428a.

All examples of Nos. 423A-423E must be accompanied by certificates of authenticity issued by a recognized expertizing committee. Fakes made from perf 12, perf 10 and imperfs exist.

1914 **Wmk. 190** ***Perf. 12x10***

No.	Description	Unused	Used
423A	A140 1c **green**	*14,000.*	*5,500.*
	Never hinged	—	
	Pair	—	*16,000.*
	Block of 4	—	*30,000.*
	On postcard		*11,000.*
	On cover, pair		*17,500.*

Formerly No. 424a. Eighteen unused and 52 used examples are recorded. Value for unused is for a sound stamp with perfs touching or just cutting the design. Value for used is for a sound stamp in the grade of fine-very fine. Of the used examples, 23 are precanceled Quincy IL (very scarce) or Chicago (usually inverted). The unused block of four, used block of four and pair on cover are each unique (top stamp of pair on cover with small piece missing and valued thus). Both the unused and used blocks have perforations slightly cutting into the design of each stamp at top. Values are for blocks with such centering.

No.	Description	Unused	Used
423B	A140 2c **rose red,** type I	*175,000.*	*12,500.*

Formerly No. 425d. One unused (a plate #7082 single) and 31 used examples are recorded. Value for used is for a sound stamp in the grade of fine-very fine. There are no precancels known on this issue.

No.	Description	Unused	Used
423C	A140 5c **blue**		*16,000.*
	Pair		—

Formerly No. 428a. 25 used examples are recorded. No unused examples are recorded. Three examples are precanceled: Tampa FL (2) and Rahway NJ (1). Value is for a sound stamp in the grade of fine-very fine. The pair is unique (one stamp creased, the other with a small tear).

Earliest documented use: April 14, 1915 (dated cancel on off-cover stamp).

1914 **Wmk. 190** ***Perf. 10x12***

No.	Description	Unused	Used
423D	A140 1c **green**		*9,000.*
	On postcard		*22,500.*

Formerly No. 424b. 56 used examples are recorded. No unused examples are recorded.The majority of stamps are precanceled Dayton OH (most common), Buffalo NY, and Elkhart IN (last two extremely scarce). Value is for a sound stamp in the grade of fine-very fine. The use on postcard is unique.

Earliest documented use: Dec. 19, 1914.

No.	Description	Unused	Used
423E	A140 2c **rose red,** type I		—

Formerly No. 425c. Only one used example has been certified (by the Philatelic Foundation). It is well centered, has a machine cancel, and has small thinning and a crease.

Plates of 400 subjects in four panes of 100 each.

Type of plate number and imprint used for the 12 special 1c and 2c plates designed for the production of coil stamps.

1913-15 **Wmk. 190** ***Perf. 10***

No.	Description	Unused	Used
424	A140 1c **green,** *Sept. 5, 1914*	2.25	.25
	bright green	2.25	.25
	deep green	2.25	.25
	yellowish green	2.25	.25
	Never hinged	4.75	
	On cover		.25
	Block of 4	9.50	1.50
	P# block of 6	60.00	
	Never hinged	90.00	
	Block of 10 with imprint "COIL STAMPS" and number (6581-82, 85, 89)	175.00	
	Never hinged	350.00	
	L or R P# block of 6 without imprint "COIL STAMPS" (#6581-82, 85, 89)	*850.00*	
	Cracked plate	—	—
	Double transfer	4.75	—
c.	Vert. pair, imperf. horiz.	*3,000.*	*2,750.*
	Never hinged	*4,500.*	
d.	Booklet pane of 6 ('13)	5.25	*7.50*
	Never hinged	8.75	
f.	Vert. pair, imperf. between and with straight edge at top	*13,000.*	

For former Nos. 424a and 424b, see Nos. 423A and 423D.

The unique example of No. 424f is never hinged, and it is valued thus.

Earliest documented uses: Oct. 11, 1914 (No. 424); Dec. 18, 1913 (No. 424d single); Sept. 24, 1915 (block with "COIL STAMPS" and plate number in selvage).

Research has proven beyond doubt that all examples of the previously listed No. 424e, booklet pane of 6, imperforate and without gum, are unissued fabrications made from an ungummed press sheet on stamp paper once undoubtedly housed in the Smithsonian philatelic collection.

No.	Description	Unused	Used
425	A140 2c **rose red,** type I, *Sept. 5, 1914*	2.10	.25
	dark rose red	2.10	.25
	carmine rose	2.10	.25
	carmine	2.10	.25
	dark carmine	2.10	.25
	scarlet	2.10	.25
	red	2.10	.25
	Never hinged	4.25	
	On cover		.25
	Block of 4	8.75	1.50
	P# block of 6	40.00	
	Never hinged	75.00	
	Block of 10 with imprint "COIL STAMPS" and number (6568, 70-72)	175.00	
	Never hinged	350.00	
	Cracked plate	9.50	—
	Double transfer	—	—
e.	Booklet pane of 6, *1913*	17.50	*25.00*
	Never hinged	30.00	

For former Nos. 425c and 425d, see Nos. 423E and 423B.

The aniline inks used on some printings of Nos. 425, 426 and 435a caused a pink tinge to permeate the paper and appear on the back. These are called "pink backs."

Earliest documented uses: Oct. 27, 1914 (No. 425); Dec. 23, 1913 (No. 425e pair).

No.	Description	Unused	Used
426	A140 3c **deep violet,** type I, *Sept. 18, 1914*	14.00	1.25
	violet	15.00	1.25
	bright violet	15.00	1.25
	reddish violet	15.00	1.25
	Never hinged	32.50	
	On cover		3.50
	Block of 4	57.50	11.00
	P# block of 6	250.00	
	Never hinged	400.00	

See "pink backs" note after No. 425.

Earliest documented use: Oct. 14, 1914.

No.	Description	Unused	Used
427	A140 4c **brown,** *Sept. 7, 1914*	32.50	.90
	dark brown	32.50	.90
	orange brown	32.50	.90
	yellowish brown	32.50	.90
	Never hinged	75.00	
	On cover		5.00
	Block of 4	135.00	8.50
	P# block of 6	475.00	
	Never hinged	775.00	
	Double transfer	42.50	—

Earliest documented use: Jan. 2, 1915.

No.	Description	Unused	Used
428	A140 5c **blue,** *Sept. 14, 1914*	32.50	.90
	bright blue	32.50	.90
	dark blue	32.50	.90
	indigo blue	32.50	.90
	Never hinged	75.00	
	On cover		3.00
	Block of 4	135.00	8.00
	P# block of 6	425.00	
	Never hinged	650.00	

For former No. 428a, see No. 423C.

Earliest documented use: Dec. 2, 1914.

No.	Description	Unused	Used
429	A140 6c **red orange,** *Sept. 28, 1914*	45.00	2.00
	deep red orange	45.00	2.00
	pale red orange	45.00	2.00
	Never hinged	105.00	
	On cover		9.00
	Block of 4 (2mm spacing)	200.00	15.00
	Block of 4 (3mm spacing)	190.00	14.00
	P# block of 6, Impt. & star	425.00	
	Never hinged	725.00	
	P# block of 6	525.00	
	Never hinged	875.00	

No.	Description	Unused	Used
430	A140 7c **black,** *Sept. 10, 1914*	80.00	4.75
	gray black	80.00	4.75
	intense black	80.00	4.75
	Never hinged	180.00	
	On cover		37.50

Block of 4 350.00 40.00
P# block of 6 1,000.
Never hinged 1,650.

Earliest documented use: April 14, 1915.

431 A148 8c **pale olive green,** *Sept. 26, 1914* 30.00 3.00
olive green 30.00 3.00
Never hinged 72.50
On cover 8.00
Block of 4 130.00 22.50
P# block of 6, Impt. & "A" 450.00
Never hinged 725.00
P# block of 6, "A" 550.00
Never hinged 900.00
Double transfer — —
a. Double impression —

Earliest documented use: Jan. 20, 1915.

432 A148 9c **salmon red,** *Oct. 6, 1914* 40.00 8.00
dark salmon red 40.00 8.00
Never hinged 95.00
On cover 27.50
Block of 4 170.00 70.00
P# block of 6 725.00
Never hinged 1,150.

Earliest documented use: Oct. 7, 1915 (dated cancel on off-cover block of 4); Feb. 25, 1916 (on cover).

433 A148 10c **orange yellow,** *Sept. 9, 1914* 40.00 1.00
golden yellow 40.00 1.00
Never hinged 95.00
On cover 7.50
Block of 4 170.00 6.00
P# block of 6, Impt. & "A" 650.00
Never hinged 1,100.
P# block of 6, "A" 950.00
Never hinged 1,600.
P# block of 6 825.00
Never hinged 1,400.

Earliest documented use: Nov. 13, 1914.

434 A148 11c **dark green,** *Aug. 12, 1915* 20.00 8.00
bluish green 20.00 8.00
Never hinged 50.00
On cover 25.00
Block of 4 85.00 65.00
P# block of 6 300.00
Never hinged 475.00

Earliest documented use: Sept. 23, 1915.

435 A148 12c **claret brown,** *Sept. 10, 1914* 22.50 5.50
deep claret brown 22.50 5.50
Never hinged 60.00
On cover 17.50
Block of 4 100.00 45.00
P# block of 6 350.00
Never hinged 525.00
Double transfer 32.50 —
Triple transfer 37.50 —
a. 12c **copper red** 27.50 6.50
Never hinged 67.50
On cover 20.00
Block of 4 120.00 50.00
P# block of 6 350.00
Never hinged 550.00

All so-called vertical pairs, imperf. between, have at least one perf. hole or "blind perfs" between the stamps.
See "pink backs" note after No. 425.

Earliest documented use: Feb. 22, 1915.

437 A148 15c **gray,** *Sept. 16, 1914* 110.00 8.00
dark gray 110.00 8.00
Never hinged 250.00
On cover 52.50
Block of 4 500.00 70.00
P# block of 6, Impt. & "A" 1,050.
Never hinged 2,100.
P# block of 6, "A" 1,225.
Never hinged 2,250.
P# block of 6 1,125.
Never hinged 2,150.

Earliest documented use: May 6, 1915.

438 A148 20c **ultramarine,** *Sept. 19, 1914* 185.00 7.00
dark ultramarine 185.00 7.00
Never hinged 425.00
On cover *150.00*
Block of 4 775.00 45.00
P# block of 6 3,250.
Never hinged *5,500.*

Earliest documented use: Nov. 28, 1914.

439 A148 30c **orange red,** *Sept. 19, 1914* 210.00 20.00
dark orange red 210.00 20.00
Never hinged 475.00
On cover *250.00*
Block of 4 900.00 135.00
P# block of 6 *4,000.*
Never hinged *6,750.*

Earliest documented use: Feb. 13, 1915.

440 A148 50c **violet,** *Dec. 10, 1915* 425.00 20.00
Never hinged 1,000.
On cover *1,750.*
Block of 4 1,900. 135.00
P# block of 6 *13,000.*
Never hinged —
Nos. 424-440 (16) 1,291. 90.80

The values for used coil singles, pairs and line pairs are for examples with contemporaneous cancels that can be authenticated by expertizing committees. Used coils with cancels most commonly from the 1950s exist, and these and stamps with other non-contemporaneous cancels sell for less than the values shown.

COIL STAMPS

1914 ***Perf. 10 Horizontally***

441 A140 1c **green,** *Nov. 14, 1914* 1.00 *1.50*
deep green 1.00 *1.50*
Never hinged 2.00
On cover 2.75
Pair 2.75 *7.00*
Never hinged 5.75
Guide line pair 8.00 *40.00*
Never hinged 17.50

442 A140 2c **carmine,** type I, *July 22, 1914* 10.00 *45.00*
deep carmine 10.00 *45.00*
Never hinged 22.50
On cover 60.00
Pair 25.00 *130.00*
Never hinged 55.00
Guide line pair 60.00 *300.00*
Never hinged 130.00

See Nos. 408V-409V in the Imperforate Flat Plate Coil Stamps section of this catalogue for the imperforate counterparts to these perforated coil stamps.

1914 ***Perf. 10 Vertically***

443 A140 1c **green,** *May 29, 1914* 30.00 *45.00*
deep green 30.00 *45.00*
Never hinged 65.00
On cover 60.00
Pair 75.00 *135.00*
Never hinged 160.00
Guide line pair 155.00 *250.00*
Never hinged 325.00

Earliest documented use: June. 19, 1914.

444 A140 2c **carmine,** type I, *Apr. 25, 1914* 50.00 40.00
deep carmine 50.00 40.00
red 50.00 40.00
Never hinged 120.00
On cover 57.50
Pair 120.00 125.00
Never hinged 250.00
Guide line pair 300.00 210.00
Never hinged 650.00
a. 2c **lake** *2,000.*

Earliest documented use: May 19, 1914.

See Nos. 408H-409H in the Imperforate Flat Plate Coil Stamps section of this catalogue for the imperforate counterparts to these perforated coil stamps.

445 A140 3c **violet,** type I, *Dec. 18, 1914* 210.00 *250.00*
deep violet 210.00 250.00
Never hinged 500.00
On cover *500.00*
Pair 500.00 *750.00*
Never hinged 1,100.
Guide line pair 1,200. *2,750.*
Never hinged 2,600.

Earliest documented use: August 13, 1915.

446 A140 4c **brown,** *Oct. 2, 1914* 130.00 *150.00*
Never hinged 280.00
On cover 200.00
Pair 300.00 *425.00*
Never hinged 650.00
Guide line pair 700.00 *1,250.*
Never hinged 1,550.

Earliest documented use: June 4, 1915.

447 A140 5c **blue,** *July 30, 1914* 45.00 *110.00*
Never hinged 100.00
On cover 140.00
Pair 105.00 *375.00*
Never hinged 220.00
Guide line pair 240.00 *950.00*
Never hinged 525.00

Earliest documented use: May 9, 1916.

Beware of plentiful fakes in the marketplace of Nos. 441-447, made by fraudulently perforating imperforate stamps or by fraudulently trimming perforations off fully perforated stamps.

ROTARY PRESS STAMPS

The Rotary Press Stamps are printed from plates that are curved to fit around a cylinder. This curvature produces stamps that are slightly larger, either horizontally or vertically, than those printed from flat plates. Designs of stamps from flat plates measure about 18½-19mm wide by 22mm high.

When the impressions are placed sidewise on the curved plates the designs are 19½-20mm wide; when they are placed vertically the designs are 22½ to 23mm high. A line of color (not a guide line) shows where the curved plates meet or join on the press.

Rotary Press Coil Stamps were printed from plates of 170 subjects for stamps coiled sidewise, and from plates of 150 subjects for stamps coiled endwise.

Double paper varieties of Rotary Press stamps are not listed in this catalogue. Collectors are referred to the note on "Rotary Press Double Paper" in the "Information for Collectors" in the front of the catalogue.

ROTARY PRESS COIL STAMPS

Stamp designs: 18½-19x22½mm

1915 ***Perf. 10 Horizontally***

448 A140 1c **green,** *Dec., 1915* 7.50 *17.50*
light green 7.50 *17.50*
Never hinged 16.00
On cover 30.00
Pair 17.50 *50.00*
Never hinged 40.00
Joint line pair 60.00 *250.00*
Never hinged 125.00

Earliest documented use: Dec. 11, 1915.

TYPE II

TWO CENTS
Type II. Shading lines in ribbons as on type I.
The toga button, rope and rope shading lines are heavy.
The shading lines of the face at the lock of hair end in a strong vertical curved line.
Used on rotary press printings only.

TYPE III

Type III. Two lines of shading in the curves of the ribbons.
Other characteristics similar to type II.
Used on rotary press printings only.

449 A140 2c **red,** type I, *1915* 2,500. 600.00
Never hinged 5,500.
carmine rose, type I 2,750.
On cover, type I 1,500.
Pair, type I 6,000. *8,000.*
Never hinged *12,500.*
Joint line pair, type I *13,500.* *25,000.*
Never hinged *28,000.*

Earliest documented uses: Oct. 29, 1915 (on cover front or dated cancel on off-cover stamp); Nov. 4, 1915 (on cover).

450 A140 2c **carmine,** type III, *1915* 12.50 *25.00*
carmine rose, type III 12.50 *25.00*
red, type III 12.50 *25.00*
Never hinged 27.50
On cover, type III 45.00
Pair, type III 30.00 *70.00*
Never hinged 65.00
Joint line pair, type III 240.00 *300.00*
Never hinged 550.00

Earliest documented use: Dec. 10, 1915 (dated cancel tying stamp to piece); Dec. 21, 1915 (on cover).

1914-16 *Perf. 10 Vertically*

Stamp designs: 19½-20x22mm

452 A140 1c **green,** *Nov. 11, 1914*	10.00	*17.50*
Never hinged	21.00	
On cover		30.00
Pair	25.00	*55.00*
Never hinged	55.00	
Joint line pair	75.00	*200.00*
Never hinged	160.00	

Earliest documented use: Nov. 25, 1914.

453 A140 2c **carmine rose,** type I, *July 3, 1914*	140.00	45.00
Never hinged	300.00	
On cover, type I		55.00
Pair, type I	300.00	140.00
Never hinged	625.00	
Joint line pair, type I	675.00	*600.00*
Never hinged	1,450.	
Cracked plate, type I	—	—

Earliest documented use: Sept. 26, 1914.

454 A140 2c **red,** type II, *June, 1915*	70.00	22.50
carmine, type II	70.00	22.50
Never hinged	160.00	
On cover, type II		50.00
Pair, type II	165.00	70.00
Never hinged	360.00	
Joint line pair, type II	400.00	*600.00*
Never hinged	850.00	

Earliest documented use: July 7, 1915.

455 A140 2c **carmine,** type III, *Dec. 1915*	8.00	3.50
carmine rose, type III	8.00	3.50
Never hinged	18.00	
On cover, type III		8.00
Pair, type III	20.00	*27.50*
Never hinged	42.50	
Joint line pair, type III	47.50	*175.00*
Never hinged	105.00	

Earliest documented use: Dec. 15, 1915.

Fraudulently altered examples of Type III (Nos. 455, 488, 492 and 540) have had one line of shading scraped off to make them resemble Type II (Nos. 454, 487, 491 and 539).

---

456 A140 3c **violet,** type I, *Feb. 2, 1916*	225.00	170.00
deep violet	225.00	170.00
red violet	225.00	170.00
Never hinged	500.00	
On cover		250.00
Pair	550.00	650.00
Never hinged	1,150.	
Joint line pair	1,250.	*3,000.*
Never hinged	2,600.	

Earliest documented use: Apr. 13, 1916.

457 A140 4c **brown,** *1915*	25.00	30.00
light brown	25.00	30.00
Never hinged	55.00	
On cover		50.00
Pair	60.00	95.00
Never hinged	140.00	
Joint line pair	160.00	*275.00*
Never hinged	325.00	
Cracked plate	35.00	—

Earliest documented use: Nov. 5, 1915.

458 A140 5c **blue,** *Mar. 9, 1916*	27.50	30.00
Never hinged	60.00	
On cover		50.00
Pair	67.50	95.00
Never hinged	150.00	
Joint line pair	160.00	*250.00*
Never hinged	350.00	
Double transfer	—	—

Earliest documented use: Apr. 6, 1916.

Horizontal Coil

1914, June 30 *Imperf.*

459 A140 2c **carmine,** type I	200.	*1,300.*
Never hinged	300.	
Pair	425.	*3,500.*
Never hinged	650.	
Joint line pair, with crease	500.	—
Never hinged	875.	
Joint line pair, without crease	850.	*50,000.*
Never hinged	1,500.	

Most line pairs of No. 459 are creased. The value for joint line pair with crease is for a pair creased vertically between the stamps, but not touching the design.

When the value for a used stamp is higher than the unused value, the stamp must have a contemporaneous cancel. Valuable stamps of this type should be accompanied by certificates of authenticity issued by recognized expertizing committees. The used value for No. 459 is for an example with such a certificate.

Beware of examples of No. 453 with perforations fraudulently trimmed to resemble single examples of No. 459.

Earliest documented use: Dec. 1914 (dated cancel on a used joint line pair, off cover).

FLAT PLATE PRINTINGS

1915 **Wmk. 191** *Perf. 10*

460 A148 $1 **violet black,** *Feb. 8*	650.	140.
Never hinged	1,450.	
On cover		*12,000.*
Block of 4	2,400.	750.
Margin block of 4, arrow, R or L	3,000.	
P# block of 6, Impt. & "A"	*11,000.*	
Never hinged	*17,000.*	
Double transfer (5782 L. 66)	800.	175.

Earliest documented uses: May 25, 1916 (dated cancel on stamp on mailing tag); June 2, 1916 (unique usage on cover is from Shanghai, China).

Wmk. 190 *Perf. 11*

461 A140 2c **pale car. red,** type I, *June 17*	150.	*375.*
Never hinged	325.	
On cover		*1,200.*
Block of 4	650.	*3,000.*
P# block of 6	*1,500.*	
Never hinged	*2,600.*	

Beware of fraudulently perforated examples of No. 409 being offered as No. 461.

See note on used stamps following No. 459.

Earliest documented use: June 24, 1915.

VALUES FOR VERY FINE STAMPS

Please note: Stamps are valued in the grade of Very Fine unless otherwise indicated.

FLAT PLATE PRINTINGS

Plates of 400 subjects in four panes of 100 each for all values 1c to 50c inclusive.

Plates of 200 subjects in two panes of 100 each for $1, $2 and $5 denominations.

The Act of Oct. 3, 1917, effective Nov. 2, 1917, created a 3 cent rate. Local rate, 2 cents.

1916-17 **Unwmk.** *Perf. 10*

462 A140 1c **green,** *Sept. 27, 1916*	7.00	.35
light green	7.00	.35
dark green	7.00	.35
bluish green	7.00	.35
Never hinged	16.00	
On cover		.50
Block of 4	30.00	3.25
P# block of 6	160.00	
Never hinged	275.00	
Experimental bureau precancel, New Orleans		10.00
Experimental bureau precancel, Springfield, Mass.		10.00
Experimental bureau precancel, Augusta, Me.		25.00
a. Booklet pane of 6, *Oct. 15, 1916*	9.50	*12.50*
Never hinged	16.00	
Cracked plate at right (Plate 7449, pane 9)	250.00	—
Never hinged	350.00	
Cracked plate at left (Plate 7449, pane 10)	310.00	
Never hinged	425.00	

Earliest documented uses: Oct. 3, 1916 (No. 462); Apr. 5, 1917 (No. 462a single).

463 A140 2c **carmine,** type I, *Sept. 1916*	4.50	.40
dark carmine	4.50	.40
rose red	4.50	.40
Never hinged	10.00	
On cover		.45
Block of 4	20.00	3.50
P# block of 6	150.00	
Never hinged	250.00	
Double transfer	6.50	—
Experimental bureau precancel, New Orleans		*500.00*
Experimental bureau precancel, Springfield, Mass.		22.50
a. Booklet pane of 6, *Oct. 8, 1916*	110.00	*110.00*
Never hinged	180.00	

See No. 467 for P# block of 6 from plate 7942.

Earliest documented uses: Sept. 12, 1916 (No. 463).

464 A140 3c **violet,** type I, *Nov. 11, 1916*	65.00	17.50
deep violet	65.00	17.50
Never hinged	165.00	
On cover		40.00
Block of 4	300.00	150.00
P# block of 6	1,500.	
Never hinged	2,500.	
Double transfer in "CENTS"	*90.00*	—
Experimental bureau precancel, New Orleans		*1,000.*
Experimental bureau precancel, Springfield, Mass.		200.00

Beware of fraudulently perforated examples of No. 483 being offered as No. 464.

Earliest documented use: Mar. 9, 1917.

465 A140 4c **orange brown,** *Oct. 7, 1916*	45.00	2.25
deep brown	45.00	2.25
brown	45.00	2.25
Never hinged	105.00	
On cover		10.00
Block of 4	200.00	22.50
P# block of 6	800.00	
Never hinged	1,350.	
Double transfer	—	—
Experimental bureau precancel, Springfield, Mass.		175.00

466 A140 5c **blue,** *Oct. 17, 1916*	65.00	2.25
dark blue	65.00	2.25
Never hinged	150.00	
On cover		12.00
Block of 4	270.00	22.50
P# block of 6	950.00	
Never hinged	1,600.	
Experimental bureau precancel, Springfield, Mass.		175.00

Earliest documented use: Dec. 7, 1916.

467 A140 5c **carmine** (error in plate of 2c)	425.00	*3,000.*
Never hinged	800.00	
On cover		*5,000.*
Block of 9, #467 in middle	900.00	*3,500.*
Never hinged	1,550.	
Block of 12, two middle stamps #467	1,750.	*5,000.*
Never hinged	2,900.	
P# block of 6 2c stamps (#463), P#7942	140.00	
Never hinged	250.00	

No. 467 is an error caused by using a 5c transfer roll in re-entering three subjects: 7942 UL 74, 7942 UL 84, 7942 LR 18; the balance of the subjects on the plate being normal 2c entries. No. 467 imperf. is listed as No. 485. The error perf 11 on unwatermarked paper is No. 505.

The first value given for the error in blocks of 9 and 12 is for blocks with the error stamp(s) never hinged. The second value given is for blocks in which all stamps are never hinged. See note on used stamps following No. 459.

Earliest documented use: May 22, 1917.

468 A140 6c **red orange,** *Oct. 10, 1916*	80.00	8.00
Never hinged	180.00	
On cover		35.00
Block of 4	340.00	70.00
P# block of 6	1,350.	
Never hinged	2,500.	
Double transfer	—	—
Experimental bureau precancel, New Orleans		*2,500.*
Experimental bureau precancel, Springfield, Mass.		175.00

Earliest documented use: Feb. 27, 1917 (dated cancel on off-cover block of 4); April 19, 1917 (on cover).

469 A140 7c **black,** *Oct. 10, 1916*	110.00	13.00
gray black	110.00	13.00
Never hinged	250.00	
On cover		45.00
Block of 4	460.00	125.00
P# block of 6	1,350.	
Never hinged	2,500.	
Experimental bureau precancel, Springfield, Mass.		175.00

Earliest documented use: Feb. 19, 1917.

470 A148 8c **olive green,** *Nov. 13, 1916*	50.00	7.00
dark olive green	50.00	7.00
Never hinged	115.00	
On cover		25.00
Block of 4	210.00	60.00
P# block of 6, Impt. & "A"	550.00	
Never hinged	900.00	
P# block of 6, "A"	600.00	
Never hinged	1,050.	
Experimental bureau precancel, Springfield, Mass.		165.00

Earliest documented use: Dec. 29, 1916 (dated cancel on off-cover block of 4); Feb. 13, 1917 (on cover).

471 A148 9c **salmon red,** *Nov. 16, 1916*	55.00	17.50
Never hinged	125.00	
On cover		40.00
Block of 4	230.00	140.00
P# block of 6	750.00	
Never hinged	1,250.	
Experimental bureau precancel, Springfield, Mass.		150.00

Earliest documented use: Aug. 6, 1917.

472 A148 10c **orange yellow,** *Oct. 17, 1916*	100.00	3.00
Never hinged	230.00	
On cover		8.50
Block of 4	425.00	17.50
P# block of 6	1,350.	
Never hinged	2,250.	
Experimental bureau precancel, Springfield, Mass.		160.00

Earliest documented use: Oct. 24, 1916.

473 A148 11c **dark green,** *Nov. 16, 1916*	42.50	19.00
Never hinged	90.00	
On cover		47.50
Block of 4	180.00	140.00
P# block of 6	360.00	
Never hinged	625.00	
Experimental bureau precancel, Springfield, Mass.		*575.00*

Earliest documented use: Apr. 13, 1917.

474 A148 12c **claret brown,** *Oct. 1916*	47.50	8.00
Never hinged	110.00	
On cover		22.50
Block of 4	210.00	55.00
P# block of 6	625.00	
Never hinged	1,050.	
Double transfer	62.50	9.00
Triple transfer	75.00	12.00
Experimental bureau precancel, Springfield, Mass.		200.00

Earliest documented uses: Oct. 6, 1916 (dated cancel on off-cover pair); Oct. 13, 1916 (on cover).

475 A148 15c **gray,** *Nov. 16, 1916*	170.00	15.00
dark gray	170.00	15.00
Never hinged	375.00	
On cover		85.00
Block of 4	725.00	120.00
P# block of 6	3,000.	
Never hinged	5,250.	
P# block of 6, Impt. & "A"	*8,000.*	
Experimental bureau precancel, Springfield, Mass.		150.00

Earliest documented use: Mar. 2, 1917.

476 A148 20c **light ultramarine,** *Dec. 5, 1916*	200.00	17.50
ultramarine	200.00	17.50
Never hinged	475.00	
On cover		*725.00*
Block of 4	850.00	130.00
P# block of 6	3,400.	
Never hinged	*5,750.*	
Experimental bureau precancel, Springfield, Mass.		125.00
476A A148 30c **orange red**	*2,000.*	
Never hinged	*4,250.*	
Block of 4	*10,000.*	
Never hinged	*20,000.*	
P# block of 6	*30,000.*	
Never hinged	*50,000.*	

No. 476A is valued in the grade of fine.

477 A148 50c **light violet,** *Mar. 2, 1917*	850.	80.00
Never hinged	2,000.	
On cover		*2,250.*
Block of 4	3,750.	575.00
P# block of 6	*60,000.*	
Never hinged	—	

Earliest documented use: Aug. 31, 1917.

478 A148 $1 **violet black,** *Dec. 22, 1916*	600.	27.50
Never hinged	1,400.	
On cover		*3,000.*
Block of 4	2,600.	200.00
Margin block of 4, arrow, R or L	2,800.	
P# block of 6, Impt. & "A"	*10,000.*	
Never hinged	*17,500.*	
Double transfer (5782 L 66)	675.	30.00

Earliest documented use: May 24, 1917 (on large part of parcel label).

TYPES OF 1902-03 ISSUE

1917, Mar. 22 Unwmk. *Perf. 10*

479 A127 $2 **dark blue**	210.00	40.00
Never hinged	475.00	
On cover (other than first flight or Zeppelin)		*1,250.*
On first flight cover		*350.00*
On Zeppelin flight cover		*750.00*
Block of 4	925.00	325.00
Margin block of 4, arrow, R or L	1,050.	
P# block of 6	4,000.	
Never hinged	*6,500.*	
Double transfer		

Earliest documented use (on large piece of reg'd parcel wrapper): Apr. 6, 1917.

480 A128 $5 **light green**	170.00	35.00
Never hinged	375.00	
On cover		*1,250.*
Block of 4	750.00	280.00
Margin block of 4, arrow, R or L	850.00	
P# block of 6	3,000.	—
Never hinged	*5,000.*	

Earliest documented use: Apr. 6, 1917 (on large piece of reg'd parcel wrapper).

Earliest documented use dates for imperforates are for the imperforate sheet stamps, not for imperforate stamps with vending and affixing machine perforations or for flat plate imperforate coil stamps. EDU dates for VAMP and flat plate imperf coil stamps are shown in their respective sections later in the catalogue.

1916-17 *Imperf.*

481 A140 1c **green,** *Nov. 1916*	1.25	.95
bluish green	1.25	.95
deep green	1.25	.95
Never hinged	1.90	
On cover		1.50
Pair	2.60	2.00
Never hinged	4.00	
Block of 4	5.25	4.00
Corner margin block of 4	5.50	4.25
Margin block of 4, arrow	3.75	4.40
Center line block	10.00	8.50
Never hinged	16.50	
P# block of 6	30.00	—
Never hinged	45.00	
Margin block of 6, Electrolytic (Pl. 13376)	450.00	
Never hinged	800.00	
Margin block of 6, Electrolytic (Pl. 13377)	1,000.	
Never hinged	1,500.	
Single, Electrolytic	5.00	
Never hinged	10.00	
Double transfer	2.75	2.75

Earliest documented use: Nov. 17, 1916.

During September 1921, the Bureau of Engraving and Printing issued a 1c stamp printed from experimental electrolytic plates made in accordance with a patent granted to George U. Rose. Tests at that time did not prove satisfactory, and the method was discontinued. Four plates were made: 13376, 13377, 13389 and 13390, from which stamps were issued. They are difficult to distinguish from the normal varieties, but can be authenticated by experts. Singles and blocks must be certified. (See No. 498).

TYPE Ia

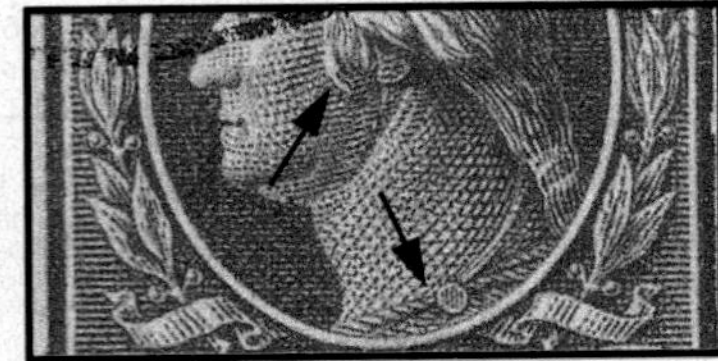

TWO CENTS

Type Ia. The design characteristics are similar to type I except that all of the lines of the design are stronger.

The toga button, toga rope and rope shading lines are heavy.

The latter characteristics are those of type II, which, however, occur only on impressions from rotary plates.

Used only on flat plates 10208 and 10209.

482 A140 2c **carmine,** type I, *Dec. 8, 1916*	1.50	1.30
deep carmine	1.50	1.30
carmine rose	1.50	1.30
deep rose	1.50	1.30
Never hinged	2.60	
On cover		2.50
Pair	3.20	2.75
Never hinged	5.50	
Block of 4	6.50	6.50
Corner margin block of 4	6.75	*6.75*
Margin block of 4, arrow	7.00	*7.00*
Center line block	9.50	*10.00*
Never hinged	15.00	
P# block of 6	30.00	—
Never hinged	45.00	
Cracked plate	—	—

Earliest documented use: Dec. 16, 1916.

See No. 485 for P# block of 6 from plate 7942.

482A A140 2c **deep rose,** type Ia	—	*65,000.*
On cover		*70,000.*
Pair		*140,000.*

Earliest documented use: Feb. 17, 1920.

The imperforate, type Ia, was issued but all known examples were privately perforated with large oblong perforations at the sides (Schermack type III). See the vending and affixing machine perforations section of this catalogue.

The No. 482A pair is unique.

TYPE II

THREE CENTS

Type II. The top line of the toga rope is strong and the rope shading lines are heavy and complete.

The line between the lips is heavy.

Used on both flat plate and rotary press printings.

483 A140 3c **violet,** type I, *Oct. 13, 1917*	12.00	10.00
light violet	12.00	10.00
Never hinged	24.00	
On cover		25.00
Pair	25.00	22.50
Never hinged	50.00	
Block of 4	50.00	45.00
Corner margin block of 4	52.50	47.50
Margin block of 4, arrow	55.00	50.00
Center line block	80.00	75.00
Never hinged	140.00	
P# block of 6	125.00	—
Never hinged	200.00	
Double transfer	20.00	—
Triple transfer		—

Earliest documented use: Nov. 8, 1917.

484 A140 3c **violet,** type II	10.00	8.00
deep violet	10.00	8.00
Never hinged	20.00	
On cover		14.00
Pair	21.00	17.00
Never hinged	42.50	
Block of 4	42.50	35.00
Corner margin block of 4	45.00	37.50
Margin block of 4, arrow	47.50	40.00
Center line block	75.00	67.50
Never hinged	140.00	
P# block of 6	95.00	—
Never hinged	160.00	
Double transfer	14.00	—

Earliest documented use: Apr. 30, 1918.

485 A140 5c **carmine** (error), *Mar. 1917*	*9,000.*	
Never hinged	*13,000.*	
Block of 9, #485 in middle	*16,500.*	
Never hinged	*22,000.*	
Block of 12, two middle stamps #485	*25,000.*	
Never hinged	*32,500.*	
P# block of six 2c stamps (#482), P#7942	130.00	
Never hinged	220.00	

No. 485 is usually seen either as the center stamp in a block of 9 with 8 No. 482 (the first value given being with No. 485 never hinged) or as two center stamps in a block of 12 (the first value given being with both examples of No. 485 never hinged). A second value is given for each block with all stamps in the block never hinged.

See note under No. 467.

ROTARY PRESS COIL STAMPS

(See note over No. 448)

1916-18 *Perf. 10 Horizontally*

Stamp designs: 18½-19x22½mm

486 A140 1c **green,** *Jan. 1918*	.85	.85
yellowish green	.85	.85
Never hinged	1.75	
On cover		1.15
Pair	2.00	*2.50*
Never hinged	4.25	
Joint line pair	4.50	*15.00*
Never hinged	9.50	
Cracked plate	—	—
Double transfer	2.25	—

Earliest documented use: June 30, 1918.

487 A140 2c **carmine,** type II, *Nov. 15, 1916*	12.50	14.00
Never hinged	27.50	
On cover		19.00
Pair	30.00	37.50
Never hinged	65.00	
Joint line pair	120.00	*140.00*
Never hinged	275.00	
Cracked plate		*600.00*

Earliest documented use: Sept. 21, 1917.

(See note after No. 455)

488 A140 2c **carmine,** type III, *1916*	3.00	*5.00*
carmine rose	3.00	*5.00*
Never hinged	6.50	
On cover		7.00
Pair	8.00	*17.50*
Never hinged	17.50	
Joint line pair	40.00	*110.00*
Never hinged	90.00	
Cracked plate	12.50	10.00

Earliest documented use: Feb. 12, 1917.

489 A140 3c **violet,** type I, *Oct. 10, 1917*	4.50	2.25
dull violet	4.50	2.25
bluish violet	4.50	2.25
Never hinged	10.00	
On cover		3.50
Pair	10.50	9.00

WEISZ STAMPS & COVERS
APPRAISALS, BUYING AND SELLING

We're Always Buying
Accepting Want-Lists

U.S. Stamps & Postal History
U.S. FDCs, Flights and Events
P.O. Box 15559, New Orleans, LA 70175
773.914.4332
weiszcovers@yahoo.com
www.douglasweisz.com

Never hinged 22.50
Joint line pair 32.50 *40.00*
Never hinged 70.00

Earliest documented use: Nov. 23, 1917.

Rosette plate crack on head

1916-22 ***Perf. 10 Vertically***

Stamp designs: 19½-20x22mm

490 A140 1c **green,** *Nov. 17, 1916* .50 *.60*
yellowish green .50 *.60*
Never hinged 1.05
On cover .80
Pair 1.25 *2.25*
Never hinged 2.60
Joint line pair 3.25 *12.50*
Never hinged 7.00
Double transfer — —
Cracked plate (horizontal) 7.50 —
Cracked plate (vertical) retouched 9.00 —
Rosette plate crack on head *60.00* —
a. Small holes, pair — —
Joint line pair — —

Earliest documented use: No. 490: Jan. 3, 1917 (dated cancel on off-cover pair); Feb. 14, 1917 (on cover).

491 A140 2c **carmine,** type II, *Nov. 17, 1916* 2,500. 800.00
Never hinged 5,250.
On cover, type II 1,100.
Pair, type II 5,750. 3,750.
Never hinged *12,500.*
Joint line pair, type II *13,000. 20,000.*
Never hinged *26,000.*

Earliest documented use: Dec. 19, 1916 (dated cancel on off-cover rejoined pair); Jan. 2, 1917 (on cover).

See note after No. 455.

492 A140 2c **carmine,** type III 9.00 1.00
carmine rose, type III 9.00 1.00
Never hinged 19.00
On cover, type III 1.40
Pair, type III 21.50 5.00
Never hinged 45.00
Joint line pair, type III 55.00 *35.00*
Never hinged 115.00
Double transfer, type III — —
Cracked plate — —
a. Small holes, joint line pair — —

Earliest documented use: Jan. 13, 1917 (No. 492).

493 A140 3c **violet,** type I, *July 23, 1917* 14.00 4.50
reddish violet, type I 14.00 4.50
Never hinged 30.00
On cover, type I 8.00
Pair, type I 35.00 12.50
Never hinged 75.00
Joint line pair, type I 110.00 *90.00*
Never hinged 230.00

Earliest documented use: Nov. 2, 1917.

494 A140 3c **violet,** type II, *Feb. 4, 1918* 10.00 2.50
dull violet, type II 10.00 2.50
gray violet, type II 10.00 2.50
Never hinged 21.50
On cover, type II 4.00
Pair, type II 24.00 9.00
Never hinged 50.00
Joint line pair, type II 75.00 22.50
Never hinged 160.00

Earliest documented use: Apr. 16, 1918.

495 A140 4c **orange brown,** *Apr. 15, 1917* 10.00 7.00
Never hinged 21.50
On cover 10.00
Pair 24.00 20.00
Never hinged 50.00
Joint line pair 75.00 45.00
Never hinged 160.00
Cracked plate 25.00 —
a. Small holes, pair — —
Joint line pair —

Earliest documented use: June 20, 1917 (No. 495).

496 A140 5c **blue,** large holes, *Jan. 15, 1919* 3.25 2.50
Never hinged 7.00
On cover 3.00
Pair 8.00 10.00
Never hinged 17.50
Joint line pair 30.00 22.50
Never hinged 65.00
a. Small holes — —
Pair *225.00* —
Never hinged *550.00*
Joint line pair —
Never hinged —

See note concerning large and small perforation holes following No. 1053.

Earliest documented use: April 15, 1919.

497 A148 10c **orange yellow,** *Jan. 31, 1922* 17.50 17.50
Never hinged 35.00
On cover 22.50
Pair 40.00 *57.50*
Never hinged 85.00
Joint line pair 120.00 *200.00*
Never hinged 260.00

Earliest documented use: Jan. 31, 1922 (FDC).

Blind Perfs

Listings of imperforate-between varieties are for examples which show no trace of "blind perfs," traces of impressions from the perforating pins which do not cut into the paper.

Some unused stamps have had the gum removed to eliminate the impressions from the perforating pins. These stamps do not qualify as the listed varieties.

TYPES OF 1913-15 ISSUE

FLAT PLATE PRINTINGS

Plates of 400 subjects in four panes of 100.

1917-19 **Unwmk.** ***Perf. 11***

498 A140 1c **green,** *Mar. 1917* .35 .25
light green .35 .25
dark green .35 .25
yellowish green .35 .25
Never hinged .75
On cover .30
Block of 4 1.40 1.50
P# block of 6 22.50
Never hinged 35.00
Margin block of 6, Electrolytic (Pl, 13376-7, 13389-90) *See note after No. 481* *1,250.*
Never hinged *2,000.*
Single, Electrolytic (See note after No. 481) *25.00*
Never hinged *50.00*
Single, Electrolytic, pl. #13390, on postcard —
Cracked plate (10656 UL and 10645 LR) 35.00 —
Double transfer 5.50 2.00
a. Vertical pair, imperf. horiz. 800.00
Never hinged *1,600.*
b. Horizontal pair, imperf. between 600.00
Never hinged *1,350.*
c. Vertical pair, imperf. between *700.00* —
d. Double impression 250.00 *3,750.*
e. Booklet pane of 6, *March 1917* 2.50 *2.00*
Never hinged 4.25
f. Booklet pane of 30, *Aug. 1917* *1,050. 12,500.*
Never hinged *1,700.*
g. Perf. 10 at top or bottom *15,000. 20,000.*
Never hinged *27,500.*

Earliest documented use: March 30, 1917 (No. 498e booklet pair); Aug. 8, 1917 (No. 498f single).

No. 498g used is valued in the grade of fine. No. 498g also known as a transitional stamp gauging 10 at left bottom and 11 at right bottom (bottom center stamp in a plate block of 6).

No. 499g, Stamp 15mm Wide

Recut In Hair, Type I

499 A140 2c **rose,** type I, *Mar. 1917* .35 .25
dark rose, type I .35 .25
carmine rose, type I .35 .25
deep rose, type I .35 .25
Never hinged .75
On cover, type I .30
Block of 4, type I 1.40 1.50
P# block of 6, type I 22.50
Never hinged 35.00
Cracked plate, type I — —
Recut in hair, type I *1,750. 2,300.*
Never hinged *3,500.*
Double transfer, type I 6.00 —
a. Vertical pair, imperf. horiz., type I 1,000.
Never hinged 2,000.
b. Horiz. pair, imperf. vert., type I *550.00 600.00*
Never hinged *1,100.*
c. Vert. pair, imperf. btwn., type I *900.00 300.00*
e. Booklet pane of 6, type I, *Mar. 31, 1917* 4.00 *2.50*
Never hinged 6.75
f. Booklet pane of 30, type I, *Aug. 1917* *20,000.* —
Never hinged *29,000.*
g. Double impression, type I 200.00 *2,000.*
Never hinged *400.00*
On cover —
As "g," stamp design 15mm wide *1,000.*
Never hinged *1,500.*
h. 2c **lake,** type I 500.00 800.00
Never hinged *1,000.*
On cover —
i. As "e," single stamp, **lake** —

No. 499b is valued in the grade of fine. No 499g used is valued in the grade of fine.

See No. 505 for P# block of 6 from plate 7942.

No. 499h occurs in two different lake shades. The true lake is similar to the lake on other lake shades noted elsewhere in this catalogue. A somewhat more common lake shade is known as "Boston lake," and it is a very distinctive and duller lake shade. Certificates of authenticity recommended for these and all listed lake shades.

Earliest documented uses: Mar. 27, 1917 (No. 499); July 19, 1917 (No. 499e single); Aug. 7, 1917 (No. 499f single).

500 A140 2c **deep rose,** type Ia 250.00 240.00
Never hinged 550.00
On cover, type Ia *650.00*
Block of 4, type Ia 1,100. *1,500.*
P# block of 6, type Ia 2,000.
Never hinged 3,750. —
P# block of 6, two stamps type I (P# 10208 LL) *15,000.*
Never hinged *22,500.*
Pair, types I and Ia (10208 LL 95 or 96) *1,500.*

Earliest documented use: Dec. 15, 1919.

No. 500 exists with imperforate top sheet margin. Examples have been altered by trimming perforations. Some also have faked Schermack perfs.

501 A140 3c **light violet,** type I, *Mar. 1917* 9.00 .40
violet, type I 9.00 .40
dark violet, type I 9.00 .40
reddish violet, type I 9.00 .40
Never hinged 20.00
On cover, type I .50
Block of 4, type I 37.50 4.00
P# block of 6, type I 140.00
Never hinged 240.00
Double transfer, type I 11.00
b. Bklt. pane of 6, type I, *Oct. 17, 1917* 75.00 *80.00*
Never hinged 125.00
c. Vert. pair, imper. horiz., type I *2,100.*
Never hinged *3,250.*
d. Double impression *3,500. 3,500.*
Never hinged *5,000.*

Earliest documented uses: Mar. 29, 1917 (No. 501); Feb. 8, 1918 (No. 501b single).

No. 501d is valued in the grade of fine.

502 A140 3c **dark violet,** type II 12.00 .75
violet, type II 12.00 .75
Never hinged 27.50
On cover, type II 1.00
Block of 4, type II 50.00 5.50
P# block of 6, type II 160.00
Never hinged 275.00
b. Bklt. pane of 6, type II, *Feb. 25, 1918* 60.00 *75.00*
Never hinged 100.00
c. Vert. pair, imperf. horiz., type II *1,400. 850.00*
Never hinged *2,750.*
On cover *1,400.*
d. Double impression 800.00 *1,000.*
Never hinged 1,600.
e. Perf. 10 at top or bottom *15,000. 30,000.*
Never hinged *21,500.*

Earliest documented uses: Jan. 30, 1918 (No. 502); June 12, 1918 (No. 502b single).

503 A140 4c **brown,** *Mar. 1917* 8.50 .40
dark brown 8.50 .40
orange brown 8.50 .40
yellow brown 8.50 .40
Never hinged 19.00
On cover 2.10
Block of 4 35.00 3.50
P# block of 6 150.00
Never hinged 250.00
Double transfer 14.00 —
b. Double impression —

504 A140 5c **blue,** *Mar. 1917* 7.50 .35
light blue 7.50 .35
dark blue 7.50 .35
Never hinged 17.00
On cover .45
Block of 4 32.50 3.00
P# block of 6 140.00
Never hinged 225.00
Double transfer 10.00 —
a. Horizontal pair, imperf. between *20,000.* —
b. Double impression *1,750. 1,600.*

Earliest documented use: June 5, 1917.

505 A140 5c **rose** (error) 325.00 *600.00*
Never hinged 625.00
On cover 2,250.
Block of 9, middle stamp #505 650.00 *1,100.*
Never hinged 1,000.
Block of 12, two middle stamps #505 1,200. *3,000.*
Never hinged 1,850.
P# block of six 2c stamps (#499), P# 7942 40.00
Never hinged 70.00

Earliest documented use: Mar. 27, 1917.

Value notes under No. 467 also apply to No. 505.

No. 506b

506 A140 6c **red orange,** *Mar. 1917* 11.00 .40
orange 11.00 .40
Never hinged 25.00
On cover 2.50
Block of 4 47.50 4.00
P# block of 6 180.00
Never hinged 300.00
Double transfer — —
a. Perf. 10 at top or bottom *30,000.* *8,000.*
b. Double impression, never hinged *2,000.*

No. 506a also exists as a transitional stamp gauging partly perf 10 and partly perf 11 at top. Value thus the same as normal 506a.

No. 506b is a partial double impression. Two authenticated examples are documented.

507 A140 7c **black,** *Mar. 1917* 24.00 1.25
gray black 24.00 1.25
intense black 24.00 1.25
Never hinged 55.00
On cover 7.75
Block of 4 100.00 12.50
P# block of 6 250.00
Never hinged 450.00
Double transfer — —

508 A148 8c **olive bister,** *Mar. 1917* 11.00 .65
dark olive green 11.00 .65
olive green 11.00 .65
Never hinged 25.00
On cover 2.75
Block of 4 47.50 6.50
P# block of 6, Impt. & "A" 170.00
Never hinged 285.00
P# block of 6, "A" 220.00
Never hinged 370.00
P# block of 6 140.00
Never hinged 240.00
b. Vertical pair, imperf. between — —
c. Perf. 10 at top or bottom *9,000.*

509 A148 9c **salmon red,** *Mar. 1917* 11.00 1.60
salmon 11.00 1.60
Never hinged 25.00
On cover 13.00
Block of 4 47.50 18.00
P# block of 6 150.00
Never hinged 250.00
Double transfer 18.00 4.50
a. Perf. 10 at top or bottom *7,500.*
Never hinged *37,500.*

No. 509a also exists as a transitional stamp gauging partly perf 10 and partly perf 11 at top or bottom. Value thus the same as normal 509a.

Earliest documented use: Nov. 23, 1917.

510 A148 10c **orange yellow,** *Mar. 1917* 15.00 .25
golden yellow 15.00 .25
Never hinged 34.00
On cover 2.00
Block of 4 62.50 2.00
P# block of 6, "A" 290.00
Never hinged 475.00
P# block of 6 200.00
Never hinged 325.00
a. 10c **brown yellow** *1,400.*
Never hinged *3,250.*

Earliest documented use: Mar. 27, 1917.

511 A148 11c **light green,** *May 1917* 7.50 2.25
green 7.50 2.25
Never hinged 17.00
dark green 8.50 2.25
Never hinged 18.00
On cover 8.50
Block of 4 32.50 20.00
P# block of 6 150.00
Never hinged 260.00
Double transfer 11.00 3.00
a. Perf. 10 at top or bottom *4,000.* *3,750.*
Never hinged *7,500.*
Block of 4, two stamps No. 511a — *9,500.*
P# block of 6, top, bottom 3 stamps No. 511a *25,000.*

No. 511a also exists as a transitional stamp gauging partly perf 10 and partly perf 11 at top or bottom. Value thus the same as normal 511a.

512 A148 12c **claret brown,** *May 1917* 7.50 .40
Never hinged 17.00
On cover 4.00
Block of 4 32.50 3.75
P# block of 6 150.00
Never hinged 260.00
Double transfer 11.00 —
Triple transfer 20.00 —
a. 12c **brown carmine** 8.50 .50
Never hinged 19.00
On cover 4.50
Block of 4 36.00 4.50
P# block of 6 150.00
Never hinged 260.00
b. Perf. 10 at top or bottom *25,000.* *15,000.*
On cover —

Earliest documented use: Aug. 15, 1917 (No. 512a); Aug. 26, 1924 (No. 512b).

513 A148 13c **apple green,** *Jan. 10, 1919* 9.50 5.50
pale apple green 9.50 5.50
Never hinged 21.00
deep apple green 11.50 6.00
Never hinged 26.00
On cover 19.00
Block of 4 40.00 45.00
P# block of 6 140.00
Never hinged 240.00

Earliest documented use: Jan. 25, 1919.

514 A148 15c **gray,** *May 1917* 32.50 1.40
dark gray 32.50 1.40
Never hinged 75.00
On cover 25.00
Block of 4 140.00 12.50
P# block of 6 550.00 —
Never hinged 900.00
Double transfer — —
a. Perf. 10 at bottom *10,000.*

Earliest documented use: Nov. 15, 1917.

No. 515c

515 A148 20c **light ultramarine,** *May 1917* 40.00 .45
gray blue 40.00 .45
Never hinged 85.00
deep ultramarine 45.00 .55
Never hinged 95.00
On cover 75.00
Block of 4 175.00 3.50
P# block of 6 600.00
Never hinged 1,000.
Double transfer — —
b. Vertical pair, imperf. between *1,750.* *3,250.*
c. Double impression *1,250.*
Never hinged *2,500.*
d. Perf. 10 at top or bottom — *12,500.*

No. 515b is valued in the grade of fine.

Beware of pairs with blind perforations inside the design of the top stamp that are offered as No. 515b.

No. 515c is a partial double impression.

Earliest documented use: May 4, 1918.

516 A148 30c **orange red,** *May 1917* 27.50 1.50
dark orange red 27.50 1.50
Never hinged 65.00
On cover 150.00
Block of 4 120.00 12.50
P# block of 6 600.00
Never hinged 925.00
Double transfer —
Dropped transfer (6921 LL 49) *1,150.*
a. Perf. 10 at top or bottom *20,000.* *15,000.*
Never hinged *37,500.*
b. Double impression —

No. 516a used is valued in the grade of fine.

Earliest documented use: Jan. 12, 1918.

517 A148 50c **red violet,** *May 1917* 45.00 .75
Never hinged 110.00
violet 55.00 .75
Never hinged 135.00
light violet 57.50 .75
Never hinged 145.00
On cover *400.00*
Block of 4 200.00 5.00
P# block of 6 1,600.
Never hinged 2,550.
Double transfer 85.00 1.75
b. Vertical pair, imperf. between & with natural straight edge at bottom *6,000.*
c. Perf. 10 at top or bottom *17,500.*

No. 517b is valued in average condition and may be a unique used pair (precanceled). The editors would like to see authenticated evidence of an unused pair.

Earliest documented use: Dec. 28, 1917 (on registry tag).

518 A148 $1 **violet brown,** *May 1917* 37.50 1.50
violet black 37.50 1.50
Never hinged 95.00
On cover *550.00*
Block of 4 165.00 12.50
Margin block of 4, arrow right or left 220.00
P# block of 6, Impt. & "A" 1,300. —
Never hinged 2,100.
Double transfer (5782 L. 66) 57.50 2.00
b. $1 **deep brown** *1,900.* *1,250.*
Never hinged *4,000.*
Block of 4 *9,000.* *5,500.*
P# block of 6, Impt. & "A," never hinged *32,500.*
Nos. 498-504,506-518 (20) 566.70 260.30

Earliest documented use: May 19, 1917.

No. 518b is valued in the grade of fine to very fine.

TYPE OF 1908-09 ISSUE

1917, Oct. 10 **Wmk. 191** ***Perf. 11***

This is the result of an old stock of No. 344 which was returned to the Bureau in 1917 and perforated with the then current gauge 11. Only lower left panes of No. 344 were perforated 11, and therefore only left and bottom plate blocks exist.

519 A139 2c **carmine** 425.00 *1,800.*
Never hinged 900.00
On cover *3,500.*
Block of 4 1,900. *9,250.*
P# block of 6, T V, Impt. 3,500. —
Never hinged *6,500.*

Beware of examples of No. 344 fraudulently perforated and offered as No. 519. Obtaining a certificate from a recognized expertizing committee is strongly recommended.

Warning: See note following No. 459 regarding used stamps.

Earliest documented use: Oct. 10, 1917.

Franklin — A149

Plates of 100 subjects.

1918, Aug. **Unwmk.** ***Perf. 11***

523 A149 $2 **orange red & black** 500. 240.
red orange & black 500. 240.
Never hinged 1,100.
On cover *2,000.*
Block of 4 2,100. 1,300.
Margin block of 4, arrow 2,200.

UNITED STATES
Whatever You Collect, HGPI Can Help!
Classic to Modern Collectors
Classics - Early Commems - Wash/Frank - Farleys
Mint to 2017 - Modern Imperfs
C13-15 Graf Zeppelins - Shanghais - Ducks
Savings Stamps - Cut Squares - Errors
Confederates & US Possessions + Trust Territories
WANT LISTS INVITED FOR ALL 1847 TO DATE!
Large stock of Wholesale & Promotional Stamps & Covers.
View 1000's of U.S. Stamps & Covers in our Web Store at http://bit.ly/US-Stamps
Topical & Issue Collectors
Autographed Plate Blocks-Photo Essays
Cacheted Artwork including Artmaster, Artcraft, Ralph Dyer, Jack Davis, Kolor Kover, Colorano
Autographed Covers-Fancy Cancel Covers
John DuPont Collection Mint Sheets
Dignitary Presentation Folders
WE BUY!
Especially needed: #1-2, 230-245, 285-92, 323-7, C13-15, all grades.
Discount Postage Available!
www.HGITNER.com
1-800-94-STAMP
Henry Gitner Philatelists, Inc.
HGPI
P.O. Box 3077-S, Middletown, NY 10940
Tel: 845-343-5151 Fax: 845-343-0068
PayPal

Toll Free: 1-800-947-8267
E-mail: hgitner@hgitner.com

Center line block	2,400.	1,400.
P# block of 8, 2# & arrow	*13,000.*	—
Never hinged	*22,500.*	

Earliest documented use: Dec. 17, 1918.

524 A149 $5 **deep green & black**	160.	35.
Never hinged	340.	
On cover		*2,500.*
Block of 4	675.	225.
Margin block of 4, arrow	700.	240.
Center line block	950.	260.
P# block of 8, 2# & arrow	3,500.	
Never hinged	*5,000.*	

Earliest documented use: Mar. 10, 1919 (strip of nine with Nos. 516, 517 and 537 on piece); Mar. 20, 1920 (on cover).

For other listing of design A149 see No. 547.

TYPES OF 1917-19 ISSUE

Plates of 400, 800 or 1600 subjects in panes of 100 each, as follows:

No. 525 — 400 and 1600 subjects
No. 526 — 400, 800 and 1600 subjects
No. 529 — 400 subjects
No. 531 — 400 subjects
No. 532 — 400, 800 and 1600 subjects
No. 535 — 400 subjects
No. 536 — 400 and 1600 subjects

1918-20 Unwmk. OFFSET PRINTING *Perf. 11*

525 A140 1c **gray green,** *Dec. 1918*	2.50	.90
Never hinged	6.00	
emerald	7.50	1.25
Never hinged	17.50	
On cover		1.75
Block of 4	10.50	6.00
P# block of 6	30.00	
Never hinged	50.00	
"Flat nose"	—	
a. 1c **dark green**	10.00	1.75
Never hinged	25.00	
c. Horizontal pair, imperf. between	*750.00*	*650.00*
d. Double impression	40.00	*750.00*
Never hinged	90.00	

No. 525c is valued in the grade of fine and with natural straight edge at right, as virtually all recorded examples come thus. No. 525d used is valued in the grade of very good.

Earliest documented use: Dec. 24, 1918.

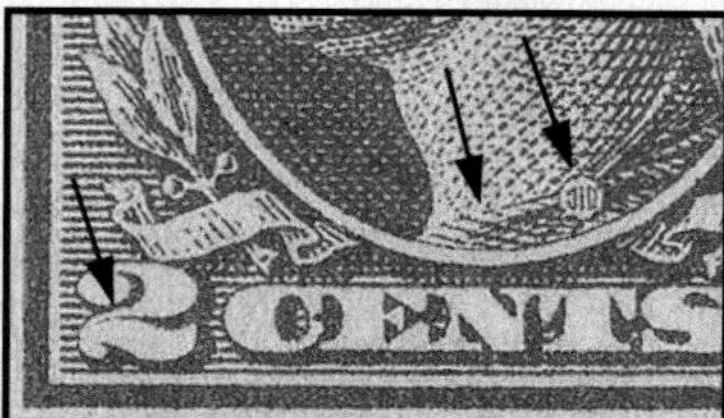

TYPE IV

TWO CENTS

Type IV — Top line of the toga rope is broken.

The shading lines in the toga button are so arranged that the curving of the first and last form "D (reversed) ID."

The line of color in the left "2" is very thin and usually broken.

Used on offset printings only.

TYPE V

Type V — Top line of the toga is complete.

There are five vertical shading lines in the toga button.

The line of color in the left "2" is very thin and usually broken.

The shading dots on the nose are as shown on the diagram.

Used on offset printings only.

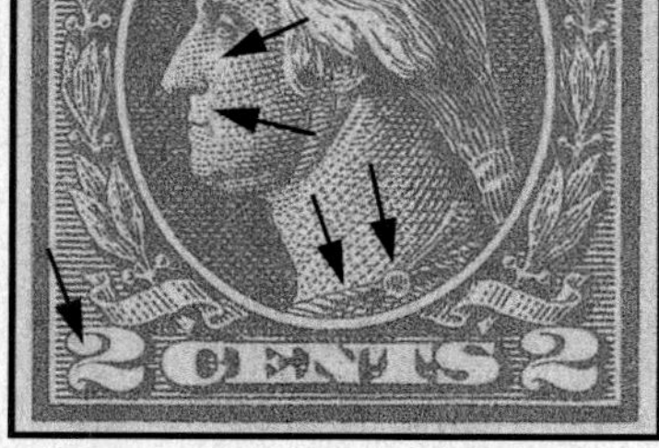

TYPE Va

Type Va — Characteristics are the same as type V except in the shading dots of the nose. The third row of dots from the bottom has four dots instead of six. The overall height is ⅓mm shorter than the other types.

Used on offset printings only.

TYPE VI

Type VI — General characteristics the same as type V except that the line of color in the left "2" is very heavy.

Used on offset printings only.

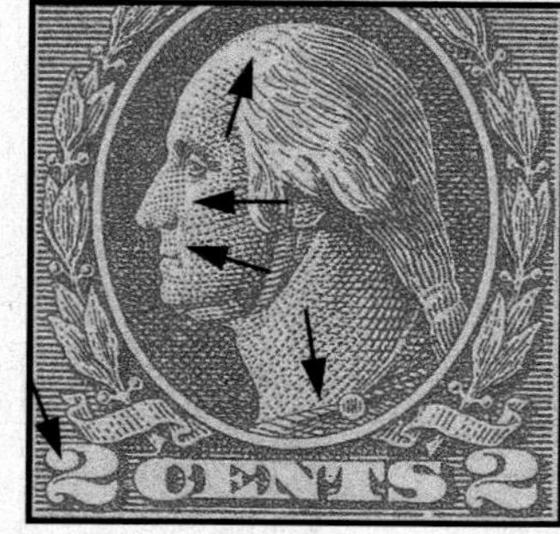

TYPE VII

Type VII — The line of color in the left "2" is invariably continuous, clearly defined and heavier than in type V or Va but not as heavy as type VI.

An additional vertical row of dots has been added to the upper lip.

Numerous additional dots have been added to the hair on top of the head.

Used on offset printings only.

Dates of issue of types after type IV are not known but official records show the first plate of each type to have been certified as follows:

Type IV, Mar. 6, 1920
Type V, Mar. 20, 1920
Type Va, May 4, 1920
Type VI, June 24, 1920
Type VII, Nov. 3, 1920

526 A140 2c **carmine,** type IV, *1920*	25.00	4.00
rose carmine, type IV	25.00	4.00
Never hinged	57.50	
On cover, type IV		11.00
Block of 4, type IV	110.00	30.00
P# block of 6, type IV	240.00	
Never hinged	450.00	
Gash on forehead, type IV	60.00	—
Never hinged	125.00	
Malformed "2" at left, type IV (10823 LR 93)	40.00	6.00

Earliest documented use: Mar. 15, 1920 (FDC).

527 A140 2c **carmine,** type V, *1920*	18.00	1.25
bright carmine, type V	18.00	1.25
rose carmine, type V	18.00	1.25
Never hinged	40.00	
On cover, Type V		2.75
Block of 4, type V	77.50	10.00
P# block of 6, type V	185.00	
Never hinged	350.00	
Line through "2" & "EN," type V	35.00	—
Never hinged	75.00	
a. Double impression, type V	100.00	—
Never hinged	225.00	
b. Vert. pair, imperf. horiz., type V	*850.00*	
c. Horiz. pair, imperf. vert., type V	*1,000.*	—

Earliest documented use: Apr. 16, 1920.

528 A140 2c **carmine,** type Va, *1920*	8.00	.40
Never hinged	20.00	
On cover, type Va		.75
Block of 4, type Va	35.00	3.50
P# block of 6, type Va	100.00	
Never hinged	175.00	
P# block of 6, monogram over P#	200.00	
Never hinged	300.00	
Retouches in "P" of Postage type Va	*52.50*	—
Retouched on toga, type Va	—	—
Variety C"R"NTS, type Va	*37.50*	
Never hinged	85.00	
Top margin P# block of 6 containing the C"R"NTS variety, type Va	*450.00*	
c. Double impression, type Va	60.00	
Never hinged	150.00	
g. Vert. pair, imperf. between	*3,250.*	

Earliest documented use: June 18, 1920.

528A A140 2c **carmine,** type VI, *1920*	47.50	2.00
bright carmine, type VI	47.50	2.00
Never hinged	115.00	
On cover, type VI		3.75
Block of 4, type VI	200.00	15.00
P# block of 6, type VI	425.00	

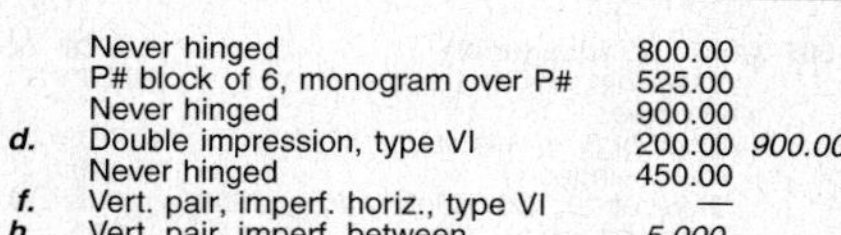

Never hinged	800.00	
P# block of 6, monogram over P#	525.00	
Never hinged	900.00	
d. Double impression, type VI	200.00	*900.00*
Never hinged	450.00	
f. Vert. pair, imperf. horiz., type VI	—	
h. Vert. pair, imperf. between	*5,000.*	

Earliest documented use: July 30, 1920.

Counterfeits exist of No. 528A. See the Postal Counterfeits section of this catalog.

528B A140 2c **carmine,** type VII, *1920*	20.00	.75
Never hinged	50.00	
On cover, type VII		1.00
Block of 4, type VII	85.00	6.00
P# block of 6, type VII	200.00	
Never hinged	375.00	
Gash on cheek, type VII	*300.00*	—
Retouched on cheek, type VII	*750.00*	—
Vertical plate scratch through face, type VII	*200.00*	
e. Double impression, type VII	77.50	*400.00*

No. 528Be used is valued in the grade of very good to fine.

Earliest documented use: Nov. 10, 1920.

TYPE III

THREE CENTS

Type III — The top line of the toga rope is strong but the 5th shading line is missing as in type I.

Center shading line of the toga button consists of two dashes with a central dot.

The "P" and "O" of "POSTAGE" are separated by a line of color.

The frame line at the bottom of the vignette is complete.

Used on offset printings only.

TYPE IV

Type IV — The shading lines of the toga rope are complete.

The second and fourth shading lines in the toga button are broken in the middle and the third line is continuous with a dot in the center.

The "P" and "O" of "POSTAGE" are joined.

The frame line at the bottom of the vignette is broken.

Used on offset printings only.

529 A140 3c **violet,** type III, *Mar. 1918*	3.50	.50
light violet, type III	3.50	.50
dark violet, type III	3.50	.50
Never hinged	7.75	
On cover, type III		.60
Block of 4, type III	14.50	4.00
P# block of 6, type III	75.00	
Never hinged	125.00	
a. Double impression, type III	50.00	*800.00*
Never hinged	115.00	
b. Printed on both sides, type III	*2,500.*	

No. 529a used is valued in the grade of very good.

Earliest documented use: Apr. 4, 1918 (No. 529); June 24, 1918 (No. 529a).

530 A140 3c **purple,** *June 1918* type IV	2.00	.30
light purple, type IV	2.00	.30
deep purple, type IV	2.00	.30
violet, type IV	2.00	.30
Never hinged	4.50	
On cover, type IV		.35
Block of 4, type IV	8.50	2.00
P# block of 6, type IV	32.50	
Never hinged	55.00	
"Blister" under "U.S.," type IV	5.00	—

	Recut under "U.S.," type IV	5.00	—
a.	Double impression, type IV	40.00	*750.00*
	Never hinged	90.00	
	On cover		*1,500.*
b.	Printed on both sides, type IV	*750.00*	
	Never hinged	*1,100.*	
c.	Triple impression, type IV	*1,750.*	—
	Nos. 525-530 (8)	126.50	10.10

No. 530a used is valued in the grade of fine.

Earliest documented use: June 30, 1918.

Earliest documented use dates for imperforates are for the imperforate sheet stamps, not for imperforate stamps with vending and affixing machine perforations or for flat plate imperforate coil stamps. EDU dates for VAMP and flat plate imperf coil stamps are shown in their respective sections later in the catalogue.

1918-20 *Imperf.*

Dates of issue of 2c types are not known, but official records show that the first plate of each type known to have been issued imperforate was certified as follows:
Type IV, Mar. 1920
Type V, May 4, 1920
Type Va, May 25, 1920
Type VI, July 26, 1920
Type VII, Dec. 2, 1920

531	A140 1c **green,** *Jan. 1919*	12.00	12.00
	gray green	12.00	12.00
	emerald	12.00	12.00
	Never hinged	21.00	
	On cover		17.50
	Pair	25.00	52.50
	Never hinged	47.50	
	Block of 4	52.50	75.00
	Corner margin block of 4	55.00	—
	Margin block of 4, arrow	57.50	80.00
	Center line block	85.00	*90.00*
	Never hinged	150.00	
	P# block of 6	125.00	—
	Never hinged	200.00	

Earliest documented use: Mar. 17, 1919 (dated cancel on off-cover plate block); April 7, 1919 (cover).

532	A140 2c **carmine rose,** type IV, *1920*	37.50	*42.50*
	Never hinged	70.00	
	On cover		75.00
	Pair	75.00	*120.00*
	Never hinged	160.00	
	Block of 4	155.00	*250.00*
	Corner margin block of 4	165.00	
	Margin block of 4, arrow	170.00	
	Center line block	240.00	
	Never hinged	425.00	
	P# block of 6	370.00	—
	Never hinged	625.00	

Earliest documented use: July 22, 1920 (dated cancel on used pair); April 12, 1923 (on cover).

533	A140 2c **carmine,** type V, *1920*	110.00	*150.00*
	Never hinged	175.00	
	On cover		225.00
	Pair	225.00	*350.00*
	Never hinged	400.00	
	Block of 4	450.00	*650.00*
	Corner margin block of 4	460.00	*700.00*
	Margin block of 4, arrow	475.00	*700.00*
	Center line block	750.00	*775.00*
	Never hinged	1,300.	
	P# block of 6	1,100.	—
	Never hinged	1,800.	
	Line through "2" and "EN," type V	225.00	
	Never hinged	450.00	

Earliest documented use: Sept. 29, 1920 (dated cancel on off-cover center line block of 4).

534	A140 2c **carmine,** type Va, *1920*	15.00	*15.00*
	carmine rose	15.00	*15.00*
	Never hinged	26.00	
	On cover		17.50
	Pair	31.00	*35.00*
	Never hinged	55.00	
	Block of 4	63.00	*70.00*
	Corner margin block of 4	67.50	
	Margin block of 4, arrow	70.00	*72.50*
	Center line block	80.00	*100.00*
	Never hinged	130.00	
	P# block of 6	130.00	—
	Never hinged	200.00	
	Block of 6, monogram over P#	225.00	
	Never hinged	360.00	

Earliest documented use: June 24, 1920.

534A	A140 2c **carmine,** type VI, *1920*	40.00	*40.00*
	Never hinged	75.00	
	On cover		45.00
	Pair	85.00	85.00
	Never hinged	160.00	
	Block of 4	175.00	230.00
	Corner block of 4	180.00	250.00
	Block of 4, arrow	185.00	—
	Center line block	260.00	*300.00*
	Never hinged	475.00	
	P# block of 6	400.00	—
	Never hinged	650.00	

Earliest documented use: Aug. 31, 1920.

534B	A140 2c **carmine,** type VII, *1920*	2,000.	1,500.
	Never hinged	3,750.	
	On cover		*5,000.*
	Pair	4,100.	*4,500.*
	Never hinged	7,750.	
	Block of 4	8,250.	*7,250.*
	Corner margin block of 4	8,500.	
	Margin block of 4, arrow	8,750.	
	Center line block	*11,000.*	
	Never hinged	16,000.	
	P# block of 6	*17,500.*	
	Never hinged	*25,000.*	

Earliest documented use: Oct. 1, 1921 (dated cancel on on-piece pair); Mar. 22, 1923 (on cover). A cover purported to be an Oct. 20, 1920, usage is believed to exist. The editors would like to see authenticated evidence of its genuineness.

Beware of perforated 2c offset stamps that may have been fraudulently trimmed to resemble Nos. 532-534B.

Examples of the 2c type VII with Schermack type III vending machine perforations have been cut down at sides to simulate the rarer No. 534B imperforate. The No. 534B with Schermack type III perforations is much less expensive than the fully imperforate No. 534B listed here.

535	A140 3c **violet,** type IV, *1918*	10.00	6.00
	Never hinged	18.00	
	On cover		12.50
	Pair	21.00	15.00
	Never hinged	37.50	
	Block of 4	41.00	32.50
	Corner margin block of 4	42.50	35.00
	Margin block of 4, arrow	45.00	35.00
	Center line block	67.50	*50.00*
	Never hinged	110.00	
	P# block of 6	85.00	—
	Never hinged	130.00	
a.	Double impression	100.00	—
	Never hinged	200.00	
	Nos. 531-534A,535 (6)	224.50	265.50

Earliest documented use: Sept. 30, 1918.

Cancellation

Haiti —

1919, Aug. 12 *Perf. 12½*

536	A140 1c **gray green**	20.00	*35.00*
	Never hinged	45.00	
	On postcard, single		225.00
	On cover, pair		300.00
	Block of 4	85.00	*175.00*
	P# block of 6	250.00	
	Never hinged	400.00	
a.	Horiz. pair, imperf. vert.	*1,000.*	

Earliest documented use: Aug. 18, 1919.

VICTORY ISSUE

Victory of the Allies in World War I

"Victory" and Flags of Allies — A150

Designed by Clair Aubrey Huston

FLAT PLATE PRINTING

Plates of 400 subjects in four panes of 100 each

1919, Mar. 3 Unwmk. Engr. *Perf. 11*

537	A150 3c **violet**	10.00	3.25
	Never hinged	20.00	
	On cover		11.00
	Block of 4	42.50	17.50
	P# block of 6	260.00	
	Never hinged	350.00	
	Double transfer	—	—
a.	3c **deep red violet**	*1,250.*	*1,750.*
	Never hinged	*2,300.*	
	On cover		—
	Block of 4	*5,250.*	*11,000.*
	P# block of 6	*10,000.*	
	Never hinged	*16,000.*	
b.	3c **light reddish violet**	150.00	50.00
	Never hinged	300.00	
	On cover		250.00
	Block of 4	650.00	250.00
	P# block of 6	1,500.	
	Never hinged	2,500.	
c.	3c **red violet**	200.00	60.00
	Never hinged	400.00	
	On cover		275.00
	Block of 4	875.00	
	P# block of 6	1,750.	
	Never hinged	2,750.	

No. 537a is valued in the grade of fine.

Earliest documented date: Mar. 3, 1919 (FDC).

REGULAR ISSUE

ROTARY PRESS PRINTINGS

(See note over No. 448)

1919 Unwmk. *Perf. 11x10*

Issued in panes of 170 stamps (coil waste), later in panes of 70 and 100 (#538, 540)

Stamp designs: 19½-20x22-22¼mm

538	A140 1c **green,** *June*	10.00	9.00
	yellowish green	10.00	9.00
	bluish green	10.00	9.00
	Never hinged	23.00	
	On cover		22.50
	Block of 4	42.50	*55.00*
	P# block of 4 & "S 30"	95.00	
	Never hinged	160.00	
	P# block of 4	110.00	
	Never hinged	180.00	
	P# block of 4, star	140.00	
	Never hinged	225.00	
	Double transfer	16.00	—
a.	Vert. pair, imperf. horiz.	60.00	*125.00*
	Never hinged	125.00	
	Block of 4	130.00	*300.00*
	Never hinged	275.00	
	P# block of 4	900.00	
	Never hinged	1,375.	

No. 538a used is valued with a contemporaneous cancel. A certificate of authenticity is advised.

Earliest documented use: June 28, 1919 (No. 538); Sept. 5, 1927 (No. 538a).

539	A140 2c **carmine rose,** type II	2,700.	*17,500.*
	Never hinged	4,250.	
	On cover, type II		*60,000.*
	Block of 4, type II	*12,000.*	*75,000.*
	P# block of 4, type II, & "S 20"	*17,500.*	
	Never hinged	*25,000.*	

No. 539 is valued in the grade of fine.

(See note after No. 455.)

Earliest documented use: June 30, 1919. This is the unique usage on cover. The used block of four also is unique.

540	A140 2c **carmine rose,** type III, *June 14*	12.00	9.50
	carmine	12.00	9.50
	Never hinged	27.50	
	On cover, type III		25.00
	Block of 4, type III	50.00	*60.00*
	Never hinged	115.00	
	P# block of 4, type III, & "S 30"	105.00	
	Never hinged	175.00	
	P# block of 4, type III, & "S 30" inverted	450.00	
	Never hinged	725.00	
	P# block of 4, type III	105.00	
	Never hinged	175.00	
	P# block of 4, type III, star	160.00	
	Never hinged	275.00	
	Double transfer, type III	21.00	—

Earliest documented use: June 17, 1919.

a.	Vert. pair, imperf. horiz., type III	60.00	*140.00*
	Never hinged	125.00	
	Block of 4	130.00	*350.00*
	Never hinged	275.00	
	P# block of 4, type III	1,000.	
	Never hinged	1,500.	
	P# block of 4, type III, Star	1,050.	
	Never hinged	1,600.	
b.	Horiz. pair, imperf. vert., type III	*2,000.*	

No. 540a used is valued with a contemporaneous cancel. A certificate of authenticity is advised.

Earliest documented use: June 17, 1919 (No. 540); Nov. 4, 1922 (No. 540a).

541	A140 3c **violet,** type II, *June 14*	40.00	37.50
	gray violet, type II	40.00	37.50
	Never hinged	100.00	
	On cover		100.00
	Block of 4	170.00	*260.00*
	P# block of 4	360.00	
	Never hinged	625.00	

Earliest documented use: June 14, 1919 (FDC).

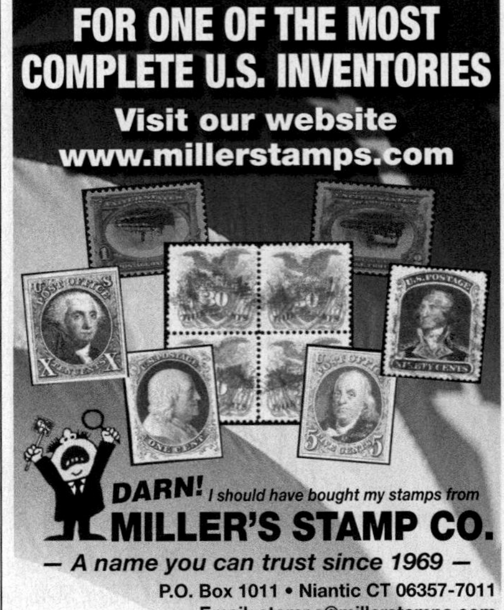

FOR ONE OF THE MOST
COMPLETE U.S. INVENTORIES
Visit our website
www.millerstamps.com
DARN! I should have bought my stamps from
MILLER'S STAMP CO.
— A name you can trust since 1969 —
P.O. Box 1011 • Niantic CT 06357-7011
Email: stamps@millerstamps.com
Phone: 860-908-6200

2020 EDITION SPECIAL FEATURE

1928 Era "Special" Booklet Paper Variety Stamps Now listed in the Scott catalogue

Robert G. Rufe

THE STAMPS: There are eleven popular U.S. issues, specifically Scott Nos. 563, 564, 566, 567, 568, 569, C11, E13, QE1, QE2 and QE3, with well-documented paper varieties that are relatively unknown to the general collector. These same paper varieties, however, have long been included in most exhibits of the series in which they appear – the Fourth Bureau definitive series, the Beacon Air Mail, and U.S. Special Delivery and Special Handling issues. The newly listed stamps within these pages will carry the following numbers: 563b, 564b, 566a, 567b, 568a, 569a, C11b, E13a, QE1b, QE2b, QE3b.

INTRODUCTION: Eleven varieties of well-known U.S. stamps are added to this year's edition to recognize their production for a limited period in 1928 on "Special" Booklet Paper. This "Special" paper consisted of leftover flat sheets of paper from stocks specified, purchased and intended for booklet pane production by the Bureau of Engraving and Printing (BEP). The newly-listed varieties are readily identifiable, and many collectors have recognized these stamps and added them to their collections since first reported by Hugh M. Southgate in 1940.

After the last print run of booklet panes on the flat plate press (the Lindbergh booklet pane, Scott C10a), the BEP had significant remaining inventory of "Special" Booklet Paper. These remnant booklet paper stocks were redirected to ordinary sheet stamp production on flat plate presses. All subsequent booklet pane production was on rotary presses. The C10a booklet stamps were last at press on April 10, 1928, and the first sheet stamps to utilize "Special" Booklet Paper, the new Special Handling service stamps, first went to press on June 22, 1928.

BACKGROUND: Why the "Special" Paper? Sheet stamps were printed on paper whose normal grain orientation was vertical, meaning that after stamps were printed on moistened paper, the designs had a tendency to shrink horizontally as the paper dried. Stamp paper shrinks approximately four times more across the grain than with the grain, meaning that sheet stamps shrink more horizontally than vertically. Accordingly, for producing booklet panes, the BEP ordered "Special" Paper with the grain running horizontally, to assure greater stability in the horizontal dimension.

RATIONALE FOR LISTING: Definitive stamps which have been printed AND issued in both sheet stamp and booklet formats have traditionally carried major and minor catalog numbers, respectively. However, sheet

Figure 1. Horizontal dimension comparison of "Special" Booklet Paper (top) vs. regular orientation paper (bottom). These are the three Fourth Bureau "ordinary" stamps in vertical format, 563b, 564b and 566a.

Figure 2. The three horizontal format stamps are turned 90° for consistent comparison with images in Figure 1. In this orientation, the "Special" Booklet Paper varieties (upper blocks) are again wider than the regular paper stamps (lower blocks). In their conventional horizontal orientation, "Special" Booklet Paper varieties of these three horizontal format stamps are very slightly narrower than their corresponding sheet stamps.

stamps printed on "Special" Booklet Paper but NOT issued as booklets have not previously been listed. The newly listed paper varieties are recognizably different from their sheet stamp counterparts, and the identification guidelines which follow will highlight the differences.

HISTORICAL DEVELOPMENT: The BEP had gone to great lengths to improve centering of images on booklet pane stamps by specifying paper properties that would control shrinkage of central design images. Their solution was to print booklet stamps on paper with the grain orientation turned 90° to control shrinkage, improve centering, and keep booklets in registration as they were interleaved, covered, bound stapled and trimmed.

The BEP demonstrated its frugality by using remnant paper when flat press sheet supplies were no longer required for booklets as booklet production was transitioned to the rotary press. Somewhat analogous to Coil Waste issues, these eleven sheet stamps were produced from "Booklet Remnant" paper stocks as a cost and resource savings measure. Since the "Special" Booklet Paper varieties were not discovered until about ten years after their production, most of these stamps were used for routine postal purposes. Southgate did not report on the Special Handling issue at all, not realizing the entire run of these new denomination printings in 1928 was on "Special" Booklet Paper, having been completed before the dates he was given.

IDENTIFICATION: With care and a bit of practice, identification is straightforward. Many collectors use inexpensive templates to overlay a known stamp on the candidate. First, one must be sure to begin with the proper stamp. In all cases these will be flat plate press, perf 11 stamps – no rotary press issues, and nothing with perf. 10½! Plate blocks are typically shown in technical presentations because they make for the simplest introduction. The differences in shrinkage across two or three stamps is usually dramatic.

Three of the eleven stamps, the Fourth Bureau Nos. 563b, 564b and 566a "ordinaries," are identified in the same manner that Washington-Franklin sheet stamps are separated from booklet pane stamps, i.e., the booklet stamps are slightly wider and shorter than the sheet stamps for vertical format issues in this series as shown in Figure 1.

The Fourth Bureau horizontal format stamps, Nos. 567b, 568a and 569a, are identified similarly, but in the perpendicular orientation, i.e., these are slightly narrower and taller than their sheet stamp counterparts. Figure 2.

The remaining five special issue stamps, or "Back-of-the-Book" issues, Nos. C11b, E13a, QE1b, QE2b and QE3b, are all horizontal format stamps normally printed on paper with the grain running vertically, so that they are the easiest to identify – the vertical design shrinkage on "Special" Booklet Paper with a horizontal grain direction is minimal compared to paper in the normal orientation, but the horizontal difference in width is striking. Figure 3.

One elementary "low-tech" observation may help with identification. In a humid environment, stamps will shrink and curl across the grain, allowing confirmation of the

Figure 3. Horizontal dimension comparison of "Special" Booklet Paper (C11b top; E13a bottom) vs. regular sheet stamp paper. These are just two of the five Special Service "Back-of-the-Book" stamps in horizontal format. All the 1928 Special Handling stamps, Nos. QE1b, QE2b and QE3b were printed on "Special" Booklet Paper.

Figure 4. Plain water sprayed with an atomizer on to the reverse side of a used QE2b first day plate block illustrates dramatic shrinkage across the horizontal grain direction.

direction of the paper grain. The horizontal grain direction of Special Handling stamps was one key in determining that all the 1928 stamps were on "Special" Booklet Paper. Figure 4.

CHALLENGE FACTOR: "Special" Booklet Paper stamps are scarcer than their regular paper counterparts. Southgate reported the actual production of stamps on "Special" paper from BEP printing records, and as a percentage of total stamps printed for each issue as reported by Gary Griffith, these are:

563b (13%), 564b (14%), 566a (3%), 567b (Not Reported), 568a (12%), 569a (15%), C11b (Not Reported), E13a (5%), QE1b (100%), QE2b (100%), QE3b (100%).

Plate numbers are helpful, but not definitive. "Special" Booklet Paper printings were limited to certain known plate numbers, but all these plates were also used for normal sheet stamps. Table 1.

While identification is straightforward, care must be exercised in the evaluation of multiples for the Fourth Bureau issues, since margin gaps changed with the introduction of star plates; some issues will have both 2.5 mm. and 3.0 mm. gaps between stamps horizontally within the same sheet.

The Beacon Air Mail, No. C11b, may present the only significant challenge for study, since many plate numbers were used on "Special" Booklet Paper for both the red frame and blue vignette passes. Accordingly, many

Table 1. "Special" Booklet Paper - Plate Numbers at Press from BEP Records

Scott No.	Denom.	Plate Numbers and Notes
563b	11¢	17617, 17618, 17619, 17620 - All narrow gauge margins
564b	12¢	18921, 18922, 18923, 19442 - All wide gauge margins, no stars
566a	15¢	17430, 17431, 17432, 17433 - All wide gauge margin, 5-point star plates
567b	20¢	18672, 18673, 18674, 18675, 18688, 18689 - Wide gauge, star plates
568a	25¢	14062, 14063, 14064, 14065 - All narrow gauge margins
569a	30¢	17446, 17447, 17448, 17449 - All wide gauge margins, no stars
C11b	5¢	Red (Frame) Nos. 19571//19626; Blue (Vignette) Nos. 19545//19619
E13a	15¢	16833, 16834, 16835, 16836
QE1b	10¢	19553, 19554, 19555, 19556
QE2b	15¢	19557, 19558, 19559, 19560
QE3b	20¢	19541, 19542, 19543, 19544

Table 1. Stamps and plate numbers which consumed the remnant inventory of "Special" Booklet Paper.

combinations of numbers are possible, and determining the scarcity or rarity of specific numbers and combination of numbers has not been attempted.

For the Special Handling issues, these listings finally allow collectors to identify and properly catalog the three paper varieties for this longest-running flat plate production issue at the BEP. All printings after 1928 until mid-1955 were on regular sheet stamp paper with vertical grain (Nos. QE1, QE2 & QE3); the 1955 printings were an "experimental" printing on an entirely different, low-moisture content, "dry" paper (Nos. QE1a, QE2a & QE3a).

MARKET CONSIDERATIONS: Since these varieties were not researched nor reported until well after their printing, no large stocks were sought nor are expected to exist. The varieties will be found randomly among these eleven issues in dealers' and collectors' holdings, and in some cases, in specialists' exhibits. As a comment regarding scarcity, the late Robert Markovits, a Special Delivery specialist, reported his exhibit copy of a, now, E13a plate block to be unique. While this Special Feature article was being written, a second No. E13a plate block was reported and authenticated. My mentor on this subject, the late Wallace B. Cleland, shared with me that he had only ever found two plate number singles of the No. E13a. In 15 years of searching, I have yet to locate a top margin plate block of either No. 567b or 569a. The 11¢ Hayes, No. 563b, seems to be the most readily found, perhaps because it is the lowest denomination of the ordinary stamps on "Special" Booklet Paper.

Traditionally, pricing for plate blocks of the Fourth Bureaus and the No. C11b Beacon Air Mail on "Special" Booklet Paper have been double the base price of the sheet stamp, ranging up to five times for the Special Delivery No. E13a. Supply and demand will bring about changes in these initial valuing estimates as market forces prompt collectors to examine their stamps for these varieties and catalog presence stimulates interest in this fascinating specialty.

BIBLIOGRAPHY:

1. Southgate, Hugh M., Read by Hon. David D. Caldwell, "A Study of Shrinkage - The 'Special' Paper Printing of 1928," The Congress Book, 1939, pp. 27-32.

2. Southgate, Hugh M., "The 'Special' Paper Printing of 1928," The Bureau Specialist, January 1940, pp. 12-16.

3. Cleland, Wallace B., The B. I. A. Plate Number Checklist, Revised, 1990.

4. Cleland, Wallace B., "The 'Special' Paper Printings of 1928," The United States Specialist, September 2000, pp. 397-401.

5. Cleland, Wallace B., "E13 Special Delivery on 'Special Paper,'" The United States Specialist, August 2003, p. 373.

6. Cleland, Wallace B., "Size Differences Between Wet and Dry Printings from Flat Plates," The United States Specialist, November 2003, pp. 519-525, and June 2004, pp. 283, 284.

7. Griffith, Gary, United States Stamps 1922-1926, Linn's Stamp News, 1997, pp. 65, 70, 78, 81, 84, 87, 279.

8. Griffith, Gary, United States Stamps 1927-1932, Linn's Stamp News, 2001, pp. 115-9, 121.

9. Lawrence, Ken, "The Lindbergh Air Mail booklet stamp of 1928," Scott Stamp Monthly, September 2004, p. 14.

10. Cleland, Wallace B., 2012 Durland Standard Plate Number Catalog, "Special Paper," p. 58; "Narrow Gauge," p. 58.

11. Rufe, Robert G., "Special Handling Stamps on Special Booklet Paper – Who Knew?" The United States Specialist, March 2014, pp. 103-112.

12. Silver, Philip, "Another Visit with the U. S Beacon Air Mail Stamp of 1928," Collectors Club Philatelist, May-June 1985, pp. 151-166.

COLLECTING NECESSITIES

APAK STAMP DRYING BOOK

Removing stamps from covers has never been easier. With the specially coated paper, stamps pop right off. Stamps are flat, dry and ready for mounting. There are 10 glossy sheets sandwiched between 11 sheets of commercial grade blotting paper. Use this book over and over again for clean and easy stamp removal.

Item	*Retail*	*AA**
DB10	$18.99	**$16.99**

STOCK PAGE BINDER & SLIPCASE

Keep all your stock pages neat and tidy with binder and matching slipcase. Available in two colors.

Item		*Retail*	*AA**
SSBSBK	Black	$21.99	**$17.99**
SSBSBL	Blue	$21.99	**$17.99**

HAGNER STOCK SHEETS

The original Hagner Stock sheets are made from archival quality pH board and feature pure polyester film pockets that are glued to each page with special chemically inert glue. For more than 40 years, collectors all over the world have come to rely on Hagner stock sheets for their long-term stamp protection. Available in black only. **Sold in packages of 5.**

	Retail	*AA**
Single Sided Sheets	$7.25	**$6.50**
Double Sided Sheets	$11.75	**$8.99**

1 Pocket 242 mm		4 Pockets 58 mm		7 Pockets 31 mm	
HGB01	Black	HGB04	Black	HGB07	Black
HGB11*	Black	HGB44*	Black	HGB77*	Black
2 Pockets 119 mm		5 Pockets 45 mm		8 Pockets 27 mm	
HGB02	Black	HGB05	Black	HGB08	Black
HGB22*	Black	HGB55*	Black	HGB88*	Black
3 Pockets 79 mm		6 Pockets 37 mm		Multi-Pockets	
HGB03	Black	HGB06	Black	HGB09	Black
HGB33*	Black	HGB66*	Black	HGB99*	Black

*** Item number for double sided sheet.***

Ordering Information

***AA prices** apply to paid subscribers of Amos Media titles, or orders placed online. Prices, terms and product availability subject to change. Taxes will apply in CA, OH, & IL.

Shipping & Handling:

United States: Orders under $10 are only $3.99; Orders over $10 are 10% of order total. Minimum charge $7.99; Maximum Charge $45.00. **Canada:** 20% of order total. Minimum charge $19.99; Maximum charge $200.00. **Foreign:** Orders are shipped via FedEx Intl. or USPS and billed actual freight.

AMOS ADVANTAGE

Call 800-572-6885

Outside U.S. & Canada call: (937) 498-0800

www.AmosAdvantage.com

Mail to: Amos Media, P.O. Box 4129, Sidney, OH 45365

1920, May 26 *Perf. 10x11*

Plates of 400 subjects in four panes of 100.

Stamp design: 19x22½-22¾mm

542	A140 1c **green**	12.50	1.50
	bluish green	12.50	1.50
	Never hinged	30.00	
	On cover		5.50
	Block of 4	55.00	12.50
	Vertical margin block of 6, P# opposite center horizontal row	165.00	
	Never hinged	300.00	

Earliest documented use: May 26, 1920 (FDC).

1921, May *Perf. 10*

Plates of 400 subjects in four panes of 100 each

Stamp design: 19x22½mm

543	A140 1c **green**	.70	.40
	deep green	.70	.40
	Never hinged	1.75	
	On cover		.45
	Block of 4	2.80	2.00
	Vertical margin block of 6, P# opposite center horizontal row	32.50	
	Never hinged	57.50	
	Corner margin block of 4, P# only	20.00	
	Never hinged	35.00	
	Double transfer	—	—
	Triple transfer	—	—
a.	Horizontal pair, imperf. between	*4,500.*	

Earliest documented use: May 21, 1921.

1922 *Perf. 11*

Rotary press sheet waste

Stamp design: 19x22½mm

544	A140 1c **green**	*22,500.*	*3,500.*
	Never hinged	*35,000.*	
	On cover		*6,500.*

No. 544 is valued in the grade of fine.

Earliest documented use: Dec. 17, 1922.

1921, May

Issued in panes of 170 stamps (coil waste), later in panes of 70 and 100

Stamp designs: 19½-20x22mm

545	A140 1c **green**	180.00	200.00
	yellowish green	180.00	210.00
	Never hinged	475.00	
	On cover		*1,800.*
	Block of 4	750.00	*1,050.*
	P# block of 4, "S 30"	1,100.	
	Never hinged	2,250.	
	P# block of 4	1,150.	
	Never hinged	2,250.	
	P# block of 4, star	1,200.	
	Never hinged	2,300.	

Earliest documented use: June 25, 1921.

546	A140 2c **carmine rose,** type III	105.00	*190.00*
	deep carmine rose	105.00	*190.00*
	Never hinged	230.00	
	On cover		*800.00*
	Block of 4	450.00	*1,000.*
	P# block of 4, "S 30"	700.00	
	Never hinged	1,300.	
	P# block of 4	775.00	
	Never hinged	1,450.	
	P# block of 4, star	800.00	
	Never hinged	1,500.	
	Recut in hair	140.00	*210.00*
a.	Perf. 10 on left side	*7,500.*	*17,500.*

No. 546a used is valued in the grade of very good. It is unique used.

Earliest documented use: May 5, 1921.

FLAT PLATE PRINTING

Plates of 100 subjects

1920, Nov. 1 *Perf. 11*

547	A149 $2 **carmine & black**	110.	35.
	Never hinged	240.	
	On cover (commercial)		1,000.
	On flown cover (philatelic)		250.
	Block of 4	440.	180.
	Margin block of 4, arrow	480.	
	Center line block	750.	—
	Margin block of 8, two P#, & arrow	3,750.	
	Never hinged	6,000.	
a.	$2 **lake & black**	190.	35.
	Never hinged	400.	

Earliest documented use: Dec. 6, 1920 (on piece).

From No. 548 forward, almost all U.S. stamps have had officially designated first days of sale and use. Therefore, from this point, earliest documented uses are given only for those stamps for which there were not designated first days of sale. For first day covers, see the First Day Cover section later in the catalogue.

PILGRIM TERCENTENARY ISSUE

Landing of the Pilgrims at Plymouth, Mass.

The "Mayflower" — A151

Landing of the Pilgrims — A152

Signing of the Compact — A153

Designed by Clair Aubrey Huston

Plates of 280 subjects in four panes of 70 each

1920, Dec. 21 **Unwmk.** *Perf. 11*

548	A151 1c **green**	3.75	2.00
	dark green	3.75	2.00
	Never hinged	9.25	
	On cover		3.50
	Block of 4	16.00	13.00
	P# block of 6	62.50	
	Never hinged	95.00	
	Double transfer	—	—
549	A152 2c **carmine rose**	5.00	1.60
	carmine	5.00	1.60
	rose	5.00	1.60
	Never hinged	12.00	
	On cover		2.50
	Block of 4	21.00	9.00
	P# block of 6	80.00	
	Never hinged	125.00	
	Cancellation		
	China		—
550	A153 5c **deep blue**	30.00	12.50
	dark blue	30.00	12.50
	Never hinged	65.00	
	On cover		22.50
	Block of 4	140.00	75.00
	P# block of 6	425.00	
	Never hinged	675.00	
	Nos. 548-550 (3)	38.75	16.10
	Nos. 548-550, never hinged	97.50	

IMPORTANT INFORMATION REGARDING VALUES FOR NEVER-HINGED STAMPS

Collectors should be aware that the values given for never-hinged stamps from No. 182 on are for stamps in the grade of very fine, just as the values for all stamps in the catalogue are for very fine stamps unless indicated otherwise. The never-hinged premium as a percentage of value will be larger for stamps in extremely fine or superb grades, and the premium will be smaller for fine-very fine, fine or poor examples. This is particularly true of the issues of the late-19th and early-20th centuries.

VALUES FOR NEVER-HINGED STAMPS PRIOR TO SCOTT 182

This catalogue does not value pre-1879 stamps in never-hinged condition. Premiums for never-hinged condition in the classic era invariably are even larger than those premiums listed for the 1879 and later issues. Generally speaking, the earlier the stamp is listed in the catalogue, the larger will be the never-hinged premium.

NEVER-HINGED PLATE BLOCKS

Values given for never-hinged plate blocks are for blocks in which all stamps have original gum that has never been hinged and has no disturbances, and all selvage, whether gummed or ungummed, has never been hinged.

For values of the most popular U.S. stamps in various conditions, including never hinged from No. 182 on, and in the grades of very good, fine, fine to very fine, very fine, very fine to extremely fine, extremely fine, extremely fine to superb, and superb, see the *Scott Stamp Values U.S. Specialized by Grade*, updated and issued each year as part of this U.S. specialized catalogue. This section is located after Postage and before Semi-Postal Stamps.

REGULAR ISSUE

Nathan Hale — A154

Franklin — A155

Warren G. Harding — A156

Washington — A157

Lincoln — A158

Martha Washington — A159

Theodore Roosevelt — A160

Garfield — A161

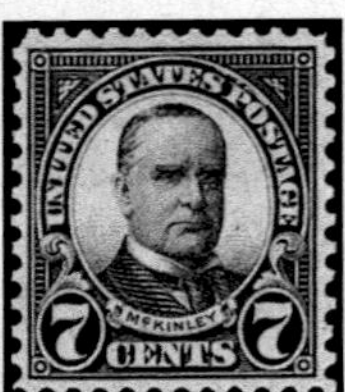

McKinley — A162

Grant — A163

Jefferson — A164

Monroe — A165

Rutherford B. Hayes — A166

Grover Cleveland — A167

American Indian — A168

Statue of Liberty — A169

Golden Gate — A170

Niagara Falls — A171

American Buffalo — A172

Arlington Amphitheater — A173

Lincoln Memorial — A174

United States Capitol — A175

Head of Freedom Statue, Capitol Dome — A176

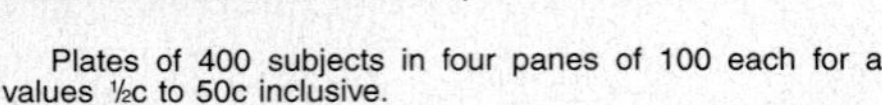
Plates of 400 subjects in four panes of 100 each for all values ½c to 50c inclusive.

Plates of 200 subjects for $1 and $2. The sheets were cut along the horizontal guide line into two panes, upper and lower, of 100 subjects each.

Plates of 100 subjects for the $5 denomination, and sheets of 100 subjects were issued intact.

The Bureau of Engraving and Printing in 1925 in experimenting to overcome the loss due to uneven perforations, produced what is known as the "Star Plate." The vertical rows of designs on these plates are spaced 3mm apart in place of 2¾mm as on the regular plates. Most of these plates were identified with a star added to the plate number.

Designed by Clair Aubrey Huston.

"Special" Booklet Paper

For a limited period of time in 1928 the Bureau of Engraving and Printing produced eleven stamps on "special" booklet paper, being sheets of paper specifically ordered and purchased for booklet pane production. A significant inventory of this paper remained when the BEP stopped printing booklets on the flat plate press and began printing all booklets on rotary presses. The "special" booklet paper had the grain running horizontally rather than the vertical grain paper normally used for sheet stamps. After being produced on moistened paper, stamps shrank four times more across the grain than with the grain. Thus, the stamps printed on "special" booklet paper shrank differently when dried than stamps printed on normal stamp paper, and the differences in design dimensions are readily identifiable.

The eleven stamps involved, with their minor-lettered numbers, are Nos. 563b, 564b, 566a, 567b, 568a, 569a, C11b, E13a, QE1b, QE2b and QE3b. All of the first printings of Nos. QE1b, QE2b and QE3b were printed on "special" booklet paper.

Nos. 563b, 564b and 566a are slightly wider and shorter than the varieties printed on normal paper; Nos. 567b, 568a and 569a are slightly narrower and taller than their counterparts; and Nos. C11b, E13a, QE1b, QE2b and QE3b are slightly shorter and noticeably wider than their counterparts.

FLAT PLATE PRINTINGS

1922-25		**Unwmk.**		***Perf. 11***
551	A154	½c **olive brown,** *Apr. 4, 1925*	.25	.25
		pale olive brown	.25	.25
		deep olive brown	.25	.25
		Never hinged	.50	
		On 1c stamped envelope (3rd class)		2.50
		Block of 4	1.00	.50
		P# block of 6	15.00	
		Never hinged	25.00	
		"Cap" on fraction bar (Pl. 17041)	12.50	2.00
552	A155	1c **deep green,** *Jan. 17, 1923*	1.25	.25
		green	1.25	.25
		pale green	1.25	.25
		Never hinged	2.75	
		On postcard		.25
		Block of 4	5.50	.40
		P# block of 6	37.50	
		Never hinged	55.00	
		Double transfer	3.25	—
a.		Booklet pane of 6, *Aug. 11, 1923*	7.50	*4.00*
		Never hinged	12.50	

Earliest documented use: Dec. 21, 1923 (No. 552a pair).

553	A156	1½c **yellow brown,** *Mar. 19, 1925*	2.00	.25
		pale yellow brown	2.00	.25
		brown	2.00	.25
		Never hinged	4.10	
		On 3rd class cover		2.25
		Block of 4	8.25	1.10
		P# block of 6	67.50	—
		Never hinged	87.50	
		Double transfer	—	—
554	A157	2c **carmine,** *Jan. 15, 1923*	1.10	.25
		light carmine	1.10	.25
		deep claret		—
		Never hinged	2.50	
		On cover		.25
		Block of 4	4.75	.40
		P# block of 6	42.50	
		Never hinged	55.00	
		P# block of 6 & small 5-point star, top only	550.00	
		Never hinged	850.00	
		P# block of 6 & large 5-point star, side only	65.00	
		Never hinged	97.50	
		Same, large 5-point star, top	600.00	
		Never hinged	1,250.	
		Same, large 6-point star, top	950.00	
		Never hinged	1,850.	
		Same, large 6-point star, side only (Pl. 17196)	1,000.	
		Never hinged	1,750.	
		Double transfer	2.40	.80
a.		Horiz. pair, imperf. vert.	*250.00*	
b.		Vert. pair, imperf. horiz.	*6,000.*	
		Never hinged	*10,000.*	
c.		Booklet pane of 6, *Feb. 10, 1923*	7.00	*3.00*
		Never hinged	12.00	
d.		Perf. 10 at top or bottom	*12,500.*	*8,500.*
		Never hinged	*15,000.*	
		On cover		*20,000.*

Virtually all top plate blocks of No. 554 with the 5-point star have narrow top selvage. Plate blocks with wide top selvage are rare and are worth much more.

Buying & Selling Specialized
UNITED STATES & POSSESSIONS
www.northstamp.com
www.stores.ebay.com/northstamp
• 38 Different U.S. Categories
• 32,000+ Stamps and Covers

PLUS
New Video!
"How To Sell Your Stamp Collection"

Check website for Monthly Coupons/Promotions
NORTHLAND
International Trading, LLC
Box 34
Verona, NJ 07044
800-950-0058

It is known that a full pane of No. 554 exists (or existed) with a spliced vertical tear, leaving three vertical columns of imperforate stamps at right. The editors would like to know if this pane, or parts of this pane, are still in existence and in collector or dealer hands.

Earliest documented uses: Feb. 10, 1923 (No. 554c single); Nov. 23, 1923 (No. 554d).

555 A158 3c **violet,** *Feb. 12, 1923* 13.00 1.20
deep violet 15.00 1.20
dark violet 15.00 1.20
red violet 13.00 1.20
bright violet 13.00 1.20
Never hinged 27.50
On cover with 2c (single UPU rate) 7.50
Block of 4 55.00 9.00
P# block of 6 240.00
Never hinged 400.00

556 A159 4c **yellow brown,** *Jan. 15, 1923* 16.00 .50
brown 16.00 .50
Never hinged 35.00
On cover 9.00
Block of 4 70.00 3.00
P# block of 6 250.00
Never hinged 375.00
Double transfer — —
a. Vert. pair, imperf. horiz. *12,500.*
b. Perf. 10 at top or bottom *3,500.* *22,500.*

No. 556a is unique. It resulted from a sheet that was damaged and patched during production.

No. 556b used also exists as a transitional stamp gauging 10 at left top and 11 at right top. Value the same.

557 A160 5c **dark blue,** *Oct. 27, 1922* 16.00 .30
deep blue 16.00 .30
Never hinged 35.00
On UPU-rate cover 6.00
Block of 4 70.00 2.00
P# block of 6 250.00
Never hinged 375.00
Double transfer (15571 UL 86) — *350.00*
a. Imperf., pair *2,000.*
Never hinged *4,000.*
P# block of 6 *29,000.*
b. Horiz. pair, imperf. vert. —
c. Perf. 10 at top or bottom — *9,500.*
On cover *17,500.*

Earliest documented use: Nov. 12, 1923 (No. 557c).

558 A161 6c **red orange,** *Nov. 20, 1922* 30.00 1.00
pale red orange 30.00 1.00
Never hinged 65.00
Pair on special delivery cover 17.50
Block of 4 125.00 7.50
P# block of 6 400.00
Never hinged 600.00
Double transfer (Plate 14169 LR 60 and 70) 55.00 2.00
Same, recut 55.00 2.00

559 A162 7c **black,** *May 1, 1923* 7.25 .75
gray black 7.25 .75
Never hinged 15.50
On registered cover with other values 27.50
Block of 4 32.50 6.00
P# block of 6 120.00
Never hinged 170.00
Double transfer — —

560 A163 8c **olive green,** *May 1, 1923* 37.50 1.00
pale olive green 37.50 1.00
Never hinged 80.00
Pair on airmail cover 12.50
Block of 4 160.00 7.50
P# block of 6 575.00
Never hinged 850.00
Double transfer — —

561 A164 9c **rose,** *Jan. 15, 1923* 11.00 1.25
pale rose 11.00 1.25
Never hinged 25.00
On registered cover with other values 22.50
Block of 4 47.50 9.00
P# block of 6 250.00
Never hinged 375.00
Double transfer — —

562 A165 10c **orange,** *Jan. 15, 1923* 13.50 .35
pale orange 13.50 .35
Never hinged 30.00
On special delivery cover with 2c 6.00
Block of 4 60.00 2.00
P# block of 6 275.00
Never hinged 400.00
a. Vert. pair, imperf. horiz. *2,000.*
Never hinged *3,250.*
b. Imperf., pair *5,750.*
Block of 4 *6,250.*
P# block of 6 *24,000.*
c. Perf. 10 at top or bottom *60,000.* *15,000.*
Pair *50,000.*

No. 562a is valued in the grade of fine, with gum and without blue defacing lines. No. 562b is valued without gum and without blue pencil defacing lines. No. 562c is valued in the grade of fine.

563 A166 11c **greenish blue,** *Oct. 4, 1922* 1.25 .60
Never hinged 2.75
light blue 1.60 .60
Never hinged 3.25
On registered cover with other values 12.50
Block of 4 5.50 3.50
P# block of 6 55.00
Never hinged 70.00
a. 11c **light bluish green** 1.25 .60
light yellow green 1.25 .60
Never hinged 2.75
On registered cover with other values 14.00
Block of 4 5.50 4.00
P# block of 6 40.00
Never hinged 60.00
b. 11c **light bluish green,** printed on "special" booklet paper, *1928* (see note before #551) 1.75 .90
Never hinged 4.00
On registered cover with other values 25.00
Block of 4 45.00
P# block of 6 90.00
Never hinged 120.00
d. Imperf., pair *20,000.*

Many other intermediate shades exist for Nos. 563 and 563a, all falling within the blue or green color families.

564 A167 12c **brown violet,** *Mar. 20, 1923* 4.75 .35
deep brown violet 4.75 .35
Never hinged 10.50
On special delivery cover 12.50
Block of 4 21.00 3.00
P# block of 6 115.00
Never hinged 160.00
P# block of 6 & large 5 point star, side only 150.00
Never hinged 225.00
P# block of 6 & large 6 point star, side only 250.00
Never hinged 400.00
Double transfer, (14404 UL 73 & 74) 11.00 1.10
a. Horiz. pair, imperf. vert. *3,750.*
b. Printed on "special" booklet paper, *1928* (see note before #551) 10.00 1.00
Never hinged 25.00
On special delivery cover 25.00
Block of 4 45.00
P# block of 6 300.00
Never hinged 500.00

565 A168 14c **blue,** *May 1, 1923* 4.25 .90
deep blue 4.25 .90
Never hinged 9.50
On registered cover with other values 15.00
Block of 4 18.00 7.50
P# block of 6 80.00
Never hinged 120.00
Double transfer — —

Horizontal pairs of No. 565 are known with spacings up to 3mm instead of 2mm between. These are from the 5th and 6th vertical rows of the right panes of Plate 14515 and also between stamps Nos. 3 and 4 of the same pane. A plate block of Pl. 14512 is known with 3mm spacing.

566 A169 15c **gray,** *Nov. 11, 1922* 16.00 .30
light gray 16.00 .30
Never hinged 35.00
On registered cover with 2c 3.50
Block of 4 70.00 2.00
P# block of 6 275.00
Never hinged 400.00
P# block of 6 & large 5 point star, side only 550.00
Never hinged 825.00
a. Printed on "special" booklet paper, *1928* (see note before #551) 30.00 2.00
Never hinged 65.00
On cover 12.00
Block of 4 130.00
P# block of 6 450.00
Never hinged 650.00

567 A170 20c **carmine rose,** *May 1, 1923* 16.00 .30
deep carmine rose 16.00 .30
Never hinged 35.00
On registered UPU-rate cover 12.50
Block of 4 70.00 2.00
P# block of 6 275.00
Never hinged 400.00
P# block of 6 & large 5 point star, side only 575.00
Never hinged 850.00
a. Horiz. pair, imperf. vert. *2,500.*
Never hinged *5,000.*
b. Printed on "special" booklet paper, *1928* (see note before #551) 35.00 3.00
Never hinged 70.00
On registered UPU-rate cover 20.00
Block of 4 150.00
P# block of 6 500.00
Never hinged 900.00

No. 567a is valued in the grade of fine.

"Bridge over Falls" plate scratches

568 A171 25c **yellow green,** *Nov. 11, 1922* 13.50 .75
green 13.50 .75
deep green 13.50 .75
Never hinged 30.00
On contract airmail cover 27.50
Block of 4 60.00 6.00
P# block of 6 300.00
Never hinged 425.00
Double transfer — —
Plate scratches ("Bridge over Falls") (17445 LL 26) *475.00* —
Never hinged *675.00*
a. Printed on "special" booklet paper, *1928* (see note before #551) 35.00 2.25
Never hinged 75.00
On contract airmail cover 35.00
Block of 4 150.00
P# block of 6 475.00
Never hinged 675.00
b. Vert. pair, imperf. horiz. *3,250.*
c. Perf. 10 at one side *5,000.* *11,000.*
Never hinged *7,500.*

No. 568b is valued in the grade of fine. No. 568c used is valued in the grade of fine.

Double Transfer at lower right

569 A172 30c **olive brown,** *Mar. 20, 1923* 22.50 .60
Never hinged 50.00
On registered cover with other values 20.00
Block of 4 100.00 5.00
P# block of 6 325.00
Never hinged 475.00
Double transfer at lower right (16065 UR 52) 450.00 —
Double transfer at left (14438 LR 79) — —
a. Printed on "special" booklet paper, *1928* (see note before #551) 45.00 3.50
Never hinged 100.00
On registered cover with other values 35.00
Block of 4 200.00
P# block of 6 500.00
Never hinged 900.00

570 A173 50c **lilac,** *Nov. 11, 1922* 32.50 .40
dull lilac 32.50 .40
Never hinged 70.00
On Federal airmail cover 27.50
Block of 4 140.00 2.00
P# block of 6 550.00
Never hinged 750.00

571 A174 $1 **violet brown,** *Feb. 12, 1923* 35.00 .80
Never hinged 75.00
violet black 42.50 1.00
Never hinged 85.00
On post-1932 registered cover with other values 27.50
Block of 4 150.00 4.50
Margin block of 4, arrow, top or bottom 160.00
P# block of 6 300.00
Never hinged 525.00
Double transfers, Pl. 18642 L 30 and Pl. 18682 90.00 2.00

572 A175 $2 **deep blue,** *Mar. 20, 1923* 55.00 9.00
Never hinged 120.00
On post-1932 registered cover with other values 55.00
Block of 4 240.00 65.00
Margin block of 4, arrow, top or bottom 300.00
P# block of 6 700.00
Never hinged 1,000.

573 A176 $5 **carmine & blue,** *Mar. 20, 1923* 90.00 15.00
Never hinged 180.00
On post-1932 registered cover with other values 175.00
Block of 4 380.00 95.00
Margin block of 4, arrow 400.00
Center line block 460.00 *105.00*
Never hinged 825.00
P# block of 8, two P# & arrow 1,650. —
Never hinged 2,600.
a. $5 **carmine lake & dark blue** 175.00 30.00
Never hinged 350.00
On post-1932 registered cover with other values 190.00
Block of 4 800.00 175.00
Margin block of 4, arrow 825.00
Center line block 900.00 *225.00*
Never hinged 1,600.
P# block of 8, two P# & arrow 2,500.
Never hinged 3,750.
Nos. 551-573 (23) 439.60 36.35
Nos. 551-573, never hinged 940.60

For other listings of perforated stamps of designs A154 to A173 see:
Nos. 578 & 579, Perf. 11x10
Nos. 581-591, Perf. 10
Nos. 594-596, Perf. 11
Nos. 632-642, 653, 692-696, Perf. 11x10½
Nos. 697-701, Perf. 10½x11
This series also includes #622-623 (perf. 11), 684-687 & 720-723.

Plate Blocks

Scott values for plate blocks printed from flat plates are for very fine side and bottom positions. Top position plate blocks with full wide selvage sell for more.

Earliest documented use dates for imperforates are for the imperforate sheet stamps, not for imperforate stamps with vending and affixing machine perforations or for flat plate imperforate coil stamps. EDU dates for VAMP and flat plate imperf coil stamps are shown in their respective sections later in the catalogue.

1923-25 *Imperf.*

Stamp design 19¼x22¼mm

No.	Description	Unused	Used
575	A155 1c **green,** *Mar. 1923*	5.00	5.00
	deep green	5.00	5.00
	Never hinged	11.00	
	On commercial cover		*100.00*
	On philatelic cover		8.50
	Pair	11.00	*12.50*
	Never hinged	24.00	
	Block of 4	22.00	27.50
	Corner margin block of 4	25.00	*27.50*
	Corner margin block of 4 (UR), "O" in selvage	—	
	Margin block of 4, arrow	27.00	*30.00*
	Center line block	40.00	40.00
	Never hinged	70.00	
	P# block of 6	80.00	—
	Never hinged	115.00	

Earliest documented use: Mar. 16, 1923.

No.	Description	Unused	Used
576	A156 1½c **yellow brown,** *Apr. 4, 1925*	1.25	*1.50*
	pale yellow brown	1.25	*1.50*
	brown	1.25	*1.50*
	Never hinged	2.70	
	On commercial cover		*25.00*
	On philatelic cover		6.00
	Pair	2.75	*3.75*
	Never hinged	6.00	
	Block of 4	5.75	*8.50*
	Corner margin block of 4	6.00	*9.00*
	Margin block of 4, arrow	6.25	*10.00*
	Center line block	11.00	*20.00*
	Never hinged	20.00	
	P# block of 6	30.00	—
	Never hinged	45.00	
	Double transfer	—	—

The 1½c A156 Rotary press imperforate is listed as No. 631.

No.	Description	Unused	Used
577	A157 2c **carmine**	1.30	1.25
	light carmine	1.30	1.25
	Never hinged	2.90	
	On commercial cover		*20.00*
	On philatelic cover		6.00
	Pair	2.80	3.00
	Never hinged	6.00	
	Block of 4	5.75	7.00
	Corner margin block of 4	6.00	*8.00*
	Margin block of 4, arrow	6.25	*10.00*
	Center line block	13.00	*15.00*
	Never hinged	22.50	
	P# block of 6	30.00	—
	Never hinged	45.00	
	P# block of 6, large 5 point star	175.00	—
	Never hinged	250.00	
a.	2c **carmine lake**		—
	Nos. 575-577 (3)	7.55	7.75
	Nos. 575-577, never hinged	16.60	

ROTARY PRESS PRINTINGS

(See note over No. 448)

Issued in sheets of 70, 100 or 170 stamps, coil waste of Nos. 597, 599

Stamp designs: 19¾x22¼mm

1923 *Perf. 11x10*

No.	Description	Unused	Used
578	A155 1c **green**	75.00	*160.00*
	Never hinged	150.00	
	On cover		*700.00*
	Block of 4	325.00	*1,000.*
	P# block of 4, star	1,000.	
	Never hinged	1,500.	

Earliest documented use: Nov. 7, 1923.

No.	Description	Unused	Used
579	A157 2c **carmine**	70.00	*140.00*
	deep carmine	70.00	*140.00*
	Never hinged	140.00	
	Block of 4	300.00	*1,750.*
	On cover		*400.00*
	P# block of 4, star	550.00	
	Never hinged	900.00	
	Recut in eye, plate 14731	*110.00*	150.00

Earliest documented use: Feb. 20, 1923.

Warning: See note following No. 459 regarding used stamps.

Plates of 400 subjects in four panes of 100 each

Stamp designs: 19¼x22½mm

1923-26 *Perf. 10*

No.	Description	Unused	Used
581	A155 1c **green,** *Apr. 21, 1923*	10.00	.75
	yellow green	10.00	.75
	pale green	10.00	.75
	Never hinged	21.00	
	On postcard		.85
	On 3rd class cover		1.75
	Block of 4	42.50	4.50
	P# block of 4	175.00	
	Never hinged	250.00	

Earliest documented use: May 18, 1923.

No.	Description	Unused	Used
582	A156 1½c **brown,** *Mar. 19, 1925*	6.00	.65
	dark brown	6.00	.65
	Never hinged	13.00	
	On 3rd class cover		6.00
	Block of 4	26.00	4.00
	P# block of 4	85.00	
	Never hinged	125.00	
	Pair with full horiz. gutter btwn.	*350.00*	
	Pair with full vert. gutter btwn.	*350.00*	

No. 582 was available in full sheets of 400 subjects but was not regularly issued in that form.

No.	Description	Unused	Used
583	A157 2c **carmine,** *Apr. 14, 1924*	3.00	.30
	deep carmine	3.00	.30
	Never hinged	6.25	
	On cover		2.50
	Block of 4	14.00	2.00
	P# block of 4	70.00	
	Never hinged	110.00	
a.	Booklet pane of 6, *Aug. 27, 1926*	110.00	*150.00*
	Never hinged	200.00	

Earliest documented use (unprecanceled): May 15, 1924.

No.	Description	Unused	Used
584	A158 3c **violet,** *Aug. 1, 1925*	27.50	3.00
	Never hinged	60.00	
	On cover with 2c (single UPU rate)		6.50
	Block of 4	130.00	17.50
	P# block of 4	275.00	
	Never hinged	425.00	
585	A159 4c **yellow brown,** *Mar. 1925*	17.50	.65
	deep yellow brown	17.50	.65
	Never hinged	37.50	
	On cover		15.00
	Block of 4	77.50	4.00
	P# block of 4	275.00	
	Never hinged	425.00	
586	A160 5c **blue,** *Dec. 1924*	17.50	.40
	deep blue	17.50	.40
	Never hinged	37.50	
	On UPU-rate cover		6.00
	Block of 4	77.50	3.00
	P# block of 4	275.00	
	Never hinged	425.00	
	Double transfer	—	—
a.	Horizontal pair, imperf. vertically		*7,500.*

No. 586a is unique, precanceled, with average centering and small faults, and it is valued as such.

No.	Description	Unused	Used
587	A161 6c **red orange,** *Mar. 1925*	9.25	.60
	pale red orange	9.25	.60
	Never hinged	20.00	
	On registered cover with other values		15.00
	Block of 4	40.00	4.00
	P# block of 4	225.00	
	Never hinged	325.00	
588	A162 7c **black,** *May 29, 1926*	12.50	6.25
	Never hinged	26.00	
	On registered cover with other values		30.00
	Block of 4	57.50	45.00
	P# block of 4	275.00	
	Never hinged	425.00	
589	A163 8c **olive green,** *May 29, 1926*	27.50	4.50
	pale olive green	27.50	4.50
	Never hinged	57.50	
	On airmail cover		22.50
	Block of 4	125.00	25.00
	P# block of 4	300.00	
	Never hinged	450.00	
590	A164 9c **rose,** *May 29, 1926*	6.00	2.50
	Never hinged	12.50	
	On registered cover with other values		22.50
	Block of 4	26.00	17.50
	P# block of 4	150.00	
	Never hinged	225.00	
591	A165 10c **orange,** *June 8, 1925*	40.00	.50
	Never hinged	85.00	
	On airmail cover		17.50
	Block of 4	200.00	3.00
	P# block of 4	475.00	
	Never hinged	750.00	
	Nos. 581-591 (11)	176.75	20.10
	Nos. 581-591, never hinged	371.25	

Bureau Precancels: 1c, 64 diff., 1½c, 76 diff., 2c, 58 diff., 3c, 41 diff., 4c, 36 diff., 5c, 38 diff., 6c, 36 diff., 7c, 18 diff., 8c, 18 diff., 9c, 13 diff., 10c, 39 diff.

Issued in sheets of 70 or 100 stamps, coil waste of Nos. 597, 599

Stamp designs approximately 19¾x22¼mm

1923 *Perf. 11*

No.	Description	Unused	Used
594	A155 1c **green**	*35,000.*	*10,500.*
	With gum	*65,000.*	
	On cover		*17,500.*
	Pair		*25,000.*

The main listing for No. 594 unused is for an example without gum; both unused and used are valued with perforations just touching frameline on one side.

Earliest documented use: Mar. 25, 1924.

No.	Description	Unused	Used
595	A157 2c **carmine**	240.00	*375.00*
	deep carmine	240.00	*375.00*
	Never hinged	450.00	
	On cover		550.00
	Block of 4	1,050.	*1,750.*
	P# block of 4, star	2,100.	—
	Never hinged	3,000.	
	Recut in eye, plate 14731		—

Earliest documented uses: Mar. 31, 1923 (dated cancel on off-cover pair of stamps); June 29, 1923 (on cover).

Rotary press sheet waste

Stamp design approximately 19¼x22½mm

No.	Description	Unused	Used
596	A155 1c **green,** machine cancel		*250,000.*
	With Bureau precancel		*200,000.*

Fifteen examples of No. 596 are recorded, all used. Ten of the fifteen carry the Bureau precancel "KANSAS CITY/MO" between lines, only two or three of the non-precenceled example are completely sound, and only three or four of the precanceled examples are completely sound. Values are for sound stamps in the grade of fine.

COIL STAMPS

ROTARY PRESS

1923-29 ***Perf. 10 Vertically***

Stamp designs approximately 19¾x22¼mm

No.	Description	Unused	Used
597	A155 1c **green,** *July 18, 1923*	.30	.25
	yellow green	.30	.25
	grayish green	—	—
	Never hinged	.60	
	Three on cover		2.25
	Pair	.65	.25
	Never hinged	1.40	
	Joint line pair	2.00	.75
	Never hinged	4.00	
	Gripper cracks	2.60	1.00
	Double transfer	2.60	1.00
598	A156 1½c **brown,** *Mar. 19, 1925*	.90	.25
	deep brown	.90	.25
	Never hinged	1.80	
	On 3rd class cover		6.00
	Pair	1.90	.25
	Never hinged	3.80	
	Joint line pair	4.50	.75
	Never hinged	9.00	

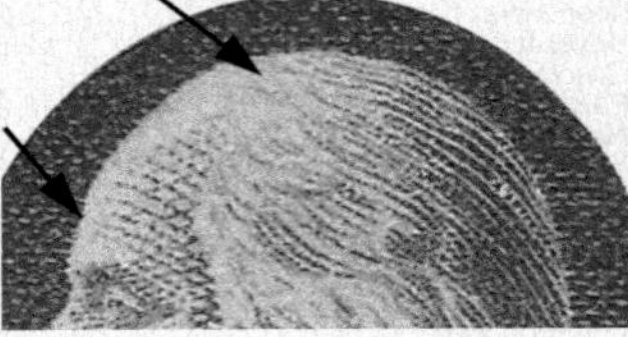

Type I

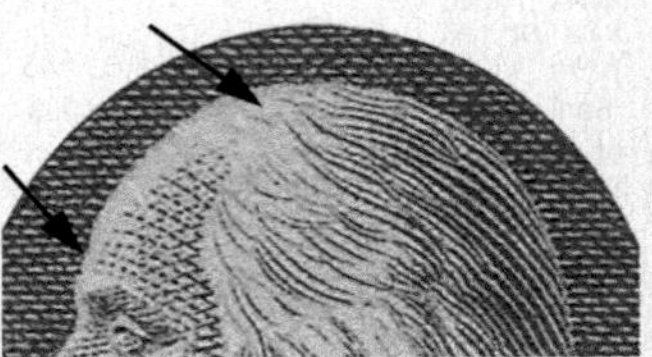

Type II

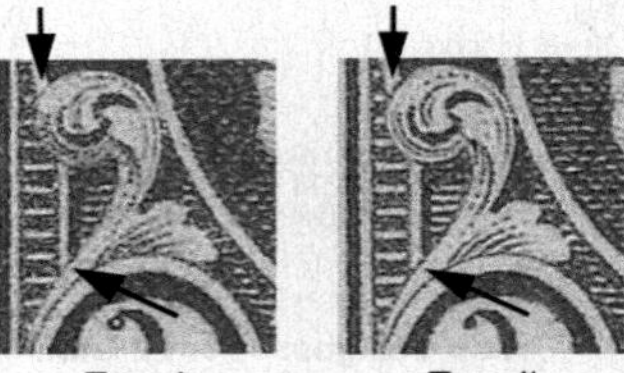

Type I Type II

QUALITY
U.S. STAMPS

From #1 to Date
Specializing in the
Modern Varieties

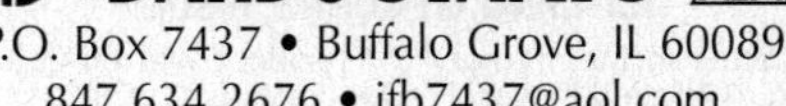

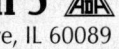

P.O. Box 7437 • Buffalo Grove, IL 60089
847.634.2676 • jfb7437@aol.com
www.BardoStamps.com

TYPE I. No line outlining forehead. No heavy hair lines at top center of head. Outline of left acanthus scroll generally faint at top and toward base at left side.

TYPE II. Thin line outlining forehead. Three heavy hair lines at top center of head; two being outstanding in the white area. Outline of left acanthus scroll very strong and clearly defined at top (under left edge of lettered panel) and at lower curve (above and to left of numeral oval). This type appears only on Nos. 599A and 634A.

No.	Description	Unused	Used
599	A157 2c **carmine,** type I, *Jan. 1923*	.35	.25
	deep carmine, type I	.35	.25
	Never hinged	.70	
	On cover		1.10
	Pair, type I	.75	.25
	Never hinged	1.50	
	Joint line pair, type I	2.25	1.00
	Never hinged	4.50	
	Double transfer, type I	1.90	1.00
	Gripper cracks, type I	2.30	2.00
b.	2c **carmine lake,** type I, never hinged	*300.00*	—
	Pair, never hinged	*650.00*	
	Joint line pair		*700.00*
	Never hinged	*950.00*	

Earliest documented use: Jan. 10, 1923 (precanceled version).

No.	Description	Unused	Used
599A	A157 2c **carmine,** type II, *Mar. 1929*	100.00	16.00
	Never hinged	200.00	
	On cover		32.50
	Pair, type II	210.00	60.00
	Never hinged	425.00	
	Joint line pair, type II	550.00	400.00
	Never hinged	1,150.	
	Joint line pair, types I & II	700.00	*1,000.*
	Never hinged	1,350.	

Earliest documented use: Mar. 29, 1929.

No.	Description	Unused	Used
600	A158 3c **violet,** *May 10, 1924*	6.25	.25
	deep violet	6.25	.25
	Never hinged	12.50	
	On cover		6.00
	Pair	13.00	.45
	Never hinged	26.00	
	Joint line pair	30.00	4.00
	Never hinged	60.00	
	Cracked plate	—	1.00
601	A159 4c **yellow brown,** *Aug. 5, 1923*	3.75	.35
	brown	3.75	.35
	Never hinged	7.50	
	On cover		14.00
	Pair	8.25	.95
	Never hinged	16.50	
	Joint line pair	27.50	10.00
	Never hinged	55.00	

Earliest documented use: Sept. 14, 1923.

No.	Description	Unused	Used
602	A160 5c **dark blue,** *Mar. 5, 1924*	1.75	.25
	Never hinged	3.50	
	On UPU-rate cover		6.00
	Pair	3.75	.35
	Never hinged	7.50	
	Joint line pair	11.00	3.00
	Never hinged	22.50	
603	A165 10c **orange,** *Dec. 1, 1924*	3.50	.25
	Never hinged	7.00	
	On special delivery cover with 2c		22.50
	Pair	8.00	.25
	Never hinged	16.00	
	Joint line pair	25.00	4.50
	Never hinged	50.00	

The 6c design A161 coil stamp is listed as No. 723.

Bureau Precancels: 1c, 296 diff., 1½c, 188 diff., 2c, type I, 113 diff., 2c, type II, Boston, Detroit, 3c, 62 diff., 4c, 34 diff., 5c, 36 diff., 10c, 32 diff.

1923-25 ***Perf. 10 Horizontally***

Stamp designs: 19¼x22½mm

No.	Description	Unused	Used
604	A155 1c **green,** *July 19, 1924*	.40	.25
	yellow green	.40	.25
	Never hinged	.80	
	Three on cover		6.00
	Pair	.85	.25
	Never hinged	1.70	
	Joint line pair	3.50	1.25
	Never hinged	7.00	
605	A156 1½c **yellow brown,** *May 9, 1925*	.40	.25
	brown	.40	.25
	Never hinged	.80	
	On 3rd class cover		17.50
	Pair	.85	.35
	Never hinged	1.70	
	Joint line pair	3.50	*4.00*
	Never hinged	7.00	
606	A157 2c **carmine,** *Dec. 31, 1923*	.40	.25
	Never hinged	.80	
	On cover		3.50
	Pair	.85	.45
	Never hinged	1.70	
	Joint line pair	2.50	*3.50*
	Never hinged	5.00	
	Cracked plate	5.25	2.00
a.	2c **carmine lake**	*75.00*	—
	Never hinged	*150.00*	
	Pair	*170.00*	
	Never hinged	*350.00*	
	Joint line pair, never hinged	*775.00*	
	Nos. 597-599,600-606 (10)	18.00	2.60
	Nos. 597-599, 600-606, never hinged	36.00	

HARDING MEMORIAL ISSUE

Tribute to the memory of President Warren G. Harding, who died in San Francisco, Aug. 2, 1923.

Warren Gamaliel Harding — A177

Plates of 400 subjects in four panes of 100 each

FLAT PLATE PRINTING

Stamp designs: 19¼x22¼mm

1923 ***Perf. 11***

No.	Description	Unused	Used
610	A177 2c **black,** *Sept. 1, 1923*	.50	.25
	intense black	.50	.25
	grayish black	.50	.25
	Never hinged	1.00	
	On cover		.30
	P# block of 6	30.00	—
	Never hinged	47.50	
	Double transfer	2.40	1.00
a.	Horiz. pair, imperf. vert.	*2,000.*	
b.	Imperf. (error), P#14870 block of 6	*25,000.*	

No. 610a is valued in the grade of fine.

No. 610b comes from left side error panes found in a normal pad of No. 610 stamps before No. 611 was issued. Two left side plate blocks and one top position plate block are recorded. Plate #14870 was not used to print No. 611. Loose stamps separated from the top and left plate blocks are indistinguishable from No. 611.

Imperf

No.	Description	Unused	Used
611	A177 2c **black,** *Nov. 15, 1923*	4.50	4.00
	Never hinged	9.00	
	On philatelic cover		8.00
	On commercial cover		15.00
	Pair	10.00	10.00
	Never hinged	20.00	
	Corner margin block of 4	22.00	22.50
	Margin block of 4, arrow	22.00	22.50
	Center line block	65.00	40.00
	Never hinged	110.00	
	P# block of 6	70.00	—
	Never hinged	90.00	

ROTARY PRESS PRINTING

Stamp designs: 19¼x22½mm

Perf. 10

No.	Description	Unused	Used
612	A177 2c **black,** *Sept. 12, 1923*	15.00	1.75
	gray black	15.00	1.75
	Never hinged	32.50	
	On cover		3.25
	P# block of 4	300.00	
	Never hinged	500.00	
	Pair with full vertical gutter between	*350.00*	

Perf. 11

No.	Description	Unused	Used
613	A177 2c **black**		*35,000.*
	Pair		*80,000.*

No. 613 was produced from rotary press sheet waste. It is valued in the grade of fine.

HUGUENOT-WALLOON TERCENTENARY ISSUE

300th anniversary of the settling of the Walloons, and in honor of the Huguenots.

Ship "Nieu Nederland" A178

Walloons Landing at Fort Orange (Albany) — A179

Jan Ribault Monument at Duval County, Fla. — A180

"Broken Circle" flaw

Designed by Clair Aubrey Huston

FLAT PLATE PRINTINGS

Plates of 200 subjects in four panes of 50 each

1924, May 1 ***Perf. 11***

No.	Description	Unused	Used
614	A178 1c **dark green**	2.30	*3.00*
	green	2.30	*3.00*
	Never hinged	4.25	
	On cover		4.50
	P# block of 6	40.00	—
	Never hinged	60.00	
	Double transfer	6.00	6.00
615	A179 2c **carmine rose**	3.75	2.25
	dark carmine rose	3.75	2.25
	Never hinged	7.00	
	On cover		3.50
	P# block of 6	60.00	—
	Never hinged	85.00	
	Double transfer	12.00	3.50
616	A180 5c **dark blue**	15.00	13.00
	deep blue	15.00	13.00
	Never hinged	27.50	
	On UPU-rate cover		20.00
	P# block of 6	250.00	—
	Never hinged	375.00	
	Added line at bottom of white circle around right numeral, "broken circle" plate flaw (15754 UR 2, 3, 4, 5)	60.00	20.00
	Nos. 614-616 (3)	21.05	18.25
	Nos. 614-616, never hinged	38.75	

LEXINGTON-CONCORD ISSUE

150th anniv. of the Battle of Lexington-Concord.

Washington at Cambridge A181

"Birth of Liberty," by Henry Sandham A182

The Minute Man, by Daniel Chester French — A183

Plates of 200 subjects in four panes of 50 each

1925, Apr. 4 ***Perf. 11***

No.	Description	Unused	Used
617	A181 1c **deep green**	2.00	2.50
	green	2.00	2.50
	Never hinged	3.75	
	On cover		3.75
	P# block of 6	40.00	—
	Never hinged	67.50	
618	A182 2c **carmine rose**	3.50	4.00
	pale carmine rose	3.50	4.00
	Never hinged	6.50	
	On cover		5.50
	P# block of 6	60.00	—
	Never hinged	85.00	
619	A183 5c **dark blue**	14.00	13.00
	blue	14.00	13.00
	Never hinged	26.00	
	On UPU-rate cover		20.00
	P# block of 6	200.00	—
	Never hinged	275.00	
	Line over head (16807 LL 48)	42.50	19.00
	Nos. 617-619 (3)	19.50	19.50
	Nos. 617-619, never hinged	36.25	

NORSE-AMERICAN ISSUE

Arrival in New York, on Oct. 9, 1825, of the sloop "Restaurationen" with the first group of immigrants from Norway.

Sloop "Restaurationen"
A184

Viking Ship
A185

Designed by Clair Aubrey Huston.

Plates of 100 subjects.

1925, May 18		*Perf. 11*
620 A184 2c **carmine & black**	3.00	2.75
deep carmine & black	3.00	2.75
Never hinged	6.00	
On cover		4.50
Margin block of 4, arrow	15.00	
Center line block	20.00	
Never hinged	37.50	
P# block of 8, two P# & arrow	160.00	—
Never hinged	275.00	
P# block of 8, carmine & arrow; black P# omitted	*3,250.*	—
621 A185 5c **dark blue & black**	9.00	9.00
Never hinged	19.00	
On UPU-rate cover		17.50
Margin block of 4, arrow	52.50	
Center line block	65.00	
Never hinged	115.00	
P# block of 8, two P# & arrow	450.00	—
Never hinged	700.00	

REGULAR ISSUE

Benjamin
Harrison — A186

Woodrow
Wilson — A187

Plates of 400 subjects in four panes of 100.

1925-26		*Perf. 11*
622 A186 13c **green,** *Jan. 11, 1926*	9.00	.75
light green	9.00	.75
Never hinged	19.00	
On registered cover with other values		17.50
P# block of 6	210.00	—
Never hinged	300.00	
P# block of 6, large 5 point star, right side only	*2,100.*	—
Never hinged	*3,000.*	
623 A187 17c **black,** *Dec. 28, 1925*	9.00	.30
gray black	9.00	.30
Never hinged	19.00	
On registered cover		6.00
P# block of 6	250.00	—
Never hinged	325.00	

Plate Blocks

Scott values for plate blocks printed from flat plates are for very fine side and bottom positions. Top position plate blocks with full wide selvage sell for more.

SESQUICENTENNIAL EXPOSITION ISSUE

Sesquicentennial Exposition, Philadelphia, Pa., June 1 - Dec. 1, 1926, and 150th anniv. of the Declaration of Independence.

Liberty
Bell — A188

Designed by Clair Aubrey Huston.

Plates of 200 subjects in four panes of 50.

1926, May 10		*Perf. 11*
627 A188 2c **carmine rose**	2.25	.50
Never hinged	4.00	
On cover		1.00
On cover, Expo. station machine canc.		7.50
On cover, Expo. station duplex hand-stamp canc.		35.00
P# block of 6	35.00	—
Never hinged	50.00	
Double transfer	—	—

ERICSSON MEMORIAL ISSUE

Unveiling of the statue of John Ericsson, builder of the "Monitor," by the Crown Prince of Sweden, Washington, D.C., May 29, 1926.

Statue of John
Ericsson — A189

Designed by Clair Aubrey Huston.

Plates of 200 subjects in four panes of 50.

1926, May 29		*Perf. 11*
628 A189 5c **gray lilac**	5.00	3.25
Never hinged	8.50	
On UPU-rate cover		8.00
P# block of 6	57.50	—
Never hinged	82.50	

BATTLE OF WHITE PLAINS ISSUE

150th anniv. of the Battle of White Plains, N. Y.

Alexander Hamilton's
Battery — A190

Designed by Clair Aubrey Huston.

Plates of 400 subjects in four panes of 100.

1926, Oct. 18		*Perf. 11*
629 A190 2c **carmine rose**	1.60	1.70
Never hinged	2.75	
On cover		2.25
P# block of 6	35.00	—
Never hinged	50.00	

INTERNATIONAL PHILATELIC EXHIBITION ISSUE
Souvenir Sheet

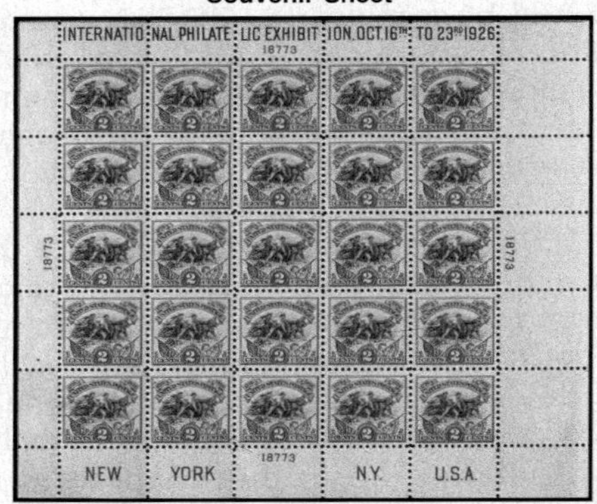

A190a

Illustration reduced.

Plates of 100 subjects in four panes of 25 each, separated by one inch wide gutters with central guide lines.

Condition valued:

Centering: Overall centering will average very fine, but individual stamps may be better or worse.

Perforations: No folds along rows of perforations.

Gum: There may be some light gum bends but no gum creases.

Hinging: There may be hinge marks in the selvage and on up to two or three stamps, but no heavy hinging or hinge remnants (except in the ungummed portion of the wide selvage.

Margins: Top panes should have about ½ inch bottom margin and 1 inch top margin.

Bottom panes should have about ½ inch top margin and just under ¾ inch bottom margin. Both will have one wide side (usually 1 inch plus) and one narrow (½ inch) side margin. The wide margin corner will have a small diagonal notch on top panes.

1926, Oct. 18		*Perf. 11*
630 A190a 2c **carmine rose,** pane of 25	275.00	*450.00*
Never hinged	500.00	
On cover		—

United States & United Nations

We Specialize in:

- Mint and Used Singles
- Plate Blocks
- Booklet Panes
- Modern Sheets
- Envelopes
- Postal Cards
- Plate Number Coils

at competitive prices!

COMPLETE LINE of Discount Stamp Collecting Supplies

Features a shopping cart with 10,000 items

GOLDEN VALLEY MINNESOTA STAMP CO.

2525 Nevada Ave N #101
Golden Valley, MN 55427

1-800-747-3144

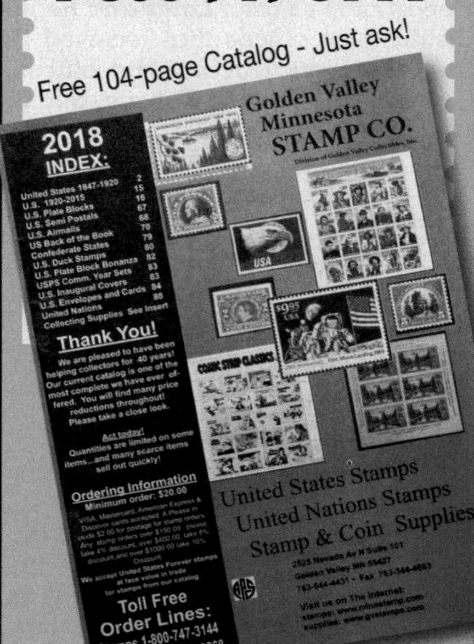

2020 EDITION SPECIAL FEATURE

Values for Kansas-Nebraska covers debut in 2020 Scott U.S. Specialized catalog

Vicky and Mick Hadley

The 2020 edition of the Scott *Specialized Catalogue of United States Stamps and Covers* includes for the first time on-cover values for the 1929 definitive (regular-issue) stamps overprinted "Kans." and "Nebr.," for use in Kansas and Nebraska.

The Kansas stamps are listed as Scott 658-668, and the Nebraska stamps are Scott 669-679. Before providing details regarding postal history associated with these fascinating stamps, some historical context is necessary.

Purpose and history of the Kansas and Nebraska stamps

The "Kans." and "Nebr." overprints were presented as a security measure to track the stamps should they be stolen from the post office. After our review of the Bureau of Engraving and Printing archives provided by the National Postal Museum in Washington, D.C., and the discovery of two official letters sent in May 1929 and July 1929 to the postmaster of the Wisner, Neb., post office, it was discovered that the overprinting was part of a broader experiment to reduce the overhead expense of stamp requisitions.

Specifically, postmasters were expected to requisition a year's supply of each of the stamps to reduce "the overhead in the matter of requisition and shipping expense sufficiently to care for the increased cost of manufacture" of the overprinted stamps. The requirement eliminated the quarterly requisitions and "emergency requests" for additional stamp stock if a supply was depleted early. The expected expense reduction ultimately would be a major savings to the U.S. Post Office Department. Based on the BEP cost of ½¢ per 1,000 stamps, the estimated cost was $12,500 for the entire printing. Smaller post offices with limited storage capacity could, with permission, request a six-month supply of stamps.

According to the 1929 edition of the U.S. Post Office Department's *Postal Laws and Regulations*, there were 862 district post offices that received the overprinted stamps from the central accounting offices in Topeka, Kan., and Omaha, Neb.: 464 in Kansas, and 398 in Nebraska. These post offices serviced a city and rural population of 2,560,000

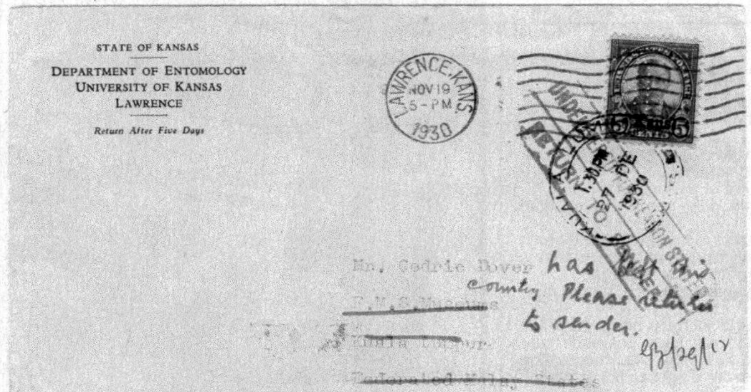

Figure 1. A single 5¢ Kansas stamp properly pays the international letter rate on this cover sent Nov. 19, 1930, from Lawrence, Kan., to Kuala Lumpur.

Figure 2. A pair of 10¢ Nebraska stamps combine to pay the 2¢ postage, 3¢ return receipt fee and 15¢ registry fee on this cover mailed March 14, 1930, from Dixon, Neb., to Hartington, Neb.

between the two states. The average number of patrons was fewer than 3,000 for each post office. The largest cities (including the central accounting offices) in Kansas (Topeka, Kansas City and Wichita) and Nebraska (Omaha and Lincoln) were to use regular non-overprinted stamps.

The entire Kansas and Nebraska issue was done in one printing. A total of 227,170,000 stamps were produced. The 1¢, 1½¢ and 2¢ printing total for both states combined was 199,470,000 stamps. The 3¢ through the 10¢ denominations for both states combined accounted for the remaining 27,700,000 stamps. This represented an average of 1,731,250 for each of those eight higher denominations for both states. An unknown quantity was kept for the philatelic window in Washington, D.C., for collector orders. The USPOD expected to make a $40,000 profit from this supply.

Production of the stamps

The Kansas and Nebraska overprints were printed on the Bureau's Stickney rotary press using the plates for the 1¢ through the 10¢ 1926-27 definitive (regular-issue) stamps. After printing the stamp design and before the gumming process, an attachment to the press printed the overprint on the stamps using electrotype plates.

Due to the moisture content of the paper, air temperature, poor synchronization with the stamp printing process and other factors, the position of the overprint continually shifted on the face of the stamp design. To deal with these factors, a manually turned wheel on the side of the precancel device adjusted the position of the overprint vertically on the face of the stamps. The pressman used this wheel to keep the overprint in proper position.

Because the paper web (roll) was printed at about 60 feet per minute, the pressman would only have about one second to view a printed pane of 100 stamps. Normal vertical spacing of the overprints within a pane of stamps was 22 millimeters between rows.

If not adjusted, the overprint moved up or down the web of stamps, and the 32mm wide gutter spacing that allowed

for cutting the web into sheets of 400 (four panes of 100 stamps) would fall on the pane of stamps instead of the gutter. When this occurred, a wide-space variety — 32mm vertical spacing between overprints — resulted. If not further corrected, this 32mm spacing would bridge a stamp and cause an overprint missing error.

Upon inspection, during the process of perforating the gummed, printed web and cutting it into 400-subject sheets, most of these errors were found and removed. These 400-subject sheets were then stacked in piles of 100 sheets between pasteboard covers, wire-stapled together at the edges, and guillotine-sliced into pads of 100 panes of 100 subjects each. After wrapping they were shipped to the central accounting offices for distribution to the district post offices.

Postal History

Values for Kansas-Nebraska covers given in the Scott U.S. Specialized catalog are for Kansas and Nebraska usages paying the most common rates — either solo or in combination with other stamps. When acquiring postal history of these stamps, there are a few points to consider. The most desirable covers originate from within Kansas or Nebraska during a period from early May 1929 through 1931, while the stamps were still in stock in post offices.

Some smaller post offices still had a stock of some denominations into 1932, but this was not common. Most of the unsold stamps had been scooped up by collectors and dealers or shipped back to the central accounting offices at that point.

Some desirable uses from outside of Kansas and Nebraska exist. For example, mail-order businesses would allow customers to pay for small orders with postage stamps; these firms would then use the stamps on their outgoing mail.

The low-denomination (1¢, 1½¢, 2¢) Kansas-Nebraska stamps are plentiful on cover and constitute the bulk of the mail. However, covers franked with 3¢ through 10¢ stamps paying the proper rates are very difficult, especially solo uses. Figure 1 pictures a solo use of the 5¢ Kansas stamp on a cover mailed Nov. 19, 1930, from Lawrence, Kan., to Kuala Lumpur. Note the "UK" perfin of the sender on the stamp: the University of Kansas. A handstamp and docketing indicate the cover was eventually returned to the sender. Illustrated in Figure 2 is a cover sent March 14, 1930, from Dixon, Neb., to Hartington, Neb. The pair of 10¢ Nebraska stamps paid the 2¢ postage, 3¢ return receipt fee and 15¢ registry fee.

Due to the small populations of the states and small towns in rural settings, covers paying special services such as registry and special delivery that required higher denominations were not plentiful. Only a small supply of the higher denominations was required even though a year's supply was to be requisitioned.

Kansas-Nebraska covers to foreign destinations are also quite elusive. Various ethnic groups that settled in the area corresponded back to their homelands. Germans represented the largest immigrant population for Kansas and Nebraska. A smaller group of Czechoslovakian and Swedish families also settled in Kansas and Nebraska. Overall, covers to Germany seem to be the most prevalent.

Other very difficult uses of any denomination on cover are perfins and precancels. Our census shows fewer than 60 Kansas-Nebraska perfin covers. Even though there were a large number of collector-inspired Kansas-Nebraska precancels, legitimate use of these on cover is similarly scarce.

Scott-Schaubek U.S. Hingeless Album

Don't mess with measuring or cutting mounts again. Get the Scott National album with Scott Numbers in Schaubek Hingeless format. The Scott/Schaubek U.S. Album features spaces for every major U.S. stamp listed in the Scott Catalogue.

Item		Retail	AA*
HUSA01	1845-1934	$299.95	**$224.99**
HUSA02	1935-1976	$299.95	**$224.99**
HUSA03	1977-1993	$299.95	**$224.99**
HUSA04	1994-2000	$299.95	**$224.99**
HUSA05	2001-2004	$199.95	**$148.49**
HUSA06	2005-2009	$249.99	**$179.99**
HUSA07	2010-2015	$249.99	**$179.99**
HUSA2016	2016	$78.99	**$67.99**
HUSA2017	2017	$78.99	**$67.99**

Item		Retail	AA*
HUSA2018	2018	$78.99	**$67.99**
HRB001	Binder	$39.99	**$34.99**
HRS001	Slipcase	$15.00	**$12.99**

U.S. ALBUM SET

Specially priced set includes the pages from 1845-2015, plus binders, slipcases and labels.

Item	Retail	AA*
HUSASET	$2,100.00	**$1,680.00**

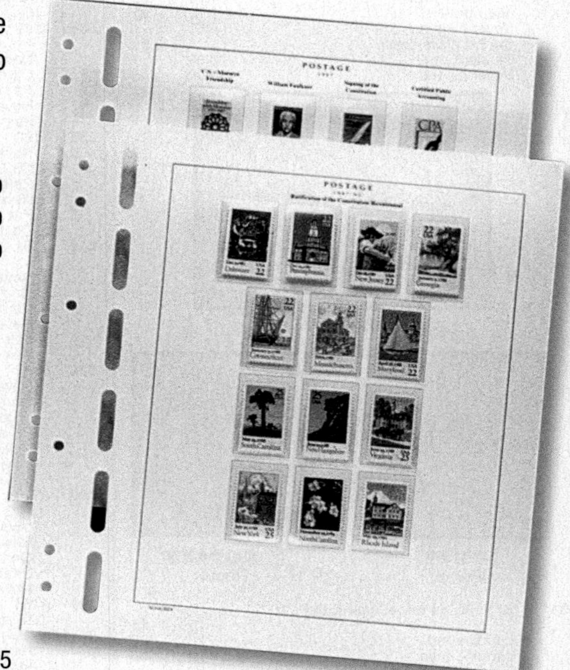

www.AmosAdvantage.com

Call 1-800-572-6885

Outside U.S. & Canada 937-498-0800 • Mail to: P.O. Box 4129, Sidney OH 45365

TERMS & CONDITIONS:*AA prices apply to paid subscribers of Amos Media publications, or orders placed online. Prices, terms and product availability subject to change. Taxes will apply in CA, OH & IL.
SHIPPING & HANDLING: United States: Orders under $10 are only $3.99. 10% of order over $10 total. Minimum Freight Charge $7.99; Maximum Freight Charge $45.00. **Canada:** 20% of order total. Minimum Freight Charge $19.99; Maximum Freight Charge $200.00.
Foreign: Orders are shipped via FedEx Economy International or USPS and billed actual freight. Brokerage, Customs or duties are the responsibility of the customer.

Dot over first "S" of "States" 18774 LL 9 or 18773 LL 11, sheet 350.00 *500.00*
Never hinged 575.00

Issued in panes measuring 158-160¼x136-146½mm containing 25 stamps with inscription "International Philatelic Exhibition, Oct. 16th to 23rd, 1926" in top margin.

VALUES FOR VERY FINE STAMPS
Please note: Stamps are valued in the grade of Very Fine unless otherwise indicated.

TYPES OF 1922-26 ISSUE
REGULAR ISSUE
ROTARY PRESS PRINTINGS
(See note above No. 448.)
Plates of 400 subjects in four panes of 100 each
Stamp designs 19¼x22½mm

1926, Aug. 27 ***Imperf.***

631 A156 1½c **yellow brown** 2.00 1.70
light brown 2.00 1.70
Never hinged 3.00
On philatelic cover 12.50
Pair 4.25 4.00
Never hinged 6.25
Pair, vert. gutter between 4.75 *5.00*
Pair, horiz. gutter between 4.75 *5.00*
Margin block with dash (left, right, top or bottom) 11.00 *14.00*
Center block with crossed gutters and dashes 35.00 *40.00*
Never hinged 55.00
P# block of 4 55.00 —
Never hinged 75.00
Without gum breaker ridges 50.00
Pair, vert. gutter between *125.00*
Pair, horiz. gutter btwn. *125.00*
Margin block with dash (left right, top or bottom) *350.00*
Center block with crossed gutters and dashes *700.00*
Never hinged *1,050.*
P# block of 4 450.00
Never hinged 700.00

1926-34 ***Perf. 11x10½***

632 A155 1c **green,** *June 10, 1927* .25 .25
yellow green .25 .25
Never hinged .35
Three on cover 1.25
P# block of 4 2.00 —
Never hinged 3.25
Pair with full vertical gutter btwn. 150.00 —
Cracked plate — —
a. Booklet pane of 6, *Nov. 2, 1927* 5.00 *4.00*
Never hinged 8.00
b. Vertical pair, imperf. between *3,000.* *3,250.*
Never hinged *5,500.*
c. Horiz. pair, imperf. between *5,000.*

No. 632b is valued in the grade of fine. No. 632c is valued in the grade of fine and never hinged. It is possibly unique.

633 A156 1½c **yellow brown,** *May 17, 1927* 1.70 .25
deep brown 1.70 .25
Never hinged 2.60
On 3rd class cover 2.50
P# block of 4 70.00 —
Never hinged 115.00

Normal

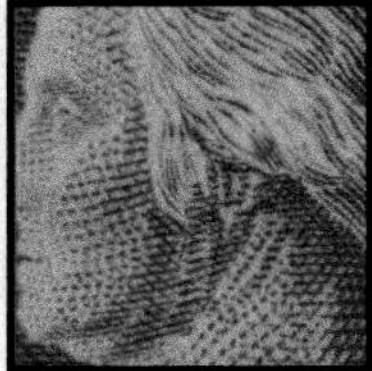

"Long ear" Recut

"Smiling George" Recut

634 A157 2c **carmine,** type I, *Dec. 10, 1926* .25 .25
carmine red .25 .25
carmine rose .25 .25
Never hinged .30
On cover .35
P# block of 4, type I, # opposite corner stamp 3.75 —
Never hinged 6.50
Vertical P# block of 10, # opposite 3rd horizontal row from top or bottom (Experimental Electric Eye plates) 7.50 —
Never hinged 12.50
Margin block of 4, Electric Eye marking .45 .25
Pair with full vertical gutter between 200.00
Recut ("long ear"), type I, 20342 UR 34 *90.00* —
Never hinged *175.00*
Gash and recut ("smiling George"), type I, 21423 UL 23 *120.00* —
Never hinged 250.00
Recut face, type I, 20234 LL 58 —
b. 2c **carmine lake**, type I *180.00* *500.00*
Never hinged *425.00*
P# block of 4 *2,250.*
Never hinged *4,250.*
c. Horizontal pair, type I, imperf. between *6,000.*
d. Booklet pane of 6, **carmine**, type I, *Feb. 25, 1927* 1.50 1.50
Never hinged 2.50
e. As "d," **carmine lake** *400.00* *1,000.*
Never hinged *750.00*
f. 2c **lake**, type I, on cover —

No. 634, Type I, exists on a thin, tough experimental paper.
No. 634c is valued in the grade of fine.

Earliest documented use: FDC (No. 634); Dec. 20, 1929 (No. 634b).

Counterfeits exist of No. 634. See the Postal Counterfeits section of this catalog.

634A A157 2c **carmine,** type II, *Dec. 1928* 300.00 13.50
Never hinged 600.00
On cover 21.00
P# block of 4, type II 2,000. —
Never hinged 3,000.
Pair with full horiz. gutter btwn. 750.00 —
Never hinged *1,250.*
Pair with full vert. gutter btwn. 750.00 —
Never hinged *1,250.*
Center block with crossed gutters 2,750.
Never hinged *4,250.*

Earliest documented use: Dec. 15, 1928.

An unused, never-hinged block of four in a distinctive dark carmine shade was authenticated as genuine in 2013. To date, unused (hinged) examples and used examples have not been reported. This shade is likely extremely scarce, and the editors would like to receive reports of additional examples.

No. 634A, Type II, was available in full sheet of 400 subjects but was not regularly issued in that form.

635 A158 3c **violet,** *Feb. 3, 1927* .75 .25
Never hinged 1.20
On cover 2.00
P# block of 4 17.50 —
Never hinged 35.00
a. 3c **bright violet,** *Feb. 7, 1934* re-issue, Plates 21185 & 21186 .35 .25
Never hinged .45
On cover .25
P# block of 4 10.00 —
Never hinged 18.00
Gripper cracks 3.25 2.00

636 A159 4c **yellow brown,** *May 17, 1927* 1.90 .25
Never hinged 3.00
On cover 8.00
P# block of 4 65.00 —
Never hinged 92.50
Pair with full vert. gutter btwn. *200.00*

637 A160 5c **dark blue,** *Mar. 24, 1927* 1.90 .25
Never hinged 3.00
On UPU-rate cover 4.50
P# block of 4 12.50 —
Never hinged 17.50
Pair with full vert. gutter btwn. *275.00*
Double transfer — —

638 A161 6c **red orange,** *July 27, 1927* 2.00 .25
Never hinged 3.20
On airmail cover 6.00
P# block of 4 15.00 —
Never hinged 20.00
Pair with full horiz. gutter btwn. —
Pair with full vert. gutter btwn. *300.00*

639 A162 7c **black,** *Mar. 24, 1927* 2.00 .25
Never hinged 3.20
On registered cover with other values 15.00
P# block of 4 15.00 —
Never hinged 20.00
a. Vertical pair, imperf. between 550.00 400.00
Never hinged 1,000.

640 A163 8c **olive green,** *June 10, 1927* 2.00 .25
olive bister 2.00 .25
Never hinged 3.20
On airmail cover 8.00
P# block of 4 15.00 —
Never hinged 20.00

641 A164 9c **rose,** *May 17, 1927* 1.90 .25
salmon rose 1.90 .25
orange red, *1931* 1.90 .25
Never hinged 3.00
On registered cover with other values 8.00
P# block of 4 12.50 —
Never hinged 17.50
Pair with full vert. gutter btwn. —

642 A165 10c **orange,** *Feb. 3, 1927* 3.25 .25
Never hinged 5.50
On special delivery cover with 2c 6.00
P# block of 4 17.00 —
Never hinged 22.50
Double transfer — —
Nos. 632-634,635-642 (11) 17.90 2.75
Nos. 632-634, 635-642 never hinged 28.00

The 1½c, 2c, 4c, 5c, 6c, 8c imperf. (dry print) are printer's waste.

See No. 653.

Bureau Precancels: 1c, 292 diff., 1½c, 147 diff., 2c, type I, 99 diff., 2c, type II, 4 diff., 3c, 101 diff., 4c, 60 diff., 5c, 91 diff., 6c, 78 diff., 7c, 66 diff., 8c, 78 diff., 9c, 60 diff., 10c, 97 diff.

VERMONT SESQUICENTENNIAL ISSUE

Battle of Bennington, 150th anniv. and State independence.

Green Mountain Boy — A191

FLAT PLATE PRINTING
Plates of 400 subjects in four panes of 100.

1927, Aug. 3 ***Perf. 11***

643 A191 2c **carmine rose** 1.20 .80
Never hinged 2.00
On cover 1.50
P# block of 6 32.50 —
Never hinged 45.00

BURGOYNE CAMPAIGN ISSUE

Battles of Bennington, Oriskany, Fort Stanwix and Saratoga.

"The Surrender of General Burgoyne at Saratoga," by John Trumbull A192

Plates of 200 subjects in four panes of 50.

1927, Aug. 3 ***Perf. 11***

644 A192 2c **carmine rose** 3.00 2.10
Never hinged 5.25
On cover 3.00
P# block of 6 32.50 —
Never hinged 42.50

VALLEY FORGE ISSUE

150th anniversary of Washington's encampment at Valley Forge, Pa.

Washington at Prayer — A193

Plates of 400 subjects in four panes of 100.

1928, May 26 ***Perf. 11***

645 A193 2c **carmine rose** 1.15 .50
Never hinged 1.80
On cover .75
P# block of 6 25.00 —
Never hinged 37.50
a. 2c **lake** —
Never hinged —

BATTLE OF MONMOUTH ISSUE

150th anniv. of the Battle of Monmouth, N.J., and "Molly Pitcher" (Mary Ludwig Hayes), the heroine of the battle.

No. 634 Overprinted

ROTARY PRESS PRINTING

1928, Oct. 20 *Perf. 11x10½*

646 A157 2c **carmine** 1.00 1.00
Never hinged 1.60
On cover 1.60
P# block of 4 37.50 —
Never hinged 52.50
Wide spacing, vert. pair 50.00 —
a. "Pitcher" only *675.00*
b. 2c **carmine lake** *2,500.*

No. 646a is valued in the grade of fine.

Normally the overprints were placed 18mm apart vertically, but pairs exist with a space of 28mm between the overprints.

HAWAII SESQUICENTENNIAL ISSUE

Sesquicentennial Celebration of the discovery of the Hawaiian Islands.

Nos. 634 and 637 Overprinted

ROTARY PRESS PRINTING

1928, Aug. 13 *Perf. 11x10½*

647 A157 2c **carmine** 4.00 4.00
Never hinged 7.25
On cover 5.75
P# block of 4 110.00 —
Never hinged 180.00
Wide spacing, vert. pair 125.00
648 A160 5c **dark blue** 11.00 12.50
Never hinged 21.50
On cover 20.00
P# block of 4 200.00 —
Never hinged 375.00

Nos. 647-648 were sold at post offices in Hawaii and at the Postal Agency in Washington, D.C. They were valid throughout the nation.

Normally the overprints were placed 18mm apart vertically, but pairs exist with a space of 28mm between the overprints.

AERONAUTICS CONFERENCE ISSUE

Intl. Civil Aeronautics Conf., Washington, D.C., Dec. 12 - 14, 1928, and 25th anniv. of the 1st airplane flight by the Wright Brothers, Dec. 17, 1903.

Wright Airplane
A194

Globe and Airplane
A195

"Prairie Dog" plate flaw

FLAT PLATE PRINTING

Plates of 200 subjects in four panes of 50.

1928, Dec. 12 *Perf. 11*

649 A194 2c **carmine rose** 1.10 .80
Never hinged 1.75
On cover 1.50
P# block of 6 11.50 —
Never hinged 17.50
650 A195 5c **blue** 4.50 3.25
Never hinged 7.00
On UPU-rate cover 5.00
P# block of 6 42.50 —
Never hinged 60.00
Plate flaw "prairie dog" (19658 LL 50) 30.00 12.50

GEORGE ROGERS CLARK ISSUE

150th anniv. of the surrender of Fort Sackville, the present site of Vincennes, Ind., to Clark.

Surrender of Fort Sackville
A196

Plates of 100 subjects in two panes of 50.

1929, Feb. 25 *Perf. 11*

651 A196 2c **carmine & black** .70 .50
deep carmine & black .70 .50
Never hinged 1.15
On cover 1.00
Margin block of 4, arrow (line only) right or left 3.25
P# block of 6, two P# & "Top" 11.00 —
Never hinged 20.00
P# block of 10, red P# only — —
Double transfer (19721 R 14, 29 & 44) 4.25 2.25

TYPE OF 1922-26 ISSUE

REGULAR ISSUE

ROTARY PRESS PRINTING

Plates of 400 subjects in four panes of 100.

1929, May 25 *Perf. 11x10½*

653 A154 ½c **olive brown** .25 .25
Never hinged .35
On 1c stamped envelope (3rd class) 1.00
P# block of 4 2.00 —
Never hinged 3.00
Damaged plate, (19652 LL 72) 2.00 1.00
Retouched plate, (19652 LL 72) 2.00 1.00
Pair with full horiz. gutter btwn. *150.00*

Bureau Precancels: 99 diff.

ELECTRIC LIGHT'S GOLDEN JUBILEE ISSUE

Invention of the 1st incandescent electric lamp by Thomas Alva Edison, Oct. 21, 1879, 50th anniv.

Edison's First Lamp — A197

Designed by Alvin R. Meissner.

FLAT PLATE PRINTING

Plates of 400 subjects in four panes of 100.

1929 *Perf. 11*

654 A197 2c **carmine rose,** *June 5* .65 .65
Never hinged 1.10
On cover 1.10
P# block of 6 25.00 —
Never hinged 40.00
a. 2c **lake** —

ROTARY PRESS PRINTING

Perf. 11x10½

655 A197 2c **carmine rose,** *June 11* .65 .25
Never hinged 1.10
On cover .25
P# block of 4 32.50 —
Never hinged 45.00

ROTARY PRESS COIL STAMP

Perf. 10 Vertically

656 A197 2c **carmine rose,** *June 11* 10.00 1.75
Never hinged 20.00
On cover 2.75
Pair 22.50 4.00
Never hinged 45.00
Joint line pair 55.00 27.50
Never hinged 110.00

SULLIVAN EXPEDITION ISSUE

150th anniversary of the Sullivan Expedition in New York State during the Revolutionary War.

Major General John Sullivan — A198

FLAT PLATE PRINTING

Plates of 400 subjects in four panes of 100.

1929, June 17 *Perf. 11*

657 A198 2c **carmine rose** .55 .55
Never hinged .95
On cover 1.00
P# block of 6 17.50 —
Never hinged 27.50
a. 2c **lake** 375.00 250.00
Never hinged 625.00
P# block of 6 *2,500.*
Never hinged *3,500.*
b. Vert. pair, imperf. btwn. *4,000.*

The unique No. 657b resulted from a paper foldover before perfing, and it has angled errant perfs from another row of horiz. perfs through the left side of the stamps.

REGULAR ISSUE

Nos. 632 to 642 Overprinted

Officially issued May 1, 1929.

Some values known canceled as early as Apr. 15.

This special issue was authorized as a measure of preventing losses from post office burglaries. Approximately a year's supply was printed and issued to postmasters. The P.O. Dept. found it desirable to discontinue the State overprinted stamps after the initial supply was used.

On-cover values are for commercial contemporaneous (1929-31) uses from Kansas or Nebraska. Later (post 1932) uses and philatelic uses such as first-flight commemorations sell for less.

ROTARY PRESS PRINTING

1929, May 1 *Perf. 11x10½*

658 A155 1c **green** 2.50 2.00
Never hinged 5.00
On cover 6.50
Single franking on drop letter 15.00
Pair on first-class letter 15.00
P# block of 4 60.00 —
Never hinged 85.00
Wide spacing, pair 32.50
a. Vertical pair, one without ovpt. *300.00*
Never hinged *500.00*
659 A156 1½c **brown** 3.25 2.90
Never hinged 6.50
Pair on first-class (after July 6, 1932) letter 20.00
Single franking on third-class unsealed advertising cover 25.00

Quality Stamps, Super Prices!
Spruce Hill Studios
See all our latest offerings on the APS website:
stampstore.org Seller ID 738268
US (all categories), Philippines, Canal Zone, Cuba, PR, Australia, Canada, French Colonies and more.
603-586-4460
email shsmc@together.net

Single franking on third-class greeting card with contents — 30.00
P# block of 4 60.00 —
Never hinged 85.00
Wide spacing, pair 70.00
a. Vertical pair, one without ovpt. *475.00*

660 A157 2c **carmine** 4.00 1.00
Never hinged 7.50
On cover 6.00
Single franking on UPU treaty rate cover *90.00*
P# block of 4 60.00 —
Never hinged 80.00
Wide spacing, pair 55.00

661 A158 3c **violet** 17.50 15.00
Never hinged 35.00
On domestic airmail cover *90.00*
On registered cover with return receipt *150.00*
Single franking on UPU postcard *200.00*
Single franking on first-class (after July 6, 1932) cover *45.00*
P# block of 4 250.00 —
Never hinged 325.00
a. Vertical pair, one without ovpt. *600.00*
Never hinged *800.00*

662 A159 4c **yellow brown** 17.50 9.00
Never hinged 35.00
Single franking on double-weight first-class letter *95.00*
Single franking on double-weight UPU treaty rate cover *130.00*
P# block of 4 225.00 —
Never hinged 300.00
a. Vertical pair, one without ovpt. *500.00*

663 A160 5c **deep blue** 12.50 9.75
Never hinged 25.00
Single franking on domestic airmail cover *95.00*
Single franking on UPU cover to Germany *80.00*
Single franking on UPU cover to other destinations *160.00*
On registered or special delivery cover *135.00*
P# block of 4 200.00 —
Never hinged 300.00

664 A161 6c **red orange** 25.00 18.00
Never hinged 50.00
On registered or special delivery cover *145.00*
Single franking on triple-weight first-class cover *175.00*
P# block of 4 450.00 —
Never hinged 600.00

665 A162 7c **black** 25.00 27.50
Never hinged 50.00
On registered or special delivery cover *175.00*
P# block of 4 500.00 —
Never hinged 700.00

666 A163 8c **olive green** 72.50 65.00
Never hinged 145.00
On registered or special delivery cover *300.00*
Single franking on quadruple-weight first-class letter *275.00*
Single franking on double-weight UPU foreign letter rate cover *375.00*
P# block of 4 700.00 —
Never hinged 925.00

667 A164 9c **light rose** 14.00 11.50
Never hinged 27.50
On registered or special delivery cover *235.00*
P# block of 4 275.00 —
Never hinged 375.00

668 A165 10c **orange yellow** 22.50 12.50
Never hinged 45.00
On registered special delivery cover *185.00*
Pair on registered first-class cover with return receipt *225.00*
P# block of 4 375.00 —
Never hinged 525.00
Pair with full horizontal gutter between *4,750.*
Nos. 658-668 (11) 216.25 174.15
Nos. 658-668, never hinged 431.50

See notes following No. 679.

Overprinted

1929, May 1

669 A155 1c **green** 3.25 2.25
Never hinged 6.50
On cover 6.50
Single franking on drop letter 15.00
Pair on first-class letter 15.00
P# block of 4 60.00 —
Never hinged 80.00
Wide spacing, pair 60.00 —
b. No period after "Nebr." (19338, 19339 UR 26, 36 and 19339 LR 26, 36) 50.00

670 A156 1½c **brown** 3.00 2.50
Never hinged 6.00
Pair on first-class (after July 6, 1932) letter 20.00
Single franking on third-class unsealed advertising cover 25.00
Single franking on third-class greeting card with contents 30.00
P# block of 4 65.00 —
Never hinged 95.00
Wide spacing, pair 60.00

671 A157 2c **carmine** 3.00 1.30
Never hinged 6.00
On cover 6.00
Single franking on UPU treaty rate cover *90.00*
P# block of 4 60.00 —
Never hinged 85.00
Wide spacing, pair 75.00

672 A158 3c **violet** 11.00 12.00
Never hinged 22.00
On domestic airmail cover *90.00*
On registered cover with return receipt *150.00*
Single franking on UPU postcard *200.00*
Single franking on first-class (after July 6, 1932) cover *45.00*
P# block of 4 260.00 —
Never hinged 350.00
Wide spacing, pair 175.00
a. Vertical pair, one without ovpt. *500.00*

673 A159 4c **yellow brown** 17.50 15.00
Never hinged 35.00
Single franking on double-weight first-class letter *95.00*
Single franking on double-weight UPU treaty rate cover *130.00*
P# block of 4 275.00 —
Never hinged 375.00
Wide spacing, pair 175.00

674 A160 5c **deep blue** 15.00 15.00
Never hinged 30.00
Single franking on domestic airmail cover *95.00*
Single franking on UPU cover to Germany *80.00*
Single franking on UPU cover to other destinations *160.00*
On registered or special delivery cover *135.00*
P# block of 4 300.00 —
Never hinged 400.00

675 A161 6c **red orange** 35.00 24.00
Never hinged 70.00
On registered or special delivery cover *145.00*
Single franking on triple-weight first-class cover *175.00*
P# block of 4 525.00 —
Never hinged 750.00

676 A162 7c **black** 22.50 18.00
Never hinged 45.00
On registered or special delivery cover *175.00*
P# block of 4 325.00 —
Never hinged 500.00

677 A163 8c **olive green** 30.00 25.00
Never hinged 60.00
On registered or special delivery cover *300.00*
Single franking on quadruple-weight first-class letter *275.00*
Single franking on double-weight UPU foreign letter rate cover *375.00*
P# block of 4 400.00 —
Never hinged 550.00
Wide spacing, pair 150.00
Never hinged 225.00

678 A164 9c **light rose** 35.00 27.50
Never hinged 70.00
On registered or special delivery cover *235.00*
P# block of 4 500.00 —
Never hinged 675.00
Wide spacing, pair 160.00
a. Vertical pair, one without ovpt. *750.00*

679 A165 10c **orange yellow** 90.00 22.50
Never hinged 180.00
On registered special delivery cover *185.00*
Pair on registered first-class cover with return receipt *225.00*
P# block of 4 925.00 —
Never hinged 1,150.
Nos. 669-679 (11) 265.25 165.05
Nos. 669-679, never hinged 530.50

Nos. 658-661, 669-673, 677-678 are known with the overprints on vertical pairs spaced 32mm apart instead of the normal 22mm.

Important: Nos. 658-679 with original gum have either one horizontal gum breaker ridge per stamp or portions of two at the extreme top and bottom of the stamps, 21mm apart. Multiple complete gum breaker ridges indicate a fake overprint. Absence of the gum breaker ridge indicates either regumming or regumming and a fake overprint.

BATTLE OF FALLEN TIMBERS ISSUE

Memorial to Gen. Anthony Wayne and for 135th anniv. of the Battle of Fallen Timbers, Ohio.

General Wayne Memorial — A199

FLAT PLATE PRINTING

Plates of 400 subjects in four panes of 100.

1929, Sept. 14 ***Perf. 11***

680 A199 2c **carmine rose** .65 .65
deep carmine rose .65 .70
Never hinged 1.00
On cover 1.10
P# block of 6 20.00 —
Never hinged 30.00

OHIO RIVER CANALIZATION ISSUE

Completion of the Ohio River Canalization Project, between Cairo, Ill. and Pittsburgh, Pa.

Lock No. 5, Monongahela River — A200

Plates of 400 subjects in four panes of 100.

1929, Oct. 19 ***Perf. 11***

681 A200 2c **carmine rose** .55 .55
Never hinged .90
On cover 1.10
P# block of 6 12.50 —
Never hinged 20.00
a. 2c **lake** *425.00* —
Never hinged *650.00*
P# block of 6, never hinged —
b. 2c **carmine lake**, never hinged —

MASSACHUSETTS BAY COLONY ISSUE

300th anniversary of the founding of the Massachusetts Bay Colony.

Massachusetts Bay Colony Seal — A201

Plates of 400 subjects in four panes of 100.

1930, Apr. 8 ***Perf. 11***

682 A201 2c **carmine rose** .65 .50
Never hinged .95
On cover 1.00
P# block of 6 20.00 —
Never hinged 26.00

CAROLINA-CHARLESTON ISSUE

260th anniv. of the founding of the Province of Carolina and the 250th anniv. of the city of Charleston, S.C.

Gov. Joseph West and Chief Shadoo, a Kiowa — A202

Plates of 400 subjects in four panes of 100.

1930, Apr. 10 ***Perf. 11***

683 A202 2c **carmine rose** 1.00 1.00
Never hinged 1.50
On cover 1.40
P# block of 6 37.50 —
Never hinged 50.00

TYPES OF 1922-26 ISSUE REGULAR ISSUE

Harding — A203

Taft — A204

REGULAR ISSUE
ROTARY PRESS PRINTING

1930 ***Perf. 11x10½***

684 A203 1½c **brown,** *Dec.1* .50 .25
yellow brown .50 .25
Never hinged .70
On 3rd class cover 2.00
P# block of 4 2.25 —
Never hinged 2.75

Pair with full horiz. gutter btwn. *175.00*
Pair with full vert. gutter btwn. —
685 A204 4c **brown,** *June 4* .80 .25
deep brown .80 .25
Never hinged 1.25
On cover 5.00
P# block of 4 15.00 —
Never hinged 20.00
Gouge on right "4" (20141 UL 24) 2.50 .65
Recut right "4" (20141 UL 24) 2.50 .65
Pair with full horiz. gutter btwn. —

Bureau Precancels: 1½c, 96 diff., 4c, 46 diff.

ROTARY PRESS COIL STAMPS
Perf. 10 Vertically

686 A203 1½c **brown,** *Dec. 1* 1.75 .25
Never hinged 2.60
On 3rd class cover 5.00
Pair 3.75 .30
Never hinged 5.75
Joint line pair 7.50 .75
Never hinged 11.50
687 A204 4c **brown,** *Sept. 18* 3.00 .45
Never hinged 4.50
On cover 10.00
Pair 6.25 1.00
Never hinged 9.50
Joint line pair 11.00 2.50
Never hinged 22.00

Bureau Precancels: 1½c, 107 diff., 4c, 23 diff.

BRADDOCK'S FIELD ISSUE

175th anniversary of the Battle of Braddock's Field, otherwise the Battle of Monongahela.

Statue of George Washington — A205

Designed by Alvin R. Meissner.

FLAT PLATE PRINTING
Plates of 400 subjects in four panes of 100.

1930, July 9 ***Perf. 11***
688 A205 2c **carmine rose** .85 .85
Never hinged 1.30
On cover 1.00
P# block of 6 30.00 —
Never hinged 40.00

VON STEUBEN ISSUE

Baron Friedrich Wilhelm von Steuben (1730-1794), participant in the American Revolution.

General von Steuben — A206

FLAT PLATE PRINTING
Plates of 400 subjects in four panes of 100.

1930, Sept. 17 ***Perf. 11***
689 A206 2c **carmine rose** .50 .50
Never hinged .75
On cover 1.05
P# block of 6 16.00 —
Never hinged 25.00
a. Imperf., pair *2,000.*
Never hinged *3,000.*
P# block of 6 *12,500.*
b. 2c **carmine lake,** never hinged *950.00*

The No. 689a plate block is unique but damaged. The value is for the item in its damaged condition.

PULASKI ISSUE

150th anniversary (in 1929) of the death of Gen. Casimir Pulaski, Polish patriot and hero of the American Revolutionary War.

General Casimir Pulaski — A207

Plates of 400 subjects in four panes of 100.

1931, Jan. 16 ***Perf. 11***
690 A207 2c **carmine rose** .30 .25
deep carmine rose .30 .25
Never hinged .40
On cover .50
P# block of 6 10.00 —
Never hinged 15.00

TYPE OF 1922-26 ISSUES
REGULAR ISSUE
ROTARY PRESS PRINTING

1931 ***Perf. 11x10½***
692 A166 11c **light blue,** *Sept. 4* 2.50 .25
Never hinged 3.75
On registered cover with other values 10.00
P# block of 4 15.00 —
Never hinged 25.00
Retouched forehead (20617 LL 2, 3) 30.00 2.50
693 A167 12c **brown violet,** *Aug. 25* 5.00 .25
violet brown 5.00 .25
Never hinged 8.00
Pair on registered cover 8.00
P# block of 4 22.50 —
Never hinged 35.00
694 A186 13c **yellow green,** *Sept. 4* 2.25 .25
light yellow green 2.25 .25
blue green 2.25 .25
Never hinged 3.50
On special delivery cover 27.50
P# block of 4 15.00 —
Never hinged 27.50
Pair with full vert. gutter btwn. 150.00
695 A168 14c **dark blue,** *Sept. 8* 4.00 .60
Never hinged 6.25
On registered cover with other values 20.00
P# block of 4 24.00 —
Never hinged 37.50
696 A169 15c **gray,** *Aug. 27* 7.75 .25
dark gray 8.00 .25
Never hinged 12.00
On registered cover with 3c 5.00
P# block of 4 40.00 —
Never hinged 55.00

Perf. 10½x11

697 A187 17c **black,** *July 25* 4.75 .25
Never hinged 7.25
On registered cover 5.00
P# block of 4 37.50 —
Never hinged 50.00
698 A170 20c **carmine rose,** *Sept. 8* 7.75 .25
Never hinged 12.50
On registered UPU-rate cover 12.50
P# block of 4 40.00 —
Never hinged 60.00
Double transfer (20538 LR 26) 20.00 —
699 A171 25c **blue green,** *July 25* 8.00 .25
Never hinged 13.00
On Federal airmail cover 20.00
P# block of 4 40.00 —
Never hinged 60.00
700 A172 30c **brown,** *Sept. 8* 12.50 .25
Never hinged 21.00
On Federal airmail cover 17.50
P# block of 4 70.00
Never hinged 95.00
Retouched in head (20552 UL 83) 30.00 1.00
Cracked plate (20552 UR 30) 27.50 1.00
701 A173 50c **lilac,** *Sept. 4* 30.00 .25
red lilac 30.00 .25
Never hinged 50.00
On Federal airmail cover 25.00
P# block of 4 160.00 —
Never hinged 230.00
Nos. 692-701 (10) 84.50 2.85
Nos. 692-701, never hinged 137.25

Bureau Precancels: 11c, 33 diff., 12c, 33 diff., 13c, 28 diff., 14c, 27 diff., 15c, 33 diff., 17c, 29 diff., 20c, 37 diff., 25c, 29 diff., 30c, 31 diff., 50c, 28 diff.

RED CROSS ISSUE

50th anniversary of the founding of the American Red Cross Society.

"The Greatest Mother" — A208

FLAT PLATE PRINTING
Plates of 200 subjects in two panes of 100.

1931, May 21 ***Perf. 11***
702 A208 2c **black & red** .25 .25
Never hinged .35
Margin block of 4, arrow right or left 1.10
P# block of 4, two P# 2.25 —
Never hinged 3.25
Double transfer 1.50 .50
a. Red cross missing (FO) *40,000.*

The cross tends to shift, appearing in many slightly varied positions.
One example of No. 702a is documented; believed to be unique. Value reflects most recent sale price at auction in 1994.

YORKTOWN ISSUE

Surrender of Cornwallis at Yorktown, 1781.

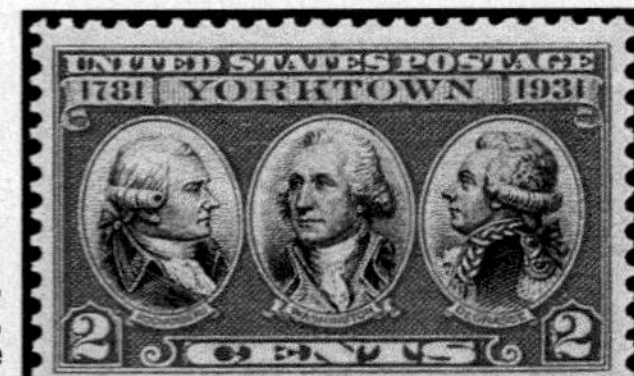

Rochambeau, Washington, de Grasse A209

First Plate Layout — Border and vignette plates of 100 subjects in two panes of 50 subjects each. Plate numbers between 20461 and 20602.
Second Plate Layout — Border plates of 100 subjects in two panes of 50 each, separated by a 1 inch wide vertical gutter with central guide line and vignette plates of 50 subjects. Plate numbers between 20646 and 20671.
Issued in panes of 50 subjects.

1931, Oct. 19 ***Perf. 11***
703 A209 2c **carmine rose & black** .35 .25
Never hinged .50
Margin block of 4, arrow marker, right or left 1.70
Center line block 1.80
P# block of 4, 2# 3.00 —
Never hinged 4.00
P# block of 4, 2# & arrow & marker block 3.00 —
Never hinged 4.00
P# block of 6, 2# & "TOP," arrow & marker 3.50 —
Never hinged 4.50
P# block of 8, 2# & "TOP" 3.75 —
Never hinged 5.00
Double transfer 1.75 .75
a. 2c **lake & black** 4.50 .75
Never hinged 6.25
b. 2c **dark lake & black** *400.00*
Never hinged *750.00*
P# block of 4, 2# *2,250.*
Never hinged *3,750.*
c. Horiz. pair, imperf. vertically *7,000.*
Never hinged *8,500.*
Center line block of 10 *35,000.*
P# block of 10, top, 2#, arrow, marker and "TOP," block *37,500.*
P# block of 10, bottom, 2#, arrow and marker *35,000.*

No. 703c is valued in the grade of fine.

BUYING
AND SELLING
ALL U.S. STAMPS
$ TOP PRICES PAID $
If it is listed in the Scott Catalog, we NEED it!
SHIP IT TO US TODAY!!
SHEETS — COLLECTIONS
POSTAGE — ACCUMULATIONS
PLATE BLOCKS — BETTER SINGLES
ANYTHING and EVERYTHING
Fair Honest Dealings
Call With Description OR For Fastest Service Ship Insured With Phone #
20+ Years Experience
FREE UNITED STATES Pricelist
WE ALSO SELL
Check out our website!
www.MALACK.com
Steve Malack Stamps
P.O. Box 5628 Endicott, NY 13763
607-862-9441 (Phone/Fax) EMAIL: STEVE@MALACK.com
SEE OUR OTHER AD ON PAGE 17

WASHINGTON BICENTENNIAL ISSUE

200th anniversary of the birth of George Washington. Various Portraits of George Washington.

By Charles Willson Peale, 1777 — A210

From Houdon Bust, 1785 — A211

By Charles Willson Peale, 1772 — A212

By Gilbert Stuart, 1796 — A213

By Charles Willson Peale, 1777 — A214

By Charles Peale Polk — A215

By Charles Willson Peale, 1795 — A216

By John Trumbull, 1792 — A217

By John Trumbull, 1780 — A218

By Charles B. J. F. Saint Memin, 1798 — A219

By W. Williams, 1794 — A220

By Gilbert Stuart, 1795 — A221

Broken Circle

ROTARY PRESS PRINTINGS

Plates of 400 subjects in four panes of 100 each

1932, Jan. 1 *Perf. 11x10½*

704 A210 ½c **olive brown**	.25	.25
Never hinged	.35	
P# block of 4	5.00	—
Never hinged	10.00	
Broken circle (20560 UR 8)	2.00	.50
705 A211 1c **green**	.25	.25
Never hinged	.35	
P# block of 4	4.00	—
Never hinged	5.50	
Gripper cracks (20742 UL and UR)	2.75	1.75
706 A212 1½c **brown**	.45	.25
Never hinged	.60	
P# block of 4	14.00	—
Never hinged	27.50	

Cracked Plate

Broken "E" Plate Flaw

707 A213 2c **carmine rose**	.30	.25
Never hinged	.45	
P# block of 4	1.40	—
Never hinged	2.20	
Pair with full vert. gutter between	—	
Cracked plate (20768 UL 1)	—	—
Broken "E" plate flaw (20772 UR 8)	—	—
Gripper cracks (20752 LR, 20755 LL & LR, 20756 LL, 20774 LR, 20792 LL & LR, 20796 LL & LR)	1.75	.65

Double Transfer

Nº 708
3 Cent Bicentennial
BROKEN TOP FRAME
L.L. 20847 - Stamp Nº 8
King

Broken Frame Line

708 A214 3c **purple**	.55	.25
Never hinged	.80	
P# block of 4	15.00	—
Never hinged	20.00	
Double transfer	1.75	.65
Broken top frame line (20847 LL 8)	5.00	1.00

Retouch in Eyes — 4c

709 A215 4c **light brown**	.60	.25
Never hinged	.85	
P# block of 4	5.00	—
Never hinged	7.00	
Double transfer (20568 LR 60)	2.00	.25
Spot between eyes plate defect (20568 LR 89)	5.00	1.00
Retouch in eyes (20568 LR 89)	3.00	.50
P# block of 4 with variety	—	
Broken bottom frame line (20568 LR 100)	2.50	.75
P# block of 4 with broken bottom frame line (20568 LR 100)	12.50	
P# block of 4 with spot between eyes (20568 LR 89) and broken bottom frame line (20568 LR 100)	20.00	

Gash On Forehead — 5c

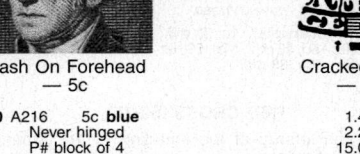

Cracked Plate — 5c

710 A216 5c **blue**	1.40	.25
Never hinged	2.25	
P# block of 4	15.00	—
Never hinged	22.50	
Plate defect over right eye (Gash on Forehead - 20636 LR 8)	25.00	—
Cracked plate (20637 UR 80)	10.00	1.10

No. 710 Gash on Forehead variety is progressive in several degrees of severity.

711 A217 6c **red orange**	2.75	.25
Never hinged	4.50	
P# block of 4	50.00	—
Never hinged	70.00	

Double Transfer

712 A218 7c **black**	.60	.25
Never hinged	.85	
P# block of 4	8.50	—
Never hinged	12.00	
Double transfer (20563 UL 1 or 20564 LL 91)	7.50	.50
P# block of 4 with variety	17.50	
713 A219 8c **olive bister**	2.50	.50
Never hinged	4.00	
P# block of 4	47.50	—
Never hinged	60.00	
Pair with full vert. gutter between	—	
714 A220 9c **pale red**	2.00	.25
orange red	2.00	.25
Never hinged	3.25	
P# block of 4	32.50	—
Never hinged	45.00	
715 A221 10c **orange yellow**	9.00	.25
Never hinged	15.00	
P# block of 4	85.00	—
Never hinged	110.00	
Nos. 704-715 (12)	20.65	3.25
Nos. 704-715, never hinged	33.25	

OLYMPIC WINTER GAMES ISSUE

3rd Olympic Winter Games, held at Lake Placid, N.Y., Feb. 4-13, 1932.

Skier — A222

FLAT PLATE PRINTING

Plates of 400 subjects in four panes of 100.

1932, Jan. 25 *Perf. 11*

716 A222 2c **carmine rose**	.35	.25
carmine	.35	.25
Never hinged	.55	
P# block of 6	8.00	—
Never hinged	11.00	
Cracked plate (20823 UR 41, 42; UL 48, 49, 50)	5.00	1.65
Recut (20823 UR 61)	3.50	1.50
Colored "snowball" (20815 UR 64)	25.00	5.00
a. 2c **lake**	*500.00*	
Never hinged	*1,000.*	
carmine lake	—	
Never hinged	—	

No. 716a should be accompanied by a certificate of authenticity issued by a recognized exertizing committee.

ARBOR DAY ISSUE

1st observance of Arbor Day in the state of Nebraska, Apr. 1872, 60th anniv., and cent. of the birth of Julius Sterling Morton, who conceived the plan and the name "Arbor Day," while he was a member of the Nebraska State Board of Agriculture.

Boy and Girl Planting Tree — A223

ROTARY PRESS PRINTING

Plates of 400 subjects in four panes of 100.

1932, Apr. 22 *Perf. 11x10½*

717 A223 2c **carmine rose**	.25	.25
Never hinged	.35	
P# block of 4	5.50	—
Never hinged	7.00	

OLYMPIC GAMES ISSUE

Issued in honor of the 10th Olympic Games, held at Los Angeles, Calif., July 30 to Aug. 14, 1932.

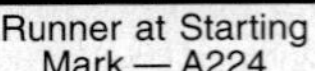
Runner at Starting Mark — A224

Myron's Discobolus — A225

Designed by Victor S. McCloskey, Jr.

ROTARY PRESS PRINTING
Plates of 400 subjects in four panes of 100.

1932, June 15 — ***Perf. 11x10½***

718 A224 3c **purple** 1.50 .25
deep purple 1.50 .25
Never hinged 2.00
P# block of 4 12.00 —
Never hinged 17.00
Gripper cracks (20906 UL 1) 4.25 .75
P# block of 4 with variety —

719 A225 5c **blue** 2.25 .25
deep blue 2.25 .25
Never hinged 2.90
P# block of 4 17.50 —
Never hinged 25.00
Gripper cracks (20868 UL & UR) 4.25 1.00

Washington, by Gilbert Stuart — A226

REGULAR ISSUE

ROTARY PRESS PRINTING
Plates of 400 subjects in four panes of 100.

1932 — ***Perf. 11x10½***

720 A226 3c **purple,** *June 16* .35 .25
light purple .35 .25
Never hinged .45
P# block of 4 1.75 —
Never hinged 2.25
Double transfer 1.00 .30
Recut face (20986 UR 15) 4.00 1.00
Gripper cracks 1.25 .30
Pair with full vert. gutter btwn. *200.00*
Pair with full horiz. gutter btwn. *200.00*
b. Booklet pane of 6, *July 25* 35.00 *12.50*
Never hinged 60.00
c. Vertical pair, imperf. between *725.00* *1,750.*
Never hinged *1,450.*

Bureau Precancels: 64 diff.

ROTARY PRESS COIL STAMPS

1932 — ***Perf. 10 Vertically***

721 A226 3c **purple,** *June 24* 2.75 .25
light purple 2.75 .25
Never hinged 3.50
Pair 5.75 .25
Never hinged 7.50
Joint line pair 10.00 1.50
Never hinged 13.00
Gripper cracks — —
Recut face (20995, pos. 29) — —
Recut lines around eyes — —

Perf. 10 Horizontally

722 A226 3c **purple,** *Oct. 12* 1.50 .35
light purple 1.50 .35
Never hinged 2.00
Pair 3.25 .80
Never hinged 4.25
Joint line pair 6.25 2.75
Never hinged 8.00

Bureau Precancels: No. 721, 46 diff.

TYPE OF 1922-26 ISSUES

1932, Aug. 18 — ***Perf. 10 Vertically***

723 A161 6c **deep orange** 11.00 .30
Never hinged 15.00
Pair 24.00 .70
Never hinged 32.50
Joint line pair 60.00 5.00
Never hinged 82.50

Bureau Precancels: 5 diff.

WILLIAM PENN ISSUE

250th anniv. of the arrival in America of Penn (1644-1718), English Quaker and founder of Pennsylvania.

William Penn — A227

FLAT PLATE PRINTING
Plates of 400 subjects in four panes of 100 each

1932, Oct. 24 — ***Perf. 11***

724 A227 3c **purple** .45 .25
Never hinged .60
P# block of 6 7.50 —
Never hinged 12.50
a. Vert. pair, imperf. horiz. —

DANIEL WEBSTER ISSUE

Daniel Webster (1782-1852), Statesman — A228

FLAT PLATE PRINTING
Plates of 400 subjects in four panes of 100.

1932, Oct. 24 — ***Perf. 11***

725 A228 3c **purple** .45 .25
light purple .45 .25
Never hinged .60
P# block of 6 15.00 —
Never hinged 20.00

GEORGIA BICENTENNIAL ISSUE

200th anniv. of the founding of the Colony of Georgia, and honoring Oglethorpe, who landed from England, Feb. 12, 1733, and personally supervised the establishing of the colony.

Gen. James Edward Oglethorpe — A229

FLAT PLATE PRINTING
Plates of 400 subjects in four panes of 100.

1933, Feb. 12 — ***Perf. 11***

726 A229 3c **purple** .50 .25
Never hinged .65
P# block of 6 9.00 —
Never hinged 15.00
P# block of 10, "C.S." in selvage 12.00
Never hinged 18.00
Bottom margin block of 20, no P# —

PEACE OF 1783 ISSUE

150th anniv. of the issuance by George Washington of the official order containing the Proclamation of Peace marking officially the ending of hostilities in the War for Independence.

Washington's Headquarters at Newburgh, N.Y. — A230

ROTARY PRESS PRINTING
Plates of 400 subjects in four panes of 100 each

1933, Apr. 19 — ***Perf. 10½x11***

727 A230 3c **violet** .25 .25
Never hinged .30
P# block of 4 3.00 —
Never hinged 5.50

No. 727 was not regularly issued in full sheets of 400 with gum. Gutter pairs and blocks with crossed gutters come from a very few non-issued full sheets. Those varieties should not be confused with similar pairs and blocks without gum, which are from the No. 752 Special Printing.

See No. 752 in the Special Printings following No. 751.

CENTURY OF PROGRESS ISSUES

"Century of Progress" Intl. Exhibition, Chicago, which opened June 1, 1933, and centenary of the incorporation of Chicago as a city.

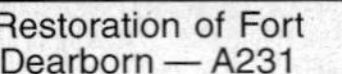
Restoration of Fort Dearborn — A231

Federal Building — A232

ROTARY PRESS PRINTING
Plates of 400 subjects in four panes of 100.

1933, May 25 — ***Perf. 10½x11***

728 A231 1c **yellow green** .25 .25
Never hinged .30
On card, Expo. station machine canc. 1.00
On card, Expo. station duplex hand-stamp canc. 3.00
P# block of 4 1.75 —
Never hinged 3.00
Gripper cracks (21133 UR & LR) 2.00 —

729 A232 3c **purple** .25 .25
Never hinged .35
On cover, Expo. station machine canc. 2.00
On cover, Expo. station duplex hand-stamp canc. 5.00
P# block of 4 2.40 —
Never hinged 4.00

Nos. 728 and 729 were not regularly issued in full sheets of 400 with gum. Gutter pairs and blocks with cross gutters and dashes, with gum, exist from a very few non-issued sheets that were retained by Postmaster General James A. Farley.

AMERICAN PHILATELIC SOCIETY ISSUE

SOUVENIR SHEETS

A231a

A232a

Illustrations reduced.

FLAT PLATE PRINTING

Plates of 225 subjects in nine panes of 25 each.

1933, Aug. 25 ***Imperf.***

Without Gum

730 A231a 1c **deep yellow green,** pane of 25 — 20.00 *25.00*
- ***a.*** Single stamp — .70 .50
  - Single on card, Expo. station machine canc. — 1.50
  - Single on card, Expo. station duplex handstamp canc. — 5.00

731 A232a 3c **purple,** pane of 25 — 20.00 *22.50*
- ***a.*** Single stamp — .65 .50
  - Single on cover, Expo. station machine canc. — 3.00
  - Single on cover, Expo. station duplex handstamp canc. — 7.50

Issued in panes measuring 134x120mm containing twenty-five stamps, inscribed in the margins:

PRINTED BY THE TREASURY DEPARTMENT, BUREAU OF ENGRAVING AND PRINTING, — UNDER AUTHORITY OF JAMES A. FARLEY, POSTMASTER-GENERAL, AT CENTURY OF PROGRESS, — IN COMPLIMENT TO THE AMERICAN PHILATELIC SOCIETY FOR ITS CONVENTION AND EXHIBITION — CHICAGO, ILLINOIS, AUGUST, 1933. PLATE NO. 21145.

Also used were plates 21159 (1c), 21146 and 21160 (3c). Each different plate number used is inscribed in the bottom selvage of the respective souvenir sheets.

See Nos. 766-767 in the Special Printings following No. 751.

NATIONAL RECOVERY ACT ISSUE

Issued to direct attention to and arouse the support of the nation for the National Recovery Act.

Group of Workers — A233

ROTARY PRESS PRINTING

Plates of 400 subjects in four panes of 100.

1933, Aug. 15 ***Perf. 10½x11***

732 A233 3c **purple** — .25 .25
- Never hinged — .30
- P# block of 4 — 1.50 —
- Never hinged — 2.00
- Gripper cracks (21151 UL & UR, 21153 UR & LR) — 1.50 —
- Recut at right (21151 UR 47) — 4.00

BYRD ANTARCTIC ISSUE

Issued in connection with the Byrd Antarctic Expedition of 1933 and for use on letters mailed through the Little America Post Office established at the Base Camp of the Expedition in the territory of the South Pole.

A Map of the World (on van der Grinten's Projection) — A234

Designed by Victor S. McCloskey, Jr.

FLAT PLATE PRINTING

Plates of 200 subjects in four panes of 50 each

1933, Oct. 9 ***Perf. 11***

733 A234 3c **dark blue** — .50 .50
- Never hinged — .60
- P# block of 6 — 12.00 —
- Never hinged — 15.00
- Double transfer (21167 LR 2) — 2.75 1.00

In addition to the postage charge of 3 cents, letters sent by the ships of the expedition to be canceled in Little America were subject to a service charge of 50 cents each.

See No. 753 in the Special Printings following No. 751.

KOSCIUSZKO ISSUE

Kosciuszko (1746-1817), Polish soldier and statesman served in the American Revolution, on the 150th anniv. of the granting to him of American citizenship.

Statue of General Tadeusz Kosciuszko — A235

Designed by Victor S. McCloskey, Jr.

FLAT PLATE PRINTING

Plates of 400 subjects in four panes of 100 each

1933, Oct. 13 ***Perf. 11***

734 A235 5c **blue** — .55 .25
- Never hinged — .65
- P# block of 6 — 22.00 —
- Never hinged — 28.00
- Cracked plate — —
- ***a.*** Horizontal pair, imperf. vertically — *1,750.*
  - Never hinged — *2,750.*
  - P# block of 8 — *35,000.*

The No. 734a plate block is unique but damaged.

NATIONAL STAMP EXHIBITION ISSUE

SOUVENIR SHEET

A235a

Illustration reduced.

TYPE OF BYRD ISSUE

Plates of 150 subjects in 25 panes of six each.

1934, Feb. 10 ***Imperf.***

Without Gum

735 A235a 3c **dark blue,** pane of 6 — 10.00 9.00
- ***a.*** Single stamp — 1.60 1.25

Issued in panes measuring 87x93mm containing six stamps, inscribed in the margins: "Printed by the Treasury Department, Bureau of Engraving and Printing, under authority of James A. Farley, Postmaster General, in the National Stamp Exhibition of 1934. New York, N. Y., February 10-18, 1934. Plate No. 21184." Plate No. 21187 was used for sheets printed at the Exhibition, but all these were destroyed.

See No. 768 in the Special Printings following No. 751.

MARYLAND TERCENTENARY ISSUE

300th anniversary of the founding of Maryland.

"The Ark" and "The Dove" — A236

Designed by Alvin R. Meissner.

FLAT PLATE PRINTING

Plates of 400 subjects in four panes of 100.

1934, Mar. 23 ***Perf. 11***

736 A236 3c **carmine rose** — .30 .25
- Never hinged — .40
- P# block of 6 — 6.25 —
- Never hinged — 9.50
- Double transfer (21190 UL 1) — — —
- ***a.*** Horizontal pair, imperf between — *4,000.*
- ***b.*** 3c **lake** — *1,000.* —
- ***c.*** 3c **carmine lake,** never hinged — —

The unique No. 736a resulted from a paper foldover before perfing, and it has angled errant perfs from another column of vert. perfs through the upper-left corner of the left stamp.

MOTHERS OF AMERICA ISSUE

Issued to commemorate Mother's Day.

Adaptation of Whistler's Portrait of his Mother — A237

Designed by Victor S. McCloskey, Jr.

Plates of 200 subjects in four panes of 50.

ROTARY PRESS PRINTING

1934, May 2 ***Perf. 11x10½***

737 A237 3c **purple** — .25 .25
- Never hinged — .30
- P# block of 4 — 1.00 —
- Never hinged — 1.30

FLAT PLATE PRINTING

Perf. 11

738 A237 3c **purple** — .25 .25
- Never hinged — .30
- P# block of 6 — 4.50 —
- Never hinged — 6.50

See No. 754 in the Special Printings following No. 751.

WISCONSIN TERCENTENARY ISSUE

Arrival of Jean Nicolet, French explorer, on the shores of Green Bay, 300th anniv. According to historical records, Nicolet was the 1st white man to reach the territory now comprising the State of Wisconsin.

Nicolet's Landing A238

Designed by Victor S. McCloskey, Jr.

FLAT PLATE PRINTING

Plates of 200 subjects in four panes of 50.

1934. July 7 ***Perf. 11***

739 A238 3c **purple** — .25 .25
- violet — .25 .25
- Never hinged — .40
- P# block of 6 — 3.50 —
- Never hinged — 5.00
- ***a.*** Vert. pair, imperf. horiz. — *575.00*
  - Never hinged — *1,050.*
- ***b.*** Horiz. pair, imperf. vert. — *1,000.*
  - Never hinged — *1,750.*
  - P# block of 10 — *6,500.*

See No. 755 in the Special Printings following No. 751.

NATIONAL PARKS YEAR ISSUE

El Capitan, Yosemite (California) — A239

Old Faithful, Yellowstone (Wyoming) — A243

View of Grand Canyon (Arizona) A240

Mt. Rainier and Mirror Lake (Washington) A241

Cliff Palace, Mesa Verde Park (Colorado) A242

Crater Lake (Oregon) A244

Great Head, Acadia Park (Maine) A245

Great White Throne, Zion Park (Utah) — A246

Great Smoky Mountains (North Carolina) — A248

Mt. Rockwell (Mt. Sinopah) and Two Medicine Lake, Glacier National Park (Montana) A247

FLAT PLATE PRINTING

Plates of 200 subjects in four panes of 50.

1934		**Unwmk.**	***Perf. 11***	
740	A239	1c **green,** *July 16*	.25	.25
		light green	.25	.25
		Never hinged	.40	
		P# block of 6	1.80	—
		Never hinged	2.50	
		Recut	1.50	.50
a.		Vert. pair, imperf. horiz., with gum	*1,750.*	
		Never hinged	*3,000.*	
741	A240	2c **red,** *July 24*	.30	.25
		orange red	.30	.25
		Never hinged	.40	
		P# block of 6	1.55	—
		Never hinged	2.00	
		Double transfer	1.25	—
a.		Vert. pair, imperf. horiz., with gum	*800.00*	
		Never hinged	*1,450.*	
		P# block of 6	—	
b.		Horiz. pair, imperf. vert., with gum	*900.00*	
		Never hinged	*1,600.*	
		P# block of 6	*3,500.*	
		Never hinged	*4,750.*	
c.		Imperf. P# 21261 block of 20	*7,500.*	

No. 741c is a unique bottom margin plate #21261 block of 20. This plate was not used to print the imperforate Farley special printing, No. 757. Loose stamps separated from this block or from other possible imperforate No. 741 Plate #21261 blocks are indistinguishable from gummed examples of No. 757.

742	A241	3c **purple,** *Aug. 3*	.40	.25
		Never hinged	.50	
		P# block of 6	2.25	—
		Never hinged	3.00	
		Recut	1.50	—
a.		Vert. pair, imperf. horiz., with gum	*1,000.*	
		Never hinged	*1,850.*	
		P# block of 6	—	
743	A242	4c **brown,** *Sept. 25*	.50	.40
		light brown	.50	.40
		Never hinged	.70	
		P# block of 6	6.50	—
		Never hinged	8.00	
a.		Vert. pair, imperf. horiz., with gum	*3,500.*	
		Never hinged	*8,000.*	
744	A243	5c **blue,** *July 30*	.80	.65
		light blue	.80	.65
		Never hinged	1.10	
		P# block of 6	9.00	—
		Never hinged	11.00	
a.		Horiz. pair, imperf. vert., with gum	*1,500.*	
		Never hinged	*4,000.*	
		P# block of 6	—	
745	A244	6c **dark blue,** *Sept. 5*	1.20	.85
		Never hinged	1.65	
		P# block of 6	15.00	—
		Never hinged	20.00	
746	A245	7c **black,** *Oct. 2*	.80	.75
		Never hinged	1.10	
		P# block of 6	9.00	—
		Never hinged	12.00	
		Double transfer	3.25	1.40
a.		Horiz. pair, imperf. vert., with gum	*1,250.*	
		Never hinged	*2,000.*	
		P# block of 6, never hinged	*6,000.*	
747	A246	8c **sage green,** *Sept. 18*	1.75	1.50
		Never hinged	2.70	
		P# block of 6	15.00	—
		Never hinged	25.00	
748	A247	9c **red orange,** *Aug. 27*	1.60	.65
		orange	1.60	.65
		Never hinged	2.40	
		P# block of 6	15.00	—
		Never hinged	20.00	
749	A248	10c **gray black,** *Oct. 8*	3.25	1.25
		gray	3.25	1.25
		Never hinged	5.00	
		P# block of 6	21.00	—
		Never hinged	30.00	
		Nos. 740-749 (10)	10.85	6.80
		Nos. 740-749, never hinged	15.95	
		Nos. 740-749, P# blks of 6	100.00	

In 1934, Postmaster General James A. Farley had full sheets of Nos. 727, 729, 730, 735, 738, 739, 740-749, 750-751 and CE1 delivered to himself and "gifted" most of these to friends and family, including President Franklin Roosevelt, Secretary of the Interior Harold Ickes, Third Assistant Postmaster General Clinton Eilenberger, and others. Nos. 738, 739 and 740-749 were delivered imperforate, and the souvenir sheets Nos. 730-731, 735 and 750-751 were delivered uncut. Nos. 740-749 and 750-751 were delivered with gum, the others without gum.

The sheets of these stamps were signed in the selvage by Farley and/or the recipients. As a result, stamps from these sheets can be and have been certified by expertizing committees as varieties of the original issues rather the 1935 Special Printings (Nos. 752-771) known as "Farley's Follies."

Sheets of these 1934 varieties have reached the marketplace from the sheets given to Roosevelt, Ickes and Eilenberger. As unissued varieties that were improperly distributed through private gifts from Postmaster General Farley rather than sold across the counter by the Post Office Department, these varieties are not listed in the Scott catalogs.

Imperforate varieties of the 2c and 5c exist as errors of the perforated Parks set, but are virtually impossible to distinguish from gummed examples from the imperforate sheets of 200.

Also, beware of fakes of the part-perforate errors of Nos. 740-749, including those with gum (see "without gum" note before No. 752.)

AMERICAN PHILATELIC SOCIETY ISSUE

SOUVENIR SHEET

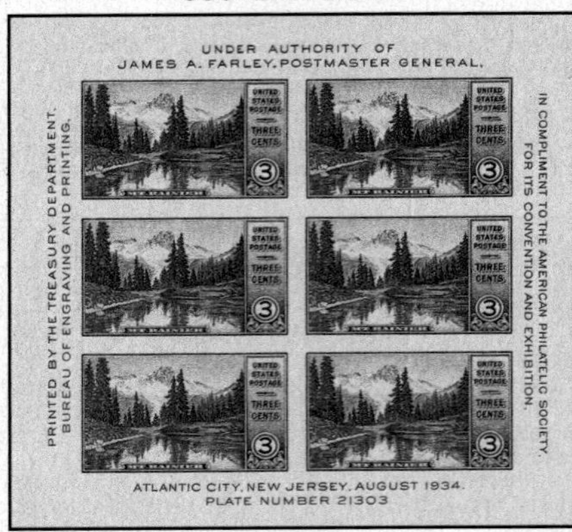

A248a

Illustration reduced.

Plates of 120 subjects in 20 panes of 6 stamps each.

1934, Aug. 28			***Imperf.***	
750	A248a	3c **purple,** pane of 6	20.00	*27.50*
		Never hinged	30.00	
a.		Single stamp	3.25	3.25
		Never hinged	4.00	

Issued in panes measuring approximately 98x93mm containing six stamps, inscribed in the margins: PRINTED BY THE TREASURY DEPARTMENT, BUREAU OF ENGRAVING AND PRINTING, — UNDER AUTHORITY OF JAMES A. FARLEY, POSTMASTER GENERAL, — IN COMPLIMENT TO THE AMERICAN PHILATELIC SOCIETY FOR ITS CONVENTION AND EXHIBITION, — ATLANTIC CITY, NEW JERSEY, AUGUST, 1934. PLATE NO. 21303.

See No. 770 in the Special Printings following No. 751.

TRANS-MISSISSIPPI PHILATELIC EXPOSITION ISSUE

SOUVENIR SHEET

A248b

Illustration reduced.

Plates of 120 subjects in 20 panes of 6 stamps each.

1934, Oct. 10 ***Imperf.***

751 A248b 1c **green,** pane of 6 10.00 12.50
Never hinged 15.00
a. Single stamp 1.65 1.60
Never hinged 2.25

Issued in panes measuring approximately 92x99mm containing six stamps, inscribed in the margins: PRINTED BY THE TREASURY DEPARTMENT, BUREAU OF ENGRAVING AND PRINTING, — UNDER AUTHORITY OF JAMES A. FARLEY, POSTMASTER GENERAL, — IN COMPLIMENT TO THE TRANS-MISSISSIPPI PHILATELIC EXPOSITION AND CONVENTION, OMAHA, NEBRASKA, — OCTOBER, 1934. PLATE NO. 21341.

See No. 769 in the Special Printings that follow.

SPECIAL PRINTING

(Nos. 752-771 inclusive)

"Issued for a limited time in full sheets as printed, and in blocks thereof, to meet the requirements of collectors and others who may be interested." — From Postal Bulletin No. 16614.

Issuance of the following 20 stamps in complete sheets resulted from the protest of collectors and others at the practice of presenting, to certain government officials, complete sheets of unsevered panes, imperforate (except Nos. 752 and 753) and generally ungummed.

Designs of Commemorative Issues

Without Gum

NOTE: In 1940 the P.O. Department offered to and did gum full sheets of Nos. 756-765 and 769-770 sent in by owners. No other Special Printings were accepted for gumming.

TYPE OF PEACE ISSUE

Issued in sheets of 400, consisting of four panes of 100 each, with vertical and horizontal gutters between and plate numbers at outside corners at sides.

ROTARY PRESS PRINTING

1935, Mar. 15 **Unwmk.** ***Perf. 10½x11***

752 A230 3c **purple** .25 .25
Pair with horiz. gutter between 5.75 —
Pair with vert. gutter between 9.50 —
Gutter block of 4 with dash (left or right) 15.00 —
Gutter block of 4 with dash (top or bottom) 20.00 —
Center block with crossed gutters and dashes 60.00 —
P# block of 4 27.50 —

TYPE OF BYRD ISSUE

Issued in sheets of 200, consisting of four panes of 50 each, with vertical and horizontal guide lines in gutters between panes, and plate numbers centered at top and bottom of each pane. This applies to Nos. 753-765 and 771.

FLAT PLATE PRINTING

Perf. 11

753 A234 3c **dark blue** .50 .45
Pair with horiz. line between 2.00 —
Pair with vert. line between 32.50 —
Margin block of 4, arrow & guide line (left or right) 8.00 —
Margin block of 4, arrow & guideline (top or bottom) 70.00 —
Center line block 75.00 75.00
P# block of 6, number at top or bottom 15.00 —

No. 753 is similar to No. 733. Positive identification is by blocks or pairs showing guide line between stamps. These lines between stamps are found only on No. 753.

TYPE OF MOTHERS OF AMERICA ISSUE

Issued in sheets of 200

FLAT PLATE PRINTING

Imperf

754 A237 3c **deep purple** .60 .60
Pair with horiz. line between 1.75 —
Pair with vert. line between 1.50 —
Margin block of 4, arrow & guideline (left or right) 3.75 —
Margin block of 4, arrow & guideline (top or bottom) 3.25 —
Center line block 7.25 —
P# block of 6, number at top or bottom 11.00 —

TYPE OF WISCONSIN ISSUE

Issued in sheets of 200

FLAT PLATE PRINTING

Imperf

755 A238 3c **deep purple** .60 .60
Pair with horiz. line between 1.75 —
Pair with vert. line between 1.50 —
Margin block of 4, arrow & guideline (left or right) 3.75 —
Margin block of 4, arrow & guideline (top or bottom) 3.25 —
Center line block 8.00 —
P# block of 6, number at top or bottom 11.00 —

TYPES OF NATIONAL PARKS ISSUE

Issued in sheets of 200

FLAT PLATE PRINTING

Imperf

756 A239 1c **green** .25 .25
With original gum, never hinged 1.60
Pair with horiz. line between .55 —
With original gum, never hinged 4.25
Pair with vert. line between .65 —
With original gum, never hinged 5.75
Margin block of 4, arrow & guideline (left or right) 1.25 —
With original gum, never hinged 9.00
Margin block of 4, arrow & guideline (top or bottom) 1.50 —
With original gum, never hinged 13.00
Center line block 3.25 —
With original gum, never hinged 27.50
P# block of 6, number at top or bottom 4.25 —
With original gum, never hinged 37.50

See note above No. 766.

757 A240 2c **red** .25 .25
With original gum, never hinged 1.75
Pair with horiz. line between .70 —
With original gum, never hinged 7.00
Pair with vert. line between .55 —
With original gum, never hinged 5.00
Margin block of 4, arrow & guideline (left or right) 1.60 —
With original gum, never hinged 17.50
Margin block of 4, arrow & guideline (top or bottom) 1.25 —
With original gum, never hinged 11.50
Center line block 4.25 —
With original gum, never hinged 35.00
P# block of 6, number at top or bottom 5.50 —
With original gum, never hinged 47.50
Double transfer —

758 A241 3c **deep purple** .50 .45
With original gum, never hinged 4.00
Pair with horiz. line between 1.40 —
With original gum, never hinged 15.00
Pair with vert. line between 1.25 —
With original gum, never hinged 12.00
Margin block of 4, arrow & guideline (left or right) 3.10 —
With original gum, never hinged 35.00
Margin block of 4, arrow & guideline (top or bottom) 2.75 —
With original gum, never hinged 26.00
Center line block 5.25 —
With original gum, never hinged 47.50
P# block of 6, number at top or bottom 12.50 —
With original gum, never hinged 130.00

759 A242 4c **brown** 1.00 .95
With original gum, never hinged 8.00
Pair with horiz. line between 2.75 —
With original gum, never hinged 30.00
Pair with vert. line between 2.25 —
With original gum, never hinged 22.50
Margin block of 4, arrow & guideline (left or right) 5.75 —
With original gum, never hinged 65.00
Margin block of 4, arrow & guideline (top or bottom) 4.75 —
With original gum, never hinged 47.50
Center line block 8.75 —
With original gum, never hinged 100.00
P# block of 6, number at top or bottom 20.00 —
With original gum, never hinged 150.00

760 A243 5c **blue** 1.60 1.40
With original gum, never hinged 12.00
Pair with horiz. line between 3.75 —
With original gum, never hinged 35.00
Pair with vert. line between 4.50 —
With original gum, never hinged 45.00
Margin block of 4, arrow & guideline (left or right) 8.00 —
With original gum, never hinged 70.00
Margin block of 4, arrow & guideline (top or bottom) 10.00 —
With original gum, never hinged 92.50
Center line block 16.00 —
With original gum, never hinged 140.00
P# block of 6, number at top or bottom 27.50 —
With original gum, never hinged 230.00
Double transfer —

761 A244 6c **dark blue** 2.40 2.25
With original gum, never hinged 19.00
Pair with horiz. line between 6.00 —
With original gum, never hinged 70.00
Pair with vert. line between 5.00 —
With original gum, never hinged 50.00
Margin block of 4, arrow & guideline (left or right) 12.00 —
With original gum, never hinged 140.00
Margin block of 4, arrow & guideline (top or bottom) 11.00 —
With original gum, never hinged 120.00
Center line block 18.00 —
With original gum, never hinged 180.00
P# block of 6, number at top or bottom) 35.00 —
With original gum, never hinged 340.00

762 A245 7c **black** 1.60 1.40
With original gum, never hinged 12.00
Pair with horiz. line between 4.25 —
With original gum, never hinged 45.00
Pair with vert. line between 3.75 —
With original gum, never hinged 37.50
Margin block of 4, arrow & guideline (left or right) 9.25 —
With original gum, never hinged 95.00
Margin block of 4, arrow & guideline (top or bottom) 8.25 —
With original gum, never hinged 85.00
Center line block 14.00 —
With original gum, never hinged 135.00
P# block of 6, number at top or bottom 30.00 —
With original gum, never hinged 280.00
Double transfer —

763 A246 8c **sage green** 1.90 1.50
With original gum, never hinged 12.50
Pair with horiz. line between 5.25 —
With original gum, never hinged 37.50
Pair with vert. line between 4.25 —
With original gum, never hinged 50.00
Margin block of 4, arrow & guideline (left or right) *12.50* —
With original gum, never hinged 85.00
Margin block of 4, arrow & guideline (top or bottom) *15.00* —
With original gum, never hinged 80.00
Center line block 20.00 —
With original gum, never hinged 175.00
P# block of 6, number at top or bottom 35.00 —
With original gum, never hinged 350.00

764 A247 9c **red orange** 2.00 1.75
With original gum, never hinged 14.00
Pair with horiz. line between 5.00 —
With original gum, never hinged 50.00
Pair with vert. line between 4.50 —
With original gum, never hinged 42.50
Margin block of 4, arrow & guideline (left or right) 11.50 —
With original gum, never hinged 125.00
Margin block of 4, arrow & guideline (top or bottom) 10.50 —
With original gum, never hinged 97.50
Center line block 22.50 —
With original gum, never hinged 210.00
P# block of 6, number at top or bottom 40.00 —
With original gum, never hinged 400.00

765 A248 10c **gray black** 4.00 3.50
With original gum, never hinged 27.50
Pair with horiz. line between 9.00 —
With original gum, never hinged 82.50
Pair with vert. line between 10.50 —
With original gum, never hinged 115.00
Margin block of 4, arrow & guideline (left or right) 20.00 —
With original gum, never hinged 175.00
Margin block of 4, arrow & guideline (top or bottom) 24.00 —
With original gum, never hinged 240.00
Center line block 30.00 —
With original gum, never hinged 275.00
P# block of 6, number at top or bottom 45.00 —
With original gum, never hinged 475.00
Nos. 756-765 (10) 15.50 13.70
Nos. 756-765, with original gum, never hinged 114.35
Nos. 756-765, P# blocks of 6 254.75

Hinged examples of Nos. 756-765 and 769-770 with original gum sell for approximately half the values shown for never-hinged stamps.

SOUVENIR SHEETS

Note: Single items from these sheets are identical with other varieties, 766 and 730, 766a and 730a, 767 and 731, 767a and 731a, 768 and 735, 768a and 735a, 769a and 756, 770a and 758.

Positive identification is by blocks or pairs showing wide gutters between stamps. These wide gutters occur only on Nos. 766-770 and measure, horizontally, 13mm on Nos. 766-767; 16mm on No. 768, and 23mm on Nos. 769-770.

TYPE OF CENTURY OF PROGRESS ISSUE

Issued in sheets of 9 panes of 25 stamps each, with vertical and horizontal gutters between panes.

FLAT PLATE PRINTING

Imperf

766	A231a 1c **yellow green,** pane of 25	27.50	30.00
a.	Single stamp	.80	.50
	Pair with horiz. gutter between	5.00	—
	Pair with vert. gutter between	7.00	—
	Block with crossed gutters	20.00	
	Block of 50 stamps (two panes)	65.00	
767	A232a 3c **deep purple,** pane of 25	25.00	25.00
a.	Single stamp	.70	.50
	Pair with horiz. gutter between	5.00	—
	Pair with vert. gutter between	6.50	—
	Block with crossed gutters	20.00	—
	Block of 50 stamps (two panes)	65.00	

NATIONAL EXHIBITION ISSUE TYPE OF BYRD ISSUE

Issued in sheets of 25 panes of 6 stamps each, with vertical and horizontal gutters between panes.

FLAT PLATE PRINTING

Imperf

768	A235a 3c **dark blue,** pane of 6	20.00	15.00
a.	Single stamp	2.80	2.40
	Pair with horiz. gutter between	7.00	—
	Pair with vert. gutter between	8.00	—
	Block of 4 with crossed gutters	20.00	—
	Block of 12 stamps (two panes)	45.00	
	Top margin single with "F" and "C.S." in selvage		—

TYPES OF NATIONAL PARKS ISSUE

Issued in sheets of 20 panes of 6 stamps each, with vertical and horizontal gutters between panes.

FLAT PLATE PRINTING

Imperf

769	A248b 1c **green,** pane of 6	11.00	11.00
	With original gum, never hinged	80.00	
a.	Single stamp	1.85	1.80
	Pair with horiz. gutter between	5.50	—
	With original gum, never hinged	40.00	
	Pair with vert. gutter between	7.50	—
	With original gum, never hinged	65.00	
	Block of 4 with crossed gutters	15.00	—
	With original gum, never hinged	120.00	
	Block of 12 stamps (two panes)	25.00	
770	A248a 3c **deep purple,** pane of 6	30.00	24.00
	With original gum, never hinged	275.00	
a.	Single stamp	3.25	3.10
	Pair with horiz. gutter between	12.00	—
	With original gum, never hinged	130.00	
	Pair with vert. gutter between	10.50	—
	With original gum, never hinged	100.00	
	Block of 4 with crossed gutters	27.50	—
	With original gum, never hinged	300.00	
	Block of 12 stamps (two panes)	65.00	

Hinged examples of Nos. 769-770 with original gum sell for approximately half the values shown for never-hinged stamps.

TYPE OF AIR POST SPECIAL DELIVERY

Issued in sheets of 200, with vertical and horizontal guide lines between panes.

FLAT PLATE PRINTING

Imperf

771	APSD1 16c **dark blue**	2.50	2.60
	Pair with horiz. line between	7.75	—
	Pair with vert. line between	6.50	—
	Margin block of 4, arrow & guideline (left or right)	17.50	—
	Margin block of 4, arrow & guideline (top or bottom)	15.00	—
	Center line block	65.00	—
	P# block of 6, number at top or bottom	55.00	—

Catalogue values for unused stamps in this section, from this point to the end, are for Never Hinged items.

VALUES FOR HINGED STAMPS AFTER NO. 771

This catalogue does not value unused stamps after No. 771 in hinged condition. Hinged unused stamps from No. 772 to the present are worth considerably less than the values given for unused stamps, which are for never-hinged examples.

CONNECTICUT TERCENTENARY ISSUE

300th anniv. of the settlement of Connecticut.

The Charter Oak — A249

Defect in Cent Sign

ROTARY PRESS PRINTING

Plates of 200 subjects in four panes of 50.

1935, Apr. 26 **Unwmk.** ***Perf. 11x10½***

772	A249 3c **rose purple**	.35	.25
	deep rose purple	.35	.25
	P# block of 4	2.25	—
	Defect in cent sign (21395 UR 4)	5.00	4.00

CALIFORNIA PACIFIC EXPOSITION ISSUE

California Pacific Exposition at San Diego.

View of San Diego Exposition A250

ROTARY PRESS PRINTING

Plates of 200 subjects in four panes of 50.

1935, May 29 **Unwmk.** ***Perf. 11x10½***

773	A250 3c **purple**	.35	.25
	On cover, Expo. station machine canc. (non-first day)		*2.50*
	On cover, Expo. station duplex hand-stamp canc. (non-first day)		*20.00*
	P# block of 4	1.50	—
	Pair with full vertical gutter between	—	

BOULDER DAM ISSUE

Dedication of Boulder Dam.

Boulder Dam (Hoover Dam) — A251

FLAT PLATE PRINTING

Plates of 200 subjects in four panes of 50.

1935, Sept. 30 **Unwmk.** ***Perf. 11***

774	A251 3c **purple**	.35	.25
	deep purple	.35	.25
	P# block of 6	2.50	—

MICHIGAN CENTENARY ISSUE

Advance celebration of Michigan Statehood centenary.

Michigan State Seal — A252

Designed by Alvin R. Meissner.

ROTARY PRESS PRINTING

Plates of 200 subjects in 4 panes of 50.

1935, Nov. 1 **Unwmk.** ***Perf. 11x10½***

775	A252 3c **purple**	.35	.25
	P# block of 4	2.25	—

TEXAS CENTENNIAL ISSUE

Centennial of Texas independence.

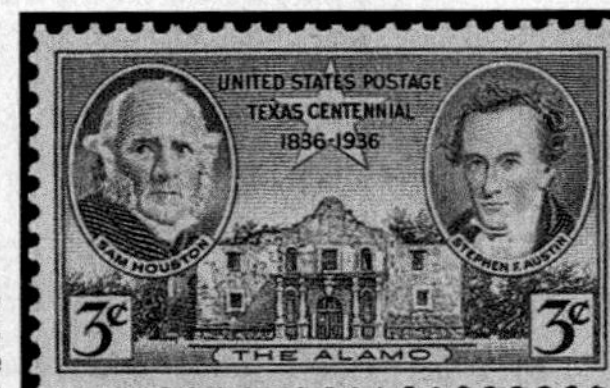

Sam Houston, Stephen F. Austin and the Alamo — A253

Designed by Alvin R. Meissner.

ROTARY PRESS PRINTING

Plates of 200 subjects in four panes of 50.

1936, Mar. 2 **Unwmk.** ***Perf. 11x10½***

776	A253 3c **purple**	.35	.25
	On cover, Expo. station machine canc.		2.00
	On cover, Expo. station duplex hand-stamp canc.		*40.00*
	P# block of 4	2.00	—
	Pair with full horizontal gutter between	*225.00*	

RHODE ISLAND TERCENTENARY ISSUE

300th anniv. of the settlement of Rhode Island.

Statue of Roger Williams — A254

ROTARY PRESS PRINTING

Plates of 200 subjects in four panes of 50.

1936, May 4 **Unwmk.** ***Perf. 10½x11***

777	A254 3c **purple**	.35	.25
	bright purple	.35	.25
	P# block of 4	2.00	—
	Pair with full gutter between	*200.00*	

THIRD INTERNATIONAL PHILATELIC EXHIBITION ISSUE

SOUVENIR SHEET

A254a

Illustration reduced.

Plates of 120 subjects in thirty panes of 4 each.

FLAT PLATE PRINTING

1936, May 9 **Unwmk.** ***Imperf.***

778	A254a **purple,** pane of 4	1.75	1.25
a.	3c Type A249	.40	.30
b.	3c Type A250	.40	.30
c.	3c Type A252	.40	.30
d.	3c Type A253	.40	.30

Issued in panes measuring 98x66mm containing four stamps, inscribed in the margins: "Printed by the Treasury Department, Bureau of Engraving and Printing, under authority of James A. Farley, Postmaster General, in compliment to the third International Philatelic Exhibition of 1936. New York, N. Y., May 9-17, 1936. Plate No. 21557."

Also used was plate 21558. Each different plate number used is inscribed in the bottom selvage of the respective souvenir sheets.

ARKANSAS CENTENNIAL ISSUE

100th anniv. of the State of Arkansas.

Arkansas Post, Old and New State Houses A255

ROTARY PRESS PRINTING

Plates of 200 subjects in four panes of 50.

1936, June 15 Unwmk. *Perf. 11x10½*

782 A255 3c **purple**	.35	.25
P# block of 4	2.00	—

OREGON TERRITORY ISSUE

Opening of the Oregon Territory, 1836, 100th anniv.

Map of Oregon Territory A256

ROTARY PRESS PRINTING

Plates of 200 subjects in four panes of 50.

1936, July 14 Unwmk. *Perf. 11x10½*

783 A256 3c **purple**	.35	.25
P# block of 4	1.25	—
Double transfer (21579 UL 3)	4.00	2.50

SUSAN B. ANTHONY ISSUE

Susan Brownell Anthony (1820-1906), woman-suffrage advocate, and 16th anniv. of the ratification of the 19th Amendment which grants American women the right to vote.

Susan B. Anthony — A257

ROTARY PRESS PRINTING

Plates of 400 subjects in four panes of 100.

1936, Aug. 26 Unwmk. *Perf. 11x10½*

784 A257 3c **purple**	.25	.25
rose purple	.25	.25
P# block of 4	1.10	—
Period missing after "B" (21590 LR 100)	4.00	2.00
P# block of 4 (21590 LR)	6.50	

ARMY ISSUE

Issued in honor of the United States Army.

Generals George Washington, Nathanael Greene and Mt. Vernon A258

Maj. Gen. Andrew Jackson, Gen. Winfield Scott and the Hermitage A259

Generals William T. Sherman, Ulysses S. Grant and Philip H. Sheridan A260

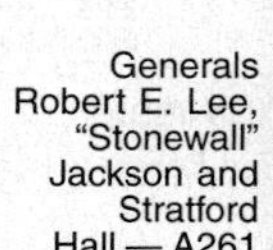

Generals Robert E. Lee, "Stonewall" Jackson and Stratford Hall — A261

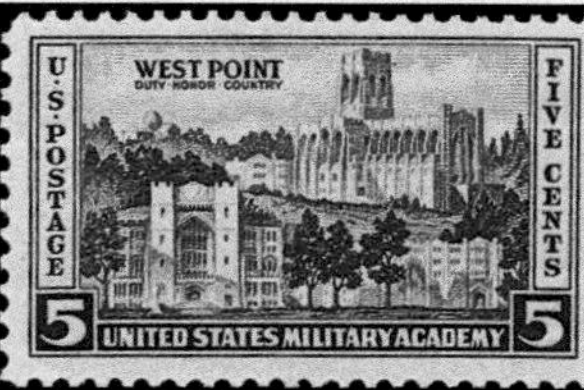

U. S. Military Academy, West Point — A262

ROTARY PRESS PRINTING

Plates of 200 subjects in four panes of 50.

1936-37 Unwmk. *Perf. 11x10½*

785 A258 1c **green,** *Dec. 15, 1936*	.30	.25
yellow green	.30	.25
P# block of 4	1.20	—
Pair with full vertical gutter between	500.00	
786 A259 2c **carmine,** *Jan. 15, 1937*	.30	.25
P# block of 4	1.20	—
787 A260 3c **purple,** *Feb. 18, 1937*	.40	.25
P# block of 4	2.50	—
788 A261 4c **gray,** *Mar. 23, 1937*	.60	.25
P# block of 4	7.50	—
789 A262 5c **ultramarine,** *May 26, 1937*	.75	.25
P# block of 4	6.50	—
Nos. 785-789 (5)	2.35	1.25

NAVY ISSUE

Issued in honor of the United States Navy.

John Paul Jones and John Barry — A263

Stephen Decatur and Thomas MacDonough A264

Admirals David G. Farragut and David D. Porter — A265

Admirals William T. Sampson, George Dewey and Winfield S. Schley A266

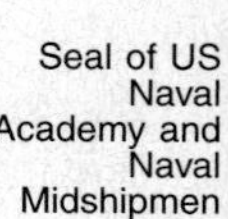

Seal of US Naval Academy and Naval Midshipmen A267

ROTARY PRESS PRINTING

Plates of 200 subjects in four panes of 50.

1936-37 Unwmk. *Perf. 11x10½*

790 A263 1c **green,** *Dec. 15, 1936*	.30	.25
yellow green	.30	.25
P# block of 4	1.20	—
791 A264 2c **carmine,** *Jan. 15, 1937*	.30	.25
P# block of 4	1.20	—
792 A265 3c **purple,** *Feb. 18, 1937*	.40	.25
P# block of 4	1.60	—
793 A266 4c **gray,** *Mar. 23, 1937*	.60	.25
P# block of 4	8.50	—
794 A267 5c **ultramarine,** *May 26, 1937*	.75	.25
P# block of 4	8.00	—
Pair with full vert. gutter btwn.	—	
Nos. 790-794 (5)	2.35	1.25

ORDINANCE OF 1787 SESQUICENTENNIAL ISSUE

150th anniv. of the adoption of the Ordinance of 1787 and the creation of the Northwest Territory.

Manasseh Cutler, Rufus Putnam and Map of Northwest Territory A268

ROTARY PRESS PRINTING

Plates of 200 subjects in four panes of 50.

1937, July 13 Unwmk. *Perf. 11x10½*

795 A268 3c **rose purple**	.30	.25
P# block of 4	1.75	—

VIRGINIA DARE ISSUE

350th anniv. of the birth of Virginia Dare, 1st child born in America of English parents (Aug. 18, 1587), and the settlement at Roanoke Island.

Virginia Dare and Parents — A269

FLAT PLATE PRINTING

Plates of 192 subjects in four panes of 48 each, separated by 1¼ inch wide gutters with central guide lines.

1937, Aug. 18 Unwmk. *Perf. 11*

796 A269 5c **gray blue**	.35	.25
P# block of 6	6.50	—

SOCIETY OF PHILATELIC AMERICANS ISSUE

SOUVENIR SHEET

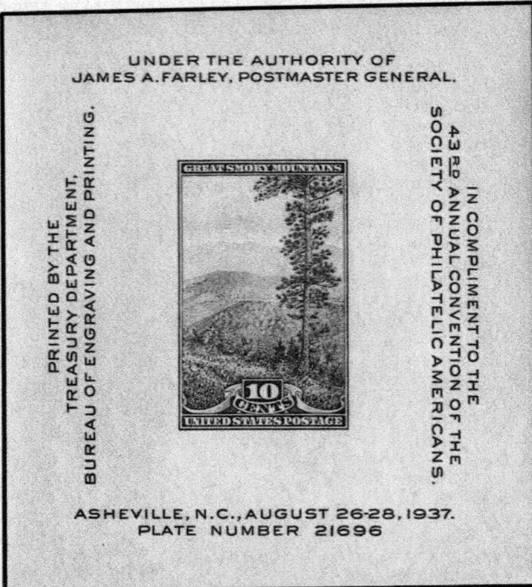

A269a

Illustration reduced.

TYPE OF NATIONAL PARKS ISSUE

Plates of 36 subjects

FLAT PLATE PRINTING

1937, Aug. 26 **Unwmk.** ***Imperf.***

797 A269a 10c **blue green** .60 .40

Issued in panes measuring 67x78mm, inscribed in margins: "Printed by the Treasury Department, Bureau of Engraving and Printing — Under the Authority of James A. Farley, Postmasster General — In Compliment to the 43rd Annual Convention of the Society of Philatelic Americans - Asheville, N.C., August 26-28, 1937. Plate Number 21695."

Also used was plate 21696. Each different plate number used is inscribed in the bottom selvage of the respective souvenir sheets.

CONSTITUTION SESQUICENTENNIAL ISSUE

150th anniversary of the signing of the Constitution on September 17, 1787.

"Adoption of the Constitution" A270

ROTARY PRESS PRINTING

Plates of 200 subjects in four panes of 50.

1937, Sept. 17 **Unwmk.** ***Perf. 11x10½***

798 A270 3c **bright reddish purple** .40 .25
P# block of 4 2.00 —

TERRITORIAL ISSUES

Hawaii

Statue of Kamehameha I, Honolulu — A271

Alaska

Mt. McKinley A272

Puerto Rico

La Fortaleza, San Juan — A273

Virgin Islands

Charlotte Amalie Harbor, St. Thomas A274

ROTARY PRESS PRINTING

Plates of 200 subjects in panes of 50.

1937 **Unwmk.** ***Perf. 10½x11***

799 A271 3c **violet,** *Oct. 18* .35 .25
P# block of 4 2.00 —

Perf. 11x10½

800 A272 3c **violet,** *Nov. 12* .40 .25
P# block of 4 2.25 —
Pair with full gutter between —

801 A273 3c **bright purple,** *Nov. 25* .40 .25
P# block of 4 2.25 —

802 A274 3c **rose violet,** *Dec. 15* .40 .25
P# block of 4 2.25 —
Pair with full vertical gutter between *275.00*
Nos. 799-802 (4) 1.55 1.00

PRESIDENTIAL ISSUE

Benjamin Franklin — A275

George Washington — A276

Martha Washington — A277

John Adams — A278

Thomas Jefferson — A279

James Madison — A280

The White House — A281

James Monroe — A282

John Quincy Adams — A283

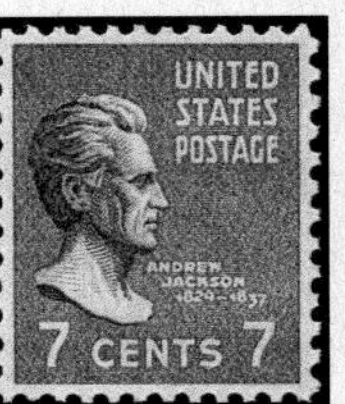

Andrew Jackson — A284

Martin Van Buren — A285

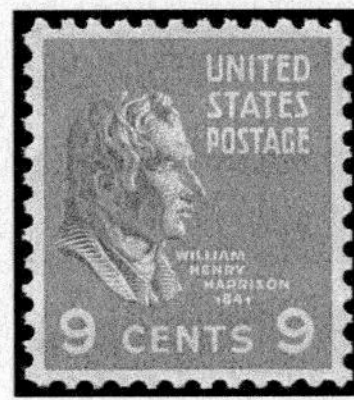

William H. Harrison — A286

John Tyler — A287

James K. Polk — A288

Zachary Taylor — A289

Millard Fillmore — A290

Franklin Pierce — A291

James Buchanan — A292

Abraham Lincoln — A293

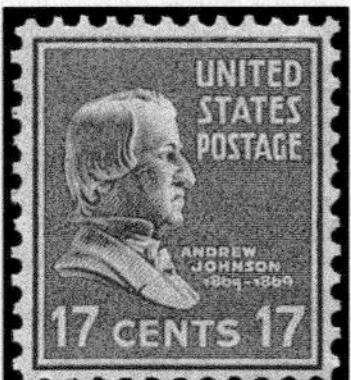

Andrew Johnson — A294

Ulysses S. Grant — A295

Rutherford B. Hayes — A296

James A. Garfield — A297

Chester A. Arthur — A298

Grover Cleveland — A299

Benjamin Harrison — A300

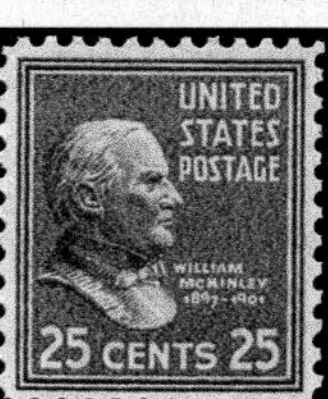

William McKinley — A301

Theodore Roosevelt — A302

William Howard Taft — A303

Woodrow Wilson — A304

Warren G. Harding — A305

Calvin Coolidge — A306

ROTARY PRESS PRINTING

Ordinary and Electric Eye (EE) Plates of 400 subjects in four panes of 100. (For details of EE Markings, see Information for Collectors in first part of this Catalogue.)

1938 Unwmk. ***Perf. 11x10½***

803 A275 ½c **deep orange,** *May 19* .25 .25
On cover 2.50
P# block of 4 .50 —
804 A276 1c **green,** *Apr. 25* .25 .25
light green .25 .25
On cover .50
Single franking on local cover at non-carrier post office 50.00
Single franking on certificate of mailing, btwn. 1938 and Feb. 1, 1954 10.00
P# block of 4 1.10 —
Pair with full vert. gutter btwn. *160.00* —
b. Booklet pane of 6 2.00 *.50*
On domestic airmail cover 75.00
c. Horiz. pair, imperf between (from booklet pane) —
805 A277 1½c **bister brown,** *May 5* .25 .25
buff ('43) .25 .25
On cover .50
Single franking on int'l printed matter cover 25.00
Single franking on pre-1949 domestic third-class (up to 2 ozs) cover 10.00
P# block of 4 .50 —
Pair with full horiz. gutter btwn. *175.00*
Pair with full vert. gutter btwn. —
b. Horiz. pair, imperf. between 100.00 20.00

No. 805b unused is not precanceled. Precanceled examples are considered used and are valued in the used column. They are valued with gum; pairs without gum are worth less.

806 A278 2c **rose carmine,** *June 3* .25 .25
rose pink ('43) .25 .25
On cover .50
Single franking on post-1949 third-class (up to 2 ozs.) cover 10.00
Single franking on local cover at carrier post office 10.00
Single franking on local cover at non-carrier post office *125.00*
P# block of 4, # opposite corner stamp 1.10 —
Vertical margin block of 10, P# opposite 3rd horizontal row (Experimental EE plates) 12.00
Recut at top of head, Pl. 22156 U.L. 3 3.00 1.50
Pair with full horiz. gutter btwn. *125.00*
Pair with full vert. gutter btwn. —
b. Booklet pane of 6 5.50 *1.00*
On double-weight domestic airmail cover *300.00*
807 A279 3c **light violet,** *June 16* .25 .25
violet .25 .25
On cover .50
Single franking on private carrier cover *150.00*
Single franking on int'l surface mail postcard until 1953 15.00
Single franking on first-class cover to UPU countries of the Americas and Spain 20.00
Single franking on post-1949 double-weight third-class cover *50.00*
Single franking on penalty-permit cover with return receipt *125.00*
Single franking on certificate of mailing, btwn. Feb. 1, 1954, and July 1, 1957 *50.00*
P# block of 4, # opposite corner stamp 1.10 .25
Vertical margin block of 10, P# opposite 3rd horizontal row (Experimental EE plates) 125.00
Pair with full vert. gutter btwn. *150.00*
Pair with full horiz. gutter btwn. *200.00*
a. Booklet pane of 6 8.50 *2.00*
Horiz. booklet pair with full vert. gutter between —
b. Horiz. pair, imperf. between *2,000.* —
c. Imperf., pair *3,500.*
d. As "a," imperf between vert. *5,000.*

No. 807d is a booklet pane of nine, the error resulting from a foldover and miscutting.

Counterfeits exist of No. 807. See the Postal Counterfeits section of this catalog.

808 A280 4c **bright rose purple,** *July 1* .75 .25
rose purple ('43) .75 .25
On cover 3.00
Single franking on domestic third-class cover 25.00
Single franking on domestic airmail postcard 25.00
Single franking on penalty-permit cover with return receipt *200.00*
Single franking on post-1949 third-class cover *125.00*
Single franking on international surface postcard 30.00
P# block of 4 3.25 —
809 A281 4½c **dark gray,** *July 11* .40 .25
gray ('43) .40 .25
On cover 20.00
Single franking on triple-weight third-class cover 75.00
Single franking on third-class cover with minimum insurance *125.00*
P# block of 4 2.00 —
810 A282 5c **bright blue,** *July 21* .35 .25
light blue .35 .25
On cover 1.00
Single franking on UPU surface cover 10.00
Single franking on domestic airmail cover 30.00
Single franking paying dead letter office return fee *75.00*
Single franking on certificate of mailing, after July 1, 1957 *150.00*
P# block of 4 1.75 —
Pair with full vert. gutter btwn. *1,350.*
811 A283 6c **red orange,** *July 28* .40 .25
On cover 1.00
Single franking on double-weight first-class cover 15.00
Single franking on 1944-45 airmail cover to POW 75.00
P# block of 4 2.00 —
Pair with full vert. gutter btwn. *1,200.*
812 A284 7c **sepia,** *Aug. 4* .40 .25
violet brown .40 .25
On cover 10.00
Single franking on 1958 domestic airmail cover 75.00
Single franking on domestic third-class cover 75.00
Single franking on penalty permit cover with return receipt *300.00*
P# block of 4 2.00 —
813 A285 8c **olive green,** *Aug. 11* .40 .25
light olive green ('43) .40 .25
bright olive green .40 .25
olive ('42) .40 .25
On cover 3.00
Single franking on domestic airmail cover 10.00
Single franking on pre-1953 double-weight UPU surface cover 75.00
Single franking on post-1953 UPU surface cover 25.00
P# block of 4 2.25 —
814 A286 9c **rose pink,** *Aug. 18* .45 .25
pink ('43) .45 .25
On cover 3.00
Single franking on triple-weight first-class cover 25.00
P# block of 4 2.25 —
Pair with full vert. gutter btwn. —
815 A287 10c **brown red,** *Sept. 2* .40 .25
pale brown red ('43) .40 .25
On cover 2.00
Single franking on airmail cover to the Caribbean 10.00
Single franking on international airmail postcard 25.00
Single franking on aerogramme or private air letter *500.00*
Single franking on airmail cover from Midway Island to Hawaii *250.00*
P# block of 4 2.25 —
816 A288 11c **ultramarine,** *Sept. 8* .75 .25
bright ultramarine .75 .25
dull ultramarine .75 .25
On cover 5.00
Single franking on international airmail postcard *150.00*
Single franking on surface mail cover with airmail surcharge in US and Europe *600.00*
Single franking on pre-1953 three-ounce UPU surface cover *500.00*
P# block of 4 3.50 —
817 A289 12c **bright mauve,** *Sept. 14* 1.00 .25
On cover 3.00
Single franking on 1938-44 double-weight domestic airmail cover 30.00
Single franking on quadruple-weight first-class cover 40.00
Single franking on local special delivery cover *125.00*
Single franking on international printed-matter cover *100.00*
Single franking on post-1953 double-weight UPU surface cover *250.00*
P# block of 4 4.50 —
818 A290 13c **blue green,** *Sept. 22* 1.30 .25
deep blue green 1.30 .25
On cover 5.00
Single franking on special delivery cover 75.00
P# block of 4 7.00 —
819 A291 14c **blue,** *Oct. 6* 1.00 .25
On cover 15.00
Single franking on 1958 double-weight domestic airmail cover *750.00*
Single franking on parcel post cover *200.00*
Single franking on pre-1953 four-ounce UPU surface cover *650.00*
P# block of 4 5.00 —
820 A292 15c **blue gray,** *Oct. 13* .80 .25
On cover 5.00
Single franking on 1945-46 airmail cover to or from Hawaii 25.00
Single franking on international airmail cover 15.00
P# block of 4 4.00 —
821 A293 16c **black,** *Oct. 20* 1.50 .25
On cover 15.00
Single franking on first-class special delivery cover *130.00*
Single franking on airmail special delivery cover *100.00*
Single franking on pre-1944 double-weight first-class special delivery cover *150.00*
Single franking on double-weight airmail cover *125.00*
P# block of 4 7.00 —
822 A294 17c **rose red,** *Oct. 27* 1.00 .25
deep rose red 1.10 .25
On cover 10.00
Single franking on local registered cover 50.00
P# block of 4 5.00 —
823 A295 18c **brown carmine,** *Nov. 3* 2.25 .25
rose brown ('43) 2.25 .25
On cover 5.00
Single franking on registered first-class cover 10.00
Single franking on 1938-44 triple-weight airmail cover *100.00*
Single franking on airmail special delivery cover *150.00*
P# block of 4 12.00 —
824 A296 19c **bright mauve,** *Nov. 10* 1.30 .35
On cover 20.00
Single franking on parcel post cover *250.00*
Single franking on registered cover with unindemnified excess value *500.00*
Single franking on double-weight local registered cover *700.00*

Single franking on double-weight first-class special delivery cover — 1,500.
P# block of 4 7.00 —

825 A297 20c **bright blue green,** *Nov. 10* 1.20 .25
deep blue green ('43) 1.20 .25
On cover 3.00
Single franking on airmail cover to or from Hawaii 10.00
Single franking on registered local letter with return receipt *60.00*
P# block of 4 5.50 —
Pair with full horiz. gutter btwn. —
Pair with full vert. gutter btwn. —

826 A298 21c **dull blue,** *Nov. 22* 1.30 .25
On cover 10.00
Single franking on registered airmail cover 25.00
Single franking on double-weight first-class registered cover 35.00
On 1944-46 airmail special delivery cover *150.00*
On 1949-51 airmail special delivery cover *200.00*
P# block of 4 7.00 —

827 A299 22c **vermilion,** *Nov. 22* 1.20 .40
On cover 20.00
Single franking on insured third-class cover *350.00*
Single franking on registered cover with return receipt and unindemnified excess value *750.00*
Single franking on registered local cover with return receipt *2,000.*
P# block of 4 8.00 —

828 A300 24c **gray black,** *Dec. 2* 3.25 .25
On cover 5.00
Single franking on registered penalty cover with return receipt 50.00
Single franking on 1944-46 triple-weight airmail cover *175.00*
Single franking on 1938-44 quadruple-weight airmail cover *150.00*
P# block of 4 14.50 —

829 A301 25c **deep red lilac,** *Dec. 2* 1.20 .25
rose lilac ('43) 1.20 .25
On cover 5.00
Single franking on airmail cover to Asia, Africa and Australia 25.00
P# block of 4 5.50 —
Pair with full vert. gutter btwn. *900.00*

830 A302 30c **deep ultra,** *Dec. 8* 3.50 .25
On cover 5.00
Single franking on airmail cover to Europe 25.00
Single franking on cover to or from Midway Island *175.00*
P# block of 4 16.00 —
a. 30c **blue** 20.00 —
P# block of 4 100.00
b. 30c **deep blue** *250.00* —
P# block of 4 *1,400.* —

831 A303 50c **mauve,** *Dec. 8* 5.50 .25
On cover 10.00
Single franking on airmail cover to the Philippines 50.00
Single franking on double-weight airmail cover to Asia, Africa and Australia 60.00
Single franking on airmail cover from Hawaii to Europe *350.00*
P# block of 4 25.00 —

Bureau Precancels: ½c, 199 diff., 1c, 701 diff., 1½c, 404 diff., 2c, 161 diff., 3c, 87 diff., 4c, 30 diff., 4½c, 27 diff., 5c, 44 diff., 6c, 45 diff., 7c, 44 diff., 8c, 44 diff., 9c, 38 diff., 10c, 43 diff.

Also, 11c, 41 diff., 12c, 33 diff., 13c, 28 diff., 14c, 23 diff., 15c, 38 diff., 16c, 6 diff., 17c, 27 diff., 18c, 5 diff., 19c, 8 diff., 20c, 39 diff., 21c, 5 diff., 22c, 4 diff., 24c, 8 diff., 25c, 23 diff., 30c, 27 diff., 50c, 24 diff.

FLAT PLATE PRINTING
Plates of 100 subjects

1938 ***Perf. 11***

832 A304 $1 **purple & black,** *Aug. 29* 7.00 .25
On cover 10.00
On registered bank tag 5.00
Single franking on double-weight airmail cover to the Philippines *125.00*
Single franking on quadruple-weight airmail cover to Asia, Africa and Australia *300.00*
Single franking on quintuple-weight airmail cover to or from Hawaii *275.00*
Margin block of 4, bottom or side arrow 30.00 —
Center line block 32.50 *4.00*
Top P# block of 4, 2# 32.50 —
Top P# block of 20, 2#, arrow, 2 TOP, 2 registration markers and denomination 160.00 —
a. Vert. pair, imperf. horiz. *1,100.*
Top P# blk of 8, imperf horiz. *7,500.*
b. Watermarked USIR ('51) 200.00 65.00
Hinged 120.00
Center line block *1,700.*
P# block of 4, 2# *2,000.*
Top P# block of 20, 2#, arrow, 2 TOP, 2 registration markers and denomination 5,000.
c. $1 **red violet & black,** *Aug. 31, 1954* 6.00 .25
On cover 30.00
On registered bank tag 10.00
Single franking on quadruple-weight airmail cover to Asia, Africa and Australia *200.00*
Top or bottom P# block of 4, 2# 30.00 —
d. As "c," vert. pair, imperf. horiz. *900.00*
e. Vertical pair, imperf. between *7,500.*
f. As "c," vert. pair, imperf. btwn. *10,000.*
g. As "c," **bright magenta & black** *70.00* 50.00
Top or bottom P# block of 4, 2# *400.00*
h. As No. 832, **red violet & black** — —
Top or bottom P# block of 4, 2# —

No. 832c is dry printed from 400-subject flat plates on thick white paper with smooth, colorless gum.

No. 832g is the far end of the color spectrum for the No. 832c stamp, trending toward a more pinkish shade, but the shade is not pink. No. 832g is known in bright magenta and in deep bright magenta; both shades qualify as No. 832g.

No. 832h is a shade variety of the wet printing (No. 832), but the shade essentially matches the red violet normally seen on the dry printing (No. 832c).

833 A305 $2 **yellow green & black,** *Sept. 29* 16.00 3.75
green & black ('43) 16.00 3.75
On cover 400.00
On registered bank tag 25.00
Single franking on airmail cover to the Philippines *2,000.*
Single franking on registered airmail cover to Europe *3,000.*
Margin block of 4, bottom or side arrow 70.00 —
Center line block 80.00 35.00
Top P# block of 4, 2# 85.00 —
Top P# block of 20, 2#, arrow, 2 TOP, 2 registration markers and denominations 400.00 —
Top P# block of 20, 2#, black # and marginal markings only (yellow green # and markings omitted) *15,000.*

834 A306 $5 **carmine & black,** *Nov. 17* 75.00 3.00
Hinged 40.00
On cover *1,500.*
On registered bank tag 25.00
dark red & black *700.00 450.00*
Margin block of 4, bottom or side arrow 325.00 —
Center line block 350.00 *25.00*
Top P# block of 4, 2# 325.00 —
Top P# block of 20, 2#, arrow, 2 TOP, 2 registration markers and denominations 2,000.
a. **$5 red brown & black** *3,000. 7,000.*
Hinged *1,850.*
Top P# block of 4, 2# *15,000.*
Hinged *9,500.*
Nos. 803-834 (32) 130.85 14.50
Nos. 803-834, P# blocks of 4 670.95

Top plate number blocks of Nos. 832, 833 and 834 are found both with and without top arrow or registration markers.

No. 834 can be chemically altered to resemble Scott 834a. No. 834a should be purchased only with competent expert certification.

Watermarks
All stamps from No. 835 on are unwatermarked.

CONSTITUTION RATIFICATION ISSUE

150th anniversary of the ratification of the United States Constitution.

Old Courthouse, Williamsburg, Va. — A307

ROTARY PRESS PRINTING
Plates of 200 subjects in four panes of 50.

1938, June 21 ***Perf. 11x10½***

835 A307 3c **deep violet** .45 .25
P# block of 4 3.50 —

SWEDISH-FINNISH TERCENTENARY ISSUE

Tercentenary of the founding of the Swedish and Finnish Settlement at Wilmington, Delaware.

"Landing of the First Swedish and Finnish Settlers in America," by Stanley M. Arthurs — A308

FLAT PLATE PRINTING
Plates of 192 subjects in four panes of 48 each, separated by 1¼ inch wide gutters with central guide lines.

1938, June 27 ***Perf. 11***

836 A308 3c **bright reddish purple** .35 .25
P# block of 6 2.25 —

NORTHWEST TERRITORY SESQUICENTENNIAL

"Colonization of the West," by Gutzon Borglum — A309

ROTARY PRESS PRINTING
Plates of 400 subjects in four panes of 100.

1938, July 15 ***Perf. 11x10½***

837 A309 3c **bright rose purple** .30 .25
P# block of 4 5.00 —

IOWA TERRITORY CENTENNIAL ISSUE

Old Capitol, Iowa City — A310

ROTARY PRESS PRINTING
Plates of 200 subjects in four panes of 50.

1938, Aug. 24 ***Perf. 11x10½***

838 A310 3c **violet** .40 .25
P# block of 4 6.00 —
Pair with full vertical gutter between —

TYPES OF 1938
REGULAR ISSUE
ROTARY PRESS COIL STAMPS

1939, Jan. 20 ***Perf. 10 Vertically***

839 A276 1c **green** .30 .25
light green .30 .25
On cover .50
Pair .60 .50
Joint line pair 1.40 .70
Small holes —
Pair —
Joint line pair —

840 A277 1½c **bister brown** .30 .25
buff .30 .25
On cover 2.00
Single franking on third-class cover 15.00
Pair .60 .50
Joint line pair 1.50 .75
Small holes — —
Pair — —
Joint line pair —

841 A278 2c **rose carmine** .40 .25
On cover 2.00
Single franking on local cover 20.00
Pair .80 .50
Joint line pair 1.75 .85
Small holes —
Pair —
Joint line pair —

842 A279 3c **light violet,** large holes .50 .25
violet .50 .25
On cover .50
Pair 1.00 .50
Joint line pair 2.00 1.00
Gripper cracks —
Thin translucent paper 2.50 —
Small holes —
Pair —
Joint line pair —

See note concerning large and small perforation holes following No. 1053.

843 A280 4c **red violet** 7.50 .40
On cover 5.00
Single franking on domestic first-class cover 75.00
Single franking on domestic third-class cover 60.00
Single franking on domestic airmail postcard *100.00*
Single franking on international postcard *125.00*
Pair 16.50 .90
Joint line pair 27.50 12.50
Small holes —
Pair —
Joint line pair —

844 A281 4½c **dark gray** .70 .40
On cover 25.00
Single franking on triple-weight third-class cover *200.00*

Single franking on third-class cover with minimum insurance *300.00*
Pair 1.50 .90
Joint line pair 5.00 2.25
Small holes —
Pair —
Joint line pair —

845 A282 5c **bright blue** 5.00 2.50
On cover 15.00
Single franking on domestic airmail cover 75.00
Single franking on UPU surface cover *125.00*
Pair 10.50 .75
Joint line pair 27.50 5.00
Small holes —
Pair —
Joint line pair —

846 A283 6c **red orange** 1.10 .55
On cover 5.00
Single franking on domestic airmail cover 10.00
Pair 2.25 .50
Joint line pair 7.50 1.50
Small holes —
Pair —
Joint line pair —

847 A287 10c **brown red** 11.00 1.00
On cover *100.00*
Single franking on international airmail postcard *1,200.*
Single franking on airmail cover the Carribean and Central and South America *2,000.*
Pair 24.00 2.50
Joint line pair 42.50 10.00
Small holes —
Pair —
Joint line pair —

Bureau Precancels: 1c, 269 diff., 1½c, 179 diff., 2c, 101 diff., 3c, 46 diff., 4c, 13 diff., 4½c, 3 diff., 5c, 6 diff., 6c, 8 diff., 10c, 4 diff.

1939, Jan. 27 ***Perf. 10 Horizontally***

848 A276 1c **green** .85 .25
On cover 1.00
Single franking on domestic postcard 6.00
Pair 1.75 .50
Joint line pair 2.75 1.25
Small holes —
Pair —
Joint line pair —

849 A277 1½c **bister brown** 1.25 .30
On cover 20.00
Single franking on third-class cover 60.00
Pair 2.50 .65
Joint line pair 4.50 2.00
Small holes —
Pair —
Joint line pair —

850 A278 2c **rose carmine** 2.50 .40
On cover 5.00
Single franking on third-class cover 50.00
Pair 5.00 .90
Joint line pair 7.50 3.50
Small holes —
Pair —
Joint line pair —

851 A279 3c **light violet** 2.50 .40
violet 2.50 .40
On cover 15.00
Single franking on domestic first-class cover 30.00
Pair 5.00 .90
Joint line pair 8.50 3.75
Thin translucent paper
Same, joint line pair *750.00*
Small holes —
Pair —
Joint line pair —
Nos. 839-851 (13) 33.90 7.20
Nos. 839-851, joint line pairs (13) 139.90 29.65

GOLDEN GATE INTL. EXPOSITION, SAN FRANCISCO

"Tower of the Sun" — A311

ROTARY PRESS PRINTING
Plates of 200 subjects in four panes of 50.

1939, Feb. 18 ***Perf. 10½x11***

852 A311 3c **bright purple** .30 .25
On cover, Expo. station machine canc. (non-first day) 3.00
On cover, Expo. station duplex handstamp canc. (non-first day) 15.00
P# block of 4 1.50 —

NEW YORK WORLD'S FAIR ISSUE

Trylon and Perisphere — A312

ROTARY PRESS PRINTING
Plates of 200 subjects in four panes of 50.

1939, Apr. 1 ***Perf. 10½x11***

853 A312 3c **violet** .30 .25
On cover, Expo. station machine canc. (non-first day) 3.00
On cover, Expo. station duplex handstamp canc. 10.00
P# block of 4 2.00 —

WASHINGTON INAUGURATION ISSUE

Sesquicentennial of the inauguration of George Washington as First President.

Washington Taking Oath of Office, Federal Building, New York City — A313

FLAT PLATE PRINTING
Plates of 200 subjects in four panes of 50.

1939, Apr. 30 ***Perf. 11***

854 A313 3c **bright purple** .60 .25
P# block of 6 3.50 —

BASEBALL CENTENNIAL ISSUE

Sandlot Baseball Game — A314

Designed by William A. Roach.

ROTARY PRESS PRINTING
Plates of 200 subjects in four panes of 50.

1939, June 12 ***Perf. 11x10½***

855 A314 3c **violet** 1.75 .25
P# block of 4 7.50 —

PANAMA CANAL ISSUE

25th anniv. of the opening of the Panama Canal.

Theodore Roosevelt, Gen. George W. Goethals and Ship in Gaillard Cut — A315

Designed by William A. Roach.

FLAT PLATE PRINTING
Plates of 200 subjects in four panes of 50.

1939, Aug. 15 ***Perf. 11***

856 A315 3c **reddish purple** .40 .25
P# block of 6 3.50 —

PRINTING TERCENTENARY ISSUE

Issued in commemoration of the 300th anniversary of printing in Colonial America. The Stephen Daye press is in the Harvard University Museum.

Stephen Daye Press — A316

Designed by William K. Schrage.

ROTARY PRESS PRINTING
E.E. Plates of 200 subjects in four panes of 50.

1939, Sept. 25 ***Perf. 10½x11***

857 A316 3c **violet** .25 .25
P# block of 4 1.00 —

50th ANNIVERSARY OF STATEHOOD ISSUE

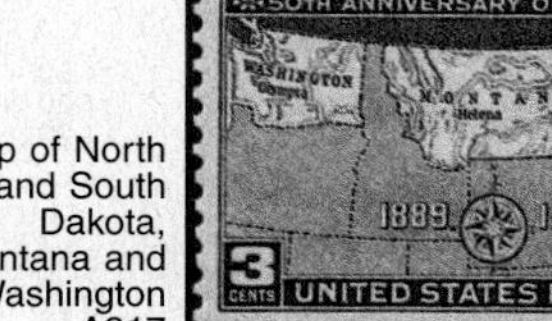

Map of North and South Dakota, Montana and Washington — A317

ROTARY PRESS PRINTING
E.E. Plates of 200 subjects in four panes of 50.

1939, Nov. 2 ***Perf. 11x10½***

858 A317 3c **rose purple** .35 .25
P# block of 4 2.25 —

FAMOUS AMERICANS ISSUES

ROTARY PRESS PRINTING
E.E. Plates of 280 subjects in four panes of 70.

AMERICAN AUTHORS

Washington Irving — A318

James Fenimore Cooper — A319

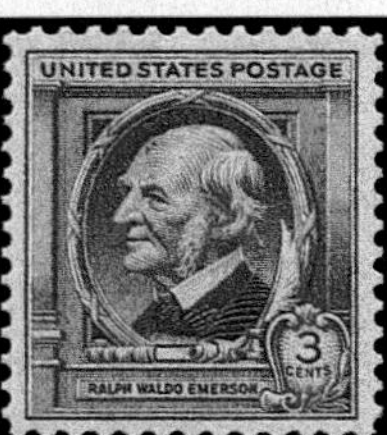

Ralph Waldo Emerson — A320

Louisa May Alcott — A321

Samuel L. Clemens (Mark Twain) — A322

1940 ***Perf. 10½x11***

859 A318 1c **bright blue green,** *Jan. 29* .25 .25
P# block of 4 1.00 —

860 A319 2c **rose carmine,** *Jan. 29* .25 .25
P# block of 4 1.25 —
861 A320 3c **bright purple,** *Feb. 5* .25 .25
P# block of 4 1.25 —
862 A321 5c **ultramarine,** *Feb. 5* .35 .25
P# block of 4 8.00 —
863 A322 10c **dark brown,** *Feb. 13* 1.75 1.20
P# block of 4 22.50 —
Nos. 859-863 (5) 2.85 2.20

AMERICAN POETS

Henry Wadsworth Longfellow — A323

John Greenleaf Whittier — A324

James Russell Lowell — A325

Walt Whitman — A326

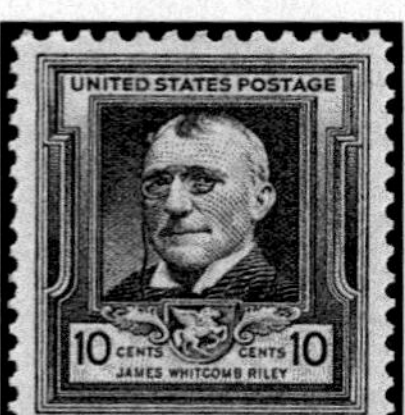

James Whitcomb Riley — A327

864 A323 1c **bright blue green,** *Feb. 16* .25 .25
P# block of 4 2.00 —
865 A324 2c **rose carmine,** *Feb. 16* .25 .25
P# block of 4 1.75 —
866 A325 3c **bright purple,** *Feb. 20* .25 .25
P# block of 4 2.25 —
867 A326 5c **ultramarine,** *Feb. 20* .50 .25
P# block of 4 8.50 —
868 A327 10c **dark brown,** *Feb. 24* 1.75 1.25
P# block of 4 22.50 —
Nos. 864-868 (5) 3.00 2.25

AMERICAN EDUCATORS

Horace Mann — A328

Mark Hopkins — A329

Charles W. Eliot — A330

Frances E. Willard — A331

Booker T. Washington — A332

869 A328 1c **bright blue green,** *Mar. 14* .25 .25
P# block of 4 2.25 —
870 A329 2c **rose carmine,** *Mar. 14* .25 .25
P# block of 4 1.75 —
871 A330 3c **bright purple,** *Mar. 28* .25 .25
P# block of 4 2.00 —
872 A331 5c **ultramarine,** *Mar. 28* .50 .25
P# block of 4 8.00 —
873 A332 10c **dark brown,** *Apr. 7* 2.25 1.10
P# block of 4 22.50 —
Nos. 869-873 (5) 3.50 2.10

AMERICAN SCIENTISTS

John James Audubon — A333

Dr. Crawford W. Long — A334

Luther Burbank — A335

Dr. Walter Reed — A336

Jane Addams — A337

874 A333 1c **bright blue green,** *Apr. 8* .25 .25
P# block of 4 1.00 —
875 A334 2c **rose carmine,** *Apr. 8* .25 .25
P# block of 4 1.00 —
876 A335 3c **bright purple,** *Apr. 17* .25 .25
P# block of 4 1.10 —
877 A336 5c **ultramarine,** *Apr. 17* .50 .25
P# block of 4 5.50 —
878 A337 10c **dark brown,** *Apr. 26* 1.50 .85
P# block of 4 15.00 —
Nos. 874-878 (5) 2.75 1.85

AMERICAN COMPOSERS

Stephen Collins Foster — A338

John Philip Sousa — A339

Victor Herbert — A340

Edward A. MacDowell — A341

Ethelbert Nevin — A342

879 A338 1c **bright blue green,** *May 3* .25 .25
P# block of 4 1.00 —
880 A339 2c **rose carmine,** *May 3* .25 .25
P# block of 4 1.00 —
881 A340 3c **bright purple,** *May 13* .25 .25
P# block of 4 1.10 —
882 A341 5c **ultramarine,** *May 13* .50 .25
P# block of 4 9.00 —
883 A342 10c **dark brown,** *June 10* 3.75 1.35
P# block of 4 20.00 —
Nos. 879-883 (5) 5.00 2.35

AMERICAN ARTISTS

Gilbert Charles Stuart — A343

James A. McNeill Whistler — A344

Augustus Saint-Gaudens — A345

Daniel Chester French — A346

Frederic Remington — A347

884 A343 1c **bright blue green,** *Sept. 5* .25 .25
P# block of 4 1.00 —
885 A344 2c **rose carmine,** *Sept. 5* .25 .25
P# block of 4 1.00 —
886 A345 3c **bright purple,** *Sept. 16* .30 .25
P# block of 4 1.50 —
887 A346 5c **ultramarine,** *Sept. 16* .50 .25
P# block of 4 8.00 —
888 A347 10c **dark brown,** *Sept. 30* 1.75 1.25
P# block of 4 15.00 —
Nos. 884-888 (5) 3.05 2.25

AMERICAN INVENTORS

Eli Whitney — A348

Samuel F. B. Morse — A349

Cyrus Hall McCormick — A350

Elias Howe — A351

Alexander Graham Bell — A352

889 A348 1c **bright blue green,** *Oct. 7*	.25	.25
P# block of 4	2.25	—
890 A349 2c **rose carmine,** *Oct. 7*	.30	.25
P# block of 4	2.00	—
891 A350 3c **bright purple,** *Oct. 14*	.30	.25
P# block of 4	1.50	—
892 A351 5c **ultramarine,** *Oct. 14*	1.10	.30
P# block of 4	11.00	—
893 A352 10c **dark brown,** *Oct. 28*	11.00	2.00
P# block of 4	40.00	—
Nos. 889-893 (5)	12.95	3.05
Nos. 859-893 (35)	33.10	16.05
Nos. 859-893, P# blocks of 4	245.70	

PONY EXPRESS, 80th ANNIV. ISSUE

Pony Express Rider — A353

ROTARY PRESS PRINTING

E.E. Plates of 200 subjects in four panes of 50.

1940, Apr. 3 ***Perf. 11x10½***

894 A353 3c **henna brown**	.50	.25
P# block of 4	3.50	—

PAN AMERICAN UNION ISSUE

Founding of the Pan American Union, 50th anniv.

The Three Graces (Botticelli) — A354

ROTARY PRESS PRINTING

E.E. Plates of 200 subjects in four panes of 50.

1940, Apr. 14 ***Perf. 10½x11***

895 A354 3c **bright rose purple**	.30	.25
P# block of 4	2.75	—

IDAHO STATEHOOD, 50th ANNIV.

Idaho State Capitol A355

ROTARY PRESS PRINTING

E.E. Plates of 200 subjects in four panes of 50.

1940, July 3 ***Perf. 11x10½***

896 A355 3c **bright mauve**	.35	.25
P# block of 4	2.25	—

WYOMING STATEHOOD, 50th ANNIV.

Wyoming State Seal — A356

ROTARY PRESS PRINTING

E.E. Plates of 200 subjects in four panes of 50.

1940, July 10 ***Perf. 10½x11***

897 A356 3c **brown violet**	.35	.25
P# block of 4	2.25	—

CORONADO EXPEDITION, 400th ANNIV.

"Coronado and His Captains" Painted by Gerald Cassidy A357

ROTARY PRESS PRINTING

E.E. Plates of 200 subjects in four panes of 50.

1940, Sept. 7 ***Perf. 11x10½***

898 A357 3c **bright violet**	.35	.25
P# block of 4	2.25	—

NATIONAL DEFENSE ISSUE

Statue of Liberty — A358

90-millimeter Anti-aircraft Gun — A359

Torch of Enlightenment — A360

ROTARY PRESS PRINTING

E.E. Plates of 400 subjects in four panes of 100

1940, Oct. 16 ***Perf. 11x10½***

899 A358 1c **bright blue green**	.25	.25
P# block of 4	1.00	—
Cracked plate (22684 UR 10)	3.00	
Gripper cracks	3.00	
Pair with full vert. gutter between	*200.00*	
a. Vertical pair, imperf. between	*600.00*	—
b. Horizontal pair, imperf. between	32.50	—

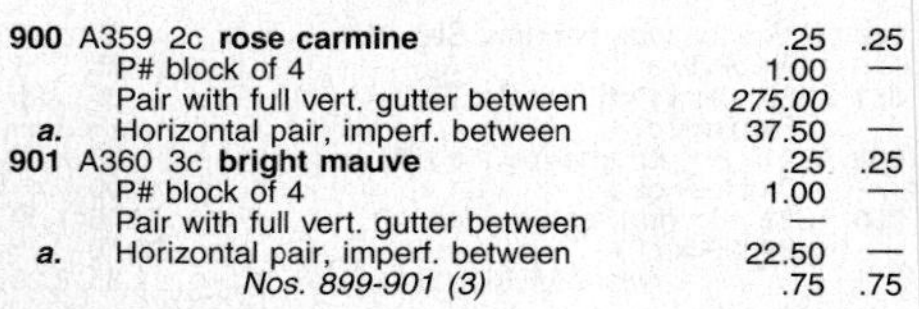

900 A359 2c **rose carmine**	.25	.25
P# block of 4	1.00	—
Pair with full vert. gutter between	*275.00*	
a. Horizontal pair, imperf. between	37.50	—
901 A360 3c **bright mauve**	.25	.25
P# block of 4	1.00	—
Pair with full vert. gutter between	—	
a. Horizontal pair, imperf. between	22.50	—
Nos. 899-901 (3)	.75	.75

Bureau Precancels: 1c, 316 diff., 2c, 25 diff., 3c, 22 diff.

THIRTEENTH AMENDMENT ISSUE

75th anniv. of the 13th Amendment to the Constitution abolishing slavery.

Emancipation Monument; Lincoln and Kneeling Slave, by Thomas Ball — A361

Designed by William A. Roach.

ROTARY PRESS PRINTING

E.E. Plates of 200 subjects in four panes of 50.

1940, Oct. 20 ***Perf. 10½x11***

902 A361 3c **violet**	.50	.25
dark violet	.50	.25
P# block of 4	3.50	—

VERMONT STATEHOOD, 150th ANNIV.

State Capitol, Montpelier A362

Designed by Alvin R. Meissner.

ROTARY PRESS PRINTING

E.E. Plates of 200 subjects in four panes of 50.

1941, Mar. 4 ***Perf. 11x10½***

903 A362 3c **light violet**	.45	.25
P# block of 4	3.00	—

KENTUCKY STATEHOOD, 150th ANNIV.

Daniel Boone and Three Frontiersmen, from Mural by Gilbert White — A363

Designed by William A. Roach.

ROTARY PRESS PRINTING

E.E. Plates of 200 subjects in four panes of 50.

1942, June 1 ***Perf. 11x10½***

904 A363 3c **purple**	.30	.25
P# block of 4	1.75	—

WIN THE WAR ISSUE

American Eagle — A364

ROTARY PRESS PRINTING

E.E. Plates of 400 subjects in four panes of 100.

1942, July 4 ***Perf. 11x10½***

905 A364 3c **bright lilac** .25 .25
light violet .25 .25
P# block of 4 2.25 —
Pair with full vert. gutter between *200.00*
Pair with full horiz. gutter between *600.00*
b. 3c **reddish purple** *750.00 500.00*

Bureau Precancels: 26 diff.

All examples of No. 905b are precanceled either Los Angeles, Calif., Fremont, Ohio, or St. Paul, Minn. Value is for Los Angeles, which is the more common. Value of Fremont, unused, $1,500. Value of St. Paul, used (without gum), $2,500. The stamps with St. Paul precancel are slightly less reddish than Los Angeles or Fremont, but they are in the same reddish purple/purple color family.

CHINESE RESISTANCE ISSUE

Issued to commemorate the Chinese people's five years of resistance to Japanese aggression.

Map of China, Abraham Lincoln and Sun Yat-sen, Founder of the Chinese Republic A365

ROTARY PRESS PRINTING

E.E. Plates of 200 subjects in four panes of 50.

1942, July 7 ***Perf. 11x10½***

906 A365 5c **bright blue** *4.00* .50
P# block of 4 *22.00* —

ALLIED NATIONS ISSUE

Allegory of Victory — A366

Designed by Leon Helguera.

ROTARY PRESS PRINTING

E.E. Plates of 400 subjects in four panes of 100.

1943, Jan. 14 ***Perf. 11x10½***

907 A366 2c **rose carmine** .25 .25
P# block of 4 1.00 —
Pair with full vert. or horiz. gutter between *225.00*

Bureau Precancels: Denver, Baltimore.

FOUR FREEDOMS ISSUE

Liberty Holding the Torch of Freedom and Enlightenment — A367

Designed by Paul Manship.

ROTARY PRESS PRINTING

E.E. Plates of 400 subjects in four panes of 100.

1943, Feb. 12 ***Perf. 11x10½***

908 A367 1c **bright blue green** .25 .25
P# block of 4 1.00 —

Bureau Precancels: 20 diff.

OVERRUN COUNTRIES ISSUE

Due to the failure of the printers to divulge detailed information as to printing processes used, the editors omit listings of irregularities, flaws and blemishes which are numerous in this issue. Exceptions are made for certified double impressions, the widely recognized "KORPA" variety, and "reverse" vs. "normal" printings of the flag colors.

Flag of Poland A368

Printed by the American Bank Note Co.

FRAMES ENGRAVED, CENTERS OFFSET LETTERPRESS

ROTARY PRESS PRINTING

Plates of 200 subjects in four panes of 50.

1943-44 ***Perf. 12***

909 A368 5c **blue violet, bright red & black,** *June 22, 1943* .25 .25
Margin block of 4, Inscribed "Poland" 3.50 —
Top margin block of 6, with red & blue violet guide markings and "Poland" 4.75 —
Bottom margin block of 6, with red & black guide markings 1.65 —
a. Double impression of "Poland" *200.00*
b. Double impression of black flag color and red "Poland" —
c. Reverse printing of flag colors (bright red over black) *25.00 150.00*

Flag of Czechoslovakia — A368a

910 A368a 5c **blue violet, blue, bright red & black,** *July 12, 1943* .25 .25
Margin block of 4, inscribed "Czechoslovakia" 2.75 —
Top margin block of 6, with red & blue violet guide markings and "Czechoslovakia" 3.25 —
a. Double impression of "Czechoslovakia" *600.00*
b. Reverse printing of flag colors (blue and bright red over black) — *150.00*
c. Partial reverse printing of flag colors (bright red over black and black over blue) —

Flag of Norway — A368b

911 A368b 5c **blue violet, dark rose, deep blue & black,** *July 27, 1943* .25 .25
Margin block of 4, inscribed "Norway" 1.30 —
Bottom margin block of 6 with dark rose & blue violet guide markings 1.65 —
a. Double impression of "Norway" *225.00*
b. Reverse printing of flag colors (dark rose and deep blue over black) —

Flag of Luxembourg — A368c

912 A368c 5c **blue violet, dark rose, light blue & black,** *Aug. 10, 1943* .25 .25
Margin block of 4, inscribed "Luxembourg" 1.30 —
Top margin block of 6 with light blue & blue violet guide markings & "Luxembourg" 1.65 —
a. Double impression of "Luxembourg" —
b. Reverse printing of flag colors (dark rose and light blue over black) — —
c. Partial reverse printing of flag colors (dark rose over black and black over light blue) —

Flag of Netherlands — A368d

913 A368d 5c **blue violet, dark rose, blue & black,** *Aug. 24, 1943* .25 .25
Margin block of 4, inscribed "Netherlands" 1.25 —
Bottom margin block of 6 with blue & blue violet guide markings 1.65 —
a. Reverse printing of flag colors (dark rose and blue over black) — *150.00*
b. Partial reverse printing of flag colors (blue over black and black over dark rose) .25 .25
c. Double impression of black 90.00

Flag of Belgium — A368e

914 A368e 5c **blue violet, dark rose, yellow & black,** *Sept. 14, 1943* .25 .25
Margin block of 4, inscribed "Belgium" 1.10 —
Top margin block of 6, with yellow & blue violet guide markings and "Belgium" 1.50 —
a. Double impression of "Belgium" *200.00*
b. Reverse printing of flag colors (red and yellow over black) .25 .25
c. Partial reverse printing of flag colors (yellow over black and black over red) —

Flag of France — A368f

915 A368f 5c **blue violet, deep blue, dark rose & black,** *Sept. 28, 1943* .25 .25
Margin block of 4, inscribed "France" 1.25 —
Bottom margin block of 6 with dark rose & blue violet guide markings 1.65 —
a. Reverse printing of flag colors (deep blue and dark rose over black) *20.00 150.00*
b. Partial reverse printing of flag colors (dark rose over black and black over deep blue) —

Flag of Greece — A368g

916 A368g 5c **blue vio, pale blue, grnsh blue & blk,** reverse printing of flag colors (pale blue flag stripes over pale blue shading), *Oct. 12, 1943* .50 .25
Margin block of 4, inscribed "Greece" 6.50 —
Top margin block of 6 with pale blue & blue violet guide markings & "Greece" 11.50 —
a. "Normal" printing of flag colors (dark blue shading over pale blue flag stripes) — —

Flag of Yugoslavia — A368h

Normal

Reverse Printing of Flag Colors

917 A368h 5c **blue violet, blue, dark rose & black,** *Oct. 26, 1943* .40 .25
Margin block of 4, inscribed "Yugoslavia" 4.25 —
Bottom margin block of 6 with dark rose & blue violet guide markings 2.60 —
a. Reverse printing of flag colors (blue and dark rose over black) *20.00* —
b. Double impression of black *250.00* *200.00*
c. Partial reverse printing of flag colors (dark rose over black and black over blue) —

Flag of Albania — A368i

918 A368i 5c **blue violet, dark red & black,** *Nov. 9, 1943* .25 .25
Margin block of 4, inscribed "Albania" 4.25 —
Top margin block of 6, with dark red & blue violet guide markings & "Albania" 6.50 —
a. Double impression of "Albania" — *600.00*
b. Reverse printing of flag colors (red over black) — —

Flag of Austria — A368j

919 A368j 5c **blue violet, red & black,** *Nov. 23, 1943* .30 .25
Margin block of 4, inscribed "Austria" 3.50 —
Bottom margin block of 6, with red & blue violet guide markings 2.00 —
a. Double impression of "Austria" *225.00*
b. Reverse printing of flag colors (red over black) —
c. Double impression of black —

Flag of Denmark — A368k

920 A368k 5c **blue violet, red & black,** *Dec. 7, 1943* .30 .25
Margin block of 4, inscribed "Denmark" 5.25 —
Top margin block of 6, with red & blue violet guide markings & "Denmark" 6.00 —
a. Reverse printing of flag colors (red over black) — *150.00*
b. 5c **blue violet, red & gray** .30 .25
c. As "b," reverse printing of flag colors (red over gray) — —

Flag of Korea — A368m

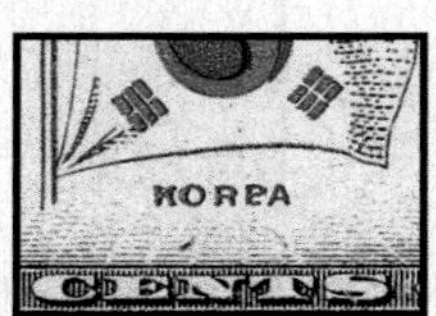

"KORPA" plate flaw

921 A368m 5c **blue violet, red, light blue & gray,** reverse printing of flag colors (light blue over gray), *Nov. 2, 1944* .25 .25
Margin block of 4, inscribed "Korea" 4.50 —
Top margin block of 6 with blue & black guide markings and "Korea" 5.25 —
"KORPA" plate flaw 22.50 12.50
a. Double impression of light blue (including "Korea") —
b. "Normal" printing of flag colors (gray over light blue) .25 .25
c. Double impression of red — —

The "P" of "KORPA" is actually a mangled "E." Occurs only on some panes, position 26.

Nos. 909-921 (13) 3.75 3.25
Nos. 909-921, Name blocks of 4 43.60

TRANSCONTINENTAL RAILROAD ISSUE

Completion of the 1st transcontinental railroad, 75th anniv.

"Golden Spike Ceremony" Painted by John McQuarrie A369

ENGRAVED
ROTARY PRESS PRINTING
E.E. Plates of 200 subjects in four panes of 50.

1944, May 10 ***Perf. 11x10½***
922 A369 3c **violet** .25 .25
P# block of 4 2.50 —

STEAMSHIP ISSUE

1st steamship to cross the Atlantic, 125th anniv.

"Savannah" A370

ROTARY PRESS PRINTING
E.E. Plates of 200 subjects in four panes of 50.

1944, May 22 ***Perf. 11x10½***
923 A370 3c **violet** .25 .25
P# block of 4 1.25 —

TELEGRAPH ISSUE

1st message transmitted by telegraph, cent.

Telegraph Wires and Morse's First Transmitted Words "What Hath God Wrought" A371

ROTARY PRESS PRINTING
E.E. Plates of 200 subjects in four panes of 50.

1944, May 24 ***Perf. 11x10½***
924 A371 3c **bright purple** .25 .25
P# block of 4 1.00 —

PHILIPPINE ISSUE

Final resistance of the US and Philippine defenders on Corregidor to the Japanese invaders in 1942.

Aerial View of Corregidor, Manila Bay — A372

ROTARY PRESS PRINTING
E.E. Plates of 200 subjects in four panes of 50.

1944, Sept. 27 ***Perf. 11x10½***
925 A372 3c **deep violet** .25 .25
P# block of 4 1.50 —

MOTION PICTURE, 50th ANNIV.

Motion Picture Showing for Armed Forces in South Pacific — A373

ROTARY PRESS PRINTING
E.E. Plates of 200 subjects in four panes of 50.

1944, Oct. 31 ***Perf. 11x10½***
926 A373 3c **deep violet** .25 .25
P# block of 4 1.00 —

FLORIDA STATEHOOD, CENTENARY

State Seal, Gates of St. Augustine and Capitol at Tallahassee A374

ROTARY PRESS PRINTING
E.E. Plates of 200 subjects in four panes of 50.

1945, Mar. 3 ***Perf. 11x10½***
927 A374 3c **bright red violet** .25 .25
P# block of 4 1.40 —

UNITED NATIONS CONFERENCE ISSUE

United Nations Conference, San Francisco, Calif.

"Toward United Nations, April 25, 1945" — A375

ROTARY PRESS PRINTING

E.E. Plates of 200 subjects in four panes of 50.

1945, Apr. 25 *Perf. 11x10½*

928 A375 5c **ultramarine** .25 .25
P# block of 4 1.00 —

IWO JIMA (MARINES) ISSUE

Battle of Iwo Jima and honoring the achievements of the US Marines.

Marines Raising American Flag on Mount Suribachi, Iwo Jima, from a photograph by Joe Rosenthal — A376

ROTARY PRESS PRINTING

E.E. Plates of 200 subjects in four panes of 50.

1945, July 11 *Perf. 10½x11*

929 A376 3c **yellow green** .30 .25
P# block of 4 2.00 —

FRANKLIN D. ROOSEVELT ISSUE

Franklin Delano Roosevelt (1882-1945).

Roosevelt and Hyde Park Residence A377

Roosevelt and the "Little White House" at Warm Springs, Ga. — A378

Roosevelt and White House — A379

Roosevelt, Map of Western Hemisphere and Four Freedoms A380

ROTARY PRESS PRINTING

E.E. Plates of 200 subjects in four panes of 50.

1945-46 *Perf. 11x10½*

930 A377 1c **blue green,** *July 26, 1945* .25 .25
P# block of 4 1.00 —
931 A378 2c **carmine rose,** *Aug. 24, 1945* .25 .25
P# block of 4 1.00 —
932 A379 3c **purple,** *June 27, 1945* .25 .25
P# block of 4 1.00 —
933 A380 5c **bright blue,** *Jan. 30, 1946* .25 .25
P# block of 4 1.00 —
Nos. 930-933 (4) 1.00 1.00

ARMY ISSUE

Achievements of the US Army in World War II.

United States Troops Passing Arch of Triumph, Paris — A381

ROTARY PRESS PRINTING

E.E. Plates of 200 subjects in four panes of 50.

1945, Sept. 28 *Perf. 11x10½*

934 A381 3c **olive** .25 .25
P# block of 4 1.00 —

NAVY ISSUE

Achievements of the U.S. Navy in World War II.

United States Sailors — A382

ROTARY PRESS PRINTING

E.E. Plates of 200 subjects in four panes of 50.

1945, Oct. 27 *Perf. 11x10½*

935 A382 3c **blue** .25 .25
P# block of 4 1.00 —

COAST GUARD ISSUE

Achievements of the US Coast Guard in World War II.

Coast Guard Landing Craft and Supply Ship — A383

ROTARY PRESS PRINTING

E.E. Plates of 200 subjects in four panes of 50.

1945, Nov. 10 *Perf. 11x10½*

936 A383 3c **bright blue green** .25 .25
P# block of 4 1.00 —

ALFRED E. SMITH ISSUE

Alfred E. Smith, Governor of New York — A384

ROTARY PRESS PRINTING

E.E. Plates of 400 subjects in four panes of 100.

1945, Nov. 26 *Perf. 11x10½*

937 A384 3c **purple** .25 .25
P# block of 4 1.00
Pair with full vert. gutter btwn. —
Pair with full horiz. gutter btwn. *300.00*

TEXAS STATEHOOD, 100th ANNIV.

Flags of the United States and the State of Texas — A385

ROTARY PRESS PRINTING

E.E. Plates of 200 subjects in four panes of 50.

1945, Dec. 29 *Perf. 11x10½*

938 A385 3c **dark blue** .25 .25
P# block of 4 1.00 —

MERCHANT MARINE ISSUE

Achievements of the US Merchant Marine in World War II.

Liberty Ship Unloading Cargo — A386

ROTARY PRESS PRINTING

E.E. Plates of 200 subjects in four panes of 50.

1946, Feb. 26 *Perf. 11x10½*

939 A386 3c **blue green** .25 .25
P# block of 4 1.00 —

VETERANS OF WORLD WAR II ISSUE

Issued to honor all veterans of World War II.

Honorable Discharge Emblem — A387

ROTARY PRESS PRINTING

E.E. Plates of 400 subjects in four panes of 100.

1946, May 9 *Perf. 11x10½*

940 A387 3c **dark violet** .25 .25
P# block of 4 1.00 —
Pair with full vert. gutter btwn. *225.00*

TENNESSEE STATEHOOD, 150th ANNIV.

Andrew Jackson, John Sevier and State Capitol, Nashville A388

ROTARY PRESS PRINTING

E.E. Plates of 200 subjects in four panes of 50.

1946, June 1 *Perf. 11x10½*

941 A388 3c **dark violet** .25 .25
P# block of 4 1.00 —

IOWA STATEHOOD, 100th ANNIV.

Iowa State Flag and Map — A389

ROTARY PRESS PRINTING

E.E. Plates of 200 subjects in four panes of 50.

1946, Aug. 3 *Perf. 11x10½*

942 A389 3c **deep blue** .25 .25
P# block of 4 1.00 —

SMITHSONIAN INSTITUTION ISSUE

100th anniversary of the establishment of the Smithsonian Institution, Washington, D.C.

Smithsonian Institution A390

ROTARY PRESS PRINTING

E.E. Plates of 200 subjects in four panes of 50.

1946, Aug. 10 ***Perf. 11x10½***

943 A390 3c **violet brown** .25 .25

P# block of 4 1.00 —

KEARNY EXPEDITION ISSUE

100th anniversary of the entry of General Stephen Watts Kearny into Santa Fe.

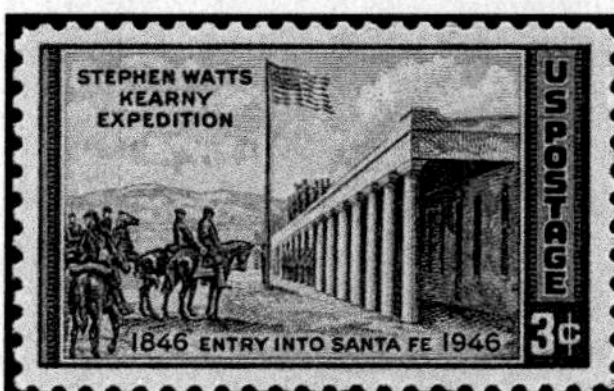

"Capture of Santa Fe" by Kenneth M. Chapman A391

ROTARY PRESS PRINTING

E.E. Plates of 200 subjects in four panes of 50.

1946, Oct. 16 ***Perf. 11x10½***

944 A391 3c **brown violet** .25 .25

P# block of 4 1.00 —

THOMAS A. EDISON ISSUE

Thomas A. Edison (1847-1931), Inventor — A392

ROTARY PRESS PRINTING

E.E. Plates of 280 subjects in four panes of 70.

1947, Feb. 11 ***Perf. 10½x11***

945 A392 3c **bright red violet** .25 .25

P# block of 4 1.00 —

JOSEPH PULITZER ISSUE

Joseph Pulitzer (1847-1911), Journalist, and Statue of Liberty A393

Designed by Victor S. McCloskey, Jr.

ROTARY PRESS PRINTING

E.E. Plates of 200 subjects in four panes of 50.

1947, Apr. 10 ***Perf. 11x10½***

946 A393 3c **purple** .25 .25

P# block of 4 1.00 —

POSTAGE STAMP CENTENARY ISSUE

Centenary of the first postage stamps issued by the United States Government

Washington and Franklin, Early and Modern Mail-carrying Vehicles A394

Designed by Leon Helguera.

ROTARY PRESS PRINTING

E.E. Plates of 200 subjects in four panes of 50.

1947, May 17 ***Perf. 11x10½***

947 A394 3c **deep blue** .25 .25

P# block of 4 1.00 —

CENTENARY INTERNATIONAL PHILATELIC EXHIBITION ISSUE

SOUVENIR SHEET

A395

Illustration reduced.

FLAT PLATE PRINTING

Plates of 30 subjects

1947, May 19 ***Imperf.***

948 A395 Pane of 2 .55 .45

a. 5c **blue**, type A1 .25 .25

b. 10c **brown orange**, type A2 .25 .25

Pane inscribed below stamps: "100th Anniversary United States Postage Stamps" and in the margins:

"PRINTED BY THE TREASURY DEPARTMENT, BUREAU OF ENGRAVING AND PRINTING. — UNDER AUTHORITY OF ROBERT E. HANNEGAN, POSTMASTER GENERAL. — IN COMPLIMENT TO THE CENTENARY INTERNATIONAL PHILATELIC EXHIBITION. — NEW YORK, N.Y., MAY 17-25, 1947."

Pane size varies: 96-98x66-68mm.

DOCTORS ISSUE

Issued to honor the physicians of America.

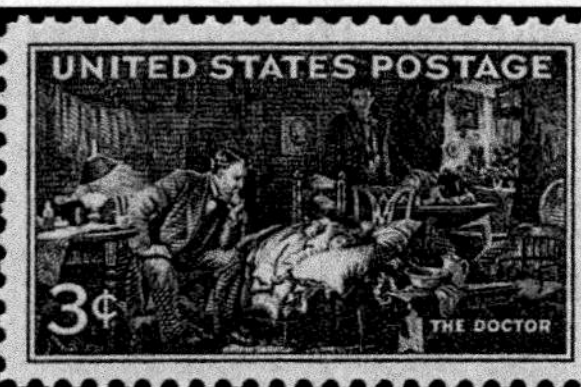

"The Doctor" by Sir Luke Fildes — A396

Designed by Charles R. Chickering.

ROTARY PRESS PRINTING

E.E. Plates of 200 subjects in four panes of 50.

1947, June 9 ***Perf. 11x10½***

949 A396 3c **brown violet** .25 .25

P# block of 4 1.00 —

UTAH ISSUE

Centenary of the settlement of Utah.

Pioneers Entering the Valley of Great Salt Lake — A397

Designed by Charles R. Chickering.

ROTARY PRESS PRINTING

E.E. Plates of 200 subjects in four panes of 50.

1947, July 24 ***Perf. 11x10½***

950 A397 3c **dark violet** .25 .25

P# block of 4 1.00 —

U.S. FRIGATE CONSTITUTION ISSUE

150th anniversary of the launching of the U.S. frigate Constitution ("Old Ironsides").

Naval Architect's Drawing of Frigate Constitution A398

Designed by Andrew H. Hepburn.

ROTARY PRESS PRINTING

E.E. Plates of 200 subjects in four panes of 50.

1947, Oct. 21 ***Perf. 11x10½***

951 A398 3c **blue green** .25 .25

P# block of 4 1.00 —

EVERGLADES NATIONAL PARK ISSUE

Dedication of the Everglades National Park, Florida, Dec. 6, 1947.

Great White Heron and Map of Florida — A399

Designed by Robert I. Miller, Jr.

ROTARY PRESS PRINTING

E.E. Plates of 200 subjects in four panes of 50.

1947, Dec. 5 ***Perf. 10½x11***

952 A399 3c **bright green** .25 .25

P# block of 4 1.00 —

GEORGE WASHINGTON CARVER ISSUE

5th anniversary of the death of Dr. George Washington Carver, (1864-1943), botanist.

Dr. George Washington Carver — A400

ROTARY PRESS PRINTING

E.E. Plates of 280 subjects in four panes of 70.

1948, Jan. 5 ***Perf. 10½x11***

953 A400 3c **bright red violet** .25 .25

P# block of 4 1.00 —

CALIFORNIA GOLD CENTENNIAL ISSUE

Sutter's Mill, Coloma, California A401

Designed by Charles R. Chickering.

ROTARY PRESS PRINTING

E.E. Plates of 200 subjects in four panes of 50.

1948, Jan. 24 ***Perf. 11x10½***

954 A401 3c **dark violet** .25 .25

P# block of 4 1.00 —

MISSISSIPPI TERRITORY ISSUE

Mississippi Territory establishment, 150th anniv.

Map, Seal of Mississippi Territory and Gov. Winthrop Sargent A402

Designed by William K. Schrage.

ROTARY PRESS PRINTING

E.E. Plates of 200 subjects in four panes of 50.

1948, Apr. 7 ***Perf. 11x10½***

955 A402 3c **brown violet**	.25	.25
P# block of 4	1.00	—

FOUR CHAPLAINS ISSUE

George L. Fox, Clark V. Poling, John P. Washington and Alexander D. Goode, the 4 chaplains who sacrificed their lives in the sinking of the S.S. Dorchester, Feb. 3, 1943.

Four Chaplains and Sinking S.S. Dorchester A403

Designed by Charles R. Chickering.

ROTARY PRESS PRINTING

E.E. Plates of 200 subjects in four panes of 50.

1948, May 28 ***Perf. 11x10½***

956 A403 3c **gray black**	.25	.25
P# block of 4	1.00	—

WISCONSIN STATEHOOD, 100th ANNIV.

Map on Scroll and State Capitol — A404

Designed by Victor S. McCloskey, Jr.

ROTARY PRESS PRINTING

E.E. Plates of 200 subjects in four panes of 50.

1948, May 29 ***Perf. 11x10½***

957 A404 3c **dark violet**	.25	.25
P# block of 4	1.00	—

SWEDISH PIONEER ISSUE

Centenary of the coming of the Swedish pioneers to the Middle West.

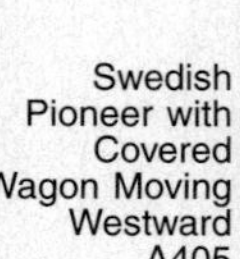

Swedish Pioneer with Covered Wagon Moving Westward A405

Designed by Charles R. Chickering.

ROTARY PRESS PRINTING

E.E. Plates of 200 subjects in four panes of 50.

1948, June 4 ***Perf. 11x10½***

958 A405 5c **deep blue**	.25	.25
P# block of 4	1.00	—

PROGRESS OF WOMEN ISSUE

Century of progress of American Women.

Elizabeth Stanton, Carrie Chapman Catt and Lucretia Mott — A406

Designed by Victor S. McCloskey, Jr.

ROTARY PRESS PRINTING

E.E. Plates of 200 subjects in four panes of 50.

1948, July 19 ***Perf. 11x10½***

959 A406 3c **dark violet**	.25	.25
P# block of 4	1.00	—

WILLIAM ALLEN WHITE ISSUE

William Allen White (1868-1944), Writer and Journalist — A407

ROTARY PRESS PRINTING

E.E. Plates of 280 subjects in four panes of 70.

1948, July 31 ***Perf. 10½x11***

960 A407 3c **bright red violet**	.25	.25
P# block of 4	1.00	—

UNITED STATES-CANADA FRIENDSHIP ISSUE

Century of friendship between the US and Canada.

Niagara Railway Suspension Bridge — A408

Designed by Leon Helguera, modeled by V. S. McCloskey, Jr.

ROTARY PRESS PRINTING

E.E. Plates of 200 subjects in four panes of 50.

1948, Aug. 2 ***Perf. 11x10½***

961 A408 3c **blue**	.25	.25
P# block of 4	1.00	—

FRANCIS SCOTT KEY ISSUE

Francis Scott Key (1779-1843), Maryland lawyer and author of "The Star-Spangled Banner" (1813).

Francis Scott Key and American Flags of 1814 and 1948 — A409

Designed by Victor S. McCloskey, Jr.

ROTARY PRESS PRINTING

E.E. Plates of 200 subjects in four panes of 50.

1948, Aug. 9 ***Perf. 11x10½***

962 A409 3c **rose pink**	.25	.25
P# block of 4	1.00	—

SALUTE TO YOUTH ISSUE

Issued to honor the Youth of America and to publicize "Youth Month," September, 1948.

Girl and Boy Carrying Books — A410

ROTARY PRESS PRINTING

E.E. Plates of 200 subjects in four panes of 50.

1948, Aug. 11 ***Perf. 11x10½***

963 A410 3c **deep blue**	.25	.25
P# block of 4	1.00	—

OREGON TERRITORY ISSUE

Centenary of the establishment of Oregon Territory.

John McLoughlin, Jason Lee and Wagon on Oregon Trail — A411

ROTARY PRESS PRINTING

E.E. Plates of 200 subjects in four panes of 50.

1948, Aug. 14 ***Perf. 11x10½***

964 A411 3c **brown red**	.25	.25
P# block of 4	1.00	—

HARLAN F. STONE ISSUE

Harlan Fiske Stone (1872-1946) of New York, Associate Justice of the Supreme Court, 1925-1941, and Chief Justice, 1941-1946 — A412

ROTARY PRESS PRINTING

E.E. Plates of 280 subjects in four panes of 70.

1948, Aug. 25 ***Perf. 10½x11***

965 A412 3c **bright red violet**	.25	.25
P# block of 4	1.00	—

PALOMAR MOUNTAIN OBSERVATORY ISSUE

Dedication, August 30, 1948.

Observatory, Palomar Mountain, California — A413

Designed by Victor S. McCloskey, Jr.

ROTARY PRESS PRINTING

E.E. Plates of 280 subjects in four panes of 70.

1948, Aug. 30 ***Perf. 10½x11***

966 A413 3c **blue**	.25	.25
P# block of 4	1.00	—
a. Vert. pair, imperf. between	*300.00*	

CLARA BARTON ISSUE

Clara Barton (1821-1912), Founder of the American Red Cross in 1882 — A414

Designed by Charles R. Chickering.

ROTARY PRESS PRINTING

E.E. Plates of 200 subjects in four panes of 50.

1948, Sept. 7 ***Perf. 11x10½***

967 A414 3c **rose pink** .25 .25
P# block of 4 1.00 —

POULTRY INDUSTRY CENTENNIAL ISSUE

Light Brahma Rooster A415

Designed by Charles R. Chickering.

ROTARY PRESS PRINTING

E.E. Plates of 200 subjects in four panes of 50.

1948, Sept. 9 ***Perf. 11x10½***

968 A415 3c **sepia** .25 .25
P# block of 4 1.10 —

GOLD STAR MOTHERS ISSUE

Issued to honor the mothers of deceased members of the United States armed forces.

Star and Palm Frond — A416

Designed by Charles R. Chickering.

ROTARY PRESS PRINTING

E.E. Plates of 200 subjects in four panes of 50.

1948, Sept. 21 ***Perf. 10½x11***

969 A416 3c **orange yellow** .25 .25
P# block of 4 1.00 —

FORT KEARNY ISSUE

Establishment of Fort Kearny, Neb., centenary.

Fort Kearny and Pioneer Group — A417

ROTARY PRESS PRINTING

E.E. Plates of 200 subjects in four panes of 50.

1948, Sept. 22 ***Perf. 11x10½***

970 A417 3c **violet** .25 .25
P# block of 4 1.00 —

VOLUNTEER FIREMEN ISSUE

300th anniv. of the organization of the 1st volunteer firemen in America by Peter Stuyvesant.

Peter Stuyvesant, Early and Modern Fire Engines A418

ROTARY PRESS PRINTING

E.E. Plates of 200 subjects in four panes of 50.

1948, Oct. 4 ***Perf. 11x10½***

971 A418 3c **bright rose carmine** .25 .25
P# block of 4 1.00 —

INDIAN CENTENNIAL ISSUE

Centenary of the arrival in Indian Territory, later Oklahoma, of the Five Civilized Indian Tribes: Cherokee, Chickasaw, Choctaw, Muscogee and Seminole.

Map of Indian Territory and Seals of Five Tribes — A419

ROTARY PRESS PRINTING

E.E. Plates of 200 subjects in four panes of 50.

1948, Oct. 15 ***Perf. 11x10½***

972 A419 3c **dark brown** .25 .25
P# block of 4 1.00 —

ROUGH RIDERS ISSUE

50th anniversary of the organization of the Rough Riders of the Spanish-American War.

Statue of Capt. William O. (Bucky) O'Neill by Solon H. Borglum A420

Designed by Victor S. McCloskey, Jr.

ROTARY PRESS PRINTING

E.E. Plates of 200 subjects in four panes of 50.

1948, Oct. 27 ***Perf. 11x10½***

973 A420 3c **violet brown** .25 .25
P# block of 4 1.20 —

JULIETTE LOW ISSUE

Low (1860-1927), founder of the Girl Scouts of America. Mrs. Low organized the 1st Girl Guides troop in 1912 at Savannah. The name was changed to Girl Scouts in 1913 and headquarters moved to New York.

Juliette Gordon Low and Girl Scout Emblem A421

Designed by William K. Schrage.

ROTARY PRESS PRINTING

E.E. Plates of 200 subjects in four panes of 50.

1948, Oct. 29 ***Perf. 11x10½***

974 A421 3c **blue green** .25 .25
P# block of 4 1.00 —

WILL ROGERS ISSUE

Will Rogers, (1879-1935), Humorist and Political Commentator. — A422

ROTARY PRESS PRINTING

E.E. Plates of 280 subjects in four panes of 70.

1948, Nov. 4 ***Perf. 10½x11***

975 A422 3c **bright red violet** .25 .25
P# block of 4 1.00 —

FORT BLISS CENTENNIAL ISSUE

Fort Bliss, El Paso, Texas, and Rocket Firing — A423

Designed by Charles R. Chickering.

ROTARY PRESS PRINTING

E.E. Plates of 280 subjects in four panes of 70.

1948, Nov. 5 ***Perf. 10½x11***

976 A423 3c **henna brown** .25 .25
P# block of 4 1.00 —

MOINA MICHAEL ISSUE

Moina Michael (1870-1944), educator who originated (1918) the Flanders Field Poppy Day idea as a memorial to the war dead.

Moina Michael and Poppy Plant — A424

ROTARY PRESS PRINTING

E.E. Plates of 200 subjects in four panes of 50.

1948, Nov. 9 ***Perf. 11x10½***

977 A424 3c **rose pink** .25 .25
P# block of 4 1.00 —

GETTYSBURG ADDRESS ISSUE

85th anniversary of Abraham Lincoln's address at Gettysburg, Pennsylvania.

Abraham Lincoln and Quotation from Gettysburg Address A425

Designed by Charles R. Chickering.

ROTARY PRESS PRINTING

E.E. Plates of 200 subjects in four panes of 50.

1948, Nov. 19 ***Perf. 11x10½***

978 A425 3c **bright blue** .25 .25
P# block of 4 1.25 —

AMERICAN TURNERS ISSUE

Formation of the American Turners Soc., cent.

Torch and Emblem of American Turners — A426

Designed by Alvin R. Meissner.

ROTARY PRESS PRINTING

E.E. Plates of 200 subjects in four panes of 50.

1948, Nov. 20 ***Perf. 10½x11***

979 A426 3c **carmine** .25 .25
P# block of 4 1.00 —

JOEL CHANDLER HARRIS ISSUE

Joel Chandler Harris (1848-1908), Georgia Writer, Creator of "Uncle Remus" and newspaperman. — A427

ROTARY PRESS PRINTING

E.E. Plates of 280 subjects in four panes of 70.

1948, Dec. 9 ***Perf. 10½x11***

980 A427 3c **bright red violet** .25 .25
P# block of 4 1.00 —

MINNESOTA TERRITORY ISSUE

Establishment of Minnesota Territory, cent.

Pioneer and Red River Oxcart — A428

ROTARY PRESS PRINTING

E.E. Plates of 200 subjects in four panes of 50.

1949, Mar. 3 ***Perf. 11x10½***

981 A428 3c **blue green** .25 .25
P# block of 4 1.00 —

WASHINGTON AND LEE UNIVERSITY ISSUE

Bicentenary of Washington and Lee University.

George Washington, Robert E. Lee and University Building, Lexington, Va. — A429

ROTARY PRESS PRINTING

E.E. Plates of 200 subjects in four panes of 50.

1949, Apr. 12 ***Perf. 11x10½***

982 A429 3c **ultramarine** .25 .25
P# block of 4 1.00 —

PUERTO RICO ELECTION ISSUE

First gubernatorial election in the Territory of Puerto Rico, Nov. 2, 1948.

Puerto Rican Farmer Holding Cogwheel and Ballot Box — A430

ROTARY PRESS PRINTING

E.E. Plates of 200 subjects in four panes of 50.

1949, Apr. 27 ***Perf. 11x10½***

983 A430 3c **green** .25 .25
P# block of 4 1.00 —

ANNAPOLIS TERCENTENARY ISSUE

Founding of Annapolis, Maryland, 300th anniv.

James Stoddert's 1718 Map of Regions about Annapolis, Redrawn A431

ROTARY PRESS PRINTING

E.E. Plates of 200 subjects in four panes of 50.

1949, May 23 ***Perf. 11x10½***

984 A431 3c **aquamarine** .25 .25
P# block of 4 1.00 —

G.A.R. ISSUE

Final encampment of the Grand Army of the Republic, Indianapolis, Aug. 28 - Sept. 1, 1949.

Union Soldier and G.A.R. Veteran of 1949 — A432

Designed by Charles R. Chickering.

ROTARY PRESS PRINTING

E.E. Plates of 200 subjects in four panes of 50.

1949, Aug. 29 ***Perf. 11x10½***

985 A432 3c **bright rose carmine** .25 .25
P# block of 4 1.00 —

EDGAR ALLAN POE ISSUE

Edgar Allan Poe (1809-1849), Boston-born Poet, Story Writer and Editor — A433

Inner Frame Line Missing

ROTARY PRESS PRINTING

E.E. Plates of 280 subjects in four panes of 70.

1949, Oct. 7 ***Perf. 10½x11***

986 A433 3c **bright red violet** .25 .25
P# block of 4 1.00 —
Thin outer frame line at top, inner line missing (24143 LL 42) 6.00

AMERICAN BANKERS ASSOCIATION ISSUE

75th anniv. of the formation of the Association.

Coin, Symbolizing Fields of Banking Service A434

Designed by Charles R. Chickering.

ROTARY PRESS PRINTING

E.E. Plates of 200 subjects in four panes of 50.

1950, Jan. 3 ***Perf. 11x10½***

987 A434 3c **yellow green** .25 .25
P# block of 4 1.00 —

SAMUEL GOMPERS ISSUE

Samuel Gompers (1850-1924), British-born American Labor Leader — A435

ROTARY PRESS PRINTING

E.E. Plates of 280 subjects in four panes of 70.

1950, Jan. 27 ***Perf. 10½x11***

988 A435 3c **bright red violet** .25 .25
P# block of 4 1.00 —

NATIONAL CAPITAL SESQUICENTENNIAL ISSUE

150th anniversary of the establishment of the National Capital, Washington, D.C.

Statue of Freedom on Capitol Dome — A436

Executive Mansion A437

Supreme Court Building A438

United States Capitol — A439

ROTARY PRESS PRINTING

E.E. Plates of 200 subjects in four panes of 50.

1950 ***Perf. 10½x11, 11x10½***

989 A436 3c **bright blue,** *Apr. 20* .25 .25
P# block of 4 1.00 —
990 A437 3c **deep green,** *June 12* .25 .25
P# block of 4 1.00 —
991 A438 3c **light violet,** *Aug. 2* .25 .25
P# block of 4 1.00 —
992 A439 3c **bright red violet,** *Nov. 22* .25 .25
P# block of 4 1.20 —
Gripper cracks (24285 UL 11) 4.50 3.00
Nos. 989-992 (4) 1.00 1.00

RAILROAD ENGINEERS ISSUE

Issued to honor the Railroad Engineers of America. Stamp portrays John Luther (Casey) Jones (1864-1900), locomotive engineer killed in train wreck near Vaughn, Miss.

"Casey" Jones and Locomotives of 1900 and 1950 — A440

ROTARY PRESS PRINTING

E.E. Plates of 200 subjects in four panes of 50.

1950, Apr. 29 ***Perf. 11x10½***

993 A440 3c **violet brown** .25 .25
P# block of 4 1.00 —

KANSAS CITY, MISSOURI, CENTENARY ISSUE

Kansas City, Missouri, incorporation.

Kansas City Skyline, 1950 and Westport Landing, 1850 — A441

ROTARY PRESS PRINTING

E.E. Plates of 200 subjects in four panes of 50.

1950, June 3 *Perf. 11x10½*

994 A441 3c **violet**	.25	.25
P# block of 4	1.00	—

BOY SCOUTS ISSUE

Honoring the Boy Scouts of America on the occasion of the 2nd National Jamboree, Valley Forge, Pa.

Three Boys, Statue of Liberty and Scout Badge A442

ROTARY PRESS PRINTING

E.E. Plates of 200 subjects in four panes of 50.

1950, June 30 *Perf. 11x10½*

995 A442 3c **sepia**	.25	.25
P# block of 4	1.00	—

INDIANA TERRITORY ISSUE

Establishment of Indiana Territory, 150th anniv.

Gov. William Henry Harrison and First Indiana Capitol, Vincennes A443

ROTARY PRESS PRINTING

E.E. Plates of 200 subjects in four panes of 50.

1950, July 4 *Perf. 11x10½*

996 A443 3c **bright blue**	.25	.25
P# block of 4	1.00	—

CALIFORNIA STATEHOOD ISSUE

Gold Miner, Pioneers and S.S. Oregon A444

ROTARY PRESS PRINTING

E.E. Plates of 200 subjects in four panes of 50.

1950, Sept. 9 *Perf. 11x10½*

997 A444 3c **yellow orange**	.25	.25
P# block of 4	1.00	—

UNITED CONFEDERATE VETERANS FINAL REUNION ISSUE

Final reunion of the United Confederate Veterans, Norfolk, Virginia, May 30, 1951.

Confederate Soldier and United Confederate Veteran A445

ROTARY PRESS PRINTING

E.E. Plates of 200 subjects in four panes of 50.

1951, May 30 *Perf. 11x10½*

998 A445 3c **gray**	.25	.25
P# block of 4	1.00	—

NEVADA CENTENNIAL ISSUE

Centenary of the settlement of Nevada.

Carson Valley, c. 1851 — A446

Designed by Charles R. Chickering.

ROTARY PRESS PRINTING

E.E. Plates of 200 subjects in four panes of 50.

1951, July 14 *Perf. 11x10½*

999 A446 3c **light olive green**	.25	.25
P# block of 4	1.00	—

LANDING OF CADILLAC ISSUE

250th anniversary of the landing of Antoine de la Mothe Cadillac at Detroit.

Detroit Skyline and Cadillac Landing A447

ROTARY PRESS PRINTING

E.E. Plates of 200 subjects in four panes of 50.

1951, July 24 *Perf. 11x10½*

1000 A447 3c **blue**	.25	.25
P# block of 4	1.00	—

COLORADO STATEHOOD, 75th ANNIV.

Colorado Capitol, Mount of the Holy Cross, Columbine and Bronco Buster by Proctor A448

ROTARY PRESS PRINTING

E.E. Plates of 200 subjects in four panes of 50.

1951, Aug. 1 *Perf. 11x10½*

1001 A448 3c **blue violet**	.25	.25
P# block of 4	1.00	—

AMERICAN CHEMICAL SOCIETY ISSUE

75th anniv. of the formation of the Society.

A.C.S. Emblem and Symbols of Chemistry A449

ROTARY PRESS PRINTING

E.E. Plates of 200 subjects in four panes of 50.

1951, Sept. 4 *Perf. 11x10½*

1002 A449 3c **violet brown**	.25	.25
P# block of 4	1.00	—

BATTLE OF BROOKLYN, 175th ANNIV.

Gen. George Washington Evacuating Army; Fulton Ferry House at Right — A450

ROTARY PRESS PRINTING

E.E. Plates of 200 subjects in four panes of 50.

1951, Dec. 10 *Perf. 11x10½*

1003 A450 3c **violet**	.25	.25
P# block of 4	1.00	—

BETSY ROSS ISSUE

200th anniv. of the birth of Betsy Ross, maker of the first American flag.

"Birth of Our Nation's Flag," by Charles H. Weisgerber — Betsy Ross Showing Flag to Gen. George Washington, Robert Morris and George Ross — A451

ROTARY PRESS PRINTING

E.E. Plates of 200 subjects in four panes of 50.

1952, Jan. 2 *Perf. 11x10½*

1004 A451 3c **carmine rose**	.25	.25
P# block of 4	1.00	—

4-H CLUB ISSUE

Farm, Club Emblem, Boy and Girl — A452

ROTARY PRESS PRINTING

E.E. Plates of 200 subjects in four panes of 50.

1952, Jan. 15 *Perf. 11x10½*

1005 A452 3c **blue green**	.25	.25
P# block of 4	1.00	—

B. & O. RAILROAD ISSUE

125th anniv. of the granting of a charter to the Baltimore and Ohio Railroad Company by the Maryland Legislature.

Charter and Three Stages of Rail Transportation A453

ROTARY PRESS PRINTING

E.E. Plates of 200 subjects in four panes of 50.

1952, Feb. 28 *Perf. 11x10½*

1006 A453 3c **bright blue**	.25	.25
P# block of 4	1.00	—

A. A. A. ISSUE

50th anniversary of the formation of the American Automobile Association.

School Girls and Safety Patrolman Automobiles of 1902 and 1952 — A454

ROTARY PRESS PRINTING

E.E. Plates of 200 subjects in four panes of 50.

1952, Mar. 4 ***Perf. 11x10½***

1007 A454 3c **deep blue** .25 .25
P# block of 4 1.00 —

NATO ISSUE

Signing of the North Atlantic Treaty, 3rd anniv.

Torch of Liberty and Globe — A455

ROTARY PRESS PRINTING

E.E. Plates of 400 subjects in four panes of 100.

1952, Apr. 4 ***Perf. 11x10½***

1008 A455 3c **deep violet** .25 .25
P# block of 4 1.00 —

GRAND COULEE DAM ISSUE

50 years of Federal cooperation in developing the resources of rivers and streams in the West.

Spillway, Grand Coulee Dam — A456

ROTARY PRESS PRINTING

E.E. Plates of 200 subjects in four panes of 50.

1952, May 15 ***Perf. 11x10½***

1009 A456 3c **blue green** .25 .25
P# block of 4 1.00 —

LAFAYETTE ISSUE

175th anniversary of the arrival of Marquis de Lafayette in America.

Marquis de Lafayette, Flags, Cannon and Landing Party — A457

Designed by Victor S. McCloskey, Jr.

ROTARY PRESS PRINTING

E.E. Plates of 200 subjects in four panes of 50.

1952, June 13 ***Perf. 11x10½***

1010 A457 3c **bright blue** .25 .25
P# block of 4 1.00 —

MT. RUSHMORE MEMORIAL ISSUE

Dedication of the Mt. Rushmore National Memorial in the Black Hills of South Dakota, 25th anniv.

Sculptured Heads on Mt. Rushmore — A458

Designed by William K. Schrage.

ROTARY PRESS PRINTING

E.E. Plates of 200 subjects in four panes of 50.

1952, Aug. 11 ***Perf. 10½x11***

1011 A458 3c **blue green** .25 .25
P# block of 4 1.00 —

ENGINEERING CENTENNIAL ISSUE

American Society of Civil Engineers founding.

George Washington Bridge and Covered Bridge of 1850's — A459

ROTARY PRESS PRINTING

E.E. Plates of 200 subjects in four panes of 50.

1952, Sept. 6 ***Perf. 11x10½***

1012 A459 3c **violet blue** .25 .25
P# block of 4 1.00 —

SERVICE WOMEN ISSUE

Women in the United States Armed Services.

Women of the Marine Corps, Army, Navy and Air Force — A460

ROTARY PRESS PRINTING

E.E. Plates of 200 subjects in four panes of 50.

1952, Sept. 11 ***Perf. 11x10½***

1013 A460 3c **deep blue** .25 .25
P# block of 4 1.00 —

GUTENBERG BIBLE ISSUE

Printing of the 1st book, the Holy Bible, from movable type, by Johann Gutenberg, 500th anniv.

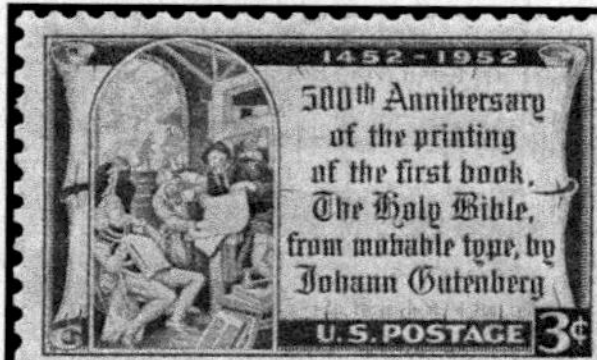

Gutenberg Showing Proof to the Elector of Mainz — A461

ROTARY PRESS PRINTING

E.E. Plates of 200 subjects in four panes of 50.

1952, Sept. 30 ***Perf. 11x10½***

1014 A461 3c **violet** .25 .25
P# block of 4 1.00 —

NEWSPAPER BOYS ISSUE

Newspaper Boy, Torch and Group of Homes A462

ROTARY PRESS PRINTING

E.E. Plates of 200 subjects in four panes of 50.

1952, Oct. 4 ***Perf. 11x10½***

1015 A462 3c **violet** .25 .25
P# block of 4 1.00 —

RED CROSS ISSUE

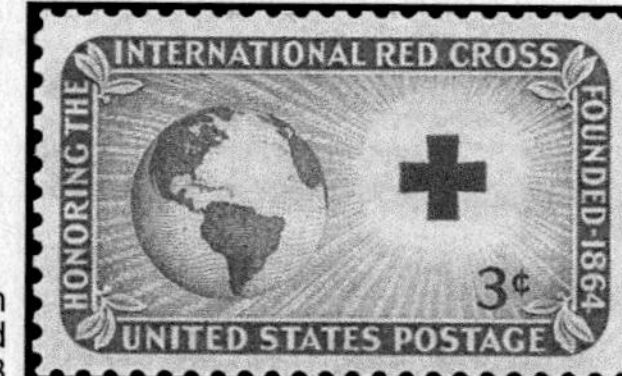

Globe, Sun and Cross — A463

ROTARY PRESS PRINTING

Cross Typographed

E.E. Plates of 200 subjects in four panes of 50.

1952, Nov. 21 ***Perf. 11x10½***

1016 A463 3c **deep blue & carmine** .25 .25
P# block of 4 1.00 —

NATIONAL GUARD ISSUE

National Guardsman, Amphibious Landing and Disaster Service A464

ROTARY PRESS PRINTING

E.E. Plates of 200 subjects in four panes of 50.

1953, Feb. 23 ***Perf. 11x10½***

1017 A464 3c **bright blue** .25 .25
P# block of 4 1.00 —

OHIO STATEHOOD, 150th ANNIV.

Ohio Map, State Seal, Buckeye Leaf — A465

ROTARY PRESS PRINTING

E.E. Plates of 280 subjects in four panes of 70.

1953, Mar. 2 ***Perf. 11x10½***

1018 A465 3c **chocolate** .25 .25
P# block of 4 1.00 —

WASHINGTON TERRITORY ISSUE

Organization of Washington Territory, cent.

Medallion, Pioneers and Washington Scene — A466

ROTARY PRESS PRINTING

E.E. Plates of 200 subjects in four panes of 50.

1953, Mar. 2 ***Perf. 11x10½***

1019 A466 3c **green** .25 .25
P# block of 4 1.00 —

LOUISIANA PURCHASE, 150th ANNIV.

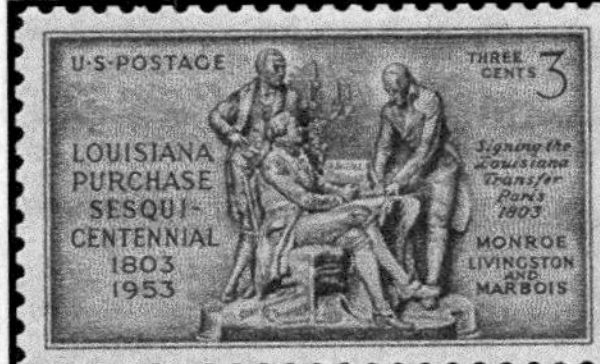

James Monroe, Robert R. Livingston and Marquis Francois de Barbé-Marbois A467

ROTARY PRESS PRINTING

E.E. Plates of 200 subjects in four panes of 50.

1953, Apr. 30 ***Perf. 11x10½***

1020 A467 3c **violet brown** .25 .25
P# block of 4 1.00 —

OPENING OF JAPAN CENTENNIAL ISSUE

Centenary of Commodore Matthew Calbraith Perry's negotiations with Japan, which opened her doors to foreign trade.

Commodore Matthew C. Perry and First Anchorage off Tokyo Bay — A468

ROTARY PRESS PRINTING

E.E. Plates of 200 subjects in four panes of 50.

1953, July 14 ***Perf. 11x10½***

1021 A468 5c **green** .25 .25
P# block of 4 1.00 —

AMERICAN BAR ASSOCIATION, 75th ANNIV.

Section of Frieze, Supreme Court Room — A469

ROTARY PRESS PRINTING

E.E. Plates of 200 subjects in four panes of 50.

1953, Aug. 24 ***Perf. 11x10½***

1022 A469 3c **rose violet** .25 .25
P# block of 4 1.00 —

SAGAMORE HILL ISSUE

Opening of Sagamore Hill, Theodore Roosevelt's home, as a national shrine.

Home of Theodore Roosevelt A470

ROTARY PRESS PRINTING

E.E. Plates of 200 subjects in four panes of 50.

1953, Sept. 14 ***Perf. 11x10½***

1023 A470 3c **yellow green** .25 .25
P# block of 4 1.00 —

FUTURE FARMERS ISSUE

25th anniversary of the organization of Future Farmers of America.

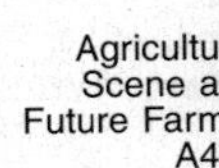

Agricultural Scene and Future Farmer A471

ROTARY PRESS PRINTING

E.E. Plates of 200 subjects in four panes of 50.

1953, Oct. 13 ***Perf. 11x10½***

1024 A471 3c **deep blue** .25 .25
P# block of 4 1.00 —

TRUCKING INDUSTRY ISSUE

50th anniv. of the Trucking Industry in the US.

Truck, Farm and Distant City — A472

ROTARY PRESS PRINTING

E.E. Plates of 200 subjects in four panes of 50.

1953, Oct. 27 ***Perf. 11x10½***

1025 A472 3c **violet** .25 .25
P# block of 4 1.00 —

GENERAL PATTON ISSUE

Honoring Gen. George S. Patton, Jr. (1885-1945), and the armored forces of the US Army.

Gen. George S. Patton, Jr., and Tanks in Action — A473

ROTARY PRESS PRINTING

E.E. Plates of 200 subjects in four panes of 50.

1953, Nov. 11 ***Perf. 11x10½***

1026 A473 3c **blue violet** .25 .25
P# block of 4 1.00 —

NEW YORK CITY, 300th ANNIV.

Dutch Ship in New Amsterdam Harbor A474

ROTARY PRESS PRINTING

E.E. Plates of 200 subjects in four panes of 50.

1953, Nov. 20 ***Perf. 11x10½***

1027 A474 3c **bright red violet** .25 .25
P# block of 4 1.00 —

GADSDEN PURCHASE ISSUE

Centenary of James Gadsden's purchase of territory from Mexico to adjust the US-Mexico boundary.

Map and Pioneer Group — A475

ROTARY PRESS PRINTING

E.E. Plates of 200 subjects in four panes of 50.

1953, Dec. 30 ***Perf. 11x10½***

1028 A475 3c **copper brown** .25 .25
P# block of 4 1.00 —

COLUMBIA UNIVERSITY, 200th ANNIV.

Low Memorial Library A476

ROTARY PRESS PRINTING

E.E. Plates of 200 subjects in four panes of 50.

1954, Jan. 4 ***Perf. 11x10½***

1029 A476 3c **blue** .25 .25
P# block of 4 1.00 —

Wet and Dry Printings

In 1953 the Bureau of Engraving and Printing began experiments in printing on "dry" paper (moisture content 5-10 per cent). In previous "wet" printings the paper had a moisture content of 15-35 per cent.

The new process required a thicker, stiffer paper, special types of inks and greater pressure to force the paper into the recessed plates. The "dry" printings show whiter paper, a higher sheen on the surface, feel thicker and stiffer, and the designs stand out more clearly than on the "wet" printings.

Nos. 832c and 1041 (flat plate) were the first "dry" printings to be issued of flat-plate, regular-issue stamps. No. 1063 was the first rotary press stamp to be produced entirely by "dry" printing. Nos. QE1a, QE2a and QE3a, RF26A and RW21 (all flat plate) were the first "dry" printings of back-of-the-book issue stamps.

Stamps printed by both the "wet" and "dry" process are Nos. 1030, 1031, 1035, 1035a, 1036, 1039, 1049, 1050-1052, 1054, 1055, 1057, 1058, C34-C36, C39, C39a, J78, J80-J84, QE1-QE3, RF26-RF28, S1, S1a, S2, S2a, S3. The "wet" printed 4c coil, No. 1058b, exists only Bureau precanceled.

In the Liberty Issue listings that follow, wet printings are listed first, followed by dry printings, except for Nos. 1058 and 1058b. Where only one type of printing of a stamp is indicated, it is "dry."

All postage stamps have been printed by the "dry" process since the late 1950s.

LIBERTY ISSUE

Benjamin Franklin — A477

George Washington — A478

Palace of the Governors, Santa Fe — A478a

Mount Vernon — A479

Thomas Jefferson — A480

Bunker Hill Monument and Massachusetts Flag, 1776 — A481

Statue of Liberty — A482

Abraham Lincoln — A483

The Hermitage, Home of Andrew Jackson, near Nashville — A484

James Monroe — A485

Theodore Roosevelt — A486

Woodrow Wilson — A487

Statue of Liberty — A488

Statue of Liberty — A489

The Alamo, San Antonio — A490

Independence Hall — A491

Statue of Liberty — A491a

Benjamin Harrison — A492

John Jay — A493

Monticello, Home of Thomas Jefferson, near Charlottesville, Va. — A494

Paul Revere — A495

Robert E. Lee — A496

John Marshall — A497

Susan B. Anthony — A498

Patrick Henry — A499

Alexander Hamilton — A500

ROTARY PRESS PRINTING

E.E. Plates of 400 subjects in four panes of 100

1954-68 ***Perf. 11x10½***

1030 A477 ½c **red orange,** wet printing, *Oct. 20, 1955* .25 .25
On cover 1.50
P# block of 4 1.00 —
a. ½c **red orange**, dry printing, *May 1958* .25 .25
On cover 1.50
P# block of 4 (#25980 and up) 1.00 —

Counterfeits exist of No. 1030. See the Postal Counterfeits section of this catalog.

1031 A478 1c **dark green**, wet printing, *Aug. 28, 1954* .25 .25
On cover 1.50
P# block of 4 1.00 —
b. 1c **dark green**, dry printing, *Mar. 1956* .25 .25
On cover 1.50
P# block of 4 (#25326 and up) 1.00 —
Pair with full vert. gutter between *150.00*
Pair with full horiz. gutter between *150.00*

Perf. 10½x11

1031A A478a 1¼c **turquoise**, *June 17, 1960* .25 .25
On cover 1.00
P# block of 4 1.00 —

1032 A479 1½c **brown carmine**, *Feb. 22, 1956* .25 .25
On cover 1.00
Precanceled single on bulk rate cover 3.00
P# block of 4 1.00 —

Perf. 11x10½

1033 A480 2c **carmine rose**, *Sept. 15, 1954* .25 .25
On cover .50
Single franking on noncarrier drop-rate cover *125.00*
P# block of 4 1.00 —
Pair with full vert. gutter btwn. —
Pair with full horiz. gutter btwn. —
a. Silkote paper *275.*
P# block of 4 *2,000.*
Single franking on third-class cover *15,000.*

Silkote paper was used in 1954 for an experimental printing of 50,000 stamps. The stamps were put on sale at the Westbrook, Maine post office in Dec. 17, 1954. Only plates 25061 and 25062 were used to print No. 1033a (these plates also used to print No. 1033 on normal paper). Competent expertization is required for No. 1033a.

1034 A481 2½c **gray blue**, *June 17, 1959* .25 .25
On cover 1.00
P# block of 4 1.00 —

1035 A482 3c **deep violet**, wet printing, *June 30, 1954* .25 .25
On cover .50
Single franking on noncarrier drop-rate cover *350.00*
P# block of 4 1.00 —
a. Booklet pane of 6, *June 30, 1954* 3.50 *1.25*
b. Horiz. pairs, imperf. btwn in #1035a with foldover (two pairs recorded in two full panes) or miscut (three pairs from pane) *5,000.*
c. 3c **deep violet**, dry printing .25 .25
On cover .50
Single franking on certificate of mailing 10.00
P# block of 4 (#25235 and up) 1.00 —
Pair with full vert. gutter between *150.00*
Pair with full horiz. gutter between *150.00*
d. Booklet pane of 6, dry printing 4.50 *1.50*
e. Tagged, *July 6, 1966* .35 .25
On cover 25.00
P# block of 4 5.75 —
f. Imperf., pair *3,000.*
g. Horiz. pair, imperf. between *1,000.*

No. 1057b measures about 19½x22mm; No. 1035f, about 18¾x22½mm.

1036 A483 4c **red violet,** wet printing, *Nov. 19, 1954* .25 .25
On cover .50
Single franking on noncarrier drop-rate cover *400.00*
P# block of 4 1.00 —
a. 4c **red violet**, dry printing .25 .25
On cover .50
P# block of 4 (#25445 and up) 1.00 —
Pair with full vert. gutter between *600.00*
Pair with full horiz. gutter between *850.00*
b. Booklet pane of 6, *July 31, 1958* 2.75 *1.25*
c. As "b," imperf. horiz. *10,000.*
d. Horiz. pair, imperf between *4,150.*
e. Tagged, *Nov. 2, 1963* .65 .40
On cover 30.00
P# block of 4 9.00 —

No. 1036d resulted from a booklet pane foldover after perforating and before cutting into panes.

Counterfeits exist of No. 1036. See the Postal Counterfeits section of this catalog.

Perf. 10½x11

1037 A484 4½c **blue green,** *Mar. 16, 1959* .25 .25
On cover 5.00
Single franking on third-class cover 15.00
P# block of 4 1.00 —

Perf. 11x10½

1038 A485 5c **deep blue**, *Dec. 2, 1954* .25 .25
On cover 3.00
Single franking on certificate of mailing 20.00
Precanceled single franking on international printed matter cover 20.00
P# block of 4 1.00 —
Pair with full vert. gutter btwn. *200.00*

1039 A486 6c **carmine**, wet printing, *Nov. 18, 1955* .40 .25
On cover 1.00
P# block of 4 2.00 —
Pair with full vert. gutter btwn. *2,750.*
a. 6c **carmine**, dry printing .25 .25
On cover 1.00
P# block of 4 (#25427 and up) 1.20 —
b. Imperf, block of 4 (unique) *23,000.*

1040 A487 7c **rose carmine**, *Jan. 10, 1956* .25 .25
On cover 1.00
P# block of 4 1.00 —
a. 7c **dark rose carmine** .25 .25
P# block of 4 1.20 —

FLAT PLATE PRINTING

Plates of 400 subjects in four panes of 100 each

Size: 22.7mm high

Perf. 11

1041 A488 8c **dark violet blue & carmine,** *Apr. 9, 1954* .25 .25
On cover 2.00
P# block of 4, 2# 1.80 —
Corner P# block of 4, blue # only *2,000.*
Corner P# block of 4, red # only —
a. Double impression of carmine *575.00* —

FLAT PRINTING PLATES
Frame: 24912-13-14-15, 24926, 24929-30, 24932-33.
Vignette: 24916-17-18-19-20, 24935-36-37, 24939.
See note following No. 1041B.

ROTARY PRESS PRINTING

Plates of 400 subjects in four panes of 100 each

Size: 22.9mm high

Perf. 11

1041B A488 8c **dark violet blue & carmine,** *Apr. 9, 1954* .40 .25
On cover 2.00
P# block of 4, 2# 4.25 —

ROTARY PRINTING PLATES
Frame: 24923-24, 24928, 24940, 24942.
Vignette: 24927, 24938.
No. 1041B is slightly taller than No. 1041, about the thickness of one line of engraving.

GIORI PRESS PRINTING

Plates of 400 subjects in four panes of 100 each

Redrawn design

Perf. 11

1042 A489 8c **dark violet blue & carmine rose,** *Mar. 22, 1958* .25 .25
On cover 2.00
P# block of 4 1.00 —

The 8c John J. Pershing stamp, formerly No. 1042A, is now included with the regular issue of 1961-66. See No. 1214.

ROTARY PRESS PRINTING

E.E. Plates of 400 subjects in four panes of 100 each

Perf. 10½x11

1043 A490 9c **rose lilac,** *June 14, 1956* .30 .25
On cover 3.00
P# block of 4 1.50 —
a. 9c **dark rose lilac** .30 .25
P# block of 4 1.50 —

1044 A491 10c **rose lake,** *July 4, 1956* .30 .25
On cover 2.00
Single franking on private aerogramme *300.00*
P# block of 4 1.25 —
b. 10c **dark rose lake** .25 .25
P# block of 4 1.00 —
d. Tagged, *July 6, 1966* 2.00 1.00
On cover 30.00
P# block of 4 *35.00* —

No. 1044b is from later printings and is on a harder, whiter paper than No. 1044.

Counterfeits exist of No. 1044. See the Postal Counterfeits section of this catalog.

GIORI PRESS PRINTING

Plates of 400 subjects in four panes of 100.

Perf. 11

1044A A491a 11c **carmine & dark violet blue,** *June 15, 1961* .30 .25
On cover 2.00
Single franking on international airmail postcard 5.00
Single franking on private aerogram 50.00
P# block of 4 1.40 —
c. Tagged, *Jan. 11, 1967* 3.00 1.60
On cover *200.00*
P# block of 4 *60.00* —

ROTARY PRESS PRINTING

E.E. Plates of 400 subjects in four panes of 100 each

Perf. 11x10½

1045 A492 12c **red,** *June 6, 1959* .35 .25
On cover 3.00
P# block of 4 1.60 —
a. Tagged, *1968* .35 .25
On cover 30.00
Single franking on third-class cover *75.00*
P# block of 4 4.00 —

1046 A493 15c **rose lake,** *Dec. 12, 1958* .60 .25
On cover 3.00
Single franking on international airmail cover 10.00
P# block of 4 2.75 —
a. Tagged, *July 6, 1966* 1.10 .80
On cover 25.00
P# block of 4 13.00

Perf. 10½x11

1047 A494 20c **ultramarine,** *Apr. 13, 1956* .50 .25
On cover 3.00
Single franking on double-weight airmail cover to Central America 50.00
P# block of 4 2.25 —
a. 20c **deep bright ultramarine** .50 .25
P# block of 4 2.25 —

No. 1047a is from later printings and is on a harder, whiter paper than No. 1047.

Perf. 11x10½

1048 A495 25c **green,** *Apr. 18, 1958* 1.00 .75
On cover 2.00
Single franking on airmail cover to Asia 10.00
P# block of 4 4.25 —

1049 A496 30c **black,** wet printing, *Sept. 21, 1955* 1.20 .75
On cover 2.00
P# block of 4 5.25 —
a. 30c **black,** dry printing, *June 1957* .90 .25
On cover 2.00
Single franking on international airmail cover 10.00
P# block of 4 (#25487 and up) 4.00 —
b. 30c **intense black** .80 .25
P# block of 4 3.75 —

No. 1049b is from later printings and is on a harder, whiter paper than Nos. 1049 or 1049a.

Counterfeits exist of No. 1049. See the Postal Counterfeits section of this catalog.

1050 A497 40c **brown red,** wet printing, *Sept. 24, 1955* 1.75 .25
On cover 5.00
P# block of 4 9.00 —
a. 40c **brown red,** dry printing, *Apr. 1958* 1.50 .25
On cover 5.00
Single franking on international airmail cover 50.00
P# block of 4 (#25571 and up) 7.00 —

Cracked Plate

1051 A498 50c **bright purple,** wet printing, *Aug. 25, 1955* 1.75 .25
On cover 10.00
P# block of 4 11.00 —
Cracked plate (25231 UL 1) *17.50* —
P# block of 4, UL stamp cracked plate *25.00* —
a. 50c **bright purple,** dry printing, *Apr. 1958* 1.50 .25
On cover 10.00
Single franking on international airmail cover 40.00
P# block of 4 (#25897 and up) 7.00 —

1052 A499 $1 **purple,** wet printing, *Oct. 7, 1955* 5.00 1.00
On cover 25.00
P# block of 4 21.00 —
a. $1 **purple,** dry printing, *Oct. 1958* 4.50 .25
On cover 25.00
Single franking on international airmail cover *150.00*
P# block of 4 (#25541 and up) 18.00 —

Counterfeits exist of No. 1052. See the Postal Counterfeits section of this catalog.

FLAT PLATE PRINTING

Plates of 400 subjects in four panes of 100.

Perf. 11

1053 A500 $5 **black,** *Mar. 19, 1956* 47.50 6.75
On registered bank tag 25.00
On air parcel-post tag 75.00
On commercial cover *1,800.*
Single franking on registered cover *7,000.*
P# block of 4 210.00 —
Nos. 1030-1053 (27) 64.60 15.00

Bureau Precancels: ½c, 37 diff., 1c, 113 diff., 1¼c, 142 diff., 1½c, 45 diff.

2c, 86 diff., 2½c, 123 diff., 3c, 106 diff., 4c, 95 diff., 4½c, 23 diff., 5c, 20 diff., 6c, 23 diff., 7c, 16 diff.

Also, No. 1041, 12 diff., No. 1042, 12 diff., 9c, 15 diff., 10c, 16 diff., 11c, New York, 12c, 6 diff.

15c, 12 diff., 20c, 20 diff., 25c, 11 diff., 30c, 17 diff., 40c, 10 diff., 50c, 19 diff., $1, 5 diff.

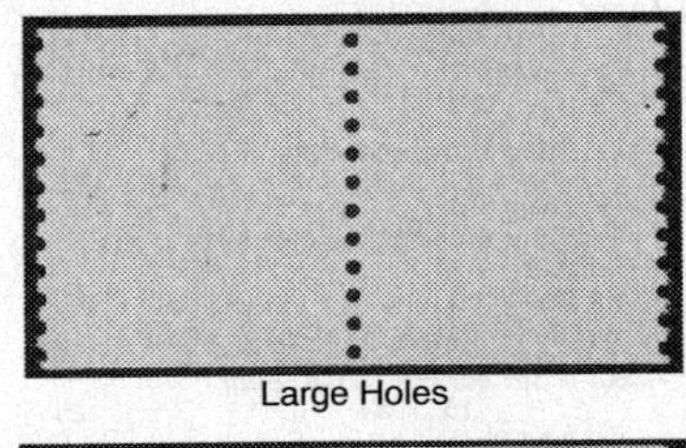
Large Holes

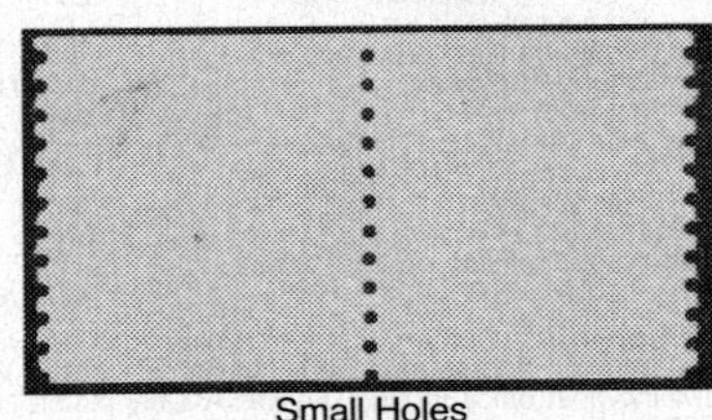
Small Holes

With the change from 384-subject plates to 432-subject plates the size of the perforation holes was reduced. While both are perf. 10 the later holes are smaller than the paper between them. The difference is most noticeable on pairs.

Gripper Crack

ROTARY PRESS COIL STAMPS

1954-80 ***Perf. 10 Vertically***

1054 A478 1c **dark green,** large holes, wet printing, *Oct. 8, 1954* .60 .25
On cover 3.00
Pair 1.20 .40
Joint line pair 2.75 .90
Gripper crack — —
b. 1c **dark green,** large holes, dry printing, *Aug. 1957* 1.00 .25
On cover 3.00
Pair 2.00 .50
Joint line pair 4.00 .65
Small holes, dry printing, *Feb. 1960* .25 .25
On cover 3.00
Pair .50 .50
Joint line pair 1.00 .65
c. Imperf., pair — —

Perf. 10 Horizontally

1054A A478a 1¼c **turquoise,** *June 17, 1960,* small holes .25 .25
On cover 2.00
Pair .50 .50
Joint line pair 2.25 1.00
Large holes *3.50* .25
Pair *7.00* .50
Joint line pair *90.00* 1.25
d. Imperf., pair —
Joint line pair —

All examples of No. 1054Ad are precanceled "SEATTLE/WASH." No. 1054A with large holes exists non-precanceled as well as precanceled. The values shown are for the non-precanceled variety; precanceled stamps with large holes are quite common.

Perf. 10 Vertically

1055 A480 2c **carmine rose,** large holes, wet printing, *Oct. 22, 1954* .60 .25
On cover .50
Pair 1.20 .50
Joint line pair 3.50 .60
Small holes —
Pair —
Joint line pair —
a. 2c **carmine rose,** large holes, dry printing, *May 1957* .35 .25
On cover .50
Pair .80 .50
Joint line pair 1.50 .60
Small holes, *Aug. 1961* 7.00 .25
Pair 17.50 .50
Joint line pair 50.00 .60
b. Tagged, small holes, shiny gum, *May 6, 1968* .25 .25
On cover 2.00
Pair .50 .50
Joint line pair .75 .60
Dull gum, tagged, small holes .75
Pair 1.50
Joint line pair 6.00
Large holes, *May 6, 1968* —
c. Imperf., pair, untagged, shiny gum (Bureau precanceled, Riverdale, MD) *325.00*
Joint line pair *1,200.*
d. Imperf. pair, tagged, shiny gum *425.00*
Joint line pair *1,100.*

1056 A481 2½c **gray blue,** large holes *Sept. 9, 1959* .30 .25
On cover 2.00
Pair .60 .50
Joint line pair 3.50 1.75
Small holes, *Jan. 1961* *400.00* *100.00*
Pair *850.00* *200.00*
Joint line pair *3,000.* *400.00*

No. 1056 with small holes only known with Bureau precancels. It was against postal regulations to make mint precanceled stamps available other than to permit holders for their use. Resale was prohibited. Since some mint examples do exist in the marketplace, values are furnished here.

1057 A482 3c **deep violet,** large holes, wet printing, *July 20, 1954* .35 .25
On cover .50
Pair .80 .50
Joint line pair 2.75 .60
Small holes, *Jan. 1961* —
Pair —
Joint line pair —
a. 3c **deep violet,** large holes, dry printing, *Oct. 1956* .35 .25
On cover .50
Pair .80 .50
Joint line pair 2.75 .60
Gripper cracks
Small holes, *Mar. 1958* .25 .25
Pair .25 .50

	Joint line pair	.55	.60
b.	Imperf., pair	*1,250.*	*800.00*
	Joint line pair	*2,750.*	—
c.	Tagged, small holes, Look magazine printing, *Oct. 1966*	8.00	4.00
	On "Look" cover		*10,000.*
	Pair	17.50	8.00
	Joint line pair	*350.00*	
d.	Tagged, small holes, philatelic printing, *June 26, 1967*	1.00	.50
	On cover		*250.00*
	Pair	3.00	1.00
	Joint line pair	25.00	—

Earliest documented use: Dec. 29, 1966 (No. 1057c).

No. 1057b measures about 19½x22mm; No. 1035f, about 18¾x22½mm.

The second tagged printing (No. 1057d) was a "philatelic reprint" made when the original stock of tagged stamps was exhausted. The original tagged printing (No. 1057c, specially printed for "Look" magazine) has a less intense color, the impression is less sharp and the tagging is brighter.

The reprint was printed on a slightly fluorescent paper, while the original paper is dead under longwave UV light.

1058 A483	4c **red violet,** large holes, dry printing, *July 31, 1958*	.75	.25
	On cover		.50
	Pair	1.60	.50
	Joint line pair	2.50	.60
	Small holes	.25	.25
	Pair	.55	.50
	Joint line pair	.75	.60
a.	Imperf., pair	75.00	70.00
	Joint line pair	*225.00*	
b.	4c **red violet,** large holes, wet printing, (Bureau precanceled)	*22.50*	2.25
	On cover		2.50
	Pair	*47.50*	—
	Joint line pair	*300.00*	

It was against postal regulations to make mint precanceled examples of No. 1058b available other than to permit holders for their use. Resale was prohibited. Since some mint examples do exist in the marketplace, values are furnished here.

Perf. 10 Horizontally

1059 A484	4½c **blue green,** large holes, *May 1, 1959*	1.50	1.00
	On cover		15.00
	Single franking on third-class cover		*200.00*
	Pair	3.25	2.25
	Joint line pair	14.00	3.00
	Small holes	12.00	—
	Pair	35.00	—
	Joint line pair	*450.00*	—

Perf. 10 Vertically

1059A A495	25c **green,** *Feb. 25, 1965*	.50	.30
	On cover		2.00
	Pair	1.00	.60
	Joint line pair	2.00	1.20
b.	Tagged, shiny gum, *Apr. 3, 1973*	.80	.25
	On cover		2.00
	Pair	1.60	.50
	Joint line pair	3.25	1.25
	Thin translucent paper	—	—
	Tagged, dull gum, *1980*	4.00	
	Pair	8.00	
	Joint line pair	12.00	
c.	Imperf., pair, untagged	—	
	Joint line pair	—	
d.	Imperf., pair, tagged	30.00	
	Joint line pair	60.00	

Value for No. 1059Ad is for fine centering.

Bureau Precancels: 1c, 118 diff., 1¼c, 105 diff., 2c, 191 diff., 2½c, 94 diff., 3c, 142 diff., 4c, 83 diff., 4½c, 23 diff.

The editors question the existence of No. 1059Ac. Evidence of its existence is necessary to maintain this listing.

NEBRASKA TERRITORY ISSUE

Establishment of the Nebraska Territory, centenary.

"The Sower," Mitchell Pass and Scotts Bluff — A507

ROTARY PRESS PRINTING

E.E. Plates of 200 subjects in four panes of 50.

1954, May 7 ***Perf. 11x10½***

1060 A507 3c **violet**		.25	.25
P# block of 4		1.00	—

KANSAS TERRITORY ISSUE

Establishment of the Kansas Territory, centenary.

Wheat Field and Pioneer Wagon Train — A508

ROTARY PRESS PRINTING

E.E. Plates of 200 subjects in four panes of 50.

1954, May 31 ***Perf. 11x10½***

1061 A508 3c **brown orange**		.25	.25
P# block of 4		1.00	—

GEORGE EASTMAN ISSUE

Eastman (1854-1932), inventor of photographic dry plates, flexible film and the Kodak camera; Rochester, N.Y., industrialist. — A509

ROTARY PRESS PRINTING

E.E. Plates of 280 subjects in four panes of 70.

1954, July 12 ***Perf. 10½x11***

1062 A509 3c **violet brown**		.25	.25
P# block of 4		1.00	—

LEWIS AND CLARK EXPEDITION

150th anniv. of the Lewis and Clark expedition.

Meriwether Lewis, William Clark and Sacagawea Landing on Missouri Riverbank A510

ROTARY PRESS PRINTING

E.E. Plates of 200 subjects in four panes of 50.

1954, July 28 ***Perf. 11x10½***

1063 A510 3c **violet brown**		.25	.25
P# block of 4		1.00	—

PENNSYLVANIA ACADEMY OF THE FINE ARTS ISSUE

150th anniversary of the founding of the Pennsylvania Academy of the Fine Arts, Philadelphia.

Charles Willson Peale in his Museum, Self-portrait — A511

ROTARY PRESS PRINTING

E.E. Plates of 200 subjects in four panes of 50.

1955, Jan. 15 ***Perf. 10½x11***

1064 A511 3c **rose brown**		.25	.25
P# block of 4		1.00	—

LAND GRANT COLLEGES ISSUE

Centenary of the founding of Michigan State College and Pennsylvania State University, first of the land grant institutions.

Open Book and Symbols of Subjects Taught — A512

ROTARY PRESS PRINTING

E.E. Plates of 200 subjects in four panes of 50.

1955, Feb. 12 ***Perf. 11x10½***

1065 A512 3c **green**		.25	.25
P# block of 4		1.00	—

ROTARY INTERNATIONAL, 50th ANNIV.

Torch, Globe and Rotary Emblem A513

ROTARY PRESS PRINTING

E.E. Plates of 200 subjects in four panes of 50.

1955, Feb. 23 ***Perf. 11x10½***

1066 A513 8c **deep blue**		.25	.25
P# block of 4		1.25	—

ARMED FORCES RESERVE ISSUE

Marine, Coast Guard, Army, Navy and Air Force Personnel A514

ROTARY PRESS PRINTING

E.E. Plates of 200 subjects in four panes of 50.

1955, May 21 ***Perf. 11x10½***

1067 A514 3c **bright red violet**		.25	.25
P# block of 4		1.00	—

NEW HAMPSHIRE ISSUE

Sesquicentennial of the discovery of the "Old Man of the Mountains."

Great Stone Face — A515

ROTARY PRESS PRINTING

E.E. Plates of 200 subjects in four panes of 50.

1955, June 21 ***Perf. 10½x11***

1068 A515 3c **green**		.25	.25
P# block of 4		1.00	—

SOO LOCKS ISSUE

Centenary of the opening of the Soo Locks.

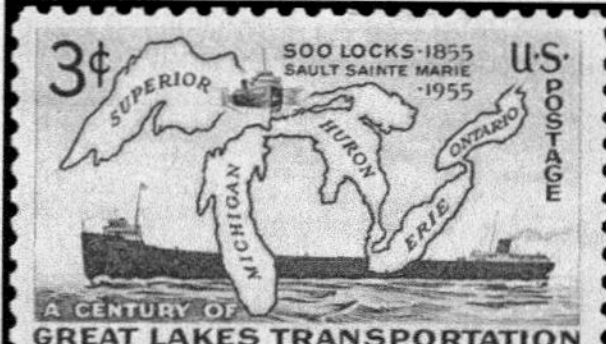

Map of Great Lakes and Two Steamers A516

ROTARY PRESS PRINTING
E.E. Plates of 200 subjects in four panes of 50.

1955, June 28 ***Perf. 11x10½***
1069 A516 3c **blue** .25 .25
P# block of 4 1.00 —

ATOMS FOR PEACE ISSUE

Issued to promote an Atoms for Peace policy.

Atomic Energy Encircling the Hemispheres A517

Designed by George R. Cox.

ROTARY PRESS PRINTING
E.E. Plates of 200 subjects in four panes of 50.

1955, July 28 ***Perf. 11x10½***
1070 A517 3c **deep blue** .25 .25
P# block of 4 1.10 —

FORT TICONDEROGA ISSUE

Bicentenary of Fort Ticonderoga, New York.

Map of the Fort, Ethan Allen and Artillery A518

Designed by Enrico Arno.

ROTARY PRESS PRINTING
E.E. Plates of 200 subjects in four panes of 50.

1955, Sept. 18 ***Perf. 11x10½***
1071 A518 3c **light brown** .25 .25
P# block of 4 1.10 —

ANDREW W. MELLON ISSUE

Andrew W. Mellon (1855-1937), US Secretary of the Treasury (1921-32), Financier and Art Collector — A519

Designed by Victor S. McCloskey, Jr.

ROTARY PRESS PRINTING
E.E. Plates of 280 subjects in four panes of 70.

1955, Dec. 20 ***Perf. 10½x11***
1072 A519 3c **rose carmine** .25 .25
P# block of 4 1.10 —

BENJAMIN FRANKLIN ISSUE

250th anniv. of the birth of Benjamin Franklin.

"Franklin Taking Electricity from the Sky," by Benjamin West — A520

Designed by Charles R. Chickering.

ROTARY PRESS PRINTING
E.E. Plates of 200 subjects in four panes of 50.

1956, Jan. 17 ***Perf. 10½x11***
1073 A520 3c **bright carmine** .25 .25
P# block of 4 1.10 —

BOOKER T. WASHINGTON ISSUE

Washington (1856-1915), black educator, founder and head of Tuskegee Institute in Alabama.

Log Cabin — A521

Designed by Charles R. Chickering.

ROTARY PRESS PRINTING
E.E. Plates of 200 subjects in four panes of 50.

1956, Apr. 5 ***Perf. 11x10½***
1074 A521 3c **deep blue** .25 .25
P# block of 4 1.00 —

FIFTH INTERNATIONAL PHILATELIC EXHIBITION ISSUES

FIPEX, New York City, Apr. 28 - May 6, 1956.

SOUVENIR SHEET

A522

Illustration reduced.

FLAT PLATE PRINTING
Plates of 24 subjects

1956, Apr. 28 ***Imperf.***
1075 A522 Pane of 2 1.20 1.50
a. A482 3c deep violet .75 .60
b. A488 8c dark violet blue & carmine .85 .75

No. 1075 measures 108x73mm. Nos. 1075a and 1075b measure 24x28mm.

Inscriptions printed in dark violet blue; scrolls and stars in carmine.

New York Coliseum and Columbus Monument A523

Designed by William K. Schrage.

ROTARY PRESS PRINTING
E.E. Plates of 200 subjects in four panes of 50.

1956, Apr. 30 ***Perf. 11x10½***
1076 A523 3c **deep violet** .25 .25
P# block of 4 1.10 —

WILDLIFE CONSERVATION ISSUE

Issued to emphasize the importance of Wildlife Conservation in America.

Wild Turkey A524

Pronghorn Antelope A525

King Salmon — A526

Designed by Robert W. (Bob) Hines.

ROTARY PRESS PRINTING
E.E. Plates of 200 subjects in four panes of 50.

1956 ***Perf. 11x10½***
1077 A524 3c **rose lake,** *May 5* .25 .25
P# block of 4 1.00 —
1078 A525 3c **brown,** *June 22* .25 .25
P# block of 4 1.00 —
1079 A526 3c **blue green,** *Nov. 9* .25 .25
P# block of 4 1.00 —
Nos. 1077-1079 (3) .75 .75

PURE FOOD AND DRUG LAWS, 50th ANNIV.

Harvey Washington Wiley — A527

Designed by Robert L. Miller

ROTARY PRESS PRINTING
E.E. Plates of 200 subjects in four panes of 50.

1956, June 27 ***Perf. 10½x11***
1080 A527 3c **dark blue green** .25 .25
P# block of 4 1.00 —

WHEATLAND ISSUE

Pres. Buchanan's Home, Lancaster, Pa. — A528

ROTARY PRESS PRINTING
E.E. Plates of 200 subjects in four panes of 50.

1956, Aug. 5 ***Perf. 11x10½***
1081 A528 3c **black brown** .25 .25
P# block of 4 1.00 —

LABOR DAY ISSUE

Mosaic, AFL-CIO Headquarters — A529

Designed by Victor S. McCloskey, Jr.

ROTARY PRESS PRINTING

E.E. Plates of 200 subjects in four panes of 50.

1956, Sept. 3 ***Perf. 10½x11***

1082 A529 3c **deep blue** .25 .25
P# block of 4 1.00 —

NASSAU HALL ISSUE

200th anniv. of Nassau Hall, Princeton University.

Nassau Hall, Princeton, N.J. — A530

ROTARY PRESS PRINTING

E.E. Plates of 200 subjects in four panes of 50.

1956, Sept. 22 ***Perf. 11x10½***

1083 A530 3c **black**, *orange* .25 .25
P# block of 4 1.00 —

DEVILS TOWER ISSUE

Issued to commemorate the 50th anniversary of the Federal law providing for protection of American natural antiquities. Devils Tower National Monument, Wyoming, is an outstanding example.

Devils Tower — A531

Designed by Charles R. Chickering.

ROTARY PRESS PRINTING

E.E. Plates of 200 subjects in four panes of 50.

1956, Sept. 24 ***Perf. 10½x11***

1084 A531 3c **violet** .25 .25
P# block of 4 1.00 —
Pair with full horiz. gutter btwn. *400.00*

CHILDREN'S ISSUE

Issued to promote friendship among the children of the world.

Children of the World — A532

Designed by Ronald Dias.

ROTARY PRESS PRINTING

E.E. Plates of 200 subjects in four panes of 50.

1956, Dec. 15 ***Perf. 11x10½***

1085 A532 3c **dark blue** .25 .25
P# block of 4 1.00 —

ALEXANDER HAMILTON (1755-1804)

Alexander Hamilton and Federal Hall — A533

Designed by William K. Schrage.

ROTARY PRESS PRINTING

E.E. Plates of 200 subjects in four panes of 50.

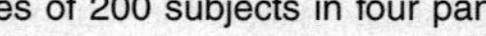

1957, Jan. 11 ***Perf. 11x10½***

1086 A533 3c **rose red** .25 .25
P# block of 4 1:00 —

POLIO ISSUE

Honoring "those who helped fight polio," and on for 20th anniv. of the Natl. Foundation for Infantile Paralysis and the March of Dimes.

Allegory — A534

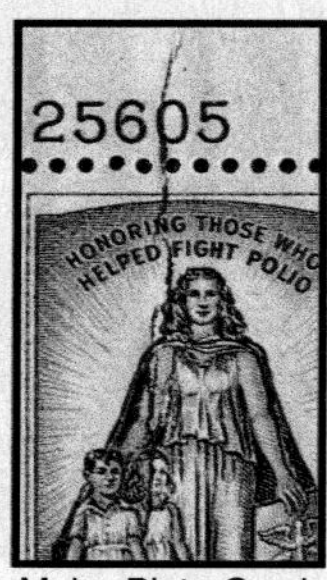

Major Plate Crack

Designed by Charles R. Chickering.

ROTARY PRESS PRINTING

E.E. Plates of 200 subjects in four panes of 50.

1957, Jan. 15 ***Perf. 10½x11***

1087 A534 3c **red lilac** .25 .25
P# block of 4 1.00 —
Major plate crack (25605 UL 1) —

COAST AND GEODETIC SURVEY ISSUE

150th anniversary of the establishment of the Coast and Geodetic Survey.

Flag of Coast and Geodetic Survey and Ships at Sea — A535

Designed by Harold E. MacEwen.

ROTARY PRESS PRINTING

E.E. Plates of 200 subjects in four panes of 50.

1957, Feb. 11 ***Perf. 11x10½***

1088 A535 3c **dark blue** .25 .25
P# block of 4 1.00 —

ARCHITECTS ISSUE

American Institute of Architects, centenary.

Corinthian Capital and Mushroom Type Head and Shaft — A536

Designed by Robert J. Schultz.

ROTARY PRESS PRINTING

E.E. Plates of 200 subjects in four panes of 50.

1957, Feb. 23 ***Perf. 11x10½***

1089 A536 3c **red lilac** .25 .25
P# block of 4 1.00 —

STEEL INDUSTRY ISSUE

Centenary of the steel industry in America.

American Eagle and Pouring Ladle — A537

Designed by Anthonio Petruccelli.

ROTARY PRESS PRINTING

E.E. Plates of 200 subjects in four panes of 50.

1957, May 22 ***Perf. 10½x11***

1090 A537 3c **bright ultramarine** .25 .25
P# block of 4 1.00 —

INTERNATIONAL NAVAL REVIEW ISSUE

Issued to commemorate the International Naval Review and the Jamestown Festival.

Aircraft Carrier and Jamestown Festival Emblem A538

Designed by Richard A. Genders.

ROTARY PRESS PRINTING

E.E. Plates of 200 subjects in four panes of 50.

1957, June 10 ***Perf. 11x10½***

1091 A538 3c **blue green** .25 .25
P# block of 4 1.00 —

OKLAHOMA STATEHOOD, 50th ANNIV.

Map of Oklahoma, Arrow and Atom Diagram A539

Designed by William K. Schrage.

ROTARY PRESS PRINTING

E.E. Plates of 200 subjects in four panes of 50.

1957, June 14 ***Perf. 11x10½***

1092 A539 3c **dark blue** .25 .25
P# block of 4 1.00 —

SCHOOL TEACHERS ISSUE

Teacher and Pupils — A540

ROTARY PRESS PRINTING

E.E. Plates of 200 subjects in four panes of 50.

1957, July 1 ***Perf. 11x10½***

1093 A540 3c **rose lake** .25 .25
P# block of 4 1.00 —

FLAG ISSUE

"Old Glory" (48 Stars) — A541

Designed by Victor S. McCloskey, Jr.

GIORI PRESS PRINTING

Plates of 200 subjects in four panes of 50.

1957, July 4 ***Perf. 11***

1094 A541 4c **dark blue & deep carmine** .25 .25
P# block of 4 1.00 —

SHIP BUILDING ISSUE

350th anniversary of shipbuilding in America.

"Virginia of Sagadahock" and Seal of Maine — A542

Designed by Ervine Metzel, Mrs. William Zorach, A. M. Main, Jr., and George F. Cary II.

ROTARY PRESS PRINTING

E.E. Plates of 280 subjects in four panes of 70.

1957, Aug. 15 ***Perf. 10½x11***

1095 A542 3c **deep violet** .25 .25
P# block of 4 1.00 —

CHAMPION OF LIBERTY ISSUE

Magsaysay (1907-57), Pres. of the Philippines.

Ramon Magsaysay — A543

Designed by Arnold Copeland, Ervine Metzl and William H. Buckley.

GIORI PRESS PRINTING

Plates of 192 subjects in four panes of 48 each.

1957, Aug. 31 ***Perf. 11***

1096 A543 8c **carmine, ultramarine & ocher** .25 .25
P# block of 4, 2# 1.00 —
P# block of 4, ultra. # omitted —

LAFAYETTE BICENTENARY ISSUE

Marquis de Lafayette (1757-1834) — A544

Designed by Ervine Metzl.

ROTARY PRESS PRINTING

E.E. Plates of 200 subjects in four panes of 50.

1957, Sept. 6 ***Perf. 10½x11***

1097 A544 3c **rose lake** .25 .25
P# block of 4 1.00 —

WILDLIFE CONSERVATION ISSUE

Issued to emphasize the importance of Wildlife Conservation in America.

Whooping Cranes — A545

Designed by Bob Hines and C.R. Chickering.

GIORI PRESS PRINTING

Plates of 200 subjects in four panes of 50.

1957, Nov. 22 ***Perf. 11***

1098 A545 3c **blue, ocher & green** .25 .25
P# block of 4 1.00 —

RELIGIOUS FREEDOM ISSUE

300th anniv. of the Flushing Remonstrance.

Bible, Hat and Quill Pen — A546

Designed by Robert Geissmann.

ROTARY PRESS PRINTING

E.E. Plates of 200 subjects in four panes of 50.

1957, Dec. 27 ***Perf. 10½x11***

1099 A546 3c **black** .25 .25
P# block of 4 1.00 —

GARDENING HORTICULTURE ISSUE

Issued to honor the garden clubs of America and in connection with the centenary of the birth of Liberty Hyde Bailey, horticulturist.

"Bountiful Earth" — A547

Designed by Denver Gillen.

ROTARY PRESS PRINTING

E.E. Plates of 200 subjects in four panes of 50.

1958, Mar. 15 ***Perf. 10½x11***

1100 A547 3c **green** .25 .25
P# block of 4 1.00 —

BRUSSELS EXHIBITION ISSUE

Issued in honor of the opening of the Universal and International Exhibition at Brussels, April 17.

US Pavilion at Brussels A551

Designed by Bradbury Thompson.

ROTARY PRESS PRINTING

E.E. Plates of 200 subjects in four panes of 50.

1958, Apr. 17 ***Perf. 11x10½***

1104 A551 3c **deep claret** .25 .25
On cover, Expo. station ("U.S. Pavilion") canc. 3.00
P# block of 4 1.00 —

JAMES MONROE ISSUE

James Monroe (1758-1831), 5th President of the US — A552

Designed by Frank P. Conley.

ROTARY PRESS PRINTING

E.E. Plates of 280 subjects in four panes of 70.

1958, Apr. 28 ***Perf. 11x10½***

1105 A552 3c **purple** .25 .25
P# block of 4 1.00 —

MINNESOTA STATEHOOD, 100th ANNIV.

Minnesota Lakes and Pines — A553

Designed by Homer Hill.

ROTARY PRESS PRINTING

E.E. Plates of 200 subjects in four panes of 50.

1958, May 11 ***Perf. 11x10½***

1106 A553 3c **green** .25 .25
P# block of 4 1.00 —

GEOPHYSICAL YEAR ISSUE

International Geophysical Year, 1957-58.

Solar Disc and Hands from Michelangelo's "Creation of Adam" — A554

Designed by Ervine Metzl.

GIORI PRESS PRINTING

Plates of 200 subjects in four panes of 50.

1958, May 31 ***Perf. 11***

1107 A554 3c **black & red orange** .25 .25
P# block of 4 1.00 —

GUNSTON HALL ISSUE

Issued for the bicentenary of Gunston Hall and to honor George Mason, author of the Constitution of Virginia and the Virginia Bill of Rights.

Gunston Hall, Virginia A555

Designed by Rene Clarke.

ROTARY PRESS PRINTING

E.E. Plates of 200 subjects in four panes of 50.

1958, June 12 ***Perf. 11x10½***

1108 A555 3c **light green** .25 .25
P# block of 4 1.00 —

MACKINAC BRIDGE ISSUE

Dedication of Mackinac Bridge, Michigan.

Mackinac Bridge — A556

Designed by Arnold J. Copeland.

ROTARY PRESS PRINTING

E.E. Plates of 200 subjects in four panes of 50.

1958, June 25 ***Perf. 10½x11***

1109 A556 3c **bright greenish blue** .25 .25
P# block of 4 1.00 —

CHAMPION OF LIBERTY ISSUE

Simon Bolívar, South American freedom fighter.

Simon Bolívar — A557

ROTARY PRESS PRINTING

E.E. Plates of 280 subjects in four panes of 70.

1958, July 24 ***Perf. 10½x11***

1110 A557 4c **olive bister** .25 .25
P# block of 4 1.00 —

GIORI PRESS PRINTING

Plates of 288 subjects in four panes of 72 each.

Perf. 11

1111 A557 8c **carmine, ultramarine & ocher** .25 .25
P# block of 4, 2# 1.25 —
P# block of 4, ocher # only —

ATLANTIC CABLE CENTENNIAL ISSUE

Centenary of the Atlantic Cable, linking the Eastern and Western hemispheres.

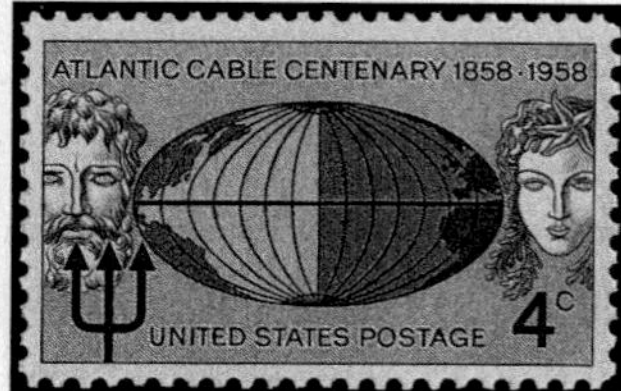

Neptune, Globe and Mermaid A558

Designed by George Giusti.

ROTARY PRESS PRINTING

E.E. Plates of 200 subjects in four panes of 50.

1958, Aug. 15 ***Perf. 11x10½***

1112 A558 4c **reddish purple** .25 .25
P# block of 4 1.00 —

LINCOLN SESQUICENTENNIAL ISSUE

Sesquicentennial of the birth of Abraham Lincoln. No. 1114 also for the centenary of the founding of Cooper Union, New York City. No. 1115 marks the centenary of the Lincoln-Douglas Debates.

Lincoln by George Healy — A559

Lincoln by Gutzon Borglum — A560

Lincoln and Stephen A. Douglas Debating, from Painting by Joseph Boggs Beale — A561

Daniel Chester French Statue of Lincoln as Drawn by Fritz Busse — A562

Designed by Ervine Metzl.

ROTARY PRESS PRINTING

E.E. Plates of 200 subjects in four panes of 50.

1958-59 ***Perf. 10½x11***

1113 A559 1c **green,** *Feb. 12, 1959* .25 .25
P# block of 4 .50 —
1114 A560 3c **dark rose,** *Feb. 27, 1959* .25 .25
P# block of 4 1.00 —

Perf. 11x10½

1115 A561 4c **sepia,** *Aug. 27, 1958* .25 .25
P# block of 4 1.00 —
1116 A562 4c **dark blue,** *May 30, 1959* .25 .25
P# block of 4 1.00 —
Nos. 1113-1116 (4) 1.00 1.00

CHAMPION OF LIBERTY ISSUE

Lajos Kossuth, Hungarian freedom fighter.

Lajos Kossuth — A563

ROTARY PRESS PRINTING

E.E. Plates of 280 subjects in four panes of 70.

1958, Sept. 19 ***Perf. 10½x11***

1117 A563 4c **green** .25 .25
P# block of 4 1.00 —

GIORI PRESS PRINTING

Plates of 288 subjects in four panes of 72 each.

Perf. 11

1118 A563 8c **carmine, ultramarine & ocher** .25 .25
P# block of 4, 2# 1.00 —

FREEDOM OF PRESS ISSUE

Honoring Journalism and freedom of the press in connection with the 50th anniv. of the 1st School of Journalism at the University of Missouri.

Early Press and Hand Holding Quill — A564

Designed by Lester Beall and Charles Goslin.

ROTARY PRESS PRINTING

E.E. Plates of 200 subjects in four panes of 50.

1958, Sept. 22 ***Perf. 10½x11***

1119 A564 4c **black** .25 .25
P# block of 4 1.00 —

OVERLAND MAIL ISSUE

Centenary of Overland Mail Service.

Mail Coach and Map of Southwest US — A565

Designed by William H. Buckley.

ROTARY PRESS PRINTING

E.E. Plates of 200 subjects in four panes of 50.

1958, Oct. 10 ***Perf. 11x10½***

1120 A565 4c **crimson rose** .25 .25
P# block of 4 1.00 —

NOAH WEBSTER ISSUE

Webster (1758-1843), lexicographer and author.

Noah Webster — A566

Designed by Charles R. Chickering.

ROTARY PRESS PRINTING

E.E. Plates of 280 subjects in four panes of 70.

1958, Oct. 16 ***Perf. 10½x11***

1121 A566 4c **dark carmine rose** .25 .25
P# block of 4 1.00 —

FOREST CONSERVATION ISSUE

Issued to publicize forest conservation and the protection of natural resources and to honor Theodore Roosevelt, a leading forest conservationist, on the centenary of his birth.

Forest Scene — A567

Designed by Rudolph Wendelin.

GIORI PRESS PRINTING

Plates of 200 subjects in four panes of 50.

1958, Oct. 27 *Perf. 11*

1122 A567 4c **green, yellow & brown**	.25	.25
P# block of 4	1.00	—

FORT DUQUESNE ISSUE

Bicentennial of Fort Duquesne (Fort Pitt) at future site of Pittsburgh.

British Capture of Fort Duquesne, 1758; Brig. Gen. John Forbes on Litter, Colonel Washington Mounted A568

Designed by William H. Buckley and Douglas Gorsline.

ROTARY PRESS PRINTING

E.E. Plates of 200 subjects in four panes of 50.

1958, Nov. 25 *Perf. 11x10½*

1123 A568 4c **blue**	.25	.25
P# block of 4	1.00	—

OREGON STATEHOOD, 100th ANNIV.

Covered Wagon and Mt. Hood — A569

Designed by Robert Hallock.

ROTARY PRESS PRINTING

E.E. Plates of 200 subjects in four panes of 50.

1959, Feb. 14 *Perf. 11x10½*

1124 A569 4c **blue green**	.25	.25
P# block of 4	1.00	—

CHAMPION OF LIBERTY ISSUE

San Martin, So. American soldier and statesman.

José de San Martin — A570

ROTARY PRESS PRINTING

E.E. Plates of 280 subjects in four panes of 70.

1959, Feb. 25 *Perf. 10½x11*

1125 A570 4c **blue**	.25	.25
P# block of 4	1.00	—
a. Horiz. pair, imperf. between	*900.00*	

GIORI PRESS PRINTING

Plates of 288 subjects in four panes of 72 each.

Perf. 11

1126 A570 8c **carmine, ultramarine & ocher**	.25	.25
P# block of 4	1.10	—

NATO ISSUE

North Atlantic Treaty Organization, 10th anniv.

NATO Emblem — A571

Designed by Stevan Dohanos.

ROTARY PRESS PRINTING

E.E. Plates of 280 subjects in four panes of 70.

1959, Apr. 1 *Perf. 10½x11*

1127 A571 4c **blue**	.25	.25
P# block of 4	1.00	—

ARCTIC EXPLORATIONS ISSUE

Conquest of the Arctic by land by Rear Admiral Robert Edwin Peary in 1909 and by sea by the submarine "Nautilus" in 1958.

North Pole, Dog Sled and "Nautilus" A572

Designed by George Samerjan.

ROTARY PRESS PRINTING

E.E. Plates of 200 subjects in four panes of 50.

1959, Apr. 6 *Perf. 11x10½*

1128 A572 4c **bright greenish blue**	.25	.25
P# block of 4	1.00	—

WORLD PEACE THROUGH WORLD TRADE ISSUE

Issued in conjunction with the 17th Congress of the International Chamber of Commerce, Washington, D.C., April 19-25.

Globe and Laurel — A573

Designed by Robert Baker.

ROTARY PRESS PRINTING

E.E. Plates of 200 subjects in four panes of 50.

1959, Apr. 20 *Perf. 11x10½*

1129 A573 8c **rose lake**	.25	.25
P# block of 4	1.00	—

SILVER CENTENNIAL ISSUE

Discovery of silver at the Comstock Lode, Nevada.

Henry Comstock at Mount Davidson Site — A574

Designed by Robert L. Miller and W.K. Schrage.

ROTARY PRESS PRINTING

E.E. Plates of 200 subjects in four panes of 50.

1959, June 8 *Perf. 11x10½*

1130 A574 4c **black**	.25	.25
P# block of 4	1.00	—

ST. LAWRENCE SEAWAY ISSUE

Opening of the St. Lawrence Seaway.

Great Lakes, Maple Leaf and Eagle Emblems A575

Designed by Arnold Copeland, Ervine Metzl, William H. Buckley and Gerald Trottier.

GIORI PRESS PRINTING

Plates of 200 subjects in four panes of 50.

1959, June 26 *Perf. 11*

1131 A575 4c **red & dark blue**	.25	.25
P# block of 4	1.00	—
Pair with full horiz. gutter btwn.	—	

See Canada No. 387.

49-STAR FLAG ISSUE

U.S. Flag, 1959 — A576

Designed by Stevan Dohanos.

GIORI PRESS PRINTING

Plates of 200 subjects in four panes of 50.

1959, July 4 *Perf. 11*

1132 A576 4c **ocher, dark blue & deep carmine**	.25	.25
P# block of 4	1.00	—

SOIL CONSERVATION ISSUE

Issued as a tribute to farmers and ranchers who use soil and water conservation measures.

Modern Farm — A577

Designed by Walter Hortens.

GIORI PRESS PRINTING

Plates of 200 subjects in four panes of 50.

1959, Aug. 26 *Perf. 11*

1133 A577 4c **blue, green & ocher**	.25	.25
P# block of 4	1.00	—

PETROLEUM INDUSTRY ISSUE

Centenary of the completion of the nation's first oil well at Titusville, Pa.

Oil Derrick — A578

Designed by Robert Foster.

ROTARY PRESS PRINTING

E.E. Plates of 200 subjects in four panes of 50.

1959, Aug. 27 *Perf. 10½x11*

1134 A578 4c **brown**	.25	.25
P# block of 4	1.00	—

DENTAL HEALTH ISSUE

Issued to publicize Dental Health and for the centenary of the American Dental Association.

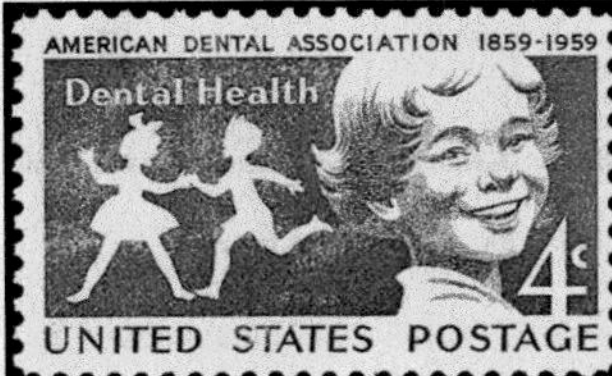

Children A579

Designed by Charles Henry Carter.

ROTARY PRESS PRINTING
E.E. Plates of 200 subjects in four panes of 50.

1959, Sept. 14 *Perf. 11x10½*
1135 A579 4c **green** .25 .25
P# block of 4 1.00 —

No. 1135 exists tagged as a Pitney-Bowes tagging essay.

CHAMPION OF LIBERTY ISSUE

Ernst Reuter, Mayor of Berlin, 1948-53.

Ernst Reuter — A580

ROTARY PRESS PRINTING
E.E. Plates of 280 subjects in four panes of 70.

1959, Sept. 29 *Perf. 10½x11*
1136 A580 4c **gray** .25 .25
P# block of 4 1.00 —

GIORI PRESS PRINTING
Plates of 288 subjects in four panes of 72 each.
Perf. 11

1137 A580 8c **carmine, ultramarine & ocher** .25 .25
P# block of 4 1.10 —
a. Ocher missing (EP) *3,000.*
b. Ultramarine missing (EP) *3,750.*
c. Ocher & ultramarine missing (EP) *4,000.*
d. All colors missing (EP) *2,000.*

DR. EPHRAIM McDOWELL ISSUE

Honoring McDowell (1771-1830) on the 150th anniv. of the 1st successful ovarian operation in the US, performed at Danville, Ky., 1809.

Dr. Ephraim McDowell — A581

Designed by Charles R. Chickering.

ROTARY PRESS PRINTING
E.E. Plates of 280 subjects in four panes of 70.

1959, Dec. 3 *Perf. 10½x11*
1138 A581 4c **rose lake** .25 .25
P# block of 4 1.00 —
a. Vert. pair, imperf. btwn. *375.00*
b. Vert. pair, imperf. horiz. *200.00*

VALUES FOR HINGED STAMPS AFTER NO. 771
This catalogue does not value unused stamps after No. 771 in hinged condition. Hinged unused stamps from No. 772 to the present are worth considerably less than the values given for unused stamps, which are for never-hinged examples.

AMERICAN CREDO ISSUE

Issued to re-emphasize the ideals upon which America was founded and to honor those great Americans who wrote or uttered the credos.

Quotation from Washington's Farewell Address, 1796 — A582

Benjamin Franklin Quotation A583

Thomas Jefferson Quotation A584

Francis Scott Key Quotation A585

Abraham Lincoln Quotation A586

Patrick Henry Quotation A587

Designed by Frank Conley.

GIORI PRESS PRINTING
Plates of 200 subjects in four panes of 50.

1960-61 *Perf. 11*
1139 A582 4c **dark violet blue, & carmine,** *Jan. 20, 1960* .25 .25
P# block of 4 1.00 —
1140 A583 4c **olive bister & green,** *Mar. 31, 1960* .25 .25
P# block of 4 1.00 —
1141 A584 4c **gray & vermilion,** *May 18, 1960* .25 .25
P# block of 4 1.00 —
1142 A585 4c **carmine & dark blue,** *Sept. 14, 1960* .25 .25
P# block of 4 1.00 —
1143 A586 4c **magenta & green,** *Nov. 19, 1960* .25 .25
P# block of 4 1.00 —
Pair with full horiz. gutter between 525.00
1144 A587 4c **green & brown,** *Jan. 11, 1961* .25 .25
P# block of 4 1.00 —
Nos. 1139-1144 (6) 1.50 1.50

BOY SCOUT JUBILEE ISSUE

50th anniv. of the Boy Scouts of America.

Boy Scout Giving Scout Sign — A588

Designed by Norman Rockwell.

GIORI PRESS PRINTING
Plates of 200 subjects in four panes of 50.

1960, Feb. 8 *Perf. 11*
1145 A588 4c **red, dark blue & dark bister** .25 .25
P# block of 4 1.00 —

No. 1145 exists tagged as a Pitney-Bowes tagging essay.

OLYMPIC WINTER GAMES ISSUE

Opening of the 8th Olympic Winter Games, Squaw Valley, Feb. 18-29, 1960.

Olympic Rings and Snowflake — A589

Designed by Ervine Metzl.

ROTARY PRESS PRINTING
E.E. Plates of 200 subjects in four panes of 50.

1960, Feb. 18 *Perf. 10½x11*
1146 A589 4c **dull blue** .25 .25
P# block of 4 1.00 —

CHAMPION OF LIBERTY ISSUE

Issued to honor Thomas G. Masaryk, founder and president of Czechoslovakia (1918-35), on the 110th anniversary of his birth.

Thomas G. Masaryk — A590

ROTARY PRESS PRINTING
E.E. Plates of 280 subjects in four panes of 70.

1960, Mar. 7 *Perf. 10½x11*
1147 A590 4c **blue** .25 .25
P# block of 4 1.00 —
a. Vert. pair, imperf. between *1,900.*

GIORI PRESS PRINTING
Plates of 288 subjects in four panes of 72 each.
Perf. 11

1148 A590 8c **carmine, ultramarine & ocher** .25 .25
P# block of 4 1.00 —
a. Horiz. pair, imperf. between —

WORLD REFUGEE YEAR ISSUE

World Refugee Year, July 1, 1959-June 30, 1960.

Family Walking Toward New Life — A591

Designed by Ervine Metzl.

ROTARY PRESS PRINTING
E.E. Plates of 200 subjects in four panes of 50.

1960, Apr. 7 *Perf. 11x10½*
1149 A591 4c **gray black** .25 .25
P# block of 4 1.00 —

WATER CONSERVATION ISSUE

Issued to stress the importance of water conservation and to commemorate the 7th Watershed Congress, Washington, D.C.

Water: From Watershed to Consumer A592

Designed by Elmo White.

GIORI PRESS PRINTING

Plates of 200 subjects in four panes of 50.

1960, Apr. 18 ***Perf. 11***

1150 A592 4c **dark blue, brown orange & green** .25 .25
P# block of 4 1.00 —
a. Brown orange missing (EP) *2,750.*

SEATO ISSUE

South-East Asia Treaty Organization and for the SEATO Conf., Washington, D.C., May 31-June 3.

SEATO Emblem — A593

Designed by John Maass.

ROTARY PRESS PRINTING

E.E. plates of 280 subjects in four panes of 70.

1960, May 31 ***Perf. 10½x11***

1151 A593 4c **blue** .25 .25
P# block of 4 1.00 —
a. Vertical pair, imperf. between *125.00*

AMERICAN WOMAN ISSUE

Issued to pay tribute to American women and their accomplishments in civic affairs, education, arts and industry.

Mother and Daughter A594

Designed by Robert Sivard.

ROTARY PRESS PRINTING

E.E. Plates of 200 subjects in four panes of 50.

1960, June 2 ***Perf. 11x10½***

1152 A594 4c **deep violet** .25 .25
P# block of 4 1.00 —

50-STAR FLAG ISSUE

US Flag, 1960 — A595

Designed by Stevan Dohanos.

GIORI PRESS PRINTING

Plates of 200 subjects in four panes of 50.

1960, July 4 ***Perf. 11***

1153 A595 4c **dark blue & red** .25 .25
P# block of 4 1.00 —

PONY EXPRESS CENTENNIAL ISSUE

Pony Express Rider — A596

Designed by Harold von Schmidt.

ROTARY PRESS PRINTING

E.E. Plates of 200 subjects in four panes of 50.

1960, July 19 ***Perf. 11x10½***

1154 A596 4c **sepia** .25 .25
P# block of 4 1.00 —

EMPLOY THE HANDICAPPED ISSUE

Promoting the employment of the physically handicapped and publicizing the 8th World Congress of the Intl. Soc. for the Welfare of Cripples, New York City.

Man in Wheelchair Operating Drill Press — A597

Designed by Carl Bobertz.

ROTARY PRESS PRINTING

E.E. Plates of 200 subjects in four panes of 50.

1960, Aug. 28 ***Perf. 10½x11***

1155 A597 4c **dark blue** .25 .25
P# block of 4 1.00 —

WORLD FORESTRY CONGRESS ISSUE

5th World Forestry Cong., Seattle, Wash., Aug. 29-Sept. 10.

World Forestry Congress Seal — A598

ROTARY PRESS PRINTING

E.E. Plates of 200 subjects in four panes of 50.

1960, Aug. 29 ***Perf. 10½x11***

1156 A598 4c **green** .25 .25
P# block of 4 1.00 —

MEXICAN INDEPENDENCE, 150th ANNIV.

Independence Bell — A599

Designed by Leon Helguera and Charles R. Chickering.

GIORI PRESS PRINTING

Plates of 200 subjects in four panes of 50.

1960, Sept. 16 ***Perf. 11***

1157 A599 4c **green & rose red** .25 .25
P# block of 4 1.00 —

See Mexico No. 910.

US-JAPAN TREATY ISSUE

Centenary of the United States-Japan Treaty of Amity and Commerce.

Washington Monument and Cherry Blossoms — A600

Designed by Gyo Fujikawa.

GIORI PRESS PRINTING

Plates of 200 subjects in four panes of 50.

1960, Sept. 28 ***Perf. 11***

1158 A600 4c **blue & pink** .25 .25
P# block of 4 1.00 —

CHAMPION OF LIBERTY ISSUE

Jan Paderewski, Polish statesman and musician.

Ignacy Jan Paderewski — A601

ROTARY PRESS PRINTING

E.E. Plates of 280 subjects in four panes of 70.

1960, Oct. 8 ***Perf. 10½x11***

1159 A601 4c **blue** .25 .25
P# block of 4 1.00 —

GIORI PRESS PRINTING

Plates of 288 subjects in four panes of 72 each.

Perf. 11

1160 A601 8c **carmine, ultramarine & ocher** .25 .25
P# block of 4 1.00 —

SENATOR TAFT MEMORIAL ISSUE

Senator Robert A. Taft (1889-1953) of Ohio.

Robert A. Taft — A602

Designed by William K. Schrage.

ROTARY PRESS PRINTING

E.E. Plates of 280 subjects in four panes of 70.

1960, Oct. 10 ***Perf. 10½x11***

1161 A602 4c **dull violet** .25 .25
P# block of 4 1.00 —

WHEELS OF FREEDOM ISSUE

Issued to honor the automotive industry and in connection with the National Automobile Show, Detroit, Oct. 15-23.

Globe and Steering Wheel with Tractor, Car and Truck — A603

Designed by Arnold J. Copeland.

ROTARY PRESS PRINTING
E.E. Plates of 200 subjects in four panes of 50.

1960, Oct. 15 ***Perf. 11x10½***

1162 A603 4c **dark blue**	.25	.25
P# block of 4	1.00	—

BOYS' CLUBS OF AMERICA ISSUE

Boys' Clubs of America movement, centenary.

Profile of Boy — A604

Designed by Charles T. Coiner.

GIORI PRESS PRINTING
Plates of 200 subjects in four panes of 50.

1960, Oct. 18 ***Perf. 11***

1163 A604 4c **indigo, slate & rose red**	.25	.25
P# block of 4	1.00	—

FIRST AUTOMATED POST OFFICE IN THE US ISSUE

Publicizing the opening of the 1st automated post office in the US at Providence, R.I.

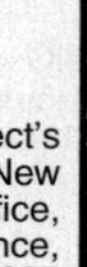

Architect's Sketch of New Post Office, Providence, R.I. — A605

Designed by Arnold J. Copeland and Victor S. McCloskey, Jr.

GIORI PRESS PRINTING
Plates of 200 subjects in four panes of 50.

1960, Oct. 20 ***Perf. 11***

1164 A605 4c **dark blue & carmine**	.25	.25
P# block of 4	1.00	—
a. Red missing (PS)	*250.00*	

CHAMPION OF LIBERTY ISSUE

Baron Karl Gustaf Emil Mannerheim (1867-1951), Marshal and President of Finland.

Baron Gustaf Mannerheim — A606

ROTARY PRESS PRINTING
E.E. Plates of 280 subjects in four panes of 70.

1960, Oct. 26 ***Perf. 10½x11***

1165 A606 4c **blue**	.25	.25
P# block of 4	1.00	—

GIORI PRESS PRINTING
Plates of 288 subjects in four panes of 72 each.
Perf. 11

1166 A606 8c **carmine, ultramarine & ocher**	.25	.25
P# block of 4	1.00	—

CAMP FIRE GIRLS ISSUE

50th anniv. of the Camp Fire Girls' movement and in connection with the Golden Jubilee Convention celebration of the Camp Fire Girls.

Camp Fire Girls Emblem — A607

Designed by H. Edward Oliver.

GIORI PRESS PRINTING
Plates of 200 subjects in four panes of 50.

1960, Nov. 1 ***Perf. 11***

1167 A607 4c **dark blue & bright red**	.25	.25
P# block of 4	1.00	—

CHAMPION OF LIBERTY ISSUE

Giuseppe Garibaldi (1807-1882), Italian patriot and freedom fighter.

Giuseppe Garibaldi — A608

ROTARY PRESS PRINTING
E.E. Plates of 280 subjects in four panes of 70.

1960, Nov. 2 ***Perf. 10½x11***

1168 A608 4c **green**	.25	.25
P# block of 4	1.00	—

GIORI PRESS PRINTING
Plates of 288 subjects in four panes of 72 each.
Perf. 11

1169 A608 8c **carmine, ultramarine & ocher**	.25	.25
P# block of 4	1.00	—

SENATOR GEORGE MEMORIAL ISSUE

Walter F. George (1878-1957) of Georgia.

Walter F. George — A609

Designed by William K. Schrage.

ROTARY PRESS PRINTING
E.E. Plates of 280 subjects in four panes of 70.

1960, Nov. 5 ***Perf. 10½x11***

1170 A609 4c **dull violet**	.25	.25
P# block of 4	1.00	—

ANDREW CARNEGIE ISSUE

Carnegie (1835-1919), industrialist & philanthropist.

Andrew Carnegie — A610

Designed by Charles R. Chickering.

ROTARY PRESS PRINTING
E.E. Plates of 280 subjects in four panes of 70.

1960, Nov. 25 ***Perf. 10½x11***

1171 A610 4c **deep claret**	.25	.25
P# block of 4	1.00	—

JOHN FOSTER DULLES MEMORIAL ISSUE

Dulles (1888-1959), Secretary of State (1953-59).

John Foster Dulles — A611

Designed by William K. Schrage.

ROTARY PRESS PRINTING
E.E. Plates of 280 subjects in four panes of 70.

1960, Dec. 6 ***Perf. 10½x11***

1172 A611 4c **dull violet**	.25	.25
P# block of 4	1.00	—

ECHO I — COMMUNICATIONS FOR PEACE ISSUE

World's 1st communications satellite, Echo I, placed in orbit by the Natl. Aeronautics and Space Admin., Aug. 12, 1960.

Radio Waves Connecting Echo I and Earth — A612

Designed by Ervine Metzl.

ROTARY PRESS PRINTING
E.E. Plates of 200 subjects in four panes of 50.

1960, Dec. 15 ***Perf. 11x10½***

1173 A612 4c **deep violet**	.25	.25
P# block of 4	1.00	—

CHAMPION OF LIBERTY ISSUE

Mohandas K. Gandhi, leader in India's struggle for independence.

Mahatma Gandhi — A613

ROTARY PRESS PRINTING
E.E. Plates of 280 subjects in four panes of 70.

1961, Jan. 26 ***Perf. 10½x11***

1174 A613 4c **red orange**	.25	.25
P# block of 4	1.00	—

GIORI PRESS PRINTING
Plates of 288 subjects in four panes of 72 each.
Perf. 11

1175 A613 8c **carmine, ultramarine & ocher**	.25	.25
P# block of 4	1.00	—

RANGE CONSERVATION ISSUE

Issued to stress the importance of range conservation and to commemorate the meeting of the American Society of Range Management. "The Trail Boss" from a drawing by Charles M. Russell is the Society's emblem.

The Trail Boss and Modern Range — A614

Designed by Rudolph Wendelin.

GIORI PRESS PRINTING

Plates of 200 subjects in four panes of 50.

1961, Feb. 2 ***Perf. 11***

1176 A614 4c **blue, slate & brown orange**	.25	.25
P# block of 4	1.00	—

HORACE GREELEY ISSUE

Horace Greeley (1811-1872), Publisher and Editor — A615

Designed by Charles R. Chickering.

ROTARY PRESS PRINTING

E.E. Plates of 280 subjects in four panes of 70.

1961, Feb. 3 ***Perf. 10½x11***

1177 A615 4c **dull violet**	.25	.25
P# block of 4	1.00	—

CIVIL WAR CENTENNIAL ISSUE

Centenaries of the firing on Fort Sumter (No. 1178), the Battle of Shiloh (No. 1179), the Battle of Gettysburg (No. 1180), the Battle of the Wilderness (No. 1181) and the surrender at Appomattox (No. 1182).

Sea Coast Gun of 1861 — A616

Rifleman at Battle of Shiloh, 1862 — A617

Blue and Gray at Gettysburg, 1863 — A618

Battle of the Wilderness, 1864 — A619

Appomattox, 1865 — A620

Designed by Charles R. Chickering (Sumter), Noel Sickles (Shiloh), Roy Gjertson (Gettysburg), B. Harold Christenson (Wilderness), Leonard Fellman (Appomattox).

ROTARY PRESS PRINTING

E.E. Plates of 200 subjects in four panes of 50.

1961-65 ***Perf. 11x10½***

1178 A616 4c **light green,** *Apr. 12, 1961*	.25	.25
P# block of 4	1.00	—
1179 A617 4c **black,** *peach blossom, Apr. 7, 1962*	.25	.25
P# block of 4	1.00	—

GIORI PRESS PRINTING

Plates of 200 subjects in four panes of 50.

Perf. 11

1180 A618 5c **gray & blue,** *July 1, 1963*	.25	.25
P# block of 4	1.00	—
1181 A619 5c **dark red & black,** *May 5, 1964*	.25	.25
P# block of 4	1.00	—
Margin block of 4, Mr. Zip and "Use Zip Code"	1.00	—
1182 A620 5c **Prus. blue & black,** *Apr. 9, 1965*	.30	.25
P# block of 4	1.25	—
Margin block of 4, Mr. Zip and "Use Zip Code"	1.25	—
a. Horiz. pair, imperf. vert.	*3,500.*	
Nos. 1178-1182 (5)	1.30	1.25

KANSAS STATEHOOD, 100th ANNIV.

Sunflower, Pioneer Couple and Stockade A621

GIORI PRESS PRINTING

Plates of 200 subjects in four panes of 50.

1961, May 10 ***Perf. 11***

1183 A621 4c **brown, dark red & green,** *yellow*	.25	.25
P# block of 4	1.00	—

SENATOR NORRIS ISSUE

Senator George W. Norris of Nebraska, and Norris Dam — A622

Designed by Charles R. Chickering.

ROTARY PRESS PRINTING

E.E. Plates of 200 subjects in four panes of 50.

1961, July 11 ***Perf. 11x10½***

1184 A622 4c **blue green**	.25	.25
P# block of 4	1.00	—

NAVAL AVIATION, 50th ANNIV.

Navy's First Plane (Curtiss A-1 of 1911) and Naval Air Wings — A623

Designed by John Maass.

ROTARY PRESS PRINTING

E.E. Plates of 200 subjects in four panes of 50.

1961, Aug. 20 ***Perf. 11x10½***

1185 A623 4c **blue**	.25	.25
P# block of 4	1.00	—
Pair with full vert. gutter btwn.	*150.00*	

WORKMEN'S COMPENSATION ISSUE

50th anniv. of the 1st successful Workmen's Compensation Law, enacted by the Wisconsin legislature.

Scales of Justice, Factory, Worker and Family — A624

Designed by Norman Todhunter.

ROTARY PRESS PRINTING

E.E. Plates of 200 subjects in four panes of 50.

1961, Sept. 4 ***Perf. 10½x11***

1186 A624 4c **ultramarine,** *grayish*	.25	.25
P# block of 4	1.00	—
P# block of 4 inverted	1.10	—

FREDERIC REMINGTON ISSUE

Remington (1861-1909), artist of the West. The design is from an oil painting, Amon Carter Museum of Western Art, Fort Worth, Texas.

"The Smoke Signal" — A625

Designed by Charles R. Chickering.

GIORI PRESS PRINTING

Panes of 200 subjects in four panes of 50.

1961, Oct. 4 ***Perf. 11***

1187 A625 4c **multicolored**	.25	.25
P# block of 4	1.00	—

REPUBLIC OF CHINA ISSUE

50th anniversary of the Republic of China.

Sun Yat-sen — A626

ROTARY PRESS PRINTING

E.E. Plates of 200 subjects in four panes of 50.

1961, Oct. 10 ***Perf. 10½x11***

1188 A626 4c **blue**	.35	.25
P# block of 4	1.50	—

NAISMITH — BASKETBALL ISSUE

Honoring basketball and James Naismith (1861-1939), Canada-born director of physical education, who invented the game in 1891 at Y.M.C.A. College, Springfield, Mass.

Basketball — A627

Designed by Charles R. Chickering.

ROTARY PRESS PRINTING

E.E. Plates of 200 subjects in four panes of 50.

1961, Nov. 6 *Perf. 10½x11*

1189 A627 4c **brown** .25 .25
P# block of 4 1.00 —

NURSING ISSUE

Issued to honor the nursing profession.

Student Nurse Lighting Candle — A628

Designed by Alfred Charles Parker.

GIORI PRESS PRINTING

Plates of 200 subjects in four panes of 50.

1961, Dec. 28 *Perf. 11*

1190 A628 4c **blue, green, orange & black** .25 .25
P# block of 4, 2# 1.00 —

NEW MEXICO STATEHOOD, 50th ANNIV.

Shiprock A629

Designed by Robert J. Jones.

GIORI PRESS PRINTING

Plates of 200 subjects in four panes of 50.

1962, Jan. 6 *Perf. 11*

1191 A629 4c **lt. blue, maroon & bister** .25 .25
P# block of 4 1.00 —

ARIZONA STATEHOOD, 50th ANNIV.

Giant Saguaro Cactus — A630

Designed by Jimmie E. Ihms and James M. Chemi.

GIORI PRESS PRINTING

Plates of 200 subjects in four panes of 50.

1962, Feb. 14 *Perf. 11*

1192 A630 4c **carmine, violet blue & green** .25 .25
P# block of 4 1.00 —

PROJECT MERCURY ISSUE

1st orbital flight of a US astronaut, Lt. Col. John H. Glenn, Jr., Feb. 20, 1962.

"Friendship 7" Capsule and Globe — A631

GIORI PRESS PRINTING

Plates of 200 subjects in four panes of 50.

1962, Feb. 20 *Perf. 11*

1193 A631 4c **dark blue & yellow** .25 .25
P# block of 4 1.00 —

Imperfs. are printers waste.

MALARIA ERADICATION ISSUE

World Health Organization's drive to eradicate malaria.

Great Seal of US and WHO Symbol A632

Designed by Charles R. Chickering.

GIORI PRESS PRINTING

Plates of 200 subjects in four panes of 50.

1962, Mar. 30 *Perf. 11*

1194 A632 4c **blue & bister** .25 .25
P# block of 4 1.00 —

CHARLES EVANS HUGHES ISSUE

Hughes (1862-1948), Governor of New York, Chief Justice of the US.

Charles Evans Hughes — A633

Designed by Charles R. Chickering.

ROTARY PRESS PRINTING

E.E. Plates of 200 subjects in four panes of 50.

1962, Apr. 11 *Perf. 10½x11*

1195 A633 4c **black,** *buff* .25 .25
P# block of 4 1.00 —

SEATTLE WORLD'S FAIR ISSUE

"Century 21" International Exposition, Seattle, Wash., Apr. 21-Oct. 21.

"Space Needle" and Monorail — A634

Designed by John Maass.

GIORI PRESS PRINTING

Plates of 200 subjects in four panes of 50.

1962, Apr. 25 *Perf. 11*

1196 A634 4c **red & dark blue** .25 .25
On cover, "Century 21" Expo. cancel 5.00
On cover, "Space Needle" Expo. cancel 2.00
P# block of 4 1.00 —

LOUISIANA STATEHOOD, 150th ANNIV.

Riverboat on the Mississippi A635

Designed by Norman Todhunter.

GIORI PRESS PRINTING

Plates of 200 subjects in four panes of 50.

1962, Apr. 30 *Perf. 11*

1197 A635 4c **blue, dark slate green & red** .25 .25
P# block of 4 1.00 —

HOMESTEAD ACT, CENTENARY

Sod Hut and Settlers A636

Designed by Charles R. Chickering.

ROTARY PRESS PRINTING

E.E. Plates of 200 subjects in four panes of 50.

1962, May 20 *Perf. 11x10½*

1198 A636 4c **slate** .25 .25
P# block of 4 1.00 —

GIRL SCOUTS ISSUE

50th anniversary of the Girl Scouts of America.

Senior Girl Scout and Flag — A637

Designed by Ward Brackett.

ROTARY PRESS PRINTING

E.E. Plates of 200 subjects in four panes of 50.

1962, July 24 *Perf. 11x10½*

1199 A637 4c **rose red** .25 .25
P# block of 4 1.00 —
Pair with full vertical gutter between *250.00*

SENATOR BRIEN McMAHON ISSUE

McMahon (1903-52) of Connecticut had a role in opening the way to peaceful uses of atomic energy through the Atomic Energy Act establishing the Atomic Energy Commission.

Brien McMahon and Atomic Symbol A638

Designed by V. S. McCloskey, Jr.

ROTARY PRESS PRINTING

E.E. Plates of 200 subjects in four panes of 50.

1962, July 28 *Perf. 11x10½*

1200 A638 4c **purple** .25 .25
P# block of 4 1.00 —

APPRENTICESHIP ISSUE

National Apprenticeship Program and 25th anniv. of the National Apprenticeship Act.

Machinist Handing Micrometer to Apprentice A639

Designed by Robert Geissmann.

ROTARY PRESS PRINTING
E.E. Plates of 200 subjects in four panes of 50.

1962, Aug. 31 *Perf. 11x10½*
1201 A639 4c **black,** *yellow bister* .25 .25
P# block of 4 1.00 —

SAM RAYBURN ISSUE

Sam Rayburn (1882-1961), Speaker of the House of Representatives — A640

Designed by Robert L. Miller.

GIORI PRESS PRINTING
Plates of 200 subjects in four panes of 50.

1962, Sept. 16 *Perf. 11*
1202 A640 4c **dark blue & red brown** .25 .25
P# block of 4 1.00 —

DAG HAMMARSKJOLD ISSUE

UN Headquarters and Dag Hammarskjold, UN Sec. Gen., 1953-61 A641

Designed by Herbert M. Sanborn.

GIORI PRESS PRINTING
Plates of 200 subjects in four panes of 50.

1962, Oct. 23 *Perf. 11*
1203 A641 4c **black, brown & yellow** .25 .25
P# block of 4, 2# 1.00 —
a. Yellow inverted, on cover, see note —
Vert. pair, on piece *4,250.*

No. 1203a can only be collected on a cover postmarked before Nov. 16, 1962 (the date the Hammarskjold Special Printing, No. 1204, was issued), or tied on dated piece (unique used pair). Covers are known machine postmarked Cuyahoga Falls, Ohio, Nov. 14, 1962, and notarized in the lower left corner by George W. Schwartz, Notary Public. Other covers are reported postmarked Oct. 26, 1962, Brooklyn, NY, Vanderveer Station. Unaddressed, uncacheted first day covers also exist. Other covers may exist. All covers must be accompanied by certificates from recognized expertizing committees. Value of first-day cover, $3,000.

An unused pane of 50 was signed in the selvage by ten well-known philatelists attesting to its genuineness. This pane was donated to the American Philatelic Society in 1987.

An unknown number of "first day covers" exist bearing Artmaster cachets. These were contrived using examples of No. 1204.

Hammarskjold Special Printing

No. 1204 was issued following discovery of No. 1203 with yellow background inverted.

GIORI PRESS PRINTING
Plates of 200 subjects in four panes of 50.

1962, Nov. 16 *Perf. 11*
1204 A641 4c **black, brown & yel** (yellow inverted) .25 .25
P# block of 4, 2#, yellow # inverted 1.00 —

The inverted yellow impression is shifted to the right in relation to the black and brown impression. Stamps of first vertical row of UL and LL panes show no yellow at left side for a space of 11-11½mm in from the perforations.

Stamps of first vertical row of UR and LR panes show vertical no-yellow strip 9¾mm wide, covering UN Building. On all others, the vertical no-yellow strip is 3½mm wide, and touches UN Building.

CHRISTMAS ISSUE

Wreath and Candles — A642

Designed by Jim Crawford.

GIORI PRESS PRINTING
Plates of 400 subjects in four panes of 100.
Panes of 90 and 100 exist without plate numbers due to provisional use of smaller paper.
Value per pane thus $50.

1962, Nov. 1 *Perf. 11*
1205 A642 4c **green & red** .25 .25
P# block of 4 1.00 —

HIGHER EDUCATION ISSUE

Higher education's role in American cultural and industrial development and the centenary celebrations of the signing of the law creating land-grant colleges and universities.

Map of U.S. and Lamp — A643

Designed by Henry K. Bencsath.

GIORI PRESS PRINTING
Plates of 200 subjects in panes of 50.

1962, Nov. 14 *Perf. 11*
1206 A643 4c **blue green & black** .25 .25
P# block of 4, 2# 1.00 —

WINSLOW HOMER ISSUE

Homer (1836-1910), painter, showing his oil, "Breezing Up," which hangs in the National Gallery, Washington, D.C.

"Breezing Up" — A644

Designed by Victor S. McCloskey, Jr.

GIORI PRESS PRINTING
Plates of 200 subjects in four panes of 50.

1962, Dec. 15 *Perf. 11*
1207 A644 4c **multicolored** .25 .25
P# block of 4 1.00 —
a. Horiz. pair, imperf. btwn. and at right *7,000.*

FLAG ISSUE

Flag over White House — A645

Designed by Robert J. Jones.

GIORI PRESS PRINTING
Plates of 400 subjects in four panes of 100.

1963-66 *Perf. 11*
1208 A645 5c **blue & red,** *Jan. 9, 1963* .25 .25
P# block of 4 1.00 —
Pair with full horiz. gutter between —
a. Tagged, *Aug. 25, 1966* .25 .25
P# block of 4 2.25 —
b. Horiz. pair, imperf. between, tagged *2,250.*

Beware of pairs with faint blind perfs between offered as No. 1208b.

REGULAR ISSUE

Andrew Jackson — A646

George Washington — A650

John J. Pershing — A651

Designed by William K. Schrage.

ROTARY PRESS PRINTING
E.E. Plates of 400 subjects in four panes of 100.

1961-66 *Perf. 11x10½*
1209 A646 1c **green,** *Mar. 22, 1963* .25 .25
P# block of 4 1.00 —
Pair with full vert. gutter btwn. —
a. Tagged, *July 6, 1966* .25 .25
P# block of 4 .50 —
1213 A650 5c **dark blue gray,** *Nov. 23, 1962* .25 .25
P# block of 4 1.00 —
Pair with full vert. gutter btwn. *250.00*
Pair with full horiz. gutter btwn. *425.00*
a. Booklet pane of 5 + label 2.00 *2.00*
b. Tagged, *Oct. 28, 1963* .50 .25
P# block of 4 4.50 —
c. As "a," tagged, *Oct. 28, 1963* 2.00 *1.50*
d. Horiz. pair, imperf. between, in #1213a with foldover or miscut *1,750.*

Counterfeits exist of No. 1213. See the Postal Counterfeits section of this catalog.

1214 A651 8c **brown,** *Nov. 17, 1961* .25 .25
P# block of 4 1.00

Bureau Precancels: 1c, 10 diff., 5c, 18 diff., 8c, 16 diff.

No. 1213d resulted from a paper foldover after perforating and before cutting into panes. At least six individually unique panes exist, including at least one that contains two error pairs. Recent auction prices for panes have ranged between $1,400 and $4,000.

COIL STAMPS
(Rotary Press)

1962-66 *Perf. 10 Vertically*
1225 A646 1c **green,** *May 31, 1963* .40 .25
Pair .80 .25
Joint line pair 2.25 .25
a. Tagged, *July 6, 1966* .40 .25
Joint line pair .90 .25
1229 A650 5c **dark blue gray,** *Nov. 23, 1962* 1.50 .25
Pair 3.00 .25
Joint line pair 4.00 .35
a. Tagged, *Oct. 28, 1963* 2.50 .25
Joint line pair 12.00 .25
b. Imperf., pair *300.00*
Joint line pair *900.00*

Bureau Precancels: 1c, 5 diff., 5c, 14 diff.

See Luminescence note in "Basic Stamp Information" in the introduction.

CAROLINA CHARTER ISSUE

Tercentenary of the Carolina Charter granting to 8 Englishmen lands extending coast-to-coast roughly along the present border of Virginia to the north and Florida to the south. Original charter on display at Raleigh.

First Page of Carolina Charter A662

Designed by Robert L. Miller.

GIORI PRESS PRINTING

Plates of 200 subjects in four panes of 50.

1963, Apr. 6 ***Perf. 11***

1230 A662 5c **dark carmine & brown** .25 .25
P# block of 4 1.00 —

FOOD FOR PEACE-FREEDOM FROM HUNGER ISSUE

American "Food for Peace" program and the "Freedom from Hunger" campaign of the FAO.

Wheat — A663

Designed by Stevan Dohanos.

GIORI PRESS PRINTING

Plates of 200 subjects in four panes of 50.

1963, June 4 ***Perf. 11***

1231 A663 5c **green, buff & red** .25 .25
P# block of 4 1.00 —

WEST VIRGINIA STATEHOOD, 100th ANNIV.

Map of West Virginia and State Capitol A664

Designed by Dr. Dwight Mutchler.

GIORI PRESS PRINTING

Plates of 200 subjects in four panes of 50.

1963, June 20 ***Perf. 11***

1232 A664 5c **green, red & black** .25 .25
P# block of 4 1.00 —

EMANCIPATION PROCLAMATION ISSUE

Centenary of Lincoln's Emancipation Proclamation freeing about 3,000,000 slaves in 10 southern states.

Severed Chain — A665

Designed by Georg Olden.

GIORI PRESS PRINTING

Plates of 200 subjects in four panes of 50.

1963, Aug. 16 ***Perf. 11***

1233 A665 5c **dark blue, black & red** .25 .25
P# block of 4 1.00 —

ALLIANCE FOR PROGRESS ISSUE

2nd anniv. of the Alliance for Progress, which aims to stimulate economic growth and raise living standards in Latin America.

Alliance Emblem A666

Designed by William K. Schrage.

GIORI PRESS PRINTING

Plates of 200 subjects in four panes of 50.

1963, Aug. 17 ***Perf. 11***

1234 A666 5c **ultramarine & green** .25 .25
P# block of 4 1.00 —
Pair with full vert. gutter between *750.00*

CORDELL HULL ISSUE

Hull (1871-1955), Secretary of State (1933-44).

Cordell Hull — A667

Designed by Robert J. Jones.

ROTARY PRESS PRINTING

E.E. Plates of 200 subjects in four panes of 50.

1963, Oct. 5 ***Perf. 10½x11***

1235 A667 5c **blue green** .25 .25
P# block of 4 1.00 —

ELEANOR ROOSEVELT ISSUE

Mrs. Franklin D. Roosevelt (1884-1962).

Eleanor Roosevelt A668

Designed by Robert L. Miller.

ROTARY PRESS PRINTING

E.E. Plates of 200 subjects in four panes of 50.

1963, Oct. 11 ***Perf. 11x10½***

1236 A668 5c **bright purple** .25 .25
P# block of 4 1.00 —

SCIENCE ISSUE

Honoring the sciences and in connection with the centenary of the Natl. Academy of Science.

"The Universe" A669

Designed by Antonio Frasconi.

GIORI PRESS PRINTING

Plates of 200 subjects in four panes of 50.

1963, Oct. 14 ***Perf. 11***

1237 A669 5c **Prussian blue & black** .25 .25
P# block of 4 1.00 —

CITY MAIL DELIVERY ISSUE

Centenary of free city mail delivery.

Letter Carrier, 1863 — A670

Designed by Norman Rockwell.

GIORI PRESS PRINTING

Plates of 200 subjects in four panes of 50.

1963, Oct. 26 **Tagged** ***Perf. 11***

1238 A670 5c **gray, dark blue & red** .25 .25
P# block of 4 1.00 —
a. Tagging omitted 10.00

RED CROSS CENTENARY ISSUE

Cuban Refugees on S.S. Morning Light and Red Cross Flag — A671

Designed by Victor S. McCloskey, Jr.

GIORI PRESS PRINTING

Plates of 200 subjects in four panes of 50.

1963, Oct. 29 ***Perf. 11***

1239 A671 5c **bluish black & red** .25 .25
P# block of 4 1.00 —

CHRISTMAS ISSUE

National Christmas Tree and White House — A672

Designed by Lily Spandorf; modified by Norman Todhunter.

GIORI PRESS PRINTING

Plates of 400 subjects in four panes of 100.

1963, Nov. 1 ***Perf. 11***

1240 A672 5c **dark blue, bluish black & red** .25 .25
P# block of 4 1.00 —
a. Tagged, *Nov. 2, 1963* .65 .50
P# block of 4 5.00 —
Pair with full horiz. gutter between —
b. Horiz. pair, imperf between *7,500.*
c. Red missing (PS) —

JOHN JAMES AUDUBON ISSUE

Audubon (1785-1851), ornithologist and artist. The birds pictured are actually Collie's magpie jays. See No. C71.

"Columbia Jays" by Audubon — A673

Designed by Robert L. Miller.

GIORI PRESS PRINTING

Plates of 200 subjects in four panes of 50.

1963, Dec. 7 *Perf. 11*

1241 A673 5c **dark blue & multicolored** .25 .25
P# block of 4 1.00 —

SAM HOUSTON ISSUE

Houston (1793-1863), soldier, president of Texas, US senator.

Sam Houston — A674

Designed by Tom Lea.

ROTARY PRESS PRINTING

E.E. Plates of 200 subjects in four panes of 50.

1964, Jan. 10 *Perf. 10½x11*

1242 A674 5c **black** .25 .25
P# block of 4 1.00 —
Margin block of 4, Mr. Zip and "Use Zip Code" 1.00 —

CHARLES M. RUSSELL ISSUE

Russell (1864-1926), painter. The design is from a painting, Thomas Gilcrease Institute of American History and Art, Tulsa, Okla.

"Jerked Down" — A675

Designed by William K. Schrage.

GIORI PRESS PRINTING

Plates of 200 subjects in four panes of 50.

1964, Mar. 19 *Perf. 11*

1243 A675 5c **multicolored** .25 .25
P# block of 4 1.00 —
Margin block of 4, Mr. Zip and "Use Zip Code" 1.00 —

NEW YORK WORLD'S FAIR ISSUE

New York World's Fair, 1964-65.

Mall with Unisphere and "Rocket Thrower" by Donald De Lue — A676

Designed by Robert J. Jones.

ROTARY PRESS PRINTING

E.E. Plates of 200 subjects in four panes of 50.

1964, Apr. 22 *Perf. 11x10½*

1244 A676 5c **blue green** .25 .25
On cover, Expo. station machine cancel (non-first day) 2.00
On cover, Expo. station handstamp cancel (non-first day) 10.00
P# block of 4 1.00 —
Margin block of 4, Mr. Zip and "Use Zip Code" 1.00 —
a. All color omitted —

On No. 1244a, a clear albino impression of the design is present.

JOHN MUIR ISSUE

Muir (1838-1914), naturalist and conservationist.

John Muir and Redwood Forest — A677

Designed by Rudolph Wendelin.

GIORI PRESS PRINTING

Plates of 200 subjects in four panes of 50.

1964, Apr. 29 *Perf. 11*

1245 A677 5c **brown, green, yellow green & olive** .25 .25
P# block of 4 1.00 —

KENNEDY MEMORIAL ISSUE

President John Fitzgerald Kennedy, (1917-1963).

John F. Kennedy and Eternal Flame — A678

Designed by Raymond Loewy/William Snaith, Inc.

Photograph by William S. Murphy.

ROTARY PRESS PRINTING

E.E. Plates of 200 subjects in four panes of 50.

1964, May 29 *Perf. 11x10½*

1246 A678 5c **blue gray** .25 .25
P# block of 4 1.00 —

NEW JERSEY TERCENTENARY ISSUE

300th anniv. of English colonization of New Jersey. The design is from a mural by Howard Pyle in the Essex County Courthouse, Newark, N.J.

Philip Carteret Landing at Elizabethtown, and Map of New Jersey — A679

Designed by Douglas Allen.

ROTARY PRESS PRINTING

E.E. Plates of 200 subjects in four panes of 50.

1964, June 15 *Perf. 10½x11*

1247 A679 5c **brt ultramarine** .25 .25
P# block of 4 1.00 —
Margin block of 4, Mr. Zip and "Use Zip Code" 1.00 —

NEVADA STATEHOOD, 100th ANNIV.

Virginia City and Map of Nevada A680

Designed by William K. Schrage.

GIORI PRESS PRINTING

Plates of 200 subjects in four panes of 50.

1964, July 22 *Perf. 11*

1248 A680 5c **red, yellow & blue** .25 .25
P# block of 4 1.00 —
Margin block of 4, Mr. Zip and "Use Zip Code" 1.00 —

REGISTER AND VOTE ISSUE

Campaign to draw more voters to the polls.

Flag — A681

Designed by Victor S. McCloskey, Jr.

GIORI PRESS PRINTING

Plates of 200 subjects in four panes of 50.

1964, Aug. 1 *Perf. 11*

1249 A681 5c **dark blue & red** .25 .25
P# block of 4 1.00 —
Margin block of 4, Mr. Zip and "Use Zip Code" 1.00 —

SHAKESPEARE ISSUE

William Shakespeare (1564-1616).

William Shakespeare — A682

Designed by Douglas Gorsline.

ROTARY PRESS PRINTING

E.E. Plates of 200 subjects in four panes of 50.

1964, Aug. 14 *Perf. 10½x11*

1250 A682 5c **black brown,** *tan* .25 .25
P# block of 4 1.00 —
Margin block of 4, Mr. Zip and "Use Zip Code" 1.00 —

DOCTORS MAYO ISSUE

Dr. William James Mayo (1861-1939) and his brother, Dr. Charles Horace Mayo (1865-1939), surgeons who founded the Mayo Foundation for Medical Education and Research in affiliation with the Univ. of Minnesota at Rochester. Heads on stamp are from a sculpture by James Earle Fraser.

Drs. William and Charles Mayo — A683

ROTARY PRESS PRINTING

E.E. Plates of 200 subjects in four panes of 50.

1964, Sept. 11 *Perf. 10½x11*

1251 A683 5c **green**	.25	.25
P# block of 4	1.00	—
Margin block of 4, Mr. Zip and "Use Zip Code"	1.00	—

AMERICAN MUSIC ISSUE

50th anniv. of the founding of the American Society of Composers, Authors and Publishers (ASCAP).

Lute, Horn, Laurel, Oak and Music Score — A684

Designed by Bradbury Thompson.

GIORI PRESS PRINTING

Plates of 200 subjects in four panes of 50.

1964, Oct. 15 *Perf. 11*

Gray Paper with Blue Threads

1252 A684 5c **red, black & blue**	.25	.25
P# block of 4	1.00	—
Margin block of 4, Mr. Zip and "Use Zip Code"	1.00	—
a. Blue omitted	*650.00*	
b. Blue missing (PS)	—	

Beware of examples offered as No. 1252a which have traces of blue.

HOMEMAKERS ISSUE

Honoring American women as homemakers and for the 50th anniv. of the passage of the Smith-Lever Act. By providing economic experts under an extension service of the U.S. Dept. of Agriculture, this legislation helped to improve homelife.

Farm Scene Sampler A685

Designed by Norman Todhunter.

Plates of 200 subjects in four panes of 50.

Engraved (Giori Press); Background Lithographed

1964, Oct. 26 *Perf. 11*

1253 A685 5c **multicolored**	.25	.25
P# block of 4	1.00	—
Margin block of 4, Mr. Zip and "Use Zip Code"	1.00	—

CHRISTMAS ISSUE

Holly — A686

Mistletoe — A687

Poinsettia — A688

Sprig of Conifer — A689

Designed by Thomas F. Naegele.

GIORI PRESS PRINTING

Plates of 400 subjects in four panes of 100.

Panes contain 25 subjects each of Nos. 1254-1257

1964, Nov. 9 *Perf. 11*

1254 A686 5c **green, carmine & black**	.25	.25
a. Tagged, *Nov. 10*	.75	.50
b. Printed on gummed side	*1,850.*	
c. All color missing (FO)	2,000.	
1255 A687 5c **carmine, green & black**	.25	.25
a. Tagged, *Nov. 10*	.75	.50
1256 A688 5c **carmine, green & black**	.25	.25
a. Tagged, *Nov. 10*	.75	.50
1257 A689 5c **black, green & carmine**	.25	.25
a. Tagged, *Nov. 10*	.75	.50
b. Block of 4, #1254-1257	1.00	1.00
P# block of 4	1.00	—
Margin block of 4, Zip and "Use Zip Code"	1.00	—
c. Block of 4, tagged	3.00	2.25
P# block of 4	6.00	—
Zip block of 4	3.25	—

No. 1254b resulted from a paper foldover before printing and perforating.

No. 1254c is unique and is in a block of four with the other three stamps missing parts of the designs.

VERRAZANO-NARROWS BRIDGE ISSUE

Opening of the Verrazano-Narrows Bridge connecting Staten Island and Brooklyn.

Verrazano-Narrows Bridge and Map of New York Bay — A690

ROTARY PRESS PRINTING

E.E. Plates of 200 subjects in four panes of 50.

1964, Nov. 21 *Perf. 10½x11*

1258 A690 5c **blue green**	.25	.25
P# block of 4	1.00	—
Margin block of 4, Mr. Zip and "Use Zip Code"	1.00	—

FINE ARTS ISSUE

Abstract Design by Stuart Davis — A691

GIORI PRESS PRINTING

Plates of 200 subjects in four panes of 50.

1964, Dec. 2 *Perf. 11*

1259 A691 5c **ultra., black & dull red**	.25	.25
P# block of 4, 2#	1.00	—
Margin block of 4, Mr. Zip and "Use Zip Code"	1.00	—

AMATEUR RADIO ISSUE

Issued to honor the radio amateurs on the 50th anniversary of the American Radio Relay League.

Radio Waves and Dial — A692

Designed by Emil J. Willett.

ROTARY PRESS PRINTING

E.E. Plates of 200 subjects in four panes of 50.

1964, Dec. 15 *Perf. 10½x11*

1260 A692 5c **red lilac**	.25	.25
P# block of 4	1.00	—
Margin block of 4, Mr. Zip and "Use Zip Code"	1.00	—

BATTLE OF NEW ORLEANS ISSUE

Battle of New Orleans, Chalmette Plantation, Jan. 8-18, 1815, established 150 years of peace and friendship between the US and Great Britain.

General Andrew Jackson and Sesquicentennial Medal — A693

Designed by Robert J. Jones.

GIORI PRESS PRINTING

Plates of 200 subjects in four panes of 50.

1965, Jan. 8 *Perf. 11*

1261 A693 5c **deep carmine, violet blue & gray**	.25	.25
P# block of 4	1.00	—
Margin block of 4, Mr. Zip and "Use Zip Code"	1.00	—

PHYSICAL FITNESS-SOKOL ISSUE

Publicizing the importance of physical fitness and for the centenary of the founding of the Sokol (athletic) organization in America.

Discus Thrower — A694

Designed by Norman Todhunter.

GIORI PRESS PRINTING

Plates of 200 subjects in four panes of 50.

1965, Feb. 15 *Perf. 11*

1262 A694 5c **maroon & black**	.25	.25
P# block of 4	1.00	—
Margin block of 4, Mr. Zip and "Use Zip Code"	1.00	—

CRUSADE AGAINST CANCER ISSUE

Issued to publicize the "Crusade Against Cancer" and to stress the importance of early diagnosis.

Microscope and Stethoscope — A695

Designed by Stevan Dohanos.

GIORI PRESS PRINTING

Plates of 200 subjects in four panes of 50.

1965, Apr. 1 *Perf. 11*

1263 A695 5c **black, purple & red orange**	.25	.25
P# block of 4, 2#	1.00	—
Margin block of 4, Mr. Zip and "Use Zip Code"	1.00	—

CHURCHILL MEMORIAL ISSUE

Sir Winston Spencer Churchill (1874-1965), British statesman and World War II leader.

Winston Churchill — A696

Designed by Richard Hurd.

ROTARY PRESS PRINTING

E.E. Plates of 200 subjects in four panes of 50.

1965, May 13 ***Perf. 10½x11***

1264 A696 5c **black** .25 .25
P# block of 4 1.00 —
Margin block of 4, Mr. Zip and "Use Zip Code" 1.00 —

MAGNA CARTA ISSUE

750th anniversary of the Magna Carta, the basis of English and American common law.

Procession of Barons and King John's Crown — A697

Designed by Brook Temple.

GIORI PRESS PRINTING

Plates of 200 subjects in four panes of 50.

1965, June 15 ***Perf. 11***

1265 A697 5c **black, yellow ocher & red lilac** .25 .25
P# block of 4, 2# 1.00 —
Margin block of 4, Mr. Zip and "Use Zip Code" 1.00 —
Corner block of 4, black # omitted —

INTERNATIONAL COOPERATION YEAR

ICY, 1965, and 20th anniv. of the UN.

International Cooperation Year Emblem A698

Designed by Herbert M. Sanborn and Olav S. Mathiesen.

GIORI PRESS PRINTING

Plates of 200 subjects in four panes of 50.

1965, June 26 ***Perf. 11***

1266 A698 5c **dull blue & black** .25 .25
P# block of 4 1.00 —
Margin block of 4, Mr. Zip and "Use Zip Code" 1.00 —

SALVATION ARMY ISSUE

Centenary of the founding of the Salvation Army by William Booth in London.

A699

Designed by Sam Marsh.

GIORI PRESS PRINTING

Plates of 200 subjects in four panes of 50.

1965, July 2 ***Perf. 11***

1267 A699 5c **red, black & dark blue** .25 .25
P# block of 4 1.00 —
Margin block of 4, Mr. Zip and "Use Zip Code" 1.00 —

DANTE ISSUE

Dante Alighieri (1265-1321), Italian poet.

Dante after a 16th Century Painting — A700

Designed by Douglas Gorsline.

ROTARY PRESS PRINTING

E.E. Plates of 200 subjects in four panes of 50.

1965, July 17 ***Perf. 10½x11***

1268 A700 5c **maroon,** *tan* .25 .25
P# block of 4 1.00 —
Margin block of 4, Mr. Zip and "Use Zip Code" 1.00 —

HERBERT HOOVER ISSUE

President Herbert Clark Hoover, (1874-1964).

Herbert Hoover — A701

Designed by Norman Todhunter; photograph by Fabian Bachrach, Sr.

ROTARY PRESS PRINTING

E.E. Plates of 200 subjects in four panes of 50.

1965, Aug. 10 ***Perf. 10½x11***

1269 A701 5c **rose red** .25 .25
P# block of 4 1.00 —
Margin block of 4, Mr. Zip and "Use Zip Code" 1.00 —

ROBERT FULTON ISSUE

Fulton (1765-1815), inventor of the 1st commercial steamship.

Robert Fulton and the Clermont A702

Designed by John Maass; bust by Jean Antoine Houdon.

GIORI PRESS PRINTING

Plates of 200 subjects in four panes of 50.

1965, Aug. 19 ***Perf. 11***

1270 A702 5c **black & blue** .25 .25
P# block of 4 1.00 —
Margin block of 4, Mr. Zip and "Use Zip Code" 1.00 —

FLORIDA SETTLEMENT ISSUE

400th anniv. of the settlement of Florida, and the 1st permanent European settlement in the continental US, St. Augustine, Fla.

Spanish Explorer, Royal Flag of Spain and Ships — A703

Designed by Brook Temple.

GIORI PRESS PRINTING

Plates of 200 subjects with four panes of 50.

1965, Aug. 28 ***Perf. 11***

1271 A703 5c **red, yellow & black** .25 .25
P# block of 4, 3# 1.00 —
Margin block of 4, Mr. Zip and "Use Zip Code" 1.00 —
a. Yellow omitted *200.00*

See Spain No. 1312.

TRAFFIC SAFETY ISSUE

Issued to publicize traffic safety and the prevention of traffic accidents.

Traffic Signal — A704

Designed by Richard F. Hurd.

GIORI PRESS PRINTING

Plates of 200 subjects in four panes of 50.

1965, Sept. 3 ***Perf. 11***

1272 A704 5c **emerald, black & red** .25 .25
P# block of 4, 2# 1.00 —
Margin block of 4, Mr. Zip and "Use Zip Code" 1.00 —

JOHN SINGLETON COPLEY ISSUE

Copley (1738-1815), painter. The portrait of the artist's daughter is from the oil painting "The Copley Family," which hangs in the National Gallery of Art, Washington, D.C.

Elizabeth Clarke Copley — A705

Designed by John Carter Brown.

GIORI PRESS PRINTING
Plates of 200 subjects in four panes of 50.

1965, Sept. 17 ***Perf. 11***

1273 A705 5c **black, brown & olive**	.25	.25
P# block of 4	1.00	—
Margin block of 4, Mr. Zip and "Use Zip Code"	1.00	—

INTERNATIONAL TELECOMMUNICATION UNION, 100th ANNIV.

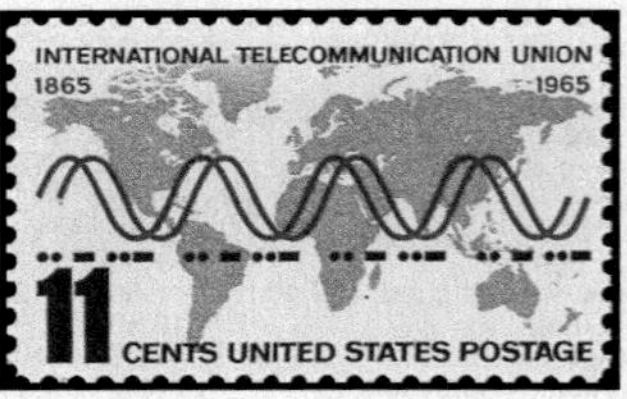

Galt Projection World Map and Radio Sine Wave — A706

Designed by Thomas F. Naegele.

GIORI PRESS PRINTING
Plates of 200 subjects with four panes of 50.

1965, Oct. 6 ***Perf. 11***

1274 A706 11c **black, carmine & bister**	.35	.25
P# block of 4, 2#	1.60	—
Margin block of 4, Mr. Zip and "Use Zip Code"	1.50	—

ADLAI STEVENSON ISSUE

Adlai Ewing Stevenson (1900-65), governor of Illinois, US ambassador to the UN.

Adlai E. Stevenson — A707

Designed by George Samerjan; photograph by Philippe Halsman.

LITHOGRAPHED, ENGRAVED (Giori)
Plates of 200 subjects in four panes of 50.

1965, Oct. 23 ***Perf. 11***

1275 A707 5c **pale blue, black, carmine & violet blue**	.25	.25
P# block of 4	1.10	—

CHRISTMAS ISSUE

Angel with Trumpet, 1840 Weather Vane — A708

Designed by Robert Jones.

After a watercolor by Lucille Gloria Chabot of the 1840 weather vane from the People's Methodist Church, Newburyport, Mass.

GIORI PRESS PRINTING
Plates of 400 subjects in four panes of 100.

1965, Nov. 2 ***Perf. 11***

1276 A708 5c **carmine, dark olive green & bister**	.25	.25
P# block of 4	1.00	—
Margin block of 4, Mr. Zip and "Use Zip Code"	1.00	—
Pair with full vert. gutter btwn.	*400.00*	
a. Tagged, *Nov. 15*	.75	.25
P# block of 4	5.50	—
Zip block of 4	3.50	—

PROMINENT AMERICANS ISSUE

Thomas Jefferson — A710

Albert Gallatin — A711

Frank Lloyd Wright and Guggenheim Museum, New York — A712

Francis Parkman — A713

Abraham Lincoln — A714

George Washington — A715

George Washington (redrawn) — A715a

Franklin D. Roosevelt — A716

Albert Einstein — A717

Andrew Jackson — A718

Henry Ford and 1909 Model T — A718a

John F. Kennedy — A719

Oliver Wendell Holmes — A720

Type III — A720a

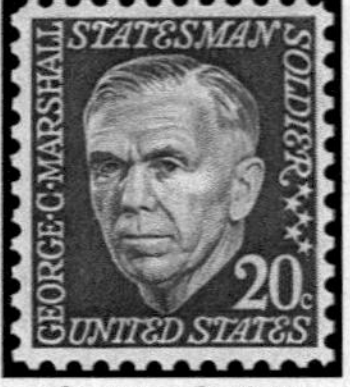

George Catlett Marshall — A721

Frederick Douglass — A722

John Dewey — A723

Thomas Paine — A724

Lucy Stone — A725

Eugene O'Neill — A726

John Bassett Moore — A727

Designers: 1c, Robert Geissmann, after portrait by Rembrandt Peale. 1¼c, Robert Gallatin. 2c, Patricia Amarantides;

QUALITY
U.S. STAMPS

From #1 to Date
Specializing in the
Modern Varieties

P.O. Box 7437 • Buffalo Grove, IL 60089
847.634.2676 • jfb7437@aol.com
www.BardoStamps.com

photograph by Blackstone-Shelburne. 3c, Bill Hyde. 4c, Bill Hyde; photograph by Mathew Brady. 5c, Bill Hyde, after portrait by Rembrandt Peale. 5c, No. 1283B, Redrawn by Stevan Dohanos. 6c, 30c, Richard L. Clark. 8c, Frank Sebastiano; photograph by Philippe Halsman. 10c, Lester Beall. 12c, Norman Todhunter. 13c, Stevan Dohanos; photograph by Jacques Lowe. 15c, Richard F. Hurd. 20c, Robert Geissmann. 25c, Walter DuBois Richards. 40c, Robert Geissmann, after portrait by John Wesley Jarvis. 50c, Mark English. $1, Norman Todhunter. $5, Tom Laufer.

Types of 15c:

I. Necktie barely touches coat at bottom; crosshatching of tie strong and complete. Flag of "5" is true horizontal. Crosshatching of "15" is colorless when visible.

II. Necktie does not touch coat at bottom; LL to UR crosshatching lines strong, UL to LR lines very faint. Flag of "5" slants down slightly at right. Crosshatching of "15" is colored and visible when magnified.

III. Used only for No. 1288B; smaller in overall size and "15¢" is ¾mm closer to head.

ROTARY PRESS PRINTING

E.E. Plates of 400 subjects in four panes of 100

1965-78 ***Perf. 11x10½, 10½x11***

1278 A710 1c **green,** tagged, shiny gum, *Jan. 12, 1968* .25 .25
On cover 4.00
P# block of 4 .50 —
Margin block of 4, "Use Zip Codes" .50 —
Dull gum (from bklt. pane) .25
a. Booklet pane of 8, shiny gum, *Jan. 12, 1968* 1.00 .75
Dull gum 1.75
b. Bklt. pane of 4+2 labels, *May 10, 1971* .75 .60
c. Untagged (Bureau precanceled) 6.25 1.25
P# block of 4 175.00
Margin block of 4, "Use Zip Codes" 30.00
d. Tagging omitted (not Bureau precanceled), shiny gum 4.00 —
dull gum —
e. As "a," dull gum, tagging omitted *85.00*

1279 A711 1¼c **light green,** *Jan. 30, 1967* .25 .25
On cover 6.00
Single franking on third-class nonprofit cover *125.00*
P# block of 4 3.50 —

1280 A712 2c **dark blue gray,** tagged, shiny gum, *June 8, 1966* .25 .25
On cover 4.00
Single franking on third-class nonprofit cover 10.00
Single franking on certificate of mailing *100.00*
P# block of 4 .50 —
Margin block of 4, "Use Zip Codes" .50 —
Pair with full vert. gutter between —
Dull gum (from bklt. pane) .25
a. Bklt. pane of 5 + label, *Jan. 8, 1968* 1.25 .80
b. Untagged (Bureau precanceled) 1.35 .40
P# block of 4 27.50
Margin block of 4, "Use Zip Codes" 7.50
c. Bklt. pane of 6, shiny gum, *May 7, 1971* 1.00 .75
Dull gum 1.10
d. Tagging omitted (not Bureau precanceled) 4.00 —

1281 A713 3c **violet,** tagged, *Sept. 16, 1967* .25 .25
On cover 4.00
Single franking on third-class nonprofit cover 15.00
P# block of 4 .50 —
Margin block of 4, "Use Zip Codes" .50 —
Pair with full horiz. gutter between —
a. Untagged (Bureau precanceled) 3.00 .75
P# block of 4 —
Margin block of 4, "Use Zip Codes" 30.00
b. Tagging omitted (not Bureau precanceled) 6.00 —

1282 A714 4c **black,** *Nov. 19, 1965* .25 .25
On cover 4.00
Single franking on third-class cover 5.00
Single franking on third-class bulk-rate cover 30.00
P# block of 4 1.00 —
a. Tagged, *Dec. 1, 1965* .25 .25
P# block of 4 1.00 —
Pair with full horiz. gutter between *800.00*

1283 A715 5c **blue,** *Feb. 22, 1966* .25 .25
On cover 2.00
Single franking on int'l surface printed-matter cover 15.00
Single franking on certificate of mailing 20.00
P# block of 4 1.00 —
a. Tagged, *Feb. 23, 1966* .25 .25
P# block of 4 1.00 —
Pair with full vert. gutter between *350.00*

1283B A715a 5c **blue,** tagged, shiny gum, *Nov. 17, 1967* .25 .25
On cover 2.00
Single franking on third-class bulk-rate cover 10.00
P# block of 4 1.00 —
Pair with full horiz. gutter between *175.00*
Dull gum .25
P# block of 4 1.40
d. Untagged (Bureau precanceled) 12.50 1.00
P# block of 4 —
e. Tagging omitted (not Bureau precanceled), shiny gum 6.00
Dull gum 5.50

No. 1283B is redrawn; highlights, shadows softened.

1284 A716 6c **gray brown,** *Jan. 29, 1966* .25 .25
On cover 2.00
Single franking on third-class cover 10.00
P# block of 4 1.00 —
Margin block of 4, "Use Zip Codes" (Bureau precanceled) 3.00
Pair with full horiz. gutter between *150.00*
Pair with full vert. gutter between *150.00*
a. Tagged, *Dec. 29, 1966* .25 .25
P# block of 4 1.00 —
Margin block of 4, "Use Zip Codes" 1.00 —
b. Booklet pane of 8, *Dec. 28, 1967* 1.50 1.00
c. Bklt. pane of 5+ label, *Jan. 9, 1968* 1.40 1.00
d. Horiz. pair, imperf. between *2,250.*
e. As "b," tagging omitted *90.00*

For untagged sheet stamps, "Use Zip Codes" and "Mail Early in the Day" marginal markings are found only on panes with Bureau precancels.

Counterfeits exist of No. 1284. See the Postal Counterfeits section of this catalog.

1285 A717 8c **violet,** *Mar. 14, 1966* .25 .25
On cover 4.00
Single franking on first-class cover 4.00
Single franking on third-class cover 15.00
Single franking on international surface-rate postcard —
P# block of 4 1.00 —
a. Tagged, *July 6, 1966* .25 .25
P# block of 4 1.10 —
Margin block of 4, "Use Zip Codes" 1.00 —

1286 A718 10c **lilac,** tagged, *Mar. 15, 1967* .25 .25
On cover 4.00
Single franking on int'l surface postcard 10.00
P# block of 4 1.10 —
Margin block of 4, "Use Zip Codes" 1.00 —
b. Untagged (Bureau precanceled) 55.00 1.75
P# block of 4 —
Margin block of 4, "Use Zip Codes" 275.00
e. Tagging omitted (not Bureau precanceled) 10.00

1286A 718a 12c **black,** tagged, *July 30, 1968* .25 .25
On cover 8.00
Single franking on domestic surface postcard 8.00
Single franking on int'l surface postcard 15.00
P# block of 4 1.30 —
Margin block of 4, "Use Zip Codes" 1.00 —
c. Untagged (Bureau precanceled) 4.75 1.00
P# block of 4 145.00
Margin block of 4, "Use Zip Codes" 27.50
d. Tagging omitted (not Bureau precanceled) 35.00

1287 A719 13c **brown,** tagged, *May 29, 1967* .30 .25
On cover 8.00
Single franking on int'l airmail postcard 10.00
Single franking on first-class airmail cover 15.00
Single franking on int'l surface cover 15.00
P# block of 4 1.50 —
Pair with full horiz. gutter between *500.00*
a. Untagged (Bureau precanceled) 6.00 1.00
P# block of 4 100.00
b. Tagging omitted (not Bureau precanceled) *15.00* —

Counterfeits exist of No. 1287. See the Postal Counterfeits section of this catalog.

1288 A720 15c **magenta,** type I, tagged, *Mar. 8, 1968* .30 .25
On cover 4.00
Single franking on first-class cover 4.00
Single franking on certificate of mailing 15.00
P# block of 4 1.25 —
Margin block of 4, "Use Zip Codes" 1.25 —
Pair with full horiz. gutter between *200.00*
Pair with full vert. gutter between *325.00*
a. Untagged (Bureau precanceled) .75 .75
P# block of 4 29.50
Margin block of 4, "Use Zip Codes" 7.50
d. Type II .55 .25
On cover 4.00
P# block of 4 8.00 —
Zip block of 4 3.50 —
Pair with full vert. gutter between —
f. As "d," tagging omitted (not Bureau precanceled) 7.50 —
h. As No. 1288, tagging omitted (not Bureau precanceled) 40.00

Imperforates exist from printer's waste.

Counterfeits exist of No. 1288. See the Postal Counterfeits section of this catalog.

Earliest documented use: July 16, 1979 (No. 1288d).

Values for No. 1288a are for the bars-only precancel. Also exists with city precancels, and worth more thus.

The existence of the No. 1288d pair with vert. gutter between has been questioned by specialists. The editors would like to see evidence of its existence.

1288B A720a 15c **magenta,** type III, tagged, perf. 10 (from blkt. pane) .35 .25
On cover 6.00
c. Booklet pane of 8, *June 14, 1978* 2.80 1.75
e. As "c," vert. imperf. between *1,500.*
g. Tagging omitted *10.00* —
i. As "c," tagging omitted *80.00* *50.00*

No. 1288B issued in booklets only. All stamps have one or two straight edges. Plates made from redrawn die.

1289 A721 20c **deep olive,** shiny gum, *Oct. 24, 1967* .40 .25
On cover 2.00
Single franking on int'l airmail cover to Europe 15.00
Single franking on domestic airmail cover 10.00
Single franking on int'l surface cover 20.00
P# block of 4 1.75 —
Margin block of 4, "Use Zip Codes" 1.65 —
a. Tagged, shiny gum, *Apr. 3, 1973* .40 .25
P# block of 4 1.75 —
Zip block of 4 1.65 —
Dull gum .45
P# block of 4 2.10
Zip block of 4 1.90
b. 20c **black olive,** tagged, dull gum .50 .25
P# block of 4 3.50 —
Zip block of 4 2.25 —
c. As "a," double impression *500.00*

1290 A722 25c **rose lake,** *Feb. 14, 1967* .55 .25
On cover 2.00
Single franking on int'l airmail cover to Asia 15.00
P# block of 4 2.25 —
Margin block of 4, "Use Zip Codes" 2.20 —
a. Tagged, shiny gum, *Apr. 3, 1973* .45 .25
P# block of 4 2.00 —
Zip block of 4 1.90 —
Dull gum .45
P# block of 4 2.00
Zip block of 4 1.90
b. 25c **magenta** *15.00* —
On cover —
P# block of 4 *125.00*

Shades of No. 1290 rose lake exist that tend toward magenta, but are not. Competent identification is important for No. 1290b.

1291 A723 30c **red lilac,** *Oct. 21, 1968* .65 .25
On cover 10.00
Single franking on double-weight airmail cover to Central/South America 15.00
P# block of 4 2.90 —
Margin block of 4, "Use Zip Codes" 2.70 —
a. Tagged, *Apr. 3, 1973* .50 .25
P# block of 4 2.25 —
Zip block of 4 2.10 —

1292 A724 40c **blue black,** shiny gum, *Jan. 29, 1968* .80 .25
On cover 6.00
Single franking on double-weight airmail cover to Europe 10.00
P# block of 4 3.25 —
Margin block of 4, "Use Zip Codes" 3.25 —
a. Tagged, shiny gum, *Apr. 3, 1973* .75 .25
P# block of 4 3.75 —
Zip block of 4 3.00 —
Dull gum .75
P# block of 4 3.00
Zip block of 4 3.00
b. As "a" with dull gum, tagging omitted —

1293 A725 50c **rose magenta,** *Aug. 13, 1968* 1.00 .25
On cover 4.00
Single franking on double-weight airmail cover to Asia 20.00
P# block of 4 4.25 —
Margin block of 4, "Use Zip Codes" 4.00 —
Pair with full vert. gutter btwn. —
a. Tagged, *Apr. 3, 1973* .80 .25
P# block of 4 3.50 —
Zip block of 4 3.25 —
Pair with full horiz. gutter btwn. —

Counterfeits exist of No. 1293. See the Postal Counterfeits section of this catalog.

1294 A726 $1 **dull purple,** *Oct. 16, 1967* 2.25 .25
On cover 5.00
Single franking on registered airmail cover 10.00
Single franking on quadruple-weight int'l airmail cover to Asia 20.00
P# block of 4 10.00 —

Margin block of 4, "Use Zip Codes" 9.25 —
a. Tagged, *Apr. 3, 1973* 1.75 .25
P# block of 4 7.25 —
Zip block of 4 7.00 —
b. **black violet** 100.00 *350.00*
P# block of 4 *1,100.*
Zip block of 4 *450.00*

1295 A727 $5 **gray black,** *Dec. 3, 1966* 10.00 2.25
On cover 20.00
Single franking on registered first-class cover *500.00*
Single franking on fourth-class cover *750.00*
P# block of 4 42.50 —
a. Tagged, *Apr. 3, 1973* 8.50 2.00
P# block of 4 35.00 —
Nos. 1278-1295 (21) 19.35 7.25
Nos. 1278-1288, 1289-1295, P# blocks of 4 (20) 78.65

Counterfeits exist of No. 1295. See the Postal Counterfeits section of this catalog.

Bureau Precancels: 1c, 19 diff., 1¼c, 14 diff., 2c, 41 diff., 3c, 11 diff., 4c, 49 diff., No. 1283, 7 diff., No. 1283B, 29 diff., 6c, 35 diff., 8c, 18 diff., 10c, 12 diff., 12c, 3 diff., 13c, 3 diff., No. 1288a, 9 diff., 20c, 14 diff., 25c, 9 diff., 30c, 14 diff., 40c, 7 diff., 50c, 14 diff., $1, 8 diff.

See Luminescence note in the catalogue introduction.

COIL STAMPS

1967-75 Tagged *Perf. 10 Horizontally*

1297 A713 3c **violet,** shiny gum, *Nov. 4, 1975* .25 .25
On cover 3.00
Pair .50 .50
Joint line pair .60 .60
Dull gum .75
Joint line pair 3.00
a. Imperf., pair, shiny gum 22.50
Imperf., joint line pair 45.00
Imperf, pair, dull gum 22.50
Imperf, joint line pair 45.00
b. Untagged (Bureau precanceled), shiny gum .40 .25
Single franking on third-class nonprofit cover 5.00
Pair .80 .50
Joint line pair 62.50 3.75
Dull gum .25
Pair .50
Joint line pair 3.75
c. As "b," imperf. pair 8.00 —
Single franking on nonprofit carrier cover 5.00
Joint line pair 20.00

No. 1297c is precanceled "Nonprofit Org. / CAR RT SORT."

1298 A716 6c **gray brown,** *Dec. 28, 1967* .25 .25
On cover 4.00
Single franking on third-class cover 10.00
Pair .50 .50
Joint line pair 1.10 .60
a. Imperf., pair *1,500.*
Imperf., joint line pair *4,500.*
b. Tagging omitted 3.50

Bureau Precancels: 3c, 9 diff.

Franklin D. Roosevelt — A727a

Revised design by Robert J. Jones and Howard C. Mildner.

COIL STAMPS

1966-81 Tagged *Perf. 10 Vertically*

1299 A710 1c **green,** *Jan. 12, 1968* .25 .25
On cover 4.00
Pair .50 .50
Joint line pair .60 .60
a. Untagged (Bureau precanceled) 8.00 1.75
Pair 17.50 4.00
Joint line pair *290.00* —
b. Imperf., pair *22.50* —
Imperf., joint line pair *50.00*
c. Tagging omitted (not Bureau pre-canceled) —

1303 A714 4c **black,** *May 28, 1966* .25 .25
On cover 8.00
Pair .50 .50
Joint line pair .75 .60
a. Untagged (Bureau precanceled) 8.75 .75
Pair 19.00 1.75
Joint line pair *250.00* —
b. Imperf., pair *600.00*
Imperf., joint line pair *1,300.*
c. Tagging omitted (not Bureau pre-canceled) *15.00* —

1304 A715 5c **blue,** shiny gum, *Sept. 8, 1966* .25 .25
On cover 3.00
Pair .50 .50
Joint line pair .75 .60
Dull gum .75
Joint line pair 5.00
a. Untagged (Bureau precanceled) 6.50 .65
Single franking on third-class bulk rate cover 6.00
Pair 14.00 1.40
Joint line pair *175.00* —
b. Imperf., pair *110.00*
Joint line pair *250.00*
e. As "a," imperf., pair *250.00*
Joint line pair *800.00*
f. Tagging omitted (not Bureau pre-canceled) — —

No. 1304b is valued in the grade of fine.

No. 1304e is precanceled Mount Pleasant, Iowa. Also exists from Chicago, Illinois; value $1,500 for pair.

1304C A715a 5c **blue,** *Jan., 1981* .25 .25
On cover 3.00
Pair .50 .50
Joint line pair 1.25 —
d. Imperf., pair *375.00*
Joint line pair *675.00*

1305 A727a 6c **gray brown,** *Feb. 28, 1968* .25 .25
On cover 2.00
Single franking on third-class cover 10.00
Pair .50 .50
Joint line pair .75 .60
a. Imperf., pair 55.00
Joint line pair *115.00*
b. Untagged (Bureau precanceled) 20.00 1.00
Pair 42.50 2.25
Joint line pair *675.00* —
k. Tagging omitted (not Bureau pre-canceled) 4.00 —
m. Pair, imperf. between *250.00*
Joint line pair *500.00*

1305E A720 15c **magenta,** type I, shiny gum, *June 14, 1978* .25 .25
On cover 2.00
Pair .50 .50
Joint line pair 1.10 .60
Dull gum .75
Joint line pair 4.50
f. Untagged (Bureau precanceled, Chicago, IL) 32.50 —
Pair 75.00 —
Joint line pair *1,100.* —
g. Imperf., pair, type I, shiny gum 20.00
Joint line pair 50.00
Imperf., pair, dull gum 22.50
Joint line pair 60.00
h. Pair, imperf. between 125.00
Joint line pair *400.00*
i. Type II, dull gum 1.50 .25
On cover 2.00
Single franking on first-class cover 5.00
Joint line pair 5.00 —
j. Type II, dull gum, Imperf., pair *55.00*
Joint line pair *150.00*
l. Tagging omitted —

Earliest documented use: July 16, 1979 (No. 1305Ei).

1305C A726 $1 **dull purple,** shiny gum, *Jan. 12, 1973* 3.25 .40
blackish purple 4.00 .60
On cover 8.00
Single franking on first-class insured cover 35.00
Pair 6.50 .80
Joint line pair 9.50 1.50
Dull gum 4.75
Pair 9.50
Joint line pair 15.00
d. Imperf., pair *1,250.*
Joint line pair *3,000.*
Nos. 1297-1305C (9) 5.25 2.40

Bureau Precancels: 1c, 5 diff., 4c, 35 diff., No. 1304a, 45 diff., 6c, 30 diff.

MIGRATORY BIRD TREATY ISSUE

Migratory Birds over Canada-US Border A728

Designed by Burt E. Pringle.

GIORI PRESS PRINTING

Plates of 200 subjects in four panes of 50.

1966, Mar. 16 *Perf. 11*

1306 A728 5c **black, crimson & dark blue** .25 .25
P# block of 4, 2# 1.00 —
Margin block of 4, Mr. Zip and "Use Zip Code" 1.00 —

HUMANE TREATMENT OF ANIMALS ISSUE

Issued to promote humane treatment of all animals and for the centenary of the American Society for the Prevention of Cruelty to Animals.

Mongrel A729

Designed by Norman Todhunter.

LITHOGRAPHED, ENGRAVED (Giori)

Plates of 200 subjects in four panes of 50.

1966, Apr. 9 *Perf. 11*

1307 A729 5c **orange brown & black** .25 .25
P# block of 4 1.00 —
Margin block of 4, Mr. Zip and "Use Zip Code" 1.00 —

INDIANA STATEHOOD, 150th ANNIV.

Sesquicentennial Seal; Map of Indiana with 19 Stars and old Capitol at Corydon — A730

Designed by Paul A. Wehr.

GIORI PRESS PRINTING

Plates of 200 subjects in four panes of 50.

1966, Apr. 16 *Perf. 11*

1308 A730 5c **ocher, brown & violet blue** .25 .25
P# block of 4, 2# 1.00 —
Margin block of 4, Mr. Zip and "Use Zip Code" 1.00 —

AMERICAN CIRCUS ISSUE

Issued to honor the American Circus on the centenary of the birth of John Ringling.

Clown — A731

Designed by Edward Klauck.

GIORI PRESS PRINTING

Plates of 200 subjects in four panes of 50.

1966, May 2 *Perf. 11*

1309 A731 5c **multicolored** .25 .25
P# block of 4, 2# 1.00 —
Margin block of 4, Mr. Zip and "Use Zip Code" 1.00 —

SIXTH INTERNATIONAL PHILATELIC EXHIBITION ISSUES

Sixth International Philatelic Exhibition (SIPEX), Washington, D.C., May 21-30.

Stamped Cover — A732

Designed by Thomas F. Naegele.

LITHOGRAPHED, ENGRAVED (Giori)
Plates of 200 subjects in four panes of 50.

1966 ***Perf. 11***
1310 A732 5c **multicolored**, *May 21* .25 .25
P# block of 4 1.00 —
Margin block of 4, Mr. Zip and "Use Zip Code" 1.00 —

Souvenir Sheet

A733

Designed by Brook Temple.

Plates of 24 subjects
Imperf
1311 A733 5c **multicolored**, *May 23* .25 .25

No. 1311 measures 108x74mm. Below the stamp appears a line drawing of the Capitol and Washington Monument. Marginal inscriptions and drawing are green.

BILL OF RIGHTS, 175th ANNIV.

"Freedom" Checking "Tyranny" — A734

Designed by Herbert L. Block (Herblock).

GIORI PRESS PRINTING
Plates of 200 subjects in four panes of 50.

1966, July 1 ***Perf. 11***
1312 A734 5c **carmine, dark & light blue** .25 .25
P# block of 4, 2# 1.00 —
Margin block of 4, Mr. Zip and "Use Zip Code" 1.00 —

POLISH MILLENNIUM ISSUE

Adoption of Christianity in Poland, 1000th anniv.

Polish Eagle and Cross — A735

Designed by Edmund D. Lewandowski.

ROTARY PRESS PRINTING
E.E. Plates of 200 subjects in four panes of 50.

1966, July 30 ***Perf. 10½x11***
1313 A735 5c **red** .25 .25
P# block of 4 1.00 —
Margin block of 4, Mr. Zip and "Use Zip Code" 1.00 —

Tagging Extended

During 1966, experimental use of tagged stamps was extended to the Cincinnati Postal Region covering offices in Indiana, Kentucky and Ohio. To supply these offices about 12 percent of the following nine issues (Nos. 1314-1322) were tagged.

NATIONAL PARK SERVICE ISSUE

50th anniv. of the Natl. Park Service of the Interior Dept. The design "Parkscape U.S.A." identifies Natl. Park Service facilities.

National Park Service Emblem A736

Designed by Thomas H. Geismar.

LITHOGRAPHED, ENGRAVED (Giori)
Plates of 200 subjects in four panes of 50.

1966, Aug. 25 ***Perf. 11***
1314 A736 5c **yellow, black & green** .25 .25
P# block of 4 1.00 —
Margin block of 4, Mr. Zip and "Use Zip Code" 1.00 —
a. Tagged, *Aug. 26* .35 .35
P# block of 4 2.25 —
Zip block of 4 1.50 —

MARINE CORPS RESERVE ISSUE

US Marine Corps Reserve founding, 50th anniv.

Combat Marine, 1966; Frogman; World War II Flier; World War I "Devil Dog" and Marine, 1775 — A737

Designed by Stella Grafakos.

LITHOGRAPHED, ENGRAVED (Giori)
Plates of 200 subjects in four panes of 50.

1966, Aug. 29 ***Perf. 11***
1315 A737 5c **black, bister, red & ultra** .25 .25
P# block of 4 1.00 —
Margin block of 4, Mr. Zip and "Use Zip Code" 1.00 —
a. Tagged .40 .25
P# block of 4 2.25 —
Zip block of 4 1.70 —
b. Black & bister (engraved) missing (EP) *16,000.*

GENERAL FEDERATION OF WOMEN'S CLUBS ISSUE

75 years of service by the General Federation of Women's Clubs.

Women of 1890 and 1966 — A738

Designed by Charles Henry Carter.

GIORI PRESS PRINTING
Plates of 200 subjects in four panes of 50.

1966, Sept. 12 ***Perf. 11***
1316 A738 5c **black, pink & blue** .25 .25
P# block of 4, 2# 1.00 —
Margin block of 4, Mr. Zip and "Use Zip Code" 1.00 —
a. Tagged, *Sept. 13* .40 .25
P# block of 4, 2# 2.25 —
Zip block of 4 1.70 —

AMERICAN FOLKLORE ISSUE
Johnny Appleseed

Issued to honor Johnny Appleseed (John Chapman 1774-1845), who wandered over 100,000 square miles planting apple trees, and who gave away and sold seedlings to Midwest pioneers.

Johnny Appleseed — A739

Designed by Robert Bode.

GIORI PRESS PRINTING
Plates of 200 subjects in four panes of 50.

1966, Sept. 24 ***Perf. 11***
1317 A739 5c **green, red & black** .25 .25
P# block of 4, 2# 1.00 —
Margin block of 4, Mr. Zip and "Use Zip Code" 1.00 —
Pair with full horiz. gutter between —
a. Tagged, *Sept. 26* .40 .25
P# block of 4, 2# 2.25 —
Zip block of 4 1.70 —

BEAUTIFICATION OF AMERICA ISSUE

Issued to publicize President Johnson's "Plant for a more beautiful America" campaign.

Jefferson Memorial, Tidal Basin and Cherry Blossoms A740

Designed by Miss Gyo Fujikawa.

GIORI PRESS PRINTING
Plates of 200 subjects in four panes of 50.

1966, Oct. 5 ***Perf. 11***
1318 A740 5c **emerald, pink & black** .25 .25
P# block of 4, 2# 1.00 —
Margin block of 4, Mr. Zip and "Use Zip Code" 1.00 —
a. Tagged .40 .25
P# block of 4, 2# 2.25 —
Zip block of 4 1.70 —

Compare with No. 4716c.

GREAT RIVER ROAD ISSUE

Issued to publicize the 5,600-mile Great River Road connecting New Orleans with Kenora, Ontario, and following the Mississippi most of the way.

Map of Central United States with Great River Road — A741

Designed by Herbert Bayer.

LITHOGRAPHED, ENGRAVED (Giori)
Plates of 200 subjects in four panes of 50.

1966, Oct. 21
1319 A741 5c **vermilion, yellow, blue & green** .25 .25
P# block of 4 1.00 —
Margin block of 4, Mr. Zip and "Use Zip Code" 1.00 —

a.	Tagged, *Oct. 22*	.45	.25
	P# block of 4	2.50	—
	Zip block of 4	1.90	—

SAVINGS BOND-SERVICEMEN ISSUE

25th anniv. of US Savings Bonds, and honoring American servicemen.

Statue of Liberty and "Old Glory" — A742

Designed by Stevan Dohanos, photo by Bob Noble.

LITHOGRAPHED, ENGRAVED (Giori)
Plates of 200 subjects in four panes of 50.

1966, Oct. 26 ***Perf. 11***

1320	A742 5c **red, dark blue, light blue & black**	.25	.25
	P# block of 4	1.00	—
	Margin block of 4, Mr. Zip and "Use Zip Code"	1.00	—
a.	Tagged, *Oct. 27*	.40	.25
	P# block of 4	2.00	—
	Zip block of 4	1.70	—
b.	Red, dark blue & black missing (EP)	*3,750.*	
c.	Dark blue (engr.) missing (EP)	*5,000.*	

CHRISTMAS ISSUE

Madonna and Child, by Hans Memling — A743

Designed by Howard C. Mildner.

Modeled after "Madonna and Child with Angels," by the Flemish artist Hans Memling (c.1430-1494), Mellon Collection, National Gallery of Art, Washington, D.C.

LITHOGRAPHED, ENGRAVED (Giori)
Plates of 400 subjects in four panes of 100.

1966, Nov. 1 ***Perf. 11***

1321	A743 5c **multicolored**	.25	.25
	P# block of 4	1.00	—
	Margin block of 4, Mr. Zip and "Use Zip Code"	1.00	—
a.	Tagged, *Nov. 2*	.40	.25
	P# block of 4	2.00	—
	Zip block of 4	1.70	—

MARY CASSATT ISSUE

Cassatt (1844-1926), painter. The painting "The Boating Party" is in the Natl. Gallery of Art, Washington, D.C.

"The Boating Party" — A744

Designed by Robert J. Jones.

GIORI PRESS PRINTING
Plates of 200 subjects in four panes of 50.

1966, Nov. 17 ***Perf. 11***

1322	A744 5c **multicolored**	.25	.25
	P# block of 4, 2#	1.00	—
	Margin block of 4, Mr. Zip and "Use Zip Code"	1.00	—
a.	Tagged	.40	.25
	P# block of 4, 2#	2.00	—
	Zip block of 4	1.70	—

NATIONAL GRANGE ISSUE

Centenary of the founding of the National Grange, American farmers' organization.

Grange Poster, 1870 — A745

Designed by Lee Pavao.

GIORI PRESS PRINTING
Plates of 200 subjects in four panes of 50.

1967, Apr. 17 **Tagged** ***Perf. 11***

1323	A745 5c **orange, yellow, brown, green & black**	.25	.25
	P# block of 4, 2#	1.00	—
	Margin block of 4, Mr. Zip and "Use Zip Code"	1.00	—
a.	Tagging omitted	*6.00*	—

Phosphor Tagging

From No. 1323 onward, all postage issues are tagged, unless otherwise noted.

Inadvertent omissions of tagging occurred on Nos. 1238, 1278, 1281, 1298 and 1305. In addition many tagged issues from 1967 on exist with tagging unintentionally omitted, and these errors are listed herein.

CANADA CENTENARY ISSUE

Centenary of Canada's emergence as a nation.

Canadian Landscape A746

Designed by Ivan Chermayeff.

GIORI PRESS PRINTING
Plates of 200 subjects in four panes of 50.

1967, May 25 **Tagged** ***Perf. 11***

1324	A746 5c **lt. blue, dp. green, ultra, olive & black**	.25	.25
	On cover, Expo. station ("U.S. Pavilion") machine canc.		1.00
	On cover, Expo. station handstamp canc.		2.50
	P# block of 4, 2#	1.00	—
	Margin block of 4, Mr. Zip and "Use Zip Code"	1.00	—
a.	Tagging omitted	*7.50*	—

ERIE CANAL ISSUE

150th anniversary of the Erie Canal ground-breaking ceremony at Rome, N.Y. The canal links Lake Erie and New York City.

Stern of Early Canal Boat — A747

Designed by George Samerjan.

LITHOGRAPHED, ENGRAVED (Giori)
Plates of 200 subjects in four panes of 50.

1967, July 4 **Tagged** ***Perf. 11***

1325	A747 5c **ultra, grnsh blue, blk & crim**	.25	.25
	P# block of 4	1.00	—
	Margin block of 4, Mr. Zip and "Use Zip Code"	1.00	—
a.	Tagging omitted	*20.00*	—

"SEARCH FOR PEACE" — LIONS ISSUE

Issued to publicize the search for peace. "Search for Peace" was the theme of an essay contest for young men and women sponsored by Lions International on its 50th anniversary.

Peace Dove — A748

Designed by Bradbury Thompson.

GIORI PRESS PRINTING
Plates of 200 subjects in four panes of 50.

1967, July 5 **Tagged** ***Perf. 11***

Gray Paper with Blue Threads

1326	A748 5c **blue, red & black**	.25	.25
	P# block of 4	1.00	—
	Margin block of 4, Mr. Zip and "Use Zip Code"	1.00	—
a.	Tagging omitted	*10.00*	—

HENRY DAVID THOREAU ISSUE

Henry David Thoreau (1817-62), Writer — A749

Designed by Leonard Baskin.

GIORI PRESS PRINTING
Plates of 200 subjects in four panes of 50.

1967, July 12 **Tagged** ***Perf. 11***

1327	A749 5c **carmine, black & blue green**	.25	.25
	P# block of 4	1.00	—
	Margin block of 4, Mr. Zip and "Use Zip Code"	1.00	—
a.	Tagging omitted	*200.00*	
b.	Carmine missing (PS)	—	

NEBRASKA STATEHOOD, 100th ANNIV.

Hereford Steer and Ear of Corn — A750

Designed by Julian K. Billings.

LITHOGRAPHED, ENGRAVED (Giori)
Plates of 200 subjects in four panes of 50.

1967, July 29 **Tagged** ***Perf. 11***

1328	A750 5c **dark red brown, lemon & yellow**	.25	.25
	P# block of 4	1.00	—
	Margin block of 4, Mr. Zip and "Use Zip Code"	1.00	—
a.	Tagging omitted	*7.50*	—

VOICE OF AMERICA ISSUE

25th anniv. of the radio branch of the United States Information Agency (USIA).

Radio Transmission Tower and Waves — A751

Designed by Georg Olden.

LITHOGRAPHED, ENGRAVED (Giori)
Plates of 200 subjects in four panes of 50.

1967, Aug. 1 **Tagged** ***Perf. 11***

1329 A751 5c **red, blue, black & carmine** .25 .25
P# block of 4 1.00 —
Margin block of 4, Mr. Zip and "Use Zip Code" 1.00 —
a. Tagging omitted *20.00* —

AMERICAN FOLKLORE ISSUE

Davy Crockett (1786-1836), frontiersman, hunter, and congressman from Tennessee who died at the Alamo.

Davy Crockett and Scrub Pine — A752

Designed by Robert Bode.

LITHOGRAPHED, ENGRAVED (Giori)
Plates of 200 subjects in four panes of 50.

1967, Aug. 17 **Tagged** ***Perf. 11***

1330 A752 5c **green, black, & yellow** .25 .25
P# block of 4 1.00 —
Margin block of 4, Mr. Zip and "Use Zip Code" 1.00 —
a. Vertical pair, imperf. between *7,500.*
b. Green (engr.) missing (FO) —
c. Black & green (engr.) missing (FO) —
e. Tagging omitted *10.00* —

A foldover on a pane of No. 1330 resulted in one example each of Nos. 1330b-1330c. Part of the colors appear on the back of the selvage and one freak stamp. An engraved black-and-green-only impression appears on the gummed side of one almost-complete "stamp."

ACCOMPLISHMENTS IN SPACE ISSUE

US accomplishments in space. Printed with continuous design in horizontal rows of 5. In the left panes the astronaut stamp is 1st, 3rd and 5th, the spaceship 2nd and 4th. This arrangement is reversed in the right panes.

Space-Walking Astronaut — A753

Gemini 4 Capsule — A754

Designed by Paul Calle.

LITHOGRAPHED, ENGRAVED (Giori)
Plates of 200 subjects in four panes of 50.

1967, Sept. 29 **Tagged** ***Perf. 11***

1331 A753 5c **multicolored** .55 .25
a. Tagging omitted *25.00* —
1332 A754 5c **multicolored** .55 .25
P# block of 4 2.50 —
Margin block of 4, Mr. Zip and "Use Zip Code" 2.40 —
Plate flaw (red stripes of flag on capsule omitted; 29322, 29325 UL 19) 200.00
a. Tagging omitted *25.00* —
b. Pair, #1331-1332 1.25 1.25
c. As "b," tagging omitted *60.00* —

URBAN PLANNING ISSUE

Publicizing the importance of Urban Planning in connection with the Intl. Conf. of the American Institute of Planners, Washington, D.C., Oct. 1-6.

View of Model City — A755

Designed by Francis Ferguson.

LITHOGRAPHED, ENGRAVED (Giori)
Plates of 200 subjects in four panes of 50.

1967, Oct. 2 **Tagged** ***Perf. 11***

1333 A755 5c **dark blue, light blue & black** .25 .25
P# block of 4 1.00 —
Margin block of 4, Mr. Zip and "Use Zip Code" 1.00 —
a. Tagging omitted *50.00* —

FINNISH INDEPENDENCE, 50th ANNIV.

Finnish Coat of Arms — A756

Designed by Bradbury Thompson.

ENGRAVED (Giori)
Plates of 200 subjects in four panes of 50.

1967, Oct. 6 **Tagged** ***Perf. 11***

1334 A756 5c **blue** .25 .25
P# block of 4 1.00 —
Margin block of 4, Mr. Zip and "Use Zip Code" 1.00 —
a. Tagging omitted *100.00*

THOMAS EAKINS ISSUE

Eakins (1844-1916), painter and sculptor. The painting is in the Natl. Gallery of Art, Washington, D.C.

"The Biglin Brothers Racing" (Sculling on Schuylkill River, Philadelphia) A757

Printed by Photogravure & Color Co., Moonachie, N.J.

PHOTOGRAVURE
Plates of 200 subjects in four panes of 50.

1967, Nov. 2 **Tagged** ***Perf. 12***

1335 A757 5c **gold & multicolored** .25 .25
P# block of 4, 6# 1.00 —
a. Tagging omitted *40.00* —

Plate number blocks from upper left or lower left panes show clipped corner of margin.

CHRISTMAS ISSUE

Madonna and Child, by Hans Memling — A758

LITHOGRAPHED, ENGRAVED (Giori)
Plates of 200 subjects in four panes of 50.

1967, Nov. 6 **Tagged** ***Perf. 11***

1336 A758 5c **multicolored** .25 .25
P# block of 4 1.00 —
Margin block of 4, Mr. Zip and "Use Zip Code" 1.00 —
a. Tagging omitted *5.50* —

See note on painting above No. 1321.

MISSISSIPPI STATEHOOD, 150th ANNIV.

Magnolia A759

Designed by Andrew Bucci.

GIORI PRESS PRINTING
Plates of 200 subjects in four panes of 50.

1967, Dec. 11 **Tagged** ***Perf. 11***

1337 A759 5c **brt. greenish blue, green & red brown** .25 .25
P# block of 4, 2# 1.00 —
Margin block of 4, Mr. Zip and "Use Zip Code" 1.00 —
a. Tagging omitted *10.00* —

FLAG ISSUE

Flag and White House — A760

Designed by Stevan Dohanos.

GIORI PRESS PRINTING
Plates of 400 subjects in four panes of 100.

1968, Jan. 24 **Tagged** ***Perf. 11***
Size: 19x22mm

1338 A760 6c **dark blue, red & green** .25 .25
P# block of 4 1.00 —
Margin block of 4, "Use Zip Code" 1.00 —
Pair with full vert. gutter btwn. —
k. Vert. pair, imperf. btwn. *250.00* *150.00*
m. Tagging omitted *4.50* —
s. Red missing (FO) —
u. Vert. pair, imperf horiz. *275.00*
v. All color omitted —

No. 1338s is unique.

Beware of regumming on No. 1338u. Most examples have had the gum washed off to make it difficult or impossible to detect blind perfs. Check carefully for blind perfs. Value is for pair with original gum.

On No. 1338v, an albino impression of the engraved plate is present.

COIL STAMP

MULTICOLOR HUCK PRESS

1969, May 30 **Tagged** ***Perf. 10 Vertically***
Size: 18¼x21mm

1338A A760 6c **dark blue, red & green** .25 .25
Pair .50 .50
b. Imperf., pair *350.00*
q. Tagging omitted *10.00* —

MULTICOLOR HUCK PRESS
Panes of 100 (10x10) each

1970-71 **Tagged** ***Perf. 11x10½***
Size: 18¼x21mm

1338D A760 6c **dark blue, red & green,** *Aug. 7, 1970* .25 .25
Margin block of 20+ 4.00 —
e. Horiz. pair, imperf. between *115.00*
n. Tagging omitted *5.00* —
1338F A760 8c **dark blue, red & slate green,** *May 10, 1971* .25 .25
Margin block of 20+ 3.50 —
i. Imperf., vert. pair 35.00
j. Horiz. pair, imperf. between 45.00
o. Tagging omitted *5.00* —
p. Slate green omitted *300.00*
t. Horiz. pair, imperf. vertically —

+ Margin blocks of 20 come in four versions: (1) 2 P#, 3 ME, 3 zip; (2) 3 P#, 2 ME, 2 zip; (3) 2 P#, 3 ME, 2 zip; (4) 3 P#, 2 ME, 3 zip.

COIL STAMP
MULTICOLOR HUCK PRESS

1971, May 10 **Tagged** ***Perf. 10 Vertically***
Size: 18¼x21mm

1338G A760 8c **dk blue, red & slate green** .30 .25
Pair .60 .50
h. Imperf., pair *45.00*
r. Tagging omitted *5.00* —

ILLINOIS STATEHOOD, 150th ANNIV.

Farm Buildings and Fields of Ripening Grain — A761

Designed by George Barford.

LITHOGRAPHED, ENGRAVED (Giori)
Plates of 200 subjects in four panes of 50.

1968, Feb. 12 **Tagged** ***Perf. 11***
1339 A761 6c **dk blue, blue, red & ocher** .25 .25
P# block of 4 1.00 —
Margin block of 4, Mr. Zip and "Use Zip Code" 1.00 —
a. Tagging omitted *170.00*

HEMISFAIR '68 ISSUE

HemisFair '68 exhibition, San Antonio, Texas, Apr. 6-Oct. 6, for the 250th anniv. of San Antonio.

Map of North and South America and Lines Converging on San Antonio — A762

Designed by Louis Macouillard.

LITHOGRAPHED, ENGRAVED (Giori)
Plates of 200 subjects in four panes of 50.

1968, Mar. 30 **Tagged** ***Perf. 11***
1340 A762 6c **blue, rose red & white** .25 .25
On cover, Expo. station machine canc. 10.00
On cover, Expo. roller canc. 25.00
P# block of 4 1.00 —
Margin block of 4, Mr. Zip and "Use Zip Code" 1.00 —
a. White omitted *650.00*

AIRLIFT ISSUE

Issued to pay for airlift of parcels from and to US ports to servicemen overseas and in Alaska, Hawaii and Puerto Rico. Valid for all regular postage. On Apr. 26, 1969, the Post Office Department ruled that henceforth No. 1341 "may be used toward paying the postage or fees for special services on *airmail* articles."

Eagle Holding Pennant A763

Designed by Stevan Dohanos.

After a late 19th century wood carving, part of the Index of American Design, National Gallery of Art.

LITHOGRAPHED, ENGRAVED (Giori)
Plates of 200 subjects in four panes of 50.

1968, Apr. 4 **Untagged** ***Perf. 11***
1341 A763 $1 **sepia, dk. blue, ocher & brown red** 2.00 1.25
P# block of 4 8.25 —
Margin block of 4, Mr. Zip and "Use Zip Code" 8.00 —
Pair with full horiz. gutter btwn. —

"SUPPORT OUR YOUTH" — ELKS ISSUE

Support Our Youth program, and honoring the Benevolent and Protective Order of Elks, which extended its youth service program in observance of its centennial year.

Girls and Boys — A764

Designed by Edward Vebell.

LITHOGRAPHED, ENGRAVED (Giori)
Plates of 200 subjects in four panes of 50.

1968, May 1 **Tagged** ***Perf. 11***
1342 A764 6c **ultramarine & orange red** .25 .25
P# block of 4 1.00 —
Margin block of 4, Mr. Zip and "Use Zip Code" 1.00 —
a. Tagging omitted 10.00 —

LAW AND ORDER ISSUE

Publicizing the policeman as protector and friend and to encourage respect for law and order.

Policeman and Boy — A765

Designed by Ward Brackett.

GIORI PRESS PRINTING
Plates of 200 subjects in four panes of 50 each

1968, May 17 **Tagged** ***Perf. 11***
1343 A765 6c **chalky blue, black & red** .25 .25
P# block of 4 1.00 —
Margin block of 4, Mr. Zip and "Use Zip Code" 1.00 —
a. Tagging omitted *175.00 90.00*

REGISTER AND VOTE ISSUE

Campaign to draw more voters to the polls. The weather vane is from an old house in the Russian Hill section of San Francisco, Cal.

Eagle Weather Vane — A766

Designed by Norman Todhunter and Bill Hyde; photograph by M. Halberstadt.

LITHOGRAPHED, ENGRAVED (Giori)
Plates of 200 subjects in four panes of 50.

1968, June 27 **Tagged** ***Perf. 11***
1344 A766 6c **black, yellow & orange** .25 .25
P# block of 4 1.00 —
Margin block of 4, Mr. Zip and "Use Zip Code" 1.00 —
a. Tagging omitted —

HISTORIC FLAG SERIES

Flags carried by American colonists and by citizens of the new United States. Printed se-tenant in vertical columns of 10. The flag sequence on the 2 upper panes is as listed. On the 2 lower panes the sequence is reversed with the Navy Jack in the 1st row and the Fort Moultrie flag in the 10th.

Ft. Moultrie, 1776 — A767

Ft. McHenry, 1795-1818 A768

Washington's Cruisers, 1775 — A769

Bennington, 1777 — A770

Rhode Island, 1775 — A771

First Stars and Stripes, 1777 — A772

Bunker Hill, 1775 — A773

Grand Union, 1776 — A774

Philadelphia Light Horse, 1775 — A775

First Navy Jack, 1775 — A776

ENGR. (Giori) (#1345-1348, 1350);
ENGR. & LITHO. (#1349, 1351-1354)
Plates of 200 subjects in four panes of 50.

1968, July 4 **Tagged** ***Perf. 11***

1345	A767 6c **dark blue**	.40	.25
1346	A768 6c **dark blue & red**	.40	.25
1347	A769 6c **dark blue & olive green**	.30	.25
1348	A770 6c **dark blue & red**	.30	.25
1349	A771 6c **dark blue, yellow & red**	.30	.25
1350	A772 6c **dark blue & red**	.30	.25
1351	A773 6c **dark blue, olive green & red**	.30	.25
1352	A774 6c **dark blue & red**	.30	.25
1353	A775 6c **dark blue, yellow & red**	.30	.25
1354	A776 6c **dark blue, red & yellow**	.30	.25
a.	Strip of ten, #1345-1354	3.25	*3.25*
	P# block of 20, inscriptions, #1345-1354	6.75	—
b.	#1345b-1354b, any single, tagging omitted	*65.00*	
c.	As "a," imperf	*4,500.*	
d.	As "a," tagging omitted	*650.00*	

WALT DISNEY ISSUE

Walt Disney (1901-1966), cartoonist, film producer and creator of Mickey Mouse.

Walt Disney and Children of the World — A777

Designed by C. Robert Moore.

Designed after portrait by Paul E. Wenzel.
Printed by Achrovure Division of Union-Camp Corp., Englewood, N.J.

PHOTOGRAVURE
Plates of 400 subjects in eight panes of 50.

1968, Sept. 11 **Tagged** ***Perf. 12***

1355	A777 6c **multicolored**	.40	.25
	P# block of 4, 5#	1.75	—
	P# block of 4, 5#, 5 dashes	1.75	—
	Margin block of 4, Mr. Zip and "Use Zip Code"	1.60	—
a.	Ocher omitted ("Walt Disney," "6c," etc.)	*350.00*	—
b.	Vert. pair, imperf. horiz.	*575.00*	
c.	Imperf., pair	*425.00*	
d.	Black omitted	*1,750.*	
e.	Horiz. pair, imperf. between	*5,000.*	
f.	Blue omitted	*1,500.*	
g.	Tagging omitted	*17.50*	—

FATHER MARQUETTE ISSUE

Father Jacques Marquette (1637-1675), French Jesuit missionary, who together with Louis Jolliet explored the Mississippi River and its tributaries.

Father Marquette and Louis Jolliet Exploring the Mississippi A778

Designed by Stanley W. Galli.

LITHOGRAPHED, ENGRAVED (Giori)
Plates of 200 subjects in four panes of 50.

1968, Sept. 20 **Tagged** ***Perf. 11***

1356	A778 6c **black, apple green & orange brown**	.25	.25
	P# block of 4	1.00	—
	Margin block of 4, Mr. Zip and "Use Zip Code"	1.00	—
a.	Tagging omitted	*7.50*	—

AMERICAN FOLKLORE ISSUE

Daniel Boone (1734-1820), frontiersman and trapper.

Pennsylvania Rifle, Powder Horn, Tomahawk Pipe and Knife — A779

Designed by Louis Macouillard.

LITHOGRAPHED, ENGRAVED (Giori)
Plates of 200 subjects in four panes of 50.

1968, Sept. 26 **Tagged** ***Perf. 11***

1357	A779 6c **yellow, deep yellow, maroon & black**	.25	.25
	P# block of 4	1.00	—
	Margin block of 4, Mr. Zip and "Use Zip Code"	1.00	—
a.	Tagging omitted	*275.00*	

ARKANSAS RIVER NAVIGATION ISSUE

Opening of the Arkansas River to commercial navigation.

Ship's Wheel, Power Transmission Tower and Barge — A780

Designed by Dean Ellis.

LITHOGRAPHED, ENGRAVED (Giori)
Plates of 200 subjects in four panes of 50.

1968, Oct. 1 **Tagged** ***Perf. 11***

1358	A780 6c **bright blue, dark blue & black**	.25	.25
	P# block of 4	1.00	—
	Margin block of 4, Mr. Zip and "Use Zip Code"	1.00	—
a.	Tagging omitted	*200.00*	

LEIF ERIKSON ISSUE

Leif Erikson, 11th century Norse explorer, called the 1st European to set foot on the American continent, at a place he called Vinland. The statue by the American sculptor A. Stirling Calder is in Reykjavik, Iceland.

Leif Erikson by A. Stirling Calder — A781

Designed by Kurt Weiner.

LITHOGRAPHED & ENGRAVED
Plates of 200 subjects in four panes of 50.

1968, Oct. 9 **Tagged** ***Perf. 11***

1359	A781 6c **light gray brown & black brown**	.25	.25
	P# block of 4	1.25	—
	Margin block of 4, Mr. Zip and "Use Zip Code"	1.00	—

The luminescent element is in the light gray brown ink of the background. The engraved parts were printed on a rotary currency press.

CHEROKEE STRIP ISSUE

75th anniversary of the opening of the Cherokee Strip to settlers, Sept. 16, 1893.

Racing for Homesteads in Cherokee Strip, 1893 — A782

Designed by Norman Todhunter.

ROTARY PRESS PRINTING
E.E. Plates of 200 subjects in four panes of 50.

1968, Oct. 15 **Tagged** ***Perf. 11x10½***

1360	A782 6c **brown**	.25	.25
	P# block of 4	1.10	—
	Margin block of 4, Mr. Zip and "Use Zip Code"	1.00	—
a.	Tagging omitted	*10.00*	—

JOHN TRUMBULL ISSUE

Trumbull (1756-1843), painter. The stamp shows Lt. Thomas Grosvenor and his attendant Peter Salem. The painting hangs at Yale University.

Detail from "The Battle of Bunker's Hill" — A783

Modeled by Robert J. Jones.

LITHOGRAPHED, ENGRAVED (Giori)
Plates of 200 subjects in four panes of 50.

1968, Oct. 18 **Tagged** ***Perf. 11***

1361	A783 6c **multicolored**	.25	.25
	P# block of 4	1.00	—
	Margin block of 4, Mr. Zip and "Use Zip Code"	1.00	—
a.	Tagging omitted	*125.00*	—
b.	Black (engr.) missing (FO)	*11,000.*	—

WATERFOWL CONSERVATION ISSUE

Wood Ducks — A784

Designed by Stanley W. Galli.

LITHOGRAPHED, ENGRAVED (Giori)
Plates of 200 subjects in four panes of 50.

1968, Oct. 24 **Tagged** ***Perf. 11***

1362	A784 6c **black & multicolored**	.25	.25
	P# block of 4	1.00	—
	Margin block of 4, Mr. Zip and "Use Zip Code"	1.00	—
a.	Vertical pair, imperf. between	*250.00*	—
b.	Red & dark blue omitted	*350.00*	
c.	Red omitted		*1,750.*

Dangerous fakes exist of Nos. 1362b and 1362c. Authentication by experts is required.

CHRISTMAS ISSUE

"The Annunciation" by the 15th century Flemish painter Jan van Eyck is in the National Gallery of Art, Washington, D.C.

Angel Gabriel, from "The Annunciation" by Jan van Eyck — A785

Designed by Robert J. Jones.

ENGRAVED (Multicolor Huck press)
Panes of 50 (10x5)

1968, Nov. 1 **Tagged** ***Perf. 11***

1363	A785 6c **multicolored**	.25	.25
	P# block of 10 (see note)	2.50	—
a.	Untagged, *Nov. 2*	.25	.25
	P# block of 10 (see note)	2.50	—
b.	Imperf., pair, tagged	*140.00*	
c.	Light yellow omitted	*50.00*	—
d.	Imperf., pair, untagged	*200.00*	

P# blocks come in two versions: (1) 7 P#, 3 ME; (2) 8 P#, 2 ME.

AMERICAN INDIAN ISSUE

Honoring the American Indian and to celebrate the opening of the Natl. Portrait Gallery, Washington, D.C. Chief Joseph (Indian name, Thunder Traveling over the Mountains), a leader of the Nez Percé, was born in eastern Oregon about 1840 and died at the Colville Reservation in Washington State in 1904.

Chief Joseph, by Cyrenius Hall — A786

Designed by Robert J. Jones; lettering by Crimilda Pontes.

LITHOGRAPHED, ENGRAVED (Giori)
Plates of 200 subjects in four panes of 50.

1968, Nov. 4 **Tagged** ***Perf. 11***

1364	A786 6c **black & multi**	.25	.25
	P# block of 4	1.00	—
	Margin block of 4, Mr. Zip and "Use Zip Code"	1.00	—
a.	Tagging omitted	—	—

BEAUTIFICATION OF AMERICA ISSUE

Publicizing the Natural Beauty Campaign for more beautiful cities, parks, highways and streets. In the left panes Nos. 1365 and 1367 appear in 1st, 3rd and 5th place, Nos. 1366 and 1368 in 2nd and 4th place. This arrangement is reversed in the right panes.

Capitol, Azaleas and Tulips — A787

Washington Monument, Potomac River and Daffodils A788

Poppies and Lupines along Highway A789

Blooming Crab Apples Lining Avenue A790

Designed by Walter DuBois Richards.

LITHOGRAPHED, ENGRAVED (Giori)
Plates of 200 subjects in four panes of 50.

1969, Jan. 16 **Tagged** ***Perf. 11***

1365	A787 6c **multicolored**	.25	.25
1366	A788 6c **multicolored**	.25	.25
1367	A789 6c **multicolored**	.25	.25
1368	A790 6c **multicolored**	.25	.25
a.	Block of 4, #1365-1368	1.00	*1.25*
	P# block of 4	1.10	—
	Margin block of 4, Mr. Zip and "Use Zip Code"	1.00	—
b.	#1365b-1368b, tagging omitted, any single	*75.00*	
c.	As "a," tagging omitted	325.00	

Compare with Nos. 4716a, 4716b, 4716d, 4716e.

AMERICAN LEGION, 50th ANNIV.

Eagle from Great Seal — A791

Designed by Robert Hallock.

LITHOGRAPHED, ENGRAVED (Giori)
Plates of 200 subjects in four panes of 50.

1969, Mar. 15 **Tagged** ***Perf. 11***

1369	A791 6c **red, blue & black**	.25	.25
	P# block of 4	1.00	—
	Margin block of 4, Mr. Zip and "Use Zip Code"	1.00	—
a.	Tagging omitted	*225.00*	

AMERICAN FOLKLORE ISSUE

Grandma Moses (Anna Mary Robertson Moses, 1860-1961), primitive painter of American life.

July Fourth, by Grandma Moses — A792

Designed by Robert J. Jones.

LITHOGRAPHED, ENGRAVED (Giori)
Plates of 200 subjects in four panes of 50.

1969, May 1 **Tagged** ***Perf. 11***

1370	A792 6c **multicolored**	.25	.25
	P# block of 4	1.00	—
	Margin block of 4, Mr. Zip and "Use Zip Code"	1.00	—
a.	Horizontal pair, imperf. between	*140.00*	—
b.	Engraved black ("6c U.S. Postage") & Prus. blue ("Grandma Moses") omitted	*400.00*	
c.	Tagging omitted	10.00	—

Beware of pairs with blind perfs. being offered as No. 1370a.

No. 1370b often comes with mottled or disturbed gum. Such stamps sell for about two-thirds as much as examples with perfect gum.

APOLLO 8 ISSUE

Apollo 8 mission, which 1st put men into orbit around the moon, Dec. 21-27, 1968. The astronauts were: Col. Frank Borman, Capt. James Lovell and Maj. William Anders.

Moon Surface and Earth — A793

Designed by Leonard E. Buckley after a photograph by the Apollo 8 astronauts.

LITHOGRAPHED, ENGRAVED (Giori)
Plates of 200 subjects in four panes of 50.

1969, May 5 **Tagged** ***Perf. 11***

1371	A793 6c **black, blue & ocher**	.25	.25
	P# block of 4	1.00	—
	Margin block of 4, Mr. Zip and "Use Zip Code"	1.00	—
a.	Tagging omitted	—	

Imperfs. exist from printer's waste.

W.C. HANDY ISSUE

Handy (1873-1958), jazz musician and composer.

William Christopher Handy — A794

Designed by Bernice Kochan.

LITHOGRAPHED, ENGRAVED (Giori)
Plates of 200 subjects in four panes of 50.

1969, May 17 **Tagged** ***Perf. 11***

1372 A794 6c **violet, deep lilac & blue** .25 .25
P# block of 4 1.00 —
Margin block of 4, Mr. Zip and "Use Zip Code" 1.00 —
a. Tagging omitted 10.00 —

CALIFORNIA SETTLEMENT, 200th ANNIV.

Carmel Mission Belfry — A795

Designed by Leonard Buckley and Howard C. Mildner.

LITHOGRAPHED, ENGRAVED (Giori)
Plates of 200 subjects in four panes of 50.

1969, July 16 **Tagged** ***Perf. 11***

1373 A795 6c **orange, red, black & light blue** .25 .25
P# block of 4 1.00 —
Margin block of 4, Mr. Zip and "Use Zip Code" 1.00 —
a. Tagging omitted 10.00 —
b. Red (engr.) missing (CM) *400.00*

JOHN WESLEY POWELL ISSUE

Powell (1834-1902), geologist who explored the Green and Colorado Rivers 1869-75, and ethnologist.

Major Powell Exploring Colorado River, 1869 — A796

Designed by Rudolph Wendelin.

LITHOGRAPHED, ENGRAVED (Giori)
Plates of 200 subjects in four panes of 50.

1969, Aug. 1 **Tagged** ***Perf. 11***

1374 A796 6c **black, ocher & light blue** .25 .25
P# block of 4 1.00 —
Margin block of 4, Mr. Zip and "Use Zip Code" 1.00 —
a. Tagging omitted 10.00 —

ALABAMA STATEHOOD, 150th ANNIV.

Camellia and Yellow-shafted Flicker — A797

Designed by Bernice Kochan

LITHOGRAPHED, ENGRAVED (Giori)
Plates of 200 subjects in four panes of 50.

1969, Aug. 2 **Tagged** ***Perf. 11***

1375 A797 6c **magenta, rose red, yellow, dark green & brown** .25 .25
P# block of 4 1.00 —
Margin block of 4, Mr. Zip and "Use Zip Code" 1.00 —
a. Tagging omitted *160.00* —

BOTANICAL CONGRESS ISSUE

11th Intl. Botanical Cong., Seattle, Wash., Aug. 24-Sept. 2. In left panes Nos. 1376 and 1378 appear in 1st, 3rd and 5th place; Nos. 1377 and 1379 in 2nd and 4th place. This arrangement is reversed in right panes.

Douglas Fir (Northwest) A798

Lady's-slipper (Northeast) A799

Ocotillo (Southwest) A800

Franklinia (Southeast) A801

Designed by Stanley Galli.

LITHOGRAPHED, ENGRAVED (Giori)
Plates of 200 subjects in four panes of 50.

1969, Aug. 23 **Tagged** ***Perf. 11***

1376 A798 6c **multicolored** .35 .25
1377 A799 6c **multicolored** .35 .25
1378 A800 6c **multicolored** .35 .25
1379 A801 6c **multicolored** .35 .25
a. Block of 4, #1376-1379 1.40 *1.75*
P# block of 4 1.50 —
Margin block of 4, Mr. Zip and "Use Zip Code" 1.45 —

DARTMOUTH COLLEGE CASE ISSUE

150th anniv. of the Dartmouth College Case, which Daniel Webster argued before the Supreme Court, reasserting the sanctity of contracts.

Daniel Webster and Dartmouth Hall — A802

Designed by John R. Scotford, Jr.

ROTARY PRESS PRINTING
E.E. Plates of 200 subjects in four panes of 50.

1969, Sept. 22 **Tagged** ***Perf. 10½x11***

1380 A802 6c **green** .25 .25
P# block of 4 1.00 —
Margin block of 4, Mr. Zip and "Use Zip Code" 1.00 —

PROFESSIONAL BASEBALL, 100th ANNIV.

Batter — A803

Designed by Alex Ross.

LITHOGRAPHED, ENGRAVED (Giori)
Plates of 200 subjects in four panes of 50.

1969, Sept. 24 **Tagged** ***Perf. 11***

1381 A803 6c **yellow, red, black & green** .45 .25
P# block of 4 2.00 —
Margin block of 4, Mr. Zip and "Use Zip Code" 1.90 —
a. Black omitted ("1869-1969, United States, 6c, Professional Baseball") *500.00*
b. Tagging omitted —
c. Double impression of black (engr.) *5,750.*

INTERCOLLEGIATE FOOTBALL, 100th ANNIV.

Football Player and Coach — A804

Designed by Robert Peak.

LITHOGRAPHED, ENGRAVED (Giori)
Plates of 200 subjects in four panes of 50.

1969, Sept. 26 **Tagged** ***Perf. 11***

1382 A804 6c **red & green** .25 .25
P# block of 4 1.10 —
Margin block of 4, Mr. Zip and "Use Zip Code" 1.00 —
a. Tagging omitted — —
b. Vert. pair, imperf horiz. *5,750.*
c. Double impression *2,500.*

The engraved parts were printed on a rotary currency press.
No. 1382b is unique.
Two examples of No. 1382c are recorded, with the double impression on the left part of the left stamps within a lower left plate block of 4. Value given is for the plate block.

DWIGHT D. EISENHOWER ISSUE

U.S. 6c POSTAGE
DWIGHT D. EISENHOWER

Dwight D. Eisenhower, 34th President (1890-1969) — A805

Designed by Robert J. Jones; photograph by Bernie Noble.

GIORI PRESS PRINTING
Plates of 128 subjects in 4 panes of 32 each.

1969, Oct. 14 **Tagged** ***Perf. 11***

1383 A805 6c **blue, black & red** .25 .25
P# block of 4 1.00 —
Margin block of 4, Mr. Zip and "Use Zip Code" 1.00 —
a. Tagging omitted —
b. Blue ("U.S. 6c Postage") missing (PS) *600.00*

CHRISTMAS ISSUE

The painting, painted about 1870 by an unknown primitive artist, is the property of the N.Y. State Historical Association, Cooperstown, N.Y.

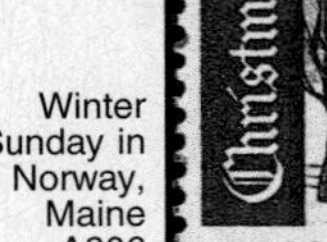

Winter Sunday in Norway, Maine A806

Designed by Stevan Dohanos.

ENGRAVED (Multicolor Huck)
Panes of 50 (5x10)

1969, Nov. 3 Tagged *Perf. 11x10½*

1384	A806 6c **dark green & multicolored**	.25	.25
	P# block of 10, 5#, 2-3 zip, 2-3 Mail Early	2.00	—
	Precancel	.60	.25
b.	Imperf., pair	*700.00*	
c.	Light green omitted	30.00	
d.	Light green, red & yellow omitted	*600.00*	—
e.	Yellow omitted	*1,500.*	
f.	Tagging omitted	*5.00*	—
g.	Red & yellow omitted	*2,250.*	
h.	Light green and yellow omitted	*500.00*	
i.	Light green and red omitted	—	
j.	Vert. pair, top stamp Baltimore precancel, bottom stamp precancel missing (FO)	—	
k.	Baltimore precancel printed on gum side	*150.00*	
l.	Baltimore precancel, vert. pair, one stamp missing precancel, other stamp with precancel printed inverted on reverse (FO)	*500.00*	
m.	Inverted Baltimore precancel	*200.00*	
n.	Baltimore precancel printed inverted on reverse (FO)	*150.00*	
o.	Baltimore precancel, tagging omitted	*50.00*	
p.	Double impression of New Haven precancel	—	
q.	Inverted Memphis precancel	*100.00*	
r.	Memphis precancel, tagging omitted	—	
s.	New Haven precancel, tagging omitted	—	

The precancel value applies to the least expensive of experimental precancels printed locally in four cities, on tagged stamps, with the names between lines 4½mm apart: in black or green, "ATLANTA, GA" and in green only "BALTIMORE, MD," "MEMPHIS, TN" and "NEW HAVEN, CT." They were sold freely to the public and could be used on any class of mail at all post offices during the experimental program and thereafter.

Most examples of No. 1384c show orange where the offset green was. Value is for this variety. Examples without orange sell for more.

On No. 1384i, almost all of the yellow is also omitted. Do not confuse with No. 1384d.

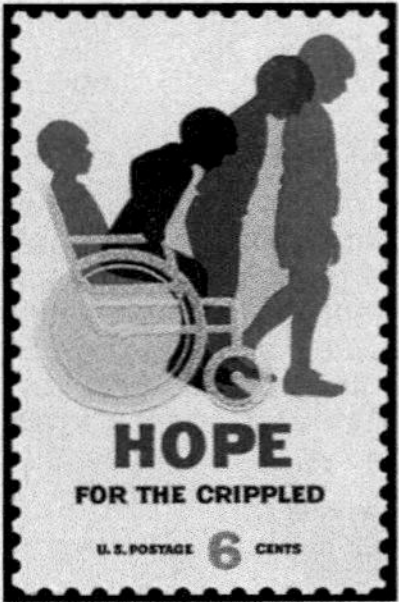

Cured Child — A807

HOPE FOR CRIPPLED ISSUE

Issued to encourage the rehabilitation of crippled children and adults and to honor the National Society for Crippled Children and Adults (Easter Seal Society) on its 50th anniversary.

Designed by Mark English.

LITHOGRAPHED, ENGRAVED (Giori)
Plates of 200 subjects in four panes of 50.

1969, Nov. 20 Tagged *Perf. 11*

1385	A807 6c **multicolored**	.25	.25
	P# block of 4	1.00	—
	Margin block of 4, Mr. Zip and "Use Zip Code"	1.00	—
a.	Tagging omitted	—	

WILLIAM M. HARNETT ISSUE

"Old Models" — A808

Harnett (1848-1892), painter. The painting hangs in the Museum of Fine Arts, Boston.

Designed by Robert J. Jones.

LITHOGRAPHED, ENGRAVED (Giori)
Plates of 128 subjects in 4 panes of 32 each.

1969, Dec. 3 Tagged *Perf. 11*

1386	A808 6c **multicolored**	.25	.25
	P# block of 4	1.00	—
	Margin block of 4, Mr. Zip and "Use Zip Code"	1.00	—
a.	Red (engr.) missing (CM)	—	

NATURAL HISTORY ISSUE

Centenary of the American Museum of Natural History, New York City. Nos. 1387-1388 alternate in 1st row, Nos. 1389-1390 in 2nd row. This arrangement is repeated throughout the pane.

American Bald Eagle — A809

African Elephant Herd — A810

Tlingit Chief in Haida Ceremonial Canoe — A811

Brontosaurus, Stegosaurus and Allosaurus from Jurassic Period — A812

Designers: No. 1387, Walter Richards; No. 1388, Dean Ellis; No. 1389, Paul Rabut; No. 1390, detail from mural by Rudolph Zallinger in Yal Peabody Museum, adapted by Robert J. Jones.

LITHOGRAPHED, ENGRAVED (Giori)
Plates of 128 subjects in 4 panes of 32 each (4x8).

1970, May 6 Tagged *Perf. 11*

1387	A809 6c **multicolored**	.25	.25
1388	A810 6c **multicolored**	.25	.25
1389	A811 6c **multicolored**	.25	.25
1390	A812 6c **multicolored**	.25	.25
a.	Block of 4, #1387-1390	1.00	*1.00*
	P# block of 4	1.10	—
	Margin block of 4, Mr. Zip and "Use Zip Code"	1.00	—
b.	As "a," tagging omitted	—	—

MAINE STATEHOOD, 150th ANNIV.

The painting hangs in the Metropolitan Museum of Art, New York City.

The Lighthouse at Two Lights, Maine, by Edward Hopper A813

Designed by Stevan Dohanos.

LITHOGRAPHED, ENGRAVED (Giori)
Plates of 200 subjects in four panes of 50.

1970, July 9 Tagged *Perf. 11*

1391	A813 6c **black & multi**	.25	.25
	P# block of 4	1.00	—
	Margin block of 4, Mr. Zip and "Use Zip Code"	1.00	—
a.	Tagging omitted	*175.00*	—

WILDLIFE CONSERVATION ISSUE

American Buffalo — A814

Designed by Robert Lougheed.

ROTARY PRESS PRINTING
E.E. Plates of 200 subjects in four panes of 50.

1970, July 20 Tagged *Perf. 11x10½*

1392	A814 6c **black,** *light brown*	.25	.25
	P# block of 4	1.00	—
	Margin block of 4, Mr. Zip and "Use Zip Code"	1.00	—

REGULAR ISSUE
Dwight David Eisenhower

Dot between "R" and "U" — A815

No Dot between "R" and "U" — A815a

Benjamin Franklin — A816

U.S. Postal Service Emblem — A817

Fiorello H. LaGuardia A817a

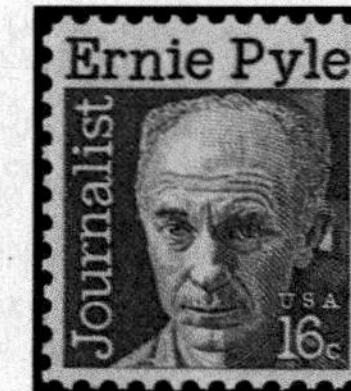

Ernest Taylor Pyle — A818

Dr. Elizabeth Blackwell — A818a

Amadeo P. Giannini A818b

Designers: Nos. 1393-1395, 1401-1402, Robert Geissman; photograph by George Tames. 7c, Bill Hyde. No. 1396, Raymond Loewy/William Smith, Inc. 14c, Robert Geissman; photograph by George Fayer. 16c, Robert Geissman; photograph by Alfred Eisenstadt. 18c, Robert Geissman; painting by Joseph Kozlowski. 21c, Robert Geissman.

ROTARY PRESS PRINTING

E.E. Plates of 400 subjects in four panes of 100.

1970-74 **Tagged** ***Perf. 11x10½***

1393 A815 6c **dark blue gray,** shiny gum, *Aug. 6, 1970* .25 .25
On cover 2.00
Single franking on certificate of mailing *100.00*
P# block of 4 1.00 —
Margin block of 4, "Use Zip Codes" 1.00 —
Dull gum .25
P# block of 4 1.40
Zip block of 4 1.00
a. Booklet pane of 8, shiny gum 2.00 2.00
Dull gum 2.25
b. Booklet pane of 5 + label 1.40 1.40
c. Untagged (Bureau precanceled) 12.75 3.00
P# block of 4 *175.00*
Margin block of 4, "Use Zip Codes" 75.00
g. Tagging omitted (not Bureau precanceled) *150.00* —
h. As "a," tagging omitted, shiny gum *250.00* —
Dull gum *325.00*

Counterfeits exist of No. 1393. See the Postal Counterfeits section of this catalog.

Perf. 10½x11

1393D A816 7c **bright blue,** shiny gum, *Oct. 20, 1972* .25 .25
On cover 4.00
Single franking on first-class postcard 8.00
P# block of 4 1.00 —
Margin block of 4, "Use Zip Codes" 1.00 —
Dull gum .25
P# block of 4 1.25
Zip block of 4 1.00
e. Untagged (Bureau precanceled) 4.25 1.00
P# block of 4 52.50
Margin block of 4, "Use Zip Codes" 22.50
f. Tagging omitted (not Bureau precanceled) 5.00 —

GIORI PRESS PRINTING

Plates of 400 subjects in four panes of 100.

Perf. 11

1394 A815a 8c **black, red & blue gray,** *May 10, 1971* .25 .25
On cover 2.00
P# block of 4 1.00 —
Margin block of 4, "Use Zip Codes" 1.00 —
Pair with full vert. gutter btwn. —
a. Tagging omitted 5.00 —
b. Red missing (PS) *150.00*
c. Red missing (FO) *1,250.*
d. Red and blue gray missing (PS) —
e. Red and blue gray missing (FO or preprinting paper crease) *1,000.*
f. All colors and tagging missing (FO) *1,000.*
g. Printed on gum side, tagged *1,000.*

No. 1394f must be collected se-tenant with No. 1394c, 1394e, or with a partially printed No. 1394.

Counterfeits exist of No. 1394. See the Postal Counterfeits section of this catalog.

ROTARY PRESS PRINTING

Perf. 11x10½ on 2 or 3 Sides

1395 A815 8c **deep claret,** shiny gum (from blkt. pane) .25 .25
Dull gum .25
On cover 2.00
a. Booklet pane of 8, shiny gum, *May 10, 1971* 2.00 2.00
b. Booklet pane of 6, shiny gum, *May 10, 1971* 1.50 1.50
c. Booklet pane of 4 + 2 labels, dull gum, *Jan. 28, 1972* 1.65 1.10
d. Booklet pane of 7 + label, dull gum, *Jan. 28, 1972* 1.90 1.90
e. Vert. pair, imperf. between, in #1395a or 1395d with foldover *750.00*
f. As "a," tagging omitted — —
g. As "b," tagging omitted *80.00* —
h. As "c," tagging omitted *55.00* —
i. As "d," tagging omitted —
j. As No. 1395, tagging omitted 7.50 —
dull gum 7.50 —

No. 1395 was issued only in booklets.

At least 4 pairs of No. 1395e are recorded from 3 panes (one No. 1395a and two 1395d) with different foldover patterns. A pane of No. 1395d also is known with a foldover resulting in a vertical pair of stamp and label, imperf between.

PHOTOGRAVURE (Andreotti)

Plates of 400 subjects in four panes of 100.

Perf. 11x10½

1396 A817 8c **multicolored,** *July 1, 1971* .25 .25
P# block of 12, 6# 2.50
P# block of 20, 6#, "Mail Early in the Day," "Use Zip Codes" and rectangular color contents (UL pane) 4.00
Margin block of 4, "Use Zip Codes" 1.00 —

ROTARY PRESS PRINTING

E.E. Plates of 400 subjects in four panes of 100.

1397 A817a 14c **gray brown,** *Apr. 24, 1972* .25 .25
On cover 10.00
Single franking on airmail postcard 30.00
Single franking on int'l printed-matter surface cover 25.00
P# block of 4 1.10 —
Margin block of 4, "Use Zip Codes" —
a. Untagged (Bureau precanceled) *100.00* 17.50
P# block of 4 —
Margin block of 4, "Use Zip Codes" —
1398 A818 16c **brown,** *May 7, 1971* .35 .25
On cover 6.00
Single franking on double-weight airmail cover 40.00
Single franking on third-class cover *70.00*
P# block of 4 2.50 —
Margin block of 4, "Use Zip Codes" 1.50 —
a. Untagged (Bureau precanceled) 22.50 5.00
P# block of 4 —
Margin block of 4, "Use Zip Codes" 175.00
b. Tagging omitted (not Bureau precanceled) *125.00* —
1399 A818a 18c **violet,** *Jan. 23, 1974* .35 .25
On cover 10.00
Single franking on int'l surface cover 30.00
Single franking on int'l airmail postcard 30.00
Single franking on double-weight third-class cover *60.00*
P# block of 4 1.50 —
Margin block of 4, "Use Zip Codes" 1.40 —
1400 A818b 21c **green,** *June 27, 1973* .40 .25
On cover 10.00
Single franking on int'l airmail cover 15.00
P# block of 4 1.65 —
Margin block of 4, "Use Zip Codes" 1.60 —
Nos. 1393-1400 (9) 2.60 2.25

Bureau Precancels: 6c, 6 diff., 7c, 13 diff., No. 1394, 24 diff., 14c, 3 diff., 16c, NYC, 3 diff. Greensboro, NC.

COIL STAMPS

ROTARY PRESS PRINTING

1970-71 **Tagged** ***Perf. 10 Vert.***

1401 A815 6c **dark blue gray,** shiny gum, *Aug. 6, 1970* .25 .25
On cover 2.00
Pair .50 .50
Joint line pair .60 .60
Dull gum .85
Joint line pair 7.00
a. Untagged (Bureau precanceled) 19.50 3.00
Pair 42.50 6.50
Joint line pair *525.00* —
b. Imperf., pair *2,500.*
Joint line pair —
1402 A815 8c **deep claret,** *May 10, 1971* .25 .25
On cover 2.00
Single franking on third-class bulk qty discount cover 10.00
Pair .50 .50
Joint line pair .60 .60
a. Imperf., pair 37.50
Joint line pair 70.00
b. Untagged (Bureau precanceled) 6.75 .75
Pair 15.00 1.60
Joint line pair *185.00* —
c. Pair, imperf. between *6,250.*

No. 1401b often found with small faults and/or without gum. Such examples sell for considerably less.

Bureau Precancels: 6c, 4 diff., 8c, 34 diff.

EDGAR LEE MASTERS ISSUE

Edgar Lee Masters (1869-1950), Poet — A819

Designed by Fred Otnes.

LITHOGRAPHED, ENGRAVED (Giori)

Plates of 200 subjects in four panes of 50.

1970, Aug. 22 **Tagged** ***Perf. 11***

1405 A819 6c **black & olive bister** .25 .25
P# block of 4 1.00 —
Margin block of 4, Mr. Zip and "Use Zip Code" 1.00 —
a. Tagging omitted 140.00 —

WOMAN SUFFRAGE ISSUE

50th anniversary of the 19th Amendment, which gave the vote to women.

Suffragettes, 1920, and Woman Voter, 1970 — A820

Designed by Ward Brackett.

GIORI PRESS PRINTING

Plates of 200 subjects in four panes of 50.

1970, Aug. 26 **Tagged** ***Perf. 11***

1406 A820 6c **blue** .25 .25
P# block of 4 1.00 —
Margin block of 4, Mr. Zip and "Use Zip Code" 1.00 —

SOUTH CAROLINA ISSUE

300th anniv. of the founding of Charles Town (Charleston), the 1st permanent settlement of South Carolina. Against a background of pine wood the line drawings of the design represent the economic and historic development of South Carolina: the spire of St. Phillip's Church, Capitol, state flag, a ship, 17th century man and woman, a Fort Sumter cannon, barrels, cotton, tobacco and yellow jasmine.

Symbols of South Carolina A821

Designed by George Samerjan.

LITHOGRAPHED, ENGRAVED (Giori)

Plates of 200 subjects in four panes of 50.

1970, Sept. 12 **Tagged** ***Perf. 11***

1407 A821 6c **bister, black & red** .25 .25
P# block of 4 1.00 —
Margin block of 4, Mr. Zip and "Use Zip Code" 1.00 —

STONE MOUNTAIN MEMORIAL ISSUE

Dedication of the Stone Mountain Confederate Memorial, Georgia, May 9, 1970.

Robert E. Lee, Jefferson Davis and "Stonewall" Jackson
A822

Designed by Robert Hallock.

GIORI PRESS PRINTING
Plates of 200 subjects in four panes of 50.

1970, Sept. 19 **Tagged** ***Perf. 11***

1408 A822 6c **gray**		.25	.25
	P# block of 4	1.00	—
	Margin block of 4, Mr. Zip and "Use Zip Code"	1.00	—

FORT SNELLING ISSUE

150th anniv. of Fort Snelling, Minnesota, an important outpost for the opening of the Northwest.

Fort Snelling, Keelboat and Tepees
A823

Designed by David K. Stone.

LITHOGRAPHED, ENGRAVED (Giori)
Plates of 200 in four panes of 50.

1970, Oct. 17 **Tagged** ***Perf. 11***

1409 A823 6c **yellow & multicolored**		.25	.25
	P# block of 4	1.00	—
	Margin block of 4, Mr. Zip and "Use Zip Code"	1.00	—
a.	Tagging omitted	—	—

ANTI-POLLUTION ISSUE

Issued to focus attention on the problems of pollution.

In left panes Nos. 1410 and 1412 appear in 1st, 3rd and 5th place; Nos. 1411 and 1413 in 2nd and 4th place. This arrangement is reversed in right panes.

Globe and Wheat — A824

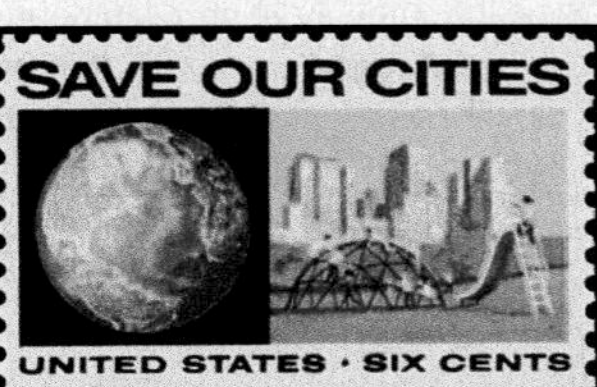

Globe and City — A825

Globe and Bluegill
A826

Globe and Seagull
A827

Designed by Arnold Copeland and Walter DuBois Richards. Printed by Bureau of Engraving and Printing at Guilford Gravure, Inc., Guilford, Conn.

PHOTOGRAVURE
Plates of 200 subjects in four panes of 50.

1970, Oct. 28 **Tagged** ***Perf. 11x10½***

1410 A824 6c **multicolored**		.25	.25
1411 A825 6c **multicolored**		.25	.25
1412 A826 6c **multicolored**		.25	.25
1413 A827 6c **multicolored**		.25	.25
a.	Block of 4, #1410-1413	1.00	*1.25*
	P# block of 10, 5#	2.50	—
	Margin block of 4, Mr. Zip and "Use Zip Code"	1.10	—

CHRISTMAS ISSUE

In left panes Nos. 1415 and 1417 appear in 1st, 3rd and 5th place; Nos. 1416 and 1418 in 2nd and 4th place. This arrangement is reversed in right panes.

Nativity, by Lorenzo Lotto — A828

Tin and Cast-iron Locomotive
A829

Toy Horse on Wheels
A830

Mechanical Tricycle
A831

Doll Carriage
A832

Designers: No. 1414, Howard C. Mildner, from a painting by Lorenzo Lotto (1480-1556) in the National Gallery of Art, Washington, D.C. Nos. 1415-1418, Stevan Dohanos, from a drawing (locomotive) by Charles Hemming and from "Golden Age of Toys" by Fondin and Remise.
Printed by Guilford Gravure, Inc., Guilford, Conn.

PHOTOGRAVURE
Plates of 200 subjects in four panes of 50.

1970, Nov. 5 **Tagged** ***Perf. 10½x11***

1414 A828 6c **multicolored**		.25	.25
	P# block of 8, 4#	1.10	—
	Margin block of 4, Mr. Zip and "Use Zip Code"	.50	—
a.	Precanceled	.25	.25
	P# block of 8, 4#	2.00	—
	Margin block of 4, Mr. Zip and "Use Zip Code"	1.00	—
b.	Black omitted	*400.00*	
c.	As "a," blue omitted	*1,100.*	
d.	Type II	.25	.25
	P# block of 8, 4#	3.25	—
	Zip block of 4	1.00	—
e.	Type II, precanceled	.25	.25
	P# block of 8, 4#	4.25	—
	Zip block of 4	1.25	—

No. 1414 has a slightly blurry impression, snowflaking in the sky and no gum breaker ridges. No. 1414d has shiny surfaced paper, sharper impression, no snowflaking and vertical and horizontal gum breaker ridges.

No. 1414a has a slightly blurry impression, snowflaking in the sky, no gum breaker ridges and the precancel is grayish black. No. 1414e has sharper impression, no snowflaking, gum breaker ridges and the precancel is intense black.

Perf. 11x10½

1415 A829 6c **multicolored**		.30	.25
a.	Precanceled	.65	.25
b.	Black omitted	*1,750.*	
c.	Tagging omitted	—	—
1416 A830 6c **multicolored**		.30	.25
a.	Precanceled	.65	.25
b.	Black omitted	1,750.	
c.	Imperf., pair (#1416, 1418)		*2,500.*
d.	Tagging omitted	—	
1417 A831 6c **multicolored**		.30	.25
a.	Precanceled	.65	.25
b.	Black omitted	*1,750.*	
c.	Tagging omitted	—	—
1418 A832 6c **multicolored**		.30	.25
a.	Precanceled	.65	.25
b.	Block of 4, #1415-1418	1.25	*1.40*
	P# block of 8, 4#	3.00	—
	Margin block of 4, Mr. Zip and "Use Zip Code"	1.25	—
c.	As "b," precanceled	3.75	*3.50*
	P# block of 8, 4P#	5.50	—
	Margin block of 4, Mr. Zip and "Use Zip Code"	3.00	—
d.	Black omitted	*1,750.*	
e.	As "b," black omitted	*8,000.*	
f.	As "b," black omitted on #1417 & 1418	*4,000.*	
g.	P# block of 8, black omitted on #1415 & 1416	*4,000.*	
h.	As "b," tagging omitted on #1415 and 1417	—	
i.	Tagging omitted	—	
	Nos. 1415-1418 (4)	1.20	1.00

Nos. 1415-1418 and 1415a-1418a are known both without gum breaker ridges (common) and with gum breaker ridges (scarce).

The precanceled stamps, Nos. 1414a-1418a, were furnished to 68 cities. The plates include two straight (No. 1414a) or two wavy (Nos. 1415a-1418a) black lines that make up the precancellation. Unused values are for stamps with gum and used values are for stamps with an additional cancellation or without gum.

UNITED NATIONS, 25th ANNIV.

"UN" and UN Emblem
A833

Designed by Arnold Copeland.

LITHOGRAPHED, ENGRAVED (Giori)
Plates of 200 subjects in four panes of 50.

1970, Nov. 20 **Tagged** ***Perf. 11***

1419 A833 6c **black, verm & ultra**		.25	.25
	P# block of 4	1.00	—
	Margin block of 4, Mr. Zip and "Use Zip Code"	1.00	—
	Pair with full horiz. gutter btwn.	—	
a.	Tagging omitted	*75.00*	—

LANDING OF THE PILGRIMS ISSUE

350th anniv. of the landing of the Mayflower.

Mayflower and Pilgrims — A834

Designed by Mark English.

LITHOGRAPHED, ENGRAVED (Giori)

Plates of 200 subjects in four panes of 50.

1970, Nov. 21 **Tagged** ***Perf. 11***

1420 A834 6c **blk, org, yel, magenta, bl & brn** .25 .25
P# block of 4 1.00 —
Margin block of 4, Mr. Zip and "Use Zip Code" 1.00 —
a. Orange & yellow omitted *525.00*
b. Tagging omitted — —

DISABLED AMERICAN VETERANS AND SERVICEMEN ISSUE

No. 1421 for the 50th anniv. of the Disabled Veterans of America Organization; No. 1422 honors the contribution of servicemen, particularly those who were prisoners of war, missing or killed in action. Nos. 1421-1422 are printed se-tenant in horizontal rows of 10.

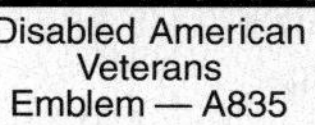

Disabled American Veterans Emblem — A835

A836

Designed by Stevan Dohanos.

LITHOGRAPHED, ENGRAVED (Giori)

Plates of 200 subjects in four panes of 50.

1970, Nov. 24 **Tagged** ***Perf. 11***

1421 A835 6c **dark blue, red & multicolored** .25 .25

ENGRAVED

1422 A836 6c **dark blue, black & red** .25 .25
a. Pair, #1421-1422 .50 .50
P# block of 4 1.00 —
Margin block of 4, Mr. Zip and "Use Zip Code" 1.00 —
b. As "a," tagging omitted 90.00 —

AMERICAN WOOL INDUSTRY ISSUE

450th anniv. of the introduction of sheep to the North American continent and the beginning of the American wool industry.

Ewe and Lamb — A837

Designed by Dean Ellis.

LITHOGRAPHED, ENGRAVED (Giori)

Plates of 200 subjects in four panes of 50.

1971, Jan. 19 **Tagged** ***Perf. 11***

1423 A837 6c **multicolored** .25 .25
P# block of 4 1.00 —
Margin block of 4, Mr. Zip and "Use Zip Code" 1.00 —
a. Tagging omitted 11.00 —
b. Teal blue ("United States") missing (CM) *400.00*

GEN. DOUGLAS MacARTHUR ISSUE

MacArthur (1880-1964), Chief of Staff, Supreme Commander for the Allied Powers in the Pacific Area during World War II and Supreme Commander in Japan after the war.

Gen. Douglas MacArthur — A838

Designed by Paul Calle; Wide World photograph.

GIORI PRESS PRINTING

Plates of 200 subjects in four panes of 50.

1971, Jan. 26 **Tagged** ***Perf. 11***

1424 A838 6c **black, red & dark blue** .25 .25
P# block of 4 1.00 —
Margin block of 4, Mr. Zip and "Use Zip Code" 1.00 —
a. Red missing (PS) —
b. Tagging omitted *300.00* —
c. Blue missing (PS) —

BLOOD DONOR ISSUE

Salute to blood donors and spur to increased participation in the blood donor program.

"Giving Blood Saves Lives" — A839

Designed by Howard Munce.

LITHOGRAPHED, ENGRAVED (Giori)

Plates of 200 subjects in four panes of 50.

1971, Mar. 12 **Tagged** ***Perf. 11***

1425 A839 6c **blue, scarlet & indigo** .25 .25
P# block of 4 1.00 —
Margin block of 4, Mr. Zip and "Use Zip Code" 1.00 —
a. Tagging omitted 10.00 —

MISSOURI STATEHOOD, 150th ANNIV.

The stamp design shows a Pawnee facing a hunter-trapper and a group of settlers. It is from a mural by Thomas Hart Benton in the Harry S Truman Library, Independence, Mo.

"Independence and the Opening of the West," Detail, by Thomas Hart Benton — A840

Designed by Bradbury Thompson.

PHOTOGRAVURE (Andreotti)

Plates of 200 subjects in four panes of 50.

1971, May 8 **Tagged** ***Perf. 11x10½***

1426 A840 8c **multicolored** .25 .25
P# block of 12, 6# 3.00 —
Margin block of 4, Mr. Zip and "Use Zip Code" 1.00 —
a. Tagging omitted — —

See note on Andreotti printings and their color control markings in Information for Collectors under Printing, Photogravure.

WILDLIFE CONSERVATION ISSUE

Nos. 1427-1428 alternate in first row, Nos. 1429-1430 in second row. This arrangement repeated throughout pane.

Trout A841

Alligator — A842

Polar Bear and Cubs A843

WILDLIFE CONSERVATION 8c UNITED STATES CALIFORNIA CONDOR

California Condor — A844

Designed by Stanley W. Galli.

LITHOGRAPHED, ENGRAVED (Giori)

Plates of 128 subjects in 4 panes of 32 each (4x8).

1971, June 12 **Tagged** ***Perf. 11***

1427 A841 8c **multicolored** .25 .25
a. Red omitted *1,250.*
b. Green (engr.) omitted —
1428 A842 8c **multicolored** .25 .25
1429 A843 8c **multicolored** .25 .25
1430 A844 8c **multicolored** .25 .25
a. Block of 4, #1427-1430 1.00 1.00
P# block of 4 1.25 —
Margin block of 4, Mr. Zip and "Use Zip Code" 1.00 —
b. As "a," light green & dark green omitted from #1427-1428 *3,250.*
c. As "a," red omitted from #1427, 1429-1430 *3,000.*
d. As "a," tagging omitted —

ANTARCTIC TREATY ISSUE

Map of Antarctica A845

Designed by Howard Koslow.

Adapted from emblem on official documents of Consultative Meetings.

GIORI PRESS PRINTING

Plates of 200 subjects in four panes of 50.

1971, June 23 **Tagged** ***Perf. 11***

1431 A845 8c **red & dark blue** .25 .25
P# block of 4 1.00 —
Margin block of 4, Mr. Zip and "Use Zip Code" 1.00 —
a. Tagging omitted *10.00*
b. Both colors missing (EP) *500.00*

No. 1431b should be collected se-tenant with a normal stamp and/or a partially printed stamp.

AMERICAN REVOLUTION BICENTENNIAL

Bicentennial Commission Emblem — A846

Designed by Chermayeff & Geismar.

LITHOGRAPHED, ENGRAVED (Giori)

Plates of 200 subjects in four panes of 50.

1971, July 4 **Tagged** ***Perf. 11***

1432 A846 8c **gray, red, blue & black** .25 .25
P# block of 4 1.25 —
Margin block of 4, Mr. Zip and "Use Zip Code" 1.00 —
a. Gray & black missing (EP) *325.00*
b. Gray ("U.S. Postage 8c") missing (EP) *650.00*
c. Tagging omitted 125.00

JOHN SLOAN ISSUE

John Sloan (1871-1951), painter. The painting hangs in the Phillips Gallery, Washington, D.C.

The Wake of the Ferry — A847

Designed by Bradbury Thompson.

LITHOGRAPHED, ENGRAVED (Giori)

Plates of 200 subjects in four panes of 50.

1971, Aug. 2 **Tagged** ***Perf. 11***

1433 A847 8c **multicolored** .25 .25
P# block of 4 1.00 —
Margin block of 4, Mr. Zip and "Use Zip Code" 1.00 —
a. Tagging omitted —
b. Red engr. ("John Sloan" and "8") missing (CM) *950.00*

SPACE ACHIEVEMENT DECADE ISSUE

Decade of space achievements and the Apollo 15 moon exploration mission, July 26-Aug. 7. In the left panes the earth and sun stamp is 1st, 3rd and 5th, the rover 2nd and 4th. This arrangement is reversed in the right panes.

Earth, Sun and Landing Craft on Moon — A848

Lunar Rover and Astronauts A849

Designed by Robert McCall.

LITHOGRAPHED, ENGRAVED (Giori)

Plates of 200 subjects in four panes of 50.

1971, Aug. 2 **Tagged** ***Perf. 11***

1434 A848 8c **black, blue, gray, yellow & red** .25 .25
a. Tagging omitted *45.00*
1435 A849 8c **black, blue, gray, yellow & red** .25 .25
a. Tagging omitted *45.00*
b. Pair, #1434-1435 .50 .50
P# block of 4 1.00 —
Margin block of 4, Mr. Zip and "Use Zip Code" 1.00 —
c. As "b," tagging omitted *125.00*
d. As "b," blue & red (litho.) omitted *950.00*

EMILY DICKINSON ISSUE

Emily Elizabeth Dickinson (1830-1886), Poet — A850

Designed by Bernard Fuchs after a photograph.

LITHOGRAPHED, ENGRAVED (Giori)

Plates of 200 subjects in four panes of 50.

1971, Aug. 28 **Tagged** ***Perf. 11***

1436 A850 8c **multicolored**, *greenish* .25 .25
P# block of 4 1.00 —
Margin block of 4, Mr. Zip and "Use Zip Code" 1.00 —
a. Black & olive (engr.) omitted *500.00*
b. Pale rose missing (EP) *5,000.*
c. Red omitted —
d. Tagging omitted 130.00 —

SAN JUAN ISSUE

450th anniversary of San Juan, Puerto Rico.

Sentry Box, Morro Castle, San Juan — A851

Designed as a woodcut by Walter Brooks.

LITHOGRAPHED, ENGRAVED (Giori)

Plates of 200 subjects in four panes of 50.

1971, Sept. 12 **Tagged** ***Perf. 11***

1437 A851 8c **pale brown, black, yellow, red brown & dark brown** .25 .25
P# block of 4 1.50 —
Margin block of 4, Mr. Zip and "Use Zip Code" 1.10 —
a. Tagging omitted *10.00* —
b. Dark brown (engr.) omitted *1,500.* —

No. 1437b used is a 1971 on-cover single expertized in 2014.

VALUES FOR HINGED STAMPS AFTER NO. 771

This catalogue does not value unused stamps after No. 771 in hinged condition. Hinged unused stamps from No. 772 to the present are worth considerably less than the values given for unused stamps, which are for never-hinged examples.

PREVENT DRUG ABUSE ISSUE

Drug Abuse Prevention Week, Oct. 3-9.

Young Woman Drug Addict — A852

Designed by Miggs Burroughs.

PHOTOGRAVURE (Andreotti)

Plates of 200 subjects in four panes of 50.

1971, Oct. 4 **Tagged** ***Perf. 10½x11***

1438 A852 8c **blue, deep blue & black** .25 .25
P# block of 6, 3# 1.00 —
Margin block of 4, "Use Zip Code" 1.00 —
a. Tagging omitted —

CARE ISSUE

25th anniversary of CARE, a US-Canadian Cooperative for American Relief Everywhere.

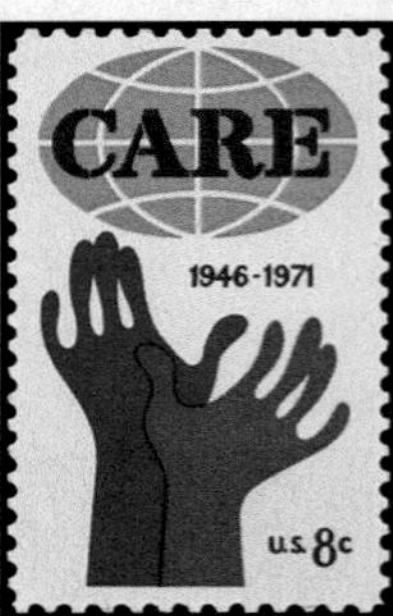

Hands Reaching for CARE — A853

Designed by Soren Noring

PHOTOGRAVURE (Andreotti)

Plates of 200 subjects in four panes of 50.

1971, Oct. 27 **Tagged** ***Perf. 10½x11***

1439 A853 8c **blue, blk, vio & red lilac** .25 .25
P# block of 8, 4# 1.75 —
Margin block of 4, Mr. Zip and "Use Zip Code" 1.00 —
a. Black omitted *1,100.*
b. Tagging omitted 5.00 —

HISTORIC PRESERVATION ISSUE

Nos. 1440-1441 alternate in 1st row, Nos. 1442-1443 in 2nd row. This arrangement is repeated throughout the pane.

Decatur House, Washington, D.C. — A854

Whaling Ship Charles W. Morgan, Mystic, Conn. — A855

Cable Car, San Francisco — A856

San Xavier del Bac Mission, Tucson, Ariz. — A857

Designed by Melbourne Brindle.

LITHOGRAPHED, ENGRAVED (Giori)

1971, Oct. 29	**Tagged**		***Perf. 11***	
1440	A854 8c **black brown & ocher,** *buff*		.25	.25
1441	A855 8c **black brown & ocher,** *buff*		.25	.25
1442	A856 8c **black brown & ocher,** *buff*		.25	.25
1443	A857 8c **black brown & ocher,** *buff*		.25	.25
a.	Block of 4, #1440-1443		1.00	*1.00*
	P# block of 4		1.00	—
	Margin block of 4, Mr. Zip and "Use Zip Code"		1.00	—
b.	As "a," black brown omitted		*800.00*	
c.	As "a," ocher omitted		*2,500.*	
d.	As "a," tagging omitted		*75.00*	

CHRISTMAS ISSUE

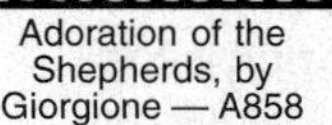

Adoration of the Shepherds, by Giorgione — A858

"Partridge in a Pear Tree" — A859

Designers: No. 1444, Bradbury Thompson, using a painting by Giorgione in the National Gallery of Art, Washington, D.C. No. 1445, Jamie Wyeth.

PHOTOGRAVURE (Andreotti)

Plates of 200 subjects in four panes of 50.

1971, Nov. 10	**Tagged**	***Perf. 10½x11***	
1444	A858 8c **gold & multi**	.25	.25
	P# block of 12, 6#	1.80	—
	Margin block of 4, Mr. Zip and "Use Zip Code"	1.00	—
a.	Gold omitted	*350.00*	
b.	Tagging omitted	—	
1445	A859 8c **dark green, red & multicolored**	.25	.25
	P# block of 12, 6#	1.80	
	Margin block of 4, Mr. Zip and "Use Zip Code"	1.00	—

SIDNEY LANIER ISSUE

Lanier (1842-81), poet, musician, lawyer, educator.

Sidney Lanier — A860

Designed by William A. Smith.

GIORI PRESS PRINTING

Plates of 200 subjects in four panes of 50.

1972, Feb. 3	**Tagged**	***Perf. 11***	
1446	A860 8c **black, brown & light blue**	.25	.25
	P# block of 4	1.00	—
	Margin block of 4, Mr. Zip and "Use Zip Code"	1.00	—
a.	Tagging omitted	60.00	

PEACE CORPS ISSUE

Peace Corps Poster, by David Battle — A861

Designed by Bradbury Thompson.

PHOTOGRAVURE (Andreotti)

Plates of 200 subjects in four panes of 50.

1972, Feb. 11	**Tagged**	***Perf. 10½x11***	
1447	A861 8c **dark blue, light blue & red**	.25	.25
	P# block of 6, 3#	1.50	—
	Margin block of 4, Mr. Zip and "Use Zip Code"	1.00	—
a.	Tagging omitted	5.00	

NATIONAL PARKS CENTENNIAL ISSUE

Centenary of Yellowstone National Park, the 1st National Park, and of the entire National Park System. See No. C84.

A862 A863

A864 A865

Cape Hatteras National Seashore

Wolf Trap Farm, Va. — A866

Old Faithful, Yellowstone — A867

Mt. McKinley, Alaska — A868

Designers: 2c, Walter D. Richards; 6c, Howard Koslow; 8c, Robert Handville; 15c, James Barkley.

LITHOGRAPHED, ENGRAVED (Giori)

1972	**Tagged**	***Perf. 11***	
	Plates of 400 subjects in 4 panes of 100 each		
1448	A862 2c **black & multi.,** *Apr. 5*	.25	.25
1449	A863 2c **black & multi.,** *Apr. 5*	.25	.25
1450	A864 2c **black & multi.,** *Apr. 5*	.25	.25
1451	A865 2c **black & multi.,** *Apr. 5*	.25	.25
a.	Block of 4, #1448-1451	.50	.50
	P# block of 4	.60	—
	Margin block of 4, "Use Zip Codes"	.50	—
b.	As "a," black (litho.) omitted	*1,000.*	
c.	As "a," tagging omitted	*150.00*	
	Plates of 200 subjects in four panes of 50 each		
1452	A866 6c **black & multicolored,** *June 26*	.25	.25
	P# block of 4	1.00	—
	Margin block of 4, Mr. Zip and "Use Zip Code"	1.00	—
a.	Tagging omitted	*10.00*	
	Plates of 128 subjects in four panes of 32 (8x4)		
1453	A867 8c **blk, blue, brn & multi,** *Mar. 1*	.25	.25
	P# block of 4	1.00	—
	Margin block of 4, Mr. Zip and "Use Zip Code"	1.00	—
a.	Tagging omitted	140.00	
	Plates of 200 subjects in four panes of 50 each		
1454	A868 15c **black & multi.,** *July 28*	.30	.25
	P# block of 4	1.30	—
	Margin block of 4, Mr. Zip	1.25	—
a.	Tagging omitted	150.00	
b.	Yellow omitted	*3,000.*	

FAMILY PLANNING ISSUE

Family — A869

LITHOGRAPHED, ENGRAVED (Giori)

Plates of 200 subjects in four panes of 50.

1972, Mar. 18	**Tagged**	***Perf. 11***	
1455	A869 8c **black & multicolored**	.25	.25
	P# block of 4	1.00	—
	Margin block of 4, Mr. Zip and "Use Zip Code"	1.00	—
a.	Yellow omitted	*300.00*	
c.	Dark brown missing (FO)	*9,500.*	
d.	Tagging omitted	*275.00*	

AMERICAN BICENTENNIAL ISSUE
Colonial American Craftsmen

In left panes Nos. 1456 and 1458 appear in 1st, 3rd and 5th place; Nos. 1457 and 1459 in 2nd and 4th place. This arrangement is reversed in right panes.

Glass Blower — A870

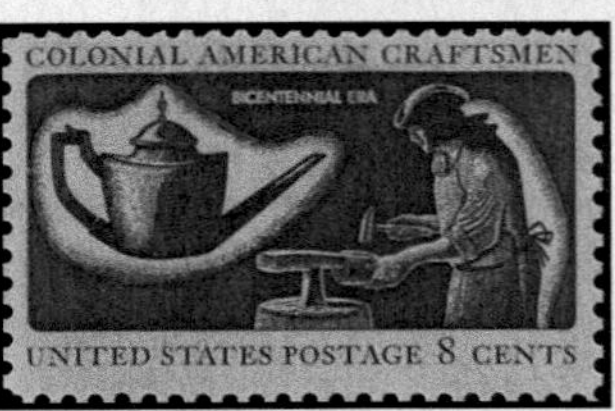

Silversmith A871

Wigmaker A872

Hatter — A873

Designed by Leonard Everett Fisher.

ENGRAVED

E.E. Plates of 200 subjects in four panes of 50.

1972, July 4	Tagged	Perf. 11x10½	
1456 A870 8c **deep brown,** *dull yellow*		.25	.25
1457 A871 8c **deep brown,** *dull yellow*		.25	.25
1458 A872 8c **deep brown,** *dull yellow*		.25	.25
1459 A873 8c **deep brown,** *dull yellow*		.25	.25
a. Block of 4, #1456-1459		1.00	1.00
P# block of 4		1.00	—
Margin block of 4, Mr. Zip and "Use Zip Code"		1.00	—
b. As "a," tagging omitted		*150.00*	

Margin includes Bicentennial Commission emblem and inscription: USA BICENTENNIAL / HONORS COLONIAL / AMERICAN CRAFTSMEN.

OLYMPIC GAMES ISSUE

11th Winter Olympic Games, Sapporo, Japan, Feb. 3-13 and 20th Summer Olympic Games, Munich, Germany, Aug. 26-Sept. 11. See No. C85.

Bicycling and Olympic Rings — A874

Bobsledding and Olympic Rings — A875

Running and Olympic Rings — A876

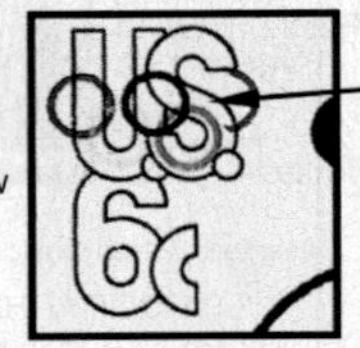

"Broken red ring" Cylinder Flaw

Designed by Lance Wyman.

PHOTOGRAVURE (Andreotti)

Plates of 200 subjects in four panes of 50.

1972, Aug. 17	Tagged	Perf. 11x10½	
1460 A874 6c **black, blue, red, emerald & yellow**		.25	.25
P# block of 10, 5#		1.50	—
Margin block of 4, Mr. Zip and "Use Zip Code"		1.00	—
Cylinder flaw (broken red ring) (33313 UL 43)		10.00	
1461 A875 8c **black, blue, red, emerald & yellow**		.25	.25
P# block of 10, 5#		1.75	—
Margin block of 4, Mr. Zip and "Use Zip Code"		1.00	—
a. Tagging omitted		7.50	
1462 A876 15c **black, blue, red, emerald & yel**		.30	.25
P# block of 10, 5#		3.00	—
Margin block of 4, Mr. Zip and "Use Zip Code"		1.20	—
a. Tagging omitted		—	
Nos. 1460-1462 (3)		.80	.75

PARENT TEACHER ASSN., 75th ANNIV.

Blackboard A877

Designed by Arthur S. Congdon III.

PHOTOGRAVURE (Andreotti)

Plates of 200 subjects in four panes of 50.

1972, Sept. 15	Tagged	Perf. 11x10½	
1463 A877 8c **yellow & black**		.25	.25
P# block of 4, 2#		1.00	—
P# block of 4, yellow # reversed		1.00	—
Margin block of 4, Mr. Zip and "Use Zip Code"		1.00	—
a. Tagging omitted		*175.00*	

WILDLIFE CONSERVATION ISSUE

Nos. 1464-1465 alternate in 1st row, Nos. 1468-1469 in 2nd row. This arrangement repeated throughout pane.

Fur Seals A878

Cardinal — A879

Brown Pelican — A880

Bighorn Sheep — A881

Designed by Stanley W. Galli.

LITHOGRAPHED, ENGRAVED (Giori)

Plates of 128 subjects in 4 panes of 32 (4x8).

1972, Sept. 20	Tagged	Perf. 11	
1464 A878 8c **multicolored**		.25	.25
1465 A879 8c **multicolored**		.25	.25
1466 A880 8c **multicolored**		.25	.25
1467 A881 8c **multicolored**		.25	.25
a. Block of 4, #1464-1467		1.00	*1.00*
P# block of 4		1.10	—
Margin block of 4, Mr. Zip and "Use Zip Code"		1.00	—
b. As "a," brown omitted		*2,750.*	
c. As "a," green & blue omitted		*2,750.*	
d. As "a," red & brown omitted		*3,250.*	
e. As "a," tagging omitted		*300.00*	

MAIL ORDER BUSINESS ISSUE

Centenary of mail order business, originated by Aaron Montgomery Ward, Chicago. Design based on Headsville, W.Va., post office in Smithsonian Institution, Washington, D.C.

Rural Post Office Store — A882

Designed by Robert Lambdin.

PHOTOGRAVURE (Andreotti)

Plates of 200 subjects in four panes of 50.

1972, Sept, 27	Tagged	Perf. 11x10½	
1468 A882 8c **multicolored**		.25	.25
P# block of 12, 6#		1.75	—
Margin block of 4, Mr. Zip and "Use Zip Code"		1.00	—

The tagging on No. 1468 consists of a vertical bar of phosphor 10mm wide.

OSTEOPATHIC MEDICINE ISSUE

75th anniv. of the American Osteopathic Assoc., founded by Dr. Andrew T. Still (1828-1917), who developed the principles of osteopathy in 1874.

Man's Quest for Health — A883

Designed by V. Jack Ruther.

PHOTOGRAVURE (Andreotti)

Plates of 200 subjects in four panes of 50.

1972, Oct. 9	**Tagged**	***Perf. 10½x11***	
1469	A883 8c **multicolored**	.25	.25
	P# block of 6, 3#	1.10	—
	Margin block of 4, Mr. Zip and "Use Zip Code"	1.00	—

AMERICAN FOLKLORE ISSUE

Tom Sawyer, by Norman Rockwell — A884

Designed by Bradbury Thompson.

LITHOGRAPHED, ENGRAVED (Giori)

Plates of 200 subjects in four panes of 50.

1972, Oct. 13	**Tagged**	***Perf. 11***	
1470	A884 8c **black, red, yellow, tan, blue & rose red**	.25	.25
	P# block of 4	1.00	—
	Margin block of 4, Mr. Zip and "Use Zip Code"	1.00	—
a.	Horiz. pair, imperf. between	*6,750.*	
b.	Red & black (engr.) omitted	*800.00*	
c.	Yellow & tan (litho.) omitted	*1,100.*	
d.	Tagging omitted	*110.*	
e.	Red (engr. 8c) missing (CM)	*750.*	

CHRISTMAS ISSUE

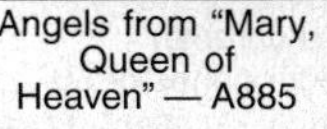

Angels from "Mary, Queen of Heaven" — A885

Santa Claus — A886

Designers: No. 1471, Bradbury Thompson, using detail from a painting by the Master of the St. Lucy legend, in the National Gallery of Art, Washington, D.C. No. 1472, Stevan Dohanos.

PHOTOGRAVURE (Andreotti)

Plates of 200 subjects in four panes of 50.

1972, Nov. 9	**Tagged**	***Perf. 10½x11***	
1471	A885 8c **multicolored**	.25	.25
	P# block of 12, 6#	1.75	—
	Margin block of 4, Mr. Zip and "Use Zip Code"	1.00	—
a.	Pink omitted	*100.00*	
b.	Black omitted	*2,500.*	
1472	A886 8c **multicolored**	.25	.25
	P# block of 12, 6#	1.75	—
	Margin block of 4, Mr. Zip and "Use Zip Code"	1.00	—
a.	Tagging omitted	—	

PHARMACY ISSUE

Honoring American druggists in connection with the 120th anniversary of the American Pharmaceutical Association.

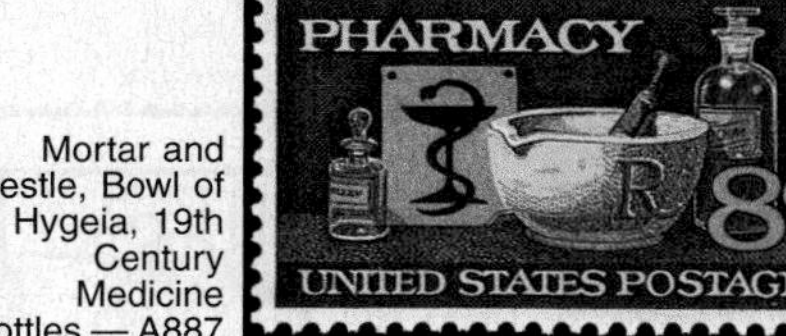

Mortar and Pestle, Bowl of Hygeia, 19th Century Medicine Bottles — A887

Designed by Ken Davies.

LITHOGRAPHED, ENGRAVED (Giori)

Plates of 200 subjects in four panes of 50.

1972, Nov. 10	**Tagged**	***Perf. 11***	
1473	A887 8c **black & multi**	.25	.25
	P# block of 4	1.00	—
	Margin block of 4, Mr. Zip and "Use Zip Code"	1.00	—
a.	Blue & orange omitted	*600.00*	
b.	Blue omitted	*1,250.*	
c.	Orange omitted	*1,250.*	
d.	Tagging omitted	225.00	—
e.	Vertical pair, imperf horiz.	*2,000.*	

STAMP COLLECTING ISSUE

Issued to publicize stamp collecting.

U.S. No. 1 under Magnifying Glass — A888

Designed by Frank E. Livia.

LITHOGRAPHED, ENGRAVED (Giori)

Plates of 160 subjects in four panes of 40.

1972, Nov. 17	**Tagged**	***Perf. 11***	
1474	A888 8c **multicolored**	.25	.25
	P# block of 4	1.00	—
	Margin block of 4, Mr. Zip and "Use Zip Code"	1.00	—
a.	Black (litho.) omitted	*325.00*	
b.	Tagging omitted	4.50	

Counterfeits exist of No. 1474. See the Postal Counterfeits section of this catalog.

LOVE ISSUE

"Love," by Robert Indiana A889

Designed by Robert Indiana.

PHOTOGRAVURE (Andreotti)

Plates of 200 subjects in four panes of 50.

1973, Jan. 26	**Tagged**	***Perf. 11x10½***	
1475	A889 8c **red, emerald & violet blue**	.25	.25
	P# block of 6, 3#	1.00	—
	Margin block of 4, Mr. Zip and "Use Zip Code"	1.00	—

AMERICAN BICENTENNIAL ISSUE

Communications in Colonial Times

Printer and Patriots Examining Pamphlet A890

Posting a Broadside A891

Postrider A892

Drummer A893

Designed by William A. Smith.

GIORI PRESS PRINTING

Plates of 200 subjects in four panes of 50.

1973	**Tagged**	***Perf. 11***	
1476	A890 8c **ultra, greenish blk & red,** *Feb. 16*	.25	.25
	P# block of 4	1.00	—
	Margin block of 4, Mr. Zip and "Use Zip Code"	1.00	—
a.	Tagging omitted	45.00	
b.	Red missing (PS)	*300.00*	
1477	A891 8c **black, vermilion & ultra,** *Apr. 13*	.25	.25
	P# block of 4	1.00	—
	Margin block of 4, Mr. Zip and "Use Zip Code"	1.00	—
	Pair with full horiz. gutter btwn	*500.00*	
a.	Tagging omitted	—	

LITHOGRAPHED, ENGRAVED (Giori)

1478	A892 8c **blue, black, red & green,** *June 22*	.25	.25
	P# block of 4	1.00	—
	Margin block of 4, Mr. Zip and "Use Zip Code"	1.00	—
a.	Red missing (CM)	—	
1479	A893 8c **blue, black, yellow & red,** *Sept. 28*	.25	.25
	P# block of 4	1.00	—
	Margin block of 4, Mr. Zip and "Use Zip Code"	1.00	—
a.	Blue missing (CM)	—	
b.	Red missing (CM)	—	
	Nos. 1476-1479 (4)	1.00	1.00

Margin of Nos. 1477-1479 includes Bicentennial Commission emblem and inscription.

AMERICAN BICENTENNIAL ISSUE

Boston Tea Party

In left panes Nos. 1480 and 1482 appear in 1st, 3rd and 5th place, Nos. 1481 and 1483 appear in 2nd and 4th place. This arrangement is reversed in right panes.

British Merchantman A894

British Three-master A895

Boats and Ship's Hull — A896

Boat and Dock — A897

Designed by William A. Smith.

LITHOGRAPHED, ENGRAVED (Giori)
Plates of 200 subjects in four panes of 50.

1973, July 4	**Tagged**		**Perf. 11**
1480	A894 8c **black & multicolored**	.25	.25
1481	A895 8c **black & multicolored**	.25	.25
1482	A896 8c **black & multicolored**	.25	.25
1483	A897 8c **black & multicolored**	.25	.25
a.	Block of 4, #1480-1483	1.00	1.00
	P# block of 4	1.00	—
	Margin block of 4, Mr. Zip and "Use Zip Code"	1.00	—
b.	As "a," black (engraved) omitted	*950.00*	
c.	As "a," black (litho.) omitted	*900.00*	
d.	As "a," tagging omitted	*200.00*	—
e.	As "a," dk blue omitted	*1,500.*	*750.00*
	On cover		—

Margin includes Bicentennial Commission emblem and inscription.

AMERICAN ARTS ISSUE

George Gershwin (1898-1937), composer (No. 1484); Robinson Jeffers (1887-1962), poet (No. 1485); Henry Ossawa Tanner (1859-1937), black painter (No. 1486); Willa Cather (1873-1947), novelist (No. 1487).

Gershwin, Sportin' Life, Porgy and Bess — A898

Robinson Jeffers, Man and Children of Carmel with Burro — A899

Henry Ossawa Tanner, Palette and Rainbow A900

Willa Cather, Pioneer Family and Covered Wagon A901

Designed by Mark English.

PHOTOGRAVURE (Andreotti)
Plates of 160 subjects in four panes of 40.

1973	**Tagged**		**Perf. 11**
1484	A898 8c **dp. green & multi.,** *Feb. 28*	.25	.25
	P# block of 12, 6#	2.00	—
	Margin block of 4, Mr. Zip, "Use Zip Code" and "Mail Early in the Day"	1.00	—
	P# block of 16, 6#, Mr. Zip and slogans	3.00	—
a.	Vertical pair, imperf. horiz.	*160.00*	
1485	A899 8c **Prussian blue & multi.,** *Aug. 13*	.25	.25
	P# block of 12, 6#	2.00	—
	Margin block of 4, Mr. Zip, "Use Zip Code" "Mail Early in the Day"	.60	—
	P# block of 16, 6#, Mr. Zip and slogans	3.00	—
a.	Vertical pair, imperf. horiz.	*160.00*	
1486	A900 8c **yellow brown & multi.,** *Sept. 10*	.25	.25
	P# block of 12, 6#	2.00	—
	Margin block of 4, Mr. Zip, "Use Zip Code" "Mail Early in the Day"	1.00	—
	P# block of 16, 6#, Mr. Zip and slogans	3.00	—
1487	A901 8c **deep brown & multi.,** *Sept. 20*	.25	.25
	P# block of 12, 6#	2.50	—
	Margin block of 4, Mr. Zip, "Use Zip Code" "Mail Early in the Day"	1.00	—
	P# block of 16, 6#, Mr. Zip and slogans	3.00	—
a.	Vertical pair, imperf. horiz.	*175.00*	
	Nos. 1484-1487 (4)	1.00	1.00

COPERNICUS ISSUE

Nicolaus Copernicus (1473-1543), Polish Astronomer — A902

Designed by Alvin Eisenman after 18th century engraving.

LITHOGRAPHED, ENGRAVED (Giori)
Plates of 200 subjects in four panes of 50.

1973, Apr. 23	**Tagged**		**Perf. 11**
1488	A902 8c **black & orange**	.25	.25
	P# block of 4	1.00	—
	Margin block of 4, Mr. Zip and "Use Zip Code"	1.00	—
a.	Orange omitted	*400.00*	
b.	Black (engraved) omitted	*600.00*	
c.	Tagging omitted	*125.00*	

The orange can be chemically removed. Expertization of No. 1488a is required.

POSTAL SERVICE EMPLOYEES ISSUE

A tribute to US Postal Service employees. Nos. 1489-1498 are printed se-tenant in horizontal rows of 10. Emerald inscription on back, printed beneath gum in water-soluble ink, includes Postal Service emblem, "People Serving You" and a statement, differing for each of the 10 stamps, about some aspect of postal service.

Each stamp in top or bottom row has a tab with blue inscription enumerating various jobs in postal service.

Stamp Counter — A903

Mail Collection — A904

Letter Facing on Conveyor Belt — A905

Parcel Post Sorting — A906

Mail Canceling — A907

Manual Letter Routing — A908

Electronic Letter Routing — A909

Loading Mail on Truck — A910

Mailman — A911

Rural Mail Delivery — A912

Designed by Edward Vebell.

PHOTOGRAVURE (Andreotti)

Plates of 200 subjects in four panes of 50.

1973, Apr. 30 Tagged ***Perf. 10½x11***

1489 A903 8c **multicolored** .25 .25
1490 A904 8c **multicolored** .25 .25
1491 A905 8c **multicolored** .25 .25
1492 A906 8c **multicolored** .25 .25
1493 A907 8c **multicolored** .25 .25
1494 A908 8c **multicolored** .25 .25
1495 A909 8c **multicolored** .25 .25
1496 A910 8c **multicolored** .25 .25
1497 A911 8c **multicolored** .25 .25
1498 A912 8c **multicolored** .25 .25
a. Strip of 10, #1489-1498 2.50 2.50
P# block of 20, 5# and 10 tabs 4.00 —
b. As "a," tagging omitted *250.00* —

The tagging on Nos. 1489-1498 consists of a ½-inch horizontal band of phosphor.

HARRY S. TRUMAN ISSUE

Harry S Truman, 33rd President, (1884-1972) — A913

Designed by Bradbury Thompson; photograph by Leo Stern.

GIORI PRESS PRINTING

Plates of 128 subjects in four panes of 32 each.

1973, May 8 Tagged ***Perf. 11***

1499 A913 8c **carmine rose, black & blue** .25 .25
P# block of 4 1.00 —
a. Tagging omitted 7.50

ELECTRONICS PROGRESS ISSUE

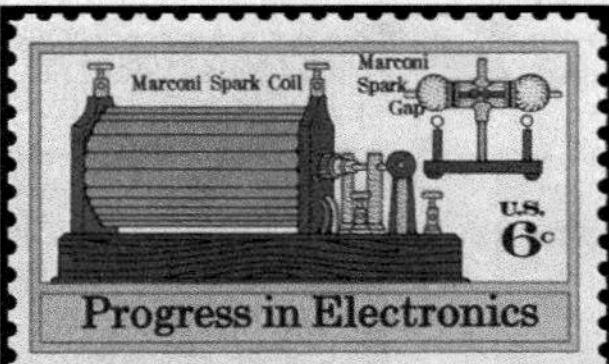

Marconi's Spark Coil and Spark Gap — A914

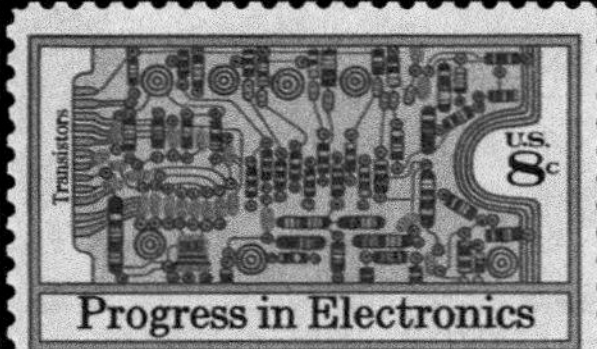

Transistors and Printed Circuit Board — A915

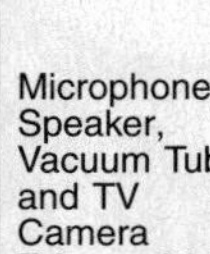

Microphone, Speaker, Vacuum Tube and TV Camera Tube — A916

Designed by Walter and Naiad Einsel.

LITHOGRAPHED, ENGRAVED (Giori)

Plates of 200 subjects in four panes of 50.

1973, July 10 Tagged ***Perf. 11***

1500 A914 6c **lilac & multicolored** .25 .25
P# block of 4 1.00 —
Margin block of 4, Mr. Zip and "Use Zip Code" 1.00 —
a. Tagging omitted 90.00
1501 A915 8c **tan & multicolored** .25 .25
P# block of 4 1.00 —
Margin block of 4, Mr. Zip and "Use Zip Code" 1.00 —
a. Black (inscriptions & "U.S. 8c") omitted *300.00*
b. Tan (background) & lilac omitted *600.00*
c. Tagging omitted *175.00*

Many examples of No. 1501b are hinged. Value about one-half never hinged value.

1502 A916 15c **gray green & multicolored** .30 .25
P# block of 4 1.30 —
Margin block of 4, Mr. Zip and "Use Zip Code" 1.20 —
a. Black (inscriptions & "U.S. 15c") omitted *850.00*
Nos. 1500-1502 (3) .80 .75

See No. C86.

LYNDON B. JOHNSON ISSUE

Lyndon B. Johnson, 36th President (1908-1973) — A917

Designed by Bradbury Thompson, portrait by Elizabeth Shoumatoff.

PHOTOGRAVURE (Andreotti)

Plates of 128 subjects in four panes of 32 each.

1973, Aug. 27 Tagged ***Perf. 11***

1503 A917 8c **black & multicolored,** *Aug. 27* .25 .25
P# block of 12, 6# 2.50 —
a. Horiz. pair, imperf. vert. *200.00*

RURAL AMERICA ISSUE

Centenary of the introduction of Aberdeen Angus cattle into the US (#1504); of the Chautauqua Institution (#1505); and of the introduction of hard winter wheat into Kansas by Mennonite immigrants (#1506).

Angus and Longhorn Cattle — A918

Chautauqua Tent and Buggies A919

Wheat Fields and Train — A920

No. 1504 modeled by Frank Waslick after painting by F. C. "Frank" Murphy. Nos. 1505-1506 designed by John Falter.

LITHOGRAPHED, ENGRAVED (Giori)

Plates of 200 subjects in four panes of 50.

1973-74 Tagged ***Perf. 11***

1504 A918 8c **multicolored,** *Oct. 5, 1973* .25 .25
P# block of 4 1.00 —
Margin block of 4, Mr. Zip and "Use Zip Code" 1.00 —
a. Green & red brown omitted *600.00*
b. Vert. pair, imperf. between *5,000.*
c. Tagging omitted 100.00
d. Blue (engr.) missing (PS) —
1505 A919 10c **multicolored,** *Aug. 6, 1974* .25 .25
P# block of 4 1.00 —
Margin block of 4, Mr. Zip and "Use Zip Code" 1.00 —
a. Black (litho.) omitted *1,750.*
b. Tagging omitted —
1506 A920 10c **multicolored,** *Aug. 16, 1974* .25 .25
P# block of 4 1.00 —
Margin block of 4, Mr. Zip and "Use Zip Code" 1.00 —
a. Black and blue (engr.) omitted *450.00*
b. Tagging omitted 100.00
Nos. 1504-1506 (3) .75 .75

CHRISTMAS ISSUE

Small Cowper Madonna, by Raphael — A921

Christmas Tree in Needlepoint — A922

Designers: No. 1507, Bradbury Thompson, using a painting in the National Gallery of Art, Washington, D.C. No. 1508, Dolli Tingle.

PHOTOGRAVURE (Andreotti)

Plates of 200 subjects in four panes of 50.

1973, Nov. 7 Tagged ***Perf. 10½x11***

1507 A921 8c **multicolored** .25 .25
P# block of 12, 6# 2.00 —
Margin block of 4, Mr. Zip and "Use Zip Code" 1.00 —
Pair with full vert. gutter btwn. —
1508 A922 8c **multicolored** .25 .25
P# block of 12, 6# 2.00 —
Margin block of 4, Mr. Zip and "Use Zip Code" 1.00 —
Pair with full horiz. gutter btwn. —
a. Vertical pair, imperf. between *225.00*

The tagging on Nos. 1507-1508 consists of a 20x12mm horizontal bar of phosphor.

50-Star and 13-Star Flags — A923

Jefferson Memorial and Signature — A924

Mail Transport — A925

Liberty Bell — A926

Designers: No. 1509, Ren Wicks. No. 1510, Dean Ellis. No. 1511, Randall McDougall. 6.3c, Frank Lionetti.

MULTICOLOR HUCK PRESS

Panes of 100 (10x10)

1973-74 Tagged ***Perf. 11x10½***

1509 A923 10c **red & blue,** *Dec. 8, 1973* .25 .25
P# block of 20, 4-6#, 2-3 "Mail Early" and 2-3 "Use Zip Code" 4.25 —
a. Horizontal pair, imperf. between *40.00* —
b. Blue omitted *150.00* —
c. Imperf., vert. pair *450.00*
d. Horiz. pair, imperf. vert. *900.00*
e. Tagging omitted *10.00*
f. Vert. pair, imperf between —

No. 1509 exists imperf and with red omitted from printer's waste.

Counterfeits exist of No. 1509. See the Postal Counterfeits section of this catalog.

ROTARY PRESS PRINTING

E.E. Plates of 400 subjects in four panes of 100.

1510 A924 10c **blue,** *Dec. 14, 1973* .25 .25
P# block of 4 1.00 —
Margin block of 4, "Use Zip Codes" 1.00 —
a. Untagged (Bureau precanceled) 4.00 1.00
P# block of 4 50.00
Margin block of 4, "Use Zip Codes" 25.00
b. Booklet pane of 5 + label 1.65 1.25
c. Booklet pane of 8 2.00 2.00
Pair of bklt panes with full vert. gutter btwn. *1,750.*
Pair of bklt. singles with full vert. gutter btwn. 500.00
d. Booklet pane of 6, *Aug. 5, 1974* 5.00 1.75
e. Vert. pair, imperf. horiz. *300.00*
f. Vert. pair, imperf. btwn., in #1510c with miscut or with foldover *450.00*
g. As No. 1510, tagging omitted (not Bureau precanceled) 10.00
h. As "c," tagging omitted — —
i. As "b," double booklet pane of 10 plus stamps with 2 horiz. pairs imperf. btwn. plus stamp and label imperf. btwn. (FO) *1,750.*
j. As "d," tagging omitted —

Counterfeits exist of No. 1510. See the Postal Counterfeits section of this catalog.

Bureau Precancels: 10 different.

No. 1510 varieties and 1510f resulted from paper foldovers after perforating and before cutting into booklet panes.

PHOTOGRAVURE (Andreotti)

Plates of 400 subjects in four panes of 100.

1511 A925 10c **multicolored,** *Jan. 4, 1974* .25 .25
P# block of 8, 4# 2.00 —
Margin block of 4, "Use Zip Codes" 1.00 —
Pair with full horiz. gutter btwn. —
a. Yellow omitted *40.00*

Beware of stamps with yellow chemically removed offered as No. 1511a.

COIL STAMPS
ROTARY PRESS PRINTING

1973-74 Tagged *Perf. 10 Vert.*

1518 A926 6.3c **brick red,** *Oct. 1, 1974* .25 .25
Pair .50 .50
Joint line pair .80 —
a. Untagged (Bureau precanceled) .35 .25
Pair .70 .50
Joint line pair 1.65 1.65
b. Imperf., pair *130.00*
Joint line pair *375.00*
c. As "a," imperf., pair *75.00*
Joint line pair *175.00*

A total of 129 different Bureau precancels were used by 117 cities.

No. 1518c is precanceled Washington, DC. Columbus, Ohio and Garden City, N.Y. Values for Columbus pair $400, for Garden City pair $850.

MULTICOLOR HUCK PRESS

1519 A923 10c **red & blue,** *Dec. 8, 1973* .25 .25
Pair .50 .50
a. Imperf., pair 35.00
b. Tagging omitted *9.00*

Huck press printings often show parts of a joint line, but this feature is not consistent.

ROTARY PRESS PRINTING

1520 A924 10c **blue,** *Dec. 14, 1973* .25 .25
Pair .50 .50
Joint line pair .75 —
a. Untagged (Bureau precanceled) 5.50 1.25
Pair 12.00 2.75
Joint line pair *185.00* —
b. Imperf., pair 30.00
Joint line pair 50.00
c. Tagging omitted —

Bureau Precancels: No. 1520a, 14 diff.

VETERANS OF FOREIGN WARS ISSUE

75th anniversary of Veterans of Spanish-American and Other Foreign Wars.

Emblem and Initials of Veterans of Foreign Wars — A928

Designed by Robert Hallock.

GIORI PRESS PRINTING

Plates of 200 subjects in 4 plates of 50.

1974, Mar. 11 Tagged *Perf. 11*

1525 A928 10c **red & dark blue** .25 .25
P# block of 4 1.00 —
Margin block of 4, Mr. Zip and "Use Zip Code" 1.00 —
a. Tagging omitted *90.00*
b. Blue missing (PS) —

ROBERT FROST ISSUE

Robert Frost (1873-1963), Poet — A929

Designed by Paul Calle; photograph by David Rhinelander.

ROTARY PRESS PRINTING

E.E. Plates of 200 subjects in four panes of 50.

1974, Mar. 26 Tagged *Perf. 10½x11*

1526 A929 10c **black** .25 .25
P# block of 4 1.00 —
Margin block of 4, Mr. Zip and "Use Zip Code" 1.00 —

EXPO '74 WORLD'S FAIR ISSUE

EXPO '74 World's Fair "Preserve the Environment," Spokane, Wash., May 4-Nov. 4.

"Cosmic Jumper" and "Smiling Sage" — A930

Designed by Peter Max.

PHOTOGRAVURE (Andreotti)

Plates of 160 subjects in four panes of 40.

1974, Apr. 18 Tagged *Perf. 11*

1527 A930 10c **multicolored** .25 .25
On cover, Expo. station handstamp canc. 12.50
P# block of 12, 6# 3.00 —
Margin block of 4, Mr. Zip, "Use Zip Code" and "Mail Early in the Day" 1.00 —
P# block of 16, 6#, Mr. Zip and slogans 4.00 —

HORSE RACING ISSUE

Kentucky Derby, Churchill Downs, centenary.

Horses Rounding Turn — A931

Designed by Henry Koehler.

PHOTOGRAVURE (Andreotti)

Plates of 200 subjects in four panes of 50.

1974, May 4 Tagged *Perf. 11x10½*

1528 A931 10c **yellow & multicolored** .25 .25
P# block of 12, 6# 3.25 —
Margin block of 4, Mr. Zip and "Use Zip Code" 1.10 —
a. Blue ("Horse Racing") omitted *650.00*
b. Red ("U.S. postage 10 cents") omitted *1,750.*
c. Tagging omitted 90.00

Beware of stamps offered as No. 1528b that have traces of red.

SKYLAB ISSUE

First anniversary of the launching of Skylab I, honoring all who participated in the Skylab project.

Skylab — A932

Designed by Robert T. McCall.

LITHOGRAPHED, ENGRAVED (Giori)

Plates of 200 subjects in four panes of 50.

1974, May 14 Tagged *Perf. 11*

1529 A932 10c **multicolored** .25 .25
P# block of 4 1.00 —
Margin block of 4, Mr. Zip and "Use Zip Code" 1.00 —
a. Vert. pair, imperf. between —
b. Tagging omitted *10.00*
c. Vert. pair, imperf. horiz. —
d. Double impression of magenta —

UNIVERSAL POSTAL UNION ISSUE

UPU cent. In the 1st row Nos. 1530-1537 are in sequence as listed. In the 2nd row Nos. 1534-1537 are followed by Nos. 1530-1533. Every row of 8 and every horizontal block of 8 contains all 8 designs. The letter writing designs are from famous works of art; some are details. The quotation on every second stamp, "Letters mingle souls," is from a letter by poet John Donne.

Michelangelo, from "School of Athens," by Raphael, 1509 — A933

"Five Feminine Virtues," by Hokusai, c. 1811 — A934

"Old Scraps," by John Fredrick Peto, 1894 — A935

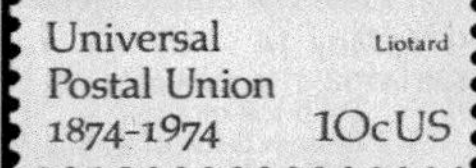

"The Lovely Reader," by Jean Etienne Liotard, 1746 — A936

"Lady Writing Letter," by Gerard Terborch, 1654 — A937

Inkwell and Quill, from "Boy with a Top," by Jean-Baptiste Simeon Chardin, 1738 — A938

Mrs. John Douglas, by Thomas Gainsborough, 1784 — A939

Don Antonio Noriega, by Francisco de Goya, 1801 — A940

Designed by Bradbury Thompson.

PHOTOGRAVURE (Andreotti)

Plates of 128 subjects in four panes of 32 each.

1974, June 6	**Tagged**	***Perf. 11***	
1530 A933 10c **multicolored**		.25	.25
1531 A934 10c **multicolored**		.25	.25
1532 A935 10c **multicolored**		.25	.25
1533 A936 10c **multicolored**		.25	.25
1534 A937 10c **multicolored**		.25	.25
1535 A938 10c **multicolored**		.25	.25
1536 A939 10c **multicolored**		.25	.25
1537 A940 10c **multicolored**		.25	.25
a. Block or strip of 8 (#1530-1537)		2.00	2.00
P# block of 16, 5#, "Mail Early in the Day," Mr. Zip and "Use Zip Code"		3.50	—
P# block of 10, 5#; no slogans		2.50	—
b. As "a," (block), imperf. vert.		*2,500.*	

MINERAL HERITAGE ISSUE

The sequence of stamps in 1st horizontal row is Nos. 1538-1541, 1538-1539. In 2nd row Nos. 1540-1541 are followed by Nos. 1538-1541.

Petrified Wood A941

Tourmaline — A942

Amethyst A943

Rhodochrosite — A944

Designed by Leonard F. Buckley.

LITHOGRAPHED, ENGRAVED (Giori)

Plates of 192 subjects in four panes of 48 (6x8).

1974, June 13	**Tagged**	***Perf. 11***	
1538 A941 10c **blue & multicolored**		.25	.25
a. Light blue & yellow (litho.) omitted		—	
1539 A942 10c **blue & multicolored**		.25	.25
a. Light blue (litho.) omitted		—	
b. Black & purple (engr.) omitted		—	
1540 A943 10c **blue & multicolored**		.25	.25
a. Light blue & yellow (litho.) omitted		—	
1541 A944 10c **blue & multicolored**		.25	.25
a. Block or strip of 4, #1538-1541		1.00	1.00
P# block of 4		1.00	—
Margin block of 4, Mr. Zip and "Use Zip Code"		1.00	—
b. As "a," light blue & yellow (litho.) omitted		*900.00*	—
c. Light blue (litho.) omitted		—	
d. Black & red (engr.) omitted		—	
e. Block of 4, two right stamps being Nos. 1539b and 1541d		*7,000.*	
f. As "a," tagging omitted		*225.00*	

No. 1541e is usually collected as a transition block of six or larger.

KENTUCKY SETTLEMENT, 200th ANNIV.
Fort Harrod, first settlement in Kentucky.

Covered Wagons at Fort Harrod — A945

Designed by David K. Stone.

LITHOGRAPHED, ENGRAVED (Giori)

Plates of 200 subjects in four panes of 50.

1974, June 15	**Tagged**	***Perf. 11***	
1542 A945 10c **green & multicolored**		.25	.25
P# block of 4		1.00	—
Margin block of 4, Mr. Zip and "Use Zip Code"		1.00	—
a. Dull black (litho.) omitted		*400.00*	
b. Green (engr. & litho.), black (engr. & litho.) & blue missing (EP)		*1,750.*	
c. Green (engr.) missing (EP)		*3,000.*	

d.	Green (engr.) & black (litho.) missing (EP)	—	
e.	Tagging omitted	150.00	
f.	Blue (litho.) omitted	—	

No. 1542f was caused by an occurrence that seems to be unique for U.S. total color omitted/missing errors. According to the BEP, oil on the printing blanket made a small area unreceptive to the blue ink. No blue at all was printed on one unique error stamp.

AMERICAN REVOLUTION BICENTENNIAL ISSUE
First Continental Congress

Nos. 1543-1544 alternate in 1st row, Nos. 1545-1546 in 2nd row. This arrangement is repeated throughout the pane.

Carpenters' Hall, Philadelphia A946

"We ask but for peace . . ." A947

"Deriving their just powers . . ." A948

Independence Hall — A949

Designed by Frank P. Conley

GIORI PRESS PRINTING

Plates of 200 subjects in four panes of 50.

1974, July 4 **Tagged** ***Perf. 11***

1543	A946 10c **dark blue & red**	.25	.25
1544	A947 10c **gray, dark blue & red**	.25	.25
1545	A948 10c **gray, dark blue & red**	.25	.25
1546	A949 10c **red & dark blue**	.25	.25
a.	Block of 4, #1543-1546	1.00	1.00
	P# block of 4	1.00	—
	Margin block of 4, Mr. Zip and "Use Zip Code"	1.00	—
b.	As "a," tagging omitted	*65.00*	

Margin includes Bicentennial Commission emblem and inscription.

ENERGY CONSERVATION ISSUE

Publicizing the importance of conserving all forms of energy.

Molecules and Drops of Gasoline and Oil — A950

Designed by Robert W. Bode.

LITHOGRAPHED, ENGRAVED (Giori)

Plates of 200 subjects in four panes of 50.

1974, Sept. 23 **Tagged** ***Perf. 11***

1547	A950 10c **multicolored**	.25	.25
	P# block of 4	1.00	—
	Margin block of 4, Mr. Zip and "Use Zip Code"	1.00	—
a.	Blue & orange omitted	*400.00*	
b.	Orange & green omitted	*275.00*	
c.	Green omitted	*400.00*	
d.	Tagging omitted	10.00	

AMERICAN FOLKLORE ISSUE
Legend of Sleepy Hollow

The Headless Horseman in pursuit of Ichabod Crane from "Legend of Sleepy Hollow," by Washington Irving.

Headless Horseman and Ichabod A951

Designed by Leonard Everett Fisher.

LITHOGRAPHED, ENGRAVED (Giori)

Plates of 200 subjects in four panes of 50.

1974, Oct. 10 **Tagged** ***Perf. 11***

1548	A951 10c **dk bl, blk, org & yel**	.25	.25
	P# block of 4	1.00	—
	Margin block of 4, Mr. Zip and "Use Zip Code"	1.00	—
a.	Tagging omitted	*225.00*	—

RETARDED CHILDREN ISSUE

Retarded Children Can Be Helped, theme of annual convention of the National Association of Retarded Citizens.

Retarded Child — A952

Designed by Paul Calle.

GIORI PRESS PRINTING

Plates of 200 subjects in four panes of 50.

1974, Oct. 12 **Tagged** ***Perf. 11***

1549	A952 10c **brown red & dark brown**	.25	.25
	P# block of 4	1.00	—
	Margin block of 4, Mr. Zip and "Use Zip Code"	1.00	—
a.	Tagging omitted	11.00	

WARNING: DO NOT SOAK Ⓢ

Beginning with No. 1552, the first U.S. self-adhesive stamp, the symbol shown above, a black "S" inside a red circle, accompanies listings or appears in footnotes for self-adhesive stamps that will not separate from paper or otherwise do not respond well to a standard warm-water soak. In general, the symbol appears with the issue title, or on the listing line, next to the color description. The editors strongly recommend that such stamps be collected on piece.

CHRISTMAS ISSUE

Angel — A953

"The Road-Winter," by Currier and Ives — A954

Designers: No. 1550, Bradbury Thompson, using detail from the Pérussis altarpiece painted by anonymous French artist, 1480, in Metropolitan Museum of Art, New York City. No. 1551, Stevan Dohanos, using Currier and Ives print from drawing by Otto Knirsch.

PHOTOGRAVURE (Andreotti)

Plates of 200 subjects in four panes of 50.

1974, Oct. 23 **Tagged** ***Perf. 10½x11***

1550	A953 10c **multicolored**	.25	.25
	P# block of 10, 5#	2.50	—
	Margin block of 4, Mr. Zip and "Use Zip Code"	1.00	—
	Perf. 11x10½		
1551	A954 10c **multicolored**	.25	.25
	P# block of 12, 6#	3.00	—
	Margin block of 4, Mr. Zip and "Use Zip Code"	1.00	—
a.	Buff omitted	12.50	
b.	Tagging omitted	*175.00*	

No. 1551a is difficult to identify. Competent expertization is necessary.

Dove Weather Vane atop Mount Vernon — A955

Designers: Don Hedin and Robert Geissman.

Die Cut, Paper Backing Rouletted

1974, Nov. 15 **Untagged**

Self-adhesive; Inscribed "Precanceled"

1552	A955 10c **multicolored** Ⓢ	.25	.25
	P# block of 20, 6#, 5 slogans	4.50	
	P# block of 12, 6#, 5 different slogans	3.00	
	Nos. 1550-1552 (3)	.75	.75

Unused value of No. 1552 is for stamp on rouletted paper backing as issued. Used value is for stamp on piece, with or without postmark. **Most examples are becoming discolored from the adhesive. The Catalogue value is for discolored examples.**

Die cutting includes crossed slashes through dove, applied to prevent removal and re-use of the stamp. The stamp will separate into layers if soaked.

Two different machines were used to roulette the sheet.

See note after No. 1549.

AMERICAN ARTS ISSUE

Benjamin West (1738-1820), painter (No. 1553); Paul Laurence Dunbar (1872-1906), poet (No. 1554); David (Lewelyn) Wark Griffith (1875-1948), motion picture producer (No. 1555).

Self-portrait — A956

A957

A958

Designers: No. 1553, Bradbury Thompson; No. 1554, Walter D. Richards; No. 1555, Fred Otnes.

PHOTOGRAVURE (Andreotti)

Plates of 200 subjects in four panes of 50.

1975 **Tagged** ***Perf. 10½x11***

1553 A956 10c **multicolored**, *Feb. 10* .25 .25
P# block of 10, 5# 2.50 —
Margin block of 4, Mr. Zip and "Use Zip Code" 1.00 —

Perf. 11

1554 A957 10c **multicolored**, *May 1* .25 .25
P# block of 10, 5# 2.50 —
Margin block of 4, Mr. Zip and "Use Zip Code" 1.00 —
a. Imperf., pair *800.00*
b. Tagging omitted *350.00*

LITHOGRAPHED, ENGRAVED (Giori)

Perf. 11

1555 A958 10c **brown & multicolored**, *May 27* .25 .25
P# block of 4 1.00 —
Margin block of 4, Mr. Zip and "Use Zip Code" 1.00 —
a. Brown (engr.) omitted *450.00*
b. Tagging omitted *175.00*
Nos. 1553-1555 (3) .75 .75

SPACE ISSUES

US space accomplishments with unmanned craft. Pioneer 10 passed within 81,000 miles of Jupiter, Dec. 10, 1973. Mariner 10 explored Venus and Mercury in 1974 and Mercury again in 1975.

Pioneer 10 Passing Jupiter A959

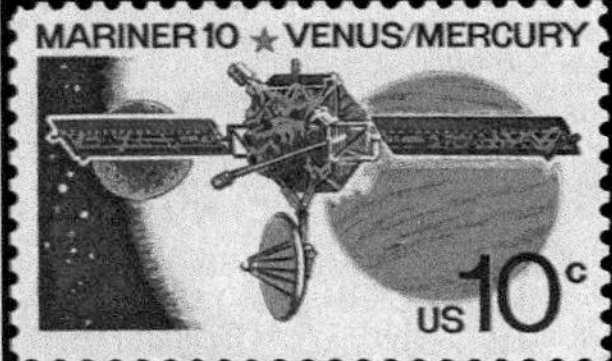

Mariner 10, Venus and Mercury A960

Designed by Robert McCall (No. 1556); Roy Gjertson (No. 1557).

LITHOGRAPHED, ENGRAVED (Giori)

Plates of 200 subjects in four panes of 50.

1975 **Tagged** ***Perf. 11***

1556 A959 10c **light yellow, dark yellow, red, blue & 2 dark blues**, *Feb. 28* .25 .25
P# block of 4 1.00 —
Margin block of 4, Mr. Zip and "Use Zip Code" 1.00 —
a. Red & dark yellow omitted *750.00*
b. Dark blues (engr.) omitted *450.00*
c. Tagging omitted *12.50*
d. Dark yellow omitted —

Imperfs. exist from printer's waste.

1557 A960 10c **black, red, ultra & bister**, *Apr. 4* .25 .25
P# block of 4 1.00 —
Margin block of 4, Mr. Zip and "Use Zip Code" 1.00 —
a. Red omitted *275.00*
b. Ultramarine & bister omitted *850.00*
c. Tagging omitted *12.50*
d. Red missing (PS) *525.00*

COLLECTIVE BARGAINING ISSUE

Collective Bargaining law, enacted 1935, in Wagner Act.

"Labor and Management" A961

Designed by Robert Hallock.

PHOTOGRAVURE (Andreotti)

Plates of 200 subjects in four panes of 50.

1975, Mar. 13 **Tagged** ***Perf. 11***

1558 A961 10c **multicolored** .25 .25
P# block of 8, 4# 2.00 —
Margin block of 4, Mr. Zip and "Use Zip Code" 1.00 —

Imperforates exist from printer's waste.

AMERICAN BICENTENNIAL ISSUE

Contributors to the Cause

Sybil Ludington, age 16, rallied militia, Apr. 26, 1777; Salem Poor, black freeman, fought in Battle of Bunker Hill; Haym Salomon, Jewish immigrant, raised money to finance Revolutionary War; Peter Francisco, Portuguese-French immigrant, joined Continental Army at 15. Emerald inscription on back, printed beneath gum in water-soluble ink, gives thumbnail sketch of portrayed contributor.

Sybil Ludington A962

Salem Poor — A963

Haym Salomon A964

Peter Francisco A965

Designed by Neil Boyle.

PHOTOGRAVURE (Andreotti)

Plates of 200 subjects in four panes of 50.

1975, Mar. 25 **Tagged** ***Perf. 11x10½***

1559 A962 8c **multicolored** .25 .25
P# block of 10, 5# 2.50 —
Margin block of 4, Mr. Zip and "Use Zip Code" 1.00 —
a. Back inscriptions omitted *110.00*
1560 A963 10c **multicolored** .25 .25
P# block of 10, 5# 2.50 —
Margin block of 4, Mr. Zip and "Use Zip Code" 1.00 —
a. Back inscription omitted *110.00*
b. Black missing (PS) —
1561 A964 10c **multicolored** .25 .25
P# block of 10, 5# 2.50 —
Margin block of 4, Mr. Zip and "Use Zip Code" 1.00 —
a. Back inscription omitted *110.00*
1562 A965 18c **multicolored** .35 .25
P# block of 10, 5# 3.60 —
Margin block of 4, Mr. Zip and "Use Zip Code" 1.45 —
Nos. 1559-1562 (4) 1.10 1.00

On No. 1560, two black plates were used. No. 1560b is missing the impression from one of those plates ("Salem Poor - U.S. Bicentennial symbol - Gallant Soldier") due to an upward shift of the horizontal perforations.

Dangerous fakes exist of No. 1561 with red apparently omitted. Professional authentication is mandatory in order to establish such a stamp as a genuine error.

Lexington-Concord Battle, 200th Anniv.

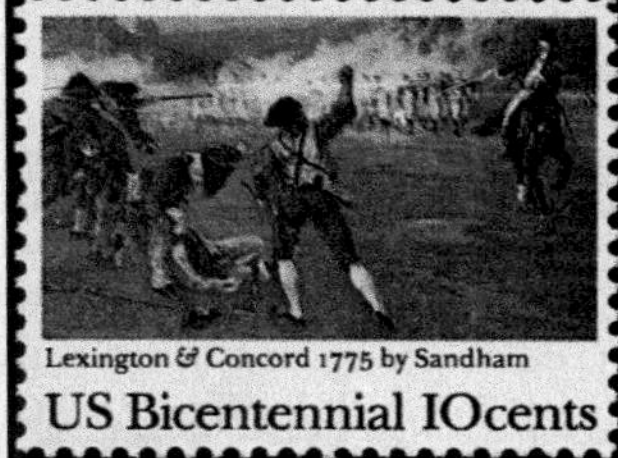

"Birth of Liberty," by Henry Sandham A966

Designed by Bradbury Thompson.

PHOTOGRAVURE (Andreotti)

Plates of 160 subjects in four panes of 40.

1975, Apr. 19 **Tagged** ***Perf. 11***

1563 A966 10c **multicolored** .25 .25
P# block of 12, 6# 2.50 —
Margin block of 4, Mr. Zip, "Use Zip Code" and "Mail Early in the Day" 1.00 —
P# block of 16, 6 P#, Mr. Zip and slogans 3.40 —
a. Vert. pair, imperf. horiz. *300.00*

Bunker Hill Battle, 200th Anniv.

Battle of Bunker Hill, by John Trumbull — A967

Designed by Bradbury Thompson.

PHOTOGRAVURE (Andreotti)

Plates of 160 subjects in four panes of 40.

1975, June 17 **Tagged** ***Perf. 11***

1564 A967 10c **multicolored** .25 .25
P# block of 12, 6# 2.50 —
Margin block of 4, Mr. Zip, "Use Zip Code" and "Mail Early in the Day" 1.00 —
P# block of 16, 6#, Mr. Zip and slogans 3.40 —

Military Uniforms

Bicentenary of US Military Services. Nos. 1565-1566 alternate in one row, Nos. 1567-1568 in next row.

Soldier with Flintlock Musket, Uniform Button — A968

Sailor with Grappling Hook, First Navy Jack, 1775 — A969

Marine with Musket, Fullrigged Ship — A970

Militiaman with Musket and Powder Horn — A971

Designed by Edward Vebell.

PHOTOGRAVURE (Andreotti)

Plates of 200 subjects in four panes of 50.

1975, July 4 — Tagged — *Perf. 11*

1565	A968	10c **multicolored**	.25	.25
a.		Tagging omitted	—	
1566	A969	10c **multicolored**	.25	.25
1567	A970	10c **multicolored**	.25	.25
1568	A971	10c **multicolored**	.25	.25
a.		Block of 4, #1565-1568	1.00	1.00
		P# block of 12, 6#	2.50	—
		P# block of 20, 6#, Mr. Zip and slogans	4.50	—
		Margin block of 4, Mr. Zip and "Use Zip Code"	1.00	—
b.		As "a," tagging omitted on #1565 and 1566	—	

APOLLO SOYUZ SPACE ISSUE

Apollo Soyuz space test project, Russo-American cooperation, launched July 15; link-up, July 17. Nos. In the 1st row, No. 1569 is in 1st and 3rd space, No. 1570 is 2nd space; in the 2nd row No. 1570 is in 1st and 3rd space, No. 1569 in 2nd space, etc.

Participating US and USSR crews: Thomas P. Stafford, Donald K. Slayton, Vance D. Brand, Aleksei A. Leonov, Valery N. Kubasov.

Apollo and Soyuz after Link-up, and Earth — A972

Spacecraft before Link-up, Earth and Project Emblem — A973

Illustrations reduced.

Designed by Robert McCall (No. 1569) and Anatoly M. Aksamit of USSR (No. 1570).

PHOTOGRAVURE (Andreotti)

Plates of 96 subjects in four panes of 24 each.

1975, July 15 — Tagged — *Perf. 11*

1569	A972	10c **multicolored**	.25	.25
		Pair with full horiz. gutter btwn.	—	
1570	A973	10c **multicolored**	.25	.25
a.		Pair, #1569-1570	.50	.50
		P# block of 12, 6#	2.50	—
		Margin block of 4, Mr. Zip, "Use Zip Code"	1.00	—
		P# block of 16, 6#, Mr. Zip, "Use Zip Code"	3.40	—
		Pair with full horiz. gutter btwn.	—	
b.		As "a," tagging omitted	*30.00*	—
c.		As "a," vert. pair, imperf. horiz.	*800.00*	
d.		As "a," yellow omitted	*900.00*	

Nos. 1569-1570 totally imperforate are printer's waste.

See Russia Nos. 4339-4340.

INTERNATIONAL WOMEN'S YEAR ISSUE

International Women's Year 1975.

Worldwide Equality for Women A974

Designed by Miriam Schottland.

PHOTOGRAVURE (Andreotti)

Plates of 200 subjects in four panes of 50.

1975, Aug. 26 — Tagged — *Perf. 11x10½*

1571	A974	10c **blue, orange & dark blue**	.25	.25
		P# block of 6, 3#	1.30	—
		Margin block of 4, Mr. Zip and "Use Zip Code"	1.00	—
a.		Tagging omitted	10.00	

US POSTAL SERVICE BICENTENNIAL ISSUE

Nos. 1572-1573 alternate in 1st row, Nos. 1574-1575 in 2nd row. This arrangement is repeated throughout the pane.

Stagecoach and Trailer Truck — A975

Old and New Locomotives A976

Early Mail Plane and Jet — A977

Satellite for Transmission of Mailgrams A978

Designed by James L. Womer.

PHOTOGRAVURE (Andreotti)

Plates of 200 subjects in four panes of 50.

1975, Sept. 3 — Tagged — *Perf. 11x10½*

1572	A975	10c **multicolored**	.25	.25
1573	A976	10c **multicolored**	.25	.25
1574	A977	10c **multicolored**	.25	.25
1575	A978	10c **multicolored**	.25	.25
a.		Block of 4, #1572-1575	1.00	1.00
		P# block of 12, 6#	2.50	—
		P# block of 20, 6#, Mr. Zip and slogans	4.50	—
		Margin block of 4, Mr. Zip and "Use Zip Code"	1.00	—
b.		As "a," red "10c" omitted, tagging omitted	—	

WORLD PEACE THROUGH LAW ISSUE

A prelude to 7th World Law Conference of the World Peace Through Law Center at Washington, D.C., Oct. 12-17.

Law Book, Gavel, Olive Branch and Globe — A979

Designed by Melbourne Brindle.

GIORI PRESS PRINTING

Plates of 200 subjects in four panes of 50.

1975, Sept. 29 — Tagged — *Perf. 11*

1576	A979	10c **green, Prussian blue & rose brown**	.25	.25
		P# block of 4	1.00	—
		Margin block of 4, Mr. Zip and "Use Zip Code"	1.00	—
a.		Tagging omitted	10.00	
b.		Horiz. pair, imperf vert.	*7,500.*	
c.		All colors omitted	—	

No. 1576c is collected in a horiz. strip as two errors se-tenant with a partially printed stamp.

BANKING AND COMMERCE ISSUE

Banking and commerce in the U.S., and for the Centennial Convention of the American Bankers Association.

Designed by V. Jack Ruther.

Engine Turning, Indian Head Penny, Morgan-type Silver Dollar — A980

Seated Liberty Quarter, $20 Gold Double Eagle and Engine Turning A981

LITHOGRAPHED, ENGRAVED (Giori)

Plates of 160 subjects in four panes of 40.

1975, Oct. 6 — Tagged — *Perf. 11*

1577	A980	10c **multicolored**	.25	.25
1578	A981	10c **multicolored**	.25	.25
a.		Pair, #1577-1578	.50	.50
		P# block of 4	1.00	—
		Margin block of 4, Mr. Zip and "Use Zip Code"	1.00	—
b.		As "a," brown & blue (litho) omitted	*1,400.*	
c.		As "a," brown, blue & yellow (litho) omitted	*1,750.*	
d.		As No. 1578a, tagging omitted		—

CHRISTMAS ISSUE

Madonna and Child, by Domenico Ghirlandaio — A982

Christmas Card, by Louis Prang, 1878 — A983

Plate flaw ("d" damaged and no dot on the second "i" in "Ghirlandaio")

Designed by Stevan Dohanos.

PHOTOGRAVURE (Andreotti)

Plates of 200 subjects in four panes of 50.

1975, Oct. 14 Tagged *Perf. 11*

1579	A982 (10c) **multicolored**		.25	.25
		P# block of 12, 6#	2.50	—
		Margin block of 4, Mr. Zip and "Use Zip Code"	1.00	—
		Plate flaw ("d" damaged and no dot on the second "i" in "Ghirlandaio") (36741-36746 LL 47)	5.00	—
	a.	Imperf., pair	*75.00*	

Perf. 11.2

1580	A983 (10c) **multicolored**		.25	.25
		P# block of 12, 6#	2.50	—
		Margin block of 4, Mr. Zip and "Use Zip Code"	1.00	—
	a.	Imperf., pair	*85.00*	
	c.	Perf. 10.9	.25	.25
		P# block of 12, 6#	3.50	—
		Margin block of 4, Mr. Zip and "Use Zip Code"	1.00	—

Perf. 10.5x11.3

1580B	A983 (10c) **multicolored,**		.65	.25
		P# block of 12, 6#	14.00	—
		Margin block of 4, Mr. Zip and "Use Zip Code"	2.75	—

AMERICANA ISSUE

Inkwell and Quill — A984

Speaker's Stand — A985

Early Ballot Box — A987

Books, Bookmark, Eyeglasses — A988

Dome of Capitol — A994

Contemplation of Justice, by J. E. Fraser — A995

Early American Printing Press — A996

Torch, Statue of Liberty — A997

Liberty Bell — A998

Eagle and Shield — A999

Fort McHenry Flag (15 Stars) — A1001

Head, Statue of Liberty — A1002

Old North Church, Boston — A1003

Fort Nisqually, Wash. — A1004

Sandy Hook Lighthouse, NJ — A1005

Morris Township School No. 2, Devils Lake, ND — A1006

Iron "Betty" Lamp, Plymouth Colony, 17th-18th Centuries — A1007

Rush Lamp and Candle Holder — A1008

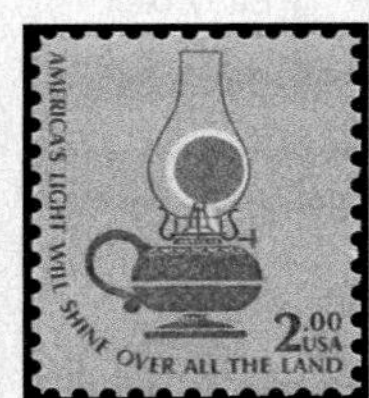

Kerosene Table Lamp — A1009

Railroad Conductor's Lantern, c. 1850 — A1010

Designed by: 2c, 4c, 15c, V. Jack Ruther Robert Hallock. 3c, Clarence Holbert. 9c, 10c, 11c, Walter Brooks. 12c, George Mercer. No. 1595, Bernard Glassman. No. 1596, James L. Womer.

ROTARY PRESS PRINTING

E.E. Plates of 400 subjects in four panes of 100.

1975-81 Tagged *Perf. 11¼x10½*

Size: 18½x22½mm

1581	A984 1c **dark blue,** *greenish,* shiny gum, *Dec. 8, 1977*		.25	.25
		P# block of 4	.50	—
		Margin block of 4, "Use Zip Code"	.25	—
		Dull gum	.25	
		P# block of 4	.50	
		Zip block of 4	.25	
		Pair with full vert. gutter btwn.	—	
	a.	Untagged (Bureau precanceled)	4.50	1.50
		P# block of 4	30.00	
		Margin block of 4, "Use Zip Codes"	18.50	
	c.	White paper, dull gum	100.00	—
	d.	Tagging omitted (not Bureau precanceled), shiny gum	7.50	
		Dull gum	7.50	
1582	A985 2c **red brown,** *greenish,* shiny gum, *Dec. 8, 1977*		.25	.25
		P# block of 4	.50	—
		Margin block of 4, "Use Zip Code"	.25	—
		Dull gum	.25	
		P# block of 4	2.50	
		Zip block of 4	1.00	
	a.	Untagged (Bureau precanceled)	4.50	1.50
		P# block of 4	30.00	
		Zip block of 4	18.50	
	b.	Cream paper, dull gum, *1981*	.25	.25
		P# block of 4	.50	
		Zip block of 4	.25	
	c.	Tagging omitted (not Bureau precanceled)	7.50	
1584	A987 3c **olive,** *greenish,* shiny gum, *Dec. 8, 1977*		.25	.25
		P# block of 4	.50	—
		Margin block of 4, "Use Zip Code"	.50	—
		Dull gum	.25	
		P# block of 4	.50	
		Zip block of 4	.50	
		Pair with full horiz. gutter btwn.	*275.00*	
	a.	Untagged (Bureau precanceled), dull gum	.75	.50
		P# block of 4	9.50	
		Zip block of 4	5.00	
	b.	Tagging omitted (not Bureau precanceled), shiny gum	10.00	
		dull gum	10.00	

Values for No. 1584a are for the lines-only precancel. Also known with city precancels, and valued at $50 thus.

1585	A988 4c **rose magenta,** *cream,* shiny gum, *Dec. 8, 1977*		.25	.25
		P# block of 4	.75	—
		Margin block of 4, "Use Zip Code"	.50	—
		Dull gum	.25	
		P# block of 4	1.10	
		Zip block of 4	1.00	
		Pair with full horiz. gutter btwn.	*150.00*	
	a.	Untagged (Bureau precanceled)	1.00	.75
		P# block of 4	13.50	
		Zip block of 4	6.00	
	b.	Tagging omitted (not Bureau precanceled), dull gum	*65.00*	
		Shiny gum	*40.00*	

The pair with horiz. gutter between also is misperfed through the stamps horizontally.

Also known with city precancels, and valued at $100 thus.

Size: 17½x20½mm

Perf. 11x10½ on 3 Sides

1590	A994 9c **slate green** (from bklt. pane #1623a), *Mar. 11, 1977*		.45	*1.00*
		Pair with full horiz. gutter between	—	
	b.	Tagging omitted	—	

Perf. 10x9¾ on 3 Sides

1590A	A994 9c **slate green** (from bklt. pane #1623Bc), *Mar. 11, 1977*		12.50	12.50

Size: 18½x22½mm

Perf. 11¼x10½

1591	A994 9c **slate green,** *gray,* shiny gum, *Nov. 24, 1975*		.25	.25
		P# block of 4	1.00	—
		Margin block of 4, "Use Zip Code"	1.00	—
		Dull gum	1.00	
		P# block of 4	5.00	
		Zip block of 4	4.25	
	a.	Untagged (Bureau precanceled)	1.75	1.00
		P# block of 4	45.00	
		Zip block of 4	8.00	
	b.	Tagging omitted (not Bureau precanceled)	6.00	

Values for No. 1591a are for the lines-only precancel. Also known with city precancels, and valued at $32.50 thus.

1592	A995 10c **violet,** *gray,* shiny gum, *Nov. 17, 1977*		.25	.25
		P# block of 4	1.00	—
		Margin block of 4, "Use Zip Code"	1.00	—
		Dull gum	.25	
		P# block of 4	1.00	
		Zip block of 4	1.00	
	a.	Untagged (Bureau precanceled, Chicago)	9.50	5.00
		P# block of 4	95.00	
		Zip block of 4	42.50	

b. Tagging omitted (not Bureau precanceled), dull gum 7.50

1593 A996 11c **orange,** *gray, Nov. 13, 1975* .25 .25
P# block of 4 1.00 —
Margin block of 4, "Use Zip Code" 1.00 —
Pair with full horiz. gutter between —
a. Tagging omitted 5.00

1594 A997 12c **red brown,** *beige, Apr. 8, 1981* .25 .25
brownish red .25 .25
P# block of 4 1.60 —
Zip block of 4 1.10 —
a. Tagging omitted 10.00

Perf. 11¼x10½ on 2 or 3 Sides

1595 A998 13c **brown** (from bklt. pane), *Oct. 31, 1975* .30 .25
a. Booklet pane of 6 2.25 1.50
b. Booklet pane of 7 + label 2.25 1.50
c. Booklet pane of 8 2.25 1.50
d. Booklet pane of 5 + label, *Apr. 2, 1976* 1.75 1.25
e. Vert. pair, imperf. btwn., in #1595c with foldover *1,100.*
f. Tagging omitted — —
g. Horiz. pair, imperf. btwn., in #1595d with foldover —
h. As "a," miscut and inserted upside down into booklet cover, imperf below bottom stamps and with "tab" at bottom —
i. As "b," tagging omitted —
j. As "d," tagging omitted —

Nos. 1595e and 1595g resulted from paper foldovers after perforating and before cutting into panes. Beware of printer's waste consisting of complete panes with perfs around all outside edges.

Counterfeits exist of No. 1595. See the Postal Counterfeits section of this catalog.

PHOTOGRAVURE (Andreotti)
Plates of 400 subjects in four panes of 100.

Perf. 11¼ Bullseye

1596 A999 13c **multicolored,** *Dec. 1, 1975* .25 .25
P# block of 12, 6# 3.25 —
P# block of 20, 6# and slogans 5.50 —
Margin block of 4, "Use Zip Code" 1.00 —
Pair with full horiz. gutter btwn. *150.00*
a. Imperf., pair *40.00* —
b. Yellow omitted *75.00*
d. Line perforated 11 *27.50* —
P# block of 12, 6# *350.00* —

On No. 1596 the entire sheet is perforated at one time so the perforations meet perfectly at the corners of the stamp. On No. 1596d the perforations do not line up perfectly.

ENGRAVED (Combination Press)
Plates of 460 subjects (20x23) in panes of 100 (10x10)

Perf. 11x11¼

1597 A1001 15c **gray, dark blue & red,** large block tagging, *June 30, 1978* .30 .25
P# block of 6 1.90 —
P# block of 20, 1-2# 6.50 —
a. Small block tagging .30 .25
P# block of 6 1.90 —
P# block of 20, 1-2# 6.50 —
b. Gray omitted *300.00*
c. Vert. pair, imperf btwn and with natural straight edge at bottom *350.00*
d. Tagging omitted 5.00
e. Imperf., vert. pair *15.00*
f. As "e," tagging omitted —

Plate number appears 3 times on each plate of 23 rows. With no separating gutters, each pane has only left or right sheet margin. Plate numbers appear on both margins; there are no slogans.

ENGRAVED

Perf. 11x10½ on 2 or 3 Sides

1598 A1001 15c **gray, dark blue & red** (from bklt. pane), *June 30, 1978* .40 .25
a. Booklet pane of 8 3.75 1.50

Perf. 11¼x10½

1599 A1002 16c **blue,** *Mar. 31, 1978* .35 .25
P# block of 4 1.90 —
Margin block of 4, "Use Correct Zip Code" 1.40 —

1603 A1003 24c **red,** *blue, Nov. 14, 1975* .50 .25
P# block of 4 2.25 —
Margin block of 4, "Use Zip Code" 2.00 —
a. Tagging omitted 7.50
b. **red,** *greenish blue* .50 .25
P# block of 4 2.25 —
Margin block of 4, "Use Zip Code" 2.00

1604 A1004 28c **brown,** *blue,* shiny gum, *Aug. 11, 1978* .55 .25
P# block of 4 3.00 —
Margin block of 4, "Use Correct Zip Code" 2.25 —
Dull gum 1.10
P# block of 4 10.00
Zip block of 4 5.00

1605 A1005 29c **blue,** *light blue,* shiny gum, *Apr. 14, 1978* .60 .25
P# block of 4 3.00 —
Margin block of 4, "Use Correct Zip Code" 2.40 —
Dull gum 2.00
P# block of 4 15.00
Zip block of 4 9.00

1606 A1006 30c **green,** *blue, Aug. 27, 1979* .55 .25
P# block of 4 2.40 —
Margin block of 4, "Use Correct Zip Code" 2.25 —
a. Tagging omitted 55.00

LITHOGRAPHED AND ENGRAVED

Perf. 11

1608 A1007 50c **tan, black & orange,** *Sept. 11, 1979* .85 .25
P# block of 4 3.75 —
Margin block of 4, "Use Correct Zip Code" 3.50 —
a. Black omitted *375.00*
b. Vert. pair, imperf. horiz. *1,200.*
c. Tagging omitted 20.00

Beware of examples offered as No. 1608b that have blind perfs.

1610 A1008 $1 **tan, brown, orange & yellow,** *July 2, 1979* 2.00 .25
P# block of 4 8.50 —
Margin block of 4, "Use Correct Zip Code" 8.00 —
Pair with full vert. gutter btwn. —
a. Brown (engraved) omitted *175.00*
b. Tan, orange & yellow omitted *175.00*
c. Brown (engraved) inverted *17,000.*
d. Tagging omitted *20.00*

1611 A1009 $2 **tan, dark green, orange & yellow,** *Nov. 16, 1978* 3.75 .75
dark tan, dark green, orange & yellow 3.75 .75
P# block of 4 16.00 —
Margin block of 4, "Use Correct Zip Code" 15.00 —
a. Tagging omitted — —

1612 A1010 $5 **tan, red brown, yellow & orange,** *Aug. 23, 1979* 8.50 1.75
P# block of 4 36.00 —
Margin block of 4, "Use Correct Zip Code" 34.00 —
Nos. 1581-1612 (23) 33.85 20.75

Nos. 1590, 1590A, 1595, 1598, 1623 and 1623b were issued only in booklets. All stamps have one or two straight edges.

Bureau Precancels: 1c, 3 diff., 2c, Chicago, Greensboro, NC, 3c, 6 diff., 4c, Chicago, lines only, No. 1591a, 4 diff., No. 1596, 5 diff., 30c, lines only, 50c, 3 spacings, lines only, $1, 2 spacings, lines only. The 30c, 50c, $1 and No. 1596 are precanceled on tagged stamps.

Six-string Guitar — A1011

Saxhorns — A1012

Drum — A1013

Steinway Grand Piano, 1857 — A1014

Designers: 3.1c, George Mercer. 7.7c, Susan Robb. 7.9c, Bernard Glassman. 10c, Walter Brooks. 15c, V. Jack Ruther.

COIL STAMPS
ENGRAVED

1975-79 ***Perf. 10 Vertically***

1613 A1011 3.1c **brown,** *yellow, Oct. 25, 1979* .25 .25
Pair .50 .50
Joint line pair 1.25 —
a. Untagged (Bureau precanceled, lines only) .35 .35
Pair .70 .70
Joint line pair 7.00 —
b. Imperf., pair *850.00*
Joint line pair —

1614 A1012 7.7c **brown,** *bright yellow, Nov. 20, 1976* .25 .25
Pair .50 .50
Joint line pair .90 —
a. Untagged (Bureau precanceled) .40 .30
Pair .80 .60
Joint line pair 3.25 —
b. As "a," imperf., pair *1,250.*
Joint line pair *3,000.*

A total of 160 different Bureau precancels were used by 153 cities.

No. 1614b is precanceled Washington, DC. Also exists with Marion, OH precancel; value $1,950 for pair.

1615 A1013 7.9c **carmine,** *yellow,* shiny gum, *Apr. 23, 1976* .25 .25
Pair .50 .50
Joint line pair .75 —
Dull gum 1.00
Pair 2.00
Joint line pair 6.00
a. Untagged (Bureau precanceled), shiny gum .40 .40
Pair .80 .80
Joint line pair 2.75 —
Dull gum .45
Pair .90
Joint line pair 4.50
b. Imperf., pair *300.00*

A total of 109 different Bureau precancels were used by 107 cities plus two types of CAR. RT./SORT.

1615C A1014 8.4c **dark blue,** *yellow,* shiny gum, *July 13, 1978* .25 .25
Pair .50 .50
Joint line pair 3.25 .60
d. Untagged (Bureau precanceled), shiny gum .50 .40
Pair 1.00 .80
Joint line pair 4.25 —
Dull gum .40
Pair .80
Joint line pair 3.25
e. As "d," pair, imperf. between 45.00
Joint line pair *110.00*
f. As "d," imperf. pair, shiny gum 15.00
Joint line pair *35.00*
Dull gum *15.00*
Joint line pair *35.00*

A total of 145 different Bureau precancels were used by 144 cities.

No. 1615Ce is precanceled with lines only. No. 1615Cf is precanceled with lines only (value shown) and also exists in pairs precanceled Newark, N.J. ($25.), Brownstown, Ind. ($900), Oklahoma City, Okla. ($1,500.) and Washington, DC ($900).

1616 A994 9c **slate green,** *gray, Mar. 5, 1976* .25 .25
Pair .50 .50
Joint line pair .90 —
a. Imperf., pair *125.00*
Joint line pair *260.00*
b. Untagged (Bureau precanceled), shiny gum 1.15 .75
Pair 2.30 1.50
Joint line pair 42.50 —
Dull gum .75
Pair 1.50
Joint line pair 19.50
c. As "b," imperf., pair *600.00*
Joint line pair —

Values for No. 1616b with shiny gum are for the lines-only precancel. Also known with city precancels, and worth more thus.

No. 1616c is precanceled Pleasantville, NY.

1617 A995 10c **violet,** *gray,* shiny gum, *Nov. 4, 1977* .25 .25
Pair .50 .50
Joint line pair 1.00 —
Dull gum .30
Pair .60
Joint line pair 2.50
a. Untagged (Bureau precanceled, shiny gum) 42.50 1.35
Pair 90.00 2.75
Joint line pair *1,150.* —
Dull gum 1.35
Pair 2.75
Joint line pair 47.50
b. Imperf., pair, shiny gum 80.00
Joint line pair, shiny gum *150.00*
Imperf., pair, dull gum 55.00
Joint line pair, dull gum *115.00*
c. As "a," imperf pair, dull gum *3,750.*
Joint line pair, dull gum *4,750.*

1618 A998 13c **brown,** shiny gum, *Nov. 25, 1975* .25 .25
Pair .50 .50
Joint line pair .75 —
Dull gum 1.50
Pair 3.00
Joint line pair 9.00
a. Untagged (Bureau precanceled), shiny gum 5.75 .75
Pair 12.00 1.50
Joint line pair 100.00 —
Dull gum .75
Pair 1.50
Joint line pair 32.50
b. Imperf., pair 22.50
Joint line pair 45.00
g. Pair, imperf. between *600.00*
h. As "a," imperf., pair —
j. As No. 1618, shiny gum, tagging omitted —

Values for No. 1618a with shiny gum are for the lines-only precancel. Also known with city precancels, and worth more thus. No. 1618a with dull gum and lines-only precancel is extremely scarce and is worth much more than the values shown.

1618C A1001 15c **gray, dark blue & red,** small block tagging, *June 30, 1978* .75 .25
Pair 1.50 .50
d. Imperf., pair, small block tagging 20.00
e. Pair, imperf. between *100.00*
f. Gray omitted 30.00
i. Tagging omitted 65.00
k. As "d," tagging omitted —

l. Large block tagging .90 .35
Pair 1.80 .70
1619 A1002 16c **ultramarine,** overall tagging, *Mar. 31, 1978* .35 .25
Pair .70 .50
Joint line pair 1.75 —
a. Block tagging .50 .25
Pair 1.00 .50
Nos. 1613-1619 (9) 2.85 2.25

No. 1619a (the B press printing) has a white background without bluish tinge, is a fraction of a millimeter smaller than No. 1619 (the Cottrell press printing) and has no joint lines.
Bureau Precancels: 9c, 7 diff., 10c, 3 diff., 13c, 12 diff.
See Nos. 1811, 1813, 1816.

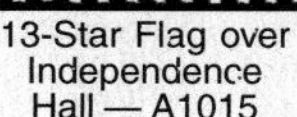

13-Star Flag over Independence Hall — A1015

Flag over Capitol — A1016

Designers: No. 1622, Melbourne Brindle. No. 1623, Esther Porter.

Panes of 100 (10x10) each.

1975-81 ***Perf. 11x10¾***
1622 A1015 13c **dk blue, red & brown red,** *Nov. 15, 1975* .25 .25
P# block of 20, 2-3#, 2-3 Zip, 2-3 Mail Early 6.00 —
a. Horiz. pair, imperf. between 40.00
b. Vertical pair, imperf. *300.00*
e. Horiz. pair, imperf. vert. —
f. Tagging omitted 9.00
g. As "a," tagging omitted —

No. 1622 was printed on the Multicolored Huck Press. Plate markings are at top or bottom of pane. It has large block tagging and nearly vertical multiple gum ridges.
See note after No. 1338F for marginal markings.

Perf. 11¼
1622C A1015 13c **dk blue, red & brown red,** *1981* 1.00 .25
P# block of 20, 1-2#, 1-2 Zip 35.00 —
P# block of 6 25.00 —
d. Vertical pair, imperf 100.00
h. As "d," tagging omitted —

No. 1622C was printed on the Combination Press. Plate markings are at sides of pane. It has small block tagging and shiny flat gum.
See note after No. 1703.

BOOKLET STAMPS

Perf. 11x10½ on 2 or 3 Sides
1977, Mar. 11 **Engr.**
1623 A1016 13c **blue & red** .25 .25
a. Booklet pane, 1 #1590 + 7 #1623 2.25 2.00
d. Pair, #1590 & #1623 .70 *1.25*
f. Tagging omitted —
g. As "a," tagging omitted —

Perf. 10x9¾ on 2 or 3 Sides
1623B A1016 13c **blue & red** .65 .75
c. Booklet pane, 1 #1590A + 7 #1623B 15.00 15.00
e. Pair, #1590A & #1623B 14.00 14.00

COIL STAMP

1975, Nov. 15 ***Perf. 10 Vertically***
1625 A1015 13c **dk blue, red & brown red** .35 .25
Pair .70 .50
a. Imperf., pair 20.00
b. Tagging omitted —

No. 1625 was printed on both the Huck and "B" presses. Huck press printings have pebbled gum (gummed on press), while "B" press printings have smooth gum (pregummed paper). Huck press printings often show portions of a joint line, but this feature is not consistent. Values for coils and imperf coils the same for both varieties.

AMERICAN BICENTENNIAL ISSUE
The Spirit of '76

Designed after painting by Archibald M. Willard in Abbot Hall, Marblehead, Massachusetts. Nos. 1629-1631 printed in continuous design.
Left panes contain 3 No. 1631a and one No. 1629; right panes contain one No. 1631 and 3 No. 1631a.

Drummer Boy — A1019

Old Drummer — A1020

Fifer — A1021

Designed by Vincent E. Hoffman.

PHOTOGRAVURE (Andreotti)
Plates of 200 subjects in four panes of 50.

1976, Jan. 1 **Tagged** ***Perf. 11***
1629 A1019 13c **blue violet & multi** .25 .25
a. Imperf., vert. pair —
1630 A1020 13c **blue violet & multi** .25 .25
1631 A1021 13c **blue violet & multi** .25 .25
a. Strip of 3, #1629-1631 .75 .75
P# block of 12, 5# 3.50 —
P# block of 20, 5#, slogans 5.75 —
b. As "a," imperf. *700.00*
c. Imperf., vert. pair, #1631 *500.00*

INTERPHIL ISSUE

Interphil 76 International Philatelic Exhibition, Philadelphia, Pa., May 29-June 6.

"Interphil 76" A1022

Designed by Terrence W. McCaffrey.

LITHOGRAPHED, ENGRAVED (Giori)
Plates of 200 subjects of four panes of 50.

1976, Jan. 17 **Tagged** ***Perf. 11***
1632 A1022 13c **dark blue & red (engr.), ultra. & red (litho.)** .25 .25
P# block of 4 1.00 —
Margin block of 4, Mr. Zip and "Use Zip Code" 1.00 —
a. Dark blue & red (engr.) missing (CM) —
b. Tagging omitted 75.00 —
c. Red (engr,) missing (CM) —

AMERICAN BICENTENNIAL ISSUE

Illustration reduced.

Designed by Walt Reed.

PHOTOGRAVURE (Andreotti)
Plates of 200 subjects in four panes of 50.

1976, Feb. 23 **Tagged** ***Perf. 11***
1633 A1023 13c Delaware .30 .25
1634 A1024 13c Pennsylvania .30 .25
1635 A1025 13c New Jersey .30 .25
1636 A1026 13c Georgia .30 .25
1637 A1027 13c Connecticut .30 .25
1638 A1028 13c Massachusetts .30 .25
1639 A1029 13c Maryland .30 .25
1640 A1030 13c South Carolina .30 .25
1641 A1031 13c New Hampshire .30 .25
1642 A1032 13c Virginia .30 .25
1643 A1033 13c New York .30 .25
1644 A1034 13c North Carolina .30 .25
1645 A1035 13c Rhode Island .30 .25
1646 A1036 13c Vermont .30 .25
1647 A1037 13c Kentucky .30 .25
1648 A1038 13c Tennessee .30 .25
1649 A1039 13c Ohio .30 .25
1650 A1040 13c Louisiana .30 .25
1651 A1041 13c Indiana .30 .25
1652 A1042 13c Mississippi .30 .25
1653 A1043 13c Illinois .30 .25
1654 A1044 13c Alabama .30 .25
1655 A1045 13c Maine .30 .25
1656 A1046 13c Missouri .30 .25
1657 A1047 13c Arkansas .30 .25
1658 A1048 13c Michigan .30 .25
1659 A1049 13c Florida .30 .25
1660 A1050 13c Texas .30 .25
1661 A1051 13c Iowa .30 .25
1662 A1052 13c Wisconsin .30 .25
1663 A1053 13c California .30 .25
1664 A1054 13c Minnesota .30 .25
1665 A1055 13c Oregon .30 .25
1666 A1056 13c Kansas .30 .25
1667 A1057 13c West Virginia .30 .25
a. Tagging omitted —
1668 A1058 13c Nevada .30 .25
1669 A1059 13c Nebraska .30 .25
1670 A1060 13c Colorado .30 .25
1671 A1061 13c North Dakota .30 .25
1672 A1062 13c South Dakota .30 .25
1673 A1063 13c Montana .30 .25
1674 A1064 13c Washington .30 .25
1675 A1065 13c Idaho .30 .25
1676 A1066 13c Wyoming .30 .25
1677 A1067 13c Utah .30 .25
1678 A1068 13c Oklahoma .30 .25
1679 A1069 13c New Mexico .30 .25
1680 A1070 13c Arizona .30 .25
1681 A1071 13c Alaska .30 .25
1682 A1072 13c Hawaii .30 .25
a. Pane of 50 17.50 15.00

TELEPHONE CENTENNIAL ISSUE

Centenary of first telephone call by Alexander Graham Bell, March 10, 1876.

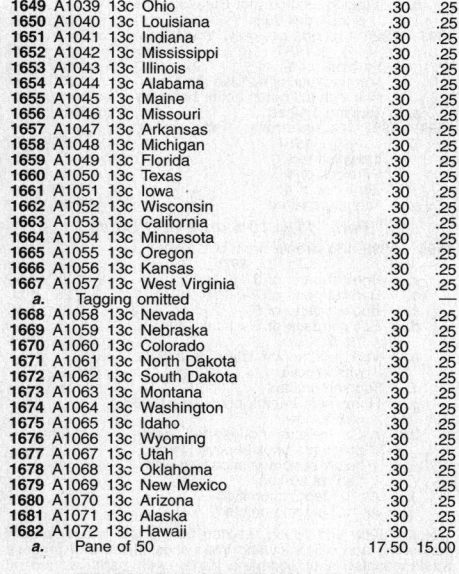

Bell's Telephone Patent Application, 1876 — A1073

Designed by George Tscherny.

ENGRAVED (Giori)
Plates of 200 subjects in four panes of 50.

1976, Mar. 10 **Tagged** ***Perf. 11***
1683 A1073 13c **black, purple & red,** *tan* .25 .25
P# block of 4 1.10 —
Margin block of 4, Mr. Zip and "Use Zip Code" 1.00 —
a. Black & purple missing (EP) *450.00*
b. Red missing (EP) —
c. All colors missing (EP) —
d. Tagging omitted —

On No. 1683a, the errors have only tiny traces of red present, so are best collected as a horiz. strip of 5 with 2 or 3 error stamps. No. 1683c also must be collected as a transitional strip.

COMMERCIAL AVIATION ISSUE

50th anniversary of first contract airmail flights: Dearborn, Mich. to Cleveland, Ohio, Feb. 15, 1926; and Pasco, Wash. to Elko, Nev., Apr. 6, 1926.

Ford-Pullman Monoplane and Laird Swallow Biplane A1074

Designed by Robert E. Cunningham.

PHOTOGRAVURE (Andreotti)
Plates of 200 subjects in four panes of 50 each

1976, Mar. 19 **Tagged** ***Perf. 11***
1684 A1074 13c **blue & multicolored** .25 .25
P# block of 10, 5# 2.75 —
Margin block of 4, Mr. Zip and "Use Zip Code" 1.00 —
a. Tagging omitted —

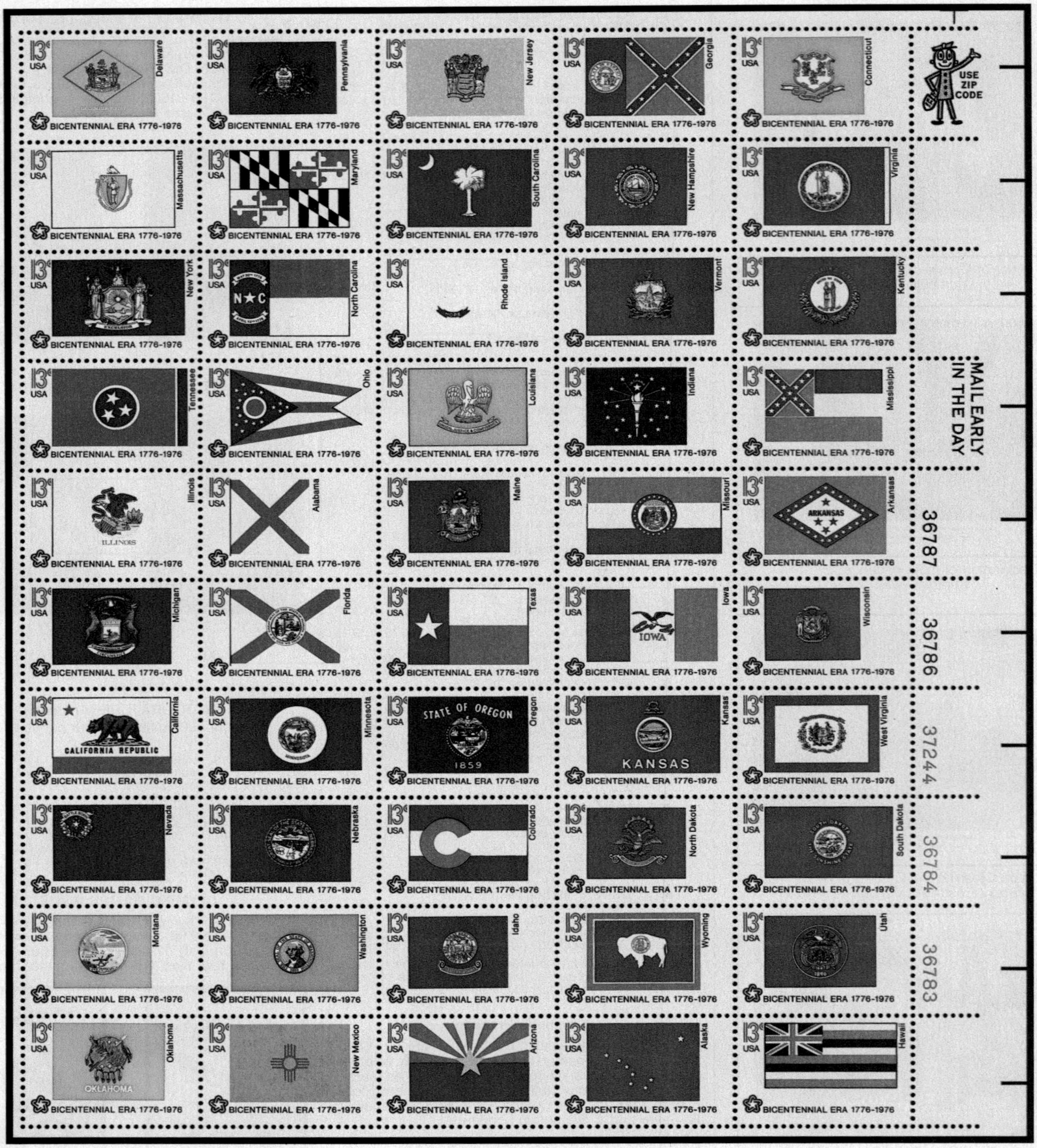

State Flags A1023-A1072

CHEMISTRY ISSUE

Honoring American chemists, in conjunction with the centenary of the American Chemical Society.

Various Flasks, Separatory Funnel, Computer Tape — A1075

Designed by Ken Davies.

PHOTOGRAVURE (Andreotti)

Plates of 200 subjects in four panes of 50.

1976, Apr. 6	**Tagged**	***Perf. 11***	
1685 A1075 13c **multicolored**		.25	.25
P# block of 12, 6#		3.25	—
Margin block of 4, Mr. Zip and "Use Zip Code"		1.00	—
Pair with full vert. gutter btwn.		—	

AMERICAN BICENTENNIAL ISSUES

SOUVENIR SHEETS

Designs, from Left to Right, No. 1686: a, Two British officers. b, Gen. Benjamin Lincoln. c, George Washington. d, John Trumbull, Col. Cobb, von Steuben, Lafayette, Thomas Nelson. e, Alexander Hamilton, John Laurens, Walter Stewart (all vert.).

No. 1687: a, John Adams, Roger Sherman, Robert R. Livingston. b, Jefferson, Franklin. c, Thomas Nelson, Jr., Francis Lewis, John Witherspoon, Samuel Huntington. d, John Hancock, Charles Thomson. e, George Read, John Dickinson, Edward Rutledge (a, d, vert., b, c, e, horiz.).

No. 1688: a, Boatsman. b, Washington. c, Flag bearer. d, Men in boat. e, Men on shore (a, d, horiz., b, c, e, vert.).

No. 1689: a, Two officers. b, Washington. c, Officer, black horse. d, Officer, white horse. e, Three soldiers (a, c, e, horiz., b, d, vert.).

Surrender of Cornwallis at Yorktown, by John Trumbull — A1076

Declaration of Independence, by John Trumbull — A1077

Washington Crossing the Delaware, by Emmanuel Leutze / Eastman Johnson — A1078

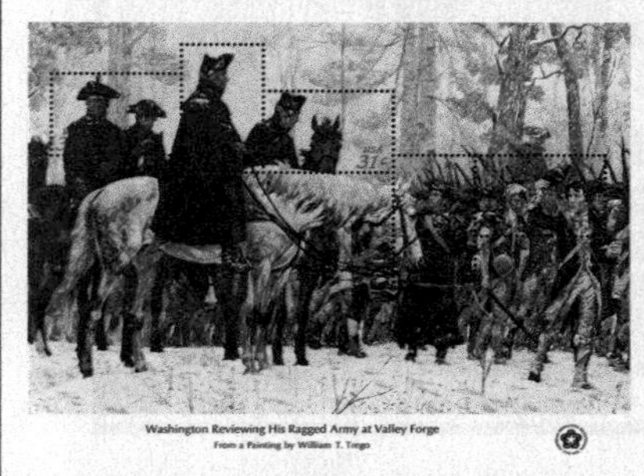

Washington Reviewing Army at Valley Forge, by William T. Trego — A1079

Illustrations reduced.

Designed by Vincent E. Hoffman.

LITHOGRAPHED

Plates of 30 subjects in six panes of 5 each.

1976, May 29 **Tagged** ***Perf. 11***

1686	A1076 Pane of 5	2.75	2.25
a.-e.	13c **multicolored**	.40	.40
f.	"USA/13c" omitted on "b," "c" & "d," imperf, tagging omitted	—	1,750.
g.	"USA/13c" omitted on "a" & "e"	500.00	300.00
h.	Imperf., tagging omitted		2,500.
i.	"USA/13c" omitted on "b," "c" & "d"	500.00	
j.	"USA/13c" double on "b"	—	
k.	"USA/13c" omitted on "c" & "d"	750.00	
l.	"USA/13c" omitted on "e"	475.00	
m.	"USA/13c" omitted, imperf., tagging omitted		—
n.	As "g," imperf., tagging omitted		—
o.	"USA/13c" missing on "a" (PS)	450.00	
p.	As No. 1686, tagging omitted		—
q.	"USA/13c" omitted on "a"	750.00	
r.	Imperf., tagged		—
s.	"USA/13c" missing on "b" and "d" (PS)	—	
1687	A1077 Pane of 5	3.75	3.25
a.-e.	18c **multicolored**	.50	.50
f.	Design & marginal inscriptions omitted	2,500.	
g.	"USA/18c" omitted on "a" & "c"	550.00	—
h.	"USA/18c" omitted on "b," "d" & "e"	350.00	
i.	"USA/18c" omitted on "d"	425.00	475.00
j.	Black omitted in design	1,500.	
k.	"USA/18c" omitted, imperf., tagging omitted	1,500.	
m.	"USA/18c" omitted on "b" & "e"	500.00	
n.	"USA/18c" omitted on "b" & "d"	1,000.	
p.	Imperf. (tagged)	1,000.	
q.	"USA/18c" missing on "c" (CM)	—	
r.	Yellow omitted	5,000.	
s.	"USA/18c" missing on "a," "c" and "d" (PS)	—	
t.	"USA/18c" missing on "a" and "d" (PS)	300.00	
u.	"USA/18c" omitted on "a"	5,000.	
1688	A1078 Pane of 5	4.75	4.25
a.-e.	24c **multicolored**	.65	.65
f.	"USA/24c" omitted, imperf., tagging omitted	950.00	
g.	"USA/24c" omitted on "d" & "e"	400.00	400.00
h.	Design & marginal inscriptions omitted	2,500.	
i.	"USA/24c" omitted on "a," "b" & "c"	400.00	400.00
j.	Imperf., tagging omitted	1,250.	
k.	"USA/24c" of "d" & "e" inverted	12,500.	
l.	As "i," imperf, tagging omitted	3,250.	—
m.	Tagging omitted on "e" and "f"	—	
n.	As No. 1688, perfs inverted and reversed	7,500.	
o.	As No. 1688, tagging omitted	850.00	
p.	"USA/24c" missing on "d" and "e" (CM)	—	
q.	"USA/24c" omitted on "b" and "c"	—	
r.	"USA/24c" omitted on "a"	400.00	
s.	As No. 1688, imperf.	1,250.	
1689	A1079 Pane of 5	5.75	5.25
a.-e.	31c **multicolored**	.80	.80
f.	"USA/31c" omitted, imperf.	950.00	
g.	"USA/31c" omitted on "a" & "c"	375.00	
h.	"USA/31c" omitted on "b," "d" & "e"	450.00	—
i.	"USA/31c" omitted on "e"	375.00	
j.	Black omitted in design	1,450.	
k.	Imperf., tagging omitted		2,000.
l.	"USA/31c" omitted on "b" & "d"	300.00	
m.	"USA/31c" omitted on "a," "c" & "e"	750.00	
n.	As "m," imperf., tagging omitted	—	
p.	As "h," imperf., tagging omitted		1,250.
q.	As "g," imperf., tagging omitted	2,500.	
r.	"USA/31c" omitted on "d" & "e"	600.00	
s.	As "f," tagging omitted	2,000.	
t.	"USA/31c" omitted on "d"	500.00	
u.	As No. 1689, tagging omitted	—	
v.	As No. 1689, perfs and tagging inverted	10,000.	
w.	"USA/31c" missing on "a," "b," "c" and "d" (PS)	500.00	
x.	"USA/31c" missing on "e" (CM)	—	
y.	"USA/31c" omitted on "a"	—	
	Nos. 1686-1689 (4)	17.00	

Issued in connection with Interphil 76 International Philatelic Exhibition, Philadelphia, Pa., May 29-June 6. Size of panes: 203x152mm; size of stamps: 25x39½mm, 39½x25mm.

Benjamin Franklin

American Bicentennial: Benjamin Franklin (1706-1790), deputy postmaster general for the colonies (1753-1774) and statesman. Design based on marble bust by anonymous Italian sculptor after terra cotta bust by Jean Jacques Caffieri, 1777. Map published by R. Sayer and J. Bennett in London.

Franklin and Map of North America, 1776 — A1080

Designed by Bernard Reilander (Canada).

LITHOGRAPHED, ENGRAVED (Giori)

Plates of 200 subjects in four panes of 50.

1976, June 1 **Tagged** ***Perf. 11***

1690	A1080 13c **multicolored**	.25	.25
	P# block of 4	1.10	—
	Margin block of 4, Mr. Zip and "Use Zip Code"	1.00	—
a.	Light blue omitted	150.00	
b.	Tagging omitted	10.00	

See Canada No. 691.

Declaration of Independence

Designed after painting of Declaration of Independence, by John Trumbull, in the Rotunda of the Capitol, Washington, D.C. Nos. 1691-1694 printed in continuous design. Left panes contain 10 No. 1694a and 5 each of Nos. 1691-1692; right panes contain 5 each of Nos. 1693-1694 and 10 No. 1694a.

A1081

A1082

A1083

A1084

Designed by Vincent E. Hoffman.

PHOTOGRAVURE (Andreotti)

Plates of 200 subjects in four panes of 50.

1976, July 4 **Tagged** ***Perf. 11***

1691	A1081 13c **multicolored**	.30	.25
1692	A1082 13c **multicolored**	.30	.25
1693	A1083 13c **multicolored**	.30	.25
1694	A1084 13c **multicolored**	.30	.25
a.	Strip of 4, #1691-1694	1.20	1.10
	P# block of 20, 5#, "Mail Early in the Day," Mr. Zip and "Use Zip Code"	7.00	—
	P# block of 16, 5#, "Mail Early in the Day"	6.50	—
	Margin block of 4, Mr. Zip and "Use Zip Code"	1.25	—

OLYMPIC GAMES ISSUE

12th Winter Olympic Games, Innsbruck, Austria, Feb. 4-15, and 21st Summer Olympic Games, Montreal, Canada, July 17-Aug. 1. Nos. 1695-1696 alternate in one row, Nos. 1697-1698 in other row.

Diving — A1085

Skiing — A1086

Running — A1087

Skating — A1088

Designed by Donald Moss.

PHOTOGRAVURE (Andreotti)

Plates of 200 subjects in four panes of 50.

1976, July 16 Tagged *Perf. 11*

1695 A1085 13c **multicolored**	.30	.25
1696 A1086 13c **multicolored**	.30	.25
1697 A1087 13c **multicolored**	.30	.25
1698 A1088 13c **multicolored**	.30	.25
a. Block of 4, #1695-1698	1.20	1.20
P# block of 12, 6#	4.00	—
P# block of 20, 6#, Mr. Zip and slogans	8.75	—
Margin block of 4, Mr. Zip and "Use Zip Code"	1.40	—
b. As "a," imperf.	*375.00*	

CLARA MAASS ISSUE

Clara Louise Maass (1876-1901), volunteer in fight against yellow fever, birth centenary.

Clara Maass and Newark German Hospital Pin — A1089

Designed by Paul Calle.

PHOTOGRAVURE (Andreotti)

Plates of 160 subjects in four panes of 40.

1976, Aug. 18 Tagged *Perf. 11*

1699 A1089 13c **multicolored**	.25	.25
P# block of 12, 6#	4.00	—
Margin block of 4, Mr. Zip, "Use Zip Code" and "Mail Early in the Day"	1.00	—
a. Horiz. pair, imperf. vert.	*350.00*	
b. Dark blue missing (PS)	*700.00*	

On No. 1699, two blue plates were used. No 1699b is missing the dark blue ("She gave her life") at bottom due to an upward shift of the horizontal perforations.

ADOLPH S. OCHS ISSUE

Adolph S. Ochs (1858-1935), Publisher of the New York Times, 1896-1935 — A1090

Designed by Bradbury Thompson; photograph by S. J. Woolf.

GIORI PRESS PRINTING

Plates of 128 subjects in four panes of 32 (8x4).

1976, Sept. 18 Tagged *Perf. 11*

1700 A1090 13c **black & gray**	.25	.25
P# block of 4	1.10	—
Margin block of 4, Mr. Zip and "Use Zip Code"	1.00	—
a. Tagging omitted	*45.00*	—

CHRISTMAS ISSUE

Nativity, by John Singleton Copley A1091

"Winter Pastime," by Nathaniel Currier A1092

Designers: No. 1701, Bradbury Thompson after 1776 painting in Museum of Fine Arts, Boston. No. 1702, Stevan Dohanos after 1855 lithograph in Museum of the City of New York.

PHOTOGRAVURE (Andreotti)

Plates of 200 subjects in four panes of 50.

1976, Oct. 27 Tagged *Perf. 11*

1701 A1091 13c **multicolored**	.25	.25
P# block of 12, 6#	3.25	—
Margin block of 4, Mr. Zip and "Use Zip Code"	1.00	—
a. Imperf., pair	*85.00*	
1702 A1092 13c **multi,** overall tagging	.25	.25
P# block of 10, 5#	2.75	—
Margin block of 4, Mr. Zip and "Use Zip Code"	1.00	—
a. Imperf., pair	*75.00*	

COMBINATION PRESS

Plates of 230 (10x23) subjects in panes of 50 (5x10)

Tagged, Block

1703 A1092 13c **multicolored**	.25	.25
P# block of 20, 5-8#	6.00	—
a. Imperf., pair	*75.00*	
b. Vert. pair, imperf. between	*275.00*	
c. Tagging omitted	17.50	
d. Red omitted	*500.00*	
e. Yellow omitted	—	

No. 1702 has overall tagging. Lettering at base is black and usually ½mm below design. As a rule, no "snowflaking" in sky or pond. Pane of 50 has margins on 4 sides with slogans. Plate Nos. 37465-37478.

No. 1703 has block tagging the size of printed area. Lettering at base is gray black and usually ¾mm below design. "Snowflaking" generally in sky and pond. Plate Nos. 37617-37621 or 37634-37638.

Examples of No. 1703 are known with various amounts of red or yellow missing. Nos. 1703d-1703e are stamps with the colors totally omitted. Expertization is recommended.

COMBINATION PRESS

Cylindrical plates consist of 23 rows of subjects, 10 across for commemoratives (230 subjects), 20 across for definitives (460 subjects), with selvage on the two outer edges only. Guillotining through the perforations creates individual panes of 50 or 100 with selvage on one side only.

Failure of the guillotine to separate through the perforations resulted in straight edges on some stamps. Perforating teeth along the center column and the tenth rows were removed for issues released on or after May 31, 1984 (the 10c Richard Russell, for definitives; the 20c Horace Moses, for commemoratives), creating panes with straight edged stamps on three sides.

Three sets of plate numbers, copyright notices (starting with No. 1787), and zip insignia (starting with No. 1927) are arranged identically on the left and right sides of the plate so that each pane has at least one of each marking. The markings adjacent to any particular row are repeated either seven or eight rows away on the cylinder.

Fifteen combinations of the three marginal markings and blank rows are possible on panes.

AMERICAN BICENTENNIAL ISSUE
Washington at Princeton

Washington's Victory over Lord Cornwallis at Princeton, N.J., bicentenary.

Washington, Nassau Hall, Hessian Prisoners and 13-star Flag, by Charles Willson Peale — A1093

Designed by Bradbury Thompson.

PHOTOGRAVURE (Andreotti)

Plates of 160 subjects in four panes of 40.

1977, Jan. 3 Tagged *Perf. 11*

1704 A1093 13c **multicolored**	.25	.25
P# block of 10, 5#	2.75	—
Margin block of 4, Mr. Zip and "Use Zip Code", "Mail Early in the Day"	1.00	—
a. Horiz. pair, imperf. vert.	*425.00*	
b. Black (inscriptions) missing (PS)	—	

SOUND RECORDING ISSUE

Centenary of the invention of the phonograph by Thomas Alva Edison and development of sophisticated recording industry.

Tin Foil Phonograph A1094

Designed by Walter and Naiad Einsel.

LITHOGRAPHED, ENGRAVED (Giori)

Plates of 200 subjects in four panes of 50.

1977, Mar. 23 Tagged *Perf. 11*

1705 A1094 13c **black & multicolored**	.25	.25
P# block of 4	1.10	—
Margin block of 4, Mr. Zip and "Use Zip Code"	1.00	—
a. Tagging omitted	—	

AMERICAN FOLK ART SERIES
Pueblo Pottery

Pueblo art, 1880-1920, from Museums in New Mexico, Arizona and Colorado.

Nos. 1706-1709 are printed in blocks and strips of 4 in panes of 40. In the 1st row Nos. 1706-1709 are in sequence as listed. In the 2nd row Nos. 1708-1709 are followed by Nos. 1706-1709, 1708-1709.

Zia Pot — A1095

San Ildefonso Pot — A1096

Hopi Pot — A1097

Acoma Pot — A1098

Designed by Ford Ruthling.

PHOTOGRAVURE (Andreotti)
Plates of 160 subjects in four panes of 40.

1977, Apr. 13	**Tagged**	***Perf. 11***	
1706 A1095 13c **multicolored**		.25	.25
1707 A1096 13c **multicolored**		.25	.25
1708 A1097 13c **multicolored**		.25	.25
1709 A1098 13c **multicolored**		.25	.25
a. Block or strip of 4, #1706-1709		1.00	1.00
P# block of 10, 5#		2.75	—
P# block of 16, 5#; Mr. Zip and slogans		4.25	—
Margin block of 6, Mr. Zip and "Use Zip Code" "Mail Early in the Day"		1.50	—
b. As "a," imperf. vert.		*1,100.*	

LINDBERGH FLIGHT ISSUE

Charles A. Lindbergh's solo transatlantic flight from New York to Paris, 50th anniversary.

Spirit of St. Louis — A1099

Designed by Robert E. Cunningham.

PHOTOGRAVURE (Andreotti)
Plates of 200 subjects in four panes of 50.

1977, May 20	**Tagged**	***Perf. 11***	
1710 A1099 13c **multicolored**		.25	.25
P# block of 12, 6#		3.25	—
Margin block of 4, Mr. Zip and "Use Zip Code"		1.00	—
a. Imperf., pair		*700.00*	
b. Tagging omitted		—	

Beware of private overprints on No. 1710.

COLORADO STATEHOOD ISSUE

Issued to honor Colorado as the "Centennial State." It achieved statehood in 1876.

Columbine and Rocky Mountains — A1100

Designed by V. Jack Ruther.

PHOTOGRAVURE (Andreotti)
Plates of 200 subjects in four panes of 50.

1977, May 21	**Tagged**	***Perf. 11***	
1711 A1100 13c **multicolored**		.25	.25
P# block of 12, 6#		3.25	—
Margin block of 4, Mr. Zip and "Use Zip Code"		1.00	—
a. Horiz. pair, imperf. between and with natural straight edge at right		*650.00*	
b. Horiz. pair, imperf. vertically		*500.00*	
c. Perf. 11.2		.75	.25
P# block of 12, 6#		20.00	

Perforations do not run through the sheet margin on about 10 percent of the sheets of No. 1711.

BUTTERFLY ISSUE

Nos. 1712-1713 alternate in 1st row, Nos. 1714-1715 in 2nd row. This arrangement is repeated throughout the pane. Butterflies represent different geographic US areas.

Swallowtail A1101

Checkerspot A1102

Dogface A1103

Orange-Tip A1104

Designed by Stanley Galli.

PHOTOGRAVURE (Andreotti)
Plates of 200 subjects in four panes of 50.

1977, June 6	**Tagged**	***Perf. 11***	
1712 A1101 13c **tan & multicolored**		.25	.25
1713 A1102 13c **tan & multicolored**		.25	.25
1714 A1103 13c **tan & multicolored**		.25	.25
1715 A1104 13c **tan & multicolored**		.25	.25
a. Block of 4, #1712-1715		1.00	1.00
P# block of 12, 6#		3.25	—
P# block of 20, 6#, Mr. Zip and slogans		5.50	—
Margin block of 4, Mr. Zip and "Use Zip Code"		1.05	—
b. As "a," imperf. horiz.		*9,500.*	

AMERICAN BICENTENNIAL ISSUES
Marquis de Lafayette

200th anniversary of Lafayette's Landing on the coast of South Carolina, north of Charleston.

Marquis de Lafayette — A1105

Designed by Bradbury Thompson.

GIORI PRESS PRINTING
Plates of 160 subjects in four panes of 40.

1977, June 13	**Tagged**	***Perf. 11***	
1716 A1105 13c **blue, black & red**		.25	.25
P# block of 4		1.10	—
Margin block of 4, Mr. Zip and "Use Zip Code"		1.00	—
a. Red missing (PS)		*300.00*	

Skilled Hands for Independence

Nos. 1717-1718 alternate in 1st row, Nos. 1719-1720 in 2nd row. This arrangement is repeated throughout the pane.

Seamstress A1106

Blacksmith A1107

the WHEELWRIGHT
for INDEPENDENCE USA 13c
Wheelwright A1108

Leatherworker A1109

Designed by Leonard Everett Fisher.

PHOTOGRAVURE (Andreotti)
Plates of 200 subjects in four panes of 50.

1977, July 4	**Tagged**	***Perf. 11***	
1717 A1106 13c **multicolored**		.25	.25
1718 A1107 13c **multicolored**		.25	.25
1719 A1108 13c **multicolored**		.25	.25
1720 A1109 13c **multicolored**		.25	.25
a. Block of 4, #1717-1720		1.00	1.00
P# block of 12, 6#		3.25	
P# block of 20, 6#, Mr. Zip and slogans		5.50	—
Margin block of 4, Mr. Zip and "Use Zip Code"		1.05	—

PEACE BRIDGE ISSUE

50th anniversary of the Peace Bridge, connecting Buffalo (Fort Porter), N.Y. and Fort Erie, Ontario.

Peace Bridge and Dove — A1110

Designed by Bernard Brussel-Smith (wood-cut).

ENGRAVED

Plates of 200 subjects in four panes of 50.

1977, Aug. 4 **Tagged** ***Perf. 11x10½***

1721	A1110	13c **blue**	.25	.25
		P# block of 4	1.10	—
		Margin block of 4, Mr. Zip and "Use Zip Code"	1.00	—

AMERICAN BICENTENNIAL ISSUE
Battle of Oriskany

200th anniv. of the Battle of Oriskany, American Militia led by Brig. Gen. Nicholas Herkimer (1728-77).

Herkimer at Oriskany, by Frederick Yohn — A1111

Designed by Bradbury Thompson after painting in Utica, N.Y. Public Library.

PHOTOGRAVURE (Andreotti)

Plates of 160 subjects in four panes of 40.

1977, Aug. 6 **Tagged** ***Perf. 11***

1722	A1111	13c **multicolored**	.25	.25
		P# block of 10, 5#	2.75	—
		Margin block of 6, Mr. Zip and "Use Zip Code" and "Mail Early in the Day"	1.50	—

ENERGY ISSUE

Conservation and development of nation's energy resources. Nos. 1723-1724 se-tenant vertically.

"Conservation" A1112

"Development" A1113

Designed by Terrance W. McCaffrey.

PHOTOGRAVURE (Andreotti)

Plates of 160 subjects in four panes of 40.

1977, Oct. 20 **Tagged** ***Perf. 11***

1723	A1112	13c **multicolored**	.25	.25
1724	A1113	13c **multicolored**	.25	.25
a.		Pair, #1723-1724	.50	.50
		P# block of 12, 6#	3.25	—
		Margin block of 4, Mr. Zip, "Use Zip Code" and "Mail Early in the Day"	1.00	—

ALTA CALIFORNIA ISSUE

Founding of El Pueblo de San José de Guadalupe, first civil settlement in Alta California, 200th anniversary.

Farm Houses A1114

Designed by Earl Thollander.

LITHOGRAPHED, ENGRAVED (Giori)

Plates of 200 subjects in four panes of 50.

1977, Sept. 9 **Tagged** ***Perf. 11***

1725	A1114	13c **black & multicolored**	.25	.25
		P# block of 4	1.10	—
		Margin block of 4, Mr. Zip and "Use Zip Code"	1.00	—
a.		Tagging omitted	*250.00*	—

AMERICAN BICENTENNIAL ISSUE
Articles of Confederation

200th anniversary of drafting the Articles of Confederation, York Town, Pa.

Members of Continental Congress in Conference A1115

Designed by David Blossom.

ENGRAVED (Giori)

Plates of 200 subjects in four panes of 50.

1977, Sept. 30 **Tagged** ***Perf. 11***

1726	A1115	13c **red & brown,** *cream*	.25	.25
		P# block of 4	1.10	—
		Margin block of 4, Mr. Zip and "Use Zip Code"	1.00	—
a.		Tagging omitted	100.00	
b.		Red omitted	*500.00*	
c.		Red & brown omitted	*300.00*	

No. 1726b also has most of the brown omitted. No. 1726c must be collected as a transition multiple, certainly with No. 1726b and preferably also with No. 1726.

TALKING PICTURES, 50th ANNIV.

Movie Projector and Phonograph A1116

Designed by Walter Einsel.

LITHOGRAPHED, ENGRAVED (Giori)

Plates of 200 subjects in four panes of 50.

1977, Oct. 6 **Tagged** ***Perf. 11***

1727	A1116	13c **multicolored**	.25	.25
		P# block of 4	1.10	—
		Margin block of 4, Mr. Zip and "Use Zip Code"	1.00	—

AMERICAN BICENTENNIAL ISSUE
Surrender at Saratoga

200th anniversary of Gen. John Burgoyne's surrender at Saratoga.

Surrender of Burgoyne, by John Trumbull A1117

Designed by Bradbury Thompson.

PHOTOGRAVURE (Andreotti)

Plates of 160 subjects in four panes of 40.

1977, Oct. 7 **Tagged** ***Perf. 11***

1728	A1117	13c **multicolored**	.25	.25
		P# block of 10, 5#	2.75	—
		Margin block of 6, Mr. Zip, "Use Zip Code" and "Mail Early in the Day"	1.50	—
a.		Tagging omitted	—	

CHRISTMAS ISSUE

Washington at Valley Forge — A1118

Rural Mailbox — A1119

Designers: No. 1729, Stevan Dohanos, after painting by J. C. Leyendecker. No. 1730, Dolli Tingle.

PHOTOGRAVURE (Combination Press)

Plates of 460 subjects (20x23) in panes of 100 (10x10).

1977, Oct. 21 **Tagged** ***Perf. 11***

1729	A1118	13c **multicolored**	.25	.25
		P# block of 20, 5-8#	5.75	—
a.		Imperf., pair	*50.00*	

See Combination Press note after No. 1703.

PHOTOGRAVURE (Andreotti)

Plates of 400 subjects in 4 panes of 100.

1730	A1119	13c **multicolored**	.25	.25
		P# block of 10, 5#	2.75	—
		Margin block of 4, Mr. Zip and "Use Zip Code"	1.00	—
		Pair with full vert. gutter btwn.	—	
a.		Imperf., pair	*175.00*	

CARL SANDBURG ISSUE

Carl Sandburg (1878-1967), poet, biographer and collector of American folk songs, birth centenary.

Carl Sandburg, by William A. Smith, 1952 — A1120

Designed by William A. Smith.

GIORI PRESS PRINTING

Plates of 200 subjects in four panes of 50.

1978, Jan. 6 **Tagged** ***Perf. 11***

1731	A1120	13c **black & brown**	.25	.25
		P# block of 4	1.25	—
		Margin block of 4, Mr. Zip	1.05	—
a.		Brown omitted	*1,750.*	
b.		Tagging omitted	*225.00*	
c.		All colors omitted	—	

No. 1731c is tagged and has a faint black tagging ghost. Authentication is advised.

CAPTAIN COOK ISSUE

Capt. James Cook, 200th anniversary of his arrival in Hawaii, at Waimea, Kauai, Jan. 20, 1778, and of his anchorage in Cook Inlet, near Anchorage, Alaska, June 1, 1778. Nos. 1732-1733 printed in panes of 50, containing 25 each of Nos. 1732-1733 including 5 No. 1733b.

Capt. Cook, by Nathaniel Dance — A1121

"Resolution" and "Discovery," by John Webber A1122

Designers: No. 1732, Robert F. Szabo. No. 1733, Jak Katalan.

GIORI PRESS PRINTING

Plates of 200 subjects in four panes of 50.

1978, Jan. 20 **Tagged** ***Perf. 11***

1732 A1121 13c **dark blue** .25 .25
1733 A1122 13c **green** .25 .25
a. Vert. pair, imperf. horiz. *1,000.*
b. Pair, #1732-1733 .50 .50
P# block of 4, #1732 or 1733 1.10 —
Margin block of 4, Mr. Zip, #1732 or 1733 1.05 —
P# block of 20, 10 each #1732-1733, P# and slogans 5.25 —
c. As "b," imperf. between *4,000.*
d. As "b," tagging omitted *250.00*

Indian Head Penny, 1877 — A1123

Eagle — A1124

Red Masterpiece and Medallion Roses — A1126

ENGRAVED (Giori)

Plates of 600 subjects in four panes of 150.

1978 **Tagged** ***Perf. 11***

1734 A1123 13c **brown & blue green,** *bister, Jan. 11, 1978* .25 .25
P# block of 4 1.10 —
Margin block of 4, "Use Correct Zip Code" 1.00 —
Vert. pair with full horiz. gutter between —
a. Horiz. pair, imperf. vert. *175.00*
b. Tagging omitted *175.00*

PHOTOGRAVURE (Andreotti)

Plates of 400 subjects in four panes of 100.

1735 A1124 (15c) **orange,** *May 22, 1978* .30 .25
P# block of 4 1.40 —
Margin block of 4, "Use Zip Code" 1.25 —
Vert. pair with full horiz. gutter between —
a. Imperf., pair *70.00*
b. Vert. pair, imperf. horiz. *500.00*
c. Perf. 11.2 .35 .25
P# block of 4 1.80 —
Zip block of 4 1.50 —

BOOKLET STAMPS

ENGRAVED

Perf. 11x10½ on 2 or 3 Sides

1736 A1124 (15c) **orange** .30 .25
a. Booklet pane of 8, *May 22, 1978* 2.50 1.50
b. As "a," tagging omitted —
c. Vert. pair, imperf. btwn., in #1736a with foldover *1,000.*
d. As No. 1736, tagging omitted —

Perf. 10 on 2 or 3 Sides

1737 A1126 15c **multicolored** .30 .25
a. Booklet pane of 8, *July 11, 1978* 2.50 2.00
b. Imperf, pair *450.00*
c. As "a," imperf *2,250.*
d. As "a," tagging omitted *60.00*
e. As No. 1737, tagging omitted 6.50

A1127 A1128 A1129

A1130 A1131

Designed by Ronald Sharpe.

BOOKLET STAMPS

ENGRAVED

1980, Feb. 7 **Tagged** ***Perf. 11 on 2 or 3 Sides***

1738 A1127 15c **sepia,** *yellow* .30 .25
1739 A1128 15c **sepia,** *yellow* .30 .25
1740 A1129 15c **sepia,** *yellow* .30 .25
1741 A1130 15c **sepia,** *yellow* .30 .25
1742 A1131 15c **sepia,** *yellow* .30 .25
a. Booklet pane of 10, 2 each #1738-1742 3.50 3.00
b. Strip of 5, #1738-1742 1.50 1.40

COIL STAMP

1978, May 22 ***Perf. 10 Vert.***

1743 A1124 (15c) **orange** .30 .25
Pair .60 .25
Joint line pair .75 —
a. Imperf., pair 65.00
Joint line pair 140.00

No. 1743a is valued in the grade of fine.

BLACK HERITAGE SERIES

Harriet Tubman (1820-1913), born a slave, helped more than 300 slaves escape to freedom.

Harriet Tubman and Cart Carrying Slaves — A1133

Designed by Jerry Pinkney after photograph.

PHOTOGRAVURE (Andreotti)

Plates of 200 subjects in four panes of 50.

1978, Feb. 1 **Tagged** ***Perf. 10½x11***

1744 A1133 13c **multicolored** .25 .25
P# block of 12, 6# 3.25 —
Margin block of 4, Mr. Zip 1.00 —

AMERICAN FOLK ART SERIES

Quilts

Nos. 1745-1746 alternate in 1st row, Nos. 1747-1748 in 2nd.

Basket Design

A1134

A1135

A1136

A1137

Designed by Christopher Pullman after 1875 quilt made in New York City. Illustration reduced.

PHOTOGRAVURE (Andreotti)

Plates of 192 subjects in four panes of 48 (6x8).

1978, Mar. 8 **Tagged** ***Perf. 11***

1745 A1134 13c **multicolored** .25 .25
1746 A1135 13c **multicolored** .25 .25
1747 A1136 13c **multicolored** .25 .25
1748 A1137 13c **multicolored** .25 .25
a. Block of 4, #1745-1748 1.00 1.00
P# block of 12, 6# 3.25 —
P# block of 16, 6#, Mr. Zip and copyright 4.50 —
Margin block of 4, Mr. Zip, copyright 1.05 —

AMERICAN DANCE ISSUE

Nos. 1749-1750 alternate in 1st row, Nos. 1751-1752 in 2nd.

Ballet A1138